THE
OXFORD DICTIONARY
OF THE
CHRISTIAN CHURCH

THE
OXFORD DICTIONARY
OF THE
CHRISTIAN CHURCH

Edited by

F. L. CROSS

*Lady Margaret Professor of Divinity in
the University of Oxford and
Canon of Christ Church*

LONDON
OXFORD UNIVERSITY PRESS
NEW YORK   TORONTO

Oxford University Press, Ely House, London W.1

GLASGOW NEW YORK TORONTO MELBOURNE WELLINGTON
CAPE TOWN SALISBURY IBADAN NAIROBI LUSAKA ADDIS ABABA
BOMBAY CALCUTTA MADRAS KARACHI LAHORE DACCA
KUALA LUMPUR HONG KONG

First Published 1957
Reprinted (with corrections) 1958, 1961, 1963 *and* 1966

PRINTED IN GREAT BRITAIN

PREFACE

THE Christian Church has been so closely interwoven with the course of Western civilization that her history, life, and institutions are matters of deep concern not only to those who through Holy Baptism have been admitted to membership in the Body of Christ, but to all who take an intelligent interest in contemporary culture. The present *Dictionary* has been compiled in order to bring together, in a concise and handy form, as large a body of information as possible directly bearing on the Christian Church. It is addressed to the needs not merely of those whose primary vocation lies in the Christian ministry or in the professional study of theology or church history, nor even only to the general body of professing Christians who seek information about their faith and its growth, but to the educated public as a whole. For this and other reasons technicalities have been avoided, and it is hoped that throughout the entries are so written as to be immediately intelligible to the layman. If the *Dictionary* has any apologetic purpose, it seeks to achieve it solely through the objective presentation of fact.

The scope of the *Dictionary* need not be outlined here, as it will be discovered most readily from a rapid perusal of its pages. If a historical treatment predominates, the employment of this method will need no defence in the case of a faith which is so evidently rooted in history as is Christianity. The attempt has been made to give due and proportionate attention to the several parts and aspects of a vast field, covering over nineteen centuries. But history, as modern studies in its structure by Wilhelm Dilthey, Ernst Troeltsch, and a host of others have made abundantly clear, is by its nature selective, and a discipline in which the employment of objective canons, for example on a statistical basis, is an intrinsically unattainable ideal. If in the present work fuller attention has been paid to Western Christendom than to later Eastern Orthodoxy, to Christianity in Britain than to that of the Continent, to the events of the nineteenth century than to those of the tenth, this disproportion is only relative. In any case it may be presumed that the reader will welcome fuller information on matters at closer range. If, on the other hand, to some readers outside Europe it seems that insufficient attention has been given to the non-European lands where Christianity is now firmly planted, it must be recalled that the Church's connexion with Mediterranean and European countries is of far longer standing, and this fact is necessarily reflected in the subject-matter of a work in which the treatment is historical.

Perhaps some readers will look for a rather fuller treatment of Biblical matters in a *Dictionary of the Christian Church* than will be found here; and reasonably. The importance of the Bible throughout the history of the Church—and especially whenever she has been fully alive to her theological vocation—has always been fundamental. But it would have been impossible to give any adequate treatment of Biblical subjects in the present work without making disproportionate demands on space. There seemed the less need for doing so in view of the abundance of Biblical aids in the form of dictionaries (lexical, factual, and theological), concordances, and compendious commentaries of varying dimensions. These works are readily accessible in libraries. But as they are seldom privately possessed except by the clergy and others with a direct interest in theological studies, it was felt that some information of an elementary kind would be welcomed by a considerable body of lay people whose needs the *Dictionary* might be expected to serve. It is primarily for such readers that the entries on Biblical subjects are included.

A notable constituent of the *Dictionary* is the Bibliographies in small type at the end of the articles. To enable the reader to use these to the best advantage it may be of service to add a few details about their construction and purpose. They were mostly compiled independently of the articles, and their form, it must be confessed, was devised as the *Dictionary* developed, so that complete consistency has not been achieved. They do not set out to record (as is not infrequently the case in dictionary works) the sources which the compiler happens to have found specially useful. Their purpose, rather, is to record the principal items of primary and permanent interest bearing on the subject of the entry. The reader is asked, therefore, not to be too hasty in his strictures when he finds a work listed which the best critics assure him is 'superseded'. Still less must he suppose that the inclusion of a book implies an editorial *nihil obstat*. It is sufficiently familiar that a bad book has sometimes had great intrinsic importance in relation to a particular subject; and since the historical student may need to discover details of such a book, they have been included. Careful attention has also been given to recording the original date of publication of all items, partly to enable the bibliographies to be used by those interested in the authors as well as the contents of the books. Unless the contrary is expressly stated, the date given is always to be taken as that of the first edition. For those who want further readily accessible material, either by way of bibliography or on the subject itself, a liberal citation of articles in the larger standard dictionaries and encyclopaedic works has been made on a selective basis. Our own experience of dictionary works is that *P.R.E.*[1] is to be especially commended for its thoroughness and accuracy, *D.T.C.* for its amplitude, and *E.C.* for its modernity. We have found no reason to contest what appears to be the general verdict about the limitations of *D.A.C.L.* But that dictionary, despite its inaccuracies, is so often the only pointer to further material on archaeological and liturgical matters that we have frequently cited it. With use, the reader will perhaps accustom himself to finding guidance from the bibliography also by its omissions. Thus, where in the case of a person no biography is recorded, it can ordinarily be assumed that none is known to the Editor.

We hope, finally, that the inclusion of this relatively extensive bibliography needs no apology. Those who pursue theological and historical studies rarely possess a large private library in these days, and are more than hitherto dependent on public libraries, often at some distance. It is believed that the *Dictionary* will put the student of church history in possession of a larger body of bibliographical material than any other work of similar compass. If a good deal of this information will be rarely, if ever, wanted by many users of the *Dictionary*, this is a common phenomenon in a reference book. The same is true of *Bradshaw* or *Whitaker* or *Crockford*.

In the construction of the *Dictionary* constant use has naturally been made of the standard sets of texts, historical collections, and histories, as well as the larger dictionaries, encyclopaedias, chronological tables, gazetteers, atlases, and other works of reference. Where any question of accuracy arose, the attempt was always made to

---

[1] The full titles corresponding to these and the many other abbreviations used will be found in the 'List of Abbreviations', pp. xiii-xix.

verify details from first-hand sources. The extent to which this process could be carried had obvious limits. Where there are many hundreds of opportunities for error on every page, doubtless many inaccuracies survive. But it may be worth pointing out that in some instances considerable labour has been involved in the establishment of a single reference or date; and hence where such, as given in this *Dictionary*, differs from that currently found elsewhere, while it might be prudent to treat it with reserve, it would be mistaken to conclude that it was necessarily wrong.

It is unnecessary to recount in detail the stages by which the *Dictionary* has assumed its present shape. It owes its inception to Mr. G. F. J. Cumberlege of the Oxford University Press, who invited the Editor to undertake the work as long ago as 1939. Reference to the list of Contributors on pp. x-xii will show that it is the work of many hands, among them several scholars of high distinction. Roughly half the entries, including most of those of major importance, were drafted by these Contributors working independently. The rest, together with the bibliographies, were compiled by the Editor and his immediate associates. In some cases the reader who is versed in contemporary theological literature will have little difficulty in identifying the authorship of certain articles. But in order to secure the maximum uniformity it was agreed at the outset that all contributions should be subject to such editorial modification and reconstruction as seemed desirable, and that anonymity should be preserved. In the event many of the articles in the *Dictionary* are the work of several hands.

A consequence of this method of composition is that revision has been continuous. The material as put at the Editor's disposal needed welding, as far as possible, into a unity. By the close interrelation of the articles much economy of space has been achieved. In this connexion the Publisher generously allowed a great deal of recasting in the proof stage. The Editor is conscious that with the expenditure of further time and labour this process could with profit have been carried further, especially, he believes, in the earlier sections of the work. But a year or so ago it seemed to the Press and the Editor alike that the time had come to eschew further revision and to start the book on its way. In a dictionary (and particularly in one on a new pattern) perfection is an unattainable ideal. If in its future editions this work is to be less imperfect, the Editor must look to the goodwill of his readers to inform him of points needing correction.

There remains the happy task of expressing my own thanks, and also, I doubt not, those of future users of the *Dictionary*, to the very large company of those who in innumerable ways have contributed to its making. It is possible to mention by name only a few of them.

There are, first, my immediate associates. In the earliest stages of the work I had as a collaborator in the Editorship my then colleague the Rev. T. M. Parker, *cuius eruditionis fontes plurimi gustavimus exhausit nemo.*[1] Though he had a decisive formative influence on the *Dictionary*, he was, alas, soon compelled to withdraw by pressure of other work. At this period valuable assistance was also given by the Rev. H. J. Sutters who, among other labours, compiled the original list of entries. During several of the War years, when progress was necessarily slow, Miss Hilda C. Graef, now known

[1] Words originally applied to F. E. Brightman, an earlier Librarian of Pusey House, by C. H. Turner.

as the biographer of Therese Neumann and Edith Stein, drafted or revised a great number of the early entries; and it was to her, more than to anyone else, that the possession of a continuous first draft was due. In the herculean task of finally producing from a vast assemblage of material a work which had form, unity, and completeness, my principal debt is to Miss Elizabeth A. Livingstone. For over five years the *Dictionary* has engaged her devoted and untiring energies. No problem that arose could be allowed to rest until it had been pursued to its limits, whether by research, correspondence, or personal interviews, and in some cases by all three means; and in this connexion abundant thanks are also due to the large body of those who have generously responded to Miss Livingstone's inquiries. The drafting of the bibliographies is almost wholly due to the same collaborator. There are relatively few of the books or articles cited which Miss Livingstone has not handled, or, where this proved impossible, pursued to an unimpeachable source; and, it need hardly be said, there are a vast number of others which, though examined, have been passed by unrecorded, either through the exigencies of space or through their want of permanent interest. This task has involved the consultation of what must be almost, if not quite, a record number of books in public libraries; and it would be impossible not to mention our indebtedness to the staffs of the Bodleian Library and of the Reading Room of the British Museum, on whom the compilation of the *Dictionary* has imposed (in the literal sense as well as in others) many very heavy burdens. At the Bodleian Library, particular thanks are due to Mr. R. G. Chapman, M.A., Mr. R. J. Key, M.A., and Miss Angela M. Jackson.

At a comparatively early stage in the work, the Press invited Professor F. M. Powicke and the Rev. Professor S. L. Greenslade to report on and, as far as opportunity allowed, to read the proofs. Professor Powicke's valuable comments on the earlier drafts of the medieval articles preserved us from many pitfalls, while Professor Greenslade, who scrutinized the whole work, made innumerable suggestions which were of untold service. It must be insisted, however, that so many modifications have been made in the text since these two scholars concluded their task several years ago, that they must not be held in any way responsible for errors. In the later stages of the work much assistance was received with the medieval articles from Dr. R. W. Hunt, the Keeper of Western Manuscripts at the Bodleian Library, and, in the matter of the medieval bibliographies, from Dr. Daniel Callus, O.P. The Editor hopes that in consequence of this abundant assistance even specialists in medieval studies will find the work a useful reference book. In Semitic matters, where the Editor's own incompetence has made him much in need of guidance, he has also to thank Professors G. R. Driver, C. A. Simpson, and H. F. D. Sparks, and Mr. O. H. M. Lehmann for help on specific points.

A word of special thanks is due for help of another kind. With a generosity which would be unbelievable to those who do not know him, Mr. Samuel Gurney went through the whole of the galley proofs, almost line by line, assiduously checking references against standard works and producing lively comments and suggestions from his wide store of learning about all things ecclesiastical and unecclesiastical.

It need hardly be said that the production of the *Dictionary* has involved a great deal of typing and other secretarial work. Usually each article needed to be drafted many times before it was in the right form for the printer. In this connexion thanks are due to some of those already mentioned as well as to Miss G. I. Johns, to Mrs. M. Bridge, and to Mrs. J. Barnicoat, among others.

Finally, a word of thanks must be said to the Oxford University Press and their printers. The Editor had the good fortune to have a publisher with unique experience in Dictionaries. To learn that the construction of a dictionary is not the wholly humdrum task of Dr. Johnson's lexicographer, the reader need but turn to the fascinating Preface to the new *Liddell and Scott*. If the finished work is not quite the companionable and attractive book that I believe Mr. Cumberlege originally envisaged, this is because it became clear, as the work proceeded, that it was not within the present Editor's capacity to produce it. But I am grateful to him for his generous and continuous interest in the work until he retired from the Press last September, and also to all other members of the staff of Amen House who have been concerned with the *Dictionary* since its inception. The printers, Messrs. R. & R. Clark of Edinburgh, have earned the gratitude of the Press, the readers of the *Dictionary*, and myself by their patience and accuracy at every stage of the long and complicated process of production, and through them the Scottish, as well as the English, tradition of academic printing and publishing has contributed to this book.

F. L. CROSS

CHRIST CHURCH,
    OXFORD
  May 1957

NOTE TO SECOND IMPRESSION

In the event the *Dictionary* was published on 10 October last. I am grateful to the public for their generous reception of it and also to the many correspondents who have sent me, either personally or through the publishers, suggestions and lists of *corrigenda*. The urgent demand for a reprint, for which copy had to be sent to the printers in January and the proofs passed in March, will explain why certain matters raised by correspondents have had to be held over. The present reprint contains some bibliographical additions and a large number of corrections. Of the latter many are typographical and all but a few of a minor character.

F. L. C.

CHRIST CHURCH,
    OXFORD
  April 1958

NOTE TO FOURTH IMPRESSION

The present reprint contains two new entries, a number of bibliographical additions, mainly of recent publications, and some corrections of minor matters.

F. L. C.

CHRIST CHURCH,
    OXFORD
  April 1963

LIST OF CONTRIBUTORS

N. J. ABERCROMBIE, M.A., D.Phil., sometime Editor of the *Dublin Review*

The Rev. A. W. ADAMS, M.A., B.D., Fellow and Dean of Divinity, Magdalen College, Oxford

The Rev. J. BACKHOUSE, B.A., Maghull, Liverpool

The Rev. M. B. BANISTER, M.A., Vicar of Long Eaton, Derbys.

Miss R. BARBOUR, M.A., Assistant in the Department of Western Manuscripts, Bodleian Library, Oxford

The Rev. C. K. BARRETT, M.A., D.D., Senior Lecturer in Theology in the University of Durham

†The Rev. J. V. BARTLET, D.D., sometime Professor of Church History, Mansfield College, Oxford

Miss E. BLACKBURN, Wakefield

The Rev. ANDREW BLAIR, C.R., M.A., Prior of the House of the Resurrection, Mirfield

The Rev. H. S. BOX, B.D., Ph.D., Vicar of St. Barnabas, Bexhill

The Rev. H. R. T. BRANDRETH, Chaplain of St. George's Anglican Church, Paris

The Rev. DANIEL CALLUS, O.P., M.A., D.Phil., Blackfriars, Oxford

The Rev. A. C. CANNER, M.A., Vicar of Tintagel, Cornwall

The Rev. R. E. CANT, M.A., Canon Residentiary and Chancellor of York

The Rev. E. F. CARPENTER, M.A., B.D., Ph.D., Canon of Westminster

The Rt. Rev. H. J. CARPENTER, D.D., Lord Bishop of Oxford

The Rev. W. J. CRATCHLEY, M.A., D.D., Ph.D., Vicar of St. Mark's, Swindon, and Honorary Canon of Bristol

The Rev. F. L. CROSS, D.Phil., D.D., Lady Margaret Professor of Divinity and Canon of Christ Church, Oxford

The Rev. V. A. DEMANT, M.A., D.Litt., Regius Professor of Moral and Pastoral Theology and Canon of Christ Church, Oxford

The Rev. D. R. DENDY, M.A., B.D., Headmaster of the Cathedral Choir School, Oxford

A. G. DICKENS, M.A., Professor of History, University of Hull

The Rev. J. C. DICKINSON, M.A., B.Litt., Fellow and Chaplain of Pembroke College, Cambridge

The Rev. H. H. FARMER, M.A., D.D., Fellow of Peterhouse and Norris-Hulse Professor of Divinity, Cambridge

Mrs. RUTH FRAENKEL, Ph.D., Oxford.

†The Rev. R. S. FRANKS, M.A., D.Litt., sometime Principal of Western College, Bristol

Miss H. C. GRAEF, sometime Senior Assistant on the *Lexicon of Patristic Greek*, Oxford

The Rev. K. GRAYSTON, M.A., Professor in New Testament Language and Literature, Didsbury College, Bristol

The Rev. V. H. H. GREEN, M.A., B.D., Fellow and Chaplain of Lincoln College, Oxford

The Rev. S. L. GREENSLADE, D.D., Van Mildert Professor of Divinity and Canon of Durham

Miss E. M. GRINLING, M.A., Girton College, Cambridge

SAMUEL GURNEY, M.A., Trinity College, Oxford

The Rev. R. J. HAMMER, M.A., B.D., M.Th., Professor at Nippon Sei Ko Kwai Central Theological College, Tokyo

The Very Rev. F. P. HARTON, B.D., Dean of Wells

The Rev. J. P. HODGES, M.A., Rector of Streatham

The Rev. F. HOOD, M.A., Vicar of St. Mary Aldermary, London, and Canon of Monmouth

G. N. S. HUNT, M.A., Wadham College, Oxford

R. W. HUNT, M.A., D.Phil., Keeper of Western Manuscripts, Bodleian Library, and Fellow of Balliol College, Oxford

Mrs. H. T. JENKINS, M.A., B.Litt., Assistant Editor, *Victoria County History of Oxfordshire*

The Rev. S. A. C. JOHN, M.A., Vicar of St. Philip's, Sydenham

The Rev. E. W. KEMP, M.A., B.D., Fellow and Chaplain of Exeter College, Oxford, and Canon and Prebendary of Caistor in Lincoln Cathedral

LIST OF CONTRIBUTORS

†Sir FREDERIC KENYON, K.C.B., sometime Director and Principal Librarian, British Museum, London

The Rev. G. D. KILPATRICK, D.D., Dean Ireland's Professor of Exegesis of Holy Scripture, Oxford

The Rev. H. P. KINGDON, M.A., Vicar of Chewton Mendip, Som., and Lecturer at Wells Theological College

The Rev. GEORGE KNIGHT, M.A., Chaplain, R.N.

The Rev. H. KNIGHT, B.D., D.Phil., sometime Assistant Master, the King's School, Canterbury

The Rev. G. W. H. LAMPE, D.D., Edward Cadbury Professor of Theology, University of Birmingham

†The Rev. A. C. LAWSON, D.D., sometime Vicar of St. Michael's, Shrewsbury

O. H. M. LEHMANN, B.Litt., M.A., St. Catherine's Society, Oxford

Miss E. A. LIVINGSTONE, M.A., St. Anne's College, Oxford

The Rev. J. MACDONALD, M.A., Librarian of Pusey House, Oxford

D. M. MACKINNON, M.A., Regius Professor of Moral Philosophy, Aberdeen

The Rev. W. W. S. MARCH, M.A., B.D., Vicar of Eastbourne

The Rev. E. L. MASCALL, D.D., Student of Christ Church, Oxford

The Rev. R. L. P. MILBURN, M.A., Fellow and Chaplain of Worcester College, Oxford

The Rev. L. MINHINNICK, M.A., Vicar of St. Mark's, Birkenhead

The Rt. Rev. R. C. MORTIMER, D.D., Lord Bishop of Exeter

The Rev. C. B. MOSS, D.D., sometime Vice-Principal, St. Boniface College, Warminster.

The Rev. R. W. NICHOLLS, B.A., A.K.C., Vicar of St. Patrick's, Hove

The Rev. D. NICHOLSON, M.A., Vice-Principal of Edinburgh Theological College

The Rev. T. M. PARKER, D.D., Fellow and Chaplain of University College, Oxford

The Rev. E. A. PAYNE, D.D., General Secretary, Baptist Union of Great Britain and Ireland

†The Rev. A. F. SCOTT PEARSON, D.Litt., Professor of Ecclesiastical History and Symbolics, Presbyterian College, Belfast

Miss V. POHLE, Liverpool

Sir MAURICE POWICKE, M.A., D.Litt., sometime Regius Professor of Modern History, Oxford

†The Rev. G. L. PRESTIGE, D.D., sometime Canon and Treasurer of St. Paul's Cathedral, London

The Rev. A. A. H. RADICE, M.A., Rector of Hepworth, Suffolk

The Rev. E. C. RATCLIFF, M.A., Ely Professor of Divinity, Cambridge, and Canon of Ely

Miss M. E. REEVES, M.A., Fellow of St. Anne's College, Oxford

†The Rev. C. F. ROGERS, M.A., sometime Professor of Pastoral Theology, King's College, London

D. M. ROGERS, M.A., D.Phil., Assistant in the Department of Printed Books, Bodleian Library, Oxford

The Rev. H. P. SAUNDERS, M.A., sometime Principal of Ely Theological College and Canon of Ely

The Rt. Rev. J. L. SCHUSTER, M.A., Lord Bishop of St. John's, Kaffraria

†The Rev. W. B. SELBIE, D.D., sometime Principal of Mansfield College, Oxford

The Rev. E. N. C. SERGEANT, M.A., Vicar of Great and Little Tew, Oxon.

The Rev. C. A. SIMPSON, D.D., Regius Professor of Hebrew and Canon of Christ Church, Oxford

The Rev. C. D. SMITH, M.A., Vicar of St. Peter's, Streatham

The Rev. H. F. D. SPARKS, D.D., Oriel Professor of the Interpretation of Holy Scripture, Oxford

†The Rev. D. STONE, D.D., sometime Principal of Pusey House, and Honorary Canon of Christ Church, Oxford

The Rev. G. M. STYLER, M.A., Fellow of Corpus Christi College, Cambridge

The Rev. H. J. SUTTERS, M.A., Vicar of Coleford, Bath

The Rev. N. SYKES, D.Phil., D.D., Dixie Professor of Ecclesiastical History, Cambridge

The Rev. H. EDWARD SYMONDS, C.R., D.D., Mirfield

The Rev. J. P. THORNTON-DUESBERY, M.A., Master of St. Peter's Hall, Oxford

The Rev. H. E. W. TURNER, D.D., Lightfoot Professor of Divinity and Canon of Durham

LIST OF CONTRIBUTORS

K. C. TURPIN, B.Litt., M.A., Provost of Oriel College, Oxford

The Rev. A. R. VIDLER, Litt.D., Fellow and Dean of King's College, Cambridge

The Rev. F. E. VOKES, M.A., B.D., Professor of Theology and Hebrew, St. David's College, Lampeter

The Rev. H. K. WHITE, M.A., sometime Librarian of Pusey House, Oxford

The Rev. W. A. WHITEHOUSE, B.Litt., M.A., Reader in Divinity, University of Durham

The Rev. D. E. H. WHITELEY, M.A., Fellow and Chaplain of Jesus College, Oxford

†The Rev. W. T. WHITLEY, M.A., LL.D., sometime Principal of Melbourne Baptist College, Victoria, Australia.

The Rev. B. J. WIGAN, M.A., Rector of Little Berkhamsted, Herts

The Ven. C. WITTON-DAVIES, M.A., Archdeacon of Oxford

H. G. WOOD, D.D., sometime Professor of Theology, University of Birmingham

xii

ABBREVIATIONS

(A) The most common abbreviations, used throughout the book

AV   Authorized Version [i.e. King James Version, 1611].
BCP   Book of Common Prayer.
C of E   Church of England.
NT   New Testament.
OT   Old Testament.
RC   Roman Catholic.
RV   [English] Revised Version (NT, 1881 ; OT, 1885 ; Apocrypha, 1895).

An asterisk (*) preceding a word indicates a relevant article in the Dictionary under that (or a closely similar) heading.

It is recommended that the present Dictionary should be quoted as *O.D.C.C.*

(B) Further abbreviations, mainly bibliographical

[The editions mentioned are those cited in the *Dictionary*]

A.A.S.   *Acta Apostolicae Sedis* (Rome, 1909 ff.).

AA.SS.   **Acta Sanctorum* (Antwerp, 1643 ff.).

Abh. (Bayr.)   *Abhandlungen der philosophisch-philologischen (und historischen) Classe der (königlich) bayerischen Akademie der Wissenschaften* (Munich, 1835 ff.).

Abh. (Berl.)   *Abhandlungen der (königlichen) preussischen [from 1947 deutschen] Akademie der Wissenschaften* (Berlin, 1815–1907; philosoph.-hist. Kl., ib., 1908–49).

Abh. (Gött.)   *Abhandlungen der (königlichen) Gesellschaft (Academie) der Wissenschaften zu Göttingen.* Philolog.-hist. Kl., N.F. (Berlin, 1897 ff.).

Abh. (Sächs.)   *Abhandlungen der philologisch-historischen Classe der (königlich) sächsischen Gesellschaft (Akademie) der Wissenschaften* (Leipzig, 1850 ff.).

A.C.O.   *Acta Conciliorum Oecumenicorum*, ed. E. *Schwartz (Strassburg, 1914 ff.).

A.C.W.   Ancient Christian Writers. The Works of the Fathers in Translation, ed. J. Quasten–J. C. Plumpe (Westminster, Maryland–London, 1946 ff.).

A.F.H.   *Archivum Franciscanum Historicum* (Quaracchi, 1908 ff.).

A.H.M.A.   *Analecta Hymnica Medii Aevi*, ed. G. M. Dreves, S.J., and C. Blume, S.J. (55 vols., Leipzig, 1886–1922).

Altaner   B. Altaner, *Patrologie*. Leben, Schriften und Lehre der Kirchenväter (ed. 1950).

A.M.   **Hymns Ancient and Modern* (London, Standard Edition, 1916).

Anal. Boll.   *Analecta Bollandiana* (Paris and Brussels, 1882 ff.).

A.N.C.L.   Ante-Nicene Christian Library (Edinburgh, 1864 ff.).

A.S.S.   *Acta Sanctae Sedis* (41 vols., Rome, 1865–1908).

Bardenhewer i   O. *Bardenhewer, *Geschichte der altkirchlichen Literatur* i (ed. 2, 1913).
Bardenhewer ii O. *Bardenhewer, *Geschichte der altkirchlichen Literatur* ii (ed. 2, 1914).
Bardenhewer iii O. *Bardenhewer, *Geschichte der altkirchlichen Literatur* iii (ed. 1, 1912).
Bardenhewer iv O. *Bardenhewer, *Geschichte der altkirchlichen Literatur* iv (1924).
Bardenhewer v   O. *Bardenhewer, *Geschichte der altkirchlichen Literatur* v (1932).

Ber. (Sächs.)   *Berichte über die Verhandlungen der (königlich) sächsichen Gesellschaft (Akademie) der Wissenschaften zu Leipzig.* Philologisch-historische Classe (Leipzig, 1849 ff.).

Bettenson   H. Bettenson (ed.), *Documents of the Christian Church* (World's Classics, London, 1943). [Also publd., with different pagination, in Galaxy Edition, New York, 1947.]

xiii

B.G.P.M.	*Beiträge zur Geschichte der Philosophie des Mittelalters.* Texte und Untersuchungen, begründet von C. Baeumker. Münster i.W., 1891 ff. (Supplementbände, 1913 ff.).
B.H.G.	*Bibliotheca Hagiographica Graeca*, ediderunt Socii Bollandiani (ed. 2, Brussels, 1909).
B.H.L.	*Bibliotheca Hagiographica Latina Antiquae et Mediae Aetatis*, ediderunt Socii Bollandiani (Subsidia Hagiographica, vi ; 2 vols., Brussels, 1898–1901 ; +Supplement, ib., xii ; 1911).
B.H.O.	*Bibliotheca Hagiographica Orientalis*, ediderunt Socii Bollandiani (Subsidia Hagiographica, x ; Brussels, 1910).
Braun, A.G.	J. Braun, S.J., *Das christliche Altargerät* (1932).
Braun, C.A.	J. Braun, S.J., *Der christliche Altar* (2 vols., 1924).
Braun, L.G.	J. Braun, S.J., *Die liturgische Gewandung im Occident und Orient nach Ursprung und Entwicklung, Verwendung und Symbolik* (1907).
Braun, L.P.	J. Braun, S.J., *Die liturgischen Paramente in Gegenwart und Vergangenheit* (ed. 2, 1924).
Bremond	H. *Bremond, *Histoire littéraire du sentiment religieux en France depuis la fin des guerres de religion jusqu'à nos jours* (11 vols., 1916–33+ index, 1936).
Brightman, L.E.W.	F. E. *Brightman, *Liturgies Eastern and Western*, vol. i. Eastern (1896; all publd.).
B.Z.	*Byzantinische Zeitschrift* (Leipzig, 1892 ff.).
Camb. Bib.	The Cambridge Bible for Schools (1878–1936 ; R.V., 1903–30).
C. Anc. H.	*The Cambridge Ancient History*, ed. J. B. Bury, S. A. Cook, F. E. Adcock, M. P. Charlesworth, and N. H. Baynes (12 vols., 1923–39).
C.B.E.L.	*The Cambridge Bibliography of English Literature*, ed. F. W. Bateson (4 vols., Cambridge, 1940).
C.E.	*Catholic Encyclopedia* (15 vols. + Index, New York, 1907–14).
Cent. Bib.	The Century Bible, ed. W. F. Adeney (34 vols., Edinburgh, 1901–22).
C.G.T.	The Cambridge Greek Testament for Schools (and Colleges) [ed. J. J. S. Perowne and others (20 vols., Cambridge, 1881–1933)].
C.H.S.	*Church Historical Society.
C.I.C.	*Codex Iuris Canonici (1918).
Clar. Bib.	The Clarendon Bible (Oxford, 1922 ff.).
C. Med. H.	*Cambridge Medieval History*, planned by J. B. Bury, ed. H. M. Gwatkin, J. P. Whitney and others (8 vols., 1911–36, and vol. of maps, 1936).
C.M.H.	*Cambridge Modern History*, planned by Lord *Acton, ed. A. W. Ward, G. W. Prothero, and S. Leathes (12 vols., 1902–10+ index, 1911 and atlas, 1912).
C.Q.R.	*Church Quarterly Review* (London, 1875 ff.).
C.R.S.	*Catholic Record Society (London, 1905 ff.).
C.S.C.O.	Corpus Scriptorum Christianorum Orientalium (Paris, &c., 1903 ff.).
C.S.E.L.	Corpus Scriptorum Ecclesiasticorum Latinorum (Vienna, 1866 ff.).
C.S.H. Byz.	Corpus Scriptorum Historiae Byzantinae (49 vols., Bonn, 1828–78).
D.A.C.	*Dictionary of the Apostolic Church*, ed. J. *Hastings (2 vols., 1915–18).
D.A.C.L.	*Dictionnaire d'Archéologie Chrétienne et de Liturgie*, ed. F. *Cabrol, O.S.B., and H. *Leclercq, O.S.B. (15 vols., 1907–53).
Darlow–Moule	T .H. Darlow–H. F. Moule, *Historical Catalogue of the Printed Editions of Holy Scripture in the Library of the British and Foreign Bible Society* (2 vols. bound in 4, 1905–11).
D.C.A.	*Dictionary of Christian Antiquities*, ed. W. Smith and S. Cheetham (2 vols., 1875–80).
D.C.B.	*Dictionary of Christian Biography*, ed. W. Smith and H. Wace (4 vols., 1877–87).
D.C.G.	*Dictionary of Christ and the Gospels*, ed. J. *Hastings (2 vols., 1906–8).
D.D.C.	*Dictionnaire de Droit Canonique*, ed. R. Naz (1935 ff.).
D.E.C.H.	*Dictionary of English Church History*, ed. S. L. Ollard and G. Crosse (1912).
D.E.C.H. (ed. 3, 1948)	*Dictionary of English Church History*, ed. 3 by S. L. Ollard, G. Crosse, and M. F. Bond (1948).

Dekkers	E. Dekkers, O.S.B.–A. Gaar (edd.), *Clavis Patrum Latinorum qua in novum Corpus Christianorum edendum Optimas quasque Scriptorum Recensiones . . . recludit* (Sacris Eruditi, iii ; Sint Pietersabdij, Steenbrugge, 1951).
Denz.–Bann.	H. Denzinger, *Enchiridion Symbolorum Definitionum et Declarationum de Rebus Fidei et Morum,* ed. 28 after that of C. Bannwart, S.J., and I. B. Umberg, S.J., by C. Rahner, S.J. (Freiburg i.Br., 1952).
D.H.G.E.	*Dictionnaire d'Histoire et de Géographie Ecclésiastiques,* ed. A. Baudrillart and others (1912 ff.).
Dict. Amer. Biog.	*Dictionary of American Biography,* published under the Auspices of the American Council of Learned Societies, ed. A. Johnson and others (20 vols., 1928–36 + index, 1937, and Supplement, 1944).
Dict. Bibl.	*Dictionnaire de la Bible,* ed. F. Vigouroux, P.S.S. (5 vols., 1895–1912).
Dict. Bibl., Suppl.	*Dictionnaire de la Bible,* Supplément ed. L. Pirot (1928 ff.).
Dict. Sp.	*Dictionnaire de Spiritualité,* ed. M. Viller, S.J., and others (1937 ff.).
D.N.B.	*Dictionary of National Biography,* founded by G. Smith, ed. L. Stephen and S. Lee (63 vols., 1885–1900). [Also repr., with some corrections, in 21 vols., 1908–9.]
D.N.B., Suppl.	*Dictionary of National Biography,* Supplement, ed. S. Lee (3 vols., 1901). [Also repr. in 1 vol., 1909.]
D.N.B., 1901–1911	*Dictionary of National Biography, Supplement January 1901–December 1911,* ed. S. Lee (3 vols., 1912).
D.N.B., 1912–1921	*Dictionary of National Biography, 1912–1921,* ed. H. W. C. Davis and J. R. H. Weaver (1927).
D.N.B., 1922–1930	*Dictionary of National Biography, 1922–1930,* ed. J. R. H. Weaver (1937).
D.N.B., 1931–1940	*Dictionary of National Biography, 1931–1940,* ed. L. G. Wickham Legg (1949).
D.N.B., 1941–1950	*Dictionary of National Biography, 1941–1950,* ed. L. G. Wickham Legg and E. T. Williams (1959).
D.T.C.	*Dictionnaire de Théologie Catholique,* ed. A. Vacant, E. Mangenot, and É. Amann (15 vols., 1903–50).
Duchesne	[see *L.P.*].
E.B. (ed. 11)	*Encyclopaedia Britannica,* ed. 11 (28 vols. and Index, 1910–11).
E.Bi.	*Encyclopaedia Biblica,* ed. T. K. Cheyne and J. S. Black (4 vols., 1899–1903).
E.C.	*Enciclopedia Cattolica,* ed. P. Paschini and others (12 vols., 1949–54).
E.E.T.S.	Early English Text Society (London, 1894 ff.).
E.H.	Exegetisches Handbuch zum Alten Testament, ed. J. Nickel (Münster i.W., 1911 ff.).
E.H.	*English Hymnal (London, 1906).
E.H.R.	*English Historical Review* (London, 1886 ff.).
E.J.	*Encyclopaedia Judaica,* ed. J. Klatzkin and others (10 vols., Berlin, 1928–34).
E.L.	*Ephemerides Liturgicae* (Rome, 1887 ff.).
É.O.	*Échos d'Orient* (Paris, 39 vols., 1897–1942).
E.O.M.I.A.	*Ecclesiae Occidentalis Monumenta Iuris Antiquissima,* ed. C. H. *Turner (Oxford, 1899 ff.).
Fliche–Martin	A. Fliche–V. Martin (edd.), *Histoire de l'Église depuis les origines jusqu'à nos jours* (Paris, 1935 ff.).
G.C.S.	Die griechischen christlichen Schriftsteller der ersten drei Jahrhunderte (Leipzig, 1897–1941; Berlin and Leipzig, 1953; Berlin, 1954 ff.).
Gee–Hardy	H. Gee–W. J. Hardy (edd.), *Documents Illustrative of English Church History* (1896).
Gel. Anz. (Gött.)	*Göttingische gelehrte Anzeigen unter der Aufsicht der (königl.) Gesellschaft (Academie) der Wissenschaften* (Göttingen, 1884 ff.).
Hardouin	J. *Hardouin [Harduinus], *Acta Conciliorum et Epistolae Decretales, ac Constitutiones Summorum Pontificum* (12 vols., Paris, '1714–15').
Hardy	T. D. Hardy, *Descriptive Catalogue of Materials Relating to the History of Great Britain and Ireland to the End of the Reign of Henry VII* (3 vols. bound in 4, Rolls Series, 1862–71).
H.A.T.	Handbuch zum Alten Testament, ed. O. Eissfeldt (Tübingen, 1934 ff.).

Hb.N.T.	Handbuch zum Neuen Testament, begründet von H. *Lietzmann (1908 ff.).
H.B.S.	*Henry Bradshaw Society (1891 ff.).
H.D.B.	J. *Hastings (ed.), *Dictionary of the Bible* (4 vols., 1898–1902, with extra vol., 1904).
H.E.	*Historia Ecclesiastica.*
Hefele–Leclercq	C. J. *Hefele (tr. into Fr. by H. *Leclercq, O.S.B.), *Histoire des conciles d'après les documents originaux* (1907 ff.).
Heimbucher	M. Heimbucher, *Die Orden und Kongregationen der katholischen Kirche*, i (ed. 3, 1933), ii (1934).
H.E.R.E.	J. *Hastings (ed.), *Encyclopaedia of Religion and Ethics* (12 vols. + Index, 1908–26).
Hist. J.	*Historisches Jahrbuch* (Münster i.W., 1880–82; Munich, 1883–1930; Cologne, 1931–50; Munich and Freiburg i.Br., 1950 ff.).
H.K.A.T.	Handkommentar zum Alten Testament, ed. W. Nowack (18 vols., Göttingen, 1892–1933).
H.T.R.	*Harvard Theological Review* (New York, 1908 f.; Cambridge, Mass., 1910 ff.).
H.T.S.	Harvard Theological Studies (Cambridge, Mass., 1916 ff.).
H.U.L.	Home University Library (London, 1911 ff.).
H.Z.	*Historische Zeitschrift* (Munich, &c., 1859 ff.).
I.C.C.	International Critical Commentary (London, 1895 ff.).
I.L.S.	*Inscriptiones Latinae Selectae*, ed. H. Dessau (3 vols. in 5, Berlin, 1892–1916).
Jaffé	P. Jaffé, *Regesta Pontificum Romanorum ab Condita Ecclesia ad Annum post Christum Natum MCXCVIII*, ed. 2 by G. Wattenbach (2 vols., Leipzig, 1885–8).
J.E.	*Jewish Encyclopedia*, ed. I. Singer and others (12 vols., New York and London, 1901–6).
J.E.H.	*Journal of Ecclesiastical History* (London, 1950 ff.).
J.L.W.	*Jahrbuch für Liturgiewissenschaft* (Münster i.W., 1921–41).
J.Q.R.	*Jewish Quarterly Review* (London, 1888–1908; Philadelphia, 1910 ff.).
J.T.S.	*Journal of Theological Studies* (London, 1900–5; Oxford, 1906–49; N.S., Oxford, 1950 ff.).
Jungmann (1952)	J. A. Jungmann, S.J., *Missarum Sollemnia*. Eine genetische Erklärung der römischen Messe (2 vols., ed. 1952).
Jungmann (Eng. tr.)	J. A. Jungmann, S.J., *The Mass of the Roman Rite* (Eng. tr. of preceding, 2 vols., New York, 1951–5).
K.A.T.	Kommentar zum Alten Testament, ed. E. Sellin (Leipzig, 1913 ff.).
K.E.H.	Kurzgefasstes exegetisches Handbuch zum Alten Testament (Leipzig, 1838 ff.).
K.E.K.	Kritisch-exegetischer Kommentar über das Neue Testament, ed. H. A. W. *Meyer (16 vols., Göttingen, 1832–52; Eng. tr., 20 vols., 1873–95; also subsequent edd.).
K.H.A.T.	Kurzer Hand-Commentar zum Alten Testament, ed. K. Marti (21 vols., Freiburg i.B., 1897–1906).
Kidd	B. J. Kidd (ed.), *Documents Illustrative of the Continental Reformation* (1911).
Krumbacher	K. Krumbacher, *Geschichte der byzantinischen Literatur von Justinian bis zum Ende des oströmischen Reiches, 527–1453* (ed. 2, 1897).
L.A.C.T.	*Library of Anglo-Catholic Theology (97 vols., Oxford, 1841–63).
Latourette	K. S. Latourette, *History of the Expansion of Christianity* (7 vols., New York and London, 1938–45).
Lauchert	F. Lauchert, *Die Kanones der wichtigsten altkirchlichen Concilien* (1896).
L.F.	*Library of the Fathers (43 vols., Oxford, 1838–74).
L.L.E.	Library of Liturgiology and Ecclesiology for English Readers, ed. V. Staley.
Loeb	Loeb Classical Library (London and Cambridge, Mass., 1912 ff.).

L.P. (Duchesne)	Le *Liber Pontificalis*, ed. L. *Duchesne (Bibliothèque des Écoles Françaises d'Athènes et de Rome, 2 vols., 1886–92).
L.Th.K.	Lexikon für Theologie und Kirche, ed. M. Buchberger (10 vols., 1930–1938).
McNeile	A. H. McNeile, *An Introduction to the Study of the New Testament* (ed. 2 by C. S. C. Williams, 1953).
Mai, *N.P.B.*	A. *Mai (ed.), *Nova Patrum Bibliotheca* (8 vols., Rome, 1844–71).
Mai, *S.R.*	A. *Mai (ed.), *Spicilegium Romanum* (10 vols., Rome, 1839–44).
Mai, *S.V.N.C.*	A. *Mai (ed.), *Scriptorum Veterum Nova Collectio e Vaticanis Codicibus edita* (10 vols., Rome, 1825–38).
Manitius	M. Manitius, *Geschichte der lateinischen Literatur des Mittelalters* (Handbuch der klassischen Altertumswissenschaft, ed. I. von Müller, ix, Abt. 2, 3 vols., 1911–31).
Mann	H. K. Mann, *The Lives of the Popes in the (Early) Middle Ages* (18 vols., bound in 19, 1902–32).
Mansi	J. D. *Mansi, *Sacrorum Conciliorum Nova et Amplissima Collectio* (31 vols., Florence, 1759–98).
M.G.H.	Monumenta Germaniae Historica.
Mirbt	C. Mirbt, *Quellen zur Geschichte des Papsttums und des römischen Katholizismus* (ed. 4, 1924).
Moff. Comm.	The Moffatt Commentaries.
N.A.	*Neues Archiv der Gesellschaft für ältere deutsche Geschichtskunde zur Beförderung einer Gesammtausgabe der Quellenschriften deutscher Geschichte des Mittelalters* (Hanover, 1876–1922; Berlin, 1922–35).
Nachr. (Gött.)	*Nachrichten von der (königlichen) Gesellschaft (Academie) der Wissenschaften zu Göttingen.* Philolog.-hist. Kl. (Göttingen, 1894 ff.).
N.F.	Neue Folge.
N.P.B.	[see Mai.].
N.P.N.C.F.	Nicene and Post-Nicene Christian Fathers (New York, 1887–92 ; Oxford, 1890–1900).
N.S.	New Series.
O.C.	*Oriens Christianus* (Leipzig, 1901 ff. For details see p. 991).
O.C.D.	*The Oxford Classical Dictionary*, ed. M. Cary–J. D. Denniston–J. W. Duff–A. D. Nock–H. H. Scullard (1949).
O.C.P.	*Orientalia Christiana Periodica* (Rome, 1935 ff.).
O.E.D.	*A New [Oxford] English Dictionary on Historical Principles* founded mainly on the Materials collected by The Philological Society, ed. J. A. H. Murray–H. Bradley–W. A. Craigie–C. T. Onions (10 vols. + supplement, 1884–1933).
O.H.S.	Oxford Historical Society (Oxford, 1885 ff.).
Pastor	L. *Pastor, *The History of the Popes from the Close of the Middle Ages*, Eng. tr. (40 vols., 1891–1954).
P.B.D. (1912)	*Prayer Book Dictionary*, ed. G. Harford, M. Stevenson, and J. W. Tyrer (1912).
P.B.D. (1925)	*Prayer Book Dictionary*, ed. G. Harford, M. Stevenson, and J. W. Tyrer (ed. 1925).
PG	*Patrologia Graeca*, ed. J. P. *Migne (162 vols., Paris, 1857–66).
PL	*Patrologia Latina*, ed. J. P. *Migne (221 vols., Paris, 1844–64).
P.O.	*Patrologia Orientalis*, ed. R. Graffin and F. Nau (Paris, 1907 ff.).
Pourrat	P. Pourrat, P.S.S., *La Spiritualité chrétienne* (4 vols., 1918–28).
P.R.E. (ed. 3)	*Realencyklopädie für protestantische Theologie und Kirche*, begründet von J. J. Herzog, ed. 3 by A. Hauck (21 vols., 1898–1908 + Register, 1909, and Ergänzungen und Nachträge, 2 vols., 1913).
P.W.	A. Pauly, *Real-Encyclopädie der classichen Altertumswissenschaft*, ed. G. Wissowa (1893 ff.).
Quétif–Échard	J. Quétif, O.P.–J. Échard, O.P., *Scriptores Ordinis Praedicatorum Recensiti* (2 vols., Paris, 1719–21).
Raby	F. J. E. Raby, *A History of Christian Latin Poetry from the Beginnings to the Close of the Middle Ages* (1927).

Raby (1953)	F. J. E. Raby, *A History of Christian Latin Poetry from the Beginnings to the Close of the Middle Ages* (ed. 2, 1953).
R.A.C.	*Reallexikon für Antike und Christentum*. Sachwörterbuch zur Auseinandersetzung des Christentums mit der antiken Welt in Verbindung mit F. J. Dölger–H. Lietzmann und unter besonderer Mitwirkung von J. H. Waszink–L. Wenger herausgegeben von T. Klauser (Stuttgart, 1950 ff.).
R. Bén.	*Revue Bénédictine* (vols. i–v publ. under the title *Le Messager des Fidèles*; Lille and Bruges, 1884; Maredsous, 1885 ff.).
R. Bibl.	*Revue Biblique* (Paris, 1892 ff.).
Rech. S.R.	*Recherches de Science Religieuse* (Paris, 1910 ff.).
Rev. S.R.	*Revue des Sciences Religieuses* (Paris, 1921 f.; Strassburg and Paris, 1923 f.; Strassburg, 1925 ff.).
R.G.G.	*Die Religion in Geschichte und Gegenwart*, ed. 2 by H. Gunkel and L. Zscharnack (5 vols., 1927–31).
R.H.	*Revue Historique* (Paris, 1876 ff.).
R.H.E.	*Revue d'Histoire Ecclésiastique* (Louvain, 1900 ff.).
R.H.P.R.	*Revue d'Histoire et de Philosophie religieuses* (Strassburg, 1921–4; Strassburg–Paris, 1925–49; Paris, 1950 ff.).
Riv. A.C.	*Rivista di Archeologia Cristiana* (Rome, 1924 ff.).
Rohault	C. Rohault de Fleury, *La Messe*. Études archéologiques sur ses monuments (8 vols., 1883–9).
R.Q.	*Römische Quartalschrift für die christliche Alterthumskunde und für Kirchengeschichte* (47 vols., Rome, 1887–1937 + 28 Supplementhefte, 1893–1931).
R.Q.H.	*Revue des Questions Historiques* (Paris, 1866–1933; Blois, 1933; Paris, 1934; Blois, 1935 f.; Bourges, 1937 ff.).
R.S.P.T.	*Revue des Sciences Philosophiques et Théologiques* (Kain–Paris, 1907–12; Paris, 1913 ff.).
R.T.A.M.	*Recherches de Théologie Ancienne et Médiévale* (Louvain, 1929 ff.).
Sb. (Bayr.)	*Sitzungsberichte der (königlich) bayerischen Akademie der Wissenschaften (zu München)* (Munich, 1860–71; philosoph.-philolog. und hist. Cl., 1871–1930; philosoph.-hist. Abt. 1930 ff.).
Sb. (Berl.)	*Sitzungsberichte der (königlichen) preussischen [from 1948 deutschen] Akademie der Wissenschaften zu Berlin* (Berlin, 1882–1921; philosoph. hist. Kl., 1922–49).
Sb. (Heid.)	*Sitzungsberichte der Heidelberger Akademie der Wissenschaften. Philosoph.-hist. Kl.* (Heidelberg, 1910 ff.).
Sb. (Wien)	*Sitzungsberichte der (kaiserlichen) Akademie der Wissenschaften (in Wien)*. Hist.-philolog. or Philolog.-hist. Kl. (Vienna, 1848 ff.).
S.C.	*Sources Chrétiennes* (Paris, 1940 ff.).
Schottenloher	K. Schottenloher, *Bibliographie zur deutschen Geschichte im Zeitalter der Glaubensspaltung, 1517–1585* (6 vols., 1933–40).
Sommervogel	Augustin de Backer, S.J.–Aloys de Backer, S.J.–A. Carayon, S.J., *Bibliothèque de la Compagnie de Jésus*, ed. C. Sommervogel, S.J. (10 vols., 1890–1909).
S.P.C.K.	Society for Promoting Christian Knowledge. (See p. 1278 f.)
S.P.G.	Society for the Propagation of the Gospel. (See p. 1280.)
S.R.	[see Mai].
S.S.L.	*Spicilegium Sacrum Lovaniense*. Études et documents (Louvain, 1922 ff.).
S.T.	*Studi e Testi* (Rome, 1900 ff.).
Stammler	W. Stammler and others (edd.), *Die Deutsche Literatur des Mittelalters*. Verfasserlexikon (5 vols., 1933–55).
S.V.N.C.	[see Mai.]
Teub.	*Bibliotheca Scriptorum Graecorum et Romanorum Teubneriana* (Leipzig, 1849 ff.).
Th.Q.	*Theologische Quartalschrift* (Tübingen, 1831–1928; various places 1929 ff.).
T.L.S.	*The Times Literary Supplement* (London, 1902 ff.).

T.L.Z.	*Theologische Literaturzeitung* (Leipzig, 1876 ff. + Bibliographisches Beiblatt, ib., 1922 ff.).
T.U.	**Texte und Untersuchungen zur Geschichte der altchristlichen Literatur*, begründet von O. von Gebhardt und A. *Harnack (Leipzig, 1882 ff.).
Turner	[see *E.O.M.I.A.*].
T.W.B.	*Theologisches Wörterbuch zum Neuen Testament*, ed. G. Kittel (1933 ff.).
Überweg i	F. Überweg, *Grundriss der Geschichte der Philosophie* i (ed. 12 by K. Praechter, 1926).
Überweg ii	F. Überweg, *Grundriss der Geschichte der Philosophie* ii (ed. 11 by B. Geyer, 1928).
Überweg iii	F. Überweg, *Grundriss der Geschichte der Philosophie* iii (ed. 12 by M. Frischeisen-Köhler and W. Moog, 1924).
Überweg iv	F. Überweg, *Grundriss der Geschichte der Philosophie* iv (ed. 12 by T. K. Oesterreich, 1923).
Überweg v	F. Überweg, *Grundriss der Geschichte der Philosophie* v (ed. 12 by T. K. Oesterreich, 1928).
V.C.	*Vigiliae Christianae.* A Review of early Christian Life and Language (Amsterdam, 1947 ff.).
V.C.H.	*Victoria County History* (London, 1900 ff.).
Vulg. *or* Vg.	*Vulgate.
West. Comm.	Westminster Commentaries [until 1903, ' Oxford Commentaries '], ed. W. *Lock, &c. (London, 1899 ff.).
Z.A.T.W.	*Zeitschrift für die alttestamentliche Wissenschaft (und die Kunde des nachbiblischen Judentums)* (Giessen, 1881–1932; Berlin, 1933 ff. + Beihefte, Giessen, 1896–1934, Berlin, 1936 ff.).
Z.K.G.	*Zeitschrift für Kirchengeschichte* (Gotha, 1877–1930, Stuttgart, 1931 ff.).
Z.K.T.	*Zeitschrift für katholische Theologie* (Innsbruck, 1877–1940; Vienna, 1947 ff.).
Z.N.T.W.	*Zeitschrift für die neutestamentliche Wissenschaft und die Kunde des Urchristentums* (Giessen, 1900–32; Berlin, 1933 ff. + Beihefte, Giessen, 1923–34; Berlin, 1936 ff.).

(C) Biblical Books

OT : Gen., Exod., Lev., Num., Deut., Jos., Jgs., Ruth, 1, 2 Sam. (=1, 2 Reg., Vulg.), 1, 2 Kgs. (=3, 4 Reg., Vulg.), 1, 2 Chron. (=1, 2 Paralip., Vulg.), Ez. (=1 Esd., Vulg.), Neh. (=2 Esd., Vulg.), Est., Job, Pss., Prov., Eccles., Song of Songs (=Cant., Vulg.), Is. (=Es., Vulg.) .Jer., Lam., Ezek., Dan., Hos., Joel, Am., Obad., Jon., Mic., Nah., Hab., Zeph., Hag. Zech., Mal.

Apocrypha : 1, 2 Esd. (=3, 4 Esd., Vulg.), Tob., Judith, Rest of Est., Wisd. Sol., Ecclus. (=Sirach), Bar., S. of III Ch., Sus., Bel, Pr. Man., 1, 2 Macc.

NT : Mt., Mk., Lk., Jn. Acts, Rom., 1, 2 Cor., Gal., Eph., Phil., Col., 1, 2 Thess., 1, 2 Tim., Tit., Philem., Heb., Jas., 1, 2 Pet., 1, 2, 3 Jn., Jude, Rev. (=Apoc., Vulg.)

A

AARON. In Hebrew tradition *Moses' brother. He is first mentioned in the narrative of Moses' vision on Mt. Horeb (Ex. 4.14), when Jehovah assigns him to Moses as his assistant. Jehovah afterwards appointed him and his descendants to be priests (Ex. 28 and 29; Num. 8 and 18), an office he kept despite his share in setting up the golden calf (Ex. 32. 1–6). The power of his priestly intercession is emphasized in the story of his staying a plague (Num. 16. 43–8), and his authority is miraculously confirmed by the budding rod (Num. 17. 1–8). Aaron's priesthood, whose chief function was the offering of acceptable sacrifice to God, gave him a unique position. He was the head of his sons and the Levites; he alone offered incense in the Holy of Holies and mediated between God and the people; and, like a king, he was anointed and crowned with diadem and tiara. (Ex. 28). He is thus in Christian theology a type of Christ. This conception of Aaron as at once foreshadowing and being replaced by Him is worked out in the Ep. to the Hebrews, where the superiority of the perfect sacrifice of Calvary to the animal sacrifices of the Aaronic priesthood is established. For critical theories on the growth of the Aaronic priesthood, see modern works on the OT.

R. H. *Kennett, 'The Origin of the Aaronite Priesthood', in *J.T.S.*. vi (1904–5), pp. 161–86. See also A. H. McNeile, ib., vii (1905–6), pp. 1–9, and R. H. Kennett, ib., pp. 620–4.

ABAILARD. See *Abelard*.

ABBA. The Aramaic word for 'Father'. It occurs three times in the NT, Mk. 14. 36, Rom. 8. 15, and Gal. 4. 6, in each case with its Greek equivalent ('Αββᾶ, ὁ Πατήρ, 'Abba, Father').

ABBÉ. A French term, originally restricted to the *abbot of a monastery, but in modern times applied to every person wearing secular ecclesiastical dress. The extension of meaning took place in the 16th cent., when the Concordat of 1516 authorized Francis I to nominate secular priests abbots 'in *commendam'. As the number of nominations far exceeded the abbacies available, many 'abbés', who often were not even in major orders, devoted themselves to other work, e.g. educational and literary pursuits, whence the term was transferred to secular clerics in general. To-day such clerics are correctly addressed as 'M. l'Abbé'.

ABBESS. The superior of certain communities of nuns following the *Benedictine rule, though the title is extended to the superiors of orders of *canonesses and (esp.) to those of the Second *Franciscan Order. The earliest known use of the title (Lat. *abbatissa*) is in a sepulchral inscription (514) on the site of an ancient convent near the basilica of St. Agnes extra muros at *Rome. A nun must now be forty years of age and ten years professed before she can be elected. She then receives the same episcopal benediction as an abbot, though this cannot in her case convey any power resembling that of the keys. Except in the Franciscan Order, the office is held for life and confers the right to the ring and staff. In the Middle Ages wide powers were claimed by certain abbesses, e.g. the Abbess of Conversano on election, vested in a mitre, received the homage of the local clergy, while *Innocent III had to forbid the Abbesses of Burgos and Palentia from hearing the confessions of their nuns. In England abbesses attended councils on several occasions, e.g. St. *Hilda was present at *Whitby in 664. The Council of *Trent put an end to most special prerogatives, and now Canon Law (C.I.C., can. 535) subordinates the abbess in certain respects to the bishop of the diocese.

A. Tamburinius, O.S.B., *De Jure Abbatissarum et Monialium* (Rome, 1638). Eileen Power, *Medieval English Nunneries*, c. 1275 to 1535 (1922), pp. 42–95. K. H. Schäfer, *Die Kanonissenstifter im deutschen Mittelalter* (Kirchenrechtliche Abhandlungen, Hftt. 43–4; 1907), pp. 140–5. Pie de Langogne, O.F.M.Cap., in *D.T.C.*, i (1903) cols. 17–22, s.v. 'Abbesses'; F. Oliger, O.F.M., in *E.C.*, i (1948), cols. 17–19, s.v. 'Abbadessa'. J. Baucher, O.S.B., in *D.D.C.*, i (1935), cols. 62–71, s.v. 'Abbesses'.

ABBO, St. (c. 945–1004), otherwise 'Abbon', Abbot of *Fleury. He was born nr. Orleans, entered the Benedictine abbey of Fleury, and studied at *Paris, *Reims, and Fleury. From 985 to 987 he was in charge of studies at the monastery school of Ramsey, at the same time helping *Oswald, Abp. of *York, in the restoration of monasticism in England. He was elected Abbot of Fleury in 988. He supported the *Cluniac Reform and was an ardent defender of Papal authority and of the freedom of the monasteries from both episcopal and secular interference. He was killed in a revolt occasioned by the reform of the priory of La Réole in Gascony. His correspondence is a valuable source for the relations between France and the Papacy during the reign of Robert the Pious. He also issued writings on mathematics and astronomy and an Epitome of the Lives of the Popes. Feast day, 13 Nov.

Works and Letters in J. P. Migne, *PL*, cxxxix, 417–578 (incomplete). The principal authority is the Vita by a monk Aimonus repr. from the *Acta Sanctorum Ordinis Sancti Benedicti* in J. P. Migne, l.c., 375–414. J. B. Pardiac, *Histoire de Saint Abbon, Abbé de Fleury-sur-Loire* (1872). H. Bradley, 'On the Text of Abbo of Fleury's *Quaestiones Grammaticales*' in *Proceedings of the British Academy*, x (1921–3), pp. 173–80; A. Van de Vyver, 'Les Œuvres inédites d'Abbon de Fleury' in *R.Bén.*, xlvii (1935), pp. 125–69. A. Fliche, *La Réforme grégorienne*, i (S.S.L. vi; 1924), pp. 47–60. U. Berlière, O.S.B., in *D.H.G.E.*, i (1912), cols. 49–51, s.v. 'Abbon de Fleury', with details of his works and edd. of them. A. Amanieu in *D.D.C.*, i (1935), cols. 71–6, s.v. 'Abbon de Fleury'.

ABBOT (from Syriac *Abba*, i.e. Father; Lat. *Abbas*). In the W. Church it is the official title of the superior of a large religious house belonging either to one of the orders of the *Benedictine family (e.g. *Cistercian and *Trappists) or to certain orders of *Canons Regular (e.g. Canons Regular of the *Lateran and *Premonstratensians). Acc. to the Rule of St. *Benedict, the abbot is to be regarded as the father of his monastic family, and as such has far-reaching powers in the government of his house, the rules of which he may regulate in accordance with the needs of climate, customs of the times, &c. He is elected, normally for life, by the monks of his abbey, but in the Middle Ages temporal rulers frequently usurped the right of appointment. Within three months of his election he must receive a solemn benediction (C.I.C., can. 625), regarded as a *sacramental, acc. to his status either from the diocesan bishop, or, if he is an 'Abbot *nullius', from any bishop, or, in the case of some privileged abbeys, from another abbot. Most abbots are 'abbates regiminis', i.e. they are entrusted with the government of their monastery and exempt from episcopal jurisdiction. The 'abbates nullius [*sc*. dioecesis]' have either episcopal jurisdiction in their territory, or at least special privileges in the administration of the Sacraments, e.g. they may confer *confirmation and *minor orders in their territory, whereas the 'abbates regiminis' may give the tonsure and confer minor orders only on the professed monks of their houses. The 'titular abbots' hold the title of an abbey no longer in existence, and exercise none of the functions of an abbot. The insignia of office are the same as those of a bishop, viz. *mitre, *crozier, *ring, &c. They are old privileges that gradually came into use from the beginning of the Middle Ages, as was also their assistance at Church Councils (since the 8th Council of *Toledo in 653). The ancient distinction between mitred abbots (in pre-Reformation England, peers of Parliament) and others therefore does not now exist. The superiors of certain prominent monasteries have the name of 'Archabbot', and, in addition, the presiding abbot of a *Congregation (q.v.) is often known as the 'Abbot President' or 'Abbot General'. Since 1893 the Benedictine Order has had an 'Abbot Primate' who presides over the whole order. In the RC Church the election, rights, and duties of abbots are regulated by canon law (C.I.C., esp. cans. 319–27). The corresponding rank in the E. Church is *Hegoumen or *Archimandrite (q.v.).

Chs. 2, 3, 46, and 64 of the 'Rule of St. Benedict' are esp. concerned with the Abbot; Comm. on the rule by P. Delatte, O.S.B. (Eng. tr. by J. McCann, O.S.B., 1921), pp. 35–60, 358–60, 441–55 and passim; see also other comm. to rule cited under *Benedict, St., Rule of*. A. Tamburinius, O.S.B., *De Iure Abbatum* (3 vols., Lyons, 1640). F. A. *Gasquet, *English Monastic Life* (The Antiquary's Books, 1904), pp. 42–52; [E.] C. Butler, O.S.B., *Benedictine Monachism* (1919), pp. 184–99; [M.] D. Knowles, O.S.B., *The Monastic Order in England* (1940), esp. pp. 395–410. F. Chamard, O.S.B., 'Les Abbés au moyen-âge' in *R.Q.H.*, xxxiii (1885), pp. 71–108. Pie de Langogne, O.F.M.Cap., in *D.T.C.*, i (1903), cols. 10–17, s.v. 'Abbés', with reff. and bibl.; G. Creusen, S.J., J. Monay, O.F.M., F. M. Cappello, S.J., in *E.C.*, i (1949), cols. 9–15, s.v. 'Abate', with bibl. J. M. Besse in *D.A.C.L.*, i (1907), cols. 39–42, s.v. 'Abbé'. J. Baucher, O.S.B., in *D.D.C.*, i (1935), cols. 29–62, s.v. 'Abbés'.

ABBOT OF MISRULE. See *Misrule, Lord of*.

ABBOT, EZRA (1819–84), Biblical scholar. A native of Maine, U.S.A., and a *Unitarian by belief, in 1856 he became assistant librarian at Harvard university and in 1872 professor of NT at the Harvard divinity school. In 1871 he was appointed one of the original members of the American NT Revision Company in charge of the *RV, where his judgement exercised great influence. Several of his textual researches were incorporated into C. R. *Gregory's *Prolegomena* (1890) to the 8th (last) edition of C. *Tischendorf's Greek NT. Though extreme care for detail much restricted the extent of his own publications, his work bore fruit in the writings of many others, who sought his assistance. His other writings included 'The Authorship of the Fourth Gospel. External Evidences', an able defence of the Johannine authorship in the *Unitarian Review* (1880), and a very thorough discussion of the punctuation of Rom. 9. 5 in the *Journal of the Society of Biblical Literature and Exegesis* for 1883. These items, as well as several other of his papers, were reprinted after his death in *Critical Essays* (1888).

Ezra Abbot (Cambridge, Mass., 1884), with pref. by S. J. Barrows, addresses by J. H. Thayer (pp. 28–60) and others, memorial tributes, short biogr. note (p. 7), and list of Abbot's publications (pp. 69–73). B. W. Bacon in *Dict. Amer. Biog.* (1928), p. 10 f.

ABBOT, GEORGE (1562–1633), Abp. of *Canterbury. A native of Guildford, he was educated and later taught at Balliol College, Oxford. In 1597 he became master of University College, Oxford, and in 1600, 1603, and 1605 he was vice-chancellor. In 1600 he also became Dean of *Winchester. He displayed from an early date strong *Puritan sympathies which brought him increasingly into conflict with the rising party of High Churchmen in the university, esp. W. *Laud. In 1606 his unqualified defence of hereditary monarchy against J. *Overall gained him royal favour, and this favour was increased after a mission to Scotland (1608) in which he succeeded in persuading Scotland of the lawfulness of episcopacy and in arranging a union between the two Churches. Preferments followed rapidly. In 1609 he was made Bp. of *Lichfield and Coventry; later in the year he was translated to London; and in 1611 he became Abp. of Canterbury. As his long Archiepiscopate was marked by the decline of Puritanism among the influential classes, Abbot found himself forced to fight a losing cause. He was severe on RCs and correspondingly partial to *Calvinists. Thus he encouraged the King's endeavours to secure the dismissal of C. *Vorstius as an *Arminian from his chair at *Leyden; he arranged for the settlement of M. A. *de Dominis, the apostate Abp. of Spalato, in English benefices; he refused to allow the 'Book of *Sports' to be read in Croydon Church; and he ensured that England was represented at the Synod of *Dort (1618). The strong line he took in the Essex nullity suit

(1616), however, in which he upheld justice against the King and others in high position, won him deserved respect and a temporary popularity among Anglicans of all schools. His unhappiness culminated in the curious consequences of an accident while hunting at Bramshill, Hants, in 1622. Having accidentally shot a gamekeeper, Abbot was considered by some of his fellow-bishops to have become irregular as a man of blood. When the case was tried by a commission of six bishops and four laymen, and opinion was equally divided as to the irregularity, James gave his decision in Abbot's favour. On 24 Dec. James signed on his behalf a formal dispensation and Abbot resumed his duties, and in 1625 he crowned *Charles I. His writings include a widely circulated *Geography, or a Brief Description of the Whole World* (1599), and an *Exposition on the Prophet Jonah* (1600).

His elder brother, ROBERT ABBOT (1560–1617) was Bp. of *Salisbury from 1615 till his death.

Life of George Abbot by W. Oldys in *Biographia Britannica*, i (1747), repr. separately, Guildford, 1777. J. Rushworth, 'The Sequestration of Archbishop Abbot from all his Ecclesiastical Offices in 1627', orig. issued in his *Historical Collections* (1659–1701), repr. in E. Arber, *An English Garner*, iv (1882). Modern life by P. A. Welsby (London, S.P.C.K., 1962). S. L. Lee in *D.N.B.*, i (1885), pp. 5–20, s.v.

ABBOTT, EDWIN ABBOTT (1838–1926), Anglican schoolmaster and scholar. He was educated at the City of London School and St. John's College, Cambridge, and in 1863 ordained priest. Becoming head master of his old school in 1865, he introduced methods of teaching in classical, literary, and scientific subjects unsurpassed in their day. In 1889 he resigned to devote himself to theological study. His writings, largely addressed to a public not reached by technical books of theology, included the three romances *Philochristus*, the life of Christ from the standpoint of a 1st cent. disciple (1878), *Onesimus* (1882), and *Silanus* (1906); and, of a less popular kind, *The Kernel and the Husk* (1886) and *Philomythus* (1891). He also issued a long series of works on the philology and literary problems of the Gospels, among them his *Johannine Vocabulary* (1905) and *Johannine Grammar* (1906). His other writings include studies in F. *Bacon (a critical monograph, *Bacon and Essex*, 1877, and an Introduction to his 7th edition of Bacon's *Essays*, 1886), *The Anglican Career of Cardinal* [J. H.] *Newman (2 vols., 1892; hostile), *St. *Thomas of *Canterbury. His Death and Miracles* (2 vols., 1898), and, esp. in his earlier years, a large number of school textbooks.

L. R. Farnell in *D.N.B.*, 1922–1930 (1937), pp. 1–3, s.v.

ABBREVIATOR. An official of the Roman chancery, whose principal duty was the preparation of letters and writs for the collation of Church dignities. He was so named from the extensive abbreviations employed in Papal documents. *Pius II erected the abbreviators into a college of prelates divided into three ranks (1463). In 1814 Pius VII abolished the

junior ranks, and in 1908, when *Pius X reorganized the chancery, the college as a whole was suppressed and its functions transferred to a group of *Protonotaries (*protonotarii apostolici participantes*).

ABDH-ISHO. See *Ebedjesus*.

À BECKET, St. THOMAS. See *Becket, St. Thomas*.

ABEL. Acc. to Gen. 4. 2, the second son of *Adam and *Eve, who became a shepherd, whilst his brother Cain cultivated the land. He was slain by Cain, jealous that Abel's sacrifice of the firstlings of his flock had been accepted by Jehovah, whereas his own was rejected (Gen. 4. 3 ff.). Gen. 4 contains the only mentions of him in the OT. In the NT our Lord places him at the beginning of the line of prophets who were killed ('from the blood of righteous Abel', Mt. 23. 35), and the author of *Heb., who attributes the acceptance of his sacrifice to his faith (11. 4), opposes his blood to that of Christ 'that speaketh better than that of Abel' (12. 24; cf. also 1 Jn. 3. 12). The Fathers, who frequently commented on his story, regarded him as a type of Christ, the principal point of comparison being his innocent life as a shepherd, his accepted sacrifice, and his violent death. As the first of martyrs he also sometimes stands for the persecuted Christians, belonging to the city which is in heaven (St. *Augustine, *De Civ. Dei*, xv. i). In the Liturgy, his name is mentioned with those of *Abraham and *Melchizedek in the *Canon of the Roman Mass, and in the prayers for the dying, where he is the first helper invoked to assist the soul. See also *Abelites*.

V. Aptowitzer, *Kain und Abel in der Agada, den Apokryphen, der hellenistischen, christlichen und muhammedanischen Literatur* (1922). E. Palis in *Dict. Bibl.*, 1 (1895), cols. 28–30, s.v.; J. Lewinsohn, I. Chanoch, and B. Heller in *Encyclopaedia Judaica*, i (Berlin, 1928), cols. 207–14, s.v. with bibl. See also Commentaries on Gen.

ABELARD, PETER (1079–1142), philosopher and theologian. (This, the conventional spelling, is certainly wrong. Some modern historians adopt the more accurate form **Abailard**.) He was born at Pallet, nr. Nantes, of Breton parents. The pupil successively of *Roscellinus, *William of Champeaux, and *Anselm of Laon, he early showed evidence of a lively, restless, and independent mind which brought him into frequent conflict with his masters. His brilliant refutation of the extreme *Realism of William of Champeaux at once established his reputation as a teacher. He continued to lecture at Paris to large audiences of enthusiastic students first in dialectics and later in theology, until his career was cut short in 1118 by the tragic issue of his love affair with Héloïse, the niece of Fulbert, Canon of Notre-Dame. After his retirement to the monastery of St.-Denis, attacks were made upon the orthodoxy of his teaching about the Trinity, and at the Council of

*Soissons (1121) he was condemned unheard and a book of his on the subject (acc. to R. Stölzle the 'De Unitate et Trinitate Divina') was burnt. His criticism of the legend of St. *Dionysius, the patron of the abbey, made it necessary for him to flee from the wrath of the monks and he now established a small oratory called the Paraclete near Troyes. In 1125 he became Abbot of St.-Gildas. He resumed his career as a teacher at Paris *c.* 1136, where he had among his pupils *Arnold of Brescia and *John of Salisbury. At about this time St. *Bernard of Clairvaux denounced his teaching to the bishops of France. In 1141 (acc. to J. G. Sikes, 1140) several propositions selected from his writings were condemned at the Council of *Sens and St. Bernard secured the confirmation of the sentence by Pope *Innocent II. Abelard was eventually reconciled to St. Bernard and spent the rest of his life at Cluny, where he was well received by *Peter the Venerable. He died at the Cluniac priory of St.-Marcel, near Chalon-sur-Saône.

The range and variety of Abelard's gifts are reflected in his writings. His philosophical works include 'Scito te ipsum' (on Ethics), a 'Dialectica', and some 'Glossulae' on *Porphyry. His 'Sic et Non', a collection of apparently contradictory excerpts from the Scriptures and the Fathers on a large number of questions, exercised a decisive influence on the history of Scholastic method. Its purpose was to stimulate its readers to resolve the seeming contradictions, not (as has been popularly supposed) to discredit the principle of authority. In his treatise 'Theologia Summi Boni' (*c.* 1120) Abelard applied his dialectical principles to the doctrine of the Trinity, and after condemnation in 1121 defended himself in 'Theologia Christiana' (1123–4). In his Commentary on Romans he expounded his doctrine of the Atonement. His own personal history is contained in the 'Historia Calamitatum' and in his letters to Héloïse. He was also the author of several hymns, among them the well-known 'O Quanta Qualia' ('O what the joy and the glory must be'), written for Vespers on Saturday which, with its characteristic combination of devotional feeling and dialectical play, hymns the joys of the endless Sabbath in heaven.

Abelard's philosophical and theological doctrines were to a great extent determined by his early interest in the problem of universals. Against the exaggerated Realism of his time, he maintained that the only existents were the individuals and that from them the elements of human language ('voces' or 'nomina') are derived by abstraction. It is wholly mistaken to consider the 'vox' or 'nomen' as a thing ('res'), since no individual thing can be predicated of a subject. The sole function of the universal is logical. To explain the fact that any name, say 'man', has reference to a common factor in various individuals, Abelard elaborated a psychological theory, largely derived from *Aristotle, acc. to which by the 'nomen' the 'natura rei' was apprehended, while what was properly individual

and particular remained as a residue outside the logical process. In the result he reached a position between the extreme Realism of William of Champeaux and the crude *Nominalism of Roscellinus. In his ethics he held that sin consisted wholly in contempt for the wishes of God; and this emphasis on intention led to a practical ignoring of the distinction between good and evil acts. Unlike the 13th cent. moralists, he was free from the dominion of Aristotle's Ethics, which were unknown to him except through a few scattered references in *Boethius. This stress on intention assisted him also towards an exemplarist theory of the Atonement, acc. to which the suffering Christ was our supreme example, though little more.

His intellectual independence and dialectical methods naturally aroused the opposition of authoritarian mystics like St. Bernard, but his influence, through his lectures even more than through his writings, was enormous. His success came rather through the brilliance and freshness with which he handled particular problems than in the propagation of an elaborated system. In his application of reason to the deepest mysteries of the faith, notably the doctrine of the Trinity, he showed a daring which merited the censure of his contemporaries, though his distrust of authority where it was genuinely traditional must not be exaggerated.

There is no complete edition of Abelard's works, which have indeed only slowly come to light in modern times. Early ed. by A. Du Chesne (2 vols., Paris, 1616), repr., with additions, in J. P. Migne, *PL*, clxxviii; modern collections of *Ouvrages inédites* by V. Cousin (Paris, 1836) and *Opera hactenus seorsim edita* by id. (2 vols., ib., 1849–59). Crit. ed. of hymns by G. M. Dreves, S.J. (ib., 1891). 'Theologia Summi Boni' first pr. by R. Stölzle (under the title 'De Unitate et Trinitate Divina', Freiburg i.Br., 1891); crit. ed. by H. Ostlender (B.G.P.M., xxxv, Hftt. 2/3; 1939). Gloss on Logic first pr. by P. Geyer (ib., xxi, Hftt. 1/4; 1919–33); supplement by M. Dal Pra (Rome, 1954). 'Dialectica' ed. L. M. de Rijk (Assen, 1956). P. Ruf–M. *Grabmann (edd.), *Ein neuaufgefundenes Bruchstück der Apologia Abaelards* (*Sb.* (Bayr., 1930), Hft. 5). Eng. tr. of *Ethics* by J. R. McCallum (Oxford, 1935) and of correspondence with Héloïse by C. K. S. Moncrieff (London, 1925). Principal modern study by J. G. Sikes (Cambridge, 1932), with bibl. E. *Gilson, *Héloïse et Abélard* (1938). J. Cottiaux, 'La Conception de la théologie chez Abélard' in *R.H.E.*, xxvii (1932), pp. 247–95, 533–51, 788–828. A. M. Landgraf, *Einführung in die Geschichte der theologischen Literatur der Frühscholastik* (1948), pp. 62–73, for bibl. to date. E. Portalié in *D.T.C.*, i (1903), cols. 36–55; E. Vacandard in *D.E.G.E.*, i (1912), cols. 71–91.

ABELITES, also Abelians and Abelonians. A small African sect which originated in the diocese of Hippo and is known only from St. *Augustine (*De Haer.* lxxxvii). Admitting marriage and, indeed, holding it to be obligatory, its members lived in complete continence after the alleged example of *Abel. They perpetuated their existence by each husband and wife adopting a boy and a girl. By St. Augustine's time it had ceased to exist as a sect, the few surviving Abelite families having been received back into the Church.

ABERCIUS, Inscription of. The Greek epitaph of Abercius Marcellus, Bp. of Hieropolis (not Hierapolis), in Phrygia Salutaris

(d. *c.* 200). Discovered by W. M. *Ramsay in 1883, it had been composed and apparently set up by Abercius over his future tomb. It mentions his travels to Rome and Nisibis and, making allusive use of early Christian symbolism, gives Abercius' testimony to the currency everywhere of the Eucharist. The inscription, which was presented by the Sultan Abdul Hamid to *Leo XIII, is now in the *Lateran Museum. The attempts of certain scholars (e.g. G. Ficker, A. Dieterich) to maintain that Abercius was a pagan priest, not a Christian bishop, have now been abandoned.

The 'Life of Abercius', which exists in three recensions, is of much later date. It attributes to Abercius a 'Book of Teaching' (βίβλον διδασκαλίας) as well as a letter to the Emp. *Marcus Aurelius, and also incorporates the text of the Inscription. The original form of this 'Life' was apparently written at Hieropolis towards the end of the 4th cent. Despite J. B. *Pitra's defence, the *Vita* appears to be of no independent historical value. Abercius is commemorated in both E. and W. as a saint. Feast day, 22 Oct.

The Greek text with Eng. trans. is in J. B. *Lightfoot, *The Apostolic Fathers* (1889), II, i, pp. 492–501. W. Lüdtke–T. Nissen, *Die Grabschrift des Aberkios. Ihre Überlieferung und ihr Text* (Bibl. Teub., 1910). The text of the Lives is in *S. Abercii Vita*, ed. T. Nissen (Bibl. Teub., 1912). More recent literature in J. Quasten, *Monumenta Eucharistica et Liturgica Vetustissima* (Bonn, 1935), i, pp. 21-4 (with text).

ABGAR, Legend of. An old tradition ascribes to Abgar V (4 B.C. to A.D. 50), one of the kings of *Edessa, an exchange of letters with our Lord. The king, being ill, wrote to Christ asking Him to visit and heal him, who, though declining to come Himself, promised that, after His Ascension, He would send a disciple to cure the king and preach the Gospel to the people. In one version of the story is added a special blessing for Edessa. The legend is reported in variant forms by *Eusebius (*HE*, I. xiii) and in the 'Doctrine of *Addai'. In the account of Eusebius the letter is followed by a recital of the mission of *Thaddaeus, one of the Seventy, who is sent by St. *Thomas 'who is also called Jude', heals the king and converts many inhabitants of the city. Acc. to the 'Pilgrimage of *Etheria', the letter of Christ, written in Syriac on parchment, was preserved at Edessa; there existed many copies of it to which were ascribed miraculous powers of healing and protection. Among the later additions to this very popular legend is the story that, together with the letter, Christ also sent His portrait, miraculously imprinted on canvas. The legend, which probably originated some time after the conversion of Abgar IX (179–214), was accepted as authentic in the E., but widely rejected in the W. and the letter placed among the apocryphal books by the *Gelasian Decree. It has, however, found defenders even in modern times both among Catholics and Protestants.

R. A. Lipsius, *Die edessenische Abgarsage kritisch untersucht* (1880); L. J. Tixeront, *Les Origines de l'Église d'Édesse et la légende d'Abgar* (1888); E. von Dobschütz, 'Der Briefwechsel zwischen Abgar und Jesus' in *Zeitschrift für wissenschaftliche Theologie*, 43 (1900), pp. 422–86.

ABJURATION. The act of renouncing any idea, person, or thing to which one has previously adhered. Acc. to canon law it is an external retractation, made before witnesses, of errors contrary to Catholic faith and unity, such as apostasy, heresy, and schism. There are examples of it in the reconciliation of penitents during the first centuries, in the history of ecclesiastical legislation of the Middle Ages, and in the practice of the *Inquisition, which imposed abjuration on formal heretics as well as on suspects. To-day the term is usually restricted to the public retractation imposed on those abandoning an 'acatholic' faith, esp. Protestantism, in order to be received into the Catholic Church. Acc. to the 'Form for the Reception of a Convert', used in the RC Church in this country, only an unspecified abjuration is required after the formal profession of faith. It is enforced as a guarantee of the sincerity of the conversion and as a help for future perseverance.

The Greek Church has also set forms of abjuration, esp. for *Manichaeans, *Jews, and *Mohammedans, containing short descriptions of the errors renounced. There also exist numerous formulae for RCs seeking admission to the Greek Church, renouncing esp. the *Filioque and the Council of *Florence (1439), to which has been added more recently a special anathema against Papal *Infallibility. During the last three centuries there have been many conversions from Protestantism to Orthodoxy, for which are required abjurations of the *Double Procession, and also of the denials of the *Real Presence, the priesthood, the cult of the saints and images, and other Protestant tenets.

ABJURATION, Oath of. This oath for renouncing the Stuart dynasty, to be sworn by everyone who took office, civil, military, or spiritual, was first proposed in 1690, but not made compulsory until 1701 by 13 Will. III, c. 6. It was reimposed by 1 Geo. I, c. 13 and 6 Geo. III, c. 53. In 1778 it was imposed on RCs in England as a condition of the removal of various disabilities. Among the matters to be abjured were the claims of the Pretender, the temporal power of the Pope and his right to depose, and the tenets that heretics may lawfully be put to death, and that faith need not be kept with them. Its imposition was finally abolished in 1858 and its place taken by a new form of the Oath of *Allegiance.

ABLUTIONS. (1) The washing of fingers and chalice by the celebrant after the Communion in the Mass. The ceremony became part of the Eucharistic rite in the 10th or 11th cent. Its performance varied; the chalice usually received only one ablution with wine, and the fingers were rinsed either with wine or with water or, later, with both. In the RC Church the rite was finally regulated in the *Missal of *Pius V, which prescribes a twofold ablution of the chalice first with wine, then with wine and water, the ablution of the fingers with wine and water being connected with the latter. In the *Mozarabic and Greek rites the ablutions are performed privately after the Mass; in the other E. rites, however, as in the Roman, immediately after the Communion and before the concluding prayers. The development of the ceremony is a consequence of the belief in the Eucharistic Presence and an expression of reverence due to Christ present under the Sacred Species.

(2) In the RC Church the rinsing of the mouth after the reception of the Bl. Sacrament with wine by the new priests in the Ordination Mass, and with water at the Communion of the Sick. The W. custom is probably connected with the medieval practice of giving the communicants a draught of unconsecrated wine immediately after Communion to cleanse the mouth. A similar custom exists in the E., where in many places the communicants receive unconsecrated wine after Communion at the Liturgy. These various ceremonies may be survivals of Communion in both kinds or (less probably) of the ancient *Agape.

On (1), W. Lockton, *The Treatment of the Remains at the Eucharist* (1920).

ABORTION. The practice of abortion has been consistently condemned by Christian moralists. It is already forbidden by the Council of *Elvira (c. 306, can. 61). The practice is also treated in most modern codes of civil law as a criminal offence. Even in Soviet Russia, where its use has been permitted, this liberty has been much restricted in recent years.

With therapeutic abortion, however, there is less unanimity. In the civil law of most countries it is sanctioned under varying restrictions. In English law it is tolerated only when considered by the physician necessary to save the mother's life, though a modern legal decision (*Rex* v. *Bourne,* 1938) has interpreted this as extending to cases where grave damage to the health or sanity of the mother is anticipated. Christian opinion is divided. A large body of non-Catholic moralists approve of the civil law on the ground that the life of the mother is more important than that of the unborn child. Catholic moral theologians, on the other hand, hold that therapeutic abortion as an end in itself is always unlawful. An operation intended primarily for some other purpose than the destruction of the foetus, which may actually result in its death, is, however, considered permissible on the ground that, for sufficient reason, it is lawful to perform an action in itself good or indifferent from which two results, a good and a bad, may follow. The principle underlying the Catholic attitude is the belief that it is never lawful to kill the innocent directly.

Present regulations of RC Church summarized in the *CIC,* cans. 2350, para. 1, and 985, No. 4. H. Davis, S.J., *Moral and Pastoral Theology,* ii (1935), pp. 138-58, and iv (1935) p. 483 f. S. du Moriez, *L'Avortement* (1912). A. E. Crawley in *H.E.R.E.,* vi (1913), pp. 54-7, s.v. 'Foeticide'; A. Beugnet in *D.T.C.,* i (1903), cols. 2644-52, s.v. 'Avortement'; C. Coppens in *C.E.,* i (1907), pp. 46-9, s.v.; J. Delmaille in *D.D.C.,* i (1935), cols. 1536-61, s.v. 'Avortement', with bibl.

ABRAHAM, sometimes in the form **Abram,** Hebrew patriarch. He apparently lived at the time of Hammurabi (between 2100 and 2000 B.C.), whom most modern scholars identify with the Amraphel of Gen. 14. 1. His life is described in Gen. 11. 26-25. 18. Born at Ur in Chaldaea, he went to Haran under a Divine inspiration (Gen. 15. 7) and, having received another call (Gen. 12. 1), proceeded to Canaan. Famine then drove him into Egypt. On his return he saved his nephew Lot from the captivity of Chedorlaomer, king of Elam, and was blessed by *Melchizedek, king of Salem. Then Jehovah promised him a son by his wife Sarah and an innumerable posterity, confirming His promises by a Covenant. After the birth of his son *Isaac, Abraham's faith was put to a severe test by a command to sacrifice his son. When Abraham had shown his readiness even for this act of obedience, a ram was substituted before the sacrifice was actually offered, and Abraham was rewarded by the formal renewal of God's promises.

The Christian Church has always recognized in Abraham her spiritual ancestor on account of his faith, a conception worked out by St. Paul (Rom. 4. 11, Gal. 3. 7), St. James (2. 21-23), and the author of Hebrews (11. 8-10). The Fathers, e.g. St. *Clement of Rome and St. *Ambrose, exalted his generous obedience in leaving his homeland; and St. Augustine loved to compare it to the following of the Word practised by the Apostles. Later spiritual writers see in it a type of the religious vocation of the individual soul. His sacrifice particularly furnished the Fathers with a model of perfect submission to the will of God even in the severest trials. It came to prefigure the death of Christ, and many writers, e.g. *Tertullian, *Origen, St. *Cyril of Alexandria, and *Theodoret, draw out all the similarities, e.g. the ram that is killed signifies the humanity, and Isaac who remains alive the Divinity of our Lord. In the *Canon of the Mass, and in St.*Thomas' prose for the Feast of *Corpus Christi, '*Lauda Sion', the immolation of Isaac prefigures the Sacrifice of the Mass.

The term 'Abraham's bosom' is of Rabbinic origin and used by our Lord in the parable of Dives and Lazarus (Lk. 16. 22). Acc. to St. *Augustine, it is not to be taken literally but signifies the place of repose where Abraham is. In RC terminology it is identified either with the *Limbo of the Patriarchs, a place where the saintly souls of the Old Covenant enjoyed peace while awaiting the perfect happiness of heaven, or with heaven itself.

C. L. Woolley, *Abraham.* Recent Discoveries and Hebrew Origins (1936). P. Dhorme, 'Abraham dans le cadre de l'histoire' in *R. Bibl.,* xxxvii (1928), pp. 367-85 and 481-511; xl (1931), pp. 364-74 and 503-18. E. Mangenot in *Dict. Bibl.,* i (1895), cols. 74-85, s.v.; F. *Cabrol, O.S.B., in *D.A.C.L.,* i (pt. 1; 1907), cols. 111-27, s.v.; L. Pirot in *Dict. Bibl.* Suppl., i (1928), cols. 8-28, s.v., with bibl. On the phrase 'Abraham's Bosom', see R. Meyer in *T.W.B.,* iii (1938), pp. 824 6, s.v. κόλπος, with bibl.

ABRAHAM, Apocalypse of. Jewish apocryphal writing, probably late 1st cent. The opening chapters (1-8) are a *Midrash on

*Abraham's conversion from idolatry. The rest of the book (9–32) describes a series of visions seen by Abraham in the heavens, showing the nature of sin and the Fall and its issue in God's destruction of the *Jerusalem Temple (A.D. 70). The book ends (32) with a promise that God will deliver His chosen. The work almost certainly goes back, through a lost Greek version, to a Hebrew or Aramaic original; but the text survives, apart from its embodiment in late comprehensive Slavonic works on the O.T. known as the 'Palaeas', only in a Slavonic version, preserved in Moscow ('Codex Sylvester'). In its present form the book shows traces of Christian, and esp. *Gnostic, adaptation.

The Slavonic text has been publd. twice—by two Russian scholars, N. Tikhonravov (Moscow, 1863) and J. Sreznevsky (Petrograd, 1863). A facsimile edition was issued at Petrograd in 1890. G. N. Bonwetsch, *Die Apocalypse Abrahams* (1897; with Ger. trans.). G. H. Box, *The Apocalypse of Abraham* (S.P.C.K. texts, 1918; Eng. trans.).

ABRAHAM, Testament of. A Hellenistic apocryphal writing. It describes how the aged *Abraham, unwilling to face death, is taken to heaven by the Archangel *Michael, who reveals to him the sinful doings of dwellers on the earth. Abraham then has a vision of the two roads leading to hell and paradise and learns how most men choose the former. After praying for the forgiveness of sinners, he is brought back to earth and finally borne by the Angel of Death to paradise. The Testament exists in two Greek recensions (apparently its original language), as well as in Rumanian, Arabic, Ethiopic, and Coptic versions. In the last three of these versions it is supplemented by 'Testaments' of Isaac and of Jacob. Its few certainly Christian passages are generally thought to be interpolations in an originally Jewish work.

M. R. James, 'The Testament of Abraham. The Greek Text now first edited' in Cambridge *Texts and Studies*, ii, No. 2 (1892). There is an Eng. trans. by G. H. Box, with an Appendix containing a translation of the Coptic Version of the Testaments of Isaac and Jacob by S. Gaselee (S.P.C.K., 1927).

ABRAHAM ECCHELLENSIS (1600–64), *Maronite scholar. A native of Hekel or Ecchel on Mt. Lebanon, he studied at the Maronite College in *Rome and afterwards taught oriental languages at the *Propaganda. From 1630 to 1642 he was at the Collège Royal in Paris. From 1642 to 1645 he was back in Rome, from 1645 to 1653 again in Paris, and finally, from 1653 till his death in Rome. He published several important works on oriental languages, among them an edition of 84 spurious Arabic *Nicene Canons (1645) and Syriac and Arabic versions of 3 Macc. and of Ruth for the Paris *Polyglott. His other writings include a collection of documents relating to St. *Antony (1646); *Chronicon Orientale* (1653); *Concordantia Nationum Christianarum Orientalium in Fidei Catholicae Dogmate* (1655) in conjunction with L. *Allatius; *De Origine Nominis Papae* (1660);

and some letters to J. *Morinus on the Oriental Liturgies (publd. by Morinus, 1682).

J. Lamy in *D.T.C.*, i (1903), cols. 116–18, L. Petit in *D.H.G.E.*, i (1912), cols. 169–71, both s.v.

ABRAHAMS, ISRAEL (1858–1925), Rabbinic scholar. Educated at University College, London, he was appointed reader in Talmudic and Rabbinic literature at Cambridge in 1902. He became prominent as a leader of 'Liberal Judaism'. In his later years he applied himself esp. to the study of Christian origins in their relation to their Rabbinic background, setting out his conclusions in two series of *Studies in Pharisaism and the Gospels* (1917, 1924). From 1889 to 1907 he edited (with C. J. Goldsmid Montefiore, 1858-1938) the *Jewish Quarterly Review*.

G. A. Kohut (ed.), *Jewish Studies in Memory of Israel Abrahams* (New York, 1927), with select bibl. of Abraham's works, pp. xix–xlvii; suppl. bibl. by S. Levy in *Jewish Historical Society of England, Miscellanies* iii (1937), pp. 41–6. H. Loewe, *Israel Abrahams* (1944).

ABSOLUTE IDEALISM. The philosophical system of G. W. F. *Hegel and his followers. It is 'idealistic' in the sense that it conceives the whole of reality to be the expression of an Idea, while it is termed 'absolute' in contrast with the 'Subjective Idealism' of such thinkers as G. *Berkeley and J. G. *Fichte, who accord priority to the subjective elements in experience. In recent British philosophy the doctrine is associated esp. with the names of F. H. *Bradley and B. *Bosanquet, through whose writings it came to exercise a pervasive influence on British speculative thought, including philosophical theology, in the decades immediately preceding World War I.

For its influence on British theology see C. C. J. *Webb, *A Study of Religious Thought in England from 1850* (1933).

ABSOLUTION. The formal act of a priest or bishop pronouncing the forgiveness of sins by Christ to those who are qualified by penitence to receive it. In the NT the grace of forgiveness flows from the Person of Christ, who is Mediator and Redeemer (Mk. 2. 5–11). The traditional Catholic doctrine is that this grace of forgiveness is now normally imparted on earth to repentant sinners by means of the ordained ministry, though this belief is commonly denied among Protestants. In the early Church absolution was given publicly to reconciled sinners after public penance. Private confession and absolution, which began as a devotional custom in certain Celtic monasteries, later became the usual method of obtaining remission of sins.

Two methods of absolution have been, and still are, in use — the indicative and the precatory. By *indicative* is meant the use by the absolver of such formulae as 'I absolve thee', whereas in *precatory* methods of absolution the priest prays formally that God will absolve an individual or a congregation. In the E., the precatory form is employed even in the absolution of individuals, though in the

Russian Church, and possibly elsewhere, the indicative is added. The RC Church uses the indicative for individuals (adding the precatory, but holding it insufficient if used alone) and the precatory for liturgical purposes. The Anglican BCP implies a use similar to the Roman (see the Office for the *Visitation of the Sick, compared with the Communion Office and the Forms of Prayer for use at *Sea), but in Morning and Evening Prayer a new form is provided, which is usually held to be only *declaratory*, i.e. the pronouncement that God forgives those who repent.

A. Villien in *D.D.C.*, i (1935), cols. 120–3. See also bibl. under *Penance*.

ABSOLUTION PRAYER. A prayer of this name is found in the Divine Office after the Psalms and before the lessons of each *nocturn. The name has been derived from *absolutio* in the sense of completion, on the ground that the prayer ends a section of the office; but the prayer does not appear in its present form until the 13th cent. when *absolutio* was already a technical term, and further, one of the prayers is of a penitential character.

ABSOLUTIONS OF THE DEAD. The title given to the service in the RC Church said after the *Requiem Mass in the presence of the body before it is taken from the church. It may also be said even though the body is not present. The title is derived from the occurrence of the word 'absolve' in two of the prayers. The service consists of prayers for the departed soul, and the censing and aspersing of the body during the saying of the *Pater. One of the concluding prayers is found in the earliest Gregorian MSS., but the service as a whole is medieval. An account of a funeral by St. *Theodore, Abp. of Canterbury (d. 690), definitely excludes it.

ABSTINENCE. A penitential practice, consisting in abstaining from the use of certain kinds of food. It is thus commonly distinguished from *fasting (q.v.), which means the refusal of all, or all but a strictly limited quantity of, food, irrespective of its kind. It is practised among most peoples in different forms and for various reasons, e.g. among Egyptians, Indians, Greeks, Arabs. The Jewish Law contained elaborate food prohibitions (Lev. 11), which, however, were abrogated by the New Dispensation, the only apparent exceptions being blood and things strangled (Acts 15). From early Christian times, however, other kinds of abstinence were practised, esp. among the hermits. Thus St. *Antony and his followers abstained from all food save bread, salt, and water, and *Pachomius and the Egyptian monks followed a similar diet. It was carried to excess in several early heretical sects who taught dualistic doctrines, e.g. the *Manichees and various other *Gnostic bodies. In the W. more or less severe abstinence throughout the year is practised by most contemplative orders, such as *Carthusians, *Carmelites, and some *Benedictine congregations. Both in E. and W. the Friday abstinence of all Christians in commemoration of the Passion was in use from early times. It is mentioned by *Clement of Alexandria and *Tertullian as an established custom, and was extended to Saturday in the W. at about the same time. The practice was attacked by *Jovinian in the 4th cent., and later by the *Reformers, who considered it to be contrary to the Gospel.

Acc. to modern RC practice abstinence from flesh-meat is observed on all Fridays of the year except when they coincide with Holy Days of *Obligation, on all Wednesdays in *Lent, on the *Ember Wednesdays, and certain *Vigils and *Rogation Days. The Saturday abstinence, which has its roots in *patristic times and the Middle Ages, is dispensed by Papal indult in many countries, including England and Wales and the U.S.A. The precept of abstinence is considered to fall under the *Commandments of the Church and to bind under grave sin all persons who have the use of reason after the seventh year of age. It is, however, dispensed in cases of sickness, poverty, heavy labour, in times of war, and in other circumstances, when it could not be observed without grave inconvenience. In the Greek and other E. Churches the practice of abstinence (ξηροφαγία, 'dry food') is far more rigid. It extends to all Wednesdays and Fridays of the year, all days of the Major (Lent) Fast including Sundays, and several other periods, bringing up the number of days of abstinence to about 150; and not only meat, but fish, eggs, milk, cheese, oil, and wine are also forbidden. In the C of E, though there is nothing formally enjoined in the matter of abstinence as distinct from fasting, the Friday abstinence has never been completely abolished. Its wider observance in recent times has been due esp. to the *Oxford Movement. See also *Fasts and Fasting*.

Artt. s.v. in *D.T.C.*, i (1903), cols. 261–77 (several authors). See also bibl. to *Fasting*.

ABUNA (Eth. and Arab. *Abu-na*, 'our father'). The Patriarch of the *Abyssinian Church.

ABYSSINIAN CHURCH. See *Ethiopian Church*.

ACACIAN SCHISM. In the *Monophysite Controversy, a temporary schism (482–519) between *Rome and the East, which arose out of the Emp. *Zeno's *Henoticon (q.v.). It began during the Patriarchate of Acacius (471–489) at *Constantinople. Despite the attempts of Flavitas (490) and Euphemius (490–6), Acacius' successors, to heal it, it continued till the accession of Justin (518).

On Acacius, see M. Jugie, A.A., in *D.H.G.E.*, i (1912), cols. 244–8, s.v. G. Bardy in Fliche–Martin, iv (1945), pp. 290–320. E. *Schwartz, *Publizistische Sammlungen zum Acacianischen Schisma* in *Abh.* (Bayr.), 1934, Heft 10.

ACACIUS OF CAESAREA (d. 366), *Arian theologian. A disciple of *Eusebius Pamphili and his successor in the see of *Caesarea (in Palestine) in 340, he was a representative of strict Arianism. Under the Emp. *Constantius he was pronounced deposed by the Council of *Sardica (343) and became one of the principal representatives of the *Homoeans. He proposed a Homoean Creed at the Council of *Seleucia in 359 and drew up the acts (now lost) of the Homoean Synod of Constantinople in 360. Under *Jovian he signed the Creed of *Nicaea at Antioch in 363, but returned to Arianism under Valens. He was deposed in 365 by the Semiarian Synod of Lampsacus. Among his works were 17 vols. on Eccles. and other treatises, which now exist only in fragments. His followers ('Acacians') were for a short time (357–61) a distinct and important theological party.

The main sources are *Jerome, *De Vir. Ill.* 98, and *Socrates, *H.E.* ii. 4, together with St. Jerome's letters. Part of a polemical treatise against *Marcellus of Ancyra is preserved by *Epiphanius, *Haer.* lxxii. 6–10. Fragments on the Ep. to the *Romans ed. by K. Staab, *Pauluskommentare aus der griechischen Kirche* (1933), pp. 53–6. R. Devreesse, 'Anciens Commentateurs grecs de l'Octateuque' in *R. Bibl.* xliv (1935), pp. 186–9.

ACARIE, Mme (1566–1618), 'Mary of the Incarnation', foundress of the *Carmelites of the Reform in France. The daughter of a wealthy bourgeois family, Barbe Jeanne Avrillot was educated at the convent of Longchamps, nr. Mount Valérien, where she showed signs of exceptional piety. Although anxious to enter the cloister, in 1584 she married, in obedience to her parents, Pierre Acarie, Vicomte de Villemore, to whom she became a devoted wife. A French trans. (1601) of Francisco de Ribera's Life of St. *Teresa made a deep impression on her; and, strengthened by visions in the belief that it was her vocation to introduce the Carmelites into France, she persuaded Mlle de Longueville to obtain the consent of the King and actively assisted in the establishment of the Carmel of Paris in 1603. She also assisted Mme de Sainte-Beuve in establishing the *Ursulines and encouraged P. de *Bérulle in the foundation of the *Oratory. After the death of her husband (1613) she was received as a lay sister in the Carmel at Amiens. In 1615 she was professed under the name of 'Mary of the Incarnation' and in 1616 transferred to Pontoise to reform the finances of the house.

Mme Acarie was renowned for her charity and greatly respected as a spiritual adviser. She was the subject of numerous ecstasies and the frequent recipient of visions, but, since she has left no record of her experiences, it is difficult to assess the quality of her mysticism. She was held in high repute by St. *Francis de Sales and beatified in 1791. Feast day, 18 Apr.

A. Duval, *La Vie admirable de Sœur Marie de l'Incarnation* (1641). J. A. B. Boucher, *Vie de la Bienheureuse Sœur Marie de l'Incarnation* (1800). Bruno de J[ésus] M[arie], O.C.D., *La Belle Acarie, Bienheureuse Marie de l'Incarnation* (1942), with bibl.; L. C. Sheppard, *Barbe Acarie* (1953). Bremond, ii (1916), pp. 193–262. Eng. tr., ii (1930), pp. 145–94. Further life by E. de Broglie ('Les Saints', 1903).

ACATHISTUS (Gk. ἀκάθιστος, 'not sitting', because it was sung standing), famous liturgical

hymn in honour of the BVM, sung in the Greek Church on the Saturday of the fifth week of *Lent. It consists of 24 stanzas of varying length, each beginning with one of the 24 letters of the alphabet. The beautiful text is based on the Gospel narratives of the Nativity. The authorship of the hymn is doubtful. Acc. to a widespread belief it was composed by *Sergius, the *Monothelite Patr. of *Constantinople, in thanksgiving for the deliverance of his city from the Avars and Slavs in 626. It has also been assigned to George Pisides. But acc. to a 9th cent. MS. of *St. Gall it was written by the Patr. *Germanus, who, after the defeat of the Mohammedans before the capital in 717–18, instituted a special feast in which the Acathistus was to be sung; and this statement is accepted by some modern scholars.

The Acathistus is printed in J. P. Migne, *PG*, xcii, 1335–1348, among the works of George Pisides. There are critical editions by J. B. *Pitra in *Analecta Sacra*, i (1876), and by W. Christ and M. Paranikas in *Anthologia Carminum Christianorum* (1871). D. Attwater, *The Akathistos Hymn*. Translated from the original Greek. With historical and liturgical notes (1934).

ACCEPTANTS. Those who 'accepted' the bull '*Unigenitus' (1713) in the *Jansenist controversy, as contrasted with the 'Appellants' who appealed against it.

ACCEPTILATION. Originally a term in Roman law for verbal release from a verbal obligation, it was adopted by the *Scotist theologians for the doctrine that the sacrifice of Christ derives its value as a satisfaction from its arbitrary acceptance by God.

ACCESSION SERVICE, The. The form of prayer for use on the anniversary of the accession of the reigning sovereign, printed at the end of the BCP. Such forms have been in use in England and Wales since 1576. The Order is put out by the Sovereign in Council. Strictly it has no other authority and is not part of the BCP, though can. ii of the 1640 canons recognizes the service. No service was issued for *Charles II's reign, as 30 Jan., the date of his *de jure* accession, was provided for by the commemoration of King *Charles the Martyr. Various revisions have been made from time to time. The last and most comprehensive, that of 1901, is the model of the service still in use. Here provision is made (1) for special forms of Morning and Evening Prayer (with proper Psalms, Lessons, &c.); (2) for a proper Collect, Epistle, and Gospel at the Eucharist; and (3) for a separate service, opening with the *Te Deum. A fresh Order in Council is issued at the beginning of every reign, and when modifications are required through other changes in the Royal Family. Since 1936, the first revision after the disestablishment of the Church of *Wales, the use of the service has been ordered only for churches in the provinces of *Canterbury and *York.

For the forms put out in 1576 and 1578, see W. K. Clay (ed.), *Liturgies and Occasional Forms of Prayer set forth in*

the Reign of Queen Elizabeth (*Parker Soc., 1847), pp. 548–61.
D. Maclean in *P.B.D.* (1912), p. 2.

ACCIDENT. In medieval philosophy, following *Aristotle, an entity whose essential nature it is to inhere in another entity as a subject ('ens in alio'). It is thus to be contrasted with a substance ('ens per se').

The term has played an important part in Eucharistic doctrine since the *Schoolmen evolved the theory of the 'accidentia sine subjecto' ('accidents without a subject') to elucidate the mystery of the Presence. The concept was used to explain how, after the changing of the substances of the bread and wine into those of the Body and Blood of Christ, the accidents of the former, e.g. quantity, colour, taste, &c., continued to exist and be perceptible by the senses. St. *Thomas, e.g., taught (*Summa Theol.* iii, q. 77) that after the consecration through miraculous Divine intervention the accident of quantity continued to exist without inhering in a substance and that in this accident the other accidents inhered in a natural manner. By the end of the 14th cent. the explanation in terms of accidents had come to be widely accepted, but J. *Wycliffe and J. *Huss, as well as M. *Luther and the *Reformers generally, rejected it. The Council of *Trent taught the continuance of the 'species' of bread and wine after consecration, but without mention of accidents. The doctrine of the 'accidentia sine subjecto', though very generally accepted among RC theologians, has in fact never been formally defined. See also *Transubstantiation*.

P. Mielle in *D.T.C.*, i (1903), cols. 302–4; C. Fabro in *E.C.*, i (1949), col. 191 f., with bibl. Full discussion of accidents in Eucharistic theology by F. Jansen, S.J., in *D.T.C.*, v (1913), cols. 1368–1452, s.v. 'Eucharistiques (Accidents)', with bibl.

ACCIDIE (Gk. ἀκηδία, 'negligence', 'indifference'). In its general sense the word is used several times in the *Septuagint (e.g. Ps. 119. 28, Is. 61. 3), but later its meaning was modified to convey sadness, spiritual torpor, and sloth, as in *Hermas (*Vis.* III, xi. 3). In this sense it figures as one of the capital vices in the lists of the spiritual writers of antiquity and the Middle Ages. The classical description of it, given by *Cassian (*Instit.* x. 2), depicts it as a state of restlessness and inability either to work or pray. It is treated at length by St. *Thomas Aquinas (IIᵃ IIᵃᵉ, q. 35) and mentioned in the '*Ancren Riwle' and the writings of Richard *Rolle of Hampole. Accidie is generally regarded as affecting particularly monks and hermits, who are more liable to it than other persons owing to the outward monotony of their life. Assiduous prayer is recommended as the best remedy for it. The term received a new lease of life in England through the influence of F. *Paget, who, in his 'Introductory Essay Concerning Accidie' in *The Spirit of Discipline* (1891), studied it in a number of ancient and modern authors as well as in its modern manifestations.

ACCOMMODATION. In theology, the adaptation of a text or teaching to altered circumstances.

(1) It is sometimes used to connote the giving to a text in Scripture a meaning not intended by the writer, e.g. St. *Matthew's application of 'Out of Egypt have I called my son' (Hos. 11. 1; cf. Mt. 2. 15) to Christ where 'son' meant originally the nation of Israel, or the reference in the Roman Mass of Pharaoh's words 'Ite ad Joseph' ('Go to Joseph', Gen. 41. 55) to the Lord's Foster-father. This usage of the word is mainly found in RC writers.

(2) 'Accommodation' (Ger. *Herablassung*, lit. 'condescension'; also *Akkommodation*) was also used by liberal German theologians of the 18th cent. to expound the mode of Divine communication through the Bible. J. S. *Semler and other exegetes maintained that beside the timeless and unchangeable element in Scripture, there were passages in which the Divine revelation was accommodated to the human understanding by being clothed in transitory forms. Such accommodation was met with esp. in the teaching of Christ. His explicit words and implicit assumptions about, e.g., the authorship of particular parts of the OT, the Messianic character of certain prophecies, or the objective reality of demon-possession, were explained, not as the necessary limitations of His human knowledge consequent on the reality of the Incarnation, but as the deliberate adjustment of His words and actions to the ideas and beliefs of contemporary Judaism. Under the influence of the rationalistic tendencies of the *Aufklärung this form of exegesis often reduced the core of eternal truth to small proportions; e.g. the NT teaching on the *Atonement was explained as merely 'accommodation' to Jewish thought-forms and therefore without validity for later ages.

(3) The word is also used in a more general sense of the teaching by Christians of part only of the truth for the sake of prudence, or of the modification of the form of Christian teaching to secure its more ready acceptance. A notable instance of accommodation in this sense was the practice of the *Jesuit missionaries in China to use the word '*t'ien*' for God and to allow converts to continue in practices akin to ancestor-worship. Such accommodation was forbidden in 1715 by Clement XI and again in 1742 by *Benedict XIV. The method of 'reserve' advocated by I. *Williams in No. 80 of *Tracts for the Times*, entitled *On Reserve in Communicating Religious Knowledge*, has certain affinities with this form of 'accommodation'; but here the chief motive for adjustment was the need for reverence in speaking of sacred subjects.

ACELDAMA (RV, AKELDAMA). 'The field of blood', a piece of land in the neighbourhood of *Jerusalem, so named (1) acc. to Mt. 27. 8, because it was bought with the price of the Lord's blood; but (2) acc. to Acts 1. 18 f., because it was the scene of *Judas' tragic end.

ACOEMETAE (Gk. ἀκοίμηται, 'sleepless ones'). A celebrated body of Orthodox monks. They were founded *c.* 400 by Abbot Alexander (*c.* 350 – *c.* 430), who, after having established a monastery on the Euphrates, went to *Constantinople where he established a religious house whose monks were to observe absolute poverty, do no manual work, exercise a vigorous apostolate by means of missions, and keep up perpetual psalmody in alternating choirs. These ideas, which were complete novelties in Byzantine monasticism, attracted a great number of monks from other convents. They provoked, however, such hostility from the Patr. *Nestorius and others that Alexander was driven from Constantinople and, after many difficulties, founded a monastery on these lines at Gomon in Bithynia. Under his successor it was transferred to the modern Tchiboukli, on the middle Bosphorus, where the monks were first given by the populace their name of 'Acoemetae', which they henceforth kept. The Acoemetae, many of whom were taken for other foundations, e.g. *Studios, became ardent defenders of orthodoxy against the *Monophysites, their most famous member being their abbot St. Marcellus who signed the condemnation of *Eutyches at Constantinople in 448. In their struggle against Eutychianism, however, the monks later fell into the *Nestorian heresy for which they were excommunicated by Pope John II in 534. There are few mentions of them after this period. At an uncertain date they transferred their monastery to Constantinople where they are mentioned in the 12th cent. As early as the time of Marcellus they had modified the exaggerated poverty enjoined by Alexander, and later possessed one of the most famous monastic libraries in the East.

Life of St. Alexander in *A.A.SS.*, Jan. I (1643), pp. 1018–1029. [E.] Marin, *Les Moines de Constantinople depuis la fondation de la ville jusqu'à la mort de Photius, 330–898* (1897), passim. J. Pargoire, A.A., 'Un Mot sur les Acémètes' in *É.O.*, ii (1898), pp. 304–8 and 365–72. E. Marin in *D.T.C.*, i (1903), cols. 304–8, J. Pargoire, A.A., in *D.A.C.L.*, i (1907), cols. 307–21, S. Vailhé, A.A., in *D.H.G.E.*, i (1912), cols. 272–82, all s.v. 'Acémètes', with bibl.

ACOLYTE. The highest of the four *Minor Orders of the Latin Church. The duties of acolytes are to light the altar candles, to carry candles in procession, to prepare the wine and water for Mass, and to assist the Sacred Ministers at Mass. They are first mentioned at *Rome in A.D. 251 and about this time were subjected to the regional *deacons, probably six to each region. In the early '*Ordines Romani' they have a multitude of duties including that of carrying the Eucharist. Gradually the *subdeacons and acolytes absorbed most of the functions of the other Minor Orders at Mass and Baptism. Some acolytes also became palace officers or secretaries to the Pope. The office of acolyte is also found in Africa in the time of St. *Cyprian but seldom elsewhere in the W. in the early centuries. It is not known as a separate order in the E. In modern practice the functions of acolytes in church are very frequently performed by lay persons.

J. *Morinus, *Commentarius de Sacris Ecclesiae Ordinationibus*, ii (Paris, 1655), pp. 197 f., 236–9 and passim. F. Wieland, *Die genetische Entwicklung der sog. Ordines Minores in den drei ersten Jahrhunderten* (R.Q., Suppl. Hft. vii; 1897), pp. 48–54 and 154–61. H. *Leclercq, O.S.B., in *D.A.C.L.*, i (pt. 1; 1907), cols. 348–56; F. [Philip] Oppenheim, O.S.B., in *E.C.* i (1949), col. 198 f.

ACOSMISM (Gk. ά privative, and κόσμος, the 'ordered universe'). An extreme form of *pantheism (q.v.) which asserts that the totality of individual things is nothing but a manifestation of the *Absolute and has no real being. It may be contrasted with those forms of pantheism which conceive of the Absolute as in some sense ingredient into individual things. The term was used by G. W. F. *Hegel, who apparently coined the word (*Encyclopädie*, § 50) to describe B. *Spinoza's system.

ACQUAVIVA, CLAUDIUS. See *Aquaviva, Claudius*.

ACT, Human. In moral theology the term denotes the free and voluntary actions of a human being done with knowledge and attention. To such acts alone can moral praise or blame be accorded, since those which fall below this level are not full expressions of the will of man, as a being endowed with freewill. An act can be made less than human by (1) ignorance, in so far as this is not the fault of the person acting (see *Invincible Ignorance*), (2) force or constraint applied by an outside agent, (3) passion, in so far as its influence is independent of the will, (4) fear, if sufficient seriously to cloud the mind, or (5) habit, in so far as it destroys advertence to what one is doing.

ACTA APOSTOLICAE SEDIS. The official gazette of the *Vatican, founded by *Pius X in the decree, 'Promulgandi Pontificias Constitutiones' (29 Sept. 1908). Publication began in Jan. 1909. About twelve issues appear each year.

ACTA SANCTORUM. The celebrated series of lives of the saints, arranged in the order of their feasts in the ecclesiastical year, which was begun by the *Bollandists, a small body of *Jesuit scholars, in the 17th cent. The plan was conceived by H. Rosweyde (d. 1629), who saw, however, none of it completed. The first two vols. (Jan.) were published at Antwerp in 1643. By the date of the suppression of the order (1773), 50 vols. (to 7 Oct.) had been brought out. Three further vols. were edited by former Jesuits, *Premonstratensians, and others shortly afterwards, and in 1837 the work was resumed by the Society. In 1930 it had reached 10 Nov.

New ed. of the vols. from Jan. I to Oct. VI ed. by J. Carnandet, Paris, 1863–8. See also bibl. to *Bollandists*.

ACTA SANCTORUM ORDINIS SANCTI BENEDICTI. The history of the saints of the *Benedictine Order, of which J. *Mabillon published the first volume in 1668. It was completed in 1701.

Repr. by the Benedictines of *Solesmes (Macon, 1935 ff.).

ACTION (Lat. *actio*). A name once applied to the whole Mass either as a single sacrificial action or possibly as a contraction of the phrase *gratiarum actio*, i.e. 'thanksgiving', 'Eucharist'. Later it was applied in a more restricted sense to the *Canon of the Mass as the sacrificial action *par excellence*. The phrase survives in the Roman Missal in the heading of the *Communicantes* prayer, 'Infra actionem'.

ACTION FRANÇAISE. This French political movement was begun in 1899 by the brilliant writer Charles Maurras. Though a freethinker personally, he regarded Catholicism as essential to French civilization which had the duty of maintaining the classical Greco-Roman tradition. He attacked the methods of 19th cent. democracy, as exemplified in the Third Republic, and preached a monarchist crusade. His movement attracted many followers and produced a daily paper, *L'Action française*, of which Léon Daudet, another clever publicist, was editor. Conducted with great *élan* and skill, the movement included many Catholics who were willing to co-operate with Maurras in the general cause despite his unbelief. Efforts made to have the movement condemned at Rome were suspended owing to its popularity and the confusion of the war of 1914–18 and its aftermath, but finally in 1926 the co-operation of RCs in the movement was forbidden by *Pius XI and its paper put on the *Index. Difficulty was experienced in persuading some of the French hierarchy and the older school of Catholic laity (who, despite the exhortations of *Leo XIII to 'rally to' the Republic, remained set in traditional Royalism) to accept the condemnation, but the opposition was overcome and the movement has since languished.

The literature is scattered. D. Gwynn, *The 'Action Française' Condemnation* (1928). J. *Maritain, *Une Opinion sur Charles Maurras et le devoir des Catholiques* (1926); id., *La Primauté du spirituel* (1927). P. Doncœur and others, *Pourquoi Rome a parlé* (1927). A. da Langasco in *E.C.*, i (1949), cols. 255–8, with useful bibl. and bibliog. reff.

ACTION SERMON. Among Scottish *Presbyterians, the sermon preached before the administration of the Lord's Supper. J. *Calvin used the expression *action de grâce* for the thanksgiving which followed Communion, and from this use J. *Knox probably took it as a name for the whole service. The sermon has now become less important than the prayers preceding Communion, and is frequently omitted.

ACTON, JOHN. See *Ayton, John*.

ACTON, JOHN EMERICH EDWARD DALBERG, first Baron Acton (1834–1902), historian. Born at Naples of an old English

RC stock, he was educated at *Paris, Oscott (under N. *Wiseman), and Munich, where he formed a lifelong friendship with J. J. I. von *Döllinger. He was debarred from Cambridge by the unrepealed religious tests. From his early years an ardent liberal in politics, he became Whig M.P. for Carlow in 1859, and was thus brought into relations with W. E. *Gladstone, whom he much admired. He also became actively interested in the cause of religious liberty, taking over from J. H. *Newman in 1859 the editorship of the RC *Rambler* (from 1862, *Home and Foreign Review*) in defence of liberal views. His own contributions reflected his immense range of knowledge, but the threat of a Papal veto owing to its anti-*Ultramontane tendencies led him to suspend it in 1864. Henceforward he endeavoured to resist the movement towards Ultramontanism in the RC Church. He strongly opposed the *.*Syllabus Errorum* (1864), and in 1869 went to Rome to organize resistance to the definition of Papal Infallibility at the *Vatican Council, working in close conjunction with Döllinger when publishing in the *Allgemeine Zeitung* the famous series of letters under the signature '*Quirinus'. But he never formally broke with the RC Church, and in 1874 in some letters to *The Times* publicly explained his position on the basis of Gladstone's pamphlet on *The Vatican Decrees*. In his later years Acton's main energies were devoted to encouraging the study of modern history. He helped to found (1886), and often contributed to, the *English Historical Review*. In 1895 Lord Rosebery appointed him regius professor of modern history at Cambridge in succession to Sir John *Seeley, where he delivered his famous inaugural lecture on the study of history (reprinted in *Lectures on Modern History*, ed. by J. N. *Figgis and R. V. Laurence, 1906). His last great work was to plan the *Cambridge Modern History* (12 vols. and index, 1901–11), for which he wrote the Introductory chapter, though most of the work was not published till after his death. His posthumously published writings include *Historical Essays and Studies* (1907), *The History of Freedom* (1907), and *Lectures on the French Revolution* (1910), books partly based on studies which grew out of a long-projected, but never executed, 'History of Liberty'. The three collections of his letters—the *Letters to Mrs. Drew* (Gladstone's daughter) (1903), and those edited respectively by F. A. *Gasquet and J. N. Figgis—give a vivid impression of his personality.

Letters of Lord Acton to Mary, daughter of the Right Hon. W. E. Gladstone, ed. with Introd. Memoir (pp. xi–lxxvii) by H. Paul (1904); F. A. Gasquet, O.S.B., *Lord Acton and his Circle* [1906]; J. N. Figgis and R. V. Laurence (edd.), *Selections from the Correspondence of the First Lord Acton* (1917). D. Mathew, *Acton* (1946); G. Himmelfarb, *Lord Acton. A Study in Conscience and Politics* (1952). Studies by U. Noack (Frankfurt, 1935, 1936, and 1947). Bibl. in W. A. Shaw, *A Bibliography of the Historical Works of Dr. Creighton*, &c. (Royal Historical Society, 1903), pp. 3–63.

ACTS OF THE APOSTLES, THE. The fifth book of the NT, written by St. *Luke, the author of the Third Gospel. It traces the progress of the Christian Church from the Ascension of our Lord to St. *Paul's first visit to *Rome. The identity of authorship between the Third Gospel and Acts is undisputed; and there are good grounds for holding that both are the work of St. Luke, the companion of St. Paul, mentioned in Col. 4. 14, Philem. 24, and 2 Tim. 4. 11. This is definitely stated by Christian writers from the latter part of the 2nd cent. onwards, e.g. the *Muratorian Canon, St. *Irenaeus, *Clement of Alexandria, and *Tertullian. The argument from the use of medical language in Luke–Acts to prove that the writer was a physician (cf. Col. 4. 14) has been shown by L. J. Cadbury to be insufficient, though the terminology is fully consistent with medical authorship. The accuracy of the author in many places where Acts and profane history meet on common ground has been vindicated by modern archaeological finds, notably through the researches of Sir William *Ramsay. The chief difficulties the Lucan authorship has to face come from certain alleged inconsistencies between Acts and the Pauline Epistles; but, given their different aims, these are not insuperable.

Scholars are far less unanimous on the question of date. Two different views were already held in antiquity. Acc. to the so-called *Anti-Marcionite 'Prologue of Luke' (probably c. 160–80), Acts was written in Achaia some time after the death of St. Paul. The more common early opinion dated the book at the end or shortly after the Apostle's first Roman captivity. *Eusebius based this view chiefly on 2 Tim. 4. 16 ff. Among modern exegetes it is followed by A. *Harnack, who considered it unlikely that Acts would have omitted any mention of St. Paul's martyrdom if it had already taken place. A third view, held by several modern scholars, favours a date between 90 and 95, on the grounds that certain parallels between Luke–Acts and the writings of *Josephus demand that the author should have either read Josephus' 'Antiquities' (93) or heard his lectures in Rome (90). This argument, however, is not altogether convincing. The majority of critics favour a date between 70 and 80, which is considered late enough to account for the supposedly idealized picture of the nascent Church. In any case a date prior to the Domitianic persecution (c. 95) seems demanded, as after this the favourable attitude of Acts towards the Roman authorities would be difficult to understand.

The sources used by the author are oral and perhaps written traditions; the apparent existence of doublets in the earlier chapters has been thought to support this latter hypothesis, and several scholars, e.g. A. Harnack, have claimed success in separating these sources. Acc. to C. C. Torrey, Acts 1.2 – 15.35 is St. Luke's translation of a single Aramaic document emanating from Jerusalem which was concerned to show the universal mission of Christianity. The so-called 'We-sections' (Acts 16. 10–17; 20. 5–15; 21. 1–17; 27. 1 – 28. 16, to which *Codex Bezae adds 11. 27) are now generally believed to come from the author's own travel diary, thus revealing him as an eye-witness of many of the events he relates.

The text of Acts, which has come down to us in two recensions, presents a difficult critical problem. The shorter text is represented by most of the great Uncial MSS., e.g. the *Codices Sinaiticus, Vaticanus and Alexandrinus, the other, longer, text by the so-called '*Western text', esp. Codex Bezae. Several theories have been put forward to account for this divergence. Acc. to one view, represented e.g. by F. *Blass and T. *Zahn, Luke himself issued his work in two versions; acc. to another, which is much more widely held, the original text was expanded and smoothed over by some writer versed in tradition early in the 2nd cent.

The Book of Acts may be conveniently divided (after C. H. *Turner) into six parts, tracing the progress of Christianity from *Jerusalem to Rome. 1.1–6.7 describes the Jerusalem Church and the preaching of St. *Peter; 6.8–9.31 the extension of the Church throughout Palestine and the preaching of St. *Stephen; 9.32–12.24 the extension of the Church to *Antioch and the conversion of Cornelius; 12.25–16.5 St. Paul's mission to Galatia and the Council of Jerusalem; 16.6–19.20 the conversions of Macedonia, Greece, and Asia; and 19. 21 to the end describes the extension of the Church to Rome and Paul's journey thither as a prisoner.

The book emphasizes the Divine origin of Christianity, which is attested by the Apostles and their miracles and martyrdoms. In their discourses with the Jews they affirm that Jesus is the Messiah (2. 36, 4. 27, 9. 22, &c.), proclaimed as such by His Resurrection, of which they are the authorized witnesses (e.g. 1. 22, 3. 15), and foretold in the OT (2. 24–36, 13. 16–38). The most striking proofs of the Divine origin of the infant Church are the miraculous intervention of the Holy Ghost in her foundation (2. 1–5), the fervent charity of the first Christians (2. 44–7), the rapid propagation of Christianity, and the Divine help given to the Apostles, esp. to St. Peter and St. Paul (chs. 12 and 16). The Trinitarian dogma is already there in germ, although the Personality of the Holy Ghost is not yet fully recognized. Belief in the Divinity of Christ is implicit in the Book, e.g., in the passage on the Blood of God (20. 28), through whose grace all men, whether Jews or Gentiles, must be saved (15. 11). Sins are effaced by Baptism (2. 38), the newly baptized receive the Holy Ghost in Confirmation (8. 15–17, 19. 6), and all the faithful remain in fellowship in 'the breaking of bread' (ἡ κλάσις τοῦ ἄρτου, 2. 42; cf. 2. 46, 20. 7), the term used in Acts for the Eucharistic rite. Thus, acc. to Acts, the Church has her special rites from the beginning, by which Christianity is distinguished from Judaism. This distinction becomes noticeable esp. with the conversion of pagans (ch. 11) and through the decision of the Council of Jerusalem (ch. 15) to abrogate certain of the Mosaic observances. The infant Church seems to have been governed first only by the Apostles (2. 42, 4. 33), to whom the 'Seven' were added later (6. 1–6) as well as elders (πρεσβύτεροι, 14. 23, 15. 2, &c.) and bishops (ἐπίσκοποι, 20. 28), the latter two evidently not yet being distinguished. Thus Acts presents a fairly complete picture of the beginnings of the Church in its progress from Jerusalem to Rome, which, after the exaggerations of the *Tübingen School have been discarded, is now generally regarded as reliable.

Modern Commentaries by T. E. Page (London, 1886); R. B. Rackham, C.R. (West. Comm., 1901); E. Preuschen (Hb.N.T., 1912); A. *Loisy (Paris, 1920); A. W. F. Blunt (Clar. Bib., 1922); E. Jacquier (Paris, 1927); F. J. Foakes Jackson (Moff. Comm., 1931) and C. S. C. Williams (Black's New Testament Commentaries, 1957). A. *Harnack, Die Apostelgeschichte (1908; Eng. tr., 1909), and other works; C. C. Torrey, The Composition and Date of Acts (Harvard Theological Studies, No. 1, 1916); F. J. Foakes Jackson–K. *Lake (edd.), The Beginnings of Christianity (5 vols., 1920–33); W. L. Knox, St. Paul and the Church of Jerusalem (1925); H. J. Cadbury, The Making of Luke–Acts (1927); A. C. Clark, The Acts of the Apostles (1933; on the text); W. L. Knox, The Acts of the Apostles (1948). McNeile, pp. 92–123, with further bibl.

ACTS OF THE MARTYRS.

Of the numerous separate accounts of early Christian martyrdoms of varying authenticity, the most reliable are those that follow the official short-hand reports of the trials. Very few of these, however, have survived, perhaps the most perfect specimen of this type being the 'Acta Proconsularia' of St. *Cyprian. A second category, the so-called 'Passiones', are the stories of martyrdoms written by Christian authors and based on eyewitness accounts. To this type belong the 'Martyrdoms' of St. *Ignatius, of St. *Polycarp, of the Martyrs of Lyons, the famous 'Passion of St. *Perpetua and St. Felicitas', the 'Passion of St. *Irenaeus', and others. In all these the miraculous element is much restricted, a feature which did not appeal to the popular taste. In their later versions the sober account of the original was frequently embellished with miraculous and other apocryphal or legendary material, e.g. in the cases of St. Perpetua, the *Scillitan Martyrs, and other authentic Acts. A third category belongs completely to the realm of legend, with probably no historical kernel whatever. Such are the Acts of St. *Catherine of Alexandria and those of St. *George.

*Eusebius of Caesarea was probably the first Christian author to produce a collection of Acts of Martyrs; his great work, the Συναγωγὴ τῶν Ἀρχαίων Μαρτυρίων, is unfortunately lost, but a smaller one on the Palestinian martyrs survives in Greek fragments and in a complete Syriac version. In the W. Church the Acts of the Martyrs were carefully collected and used in the Liturgy from early times, as is testified by St. *Augustine.

The most comprehensive collection is contained in the *Bollandist *Acta Sanctorum. Another well-known set is that of T. *Ruinart, Acta Primorum Martyrum Sincera et Selecta (1689). Critical studies appear in the Analecta Bollandiana and in the many writings of H. *Delehaye. A useful English selection is E. C. C. Owen, Some Authentic Acts of the Early Martyrs (1927).

ACTS OF Sts. PAUL AND THECLA.
See Paul and Thecla, Acts of Sts.

ACTS OF St. PETER.
See Peter, Acts of St.

ACTS OF PILATE.
See Pilate, Acts of.

ACTUAL GRACE.
See Grace.

ACTUAL SIN.
A sin, whether of commission or omission, which is the outcome of a free personal act of the individual will. In Christian theology it is contrasted with *Original Sin (q.v.). See also Sin.

ACTUS PURUS
(Lat., 'Pure Actuality'). The scholastic term for the absolute perfection of God. It depends upon the *Aristotelian distinction between potentiality and actuality. Potentiality, as the aptitude to change, is the mark of all created things, even Angels, because their existence is contingent upon the action of a creator. It is thus the mark of imperfection. God alone, as being free from change, and being all that He can be, is free from potentiality, and may therefore be described as pure actuality. The distinction between potentiality and actuality is the foundation of the first of the five scholastic arguments for the existence of God (see Quinque Viae).

ADALBERT OF BREMEN
(c. 1000–72), German Archbishop. He was the descendant of a noble Saxon family. In 1032 he became canon at Bremen, later provost of Halberstadt Cathedral, and in 1045 Abp. of Bremen-Hamburg. He was an energetic promoter of missionary activities, esp. in the Nordic countries, Scandinavia, Iceland, Greenland, and the Orkneys, and planned to become Patriarch of the North. In 1053 *Leo IX nominated him Papal Vicar and Legate of the Nordic nations. During the minority of Henry IV he gradually gained considerable influence over the young king, who loaded him with rich counties and abbeys. In 1066 Henry was compelled to dismiss him from his court by the jealousy of enemies, who also invaded his archbishopric and robbed him of his possessions. In 1069 he was recalled by Henry and part of his property restored. His last years were darkened by the invasion of the pagan Wends who destroyed Hamburg in 1071–2.

Contemporary account by Adam of Bremen (d. c. 1085) in his Gesta Hammaburgensis Ecclesiae Pontificum (ed. J. M. Lappenberg in M.G.H., Scriptores, vii, 1846, pp. 335–67). G. Meyer von Knonau, Jahrbücher des deutschen Reiches unter Heinrich IV und Heinrich V, ii (1894), pp. 121–47. C. Gründhagen, Adalbert, Erzbischof von Hamburg und die Idee eines nordischen Patriarchats (1854). E. Aurelius, 'Adalbert, Arkebiskop af Hamburg-Bremen' in Kyrkohistorisk Årsskrift, i (1900), pp. 205–24. W. Biereye, 'Die Urkunden des Erzbischofs Adalberts von Bremen' in Zeitschrift des Vereins für Hamburgische Geschichte, xx (1915), pp. 28–99. J. Metzler in L.Th.K., i (1930), col. 79 f., s.v.

ADAM.
In traditional theology, the first man. The etymology is disputed. In Genesis there are two accounts of his creation—1. 26–31,

attributed to a Priestly editor (P), and 2. 5–7, attributed to the Yahwist (J); the stories of his Fall and subsequent history (Gen. 2.15–4.1 and 25) are all J material. Acc. to the P account, Adam was created on the sixth day, after the animals (1. 26); was made in the image and likeness of God (1. 26 f.); commanded to multiply; and given dominion over the earth (1. 28–30). The J account, more anthropomorphic, assigns his creation to the time when the earth was still void. It describes God's breathing into Adam's nostrils the breath of life (2. 7), the creation of *Eve from Adam's rib (2. 21 f.), and Adam's work in the garden of Eden, with its Tree of Knowledge and forbidden fruit (2. 17). Ch. 3 narrates Adam's *Fall (q.v.), the curse laid on him, and the expulsion from Paradise.

Traditional theology has utilized the Scriptural statements in its doctrine of man and his relation to God. As the father of the human race Adam has been held to have been endowed with great intellectual gifts, enabling him, e.g., to give names to all the animals (2. 19 f.). He was also held to possess infused knowledge (Ecclus. 17. 6 f.). The Councils of *Orange (529, can. 19) and of *Trent (sess. 5, cans. 1 and 2) defined that he was created in the state of sanctifying grace in conformity with the belief that Christ, the *Second Adam (Rom. 5. 14 and 1 Cor. 15. 45), restored mankind to the state of righteousness which had been lost by the first Adam. This state of grace has been held to consist with certain preternatural privileges, such as the absence of concupiscence, and the possession of immortality and impassibility, which were bestowed on Adam in his original condition. It was through the Fall that these prerogatives were lost.

Acc. to Christian tradition, Christ delivered Adam from *Limbo. The notion of *Tatian and the *Encratites that Adam had been damned was rejected by St. *Irenaeus, who taught that Christ's victory over the old Serpent would not have been complete had He not delivered Adam from his power. Acc. to a Jewish tradition, taken up by St. *Jerome and long accepted in the W., he was buried at Hebron. This supposition gradually gave way to another, first found in *Origen and widespread esp. in the E., which placed his tomb on *Calvary, so that at the Crucifixion the Blood of the Second Adam was poured out over the head of the First. St. *Augustine (In Ps. xcv [xcvi], No. 15) found in the four letters of Adam's name allusion to the four points of the compass (Anatole, Dysis, Arctos, Mesembria) and hence a sign of his identity with fallen humanity scattered over the whole world. The E. Churches give a public cult to Adam and Eve, whose feast is kept by the Greeks on the Sunday before *Christmas.

J. Jeremias in T.W.B., i (1933), pp. 141–3; D. *Stone 'Lexicon of Patristic Greek: Ἀδάμ' in J.T.S., xxiv (1922–3), pp. 473–5. X. Le Bachelet in D.T.C., i (1903), cols. 368–86, with bibl. H. *Leclercq, O.S.B., in D.A.C.L., i (pt. 1; 1907), cols. 509–19, s.v. 'Adam et Ève'.

ADAM OF MARSH, 'Adam de Marisco' (d. c. 1258), English *Franciscan theologian. He

was probably a native of Somerset, educated at *Oxford, and after being ordained priest received the living of *Wearmouth from his uncle, Richard, Bp. of *Durham. Probably c. 1230 he entered the Franciscan Order at *Worcester and later was sent to Oxford. In 1239 he took part in the General Chapter of the order at Pisa, and in 1245 he accompanied Robert *Grosseteste, his lifelong friend, to the Council of *Lyons. Despite the plans of the French to give him a chair at the university of *Paris he returned to Oxford, where, from c. 1247, he was regent of the Franciscan house of studies. Apart from his work as a scholar he exercised great influence in English political and social life. Together with *Grosseteste and Simon de Montfort he defended the national liberties, and his advice was frequently sought by the most influential men of the country, among them Henry III and *Boniface, Abp. of *Canterbury. In 1256 both Henry and Boniface endeavoured to have him appointed to the see of *Ely, but the monks of Ely objected and obtained a Papal decision in their favour. Besides letters, he probably also wrote commentaries on Cant. and Heb. His learning, highly esteemed, e.g. by Roger *Bacon, gained him the title of 'Doctor Illustris'.

Letters ed. J. S. Brewer, Monumenta Franciscana, i (R.S., 1858), pp. 77–489, with introd., pp. lxxvi–ci. The other principal source is the mid-13th cent. Tractatus de Adventu Fratrum Minorum in Angliam of Thomas of Eccleston, O.F.M., esp. Collationes xi, xiii f., ed. A. G. Little (Collection d'Études et de Documents vii, 1909), pp. 22 f., 63 f., 88, 105 f. A. G. Little, The Grey Friars in Oxford (Oxford Historical Society, xx, 1892), pp. 134–9; id., 'The Franciscan School at Oxford in the Thirteenth Century' in A.F.H., xix (1926), pp. 803–74, esp. pp. 831–7. M. *Creighton in D.N.B., i (1855), p. 79, s.v.

ADAM OF ST.-VICTOR (d. between 1177 and 1192), *sequence writer. Probably a Breton by birth ('Brito', possibly=British), he was educated at *Paris, and c. 1130 entered the abbey of St.-Victor (see Victorines). His fame rests upon the large number of sequences, including some of the earliest and finest, ascribed to him; they combine facility of treatment with liturgical austerity and doctrinal precision. Those assigned to him include Heri Mundus Exultavit (for Feast of St. *Stephen; Eng. tr. in A.M. 64); Verbi Vere Substantivi (for Feast of St. *John Evangelist); Zyma Vetus Expurgetur (for *Easter); Salve Mater Salvatoris; Plausu Chorus Laetabundo (Eng. tr. in E.H. 179 and A.M. 621) and Supernae Matris Gaudia (Eng. tr. in E.H. 200). A number of prose works, including a dictionary of difficult Biblical words, have also been ascribed to him.

A number of sequences attributed to him were printed by J. Clichtoveus, Elucidatorium Ecclesiasticum (Paris, 1515), pp. 154–200; seventy further sequences, preserved in MS. at the Abbey of St.-Victor, were transferred at its dissolution to the Bibliothèque Nationale; full ed. by L. Gautier (2 vols., Paris, 1858–9), with introd. in vol. i, pp. xv–clxxxv; text repr., with Eng. tr., by D. S. Wrangham (3 vols., London, 1881); further ed. by E. Misset–P. Aubry (Paris, 1900), with crit. study pp. 3–166 (very critical of ascription to Adam of St.-Victor). Crit. ed. of text by C. Blume, S.J.–H. M. Bannister (edd.), Liturgische Prosen des Übergangsstiles und der zweiten Epoche insbesondere die dem Adam von Sanct Victor zugeschriebenen (A.H.M.A., liv, 1915); see also C. Blume, S.J., Liturgische Prosen zweiter Epoche auf

Feste der Heiligen (ib., lv, 1922), pp. vii–ix, with reff. Raby, pp. 348–55, with further bibl. p. 482. P. Lejay in *D.T.C.*, i (1903), col. 388 f., s.v.

ADAMANTIUS (early 4th cent.), Greek anti-*Gnostic writer. He was the author of the Dialogue, 'De recta in Deum fide', prob. from internal evidence a product of Asia Minor or Syria, but nothing further is known of him. St. *Basil the Great and St. *Gregory Nazianzen wrongly identify him with *Origen. The Dialogue, in five books, is a disputation first with two disciples of *Marcion, and then with followers of *Bardesanes and *Valentinus. At the end, Eutropius, a pagan arbitrator, gives the palm of victory to Adamantius. The work was translated into Latin by *Rufinus.

Ed. *princeps* by J. R. Wetstein (Basle, 1674), repr. in edd. of *Origen (e.g. *PG*, xi, 1711–1884). Rufinus' Lat. text, which survives only in a 12th-cent. MS at Schlettstadt, formerly at Hirschau, was first publd. by C. P. *Caspari, *Kirchenhistorische Anecdota* (Christiania, 1883), i, pp. 1–129. Crit. ed., with Rufinus' Lat., by W. H. van de Sande Bakhuyzen (G.C.S., 1901).

ADAMITES. A small Christian sect, first mentioned by St. *Epiphanius (*Haer.* 52) and St. *Augustine (*Haer.* 31), who aimed at returning to man's primitive innocence in Paradise by the practice of nudity. They are perhaps to be identified with a group of *Carpocratians referred to by St. *Clement of Alexandria (*Strom.* III. ii) who advocated community of wives and sexual promiscuity. In more recent times, small groups among the *Waldenses, Dutch *Anabaptists, and others, also calling themselves 'Adamites', have advocated similar doctrines and practices.

G. Bareille in *D.T.C.*, i (1903), col. 391 f., s.v.

ADAMNAN, St. (*c.* 624–704), Abbot of *Iona. He was educated by the monks of St. *Columba at his native place of Drumhome (Co. Donegal), and in 650 became a novice at the monastery of Iona, where he was elected abbot in 679. A visit to the abbey of *Wearmouth led him to accept the Roman dating of *Easter, but through the resistance of his monks he was unable to introduce it at Iona. He was more successful, however, in furthering the Roman observance in Ireland, which he visited three times. On the last of these visits he caused the Synod of Tara (697) to adopt a law forbidding women and children to be made prisoners of war, called after him the 'Canon of Adamnan'. He was one of the greatest scholars that Iona produced; his 'Life of St. Columba' (ed. J. T. Fowler, 1894), though containing much fabulous material, is of very great historic value. He also wrote an account of a pilgrim's visit to Palestine, 'De Locis Sanctis' (ed. by P. Geyer in the Vienna 'Corpus Scriptorum', vol. xxxix, 1898). He was greatly venerated in Scotland and in Ireland, in the latter country under the name of St. Eunan. Feast day, 23 Sept.

The chief authority for his life is *Bede, *H.E.*, v, 15 f. and 21; notes to ed. by C. Plummer, ii (Oxford, 1896), pp. 300–4. Irish life in O. J. Bergin–R. I. Best–K. Meyer–J. G. O'Keeffe

(edd.). *Anecdota from Irish Manuscripts*, ii (Halle and Dublin, 1908), pp. 10–20, with Eng. tr. and notes by M. Joynt in *Celtic Review*, v (1908), pp. 97–107. Further material noted in C. Plummer, *Miscellanea Hagiographica Hibernica* (Studia Hagiographica, xv, 1925), pp. 198–200 and 226. Crit. ed. of life of St. Columba, with Eng. tr., by A. O. Anderson and Margaret O. Anderson (London, 1961). J. T. Gilbert in *D.N.B.*, i (1885), p. 92 f., s.v.

ADAMSON, PATRICK (1537–92), Abp. of St. Andrews. Educated at Perth Grammar School and St. Andrews university, he was minister at Ceres from 1563 to 1566. He then went abroad for some years, living in France and for a time also at *Geneva, where he studied *Calvinist theology under T. *Beza. He was imprisoned for six months for describing the infant son of *Mary Queen of Scots as 'serenissimus princeps' of Scotland, England, France, and Ireland. After his return he published a catechism of his own compilation as well as a Latin version of the '*Scottish Confession' (1572). Appointed in 1576 Abp. of St. Andrews in succession to John Douglas (1571–6), he now became involved in a long controversy with the *Presbyterian party. In 1583 some sermons preached before *James VI (I) led to his winning the royal favour and becoming Ambassador at *Elizabeth's court later in the same year. During his stay in London he used his great powers of oratory to bring discredit on the Presbyterian party. Strongly supported by the King, he returned to Scotland in May 1584, but his disfavour with the *General Assembly continued to increase, and his *Declaration of the King's Majesty's Intention in the late Acts of Parliament* (1585) provoked much hostility. At the synod of Fife (April 1586), James Melville, the nephew of Andrew *Melville and professor of theology at St. Andrews, made a fierce attack on his character and opinions and, though Adamson brought the matter before the King, the synod excommunicated him. Further charges were made on his character at the meeting of the General Assembly in 1587, and in the following year Adamson lost the King's favour. Adamson now sought the support of A. Melville and is credited with a *Recantation* of his earlier *Declaration*, though there are grounds for believing the Recantation to be spurious. His writings include Latin renderings of the Lamentations of Jeremiah and of the Book of Revelation (both 1590).

The most reliable authority is D. Calderwood, *History of the Kirk of Scotland* (1678; crit. ed. from unpubld. MSS. by T. Thomson, Woodrow Society, esp. vols. i–v, 1842–4). There is also a life by T. Wilson appended to his ed. of Adamson's *De Sacro Pastoris Munere* (1619; sep. pagination). A. H. Bullen in *D.N.B.*, i (1885), pp. 111–15, s.v.

ADDAI. The traditional founder of the Church at *Edessa. In Syriac tradition he was one of the 72 (al. 70) disciples of Lk. 10. 1. It seems probable that the name is philologically the same as '*Thaddaeus', with whom *Eusebius (*H.E.*, 1.xii. 3) actually identifies him. Acc. to the 'Doctrine of Addai' (q.v.) he was sent by St. *Thomas the Apostle to heal King *Abgar (q.v.). F. C. *Burkitt has identified him with *Tatian (2nd cent.) of whom no independent memory survived in the Syriac

Church, holding that the tradition that Addai belonged to the 1st cent. was of later date.

His historical existence is defended by E. Sachau, *Die Chronik von Arbela* (1915); F. C. Burkitt in *J.T.S.*, xxv (1923–4), p. 130. See also bibl. to foll. entry.

ADDAI, The Doctrine of. A Syriac writing, preserved *in toto* only in a single Petrograd MS., which describes how King *Abgar (q.v.) was brought into contact with Christ and *Addai was sent to *Edessa to convert him. It probably dates from *c.* 400, but seems to depend on older sources, notably the document used in Eusebius *H.E.*, i. xiii. 6–8. An Armenian version also survives. Part of the Syriac text was published by W. *Cureton in his *Ancient Syriac Documents* (1864) and the whole by G. Phillips in *The Doctrine of Addai the Apostle* (1876). The historicity of the narrative, defended by many older scholars (e.g. C. *Baronius, Le N. *Tillemont, W. *Cave, J. E. *Grabe, Cureton, G. Phillips), has now been generally abandoned.

There are Eng. trr. in the edd. of both Cureton and Phillips. L. J. Tixeront, *Les Origines de l'Église d'Édesse et la légende d'Abgar* (1888), pp. 20–159. Bardenhewer, i, pp. 591–6, and iv, p. 326. Altaner, pp. 57 f.

ADDAI AND MARI, Liturgy of. The Syriac Liturgy which is still the normal rite of the *Nestorian Christians. The rite was probably composed *c.* 200 for the Syriac-speaking Church at *Edessa, which looked back to *Addai and his disciple, Mari, as their founders, its Greek influences apparently being much later modifications. Though no MSS. of it go beyond the 16th cent., there is little doubt that it preserves the original structure of the rite and is thus of the highest importance for the early history of the Liturgy. Notable points about the *Anaphora, in its original form, are its address to Christ (not to God the Father) and the absence of any Words of Institution.

The *editio princeps* of the Syriac text is in *Liturgia Sanctorum Apostolorum Adaei et Maris* (Urmi, 1890–2). For Eng. trans., see F. E. *Brightman, *Liturgies Eastern and Western*, i (1896), pp. 245–305. G.P. Badger, *The Nestorians and their Rituals* (1852), esp. ii, pp. 215–43; E. C. Ratcliff, 'The Original Form of the Anaphora of Addai and Mari. A Suggestion' in *Journal of Theological Studies*, xxx (1929), pp. 23–32; G. Dix, O.S.B., *The Shape of the Liturgy* (1945), esp. pp. 177–87.

ADELARD OF BATH (early 12th cent.), English Scholastic philosopher. Few facts about his life survive, but he is known to have studied at Tours and Laon and to have travelled widely in Europe as well as in N. Africa and Asia Minor. He translated the 'Elements' of Euclid, and in his 'Quaestiones Naturales' defended Democritus' theory of atoms as well as the Aristotelian proof of God's existence from motion. In his principal work, 'De Eodem et Diverso' (between 1105 and 1116), written in epistolary form, Adelard developed a theory of the Liberal Arts and also attempted to reconcile the *Platonic and *Aristotelian doctrines of *universals, holding that in reality the universal and the particular

were identical, and distinct only in our mode of apprehending them.

Adelard's 'De Eodem et Diverso', ed. H. Willner (B.G.P.M., iv, Hft. 1; 1903); 'Quaestiones Naturales', ed. M. Müller (ib., xxxi, Hft. 2; 1934). F. J. P. Bliemetzrieder, *Adelhard von Bath* (Munich, 1935). C. H. Haskins, 'Adelard of Bath' in *E.H.R.*, xxvi (1911), pp. 491–8. U. Berlière, O.S.B., in *D.H.G.E.*, i (1912), col. 522 f., with details of works, publd. and unpubld.

ADESTE FIDELES. Anonymous Christmas hymn, probably written in the 17th or 18th cent., of French or German authorship. Its most popular tune has been doubtfully ascribed to John Reading, the 17th cent. organist of *Winchester Cathedral. It has been frequently translated, the best-known version being that by F. *Oakeley, 'O come, all ye faithful, joyfully triumphant'.

J. Stéphan, O.S.B., *The 'Adeste Fideles'*, A Study on its Origin and Development (Buckfast Abbey, 1947; enlarged Fr. ed., 1949).

ADHERENTS. In the Church of *Scotland, baptized persons who, although non-communicants, are intimately connected with a congregation. If parishioners and seat-holders over 21 years of age, they have the right to be placed on the electoral register. This right is controlled by the *kirk-session to whose jurisdiction they are subject.

ADIAPHORISTS (from Gk. ἀδιάφορα, 'things indifferent'). A party in German Protestantism which held that certain rites and actions were matters of indifference. The first controversy on the subject broke out in connexion with the *Leipzig Interim (1548). In this compromise between the theologians of *Wittenberg, esp. P. *Melanchthon, and the ecclesiastical and civil authorities of Saxony, the Wittenberg group declared certain Catholic practices such as *Confirmation and *Extreme Unction, the *Mass without *Transubstantiation, and the Veneration of Saints 'adiaphora', i.e. matters on which concessions might be made in the interest of peace without prejudice to Protestant doctrine. This policy was fiercely opposed by M. *Flacius Illyricus, who, in his *De Veris et Falsis Adiaphoris* (1549), stressed the dangers to integral *Lutheranism of these concessions. The controversy continued till after the Peace of *Augsburg (1555) and was brought to an end only by Article 10 of the Formula of *Concord (1577), which ruled that in times of persecution concessions were not to be made, but otherwise ceremonies not commanded or forbidden by Scripture might be altered acc. to the decisions of individual Churches.

Another controversy on 'adiaphora' broke out in the latter half of the 17th cent. between the Pietistical followers of P. J. *Spener and A. H. *Francke, who declared all worldly pleasures such as theatres and dances to be sinful in themselves, and the orthodox Lutherans who held them to be indifferent and therefore permitted. A harmonizing of the two points of view was later given by F. D. E. *Schleiermacher, who, though denying the conception of matters of indifference, considered ordinary pleasures part of the whole of human life and therefore not only permissible but even demanded by duty.

F. H. R. Frank, *Die Theologie der Concordienformel historisch-diplomatisch entwickelt und beleuchtet*, iv (1865) pp. 1–120. A. *Ritschl, *Geschichte des Pietismus*, ii (1884), pp. 174–83. J. Gottschick in *P.R.E.* (ed. 3), i (1896), pp. 168–79, s.v. 'Adiaphora'; E. T. Horn in *H.E.R.E.*, i (1908), pp. 91–3, s.v. 'Adiaphorism'.

AD LIMINA APOSTOLORUM, i.e., lit., 'to the thresholds of the Apostles'. Pilgrimages 'ad limina Apostolorum', *sc.* to the tombs of St. *Peter and St. *Paul in *Rome, usually undertaken in fulfilment of a vow, were very popular in the Middle Ages. In modern times the term is ordinarily used in a technical sense, denoting the obligation of RC bishops to pay regular visits to Rome to venerate the tombs of the Apostles and to report on the state of their dioceses to the Pope. This custom originated in the decree of a Roman synod (743) which enjoined such visits on all bishops who had been ordained at Rome (can. 4). *Gregory VII extended this obligation to all metropolitans of the W., and from the 13th cent. it was imposed on all bishops consecrated by the Pope himself or by his special representative. *Sixtus V, by the bull 'Romanus Pontifex' of 20 Dec. 1584, required the visit from all bishops every three to ten years, acc. to the distance of their dioceses. Acc. to the revised regulation of Pius X (1909), which was taken over into the *CIC* (cans. 299, 341, 342), all Ordinaries and Vicars Apostolic who have jurisdiction must perform the Visitatio ad Limina Apostolorum either personally or by representative every five years if their dioceses are in Europe, and every ten years if they are beyond.

F. M. Cappello, *De Visitatione Liminum* (2 vols., 1912–13).

ADMONITION TO PARLIAMENT, The. (1572). A manifesto against all ecclesiastical and university dignitaries and demanding a non-episcopal constitution for the English Church. It attacked *inter alia* the use of wafer-bread at the Communion, then still current, reception of the Sacrament kneeling, and the admission of Papists to Communion, and demanded the restoration of excommunication. Apparently a composite document, it was issued anonymously from unknown presses, and very widely and eagerly read. The responsibility for it was saddled on two London *Puritan clergymen, John Field and Thomas Wilcox, who sought to present it to Parliament; but both were committed to Newgate on 7 July 1572. When the Bishops inveighed against the *Admonition*, it was vigorously defended in the *Second Admonition to the Parliament* ascribed to T. *Cartwright. Both the *Admonition* and this defence of it were suppressed by a royal proclamation on 11 June 1573, and Cartwright, on the issue of a warrant for his arrest, was compelled to leave the country. The controversy was the immediate occasion of R. *Hooker's *Ecclesiastical Polity* (1594–7).

Text in *Puritan Manifestoes*, ed. by W. H. *Frere and C. E. Douglas (C.H.S., lxxii, 1907), pp. 5–19; Second Ad-

monition, ib., pp. 79–133. D. J. McGinn, *Admonition Controversy* (Rutgers University Studies in English, v, New Brunswick, 1949).

ADO, Martyrology of. The *martyrology compiled in 858 by St. Ado (*c.* 800–75), then a *Benedictine monk, later Abp. of Vienne. Acc. to Ado, his basis was an ancient Roman martyrology ('Martyrologium Romanum Parvum') which he had discovered at *Ravenna, but this work, which is full of blunders, was certainly spurious and may even have been fabricated by Ado himself. The highly convenient plan and arrangement of the compilation were the pattern for later martyrologies. It directly influenced the Martyrology of *Usuard and mediately the '*Roman Martyrology', and was thus the source of most of the merits and defects of its successors.

The Martyrology of Ado was edited by H. Rosweyde in 1613 (reprinted in J. P. Migne, *PL*, cxxiii, 139–436), and by D. Giorgi (Rome, 1745). H. *Quentin, *Les Martyrologes historiques* (1908).

ADONAI (Heb. אֲדֹנָי, plur., probably 'majestatis', of אָדוֹן, 'master', 'Lord'). Divine name, frequently used in the OT. Apart from its use in the Hebrew Bible, the Jews also employed and read it as a substitute for the unutterable name of Jehovah, which, in the texts, is usually pointed with the vowel signs proper to Adonai. The *Gnostics employed it as a name for one of their aeons.

In the Christian Liturgy the term is applied esp. to the Second Person of the Trinity in the great antiphon to the Magnificat for 18 Dec., 'O Adonai' (see *O-Antiphons*).

G. H. *Dalman, *Studien zur biblischen Theologie*. Der Gottesname Adonaj und seine Geschichte (1889).

ADOPTIANISM. (1) The heresy, originating in Spain in the 8th cent., acc. to which Christ, in His humanity, is not the true, but only the adoptive, Son of God. Its chief representatives were *Elipandus, Abp. of *Toledo, and *Felix, Bp. of Urgel. The heresy probably arose out of Elipandus' fight against the error of Migetius, who rejected all distinction between the Second Person of the Trinity and the Incarnate Christ, and its development was perhaps assisted by the fact that a quasi-*Nestorian theology would be more acceptable than orthodox doctrine to the Moors, then in possession of Toledo. Elipandus upheld a distinction between the 'Logos, as the true natural and eternal Son of God, and Christ, the adoptive Son, who is Son only metaphorically, because the Word 'adopted' the humanity, thereby attaching the filiation to the nature rather than to the Person of Christ. He was supported by Felix of Urgel, who recanted, however, at a synod held at Ratisbon in 792. Having repeated his abjuration before the Pope, Felix returned to his diocese, but again fell into error and was obliged to flee. The Spanish bishops sided with Elipandus and tried to prove their views from Scripture and the Fathers. After they had communicated to the Pope a letter they had sent to *Charlemagne, the latter called the Council of Frankfurt (794), where the bishops attacked the Spanish arguments in two documents. These, together with a third drawn up by *Hadrian I, were sent to Spain. A reply from Felix in favour of the heresy provoked *Alcuin's famous seven books 'Contra Felicem', and in 799 *Leo III called a synod at *Rome which anathematized Felix. In the same year, after a long dispute, he once more recanted. Elipandus, however, remained firm, and Alcuin wrote another treatise against him. The archbishop died soon afterwards and the heresy disappeared.

It was revived, however, in the 12th cent. in a modified form by *Abelard, *Gilbert de La Porrée, and others, who, through identifying the rational nature with the Person, arrived also at Adoptianist views. In later times several attempts were made, e.g. by *Duns Scotus, *Durandus, F. *Suarez, and others, to interpret in an orthodox sense the statement that Jesus as Man is the adopted Son of God, but these theories were all rejected as subversive of a sound Christology.

(2) Through the influence of A. *Harnack's *Dogmengeschichte* the term (usually spelt 'Adoptionism') has also been frequently applied to the heretical stream in early Greek theology which regarded Christ as a man gifted with Divine powers. This view, first represented by the *Ebionites, was later developed by the *Monarchians, e.g. *Theodotus and *Paul of Samosata. *Theodore of Mopsuestia, *Nestorius, and the *Antiochene School in general also tend to what may be called, in a rather loose sense, an Adoptionist Christology.

On (1), see C. W. F. Walch, *Historia Adoptianorum* (Göttingen, 1755); Hefele–Leclercq, III, ii (1910), pp. 1001–1060. É. Amann, 'L'Adoptianisme espagnol du VIIIe siècle' in *Rev. S.R.*, xvi (1936), pp. 281–317. H. Quilliet in *D.T.C.*, i (1903), cols. 403–13, and M. Jugie, A.A., in *E.C.*, i (1949), cols. 327–30, both s.v.

ADORATION. In strict terminology the expression, from the Lat. *adoratio*, is equivalent to the Greek theological term λατρεία, designating an act of worship due to God alone. If used more loosely, however, it also covers the Greek προσκύνησις, which, in early times, was used for adoration of God as well as for veneration such as is paid to persons or objects of sacred character. In this second sense it was frequently used among E. peoples and also in the Bible, e.g. in the narrative of Joseph and his brethren (Gen. 43. 26), whereas in the first sense it is used, e.g., in the Second Commandment. Our Lord inculcates that adoration (προσκύνησις) is due to God alone (Mt. 4. 10). He Himself is frequently adored (e.g. Jn. 9. 38), whereas, on the other hand, St. *Peter refuses the adoration of Cornelius (Acts 10. 25 f.). The Divine prerogative of adoration was emphasized esp. by the early Christian martyrs, who refused to 'adore' the statues of the Emperor. It was claimed for the Son and the Holy Ghost, e.g. by *Justin Martyr, *Origen, and other early Fathers, a fact which shows the equality of the Three Divine Persons, whereas it is denied to all creatures, not excepting the BVM. Until the 5th cent.

Christians seem not to have distinguished between λατρεία and προσκύνησις. But the increasing veneration of images and the ensuing *Iconoclastic Controversy necessitated a stricter terminology. The Second Council of *Nicaea (787) reserved the term λατρεία to the worship of God alone, whereas προσκύνησις might be applied also to the cult of creatures. After some controversy this distinction was accepted also in the W., and from the age of Scholasticism W. theologians term adoration of God ''latria', but veneration of creatures ''dulia' (Gk. δουλεία).

The principal act of adoration in Christian worship is the offering of sacrifice, which is the exclusive prerogative of God, but it will normally be accompanied by such secondary acts as prayers of praise, prostrations, &c. The adoration paid to the Bl. Sacrament depends on the doctrine of the Real Presence, among its most striking manifestations being the practices of the *Forty Hours and of Perpetual Adoration, cultivated by many religious congregations. In the C of E a service of Eucharistic devotion, sometimes resembling the RC *Benediction service, is also frequently termed 'Adoration'.

A. Molien in *Dict. Sp.*, i (1937), cols. 210–22, s.v., with bibl.

ADORO TE DEVOTE. Eucharistic hymn, attributed by the MSS. to St. *Thomas Aquinas, though his authorship has been contested. It is a simple, but very personal and deeply felt, prayer to the Lord hidden under the sacramental species. Unlike St. Thomas' other Eucharistic hymns, it was not written for the Office of *Corpus Christi. It is, however, printed in the Roman *Missal and *Breviary among the 'Orationes pro Opportunitate Sacerdotis Dicendae'. There are numerous English translations, the most famous of which, found in several slightly varying forms, is that by J. R. Woodford (1850), Bp. of *Ely, 'Thee we adore, O hidden Saviour'.

Crit. ed. of text by C. M. Dreves (ed.), *Lateinische Hymnendichter des Mittelalters*, ii (A.H.M.A. 1; 1907), pp. 589–91. A. *Wilmart, O.S.B., 'La Tradition littéraire et textuelle de "l'Adoro te devote"' in *R.T.A.M.*, i (1929), pp. 21–40 and 149–76; repr. in Wilmart's *Auteurs spirituels et textes dévots* (1932), pp. 361–414 (ch. xii). F. J. E. Raby, 'The Date and Authorship of the Poem *Adoro Te Devote*' in *Speculum*, xx (1945), pp. 236–8.

ADRIAN I, IV, VI. See *Hadrian I, IV, VI*.

ADVENT (Lat. *Adventus*, 'coming', i.e. of Christ). The ecclesiastical season immediately before *Christmas. In W. Christendom Advent Sunday, i.e. the first day of Advent, is the Sunday nearest to St. Andrew's Day (30 Nov.). Four Sundays in Advent thus always precede Christmas Day. In the E. Advent is a much longer season, beginning in the middle of Nov. Advent Sunday is also the day on which the ecclesiastical year begins. The first clear references to the season in the W. come from the latter half of the 6th cent. In the *Gelasian Sacramentary Advent Collects, Epistles, and Gospels are provided for the five Sundays preceding Christmas and for the corresponding Wednesdays and Fridays. The Wednesday and Friday *propers of the Mass remained in England until the BCP of 1549.

Advent was formerly kept as *Lent, but with less strictness. In the W. fasting is no longer formally ordered, though festivities are discouraged and the solemn character of the season is marked by the liturgical use of purple (except on the Third Sunday, '*Gaudete', q.v., when rose-coloured vestments are tolerated), and, in the Roman Missal, by the omission of Gloria in Excelsis at the Sunday Masses. At High Mass, the *deacon and *sub-deacon wear, as in Lent, folded chasubles instead of the usual dalmatic and tunicle. Marriages are not normally solemnized. The season is observed as a time of preparation not only for Christmas but also for the Second Coming of Christ as Judge at the Last Day.

M. Jugie, A.A., 'La Première Fête mariale en orient et occident, l'Avent primitif' in É.O., xxvi (1923), pp. 130–52; B. Botte, O.S.B., Les Origines de la Noël et de l'Épiphanie (Louvain, 1932), pp. 263–84; J. A. Jungmann, S.J., Gewordene Liturgie (1941), pp. 232–94 ('Advent und Voradvent'). F. *Cabrol, O.S.B., in D.A.C.L., i (1907), cols. 3223–30, s.v. 'Avent'; F. Mershman in C.E., i (1907), pp. 165 f.; E. Cattaneo in E.C., ii (1949), cols. 560–2, s.v. 'Avvento'.

ADVENTISTS. Various Christian groups which hold in common that the Second Coming of Christ is to be expected immediately. As a denomination the Adventists date from 1831, when William Miller (1782–1849) first began to proclaim at Dresden, N.Y., U.S.A., the imminence of the Second Coming. On the basis of study of dates in the OT he came to fix the Second Coming in 1843–4. He made converts from many Christian bodies; premillennium conferences were held; and a paper called The Midnight Cry started. After the year had passed uneventfully, various later dates were suggested. Miller himself always maintained that the Coming was imminent, though in his later years he became less ready to pronounce dates. Differences of opinion as to the date of the Second Advent and also on the question of the immortality of the soul produced schisms. The 'Evangelical Adventists' who were the original body, and retained a Catholic belief in the after-life, have died out. The chief bodies now are the 'Second Advent Christians' and the 'Seventh Day Adventists' (q.v.).

D. T. Taylor, The Reign of Christ on Earth (Boston, 1855; ed. H. L. Hastings, London, 1882). H. C. Sheldon, Studies in Recent Adventism (New York, 1915). K. Allgermissen, Die Adventisten (1928); A. Rettaroli, Protestanti avventisti (1941). See also bibl. to Seventh Day Adventists.

ADVERTISEMENTS, Book of. The book entitled Advertisements, partly for due Order in the public Administration of Common Prayers and using the Holy Sacraments, and partly for the Apparel of all Persons Ecclesiastical by virtue of the Queen's Majesty's Letters commanding the same, issued in Mar. 1566 by Abp. M. *Parker. Of 39 items in all, it ordered inter alia the use of the surplice (in place of the traditional Mass vestments) in the Eucharist and kneeling at the reception of Communion, and disallowed the *Sign of the Cross in Baptism. It has long been disputed whether this book of Advertisements is to be understood as the 'other order' in the paragraph in the Act of *Uniformity of 1559 providing that the Ornaments (see *Ornaments Rubric) in use in the second year of Edward VI should be retained 'until other order shall therein be taken by the authority of the Queen's Majesty'. Though the 19th cent. courts upheld that the Advertisements were covered by the Act of 1559, there are good grounds for questioning this opinion, one of the most cogent being the survival of the rubric in the BCP of 1662.

Text in H. Gee – W. J. Hardy, Documents illustrative of English Church History (1896), No. lxxxi (pp. 467-75).

ADVOCATUS DIABOLI (Lat., 'Devil's Advocate'). A popular term for the '*Promotor Fidei' (q.v.).

ADVOWSON. The right of appointing a clergyman to a parish or other ecclesiastical benefice. Advowsons are of two kinds: (1) 'Collative', when they are held by the *Ordinary under whose jurisdiction the benefice is, normally the bishop of the diocese; and (2) 'Presentative', when they are held by some other person ('patron'), who presents the nominee for institution. In the latter case the patron, who may be clerical or lay, an individual or a corporation, does not possess the right of putting his candidate in spiritual or even legal possession of the office. He presents him to the bishop or other ecclesiastical superior for *institution and *induction (qq.v.), and the latter may for due cause reject the nominee. The right of Advowson is historically the survival of an originally much more extensive control exercised by the feudal lord over churches on his estates, which goes back in turn to the time when the pagan priest, in Teutonic Europe the predecessor of the Christian priest, was the feudal dependant of the lord.

In most RC countries Advowson has died out, though it survives in a few places. In the C of E, where it still exists, its exercise is governed by English civil law, which since the time of the Constitutions of *Clarendon (1164) has succeeded in maintaining control of this valuable right. Thus a bishop who without legal cause refuses to accept a patron's nominee can be compelled to do so by an action of *Quare impedit in the civil courts. In the 14th cent. the Papal method of overriding these rights of private patronage by means of *Provisions was fought by the State in the Statute of Provisors (1351). In the C of E the right of Advowson may be held by anyone who is not a RC or an alien.

An Advowson is treated by English law as a right of property which can be transferred by gift or sale. The scandals to which this fact has sometimes given rise have led to recent attempts to limit the right of presentation itself and the power to alienate it. In the

Church of *Scotland the rights of private patronage were resisted by a large party in the Kirk and were the chief cause of the secessions which eventually produced the Free Kirk (1843).

AEGIDIUS, St. See *Giles, St.*

AEGIDIUS ROMANUS. See *Giles of Rome.*

A.E.G.M. See *Anglican Evangelical Group Movement.*

AELFHEAH, St. See *Alphege, St.*

AELFRIC (*c.* 955–*c.* 1020), 'the Grammarian', Abbot of Eynsham. Having entered the *Benedictine abbey at *Winchester under *Ethelwold, who implanted in him the ideals of St. *Dunstan's monastic reform, he became the greatest scholar and the literary leader of the English Benedictine revival. In 987 he was transferred to the newly founded abbey at Cerne Abbas in Dorset and here issued two sets of homilies in English, dealing respectively with the events of the liturgical year and with doctrinal and historical subjects. The latter series gained a revived notoriety at the time of the Reformation, as Aelfric not only denied the *Immaculate Conception of the BVM but was also held to have maintained a view of the Eucharist incompatible with *Transubstantiation. In his Eucharistic theology he was probably influenced by *Ratramnus, though his unorthodoxy was apparently much exaggerated. The use of alliterative prose which marked these homilies was developed in a third series on the 'Lives of the Saints', where the arrangement is commonly as verse. In 1005 he was appointed the first Abbot of Eynsham in Oxfordshire. His writings of this period include an abridgement of Ethelwold's 'De Consuetudine Monachorum', a Latin Life of Ethelwold, and an English rendering of *Bede's 'De Temporibus'. His greatest claim to fame was his provision of books with real literary merit for the rural clergy in their native language.

W. Skeat (ed.), *Aelfric's Lives of the Saints* (E.E.T.S., lxxvi, lxxxii, xciv, and cxiv bound in 2 vols., 1881–90), C. L. White, *Aelfric.* A new Study of his Life and Writings (Yale Studies in English, ii, 1898); S. H. Gem, *An Anglo-Saxon Abbot.* Aelfric of Evesham (1912). M. M. Dubois, *Aelfric, sermonnaire, docteur et grammairien* (Paris, 1942), with full bibl.

AELIA CAPITOLINA. The new city which Hadrian built in *c.* 130 on the site of *Jerusalem (destroyed A.D. 70). It was so named after the Emperor himself (Publius Aelius Hadrianus) and Jupiter Capitolinus. Statues to both Hadrian and Jupiter were erected in the area of the Temple. Its exact limits are unknown, but it probably extended as far as the present N. wall of Jerusalem and included the northern part of the Western hill.

[L.] H. Vincent, O.P.–F. M. Abel, O.P., *Jerusalem,* ii (1914–26), pp. 1–39, with map as planche i.

AELRED, St. See *Ailred, St.*

AENEAS OF GAZA (d. 518), Christian philosopher. He studied under Hierocles, the *Neoplatonist, at *Alexandria, and became a strong supporter of *Platonist and *Neoplatonist doctrines. In his dialogue 'Theophrastus', he defended the immortality of the soul and the resurrection of the body, though he rejected such tenets of Platonism as conflicted with orthodox Christian doctrine, e.g. the pre-existence of the soul and the eternity of the world. 25 of his letters have also survived. With *Procopius of Gaza and *Zacharias Scholasticus, he made up the 'Gaza Triad'.

Gk. text of the 'Theophrastus' in A. *Gallandi, *Bibliotheca Veterum Patrum,* x (1774), pp. 629–64, repr. J. P. Migne, *PG,* lxxxv, 865–1004. Letters ed. R. Hercher, *Epistolographi Graeci* (Paris, 1873), pp. 24–32. Studies by G. Schalkhausser (Erlangen, 1898) and S. Sikorski (Trebnitz, [1908]).

AENEAS SILVIUS PICCOLOMINI. See *Pius II.*

AENGUS, ST. See *Oengus, St.*

AEQUIPROBABILISM. See *Equiprobabilism.*

AERIUS (4th cent.), presbyter of Pontus. He was at first an associate of *Eustathius, later (from 355) Bp. of Sebaste, with whose ascetic movement he was closely identified and by whom he was ordained; but later (*c.* 360) the two quarrelled. Acc. to St. *Epiphanius (*Haer.* 75), from whom our knowledge of him is mainly derived, he maintained that there was no distinction between the function and rank of bishops and priests; that the observance of *Easter was a Jewish superstition (1 Cor. 5. 7); that prescribed fasts were wrong; and that it was useless to pray and give alms for the dead. Hence his followers refused to fast even in *Holy Week, though they observed a purely voluntary fast on *Sundays. Aerius was also charged by Epiphanius with being an *Arian. His followers (Aerians) are mentioned by St. *Philaster (*Haer.* 72) and by St. *Augustine (*Haer.* 53), but appear to have died out soon after his death. Aerius has prob. received from modern controversialists (*Bellarmine; some 17th-cent. Anglicans) more attention than his importance merits.

V. Ermoni in *D.H.G.E.,* i (1912), col. 663, and A. Bigelmair in *L.Th.K.,* i (1930), col. 113.

AETERNI PATRIS. The encyclical of *Leo XIII (4 Aug., 1879), commending to the Church the study of philosophy, and esp. of the works of St. *Thomas Aquinas. It gave the impetus to the subsequent revival of Scholastic philosophy.

Text in *Acta Leonis XIII* (1887), pp. 88–108; Eng. tr. in J. *Maritain, *St. Thomas Aquinas* (1931), pp. 189–214. B. Chocarne, *S. Thomas d'Aquin et l'encyclique Aeterni Patris de S.S. le Pape Léon XIII* (1884).

AETHELBERT, AETHELBURGH. See *Ethelbert, Ethelburga,* &c.

AETIUS (d. *c.* 370). A Christian sophist who carried the principles of *Arianism to their furthest limits. His enemies, by a play on his name, surnamed him ἄθεος, 'the godless one'. Originally a craftsman of *Antioch, he travelled to *Alexandria where he became a subtle dialectician and skilled in the philosophy of *Aristotle. Under the Emp. *Julian (361–3) he was ordained a bishop by the Arians without fixed see. He and his followers, also known as *Anomoeans, asserted the total unlikeness of the Son to the Father. A short writing of his (συνταγμάτιον περὶ ἀγεννήτου θεοῦ καὶ γεννητοῦ) is preserved by *Epiphanius (*Haer.* 76. 11).

G. Bardy, 'L'Héritage littéraire d'Aétius' in *R.H.E.*, xxiv (1928), pp. 807–27; V. Grumel, 'Les Textes monothélites d'Aétius' in *É.O.*, xxxii (1929), pp. 159–66.

AFFECTIVE PRAYER. A stage in the development of prayer at which less use of the intellect and imagination is made than by beginners, and the soul is chiefly engaged in making acts of the will, to unite itself more closely to God.

AFFINITY. In moral theology, relationship created by marriage. It arises from a valid marriage, whether consummated or not, and is held to form an impediment to subsequent marriage between the one party and certain blood relations of the other. The impediment is not extinguished by death. In the C of E the sphere of affinity is regulated by the 'Table of *Kindred and Affinity' (q.v.) of 1563, authorized by can. 99 of 1603 on the basis of Lev. 18, which superseded the complicated rules of the medieval canonists. Marriages within the prohibited degrees were voidable in civil law until 1835, when Lord *Lyndhurst's Marriage Act (5 & 6 Will. IV, c. 54) rendered them *ipso facto* void. The Act of 1907 (7 Edw. VII, c. 47) legalized marriage with a deceased wife's sister (see *Deceased Wife's Sister's Marriage Act*) and these provisions were considerably extended by Acts of 1921 and 1931, which included notably unions with a niece by marriage. All these provisions refer to marriages terminated by death, and not by divorce. In 1947 Convocation amended Canon 99 to bring the law of the Church into conformity with that of the state. The RC rulings will be found in the *Codex Iuris Canonici* (cans. 97, 1042, 1077). RC canon law (*CIC*, § 1079) still recognizes spiritual affinity, which arises between the godparent and the baptized; but it is easily dispensed.

P. Dib in *D.D.C.*, i (1935), cols. 264–85, s.v. 'Affinité'; A. Liuzzi in *E.C.*, i (1949), cols. 366–8, s.v. 'Affinità', with further bibl. See also bibl. to *Prohibited Degrees*.

AFFIRMATION. In English civil law, a solemn declaration in place of an oath made by those who have conscientious objection to being sworn, either because of their religious convictions or because they have no religious belief. It may only be administered when the oath is refused.

In the 17th cent. *Quakers suffered severe persecution for refusing to be sworn. The *Toleration Act of 1689 began the process of relief by allowing 'certain persons, dissenters from the Church of England', to make an affirmation of allegiance, and in 1691 a similar concession was made in respect of the Oath of Supremacy in *Ireland (2 & 3 Will. & Mary, c. 2). The position was regularized for the 'people called Quakers' by an Act of 1696 (7 & 8 Will. & Mary, c. 34), which expressly granted them the general right of making an affirmation in place of an oath. This permission was limited, however, to official oaths and criminal proceedings were exempted. This last restriction was removed by two Acts of 1833, the 'Quakers and Moravians Act' (2 & 3 Will. IV, c. 49) and the 'Separatists Affirmation Act' (3 Will. IV, c. 82); in 1838 (1 & 2 Vict., c. 77) the exemption was extended to include former adherents of those sects. In 1854 the 'Common Law Procedure Act' (17 & 18 Vict., c. 125) allowed the right of affirmation to all who conscientiously objected to being sworn. This was not construed to include atheists, who, though allowed by the Evidence Act of 1869 (32 & 33 Vict., c. 68) and the Evidence Amendment Act of 1870 (33 & 34 Vict., c. 49) to give oral evidence on affirmation, were only finally freed of their disabilities by the 'Oaths Act' of 1888 (51 & 52 Vict., c. 46), which provided for depositions by atheists.

In practice the right to affirm is little used except by Quakers, as the Act requires unbelievers to make public profession of their atheism.

AFFUSION (or, occasionally, 'Infusion'). The method of *baptism now ordinarily practised in the W. Church whereby water is poured over the head of the candidate. It did not become general until the later Middle Ages, *immersion and *submersion being the usual methods in earlier times. The change was doubtless due to the wish to avoid possible dangers to the candidate's health. It was perhaps adopted from the first in cases where immersion was not easily possible, e.g. on the Day of *Pentecost (Acts 2. 41) or in the gaoler's house at Philippi (Acts 16. 33). In the BCP it is a recognized alternative to immersion. See also *Aspersion*.

AFRAATES. See *Aphraates*.

AFRICA. See *South Africa, Christianity in; U.M.C.A.; West Africa, Christianity in.*

AFRICA, The Church in Roman. How Christianity spread to Roman 'Africa' (i.e. roughly Tripoli, Tunisia, Algeria, and Morocco) is unknown. The earliest evidence is that of the '*Acta' of the *Scillitan martyrs (180); and the '*Passion' of St. *Perpetua (203) and the works of *Tertullian (197–*c.* 220) reveal a Church widespread and organized. While Roman Christians were still speaking Greek, the African Church was already using a Latin Bible and liturgy. By *Cyprian's time (*c.* 250) there were fully 100 bishops, under the primacy of Carthage. The Romanized towns and the coastal regions were the chief, but not the only, areas of evangelization; and, though sees were more frequent in Africa Proconsularis and Numidia, parts of Mauretania had been touched. *Persecution by the Emp. *Decius (250) weakened the Church, leading to controversy over the readmission of lapsed members and to the *Novatianist schism, which in turn produced controversy with Rome over rebaptism. But, led by Cyprian, the faithful recovered strength and withstood fresh persecution under the Emp. Valerian (258). At the end of the century Africa added *Arnobius and *Lactantius to the as yet short roll of Latin theologians.

The 4th cent. saw the partly theological, partly social struggle against *Donatism, arising out of *Diocletian's persecution; the writings of *Tyconius and *Optatus; and the rise of St. *Augustine. Notable features of this period were the war against paganism, the growth of monasticism, African resistance to Papal claims, and the series of African Councils, the canons of which were incorporated into both Greek and Latin *canon law.

Such achievements were ended by the Vandal invaders (429), whose *Arian kings normally repressed Catholic Christianity, with intermittent toleration as when Hilderic allowed an important council to assemble in 525. The chief writers of this later period were the historian *Victor Vitensis, the poet Dracontius, *Vigilius of Thapsus, and *Fulgentius of Ruspe. The reconquest (534) by *Justinian's general, Belisarius, restored orthodoxy, and some African theologians, notably Facundus, were prominent in defence of the *Three Chapters; while monasticism became strong and canonists again active. Later still, *Gregory I (590–604) corresponded with African bishops, the Berber tribes were gradually converted, and, in *c.* 640, Africa strongly challenged *Monothelitism. But at the end of the 7th cent. the Arab conquest (Carthage fell in 698) reduced to a shadow the Church which had bred so many martyrs and thinkers. Its ruined shrines are now being uncovered.

The best lit. is in French. H. *Leclercq, O.S.B., *L'Afrique chrétienne* (2 vols., 1904); P. Monceaux, *Histoire littéraire de l'Afrique chrétienne* (7 vols., 1901–23). S. A. Morcelli, *Africa Christiana* (3 vols., Brescia, 1816–17); J. Mesnage, *L'Afrique chrétienne* (1912; on topography); E. Buonaiuti, *Il cristianesimo nell' Africa romana* (Bari, 1928). H. Leclercq, O.S.B., in *D.A.C.L.*, i (1907), cols. 575–775, s.v. 'Afrique'. M. Scaduto in *E.C.*, i (1948), cols. 393–8, s.v. 'Africa, III: Storia cristiana antica'.

AFRICANUS, SEXTUS JULIUS. See *Julius Africanus*, Sextus.

AGABUS, St., prophet. He is mentioned in Acts as foretelling the famine (A.D. 44–8) under Claudius (11. 28) and St. Paul's imprisonment (21. 10). In the E Church he is held to be one of the seventy disciples (Lk. 10. 1) and dignified as an Apostle. Feast day, in the E. 8 Mar.; in the W. 13 Feb.

AGAPE (Gk. ἀγάπη, 'love'). (1) The word, which prob. first occurs in the *Septuagint, is believed to have been coined by the sacred

authors from the verb ἀγαπάω, to avoid the sensual associations of the ordinary Greek noun ἔρως. It is used only twice in the Synoptics (Mt. 24. 12, Lk. 11. 42), but often in St. John and the Pauline (esp. 1 Cor. 13) and Johannine Epistles, and always of the love of God or Christ, or of the love of Christians for one another. From the Scriptures it passed into the vocabulary of the Greek Fathers; it is usually translated in Latin by 'caritas', hence the original meaning of 'charity' in English.

(2) The term is applied also to the common religious meal which seems to have been in use in the early Church in close relation to the Eucharist. The classic NT ref. is 1 Cor. 11. 17–34, where abuses which accompanied the common meals that preceded the Eucharist are condemned. The most important early documents held to attest the practice are St. *Ignatius' ref. to the Christian love-feasts in his letter to the Smyrnæans (8), and esp. *Pliny's letter to Trajan. The latter contains a description of two separate Christian meetings, the one an early morning assembly for prayer, traditionally regarded as a Eucharistic celebration, the other an ordinary meal, believed to be the Agape. The 'Apologies' of *Justin Martyr, however, deal only with the Eucharist and make no mention of the Agape. On the other hand, *Tertullian seems to refer to it explicitly in his *Apology* (39). It is generally agreed that the connexion of the Agape with the Eucharist almost ceased from the time of St. *Cyprian, the Eucharist being celebrated fasting in the morning, and the Agape in the evening. The Agape seems also to have become more and more a charity supper and is described as such by St. *Augustine. Though still mentioned at the Trullan Council (692), it had fallen into disuse by the end of the patristic age.

(1) A. Nygren, *Den Kristna Kärlekstanken genom tiderna*. Eros och Agape (2 vols., 1930–6; Eng. tr. (*Agape and Eros*) in 3 vols., 1932–9, pt. i by A. G. Hebert, S.S.M., and pt. ii, 2 vols., by P. S. Watson; new tr. by P. S. Watson, 1953). V. Warnack, *Agape. Die Liebe als Grundmotiv der neutestamentlichen Theologie* (1951).

(2) Apart from 1 Cor. 11, the chief NT texts are Acts 2. 42, 2. 46; Acts 6; Acts 20. 7, 20. 11; 2 Pet. 2. 13; Jude 12. Cf. also *Did.*, 9 and 10 (acc. to F. *Kattenbusch, T. *Zahn, G. *Dix, ref. here to *Agape*; acc. to P. Batiffol, H. *Lietzmann, K. Völker ref. to Eucharist); Ignatius, *Smyrn.*, 6. 8, 8. 2, and 12. 2, *Trall.*, 2. 3, *Magn.*, 1. 1, &c.; Pliny, *Ep. ad Traj.*, x. 97; Justin, *Apol.*, i. 65 f.; **Epist. Apost.*, 15; *Tertullian, *Apol.*, 39; St. *Cyril Alex., *Paedag.*, ii. 1; St. *Hippolytus, **Apost. Trad.*, xxvi. J. F. Keating, *The Agape and the Eucharist in the Early Church* (1901); P. Batiffol in *D.T.C.*, i (1901), cols. 551–6, s.v.; id., *Études d'histoire et de théologie positive*, Sér. 1 (ed. 7), pp. 283–325; W. O. E. Oesterley, *The Jewish Background of the Christian Liturgy* (1925), pp. 194–204; H. *Lietzmann, *Messe und Herrenmahl* (1926), pp. 197–210, 230–50; K. Völker, *Mysterium und Agape. Die gemeinsamen Mahlzeiten in der alten Kirche* (1926); J. M. Hanssens, S.J., 'L'Agape et l'Eucharistie' in *E.L.*, xli (1927), pp. 525–48, xlii (1928), pp. 545–74, xliii (1929), pp. 177–98 and 520–9; A. Arnold, *Der Ursprung des christlichen Abendmahls im Lichte der neuesten liturgiegeschichtlichen Forschung* (1937); G. *Dix, O.S.B., in *The Shape of the Liturgy* (1944), pp. 82–102. See also H. *Leclercq, O.S.B., in *D.A.C.L.*, i (pt. 1, 1907), cols. 775–848 (holds the Agape was a funeral meal), J. Sauer in *L.Th.K.*, i (1930), cols. 122–4, and A. Romeo in *E.C.*, i (1949), cols. 420–5.

AGAPEMONE, Church of the. A small English sect of the 19th cent. It was founded by H. J. Prince (1811–99), a former student of St. David's College, Lampeter, who had been

ordained in the C of E in 1840 and served as curate at Charlynch nr. Bridgwater in Somerset. There, together with his rector, Samuel Starky, he started a revivalist movement which soon resulted in illusions of the grossest kind. After being inhibited successively by several bishops, he and Starky left the C of E and began a ministry of their own, asserting that they were the Holy Ghost personified, the Two Witnesses of Rev. 11, or *Elijah. In 1849 they opened the 'Agapemone' in the village of Spaxton, being amply supported by their followers, who believed Prince to be a Divine being. The morals of the sect soon began to give grave scandal and a trial ensued revealing the licentiousness of Prince and his followers. In 1890 there was a period of renewed activity, when the sect conducted a successful campaign at Clapton, calling themselves the 'Children of the Resurrection', under J. H. Smyth-Pigott, the successor of Prince to the leadership, who proclaimed himself to be Christ. The sect vanished in the beginning of the 20th cent.

Material on the Agapemonites is to be found in Prince's own writings, e.g. *A Hook in the Nose of Leviathan* (1877) and *The Man Christ Jesus* (1886), as well as in those of his opponents, among which are J. G. Dick, *A Word of Warning* (1845), and O. Piers, *The Door not Shut* (1846).

AGAPETAE (Gk. ἀγαπηταί, 'beloved'). Another name for *Subintroductae.

AGAPETUS, St. (d. 536), Pope from 535. He was a strong defender of orthodoxy. In 536 he visited *Constantinople where, in spite of Imperial opposition from *Justinian and Theodora, he deposed Anthimus, the *Monophysite Patr. of *Constantinople, and consecrated *Mennas as his successor. He died soon afterwards, after a reign of ten months. Feast day, in the E. 22 April (day of death), in the W. 20 Sept.

Letters and other items in J. P. Migne, *PL*, lxvi, 35-80. Jaffé, i, pp. 113-15. *L.P.* (Duchesne), i, pp. 287-9. H. I. Marrou, 'Autour de la bibliothèque du Pape Agapit' in *Mélanges d'Archéologie et d'Histoire*, xlviii (1931), pp. 124-69. J. P. Kirsch in *D.H.G.E.*, i (1912), cols. 887-90, s.v. I. Daniele in *E.C.*, i (1948), col. 428 f., s.v. 'Agapeto I', with bibl.

AGATHA, St. A virgin martyred at Catania in Sicily. In the 5th and succeeding cents. she was held in great veneration. Her name occurs in the *Canon of the Roman Mass and in the ancient *martyrologies; and two early churches were dedicated to her in Rome. The date of her death is quite uncertain, and the *acts of her martyrdom, which derive from the beginning of the 6th cent., are legendary. Besides being the patron saint of the city of Catania and of bell-founders, she is invoked against fire. Feast day, 5 Feb.

'Acta' in *AA.SS.*, Feb. I (1658), pp. 598-602. S. Romeo, *S. Agata, V. e M. e il suo culto* (Catania, 1922). V. L. Kennedy, C.S.B., *The Saints of the Canon of the Mass* (Studi di Antichità Cristiana, xiv, Rome, 1938), pp. 169-73; F. di Capua, 'La concezione agonistica del martirio nei primi secoli del cristianesimo e l'introito della messa di S. Agata' in *E.L.*, lxi (1947), pp. 229-40. On the early Roman church (mentioned by St. *Gregory the Great, *Dialog.*, iii. 30) dedicated to her see C. Huelsen, C. Cecchelli and others, *S. Agata dei Goti* (Monografie sulle chiese di Roma, I, 1924). J. P.

Kirsch in *C.E.*, i (1907), p. 203 f., s.v.; P. Allard in *D.A.C.L.*, i (pt. 1; 1907), cols. 848-50, s.v., with further bibl.; M. Scaduto and P. Toschi in *E.C.*, i (1948), cols. 432-6, s.v. 'Agata', with bibl.

AGATHANGELOS. The reputed first historian of *Armenia, who professes to be the author of a Life of St. *Gregory the Illuminator (q.v.). Perhaps 'Agathangelos' is only a pseudonym of an Armenian Christian, proclaiming to his countrymen the 'good tidings' of their conversion. The writer asserts that he was contemporary of St. Gregory and wrote his Life at the command of King Tiridates (c. 238-314). A. von Gutschmid claimed to have proved that the Armenian text dates from c. 450, but argued the use of earlier reliable sources. The Greek text is secondary to the Armenian.

Editions of the Armenian text have appeared at *Constantinople (1709 and 1824), *Venice (1835 and 1862), and Tiflis (1882). The Greek text is in the *Acta Sanctorum*, Sept. VIII (1762), pp. 320-402; it was re-edited by P. de Lagarde in the *Abhandlungen* of the Göttingen Academy, xxxv (1887). A. von Gutschmid, 'Agathangelos' in the *Zeitschrift der deutschen morgenländischen Gesellschaft*, xxxi (1877), pp. 1-60.

AGATHIAS (c. 536-c. 582), poet and historian. He practised as an advocate at *Constantinople. His Περὶ τῆς Ἰουστινιανοῦ Βασιλείας is our principal authority for the history of the years 552-8 of the reign of *Justinian. He also made a collection of contemporary epigrams (including several of his own) and wrote erotic myths in nine books of Δαφνιακά. It is doubtful if he was a Christian.

'History' first ed. with notes and Lat. tr. by B. Vulcanius (Leyden, 1594), with 'Epigrammata Graeca' appended. Crit. edd. by B. G. Niebuhr (C.S.H. Byz., 1828; repr. J. P. Migne, *PG*, lxxxviii, 1269-1596) and L. Dindorf (Teubn., 1871). Krumbacher, pp. 240-3, with bibl.

AGATHO (c. 577-681), Pope from 678. He was a Sicilian by birth. In 680 he held a council at Rome against the *Monothelites, the doctrinal formula set forth at which was adopted at the Sixth Oecumenical Council of *Constantinople. He also took up the cause of St. *Wilfred of York in his dispute with *Theodore, Abp. of *Canterbury, and the King of Northumbria, and furthered the spread of the Roman Liturgy in England. Feast day, 10 Jan.

Jaffé, i, pp. 238-40. *L.P.* (Duchesne), i, pp. cclvii and 350-8. A. Vacant-H. Quentin, O.S.B., in *D.T.C.*, i (1903), cols. 559-63, s.v.; J. P. Kirsch in *D.H.G.E.*, i (1912), cols. 916-18, s.v.; E. Daniels in *E.C.*, i (1948), cols. 436-8, s.v 'Agatone, Papa', with bibl.

AGDE, Council of (*Concilium Agathense*). A Council held in 506 at Agde in the S. of France under the presidency of St. *Caesarius of Arles. Its 47 genuine canons deal with such subjects as clerical celibacy, the canonical age for ordination, the relations of a bishop and his diocesan synod, church property, public peace, and the religious obligations of the faithful.

Hardouin, ii, cols. 995-1006; Hefele-Leclercq, ii (2; 1908), pp. 973-1002. F. *Cabrol in *D.A.C.L.*, i (1907), 871-7, s.v.

AGE, Canonical. The age, fixed by *canon law, at which a person becomes capable of undertaking special duties, of enjoying special privileges, or of entering specified new states of life. The term is esp. used in connexion with *ordination, for which in the C of E the canonical age for a deacon is 'twenty-three . . . unless he have a *faculty'; for a priest 'full four and twenty years'; and for a bishop 'fully thirty years'.

'AGE OF REASON'. (1) The normal age at which a child may be supposed to become wholly responsible for his conduct, and therefore capable of *mortal sin. In RC moral theology this age is held to be reached at about seven years.
(2) A name sometimes applied to the 18th cent., when the prevailing tendency in philosophy and religion was rationalistic and opposed to all belief in the supernatural. W. *Cave described it as the *saeculum rationalisticum.*

AGENDA (Lat.), 'things to be performed'.
(1) A term occasionally found in English 17th cent. divines for matters of religious practice as opposed to those of belief (*credenda*).
(2) In certain primitive (particularly African liturgies it is used of the central part of the *Mass, elsewhere called the *Canon, Prex, *Anaphora,* &c. In the Council of *Carthage of 390 (can. 9), it is used of the Eucharist as a whole.
(3) Among German-speaking Protestants on the Continent, the term is in regular use for the prescribed forms of service.

AGIOS O THEOS (Gk. ἅγιος ὁ θεός, 'Holy God'). An anthem, so named from its first words, which occurs in the E. liturgies. It has survived, in the original Greek, in the Roman Good Friday Liturgy (Mass of the *Presanctified), where it is sung during the *Veneration of the Cross. See also *Trisagion.*

AGNELLUS OF PISA, Bl. (c. 1195–1236), founder of the English *Franciscan Province. He was received into the Order at Pisa, his native city, by St. *Francis, who sent him to *Paris to erect a convent. Later he returned to Italy. In 1224 he was despatched to England, and on 12 Sept. arrived at Dover with eight other friars, four of them English. Shortly afterwards he established friaries at *Canterbury and at *Oxford. He engaged R. *Grosseteste to teach in the latter, which (though Agnellus himself was not a scholar) rapidly became a famous centre of learning. He exercised considerable political influence in the conflict between Henry III and the Earl Marshal. Until the Reformation his remains were venerated at Oxford. His cultus was confirmed by *Leo XIII in 1892. His feast is kept on 13 Mar. and (in the Order) on 7 May.

The principal authority is Thomas of Eccleston, *Tractatus de Adventu Fratrum Minorum in Angliam* (ed. A. G. Little, 'Collection d'Études et de Documents', vii; Paris, 1909; with relevant passages from the Chronicle of Lanercost and Bartholomew of Pisa's Liber Conformitatum in appendices); Eng. tr. of the Tractatus by Father Cuthbert, O.S.F.C. (London, 1903). C. Mariotti, O.F.M., *Il B. Agnello da Pisa ed. i Frati Minori in Inghilterra* (1895); Father Gilbert, O.S.F.C., *B. Agnellus and the English Grey Friars* (1937). E. Hutton, *The Franciscans in England, 1224–1538* (1926), pp. 9–134, passim. Antoine de Sérent, O.F.M., in *D.H.G.E.,* i (1912), col. 907 f., s.v., with further reff.

AGNELLUS, ANDREAS (805 – c. 846), historian of *Ravenna. He had the title of Abbot, but appears to have remained a secular priest. His principal writing, 'Liber Pontificalis Ecclesiae Ravennatis', is an elaborate account of the see, modelled on the '*Liber Pontificalis' which traces the history from St. *Apollinarius to his own age. It is full of historical errors, but also embodies valuable information about the buildings and customs of Ravenna, esp. in Agnellus' own time. The work was written largely to support the claims of Ravenna against *Rome. He has often been confused with St. Agnellus, Abp. of Ravenna (c. 556–c. 566).

Editio princeps of the *Liber Pontificalis Ecclesiae Ravennatis* was publ. in 2 vols., Leipzig, 1708; crit. ed. by O. Holder-Egger in *M.G.H.,* Scriptores Rerum Langobardicarum et Italicarum Saec. VI–IX (1878), pp. 265–391; also ed. A. Testi Rasponi in *Rerum Italicarum Scriptores* founded by L. A. *Muratori, ed. 2 cont. by C. Carducci–V. Fiorini, II, iii (1924 ff.). F. Lanzoni, 'Il "Liber Pontificalis" Ravennate' in *Rivista di Scienze Storiche,* i (1909), pp. 345–70, 425–464; and 570–92; also publ. separately. A. Ferrua, S.J., in *E.C.,* i (1948), cols. 465–7, s.v. 'Agnello di Ravenna'.

AGNES, St. She has been venerated as a virgin in Rome since the 4th cent., but the early legends of her martyrdom vary considerably, and nothing certain can be deduced as to the date or manner of her death. A *basilica was built in c. 350 on the Via Nomentana on the site of her remains. Her name occurs in the Roman *Canon of the Mass and in all *martyrologies both in E. and W., though on different days. In art she is represented with a lamb, no doubt on account of the similarity of 'agnus' with 'Agnes', and the archiepiscopal *pallium is made from the wool of two lambs, blessed each year in her basilica on her feast (21 Jan.). In the Roman Calendar a second feast is kept on the octave day, 28 Jan.

Lat. text of her Acta, ascribed to St. *Ambrose, in *AA.SS.,* Jan. II (1643), pp. 351–4; F. de' Cavalieri, *S. Agnese nella tradizione e nella leggenda* (*R.Q.,* Suppl. x, 1899), with Gr. texts, pp. 71–92. L. de Kerval, *Une Fleur des catacombes. Saint Agnès dans la légende et dans l'histoire* (1901). F. Jubaru, S.J., *Sainte Agnès vierge et martyre de la voie Nomentane d'après de nouvelles recherches* (1907), on which see F. de' Cavalieri, *Hagiographica* (S.T., xix, 1908), pp. 141–64. A. J. Denomy, C.S.B. (ed.), *The Old French Lives of Saint Agnes and Other Vernacular Versions of the Middle Ages* (Harvard Studies in Romance Languages, xiii, 1938), with full introd., pp. 4–38, and hagiographical bibl., pp. 263–5. Popular studies by T. Shearman on the cult; London, 1904), by A. Smith, C.R.L. (London, 1906), and by F. Jubaru, S.J. (Paris, 1914). P. Allard and H. *Leclercq in *D.A.C.L.,* i (1907), cols. 915–65, with bibl. A. P. Frutaz in *E.C.,* i (1948), cols. 467–74, s.v. 'Agnese', with further bibl.

AGNOETAE (Gk. ἀγνοέω, 'to be ignorant of'). A *Monophysite sect founded by Themistius, a deacon of *Alexandria (6th cent.; hence also 'Themistians'). On the basis of Mk. 13. 32, Jn. 11. 34, &c., they attributed ignorance to the human soul of Christ. Till recently it has commonly been supposed, but apparently wrongly, that they ascribed ignorance also to the Godhead of Christ. Their teaching was attacked by Eulogius, Patr. of Alexandria, in 598–9, and also declared heretical by Pope *Gregory I.

P. *Schaff in *D.C.B.*, i (1877), pp. 62 f., s.v.; J. P. Junglas in *L.Th.K.*, i (1930), col. 142, s.v., with patristic reff. and bibl.

AGNOSTICISM. The doctrine that only material phenomena can be the subject of real knowledge and that all knowledge of such entities as a Divine Being, immortality, and a supernatural world is impossible. The invention of the word has been commonly ascribed, on the authority of R. H. *Hutton, to T. H. *Huxley, who is said to have coined it, on the basis of Acts 17. 23, in 1869 at a private meeting of a group which later developed into the *Metaphysical Society. The title was esp. affected in the later 19th cent. by persons of sceptical inclinations who wished to avoid professing dogmatic atheism. As an elaborated theory it had close similarities with the doctrine of the *Unknowable of H. *Spencer, and was also akin to the teaching of W. Hamilton (1805–1865) on the *Unconditioned. In popular usage the word came to be applied to all forms of scepticism.

J. Ward, *Naturalism and Agnosticism* (*Gifford Lectures for 1896–8; 1899).

AGNUS DEI. (1) The formula beginning with the words 'O Lamb of God' recited three times by the priest in the Latin liturgy shortly before the Communion. The Scriptural basis is Jn. 1. 29 (itself derived from Is. 53. 7), but the repetition is first found in the *Gloria in excelsis, introduced at Rome for episcopal Masses by Pope *Symmachus (498–514). Its independent use is ascribed by the *Liber Pontificalis to *Sergius I (687–701), a Syrian, who ordered it to be sung at the time of the Fraction. Its origin may have been a practical protest by Sergius against can. 82 of the *Trullan Council (692) forbidding the representation of Our Lord under the form of a lamb. Originally recited once only, by the beginning of the 11th cent. it was said three times, though the third 'have mercy upon us' was changed to 'grant us peace', whether as a preparation for the *Kiss of Peace or, as *Innocent III says, because of the calamities afflicting the Church, is uncertain. In the Middle Ages the Agnus, like the *Kyrie, was extensively interpolated. On *Good Friday and *Holy Saturday it is omitted, while in *Requiems 'grant them rest' is substituted for the second part. It is now not uncommonly used in the C of E where its legality was upheld by the *Lincoln Judgement.

(2) A wax medallion bearing the figure of a lamb, blessed by the Pope in the first year of his pontificate and every 7th year afterwards. These objects of devotion are first heard of early in the 9th cent. at Rome, where the Archdeacon manufactured them on Holy Saturday from the remnants of the previous year's *paschal candle. They may represent a Christian substitute for a pagan charm. Agnus Dei's are also made of a mixture of wax and dust believed to be that of the bones of martyrs.

On (1), L. *Duchesne (ed.), *L.P.*, i, p. 376. F. *Cabrol, O.S.B., in *D.A.C.L.*, i (1907), cols. 965–9, s.v., and Jungmann (1950), ii, pp. 413–22.
On (2), E. Mangenot in *D.T.C.*, i (1903), cols. 605–13, s.v., with bibl. W. Henry in *D.A.C.L.*, i (1907), cols. 969–971, s.v.

AGOBARD (c. 779–840), Abp. of Lyons. Appointed coadjutor to Leidrad of Lyons in 813, he succeeded to his see in 816. His opposition to the schemes of the Empress Judith led to his deposition at the Council of Thionville (835), but he was reinstated two years later. He was a versatile scholar whose works were marked by much originality. He attacked the excessive veneration of images, trial by ordeal, the belief in witchcraft, and the 'absurd opinion of the vulgar concerning hail and thunder' (that it was due to magic). His theological writings, mainly directed against the *Adoptianist heresy, included a treatise against *Felix of Urgel. He also attacked the liturgical speculations of *Amalarius of Metz.

Works first published by P. Masson (Paris, 1605) and re-ed. by S. *Baluzius (2 vols. bound in 1, Paris, 1666), repr. in J. P. Migne, *PL*, civ, 159–352. Crit. edd. of his 'Libri duo pro filiis et contra Iudith uxorem Ludovici Pii' by G. Waitz in *M.G.H.*, Scriptores XV, i (1887), pp. 274–9; of his letters by E. Dümmler, ib., Epistolae V (1898), pp. 150–239, and of the 'Carmen ad Agobardum Archiepiscopum missum', also by E. Dümmler, ib., Poetae II (1883), p. 118 f. [A.] Bressolles, *Saint Agobard*, évêque de Lyon (L'Église et l'État au moyen-âge IX, 1949). R. Foss, 'Leben und Schriften Agobards, Erzbischofs von Lyon' in *Beiträge zur Förderung christlicher Theologie*, Jahrg. I, Heit 3 (1897), pp. 101–44; R. Jud, O.S.B., 'Agobards von Lyon theologische Stellung nach seinen Schriften' in *Veröffentlichungen aus dem kirchenhistorischen Seminar München*, Reihe III, nr. 1 (Festgabe Alois Knöpfler, 1907), pp. 126–44. Short studies by L. Rozier (Montauban, 1891), F. Wiegand (Erlangen and Leipzig, 1901), and F. Leonardi (Vienna, 1927). [A.] Bressolles, *Saint Agobard, évêque de Lyon, 769–840*. Doctrine et action politique d'Agobard (1934).

AGONIZANTS (from Med. Lat. *agonizo*, 'to be at the point of death'). The fraternity, also known as 'Camillians' which was founded by St. *Camillus de Lellis (q.v.) at *Rome in 1586. In 1591 the Order was given a rule by Gregory XIV, and soon grew rapidly in riches and popularity. Its work has always been to minister to the sick and dying.

Heimbucher, ii (ed. 3, 1934), pp. 114–19 and 664 f.

AGRAPHA (i.e. 'unwritten [sayings]'). A name given esp. to the sayings of Christ not contained in the four canonical Gospels. Some occur in various NT MSS. (e.g. Lk. 6. 4 in the *Codex Bezae); one in Acts (20. 35); others in early tradition, e.g. in the 'Gospel acc. to the *Hebrews'; and others in the writings of the fathers, and in, e.g., the *Oxyrhynchus papyri.

A. Resch, *Agrapha*. Aussercanonische Evangelienfragmente (T.U., v, Heft 4; 1889); id., *Agrapha*. Aussercanonische Schriftfragmente (ib., xxx, Hftt. 3–4, 1906). J. H. *Ropes, *Die Sprüche Jesu die in den kanonischen Evangelien nicht überliefert sind* (ib., xiv, Hft. 2, 1896). B. Jackson, *Twenty-Five Agrapha* (1900; incl. Eng. tr.). M. R. James, *The Apocryphal New Testament* (1924), pp. 33–7. U. Holzmann, S.J., 'Unbeachtete patristische Agrapha' in

Z.K.T., xxxviii (1914), pp. 113–43, xxxix (1915), pp. 98–118 and 801–3; E. Jacquier, 'Les Sentences du Seigneur extra-canoniques (Les Agrapha)' in *R. Bibl.*, xxv (1918), pp. 93–135. F. *Cabrol, O.S.B., in *D.A.C.L.*, i (1907), cols. 979–84, s.v.; J. H. Ropes in *H.D.B.*, extra vol. (1904), pp. 343–52, s.v., with good bibl. L. Vaganay in *Dict. Bibl.*, Suppl. i (1928), cols. 158–98, s.v.; A. Romeo in *E.C.*, i (1948), cols. 568–70, s.v. 'Agraphon'. R. Dunkerley, *Beyond the Gospels* (Pelican Books, 1957).

AGRICOLA, JOHANN (*c.* 1494–1566), German Protestant reformer. A native of Eisleben, he studied under M. *Luther at *Wittenberg and in 1519 accompanied him to the *Leipzig Disputation. Afterwards he worked as a reformer at Frankfurt and Eisleben. In 1536 he began to teach at Wittenberg, where he was welcomed by Luther until, after a brief interval, he became a supporter of *Antinomianism and a violent controversy with Luther ensued. In 1540 he removed to Berlin, where he published a recantation which few save Luther refused to accept. Joachim II, Elector of Brandenburg, appointed him to the offices of *General-superintendent and court preacher, which he filled actively and influentially till his death. He was associated with J. von Pflug and M. Helding in the preparation of the *Augsburg Interim of 1548, and tried, but in vain, to conclude the controversy of the *Adiaphorists. He is also remembered as the first person to publish collections of German proverbs (1528, 1529, 1548).

Life by G. Kawerau (Berlin, 1881). G. Loesche, 'Eine Johann Agricola-Urkunde' in *Z.K.G.*, xlii (1923), p. 396 f. Schottenloher, i (1933), p. 5 f. (Nos. 130–49).

AGRIPPA VON NETTESHEIM, HEINRICH CORNELIUS (1486–1535), scholar and adventurer. After studying at *Cologne and *Paris (1506), he fought in the service of the King of Spain in 1508. In 1509 he lectured on occult sciences and Hebrew at Dôle, where he was attacked for teaching heresy, and in 1510 fled to England. From 1511 to 1517 he was in Lombardy. Here he attended the schismatical Council of *Pisa (1511) as a theologian in the service of the Emp. Maximilian, and later lectured on the *Hermetica* at Pavia and Turin. From *c.* 1518, when he became councillor and orator of Metz, he interested himself in the Reformation with many of the aims of which he sympathized, though he condemned the excesses of M. *Luther. In 1524 he was appointed physician to Louise of Savoy but soon fell into disgrace. In 1529 he became historiographer of the Emp. *Charles V, and in the next years published his two most important works, *De Incertitudine et Vanitate Scientiarum et Artium* (1530) and *De Occulta Philosophia* (1531). The second, which in date of writing is the earlier, having probably been completed *c.* 1510, attempts to establish the mutual interrelation of all things, the knowledge of which constitutes the true science or ' magic ' known only to the chosen few. This knowledge is based simultaneously on nature, Revelation, and the mystic sense of Scripture, and, on condition of detaching ourselves entirely from the world of sense, gives us the key to governing and turning to our use the forces of the universe. The *De Incertitu-*

dine, on the other hand, written in a profoundly sceptical spirit, is hostile to all science and scholarship. Confining truth to the Bible alone, it violently attacked *Scholasticism, known to Agrippa only in its decadent contemporary form, as well as many institutions of the Church, such as the cult of saints and relics. The publication of these works earned him a year's imprisonment, but his death, in 1535, saved him from further consequences of his audacious doctrines. In his later years he was closely associated with *Hermann of Wied, the reforming Abp. of Cologne.

Works (2 vols., Lyons, no date; repr. Lyons, 1600). H. Morley, *The Life of Henry Cornelius Agrippa von Nettesheim* (2 vols., 1856); A. Prost, *Les Sciences et les arts occultes au seizième siècle*. Cornelius Agrippa, sa vie et ses œuvres (2 vols., 1881); J. Orsier, *Henri Cornélis Agrippa* (1911).

AHIKAR LEGEND. A story which occurs in various forms but in essence tells of a Grand Vizier of Sennacherib, Ahikar the Wise, against whom his adopted son, Nadan, plotted and received appropriate retribution. The legend was widely spread in the East. It is met with in the Elephantine papyri and in Rumanian, Slavonic, Armenian, Arabic, and Syriac literature. Since G. Hoffmann (1880) pointed out the identity of 'Achiacharus', *Tobit's nephew (Tob., i. 21), with 'Ahikar', its influence on the Book of Tobit has been universally admitted.

F. C. Conybeare, J. R. Harris, and A. S. Lewis, *The Story of Ahikar from the Syriac, Arabic, Armenian, Ethiopic, Greek and Slavonic Versions* (1898); R. H. *Charles, *The Apocrypha and Pseudepigrapha of the OT*, ii (1913), pp. 715–84; F. Nau, *Histoire et sagesse d'Ahikar l'Assyrien* (1909).

AIDAN, St. (d. 651), monk of *Iona and Bp. of *Lindisfarne. At the request of St. *Oswald, King of Northumbria, he was sent from Iona to revive the missionary work of *Paulinus. Consecrated bishop in 635, he established his headquarters on the island of Lindisfarne, whence he made long journeys on the mainland, strengthening the Christian communities and founding new missionary outposts. The Christian practices taught by Aidan were those of the *Celtic Church. He carefully educated a group of twelve English boys to be future ecclesiastical leaders of their people, among them St. *Chad. His asceticism and gentleness won rapid success for his mission, and his personal relations with Oswald (d. 642) and Oswald's successor, St. *Oswin (d. 651), were close and intimate. He is said to have died of grief at the murder of Oswin. Feast day, 31 Aug.

The principal authority is *Bede, *H.E.*, iii, 3, 5 f., 14–17, 25; notes to ed. by C. Plummer, ii (Oxford, 1896), esp. pp. 136 and 164–7. A. C. Fryer, *Aidan, the Apostle of the North* [1884]. J. B. *Lightfoot, *Leaders in the Northern Church* (Sermons, 1890), pp. 39–54. Elizabeth W. Grierson, *The Story of the Northumbrian Saints, S. Oswald, S. Aidan, S. Cuthbert* (1913), pp. 45–69. W. *Bright, *Chapters of Early English Church History* (1878), pp. 134–46 and 163 f.

AILLY, PIERRE DE. See *D'Ailly, Pierre*.

AILRED, St. (1109–67), also 'Aelred', the 'Bernard of the North', Abbot of *Rievaulx. The son of a Saxon priest of *Hexham, he was for some years at the court of King David of

Scotland, son of St. *Margaret. He entered the *Cistercian house at Rievaulx *c.* 1133, became Abbot of Revesby in 1143, and Abbot of Rievaulx in 1147. In 1163 Ailred was present at the translation of the body of St. *Edward the Confessor in *Westminster Abbey, and later he wrote his Life. His theological writings, which are a successful combination of mysticism and speculative theology, won him the name of the 'English St. Bernard'. The most important are his 'Speculum Caritatis' and 'De Spirituali Amicitia', the latter a kind of spiritual counterpart to Cicero's 'De Amicitia'. His Life was written by his pupil, Walter Daniel. Feast day, 12 Jan., also 3 Mar.

'Opera Ascetica' in B. Tissier, *Bibliotheca Patrum Cisterciensium*, v (Bono-Fonte, 1662), pp. 162–388; *Opera Historica* in R. Twysden, *Historiae Anglicanae Scriptores Decem* (London, 1652), cols. 337–422; both repr. in J. P. Migne, *PL*, cxcv, 209–796. A. *Wilmart, O.S.B., 'L'Oraison pastorale de l'Abbé Aelred' (which prints for the first time a prayer in Jesus Coll., Cambridge, MS. 34, fol. 97r–99r) in *R. Bén.*, xxxvii (1925), pp. 263–72, with correction ib., xli (1929), p. 74. F. M. Powicke, 'Aelred of Rievaulx and his Biographer Walter Daniel' in *The Bulletin of the John Rylands Library*, vi (1921), pp. 310–51 and 452–521, repr. [1922]; id. (ed.), *The Life of Ailred of Rievaulx by Walter Daniel* (tr. and notes; 1950).

'AIN KARIM. A village about 5 miles W. of *Jerusalem, in the hill country, traditionally regarded as the home of *Zacharias and *Elizabeth, the birthplace of St. *John Baptist, and the scene of the *Visitation.

AISLE (Fr. *aile*, 'wing'). Commonly any extension of the nave of a church made by the piercing of its side walls with a series of arches and the building on of an extension with a separate and lower roof, for the purpose of increased accommodation. Less frequently a similar extension of the chancel or transept. It is often, but quite wrongly, used of a gangway up the centre of the nave or elsewhere; and the corresponding expression 'centre aisle' is a contradiction in terms.

AKHMÎM FRAGMENT. A fragment of a Greek MS. discovered by U. Bouriant in the winter of 1886–7 in a Christian tomb at Akhmîm in Egypt, containing a scrap of the Gospel of Peter (see *Peter, Gospel of*), another of the Apocalypse of Peter (see *Peter, Apocalypse of*), and considerable portions of the Greek Book of *Enoch. The MS. (prob. 8th cent.) is now at Cairo.

Text of Enoch ed. U. Bouriant in *Mémoires publiés par les membres de la Mission Archéologique Française au Caire*, ix (1892), pp. 111–46; of the Gospel and Apocalypse of Peter ed. A. Lods, ib., pp. 219–28. H. B. *Swete, *The Akhmim Fragment of the Apocryphal Gospel of St. Peter* (1893); L. Vaganay, *L'Evangile de Pierre* (1930), esp. pp. 12–82.

AKIBA or AQIBA (*c.* 50–132), Jewish Rabbi. Akiba ben Joseph was the most influential rabbi of his generation. As teacher of the renowned Rabbi Meir he prob. much influenced the *Mishnah. He actively supported the revolt of *Bar-Cochba, recognizing his claims as Messiah. He was taken prisoner by the Romans and burnt alive. *Aquila's version of the OT was probably a product of the School of Akiba.

L. Finkelstein, *Akiba. Saint and Martyr* (New York, 1936). J. Bornstein in *E.J.*, ii (1928), cols. 7–22, incl. bibl.

AKOIMETAE. See *Acoemetae*.

ALACOQUE, St. MARGARET MARY. See *Margaret Mary Alacoque, St.*

ALAIN OF LILLE (*c.* 1128–1203), also 'Alanus ab Insulis', Alain de l'Isle, theologian and eclectic philosopher. He was sometimes known as 'doctor universalis'. Of his life little is known except that he studied in Paris, took part in the Third *Lateran Council (1179), and eventually entered the monastery at *Cîteaux. He held a rationalist-mystical view of the relation of philosophy and religion, maintaining that all the truths of religion are discoverable by unaided reason. His mysticism was based on his philosophy, chiefly a mixture of Pythagoreanism and *Neoplatonism, in which a curious feature is his belief in 'Nature' as a mediator in creation between God and matter. He was also much influenced by *Boethius. The 'Ars Fidei Catholicae', an attempt to confute non-Christians on rational grounds alone, which until recently was attributed to him, has been shown by M. *Grabmann to be the work of Nicholas of Amiens.

Collections of his works by C. de Visch (Antwerp, 1654) and, with additions, in the *Bibliotheca Scriptorum Ordinis Cisterciensis* (ib., 1654) and J. P. Migne, *PL*, ccx; but many still remain unpublished. There are Eng. trr. of *The Complaint of Nature*, by D. M. Moffat (Yale Studies in English, xxxvi, New York, 1908) and, with notes, of his *Anticlaudian*, by W. H. Cornog (Philadelphia, 1935). A. Dupuis, *Alain de Lille* (Lille, 1859). M. B. Haureau, 'Mémoire sur la vie et quelques œuvres d'Alain de Lille' in *Mémoires de l'Institut National de France, Académie des Inscriptions et Belles-Lettres*, xxxii (1886), pp. 1–27. M. Baumgartner, *Die Philosophie des Alanus de Insulis* (B.G.P.M., iv, Hft. 2; 1896). M. Grabmann, *Die Geschichte der scholastischen Methode*, ii (1911), pp. 452–76. Überweg, ii, 245–7, with bibl., p. 706. P. Braun in *D.T.C.*, i (1903), cols. 656–8; M. Jacquin in *D.H.G.E.*, i (1912), cols. 1290–304; J. M. Canivez in *Dict. Sp.*, i (1927), cols. 270–2, all s.v.; A. Maier in *E.C.*, i (1948), cols. 622–4, s.v. 'Alano di Lilla'.

ALANE, ALEXANDER. See *Alesius, Alexander*.

ALAPA. According to W. usage, the light blow delivered by the bishop on the cheek (*leviter in maxilla caedit*) of those being confirmed. It is perhaps an imitation of the blow with the sword by which a young Teutonic warrior was dubbed a knight and, if so, symbolizes the spiritual warfare which lies ahead of the candidate.

ALARIC (*c.* 370–410), Visigothic chief. A member of one of the noblest Gothic families, he served as general of the barbarian auxiliaries under the Emp. *Theodosius I. On the latter's death, he hoped for a more important and regular position in the Empire, and, being disappointed in this, determined to conquer a kingdom for himself. Both E. and W. emperors failed to deal adequately with him in negotiation and battle, and three times, in

408, 409, and 410, he besieged *Rome. After the last siege, the city was entered on 24 Aug. 410, and thus conquered for the first time by a Gothic king. This event, which caused consternation throughout the Empire, was the immediate occasion of St. *Augustine's *City of God*. Like most of the Goths, Alaric was an *Arian by religion.

The chief authorities are his contemporaries *Orosius, Claudian, *Zosimus, and Jordanus.

A LASCO, JOHN. See *Laski, John A.*

ALB. A white linen garment, reaching from the neck to the ankles with tight-fitting sleeves and held in at the waist by a girdle, worn by the ministers at Mass. It is derived from the under-tunic common in the Roman and Greek world. It has been used in Christian worship from an early date, but it was not regarded as a specifically liturgical garment until long after the other Eucharistic Vestments. Sometimes it is ornamented, near the hem, with strips of embroidery or other coloured material, known as 'apparels'. The alb is taken to symbolize purity, and the celebrant says 'Make me white . . .' when he puts it on. Albs of silk and in colours have also sometimes been used.

Braun, *L.G.*, pp. 57–92 (ch. 3). C. Callewaert, 'De Alba Liturgica' in *Collationes Brugenses*, xxv (1925), pp. 370–4, repr. in his *Sacris Erudiri* (Steenbrugge, 1940), No. xx, pp. 211–14.

ALBAN, St., the first British martyr ('Protomartyr Anglorum'). He is traditionally associated with the *Diocletianic persecution (*c.* 305). Acc. to *Bede (*Eccl. Hist.* i, 7), he was a pagan of Verulamium (now *St. Albans in Herts) who was converted and baptized by a fugitive priest whom he sheltered. When the governor sent soldiers to search the house, Alban disguised himself in the priest's cloak, was arrested, and condemned to martyrdom. The priest, traditionally named Amphibalus from some confusion with the cloak (*amphibalus*), is said to have been stoned to death a few days later at Redbourn. St. Alban is commemorated by *Venantius Fortunatus (*c.* 580) in the line *Albanum egregium fecundia Britannia profert*. His shrine still stands in St. Albans Abbey. He is not to be identified with the St. Alban venerated at Cologne. His feast is 22 June, though the BCP (probably by a misreading of xxii as xvii) commemorates him on 17 June.

AA.SS., Jun. IV (1707), pp. 146–70; W. Meyer, 'Die Legende des h. Albanus des Protomartyr Angliae in Texten vor Beda' in *Abh.* (Gött.), N.F., viii (1904), n. i. For various forms of the legend see Hardy, i, pp. 3–30. W. Levison, 'St. Alban and St. Albans' in *Antiquity*, xv (1941), pp. 337–59.

ALBAN, ST., AND ST. SERGIUS, Fellowship of. An organization which exists to promote understanding and intercourse between the Churches of England and Russia, by prayer, services, meetings, conferences, and the publication of a periodical, *Sobornost*.

The Journal of the Fellowship of S. Alban and S. Sergius. Quarterly (London, 1928–33, typewritten; 1934 printed);

Sobornost (ib., 1935 ff.). N. Zernov in R. Rouse–S. C. Neill (edd.), *A History of the Ecumenical Movement, 1517–1948* (1954), pp. 662–4.

ALBANIA, Christianity in. Christianity probably reached what is now Albania at an early date through traders from Epirus and Macedonia, but with the fall of the W. Empire in the 5th and 6th cents. its influence was largely destroyed. In the Dark Ages, the native Illyrians, who at that time became known as Albanians, were made subject first to the Byzantine court, and so to Eastern Orthodox Christianity (840), and later to Slav invaders from the north. At the religious schism between E. and W. a section of Albanians transferred their religious allegiance from *Constantinople to *Rome. In 1389 the medieval Serbian Empire, into which the Albanians were later incorporated, fell to the Turks, who overran the country. Nevertheless, for ninety years resistance was effectively made to the Turkish power, esp. under Iskander Bey (1403–67), a national leader who maintained an independent kingdom in Upper Albania from 1443 till his death. He also encouraged his followers to abandon Orthodoxy for Rome. Many remained faithful to Orthodoxy, however, and under centuries of Turkish rule the proportion of Orthodox to Latins increased. Although the Turks, who finally subjugated Albania in 1521, treated the Albanians as allies rather than subjects, imperial favour was dependent upon the profession of *Mohammedanism, and there was much apostasy. Local Turkish lords indulged for centuries in every kind of persecution. In 1913 Albania became independent.

W. Peacock, *Albania*. The Foundling State of Europe (1914). D. Attwater, *The Dissident Eastern Churches* (Milwaukee, Wisc., [1937]), pp. 155 f.

ALBERT OF BRANDENBURG (1490–1545), Cardinal Abp. and Elector of Mainz. After studying at Frankfurt-on-Oder, he was successively a prebendary of Mainz (1509), Abp. of Magdeburg (1513), and Abp. of Mainz (1514). In 1518 he was created cardinal. Entrusted by *Leo X in 1517 with the publication in Saxony and Brandenburg of the Indulgence for St. Peter's in *Rome, he secured the services of the notorious Dominican, J. *Tetzel, to preach it. He was himself a man of liberal ideas and a friend of the humanists, notably of *Ulrich von Hutten, even favouring the Reformation in its first stages and encouraging the publication of books in its support. After an admonition from Leo X, Albert gradually changed his attitude. Having again wavered during the Peasant War (1525), he finally threw in his lot with the Papacy at the Dessau Meeting (1525) and was henceforward its resolute defender, though he tried to discourage extreme measures against the Protestants. In 1538 he took part in the Nuremberg Meeting which opposed the League of *Schmalkalden. In 1542 he became, through the influence of the *Jesuit Peter Faber, who resided in his diocese for a year, a warm admirer of the new Order, and in his last years worked strenuously on its behalf.

J. H. Hennes, *Albrecht von Brandenburg, Erzbischof von Metz und Magdeburg* (1858); J. May, *Der Kurfürst, Cardinal und Erzbischof Albrecht II von Mainz und Magdeburg* (2 vols., 1865–75). T. Kolde in *P.R.E.* (ed. 3), i (1896), pp. 306–10, s.v. 'Albrecht von Mainz'. Full bibl. in Schottenloher, iii (1936), pp. 275–8.

ALBERT OF PRUSSIA (1490–1568). The last Grand Master of the *Teutonic Order, and first Hohenzollern Duke of Prussia. He was converted to Protestantism, and, supported by the counsel of M. *Luther, determined to make Prussia a hereditary duchy. In 1525 he achieved this end, but he was obliged to recognize the Polish king as suzerain. He encouraged education, established schools in his duchy, and founded the university of Königsberg in 1544, where he appointed A. *Osiander professor in 1549. After the quarrel between the latter and P. *Melanchthon over *justification by faith, a strict form of Lutheranism was established in his dominions.

J. Voigt, *Briefwechsel der berühmtesten Gelehrten des Zeitalters der Reformation mit Herzog Albrecht von Preussen* (Königsberg, 1841). E. Joachim, *Die Politik des letzten Hochmeisters in Preussen, Albrecht von Brandenburg* (Publicationen aus den k. Preuss. Staatsarchiven l, lviii, lxi, 1892–1895). K. Lohmeyer, *Herzog Albrecht von Preussen* (Danzig, 1890). C. F. D. Erdmann in *P.R.E.* (ed. 3), i (1896), pp. 310–23, s.v. 'Albrecht von Preussen', with bibl. Full bibl. in Schottenloher, iii (1936), pp. 412–20.

ALBERTUS MAGNUS, St. (*c.* 1200–1280), medieval theologian. He entered the newly founded *Dominican order at Padua in 1223. After teaching in the schools of Hildesheim, Ratisbon, Cologne (where St. *Thomas Aquinas was his pupil), and elsewhere, he lectured at Paris from 1245, returned to Cologne in 1248 to organize the Dominican *studium generale*, and from 1254 to 1257 was Provincial of the German province. In 1256 he wrote a book against *Averroism, at the request of Pope Alexander IV (*De unitate intellectus contra Averroem*). In 1260 he became Bp. of Ratisbon, but soon resigned in order to devote himself to literary work. He attended the Council of *Lyons of 1274, and in 1277 defended at Paris the doctrines of his pupil Aquinas.

Albertus Magnus was possessed of vast learning and was a voluminous if at times unsystematic and somewhat inconsistent writer. His principal works include a 'Summa Theologiae' (never completed), a 'Summa de Creaturis', and a commentary on the 'Sentences' of *Peter Lombard. He was much influenced by Jewish and Arabic writers as well as by *Aristotle and the older *Augustinian school of thought (e.g. belief in *rationes seminales*) and foreshadowed Aquinas' synthesis of philosophy and theology. He sought on the basis of his immense knowledge and powers of observation a complete reform of the science of his time, but his writings contain innumerable digressions and lack the organic unity of those of his pupil. His exegesis is difficult to construe by reason of his extensive paraphrasing. Dante puts him with Aquinas

among the great lovers of wisdom (*spiriti sapienti*). He was beatified in 1622, and canonized and proclaimed a *doctor ecclesiae* by *Pius XI in 1931. Feast day, 15 Nov.

Works ed. P. Jammy (21 vols., Lyons, 1651); mod. ed. A. Borgnet (38 vols., Paris, 1890–9). Ps.-Albertian *De Adhaerendo Deo* tr. into Eng. (London, 1654; mod. edd. 1850 and 1949). P. de Loë, O.P. (ed.), 'De Vita et Scriptis Beati Alberti Magni' in *Anal. Boll.*, xix (1900), pp. 257–84, xx (1901), pp. 273–316, and xxi (1902), pp. 361–71. J. Sighart, *Albertus Magnus* (1857; Eng. tr., 1876). G. von Hertling, *Albertus Magnus*. Beiträge zu seiner Würdigung (B.G.P.M., xiv, Hfte. 5–6, 1914); F. Pelster, S.J., *Kritische Studien zum Leben und zu den Schriften Alberts des Grossen* (1920); F. Strunz, *Albertus Magnus* (1926); H. Wilms, O.P., *Albertus der Grosse* ([1930]; Eng. tr., 1933); H. C. Scheeben, *Albertus der Grosse*. Zur Chronologie seines Lebens (Quellen und Forschungen zur Geschichte des Dominikanerordens in Deutschland, xxvii, 1931); G. Meersseman, O.P., *Introductio in Opera Omnia B. Alberti Magni O.P.* (Bruges, 1931). H. Laurent, O.P.–M. J. Congar, O.P., 'Essai de bibliographie albertienne' in *Rev. Thomiste*, xxxvi (1931), pp. 422–68. Überweg, ii, pp. 400–16 and 739–42, and A. Walz, O.P., in *E.C.*, i (1948), cols. 698–705, s.v., both with bibl. Crit. ed. of Works by B. Geyer and others (Münster i.W., 1955 ff.).

ALBIGENSES. A heretical sect, so named from the city of Albi in the department of Tarn, which appeared in the south of France early in the 11th cent. In other parts of Europe they are frequently called '*Cathari' (q.v.). Acc. to their teaching, which was a form of *Manichaean dualism, there are two eternal principles of good and evil, spirits having been created by the good, matter by the bad principle. When part of the spirits fell from their original goodness they were imprisoned in bodies as a punishment, wandering from one to the other ('metempsychosis') until they had completed their expiation and merited heaven. Though retaining the NT and the prophetic parts of the OT, the Albigenses interpreted them as allegories, teaching that Christ was an angel with a phantom body who, consequently, did not suffer nor rise again, and whose redemptive work consisted only in teaching man the true (i.e. Albigensian) doctrine. The Catholic Church, by taking the NT allegories literally, had been corrupted and was doing the work of the devil.

Rejecting the sacraments, the doctrines of hell, purgatory, and the resurrection of the body, the Albigenses were animated by an implacable hatred against the Church. Believing that all matter was bad, their moral doctrine was of extreme rigorism, condemning marriage, the use of meat, milk, eggs, and other animal produce, and recommending a form of suicide by starvation called 'endura'. As, however, these ideals were too austere for the majority of men and women, they distinguished two classes, the 'perfect', who received the 'consolamentum', i.e. baptism of the Holy Spirit by imposition of hands, and kept the precepts in all their rigour, and the ordinary 'believers' who were allowed to lead normal lives but promised to receive the 'consolamentum' when in danger of death; if they recovered, they were obliged to lead the life of the 'perfect' or die by 'endura'.

The Albigenses, who because of their unsocial doctrines were a menace not only to the faith of the Church but to ordered society, were condemned by successive Councils, at *Reims in 1148 and at *Verona in 1184, and at the Fourth *Lateran Council of 1215 Catholic doctrine was defined with special reference to their errors. The heresy, however, spread rapidly, since the 'perfect' gained a hold on the people by the austerity of their lives which contrasted with the laxity of many of the Catholic clergy. *Innocent III sought to convert them by several missions, entrusted to the *Cistercians and later to St. *Dominic, which were all unsuccessful. At last, after the assassination of the Papal legate Peter of Castelnau in 1208, the Pope decided upon a *Crusade against them, the leader of which was Simon de Montfort. The actual Crusade, often conducted with great cruelty, ended in 1218, the year of Montfort's death, the outstanding events being the massacre of Béziers in 1209, and the battle of Muret in 1213, where Simon decisively defeated Peter of Aragon, their leader. From 1219 to the treaty of Paris in 1229 the war was mainly a fight for the incorporation of Languedoc into France. In 1233 *Gregory IX charged the Dominican *Inquisition with the final extirpation of the heresy, of which no trace was left at the end of the 14th cent.

The main sources are the records of the prosecutions. C. Douais (ed.), *Les Sources de l'histoire de l'inquisition dans le midi de la France* (1881); id., *Documents pour servir à l'histoire de l'inquisition dans Languedoc* (2 vols., 'Société de l'Histoire de France', 1900). C. Schmidt, *Histoire et doctrine de la secte des Cathares ou Albigeois* (1849); C. Douais, *Les Albigeois. Leurs origines. Action de l'Église au* XIIe *siècle* (1879). H. J. Warner, *The Albigensian Heresy* (2 vols., 1922–8); E. G. A. Holmes, *The Albigensian or Catharist Heresy* (1925). É. Vacandard, 'Les Origines de l'hérésie albigeoise' in *R.Q.H.*, lv (1894), pp. 50–83. A. Luchaire, *Innocent III*: ii, La Croisade des Albigeois (1905). J. Guiraud in *D.H.G.E.*, i (1912), cols. 1619–94. For more recent work, see bibl. to *Cathari*.

ALBRIGHT BRETHREN. See *Evangelical Association.*

ALCORAN. See *Koran.*

ALCUIN (c. 735–804), the inspirer of the *Carolingian Renaissance. He was educated in his native *York, at the cathedral school, of which he became master in 766. After meeting *Charlemagne at Parma in 781 he became his adviser in religious and educational matters. As royal tutor he established a palace library, and becoming Abbot of Tours in 796, set up there an important school and library. He used the dialogue method for instruction, and made *Boethius, *Augustine, and the grammarians the chief subjects of study. Among his more famous pupils were *Amalarius of Metz and *Rabanus Maurus. His own works consist of educational manuals, poetry in the style of *Fortunatus (including a history of the church of York), an attack on the *Adoptianist heresy of *Felix of Urgel (who opposed him at the Council of Frankfurt), and letters which give a valuable insight into Carolingian society. He revised the Roman lectionary in Gaul and added an appendix to the *Sacramentary sent by Pope *Hadrian to *Charlemagne, reconciling it with the surviving Gallican customs.

Collected edd. of his works by A. Quercetanus (Paris, 1617) and Frobenius Forster (2 vols., Ratisbon, 1777) repr. in J. P. Migne, *PL*, c and ci; additions in P. Jaffé (ed. W. Wattenbach–E. L. Duemmler), *Monumenta Alcuiniana* (Bibliotheca Rerum Germanicarum, vi, Berlin, 1873). There is an early Life written between 823 and 829 printed among his works (J. P. Migne, *PL*, c, 89–106). E. Dümmler, 'Zur Lebensgeschichte Alchvins' in *N.A.*, xviii (1893), pp. 53–70. K. Werner, *Alcuin und sein Jahrhundert* (1876); A. Kleinclausz, *Alcuin* (Annales de l'Université de Lyon, 3e Sér., Lettres, fasc. xv; 1948). C. J. B. Gaskoin, *Alcuin.* His Life and Work (1904); E. M. Wilmot-Buxton, *Alcuin* (Catholic Thought and Thinkers, 1922); E. S. Duckett, *Alcuin.* Friend of Charlemagne (New York, 1951). M. Roger, *L'Enseignement des lettres classiques d'Ausone à Alcuin* (1905), pp. 318–402 passim and 440–8; W. Levison, *England and the Continent in the Eighth Century* (1946), pp. 148–75. F. *Cabrol, O.S.B., 'Les Écrits liturgiques d'Alcuin' in *R.H.E.*, xix (1923), pp. 507–21. A. L. Poole in *D.E.C.H.*, pp. 12 f., s.v.; P. Moncelle in *D.H.G.E.*, ii (1914), cols. 30-40, s.v. Study by G. Ellard, S.J. (Chicago, 1956).

ALCUIN CLUB. An Anglican society founded in 1897 'to encourage and assist in the practical study of ceremonial, and the arrangement of churches, their furniture and ornaments, in accordance with the rubrics of the BCP, strict obedience to which is the guiding principle of the Club'. It has issued several series of publications, most of them dealing with the liturgical subjects. In 1923–4 it put out proposals for a revised BCP, sometimes known (from the colour of the wrappers) as the 'Orange Book'.

The Alcuin Club's Publications include Tracts (London, 1897 ff.), Collections (ib., 1899 ff.), and Prayer Book Revision Pamphlets (1912 ff.).

ALDHELM, St. (d. 709), first Bp. of Sherborne. The details of his life are uncertain as they derive from the two late (12th cent.) writers Faricius of Abingdon and *William of Malmesbury. He was a near relation of Ine, King of Wessex. c. 675 he became Abbot of Malmesbury and in 705 Bp. of the new diocese of Sherborne, when the old see of Wessex was divided. He took a prominent part in the reforming movement initiated by Abp. *Theodore and the monk Hadrian, and founded some monasteries as well as several churches. Traditionally he was supposed to have dedicated the small church at Bradford-on-Avon to St. Lawrence, but it is probably of much later date (? c. A.D. 1000). Much of his Latin writing, composed in a turgid style and full of crudities, survives to attest his learning. He was held in high repute as a poet, but none of his English poems have been preserved. Feast day, 25 May.

Works, with Vita by Fabricius, ed. J. A. Giles (Oxford, 1844), repr. J. P. Migne, *PL*, lxxxix, 63–314. Modern ed. of Works by R. Ehwald in *M.G.H.*, Auctores Antiquissimi, xv (1913–19). Life by *William of Malmesbury, ed. N. E. S. A. Hamilton, *Gesta Pontificum Anglorum*, Book v (R.S., 1870), pp. 330–443. G. F. Browne, *St. Aldhelm* (1903); W. B. Wildman, *Life of St. Ealdhelm* (1905). See also A. S. Cook, *Sources for the Biography of Aldhelm* (Transactions of the Connecticut Academy of Arts and Sciences, xxviii, 1927).

ALDRICH, HENRY (1647–1710), Dean of *Christ Church. Educated at Westminster and at Christ Church, Oxford, he became Canon of Christ Church in 1682, and in 1689, as an opponent of the High Church party and

as a supporter of the Revolution, was appointed to succeed the RC dean, J. Massey. In 1692 he became vice-chancellor. He was remarkable for his versatility. His *Artis Logicae Compendium* (1691; revised by H. L. *Mansel, 1849) remained a standard textbook until the end of the 19th cent. He was a skilful architect, and Peckwater Quadrangle and other buildings in Oxford are ascribed to him. He also composed several anthems largely based on Italian models, was the author of a manual of heraldry, and learned in chemistry.

H. L. Thompson, *Christ Church* (1900), pp. 112–24; E. F. A. Suttle, 'Henry Aldrich, Dean of Christ Church' in *Oxoniensia*, v (1940), pp. 115–32; W. G. Hiscock, *A Christ Church Miscellany* (1946), pp. 17–37.

ALEANDER, GIROLAMO (1480–1542), humanist scholar. In 1508 he introduced Greek studies into France, and in 1513 became rector of the University of Paris. The important part that he took in the history of the Reformation began with his appointment by *Leo X as one of the two Papal envoys commissioned to present M. *Luther with the Bull '*Exsurge Domine', and to negotiate with the Emperor for support against him. In his Ash Wednesday sermon (13 Feb. 1521) at the Diet of *Worms, he vigorously denounced Luther and demanded his condemnation without trial. Unlike many at Rome, Aleander was never in doubt either as to the fact of Luther's popularity in Germany or as to the pressing need for disciplinary reform in the Church. In 1524 he was appointed Abp. of Brindisi and in 1538 a cardinal.

T. Brieger, *Aleander und Luther, 1521* (Gotha, 1884). W. Friedensburg (ed.), *Legation Aleanders 1538–1539* (Nuntiaturberichte aus Deutschland, iii–iv, 1893). P. Kalkoff, *Die Depeschen des Nuntius Aleander vom Wormser Reichstage* (1886; ed. 2, 1897); A. Hausrath, *Aleander und Luther auf dem Reichstage zu Worms* (1897). J. Paquier, *Jérome Aléandre de sa naissance à la fin de son séjour à Brindes, 1480–1529* (1900). P. Kalkoff, *Aleander gegen Luther* (1908); id., 'Zur Charakteristik Aleanders' in *Z.K.G.*, xliii (1924), pp. 209–19. T. Brieger in *P.R.E.* (ed. 3), i (1896), pp. 328–332. Further bibl. in Schottenloher, i (1933), pp. 11–13.

ALEMBERT, J. Le R. D'. See *D'Alembert, J. Le R.*

ALEPH (א). The first letter of Hebrew alphabet, numerically equivalent to one. Textual critics use it to denote the *Codex Sinaiticus.

ALESIUS, ALEXANDER (1500–65), alternatively 'Aless' or 'Alane', Scottish *Lutheran divine. A native of Edinburgh, he studied at St. Andrews, where he became a canon. Selected in 1527 to confute Patrick *Hamilton, who had become an adherent of Lutheran doctrines, he was himself won over by Hamilton's arguments and steadfastness at the stake (1528), and shortly after delivered a Latin sermon at St. Andrews attacking the morals of the clergy for which he was imprisoned. In 1532 he escaped to Germany, where in 1533 he made the acquaintance of M. *Luther and P. *Melanchthon at *Wittenberg and signed the *Augsburg Confession. In the same year he wrote against a Scottish decree forbidding

the laity to read the Bible and in 1534 he was excommunicated at Holyrood. In 1535 he brought a letter to England from Melanchthon to *Henry VIII. On his arrival he was warmly welcomed, esp. by T. *Cranmer, and T. *Cromwell, the new chancellor, made him a divinity lecturer at Cambridge. The opposition to his Protestantism, however, soon caused him to leave Cambridge and for a time he practised in London as a physician, where at Cromwell's request he disputed with J. Stokesly, Bp. of London, on the number of the Sacraments. After the passing of the Act of *Six Articles (1539) he left again for Germany and in 1540 became professor of theology at Frankfurt-on-the-Oder. After various other academic offices and missions in the cause of the Reformation, he revisited England under *Edward VI, when he was employed by Cranmer to translate parts of the First BCP of 1549 into Latin (publd. Leipzig, 1551) for the information of M. *Bucer and *Peter Martyr. He was the author of many exegetical and controversial writings.

J. Thomasius, *Orationes* (Leipzig, 1683), Oratio XIV, delivered at Leipzig on 20 April 1661, pp. 300–22. A. W. Ward in *D.N.B.*, i (1885), pp. 254–9, s.v., with further reff.

ALEXANDER, St. (d. 328), Bp. of *Alexandria from 313. He was actively concerned in putting down the *Meletian and *Arian schisms. At a council of his clergy at Alexandria c. 321 he excommunicated *Arius, one of his presbyters, who shortly before had begun to propagate his doctrines. He then got into touch with the leading theologian of the West, Bp. *Hosius of Cordova, and, with the energetic support of his deacon *Athanasius (who was shortly afterwards to succeed him in his see), took a leading part at the Council of *Nicaea. Two of his Epistles survive (*Theodoret, *H.E.*, I. iv; *Socrates, *H.E.*, I. vi). Feast day, in the West, 26 Feb.; in the *Coptic Church, 22 April.

Other writings ascribed to him, preserved in Syriac or Coptic, include a 'Sermo de Anima et Corpore deque Passione Domini' first ed. from Vat. syr. 368 in Mai, *N.B.P.*, ii, pp. 529–39. Collected ed. of his writings in J. P. Migne, *PG*, xviii, 523–608. Crit. ed. of Epp. in H. G. Opitz (ed.), *Athanasius Werke*, iii (1 f.; 1934–5), pp. 6–11, 19–31. The disputed question as to the order of his two Epistles is examined in V. Hugger, 'Wie sind die Briefe Alexanders von Alexandrien chronologisch zu ordnen?' in *T.Q.*, xci (1909), pp. 66–86; G. Loeschcke, 'Zur Chronologie der beiden grossen antiarianischen Schreiben des Alexander von Alexandrien' in *Z.K.G.*, xxxi (1910), pp. 584–6; and elsewhere. G. Bardy, 'Saint Alexandre d'Alexandrie a-t-il connu la Thalie d'Arius?' in *Rev. S.R.*, vi (1926), pp. 527–32. Bardenhewer, iii, pp. 34–41.

ALEXANDER II (d. 1073), 'Anselm of Lucca', Pope from 1061. A native of Baggio, nr. *Milan, after studying under *Lanfranc at Bec, he supported the *Pataria*, or popular party seeking the reform of the clergy. In order to dispose of him the Abp. of Milan sent him on a mission to the Emp. Henry III (1039–1056). In 1057 he became Bp. of Lucca. Elected Pope in 1061 with the support of Hildebrand (later *Gregory VII), he was enthroned without obtaining the support of the Emp. Henry IV (1056–1106), who had an anti-Pope (Honorius II) elected. Although the schism continued until Honorius' death (1072), Alexander was generally recognized, except in Parma, after the Synod of Mantua of 1064. As Pope he tried to realize the ideals of the reforming party. He dispatched legates to Lombardy, France, Spain, and England and held four synods at Rome. He renewed the decrees against simony and enforcing clerical celibacy, adding a prohibition against attendance at the Mass of an incontinent priest, laid down regulations for the freedom of episcopal elections, forbade lay-investiture and legislated on marriage. He took strong action to enforce these measures, summoning to Rome the Abps. of Mainz and Cologne and the Bp. of Bamberg, and deposing the Abp. of Milan for simony. He strengthened the influence of the Papacy by insisting on personal attendance at Rome before conferring the *pallium, and he persuaded Philip I of France to accord the same significance to Papal decrees as to canons. His blessing was asked and given to William of Normandy's invasion of England (1066). The last important act of his pontificate was his excommunication of the advisers of the Emp. Henry IV. He is not to be confounded with (St.) *Anselm of Lucca (c. 1036–88, q.v.).

146 genuine and six doubtful letters or bulls printed in J. P. Migne, PL, cxlvi, 1279–1430. O. Delarc, Saint Grégoire VII et la réforme de l'Église au XIᵉ siècle, ii (1889), pp. 161–526. A. Fliche, La Réforme grégorienne, i (S.S.L., fasc. vi, 1924), pp. 341–84; Mann, vi (1925), pp. 261–369; A. Fliche in Fliche–Martin, viii (1944), pp. 31–54. H. Hemmer in D.T.C., i (1903), cols. 709–11, s.v. 'Alexandre II'; V. Ermoni in D.H.G.E., ii (1914), cols. 206–8, s.v. 'Alexandre II'; P. Paschini in E.C., i (1948), cols. 788–90, s.v. 'Alessandro II', each with bibl.

ALEXANDER III (d. 1181), Pope. Orlando ('Roland') Bandinelli was at first a Professor at *Bologna where he achieved considerable reputation as a canonist. He exercised a strong influence on *Hadrian IV, whom he succeeded in 1159. An *antipope, Victor IV, was immediately set up and supported by the Emp. *Frederick I (Barbarossa). The schism lasted for 17 years and was ended only by the unconditional surrender of the Emperor at Venice in 1177. During the schism, Alexander lived mostly in France, where he was brought into close contact with Henry II of England in the affair of *Becket. The Pope as a subtle diplomatist was embarrassed by the impetuous Archbishop, but showed himself very firm in imposing penance upon Henry for Becket's murder. In 1179 he assembled and presided over the Third *Lateran Council, one of the most important measures of which was to vest the exclusive right of electing a Pope in a two-thirds majority of the cardinals. As a scholar, Alexander's reputation rests upon his commentary on the '*Decretum' of *Gratian and the 'Sententiae Rolandi', the latter a theological work strongly under the influence of *Abelard. He strongly encouraged the scholastic revival of the 12th cent. The city of Alessandria, founded in the plain of Lombardy at this time, was named after him in gratitude for his support of the liberties of the Lombard Communes against Barbarossa.

Much of his Correspondence in J. P. Migne, PL, cc; further letters and information on his part in the Becket controversy in J. C. Robertson–J. B. Sheppard (edd.), Materials for the History of Thomas Becket, v–vii (R.S., 1881–5); see also Jaffe–Wattenbach, ii, pp. 145–418. The chief authority up to 1178 is the life by Card. Boson, his favourite Cardinal, in L.P. (Duchesne), ii, pp. 397–446; further life by G. F. Loredano (Venice, 1637; often repr.)). H. Reuter, Geschichte Alexanders des Dritten und der Kirche seiner Zeit (3 vols., 1845); H. Kerner, Papst Alexander III (1874); W. Ohnsorge, Die Legaten Alexander III im ersten Jahrzehnt seines Pontifikats, 1159–1169 (Historische Studien, Hft. clxxv; 1928). U. Stutz, Papst Alexander III gegen die Freiung Langobardischer Eigenkirchen in Abh. (Berl.), 1936, No. 6. Mann, x (1925), pp. 1–238, with full reff. E. Portalié, S.J., and H. Moureau in D.T.C., i (1903), cols. 711–21, s.v.; V. Ermoni (Lazarite) in D.H.G.E., ii (1914), cols. 208–14; F. Liuzzi in E.C., i (1948), cols. 790–2, s.v. 'Alessandro III'.

ALEXANDER V (c. 1339–1410), Pope. Peter of Candia (Crete), also 'Peter Philarges', having become a *Franciscan, studied at Oxford and later was a Master of Theology at Paris (1381) where he lectured on the *Sentences. His academic career was brought to an end by preferment. He became Bp. successively of Piacenza (1386), Vicenza (1387), Novara (1389), Abp. of Milan (1402); and in 1409 at the Council of *Pisa he was unanimously elected to fill the Papal chair, presumed vacant, despite the two existing claimants. His strong character and extensive learning aroused great hopes; but he died after ten months. RC theologians still dispute whether he can claim a place in the true Papal succession. His importance in medieval thought has recently been increasingly recognized. His surviving 'Commentary on the Sentences' shows marked *nominalistic leanings.

M. Renières, Ἱστορικαὶ μελέται. Ὁ Ἕλλην πάπας Ἀλέξανδρος εʹ (Athens, 1881). F. *Ehrle, Der Sentenzenkommentar Peters von Candia des Pisaner Papstes Alexanders V (Franziskanische Studien, Beiheft ix, 1925). Pastor, i (1891), p. 190 f. L. Salembier in D.T.C., i (1903), cols. 772–4; A. Clerval in D.H.G.E., ii (1914), cols. 216–18; P. Paschini in E.C., i (1948), col. 794 f., s.v. 'Alessandro V'.

ALEXANDER VI (1431–1503), Pope from 1492. Rodrigo Borgia, a Spaniard by birth and nephew of Pope Calixtus III (1455–8), who created him a Cardinal in 1456, after studying at *Bologna, was appointed Chancellor of the Roman Church in 1457. He exercised considerable influence under Paul II (1464–71), and was largely responsible for the election of *Sixtus IV (1471). His own election having been secured largely through bribery, the course of his pontificate was determined almost solely by political and family considerations, esp. his favouritism of his son, Caesar. Among the most notable acts of his pontificate were the series dividing the New World between *Spain and *Portugal (1493–4), his prosecution and execution of G. *Savonarola in 1498, the *Jubilee which he organized in 1500 and the crusade against the Moors (1499–1500). A man of immoral life, he was an astute politician and generous patron of artists, esp. D. Bramante, G. and A. Sangallo and ' Pinturicchio'. Under him the Leonine city was largely replanned and the castle of Sant' Angelo rebuilt.

P. de Roo (ed.), Materials for a History of Pope Alexander VI, his Relatives and his Times (5 vols., Brussels, 1924).

V. Nemec, *Papst Alexander VI* (1879); A. Leonetti, *Papa Alessandro VI* (3 vols., with documents, 1880); L'Abbé Clément de Vebron, *Les Borgia*, Histoire du Pape Alexandre VI, de César et de Lucrèce Borgia (1882); J. Schnitzer, *Der Tod Alexanders VI*. Eine quellenkritische Untersuchung (1929); O. Ferrara, *El Papa Borgia* (1943; Eng. tr. 1942). H. Vander Linden, 'Alexander VI and the Demarcation of the Maritime and Colonial Domains of Spain and Portugal, 1493–1494' in *American Historical Review*, xxii (1917), pp. 1–20. Pastor, v (1898), pp. 375–523, and vi (1898), pp. 3–181. J. F. Loughlin in *C.E.*, i (1907), pp. 289–94; J. Paquier in *D.T.C.*, i (1903), cols. 724–7; P. Richard in *D.H.G.E.*, ii (1914), cols. 218–29, all s.v.; G. M. Pou y Marti in *E.C.*, i [c. 1949], cols. 795–801, s.v. 'Alessandro VI'.

ALEXANDER VII (1599–1667), Pope from 1655. Fabio Chigi was a native of Siena, where he studied philosophy, law, and theology. In 1626 he entered upon an ecclesiastical career at *Rome. After being *Inquisitor of Malta, he became Papal Nuntius at *Cologne in 1639. As such he followed the negotiations of the Peace of *Westphalia and protested against several of its clauses. After his return to Rome (1651), he was created cardinal in 1652 and became Papal secretary of state. During the first year of his pontificate he showed himself an enemy of nepotism, but in 1656 he gave way to the pressure of his advisers, who feared a weakening of the Papal position through the absence of his family, and called his brother and nephews to Rome. As a theologian he was of strongly anti-*Jansenistic views, and, to make Jansenist subterfuges impossible, condemned in 1665 the five propositions drawn from *Augustinus in the sense in which C. *Jansenius had meant them. In this attitude he was supported by Louis XIV, though political troubles arose between the Pope and the King, owing to a dispute between the Papal *entourage* and the French ambassador. Louis thereupon seized *Avignon and Venaissin, and threatened to invade the States of the Church, and Alexander had to sign the humiliating peace of Pisa in 1664. Following the controversy on *Probabilism, he condemned, in 1665 and 1666, 45 *Laxist propositions, though not the Probabilist system. He was a friend of the *Jesuits, esp. of Cardinal Sforza Pallavicini, the historian of the Council of *Trent, and he procured the readmission of the order to the republic of *Venice. He also did much for the embellishment and modernization of Rome.

S. Pallavicini, S.J., *Della vita di Alessandro VII* (only to 1659; 2 vols., 1839–40). C. Gérin, 'L'Ambassade de Créquy à Rome et le traité de Pise, 1662–1664' in *R.Q.H.*, xxviii (1880), pp. 79–151. Pastor, xxxi (1940), pp. 1–313. H. Hemmer–E. Deshayes in *D.T.C.*, i (1903), cols. 727–47, s.v.; P. Richard in *D.H.G.E.*, ii (1914), cols. 229–44, s.v.; C. Incisa della Rocchetta in *E.C.*, i (1948), cols. 801–3, s.v. 'Alessandro VII'; each with bibl.

ALEXANDER VIII (1610–91), Pope from 1689. Pietro Ottoboni, the descendant of a noble Venetian family, studied at Padua, where he became a doctor of canon and civil law in 1627. Having been an auditor of the *Rota for 14 years, he was created cardinal by *Innocent X in 1652, and subsequently became Bp. of Brescia. After his election to the Papacy in 1689, he effected a reconciliation with Louis XIV, who, in 1690, gave back *Avignon and Venaissin, which he had taken from *Alexander VII. His most important doctrinal decisions were the condemnations of the Four *Gallican Propositions of 1682 and of 31 propositions of C. *Jansenius, both in 1690. In the same year he also condemned the doctrine of *Philosophical Sin. Despite the condemnation of Gallicanism his relations with France remained satisfactory. During his short pontificate he helped his native city of *Venice against the Turks, and brought about several social improvements in the States of the Church by a diminution of taxes and an increase of cheap food imports. He also enriched the *Vatican Library by the purchase of the valuable MSS. ('Reginenses') of Queen *Christina of Sweden.

S. Freiherr von Bischoffshausen, *Papst Alexander VIII und der Wiener Hof, 1689–1691* (1900); C. Gérin, 'Le Pape Alexandre VIII et Louis XIV d'après des documents inédits' in *R.Q.H.*, xxii (1877), pp. 135–210; E. Michaud, *La Politique de compromis avec Rome en 1689*. Le Pape Alexandre VIII et le Duc de Chaulines d'après les correspondances diplomatiques inédites du Ministère des Affaires étrangères de France (1888). M. Dubruel. 'Le Pape Alexandre VIII et les affaires de France' in *R.H.E.*, xv (1914), pp. 282–302 and 495–514. Pastor, xxxii (1940), pp. 525–60. H. Hemmer and X. Le Bachelet in *D.T.C.*, i (1905), cols. 747–63, s.v.; P. Richard in *D.H.G.E.*, ii (1914), cols. 244–51, s.v.; P. Dalla Torre in *E.C.*, i (1948), col. 803–5, s.v. 'Alessandro VIII'; each with bibl.

ALEXANDER OF HALES (c. 1170–1245), the 'Doctor Irrefragabilis'. Born at Hales in Gloucestershire, he was educated, and later taught, at *Paris. In 1236 he joined the *Franciscan Order without renouncing (as was the custom) his teaching chair. The 'Summa Theologiae' traditionally ascribed to him has been shown to be a later compilation by the Franciscan theologians of Paris incorporating extracts from John de La Rochelle, St. *Bonaventura, William of Melitona and others, besides considerable material from the writings of Alexander himself. In conjunction with John de La Rochelle and others, he also wrote an 'Expositio in Regulam S. Francisci' (1242). His other genuine works include glosses on the *Sentences of *Peter Lombard, which dates from his secular period, and a series of 'Quaestiones'.

His *Summa Theologica* was first publd. at Venice, 1475, under the name of Thomas of Hales; crit. ed. by the Franciscans of Quaracchi (4 vols., 1924–48), with invaluable prolegomena by V. Doucet, O.F.M., in vol. iv, pp. xiii–ccclxx. Gloss ed. idd. (Bibliotheca Francescana Scholastica Medii Aevi, xii–xv; 1951 ff.). An ed. of the *Quaestiones* in preparation (1956); summary of contents by F. M. Henquinet, O.F.M., 'Les Questions inédites d'Alexandre de Hales sur les Fins dernières' in *R.T.A.M.*, x (1938), pp. 56–78, 153–72, 268–78; id., 'De Centum et Septem Quaestionibus Halesianis Codicis Tudertinen. 121' in *Antonianum*, xiii (1938), pp. 335–66, 489–514. I. Herscher, O.F.M., 'A Bibliography of Alexander of Hales' in *Franciscan Studies*, xxvi (1945), pp. 435–54. V. Doucet, O.F.M., in *E.C.*, i (1948), cols. 784–7, s.v. 'Alessandro di Hales', with further bibl.

ALEXANDER OF LYCOPOLIS (3rd cent.), writer against *Manichaeism. He was probably a pagan who became a Manichaean and later a Christian, though some modern scholars, notably L. S. le N. *Tillemont and, more recently, A. Brinkmann, contend that he never embraced Christianity. Acc. to *Photius (*Contra Manichaeos*, i, 11) he became a bishop.

His fame rests on his treatise against the Manichaeans, Πρὸς τὰς Μανιχαίου δόξας, in which he praises the simplicity and efficacy of the Christian philosophy and contrasts it with the illogical and contradictory doctrines of the Manichaeans. Though his style and thought are often obscure, the work is a primary source for the study of Manichaeism.

The treatise, first publd. by F. *Combefis in 1672, is reprinted in J. P. Migne, *PG*, xviii, 411–48. A. Brinkmann, *Alexandri Lycopolitani contra Manichaei opiniones disputatio* (1895).

ALEXANDER NATALIS. See *Natalis, Alexander.*

ALEXANDER, MICHAEL SOLOMON (1799–1845), first Anglican bishop in *Jerusalem. Born in Schönlanke in Posen, he was trained in strictly orthodox *Judaism and became a teacher of German and the *Talmud. He came to England in 1820 and here was brought into personal contact with Christianity, was suspended from his duties as rabbi, and baptized in 1825. Upon his ordination in 1827 he joined the London Society for Promoting Christianity among the Jews and served as a missionary in Danzig from 1827 to 1830. From 1830 to 1841 he had a mission in London, and from 1832 was also professor of Hebrew at *King's College. Here he took an active part in revising the Hebrew NT and also translated the BCP into Hebrew. On the establishment of the Anglican bishopric at Jerusalem, he was selected and consecrated as first bishop of the see (1841), where his short term of service was successful alike among Arabs and Jews. See also *Jerusalem, Anglican Bishopric in.*

Autobiogr. account of his conversion appended to J. Hatchard, *The Predictions and Promises of God Respecting Israel* (sermon, 1825), pp. 37–40. J. F. A. De la Roi, *Michael Solomon Alexander, der erste evangelische Bischof in Jerusalem* (1897).

ALEXANDRIAN THEOLOGY. The theology of the early Church at Alexandria came markedly under the influence of that Platonic tradition of philosophy which, beginning in the Graeco-Jewish period, was taken into the Christian system of thought by the *Apologists, and later by *Clement of Alexandria, *Origen, and the *Catechetical School. The effect of Origen upon later Alexandrian theologians was overmastering. The Platonic sense of the reality of the spiritual world and the ready tolerance of *dualism are seen in the stress laid by Alexandrian writers upon the transcendence of God, upon the essential Godhead of all Three Persons, and upon the Divine Nature in the Incarnate Christ. Thus it was that the opposition to characteristically *Antiochene heresies, such as the overemphasis on the humanity of Christ which produced *Adoptionism and *Nestorianism, came chiefly from Alexandrians such as St. *Athanasius and St. *Cyril.

The Alexandrians, however, in their anxiety to maintain that the distinction between the Persons of the Trinity was more than purely functional, tended considerably towards tritheism, into which Origen himself is generally held to have fallen. Their emphasis upon the separateness of the Three Persons produced a type of theology called by F. *Loofs 'Pluralist-Trinitarian'. In their account of the Person of Christ they stressed His divinity, and even the orthodox among them (e.g. St. *Cyril) did not hesitate to say of the Incarnate Christ that 'God suffered', while the less orthodox, beginning with *Apollinarius, frankly refused to believe in any true humanity in Christ, holding that His highest human faculties were simply replaced by the Divine Nature, so that He could neither be tempted nor suffer. *Monophysitism must be considered an extreme form of the Alexandrian school of thought, which, by verbal adherence to Cyril's language, taught that there was only one nature in Christ, a view which practically nullified His humanity; while *Monothelitism, in the 7th cent., carried on the same tradition in different terms, by asserting the unity of Christ's Divine and Human Will.

In their exegesis of Scripture the Alexandrians were strongly drawn to mystical and allegorical exposition, in contrast with the literal and historical method of Antioch.

C. *Bigg, *The Christian Platonists of Alexandria.* The *Bampton Lectures for 1886 (ed. F. E. *Brightman, 1913); W. R. Inge, 'Alexandrian Theology' in *H.E.R.E.* s.v.; R. B. Tollinton, *Alexandrine Teaching on the Universe* (1932); E. Molland, *The Conception of the Gospel in the Alexandrian Theology* (Oslo, 1938); R. V. Sellers, *Two Ancient Christologies* (1940).

ALFORD, HENRY (1810–71), Dean of *Canterbury. He entered Trinity College, Cambridge, in 1829, and was elected fellow in 1834. In 1835 he became vicar of Wymeswold, Leicestershire. From 1853 to 1857 he ministered to a large congregation at Quebec Chapel, Marylebone, and then became Dean of Canterbury, where he remained till his death. His most important work was an edition of the Greek NT (1849–61), in which he united freshness of treatment with wide learning. He also translated the 'Odyssey', wrote several well-known hymns (among them, 'Come, ye thankful people, come' and 'Ten thousand times ten thousand'), edited the writings of J. *Donne (1839), published some original verse, and was the first editor of the *Contemporary Review.*

Poetical Works, 2 vols., 1845. Life, Journal and Letters, ed. by Fanny Alford, his widow (1873).

ALFRED THE GREAT (849–99), King of Wessex from 871. He was born at Wantage. Apart from his defeat of the Danes, which contributed materially to the maintenance of Christianity in England, Alfred is chiefly memorable in Church History for the care with which he promoted ecclesiastical reform and the revival of learning. Himself a man of considerable education, he gathered round him a band of scholars from England, Wales, and the Continent, and with their help translated a number of the most popular Latin works of the time, among them the 'Dialogues' and 'Pastoral

Rule' of *Gregory the Great, the 'Consolations' of *Boethius, the 'History' of *Orosius, and the 'Soliloquies' of St. *Augustine. He founded monastic communities at Shaftesbury and Athelney, made plans for one at *Winchester, and seems to have contemplated subdivision of the dioceses of Wessex, although this latter scheme did not materialize until ten years after his death, when one of his disciples, Abp. Plegmund, consecrated seven bishops for *Winchester, Ramsbury, *Sherborne, *Wells, *Crediton, *Dorchester, and the South Saxons. The time was not ripe for his proposals for monastic reform and they met with little success, but his literary works had a considerable influence. He has been remembered for a thousand years as one who did his utmost for the education of his clergy and nobles, and, in his own life, the pattern of a Christian king.

Mod. Eng. tr. as *The Whole Works of King Alfred the Great*, with preliminary essays, ed. J. A. Giles (3 vols. bound in 2, London, 1858), incl. orig. text of poems; crit. edd. of Alfred's versions of Gregory's Pastoral Rule by H. Sweet (E.E.T.S., xlv and l, 1871–2), of Orosius part i by id. (ib., lxxix, 1883), of the Proverbs by E. Borgström (Lund, 1908) and of the Soliloquies of St. Augustine by W. Endter (Bibliothek der Angelsächsischen Prosa, xi, Hamburg, 1922). Further edd. and works of criticism in *C.B.E.L.*, i, pp. 85–8. The primary sources for his life are the contemporary biography by Asser (crit. ed. by W. H. Stevenson, Oxford, 1904) and the 'Anglo-Saxon Chronicle', sub annis 853–901. C. Plummer, *The Life and Times of Alfred the Great* (Ford Lectures for 1901, 1902), with bibl. reff. Other lives by R. Pauli (Berlin, 1851; Eng. tr., 1852) and B. A. Lees (New York and London, 1919). On his reign, R. H. Hodgkin, *A History of the Anglo-Saxons*, ii (1935), pp. 537–688; F. M. Stenton, *Anglo-Saxon England* (1943), pp. 246–73.

ALITURGICAL DAYS. Days on which the Eucharist may not be celebrated. In the Roman rite there are now two such days, *Good Friday and Holy Saturday; in the Eastern Church there are many more.

ALL SAINTS' DAY. The feast, kept in the W. on 1 Nov., to celebrate all the Christian saints, known and unknown. Reference to such a feast occurs in St. *Ephrem Syrus (d. 373), while in St. *Chrysostom (d. 407) it is assigned to a definite day, viz. the first Sunday after *Pentecost, that still observed in the E. This same day was apparently associated with the saints also at *Rome in the 6th cent.; but in the W. the feast did not become firmly established until the consecration of the Pantheon at Rome (*dedicatio S. Mariae ad martyres*) to Christian usage by Boniface IV on 13 May 609 or 610. From then on an annual commemoration of 'All Saints' was made on 13 May. Its observance on 1 Nov. appears to date from the time of Gregory III (d. 741) who dedicated on that day a chapel in the basilica of St. Peter to 'All the Saints'. Gregory IV (d. 844) ordered its universal observance and Sixtus IV (d. 1484) added the Octave. In the calendar in the proposed revision of the BCP of 1927–8, the Octave Day (8 Nov.) is assigned to the 'Saints, Martyrs, and Doctors of the Church of England'.

Serm. of St. *Chrysostom, *Laudatio Sanctorum Omnium* (J. P. Migne, *PG*, l. 705–12). L. Eisenhofer, *Handbuch der katholischen Liturgik*, i (1932), p. 606 f. G. Löw in *E.C.*, ix (1952), cols. 86–90, s.v. 'Ognissanti'.

ALL SOULS' DAY. The commemoration of the souls of the faithful departed on 2 Nov., the day following *All Saints' Day. (When 2 Nov. is a Sunday, however, All Souls' Day is 3 Nov.) Its observance became universal through the influence of *Odilo of Cluny, who in 998 commanded its annual celebration in the *Benedictine houses of his congregation. Priests of the Latin rite are permitted to celebrate three Masses on All Souls' Day (a privilege confined to this day and *Christmas). The Mass contains the famous sequence, '*Dies Irae'.

The 'Statutum Odilonis pro Defunctis' is printed in J. P. Migne, *PL*, cxlii, 1037 f. The commemoration is first met with at Rome in the 14th cent. (*Ordo Romanus XIV, no. 101). For the Apostolic Constitution of *Benedict XV (10 Aug. 1915) permitting the three Masses on the day, see *A.A.S.*, vii (1915), pp. 401–4.

ALLAH. An Arabic word used by all Moslems as the name of God. The word is a combination of '*al* (the definite article) and *ilah* ('god'), and was probably first used among the Arabs when passing from polytheism to monolatry to indicate that their own God was the supreme God. The Moslem use of the word may be interpreted to mean 'The Only God'. In Moslem belief, God has 99 further names, each of which is represented by a bead on their rosary, the hundredth and largest of them representing the name Allah itself.

ALLATIUS, LEO (1586–1669), Greek RC theologian and historian. He was a native of Chios. In 1622 he supervised the transference of the valuable collection of Palatinate MSS. from Heidelberg to the Vatican Library, of which he became custodian in 1661. A zealous advocate of reunion between the Orthodox and RC Churches, he wrote several works seeking to establish the unity in essential doctrine between them, the chief being his *De ecclesiae occidentalis atque orientalis perpetua consensione libri III* (Cologne, 1648). He also wrote extensively on *patristics.

List of his writings in H. Hurter, S.J., *Nomenclator Literarius*, iv (ed. 3, 1910), cols. 122–30. MS. *Vita* by S. Gradi, partly printed in A. *Mai, *N.P.B.*, VI (2; 1853), pp. v–xxviii. C. Mazzi, 'Leone Allacci e la Palatina di Heidelberg' in *Propugnatore* (Bologna), xxiv (1891: 1), pp. 261–307; xxv (1892: 1), pp. 130–206, 315–88; xxv (1892: 2), pp. 370–400. L. Petit, A.A., in *D.T.C.*, i (1903), cols. 830–3, s.v.

ALLEGIANCE, Oath of. The oath to the King taken by the clergy of the C of E under an Act of 1868 (31 & 32 Vic. cap. 72) at their ordination to the diaconate and to the priesthood, and on admission to a benefice. It replaces the acknowledgement of the sovereign as Supreme Governor in things or causes, spiritual or temporal, which had been required by Canon 36 of 1604 until the canon was amended in 1865. It is now a statutory obligation, imposed by the civil power alone, and not by canon.

ALLEGORY. Acc. to St. *Augustine, a mode of speech in which one thing is understood by another (*De Trin.* xv, ix, 15). It differs from the *parable in its more systematic presentation of the different features of the idea it illustrates as well as in its contents, which are concerned with the exposition of theoretical truths rather than with practical exhortation. Though not so frequent as parables, there are instances of allegories in the Bible, e.g. that of the vine in Is. 5. 1–6 and Ps. 80. 8–16.

The allegorical interpretation of Scripture is a particular method of exegesis which, acc. to *Philo, was practised in the Palestinian Rabbinical schools. It was frequently applied to the OT by NT writers, the term itself being used by St. Paul in Gal. 4. 24, 'which things contain an allegory' (ἅτινά ἐστιν ἀλληγορούμενα). Acc. to St. Augustine (loc. cit.), the allegories which the NT writers find in the OT are not mere rhetorical figures but historical facts ('non in verbis sed in facto'), God, as the author of Scripture, having foreordained certain facts recorded in the Bible in such a manner as to be, apart from historical reality, also a prophetic announcement of future events. Thus St. Paul sees the relations between the Church and the Synagogue prefigured in the story of Isaac and Ishmael, and Christ in Adam or in the Paschal Lamb. The early Fathers continued to use this method of interpretation which is found, e.g. in the 'Ep. of *Barnabas', St. *Clement of Rome, St. *Irenaeus, and *Tertullian. It was developed and carried to excess by the School of *Alexandria, which would see an allegorical meaning in almost every passage of the Bible and sometimes deny a literal sense altogether. *Clement of Alexandria distinguished a literal, mystical, moral, and prophetical interpretation, and *Origen the literal, moral, and spiritual sense, corresponding to the human body, soul, and spirit. The School of *Antioch, on the other hand, though not completely rejecting the allegorical interpretation, used it very sparingly, preferring the historical sense, e.g. St. John *Chrysostom. The Latin Fathers, esp. St. *Ambrose and St. *Augustine, hold an intermediate position, admitting a literal as well as an allegorical significance for a great number of OT narratives. *Cassian (Collat. xiv, 8), following Clement of Alexandria, established the division which remained classical throughout the Middle Ages, in distinguishing four senses, viz. the literal, the allegorical strictly so called, applying the passage to Christ and the Church Militant, the tropological or moral, understanding it of the soul and its virtues, and the anagogical, applying it to the heavenly realities. This method was taken up by the Schoolmen and is still used in the RC Church.

The 16th cent. Reformers, M. *Luther, P. *Melanchthon, J. *Calvin, and others, explicitly repudiated all allegorical interpretation, acc. to their guiding principle 'Scriptura scripturae interpres'. This has remained the usual attitude of Protestant exegetes to the present day. It has, however, been realized in recent times by some scholars that if the doctrine of the Inspiration of Scripture is to be maintained, the complete rejection of the allegorical interpretation leads to serious difficulties, e.g. in the case of the so-called *Imprecatory Psalms.

J. Geffcken in H.E.R.E., i (1908), pp. 327–31.

ALLELUIA (Heb. הַלְלוּיָה, 'Praise ye Yah'), liturgical expression of praise. It occurs in a number of Psalms, esp. in Pss. 111–17, where its position indicated that it was chanted as a kind of *antiphon by the choir of the *Levites. It is found elsewhere in the Bible only in Tobit (13. 18) and the Book of Rev. (19. 1, 3, 4, 6), in both places as the chant of the saints in heaven. It was taken over into the liturgy of the Church at an early date. In the W. it became the characteristic expression of joy and was therefore sung esp. in *Paschaltide, as is witnessed by St. *Augustine (Serm. 252, De diebus paschalibus, xxiii, 9), but whether, as Sozomen (Hist. Eccl. vii, 19) affirms, it was restricted at *Rome to *Easter Day or not, remains doubtful. The Roman usage was regulated by St. *Gregory the Great, who ordered the Alleluia to be said at Mass and the Office throughout the year except in the penitential time between *Septuagesima and Easter. It was later omitted also in funeral offices. In the Greek Church, on the other hand, it remained a part of all offices, and its omission at certain times was made one of the grievances of the E. Church against the W. in the struggle which led to the schism of the 11th century.

Acc. to the Roman Rite the Alleluia is sung at all Masses except those between Septuagesima and Easter, the ferial Masses of *Advent, *Ember Day and *Vigil Masses outside Paschaltide, and *Requiems. It is chanted after the *Gradual, and normally consists of a twofold Alleluia, a verse from Scripture, and another Alleluia. In Paschaltide another verse with its Alleluia is added and the Gradual omitted, and both in the Mass and the Divine Office Alleluias are inserted in many places. The name 'Alleluia Saturday' is sometimes applied to Holy Saturday because, to mark the return of the Alleluia after its absence since Septuagesima, the celebrant solemnly intones it three times, each time at a higher pitch. In the E. a hymn called the '*Cherubic Hymn' or 'Cherubicon', which contains the Alleluias, is now sung at the *Great Entrance; and the Alleluia is also sung before the Gospel. In the *Ambrosian Rite the form 'Hallelujah' is used.

On the orig. use of the word, cf. F. H. Woods in H.D.B., ii (1899), p. 287. T. Nöldeke, 'Halleluya' in Beihefte zur Z.A.T.W., xxxiii (1918), pp. 375–80. L. Eisenhofer, Grundriss der Liturgik des römischen Ritus (ed. 5, 1950), pp. 47 and 122. F. *Cabrol, O.S.B., in D.A.C.L., i (1907), cols. 1226–46, s.v. 'Alleluia (ii: Acclamation liturgique)'. On the Alleluia Chant in the Mass, see Jungmann (1952), i, pp. 539–65.

ALLELUYATIC SEQUENCE. A name popularly given to the hymn 'Cantemus cuncti melodium' ('The strain upraise of joy and praise, Alleluia', Eng. Hymnal, No. 494), on account of its frequent repetition of 'Alleluia'. It was written c. the 9th cent., and used before or at *Septuagesima for the 'farewell to Alleluia', since, acc. to traditional liturgical practice, the word Alleluia, as an expression of joy, is not used between Septuagesima and *Easter. The words are based on Ps. 147.

Crit. ed. of text by C. Blume, S. J.–H. Bannister (edd.), *Thesauri Hymnologici Prosarium* (A.H.M.A., liii; 1911), pp. 60–2. W. A. Shoults and J. Julian in J. Julian (ed.), *Dictionary of Hymnology* (ed. 2, 1907), p. 203 f., s.v. 'Cantemus Cuncti Melodium Nunc'.

ALLEN, WILLIAM (1532–94), Cardinal. He was a fellow of Oriel College, Oxford, and later Principal of St. Mary's Hall. In 1561 he left England for Louvain, returned in the next year, and was finally forced to leave the country in 1565. From that time he concentrated on the work of training RC mission priests for the conversion of England, believing that the majority of English people were still Catholic at heart, and that Protestantism was only a temporary phase of opinion. He founded colleges for this work at *Douai (1568), *Rome (1575–8), and Valladolid (1589). From the press at Douai there issued a stream of RC propaganda, and the *Douai version of the Bible was produced under his inspiration. By supporting Philip II's invasion of England in 1588, however, he incurred the serious hostility of many English RCs. Towards the end of his life he was appointed Abp. of Malines, but his appointment was never confirmed. He ended his days at the English college at Rome which he had founded.

Modern reprint of his *Brief History of the Glorious Martyrdom of Twelve Reverend Priests, Father Edmund Campion and his Companions*, by J. H. Pollen, S.J. (1908). *The Letters and Memorials of William Cardinal Allen (1532–1594)*, ed. with hist. introd. by T. F. Knox, Cong. Orat. (Records of the English Catholics under the Penal Laws, ii, 1882). 'Some Correspondence of Cardinal Allen, 1579–85, from the Jesuit Archives' contributed by P. Ryan, S.J., to the C.R.S., *Miscellanea*, vii (C.R.S., ix, 1911), pp. 12–105. Life by Bede Camm, O.S.B. (1908). M. Haile, *An Elizabethan Cardinal* (1914). A Bellesheim, *Wilhelm Cardinal Allen (1532–1594) und die englischen Seminare auf dem Festlande* (1885).

ALLESTREE, RICHARD (1619–81), Anglican divine. He was educated at *Christ Church, Oxford, where Richard Busby (afterwards Headmaster of Westminster) was his tutor. For a time he served in the royalist forces and throughout his life remained loyal in support of the Stuart cause. During the Commonwealth he assisted J. *Fell in continuing the C of E service in a private dwelling-house in Oxford. From 1663 to 1679 he was Regius Professor of Divinity at Oxford and in 1665 he also became Provost of Eton. He is best remembered as the probable author of the *'Whole Duty of Man'.

Collected ed. of *The Works of the Learned and Pious Author of The Whole Duty of Man* (2 parts, Oxford, 1684). Anon. life by J. Fell prefixed to *Forty Sermons* (1684: no pagination); repr. separately, 1848.

ALLIES, THOMAS WILLIAM (1813–1903), theologian. From 1833 to 1841 he was a fellow of Wadham College, Oxford. He became closely associated with the leaders of the *Oxford Movement, esp. E. B. *Pusey; but having begun to doubt the Anglican position during travels abroad in 1845 and 1847 (described in his *Journal in France* [1848]), he

joined the RC Church after the *Gorham Judgement. He was a man of wide learning, and in his later life a prominent apologist for Roman Catholicism both by lectures and writings. His books include *The Church of England cleared from the Charge of Schism* (1846) and *The See of St. Peter* (1850).

Mary H. Allies (daughter), *Thomas William Allies* (1907; repr., with additional appendices, 1924).

ALMACHIUS, St. See *Telemachus, St.*

ALMERY. An obsolete form of the word '*Aumbry' (q.v.).

ALMONER. An officer who has the duty of dispensing alms. Very frequently he is in holy orders. The Lord High Almoner of the King of England, who has the disposing of the King's alms and on *Maundy Thursday, in the absence of the King, distributes the royal 'maundy', is usually a bishop. In France *aumônier* is used in a more general sense of 'chaplain'.

ALMUCE, alternatively 'Amice' or 'Amess'. An item of ecclesiastical costume, usually a cape lined with fur, worn in certain religious orders. Its use can be traced back to the 12th cent. In more recent times it has been worn esp. by canons in *France, who carry their almuce as a mark of dignity over the left arm. The word 'amice' (Lat. *almutia*) in this sense is independent in derivation from that of the *amice (q.v.) worn at the Eucharist, though the two have often been confused.

ALOGI. A group of heretics in Asia Minor (c. A.D. 170). They seem to have been strongly opposed to *Montanism and to have ascribed the Gosp. and Rev. of St. John to *Cerinthus, but their exact doctrines are not easy to ascertain. Acc. to *Epiphanius (*Haer.* 51), they denied the divinity of the Holy Ghost and of the Logos. The word '*Alogi*' (ἄλογοι) was coined for them by their opponents, who used it in the double sense of 'unreasonable' and 'disbelievers in the Logos'.

V. Rose, O.P., 'Question johannine. Les Aloges asiatiques et les aloges romains' in *R. Bibl.*, vi (1897), pp. 516–534. A. Bludau, *Die ersten Gegner der Johannes-Schriften* (Biblische Studien, xxii, Hftt. 1 and 2; 1925). G. Bareille in *D.T.C.*, i (1903), cols. 898–901, s.v., with further reff.

ALOYSIUS GONZAGA, St. (1568–91), patron of RC youth. Of noble descent, he was destined for a military career, and from 1577 to 1579 was at Florence as a page at the court of Francesco de' Medici, where he first began to feel a vocation to religion. After joining the suite of Mary of Austria in 1581, he followed her to Spain, but in 1584 he returned to Italy, where, in the face of great opposition, he entered the novitiate of the *Jesuits in 1585. He made his vows in 1587, and died, at the age of 23, a victim to his labours among the plague-stricken of Rome. He was canonized in 1726. Feast day, 21 June.

Opera Omnia, partim Italice, partim Latine (incomplete) ed. A. Heuser (Bibliotheca Mystica et Ascetica, iii, Cologne, etc., 1850). Works listed in Sommervogel, iii (1892), cols. 1575–81, and ix (1900), col. 420. Life by his contemporary and associate, V. Cepari, S.J. (Rome, 1606; Lat. tr., Cologne, 1608; Eng. tr., Paris, 1627); ed., with additional matter, by A. Schroeber, S.J. (Einsiedeln, 1891; Eng. tr., 1891). The account in *A.A.SS.*, Jun. IV (1707), pp. 847–1167, utilizes the process of beatification. C. C. Martindale, S.J., *The Vocation of Aloysius Gonzaga* (1927), with bibl. Other lives by E. H. Thompson (London, 1867), M. Meschler, S.J. (Paris, 1891; Eng. tr., 1911), F. Crispolti (Mantua, 1924) and A. Koch, S.J. (Innsbruck, 1927; Eng. tr., 1928).

ALPHA AND OMEGA (Α and Ω). The
first and last letters of the Greek alphabet, used in the Christian Church to denote God's eternity and infinitude. In the NT they are found in Rev. 1. 8, 21. 6, and also in 22. 13 (of Christ). Their adoption is probably derived from the Heb. use of the word 'truth', אמת, the first and last letters of which are the first and last letters of the Heb. alphabet.

G. Kittel in *T.W.B.*, i (1933), pp. 1–3, s.v., with reff. F. *Cabrol, O.S.B., in *D.A.C.L.*, i (pt. 1; 1907), cols. 1–25, s.v.

ALPHEGE, St. (954–1012), also Aelfheah,
Abp. of *Canterbury. A monk of Deerhurst and then Abbot of Bath, he became Bp. of *Winchester in 984 and was translated to Canterbury in 1006. He held the Council of Enham (1009?) at which certain disciplinary canons were passed. He was murdered by the Danes during a drunken feast because he would not ransom himself at the expense of his poor tenants, and was therefore regarded as a martyr. Feast day, 19 Apr.

Life by Osbern, monk of Canterbury (d. *c.* 1090), in [H. Wharton] *Anglia Sacra*, ii (1691), pp. 122–42, with Osbern's account of translation of Alphege's relics from London to Canterbury (1023), pp. 143–7. E. A. Freeman, *The History of the Norman Conquest*, i (1867), pp. 387–9, with note on sources in ed. 3 (1877), pp. 673–8.

ALPHONSUS LIGUORI, St. (1696–1787),
founder of the *Redemptorists and moral theologian. The son of a Neapolitan noble, Giuseppe dei Liguori, Alfonso Maria dei Liguori was born at Marianella near Naples. After taking the degree of Doctor of Laws at the age of 16, he practised with marked success at the bar for eight years; but in 1723 the loss, by an oversight, of an important suit in which a Neapolitan noble was suing the Grand Duke of Tuscany for £100,000 convinced him of the transitoriness of worldly glory and he withdrew from his profession. He received the tonsure, joined an association of mission preachers, was ordained priest in 1726, and became a successful evangelist in the country around Naples. In 1729 he took up residence in a missionary college in Naples where he made the close friendship of Tomaso Falcoia (1663–1743), of the congregation of the *Pii Operarii*, who had taken part in the foundation (1719) of a conservatorium for religious women at Scala, near Amalfi, and was to exercise great influence on him. When in 1730 Falcoia became Bp. of Castellamare, the diocese in which Scala was situated, Alphonsus moved to Scala, in 1731 reorganized the nuns (the first house of 'Redemptoristines'), and then in 1732 founded the 'Congregation of the Most Holy Redeemer' or 'Redemptorists' (q.v.) for men in a neighbour-

ing hospice. Originally there were seven postulants under Alphonsus' guidance, who devoted themselves to pastoral work among the poor in the country districts. Falcoia was technically their director until his death (1743), when Alphonsus was formally elected Superior-General; but, owing to internal dissensions, growth was slow. In 1745 Alphonsus wrote the first of his many devotional and spiritual works. In 1749 *Benedict XIV approved the rule and institute for men and in 1750 the corresponding ones for women. In 1762 Alphonsus accepted with much reluctance the see of Sant' Agata dei Goti, in the province of Beneventum (he had declined the Archbishopric of Palermo in 1747). Here, continuing to live an austere life, he was largely engaged in literary and missionary labours. In 1775 he resigned his see on the plea of ill-health and retired to Nocera. But he lived another twelve years, and became involved in much controversy arising from the affairs of his Order. His last years were clouded by severe spiritual trials and darkness.

Alphonsus sought to commend the Gospel to a sceptical age by gentle and direct methods. Spurning the florid oratory of his contemporaries, he preached simply and to the heart and believed that the rigorism of the contemporary confessional (largely under *Jansenist influences) repelled rather than won back the sinful. He set out these ideals in a system of Moral Theology, first outlined in his *Annotations* to Hermann Busembaum (a much esteemed Jesuit casuist, 1600–68), published at Naples in 1748. This teaching he recast in his celebrated *Theologia Moralis* (2 vols., 1753 and 1755), of which seven further editions appeared before his death, as well as a number of compendiums, e.g. the *Homo Apostolicus* (1759). In the debate as to how far it is allowable to follow any 'probable' opinion in matters of conduct, Alphonsus, in contradistinction to the Jesuits, developed the system known as *Equiprobabilism (q.v.).

His innumerable devotional writings include (Eng. titles) *Visits to the Blessed Sacrament and the Blessed Virgin* (1745), *The Glories of Mary* (1750), *Novena of Christmas* (1758), *Novena of the Heart of Jesus* (1758), *The Great Means of Prayer* (1759), *The True Spouse of Jesus Christ* (1760), and *The Way of Salvation* (1767). They became very popular and remained in general use down to the later 19th cent. There is no doubt that they fostered devotion; but their exuberance became a frequent target of criticism, esp. by Protestant writers.

Alphonsus was beatified in 1816, canonized in 1839, and declared a *doctor ecclesiae* by *Pius IX in 1871. Feast day, 2 Aug.

The primary source is A. M. Tannoia, C.SS.R., *Della vita ed istituto del venerabile Alfonso Maria Liguori* (3 vols., 1799–1802). This should be corrected in its details by the scholarly Life by K. Dilgskron, C.SS.R. (Germ.; Regensburg and New York, 1887). More recent Life by A. C. Berthe, C.SS.R. (Paris, 2 vols., 1900; Eng. trans. with important corrections by H. Castle, C.SS.R., 2 vols., 1905). His Letters were edited by P. Kuntz, C.SS.R. (3 vols., Rome, 1887). There are many editions of his *Theologia Moralis* and his popular devotional works. On Alphonsus' spiritual teaching, see P. Pourrat, S.J., *La Spiritualité chrétienne*, iv, 449–91.

F. Meyrick, *Moral and Devotional Theology of the Church of Rome, according to the authoritative Teaching of S. Alfonso de' Liguori* (1857; hostile).

ALTAR (Gk. θυσιαστήριον; Lat. *altare, ara*). The word was used of the Eucharistic table (if not already in Heb. 13. 10) in *Ignatius, *Tertullian, and *Cyprian, and this usage has been general in Catholic Christianity ever since. At the *Reformation, however, it gave rise to much controversy owing to the disputes concerning the doctrine of the *sacrifice of the Mass, of which the (stone) altar was taken as a natural symbol. The present English BCP avoids the term, but it was never rejected in England by authority.

The earliest altars were doubtless of wood, being the tables in private houses normally used for domestic purposes, and *Optatus, *Augustine, and others mention wooden altars in the 4th and 5th cents. No doubt the custom of celebrating the Eucharist on the tombs of martyrs first caused stone altars to come in. After the persecutions it became common to enclose the relics of martyrs in altars, and this practice now prevails everywhere in the RC Church. For centuries there was only one altar in each Christian church, but the practice of celebrating private *Masses caused others to be added, the original altar being then known as the 'High Altar', and it became customary for each of these additional altars to be dedicated to some saint other than that to which the church itself is dedicated. In the E. Ch., where private Masses are unknown, churches commonly have only one altar, though the E. regulation that the Eucharist must always be offered on a 'fasting altar' explains the occasional occurrence of two altars in the same church, to allow for two Masses on a single day. The Roman rite forbids the celebration of Mass except on an altar blessed by the bishop, but the use of a 'portable altar' (*altare portatile*), of much smaller dimensions than the fixed ones, is permitted.

It is now customary for altars to be covered with three cloths (which first appear in the 9th cent.) and to be ornamented with a cross and candlesticks. Before the 10th cent. these ornaments were not placed on the altar, but the cross surmounted the *ciborium magnum which covered the altar, and the candles were held round during the Eucharist or suspended in candelabra from the ciborium (see foll. entry).

In the C of E the legality of stone altars was disputed in the 19th cent., but in recent times their use has become fairly common.

Comprehensive collection of material in J. Braun's two works (*C.A.* and *A.G.*). Rohault, i, pp. 93–240, with pll. xxiii–lxxxix. E. *Bishop, *Liturgica Historica* (1918), No. ii, On the History of the Christian Altar', pp. 20–38. W. H. St. J. Hope (ed.), *English Altars from Illuminated Manuscripts* (*Alcuin Club Collections, i; 1899); P. *Dearmer, *Fifty Pictures of Gothic Altars* (ib., x; 1910). H. *Leclercq, O.S.B., in *D.A.C.L.*, i (1907), cols. 3155–89, s.v. 'Autel', with bibl.

ALTAR LIGHTS. The use of candles on the Christian altar seems to derive from the lighted candles which were carried in early times before the Pope as a mark of honour and at first placed on the floor behind the altar. The custom of placing them upon the altar is not definitely attested before c. 1175, when two candles flanking an altar cross are mentioned as 'the present custom' of the Papal chapel. Subsequently mention is made of seven or more candles, acc. to the dignity of the feast, though one candle alone, to light the Missal, was also frequent. Cranmer's *Visitation Articles (1547) implied the permissibility of two altar lights. *Edward VI's 2nd *Injunction (1549) prohibited them, but they have now been widely restored in England. The *Lincoln Judgement (1890) recognized the legality in the C of E of two altar candles. Ordinarily altar candles are of white wax, but the W. rubrics prescribe yellow ('unbleached') candles for *requiem masses and the *Good Friday liturgy.

Braun, *A.G.*, 'Die Altarleuchter', pp. 492–530; E. *Bishop, *Liturgica Historica* (1918), 'Of Six Candles on the Altar: An Enquiry', pp. 301–13. [*E. De L.*] *Read and Others v. the Lord Bishop of Lincoln.* Judgement, 21 Nov. 1890 (1890). [J. F. Russell–] V. Staley (ed.), *Hierurgia Anglicana.* Documents and Extracts (L.L.E.) pt. i (1902), pp. 48–201 passim. D. R. Dendy, *The Use of Lights in Christian Worship* (1959).

ALTAR RAILS. Rails to protect the altar from profanation were widely introduced into English churches in the early years of *Elizabeth I, when the rood-screens and their protecting doors were removed. The *Puritans disliked them as implying that the altar was specially sacred, and in many cases they were taken out again. In his Archiepiscopal Visitation (1634), W. *Laud ordered altars which had been removed into the body of the church to be restored to the east wall and required their protection by altar rails, at which the communicants were to receive the Sacrament; and many fine examples of altar rails date from this period. Their removal, however, was again ordered by Parliament in 1641, and they finally came back at the Restoration in 1660.

Francis Bond, *The Chancel of English Churches* (1916), pp. 131–9.

ALTAR OF REPOSE. See *Repose, Altar of.*

ALUMBRADOS (also 'Illuminati', i.e. 'enlightened'). A loosely knit group of spiritual persons in *Spain in the 16th cent. They led a retired life given to prayer and contemplation, and their practices were propagated esp. by the reformed *Franciscans, St. *John of Avila, and some members of the *Jesuit Order. Whether or not several of them were doctrinally unorthodox is uncertain; but some members of the movement were spiritually unbalanced and exercised an unhealthy influence on those whom they excited by their pretended visions and revelations. They were severely treated by the *Inquisition, though many of their adherents were saintly men and women and some were later even canonized. In 1527 St. *Ignatius Loyola, while a student at Salamanca, was charged with showing them sympathy.

M. Menéndez y Pelayo, *Historia de los heterodoxos españoles*, ii [c. 1880], pp. 521–58; E. Colunga, O.P., 'Intelectualistas y místicos en la teología española del siglo xvi' in *La Ciencia Tomista*, x (1914–15), pp. 223–42; J. Baruzi, *Saint Jean de la Croix et le problème de l'expérience mystique* (1924), pp. 251–69; Bremond, viii (1928), pp. 196–227, with bibl. G. Constant in *D.H.G.E.*, ii (1914), s.v., with bibl.

AMALARIUS OF METZ

AMALARIUS OF METZ (*c.* 780–850 [or 851]), liturgical scholar. He is perhaps (so J. *Sirmond and many subsequent historians) to be distinguished from Amalarius, Bp. of Trier (*c.* 809–16). A pupil and admirer of *Alcuin, he was a prominent figure in the *Carolingian Renaissance, and in 835 he was appointed to administer the see of Lyons during the absence of its Abp. *Agobard. His principal treatise, the 'De ecclesiasticis officiis' (in four books), which was partly an attempt to further the fusion of Roman and *Gallican ceremonial practices, exercised great influence in the Middle Ages and remains a fundamental source for the history of liturgy. Its explanations of ritual are sometimes highly fantastic and artificial, and at the synod of Quiercy in 838 some of its contents were pronounced heretical. Among his other surviving writings are a small treatise on the ceremonies of *Baptism and an 'Eclogae de officio missae', a description of the Roman Pontifical Mass. He compiled an *antiphonary which has not survived.

His 'Regula Canonicorum et Sanctimonialium', 'Eclogae de Officio Missae' and 'Epistolae' in J. P. Migne, *PL*, cv, 815–1340; crit. edd. of his 'Epistolae' by E. Duemmler in *M.G.H.* Epistolae v (1899), pp. 240–724, of his 'Opera Liturgica Omnia' by J. M. Hanssens, S.J., *S.T.*, cxxxviii–cxl (1948–50), with bibl. J. *Sirmond, S.J., 'De Duobus Amalariis' in *Opera Varia*, iv (Paris, 1696), cols. 641–7. R. Mönchemeier, *Amalar von Metz* (Kirchengeschichtliche Studien, i, Hft. 3–4, 1893); G.*M[orin], O.S.B., 'La Question des deux Amalaire' in *R. Bén.*, viii (1891), pp. 433–42; id., 'Amalaire. Esquisse biographique', ib., ix (1892), pp. 337–51; id., 'Encore la question des deux Amalaire. Réponse à l'objection de M. Mönchemeier', ib., xi (1894), pp. 241–3. E. Dabroise in *D.A.C.L.*, i (1907), cols. 1323–30, s.v.

AMALRIC

AMALRIC (d. *c.* 1207), scholastic philosopher. He was a native of Bena, near *Chartres, and taught at *Paris. In a series of *pantheistic doctrines, which had many points of contact with those of *Erigena, he maintained (*inter alia*) that God was the one essence underlying all created beings (*deum esse essentiam omnium creaturarum et esse omnium*) and that those who remain in the love of God cannot sin. He founded a sect, the 'Amalricians', who further developed his teachings. His leading theses were expressly condemned by a synod at Paris in 1210 and again at the *Lateran Council of 1215. See also *David of Dinant*.

The principal sources are *Caesarius of Heisterbach, *Dialogus Miraculorum* (ed. J. Strange, Cologne, 1851, pp. 304–7) and Martin Oppaviensis, *Chronicon Pontificum et Imperatorum* (ed. L. Weiland in *M.G.H.*, Scriptores, xxii, 1872, p. 438). C. Baeumker (ed.), 'Contra Amaurianos. Ein anonymer wahrscheinlich dem Garnerius von Rochefort zugehöriger Traktat gegen die Amalrikaner aus dem Anfang des XIII. Jahrhunderts' in *B.G.P.M.*, xxiv (1926), Hfft. 5–6. G. C. Capelle, *Autour du décret de 1210*, III, Amaury de Bène, étude sur son panthéisme formel (Bibliothèque Thomiste, xvi, 1932). See also Überweg, ii, 250 f., with bibl., p. 707 f.

AMANA SOCIETY

AMANA SOCIETY. A Christian sect, otherwise known as the Community of True Inspiration. It originated in Germany in 1714, under the influence of the writings of

E. L. Grüber and J. F. Rock, who were deeply imbued with *Pietist views, but centred all their teaching in the doctrine of present-day inspiration. A large part of the body sailed for America in 1842. In 1855 they finally settled at Amana, Iowa, and were granted a formal constitution under the laws of the state in 1859. They survive as a small communistic community.

W. R. Perkins–B. L. Wick, *History of the Amana Society, or Community of True Inspiration* (State University of Iowa Publications. Historical Monograph, i, 1891); B.M.H. Shambaugh, *Amana*. The Community of True Inspiration (Iowa, 1908); id., *Amana That Was and Amana That Is* (Iowa, 1932). B. M. H. Shambaugh in *H.E.R.E.*, i (1908), pp. 358–69, s.v.

AMANDUS, St.

AMANDUS, St. (d. *c.* 675), Merovingian Apostle of Flanders. Born near Nantes, in early manhood he made his way to Tours, and then to Bourges, where he lived an ascetic life under the direction of St. Austregisilus, the Bishop. In 628, having been consecrated Bishop at the behest of Clothaire II without any fixed see, he began active missionary work in Flanders and Carinthia, and in 633 founded two monasteries at Ghent under the patronage of St. *Peter (one of them taking the name of St. Bavon, the benefactor). Later he founded a large monastery at Elnon, near Tournai, of which he was in his last years Abbot; afterwards it was known as St.-Amand. He is said, but on very doubtful authority, to have been Bp. of Maestricht from 649 to 652. His 'Testamentum' survives, but otherwise the evidence for his life is not very trustworthy. Feast day, 6 Feb.

Testamentum ed. by B. Krusch in *M.G.H.*, Scriptores Rerum Merovingicarum, v (1910), pp. 483–5. One recension of the Vita Amandi, attributed to Amandus's disciple, Baudemundus, pr. in *AA.SS.*, Feb. I (1658), pp. 848–72; another by B. Krusch, op. cit., pp. 428–49; the ascription to Baudemundus is denied by Krusch, who considers the life to be late 8th cent. (ib., pp. 395–428). Further life by Milo, a monk of St. Amand (*c.* A.D. 845–55), ed. L. Traube, *M.G.H.* Poetae, iii (1896), pp. 567–610; prose suppl. ed. B. Krusch, op. cit., pp. 450–85. L. Van der Essen, *Étude critique et littéraire sur les Vitae des saints mérovingiens de l'ancienne Belgique* (1907), pp. 336–49. E. de Moreau, S.J., *Saint Amand* (Museum Lessianum. Section Missiologique, vii, 1927), with bibl.

AMAURY. See Amalric.

AMBO

AMBO. A raised platform in a Christian *basilica, from which the Scriptures could be read to the people and litanies and other public parts of the liturgy conducted. Originally there was only one, but later two were built, one for the Epistle and one for the Gospel, on the south and north sides respectively. Several early examples survive, but after the 14th cent. they were replaced by the pulpit. Recently there has been a tendency in some places to reintroduce them.

Rohault, iii (1883), pp. 1–72; H. *Leclercq, O.S.B., in *D.A.C.L.*, i (1907), cols. 1330–47, s.v. 'Ambon'. with reff.

AMBROSE, St.

AMBROSE, St. (*c.* 339–97), Bp. of *Milan. He was born at Trier, the son of the Praetorian Prefect of Gaul. After practising in the Roman law-courts he was appointed, *c.* 370, governor of Aemilia-Liguria, with his seat at Milan. On the death in 374 of *Auxentius, the Arian

Bp. of Milan, the Catholic laity demanded that Ambrose should succeed him. He was then a Christian by belief, but unbaptized, i.e. only a *catechumen. With some hesitation he accepted the see, was baptized and ordained, and first devoted himself to the study of theology under the guidance of his former tutor, *Simplicianus. As bishop he was famous as a preacher, and outstanding as a jealous upholder of orthodoxy. To him was partly due the conversion of St. *Augustine (386), who greatly revered him. Events brought him into close touch with the rulers of the Western Empire—*Gratian, Maximus, Justina (mother of Valentinian II), and *Theodosius I. He combated paganism and *Arianism, maintained the independence of the Church against the civil power, and championed morality, e.g. in protesting against the execution of *Priscillianist heretics under Maximus, and in excommunicating the Emp. *Theodosius for a massacre at *Thessalonica. His most notable work, 'De Officiis Ministrorum', is a treatise on Christian ethics, based on Cicero, with special reference to the clergy. The rest consist largely of the substance of sermons or instruction given to candidates for baptism, on the Faith and Sacraments. Knowledge of Greek enabled him to introduce much E. theology into the West. He also wrote on ascetical subjects, and did much to encourage monasticism in N. Italy. His Letters are of great historical value. He is also the author of several well-known Latin hymns, and recent scholarship (H. Brewer and A. E. Burn) has attributed to him the so-called *Athanasian Creed.

With St. *Jerome, St. Augustine and St. *Gregory the Great, St. Ambrose is one of the four traditional Doctors of the Latin Church. Feast day, 7 Dec.; in the BCP calendar, 4 Apr.

Editio princeps of his Works, Venice, 1485. Benedictine ed. [F. du Frische–N. le Nourry], 2 vols., Paris, 1686–90; repr. in J. P. Migne, *PL*, xiv–xvii. Crit. ed. by C. Schenk, M. Petschenig, &c. (C.S.E.L., 1902 ff.). Life by Paulinus, his secretary at the time of his death, in J. P. Migne, op. cit., xiv, 27–46. F. H. Dudden, *The Life and Times of St. Ambrose* (2 vols., 1935). M. Ihm, *Studia Ambrosiana* (1890). H. F. v. Campenhausen, *Ambrosius von Mailand als Kirchenpolitiker* (1929); J. R. Palanque, *Saint Ambroise et l'empire romain* (1933). *Ambrosiana. Scritti di storia, archeologia ed arte pubblicati nel XVI centenario della nascita di Sant' Ambrogio, CCCXL-MCMXL* (1942). R. H. *Connolly, *The Explanatio Symboli ad Initiandos, A Work of Saint Ambrose.* (Texts and Studies, x; 1952). P. de Labriolle, *Histoire de la littérature chrétienne* (1920), pp. 351–82 (Eng. tr., 1924, pp. 263–86). Bardenhewer, iii (ed. 2, 1923), pp. 498–547; Altaner (1951), pp. 329–41, both with detailed bibl. See also bibls. to *De Sacramentis* and *Athanasian Creed*.

AMBROSE, St., OF CAMALDOLI. See *Traversari, Ambrogio.*

AMBROSE, ISAAC (1604–64), *Puritan divine. The son of a Lancashire clergyman, he was born at Ormskirk, Lancs, educated at Brasenose College, Oxford, and ordained priest before 1627. After serving cures at Castleton, Derby, and Clapham, Yorks (from 1629), he became one of the King's four Preachers in Lancashire (from 1634) and resided at Garstang, near Preston. In 1641 he became a *Presbyterian and subsequently took a prominent part in the seventh Lancashire Classis, several times acting as Moderator. He was twice taken prisoner by the royal army, and, on the fall of Bolton in 1644, moved to Leeds. He served on the committee for the ejection of 'scandalous and ignorant ministers and schoolmasters', but was forced by the deposed ministers to go to London in 1649. In 1650 he was still ministering in Preston. From 1654 he resided at Garstang, whence he was ejected in 1662.

He was a man of peaceful disposition, who spent a month each year in solitary meditation, prayer and study. After an illness he determined to write a devotional description of what the Lord had done for his soul. Written in 1653, it was published in 1658 under the title, *Looking unto Jesus, or the Soul's Eyeing of Jesus as Carrying on the Great Work of Man's Salvation.* The work, which emphasized the unity of the Person of Christ in the Incarnation, is marked by a deep piety, combined with vividness and freshness of imagination. His other publications include *Prima, Media, and Ultima, the First, Middle and Last Things: in Three Treatises* (1650); *Redeeming the Time* (1658); funeral sermon on Lady Hoghton; and *War with Devils—Ministration of Angels* (1661).

Complete Works ed., London, 3 parts, 1674–89; new ed., 2 vols., Manchester, 1812. A. *Wood, *Athenae Oxonienses* (ed. P. Bliss), iii (1817), cols. 659–61.

AMBROSIAN RITE. The rite used in the old archiepiscopal province of *Milan and one of the very few non-Roman rites which survive in the RC Church in the W. Its name is derived from St. *Ambrose, Bp. of Milan, but there is no definite evidence of connexion with him. Although for many centuries now it has contained the Roman *Canon of the Mass, it differs widely from the Roman rite. Thus, the *offertory takes place before and not after the Creed (as in the Roman rite) and is accompanied by a procession (see Vecchioni). Three important theories of the origin of the rite have been put forward: (1) It is merely a development of the present Roman rite; (2) it is an older Western rite which has survived only at Milan; (3) it is an Oriental rite introduced at Milan by the Greek and Arian Bishop *Auxentius (or one of the other six Greek bishops who appear among the ten predecessors of St. Ambrose) which, purged of heresy (it is suggested) by St. Ambrose, became the parent of the whole family of *Gallican rites. This last theory (originated by L. *Duchesne) was widely held in the earlier years of the 20th cent., but it is now commonly regarded as of purely Western ancestry.

The Ambrosian Missal was first ed. at Milan in 1475. That now in current use appeared in 1902; crit. ed. by A. Ratti (*Pius XI)–M. Magistretti, Milan, 1913. Eng. tr. by E. G. C. F. Atchley (London, 1909). M. Magistretti (ed.), *Beroldus, sive Ecclesiae Ambrosianae Mediolanensis Kalendarium et Ordines Saec. XII* (Milan, 1894); id., *Monumenta Veteris Liturgiae Ambrosianae* (3 vols., ib., 1897–1905) and other works. F. Magani, *L' antica liturgia romana* (1897–1899). W. C. Bishop, *The Mozarabic and Ambrosian Rites*

(*Alcuin Club Tracts, xv, 1924), pp. 98–134. A. Paredi, *I prefazi ambrosiani*. (Pubbl. Univ. Catt. del Sacro Cuore, ser. 4, xxv, Milan, 1937). L. Duchesne, *Origines du culte chrétien* (1889), ch. iii, pp. 81–99; Eng. tr. (1903), pp. 86–105. A. A. King, *Notes on the Catholic Liturgies* (1930), ch. vi, pp. 211–48. P. Lejay in *D.A.C.L.*, i (1907), cols. 1373–442, s.v. 'Ambrosien (Rit)'. Further bibl. in A. *Baumstark, *Liturgie comparée*, ed. 3 by B. Botte, O.S.B. (Irénikon, 1953), pp. 235–7.

AMBROSIANA. The Ambrosian Library at Milan, founded *c.* 1605 by Federico Borromeo (1564–1631), was one of the first large libraries to be open to the public without distinction. The books were originally protected from theft by the severest ecclesiastical faculties, the removal of a book being a sin from which only the Pope could absolve. Borromeo sent agents all over the world to collect MSS., and *c.* 1803 it received many ancient MSS. from the library at *Bobbio. *Pius XI (Achille Ratti) was Librarian of the Ambrosiana from 1888 to 1912 (Prefect from 1907).

A. Martini and D. Bassi, *Catalogus Codicum Graecorum Bibliothecae Ambrosianae* (Milan, 2 vols., 1906); A. Rivolta, *Catalogo dei Codici pinelliani dell' Ambrosiana* (1932). Mai, *S.R.*, v (1841), pp. 24–50, 'De Nonnullis Codicibus Bibliothecae Ambrosianae'; E. Griffini, 'Lista dei manoscritti arabi nuovi fondo della Biblioteca Ambrosiana di Milan' in *Rivista degli Studi Orientali*, iii (1910), pp. 253–78. A. Saba, 'La biblioteca Ambrosiana' in *Aevum*, vi (1932), pp. 531–620.

AMBROSIASTER. The name given (first by D. *Erasmus) to the author of a set of Latin commentaries on the thirteen Epp. of St. Paul, ascribed in all the manuscripts but one, and by most medieval writers, to *Ambrose. St. *Augustine and certain Irish authorities quote that on Romans as by 'Sanctus Hilarius'. Their ascription to Ambrose, which was first questioned in modern times by Erasmus, is now universally denied, and various persons have been suggested as their author, e.g. Isaac, an ex-Jew, who relapsed into Judaism, and opposed *Damasus in 374; 'Hilary the Deacon'; Hilary, a layman and Proconsul of Africa; and *Evagrius of Antioch. The commentaries are on the *Old Latin text of the Epistles and thus an important witness to the pre-Vulgate text. The writer avoids allegory, is practical, and has a good sense of history. Ambrosiaster is almost certainly also the author of 'Quaestiones Veteris et Novi Testamenti', wrongly ascribed to Augustine, and possibly of the 'Mosaicarum et Romanarum Legum Collectio'.

Commentaries in J. P. Migne, *PL*, xvii, 45–508. 'Quaestiones', ed. A. *Souter, *CSEL*, l (1908) A. Souter, 'A Study of Ambrosiaster' in *Camb. Texts and Studies*, vii, 4 (1905); id., *The Earliest Latin Commentaries on the Epistles of St. Paul* (1927).

AMBULATORY. The 'walking-space' which arises when an apsidal sanctuary in certain churches of the Norman period is surrounded by continuous *aisles. The ambulatory is bounded on one side by the arches of the sanctuary, and on the other may give access to a series of chapels of a later date.

A.M.D.G. ('*Ad Maiorem Dei Gloriam*', 'To the greater glory of God'). The motto of the *Jesuits, but it also frequently appears elsewhere in Christian use.

AMEN (Heb. אָמֵן; Gk. ἀμήν). A Hebrew word meaning 'verily'. It is used to express assent by Jews (Dt. 27. 15 ff.) and Christians (1 Cor. 14. 16) at the end of religious formulae, prayers, hymns, and creeds. Cf. the *Catechism of the BCP: 'and therefore I say, Amen, so be it'.

H. Schlier in *T.W.B.*, i (1933), pp. 339–42, s.v. 'ἀμήν', with reff.; W. Bauer, *Griechisch-deutsches Wörterbuch zu den Schriften des N.T.* (ed. 4, 1952), col. 82 f., s.v. 'ἀμήν', with reff. F. *Cabrol in *D.A.C.L.*, i (1907), cols. 1554–73, s.v.; I. Cecchetti in *E.C.*, i (1949), cols. 1030–32, s.v.

AMERICANISM. A movement propagated in the last decade of the 19th cent. among American RCs by I. T. *Hecker with a view to adapting as far as possible the external life of the Church to supposed modern cultural ideals. Stress was laid on the value of the 'active' virtues (e.g. humanitarianism, eugenic reform, democracy), and the 'passive' attitudes such as humility and subjection to authority were depreciated. It was also urged that the Church should relax as far as possible the rigour of her requirements on converts, emphasize what was held in common by RCs and other Christians, and minimize points of difference. In an Apostolic Letter, 'Testem Benevolentiae' (22 Jan. 1899), addressed to Cardinal J. Gibbons, Abp. of Baltimore, *Leo XIII condemned it in moderate but quite definite terms; and in consequence it quickly disappeared.

'Testem Benevolentiae' in *Acta Leonis XIII*, vii (1906), pp. 223–33. J. Ireland, *The Church and Modern Society* (Chicago, 1897); A. J. Delattre, *Un Catholicisme américain* (Namur, 1898); A. Houtin, *L'Américanisme* (Namur, 1904); J. Rivière, *Le Modernisme dans l'Église* (1929), pp. 109–38; [E.] Lecanuet, *La Vie dans l'Église sous Léon XIII* (1930), ch. xiii, 'L'Américanisme en France', pp. 544–602. See also bibl. under *Hecker*.

AMES, WILLIAM (1576–1633), *Calvinist moral theologian and controversialist. Educated at Christ's College, Cambridge, where his tutor was W. *Perkins, he became an extreme *Puritan, refusing to wear the surplice in his college chapel and in 1609 attacking card-playing in a sermon. Leaving Cambridge *c.* 1610, he settled for a time at Colchester and then moved to Holland. Here he took a prominent part in the *Remonstrant controversies and became recognized by the Calvinists as one of their best theologians. In 1622 he became professor of theology at Franeker, where he attracted hearers from all parts of Protestant Europe. A few months before his death he gave up his professorship for reasons of health and took charge of the English congregation at Rotterdam. His most important work, *De Conscientia, eius Jure et Casibus* (1632), is one of the few Protestant treatises on *casuistry and was long held in high repute for its incisive decisions. Of his theological works, the principal was *Medulla Theologiae* (ed. 1, 1627), a systematical exposition of Calvinist principles. Among his controversial writings were *Bellarminus Enervatus* (4 vols., 1628) and *Animadversiones in Synodalia* (1629).

His *Latin Works* were edited, with a Life, by M. Nethenus (5 vols., Amsterdam, 1658).

AMICE (Lat. *amictus*). A linen cloth, square or oblong in shape, with strings attached. In the W. Church it is worn round the neck by the priest when celebrating the Eucharist, and by other ministers who wear the *alb. Its original significance is obscure. Since the bishop conveys the amice to the *sub-deacon at his ordination with the admonition that it signifies the 'castigatio vocis', it is natural to suppose that it was originally a sort of scarf to protect the throat. On the other hand, in the prayers said before Mass when the amice is being put on, it is referred to as 'galea salutis' ('helmet of salvation'), from which it would be natural to deduce that it was originally a head covering. This view is supported by the fact that certain religious orders still wear the amice in the form of a head covering when approaching the altar for Mass, and during parts of the service. In some orders (e.g. the *Benedictine) the amice has the shape of a hood and is worn in such a way as to form an outer covering for the hood of the religious habit. In the E. the amice as such is not used, but it is customary for some priests to use an ordinary handkerchief in the same way, as a practical method of preventing the vestments becoming stained by perspiration. See also *Almuce*.

Braun, *L.G.*, ch. i, pp. 21–52.

AMIDAH. See *Eighteen Benedictions*.

AMMON, St. (d. *c.* 350) (also **AMUN**), Egyptian hermit. One of the most celebrated ascetics of the *Nitrian desert, he is mentioned by St. *Athanasius in his *Vita Antonii*. On St. *Anthony's advice he sought to bring his monks together under his immediate supervision. Feast day, 4 Oct.

Other sources include *Palladius, *Lausiac History*, ch. 8, and the *Historia Monachorum*, ch. 29. Introd. by C. Byeus, S.J., to extract from Palladius in *AA.SS.*, Oct. II (1768), pp. 413–21. I. G. Smith in *D.C.B.*, i (1877), p. 102, s.v.

AMMONIAN SECTIONS. Divisions found in the margins of nearly all Gk. and Lat. MSS. of the Four Gospels, devised to illustrate the parallelism between corresponding passages in the different Gospels. Until recently they were generally held to be the work of *Ammonius Saccas, but it is more likely that they were compiled by *Eusebius of Caesarea in connexion with his canons. They were of great use in identifying passages before the now current division into chapters and verses became established.

Bardenhewer, *G.A.L.*, ii (ed. 2, 1914), pp. 198–202. J. W. Burgon, *The Last Twelve Verses of the Gospel according to St. Mark* (1871), pp. 125–32, 295–312. G. H. Gwilliam, 'The Ammonian Sections, Eusebian Canons, and Harmonizing Tables in the Syriac Tetra-evangelium' in *Studia Biblica et Ecclesiastica*, ii (1890), pp. 241–72.

AMMONIUS SACCAS (*c.* A.D. 175–242). The reputed founder of *Neoplatonism. An Alexandrian by birth, he was held in high repute as a teacher, and appears to have considerably influenced *Plotinus, who, on hearing a discourse of Ammonius, remarked,

'This is the man I was looking for' (τοῦτον ἐζήτουν). Acc. to *Porphyry (in *Eusebius, *H.E.* v. xix), who also states (probably wrongly) that Ammonius was a lapsed Christian, he had *Origen (but perhaps not the Christian Origen) among his pupils. He is said to have committed none of his teachings to writing. (See also previous entry.)

H. von Arnim, 'Quelle der Ueberlieferung über Ammonius Sakkas' in *Rheinisches Museum für Philologie*, N.F., xlii (1887), pp. 276–85; E. Zeller, 'Ammonius Sakkas und Plotinus' in *Archiv für Geschichte der Philosophie*, vii (1894), pp. 295–312. Überweg, i, pp. 593–5, with further bibl. p. 188*. Art. (unsigned) in *E.B.* (ed. 11), i (1910), p. 864, s.v.

AMOS, Book of. Amos was the first in time of the canonical prophets of the OT. A herdman of Tekoa and a dresser of sycamore trees who exercised his ministry in Israel 'in the days of Uzziah king of Judah, and in the days of Jeroboam the son of Joash king of Israel' (1. 1), i.e. between 760 and 750 B.C, he asserted that it was not by descent or profession that he was a prophet and that Jehovah had simply taken him from following the flock (7. 14 f.). His message was delivered at a time when, owing to the prosperity which had come from a period of freedom from outside invasion, the leaders of the nation were given to luxury, wealth was being accumulated in a way that led to injustice and oppression of the poor, and the religion of Jehovah was being debased. Amos found his mission in denouncing these low conceptions of God. He urged the importance of social justice and the threat of coming judgement. Although he apparently did not proclaim belief in an explicit monotheism, he insisted that God was the Lord of nature and of nations, revealing His power in history, particularly in His chosen people. He may thus be regarded as the precursor of *Deutero-Isaiah. Further, he asserted that the covenant-relationship which exists between God and His chosen people is rooted in, and influenced by, the righteousness of God, so that 'the Day of the Lord' to which the Hebrews looked forward as the beginning of a Golden Age would be a day of justice, when Israel would be humiliated and receive the due reward of iniquity.

Modern commentaries by S. R. *Driver (on Joel and Amos, Camb. Bibl., 1897, pp. 93–239; revised ed., 1915, pp. 95–245), W. R. Harper (on Amos and Hosea, I.C.C., 1905), E. A. Edghill (West. Comm., 1914), L. Köhler (Zürich, 1917), R. S. Cripps (London, 1929) and N. H. Snaith (Study Notes on Bible Books, 2 parts, 1945–6).

AMPHIBALUM (or **–US**). (1) A *Gallican name for the *chasuble; (2) the *birrus*, a garment put on first and covering the head, and perhaps to be identified with the *amictus*, or *amice. Acc. to tradition, St. Amphibalus was the name of a martyr closely associated with St. *Alban.

AMPHILOCHIUS, St. (*c.* 340–395), Bp. of Iconium from 373. A cousin of *Gregory Nazianzus, he stood in close personal relations with all the *Cappadocian Fathers. He was present at a council of Iconium in 376 in which the full Divinity of the Holy Spirit was zealously defended, and was head of the Council of Side in 390 which excommunicated the *Messalians. Most of his surviving writings are in a fragmentary condition; but a few are complete, including some sermons. Feast day, 23 Nov.

Fragments in J. P. Migne, *PL*, xxxix, 97 ff. (incomplete). K. Holl, *A. v. Ikonium in seinem Verhältnis zu den grossen Kappadoziern* (1904); G. Ficker, *Amphilochiana* I (1906, all publd.).

AMPULLA. Lat., a globular vessel for holding liquid. The term is used of three classes of objects.

(1) Of certain bottle-shaped vessels, usually of glass, found at tombs in the *catacombs. Such have often been known as 'ampullae sanguinis' from an identification, going back to the 17th cent., of the dark-red sediment frequently found in them with the blood of a martyr. But their date (4th cent. onwards), the proportion found in the graves of small children, the discovery of similar ampullae at Jewish catacombs, e.g. on the *Via Labicana*, together with the scientific analysis of their contents, have discredited this view. It would appear rather that they were used to preserve drops of the perfume poured on the bodies of the dead.

(2) Of certain coarsely made vases of baked clay often bearing the image or symbol of the saint, which were used to preserve oil from the lights burnt in *martyria*. A number sent by Pope *Gregory I from the tombs of Roman martyrs are preserved at the Cathedral at Monza. Those brought by pilgrims from the tomb of St. *Menas in Egypt are esp. common.

(3) Of vessels to preserve the sacramental oils. They are referred to e.g. in St. *Optatus of Milevis (*Contra Donatistas*, ii, 19) and the *Gregorian Sacramentary. The most famous of such ampullae is the 'Sainte Ampoule' which, acc. to a legend in Flodoard (10th cent.), already mentioned by *Hincmar (d. 882), was brought by a dove at the prayers of St. *Remigius for the baptism of Clovis in 496. It was preserved at Reims and used at the coronation of French kings until the Revolution. Although it was broken in 1793, a fragment was preserved and used at the coronation of Charles X (1824). It appears to have been made of a metal similar to tin and engraven with a representation of the Adoration of the Magi and Shepherds. Similar legends of the miraculous origin of ampullae are found elsewhere in Europe. That among the English coronation regalia is in the unusual form of an eagle with outstretched wings. It dates from 1660 and was prob. copied from an earlier one, which, acc. to legend, was entrusted by the BVM to St. *Thomas of Canterbury.

O. M. Dalton, *Catalogue of Christian Antiquities of the British Museum* (1901), pp. 154–9; C. M. Kaufmann, *Zur ikonographie der Menas-Ampullen* (1910); C. Cechelli, 'Note iconografiche su alcune ampolle bobbiesi' in *R.A.C.*, iv (1927), pp. 15–39. H. *Leclercq, O.S.B., in *D.A.C.L.*, i (pt. 2; 1907), cols. 1722–78, s.v. 'Ampoules' and E. Josi in *E.C.*, i (1949), cols. 1113–15, s.v. 'Ampolla'. On (3), Sir Francis Oppenheimer, *The Legend of the Ste. Ampoule* (1953).

AMSDORF, NIKOLAUS VON (1483–1565), *Lutheran theologian. A native of Torgau, he studied at Leipzig and Wittenberg, where he became lecturer in philosophy and theology and canon in 1508. In 1517 he joined M. *Luther, whom he accompanied to the Disputation at Leipzig in 1519 and to the Diet of *Worms in 1521. In 1524 he went to Magdeburg to lead the Protestant opposition against the Catholic clergy and to reform the services on Wittenberg lines. In 1528 and 1531 he did the same for Goslar. In 1534 he was responsible for Luther's renewed dispute with *Erasmus. He later quarrelled with P. *Melanchthon and M. *Bucer and alienated the Emperor during the Colloquy of *Ratisbon in 1541. In the same year he was appointed Bp. of Naumburg by the Elector of Saxony against the candidate of the Cathedral chapter and the wishes of the Emperor, but had to give up the appointment after the war of *Schmalkalden (1547) and went to Eisenach. He was a violent opponent of the *Leipzig Interim, and, with *Flacius Illyricus, became a leader of the intransigent Lutheran party against the *Adiaphorists (q.v.). During the *Synergist controversy he maintained against P. Major, J. Pfeffinger, and others not only the uselessness but the actual harmfulness of good works, but did not subscribe to the teaching of Flacius Illyricus on sin as the substance of natural man. His one-sided interpretation of Luther caused a split within the Lutheran party, and his teaching on the harmfulness of good works was criticized in the Formula of *Concord.

There is no adequate biography; short Life by T. Pressel (Elberfeld, 1862). C. Eichhorn, '*Amsdorfiana aus dem codex chartaceus nr. 43 der Dorpater Universität-Bibliothek*' in *Z.K.G.*, xxii (1901), pp. 605–46. O. H. Nébe, *Reine Lehre. Zur Theologie des Niklas von Amsdorff* (1935). Dr. Schwarz–G. Kawerau in *P.R.E.* (ed. 3), i (1896), pp. 464–7.

AMSTERDAM ASSEMBLY, The (1948). The Assembly in the Concertgebouw, Amsterdam, from 22 Aug. to 4 Sept. which formally constituted the '*World Council of Churches' (q.v.). The Church leaders present included Marc Boegner, Pastor of Passy and President of the Protestant Federation of France; Erling Eidem, *Lutheran Abp. of Upsala; Geoffrey Fisher, Abp. of Canterbury; Strenopoulos Germanos, Abp. of Thyateira, under the *Oecumenical Patriarch; and J. R. *Mott (q.v.). The theme of the discussions was 'Man's Disorder and God's Design', under the four separate heads 'The Universal Church in God's Design' (by G. *Aulen, K. *Barth, G. Florovsky, R. *Niebuhr, E. Schlink, O. Tomkins, W. A. Visser 't Hooft, etc.), 'The Church's Witness to God's Design' (by E. *Brunner, W. M. Horton, H. Kraemer, S. C. Neill, P. Tillich, etc.), 'The Church and the Disorder of Society' (by Kathleen Bliss, E. Brunner, R. Niebuhr, J. H. Oldham, etc.), and 'The Church and International Disorder' (by E. Brunner, J. F. Dulles, J. L. Hromadka, etc.).

The Official Report, with the 4 vols. under the separate titles named above, was issued in 1948–9. H. G. G. Herklots, *Amsterdam, 1948* (1948; popular).

ANABAPTISTS ('re-baptizers', from Gk. ἀνά and βαπτίζω). The comprehensive designation of various groups on the Continent who in the 16th cent. refused to allow their children to be baptized and reinstituted the baptism of believers. Their refusal to admit that infant baptism was true baptism led to the nickname. The main groups to be distinguished are: (1) Thomas *Münzer (1490?–1525) and the *Zwickau Prophets who appeared in *Wittenberg in 1521. Münzer sympathized with the *Peasants' Revolt (1525) and taught a doctrine of the *Inner Light which reappeared later in the *Quakers. (2) The Swiss Brethren, who reintroduced believers' baptism as the basis of Church fellowship in Zürich in 1525 and who also taught doctrines of non-resistance and the rejection of Christian participation in the magistracy. Their views quickly spread in the Swiss valleys, and into the Rhineland and SW Germany. To this group belonged Balthasar *Hübmaier (c. 1485–1528) and, for a time, Hans Denck (1495?–1527). (3) Communities which found asylum in Moravia and, under the leadership of Jacob Hutter (d. 1536), established settlements based on the common ownership of property. After many sufferings and wanderings certain of their descendants, now known as Hutterites or Hutterian Brethren, are to be found in the United States. (4) Melchiorites or Hoffmanites, that is, Anabaptists influenced by Melchior *Hoffmann (1498–1543), mainly in NW Germany and the Low Countries. Hoffmann taught an unorthodox Christology of a *Docetic kind and probably also encouraged *chiliastic hopes. (5) A group of Anabaptist refugees from Münster who in 1533–5 attempted to establish a Kingdom of the Saints under the leadership first of Jan Mattys (d. 1534) and then of Jan Bockelson (John of *Leyden, 1510–36). During the siege of the city a form of polygamy was introduced, and the grave excesses and fanaticism brought ill-odour on the whole of the left-wing movement. (6) The *Mennonites, shepherded and reorganized in Holland and Friesland by Menno Simons after the Münster episode. Their views were similar to those of the Swiss Brethren, with pacifism and non-resistance strongly emphasized. They later became in Holland an influential community of rather liberal theological views and also spread to other continental lands and to America. In all they now number 500,000.

Miguel *Servetus is sometimes classed among the Anabaptists, but he was not the organizer of churches as were those listed above. Faustus *Socinus also rejected infant baptism, and Socinian influences are to be traced on some of the later Mennonites.

The Anabaptists were vigorously denounced by M. *Luther, H. *Zwingli, and J. *Calvin and severely persecuted by both Roman Catholics and Protestants. Those put to death probably ran into tens of thousands. Down to modern times they have suffered from too hostile criticism; and Anabaptist hymnology and martyrology are only now receiving sympathetic and scholarly study.

There were Anabaptists in England as early as 1534, but throughout the 16th cent. Anabaptist views seem to have been mainly confined to refugees from the Low Countries. The early *Separatists and *Brownists, however, were probably influenced by them, and John *Smyth was certainly in close touch with the Mennonites. In the 17th and 18th cents. Baptists were often described as Anabaptists, but the name had then become one of abuse with evil associations and was, as such, repudiated.

Quellen zur Geschichte der Wiedertäufer (Quellen und Forschungen zur Reformationsgeschichte, vols. xii, xvi, xxiii, etc., 1950 ff., vol. i (xii) by G. Bossert, *Herzogtum Württemberg*, vol. ii (xvi) by K. Schornbaum, *Markgraftum Brandenburg*). L. Keller, *Geschichte der Wiedertäufer und ihres Reiches zu Münster* (1880); R. Heath, *Anabaptism from its Rise at Zwickau to its Fall at Münster, 1521–1536* (1895). H. S. Burrage, *History of the Anabaptists in Switzerland* (American Baptist Publications Society; Philadelphia, 1882); E. B. Bax, *The Social Side of the Reformation in Germany*, iii ('The Rise and Fall of the Anabaptists', 1903). R. J. Smithson, *The Anabaptists*. Their Contribution to our Protestant Heritage (1935). G. Uhlhorn in *P.R.E.* (ed. 3), i (1896), pp. 481–5, s.v. 'Anabaptisten'; W. Koehler in *R.G.G.* (ed. 2), v (1931), cols. 1915–17, s.v. 'Wiedertäufer', both with bibl.

ANACLETUS, St. (1st cent.), also 'Anencletus', Gk. ἀνέγκλητος, i.e. 'blameless', early Bp. of *Rome. He is probably to be identified with 'Cletus' (so *Irenaeus, *Eusebius, *Optatus, *Augustine), though the *Liberian Catalogue and the *Liber Pontificalis distinguish them. He followed St. *Linus (the successor of St. *Peter) and preceded St. *Clement of Rome (d. c. 96). Nothing further is known of him, though tradition attributes the division of Rome into 25 parishes to him. The feast of St. Cletus (with St. Marcellinus, d. c. 304) is kept on 26 Apr.

Jaffé, i, p. 1 f. *L.P.* (Duchesne), i, pp. lxix f. and 125. H. Hemmer in *D.T.C.*, i (1903), col. 1141 f., s.v. 'Anaclet'; J. P. Kirsch in *D.H.G.E.*, ii (1914), col. 1407 f., s.v. 'Anaclet'; P. Goggi in *E.C.*, i (1948), col. 1126, s.v. 'Anacleto'.

ANAKEPHALAIOSIS. See *Recapitulation*.

ANALECTA BOLLANDIANA. A quarterly review which has been issued since 1882 by the *Bollandists. It is devoted to hagiographical studies and research and from time to time prints hitherto unpublished documents.

ANALOGY. A method of predication whereby concepts derived from a familiar object are made applicable to a relatively unknown object in virtue of some similarity between the two otherwise dissimilar objects (called 'analogues'). Thus it is by 'analogy' that it is possible for the human intellect to speak of the 'justice' of God, for though God's justice is not totally dissimilar from justice as met with in human experience, it is certainly not identical with it. In this way the employment of analogy enables the theologian and the philosopher to avoid the Scylla of 'anthropomorphism', which by the use of 'univocal' concepts assumes the unqualified similarity between God and man, and the Charybdis of 'symbolism', which by the use of 'equivocal' concepts tends to presuppose their total dissimilarity. It should be noted that theologians in the tradition of St. *Thomas and *Cajetan who employ the method of analogy regard the errors of the 'symbolists' as less grievous than those of the 'anthropomorphists'. The legitimate employment on their view of the *via eminentiae presupposes the prior use of the *via negativa.

J. M. Ramírez, O.P., 'De Analogia secundum Doctrinam Aristotelico-Thomisticam' in *La Ciencia tomista*, xxiv (1921), pp. 20–40, and xxv (1922), pp. 17–38; B. de Solage, O.P., *Dialogue sur l'analogie* (1946). T. L. Penido, O.P., *Le Rôle de l'analogie en théologie dogmatique* (1931). A. Chollet in *D.T.C.*, i (1903), cols. 1142–54, and P. Parente in *E.C.*, i (1949), cols. 1138–40.

ANALOGY OF RELIGION, The (1736).

J. *Butler's famous book, the purpose and scope of which was indicated by its title, *The Analogy of Religion, Natural and Revealed, to the Constitution and Course of Nature*, was addressed to inquirers who, while conscious of order and regularity in Nature (which were ascribed by many of his *Deistical contemporaries to a transcendent Deity who was believed to have no interest in human affairs), were unconvinced of the claims of religion. Its two parts seek to establish the analogy and conformity of Natural and Revealed Religion respectively with what is observable in Nature.

Part I begins with a defence of the immortality of the soul, arguing that changes in the conditions of its life are of a piece with the visible changes experienced by the human body (ch. 1). There follows a defence of rewards and punishments (ch. 2) and of God's moral government of the world (ch. 3), and a discussion of the conditions and purposes of the state of probation that is allotted to each individual (chs. 4 and 5). In ch. 6 it is argued that the doctrine of necessity is no hindrance to religious belief, and in ch. 7 that our ignorance of the whole scheme of Providence should remove the grounds of perplexity concerning the Divine government of the world.

In Part II Butler turns to Revealed Religion. After stressing the importance of Revelation, if it be a fact, for human life (ch. 1), he argues against the supposed objection to it as miraculous (ch. 2). Its supernatural character, however, does not rule out theological speculation about it. It is within the competence of reason to judge not only of the meaning but also of the morality and evidence of Revelation (ch. 3). He goes on to urge that as Conscience, no less than the Bible, is a gift of God, no dictum of Scripture can offer any pretext for evading the demands of the moral imperative. Any apparent immoralities or inconsistencies in the Bible cannot be real (ch. 4). Redemption is wrought by the Death of Christ (ch. 5). The evidence for the Christian Revelation may not amount to demonstration, but this is no objection, for here as elsewhere probability is the guide of life (ch. 6). The work concludes with some account of the particular evidences for Christianity derived from miracles and prophecy (ch. 7) and a final defence of the mode of arguing from analogy (ch. 8).

The book is remarkable for the closely knit texture of its argument. Despite the absence of any direct reference to the Deists, in the long run it did more to discredit the movement than the vast body of polemical literature, now forgotten, which sought to grapple with its upholders directly.

Of modern editions the best is that of W. E. *Gladstone (1896).

ANAMNESIS (Gk. ἀνάμνησις, 'memorial').

The word, which is used in the narrative of the Eucharist in the NT (1 Cor. 11. 24 f., Lk. 22. 19), is employed by liturgists for the commemoration of the Passion, Resurrection, and Ascension of Christ, which in most liturgies is included in the Eucharistic *Canon after the Words of Institution.

Jungmann (ed. 3, 1952), i, pp. 271–81. O. Casel, O.S.B., 'Das Mysteriengedächtnis der Massliturgie im Lichte der Tradition' in *J.L.W.*, vi (1926), pp. 113–204. N. A. Dahl, 'Anamnesis. Mémoire et commémoration dans le christianisme primitif' in *Studia Theologica* (Lund), i (1948), pp. 69–95. B. Botte, O.S.B., 'Problèmes de l'Anamnèse' in *J.E.H.*, v (1954), pp. 16–24. F. *Cabrol, O.S.B., in *D.A.C.L.*, i (pt. 2; 1907), cols. 1880–96.

ANANIAS AND SAPPHIRA.

The man and his wife who, when the Apostolic Church experimented with community of goods, held back some of their property, and, on being challenged in turn by St. Peter, suddenly fell dead. The story is in Acts 5. 1–11.

ANAPHORA (Gk. ἀναφορά, lit. 'offering',)

The central prayer in the Eucharistic Liturgy. containing the *Consecration, the *Anamnesis, and the *Communion. It thus covers more than the *Canon, of which the Communion is not considered to be a part. The traditional order of its parts is *Sursum Corda (usually introduced by some form of benediction), *Sanctus, Memorial of the Incarnation, Words of *Institution, *Epiclesis (not found in Roman and derived Liturgies), and sometimes an Intercession. Among the oldest known Anaphoras are that in the '*Apostolic Tradition' of *Hippolytus and that of *Serapion, Bp. of Thmuis.

ANASTASIA, St. (c. 304), martyr.

A curious liturgical interest attaches to this saint as, though originally unconnected with *Rome, she is mentioned in the Roman *Canon of the Mass and commemorated in the Second Mass for *Christmas Day. She was apparently martyred at Sirmium in Pannonia, whence her relics were translated to *Constantinople by St. *Gennadius (458–71) and interred in the church of the Anastasis, founded by St. *Gregory Nazianzen. Hence the cultus spread, probably through the agency of Byzantine officials, to the ancient church near the Circus Maximus known as the *titulus Anastasiae* (perhaps from the name of its founder) and the only church near the imperial palace; the dedication was now understood of the Sirmian saint; and the Pope celebrated here the stational Mass of Dawn on Christmas Day. Acc. to later and quite untrustworthy legends, Anastasia was a Roman lady of noble birth, the wife of a pagan Publius and a spiritual disciple of St. *Chrysogonus, and was martyred on the island of Palmaria. Feast day, 25 Dec.

'Acta' discussed in H. *Delehaye, S.J., *Étude sur le légendier romain* (Subsidia Hagiographica, xxiii, 1936), pp. 151–71. L. *Duchesne, 'Notes sur la topographie de Rome au moyen âge', No. III, 'Sainte-Anastasie', in *Mélanges d'archéologie et d'histoire*, vii (1887), pp. 387–413; H. Grisar, S.J., 'S. Anastasia di Roma' in *Analecta Romana*, i (1899), pp. 595–610; J. P. Kirsch, *Die römischen Titelkirchen im Altertum* (1918), pp. 18–23 ('Titulus Anastasiae').

ANASTASIS (Gk. ἀνάστασις, 'resurrection'). From the first the word was used of the resurrection both of Christ Himself and of mankind in general. There were early churches dedicated to the Anastasis (of Christ) at *Jerusalem and *Constantinople; and it is possible (but see previous entry) that the present church of 'St. Anastasia' at *Rome, at the foot of the Palatine Hill, originally had that dedication.

ANASTASIUS (d. *c.* 700) ('Anastasius Sinaita'), abbot of the monastery of St. Catherine on Mount *Sinai. A strong supporter of orthodoxy against all forms of heresy, he is believed to have attacked *monophysitism at *Alexandria as early as 640, and it was against the same heresy that his most important treatise, the 'Hodegos' (Gk. ὁδηγός, i.e. 'Guide'), was primarily directed. The 154 'Questions and Answers' included in editions of his writings are not in their present form his work.

The fullest collection of his works is in J. P. Migne, *PG*, lxxxix, 35–1288; further works under the title 'Anastasiana' in J. B. *Pitra, *Iuris Ecclesiastici Graecorum Historia et Monumenta*, ii (1868), pp. 238–94. J. B. Kumpfmüller, *De Anastasio Sinaita* (Würzburg, 1865). T. Spacil, S.J., 'La teologia di S. Anastasio Sinaita' in *Bessarione*, xxvi (1922), pp. 157–78, and xxvii (1923), pp. 14–44. G. Bardy, 'La Littérature patristique des "*Quaestiones et Responsiones*" sur l'écriture sainte: Anastase le Sinaite' in *R. Bibl.*, xlii (1933), pp. 339–43. Bardenhewer, v, pp. 41–6; Altaner, p. 473, with bibl. G. Bardy in *Dict. Sp.*, i (1937), col. 546 f., s.v.; M. Jugie, A.A., in *E.C.*, i (1949), col. 1157 f., s.v. 'Anastasio'.

ANASTASIUS BIBLIOTHECARIUS (9th cent.), scholar. Apparently a native of Rome, he was educated by Greek monks with whom he retained close associations. In Aug. 855 he allowed the Imperial party to proclaim him Anti-Pope against Benedict III, but soon proved himself too rash and undisciplined for the office and was disowned by his supporters a month later. He was the best Greek scholar of his age in the W. Nicholas I gave him the Abbacy of St. Maria in Trastevere, while later Popes made them their Librarian (hence 'Bibliothecarius') and rewarded him with important posts in the Chancery where he tried to stem the threatening schism in the E. He attended the final session of the Eighth *Oecumenical Council (869) and later (871) translated its Acts into Latin. In 873 he translated the Acts of the Seventh Council (787). Among his other writings are a *Chronographia Tripartita*, based on earlier Byzantine historians, and several works on Dogmatic Theology.

A. Lapôtre, *De Anastasio Bibliothecario sedis apostolicae* (Paris, 1885). E. Perels, *Papst Nikolaus I und Anastasius*

Bibliothecarius (1920). J. *Hergenröther, *Photius, Patriarch von Constantinopel*, ii (1867), pp. 228–41. C. Laehr, 'Die Briefe und Prologe des Bibliothekars' in *N.A.*, xlvii (1928), pp. 416–68. Duchesne, *L.P.*, i, p. xxxv (on his reputed authorship of the *Liber Pontificalis*).

ANATHEMA (Gk. ἀνάθεμα, lit. 'suspended', 'set up above'). It is the equivalent of the Heb. word חֵרֶם, the root meaning of which is 'to cut off', 'curse', 'separate'. In the OT the term is used of votive offerings, e.g. Lev. 21. 5; but more often of things 'devoted to God', and hence 'under a ban' (e.g. in Deut. 7. 26), i.e. not for common use (cf. Lev. 27. 28 f.). Thus people, animals, cities, nations, and things could all become 'anathema', which frequently involved complete extermination (cf. Joshua 6, Deut. 7. 1 f., 1 Sam. 15). The practice was later alleviated, and after the Exile was normally confined to exclusion from the community and loss of goods. In this form it survived until the times of our Lord (e.g. Mt. 18. 17, Jn. 9. 22, though the term itself is not used in these and similar Gospel passages). St. *Paul uses the word to denote separation from the Christian community inflicted for sins such as preaching a gospel other than his (Gal. 1. 8 f.) or for not loving the Lord (1 Cor. 16. 22), whereas in other passages it simply means malediction (e.g. 1 Cor. 12. 3).

In the post-Apostolic Church the earliest recorded instance of anathematizing offenders is at the Council of *Elvira (*c.* 306). It soon became the regular procedure against heretics. In 431, St. *Cyril of Alexandria issued his famous twelve anathematisms against Nestorius. From the 6th cent. anathematization began to be distinguished from excommunication. *Gratian explained that the latter involved only exclusion from the Sacraments and worship, whereas the former was complete separation from the Body of the faithful (*Decretum*, Bk. ii, can. 106), a distinction which was closely akin to *Gregory IX's distinction of 'Major' and 'Minor' Excommunication. In practice the distinction lost its meaning, apart from the solemn ceremony which is used for anathemas. Acc. to the *Pontifical ('Ordo excommunicandi et absolvendi'), sentence is pronounced by the Bishop, vested in a purple cope and surrounded by twelve priests who bear lighted candles, which are thrown to the ground when sentence has been uttered.

J. Behm in *T.W.B.*, i (1933), p. 356 f. L. Brun, *Segen und Fluch im Urchristentum* (Oslo, 1931). A. Vacant in *D.T.C.*, i (1903), cols. 1168–71 and A. Amanieu in *D.D.C.*, i (1935), cols. 512–16, with bibl.

ANATOLIUS, St. (d. *c.* 282), Bp. of Laodicea. He was a native of *Alexandria, where he established a school of *Aristotelian philosophy and obtained a seat in the senate. During the siege of the Alexandrian suburb Brychion, in the revolt under the Prefect Aemilian (262), Anatolius devised a successful stratagem to relieve his fellow-Christians. Soon afterwards he was consecrated, apparently as coadjutor-bishop, by Theotecnus, Bp. of *Caesarea in Palestine, and in 268, on his way to the Synod at *Antioch to deal with

*Paul of Samosata, made Bp. of Laodicea. Though a man of great learning and held in high repute by *Eusebius (*HE*, VII, xxxii, 6–12) and St. *Jerome (*De Viris Ill.* lxxiii), his writings were few. They included a treatise on the date of Easter (Περὶ τοῦ Πάσχα), based on the 19-year cycle still used, from which Eusebius (loc. cit.) quotes a passage, and a work in 10 Books on the Elements of Arithmetic (Ἀριθμητικαὶ εἰσαγωγαί), of which fragments survive (J. P. *Migne, *PG*, x, 231–6). It seems that the attribution to Anatolius of the 'Liber Anatoli de Ratione Paschali' (acc. to B. Krusch, compiled in England in the 6th cent.; acc. to C. H. *Turner, at *Iona between 580 and 600) is mistaken. Feast day, 3 July.

The 'Liber Anatoli de Ratione Paschali' was first published by A. Bucher, S.J., *De Doctrina Temporum Commentarius* (Antwerp, 1634; reprinted in J. P. Migne, *PL*, x, 209–232). A new edition was issued by B. Krusch, *Studien zur christlich-mittelalterlichen Chronologie*. Der 84-jährige Osterzyklus und seine Quellen (1880). C. H. Turner, 'The Paschal Canon of "Anatolius of Laodicea"' in the *English Historical Review*, x (1895), pp. 699–710; E. *Schwartz, *Christliche und jüdische Ostertafeln* (1905).

ANCHORITE (*m.*), **ANCHORESS** (*f.*) (Gk. ἀναχωρέω, 'to withdraw'). A person who withdraws from the world to live a solitary life of silence, prayer, and mortification. Technically the term covers *coenobites as well as *hermits, but it is commonly restricted to the latter, i.e. persons who live entirely alone. The word, in distinction from 'hermit', is now used esp. of one who lives in strictly confined quarters (his 'cell'). In the early Church this way of life was at the will of the anchorite, who was free to leave his retirement if necessary, but later it was recognized and ordered acc. to rules by the Church, the bishop himself enclosing the anchorite, who was thenceforward confined within the walls of his cell. In the later Middle Ages an anchorite's cell was sometimes attached to parish churches.

R. M. Clay, *The Hermits and Anchorites of England* (1914), pp. 73–198 and 203–63.

ANCIENT OF DAYS. A designation of Jehovah found in Dan. 7. 9, 13, and 22. In the original Aramaic (יוֹמִין עַתִּיק) the expression here used should be translated literally 'one aged in days'. It conveyed no idea of eternity, but apparently described the Deity under the figure of an old man.

ANCREN RIWLE ('Regula Inclusarum'). An English treatise on the spiritual life, probably written between 1190 and 1230, and variously ascribed to Simon of Ghent, Richard *Poore (Bps. of *Sarum), Roger *Bacon, and St. *Gilbert of Sempringham. It is chiefly concerned with a rule of prayer, and is marked by a wise discretion and spiritual insight. It is not solely a rule for *anchoresses as its title implies, but is intended for others beside solitaries.

B.M. Cotton MS. Nero A. XIV, collated with other MSS., ed. by J. Morton (Camden Society, lvii, 1853), incl. modern Eng. vers.; also ed. M. B. Salu, with introd. by G. Sitwell ('Orchard Books', 1955). Crit. edd. of Eng. Text by M. Day from the B.M. Cotton MS. Nero A. XIV (*E.E.T.S.*, Orig. Ser., ccxxv, 1952); from B.M. MS. Roy. 8 c, I by A. C. Baugh (ib., ccxxxii, 1956), of the Lat. vers. by C. D'Evelyn from Merton Coll. MS. 44 and B.M. Cotton MS. Vitellius E. VII (ib., ccxvi, 1944), and of the Fr. vers. by J. A. Herbert from the B.M. Cotton MS. Vitellius F. VII (ib., ccxix, 1944). Hope Emily Allen, 'On the Author of the *Ancren Riwle*' in *Publications of the Modern Language Association of America*, xliv (1929), pp. 635–80; further notes by id. in *The Modern Language Review*, xiv (1919), p. 209 f.; xvii (1922), p. 403; xviii (1923), pp. 1–8, and xix (1924), p. 95; xxiv (1929), pp. 1–15; in *T.L.S.*, 1936, p. 863, and in [P. W. Long, ed.] *Essays and Studies in Honour of Carleton Brown* (New York, 1940), pp. 183–219.

ANCYRA (also **Angora**, now **Ankara**). Among the important early Church synods held here were:

(1) 314. A council of from 12 to 18 bishops from Asia Minor and Syria. It dealt with the question of the *'lapsi'. In its first nine canons ecclesiastical penalties were allotted acc. to the gravity and scandal of the lapse, but eventual reconciliation was granted to all. The remaining canons (10–25), which were concerned with various other offences, are of importance in the development of the *penitential system. Canon 13 has caused some controversy since it seems to favour ordination by presbyters.

(2) 358. A council of the *Semi-Arians under the presidency of *Basil of Ancyra, which rejected both extreme Arian teaching and also the Nicene *Homoousios ('of one substance'), and asserted that the Son was 'like in substance' to the Father.

(3) 375. An Arian synod, at which Gregory of Nyssa was deposed.

On (1), Hardouin, i, cols. 269–82; Mansi, ii, cols. 513–40. Canons also in Lauchert, pp. 29–34; crit. ed. of Lat. texts in C. H. *Turner, *E.O.M.I.A.*, II i (1907). Hefele–Leclercq, i (1; 1907), pp. 298–326. R. B. Rackham, 'The Text of the Canons of Ancyra' in *Studia Biblica et Ecclesiastica*, iii (Oxford, 1891), pp. 139–216. C. H. Turner, 'Canon xiii of Ancyra' in C. *Gore, *The Church and the Ministry* (new ed., 1919), pp. 327–30.

ANDREW, St., *Apostle. He was the brother of St. *Peter, with whom he appears in the Gospels (Mk. 1. 16–20, 29, &c.). Though not a member of the inner band of three (Peter, *James, and *John), several incidents concerning him are recorded (Jn. 1. 35–42, Mt. 4. 18–20, Jn. 6. 8 f., Mk. 13. 3 f., &c.). *Eusebius (*H.E.*, III. i. 1) states that he later went to Scythia. Acc. to a late and unreliable tradition he was martyred at Patras, in Achaia, in 60. The *Muratorian Fragment connects him with the writing of St. John's Gospel. The tradition of the form of St. Andrew's Cross (a cross like the Gk. X) cannot be traced back further than the 14th cent. Feast day 30 Nov. In the Anglican Communion, St. Andrewstide is widely observed by intercessions for foreign missions. Since c. 750 he has been regarded as the patron saint of Scotland. See also following entry.

M. R. James in *H.D.B.*, i (1898), p. 92 f., s.v. On St. Andrew's connexion with Scotland, W. F. Skene, *Celtic Scotland*, i (1876), pp. 296–99, with reff. to orig. sources. Cf. also foll. bibl.

ANDREW, Acts of St. An apocryphal book dating probably from the early 3rd cent., and once held in great favour among the

*Gnostic heretics. In its original form it no longer survives, though a fragment of the work is contained in cod. Vat. gr. 808 and *Gregory of Tours gives a long epitome of it. It depicts the apostle as imprisoned at Patras, and prosecuted for his advocacy of ascetic practices. The 'Martyrdom' of St. Andrew, a variant text of part of the work, describes the Apostle's death by crucifixion, but without mention of the 'St. Andrew's cross' (see previous entry).

The Greek text is in R. A. Lipsius–M. Bonnet, *Acta Apocrypha*, ii, 1 ff. M. R. James, *The Apocryphal NT* (1924), pp. 337–63.

ANDREW OF CRETE, St. (*c.* 660–740), theologian and hymn writer. A native of Damascus, he became Abp. of Gortyna in Crete *c.* 692. In 712 he lapsed into *Monothelitism, but retracted in the following year. He wrote many hymns, notably a series of '*canons', of which form of composition he is said to have been the inventor. His most famous piece, the 'Great Canon' (ὁ μέγας κανών), contains no less than 250 strophes. A considerable number of his homilies have also survived. Feast day, 4 July. (He is not to be confounded with St. Andrew of Crete, 'the Colybite', d. 766; Feast day, 20 Oct.)

Opera, with Lat. tr., ed. by F. Combefis, O.P., Paris, 1644; repr. from A. *Gallandi in J. P. Migne, *PG*, xcvii, 805–1444. S. Vailhé, A.A., 'St. André de Crète' in *E.O.*, v (1902), pp. 378–87. A. Heisenberg, 'Ein jambisches Gedicht des Andreas von Kreta' in *B.Z.*, x (1901), pp. 505–14. Bardenhewer, *G.A.L.*, v (1932), pp. 152–7, and Altaner (1951), p. 480, both with further bibl.

ANDREWES, LANCELOT (1555–1626), Bp. of *Winchester. Born in the parish of All Hallows, Barking, he was educated at Merchant Taylors' School and Pembroke Hall, Cambridge, where he was elected Fellow in 1576 and catechist in 1580. He was a devoted scholar, hard-working and accurate, who became the master of fifteen languages. In 1589 he became vicar of St. Giles, Cripplegate, and in the same year, in succession to W. *Fulke, Master of Pembroke Hall. His incumbency at Cripplegate was attached to a prebend at *St. Paul's where his remarkable preaching abilities first attracted notice. *Elizabeth offered him two bishoprics (*Salisbury, *Ely); but he declined both owing to conditions which involved the alienation of some of the revenues. In 1601 he became Dean of *Westminster. Under *James I (1603), who held Andrewes in high esteem, he rapidly rose. He became Bp. of *Chichester in 1605, of Ely in 1609, and of *Winchester in 1619. In 1604 he took a leading part in the *Hampton Court Conference, which appointed him one of the translators of the *Authorized Version of the Bible; he was largely responsible for the Pentateuch and the historical Books. In the next years he became involved in the controversy over the Oath of Allegiance, imposed after the *Gunpowder Plot (1605). When St. Robert *Bellarmine, under the pseudonym of 'Matthaeus Tortus' (his almoner), had attacked King James' *Apology for the Oath* (1608), Andrewes wrote a vigorous and able reply under the title *Tortura Torti*

(1609). After a further attack on the King by Bellarmine, who now wrote in his own name, Andrewes issued a second work, *Responsio ad Apologiam Cardinalis Bellarmini* (1610). In 1613 he sat on the commission which investigated the Essex nullity suit where he was one of the seven members who voted for the divorce. In 1617 he accompanied James I to Scotland in an attempt to persuade the Scots to accept episcopacy. Later he was put on the commission on the irregularity of G. *Abbot, Abp. of *Canterbury, who had accidentally shot a gamekeeper while hunting (Oct. 1621). He died at Winchester House, *Southwark, on 26 Sept. 1626 and was buried in the parish church of St. Saviour and St. Mary Overy, now Southwark Cathedral.

Theologically, Andrewes was one of the principal influences in the formation of a distinctive Anglican theology, which, in reaction from the rigidity of Puritanism, should be reasonable in outlook and Catholic in tone. Convinced that true theology must be built on sound learning, he cultivated the friendship of such divines as R. *Hooker and G. *Herbert, as well as of liberal scholars from abroad, e.g. I. *Casaubon, P. *Du Moulin, and H. *Grotius. He opposed the *Lambeth Articles (1595), though at the time he was chaplain to Abp. J. *Whitgift. Probably his known aversion to Calvinism explains his absence from the Anglican delegation to the Synod of *Dort (1618). He held a high doctrine of the Eucharist, emphasizing that in the sacrament we receive the true body and blood of Christ and constantly using sacrificial language of the rite. He wanted the C of E to express its worship in an ordered ceremonial, and in his own chapel used the mixed chalice, incense and altar-lights.

But in his lifetime Andrewes' fame rested esp. on his preaching. He regularly preached at court on the greater Church feasts; and his 'Ninety-Six Sermons', first publd. in a collected edition by W. *Laud and J. Buckeridge in 1629, remain a classic of Anglican homiletic works. They are characterized by verbal conceits, a minute and (to modern feeling) overworked analysis of the text, and with constant Greek and Latin quotations. His famous *Preces Privatae*, a collection of his devotions gradually compiled for his personal use, were first published by R. Drake in 1648. They were issued in a revised and much improved edition by F. E. *Brightman in 1903. His *Pattern of Catechistical Doctrine* (1630; also posthumous) was based on lectures delivered at Pembroke Hall, Cambridge.

His Works ed. by J. P. Wilson and J. Bliss in *L.A.C.T.* (11 vols., 1841–54). Brief life by Henry Isaacson (1581–1654), Andrewes' pupil, amanuensis, and intimate friend (London, 1650 [1651]; new ed. by S. Isaacson, London, 1829; also incl. in works). Other lives by A. T. Russell (Cambridge, 1860) and R. L. *Ottley (London, 1894). R. W. *Church, 'Lancelot Andrewes' in A. Barry (ed.), *Masters of English Theology* (1877), pp. 61–112. T. S. *Eliot, *For Lancelot Andrewes. Essays on Style and Order* (1928), ch. i, pp. 13–32. Selections in P. E. More–F. L. Cross, *Anglicanism* (1935). Study by P. A. Welsby (London, S.P.C.K., 1958). J. H. Overton in *D.N.B.*, i (1885), pp. 401–5, s.v.

ANENCLETUS, St. See *Anacletus, St.*

ANGEL (from Gk. ἄγγελος, 'messenger'). The belief in angels is amply attested in the Bible, both in the OT and NT. They are represented as an innumerable multitude (e.g. Gen. 32. 2; Dan. 7. 10) of beings intermediate between God and man. In the older books interest is chiefly confined to their mission (cf. Gen. 16. 7 ff.; Jgs. 6. 11 ff.), whereas in the later ones their nature is more clearly defined. In Isaiah's vision (Is. 6) and in Job they form the heavenly court and sing the praises of God, whose commands they obediently perform for nations (Dan. 10. 13 and 21, 12. 1) as well as for individuals, and even three proper names, *Michael (Dan. 10. 13), *Gabriel (Dan. 8. 16), and *Raphael (Tob. 7. 8), are recorded. In *Philo and the Jewish apocryphal writings, esp. *Enoch, angelology is highly developed, and angels, being the constant intermediators between God and man, were also regarded as the promulgators of the Law, a view accepted by the NT writers (Acts 7. 53, Gal. 3. 19, Heb. 2. 2). Our Lord Himself sanctioned the popular belief. Acc. to His teaching the angels are spiritual beings (Mt. 22. 30) who enjoy always the vision of God in heaven (Mt. 18. 10) and will accompany Him at His Second Coming (Mt. 16. 27). The NT authors represent Christ as surrounded by angels at the most important periods of His life. They announce His Incarnation (Mt. 1. 20, 24) and His Birth (Lk. 2. 9–15); they minister to Him in the desert (Mt. 4. 11), strengthen Him in His agony (Lk. 22. 43), would be ready to defend Him when He is captured (Mt. 26. 53), and are the first witnesses of His Resurrection (Mt. 28. 2–7; Jn. 20. 12 f.). In Rev. the role of angels is paramount; their worship in heaven is the prototype of the worship of the Church, and their ministry at the end of the world is the visionary development of our Lord's teaching. On the other hand, the dangers of an exaggerated cult paid to them by some heretical sects in the early days of Christianity are reflected in St. Paul's Ep. to the Col. (2. 18) and perhaps also in Heb. which lays special emphasis on the superiority of Christ to the angels (1. 4 ff.).

In the first cents., while the great Trinitarian and Christological doctrines were being worked out, interest in angels was comparatively peripheral. Their existence, it is true, was accepted by the Fathers as a truth of faith; their immaterial and spiritual nature, however, was not fully recognized except by *Dionysius the Areopagite and St. *Gregory the Great. *Origen attributed to them an ethereal body, an opinion which seems to have been shared by St. *Augustine. There was similar uncertainty on the subject of their present state. St. *Ignatius of Antioch had affirmed that they must believe in the Blood of Christ in order to be saved (*Smyrn.* 6. 1), and Origen held the good angels to be no less capable of falling than the demons were of being saved. This teaching was rejected by most of the orthodox Fathers, though traces of it are to be found in *Didymus, *Cyril of Jerusalem, and others. Perhaps the greatest interest was taken in the

question of the angelic orders, raised by the two enumerations of St. Paul in Eph. 1. 21 and Col. 1. 16 respectively. By amalgamating both passages five different ranks were arrived at, to which were sometimes added 'Angels' (here understood as a separate species of beings) and '*Archangels' (so *Irenaeus), and also the *Seraphim of Is. 6. 2 and the *Cherubim of Ez. 1. 5; but their number and order were only fixed by Dionysius in his 'Celestial Hierarchies', where they are arranged in three hierarchies containing three choirs each, in the order of Seraphim, Cherubim and Thrones, Dominations, Virtues and Powers, Principalities, Archangels and Angels. Of these only the last two choirs have an immediate mission to men.

In the Middle Ages Dionysius' speculative doctrine was taken over and developed by the Schoolmen, and a treatise on angels became an integral part of the Commentaries on the 'Sentences' of *Peter Lombard from the 13th cent. onwards. The doctrines of St. *Thomas and *Duns Scotus were foreshadowed by St. *Albert the Great and St. *Bonaventure respectively. St. Thomas and all the Schoolmen after him are at one on the point that angels are intelligences not destined to be united to a body, and thereby differ from the human soul. Acc. to St. Thomas they are not composed of 'form' and 'matter', but are subsistent forms, each differing from the other and forming a species in himself. From their immateriality follows that they are by nature immortal and incorruptible; having neither extension nor dimensions they cannot be in a place, but can move and act on material beings by applying their power to the place in which they want to be. Duns Scotus, on the other hand, regards angels as composite beings consisting of form and matter, though the latter is not corporeal. There may be several angels in the same species, and several angels may occupy the same place. The angelic mode of knowledge had already been discussed by St. Augustine (*Civ. Dei*, 11. 29), from whom St. Thomas took over the distinction between 'scientia matutina' and 'scientia vespertina', the former being supernatural knowledge which sees its objects in the Divine Word, and the latter natural, which knows individual things not, indeed, as man, through the senses, but through the intelligible species infused into the angelic intelligence at its creation. St. Thomas held that its proper object was the immaterial, and its mode not discursive reasoning, but the intuitive perception of conclusions in their principles, a view contested by Duns Scotus, and later by F. *Suarez, who held that angels can reason. On the question of the Fall, St. Thomas taught that the angelic will is such that one good or bad act fixes him irrevocably in good or evil, whereas Duns Scotus regarded a succession of acts as necessary. On several other points both schools of thought were in agreement. Thus most Scholastics taught that the angels were created at the same time as the material universe, that they were elevated to a state of grace in order to undergo a test followed either by super-natural beatitude or eternal damnation, and that the chief Divine mysteries, esp. the Incarnation, were then revealed to them. In the question of the hierarchy they all followed Dionysius more or less closely.

The teaching of post-medieval theologians runs on the lines of a Thomist-Scotist synthesis as developed by Suarez. The RC Church has made few pronouncements on the subject. While Catholic Christianity in general teaches the existence of angels, their perfect spirituality and their creation before man, and enjoins a cult similar to that given to the saints, Protestants have tended to shrink from definition and speculation in the matter. See also *Guardian Angels*.

F. Suarez, S.J., *Summa Theologiae de Deo Rerum Omnium Creatore*, pars secunda, 'De Angelis' (Lyons, 1620). J. Turmel, 'Histoire de l'angélologie des temps apostolique à la fin du Vᵉ siècle' in *Revue d'histoire et de littérature religieuses*, iii (1898), pp. 531–52; id., 'L'Angélologie depuis le faux Denys l'Aréopagite', ib., iv (1899), pp. 217–38, 289–309, 414–34, 537–62; G. Bareille, 'Le Culte des anges à l'époque des pères de l'Église' in *Revue Thomiste*, viii (1900), pp. 40–49. A. Davidson in *H.D.B.*, i (1900), pp. 93–7, s.v.; A. Vacant, G. Bareille, L. Petit, J. Parisot, J. Miskgian in *D.T.C.*, i (1903), cols. 1189–1272, s.v. 'Anges'; H. L. Pass in *H.E.R.E.*, iv (1911), pp. 578–83, s.v. 'Demons and Spirits (Christian)'; A. Lemennoyer, O.P. in *Dict. Bibl.*, Suppl. i (1928), cols. 255–62, s.v. Angélologie'; J. Duhr in *Dict. Sp.*, i (1937), cols. 580–625, s.v. 'Anges', all with bibl. For representation in art, H. *Leclercq, O.S.B., in *D.A.C.L.*, i (1907), cols. 2080–2161, s.v. 'Anges' with bibl. and J. Villette, *L'Ange dans l'art d'Occident du XIIᵉ au XVIᵉ siècle* (1940), with bibl.

ANGELA OF FOLIGNO, Bl. (c. 1248–1309), Umbrian mystic.

She came of a wealthy family and spent almost her whole life at Foligno. After the death of her husband she was converted to a life of austerity and prayer and later became a *Franciscan tertiary. She was the recipient of frequent visions, esp. relating to the Lord's Passion. The accounts of them, taken down from dictation by her confessor, Brother Arnold, and later circulated as 'Liber Visionum et Instructionum', reflect early Franciscan piety at its highest. Angela was beatified by Innocent XII in 1693. Feast day, 4 Jan. (in the Franciscan Order, 30 Mar.).

Her 'Liber Visionum', publ. at Alcalá 1502, ed. L. P. Rosello (Venice, c. 1510); also Paris, 1598, and Cologne, 1601; ed. with notes by J. H. Lammertz (*Bibliotheca Mystica et Ascetica*, v, Cologne, 1851). Crit. edd. after the MS. Assisi 342 by P. Doncœur, S.J.–M. Faloci Pulignani (Bibliothèque d'Ascétique et de Mystique ii, Paris, 1926) and, with Fr. tr., ed. M. J. Ferré–L. Baudry (Paris, 1927). Eng. tr. by A. P. J. Cruikshank (anon.; 1871) and M. G. Steegman, with preface by A. Thorold ('1909' [1908]). L. Leclève, *Sainte Angèle de Foligno* (1936).

ANGELA MERICI, St. (1474–1540),

foundress of the *Ursulines. She lived most of her mature life at Brescia. In her early years she was a Franciscan *tertiary. After devoting some years to the education of young girls and the care of sick women, she made a pilgrimage to Palestine in 1524–5 during which she was smitten with blindness for a time. As the result of visions she founded at Brescia in 1535 a religious community for women which she named after her patron, St. Ursula. In 1537 she herself was elected superior. She was canonized in 1807. Feast day, 31 May.

The earliest biography, compiled by G. B. Nazari in 1560, is printed as an appendix to G. Bertoletti, *Storia di S. Angela Merici, 1474–1540* (Brescia, 1923). Later lives by O. Gondi, S.J. (Sabbia, 1660) and C. Doneda (Brescia, 1768). *Ste Angèle Merici et l'ordre des Ursulines*, par une religieuse du même ordre (2 vols., 1922); Sister M[ary] Monica, O.S.U., *Angela Merici and her Teaching Idea, 1474–1540* (New York, 1927), with bibl. Other studies by C. M. Salvatori, S.J. (Rome, 1807), V. Postel (Paris, 1878), B. O'Reilly (London, 1880), M. V. Neusee, O.S.U. (Innsbruck, 1893; ed. 2, Freiburg i.Br., 1912), and W. E. Hubert (Mainz, 1891).

ANGELIC DOCTOR, The.

A title applied from medieval times to St. *Thomas Aquinas in reference to 'the almost angelic quality of his intellect' (Motu Proprio, *Doctoris Angelici*, 29 June 1914). See also *Doctors, Scholastic*.

ANGELIC HYMN. (Lat. *hymnus angelicus*).

Another name for the *Gloria in excelsis (q.v.), the opening words of which are the hymn of the angelic host at *Bethlehem (Lk. 2. 14).

ANGELICO, FRA (1387–1455), Blessed

Fra Angelico Giovanni da Fiesole, painter of the Florentine school. He joined the *Dominican Order in 1407, and did his first work in art in illuminating MSS. Between 1409 and 1418 the struggles of the *Great Schism made it necessary for him to be away from his own community house at Fiesole, and he stayed first at Foligno, and then at Cortona, where are some of his greatest pictures. In middle life he undertook the decoration of the convent of San Marco at Florence and the frescoes of two chapels in the *Vatican. He is said to have been offered the Abpric. of Florence, but to have declined it in order to devote himself wholly to his art. His greatest artistic talents lay in his use of brilliant colour and his powers of decoration.

L. Douglas, *Fra Angelico* (London, 1902); J. Pope-Hennessy, *Fra Angelico* (London, 1952).

ANGELS OF THE CHURCHES.

The seven angels of the Churches of *Ephesus, Smyrna, Pergamum, Thyatira, Sardis, Philadelphia, and Laodicea mentioned in Rev. 1–3. To whom or what is the reference is much disputed. If the angels are men they may be bishops occupying their sees; if not, they are perhaps the spiritual protectors of the respective churches.

H. M. Gwatkin in *H.D.B.*, i (1900), col. 97, s.v.; W. M. Ramsay, *The Letters to the Seven Churches of Asia* (1904), pp. 69–72.

ANGELUS.

In the W. Church, the devotion consisting in the repetition thrice daily (early morning, noon, and evening) of three *Ave Marias with *versicles and a *collect as a memorial of the Incarnation. A bell is rung three times for each Ave and nine times for the collect. The name comes from the first word of the opening versicle in the Latin. During *Eastertide its place is taken by a devotion beginning with the verse, 'Regina coeli laetare, alleluia'. Its history is obscure. The use of a similar devotion, recited at night to a bell, was adopted in Germany in the 13th cent. The morning Angelus first appears in the 14th cent., while the earliest evidence for the midday Angelus is from the 15th cent. The devotion did not come into general use until the 17th cent. The evening Angelus bell is commonly known in Italy as the 'Ave Maria'.

H. Thurston, S.J., 'Our Popular Devotions', Sect. v: 'The Angelus', in *The Month*, xcviii (1901), pp. 483–99, 607–16; xcix (1902), pp. 61–73, 518–32; also c (1902), p. 89 f. T. Esser, O.P., 'Geschichte des englischen Grusses' in *Hist. J.*, v (1884), pp. 88–116; id., 'Das Ave-Maria-Läuten und der "Engel des Herrn" in ihrer geschichtlichen Entwickelung', ib., xxiii (1902), pp. 22–51, 247–69, 775–825. Hefele-Leclercq, v (2; 1913), Appendice IV, 'Sur la salutation angélique prescrite par le canon 7 du Concile de Béziers en 1246', pp. 1734–59. U. Berlière in *D.T.C.*, i (pt. i; 1903), cols. 1273–7, s.v. 'Angélique (Salutation)'; H. Thurston, S.J., in *Dict. Sp.*, i (1937), col. 1164 f., s.v. 'Ave Maria', both with bibl.

ANGELUS SILESIUS (1624–77), **(Johannes Scheffler)**, mystical poet and controversialist. The son of a Lutheran Polish noble, he became (*c.* 1649) court physician to the Duke of Oels, in Silesia. In 1653 he became a RC, and thenceforward devoted his time and energies to writing. In 1661 he was ordained priest. His chief fame lies in his mystical poems, published under the titles of *Heilige Seelenlust* (1657) and *Der Cherubinische Wandersmann* (1675; 1st ed. with different title, 1657). The former interprets the spiritual life with the imagery of the Song of Solomon; the latter was written under the deep influence of *Eckhart. He also began in 1663 a series of 55 controversial tracts in which he attacked various Christian sects. Some of these were collected in his *Ecclesiologia* (1677).

Editions of his works by H. L. Held (3 vols., 1921; ed. 2, 1924) and G. Ellinger (2 vols. [1924]). J. E. C. Flitch, *Angelus Silesius* (selected Eng. translations, 1932).

ANGLICAN AND EASTERN CHURCHES ASSOCIATION. A body founded in 1906 to pray and work for the reunion of the Eastern Orthodox Churches and the Anglican Communion. Its original name was the 'Anglican and Eastern Orthodox Churches Union'.

ANGLICAN CHANT. The music of the Psalms, as widely used in the Anglican Communion. It consists of a tune in barred music, harmonized, in which the first part of each half-verse is sung on a reciting note, and the concluding words fitted to a tune in metrical rhythm. It developed out of the plainchant psalm-tones about the end of the 17th cent., harmony and more rigid time being introduced; and it became widely popular about the middle of the 19th, when parish churches began to copy the choral services of cathedrals. In the 20th cent. a movement began to adapt the Anglican chant to a less rigid time, in order to avoid distortion of the words, and various methods, such as rearrangements of verses, the use of speech-rhythm, &c., have been employed to this end; but no wholly satisfactory plan has yet been devised. The Anglican chant is still very widely used, but there has been, since the middle of the 19th cent., a parallel revival of *plainchant.

R. *Bridges in *P.B.D.* (1912), pp. 171–81, s.vv. 'Chant Anglican' and 'Chanting'; C. S. Phillips, *The Singing Church* (1945), pp. 112 f. and 201–10.

ANGLICAN COMMUNION, The. The Church in communion with, and recognizing the leadership of, the see of *Canterbury, whether in England or abroad. It consists of the *Church of England (the only part still retaining State Establishment), the Church of *Ireland, the Church in *Wales, the Episcopal Church in *Scotland, the *Protestant Episcopal Church in the U.S.A., the Church of Pakistan, *India, *Burma, and *Ceylon, the *Canadian Church, the Church of the *W. Indies, the *Australian Church, the Church of *New Zealand, the Church of the Province of *S. Africa, the Province of W. Africa, the Nippon Sei Ko Kwai (*Japan), and various missionary dioceses under the Abp. of Canterbury's direct jurisdiction. Communication with Anglican dioceses in China was practically cut off by the rise of Communism, and their position is uncertain.

For the first 250 years after the *Reformation, the Anglican Communion, except for the Episcopal Church in Scotland (disestablished from the days of *William III), consisted solely of the State Church of England, Ireland, and Wales. Efforts to found sees in the colonies were hindered by supposed legal objections, and priests working there, who were for the most part state chaplains rather than missionaries, were placed under the jurisdiction of the Bp. of *London. In 1784 the Scottish bishops accepted an invitation to consecrate S. *Seabury as the first bishop of the American Church, and after an Act (26 Geo. III, *c.* 84[2]) had been passed in 1786 which made possible the consecration in England of bishops for sees abroad, three more American bishops were consecrated by the English Archbishops in 1787. The Protestant Episcopal Church of the United States thus came into being as an autonomous body in full communion with Canterbury, and in 1789 produced its own revised edition of the BCP.

Meanwhile in 1787 the first Bp. of Nova Scotia (C. Inglis) was consecrated, with jurisdiction over British N. America, and new sees were shortly afterwards set up in this area. In 1814, T. F. *Middleton was consecrated the first Bp. of Calcutta, a diocese later extended to cover India, Ceylon, the E. Indies, and New S. Wales, but soon divided by the creation of the sees of Madras (1835) and Bombay (1837), and the appointment of W. Broughton as first Bp. of Australia in 1836. The diocese of New Zealand was set up in 1841, with G. A. *Selwyn as its first bishop.

In the same year the Colonial Bishoprics' Council, through the efforts of C. J. *Blomfield, Bp. of London, was formed and a great increase in the number of overseas bishoprics followed. Provincial organization began in 1835, when the Bp. of Calcutta became Metropolitan of India; it was extended to Australia in 1847, to S. Africa in 1853, to New Zealand in 1858, and to Canada in 1860. During the same period diocesan and provincial synods began to meet, and towards the end of the 19th cent. the title of Abp. was assumed by some of the metropolitans. In 1855 for the first time an Anglican (non-U.S.) bishop was consecrated outside the British Isles. Gradually complete independence both of the state and of the jurisdiction of Canterbury was secured by those dioceses with provincial organization. Other dioceses, though free from state establishment, depend directly upon Canterbury, and are subject to the Abp. of Canterbury's jurisdiction. The Church of Ireland was disestablished in 1869, that in Wales in 1920, and the Church of India in 1928. Outside the British Empire a few Anglican sees have been founded, (e.g.) in China and Japan (where English, Canadian, and American missions work together); in *Jerusalem, Iran, and Egypt; and in scattered places elsewhere, e.g. Madagascar. The diocese of Gibraltar includes Anglican chaplaincies in S. Europe.

Anglican bishops meet periodically as a body at the *Lambeth Conference (q.v.) which was instituted in 1867 by Abp. C. T. *Longley. The conference cannot legislate or make decisions in the name of the Church, but its published reports indicate the opinions of the contemporary Anglican episcopate as a whole.

H. Lowther Clarke, *Constitutional Church Government in the Dominions beyond the Seas and in other Parts of the Anglican Communion* (1924). J. W. C. Wand (ed.), *The Anglican Communion.* A Survey (1948). For current information see *The Official Year Book of the Church of England.* The Eucharistic rites of the various branches of the Anglican Communion are collected in B. [J.] Wigan (ed.), *The Liturgy in English* (1962).

ANGLICAN EVANGELICAL GROUP MOVEMENT.

An association of the Anglican clergy and laity holding *Liberal Evangelical views. The movement originated in 1906 as a private body with the title of the 'Group Brotherhood', led by J. C. Wright (then Canon of Manchester), F. S. Guy Warman (then Vicar of Birkenhead, later Bp. of Manchester), and J. E. Watts-Ditchfield (then Vicar of St. James - the - less, Bethnal Green, later Bp. of Chelmsford), and arose from the desire of some of the younger Evangelicals to free Evangelicalism from what they regarded as an unduly conservative interpretation of Christianity, to welcome the help of science and criticism in the search for truth, and to infuse more dignity and beauty into worship. In 1923 the movement adopted its present title and became public, with Canon V. F. Storr (d. 1940) as its chief leader. Its members are pledged to study the social and economic implications of the Gospel, and to work for effective unity among all Christian people. Its activities include group study and the holding of retreats and conventions, esp. an annual conference which for many years met at Cromer, for the deepening of spiritual life.

T. G. Rogers (ed.), *Liberal Evangelicalism.* By Members of the Church of England (1923).

ANGLICAN ORDINATIONS.

Until the subject was removed from the sphere of public discussion in the RC Church by *Leo XIII's Bull '*Apostolicae Curae' (1896), there was diversity of opinion in that Communion on the *validity of the Orders of *Bishop, *Priest, and *Deacon conferred by the Reformation *Ordinals of the C of E. The grounds on which their validity has been and is attacked fall into two classes: (a) Attacks on the actual historical continuity by the laying-on of hands. These usually assert either that Abp. M. *Parker was not himself consecrated or that his principal consecrator, W. *Barlow, had not been consecrated. Only rarely is either of these theses nowadays maintained by scholars; and even if the succession had been lost with Parker, it would have been restored with W. *Laud from whom the present English episcopate derives, and who was consecrated by bishops, some of whom were in the undisputed Irish and Italian successions. (b) Attacks on the sufficiency of the *Ordinal introduced under *Edward VI. These have been of two kinds: (1) Assertions that the omission of the *porrectio instrumentorum* (see *Instruments, Tradition of the*) and other ceremonies renders the rite invalid. The recognition that such ceremonies were not in use in the early Church has led this objection to be abandoned. (2) The arguments of Leo XIII that the *intention of the Anglican Church as expressed in the rite is defective because there are no acts or words explicitly conferring the power for priests to offer sacrifice, and that the acts and words formerly used for this purpose were omitted by the Reformers. To this charge the Abps. of Canterbury and York replied in an Encyclical Letter, dated 29 Mar. 1897, in which they argued that the Anglican Church makes it clear that she intends to confer the Office instituted by Christ and all that it contains; they contended that the C of E teaches the doctrine of the *Eucharistic Sacrifice in terms at least as explicit as those of the *Canon of the Roman Mass; and finally they pointed out that the words and acts required by the Pope are not found in the earliest Roman Ordinals, so that if their omission renders an Ordination invalid, the Orders of the Church of Rome are on no surer footing than those of the C of E. It has also been made a ground of complaint against the Edwardine Ordinal that the *formulae* for the Ordination of bishop and priest are the same, 'Accipe Spiritum Sanctum'; but to this objection it is replied that the intention to distinguish between the two is sufficiently expressed in the existence of two separate services, the contents of the services themselves, and the Preface to the Ordinal.

The validity of Anglican Orders has been recognized by the *Old Catholics, and many parts of the Eastern Orthodox Church hold that they are as valid as those of the RC Church.

Besides the official documents mentioned, there were several important pamphlets issued by the Church Historical Society (S.P.C.K.) publ. *c.* 1896. E. Denny–T. A. *Lacey, *De Hierarchia Anglicana Dissertatio Apologetica* (1895); T. A. Lacey, *A Roman Diary and other Documents* (1910); Viscount *Halifax, *Leo XIII and Anglican Orders* (1912); G. *Dix, *The Question of Anglican Orders* (1944); C. Androutsos, *The Validity of English Ordinations from an Orthodox Catholic Point of View* (1909); C. Papadopoulos, *The Validity of Anglican Ordinations* (Eng. tr., 1931); L. Marchal in *D.T.C.*, xi, 2 (1932), with bibl.

ANGLICANISM. This word properly applies to the system of doctrine and practice upheld by those Christians who are in religious communion with the see of *Canterbury. But it is esp. used, in a somewhat more restricted sense, of that system in so far as it emphasizes its claim to possess a religious outlook distinguishable from that of other Christian communions both Catholic and Protestant. The original formulation of Anglican principles is to be sought in the reign of *Elizabeth rather than in that of *Henry VIII or *Edward VI, for it was under her that a *via media between the opposing factions of *Rome and *Geneva became a political necessity and Anglicanism as a doctrinal system came into existence. Its formularies, in what is substantially their present form, also date from Elizabeth's reign, and the Elizabethan BCP was the focus of the controversies of the 17th cent., the subsequent alterations in the Book being of little theological significance.

The 17th cent., however, was the golden age of Anglicanism, and in the lives and writings of L. *Andrewes, W. *Laud, A. *Sparrow, H. *Thorndike, T. *Ken, and many others, often known collectively as the 'Caroline Divines', the Church of England at once confirmed her rejection of the claims of Rome and refused to adopt the theological system of the Continental reformers. The historic episcopate was preserved, even though many, e.g. R. *Hooker (the greatest of the Elizabethans), did not regard it as of divine institution. The legitimacy, and to some degree, even the necessity, of ecclesiastical development was not denied, but its extent was held to be limited by the appeal to Scripture, as containing all things necessary to eternal salvation. Truth was therefore to be sought from the joint testimony of Scripture and ecclesiastical authority, which in its turn was to be based on the traditions of the first four centuries.

At the Restoration of 1660 the school of W. *Laud (d. 1645) triumphed; but its influence was partly lost to the Church by the secession in 1690 of the *Nonjurors (one archbishop, six bishops, about four hundred of the clergy, and the indeterminate number of lay people who adhered to them), which deprived her of many successors of the men who had shaped her formularies and defended her claim to be something more than a product of the Reformation. From the point of view of historic Anglicanism the loss was the more serious as it took place at a time when the C of E needed all her resources of learning and piety to resist the secular learning of the oncoming 18th cent. Though the attacks of the *Deists and rationalists were in fact repelled, Anglicanism was in decline until the rise of the *Oxford Movement. The *Evangelical Revival did much to renew the spiritual life of the Church, but its ideals departed from those of the traditional ethos of the C of E though Evangelicals have continued to form a large party in the Church. In the 18th cent. Evangelicalism also took little account of the intellectual atmosphere of its age. It was the leaders of the *Oxford Movement who advanced once more, and, indeed, often went beyond, the claims of the Caroline Divines. As the influence of the Movement extended it was in some measure affected by the *Ultramontanism which in the 19th cent. triumphed in the RC Church. In England it issued in a tendency to minimize the distinctive features of the national Church in the endeavour to secure for her a fuller participation in the life of Catholic Christendom at large. On the other hand, the C of E tolerated, esp. in the later years of the 19th cent. and the earlier years of the 20th, a considerable infiltration of *Liberalism.

P. E. More–F. L. Cross, *Anglicanism.* The Thought and Practice of the Church of England illustrated from the Religious Literature of the Seventeenth Century (1935). A. C. *Headlam, *The Church of England* (1924); H. H. *Henson, *The Church of England* (1939); C. M. Ady, *The English Church* (1940); A. T. P. Williams, *The Anglican Tradition in the Life of England* (1947); C. F. Garbett, *The Claims of the Church of England* (1947). F. M. Powicke, *The Reformation in England* (1941); J. H. Overton, *Life in the English Church, 1660–1714* (1885); S. C. Carpenter, *Church and People, 1789–1889* (1933). The ethos and spirit of recent Anglicanism can be studied in biographies, *e.g.* of A. C. *Tait, E. W. *Benson, M. *Creighton, R. T. *Davidson, C. *Gore, C. G. *Lang, W. *Temple, and H. H. Henson. J. W. C. Wand, *Anglicanism in History and Today* (1961).

ANGLO-CATHOLIC CONGRESSES. A series of congresses held in London in 1920, 1923, 1927, 1930, and 1933, to further the cause of *Anglo-Catholicism. A later Congress on a more limited scale was held in London in 1948.

Reports issued after each Congress, the first ed. by D. *Stone (1920).

ANGLO - CATHOLICISM. The modern name of the more advanced section of the *High Church movement in the C of E. From 1838, when the word first appears, its employment became general. (The *Tractarian designation of their series of reprints of 17th cent. divines as the 'Library of Anglo-Catholic Theology' [1841 ff.] has often led to the erroneous supposition that the word 'Anglo-Catholic' was much older; the Lat. *Anglo-Catholicus,* however, occurs in the 17th cent.) Anglo-Catholics emphasize the dogmatic and sacramental aspects of the Christian Creed and life, and the historic continuity of the existing C of E with that of the Middle Ages; and they have generally wished to establish as close an agreement as was possible without sacrifice of essential principles between the doctrine and practice of the C of E and those of the other Churches of Catholic Christendom. Like other High Churchmen, they have always maintained that their principles alone rightly express the faith of the C of E.

W. L. Knox, O.G.S., *The Catholic Movement in the Church of England* (1923); D. *Stone, *The Faith of an English Catholic* (1926).

ANGLO-SAXON CHURCH. By this title is meant the Church in England from the end of the 6th cent. to the Norman Conquest (1066). During the 6th and 7th cents. England was being evangelized from two sides.

In 597 the Roman mission of St. *Augustine landed at Thanet in the south and sees were quickly set up at *Canterbury, *London, *Rochester, and *York. In the north, the Celtic St. *Aidan established himself at *Lindisfarne c. 635. For a time the work of the missions was hindered by disputes over differences in such customs as the date of observing Easter and the cutting of the *tonsure. But in 664 union between north and south was virtually achieved at the Synod of *Whitby, and in 669 *Theodore of Tarsus arrived as Abp. of Canterbury and began his great work of reform and organization. Further important synods of the English bishops were held at *Hertford in 673 and *Hatfield in 680, and many new dioceses were formed. In 787, at a synod presided over by two papal legates, *Lichfield was made an archbishopric, but the arrangement lasted for only sixteen years. The Danish invasions were a great blow to the Church, although the victory of *Alfred secured the nominal acceptance of Christianity by the invaders. In the 10th cent., reforms were initiated by St. *Dunstan and a closer connexion with the Continent established. At the Norman Conquest, most of the surviving Anglo-Saxon bishops were removed, but the most outstanding of them, St. *Wulfstan, continued at *Worcester till his death in 1095.

Monasticism was very strong in the Anglo-Saxon Church, most of the work of evangelization being done by monks, and it is to this period that we may trace the origin of the English custom of having cathedrals with monastic chapters. Double monasteries of men and women, often under the rule of an abbess, were not uncommon during the period, but most of them had disappeared by the Conquest. The connexion between Church and State was particularly close. The conversion of a district usually began in the royal palace; bishoprics were conterminous with tribal areas; and it is very often difficult to decide whether a particular assembly was primarily ecclesiastical or secular. In some of these respects, however, the Anglo-Saxon Church did not differ from many Continental Churches of the time. Despite a popular belief to the contrary, relations between the Anglo-Saxon Church and the rest of W. Christendom seem to have been constant and good.

W. *Bright, Chapters of Early English Church History (3rd ed., 1897); W. Hunt, The English Church from its Foundation to the Norman Conquest (1899); R. H. Hodgkin, A History of the Anglo-Saxons (2 vols., 1935); F. M. Stenton, Anglo-Saxon England (1943). Margaret Deanesly, The Pre-Conquest Church in England (1961); id., Sidelights on the Anglo-Saxon Church (1962); J. Godfrey, The Church in Anglo-Saxon England (1962).

ANIMA CHRISTI (Lat., 'Soul of Christ'), the well-known prayer, beginning

Soul of Christ, sanctify me,
Body of Christ, save me,

used esp. as a private Eucharistic devotion. From its use at the outset of the *Spiritual Exercises it has been traditionally ascribed to St. *Ignatius Loyola ('Aspirationes S. Ignatii ad Sanctissimum Redemptorem'), but is really very

much older. It appears to date from the early 14th cent. (not 12th cent., as L. Eisenhofer). John XXII (d. 1334; probably not its author, despite G. M. Dreves) enriched it with indulgences. Early occurrences of it are in the Brit. Mus. MS. Harl. 1260, f. 158 (A.D. 1370); a prayer-book of Card. Peter of Luxembourg (d. 1387), preserved at *Avignon; and on an inscription of Moorish workmanship on the gates of the Alcazar at Seville (c. 1364).

H. Thurston, S.J., 'The Anima Christi' in Month, cxxv (1915), pp. 493–505; repr. in his Familiar Prayers, ed. P. Grosjean, S.J. (1953), ch. iii, pp. 38–53. D. Prideaux, O.S.B., 'A Note on the Prayer "Anima Christi"' in Laudate, i (1923), pp. 9–21. H. L. Pass, Anima Christi. A Little Treatise on the Spiritual Life (1934), esp. pp. 293–302. P. Schepens, 'Pour l'histoire de la prière Anima Christi' in Nouvelle Revue théologique, lxii (1935), pp. 699–710. H. Thurston, S.J., in Dict. Sp., i (1937), cols. 670–2, s.v., with further bibl.

ANIMISM. The belief, widespread among primitive peoples, that certain material objects, e.g. trees and stones, are possessed by spirits which are the cause of their movements and characteristic qualities. Echoes of animism are found in the OT, e.g. *Jacob's treatment of the stone at Bethel as if it were divine (Gen. 28. 22). Anti-Christian writers have sometimes held all worship of a personal god, particularly if connected with special holy places, to be a survival of primitive animism; while the Christian need not deny that in early times animistic ideas assisted, e.g. the growth of such beliefs as *immortality.

E. B. Tylor, Primitive Culture (2 vols., 1871), chs. xi-xvii. G. d'Alviella in H.E.R.E., i (1908), pp. 535–7, s.v. See also bibl. to Anthropology.

ANNA COMNENA (b. 1083; d. after 1148). The daughter of the Emperor Alexius I, Comnenus, and Irene, she was one of the earliest women historians and among the most outstanding writers of the Byzantine age. Having conspired unsuccessfully after her father's death to depose her brother, John, in the interests of her husband, Nicephorus Bryennius, she retired to a convent where she wrote a history of her father's reign, the 'Alexiad' ('Αλεξιάς). This work, finished in 1148, is less a history than an apology or panegyric, being full of extravagant adulation and almost devoid of critical judgement. It is, however, of great interest as a representation of the Orthodox hostility to the W. Church and to the *Crusades as a menace to the E. Empire. She praises Alexius's persecution of the *Bogomil heretics which culminated in the execution of Basilius, their leader.

The best edns. of the Alexiad are those of A. Reifferscheid, 2 vols., Teubner, 1884) and B. Leib (3 vols., 1937–45; with Fr. trans.). Eng. trans. of the Alexiad by E. A. S. Dawes (1928). G. Buckler, Anna Comnena (1929).

ANNAS. The Jewish *High priest from A.D. 6 (or 7) to 15. In the latter year he was deposed by the procurator, Valerius Gratus, and succeeded by his son-in-law, *Caiaphas, though, as appears from Lk. 3. 2, Jn. 18. 13, and Acts 4. 6, he continued to be regarded as having at least a share in his former office, and was perhaps regarded by strict Jews as the lawful High Priest. Acc. to Jn. 18. 13, Jesus, after His arrest, was first brought to Annas and had a preliminary trial in his palace before being sent on to Caiaphas. In Acts 4. 6 he takes a leading part in the trial of the Apostles at Jerusalem.

ANNATES (Lat. *annatae*, from *annus*, 'year'.) The first year's revenue of an ecclesiastical benefice, paid to the Papal curia. The practice became general through the increase of direct Papal nomination to livings in the 13th cent. The actual term 'annata' was at first applied only to the tax paid upon minor benefices, but in the 15th cent. it came to be used also of the 'servitia' paid on bishoprics and the headships of monasteries. The payment of annates from English benefices to the Holy See was conditionally restrained in 1532 and transferred to the crown in 1534 under the Annates Statute (25 Hen. VIII, *c.* 20). They were finally converted into '*Queen Anne's Bounty' in 1704.

W. E. Lunt, *Papal Revenues in the Middle Ages* (New York, 2 vols., 1934), esp. vol. i, pp. 93–9, and vol. ii, pp. 315–72, with full reff. J. P. Kirsch in *C.E.*, i (1907), p. 537 f., with bibl.

ANNE, St., Mother of the BVM. Her name (not found in the Bible) and the legend of her life occur already in the *Protevangelium of James (2nd cent.). A church was erected at *Constantinople in her honour by the Emp. *Justinian I (d. 565) and relics and pictures at *Rome (S. Maria Antiqua) date from the 8th cent. In the 10th cent. her feast was observed at Naples and it was widely current in the W. by 1350. Urban VI expressly ordered it for all England, to popularize the marriage of Richard II to Anne of Bohemia (Jan. 1382). By the end of the Middle Ages the cult had become extremely popular and was an object of special attack by M. *Luther and other Reformers. In 1584 it was ordered for the Universal Church, and Gregory XV even made it a *Feast of Obligation. The feast is now observed with esp. devotion in *Canada and also in Brittany (of which country she is Patroness). Feast day in the W., 26 July; in the E., 25 July.

The primary source is the Protevangelium Jacobi, i–viii. B. Kleinschmidt, O.F.M., *Die heilige Anna, ihre Verehrung in Geschichte, Kunst und Volkstum* (Forschungen zur Volkskunde, 1930). H. M. Bannister, 'The Introduction of the Cultus of St. Anne into the West' in *E.H.R.*, xviii (1903), pp. 107–12. Further study of the cult by P. V. Charland, O.P. (Quebec, 1904).

ANNE (1665–1714), Queen of Great Britain and Ireland. She was the second daughter of *James II, but was brought up as an Anglican, and in 1702 succeeded her brother-in-law, *William III, her brother, James, being excluded from the succession as a RC. Her political views varied during her reign, but in religious matters she remained consistently true to the *High Church tradition of her grandfather, *Charles I. Early in her reign (1704) she created for the Church '*Queen Anne's

Bounty'. She attempted, by exercise of her right of nominating bishops, to introduce a High Church and Tory element on the Bench, which at her accession was composed almost entirely of Whigs and *Latitudinarians, out of sympathy with the predominantly High Church inferior clergy. She strongly supported the *Occasional Conformity Bill, first introduced into Parliament in 1702, to end the scandal of Dissenters' qualifying for public office by occasional communion in their parish churches; but the bill was not passed till the end of her reign, when there was a decided Tory majority in the Commons. In 1710 she was present at the trial of H. *Sacheverell, which achieved the discomfiture of the Whigs at the ensuing elections, and she was thought by the general public to be a strong supporter of the accused. The Tory ascendancy of 1711–14 was used for political measures against Dissent (such as the *Schism Act of 1714), instead of constructive enactments, and it did not long survive the Queen's death. Though the power of the Latitudinarian party in the Church, dominant at her accession, was somewhat checked during her reign and the Caroline High Church tradition revived, the success of her policy was weakened by the effects of the secession of the *Nonjurors, as well as by the political incompetence of the Tory party, who alone gave it active support. In the next reign it was almost destroyed by the association of High Churchmanship with *Jacobitism.

Beatrice C. Brown (ed.), *The Letters and Diplomatic Instructions of Queen Anne* (1935). *The Life of Her Late Majesty Queen Anne* (anon., 2 vols., 1721). A. Boyer, *The History of the Reign of Queen Anne* (11 vols., 1703–13). G. M. Trevelyan, *England under Queen Anne* (3 vols., 1930–1934). Studies by Agnes Strickland ('Lives of the Queens of England', xi, 1847, pp. 341–440 and xii, 1848), H. Paul (London, 1906), 'L. Melville' (pseud. for L. S. Benjamin, London, 1930), M. R. Hopkinson (London, 1934), and N. Connell (London, 1937).

ANNE'S BOUNTY, Queen. See *Queen Anne's Bounty*.

ANNEXED BOOK, The. A name given to the actual BCP annexed to the Act of *Uniformity of 1662, which prescribed the use throughout the realm of 'true and perfect copies' of it. The MS. original was a fair copy made from the 'Convocation Book' (i.e. the text finally approved by Convocation in 1661), which was signed by the members of Convocation, and then presented to Parliament.

A *Facsimile of the BCP signed by Convocation, Dec. 20, 1661, and attached to the Act of Uniformity, 1662*, was publ. in 1891.

ANNIHILATIONISM. See *Conditional Immortality*.

ANNO DOMINI (Lat.), 'in the year of the Lord'. The current system of dating by 'A.D.', based on the supposed year of the Birth of Christ, was devised by *Dionysius Exiguus (d. *c.* 550). It is now commonly held that the actual Birth was several years earlier, between 7 and 4 B.C., since it is established that Herod the Great died (cf. Mt. 2. 19) in the latter year.

Some authorities, however, have preferred the date A.D. 6, the date usually given to the great taxing under Quirinius (Lk. 2. 1 f.). See also *Chronology* (Biblical).

ANNUNCIATION OF THE BVM. The

feast, observed on 25 Mar. ('Lady Day'), commemorates the announcement of the Incarnation by the angel *Gabriel to the Virgin and the conception of Christ in her womb (Lk. 1. 26–38). The date depends on that of Christ's Nativity (25 Dec.), itself not fixed until a comparatively late period in Christian history. The homilies of the Patr. *Proclus of Constantinople may imply its observance in the E. *c.* 430, but the first authentic reference to the festival in the W. is in the *Gelasian Sacramentary. In the Acts of the Council *in *Trullo* (692) it is exempted from the ban on feasts in *Lent, while in Spain the observance was long kept on 18 Dec., to prevent its occurrence in Lent. By the 8th cent. its observance in the W. had become universal. In the BCP it is a '*red letter' day and in the Table of Proper Lessons is described as the 'Annunciation of Our Lady', the only place where the Book uses this title of the Virgin.

St. *Bernard's famous Homilies 'Super *Missus Est*' are repr. in J. P. Migne, *PL*, clxxxiii, 55–88. On the Lucan narrative see O. *Bardenhewer, 'Maria Verkündigung: ein Kommentar' in *Biblische Studien*, x (1905), pp. 449–621. On the spread of the Feast, S. Vailhé, A.A., 'Origines de la fête de l'Annonciation' in *É.O.*, ix (1906), pp. 138–45; M. Jugie, A.A., 'La Première Fête mariale en Orient et en Occident: l'avent primitif' in ib., xxvi (1923), pp. 130–52. I. Cecchetti, 'L' Annunciazione. Il racconto biblico e la festa liturgica' in *Bolletino Ceciliano*, xxxviii (1943), pp. 46–8 and 98–114.

ANOINTING. A ceremonial action per-

formed on persons and things to separate them from profane use and obtain on their behalf the infusion of Divine grace. The ceremonial use of oil is common to many religions, e.g. Hinduism, the worship of ancient Greece and Rome, and many primitive peoples. In the OT priests and kings are anointed to symbolize their sanctity and endowment with the Spirit of God; hence the future deliverer of Israel was designated the 'Messiah' or 'Anointed One', and this title was taken over by the Apostles and appears in the NT in its Greek form 'Christ' (Χριστός). In the NT anointing is used as a charismatic means of healing (e.g. Mk. 6. 13) and combined with prayer in Jas. 5. 14 (see *Unction*). The Church from early times made sacramental use of it in the rites of *Baptism, *Confirmation, and *Ordination (qq.v.) as well as in the consecration of churches, altars, bells, &c. The anointing of kings, which is first met with in the 7th cent., was influenced immediately by the OT (see *Coronation*).

A. Macalister in *H.D.B.*, i (1898), pp. 100–2, s.v.; F. *Cabrol, O.S.B., in *D.A.C.L.*, vi (pt. 2; 1925), cols. 2777–91, s.v. 'Huile'; W. Deinhardt in *L.Th.K.*, ix (1937), col. 111 f., s.v. 'Salbung', all with bibl. See also bibl. to *Chrism*.

ANOMOEANS. The extreme *Arians of

the 4th cent., so called from their doctrine that the Son was totally unlike (ἀνόμοιος) the

Father. Their leaders were *Aetius and *Eunomius. They were also known as 'Aetians and '*Exoucontians'.

ANSCHAR, St. See *Anskar, St.*

ANSELM, St. (*c.* 1033–1109), Abp. of

*Canterbury. He was the son of a Lombard landowner and a native of Aosta. After several years of undisciplined life he crossed the Alps into *France in 1056 and in 1059 entered the monastic school at *Bec in Normandy, then directed by *Lanfranc of Pavia, his fellow-countryman. Here he was persuaded by Lanfranc and Mauritius, Abp. of Rouen, to take monastic vows (1060) and in 1063 he succeeded Lanfranc as prior. His strong character and remarkable intellectual abilities gained him a high reputation as a teacher and spiritual director. His principal writings, the *Monologium*, the *De Veritate*, the *De Libero Arbitrio*, the *De Casu Diaboli*, the *Proslogium* (but acc. to D. Knowles, written when he was Abp. of Canterbury) and the *Liber Apologeticus pro Insipiente*, all appear to date from the Bec period. When Abbot Herluin died in 1078, Anselm succeeded to the Abbacy of Bec. From now on he paid several visits to England, where he renewed his acquaintance with Lanfranc and won the respect of William I and many of the barons. On Lanfranc's death (1089) it was the general wish of the English clergy that Anselm should succeed to the primacy; but his refusal to compromise the spiritual independence of the office led Rufus to withhold his consent and only when the king was gravely ill at *Gloucester (1093) did Anselm finally leave Bec for his see. On Rufus' recovery, conflict between King and Archbishop broke out again, technically over the question of the recognition of Pope *Urban II (against the Imperial anti-Pope Wibert, who had Rufus' support), but in fact over the spiritual rights of the Church. Despite the pleadings of barons and bishops, Anselm refused to submit at the Council of Rockingham in 1095. His courageous stand won over the barons, while the King agreed to acknowledge Urban, but still hoped that Anselm would resign, or at least consent to receive the *pallium from his hands. On Anselm's refusal, other charges were fabricated against him and in 1097 he left the country and made his way to Urban at Rome. To this period belongs his famous study on the *Atonement, the *Cur Deus Homo?* In 1098 he attended the Council of Bari at Urban's request and defended the *Double Procession against the Greeks with the arguments embodied in his *De Processione Sancti Spiritus*. At a Council at Rome in 1099, he formally recognized the impropriety of lay *investiture. After Rufus' death (2 Aug. 1100), he was recalled to England by Henry I, where he received a warm welcome from the populace; but in his relations with the Crown Anselm stood by his principles, refusing to renew the homage which he had paid to Rufus or to consecrate bishops whom Henry had invested. On the King's refusal to give way, he again went into exile in 1103. The somewhat more tolerant outlook of Urban's successor, Paschal II (1099–1118), helped to resolve the conflict and in 1107 Anselm returned to his see. In his last years he introduced many reforms, encouraging regular synods, enforcing clerical *celibacy and suppressing the slave trade. He also actively supported the creation of the new diocese of *Ely.

Both as theologian and philosopher, Anselm has a foremost place among the earlier Scholastic thinkers. He was the most luminous and penetrating intellect between St. *Augustine and St. *Thomas Aquinas (J. de Ghellinck, S.J.; D. Knowles, O.S.B.). He differed from most of his predecessors in preferring to defend the faith by intellectual reasoning to employing arguments built on Scriptural and other written authorities. The object of his *Monologium* and *De Veritate* was to establish the being of God solely from the consideration of truth and goodness as intellectual notions, without appeal to empirical fact. It led to his equation of God with the *Platonic 'Idea of the Good'. In the *Proslogium* this reasoning was given the more systematic form of the *Ontological Argument (q.v.). Anselm here maintained that if we mean by God (as he held that we do) 'that than which nothing greater can be conceived' (*id quo nihil majus cogitari possit*), then we cannot conceive of this entity except as existing. His *Liber Apologeticus pro Insipiente* was a reply to his objector, Gaunilo, a monk of Marmoutier, who had retorted with the Psalmist's fool 'There is no God' (Ps. 14. 1). Like St. Augustine, Anselm saw in faith the precondition of the right use of reason ('credo ut intelligam'); but it yet remains our duty, so far as we can, to exercise our minds on the apprehension of revealed truth. These Platonic doctrines put Anselm in the front rank of the medieval *Realists and have also made him a forerunner of R. *Descartes. His *Cur Deus Homo?* was the most considerable contribution to the theology of the Atonement in the Middle Ages. It interpreted the doctrine in terms of the satisfaction due to the outraged majesty of God and strongly repudiated the notion, current since *Origen and St. *Gregory of Nyssa, that the devil had rights over fallen man which it was a leading purpose of the Cross to satisfy. He was also the author of many letters, including a correspondence with Gilbert Crispin, Abbot of *Westminster (1085–1117), but there seem no sufficient grounds for believing that the hymns which some modern scholars have attributed to him are his.

Feast day, 21 April. In 1720 he was declared by *Clement XI a 'Doctor of the Church'.

First satisfactory ed. of Anselm's Works that of the *Maurist, G. Gerberon, O.S.B. (Paris, 1675); repr. in J. P. Migne, *PL*, clviii and clix. Crit. ed. by F. S. Schmitt, O.S.B. (begun Seckau, 1938; repr. and continued, Edinburgh, 1946 ff.). Eng. trr. of his 'Devotions' (Proslogion, &c.), ed. C. C. J. *Webb, London, 1903; of *Cur Deus Homo?*, London, 1886; also London, 1889. The chief sources for his Life are the 'Historia Novorum' and 'Vita Anselmi' of

*Eadmer, Anselm's chaplain; crit. edd. by M. Rule, 'Rolls Series', vol. 81, 1884. Modern Lives by R. W. *Church (London, 1870), M. Rule (2 vols., London, 1883), J. M. Rigg (London, 1896). On his philosophy, F. Baeumker, *Die Lehre Anselms von Canterbury über den Willen und seine Wahlfreiheit* (1912); C. C. J. *Webb, *Studies in the History of Natural Theology* (1915), pp. 156–98; C. Filliatre, *La Philosophie d'Anselme de Cantorbéry* (1920); A. Koyré, *L'Idée de Dieu dans la philosophie de St. Anselme* (1923); A. Kolping, *Anselms Proslogion—Beweis der Existenz Gottes* (1939); J. L. Springer, *Argumentum Ontologicum*. Existentieele Interpretatie van het speculatieve Godsbewijs in het Proslogion van S. Anselmus (1947). On his doctrine of the Atonement, E. A. Peloux, *La Doctrine de la rédemption d'après Anselme de Cantorbéry* (1887); L. Heinrichs, *Die Genugtuungstheorie des hl. Anselmus von Canterbury neu dargestellt und dogmatisch geprüft* (1909); G. C. Foley, *Anselm's Theory of the Atonement* (1909). Überweg, pp. 192–203 and 698–700. J. Bainvel in *D.T.C.*, i (1903), cols. 1327–60.

ANSELM OF LAON (d. 1117), 'Laudunensis', theologian. He was educated at *Bec under St. *Anselm of Canterbury. Towards the end of the 11th cent., with the assistance of his brother Radolf, he established a school at Laon, which became famous and attracted such well-known scholars as *William of Champeaux and *Abelard. The theological influence of Anselm was widespread. His teaching was given in commentaries on Books of the Bible, with discussions in elementary *quaestio* form, but no texts are known to survive except a few detached 'Sententiae'. Anselm also played a part in laying the foundations of the standard commentaries on the Bible, later known as the 'Glossa Interlinearis'.

Writings in J. P. Migne, *PL*, clxii, 1187–227 and 1499–593; the *Enarrationes in Evangelium Matthaei* here (cols. 1227–1499) are wrongly assigned to him; his commentary on Matt. survives only in an unpublished MS. at Alençon (cod. 28). F. P. Bliemetzrieder, *Anselms von Leon Systematische Sentenzen* (B.G.P.M., xviii, Hftt. 2–3; 1919), with text. J. de Ghellinck, S.J., 'The Sentences of Anselm of Laon and their Place in the Codification of Theology during the XIIth Century' in *Irish Theological Quarterly*, vi (1911), pp. 427–41. R. Silvain, 'La Tradition des sentences d'Anselme de Laon' in *Archives d'histoire doctrinale et littéraire du moyen-âge* xvi (1948), pp. 1–52. O. Lottin, O.S.B., 'Aux origines de l'école théologique d'Anselme de Laon' in *R.T.A.M.*, x (1938), pp. 101–22; id., 'Nouveaux Fragments théologiques de l'école d'Anselme de Laon', ib., xi (1939), pp. 242–59, 305–23, xii (1940), pp. 49–77, xiii (1946), pp. 202–21, 261–81, xiv (1947), pp. 5–31 and 157–85. M. *Grabmann, *Die Geschichte der scholastischen Methode*, ii (1911), pp. 136–68.

ANSELM OF LUCCA, Pope (d. 1073). See *Alexander II*.

ANSELM OF LUCCA, St. (c. 1036–1086). He is not to be confused with his uncle, *Alexander II (q.v., also 'Anselm of Lucca'), by whom he was nominated to the see of Lucca in 1071. After hesitation he accepted investiture from *Henry IV, but repented, resigned his bishopric, and retired to the *Cluniac monastery at Polirone, near Mantua. Later, at the insistence of *Gregory VII, he returned to his see, where he lived an austere life and sought to impose strict discipline on an unwilling chapter. The resulting friction led to his expulsion by the Emperor and the Antipope, Guibert, c. 1080. In his last years he was Papal Legate in Lombardy. He wrote a treatise against lay investiture ('Contra Guibertum et Sequaces ejus') and made a famous collection of canons, later incorporated in *Gratian's 'Decretum'. Feast day, 18 Mar.

His *Liber contra Guibertum, Collectio Canonum* and extracts from his *Collectanea* are repr. in J. P. Migne, *PL*, cxviii, 445–536; crit. ed. of his *Collectio Canonum* by F. Thaner (Innsbruck, 2 fascc. 1906–11). The principal authority for his life is the Vita attributed to Bardo, *primicerius of Lucca Cathedral; crit. ed. by R. Wilmans in *M.G.H.*, Scriptores, xii (1856), pp. 1–35. There are also two metrical lives, the one by Rangerius, Bp. of Lucca, in 1099, publ. by V. de la Fuente (Madrid, 1870); the other by Donizzio, also practically contemporary, ed. W. Arndt in *M.G.H.*, Scriptores, xx (1868), pp. 692–6. A. Overmann, 'Die *Vita Anselmi Lucensis Episcopi* des Rangerius' in *N.A.*, xxi (1896), pp. 403–40. B. Schmeidler–G. Schwartz, 'Kleine Studien zu den Viten des Bischofs Anselm und zur Geschichte des Investiturstreits in Lucca', ib., xliii (1920), pp. 515–50, esp. pp. 515–43 and 549 f. A. Rota, S.J., *Notizie istoriche di S. Anselmo* (Verona, 1733). R. Montanari, *La 'Collectio Canonum' di S. Anselmo di Lucca e la riforma gregoriana* (Mantua, 1941). A. Amanieu in *D.D.C.*, i (1935), cols. 567–78, s.v. 'Anselme de Lucques (Collection d')'. P. Richard in *D.H.G.E.*, iii (1924), cols. 489–93, s.v. 'Anselme de Lucques'.

ANSKAR, St. (801–65), the 'Apostle of the North'. A native of Picardy, he became a monk at *Corbie. Thence he went to Westphalia, and later to *Denmark whose king had been recently converted. He established a school in Schleswig, but was soon expelled by the local heathen. He then went to *Sweden, where he built the first Christian Church. *C.* 832 he was appointed by Gregory IV Bp. of Hamburg and *c.* 848 first Abp. of Bremen. In 854 he was in Denmark again, converted Erik, King of Jutland, and did much to mitigate the horrors of the slave trade. After his death the Scandinavian countries relapsed completely into paganism. In Germany he is also known as 'St. Scharies'. Feast day, 3 Feb.

The principal authority is the life attributed to Rimbert, his successor in the see of Bremen (crit. ed. by G. Waitz in Scriptores Rerum Germanicarum, 1884; Eng. tr., with introd. notes and bibl., by C. H. Robinson, 1921). W. Levison, 'Die echte und die verfälschte Gestalt von Rimberts Vita Anskarii' in *Zeitschrift des Vereins für Hamburgische Geschichte*, xxiii (1919), pp. 89–146. G. H. Kippel, *Historische Forschungen und Darstellungen*, ii, Lebensbeschreibung des Erzbischofs Ansgar (1845), with text of St. Anskar's 'Pigmenta', pp. 230–50, and other important docc. in appendices. A. Tappehorn, *Leben des heiligen Ansgar, Apostels von Dänemark und Schweden* (1863); E. de Moreau, S.J., *Saint Anschaire* (Museum Lessianum, Section Missiologique, xii; 1930). H. Bihlmeyer, O.S.B., 'Der hl. Ansgar', in *Studien und Mitteilungen aus des Benediktiner und Zisterzienser-Orden*, xxv (1904), pp. 154–72. G. Dehio, *Geschichte des Erzbistums Hamburg-Bremen bis zum Ausgang der Mission*, i (1877), pp. 42–92. G. Allmang in *D.H.G.E.*, iii (1924), cols. 435–41, s.v. 'Anschaire'.

ANSON BY-LAW, The. The law allowing a child to be withdrawn from a primary school during any time allotted to religious observance or instruction if the parent so desires and if arrangement has been made for him to attend religious observance or instruction elsewhere. It was so named after Sir William Reynell Anson (1843–1914), who was Parliamentary Secretary to the Board of Education when the Education Act of 1902 was passed. The Education Act of 1936 made the principles of this By-law everywhere applicable, and similar provision was made by the Act of 1944 (7 & 8 Geo. VI, c. 31, sect. 25).

ANTE-CHAPEL. A small addition westwards in some college chapels which were built on the model of a monastic choir. It is structurally a truncated nave, added to give technical completeness to the building and thus avoid the architectural anomaly of a chancel *in vacuo.*

ANTE-COMMUNION. In the C of E the earlier portion of the service of Holy Communion down to and including the Prayer for the Church Militant, esp. when recited without the remainder of the service. The essential parts of the full rite (offering and consecration of the Bread and Wine and the Communion of the celebrant) being omitted, it is in no sense a real Eucharist. Analogies have been found for it elsewhere in the Mass of the *Presanctified and the 'Dry Mass', but liturgically the only real parallel is the 'Mass of the Catechumens' in the early Church.

ANTELAPSARIANISM. See *Supralapsarianism.*

ANTEPENDIUM. A vesture or *frontal, varying in colour acc. to the ecclesiastical season, which hangs in front of the altar.

ANTHEM. The Anglicized form of the word *antiphon. It was used originally of a hymn sung alternately by two choirs; but in current English it is commonly applied to sacred vocal music set to Scriptural words. In the BCP it has the meanings *antiphon (as in the preface 'Concerning the Service of the Church'), *canticle (so applied to the Easter 'Anthems', e.g., and by implication to Ps. 95), and its usual modern sense. In the Anglican service, the proper place for the anthem is after the third collect at Morning and Evening Prayer, as prescribed by the 1662 rubric at this point.

E. H. Fellowes, *English Cathedral Music from Edward VI to Edward VII* (1941). A. M. Y. Baylay–J. S. Heap–H. Goss-Custard in *P.B.D.* (1925), pp. 25–9, s.v.

ANTHONY, St. See *Antony, St.*

ANTHROPOLOGY. In its more exact sense as used by theologians the study of man as contrasted, e.g., with that of God, or of angels, and more particularly the study 'of his creation, elevation to supernatural status, and his fall' (A. *Tanquerey). It enables the Christian apologist to exhibit the true nature and end of man, and his superior status to the animal creation, as against views which represent him as a purely biological species, or an economic unit, or a mass of psychological reflexes. This, the traditional meaning of the word, has been revived in theological discussion in the present century.

In popular usage, however, esp. since the middle of the 19th cent., the word has been widely used for the science which studies the life and environment of primitive man. So understood, it may be considered to consist of two parts, viz. Physical and Cultural Anthropology. The former relates to man's biological history, and for this branch the most valuable evidence includes the few skeletons and fragments which have by accident escaped disintegration. Among these are the celebrated Java ape-man's calvaria, two molar teeth, and left femur, discovered in 1891–2. Cultural Anthropology, on the other hand, studies the remains of man's handicraft-work and the marks he has made upon his surroundings, in order to gain impressions of his social and cultural history in his primitive development.

(1) In the former sense, the subject finds its place in all manuals of dogmatic theology. See bibl. to *Theology*.

(2) From the large modern literature, the foll. items may be mentioned as historically imp.: J. C. Prichard, *Natural History of Man* (1843); T. H. *Huxley, *Man's Place in Nature* (1863); E. B. Tylor, *Early History of Mankind* (1865); id., *Primitive Culture* (1871); A. de Quatrefages, *Unité de l'espèce humaine* (1867; Eng. tr., 1879), A. H. Keane, *Ethnology* (1896); id., *Man, Past and Present* (1899). Popular acct. in R. R. Marett, *Anthropology* (H.U.L., 1912). R. Munro in *H.E.R.E.*. i (1908), pp. 561–73, and E. J. and E. K. Miller in *Chambers's Encyclopaedia* (1950), i, pp. 453–8, s.v.

ANTHROPOMORPHISM. The attribution to God of human characteristics. This tendency arises out of the conditions of human knowledge which originates in sense perception. In its crudest forms it is most prominent in primitive and polytheistic religions, and from the point of view of Greek philosophy it was already ridiculed by Xenophanes. Scripture, esp. in the earlier books of the OT (e.g. Gen. 3. 8, 32. 24 ff., Exod. 4. 24), in order to be intelligible to less developed minds, frequently uses anthropomorphic language, which is in most cases clearly metaphorical. In Christian philosophy, on the other hand, seemingly anthropomorphic conceptions such as personality, will, &c., are predicated of God, though in a way different from that in which they are used of creatures. Without the use of these or similar modes of expression, any developed exposition of the nature and attributes of God would be impossible.

ANTHROPOSOPHY. A religious system evolved by R. *Steiner (q.v.) from neo-Indian theosophy, but placing man instead of God in its centre. It aims at leading man by a certain discipline of 'concentration' and 'meditation' towards an 'intuition' in which the lower ego receives the vision of the higher self. Anthroposophy teaches a highly elaborated and fantastic doctrine of the origin of the world, the various epochs of mankind, the 'sun being' ('Sonnenwesen') Christ, reincarnation, and 'Karma'. It has found adherents in Germany as well as in Britain and America, esp. among those in search of religious experiences outside the normal channels of Church life. It was condemned by the RC Church in 1919.

G. Kaufmann, *Fruits of Anthroposophy* (1922); H. Leisegang, *Die Grundlagen der Anthroposophie* (1924); A. F. Stolzenburg, *Anthroposophie und Christentum* (1925).

ANTIBURGHER. A member of the group in the Secession Church in Scotland which separated in 1747 from the *'Burgher' group because it refused to admit that an adherent of that Church could take the civil 'Burgess Oath'.

ANTICHRIST. The prince of Christ's enemies. In the NT he is referred to by name only 1 Jn. 2. 18, 22, 4. 3, and 2 Jn. 7 (where he is identified with those who deny the Incarnation). Many see him, however, in the strange beasts of Rev., sometimes thought to represent Rome, and in 'the man of sin' of 2 Thess. 2. 3–10 who will appear after a great apostasy before 'the day of the Lord' and sit in God's sanctuary, claiming to be God, but will be finally slain by Christ. Some have maintained that there was a Jewish Antichrist legend which was adopted and expanded by Christians; others have connected Antichrist not with a person but with an evil principle; yet others have seen in Antichrist a reference to some historical person—*Caligula, *Simon Magus, or *Nero. The attempt of Caligula to set up his statue in the Temple at Jerusalem, and the deification of the Emperor and Emperor-worship, suggested strongly that Antichrist would come from imperial Rome; and the effect of the Neronian persecutions, particularly in view of Rev. 17. 8, 13. 3, and the uncertainty concerning Nero's grave, led men to expect Nero to return from the tomb. Acc. to *Jerome and *Augustine, many believed that St. John the Divine was not dead but sleeping, waiting to testify against *Nero redivivus* as Antichrist. In the 4th cent. Antichrist was sometimes identified with the *Arian heresy, whilst *Cyril of Jerusalem states that he will be a magician who will take control of the Roman Empire, claim to be Christ, deceive the Jews by pretending to be the Son of David and rebuilding the Temple, and who, after persecuting the Christians, will be slain at the Second Advent by the Son of God (*Cat. Lect.* xv.11–15). Since the Reformation, the identification of the Pope with Antichrist has been frequently made, esp. in the less educated circles of Protestantism.

W. *Bousset, *Der Antichrist* (1895; Eng. tr. 1896).

ANTICLERICALISM. A liberal movement in politics and religion which affected many parts of Europe in the 19th cent. Although the movement had roots in the religious indifference and scepticism of the 18th cent., it first became an active political force through the French Revolution. In general, it was opposed to any dogmatic or denominational form of Christianity, maintaining that the established order in Church affairs was simply a bulwark of the political reaction and tyranny which it aimed to overthrow. It directed its attack esp. on the RC Church and its civil privileges. In France the establishment of the RC religion was overthrown in 1792–3, although those of the clergy who were prepared to submit to the directions of the State were otherwise left unmolested; but by the *Concordat of 1801 an agreement was reached between Church and State, which, though not fully implemented until after the fall of Napoleon in 1815, restored the full liberty and ascendancy of Catholicism. But a strong anticlerical party remained, which grew in influence after the revolution of 1871, until finally in 1905 the state ceased to recognize the RC religion, or to grant any privileges to its representatives, while in some respects, e.g. the suppression of certain religious orders, a definitely hostile position was taken up. In *Belgium the revolution of 1830 was the joint work of Catholics and liberals, and the result was that, for some years after the independent monarchy had been set up, these parties, in other countries mutually and actively hostile, agreed to work together. But the arrangement broke down, the liberals gradually gaining the upper hand. In 1884, however, the Catholics won a decisive victory at the elections, and the dominant position they then secured has won their freedom from anticlerical restrictions ever since. In *Spain and *Portugal there were various anticlerical movements between 1830 and 1870, which were concerned chiefly to combat the influence of the papal curia and legates, to secure ecclesiastical appointments to the crown, and to suppress various religious orders; while in Spanish America some of the new republics, on gaining their independence, showed a certain anticlerical bias. Both in Spain and Portugal Church and State came to terms in the latter half of the century, though the revolutions of 1910 in Portugal and 1931 in Spain brought a recrudescence of anticlericalism, as did the establishment of a Communist Government in *Mexico. The growth of the nationalist movement in Italy from c. 1840 to the establishment of the Kingdom of Italy in 1871 went hand in hand with anticlericalism, as the civil Papal state was itself ruled by a reactionary government, which gave active support to the Austro-Hungarian empire and to the local arbitrary rulers; but after 1871 the triumph of the new order led to no strongly anti-ecclesiastical results apart from the suppression of the temporal power of the Vatican, and this was formally restored by the *Lateran Treaty of 1929 within the limits of the Vatican itself, which then became an independent state.

For anticlericalism in France, E. Lecanuet, *L'Église de France sous la Troisième République* (2 vols., 1907–10), esp. vol. ii, ch. 8; E. Faguet, *L'Anticléricalisme* (1906).

ANTIDIDAGMA, The. The reply issued in 1544 by the cathedral chapter of *Cologne to the plan set out by Abp. *Hermann of Wied in his *Consultatio* to reform Catholic practice. It was a moderate restatement of traditional principles and apparently mainly the work of J. Gropper. Its language exercised a certain influence on the BCP of 1549.

The work orig. appeared in German early in 1544 with the title *Christliche und katholische Gegenberichtung eines ehrwürdigen Domcapitals zu Köln wider das Buch der genannten Reformation.* The Lat. version, which followed soon afterwards, had a long title beginning *Antididagma, seu Christianae et Catholicae Religionis per . . . Canonicos Metropolitanae Ecclesiae Colonien. Propugnatio* (Cologne, 1544; repr. Paris 1549). F. E. *Brightman, *The English Rite*, i (1915), p. xlviii f.

ANTILEGOMENA (Gk. τὰ ἀντιλεγόμενα). The word is used by *Eusebius of Caesarea (*H.E.* III, xxv, 3 f.) of those Scriptural books of which the claim to be considered a part

of the NT canon was disputed. He subdivided them into (1) those 'generally recognized' (γνώριμοι), viz. Jas., Jude, 2 Pet., 2 and 3 Jn.; and (2) the 'spurious' (νόθοι), viz. the 'Acts of Paul', the 'Shepherd of *Hermas', the Apoc. of *Peter', the 'Ep. of *Barnabas', the '*Didache', and (perhaps) the 'Rev. of St. John'.

ANTI-MARCIONITE PROLOGUES, The. A set of short introductory prologues, prefixed to the Gospels of Mk., Lk., and Jn. (that to Mt. has presumably been lost), which are contained in some 40 MSS. of the Vulgate. They were written in Greek, but only that to Luke has survived in its original language. D. de Bruyne and A. *Harnack held that they were the earliest of the extant Gospel Prologues, dating from the latter half of the 2nd cent., and thus threw important light on the origins of the Gospels. They are perhaps considerably later.

Text in A. *Huck–H. *Lietzmann–F. L. Cross, *A Synopsis of the First Three Gospels* (Tübingen, 1936), p. viii. D. de Bruyne, O.S.B., 'Les Plus Anciens Prologues latins des évangiles' in *R. Bibl.*, xl (1928), pp. 193–214; A. *Harnack, 'Die ältesten Evangelien-Prologe und die Bildung des Neuen Testaments' in *Sb.* (Berl.), xxiv (1928), pp. 322–41; E. Gutwenger, 'The Anti-Marcionite Prologues' in *Theological Studies*, vii (1946), pp. 393–409. See also J. Quasten, *Patrology*, i (Utrecht, 1953), p. 210 f., with further bibl.

ANTIMINSION also 'Antimension' (Gk. ἀντιμήνσιον, 'instead of a table'). In the E. Church, the portable altar, consisting of a cloth of silk or linen, decorated with representations of the Passion, and usually of the entombment of Christ, and containing relics. It was originally intended for use when there was no properly consecrated altar, but is now always used, even on consecrated altars, in the manner of the Western *corporal, with another and true corporal, the *eileton, on the top of it. It is first met with at about the beginning of the 9th cent.

ANTINOMIANISM. A general name for the view that Christians are by grace set free from the need of observing any moral law. It was attributed to St. *Paul by his opponents (Rom. 3. 8) because of his disparagement of the Mosaic Law in favour of the Law of the New Covenant 'written in the heart' —an internal impulse towards good—and strenuously repudiated by him. The charge of antinomianism was justly made against many of the *Gnostic sects, e.g. the *Nicolaitans and the *Ophites, who held that as matter was so sharply opposed to spirit, bodily actions were indifferent and therefore licentiousness was wholly admissible. At the Reformation, antinomian teaching was revived, e.g. by the *Anabaptists and J. *Agricola, as following from the *Lutheran doctrine of *justification by faith. In England some antinomian sects developed under the Commonwealth.

ANTINOMY. In philosophy, one of a pair of mutually conflicting laws or sequences of thought ('thesis' and 'antithesis'), each of which possesses, or appears to possess, equal validity. In the *Critique of Pure Reason* (1781), I. *Kant elaborated four antinomies, the purpose of which was to show the inconsistencies to which the understanding is driven when it applies itself to philosophical speculation and thus to demonstrate the impossibility of theoretical metaphysics. Their subjects are (1) the spatial and temporal limitations of the physical world; (2) the divisibility of substances; (3) causality and freedom; and (4) the relation of the First Cause to the world.

ANTIOCH. In size and importance, Antioch in Syria was the third city of the Roman Empire. As appears from Acts, a Christian community existed there from almost the earliest days, and it was here that the disciples of Christ were first called 'Christians' (Acts 11. 26). The community strongly supported St. Paul's anti-Judaizing policy. Acc. to tradition, the first bishop of the city was St. *Peter, and by the beginning of the 2nd cent. the Church had a well-established organization, with the celebrated St. *Ignatius as its bishop. From the 4th cent., the see ranked after Rome and Alexandria as the 3rd patriarchial see of Christendom, reaching its greatest extent of jurisdiction at the end of that cent. Gradually, however, the rise in power of the see of *Constantinople, and to a less extent the erection of *Jerusalem into a Patriarchate, reduced the importance of Antioch, and its influence also suffered later from the *Nestorian and *Monophysite schisms (the latter supported by the civil power of the Saracens). At the Great Schism of 1054, the patriarchate supported Constantinople, but in 1100 the Orthodox Patriarch of Antioch withdrew to Constantinople, and the Crusaders appointed a Latin Patriarch. From the 14th cent. the Latin Patriarchate has been only titular. The Orthodox Patriarch now resides at Damascus, the most important city in Syria. Other patriarchs, *Uniat and Monophysite, take the title of Antioch, though these also do not reside there. A small Turkish township now exists on the site, where excavations were carried out by a Franco-American expedition in 1931–9. See also *Antiochene Theology* (below).

M. Lequien, *Oriens Christianus*, ii (Paris, 1740), cols. 669–1076, and iii (ib., 1740), cols. 1153–240. J. M. *Neale, *A History of the Holy Eastern Church*, v, 'The Patriarchate of Antioch' (1873). E. S. Bouchier, *A Short History of Antioch*, 300 B.C.–A.D. 1268 (1921). V. Schultze, *Altchristliche Städte und Landschaften*, iii, 'Antiocheia' (1930). R. Devreesse, *Le Patriarchat d'Antioche depuis la paix de l'Église jusqu'à la conquête arabe* (1945). G. W. Elderkin–R. Stillwell and others, *Antioch-on-the-Orontes* (Publications of the Committee for the Excavation of Antioch and its Vicinity; vols. i–iii (Princeton, etc., 1934–41, on excavations of 1934–9); subsequent vols. 1942 ff.). C. R. Morey, *The Mosaics of Antioch* (1938). C. Karalevskij in *D.H.G.E.*, iii (1924), cols. 563–703, s.v. 'Antioche' with detailed bibl. G. M. Perrella–E. Josi–G. Hofmann, S.J. in *E.C.* i (1949), cols. 1455–60, and A. Raes, S.J.–A. Romeo, ib., cols. 1471–1479, s.v. 'Antioco' with further bibl. G. Downey, *A History of Antioch in Syria from Seleucus to the Arab Conquest* (Princeton, 1961).

ANTIOCH, Council of (341). The 'Dedication Council' ('concilium in encaeniis') held on the occasion of the consecration of *Constantine's 'Golden Church' at *Antioch, was the first of the many 4th cent. councils in which efforts were made to abandon strict *Nicene theology. It was attended by 97 bishops besides the Emp. *Constantius himself. No less than four creeds were put forward, all of them defective from the standpoint of orthodoxy since they were intended not to supplement, but to replace, that of *Nicaea. The 25 (mainly disciplinary) 'Canons of Antioch' preserved in many of the ancient collections, both Greek and Latin, are generally supposed to have been the work of this Council, though some historians (e.g. the *Ballerini, L. *Duchesne, and C. H. *Turner) have argued that they really belong to a Council held at Antioch in 330.

Hardouin, i, cols. 589–610; Mansi, ii (1759) cols. 1305–50. Canons also in Lauchert, pp. 43–50; crit. ed. of Lat. texts in C. H. *Turner, *E.O.M.I.A.*, II, ii (1913), pp. 215–320. Hefele–Leclercq, i (2; 1907), pp. 702–33. E. *Schelstrate, *Sacrum Antiochenum Concilium* (Antwerp, 1681); P. and H. Ballerini, *S. Leonis Opera*, iii (1757), pp. xxv–xxx, repr. in J. P. Migne, *PL*, lvi, 37–41; L. *Duchesne, *Histoire ancienne de l'Église*, ii (1907), p. 211 n. E. *Schwartz, 'Zur Geschichte des Athanasius, IX' in *Nch.* (Gott.) 1911, pp. 469–522. G. Bardy in *D.D.C.*, i (1935), cols. 589–98, s.v. 'Antioche (Concile et Canons d')'. For the Creeds connected with the Council, see J. N. D. Kelly, *Early Christian Creeds* (1950), pp. 263–74; also G. Bardy, *Recherches sur S. Lucien d'Antioche et son école* (1936), pp. 85–132.

ANTIOCHENE THEOLOGY. The theology of the early Christian Church of Antioch was sometimes complementary, sometimes opposed, to that of *Alexandria. Its tendency was *Aristotelian and historical, in contrast with the more *Platonic and mystical tradition characteristic of Egypt. The tradition is seen in heretics and orthodox alike, from *Paul of Samosata, through *Lucian of Antioch and *Marcellus of Ancyra, down to *Chrysostom, *Theodore of Mopsuestia, *Nestorius, *Theodoret, and the later anti-Monophysite writers. Antiochene exegesis of Scripture was historical, and, unlike Alexandrian, looked not for a hidden meaning in the text, but for the sense intended by the inspired writer. It was likewise critical, holding some parts of the Bible to be of more value than others. The doctrine of the Trinity prevalent in this school of thought was what F. *Loofs calls the 'Economic-Trinitarian' (from the word οἰκονομία, i.e. 'Divine plan of salvation'), in which the Three Persons are distinguished only by their modes of operation. In such teaching on the Godhead there is an obvious similarity to *Sabellianism, but the Antiochenes hotly rejected the identification of the two views. In spite of their Seleucid history, they had retained much of their original Semitic outlook; and this fact perhaps helps to account for their insistence on the oneness of God and their abhorrence of whatever appeared in the slightest degree to savour of tritheism. They did not use the term 'Son' of the pre-existent *Logos, but restricted its application to the historical Christ. The Holy Ghost, again, is the Spirit of the Son as well as of the Father, but (at least for Paul of Samosata) the Spirit of the *Incarnate* Son, who is Man as well as God.

The divergence between Antioch and Alexandria is most marked, however, when we come to the Christological controversies of the 5th cent. On this question the historical bent of the former made it emphasize the humanity of Christ. The tendency of the school was to incline towards belief in a loose union of the Divine and human natures in Christ; and this looseness appeared to their opponents to be even greater than it actually was on account of certain terminological ambiguities. The need of human moral effort was strongly urged— a fact which well explains the sympathy of *Nestorius for the *Pelagians—and some interpreted predestination as being due to foreseen merits. The tradition was discredited after the Council of *Ephesus (431), and did not altogether recover its prestige when the opposing tendency, which produced *Apollinarianism and *Eutychianism, fell into disrepute.

F. Loofs, *Paulus von Samosata* (1924); R. V. Sellers, *Two Ancient Christologies* (1940).

ANTIOCHUS EPIPHANES (d. 163 B.C.),
King of Syria from 175 B.C. (The epithet 'Epiphanes' means 'illustrious'.) His policy of attaining political unity by propagating Greek culture met with violent resistance from the Jews. He succeeded, however, in using as his pawns the high-priests Jason and Menelaus, who had in turn bought the *high-priesthood from him. In 170 B.C. he attacked *Jerusalem and spoiled the Temple, and in 168 B.C. made a renewed and fiercer onslaught in a determination to exterminate Judaism. Jewish customs were forbidden under penalty of death, the Temple defiled, and pagan cults instituted. This led to the *Maccabean revolt, after which Antiochus retired to Persia, where he died. His policy and actions are described in the Books of the Maccabees.

The chief Biblical reff. are Dan. 11. 11–45; 1 Macc. 1. 11–67, 2. and 3., and 6. 1–16; and 2 Macc. 4. 7–9. 29. The other authorities include Livy (xli. 20), Polybius (xxvi. 1; xxix. 24–7; xxxi. 9; xxxviii. 18–20,; etc.), and Diodorus Siculus (xxix. 32, xxxi. 16. and xxxiv. 1), as well as *Josephus. E. R. Bevan, *The House of Seleucus*, ii (1902), pp. 126–77; id., *Jerusalem under the High Priests* (1904), pp. 74–90. F. M. Abel, O.P., 'Antiochus Epiphanes' in *Vivre et penser*, i (1941; war-time title of *R. Bibl.*), pp. 231–54.

ANTIPAS, HEROD. See *Herod Family*.

ANTIPHON (Gk. ἀντίφωνον, orig. 'something sung alternately by two choirs'). In the W. Church, sentences, usually from Scripture, recited before and after the *Psalms and *Canticles in the Divine Office. They vary with the season or feast, and are often intended to indicate the spirit in which the (invariable) Psalms and Canticles are to be sung. On feasts of double rank they are 'doubled' (i.e. recited completely before and after the Psalms or Canticles), but on other occasions the first words only are said before the Psalm and the whole afterwards. The name is also applied to the Four Anthems of Our Lady, sung, acc. to season, at the close of the greater choir Offices. In the E. Church the word is used in a different sense, and applied to the three anthems sung antiphonally in the early part of the Eucharistic Liturgy, and varying acc. to the feast or season. There are also antiphons at *vespers and *mattins, consisting of psalms sung antiphonally, and at other offices and functions. Such antiphonal singing may either be divided between two choirs or else between a soloist and the choir, and may either consist of verses sung thus in alternation, or of a psalm broken at intervals by a refrain. See also *Anthem*.

ANTIPHONAL, also 'Antiphonary'. Orig. the liturgical book in the W. Church containing all parts both of the Choir *Office and of the *Mass which were sung by the choir antiphonally. It therefore included the '*Graduale'. In later times the Office ('Antiphonarium officii') and Mass ('Antiphonarium missae') portions were separated, and in current usage the word is restricted to the former book. Down to 1903, the official edition of the antiphonary in the RC Church, was the 'Ratisbon edition', commended by *Pius IX and *Leo XIII, when it was ordered to be replaced by the 'Vatican edition'.

ANTIPOPE. A person set up as Bp. of Rome in opposition to the person already holding the see or lawfully elected to it. There have been about twenty-five antipopes in the history of the Church.

ANTITRINITARIANISM. A term used to denote various professedly Christian systems which agree only in rejecting the Catholic doctrine of the *Trinity. Such were those of the *Ebionite Jewish Christians of the 1st cent., who thought that to recognize Christ as God would involve the abandonment of *monotheism; the *Gnostic sects of the 2nd, who subordinated Christ to God as being merely a manifestation of the Father, instead of a co-equal Person (see *Subordinationism*); and the Monarchian *Modalists who refused to admit distinct Persons within the Trinity, regarding the Son and Holy Ghost as aspects of the Father's Being. The *Arian view of Christ's Person, which in all its forms fell short of conceding Him full divinity, is also antitrinitarian. In the Middle Ages several obscure pseudo-mystical and pantheistic sects held antitrinitarian views. For the better known post-Reformation forms of Antitrinitarianism, see under *Socinus and *Unitarianism. Unitarianism is the most radical form in which it survives to-day.

ANTONELLI, GIACOMO (1806–76),
Cardinal Secretary of State. He never proceeded beyond the diaconate, to which he was ordained in 1840. After holding various offices under *Gregory XVI, he was created a *cardinal by *Pius IX on his accession (1847). In 1848 he arranged the flight of the Pope to *Gaeta, where he was appointed Secretary of State. Returning to Rome in 1850, he

influenced the Pope in favour of a reactionary and ultramontane policy, and virtually became the temporal ruler of Rome up to 1870, being nicknamed the 'Red Pope'. He opposed the convening of the *Vatican Council, and while it was sitting advised the Pope to drop the *Infallibility question. After 1870 he was chiefly concerned with maintaining the claims of the papacy in its struggle with the *Risorgimento*. A statesman rather than a prelate, he was loaded with praise by his friends, but regarded as unscrupulous by his enemies.

Short biog. sketch by A. de Waal (Bonn, 1876). V. Vetere, *I ventidue anni del Cardinale Antonelli* (1871). P. Richard in *D.H.G.E.*, iii (1924), cols. 832-7.

ANTONIANS. Several communities claiming the patronage of, or descent from, St. *Antony of Egypt.

(1) The original disciples of St. *Antony in the desert, with whom the present Antonians of the *Maronites [(3) below] in the Near East claim (but on insufficient historical evidence) continuity.

(2) A congregation founded by Gaston de Dauphiné in 1095, which spread through France, Spain, and Italy, and survived till the French Revolution. They were known as the 'Hospital Brothers of Saint Antony'.

(3) An order in the *Armenian Church, founded in the 17th cent. to maintain the connexion with the RC Church. There are also Antonians among the Chaldean and Maronite *Uniats, and the monastery of Mount *Sinai among the Orthodox claims to follow the rule of St. Antony.

(4) A congregation founded in Flanders in 1615.

The name was also taken by an antinomian sect founded in Switzerland in 1802 by a certain Anton Unternäher (1759-1824; hence the name) who pretended to be the redeemer of mankind.

ANTONINUS, St. (1389-1459), also 'Antonino', Abp. of Florence. At the age of 16 he joined the *Dominican Order. After making his novitiate at Cortona in company with Fra *Angelico and Fra *Bartolommeo, he governed in turn the convents of his order at Rome, Naples, Cajeta, Cortona, Siena, Fiesole, and Florence, promoting everywhere the reforms of Bl. John Dominic (1376-1419), with a view to restoring the primitive rule. In 1436 he established the famous Convent of San Marco at Florence, and, with the munificence of Cosimo de' Medici, built the adjoining church. In 1446 he was made Abp. of Florence by *Eugenius IV. By his integrity and wisdom he became the counsellor of popes and statesmen, and by his care for the sick and needy in times of plague and famine endeared himself to the people. As a writer he was distinguished for his 'Summa theologica moralis', several treatises on the Christian life, and a general history of the world. As an economist, he was among the first to adapt Catholic traditions to modern conditions,

maintaining that money invested in business was true capital and that it was not therefore necessarily wrong to receive interest on it. Feast day, 10 May.

His works are listed in Quétif–Echard, i (1719), p. 818 f., and ii (1721), p. 823. *Summa Theologica* (first publ. Venice, 1477–9), ed. P. *Ballerini (Verona, 1740). R. Morçay (ed.), *Chroniques de Saint Antonin*. Fragments originaux du titre xxii, 1378–1459 (1913). Life by Francesco di Castiglione, a member of Antoninus' household, printed in *A A.SS.*, Mai. I (1680), pp. 313–25, with almost contemporary additions by Leonard de Suburti, O.P., pp. 326–34, and account, with extracts, of the Process of Canonization, pp. 335–51. R. Morçay, *Saint Antonin archevêque de Florence, 1389–1459* (1914). C. Ilgner, *Die volkswirtschaftlichen Anschauungen Antonins von Florenz, 1389–1459* (1904). B. Jarrett, O.P., *S. Antonino and Medieval Economics* (1914). J. B. Walker, *The 'Chronicles' of Saint Antoninus* (Catholic University of America, Studies in Medieval History, vi, 1934). Further lives by A. Masseron ('Les Saints', 1926) and P. Bargellini (Brescia, 1947; popular).

ANTONY, St., of Egypt (251?–356), hermit. C. 269 Antony gave away his possessions, and devoted himself to a life of asceticism, and c. 285 retired completely into the desert, where he is said to have fought with demons under the guise of wild beasts. The holiness and ordered discipline of his life, seen in contrast to the wickedness of the contemporary world, and also compared with the more eccentric austerities of other solitaries, attracted a number of disciples; and c. 305 he came out of his solitude to organize them into a community of hermits who lived under rule (an innovation) but with little common life comparable to that of the later religious orders. Antony retired again into solitude c. 310, but later exercised his influence in support of the Nicene party in the *Arian controversy, in which he was closely associated with St. *Athanasius. Towards the end of his life, the numbers of those who turned to the solitary life of the desert increased as a result of the secularization of the Church, and his authority grew correspondingly. The evidence for his life is the 'Vita Antonii' by St. Athanasius, the authenticity of which has sometimes been doubted. Feast day, 17 Jan.

The seven Epp. of Antony, mentioned by *Jerome (*De vir. ill.*, 88) and surviving *in toto* only in a Lat. tr. printed in J. P. Migne, *PG*, xl, 977–1000, are prob. genuine; the collection of twenty *Epp.* printed ib., 999–1066, a working over of the earlier set through the Arab., appears to contain nothing further authentic. A letter to Abbot Theodore and his monks 'On proper Repentance' (*PG*, xl, 1065) seems to be genuine; but the twenty Sermons (xl, 961–78) and the so-called 'Rule of St. Antony' (xl, 1065–79) are spurious. The authenticity of the *Vita* by Athanasius (*PG*, xxvi, 835–978) was attacked by H. Weingarten, 'Der Ursprung des Mönchtums im nachconstantinischen Zeitalter', in *Z.K.G.*, i (1877), pp. 1–35, 545–74; but since the reply by A. Eichhorn, *Athanasii de Vita Ascetica Testimonia Collecta* (Halle, 1886), it has been generally accepted; early tr. by *Evagrius of Antioch. For the extensive modern lit. on Antony (esp. imp. that of G. Garitte), see B. Altaner, *Patrologie* (ed. 2, 1950), p. 224 f. and (on the Vita Antonii) p. 235. J. List, *Das Antoniusleben des hl. Athanasius des Grossen* (Athens, 1930). L. Bouyer, Cong. Or., *La Vie de Saint Antoine* (1950).

ANTONY, St., of Padua (1195–1231), *Franciscan friar. Born at Lisbon of noble family, he was educated at Lisbon Cathedral School. In 1210 he joined the *Augustinian Canons near Lisbon, being transferred at his own request in 1212 to Coimbra, where he engaged in study. When the relics of some Franciscans killed in Morocco were brought to Coimbra in 1220, he was filled with a desire for martyrdom. Obtaining his release, in 1220 or 1221 he received the *Franciscan habit in the chapel of St. Antony at Olivares, near Coimbra, prob. at this time changing his name from Ferdinand to Antony. He sailed to Morocco, but was forced by illness to return to Europe. He attended the General Chapter at *Assisi in 1221, and was sent to the hermitage of San Paolo near Forlì. When he was suddenly called upon to preach at an ordination at Forlì, his unexpected eloquence and learning were discovered. He was immediately recalled and, with the approval of St. *Francis, appointed lector in theology to the Order, being the first to hold the post. He taught at *Bologna in 1222, Montpellier in 1224, and later at Toulouse. He was appointed Guardian of Puy in 1224, Custodian at Limoges in 1226, and possibly Provincial of Emilia or Romagna in 1227, but was released from office in 1230 to devote himself more fully to preaching. He spent the rest of his life near Padua, where his relics have always been venerated. He was canonized in 1232. Feast day, 13 June.

St. Antony's preaching gained a considerable reputation during his life; it was largely directed against the vices of usury and avarice; it also met with notable success among the heretics of France and northern Italy. Possibly during his life, and certainly after his death, he was widely regarded as a worker of miracles. His cultus, always popular, further developed in the late 19th cent. He is chiefly invoked for the return of lost property, possibly because of the incident related in the *Chronica XXIV Generalium* (no. 21) of the novice who ran away with a Psalter which St. Antony was using and was forced by an alarming apparition to return it. He is also the patron of the poor, alms given to obtain his intercession being known since *c.* 1870 as 'St. Antony's Bread'; and he is believed to protect the pregnant and travellers. In early art he is usually depicted with a book or lily, symbolizing his knowledge of Scripture, or occasionally with an ass, which is supposed to have knelt before the Blessed Sacrament upheld by St. Antony; later, he is represented holding the Holy Child.

Collections of his sermons were publ. at Paris in 1520 and 1521; collected ed. of his works by J. de La Haye (ed.), *Sancti Francisci Assisiatis . . . nec non Sancti Antonii Paduani Opera Omnia* (ib., 1641), pp. 97–792; additional sermons ed. A. Pagus, O.F.M. (Avignon, 1684). Modern Eng. tr. of his *Moral Concordances* by J. M. *Neale (London, 1856). The most important source for his life is the *Legenda Prima* written shortly after his death; crit. ed., with later appendix, by L. de Kerval in *Collection d'Études et de Documents*, v (1904), pp. 1–157, with notes on other sources, pp. 237–71. Id., *L'Évolution et le développement du merveilleux dans les légendes de S. Antoine de Padua* (Opuscules de Critique Historique, xii, xiii, and xiv, 1906). E. Gilliat-Smith, *Saint Anthony of Padua according to his Contemporaries* (1926); R. M. Huber, O.F.M., *St. Anthony of Padua, Doctor of the Church Universal* (Milwaukee, 1945). Other lives by A. Lépître ('Les Saints', 1901; Eng. tr., 1902), V. Facchinetti (Milan, 1925; Fr. tr., 1926), N. Vian (Milan, 1934; Eng. tr., 1936), and R.Maloney, O.F.M. (more popular; Dublin, 1931). R. Pratesi, O.F.M., in *E.C.*, i (1948), cols. 1548–54, with further reff.

APELLES (2nd cent.), founder of a *Gnostic sect. Our slight knowledge of him comes mainly from fragments of his antagonist, Rhodo (in *Eusebius, *HE*, v, xiii), and reff. in *Tertullian's *De Praescriptione* (xxx; xxxiv). Originally a disciple of *Marcion at *Rome, he taught at *Alexandria and later returned to Rome, where he came under the influence of a visionary Philumene, whose oracles he collected. He embodied his system in an extended work, Συλλογισμοί. He modified Marcion's dualism in an endeavour to defend a less *Docetic doctrine of the Person of Christ. Christ came down from the good God, who was not himself the creator of the world, however, and really lived and really suffered in a body miraculously formed out of the elements. Those who believed in Christ would gain salvation not by knowledge alone or by faith alone, but by good works. Tertullian wrote a book against him, now lost.

For sources, see A. *Harnack, *Marcion* (T.U., xlv, 1921), pp. 213–30, and Beilage VII (pp. 123*–339*). G. Bareille in *D.T.C.*, i (1903), cols. 1455–7.

APHRAATES (early 4th cent.), the first of the *Syriac Church fathers. He was a monk, probably also a bishop (of an unknown see), and almost certainly suffered persecution at the hands of King Sapor the Great (309–79). Our knowledge of him comes from 23 treatises which he wrote between 336 and 345, usually, but inaccurately, known as his 'Homilies'. The first 22 are tractates, arranged on an acrostic plan, each beginning with a different letter of the alphabet, and give a survey of the Christian faith. The 23rd, of the nature of an appendix, is a short treatise 'On the berry' (Is. 65. 8). His writings show that he attached importance to asceticism, esp. celibacy, and that, at least in intention, he was orthodox in his theology. His works throw valuable light on early Christianity in Persia and on the text of the N.T. He was known as 'the Persian Sage'.

Syr. text of Homilies ed. by W. Wright (London, 1869) and, with Lat. tr., by J. Parisot, O.S.B. (Patr. Syr., i, 2 ptt. 1894–1907). Germ. tr. by G. Bert (T.U., iii, Hftt. 3–4; 1888); Eng. tr. of eight Homm. by J. Gwynn in *N.P.N.C.F.*, Ser. 2, xiii (1898), pp. 345–412. R. H. *Connolly, 'Aphraates and Monasticism' in *J.T.S.*, vi (1905), pp. 522–39; reply by F. C. *Burkitt, ib., vii (1906), pp. 10–15. I. Ortis de Urbina, S.J., *Die Gottheit Christi bei Afrahat* (Orientalia Christiana, vol. xxxi, fasc. i (Num. 87); 1933). Bardenhewer, iv, pp. 327–40; A. *Baumstark, *Geschichte der syrischen Literatur* (1922), pp. 30–32, with reff. to earlier works.

APHTHARTODOCETAE. One of the divisions of the *Monophysites (q.v.). They were founded by *Julian, Bp. of Halicarnassus, and are hence known also as 'Julianists'. They taught that from the first moment of the Incarnation the earthly body of Christ was in its nature incorruptible (ἄφθαρτος), impassible, and immortal, though this fact did not preclude Him from accepting suffering and death by a free act of His will. The doctrine was attacked (on grounds acceptable also to Catholic orthodoxy) by *Severus, the Monophysite Patr. of Antioch, as incompatible with belief in the true humanity of Christ.

R. Draguet, *Julien d'Halicarnasse et sa controverse avec Sévère* (1924).

APIARIUS. A priest of the diocese of Sicca in proconsular Africa, who was deposed by his bishop for misconduct. The incident is important in connexion with the growth of Papal jurisdiction. Apiarius appealed to Pope *Zosimus (417–18), who thereupon ordered him to be reinstated. In consequence a council held at *Carthage in May 418 forbade appeals beyond the sea. The Pope protested at this decree, and the case dragged on for some years. C. 423 Apiarius was again excommunicated, and again appealed to Rome with the same result. The incident also led to a fresh examination of the authority attaching to the *Sardican Canons and thus indirectly had a decisive influence on the beginnings of the codification of *canon law.

Hefele–Leclercq, ii, pp. 196–215 passim, with bibl. note p. 196. Fliche–Martin, iv, pp. 253 f. and 257 with reff. A. Audollent in *D.H.G.E.*, iii (1924), cols. 951–4, s.v., with bibl.

APOCALYPSES. See *Abraham, Apocalypse of; Baruch, Apocalypse of; Revelation, Book of.*

APOCALYPTIC LITERATURE. The word 'apocalypse' (ἀποκάλυψις) means a 'revelation' or 'unveiling', so that an apocalyptic book claims to reveal things which are normally hidden and to unveil the future. The Jewish Apocalyptic books belong approximately to the period 200 B.C.–A.D. 100 and deal with the end of the present world order and with the next world. Whereas the Israelite Prophets were primarily preachers, concerned with current problems of their own generation and nation, the Apocalyptists were preeminently writers, directing their attention towards the end of things and to the destiny of the world in general. The origins and growth of this literature were due to the history of Palestine's conflicts with other nations and to the conviction that trust in military power was useless. As the nation continued to be subjected to foreign domination, it despaired of ever attaining political supremacy, and the conclusion was drawn that God would eventually intervene, destroy Israel's enemies, and set up His Kingdom on earth.

Apocalyptic Literature proper begins with the Book of *Daniel, probably written during the persecution of *Antiochus Epiphanes (175–163 B.C.) to comfort the Jews in their distress and to assure them of the approaching Divine intervention, though the beginnings of Apocalyptic tendencies can be seen in the prophetic writings (e.g. Joel 2, Is. 65, Amos 5. 16–20, 9. 11–15, Is. 24–7, Is. 33, Zech. 12–14, Ezek. 38, 39), where there are frequent references to the approaching 'day of the Lord'. The Apocalyptic writings, in the technical sense, are always pseudonymous and written in the names of Israel's past heroes, a circumstance probably to be ascribed to the fact that, owing to the supremacy of the Law (which was regarded as containing the complete and final revelation of the Divine will), the only way to secure a hearing after the formation of the earliest form of the OT *Canon in the 3rd cent. B.C. was to attribute these writings to some famous person of the pre-legal period.

Important Jewish Apocalyptic writings outside the OT (to which reference has just been made) are the Book of *Enoch, the Book of the Secrets of Enoch, the Apocalypse of *Baruch, the Fourth Book of *Ezra, the Assumption of *Moses, the Book of *Jubilees, the Ascension of *Isaiah, and the *Testament of the Twelve Patriarchs.

In the NT, the element of Apocalyptic appears in various places. The two most important Christian Apocalypses are Rev. and the (non-canonical) 'Apocalypse of *Peter'. Whatever interpretation the Lord Himself wished His disciples to put upon His Apocalyptic utterances, it is clear that, at least in the earlier part of the Apostolic age, a speedy Second Coming of Christ was expected (see, e.g., Mt. 24 and 25, Mk. 13, Lk. 21, 1 Thess. 4, 1 Cor. 15 for typical Apocalyptic passages). 2 Pet. and Rev. probably belong to a slightly later period, when severe persecution was troubling the Church.

Most of the Jewish Apocalyptic writings not in the OT will be found in R. H. *Charles, *The Apocrypha and Pseudepigrapha of the OT* (2 vols., 1913).

APOCATASTASIS. The Greek name (ἀποκατάστασις) for the doctrine that ultimately all free moral creatures—angels, men, and devils—will share in the grace of salvation. It is to be found in *Clement of Alexandria, in *Origen and in St. *Gregory of Nyssa. It was strongly attacked by St. *Augustine of Hippo and formally condemned in the first anathema against *Origenism, probably put out by the Council of *Constantinople in A.D. 543. In more modern times the doctrine has been defended by certain *Anabaptists, *Moravians, *Christadelphians (modified in some of these by a form of *conditional immortality), and also by certain individual theologians, of whom perhaps the most important is F. D. E. *Schleiermacher. Such teaching is also known as *Universalism.

APOCRISIARIUS (from Gk. ἀποκρίνομαι 'to answer, make response'). An ecclesiastical deputy or other official of high rank.

(1) The envoys used by the Patriarchates as their diplomatic representatives in other patriarchal cities or at imperial courts. *Apocrisiarii* were at first, from the 5th cent., sent on specific missions, but by the 9th cent. at any rate they had acquired the character of permanent legates. In recent years the *Oecumenical Patriarch has appointed an 'apocrisiarius' to the Abp. of *Canterbury.

(2) The title was also used of the senior court chaplains of the Frankish courts, also known as 'archicapellani'.

APOCRYPHA, The (Gk. τὰ ἀπόκρυφα (plur.), 'the hidden [things]'). The Biblical Books received by the early Church as part of the Gk. version of the OT, but not included in the Heb. Bible, being excluded by the non-Hellenistic Jews from their *Canon. Their position in Christian usage has been somewhat ambiguous. In the *Vulgate and versions derived from it they are mostly part of the OT; but in the AV, RV, and other non-Roman modern versions, they either form a separate section between the OT and NT, or are omitted altogether. They comprise (in the order of the AV): 1 Esdras, Tobit, Judith, the Rest of Esther, the Wisdom of Solomon, Ecclesiasticus, Baruch with the Epistle of Jeremy, the Song of the Three Holy Children, the History of Susanna, Bel and the Dragon, the Prayer of Manasses, and 1 and 2 Maccabees (qq.v.).

The Church received these writings from Hellenistic Judaism, esp. that of *Alexandria. In the *Septuagint (LXX), which incorporated all except 2 Esd., they were in no way differentiated from the other Books of the OT. The narrative Books (1 Esd., Tobit, Judith, 1 and 2 Macc.) are grouped in the principal MSS with the later historical Books 1 Chron.-Esth., the Wisdom Books (Wisd., Ecclus.) with Prov., etc., and Pr. of Man. is appended to the Psalter. The three items, Song of III Ch., Susanna, and Bel and Dragon (collectively known as 'the Additions to Daniel') are here integral parts of the Book of Dan., being the parts of the Gk. text to which nothing corresponds in the Heb. Similarly the disjointed chapters (by no means a complete Book) appearing in the Eng. versions of the Apocrypha as 'the Rest of Esther' are here simply the portions of the Gk. text of Esth. not found in the Heb. Baruch and Ep. of Jer. are appended in LXX MSS. to Jer., though not derived from the Heb. Book. Under the name of 'Esdras' (the Gk. form of Heb. 'Ezra') the LXX contains two Books: one ('Εσδρας α', i.e. '1 Ezra') corresponds to portions of (the Heb.) 2 Chron., Ezr., and Neh., but contains also a passage (1 Esd. 3. 1-5. 6.) not found there; the other ('Εσδρας β', i.e. '2 Ezra') is a faithful rendering of Ezr. and Neh. The latter therefore is regarded as the LXX version of these OT Books, while the former, which diverges from the Heb., appears among the Apocrypha as '1 Esdras'. The '2 Esdras' of the Apocrypha is a different work altogether. It is not extant in Gk. and found only in Latin MSS.; but it was doubtless translated from the Gk., and is, like the rest, of Jewish origin. This last is also known as the 'Ezra Apocalypse'.

In date of writing, the Books of the Apocrypha derive from the period 300 B.C.-A.D. 100 approx., and mostly from 200 B.C.-A.D. 70, i.e. before the definite separation of the Church from Judaism. In this period, though the *Canon of the Jewish Scriptures was closed as far as the 'Law' and the 'Prophets' were concerned, it was still possible for works which came to be known technically as 'Writings' to claim the status of Scripture, and some of the

Canonical Books of the OT (e.g. Dan.) date from this period. Some of the Apocrypha, e.g. Ecclus. (cf. the Prologue to the Book), being written originally in Heb., might have gained canonical status, but did not; others (e.g. 2 Macc.), being written in Gk., were never current among Aramaic-speaking Jews. When the Hebrew Canon of Scripture was finally settled (traditionally at the Synod of *Jamnia, c. A.D. 100), the Heb. text of the excluded Books ceased to be copied. With the exception of fragments recovered in modern times, e.g. considerable portions of Ecclus. discovered in an ancient *genizah, this has hence been lost. On the other hand, the Gk. survived because of its use by Christians, who at first received all the Books of the Septuagint equally as Scripture. Though no Book of the Apocrypha is quoted in the NT, *Clement of Rome and other early Fathers, notably *Clement of Alexandria and *Origen, cite them frequently. The considerable use made of them by Christians for apologetic purposes, e.g. of texts held to refer to such Christian doctrines as the Incarnation and the Eternal Generation of the *Wisdom (equated with the Word (*Logos), i.e. Son) of God (Wis. 7. 26), may have contributed to the Jewish rejection of the Books. In the later Gk. version of the Scriptures made by the Jew *Aquila (q.v.), the Heb. Canon was followed exactly.

Down to the 4th cent. the Church generally accepted all the Books of the Septuagint as canonical. Gk. and Lat. Fathers alike *Irenaeus, *Tertullian, *Cyprian) cite both classes of Books without distinction. In the 4th cent., however, many Gk. Fathers (e.g. *Eusebius, *Athanasius, *Cyril of Jerusalem, *Epiphanius, *Gregory of Nazianzus), came to recognize a distinction between those canonical in Heb. and the rest, though the latter were still customarily cited as Scripture. St. *Jerome, through his Eastern contacts and his Heb. studies, accepted this distinction, and introduced the term 'apocrypha' for the latter class, which he also described as the 'libri ecclesiastici' as distinguished from the 'libri canonici'. But with a few exceptions (e.g. *Hilary, *Rufinus), W. writers (esp. *Augustine) continued to consider all as equally canonical. In the E. Church opinion varied, and for some centuries the Books continued to be widely accepted; but at the Synod of *Jerusalem in 1672 it was decided that Tobit, Judith, Ecclus., and Wisd. alone were to be regarded as canonical. Opinion in the W. also was not unanimous, some authorities considering certain books uncanonical; but, despite Jerome's distinction, all, including '2 Esdras' (see above), were commonly included in the Vulgate and cited as Scripture. (In the Vulgate, 'I, II Esdras' = Ezr. and Neh. (from the Heb.); 'III Esdras' = '1 Esdras' (i.e. 'Εσδρας α' (of the LXX); and 'IV Esdras' = '2 Esdras' (the Ezra Apocalypse).)

At the Reformation, Protestant leaders, ignoring the traditional acceptance of all the Books of the LXX in the early Church and desiring to return to Biblical authority purged of medieval tradition, refused the status of inspired Scripture to those Books of the Vulg. not to be found in the Heb. Canon. M. *Luther, however, included the Apocrypha (except 1 and 2 Esd.) as an appendix to his translation of the Bible (1534), and in his preface allowed them to be 'useful and good to be read'. The Geneva translators (see *Bible*, English versions) translated them, with a preface recognizing their value for 'knowledge of history and instruction of godly manners', and the C of E, in the *Thirty-nine Articles (1562) (Art. VI), stated that 'the Church doth read [them] for example of life and instruction of manners; but yet it doth not apply them to establish any doctrine'. At the Council of *Trent (Sess. IV, 8 April 1548), the full canonicity of the Books was confirmed, with the exception of 1 and 2 (i.e. III and IV) Esdras and Pr. of Man., which were placed henceforth in an appendix to the Vulgate, after the NT. This decision was confirmed for the RC Church by the *Vatican Council (1870). In the C of E, in accordance with Art. VI, the Apocrypha, as a separate section between the OT and NT, were included as an integral part of the *Authorized Version of 1611. Under Puritan ascendancy, however, it was declared in the *Westminster Confession (1646–7) that the Apocrypha were not 'to be otherwise approved or made use of than other human writings'. The common attitude to them in Great Britain, maintained officially by the Church of *Scotland and favoured by nonconformists, was of rejection or at least suspicion, and this, perhaps combined with Anglican apathy, and reinforced by the decision of the *British and Foreign Bible Society not to distribute Bibles containing them, led to their general omission from the editions commonly sold. In the BCP of 1662, portions of some of them were included in the Lectionary, and this was continued in the Lectionary of 1871 as far as Wisd., Ecclus., and Baruch were concerned. In the Revised Lectionary of 1922 portions of Pr. of Man., 1 and 2 Macc., and Tobit were also included.

With the growth of a historical perspective in Biblical studies in the 19th cent., and the increased knowledge and interest in Hellenistic and non-biblical background of the NT, the great value of the Apocrypha as historical sources came to be generally recognized, and there came also a new recognition of their religious value. Historically they are invaluable for the light which they throw on the period between the end of the OT historical narrative in Ezra-Neh. (c. 400 B.C.) and the opening of the NT. They witness to the rise of the belief in eternal life and in the resurrection of the body, championed by the Pharisees in the NT period (cf. Mk. 12. 18–27, Acts 23. 6–9), and as touching questions that were very much alive in the Apostolic Age (e.g. the Jewish Law, good works, sin and its origin in the *Fall, eschatology); and as having been read as Scripture by the pre-Nicene Church and many post-Nicene Fathers, they have gained increasing respect even from those who

do not hold them to be equally canonical with the rest of the OT.

Revision of AV Eng. tr., with crit. comm. ed. H. *Wace. (Speaker's Commentary, 2 vols., 1888), with valuable 'General Introduction' by G. *Salmon, i, pp. ix–xlvi; Eng. tr., with full introd., bibl., and notes, also in R. H. *Charles, *The Apocrypha and Pseudepigrapha of the Old Testament*, i (1913). O. F. Fritzsche–C. L. W. Grimm, *Kurzgefasstes exegetisches Handbuch zu den Apocryphen des Alten Testaments* (6. Lief., 1851–60). L. E. T. André, *Les Apocryphes de l'Ancien Testament* (Florence, 1903). W. O. E. Oesterley, *The Books of the Apocrypha*. Their Origin, Teaching and Contents (1914); id., *An Introduction to the Books of the Apocrypha* (1935). R. H. Malden, *The Apocrypha* (1936; brief). E. J. Goodspeed, *The Story of the Apocrypha* (Chicago, 1939). W. H. Daubney, *The Use of the Apocrypha in the Christian Church* (1900). H. M. Hughes, *The Ethics of Jewish Apocryphal Literature* [1909]; R. T. Herford, *Talmud and Apocrypha*. A Comparative Study of the Jewish Ethical Teaching in the Rabbinical and non-Rabbinical Sources in the Early Centuries (1933). R. H. Pfeiffer, *History of New Testament Times with an Introduction to the Apocrypha* (New York, 1949; London, 1954), pp. 233–522. B. M. Metzger, *An Introduction to the Apocrypha* (New York, 1957). E. *Schürer in *P.R.E.* (ed. 3), i (1896), pp. 622–53, s.v. 'Apokryphen des Alten Testaments'.

APOCRYPHAL NEW TESTAMENT. A modern title for various early Christian books outside the *Canon of the NT, which are similar in general form to the corresponding canonical Scriptures. The epithet 'apocryphal' here does not of itself imply inaccuracy, unauthenticity, or unorthodoxy.

Gospels. Many of these exist. It is possible that in a few places some of these embody trustworthy oral traditions, e.g. the *Gospels Acc. to the Hebrews* and *Acc. to the Egyptians* and that *of Peter*. Others such as the *Gospels of Marcion*, *of the Twelve Apostles*, *of Thomas*, and *of Philip* were intended to support heretical and esp. *Gnostic views. A third group set out to satisfy popular curiosity with tales of the Childhood of Christ, His Passion, and His post-Resurrection life; their contents were often patently garrulous and their ideas not infrequently immoral. To this group belongs the *Childhood Gospel of Thomas*, the Arabic *Gospel of the Childhood*, the *History of Joseph the Carpenter*, and the *Departure of Mary*; and for the later part the *Gospel of Nicodemus* (sometimes called the *Acts of Pilate*) and the *Legend of * Abgar*. Most of these works lie between the late 1st and early 3rd cents.

Acts. Of the Apocryphal Acts, the most important are those of *Peter, Paul, John, Andrew*, and *Thomas*, all probably late 2nd cent. They are sometimes known collectively as the 'Leucian Acts', because all were ascribed by *Photius to one Leucius Charinus; but wide differences of style, matter, and doctrinal standpoint forbid the assumption of common authorship. Their subject-matter is partly made up of stories parallel to and perhaps inspired by the canonical Acts of the Apostles, partly credible oral traditions, partly evident romance. The *Acts of Paul* (from which the *Acts of Paul and Thecla*, which was current as a separate work, was later extracted) is not markedly heretical; but nearly all the others in varying degrees reflect current heretical influences.

Epistles and Other Writings. Of the non-canonical epistles the best known are those of *Clement* ('ep. 1') and *Barnabas* (qq.v.; c. A.D. 100) though these hardly come under the title as ordinarily used. Among others are the spurious Epp. of St. Paul *To the Corinthians* and *To the Laodiceans*. There are also various apocryphal apocalypses besides the Revelation of St. John, which itself long remained on the borders of the NT canon.

M. R. James, *The Apocryphal New Testament* (1924; the principal texts in Eng. trans.). C. *Tischendorf, ed., *Evangelia Apocrypha* (Leipzig, 1853; ed. 2, 1876). R. A. Lipsius-M. Bonnet, *Acta Apostolorum Apocrypha* (Leipzig, 1891–1903). M. R. James, *Anecdota Apocrypha* (Cambridge 'Texts and Studies', 1893 and 1897). See also literature under separate items.

APODEIPNON (Gk. ἀπόδειπνον). In the E. Church, the late evening liturgical service which is the counterpart of *Compline in the West.

APOLLINARIS, St. (date unknown), first Bp. of *Ravenna. The earliest mention of him is in a sermon of St. Peter *Chrysologus (d. c. 450), who styles him a martyr; but the principal authority is some (historically worthless) 7th cent. *acta* which put him in the 1st cent. and make him a disciple of St. *Peter at Antioch. His body was venerated in early times at Classe, near Ravenna, the supposed scene of his sufferings, later in the cathedral of Ravenna itself. His name still occurs in the canon of the *Ambrosian Rite. Feast day, 23 July. See also *Ravenna*.

AA.SS. Jul. V (1727), pp. 328–85. incl. medieval accounts of the translation of his relics. F. Lanzoni, *Le origini delle diocesi antiche d' Italia*. Studio critico (S.T., 35, 1923), pp. 452–75 (on Ravenna, with bibl. reff.). E. Will, *Saint Apollinaire de Ravenne* (1936); G. Lucchesi, *Note agiografiche sui primi vescovi di Ravenna* (Faenza, 1941). H. *Delehaye, S.J., 'L'Hagiographie ancienne de Ravenne' in *Anal. Boll.*, xlvii (1929), pp. 5–30.

APOLLINARIS SIDONIUS. See *Sidonius Apollinaris*.

APOLLINARIUS, CLAUDIUS (2nd cent.), Bp. of Hierapolis, early Christian *Apologist. His writings included a 'Defence of the Faith', presented to Marcus Aurelius (prob. in 172), treatises 'Against the Pagans' (Πρὸς Ἕλληνας), on 'Truth' (Περὶ Ἀληθείας), and on *Easter (Περὶ τοῦ Πάσχα), and a work against the *Montanists. Apart from a few fragments, all his writings are lost. Feast day, 8 Jan.

The chief authority is *Eusebius, *HE*, iv, xxvii, and v, xix. The fragments are collected in M. J. *Routh, *Reliquiae Sacrae*, i (ed. 2), pp. 155–74, and in J. C. T. Otto, *Corpus Apologetarum Christianorum*, ix (1872), pp. 479–95.

APOLLINARIUS and APOLLINARIANISM. *Apollinarius* (or *Apollinaris*) ('the Younger', c. 310–c. 390) was the son of a grammarian of Berytus, also named Apollinarius ('the Elder'), in conjunction with whom he rewrote much of the Bible in classical forms when the Emp. *Julian (361–3) forbade Christians to use the pagan classics. A vigorous advocate of orthodoxy against the *Arians, he became Bp. of Laodicea c. 360 and was a close friend of St. *Athanasius (whom he had received on his return from exile in 346). Teaching akin to that of Apollinarius was condemned at the Council of *Alexandria in 362, but soon afterwards he explained himself satisfactorily. His characteristic Christological teaching, which was little known before 371, was explicitly condemned by synods at Rome in 374–80 and by the Council of *Constantinople of 381. Apollinarius himself seceded from the Church c. 375, and from 381 the State forbade Apollinarian public worship. Of his many works only fragments remain, mostly under other writers' names.

Of Apollinarius' extensive writings, most have been lost. Among his dogmatic works which survive under the false names of orthodox writers are (1) a 'Detailed Confession of Faith' (ἡ κατὰ μέρος πίστις), attributed to St. *Gregory Thaumaturgus; (2) 'Quod unus sit Christus', 'De Incarnatione Dei Verbi' and a Profession of Faith addressed to the Emp. *Jovian, all attributed to St. *Athanasius; (3) three writings under the name of Pope *Julius (337–52). Another dogmatic work (Ἀπόδειξις) can be partially reconstructed from St. *Gregory of Nyssa's attack on it in his 'Antirrheticus'. Fragments of his many Commentaries on the OT and NT, as well as of his apologetic works against *Porphyry (in 30 Books) and the Emp. *Julian, have also been preserved, largely in *catenae*. A Paraphrase of the Pss. in hexameters is of doubtful authenticity.

The objects of *Apollinarianism*, the first great Christological heresy, were (1) to assert the unity of Godhead and manhood in Christ, (2) to teach the full Deity of Christ, and (3) to avoid teaching that there was a moral development in Christ's life. To gain these ends, Apollinarius asserted that in man there coexist body, soul, and spirit. In Christ, however, were to be found the human body and soul, but no human spirit, the spirit being replaced by the Divine *Logos. Thus while He possessed perfect Godhead, He lacked complete manhood. It has been argued (G. A. *Dorner, R. L.*Ottley, H. M. Relton), indeed, that Apollinarius may have met the objection that Christ's manhood was not complete by saying that the Logos was the prototype of all human spirits and so could replace the spirit without detriment to the humanity; but this interpretation of his teaching rests mainly on its misunderstanding by St.*Gregory of Nyssa (so C. E. Raven, G. L. Prestige). Much confusion was created as the controversy developed through want of agreement as to the use of terms 'Person' and 'Nature', and as to whether the human personality is to be divided into body and soul, or into body, soul, and spirit. The fundamental objection to Apollinarius' teaching from the point of view of Catholic orthodoxy is that if there is no complete manhood in Christ, He is not a perfect example for us, nor did He redeem the whole of human nature but only its spiritual elements.

Texts in H. Lietzmann, *Apollinaris von Laodicea und seine Schule*. Texte und Untersuchungen, i (Tübingen, 1904; all publd.); this supersedes the collection of texts in J. Dräseke, *Apollinaris von Laodicea* (T.U., No. vii, Hft. 3 and 4, 1892; conclusions generally rejected). Additional texts: A. Ludwich, *Metaphrasis Psalmorum* (ed. Teubner, 1912);

K. Staab, *Pauluskommentare aus der griechischen Kirche* (1933), pp. 57–82; H. de Riedmatten, O.P., 'Les Fragments d'Apollinaire à l' "Éranistes"' in *Das Konzil von Chalkedon. Geschichte und Gegenwart* (ed. A. Grillmeier, S.J., and H. Bacht, S.J.), i (1951), pp. 203–12. G. Voisin, *L'Apollinarisme* (1901); R. Aigrain in *D.H.G.E.*, iii (1924), cols. 962–82, s.v.; C. E. Raven, *Apollinarianism* (1923); G. L. Prestige, *Fathers and Heretics* (Bampton Lectures for 1940; 1940), Lect. v, pp. 193–246. On the Psalm Metaphrasis, see J. Golega, 'Verfasser und Zeit der Psalterparaphrase des Apolinarios' in *B.Z.*, xxxix (1939), pp. 1–22 (author perhaps presbyter Marcianus, d. at Constantinople after 471). G. L. Prestige, *St. Basil the Great and Apollinaris of Laodicea*, ed. H. Chadwick (London, S.P.C.K., 1956). Important study by H. de Riedmatten (in preparation, 1956).

APOLLONIUS OF TYANA (d. *c.* 98),

Neopythagorean philosopher. His virtuous life and reforming religious tendencies were constantly exaggerated after his death, until it became possible for anti-Christian writers to compose biographies of him consciously parallel with the Gospel life of Christ. The Life of him by Flavius Philostratus (*c.* 220), though perhaps not inspired by this motive, furnished by its exaggeration and pretensions matter for anti-Christians in later times, and in particular for Hierocles, Governor of Bithynia *c.* 303, who wrote a Life of Apollonius which called forth a refutation from *Eusebius of Caesarea. In modern times opponents of Christianity have occasionally used Philostratus to disparage the uniqueness of the Christian Gospel, but the alleged parallels are generally admitted to be unconvincing.

There is a convenient edition of Philostratus' *Vita Apollonii* in the Loeb Classical Library (2 vols., 1912, ed. by F. C. Conybeare). Also Eng. tr., with valuable introduction, by J. S. Phillimore (2 vols., 1912).

APOLLOS.

A 'learned' Jew of Alexandria, 'mighty in the scriptures' (Acts 18. 24). He was originally a follower of 'the baptism of John [the Baptist]', but his Christian education was completed *c.* 54 at *Ephesus by *Priscilla and Aquila. He then preached at Corinth, where some Christians wished to set him up as a rival to St. Paul (Acts 18. 24, 1 Cor. 3. 4, &c.). It has been supposed by some (e.g. M. *Luther) that he was the author of the epistle to the Hebrews.

APOLOGETICS.

The defence of the Christian faith on intellectual grounds by trained theologians and philosophers. Historically this work began with the presentation of the case for Christianity to non-Christians by the 2nd cent. *Apologists, but its task soon included also the defence of orthodox teaching against those who dissent from it. The present function of Christian apologetics is considered to be esp. dispassionately to set down the rational ground of the faith, without necessarily having any particular antagonist in view. So understood, the scope of Christian apologetics falls into three parts: (1) to show that it is more reasonable to have a religion than not; (2) to show that Christianity can give a more rational account of itself than any other religion; (3) to show that it is more reasonable to profess orthodox Christianity than any other form. It is not generally claimed that the

essential truth of Christianity is certainly demonstrable by purely logical or scientific methods, but it is maintained that it is possible to show by these means that its acceptance is entirely in accordance with the demands of reason.

A. B. *Bruce, *Apologetics* (1892); J. Baillie, *Our Knowledge of God* (1939); A. Richardson, *Christian Apologetics* (1947). K. Werner, *Geschichte der apologetischen und polemischen Literatur der christlichen Theologie* (5 vols., 1861–7); O. Zöckler, *Geschichte der Apologie des Christentums* (1907). A. d'Alès (ed.), *Dictionnaire apologétique de la foi catholique* (4 vols., ed. 4, 1911–28). T. W. Crafer, in *H.E.R.E.*, i (1908), cols. 611–22, s.v.

APOLOGIA PRO VITA SUA (1864). J. H.

*Newman's 'history of [his] religious opinions' down to his reception into the RC Church, 9 Oct. 1845. It is a primary historical source for the *Oxford Movement, not least because of the letters and other historical documents which it contains. The moving and tragic work, one of the greatest autobiographies in the language, was provoked by a gibe of C. *Kingsley in *Macmillan's Magazine* for January 1864 (cited s.v. *Kingsley*). Early in Feb. 1864 Newman published in a pamphlet some correspondence with Kingsley and the publisher over the passage with the title *Mr. Kingsley and Dr. Newman*. Kingsley promptly issued a reply ('*What, then, does Dr. Newman mean?*'). The *Apologia*, Newman's answer, was orig. issued in weekly parts.

Many reprints, e.g. in *Everyman's Library* (1912). Crit. ed., with introd. by Wilfrid Ward, London (O.U.P.), 1913; reissued 1931. Fr. tr., with introd. and notes, by M. Nédoncelle, Paris, 1939. C. H. Collette, *Dr. Newman and his Religious Opinions* (1866; anti-Roman critique). W. E. Houghton, *The Art of Newman's Apologia* (New Haven, U.S.A., 1945).

APOLOGISTS.

The name esp. given to the Christian writers who (*c.* 120–220) first addressed themselves to the task of making a reasoned defence and recommendation of their faith to outsiders. They include *Aristides, *Justin Martyr, *Tatian, *Athenagoras, *Theophilus, *Minucius Felix, and *Tertullian. They belonged to the period when Christianity was first making converts among the educated classes, and was also in conflict with the State over its very right to exist. Their object was to gain a fair hearing for Christianity and to dispel popular slanders and misunderstandings, and to provide for this purpose some account of Christian belief and practice. They had to meet (1) pagan philosophy and the general outlook which it influenced, and (2) the specifically Jewish objections. They devoted much attention to the application of OT prophecy to Christianity, and to the position of the divinity of Christ in relation to monotheism, and esp. in connexion with the latter doctrine elaborated the teaching on the *Logos and won for it a permanent place in Christian theology. Except for Tertullian, they were not primarily theologians. Their method was to exhibit Christianity to emperors and to the public as politically harmless and morally and culturally superior to paganism.

Collected crit. ed. of texts by J. C. T. Otto, *Corpus Apologetarum* (9 vols., Jena, 1847–72; ed. 3 of vols. 1–5 [*Justin], 1876–81; more recent text (except Theophilus) in E. J. Goodspeed, *Die ältesten Apologeten* (1914). Eng. trr. in A.N.C.L. (various authors and dates). E. J. Goodspeed, *Index Apologeticus* (Leipzig, 1912; vocabulary). J. Geffcken, *Zwei griechische Apologeten* (1907; Aristides and Athenagoras); A. Puech, *Les Apologistes grecs du deuxième siècle de notre ère* (1912); M. Pellegrino, *Studi su l' antica apologetica* (1947). V. A. Spence Little, *The Christology of the Apologists* (1934). See also standard Patrologies and bibls. under separate Apologists.

APOLYSIS and APOLYTIKION (Gk. ἀπόλυσις and ἀπολυτίκιον). Respectively the dismissal-blessing and dismissal-prayer in the E. rites, both said by the priest at the end of the Liturgy and certain offices.

APOPHTHEGM. A designation used by R. *Bultmann and other *Form-critics for those items in the Gospels which M. *Dibelius describes as '*Paradigms'. The term had been used previously for stories of a similar type in secular Greek literature.

APOPHTHEGMATA PATRUM. A collection of sayings of the Egyptian monks, arranged alphabetically acc. to the speakers. It dates from the 4th–5th cents. and throws much light on their lives and ideals. As a large proportion are sayings of one Poemen (who lived well into the 5th cent.), the work may have been compiled by his followers. It was known to John *Moschus (d. 619), to *Cyril of Scythopolis (d. *c.* 560), and perhaps also to *Socrates Scholasticus (d. after 450) and *Cassian (d. *c.* 435).

The most widely diffused collection is that first printed by J. B.*Cotelier, *Ecclesiae Graecae Monumenta*, i (1677), pp. 338–712 (repr. J. P. Migne, *PG*, lxv. 71–440). Other collections in Cod. Burney 50 of the Brit. Mus. and a Lat. version publd. by H. Rosweyde, S.J., as Bk. vii of his *Vitae Patrum* (1617; this and other texts repr. in *PL*, lxxiii and lxxiv). W. *Bossuet, *Apophthegmata*. Studien zur Geschichte des ältesten Mönchtums (ed. T. Hermann and G. Krüger, 1923). Further bibl. in B. Altaner, *Patrologie* (ed. 2, 1950), p. 190.

APOSTASY. In the discipline of the early Church the term was used of the abandonment of Christianity, which was, with murder and fornication, one of the three sins at first accounted unpardonable, if committed by a baptized person, and later pardonable only after public penance. In modern RC usage it has been customary, following the usage of *Benedict XIV, to employ the word in three senses: (a) apostasy from the faith, or from the RC Church; (b) apostasy from Holy Orders, by a cleric; (c) apostasy of a monk or nun from the religious life. It should be noted that in the case of (a) Roman discipline brands the children of the apostate with certain disabilities, as well as himself. In non-technical language, the word is generally used only of the entire abandonment of Christianity.

On Apostasy in the early Church see bibl. on *Lapsi*. Modern RC legislation in *C.I.C.*, cans. 1325 (par. 2), 1065 and 1240, and, in the case of religious, cans. 644–6.

APOSTIL. See *Postil*.

APOSTLE (Gk. ἀπόστολος). (1) The title given in the Gospels, and later, to the twelve chief disciples of Christ (e.g. Mt. 10. 2, Lk. 22. 14, Acts 1. 2). The lists of names given in the Gospels and Acts vary slightly, a fact probably to be explained by the application of different names to the same persons, rather than by actual discrepancy. After the suicide of *Judas Iscariot, his place was taken by *Matthias, and the term 'Apostle' is also applied to him, as well as, in the Acts and Epp., to *Paul and *Barnabas. It is possible that the term was used in the second generation of Christians of a wider circle of Church officials. In modern usage the term is sometimes applied to the leader of the first Christian mission to a country, e.g., to St.*Patrick, the 'Apostle of Ireland', Sts. *Cyril and Methodius, the 'Apostles of the Slavs', and many others. Where the traditional beliefs of the operation of grace and authority in the Christian Church are maintained, it is through the original twelve Apostles that this grace and authority is held to descend from Christ, and from them to their lawfully appointed successors. (See *Apostolic Succession*, *Episcopacy*.) Acc. to later traditions, all the twelve Apostles, except St. John, were also martyrs.

(2) A name given to the Epistle read in the E. Liturgy. It is always a portion of an epistle of one of the apostles or is taken from Acts, and never, as in Western rites on occasion, an extract from the OT. The word is also used for the book which contains these readings set out as appointed.

(3) An official in the *Catholic Apostolic Church.

On (1) J. B.*Lightfoot *St. Paul's Epistle to the Galatians* (1865), pp. 89–97. ('On the Name and Office of Apostle'). K. E. *Kirk (ed.), *The Apostolic Ministry*. Essays on the History and the Doctrine of Episcopacy (1946). H. Vogelstein, 'The Development of the Apostolate in Judaism and its Transformation in Christianity' in *Hebrew Union College Annual*, ii (1925), pp. 99–123. K. H. Rengstorf in *T.W.B.*, i (1933), pp. 406–48, s.v. ἀπόστολος, with full bibl. G. Saas, *Apostelamt und Kirche*. Eine theologisch-exegetische Untersuchung des paulinischen Apostelbegriffs (1939); A. Fridrichsen, *The Apostle and his Message* (Uppsala, 1947); H. von Campenhausen, 'Der urchristliche Apostelbegriff' in *Studia Theologica* (Lund), i (1948), pp. 96–130. A Verheul, 'De Moderne Exegese over ἀπόστολος' in *Sacris Erudiri*, i (1948), pp. 380–96.

APOSTLE OF ENGLAND, The. St. *Augustine of *Canterbury (q.v.).

APOSTLE OF THE GENTILES, The. St.*Paul. The title does not occur in the NT; but cf. Gal. 2. 7.

APOSTLE OF ROME, The. Title of St. *Philip Neri, (q.v.).

APOSTLES' CREED, The. A statement of faith used only in the W. Church. Like other ancient *Creeds, it falls into three sections, concerned with God, Jesus Christ, and the Holy Spirit, and appears to be based structurally on Mt. 28. 19. It is terse in expression, and lacks theological explanations. Though

its affirmations can be supported by NT evidence, the formula itself is not of apostolic origin. Its title is first found *c.* 390, and soon afterwards the legend appears that it was a joint composition by the twelve Apostles. An 8th cent. writer is the first to quote it exactly in its present form, but local baptismal confessions in use at Rome and in other W. Churches in the 4th cent. already approximate to the present Creed, with minor variations and the lack of a few words and phrases. Some scholars hold that in this shorter form the Creed was in use at Rome by 150, others that the 4th cent. Creed grew more gradually from an earlier threefold confession of nine clauses by additions to the central section. By the early Middle Ages the complete form was everywhere used at baptism in the W., and the practice of reciting it in daily services soon began. Both uses continue. Thus in the BCP it is used daily in the services of *Mattins and *Evensong, except on the thirteen days in the year on which the *Athanasian Creed is prescribed to be said in its place at Mattins.

A. E. Burn, *The Apostles' Creed* ('Oxford Church Text Books', 1906); J. N. D. Kelly, *Early Christian Creeds* (1950), esp. pp. 368–434. F.*Kattenbusch, *Das apostolische Symbol* (2 vols., 1894–1900). T.*Zahn, *Das apostolische Symbolum* (1893; Eng. tr., 1899); A.*Harnack, 'Apostolisches Symbolum' in *P.R.E.* (ed. 3), i (1897), pp. 741–55 (Eng. tr. as sep. work, *The Apostles' Creed* 1901); E. Vacandard, 'Les Origines du symbole des apôtres' in *R.Q.H.*, lxvii (1899), pp. 329–77; A. C. McGiffert, *The Apostles' Creed* (1902); H.*Lietzmann, 'Die Anfänge des Glaubensbekenntnisses' in *Festgabe . . . A. Harnack* (1921), pp. 226–42, id. in *R.G.G.* (ed. 2), i. (1927), col. 443–6. P. Feine, *Die Gestalt des apostolischen Glaubensbekenntnisses in der Zeit des Neuen Testaments* (1925). J. de Ghellinck, S.J., *Patristique et moyen-âge*, i: Les Recherches sur les origines du symbole des apôtres (1946; ed. 2, 1949), fundamental with full summary of modern literature. See also bibl. to *Old Roman Creed.*

APOSTLES, Doctrine of the Twelve. See *Didache.*

APOSTLES, Epistle of the. See *Testament of Our Lord in Galilee.*

APOSTLESHIP OF PRAYER, The. A RC pious association under the guidance of the *Jesuit Order, with special devotion to the *Sacred Heart of Jesus. There are three degrees of membership, acc. to the rule of devotion undertaken. It was founded at Vals, France, in 1844 by F. X. Gautrelet, and in 1879 received from the Pope formal statutes, which were revised in 1896.

APOSTOLIC AGE, The. A modern title in use esp. among Biblical scholars for the first period in the history of the Christian Church, approximately falling within the lifetime of the *Apostles (q.v.). Great importance is attached, esp. by Protestants, to the practices and beliefs of the Church during this period.

APOSTOLIC CANONS, The. A series of 85 canons attributed to the Apostles. They form the concluding chapter (viii. 47) of the '*Apostolic Constitutions', the author of which (late 4th cent.) probably compiled them him-

self. Most of them deal with the ordination, the official responsibilities, and the moral conduct of the clergy, though a few are concerned with the duties of Christians in general. Twenty of the set are based on canons of *Antioch (? 341). The first 50 were translated into Latin in the 6th cent. by *Dionysius Exiguus, and thus became part of the early canon law of the Western Church, while the *Trullan Council (692) (though it condemned the 'Apostolic Constitutions' as a whole) secured their formal recognition in the East.

F. X. Funk, *Didascalia et Constitutiones Apostolorum* (1905), i, 564–93; Eng. trans. in the *Ante-Nicene Christian Library*, vol. xvii, pp. 257–69.

APOSTOLIC CHURCH ORDER, The. An early Christian document, containing regulations on various matters of moral and ecclesiastical practice. It is so named because its contents are ascribed to the various Apostles, who speak at a reputed council at which Mary and Martha were present. It is thought to have been composed in Egypt *c.* A.D. 300. The document was evidently the work of a very eccentric or ignorant compiler, as it treats 'Peter' and 'Cephas' as different persons and deals with *Readers as though they ranked between *Presbyters and *Deacons. It contains a text of the *Two Ways parallel to, or based on, that in the *Didache. It was originally written in Greek, but it survives also in Latin and in several Oriental versions.

The Greek text was first edited by J. W. Bickell, *Geschichte des Kirchenrechts* (1843), pp. 107–32. The Latin is in E. Hauler, *Didascaliae apostolorum fragmenta Ueronensia Latina*, fasc. 1 (1900), pp. 92–101. A.*Harnack, *Sources of the Apostolic Canons* [= the 'Apostolic Church Order', the Eng. trans. having a very misleading title] (1895).

APOSTOLIC CONSTITUTIONS, The. A collection of ecclesiastical law dating from the latter half of the 4th cent. and almost certainly of Syrian *provenance.* The full title is 'Ordinances of the Holy Apostles through Clement'. Of its eight books I to VI are based on the '*Didascalia'; VII, 1–32 on the '*Didache'; VII, 33–49 is liturgical material; VIII, 1–2 may be connected with *Hippolytus' 'Concerning Spiritual Gifts'; VIII, 3–27 is an elaborate version of the Antiochene Liturgy; VIII, 28–46 are canons; while VIII, 47 is the '*Apostolic Canons', perhaps added to the work later. There are good grounds for identifying the compiler with the 4th cent. interpolator of St. *Ignatius' Epp., and there are also some indications that he was an *Arian. The work is a valuable witness to the religious practices and beliefs of its period.

Ed. princeps by F. *Torres, Venice, 1563, repr. by J. B. *Cotelier in *Patres Apostolici*, i (1672) with new Lat. tr. Later edd. by W. Ueltzen (Schwerin, 1853), P. A. *Lagarde (Leipzig, 1862) and F. X. Funk (Paderborn, 1905). J. P. Migne, *PG*, i, 555–1156 (from Cotelier). Liturgy in Book VIII also pr. in Brightman, *L.E.W.*, pp. 3–30, with introd. pp. xvii–xlvii. Eng. tr. by J. Donaldson in A.N.C.L., xvii (1870), pt. 2. F. X. Funk, *Die apostolischen Konstitutionen* (1891), and later works. F. Nau in *D.T.C.*, iii (1908), cols. 1520–37, s.v. 'Constitutions apostoliques'; H. *Leclercq, O.S.B., in *D.A.C.L.*, iii (pt. 2; 1914), cols. 2732–95, s.v.

'Constitutions apostoliques'. Altaner (1950), p. 43 f., with later bibl.

APOSTOLIC DELEGATE. A person appointed by the Pope to keep the *Vatican informed of ecclesiastical matters in the territory which the *Holy See has assigned to him. He is not a diplomatic official, his status being purely ecclesiastical. The Vatican appointed an Apostolic Delegate to Great Britain for the first time in 1938 in the person of Mgr. William Godfrey (b. 1889).

APOSTOLIC FATHERS, The. The title given since the later 17th cent. to those Fathers of the age immediately succeeding the NT period whose works in whole or in part have survived. They are *Clement of Rome, *Ignatius, *Hermas, *Polycarp, and *Papias, and the authors of the 'Ep. of *Barnabas', of the 'Ep. to *Diognetus', of '2 *Clement', and of the '*Didache'. In modern printed editions the 'Martyrdoms' of Clement, Ignatius, and Polycarp are sometimes included with them. Some of these writings hovered for a time on the edge of the NT canon, Herm. and Barn., e.g. being found in the *Codex Sinaiticus and 1 Clem. in the *Codex Alexandrinus. Though full of reminiscences of the NT, they are on an altogether lower spiritual level.

J. B.*Cotelier, *SS. Patrum qui Temporibus Apostolicis floruerunt . . . Opera* (Paris, 1672). J. P. Migne, *PG*, i–ii. Collected modern edd. by O. Gebhardt, A. *Harnack and T.*Zahn (3 vols., Leipzig, 1875–7; ed. minor, ib., 1877); by J. B.*Lightfoot (5 vols., 1885–90, fine ed. of Clement, Ignatius, and Polycarp only, with full comm. and notes; ed. of texts, with Eng. tr., in one vol., 1891); by F. X. Funk (2 vols., Tübingen, 1878–81); by K.*Lake (Loeb, 2 vols., 1917–19, with Eng. tr.); and by K. Bihlmeyer (Tübingen, 1924). Eng. tr. also in *Ante-Nicene Christian Library* (1867). For edd. and transs. of individual Fathers, see the sep. entries. For vocabulary, E. J. Goodspeed, *Index Patristicus sive Clavis Patrum Apostolicorum* (Leipzig, 1907). A. *Hilgenfeld, *Die apostolischen Väter* (1853); D. Völter, *Die apostolischen Väter* (2 vols., Leiden, 1904–10). *The New Testament in the Apostolic Fathers* (ed. Oxford Society of Hist. Theology, 1905). For doctrine, see L. J. Tixeront, *Histoire des dogmes*, i (1905), ch. iii, pp. 115–63 (Eng. tr., 1910, pp. 104–48). T. F. Torrance, *The Doctrine of Grace in the Apostolic Fathers* (1948). J. Lawson, *A Theological and Historical Introduction to the Apostolic Fathers* (1961).

APOSTOLIC KING, The. A title traditionally borne by the King of Hungary. It is supposed to have been conferred on the first King, Stephen I (d. 1038), by Pope *Sylvester II on account of his apostolic zeal. He was also known as 'His Apostolic Majesty'.

APOSTOLIC SEE, The. The see of Rome, so called from its traditional association with the two Apostles, St. *Peter and St. *Paul.

APOSTOLIC SUCCESSION. The method whereby the ministry of the Christian Church is held to be derived from the apostles by a continuous succession. It has usually been associated with an assertion that the succession has been maintained by a series of bishops. These bishops have been regarded as succeeding the apostles because : (1) they perform the functions of the apostles; (2) their commission goes back to the apostles; (3) they succeed one

another in the same sees, the derivation of which may be traced back to the communion of the apostles; and (4) by some writers because through their consecration to the episcopal office they inherit from the apostles the transmission of the Holy Ghost which empowers them for the performance of their work. The fact of the succession of the ministry from the apostles, and of the apostles from Christ, was strongly emphasized by *Clement of Rome before the end of the 1st cent.; and the necessity for it has been very widely taught within the historic Church. The fact of continuity in the succession has occasionally been disputed; and the necessity has been denied by most Protestant writers, and asserted only with qualifications by some other theologians.

A. W. Haddan, *Apostolical Succession in the Church of England* (1869); C. *Gore, *The Ministry of the Christian Church* (1889; ed. C. H. Turner, 1919); A. C. *Headlam in *The Prayer Book Dictionary* (1912 and 1925); C. H. *Turner in *Essays on the Early History of the Church and the Ministry*, edited by H. B.*Swete (1918; ed. 2, 1921); K. E.*Kirk (ed.), *The Apostolic Ministry* (1946). A. Ehrhardt, *The Apostolic Succession in the First Two Centuries of the Church* (1953). E. Benz, *Bischofsamt und apostolische Sukzession im deutschen Protestantismus* (1953).

APOSTOLIC TRADITION, The. (Gk. ἡ ἀποστολικὴ παράδοσις). The document formerly known as the '*Egyptian Church Order', now generally held to be the work of St. *Hippolytus. The treatise is apparently referred to in the words περὶ χαρισμάτων ἀποστολικὴ παράδοσις which occur in the list of writings attributed to Hippolytus on the statue of him preserved in the *Lateran Museum at Rome. It contains a detailed description of rites and practices presumably in use at Rome in the early 3rd cent. The main source for the text is a Latin codex at *Verona (lv[53]), though in a much modified form it has been incorporated into many later documents which have survived in a variety of Eastern languages. The Verona text was first published by E. Hauler in 1900, but the credit for establishing its Hippolytan authorship belongs to R. H. *Connolly, and, in a less degree, to E. *Schwartz.

The authorities for the text are in Copt. (Sah. and Boh.), Eth., Arab., and Lat.; also its workings-over in *Apostolic Constitutions, vii, and in *Testamentum Domini (extant in Syr.). The text was first publd. in Eth. in J. *Ludolf, *Ad suam Historiam Aethiopicam Commentarius* (Frankfurt a.M., 1691), in Lat. in E. Hauler, *Didascaliae Apostolorum Fragmenta Veronensia* (Leipzig, 1900). E.*Schwartz, *Über die Pseudoapostolischen Kirchenordnungen* (Strassburg, 1910); R. H. Connolly, *The So-called Egyptian Church Order and Derived Documents* (Camb. Texts and Studies, viii, 4, 1916). Crit. text (Engl.) ed. G.*Dix, O.S.B., (with textual evidence well set out; S.P.C.K., 1937); other edd. by B. S. Easton (Cambridge, 1934) and B. Botte, O.S.B. (S.C. 11, 1946). H. Elfers, *Die Kirchenordnung Hippolyts von Rom* (1938). R. Lorentz, *De egyptische Kerkenordeningen en Hippolytus van Rome* (denies Hippolytean authorship; Haarlem, 1929). B. Botte, 'L'Authenticité de la Tradition apostolique de S. Hippolyte' in *Recherches de Théologie ancienne et médiévale*, xvi (1949), pp. 177–85.

APOSTOLICAE CURAE. The encyclical of Pope *Leo XIII, issued on 13 Sept. 1896, in which Anglican Orders were condemned as invalid through defect both of form and intention. A 'Responsio' was issued in

1897 by the Abps. of Canterbury and York. For the history of the question see *Anglican Ordinations*.

The text is in *Leonis Papae XIII Allocutiones, Epistolae, Constitutiones*, vi (1900), pp. 198–210. Bettenson, pp. 382–3.

APOSTOLICI (Lat.), 'Apostolics'. Among the several sects and religious bodies to whom this title has been applied, either by themselves or by others, are:

(1) Some *Gnostic communities of the 2nd–4th cents. They are described by *Epiphanius (*Haer.* 61).

(2) An ascetic body which flourished in the 12th cent. around Cologne and at Périgueux in France. They rejected marriage, oaths, and the use of flesh-meat, and attacked many Catholic doctrines. St. *Bernard of Clairvaux preached against them.

(3) A sect begun at Parma in 1260 by one Gerard Segarelli. It drew its inspiration from the *Franciscan teaching on poverty. It was condemned at Rome in 1286 and again in 1291, and in 1300 Segarelli was burnt to death at Parma. Shortly afterwards the sect was revived under Fra Dolcino, who expounded apocalyptic doctrines derived from *Joachim of Flora. In 1307 he, too, was burnt at the stake.

(4) The name has also been assumed by certain Protestant groups, e.g. some *Anabaptist sects.

APOSTOLICITY. One of the four marks of the Church set forth in the *Nicene Creed ([*Credo*] *in unam sanctam catholicam et apostolicam ecclesiam*). On a Catholic view, the word means identifiable with the Church of the Apostles by succession (see *Apostolic Succession*) and continuity of doctrine, to which RCs would add by communion with the 'see of Peter'. By Protestants it is generally understood to mean 'primitive', in contrast with real or supposed corruptions of post-apostolic times. (See also *Notes of the Church*.)

APOSTOLICUM. A name given, esp. on the Continent, to the *Apostles' Creed.

APOTHEOSIS (Gk. ἀποθέωσις, from θεός, 'god'). The pagan custom of regarding as gods emperors and certain other persons, at first only after their death, but from the time of Domitian (A.D. 81–96) even in their lifetime. This idea of deification has sometimes been thought to be connected with the origins of Christian canonization, a theory which finds a measure of support in the medieval use of the Latin 'divus' as a title of the saints. Theologically, however, there is the essential difference that the saints are not reckoned to be more than human. Rarely in *Gnosticism, and once in *Gregory Thaumaturgus, the word ἀποθέωσις is used in the sense of 'union with God'; but this idea of 'divination' through religious union, though common in Eastern Christian mysticism and theology, is much more generally described as θέωσις or θεοποίησις.

E. Strong, *Apotheosis and After Life* (1915). F. Cumont, 'L'Aigle funéraire des Syriens et l'apothéose des empereurs' in *Revue historique des Religions*, lxii (1910), pp. 119–64; repr. with additions in his *Études syriennes* (1917), pp. 35–118. G. Wissowa, *Religion und Kultus der Römer* (1902), pp. 282–89 ('Dea Roma und die Divi Imperatores'). F. Hiller in P.W., ii (1895), cols. 184–8, s.v., and E. R. Bevan in *H.E.R.E.*, iv (1911), pp. 525–33, s.v. 'Deification (Greek and Roman)', with bibl.

APPARITIONS OF THE BVM, The. The eighteen manifestations of the BVM to St. *Bernadette (q.v.) in the grotto near *Lourdes between 11 Feb. and 16 July 1858. They are commemorated in the RC Church on 11 Feb. by a Feast which has been of universal observance since 1907.

APPARITOR. An officer chosen by an ecclesiastical judge to summon persons to appear before, and to execute the orders and decrees of, his court. When apparitors hold their office by patent, the judge cannot remove them at his discretion. Their number and privileges were restricted by a *canon (138) of 1603. They were also anciently called 'Summoners' or 'Sumners'.

APPEALS. Applications from a lower to a higher judicial authority, a term commonly used in connexion with the ecclesiastical *courts. Appeals by clergy and laity to authorities higher than their diocesans were based upon Roman civil law and regulated by several councils from *Nicaea (325) to *Trent (1545–63). During the Middle Ages appeal to the Papal *Curia from the English ecclesiastical courts occasioned intermittent friction between Church and State. From the time of *Henry II, the Kings of England attempted to limit appeals to Rome, until in 1534 Henry VIII abolished them, substituting the Court of *Delegates as final arbiter in ecclesiastical causes.

APPEARANCE. A word once popular in philosophy through the use made of it by F. H. *Bradley in his *Appearance and Reality* (1893). Acc. to Bradley, the only reality is an absolute all-inclusive experience ('the richer for every discord'), and everything other than this, including morality and religion, is convicted on analysis of contradiction and hence assigned to the realm of 'appearance'. In a somewhat different sense, the word is also used of those elements in our knowledge which we obtain through our senses. It is this meaning which is found in the *Platonist emphasis on the need for 'saving the appearances' (σώζειν τὰ φαινόμενα, *Proclus, Hyp. 5. 10), i.e. for securing that the facts of sense-observation have their due place in any rationalized theory or system about the world.

APPELLANTS. (1) The 31 RC secular priests, headed by William Bishop (*c.* 1553–1624), titular Bp. of *Chalcedon from 1623, who appealed to *Rome in 1599 for the cancellation of G. *Blackwell's appointment as

*Archpriest and superior of the mission on the ground that his pro-*Jesuit policy was damaging the RC cause in England. Since Card. W. *Allen's death (1594), the English RCs had become divided into an extreme party, mostly Jesuits, under R. *Parsons, who wished to destroy *Elizabeth's government, and the remainder who were politically loyal; and Blackwell's appointment in 1598 had brought matters to a head. The original Appeal was a failure. But, as Blackwell persevered in his policy, the seculars made further Appeals in 1601 and 1602, the third time with the support of the French ambassador. Blackwell was reprimanded, his connexion with the Jesuits severed, and several Appellant priests put on the controlling council. On his return, Bishop drew up a 'Protestation of Allegiance' to Elizabeth (31 Jan. 1603) in which he and 12 other priests formally repudiated the use of political means for the conversion of England. The controversy came to an end when in 1608 Blackwell himself took the Oath of Allegiance to *James I.

(2) The name assumed by those of *Jansenist sentiments who, after the condemnation by '*Unigenitus' (1713) of 101 of P. *Quesnel's propositions, tried to prevent its acceptance. Their most important representative was Card. L. A. *de Noailles, the Abp. of *Paris, who was joined by 12 bishops, the *Sorbonne, and several other universities. They carried on a prolonged literary controversy by pamphlets and appealed against the Papal decree to a future General Council. In 1718 they were condemned and excommunicated by the bull 'Pastoralis Officii' and from 1720 were attacked also by the French court. With the submission of de Noailles in 1728, the Appellants lost their chief support and soon sank into insignificance.

On (1), T. G. Law (ed.), *The Archpriest Controversy. Documents relating to the Dissensions of the Roman Catholic Clergy, 1597–1602* (Camden Society, N.S., lxvi and lxviii, 1896–8).

On (2), see bibl. to *Jansenism*.

APPIAN WAY, The (Lat., *Via Appia*). The famous road constructed by the censor Appius Claudius Caecus in 312 B.C. from *Rome to the S. of Italy. It was orig. carried as far as Capua, but later taken through to Brindisi. After disembarking at Puteoli, St. *Paul travelled on the Appian Way on his first journey to Rome, being met (Acts 28. 15) by groups of Christian disciples at 'Appii Forum' (43 miles) and *Three Taverns (33 miles from Rome).

Owing to the construction of the Via Appia Nuova, for the first few miles out of Rome the old road remains much as it was in ancient times. It is still flanked by many monuments, mostly tombs. The Christian sanctuaries and remains along it include the '*Domine, Quo Vadis?' chapel (q.v.); the *catacombs of St. *Callistus (the burying place of most of the Popes in the 3rd cent.) and of Praetextatus; and the basilica of St. *Sebastian (near the reputed resting-place of the remains of St. *Peter and St. Paul during the persecution of Valerian, 258).

APPROPRIATION. The practice common in the Middle Ages of permanently annexing to a monastery the *tithes and other endowments which were intended for parochial use. See also *Impropriation*.

APRON. The 'apron' which is part of the distinctive dress of Anglican bishops, deans and archdeacons is really a shortened form of the *cassock, extending to the knees. Formerly this dress was widely worn on the Continent, but in the 19th cent. its use was very much restricted by *Pius IX.

APSE. A semicircular or polygonal eastern end to a chancel. This was a universal feature of the primitive *basilican type of church architecture, adapted from the model of Roman public buildings. The altar stood in the chord of the apse, with the seats of the bishop and presbyters in the curved space behind. It was introduced into England by St. *Augustine's mission, but the Celtic square-ended chancel continued to prevail. The Norman builders again favoured the apse, but in later building there was a general reversion to the indigenous square-end, only a few examples of apsidal sanctuaries still remaining, e.g. at *Norwich Cathedral. See *Basilica*.

A.P.U.C. ('Association for the Promotion of the Unity of Christendom'). A society formed in 1857 in F. G. *Lee's rooms to further the cause of reunion, esp. between the C of E and Rome. Its members were required to say daily the prayer for the unity of the Church in the Latin Missal. It owed its foundation chiefly to A. M. Phillipps *de Lisle, a leading RC layman, who had earlier (c. 1838) established a 'Society for Prayers for the Conversion of England'; and it included Anglicans (among them A. P. *Forbes) and also some Easterns. It was condemned by the *Holy Office in 1864 and RCs were then compelled to withdraw from it.

The organ of the Association was *The Union Review* (1863–75). For details see the lives of A. M. P. de Lisle, F. G. Lee, J. H. *Newman (by Wilfrid Ward) and H. E. *Manning.

AQUARIANS (Lat. *Aquarii*, from *aqua*, 'water'). A name given by *Philaster (*Haer*. 77) and *Augustine (*Haer*. 64) to a sect or sects which, for ascetic or other reasons, used water instead of wine in the Eucharist. They were sometimes known as 'Hydroparastatae' (Gk. Ὑδροπαραστάται, 'those who advocate water').

AQUAVIVA, CLAUDIUS (1543-1615), fifth General of the *Jesuit Order. The son of the Duke of Atri, in the Abruzzi, he studied civil and canon law at Perugia, and entered the Jesuit novitiate in *Rome in 1567. After being provincial at Naples and Rome, he was elected Superior General of the order in 1581. His remarkable gifts, which made him a born ruler and a great statesman, led to the consolidation of the Society and its subsequent far-reaching influence. During the first years of his generalship he was faced with many difficulties, among them the persecutions in England, the *Huguenot troubles in France, the expulsion of the Jesuits from *Venice and other places, and esp. the Spanish schism within the order, organized by G. *Vasquez and supported by *Philip II and the Pope. In the course of the schism the General was denounced in Rome, but he convinced the Pope of the imprudence of the revolt. He again successfully appealed to the Pope when the Inquisition wanted to examine the constitutions of the order. The position became serious, however, when *Sixtus V, who had always been hostile to the order, wished to alter its entire organization; but the plan was frustrated by the Pope's death. During Aquaviva's generalship the Society developed considerably, esp. in its missionary activities. It was implicated in several theological controversies, among them the famous dispute with the *Dominicans on *Grace. Apart from the exterior organization of the order, Aquaviva strengthened its inner life; he ordered the drawing-up of the famous "Ratio Studiorum' as well as a comprehensive interpretation of St. *Ignatius' 'Spiritual Exercises'; and he fostered their spirit in many encyclical letters, stressing the need of combining the active life with prayer and meditation.

Works listed in Sommervogel, i (1890), cols. 480–91, and viii (1898), col. 1669 f. J. de Guibert, S.J., ' La Généralat de Claude Aquaviva (1581–1615). Sa place dans l'histoire de la spiritualité de la Compagnie de Jésus' in *Archivum Historicum Societatis Jesu*, x (1941), pp. 59–93. A. Astrain, S.J., *Historia de la Compañía de Jesús*, vols. iii (1910), pt. 2, and iv (1913). E. Rivière in *D.H.G.E.*, i (1912), cols. 354–8, s.v. 'Acquaviva', and P. Dudon in *Dictionnaire de spiritualité*, i (1937), cols. 829–34, s.v., both with bibl.

AQUILA, St. See *Priscilla, St.*

AQUILA, Version of. Greek version of the OT. It was the work of Aquila, a native of Sinope in Pontus, who lived under Hadrian (117–38). Acc. to St. *Epiphanius (*Mens. et Pond.* 14), he was a relative of the Emperor and was converted to Christianity during a stay in *Jerusalem, but, having refused to give up his astrological studies, he was excommunicated and became a proselyte to Judaism. Having become a disciple of the *Rabbis, from whom he learned Hebrew and the rabbinical method of exegesis, he used this knowledge to make a Greek translation of the OT, intended to replace the *Septuagint which had been adopted by the Christians. This translation, which was finished probably *c.* 140, was extremely literal; it attempted to reproduce even the etymology of the Hebrew words and particles that cannot be translated. This procedure frequently obscured the sense; but the fidelity of Aquila's version to the Hebrew original was admitted by the Fathers most competent to judge, such as *Origen and *Jerome.

Surviving fragments of Aquila's version ed. F. *Field in *Origenis Hexaplorum quae supersunt* (2 vols., Oxford, 1871–1875); more recently discovered passages ed. G. Mercati, *Un palimpsesto ambrosiano dei salmi esapli* (Turin, 1896), and F. C. *Burkitt, *Fragments of the Book of Kings according to the Translation of Aquila* (1897, with pref. by C. Taylor; texts from the Cairo Geniza). M. Abrahams, *Aquila's Greek Version of the Hebrew Bible* (1919); A. E. Silverstone, *Aquila and Onkelos* (Publications of the University of Manchester. Semitic Languages Series, No. 1, 1931; claims to identify Aquila with Onkelos). H. B. *Swete, *An Introduction to the Old Testament in Greek* (1900), pp. 31–42. E. *Schürer, *Geschichte des jüdischen Volkes im Zeitalter Jesu Christi*, iii (ed. 4, 1909), pp. 435–9, with bibl. to date. C. Taylor in *D.C.B.*, iii (1882), p. 17 f., s.v. 'Hexapla, 3'.

AQUINAS, St. Thomas. See *Thomas Aquinas, St.*

ARABIC VERSIONS OF THE NEW TESTAMENT. Several are known, but none seems to antedate the age of *Mohammed. They were made in some cases direct from the Greek, in others through the *Syriac and Coptic (*Bohairic) versions. The oldest surviving MS. (8th cent.) is a translation from the Syriac *Peshitta. Not until the 13th cent. was an Arabic version sponsored by ecclesiastical authority; but in that cent. two official revisions were made at *Alexandria. The later of these, the so-called 'Alexandrian Vulgate', is that followed in modern printed Arabic editions of the NT.

The NT was ed. by T. Erpenius at Leyden, 1616. The Gospels alone were pr. at Rome, 1590 (colophon, 1591); and, with Lat. tr., 1591; crit. ed. P. de Lagarde (Leipzig, 1864). I. Guidi, 'Le traduzioni degli evangelii in arabo e in etiopico' in *Atti della R. Accademia dei Lincei*, Serie Quarta, Classe di Scienze Morali, Storiche et Filologiche iv, i (1888), pp. 5–37. C. Peters, 'Proben eines bedeutsamen arabischen Evangelien-Textes' in *O.C.*, Ser. 3, xi (1936), pp. 188–211 (texts, with Germ. tr., pp. 196–211). G. Graf, 'Arabische Übersetzungen der Apokalypse' in *Biblica*, x (1929), pp. 170–94. F. C. *Burkitt in *H.D.B.*, i (1898), 136–8, s.v.

ARAMAIC. The Semitic language which was the vernacular in Palestine in the time of Christ, and which He Himself almost certainly used. It had long been spoken by the Arameans in N. Syria and in Mesopotamia, and came to be used increasingly throughout the Levant for commercial and diplomatic transactions (cf. 2 Kgs. 18. 26). In later OT times it more and more ousted Hebrew as the language of Palestine. A few sections of the OT itself (Ezra 4. 8–6. 18, 7. 12–26; Dan. 2. 4–7. 28; Jer. 10. 11) are written in Aramaic and by NT times Hebrew was cultivated only by the learned. To satisfy the needs of the people, the Hebrew Scriptures were issued in the form of Aramaic paraphrases, known as the *Targums. *Syriac (q.v.) is another form of the same language, and Mandaic is closely allied to it. In the NT there are many places where the Greek reflects the Aramaic modes of thought or background of the writers, and occasionally Aramaic words are preserved, e.g. Mk. 5. 41, 7. 34, 15. 34. A few scholars have maintained that some of the NT books, e.g. Jn. (so C. F. *Burney), or even all the Gospels (so C. C. Torrey), were originally written in Aramaic and that our extant text is a translation. See also *Chaldee.

C. Brockelmann, *Grundriss der vergleichenden Grammatik der semitischen Sprachen* (2 vols., 1908–13); F. Rosenthal, *Die aramaistische Forschung seit Theodor Nöldekes Veröffentlichungen* (1939). H. Bauer-P. Leander, *Grammatik des Biblisch-Aramäischen* (1927). H. H. Rowley, *The Aramaic of the Old Testament* (1929). M. Black, *An Aramaic Approach to the Gospels and Acts* (1946). W. B. Stevenson, *Grammar of Palestinian Jewish Aramaic* (1924); G.*Dalman, *Grammatik des jüdisch-palästinischen Aramäisch* (1894; ed. 2, revised, 1905); F. Schulthess-E. Littmann, *Grammatik des christlich-palästinischen Aramäisch* (1924). A. Dupont-Sommer, *Les Araméens* (1949). For full bibl. H. Fleisch, *Introduction à l'étude des langues sémitiques* (1947), pp. 71–87.

ARBUTHNOTT, Missal of. A Scottish MS. missal dated 1491, now in the Paisley Museum. It survives complete, on 244 leaves. It corresponds closely with the typical edition of 1498 of the *Sarum Missal, with differences chiefly in the *Propers for Saints. It also contains some *sequences not found in the English pre-Reformation uses. As the only surviving specimen of the Medieval Scottish Use, the MS. is of unique value.

Ed. G. H. *Forbes, *Liber Ecclesie Beati Terrenani de Arbuthnott* (Burntisland, 1864).

ARCHAEOLOGY, Christian. The term 'archaeology' was formerly used to distinguish the description of early Christian institutions (e.g. the officers of the Church, its liturgies, law, social life, financial and territorial organization) from the narrative history of persons and events. Of such work, J. *Bingham's *Antiquities of the Christian Church* (1708–22) is the classic English example. Nowadays it commonly denotes the study of Christian monuments, as distinct from documents, for the light which they can be made to throw upon Christian antiquity, apart from their aesthetic value or place as works of art. In this context, 'antiquity' may be somewhat arbitrarily determined as the first six centuries of Christianity. As in other branches of archaeology, sites are excavated, inscriptions reconstructed, methods of building studied, forms of ornament and lettering classified, and the pedigree of pictorial themes traced (*iconography); but pottery is much less important, while the *catacombs set special problems. The main classes of early Christian monuments are cemeteries, buildings (chiefly churches, baptisteries, and monasteries), sculpture (including ivories), paintings, mosaic, textiles, liturgical implements, and such miscellaneous objects as glass, lamps, medals, and rings. Epigraphy, the study of *inscriptions, is a special branch of archaeology.

The foundations of Christian archaeology were laid by the study of the Roman catacombs which, almost forgotten for a thousand years, began to be rediscovered in the 16th cent. Its first great achievement, A. Bosio's *Roma sotterranea*, was published in 1632. Scholars of the next century applied themselves rather to classical monuments; but G. B. *de Rossi, whose great *Roma sotterranea Cristiana* began to appear in 1864, brought truly scientific methods into Christian archaeology. The Pontificio Istituto di Archeologia Cristiana at Rome is now exploring the catacombs systematically. Their frescoes have been minutely studied by J. Wilpert, who also published a *corpus* of the ancient mosaics in the Roman churches. The churches themselves are being described in a series of monographs.

Besides Rome, *Ravenna is a treasure-house of Christian monuments. Syria has proved rich in remains of churches, Egypt in monastic ruins. French excavation in N. Africa, supplemented by Italian research in Tripolitania, has recovered from the sand churches, baptisteries, mosaics, and tombstones in great numbers. Asia Minor, where pioneer work was done by W. M.*Ramsay, has yet much to disclose. The rapid progress of discovery and elucidation can be studied in the *Rivista di Archeologia cristiana* (from 1924). See also *Dura-Europos*.

The evidence of monuments alone is limited, but, used with the documents, it considerably increases our knowledge of the early Church. Little is added to the history of particular events and persons, for Christian inscriptions rarely contain the detail found in pagan ones. Yet much can be gleaned which the available literary sources omit. From the size, character, and development of cemeteries and churches we gather some idea of the growth, resources, and even the racial composition of individual communities, while their incidence helps us to trace the expansion of Christianity in each area. Paintings, mosaics, and sarcophagi illustrate beliefs, the pairing of OT and NT subjects being especially noteworthy. Archaeological material also assists liturgical and hagiographical studies, and provides evidence of the strength of Roman or non-Roman influences in regional churches. Early Christian history is not especially dependent upon archaeological methods, but future work should throw increasing light on the religious life of the ordinary layman, too often neglected by ecclesiastical historians, ancient and modern.

The following general guides contain fuller lists of books: W. Lowrie, *Monuments of the Early Church* (1901); H. *Leclercq, *Manuel d'archéologie chrétienne* (2 vols., 1907); *British Museum: A Guide to the Early Christian and Byzantine Antiquities* (2nd ed., 1921); J. Strzygowski, *Origins of Christian Church Art* (E.T., 1923); W. Smith and S. Cheetham, *Dictionary of Christian Antiquities* (2 vols., 1875–80); F. *Cabrol–H. Leclercq, *Dictionnaire d'archéologie chrétienne et de liturgie* (15 vols., 1907–53); R. Aigrain, *Archéologie chrétienne* (1941).

ARCHANGEL (Gk. ἀρχάγγελος, 'chief angel'). In the NT the word occurs only twice, at Jude v. 9, where *Michael is referred to as 'the Archangel', and at 1 Thess. 4. 16 ('the voice of the archangel'). In Christian tradition *Gabriel and *Raphael are also commonly reckoned with Michael among the archangels. Acc. to traditional angelology, as expounded by Pseudo-*Dionysius the Areopagite, the archangels belong to the third and lowest hierarchy of the angelic beings. See also *Angel*.

ARCHBISHOP. (Gk. ἀρχιεπίσκοπος). In the 4th and 5th cents. the title was applied to the *patriarchs and holders of other outstanding sees. Later its use was extended to *metropolitans (or *primates) having jurisdiction over an ecclesiastical province. In the Latin Church it has now almost become a title of honour for a bishop of a distinguished see.

See bibl. to *Bishops*.

ARCHDEACON. A cleric having a defined administrative authority delegated to him by the bishop in the whole or part of the diocese. The territory assigned to him is known as an archdeaconry and gives him a territorial title, e.g. 'Archdeacon of Lindsey'. In the C of E and other Churches of the Anglican Communion an Archdeacon is styled 'Venerable'. The duties of archdeacons vary widely but they usually include a general disciplinary supervision of the clergy of their archdeaconry and a more particular care over the temporal administration of its ecclesiastical property. Thus they usually *induct parish priests to new benefices and admit *churchwardens to their offices. Originally, as the name implies, an archdeacon was merely the chief of the *deacons who assisted diocesan bishops in their work. They were in deacon's orders and gradually acquired what was almost a right of succession to the episcopal throne. The transition from this to the present position of archdeacons was accomplished by the 9th cent. but the steps by which it came about are not clear. In England since 1662 an archdeacon must be in priest's orders, and since 1840 must have been so for six years. The Anglican *Ordinal presupposes that among his functions the examination and presentation of candidates for *Ordination.

J. *Bingham, *Origines Ecclesiasticae*, Book II, ch. 21 (1708), pp. 287–301. A. Gréa, 'Essai historique sur les archidiacres' in *Bibliothèque de l'École des Chartes*, xii (1851), pp. 39–67 and 215–47: F. X. Glasschröder, 'Zur Geschichte des Archidiakonates' in S. Ehses (ed.), *Festschrift zum elfhundertjährigen Jubiläum des Deutschen Campo in Rom* (1897), pp. 139–49. R. *Phillimore, *The Ecclesiastical Law of the Church of England*, i (ed. 2 by W. G. F. Phillimore, 1895), esp. pp. 194–207 (see also index); H. W. Cripps, *A Practical Treatise on the Law Relating to the Church and Clergy* (ed. 8 by K. M. Macmorran, 1937), pp. 28 and 87–93. J. P. Kirsch in *C.E.*, i (1907), p. 693 f., s.v. E. W. Watson in *D.E.C.H.*, pp. 18–21, s.v. A. Koeniger in *L.Th.K.*, i (1930), cols. 615–17, s.v. 'Archidiakon', with modern bibl. on early and medieval archdeacons (mainly very specialized); A. Amanieu in *D.D.C.*, i (1935), cols. 948–1004, s.v. 'Archidiacre', with extensive bibl.

ARCHDIOCESE. A diocese of which the holder is *ex officio* *Archbishop, e.g. *Canterbury. The word is used esp. of RC Archdioceses, e.g. *Westminster.

ARCHES, Court of. The *Consistory Court of the province of *Canterbury which formerly met in *Bow Church ('S. Maria de Arcubus'). Originally it was presided over by the Archbishop's *Official Principal, but later the office was combined with that of the 'Dean of Arches' (the judge of the Archbishop's 'Court of Peculiars' which sat in the same church) under the second title. Appeals are allowed from the diocesan Consistory Courts of the Province of Canterbury to the Court of Arches. Formerly an appeal from this Court lay only to the Pope; in 1534, by the Act for the Submission of the Clergy and the Restraint of Appeals, this was transferred to the King in Chancery. Since 1874 the Dean of Arches has also been president of the corresponding Chancery Court of York as well as of the secular court set up by the *Public Worship Regulation Act (1874).

Very few medieval records of the Court are known; those from the *Restoration to 1914, with a few exceptions, are catalogued in M. D. Slatter, *Lists of the Records of the Court of Arches deposited for Temporary Safe Keeping in the Bodleian Library in 1941* (1951; not publd. but widely circulated). M. *Parker, *De Antiquitate Britannicae Ecclesiae* (1605), pp. 30–33. W. S. Holdsworth, *A History of English Law*, i (1903), p. 371. Irene J. Churchill, *Canterbury Administration* (2 vols., 1933), vol. i, pp. 424–69, and vol. ii, App. i, pp. 186–210.

ARCHIMANDRITE (Gk. ἀρχιμανδρίτης). The term, which was in use in the E. Church from the 4th cent., was applied originally to the head of a monastery, and was thus the equivalent of the Western 'abbot'. Later, it came to be used esp. of the superior of a group of several monasteries, such as the groups at Mt. *Athos or Mt. Olympus. Nowadays the word is still used in this sense, but also of high administrative officials in the E. Church. Archimandrites of both kinds rank next after bishops. Although it is a general principle that Orthodox bishops shall be chosen from the religious orders, Archimandrites of the second kind are not infrequently appointed even if not monks.

ARCHPRIEST. An ecclesiastic in priest's orders who occupies a position of pre-eminence among other priests. From the early 5th cent. the title was applied to the senior Presbyter of a city, either by years or appointment, who performed many of the Bishop's liturgical and governmental functions in his absence or during a vacancy. In later times, while the *Archdeacon had become responsible for the governmental work of the Bishop, the Archpriest continued to perform the Bishop's sacerdotal duties in his absence. Though there is some doubt as to which was originally superior, by the 13th cent. the Archdeacon had vindicated his position. Gradually, except at *Rome, most of the work of both these officials during a vacancy was taken over by the *Vicar-General. In some continental cathedrals the Archpriest survives as a capitular dignitary.

As Christianity spread in the 4th cent. from the cities to the countryside, the title was also given, esp. in Gaul, to the cleric who presided over the groups of parishes which united for the principal Sunday Mass and other functions previously performed by the Bishop. In this sense the word is first found in the Second Council of Tours (576). With the formation of separate parishes the importance of the Archpriest declined, and most of his duties were taken over by the *rural dean.

In the RC and esp. in the Orthodox Church, the title is still one of honour, which may or may not carry any specific function. In the E. Church it is the highest rank to which a married priest can attain. The title was also given to the superior appointed by the Pope to govern the secular priests sent to England from foreign seminaries between 1598 and 1621 (see foll. entry).

A. Amanieu in *D.D.C.*, i (1935), cols. 1004–26, s.v. 'Archiprêtre', with extensive bibl.

ARCHPRIEST CONTROVERSY, The.
The dispute between the pro-*Jesuit and anti-Jesuit RC clergy in England which followed the death of Card. W. *Allen in 1594. For details, see *Appellants* (1) and *Blackwell, G.*

ARCOSOLIUM.
The word is sometimes used as an equivalent to 'sarcophagus', but properly it is applied to the particular kind of tomb, excavated in the wall of the Roman *catacombs, consisting of two halves, the lower being the actual sarcophagus, on which after the burial a marble slab was placed horizontally, and the upper an arch carved out to a depth equal to the width of this slab. Many of the martyrs, though not the earliest, are buried in such 'arcosolia', the slab coverings having been used as altars. The ornamentations of the 'arcosolia' were often beautiful and elaborate, and, in later times, complicated forms of tomb embodying several 'arcosolia' were sometimes constructed.

G. B. *de Rossi, *La Roma sotterranea cristiana*, esp. ii (1877), pp. 419 f. and 492 f. H. *Leclercq, O.S.B., in *D.A.C.L.*, i (pt. ii; 1907), cols. 2774–87, s.v., with full reff.

AREOPAGITE, The.
The mystical writer, *Dionysius (6) (? 5th cent.), so named from a wrong identification with the Dionysius who was converted by St. Paul's speech on the *Areopagus (Acts 17. 34).

AREOPAGUS, The
(Gk., Ἄρειος πάγος, 'Mars' Hill'), a spur jutting out and separated by a short saddle from the western end of the Acropolis, Athens, prob. so called from a myth that Mars had here cleared himself of the murder of Halirrhothius, the son of Neptune. The name Areopagus was also applied to an oligarchical council which, from very early times, met on the hill. Its functions appear to have been mainly judicial (esp. trials for homicide), though at times it endeavoured to exert political influence. Under the Roman Empire it seems to have been increasingly concerned with religious matters. It is not entirely clear whether, when St. *Paul was brought to the Areopagus to explain his 'new teaching' (Acts 17. 19), it was before the official court or whether the place was merely chosen as convenient for a meeting. The language of Acts suggests the latter view, though a marginal note in some MSS indicates the other alternative, which was that adopted by St. *Chrysostom. Traces of ancient stone seats on the Areopagus are still visible.

B. Keil, *Beiträge zur Geschichte des Areopags* (Sb. (Leipz.), xi. 8, 1920). W. S. Ferguson, 'Researches in Athenian and Delian Documents III' in *Klio*, ix (1909), pp. 304–40, remarks on the Council, pp. 325–30. E. Curtius, 'Paulus in Athen' in *Sb.* (Berl.), xxvi (1893), pp. 925–38; W. M. *Ramsay, *St. Paul the Traveller and Roman Citizen* (1895), pp. 243–9, with note p. 260; K. *Lake–H. J. Cadbury, in *The Beginnings of Christianity*, Part I, The Acts of the Apostles, iv (1933), pp. 212–14; M. *Dibelius, *Paulus auf dem Areopag* (Sb. (Heid.), 1938–9, Abh. 2; 1939). H. *Leclercq, O.S.B., in *D.A.C.L.*, i (pt. 2; 1907), cols. 3040–46, s.v. 'Athènes (§ ii); A. Romeo in *E.C.*, i (1949), col. 1854 f., s.v., with further bibl.

ARGENTINE, Christianity in the.
Argentina, originally a Spanish colony, obtained its complete independence in 1816 after the revolution of 1810. The state religion has always been RC, and the president of the republic must be of that faith. Papal mandates, however, are only admitted after leave from the government, and there is complete religious toleration. There are 24 dioceses divided into 9 provinces under the primacy of the Archbishop of Buenos Aires. Immigration from Europe in recent times has been chiefly from the southern countries, which are RC, so that the predominant official religion has not been changed; but there is a large body of strongly *anticlerical feeling in the country. Education is under state control.

There is much relevant material (up to 1852) in V. F. López, *Historia de la República Argentina* (10 vols., Buenos Aires, 1883–93; new ed., 1911), and P. Denis, *La République Argentine* (1920; Eng. tr. 1922), passim. R. Levene, *Lecciones de historia argentina* (ed. 11, 2 vols., Buenos Aires, 1928), esp. ch. 14 (Eng. tr., 'The Inter-American Historical Series', i, Chapel Hill, N.C., 1937, pp. 148–56). J. L. Mecham, *Church and State in Latin America. A History of Politico-Ecclesiastical Relations* (Chapel Hill, N.C., 1934), ch. 10, pp. 275–303. E. F. Every, *The Anglican Church in South America* (1915), pp. 17–40. Latourette, v (1943), pp. 83, 96, 109–111, 113, and 119–21; vii (1945), pp. 169 and 183, with bibl. reff. J. C. Zuretti, *Historia eclesiástica argentina* (Buenos Aires, 1945).

ARIANISM.
The principal heresy which denied the true Divinity of Jesus Christ, so-called after its author, *Arius (q.v.).

Arianism maintained that the Son of God was not eternal but created by the Father from nothing as an instrument for the creation of the world; and that therefore He was not God by nature, but a changeable creature, His dignity as Son of God having been bestowed on Him by the Father on account of His foreseen abiding righteousness. This teaching, though condemned by Arius's bishop *Alexander at a synod at *Alexandria (c. 320), continued to spread and to agitate the masses, until the Emp. *Constantine, anxious for the peace of the newly unified Empire, called a General Council at *Nicaea which met in 325. There the opponents of Arianism, largely under the spiritual leadership of St. *Athanasius, then a deacon at Alexandria, defined the Catholic faith in the coeternity and coequality of the Father and the Son, using the famous term '*homoousios'to express their consubstantiality, while Arius and certain heretical bishops, among them *Eusebius of Nicomedia, were banished. Constantine, at first an ardent promoter of the

Nicene faith, soon began to waver, probably owing to the influence of his sister Constantia, who favoured Arianism. In 328 the influential Eusebius of Nicomedia and the other exiled bishops were permitted to return and at once began to intrigue against the Nicene party. *Eustathius of Antioch was deposed and banished in 330, and Athanasius, since 328 Bp. of Alexandria, had to go into exile to Treves in 335. Arius himself was to be recognized as orthodox and to be received back into the Church in 336, when his sudden death prevented his reinstatement.

After the death of Constantine (337), Athanasius and some other Nicene bishops returned to their dioceses. But the new Emperor of the East, Constantius, soon openly embraced Arianism, his zeal being restrained only by his fear of his brother Constans, the ruler of the West, who protected the Catholics. In 339 Athanasius was again deprived of his see and fled to Rome, where his orthodoxy was recognized by a Council held in 341. In the same year a Council was held at *Antioch by the bishops of the East. Here the majority subscribed an attenuated form of Arianism represented by Eusebius of Nicomedia, which recommended itself for political rather than for theological reasons. The Council drew up four different statements of faith of varying admixture of error, which have in common a deliberate doctrinal vagueness, the omission or even rejection of the homoousios, and the condemnation of Arianism in its original crudeness. To restore peace to the Empire another Council was convoked by both Emperors at *Sardica in 343, which, however, the Eusebian bishops left for fear of being defeated. At Sardica Athanasius was again recognized as the rightful Bp. of Alexandria and several Arian bishops were deposed.

A short period of peace followed after Athanasius had returned to Alexandria in 346, but with the death of Constans in 350, which left Constantius sole ruler, new persecutions began for the Catholics. In 351 a Council held by the Eusebians at Sirmium drew up a new and rather vague formula intended to supersede the Creed of Nicaea, which the W. bishops were compelled to reject at Arles in 353 and at Milan in 355, Athanasius, Pope *Liberius, St. *Hilary of Poitiers and many others being exiled. The Arians, however, now split up into three major groups. The extreme party, usually called '*Anomoeans' (from ἀνόμοιος, 'dissimilar'), pressed the differences between the Father and the Son, who resemble each other at most morally; the middle party, called '*Homoeans' (from ὅμοιος, 'similar'), aimed at avoiding dogmatic precision as far as possible by affirming simply that the Son is similar to the Father 'acc. to the Scriptures'; while a third group, the '*Semi-Arians' (q.v.), favoured the term 'homoiousios' as expressing both the similarity and the distinction between the first Two Persons of the Trinity. To this last group, many of whom were almost orthodox, St. *Cyril of Jerusalem belonged for a long time. These different views were laid

down in further formulas of faith. Among them a Homoean formula, drawn up at a further Council of Sirmium (357), was accepted by a double council of E. and W. bishops who met at Seleucia and *Ariminum respectively in 359. It was of this year that St. *Jerome wrote his well-known comment: 'The whole world groaned and marvelled to find itself Arian' (Dial. adv. Lucif. 19; PL, xxiii. 172 C).

This crowning victory of Arianism was the turning point of its history, since it frightened the Semi-Arians into the ranks of orthodoxy. With the death of Constantius (361) it lost its chief supporter; Athanasius returned to Alexandria and, in 362, held a Council which facilitated the reconciliation of many of moderate views by demanding of them only the recognition of the Council of Nicaea and the rejection of Arianism. The W. under the Catholic Emp. Valentinian was soon restored to orthodoxy while in the E. its victory was retarded by the Arian Emp. Valens. Athanasius had died in 373; but the brilliant theological exposition of the Nicene faith by the three Cappadocians, St. *Basil, St. *Gregory of Nazianzus, and St. *Gregory of Nyssa, prepared the way for the final victory of orthodoxy under the Emp. *Theodosius at the Council of *Constantinople in 381. After being driven from the Empire, Arianism retained a foothold among the Teutonic tribes, esp. through *Ulphilas' *Gothic Bible and Liturgy, which prevented their rapid assimilation with their Catholic subjects when they occupied the greater part of the W. Empire and caused persecution of Catholics in N. Africa and Spain. The conversion of the Franks to Catholicism (496) was the prelude to its gradual disappearance from the religious creed of the Teutonic tribes.

The subject of necessity fills a central place in all the Church Histories of the 4th cent. (L. *Duchesne, B. J. Kidd, H. *Lietzmann, A. Fliche–A. Martin). H. M. Gwatkin, Studies of Arianism (1882; ed. 2, 1900); id., The Arian Controversy (1889). L. Maimbourg, S.J., Histoire de l'arianisme (1673; Eng. tr., 2 vols., 1728–9). P. Snellmann, Der Anfang des arianischen Streites (Helsingfors, 1904); S. Rogala, Die Anfänge des arianischen Streites (1907). G. Bardy, Recherches sur S. Lucien d'Antioche et son école (1936). J. Gummerus, Die homousianische Partei bis zum Tode des Konstantius (1900); G. Rasneur, 'L'Homoiousianisme dans ses rapports avec l'orthodoxie' in R.H.E., iv (1903), pp. 189–206 and 411–31. F. *Loofs in P.R.E. (ed. 3), ii (1897), pp. 6–45 and X. Le Bachelet in D.T.C., i (1903), cols. 1779–1863, both with full bibl.

ARIDITY. A term of *Ascetical Theology, denoting a state devoid of sensible fervour in which the soul finds it impossible, or at least very difficult, to produce the normal acts of prayer. This may be the result either of physical causes such as illness, or voluntary moral imperfections and indulgence of the passions, or, lastly (it is held), a Divinely ordained trial, normally leading to contemplation. Acc. to St. *John of the Cross, this last can be distinguished from the other two causes by three marks, viz. the absence of satisfaction in all things, whether Divine or created, a great anxiety to please God, and a continued inability to use reason or imagination in prayer. All spiritual writers agree in enjoining perseverance in prayer despite the trial of aridity and they regard it, if patiently borne, as a means of great advancement to the Christian soul.

ARIEL. A name used of *Jerusalem in Is. 29. 1. The most probable interpretation appears to be 'altar-hearth' (cf. Ezek. 43. 15).

ARIMINUM AND SELEUCIA, Synods of. Two synods to which the Emp. *Constantius summoned the Bishops of the W. and E. respectively in 359 in an attempt to settle the *Arian dispute. That at Ariminum (Rimini) was much the larger of the two assemblies, and the great majority of its adherents were orthodox. The Arian minority, however, included a group of skilled diplomats, among them *Valens and Ursacius, who succeeded in undoing the effect of the anti-Arian decision of the Council when it reached the Emperor. In consequence, under imperial pressure, the orthodox Bps. at Ariminum, who had not dispersed, were induced to recant later in the year, and in the interests of peace to subscribe an Arianizing Creed, drawn up at Nice in Thrace.

At Seleucia, under the leadership of the *Anomoeans, Acacius and Eudoxius, the Creed of Nice was also accepted.

It was these and similar events that led St. *Jerome to remark of the year 359 that 'the whole world groaned and wondered to find itself Arian' (*ingemuit totus orbis et se Arianum esse miratus est, Dial. adv. Lucif. 19, PL, xxiii, 172).

Hardouin, i (1715), cols. 711–26; Mansi, iii (1759), cols. 293–310 and 315–26. Hefele-Leclercq, i (2; 1907), pp. 929–955. G. Bardy in Fliche-Martin, iii (1936), pp. 161–9.

ARISTEAS, Letter of. A Jewish pseud-epigraphic letter written in Greek which claims to have been written by one Aristeas, an official at the court of Ptolemy Philadelphus (285–247 B.C.). It contains a legend, describing how the *Septuagint came to be miraculously written. Its composition has been variously dated between 200 B.C. and A.D. 33.

Crit. edd. of Gk. text by P. Wendland (Teubn., Leipzig, 1900) and H. St. J. Thackeray in H. B. *Swete, An Introduction to the Old Testament in Greek (1900), pp. 499–574. Eng. tr. by H. St. J. Thackeray (S.P.C.K., 1917). H. G. Meecham, The Letter of Aristeas. A Linguistic Study with special reference to the Greek Bible (Manchester Univ. Press, 1935; with repr. of Thackeray's text). J. G. Février, La Date, la composition et les sources de la lettre d'Aristée à Philocrate (Bibliothèque de l'École des Hautes Études, fasc. 242, 1924).

ARISTIDES (2nd cent.) of Athens, Christian philosopher and Apologist. Until recent times our only knowledge of him came from brief references in *Eusebius and St.*Jerome. In 1878, however, part of his 'Apology' in an *Armenian translation was published at *Venice by the *Mechitarists; and, in spite of the in-credulity of E. *Renan and others, its authen-ticity was established. In 1891 a Syriac trans-lation of the whole work, discovered in 1889 on

Mt. *Sinai, was edited by J. R. *Harris; and, in an appendix, J. A. *Robinson gave reasons for believing that the original Greek, somewhat modified and expanded, was to be found in the apology for Christianity in the 'Lives of *Barlaam and Josaphat'. Acc. to Eusebius, Aristides delivered his Apology to the Emp. *Hadrian at the same time as another apologist, *Quadratus, viz. in 124. But Dr. J. R. Harris gives strong arguments in favour of the view that these Apologies were in fact both ad-dressed to *Antoninus Pius (d. 161) early in his reign.

Aristides sought to defend the existence and eternity of God, and to show that Christians had a fuller understanding of His nature than either the barbarians, the Greeks, or the Jews, and that they alone love acc. to His precepts. Like *Justin and *Tatian, he retained the status and garb of a philosopher after his con-version. He is now credited also with a ser-mon on Lk. 23. 43. The theory of some scholars (H. Kihn, G. Krüger) that he was the author of the Ep. to *Diognetus has not, however, won general acceptance.

Eusebius, H.E., IV, iii. 3, and Chron., ad. a. 2140; Jerome, De vir. illustr., 20. Crit. ed. of Gk. text by J. Geffcken, Zwei griechische Apologeten (1907), pp. 1–96; other attempts at reconstruction of Gk. text by R. Seeberg (1893); Syr. text ed. J. R.*Harris, 'The Apology of Aristides of the Christians', with appendix with Gk. text ed. J. A. *Robin-son, in Camb. Texts and Studies, I (1) (1891); Arm. fragm. in G. B. *Pitra, Analecta Sacra, iv (1883), pp. 6–10 and 282–6. A papyrus frag. of the Gk. text has also been publd. by G. Krüger in T.L.Z., xlix (1924), p. 47 f. Eng. tr. by D. M. Kay in Ante-Nicene Christian Library. Additional vol. (1897), pp. 259–79. Bardenhewer, i (ed. 2; 1913), pp. 187–202; B. Altaner, Patrologie (ed. 2, 1950), p. 88 f.

ARISTION (1st cent.). Acc. to *Papias, as reported by *Eusebius (HE, III, xxxix, 4), he was a primary authority, with the Presbyter *John, for the traditions about the Lord. He is certainly to be distinguished from *Aristo of Pella, whom Eusebius (IV, vi, 3) cites as an authority for the *Bar Cochba revolt, though the two are identified by St. *Maximus Con-fessor. In an *Armenian MS. dated 986, [Mk.] 16. 9-20 (the concluding twelve verses of the Gospel in most texts) is attributed to 'the Presbyter Ariston'. But F. C. *Cony-beare's theory that the MS. preserves a genuine tradition which recognized Papias' Aristion as their real author has received little following.

F. C. *Conybeare, 'Aristion the Author of the Last Twelve Verses of Mark' in The Expositor, Ser. IV. viii (1893), pp. 241–54; id., 'On the Last Twelve Verses of St. Mark's Gospel' in ib., Ser. V. ii (1895), pp. 401–21; J.*Chap-man, O.S.B., 'Aristion, author of the Ep. to the Hebrews' in R. Bén. xxii (1905), pp. 50–64. Bardenhewer, i (ed. 2, 1913), p. 448 f. B. W. Bacon in D.C.G., i (1906), pp. 114–18, and E. Peterson in E.C., i (1949), col. 1908 f.

ARISTO of Pella (c. 140), early Christian *Apologist. His work has perished; but it is mentioned, without the author's name, in *Origen's 'Contra Celsum' (iv, 52), where its title is given as 'Disputation between Jason and Papiscus concerning Christ'. Jason, a baptized Jew, converts his fellow-Jew, Papis-cus, by proving the fulfilment of the Messianic prophecies in Christ. Origen defends its allegorical interpretation of the OT against the mockeries of Celsus. The 'Disputation' is first ascribed to Aristo by St.*Maximus Confessor (*Comm. in Dion. Areop. De Myst. Theol.*, i, p. 243). Acc. to *Eusebius (*HE*, IV, vi, 3), Aristo wrote an account of the destruction of *Jerusalem under Hadrian (135).

Bardenhewer, i (ed. 2, 1913), pp. 202–6, with full bibl. E. Peterson in *E.C.*, i (1949), col. 1911 f.

ARISTOBULUS, St. In Rom. 16. 10 St. *Paul sent greeting to the 'household of Aristobulus' (τοὺς ἐκ τῶν Ἀριστοβούλου). Nothing further is known of this Aristobulus, unless he be the grandson of *Herod the Great and friend of the Emp. Claudius of this name. It is possible that he came to be considered a Christian merely because of his mention in the NT. Acc. to a Spanish tradition, he made his way to Britain in the second year of the reign of *Nero and finally became Bp. of Britonia (modern Mondoñedo) in Spain. Feast day, 30 or 31 Oct.

He has sometimes been identified with an Aristobulus who, acc. to the Gk. menologies, was one of the seventy disciples (Lk. 10. 1) and brother of St. *Barnabas and whose daughter married St. *Peter. This Aristobulus was believed to have been consecrated Bishop by St. Paul and to have organized a Church in Britain; but the story is without credible authority. He was apparently the Aristobulus, 'the disciple of the Apostles', named in the Roman *Martyrology. Feast day, 15 or 16 March.

Extr. on Aristobulus from Gk. Menology in *AA.SS.*, Mart. I (1668), p. 869; cf. also ib., II (1668), pp. 374–6. R. Aigrain in *D.H.G.E.*, iv (1930), col. 194, s.v.

ARISTOBULUS of Paneas (3rd–2nd cent. B.C.), Jewish philosopher of *Alexandria who most prob. taught *c.* 170–160 B.C. (so E. *Schürer). His Commentary on the Law, fragments of which are preserved by *Eusebius (*Praep. Ev.*, VIII, x and XIII, xii and *HE*, VII, xxxii, 17), seeks to prove that the OT was the source of much Greek philosophy and by an elaborate system of allegorical interpretation to reconcile philosophical conceptions with the Jewish creed. His citation of a *Peripatetic source (in Eus. *Praep. Ev.*, XIII, xii, 10) led *Clement of Alexandria and Eusebius to assign him to that school, but it is clear that he was also influenced by *Plato and the *Pythagoreans. The eclectic character of the work has suggested doubts about its authorship, but the ascription to Aristobulus is now generally accepted. By the early Christian Fathers Aristobulus was regarded as the founder of Jewish philosophy in Alexandria.

E. Schürer, *Geschichte des jüdischen Volkes im Zeitalter Jesu Christi*, iii (ed. 4, 1909), pp. 512–22 (Eng. tr. II, iii, 1886, pp. 237–43). P. Wendland, in *J.E.*, ii (1902), p. 97 f.

ARISTOTLE (384–322 B.C.), Greek philosopher. He was the son of Nicomachus, the court physician to Amyntas II, and born at Stagirus (later Stagira) on the peninsula of Chalcidice. In 367 he went to Athens where he became a member of the scientific group gathered round *Plato. After Plato's death (347), when Speusippus became head of the Academy, Aristotle left for Asia Minor where he spent three years with his friend and former fellow-student Hermeias, who had risen to be tyrant of the cities of Assos and Atarneus in the Troad. Here he married Pythias, Hermeias' niece, and *c.* 344 removed with his wife to Mitylene in Lesbos. After Hermeias' assassination by the Persians (343), Aristotle joined the Macedonian court, and became tutor to the crown prince, afterwards Alexander the Great, then a boy of 13; of his relations with Alexander there is very little contemporary evidence. When Alexander became king (336), Aristotle returned to Athens, where the headship of Plato's Academy happened to be vacant on Speusippus' death. Aristotle, however, was not elected, the choice falling on Xenocrates of Chalcedon. Though he never wholly severed his connexion with the Academy, he opened a rival school at the Lyceum (335), to which he attracted some of the Academy's most distinguished members. Here he devoted himself for the next twelve years to lecturing, organizing the school, fostering scientific research and collecting a large library, the model for those of *Alexandria and *Pergamum. In contrast to the Academy, where the emphasis was on mathematics, Aristotle laid the principal stress on biology. From the circumstance that the instruction was given in a covered portico ('peripatos'), his school obtained the name of 'Peripatetic'. On the death of Alexander (323), the strong anti-Macedonian agitation forced Aristotle to leave Athens, whence he withdrew with his disciples to Chalcis where he died in the following year.

Aristotle, like Plato, appears to have made regular use of the dialogue in his earlier years; but lacking Plato's imaginative gifts he probably never found the form congenial. Apart from a few fragments in later writers, his dialogues have been wholly lost. The works on which his reputation rests are apparently texts based on his lecture notes and memoranda which he had prepared for his pupils. Among the chief are the two celebrated editions of the *Ethics*,—the *Nicomachean Ethics*, issued by his son Nicomachus, and the *Eudemian Ethics*, a recasting by his pupil Eudemus, a mathematician; the *Physics* of which the earlier books deal with the science of nature in general, the later ones with motion; the *Metaphysics* on the science of Being (the title, given to it because it followed the *Physics* in the Aristotelian *corpus*, first appears in Nicolaus of Damascus); the celebrated writings on logic (the *Categories, De Interpretatione*, the *Prior* and *Posterior Analytics*, the *Topics, De Sophisticis Elenchis*) collectively known as the *Organon*; and a large number of writings on natural science (among others *de Caelo, de Generatione et Corruptione, de Anima, de Partibus Animalium*); the *Politics*; the *Rhetoric*; and the *Poetics*. In 1890 a lost treatise on the *Constitution of Athens* (not before 329–8) was found among the Egyptian papyri (1st cent. A.D.); it was published in 1891 by F. G. Kenyon and is preserved in the British Museum.

Though a disciple of *Plato, his philosophical position was very different. Whereas Plato set out from the world of 'ideas', entities which he conceived as arranged in a hierarchy, at the head of which was the 'Idea of the Good', and as alone having reality, Aristotle asserted that an idea exists only as expressed in the individual object. Thus he maintained that so far from there being an idea 'tree' possessing existence in its own right, it is the union of the 'form' tree with 'matter' which makes the real individual tree. This view required a theory of causation to account for the conjunction of form and matter, and Aristotle was thus led to postulate a 'First Cause', though he did not hold this supreme cause to be personal in the Christian sense. In explaining his doctrine he analysed the four senses in which the word 'cause' may be used. A cause, he affirmed, might be 'formal', 'material', 'final', or 'efficient'. The 'material cause' is the matter upon which the form (or in the case of change, the new form) is imposed; the 'formal cause' is the form which in conjunction with matter makes the new object a distinct entity; the 'final cause' is the end which, in processes of growth or change, determines the course of the development; and the 'efficient cause' is the motive power which produces the event. For the world as a whole, Aristotle found the efficient, formal, and final causes in God, Who is the Unmoved Mover (πρῶτον κινοῦν) of all things.

The science of 'Logic' was Aristotle's creation, and within its limits his treatment covered practically the whole field, though since the latter part of the 19th cent., esp. under the influence of G. Frege and Bertrand Russell, the scope of logic has been greatly widened. Aristotle treats of concepts, judgements and propositions, the syllogism, demonstration, the problematic syllogism, and fallacies. His works on Physics have formed the basis of all subsequent study of the subject. His 'Ethics' has also had an enormous influence. He conceived the ideal life as one of moderation, contending that virtue is always a mean between two extremes—courage, e.g., being a mean between cowardice and foolhardiness.

In the early centuries of the Christian Church, Aristotle's philosophy was regarded with suspicion, largely because his teachings were thought to lead to a materialistic view of the world. This attitude was further encouraged by the high repute in which Plato, conceived as the diametrically opposed philosopher to Aristotle, was held by the Christian Fathers. *Boethius (6th cent.), however, vigorously expounded Aristotelian doctrines. In the Middle Ages, when first-hand acquaintance with Aristotle had disappeared for some centuries, knowledge of his teachings was gradually recovered from Arabic translations made by Jews and Moslems. These were translated into Latin in the 12th cent. The Church at first looked upon these works with great suspicion, but this was finally dissipated when such competent Christian philosophers as St. *Albertus Magnus and St. *Thomas Aquinas built up their systems on an avowedly Aristotelian basis. This basis has been that accepted by Latin philosophical theology in the West ever since. The thinkers of the Renaissance (and their eminent precursor, *Nicolas of Cusa) gave Platonism a new lease of life. In recent times, Thomistic Aristotelianism has again become a considerable force.

Editio princeps, by Aldine Press, 5 vols. fol., Venice, 1495–8. The best collected ed. (from which citations are normally given) is that of the Prussian Academy, ed. I. Bekker (5 vols., Berlin, 1831–70; fragments ed. V. Rose, scholia ed. C. A. Brandis, index ed. H. Bonitz); many of the early Gk. Commentaries on Aristotle publd. as a 'Supplementum Aristotelicum' to the Berlin ed. (3 vols., 1885–1903). More recent edd. Gk. text of single works, with modern commentaries, include: Ethics, ed. A. Grant (2 vols., 1857) and J. Burnet (London, 1900); Politics, ed. W. L. Newman (4 vols., Oxford, 1887–1902); De Anima, ed. R. D. Hicks (Cambridge, 1907); Metaphysics, ed. W. D. Ross (2 vols., Oxford, 1924); Physics, ed. id. (ib., 1936); Prior and Posterior Analytics, ed. id. (ib., 1949); Rhetoric, ed. E. M. Cope (3 vols., Cambridge, 1877); De Generatione et Corruptione, ed. H. H. Joachim (Oxford, 1922); Poetics, ed. A. Gudeman (Berlin, 1934). F. G. Kenyon (ed.), Aristotle on the Constitution of Athens (1891); also ed., with full introd., notes, and Gk. index, by J. E. Sandys (London, 1893). Many items also in O.C.T. Eng. trr. in 12 vols., ed. J. A. Smith and W. D. Ross (Oxford, 1908–52); several of Aristotle's works also tr. in Loeb (various dates).

On the Medieval versions of Aristotle, see G. Lacombe, Aristoteles Latinus, in 'Corpus Philosophorum Medii Aevi Academiarum Consociatarum Auspiciis et Consilio Editum' (Codicum descriptio, pars prior [esp. on MSS.; all publd. to date], Rome, 1939). M. *Grabmann, Forschungen über die lateinischen Aristoteles-Übersetzungen des XIII. Jahrhunderts (B.G.P.M., xvii, Hftt. 5–6; with bibl. A. Jourdain, Recherches sur l'âge et l'origine des traductions d'Aristote (1819); E. *Renan, Averroes et l'averroïsme (1852). Further information in Überweg, ii, pp. 342–51.

Modern studies include G. Grote, Aristotle (ed. A. Bain and G. C. Robertson, 2 vols., 1872); W. Jaeger, Aristoteles. Grundlegung einer Geschichte seiner Entwicklung (1923; Eng. tr. 1934); W. D. Ross, Aristotle (1923); J. Stenzel, Zahl und Gestalt bei Platon und Aristoteles (1924); G. R. G. Mure, Aristotle (1932); D. J. Allen, The Philosophy of Aristotle (H.U.L., 1952).

On his political doctrines E. Barker, The Political Thought of Plato and Aristotle (1906). On his relation to modern logic, J. Lukasiewicz, Aristotle's Syllogistic from the Standpoint of Modern Formal Logic (1951). R. Jolivet, 'Aristote et St. Thomas ou la notion de création' in Revue des Sciences Philosophiques et Théologiques, xix (1930), pp. 5–50, and 209–35, repr. in Essai sur les rapports entre la pensée grecque et la pensée chrétienne (1931). On his theology H. von Arnim, Die Entstehung der Gotteslehre des Aristoteles (Sb. (Wien), ccxii, Abh. 5; 1931). W. K. C. Guthrie, 'The Development of Aristotle's Theology' in Classical Quarterly, xxvii (1933), pp. 162–71. V. L. Dowdell, Aristotle and Anglican Religious Thought (Cornell Univ. Press, Ithaca, New York, 1942).

Überweg, i, pp. 347–401, with bibl. pp. 101*–122*. T. Case in E.B. (ed. 11), ii, pp. 501–22. W. D. Ross in O.C.D. (1949), pp. 94–7, with bibl.

ARIUS (c. 250–c. 336), heresiarch. There is much divergence between the authorities for his life. He was prob. a Libyan by birth and a pupil of *Lucian of Antioch; and, if *Sozomen (HE, i. 15) can be trusted, he was ordained deacon by St. *Peter, Bp. of *Alexandria (d. 312), who later excommunicated him as a member of the *Melitian sect. Under Achillas (312–13), Peter's successor, he was ordained priest and put in charge of Baucalis, one of the principal churches at Alexandria. Here he seems to have met with marked success as a preacher and been revered for his asceticism. Under the next Bishop, St. *Alexander, he came forward prob. c. 319 (not 323, as E. *Schwartz) as a champion of subordinationist teaching about the Person of Christ. The controversy quickly spread, Arius seeking support among other disciples of Lucian, notably *Eusebius of Nicomedia, while a synod at Alexandria under Alexander proceeded to excommunicate him. Shortly after his arrival in the East (Sept. 324), the Emp. *Constantine sent St. *Hosius to Alexandria to attempt a settlement; but the mission failed. Accordingly an *Oecumenical Council was convened (orig. to Ancyra), met at *Nicaea in the early summer of 325, and, largely through the influence of St. *Athanasius, condemned Arius. Arius spent the next few years in banishment in Illyria, but, owing to the Court influence of Eusebius of Nicomedia, he was recalled from exile prob. c. 334. He returned to Alexandria where Athanasius was ordered to receive him back to communion, but refused. He died suddenly in the streets of Constantinople c. 336.

Arius seems to have written little. He embodied his doctrine in popular songs, known as the Thaleia (Θάλεια, 'Banquet'), one at least composed in an acrostic form; but only fragments survive. There also exist a Letter seeking support from Eusebius of Nicomedia (ap. *Theodoret, HE, i. 4) and a statement of belief in a letter to Alexander (Athanasius, De Synodis, 16). See also Arianism.

The chief sources for his Life are the writings of Athanasius, supplemented by *Epiphanius (Haer. 69) and the Church Historians, *Rufinus, *Socrates, *Sozomen, *Philostorgius. See also bibl. to 'Arianism'.

ARK. (1) The Ark of Noah, which the Patriarch was bidden to build of gopher wood to preserve life during the *Flood, is described in Gen. 6. It was borne on the waters for a year and eleven days (Gen. 7. 11 and 8. 4) and finally rested on the 'Mountains of Ararat' (8. 4; acc. to Syr. Bible at Kurdu); and was the means whereby Noah and his family ('eight persons', 1 Pet. 3. 20) and representatives of all the living creatures were saved from the catastrophe. Critics are widely agreed that the Heb. narrative has been influenced by the *Gilgamish Epic, which describes the building of a similar vessel (tablet 11, lines 48–66). The Babylonian historian, Berossus (c. 300 B.C.), states that remains of the ark were extant in his day in Armenia and used for making amulets and bracelets.

(2) The Ark of the Covenant, the most sacred religious symbol of the Hebrew people and believed to represent the Presence of God. Acc. to the traditional accounts the Ark was carried by the Israelites from the time of the *Exodus (? 13th cent. B.C.) into the land of Canaan, and, until the *Temple was built, was kept in a holy tent or *tabernacle. It was considered to be of such sanctity that for an unauthorized person to touch it, even accidentally, was sacrilege, punishable by death (cf. e.g. 2 Sam. 6. 6). When it was permanently

lodged within the Temple of *Solomon, its home was the 'Holy of Holies', which the High Priest alone entered once a year. The Ark seems at one time to have contained only the tables of the Law (1 Kgs. 8. 9), but several traditions exist (e.g. Heb. 9. 4) of other things which were kept inside it. The Ark was apparently captured when *Jerusalem fell in 587–586 B.C., and nothing is certainly known of its later history. See also Synagogue.

Both the Ark of Noah and the Ark of the Covenant have been symbolically interpreted by the Christian Fathers and theologians. Acc. to *Tertullian, St. *Jerome, and others, the Ark of Noah typifies the Church, which, like it, is the only means of salvation, containing saints and sinners symbolized by the pure and impure animals, and being tossed about by tempests but never submerged. The Ark of the Covenant, on the other hand, is a symbol of our Lord. Acc. to St. *Thomas Aquinas the gold with which it is overlaid signifies His wisdom and charity; the golden vase it contains represents His soul, Aaron's rod His priestly dignity, and the Tables of the Law His office as law-giver. St. *Bonaventure saw in it a figure of the Eucharist; acc. to a sermon attributed to St. *Ambrose it symbolizes our Lady, in whom was enclosed the heir of the Law as the Law itself was contained in the Ark of the Covenant. In this sense the symbolism is applied in the Litany of *Loreto, where our Lady is called 'Foederis Arca'.

(1) E. Mangenot in Dict. Bibl., i (1895), cols. 923–6, s.v. 'Arche de Noé'; G. Rinaldi in E.C., i (1949), cols. 1785–7, s.v. 'Arca di Noe'. See also comm. on Gen.
(2) M. *Dibelius, Die Lade Jahwes (1906); K. *Budde, 'War die Lade Jahwes ein leerer Thron?' in Theologische Studien und Kritiken, lxxvii (1906), pp. 489–507. W. R. Arnold, Ephod and Ark (Harvard Theological Studies No. 3; 1917); K. Budde, 'Ephod und Lade' in Z.A.T.W., xxxix (1921), pp 1–42. H. Gressmann, 'Die Lade Jahwes und das Allerheiligste des salomonischen Tempels' (Beiträge zur Wissenschaft vom Alten Testament, xxvi, 1920). O. Eissfeldt, 'Lade und Stierbild' in Z.A.T.W., lviii (1940–41), pp. 190–215. H. Lesêtre in Dict. Bibl., i (1895), cols. 912–923, s.v. 'Arche d'alliance'; E. Josi in E.C., i (1949), cols. 1783–5, s.v. 'Arca (dell' alleanza)', with bibl.
H. Hurter, S.J., 'De Arca Noe, Ecclesiae Typo, Patrum Sententiae' in Opuscula Patrum Selecta, iii (Innsbruck, 1868), pp. 217–33. H. *Leclercq, O.S.B., in D.A.C.L., i (pt. 1; 1907), cols. 2709–32, s.v. 'Arche (de Noé)', with reff. H. Lesêtre, op. cit., col. 923. See also bibl. to Flood.

ARLES (Lat. Arelate), **Synods of.** At least fifteen Councils were held at Arles between 314 and 1275. The more important were:

(1) 314. Summoned by *Constantine to deal with the *Donatist schism. It passed 22 canons dealing with abuses resulting from the persecutions.

(2) 353. An *Arianizing Council.

[(2a). The 25 canons of the so-called 'Second Council of Arles' of the 5th cent. appear to be a private collection of canons based on those of earlier councils held elsewhere and not to have ever received conciliar authority.]

(3) 813. Canons passed concerning preaching and the education of the clergy.

(4) 1236. Canons passed against the *Albigensians.

(5) 1263 (earlier authorities, 1260). Condemned the doctrines of *Joachim of Flora.

(1) Hardouin, i (1715), cols. 259–70; Mansi, ii (1759), cols. 463–512. Canons also in Lauchert, pp. 26–9; crit. ed. in Turner, *E.O.M.I.A.*, I. ii. 2 (1939), pp. 372–416. Hefele–Leclercq, i (1; 1907), pp. 275–98, F. X. Funk, 'Die Zeit der ersten Synode von Arles' in *Theologische Quartalschrift*, lxxii (1890), pp. 296–304, repr. in id., *Kirchengeschichtliche Abhandlungen und Untersuchungen*, i (1897), pp. 352–8; L. *Duchesne, 'La Date du concile d'Arles' in *Mélanges d'Archéologie et d'Histoire*, x (1890), pp. 640–4. H. Schrörs, 'Drei Aktenstücke in Betreff des Konzils von Arles' in *Zeitschrift der Savigny Stiftung für Rechtsgeschichte*, xlii, Kan. Abth., xi (1921), pp. 429–39.

ARMADA, Spanish. The great fleet was intended by *Philip II of Spain for the invasion of England in the interests of RC-ism and to avenge English attacks upon Spanish trade. Its defeat after a week's fighting in the English Channel (20–27 July 1588) was hailed as a 'great deliverance' by countless Anglican preachers.

ARMAGH (Ard-Macha, 'Height of Macha', a legendary queen). Archiepiscopal see in the North of Ireland. Founded by St. *Patrick in 445, it early became the seat of a celebrated school, much frequented by Anglo - Saxon scholars. During the unsettlement of the Norman invasions, the temporal revenues of the see were usurped by the Counts of Armagh (1021–1105). Important reforms were carried through in the face of much opposition under St. Cellach (or Celsus, 1105–29) and St. *Malachy (1134–7). When Ireland passed under English domination in 1215 the see lost much of its independence. The English kings claimed the temporalities during vacancies and a share in the election of bishops. Under *Henry VIII, Abp. George Cromer (1522–43) refused to recognize the royal supremacy and opposed the reforming measures. His successor, George Dowdall (d. 1558), took the oath of supremacy and hence was not recognized by Paul III, but he too was a zealous supporter of the old faith. Under *Edward VI he left the country, and in 1552 the first Protestant bishop, Hugh Goodacre (d. 1553), was appointed. Henceforward there was both a Protestant and a RC succession, though for many generations bishops of the latter lived in exile or destitution, Oliver *Plunket (1669–81) suffering martyrdom. Among the Protestant archbishops were J. *Ussher, the famous scholar (1624–56), and Richard Robinson, first Baron Rokeby (1765–94), to whose munificence Armagh owes the archbishop's palace, a library and other public institutions. Towards the end of the 18th cent. the Catholic archbishops resumed their normal way of life. A new RC cathedral, dedicated to St. Patrick, was built (1840–1904), and many religious Orders and Congregations were established in the diocese. The present Anglican cathedral of St. Patrick is on a fortified hill, acc. to tradition given to Patrick by King Daire. It was mainly rebuilt in the 18th cent., but followed in general plan the original 13th cent. structure.

Since the later Middle Ages the Abps. of Armagh's claim to the primacy has constantly been contested by the Abps. of Dublin, both Catholic and Protestant. The long literary feud, which followed the conflict between Oliver Plunket and Peter Talbot, Abp. of Dublin in 1670, culminated in the learned work of Hugh MacMahon, *Jus Primatiale Armacanum* (1728). See also following entry.

Ambrose Coleman, O.P., in *C.E.*, i (1907), pp. 729–33, with bibl.

ARMAGH, The Book of (Lat. *Liber Ar[d]-machanus*. A celebrated 8th–9th cent. vellum codex. It contains a miscellaneous collection of documents, partly Irish and partly Latin, and some of them of the first importance for the history of Ireland. Of special interest are its two Lives of St. *Patrick, an important text of the Life of St. *Martin of Tours by *Sulpicius Severus, and a complete non-*Vulgate text of the Latin NT, in the order Gospels (Mt., Mk., Jn., Lk.), Pauline Epp., Catholic Epp., Rev., Acts. The scribe was Ferdomnach of Armagh (d. 845 or 846), who wrote at least the first part of the Book in 807 or 808. The MS., which was treated in the Middle Ages with great ceremony and apparently used in giving testimony and in the swearing of oaths, passed into private possession after the Reformation, and is now at Trinity College, Dublin (MS. no. 52). It is thus sometimes referred to by textual critics as the 'Codex Dublinensis'.

Liber Ardmachanus: The Book of Armagh, ed. with Introduction and Appendices by J. Gwynn (Dublin, 1913). For a good brief account, see J. Dunn in *C.E.*, i (1907), p. 733 f.

ARMENIA, Christianity in. The Armenians were the first nation to embrace Christianity officially. They were converted by *Gregory the Illuminator, who had been consecrated bishop by the Metropolitan of Caesarea in Cappadocia in 294, and who baptized their king Tiridates III (238–314). Gregory established the chief see at Etchmiadzin nr. Mount Ararat, and for a time the office of *Catholicos (or Primate) was hereditary in his family, and continued subject to the jurisdiction of the Metropolitan of Caesarea, who consecrated each successor. In 390 Armenia became divided between the Byzantine and Persian empires, and in 430 the monarchy disappeared, since when the Armenians have been subject to Persians, Arabs, Turks, and Russians, and their unity has consisted in the bond of race, language, literature, and religion.

In 374 the Armenians repudiated their dependence on the Church of Caesarea. In the early part of the 5th cent. St.*Isaac the Great (Catholicos *c.* 390–*c.* 440) and St.*Mesrob reformed the Church, and the Bible and the Liturgy were translated from the *Syriac into Armenian. Owing to the wars in which they were involved, the Armenians took no part in the *Monophysite troubles and were not represented at the Council of *Chalcedon in 451; but about 50 years later, partly for political reasons, they repudiated that Council, in consequence of which the Armenian Church has since been reputed Monophysite. They have never entered, however, into full communion with churches professing the Monophysite heresy.

The next 700 years was a period of persecution from Persians and Arabs. From the end of the 12th cent. until 1375 the Armenians of Little Armenia were united with Rome, during which period many W. practices were adopted from contact with the *Crusaders. The whole Armenian Church was influenced in this way. Armenia sent representatives to the Council of *Florence (1438–9), which issued the famous instruction 'Pro Armenis', on the *Sacraments. The decree of reunion, however, had few practical results.

The Armenians have suffered persecution intermittently throughout their history, and a large proportion of the whole nation has been massacred by the Turks, and later also by the Soviets, between 1893 and the present time. There are thought to be about 2½ million Armenians to-day, including about 100,000 who are in communion with Rome. The non-Roman Armenians are sometimes distinguished as 'Gregorian Armenians'. There are Armenian churches in London and Manchester, and about 100,000 Armenians in N. America.

The present organization consists of the Patriarchate of Etchmiadzin, the Catholicate of Sis, and the Patriarchates of Jerusalem and Constantinople. There are two classes of priests—the 'vardapets' or doctors, who are unmarried, and the parish priests, who, unless monks, must be married before ordination to the diaconate. Monks cannot, except by dispensation, become bishops, who are usually chosen from among the vardapets.

Their dogmas are similar to those of the Orthodox Church, and their Liturgy is substantially that of St. *Basil, in classical Armenian. The chief vestment is the chasuble (*shurtshar*), shaped like a cope. For the Eucharist, they use unleavened bread in the form of a large Latin host, and do not mix water with the wine (see *Mixed Chalice*). They give Communion in both kinds by intinction. They follow the Julian Calendar. They are unique among non-Protestant Christians in not observing *Christmas as a separate feast. Instead, they celebrate the Nativity of our Lord as part of the *Epiphany, from 5 to 13 January. They make the sign of the Cross after the manner of the Latins.

S. Weber, *Die katholische Kirche in Armenien. Ihre Begründung und Entwicklung vor der Trennung* (1903); M. Ormanian, *L'Église arménienne. Son histoire, sa doctrine, son régime, sa discipline, sa liturgie, son présent* (1910; Eng. tr. 1912). F. Tournebize, *Histoire politique et religieuse de l'Arménie* (1900 ff.). H. E. B. Lynch, *Armenia. Travels and Studies* (2 vols., 1901); J. J. M. de Morgan, *Histoire de peuple arménien* (1919; Eng. tr., Boston, Mass. [1949]). F. C. *Conybeare–A. J. Maclean (edd. and trr.), *Rituale Armenorum* (1905); A. A. King, *The Rites of Eastern Christendom* (Rome, 1948), ch. 10, pp. 521–646. J. Muyldermans, 'Le Costume liturgique arménien. Étude historique' in *Le Muséon*, xxxix (1925), pp. 253–324. On Armenian theology, M. Jugie, A.A., *Theologia Dogmatica Christianorum Orientalium ab Ecclesia Catholica Dissidentium*, v (Paris, 1935), pp. 478–89. A. *Fortescue, *The Lesser Eastern Churches* (1913), pp. 383–445; D. Attwater, *The Dissident Eastern Churches* (Milwaukee, Wisc. [1937]), pp. 293–308.

ARMENIAN VERSION OF NT. The Gospels, Acts, and Pauline Epp. were translated into Armenian in the 3rd–4th cents., probably from an Old *Syriac version. Traditionally this translation has been ascribed to Sts. Mesrop and Sahak. After the Council of *Ephesus (431), two Armenians returned from *Constantinople with 'correct' copies of the Greek Bible (i.e. with MSS. of the *Lucianic text) and proceeded to bring the then existing Armenian text into conformity. In one Armenian MS. the concluding 12 verses of Mk. (16. 9–20) are attributed to 'the presbyter *Aristion'.

Editions: Amsterdam, 1666; Venice, 1805 (by Zohrab, one of the *Mechitarist fathers). F. C. *Conybeare in F. H. A.*Scrivener's *Introduction* (1894) and arts. 'Armenian Version' in *HDB*; R. P. Blake, *H.T.R.* xxi (1928), 307–10. *Editio princeps* of whole Armenian Bible, Amsterdam, 1666; first crit. ed. by J. Zohrab, Venice, 1805. NT publd. separately Amsterdam, 1668; ed. J. Zohrab, Venice, 1789. Book of Rev. ed. F. C. *Conybeare (Text and Translation Society, iii, 1907, pp. 1–163). F. Macler, *Le Texte arménien de l'Évangile d'après Matthieu et Marc* (Annales du Musée Guimet. Bibliothèque d'Études, xxviii; 1919). S. Lyonnet, S.J., *Les Origines de la Version arménienne et le Diatessaron* (Biblica et Orientalia, xiii; 1950). F. C. Conybeare in *H.D.B.*, i (1900), p. 153 f.

ARMILL. One of the *Coronation regalia. Although the word means 'bracelet', it is applied to a garment resembling a *stole, both in the '*Liber Regalis' and in the modern Coronation Service. It has been held to signify the quasi-priestly character of the anointed king. In former times it was crossed over the breast, and was so found on the body of Edward I, when his tomb was opened in 1774. The *Lambeth MS. of *Charles I's Coronation ordered the words 'Receive the Bracelets of Sincerity and Wisdom' to be said by the prelate who placed the armill on the king. Later it was placed on the king's shoulders by the Dean of *Westminster, as one of the 'garments of salvation'. It is perhaps identical with the Greek λῶρος, a long jewelled scarf worn by the Byzantine emperors. At the Coronation of Queen Elizabeth II (1953) the use of armills in the form of bracelets was restored.

A. Taylor, *The Glory of Regality. An Historical Treatise on the Anointing and Crowning of the Kings and Queens of England* (1820), pp. 81–5. E. C. Ratcliff, *The Coronation Service of Her Majesty Queen Elizabeth II* (1953), p. 31 f.

ARMINIANISM. Jacobus Arminius (Jakob Hermandszoon), the celebrated Dutch Reformed theologian (1560–1609), was the son of Hermand Jacobszoon, a cutler of Oudewater in S. Holland. He was schooled at Utrecht and later studied for a time at Marburg. On hearing that most of his relatives had been massacred by the Spaniards, he returned to Holland and took refuge at Rotterdam. Here his evident theological abilities won him influential friends and support. He continued his theological studies at *Leyden (1576–82), at *Geneva under T. *Beza, and (for a short time) at *Basle, as well as at Padua and *Rome. On his return to Holland in 1587 he received a call to minister at Amsterdam and was ordained there in the following year. Studies in the Ep. to the Romans having led him to doubt the Calvinistic doctrine of predestination, he was accused of *Pelagianism and disloyalty to the Confessions of his Church. After an unsuccessful attempt of J. Uitenbogaert to mediate, his opposition to Calvinistic doctrines became more pronounced. An extensive correspondence with Francis Junius, professor at Leyden, and an attempted refutation (not published till after Arminius' death) of W. *Perkins' treatise on predestination led him to work out his doctrines with greater precision. He also found himself increasingly drawn into the political struggle in Holland, as his views on the absolute authority of the State brought him the support of J. van Oldenbarneveldt against the military ideals of Prince Maurice of Orange. Appointed professor at Leyden in 1603, he was at once drawn into a conflict with the zealous Calvinist F. *Gomar, who had taught at Leyden since 1594, but after a disputation at the Hague in the presence of Oldenbarneveldt on 6 May 1603, Arminius successfully cleared himself of the charges of Pelagianism and *Socinianism, and obtained possession of his chair. He now found himself at one of the chief centres of learning in Europe, with J. J. *Scaliger as his colleague and H. *Grotius as his pupil, and provided with wide opportunities for furthering his beliefs. For the rest of his life, though his temper remained conciliatory and he was steadily supported by the curators of the university, he was engaged in controversy. He made it one of his chief ends to obtain the revision of the two chief Calvinistic documents of the Dutch Church, the *Belgic Confession and *Heidelberg Catechism. But though negotiations for a National Synod for this purpose were unsuccessful he commanded widespread respect, and from 1608 H. *Grotius threw in his lot with him. The disputes continued down to the time of his death.

As a system of faith, Arminian doctrines, formally set forth in the *Remonstrance (q.v.) of 1610, were a theological reaction against the deterministic logic of Calvinism. The Arminians insisted that the Divine sovereignty was compatible with a real free-will in man; that Jesus Christ died for all men and not only for the elect; and that both the *Supralapsarian and *Sublapsarian views of *predestination were unbiblical. At first the opposition to Arminianism was led by F. Gomar. The struggle was long and bitter. Suspected of favouring the pro-Spanish party in politics, the Arminians were attacked by Prince Maurice of Orange. After their condemnation at the Synod of *Dort (1618–19), many were banished and others persecuted. By 1630 a more tolerant policy had been adopted, but it was not until 1795 that the Remonstrants were officially recognized.

As representatives of a more liberal school of theology than the strict Calvinists, the Arminians exercised considerable influence on the formation of modern Dutch and European

Protestant theology. In England the anti-Calvinistic trend in 17th cent. theology, and esp. in the Laudian revival, was widely termed 'Arminian' by its opponents, though it is doubtful if here the direct influence of Arminius' teaching was at all considerable. In the *Methodist movement J. *Wesley held an Arminian position, as contrasted with G. *Whitefield's Calvinist teaching, thus giving rise to the division in theological outlook between *Wesleyan and *Calvinistic Methodists which has persisted down to present times. On the Continent the reputation of Arminianism sank very low in the 18th cent., owing to the association which grew up between it and *Socinianism. More recently the tension between the Arminian and Calvinist trends in theology had been less acute, until the theological revival of Calvinism under the influence of K. *Barth.

J. Arminius' Theological Works, ed. Leyden, 1629 (repr. Frankfurt, 1631, 1635). Eng. tr. by J. and W. Nichols (3 vols., London, 1825–75). Lives by C. Brandt (Amsterdam, 1724; Eng. tr., 1854), J. Nichols (London, 1843), and J. H. Maronier (Amsterdam, 1905). A. W. Harrison, The Beginnings of Arminianism to the Synod of Dort (1926); id., Arminianism (1937).

ARNAULD, ANTOINE (1612–94), 'the Great Arnauld', French theologian and philosopher. He was the twentieth son of a bourgeois family, born in Paris, who, after the death of his father in 1619, came increasingly under the influence of his mother and of his sister, Angélique (see foll. entry). In 1633 he entered the *Sorbonne, where the subject of his bachelor's thesis was the doctrine of Grace. For some years he was a prominent figure in the intellectual society of Paris, but, after receiving the subdiaconate in 1638, he began to enter into association with *Port-Royal and *Saint-Cyran. He was priested in 1641 and the following day retired to Port-Royal. In 1643 he published De la fréquente communion, which with its stress on the need for thorough preparation for Communion and its emphasis on the right interior dispositions did much to propagate Jansenist principles among a wide public. The book provoked a storm from the Jesuits which necessitated Arnauld's withdrawal from public life. In the next year he published (anon.) his Apologie de M. Jansenius, a semi-official manifesto of the Jansenist theological position; and Arnauld now became the acknowledged leader of the Jansenists, writing extensively on their behalf. The publication of two outspoken Lettres . . . à un duc et pair, directed against the Jesuit method in the confessional, provoked an attack from the Sorbonne. The support of the *Dominicans and also of B. *Pascal who sought to justify Arnauld in the first of his Lettres provinciales, failed to save him, and he was censured by the Sorbonne in Jan. 1656 and in Feb. 1656 solemnly degraded; and until the 'Peace of the Church' of 1668 he remained in retirement. In 1669 he was received by Louis XIV, restored to position as a Doctor of the Sorbonne and treated as a popular hero. With P. *Nicole (q.v.) he then began a major treatise against the *Calvinists, *La Perpétuité de la foi catholique touchant l'Eucharistie* (1669–74). When the Jansenist controversy began to revive in 1679, Arnauld left France for the Netherlands, where he was joined by P. *Quesnel; and here he continued to write, until his death, against N.*Malebranche, on *Gallicanism, and on various Biblical subjects. If he was less radical than Jansen in his teaching on the all-embracing power of grace, it was to him more than to anyone else that Jansenist principles owed their diffusion.

Arnauld was the author of over 320 works. Many of his letters are in MS. in the Bibliothèque Nationale, Paris. *Œuvres de Messire Antoine Arnauld* (43 vols., Lausanne, 1775–83; with Life in vol. 43). P. *Quesnel, *Histoire abrégée de la vie et des ouvrages de M. Arnauld* (Cologne, 1695). R. Rapin, *Mémoires...sur l'Église et la société, la cour, la ville et le jansénisme, 1644–1669* (ed. L. Aubineau, 3 vols., 1865), passim. J. Brucker in *D.T.C.*, i (1903), cols. 1978–83 and J. Carreyre, P.S.S., in *D.H.G.E.*, iv (1930), cols. 447–85, both s.v. and with bibl.

ARNAULD, JACQUELINE MARIE ANGÉLIQUE (1591–1661), 'Mère Angélique', Abbess of *Port-Royal. She was the sister of Antoine *Arnauld (see preceding entry), and christened Jacqueline, but at her confirmation took the name of Angélique by which she is commonly known. Born at Paris, she was procured succession at the age of seven to the abbacy of Port-Royal, and after residence in the *Benedictine convents of St.-Antoine, Paris, and at Maubuisson, she became Abbess of Port-Royal in 1602. At first she shared without protest in the very relaxed (but not immoral) discipline of the house, until in 1608 she was converted by a sermon from a visiting *Capuchin friar. She promptly introduced drastic reforms (community of goods, enclosure, regular office, uniformity of dress, abstinence, and silence) and also laid great emphasis on the inner discipline of the spirit. In 1618 she carried through similar reforms at Maubuisson. In 1619 she fell in with St. *Francis de Sales and wished to join the *Visitation nuns, but permission being refused, she returned to Port-Royal in 1622. The community now increased rapidly in numbers and came to include Angélique's four sisters and their mother, and in 1625 Angélique moved it to a larger house in the Faubourg Saint-Jacques in Paris. A proposal of Sebastian Zamet, Bp. of Langres (Bp. 1615–55), to amalgamate the community with the reformed Benedictine house of Tard, nr. Dijon, led to serious differences, and in 1630 her sister Agnès was elected Abbess to replace her, though Angélique continued to exercise considerable influence. In the next years Angélique came under the influence of *Saint-Cyran, under whom the community became an enthusiastic upholder of *Jansenist principles and practice, and Angélique herself for long periods abstained from Communion. From 1642 to 1654 she was again Abbess. She died shortly after the signing of the Formulary of 1661. See also *Port-Royal.*

Her spiritual doctrines, based on papers written by herself or under her immediate inspiration, may be studied in *Mémoires pour servir à l'histoire de Port-Royal et à la vie de la Révérende Mère Marie-Angélique . . . Arnauld* (3 vols., Utrecht, 1742–4), *Entretiens ou conférences de la Révérende Mère Angélique Arnauld* (3 vols.; Utrecht, 1757) and other collections. Lives by G. Dall (pseud., Paris, 1893), M. Reynès-Monlaur (Paris, 1901), E. K. Sanders ('A. K. H.' [authoress' pseud.], London, 1905; new edd. under her name, London, 1914 and 1928), and J. Pannier (Issy les Moulineaux, 1931). A. Gazier, *Jeanne de Chantal et Angélique Arnauld d'après leur correspondance, 1620–1641* (Paris, 1915).

ARNDT, ERNST MORITZ (1769–1860), German patriot and poet. A native of Schoritz in the island of Rügen and of a strict Protestant family, he studied at Greifswald (1791) and Jena (1793), where he came under the influence of the *Aufklärung and of the Critical Philosophy (esp. J. G. *Fichte). Philosophical doubts led him to give up his intention of becoming a pastor in 1797. In 1800 he became lecturer in history at Greifswald university. His work, *Vom Geist der Zeit* (1806), directed against Napoleon, endangered his freedom and he fled to Sweden. During the wars from 1812 onwards he exercised a great influence by his patriotic publications. In 1818 he was appointed professor of history at the newly founded university of Bonn. In 1819 appeared a fourth part of *Vom Geist der Zeit*, in which he attacked the reactionary policy of the German princes. Suspension from his professorship followed in 1820, and for the next 20 years Arndt devoted himself to literary work. In 1840 he was reinstalled in his office by Frederick William IV.

Despite his change-over from theology to history Arndt always retained his religious interests. After a period of doubt, during which he tried to combine *Lutheranism with the contemporary German Idealistic philosophy, he began, in 1817, to occupy himself more with the Bible and the Reformation, and, under the influence of friends, esp. F. D. E. *Schleiermacher, he adopted a more definitely Christian attitude. To this period belong his hymns to Christ, among them his popular '*Ich weiss, an wen ich glaube*'. His hopes of a union between Protestants and Catholics in a German National Church were disappointed through the growing influence of *Ultramontanism, and in his later years he became one of the sturdiest representatives of German Protestantism, his most important work on the subject being *Über den gegenwärtigen Stand des Protestantismus* (1844).

Works ed. H. Rösch and others (14 vols., Leipzig and Magdeburg, 1892–1909). Lives by W. Baur (ed. 2, Hamburg, 1863), E. Langenberg (Bonn, 1865), R. Theile (Gütersloh, 1894), E. Muesebeck (vol. i, Gotha, 1914; all publd.) and P. Breitenkamp (Berlin, 1939). R. Wolfram, *Ernst Moritz Arndt und Schweden* (1933). P. Knauer, *Ernst Morits Arndt. Der grosse Erzieher der Deutschen* (1935). A. G. Pundt, *Arndt and the National Awakening in Germany* (Columbia University thesis; New York, 1939). R. Fahrer, *Arndt. Geistiges und politisches Verhalten* (1937). G. Heine, *Ernst Moritz Arndt. Der Weg eines deutschen Mannes* [1939]. U. E. W. Willers, *Ernst Moritz Arndt och hans Svenska Förbindelser. Studier i svensk-pommersk Historiografi och svensk Opinionsbildning* (1945), with portrait and bibl.

ARNDT, JOHANN (1555–1621), *Lutheran theologian and mystical writer. A devoted follower of P. *Melanchthon, he studied at

Helmstädt (1576) and *Wittenberg (1577) and later at Strassburg and Basle. In 1583 he was made pastor of Badeborn, but aroused *Calvinist hostility by his uncompromising Lutheranism. In 1590 he was compelled to move to Quedlinburg and in 1599 to Brunswick. He is chiefly remembered for his *Vier Bücher vom wahren Christentum* (1606), in which, in contrast to the prevalent forensic view of the Atonement, he dwelt on the work of Christ in the heart of man. Arndt was much venerated by the German *Pietists.

Works ed. by J. J. Rambach (8 vols., Leipzig, 1734–6). H. L. Pertz, *De Johanne Arndtio eiusque Libris qui inscribuntur: De Vero Christianismo* (Hanover, 1852). C. Ochmann, *Essai sur la vie et la doctrine de J. Arndt* (1861). F. J. Winter, *Johann Arndt, der Verfasser des 'Wahren Christentums'* (Schriften des Vereins für Reformationsgeschichte, Nos. ci-cii, 1911); W. Koepp, *Johann Arndt. Eine Untersuchung über die Mystik im Luthertum* (1912), with bibl. F. A. G. *Tholuck–W. Hölscher in *P.R.E.*, ii (1897), pp. 108–12, s.v.

ARNOBIUS (d. c. 330). A Christian apologist who flourished in the time of *Diocletian (284–305). Acc. to *Jerome, he was originally a rhetorician at Sicca in proconsular Africa. In his 'Adversus Nationes' (c. 303–310), a treatise full of curious learning, he defended the consonance of the Christian religion with the best pagan philosophy. *Lactantius was his pupil.

The *Adv. Nationes* survives in the single MS., Par. Bibl. Nat. 1661. Text first ed. by Faustus Sabaeus [Brixianus] at Rome, 1543; J. P. Migne, *PL*, v. 349–1374; crit. edd. by A. Reifferscheid in C.S.E.L. iv (Vienna, 1875) and C. Marchesi (Turin, 1934). Eng. tr. by A. H. Bryce and H. Campbell in A.N.C.L., vol. xix, 1871; more recent Eng. tr. of *Adv. Nationes* by G. E. McCracken in A.C.W. (2 vols., 1949). F. Gabarrou, *Arnobe, son œuvre* (1921); id., *Le Latin d'Arnobe* (1921); E. Rapisarda, *Arnobio* (1945). P. Monceaux, *Histoire littéraire de l'Afrique chrétienne*, iii (1905), pp. 241–6; Bardenhewer, ii (ed. 2, 1914), pp. 517–25; B. Altaner, *Patrologie* (ed. 2, 1950), p. 152 f.

ARNOBIUS JUNIOR (5th cent.). He was an African monk, who attacked St. *Augustine's doctrine of Grace in Rome c. 450. He wrote allegorizing 'Commentaries' on the Pss., some notes on the Gospels, and an anti-*Monophysite 'Conflictus cum Serapione'. G. *Morin also ascribes to him the '*Praedestinatus' (though this attribution is contested by H. v. Schubert) as well as a 'Liber ad Gregoriam', a letter to an aristocratic lady of Rome.

Editio princeps of his Commentaries by D. *Erasmus (Basle, 1522), of his 'Expositiunculae in Evangelium' by G. Cognatus [i.e. Cousin] (Basle, 1543). Complete text of the latter pr. by G. *Morin, O.S.B., in *Anecdota Maredsolana* iii (pt. 3, Maredsous and Oxford; 1903), pp. 129–51. Collected ed. in J. P. Migne, *PL*, liii, 237–692. H. von Schubert, *Der sogenannte Praedestinatus* (T.U. xxiv, Hft. 4, 1903), pp. 95–114. Bardenhewer, iv, pp. 603–6; Altaner (1950), pp. 407 f., both with further bibl. P. de Labriolle in *D.H.G.E.*, iv (1930), cols. 547–9.

ARNOLD OF BRESCIA (d. 1155), reformer. Probably a native of Brescia, Arnold studied at Paris, where, acc. to tradition, he was a pupil of *Abelard. On his return to Italy, he became a *canon regular, and at once began to attack the worldliness of the Church. He proclaimed that confession should be made not to a priest but by Christians to one another, that the sinfulness of a priest destroyed the value of the sacraments which he administered, and that spiritual persons ought not to possess worldly goods or exercise secular authority. His participation in local political disputes at Brescia forced him in 1139 to return to France, and St. *Bernard of Clairvaux secured the condemnation of his doctrines, with those of Abelard, at the Council of Sens in 1140. Arnold later (1145) made his way to Rome and there gave his support to the party which had rejected the temporal dominion of the Pope. The result was his excommunication by Eugenius III on 15 July 1148. Eventually, after the accession of the Emp. *Frederick Barbarossa, who made a treaty with the Papacy on 16 Oct. 1152, the party which Arnold supported in Rome lost control, and Arnold was captured by Barbarossa and condemned to death. He was handed over to the prefect of Rome, now returned to its obedience, and executed, and the ashes of his burnt body were thrown into the Tiber.

The primary sources for his life are the two chronicles of *Otto of Freising, the letters of St.*Bernard of Clairvaux and the *Historia Pontificalis* of *John of Salisbury; on the last, see text of R. L. Poole (Oxford, 1927), pp. lviii–lxx. R. Breyer, 'Arnold von Brescia' in *Historisches Taschenbuch*, viii (1889), pp. 121–78; K. Hampe, 'Zur Geschichte Arnolds von Brescia' in *Historische Zeitschrift*, cxxx (1924), pp. 58–69; W. v. Giesebrecht, 'Ueber Arnold von Brescia' in *Sb.* (Bayr.), iii (1873), pp. 122–54. A. Hausrath, *Arnold von Brescia* (1891). G. W. Greenaway, *Arnold of Brescia* (1931), with discussion of sources, pp. 205–10, of modern studies, pp. 211–17, and full bibl.

ARNOLD, GOTTFRIED (1666–1714), German Protestant theologian and devotional writer. A native of Annaberg in Saxony, he studied theology at *Wittenberg from 1685 to 1689, when, following the advice of P. J. *Spener, he accepted a position as private tutor at Dresden. Under Spener's influence he experienced a conversion. In 1693 he went to Quedlinburg, where he wrote his first important work, *Die erste Liebe* (1696), an enthusiastic account of the life of the first Christians, founded on his *patristic studies and esp. the work of W. *Cave. The book earned him a call to Giessen as professor of Church history in 1697, a post which he resigned in the following year because he found it too distracting. He returned to Quedlinburg, where he wrote his principal work, the *Unparteiische Kirchen- und Ketzer-Historie* (1699–1700). Though not as impartial as its title claims, it is important esp. as a history of Protestant mysticism and for its use of many out-of-the-way documents on the movement. The opposition of the official Lutheran Church led him to form close connexions with representatives of a more personal spirituality such as J. G. *Gichtel. His *Geheimnis der göttlichen Sophia* (1700) abounds in strange speculations on the androgynous nature of the first man, lost by the Fall, and recovered through Christ. After his marriage, in 1701, he devoted himself increasingly to pastoral work. In 1704 he became inspector and pastor at Werben, and in 1707 at Perleberg. His writings of this later period are devotional and less eccentric, among the most popular being *Geistliche Gestalt eines evangelischen Lehrers* (1704) and *Wahre Ab-bildung des inwendigen Christentums* (1709). He is also well known as an author of hymns, and he published translations of M.*Molinos and Mme *Guyon, and edited the works of *Angelus Silesius.

Modern edd. of his *Geistliche Lieder* by A. Knapp (Stuttgart, 1845) and R. C. Ehmann (ib., 1856; with Life, pp. 1–43). Selection ed. by E. Seeberg (Munich, 1934). F. Dibelius, *Gottfried Arnold. Sein Leben und seine Bedeutung für Kirche und Theologie* (1873); E. Seeberg, *Gottfried Arnold. Die Wissenschaft und die Mystik seiner Zeit* (1923).

ARNOLD, MATTHEW (1822–88), poet and literary critic. He was the eldest son of T. *Arnold (q.v.). Born at Laleham, Surrey, he was educated at *Winchester, Rugby, and Balliol College, *Oxford, where he won the Newdigate Prize with his poem *Cromwell* (1843). In 1845 he was elected a Fellow of Oriel College; from 1847 to 1851 he was private secretary to Lord Lansdowne; and from 1851 to 1883 a Government Inspector of Schools. From 1857 to 1867 he was also Professor of Poetry at Oxford. His powers as a poet and a critic developed somewhat slowly. *Empedocles on Etna* (1852), though poorly constructed as a dramatic work, contained some fine lyrics. In 1853 he published his *Poems* (including 'Sohrab and Rustum' and the 'Scholar Gipsy'); in 1855 his *Poems* (Second Series). 'Thyrsis' and 'Rugby Chapel' both first appeared in *New Poems* (1867). His prose writings include *On Translating Homer* (1861), *Essays in Criticism* (1865; second series, 1888), and *Culture and Anarchy* (1869). For his religious views, *St. Paul and Protestantism* (1870), *Literature and Dogma* (1873), *God and the Bible* (1875), and *Last Essays on Church and Religion* (1877) are of particular interest.

Matthew Arnold made it his mission to condemn the boorishness of the English, finding in 'culture' the cure for contemporary ills and a potent help towards the formation of human character. Religion, he held, was to be concerned with conduct and not with speculation about the nature of things. The power behind the universe is a moral one, and with it a moral tendency which resides in man is in sympathy. These truths Arnold held to be manifested in the OT belief that righteousness, which God approves, exalts a nation; but he deplored the superstitious *Bibliolatry, alien from the scientific spirit of the age, which interpreted with literalness such poetic images as the hope of the *Messiah. The religion of Jesus had shown advance by laying stress on personal rather than national conduct, and had suffused morality with emotion and, therefore, with happiness.

Collected Works, 15 vols., London, 1903–4 (with bibl. by T. B. Smart). Several collected edd. of Poems, among them 2 vols., London, 1869, and 2 vols., London, 1877. Selected Essays ed. G. K. *Chesterton (Everyman's Library, 1906). *Letters, 1848–1888* ed. G. W. E. Russell (2 vols., 1895); *Letters to Arthur Hugh Clough*, ed. H. F. Lowry (1932). *Note-Books*, ed. H. F. Lowry, K. Young and W. H. Dunn, London, 1952. Studies by G. Saintsbury ('Modern English Writers', 1899), H. W. Paul ('English Men of Letters', 1902),

G. W. E. Russell ('Literary Lives', 1904), Hugh Kingsmill (pseud., 1928), L. Trilling (New York, 1939), E. K. Brown (Toronto, 1948). Further bibl. in *C.B.E.L.*, ii (1940), pp. 265–70. R. Garnett in *D.N.B.*, Suppl. i (1901), pp. 70–75, s.v.

ARNOLD, THOMAS (1795–1842), Headmaster of Rugby. A fine classical scholar, he was a Fellow of Oriel College, Oxford, from 1815 to 1819, where he was a contemporary of John *Keble and R. D. *Hampden. In 1828 he was appointed Headmaster of Rugby. Here he aimed at fostering a system of education based on a carefully laid foundation of religious training. He made it his goal to educate the sons of middle-class parents, who began to flock into the public schools towards the close of his lifetime, into a high sense of duty, of public service, and of the importance of personal character. He believed in the essential unity of the secular and religious, of Church and state, and in the universal priesthood of the laity. He objected to the *Tractarians on the ground of their ecclesiasticism, and vigorously attacked them in an article entitled 'Dr. Hampden and the Oxford Malignants' in the *Edinburgh Review* of 1836. In 1841 he was appointed Regius Professor of Modern History at Oxford, but died while still in his prime in the following year. His ecclesiastical ideals were epitomized in his *Principles of Church Reform* (1833). He also issued works on classical subjects and some volumes of sermons.

Miscellaneous Works collected and ed. by A. P. *Stanley (London, 1845). Id., *The Life and Correspondence of Thomas Arnold* (2 vols., 1844). Other studies by Emma J. Worboise (London, 1859), J. J. Findlay (ed.; Cambridge, 1897), R. J. Campbell (1927), A. Whiteridge (London, 1928), and N. Wymer (ib., 1953). T. Walrond in *D.N.B.*, ii (1885), pp. 113–17, s.v.

ARNULF, St. (c. 580–before 655), also Arnoul, Bp. of Metz. Descended from a noble Frankish family, he rapidly rose to a high position in the court of Theodebert II, King of Austrasia (595–612), renouncing his early desire for a solitary life in order to undertake the duties of government. He took an active part in securing the accession of Clothaire II in 613. He was consecrated Bp. of Metz c. 614, and from 623 assisted Clothaire's son, Dagobert, in the government of his kingdom in the Ardennes. He took part in the Councils of Clichy (c. 626–7) and of *Reims (c. 627), and was eventually allowed to resign his see. He joined his friend Romaric in retirement in a deserted place near Remiremont in the Vosges, where he spent the rest of his life in meditation and prayer. Before he was consecrated Bishop he had been married to the daughter of the Count of Bologne. One of his sons, Clodulf, was his third successor in the see of Metz; by the marriage of the other with a daughter of Pepin of Landen, Mayor of the Palace of Austrasia, he became an ancestor of the Carolingian kings of France. Feast day, 18 July or 16 Aug.

The principal authority is an anonymous contemporary Lat. life pr. in *AA.SS.* Jul. IV (1735), pp. 435–40; a further life, mainly dependent on it, dating from the reign of Louis

II (846-79) and attributed to Umno, ib., pp. 440-45; crit. ed. of the former by B. Krusch in *M.G.H.* Scriptores Rerum Merovingicarum, ii (1888), pp. 426-46. J. Depoin, 'Grandes Figures monacales des temps mérovingiens: Saint Arnoul de Metz. Études de critique historique' in *Revue Mabillon*, xi (1921), pp. 245-58; xii (1922), pp. 13-25.

ARTEMON (also **ARTEMAS**) (3rd cent.), *Adoptionist heretic. All that is known of him is that *c.* 235 he taught at *Rome and that he was excommunicated for heretical teaching. His doctrine, which seems to have been a later development of that of the two *Theodoti, was that Christ was only a man, though He excelled the Prophets. It was attacked on the twofold basis of Scripture and the earliest Christian tradition by the author of the '*Little Labyrinth'.

ARTICLES. See *Irish Articles; Lambeth Articles; Organic Articles; Six Articles; Ten Articles; Thirteen Articles; Thirty - Nine Articles; Twelve Articles.*

ARUNDEL, THOMAS (1353-1414), Abp. of *Canterbury. A prominent politician and, with his brother, an opponent of Richard II, he was consecrated Bp. of *Ely in 1374, and translated to *York in 1388 and to *Canterbury in 1396. In 1397 he was impeached in Parliament and banished. Restored to Canterbury in 1399, he was three times Chancellor under Henry IV, and remained in possession of his see until his death. He was a prominent opponent of the *Lollards, holding a provincial council against them at *Oxford in 1408, seeking out Lollard writings, and showing himself active in the persecution carried out against them.

J.*Gairdner, *Lollardy and the Reformation in England*, i (1908), pp. 54-265 passim; K. B. McFarlane, *John Wycliffe and the Beginnings of English Nonconformity* [1953], pp. 150-5 and 161-5. J. Gairdner in *D.N.B.*, ii (1885), pp. 137-41, s.v.

ASAPH, St. (*fl.* 570), Welsh saint. He became a disciple of St. *Kentigern, when the latter was in exile at Llanelwy (later called *St. Asaph) in Wales. When Kentigern returned to Scotland, *c.* 570, Asaph succeeded him as head of the monastery of Llanelwy, and became the first Welsh bishop of the see. Nothing more is definitely known of him. Feast day, 1 May.

AA.SS. Mai. I (1680), p. 82 f. D. Lleufer Thomas in *D.N.B.*, Suppl. i (1901), p. 78 f., with bibl.

ASBURY, FRANCIS (1745-1816). One of the two first *Methodist bishops in America. Sent to America by J.*Wesley in 1771, he was very soon given supervision of all Methodist work in the country. When the American Methodists became a separate organization in 1784, he and Thomas Coke became joint superintendents. His journal from 1771 has much valuable historical matter. He continued the work of organization and administration until his death.

His *Journal* was edited at New York, 1862. W. L. Duren, *Francis Asbury* (1928).

ASCENSION OF CHRIST, The. The withdrawal of Christ into Heaven, witnessed by the Apostles (Mk. 16. 19, Lk. 24. 51, Acts 1. 9). Acc. to tradition it took place on the Mount of *Olives. Lk. 24. 50-53 has been held to imply that the Ascension happened on the evening of the day of the Resurrection, but acc. to Acts 1. 3 it occurred forty days later. There are also explicit references to it in Jn. (cf. 6. 62, 20. 17), though this Gospel has no account of the event itself, and implicit references in the rest of the NT (cf. Eph. 4. 8-10, Heb. 4. 14, 7. 26, 1 Pet. 3. 22, 1 Tim. 3. 16).

The Ascension marked the solemn close of the post-Resurrection appearances and the exaltation of Christ to the heavenly life after He had spoken to His Apostles of 'the things concerning the Kingdom of God'. Its theological significance consists in the fact that thereby Christ's human nature was taken into Heaven, whence He now exercises all power in Heaven and on earth (cf. Jn. 14. 2, Phil. 3. 21, Heb. 6. 20, Rev. 3. 21).

Ascension Day is one of the chief feasts of the Christian year. It is kept on the sixth Thursday, i.e. the 40th day, after *Easter. There is widespread evidence (e.g. in *Chrysostom, *Etheria, and *Socrates) for its celebration from the later years of the 4th cent. In early times its observance was frequently, if not always, marked by a procession, apparently to commemorate Christ's journey to the Mount of *Olives. Acc. to W. usage, the *Paschal Candle, lighted during the more important services in Eastertide, is extinguished after the Gospel at Mass on Ascension Day. In the BCP Proper Psalms (8, 15, 21; 24, 47, 108) are appointed for the day itself and a Proper Preface for use throughout the *octave.

W. Milligan, *The Ascension and Heavenly Priesthood of Our Lord* (1891); H. B. *Swete, *The Ascended Christ* (1910); V. Larrañaga, *L'Ascension de Notre-Seigneur* (Fr. trans., 1938). P. Benoît, O.P., 'L'Ascension' in *R. Bibl.* lvi. (1949), pp. 167-203, with further bibl. reff.

ASCENSION OF ISAIAH. See *Isaiah, Ascension of.*

ASCENT OF MOUNT CARMEL, The. The earliest of St.*John of the Cross's spiritual treatises, written between 1578 and 1580. It expounds the method by which the will, the intellect, and the senses in the Christian soul are purified in its approach to God. The book was written primarily for those entrusted with pastoral responsibilities.

ASCETICAL THEOLOGY. The theological discipline dealing with the so-called 'ordinary' ways of Christian perfection. It is to be distinguished, on the one hand, from *Moral Theology, which treats of the duties indispensable for salvation, and, on the other, from *Mystical Theology, whose subject is the 'extraordinary' or passive ways of the spiritual life. It is thus the science of Christian perfection in so far as this is accessible to human effort aided by grace. Its special object is charity, directed principally towards God and secondarily to one's neighbour. It is, however, a practical as well as a theoretical science, and hence treats also of the means to be employed and the dangers to be avoided if the end of the Christian life is to be attained.

As a science, Ascetical Theology is based on the teaching of Scripture and the traditions and decisions of the Church. It is usually divided into three parts corresponding to the three degrees of the spiritual life of 'beginners', 'proficient' and 'perfect', characterized by the *Purgative, *Illuminative, and *Unitive Ways respectively. Theologians are divided, however, as to whether the 'Unitive Way' is still a subject of Ascetical Theology or whether it comes under the competence of Mystical Theology. The former opinion, usually held by those tending to a rigid separation of Ascetical from Mystical Theology, postulates two kinds of unitive ways, one belonging to ascetics, the other to mysticism. The latter view is defended by those who admit only one unitive way, which, acc. to them, always belongs to the mystic state and is the normal—though not the most frequent—development of the ascetic life.

The beginning of Ascetical Theology as a science, though not yet separated from Moral and Mystical Theology in the modern sense, goes back to the patristic age (*Clement of Alexandria, and esp. *Dionysius the Areopagite). It was developed under the influence of the inquiring spirit of Scholasticism, e.g. by *Hugh of St. Victor, and then further elaborated by the great Schoolmen of the 13th cent., St. *Albert, St. *Thomas Aquinas, and St. *Bonaventure. In modern times treatises on subjects of Ascetical Theology have become very numerous. Among the most popular and influential are St. *Ignatius' *Spiritual Exercises*, St. *Francis de Sales' *Introduction to the Devout Life*, and St. *Alphonsus Liguori's *The True Spouse of Jesus Christ*. See also *Asceticism*.

G. B.*Scaramelli, *Direttorio ascetico* (1752; Eng. tr. 1870). A. Devine, *Manual of Ascetical Theology* (1902); A. Saudreau, O.P., *Les Degrés de la vie spirituelle* (Angers, 1904; Eng. tr. by Bede Camm, O.S.B., 2 vols., 1926); C. *Marmion, *Le Christ, vie de l'âme* (1914; Eng. tr., 1922), and Marmion's other works; A.*Tanquerey, *Précis de théologie ascétique et mystique* (1924); A. Farges, *Les Voies ordinaires de la vie spirituelle* (1925; Eng. tr., 1927). K. E. *Kirk, *The Vision of God* (1931); F. P. Harton, *The Elements of the Spiritual Life* (S.P.C.K., 1932); and numerous other manuals. Periodicals specially devoted to the subject include *Revue d'Ascétique et de Mystique* (Toulouse, 1920 ff.), *Zeitschrift für Aszese und Mystik* (Innsbruck, 1926 ff.) and *The Life of the Spirit* (Oxford, 1946 ff.; formerly as suppl. to *Blackfriars*); cf. also *Dictionnaire de spiritualité ascétique et mystique* (ed. M. Villier, S.J., F. Cavallera and others, fasc. i, 1932; vol. i, 1937; in progress). For literature on the history of the subject, see bibl. to foll. entry.

ASCETICISM (from Gk. ἄσκησις, 'exercise', 'training'). The term, which was already used by the *Stoics and Cynics, denotes a system of practices designed to combat vice and develop virtues, such as were employed not only by many Greek philosophers, but also in some E. religions, esp. Buddhism. In the NT the word occurs only once—as a verb, ἀσκεῖν, 'to strive'—at Acts 24. 16. In 1 Cor. 9. 25 the Christian life is compared to the games in which 'every man that striveth . . . is temperate in all things'. But the idea, present already in the OT, esp. in the *Wisdom books, is prominent throughout the NT. It is summed up in our Lord's call to His disciples: 'If any man would come after Me, let him deny himself and take up his cross and follow Me' (Mk. 8. 34), with its emphasis on the two sides of Christian asceticism, the negative one of self-denial and the positive one of the following of Christ. This invitation to practise self-abnegation is frequently reiterated, mostly in very strong terms (Mt. 10. 38 f., Jn. 12. 25), being shown to involve constant watchfulness (Mt. 24. 42, 25. 13, &c.) and fasting (Mt. 9. 15, Mk. 9. 29) and, in many cases, renunciation of all earthly possessions (Mt. 19. 21, Mk. 10. 28, Lk. 9. 57–62) and perpetual chastity (Mt. 19. 12). St. *Paul counsels the same ideal, repeatedly inculcating the necessity of keeping up the struggle against the inclinations of the 'old man' (e.g. Rom. 8. 13, 1 Cor. 9. 26 f., Col. 3. 5).

In the first three cents. Christian asceticism found expression esp. in the preparation of Christians for martyrdom and in the ideal of virginity, which in its complete consecration of soul and body to God, was put almost on a par with the former. *Clement of Alexandria and *Origen seem to have been the first Fathers to study the theoretical foundations of asceticism. Taking over from the Stoics the idea of ascetic action as a purification of the soul from its passions, they see in it a necessary means for loving God more perfectly and for attaining to contemplation. In the 3rd cent. the ascetic ideal as a particular way of life had gained adherents throughout Christendom, thus leading up to the age of the Fathers of the Desert and the beginnings of monasticism in the 4th cent. From that time the monks both in the East and in the West became leading representatives of asceticism, which was practised not only in such external exercises as abstinences, fasts, and vigils, but also in the interior abnegation required by the virtues proper to the monastic life. The monks, too, became authors of important ascetical treatises, among the most famous of such early writings being the Conferences of *Cassian and of *Dorotheus.

With the growing devotion to the humanity of Christ, esp. to His Passion, in the Middle Ages, asceticism underwent a certain modification in that it became increasingly inspired by the desire for conformation to the sufferings of the Redeemer. In contrast to the worldliness and avarice of the secular clergy, the *Mendicant orders practised and spread the ideal of voluntary poverty, and produced many treatises on the ascetical life. Early in the 15th cent. the '*Imitation of Christ' developed a new doctrine of the inner life on the basis of an exacting asceticism.

At the close of the Middle Ages there appeared a twofold reaction against the ascetical ideal, led by the scholars and artists of the *Renaissance on the one hand and by the

Protestant Reformers on the other. In the humanist revival of pagan antiquity there was little place for the spiritual combat of the Christian ascetic, whereas the *Lutheran doctrine of the total depravity of human nature and justification by faith alone undermined the theological foundations of the medieval ascetic writers. Despite these challenges the ascetical ideal, upheld by the Council of *Trent, continued to find its champions in such austere saints as *Peter of Alcántara, *John of the Cross, and later in the *Curé d'Ars, as well as in new *congregations and reformed branches of old orders such as the *Passionists or the *Trappists. At the same time a more exclusively interior and hidden asceticism of complete renunciation of the will found expression in other modern Institutes, e.g. the *Jesuit Order and the *Visitation Nuns. Among the *Puritans asceticism, in the negative sense of abstinence from particular pleasures or re-creations, was widely upheld and practised. In a more positive sense it also found an important place in *Methodism and esp. among the *Tractarian divines and their successors. It led to the wide revival of religious communities in England in the 19th cent. An exaggerated asceticism has been the mark of some sects, e.g. of the *Montanists, *Gnostics, and *Manicheans of the patristic period, and of the medieval *Cathari and *Waldenses, where it was usually combined with dualistic tendencies in theology.

Acc. to its classical Christian exponents asceticism is a necessary means of fighting the concupiscence of the flesh, of the eyes and the pride of life, mentioned in 1 Jn. 2. 16. It is also of great value as an imitation of the sacrificial life of Christ and as a means of expiation of one's own sins and those of others, in virtue of the doctrine of the Mystical Body. It springs from the love of God and aims at overcoming all the obstacles to this love in the soul. It is thus not an end in itself but essentially a preparation for the life of union with God, since, in its positive aspect, it seeks to foster the interior tendencies that serve to develop the life of charity.

M. J. Rouët de Journel, S.J.–J. Dutilleul, S.J. (edd.), *Enchiridion Asceticum* (Freiburg i.Br., 1930; mainly patristic); H. Koch, *Quellen zur Geschichte der Askese und des Mönchtums in der alten Kirche* (1933). H. Windisch in *T.W.B.*, i (1935), pp. 492–4, s.v. 'ἀσκέω'; O. Zöckler, *Kritische Geschichte der Askese* (1863; ed. 2 as *Askese und Mönchtum* 2 vols., 1897). Good historical survey in P. Pourrat, P.S.S., *La Spiritualité chrétienne* (4 vols., 1920–8). A Saudreau, *La Piété à travers les âges* (Angers, 1927). H. Strathmann, *Geschichte der frühchristlichen Askese bis zur Entstehung des Mönchtums* (1914); M. Viller, S.J.–K. Rahner, S.J., *Ascese und Mystik in der Väterzeit* (1939). L. Gougaud, O.S.B., *Dévotions et pratiques ascétiques du moyen-âge* (Collection 'Pax' xxi, 1925; Eng. tr., 1927). J. de Ghellinck, S.J., *Patristique et Moyen-Âge*, iii (1948), pp. 185–244 (Étude V: Un Programme de lectures spirituelles dans les écrits des pères). O. Zöckler in *H.E.R.E.*, ii (1907), pp. 73–80, s.v. 'Ascetism (Christian)'; J. de Guibert, S.J., M. Olphe-Galliard, S.J., M. Viller, S.J., and A. Willwoll, S.J., in *Dict. Sp.* i (1937), cols. 936–1010, s.v. 'Ascèse, Ascétisme'.

ASEITY (Lat. *aseitas*, from [*ens*] *a se*, 'being from itself'). The quality in virtue of which a being exists of and from itself alone. Acc. to Christian teaching, it is realized solely in God

and distinguishes Him from all created beings whose existence, as it issues ultimately from Him, is derivative from something outside itself (*ens ab alio*).

ASH WEDNESDAY. The first day of *Lent, six and a half weeks before *Easter. Down to the 7th cent., Lent began with *Quadragesima Sunday, as it still does in the *Ambrosian Rite. The four extra days were added later to secure the exact number of forty week-days for the fast. At one time public penitents at Rome were ceremonially admitted to begin their penance on this day; and when this discipline fell into disuse, between the 8th and 10th cents., the general penance of the whole congregation took its place. This was symbolized by the imposition of ashes, in token of mourning and penitence, upon the heads of clergy and people, a rite still ordered for Ash Wednesday in the Roman Missal. In the BCP of 1549 and in subsequent editions the *Commination Service is prescribed for this day. In the American Prayer Book of 1929 Ash Wednesday is mentioned as a special fast-day (with *Good Friday), and in the Scottish Book of 1929 it is named (together with the six days before Easter) a 'Greater Fast'.

F. *Cabrol, O.S.B., in *D.A.C.L.*, ii (1910), cols. 3037–44, s.v. 'Cendres', with bibl. H. Thurston, S.J., *Lent and Holy Week* (1904), pp. 84–99.

ASHERAH. A Hebrew feminine proper name, used in the OT of a *Canaanite goddess (1 Kgs. 15. 13, 2 Kgs. 21. 7 [RV]) and of the sacred pole erected as her symbol (1 Kgs. 16. 33, 2 Kgs. 13. 6 [RV]). (The AV consistently renders the word 'grove'; cf. LXX ἄλσος, Vulg. *lucus*.) The poles were set up near the Canaanite altars, which in early times were often built under green trees. The Israelites adopted them, along with other appurtenances of the pagan religion which they found in existence when they settled in Canaan, but their destruction was ordered in the Hebrew legislation (Deut. 7. 5, 12. 3).

P. Torge, *Aschera und Astarte.* Ein Beitrag zur semitischen Religionsgeschichte (1902). G. A. Barton in *J.E.*, ii (ed. 1925), p. 185, s.v., with bibl.

ASKE, ROBERT (d. 1537), leader of the ''Pilgrimage of Grace' (q.v.) Descended of an old Yorkshire family, he became an attorney and Fellow of Gray's Inn. On 13 Oct. 1536 he put himself at the head of the 'Pilgrimage' when the rebellion broke out in Lincolnshire. After treating on equal terms with the royal leaders sent to suppress the rising and obtaining a safe-conduct to *Henry VIII, he returned northwards early in 1537 with a promise that the grievances would be redressed. A fresh outbreak provided a pretext for a change in the outwardly conciliatory attitude of the King, and by May 1537 Aske had been seized and found himself a prisoner in the Tower of London. He was charged and condemned at Westminster for high treason, taken back to the North, and in July 1537 hanged in chains at *York.

Aske's own account of his capture in Lincs., his examination and other related documents preserved in the Public Record Office are ed. by Mary Bateson in *E.H.R.*, v (1890), pp. 330–45 and 550–73. See also bibl. to *Pilgrimage of Grace.*

ASKEW, ANNE (1521–46), Protestant martyr. Of Lincolnshire descent, she came under suspicion of heresy in 1545 on account of her beliefs about the Eucharist. Both Bp. E. *Bonner and Bp. S. *Gardiner examined her, with the purpose of making her recant, but without success. She was burnt at *Smithfield on 16 July 1546. For the facts, the chief authority is two tracts by J. *Bale.

The tracts are J. Bale, *The First Examination of the worthy Servant of God, Misstress Anne Askew* (Marburg, 1546); id. *The Latter Examination of Anne Askew* (ib., 1547); cf. also *The Account of the Sufferings of Anne Askew . . .* written by herself (London, 1849). Charles Wriothesley, *A Chronicle of England during the Reigns of the Stuarts*, ed. by W. D. Hamilton, i (Camden Society, Second Series, xi, 1875), pp. 155, 167–9. J. *Foxe, *Acts and Monuments*, ed. G. Townsend, v (1846), pp. 537–50.

ASPERGES. In the W. Church the ceremony of sprinkling *holy water over the altar and people before the principal Mass on Sundays. During the ceremony a chant from Ps. 51, 'Asperges me, Domine, hyssopo &c.' is ordinarily sung. In *Eastertide this is replaced by '*Vidi Aquam'. The ceremony certainly goes back to the 9th cent., when it is referred to by *Hincmar of Rheims in his 'Epistola synodica'. The sprinkler used for the purpose is known as the 'aspergillum', 'aspersorium', or 'goupillon'.

L. Eisenhofer, *Handbuch der katholischen Liturgik*, i (1932), pp. 476–80. C. Goeb, O.S.B., 'The Asperges' in *Orate Fratres*, ii (1927–8), pp. 338–42.

ASPERSION. The method of baptism whereby the candidate is merely sprinkled with the baptismal water. It is a variant of *affusion (in which the water is actually poured on the candidate), and is held to be permissible only in exceptional circumstances.

ASPIRANT. One who aspires to a vocation to the *religious life.

ASSEMANI (Syriac = 'Simon'). The family name of four famous *Maronite Orientalists of the 18th cent.

(1) **Joseph Simonius** (1687–1768). He was a native of Tripoli in Syria, who entered the Maronite College at *Rome in 1703. After being ordained priest he obtained a post at the *Vatican Library and was sent to collect MSS. in the East by Clement XI in 1715, and again in 1735. In 1736 he attended the first National Maronite Council where he used his influence to bring his countrymen into closer connexion with Rome. Shortly afterwards he was nominated Abp. of Tyre and Prefect of the Vatican Library. His principal work, the *Bibliotheca Orientalis* (4 vols., 1719–28), is a collection of *Syriac documents esp. on the

history of the Churches of Syria, Chaldaea, and Egypt, by which Syriac literature was introduced into the West, and which, for great parts, has not been superseded. He also edited the works of St. *Ephraim Syrus, *Opera Ephraemi* (6 vols., 1732–46), with Latin and Greek translations, and this is still the only complete edition. Among his other works are the unfinished *Kalendaria Ecclesiae Universae* (6 vols., 1755), designed as a collection of texts, inscriptions, &c., on all the saints of the world, *Italicae Historiae Scriptores* (4 vols., 1751–3), and the *Bibliotheca Juris Orientalis Canonici et Civilis* (5 vols., 1762–6).

(2) **Stephen Evodius** (1707–82), nephew of the former. He also studied at the Maronite College in Rome, was appointed missionary of the *Propaganda and travelled in Syria, Mesopotamia, and Egypt as well as in Europe, esp. in England. He assisted his uncle in cataloguing the MSS. of the Vatican Library. At the suggestion of *Benedict XIV he edited *Bibliothecae Mediceae-Laurentianae et Palatinae Codicum MSS. Orientalium Catalogus* (2 vols., 1742), *Acta Sanctorum Martyrum Orientalium et Occidentalium* (2 vols., 1748), and *Bibliothecae Apostolicae Vaticanae Codicum MSS. Catalogus.*

(3) **Joseph Aloysius** (1710–82). He was a brother of Joseph Simonius. He was professor of Syriac, later of Liturgy, at the Sapienza in Rome and edited *Codex Liturgicus Ecclesiae Universae* (13 vols., 1749–66), a valuable collection for the study of the E. liturgies; *Commentarius Criticus de Ecclesiis* (1766); and *Commentaria de Catholicis seu Patriarchis Chaldaeorum et Nestorianorum* (1775).

(4) **Simon** (1752–1821). After studying at Rome, he went to Syria as a missionary. In 1785 he became professor of Oriental languages at the seminary of Padua, and in 1807 at Padua university. He published several works on Arabic subjects, among them an 'Essay on the Origin, Cult, Literature, and Customs of the Arabs before Mohammed' (1787) and the 'Catalogue of the Naniana Library' (2 vols., 1787–92), both in Italian, containing important MS. extracts and essays on Arabic literature, coins, &c.

(1) J. Notain Daraunis (ed.), *Series Chronologica Patriarcharum Antiochiae per Josephum Simoneum Assemanum . . .* (1881), pp. 1–11. J. Debs, *Kitāb tarīkh Sūriya*, Part 4, vol. viii (Beirut, 1905), pp. 553–63. G. Levi della Vida, *Ricerche sulla formazione del più antico fondo dei manoscritti orientali della Bibliotheca Vaticana* (S.T., xcii, 1939), passim.

(2) J. Debs, op. cit., pp. 568–70. G. Levi della Vida, *op. cit.*, passim.

(3 and 4) J. Debs, op. cit., p. 570 f.

L. Petit, A.A., in *D.A.C.L.*, i (1907), cols. 2973–80, s.vv.; P. Stair in *E.C.*, i (1949), cols. 159–61, s.vv., both with bibl.

ASSEMBLIES OF THE FRENCH CLERGY (*Assemblées du Clergé de France*). The quinquennial meetings of representatives of the Catholic clergy which from the end of the 16th cent. were an established institution in France. They endured, after the secular States General had been discontinued, until the Revolution. Their functions were primarily to apportion the very heavy financial burdens laid on the clergy by the king, and incidentally to discuss ecclesiastical affairs. A very elaborate and successful technique of procedure enabled them to exercise considerable financial influence. In 1682 they incurred the disapproval of *Innocent XI by approving and adopting, at the behest of Louis XIV, the '*Gallican Articles'.

ASSENT, Declaration of. A legal undertaking imposed upon the clergy of the C of E at *Ordination (to both the diaconate and the priesthood), and on entering upon certain specified ecclesiastical offices. By it assent is required to the Book of *Common Prayer, the *Ordinal, and the *Thirty-Nine Articles, in place of the formal *subscription demanded before 1865. Assent is generally understood to imply a less definite form of adherence than subscription, but there is apparently no official explanation as to exactly what it involves. Perhaps the term may be explained as an undertaking to refrain from teaching anything directly opposed to the standard of doctrine implied, without requiring positive agreement in detail in one's personal opinions. The previous formula, demanding 'that he acknowledgeth *all and every* the articles . . . being in number all nine and thirty', was significantly omitted in 1865.

ASSES, Feast of (Lat. *Festum asinorum*). A religious celebration formerly observed at *Christmas (or in some cases on 14 Jan.) in certain French towns (e.g. Rouen, Beauvais), at which the prophecy of Balaam's ass (Num. 22) or alternatively the Flight of the Holy Family into Egypt (Mt. 2. 13–15) was dramatically represented.

T. J. Crowley in *C.E.*, i (1907), p. 798 f., s.v., with reff.

ASSISI. The city in the Umbrian Hills, famous as the birthplace of St.*Francis. In addition to the large three-storied *basilica of San Francesco (1228–53, with the remains of the saint) in the town itself, a second basilica, Sta. Maria degli Angeli, some 2 to 3 miles to the SW, shelters the little chapel known as the *Portiuncula, where the Franciscan Order originated. Other famous shrines in the neighbourhood are 'San Damiano', the small chapel in which in 1212 St. Francis admitted St.*Clare into his order, and the 'Eremo della Carceri', a favourite retreat of St. Francis in the mountains.

A. Cristofani, *Storia della città d' Assisi* (1866); L. D. Gordon, *The Story of Assisi* ('Medieval Towns Series', 1900).

ASSIZES OF JERUSALEM, The. The law-book compiled by John of Ibelin, a Cypriote, which purports to give the laws laid down by *Godfrey of Bouillon (d. 1100) for the kingdom of *Jerusalem. In fact, it is a manual of the customary law of the kingdom which had grown up under its later kings, and was compiled probably in the 13th cent. after the kingdom of Jerusalem had fallen. It is an important authority for the institutions of a French feudal kingdom in their earliest and purest form.

Text ed. G. T. de La Thaumassière (Bruges, 1690); excerpts repr. in J. P. Migne, *PL*, clv, 397–430; standard ed. publd. by le Comte Beugnot ('Recueil des historiens des croisades', 2 vols., Paris, 1841–3). F. Monnier, 'Godfrey de Bouillon et les assises de Jérusalem' in *Séances et travaux de l'Académie des Sciences Morales et Politiques*, c (1873), pp. 73–105, 663–94, and ci, N.S. i (1874), pp. 444–93; M. Grandclaude, *Étude critique sur les livres des assises de Jérusalem* (1923).

ASSOCIATIONS, Law of. The law promulgated by the French government on 1 July 1901 acc. to which no religious congregations, male or female, could be formed without authorization from the state. The congregations which had been recognized in the past were to be allowed to continue, provided they drew up an annual list of their members, property, and financial status which was to be submitted to the government authorities at request. On the other hand, the authorization of any congregation could be annulled by simple decree of the Council of Ministers, and new foundations of authorized congregations were subject to the permission of the Council of State. All congregations that had not been authorized in the past were declared dissolved, and severe punishments enacted for any circumvention of the law. In the following years the legislation became even more hostile. In 1902 congregations were forbidden to carry on any educational activities whatever. The men's orders then went into exile, while most of the women's transformed themselves into nursing congregations. The final consequence of this legislation was the complete break between Church and State in France in 1905.

Text in the *Journal officiel* for 2 July 1901, pp. 4025–7; an addendum, making its terms more stringent, ib. 5 Dec. 1902, p. 7901. The law which provoked the final break in 1905 ('Loi concernant la séparation des Églises et de l'État') is printed ib. 11 Dec. 1905, pp. 7205–9. Extracts in Mirbt, No. 646, pp. 499–501, with bibl.

ASSUMPTION OF THE BVM, The. The belief that the BVM, having completed her earthly life, was in body and soul assumed into heavenly glory ('Immaculatam Deiparam semper Virginem Mariam, expleto terrestris vitae cursu, fuisse corpore et anima ad caelestem gloriam assumptam'; definition *Munificentissimus Deus* of 1950).

It is now generally agreed that the belief was unknown in the earliest ages of the Church. St.*Ambrose (*Exposit. Evan. sec. Luc.* 2. 35; *PL*, xv, 1574) and St.*Epiphanius (*Haer.* lxxix, 11; *PG*, xlii, 716) were apparently still ignorant of it. It is first met with in certain NT apocrypha dating from the later 4th cent. onwards, some of them *Gnostic in sympathy. These texts, which bear such titles as 'The Passing Away of Mary' and 'The Obsequies of Mary', survive in Greek, Latin, Syriac, Coptic, Arabic and Ethiopic and are assigned in the MSS. to various authors, e.g. to St. *John the Evangelist and St. *Melito of Sardis.

They record the death of the BVM at *Jerusalem amid varying miraculous circumstances, in some cases alleging that her body was assumed on the way to the burial, in others that it was raised after three days. The date of the Virgin's death is variously assigned, e.g. to three or fifty years after the *Ascension. It appears that one such work was condemned in the *Decretum Gelasianum, though the condemnation may have been directed against its Gnostic teachings rather than specifically against the doctrine of the corporal assumption. A homily attributed in most MSS. to Timothy of Jerusalem (prob. 4th–5th cent.) may imply the alternative belief that the BVM was assumed in body and soul during her natural life.

The doctrine of the corporal assumption was first formulated in orthodox circles in the W. by St.*Gregory of Tours (d. 594), who accepted as historical the account attributed in MSS. to Melito. In the E. a passage in St. *Dionysius the Areopagite's Concerning the Divine Names (5th–6th cent.) was taken by *Andrew of Crete (d. 740) to mean that *Dionysius (the presumed disciple of St. *Paul) had witnessed the assumption, while the writings of St. *Germanus of Constantinople and other 7th cent. authors testify to the acceptance of the doctrine by this period. In the next cent. St. *John Damascene related that at the Council of *Chalcedon, *Juvenal, Bp. of Jerusalem, had told the Emp. Marcian and his wife *Pulcheria, who wished to possess the body of the BVM, that her death had been witnessed by all the Apostles, but that when her tomb was later opened, it was found empty. This account, which claimed the authority of Dionysius, presented the doctrine as ancient Catholic tradition; it was of particular influence in the West because of its inclusion from the 16th cent. in the Roman Breviary among the lessons for the Feast of the Octave of the Assumption.

Feasts celebrating the death of the BVM were observed in Palestine during the 5th cent., possibly at *Antioch in the 4th cent. The Greek Church was, however, divided as to the date between 18 Jan. (associating it with the *Epiphany) and 15 Aug. (prob. connecting it with the dedication of some church in her honour), until the Emp. Maurice (582–603) ordered that the latter date should be observed. In Rome, unless the Mass for the BVM given under 15 Aug. in the *Gelasian Sacramentary (which does not mention any corporal assumption) be original, it appears that one general feast in honour of Our Lady was observed until the last years of the 7th cent., viz. on 1 Jan. The Byzantine feasts of the BVM, incl. that of the Assumption, seem to have been introduced in the time of Pope *Sergius I (687–701). From Rome they spread to the countries of the Gallican rite, where a feast of Our Lady had previously been kept on 18 Jan. (the other E. date); and by the end of the 8th cent. the feast of the Assumption was universally observed in the W. on 15 Aug. In 847 Pope *Leo IV ordered that the octave be kept. In the C of E the feast disappeared from the BCP in 1549, and has not been officially restored. It has

been retained, however, in the Oxford University Calendar, and is now observed in many places.

The doctrine was prob. first upheld on grounds of deductive theology in an 8th or 9th cent. letter attributed to St. *Augustine (PL, xl, 1141–8) and was later defended by St. *Albertus Magnus, St. *Thomas Aquinas and St. *Bonaventure. *Benedict XIV declared it a probable opinion. In answer to repeated demands to the Popes from 1870 onwards, on 1 Nov. 1950 Pope* Pius XII in Munificentissimus Deus defined the doctrine and provided a new Mass for the Feast. In the E. Church belief in the corporal assumption of the BVM is general, though prob. in terms less precise than those of the Roman definition. It is there known as the Koimesis (lit. 'falling asleep').

O. Faller, S.J., De Priorum Saeculorum Silentio circa Assumptionem B. Mariae Virginis (Analecta Gregoriana, xxxvi, Sectio A.N. 5, 1946). M. R. James, The Apocryphal New Testament (1924), pp. 194–227, incl. Eng. tr. of main texts, with reff. to original edd. F. Cavallera, 'À propos d'une enquête patristique sur l'Assomption' in Bulletin de Littérature Ecclésiastique, xxvii (1926), pp. 97–116. Sermons by James of Serûg and James, Bp. of Birta, ed. A. *Baumstark, 'Zwei syrische Dichtungen auf das Entschlafen der allerseligsten Jungfrau' in Oriens Christianus, v (1905), pp. 82–125. B. *Capelle, O.S.B., 'La Fête de l'Assomption dans l'histoire liturgique' in Ephemerides Theologicae Lovanienses, iii (1926), pp. 33–45; id., 'La Fête de la Vierge à Jerusalem au Vᵉ siècle' in Le Muséon, lvi (1943), pp. 1–33; id., 'La Messe gallicane de l'Assomption, son rayonnement, ses sources' in Miscellanea Liturgica in Honorem L. Cunibert Mohlberg, i (1948), pp. 33–59; V. Grumel, 'Le Mois de Marie des Byzantins' in E.O., xxxv (1932), pp. 257–69; A. Raes, S.J., 'Aux origines de la fête de l'Assomption' in O.C.P., xii (1946), pp. 262–74. Duchesne, L.P., i (1886), p. 376. C. Piana, O.F.M., Assumptio Beatae Virginis Mariae apud Scriptores saec. XIII (1942). M. Jugie, A.A., La Mort et l'assomption de la Sainte Vierge. Étude historico-doctrinale (S.T., cxiv, 1944) with reff. G. Hentrich and R. G. de Moos (edd.), Petitiones de Assumptione Corporea B.V. Mariae in Caelum Definienda ad Sanctam Sedem Delatae (Rome, 2 vols., 1942); F. Cavallera, S.J., 'Une Somme sur l'Assomption' in Bulletin de Littérature Ecclésiastique, xlviii (1947), pp. 157–165; J. Coppens, 'La Definibilité de l'Assomption' in Ephemerides Theologicae Lovanienses, xxiii (1945), pp. 5–35. Good survey of modern lit. by F. *Heiler, 'Assumptio. Werke zur Dogmatisierung der leiblichen Himmelfahrt Marias' in T.L.Z., lxxix (1954), cols. 1–52. See also bibl. to Munificentissimus Deus.

ASSUMPTION OF MOSES, The. See Moses, The Assumption of.

ASSUMPTIONISTS (Augustinians of the Assumption). A religious congregation, founded at Nîmes in 1843 for the active religious life, and approved in 1864 by *Pius IX. Its members follow a modification of the *Augustinian rule. They have spread to many parts of the world, esp. since 1900, when their congregations in France were dispersed by state decree. Their work includes the care of asylums and schools, the dissemination of literature, and missionary work in many parts of the world. Several ancillary orders and confraternities have been formed to support their work. Their house at *Constantinople has esp. fostered the study of the theology and institutions of the E. Church, notably through its review, Échos d'Orient (1897 ff.) and a group of notable scholars (L. Petit, E. Bouvy, F. Cayré, M. Jugie, S. Salaville).

J. Monval, *Les Assomptionnistes* (1939). Heimbücher, ii, pp. 384–6. R. Janin, A.A., in *L.Th.K.*, i (1930), col. 731 f., and R. Souarn, A.A., in *E.C.*, i (1949), col. 502 f.

ASSYRIAN CHRISTIANS. A small group of *Nestorians who have survived to modern times in the confines of Asia Minor and Persia. The name 'Assyrians', despite W. A. Wigram, is almost certainly a misnomer. They derive from the Nestorian Church which came into being after the Council of *Ephesus (431) and, as a small isolated body, have been very tenacious of their traditions. They commemorate *Nestorius as a saint and refuse the title of θεοτόκος to the BVM. Until contacts were made with the W. in the 19th cent., notably through the 'Abp. of Canterbury's Assyrian Mission', they were almost wholly devoid of learning. Their liturgies include the primitive rite of '*Addai and Mari' (probably before 431), which with other liturgical texts was printed at Urmi by the Abp. of Canterbury's Mission in 1889. After the war of 1914–18, when they joined forces with Russia, their political situation became desperate; they have now been placed under the rule of Iraq. Among their literary possessions was the Syriac version of Nestorius' 'Treatise of Heracleides', originally brought to notice by H. Goussen in 1897 and first published in 1910 by P. Bedjan (Syriac) and F. Nau (Greek).

W. A. Wigram, *An Introduction to the History of the Assyrian Church . . . 100–640 A.D.* (1910); id., *The Assyrian Settlement* (1922); id., *Assyrians and their Neighbours* (1929).

ASTERISCUS (Gk. ἀστερίσκος, from ἀστήρ, 'a star'). In the Byzantine rites, a utensil consisting of two metal strips crossed and bent and placed over the blessed bread during the Liturgy to keep it from contact with the veil that covers it.

ASTERIUS (d. after 341), the 'Sophist', *Arian theologian. He was a pupil of *Lucian of *Antioch and was present at the Council of Antioch of 341. Besides his 'Syntagmation', of which fragments are preserved by St. *Athanasius and *Marcellus of Ancyra, Asterius wrote commentaries and homilies on the Pss., of which considerable portions have been recently recovered by M. Richard and E. Skard. His work throws important light on the early interests and methods of the Arian school.

His writings are listed by St. *Jerome, *De Vir. Ill.*, 94. G. Bardy, 'Astérius le Sophiste' in *R.H.E.*, xxii (1926), pp. 221–72; id., *Recherches sur S. Lucien d'Antioche et son école* (1936), pp. 316–57; M. Richard, 'Les Homélies d'Astérius sur les psaumes iv–vii' in *R. Bibl.*, xliv (1935), pp. 548–558, and id., 'Une Ancienne Collection d'homélies grecques sur les psaumes i–xv' in *Symbolae Osloenses*, xxv (1947), pp. 54–73, and E. Skard, 'Asterios von Amaseia und Asterios der Sophist' in *Symbolae Osloenses*, xx (1940), pp. 86–132; cf. ib., xxv (1947), pp. 80–2, and ib., xxvii (1949), pp. 54–69.

ASTROLOGY. The study of the supposed influence of the stars upon human fortunes. In modern usage the term is confined to 'judicial astrology', i.e. the 'science' which professes to forecast the fortunes of a man, e.g. from the positions of the stars at the moment of his birth. Astrology was much practised in the ancient world, but the influence of Christian teaching, as illustrated in St. *Augustine, *De Civ. Dei*, v. 1–8, suppressed it in the Empire, until in the 13th cent. it re-entered the West through Jewish and Arabic scholars, who for centuries had studied it in the East. The 16th cent. was the period when its influence was most powerful in Europe, among Catholics and Protestants alike. The scepticism of the 18th cent., with the growth of scientific knowledge, greatly reduced its popularity; and in England its credit was much shaken by a satirical pamphlet by J. *Swift, called *Prediction for the Year 1708*. In the present century the growth of unbelief and superstition has encouraged the revival of astrology in certain quarters.

ASTRUC, JEAN (1684–1766), physician and Pentateuchal critic. The son of a Protestant pastor, he was converted at an early age to Catholicism. In 1710 he was appointed to a medical professorship at Toulouse, and in 1717 at Montpellier. In 1729 he was nominated physician to the King of Poland, in 1730 to Louis XV of France, and in 1731 professor at the royal college at Paris. In 1753 he published anonymously his celebrated work *Conjectures sur les Mémoires originaux dont il paroît que Moyse s'est servi pour composer le Livre de la Genèse*, in which he maintained that in its present form the Book of Genesis was a piecing together of earlier documents. He based this view on the varying use of '*Elohim' and '*Jehovah' for the Divine name, and on the duplication of narratives. He did not dispute that it was *Moses who brought the documents together. Astruc also wrote a *Dissertation sur l'immortalité et sur l'immatérialité de l'âme* (1755).

An adapted Germ. tr. of the *Conjectures* was publd. at Frankfurt a.M. in 1783. A. Lods, *Jean Astruc et la critique biblique au XVIIIᵉ siècle* (1924). E. Böhmer in *P.R.E.* (ed. 3), ii (1897), pp. 162–70, s.v. Astruc's many medical publications do not call for mention here.

ASYLUM, Right of. See *Sanctuary*.

ATHANASIAN CREED, The. A profession of faith widely used in Western Christendom, and also known from its opening words as the 'Quicunque Vult'. It differs from the *Apostles' and *Nicene Creeds in form, as well as in embodying *anathemas, and is not a recognized standard of faith in the E., though it has appeared since *c.* 1780 in the Greek *Horologium, and in Russian service books from the 17th cent. Of the Protestant bodies, some (notably the *Lutherans) retain and use it; in the Latin *Breviary it is recited on certain days at *Prime; and in the Anglican BCP (where it is printed immediately before the Litany) it replaces the Apostles' Creed at Morning

Prayer on thirteen holydays, chosen apparently as being at roughly equal intervals apart.

The attribution to St. *Athanasius has been generally abandoned since the researches of G. J. *Voss (1642), chiefly on the ground that the Creed contains doctrinal expressions which arose only in later controversies. Not only is there no early authority for ascribing it to him, but it was evidently composed in Latin, not in Greek, and till modern times it has circulated solely in the W. By many recent critics it has been held to have originated in Gaul, and early Gallic theologians to whom it has been ascribed include *Vincent of *Lérins, *Hilary of Arles, and *Victricius of Rouen. The doctrines defended and the terminology used point to a time when the controversy over *Apollinarianism was acute, and before the outbreak of the *Nestorian and *Eutychian heresies to which no reference is made; and on the basis of these considerations most scholars now conclude that it was written between 381 and 428. In the present century there has been an increasing readiness to accept the thesis of H. Brewer, S.J., that it was the work of St. *Ambrose.

Its subject-matter falls into two halves, which expound respectively the doctrines of the Trinity and of the Incarnation. To the latter is added a list of the important events of Our Lord's redeeming work in a form resembling that of the Apostles' Creed. The creed is prefaced and concluded with the assertion that belief in the truths it asserts is necessary to salvation.

Since 1867 many efforts have been made in the C of E to have it removed from the service, or truncated, especial objection being made to the 'damnatory clauses' (vv. 2 and 42), but conservative opinion has generally held that, even if it may be considered desirable in the abstract that certain expressions should be explained or retranslated, in present circumstances any alteration would give the impression that something of the traditional faith was being surrendered; and in fact no alteration has been made. The BCP version, however, is in places inaccurate and misleading, partly because of mistranslation, and partly because the Reformers based their rendering on an inaccurate text. In the Anglican Churches outside England its use in worship has been considerably restricted.

A. E. Burn, The Athanasian Creed ('Oxford Church Text Books', 1912). Fuller treatment, with discussion of authorship, in G. D. W. Ommanney, Early History of the Athanasian Creed (1880); A. E. Burn, The Athanasian Creed and Early Commentaries (Texts and Studies, iv No. 1; Cambridge, 1896). G. D. W. Ommanney, A Critical Dissertation on the Athanasian Creed (1897). H. Brewer, S.J., Das sogenannte Athanasianische Glaubensbekenntnis ein Werk des hl. Ambrosius (1909). G. *Morin, O.S.B., 'À propos du Quicumque. Extraits d'homélies de S. Césaire d'Arles sous le nom de S. Athanase' in R. Bén., xxviii (1911), pp. 417–24. J. Stiglmayr, S.J., 'Das Quicumque und Fulgentius von Ruspe' in Z.K.T., xlix (1925), pp. 341–57 [Ath. Creed, work of Fulgentius]. A. E. Burn, 'The Authorship of the Quicumque Vult' in J.T.S., xxvii (1925–6), pp. 19–28. G. Morin, O.S.B., 'L'Origine du symbole d'Athanase: témoignage inédit de S. Césaire d'Arles' in R. Bén. xliv (1932), pp. 207–219. F. *Loofs in P.R.E. (ed. 3), ii (1897), pp. 177–94; J. [Giuseppe] Madoz, S.J., in E.C. x (1953), col. 411 f., s.v. 'Quicumque Vult', with bibl.

ATHANASIUS, St. (c. 296–373), Bp. of *Alexandria. Probably educated at the *Catechetical School in his native city, he became deacon and secretary to *Alexander, Bp. of Alexandria, and attended him at the Council of *Nicaea (325), succeeding him as bishop in 328. By his refusal to compromise with *Arianism, he incurred the enmity of the powerful Arianizing party in the reigns of *Constantine and *Constantius. They procured his deposition and exile to Trier in 336; he returned on the death of Constantine in 337; but in 339 he was forced to flee to *Rome, where he established close contacts with the W. Church, which continued throughout his life to support him. He was restored in 346 by the influence of Constans, the Western Emperor, against the will of Constantius, who in 356 again drove him from the see. He remained in hiding near Alexandria till the accession of *Julian (361), who, however, exiled him again in 362. He returned on Julian's death in 363, and, after yet another brief exile (365–6), helped for the rest of his life to build up the new Nicene party by whose support orthodoxy triumphed over Arianism at the Council of *Constantinople in 381. He died at Alexandria on 2–3 May, 373. See also Melitian Schism (1).

Before c. 318, while still in his twenties, he wrote two short treatises, the second of them the famous 'De Incarnatione'. In it he expounds how God the Word (*Logos), by His union with manhood, restored to fallen man the image of God in which he had been created (Gen. 1. 27), and by His death and resurrection met and overcame death, the consequence of sin. As bishop he was the greatest and most consistent theological opponent of Arianism. From 339 to 359 he wrote a series of works in defence of the faith proclaimed at Nicaea—viz. the true deity of God the Son—both meeting the Arians in theological controversy and exposing the tricks of their ecclesiastical politics. From about 361 onwards he especially sought the reconciliation of the large semi-Arian party to the Nicene term *homoousios ('of one substance'), which they were reluctant to accept. The Council of Alexandria (362), under his direction, greatly furthered this end, by clearing up misunderstandings of the terms ὑπόστασις (translated 'person') and οὐσία ('substance'). He was also concerned to uphold the deity of the Holy Spirit and the full manhood of Christ against *Macedonian and *Apollinarian tendencies. As the friend of the monks *Pachomius and *Serapion, and the biographer of *Antony, he aided the ascetic movement in Egypt and he was the first to introduce knowledge of monasticism to the W. His resolute character as well as his theology was the outstanding obstacle to the triumph of Arianism in the E. Feast-day, 2 May.

Ed. princeps of Gk. text 'ex officina Commeliniana', 2 vols., Heidelberg, 1600–1. All earlier edd. superseded by the Maurist text, ed. B. *Montfaucon, 3 vols., Paris, 1698; repr., with additions, by N. A. Giustiniani, Bp. of Padua, 4 vols., Padua, 1777; with further additions in J. P. Migne, PG, xxv–xxviii. Crit. text ed. H. G. Opitz [– W. Schneemelcher] for Berlin Academy in progress, Berlin, 1934 ff. Sep. edd. of *De Incarnatione* by A. *Robertson (London, 1882; ed. 2, 1893), F. L. Cross (London, S.P.C.K., 1939), and P. T. Camelot, O.P. (Sources chrétiennes, 1934 ff. 18. 1947; with *Contra Gentes*); of *Orations against Arians* by W. *Bright (Oxford, 1873); of *Historical Writings*, also by W. Bright (Oxford, 1881); of *Epp. to Serapion* by J. Lebon ('Sources chrétiennes 15', Paris, 1947). Festal Epp. ed. W. *Cureton (London, 1848). On the text, H. G. Opitz, *Untersuchungen zur Überlieferung der Schriften des Athanasius* (1935); indispensable. Eng. trr. of 'Select Treatises [against] the Arians' by J. H. *Newman (*L.F.*, 2 vols., 1842–4; ed. 2, much revised, 1881); A. *Robertson in N.P.N.C.F. (1892). There is no contemporary Life. Important is the 'Vita Acephala' publd. in 1738 by F. S. *Maffei (q.v.). Brief modern Life by G. Bardy ('Les Saints', Paris, 1914); also F. Lauchert, *Leben des heiligen Athanasius des Grossen* (1911). J. A. *Mohler, *Athanasius der Grosse und die Kirche seiner Zeit* (2 vols., 1827; ed. 2, 1844); L. Atzberger, *Der Logoslehre des hl. Athanasius* (1880); H. M. Gwatkin, *Studies of Arianism* (1882; ed. 2, 1900), passim; A. Stülcken, *Athanasiana* (T.U. xix. 4, 1899). Fundamental is series of papers by E. *Schwartz in *Nch.* (Gött.) ('Zur Geschichte des Athanasius', various dates, 1904–11). F. L. Cross, *The Study of St. Athanasius* (1945; lecture). G. Mueller, *Lexicon Athanasianum* (Berlin 1952).

ATHANASIUS, St. (*c.* 920–1003), the Athonite. A native of Trebizond, he became a monk in Bithynia, but migrated thence to Mount *Athos where he established (961) the first of its famous monasteries (the Lavra). His foundation, though resisted by the eremites already settled on Athos, prospered through the support of the Emperors Nicephorus Phocas and John Tzimisces (969–76). He became Abbot-General (πρῶτος) of all the communities on the Mount, of which 58, including Iveron, Vatopedi, and Esphigmenou, were in being by his death. Feast day, 5 July. (He is not to be confused with the Athanasius mentioned in the Roman Martyrology for this date, a 5th cent. deacon of *Jerusalem.)

His Typicon and Testament are pr. in P. Meyer, *Die Haupturkunden für die Geschichte der Athosklöster* (1894), pp. 102–22 and 123–30 respectively. Early Gk. life by a monk named Athanasius, ed. J. Pomialovsky (St. Petersburg, 1895); further Gk. life, based on an earlier text, ed. L. Petit, A.A., in *Anal. Boll.*, xxv (1906), pp. 5–89, with Fr. tr. by Hiéromoine Pierre in *Irénikon*, viii (1931), pp. 457–499, 667–89, ix (1932), pp. 71–95 and 240–64. R. Janin in *D.H.G.E.*, iv (1930), cols. 1376 f., s.v. See also bibl. to *Athos, Mt.*

ATHEISM (from Gk. ἄθεος, 'without God'). The word was originally used in Greece of all those who, whether they believed in God or not, disbelieved in the official gods of the state. Of such men Socrates was the classic instance. In the Roman Empire the term was applied in a similar sense by the pagans to Christians, but sometimes Christians, like St. *Polycarp, would turn the term against their persecutors.

Until the expression '*agnosticism' came into general use in the 19th cent., the term atheist was used, at least popularly, to describe also those who thought of the existence of God as an unprovable thesis. Of such there are three chief divisions: philosophical agnostics, *materialists, and *pantheists. Any of these may be atheists in the strict sense of the word, but none need be. The philosophical agnostic normally says that the evidence is not sufficient to compel us either to assert or to deny the existence of God; but it is only if he adds further that the assertion of God's existence is meaningless, and not merely rash, that he is strictly to be called an atheist. The materialist, similarly, is strictly to be called an atheist only if he asserts that nothing can exist outside a closed system of matter; but often he will not say more than that for practical purposes it is necessary to treat the material world as a closed system. The pantheist view, also, has taken many forms; but it does not become truly atheistic until it makes its immanent divinity into such a limited being that he is no longer recognizable as God in any ordinary sense of the word.

The philosophical non-theist of the present day is most frequently either a 'logical positivist' (i.e. a particular kind of agnostic) or a materialist, and it is under these two headings that we must look for current atheism. The logical positivist holds that since assertions about God are not capable of empirical verification they are meaningless; and though he may escape the charge of formal atheism in the way already suggested, he is commonly virtually open to the charge. The atheism of present-day materialism is also often practical, not speculative. An exception must be made, however, in the case of the Dialectical Materialism of Communism, which is consciously and avowedly atheist.

R. Flint, *Anti-Theistic Theories* (Baird Lecture, 1879); F. A. Lange, *Geschichte des Materialismus und Kritik seiner Bedeutung in der Gegenwart* (1866; Eng. tr., 3 vols., 1877–81); F. Mauthner, *Der Atheismus und seine Geschichte im Abendlande* (4 vols., 1920–3). A. B. Drachman, *Atheism in Pagan Antiquity* (1922). On the pagan attacks on the early Christians as 'atheists', see A. *Harnack, *Der Vorwurf des Atheismus in den drei ersten Jahrhunderten* (*T.U.*, XIII, i, 1905). For a recent philosophical defence of Atheism, see J. Laird's Gifford Lectures, I, *Theism and Cosmology* (1940); II, *Mind and Deity* (1941). C. B. Upton in *H.E.R.E.*, ii (1909), pp. 173–83; C. Fabro in *E.C.*, ii (1949), cols. 265–80.

ATHENAGORAS (2nd cent.), Christian *Apologist. He is described in the earliest MS. of his works as 'the Christian Philosopher of *Athens'. His 'Apology' or 'Supplication', addressed *c.* 177 to *Marcus Aurelius and his son Commodus, sought to rebut current calumnies against the Christians, viz. atheism (cc. 4–30), Thyestian banquets and Oedipean incest (cc. 31–36). Later he wrote a work 'On the Resurrection of the Dead' in which, after refuting objections (cc. 1–10), he sought to defend the doctrine positively (cc. 11–25). As a writer he was one of the ablest of the Apologists, lucid in style and forceful in argument. He was the first to elaborate a philosophical defence of the Christian doctrine of God as Three in One. He upheld the indissolubility of marriage, even by death.

The Gk. text is preserved in the 'Arethas Codex' (Par. gr. 451), written in A.D. 914, on which all the other MSS. depend. *Ed. princeps* by H. *Stephanus (Paris, 1557). Later edd. by P. *Maran (Paris, 1742; repr. in J. P. Migne, *PG*, vi, 887–1024), by J. C. T. Otto, *Corpus Apologetarum*, vii (1857), and by E. *Schwartz in *T.U.*, iv. 2 (1891); also, of Apol. only, in J. Geffcken, *Zwei griechische Apologeten* [Aristides and Athenagoras] (1907). A. Puech, *Les Apologistes grecs du IIᵉ siècle de notre ère* (1912), pp. 172–206. E. J. Goodspeed, *Die ältesten Apologeten* (1914). J. Quasten, *Patrology*, i (1950), pp. 229–36, with good bibl. G. Bareille in *D.T.C.*, i (1903), cols. 2210–4, s.v.; M. Pellegrino in *E.C.*, ii (1949), col. 286 f.

ATHENS. By the 1st cent. A.D. Athens had become a provincial city of the Roman Empire, important only for its schools of philosophy, to which upper-class Romans went as to a university. Its first known Christian connexion was the visit (prob. A.D. 51) of St. *Paul on his second missionary journey (Acts 17. 15–18. 1). His sermon to the *Epicureans and *Stoics, as given in Acts 17. 22–31, took the form of an academic discourse and the preacher evidently did not meet with his usual success. Among his few converts was St. *Dionysius the Areopagite (q.v.: 17. 34). Apart from this passage, the NT has no other references to Christianity at Athens, except the passing mention in 1 Thess. 3. 1.

The earliest evidence for a Christian community comes from the middle of the 2nd cent. Acc. to *Melito of Sardis (*Eusebius, *HE*, IV, xxvi, 10), Antoninus Pius (138–61) endeavoured to check the unofficial, and possibly riotous, persecution of Christians in Athens and elsewhere. At or about this time Publius, Bp. of Athens, was martyred and the Church almost extinguished; but it was revived under his successor, Quadratus. Athens appears to have been one of the earliest centres of a philosophical interpretation of Christianity and was the home of the *Apologists, *Quadratus (prob. to be distinguished from the Bishop just mentioned), *Aristides and *Athenagoras.

In the next centuries the history of the city was uneventful. The philosophical schools continued and the city was twice visited by *Origen, who is said to have combated an outbreak of heresy here. St. *Basil and St. *Gregory of Nazianzus both studied at Athens. In 529 *Justinian closed its schools as exponents of surviving paganism, and shortly afterwards the Parthenon and other temples were converted into churches. In the Byzantine period many churches and monasteries were built. After the Latin Conquest in 1204 (Fourth *Crusade) the Parthenon became the cathedral of a Western bishop using the Latin rite, while a Greek bishop and the Greek rite were allowed to continue in the lower town for the native population. When the city fell to the Turks (1456), its conquerors turned the Parthenon into a mosque, expelling all Western influence but tolerating, as elsewhere, the Greek Church. They remained in possession of the Acropolis until 1833 when the Kingdom of Greece was set up and the Orthodox Church of Greece became *autocephalous with Athens as the metropolitical see.

M. *Lequien, *Oriens Christianus*, ii (Paris, 1740), cols. 169–78, iii (1740), cols. 837–44. A. Mommsen, *Athenae Christianae* (Leipzig, 1868). F. *Gregorovius, *Geschichte der Stadt Athen im Mittelalter von der Zeit Justinians bis zur türkischen Eroberung* (2 vols., 1889). N. T. Philadelpheus, Ἱστορία τῶν Ἀθηνῶν ἐπὶ Τουρκοκρατίας ἀπὸ τοῦ 1400 μέχρι τοῦ 1800 (2 vols., Athens, 1902). V. Laurent, A. A., 'La Liste épiscopale de la métropole d'Athènes' in *Mémorial Louis Petit* (Bucarest, 1948), pp. 272–91. R. Janin, A.A., in *D.H.G.E.*, v (1931), cols. 15–42, s.v.

ATHON, JOHN. See *Ayton, John.*

ATHOS, Mount. The 'Holy Mountain'. The peninsula which projects into the Aegean Sea from the coast of Macedonia and terminates in Mount Athos has long been entirely the property of monasteries of the Eastern Orthodox Church. The first monastic settlement of which there is reliable evidence is the foundation of the monastery of the 'Lavra' by St. *Athanasius the Athonite in 962. There are now 20 virtually independent monasteries on the peninsula. Such matters as are of common concern to the whole mountain are legislated for by a council, made up of one representative from each monastery, and an executive committee of four members. The monasteries contain many valuable MSS. and works of art. A curious rule of the Athonite monks forbids women, or even female animals, to set foot on the peninsula.

R. Curzon, *Visits to Monasteries in the Levant* (1849), pt. 4, pp. 327–449. A. Riley, *Athos, or the Mountain of the Monks* (1887); P. Meyer, *Die Haupturkunden für die Geschichte der Athosklöster* (1894). G. Smurnakes, Τὸ Ἅγιον Ὄρος (Athens, 1903); R. M. Dawkins, *The Monks of Athos* (1936). G. Millet (ed.), *Monuments de l'Athos*: i, les peintures (Monuments de l'art byzantin, v, 1927). Catalogues of MSS. include S. P. Lambros, *Catalogue of the Greek Manuscripts on Mount Athos* (2 vols., Cambridge, Engl., 1895–1900) and those of S. Eustratiades–Arcadios (MSS. of the Monastery of Vatopedi; Harvard Theological Studies, Cambridge, Mass., xi, 1924) and Spyridon–S. Eustratiades (MSS. of the Laura; ib., xii, 1925). P. de Meester, O.S.B., and V. Golzio in *E.C.*, ii (1949), cols. 300–7, s.v., with bibl.

ATONEMENT (i.e. 'at-one-ment'). In Christian theology, man's reconciliation with God through the sacrificial death of Christ.

The need for such reconciliation is implicit in the OT conception of God's absolute righteousness, to which nothing impure or sinful can approach. Its achievement is here represented as dependent on an act of God Himself, whether by the Divine appointment of the sacrificial system through which uncleanness, both ritual and moral, may be purged by the shedding of blood (cf. Heb. 9. 22), or, in a Prophetic view, by the future Divine gift of a New Covenant to replace the old covenant which sinful Israel has broken (Jer. 31. 31), or, in certain passages of the Book of Is., by the action of a Divinely-sent *Servant of the Lord who is 'wounded for our transgressions' and 'bare the sin of many' (Is. 53. 5, 12). But the Prophets also insisted that without repentance the offering of sacrifice for sins was futile (Is. 1. 10–17, Hos. 6. 6).

Christ Himself, like *John the Baptist, began His ministry with a call to universal repentance for sin (Mk. 1. 4–15). While He proclaimed the uselessness of blood-sacrifices considered as a substitute for repentance (Mt. 9. 13), He spoke also of giving His life 'a ransom for many' (Mk. 10. 45) and at the institution of the *Eucharist declared the shedding of His blood to constitute 'the new covenant' (Lk. 22. 20, 1 Cor. 11. 25) and to be 'unto remission of sins' (Mt. 26. 28). He also applied to Himself the words of Is. 53 relating to the Suffering Servant (Lk. 22. 37). In St. *John's Gospel Christ is set forth as 'the Lamb of God which taketh away the sin of the world ' (Jn. 1. 29) and

His death shown in a sacrificial light by being placed in juxtaposition to the sacrifice of the *Paschal Lamb at the *Passover (Jn. 19. 14, 36). Hence in the earliest Christian preaching His death was already proclaimed to be 'for our sins' (1 Cor. 15. 3) and His work expounded on the basis of Is. 53 (Acts 8. 32–35).

For the elaboration of the doctrine, the Church owed a unique debt to St. Paul. Christ's death and resurrection were the means by which we are redeemed from the effects of Law and its transgression, namely sin, from God's condemnation, and from death. By Baptism the Christian mystically shares in Christ's death and His victory over it, viz. the resurrection, and acquires, by God's free gift, a new status of sonship or justification, and peace was made between God and man 'through the blood of His cross' (Col. 1. 20); hence the death of Christ was a propitiation (ἱλαστήριον, Rom. 3. 25). Of the other NT writers, St. Peter speaks of our redemption 'with precious blood' (1 Pet. 1. 18 f.), and the author of Hebrews makes constant use of sacrificial language in the same connexion (cf. esp. ch. 9).

The Fathers took up and developed the doctrine of the NT, and posed problems which did not come within the purview of the Biblical writers. For *Origen the death of Christ was the ransom paid to Satan, who had acquired rights over man by the Fall. This view, though rejected by St. *Gregory of Nazianzus, was accepted with various modifications by many of the Latin Fathers, among them St. *Hilary of Poitiers, St. *Augustine, and St. *Leo. But while maintaining that the devil had rights over sinful man, the exponents of this doctrine also commonly stressed the other aspect that, in trying to exercise them on the sinless Christ he abused them, and was thus himself conquered by the power of the Resurrection. Another, and to modern ideas more congenial, doctrine is that God the Son, by taking our nature upon Him, has effected a change in human nature as such. It is typified in such a saying as St. Athanasius' 'He became man that we might be made divine' (De Inc. 54). The general Patristic teaching is that Christ is our representative, not our substitute; and that the effect of His sufferings, His perfect obedience, and His resurrection extends to the whole of humanity and beyond.

In the 11–12th cents. with St. *Anselm's Cur Deus Homo the emphasis shifted. The role of Satan receded and its place was taken by the idea of satisfaction. Sin, being an infinite offence against God, required a satisfaction equally infinite. As no finite being, man or angel, could offer such satisfaction, it was necessary that an infinite being, viz. God Himself, should take the place of man and, by His death, make complete satisfaction to Divine Justice. Hence the death of Christ was not a ransom paid to the devil but a debt paid to the Father. *Abelard, on the other hand, sought the explanation in terms of love. Christ's atoning death was effective primarily through its exemplary value, namely through the response of love that Calvary evoked in the sinner.

This break with tradition, too radical to meet with much acceptance, was violently criticized by St. *Bernard. The later Scholastic teaching set out from Anselm. St. *Thomas, while accepting Anselm's satisfactional view as a correct account of what took place, denied that the method of satisfaction was imperative. However 'convenient' the method, it had no intrinsic necessity, because God might have redeemed us without exacting full satisfaction. In the circumstances, however, the satisfaction was not only adequate but superabundant, for whereas the offence against God, being perpetrated by a finite being, was only morally infinite, the satisfaction, being the work of a Divine Person, was objectively, as well as morally, infinite. This teaching, which became the current opinion among Catholic theologians, was challenged by the *Scotists and *Nominalists, who held that the Atonement was adequate, not because of its own intrinsic value, but because of its 'extrinsic acceptance' by God.

The Reformers, though leaving the core of the traditional doctrine intact, developed it in a different direction. M. *Luther rejected the Scholastic satisfaction theory and taught that Christ, in bearing by voluntary substitution the punishment due to man, was reckoned by God a sinner in his place. J. *Calvin went even further in teaching that the Saviour 'bore in His soul the tortures of a condemned and ruined man'. In reaction against the exaggerations of this 'penal theory' arose the doctrine, first defended by the *Socinians, which denied the objective efficacy of the Cross and looked upon the death of Christ as primarily an example to His followers. Notable modern exponents of this view in England were B. *Jowett and H. *Rashdall. More recently there has been a return to traditional views. The 'Patristic doctrine' has been persuasively upheld by G. Aulén (Christus Victor, 1931), for whom it is the 'classical' idea of the redemption. Under the influence of the *Barthian theology there has been a renewed stress on the objectivity of the Atonement and a determination to put the Cross rather than the Manger at the centre of the Christian Creed. It should be added finally that there has never been any official formulation in orthodox Christianity of the mystery of the Lord's Redemption and that there is every likelihood that a variety of emphases and interpretations will continue.

For the history of the doctrine, see J. Rivière, Le Dogme de la Rédemption: Essai d'Étude Historique (1905; Eng. trans., 1909); id. Le Dogme de la Rédemption: Études Critiques et Documents (1931); J. K. Mozley, The Doctrine of the Atonement (1915); R. S. Franks, The History of the Doctrine of the Work of Christ (2 vols., 1918); H. *Rashdall, The Idea of Atonement in Christian Theology (1919); L. W. Grensted, A Short History of the Doctrine of the Atonement (1920).

For the NT teaching, see J. *Denney, The Death of Christ: Its Place and Interpretation in the NT (1902); V. Taylor, Jesus and His Sacrifice: A Study of the Passion-Sayings in the Gospels (1937); id. The Atonement in New Testament Teaching (1940); id. Forgiveness and Reconciliation: A Study in New Testament Theology (1941).

For systematic presentations, see J. McLeod Campbell, The Nature of the Atonement (1856); R. W. *Dale, The Atonement (1887; orthodox *Congregationalist); J. Scott Lidgett,

The Spiritual Principle of the Atonement (1901); R. C. *Moberly, *Atonement and Personality* (1901; worked out on the basis of Vicarious Penitence, Anglican); P. T. Forsyth, *The Work of Christ* (1910); J. Rivière, *Le Dogme de la Rédemption: Étude théologique* (1914; RC); J. Denney, *The Christian Doctrine of Reconciliation* (1917; posthumous); *The Atonement in History and in Life*, ed. by L. W. Grensted (1929; Anglican Liberal Evangelical); H. Maynard Smith, *Atonement* (1925); K. E. *Kirk, 'The Atonement', in *Essays Catholic and Critical* (1926; Anglican); *The Atonement*: Papers from the Summer School of Catholic Studies held at Cambridge, July 31-Aug. 9, 1926 (1928); R. S. Franks, *The Atonement* (1934); E. *Brunner, *The Mediator* (Eng. trans., 1934); id. *The Divine Imperative* (Eng. trans., 1937); L. S. Thornton, C.R., *The Doctrine of the Atonement* (1937); O. C. *Quick, *The Gospel of the New World* (1944).

ATONEMENT, Day of. The annual Jewish fast day (יוֹם הַכִּפֻּרִים, ἡμέρα ἐξιλασμοῦ) which falls on the 10th day of the 7th month (Tishri), i.e. roughly in Oct. Its observance is regulated by Lev. 16. 23, 27–32, and Num. 29. 7–11 (acc. to the critical view of the OT, all post-Exilic). Its purpose is the cleansing of sanctuary, priesthood, and people from sin and the re-establishment of good relations between God and His chosen ones. It is the only fast which the Mosaic Law provides. Much of the ritual ordered in the OT has necessarily lapsed, e.g. the entry of the priest into the *Holy of Holies in the *Temple, the offering of incense before the Mercy Seat and its sprinkling with blood, and the scapegoat for *Azazel dispatched to the wilderness. The basis of present observance is to be found in the Tractate 'Yoma' of the *Mishnah, wholly devoted to the subject. The Day is still observed by strict abstinence from food, and many Jews who rarely attend public worship on other occasions attend the synagogue. The imagery of the Day of Atonement deeply influenced the NT author of the Ep. to the Heb., who saw in Christ the Great High Priest whose Atonement on the Cross abolished the need for the annual repetition of the observance.

S. Landersdorfer, *Studien zum biblischen Versöhnungstag* (1924). I. Elbogen, *Der jüdische Gottesdienst in seiner geschichtlichen Entwicklung* (1913), pp. 149–54. A. Z. Idelsohn, 'The Kol Nidre Tune' in *Hebrew Union College Annual*, viii-ix (1931-2), pp. 493–509. S. R. *Driver-H. A. White in *H.D.B.*, i (1898), pp. 199–202, s.v., and M. L. Margolis in *Jewish Encyclopedia*, ii (ed. 1925), cols. 284–9, s.v.

ATRIUM. The main court of the Roman house. From an early date the word was used of the forecourt attached to Christian churches, which usually consisted of a colonnaded quadrangle with a fountain in the middle. It was connected with the interior of the church by a *narthex or portico, which ran the length of one side, and by which from *c.* the 6th cent. it was replaced as the main way of approach from without. An atrium with porticoes attached to the church erected by St. *Paulinus at Tyre is described by *Eusebius (*Hist. Eccl.* x. iv, 39).

ATTERBURY, FRANCIS (1662–1732), Bp. of *Rochester. He was a Tory High Churchman. After some years of academic controversy at Christ Church, Oxford, he became Lecturer of St. Bride's, London, chaplain to *William and Mary, and preacher at Bridewell Hospital. In his (anonymous) *Letter of a Convocation Man* (1697) and his *Rights and Privileges of an English Convocation Stated and Vindicated* (1700), he became the champion of *Convocation against the Crown and of the inferior clergy against the bishops. In 1701 he became Archdeacon of Totnes, in 1704 Dean of Carlisle, in 1711 Dean of Christ Church, and in 1713 Bp. of Rochester and Dean of *Westminster. In 1723 he was deprived of all his offices and banished from the country for alleged complicity in a Jacobite plot, and he died in exile. He was regarded as the best preacher of his day.

His Memoirs and Correspondence were edited by F. Williams (2 vols., 1869). H. C. Beeching, *Francis Atterbury* (1909). J. H. Overton in *D.N.B.*, ii (1885), pp. 233–8.

ATTICUS (d. 425), Patr. of *Constantinople. A native of Sebaste in *Armenia, he was brought up in the *Pneumatomachian heresy, but after making his way to Constantinople he was converted to orthodoxy. Here be became a bitter opponent of St. *Chrysostom. On the death of Arsacius, who had held the see of Constantinople for little more than a year after Chrysostom's expulsion (June 404), Atticus succeeded to the patriarchate. After Chrysostom's death (Sept. 407), however, he made concessions to the party of his supporters and eventually readmitted Chrysostom's name to the *diptychs, much to the annoyance of St. *Cyril of Alexandria. By obtaining a rescript from Emp. *Theodosius II which put the whole of Illyria and the 'Provincia Orientalis' under his authority, he enlarged the influence of his see, though these extended rights were lost later. His writings, which are of little merit, are chiefly directed against heresy (*Nestorianism, *Pelagianism, the *Messalians). The Latin version of the recension of the *Nicene canons which he sent to the Council of *Carthage of 419 goes under his name. In the E. he is venerated as a saint. Feast days, 8 Jan. and 11 Oct.

The Lat. Version of the recension of the Nicene canons under his name is printed in Turner, *E.O.M.I.A.*, I. ii (1904), pp. 104–42; letters in J. P. Migne, *PG*, lxv, 649 f., 716–21, with further reff. 651 f.; the Syriac text of a sermon on Our Lady ed., with Fr. tr., M. Brière, in *Revue de l'Orient Chrétien*, xxxiv (1933-4), pp. 160–86, and, with Lat. tr., and other material, J. Lebon, in *Le Muséon*, xlvi (1933), pp. 167–202. The principal authorities for his life are *Socrates, *H.E.*, vii, 2, *Sozomen, *H.E.*, viii, 27, and *Palladius, *Dialogus de Vita S. Johannis Chrysostomi*, ix-xi. Life from various sources printed in *A.A.SS.*, Jan. I (1643), pp. 473–82; also ib. Aug. I (1753), p. 32 f. J. *Hergenröther, *Photius*, i (1867), pp. 43–8. G. Bardy, 'Atticus de Constantinople et Cyrille d'Alexandre' in Fliche-Martin, iv (1937), pp. 149–162. Bardenhewer, iii (1912), p. 361 f. C. Verschaffel in *D.T.C.*, i (1903), col. 2220 f., s.v.; M. T. Disdier in *D.H.G.E.*, v (1930), cols. 161–6, s.v.

ATTILA (d. 453), King of the Huns from 433. In 451 he invaded Gaul, but was checked by a defeat near Troyes. (The story that he spared the town at the request of its bishop, Lupus, is unhistorical, however.) In the next year he attacked Italy, and after ravaging the cities of the North he desisted only at the prayers of *Leo I from attempting to capture Rome. He is known in Christian legends of Latin origin, from his savagery, as the 'Scourge of God' (*flagellum Dei*), i.e. as a minister of divine vengeance. Teutonic legends, on the other hand, represent him as hospitable and magnanimous.

T. Hodgkin, *Italy and her Invaders*, ii (1880), pp. 39–202. E. Hutton, *Attila and the Huns* (1915); M. Brion, *La Vie d'Attila* (1928; Eng. tr., 1929); E. A. Thompson, *A History of Attila and the Huns* (1948) with bibl.

ATTO (c. 885–961), Bp. of Vercelli from 924. He was a canonist and theologian remarkable for his great erudition in an unlearned age. His writings included a long commentary on the Pauline Epistles (dependent on *Augustine, *Jerome, *Claudius of Turin, and others) and a collection of ecclesiastical canons. Some of his letters and sermons have also survived.

Works ed. C. Buronzo del Signore (2 vols., Vercelli, 1768), repr. J. P. Migne, *PL*, cxxxiv, 9–916. Modern ed. of his 'Polypticum', an incisive critique of affairs in N. Italy in his day (but doubtfully the work of Atto himself) with Germ. tr. by G. Goetz (*Abh.* (Sächs.), xxxvii, Hft. 2; 1922). E. Pasteris, *Attone di Vercelli ossia il più grande vescovo e scrittore italiano del secolo X*. Vita ed opere con uno studio sulle sue prose ritmiche recentemente scoperte dall' autore (1925). J. Schultz, *Atto von Vercelli, 924–961* (Diss., Göttingen, 1885). A. Fliche, *La Réforme grégorienne*, i (S.S.L., vi, 1924), pp. 61–74.

ATTRITION. The sorrow for sin which proceeds from a sense of fear rather than (as does true *contrition) from the love of God. Even so, it is held by *moral theologians to be sufficient to procure God's pardon.

AUBIGNÉ, J. H. M. D'. See *Merle d'Aubigné, J. H.*

AUBURN DECLARATION, The (1837). A statement issued in 1837 in which the principal doctrines of the American *Presbyterians of the 'New School' were set forth. It was compiled by the Rev. Baxter Dickinson (d. 1876) in reply to the charges made by the 'Old School' against the 'New School' to the effect that they had departed from the traditional *Calvinist teaching as embodied in the *Westminster standards. The statement, which was accepted in Aug. 1837 at Auburn, New York State, was made the theological basis on which the 'New School' was organized as a separate body. In 1868 the Declaration was admitted by the General Assembly of the 'Old School' to contain 'all the fundamentals of the Calvinistic Creed' and thus paved the way for the reunion of 1870. Its 16 propositions are concerned rather to rebut a number of imputed soteriological and anthropological errors than to frame a set of positive beliefs.

The text is in P. Schaff, *The Creeds of Christendom* (1877), vol. iii, pp. 777–80.

AUCTOREM FIDEI. The bull of *Pius VI, dated 28 Aug. 1794, which condemned 85 articles of the Synod of *Pistoia (1786).

Text in A. Barbèri–R. Segreti (edd.), *Bullarii Romani Continuatio*, ix (Rome, 1845), pp. 395–418; the greater part, incl. the propositions condemned, is repr. in Denz.-Bann., pp. 415–42 (Nos. 1501–99). See also bibl. to *Pistoia, Synod of*, and *Pius VI*.

AUDIANI. A 4th cent. rigorist sect founded by a layman, Audius, which separated from the Church on the ground that the clergy were too secularized. They were also accused of holding an *anthropomorphic view of the Godhead. Banished by *Constantine to Scythia, they there carried on missionary activity among the Goths.

The principal authorities are *Epiphanius, *Haer.*, 70, and *Theodoret, *H.E.*, iv, 10. L. E. Iselin, 'Audios und die Audianer' in *Jahrbücher für protestantische Theologie*, xvi (1890), pp. 298–305. G. Bareille in *D.T.C.*, i (1903), cols. 2265–7, s.v. 'Audiens', with further patristic reff.; E. Peterson in *E.C.*, ii (1949), col 389 f., s.v. 'Audi', with bibl.

AUDIENCE, Court of. Formerly the ecclesiastical court of the province of *Canterbury. Originally the Archbishop exercised his legatine jurisdiction in person, but later was assisted by assessors ('Auditors'), who were gradually reduced to one. Later still, this remaining Assessor sat at *St. Paul's as judge of the Court. In 1536 an attempt was made to abolish the Court; but it survived until the next century, when it was merged in the Court of *Arches.

M. *Parker, *De Antiquitate Britannicae Ecclesiae* (1605), pp. 30–3. W. S. Holdsworth, *A History of English Law*, i (1903), p. 371 f. Irene J. Churchill, *Canterbury Administration*, i (1933), pp. 470–99, with reff.

AUDIENCES, Pontifical. Receptions given by the Pope to visitors to *Rome and to officials having business with the Holy See. They are for the most part private, but the general public are received in large numbers three or four times a week.

AUDIENTES (Lat.), 'hearers'. In the early Church, those belonging to the first stage of the *catechumenate. When they definitely desired to commit themselves to immediate prebaptismal instruction, they were admitted to the higher order of '*competentes'.

AUDOIN, St. See *Ouen, St.*

AUDRY, St. See *Etheldreda, St.*

AUFER A NOBIS. In the Roman Mass the collect for purity said by the celebrant at the end of the *Preparation as he goes up to the altar. The text is first found in the *Leonine Sacramentary as the collect in the fourth of a collection of Masses headed 'In Natale Episcoporum'.

Jungmann (1949) i, esp. pp. 362–4 and 382–6.

AUFKLÄRUNG (Germ., 'Enlightenment'). The term is applied in a technical sense to a movement of thought which appeared in an esp.

clear-cut form in 18th-cent. Germany and is connected with the names of H. S. *Reimarus, G. E. *Lessing, and J. G. *Herder. Set within the world-wide tendency to Rationalism, characteristic of the period, the 'Aufklärung' combines opposition to all supernatural religion and belief in the all-sufficiency of human reason with an ardent desire to promote the happiness of men in this life. One of its chief ideals was religious toleration, represented by Lessing's Nathan der Weise and the policy of Frederick the Great. Most of its representatives preserved the belief in God, freedom and immortality as consonant with reason, but rejected the Christian dogma and were hostile to Catholicism as well as to Protestant orthodoxy, which they regarded as powers of spiritual darkness depriving humanity of the use of its rational faculties. Their fundamental belief in the goodness of human nature, which blinded them to the fact of sin, produced an easy optimism and absolute faith in the progress and perfectibility of human society once the principles of enlightened reason had been recognized. The spirit of the 'Aufklärung' penetrated deeply into German Protestantism, where it disintegrated faith in the authority of the Bible and encouraged Biblical criticism on the one hand and an emotional 'Pietism' on the other. In German Catholicism it had its exponents among the educated laity and the higher clergy, being favoured by the policy of *Joseph II. It directed itself esp. against the religious orders, the celibacy of the clergy, the devotion to the saints, and such popular expressions of piety as pilgrimages and the veneration of relics.

AUGSBURG, The Confession of (1530). The Lutheran confession of faith, mainly the work of P. *Melanchthon, which, after receiving M. *Luther's approval, was presented at Augsburg to the Emp., *Charles V, on 25 June 1530. To make the Lutheran position as inoffensive as possible to the Catholic party, its language was studiously moderate. In form it is divided (apart from an introductory preface) into two parts. The first epitomizes in 21 articles the essential Lutheran doctrines. Of these the 20th, which expounds the Lutheran doctrines on faith and good works, is the most elaborate. The second half reviews the abuses for which remedy is demanded, among them communion in one kind, clerical celibacy, private masses, monastic vows, and compulsory confession. After receiving it, the Emperor transmitted it to a body of RC theologians which included J. *Eck, J. *Faber, and J. *Cochlaeus, and their reply, designated the 'Confutatio pontificia', was read on 3 Aug. Melanchthon answered this with an 'Apology for the Confession', which the Emperor refused to receive.

The Confession was, from the first, an authoritative Lutheran document, and in the spring of 1531 (with a few slight changes) the editio princeps was published. In the ensuing years it was issued in a number of forms which

varied somewhat in doctrine. In 1580, when the 'Book of *Concord' was drawn up, an endeavour was made to revert to the text presented to the Diet in 1530, and this 1580 text, the so-called 'Invariata', though it differs in over 450 places (mostly of no significance) from that of the Diet, remains the chief standard of faith in the Lutheran Churches. The considerably revised text issued by Melanchthon in 1540 (the 'Variata') is accepted by the Reformed (i.e. Calvinist) Churches in certain parts of Germany.

Crit. ed. of text (Germ. and Lat.) by P. Tschackert (Leipzig, 1901); Lat. text also in Kidd, pp. 259–89 (No. 116); Lat. text, with Eng. tr., in P. *Schaff, The Creeds of Christendom, iii (1882), pp. 3–73, with discussion, i (1881), pp. 225–44. W. Gussmann, Quellen und Forschungen zur Geschichte des Augsburgischen Glaubensbekenntnisses (2 vols., 1911). A. F. C. *Vilmar, Die Augsburgishe Confession erklärt (ed. K. W. Piderit, Gütersloh, 1870). J. Ficker, Die Konfutation des Augsburgischen Bekenntnisses (on the 'Confutatio'; 1891). W. E. Nagel, Luthers Anteil an der Confessio Augustana (Beiträge zur Förderung christlicher Theologie, xxxiv, Hft. 1; 1930). Further bibl. in Schottenloher, iv (1938), pp. 35–45 (Nos. 34504–679), and on the Confutation, p. 45 f. (Nos. 34680–87a.). T. Kolde in P.R.E. (ed. 3), ii (1897), pp. 242–50, s.v.; F. Blanke in R.G.G. (ed. 2), i (1927), cols. 651–5, s.v., both with bibl.

AUGSBURG, The Interim of. The doctrinal formula accepted as the provisional basis of religious settlement between Catholics and Protestants in 1548. After a joint commission of both groups, appointed by *Charles V in Feb. 1548, had failed to reach agreement, the Emperor had a formula prepared by J. *Pflug, Bp. of Naumburg, M. Helding, suffragan Bp. of Mainz, and J. *Agricola. This doctrinal compromise in 26 articles was designed as a provisional basis till the Council of *Trent made a final settlement. The chief points yielded to the Protestants were clerical marriage and communion in both kinds. After being secretly circulated, it was accepted at the Diet of Augsburg, 30 June 1548, and rigidly executed in parts of S. Germany. In the more Protestant parts of Germany, where the Augsburg Interim failed to obtain assent, a less Catholic edict, the so-called 'Leipzig Interim', put forth by the Elector Maurice in Dec. 1548, was adopted.

Text in B. J. Kidd, No. 148, pp. 359–62. L. *Pastor, Die kirchlichen Reunionsbestrebungen während der Regierung Karls V (1879), ch. ix, pp. 345–417.

AUGSBURG, Peace of (1555). The settlement of religious affairs in the German Empire between Ferdinand I and the Electors at Augsburg on 25 Sept. 1555. It recognized the existence of both Catholicism and Lutheranism (but not Calvinism) in Germany, providing that in each land subjects should follow the religion of their ruler (cuius regio eius religio). Those not content with this settlement were permitted, after selling their property, to migrate to other lands. In the Imperial cities, both religions, if already established, were to continue. The official standard of Lutheran faith was the '*Augsburg Confession' of 1530 or any of its later recensions. Though Lutheranism then secured

official recognition it was a victory for territorialism, not toleration. All property in the
hands of Protestants at the time of the Passau
Treaty (1552) was to be confirmed to them.
This 'Peace' continued the basis of the ecclesiastical settlement in the Empire until the
Treaty of *Westphalia of 1648.

Crit. ed. of text in A. Druffel, *Beiträge zur Reichsgeschichte
1553–1555* (revised ed. by K. Brandi; Briefe und Akten zur
Geschichte des sechzehnten Jahrhunderts, iv; 1896). Eng.
tr. of the main clauses is repr. in Kidd, p. 363 f. (No. 149).
C. W. Spieker, *Geschichte des Augsburger Religionsfriedens
von 26 September 1555* (Schleiz, 1854). G. Wolf, *Der
Augsburger Religionsfriede* (Stuttgart, 1890). Further bibl.
in Schottenloher, iv (1938), p. 34 f. (Nos. 34481–503).

AUGUSTEUM. The building erected at
*Wittenberg in 1564–83 on the site of the
*Augustinian monastery at which M. *Luther
in his early life had taught. It at first served
University purposes, but after many vicissi-
tudes in the 18th cent. eventually became a
Lutheran theological seminary.

AUGUSTINE, St., of Canterbury (d. 604
or 605), missionary to Kent and first Abp. of
*Canterbury. The prior of St. Andrew's
monastery at Rome, he was in 596 dispatched
by St. *Gregory the Great, then Pope, to
refound the Church in England. He wished
to turn back while in Gaul, but, encouraged
by letters from Gregory, he finally landed in
Kent in the summer of 597. He was favourably
received and given every opportunity for his
work, and after a few months Christianity was
formally adopted by *Ethelbert, King of Kent,
whose wife Bertha had been a Christian before
marriage. The work being thus established,
Augustine went to *Arles to be consecrated
as Abp. of Canterbury. His capacity for
organization seems to have been limited, for
he wrote to ask for Gregory's direction on
the smallest points. c. 603 Augustine, with
Ethelbert's assistance, attempted to reach an
agreement with representatives of the ancient
*Celtic Church, which still survived in Britain
and was at variance with Rome on questions
of discipline and practice; but the attempt was
a failure. The final act of Augustine, prob. in
604, was to send Justus to preach west of the
Medway, with the title of *Rochester, and
*Mellitus to work, as Bp. of *London,
among the East Saxons. Feast day, 26 May
(in the modern Roman calendar, except in
England, 28).

The principal authority is *Bede, *H.E.*, i, 23–ii, 3; notes
to ed. by C. Plummer, ii (Oxford, 1896), pp. 37–81. Life by
Goscelin in *A.A.SS.*, Mai. VI (1688), pp. 375–95. Docc. of
primary importance for his mission and episcopate in A. W.
Haddan–W. *Stubbs (edd.), *Councils and Ecclesiastical
Documents Relating to Great Britain and Ireland* (1871),
pp. 3–60. A. J. Mason (ed.), *The Mission of St. Augustine
to England according to the Original Documents* (1897); A.
Brou, S.J., *S. Augustin de Canterbury et ses compagnons* (1897; Eng. tr., 1897). H. Howorth, *Saint Augustine
of Canterbury* (1913). G. F. Browne, *Augustine and his Companions* (lectures; 1895). F. *Oakeley, *The Life of St.
Augustine of Canterbury, Apostle of the English* (The Lives
of English Saints Written at the Suggestion of John Henry
Newman, 1845; ed. 2 ed. A. W. Hutton, iii, 1901, pp. 171–
464). F. M. Stenton, *Anglo-Saxon England* (Oxford History
of England, ii, 1943), pp. 103–12. M. *Creighton in *D.N.B.*,
ii (1885), pp. 255–7.

AUGUSTINE, St., of Hippo (354–430),
Bp. of Hippo Regius and one of the '*Doctors
of the Church'. Born at Tagaste in N. Africa,
of a pagan father and a Christian mother
(*Monica), he received a Christian education.
He was sent to the University of Carthage, where
he studied rhetoric with a view to becoming
a lawyer, but he soon decided to devote himself exclusively to literary pursuits. Here he
gradually abandoned what little Christianity he
possessed, and also took a mistress, to whom
he remained faithful for fifteen years. A new
stage was reached in 373, when a reading of
Cicero's (lost) 'Hortensius' aroused in him a
passionate interest in problems of philosophy.
Shortly afterwards he became a *Manichaean,
and to this religion he remained attached for
nine years. In 383 the failure of Faustus, a
celebrated Manichaean, to solve many problems
which had been puzzling him eventually disillusioned him, and when shortly afterwards
Augustine migrated to *Rome and opened a
school of rhetoric, he had ceased to be openly
a member of the sect though he was still held
captive by some of their doctrines. Disgusted
by the behaviour of his pupils at Rome, he
left the capital for a professorship at Milan,
where he soon came under the influence of the
bishop, *Ambrose. By the time he arrived
at Milan, his philosophy was probably already
that of the 'Academics', which denied the
possibility of attaining absolute truth; but a
little later he became a *Neo-Platonist and
gradually drew nearer to Christianity. The
sermons of St. Ambrose attracted him both
by their literary quality and the answers they
afforded to many of his objections to the Bible.
Simplicianus, Ambrose's tutor, recounted the
conversion of the Neo-Platonist, *Victorinus,
and it soon became apparent that the only
thing that held Augustine back was his inability to live in continence. In the summer
of 386 he heard from Pontitian the story of
the two civil servants who had become monks
after reading the Life of St. *Antony, and
very soon afterwards a glance at Rom. 13.
13 f. (in response to a Divine oracle, 'Tolle
lege'), gave him the final victory.

After some months spent in seclusion at
Cassiciacum, Augustine was baptized on
Easter Eve, 387. In 388 he returned to Africa
and established with some friends a kind of
monastery at Tagaste. While visiting the town
of Hippo Regius he was suddenly seized by
the people and presented to the aged bishop,
Valerius, for ordination. He became a priest
in 391, and although he continued to live a
monastic life he soon acquired considerable
influence in the affairs of the African Church.
In 395 he was consecrated coadjutor bishop to
Valerius, Bp. of Hippo, and from c. 396 until
his death presided as sole bishop over the see.
He died on 28 Aug. 430, when the Vandals
were besieging Hippo.

Augustine's abiding importance rests on his
penetrating understanding of Christian truth.
During his episcopate he was called upon to
deal with three heresies, all of which were
confronting the Church with problems of the

greatest moment; and it was mainly through his struggle with these three systems that his own theology was formulated. The least dangerous was Manichaeism, for its doctrines were too obviously remote from historic Christianity to have any real hope of success at that late date. But in his attack on it, Augustine laid the basis of the metaphysic which moulded the thought of the Schoolmen. He defended, against the Manichaean attempt to solve the problem of evil by positing the existence of an evil agency eternally opposed to the good God, the essential goodness of all creation. He maintained that God was the sole creator of all things and alone sustained them in being, and that evil is, properly speaking, the privation of some good which ought to be had. In the case of physical evil this results from the imperfect character of creatures; in the case of moral evil it springs from free-will.

More urgent on the practical side was the *Donatist controversy on account of the deep divisions into which it rent the African Church. It forced Augustine to carry the doctrines of the Church, the Sacraments, and Sacramental grace to a stage beyond that reached by any of his predecessors, and thereby to influence all subsequent Western theology. The Church, he maintained, was 'one' through the mutual charity of its members, and 'holy', not because her members, but because her purposes, are holy. She contains within her fold both good and evil men, and not till the last day will the latter be rooted out; and while he acknowledged that there were good men outside the Church, he seems to have thought that all who were to be saved would become members of the Church before they died. His teaching also greatly furthered the development of the distinction between '*validity' and 'regularity' in the administration of the Sacraments. In another department of theology, the same controversy forced him to consider the relation of the coercive authority of the state to the Church. He accepted the civil power as part of God's Providence, but held that it was good only in so far as it was founded on justice, which included the worship of the true God. As a corollary, he came to accept the aid of the state to punish and suppress heresy and schism, but deprecated the use of the death-penalty.

His later years were taken up largely with the *Pelagian controversy. It was c. 410 that Augustine received news that Pelagius had been attacking a sentence of his (Da quod iubes et iube quod vis) in the 'Confessions' (x, 29 [40]). A fierce controversy ensued which evoked his teaching upon the *Fall, *Original Sin, and *Predestination. Augustine maintained that man was created with certain supernatural gifts which were lost by the Fall of Adam. As a result, man suffers from a hereditary moral disease, and is also subject to the inherited legal liability for Adam's sin; and from these evils we can be saved solely by the grace of God. At times Augustine shows himself to be frankly Predestinarian. The whole human race is one mass of sin (massa peccati), out of which God has elected some souls to receive His unmerited mercy. There is no other explanation of the elect and non-elect than the inscrutable wisdom of God, and babies who die unbaptized go into everlasting perdition. This side of Augustine's teaching was strongly affected by his personal experience of the overpowering grace of God. It found its most extreme formulation in the writings which he issued at the end of his life, and exercised a great influence upon J. *Calvin and some of the other Reformers, though its details have won only limited approval from some of the most illustrious theologians both before and since the 16th cent.

In consequence of these controversies, a large proportion of Augustine's writings take a polemical form. Of his other works, the two most celebrated are the '*Confessions' and the 'City of God'. The former, the greater part of which is autobiographical and carries the story of his life down to his conversion, was written shortly before 400. The marked differences in temper between the 'Confessions' and his philosophical writings roughly contemporary with his conversion seem to compel the conclusion that in the 'Confessions' he has imposed on the facts, probably unintentionally, a considerable element of interpretation. In its power of analysing the emotional side of Christian experience in the face of sin it is unsurpassed. The impulse to the writing of the 22 books of the 'City of God', which was spread over several years (413–26), arose out of the fall of Rome to *Alaric in 410. The event had caused consternation throughout the civilized world, and Augustine, who himself was profoundly moved, conceived the book as a reply to pagans who maintained that the fall of the city was due to the abolition of the heathen worship. It led him to deal with the fundamental contrast between Christianity and the world, and has made it the supreme exposition of a Christian philosophy of history. Among his other writings are a philosophical treatise 'De Trinitate' in 15 books, a large collection of epistles (including an interesting correspondence with St. *Jerome), many sermons, and, from his earlier Christian years, a collection of philosophical dialogues. Shortly before his death he published his 'Retractations', in which he reviewed his literary work.

Augustine's influence on the course of subsequent theology has been immense. He moulded the whole of that of the Middle Ages down to the 13th cent., and even the reaction against Augustinianism with the rediscovery of *Aristotle in the 13th cent., e.g. in St. *Thomas Aquinas, was less complete than has widely been supposed. The Reformers also appealed to elements of Augustine's teaching in their attack on the Schoolmen; and later the *Jansenists invoked his authority. Without St. Augustine's massive intellect and deep spiritual perception Western theology would never have taken the shape in which it is familiar to us. Feast day, 28 Aug.

St. Augustine's earliest writings are his Dialogues (no doubt an idealization of the actual conversations in which he took part at Cassiciacum), which include *Contra Academicos*, *De Beata Vita*, *De Ordine*, *Soliloquia* and *De Immortalitate Animae* (all A.D. 386–7; J. P. Migne, *PL*, xxxii). Among his Anti-Manichaean writings are *Acta contra Fortunatum Manichaeum* (397–8), *Contra Faustum Manichaeum* (33 Bks., 397–8) and *Contra Secundinum Manichaeum* (405), all in *PL*; among his works against the Donatists, *Psalmus contra Partem Donati* (394), *Contra Epistolam Parmeniani* (400), *De Baptismo contra Donatistas* (400), and *Breviculus Collationis cum Donatistis* (411), all in *PL*, xliii; among those against the Pelagians, *De Peccatorum Meritis et Remissione* (411), *De Spiritu et Littera* (412), *De Natura et Gratia* (415), *De Gestis Pelagii* (417), *Contra Julianum* (6 Bks., 421), all in *PL*, xliv; among those against the *Semipelagians, *De Gratia et Libero Arbitrio* (420), *De Correptione et Gratia* (426), *De Praedestinatione Sanctorum* (428), and *De Dono Perseverantiae* (428), in *PL*, xliv and xlv. He also wrote a short general treatise, *De Haeresibus* (428; *PL*, xlii, 21–50). Of his Biblical writings the chief are *De Genesi ad Litteram* (12 Bks., 401–15; *PL*, xxxiv), *De Consensu Evangelistarum* (4 Bks., 400; *PL*, xxxiv), *Tractatus CXXIV in Joannis Evangelium* and *Tractatus X in Ep. Joannis* (c. 416, *PL*, xxxv), and *Enarrationes in Psalmos* (*PL*, xxxvi and xxxvii). His chief dogmatic works include *De Diversis Questionibus ad Simplicianum* (397; *PL*, xl), *De Trinitate* (15 Bks., 400–16; *PL*, xlii), *Enchiridion ad Laurentium* (423–4; *PL*, xli, 229–90), and *De Civitate Dei* (22 Bks., 413–26; *PL*, xli). The *Confessions* are in *PL*, xxxii, 583–656. Augustine also wrote many important letters, nearly all on dogmatic subjects, of which some 220 survive. To his large collection of Sermons many additions have been made in recent times, esp. through the researches of G. *Morin, O.S.B., C. Lambot, O.S.B., and A. *Wilmart, O.S.B. At the end of his life Augustine reviewed his several works in his *Retractationes* (426; *PL*, xxxii. 659–868).

First collected ed. of his Works by J. Amerbach (9 vols.), Basle, 1506). Other imp. early edd. by D. *Erasmus (10 vols., Basle, 1528–9) and the 'Theologi Lovanienses' (11 vols., Antwerp, 1577). All previous edd. were superseded by that of the *Maurists (J. Blampin, P. *Coustant, and others; 11 vols., Paris, 1679–1700, with valuable index in vol. xi); repr. frequently, incl. J. P. Migne, *PL*, xxxii–xlvii (unfortunately with varying pagination in the several Migne reprints); on the Maurist ed. see J. de Ghellinck, S.J., *Patristique et Moyen-Age*, iii (1948), pp. 339–484 (Étude viii: une Édition patristique célèbre). Since 1887 crit. ed. of individual works in the C.S.E.L. (some items, however, not up to the usual standard of this series).

Eng. trr. in the *Library of the Fathers by Marcus Dods and by P. *Schaff in 'Nicene and Post Nicene Christian Fathers' (8 vols., 1887–92).

Contemporary Life by his friend and disciple, Possidius, Bp. of Calama (*PL*, new ed. with Eng. tr. by H. T. Weiskotten, Princeton, U.S.A., 1919; Ger. tr. by A. *Harnack, Berlin, 1930). Full modern Life in ed. Ben. (repr. *PL*, xxxii, 65–578). Le N. *Tillemont, *Mémoires pour servir à l'Histoire Ecclés.*, xiii (ed. 2, 1710). Modern Lives by A. G. Kloth (2 vols., Aachen, 1840), J. J. F. Poujoulat (3 vols., Paris, 1845–6), P. Schaff (Berlin, 1854; Eng. tr., 1854), F. and P. Böhringer (2 vols., Stuttgart, 1877–8), J. Martin ('Les Grands Philosophes', Paris, 1901), G. Frhr. von Hertling ('Weltgeschichte in Karakterbildern', ed. F. Kampers, No. 1; Mainz, 1902), L. Bertrand (Paris, [1913]; Eng. tr., 1914), W. Montgomery (London, 1914), H. Pope, O.P. (London, 1937), G. Bardy (Montpellier, 1940). Studies on his early Christian period, with discussions on the contrast betw. the *Dialogues* and the *Confessions*, include H. A. Naville, *St. Augustin*. Étude sur le développement de sa pensée jusqu'à l'époque de son ordination (Geneva, 1872), F. Wörter, *Die Geistesentwicklung des hl. Aur. Augustinus bis zu seiner Taufe* (Paderborn, 1892), H. Becker, *Augustin*. Studien zu seiner geistigen Entwicklung (1908), P. Alfaric, *L'Évolution intellectuelle de S. Augustin*. I: du manichéisme au néoplatonisme (all publd., 1918), C. Boyer, S.J., *Christianisme et néoplatonisme dans la formation de Saint Augustin* (1921).

Among the countless edd., monographs, and artt. on individual treatises are: (1) CONFESSIONS: Ed. J. Gibb and W. Montgomery, 'Cambridge Patristic Texts', 1908, with valuable notes; A. Harnack, *Augustins Konfessionen*. Ein Vortrag (1888; Eng. tr., with an essay on *Monasticism*, 1901); R. L. *Ottley, *Studies in the Confessions of St. Augustine* (1919). (2) DE CIVITATE DEI: Ed. princeps, Subiaco, 1467. Ed. J. E. C. Welldon, 2 vols., S.P.C.K., 1924. Eng. trr. by John Healey (London, 1610); reissued, with introd. by E. Barker, London, 1931; ed. R. V. G. Tasker, Everyman's Library, 2 vols., 1945. J. N. *Figgis, *The Political Aspects of St. Augustine's 'City of God'* (1921); J. H. S.

Burleigh, *The City of God*. A study of St. Augustine's Philosophy (1949). (3) SERMONS: A. Regnier, *De la latinité des sermons de St. Augustin* (1886); C. Mohrmann, *Die altchristliche Sondersprache in den Sermones des hl. Augustin* (Latinitas Christianorum primaeva, fasc. 3, 1932). (4) EPISTLES: Excellent ed. by A. Goldbacher in C.S.E.L., 34(1), 1895; 34(2), 1898; 44, 1904; 57, 1911. W. Thimme, *Augustin*. Ein Lebens- und Characterbild auf Grund seiner Briefe (1910).

On his place in the history of Western civilization, cf. E. *Troeltsch, *Augustin, die christliche Antike und das Mittelalter im Anschluss an die Schrift*, De Civitate Dei (1915); H. I. Marrou, *St. Augustin et la fin de la culture antique* (1938).

On his theology and outlook generally. A. Dorner, *Augustinus, sein theologisches System und seine religionsphilosophische Anschauung* (1873); W. Cunningham, S. *Austin and his Place in the History of Christian Thought* (1886); K. Adam, *Die Eucharistielehre des hl. Augustin* (1908); J. Mausbach, *Die Ethik des hl. Augustinus* (2 vols., 1909); T. A. *Lacey, *Nature, Miracle and Sin*. A Study of St. Augustine's Conception of the Natural Order (1916); P. *Botiffol, *Le Catholicisme de S. Augustin* (2 vols., 1920); *A Monument to St. Augustine*. By various authors, London, 1930; J. Burnaby, *Amor Dei*. A Study of the Religion of St. Augustine (1938); F. van der Meer, *Augustinus de Zielzorger* (1947; Eng. tr. 1961).

Of the artt. in all dictionaries and encyclopaedic works, one of the fullest is that by E. Portalié, *D.T.C.*, i (1903), cols. 2268–472, with bibls.

AUGUSTINE OF HIPPO, Rule of St.

A title formerly applied to several documents but properly limited to that 'Regula Sancti Augustini' made famous through its adoption by the *Augustinian Canons (q.v.). From at least the 6th cent. this was in two parts—a short prologue laying down certain precise monastic observances (the 'Regula Secunda') and a longer and more general consideration of the common life (the 'Regula ad servos Dei'), which is an adaptation for the use of a religious community of men of St. Augustine's *Ep.* 211 (A.D. 423; addressed to nuns). The Rule was probably drawn up in the middle of the 5th cent. by one of Augustine's followers who composed the prologue and adapted the letter, but it is not impossible that the saint himself was the author of both. Little used in the early Middle Ages, the Rule was resuscitated in the late 11th cent. by the regular canons and quickly became the recognized standard of their order, though after the early 12th cent. the archaic prologue was often abbreviated or omitted.

The sanity of the Rule, its adaptability, and the repute of its supposed author led to its adoption by a number of monastic bodies, active and contemplative, including the *Dominicans, the *Augustinian Hermits, the *Servites, and the *Ursuline and *Visitation nuns.

The text of the 'Regula Secunda' is repr. from Augustine's *Opera*, ed. Ben., in J. P. Migne, *PL*, xxxii, 1449–52; that of the 'Regula ad Servos Dei', ib. 1377–84. Crit. ed., with discussion, by A. C. Vega, *La regla de San Agustin* (Escurial, 1933). A third rule ('Regula Consensoria') which long went under Augustine's name has been shown by D. de Bruyne, O.S.B., 'La *Regula consensoria*, une règle des moines priscillianistes' in *R. Bén.*, xxv (1908), pp. 83–8, to be a *Priscillianist work. F. Weninger, *Die Regula des hl. Augustinus* (Innsbruck, 1929); P. Mandonnet, O.P., *Saint Dominique*, ii (1937), pp. 103–272. B. *Capelle, O.S.B., 'L'Épître 211 et la règle de Saint Augustin' in *Analecta Praemonstratensia*, iii (1927), pp. 369–78; C. Lambot, O.S.B., 'La Règle de S. Augustine et de S. Césaire' in *R. Bén.*, xli (1929), pp. 333–41; M. Verheijen, O.E.S.A., 'La *Regula Sancti Augustini*' in *Vigiliae Christianae*, vii (1953), pp. 27–56. W. Hümpfner, O.E.S.A., 'Die Mönchsregel des heiligen Augustinus' in *Augustinus Magister* (Congrès International Augustinien, Paris, 21–24 septembre 1954), i (1954). pp. 241–54, with further reff. Id. in *L.Th.K.*, (1930), col. 824 f.

AUGUSTINIAN CANONS.

(They were also known as 'Austin', or 'Black' or 'Regular Canons'). Though the ideal of the *Canons Regular had been foreshadowed by various attempts in the early Church to establish a full common life for houses of clerks (notably that by St. *Augustine of Hippo), as a family of religious in the W. Church they date from the first years of the movement later known as the Gregorian Reform.

Their origin is to be found in certain communities of clerks in Northern Italy and the S. of France, who in the middle decades of the 11th cent. sought to live the common life of poverty, celibacy, and obedience, in accordance with what they believed to be the example of the early Christians. Their way of life received official approval at *Lateran synods in 1059 and 1063 and in the following cent. was widely adopted in W. Europe. By the opening decades of the 12th cent., members of these communities had come to be known as 'regular canons' (*canonici regulares*) and had generally adopted the Rule of St. Augustine (which half a cent. before was almost unknown to them; see previous entry). From now on a regular canon is almost synonymous with an Augustinian canon, i.e. one who follows the Rule of St. Augustine. From the early 12th cent., a number of independent Augustinian congregations were established of which some of the more influential, e.g. the *Victorines and the *Premonstratensians, were much influenced by *Cistercian customs. In subsequent times Augustinian canons suffered considerably from the disorders and changes of the later Middle Ages and the disturbances of the *Reformation, and many houses were suppressed and replaced by other orders, esp. the *clerks regular. But certain of the older congregations still survive in the RC Church, notably the 'Canons Regular of the Lateran' (C.R.L.), whom Pope Alexander II (1061–73) instituted in his cathedral church.

Of clerical origin, the Augustinian canons were liable to episcopal visitation and able to undertake parochial responsibilities, though this was a privilege of which they did not always make extensive use in the Middle Ages. The flexibility of their rule enabled regular canons to follow various vocations, active and contemplative. They had a notable connexion with hospitals; in London St. Bartholomew's and St. Thomas's Hospitals were formerly both Augustinian houses.

E. Amort, *Vetus Disciplina Canonicorum Regularium et Secularium ex Documentis magna parte hucusque ineditis a Temporibus Apostolicis usque ad Saeculum xvii critice et moraliter expensa* (2 vols., Venice, 1747). H. E. Salter (ed.), *Chapters of the Augustinian Canons* (Canterbury and York Society, xxix, 1922). J. C. Dickinson, *The Origins of the Austin Canons and their Introduction into England* (C.H.S., 1950). L. Hertling, S.J., 'Kanoniker, Augustinusregel und Augustinerorden' in *Z.K.T.*, liv (1930), pp. 335–59; C. Dereine, S.J., 'Vie commune, règle de Saint Augustin et chanoines réguliers au XIᵉ siècle' in *R.H.E.*, xli (1946), pp. 365–406. Heimbücher, i, pp. 392–413.

AUGUSTINIAN HERMITS or FRIARS.

A religious order founded in the Middle Ages. It was formed from several Italian congregations of hermits which, in the interests of ecclesiastical efficiency, were banded together under the Rule of St. *Augustine by Pope Alexander IV in 1256, with a constitution modelled on that of the *Dominicans. The order, which had at first made its settlements in remote places, soon tended to concentrate their work in towns, and became widely established in W. Europe. The later Middle Ages saw the rise of certain local reformed congregations of the order, to one of which, the German Reformed Congregation (1493), M. *Luther belonged. Augustinian hermits suffered considerably from the effects of the Reformation and the secularizations of later times, but they still survive—notably in parts of W. Europe and also in South America, where they undertake extensive pastoral and educational work. The 'Discalced Augustinians' (also known as 'Augustinian *Recollects') are a reformed congregation living under very severe constitutions; their first house was founded in 1588.

L. Empoli, O.E.S.A. (ed.), *Bullarium Ordinis Eremitarum S. Augustini, in quo plures Constitutiones Apostolicae ... ab Innocentio Tertio usque ad Urbanum Octavum ad eunden Ordinem spectantes collectae sunt* (Rome, 1628). Their constitutions were publ. at Venice, 1508; Rome, 1625; Rome, 1686; and subsequently. D. A. Perini, O.E.S.A., *Bibliographia Augustiniana, cum notis Biographicis.* Scriptores Itali (4 parts, [1929]–1937). A. Gwynn, S.J., *The English Austin Friars in the Time of Wyclif* (1940). Heimbücher, i, pp. 536–65, ii, p. 660, with bibl.; W. Hümpfner, O.E.S.A., in *L.Th.K.*, i (1930), cols. 816–23, s.v. 'Augustiner-Eremiten', with bibl. M. T. Disdier, A.A., in *D.H.G.E.*, v (1930), cols. 499–595, s.v. 'Augustin (Iᵉʳ Ordre dit de Saint) (Érémites)', with full bibl.

AUGUSTINIANS OF THE ASSUMPTION. See *Assumptionists*.

'AUGUSTINUS'.

The title of the treatise by Cornelius *Jansenius (d. 1638) on grace and human nature. It was published at Louvain in August 1640. Based on the anti-Pelagian works of St. *Augustine, and embodying many of the conclusions of M. *Baius, it was directed against the neo-scholastic theologians. It became the accepted exposition of the dogmatic principles of *Jansenism.

After the 'privilège' necessary for publication had been granted on 13 Feb. 1640, the work appeared at Louvain later in the same year (repr. Paris, 1641, and Rouen, 1643). Full analysis by J. Carreyre in *D.T.C.*, viii (pt. 1; 1924), cols. 330–448 (useful). N. J. Abercrombie, *The Origins of Jansenism* (1936). R. Rapin, S.J. (1621–87), *Histoire du jansénisme depuis son origine jusqu'en 1644* (first ed. E. Domenech, Paris, 1861).

AULÉN, GUSTAV (1879–), Bp. of

Strängnäs. He was appointed professor of systematic theology in the University of Lund in 1913, and consecrated Bp. of Lund in 1930. With A. Nygren (b. 1890), he was a leader of the *motivsforschung* school, which seeks to see the essential Christian truth behind a doctrine rather than to stress the actual form in which it is presented. His most important works are *Den allmänneliga kristna tron* ("The

Catholic Christian Faith', 1923), *Den kristna gudsbilden* ('The Christian Idea of God', 1927), and his Olaus *Petri Lectures for 1930, published as *Den kristna försoningstanken* ('The Christian Idea of the Atonement'), of which an abridged version has been produced in English by A. G. Hebert under the title of *Christus Victor* (1931). In these lectures Aulén defends a modified version of the 'ransom to the devil' theory of the *Atonement.

AUMBRY, also 'Ambry'. A cupboard in the wall of a church or sacristy in which, in medieval times, sacred vessels, relics, books, and sometimes, but not usually, the reserved Sacrament might be kept. Its use for the last-named purpose is forbidden by the RC Church, but is common in the Anglican Communion.

G. *Dix, *A Detection of Aumbries* (1942); E. Maffei, *La Réservation eucharistique jusqu'à la Renaissance* (1942); S. J. P van Dijk, O.F.M.–Joan H. Walker, *The Myth of the Aumbry* (1957; reply to G. Dix).

AURELIUS, St. (d. *c.* 430), Bp. of *Carthage from *c.* 391. He presided over a long series of ecclesiastical councils, mostly at Carthage. Some of the letters addressed to him by St. *Augustine (Aug. *epp.* 22, 41, 60, 174), who held him in high honour, survive. Feast day, 20 July.

AA.SS., Oct. XI (1864), pp. 852–60. A. Audollent in *D.H.G.E.*, v (1930), cols. 726–38, s.v., with bibl.

AUREOLE (Lat. *aureolus*, 'golden'). In sacred pictures, the background of gold, typifying glory, which often surrounds the figure, as distinct from the 'nimbus' (or halo), which covers only the head.

AURICULAR CONFESSION. Confession 'to the ear' [Lat. *ad auriculam*, sc. of a priest], i.e. the confession of sins to God in the presence of a priest authorized to forgive them in His Name.

AUSCULTA FILI (Lat.), 'Listen, my son'. The opening words (1) of the Rule of St. *Benedict and (2) of *Boniface VIII's bull of 5 Dec. 1301 to Philip the Fair of France.

AUSONIUS (*c.* 310–*c.* 395), Roman poet. Decimus Magnus Ausonius was a native of Burdigala (Bordeaux), where he established a school of rhetoric. *C.* 365 he became tutor to the future Emp. *Gratian, who in 379 raised him to the consulship. To judge by a few of his poems, he made at least some profession of Christianity in his mature years, though the letters (in verse) which he addressed to his former pupil, *Paulinus of Nola, to dissuade him from his project of giving up his wealth to the poor and becoming a monk, reveal little of the Christian sense of vocation. Of his 'Epigrams', three—the 'Versus paschales pro Augusto', the 'Oratio Matutina', and the 'Oratio versibus rhopalicis'—are ostensibly the work of an orthodox Christian. Of his many secular poems, perhaps the most successful

was his 'Mosella', a poem describing the region of the Moselle and the city of Trier.

Ed. princeps, Venice, 1472. Crit. edd. by C. Schenkl (*M.G.H.*, Auct. Ant. V, 2; 1883), R. Peiper (ed. Teubn., 1886), and H. G. E. White (Loeb, 2 vols., 1919–21); of his *Mosella*, by C. Hosius (Marburg, 1894). Text also in J. P. Migne, *PL*, xix, 817–958. M. J. Pattist, *Ausonius als Christ* (Amsterdam and Paris, 1925). Bardenhewer, iii, pp. 436–40. F. Marx in *P.W.*, ii (1896), cols. 2562–80, P. de Labriolle in *D.H.G.E.*, v (1931), cols. 773–9, M. Pellegrino in *E.C.*, ii (1949), cols. 416–18, and B. Altaner, *Patrologie* (ed. 2, 1950), p. 358.

AUSTIN. An older English form of '*Augustine'.

AUSTRALIA, Christianity in. The white population of Australia, since the first settlement in 1788, has always been almost entirely of British origin, and the C of E has always been the predominant religion, though no longer formally 'established'. An English chaplain (Richard Johnson) accompanied the first settlement, and some ministrations were maintained in the years following, down to the foundation of the Diocese of Australia in 1836, when W. G. Broughton, who had been Archdeacon of N.S.W. since 1829, was consecrated the first Bishop. The official connexion between Church and state was broken in N.S.W. in 1862, and in the other states shortly afterwards. But with the growth of the population the Anglican Church continued to expand, so that to-day there are over 20 dioceses in Australia. In the towns the Church is self-supporting, and indeed sends missions to Papua and Melanesia, besides supporting others in China, India, and Africa. One of the chief problems of Church work in Australia itself is the distance between farms and settlements in the Bush, and the work of the 'Bush Brotherhoods', founded in 1903 under the inspiration of B. F. *Westcott, Bp. of *Durham (d. 1901), and consisting of groups of evangelists who serve for five years, living at a common centre and working on non-parochial lines, is an attempt to deal with this difficulty. The Bush Church Aid Society, founded in 1920, does work in the same field, on more nearly parochial lines. There is still missionary work to be done among the few aborigines of the interior. The state controls primary education, but there are also Church primary schools, and most intermediate schools are under denominational control.

A majority of Australians are nominally Anglican, but about a quarter of the population is RC. In the earliest times the ministrations of RC chaplains to the convict settlers were generally forbidden, though there were many Irish political prisoners in the colony. Toleration was nominally granted in 1820, but down to 1844 prisoners were in some places compelled to attend Anglican services. W. B. *Ullathorne, who worked in Australia from 1833 till 1840, did much to excite public feeling against the abuses of the convict settlements. J. B. Polding, O.S.B., was appointed Bp. of Hiero-Caesarea (titular), with jurisdiction over Australia, in 1834, and an independent see was set up in 1841, and soon subdivided. Many Irish RCs entered Australia in the gold-rush of 1851.

*Methodism and *Presbyterianism were also unrecognized in the earliest days, though members of these bodies, which now form the most considerable non-Anglican Protestant bodies in the country, came in the first settlements. Nevertheless, Methodist missions began in 1813 and Presbyterian in 1823. Other denominations, of which the most numerous are the *Congregationalists, have entered since, but their followings are small.

H. L. Clarke, *Constitutional Church Government in the Dominions Beyond the Seas* (1924), pp. 75–167; F. Goldsmith in C. Jenkins–K. D. Mackenzie (edd.), *Episcopacy Ancient and Modern* (1930), pp. 250–61. E. Symonds, *The Story of the Australian Church* ('Colonial Church Histories', 1898); A. E. David, *Australia* ('Handbooks of Church Expansion', 1908); R. A. Giles, *The Constitutional History of the Australian Church* (1929). A. Burton, *Church Beginnings in the West* (1941); C. L. M. Hawtrey, *The Availing Struggle. A Record of the Planning and Development of the Church of England in Western Australia, 1829–1949* [c. 1950]; A. E. Clark, *The Church of Our Fathers, being the History of the Church of England in Gippsland, 1847–1947* (Melbourne, 1948).
P. F. Moran, *History of the Catholic Church in Australasia* (Sydney, [1894]); E. M. O'Brien, *The Dawn of Catholicism in Australia* (2 vols., Sydney, 1928). J. G. Murtagh, *Australia: The Catholic Chapter* (New York, 1946). H. N. Birt, O.S.B., *Benedictine Pioneers in Australia* (2 vols., 1911). H. W. Cleary in *C.E.*, ii (1907), pp. 113–20, s.v., with bibl.
R. Hamilton, *A Jubilee History of the Presbyterian Church of Victoria* (1888); J. Cameron, *Centenary History of the Presbyterian Church in New South Wales* (Sydney, 1905); R. Bardon, *The Centenary History of the Presbyterian Church of Queensland* (Brisbane, 1949). J. C. Robinson, *The Free Presbyterian Church of Australia* (Melbourne, 1947). J. Colwell, *The Illustrated History of Methodism*, Australia: 1812 to 1855. New South Wales and Polynesia: 1856 to 1902 (Sydney, etc., 1904). H. E. Hughes, *Our First Hundred Years*. The Baptist Church of South Australia (Adelaide, 1937); F. J. Wilkin, *Baptists in Victoria*. Our First Centenary, 1838–1938 (Melbourne, 1939). R. S. C. Dingle (ed.), *Annals of Achievement*. A Review of Queensland Methodism, 1847–1947 (Brisbane, 1947). F. W. Cox, *Three Quarters of a Century* (on Congregationalism in S. Australia: Adelaide, 1912).
Latourette, v, pp. 130–76, with bibl. pp. 471–506 passim, and vii, pp. 186–90, with bibl. pp. 507–31 passim.

AUTHORITY. Religious or ecclesiastical authority should be distinguished from civil. The latter is concerned to enforce obedience to the laws and regulations of the state, while the former is mainly a power to influence belief or conduct. It may be objected that opinion should be formed and the conscience guided by reason alone. But Christianity claims to be based upon revelation, i.e. it professes to know truths transcending man's natural capacities of apprehension and revealed directly or indirectly by God. These truths are not, acc. e.g. to St. *Thomas Aquinas, contrary to reason, but their discovery is for the most part beyond its reach, and, as made known by God, they have the authority of God.

The utterances of the OT prophets have authority as inspired by the Spirit of God. To Christians, who believe that Jesus Christ is God incarnate, the revelation given through Him is final and His teaching has absolute authority, though some would maintain that even here the limitations inherent in His human nature must be taken into account.

This revelation, it is held, was apprehended by the Apostles and transmitted to the Christian Church both by word of mouth and by the Apostolic writings which survive in the New Testament. As inspired by the Holy Spirit of God or Christ, their teaching has an authority second only to the utterances of Christ Himself.

This teaching is handed on by the Church, partly through *Tradition and partly through Scripture. Catholics hold that this teaching has absolute authority for the further reason that the Church is divinely guided into the whole truth of the Christian revelation by the Holy Spirit (Jn. 16. 13), and that the organs of this authoritative teaching include *General Councils and (for RCs) the Pope in his *ex-cathedra pronouncements. Protestants, however, until quite recent times, have commonly confined this authority to the Bible, guaranteed by its appeal to the individual conscience rather than by the consent of the Church. Some have gone further and recognized no teaching as authoritative unless approved in each case by the Divine Spirit operating in the individual.

Church authority has been enforced in the past by temporal penalties, but it is now generally imposed, as in primitive times before the conversion of the Roman Empire, by spiritual censures alone, esp. that of *excommunication.

J. *Martineau, *The Seat of Authority in Religion* (1890); J. *Oman, *Vision and Authority, or the Throne of St. Peter* (1902); A. *Sabatier, *Les Religions d'autorité et la religion de l'esprit* (1903; Eng. tr., 1904); A. E. J. Rawlinson, *Authority and Freedom* (1924); T. A. *Lacey, *Authority in the Church. A Study of Principles* (1928). J. Iverach in *H.E.R.E.*, ii (1909), pp. 249–54, s.v.

AUTHORIZED VERSION OF THE BIBLE. At the *Hampton Court Conference (1604) Dr. John *Rainolds (or Reynolds, 1549–1607), the *Puritan President of Corpus Christi College, Oxford, suggested that there should be a new translation of the Bible. R. *Bancroft, Bp. of London, having reluctantly concurred, *James I ordered that the work should be begun, and a strong body of revisers was formed, including the professors of Hebrew and Greek at Oxford and Cambridge and other leading scholars, about 50 in all, who sat in six groups, two at Oxford, two at Cambridge, and two at Westminster. Their instructions were to take the *Bishops' Bible as their basis, to consult all earlier versions, esp. the *Reims NT (see *Douai*) and the *Geneva Bible, to retain the old ecclesiastical terms (such as 'Church' for 'Congregation' and 'Baptism' for 'Washing'), and to exclude all marginal notes, unless required to explain some Hebrew or Greek word. Each group worked separately at first, with a special portion of the Bible assigned to it. They then sent their work to all the others for criticism, and final settlement was made at a general meeting of the chief members of each group, learned men from outside being called in to discuss cases of special difficulty. W. *Tyndale's influence through various versions down to the Bishops' Bible fixed the general tone of the translation, which is also indebted to J. *Wycliffe. The work, which began in 1607, took two years and nine months to prepare for the press, and was paid for at 30s. each man per week, and by preferment. The final MS. (now lost) was bought by Robert Barker (d. 1645), the King's Printer, for £3,500, which included the copyright. It was seen through the press by Dr. Miles Smith (d. 1624) and Bp. T. Bilson (1547–1616), and first appeared in large folio volumes, printed in black letter, with headings and chapter-summaries in Roman type, at 25s. in sheets, 30s. bound, in 1611. The 'Preface of the translators', probably by Dr. Miles Smith, explains that it is a revision, not a new translation, and that the revisers, who had the original Hebrew and Greek texts before them, steered a course between the Puritan and Roman versions. On the title-page are the words 'Appointed to be read in Churches', but it has in fact never been officially 'authorized'. It immediately superseded the Bishops' Bible, and won favour by its intrinsic merits rather than by official backing. Greek and Hebrew scholarship had increased during the past half-century; the English language had been enriched by such men as E. Spenser, P. Sidney, R. *Hooker, C. Marlowe, and W. Shakespeare; and it was the right moment for a revision. The OT reproduced the spirit of the old Hebrew, the NT became a finer piece of literature than the original Greek, and the whole is the finest specimen of English prose and the Bible of every English-speaking country. Modern editions often omit the Preface and the Apocrypha, and the current text differs considerably in orthography from the first edition of 1611. In the U.S.A. it is commonly known as the 'King James Version'.

F. H. [A.] Scrivener, *The Cambridge Paragraph Bible* (1873), Introd., pp. ix–cix; largely repr. with revisions, id., *The Authorized Edition of the English Bible, 1611. Its Subsequent Reprints and Modern Representations* (1884). B. F. Westcott, *A General View of the History of the English Bible* (ed. 3 by W. A. Wright, 1905), pp. 107–21 and 255–78; A. W. Pollard, *Records of the English Bible* (1911), pp. 37–76, with documents pp. 331–77. J. Isaacs in H. Wheeler Robinson (ed.), *The Bible in its Ancient and English Versions* (1940), pp. 196–227. R. C. *Trench, *On the Authorized Version of the New Testament in Connection with some Recent Proposals for Revision* (1858). T. H. Darlow–H. F. Moule, i (1903), pp. 133–6, with reff. See further bibl. s.v. *Bible* (English Versions).

AUTO-DA-FÉ (Portug., 'act of faith'). The ceremony of the Spanish *Inquisition at which, after a Procession, Mass, and Sermon, sentences were read and executed. Heretics were clad in the ceremonial *san-benito* (if unrepentant, grotesquely embroidered), with yellow mitre. Those sentenced to death were handed over to the secular power with an exhortation to mercy, though by *Innocent IV's bull 'Ad Extirpanda' (1252) execution had to follow within five days, and, until the last case at Seville in 1781, this was carried out by burning at the stake.

AUTO SACRAMENTAL (Sp. *auto*, 'ordinance'). A form of entertainment formerly common in Spain, analogous to the English *morality plays. These plays date from well into the medieval times, but the classical period was the 15th–16th cents., when the chief writers were J. de la Encina, G. Vicente, and, best known of all, Pedro Calderón (1600–1681). By this period the autos were always associated with the feast of *Corpus Christi, and in their later development took the form of allegorical treatments of the mystery of the Eucharist. They were preceded by a procession of the Host through the streets of the town to a space outside the house of some dignitary, where the performance was given. The procession and whole performance were at the public expense, and their magnificence was limited only by the resources of the city or town producing the play, which were strained to the utmost. Many of the plays are of considerable artistic merit, and they had a wide popularity. They were officially prohibited in 1765 by King Charles III, but for many years after this date they continued to be shown in the remoter districts.

E. González Pedroso (ed.), *Autos sacramentales desde su origen hasta fines del siglo XVII* (Biblioteca de Auctores Españoles [lviii], 1865), with introd. pp. vii–lxi. H. A. Rennert, *The Spanish Stage in the Time of Lope de Vega* (New York, 1909), esp. pp. 297–333. A. A. Parker, 'Notes on the Religious Drama in Medieval Spain and the Origins of the "Auto Sacramental"' in *Modern Language Review*, xxx (1935), pp. 170–82. Id., *The Allegorical Drama of Calderón. An Introduction to the Autos Sacramentales* (1943), with reff.

AUTOCEPHALOUS (Gk. αὐτοκέφαλος, lit. 'himself the head'). A term used in the early Church to describe bishops who were under no superior authority and thus independent both of *Patriarch and *Metropolitan. Such were the bishops of *Cyprus, the bishops of *Armenia and Iberia down to the time of *Photius, and probably the British bishops before 597. The bishops of *Ravenna may also have had such autonomy for a time. In another sense, the word was used of Eastern bishops who were directly dependent on the Patriarch, without intermediate reference to a Metropolitan, as well as of priests belonging to patriarchal dioceses. Its principal later and current use, however, is for the modern national Churches that make up the Eastern Orthodox Church which, though normally in communion with *Constantinople, are governed by their own national synods. In the same connexion it is used of the independent monastery on Mount *Sinai.

AUXENTIUS (d. 373 or 374), Arian Bp. of Milan. A Cappadocian by birth, he was ordained c. 343 by Gregory, the intruded Bp. of *Alexandria, and soon became the most prominent supporter of *Arianism in the West. Though ignorant of Latin, he was appointed to the see of Milan by *Constantius in 355. Despite condemnations for heresy at Councils at *Ariminum (359) and *Paris (360), he continued to hold his bishopric. Neither the approaches of *Hilary of Poitiers to *Valentinian on the subject in 364–5 nor *Athanasius's attack on him in 369 nor the annulling of Ariminum at Rome in 372 dislodged him, and he continued in possession of his see till his death. The influence of his teaching cannot have been great with the Milanese populace, for they enthusiastically welcomed St. *Ambrose as his orthodox successor. L. *Duchesne held that the *Ambrosian Liturgy, in his opinion the parent of the *Gallican Liturgies, owed its Eastern characteristics to Auxentius' practice.

Our knowledge of Auxentius derives from scattered reff. in St. *Athanasius, St. *Basil, St. Hilary of Poitiers, and St. *Eusebius of Vercelli. L. *Duchesne, *Origines du culte chrétien* (1889), pp. 84–9 (Eng. tr., ed. 1903, pp. 90–5).

AUXILIARY SAINTS (Lat. *auxilium*, 'assistance'). A group of fourteen saints, venerated for the supposed efficacy of their prayers on behalf of human necessities. They are: Sts. *George (23 Apr.), *Blaise (3 Feb.), *Erasmus (2 June), *Pantaleon (27 July), *Vitus (15 June), *Christopher (25 July), *Denys (9 Oct.), Cyriacus (8 Aug.), Acacius (8 May), *Eustace (20 Sept.), *Giles (1 Sept.), *Margaret (20 July), *Barbara (4 Dec.), *Catherine of Alexandria (25 Nov.).

AVANCINI, NIKOLA (1611–86), *Jesuit ascetic writer and theologian. A native of Bretz, near *Trent, he entered the Society of Jesus in 1627 and held teaching appointments at Trieste (1634), Laibach (1635) and Vienna (1641). He became successively rector of the Colleges of Passau (1664), Vienna (1666) and Gratz (1672). In 1675 he was appointed Visitor of Bohemia, in 1676 Provincial of the Austrian Province and in 1682 Assistant for the German Provinces. He had just been nominated temporary Vicar-General of the Order at his death. He wrote extensively on philosophy and theology, esp. during the earlier years of his life. His *Vita et Doctrina Jesu Christi ex Quattuor Evangelistis Collecta* (Vienna, 1665), a collection of terse and pithy daily meditations, deservedly established itself as a classic. It has been translated into most modern European languages and is still widely used, esp. by the clergy. His other published works include *Poesis Lyrica* (1659) and *Orationes* (3 vols., 1656–60).

There is a modern Eng. tr. (somewhat adapted) of Avancini's *Vita et Doctrina Jesu Christi* by K. D. Mackenzie (S.P.C.K.; 1937). Works listed in Sommervogel, i (1890), cols. 668–80, and viii (1898), col. 1711 f. E. Lamalle, S.J., in *D.H.G.E.* v (1931), col. 991 f., s.v., with bibl.; A. Fiocchi in *E.C.*, ii (1949), col. 506, s.v., with bibl.

AVE MARIA. See *Hail Mary*.

AVE MARIS STELLA. One of the most popular Marian hymns, dating at least from the 9th cent. It is contained in the 9th cent. Codex Sangallensis 95 and has been attributed to various authors, one of the most probable assignations being that to *Paul the Deacon. The rhymeless hymn is a prayer of great simplicity and beauty for the maternal intercession of the BVM. In the Roman breviary it is the Vespers hymn of the Common of Feasts of the BVM and of the Saturday Office and the Little Office of our Lady. It has frequently been paraphrased and translated, perhaps the best-known version being that by E. *Caswall, 'Hail Thou Star of Ocean'.

Crit. text, with notes, in C. Blume, S.J., (ed.), *Die Hymnen des Thesaurus Hymnologicus H. A. Daniels und andere Hymnen-Ausgaben* (A.H.M.A., li, 1908), pp. 140–2. F. B. Plaine, O.S.B., 'Hymni Marialis *Ave Maris Stella* Expositio' in *Studien und Mittheilungen aus dem Benedictiner- und Cistercienser-Orden*, xiv (1893), pp. 244–55; G. M. Dreves, S.J., 'Der Hymnus vom Meeresstern' in *Stimmen aus Maria-Laach*, l (1896), pp. 558–69.

AVE VERUM CORPUS. Short anonymous Eucharistic hymn, probably dating from the 14th cent., beginning 'Ave verum corpus, natum De Maria Virgine' ('Jesu, Word of God Incarnate, Of the Virgin Mary born'). It was sung, esp. in Italy, France, and Germany, after the *Preface or during the *Consecration at Mass, and is still frequently chanted, e.g. at *Benediction (settings by W. A. Mozart, C. Gounod, and others).

Crit. text in C. Blume, S.J.–H. M. Bannister (edd.), *Liturgische Prosen des Übergangsstiles und der zweiten Epoche insbesondere die dem Adam von Sanct Victor zugeschriebenen* (A.H.M.A., liv, 1915), No. 167, p. 257 f.

AVENCEBRON. See *Avicebron*.

AVERROISM. Averroes (Ibn Rushd, 1126–98) was the descendant of a good Mohammedan family at Cordova, where he studied theology and law, later also medicine, mathematics, and philosophy. After being cadi at Cordova and Seville, he became the friend and, in 1182, the physician of the caliph, Abu Jacub Jusuf, and also enjoyed the favour of his son, Al Mansur, until, in 1195, he was accused of heresy and exiled, but recalled shortly before his death. His chief claim to fame rests on his Commentaries on *Aristotle, for which he was known in the Middle Ages as 'The Commentator'. Though generally a faithful interpreter of the philosopher, whom he venerated as the greatest genius of all times, his Aristotelianism, like that of most Arabic philosophers, is tinged with *Neo-Platonist ideas. Acc. to him God, the Prime Mover, is entirely separated from the world, in which He exercises no Providence, while the celestial spheres are intelligences, emanating from God in a descendent series until they reach man. He taught, further, the eternity and potentiality of matter and the unity of the human intellect ('monopsychism'), i.e. the doctrine that only one intellect exists for the whole human race in which every individual participates, to the exclusion of personal immortality. He consequently interpreted the Koran allegorically, though retaining the literal interpretation as the only one suitable for the common people.

The theories of Averroes became known in Catholic Europe in the 13th cent. and began to gain ground in Paris when, in 1255, the Arts faculty prescribed the study of Aristotle. Their danger to the Christian faith being at once recognized, St. *Albert the Great, at the command of Alexander IV, wrote a refutation entitled 'De Unitate Intellectus contra Averroem' (1256). In 1257 St. Thomas Aquinas began his 'Summa contra Gentiles' in which he too attacked Averroes, whose growing influence caused Urban IV in 1263 to renew *Gregory IX's prohibition of the study of Aristotle. The head of the Averroist school in Paris was *Siger of Brabant; the chief consequences of his central doctrine, of the unity of the intellect, though taught with safeguards, were the denial of personal immortality, of the freedom of the will and of moral responsibility, and the acceptance of the eternity of the world and of the human race. Siger and his followers professed to reconcile their teaching with the dogmas of the Church by the expedient of the double truth, acc. to which they claimed to believe as theologians what they denied as philosophers. It was against this school that St. Thomas wrote his treatise 'De Unitate Intellectus contra Averroistas' in 1270, and in the same year that the Averroist errors were formally anathematized and their supporters excommunicated by the Bp. of Paris. After a further condemnation in 1277, Averroism disappeared from the university of Paris, but infiltrated again in the 14th cent. when it was taught, e.g., by John of Jandun. It survived in Italy, esp. at Padua, until the time of the Renaissance.

Good account with full bibl. by M. M. Gorce, O.P., in *D.H.G.E.*, v (1931), cols. 1032–92, s.v. Of older works, E. *Renan, *Averroès et l'averroïsme* (1852) is still useful. See also bibl. to *Siger of Brabant*, esp. works of P. Mandonnet, F. van Steenberghen, and B. Nardi. M. *Grabmann, *Der lateinische Averroismus des 13. Jahrhunderts und seine Stellung zur christlichen Weltanschauung* (Sb. (Bayr), 1931, Hft. 2). On Averroes himself, see also Überweg, ii, pp. 313–322, with bibl., p. 722 f.

AVESTA. The Sacred Books of the *Zoroastrians or Parsees, which set forth the theology and religious system of the ancient Persians. The title used by earlier modern scholars, 'Zend-Avesta', rests on a misunderstanding. The work, which was based on much older matter, was put together under Sappor II (309–79) when it reached substantially its present outline. Considerable additions were made after the Arab Conquest of Persia (637–651) and a very great deal has been lost since. The main subjects dealt with are the ritual, hymns, liturgy, and law of the Parsees, and it is divided into five sections. The comparatively short portion known as the Gathas (versified sermons), written in a slightly different dialect, appears to be the oldest part of the work and perhaps goes back to Zoroaster himself. Knowledge of the work was first brought to the W. by a French scholar, Anquetil du Perron, who journeyed to India in 1754 with the express purpose of procuring the text, and after many difficulties returned with a copy for publication in 1771.

The standard edition is that of K. F. Geldner (Stuttgart, 1885–96). Eng. trans. in *The Sacred Books of the East* (ed.

F. Max Müller), iv, xxiii, xxxi, by J. Darmesteter and L. H. Mills. Cf. art. 'Zoroaster' in *EB* (ed. 11) and *H.E.R.E.*, s.vv.

AVICEBRON (c. 1020–c. 1070). The name commonly given to the Spanish Jewish philosopher, Salomon ben Gabirol (i.e. Gabriel). He was also known as 'Avencebrol'. Medieval Christian writers wrongly supposed him to be an Arabian (Mohammedan). His system, which contained both *Aristotelian and *Neoplatonist elements, was in essence *pantheistic, and St. *Thomas Aquinas directed against him his Opusculum 15, 'De substantiis separatis'. His chief treatise, the 'Fons Vitae', was an Arabic work, written in dialogue form, which in a Latin translation became very popular in the Middle Ages. He also wrote poems and hymns.

The Arabic original of the *Fons Vitae* has been lost; extracts surviving in medieval Heb. tr. were rediscovered and ed., with Fr. tr. and important introd. on his life and works, by S. Munk, *Mélanges de philosophie juive et arabe* (1859); 12th cent. Lat. tr. ed., with introd., by C. Baeumker (*B.G.P.M.*, i, Hftt. 2–4; 1892–5). Arabic text of 'The Improvement of Moral Qualities', ed., with Eng. tr. and introd., by S. S. Wise (Columbia University Oriental Studies, New York, 1901). Modern ed. of his poems, written in Heb., by H. N. Bialik–J. H. Ravnitzki (3 vols., Berlin and Tel-Aviv, 1924–32). J. Guttmann, *Die Philosophie des Salomon ibn Gabirol (Avicebron) dargestellt und erläutert* (1899); M. Wittmann, *Die Stellung des hl. Thomas von Aquin zu Avencebrol (Ibn Gebirol)* (*B.G.P.M.* iii, Hft. 3; 1900); id., *Zur Stellung Avencebrol's (Ibn Gebirol's) im Entwicklungsgang der arabischen Philosophie* (ib. v, Hft. i; 1905). A Geiger, *Salomo Gabirol und seine Dichtungen* (1867). I. Husik, *A History of Mediaeval Jewish Philosophy* (New York, 1916), pp. 59–79. M. M. Gorce, O.P., in *D.H.G.E.*, v (1931), cols. 1104–7, s.v., with bibl.

AVICENNA (980–1037). Arabian philosopher, who also acted as the court physician to a number of Persian princes. His full name was 'Abu 'Ali al Hosain ibn 'Abdallah ibn Sina'. His teaching exercised a great influence on the earlier *Schoolmen. His philosophy was in the main *Aristotelian, but it was also much influenced by *Neo-platonism. He held that there was a hierarchy of emanations from the Godhead which mediate between God and man. Of these the most important is the 'active intellect', which Avicenna conceived as an entity in a Platonic world of ideas. The 'passive intellect', which is his name for the individual mind, can acquire ideas only by contact with the active, and is thus secondary. He distinguished, in the usual Aristotelian fashion, between necessary and contingent being, holding that God was necessary and the universe contingent; but between the two he set the world of ideas, which he held to be necessary, though not of itself, but because God has made it so. He was the author of c. 100 treatises, including a *Canon of Medicine*, which long enjoyed a great reputation and an immense encyclopaedic work, '*Ash-Shifa*' or 'Sanatio'.

His works, which were written mainly in Arabic, were known to the Middle Ages in Hebrew and (esp.) Latin trr. (the latter often made from the Heb.). Collections of his works were publ., in Lat. tr., at Venice, 1495, 1508, and 1546. A. M. Goichon, *Lexique de la langue philosophique d'Ibn Sinā (Avicenne)* (1938). C. de Vaux, *Avicenne* ('Les Grands Philosophes'; 1900). A. M. Goichon, *La Distinction de l'essence et de l'existence d'après Ibn Sinā (Avicenne)* (1937).

M. C. Hernández, *La metafisica de Avicena* (Granada, 1949); L. Gardet, *La Pensée religieuse d'Avicenne* (Études de Philosophie Médiévale, xli; 1951), with reff. to recent edd. of his religious works. W. Klein, *Die Substanzlehre Avicennas bei Thomas von Aquin auf Grund der ihm zugänglichen lateinischen Übersetzungen* (1933). E. Gilson, 'Avicenne et le point de départ de Duns Scot', in *Archives d'Histoire Doctrinale et Littéraire du Moyen-Âge*, ii (1927), pp. 89–49; 'Les Sources gréco-arabes de l'augustinisme avicennisant', ib., iv (1930), pp. 5–158. Überweg, ii, pp. 307–10. C. Brockelmann, *Geschichte der arabischen Litteratur*, i (ed. 1943), pp. 589–99, and suppl. i (1937), pp. 812–28. Details of modern edd. and further litt. in P. J. Menasce, O.P., *Arabische Philosophie* (1948), pp. 35–8. O. C. Gruner, *A Treatise on the Canon of Avicenna*, incorporating a translation of the first Book (1930). G. Sarton, *Introduction to the History of Science*, i (Baltimore, 1927), esp. pp. 709–13, with further bibl. M. M. Gorce in *D.H.G.E.*, v (1931), cols. 1107–19, s.v. with detailed bibl. Full bibl. of MSS. by G. C. Anawati, O.P. (Cairo, 1950; in Arabic). Study by S. M. Afan (London, 1958).

AVIGNON. Acc. to tradition, its first Bp. was St. Rufus, a disciple of St. *Paul. It was in the 12th cent. a centre of the *Albigenses, and for this reason its defences were dismantled by Louis VIII in 1226. From 1309 till 1377 it was the residence ('*Babylonian Captivity') of the Popes, though it did not become Papal property until 1348, when Clement VI bought it from Joanna, the Queen of Naples. After the Papal court had returned to Rome, two *antipopes, Clement VII and Benedict XIII, lived in Avignon, the latter being finally expelled in 1408.

T. Okey, *The Story of Avignon* ('Medieval Towns Series', 1911). E. Duprat, *Les Origines de l'église d'Avignon. Des origines à 879* (1909). J. Girard-P. Pansier, *La Cour temporelle d'Avignon aux XIVe et XVIe siècles* (Recherches Historiques et Documents sur Avignon, le Comtat-Venaissin et la Principauté d'Orange, i; 1909). G. Mollat, *Les Papes d'Avignon, 1305–1378* (1912). H. Labande, *Les Palais des papes et les monuments d'Avignon au XIVe siècle* (2 vols., Marseilles, 1925). J. Girard in *D.H.G.E.* v (1931), cols. 1121–53, s.v.

AVITUS, St. (d. *c.* 519), Bp. of Vienne from *c.* 490. Alcimus Ecdicius Avitus was born in Auvergne of a Roman senatorial family. Succeeding to the see of Vienne in Gaul on the death of his father, Isychius (490), he exercised an enduring influence on the ecclesiastical life of Burgundy and won the Arian King Sigismund to the acceptance of Catholic orthodoxy. He was also a strong advocate of the movement for the closer ecclesiastical union of Gaul with Rome. His deserved reputation for learning greatly impressed King *Clovis, then still a pagan. Among his surviving writings are five poems *De Mosaicae Historiae Gestis*, two complete homilies (and fragments of many others), a poem *De Virginitate*, and some 100 epistles. Feast day, 5 Feb.

Works ed. J. *Sirmond, S.J., Paris, 1643 (repr., *via* A. *Gallandi, in J. P. Migne, *PL*, lix. 191–388). Revised text by R. Peiper in *M.G.H.*, Auctores Antiquissimi VI (ii; 1883); also by U. Chevalier (Lyons, 1890). Study by A. Charaux (Paris, 1876). H. Goelzer, *Le Latin de S. Avit* (1909); M. Burckhardt, *Die Briefsammlung des Bischofs Avitus von Vienne* (1938). F. Vernet in *D.T.C.*, i (1903), cols. 2639–2644; B. Altaner, *Patrologie* (ed. 2, 1950), p. 426.

AVRILLON, JEAN BAPTISTE ÉLIE (1652–1729), French theologian and spiritual writer. He made his profession as a *Minim in 1761. Among his writings were *Réflexions*

théologiques, morales et affectives sur les attributs de Dieu (1705) and manuals for the observance of *Lent and *Advent. E. B. *Pusey published in 1844 adapted English versions of *A Guide for passing Advent holily* and *A Guide for passing Lent holily*, and in 1845, of *The Year of Affections*.

P. Pourrat, P.S.S., *La Spiritualité chrétienne*, iv (1928), pp. 333–36; J. de Guibert in *Dict. Sp.*, i (1937), col. 1185 f.

AXUM, also Aksum. The ancient religious and political capital of Abyssinia (*Ethiopia). Christianity was established here in the 4th cent. under St. *Frumentius. The city is still held in great veneration as a religious centre.

J. T. Bent, *The Sacred City of the Ethiopians. Being a record of Travel and Research in Abyssinia in 1893* (1893), esp. pp. 152–97 and 238–85. *Deutsche Aksum-Expedition* hg. von der Generalverwaltung der königlichen Museen zu Berlin (by E. Littmann, T. von Lüpke, D. Krencker, and R. Zahn; 4 vols. bound in one, Berlin, 1913). U. Monneret de Villard, *Aksum*. Ricerche di topografia generale (Analecta Orientalia, xvi; 1938). S. Puglisi, 'Primi risultati delle indagini compiute dalla missione archeologica di Aksum' in *Africa Italiana*, viii (1941), pp. 95–153. C. Conti Rossini in *D.H.G.E.*, v (1931), cols. 1257–9, s.v. 'Axoum'.

AYLIFFE, JOHN (1676–1732), English jurist. He was educated at Winchester and at New College, Oxford. His strong Whig sympathies brought him into conflict with the dominant Jacobitism of Oxford, and his *Ancient and Present State of the University of Oxford* (2 vols., 1714) led to expulsion from the university and loss of his degrees. In 1726 he published his *Parergon Iuris Canonici Anglicani* (ed. 2, 1734), arranged alphabetically, which remains a treatise of high authority. In 1734 his *New Pandect of the Civil Law* (vol. i, on Roman law; all publd.) appeared posthumously.

S. Gibson, 'A Neglected Oxford Historian' in *Oxford Essays in Medieval History Presented to Herbert Edward Salter* (1934), No. XI, pp. 234–41. G. P. Macdonell in *D.N.B.*, ii (1885), pp. 279–81, s.v.

AYTON, JOHN (d. 1350), English canonist. His name occurs in several forms, among them 'Acton' (so in *D.N.B.*), 'Athone', 'Achedune'. He was a pupil of Abp. J. *Stratford and became a canon of *Lincoln. He wrote a commentary on the 'Constitutions' of the Papal legates Otto and Ottobon, which was printed in the 1496 and later editions of W. *Lyndwood's *Provinciale*.

Besides the prefaces to the various edd. of Lyndwood, see also F. W. *Maitland, *Roman Canon Law in the Church of England* (1898), pp. 6–14, 55 and 76. S. L. Lee in *D.N.B.*, (1885), p. 67, s.v. 'Acton, John'.

AZAZEL (עֲזָאזֵל). In OT theology, the demon—originally probably a goat-deity—dwelling in the desert, to whom the 'scapegoat' of the sin-offering was dispatched (Lev. 16. 1–28). In Enoch 6, 8, 10 he is a leader of the fallen angels, a Prometheus-like instructor of mankind in crafts, and the author of all sin. In later Jewish, *Gnostic, and

*Mohammedan traditions, he is a leader of demons.

T. K. *Cheyne, 'The date and origin of the ritual of the "Scapegoat"' in *Z.A.T.W.*, xv (1895), pp. 153–6; id. in *E.Bi.*, i (1899), cols. 393–8, s.v. S. R. *Driver in *H.D.B.*, i (1898), p. 207 f., s.v. J. G. Frazer, *The Golden Bough*, vi, The Scapegoat (1913), p. 210, note 4.

AZYMITES (Lat. also 'Infermentarii'). The name given to the W. Church by the Easterns at the time of the schism of 1054, with reference to their use of unleavened bread (τὰ ἄζυμα) in the Liturgy, which, on the E. view, invalidated the rite. See also *Bread, Leavened and Unleavened*.

B

BAAL (Heb. בַּעַל, Gk. Βάαλ or Βαάλ). The word, which means literally 'lord' or 'owner', e.g. of a house (Ex. 22. 7, Jgs. 19. 22), was used esp. of the Semitic deities who were held to produce agricultural and animal fertility. The older view that there was a supreme Deity, Baal, to be identified with the sun god, rests on insufficient evidence. The debased rites which arose in connexion with Baal nature worship caused it to be vigorously attacked by the Hebrew prophets, who constantly found themselves compelled to resist attempts to fuse the worship of Jehovah with that of the local Baalim. The 'high places' at which the cultus was centred were finally destroyed through the efforts of such men as *Elijah and King Josiah. It was the abhorrence of Baal worship that in later times led the Jews to read the word 'Bosheth' ('shame') as a substitute wherever Baal occurred in the sacred text ; hence the two forms of the same name, 'Eshbaal' (1 Chr. 9. 39) and 'Ishbosheth' (2 Sam. 2, 8). See also *Bel*.

W. R. *Smith, Lectures on the Religion of the Semites (ed. 3, by S. A. *Cook, 1927), passim. L. H. Vincent, O.P., 'Le Ba'al cananéen de Beisan et sa parèdre' in R. Bibl., xxxvii (1928), pp. 512–43; id., 'La Notion biblique du haut-lieu', pt. i, ib. lv (1948), pp. 245–78. R. Dussaud, 'Le Vrai Nom de Ba'al' in Revue de l'Histoire des Religions, cxiii (1936), pp. 5–20. A. S. *Peake in H.D.B. i (1900), pp. 209–211, s.v.; B. Mariani in E.C., ii (1949), cols. 614–16, s.v., with good bibl.

BABEL, Tower of. Acc. to Gen. 11. 1–9, the tower reaching to heaven, the presumptuous construction of which was frustrated by Jehovah through confusion of languages among its builders. The story was probably inspired by the famous Babylonian temple-tower ('ziggurat') of Etemenanki, which symbolized for the Israelites the pride of the Gentile powers, destined by God to dissolution from within. The immediate purpose of the narrative, which plays upon the words Babil (Babylon) and the Heb. בָּלַל (balal, 'to confuse'), seems to have been to account for the division of languages.

Besides comm. on Genesis, cited s.v., K. *Budde, 'Einheitlichkeit und Erhaltung von Gen. 11. 1–9' in Vom Alten Testament Karl Marti zum siebzigsten Geburtstage gewidmet (Beihefte zur Z.A.T.W., xli; 1925), pp. 45–51. Recent archaeological reconstructions include R. Koldewey, Der Babylonische Turm (Mitteilungen der deutschen Orient-Gesellschaft zu Berlin, No. 59; 1918); H. Gressmann, The Tower of Babel (Hilda Stroock Lectures for 1927; posthumously ed. J. Obermann. New York, 1928); T. Dombart, Der Babylonische Turm (Der Alte Orient, xxix, Hft. 2; 1930); G. Contenau, Le Déluge babylonien suivi de Ishtar aux enfers, la Tour de Babel (Bibliothèque Historique; 1941), pp. 255–87 (revised ed. 1952, pp. 226–58, with bibl. p. 265). L. H. Vincent, O.P., 'De la tour de Babel au temple' in R. Bibl., liii (1946), pp. 403–40; A. Parrot, Ziggurats et tour de Babel (1949). A. Romeo in E.C., ii (1949), cols. 619–21, for further bibl.

BABYLAS, St. (d. c. 250), Bp. of *Antioch. C. 240 he succeeded Zebinus in the see of Antioch. St. *Chrysostom relates that he once refused an emperor (prob. *Philip the Arabian, 244–9, nominally a Christian) access to a church on the ground of an unrepented crime. He was imprisoned in the *Decian persecution and died in bonds. In 351 his remains were translated to Daphne, a suburb of Antioch, to hallow a former temple of Apollo for Christian worship. In 362 *Julian the Apostate ordered their removal when unable to obtain a reply from the oracle of Apollo, and they were brought back to Antioch with Psalms ridiculing the heathen idols. Babylas became the object of a devoted cultus at Antioch, and St. Chrysostom preached two panegyrics (untrustworthy as historical sources) in his honour. Later his cultus extended to the W., and he was celebrated both in prose and verse by St. *Aldhelm of Sherborne. Feast day, 24 Jan.

*Eusebius, H.E., VI, xxix. 4 and xxxix. 4; *Sozomen, H.E., v, 19; *Theodoret, H.E., iii, 6. Chrysostom's sermons on Babylas are in PG, l, 527–72; on their slight historical value see H. *Delehaye, S.J., Les Passions des martyrs et les genres littéraires (1921), pp. 209 and 232. Three series of Acta (all late) are printed in A.A.SS. Jan. II (1643), pp. 569–578; Aldhelm, De Virginitate Prosa, xxxiii, ed. R. Ehwald in M.G.H., Auctores Antiquissimi, xv (1919), p. 274 f., and id., De Virginitate Carmen, 11, 1035–70, ib. p. 397 f. 'Les Saints Babylas' in Anal. Boll., xix (1900), pp. 5–8.

BABYLONIAN CAPTIVITY. The captivity in Babylon whither under Nebuchadnezzar (604–562 B.C.) the Jews were deported in two batches in 597 and 586 B.C. respectively (2 Kgs. 24. 14–16 ; 25. 11). Acc. to Ez. 2, they were permitted to return after the Persian ruler, Cyrus, had captured Babylon in 538 B.C., though many of them did not return till at least a hundred years later (Neh. 1 ff.).

The expression was used metaphorically by F. *Petrarch and subsequent writers of the exile of the Popes at *Avignon from 1309 to 1377. M. *Luther's treatise on the Babylonish Captivity of the Church (1520) was a sustained attack on the 'bondage' in which the Church had been held by the withdrawal of the chalice from the laity, the doctrine of *transubstantiation, and the *Sacrifice of the Mass.

BACH, JOHANN SEBASTIAN (1685–1750), German composer. After being court organist at Weimar (1708–17) and court 'kapellmeister' at Cöthen (1717–23), he became cantor at the Thomas school at Leipzig in 1723, a post he retained till his death. His chief religious works belong to his Leipzig period, notably the two great Passions acc. to St. Matthew and to St. John and the Mass in B minor. The music, which in consummate contrapuntal art expresses deep spiritual realities, was originally used at Protestant services but is now performed almost exclusively outside Divine worship. The Passions, based upon the liturgical narratives, are interspersed with arias and chorales; the Masses are divided up into a series of separate numbers, acc. to the custom of the time, and permeated with a mysterious symbolism. The Protestant German chorale has inspired many of his motets and esp. the cantatas, designed to be musical accompaniments and interpretations of the sermon. Among Bach's other choral works the 'Magnificat' and the Christmas Oratorio are the most famous. Bach's music remained forgotten after his death until it was rediscovered in the 19th cent. by F. Mendelssohn and other 'Romantic' composers. It is now generally recognized to belong to the same great timeless tradition as that of G. P. *Palestrina and W. A. Mozart, and though it was composed in the service of the German Lutheran Church, its religious depth is confined to no denomination.

Collected ed. of his works publd. for the Bachgesellschaft (59 vols.+index 2 vols., 1851–'1899' [1900]); new ed., Kassel, &c., 1955. Letters ed. H. U. E. H. Müller von Asow (Ratisbon, 1950 ff.). Primary life by J. N. Forkel (Leipzig, 1802; Eng. tr., 1820; modern Eng. tr., 1920). Other lives by P. Spitta (2 vols., Leipzig, 1873–80; Eng. tr., 3 vols., 1884–5), K. L. Poole (London, 1882), A. *Schweitzer (in Fr., Leipzig, 1905; Eng. tr., 1911), C. H. H. Parry (London, 1909), and C. S. Terry (ib., 1928); also other works by the last author. Id. in Grove's *Dictionary of Music and Musicians* (ed. 5 by E. Blom), i (1954), pp. 293–321.

BACON, FRANCIS (1561–1626), Viscount St. Albans, philosopher, essayist, orator, and lawyer. He was the eighth and youngest son of Sir Nicholas Bacon (1509–79), *Elizabeth I's first Lord Keeper, and of a daughter of Sir Anthony Cooke (1504–76), at one time tutor to *Edward VI. Born at York House in the Strand, London, he entered Trinity College, Cambridge, in 1573, was admitted to Gray's Inn in 1576 and, after abandoning an intended diplomatic career, decided to make law his profession. Elizabeth used him as her 'learned counsel', but, in spite of frequent petitions to his uncle, Lord Burghley, and his friendship (from 1591) with Essex, he did not rise to office during her reign. In 1584 he became M.P. for Melcombe Regis and later for Taunton (1586), Liverpool (1589), Middlesex (1593), and Southampton (1597). In 1601 he played a leading part in the trial and condemnation of his former friend, issuing at the Queen's behest *A Declaration of the Practices and Treasons attempted and committed by Robert, late Earl of Essex, and his Complices* (1601).

In the Parliament of 1604, in which Bacon defended the Union and the King's retention of feudal rights, *James I realized his worth. In 1607 he became Solicitor-General, in 1608 Clerk of the Star Chamber, in 1613 Attorney-General, and in 1617 Lord Keeper. For several years there was strong rivalry between Coke and Bacon through the conflicting claims of the Courts of Common Law and Chancery. In 1618 he was made Lord Chancellor and also Viscount St. Albans. It became clear, however, that his position depended increasingly on the personal pleasure of Buckingham; and when in 1620 Parliament set up a committee to examine abuses in the Courts of Justice, Bacon was seized on as a referee for the legality of Crown patents, and, at the instigation of Coke, accused of bribery and corruption. In 1621 he was disgraced and retired into private life.

Throughout his life Bacon was strongly attracted to the problems of philosophy. His *Proficience and Advancement of Learning* (1605) was designed to sum up the stock and deficiencies of human knowledge and to insist that since man's power to control nature was in his own hands, success rested on applying the right methods. By inductions from the simplest facts of experience man could reach forward to the discovery of fundamental principles which in turn would issue in beneficial practical results. In the *Novum Organum* (1620) he expounded these ideas more systematically. Here he outlined what he termed the 'Great Instauration' and developed his well-known analysis of the fallacies which beset human thought (*idola tribus, idola specus, idola fori, idola theatri*). In 1623 followed his *De Augmentis Scientiarum*, an expanded Latin version of the book of 1605. His *New Atlantis* (1627, posthumous) described the ideal State, in which the New Philosophy would be carried through by political machinery and State guidance, aided by a college of science ('Solomon's House'). Meanwhile Bacon's *Essays* had been appearing with additions in each new edition (1597, 1612, 1625); the famous one on 'Atheism' first saw the light in 1612.

Bacon carried his empiricism into the realm of morals. He denied the existence of absolute rules of conduct or of a 'summum bonum'. But though his philosophy of experience, with its grandiose claims, attracted much attention among his contemporaries, it is less clear that it exercised the influence on later thought commonly attributed to it. It stood, however, in the main stream of English philosophical tradition. His religion was that of a discriminating, yet orthodox, member of the Church of England.

Opera Omnia, publ. in 6 vols., Amsterdam, 1661–84; standard ed. by J. Spedding-R. L. Ellis-D. D. Heath (14 vols. London, 1857–74) of which the last 7 vols. comprise the *Letters and Life of Francis Bacon* (incl. his Occasional Works, ed. J. Spedding). *Philosophical Works*, partly repr. with introd. by J. M. Robertson (London 1905). Modern edd. (with introd. and notes) of his *Essays* by E. A. *Abbott ('London Series of English Classics', 2 vols., 1876) and of his *Novum Organum* by T. Fowler (Oxford, 1878). Studies by T. Fowler ('English Philosophers', 1881), R. W. *Church ('English Men of Letters', 1884), E. A. Abbott (London, 1885), G. W. Steeves (London, 1910) I. Levine (London, 1925), Mary Sturt (London, 1932), and C. [W. S.] *Williams (London, 1933). F. H. Anderson, *The Philosophy of Francis Bacon* (Chicago, 1948); A. Levi, *Il pensiero di Francesco Bacone considerato in relazione con le filosofie della natura del rinascimento e col razionalismo cartesiano* (1925). A. E. *Taylor, *Philosophical Studies* (1934), ch. vii ('Francis Bacon', Henriette Hertz Lecture, 1926). R. W. Gibson, *Francis Bacon. A Bibliography of his Works and of Baconiana to the Year 1750* (1950).

BACON, ROGER (*c.* 1214–92), 'Doctor mirabilis', *Franciscan philosopher. (The traditional accounts of Bacon's career have been shown recently to need considerable revision.) Born at either Ilchester in Somerset or Bisley in Glos., he studied at Oxford though not, it would appear, under either St. *Edmund of

Abingdon or Robert *Grosseteste. Not later than 1236 he made his way to Paris where he was one of the first to lecture on *Aristotle (incl. the '*Liber de Causis'). Here he became interested in experimentation and, c. 1247, resigned his chair to devote himself to science. He returned to England c. 1251 and prob. then joined the Franciscan Order. It is unlikely that he was ever ordained to the priesthood or that he ever taught at Oxford. He returned to France c. 1256, but owing to ill-health had to give up his studies for some ten years.

A new stage in Bacon's career was reached in the middle sixties. Knowledge of his writings, as yet of strictly limited extent, having reached Clement IV (1265–8; formerly Abp. of Narbonne), the Pope bade him dispatch to Rome an account of his doctrines 'secretly and without delay'. Bacon accordingly set out to expound his system on an ambitious scale. He completed the 'Communia Naturalium' and the 'Communia Mathematicae', but finding the continuation of the work on these dimensions impracticable, contented himself with an epitome of his doctrine ('Tractatus Praeambulus'). The outcome was the work since known as the 'Opus Majus'. This he soon followed by the 'Opus Minus'; and both 'Opera', together with 'De Multiplicatione Speciarum' and a work on alchemy, were dispatched to the Pope c. 1268. Unfortunately Bacon did not gain the Papal commendation he hoped for, Clement having died on 29 Nov. 1268. Bacon then returned to Oxford, where he wrote, inter alia, Gk. and Heb. grammars. He also completed his 'Opus Tertium'. The three 'Opera' together were an encyclopaedic treatise, dealing with such diverse subjects as the relation between philosophy and theology, grammar, mathematics, geography, perspective, physiology, and experimental science ('domina omnium scientiarum'). To this period also belongs his 'Compendium Studii Philosophiae' (c. 1272), containing a bitter attack on the vices and ignorance of the clergy. In the 'Opus Tertium' Bacon complains of vexatious treatment from his superiors. But the common view that he suffered imprisonment following the condemnation of 219 propositions by Stephen Tempier, Bp. of Paris, on 7 Mar. 1277 is unlikely, since even if the attack were aimed at Bacon, such a decision would not have been operative in England. His last work was his unfinished 'Compendium Studii Theologiae' (1292).

It is difficult to assess Bacon's place in the history of philosophy. He was undoubtedly a writer of much originality and a man of exceptional learning. His independent views and irascible temperament brought him constant conflict; and his criticism of many medieval assumptions was a healthy challenge to conventionalism. His stress on the need for a knowledge of Gk. and Heb. for the understanding of the Scriptures showed him to be before his time. But how far he advanced beyond a mass of unrelated ideas and facts to a philosophical grasp of principles is less clear.

The extent of his experimentation is also uncertain, though there are good reasons for accepting the common view that he invented a rudimentary telescope, as well as gunpowder and the thermometer.

'Opus Maius', ed. J. H. Bridges (3 vols., Oxford, 1897–1900); 'Opus Minus', 'Opus Tertium', and 'Compendium Studii Philosophiae', ed. J. S. Brewer in Rogeri Bacon Opera quaedam hactenus inedita, i (all publd., London, 1859). 'Opus Tertium', ed. P. Duhem (Quaracchi, 1909). 'Compendium Studii Theologiae', ed. H. *Rashdall (British Society for Franciscan Studies, Aberdeen, 1911; in an appendix in the vol., A. G. Little attempts the difficult task of listing Bacon's complete works, pp. 71–112). Many items ed. (not very satisfactorily) by R. Steele and others in Opera hactenus inedita Rogeri Baconi (London and Oxford, 1905 ff.). His Gk. grammar (Oxford, C.C.C., MS. 48, s. xiv, the sole important MS.) and fragments of Heb. grammar ed. E. Nolan and S. A. Hirsch (Cambridge, 1902). A. G. Little (ed.), Roger Bacon (Commemorative Essays, 1914). Dorothea E. Sharp, Franciscan Philosophy at Oxford in the Thirteenth Century (British Society of Franciscan Studies, xvi; 1930), pp. 115–71. S. E. Easton, Roger Bacon and his Search for a Universal Science (1952). On his doctrinal system, three studies by R. Carton (Études de philosophie médiévale, vols. ii, iii, and v; 1924). F. W. Woodruff, Roger Bacon. A Biography (popular [1938]). D. A. Callus, O.P., in Chambers's Encyclopedia (ed. 1950), ii, p. 38 f. Bacon's 'Moralis Philosophia', ed. F. Delorme, O.F.M.–E. Massa (Zürich, 1953).

BAEDA. See Bede.

BAEUMER, SUITBERT. See Bäumer, Suitbert.

BAGOT, RICHARD (1782–1854), Bp. of *Bath and Wells. He was educated at Rugby and at *Christ Church, Oxford, and in 1804 elected a Fellow of All Souls. From 1829 to 1845 he was Bp. of *Oxford. His relations with the *Tractarians are his chief interest to the historian. When in a charge of 1838 he reproved them for practices 'which hitherto had ended in superstition', E. B. *Pusey addressed to him an Open Letter. After the publication of Tract 90 in 1841, Bagot induced J. H. *Newman to cease issuing the tracts altogether, but in a charge of 1842 he defended the Tractarians against current attacks, though he denounced the 'lamentable want of judgement' of the rank and file of the Movement. In 1845 he was translated at his own desire to the see of *Bath and Wells, where the closing months of his life were taken up by a controversy with G. A. *Denison, Vicar of East Brent, on Eucharistic doctrine.

S. Lee in D.N.B., ii (1885), p. 339 f., s.v., with bibl.

BAINBRIDGE, CHRISTOPHER (c. 1464–1514), Abp. of *York and cardinal. He was born at Hilton, nr. Appleby, in Westmoreland, and educated at Queen's College, Oxford, of which he became provost c. 1495. He held a number of benefices and was made Dean of *Windsor in 1505. In 1507 he was consecrated Bp. of *Durham, and translated to York in 1508. *Henry VIII sent him to *Rome as ambassador in 1509 and *Julius II created him cardinal in 1511. As such, Julius II entrusted him with a military expedition against Ferrara. In the same year (1511), Henry chose him to inform the Pope of England's adhesion to the

Holy League against France. Bainbridge died of poison administered by one of his chaplains, who accused Sylvester de Gigli, Bp. of *Worcester and resident English ambassador at Rome, of instigating him to the murder from motives of rivalry (though de Gigli was finally acquitted). A man of violent temper, Bainbridge proved himself a courageous defender of English interests at the Curia.

Liber Pontificalis Chr. Bainbridge Archiepiscopi Eboracensis, ed. W. G. Henderson (Surtees Society, lxi, 1875). *Calendar of State Papers and Manuscripts relating to English Affairs existing in the Archives and Collections of Venice and other Libraries of North Italy*, ii, ed. R. Brown (1867), passim. A. *Wood, *Athenae Oxonienses*, ii (ed. P. Bliss, 1815), cols. 702-4. J. *Gairdner in *D.N.B.*, ii (1885), p. 433 f.

BAIRD LECTURES. A series of lectures established in 1871 on the benefaction of James Baird (1802–76), a wealthy ironmaster, for the defence of orthodox *Presbyterian teaching. Each annual course is delivered at Glasgow, and also if required at one other Scottish university. The lecturer, who may be reappointed, must be a minister of the Established Church of Scotland, and the course be of at least six lectures.

BAIUS, MICHEL (1513–89), Flemish theologian. He was educated at Louvain, became principal of Standonk College in 1541, and held various appointments in the University of Louvain in the years following. Shortly after 1550 he joined John Hessels (1522–66) in asserting theological propositions on the subjects of grace and sin which were held to be unorthodox, and met with the displeasure of the Chancellor of the University and the Abp. of Malines. In 1560 eighteen of his propositions were censured by the *Sorbonne. Even so, Baius and Hessels were chosen to represent the University in 1563 at the Council of *Trent, and received the powerful protection of the King of Spain. Further publications by Baius resulted in the bull 'Ex omnibus afflictionibus' (1 Oct. 1567), in which a large number of propositions from his writings, or embodying his doctrine, were condemned, but which did not mention him by name. For the rest of his life he seems to have hesitated between loyalty to his principles and the desire to remain in the RC Church, and to have been seeking ways of verbal reconciliation between his teaching and official pronouncements. In 1579 the bull 'Provisionis Nostrae' reaffirmed that of 1567, and Baius made a formal recantation of his main views, but his subsequent writings appear to show that they still underlay his teachings.

His system, 'Baianism', is often considered an anticipation of *Jansenism. It is contained in a series of small works, in which Baius interprets in his own way the anti-*Pelagian teaching of St. *Augustine. Its main principles were: (1) That in the primitive state, innocence was not a supernatural gift of God to man, but the necessary complement of human nature itself. (2) That *original sin is not merely a privation of grace, but habitual *concupiscence, transmitted by heredity, and so even in unconscious infants is a sin or moral evil of itself. (3) That the sole work of *redemption is to enable us to recover the gifts of original innocence and live moral lives; and that this end is achieved by the substitution of charity for concupiscence as the motive for each meritorious act. The grace conferred by redemption was thus not considered to be supernatural.

Opera, ed. G. Gerberon, O.S.B., Cologne, 1696. The 18 censured propositions, together with Baius' annotations, and a further explanation of his doctrine made to the Theology Faculty at Louvain, and part of a letter of 1569, were repr. by H. Lennerz, S.J. (Pontificia Universitas Gregoriana, Textus et Documenta, Series Theologica, xxiv; 1938). J. B. Du Chesne S.J., *Histoire de baianisme ou l'hérésie de Michel Baius* (Douai, 1731). F. X. Linsenmann, *Michael Baius und die Grundlegung des Jansenismus* (Tübingen, 1867). F. X. Jansens, S.J., *Baius et le baianisme* (Museum Lessianum, Section Théologique, xviii; Louvain, 1927). H. de Lubac, S.J., 'Deux Augustiniens fourayés, Baïus et Jansénius; I, Baïus' in *Rech. S.R.*, xxi (1931), pp. 422-43. A. Lanz, S.J., 'La dottrina "De Locis Theologicis" di M. Baio in una celebra controversia del secolo XVI' in *Gregorianum*, xxii (1941), pp. 44-79 and 467-96. N. J. Abercrombie, *The Origins of Jansenism* (1936), pp. 87-93, 137-42 and passim. X. Le Bachelet, S.J., in *D.T.C.*, ii (1905), cols. 38-111, s.v.; J. F. Sollier, S.M., in *C.E.*, ii (1907), pp. 209-12, s.v. See also works cited under *Jansenism.

BAKER, AUGUSTINE (baptismal name, David) (1575–1641), *Benedictine writer on ascetical theology and history. He became a RC, entered the Benedictine Order at Padua in 1605, and was ordained priest *c*. 1615. He worked at Cambrai and *Douai, and as a chaplain in England. Of his ascetical writings the most famous survive in *Sancta Sophia, or Holy Wisdom* (2 vols., 1657), a collection made posthumously. It expounds the way of contemplation, under the headings 'Of an Internal Life in General', 'Of Mortification', and 'Of Prayer'. His important researches into the history of the origins of the *Benedictine Order in England were published in *Apostolatus Benedictinorum in Anglia* (Douai, 1626). He also left in MS. a Life of Dame Gertrude *More (q.v. for details).

Confessions, ed. J. McCann, O.S.B. (1922). Lives by P. Salvin [O.S.B.] and S. Cressy [O.S.B.], ed. by J. McCann (1933); 'Memorials' incl. his autobiography and life by Fr. Leander Prichard in *Memorials of Father Augustine Baker and other Documents relating to the English Benedictines*, ed. J. McCann and [R.] H. *Connolly (Catholic Record Society, xxxiii, 1933), pp. 1-154. J. N. Sweeney, O.S.B., *The Life and Spirit of Father Augustine Baker* (1861).

BAKER, SIR HENRY WILLIAMS, Bart. (1821–77), hymn-writer. The son of Vice-Admiral Sir Henry Loraine Baker, he was educated at Trinity College, Cambridge. From 1851 until his death he was Vicar of Monkland, near Leominster. His many hymns, written under the influence of the *High Church Movement, of which he was a devoted supporter, were marked by simplicity of expression and smoothness of rhythm. Among those which have become well known are 'The King of Love my Shepherd is' (paraphrase of Ps. 23), 'Lord, Thy Word abideth'

'There is a blessed home', and 'Shall we not love thee, Mother dear?' He was also the promoter and compiler of the original edition (1861) of *Hymns Ancient and Modern (q.v.) as well as the editor of other hymn-books and a devotional manual.

A. H. Grant in *D.N.B.*, iii (1885), p. 11.

BALDACHINO (from Ital. *Baldacco*, 'Bagdad', whence came the materials used in its construction). A canopy used to cover an altar, also called **Umbraculum** or *Ciborium. It may be made of wood, stone, or metal, in which case it is supported on pillars, or of silk or velvet when it is suspended from the ceiling or attached to the wall. It was originally surmounted by a cross, which was later placed on or behind the altar. The oldest existing example is of the 9th cent., at *Ravenna; the largest and most famous is G. L. Bernini's canopy on twisted pillars over the high altar of *St. Peter's at *Rome. The baldachino is required in the RC Church by the *Caeremoniale Episcoporum (I. 12. 13 and 14. 1), though its use is by no means general. The Reformers objected to it on the ground that it tended to make the Lord's Table a fixture, and J. *Jewel, Bp. of *Salisbury, made it a subject of controversy with the Jesuit, T. *Harding. The word is also used of the canopy over a bishop's throne, over statues, and of the movable canopy carried in processions, e.g. of the Blessed Sacrament.

Braun, *C.A.*, ii, pp. 185-9 and 262-71.

BALDWIN (d. 1190), Abp. of *Canterbury. A native of *Exeter, he entered the *Cistercian abbey of Ford, Devonshire, where he was elected abbot within a year. In 1180 he was appointed Bp. of *Worcester. In 1184 he was elected Abp. of Canterbury, but his election was contested by the monks of Christ Church, who disliked his austere ideals. When he decided to erect a college of secular priests at Hakington, nr. Canterbury, from some revenues due to Christ Church, the monks appealed to the Pope, who decided in their favour. Baldwin, upheld by the King, refused to submit, and a compromise was reached in 1189, after a long struggle, at the end of which the monks made their submission and the archbishop agreed to found his college on a site near *Lambeth. In 1190 he took part in the Crusade, but his grief at the lack of discipline of the Christian armies probably hastened his death. He bequeathed his whole fortune to the liberation of the Holy Land. Among his works, which were printed in the 'Bibliotheca Patrum Cisterciensium' (1662), are a treatise on faith, 'De commendatione Fidei', and one on the Eucharist, 'De Sacramento Altaris'. He was the first Abp. of Canterbury to secure the supremacy of his see over *Wales.

His works are repr. from B. Tissier, *Bibliotheca Patrum Cisterciensium*, in J. P. Migne, *PL*, cciv, 401-774. Some of his correspondence is ed. W. *Stubbs, *Epistolae Cantuarien-*ses (Chronicles and Memorials of the Reign of Richard I, ii; R.S., 1865, pp. 4-329 'Tempore Balwini', with introd. pp. xxxiii-lxxx passim and cxlii f.). P. Guébin, 'Deux Sermons inédits de Baldwin, archevêque de Canterbury 1184-1190' in *J.T.S.*, xiii (1912), pp. 571-4. His tour of Wales was described by *Giraldus, *Itinerarium Kambriae* (*Works*, ed. J. F. Dimock, vi, R.S., 1868, pp. 3-152. W. F. *Hook, *Lives of the Archbishops of Canterbury*, ii (1862), pp. 539-73. W. Hunt in *D.N.B.*, iii (1865), pp. 32-4, s.v.

BALE, JOHN (1495-1563), Bp. of Ossory, 'Bilious Bale'. At the age of 12, he entered the *Carmelite monastery at Norwich. Later he renounced his vow of celibacy, became a vigorous and unscrupulous defender of Reformed doctrines and a writer of miracle plays, and thereby attracted the attention of T. *Cromwell, who took him under his protection. On Cromwell's fall in 1540, he fled to Germany, where he continued writing. Returning to England on *Edward VI's accession (1547), he became Rector of Bishopstoke, Hants, and in 1552 was made Bp. of Ossory. He provoked strong opposition in Ireland by his refusal to be consecrated by the Roman rite and his radical innovations; and he was soon forced to flee to Holland. He did not come back until *Elizabeth's accession in 1559, when, feeling too old to return to Ossory, he settled at *Canterbury, where he resided till his death. Though he possessed great learning, his writings are extremely coarse and bitter. The most important of his numerous plays, *King John* (c. 1548), marks the transition from the older *morality plays to the later historical dramas. His *Illustrium majoris Britanniae Scriptorum, hoc est, Angliae Cambriae ac Scotiae Summarium* (1548-9) is an indispensable catalogue of British authors and their writings, though often inaccurate and biased.

Select Works, ed. H. Christmas (Parker Society, 1849), with biogr. notice, pp. vii-xii; *Dramatic Works*, ed. by J. S. Farmer (Early English Dramatists, 1907). His 'Index Britanniae Scriptorum' has been ed. by R. L. Poole–M. Bateson (Anecdota Oxoniensia, Med. and Mod. Series, ix, 1902), his *King John* repr. by J. H. P. Pafford (Malone Society, 1931). Much autobiographical material in *The Vocation of John Bale to the Bishopric of Ossory in Ireland, his Persecutions in the same and final Deliverance* (1553; repr. in the Harleian Miscellany, vi [1745], pp. 402-28); short life appended to that of Leland in *The Lives of John Leland, Thomas Hearne and Antony Wood* (1772; separate pagination). Modern studies by J. W. Harris (Illinois Studies in Language and Literature, xxv, pt. 3, 1940) and H. McCusker (Bryn Mawr, Pa., 1942). W. T. Davies, 'A Bibliography of John Bale' in the *Oxford Bibliographical Society Proceedings and Papers*, v (1940), pp. 201-79.

BALFOUR, ARTHUR JAMES (1848-1930), British statesman and philosopher. In 1879 he published a work intended as an apology for religious faith with the somewhat misleading title, *A Defence of Philosophic Doubt*. It endeavoured to show that all forms of human knowledge, including the natural sciences with their boasting claims, left certain basic residual problems which defied intellectual solution, and that the ultimate convictions of mankind rested on the non-rational ground of religious faith. This position Balfour developed in his *Foundations of Belief* (1895), which, in view of the eminence to which he had then risen as a statesman, attracted very wide attention. He worked out his position somewhat further in two sets of *Gifford Lectures, *Theism and Humanism* (1915) and *Theism and Thought* (1923). In public affairs, his Education Bill of 1902 provoked keen hostility from Nonconformists and in defence he published a *Letter on the Criticisms of an Opponent* [J. *Clifford] (subsequently included in his *Essays and Addresses*, ed. 3, 1905). He was a communicant in both the C of E and the Church of Scotland.

His biography was written by Blanche E. C. Dugdale, his niece (2 vols., 1936).

BALL, JOHN (d. 1381), priest. Implicated in the insurrection of Wat Tyler. Little is known of his early life. Acc. to his own account he was first at *York and later at Colchester. In 1366, when living in Essex, he was summoned before the Abp. of *Canterbury for preaching *Wycliffite doctrines of property, and the faithful were forbidden to attend his sermons. In 1376 his arrest as an excommunicated person was ordered, but his popularity continued, esp. through his teaching of the equality of bondsmen and gentry. During Tyler's insurrection (1381) he was in custody in the Archbishop's prison at Maidstone, but was freed by the rebels and brought in triumph to Canterbury. At Blackheath he preached on the famous rhyme 'When Adam dalf and Eve span, Who was then a gentilman?' and incited the populace to kill the nobles and all others opposed to his ideal of social equality. He was present at the death of Abp. *Simon of Sudbury in the Tower, and also at the meeting of Wat Tyler and the King at *Smithfield. After Tyler's death he fled to the Midlands. He was captured at Coventry and brought before Richard II at *St. Albans, where he was executed as a traitor.

The chief authorities for his life are the *Fasciculi Zizaniorum* (ed. W. W. Shirley, Rolls Series, 1858), p. 273; Thomas Walsingham, *Historia Angliana*, ii (ed. by H. T. Riley, R.S., 1864), pp. 32–4; Henry Knighton, *Chronicon*, ii (ed. by J. R. Lumby, R.S., 1895), pp. 131 f. and 139 f.   J. Gairdner in *D.N.B.*, iii (1885), p. 73 f.

BALLERINI, PIETRO (1698–1769), Patristic scholar and canonist. He was the son of a surgeon, born at *Verona, and educated by the *Jesuits there. Ordained priest in 1722, he shortly afterwards became principal of a classical school in the same city. Attention was drawn to his work on moral theology when his extreme views on *usury were condemned by Pope *Benedict XIV in his bull *Vix pervenit* (1745). In 1748 he was sent by the republic of *Venice to defend its interests at *Rome in a dispute over Aquileia. He was then commissioned by the Pope to prepare a new edition of the works of St. *Leo the Great to replace that of P. *Quesnel (1675), which had been written in the interests of *Gallicanism. This edition (3 vols., Venice, 1753–7), published in conjunction with his brother Girolamo Ballerini (1702–81), has remained the standard text of Leo; the last vol. contains a valuable collection of documents (not publd. elsewhere)

and dissertations on the early history of *canon law. The joint work of the two brothers, which owed much of its success to their fruitful co-operation, also included *Henrici Norisii Veronensis . . . Opera* (4 vols., Verona, 1729–1732) with valuable material on ecclesiastical history, *S. Zenonis, Episcopi Veronensis, Sermones* with notes (Verona, 1739), *S. Antonini, Archiepiscopi Florentini, Summa Theologica*, with life of the author (Verona, 4 parts, 1740–1741) and *Ratherii, Episcopi Veronensis, Opera* (Verona, 1765). Pietro alone also published, among other items, *Il Metodo di S. Agostino negli studi* (Verona, 1724), a history of *probabilism which seemed rather to defend the theory of *probabiliorism (Verona, 1736), an edition of the *S. Raymundi de Pennafort Summa* (Verona, 1744), a treatise on usury (Bologna, 1747) and, against *Febronianism, the *De Vi ac Ratione Primatus Romanorum Pontificum* (Verona, 1766) and the *De Potestate Ecclesiastica Summorum Pontificum et Conciliorum Generalium* (ib., 1768).

Count Giammaria Mazzuchelli, *Gli scrittori d' Italia*, ii (pt. 1; 1758), pp. 178–85, s.vv. W. Telfer, 'Additional Note B. The Ballerini' appended to art. 'The Codex Verona LX (58)' in *Harvard Theological Review*, xxxvi (1943), p. 231 f. C. Verschaffel in *D.T.C.*, ii (1905), col. 131 f., s.v.; A. de Meyer in *D.H.G.E.*, vi (1932), cols. 339–41, s.v.

BALSAMON, THEODORE (c. 1140–after 1195), Greek canonist. He was born in *Constantinople and held several ecclesiastical appointments in the capital. Before 1191 he became Greek Patriarch of *Antioch, but he never exercised his official functions as the *Crusaders put in a Latin Patriarch, and he continued to reside at Constantinople. His *Scholia*, his most important work, consists of (1) a commentary on the 'Nomocanon' of *Photius, and (2) one of the principal collections of the *canon law of the East. In the latter he expounds how the civil legislation is to be treated when it conflicts with the ecclesiastical canon.

Extant Works repr. from W. *Beveridge's Συνοδικόν (2 vols., Oxford, 1672) in J. P. Migne, *PG*, cxxxvii and cxxxviii. V. N. Beneshevich, *A Study of the Tradition of the Nomocanon of Photius and the Version of Balsamon* (in Russ.; 2 parts, St. Petersburg, 1905). Krumbacher, pp. 607–609. L. Petit, A.A., in *D.T.C.*, ii (1905), cols. 135–7, s.v., with bibl.

BALTIMORE, Councils of. A series of ecclesiastical councils, three plenary (1852–84) and ten provincial (1829–69), by which many details of the administration and discipline of the RC Church in the U.S.A. were settled. Little was decreed on doctrinal matters; but the Second Plenary Council (1866) issued some warnings against the teachings which were later generally known as *Americanism and condemned by *Leo XIII in the letter 'Testem benevolentiae' (1899).

Acts and Decrees of the three Plenary Councils publd. at Baltimore in 1853, 1868, and 1886; Decrees and other documents of the Provincial Councils in *Acta et Decreta Sacrorum Conciliorum Recentium Collectio Lacensis*, iii (Freiburg, 1875), cols. 9–122, 155–82, and 575–600 (also text of first two Plenary Councils, cols. 129–54 and 323–574).

P. Guilday, *A History of the Councils of Baltimore: 1791–1884* (New York, 1932). W. H. W. Fanning in *C.E.*, ii (1907), pp. 235–41, s.v.

BALUZE, ÉTIENNE (1630–1718), 'Balusius', ecclesiastical historian. Born at Tulle, where he was brought up in the *Jesuit College, he studied at *Toulouse. In 1656 he was called to *Paris as secretary to Peter de *Marca (d. 1662), in 1662 he became librarian to J. B. Colbert (1619–83), in 1670 professor of canon law at the Collège de France and in 1707 Director of the Collège. The political views expressed in his history of the House of Auvergne (1708) led to his banishment from Paris (1710–13). His writings include *Capitularia Regum Francorum* (1677), an edition of the Epistles of *Innocent III (1682; incomplete, since Baluze was denied access to the Vatican archives), *Conciliorum Nova Collectio* (1683), an edition of *Marius Mercator (1684), *Vitae Paparum Avenionensium* (1693; put on the Index for alleged *Gallicanism, 1698), and *Historia Tutelensis* (a history of Tulle, 1717).

New ed. of his *Vitae Paparum Avenionensium*, ed. G. Mollat (4 vols., Paris, (1916)–(1927)). R. Fage, *Les Œuvres de Baluze, cataloguées et décrites* (Tulle, 2 pts., 1882–4). C. Godard, *De Stephano Baluzio Tutelensi, Libertatum Ecclesiae Gallicanae Propugnatore* (Paris, thesis, 1901). G. Mollat, *Étude critique sur les* Vitae Paparum Avenionensium *d'Étienne Baluze* (1917). H. *Quentin, O.S.B., *Jean-Dominique Mansi et les grandes collections conciliaires* (1900), pp. 32–8 and 204–69.

BAMPTON LECTURES. By the will of John Bampton, Canon of Salisbury (d. 1751), an endowment was created for eight annual lectures to be delivered in St. Mary's, Oxford. Their subject is the exposition and defence of the Christian Faith as expressed in the Creeds, on the authority of Scripture and the Fathers. The first series was given in 1780. Since 1895 they have been delivered biennially. In recent times notable courses have been delivered by W. R. *Inge (1899), H. *Rashdall (1915), A. C. *Headlam (1920), N. P. *Williams (1924), K. E. *Kirk (1928), R. H. *Lightfoot (1934), and others. Another series of lectures ('Sarum Lectures'), open to non-Anglican speakers, has now been established from the Bampton fund; the first two lecturers were C. H. *Dodd and J. Daniélou, S.J.

BANCROFT, RICHARD (1544–1610), Abp. of *Canterbury. He was educated at Christ's College, and later at Jesus College, Cambridge. He first became well known between 1580 and 1590 as a stern opponent and persecutor of the *Puritans. In 1586 he was made treasurer of *St. Paul's Cathedral, and in 1587 Canon of *Westminster. In a sermon preached on 1 Jn. 4. 1 in 1589 at St. Paul's Cross in defence of the divine origin of episcopacy, he outspokenly condemned not only Puritanism but also *Presbyterianism. In 1597 he was appointed to the see of London, from which date, owing to J. *Whitgift's age and incapacity he virtually possessed archiepiscopal powers.

On Whitgift's death in 1604, he was translated to Canterbury. His refusal to compromise, not over-tactfully expressed, was one cause of the failure of the *Hampton Court Conference. The canons of 1604 were principally his work, and he secured their passage through *Convocation. As Abp., besides continuing relentlessly his anti-Puritan policy, he endeavoured, but without success, to secure the complete independence of the ecclesiastical courts from secular control. Shortly before his death, he assisted in the re-establishment of episcopacy in Scotland.

A. Peel (ed.), *Tracts ascribed to Richard Bancroft* (1953); R. G. Usher, *Reconstruction of the English Church* (2 vols., 1910). S. B. Babbage, *Puritanism and Richard Bancroft* (1962).

BÁÑEZ, DOMINGO (1528–1604), *Thomist theologian. In his youth he studied philosophy at Salamanca, and in 1547 made his profession in the *Dominican Order. For some years he studied under Domingo *Soto, and held professorships in the Spanish universities of Ávila, Valladolid, and elsewhere. In 1577 he returned to Salamanca, was elected to the chief chair in 1580, and acquired a great reputation as an exponent of the traditional Scholastic theology, in which he usually followed St. Thomas down to the smallest details; and he took a prominent part in the Jesuit-Dominican controversy on *Grace. He was the director and confessor of St. *Teresa of Ávila, who relied on his counsel in her own interior life, and in her reform of the *Carmelites.

Works listed in Quétif–Échard, ii (1721), p. 352 f. V. Beltrán de Heredia, O.P., 'Actuación de Maestro Domingo Báñez en la universidad de Salamanca' in *La Ciencia Tomista*, xxv (1922), pp. 64–73, 208–40, xxvi (1922), pp. 63–73, 199–223, xxvii (1923), pp. 40–51, 361–74, xxviii (1923), pp. 36–47; id., 'El Maestro Fray Domingo Báñez y la inquisición española', ib., xxxvii (1928), pp. 289–309, xxxviii (1928), pp. 35–58, 171–86; id., 'Valor doctrinal de las lecturas del P. Báñez', ib., xxxix (1929), pp. 60–81; id., 'Vindicando la memoria del Maestro fray Domingo Báñez', ib., xl (1929), pp. 312–22; id., 'El Maestro Domingo Báñez', ib., xlvii (1933), pp. 26–39, 162–79. M. Lépée, *Báñez et Sainte Thérèse* 1947), esp. pp. 34–74, with bibl. p. 7 f. P. Mandonnet, O.P. in *D.T.C.*, ii (1905), cols. 140–5, s.v.; R. M. Martin, O.P., in *D.H.G.E.*, vi (1932), cols. 492–4, s.v., both with bibl.

BANGOR. Of the many places of this name, the three best known are:

(1) 'Bangor Fawr' in Carnarvonshire. The see was traditionally founded by the abbot-bishop, St. *Deiniol (d. 584?), but scarcely anything is known of it till Norman times. The cathedral was rebuilt by Bp. Anian (1267–1305) who baptized Edward II, but was burnt in 1402 by Owen Glendower, and lay in ruins until Bp. Henry Deane (d. 1503) began to rebuild the choir. The work was completed by Bp. Thomas Skevington (d. 1533), who had previously been Abbot of *Beaulieu. From 1716 to 1721 the see was filled by the notorious B. *Hoadley. (See also *Bangor, Use of*).

(2) 'Bangor Iscoed' in Flintshire. Here stood the greatest monastery of Wales, which at one time held 2,000 monks. The early

history of this Bangor is also uncertain; but its monks are known to have refused to co-operate with St. *Augustine at the close of the 6th cent. In 603 the Saxons under Ethelfrid of Northumbria put to death 1,200 of its monks. Little or nothing of the abbey exists to-day.

(3) Bangor in Co. Down, Ireland. St. *Comgall founded an abbey here in 559, from which many daughter monasteries arose, so that at his death (601) he ruled 3,000 monks. It was the original home of St. *Columbanus and St. *Gall. After it had been plundered by the Danes in 824 it remained derelict until rebuilt on a magnificent scale in the 12th cent. It soon decayed again, however. From 1469 *Franciscans were in possession, and a century later the *Augustinians. Very little of the abbey remains.

See also foll. entries.

On (1), B. Willis, *Survey of the Cathedral Church of Bangor* (1721). A. I. Pryce, *The Diocese of Bangor in the XVIth Century, being a Digest of the Registers of the Bishops, 1512-1646* (Bangor, 1923); *The Diocese of Bangor during the Three Centuries, 1600-1899* (Cardiff, 1929). Rose Graham in *D.H.G.E.*, vi (1932), col. 494 f., s.v.
On (2), Rose Graham in *D.H.G.E.*, vi (1932), col. 502, s.v.
On (3), F. O'Brian, O.F.M., in *D.H.G.E.*, vi (1932), cols. 497-502, s.v.

BANGOR, Antiphonary of.

This *Antiphonary, written in the monastery at the Irish Bangor between 680 and 691, passed to *Bobbio, whence Federigo Borromeo transferred it in 1609 to the *Ambrosiana at Milan (where it is now Cod. C.5 inf.). It is the only surviving liturgical authority for the choir office in the Celtic Church. The familiar hymn 'Sancti venite, Christi Corpus sumite' (Eng. trans. by J. M. *Neale 'Draw nigh and take the body of the Lord', *English Hymnal* 307) is taken from this source.

Crit. ed. by F. E. Warren (H.B.S., iv and x; 1893-5). F. *Cabrol, O.S.B., in *D.A.C.L.*, ii (pt. 1; 1910), cols. 183-91. See also bibl. to *Celtic Church*.

BANGOR, Use of.

Of the pre-Reformation liturgical 'Use of [Welsh] Bangor' referred to by T. *Cranmer in the preface to the 1549 BCP (see *Concerning the Service of the Church*) nothing definite can be discovered. It is likely that it preserved ancient Celtic elements and a calendar rich in Welsh saints. Earlier liturgists thought that it had survived in a MS. Missal in use at Oswestry (then in the diocese of St. Asaph) in 1554; but it now seems clear that this missal attests a predominantly *'Sarum Use'.

BANGORIAN CONTROVERSY, The.

The dispute which followed the sermon preached by B. *Hoadly, Bp. of *Bangor, on 31 Mar. 1717 before George I on 'The Nature of the Kingdom of Christ', endeavouring to prove from the text, 'My kingdom is not of this world' (Jn. 18. 36), that the Gospels afford no warrant for any visible Church authority. The subject is said to have been suggested by the King. The sermon, which was immedi-

ately published, provoked a large number of pamphlets attacking Hoadly. Among his more formidable antagonists were W. *Law, in his *Three Letters to the Bishop of Bangor* (1717-1719), and T. *Sherlock. On 3 May 1717 the Lower House of *Convocation appointed a committee to consider the sermon, which reported on 10 May. When the Lower House resolved to send its findings to the Upper House, the King, to save Hoadly from synodical condemnation, which would have emphasized the opposition of the clergy to the government, prorogued Convocation, which did not meet again, except formally, until 1852.

The fullest bibliography is that by T. Herne, 'An Account of all the considerable pamphlets that have been published on either Side in the Present Controversy between the Bishop of Bangor, and Others to the End of the Year MDCCXIX' in *The Works of Benjamin Hoadley*, publd. by his son John Hoadley (1773), ii, pp. 381-401, and i, pp. 689-701. See also ib., ii, pp. 379-990 and passim; J. O. Nash-C. *Gore, *William Law's Defence of Church Principles* (Westminster Library [1893]).

BANNERS, Processional.

A banner was originally the standard of a king or prince providing a rallying point for his forces in battle. Christians of the 7th cent. had seen the symbolism of this, and were using crosses with red streamers (*vexilla*) attached for street processions in Rome. (Cf. the contemporary hymn *Vexilla Regis prodeunt*.) Medieval banners bore the armorial designs of knights and were not apparently used exclusively for Church functions.

BANNS OF MARRIAGE.

The custom of announcing a forthcoming marriage during Divine Service was probably taken over from pre-Christian practice, but it seems to have developed esp. after *Charlemagne's order for inquiry before marriage into possible consanguinity between the parties. The practice was enjoined by the Synod of *Westminster of 1200 and the *Lateran Council of 1215. The BCP regards the publication of banns as the normal prelude to marriage, though the obtaining of a licence is a civil and canonical equivalent. Under the Marriage Act of 1823 they must be published in an audible manner in the parish church or in some public chapel on three Sundays preceding the marriage. If the persons to be married dwell in different parishes or chapelries, publication must take place in both. The clergyman is entitled to seven days' notice of the first publication; and if the marriage is not solemnized within three months, republication is necessary. In certain circumstances, banns may be published by a *lay reader. See also *Marriage Licenses*.

H. W. Cripps, *A Practical Treatise on the Law relating to the Church and Clergy* (ed. 8 by K. M. Macmorran, 1937), pp. 540-7 and 551.

BAPTISM.

The *Sacramental rite which admits a candidate to the Christian Church. Acc. to Jn. 3. 5, Christ announced the necessity of a spiritual regeneration 'of water and the

Spirit' in His conversation with Nicodemus, and it has been commonly held that He instituted the Sacrament either at an unspecified date before His Passion or after His Resurrection, when He gave the disciples the command to baptize in the threefold Name (Mt. 28. 19). Many modern critics, indeed, have denied the institution of the Sacrament by Christ, together with the historicity of Mt. 28. 19, and even in a few cases the authenticity of the text. Orthodox Christians, however, have from the beginning attached the highest importance to Baptism and believed that in doing so they were carrying out the command of Christ. Counterparts to Christian Baptism in its outward form have been found in the initiation rites of Jewish proselytes as well as of the mystery religions, and Christians have often seen the Sacrament foreshadowed in the Flood, in the passage through the Red Sea, in the rite of circumcision, and in other OT figures. The two constituent parts of the Sacrament, water and the Trinitarian formula, are both contained in the NT (Jn. 3. 5, Mt. 28. 19). It has been suggested on the basis of several passages in Acts (2. 38, 10. 48, 19. 5) that Baptism in the primitive Church was 'in the Name of the Lord Jesus'. The fact, however, that at least from the end of the 1st cent. Baptism has been regularly administered in the threefold Name has led many theologians to another interpretation acc. to which these passages are not a baptismal formula but are intended to distinguish between the Christian Baptism and that of John. From our Lord's words to Nicodemus it would seem that Baptism is necessary for salvation. It must be preceded by faith (Acts 8. 13, 10. 33) and repentance (Acts 2. 38), and acc. to St. Paul effects and represents the believer's union with Christ through which he participates in His death and resurrection (Rom. 6. 4), is cleansed from his sins (1 Cor. 6. 11), and incorporated into the Body of Christ (1 Cor. 12. 13). Though Infant Baptism is not mentioned in the NT it is perhaps implied in passages such as Mt. 19. 14, Acts 16. 33, and 1 Tim. 2. 4. See *Infant Baptism*.

The rites of Baptism were developed in the early Church. In the 'Two Ways' of the *Didache* the principal duties of the candidates for Baptism and the method of administering it by triple immersion or infusion on the head are outlined. This triple immersion is also attested by *Tertullian (Adversus Prax.* 26), who in his *De Baptismate* and *De Corona Militis* describes the other parts of the rite, such as the preparatory fast and vigil, the confession of sins, the renunciation of the devil and, after the immersion, the imposition of hands and the symbolic meal of milk and honey. In the early Church Baptism was normally conferred by the Bishop, and closely associated with *Confirmation and the Eucharist. From the 2nd–4th cents. it was given only at *Easter and *Pentecost; in the 4th cent. the Feast of the *Epiphany was introduced as an additional date in the East, whence it passed to Sicily, Africa, and Spain. In Spain and Gaul *Christmas and certain other Feasts were also added, though the Popes St. *Siricius and St. *Leo protested against these innovations. In cases of necessity, however, Baptism might be administered at any time and by any Christian, though, acc. to Tertullian, the *Apostolic Constitutions*, and the 'Fourth Council of *Carthage', not by women. A practice which was very general in the first four or five cents. was the delay of Baptism till death was believed to be imminent, for fear of the responsibilities incurred by it. In this case Baptism was conferred without ceremonies, but regarded as inferior to regular Baptism and constituted a canonical impediment debarring the persons thus baptized, who were called 'clinici' (Gk. κλίνη, 'bed'), from ordination to the priesthood. Clinical Baptism gradually fell into desuetude owing esp. to the increasing practice of Infant Baptism and the development of the penitential system.

The theology of Baptism was elucidated by the 3rd cent. controversy on the validity of heretical Baptism. The general practice of the Church in the West came to be to admit persons baptized in heretical sects by mere imposition of hands. Probably on account of a passage from Tertullian (*De Baptismo*, 15), which asserted that the true Baptism was to be found only in the Catholic Church, the Church in N. Africa followed the custom of re-baptizing heretics. This practice was strongly supported by St. *Cyprian and confirmed by two Councils at Carthage in 255 and 256. When the decisions of the latter were submitted to Pope St. *Stephen he refused to sanction rebaptism and also threatened the African bishops with excommunication if they continued the practice. The controversy was stopped by the deaths of Stephen (257) and Cyprian (258) and a fresh outbreak of persecution, though each party continued to follow its own custom. The dispute was revived in the beginning of the 4th cent. by the *Donatists, who held Baptism to be invalid if conferred by a heretical or even an unworthy Catholic minister. The Council of *Arles in 314 opposed this view by declaring heretical Baptism valid if conferred in the name of the Trinity, and this teaching came to be generally accepted by the whole Church esp. through the influence of St. *Augustine. He established the dependence of the validity of the Sacrament on the correct form prescribed by Christ, regardless of the faith or worthiness of the minister ('*non cogitandum quis det, sed quid det*'). In defending the propriety of Infant Baptism against the *Pelagians, he also maintained that one of the chief effects of the Sacrament was the removal of the stain of *Original Sin on the soul which bars even the new-born child from the Kingdom of Heaven, thereby developing earlier teaching from NT times, acc. to which the remission of Actual Sins, the infusion of grace and the incorporation into the Church had been generally recognized as results of Baptism. The doctrine of the Baptismal *character (Gk. σφραγίς) marking the baptized soul in a special way, which had been adumbrated by *Hermas and in the 'Acts of *Thomas' and developed in the 4th cent. by St. *Cyril of Jerusalem, was also perfected by St. Augustine. He held that the Holy Spirit produced in Baptism an effect independent of sanctifying grace. This 'character' marked the soul as the property of the Trinity, remained even with the apostate as the royal seal remained on a coin, and allowed the Christian soul to be recognized even in hell. The effects of Baptism were produced by God independently of the minister, '*ex opere operato*', by the application of the merits of Christ. St. Augustine allowed, however, the 'baptism of blood' by martyrdom and the 'baptism of desire' in certain cases as equivalents of the Sacrament.

The Augustinian doctrine was taken up and developed by the Schoolmen, esp. St. Thomas *Aquinas, who distinguished between the 'remote matter' of water and the 'proximate matter' of *immersion or *infusion. Though remitting both Original and Actual Sin and their punishment, Baptism did not efface the consequences of Original Sin in the natural order such as ignorance, suffering, concupiscence, and death. It conferred habitual grace, the infused virtues and the gifts of the Holy Ghost. The Baptismal character formed the Christian in the image of Christ and bestowed on him a certain participation in His priesthood.

The 16th cent. Reformers did not leave the medieval teaching on Baptism intact. The *Augsburg Confession contented itself with stating that Baptism was necessary to salvation, that by it the grace of God was offered, and that children were to be baptized and thus received into God's favour. M. *Luther sought to combine belief in the necessity of Baptism with his doctrine of justification by faith alone. Baptism was a promise of Divine grace after which a man's sins are no longer imputed to him. H. *Zwingli, on the other hand, denied the necessity of Baptism, seeing in it only a sign admitting man to the Christian community. J. *Calvin, though holding that Baptism gave man an assurance of pardon and of participation in the gifts of Christ, taught that it was efficacious only for the elect, since they alone have the faith without which the rite is worthless. The BCP preserved the traditional Catholic teaching. In the Orders for the Administration of Baptism it maintained the doctrine of Baptismal Regeneration, asserting that man is washed and sanctified with the Holy Ghost, delivered from the wrath of God, received into the ark of Christ's Church, accorded remission of sins, and made an heir of everlasting salvation. In the *Thirty-Nine Articles the teaching is less explicit, but they clearly exclude the Zwinglian view and regard Baptism as a 'sign of Regeneration' by which 'the promises of forgiveness of sin and of our adoption to be the sons of God by the Holy Ghost are visibly signed and sealed'. The doctrine of the RC Church was restated at the Council of *Trent, particular stress being laid on the fact that Baptism is not merely a sign of grace, but

actually contains and confers it on those who put no obstacle (*obex*) in its way, and that, further, it is the instrument used by God for the justification of infidels. The modern RC legislation concerning Baptism is contained in the C.I.C., cans. 737–79.

The rationalism of the 18th cent. contributed largely to the indifference towards Baptism in the Continental Protestant Churches as well as in the C of E. The revival of the Catholic doctrine of Baptismal Regeneration in the latter is due to the *Tractarian Movement, esp. E. B. *Pusey's three Tracts, Nos. 67–9. The *Gorham Case (q.v.) in 1850 attracted the attention of the general public to the question, and, though the secular authorities decided against the Catholic view, the latter has since become increasingly prevalent in the C of E. In recent times the need for some restatement of Baptismal theology has been widely felt. This has been esp. prompted by the custom of presenting for Baptism children from homes where there is little prospect of their having a Christian upbringing.

The most elaborate form of the rite in modern W. usage is in the RC Church. Here solemn Baptism may be administered at any time by the parish priest, with water which has been specially blessed on *Holy Saturday or *Whit Saturday. The chief preliminary ceremonies are the *exorcisms, the placing of *salt in the candidate's mouth, the anointing with spittle, the *renunciation of Satan, his works and his pomps, and the anointing with the '*oil of catechumens'. Then follows the declaration of faith and the triple pouring of water on the candidate's head accompanied by the Baptismal Formula. The anointing with chrism and the placing of a white veil on the candidate's head and of a candle in his hand complete the ceremony.

The rite of the C of E is much simpler. Acc. to the BCP, Baptism should be administered after the Second Lesson at Morning or Evening Prayer. After several prayers recited by the priest and a reading from the Gospel there follows the renunciation of the devil, the world, and the flesh, the confession of faith, the naming of the child by the *godparents and the *immersion in or *affusion of water, accompanied by the Baptismal formula, followed by a signing with the cross and concluding prayers. In conditional Baptism, which is given both in the RC Church and the C of E, when it is doubtful whether the candidate has already previously been validly baptized, most of the ceremonies are omitted and the Baptismal Formula is pronounced in a conditional form, beginning in the C of E 'If thou art not already baptized, I baptize thee'. See also foll. entry.

The chief Patristic authorities are *Didache, vii; *Ep. Barnabae*, xi; Tertullian, *De Baptismo*; *Cyprian, *Epistulae*; ps.-Cyprian, *De Rebaptismate*; Cyril of Jerusalem, *Catecheses*, xix–xxi; Ambrose, *De Mysteriis* and *De Sacramentis*; several treatises of Gregory of Nyssa and St. Augustine; *Pacian, *De Baptismo*; Maximus of Turin, *De Baptismo*; *Ildefonsus, *De Cognitione Baptismi*. The classical medieval treatment is in St. *Thomas Aquinas, *S.T.*, III. qq. 66–71; cf. also *Alexander of Hales, *S.T.*, IV. qq. 1–8, and St. *Bonaventura, *In quarto dist.*, 1–6.

G. *Cassander, De Baptismo Infantium Testimonia Veterum (1563); J. Busaeus, S.J., De Baptismi Necessitate (1589); W. *Wall, The History of Infant Baptism (2 vols., 1705); J. W. F. Höfling, Das Sacrament der Taufe (2 vols., 1846–8; Lutheran); E. B. Pusey, Scriptural Views of Holy Baptism (*Tracts for the Times, Nos. 67, 68, 69; all 1835); J. B. *Mozley, The Primitive Doctrine of Baptismal Regeneration (1856); id., A Review of the Baptismal Controversy (1862). J. Corblet, Histoire dogmatique, liturgique et archéologique du sacrament de baptême (2 vols., 1881–2); D. *Stone, Holy Baptism (Oxford Library of Practical Theology, 1899); H. Windisch, Taufe und Sünde im ältesten Christentum bis au, Origenes (1908); W. Heitmüller, Taufe und Abendmahl im Urchristentum (1911); A. d'Alès, Baptême et confirmation (1928; Eng. tr., 1929); R. *Reitzenstein, Die Vorgeschichte der christlichen Taufe (1929); P. Lundberg, La Typologie baptismale dans l'ancienne Église (Act. Semin. Neotest. Upsal. X, 1942); K. Barth, Die kirchliche Lehre von der Taufe (1943; Eng. tr., E. A. Payne, 1948); O. Cullmann, Die Tauflehre des Neuen Testaments (1948; Eng. tr., J. K. S. Reid, 1950); G. W. H. Lampe, The Seal of the Spirit (1951); A. Benoit, Le Baptême chrétien au second siècle. La théologie des pères (1953). J. G. Davies, The Architectural Setting of Baptism (1962).
Various authors in H.E.R.E., ii (1909), pp. 367–412 (on Christian and non-Christian Baptism), and in D.T.C., ii (1905), cols. 167–378; P. de Puniet, O.S.B., in D.A.C.L., it (pt. 1, 1910), cols. 251–346; A. Oepke, βάπτω, βαπτίζω, βαπτισμός, βάπτισμα, βαπτιστής in T.W.B., i (1933), pp. 527–544; J. Coppens in Dict. Bibl., Suppl. i (1928), cols. 852–924, all with bibls.
See also bibl. to Confirmation.

BAPTISM OF CHRIST, The. This event is recorded by the first three Evangelists and implied also by Jn., but each has significant differences of detail. Acc. to Mk. 1. 9–11, now usually considered the primary source for the event in the Gospels, Christ came to hear St. *John the Baptist and, like others, received baptism at his hands. The implied motive seems to be the deep, sympathetic interest which Jesus felt in the work of John and the fitting character of such baptism as a public profession of moral integrity. The vision of the opened heavens and the Divine Voice were the token of the Lord's Messiahship.

Among Patristic writers who regard the Lord's Baptism as instituting Christian Baptism are *Ambrose, In Luc., ii. 83, and *Chrysostom, Hom. in Mt. 12.3; cf. also St. *Thomas, S.T., III, lxvi, 2. J. Bornemann, Die Taufe Christi durch Johannes in der dogmatischen Beurteilung der christlichen Theologen der vier ersten Jahrhunderte (1896).

BAPTISTERY. A building connected with a church, in which the rite of *Baptism is administered. The earliest known baptistery is that at *Dura Europos (before A.D. 256). Another example is that at the *Lateran at *Rome, which has traditionally been held to date from the time of *Constantine I (much altered later). It is octagonal, with a low font in the centre, surrounded by eight columns and an ambulatory. The church of S. Costanza, orig. built as a tomb for the daughter of Constantine, is another round Roman edifice which was also formerly used as a baptistery. There are later examples at *Pisa, *Ravenna, Florence, Nocera, Tebessa, el-Kantara, Poitiers, and elsewhere. The erection of a separate structure was always confined to a few of the larger churches and none is later than c. 10th cent., when the practice of Baptism (by *affusion) in the church itself became virtually universal. In modern times a portion of the church, usually near the entrance, is often arranged as a baptistery.

J. Corblet, 'Des Lieux consacrés à l'administration du baptême' in Revue de l'Art Chrétien, xxiii (1877), pp. 276–81, xxiv (1877), pp. 112–82, 300–10, xxv (1878), pp. 26–49, 275–316. C. F. Rogers, 'Baptism and Christian Archaeology' in Studia Biblica et Ecclesiastica, v (Oxford, 1903), pp. 239–361, esp. pp. 321–59, passim. J. G. Davies, The Origin and Development of Early Christian Church Architecture (1952), pp. 20 f. (with plan of that at Dura Europus), 58, 101–7. On the famous Baptistery at the Lateran, see also G. B. Giovenale, Il Battistero Lateranense nelle recenti indagini della Pont. Commissione di archeologia sacra (1929). A. Nesbitt in D.C.A., i (1875), pp. 173–8; H. *Leclercq, O.S.B., in D.A.C.L., ii (pt. 1; 1910), cols. 382–469; J. Sauer in L.Th.K., i (1930), cols. 954–6; E. Josi and E. Lavagnino in E.C., ii (1949), cols. 1050–56. See also J. G. Davies, cit. s.v. 'Baptism'.

BAPTISTS. One of the largest Protestant and Free Church communions, to be found in every Continent. The total membership c. 1950 was probably some thirteen to fourteen million, with a community strength at least three times as large. They trace their origins in modern times to the action of John *Smyth, a *Separatist exile in Amsterdam who, in 1609, reinstituted the baptism of conscious believers as the basis of the fellowship of a gathered Church. But Smyth was under *Mennonite influence, and Baptist origins have often been traced back through the *Anabaptist wing of the Continental Reformation to the protests of medieval sects against prevailing baptismal theory and practice and thence to the days of the early Church and the New Testament. Smyth and his associates were concerned to re-establish the rite of baptism acc. to its NT meaning, in the interests of a true doctrine of the nature of the Church.

The first Baptist Church in England consisted of certain members of Smyth's Church who returned to London in 1612 under the leadership of Thomas *Helwys. From this a number of other churches sprang in Stuart and Commonwealth times. They were *Arminian in theology and their polity was of a connexional kind. They became known as 'General Baptists'. In 1633 the adoption of believers' baptism by a group of *Calvinistic London Separatists, who were members of the Church which had had Henry Jacob as pastor, led to the rise of 'Particular Baptist' Churches in many parts of the country. About the same time *immersion became the usual mode of baptism, instead of *affusion or sprinkling, again in obedience to the NT. Calvinistic Baptist Churches were in general independent or congregational in polity, but from Commonwealth times Associations of Churches covering wide areas of the country became general, and these Associations have continued a vital part of Baptist Church life.

Many Baptists were associated with the more radical spiritual and political movements of the 17th cent. They were pioneers in pleas for freedom of conscience and religious liberty. After the Restoration they moved closer in spirit and temper to the *Presbyterians and *Independents and became recognized as one of the *Three Denominations of Protestant

Dissenters. John *Bunyan was an outstanding figure among them and was important not only for his writings, but because he stood for local Church fellowships which should include Baptists and Paedobaptists. From the middle of the 17th cent. there were Baptist churches in the American colonies. The settlement of Roger *Williams at Providence, Rhode Island, and the Church formed there in 1639 on Baptist principles is generally regarded as the beginning of American Baptist history. A small 17th cent. group who became known as Sabbatarian or Seventh Day Baptists, and whose descendants are still represented in both England and America, regarded the Fourth Commandment as requiring services on the seventh not the first day of the week.

In the 18th cent. many of the General Baptist Churches in England came under *Unitarian influences and ultimately ceased to maintain their witness to believers' baptism. But Dan Taylor (1738–1816), under the stimulus of the *Evangelical Revival, formed a so-called New Connexion among them which maintained a vigorous life in the eastern midlands, and a century later united with the main stream of Baptist witness. The *Baptist Missionary Society, formed in 1792 by ministers of the Northamptonshire Association of Particular Baptist Churches at the call of William *Carey, initiated the modern movement of missionary expansion among Protestant Churches. Northamptonshire Baptists had been stirred by reports of the *Great Awakening in New England. This revival quickened the Baptist Churches of America and led to the beginnings of the rapid and spectacular growth of Baptists in that continent. Baptist preachers were in the van as the frontier was carried westwards. As a result of their missionary zeal Baptists became the largest religious community in many of the southern States and by c. 1950 there were some 12,000,000 Baptists in America. They are organized in four Conventions: the Southern Convention (the strongest and most conservative) and the Northern, and two Negro Conventions. Over 66 per cent of the total negro Church membership is Baptist. American Baptists have also shown enthusiasm for foreign missions, in which matter Adoniram *Judson, of *Burma, was their pioneer.

The rigid Calvinism of the 18th cent. was gradually modified not only in America, but in England, though not without some protests. There remained a number of so-called Strict Baptist Churches, strongly Calvinist in theology, and unwilling to open even the Lord's Table to other than baptized believers. In the 19th cent., however, most Baptist Churches adopted open communion; many also adopted 'open membership', thus maintaining and extending the tradition which went back to Bunyan. The increase in their numbers more than kept pace with the growth in population, and from their ranks came outstanding preachers such as Robert *Hall, C. H. *Spurgeon, Alexander *Maclaren, and John *Clifford. The Baptist General Union, formed in 1813,

was gradually transformed into the Baptist Union of Great Britain and Ireland. Its modern developments owed much to the leadership of J. H. *Shakespeare (1857–1928), who was secretary for twenty-five years. There are in Britain over 340,000 Church members, organized into 3,600 Churches, with nearly 2,000 ministers. Baptists shared in the *Free Church Council movement and are members of the Free Church Federal Council, the *British Council of Churches, and the *World Council of Churches. They have shown hesitation about schemes for organic union, partly because of their concern regarding their witness to believers' baptism; but they have always been eager for co-operation and fellowship with their fellow Christians. The Baptists of Scotland were much influenced by the life and teaching of Archibald McLean (1733–1812). He and his followers attempted a very close following of the NT in doctrine and practice and were at one time known as 'Scotch Baptists' or '*Sandemanian Baptists'. Their work provided one of the sources of the *Disciples of Christ. Baptists have been numerous in Wales since John Myles or Miles (1621–84) organized the first church at Ilston (1649) and Vavasour Powell (1617–70) acted as the leader of a band of itinerant evangelists. Their most famous preacher was Christmas Evans (1766–1838). There has been a considerable emigration of Baptists from Wales to the United States. Both Scottish and Welsh Baptists have, on the whole, been more conservative theologically and in Church practice than those of England.

In 1834 a Baptist Church was formed in Hamburg under the leadership of J. G. Oncken (1800–84) and from this came a widespread Baptist movement on the Continent of Europe. It spread from German-speaking to Slav-speaking peoples. Baptists were severely persecuted in Czarist Russia. They increased in numbers in the early years of the Soviet régime, but have more recently suffered from the general restrictions on religious freedom. Their present strength is uncertain, but probably considerable. Almost all the Baptist groups on the continent of Europe are strongly Biblicist. In 1905 a Baptist World Alliance was formed at a congress in London, with the aims of promoting unity and fellowship among the Baptists of the world, securing and defending religious freedom, and proclaiming Baptist principles. Its present headquarters is in Washington, D.C.

In spite of their variety and individualism, most Baptists have remained strongly attached to the truths of evangelical Christianity. In their worship they follow in general the Reformed tradition. Their polity is a modified form of independency. Their ministers, or pastors, receive, in most lands, a careful training. Their oldest college in Britain traces its history back to the 1679 bequest of a Bristol writing-master. Regent's Park College, of which H. Wheeler *Robinson was principal from 1920 to 1942, is now located in Oxford. Many colleges and universities in America are under Baptist auspices, and in India Carey's college at Serampore remains the only institution able to confer divinity degrees.

T. Armitage, *A History of the Baptists, traced with their Vital Principles and Practices, from the Time of our Lord and Saviour Jesus Christ, to the Year 1886* (New York and London, 1888). T. Crosby, *The History of the English Baptists from the Reformation to the Beginning of the Reign of King George I* (4 vols., 1738–40). J. Ivimey, *A History of the English Baptists* (4 vols., 1811–30). B. Evans, *The Early English Baptists* (2 vols., 1862–4). W. T. Whitley, *A History of the British Baptists* (1923); A. C. Underwood, *A History of the English Baptists* (1947). W. T. Whitley, *The Baptists of London, 1612–1928* [1928]. J. H. Rushbrooke, *The Baptists in the Continent of Europe* (1923); id., *Some Chapters of European Baptist History* (1929; new material on Russia). A. H. Newman, *A History of the Baptist Churches in the United States* (American Church History, Series ii; New York, 1894). E. R. Fitch, *The Baptists of Canada* (Toronto, 1911). H. J. Batts, *The Story of 100 Years, 1820–1920.* The History of the Baptist Church in South Africa (Cape Town, 1922). W. T. Whitley, *A Baptist Bibliography* (2 vols., 1916–22). R. G. Torbet, *History of the Baptists* (Philadelphia, Pa., 1950). W. J. McGlothlin, *Baptist Confessions of Faith* (Philadelphia, Pa. [1911]). H. Wheeler Robinson, 'Baptist Principles before the Rise of Baptist Churches' in *The Baptists of Yorkshire.* Being the Centenary Memorial Volume of the Yorkshire Baptist Association (1912), pp. 3–50. E. A. Payne, *The Fellowship of Believers.* Baptist Thought and Practice Yesterday and Today (1944). See also publications of the Baptist Historical Society, 1908 ff.; for German Baptists, see bibl. to *Tunkers*.

BAPTIST MISSIONARY SOCIETY. It was founded at Kettering, Northants, on 2 Oct. 1792. The first secretary was Andrew Fuller (1754–1815). Its first missionary, W. *Carey, to whose earnest pleading the Society owed its origin, went in 1793 to India, where the major part of the work of the Society is still done. The other main fields have been: (1) Jamaica, where William Knibb (1803–45) and other missionaries gave vigorous support to the cause of slave emancipation, (2) China, where Timothy Richard (1845–1919) was an outstanding pioneer, and (3) Cameroons and Congo. George Grenfell (1849–1906) and Holman Bentley (1855–1906) played notable parts in the opening up of the Congo. The Society now has more than 400 missionaries engaged in evangelistic, educational, and medical work.

Essays in J. B. Myers (ed.), *The Centenary Volume of the Baptist Missionary Society* (1892); others in the B.M.S. commemorative vol., *Ter-Jubilee Celebrations, 1942–4* (1945).

BARABBAS. The 'robber' (λῃστής, Jn. 18. 40) whom *Pilate released from prison to the Jews instead of Christ (Mk. 15. 6–15). It is possible (on the evidence of certain MSS.), but unlikely, that his real name was 'Jesus Barabbas', Barabbas in that case being a patronymic.

BARBARA, St. Acc. to tradition, the daughter of a pagan of Nicomedia, who on being converted to the Christian faith was handed over by her father to the prefect and martyred. A circumstantial account of her martyrdom is contained in the *Golden Legend.* She is one of the fourteen *Auxiliary Saints. Her prayers are sought esp. as a protection against thunderstorms and fire; and, by an

obvious extension of this idea, she is venerated as the patroness of artillerymen and firemen. Feast day, 4 Dec.

The earliest accounts, apparently written in Gk., are now lost; various versions in Syr., Lat., and other languages survive. A late Gk. text is printed in J. P. Migne, *PG*, cxvi, 301–16; another, prob. earlier, ed. A. Wirth, *Danae in christlichen Legenden* (Prague, etc., 1892), pp. 103–12. Syr. text ed. Agnes Smith Lewis, *Studia Sinaitica*, ix (1900), pp. 101–10, with Eng. tr., x (1900), pp. 77–84; W. Weyh, *Der syrische Barbara-Legende* (1912). Lat. text in P. Paschini, *S. Barbara.* Note agiografiche ('Lateranum', 1927), pp. 38–52, with reff. S. Peine, *St. Barbara, die Schutzheilige der Bergleute und der Artillerie, und ihre Darstellung in der Kunst* (1896). Comte de Lapparent, 'Sur quelques représentations de Sainte Barbe' in *Bulletin Monumental*, lxxxvi (1927), pp. 149–53.

BARBAROSSA. See *Frederick I*.

BARBE. (Fr. 'uncle', lit. 'the bearded'). A title of respect used by the *Waldenses of their preachers.

BARBERINI. A Roman family of Tuscan descent, several of whose members filled important offices in the Church in Italy in the 17th cent. In 1623 Maffeo Barberini was elected Pope as *Urban VIII. Francesco Barberini the elder (1597–1679), who built the fine Palazzo Barberini in Rome, founded in 1627 the 'Biblioteca Barberina', containing the famous collection of MSS. which passed to the Vatican Library in 1902. Their reckless plundering of ancient monuments for their designs, e.g. Urban VIII's conversion of the brass tubes supporting the roof of the *Pantheon into the canopy for the high altar at St. Peter's and cannons for the Castel S. Angelo, gave rise to the *mot* 'Quod non fecerunt barbari, fecerunt Barberini'.

T. H. Didier and F. Bonnard in *D.H.G.E.*, vi (1932), cols. 640–5, s.v. G. Graglia in *E.C.*, ii (1949), cols. 825–7, s.v., with bibl.

BARCLAY, JOHN (1734–98), founder of the '*Bereans' (q.v.) or 'Barclayites'. The son of a farmer at Muthill in Perthshire, he was educated at St. Andrews university, where he came under the influence of Archibald Campbell, (1691–1756), prof. of Church history, whose teaching was attracting attention through its denial of natural theology. In 1759 Barclay was licensed by the presbytery of Auchterarder, and soon afterwards became assistant to James Jobson, the incumbent of Errol, a strong Evangelical. Differences of opinion with Jobson led him to move to Fettercairn, Kincardine, in 1763, where he was appointed assistant to A. Dow and won the hearts of the parishioners through pastoral zeal and eloquence. In 1766 Barclay published *Rejoice Evermore, or Christ All in All*, in which he expounded a doctrine of immediate Divine revelation. Censure for heresy by the presbytery followed, and in consequence, despite a petition to the Crown from virtually all the parishioners, he was not appointed to succeed Dow on his death in 1772. Barclay then made his way to Edinburgh, where he gained only a small following. Unable to procure ordination in Scotland, he went to Newcastle, and here he succeeded in being regularly ordained in 1773. Returning soon afterwards to Edinburgh, he constituted a new Church, known as the Berean Assembly, from its zeal for study of the Bible (cf. Acts 17. 10 f.). He laboured on behalf of the community in considerable poverty, but with great earnestness, and continued to publish writings. The chief was a collected work (1776) containing *inter alia* his earlier *The Psalms, paraphrased according to the New Testament Interpretation* (1766), illustrating Barclay's beliefs on Scripture. In 1776 Barclay went to London to propagate his doctrines, where he seems to have met with considerable success, and established Berean communities both in London and at Bristol. He returned to Scotland in 1778, continuing to work and travel for his cause, despite very straitened conditions, till his death.

The *Works of John Barclay* [i.e. his Essays], ed. J. Thomson–D. McMillan (Glasgow, 1852), with 'A Short Account of the Early Part of the Life of Mr. John Barclay', pp. 11–21. A. Miller in *H.E.R.E.*, ii (1909), pp. 519–23, s.v. 'Bereans'.

BARCLAY, ROBERT (1648–90), Scottish *Quaker apologist. He was the son of David Barclay (1610–86) who served as a soldier under *Gustavus Adolphus, assisted in the defeat of Montrose before Inverness (1646) and was one of the thirty Scottish Members of Parliament under O. *Cromwell (1654 and 1656). Robert was born at Gordonstown, Morayshire, and educated at the (RC) Scottish College at *Paris. His father having declared his adhesion to the Quakers in 1666, Robert followed his example in 1667. He soon acquired a wide learning which, combined with considerable intellectual powers, made him the most weighty of all Quaker theologians. In 1673 he published his *Catechism and Confession of Faith*. In 1676 there followed his principal work, his 'Apology', written to support fifteen Quaker 'Theses Theologiae' which he had defended at Aberdeen and circulated in English, Latin, French, and Dutch. It was originally printed in Latin at Amsterdam as *Theologiae Verae Christianae Apologia* (1676); the English version, *Apology for the True Christian Religion, as the same is set forth and preached by the People called in Scorn 'Quakers'*, first appeared in 1678. Its impressive and eloquent defence of the doctrine of the '*Inner Light' against the sufficiency of external authorities, including the Bible, made it the classical exposition of Quaker principles. The work also included a strong attack on *Calvinism. During his travels in Holland and Germany (1676) Barclay won the sympathy of Elizabeth, the Princess Palatine, for Quaker principles; and on his return he came into favour with the Duke of York (later *James II), whom he believed to be a genuine advocate of toleration. He was thus able to be of service to W. *Penn in his foundation of Pennsylvania, and in 1683 Barclay was himself appointed governor of East New Jersey (U.S.A.) which was given a constitution

on Quaker principles. In the course of his life Barclay often suffered imprisonment for his doctrines. His other writings include *The Anarchy of Ranters* (1676), *The Apology Vindicated* (1679), and *The Possibility and Necessity of an Inward and Immediate Revelation* (1686).

His works were issued in 1692 in a collected folio volume, with the title *Truth Triumphant*. They were republd. in 3 vols. in 1717–18. The *Apology* has often been reprinted.

BAR-COCHBA (Aram. כוכבא בר, i.e. 'son of a star'; cf. Num. 24. 17). The leader of a Jewish rebellion in Palestine in A.D. 132. Its purpose was to resist the project of the Emp. *Hadrian to rebuild *Jerusalem as a Graeco-Roman city, with a temple of Jupiter on the site of the former Jewish Temple. See *Aelia Capitolina*. Bar-cochba claimed to be, and was accepted as, the Messiah. A fierce guerrilla war was waged from 132 to 135 in which both sides suffered severe losses. The name Bar-cochba is found only in Christian sources. By the Jews the name is given as Simeon.

E. *Schürer, *Geschichte des jüdischen Volkes*, i (ed. 3, 1901), pp. 682–5 and 695 (Eng. tr., i, div. 2 (1890), pp. 297–300 and 311). On MS. recently identified as his autograph, see J. T. Milik, 'Une Lettre de Siméon Bar Kokheba' in *R. Bibl.*, lx (1953), pp. 276–94.

BARDENHEWER, OTTO, (1851–1935), *Patristic scholar. Born at München-Gladbach, he was educated at Bonn and Würzburg universities, lectured at Munich from 1879 to 1884 and was professor of OT Exegesis at Münster i.W. from 1884 to 1886 and of NT Exegesis at Munich from 1886 to 1924. His *Patrologie* in a single volume appeared in 1894 (Eng. trans., 1908). This was followed by his more ambitious *Geschichte der altkirchlichen Literatur* (i, 1902, ed. 2, 1913; ii, 1903, ed. 2, 1914; iii, 1912, with additions, 1923; iv, 1924; v, 1932) which for its completeness, soundness of judgement and clarity of presentation is unsurpassed; it remains a standard work of reference. His other works include *Des heiligen Hippolytus von Rom Commentar zum Buche Daniel* (1877), *Polychronius, Bruder Theodors von Mopsuestia und Bischof von Apamea* (1879), and many contributions to *Biblische Studien*.

J. Sickenberger, *Erinnerungen an Otto Bardenhewer* (1937). E. Peterson in *E.C.*, ii (1949), col. 839 f.

BARDESANES (154–222), correctly 'Bar-Daisan', heretic. Acc. to Oriental writers, he was a native of *Edessa, who was converted to Christianity in 179, later excommunicated, and fled to Armenia *c.* 216. He probably taught a kind of astrological fatalism and was not, as traditionally supposed, a *Gnostic dualist. With the help of his son, Harmonius, he wrote a large collection of Syriac hymns through which he diffused his doctrines; and he may thus be considered the father of Syriac hymnology. A 'Dialogue of Destiny, or the Book of the Laws of the Lands' from which *Eusebius and other Christian Fathers preserve fragments (as from Περὶ εἱμαρμένης), has come down in the orig. Syriac. It is not impossible that the 'Acts of *Thomas' came from circles under his influence. Bardesanes held that Christ's Body was a phantom and that there would be no future resurrection, and apparently taught a form of emanationism. His disciples maintained a precarious existence for several centuries.

Early sources include *Eusebius, *H.E.*, IV, xxx, *Epiphanius, *Haer.*, lvi, and *Moses of Chorene (ii, 66). His 'Dialogue of Destiny', ed. W. *Cureton, *Spicilegium Syriacum* (London, 1855), pp. 1–21 (Syr.), with Eng. tr., pp. 1–34; later ed. F. Nau (Paris, 1899). A single quotation from his Hymns (150) is preserved by *Ephrem Syrus (*Opera*, ii, 483). There is a large modern literature, incl. works by A. Hahn, A. *Hilgenfeld, F. J. A. *Hort, F. C. *Burkitt, W. *Bousset, and others, much of it cited by H. E. W. Turner, *The Pattern of Christian Truth* (1954), pp. 90–4; F. Haase, *Zur Bardesanischen Gnosis* (T.U., xxxiv, 4, 1910); H. H. Schaeder, 'Bardesanes von Edessa in der Überlieferung der griechischen und syrischen Kirche' in *Z.K.G.*, li (1932), pp. 21–73. Bardenhewer, i, pp. 364–8; Altaner (1950), p. 106. F. Nau in *D.T.C.*, ii (1904), cols. 391–401, s.v.

BAR HEBRAEUS (1226–86). The name by which Abû-l-Farag̣, a *Jacobite Syrian bishop and philosopher, is commonly known. He was the son of a physician of Jewish descent who was converted to the Christian faith. After studying medicine at Antioch and Tripoli, he was consecrated bishop in 1246, and in 1264 he became Primate of the East, with his residence at the monastery of Mar Mattai near Mosul. His travels as primate enabled him to consult libraries in many distant parts, and out of the vast erudition thus acquired he composed a large *corpus* of writings in which he transmitted his predecessors' learning by condensation or reproduction. Most of his works were written in *Syriac, by that date a dead language, but a few in Arabic. They include the 'Granary of Mysteries' ('Horreum Mysteriorum'), a collection of *scholia on the Bible; the 'Cream of Science' (still unedited), a vast encyclopaedic work in which he shows himself an Aristotelian of the school of *Avicenna and the Arabs; and the 'Chronicle' which professes to give a complete history of the world from the creation.

Autobiography publ. by J. S. *Assemani, *Bibliotheca Orientalis*, ii (Rome, 1721), pp. 248–63. J. Göttsberger, *Barhebräus und seine Scholia zur heiligen Schrift* (Biblische Studien v, Hftt. 4–5, 1900). A. *Baumstark, *Geschichte der syrischen Literatur* (1922). p. 136. J. Nau in *D.T.C.*, ii (1905), cols. 401–6, s.v., with further bibl.

BARLAAM AND JOASAPH, Sts., two subjects of a popular medieval legend. It having been prophesied in the infancy of *Joasaph (or 'Josaphat'), the son of a heathen Indian king, that he would be converted to Christianity, he was shut up in a palace so that he should know nothing of the facts or evils of life. Thence he escaped, and was found and won to the Christian faith by the hermit Barlaam. For a time he ruled the kingdom with his father, but later also retired to the wilderness with Barlaam.

The story, which dates apparently from the 8th cent., was written to glorify Christian monasticism. It is divided into three parts:

(1) narrative; (2) speeches, containing expositions of Christian doctrine and quotations from early Christian writers, including the 'Apology' of *Aristides; and (3) the 'Apologues', fables or parables. It seems established that it is based on Buddhist sources. Traditionally it has been attributed (prob. rightly, acc. to J. M. Hoeck, O.S.B.) to St. *John of Damascus. See also *Joasaph, St.*

The names of Barlaam and Josaphat were added to the Roman *Martyrology by C. *Baronius. Their feast is observed on 27 Nov. In W. calendars another St. Barlaam, a martyr, is commemorated on 9 Nov.

Ed. princeps of Gk. text in J. F. Boissonade, *Anecdota Graeca*, iv (1832), pp. 1–365; repr. in J. P. Migne, *PG*, xcvi, 857–1250. Modern ed., with Eng. tr., by G. R. Woodward and H. Mattingly (Loeb, 1914). Georgian text ed. E. Takaishvili (Tiflis, 1895); Eth. text from MS. B.Mus., Or. 699, ed. E. A. Wallis Budge (2 vols., Cambridge, 1923). R. L. Wolff, 'Barlaam and Joasaph' in *Harvard Theological Review*, xxxii (1939), pp. 131–9 (ascribes work to St. Euthymius, a monk of Mt. *Athos, d. 1028). J. M. Hoeck, O.S.B., 'Stand und Aufgaben der Damaskenos-Forschung' in *O.C.P.* xvii (1951), p. 32 f. J. van den Gheyn in *D.T.C.*, ii (1905), cols. 410–16, H. *Leclercq, O.S.B., in *D.A.C.L.*, vii (pt. 2, 1927), cols. 2539–54, and G. Bardy in *D.H.G.E.*, vi (1932), cols. 813–15.

BARLOW, THOMAS (1607–91), Bp. of *Lincoln. At *Oxford he became Librarian of the *Bodleian (1642), Provost of Queen's (1657), and Lady Margaret Professor of Divinity (1660). Theologically he was a definite *Calvinist, but, by persistent trimming, he kept his offices through the many changes of the century. He became Bp. of Lincoln in 1675, but there is reason to doubt whether he ever visited his cathedral. His violent anti-Papalism found full scope in the *Popish Plot, but, on the accession of *James II, he professed his loyal affection. Undismayed, he took the oath to William III without demur. His published works include a treatise on natural theology entitled *Exercitationes aliquot metaphysicae de Deo* (1637), *Plain reasons why a Protestant of the Church of England should not turn Roman Catholic* (1688) and *Cases of Conscience* (1692).

The Genuine Remains of . . . Dr. Thomas Barlow (1693, ed. P. Pett). A. *Wood, *Athenae Oxonienses* (ed. 3, P. Bliss), iv (1820), cols. 333–41. S. Levy, 'Bishop Barlow on the "Case of the Jews" ' in *Transactions of the Jewish Historical Society of England*, iii (1899), pp. 151–6. E. Venables in *D.N.B.*, iii (1885), pp. 224–9.

BARLOW, WILLIAM (d. 1568), Bp. of *Chichester. In early life he was an *Augustinian canon, and an opponent of T. *Wolsey. He showed Protestant tendencies as early as 1529, when a series of his tracts was condemned, but he was reconciled to the court and used on diplomatic business. He became successively Bp.-elect of St. Asaph (1535–6), Bp. of *St. Davids (1536), and Bp. of *Bath and Wells (1548). Under Mary he fled abroad, but returned as Bp. of Chichester on her death. His position as chief consecrator of Abp. M. *Parker has given rise to controversy, since there is no record of his own consecration (really not surprising, however, in view of the careless keeping of the Canterbury

Register; see *Anglican Ordinations*). His views on Church and state were *Erastian in the extreme. In his *Dialogue* (1531; reprinted, 1553; new ed. by J. R. Lunn, 1897) he expressed his strong disapproval of *Lutheran opinions. He translated part of the *Apocrypha for the *Bishops' Bible.

A. S. Barnes, *Bishop Barlow and Anglican Orders*. A Study of the Original Documents (1922). C. Jenkins, 'Bishop Barlow's Consecration and Archbishop Parker's Register. With some new Documents', *J.T.S.*, xxiv (1922–1923), pp. 1-32. T. F. Tout in *D.N.B.*, iii (1885), pp. 229–31.

BARMEN DECLARATION, The (1934).

The statement drawn up at the first Synod of the *Confessing Church at Barmen from 29 to 30 May 1934, to define the belief and mission of the Church in the face of the liberal tendencies of the Nazi *German Christians. The foundation of the Church was held to be in the Revelation of God in Jesus Christ and not in any subordinate revelation in nature or history, and her primary mission was defined as to preach the Gospel of the free Grace of God. The Synod and its Declaration were deeply under the influence of K. *Barth.

Text, with full bibl., in K. D. Schmidt, *Die Bekenntnisse und grundsätzlichen Äusserungen zur Kirchenfrage*, ii (1935), section 42, pp. 91–8.

BARNABAS, St.

A Jewish *Levite of *Cyprus who became one of the earliest Christian disciples at *Jerusalem. His original name was Joseph, but he was 'surnamed Barnabas by the Apostles', the word 'Barnabas' being interpreted by St. Luke as 'son of consolation' (υἱὸς παρακλήσεως, Acts 4. 36). It was he who introduced St. *Paul, perhaps an acquaintance of long standing, to the Apostles after his conversion (Acts 9. 27), and was sent by them to inquire into the situation at *Antioch, where Christianity was being preached to Gentiles on a new scale (11. 22 ff.). Having approved, he fetched St. Paul from Tarsus to help him in the first 'missionary journey' which followed (Acts 13 and 14; see *Paul, St.*), beginning with Cyprus. Indeed, in this he was originally the leader, though St. Paul very soon became the more prominent. At the Council at Jerusalem (Acts 15) he defended the claims of the Gentile Christians, and after it returned to Antioch with St. Paul (15. 30). Owing to a dispute with St. Paul over John *Mark, 'they parted asunder one from the other' (15. 39), and Barnabas sailed for Cyprus. He probably continued to travel widely, as later St. Paul mentions him as if he were known to the *Galatians (Gal. 2. 1, 2. 13), the *Corinthians (1 Cor. 9. 6), and possibly the *Colossians (Col. 4. 10). He is the traditional founder of the Cypriot Church, and legend asserts that he was martyred at Salamis in A.D. 61. Acc. to another tradition he was one of the seventy of Lk. 10. 1, and to a third the founder of the church of Milan and its first bishop. Tertullian attributes to his authorship the Ep. to the *Hebrews. Feast day, 11 June.

A.A.SS., Jun. II (1698), pp. 420–60. Crit. ed. of his *Acta* by M. Bonnet, *Acta Philippi et Acta Thomae accedunt Acta Farnabae* (Leipzig, 1903), pp. 292–302. L. *Duchesne 'Saint Barnabé' in *Mélanges G. B. *de Rossi*. Supplément aux Mélanges d'Archéologie et d'Histoire publiés par l'École française de Rome, xii (1892), pp. 41–71.

BARNABAS, Epistle of.

An epistle of early Christian times ascribed by *Clement of Alexandria to the Apostle *Barnabas. Its Greek text was first discovered entire in the *Codex Sinaiticus. It contains a strong attack on Judaism, explaining animal sacrifices, the distinctive enactments of the Mosaic Law, and the material Temple as mistakes due to Jewish blindness and denying that they were ever God's will. The writer also maintains that the Hebrew Scriptures, so far from enjoining Judaic practices, had an esoteric sense, which he professes to reveal. In this way he succeeds in finding in the OT convincing testimonies for Christianity and against Judaism. It is very improbable that the author was really the Apostle *Barnabas. He was probably a Christian of Alexandria who wrote between A.D. 70 and 100.

For edd. and transs. of text, see bibl. to *Apostolic Fathers*. Also ed. T. Klauser (Florilegium Patristicum, fasc. i, new ed., 1940). P. Haeuser, *Der Barnabasbrief* (1912); H. Windisch, *Der Barnabasbrief* (1920; Handbuch zum N. T., Ergänzungsband, *Die apostolischen Väter*). A. L. Williams, 'The Date of the Epistle of Barnabas' in *J.T.S.*, xxxiv (1933), pp. 337–46, incl. further bibl. reff.

BARNABAS, Gospel of.

A writing in Italian, apparently forged not earlier than the 15th cent. by a native of Italy who had renounced Christianity for Islam.

Ital. text ed. with Eng. tr. by Lonsdale and Laura Ragg (Oxford, 1907). Cf. also W. E. A. Axon, 'On the Mohammedan Gospel of Barnabas' in *J.T.S.*, iii (1901–2), pp. 441–445, and Lonsdale Ragg, 'The Mohammedan "Gospel of Barnabas"' in ib., vi (1904–5), pp. 424–33. An 'Evangelium secundum Barnabam' is also listed in the ''Decretum Gelasianum' among the *spuria*; but this is prob. an independent work, now wholly lost.

BARNABITES.

A small religious order founded at Milan in 1530 by St. Antonio Maria Zaccaria (d. 1539). Officially known as the 'Clerks Regular of St. Paul', its members obtained their popular name from their church of St. Barnabas at Milan. Besides the usual monastic obligations, their rule provides for the study of St. Paul's Epistles and for education and mission work. *C.* 1950 some 35 Barnabite houses existed, mostly in Italy.

O. Premoli, Barnabite, *Storia dei Barnabiti nel cinquecento* (1913), *nel seicento* (1922), *dal 1700 al 1825* (1925). Heimbucher, ii, pp. 106–10. Further bibl. in *Enciclopedia Ecclesiastica*, i (1942), s.v. 'Barnabiti'.

BARNETT, SAMUEL AUGUSTUS (1844–1913),

Anglican social reformer. After studying law and modern history at Wadham College, *Oxford, he was ordained deacon in 1867. In 1869 he founded the Charity Organization Society. From 1873 to 1894 he was vicar of St. Jude's, Whitechapel, where his unorthodox methods (evening schools, entertainments, serving on the Board of

Guardians) at first aroused much criticism, but soon led to his recognition as a loyal priest, devoted to the religious and cultural improvement of the East End. He encouraged tutors from Oxford to come to lecture to his parishioners, and from 1884 to 1896 was the first Warden of Toynbee Hall. In 1884 he helped to found the Education Reform League, and in 1885 he became a promoter of the Artisans' Dwellings Act. Throughout his life he was active in initiating projects directed to the reform of social conditions on Christian principles and urging Christians to study them. In 1906 Barnett became a Canon of Westminster. He was much assisted in his work by his wife (Henrietta Octavia, *née* Rowland), who before marriage had been a co-worker with Octavia Hill (1838–1912). After his death 'Barnett House', for the study of social problems, was founded at Oxford in his memory. His writings include *Practicable Socialism*: Essays on Social Reform (1888), *The Service of God*: Sermons, Essays, and Addresses (1897), and *Religion and Politics* (1911).

His Life was written by his wife in 2 vols. (1918).

BARO, PETER (1534–99), anti-*Calvinist divine. Born at Étampes, he studied for the law at Bourges, where he came under the influence of the recently introduced Protestant doctrines. Abandoning law for divinity, he made his way to *Geneva, where J. *Calvin admitted him to the ministry. After returning to France, he found himself compelled to flee to England. In 1574, mainly through the influence of Burghley, he was appointed Lady Margaret professor of divinity at Cambridge. Here, despite his earlier personal associations with Calvin, he became a critic of the more predestinarian of the Calvinist doctrines. The *Lambeth Articles seem to have been drafted partly to rebut his teaching, but Baro put an anti-Calvinist sense on them and thus justified his formal assent. He also challenged W. *Perkins' teaching on predestination, then in high repute at Cambridge. But though Burghley had interposed in his favour and J. *Overall and L. *Andrewes had given him their support, Baro found it expedient to flee from Cambridge in 1596. He lived for the rest of his life in London. He can be regarded as an early leader of the movement in Anglican theology later popularly termed'*Arminianism'. His writings include *Praelectiones* on Jonah (1579), *De Fide ejusque Ortu et Natura plana ac dilucida Explicatio* (1580) and *De Praestantia et Dignitate Divinae Legis Libri Duo* (n.d.).

Abridged version of his autobiography from a Baker MS., vol. xxxix, p. 185, and other material pr. by R. Masters, *Memoirs of the Life and Writings of the late Rev. Thomas Baker* (1784), pp. 127–31.

BAROCCO. See *Baroque*.

BARONIUS, CESARE (1538–1607), ecclesiastical historian. He became a member of the *Oratory under St. *Philip Neri in 1557, and Superior in 1593. In 1596 he was made Cardinal and in 1597 Librarian of the *Vatican. His most important work, the *Annales Ecclesiastici* (12 folio volumes, 1588–1607), is a history of the Church in chapters each corresponding to a year, undertaken as a RC reply to the *Centuries of Magdeburg. At his death this work had only reached the year 1198, and various attempts, all worthless, were made to continue it, one by the Oratorians themselves. Baronius was at some pains to secure accuracy, as is clear from the long list of authorities he cites and compares. But on many matters, particularly where the E. Church is concerned, his information was scanty and in error, and throughout his critical powers failed to support his good intentions. In the 11th volume, published in 1605, he included a note supporting Papal claims in Sicily against Spain, which was published as a separate treatise after his death (Paris, 1609; Leyden, 1619), and gave much offence to Philip III. At the time of the original publication it is said to have lost Baronius the Papacy, owing to Spanish opposition. He also published two new and corrected editions of the *Roman Martyrology (1586 and 1589).

The standard ed. of his *Annales Ecclesiastici*, with the various additions and an index to the whole, is that of J. D. *Mansi and D. Georgius (38 vols., Lucca, 1738–59). Early life by H. Barnabeus, Cong. Orat. (Rome, 1651). G. Calenzio, *La vita e gli scritti del Cardinale Cesare Baronio* (1907); V. Simoncelli (ed.), *Per Cesare Baronio*. Scritti vari nel terzo centenario della sua morte (1911); G. De Libero, Cong. Orat., *Cesare Baronio, padre della storia ecclesiastica* (1936). Id. in *E.C.*, ii (1949), cols. 885–9, s.v. 'Baronio, Cesare'.

BAROQUE (Portug. *barocco*, a 'rough pearl'). The ornate style of art and architecture which flourished in Italy during the 17th and early 18th cents., and spread throughout the Continent, esp. in France and Spain. With its lofty grandeur and richness of decoration it attempted to infuse new life and religious feeling into the cold correctness of the later Renaissance, but purity of form was sometimes sacrificed to an unrestrained love of ornament. Its most notable exponents were G. L. Bernini (1598–1680), C. Maderna (1556–1629), and F. Borromini (1599–1667), but, owing to the fantastic exuberance of such architects as José Churriguera (1650–1725), the term 'baroque' came to signify anything florid or bizarre. See also *Rococo*.

C. Gurlitt, *Geschichte des Barockstiles*: i, In Italien (1887); ii, In Belgien, Holland, Frankreich, England (1888); iii, In Deutschland (1889). W. Weisbach, *Der Barock als Kunst der Gegenreformation* (1921), with plates; id., *Die Kunst des Barock in Italien, Frankreich, Deutschland und Spanien* (1924). J. Weingartner–F. Filser, *Der Geist des Barocks* (Augsburg, 1925), with plates. H. Wölfflin, *Renaissance und Barock*. Eine Untersuchung über Wesen und Entstehung des Barockstils in Italien (1888). S. Sitwell, *Southern Baroque Art* (1924), with bibl.; id., *German Baroque Art* (1927), with bibl. A. E. Brinkmann, *Barockskulptur* (Handbuch der Kunstwissenschaft, 1919). B. *Croce, *Storia della età barocca in Italia* (1929). C. Ricci in *E.B.* (ed. 14), iii (1929), p. 132 f., s.v., with useful bibl.; J. Weingartner and G. Müller in *L.Th.K.*, i (1930), cols. 981–5, s.v.; A. Prandi in *E.C.*, ii (1949), cols. 868–80, with further bibl.

BARRIER ACT. The Act passed on 8 Jan. 1697 by the General Assembly of the Church of Scotland, which requires that proposals to make any important alteration in the constitution in the Church shall first be presented in the form of overtures to the Assembly, and if passed in this form shall then be sent down to presbyteries for their consideration and opinion, and thence remitted to a future Assembly. Its purpose was to prevent hasty legislation that might prejudice the doctrine, worship, or government of the Church. The Act is still in force.

Text in *Acts of the General Assembly of the Church of Scotland, M.DC.XXXVIII.-M.DCCC.XLII.* [ed. T. Pitcairn] (1843), p. 260 f.

BARRINGTON, SHUTE (1734–1826), Bp. of *Durham. He was the youngest son of John Shute, first Viscount Barrington (1678–1734), a strong advocate of complete religious freedom for the Protestant dissenters. Educated at Eton and at Merton College, Oxford, he was ordained in 1756, and in 1761 became a canon of Christ Church. After other appointments he filled successively the sees of *Llandaff (1769), *Salisbury (1782), and *Durham (1791), and was one of the most influential bishops of his age. He made generous distribution of his large episcopal revenues. In his attitude to the Nonconformists he was less liberal than his father, deprecating any relaxation of subscription on the ground that precise articles of faith were indispensable in an Established Church. Besides issuing an edition of his father's *Miscellanea Sacra* (3 vols., 1770) he published the *Life* of his brother, William Wildman, Viscount Barrington (1814), a collection of *Sermons* (1811), and some minor works.

Brief Memoir by G. Townsend in his ed. of *The Theological Works of the first Viscount Barrington*, i (1828), pp. xliv-lix. A. H. Grant in *D.N.B.*, iii (1885), p. 294.

BARROW, HENRY (*c.* 1550–93), also Barrowe, *Congregationalist. Educated at Clare Hall, Cambridge, he was converted *c.* 1580 from the profligate life of a courtier to a strict *Puritanism of a *Brownist type. In 1586, when visiting in prison J. *Greenwood, the separatist leader, with whom he had earlier come into association, he was detained by order of Abp. J. *Whitgift, and kept in confinement till his death. He wrote in defence of separatism and congregational independence, and also engaged in controversy with R. *Browne, the *Congregationalist, who sought separation from the Established Church only as a means to a spiritual democracy, whereas Barrow appears to have held that any idea of Church order was completely corrupt. He was charged in 1590 with circulating seditious books, and three years later sentenced to be hanged. Most of his writings were printed in Holland by his friends. They included *A True Description of the Visible Congregation of the Saints, &c.* (1589) and *A Brief Discovery of the False Church* (1590). It has been argued, though with little show of probability, that Barrow was the author of the *Marprelate Tracts.

F. J. Powicke, *Henry Barrowe, Separatist, and the Exiled Church in Amsterdam* (1900).

BARROW, ISAAC (1630–77), Anglican divine, classical scholar, and mathematician. He entered Trinity College Cambridge, in 1643, and though a royalist and the son of a royalist, became a scholar in 1647, and a Fellow in 1649. From 1655 to 1659 he travelled in France, Italy, and the Near East, and on his return to England was ordained. He was appointed Professor of Greek at Cambridge in 1660, Professor of Geometry at Gresham College, London, shortly after, and the first Lucasian Professor of Mathematics at Cambridge in 1663. The last post he resigned in 1669, in favour of his pupil, I. *Newton, whose greater ability he recognized, while he himself had come to doubt whether his mathematical studies left him sufficient time for theology. Soon after this, *Charles II made him his chaplain, and in 1673 Mas·er of Trinity. The precision of a mathematician's thought is reflected in his theology, and his *Treatise on the Pope's Supremacy* (1680, posthumous) remains a work of outstanding ability. He was also one of the most successful (and lengthiest) preachers of his day.

Collected ed. of his Theological Works by J. *Tillotson (4 vols., London, 1683–7), incl. 'Some Account of the Life of Dr. Isaac Barrow' by A. H[ill]. Modern ed. by A. Napier (9 vols., Cambridge, 1859) incl. life by A. Hill, vol. i, pp. xxxvii–liv, and 'Barrow and his Academical Times as Illustrated in his Latin Works' by W. Whewell, vol. ix, pp. i–lv. Mathematical Works ed. W. Whewell (Cambridge, 1860). Further biographical Memoir by T. S. Hughes prefixed to his ed. of Barrow's Theological Works (7 vols., London, 1831), vol. i, pp. ix–xc. P. H. Osmond, *Isaac Barrow, His Life and Times* (1944). His Sermon 'Of Submission to the Divine Will' is repr. in [H.] H.[*Henson (ed.), *Selected English Sermons* (World's Classics, 1939), pp. 165–184. J. H. Overton in *D.N.B.*, iii (1885), pp. 299–305.

BARSUMAS (d. 458), *Monophysite archimandrite. He was one of the leaders of the Eutychian party at the Synod of *Constantinople of 448, at the *Latrocinium (449), and at the Council of *Chalcedon (451). To the Latrocinium, where he represented the Oriental monks at the invitation of Emp. *Theodosius II (d. 450) and sat among the Bishops, he is said to have brought a turbulent body of monks to support him; later (at Chalcedon) he was charged with responsibility for *Flavian's death. After Chalcedon he spent the rest of his life in exile.

Text of Eth. Life, with Fr. tr., ed. S. Grébaut, 'Vie de Barsoma le Syrien', in *Rev. de l'Orient Chrétien*, xiii (1908). pp. 337–45, and xiv (1909), pp. 135–42, 264–75, and 401–14. There is also an (unpubld.) Life in Syr. MSS. by his pupil, Samuel. F. Nau in *D.T.C.*, ii (1905), col. 434 f., s.v.

BARSUMAS (*c.* 420–*c.* 490), *Nestorian Bp. of Nisibis. A disciple of *Ibas of Edessa, he was present at the *Latrocinium (449), where his banishment was demanded. At an unknown date after the death of Ibas (457) he became Metropolitan of Nisibis, where with the aid of the Persian King, who welcomed him to his court, he became a keen propagandist of Nestorianism. He also strove to make his see of Nisibis independent of Seleucia-Ctesiphon. To this end he secured the deposition of Babowaï, the *Catholicos of Seleucia, and the intrusion of Acacius, his fellow-pupil at Edessa, into the see (484). But the relative position of Seleucia and Nisibis remained unsettled and caused him much trouble in the next years. He established at Nisibis an influential theological school; and when the celebrated school of *Edessa (also Nestorian) was closed in 489, Barsumas welcomed its exiles. Six of his Epistles survive.

Epp. of Barsumas, ed. O. Braun, 'Des Barsauma von Nisibis Briefe an den Katholikos Akak', in *Actes du Xe Congrès des Orientalistes, Genève, 1894* (Leyden, 1896), pt. 3, sect. 2, pp. 83–101; Ger. tr. by id., *Das Buch der Synhados* (1900), pp. 75–83. J. Labourt, *Le Christianisme dans l'empire perse sous la dynastie sassanide (224–632)* (1904), pp. 131–52. A. *Baumstark, *Geschichte der syrischen Literatur* (1922), p. 108 f. Bardenhewer, iv (1924), p. 411. F. Nau in *D.T.C.*, ii (1905), cols. 430–4, s.v.

BARTH, KARL (1886–). *Protestant theologian. He was the son of Fritz Barth (1856–1912), Prof. of NT Theology at Berne. After studying at Berne, Berlin, *Tübingen, and *Marburg, Karl Barth began as a minister at Geneva (1909–11) and was then for ten years (1911–21) pastor at Safenwil (Aargau). Here, under the shadow of the war of 1914–18 and in direct relation to his pastoral responsibility, he was led to a radical questioning of current theological notions, and wrote his 'Commentary on Romans' (*Der Römerbrief*, 1919). The originality, critical power, and actuality of its message, particularly in the pessimism of the post-war situation, at once gave him a very wide hearing among German-speaking Protestant theologians. In 1921 he became extraordinary professor at Göttingen and later Professor at Münster i.W (1925) and Bonn (1930).

On Hitler's accession to power and the outbreak of the 'Church Struggle' (1933), Barth at once threw in his lot with the *Confessing Church. As a Swiss subject he enjoyed a liberty of speech not open to a German and he had a strong backing. None the less his action demanded much courage. The formulation of Confessional theology in the *Barmen Declaration of 1934 was largely Barth's work. At the outset he held that National Socialism, being purely a matter of secular politics, was irrelevant to the Christian, provided the freedom of the Gospel was maintained. Later he came to the view that such neutrality was not possible, and vigorously attacked Nazism. On his refusal to take an oath of unconditional allegiance to the Führer, he was deprived of his chair. He left Germany and in 1935 became professor of Theology at Basle. In 1939 he was deprived of his doctorate of the University of Münster.

Barth's primary object was to lead theology away from what he believed to be the fundamentally erroneous outlook of modern religious philosophy, with its positive attitude to science,

culture, and art, its sympathy with mysticism and its stress on feeling, and to bring it back to the principles of the *Reformation. It was to be a return to the Prophetic teaching of the Bible, of which he believed that the Reformers were the most authentic exponents. Among those who specially influenced him were S. *Kierkegaard, F. M. *Dostoievski, F. *Overbeck, and the *Blumhardts. The Christian message, he held, affirmed the Supremacy and Transcendence of God, whose infinite superiority to all human aspirations meant the worthlessness of human reason. Since the *Fall, which brought man wholly under the dominion of sin, his natural capacities, including his reason, had been radically perverted, so that all 'natural theology', as expounded e.g. by the *Scholastics and the modern RC Church, as well as all religion grounded in experience, as found in, e.g., F. D. E. *Schleiermacher and the *Hegelians, has now become impossible. God's sole revelation is in Jesus Christ and the Word of God is His one and only means of communication with man. Since man is utterly dependent on Divine grace, all his boasted cultural achievements are rooted in sin.

These doctrines Barth proclaimed with passionate fervour in a style at once graphic and forceful, and in language deeply influenced by the Bible. He made them the theme of innumerable sermons and addresses, as well as of more continuous writings. In 1927 he published the beginnings of a systematic exposition of his theology in *Die christliche Dogmatik im Entwurf* I, 'Die Lehre vom Worte Gottes'; but he abandoned this work and a few years later began again on a vast scale. In 1932 there appeared the first vol. of *Die kirchliche Dogmatik* on which he was destined to be engaged for over twenty years.

After the war the University of Münster restored its doctorate to Barth (1945). In the political sphere he now declined to take up the same hostile attitude to Communism as he had hitherto done to Nazism on the ground that the Church, which must be essentially detached from politics, cannot decide in advance that Communism is necessarily evil. He has continued to act as a potent astringent influence in Protestant theology, on secondary matters (e.g. *infant baptism) often taking up provocative and sometimes unexpected positions.

In English-speaking countries, the greatest impact of 'the Barthian Theology' was in the 1930s. By the 1950s, though Barth still had professed disciples, his theological influence had become widely diffused among many who did not share his particular views nor comprise a specifically 'Barthian' movement. At the same time his personal prestige, based largely on his distinctive and forthright standpoint, has given him the position of the outstanding Protestant theologian, and perhaps the most notable Christian prophet of our times.

Barth's other works include *Das Wort Gottes und die Theologie* (collected lectures; 1924; Eng. tr., 1928), *Die Theologie und die*

Kirche (further lectures, 1928); *Credo* (an outline of dogmatics based on the *Apostles' Creed*, 1935; Eng. tr., 1936); *The Knowledge of God and the Service of God* (*Gifford Lectures, 1937–8; publd. 1938; based on the Scottish Confession of 1560); *Dogmatik in Grundriss* (Lectures delivered in Bonn, 1946; publd. 1947; Eng. tr., 1949); *Die protestantische Theologie im 19. Jahrhundert* (1947); *Die kirchliche Lehre von der Taufe* (1947; Eng. tr., 1948); *Die christliche Lehre nach dem Heidelberger Katechismus* (1948).

See also *Brunner, E.*, and *Dialectical Theology.*

The Eng. tr. of Barth's *Römerbrief* by E. C. *Hoskyns (Oxford, 1932) did much to spread knowledge of his doctrines in Britain. *Festschriften* in his honour were issued in 1936 (for his 50th birthday, ed. E. Wolf, Munich), with list of his works to date collected by C. von Kirschbaum, pp. 604–11, and trr. listed pp. 612–14; in 1946 (for his 60th birthday, 'Cahiers Théologiques de l'Actualité Protestante, Hors Série 2'; Neuchâtel–Paris); and 1947 (*Reformation Old and New*, ed. F. W. Camfield, London), with list of his chief works and Eng. trr., p. 219 f. Summary of Barth's systematic theology in O. Weber, *Karl Barth's Kirchliche Dogmatik* (1950; Eng. tr., 1953). H. von Balthasar, *Karl Barth, Darstellung und Deutung seiner Theologie* (1951). J. Hamer, O.P., *Karl Barth. L'Occasionalisme théologique de Karl Barth. Étude sur sa méthode dogmatique* (1949). Books in English include R. B. Hoyle, *The Teaching of Karl Barth* (1930); J. MacConnachie, *The Significance of Karl Barth* (1931); id., *The Barthian Theology and the Man of Today* (1933). A. Keller, *Der Weg der dialektischen Theologie durch die kirchliche Welt* (1931; Eng. tr. as *Karl Barth and Christian Unity* [1933]). C. van Til, *The New Modernism*. An Appraisal of the Theology of Barth and Brunner (1946).

BARTHOLOMEW, St.

One of the twelve Apostles. He is mentioned only in the Synoptic Gospels (Mk. 3. 18, Lk. 6. 14, Mt. 10. 3) and in Acts (1. 13). The name is a patronymic, meaning 'son of Tolmai', so that he may have had another (personal) name, and he is sometimes identified with *Nathanael (Jn. 1. 45–51, 21. 2). Acc. to *Eusebius, when *Pantaenus of Alexandria visited *India between A.D. 150 and 200, he found there 'the Gospel according to Matthew' in Hebrew, left behind by 'Bartholomew, one of the Apostles' (*H.E.* 5. 10. 3). Bartholomew is traditionally said to have been flayed alive at Albanopolis in Armenia. Feast day, 24 Aug.

A. Romeo in *E.C.*, ii (1949), cols. 916–8, s.v. 'Bartolomeo, Apostolo (I)', with bibl. See also bibl. to *Nathanael.*

BARTHOLOMEW, Gospel of St.

An apocryphal Gospel whose existence was known to *Jerome and *Bede. It has perhaps been incorporated into the 'Questions of Bartholomew' which survives in a number of Greek, Latin, and Slavonic MSS. These 'Questions' treat of the descent of Christ into hell, the Virgin's account of the Annunciation, a vision of the bottomless pit, the summons to the Devil to judgement, questions about the deadly sins, and other subjects. Their theological standpoint is Gnostic. There also exists, in Coptic, a 'Book of the Resurrection of Christ by Bartholomew the Apostle'.

A. Romeo in *E.C.*, ii (1949), col. 919 f., s.v. 'Bartolomeo, Apostolo V: Vangelo di B', with bibl. Eng. tr. in M. R. James, *Apocryphal New Testament* (1924), pp. 166–86. F. Haase, 'Zur Rekonstruktion des Bartholomäusevangeliums' in *Z.N.T.W.*, xvi (1915), pp. 93–112.

BARTHOLOMEW'S DAY, Massacre of St.

The massacre that took place on the night of 23–24 Aug. 1572, and the two following days in which, chiefly, it appears, at the instigation of *Catherine de' Medici, between 5,000 and 10,000 *Huguenots, including G. *Coligny, were put to death in Paris and other large French cities.

The massacre is discussed from different angles in all lives of *Catherine de Medici* and *Coligny, Gaspard de*, cited s.vv. J. W. Thompson, *The Wars of Religion in France, 1559–1576* (1909), pp. 448–53; F. Rocquain, *La France et Rome pendant les guerres de religion* (1924), pp. 121–45 passim. H. Bordier, *La Sainte-Barthélemy et la critique moderne* (1879); H. Wuttke, *Zur Vorgeschichte der Bartholomäusnacht* (1879); H. Baumgarten, *Vor der Bartholomäusnacht* (1882). B. L. H. Martin, *La Sainte-Barthélemy* (Épisodes Mémorables de l'Histoire de France, 1919). J. H. Mariéjol in E. Lavisse, *Histoire de France*, vi (1904), pp. 125–33, with bibl. to date, p. 114 f.

BARTHOLOMEW OF THE MARTYRS

(1514–90), Portuguese theologian. Bartholomew Fernandez, who owes his surname 'A Martyribus' to the church in which he was baptized, entered the *Dominican monastery at Lisbon in 1527. After teaching philosophy and theology in various houses of his order, he was made Bp. of Braga in 1548. In 1561 he went to *Trent, where he took a prominent part in the last nine sessions, esp. in the drafting of the decrees on the reform of the clergy, which he did his best to put into practice after his return to his diocese. In 1582 he resigned his charge and retired to the Dominican convent at Viana. He was much esteemed for his personal holiness as well as for his energy in carrying out the Tridentine reforms. Among his works is the *Stimulus Pastorum* (1564) and a *Compendium Spiritualis Doctrinae* (1582), which was translated into many languages. In 1845 he was declared Venerable by *Gregory XVI.

Opera Omnia, ed. J. D. (in religion Dom Malachie) d'Inguimbert (Rome, 2 parts bound in 1, 1734–5). Lives by *Luís of Granada and Luís de Sousa, incorporated into the Lives by L. de Cacegas (Vienna, 1619), L. Múnoz (Madrid, 1645), I. L. Le Maistre de Sacy (Paris, 1663; Eng. tr., 1880), and J. D. d'Inguimbert (Rome, 1727).

BARTHOLOMEW OF PISA (c. 1260–

1347), *Dominican theologian. He is also sometimes called 'of San Concordio' after his native place. He entered the Dominican Order in 1277, and, after studying at *Bologna and Pisa, he taught at several Dominican houses and was soon held in high reputation as a scholar. He is chiefly famous for his alphabetically arranged 'Summa de Casibus Conscientiae' (1338), also called 'Summa Pisana' or 'Summa Bartholomea'. It was much used during the 14th and 15th cents. and was later also frequently printed.

There is a description of him in 'Chronica Antiqua Conventus Sanctae Catherinae de Pisis' pr. in *Archivio Storico Italiano*, vi, par. ii, sez. iii (1845), pp. 397–633, pp. 521–9.

BARTHOLOMITES.

(1) *Armenian*. A community of *Armenian monks who fled from Armenia when the Sultan of Egypt invaded the country in 1296, and settled in

1307 at Genoa, where a church dedicated to St. Bartholomew was built for them, hence their name. Others from Armenia joined them, and they spread throughout Italy. At first they retained the Armenian Liturgy and the Rule of St. *Basil, but later, with the approval of Innocent VI (1356), they adopted the Roman Liturgy and the Rule of St. *Augustine, and wore a habit similar to that of the *Dominicans, whose privileges they were granted by Boniface IX. In the 17th cent. they began to decline and were finally suppressed by *Innocent X in 1650.

(2) *German.* A congregation of secular priests, 'Institutum clericorum saecularium in communi viventium', known also as 'Bartholomaeans', 'United Brethren', and 'Communists'. They were founded in 1640 at Tittmoning by Bartholomew Holzhauser (1613–58), a German parish priest and ecclesiastical writer, in order to revive the morals and discipline of the clergy and laity, after the decline due to the *Thirty Years War (1618–48). They lived in community under obedience to a superior, but without vows, and were entrusted with many seminaries. After receiving formal approbation from Innocent XI in 1680, they spread into England, Poland, Italy, and other European countries. Their extinction was brought about by the secularization of the German ecclesiastial states under Napoleon in 1803; and recent attempts at restoration have been without effect.

(1) [P. Hélyot], *Histoire des ordres monastiques, religieux et militaires*, i (1714), pp. 243–8. J. M. Besse in *C.E.*, ii (1907), p. 317, s.v.; C. Korolevskij in *D.H.G.E.*, vi (1932), col. 1038 f., s.v. Heimbucher, i, p. 104 f.
(2) F. Busan, O.S.B., 'Das Leben und Institut des ehrwürdigen Bartholomäus Holzhauser' in *Studien und Mitteilungen aus dem Benediktiner- und Cistercienser-Orden*, xxiii (1902), pp. 403–31 and 434–55. J. Wenner in *D.H.G.E.*, vi (1932), cols. 1039–41, s.v., with bibl. Heimbücher, ii, pp. 595–7.

BARTIMAEUS. The blind beggar healed by Christ at or near *Jericho on His last journey to *Jerusalem. He is said to have afterwards 'followed Him in the way' (Mk. 10. 46–52).

BARTOLOMMEO, FRA (*c.* 1475–1517), Florentine painter. He was an admirer and follower of *Savonarola, whose portrait he painted several times. After the latter's death, Fra Bartolommeo entered the *Dominican Order at San Marco in Florence (1498), where, except for brief absences in *Venice and *Rome, he remained for the rest of his life. His work was done esp. under the inspiration of that of Fra *Angelico, but he was also much indebted to *Leonardo da Vinci; and he became a close friend of *Raphael. Among the most famous of his works are the fresco of the 'Last Judgement' in Sta. Maria Nuova (in which he collaborated with Mariotto Albertinelli) and his 'Descent from the Cross' in the Pitti, both at Florence.

F. Knapp, *Fra Bartolommeo della Porta und die Schule von San Marco* (1903). H. von der Gabelentz, *Fra Bartolommeo und die Florentiner Renaissance* (2 vols., 1922).

H. Wölfflin, *Die klassiche Kunst. Eine Einführung in die italienische Renaissance* (1888; ed. 6 revised, 1914), ch. v, pp. 139–51; Eng. tr., 1952, pp. 140–54. J. A. Crowe and G. B. Cavalcaselle, *A History of Painting in Italy*, vi (1914), ch. iii, pp. 50–104. L. Scott, *Fra Bartolommeo and Andrea del Sarto* ('The Great Artists', 1881), pp. 1–70; further brief life by M. E. James (*Catholic Truth Society, 1902).

BARTON, ELIZABETH (*c.* 1506–34), the 'Maid of Kent'. She was a servant girl who, after an illness in 1525, had trances and claimed to utter prophecies. After inquiries and a public examination by the prior of Christ Church, Canterbury (1526), she was admitted as a nun at St. Sepulchre's Convent in the city. Her prophecies then took a political turn, consisting in personal attacks on Henry VIII for his intention to divorce his queen. In 1533, under examination by Abp. T. *Cranmer, a confession, true or false, was extorted from her that her trances were feigned, and she was prosecuted by Bill of Attainder and executed in 1534.

The main sources for her life are the Act of Attainder by which she was condemned (25 Hen. VIII, c. 12) and J. Gairdner (ed.), *Letters and Papers Foreign and Domestic of the Reign of Henry VIII*, vi (1882) and vii (1883) passim. Some material from the *Cottonian MSS. is printed by T. Wright, *Three Chapters of Letters Relating to the Suppression of the Monasteries* (Camden Society, xxvi, 1843), pp. 13–34. J. R. McKee, Cong. Orat., *Dame Elizabeth Barton, O.S.B. The Holy Maid of Kent* (1925).

BARUCH, Book of. A Book of the *Apocrypha to which is attached the 'Epistle of Jeremy', the two together, with *Lamentations, forming appendices to the Book of *Jeremiah. The book consists of (a) an introduction, which professes to have been written by Baruch, the disciple of Jeremiah, and read by him to the Jewish captives in Babylon in the 6th cent. B.C. (1. 1–14); (b) a liturgical confession (1. 15–3. 8); (c) a sermon (3. 9–4. 4); and (d) a set of canticles (4. 5–5. 9). On a critical view, the unmistakable dependence of the work upon *Daniel has led scholars to date it in post-Maccabaean times, and its liturgical use has suggested to some that it was either written or adapted for use in the cycle of sabbaths commemorating national disasters which began to be observed after the fall of *Jerusalem in A.D. 70. It is generally held that, at any rate, the earlier sections of the book were originally written in Hebrew.

Commentaries by F. H. Reusch (Freiburg i.Br., 1853) and J. J. Kneucker (Leipzig, 1879). O. C. Whitehouse in R. H. *Charles, *The Apocrypha and Pseudepigrapha of the Old Testament*, i (1913), pp. 569–95. R. R. Harwell, *The Principal Versions of Baruch* (Yale Diss., New Haven, 1915). A. A. Bevan in *E.Bi.*, i (1899), cols. 492–4; J. T. Marshall in *H.D.B.*, i (1898), pp. 251–4; both with bibl. See also bibl. to *Apocrypha*.

BARUCH, The Greek Apocalypse of ('III Baruch'). An apocryphal work, apparently of Jewish origin, but worked over by a Christian hand. It may date from the 2nd cent., and it was certainly known to *Origen (*De princ.* 2. 3. 6). The only known MS. of the Greek text is a 16th cent. minuscule in the British Museum (Add. 10073). The Apocalypse described the visions of the seven heavens which were granted to Baruch, though the last two are wanting as the MS. is defective. A *Slavonic version also exists.

Gk. text ed. M. R. James, *Apocrypha Anecdota*. Second Series (Texts and Studies, v, No. i, Cambridge, 1897), pp. 84–94. Slavonic text ed. S. Novaković (Zagreb, 1886); Eng. tr. of Slavonic text by W. R. Morfill in M. R. James, *op. cit.*, pp. 95–102. Introduction, ib., pp. li–lxxi. Eng. tr. of Gk. text, with introd. and notes, in R. H. *Charles, *The Apocrypha and Pseudepigrapha of the Old Testament*, ii (1913), pp. 527–41.

BARUCH, The Syriac Apocalypse of ('II Baruch'). A Pharisaic work which professes to have been written by Baruch, Jeremiah's secretary. It was compiled shortly after the fall of *Jerusalem in A.D. 70, and describes the capture of *Jerusalem by the Chaldeans in 586 B.C., centuries earlier, its purpose being to encourage the Jews in their new distress to stand fast. In language and ideas it has striking resemblances to IV Ezra (II *Esdras). The Apocalypse was originally composed in Greek, but the bulk of it is extant only in a single 6th cent. Syriac MS. in the '*Ambrosiana' at Milan. The theory that the book in its latest form was the work of a Christian has not been generally accepted.

Syr. text ed. by A. M. Ceriani in *Monumenta Sacra et Profana*, v (pt. 2; Milan, 1871), pp. 113–80; also by M. Kmosko in *Patrologia Syriaca* (ed. R. Graffin), ii (1907), cols. 1056–1207. Crit. study of textual tradition and presentation of text in B. Violet, *Die Apokalypsen des Esra und des Baruch in deutscher Gestalt* (G.C.S., xxxii, Leipzig, 1924). Eng. tr. with introd., notes, and indices by R. H. *Charles (London, 1896); id., *The Apocrypha and Pseudepigrapha of the Old Testament*, ii (1913), pp. 470–526. Id. in *H.D.B.*, i (1898), 249–51, s.v. 'Baruch, Apocalypse of'; J. B. Frey in *Dict. Bibl.* Suppl., i (1928), cols. 418–23, s.v. 'Apocryphes de l'Ancien Testament. 9: L'Apocalypse syriaque de Baruch'.

BASEL, Confessions and Council of. See *Basle, Confessions and Council of.*

BASHMURIC. See *Fayumic.*

BASIL, St., 'the Great' (*c.* 330–79). One of the three *Cappadocian Fathers. He was the brother of St. *Gregory of Nyssa and St. *Macrina. After being educated at Caesarea in Cappadocia, *Constantinople, and *Athens in the best pagan and Christian culture of his day, he forsook the world for the monastic life, and, after a brief period in Syria and Egypt, settled as a hermit by the river Iris near Neo-caesarea (358). Here his early friendship with St. *Gregory of Nazianzum was renewed, and they preached missions together. The Emp. *Julian (361–3), his former fellow-student at Athens, made an unsuccessful attempt to bring him to the court, but only in *c.* 364 did he leave his retirement when called by his bishop, Eusebius of Caesarea in Cappadocia, to defend orthodoxy against the Arian emperor, Valens. In 370 he was appointed to succeed Eusebius in the see of Caesarea, and held this office for the rest of his life. It brought him into the thick of further controversies with the extreme *Arian party led by *Eunomius, as well as with the *Pneumato-machi, who denied the divinity of the Holy Ghost, and with the Bps. of Rome (*Damasus) and Alexandria (*Athanasius), who refused to recognize his revered supporter, St. *Meletius, as Bp. of Antioch.

In character Basil, besides being eloquent, learned, and statesmanlike, was possessed of great personal holiness. His nature was at once sensitive and pugnacious. To these qualities he added an unusual talent for organization, and impressed on Eastern monasticism the structure and ethos which it has retained ever since. The vast series of buildings he established on the outskirts of Caesarea, which included, besides the church and episcopal residence, hospitals and hostels for the poor, who were cared for by a carefully planned system of relief, long remained a monument to his memory.

His more important writings include a large collection of letters, his treatise 'On the Holy Spirit', and his three 'Books against Eunomius'. In conjunction with *Gregory of Nazianzum he compiled the *Philocalia*, a selection of passages from the works of *Origen. In the field of doctrine he made a strong effort to reconcile the Semiarians to the formula of *Nicaea, and to show that their word *Homoiousios* ('like in substance to the Father') had the same implications as the Nicene *Homoousios* ('of one substance'). The virtual termination of the Arian controversy at the Council of *Constantinople in 381/2 shortly after his death is a tribute to his success. In some quarters he was suspected of *Apollinarianism, because he corresponded with Apollinarius, and also because in his writings he stressed the unity of the Person of Christ more than the separateness of the two natures. Feast day, 14 June. See also the following entries.

Collected Works first ed. at Basle, 1532; best ed. that of J. *Garnier, O.S.B., P. *Maran, O.S.B., Paris, 1721–30, repr., with additions, 'apud Gaume', 3 vols. in 6, Paris, 1839, and in J. P. Migne, *PG*, xxix–xxxii. Crit. edd. of *De Spiritu Sancto*, by C. F. Johnston (Oxford, 1892) and B. Pruche, O.P. (*Sources Chrétiennes*, 17, 1947); of *Epp.* by R. Deferrari (Loeb, 4 vols., 1926–34); of *Hom.*, 22 ('Ad adolescentes), by E. Sommer (Paris, 1903), A. Nardi (Turin, 1931), and F. Boulenger (Paris, 1952); of *Hom. in Hexaëm.*, by S. Giet in *Sources Chrétiennes*, 26, 1950; of *Comm. in Is.*, by P. Trevisan (2 vols., Turin, 1939). Valuable studies on text and edd. by D. Amand, O.S.B., in *R. Bén.*, lii (1940), pp. 141–61, liii (1941), pp. 119–51, liv (1942), pp. 124–44, lvi (1945), pp. 126–73. Eng. tr. of selected works by Blomfield Jackson (N.P.N.C.F., 1895). W. K. L. Clarke, *The Ascetic Works of St. Basil* (S.P.C.K., 1925). *Acta Sanctorum*, Jun. II (1698), pp. 807–958. E. Fialon, *Étude historique et littéraire sur Saint Basile* (1865); P. Allard, *Saint Basile* (1903); W. K. L. Clarke, *St. Basil the Great*. A Study in Monasticism (1913); M. M. Fox, *The Life and Times of St. Basil the Great as revealed in his Works* (Patristic Studies, No. 57, Washington, 1939). A. Cavallin, *Studien zu den Briefen des hl. Basilius* (Lund, 1944); Y. Courtonne, *Saint Basile et l'hellénisme* (1934). P. *Batiffol,'L'Ecclésiologie de S. Basile' in *E.O.*, xxv (1922), pp. 9–30; G. F. Reilly, *Imperium and Sacerdotium according to St. Basil the Great* (Washington, 1945); D. Amand, O.S.B., *L'Ascèse monastique de Saint Basile* (Maredsous, 1949). Bardenhewer, iii, pp. 130–62 and 670 f.

BASIL, Liturgy of St. The Liturgy still used in the Eastern Church on a few days in the ecclesiastical year in place of the ordinary

'Liturgy of St. *Chrysostom', viz. on the Sundays in *Lent (except *Palm Sunday), on *Maundy Thursday, and on the Eves of *Easter, of *Christmas, of *Epiphany, and on the Feast of St. *Basil (1 Jan.). In its general structure it may possibly be the work of St. Basil the Great, as there are indications that it is based on early Cappadocian practice. It has been subjected, however, to considerable modification between the date of the earliest MSS. (c. 9th cent.) and the present day, and it is likely that such changes had been going on continuously since its first compilation. Apart from some of the prayers, it agrees closely with that of St. Chrysostom (q.v.).

Text in Brightman, *L.E.W.*, pp. 309–44, 400–11; also in J. P. Migne, *PG*, xxxi. 1629–56. H. Engberding, O.S.B., *Das eucharistische Hochgebet der Basileiosliturgie* (1931). S. Euringer, *Die äthiopische Anaphora des hl. Basilius* (Rome, 1934; ed., with tr. and notes, from four MSS.). P. de Meester, O.S.B., in *D.A.C.L.*, vi (pt. 2, 1925), cols. 1596–1604 ('Authenticité des liturgies de Saint Basile et de Saint Jean Chrysostome'), s.v. 'Grecques (Liturgies)'.

BASIL, Rule of St. The monastic Rule put forward by St. *Basil the Great in 358–64 which is the basis of the usual Rule still followed by religious in the E. Church. The Rule is in two forms, the 'Regulae fusius tractatae' (55 items) and the 'Regulae brevius tractatae' (313 items), in each case set out in the form of questions and answers. While strict, it avoided giving encouragement to the more extreme austerities of the hermits of the deserts. It conceived of asceticism as a means to the perfect service of God, to be achieved in community life under obedience. Hours of liturgical prayer were laid down, and manual and other work, in the form of set tasks, enjoined. Poverty and chastity similar to that later prescribed in the West were also imposed. Children were to be trained in classes attached to the monasteries, and were to be given an opportunity of testing their vocation to the religious life. The monks were enjoined also to care for the poor. The Rule owes its present form to a revision by St. *Theodore of Studion (d. 826).

The text of the *Regulae*, together with that of the *Constitutiones Monasticae*, is in J. P. Migne, *PG* xxxi, 889–1428. See also E. F. Morison, *St. Basil and his Rule. A Study in Early Monasticism* (1912).

BASIL OF ANCYRA (4th cent.), *Arian Bp. He was a typical representative of the more moderate party of the Arians. Elected in 336 to succeed *Marcellus in the see of *Ancyra, he was himself deposed by the Council of *Sardica in 343, but reinstated by *Constantius c. 348. He took part in the Arianizing Synods of Sirmium (351), of *Ancyra (358), and Seleucia (359). His constantly increasing criticisms of the more extreme Arian doctrines, however, led their exponents to remove him from his see in 360, and banish him to Illyria, where he died. A short dogmatic treatise which he composed in conjunction with *George of Laodicea has been preserved by *Epiphanius in his *Haer.* 73, 12–22. He

was also perhaps the author of the treatise 'On Virginity' (so F. Cavallera) included among the works of St. *Basil the Great.

For the writings mentioned, see J. P. Migne, *PG*, xlii. 425–44, and xxx. 669–810. J. Gummerus, *Die homöusianische Partei bis zum Tode des Konstantius* (1900), pp. 121–34. F. Cavallera, 'Le "De Virginitate" de Basil d'Ancyre' in *R.H.E.*, vi (1905), pp. 5–14. R. Janin in *D.H.G.E.*, vi (1932), cols. 1104–7.

BASIL OF SELEUCIA (d. c. 459), Abp. of Seleucia from c. 440. He is remembered chiefly for his vacillating part in the events which preceded the Council of *Chalcedon in 451. Having condemned *Eutyches, the heresiarch, in 448, he acquiesced in his rehabilitation by the *Latrocinium in 449, but recanted shortly after and signed the *Tome of St. *Leo I in 450. A series of 41 sermons of Basil on the Scriptures (two not genuine) have been preserved; and there are a few other writings, some of them spurious, that have come down under his name.

Works in J. P. Migne, *PG*, lxxxv. 1–618; T. P. Camelot, O.P., 'Une Homélie inédite de Basile de Seleucie' in *Mélanges offerts à A. M. Desrousseaux* (1937), pp. 35–48. B. Marx, 'Der homiletische Nachlass des Basileios von Seleukia' in *O.C.P.*, vii (1941), pp. 329–69. On his 'De Vita et Miraculis S. Theclae Libri II' (Migne, l.c., 477–618), cf. H. *Delehaye, S.J., in *Anal. Boll.*, xliii (1925), pp. 49–57. Bardenhewer, iv, pp. 300–4. P. Godet in *D.T.C.*, ii (1905), col. 459 f.

BASILICA. The early form of the building used for Christian worship. It seems to have been modelled on the Roman building of the same name, which served as a law court and a commercial exchange; but some features were apparently derived from the Roman house and others from the chapels of the *catacombs, both of which had served as places of Christian worship before the conversion of the empire. The building was often approached by an '*atrium', or outer courtyard, with its colonnaded cloister. The church itself consisted of a '*narthex', or narrow porch, leading by three or more doorways into the main building. This was built with a nave and two (or even four) narrower aisles with pillars supporting horizontal architraves at first, but in later times arches. Above these rose the clerestory pierced by windows. The building was usually orientated, with the east end completed by an arch and semicircular apse, with mosaics in its vaulting. The altar, which stood out from the wall on the chord of the apse, was raised on a platform and surmounted by a canopy. Directly underneath the altar and partly below the level of the floor was the 'confessio'or chapel which sometimes contained the body of the patron Saint. While the basilica was being used for worship the bishop sat on a throne in the centre of the wall of the apse, with his clergy in a semicircle on either side. In celebrating Mass he faced the west.

To-day the title of 'basilica' is given by the Pope to certain privileged churches. Such basilicas are 'major' or 'minor'. The four 'Major Basilicas' are the Roman churches of St. John *Lateran (for the 'Patriarch of the West', the Pope), St. Peter's at the *Vatican (for the Patriarch of *Constantinople), St. Paul's outside the Walls (for the Patriarch of *Alexandria), and Sta. *Maria Maggiore (for the Patriarch of *Antioch). Each has a Papal altar, the use of which is restricted to the Pope or his immediate delegate. There are eleven 'Minor Basilicas' in Rome, and others throughout the world.

R. Krauthmeier, *Corpus Basilicarum Christianarum Romae. The Early Christian Basilicas of Rome, IV–IX Cent.* (Monumenti di Antichità Pubblicati dal Pontificio Istituto di Archeologia Cristiana, Ser. II, ii, etc., 1937 ff.). G. Dehio, 'Die Genesis der christlichen Basilika' in *Sb* (Bayr.), Jg. 1882, Hft. 2 (1882), pp. 301–41; R. Lemaire, 'L'Origine de la basilique latine' in *Annales de la Société d'Archéologie de Bruxelles*, xxv (1911), pp. 5–130; L. Bréhier, 'Les Origines de la basilique chrétienne' in *Bulletin Monumental*, lxxxvi (1927), pp. 221–49. J. G. Davies, *The Origin and Development of Early Christian Church Architecture* (1952), pp. 12–50. H.*Leclerq, O.S.B., in *D.A.C.L.*, ii (pt. 1; 1910), cols. 525–602, s.v. 'Basilique'; E. Kirchbaum, S.J., and P. Pachini–S. Mattei in *E.C.*, ii (1949), cols. 957–969, s.v.

BASILIDES.
A *Gnostic, probably of Syrian origin, who taught at *Alexandria in the second quarter of the 2nd cent., and pretended to the possession of a secret tradition transmitted from St. *Peter. He appears to have held that the supreme God, who could be described only by negatives, was separated from the world by many heavens and grades of spiritual beings; that the God of the Jews, who as a creator belonged to the lowest ranks of spiritual beings, tried to subject men to himself, and that it was in order to free them that the 'supreme God' sent into the world His Nous (mind), a spiritual being of high rank evolved from Him; that this Nous dwelt in Jesus who suffered in appearance only; and that man must follow Him to win free from matter and rise to the Supreme God. But no wholly consistent account of Basilides' teaching is possible, esp. as the authorities (*Irenaeus, *Clement of Alexandria, *Hippolytus) do not themselves agree.

Basilides wrote a 'Gospel', a commentary upon it ('exegetica' in 24 Books), and a collection of 'Psalms' or 'Odes', all lost. The chief authorities are *Irenaeus, *Adv. Haer.*, I. 24; *Clement of Alexandria, *Strom.*, passim; *Hippolytus, *Ref.*, vii. 20–7. Important art. by F. J. A. *Hort in *D.C.B.*, i (1877), pp. 268–81, s.v. J. G. W. Uhlhorn, *Das basilidianische System* (1855); P. J. G. A. Hendrix, *De Alexandrijnsche Haeresiarch Basilides* (Amsterdam, 1926). G. Bardy in *D.H.G.E.*, vi (1932), cols. 1169–75.

BASILIKON DORON
(Gk. Βασιλικὸν Δῶρον, 'a royal gift'). The title of *James I's book addressed to his eldest son, Henry (d. 1612). Its professed purpose was to guide Henry in his duties when he succeeded to the throne, but its real object was to rebuke ministers of religion who meddled in state affairs. James published it in 1599.

BASLE, Confessions of.
The [first] 'Confession of Basle', which was compiled by Oswald *Myconius (1488–1552) on the basis of a shorter formula put forward by J. *Oecolampadius in 1531, was made the basis of the reform introduced at Basle in 1534. Its theological standpoint represents a compromise between the positions of M. *Luther and H. *Zwingli. The 'First *Helvetic Confession' of 1536 is sometimes known also as the 'Second Confession of Basle'.

The text of the two confessions is in H. A. Niemeyer, *Collectio Confessionum in ecclesiis reformatis publicatarum* (Leipzig, 1840), pp. 78–122.

BASLE, Council of
(1431–49). The Council, which inherited both the tasks and the difficulties of the Council of *Constance (q.v.), was convoked by *Martin V and opened in 1431. It was presided over by Card. G. *Cesarini, who was confirmed in this office by the new Pope, *Eugenius IV. When the latter, acting on unfavourable reports, dissolved it by a bull of 18 Dec. 1431, the Council disregarded the Pope's action, which was also opposed by Cesarini, and reaffirmed the decrees of Constance on the superiority of a *General Council over the Pope. The assembly at that time consisted of only 14 bishops and abbots, apart from the inferior clergy, and, in order to enhance its authority, it introduced new regulations for procedure which gave the lower grades a majority over the bishops. It was, moreover, widely supported by the princes and the great universities, one of its best-known members being *Nicolas of Cusa, the humanist.

The Pope, pressed by the Emperor and the German princes and beset by political difficulties in Italy, by the bull 'Dudum sacrum' of 15 Dec. 1433, revoked his former decision and recognized the Council. The Council continued, however, in its anti-Papal attitude, reasserted once again the decrees of Constance, imposed many restrictions on the Papal legates, and prescribed an oath to be taken by the Pope after his election. It also attempted to regulate the nominations of cardinals and other affairs of the *Curia. In 1436 Eugenius IV denounced the usurpations of the Council in a memorandum to all Catholic princes. In 1437 the *Hussite question was settled against the Papal views by the ratification of the 'Compactata', thereby conceding to the Bohemians Communion under both kinds and several other demands. In the same year occurred the final break with the Orthodox Church over the place of the proposed council for the union. As the Pope, the Greek envoys, and the Papal minority of the Council preferred a place in Italy, Eugenius transferred the Council to *Ferrara; while those who remained at Basle deposed the Pope as a heretic and elected Amadeus VIII of Savoy as antipope (Felix V) in 1439. The renewal of the schism cost the Council its prestige, and the nations submitted one by one to Eugenius. In 1448 the Council was driven from Basle and moved to Lausanne, where Felix V abdicated, and in 1449 it submitted to the legitimate Pope.

The oecumenicity of the Council of Basle has been an object of much discussion. The *Gallicans were in favour of it, at least until its transfer to Ferrara, whereas modern RC theologians either restrict their recognition to the first 16 sessions, or, more generally, reject it altogether on the grounds of its not representing the Universal Church and the absence of Papal recognition of its acts.

Texts in Hardouin, viii–ix; Mansi, xxix (1788)–xxxi (1798). Crit. texts in *Concilium Basiliense*. Studien und Quellen zur Geschichte des Concils von Basel (ed. J. Haller and others, 1896 ff.; 8 vols. to 1936). Hefele–Leclercq, vii (pt. 2, 1916), pp. 663–1137, with extensive bibl. reff. M. Creighton, *A History of the Papacy*, ii (1882), esp. pp. 92–194. P. Lazarus, *Das Basler Konzil*. Seine Vorbereitung und Leitung, seine Gliederung und seine Behördenorganisation (Historische Studien, Heft 100; 1912). A. Zellfelder, *England und das Basler Konzil*. Mit einem Urkundenanhang (Historische Studien, Heft 113; 1913). G. Pérouse, *Le Cardinal Louis Aleman, président du concile de Bâle* (1904). J. MacCaffrey in *C.E.*, ii (1907), pp. 334–8.

BASNAGE, JACQUES (1653–1723), *Calvinist theologian and church historian. Having become in 1676 a minister at Rouen, his native town, he retired to Holland in 1685 after the revocation of the Edict of *Nantes. He later took a prominent part in Dutch affairs of state. His two most important writings are his *Histoire de la religion des églises réformées* (2 vols., 1690) and his *Histoire de l'église* (2 vols., 1699), both publd. at Rotterdam. He also wrote against J. B. *Bossuet.

G. B. Maury in *P.R.E.* (ed. 3), ii (1897), p. 441, s.v.

BASNAGE, SAMUEL (1638–1721), theologian and historian, cousin of the preceding. He also retired to Holland in 1685, where he became minister of the Walloon community at Zutphen. His two chief writings are his *De rebus sacris et ecclesiasticis exercitationes* (1692) and his *Annales politico-ecclesiastici* (3 vols., 1706), both directed against C. *Baronius.

BASSENDYNE BIBLE, The. The earliest edition of the Bible in English to be published in Scotland. In July 1575 Thomas Bassendyne (or Bassinden; d. 1577) was granted a licence by the Privy Council to print the Bible, with the stipulation that it should be ready in nine months, and in 1576 the NT appeared. The Bible was not completed, however, till 1579.

W. T. Dobson, *History of the Bassendyne Bible* (Edinburgh, 1887), esp. pp. 101–57. Darlow–Moule, i (1903), No. 119, p. 89.

BATH AND WELLS. A see of the Province of *Canterbury, of which the cathedral church is at *Wells in Somerset. The bishopric set up at Wells in 909 by King Edward the Elder was moved to Bath in 1088 by Bp. John de Villula (1088–1122); but its transference caused so much dispute between the secular canons of Wells and the monks of Bath that *c.* 1139 it was decided that both bodies should share in the election of bishops. This arrangement was finally settled by *Innocent IV in 1245 and from now on the Bishops bore the title of 'Bath and Wells'. Among notable holders of the see are R. *Fox (1492–4), T. *Wolsey (1518–23), W. *Barlow (1549–54), T.

*Ken (1685–90) and R. *Bagot (1845–54). The present abbey-church at Bath has served since the *dissolution of the monasteries as a parish church.

The following Episcopal Registers have been publd. by the Somerset Record Society: Walter Giffard, 1265–6 (xiii; 1899), John de Drokensford, 1309–29 (i; 1887), Ralph of Shrewsbury, 1329–63 (ix and x; 1896), Henry Bowett, 1401–7 (xiii; 1899), Nicholas Bubwith, 1407–24 (xxix and xxx; 1914), John Stafford, 1425–43 (xxxi and xxxii; 1915–16), Thomas Beckington, 1443–65 (xlix and l; 1934–5), Robert Stillington, 1466–91, and Richard Fox, 1492–4 (lii; 1937), Oliver King, 1496–1503, and Hadrian de Castello, 1503–18 (liv; 1939), Thomas Wolsey, 1518–23, John Clerke, 1523–41, William Knyght, 1541–7, and Gilbert Bourne, 1554–9 (lv; 1940). A Survey of the Diocesan Archives, carried out by a committee appointed by the Pilgrim Trust in 1946, was circulated in typescript among the principal record libraries of England. H. Wharton, *Anglia Sacra*, i (1691), pp. 551–77. S. H. Cassan, *Lives of the Bishops of Bath and Wells from the Earliest Times to the Present Period* (1829). On Bath Abbey, see W. *Dugdale, *Monasticon Anglicanum*, ii (ed. 1819), pp. 256–73. C. L. Marson in *D.E.C.H.*, pp. 44–6, s.v. See also bibl. to *Wells.

BATH QOL (Heb. בַּת קוֹל, 'daughter of a voice'). The term in *Rabbinic theology for a voice from Heaven such as was believed to be a regular means of God's communication with men. Such a voice is referred to in the NT at Christ's *Baptism (Mk. 1. 11) and *Transfiguration (Mk. 9. 7) and before His Passion (Jn. 12. 28), and also in Acts (9. 4, cf. 10. 13).

BATIFFOL, PIERRE (1861–1929), Church historian. A pupil of G. B. *de Rossi, from 1889 till his death he was at the École de Ste. Barbe at *Paris, except from 1898 to 1908 when he was rector of the Institut Catholique at Toulouse. His first important writings were a critical edition of the *Syntagma Doctrinae ad Monachos* included among the writings of St. *Athanasius (1890), and an important bibliographical work, *L'Abbaye de Rossano, contribution à l'histoire de la Vaticane* (1891). These were followed in 1893 by his *Histoire du Bréviaire romain* (1893; much improved ed., 1911), which exercised considerable influence on the revival of liturgical studies in France. For some years he was closely associated with the group of scholars later condemned as *Modernists. In 1902 he published the first series of his *Études d'histoire et de théologie positive* (1902) which included studies on the *Disciplina Arcani, the origins of penance, and the *Agape. A second volume, dealing with the *Eucharist, which appeared in 1905, created such a storm by its unorthodox views that Batiffol was forced to resign from his rectorship at Toulouse, and in 1911 it was placed on the *Index. In 1913 he issued a much revised edition with the separate title *L'Eucharistie, la Présence réelle et la Transubstantiation*. His later years were mainly taken up with a history of the Church and esp. of the growth of Papal power to the time of St. *Leo, of which the successive volumes were *L'Église naissante et le catholicisme* (1909; Eng. trans. *Primitive Catholicism*, 1911), *La Paix constantinienne et le catholicisme* (1914), *Le Catholicisme de Saint Augustin* (1920), and *Le Siège apostolique, 359–451* (1924). In 1928 followed

St. Grégoire le Grand (Eng. trans., 1929). His writings, if unequal in originality and historical penetration to those of his great contemporary, L. *Duchesne, with whom he shared many common interests, did much to encourage critical studies in France and esp. to introduce to his country recent German work in patristics.

J. Rivière, *Monseigneur Batiffol* (1929).

BAUER, BRUNO (1809–82), German theologian and historian. He was at first a conservative *Hegelian, and in 1835–6 scathingly reviewed D. F. *Strauss's *Leben Jesu*. But after his removal from Berlin to Bonn in 1839, his views changed; and in his *Kritik der evangelischen Geschichte des Johannes* (1840) and *Kritik der evangelischen Geschichte der Synoptiker* (3 vols., 1841–2) he went even beyond Strauss in his radical criticism of the NT, attributing the Gospel story to the imagination not, like Strauss, of the Christian community, but of a single mind. In 1842 he was deprived of his chair at Berlin; but he continued to write until his death on both historical and theological matters. His guiding principle was a belief that the origins of Christianity were to be found in Greco-Roman philosophy. He assigned the 'original Gospel' to the reign of Hadrian (117–38) and the Epp. of St. Paul to that of *Marcus Aurelius (161–80). His most important purely historical work was his *Geschichte der Politik, Kultur und Aufklärung des 18ten Jahrhunderts* (4 vols., 1843–5).

A. *Schweitzer, *Geschichte der Leben-Jesu Forschung* (ed. 2, 1913), pp. 141–61. E. Barnikol, 'Bruno Bauers Kampf gegen Religion und Christentum und die Spaltung der vormärzlichen preussischen Opposition' in *Z.K.G.*, xlvi (1927), pp. 1–34. W. Schmidt-J. Haussleiter in *P.R.E.* (ed. 3), ii (1897), pp. 444–7, and A. Meyer in *R.G.G.*, i (1927), col. 796 f.

BÄUMER, SUITBERT (1845–94), liturgical scholar. After studying at Bonn and *Tübingen, he took the *Benedictine habit at *Beuron in 1865. From 1875 to 1890 he was in exile at *Maredsous, through the *Kulturkampf. He wrote extensively on liturgical subjects, esp. in *Der Katholik* of Mainz. His chief work, *Die Geschichte des Breviers* (Freiburg i. Br., 1895; Fr. trans. by R. Biron, 2 vols., 1905), was the fruit of long and patient researches in the principal libraries of Europe. Among its theses were the liturgical importance of St. *Gregory I and the widespread influence of *Gregory VII's rite in the Papal chapel through its subsequent adoption by the *Franciscans. His other works include a Life of J. *Mabillon (1892) and a treatise on the *Apostles' Creed (1893).

U. Berlière, O.S.B., 'Dom Suitbert Baeumer, O.S.B.' in *R. Bén.*, xi (1894), pp. 481–99 (incl. list of works; pp. 497–9). R. Biron, O.S.B., 'Notice biographique' prefixed to his tr. of Bäumer's *Geschichte des Breviers* ('Histoire du bréviaire'), i (1905), pp. xiii–xiv. R. Proost in *D.A.C.L.*, ii (1910), cols. 623–6, s.v.; P. Séjourné, O.S.B., in *D.H.G.E.*, vi (1932), cols. 1474–81, s.v.

BAUMSTARK, ANTON (1872–1948), liturgist and Semitic scholar. A native of Constance, he habilitated at Heidelberg in 1898 in both Classical and Oriental Philology. From 1899 to 1905 he resided at the German Campo Santo at Rome (with J. Strzygowsky, J. Wilpert, and J. P. Kirsch as his colleagues). Later he was a schoolmaster at Sassbach in Baden (1905–21); then, simultaneously, Professor at Bonn (from 1921), Nijmegen (from 1923), and Utrecht (from 1926); and from 1930 to 1935 Professor Ordinarius in Oriental Studies at Münster i.W. In 1901 he began the periodical *Oriens Christianus* (3 Series; to 1941) in which he published much of his best work. He was also a constant contributor to the *Maria Laach *Jahrbuch für Liturgiewissenschaft* (from 1921). His separate works include: *Die Messe im Morgenland* (1906), *Festbrevier und Kirchenjahr der syrischen Jakobiten* (1910), *Die christlichen Literaturen des Orients* (2 vols., Sammlung Göschen, 1911), *Geschichte der syrischen Literatur* (1922), *Die älteste erreichbare Gestalt des 'Liber sacramentorum anni circuli' der römischen Kirche* (with C. Mohlberg, 1927), *Missale Romanum* (1930), and *Liturgie comparée*. Conférences faites au Prieuré d'Amay (1940; new ed. by B. Botte, O.S.B., 1953; Eng. ed. by F. L. Cross, 1958).

Short obituary by T. Klauser in *Ephemerides Liturgicae*, 63 (1949), pp. 185–7, followed by full bibliography by H. F. Killy (1894–1948; 546 items).

BAUR, FERDINAND CHRISTIAN (1792–1860), German Protestant theologian, founder of the *Tübingen School (q.v.). A native of Schmiden in Württemberg, he was educated at Tübingen university. From 1817 to 1826 he taught history and philology at Blaubeuren and in 1824–5 published his work, *Symbolik und Mythologie*. From 1826 until his death he was Prof. of Theology at Tübingen. A disciple of F. D. E. *Schleiermacher in his early years, he developed his characteristic doctrines under the influence of G. W. F. *Hegel's conception of history. In his work on the Pastoral Epistles, *Untersuchungen über die sog. Pastoralbriefe des Apostels Paulus* (1835), Hegelian principles were for the first time applied to the NT, primitive Christianity being represented as a struggle between divergent views, the synthesis of which was the Catholic Church. In the following years he applied these same principles to the development of Christian doctrine, esp. to the Atonement and to the Trinity and the Incarnation (*Die Lehre von der Versöhnung*, 1838; *Die christliche Lehre von der Dreieinigkeit*, 1841–3), breaking new ground by treating his subject no longer systematically but historically, and thus becoming one of the fathers of the modern history of dogma. In 1845 appeared his monograph on St. *Paul, *Paulus, der Apostel Jesu Christi* (Eng. trans., 1873–5), which roused a storm of controversy. Setting out from the thesis that the Gentile Apostle was throughout his life in violent opposition to the older disciples, Baur denied the authenticity of all Pauline Epistles except Gal., 1 and 2 Cor., and Rom., as well as the Apostolic origin of Acts. In 1847 he concluded his researches into the NT canon with a work on the Gospels, *Kritische Untersuchung über die kanonischen Evangelien*, in which he assigned the earliest date to Mt., as representing the Judaizing party, and the latest to Jn., as depicting the final reconciliation. This last Gospel reflected the *Gnostic and *Montanist controversies of the 2nd cent. and was devoid of historical value. In his later years he devoted himself chiefly to Church history, which he carried from the beginnings of Christianity to the 19th cent., the last vols. being published posthumously. Among his other writings were *Lehrbuch der christlichen Dogmengeschichte* (1847), *Das Christenthum und die christliche Kirche der drei ersten Jahrhunderte* (1853) and his *Vorlesungen über die christliche Dogmengeschichte* (ed. by his son, F. F. Baur, 4 vols., 1865–7).

H. Schmidt–J. Haussleiter in *P.R.E.* (ed. 3), ii (1897), pp. 467–83, with full list of Baur's writings (pp. 467–9) and bibl. (p. 469 f.). There are innumerable monographs on Baur and the Tübingen School, but apparently no large-scale contemporary Life. E. Zeller, *Vorträge und Abhandlungen*, i (ed. 2, 1875), pp. 390–479 (No. 11: F. C. Baur); modern life by G. Frädrich (1909). More recent literature cited by K. Bauer, *R.G.G.*, i (1927), cols. 817–20.

BAVON, St. (d. *c.* 653), also called **Allowin**. The patron saint of the cathedral and diocese of Ghent (Feast days, 1 Oct. and 1 Aug.) and of the diocese of Haarlem (Feast days, 9 Aug. and 10 May).

Three Lives are printed in *AA.SS.*, Oct. I (1765), pp. 229–253; the first, and a short extract from the third, ed. by B. Krusch in *M.G.H.*, Scriptores Rerum Merovingicarum, iv (1902), pp. 527–46. L. van der Essen in *D.H.G.E.*, vii, cols. 14 f., s.v., incl. full bibl.,

BAXTER, RICHARD (1615–91), *Puritan divine. Born at Rowton, Shropshire, he was largely self-educated. He studied first at the free school of Wroxeter, next under the nominal tutelage of Richard Wickstead, Chaplain at Ludlow Castle, and finally (1633) in London under the patronage of Sir Henry Herbert, Master of the Revels. In disgust at the frivolity of the Court he returned home to study divinity, in particular the Schoolmen. In 1634 he came into intimate contact with Joseph Symonds and Walter Cradock, two devout Nonconformist divines, who awakened his sympathies for the positive elements in dissent. In 1638 he was ordained by John Thornborough, Bp. of *Worcester, and in 1639 nominated to the Mastership of the free Grammar School at Bridgnorth, where he remained for two years, increasing his knowledge of the issues between Nonconformity and the C of E. After the promulgation of the 'Et Cetera Oath' (1640) he rejected belief in episcopacy in its current English form. In 1641 he became curate to the incumbent of Kidderminster, where amongst a corrupt and unhealthy population of hand-loom workers he continued to minister with remarkable success until 1660. So far as possible he ignored the differences between Presbyterian, Episcopalian, and Independent, and secured co-operation among the local ministers in common pastoral work. In the early part of the Civil War he temporarily joined the Parliamentary Army, preaching at Alcester on the day of the Battle of Edgehill (23 Oct. 1642). A champion of moderation, he was opposed to the *Solemn League and Covenant (1643) and also disliked O. *Cromwell's religious views. After the Battle of Naseby (14 June 1645) he became Chaplain to Colonel Edward Whalley's regiment, seeking to counteract the sectaries and to curb republican tendencies. On leaving the army (1647) he retired for a time to Rouse Lench, where he wrote his devotional classic, *The Saints' Everlasting Rest* (1650). In 1660 he played a prominent part in the recall of *Charles II; but his dissatisfaction with episcopacy led him to decline the Bishopric of *Hereford. This refusal debarred him from ecclesiastical office and he was not permitted to return to Kidderminster or to hold any living. He took a prominent part at the *Savoy Conference (1661; q.v.), for which he had prepared a 'Reformed Liturgy'; here he presented the *Exceptions to the BCP. Between 1662 and the *Declaration of Indulgence of 1687 he endured persecution, suffering at the hands of the notorious Judge Jeffreys on the questionable charge of having 'libelled the Church' in his *Paraphrase on the New Testament* (1685). He took part in the overthrow of *James II and readily complied with the Toleration Act of William and Mary. He died on 8 Dec. 1691.

Baxter left nearly 200 writings. They breathe a spirit of deep unaffected piety and reflect his love of moderation. *Gildas Salvianus, or The Reformed Pastor* (1656) illustrates the great care he took in his pastoral organization, and the *Reliquiae Baxterianae* (ed. Matthew Sylvester, 1696) is a long and careful autobiography. He also wrote several hymns, among them 'Ye holy angels bright' and 'He wants not friends that hath Thy love'.

The Practical Works of . . . Richard Baxter (London, 4 vols., 1707); new ed. with Life and examination of Baxter's writings by W. Orme (23 vols., 1830). Many of his works were reprinted in the 19th cent. Modern abridged edd. of *The Saints' Everlasting Rest*, by M. Monckton (Reunion edition [1928]), *Gildas Salvianus; or the Reformed Pastor*, by J. T. Wilkinson (1939) and of his autobiography, the *Reliquiae Baxterianae*, by J. M. L. Thomas (1925; and in Everyman's Library, 1931). *Chapters from a Christian Directory*, selected by J. Tawney with a preface by C. *Gore (1925). F. J. Powicke (ed.), with introduction by G. Unwin, 'The Reverend Baxter's last Treatise' in the *Bulletin of the John Rylands Library*, x (1926), pp. 163–218; F. J. Powicke (ed.), 'Some Unpublished Correspondence of the Rev. Richard Baxter and the Rev. John Eliot, "The Apostle to the American Indians", 1656–1682', ib., xv (1931), pp. 138–176 and 442–66. Id., *A Life of the Reverend Richard Baxter, 1615–1691* (1924); id., *The Reverend Richard Baxter Under the Cross, 1662–1691* (1927); A. R. Ladell, *Richard Baxter. Puritan and Mystic* (Studies in Church History, 1925); I. Morgan, *The Nonconformity of Richard Baxter* (1926). A. B. Grosart, *Annotated List of the Writings of Richard Baxter* (1868). J. T. Wilkinson, *Richard Baxter and Margaret Charlton. A Puritan Love Story*. Being the Breviate of the Life of Margaret Baxter, by Richard Baxter, 1681 (1928). H. Martin, *Puritanism and Richard Baxter* (1954), esp. pp. 122–92. A. B. Grosart in *D.N.B.*, iii (1885), pp. 429–37.

BAY PSALM BOOK, The. The edition of the Psalms produced at Cambridge, Massachusetts (popularly known in the U.S.A. as

'Bay State'), in 1640, and the first book to be printed in British America. It was the work of a body of *Congregationalists, among them Richard Mather (1596–1669).

B. F. Swan, 'Some Thoughts on the Bay Psalm Book of 1640, with a Census of Copies' in *The Yale University Library Gazette*, xxii (1948), pp. 51–176.

BAYEUX TAPESTRY, The. An embroidered band of linen, 231 ft. by 20 in., preserved at Bayeux in Normandy, which depicts the Norman invasion of England and the events preceding it. It was probably made for Bp. *Odo of Bayeux for use in his cathedral. In it appear Odo himself, Abp. *Stigand, and *Edward the Confessor's *Westminster Abbey, for the architecture of which it is a valuable authority. It is also an important witness to the ecclesiastical dress of the epoch.

E. Maclagan, *The Bayeux Tapestry* (King Penguin Books, 1943; ed. 2, 1945), with bibl., p. 29. F. R. Fowke, *The Bayeux Tapestry, reproduced in autotype Plates with historical Notes* (1875; smaller ed., 1898). Full bibl. in J. J. Marquet de Vasselot, *Bibliographie de la tapisserie* (1935). Excellent reproduction, with essays and bibl., in (ed.) F. M. Stenton, *The Bayeux Tapestry* (Phaedon Press, 1957).

BAYLE, PIERRE (1647–1706), sceptical writer. The son of a French Protestant minister, he became professor of philosophy and history at Rotterdam in 1681. In his *Pensées sur la comète* (1682) he argued *inter alia* that, religion and morality being independent of one another, all the private and social virtues may be equally practised by atheists. By such views, and by his championship of universal toleration (in connexion with the revocation of the Edict of *Nantes, 1685), he incurred the antagonism of influential French Protestants, and was deprived of his chair in 1693. His most famous work was his *Dictionnaire historique et critique* (1695–7; 2nd edition, enlarged, 1702). His accuracy, encyclopaedic knowledge, and sceptical temper made his work invaluable to the anti-Christian *Deists and *philosophes* of the 18th cent., both in France and in England.

Selections of his letters ed. by P. Des Maizeaux (3 vols., Rotterdam, 1714; 3 vols., Amsterdam, 1729; and 2 vols., The Hague, 1739), J. Rou (2 vols., Paris, 1857), and E. Gigas (Copenhagen, 1890). Life by P. Des Maizeaux prefixed to the *Dictionnaire historique et critique*, i (ed. 4, 1730), pp. xvii–cviii, issued separately (2 vols., 1732). Studies by L. Feuerbach (Leipzig, 1838), C. Lenient (Paris, 1855), E. Jeanmaire (Strassburg, 1862), J. Devolve (Paris, 1906), E. Smith (Albany, N.Y., 1912), and E. Lacoste (Académie-Royale de Belgique. Classe des Lettres &c, Mémoires. Collection in 8vo, xxiv, fasc. 3, 1929).

BAYLY, LEWIS (d. 1631). The author of *The Practice of Piety*. He was educated at Oxford, probably at Exeter College, and became chaplain to Henry, Prince of Wales. His *Puritan opinions gave offence at court; but he returned to favour and in 1616 became chaplain to *James I and later in the year Bp. of *Bangor. As a bishop, his opinions again made him unpopular; continual trouble with the Council led to his imprisonment in the Fleet (1621); and his laxity in ecclesiastical discipline was attacked constantly until his death. His *Practice of Piety* (ed. 3, 1613; the date of its original publication is not known) enjoyed remarkable popularity, esp. among the Puritans, and was translated into several languages; and J. *Bunyan regarded it as a great influence in his life.

Biog. Preface (inaccurate) by G. Webster to the 1842 ed. of Bayly's *Practice of Piety*. J. E. Bailey, 'Bishop Lewis Bayly and his "Practice of Piety"' in *The Manchester Quarterly*, ii (1883), pp. 221–39, repr. separately, 1883.

B.C.M.S. ('Bible Churchmen's Missionary Society'). A society formed out of the *C.M.S. when a group broke away from the parent body in 1922 in order to assert its fidelity to the traditional doctrines of the Evangelical party (in particular, to the belief in the complete inerrancy of the Scriptures), as opposed to any reinterpretation or alteration of emphasis adopted by *Liberal Evangelicals.

W. S. Hooton–J. Stafford Wright, *The First Twenty-Five Years of the Bible Churchmen's Missionary Society, 1922–47* (1947).

BEAD (Mid. Eng. 'bede'). Originally the word meant a prayer (cf. Germ. *beten*, 'to pray'), but later it was transferred to the small spherical bodies used for 'telling beads' (i.e. counting the beads of a *rosary), and hence also applied, e.g., to the parts of a necklace. 'To bid a bead' thus means 'to offer a prayer'. See also *Bidding Prayer*.

BEADLE. In the Church of Scotland an official appointed by the *session to care for the place of worship and to perform other similar functions. He is subject to the minister for direction in his duties, and hence used frequently to be known as 'the minister's man'. One of his most conspicuous tasks is to bear the books to the pulpit before divine service begins. In the newer branches of Presbyterianism he is generally called by the ambiguous title 'church officer'.

BEARD. The wearing of beards by clerics has remained the practice of the E. Church since apostolic times. From the 5th cent. onwards, however, largely under monastic influence, W. clerics adopted the practice of being clean-shaven, and at the time of *Photius, the beardlessness of the W. clergy became one of the chief points of controversy between the E. and W. From the 12th cent. a long series of prohibitions were issued by W. Councils against clerics wearing beards, but in the 15th cent. they widely came in again under the influence of secular fashion, being worn, e.g., by 16th and 17th cent. Popes. They are still worn by *Franciscans.

C. J. Seghers, 'The Practice of Shaving in the Latin Church' in *American Catholic Quarterly Review*, vii (1882), pp. 276–310. H. *Leclercq, O.S.B., in *D.A.C.L.*, ii (pt. 1; 1910), cols. 478–93, s.v. 'Barbe'. H. Thurston, S.J., in *C.E.*, ii (1907), p. 363, s.v.; S. Marsilio, O.S.B., in *E.C.*, ii, (1949), cols. 798–801, s.v. 'Barba'. K. Hilgenreiner in *L.Th.K.*, i (1930), col. 990 f., s.v. 'Bart' for further bibl.

BEARD, CHARLES (1827–88), *Unitarian divine. From 1867 he was in charge of

Renshaw Street chapel, Liverpool, and from 1864 to 1879 was editor of the *Theological Review*. Besides some fine sermons and addresses, he published several historical works. Of these the best known is his series of Hibbert Lectures for 1883, *The Reformation in its relation to Modern Thought and Knowledge*, in which, in accordance with his own sympathies, he stressed the humanistic, as against the more definitely theological, aspects of the Reformers' work.

Study in H. McLachlan, *Records of a Family, 1800–1933* (Publications of the University of Manchester, No. ccxxxix, 1935), pp. 36–75.

BEATIFIC VISION, The.
The vision of the Divine Being in heaven which, acc. to Christian theology, is the final destiny of the redeemed. Its nature and conditions were a subject of much dispute in the later Middle Ages. Benedict XII (1336) formally defined that the Divine Essence would be seen by direct intuition and face to face (*visione intuitiva et etiam faciali*), while against the *Beghards and *Beguines the Council of *Vienne of 1311 laid down that it transcended man's natural capacities and hence was supernatural, and that it was through the Divine gift of the 'light of glory' (*lumen gloriae*) that it was made accessible to him. Whereas its primary object is the vision of the Divine essence itself, it is held that the vision also extends in a secondary and complementary sense to cover all that the blessed may have a reasonable interest in knowing. Acc. to some theologians the vision is bestowed in exceptional circumstances for brief periods in this life, e.g. St. *Thomas Aquinas held that it was granted to *Moses (Ex. 34. 28–35) and St. *Paul (2 Cor. 12. 2–4).

BEATIFICATION.
In the RC Church, the act by which the Pope permits the public veneration after his death of some faithful Catholic in a particular church, diocese, country, or religious order. Very occasionally the permission to venerate a particular person in this way is extended to the whole of the RC Church. Before the 12th cent., and less generally from that date to the 17th cent., it was customary for local bishops to beatify people for their own dioceses. A person who has been beatified receives the title of 'Blessed'. In the Russian Church there is a similar process, although not bearing the same name, for authorizing the local cult of deceased Christians. See also *Canonization*.

*Benedict XIV, *De Servorum Dei Beatificatione et de Beatorum Canonizatione* (Bonn, 4 vols. bound in 5, 1734–8), passim. R. Naz in *D.D.C.*, iii (1942), cols. 10–37, s.v. 'Causes de béatification et de canonisation'; G. Löw, C.SS.R., in *E.C.*, ii (1949), cols. 1090–6, s.v. 'Beatificazione'. See also bibl. to *Canonization*.

BEATING OF THE BOUNDS.
A ceremony common in medieval England, and associated with the *Rogationtide procession round the parish. When written maps, showing parish boundaries, were hardly known, this annual perambulation was a means of impress-ing these limits on the minds of the young. The bounds were solemnly beaten with willow rods, and on occasion boys of the parish were also beaten or bumped on the ground at the boundary. The custom is known to date back to the end of the 9th or beginning of the 10th cent., and lasted on long after the religious part of the procession was abolished under *Elizabeth.

The *Injunctions of Elizabeth I (No. 18). J. H. MacMichael, 'Beating the Bounds: Its Origin' in *Notes and Queries*, 10th Series, ii (1904), p. 113 f., with short bibl. Further bibl. by J. T. Page, ib., iii (1905), p. 390 f., and by G. Potter, ib., iv (1905), p. 31.

BEATITUDES, The.
Christ's promises of coming blessings in the '*Sermon on the Mount' (Mt. 5. 3–11) and the 'Sermon on the Plain' (Lk. 6. 20–22). In Mt. there are eight (or nine) blessings of a spiritual nature, applicable to all, whereas in Lk. there are four blessings, spoken to the disciples, which relate to external conditions. In Lk. they are accompanied by four 'Woes'. The Beatitudes describe the qualities of Christian perfection and have analogies in the OT (e.g. Is. 32, 20, Ps. 1. 1) and elsewhere in the NT (e.g. Lk. 12. 37, Mt. 13. 16).

J. Dupont, O.S.B., *Les Béatitudes* (Louvain, 1954), with bibl. See also comm. to *Matthew* and *Luke*, *Gospels of*, cited s.vv.

BEATITUDES, The Mount of the.
The name traditionally given to the place where the *Sermon on the Mount is believed to have been delivered (cf. Mt. 5. 1). It has been identified since Crusading times with the mountain Karn Hattin, W. of the Sea of *Galilee.

BEATON (or BETHUNE), DAVID
(*c.* 1494–1546), Cardinal Abp. of St. Andrews. He became Abbot of Arbroath in 1523, and was sent by James V on various missions to France. In 1528 he became Keeper of the Privy Seal, Cardinal in 1538, and succeeded his uncle as Abp. of St. Andrews in 1539. On the death of James (1542) he made a bid for the regency, and in spite of his failure to secure it, acquired considerable influence over his successful competitor, the Earl of Arran. It was largely through his influence that the English plans for the subjugation of Scotland were defeated; but after his death his countrymen preferred to remember and exaggerate his actions as a persecutor, and in particular his trial and condemnation of the propagandist *G. Wishart, whose zeal for the Reformation seems to have been involved with political plottings, and designs on the Cardinal's life. He was assassinated by John Leslie at St. Andrews on 29 May 1546.

The main sources for his life are J. *Knox's *History of the Reformation*, Book i, passim, and J. *Spottiswoode, *History of the Church of Scotland* (1847–51 ed.), i, pp. 134–65. Life by J. Herkless (London, 1891).

BEAUFORT, HENRY
(*c.* 1375–1447), Cardinal and Bp. of *Lincoln and *Winchester.

He was born at Beaufort, Anjou, the son of John of Gaunt and Catherine Swynford. His parents having been married in 1396, he was declared legitimate in 1397. He was educated at Peterhouse, Cambridge, and at Queen's College, Oxford. After holding various benefices, incl. a prebend at *Lincoln from 1389, he became Dean of *Wells in 1397 and in the same year Chancellor of the Univ. of Oxford. In 1398 he was provided to the see of Lincoln. In 1403 he became Chancellor until he was translated to *Winchester in 1404, succeeding *William of Wykeham. During most of the reign of Henry IV, however, he supported the party of the Prince of Wales in opposition to the King and Abp. *Arundel. In 1407 he was declared debarred from the succession. With the accession of Henry V in 1413 he was appointed Chancellor, but resigned in 1417, ostensibly to go on a pilgrimage. On the way he attended the Council of *Constance. Here he was largely responsible for the election of Oddo Colonna as *Martin V, who issued a bull creating him Cardinal and *legatus a latere* and later granted him permission to hold the see of Winchester *in commendam* for life. Henry V, however, prevented him from accepting these favours. Appointed in 1421 as one of the guardians of Henry VI, he became Chancellor in 1424 and virtually ruled the realm for the next two years. After a serious quarrel with the Duke of Gloucester, he sought leave to go on pilgrimage again in 1426. In the same year he accepted a cardinalate, and led an unsuccessful expedition against the *Hussites; but his new office, which rendered his position ambiguous, made him very unpopular in England. In spite, however, of continued attacks by the Duke of Gloucester, esp. in 1439, he played a considerable part in foreign policy, being present at the Council of Arras in 1433 and the subsequent negotiations. After the fall of Gloucester (1441), his party was left supreme, but he personally seems to have taken little further part in politics. He died at Wolvesey Palace on Palm Sunday, 1447.

At Winchester Beaufort completed the transformation of the nave of the Cathedral, and greatly extended the Hospital of St. Cross. But he stands out by his financial ability and shrewd statesmanship rather than as a Churchman. By lending money to the King at opportune moments and high rates of (disguised) interest, he amassed a fortune which made his support indispensable to the government. In general he upheld the ideals of constitutional government and strove for peace.

L. B. Radford, *Henry Beaufort. Bishop, Chancellor, Cardinal* (1908). K. B. McFarlane, 'Henry V, Bishop Beaufort and the Red Hat 1417–1421' in *E.H.R.*, lv (1945), pp. 316–48; id., 'At the Death-Bed of Cardinal Beaufort' in *Studies in Medieval History presented to F. M. Powicke*, ed. R. W. Hunt, W. A. Pantin, and R. W. Southern (1948), pp. 405–28. See also K. H. Vickers, *Humphrey, Duke of Gloucester* (1907).

BEAUFORT, MARGARET. See *Margaret, Lady*.

BEAULIEU, Abbey of. This *Cistercian abbey in Hampshire was founded and endowed in 1204 by King John for 30 monks from *Cîteaux, and dedicated in 1246 in the presence of Henry III and his Queen, Eleanor. The abbey was from the first 'exempted' by *Innocent III, with right of sanctuary, which was sought by Ann Neville, wife of Warwick the King-Maker, Perkin Warbeck, and others. At the time of the suppression (1539) there were 32 sanctuary-men with their wives and families within the precincts. Among the portions still standing are the early English refectory (now used as the parish church), the gatehouse (now a private residence), the guest-house dormitory, and parts of the cloisters and chapter-house. Beaulieu (*Bellus locus*) has preserved its original Norman-French pronunciation of 'Bewley'.

W. J. St. John Hope and H. Breakspear, 'The Cistercian Abbey of Beaulieu' in *Archaeological Journal*, lxiii (1906), pp. 130–86. W. *Dugdale, *Monasticon Anglicanum*, v (ed. 1825), pp. 680–4.

BEC, Abbey of. This celebrated Norman abbey, situated between *Rouen and *Lisieux, was founded by Bl. Herlouin (Feast day, 26 Aug.) and consecrated by Mauger, Abp. of Rouen and uncle of William the Conqueror, in 1041. In 1060 it was much rebuilt on a much larger scale. Its notable monks included *Lanfranc (Prior, 1045–63; later Abp. of *Canterbury), St. *Anselm (Prior, 1063–78; Abbot, 1078–93; also Abp. of Canterbury); *Alexander II (Pope, 1061–73), Gundulf (Bp. of *Rochester, 1077–1108), Ernulf (also Bp. of Rochester, 1114–24) and Gilbert Crispin (Abbot of *Westminster, 1085–1117). It long enjoyed royal patronage and was visited by Henry I (1106) and Henry II (1152, 1159, 1178), Kings of England. A fire in 1263 destroyed most of the abbey; the new church built soon afterwards lasted until the 19th cent. In 1467 the Tour St. Nicholas, still extant, was constructed. After the concordat between Francis I and *Leo X in 1516, the government of the abbey passed into the hands of commendatory abbots. In 1626 it was taken over and largely rebuilt by the *Maurists. It was suppressed in 1790 and partly demolished from 1810 onwards. In the latter part of the 19th cent. the buildings attracted the interest of historians and in 1948 the Benedictine life (*Olivetan Congregation) was re-established. The abbey at one time had considerable property in England (cf. Tooting Bec); and the modern community actively promotes religious relations between France and England.

A. A. Porée, *Histoire de l'abbaye du Bec* (2 vols., Évreux, 1901). La Varende, *L'Abbaye du Bec-Hellouin*, vingt-quatre photographies de J. M. Marcel (Paris, 1951).

BECKET, St. THOMAS (?1118–70), Abp. of *Canterbury. A son of Norman settlers, Thomas studied at Paris where *Robert of Melun was among his teachers. *C.* 1141 he became a member of the household of Abp. *Theobald of Canterbury, who sent him to study law at *Bologna and Auxerre, and after ordaining him deacon, appointed him Archdeacon of Canterbury in 1154. In 1155 Henry II made him his chancellor, and his influence was enhanced by an intimate friendship with the King. He liked hunting and the display of pomp, and during a military expedition to France took a personal part in the fighting. His policy as a chancellor was generally in harmony with the wishes of the King, often against the interests of the Church; and when, in 1162, he was elected Abp. of Canterbury at the instigation of the King, he accepted the office with reluctance, knowing a break to be inevitable.

From now onwards Becket adopted a very austere style of life, resigned the chancellorship, and soon found himself in open opposition to Henry on a matter of taxation. The crucial dispute arose over the jurisdiction over criminous clerks, then reserved to the ecclesiastical courts. In 1163 Henry required the bishops to sanction beforehand his so-called 'grandfather's customs', a set of articles shortly to be drawn up, one of its objects being to transfer the trial of criminous clerks to secular courts. When the articles were made public in 1164 under the name of the 'Constitutions of *Clarendon' (q.v.), Becket firmly refused his acceptance and was immediately subjected to a series of reprisals culminating in the demand for a large sum of money in settlement of the accounts during his chancellorship. When Thomas refused, the King required a council of bishops and barons held at Northampton to pass sentence on him, but he escaped to France, appealing for justice to *Alexander III, then at Sens. During the following negotiations between the Pope, Henry, and the Archbishop, Thomas stayed at first at the *Cistercian abbey of Pontigny in Burgundy, and when the King threatened to expel all Cistercians from his dominions (1166), he moved to the *Benedictine abbey of Ste. Colombe at Sens, which was under the special protection of the French King. After he had excommunicated two of his disobedient bishops and threatened England with the interdict in 1169, a reconciliation was at last effected between him and Henry in 1170. The King promised to make amends for the coronation of his son by the Abp. of *York (Roger of Pont-l'Évêque), a flagrant infringement of the prerogatives of Canterbury, while Thomas sent Papal letters of suspension to the bishops who had assisted at the ceremony.

Becket crossed to England on 30 Nov., where he was received with popular enthusiasm. He refused, however, to absolve the Bishops, unless they swore obedience to the Pope. Henry, naturally furious, uttered some words in a fit of rage which were enough to inspire four Knights (Hugh de Morville, William de Tracy, Reginald Fitz-Urse, Richard le Breton) to make their way to Canterbury in revenge. Becket was assassinated in his cathedral in the late afternoon of 29 Dec. 1170. The murder provoked great indignation throughout Europe. Miracles were soon recorded at Becket's tomb and a widespread

cultus developed. On 21 Feb. 1173 he was canonized by Alexander III and on 12 July 1174 Henry did public penance at the shrine. Becket's remains were translated to their place in the choir (the 'Trinity Chapel') in 1220 and until the destruction of the shrine under Henry VIII (1538), it remained one of the principal pilgrimage centres of Christendom. Feast day, 29 Dec.; of his translation, 7 July.

J. C. Robertson and J. B. Sheppard, *Materials for the History of Thomas Becket* (R.S., 7 vols., 1875–85); A. L'Huillier, *St. Thomas de Cantorbéry* (2 vols., 1891); E. A. *Abbott, *St. Thomas, His Death and Miracles* (1898; rationalistic); W. H. *Hutton, *Thomas Becket, Archbishop of Canterbury* (1910; rev. ed., 1926); R. Foreville, *L'Église et la royauté en Angleterre sous Henri II Plantagenet*, 1154–1189 (1943); M. D. Knowles, 'Archbishop Thomas Becket. A Character Study' (Raleigh Lecture on History for 1949) in *Proceedings of the British Academy*, xxxv (1949), pp. 177–205; id., *The Episcopal Colleagues of Archbishop Thomas Becket* (Ford Lectures for 1949; 1951). Dramatic interpretation in T. S. *Eliot, *Murder in the Cathedral* (1935). Kate Norgate in *D.N.B.*, lvi (1898), pp. 165–73, s.v. 'Thomas'.

BECON, THOMAS (c. 1513–67), Protestant Reformer. A native of Norfolk, he was educated at Cambridge, perhaps at St. John's College, studied under H. *Latimer, and was ordained priest in 1533. He was arrested c. 1540 for preaching Protestant doctrines at Norwich and forced to recant. Having retired to Kent, he began writing copiously under the name of Theodore Basille. On the accession of *Edward VI (1547) he was appointed Chaplain to the Lord Protector; was made by T. *Cranmer one of the *Six Preachers of *Canterbury and a chaplain of Cranmer's own household; and was invited to contribute to the 'Book of *Homilies'. In 1548 he was presented to the living of St. Stephen, Walbrook. Expelled from his living on the accession of *Mary (1553), he went to Strassburg (1554) and later to Frankfurt (1555). From 1556 to 1559 he appears to have taught at *Marburg University. Returning to England soon after the accession of *Elizabeth I, he was installed as a Canon of Canterbury Cathedral in 1559 and in his last years held a succession of benefices.

Becon's writings enjoyed a very wide popularity. At first they were moderate in tone, devotional in intent, and much under *Lutheran influence. During and after his exile they grew coarser and their standpoint became *Zwinglian. Becon was usually prepared, however, to compromise on less important points, and perhaps influenced Cranmer to accept the Memorial on Kneeling at Communion (see *Black Rubric*). For the 'Book of Homilies' he wrote that 'Against Whoredom and Uncleanness' (usually known as the 'Homily against Adultery'). His numerous other works include *The Jewel of Joy* (prob. written 1547–8; earliest extant copy 1553), *The Sick Man's Salve* (composed before 1553; earliest copy 1561), and *A New Catechism* (first printed in his works). He revised them for a folio edition (3 vols., 1560–4).

Modern ed. of most of his works by J. Ayre (*Parker Society, 3 vols., 1843–44). D. S. Bailey, *Thomas Becon and the Reformation of the Church in England* (1952).

BEDA, The ('Collegio Beda'). The college at Rome where English candidates for the RC priesthood who have discovered their vocation late in life, including converts from non-Roman ministries who wish to be ordained in the RC Church, are trained.

BEDE (prayer). See *Bead*.

BEDE, St. (*c.* 673-735), 'The Venerable', Biblical scholar and 'Father of English History'. At the age of 7 he was sent to the monastery of *Wearmouth under the rule of St. *Benedict Biscop and transferred to Jarrow prob. at the time of its foundation *c.* 681. He was ordained deacon *c.* 692 (at an age much earlier than was customary) and priested when he was about 30. He visited *Lindisfarne and *York, but it is unlikely that he went outside Northumbria. From the time of his entry into the monastic life he devoted himself to the study of Scripture and to teaching and writing, becoming famous for his learning in his lifetime. His earliest works, the *De Orthographia* and the *De Arte Metrica ad Cuthbertum Levitam*, appear to have been written for the pupils of the monastery. The former is an alphabetically arranged glossary, the latter a collection of verse forms with explanations. His next work, the *De Temporibus*, was prob. written to make clear to the clergy the principles for the calculation of *Easter acc. to the Roman usage adopted by the Synod of *Whitby (664). To it he appended a chronicle of the six ages of the world, mostly adopted from St. *Isidore, which brought upon him a ridiculous charge of heresy. The work was important because, together with the *De Temporum Ratione* (written in 725) and his own historical works, it did much to establish the practice of dating events from the Incarnation. His other important scientific treatise, the *De Natura Rerum*, was prob. written about the same time; it is a cosmography based on Isidore, supplemented from Suetonius and the younger Pliny. In the intervening period he produced the greater part of his Biblical work for which he used both the *Vulgate and *Old Latin texts and often the Greek as well. His expositions, which were highly appreciated by his contemporaries and immediate successors, were founded on the writings of St. *Augustine, St. *Jerome, St. *Ambrose and St. *Gregory, but embodied some original comment. They include works on Rev., Acts, the *Catholic Epistles, Lk., Sam., Mk., Kgs., Gen. 1-20, Ez. and Neh., Exod. 24. 12-30. 21, the Song of Songs and Tobit. His historical works, for which he is in modern times best known, include the *Vita Beatorum Abbatum Benedicti, Ceolfridi, Eosterwini, Sigfridi atque Hwaethberti* (commonly called the *Historia Abbatum*), which traces the history of his monastery from its foundation to 716, his metrical *De Miraculis Sancti Cuthberti* and the more important prose *De Vita et Miraculis S. Cuthberti, Episcopi Lindisfarnensis* and, of supreme in-

terest, his *Historia Ecclesiastica Gentis Anglorum* (completed 731). This last, a primary source for early English history, owes its value to Bede's care in collecting information from those most likely to know, his meticulous listing of his authorities and the separation of historical fact from hearsay and tradition. Its interest is enhanced by the vividness of his descriptions. The *Martyrologium* which goes under his name has been so much interpolated that it is hard to distinguish the work of Bede. He also wrote a considerable amount of verse, though much that is commonly accredited to him is prob. the work of others.

To the end of his life Bede was occupied in teaching and in the recitation of the Divine Office. In a letter to Ecgberct (Bp. of York 735-66) he emphasized the importance of episcopal visitation, confirmation and frequent Communion as the remedy for the ills of the time. Less than a century after his death he was honoured with the title of Venerable, and in the 11th cent. his bones were translated to *Durham, where a stone in the cathedral still commemorates him. In 1899 Pope *Leo XIII pronounced him a '*Doctor of the Church'. Feast day, 27 May.

Complete Works publd. Paris, 1521; ed. with Eng. tr. by J. A. Giles (*Patres Ecclesiae Anglicanae*, ii-xiii, 12 vols, London, 1843-44); Lat. text repr. in J. P. Migne, *PL*, xc-xcv. Modern edd. of his *Opera Historica*, by J. Stevenson (2 vols., London, 1838-41) and C. Plummer (with notes, 2 vols., Oxford, 1896); of his prose life of St. Cuthbert by B. Colgrave, *Two Lives of St. Cuthbert* (1940), pp. 142-307 and 341-59; of his metrical life of St. Cuthbert by W. Jaager (*Palaestra*, cxcviii; 1935); of his *Expositio Actuum Apostolorum et Retractatio*, by M. L. W. Laistner (Medieval Academy of America, Publication No. 35; 1939), and of his *Opera de Temporibus*, by C. W. Jones (ib., No. 41; 1943). M. L. W. Laistner-H. H. King, *A Hand-list of Bede Manuscripts* (1943); B. Colgrave, 'The Leningrad MS. of Bede' in *The Times*, 7 Jan. 1953, p. 8, and letter of J. Stephan, O.S.B., ib., 9 Jan. 1953, p. 7. C. W. Jones, *Baedae Pseudographia*. Scientific Writings falsely ascribed to Bede (1939). A. Hamilton Thompson (ed.), *Bede*. His Life, Times and Writings. Essays in Commemoration of the Twelfth Centenary of his Death (1935). Three essays by B. *Capelle, O.S.B., M. Inguanez, O.S.B., and Beda Thum, O.S.B., *S. Beda Venerabilis* (Studia Anselmiana, fasc. vi, 1936). E. S. Duckett, *Anglo-Saxon Saints and Scholars* (New York, 1948), pp. 217-336. [Crit. ed. in *Corpus Christianorum*, 1955 ff.]

BEDLAM (='Bethlehem'). Originally the name given to the 'Hospital of St. Mary of Bethlehem', in Bishopsgate, which the Sheriff of London founded in 1247 for the housing of the clergy of St. Mary of Bethlehem when they visited Britain. It is uncertain when insane persons were first received here, but the house is mentioned as a hospital for the sick in 1330 and lunatics are definitely stated to have been there in 1402. On the *dissolution of the monasteries it passed to the London civic authorities, and in 1547 became a royal foundation for the reception of lunatics. Its place was taken in 1675 by a new hospital in Moorfields, and this again was transferred to the Lambeth Road in 1815. By an extension in meaning, the word 'Bedlam' has come to be applied to any lunatic asylum.

R. M. Clay, *The Medieval Hospitals of England* ('The Antiquary's Books'; 1909), pp. 32-4, 210, and 238. E. G. O'Donoghue, *The Story of Bethlehem Hospital from its Foundation in 1247* (1914).

BEELZEBUB. The name applied to 'the prince of devils' in the Gospels, where Christ's enemies accuse Him of 'casting out devils by Beelzebub' (Mk. 3. 22–26; cf. Mt. 12. 24–28, Lk. 11. 15–20), i.e. of acting by the power of, or of being an agent of, the evil one (cf. Mt. 10. 25), not of God. It is this direct and deliberate calling of good 'evil' which leads to the Lord's words on the sin that 'hath never forgiveness' (Mk. 3. 29, etc.).

In all the Gk. MSS. of the Gospels the form is 'Beelzebul' (Βεελζεβούλ); the form 'Beelzebub' is due to the influence of the OT, where 'Baal-zebub' is the god of the Philistine city of Ekron mentioned in 2 Kgs. 1. Neither name is found elsewhere in the Bible or contemporary sources, Jewish or pagan. 'Baal-zebub' appears to mean in Heb. 'lord of flies' and the word is so explained by ancient commentators; but the exact connexion between this and the 'Beelzebul' evidently current in *Galilee in the time of Christ and regarded as practically equivalent to '*Satan' (Mk. 3. 23), is uncertain. 'Beelzebul' is variously regarded as (a) a mere corruption in pronunciation of 'Baal-zebub', possibly influenced by an *Aramaic word meaning 'enmity', which suggested the use of this OT name for the arch-fiend; (b) derived from a Heb. word meaning 'dung', i.e. 'lord of filth'; or (c) derived from an uncommon Hebrew word for house or mansion, i.e. 'lord of the underworld'. This last suggestion, though it would give added point to the references to 'a house divided' and 'the strong man's house' in the Gospel passages (cf. 'master of the house', Mt. 10. 25), seems etymologically very improbable. The *Mishnah contains one reference to Beelzebub, understood as 'fly-god'. From the general absence of other references from Jewish literature it would seem that the term was of only local or temporary currency.

W. Foerster in *T.W.B.*, i (1933), p. 605 f., with bibl. reff. A. *Loisy, 'Beelzeboul' in *Revue d'Histoire et de Littérature Religieuses*, ix (1904), pp. 436–66. E. *Nestle in *D.C.G.*, i (1906), p. 181 f., s.v.

BÉGUINES, BÉGHARDS. The Béguines were members of certain sisterhoods, founded in the Netherlands in the 12th cent. They lived a semi-religious and somewhat austere communal life without vows, but they were free to hold private property and to leave the community and marry. Their male counterparts were the Béghards, who were usually weavers, dyers, or fullers, but who had a common purse and held no private property. These communities are said to have derived their names from Lambert le Bègue ('the stammerer'; d. 1177), a revivalist preacher at Liége. Though found mainly in the Netherlands, Béguines established themselves also in *Paris (where *Louis IX founded a Béguinage in 1264), on the Rhine, and elsewhere. The main aims of all these communities were philanthropic, esp. the service of the sick and needy, but they also devoted time to religious contemplation. They had no common rule, mother house, or superior-general. Their social doctrines, their mysticism, and their sympathies with the *Spiritual Franciscans led them to be suspected of heresy by the ecclesiastical authorities, and their teaching was condemned by the Council of *Vienne in 1311. Many of the Béghards, however, adopted a Reform and were allowed to continue by John XXII in 1321. These survived until the French Revolution. The Béguines, on the other hand, after surviving a century of persecution, had become little more than charitable institutions by the 15th cent., and were almost suppressed during the 16th cent. and again at the French Revolution, although some still exist in the Low Countries, esp. in *Belgium (Bruges, Ghent, &c.).

J. L. *Mosheim, *De Beghardis et Beguinabus Commentarius* (Leipzig, 1790), with documents. J. Greven, *Die Anfänge der Beginen* (Vorreformationsgeschichtliche Forschungen, viii, 1912). G. Kurth, 'De l'origine liégeoise des Béguines' in *Bulletin de l'Académie Royale de Belgique*. Classe des Lettres (1912), pp. 437–62; J. Greven, 'Die Ursprung des Beginenwesens. Eine Auseinandersetzung mit Godefroid Kurth' in *Hist. J.*, xxxv (1914), pp. 26–58 and 291–318. L. J. M. Philippen, *De Begijnhoven* (1918), with bibl. J. van Mierlo, S.J., in *D.H.G.E.*, vii (1934), cols. 426–41, and 457–73, s.vv. 'Bégardisme' and 'Béguinages', with bibl. E. W. McDonnell, *The Beguines and Beghards in Medieval Culture* (New Brunswick, N.J., 1954).

BEHEMOTH (Heb. בְּהֵמוֹת). This Heb. word, which occurs several times in the OT, is translated 'beast' except in Job 40. 15, where both AV and RV retain the form 'behemoth'. Here it means a particular beast, the greatest of all land animals (probably the hippopotamus), and the counterpart of the sea-beast, *Leviathan.

BEHMEN. See *Boehme, Jacob*.

BEL. Another form of 'Baal' (q.v.). In Jer. 50. 2, 51. 44 and Is. 46. 1, he is the tutelary god of Babylon, the empire which held the Jews captive.

BEL AND THE DRAGON. Two stories attached to the Book of *Daniel in certain Gk. MSS. (*Septuagint and *Theodotion) of the OT and hence included (as a single item) in the *Apocrypha of the English Bible. The former recounts (vv. 1–22; [Vulg.] Dan. 13. 65–14. 21) how Daniel convinced the Babylonian king that the lectisternia which were daily set before the image of Bel were not really consumed by the god but removed secretly by the priests, leading to the execution of the priests and the destruction of the image. The latter story (vv. 23–44; [Vulg.] Dan. 14. 22–42), which appears to be based on an ancient Semitic myth, describes how Daniel, having obtained the king's consent to attack the dragon, put it to death by throwing a large bolus into his throat. The people in their rage insisted that Daniel should be cast into a den of seven lions, whence, with the aid of the prophet *Habakkuk, who was miraculously transported from Judaea to feed him, he was saved from death and liberated. In consequence the king became a worshipper of Jehovah.

The occurrence of these stories in the Septuagint led them to be accepted by *Irenaeus, *Tertullian, *Origen, and others, but they were already questioned by *Julius Africanus. *Jerome incorporated them into the *Vulgate, though he did not conceal his doubts about them. In the AV they are entitled 'The History of the Destruction of Bel and the Dragon, cut off from the End of Daniel'. In 1894, M. Gaster announced the discovery of a story of the Dragon in *Aramaic which appeared to underlie the Gk.; his arguments were widely challenged, but many now hold, on other grounds, that the narratives are based on a Semitic original.

M. Gaster, 'The Unknown Aramaic Original of Theodotion's Additions to the Book of Daniel' in *Proceedings of the Society of Biblical Archaeology*, xvi (1894), pp. 280–90 and 312–17. Good account by T. Witton Davies in R. H. *Charles, *The Apocrypha and Pseudepigrapha of the Old Testament*, i (1913), pp. 652–64. J. A. Montgomery, '*Daniel*' (I.C.C.; 1927), p. 8 f. J. T. Marshall in *H.D.B.*, i (1898), p. 267 f. See also bibl. to *Apocrypha*.

BELGIC CONFESSION, The (1561). The 'Confession de Foi des Églises Réformées Wallonnes et Flamandes', originally drawn up in French by Guido de Brès (1522–67) on the basis of the *Gallican Confession (1559). In an attempt to conciliate the Netherlands' government it specially repudiated *Anabaptist doctrines. Its adoption in synod at Antwerp in May 1566 marked the final acceptance of Calvinistic principles in the Netherlands. It was again adopted by the Synod of *Dort in 1619.

Text in P. *Schaff, *Creeds of Evangelical Protestant Churches*, 383 ff.

BELGIUM, Christianity in. The independent history of Belgium begins with the Revolution in 1830 when she was liberated from the Netherlands. In the previous fifty years the Church had been sorely tried, first under the government of Napoleon and then under William I of *Holland (reigned 1813–44), during whose rule a Dutch Calvinist minority imposed severe restrictions on Catholics. The Revolution of 1830 had been carried through by the 'Union' of 1828 between the Belgian Liberals, a political group whose principles were based on religious free thought, and the Catholics. This Union continued to work for some years, and its last fruit was the Education Act of 1842, which allowed denominational teaching in state schools. From 1847 to 1884 the Liberals pursued an anti-Catholic policy, esp. in educational matters, which was reversed again by the elections of 1884, when the Catholics once more secured the chief voice in the government. The population of Belgium has always been predominantly Catholic. Cardinal *Mercier (1851–1926) gained a wide reputation as a national leader during the war of 1914–18, and was largely responsible for the *Malines Conversations of 1921–5 between RCs and Anglicans. In more recent times, *Jocism has been a powerful influence in Belgian Church life.

E. de Moreau, S.J., *Histoire de l'Église en Belgique* (2 vols., with suppl. vol. in collaboration with J. Deharveng and A. de Ghellinck, Museum Lessianum, Sec. Hist., i and ii, 1940–8). E. Michel, *Abbayes et monastères de Belgique*: leur importance et leur rôle dans le développement du pays (1923). H. Pirenne, *Histoire de Belgique* (7 vols., 1900–32), passim. E. de Moreau, S.J., in *D.H.G.E.*, vii (1934), cols. 519–756, s.v. 'Belgique'.

BELIAL. A Heb. word (בְּלִיַּעַל) of uncertain etymology, probably meaning 'worthlessness', 'wickedness', or 'destruction'. It is usually found in combination with a noun, e.g. 'sons of Belial' (Deut. 13. 13, 1 Sam. 2. 12, 10. 27, 25. 17, 2 Chr. 13. 7, &c.). In 2 Cor. 6. 15, the only NT ref. (where the best MSS. read Βελίαρ not Βελίαλ), St. Paul uses the word of Satan. In J. *Milton it is the name of the fallen angel who represents impurity (*Paradise Lost*, 1. 490–505, *Paradise Regained*, 2. 150).

BELLARMINE, St. ROBERT (1542–1621), theologian and controversialist. Roberto Francesco Romolo Bellarmino was born at Monte Pulciano in Tuscany. In 1560 he entered the *Jesuit Order and was ordained priest in 1570. As professor of theology at Louvain (1570), where he came into contact with non-Roman thought, he soon gained a reputation for learning and eloquence; but, partly owing to the cold climate of the north, he moved to Rome in 1576 where he became professor of controversial theology at the newly founded 'Collegium Romanum'. He was made a cardinal in 1599 and from 1602 to 1605 was Abp. of Capua. His later years were spent in the composition of works of spirituality.

His life was largely devoted to scholarship and controversy. He proved himself a vigorous and successful opponent of the Protestants, whom he sought to vanquish by reason and argument rather than by dogmatic assertion and abuse; and *James I of England engaged in controversy with him. His chief work was the *Disputationes de Controversiis Christianae Fidei adversus hujus temporis Haereticos* (3 vols., Ingolstadt, 1586–93), a systematic and clear apologia for the RC position. He also took a prominent part in the production of the revised edition of the *Vulgate, known as the Sixto-Clementine, in 1592. As regards the Papacy, he supported *Paul V in his struggle against *Venice and wrote a book against that of W. Barclay of Aberdeen (*c.* 1547–1608), denying the temporal authority of the Pope; but Bellarmine held that the Pope had only an indirect, not a direct, power in temporal matters, a view which had previously brought him into disgrace with *Sixtus V. Finally his sympathetic interest in G. *Galileo reflects his reasonableness. He was undoubtedly one of the greatest and most saintly figures in the RC Church in the latter years of the *Counter-Reformation.

He became entitled to the appellation of 'Venerable' in 1627, but further recognition was long delayed, despite frequent attempts to secure it, owing to his minimizing view of Papal authority. He was eventually canonized in 1930 and declared to be a Doctor of the Church in 1931. Feast day, 13 May.

Collected ed. of his works publd. in 7 vols., Cologne, 1617–21, vol. vii being ed. by S. Rychius; modern edd., 12 vols., Paris, 1870–4, and 8 vols., Naples, 1872; suppl. to his works ed. X. M. Le Bachelet, S.J., *Auctarium Bellarminianum* (Paris, 1913); *Opera Oratoria Postuma, adiunctis Documentis Variis ad Gubernium Animarum Spectantibus*, ed. S. Tromp, S.J. (10 vols., Rome, 1942 ff.) His autobiography, written in 1613, was pr. at the time of his attempted beatification, Rome, 1676; repr. Louvain, 1753. The primary authorities for his life are the biographies of J. Fuligatti, S.J. (Rome, 1624), D. Bartoli, S.J. (ib., 1678), and N. Frizon, S.J. (Nancy, 1708). X. M. Le Bachelet, S.J., *Bellarmin avant son cardinalat, 1524–1598* (1911), with important docc.; id., *Bellarmin et la bible sixto-clémentine* (1911), also with docc. J. Brodrick, S.J., *The Life and Works of Blessed Robert Cardinal Bellarmine* (2 vols., 1928). Other modern lives by J. P. Couderc, S.J. (2 vols., Paris, 1893), and A. M. Fiocchi (Isola del Liro, 1930); shorter studies by J. Thermes ('Les Saints', 1923) and P. Tacchi-Venturi, S.J., (Rome, 1923). E. A. Ryan, S.J., *The Historical Scholarship of Saint Bellarmine* (Université de Louvain. Recueil de Travaux publiés par les Membres des Conférences d'Histoire et de Philologie, 2ᵉ Sér., xxxv; 1936). Sommervogel, i (1890), cols. 1151–1254. R. Dudon, S.J., in *D.H.G.E.*, vii (1934), cols. 798–824, s.v. 'Bellarmin'. A. Piolanti in *E.C.*, x (1953), cols. 1043–9, s.v. 'Roberto Bellarmino' for later bibl.

BELLOC, JOSEPH HILAIRE PIERRE (1870–1953), RC historical writer and critic. Half French, he was born at St.-Cloud (nr. Versailles), educated at the *Oratory School in Birmingham under *Newman, served for a year with the French artillery, and then entered Balliol College, Oxford (1892). In 1906 he was elected Liberal M.P. for South Salford, but his fervent individualism and fear of state dominance made him critical of his party's alliance with the Socialists and he did not stand for the Second Election of 1910. He then joined G. K. *Chesterton and his brother, Cecil Chesterton, in a series of political broadsides popularly known as the 'Chesterbellocs'; and for the rest of his life he was a well-known figure in journalism, expounding Catholic economic liberalism and upholding the traditional values of European civilization as the true inheritance of the medieval system. On this general topic his chief work was *Europe and the Faith* (1912). He was the author of many historical writings which commanded attention by their brilliant and provocative style, though they were seldom contributions to serious knowledge. They include *The French Revolution* (1924), a *History of England* (1925–7), and lives of *Joan of Arc (1929), *Richelieu (1930), *Wolsey (1930), Napoleon (1932), *Charles I (1933), *Cromwell (1934), and *Milton (1935). He also wrote the popular travel-book, *The Path to Rome* (1902), some volumes of light essays, and some successful light and satirical verse.

D. Woodruff (ed.), *For Hilaire Belloc*. Essays in Honour of his 72nd Birthday (1942), incl. an essay by D. Jerrold, 'On the Influence of Hilaire Belloc', pp. 9–17. R. Braybooke, *Some Thoughts on Hilaire Belloc* (1924). R. Hamilton, *Hilaire Belloc. An Introduction to his Spirit and Work* (1945). R. Las Vergnas, *Chesterton, Belloc, Baring* (Eng. tr. by C. C. Martindale, S.J., of a series of articles in the *Revue des Deux Mondes*, with additions, 1938), pp. 50–87.

BELLS. The tradition that *Paulinus, Bp. of Nola in Campania, was the first to introduce

the bell into Christian worship (c. 420) rests on slender evidence, but it has given us two Latin words for a bell, *campana* and *nola*, unless (as is more likely) the story was invented to account for the words. St. *Gregory of Tours is the first Christian writer who mentions them frequently (c. 585). They were much used in Ireland from the 6th cent., and the famous bell of St. *Patrick survives in Dublin. Bells were used in Scotland from the 6th, and in England from the 7th cent.; and they came into general use in the Church in the 8th cent. About the 9th cent. *Crowland Abbey seems to have had a peal of bells, one of the earliest in this country, and St. *Dunstan (924–88) is known to have given bells to churches in the W. of England. From the 8th cent., bells have been blessed by a bishop with *holy water and *chrism (a ceremony popularly called the 'baptism of bells'. For centuries it has been customary to ring bells to summon the people to church and on other occasions, e.g. to announce the passing of a parishioner (the 'passing bell') or his death (as still ordered by canon 67 of the C of E), or for the ringing of the '*Angelus' or the '*De profundis'. From medieval times to the present day it has been customary for bells to bear inscriptions, sometimes in the form of a hexameter line, such as *Stella Maria maris succurre piissima nobis*. In size they vary very widely from the quite small treble to the large tenor. Thus the Great Bell of St. Paul's Cathedral (1716) weighs 17½ tons, and the bell in the Cathedral of Cologne, made out of French cannon, nearly 27 tons. Small bells are also used at the altar and rung at the Eucharist at the *Sanctus, the *Elevation, and the *Communion.

T. North, *English Bells and Bell Lore* (1888); G. S. Tyack, *A Book about Bells* [1898]. J. J. Raven, *The Bells of England* (The Antiquary's Books, 1906); H. B. Walters, *The Church Bells of England* (1913), with bibl. of English and foreign books, pp. ix–xx. H. *Leclercq, O.S.B., in *D.A.C.L.*, ii (pt. 2; 1914), cols. 1954–77, s.v. 'Cloche, clochette'.

BELL-TOWER. See *Campanile*.

BEMA (Gk. βῆμα, 'platform'). Acc. to E. usage, the space raised above the level of the *nave of a church which is shut off by the *iconostasis and contains the *altar, i.e. the counterpart of the *sanctuary in the W. The word is also used, less correctly, for the altar itself.

BENEDICAMUS DOMINO (Lat. 'Let us bless the Lord'). In the Roman rite a formula used since the 11th cent. to mark the end of the choir *offices and *Mass. The response of the congregation is 'Deo gratias' ('Thanks be to God'). In the Mass, the greeting is used only on less festal occasions (viz. when the '*Gloria in excelsis' has not been said), and then in place of the '*Ite missa est'. The substitution has been explained by the fact that on fast days *Vespers followed Mass immediately, and so the congregation was not at once dismissed. As it is not addressed to the people with the same directness as 'Ite missa est', it is not said facing them, but facing the altar.

The formula is first found in Gallican sources. Jungmann, ii (ed., 1949), pp. 526-8.

BENEDICITE (Lat. 'Bless ye [the Lord]'). The canticle or song of praise put into the mouths of Shadrach, Meshach, and Abednego, as they stood in the 'fiery furnace' before King Nebuchadnezzar. It forms part (vv. 35-66) of the 'Song of the Three Holy Children', which is added in the *Septuagint to the Hebrew *Daniel. It has been used in Christian liturgical worship from early times. *Rufinus, writing c. 406, says that it was sung by Christians throughout the world, and the Fourth Council of Toledo (633) decreed that it should be said before the *Epistle at every Mass in Spain and Gaul. It is now used at *Lauds on Sundays and festivals in the RC Church. In the BCP it is an alternative to the *Te Deum at *mattins, the 1549 Book having expressly ordered the use of this alternative in *Lent.

F. *Cabrol, O.S.B., in *D.A.C.L.*, ii (1910), cols. 660-4.

BENEDICT, St. (c. 480-c. 550), of Nursia, the 'Patriarch of Western monasticism'. Little is known of his life. Born at Nursia, he was educated at Rome, where the licentiousness of contemporary society led him to withdraw from the world and retire c. 500 to a cave at Subiaco. Here he lived as a hermit for some years. A community gradually grew up round him and he established twelve monasteries of twelve monks each, with abbots appointed by himself. Local jealousy prompted him to leave Subiaco, and, c. 525, he moved with a small band of monks to *Monte Cassino, where he remained till his death. It was here that he elaborated his plans for the reform of monasticism and composed his Rule (see foll. entry). He does not appear to have been ordained nor to have contemplated founding an order for clerics. He was buried at Monte Cassino in the same grave as his sister, St. *Scholastica. Feast day, 21 Mar.

Practically the sole source for his life is the *Dialogues* of St. *Gregory (J. P. Migne, *PL*, lxxvii, 149-430). B. Sauter, O.S.B., *Der heilige Vater Benediktus, nach St. Gregor dem Grossen* (1904), with text pp. 237-82. L. Tosti, O.S.B., *Della vita di San Benedetto* (1892; Eng. tr., 1896). I. Herwegen, O.S.B., *Der heilige Benedikt* (1917; Eng. tr., 1924); P. Renaudin, O.S.B., *Saint Benoît dans l'histoire* [1924]. J. *Chapman, O.S.B., *Saint Benedict and the Sixth Century* (1929); F. *Cabrol, O.S.B., *Saint Benoît* (1933; Eng. tr., 1934); J. McCann, O.S.B., *Saint Benedict* (1937).

BENEDICT, Oblates Regular of St. See *Oblates Regular of St. Benedict.*

BENEDICT, Rule of St. The monastic Rule drawn up by St. *Benedict of Nursia to regulate the life of his monks, originally intended to be laymen. Much in it is drawn from the earlier Rules of John *Cassian and '*Basil' (i.e. *Rufinus' fusion of Basil's two

regulae) as well as from *Caesarius of Arles; but excessive austerities are excluded, and the whole is marked by a spirit of prudent leniency. The Rule provides for patriarchal government, giving full authority and responsibility to the *abbot who is elected by vote. The vow requires residence in one place (*stabilitas loci*), obedience, and monastic virtue. The chief task of the monk as well as the centre of the community life is the performance of the *Divine Office, the *opus Dei*, from which the work, study, and private prayer that fill the rest of the day take their inspiration. Possessions are held in common, and there is no particular vow of poverty. The monasteries are thus enabled to carry out the corporal works of mercy, a fact which has had most beneficial results throughout the Middle Ages, and since.

There is an immense literature. Crit. edd. of the Rule include those of C. Butler, O.S.B. (Freiburg i.Br., 1912; ed. 3, 1935, with full bibl.), and B. Linderbauer, O.S.B. (Florilegium Patristicum, xvii; Bonn, 1928). Eng. tr., with preface by W. K. L. Clarke (S.P.C.K., London, 1931). On the textual history, L. Traube, 'Die Textgeschichte der *Regula S. Benedicti*' in *Abh.* (Bayr.) xxi [Hist. Kl.] (1898), pp. 559-731; ed. 2 by H. Plenkers, ib. xxv, Abh. 2 (1910). Commentaries by P. Delatte, O.S.B. (Paris, 1913; Eng. tr., 1921) and G. Herwegen, O.S.B. (Einsiedeln, 1944). Full bibl. in A. M. Albareda, O.S.B., *Bibliografía de la regla benedictina* (Montserrat, 1933; pp. xviii+661, 902 items). On the question, much debated recently, as to the relation of the Rule to the 'Regula Magistri', cf. A. Génestout, O.S.B., of Solesmes, 'La Règle du Maître et la règle de St. Benoît' in *Revue d'Ascétique et de Mystique*, xxi (1940), pp. 51-112 (who urges that the Prologue and first seven chs. of the Rule are dependent on the 'Regula Magistri'). Against M. Alamo, O.S.B., A. Génestout, and F. Cavallera, S.J., who have upheld the priority of the 'Regula Magistri', the contrary view has been defended by B. *Capelle, O.S.B., J. McCann, O.S.B., C. Lambot, O.S.B., and others; for bibl. on the extended discussion see B. Capelle in 'Bulletin', iii, of *R.T.A.M.* (1939), pp. 521*-523* (Nos. 1155-63), and B. Reynders, O.S.B., ib., iv (1941), p. 86 f. (Nos. 531-3); further items in J. de Ghellinck, S.J., *Patristique et Moyen-Age*, iii (1948), and in Altaner (ed. 1950), p. 434.

BENEDICT OF ANIANE, St. (c. 750-821), abbot. After serving under *Pepin and his son, *Charlemagne, he became a monk at St.-Seine, near Dijon, in 773. In 779 he founded on his own property at Aniane in Languedoc a monastery which became the centre of an extended reform of all the French monastic houses. His systematization of the *Benedictine Rule received official approval as the 'Capitulare Monasticum' at the Synod of Aachen of 817. He also made a collection of all known monastic Rules (*Codex Regularum monasticarum et canonicarum*). From c. 795 he took a vigorous part in opposing the teaching of the *Adoptianist, *Felix of Urgel. His personal life was one of severe asceticism. Feast day, 11 Feb.

His writings are in J. P. Migne, *PL*, ciii, 393-1440, with life by his disciple and friend, Ardo, repr. from the *Acta Sanctorum Ordinis Sancti Benedicti*, ib., cols. 335-84; crit. ed. of the life by G. Waitz in *M.G.H.*, Scriptores, xv (pt. 1; 1887), pp. 198-220. P. J. Nicolai, *Der heil. Benedict, Gründer von Aniane und Corneliminster* (1865). J. Narberhaus, *Benedikt von Aniane* (Beiträge zur Geschichte des alten Mönchtums und des Benediktinerordens, xvi; 1930), with bibl. W. Williams, 'St. Benedict of Aniane' in *The Downside Review*, liv (1936), pp. 357-74. O. Seebass, Ueber das Regelbuch Benedikts von Aniane' in *Z.K.G.*, xv (1895), pp. 244-60. Suzanne Dulcy, *La Règle de Saint*

Benoît d'Aniane et la réforme monastique à l'époque carolingienne (Montpellier thesis; Nîmes, 1935). P. Schmitz, O.S.B., in *D.H.G.E.*, viii (1935), cols. 177–88, s.v. 'Benoît d'Aniane', with bibl.

BENEDICT BISCOP, St. (*c.* 628–89 or 690), *Benedictine monk. Of noble Northumbrian birth, he spent his youth at the court of King Oswy. After two journeys to *Rome (the first, 653, with St. *Wilfrid), in 666 he became a monk of *Lérins. In 669 he accompanied Abp. *Theodore to *Canterbury, where he became Abbot of the monastery of St. Peter and St. Paul (later St. *Augustine's). In 674 he founded the monastery of St. Peter at *Wearmouth and in 682 that of St. Paul at Jarrow. An enthusiast for learning and art, Benedict brought back from his journeys to Rome (five in all) many paintings, relics and MSS. He also secured the services of John, the archcantor of St. Peter's, Rome, to teach in England the Roman chant. He is further reputed to have introduced into England the use of glass windows and churches built in stone. He was an enthusiastic advocate of Roman liturgical practice. His Life was written by St. *Bede who was entrusted to Benedict's care at the age of seven. Feast day, 12 Jan. He is the patron of the English Benedictines.

*Bede, *H.E.*, iv. 18 and v. 19, and *Historia Abbatum*, i; *William of Malmesbury, *Gesta Pontificum*, iv. 186, ed. by N. E. S. A. Hamilton (R.S., 1870), pp. 327–9.

BENEDICT JOSEPH LABRE, St. See *Labre, St. Benedict Joseph.*

BENEDICT XII (d. 1342), Pope from 1334. Jacques Fournier was the third of the *Avignon Popes. Of humble origin, he entered as a youth the *Cistercian abbey of Boulbonne and was later transferred to Fontfroide. Having studied at *Paris and become Master of Theology, he was installed Abbot of Fontfroide in 1311, appointed Bp. of Pamiers in 1317, and translated to Mirepoix in 1326. Created cardinal in 1327, he took part in the dogmatic controversies of the time, esp. on the questions of the poverty of Christ and on the *Beatific Vision. After being elected Pope in 1334, he at once inaugurated several ecclesiastical reforms. Himself entirely free from nepotism, he fought esp. the rapacity of the clergy, many of whom he sent back from Avignon to their dioceses without conferring benefices on them. He forbade the holding of benefices *in commendam* except in the case of cardinals and was a zealous reformer of the religious orders. He also ordered the establishment of houses of studies in every country and improved the training of novices, many of his measures being later adopted by the Council of *Trent. In the political field, where he tended to commit himself to the policy of Philip VI of France, he was less successful. French influence led his conciliatory attitude towards Louis of Bavaria to fail, and hence to the declaration of the Electors assembled at Rense to the effect

that the Emperor holds his rights not through confirmation by the Pope but through the fact of his election. Louis himself, though allying himself with France in 1341, finally wrecked all hopes of better relations between Pope and Emperor by ignoring the Pope's remonstrations and giving his son, Louis of Brandenburg, in marriage to Margaret Maultasch, who had separated from her husband without ecclesiastical dispensation. Through the war between England and France Benedict's plan for a Crusade came to nothing, and his contemplated return to Rome was frustrated by the opposition of Philip VI and the unrest in Italy, though after 1339 *Verona, *Bologna, and *Milan returned to the Papal allegiance. He also began the building of the famous palace of the Popes at Avignon. Benedict XII was a competent theologian, though his works have remained unpublished. His chief doctrinal pronouncement is the constitution 'Benedictus Deus' (1336) in which he defined the Catholic doctrine that the souls of the just who have no faults to expiate enjoy the *Beatific Vision immediately after death.

M. Vidal (ed.), *Lettres communes des papes d'Avignon. Benoît XII, 1334–1342* (Bibliothèque des Écoles Françaises d'Athènes et de Rome, Sér. III, No. 9, 3 parts, 1899–1920); G. Daumet (ed.), *Benoît XII, 1334–1342*. Lettres closes, patentes et curiales se rapportant à la France (ib., No. 2, 3 vols., 1902–11). He also wrote a Commentary on Mt., part of which was publd. by G. Lazarus (Venice, 1603) under the name of 'Benedict XI'. S. Baluse, *Vitae Paparum Avenionensium* (ed. G. Mollat, i, 1914, pp. 195–240 and 576–80). C. Jacob, *Studien über Papst Benedikt XII* (1910). J. M. Vidal, 'Notice sur les œuvres du Pape Benoît XII' in *R.H.E.*, vi (1905), pp. 557–65 and 785–810. H. Otto, 'Benedikt XII als Reformator des Kirchenstaates' in *R.Q.*, xxxvi (1928), pp. 59–110. G. Mollat, *Les Papes d'Avignon* (1912), Book i, ch. 4, and Book ii, ch. 1, pt. iv. Pastor, i (1891), pp. 83–5; X. Le Bachelet, S.J., in *D.T.C.*, ii (1905), cols. 653–704, s.v. 'Benoît XII'; L. Jadin in *D.H.G.E.*, viii (1935), cols. 116–35, s.v. 'Benoît XII'.

BENEDICT XIII (d. 1423), *Antipope at *Avignon from 1394 to 1417. Pedro de Luna was a doctor of Canon Law of great learning and austerity of life. Created *cardinal in 1375 by Gregory XI, he took part in the election of Gregory's successor, Urban VI, but later became a partisan of his Antipope, Clement VII. After Clement's death (1394) he himself was elected Antipope, largely because he promised to put an end to the schism, even if it meant abdicating. After his enthronement, however, he refused to resign, and even sustained a long siege and subsequent imprisonment in the Papal castle of Avignon in defence of his dignity. Personal negotiations with the Roman Pope, Boniface IX, and his successors Innocent VII and Gregory XII were equally unsuccessful. The Council of *Pisa, against which he had called a synod at Perpignan, deposed him in 1409, and the Council of *Constance confirmed his deposition in 1417. After this even his last adherents (Scotland, Aragon, Castile, and Sicily) left him. He shut himself up in his castle at Peñiscola near Valencia where he still claimed to be the rightful Pope until his death. As RC historians deny his rightful place in the Papal succession, the title of 'Benedict XIII' is attached to P. F. Orsini (d. 1730; see foll. entry).

Martin de Alpartil, *Chronica Actitatorum Temporibus Domini Benedicti XIII*, ed. F. Ehrle, S.J. (Quellen und Forschungen aus dem Gebiete der Geschichte, xii; 1906). S. Puig y Puig, *Episcopologio barcinonese*. Pedro de Luna, último papa de Aviñon, 1387–1430 (Barcelona, 1920). F. Ehrle, S.J., 'Aus den Akten des Afterkonzils von Perpignan 1408' in *Archiv für Literatur- und Kirchengeschichte des Mittelalters*, v (1889), pp. 387–492, and vii (1900), pp. 576–606; id., 'Neue Materialien zur Geschichte Peters von Luna (Benedikt XIII)', ib., vi (1892), pp. 138–308, and vii (1900), pp. 1–306; id. 'Die kirchenrechtlichen Schriften Peters von Luna (Benedikt XIII)', ib., vii (1900), pp. 515–75. G. Mollat, 'Épisodes du siège du palais des papes au temps de Benoît XIII (1398–1399)' in *R.H.E.*, xxiii (1927), pp. 489–501. J. A. Rubio, *La política de Benedicto XIII desde la substracción de Aragón a su obediencia hasta su destitución en el concilio de Constanza, erno de 1416 a julio de 1417* (Diss. 1926). N. Valois, *La France et le grand schisme d'occident* (4 vols., 1898–1902), passim. Pastor, i (1891), pp. 165–201 passim. E. Amann in *D.T.C.*, xii (pt. 1; 1933), cols. 2020–2029, s.v. 'Pierre de Luna'; L. Jadin in *D.H.G.E.*, viii (1935), cols. 135–63, s.v. 'Benoît XIII', with bibl.

BENEDICT XIII (1649–1730), Pope from 1724. Pietro Francesco Orsini, who entered the *Dominican Order in 1667, became a cardinal in 1672 and Abp. of Benevento in 1686. As Pope, he presided at the provincial Lateran Council of 1725, which sought to reform clerical morals; but though well-intentioned and scholarly, he was of weak character, and his policy was determined by his unscrupulous favourite, Cardinal Coscia. In 1725 he confirmed the bull '*Unigenitus', though he suffered the *Dominicans to preach a doctrine of *grace, verging on that of the *Jansenists.

Quétif-Échard, ii (1721), pp. 814–17. G. B. Pittoni, *Vita del sommo pontifice Benedetto Decimoterzo* (Venice, 1730); A. Borgia, *Benedicti XIII, Romani Pontificis Vita Commentario Excerpta* (Rome, 1741). Pastor, xxiv (1941), pp. 98–299. H. Hemmer in *D.T.C.*, ii (1905), col. 704 f., s.v., with bibl.; J. Carreyre in *D.H.G.E.*, vii (1935), col. 163 f.; C. Castiglioni in *É.C.*, ii (1949), cols. 1279–81, s.v. Benedetto XIII.

BENEDICT XIV (1675–1758), Pope from 1740. A native of *Bologna, Prospero Lorenzo Lambertini was educated at *Rome at the Collegium Clementinum. He became Consistorial Advocate in 1701, *Promotor Fidei in 1708, and assessor of the Congregation of *Rites in 1712. In 1718 he was appointed secretary of the Congregation of the *Council, in 1727 Bp. of Ancona, in 1728 cardinal, and in 1731 Abp. of Bologna. On the death of Clement XII (6 Feb. 1740), after a conclave lasting six months he was elected to the Papacy on 17 Aug.

Of wide sympathies, a clear sense of order and proportion, and a real interest in science and learning, Benedict did much to commend his office to the *Aufklärung. He was an exemplary administrator, conciliatory in his dealings with the secular powers, and esp. concerned to strengthen the moral influence of the Papacy; and his prudence and ability were respected in the courts of Europe, Protestant as well as Catholic. His *De Servorum Dei Beatificatione et Beatorum Canonizatione* (1734–8; often reprinted), which grew out of

his practical experience as 'Promotor Fidei', has remained the classical treatise on the subject. Book I contains extensive material on the history of *beatification and *canonization; Books II and III treat of the successive stages in the process including the testimonies, virtuous life and special graces (*gratis datae*) to be sought in the candidate; and Book IV deals with the requisite miracles (pt. i) and with various liturgical questions (Office and Mass of the Saint, insertion in the *Roman Martyrology, and adoption as Patron; pt. ii). Benedict also compiled an extensive work of hardly less authority on Diocesan *Synods (*De Synodo Diœcesana*, Rome, 1748; often reprinted). His own Bulls, collected in *Bullarium Benedicti XIV* (1768), frequently embodied scientific disquisitions. His other writings included an elaborate treatise on the Sacrifice of the Mass (*De Sacrosancto Missae Sacrificio*, 1748) and further works on canon law; and in 1752 he issued a standard edition of the *Caeremoniale Episcoporum* (q.v.). His Bulls dealt, *inter alia*, with the suppression of pagan practices admitted into Christianity, notably by the *Jesuits in *China ('Ex quo singulari', 1742) and *Malabar ('Omnium sollicitudinum', 1744); *usury ('Vix pervenit', 1745); *mixed marriages ('Magnae nobis admirationis', 1748); and *Jansenism ('Ex omnibus christiani orbis', 1756). To encourage historical studies, Benedict also founded a number of academies at Rome. He was buried in St. Peter's, Rome, where he is commemorated by a striking monument by Pietro Bracci.

Opera, ed. E. de Azevedo, S.J. (12 vols., Rome, 1747–8), and, with Bullarium, ed. J. Silvester (17 vols., Prato, 1839–1849); *Opera Omnia Inedita*, ed. F. Heiner (Freiburg i.Br., 1904); *Correspondance*, ed. E. Heeckeren (2 vols., Paris, 1912). Modern Eng. tr. of extracts of his *De Synodo Dioecesana* (London, 1926). Life by [L. A. de] Caraccioli (Paris, 1783). A. M. Beltanini, *Benedetto XIV e la repubblica di Venezia* (Milan, 1931). Pastor, xxxv ('1949' [1950]) and xxxvi (1950), pp. 1–142, with bibl. to date. H. Hemmer in *D.T.C.*, ii (1905), cols. 706–8, s.v. 'Benoît XIV'; R. Naz in *D.D.C.*, ii (1937), cols. 752–61, s.v. 'Benoît XIV'; J. Carreyre, P.S.S., in *D.H.G.E.*, viii (1935), cols. 164–7, s.v. 'Benoît XIV'; L. Oliger, O.F.M., in *É.C.*, ii (1949), cols. 1281–5, s.v. 'Benedetto XIV'.

BENEDICT XV (1854–1922), Pope from 1914. Giacomo P. G. B. della Chiesa was born at Pegli in the diocese of Genoa, and studied at Genoa and at the *Gregorian University, Rome. From 1883 to 1887 he was in Spain as secretary to Cardinal Rampolla, then Papal Nuncio at Madrid; and when the latter was recalled in 1887, della Chiesa returned to Rome with him, and remained there until appointed Abp. of *Bologna in 1907. On the death of *Pius X shortly after the outbreak of the war of 1914–18 he was elected to succeed him. While endeavouring to preserve the neutrality of the Holy See, he protested against inhuman methods of warfare and made several strenuous efforts to bring about peace. During his pontificate, a British representative was accredited to the Papal court for the first time since the 17th cent.

Official acts of his pontificate in *A.A.S.*, vi (1914), p. 473–xiv (1922), p. 92 (incl. the accounts of his election and funeral). Among the many lives of the Pope the fullest study in English is that of H. E. G. Rope (London, 1941). E. de Moreau, S.J., in *D.H.G.E.*, viii (1935), cols. 167–72, s.v. 'Benoît XV', with good bibl.; G. Dalla Torre in *E.C.*, ii (1949), cols. 1285–94, s.v. 'Benedetto XV', with further bibl.

BENEDICTINE ORDER. During the pontificate of *Pelagius II (579–90), after the sack of *Monte Cassino by the Lombards, the monks of St. *Benedict of Nursia (q.v.) migrated to Rome, bringing with them his Rule. *Gregory I (590–604), the successor of Pelagius, governed his own monks acc. to the same Rule. *Augustine of Canterbury and his colleagues introduced it into Britain. Such were the beginnings of Benedictine expansion in the 6th cent. It was in Britain during the 7th cent. that conflict began between the new Rule and the more austere Rule of St. *Columbanus, which was already widely extended there, and also in Gaul. Gradually the Benedictine Rule, often syncretized with more ancient rules, became the norm of monachism in England; and when Winfrid (St. *Boniface) set out early in the 8th cent. to evangelize Germany, he proceeded to establish there the Benedictine ideal. The consecration of Boniface as Abp. of Mainz (743), his foundation of *Fulda (744), and his crowning of Pepin (751) were variously significant of his achievement. His mission was one of ecclesiastical reform, and was undertaken partly by a reconstruction, on Benedictine lines, of Continental monasticism, and partly by the exaltation of the reformed regular clergy at the expense of the corrupt seculars. Up to this time the Rule of Benedict was the only visible link between the multitude of wholly autonomous abbeys; but *Benedict of Aniane pursued an ideal of closer uniformity and, with the approval of the Emp. *Louis, imposed upon the monks and nuns of the empire as a whole his 'Capitulare Monasticum' (817), tending to reform Benedictine life in the direction of greater austerity.

Henceforward, successive temporary relaxations of Benedictine discipline were invariably countered by attempts at collective reform. Such was the method of *Cluny (10th cent.), all later Cluniac houses depending upon the central policy and control of the abbots of Cluny. One consequence of this tendency was the formation of separate orders, in which the twin principles of austerity and centralization were carried further than the primitive Rule of Benedict admitted. A number of such orders appeared in the 11th cent., notably the *Camaldolese, the *Carthusian, and (chiefly through the personal influence of St. *Bernard of Clairvaux) the *Cistercian. Popes and Councils throughout the Middle Ages attempted to bring the Benedictines under one centralized constitution, on the lines of the newer orders, the fourth *Lateran Council (1215) and the bull 'Benedictina' (1336) being important moments in this development. The Benedictines themselves preferred to found local congregations as instruments of reform. The abbeys of such congregations (e.g. that of Saint Justina in Italy, founded 1412; the Bursfeld

Union in Germany, founded 1446; and later the *Maurists in France) sacrificed some degree of autonomy, but the congregations themselves remained independent of any wider organization. The *Reformation, the ecclesiastical policy of such rulers as *Joseph II, and the French Revolution, resulted in the suppression of all but a score or so of the Benedictine foundations; but since 1830 there has been a remarkable revival of the Rule in Europe and America. To-day the English Congregation alone includes between 400 and 500 choir monks, and a number of houses of other Congregations, founded in England in recent times, also continue to flourish, while modified forms of the Rule have been adopted by monks outside the Roman communion. Apart from the spiritual function of the Rule of Benedict, representing throughout the W. the norm of monastic piety, the Black Monks have rendered invaluable services to civilization, not only in preparing the social organization of the Middle Ages during the chaos of barbarian rule after the fall of the Roman Empire, but also in preserving (for instance, through the 18th cent. in France) the ideals and practice of true scholarship, and in maintaining or restoring the use of good art in the liturgical worship ('opus Dei') to which they are esp. devoted.

The Benedictine nuns, established by St. Benedict himself and his sister, St. *Scholastica, live acc. to the same Rule. In the Middle Ages they were strictly enclosed; but in modern times the Benedictine Rule became the foundation of many convents whose sisters are not enclosed and devote themselves to all kinds of charitable and educational work. Their habit is black, like that of the monks. Among their Saints are St. *Hildegard and St. *Gertrude, surnamed 'the Great'.

There is an immense literature. Good introductory accounts by G. Cyprian Alston, O.S.B., in *C.E.*, ii (1907), pp. 443–65; by Justinus Uttenweiler, O.S.B., in *L.Th.K.*, ii (1931), cols. 151–9 (good bibl. 158 f.); and by P. Schmitz, O.S.B., in *D.H.G.E.*, vii (1934), cols. 1062–1234, also C. Butler, O.S.B., *Benedictine Monachism* (1919; ed. 2, 1924). Standard sources are J. *Mabillon, O.S.B. (contd. by R. Massuet, O.S.B., T. *Ruinart, O.S.B., and E. *Martène, O.S.B.), *Annales Ordinis S. Benedicti* [480–1157] (6 vols., Paris, 1703–39), and id., *Acta Sanctorum Ordinis S. Benedicti* (9 vols., Paris, 1668–1701). C. R. F. *Montalembert, *Les Moines de l'occident* (7 vols., 1860–77; Eng. tr., 7 vols., 1861–79). I. Herwegen, O.S.B. (ed.), *Beiträge zur Geschichte des alten Mönchtums und des Benediktinerordens* (1912 ff.; 20 Hfte. to 1938). S. Hilpisch, O.S.B., *Das Benediktinertum im Wandel der Zeiten* (St. Ottilien, 1950). U. Berlière, O.S.B., *Mélanges d'histoire bénédictine* (4 vols., Maredsous, 1897–1902). P. Schmitz, O.S.B., *Histoire de l'ordre de St. Benoît* (6 vols., Maredsous, 1942–9). Heimbücher, i, pp. 154–314, and ii, pp. 650–5. On Benedictine Life in England, W. *Dugdale, *Monasticon Anglicanum* (1655–73; new ed., 1817–30), [M] David Knowles, O.S.B., *The Monastic Order in England. A History of its Development from the Times of St. Dunstan to the Fourth Lateran Council*, 943–1216 (1940; with bibl.); [M.] D. Knowles–R. N. Hadcock, *Medieval Religious Houses*, England and Wales (1953; catalogue with maps). [M.] D. Knowles and J. K. S. Saint Joseph, *Monastic Sites from the Air* (Cambridge Air Surveys, No. 1, 1952).

BENEDICTIO MENSAE. A liturgical form of grace developed in monastic circles from verses of the Psalms. Reference to it is found as early as *Cassian (*Inst. coenob.* 7. 12) and St. *Benedict (*Regula* 43). To-day the grace consists of a verse which varies acc. to the feasts, short prayers, and a blessing. After meals the prayers are preceded by a psalm and concluded by intercessions for benefactors and the dead, and the *Paternoster.

BENEDICTION. See *Blessing*.

BENEDICTION OF THE BLESSED SACRAMENT. In the W. Church a service, usually held in the afternoon or evening, which culminates in the blessing of the people with the *Reserved Sacrament in the *monstrance. A comparatively modern form of worship, it developed from the fusing of the veneration of the Host exposed out of Mass, which dated from the early part of the 14th cent., with the custom of confraternities and guilds singing evening canticles to our Lady. In the 16th and 17th cents. these devotions came to include the exposition of the *Host and the blessing of the congregation with it at the end; and the whole service, though still extra-liturgical, now follows a regular form. It is unknown in the Orthodox Church, and in the C of E is forbidden in some dioceses, allowed in modified form (as 'Adoration' or 'Devotions') in others, and in a few (esp. missionary dioceses) tolerated or actively encouraged.

Series of articles by H. Thurston, S.J., in *The Month*, xcvii (1901), pp. 587–97, xcviii (1901), pp. 58–60, 186–93, 264–76, and cvi (1905), pp. 394–404. Id., 'Benediction of the Blessed Sacrament' in *Report of the Nineteenth Eucharistic Congress, held at Westminster from 9th to 13th September 1908* (1909), pp. 452–64. A. Molien in *D.D.C.*, ii (1937), cols. 382–94, s.v.

BENEDICTIONAL. In the W. Church the liturgical book containing the formulae of the bishop's blessings formerly pronounced at Mass, esp. in Spain, France and England, before the 'Pax Domini'. The oldest extant copy appears to date from the 7th cent.

BENEDICTUS. The Song of Thanksgiving (Lk. 1. 68–79) uttered by *Zacharias at the birth of his son, St. *John Baptist. The hymn is addressed to God in thanksgiving for the fulfilment of the Messianic hopes, and to the child who is to be the Lord's forerunner. In the W. Church it is sung liturgically at *Lauds, whence it was taken over in the BCP where it finds a place in Morning Prayer. The rubric orders it to be read after the Second Lesson 'except when [it] shall happen to be read in the chapter for the day, or for the Gospel on St. John Baptist's Day', and provides Psalm 100 as an alternative.

L. Pirot in *Dict. Bibl.*, Suppl., i (1928), cols. 956–62, s.v.

BENEDICTUS QUI VENIT. The Latin form of Mt. 21. 9: 'Blessed is he that cometh in the name of the Lord'. In most of the ancient liturgies, including the Roman *Mass, it is said or sung as a hymn immediately after the *Sanctus. It was included, in a slightly altered form, in the BCP of 1549, but dropped out in the 1552 revision.

It is first found in Gaul, viz. *Caesarius of Arles, *Serm.* 73. 4. Jungmann, ii (ed. 1949), pp. 165–8.

BENEFICE. A term originally used for a grant of land for life as a reward (*beneficium*) for services. Under *canon law it came to imply an ecclesiastical office which prescribed certain duties or conditions ('spiritualities') for the due discharge of which it awarded certain revenues ('temporalities'). Parochial benefices in the C of E are of three kinds: rectories, vicarages, and perpetual curacies. In each case the duties of the incumbent include observance of the promises made at *Ordination, the showing of proper respect for his office, and due solicitude for the moral and spiritual welfare of his parishioners.

BENEFIT OF CLERGY. The exemption from trial by a secular court on being charged with felony which was accorded to the clergy in the Middle Ages. It was granted to all who were tonsured as well as to nuns. In later times benefit of clergy was allowed on a first conviction for certain offences to all who could read, on the ground that ability to read was the accepted test of a cleric. The privilege was finally abolished in England in 1827 by 7 & 8 Geo. IV, c. 28.

F. Pollock–F. W. Maitland, *The History of English Law before the Time of Edward I*, i (1895), pp. 424–40. L. C. Gabel, *Benefit of Clergy in England in the Later Middle Ages* (Smith College Studies in History, xiv, Nos. 1–4; Northampton, Mass., 1929). G. Crosse in *D.E.C.H.*, p. 53, s.v.

BENET, St. An older English form of the name of St. *Benedict.

BENGEL, JOHANNES ALBRECHT (1687–1752), *Lutheran NT scholar. He entered the Lutheran ministry in 1707, and in 1713 became professor at the seminary of Denkendorf. In 1741 he was made *Generalsuperintendent at Herbrechtingen, and in 1749 at Alpirspach. He did some work on classical and patristic literature, but his chief importance is as a textual critic and expositor of the NT. His text and *critical apparatus (1734) mark the beginning of modern scientific work in that field. Hardly less celebrated was his penetrating and pithy exegesis of the NT, published in his *Gnomon Novi Testamenti* (1742). It was much used and admired by J. *Wesley, and remains a classic.

Correspondence ed. J. C. F. Burk (great-grandson; Stuttgart, 1836). Life, also by Burk (ib., 1831; Eng. tr., 1837). Later studies by O. Wächter (Berlin, 1865), F. Nolte (Gütersloh, 1913) and R. B. Evenhuis (Wageningen, 1931). A. Hauck in *P.R.E.* (ed. 3), ii (1897) pp. 597–601, s.v.

BENNETT, WILLIAM JAMES EARLY (1804–86), Anglican *High Churchman. An upholder of *Tractarian principles, he became in 1840 priest-in-charge of St. Paul's, Knightsbridge, and in this capacity built St. Barnabas's

Pimlico (opened 1850), where he introduced what was then regarded as very advanced ceremonial. This provoked fierce opposition and mob rioting; and C. J. *Blomfield, Bp. of London, despite a certain sympathy with Bennett, became alarmed, and induced him to resign. He was instituted, however, to the vicarage of Frome Selwood, in Somerset, in 1852. In 1867 a public letter to E. B. *Pusey (*A Plea for Toleration in the Church of England*), in which he dealt with the *Real Presence in the *Eucharist, led to a series of legal actions which were significant as showing the inadequacy of the existing courts to deal with matters of doctrine. The legitimacy of his Eucharistic teaching, however, was allowed. He published many controversial and other writings.

Life by F. Bennett (London, 1909).

BEN SIRA (i.e. 'the son of Sira'). Jesus ben Sira, the author of *Ecclesiasticus (q.v.). 'Sirach' is the Greek form, the termination 'ch' indicating that the word was indeclinable.

BENSON, EDWARD WHITE (1829–96), Abp. of *Canterbury. Educated at King Edward's School, Birmingham (where he made a lifelong friendship with his fellow-pupil, J. B. *Lightfoot), and Trinity College, Cambridge, he became at first an assistant master at Rugby (1852), and then Master of the newly founded school at Wellington (1859). In 1877 he went as its first bishop to *Truro, where his vigorous and forceful character was well suited to the needs of the new diocese. In 1883 he succeeded Abp. A. C. *Tait at Canterbury, where he was intensely zealous and active in the Church's interests, but intolerant of opposition and criticism. A strong Tory, he vigorously upheld the Establishment; yet he remained a friend of W. E. *Gladstone, to whom he owed his appointment, and it was while on a visit to him that he died in Hawarden church. To deal with the ritual charges brought against E. *King, Bp. of *Lincoln, he revived the 'court of the Abp. of Canterbury', which based its decisions on the rubrics of the BCP and traditional practice in the C of E (see also *Lincoln Judgement*). His great devotion to St. *Cyprian bore fruit in *Cyprian, his Life, his Times, his Work* (1897), published a few months after his death.

His Life (2 vols., London, 1899–1900) by his son, A. C. Benson. A. J. Mason in *D.N.B.*, Supp. i (1901), pp. 171–9.

BENSON, RICHARD MEUX (1824–1915). Founder of the *Society of St. John the Evangelist ('S.S.J.E.'). Educated at *Christ Church, Oxford, of which he was a Student from 1846 to 1915, he was ordained in 1848 and in 1850 appointed Vicar of Cowley, then a village, some two miles from *Oxford, where he lived a studious, devoted life. In 1859 he was on the point of going to India on missionary work when Bp. S. *Wilberforce induced him to remain to take charge of the new suburb developing at the Oxford end of his parish.

A sermon preached by J. *Keble inspired him to found the S.S.J.E. in 1866. In 1890 he resigned his superiorship of the Society. His religious writings, mostly based on his sermons, reveal his penetrating originality and deeply spiritual mind.

'Letters' ed. G. Congreve, S.S.J.E.–W. H. Longridge, S.S.J.E. (Oxford, 1916); 'Further Letters' ed. by idd. (1920). M. V. Woodgate, *Father Benson*. Founder of the Cowley Fathers (1953). S. L. Ollard in *D.N.B.*, 1912–1921, p. 38 f.

BENSON, ROBERT HUGH (1871–1914), RC apologist. The youngest son of E. W. *Benson, Abp. of Canterbury, he was educated at Eton and Trinity College, Cambridge. In 1894 Benson was ordained, then served in the Eton mission at Hackney Wick and elsewhere, and in 1898 went to the *Community of the Resurrection at Mirfield, but was never professed. In 1903 he was received into the RC Church. After (re-)ordination in 1904, he devoted most of the remainder of his life to preaching and literary work, residing, from 1908, at Buntingford. His novels, remarkable for their vivid characterization and fervent creed, include *The Light Invisible* (1903), *By What Authority?* (1904), *The King's Achievement* (1905), *The Queen's Tragedy* (1906), *The Sentimentalists* (1906), *The Papers of a Pariah* (1907), *The Lord of the World* (1907), *The Necromancers* (1909), and *None other Gods* (1910). His published sermons include *Christ in the Church* (1911) and *The Friendship of Christ* (1912).

Spiritual Letters, with preface by A. C. Benson (brother; London, 1917). Life by C. C. Martindale, S.J (2 vols., ibid., 1916). Short Memoir by A. C. Benson (ibid., 1915). C. C. Martindale, S.J., in *D.N.B.*, 1912–1921, pp. 39–41.

BENTLEY, RICHARD (1662–1742), English classical scholar. He entered St. John's College, Cambridge, at the early age of 14. After a year as headmaster of Spalding Grammar School, he became tutor to the son of E. *Stillingfleet. In his *Boyle Lectures (1692) on the *Evidences of Natural and Revealed Religion*, as in his attack (1713) on the freethinker A. *Collins, he appeared in the role of an able apologist for Christianity. But it was as a classical scholar that he made his real mark. Before his 24th year he had started a Hexapla dictionary and in 1691 he issued a Latin letter to John *Mill as an appendix to an edition of the 'Chronicle' of *John Malalas. His brilliant restoration in this appendix of many passages where the text was corrupt revealed his great powers as a critic to the few capable to judge. In 1699 his attack on Charles Boyle in his *Dissertation on the Epistles of Phalaris* was a still more remarkable performance. During the coming years an astonishing array of works,, among them his notorious re-editing of J. *Milton's *Paradise Lost*, came from Bentley's pen. Nearly all the time, too, Bentley, who had been admitted Master of Trinity College, Cambridge, in 1700, was engaged in a bitter feud, largely provoked by his high-handed methods and reforms, with the Fellows of the College. They tried repeatedly, and almost successfully, to get their Master deposed from office, but he held it till his death.

Works, ed. Alex. Dyce (3 vols., 1836–8); J. H. Monk, *Life of Bentley* (2 vols., 1833); R. C. Jebb, *Life of Bentley* (1882); E. Hedicke, *Studia Bentleiana* (1902); A. T. Bartholomew and J. W. Clark, *Bibliography of Richard Bentley* (1908).

BERAKAH (Heb. בְּרָכָה, 'blessing'). The characteristic Jewish prayer, which takes the form of a blessing or thanksgiving to God. Hence the name 'Berakoth' is applied to the tractates of the *Talmud which contain directions about prayer, both public and private. The OT provides many examples of this type of prayer (e.g. Gen. 24. 27, Job 1. 21, Ps. 28. 6) which was carried over into Christian usage (2 Cor. 1. 3, 1 Pet. 1. 3), and there are parallelisms in ideas and phraseology between early Christian prayers and Jewish berakoth (cf. 1 Clem. 59 and the second of the *Eighteen Benedictions). It has been suggested that the use of 'Eucharist' (Gk. εὐχαριστία, one of the two translations of Heb. *berakah*) for the central Christian rite arose from the fact that the eucharistic prayer was a Christian adaptation of the Jewish berakah which was recited over a cup of wine.

BERDYAEV, NICOLAS (1874–1948), Russian philosopher and author. Originally a sceptic, of Marxist leanings, he found his way back to the Orthodox Church after the Revolution of 1905. From 1922 onwards he lived as an *émigré* in Paris. After *Christianity and Class War* (Eng. trans., 1933), *The Bourgeois Mind* (Eng. trans., 1934), and *The Fate of Man in the Modern World* (Eng. trans., 1935), he published his important *Freedom and the Spirit* (written 1927; Eng. trans., 1935). In it he attempts to adapt Christianity to the requirements of modern intellectuals and proclaims a 'spiritual Christianity' which has no need of doctrinal definitions, bourgeois morality, and set worship. His teaching has been accused of pantheist and theosophist tendencies and as essentially the religion of an aristocratic *élite*. *The Destiny of Man* (Eng. trans., 1937) contains valuable contributions to social philosophy and diagnosis. His social ethics were further elaborated in *Solitude and Society* (Eng. trans., 1938). *Spirit and Reality* (Eng. trans., 1939) is an important analysis of the spiritual needs of modern man.

M. Spinka, *Nicolas Berdyaev*. Captive of Freedom (Philadelphia [c. 1949]); O. Fielding Clarke, *Introduction to Berdyaev* (1950); G. Seaver, *Nicolas Berdyaev* (1950).

BEREANS, also known as **Barclayans** or **Barclayites**. A religious sect founded at Edinburgh in 1773 by J. *Barclay (q.v.). The name was derived from the characteristics of the Bereans mentioned in Acts 17. 10 f. Barclay taught a modified form of *Calvinism, stressing at once its supernatural and mystical aspects. Natural theology he held to be impossible, since every attempt to prove the existence of God rests on a *petitio principi*.

The sole fount of truth is Holy Scripture, which speaks throughout of Christ. The Christian, who is enabled to understand it by faith illuminated by the Holy Spirit, will find, e.g., that every single verse in the Psalms points forward to Christ or His Church. The act of faith implanted in the believer conveys assurance of salvation to him. It is thus the highest gift of God to man, and the 'blasphemy against the Holy Ghost' mentioned in the Gospels is unbelief. Any idea of a covenant-renewal at the Lord's Supper was repudiated as leading to the Romish doctrine of the Mass.

Barclay's doctrines won for a time an enthusiastic reception in a few widely scattered congregations in Scotland. Berean communities were also established in London and Bristol. After Barclay's death (1798), however, they soon melted away, and were for the most part merged in the *Congregationalists.

A. Miller in *H.E.R.E.*, ii (1909), pp. 519–23, s.v.

BERENGAR OF TOURS (*c.* 999–1088), theologian. After studying under *Fulbert of Chartres, he became 'scholasticus' of the school of St. Martin at Tours and in 1040 Archdeacon of Angers. In criticism of the somewhat carnal Eucharistic doctrines then current, Berengar professed agreement with 'the opinions of John the Scot' (*sententiae Ioannis Scoti*, i.e. of *Erigena, though very probably, by a false attribution, Berengar was referring to the work of *Ratramnus of *Corbie). On the strength of a letter which Berengar addressed to *Lanfranc and which was read at the Council of Rome in 1050, he was excommunicated. At Tours in 1054, however, and then at Rome in 1059, he recanted. But it seems that he never entirely abandoned his views, for in 1079 *Gregory VII again demanded of him, and obtained, a retractation. A disappointed man, he lived for the rest of his life as a hermit.

Berengar's more mature doctrines appear in his 'De Sacra Coena', a treatise written in reply to *Lanfranc's 'De Corpore et Sanguine Domini'. In it he denied the possibility of material change in the elements and refused to admit that the 'body of Christ is brought down from heaven and carnally present on the altar', on the ground that Christ cannot be brought down from heaven before the Last Judgement. His positive convictions are less obvious, but they were apparently based on a belief in the existence of universal ideas. He held that Christ's body, which exists only in heaven, is effective for humanity through its sacramental counterpart or type, and that Christ is present in the Eucharist not so much virtually or figuratively (although Berengar sometimes used expressions that would indicate such a view), as 'ideally'. The controversy which he provoked marked an important stage in the development of the doctrine of *Transubstantiation.

The text of Berengar's *De Sacra Coena* was discovered by G. E. *Lessing and ed. by A. F. and F. T. Vischer, Berlin, 1834. Crit. ed. by W. H. Deekenkamp (Kerkistorische

Studien ii, The Hague, 1941). A. J. Macdonald, *Berengar and the Reform of Sacramental Doctrine* (1930). D. *Stone, *A History of the Doctrine of the Eucharist* i (1909), pp. 244–59. R. W. Southern, 'Lanfranc of Bec add Berengar of Tours', in *Studies in Medieval History presented to F. M. Powicke* (1948), pp. 27–48. M. Cappuyns in *D.H.G.E.*, viii (1935), cols. 385–407, s.v., with detailed bibl.

BERESHITH (Heb. בְּרֵאשִׁית, 'in the beginning'). The first word of the Hebrew text of *Genesis and hence the Hebrew name for the Book.

BERGGRAV, EIVIND, (1884–), Bp. of Oslo. Born at Stavanger, the son of a bishop and Minister for Church and Education in the Norwegian Government, he studied at Oslo, Oxford, Cambridge, Marburg, and Lund. In 1909 he was made editor of the monthly journal *Kirke og Kultur*, and began ten years' work as a teacher. In 1919 he became pastor at Hurdalen, in 1925 prison chaplain in Oslo, and in 1929 Bp. of Hålogaland in the extreme north of Norway. In 1937 he returned to Oslo as Primate of the Norwegian Church. In earlier years he had been influenced by N. *Soderblom, Abp. of Upsala, and at Oslo he rapidly won leadership in the *Oecumenical Movement, being elected President of the World Alliance for Promoting International Friendship through the Churches in 1938 and calling a conference of Scandinavian Church leaders on the outbreak of war in 1939. After the occupation of Norway by the Nazis (9 Apr. 1940) Berggrav took an active part in organizing resistance to the Quisling Government. With six other Norwegian bishops he resigned (24 Feb. 1941) 'what the state has committed to my charge', at the same time declaring that 'the spiritual calling which has been ordained to me at the altar of God remains mine by God and by right'. Arrested on 9 Apr. he remained a solitary prisoner in a log cabin on the outskirts of Oslo until the defeat of Hitler (1945). His writings include *With God in the Darkness* (1943), an account in English of the Norwegian Church Conflict.

BERGSON, HENRI (1859–1941), French philosopher. He was born at Paris and of Jewish descent, and after gaining distinction at school in classics and the natural sciences alike, he proceeded to the École Normale Supérieure, where he fell under the spell of the activist doctrines of L. Ollé-Laprune (1839–98) and É. Boutroux (1845–1921) and in 1889 submitted for his doctorate his celebrated *Essai* (see below). In 1900 he accepted a professorship at the Collège de France, remaining there until his retirement in 1924. His intellectual brilliance and daring gained him the hearing of large audiences in many countries. In 1914 he was honoured with election to the French Academy and in 1928 with the Nobel Prize.

Believing that the way to reality was by intuition, Bergson aimed at a radical criticism of all forms of intellectualism. He held that in real life the function of the intellect is subordinate; and that in man it is intuition which accomplishes those purposes which in the lower animals are carried out by instinct. All intellectualist conceptions of reality rest on spatial patterns akin to the diagrams and clock-time of the physicist, which distort the truth and must be abandoned for a new view of time (*durée*). Reality is evolutionary and progressive. Hence the traditional philosophic systems, which in the end can never escape a static and pantheistic determinism, must give way to a new philosophy of creativity and free will in which 'the gates of the future lie ever open'. At the root of moral action lies a 'life-force' (*élan vital*), which is an impulse found at its fullest development in heroes and prophets. Bergson's doctrines thus had close affinities with the thought of W. *James and the *Pragmatists generally.

Bergson's chief works were *Essai sur les données immédiates de la conscience* (1889; Eng. trans., *Time and Free Will*, 1910); *Matière et mémoire* (1896; Eng. trans., 1911); *L'Évolution créatrice* (1907; Eng. trans., 1911); *Les Deux Sources de la morale et de la religion* (1932; Eng. trans., 1935). His influence extended far beyond professed philosophers. His ideas, in whole or in part, were welcomed by many religious thinkers (notably the RC *Modernists) who were dissatisfied with the central position assigned in traditional theology to the human intellect.

Œuvres complètes d'Henri Bergson (Geneva, 1945 ff.). Sympathetic interpretation by a disciple in H. W. Carr, *Henri Bergson. The Philosophy of Change* (1912) and id., *The Philosophy of Change* (1914). A. D. Lindsay, *The Philosophy of Bergson* (1911); D. Balsillie, *An Examination of Professor Bergson's Philosophy* (1912); A. Farges, *La Philosophie de Bergson* (1912); E. Le Roy, *Une Philosophie nouvelle*. Henri Bergson (1912; Eng. tr., 1913); J. *Maritain, *La Philosophie bergsonienne*. Études critiques (1914); J. A. Gunn, *Bergson and his Philosophy* (1920); F. Olgiati, *La filosofia di Enrico Bergson* (1912); J. Chevalier, *Bergson* (1962); A. Thibaudet, *Le Bergsonisme* (2 vols., 1929); R. Jolivet, *Essai sur le bergsonisme* (1931); A. Cresson, *Bergson* (1950). Lydie Adolphe, *La Philosophie religieuse de Bergson* (1946).

BERKELEY, GEORGE (1685–1753), philosopher and divine. He was educated at Trinity College, Dublin, of which he became Fellow in 1707. After some time spent in travelling abroad, he was appointed Dean of Derry in 1724. From 1728 to 1732 he was in America, attempting to found a missionary college in Bermuda, but the refusal of the home government to support his plan led him to abandon it. In 1734 he was made Bp. of Cloyne, a position he held until 1752, when he retired and settled in Oxford. His most important philosophical works, all of them the works of his youth, were *A New Theory of Vision* (1709), *Principles of Human Knowledge* (1710), and *Hylas and Philonous* (1713).

Berkeley is celebrated for his metaphysical doctrine, which was a form of Subjective Idealism. He held that, when we affirm material things to be real, we mean no more than that they are perceived (*esse est percipi*). Material objects, on Berkeley's view, continue to exist when not perceived by us solely because they are objects of the thought of God. The only things that exist in a primary sense are spirits, and material objects exist simply in the sense that they are perceived by spirits.

Berkeley was a philosopher rather than a theologian, but in a small work called *A Discourse on Passive Obedience* (1712) he upheld an ethical utilitarianism of a theological rather than a philosophical kind. He also wrote various short treatises on practical matters of the day.

Berkeley's chief writings have often been reprinted. New ed. by A. C. *Fraser (4 vols., incl. 'Life, Letters and Dissertation' in vol. iv, Oxford, 1871); much revised reissue, 4 vols., 1901. New crit. ed. by A. A. Luce and T. E. Jessop ('Bibliotheca Britannica Philosophica', 1948 ff.). *Selections* ed. A. C. Fraser (1874). *A New Theory of Vision and other Writings* (Everyman's Library, 1910). New Study of Berkeley's 'Common Place Book' (Brit. Mus. Add. MS. 39305) by G. A. Johnston (1930); excellent ed. of text by A. A. Luce (1944; under title *Philosophical Commentaries*). Studies of Berkeley's Life and Philosophy by A. C. Fraser ('Blackwood's Philosophical Classics', 1881), R. Metz (1925), J. M. Hone and M. M. Rossi (1931), G. D. *Hicks (1932); on the biographical side, all superseded by A. A. Luce's Life (1949). B. Rand, *Berkeley's American Sojourn* (1932); A. A. Luce, *Berkeley and Malebranche* (1934); id., *Berkeley's Immaterialism* (1945); C. D. Broad, *Berkeley's Argument about Material Substance* (Henriette Hertz Lecture, 1942). T. E. Jessop, *A Bibliography of George Berkeley* (1934). L. Stephen in *D.N.B.*, iv (1885), pp. 348–56.

BERNADETTE, St. (1844–79), peasant girl of *Lourdes. She was the daughter of François Soubirous, a miller, and the oldest child of a family of six. She was baptized as 'Marie Bernarde', but became affectionately known to her family and neighbours as 'Bernadette'. After a childhood lived in a context of poverty, at the age of 14 she received eighteen *Apparitions of the Bl. Virgin at the Massabieille Rock, near Lourdes. The first was on 11 Feb. 1858 and the last on 16 July of the same year. The Virgin, who manifested herself as the 'Immaculate Conception', revealed her presence by supernatural occurrences (esp. a miraculous spring of water) and commands (the building of a church). After a period in which Bernadette suffered much from constant questionings and publicity, she joined the Sisters of Notre-Dame at Nevers where she lived for the rest of her life. She was beatified by *Pius XI in 1925 and canonized in 1933. Feast day in France, 18 Feb. (not in the universal calendar). Her feast has also been observed on 16 Apr.

The many popular Lives include those of F. Duhourcau (Paris, 1934; Eng. tr., 1934); E. Guynot (Paris, [1937]); Margaret G. Blanton (London, 1939); F. Trochu (Paris, 1954; Eng. tr., 1957). Cf. also H. Petitot, *Histoire exacte des apparitions de N.-D. de Lourdes à Bernadette* [1935]; id., *Histoire exacte de la vie intérieure et religieuse de Ste Bernadette* [1935]. F. Werfel, *The Song of Bernadette* (novel, Eng. tr., 1942), subsequently filmed. See also bibl. to *Lourdes*.

BERNARD, St. (1090–1153), Abbot of *Clairvaux. Born of noble parents at Fontaines near Dijon, he early showed an inclination towards the monastic profession, and in 1113 with thirty other young noblemen of Burgundy, including his own brothers, he entered the monastery of Cîteaux. When two years later he was bidden by the abbot, St. *Stephen

Harding, to choose a place for a new monastery, he established a house at Clairvaux, which under his direction soon became one of the chief centres of the *Cistercian Order. Before long, Bernard was one of the most influential religious forces in Europe. In 1128 he acted as secretary to the Synod of Troyes and there obtained recognition for the Rules of the new order of Knights *Templar, which he is said himself to have drawn up. In the disputed election which followed the death of Pope Honorius II in 1130, Bernard sided with Innocent II against the antipope, Anacletus, and was eventually successful in securing Innocent's victory. As a reward the Pope showered privileges on the Cistercian Order. His power became even greater with the election of a Cistercian monk, a former pupil of his, as Pope *Eugenius III in 1145. During the next few years, he attacked the heretical teachings of *Henry of Lausanne in Languedoc and preached the Second *Crusade. The failure of the latter was a bitter disappointment to him. He was canonized in 1174, and created a '*Doctor of the Church' in 1830. Feast day, 20 Aug.

Bernard was above all else a monk. The austerities and self-mortification which he practised drew upon him the remonstrations of his friend, *William of Champeaux, but they did not avail to change his manner of life. The severely orthodox cast of his character led him to condemn *Abelard at the Council of *Sens (1140) and to attack *Gilbert de la Porrée. Indeed it was his saintliness and personality rather than the force of his intellect which made him so powerful in the Europe of his day, and found visible expression in the rapid growth of the Cistercian Order in the 12th cent. under his influence. Bernard's writings reveal a clear and penetrating grasp of theological problems, a fine eloquence of which his sermons give some suggestion, an extraordinarily intimate acquaintance with the Bible, and, above all, a faith inspired by the sublimest *mysticism. It was in his prose that his poetic feeling found expression, the widespread attribution to him of the *Rosy Sequence ('Jesu dulcis memoria') being almost certainly erroneous. In his 'De Diligendo Deo', one of the most outstanding of all medieval books on mysticism, he insisted that God should be loved simply and purely because He is God, and in his treatise 'De gratia et libero arbitrio' (in which he was much influenced by St. *Augustine) he wrote: 'Remove free-will, and there is nothing to be saved; remove grace and there is left no means of saving. The work of salvation cannot be accomplished without the co-operation of the two'. Thus the love and the grace of God, and the resultant activity of man, together made the central theme of Bernard's message to his age. If at times he appeared somewhat impetuous and obstinate, nothing could conceal the *caritas* which illumined his character and writings, and caused him to denounce the persecution of the Jews and to insist that prayer, preaching, and the life of self-denial and worship should be the *militia* of Church and state, monk and layman, alike.

Editio princeps by A. Bocard (Paris, 1508). The classical ed. is that of J. *Mabillon, O.S.B. (2 vols. fol., Paris, 1667), repr., with additions, in J. P. Migne, *PL*, clxxxii–clxxxv. J. Leclercq, O.S.B., *Etudes sur Saint Bernard et le texte de ses écrits* (Analecta Sacri Ordinis Cisterciensis, ix, fascc. 1–2; Rome, 1953). The chief sources for our knowledge of the saint are some contemporary *Lives*, pr. in J. Mabillon (also *PL*, clxxxv), esp. the 'Vita Prima' (id., cols. 225–455) and the 'Vita Secunda' (cols 469–524). Standard modern Life by E. Vacandard (2 vols., Paris, 1895); others by J. A. W. Neander (Berlin, 1813; Eng. tr., 1843), J. C. Morison (London, 1863), G. Goyau (Paris, 1929), W. W. Williams (Manchester, 1935), J. Leclercq, O.S.B. (Paris, 1948), B. S. James (London, 1957). W. W. Williams, *Studies in St. Bernard of Clairvaux* (1927); E. *Gilson, *La Théologie mystique de Saint Bernard* (1934; Eng. tr., 1940). Modern Eng. tr. of Letters by B. S. James (London, 1953). E. Vacandard in *D.T.C.*, ii (1905), cols. 761–84, and J. Schuck in *L.Th.K.*, ii (1931), cols. 197–201.

BERNARD OF CHARTRES (d. *c.* 1130). The elder brother of *Thierry of Chartres (q.v.), he was the chief formative influence on the *Platonist tradition of the school of *Chartres.

The principal authority is *John of Salisbury, esp. his *Polycraticus*, vii, 13, and *Metalogicon*, i, 5, 24, ii, 17, iii, 2, 4, and iv, 35. L. *Gilson, 'Le Platonisme de Bernard de Chartres' in *Revue néoscolastique de Philosophie*, xxv (1923), pp. 5–19.

BERNARD OF CLUNY (*c.* 1140), also Bernard of Morval or Morlass or (wrongly) Morlaix. He was a monk of *Cluny during the abbacy of *Peter the Venerable. In his day he was famous as an author of sermons and other writings, but his most enduring work is a long poem of some 3,000 lines, 'De Contemptu Mundi', written in a difficult metre (the dactylic hexameter), in which he attacks the monastic disorders of his time and stresses the transitoriness of life on earth. It is the source of many famous hymns, of which 'Brief life is here our portion', 'The world is very evil' ('Hora Novissima'), and 'Jerusalem the Golden' ('Urbs Sion aurea') are the best known. He was perhaps also the author of the 'Mariale', a celebrated poem in praise of the Blessed Virgin.

The 'De Contemptu Mundi' is pr. by T. Wright, *The Anglo-Saxon Poets and Epigrammatists of the Twelfth Century*, ii (R.S., 1872), pp. 3–102. Crit. ed. by H. C. Hoskier (London, 1929). Raby, pp. 315–19. See also A. *Wilmart, O.S.B., in *R. Bén.*, xlv (1933), pp. 249–54.

BERNARD, JOHN HENRY (1860–1927), successively Abp. of *Dublin and Provost of *Trinity College, Dublin. He came of a Kerry family and was born in Bengal. He was educated at Trinity College, Dublin, where he was elected to a fellowship in 1884 and an important lectureship in Divinity in 1886. In his earlier years, when his interests were as much philosophical as theological, he collaborated with his colleague, J. P. Mahaffy (1839–1919), in his second edition of *Kant's Critical Philosophy for English Readers* (1889); and in 1892 he published the first English version of Kant's *Kritik der Urtheilskraft*. Theologically a High Churchman, he came to fill, as time went on, a prominent place in the life of the Church of *Ireland. In 1911 he became Bp. of Ossory, and in 1915 Abp. of Dublin; and

O.D.C.C.–G

he played a notable part in the Convention on the self-government of Ireland, where he was one of the official representatives of the Protestant Church (1916–18). In 1919 he succeeded Mahaffy as Provost of Trinity College, successfully piloting the College through the revolution and its aftermath. His scholarly editions and commentaries include an English version of 'The Pilgrimage of Silvia' (see *Etheria*) for the 'Palestine Pilgrims' Text Society' (1891), the *Irish Liber Hymnorum* (with R. Atkinson, H.B.S., xiii and xiv, 1898), and commentaries on the *Pastoral Epp. (Camb. Bible, 1899) and, his most considerable work, on St. John's Gospel (posthumously ed. A. H. McNeile, 2 vols., I.C.C., 1928). His work was marked by accuracy and sound judgement rather than originality.

Life by R. H. Murray (London, 1928). On his family, see Bernard's own work, *The Bernards of Kerry* (Dublin, 1922). E. J. Gwynn in *D.N.B.*, *1922–1930* (1937), pp. 78–91.

BERNARDINES. The title popularly given to the 'Reformed Congregation of St. *Bernard', i.e. the Italian branch of the *Feuillants (q.v.).

BERNARDINO OF SIENA, St. (1380–1444). *Franciscan reformer, 'the Apostle of the Holy Name'. Born at Massa di Carrera, a town of which his father was then governor, he became a Franciscan Friar at the age of 22 and in 1438 was elected Provincial of the Friars of the Strict *Observance in Italy. In 1439 he took a prominent part at the Council of *Florence in furthering union with the Greeks. A preacher of great eloquence, to whom, said *Pius II, men listened as they might have listened to St. Paul, he made it his chief aim to regenerate the age in which he lived. He was responsible for moral reforms in many cities, and by the time of his death, although accused of heretical views on many occasions, he was perhaps the most influential religious force in Italy. He was a great promoter of devotion to the Holy *Name of Jesus. Feast day, 20 May.

Works ed. P. Rodulphius, 4 vols., Venice, 1591, and J. de la Haye, O.F.M., 4 vols., Paris, 1635. *AA.SS.*, Maius, V (1685), pp. 257*–318*. Life by Leonard Benvoglienti, dated 8 May 1446, ed. F. Van Ortroy, S.J., in *Anal. Boll.*, xxi (1902), pp. 53–80; 'Vie inédite de S. Bernadin de Sienne par un frère mineur, son contemporain', ed., id. ib., xxv (1906), pp. 304–38. Amadio Maria da Venezia, *Vita di S. Bernadino da Siena* (Venice, 1744; various later edd.). Modern lives by P. Thureau-Dangin (Paris, 1896; Eng. tr., 1906), F. Alessio (Mondovi, 1899), K. Hefele (Freiburg i.Br., 1912), A. G. F. Howell (London, 1913), V. Facchinetti, O.F.M. (Milan, 1933), and P. Bargellini (Brescia, 1933). M. Sticco, *Il pensiero di S. Bernardino da Siena* [1924]. B. Stasiewski, *Der heilige Bernadin von Siena. Untersuchungen über die Quellen seiner Biographien* (Franziskanische Studien, Beiheft xiii; 1931). M. Sticco and others, *S. Bernadino da Siena. Saggi e ricerche pubblicati nel quinto centenario della morte, 1444–1944* (Pubblicazioni dell' Università Cattolica del S. Cuore, N.S. vi; 1945). S. Tosti, O.F.M., 'Di alcuni codici delle prediche di S. Bernadino da Siena con un saggio di quelle inedite' in *A.F.H.*, xii (1919), pp. 187–263. J. Heerinckx in *Dict. Sp.*, i (1927), cols. 1518–21, s.v., with details of edd. of individual works; D. Pacetto in *E.C.*, ii (1949), cols. 1411–16, s.v., also with details of edd. of works and further bibl. *Opera* crit. ed. jussu et auctoritate P. M. Perantoni (Quaracchi, 1950 ff.).

BERNE, Theses of. Ten theological propositions, compiled by B. Haller and F. Kolb, two Berne pastors, and others, and revised by H. *Zwingli, which were made the basis of a convocation of the Swiss clergy and laity at Berne from 6 to 26 Jan. 1528. They were drawn up in defence of the Reformed theology against a set of seven theses put forward by J. *Eck in 1526. The first insists on the supremacy of the Word of God; and the remaining nine are directed against (2) *Tradition, (3) *Satisfaction, (4) the *Real Presence in the *Eucharist, (5) the *Sacrifice of the Mass, (6) Mediation through the Saints, (7) *Purgatory, (8) *Images, (9) and (10) *Celibacy. They were embodied in a decree which enforced the Reformation in Berne, 7 Feb. 1528.

Orig. Swiss-German text in E. F. K. Müller, *Die Bekenntnisschriften der reformierten Kirche* (1903), p. 20 f.; Lat. tr. (by Zwingli) in Kidd, pp. 459 f. (No. 217); Eng. tr. in P. *Schaff, *A History of the Creeds of Christendom*, i (1877), p. 365 f., with introd. and bibl., p. 364 f.

BÉRULLE, PIERRE DE (1575–1629), cardinal, diplomatist, theologian, and reformer. A native of the French province of Champagne, he was ordained priest in 1599, and from the first directed his attention to the guidance of souls and the conversion of Protestants. After much difficulty he established the reformed *Carmelites in France, and in 1611 founded the French Congregation of St. *Philip Neri's *Oratorians, thereby incurring the opposition of the *Jesuits. He secured the necessary dispensation for the marriage of Princess *Henrietta Maria to *Charles I of England in 1625, and accompanied her to England. Contrary to the wishes of *Richelieu, he reconciled Louis XIII with his mother. He was made Cardinal in 1627. His chief fame rests upon his spiritual teaching, which showed such devotion to Christ as God-made-Man that Urban VIII called him the 'Apostolus Verbi Incarnati'. The best of his writings is the *Grandeurs de Jésus* (1623).

Works ed. F. Bourgoing, Cong. Orat. (Paris, 1644), repr., with additions, by J. P. *Migne (ib., 1856). J. Dagens (ed.), *Correspondance du Cardinal Pierre de Bérulle* (Bibl. de la R.H.E., xvii, xviii, and xix, 1937–9), with Essai biographique in vol. i, pp. ix–xlv. G. Habert, *La Vie du Cardinal de Bérulle* (1646). M. Tabarand, *Histoire de Pierre de Bérulle* (2 vols., 1817). [J. F.] Nourrisson, *Le Cardinal de Bérulle* (1856). M. Houssaye, *M. de Bérulle et les Carmelites de France, 1575–1611* (1872); id., *Le Père de Bérulle et l'oratoire de Jésus, 1611–1625* (1874); id., *Le Cardinal de Bérulle et le Cardinal de Richelieu, 1625–1629* (1875). A. Molien, Cong. Orat., *Le Cardinal de Bérulle* (2 vols., 1947). Bremond, iii, pp. 3–279; Pourrat, iii, pp. 491–515.

BESSARION, JOHN (c. 1400–72), Cardinal, Greek scholar and statesman. He became a *Basilian monk in 1423; and after studying under *Gemistos Plethon (1431–6), he was made Abp. of *Nicaea in 1437 by the Emp. John VII Palaeologus. Accompanying the latter to the Council of Ferrara-*Florence in 1438, he showed great ardour for the union of the Greek and Latin Churches, a policy which made him unpopular at *Constantinople. Though the union was repudiated by many of the Greeks, he remained in communion with Rome and made his home in Italy. Here he gained the patronage of *Eugenius IV and his successors, was made Cardinal (1439); fulfilled important ecclesiastical missions, and was nearly elected Pope. Bessarion was an enthusiastic scholar and patron of scholars and, among his protégés were T. Gaza, D. Chalcondyles, and the two Lascaris, all of whom played a prominent part in the revival of Greek studies in the Italian Renaissance. He himself translated into Latin *Aristotle's 'Metaphysics' and Xenophon's 'Memorabilia', and among other works he wrote a treatise 'in Calumniatorem Platonis' directed against the Aristotelian views of George of Trebizond. Bessarion bequeathed his library, notable for its large collection of Greek MSS., to the Senate of Venice, where it is preserved in the *Marciana.

Works in J. P. Migne, *PG*, clx, 11–744. L. Mohler, *Kardinal Bessarion als Theolog, Humanist und Staatsmann* (Quellen und Forschungen aus dem Gebiete der Geschichte, xx and xxii, 1923–7), incl. Gk. text, with a Lat. tr. of his In Calumniatorem Platonis libri IV. H. Vast, *Le Cardinal Bessarion (1403–1473)*. Étude sur la chrétienté et la renaissance vers le milieu du XVᵉ siècle (1878). E. Candal, S.I., 'Bessarion Nicaenus in Concilio Florentino' in *O.C.P.*, vi (1940), pp. 417–66. L. Bréhier in *D.H.G.E.*, viii (1935), cols. 1181–99.

BETH (Heb. בֵּת, a 'house'). A word often occurring in Biblical place-names. See following entries.

BETHABARA. Acc. to Jn. 1. 28 (AV), the place 'beyond *Jordan' where St. *John the Baptist baptized, and thus presumably the scene of Christ's *Baptism. It is possibly the modern ford 'Abarah', N. of Beisan; but (a) 'abarah' means only 'crossing', and (b) many important MSS., followed by the RV, read '*Bethany beyond Jordan', and this is probably the correct text.

BETHANY. The village of Sts. *Martha and *Mary and *Lazarus (Jn. 11. 1), about two miles (Jn. 11. 18) from *Jerusalem, on the SE slopes of the Mount of *Olives (Mk. 11. 1). There Christ supped with Simon (Mk. 14. 3), and lodged during the week before His Passion (Mt. 21. 17). Its modern name is El 'Azeriyeh, i.e. 'the place of Lazarus'. 'Bethany beyond Jordan' (Jn. 1. 28 RV) is another village.

F. M. Abel, O.P., *Géographie de la Palestine*, ii (1938), p. 266 f., with reff. P. Benoit, O.P., and M. E. Boismard, O.P., 'Un Ancien Sanctuaire chrétien à Béthanie' in *R. Bibl.*, lviii (1951), pp. 200–51.

BETHEL (lit., Heb., 'House of God'). (1) Formerly the chief sanctuary in *Palestine of the *Israelite (i.e. non-Judaean) tribes. Acc. to Gen. 28. 10–22, God appeared here to *Jacob in a dream, who thereupon erected the stone on which his head had rested as a sacred pillar. On the division of the Hebrew kingdom after the death of *Solomon (1 Kgs. 12), Jeroboam I set up a 'golden calf' here (12. 28 f.), the worship continuing (cf. Am. 7. 10–13) until King Josiah abolished sacrificial worship at all sanctuaries in the kingdom except *Jerusalem in 621.

(2) The small town near Bielefeld in Westphalia which gives the popular name to the *Bodelschwinghsche Stiftungen*. These consist of homes for epileptics, training centres for deaconesses and male nurses, and a college for Protestant theological students. The aim of their founder, the *Lutheran pastor, Friedrich Bodelschwingh (1831–1910), was to relieve the lot of the mentally defective by giving them a share in the work of the community acc. to their capacity and by providing for their spiritual needs. At the same time Bethel furnished a staff of men and women willing and able to help in the social activities of the Lutheran Church. See also *Innere Mission*.

(3) A name used, esp. by certain *Methodists and *Baptists, for a place of religious worship.

BETHESDA. A pool at *Jerusalem (Jn. 5. 2; but three important MSS. (א L D) read 'Bethzatha') believed to have possessed miraculous healing properties connected with a periodical disturbance of the water. It has been variously identified, e.g. with the 'Virgin's Pool' SE of the *Temple, where a spring still bubbles intermittently.

L. H. Vincent, O.P.–F. M. Abel, O.P., *Jérusalem*. Recherches de topographie, d'archéologie et d'histoire, ii (1926), pp. 669–77, with reff. to earlier litt., and text, p. 680. C. Pronobis, 'Bethesda zur Zeit Jesu' in *Th.Q.*, cxiv (1933), pp. 181–207. L. Heidet in *Dict. Bibl.*, i (1895), cols. 1723–1732, s.v. 'Bethsaïde 3'.

BETHLEHEM. The small town five miles S. of *Jerusalem which was the native city of King *David and the birthplace of Christ. It is now an almost exclusively Christian place. It contains one of the oldest churches in Christendom, the 'Church of the Holy Nativity', built by *Constantine in 330 upon the supposed site of the Holy Birth. In spite of rebuilding by *Justinian in the 6th cent., much of the original church survives, including a mosaic pavement unearthed in 1934. Both the Orthodox and Latin Churches have rights within it. For the Council of Bethlehem (1672), see *Jerusalem, Synod of*.

L. H. Vincent, O.P.–F. M. Abel, O.P., Bethléem. *Le Sanctuaire de la Nativité* (1914). L. H. Vincent, O.P., 'Bethléem. Le Sanctuaire de la Nativité d'après les fouilles récentes' in *R. Bibl.*, xlv (1936), pp. 544–74, and xlvi (1937), pp. 93–121. R. W. Hamilton, *The Church of the Nativity, Bethlehem*. A Guide (Jerusalem, 1947). A. M. Schneider, 'Zur Baugeschichte der Geburtskirche in Bethlehem' in *Zeitschrift des deutschen Palästina-Vereins*, lxiv (1941), pp. 74–91.

BETHLEHEMITES. The name of several orders of religious, none of which now survives. *Matthew of Paris attests the existence at Cambridge of a military order dedicated to Our Lady of Bethlehem in 1257. Two centuries later, *Pius II founded a military order, dedicated to the 'Blessed Virgin Mary of Bethlehem', for the defence of the Aegean against the Turks after the fall of *Constantinople in 1453. Another order of Bethlehemites, or 'Belemites', was established *c*. A.D.

1655 in Guatemala for the purposes of tending the sick and education. See also *Bedlam*.

Heimbucher, i, pp. 608 f., 613 f. J. M. Besse, O.S.B., in *C.E.*, ii (1907), pp. 534–6.

BETHPHAGE. A village near *Bethany, with which it is always associated in the NT (Mt. 21. 1, Mk. 11. 1, Lk. 19. 29). Its exact site is uncertain.

F. M. Abel, O.P., *Géographie de la Palestine*, ii (1938), p. 279, with reff.

BETHSAIDA (lit. 'House of Fishing'). A town on the E. bank of the *Jordan at the point where it enters the Sea of Galilee. It was a predominantly Gentile city, and rebuilt by Herod Philip the tetrarch (d. A.D. 33 or 34), who renamed it 'Julias' in honour of the Roman Imperial house. Christ visited it in the course of His ministry (Mk. 8. 22, Lk. 9. 10). It has been suggested that 'Bethsaida of Galilee' (Jn. 12. 21), the home of the disciples *Philip, *Peter, and *Andrew (Jn. 1. 44), was a different place, and that, if so, this would be the city referred to at Mk. 6. 45.

F. M. Abel, O.P., *Géographie de la Palestine*, ii (1938), p. 279 f., with reff.

BETHUNE, David. See *Beaton, David*.

BETROTHAL. A free promise of future marriage between two persons. In origin the Christian betrothal ceremonies date back, both in their Jewish and Roman counterparts, to the custom of 'wife purchase'. The giving of a ring is an earnest of the man's good faith. In many countries formal betrothal before witnesses is still the custom, but in England the Church has ceased to exercise any authority in the matter, and breach of promise has become a case merely for the civil courts.

BETTING and GAMBLING. A gamble is a contract whereby the loss or gain of something of value is made wholly dependent on an uncertain event. If either of the contracting parties is in a state of certainty about the event, the gamble is invalid and fraudulent. The common forms of a gamble are bets, games of chance, and lotteries. The morality of gambling, considered as a species of recreation, is debated. Some hold it to be always illicit, but the majority of Christians regard it as permissible, though highly open to abuse. It is held on all hands, however, that for a gamble to be allowable it must conform to certain conditions. It must not be about an unlawful matter, e.g. one may not bet someone that he will not get drunk; the stake must not be excessive; and it must be for some end other than mere avarice, e.g. recreation. There is no explicit Church law proscribing gambling, except that in the RC Church it is forbidden to the clergy. The Council of *Elvira (can. 79) condemns dice, perhaps because of its pagan associations. St. *Alphonsus Liguori considers every bet at least a venial sin; but this is not the view of most RC theologians. The peculiar nature of the gambling contract and its doubtful morality is recognized by most civil codes of law, which do not allow the winner to sue at law for the gains. On the other hand they recognize it to the extent that they do not allow the loser, once he has paid, to sue for the recovery of his losses.

R. C. Mortimer, *Gambling* (1933). *Gambling, an Ethical Discussion.* A Report of Social and Industrial Commission of the Church Assembly (1950).

BEUNO, St. (d. *c.* 640), Abbot of Clynnog. He is the subject of many legends and superstitions, from which it seems impossible to disentangle any certain history. He is said to have founded monasteries in Herefordshire, but his chief mission work is believed to have been in N. Wales where his tomb was long venerated at Clynnog Vaur (Carnarvonshire). He is supposed to have restored to life St. *Winifred, his niece. He is the titular saint of the modern Jesuit College at St. Asaph, Flints. Feast day, 21 Apr.

There is a Welsh life of St. Beuno (Buchedd Beuno), of which the earliest MS. dates from 1346; Eng. tr. with notes by A. W. Wade Evans, 'Beuno Sant' in *Archaeologia Cambrensis*, lxxxv (1930), pp. 315–41. J. H. Pollen, S.J., 'Traces of a Great Welsh Saint' in *The Month*, lxxx (1894), pp. 235–47.

BEURON, Abbey of. The mother abbey of the 'Beuron Congregation' of *Benedictine monks in Hohenzollern, on the upper Danube. The present abbey and congregation were constituted in 1868, though *Augustinian Canons were established at Beuron as far back as the 11th cent. It has become famous through its work for *liturgical reform, in which it has been esp. assisted by its daughter abbey of *Maria Laach, and the creation of a school of religious art. Until 1920 the now separated Belgian abbeys of *Maredsous and Mont César (at Louvain) belonged to the Beuron Congregation.

K. T. Zingeler, *Geschichte des Klosters Beuron im Donauthale* (1890; on the Augustinian foundation). The present Benedictine Monastery is described in O. Wolff, O.S.B., *Beuron.* Bilder und Erinnerungen aus dem Mönchsleben der Jetztzeit (1889; ed. 6, 1923). J. Kreitmaier, *Beuroner Kunst.* Eine Ausdrucksform der christlichen Mystik (ed. 3, 1921). The periodical *Benediktinische Monatsschrift zur Pflege religiösen und geistigen Lebens* is publd. from Beuron (1919 ff.). Heimbücher, i, pp. 259–64, and ii, p. 653. H. S. Mayer in *L.Th.K.*, ii (1931), cols. 268–70, s.v.

BEVERIDGE, WILLIAM (1637–1708), Bp. of St. *Asaph. Educated at St. John's College, Cambridge, he was ordained deacon and priest in the same month (Jan. 1661) and at once became Vicar of Ealing. In 1672 he published his Συνοδικόν, a collection of Greek canons, which contained an abundance of (in places misguided) erudition. In the same year he became Vicar of St. Peter's, Cornhill, where he had a daily service and a Eucharist every Sunday. In 1681 he became Archdeacon of Colchester and in 1684 Prebendary of *Canterbury. When T. *Ken was deprived in 1691, Beveridge was offered (but through his *non-

juring sympathies declined) the vacated see of *Bath and Wells; and was not again offered a bishopric until 1704, when he became Bp. of St. Asaph. His principal theological work was an *Exposition of the Thirty-Nine Articles* (posthumous, 1710). Though in general a High Churchman, he embraced much of J. *Calvin's teaching on *predestination, maintaining that the number of the saved would be very small.

Collected edd. of his Works [by T. Gregory] (2 vols., fol., London, 1720), T. H. Horne (9 vols., ib., 1824) and J. Bliss (L.A.C.T., 12 vols., 1843–8); all incomplete. A. B. Grosart in *D.N.B.*, iv (1885), p. 447 f., s.v.

BEVERLEY MINSTER. The minster, which stands on the site of a Saxon church founded by St. *John of Beverley (d. 721) and is held to be one of the finest examples of Gothic architecture in Britain, is now a parish church. In the 10th cent. a college of secular canons was established here. The existing building was constructed after the destruction of the earlier church by fire in 1188. At the *Reformation, the minster was not dissolved until the Colleges and Chantries Act of 1547, as it was in the hands of secular canons. In 1713 a restoration prevented it from falling into ruin.

G. Poulson, *Beverlac*, or the Antiquities and History of the Town of Beverley, in the County of York, and of the Provostry and Collegiate Establishment of St. John's: with a minute description of the present Minster and the Church of St. Mary, and other Ancient and Modern Edifices, ii (1829); G. Oliver, *The History and Antiquities of the Town and Minster of Beverley* (1829). A. Hamilton Thompson, 'Collegiate Church of St. John the Evangelist, Beverley' in *V.C.H., Yorkshire*, ii (1913), pp. 353–9. W. *Dugdale, *Monasticon Anglicanum*, ii (ed. 1819), pp. 128–30, and vi (pt. 2; 1830), pp. 1306–12.

BEYSCHLAG, WILLIBALD (1823–1900), German Evangelical theologian. In 1856 he became Court Preacher at Karlsruhe and in 1860 Professor of Pastoral Theology at Halle. One of the leading exponents of the '*Vermittlungstheologie', he rejected the *Chalcedonian Christology, but strongly attacked the rationalistic doctrines of E. *Renan and D. F. *Strauss. In his later years he took a prominent part in ecclesiastical politics. After 1870 he helped to draw up the new constitution of the Prussian Church, and he supported the Prussian Government in the *Kulturkampf, partly by lending his aid to the cause of the '*Old Catholics'. He was also one of the chief agents in founding the *Evangelischer Bund.

Beyschlag's publications included *Karl Immanuel Nitzsch* (1871), *Der Altkatholizismus* (ed. 3, 1883), *Leben Jesu* (2 vols., 1885–6), *Neutestamentliche Theologie* (2 vols., 1891; Eng. tr., 2 vols., 1895) and *Aus meinem Leben.* Erinnerungen und Erfahrungen der jüngeren Jahre (2 vols., Halle, 1896–9). K. Pahncke in *P.R.E.* (ed. 3), xxiii (1913), pp. 192–203.

BEZA, THEODORE (1519–1605), *Calvinist theologian. De Besze (thus the original form of his name) came from an old Catholic family of Vézelay in Burgundy. He was educated by his tutor M. Wolmar, first at Orléans, later at

Bourges, where Wolmar became a Protestant and made his house a centre of the new religion, J. *Calvin being one of its frequent guests. In 1534 Wolmar returned to Germany, and from 1535 to 1539 Beza studied law at Orléans with a view to embracing an ecclesiastical career. Having soon abandoned this plan he went to *Paris, where he wrote Latin poetry and led an irregular life, as is witnessed by his Poemata Juvenilia (1548), the later editions of which he partly expurgated. In 1548 he officially renounced the Catholic religion and went to *Geneva, where he formally married Claude Desnoz, with whom he had concluded a clandestine marriage in 1544. In 1549 he became professor of Greek at Lausanne. In 1554 he defended the burning of M. *Servetus at Geneva in his treatise De Haereticis a civili Magistratu Puniendis. In 1556 he published an annotated Latin translation of the Greek NT which has often been reprinted, the best edition being that of Cambridge, 1642. In 1558 Calvin offered him a professorship at the newly founded academy at Geneva, where he published his Confession de la foi chrétienne (1560), a popular exposition of Calvinist beliefs. In 1561 he completed the edition of the Psalms begun by C. *Marot, and in the same year took a prominent part in the colloquy between Catholics and Protestants at *Poissy. Soon afterwards civil war broke out between Catholics and Protestants in France, during which he tried to procure men and arms from the Protestant German princes. In 1563 he returned to Geneva, and on the death of Calvin in the next year he became the leader of the Swiss Calvinists. In the same year (1564) he published his Vita Calvini, which is more in the nature of a panegyric than of a historically accurate biography. In 1565 he brought out his first edition of the Greek text of the NT, to which were added the Vulgate and his own Latin translation. This is the first critical edition of the Greek NT, for which he had consulted 17 MSS. as well as variants collected by H. *Stephanus and the edition published by R. *Stephanus in 1550. In 1571 he presided over the National Synod of La Rochelle, and in 1580 published the Histoire ecclésiastique des Églises réformées au royaume de France, which, however, acc. to R. Reuss, Notice bibliographique (1889), is not his own work, but a compilation of memoirs sent him from all parts of France. In 1582 Beza brought out a 2nd edition of his NT, supplemented by the '*Codex Bezae' which he had discovered at Lyons (1562), the *Peshitta, and a Latin trans. of the Arabic version. In 1597 he was visited several times by St. *Francis de Sales, who endeavoured in vain to bring him back to the RC Church.

Beza's theological opinions, which are contained esp. in the Tractationes Theologicae (1570–82), are permeated with the Calvinist spirit, and are rigidly determinist in character. He teaches the necessity of all temporal events, so that even the Fall, by which free will was completely destroyed, belongs to the eternal plan of God.

New ed. of the Histoire ecclésiastique, by G. Baum and E. Cunitz (3 vols., Paris, 1883–9). Lives by F. C. Schlosser (Heidelberg, 1809), J. W. Baum ([only to 1563] 2 vols., Berlin, 1843–51), H. Heppe (Elberfeld, 1861). C. van Proosdij (Leyden, 1895),'and H. M. Baird (Heroes of the Reformation, No. 4, 1899). On Beza and the Bible, see B. Heurtebize in Dict. Bibl., i (1895), col. 1772 f., s.v. E. Choisy, L'État chrétien à Genève au temps de Théodore de Bèze (1903). E. Choisy in P.R.E. (ed. 3), ii (1897), pp. 677–686.

B.F.B.S. See British and Foreign Bible Society.

BIASCA SACRAMENTARY. The oldest surviving MS. (10th cent.) of the *Ambrosian Rite, preserved in the *Ambrosiana (A. 24 bis inf.).

A. Ratti [*Pius XI]–G. *Mercati, Missale Ambrosianum Duplex (Milan, 1913).

BIBLE. (1) Word. The word 'Bible' is derived through the Fr. and Lat. from the Gk. βιβλία, 'books', used in the *Septuagint in such expressions as 'the Books of the Law' (1 Macc. 1. 56) and 'the holy Books' (1 Macc. 12. 9). The usual Gk. word (NT, *Philo, *Josephus) for the Jewish sacred writings, however, was not βιβλία but γραφαί ('scriptures'). But whereas γραφαί was translated into Lat. (scripturae), βιβλία was transliterated; and 'Biblia' thus became a new and distinctive term for the Holy Scriptures, denoting, as its plural form shows, a collection of books. As the Biblical books were increasingly considered a unity, the word (orig. neut. pl.) came to be understood as a fem. sing., whence the Eng. 'Bible', Fr. la Bible, etc.

(2) The Jewish Scriptures. In later times the Jews classified their Scriptures in three groups: (1) the Law (*Torah), (2) the Prophets, and (3) other Books, known collectively as the 'Writings'. The Law comprised the *Pentateuch or 'Five Books of Moses' (Gen., Exod., Lev., Num., Deut.), regarded as on a higher level than all the rest. The 'Prophets' fell into two groups, the 'Former Prophets' (Josh., Jgs., 1 and 2 Sam., and 1 and 2 Kgs.) and the 'Latter Prophets' (Is., Jer., Ezek., and the Twelve *Minor Prophets). The inclusion of the 'Former Prophets', properly historical Books, among the Prophets so far accords with the modern view which sees in them history written from an essentially prophetic point of view. The 'Writings' comprised all the remaining books of the English OT (1 and 2 Chron., Ez., Neh., Job, Pss., Prov., Eccles., Song of Songs, Ruth, Est., and Dan.) as well as some others, e.g. Ecclus., Tob., Macc., which the Jews later rejected. By the time of Christ, Jews everywhere recognized the Law and the Prophets as holy Scripture, but the exact compass of the 'Writings' was still undefined. While some, e.g. the Pss., were universally received, others, e.g. Est., which were later officially accepted, were still disputed, and others again, e.g. Ecclus., which were later rejected were not yet definitely excluded. The *Canon of the Jewish Scriptures was prob. settled at the Council of

*Jamnia (c. A.D. 100), certainly by the end of the 2nd century. As the excluded books ceased to be copied, their Hebrew text has in most cases (except for large parts of Ecclus., rediscovered in modern times) been lost.

(3) *The Greek Old Testament.* Before the Christian era the Hebrew Scriptures, including some which were later rejected from the canon, had been translated into Greek for the use of Greek-speaking Jews. This Greek Bible was extended by the inclusion of other Jewish writings of a similar kind, e.g. Wisd. Sol., which were not translations but original Greek compositions. The version of this Greek Bible in most general use was the *Septuagint (q.v.). As soon as Christianity won its footing in the Hellenistic world, this was the version in which Christians received the Jewish Scriptures; hence it was the first Christian Bible. The early separation of Christianity from Judaism caused the Christian canon before long to differ from that of the Jews. The Jewish rejection of certain books c. A.D. 100 was unheeded by the Church, which continued to reckon all books in the Septuagint as Scripture. It was only at a later date that the Church became generally conscious of its divergence here from Judaism. Then the Church designated those Books (or parts of Books) which were not in the Hebrew Canon as 'Deutero-canonical' or (as in the AV and RV) as *Apocrypha. They include some, e.g. Ecclus., Tob., Judith, 1 Macc., which it is fairly or quite certain were translations from the Heb. and others, e.g. Wisd. Sol. and 2 Macc., which are more probably original compositions by Jewish authors in Greek. Besides the Septuagint, other versions (*Symmachus, *Aquila, *Theodotion) also circulated to some extent among the Jews and in the early Christian Church.

(4) *The New Testament.* At an early date the Christian Church came to regard certain of her own writings, esp. if of Apostolic origin, as of equal authority and inspiration to those she had inherited from Judaism (cf. the collocation of St. Paul's Epp. with 'the other scriptures' in 2 Pet. 3. 16). The *Canon (q.v.) of the NT, based on the Four Gospels and the Epp. of St. Paul, came into existence largely without definition. It was formally fixed at *Rome in 382, when the Christian OT Canon (based on the Septuagint) was also defined. At *Alexandria the present Canon is already found in St. *Athanasius's *Festal Ep.* for 367.

(5) *The Latin Bible, the Apocrypha, and other Versions.* Many early Latin versions of parts of the Bible ('*Old Latin') came into use in the Christian Church esp. in Africa and Italy. The OT Books were translated not from the Hebrew but from the Greek. To remedy the confusion created by a variety of translations, St. *Jerome (later 4th cent.), encouraged by Pope *Damasus, made a fresh translation of the whole Bible, rendering the OT Books, wherever possible, from the Hebrew. (In some of the NT Books he seems to have taken over almost bodily an earlier version.) St. Jerome's version (the '*Vulgate', q.v.), which was given formal recognition at the Council of

*Trent (sess. IV), is now the authoritative Bible of the RC Church.

Jerome's task necessarily drew his attention to the Deutero-canonical Books not found in the Heb. Bible. He himself sought to exclude them from the Christian canon ('libri canonici') as 'libri ecclesiastici' or Apocrypha. But though frequent doubts as to their status continued to be raised, the Latin Church retained them and finally settled their authority at Trent (sess. IV). At the Reformation, the Protestants in their vernacular versions either omitted the Apocrypha altogether or placed them in a separate section between the OT and the NT. At the Synod of *Jerusalem in 1672 the E. Church, which had hitherto continued to use the Septuagint canon, but with some doubts about certain of the Deutero-canonical Books, rejected all but four (Tob., Judith, Ecclus., and Wisd.).

For the ancient versions other than the Septuagint and Vulgate, see *Syriac, Coptic, Ethiopic*; for the principal English versions, see foll. entry and reff. there given; for translations into other modern languages, see under the names of the translators (M. *Luther, T. *Beza, &c.).

(6) *Textual Criticism.* For this science, the object of which is to secure a text as near as possible to the wording of the original writer, the principal materials are:

For the OT (1) the Hebrew MSS.: these contain the form of text (the *Massoretic text) authoritatively established by Jewish scholars of the early Christian era: the earliest MSS. of this text (apart from parts of Is.) are of the 9th and 10th cents. A.D.; (2) the Septuagint and other Greek versions which incorporate many readings much older than those of the Massoretic text; and (3) the Vulgate and other Latin versions, also more ancient than the MSS. of the Massoretic text. See also *Dead Sea Scrolls*.

For the NT (1) innumerable Greek MSS. of which the most important (*Codex Sinaiticus, *Codex Vaticanus, &c.) are of the 4th cent. A.D. and even earlier (*Chester Beatty papyri); (2) the ancient versions, esp. the Old Syriac and the Old Latin, but also other translations in both these languages and the Coptic, Ethiopic, Armenian, Georgian, &c., versions; and (3) Patristic citations of the Scriptures. Among modern scholars who have made notable contributions to the textual criticism of the NT are C. *Tischendorf, B. F. *Westcott, F. J. A. *Hort, E. B. *Nestle and A. *Souter.

(7) *Authority and Interpretation.* The respect shown by Christ and the Apostolic Church to the Scriptures of Judaism forms the basis of the Christian attitude to the Bible. These OT Scriptures, regarded as inspired by the Holy Spirit (Lk. 24. 44, 2 Tim. 3. 15 f.), were an imperfect and partial revelation of God and a preparation for the coming of Christ, which in various ways they foretold (Heb. 1. 1 f.). If many of the ordinances which Judaism regarded as permanently valid were superseded in the Christian dispensation, the OT as a whole retained its authority, while its message was completed by the NT, so that

the two together formed a single and final record of God's revelation of Himself. Hence the OT was ordained as the possession of the Church to whom (and not to the Jews) Christians held that since the Coming of the Lord it primarily belonged.

In Patristic times the only serious challenge to this view of the Bible was that of *Marcion (q.v.), who repudiated the OT and severely curtailed the NT. After its failure the authority of the Bible was everywhere accepted. The other great heretics (e.g. *Arius) took a common stand with the orthodox and appealed (wrongly, as the Church believed) to both OT and NT in support of their doctrines. In the matter of interpretation, *allegorical methods were much in use in the Patristic, Medieval and Reformation periods. Apart from the latitude allowed by such methods of exegesis, the Divine inspiration of the Bible was generally held to require belief in the truth of all its assertions on matters not only of history, doctrine and ethics, but also of cosmology and natural science. In the earlier phases of the modern scientific movement (16th and 17th cents.) this view of inspiration was shared by Catholics and Protestants alike; and on these grounds the heliocentric teaching of *Galileo was condemned as heretical.

The difficulties in the way of maintaining this view of the Bible gave encouragement to 18th cent. *rationalism and *deism, and it was not until the 19th cent. that the critical and historical study of the Bible was seriously undertaken (J. *Wellhausen, S. R. *Driver, T. K. *Cheyne, W. *Sanday, K. *Lake, B. H. *Streeter). At first it met with much opposition, but in the later 19th and 20th cents. it was gradually accepted in the W. by most clergy and thoughtful laity outside the RC Church. More recently there are signs that, despite the rigidity of earlier official pronouncements (see *Biblical Commission*), it is coming to be widely welcomed also among RCs. It is still resisted by a certain school of Protestants (*Fundamentalists). It sets out from the belief that an ancient writing must be interpreted in its historical perspective, and related as far as possible to the circumstances of its composition and its meaning and purpose for its author and first readers. The tradition of a document's date and *provenance* must be weighed against the evidences of internal analysis and considerations of historical probability. This means comparing the Biblical books or their parts with one another, with evidence from non-Biblical writings, including the *Pseudepigrapha, and from archaeology, a process which has been assisted by the fact that external evidence became increasingly abundant and better understood in the 19th cent. By such methods many traditional opinions have been virtually overthrown, e.g. the Pentateuch is no longer attributed to the personal authorship of Moses, but ascribed to a much later period in the history of Israel (prob. 9th–4th cent. B.C.). In the NT the differences in historical value between St. *John's Gospel and the *Synoptics have been increasingly recognized. The

Fourth Gospel is probably not the report of an eye-witness (John, the son of Zebedee) nor is its author to be identified with the writer of Rev. The more important critical conclusions are now so widely accepted by those qualified to judge as to be reckoned virtually assured. They are generally recognized as the only firm foundation for a true interpretation of the Scriptures.

Since the World War of 1914–18, the approach of scholars to the NT has shifted. A 'post-critical' period has begun, in which the interest in literary and historical questions has declined. More attention is paid to the theology of the Bible and to the interrelation of different parts of the OT and the NT. There is a revived interest in the typology of the Scriptures both in Great Britain (L. S. Thornton, A. M. Farrer) and in France (J. Daniélou). Many of the Liberal assumptions regarding 'lower' and 'higher' elements in religion have been discarded before a fresh assessment of the ritual and sacramental ('priestly') elements, which it is no longer felt necessary to depreciate in contrast to the ethical ('prophetic').

TEXTS. Editions of the Hebrew OT by R. *Kittel (1905–1906; 2nd ed., 1928); *Septuagint by H. B. *Swete (1887–1894) and A. Rahlfs (2 vols., Stuttgart, 1935); Greek NT by B. F. Westcott–F. J. A. Hort (1881); E. B. Nestle (1898, new ed., 1927); A. Souter (1910; 2nd ed. 1948; text that underlying RV, apparatus only due to Souter). For English versions see foll. entry.

DICTIONARIES. W. Smith (1860-5; still useful); J. Hastings (4 vols., 1898–1902, and Extra vol., 1904, unsurpassed); *Encyclopaedia Biblica* (4 vols., 1899–1903; with some excellent and original articles, but often erratic); F. Vigouroux, *Dictionnaire de la Bible* (5 vols., 1891–1912) and Supplément (ed. L. Pirot 1928, in progress).

COMMENTARIES. Complete Commentaries ed. by J. R. Dummelow (1909) and A. S. *Peake (q.v., 1919; new ed. 1962). Also the *New Commentary*, ed. C. Gore, H. L. Goudge, A. Guillaume (SPCK, 1928; includes the Apocrypha); *Abingdon Bible Commentary*, ed. F. C. Eiselen, E. Lewis, D. G. Downey (U.S.A., 1929). Commentaries on separate books in 'Cambridge Bible', 'Century Bible', 'International Critical Commentary', 'Moffatt N.T.'. Also *The Clarendon Bible* (OT, 6 vols., 1926–48; NT in progress). *A Catholic Commentary on Holy Scripture*, ed. B. Orchard, O.S.B., R. C. Fuller and R. Russell, O.S.B. (London, 1953).

GENERAL WORKS. T. W. Manson (ed.), *A Companion to the Bible* (1939); H. Wheeler *Robinson (ed.), *The Bible in its Ancient and English Versions* (1940); G. F. Moore, *The Literature of the OT* (H.U.L., 1913; new ed., L. H. Brockington, 1948); W. O. E. Oesterley and T. H. Robinson, *Introduction to the Books of the OT* (1934); W. O. E. Oesterley, *Introduction to the Books of the Apocrypha* (1935); A. H. McNeile, *Introduction to the NT* (1927); C. H. Dodd, *The Bible To-day* (1946); *The Interpretation of the Bible*, ed. C. W. Dugmore (1944); A. Richardson, *Preface to Bible Study* (1943); A. G. Hebert, S.S.M., *The Authority of the OT* (1947). A. Robert and A. Tricot, *Initiation biblique* (1939).

BIBLE (English Versions). 1. PRE-REFORMATION VERSIONS. No complete Anglo-Saxon Bible, or even NT, exists. Translations of this period comprise (a) interlinear glosses (forming a crude word-by-word translation) of the Gospels and Pss., and (b) versions, sometimes abridged, of separate portions of the Bible, e.g. parts of Exod. 20–23 in the introductory section of King Alfred's Laws, a prose version of Pss. 1–50 (possibly by Alfred himself), and the four Gospels in West Saxon (perhaps 10th cent.). Free renderings of OT narrative passages occur in the homilies of *Aelfric (c. 992), who also translated Gen. 1–35 (36–50 having been done by another hand previously) and (with considerable omissions)

Exod. 1–Josh. 11. There are also numerous detached quotations and free renderings of other parts of the Bible in homilies.

In Middle English, from *c.* 1250 onwards, metrical versions of certain Books (esp. Gen. and Exod.), of Biblical history generally, and of the Psalter, were made. There followed in Midland and in Northern dialect prose versions of the Psalter, the latter by Richard *Rolle of Hampole.

In the 14th cent. several anonymous translations of NT books in various dialects were produced, apparently in connexion with *Lollardy and under the influence of J. *Wycliffe. But the popular view that Wycliffe himself was the first English translator of the complete Bible seems to be without foundation. There are two 'Wycliffite' versions:

(i) *MS. Bodley 959.* The greater part of the OT (i.e. as far as Bar. 3. 20, in Vulgate order) belongs to *Nicholas of Hereford, the rest of the OT and the whole of the NT to an unknown translator. Nicholas of Hereford's portion is usually dated, but on insufficient grounds, before 1382 (Synod of Blackfriars).

(ii) '*Purvey's version.*' A later revision, prob. between 1395 and 1408. The translator, commonly identified with John *Purvey, explains in the prologue his method of working 'with divers fellows and helpers' and with 'many good fellows and cunning at the correcting of the translation'.

Both these versions, esp. the former, follow the Vulgate (then the only text available), often so closely as to be detrimental to the clarity of the English. At the Council of *Oxford in 1407 the making of any fresh translations of the whole or any portion of the Bible and the use of any translation made 'in the times of John Wycliffe or since' without diocesan or synodical sanction was forbidden. Nevertheless many MSS. of the Wycliffite versions (esp. the Purvey text) continued to be made and used until the appearance of W. *Tyndale's and M. *Coverdale's work.

2. THE REFORMATION PERIOD. The Wycliffite versions, being under ecclesiastical censure, were not printed. New facilities for textual study and translation of the Bible were opened up by the printing of the Vulgate (first in 1456), the Hebrew text (1488), *Erasmus's Greek Testament (1516, with four revisions by 1535), the *Complutensian Polyglot (1522), and S. *Pagninus's literal Latin rendering of the Hebrew OT (1528). The plan of a translation of the NT from the Greek is due to W. *Tyndale and dates from *c.* 1523. He failed to obtain the patronage of C. *Tunstall, Bp. of London, but for a short while was supported by Humphrey Monmouth, a London merchant. In 1524 he fled to Germany where he probably met at *Wittenberg M. *Luther, whose German NT had appeared in 1522. The printing of Tyndale's NT (in 4to) was begun at *Cologne in 1525; but before it was complete Tyndale was forced to flee to Worms, where it was restarted and finished (in 8vo) in 1526. Subsequent editions were printed in Holland, and copies soon reached England. Tyndale then

translated the Pentateuch which was printed at Antwerp in 1529–30. His translation of Jonah appeared in 1531 and a revision of Gen. and of the NT in 1534, and of the NT again in 1535. He also translated, but never published, Josh.–2 Chron. inclusive. His NT and Pentateuch contained marginal notes, decribed by *Henry VIII as 'pestilent glosses', expressing his strongly Protestant views. Tyndale was burnt as a heretic at Vilvorde in Holland in 1536. In his prefaces, prologues, marginal references, etc., he is greatly dependent on Luther, but his translation is an independent and pioneer work, using Erasmus's Latin version of the NT, the Vulgate, and Luther's German, as well as his own interpretation of the original. His final version of the NT contains much which has passed unchanged into the Authorized Version.

In 1534 *Canterbury Convocation petitioned Henry VIII that the whole Bible might be translated into English. Though no royal command to this effect was issued, Miles *Coverdale published in 1535 a complete Bible, dedicated to the king. He based his rendering on Tyndale's where available; the other OT books he translated from the German of Luther and the Zürich version of H. *Zwingli and Leo Juda, with guidance from Pagninus and the Vulgate. He does not appear to have known Hebrew. His Psalter has remained in constant use until modern times in the BCP Version of the Psalms. In 1537 a revised English Bible known as '*Matthew's Bible' appeared. It was the first to bear the King's authorization and printed (probably in Antwerp) for the London printers, R. *Grafton and E. *Whitchurch. The ascription to 'Thomas Matthew' was nominal (the suggested identification with one Thomas Matthew of Colchester is improbable), its real editor being John *Rogers. The text consisted of Tyndale's Pentateuch, a version of Josh.–2 Chron. made from the Hebrew and hitherto unpublished (prob. also Tyndale's, cf. above), Tyndale's NT of 1535, and the remainder in Coverdale's version. Rogers's work was confined to careful editing and adaptation. For the Prayer of Manasses, omitted by Coverdale, he translated the French version of *Olivetan, from whom also he took some editorial matter. At about the same time Coverdale's Bible, previously printed abroad, was for the first time printed in England.

Further revisions of the whole Bible followed. The '*Great Bible' of 1539, printed in Paris, was issued under T. *Cromwell's patronage. In 1540 it was revised and reissued with a preface by T. *Cranmer and a notice identifying it with the 'Bible in the largest volume in English' which the *Injunction of 1538 ordered to be set up in churches. Both these revisions, which claimed on the title-page of 1539 to have been made from the Hebrew and Greek 'by the diligent study of divers excellent learned men', were by Coverdale, though they did not bear his name. Among the 'learned men' whom Coverdale had consulted was S. *Munster, who in 1534–5 had issued a literal German translation of the Hebrew. All notes and controversial matter were deliberately excluded. In 1539 R. *Taverner also published a revision of 'Matthew's Bible' based on careful attention to the Greek and to the Vulgate OT. No further translations appeared until the reign of Mary. In 1542 S. *Gardiner, Bp. of *Winchester, headed a reaction in favour of the Vulgate, and in 1546 the use of Tyndale's or Coverdale's NT was forbidden by royal decree. Under *Edward VI this policy was reversed by the Protestant movement and the English versions were again reprinted.

In the reign of *Mary, W. *Whittingham issued at Geneva in 1557 a new English NT for the Protestant exiles (for the first time divided into verses and printed in roman type). Then followed in 1559 the Psalms, and in 1560 a complete Bible, dedicated to Queen *Elizabeth. This version (the '*Geneva Bible' (q.v.), also popularly the '*Breeches Bible') was based on Tyndale and the Great Bible, but influenced by J. *Calvin and T. *Beza, as well as by the French Bibles of Lefevre and Olivetan. It had marginal notes written from an extreme Protestant viewpoint. Many of its renderings, not found in previous English versions, were later adopted into the AV.

In the reign of Elizabeth the Geneva Bible obtained great popularity in England, although it lacked the royal and ecclesiastical authorization still possessed by the Great Bible. In 1566 Abp. M. *Parker undertook a revision of the latter in co-operation with other Bishops. This new translation (the '*Bishops' Bible') was published in 1568 and revised in 1572. It copied the Geneva Bible in the adoption of verse-divisions, but the rendering was explicitly based on the Great Bible, with attention to the Greek and to the Hebrew, for which Pagninus and Munster were taken as authorities. Phrases which savoured of 'lightness or obscenity' were altered and passages considered unedifying were marked for omission in public reading. All comment, in the form of marginal notes, was eschewed. As the several revisers worked without much co-ordination, this translation varies in quality from book to book.

Though not yet acknowledging the right of the laity to read the Bible in the vernacular without special ecclesiastical sanction, the RC Church also felt the need for an acceptable English version. The NT was translated by members of the English College at Reims, largely at the instigation of W. (later Cardinal) *Allen. The chief translators were Gregory *Martin and Richard Bristow, and it was issued in 1582. The OT followed from Douai in 1609–10 (see *Douay-Reims Bible*). Both NT and OT were translated from the Vulgate, in acc. with the Council of Trent's endorsement of this version; but in the NT at least the original language was consulted. Many words and turns of phrase show the close adherence (also deliberate) of the translators to their standard, e.g. 'Pasch' (Passover), 'Azymes' (Unleavened Bread), 'supersubstantial bread' (Mt. 6. 11), 'legates of Christ' (ambassadors). But in many

places the English is vivid and direct. The Reims NT was among the versions consulted by the makers of the AV.

3. THE AUTHORIZED VERSION (1611) AND ITS SUCCESSORS. At the *Hampton Court Conference a new version of the Bible was suggested to *James I, who in the same year appointed for the task fifty-four divines, among them the Puritan J. *Rainolds, J. Bois of Cambridge, H. *Savile, J. *Overall, and L. *Andrewes. The 'Bishops' Bible' was used as a basis, but earlier English versions were taken into consideration, and the new Bible was designedly a revision rather than a completely original work. Careful marginal notes on matters of text and translation (not theology) were provided and the best resources of contemporary scholarship were utilized. The result, published in 1611, was a version of great felicity, which within a generation displaced all previous versions, and has become the only familiar, and in most cases the only known, form of the Bible to generations of English-speaking people. Beyond the royal authority under which it was made, and the statement on the title-page 'Appointed to be read in churches', no formal authorization was given to it. In the BCP of 1662 it was adopted as the text for the Epistles and Gospels, though the Psalter remained in Coverdale's version. It was carried from England to the American Colonies, and it continues in use in U.S.A., where it is known as the 'King James Version', as well as in the Dominions. See also *Authorized Version*.

The Authorized Version was not accepted entirely without criticism, but projects for further revision, e.g. that of the Long Parliament of 1653, came to nothing. Modifications in spelling, punctuation, use of capitals, etc., were unobtrusively made by editors, esp. Dr. Paris at Cambridge (1762) and B. Blayney at Oxford (1769), and the headlines of pages and the marginal references altered in different editions. The only new translations or revisions from this period were private ones. J. *Wesley's *Explanatory Notes on the New Testament* (1755) embodied a conservative revision of the AV. Other 18th-cent. translators (e.g., D. *Mace, 1729) went further in the introduction of colloquialisms or in free paraphrase into the style of contemporary elegance, esp. E. Harwood's *A Liberal Translation of the NT* (1768). Among scholarly translations of individual books was R. *Lowth's *Isaiah* (1778). The Reims–Douay version was revised by Bp. R. *Challoner (1749–50); and versions of the Pentateuch were issued by the Jewish scholars I. Delgado (1785) and D. Levi (1787).

4. THE REVISED VERSION (1881–5). The growth of Biblical scholarship and the availability of new versions for comparison, as well as changes in English usage since 1611, led to occasional expressions of dissatisfaction with the AV from the early 19th cent. e.g. in H. Hallam's *Literature of Europe* (1839) and in the *Edinburgh Review* (1855). From the middle of the century proposals for the revision of the AV were both advocated and opposed.

In 1870 the *Convocation of Canterbury took the matter up and a committee of revisers, to which non-Anglican scholars were co-opted, was appointed. They were instructed 'to introduce as few alterations as possible into the text of the AV, consistently with faithfulness' and 'to limit, as far as possible, the expression of such alterations to the language of the Authorized and earlier English versions'. No change in the text was to be finally approved except by a two-thirds majority; changes supported by only a simple majority were to be noted in the margin. The NT Company included F. J. A. *Hort, J. B. *Lightfoot, W. *Milligan, W. F. *Moulton, F. H. A. *Scrivener, B. F. *Westcott, the OT Company E. H. *Browne, A. B. *Davidson, F. *Field, C. D. Ginsburg, J. J. S. Perowne, E. H. Plumptre, N. C. *Thirlwall, and C. *Wordsworth (Bp. of Lincoln). The NT was published in 1881, the OT in 1885. The *Apocrypha was undertaken after the main work, and issued in 1895.

The Revisers followed stricter canons of translation than their predecessors of 1611, esp. in the constant use, as far as practicable, of the same English word or phrase for the same Greek or Hebrew. Though this principle caused many minor and apparently unnecessary changes, esp. in the NT, it facilitated the study of the original through the medium of the English. The Pss. and other poetical OT books were printed in lines acc. to their original structure, the rest of the text in paragraphs instead of in separate verses. The RV was widely criticized on publication and for some years after, but the work was well done within the limits set. Doubts concerning the legality of its use in Anglican public worship were countered by a resolution of Canterbury Convocation in 1899. But it has been adopted only in a minority of parish churches and cathedrals, and it is very much less in demand for private reading than the AV.

5. RECENT TRANSLATIONS. In the later 19th and earlier 20th cent. numerous translations of individual books were produced as parts of learned commentaries (e.g. the Apocrypha in R. H. *Charles's *Apocrypha and Pseudepigrapha of the Old Testament*, 1913) and separately. Many new versions of the complete NT or the whole Bible were also published, e.g. the NT of R. F. *Weymouth (1902), and the NT (1913) and OT (1924) of J. *Moffatt (complete Bible, revised, 1935). In U.S.A. the *American Standard Version*, based on the English RV with the amendments desired by the American scholars who had co-operated (by correspondence) with the English Revisers, was published in 1901. A notable private version is *The Bible, An American Translation*, by E. J. Goodspeed (NT, 1923) and J. M. Powis Smith (OT, 1935), with Apocrypha by E. J. Goodspeed (1938). In 1946 the American *Revised Standard Version* of the NT was issued by an interdenominational committee, and the complete Bible followed in 1952. This translation seeks to avoid both neologisms and archaisms by using modern English words if

they have been in use for not less than a hundred years. In England two RC versions have appeared, (1) the *Westminster Version of the Holy Scriptures*, ed. by C. Lattey and J. Keating (NT, 1935; OT incomplete), translated from the original languages, with attention to the Vulgate, and (2) the version of R. A. Knox (NT, 1945; OT, 1948–9), a completely new rendering of the Vulgate, with some regard to the Greek and Hebrew; the latter has received ecclesiastical sanction. A version in Basic English (i.e. using a limited vocabulary acc. to the principles advocated for the popularization of English among foreigners) of the NT (1941) and then of the complete Bible (1949) has been made by a committee under the direction of S. H. Hooke. In 1947, on the initiative of the Church of *Scotland, a Joint Committee of all non-RC Churches in the British Isles was set up to arrange for a new translation of the Bible into modern English (not a revision of any existing version), backed by the authority of the sponsoring Churches. Panels of translators for the OT, Apocrypha and NT, and of Literary Advisers, were appointed. The NT was published in 1961 and attracted widespread attention; and work continues.

The English Hexapla of the NT Scriptures [Wycliffe, Tyndale, Cranmer, Genevan, Anglo-Rhemish, Authorized] (1841); B. F. Westcott, *A General View of the History of the English Bible* (1868; 3rd ed. revised W. A. Wright 1905); A. W. Pollard, *Records of the English Bible* (1911); F. H. A. Scrivener, *The Authorized Edition of the English Bible* (1611). Its subsequent reprints . . . (1884); M. Deanesly, *The Lollard Bible and other Medieval Biblical Versions* (1920); H. W. *Robinson (ed.), *The Bible in its Ancient and English Versions* (1940). For printed edd., see list in Darlow-Moule. H. Pope, O.P., *English Versions of the Bible* (St. Louis, Mo., 1952). F. F. Bruce, *The English Bible*. A History of Translations (1961); F. C. Grant, *Translating the Bible* (1961).

BIBLE CHRISTIANS. One of the bodies, also known as 'Bryanites', which went to form the *United Methodist Church in 1907. It traces its origin to William O'Bryan (1778–1868), a local preacher of the *Wesleyan Methodist Church. Finding many of the villages of Devon and Cornwall in almost complete ignorance of the Gospel, he extended his very successful evangelism beyond the limits of his own circuit. In the conflict with the local Wesleyan authorities which ensued, O'Bryan, not without hesitation and regret, separated himself, and in 1815 he founded the first society of a new community at Shebbear, in N. Devon. Although faced by much opposition and persecution the new movement spread rapidly. At the end of the first year there were 567 members, and after only five years of work in the west, missionaries were sent to Kent and London. In 1831 missions were founded in Canada and Prince Edward Island; in 1846, in the United States; in 1850, in Australia.

For several years O'Bryan, as the founder of the movement, was accepted as the natural head of the Society and president of its annual Conference. His assumption of autocratic control of the property and affairs of his Churches gradually led to disputes, which were temporarily settled in 1827 by the Conference being the recognized organ of government with O'Bryan continuing as president. O'Bryan, however, was dissatisfied and in 1829 left his society; in 1831 he went to America. Later he was reconciled to the Conference, though he never rejoined it.

The Bible Christians held the doctrines common to all the branches of Methodism. When the Conference was officially constituted in 1831 provision was made for the inclusion of lay representatives. Women were admitted to the ministry equally with men, esp. in the earliest period. As it grew, the movement did notable missionary work, e.g. that of Samuel Pollard in South-west China.

In 1907 the Bible Christians united with the *Methodist New Connexion and the *United Methodist Free Churches to form the *United Methodist Church.

G. Eayrs in W. Townsend–H. B. Workman–G. Eayrs (edd.), *A New History of Methodism*, i (1909), pp. 502–13, 521–4, 543–5, ii (1909), pp. 222 f., 225 f., 474–82, and passim.

BIBLE CHURCHMEN'S MISSIONARY SOCIETY. See *B.C.M.S.*

BIBLE SOCIETY, British and Foreign.
See *British and Foreign Bible Society*.

BIBLIA PAUPERUM (Lat., 'the Bible of the Poor'). They were books composed of a series of pictures to illustrate the fulfilment of the OT in the NT, much in use in the later Middle Ages. Only a few MS. copies of them have survived. They were among the earliest books to be reproduced by printing from wood blocks.

Biblia Pauperum. Nach dem einzigen Exemplare in 50 Darstellungen, früher in Wolfenbüttel, jetzt in der Bibliothèque Nationale, herausgeg. von P. Heitz (Strassburg, 1903). Description and discussion of MSS. in H. Cornell, *Biblia Pauperum* (Stockholm, 1925). H. Engelhardt, *Der theologische Gehalt der* Biblia Pauperum (1927). F. Zoepfl in *L.Th.K.*, i (1930), col. 660 f., s.v. 'Armenbibel', with bibl.

BIBLIANDER (=Buchmann), THEODOR (c. 1504–64), Zwinglian theologian. He succeeded to H. *Zwingli's chair at Zürich University on the Reformer's death in 1531. His leanings were towards humanism. He maintained, e.g., that the heathen possessed by the law of nature a knowledge of God and attacked the *Calvinistic doctrine of *predestination. Among his chief works were a Hebrew grammar (1535), editions of the *Koran (1543) and of the *Protevangelium Jacobi (1552), and some studies in chronology (1551; 1558).

E. Egli, *Analecta Reformatoria*, ii (1901), pp. 1–144, and in *P.R.E.* (ed. 3), iii (1897), pp. 185–7, s.v.

BIBLICAL COMMISSION. A committee of cardinals, assisted by consultors, created as the central organ for the study of the Bible in the RC Church. It was instituted by *Leo XIII through the Apostolic Letter 'Vigilantiae' (30 Oct. 1902) for the double purpose of furthering Biblical studies in conformity with

the requirements of modern scholarship and of safeguarding the authority of Scripture against the attacks of exaggerated criticism. One of its chief tasks is to answer questions on Biblical matters from all over the Catholic world. Among its most notable decisions are those on the Mosaic authorship of the Pentateuch (1906), on the authenticity and historicity of the Fourth Gospel (1907), and on the Synoptic problem (1912). The decisions of the Biblical Commission are binding in conscience under pain of grave fault, i.e. they command both the exterior and interior assent of the RC clergy and the faithful. But they are not held to be infallible, and a question already decided by the Commission may be reopened if the results of new research work require it. In 1904 the Commission was given the right to confer academic degrees by *Pius X. From 1903 to 1908 its organ of publications was the *Revue Biblique* of the Jerusalem *Dominicans; since 1909 it has been the *Acta Apostolicae Sedis*.

The chief pronouncements to 1927 are printed in *Enchiridion Biblicum*. Documenta Ecclesiastica S. Scripturam Spectantia, auctoritate Pontificiae Commissionis de Re Biblica edita (Rome, 1927); also in H. Denzinger–C. Bannwart, S.J. (edd.), *Enchiridion Symbolorum* (ed. 17, 1928), Nos. 1979 f., 2110–12, 2115–19, 2121–36, 2148–78. More recently official Epp. to Abps. and Bps. of Italy, 20 Aug. 1941 (*A.A.S.*, xxxiii (1941), pp. 465–72), and to Card. Suhard of Paris, 16 Jan. 1948 (ib., xl (1948), pp. 45–8). L. Pirot in *Dict. Bibl.*, Suppl., ii (1934), cols. 103–13, s.v. 'Commission biblique', with bibl.

BIBLIOLATRY. Excessive veneration for the letter of Scripture, as found in certain *Protestants in *Reformation times and since. Cf. the cry that 'The Bible, and the Bible only, is the religion of Protestants' (based on a misunderstanding of W. *Chillingworth).

BICKELL, GUSTAV (1838–1906), Orientalist and Patristic scholar. A convert to the RC Church (1865), he was ordained priest in 1867 and was elected to professorships at Innsbruck (1874) and Vienna (1892). His Patristic writings include editions of St. *Ephraem's *Carmina Nisibena* (1866) and the works of *Isaac of Antioch (2 vols., 1873–7). In *Messe und Pascha* (1872) he maintained that the Christian Eucharistic rite had its basis in the Jewish ritual, the Liturgy of the Catechumens corresponding with the morning prayer in the synagogue and the Canon of the Mass with the Jewish passover ritual.

Biog. sketch by D. M. Müller in *Almanach der kaiserlichen Akademie der Wissenschaften*, lvi (Vienna, 1906), pp. 347–51.

BIDDING PRAYER. The form of prayer interceding for the Universal Church, the State, Clergy, Nobility and Commons, and commemorating the departed, which the Anglican Canon 55 (1604) orders to be used by preachers before the sermon. In origin it derives from the group of intercessions, usually in Litany form, which in ancient liturgies occurred after the Sermon or the Gospel. These survive in the Roman Solemn Prayers

('the Collects') of the *Good Friday Liturgy and in the isolated 'Oremus' in the ordinary Latin Mass (at the beginning of the 'Mass of the Faithful').

By the 9th cent. the priest prayed for all conditions of men and made commemoration of the departed after the sermon at Mass on Sundays and festivals. In England during the Middle Ages this was called 'Bidding the *Bedes'. These Biddings formed part of the vernacular devotions, instructions, and notices attached to the sermon, and together were known in France (where they survive in certain places) as the *Prône* (a word of uncertain origin). At first they were left to the discretion of the priest but gradually tended to assume fixed forms. The Bidding Prayer is now seldom used except in the universities, at Assize sermons, and on state occasions.

F. E. *Brightman, *The English Rite*, ii (1915), Appendix I, pp. 1020-45.

BIDDLE, JOHN (1615-62), English *Unitarian. Graduating in 1638 at Magdalen Hall, Oxford, he became shortly afterwards master of the free school at *Gloucester, where he wrote his 'XII Arguments' against the deity of the Holy Ghost. In 1645, the MS. was seized and Biddle was imprisoned for a time. In 1647, however, the 'XII Arguments' were published, and on 6 Sept. they were ordered to be burned by the hangman. Notwithstanding the ordinance of 1648, visiting with death all who denied the Trinity, he published two anti-Trinitarian tracts, but he was saved by his friends among the *Independent Parliamentarians and retired to Staffordshire, where he preached and helped to edit an edition of the *Septuagint. On the passing of the act of oblivion of 1652, his adherents, ('Biddellians', '*Socinians' or 'Unitarians') began regular Sunday worship. Biddle now published two catechisms, for which he was summoned before Parliament (1654) and again imprisoned. On release he was again put on trial, but banished by Cromwell to the Scilly Isles (1655). Returning to London on his release (1662), he was arrested, fined, and sent to prison, where he died.

Vita, said to be by J. Farrington (anon., London, 1682). J. Toulmin, *A Review of the Life, Character and Writings of the Rev. John Biddle, M.A.* (1791). A. B. Grosart in *D.N.B.*, v (1886), pp. 13-16.

BIEL, GABRIEL (c. 1420-95), scholastic philosopher. Educated at Heidelberg and Erfurt, he later joined the *Brethren of the Common Life at Butzbach, and in 1479 was appointed provost of the church at Urach. With Count Eberhard of Württemberg, he was responsible for founding the University of Tübingen, where he held the professorial chair of theology. One of the last great scholastic thinkers, he was a follower of the *nominalist thought of William of *Ockham, though he showed himself tolerant of opposite systems. His views on the relationship between the economy of commercial life and theology reflect the transitional nature of his age. Thus

he held that the 'just price' was determined by supply and demand rather than by theological maxims, and that the merchant is a useful and necessary member of society. His works included a 'Commentary on the Sentences of *Peter Lombard', an exposition of the *Canon of the Mass, and a treatise 'De potestate et utilitate monetarum'.

Most of his works exist only in edd. of 15th and 16th cents.; list in Überweg, ii, p. 604. Mod. ed. of his 'Quaestiones de Justificatione', by C. Feckes (*Opuscula et Textus*, Series Scholastica, iv, Münster i.W., 1929). Eng. tr. of his *Treatise on the Power and Utility of Moneys*, by R. B. Burke (Philadelphia and Oxford, 1930). M. *Luther, *Randbemerkungen zu Gabriel Biels* Collectorium in Quattuor Libros Sententiarum *und zu dessen* Sacri Canonis Missae Expositio (Lyons, 1514; repr. 1933). F. X. Linsenmann, 'Gabriel Biel und die Anfänge der Universität zu Tübingen' in *T.Q.*, xlvii (1865), pp. 195-226; id., 'Gabriel Biel, der letze Scholastiker, und der Nominalismus', ib., pp. 449-81 and 601-76. G. Plitt, *Gabriel Biel als Prediger geschildert* (1879). K. Feckes, *Die Rechtfertigungslehre des Gabriel Biel und ihre Stellung innerhalb der Nominalistischen Schule* (1925); id., 'Gabriel Biel, der erste grosse Dogmatiker der Universität Tübingen, in seiner wissenschaftlichen Bedeutung' in *T.Q.*, cviii (1927), pp. 50-76. J. Haller, *Die Anfänge der Universität Tübingen*, i (1927), pp. 153-73. Überweg, ii, pp. 611-13, with bibl., p. 786; M. Cappuyns, O.S.B., in *D.H.G.E.*, viii (1935), cols. 1429-35, s.v., with bibl.

BIGAMY. (1) A 'second marriage' contracted by a person whose 'first' husband or wife is still alive, when the 'first' marriage has not been declared null. The traditional view of the W. Church is that such a union is no marriage. English civil law takes the same view if a divorce has not been obtained, and, moreover, regards bigamy in such circumstances as a criminal offence. See also *Divorce*.

(2) Acc. to older usage, the term relates to a second marriage after the death of one of the partners to the first marriage. In this sense it is also known as 'digamy' (q.v.).

BIGG, CHARLES (1840-1908), Church historian. Educated at Corpus Christi College, Oxford, he was in his early life a college tutor and schoolmaster. In 1886 he delivered and published his *Bampton Lectures on *The Christian Platonists of Alexandria*, one of the finest works of English theology in the 19th cent. From 1887 to 1901 he was rector of Fenny Compton, and in 1901 succeeded W. *Bright, as Regius Prof. of ecclesiastical history at Oxford. Among his other writings are *Neoplatonism* (1895) and *The Origins of Christianity* (a history of the pre-Nicene Church, posthumous, ed. by T. B. *Strong, 1909). He also edited *The Confessions of St. Augustine* (1898) and *The Imitation of Christ* (1898).

A. Clark in *D.N.B.*, *1901-1911*, i (1912), p. 162 f., s.v.

BILNEY, THOMAS (c. 1495-1531), Protestant martyr. A member of Trinity Hall, Cambridge, he is said to have converted H. *Latimer to the doctrines of the Reformation, as well as to have had some influence on M. *Parker, the future archbishop. In 1527 he was arrested for heresy, but escaped death by recanting. Four years later he was again on trial for *Lollardism; and after recanting and relapsing he was burnt at *Norwich on 19 Aug. 1531. The grounds of his condemnation are obscure. He seems to have been perfectly orthodox on such things as *Transubstantiation and the *Sacrifice of the Mass, but to have aroused hostility by preaching violent sermons against *relics, *pilgrimages, and the cult of the Saints.

The principal authority is J. *Foxe, *Acts and Monuments* (ed. G. Townsend, iv, 1846, pp. 619–56 and 755–63). T. F. Tout in *D.N.B.*, v (1886), pp. 40–3, s.v.

BILOCATION. The presence of a person in more than one place at the same moment. Certain Saints, e.g. *Alphonsus Liguori, *Anthony of Padua, and *Philip Neri, are supposed to have been granted this gift on occasion.

BINATION. The celebration of two Masses on the same day by one priest. In the RC Church it is forbidden, except by special dispensation. In the Middle Ages the custom gave rise to scandals through priests who multiplied their Masses to obtain additional Mass stipends. The present legislation is to be found in the *Codex Iuris Canonici*, c. 806.

BINDING AND LOOSING. The power given by Christ to St. *Peter (Mt. 16. 19) and later to all the Apostles (Mt. 18. 18). It seems to be a general authority to exercise discipline over the Church, and, while some have identified it with the power of forgiving or retaining sins (Jn. 20. 23), others hold it to be a wider and more inclusive authority.

BINGHAM, JOSEPH (1668–1723), author of *The Antiquities of the Christian Church*. He was educated at Wakefield Grammar School and University College, Oxford, where he became a Fellow in 1689. He was delated to the Vice-Chancellor for a sermon preached in St. Mary's, Oxford, on 28 Oct. 1695 and on being condemned (with scant justice) for teaching the tritheistic doctrines of W. *Sherlock, resigned his Fellowship. In the same year he became rector of Headbourne Worthy, near *Winchester, and in 1712 also rector of Havant, holding the livings in plurality until his death. In 1706 he argued in *The French Church's Apology for the Church of England*, that the real affinities of the *Huguenots were with the C of E and not with the English Dissenters. He also took an active part in the controversy on lay-baptism of which he was a strong advocate. His most famous work, the *Origines Ecclesiasticae; or the Antiquities of the Christian Church* (10 vols., 1708–22), with its wealth of systematically arranged information, on the hierarchy, organization, rites, discipline, and calendar of the early Church, was the fruit of some twenty-years labours and has not been superseded. In the preface to a projected 2nd edition he advocated the reunion of the Churches on the basis of primitive episcopacy.

A Latin version was published at Halle in 1724–8 by the *Lutheran, J. H. Grischow, and a RC abridgement at Augsburg in 1788–96.

Works in 2 vols., fol., 1726; in 9 vols., with Life by his great-grandson, Richard Bingham, 1821–9.

BINITARIANISM. The belief that there are only two Persons in the Godhead instead of the three of the *Trinity, thus involving the denial of the deity of the Holy Spirit. It has been held that a few early Christian theologians, e.g. *Tertullian before he became a *Montanist, had an imperfect apprehension of the Trinity and thought in binitarian terms. The word appears to have been coined by F. *Loofs in 1898.

W. Macholz, *Spuren binitarischer Denkweisen seit Tertullian* (1902).

BIRD, WILLIAM. See *Byrd, William*.

BIRETTA. The hard square cap worn by clergy in the W. Church. In origin it was apparently a soft hat, the use of which was originally confined to the higher graduates of universities; but in the 16th cent. its use was allowed to all the clergy. Its colour is black for *priests, purple for *bishops, red for *cardinals, and white for *Premonstratensian canons and Cistercian abbots.

BIRGITTA, St., of Sweden. See *Bridget, St., of Sweden*.

BIRINUS, St. (d. 649 or 650) first Bishop of *Dorchester, near Oxford, and Apostle of the West Saxons. He was consecrated bishop by Asterius at Genoa and landed in Wessex in 634. In the following year he converted and baptized the King, Cynegils, who gave him Dorchester as his episcopal see. In 647 or 648 Birinus dedicated a church at *Winchester, the predecessor of the present cathedral. Feast day, 3 Dec. (in some places, 5 Dec.).

The MS. Lives are listed in Hardy, i, pp. 235–9. J. E. Field, *St. Berin, the Apostle of Wessex*. The History, Legends, and Traditions of the Beginning of the West Saxon Church (1902); includes discussion of primary sources. T. Varley, *St. Birinus and Wessex*. From Odin to Christ (1934).

BISCHOP, SIMON. See *Episcopius*.

BISHOP (Gk. ἐπίσκοπος, lit. 'overseer'). The highest order of ministers in the Christian Church. The word is an Anglo-Saxon corruption of *episcopus*.

In Catholic Christendom (incl. the Anglican Communion) Bishops are held to be distinguished from priests chiefly by their power to confer holy *Orders and to administer the rite of *Confirmation. They normally receive consecration at the hands of a *Metropolitan and two other bishops, and are consecrated to rule a particular diocese or part of the Church within that Metropolitan's *province. In addition to consecration two further things are necessary: election and mission. Election is the choosing of a particular person. The candidate must be of mature age (30 years in the C of E), of legitimate birth, have spent a certain period in priest's orders, and be of good character and sound doctrine. In the Roman Church election is normally performed by the Pope, who in any case has the final decision in the choice of a candidate. Elsewhere the usual method is for a Bishop to be chosen by the dean and chapter of the cathedral of the diocese or some other ecclesiastical body existing specially for this purpose. Throughout the history of the Church secular rulers have from time to time secured the right to nominate candidates to vacant sees, but theoretically this has always been subject to ecclesiastical approval. In the C of E at the present day the crown gives leave to the *dean and *chapter to proceed to an election (the document containing this permission is known as the *congé d'élire) and also nominates the person to be elected. After the election the royal assent is given to it. Should the chapter elect a person other than the one nominated, the royal assent would, presumably, be refused and the electors become subject to certain pains and penalties. When there is no recognized chapter in the diocese the crown appoints a person directly by letters patent. Mission is the conveying of the powers of a Bishop. In the C of E the Metropolitan of the province confirms the election and at the direction of the crown proceeds to the consecration. If the candidate is nominated directly by the King there is no confirmation. After consecration the new Bishop is enthroned in his cathedral and takes possession of his see. Acc. to Anglican theory this is the result of his acceptance into their company by the other Bishops. In the Roman Church a Bishop receives mission either directly from the Pope or through the Metropolitan, and every diocesan Bishop is required either in person or by an approved deputy to visit Rome every five years and report on the state of his diocese. (See *Ad Limina Apostolorum.*)

The chief duties of a modern Bishop consist in administering those Sacraments which he alone is competent to confer (*Confirmation, *Ordination), and in the general oversight of his diocese, incl. such matters as the supervision of the clergy. The Diocesan Bishop may be assisted by other Bishops who are subordinate to him and known as *suffragans (q.v.), auxiliaries, coadjutors, or assistants. In the E. Church the position and spiritual powers of the Bishop are similar to those in the West, with the exception of the additional requirement that bishops, unlike other priests, are required to be celibate. This practice virtually necessitates their recruitment from the monastic communities.

In the C of E the Diocesan Bishop exercises jurisdiction either through his *Consistory Court, over which he himself presides in theory (though he usually delegates the presidency nowadays to his *chancellor), or through commissaries appointed under the Church Discipline Act of 1840. From medieval times the English Bishops have had seats in the House of Lords; but since the Bishoprics Act of 1878 only twenty-six English Bishops (viz. the two Archbishops and the Bps. of *London, *Durham, and *Winchester *ex officio*, and twenty-one others senior by nomination to an English see) enjoy this privilege. The Bishop's connexion with his Cathedral Church, which is governed by the statutes of the various Cathedrals, varies considerably from diocese to diocese.

Among the *insignia* traditional to the Bishop (most of them now widely in use in the Anglican Communion) are the throne in his cathedral (usually on the Gospel side of the sanctuary; at *Norwich behind the high altar; see *Cathedra*), *mitre, *pastoral staff, *pectoral cross, *ring, and *caligae* (i.e. stockings and sandals). In England he is addressed as 'Right Reverend', if an Archbishop, as 'Most Reverend'. In the RC Church he is styled 'Reverendissimus et Illustrissimus'. Here, and often elsewhere, he is mentioned throughout his diocese by name in the Eucharistic prayer.

The beginnings of the Episcopate in early times have long been debated, partly because of the inconclusiveness of the NT evidence by itself, partly on account of its relevance to the many contemporary forms of Church government. It seems that at first the terms 'episcopos' and 'presbyter' were used interchangeably (cf. e.g. Acts 20. 17 and 20. 28). But for St. *Ignatius (early 2nd cent.), Bishops, Presbyters, and Deacons are already quite distinct. On the other hand, elsewhere, notably in Egypt, the threefold ministry does not seem to have established itself until considerably later. By the middle of the 2nd cent. all the leading centres of Christianity would appear to have had their Bishops, and from then until the Reformation, Christianity was everywhere organised on an episcopal basis.

The title of Bishop was retained after the Reformation in certain *Lutheran Churches, notably those of *Denmark, *Norway, *Finland, *Sweden, and Transylvania. It was temporarily restored in Prussia in 1701 and was customary in certain other German provinces such as Schleswig-Holstein; it was generally adopted for the *'Superintendents' of the German Lutheran Church in 1927. In the case of Lutheran Bishops, however, with the exception of Sweden, and Finland until 1884, the title implied no claim to Apostolic Succession or any of the peculiar powers deriving therefrom, such as are normally connected with the Catholic use of the word. The title is also in use among certain other Protestant bodies such as the *Moravians and the *Methodist Episcopal Churches of America and Africa, the former claiming Apostolic Succession although it is Presbyterian in government; the latter derives its succession from the appointments made by J. *Wesley.

See also *Apostolic Succession, Chorepiscopus, Suffragan Bishop.*

A. Barbosa, *Pastoralis Solicitudinis, siue de Officio, et Potestate Episcopi Tripartita Descriptio* (2 vols., Lyons, 1628); C. Ziegler, *De Episcopis, eorumque Juribus, Privilegiis* *et Vivendi Ratione* (Nuremberg, 1686). D. Bouix, *Tractatus de Episcopo, ubi et de Synodo Diocesana* (2 vols., Paris, 1859). R. *Phillimore, *The Ecclesiastical Law of the Church of England*, i (ed. 2, by W. G. F. Phillimore, 1895), esp. pp. 18–86; H. W. Cripps, *A Practical Treatise on the Law Relating to the Church and Clergy* (ed. 8, by K. M. Macmorran, 1937), pp. 70–86. G. Coulton in *D.E.C.H.*, pp. 58–63, s.v. The main duties and rights of modern RC bishops are laid down in *C.I.C.*, canons 329–62. E. Valton in *D.T.C.*, v (1913), cols. 1701–25, s.v. 'Évêques. Questions théologiques et canoniques', with reff. F. Claeys-Bouuaert in *D.D.C.*, v ('1951'), cols. 569–89, s.v. 'Évêques', with bibl.

There is an extensive literature on the origins of the episcopate, much of it of a high standard. For the chief original texts on the early growth of episcopacy, D. *Stone, *Episcopacy and Valid Orders in the Primitive Church* (1910). J. *Bingham, *Origines Ecclesiasticae*, Book II, chh. 1–18 (1708), pp. 49–257. The chief modern books on the subject include F. C. *Baur, *Über den Ursprung des Episcopats* (1838); J. B. *Lightfoot, 'The Christian Ministry' in id., *St. Paul's Epistle to the Philippians* (1868), pp. 179–267; E. *Hatch, *The Organization of the Early Christian Churches* (1881); C. *Gore, *The Church and the Ministry* (1889; new ed., revised by C. H. *Turner, 1919); J. Réville, *Les Origines de l'épiscopat* (1894); R. C. *Moberly, *Ministerial Priesthood* (1897); J. *Wordsworth, *The Ministry of Grace* (1901); W. M. Lindsay, *The Church and the Ministry in the Early Centuries* (1902); A. *Harnack, *Die Entstehung und Entwicklung der Kirchenverfassung und des Kirchenrechts in den zwei ersten Jahrhunderten* (1910; Eng. tr., 1910). H. B. *Swete (ed.), *Essays on the Early History of the Church and Ministry* (1918); A. J. Mason, *The Church of England and Episcopacy* (1914); B. H. *Streeter, *The Primitive Church* (1929); C. Jenkins–K. D. Mackenzie (edd.), *Episcopacy, Ancient and Modern* (1930); K. E. *Kirk (ed.). *The Apostolic Ministry* (1946); N. Sykes, *The Church of England and Non-Episcopal Churches in the Sixteenth and Seventeenth Centuries* (1948); E. R. Fairweather–R. F. Hettlinger, *Episcopacy and Reunion* (Toronto, 1952; London, 1953); K. M. Carey (ed.), *The Historic Episcopacy in the Fullness of the Church* (1954). F. Benz, *Bischofsamt und apostolische Sukzession im deutschen Protestantismus* (1953). H. M. Gwatkin in *H.D.B.*, i (1898), p. 301 f., s.v.; J. A. *Robinson in *E.Bi.*, i (1899), cols. 578–84, s.v.; D. Stone in *H.E.R.E.*, v (1912), pp. 332–7, s.v. 'Episcopacy'; F. Prat, S.J., in *D.T.C.*, v (1913), cols. 1656–1701, s.v. 'Évêques (origines de l'épiscopat)'. A. Piolanti and E. Josi in *E.C.*, xii (1954), cols. 1312–20, s.v. 'Vescovo'. W. Telfer, *The Office of a Bishop* (1962).

BISHOP, EDMUND (1846–1917), liturgist and historian. A native of Totnes, Devon, he had his schooling at *Exeter and in *Belgium. After a short time as secretary to T. *Carlyle, he held a government post from 1864 to 1885 in the Education Office, when he spent most of his leisure in research in the British Museum. In 1867 he was received into the Church of Rome. After leaving the Education Office he hoped to become a monk at *Downside Abbey; but his intention was frustrated by weak health. He continued, however, to maintain close connexions with Downside, where he made the friendship of F. A. *Gasquet who shared his liturgical interests. In 1891, in conjunction with Gasquet, he published *Edward VI and the Book of Common Prayer*; in 1908 a study of the early English calendars in the *Bosworth Psalter*; and in 1909 studies in various liturgical subjects in an appendix to R. H. *Connolly's *Liturgical Homilies of Narsai*. He also made notable contributions to the early history of the Roman liturgy, esp. the text of the *canon missae* and the history of the *Gregorian Sacramentary. Perhaps his most widely known writing was his paper on the 'Genius of the Roman Rite', originally delivered at the Historical Research Society on 8 May 1899, in which he maintained that the two chief characteristics of the Roman

rite (when divested of *Gallican accretions) were 'soberness' and 'sense'. This and many of his other papers were collected in *Liturgica Historica* (1918; posthumous).

N. J. Abercrombie, 'Bibliography of Edmund Bishop' in *T.L.S.*, li (1952), pp. 384 and 394. E. C. Butler, O.S.B., in *D.N.B.*, *1912–1921* (1927), p. 47 f. N. J. Abercrombie, 'Edmund Bishop and the Roman Breviary' in *Clergy Review*, xxxviii (1953), pp. 75–86 and 129–39. H. *Leclercq, O.S.B., in *D.A.C.L.*, ix (pt. 2; 1930), col. 1735 f., s.v. 'Liturgistes' (critical). Previous items now partly superseded by Life by N. [J.] Abercrombie (London, 1959).

BISHOPS' BIBLE, The. A new translation of the Bible, compiled at the direction of Abp. M. *Parker, and published in 1568. All *churchwardens were ordered by *Convocation to obtain a copy for their churches in 1571, and in the following year it was republished with some corrections. A novel feature of this edition was the placing of each translator's initials at the end of his part. It remained the official English version till the publication of the *Authorized Version in 1611.

BISHOPS' BOOK, The. Under the title 'The Institution of a Christen Man', this book was an exposition of the *Creed, the *Seven Sacraments, the *Decalogue, the *Lord's Prayer, and the *Ave Maria, compiled by a committee of bishops and divines in 1537. It also dealt with certain other vexed questions, among them the doctrines of *justification and *purgatory and the relation of the C of E to the Roman see. The book never received the authority of the King, who used it rather to test the temper of the people. In 1543 a revised edition was published by *Henry VIII under the title 'The *King's Book'.

The book was repr. in *Formularies of Faith set forth by Authority during the Reign of Henry VIII* (ed. C. *Lloyd, 1825), pp. 21–212. F. E. *Brightman, *The English Rite* (2 vols., 1915), Introd. (see index, p. 1064).

BISHOPS' WARS. The two brief campaigns in Scotland in 1639 and 1640. After the attempt of *Charles I to enforce the use of the Prayer Book in Scotland, the Scots had broken out into rebellion, and their avowed aim was to abolish episcopacy. The military importance of these campaigns was inconsiderable, but the need for money to conduct them obliged the King to summon the English Parliament, which had not met since 1629, and so gave his enemies in England a chance to gather their forces.

BLACK CANONS. See *Black Monks*.

BLACK FRIARS. Friars of the Order of Preachers, founded by St. *Dominic, and more generally known as 'Dominicans'. They are so named from the black *cappa* or mantle which is worn over their white habits and *scapulars.

Walter Gumbley, O.P., 'On the Name Blackfriars' in *Blackfriars*, i (1920–1), p. 54 f.

BLACK LETTER DAYS. The lesser (mainly non-Scriptural) Saints' Days (printed in black), as distinct from the major festivals, which formerly appeared in red letters in the BCP calendar. They were omitted in 1549, but four appeared in the 1552 Book and the remainder in 1561 save for St. Evurtius (added, 1604), St. Alban, and the Ven. Bede (added, 1662). In 1662 their purpose was defined by the revising bishops as the commemoration of Saints and the provision of useful calendrical notes for business purposes. The practice of distinguishing important feasts by the use of red letters goes back to the pre-Reformation service books. The Black Letter days were excluded from the Irish (1878) and American (1786) Prayer Books. A much extended list found its way into the Revised Prayer Book of 1928.

[W. *Sanday], *Minor Holy Days in the Church of England.* Primary Authorities for the Early Names [1901]. V. Staley, *The Liturgical Year.* An Explanation of the Origin, History and Significance of the Festival Days and Fasting Days of the English Church (1907), ch. xii, pp. 129–58.

BLACK MASS. The expression is used as a popular name for (1) a *Requiem, or Mass for the Dead, so called from the custom of using black vestments; and (2) a parody of the Mass celebrated with blasphemous intention, in honour of the devil.

BLACK MONKS. A name given in medieval England to the *Benedictine monks, as they were distinguished by wearing black habits. The analogous term 'Black Canons' is also found as a designation of *Augustinian canons.

BLACK RUBRIC, The. The name now commonly given to the 'Declaration on Kneeling' printed at the end of the Holy Communion service in the BCP. It is first found in the Book of 1552, when it was inserted at the last moment without Parliamentary authority. The Elizabethan edition of 1559 removed it; but it was replaced in the Book of 1662, with the significant change, however, that the words 'real and essential' were altered to 'corporal' presence, thereby indicating that its purpose was rather to guard against popular and debased medieval ideas of Eucharistic doctrine than to deny altogether Christ's presence in the Sacrament. The expression 'Black Rubric' dates only from the 19th cent. when the practice of printing the BCP with the rubrics in red was introduced and the fact that the 'Declaration' was really not a rubric at all was marked by printing it in black. In modern two-colour reprints of the BCP it will be found, however, printed in red.

J. G. Simpson in *P.B.D.* (1912), p. 105 f., s.v. See also F. E. *Brightman, *The English Rite* (2 vols., 1915), index (p. 1062), s.v. 'Declaration on Kneeling'.

BLACKWELL, GEORGE (*c.* 1545–1613), RC *Archpriest. He was educated at Trinity College, Oxford, where he was elected to a fellowship in 1566, which he subsequently gave up through his RC sympathies. In 1574 he entered the English College at *Douai and

was ordained priest in 1575. He returned to England on the RC mission in 1576. After the confusion in RC discipline that followed Card. W. *Allen's death (1594) through the absence of a supreme authority in England, Blackwell was put in control of the secular clergy by *Clement VIII, with the title of Archpriest and with 12 assistants to help him. Though not himself a *Jesuit, Blackwell pursued a strongly pro-Jesuit policy hostile to the interests of the secular clergy, who aimed at political *rapprochement* with the crown. A group of 31 *Appellants (q.v.), headed by W. Bishop, sought redress from Rome, but on 6 Apr. 1599 a reply was issued in Blackwell's favour. On the strength of it Blackwell continued his previous policy, but after two further appeals he was reproved by Clement in a letter of 5 Oct. 1602. After imprisonment for a time in 1607, he took the Oath of Allegiance to *James I, which had been formally condemned by *Paul V in 1606 and 1607, and in 1608 the Pope appointed George Birket in his place.

Reff. to Blackwell will be found in the documents of the *Archpriest Controversy (q.v.). T. Cooper in *D.N.B.*, v (1886), pp. 144–6.

BLAISE, St. See *Blasius, St.*

BLAKE, WILLIAM (1757–1827), poet, artist, and visionary. Apprenticed to an engraver from 1771 to 1778, he became, through frequent work in *Westminster Abbey, imbued with the spirit of Gothic art which remained his guiding ideal throughout his life. In 1789 he finished his *Songs of Innocence*, a collection of poems of childlike simplicity which included 'The Divine Image', where God and His image, man, are hymned as 'Mercy, Pity, Peace, and Love'. The book was engraved by hand and illustrated by coloured drawings, a technique adopted in most of his subsequent works. It was followed by *The Book of Thel* (1789) and *The Marriage of Heaven and Hell* (1793), allegorical poems full of obscure though often beautiful imagery, which Blake used to express his religious convictions. The *Songs of Experience* (1794) are a kind of complement to the *Songs of Innocence*, though on a sterner note and penetrated by a deep sense of the darker side of life, e.g. in the famous 'Tiger'. His later poetical works, written in something like free verse, are increasingly given over to theosophical speculations and unintelligible allegories. At the same time his compositions gained in artistic maturity. *c.* 1795 he produced a series of large colour prints of much imaginative power, including the magnificent 'The Elohim creating Adam', and in 1797 his illustrations of Edward Young's *Night Thoughts*. In 1804 he published his poem *Milton*, the proem of which, consists of the famous lines 'Jerusalem', much used (with the music of Hubert Parry) as a national hymn. In the following years he produced engravings for Robert Blair's *Grave* of high visionary qualities, but, like most of his drawings, not without flaws in technique. From 1808 to 1818 he was occupied with writing and illustrating his great allegorical poem *Jerusalem* in which St. *Teresa and Mme *Guyon figure among 'the gentle souls who guide the great wine-press of Love'. His unconventional religious beliefs found fresh expression in an unfinished poem, *The Everlasting Gospel*, which rejects the traditional picture of a meek and humble Christ. His greatest work, the *Inventions to the Book of Job*, completed in the last years of his life (1821–1825, publd. 1826), consists of 21 engravings showing the dealings of God with Job from the peaceful contentment of the opening scene, through the despair of the tormented Job accusing his Creator, to the rapturous bliss of his final restoration. The figures, often of elemental strength and beauty, move in the atmosphere of crude black and white contrasts which invests Blake's works with their characteristic impression of haunting unreality.

Blake's art, which spurns reason as well as nature and lives solely in the realm of imagination, was inseparable from his religion, which was itself a religion of art. Opposed to both dogma and asceticism, it flowed from a boundless sympathy with all living things which Blake identified with the forgiveness of sins proclaimed by the Gospel. Though he was little understood by his contemporaries, his visionary genius, both as a poet and an artist, has been increasingly admired since its discovery by A. C. Swinburne and interpretation by W. B. Yeats. His insistence on the supremacy of the spiritual world, though unbalanced by reason and a sound sense of reality, has acted as a powerful antidote to 19th cent. materialism.

Full bibl. in G. Keynes, *A Bibliography of William Blake* (New York, 1921); also id. in F. W. Bateson (ed.), *Cambridge Bibliography of English Literature*, ii (1940), pp. 347–50. Best ed. of Blake's Works by G. Keynes (3 vols., Nonesuch Press, 1925). Life by A. Gilchrist (2 vols., London, 1863), repr. in Everyman's Library (1942). Modern Studies by B. de Selincourt (1909), G. K. *Chesterton (1910), C. Gardner (1919), E. H. Short (1925), O. Burdett ('English Men of Letters', 1926), B. Blackstone (1949), and H. M. Margoliouth (*H.U.L.*, 1951; with useful short bibl.). G. L. Keynes, *Blake Studies* (1949). J. G. Davies, *The Theology of William Blake* (1948).

BLANDINA, St. A virgin slave girl martyred in 177 at Lyons, together with *Pothinus, the bishop of the city. Feast day, 2 June.

Her heroic courage is described in the 'Letter of the Churches of Lyons and Vienne', preserved in *Eusebius, *H.E.*, V, i, 3–63.

BLASIUS, St. Acc. to a late and historically worthless, but widely distributed legend, St. Blasius (Blaise) was Bp. of Sebaste in Armenia and martyred under *Licinius in the early 4th cent. He is said to have miraculously saved the life of a young child who was nearly choked by a fish-bone, and hence his intercessions have been sought by the sick, and esp. those with throat trouble. He is also invoked for the cure of diseases of cattle. He is one of the fourteen *Auxiliary Saints, and his cult used to be very popular in Germany. His

feast is observed in the W. on 3 Feb. (formerly 15 Feb.), in the E. on 11 Feb.

AA.SS., Feb. I (1658), pp. 331–53. His Gk. Legend is pr. in J. P. Migne, *PG*, cxvi. 817–30. J. P. Kirsch in *C.E.*, ii (1907), p. 592, with bibl., and id. in *L.Th.K.*, ii (1931), cols. 391, with further bibl.

BLASPHEMY (Gk. βλασφημία, from βλάπτω, 'to damage', and φήμη, 'reputation'). Speech, thought, or action manifesting contempt for God. In moral theology it is commonly regarded as a sin against the virtue of religion, though St. *Thomas Aquinas defined it as a sin against faith. It may be directed either immediately against God or mediately against the Church or the saints, and is by its nature a mortal sin. Blasphemy was punished by stoning in the OT (Lev. 24. 16, 1 Kgs. 21. 10), and the Code of *Justinian, as well as the medieval canon law, also prescribed severe punishments. Thus the Council of Aachen of 818 re-established the death penalty. In post-Reformation England, Blasphemy laws were passed in 1558 and reinforced in 1698. From the time of the *Aufklärung the secular authorities in most countries have regarded Blasphemy no longer as a crime against God but as an offence against society and punished it as such. In recent times repeated attempts have been made in many countries to abolish the laws against Blasphemy altogether. Thus in Great Britain only scurrilous attacks on Christianity can be sustained under the Blasphemy laws, as calculated to offend believers or even to cause a breach of the peace. Acc. to the new RC canon law Blasphemy is to be punished acc. to the decision of the *Ordinary (*CIC*, can. 2323).

BLASS, FRIEDRICH WILHELM (1843–1907), German classical scholar, who also contributed much to the philology and *textual criticism of the NT. Besides editions of Matthew (1901), Luke (1897), John (1902), and Acts (1895), he published a *Grammatik des neutestamentlichen Griechisch* (1896; Eng. trans. by H. St. J. Thackeray, 1898) and a *Philology of the Gospels* (London, 1898). He maintained that the *Western and non-Western texts of Lk. and Acts were different recensions both deriving from the same author (St. Luke), a view, however, which has found little favour among other textual critics.

W. Crönert, 'Friedrich Blass' in *Biographisches Jahrbuch für die Altertumswissenschaft*, xxxii (1909), pp. 1–32 (with list of Blass's works, pp. 30–2). For his theory of Luke-Acts, see L. J. M. Bebb in *H.D.B.*, iii (1900), p. 164 f. A. Romeo in *E.C.*, ii (1949), cols. 1716 f.

BLASTARES, MATTHEW (fl. 1335). A monk of Thessalonica who composed an alphabetical handbook of *canon law (Σύνταγμα κατὰ στοιχεῖον) as well as treatises against 'the Latins' (i.e. W. Catholics) and the Jews.

The first-named in J. P. Migne, *PG*, cxliv, 960–1400.

BLEEK, FRIEDRICH (1793–1859), German Biblical scholar. A pupil of W. M. L. *De

Wette, J. A. W. *Neander, and F. D. E. *Schleiermacher, he became professor at Bonn in 1829. He wrote a long series of critical studies on the Bible, esp. the NT, from a position on the whole conservative, strongly arguing, e.g., for the traditional authorship of St. John's Gospel. His most celebrated commentary was that on Heb. (in 3 parts, 1828, 1836, and 1840).

A. Kamphausen in *P.R.E.* (ed. 3), iii (1897), pp. 254-7, s.v.

BLEMMYDES, NICEPHORUS (1197–1272). A Greek theologian who took an active part in the attempts to reunite the E. and W. Churches in the 13th cent. From 1215 to 1221 he practised as a physician; and in 1223 was ordained priest. He wrote on a variety of subjects, including theology, physics, and geography, and also produced some poems and a monastic Rule.

His theological writings are in J. P. Migne, *PG*, cxlii, 527-1622.

BLESSED (as title). See *Beatification*.

BLESSED SACRAMENT. A term used of the Sacrament of the Eucharist, and applied both to the service itself and more esp. to the consecrated elements.

BLESSED VIRGIN, The. See *Mary, The Blessed Virgin*.

BLESSING. The authoritative pronouncement of God's favour. Instances in the OT are the blessing of Isaac (Gen. 27) and the prayer of Balaam (Num. 23 f.), both of which presuppose the automatic action of a blessing, independently of moral considerations. Later we see liturgical blessings of persons (Num. 6. 22 ff.) and of things, such as food (1 Sam. 9. 13, cf. Mt. 14. 19). In Christian practice blessing finds a frequent place in the liturgy, esp. in the blessing of the elements in consecration (so Mt. 26. 26). The blessing of the people at the end of the Mass did not become general until the later Middle Ages. Blessings are frequently given to individuals, e.g. the deacon who is to sing the Gospel, the penitent about to make a confession, and less formally outside liturgical services, by bishops and priests, and by parents to their children. The *Rituale Romanum* also provides blessings for a wide range of objects, from vestments to typewriters. In many places a custom has arisen of concluding all services with a blessing, often given at the altar. The right hand is raised to bless, and usually the *sign of the cross is made, though occasionally this is omitted. It is generally held that a deacon may not bless liturgically except when, in emergency and by express leave, he is doing some act normally performed by a priest, e.g. giving Communion outside the Liturgy. See also *Berakah*.

A. Franz, *Die kirchlichen Benediktionen im Mittelalter*

(1909). L. Eisenhofer, *Handbuch der katholischen Liturgik*, ii (1933), pp. 447-74.

BLOMFIELD, CHARLES JAMES (1786–1857), Bp. of *London. He was the son of a schoolmaster at Bury St. Edmunds, and, after a distinguished career at Trinity College, Cambridge, was ordained in 1810. In the next fourteen years he was appointed to a succession of benefices culminating in his nomination in 1824 to the see of *Chester. Here he set himself to raise the standard of clerical life and to root out abuses, esp. those of non-residence, though he himself retained his former living of St. Botolph's, Aldgate *in *commendam*. In 1828 he became Bp. of London. During his episcopate some 200 new churches were built and consecrated in his diocese, chiefly through his zeal and interest. In politics his position wavered. Though nominally a Whig, he resisted Catholic Emancipation (1829), and absented himself in the early stages of the Reform Bill, but he finally voted in its favour. His Churchmanship also seemed inconsistent. While he drove W. J. E. *Bennett from St. Paul's, Knightsbridge, and supported the *Jerusalem Bishopric scheme of 1841, he signed the protest against R. D. *Hampden's appointment to the see of *Hereford, and dissented from the judgement of the Privy Council in the *Gorham case. In 1856 he was forced by paralysis to resign his see. He was held in repute as a classic and issued editions of *Prometheus Vinctus* (1810), Callimachus (1815), Euripides (1821) and other texts.

Memoir by his son, Alfred Blomfield (2 vols., 1863).

BLONDEL, DAVID (1590–1655), French ecclesiastical historian. A native of Châlons-sur-Marne, he was educated at Sedan and at the *Genevan Academy. For most of his life he was a country pastor at Roucy, where his devotion to his flock led him to decline (1631) an offer of a chair in theology at Saumur. In 1645 he was created an 'Honorary Professor' of Saumur, with a generous annual financial grant, and in 1650 finally left Roucy to succeed G. J. *Voss at the École Illustre at Amsterdam, where he came into prominence through his liberal sympathies. He was at once a learned historian and effective controversialist. His *Pseudo-Isidorus et *Turrianus Vapulans*, perhaps his most important work, finally discredited the historicity of the '*False Decretals'. His *De la primauté en l'Église* (1641) was a defence of the Reformed ecclesiastical polity and his *Apologia pro Sententia Hieronymi de Presbyteris et Episcopis* (1646) an attack on episcopacy. He also wrote an erudite and successful criticism of the myth of Pope *Joan (in two writings, 1647 and 1657) which aroused hostility among many of his fellow-Protestants.

All his works are on the *Index. G. Bonet-Maury in *P.R.E.* (ed. 3), iii (1897), p. 261 f.; A. Lambert in *D.D.C.*, ii (1937), cols. 926 f.

BLONDEL, MAURICE (1861–1949), French philosopher. He was a native of Dijon, where he was educated at the École Normale, and later held professorships of philosophy at Montauban, Lille, and Aix-Marseille. The work that first placed him in the front rank of contemporary thinkers was *L'Action* (1893) with the significant subtitle, 'Essai d'une critique de la vie et d'une science de la pratique'. In it Blondel attempted to construct a 'philosophy of action', conceiving 'action' in its widest sense and all its ramifications, and to develop also a philosophy of the idea as well as to expound the relations between science and belief and between philosophy and religion. His analysis of action led him to conclude that the human will which produces action cannot satisfy itself, because its fundamental desire is never fulfilled by any finite good. From this point of departure he developed an argument for the being of God resting on volition, in the light of which he modified the old Scholastic proofs. God imposes Himself on the will as the first principle and the last term; we must, therefore, 'opt' either for or against Him.

The teaching of *L'Action* was amplified in several later works, e.g. *Histoire et dogme* (1904), *Le Procès de l'intelligence* (1922), and esp. *Le Problème de la philosophie catholique* (1932) and *La Pensée* (2 vols., 1934). The last-named work states his final position with regard to the intellectual aspects of experience. He here accords a greater place to abstract conceptions than in *L'Action* and affirms the legitimacy of methodical argumentation, e.g. in the rational proofs of the existence of God. Yet his position is not that of *Aristotle and St. *Thomas, but follows rather the *Platonic tradition as continued in St. *Augustine, R. *Descartes, and G. W. *Leibniz. For Blondel it is not that knowledge of creatures precedes knowledge of God, but rather it is the existence of an obscure yet positive affirmation of God that is the very condition which makes the Aristotelian and Thomist proofs possible. The problem of the supernatural also played a large part in the thought of Blondel, who was a devout Catholic. He held that the whole mental life of man was directed to the possession of God in the Beatific Vision, and consequently he attributed to unaided human reason the capacity of demonstrating its positive possibility.

Blondel's thought has been of considerable influence in modern philosophy. For several years he was closely associated with the leading figures in the *Modernist Movement, which welcomed the pragmatist aspects of his teaching; and many recent thinkers, among them R. Eucken, G. *Gentile, and F. *von Hügel, have been much indebted to him.

K. Gilbert, *Maurice Blondel's Philosophy of Action* (Univ. of North Carolina Studies in Philosophy, i, 1924); P. Archambault, *L'Œuvre philosophique de Maurice Blondel: vers un réalisme intégral* (Cahiers de La Nouvelle Journée, xii, 1928); T. Eypernon, S.J., *Le Blondélisme* (Museum Lessianum. Section Philosophique, xv, 1933); B. Romeyer, S.J., *La Philosophie religieuse de Maurice Blondel* (1943); J. Riog Gironella, S.J., *Filosofía blondeliana* (Biblioteca Filosófica de Balmesiana, Ser. 2, ii, 1944), with bibl. P. Archambault and others, *Hommage à Maurice Blondel* (La Nouvelle Journée, xii, 1946); H. Duméry, *La Philosophie de l'action*. Essai sur l'intellectualisme blondélien ('Philosophie de l'Ésprit', 1948), with preface by Blondel.

BLOUNT, CHARLES (1654–93), English *Deist. He is best known by his *Anima Mundi* (1679), a sceptical discussion of the subject of immortality, and *The Two First Books of Philostratus concerning the Life of Apollonius Tyaneus* (1680). The notes of the latter gave offence, by their attacks on 'priest-craft' and sympathy with the free thought of T. *Hobbes.

The Miscellaneous Works of Charles Blount . . . to which is prefixed the life of the author [signed Lindamour, a pseudonym of Charles Gildon] (5 parts, 1685).

BLOW, JOHN (1648–1708), composer and organist. He became one of the Children of the *Chapel Royal at the Restoration, and at an early age distinguished himself as a composer of anthems. Already in 1669 he was appointed organist of *Westminster Abbey, an office which he gave up in 1680 in favour of his greater pupil, H. *Purcell. He also held the offices of Gentleman of the Chapel Royal (1673), private musician to *James II (1685), choirmaster of *St. Paul's (1687), organist of St. Margaret's, Westminster (1695), and composer to the Chapel Royal (1699). Of his works over 100 anthems and 14 services besides secular compositions survive.

W. H. Cummings, 'Dr John Blow' in the *Quarterly Magazine of the International Music Society*, Year 10 (Leipzig, 1909), pp. 421–30; F. Bridge, *Twelve Good Musicians*, from John Bull to Henry Purcell [1920], XI, pp. 108–17. Detailed list of his works in Grove's *Dictionary of Music and Musicians*, i (ed. 4, ed. H. C. Colles, 1940), pp. 394–8, s.v.

BLOXAM, JOHN ROUSE (1807–91), Anglican ceremonialist and historian. Educated at Rugby School and at Worcester and Magdalen Colleges, *Oxford, he was ordained priest in 1833 and elected a Fellow of Magdalen in 1836. He held a succession of offices at Magdalen until appointed vicar of Upper Beeding, Sussex (1862), where he remained till his death. He associated himself closely with the *Tractarian Movement and from 1837 to 1840 was J. H. *Newman's curate at Littlemore. A careful and learned ecclesiologist, Bloxam was the real originator of the ceremonial revival in the English Church. He introduced various ornaments into Littlemore church (gilded candlesticks, wooden alms-dish, black silk stole, credence table, litany desk, &c.), which were soon afterwards copied by F. *Oakeley at the Margaret Chapel in London and thence spread and came into general use. He was also one of the first Tractarians to establish relations with RCs, though these seem to have been abruptly terminated by the secession of R. W. Sibthorp in Oct. 1841. Deeply devoted to his college, he published a Magdalen College *Register* (7 vols., 1853–81) and also compiled a valuable (unpublished) collection of college papers.

R. D. Middleton, *Magdalen Studies* (S.P.C.K., 1936), pp. 31–79; id., *Newman and Bloxam: An Oxford Friendship* (1947).

BLUMHARDT, JOHANN CHRISTOPH (1805–80), Protestant evangelist. The nephew of Christian Gottlieb Blumhardt (1779–1838), who founded the Protestant 'Basel Mission', he was born at Stuttgart, studied at *Tübingen, taught at Basel from 1830, and in 1838 became pastor at Möttlingen in Württemberg where his evangelical work attracted much attention largely through the physical cures by which it was sometimes accompanied. As his motto he took the words 'Jesus is Conqueror' (*Jesus ist Sieger*). From 1852 until his death he worked at Bad Boll, near Göppingen, which became a centre of influential international missionary work. Blumhardt's theology was developed under the influence of Swabian *Pietism (J. A. *Bengel, P. M. Hahn), but its eschatological emphasis also anticipated some elements in the *Dialectical Theology. His collected works were published in 3 vols., 1886–8.

His son, Christoph Friedrich Blumhardt (1842–1919), who took over the direction of Bad Boll after his father's death, was also a zealous missioner and a considerable theologian. Active sympathy with the needs of the working classes led him to become from 1900 to 1906 a Social Democrat member of the Württemberg diet. His writings were edited by R. Lejeune (5 vols., 1925 ff.).

E. Jäckh, *Blumhardt, Vater und Sohn und ihre Botschaft* (1924); E. *Thurneysen, *Christoph Blumhardt* (1926).

BOANERGES. The surname given by Christ (Mk. 3. 17) to *James and *John, the sons of Zebedee. The word is there stated to mean 'sons of thunder', but the derivation is quite uncertain.

BOBBIO. A small town in the Apennines, some 40 miles NE of Genoa, once the seat of an important abbey founded in 612 by St. Columbanus (who died here in 615). Its celebrated collection of early MSS. (700 of them dating from the 10th cent.), have mostly passed to the *Vatican Library, the *Ambrosiana at Milan, and Turin (several of these were destroyed in the fire of 1904). The 'Bobbio Missal', now in the Bibliothèque Nationale at Paris (B.N. 13246), is an important collection of liturgical texts, apparently of *Gallican and Irish *provenance* and dating from the 8th cent.

L. H. Cottineau, O.S.B., *Répertoire topo-bibliographique des abbayes et prieurés* (Mâcon, 1935), cols. 400–2, s.v. A. Ratti (*Pius XI), *Le ultime vicende della Biblioteca e dell' Archivio di S. Colombano di Bobbio* (1901). C. Cipolla, *Codici bobbiesi della Biblioteca Nazionale Universitaria di Torino* (Collezione paleografica bobbiese, i, 2 vols., 1907); id., G. Buzzi, *Codice diplomatico del Monastero di San Colombano di Bobbio fino all' anno MCCVIII* (3 vols., 1918); P. Collura, *La Precarolina e la Carolina a Bobbio* (1943), with reff. P. Verrua, *Bibliografia bobbiese* (Piacenza, 1936). The 'Bobbio Missal' ed., with facsimile reproduction, by E. A. Lowe (H.B.S., liii, lviii, 1917–20), with notes and studies by A. *Wilmart, O.S.B.–E. A. Lowe–H. A. Wilson (ib., lxi, 1924). A. Wilmart in *D.A.C.L.*, ii (pt. 1; 1910), cols. 935–9, s.v. 'Bobbio (Manuscrits de)'; id. ib., cols. 939–62, s.v. 'Bobbio (Missel de)'. C. Castiglioni–T. Leccisotti, O.S.B., in *E.C.*, ii (1949), cols. 1726–30, s.v., with bibl. [Also imp. study by G. *Mercati (Rome, 1934).]

BOCHART, SAMUEL (1599–1667), Biblical scholar. A native of Rouen, he studied philosophy at Sedan and theology at Saumur and in 1628 became pastor at Caen. In 1652 he accompanied P. D. *Huet to the court of *Christina of Sweden. After his return he became a member of Caen Academy. His chief works are his *Geographia Sacra* (2 pts., 1646, 1651) and the *Hierozoicon, sive Historia Animalium S. Scripturae* (2 vols., 1663); the latter esp. was drawn on by later Biblical commentators. He was a very learned oriental linguist, though his long preoccupation with Phoenician and other Semitic languages sometimes overburdened his judgement and led him to fantastic etymological conclusions.

Works publ. in 2 vols., Leyden, 1675; also ed. by J. Leusden–P. de Villemandy, with life by E. Morin (3 vols., ib., 1692). E. H. Smith, *Samuel Bochart. Recherches sur la vie et les ouvrages de cet auteur illustre* (Caen, 1833).

BODLEIAN LIBRARY. The library of the University of *Oxford. The oldest portion (15th cent.), over the Divinity School, is known as 'Duke Humphrey's Library'; but the 600 MSS. presented by Humphrey, Duke of Gloucester (d. 1447), son of Henry IV, were dispersed in 1550. The library was restocked and endowed early in the 17th cent. by Sir Thomas Bodley (d. 1613), a retired diplomat, who added the E. wing. Between 1635 and 1640 W. *Laud presented about 1300 MSS., including the 'Codex Laudianus' of Acts. Its other benefactors have included J. *Selden; Richard Rawlinson (a *non-juring bp.; d. 1755), who bequeathed nearly 5000 MSS., besides printed books and pictures; and Francis Douce (d. 1834), who left to the Bodleian his collection of illuminated service-books and other rarities. The library possesses a good collection of Patristic MSS., Oriental as well as Greek and Latin. It is one of the six libraries which under the Copyright Act can claim a presentation copy of every new work published in Great Britain.

F. Madan and H. H. E. Craster (ed.), *Summary Catalogue of the Western Manuscripts in the Bodleian Library, Oxford* (6 vols. bound in 11, 1895–1937). W. D. Macray, *Annals of the Bodleian Library, Oxford*, with a notice of the Earlier Library of the University (1868, ed. 2 enlarged, 1890); [H. H.] E. Craster, *History of the Bodleian Library 1845–1945* (1952). C. W. Wheeler (ed.), *Letters of Sir Thomas Bodley to Thomas James* (1926); *The Bodleian Library in the Seventeenth Century*. Guide to the Exhibition held during the Festival of Britain, 1951 (1951). A. Clark, *A Bodleian Guide for Visitors* (1906); F. Madan, *The Bodleian Library at Oxford* (1919).

BODY OF CHRIST, The. (1) The natural or human Body which the Lord took of Mary, and which, acc. to orthodox Christian theology, was changed but not abandoned at the Resurrection and remains for ever His in heaven.

(2) The Church (q.v.), as the community whose members are incorporated into His life in Baptism (see 1 Cor., Eph., Col., &c.), and which since *Pentecost has formed the vehicle of His redemptive activity on earth.

(3) The consecrated Bread in the *Eucharist (q.v.).

(4) The Latin form, '*Corpus Christi' (q.v.), is used as the title of a feast which since the 13th cent. has been kept in the W. Church on the

Thursday after Trinity Sunday in honour of the *Blessed Sacrament; and as a designation of churches and colleges dedicated in honour of the *Eucharist.

BOEHME, JAKOB (1575–1624), German *Lutheran theosophical author, known as 'philosophus Teutonicus'. He was the son of a farmer. At first a shepherd, he was later apprenticed to a shoemaker, and from 1599, when he was married, till 1613 followed that trade at Görlitz in Silesia. The recipient of mystical experiences, he claimed that in his writings he described only what he had learnt personally from Divine illumination. In 1612 he published his first work, *Morgenröte im Aufgang oder Aurora*, which aroused the opposition of the Lutheran pastor, Gregorius Richter, who forced the municipal authorities to intervene; and Boehme was ordered to cease writing. In 1618, however, he began a series of devotional treatises which were published under the title *Der Weg zu Christo* in 1623. As Richter continued his opposition, Boehme left Görlitz in 1624 and went to Dresden and later to the houses of several friends in Silesia, where he was much appreciated. He died soon after his return to Görlitz in the same year. His writings, most of them published posthumously, include *Die drei Prinzipien göttlichen Wesens*, an inquiry into the Divine essence; *Signatura Rerum*, containing his cosmological theories; *Mysterium Magnum*, an allegorical explanation of the Book of Genesis; and *Von Christi Testamenten*, a treatise on Baptism and the Eucharist.

Boehme is a very obscure and difficult writer who made abundant use of abstruse terminology, borrowed largely from *Paracelsus, the mystics, alchemy, and astrology; and his critics are still divided as to whether the foundation of his thought is pantheistic or dualist. Having lived from childhood in a state of religious exaltation, he believed himself called to penetrate the deepest mysteries concerning God, man, and nature. Acc. to him God, the Father, is the 'Ungrund', the indefinable matter of the universe, neither good nor evil, but containing the germs of either, unconscious and impenetrable. This 'abyss' tends to know itself in the Son, who is light and wisdom, and to expand and express itself in the Holy Ghost. The Godhead has two wills, one good and one evil, 'love' and 'wrath', which drive Him to create nature, which unfolds itself in the seven nature spirits or 'Quellgeister'. They represent (1) the desire to resist, (2) the tendency to expand, (3) the struggle between these two, (4) the transition from the inorganic to the organic world, (5) the vegetative life of the plants, (6) the animal life, and (7) man, who sums up in himself all the others. Though evil, being part of God, is necessary, yet man, whose character depends on the constellation of the stars under which his body is formed, can avoid hell by uniting himself to Christ by faith. He will then be a conqueror on earth and will ultimately replace Lucifer, the fallen angel, in the heavenly city.

Boehme has exercised a far-reaching influence, esp. in Germany and the English-speaking countries. The thinkers of German Romanticism, such as G. W. F. *Hegel, F. W. J. von *Schelling, and F. X. von Baader, acknowledge their debt to him; and in England he was a source of inspiration to P. *Sterry, the Cambridge Platonist, to the 17th–18th cent. '*Philadelphian Society', and to W. *Law. I. *Newton also wrestled with his writings for three months. His teaching was propagated by circles of disciples called 'Behmenists', who later amalgamated with the *Quakers.

A modern German edition of his Works is that by K. W. Schiebler (1831–47, reprinted 1922). A complete Eng. trans. was made by J. Ellistone and J. Sparrow (1644–62, re-edited 1762–84). C. J. Backer, *Prerequisites for the Study of Jacob Boehme* (1920); P. Hankamer, *Jakob Böhme* (1924); and R. Schrey, *Die Lehre des Jakob Böhme* (1925). For his philosophical views, E. Nobile, *Jacob Boehme ed il suo dualismo essenziale* (1928) and A. Koyré, *La Philosophie de Jacob Boehme* (1929). A German anthology is P. Hankamer *Das Böhme-Lesebuch* (1925). F. W. Dibelius in *P.R.E.* (ed. 3), iii (1897), pp. 272–6; G. W. Allen in *H.E.R.E.*, ii (1909), pp. 778–84. See also bibl. to *Martensen, H. L.

BOETHIUS, ANICIUS MANLIUS TORQUATUS SEVERINUS (c. 480–c. 524), philosopher and statesman. The son of Flavius Manlius Boethius, who was a consul in 487, he became the friend and adviser of Theodoric, and himself held the consulship in 510. His humanity and practical statesmanship are reflected in his intercession with Theodoric to avert a forced requisition of grain (*coemptio*) in Campania, and his defence of Albinus, an ex-consul, against a charge of treason. Largely as a result of the latter action he was himself accused of treason and imprisoned at Ticinum, where he was executed.

Boethius's most famous work, his 'De Consolatione Philosophiae' in five books, which was written in prison, describes how the soul attains through philosophy to knowledge of the vision of God. Despite the apparent absence of specifically Christian teaching, the treatise became very popular in the succeeding centuries, and was translated into Anglo-Saxon by King *Alfred. His more technically philosophical writings include translations of, and commentaries on, *Aristotle's περὶ ἑρμηνείας and 'Categories', and a commentary on *Victorinus Afer's translation of *Porphyry's 'Isagoge', all of them a main source of Aristotelian knowledge in the Middle Ages. (The translations of much of Aristotle's 'Organon' included in the editions of Boethius, however, are wrongly assigned to him.) He also wrote several original works on logic and school handbooks on the *quadrivium, including a textbook on music, based on Pythagoras, which retained its place in education until modern times.

It used to be much disputed whether Boethius was a Christian. But the question seems settled by the now generally admitted authenticity of the short theological treatises ascribed to him. Among these is a work on the Trinity ('De sancta trinitate') and a defence of the *Chalcedonian Christology ('Liber contra Eutychen et Nestorium'). The fact that Theodoric was an Arian caused Boethius to be regarded as a martyr of the Catholic faith. He was canonized as 'St. Severinus', and his tomb is honoured at Pavia Cathedral.

Works first ed. Venice, 1492. Several later edd. and reprr. incl. J. P. Migne, *PL*, lxiii and lxiv. Mod. edd. of *Consolatio* by R. Peiper (Bibl. Teubn., 1871), A. *Fortescue–G. Smith (London, 1926) and G. Weinberger (C.S.E.L., 67, 1934); of *In Isagogen Porphyrii Commenta*, by S. Brandt (C.S.E.L., 48, 1906); theological Tractates, ed. with Eng. tr. by H. F. Stewart and E. K. Rand (Loeb, 1918). Lane Cooper, *A Concordance of Boethius* (Medieval Academy of America, 1928). H. R. Patch, *The Tradition of Boethius. A Study of his Importance in Medieval Culture* (1935); Helen M. Barrett, *Boethius. Some Aspects of his Times and Work* (1940). P. Godet in *D.T.C.*, ii (1905), cols. 918–22. M. Cappuyns, O.S.B., in *D.H.G.E.*, ix (1937), cols. 348–80, s.v. '2. Boèce'.

BOETTICHER, PAUL ANTON. See *Lagarde, Paul Anton de.*

BOGOMILES. A dualistic sect, apparently an offshoot of the *Catharists. Their name probably derives from their founder, 'Bogomile', the Bulgarian translation of 'Theophilus', who taught between 927 and 950 in Bulgaria. The centre of the sect appears to have been Philippopolis in Thrace, whence it spread to *Constantinople, where the Emp. Alexis Comnenus had their leader burnt in 1118, and a synod ordered the destruction of their books in 1140. In spite of this the sect continued to flourish in Asia Minor and in the Balkans, until it was merged into the conquering Turks.

The Bogmiles, whose doctrines are known through the writings of *Euthymius Zygabenus, were strongly influenced by the older sects of the *Paulicians and *Euchites. They believed in a superior God, the Father, whose son Satanael revolted and was driven from heaven. Satanael created the world and Adam; but as the Father supplied Adam's soul, man belongs to God as well as to Satan. The latter then seduced Eve and was punished by being deprived of his creative power, though entrusted with the government of the world. As man fell more and more under the power of Satan, the Father sent into the world his second son, Jesus, under the appearance of a man. After conquering Satan he returned to heaven, leaving on earth his creature, the Holy Ghost, to carry on his work among the Bogomiles, the only true Christians, who are changed into ethereal bodies at death. Both Jesus and the Holy Ghost will be finally absorbed into the Father, so that only one Divine Person remains. Like other dualistic sects the Bogomiles accepted only the NT, the Psalms, and the prophetical books, believing the other parts of the OT the work of the devil. They rejected infant baptism and baptism by water, marriage, and the *Real Presence, as well as crucifixes and images and all prayers except the Our Father.

D. Obolensky, *The Bogomiles. A Study in Balkan Neo-Manchaeism* (1948), with full bibl. H. C. Puech and A. Vaillant, *Le Traité contre les Bogomiles de Cosmas le Prêtre* (1945).

BOHAIRIC (see also *Sahidic*). The dialect of *Coptic spoken in early Christian times in 'Lower Egypt', i.e. the delta of the Nile. It is so named from 'Bohaïrah', the Arabic name of Lower Egypt. As knowledge of Greek was widespread in this part of Egypt, the translation of the Scriptures was a less pressing need than farther south, and hence the Bohairic version is much later than the *Sahidic. It probably dates from c. the 6th–7th cents., and has long been, and still is, the official version of the *Coptic Church. The MSS. for the most part follow the '*Neutral' text, the oldest known MS. being a copy of the Gospels at *Oxford, dated A.D. 1173–4. 'Bohairic' is sometimes referred to as 'Memphitic', from Memphis, the principal native town in the Delta region, though the dialect seems to have originated not here but in the coast-lands near *Alexandria.

There is a critical edition of the Bohairic NT by G. Horner (Oxford, 1898–1905).

BOHEMIAN BRETHREN, later known as *'Moravian Brethren' and 'Unitas Fratrum'. They were a group of *Utraquists (q.v.) who, having for some years led an existence apart within that religious body, separated formally under the leadership of 'Brother Gregory' in 1467, in order to follow more closely the teaching of Peter Chelšický (d. c. 1460). They rejected oaths and military service, depreciated town life and private property, stressed Christian discipline, and stood for a simple, pure, and unworldly Christianity. The Brethren were organized as a Church by Lukaš of Prague, who broke with the tradition of uncompromising asceticism of the earlier Brethren, exalted faith without works, and in 1494 had the writings of Chelšický and Gregory condemned by the Synod of Rychnov. Under Lukaš's leadership the sect spread rapidly, though persecuted by the Utraquists. Their efforts to join the *Lutherans, frustrated at first by refusal to give up the celibacy of the priesthood, the Seven Sacraments, and a strict Church discipline, were successful only in 1542, after the death of Lukaš (1528), when they accepted justification by faith alone and the *Real Presence, but retained their discipline of public and private confession of sins. After the victory of Mühlberg (1547) the Emp. Ferdinand took repressive measures against them and some emigrated. Many eventually settled in Poland, where they united with the *Calvinists at the Synod of Kozminek (1555). Those who remained in Bohemia obtained the freedom to practise their cult from Maximilian II in 1575, but fixed their principal seat in Moravia, hence the other name under which they are known. In 1609 Rudolf II handed over to them the university of Prague and gave them many other rights, but after the Battle of the White Mountain (1620) they were exiled, together with their last bishop, the famous educationist A. *Comenius. The remains of the sect survived for a hundred years, and in 1721 accepted an offer of N. L. von

*Zinzendorf to join the *Herrnhuter, with whom they amalgamated. Their doctrine rested on the authority of Scripture, the interpretation of which is entrusted to the community. Each member was to realize the ideal of the Sermon on the Mount by a life of poverty and renunciation under the strict supervision of the elders. They rejected the veneration of the saints and held that the efficacy of the Sacraments depends on the dignity of the minister and the faith of the recipients. The Bohemian Brethren laid special emphasis on Church services, organization, and education. Their schools were famous and their contribution to Czech literature considerable, esp. through their complete translation of the Bible (6 vols., 1579–93). They greatly influenced *Methodism in its earlier stages.

For their later history, see under *Herrnhut* and *Moravian Brethren*.

For the bulk of the literature see bibl. to *Moravians*. J. Goll (ed.), *Quellen und Untersuchungen zur Geschichte der Böhmischen Brüder* (2 vols., Prague, 1878–82). J. T. Müller, *Geschichte der Böhmischen Brüder* (3 vols., Herrnhut, 1922–31). V. L. Tapié, *Une Église tchèque au XVe siecle*. L'Unité des frères (thesis, Paris, 1934).

BOLLANDISTS. The *Jesuit editors of the '*Acta Sanctorum', so called after John van Bolland (1596–1665), the founder and first editor of the work. The plan for a critical edition of the lives of the Saints, based on authentic sources, had been conceived by Heribert Rosweyde (1569–1629), who, however, did not live to see any of it published. Under Bolland and his successors nearly all the archives and libraries of religious houses were systematically combed for material, for which a special museum was founded at Antwerp. Work by the Bollandists was suspended when the Jesuits were suppressed in Belgium in 1773, but resumed in 1837. Among the most outstanding of recent Bollandists is H. *Delehaye. Since 1882 the *Analecta Bollandiana (q.v.) have been published as supplements.

H. Delehaye, S.J., *À travers trois siècles*. L'œuvre des Bollandistes, 1615–1915 (1920); P. Peeters, S.J., *L'Œuvre des Bollandistes* (Académie Royale de Belgique. Classe des Lettres. Mémoires. 2e Sér. (8vo), xxxix; fasc. 4; 1942). Id., *Figures bollandiennes contemporaines* (Collection Durandal No. 73; 1948). C. De Smedt, S.J., in *C.E.*, ii (1907), pp. 630–9, s.v.; M. Scaduto, S.J., in *E.C.*, ii (1949), cols. 1782–90, s.v.

BOLOGNA. The ancient Bononia, in N. Italy. In the Middle Ages its university (founded in the 11th cent.) was the chief centre in Europe for the study of canon and civil law. The city has retained since the 5th cent. its devotion to St. *Petronius (d. c. 450), an early bishop. The first general chapter of the *Dominican Order was held in the town in 1220, and in the church of S. Domenico lies the body of St. *Dominic (d. 1221).

H. *Rashdall (ed. by F. M. Powicke and A. B. Emden), *The Universities of Europe in the Middle Ages*, i (1936), ch. iv, pp. 87–268, with bibl. A. Sorbelli and L. Simeoni, *Storia della università di Bologna* (2 vols., 1940). F. Bonnard in *D.H.G.E.*, ix (1937), cols. 645–60, incl. further bibl.

BOLOGNA, Concordat of (1516). The agreement between Pope *Leo X and Francis I of France which ended the *Pragmatic Sanction of Bourges. The French king was to nominate ecclesiastics to metropolitan and cathedral churches, to abbeys, and to conventual priories, and, if certain rules were complied with, Papal confirmation was not to be refused. After two invalid nominations, however, the appointment was to lapse to the Pope.

Orig. indult, 'Primitiva illa Ecclesia', in Hardouin, ix (1714), cols. 1810–25; Leo X's supplementary bull, 'Pastor Aeternus' (19 Dec. 1516), which finally abrogated the Pragmatic Sanction of Bourges, ib., cols. 1826–31; extracts in Mirbt, No. 414, p. 252 f. L. Madelin, 'Les Premières Applications du concordat de 1516 d'après les dossiers du château Sainte-Ange' in *Mélanges d'Archéologie et d'Histoire de l'École Française de Rome*, xvii (1897), pp. 323–85.

BOLSEC, HIERONYMUS HERMES (d. 1584), Reformation theologian. Orig. a *Carmelite friar at Paris, he was obliged through the hostility to his Protestant preaching to flee to Italy, where he took refuge with the Duchess of Ferrara and began to practise as a physician. Later he took up residence in the Chablais, was brought into personal relations with J. *Calvin, and became keenly interested in the Reformer's doctrines. Soon, however, he found himself unable to accept Calvin's teaching on predestination, and after challenging it at *Geneva on 16 Oct. 1551, was handed over to the secular powers and imprisoned. When the City Council referred the matter to the three neighbouring Swiss Churches of *Basle, Zürich, and Berne, these towns gave Calvin only moderate support. But though their attitude was in fact a triumph for Bolsec, the Genevan Council dared not force Calvin's resignation, and on 22 Dec. 1551 Bolsec was banished from Geneva for ever. Calvin deemed the challenge sufficiently grave to reformulate his doctrine of predestination in the '*Consensus Genevensis'. Bolsec now began an unseemly personal attack on Calvin, carrying on his defence in the Chablais, at Berne, and at *Paris. He was present at the National Synod of Orléans in 1562, and his doctrines were again condemned at Lyons in the following year. In his last years Bolsec returned to the RC Church. His writings include very hostile Lives of Calvin (1577)—the one act of Calvin of which he approved was the burning of M. *Servetus—and of T. *Beza (1582).

E. Choisy in *P.R.E.* (ed. 3), iii (1897), p. 281 f., s.v.

BOLSENA, The Miracle of. The traditional story, familiar through Raffael's paintings in the *Vatican *stanze*, has it that when a German priest on pilgrimage to Rome was once celebrating Mass in the church of St. Cristina in the little Umbrian town of Bolsena, he was disturbed by doubts about the transubstantiation of the bread and wine, which were suddenly resolved when he saw Blood issue from the Elements and bathe the corporal. It is further narrated that when *Urban

IV had been shown the corporal, which had been conveyed to Orvieto where he was staying, he at once determined to institute the Feast of Corpus Christi and also enjoined work to begin on the cathedral of Orvieto to enshrine such a precious relic. There is no contemporary evidence for the miracle, and there is no trace of it in Urban's bull instituting the Feast.

The Miracle is first mentioned by St. *Antoninus of Florence (*Chronica*, III. tit. xix. c. 13). It is found in a fuller form in *Benedict XIV, *Commentarii duo de D. N. Jesu Christi Matrisque Eius Festis*, I (Lat. tr., 1745), p. 212.

BOMBASTUS VON HOHENHEIM, THEOPHRASTUS. See *Paracelsus*.

BONAVENTURE, St. (1221–74). Giovanni di Fidanza, *Franciscan theologian, 'Doctor seraphicus'. An Italian by birth, he entered the Franciscan Order in 1238 or 1243, and studied at *Paris under *Alexander of Hales. In 1248 he began to teach publicly, and continued to lecture at Paris till 1255. An interruption followed through opposition from the secular professors at the University; but when in 1257 the Mendicant orders were re-established in their privileges, the degree of doctor was bestowed on him. Earlier in the same year he had been elected Minister General of his order, and in this capacity he took a prominent part in settling the internal dissensions by which the order was then rent. His Life of St. *Francis was approved by his order in 1263 as the official biography of their founder, and in 1266 a general chapter at Paris decreed the destruction of all other 'legends' of the Saint. In 1271 he was mainly responsible for securing the election of *Gregory X to the Papacy. In 1273 he was created Cardinal Bp. of Albano. He took a prominent part in the events of the Council of *Lyons of 1274 and died while it was still sitting. Feast day, 14 July.

As a theologian he remained faithful to the tradition which derived from St. *Augustine and was reasserted by St. *Anselm, and had only limited sympathy with the new *Aristotelian doctrines, though he acknowledged that Aristotle's description of the facts was often correct. As against St. *Thomas, who gave a far more ready hearing to the new doctrines, St. Bonaventure held that the creation of the world in time could be demonstrated by the light of reason. He emphasized that all human wisdom was folly when compared with the mystical illumination which God sheds on the faithful Christian; and this essentially mystical theory of knowledge he set forth in his 'Itinerarium Mentis in Deum'. His most extensive and systematic work is his 'Commentary on the *Sentences' [of *Peter Lombard]. He denied the doctrine of the *immaculate conception of the BVM.

Crit. ed. of his Works by the Franciscans of Quaracchi (10 vols.; sep. index to vols. i–vi, 1882–1902). Modern Eng. tr. of his life of St. Francis (London, 1904), of three of his treatises on the spiritual and religious life (London, 1922), of The Mirror of the Blessed Life of Jesus Christ (London, 1926), and of the 'Itinerarium Mentis in Deum', tr. as *The

Franciscan Vision (London, 1937). Modern life, by L. Costelloe, O.F.M. ('The Friar Saint Series', 1911). E. Gilson, *La Philosophie de Saint Bonaventure* (Études de Philosophie Médiévale, iv, 1924; Eng. tr., 1938), with bibl. E. Longpré, O.F.M. in *D.H.G.E.*, ix (1937), cols. 741–88, s.v.; id. in *Dict. Sp.*, i (1937), cols. 1768–1843, s.v., both with bibl.

BONIFACE, St. (680–754). The 'Apostle of Germany'. Wynfrith, as he was originally called, was born at *Crediton, in Devon. In 716 he made a first, but unsuccessful, missionary journey to Frisia. Undaunted, he journeyed to Rome two years later, where he was forthwith armed with Papal authority, and in 719 on a second visit to Germany met with success in Bavaria and Thuringia and converted many of the Hessians. News of his work caused *Gregory II to demand his presence in Rome in 722, and Boniface from now on received the fullest Papal support. (The tradition that it was on this occasion that his name was changed to Boniface on the feast of St. Boniface, the Roman martyr, seems incorrect, as he apparently used the name Boniface earlier.) On his return to Germany, his courage in felling the Oak of Thor at Geismar, near Fritzlar, won him instant success, and not much later he was able to lay the foundations of a settled ecclesiastical organization for Germany. After the death of *Charles Martel (741), Boniface was given authority to carry through a reform of the whole Frankish Church, a task which he accomplished in a series of councils. c. 743 he founded the famous abbey of *Fulda. c. 747 he became Abp. of Mainz, but after a few years he resigned the see to return to his old mission in Frisia, where he met with martyrdom. His devotion to the Papacy, coupled with the success of his work, greatly assisted the spread of Papal influence N. of the Alps. Feast day, 5 June.

Opera Omnia, ed. J. A. Giles (2 vols., London, 1844); J. P. Migne, *PL*, lxxxix, 597–892. *Epp.* by E. Dümmler in *M.G.H.*, Epistolae III (1892), improved ed. by M. Tangl in ib., Epistolae Selectae I (1916). Letters tr. by E. Kylie ('The King's Classics', 1911); later ed. with introd. by E. Emerton (Columbia Univ. Press, New York, 1940). Of early Lives (ed. W. Levison in *M.G.H.*, Scriptores Rerum Germanicarum in Usum Scholarum, 1905), the most trustworthy is that by St. *Willibald. The many modern Lives (mainly Germ. and of varying merit) include those of J. C. A. Seiters (Mainz, 1845), J. P. Müller (2 vols., Amsterdam, 1869–70), G. Pfahler (Ratisbon, 1880), O. Fischer (Leipzig, 1881), B. Kuhlmann (Paderborn, 1895), G. Kurth ('Les Saints', Paris, 1902), J. M. Williamson (Ventnor, 1904), G. F. Browne (London, S.P.C.K., 1910), J. J. Laux (Freiburg i.Br., 1922), and W. Lampen (Amsterdam, 1949). 'Gedenkgabe' for the 12th centenary of his death (Fulda, 1954). See also W. Levison's Ford Lectures (1946), esp. ch. iv.

BONIFACE I, St. (d. 422). Pope from 418. Before his election to the Papacy, he had been a presbyter at Rome. Immediately on the death of *Zosimus on 26 Dec. 418, both Boniface and the archdeacon Eulalius, a rival candidate, were elected and both were consecrated on the same day (29 Dec. 418). In consequence of the dispute, Boniface did not obtain possession of the see till 10 Apr. 419, after the Emp. Honorius had decided in his favour a week earlier at *Ravenna. He did

much to restore the authority of the Papacy after the hesitating and unpopular rule of Zosimus, e.g. he firmly condemned *Pelagianism and restored the rights of the metropolitans in the S. of Gaul. He also secured the prefecture of Illyricum for his own jurisdiction when the E. Emp. *Theodosius II was endeavouring to transfer it to the obedience of the Patr. of *Constantinople. Feast day, 4 Sept.

L.P. (Duchesne), i (1886), pp. 227–9. H. Hemmer in *D.T.C.*, ii (1905), col. 988 f., s.v., with bibl.

BONIFACE VIII (c. 1234–1303), Pope from 1294. Benedict Gaetani was a native of Anagni. After studying at Todi and Spoleto he became a canon at *Paris, *Rome, and elsewhere, and in 1276 entered upon his career at the Curia, being appointed consistorial advocate and *Notary Apostolic. Having been created cardinal-deacon in 1281 and cardinal-priest in 1291, he was employed on important missions to France and Italy and took a decisive part in the abdication of St. *Celestine V. Elected Pope at Naples in 1294, he immediately went to Rome, and from the first strove to realize his double aim of the pacification of Europe and the liberation of the Holy Land from the Turks. His exertions, however, were destined to failure. After trying without success to reconcile Genoa and *Venice (1295), and to prevent the election of Frederick of Aragon as king of Sicily (1296), he became involved in his great struggle with Philip the Fair of France, which was to last until his death. In a professed attempt to stop the war between England and France by depriving the belligerents of their main financial resources, he issued the bull '*Clericis laicos' (q.v.; 25 Feb. 1296), forbidding the King to demand or receive extraordinary taxes from the clergy without Papal assent. When Philip replied by stopping all transports of gold and valuables to Rome, the Pope had to modify his claims and to concede Philip the right to decide for himself cases of necessity in which he might levy taxes without consulting him, in the letter 'Ineffabilis Amoris' (20 Sept. 1296). At the same time the Papal position was aggravated by his difficulties with the powerful family of Colonna, with whom sided the *Fraticelli, whose exaggerated teachings Boniface had proscribed. The Papal armies, however, razed the Colonna fortresses to the ground, many members of the family finding refuge in France. In 1300 the Pope was able to celebrate the Jubilee with great pomp, despite the absence of nearly all European princes. But in 1301 the struggle between Boniface and Philip broke out again when the King brought to trial the Papal legate, Bp. Bernard de Saisset, demanding his degradation and delivery to the secular power. The Pope replied by the bull '*Ausculta Fili' (5 Dec. 1301), in which he enunciated the doctrine of Papal supremacy over princes and kingdoms, attacked Philip's government, and summoned the King or his representative to a synod in Rome. It was followed by the famous bull '*Unam Sanctam' (q.v.; 18 Nov. 1302),

in which Boniface defended, with numerous patristic quotations, the jurisdiction of the Pope over all creatures. The struggle with Philip came to a head in 1303, when Philip refused to restore communications with Rome and endeavoured to bring the Pope to trial. Boniface replied by preparing a bull of excommunication, but Philip forestalled him, and William de Nogaret, at the head of a band of mercenaries, took the Pope prisoner at Anagni. Though Italian troops released him after three days, he was now broken in health and died at Rome a month later.

One of the great upholders of the absolute power of the Papacy, Boniface was the true successor of *Gregory VII and *Innocent III, but failed to understand the growth of national feeling which had taken place in the latter part of the 13th cent., and which increasingly diminished the political influence of the Popes. Among his many achievements is the compilation of the *Sext (q.v.), the embellishment of the Roman churches, and the foundation of the Roman university, the 'Sapienza' (1303).

G. Digard–M. Faucon–A. Thomas–R. Fawtier (edd.), *Les Registres de Boniface VIII* (Bibliothèque des Écoles Françaises d'Athènes et de Rome, 2ᵉ Série, iv, 4 vols., 1904–39). L. Tosti, *Storia di Bonifazio VIII e de' suoi tempi* (2 vols., 1846); H. Finke, *Aus den Tagen Bonifatius VIII* (1902); T. S. R. Boase, *Boniface VIII* (1933). M. Seidlmayer, 'Papst Bonifaz VIII und der Kirchenstaat' in *Hist. J.*, lx (1940), pp. 78–87. J. Rivière, *Le Problème de l'Église et de l'État au temps de Philippe le Bel* (*S.S.L.*, viii, 1926), passim. G. Pou y Marti, O.F.M., in *E.C.*, ii (1949), cols. 1866–75, with bibl.

BONIFACE OF SAVOY (d. 1270), Abp. of *Canterbury. He was the son of Thomas I, Count of Savoy, and through his sister's marriage became nearly related to Henry III. Having entered the *Carthusian Order while still a boy, in 1234 he was elected Bp. of Belley in Burgundy. In 1241 he was elected to succeed St. *Edmund of Abingdon as Abp. of Canterbury, but Papal confirmation was delayed and he did not reach England until 1244, when he promptly carried through several important financial reforms. In the same year he left to attend the Council of *Lyons (1245), where he was consecrated by *Innocent IV. He did not return until 1249 when he was enthroned at Canterbury on *All Saints' Day. He instituted a metropolitical visitation of his province which met with strong resistance from the clergy generally, and he retired to Rome until 1252. In his later years he was frequently abroad, returning to England for the last time in 1265. In 1269 he set out with Edward I on a crusade, but died on the way at St. Helena, Savoy. He became the subject of a cultus in Savoy (confirmed in 1830) where his feast is kept on 13 Mar.

G. Strickland, 'Ricerche storiche sopra il B. Bonifacio di Savoia, arcivescovo di Cantorbery 1207–70' in *Miscellanea di Storia Italiana*, Ser. 3, i (No. xxxii della Raccolta, 1895), pp. 349–432. M. *Creighton in *D.N.B.*, v (1886), pp. 350–2, s.v.

BONIFATIUSVEREIN (Ger. 'Boniface Society'). A society founded in 1849 under the patronage of St. *Boniface for the support of Catholics living in those parts of Germany where the population is mainly Protestant. Its work is centred at Paderborn in Westphalia.

BONN REUNION CONFERENCES. Two international conferences held at Bonn in 1874 and 1875 under the presidency of J. J. I. von *Döllinger to foster reunion between Churches which had retained the faith and order of historic Christianity. Their direction was in the hands of the newly separated *Old Catholics (though Döllinger himself never formally joined them). Others present included German Evangelicals, members of the E. Churches, and many theologians from Great Britain (including E. H. *Browne [Bp. of Winchester], H. P. *Liddon, and E. S. *Talbot) and America.

The Reports were publd. in English (London, 1875, 1876).

BONNER, EDMUND (c. 1500–1569). The last Bp. of London to die in communion with the Papacy. He was chaplain to T. *Wolsey and the only bishop who remained faithful to him till his death (1530). Despite this loyalty he retained the King's favour, and in 1538 he was appointed to the see of *Hereford, and in 1539 to that of *London. During the successive changes in Church and state he was uncompromising in defending the traditional doctrines. Under *Edward VI he was deprived for maintaining *Transubstantiation. Restored by *Mary, he played a prominent part in reconciling the country with Rome and in enforcing the laws against heresy. Under *Elizabeth he refused to take the oath under the Act of *Supremacy of 1559 and ended his days in the Marshalsea prison.

S. R. Maitland, *Essays on Subjects Connected with the Reformation in England* (1849), Nos. 17 f. and 20, pp. 345–95 and 406–76. J. *Gairdner in *D.N.B.*, v (1886), pp. 356–60, s.v., with bibl. J. P. Whitney in *D.E.C.H.*, p. 67 f., s.v.

BONOSUS (d. c. 400). A Bp. of Naïssus who denied the perpetual virginity of the BVM. His teaching was examined at a council at Capua in 391 and subsequently condemned; but Bonosus refused to submit and founded a sect (the 'Bonosians') which survived down to the 7th cent.

The earliest authority is Pope *Siricius, *ep.* 9 (ad Anysium, epis. Thessalonicensem); by an error, this letter is also ascribed to *Ambrose ('*ep.* 79'). Other sources include *Innocent I, *epp.* 16 and 17; *Marius Mercator (who, prob. mistakenly, describes Bonosus as Bp. of Sardica); Council of *Orange (538), can. 31, and *Vigilius, *ep.* 15. J. R. Palanque, *St. Ambroise et l'empire romain* (1933), pp. 259–63. E. Venables in *D.C.B.*, i (1877), p. 330 f.; F. *Loofs in *P.R.E.* (ed. 3), iii (1897), pp. 314–17, with further reff. to sources. X. Le Bachelet, S.J., in *D.T.C.*, ii (1905), cols. 1027–31.

BOOK ANNEXED, The. See *Annexed Book, The.*

BOOK OF ADVERTISEMENTS, The. See *Advertisements, The Book of.*

BOOK OF ARMAGH. See *Armagh, Book of.*

BOOK OF COMMON ORDER [PRAYER]. See *Common Order [Prayer], The Book of.*

BOOK OF CONCORD, The. See *Concord, The Formula and Book of.*

BOOK OF JUBILEES. See *Jubilees, Book of.*

BOOK OF KELLS, The. A finely ornamented MS. of the Gospels, so named from the monastery of Kells (or Kenanna) in Co. Meath, where it was written. Its script is the finest specimen of writing in an Irish hand in existence. Acc. to tradition, it belonged to St. *Columba (d. 597), but it really dates from c. 8th cent. The MS. is now at *Trinity College, Dublin (A. 1.6).

Sir Edward Sullivan, *The Book of Kells* ('The Studio', 1914; with twenty-four coloured plates). Sumptuous facsimile ed., partly in colour, by U. Graf (3 vols., Berne, 1950–1). A. Gwynn, S.J., 'Some Notes on the History of the Book of Kells' in *Irish Historical Studies*, ix (1954), pp. 131–61. J. Dunn in *C.E.*, viii (1910), p. 614 f.; and H. *Leclercq, O.S.B., in *D.A.C.L.*, viii (pt. 1, 1928), cols. 713–18, both s.v. 'Kells'.

BOOK OF LIFE. The phrase occurs in six passages in the NT: Phil. 4. 3, Rev. 3. 5, 13. 8, 17. 8, 20. 12, 15 and 21. 27. (In AV, also at 22. 19, but here all the best MS. evidence is for 'tree of life'). The conception of a heavenly register of the elect is based on ideas found in the OT (e.g. Exod. 32. 32, Is. 4. 3, Ps. 69. 28) and in the Book of *Enoch (47. 3).

BOOK OF SPORTS. See *Sports, Book of.*

BOOKS OF DISCIPLINE, The. See *Discipline, The Books of.*

BOOTH, WILLIAM (1829–1912), founder and first General of the *Salvation Army (q.v.). A native of Nottingham and of partly Jewish origin, he was apprenticed to a pawnbroker in 1842. He became a *Methodist soon after, and in 1844 he had an experience of conversion. Two years later he became a revivalist preacher. In 1849 he went to London, and in 1855 married Catherine Munford (1829–90), who shared his aspirations and became herself a famous preacher. In 1861 he left the Methodists, with whom he had come into conflict on account of his violent preaching, and established a revivalist movement of his own, called the Christian Mission, in Whitechapel, which undertook evangelistic, social, and rescue work. From 1880, when the Army spread to the U.S.A., Australia, the Continent, and elsewhere, he spent much of his life travelling and organizing and addressing meetings. In 1890 he published *In Darkest England and the Way Out* in collaboration with W. T. Stead, in which he suggested a number of remedies for the social evils of the times, including farm colonies and rescue homes. His work was encouraged by Edward VII as well as by several foreign authorities.

Booth's chief characteristic was his love for the poor, whose souls he sought to save by his preaching while at the same time ministering to their bodily needs. Though he was ignorant of theology and of a rather narrow outlook, the strength of his emotions and sympathies, combined with a shrewd commercial sense, made of his movement one of the most successful religious revivals of modern times.

In 1912, he was succeeded by his son, William Bramwell Booth (1856–1929), as General.

The Life of General Booth, by various authors (1912); H. Begbie, *Life of William Booth* (2 vols., 1920). Id. in *D.N.B.*, 1912–1921, pp. 50–2.

BOOTHS, Feast of. See *Tabernacles, Feast of.*

BORBORIANS. A sect of libertine *Gnostics which flourished from the 2nd to the 5th cents. Their doctrines and practices are described by *Epiphanius (*Haer.* 26).

BORDEAUX PILGRIM, The. The earliest known Christian pilgrim from W. Europe to the *Holy Land. He made his pilgrimage in A.D. 333–4, visiting *Constantinople and finishing his journey at Milan. His account ('Itinerarium Burdigalense') is for the most part only a list of the stages in his route, but there is a brief description of some of the sites of Palestine.

Itinerarium first publ. by P. *Pithou (n.p., 1589); crit. ed. by P. Geyer, C.S.E.L., xxxix (1889), pp. 1–33, with introd. pp. iv–viii. Eng. tr. by A. Stewart, with notes by C. W. Wilson (Palestine Pilgrims' Text Society, 1887). H. *Leclercq, O.S.B., in *D.A.C.L.*, vii (pt. 2; 1927), cols. 1853–8, s.v. 'Itinéraires', with notes of edd. and comm.; id., ib. xiv (pt. 1; 1939), cols. 76–8, s.v. 'Pèlerinages aux lieux saints'.

BORGIA, CESARE (1475–1507), Italian prince. The illegitimate son of Pope *Alexander VI, he was appointed to the Abpric. of Valencia and the cardinalate before he was 20 years of age. A few years later (1499) he was dispensed from the obligations of his orders that he might marry Charlotte d'Albert, the sister of the King of Navarre. Soon after, King Louis XII created him Duke of Valentinois and his father made him 'Captain General of the Church'. A picturesque and able soldier, Cesare proved himself unscrupulous and merciless in securing his ends, though he ruled his subjects, once they were conquered, with justice and firmness, and on his activities N. Machiavelli is said to have based his portrait of *The Prince*. Cesare recovered many of the Papal provinces which had broken away from the Holy See, and was himself proclaimed Duke of Romagna. On his father's death, an illness precluded his taking part in the elections of his successors, Pius III (who lived only a few weeks) and *Julius II. The new Pope was a resolute enemy of the Borgia family, and Cesare fled to Naples, where he was arrested and taken to Spain by order of Ferdinand of Aragon. He

escaped to Navarre, where he was employed on military service by his brother-in-law and killed while besieging the rebel castle of Viana.

E. Alvisi, *Cesare Borgia. Duca di Romagna*. Notizie e documenti (1878). Studies by C. Yriarte (2 vols., Paris, 1889; Eng. version (shortened), 1947), R. Sabatini (London, [1911]), J. L. Garner (London, 1912), and W. H. Woodward (London, 1913).

BORGIA, St. FRANCIS (1510–72), *Jesuit. The son of the Duke of Gandia, to whose title he succeeded in 1543, Francis early showed an inclination towards the religious life. *Charles V appointed him Viceroy of Catalonia, but on the death of his wife, Leonora de Castro, in 1546 he joined the Society of Jesus and in 1551 was ordained priest and disposed of his estates. He was the friend and adviser of St. *Ignatius Loyola and St. *Teresa, and proved a most active and zealous Churchman. Thus he was responsible for establishing many colleges and schools, and helped with the foundation of the 'Collegium Romanum'. He also used his influence to gain for the Jesuits a favourable reception in France. He soon won a widespread reputation for piety, was appointed Commissary General of the Jesuits for Spain, Portugal, and the Indies, and in 1565, on *Lainez's death, became the third General of the order. He died in 1572 and was canonized in 1671. Feast day, 10 Oct.

Opera Omnia, publd. at Brussels, 1675. Contemporary Lives by P. Ribadeneira, S.J. (Rome, 1596) and D. Vásquez, S.J. (unpubld.). Letters and other material in the *Monumenta Historica Societatis Jesu* (5 vols., Madrid, 1894–1911). Modern critical biographies by P. Suau ('Les Saints', Paris, 1905; more substantial work, Paris, 1910); O. Karrer, S.J. (Freiburg i.Br., 1921), with bibliography. M. Yeo, *The Greatest of the Borgias* (1936).

BORROMEO, St. CHARLES. See *Charles Borromeo, St.*

BORROW, GEORGE HENRY (1803–81), philologist and traveller. After education at Norwich Grammar School, he was articled to a firm of solicitors. His ambition was to be a writer, and soon he left the law to seek his fortune in London. He went on tramp as a tinker for several years; and from the wide experience thus gained he wrote later the descriptions of gypsy life in *Lavengro* (1851) and *Romany Rye* (2 vols., 1857). As an agent of the *British and Foreign Bible Society he travelled widely, distributing copies of the Bible. His *The Bible in Spain* (3 vols., 1843) became widely popular through its picturesque and vivacious narrative. He was also a considerable linguist who made several translations of portions of the Scriptures into little-known tongues.

W. I. Knapp, *The Life, Writings and Correspondence of George Borrow* (1899). Studies by R. A. J. Walling (1908), H. Jenkins (1912), E. Thomas (1912), C. K. Shorter (1920) and G. A. Stephen (1927).

BOSANQUET, BERNARD (1848–1923), idealist philosopher. Educated at Balliol College, Oxford where he came under the influence of T. H. *Green and R. L. Nettle-ship, he was elected a Fellow of University College in 1870 and remained there until 1881. For most of the rest of his life he lived privately at London, except from 1903 to 1908 when he was professor of moral philosophy at St. Andrews. With F. H. *Bradley he was the leading exponent of Absolute Idealism in England. Like Bradley, he showed in his teaching close affinities with G. W. F. *Hegel; but his interests were wider and his outlook more conciliatory. In logic, as for Bradley, the judgement and not the concept was the fundamental form. In his political theory he ascribed to the state, as the 'general' or 'rational will', almost limitless powers, a doctrine which met with severe criticism from L. T. Hobhouse among others. His understanding of religion was essentially *pantheistic. He conceived of it as only a stage towards metaphysics, and correspondingly of the God of religion as not more than the highest of the appearances of the Absolute; and the Incarnation at a moment in history he found meaningless. Among his many writings the chief are: *Logic, or the Morphology of Knowledge* (2 vols., 1888), *A History of Aesthetic* (1892), *A Companion to *Plato's Republic* (1895), *The Philosophical Theory of the State* (1899), *The Principle of Individuality and Value* (1912), *The Value and Destiny of the Individual* (1913), *What Religion Is* (1920), and *The Meeting of Extremes in Contemporary Philosophy* (1921).

His Life was written by his wife, Helen Bosanquet (1924). J. H. *Muirhead, *B. Bosanquet and his Friends: Letters* (1935). C. C. J. *Webb, 'Bernard Bosanquet's Philosophy of Religion' in the *Hibbert Journal*, xxii (1923–4), pp. 75–96.

BOSCO, St. JOHN (1815–88). The founder of the *Salesian Order (q.v.). The son of Piedmontese peasants, he was brought up in and around Turin, where he spent most of his life. A vision received at the age of nine (the first of many more throughout his life) aroused in him a keen interest in winning lads to the Christian faith, and in 1859 he founded the 'Pious Society of St. *Francis de Sales', commonly known as the 'Salesians'. His influence over his boys was achieved by using a minimum of restraint and discipline, combined with a careful watch over his pupils' development and the use of personal and religious encouragement. Don Bosco also actively promoted industrial schools and evening classes where young men could be apprenticed for secular vocations in a religious background. In the latter part of his life he did much to foster missionary work. He was beatified in 1929 and canonized in 1934. Feast day, 31 Jan.

C. d'Espiney, *Don Bosco* (Nice, 1881; ed. 10 with additional material, 1888). Other lives by A. Auffray, S.C. (Paris, 1929; Eng. tr., 1930), J. Jørgensen (Copenhagen, 1929; Eng. tr., 1934), H. L. Hughes (London, 1934), and H. *Ghéon (Paris, 1935; Eng. tr., 1935). L. Castano, S.D.B.– C. Testore, S.J., in *E.C.*, vi (1951), cols. 620–3, s.v. 'Giovanni Bosco'.

BOSIO, ANTONIO (c. 1576–1629), Italian archaeologist, dubbed by G. B. *de Rossi the 'Columbus of the Catacombs'. A native of

Malta, he was sent to school at Rome. After preliminary studies in philosophy and law, he gave himself up at the age of 18 to archaeology to which he devoted the rest of his life. He was the first to recognize the significance of an accidental discovery on 31 May 1578 of a subterranean burial-place on the Via Salaria. Bosio's first descent was on 10 Dec. 1593 at the Catacomb of Domitilla (though Bosio could not yet name it) on the Via Ardeatina, when, through inexperience, he lost himself and only just succeeded in finding his way out. His very extensive discoveries were described in his *Roma sotterranea* (finished 1620; not published until '1632', actually 1634 owing to delays with printing), which remained the standard work until G. B. de Rossi's researches. It was a remarkable achievement, the least satisfactory part of it being the engravings, which Bosio had entrusted to colleagues.

A. Valeri, *Cenni biografici di Antonio Bossio con documenti inediti* (1900); G. Ferretto, *Note storico-bibliografiche di archeologia cristiana* (1942), pp. 132–62. H. *Leclercq, O.S.B., in *D.A.C.L.*, ii (pt. 1; 1910), cols. 1084–93.

BOSSUET, JACQUES BÉNIGNE (1627–1704), French preacher and Bp. of Meaux. The fifth son of a judge in the Parlement of Dijon, he was educated first at the *Jesuit school at Dijon, later at Metz (whither his father had removed), and at the age of 13 appointed to a canonry in Metz cathedral. In 1642 he went to *Paris where he entered the Collège de Navarre to train for the priesthood. His oratorical gifts attracted notice through a sermon with which as a boy of 16 he entertained a *salon* at the Hôtel de Rambouillet. In 1649 he was ordained deacon and, after preparation under St. *Vincent de Paul, priest at Metz in 1652. After seven years at Metz, spent in study, controversy with the Protestants, and preaching, in 1659 he moved to Paris. Here his fame rapidly grew and he was a frequent preacher before the court. He was mainly responsible for the conversion of Marshal Turenne from Protestantism in 1668. In 1669 he was appointed Bp. of Condom in Gascony and in the same year delivered the first of his great 'Funeral Orations' (on *Henrietta Maria) which revealed to the full his powers as a pulpit orator. For the next eleven years he was tutor to the Dauphin (1670–81). During this period he published his *Exposition sur la doctrine catholique sur les matières de controverse* (1671), and also wrote (in the first place for his pupil's instruction) his *Traité de la connaissance de Dieu et de soi-même* (publd. 1722) and his *Discours sur l'histoire universelle* (1681). The latter was a compelling presentation of the Christian view of Divine overruling in history. On the completion of his duties as preceptor he was translated to the see of Meaux (1681), and now came to take an increasingly prominent part in French ecclesiastical affairs. At the Assemblée-générale du Clergé of 1682 he was mainly instrumental in securing the support of the French clergy for the moderate *Gallicanism of the Four *Gallican Articles (q.v.), which he himself drew up. In his zeal for the Catholic faith he approved of the Revocation of the Edict of *Nantes (1685) and also directed many publications against the Protestants among which his *Histoire des variations des Églises protestantes* (2 vols., 1688) was the most notable. At the same time Bossuet hoped that Christian reunion might be furthered by peaceful methods, and to this end conducted a long correspondence (1683–1700) with G. W. *Leibniz. His *Méditations sur l'Évangile* (publd. 1731) and his *Élévations sur les mystères* (publd. 1727), written in the concluding decade of his life, rank as classics of French devotional literature. In his last years the case of Mme *Guyon led him into a bitter controversy on mysticism with F. *Fénelon, and Bossuet was mainly responsible for his condemnation in 1699. His views were embodied in his *Relation sur le quiétisme* (1698). He was also a vigorous opponent of R. *Simon's theories of the Bible, notably in his *Défense de la tradition et des saints pères* (publd. 1763).

By common consent Bossuet is among the greatest preachers of all time. Not only did he possess the outward gifts which belong to the successful orator (an impressive presence, a pleasing voice, ease of manner, fitness of phrase); he also combined with them precision of thought, complete grasp of the subject and, above all, a strong hold on dogmatic truth; and to the dry light of argument he added the fire of passion. The fact that he was at his best on a large canvas made the funeral oration a form specially suited to his talents. The three on Henrietta Maria (1669), Henriette Anne d'Angleterre (1670), and the Prince de Condé (1687) will remain classics. But his real greatness as a preacher rests on the distinction he showed on less formal occasions.

Complete Works, ed. F. Lachat (31 vols., Paris, 1862–6). *Œuvres oratoires*, ed. J. Lebarq (7 vols., Lille and Paris, 1890–1921). Correspondence, ed. C. Urbain and E. Levesque (15 vols., Paris, 1909–12). Lives by L. F. de Bausset (4 vols., Paris, 1814), A. Réaume (3 vols., Paris, 1869–70), G. Lanson (Paris, 1891), A. Rébelliau ('Les Grands Écrivains français', 1900), E. K. Sanders (London, S.P.C.K., 1921), G. Baumann (Paris, 1929), W. J. Sparrow Simpson (London, S.P.C.K., 1937), and J. Calvet (Paris, 1941). A. Rébelliau, *Bossuet, historien du protestantisme* (1891); C. E. Freppel, *Bossuet et l'éloquence sacrée au XVIIe siècle* (2 vols. 1893); A. M. P. Ingold, *Bossuet et le jansénisme* (1897; ed. 2, 1904); G. Truc, *Bossuet et le classicisme religieux* (1934). F. *Cabrol, O.S.B., 'Bossuet, ses relations avec l'Angleterre' in *R.H.E.*, xxvii (1931), pp. 535–71. A. Largent in *D.T.C.*, ii (1905), cols. 1049–89; A. Levesque in *D.H.G.E.*, ix (1937), cols. 1339–91.

BOTULPH, St. (mid. 7th cent.), also Botolph, Botwulf. Acc. to the Anglo-Saxon Chronicle the founder and first abbot of a monastery at Icanhoe (or Ox-island) in 654; but it is uncertain whether this was Iken in Suffolk, where the church is dedicated to St. Botulph, or Boston (i.e. Botulph's town) in Lincs. During the Middle Ages the cult of the Saint was very popular, esp. in E. Anglia and the North, and some 70 English churches have been dedicated to him. Feast day, 17 June.

*Bede, *Historia Abbatum Auctore Anonymo*, cap. 4; notes in ed. by C. Plummer, ii (1896), p. 372. Life by Folcard printed in *AA.SS.*, Jun. III (1701), pp. 402 f. For MSS.,

editions and value of Folcard and other lives, Hardy, i, pp. 373–6. F. S. Stevenson, 'St. Botolph (Botwulf) and Iken' in the *Proceedings of the Suffolk Institute of Archaeology and Natural History*, xviii (1922), pp. 29–52.

BOUNDS, Beating of the. See *Beating of the Bounds*.

BOURCHIER, THOMAS (*c.* 1404–86), Abp. of *Canterbury. Educated at Oxford, of which University he later became Chancellor, he was appointed to the see of *Worcester in 1434, of *Ely in 1443, of Canterbury in 1454, and nominated cardinal in 1467. He became much involved in the political affairs of the time, maintaining an even balance between the conflicting interests of Lancaster and York, and retaining the favour of Edward IV. In 1457 he took a leading part in the trial of R. *Pecock, Bp. of *Chichester, for heresy. He lived to crown Henry VII king.

W. F. *Hook, *Lives of the Archbishops of Canterbury*, v (1867), pp. 268–386. J. *Gairdner in *D.N.B.*, v (1886), pp. 15–18, s.v., with ref. For his part in Pecock's condemnation see also V. H. H. Green, *Bishop Reginald Pecock* (1945), pp. 49–60.

BOURDALOUE, LOUIS (1632–1704), French preacher. He entered the *Jesuit Order in 1648, and was for many years employed in teaching humanities and morals in various provincial Jesuit houses. In 1666 he began to preach. His courses of sermons, twelve in all, delivered in Advent and Lent before *Louis XIV and his court in and after 1670, earned him the reputation of the best preacher of his time. His published sermons, though somewhat dry, exhibit excellent qualities of clarity and logical construction. Notes taken at the time of their delivery tend to confirm the impression of rhetorical power which he made upon his contemporaries. For the most part he was concerned with the moral applications of Christianity, combining an inflexible austerity of principle with a remarkable psychological tact and insight, perfected in the practice of spiritual direction.

Sermons et autres œuvres, ed. by F. Bretonneau (16 vols., Lyons, etc., 1707–34). *Œuvres complètes* (18 vols., Toulouse, 1818). Modern ed. by E. Griselle (Paris, 1919 ff.). P. M. Lauras, S.J., *Bourdaloue, sa vie et ses œuvres* (2 vols., Paris, 1881). Other lives by A. Feugère (Paris, 1874), A. A. L. Pauthe (Paris, 1900), F. Castets (2 vols., Paris, 1901–4), and E. Byrne (Paris, 1929). E. A. Blampignon, *Étude sur Bourdaloue avec quelques documents inédits, suivie d'un choix de sermons* (1886). D. N. Tarrou, *Étude sur Bourdaloue, prédicateur* (1857); E. de Ménorval, *Bourdaloue, vie d'un jésuite de la maison professe de la rue Saint-Antoine au XVIIe siècle* (1897); É. Griselle, *Bourdaloue, histoire critique de sa prédication d'après les notes de ses auditeurs et les témoignages contemporains* (3 vols., 1901–6).

BOURIGNON, ANTOINETTE (1616–80), Flemish enthusiast and adventuress. She tried to found a new ascetic order, and to run an orphanage at Liége as an *Augustinian house, both unsuccessfully. After 1662 she was estranged from organized Christianity, and came to conceive herself to be the 'woman clothed with the sun' of Rev. 12. The 'Bourignonians', a sect which believed in her pretensions, flourished in Scotland in the early part of the 18th cent.

Her collected works were issued at Amsterdam (19 vols., 1686). A. v. d. Linde, *Antoinette Bourignon. Das Licht der Welt* (Leiden, 1895).

BOUSSET, WILHELM (1865–1920), NT scholar. In 1916 he became professor of NT theology at Giessen. He made extensive investigations into the connexions of later *Judaism and early Christianity with the contemporary Hellenistic religions, and the growth of the so-called '*Religionsgeschichtliche Schule' owed much to his researches. Among his chief writings were *Der Antichrist* (1895), *Die Religion des Judentums im neutestamentlichen Zeitalter* (1903; ed. 3 by H. Gressmann, 1926), *Die Hauptprobleme der Gnosis* (1907), *Kyrios Christos* (1913), and *Apophthegmata, Studien zur Geschichte des ältesten Mönchtums* (1923, posthumous).

Bousset edited, with W. Heitmüller, the *Theologische Rundschau*, 1897–1917, and with H. *Gunkel the *Forschungen zur Religion und Geschichte des AT und NT*, 1903 ff. L. Thomas in *Dict. Bibl.*, Suppl.,, i (1928), cols. 989–92, s.v.

BOW CHURCH. The church of St. Mary-le-Bow ('Sta Maria de Arcubus') in Cheapside, so named from the stone arches of the original 11th cent. church on the site. The present church, which was badly damaged in an air raid in 1940, was built by C. *Wren after the Great Fire of 1666. It gave its name to the 'Court of *Arches' which formerly met in the vestry of the church. The confirmation of those elected bishops in the province of *Canterbury still takes place here.

See bibl. to *Arches, Court of*.

BOWDEN, JOHN WILLIAM (1798–1844), *Tractarian. A close friend and contemporary at Trinity College, Oxford, of J. H. *Newman, with whom he collaborated on a poem on 'St. Bartholomew's Eve' (1821), he became a warm supporter of the *Oxford Movement. He wrote some of the *Tracts for the Times* (Nos. 5, 29, 30, 56 and perhaps 58), many articles for the *British Critic* and a Life of *Gregory VII (1840). He also contributed six hymns to 'Lyra Apostolica' (1836).

BOWING. From very early times Christians have bowed 'at the name of Jesus', on the authority of Phil. 2. 10. How far back the custom of bowing at other times, particularly to the altar, can be traced is disputed. In the C of E, despite *Puritan objections, bowing at the Holy *Name was enjoined in Canon 18 (1604), and the practice of making their reverence and obeisance on entering and leaving the church is recommended to the people in Canon 7 (1640). The statutes of *Winchester Cathedral require that the clergy on entering and leaving the church shall 'severally bow themselves towards the altar, devoutly worshipping the Divine Majesty'.

BOY BISHOP. In medieval times it was a widespread custom, in many English monasteries, schools, and country parishes, to elect on St. *Nicholas's Day (6 Dec.) a boy who should execute till *Holy Innocents' Day (28 Dec.) various functions in church ordinarily performed by a bishop. The practice was abolished by *Henry VIII, revived by *Mary, and finally abolished by *Elizabeth. On the Continent it was never so common, though analogous celebrations sometimes took place, esp. in Germany, on the Feast of St. *Gregory the Great (12 Mar.). The intention was to express in dramatic form the reverence for childhood shewn in the Gospels.

E. K. Chambers, *The Medieval Stage* (1903), i, pp. 336–71. G. Cyprian Alston, O.S.B., in *C.E.*, ii (1907), p. 725, s.v.

BOYLE, ROBERT (1627–91). One of the leading scientists of the 17th cent., 'the father of chemistry and son of the Earl of Cork'. He took a prominent part in the foundation of the Royal Society in 1662. Besides his scientific works he wrote a long series of diffuse, but lucid, religious treatises, in which he sought to vindicate the harmony between the new scientific methods and the Christian faith. He left in his will the sum of £50 per annum for a series of eight lectures to be given in some church in London against unbelievers (the 'Boyle Lectures').

Boyle's collected works, with life, were publd. by T. Birch (5 vols., 1744). Considerable extracts from his writings in P. E. More–F. L. Cross, *Anglicanism* (SPCK, 1935), nos. 56, 89, 103, 104, 124, 350, 351.

BRABOURNE, THEOPHILUS (1590–c. 1661), English *Puritan author. In early life he appears to have officiated as a clergyman at *Norwich. In 1628 and 1631 he published two pamphlets maintaining that Saturday, not Sunday, ought to be kept as the Christian Sabbath, and for the second of these, the *Defence . . . of the Sabbath Day*, he was imprisoned for eighteen months at Newgate. The stir thus aroused was one of the reasons for *Charles I's reissue in 1633 of the 'Book of *Sports'. Under the Commonwealth Brabourne again took up the Sabbath question in a dispute with John Collings, a Presbyterian writer. At the Restoration he wrote three pamphlets in defence of the royal supremacy against the *Quakers.

B. Brook, *The Lives of the Puritans*, ii (1813), pp. 362–4. A. Gordon in *D.N.B.*, vi (1886), pp. 139–41, s.v.

BRACHIUM SAECULARE. See *Secular Arm*.

BRADFORD, JOHN (c. 1510–55), Protestant martyr. He was a native of Manchester and for a time secretary to Sir John Harrington, paymaster of the English forces in France. Seeking a more settled career, c. 1547 he began the study of law, taking chambers in the Inner Temple. Soon he abandoned this for theology and moved to St. Catharine's Hall, Cambridge, where he took his M.A. in 1549, and shortly afterwards was elected Fellow of Pembroke Hall, where J. *Whitgift was among his pupils. He was ordained deacon in 1550 by N. *Ridley, Bp. of London, who, finding him a strong supporter of the Protestant cause and a good preacher, made him his chaplain. Soon after Mary's accession (1553), he was imprisoned on a charge of sedition in the Tower where during 18 months he carried on an extensive correspondence and wrote *The Hurt of Hearing Mass* (first publd. 1580). In a trial before S. *Gardiner and others, he remained steadfast to his Protestantism and was burnt at *Smithfield on 1 July 1555.

A complete edition of his writings was published by the Parker Society (2 vols., 1848, 1853). A. H. Bullen in *D.N.B.*, vi (1886), pp. 157–9.

BRADLAUGH, CHARLES (1833–91), freethinker. He was born at Hoxton, London, the eldest son of a solicitor's clerk and brought up in the C of E. Through contact with the followers of Richard Carlile (1790–1843), a follower of T. *Paine, he became an *atheist, lost his job, and served in the army from 1850 to 1853. On leaving the army he was taken on as a lawyer's clerk. In his spare time he made a name for himself as a lecturer under the title of 'Iconoclast', becoming President of the London Secular Society (1858–90) and conducting constant lecture tours. In 1858 he supported the publishers of a defence of Felice Orsini (1819–58) for attempting to assassinate Napoleon III. From 1860 he conducted the *National Reformer* in defence of free thinking. Prosecution for its alleged sedition, followed by a legal contest as to whether Bradlaugh as an atheist could give evidence (1867–69), led to the passage of the Evidence Amendment Act in 1869. In 1866 he became a member of the Parliamentary Reform League. He also composed the first draft of the Fenian proclamation issued in 1867. In 1876, together with Mrs. A. Besant (1847–1933), who was his co-editor of the *National Reformer* from 1874 to 1885, he entered the lists in support of a Bristol publisher who had issued an American pamphlet, *Fruits of Philosophy*, and been lightly sentenced for its indecency. When Bradlaugh and Mrs. Besant reissued the pamphlet, both were sentenced heavily, but the indictment was quashed on a technical point.

In 1868 Bradlaugh stood for Parliament at Northampton, but was defeated. After two further defeats he was elected M.P. for Northampton in 1880. On the refusal of his plea to affirm or to be allowed to take the oath, he was several times excluded from the House of Commons and re-elected. He was finally allowed to take his seat under the Parliamentary Oaths Act (see *Affirmation*). In his last years he was actively interested in promoting social and political reform in *India and attended the Indian National Congress of 1889. He dissociated himself from Mrs. Besant after she became a *theosophist.

His writings, mostly in pamphlet form, include *The Bible: What it is!* (1861), *The Impeachment of the House of Brunswick* (1872), *Autobiography* (1873), *Perpetual Pensions* (1880), *John Churchill, Duke of Marlborough*

(1884), and *The Rules, Customs and Procedure in the House of Commons* (1889).

Modern ed. of *Humanity's Gain from Unbelief* and Selections from other Works (Thinker's Library, 1929). H. B. Bonner (daughter), *Charles Bradlaugh. A Record of his Life and Work*, with an Account of his Parliamentary Struggle, Politics and Teachings, by J. M. Robertson (2 vols., 1894). Other Lives by A. S. Headingley (London, 1880; rev. ed., 1883), J. M. Robertson (London, 1920), and studies issued by the Centenary Committee (*Champion of Liberty*. Charles Bradlaugh, 1933).

BRADLEY, FRANCIS HERBERT (1846–1924), exponent of Absolute Idealism. He was born at Clapham and educated at Marlborough and at University College, Oxford. From 1870 till his death he was a Fellow of Merton College, Oxford. His first important publication was his brilliant *Ethical Studies* (1876). Next followed *The Principles of Logic* (1883) and, ten years later, *Appearance and Reality* (1893), the most original work in British metaphysics in the 19th cent. Bradley argued that everywhere in the fields of natural science, ethics, religion, &c., contradictions are patent, and that therefore these realms cannot be conceived of as reality. The only true reality is to be found in an all-inclusive experience, the Absolute, wherein all contradictions, including the gulf between subject and object, are finally transcended. As the notions of personality and selfhood are riddled with contradictions, Theism and personal immortality must be rejected. In an essay on 'The Presuppositions of Critical History' (1874) he examined the foundations of historical credibility and rejected the historicity of the Gospels on the ground that their facts were without parallel in our experience. Bradley always maintained that he was indifferent to the sources of his ideas; but he was, like B. *Bosanquet, deeply indebted to G. W. F. *Hegel, partly through the medium of T. H. *Green, who had done much to encourage constructive interest in German Idealism in Oxford. Among his later works are *Essays on Truth and Reality* (1914) and a revised edition of *The Principles of Logic* (1922).

His *Essays* were collected in 2 vols., Oxford, 1935. C. A. Campbell, *Scepticism and Construction: Bradley's Sceptical Principles* (1931); R. Kagey, *The Growth of F. H. Bradley's Logic* (1931); R. W. Church, *Bradley's Dialectic* (1942).

BRADSHAW SOCIETY. See *Henry Bradshaw Society*.

BRADWARDINE, THOMAS (c. 1290–1349), Abp. of *Canterbury. Acc. to his own testimony he was a native of *Chichester. He was educated at Merton College, recently established at *Oxford, and later brought about the total exemption of the university from episcopal jurisdiction. c. 1335 Bradwardine became chaplain to Richard of Bury, Bp. of *Durham, and in 1337 chancellor of *St. Paul's Cathedral. About the same time he was made confessor to Edward III, whom he accompanied on his travels on the Continent during the wars with France. In 1346 he was one of the commissioners who tried to bring about peace between England, France, and Scotland. In 1347 he was made Archdeacon of *Lincoln. In 1349 he was consecrated Abp. of Canterbury at *Avignon, and, having returned to England, died in the same year of the Black Death.

Bradwardine was held in esteem by his contemporaries for his learning, esp. in mathematics and theology. His principal work, *De Causa Dei contra Pelagium* (ed. by H. *Savile, 1618), earned him the title of 'Doctor Profundus'. Under the influence esp. of St. *Augustine, St. *Anselm, and *Duns Scotus, he sought to build up a theological system on evident propositions, utilizing esp. the *Ontological Argument. Against the *Pelagian ideas prevalent among some contemporary theologians, he insisted on the necessity of grace and the 'irresistible' efficacy of the Divine Will, which is the cause of all action, whether necessary or contingent. By this theological Determinism he paved the way for the predestinarian thought of a *Nicholas d'Autrecourt and a John *Wycliffe. His mathematical writings include *De Arithmetica practica, De Geometria speculativa*, and *De Proportionibus*.

His *De Causa Dei contra Pelagium*, ed. H. *Savile (London, 1618), with biogr. introd. (no pagination). S. Hahn, *Thomas Bradwardine und seine Lehre von der menschlichen Willensfreiheit* (*B.G.P.M.*, v, Hft. 2; 1905). J. F. Laun, 'Thomas von Bradwardin, der Schüler Augustins und Lehrer Wiclifs' in *Z.K.G.*, xlvii (1928), pp. 333–56; Fr. tr. in *R.H.P.R.*, ix (1929), pp. 217–33. Überweg, ii, p. 622 f., with bibl., p. 788.

BRADY, NICHOLAS (1659–1726). See *Tate (Nahum) and Brady (Nicholas)*.

BRAGA, Rite of. The form of the Latin rite still in use in the cathedral of Braga (*Civitas Bracarensis*) in the N. of Portugal. There is documentary evidence for its existence from the 14th cent. and it may have owed its compilation to St. Giraldus *c.* 1100. It differs only in its details from the Roman rite. In 1924 *Pius XI confirmed the use of it throughout the archdiocese.

There is a full description in A. A. King, *Notes on the Catholic Liturgies* (1930), pp. 153–207.

BRAMHALL, JOHN (1594–1663), Abp. of *Armagh. Born near Pontefract, Yorks, he was educated at Sidney Sussex College, Cambridge, and ordained *c.* 1616. In 1633 he went to Ireland as *Strafford's chaplain and in 1634 became Bp. of Derry. Here he helped in strengthening episcopacy and maintaining the revenues of the Church of Ireland. In 1642 he retired to England and in 1644 to the Continent, returning for a brief spell to Ireland in 1648. On his permanent return at the *Restoration, he became Abp. of Armagh (1661) and exercised moderation in enforcing the Conformity Laws. He devoted his exile to replying to attacks upon the English Church from three quarters. In *Serpent Salve* (1643) he upheld episcopal and monarchical government against the democratic and presbyterian system of the Puritans, returning to the attack

in *Fair Warning against the Scottish Discipline* (1649). His *Vindication of True Liberty* (1655) was directed against the philosophical materialism and determinism of T. *Hobbes, whom he had met in *Paris; to Hobbes's *Animadversions* in reply, Bramhall answered with *Castigations of Hobbes' Animadversions* (1658), with an appendix on 'The Catching of Leviathan, the Great Whale'. In a third sphere of controversy, with Rome, he published (1653) a reply to T. B. de la Milletière's defence of *Transubstantiation (1651), upholding the Anglican doctrine of the *Real Presence. His attacks on *Ultramontanism were widely welcomed by French Catholics. In 1654 he published his celebrated *A Just Vindication of the Church of England from the Unjust Aspersion of Criminal Schism*. In response to the RC reply to this by Dr. Richard Smith, titular Bp. of *Chalcedon, Bramhall issued his *Replication* (1656), a prayer that he might live to see the Reunion of Christendom.

Collected ed. of Works, with life by H. Vesey (Dublin, 1676); modern ed. by A. W. Haddan in the L.A.C.T. (5 vols., 1842–5), with life from *Biographia Britannica* (vol. i, pp. iii–xv). Much of Bramhall's Correspondence, with other material on his episcopate, is printed in the *Report of the Manuscripts of the late Reginald Rawdon Hastings*, ed. F. Bickley (Historical MSS. Commission, lxxviii), iv (1947), pp. 55–152. W. J. Sparrow Simpson, *Archbishop Bramhall* (1927).

BRANCH THEORY OF THE CHURCH. The theory that, though the Church may have fallen into schism within itself and its several provinces or groups of provinces be out of communion with each other, each may yet be a 'branch' of the one Church of Christ, provided that it continues to hold the faith of the original undivided Church, and to maintain the *Apostolic Succession of its bishops. Such, it is contended by many Anglican theologians, is the condition of the Church at the present time, there being now three main branches, the Roman, the Eastern, and the Anglican Communions. The theory in this precise form was apparently first put forward in the 19th cent. under the inspiration of the *Oxford Movement. It is the basis of W. *Palmer's *Treatise on the Church of Christ* (1838), but only became general and popular later.

BRASSES. A form of monument in which the figure of the dead man, engraved on a flat brass panel, was let into a wall or pavement. These monuments, besides being almost imperishable, had the advantage of taking up much less room than a sculptured figure. They were much used between the 13th and 16th cents. in England, France, Germany, and the Netherlands. Many of them were destroyed by iconoclasts or carried off by plunderers at the Reformation period, but very many still remain, and give much valuable information for the history of their times, esp. about dress, vestments, &c.

H. Haines, *A Manual of Monumental Brasses comprising an Introduction to the Study of these Memorials and a List of those . . . in the British Isles* (2 vols., 1861); M. Stephenson, *A List of Monumental Brasses in the British Isles* (1926;

Appendix, 1938), incl. bibl. W. F. Creeny, *A Book of Facsimiles of Monumental Brasses on the Continent of Europe with Brief Descriptive Notes* (1884). *Oxford Portfolio of Monumental Brasses*, published by the Oxford University Brass Rubbing Society, Parts i–v (1898–1901); Series II, published by the Oxford University Archaeological Society, 1950 ff. H. W. Macklin, *The Brasses of England* ('The Antiquary's Books', 1907); A. C. Bouquet, *Church Brasses, British and Continental*. With some Notes on Incised Stone Slabs and Indents (1956), with bibl. H. Druit, *A Manual of Costume as illustrated by Monumental Brasses* (1906). More popular works include H. W. Macklin, *Monumental Brasses* (1890; frequently republd.); W. E. Gawthorp, *The Brasses of our Homeland Churches* ('The Homeland Pocket Books, No. 14', 1923).

BRAWLING. The offence of creating a disturbance in a church or churchyard. Technically the word applies to any kind of speaking in a church other than that prescribed by the BCP. Brawling has been a punishable offence in England under ecclesiastical jurisdiction since 1551, and under civil procedure since 1860. The services of non-Anglican Churches are similarly protected by the Liberty of Worship Act (1855).

BRAY, THOMAS (1656–1730), founder of the *S.P.C.K. and of the *S.P.G. (qq.v.). A native of Marton, Shropshire, he was educated at Oswestry School and All Souls College, Oxford. In 1690 he became rector of Sheldon, Warws. When an appeal from Maryland reached Henry*Compton, Bp. of London, for assistance in the colony's ecclesiastical organization, the Bishop selected Bray and made him his commissary; but legal complications long delayed his departure. Meanwhile Bray sought out missionaries to accompany him and (in view of the poverty of the clergy) worked out a scheme for the provision of free libraries in the colony. This last project met with such support that he determined to promote it also at home, where before his death he had been instrumental in establishing some 80 parochial libraries. Other of his educational and literary projects took shape in the foundation of the 'Society for Promoting Christian Knowledge' (1698). In 1699 he finally set sail for Maryland. Though well received by the governor, Bray soon found that he could better promote his purposes from Great Britain and before long returned home. Here the work of the S.P.C.K. had developed to such dimensions that Bray founded the 'Society for the Propagation of the Gospel' as a separate society for foreign missions (1701). His endeavours for the appointment of a Bishop for New England, however, were unsuccessful. In 1706 he became vicar of St. Botolph Without, Aldgate. To put the libraries on a permanent basis he created the 'Associates of Dr. Bray' (1723), which is still active. Of his writings the most widely circulated was *A Course of Lectures upon the Church Catechism* (4 vols., 1696).

E. L. Pennington, *The Reverend Thomas Bray* (Church Historical Society Publication No. vii, Philadelphia, 1934). W. K. Lowther Clarke, *Eighteenth Century Piety* (1944), ch. viii, pp. 96–100. J. H. Overton in *D.N.B.* vi (1886), pp. 239–41.

BRAY, The Vicar of. The hero of the well-known ballad whose pretended zeal for each new form of established religion from *Charles II to George I assured his tenure of his benefice. The song, which appears to date from 1720, is apparently based on an anecdote of a certain Vicar of Bray, Berks, to be read in T. *Fuller's Worthies (1662. 'This vicar, being taxed by one for being a turncoat and an inconsistent changeling, "Not so", said he, "for I always kept my principle, which is this, —to live and die the Vicar of Bray" '). Attempts to identify Fuller's cleric have not been successful. Simon Aleyn (Vicar, 1540–88) and Simon Simmonds (Aleyn's predecessor, afterwards Canon of Windsor) alone seem to fit the dates; but there is no contemporary evidence that either was the sort of cleric portrayed in the song. The suggestion that he belongs to Bray, near Dublin, is a modern conjecture wholly without support. The ballad is said to have been composed by an army officer in the time of George I.

C. Kerry, *The History and Antiquities of the Hundred of Bray, in the County of Berks* (privately printed, London, 1861), with text of ballad, ib., p. 185. An anecdote reported on p. 145 suggests that an incidental remark made by *James I to the then Vicar of Bray whom he happened to fall in with at the Bear Inn, Maidenhead ('You shall be Vicar of Bray still, I promise you'), may have been the source of the story.

BRAZEN SERPENT, The. The image set up by Moses in the wilderness, on looking at which those who had been bitten by serpents were healed (Num. 21. 8, 9). Acc. to 2 Kgs. 18. 4 it was destroyed by Hezekiah because the Israelites had been in the practice of burning incense to it. It is mentioned in the NT as a type of the crucified Christ (Jn. 3. 14).

BRAZIL, Christianity in. The conversion of Brazil was effected by *Franciscans and *Benedictines about the middle of the 16th cent. The population has ever since been almost entirely RC. The winning of independence from Portuguese rule in 1822 made no difference to the establishment of the RC faith and its financial support by the state, but in 1889, when a republic had been substituted for the empire, the Church was disestablished, the endowments discontinued, and freedom of religious belief and practice to all bodies guaranteed. But many of the civil laws at this and later dates bore the mark of RC influence.

S. Leite, S.J., *Páginas de história no Brasil* (1937), esp. ch. i, 'Influência religiosa na formação do Brasil', pp. 11–34, and passim. Id., *História da Companhia de Jesus no Brasil* (Lisbon and Rio de Janeiro, 1938 ff., 6 vols. up to 1945). C. Schlitz, S.J., 'Die Folgen der Trennung von Kirche und Staat in Brasilien' in *Stimmen aus Maria-Laach*, lxx (1906), pp. 531–92; J. Lloyd Mecham, *Church and State in Latin America*. A History of Politico-Ecclesiastical Relations (Chapel Hill, N.C., 1934), pp. 305–30. R. Bastide, 'Religion and the Church in Brazil' in T. L. Smith-A. Marchant (edd.), *Brazil*. Portrait of Half a Continent (New York, 1951), ch. xv, pp. 334–55, with bibl. Latourette, iii (1940), pp. 160–7, 236; v (1943), pp. 85 f., 96 f., 106 f., 120–3; and vii (1945), pp. 169 f., 173, 181 f. V. Fuentos in *C.E.*, ii (1907), p. 747 f., s.v., with bibl.; J. Serrano in *D.H.G.E.*, x (1938), cols. 565–89, s.v. 'Brésil'; M. Cesar de Lima in *E.C.*, iii (1950), cols. 32–5, s.v. 'Brasile'.

BREAD, Leavened and Unleavened. In the *Eucharistic rite, the Eastern Churches (except the *Armenian) customarily use leavened bread, whereas Catholics in the W. use unleavened bread. The difference in practice developed gradually; but by the time of the Schism of 1054, the divergence between E. and W. was a leading cause of dissension. In the C of E the BCP of 1549 ordered the continuance of unleavened bread, while that of 1552 permitted ('it shall suffice'), without enjoining, leavened. The '*Injunctions' of Queen *Elizabeth (1559) attempted to enforce again the use of unleavened bread, but the Book of 1661 left the rubric of 1552 practically unaltered. The *Judicial Committee of the Privy Council, however, has twice ruled that common bread is directed by the rubric. Recent revisions in various parts of the Anglican Communion expressly allow the use of either. Leavened bread is generally used by Nonconformists.

Among the earliest undisputed witnesses for unleavened bread are *Alcuin (ep. 90, ad fratres Lugdunenses, A.D. 798; *PL*, c, 289) and his pupil, *Rabanus Maurus (*Instit. Cler.* i, 31). J. *Sirmond, S.J., 'Disquisitio de Azymo', first publd. in his *Historia Poenitentiae Publicae* (Paris, 1651). R. M. Woolley, *The Bread of the Eucharist* (Alcuin Club Tracts, xi, 1897). F. *Cabrol, O.S.B., in *D.A.C.L.*, i (pt. 2; 1907), cols. 3254–60, s.v. 'Azymes', with good bibl.

BREAKSPEAR, NICOLAS. See *Hadrian IV*.

BREASTPLATE OF ST. PATRICK. An ancient Irish hymn, generally familiar through Mrs. C. F. Alexander's translation (1889), beginning 'I bind unto myself today The strong Name of the Trinity'. It was doubtless the 'Canticum Scotticum', mentioned in a note in the 'Book of *Armagh' as current before the 9th cent. Its ascription to St. *Patrick (q.v.), though possible, is uncertain. The author invokes the Trinity, Angels, Prophets, the powers of heaven and earth, and finally Christ Himself to protect him against the dominion of evil. Attention was first drawn to the hymn by G. Petrie in 1839. It was issued in a metrical English rendering, mainly the work of Whitley Stokes (1830–1909), in J. H. Todd, *St. Patrick, Apostle of Ireland* (1864).

The text survives in three ancient MSS.: (1) the 11th cent. Irish *Liber Hymnorum* at *Trinity College, Dublin, (2) a 14th or 15th cent. copy of the Tripartite Life of St. Patrick in the *Bodleian Library, Oxford (Rawl. B. 592), and (3) a MS. in the British Museum (Egerton 93). It was first publd., with an Engl. tr., by Dr. G. Petrie in 'On the History and Antiquities of Tara Hill' in *Transactions of the Royal Irish Academy*, xviii (1839), pp. 56–68; crit. edd. with metrical Eng. trr. in J. H. Bernard–R. Atkinson (edd.), *The Irish Liber Hymnorum* (H.B.S., xiii–xiv, 1898), i, pp. 133–6, and ii, pp. 49–51, with notes, pp. 208–12, and W. Stokes–J. Strachan (edd.), *Thesaurus Palaeohibernicus*, ii (1903), pp. 354–8; Eng. tr. by W. Stokes repr. in J. H. Todd, *St. Patrick, Apostle of Ireland* (1864), pp. 426–9; Eng. tr., based on that of R. Atkinson, with notes, in N. J. D. White, *St. Patrick*. His Writings and Life (S.P.C.K., 1920), pp. 61–7.

BREDA, Declaration of. The declaration made by *Charles II at Breda (Holland) on 4/14 Apr. 1660, immediately before the Restor-ation. He expressed *inter alia* his readiness to grant a 'liberty to tender consciences' among his subjects in matters of religion not affecting the peace of the kingdom.

Text in Gee–Hardy, No. cxiv, pp. 585–8. See also general works on Charles II (q.v.).

BREECHES BIBLE, The. A popular name for the *Geneva Bible of 1560 from its rendering of Gen. 3. 7, where A.V. has 'aprons'.

BREMOND, HENRI (1865–1933), French spiritual writer. He entered the *Jesuit Order in 1882, and after spending his novitiate in England was ordained priest in 1892. In 1899 he was appointed editor of the Jesuit periodical *Études*. In 1904 he left the order to devote himself entirely to literary activities. His principal work, his voluminous *Histoire littéraire du sentiment religieux en France* (11 vols., 1915–32), is a history of French spirituality chiefly in the 17th cent. in the form of a series of essays on outstanding religious person-alities. Its original and penetrating descriptions of the life of souls are illustrated by numerous quotations, often from forgotten and almost in-accessible contemporary sources. A brilliant stylist, Bremond draws captivating pictures esp. of less well-known personalities such as Mme B. A. *Acarie, J. *Surin, or the Ursuline nun, *Mary of the Incarnation. His judgement on representatives of a more active and ascetical type was in general less sympathetic. Among his other works is an essay on J. H. *Newman, *Newman, essai de biographie psychologique* (1906), and an exquisite little study, *Prière et poésie* (1926).

H. Hogarth, *Henri Bremond. The Life and Work of a Devout Humanist* (S.P.C.K., 1950). M. Martin Du Gard, *De Sainte-Beuve à Fénelon: Henri Bremond* (1927); A. Autin, *Henri Bremond* (Publicistes Chrétiens, 1947). A. *Loisy, *George Tyrrell et Henri Bremond* (1936).

BRENDAN, St. (484–577 or 583), also 'St. Brenainn', Abbot of Clonfert. The legend of the 'Navigation of St. Brendan' (c. 1050), widely popular in the Middle Ages, describes his visit to the 'northern and western islands' perhaps the Orkneys and Hebrides. The tradition that he founded the monastery of Cluain Fearta (Clonfert, in Co. Galway) may quite well be true. The churches of Brendon in Devonshire and Brancepeth in Co. Durham are dedicated to him. Feast day, 16 May. [He is to be distinguished from his contemporary St. Brendan of Birr (c. 490–573), whose feast is kept on 29 Nov.]

Lat. text of the 'Navigation of St. Brendan' pr. from ancient Paris MSS. by A. Jubinal, *La Légende latine de S. Brandaines* (1836), pp. 1–56; also ed. C. Schröder (Erlangen, 1871), and, with other material, by [Card.] P. F. Moran, *Acta Sancti Brendani* (Dublin, 1872). Old Ital. versions ed. by P. Villari, *Antiche leggende e tradizioni che illustrano la Divina commedia* (1865), pp. 82–120, repr. in G. Battelli, *Le più belle leggende cristiane* (1924), pp. 471–92. Com-parative ed. of texts by C. Wahlund, *Die altfranzösische Prosaübersetzung von Brendans Meerfahrt* (Skrifter utgifna af K. Humanistiska Vetenskaps-Samfundet i Upsala, IV, 3,1900). Tours MS. (Bibl. Municip., 1008) of Ital. version ed. E. G. R. Waters, *An Old Italian Version of the Navigatio Sancti Brendani* (Publications of Philological Society, x;

1931), with reff. D. O'Donoghue, *Brendaniana*. St. Brendan the Voyager in Story and Legend (Dublin, 1893); G. A. Little, *Brendan the Navigator*. An Interpretation (1945).

BRENT, CHARLES HENRY (1862–1929), Anglican '*Faith and Order' leader. Born at Newcastle, Ontario, Canada, he studied at Trinity College, Toronto, and was ordained priest in 1887. From 1888 to 1891 he was engaged in pastoral work in Boston, Mass. In 1901 he became the Protestant Episcopal Bp. of the Philippine Islands, and in 1918 of Western New York. From 1917 to 1919 he was the Chief of Chaplains of the American Expeditionary Force in Europe. From his first months in the Philippines Brent energetically combated the opium traffic. In 1909 he was President of the Opium Conference at Shanghai and in 1923 represented the U.S.A. on the League of Nations Narcotics Committee. In his later years his chief work was for the *Ecumenical (Faith and Order) Movement, in which he was one of the most ardent spirits. On returning from the *Edinburgh Conference of 1910 to the U.S.A. he induced the General Convention of the Protestant Episcopal Church to convene a 'World Conference on Faith and Order', and when the Conference ultimately met at *Lausanne in 1927, Brent was its President.

F. W. Kates, *Charles Henry Brent* (1948).

BRENTANO, FRANZ (1838–1917), Austrian philosopher. Ordained to the RC priesthood in 1864, he was appointed Privatdozent at Würzburg in 1866. In 1873, chiefly through intellectual difficulties about the Trinity, he separated himself from the Church. Through lectures at Vienna from 1880 to 1915 he exercised great influence on some of the leading philosophers of the next generation, among them E. *Husserl and A. von Meinong. His high regard for *Scholastic and *Aristotelian doctrines, which he had inherited from his RC training, led him to be critical of all forms of Idealism, and some of the anti-idealistic currents in 20th cent. philosophy in German-speaking countries derived directly from his teaching. His two principal writings were *Psychologie vom empirischen Standpunkt* (vol. i [all issued], 1874) and *Vom Ursprung sittlicher Erkenntnis* (1889; Eng. trans., 1902). His still unpublished works include an ambitious treatise on Theistic *Metaphysics.

A satisfactory edition of Brentano's writings is still a great desideratum.

BRENZ, JOHANN (1499–1570), reformer of Württemberg. He was born at Weildersstadt, studied at Heidelberg under *Oecolampadius, and in 1518 came under the influence of M. *Luther. In 1522 he was appointed Preacher at the church of St. Michael in Schwäbisch Hall and from now on actively supported the Reformation, preaching against the Mass and the cult of the saints. He was so successful that by the Hall *Kirchenordnung* of 1526 the Reformation in Württemberg was completed. In 1525 he refused, like Luther,

to support the insurgents in the Peasants' War. Against Oecolampadius he insisted in his *Syngramma Suevicum* (21 Oct. 1525) on the *Real Presence in the Eucharist and thus ensured the acceptance of the Lutheran teaching over the greater part of Württemberg. At the Colloquy of *Marburg (1529) he made the acquaintance of Duke Ulrich of Württemberg, who from now on gave him active support. Brenz took a leading part in the reconstitution of the university of Tübingen (1536–7). After the *Augsburg Interim (1548) Brenz was forced to leave Württemberg for a time. He was invited by T. *Cranmer to England but he refused. In 1553 he became Provost of the Stiftskirche at Stuttgart. He became involved in controversies with some of the leading *Calvinists (T. *Beza, H. *Bullinger), though in matters of Church Order he inclined to the Calvinist position. He was the author of two Catechisms (1527, 1535), many published sermons, and several controversial writings.

No modern ed. of his Works. Incomplete early ed., 8 vols. fol., Tübingen, 1576–90. T. Pressel, *Anecdota Brentiana*. Ungedruckte Briefe und Bedenken von Johannes Brenz (Tübingen, 1868). Life by J. Hartmann and C. Jaeger (2 vols., Hamburg, 1840–2). W. E. Köhler, *Bibliographia Brentiana* (Berlin, 1904); id., *Brentiana und andere Reformatoria* (Archiv für Reformationsgeschichte, Jahrgg. 9–11, 13, 14, 16, 19, 21, 22, 24, 26; 1912–29). T. Wotschke, *Brenz als Katechet* (1900). J. Hartmann and G. Bossert in *P.R.E.* (ed. 3), iii (1897), pp. 376–88, and J. Rauscher in *R.G.G.* (ed. 2), i (1927), col. 1242 f., both with bibl.

BREST-LITOVSK, Union of. The union concluded in 1596 between the *Ruthenian and the RC Churches, with the approbation of Pope *Clement VIII and Sigismund III of Poland. By it, the Metropolitan of Kiev, the Ruthenian bishops, and some millions of Christians, all of the Byzantine rite, joined the RC Church, with permission to retain their liturgy. During succeeding years the union was opposed both by Russia, which succeeded in bringing large numbers of Ruthenians back to the Orthodox Church, and also by the Latin Poles, who despised and feared Byzantine Ruthenians.

The official documents are printed by A. Theiner, *Vetera Monumenta Poloniae et Lithuaniae Gentiumque Finitimarum Historiam Illustrantia*, iii (Rome, 1863), No. clxxxv, pp. 232–49; further papal letters, pp. 269–73. E. Likowski, *Historya Unii Kościoła Ruskiego z Kościołem Rzymskim* (in Polish, Poznań, 1875); id., *Union de l'Église grecque-ruthène en Pologne avec l'Église romaine, conclue à Brest, en Lithuanie, en 1596* (1903); J. Pelesz, *Geschichte der Union der ruthenischen Kirche mit Rom von den aeltesten Zeiten bis auf die Gegenwart* (2 vols., 1881). J. Ostrowski in *D.H.G.E.*, x (1938), cols. 615–18.

BRETHREN OF THE COMMON LIFE, The (Lat. 'Fratres Communis Vitae'). An association founded in the 14th cent. to foster a higher level of Christian life and devotion. The original leader was G. de *Groote (q.v.), a canon of Utrecht, who resigned his prebend to travel through the Netherlands and preach against clerical abuses and call men to repentance. He demanded no vows from his disciples but left them free, whether clerics or laymen, to continue in their ordinary vocations. His followers developed a lofty spirituality.

They laid great stress on teaching, founding schools all over the Netherlands, and later in Germany, where a general education was offered, unsurpassed in quality and without fees. To supply books for their schools, many of their members engaged in copying MSS., and later in printing. On the death of de Groote (1384), the leadership of the Brethren was assumed by *Florentius Radwijns. Before long a group of these disciples adopted a rule and organized themselves as 'Augustinian Canons'. Among the 'Brethren' were I. *Busch, *Thomas à Kempis, Pope *Hadrian VI, and Gabriel *Biel. *Nicholas of Cusa and Rudolph Agricola (1443–85) also studied in their schools, and thus the movement exercised considerable influence on the New Learning. By the end of the 17th cent. the rise of modern universities and diocesan seminaries had led to their extinction. See also *Devotio Moderna* and *Windesheim*.

S. Kettlewell, *Thomas à Kempis and the Brethren of the Common Life* (2 vols., 1882). K. Grube, *Gerhard Groot und seine Stiftungen* (1883). E. Barnikol, *Studien zur Geschichte der Brüder von gemeinsamen Leben* (1917). A. Hyma, *The Christian Renaissance*. A History of the 'Devotio Moderna' (New York, 1925), with bibl. pp. 477–94. Pourrat, ii, pp. 381–9. S. H. Gem in *H.E.R.E.*, ii (1909), pp. 839–42, with bibl. L. Schulze in *P.R.E.* (ed. 3), iii (1897), pp. 472–507, s.v. 'Brüder des gemeinsamen Lebens', with full bibl. See also bibl. to *Devotio Moderna*.

BRETHREN OF THE FREE SPIRIT.
A name often applied by medieval writers to the members of various mystical sects which professed to be independent of ecclesiastical authority and live in the freedom of the Spirit. The teaching of these sects was usually more or less *pantheistic. They appear to date from the 13th cent., but the widespread view that they derived from *Amalric of Bena is very disputable. Probably they never had more than a rudimentary organization, if, indeed, they possessed any at all.

F. Vernet in *D.T.C.*, vi (1920), cols. 800–9, with bibl.

BRETHREN OF THE LORD, The.
References to 'the Lord's brethren', who include *James, Joseph, Simon, and *Jude, occur at Mk. 6. 3, &c., Jn. 7. 3, Acts 1. 14, 1 Cor. 9. 5. They may have been (a) sons of the Virgin *Mary and *Joseph, born after Christ. This is the most natural inference from the NT, and was accepted by *Tertullian and probably by *Hegesippus. But when put forward by *Helvidius, c. 382, it was rejected by St. *Jerome, who, apparently voicing the general opinion of the Church, maintained the perpetual virginity of the Virgin Mary. Hence St. Jerome held that (b) the Lord's 'brethren' were the sons of *Mary, 'the mother of James and Joses' (Mk. 15. 40), whom he identified with the wife of Clopas and sister of the Virgin Mary (Jn. 19. 25, R.V.). They may have been, however, (c) sons of Joseph by a former marriage (the view of St. *Epiphanius and the E. Church), or (d) acc. to a modern suggestion, sons of *Mary, 'mother of James and Joses' (not here identified with the Virgin Mary's sister), and Clopas, who acc. to

Hegesippus was the brother of Joseph. See *Marys in the NT* (3) and (4), and *Cleopas*.

J. B. *Lightfoot, *St. Paul's Epistle to the Galatians* (1865), pp. 241–74, with reff. to earlier literature. J. B. Mayor, *The Epistle of St. James* (1892), pp. v–xxv. Id., in *H.D.B.*, i (1898), pp. 320–6, s.v. with bibl.; T. *Zahn, 'Brüder und Vettern Jesu' in *Forschungen zur Geschichte des neutestamentlichen Kanons und der altkirchlichen Literatur*, vi (1900), II, pp. 225–364.

BRETSCHNEIDER, KARL GOTTLIEB
(1776–1848), German theologian. In 1816 he became *General-Superintendent at Gotha. Of his many writings, the only one of permanent interest is his *Probabilia* (1820), in which he anticipated later NT criticism by questioning the historicity of the Fourth Gospel on the grounds of its divergence from the other three. In 1834 he founded the *Corpus Reformatorum*, a series of reprints of the works of the 16th cent. Reformers, for which he himself edited the works of P. *Melanchthon.

Autobiography posthumously ed. Horst Bretschneider (Gotha, 1851); id., (ed.), *Anhang zu Karl Gottlieb Bretschneider's Selbstbiographie* (1852). K. R. Hagenbach in *P.R.E.* (ed. 3), iii (1897), pp. 389–91, s.v.

BRETT, THOMAS
(1667–1744), *Nonjuror. He was educated at Queens' and Corpus Christi Colleges, Cambridge, and ordained deacon in 1690. After holding several livings he was appointed rector of Ruckinge in 1705. Having so far had no scruples in taking the oath, he resolved, after H. *Sacheverell's trial, never to do so again. On the accession of George I (1714) he consequently resigned his living (1715) and was received as a Nonjuror by G. *Hickes, after whose death he was consecrated bishop in 1716. From 1716 to 1725 he took part in the abortive negotiations for reunion of his party with the Greek Church. He was involved in several controversies, esp. in that on the *Usages which broke out in 1715 among the Nonjurors themselves. As an eminent liturgical scholar with a particular interest in the E. liturgies, he insisted on the explicit oblation of the Eucharistic elements to the Father and on the *Epiclesis of the Holy Ghost, but reckoned the other two controversial points, viz. prayer for the dead and the mixed chalice, as of minor importance. His principal work is his *Dissertation on the Ancient Liturgies* (1720), which is still valuable, though it regards the so-called *Clementine Liturgy (i.e. *Apostolic Constitutions VIII) as authentic. Among his other works are *The Divine Right of Episcopacy* (1718), *Discourses concerning the Ever Blessed Trinity* (1720), and answers to J. *Bingham's *History of Lay Baptism* (1712) and to B. *Hoadly's *Plain Account of the Sacrament* (1735).

L. Stephen in *D.N.B.*, vi (1886), p. 285 f., s.v.

BREVIARY.
The liturgical book containing the Psalms, hymns, lessons, &c., to be recited in the Divine *Office (*horae canonicae*) of the RC Church. In early times the various parts of the *hours were distributed in different books such as the *Psaltery, *Hymnary,

*Lectionary, &c., but from the 11th cent. they began to be combined in one book. Modern breviaries are usually in four volumes, divided acc. to the four seasons of the year.

The primitive office had consisted almost exclusively of Psalms and Scripture Lessons. Its construction is still visible in the modern office for *Easter and its *octave, which lacks almost all later additions. Under the influence of St. *Ambrose, hymns and *antiphons were added, and with St. *Benedict *responsories, *canticles, *collects, and other elaborations appeared. The spread of monasticism led liturgical prayer to develop rapidly, and by the 8th cent. the cycle of hours, from *Lauds to *Compline for the Day Office, and *Matins for the Night Office, had been fixed. Originally the office allowed for the recitation of the complete Psalter each week, and the greater part of Holy Scripture during the year. But in the Middle Ages lives of the saints tended to replace the Scripture readings, and their feasts interfered with the daily succession of the Psalms. In the 16th cent. attempts at reform were made, notably by Card. F. de *Quignon (1535), but his Breviary (*Breviarium S. Crucis*) was never officially approved by the RC Church. The Council of *Trent, which provided for the abolition of the more apocryphal legends and reduced the interruption of the ferial office by the saints' days, led to the *Breviarium Romanum*, issued in Rome in 1568 under *Pius V. Smaller reforms were made under several later Popes, but the attempted general revision of *Benedict XIV was prevented by his death in 1758. Throughout the 19th cent. a thorough reform was repeatedly advocated and eventually carried out by *Pius X, who in 1911 issued the present Breviary. The Psalms, still recited every week, were redistributed, and only the greater feasts were permitted to interfere with their regular sequence. The length of the offices was also considerably shortened.

All RC priests and clerics in *major orders, as well as all professed religious whose rule prescribes it, are obliged to the daily recitation of the Breviary under pain of sin. As a rule Matins and Lauds are said on the previous day 'by anticipation'. The various religious orders have their own breviaries which differ somewhat from the Roman one, esp. in the matter of saints' days, whereas the *Benedictines have kept their more primitive traditions in the *Monastic Breviary.

J. Grancolas, *Commentaire historique sur le bréviaire romain* (2 vols., 1727). F. *Probst, *Brevier und Breviergebet* (1854); P. *Batiffol, *Histoire du bréviaire romain* (1893; Eng. tr., 1898); S. Bäumer, O.S.B., *Geschichte des Breviers* (1895; Fr. tr. with addition by R. Biron, O.S.B., 2 vols., 1905); C. Callewaert, *De Brevarii Romani Liturgia* (ed. 2; Liturgicae Institutiones, ii; Bruges, 1939). L. Eisenhofer, *Handbuch der katholischen Liturgik*, ii (1933), pp. 481–500. H. *Leclercq, O.S.B., in *D.A.C.L.*, ii (pt. 1, 1910), cols. 1262–1316, s.v., with bibl.; F. Oppenheim in *E.C.*, iii (1950), cols. 81–6, s.v., with further bibl.

BRIDE, St. (d. *c.* 523), also 'Brigid', Abbess of Kildare, 'the Mary of the Gael'. Though she is always regarded with great veneration in *Ireland, the traditions about her are conflicting and little can be said with certainty. Acc. to the common view, she was born at Faughart, near Dundalk, of parents baptized by St. *Patrick, and showed marks of sanctity from her early years. Under the direction of the Bishop St. Mel (acc. to others St. Machalleus) she took the veil, acc. to one account received episcopal orders, and founded the first nunnery in Ireland at 'Cill-Dara' (the Church of the Oak), now Kildare. By her prayers and miracles she is reputed to have exercised a potent influence on the growth of the early Irish Church. She is accounted with St. Patrick the Second Patron Saint of Ireland, and her name in the form Brigid or Bridget has become a very common Irish girl's name. Feast day, 1 Feb.

Irish life from the Book of *Lismore, ed. W. Stokes (Anecdota Oxoniensia, Mediaeval and Modern Series, v, Oxford, 1890), pp. 34–53, with Eng. tr., 182–200; Lat. lives in J. Colganus, O.F.M. (ed.), *Trias Thaumaturga* (Louvain, 1647), pp. 515–640, and in *AA.SS.*, Feb. I (1658), pp. 99–185. The hymn composed by St. Broccan Cloen (d. 650) in her honour, which is the only early authority, is ed. by J. H. *Bernard–R. Atkinson, The Irish *Liber Hymnorum*, i (H.B.S., xiii; 1898). pp. 112–28; introd. in ii (H.B.S., xiv; 1898), pp. 37 f., with Eng. tr., pp. 40–6. M. Esposito, 'On the Earliest Latin Life of St. Brigid of Kildare' in *Proceedings of the Royal Irish Academy*, xxx, Section C (1912), pp. 307–26. J. Kenney, *The Sources for the Early History of Ireland*, i (Records of Civilization, New York, 1929), pp. 356–63. T. Olden in *D.N.B.*, vi (1886), pp. 340–2, s.v. 'Brigit, St.'.

BRIDGES, ROBERT SEYMOUR (1844–1930), poet laureate. Educated at Eton and Corpus Christi College, Oxford, he practised for some years as a physician, holding various hospital appointments. Meanwhile he had been writing poetry, and in 1882 abandoned medicine to devote himself to literary interests and music. For most of the rest of his life he lived at Yattendon, Berks (1882–1904), and on Boar's Hill, Oxford (1907–30). In 1913 he became Poet Laureate. Already as a boy at Eton, he had been attracted to Catholic ideals through the influence of V. S. S. Coles (later Principal of Pusey House, Oxford) and D. M. Dolben. In mature life he tended to reject all rigid dogmatic belief, but retained strong Christian sympathies. His most considerable work, the *Testament of Beauty* (1929), was a philosophical poem in 'loose Alexandrine' metre, which sought, in language at once elevated and allusive, to reconcile scientific knowledge with Christian faith. He was also interested in Church music, and did much to raise the standard of hymnody in the English parish churches; and in the *Yattendon Hymnal* (1895–9), which embodied his ideals, he revived many fine 16th and 17th cent. melodies. His hymn-book was extensively drawn on in the *English Hymnal* (1906) and the *Oxford Hymn Book* (1908). He was also one of the founders of the 'Society for Pure English'. His other publications include *The Spirit of Man* (1915), an anthology; and the first collected edition (1918) of the *Poems* of his friend G. M. *Hopkins.

Poetical Works publ. in 6 vols., London, 1896–1905; also, omitting the eight dramas, but with other new material, ib., 1912; enlarged ed., 1936; and, incl. *Testament of Beauty*, 1954. E. Thompson, *Robert Bridges, 1844-1930* (1944). N. C. Smith, *Notes* on The Testament of Beauty (1931); G. S. Gordon, *Robert Bridges* (The Rede Lecture for 1931; 1946). N. C. Smith in *D.N.B., 1922-1930* (1937), pp. 115-19. G. L. McKay, *A Bibliography of Robert Bridges* (New York and London, 1933); S. N. Smith in *C.B.E.L.*, iii (1940), pp. 323-5.

BRIDGET OF SWEDEN, St.

BRIDGET OF SWEDEN, St. (*c.* 1303-73), founder of the *Brigittines. The daughter of one of the wealthiest landowners of Sweden, she married at the age of 13 and had eight children, one of whom was St. *Catherine of Sweden. Between 1341 and 1343 she made a pilgrimage to *Compostela with her husband, who shortly after their return died in the *Cistercian monastery at Alvastra. Thus freed from worldly ties, Bridget devoted herself assiduously to religion. *C.* 1346 she founded the Order of *Brigittines at Vadstena in Sweden. In 1349 she went to Rome to obtain confirmation for her order from the Pope, and resided there, except for occasional pilgrimages, till her death. She aided St. *Catherine of Siena in preparing the way for the return of *Gregory XI from *Avignon to Rome (1377). The revelations which she was held to have received in visions were held in great repute during the Middle Ages. She was canonized in 1391. Feast day, 8 Oct. (though she died 23 July). See also *Brigittine Order*.

Her 'Revelations' were publd. at Lübeck, 1492. The edition 'olim a Card. Turrecremata recognita et approbata, et a Consalvo Durante Epo. Ferettrano notis illustrata' (Rome, 2 vols., 1628) is considered the best. 14th-cent. Swedish tr., with other material, ed. by G. E. Klemming, *Heiliga Birgittas Uppenbarekser* (5 vols. bound in 4, Samlingar af Svenska Fornskrift Sällskapet, 1857-84); 15th cent. Eng. tr. ed. P. Cummings (*E.E.T.S.*, clxxviii, 1929). Life by Skänning and Peter of Alvastra, her confessors, ed. C. Annerstedt, *Scriptores Rerum Svecicarum Medii Aevi*, iii, pt. 2 (Upsala, 1871), pp. 185-206. Life by Birger, Abp. of Upsala, in *A.A.SS.*, Oct. IV (1780), pp. 485-93. G. E. Klemming, *Birgitta-Literatur* (1883). I. Collijn (ed.), *Acta et Processus Canonizationis Beate Birgitte* (Samlinger utgivna av Svenska Fornskrift Sällskapet, Ser. 2. Latina Skriften. Band i, Uppsala, 1924-31). Modern lives by F. J. M. A. Partridge (Quarterly Series, lxv, London, 1888), C. de Flavigny (Paris, 1892), E. Fogelkou (Stockholm, 1919; Germ. tr., 1929), E. Peacy (member of the Brigittine Order, London, [1934]) and J. Jorgensen (Copenhagen, 1943; Eng. tr., 2 vols., 1954). E. Sjöqvist–I. Cecchetti in *E.C.*, iii (1950), cols. 92-9, s.v. 'Brigida'.

BRIDGEWATER TREATISES, The.

BRIDGEWATER TREATISES, The. Eight treatises, published between 1833 and 1840 upon various aspects of 'the power, wisdom, and goodness of God, as manifested in the Creation'. They were produced under the will of the 8th Earl of Bridgewater (1756-1829), who left a sum of £8,000 to the President of the Royal Society, to be paid to one or more authors selected by him to write and publish treatises on this subject. The eight authors chosen were: T. Chalmers, J. Kidd, W. Whewell, Sir C. Bell, P. M. Roget, W. *Buckland, W. Kirby, W. Prout. The 'Ninth Bridgewater Treatise' (1837) by C. Babbage does not properly belong to the series.

BRIGGS, CHARLES AUGUSTUS

BRIGGS, CHARLES AUGUSTUS (1841-1913), OT scholar. After graduating at Union Theological Seminary, New York, he studied in Berlin, was for some years a Presbyterian pastor, and in 1874 became professor of Hebrew at Union Seminary. As editor (1880-1890) of the *Presbyterian Review* he became known as a vigorous exponent of *Higher Criticism of the OT on the lines of W. R. *Smith in Scotland. His inaugural address as professor of Biblical theology in 1891 led to his trial for heresy; and though acquitted by the New York presbytery, he was suspended by the General Assembly in 1893 from clerical functions. After taking orders in the *Protestant Episcopal Church in 1899, he devoted much energy to advocating Christian reunion. He was one of the editors both of the *International Critical Commentaries* and of the standard Hebrew *Lexicon*.

Essays in Modern Theology and Related Subjects gathered and published as a Testimonial to Charles Augustus Briggs . . . on the Completion of his Seventieth Year, January 18, 1911 (New York, 1911), with bibl. of his chief works (to 1909) by C. R. Gillett, pp. 327-47. His lectures on the *History of the Study of Theology* (delivered at the *Union Theological Seminary, New York, 1912-13) were posthumously publd. by his daughter, Emily Grace Briggs (2 vols., London, 1916). Obituary notices by H. P. Smith in *American Journal of Theology*, xvii (1913), pp. 497-508, and in *Expository Times*, xxv (1913-14), pp. 294-8. A. C. McGiffert in *Dict. Amer. Biog.*, iii (1929), p. 40 f., s.v., with further bibl.

BRIGHT, WILLIAM

BRIGHT, WILLIAM (1824-1901), Church historian and hymn-writer. He was Fellow of University College, Oxford, from 1847 to 1868, Tutor of Trinity College, Glenalmond, from 1851 to 1858, and (in succession to H. L. *Mansel) Regius professor of ecclesiastical history and Canon of Christ Church, Oxford, from 1868 until his death. He was a devoted student of the Fathers and a keen High Churchman. He wrote several well-known hymns, among them, 'We know Thee, Who Thou art' and the fine Eucharistic hymn, 'And now, O Father, mindful of the love'. He was also a forceful and vivid lecturer. His historical writings include his *History of the Church, 313-451 A.D.* (1860), *Early English Church History* (1878), and *The Age of the Fathers* (2 vols., ed. W. *Lock), 1903).

Selected Letters . . . with a Memoir, ed. B. J. Kidd (1903).

BRIGHTMAN, FRANK EDWARD

BRIGHTMAN, FRANK EDWARD (1856-1932), liturgist. From 1884 to 1903 he was a librarian of Pusey House, Oxford, and from 1902 until his death a Fellow of Magdalen. A meticulously exact scholar, he issued in 1896 *Liturgies Eastern and Western*, Vol. I, 'Eastern', a new edition of the sections on the E. Church in C. E. Hammond's book (1878) on the subject. Its learned notes were the fruit of extended researches and several journeys to monasteries in the East. (Vol. II was never published.) His *English Rite* (1915) is a laborious and valuable edition of the different versions of the BCP, arranged in parallel columns. From 1904 to 1932 he was joint-editor of the *Journal of Theological Studies*, where his wide knowledge was constantly at the disposal of the contributors. Brightman was a strong High

Churchman, whose counsel was much sought after by the leaders of the C of E.

Obituary by H. N. Bate in *Proceedings of the British Academy*, xix (1933), pp. 345–50.

BRIGID, St., of Ireland. See *Bride, St.*

BRIGITTINE ORDER (*Ordo Sanctissimi Salvatoris*). The order founded by St. *Bridget of Sweden (q.v.). Its members were originally organized in double communities of men and women, using the same chapel, and living in separate parts of the monastery; but this arrangement was given up in the 16th cent. The Brigittines are bound to poverty like other religious, except that they may possess any number of books for study. The few surviving houses are in Germany, Holland, England, and Spain. Those in Spain consist of 'Brigittines of the Recollection', who live under a special modification of the Rule made to suit Spanish conditions by the Venerable Marina de Escobar in the 17th cent. A famous English Brigittine house was that of Syon, founded at Isleworth, Middlesex, by Henry V in 1415.

[P. Helyot], *Histoire des ordres monastiques, religieux, militaires et des congrégations séculières de l'un et de l'autre sexe, qui ont esté établies jusqu'à présent*, iv (1715), pp. 25–44; Heimbucher, i, pp. 620–5. J. R. Fletcher, *The Story of the English Bridgettines of Syon Abbey* (1933). B. Williamson, *The Bridgettine Order*. Its Foundress, History and Spirit (1922; brief). P. Debongnie, C.SS.R., in *D.H.G.E.*, x (1938), cols. 728–31, s.v. 'Brigittins', with bibl.

BRITISH AND FOREIGN BIBLE SOCIETY. The largest of the Bible Societies. It was founded in London in 1804 for the printing and distribution of the Bible at home and abroad, on account of representations made to the *Religious Tract Society by Charles Williams, a preacher, of Bala. A strictly interdenominational body, by its constitution its committee is composed of 36 laymen (including 6 foreign members), the English members consisting of 15 Anglicans and 15 members of other denominations. It resisted both Bp. Herbert Marsh's wish to include the circulation of the BCP in its work, as well as the Baptist bias which William *Carey sought to introduce. It has translated the Bible (excluding the Apocrypha) into almost every known tongue.

J. Owen, *The History of the Origin and First Ten Years of the British and Foreign Bible Society* (3 vols., 1816–20); W. Canton, *A History of the British and Foreign Bible Society* (5 vols., 1904–10); G. Browne, *The History of the British and Foreign Bible Society, from its Institution in 1804 to its Jubilee in 1854* (2 vols., 1859). H. Morris, *The Founders and First Three Presidents of the Bible Society* [1895]; J. A. Patten, *These Remarkable Men* (1945). T. H. Darlow and H. F. Moule, *Historical Catalogue of the Printed Editions of Holy Scripture in the Library of the British and Foreign Bible Society* (2 vols., bound in 4, 1903–11).

BRITISH CHURCH. See *Celtic Church.*

BRITISH COUNCIL OF CHURCHES. An organization created in 1942 to further common Christian action in Great Britain. Its 'Articles of Amalgamation' (23 Sept. 1943) provide for 112 members, with official representatives of the C of E, the Church of *Scotland, the *Free Churches, the Churches of *Wales and *Ireland, the *Salvation Army, the Society of *Friends, the *Unitarian and Free Christian Churches, and five interdenominational organizations. The first President was W. *Temple, succeeded in 1945 by Abp. Geoffrey Fisher.

Articles of Amalgamation in G. K. A. Bell, *Documents on Christian Unity*. Third Series, 1930–48 (1948), No. 187.

'BRITISH CRITIC, The'. A theological quarterly which ran from 1827 to 1843. It supported the cause of the *Tractarian theologians, most of whom contributed articles to it. In its later years it came increasingly under the influence of those in the Tractarian Movement most in sympathy with Rome.

BRITISH ISRAEL THEORY. The theory that the British people is ultimately descended from the ten Israelite tribes which were taken captive into Assyria in 722–721 B.C., and thereafter wholly disappeared from Hebrew history. It is often found in conjunction with pronounced imperialist views; and though the numbers and influence of those who defend it are small, they often hold it with a persistence and enthusiasm which refuses to give a dispassionate consideration to objections urged against it. The theory meets with no support from serious ethnologists or archaeologists.

For a criticism, see H. L. Goudge, *The British Israel Theory* (1922).

BROAD CHURCH. A popular term, coined on the analogy of *High Church and *Low Church, and current esp. in the latter half of the 19th cent., for those in the C of E who objected to positive definition in theology and sought to interpret the Anglican formularies and rubrics in a broad and liberal sense. The expression appears to have been proposed originally by A. H. Clough. The existence of Broad Churchmen as a distinct party owed much to the influence of T. *Arnold and R. D. *Hampden. Characteristic representatives of the school were most of the writers for *Essays and Reviews* (1860) and A. P. *Stanley. Their successors are more commonly designated *Modernists (q.v.).

F. W. Cornish, *The English Church in the Nineteenth Century* (2 vols., 1910), esp. vol. i, pp. 186–96 and 299–316, and vol. ii, pp. 201–44. The movement is best studied, however, in the biographies of its adherents, e.g. T. Arnold, A. P. Stanley, B. *Jowett, M. *Pattison.

BROAD STOLE. A broad band of material worn *stole-wise by the deacon during part of *High Mass in certain penitential seasons. In origin it is not a stole at all, but represents a *folded chasuble, and thus goes back to the days when the deacon as well as the celebrant wore a chasuble, and folded it thus to facilitate movement. Indeed, the rubrics of the Roman Missal still enjoin the use of a real folded chasuble, the broad stole being permitted for reasons of convenience.

Braun, *L.G.*, p. 150.

BROADCASTING, Religious. In 1922 on the initiative of J. Reith (b. 1889), acting on behalf of the British Broadcasting Company, Anglican, RC, Presbyterian, and Free Church leaders formed a committee (later the 'Central Advisory Committee') which has been consulted by the Company (since 1927 Corporation) on all matters of religious broadcasting. It is now assisted by six regional religious advisory committees. The first three Heads of Religious Broadcasting were J. C. Stobart (1925–34), F. A. Iremonger (1934–9), and J. Welch (1939–47).

Beginning cautiously with hymns and sermons, religious broadcasting has come to include most types of worship. On 22 Dec. 1922 the first broadcast sermon was delivered by Preb. J. A. Mayo, rector of St. Mary's, Whitechapel. On 6 Jan. 1924 H. R. L. *Sheppard conducted in St. Martin-in-the-Fields the first service broadcast from a church. The Service of the Nine Lessons has been broadcast at Christmastide since 1928. In 1939 the First Mass of Christmas was broadcast from *Downside Abbey. On 26 Dec. 1948 the Holy Communion acc. to the rite of the C of E was first broadcast in full. On 25 Dec. 1949 the first televised service was broadcast from the chapel of the Royal Hospital, Chelsea.

Since 2 Jan. 1929 a daily service has been broadcast. It is anonymously conducted and consists of hymns, prayers, and Bible reading, and the publications issued in connexion with it include *Services for Broadcasting* (1930), *New Every Morning* (1936; Welsh ed. 1938), *Each Returning Day* (1940), and the *BBC Hymn Book* (1951).

Besides such regular programmes as 'Lift Up Your Hearts', 'Epilogue', and 'Sunday Half-hour', the B.B.C. broadcast talks, services for schools, Children's Hour prayers, and religious drama. Miss Dorothy L. Sayers' *The Man Born to be King* was written for broadcasting and first heard in 1942.

BROMPTON ORATORY. The house and church of the *Oratorians in London. The first Oratory, in King William Street, was founded in 1849, principally through the efforts of J. H. *Newman. In 1854 its members moved to Brompton Road. The present church in a somewhat florid Italian style was consecrated in 1884. It is one of the most important RC centres in London.

The London Oratory, 1849–1949 (1949); H. M. Gillett, *The Story of the London Oratory Church* (1946), incl. bibl. See also J. E. Bowden, Cong. Orat., *The Life and Letters of Frederick William Faber* (1869).

BROOKE, STOPFORD AUGUSTUS (1832–1916), *Broad Church theologian and author. He was born at Glendowan, nr. Letterkenny, Co. Donegal, and educated at Trinity College,

Dublin. Having been ordained in 1857, he became curate of St. Mary Abbots, Kensington, in 1859, where he made a name as a preacher. His Broad views brought him into conflict with the ecclesiastical authorities, and in 1863 he went to Berlin as chaplain to the Princess Royal and to the British embassy. The post, however, proved unsatisfactory; he returned to London in 1864, and in 1865 he published his widely read *Life and Letters of the Late Frederick W. Robertson*. The book reflects the outlook of the Broad Church party and was sharply attacked by the Evangelicals. In 1866 he was appointed minister of the proprietary chapel of St. James, York Street, where his preaching drew large congregations. In 1867 he became chaplain-in-ordinary to the Queen. In 1876 he published his *Primer of English Literature* which was one of the most popular works on the subject. In the same year he moved to Bedford Chapel, Bloomsbury, where he continued to engage in pastoral work even after he had left the C of E in 1880. Among the publications of this period are a *Life and Writings of Milton* (1879), a *History of Early English Literature* (1892), and volumes of sermons. In 1895 he gave up Bedford Chapel owing to ill-health, but continued his literary activities and sometimes preached in the chapels of the *Unitarians.

L. P. Jacks, *Life and Letters of Stopford Brooke* (2 vols., 1917).

BROOKS, PHILLIPS (1835–93), Bp. of Massachusetts. A native of Boston, Mass., he studied at Harvard and after a short period of teaching was ordained in the *Protestant Episcopal Church in 1859. From 1862 to 1869 he was rector of Holy Trinity, Philadelphia, where he became much attracted to the liberal religious outlook of such English theologians as F. D. *Maurice and F. W. *Robertson. In 1869 he became rector of Holy Trinity, Boston, and in 1891 Bp. of Massachusetts. The most considerable American preacher of his generation, he owed his influence to his impressive personality, wide sympathies and passionate sincerity. In 1877 he published his Yale *Lectures on Preaching* and from 1878 onwards several volumes of Sermons. He was the author of the well-known carol 'O little town of Bethlehem' (1868).

His Life and Letters were published by A. V. G. Allen (2 vols., New York, 1901). An abridged ed. was issued in 1907.

BROTHER LAWRENCE of the Resurrection (**Nicolas Herman**) (*c.* 1605–91), *Carmelite lay brother and mystic. After being a soldier and later a hermit, he entered the Carmelite monastery at *Paris in 1649, where he was given charge of the kitchen, and led a life of almost constant recollection. Lawrence's writings were edited by the Abbé de Beaufort after his death in two volumes entitled *Maximes spirituelles* (1692) and *Mœurs* *et entretiens du F. Laurent* (1694). They recommend a very elevated form of prayer consisting in the simple practice of the presence of God, whether by the imagination or the intellect. His maxims, which were highly appreciated by his contemporaries, were frequently quoted by *Fénelon in his *Défenses*.

Good modern edd. of selections of his prayers and letters under the title *La Pratique de la présence de Dieu*, with introd. and notes, by L. Van Den Bossche (Bruges, 1934) and S. M. Bouchereaux (Paris, 1948). Convenient Eng. tr. by D. Attwater (Orchard Books, Extra Series, iii; 1926).

BROTHERS HOSPITALLERS. The Order, whose members are for the most part laymen, developed out of the work for the sick of St. *John of God (d. 1550; q.v.). It began at Granada; then with the support of *Philip II hospitals were established in Madrid, Cordova, and elsewhere in Spain; and in 1572 *Pius V formally approved the Order, which adopted the *Augustinian rule. In the next decade the Hospital of St. John Calybita, established in 1584 in *Rome, became the mother-house of the Order. In addition to the three usual vows a fourth is taken to serve for life the sick in hospitals. In more recent times the Order has flourished esp. in Italy, Spain, France, and Central Europe. At present they conduct over 100 hospitals. See also *Hospitallers*.

J. Monval, *Les Frères Hospitaliers de Saint-Jean de Dieu* (1936); G. Russotto, F.B.F., *L' ordine ospedaliero di S. Giovanni di Dio* ('Fatebenefratelli') (1950); S. Montserrat Figueras, *Las actividades médico-castrenses de la inclita orden hospitalaria de San Juan de Dios* (1950). Heimbücher, i, pp. 600–11. G. Russotto, F.B.F., in *E.C.*, ix (1952), col. 416 f., s.v. 'Ospedalieri di San Giovanni di Dio', with bibl.

BROTHERS OF THE COMMON LIFE. See *Brethren of the Common Life*.

BROWN, WILLIAM ADAMS (1865–1943), *Presbyterian theologian. From 1898 to 1930 he was Roosevelt professor of systematic theology at Union Theological Seminary, New York. Belonging to the more liberal wing of American Presbyterianism, he took a prominent part in the *Oecumenical Movement and in Christian social work. His writings include *The Essence of Christianity* (1902), *Christian Theology in Outline* (1906), *Modern Theology and the Preaching of the Gospel* (1914), *The Church in America* (1922), and *Imperialistic Religion and the Religion of Democracy* (1923).

BROWNE, EDWARD HAROLD (1811–1891), Bp. of *Winchester. Educated at Eton and Emmanuel College, Cambridge, he was ordained deacon in 1836 and priest in 1837. After some parochial charges and the Vice-Principalship of St. David's College, Lampeter (1843–9), he became Norrisian professor of divinity at Cambridge in 1854, continuing to hold the living of Kenwyn (1849–57), which he exchanged in 1857 with that of Heavitree, *Exeter, and a canonry in Exeter cathedral. In 1864 he became Bp. of *Ely, and in 1873, in succession to S. *Wilberforce, Bp. of Win-

chester. Had he been younger he would probably have succeeded A. C. *Tait at *Canterbury in 1882. In 1890 he resigned his see. He was a moderating influence in the fierce conflicts aroused by *Essays and Reviews* (1860) and J. W. *Colenso's work on the *Pentateuch (1862 ff.). His theological beliefs were embodied in his *Exposition of the Thirty-Nine Articles* (2 vols., 1850–3), long a standard work among theological students. He also contributed an article on 'Inspiration' in *Aids to Faith* (1861; a reply to *Essays and Reviews*).

G. W. Kitchin, *Edward Harold Browne, D.D.* (1895).

BROWNE, GEORGE (d. 1556), Abp. of *Dublin and promoter of the Reformation in Ireland. He was originally an *Augustinian friar, but nothing is known of his life until, as Provincial of his order, he had to administer the oath of royal supremacy to the friars. In 1535 he was appointed Abp. of Dublin, and as such took an active part in the suppression of the Irish monasteries and in the union of the Irish Church with the C of E under the supremacy of the King. After the introduction of the Prayer Book of 1549 into Ireland, Browne became the head of those members of the Irish clergy who accepted the new religion and introduced the English service into Dublin Cathedral. In 1550 he found himself Primate of Ireland, owing to the translation of the primacy from the ancient see of *Armagh to that of Dublin. On the accession of *Mary, Browne had to resign his see because he was married. Of a harsh and arrogant character, Browne made many enemies and incurred the hatred of the people.

Historical Collections of the Church in Ireland during the Reigns of Kings Henry VIII, Edward VI and Queen Mary . . . set forth in the Life and Death of George Browne (1681).

BROWNE, ROBERT (*c.* 1550–1633), *Puritan separatist. He was a relative of William Cecil, Lord Burleigh, who more than once afforded him protection. Born at Tolethorpe in Rutland, Browne studied at Corpus Christi College, Cambridge, and while there came under the influence of T. *Cartwright, then advocating a *Presbyterian polity for the Church. Feeling a call to action forthwith, Browne established independent congregations at *Norwich and elsewhere. For this schismatic act he was promptly imprisoned. Having been freed by Cecil, he migrated with his Norwich flock to Middelburg in Holland; and there issued *A Book which sheweth the Life and Manner of all True Christians* (Middelburg, 1582) and *A Treatise of Reformation without Tarrying for Any* (ib., 1582). Before long Browne, who was of a quarrelsome nature, fell out with many of his congregation, and left for Scotland. Not finding the welcome he had looked for from the Scottish Church, he returned to England and published *An Answer to Mr. Cartwright's Letter for joining with the English Churches* (London, *c.* 1584). He then made a formal submission to the C of E, and became Master of St. Olave's School, *Southwark, in 1586. His changed standpoint is reflected in the title of a paper *A Reproof of Certain Schismatic Persons* (1588) of which a MS. copy is preserved at *Lambeth Palace. None the less it appears that while at Southwark he ministered to separatist congregations. In 1591 he received episcopal ordination and became Rector of Achurch, Northants. He held the benefice until his death, though there is an unexplained period (1616–26) when the entries in the parish register are in a different hand. He died in Northampton Gaol, whither he had been committed for assaulting a police constable. Browne was clearly mentally unstable; but he exercised an important influence on the beginnings of *Congregationalism, so much so that their early members were often termed 'Brownists'.

The *Reproof* mentioned in the text, a MS. of 31 pages, was discovered by Champlin Burrage in 1905 and publd. as the *Retractation of Robert Browne, Father of Congregationalism* (1907). A. Peel–L. H. Carlson (edd.), *The Writings of Robert Harrison and Robert Browne* (Elizabethan Nonconformist Texts, ii; 1953), pp. 150–531. C. Burrage, *The True Story of Robert Browne* (1906), with full list of Browne's writings and bibl. reff. Important art. by F. J. Powicke in *H.E.R.E.*, ii (1909), pp. 874–8, s.v. 'Brownism'. A. Jessop in *D.N.B.*, vii (1886), pp. 57–61.

BROWNE, SIR THOMAS (1605–82),
physician and author. After studying medicine at Oxford, Montpellier, and Padua, and receiving a doctorate at Leyden, he began to practise as a physician, and in 1637 settled at *Norwich, where he spent the rest of his life. His chief fame is due to his writings, of which the most celebrated are *Religio Medici* (1642) and *Hydriotaphia, or Urn-Burial* (1658). The former of these expounds his religious outlook, while the latter is a learned treatise on burial customs in different parts of the world. His religious views manifest a remarkable independence of judgement and 'attempt to combine daring scepticism with implicit faith in revelation' (A. H. Bullen), while he shows, probably as a result of his wide travels and sympathies, a freedom from insular prejudice rare in Englishmen of his day. But, in spite of exceptional learning and wide experience, he shared the beliefs of his age in witchcraft and alchemy, and in the Ptolemaic astronomy. He also wrote *Pseudodoxia Epidemica* (1646), *Certain Miscellany Tracts* (1683), *A Letter to a Friend upon the Occasion of the Death of his Intimate Friend* (1690), and *Christian Morals* (1716).

First collected ed. ot Works, 1686; more complete ed., with Memoir by S. Wilkin (4 vols., 1835–6). Modern crit. ed. by G. [L.] Keynes (6 vols., London, 1928–31). *Religio Medici and* [some] *Other Writings of Sir Thomas Browne*, ed. with introd. by C. H. Herford (Everyman's Library [1906]). *Christian Morals* (ed. 2, with Life by S. *Johnson, 1756; re-edited by R. S. Roberts, 1927). E. Gosse, *Sir Thomas Browne* ('English Men of Letters', 1905); O. Leroy, *Le Chevalier Thomas Browne (1605–1682). Sa vie, sa pensée et son art* (1931). Studies on his 'Religio Medici' by W. Osler in *The Library*, Ser. 2, vii (1906), pp. 1–31, and by W. Schonack (Tübingen, 1911). Bibl. by G. L. Keynes in F. W. Bateson (ed.), *C.B.E.L.*, i (1940), p. 834 f. A. H. Bullen in *D.N.B.*, vii (1886), pp. 64–72.

BROWNISTS. See *Browne, Robert.*

BRUCE, ALEXANDER BALMAIN (1831–1899), Scottish divine. Educated at Edinburgh University, he entered the Free Church ministry, and in 1875 was appointed professor in the Free Church Hall at Glasgow. In 1871 he issued his *Training of the Twelve*, the first of many books in which he sought to use the method of Gospel exegesis to present the substance of the Christian faith. This was followed by *The Humiliation of Christ* (1876), a thorough examination of the '*Kenotic theory', and *The Kingdom of God; or Christ's Teaching according to the Synoptic Gospels* (1889). The latter was much criticized in the General Assembly of the Free Church for its adoption of new principles of *Biblical Criticism, but no formal censure was passed. Among Bruce's later writings were his *Apologetics, or Christianity Defensively Stated* (1892), two series of *Gifford Lectures (for 1896–7), *St. Paul's Conception of Christianity* (1894), '*With Open Face*' (1896), commentaries on the Synoptic Gospels (*Expos. Gk. Test.*, 1897), and *The Epistle to the Hebrews* (1899). He also worked actively for the encouragement of Church music.

E. I. Carlyle in *D.N.B.* Suppl., i (1901), p. 321 f., s.v.

BRÜGGLERS. A small Swiss sect founded at Brügglen, near Berne, *c.* 1745, by two brothers, Christian and Hieronymus Kohler, probably both impostors from start to finish. They proclaimed several fantastic doctrines, asserting, e.g., that they themselves and one of their disciples, Elizabeth Kissling, were respectively incarnations of the three Persons of the Trinity, and foretold that the world would end at Christmas 1748. Their excesses and immoralities led to their exile by the Berne government in 1749, and in 1753 Hieronymus Kohler was burnt. The sect survived for a short time in remote mountainous regions.

W. Hadorn in *P.R.E.* (ed. 3), x (1901), pp. 638–41, s.v. 'Kohler, Christian und Hieronymus', with bibl.

BRUNNER, EMIL (1889–   ), Swiss *Dialectical theologian. A native of Winterthur, from 1916 to 1922 he was a pastor at Obstalden. From 1922 to 1938 he taught at Zürich and from 1938 at Princeton (U.S.A.). He was one of K. *Barth's foremost supporters in protesting against immanence in religion and Christian mysticism. But on the other hand he holds that a genuine element of truth is contained in the Catholic doctrine of *analogy, a position for which he was taken severely to task by K. Barth in his pamphlet *Nein! Antwort an Emil Brunner* (1934). His writings include *Die Mystik und das Wort* (1924); *Religionsphilosophie evangelischer Theologie* (1926; Eng. trans. *The Philosophy of Religion from the Standpoint of Protestant Theology*, 1937); *Der Mittler* (1927; Eng. trans., *The Mediator*, 1934); *Das Gebot und die Ordnungen* (1932; Eng. trans., *The Divine Imperative*, 1937); *Der Mensch im Widerspruch* (1937; Eng. trans., *Man in Revolt*, 1939). For a short time he acknow-

ledged his adherence to the *Oxford Group Movement.

BRUNO, St. (925–65). Abp. of *Cologne. The youngest son of the Emp. Henry I ('the Fowler'), he was ordained deacon in 941 or 942 and forthwith appointed abbot of the monasteries of Lorsch near Worms and of Corvei on the Weser. In 953 he became Abp. of Cologne, and as such took a leading part in furthering the ecclesiastical and temporal policy of his brother, the Emp. Otto. He remained a strong German patriot throughout his life, a true patron of learning, and by a strong policy secured the internal peace of his domains. His Life was written by the monk Ruotger. Feast day, 11 Oct. (though on other days at certain places).

Life by Ruotger pr. in *A A.SS.*, Oct. V (1786), pp. 765–86; ed. by G. H. Pertz in *M.G.H.*, Scriptores, iv (1841), pp. 252–75. H. Schrörs, 'Ruotgers Lebensgeschichte der Erzbischofs Bruno von Köln' in *Annalen des Historischen Vereins für den Niederrhein insbesondere die alte Erzdiözese Köln*, lxxxviii (1910), pp. 1–95; id., 'Die Vita Brunonis des Ruotger', ib., xc (1911), pp. 60–110; id. 'Erzbischof Bruno von Köln (953–965), eine geschichtliche Charakteristik', ib., c (1917), pp. 1–42. Full bibl. in W. Wattenbach–R. Holtzmann, *Deutschlands Geschichtsquellen im Mittelalter. Deutsche Kaiserzeit*. Band I, Hft. i (1938), pp. 88–94.

BRUNO, St. (c. 1032–1101). The founder of the *Carthusian Order. Educated at *Cologne and Rheims, he became a canon of St. Cunibert's in Cologne, whence he was recalled to be 'scholasticus' of the important cathedral school of Rheims (c. 1057). Here he had among his pupils the future Pope *Urban II. He was made chancellor of the diocese in 1075 by Manasses, the new Archbishop, a man of scandalous character, with whom he soon came into conflict. In the course of a long struggle, Bruno was forced to leave his school (1076), but he returned in 1080 when Manasses was deposed from his see. Shortly after, Bruno turned to the religious life and for a time placed himself under the direction of St. *Robert, who later founded *Cîteaux. Before long he left Robert, and with six companions went into the mountainous district near Grenoble, where, under the protection of the bishop, St. *Hugh, he laid the foundations of the *Carthusian Order (1084). In 1090 he was summoned by Pope Urban II to live in Italy and assist him with his counsel. He obeyed, but refusing the archbishopric of Reggio, retired to the wilds of Calabria and founded the monastery of La Torre, where he died. He was never formally canonized, but in 1514 his order obtained Papal leave to keep his festival (6 Oct.), The observance of the Feast was imposed on all Westerns in communion with Rome in 1623.

His Expositions on the Psalms and on the Epp. of St. Paul have been repr. by the Carthusians of Montreuil-sur-Mer, 1891–2; also in J. P. Migne, *PL*, clii and cliii. Extracts from anon. 13th cent. life (*Vita Antiquior*), together with other primary material, in *A A.SS.* Oct. III (1700), pp. 491–777. A. P. F. Lefebvre *Saint Bruno et l'ordre des Chartreux* (2 vols., 1883); H. Löbbel, *Der Stifter des Carthäuser-Ordens, der heilige Bruno aus Köln* (1899); M. M. Gorse, *Saint Bruno*. Son action et son œuvre (1902). S. Autore, O.S.B., in *D.T.C.*, ii (1905), cols. 2274–82, s.v. 'Chartreuse', with full bibl.

BRUNO, GIORDANO (1548–1600), Italian philosopher. In 1562 he joined the *Dominican Order at Naples, but on being censured for unorthodoxy, he fled in 1576. For seventeen years he moved from place to place under constant suspicion, and was in England from 1583 to 1585. Captured at Venice in 1592 by the emissaries of the *Inquisition, he was in confinement at *Rome from 1593 till, on 17 Feb. 1600, he was burnt at the stake on the Campo dei Fiori.

Under Renaissance influences Bruno became a fierce opponent of *Aristotelian doctrines and a warm admirer of N. *Copernicus. His enthusiasm for nature, however, led him to hold an extreme form of pantheistic immanentism. God was the efficient and final cause of everything, the beginning, middle, and end, the eternal and infinite. He developed this philosophy in its many consequences in his two Italian metaphysical treatises of 1584, *De la Causa, Principio, ed Uno* and *De l' Infinito, Universo, e Mondi*. In his Latin treatises, written somewhat later, he slightly modified this extreme pantheism. In the latter half of the 19th cent. the name of Bruno came to be identified with *anticlerical elements in the movement for Italian nationalism.

Latin Works ed. by J. B. Nolani (8 vols., 1889–91); Italian Works by C. *Gentile (3 vols., 1907–9). A. Riehl, *Giordano Bruno* (Leipzig, 1900); J. L. McIntyre, *Giordano Bruno* (London, 1903); C. Gentile, *Giordano Bruno nella storia della cultura* (1907); L. Olschki, *Giordano Bruno* (1927). V. Salvestrini, *Bibliographia delle opera di Giordano Bruno* (1926).

BRUYS, PIERRE DE. See *Peter of Bruys*.

BRYANITES. See *Bible Christians*.

BRYENNIOS, PHILOTHEOS (1833–1914). The discoverer of the '*Didache. A native of *Constantinople, he studied at several German universities, became professor of Church history and exegesis at Halki in 1861, director of the school in the *Phanar at Constantinople in 1867, Metropolitan of Serrae in Macedonia in 1875 and of Nicomedia in 1877. In 1873 he discovered in the library of the Hospice of the Jerusalem Monastery of the Holy Sepulchre at *Constantinople a MS. (no. 456) written in 1056 which contained some early Christian documents of the first importance, among them the Greek texts of the Ep. of *Barnabas, the 1st and 2nd Epp. of *Clement to the Corinthians, and, the most celebrated, the *Didache. He published the two Clementine Epistles in 1875 and the Didache in 1883. In 1875 he was a delegate of the E. Church at the *Bonn Reunion Conference.

Brief notice by N. Turchi in *E.C.*, iii (1950), col. 163. P. *Schaff, *The Oldest Church Manual called the 'Teaching of the Twelve Apostles'* (1885), pp. 279–96 (with autobiogr. letter from Bryennios).

BUBER, MARTIN (1878–   ), Jewish religious thinker. He was a native of Vienna, where he took his doctor's degree in 1900, and played an active part in the Zionist Movement, which he had joined in 1898. From 1906 onwards he devoted himself chiefly to religious studies. These led him to occupation with *Chasidism, whence he derived many of his ideas, e.g. those on a kind of activist mysticism and the sanctification of the daily life. From 1916 to 1924 he was editor of *Der Jude*, a leading monthly of German-speaking Jewry. In 1923 he received a call to Frankfurt university, where he lectured on Jewish theology and ethics. In 1926 he started a periodical *Die Kreatur*, with Catholic and Protestant collaborators. After the advent of A. Hitler he became professor at the university of *Jerusalem.

Among his more important writings are *Die Legende des Baalschem* (1908), *Vom Geist des Judentums* (1916), *Die Schrift* (from 1925, translation of the Bible), and *Königtum Gottes* (1932), a study of the Messianic idea. The book which has exercised the greatest influence on Protestant theologians as well as on the German Youth Movement is his small treatise *Ich und Du* (1923; Eng. trans., 1937). Written in poetical language, it studies the relationship between man and things, called by him the 'I-It' relationship, in contrast to the relation between persons, i.e. between man and man and between man and God, called the 'I-Thou' relationship.

The influence of Buber's ideas is evident esp. in the German Protestant theologians F. *Gogarten and K. *Heim, but also in recent English thinkers such as J. H. Oldham (b. 1874).

BRUYS, PIERRE DE. See Peter of Bruys.

BUCER, MARTIN (1491–1551), also spelled 'Butzer', German divine. Having entered the *Dominican Order in 1506, he began in 1518 to correspond with M. *Luther, whom he had heard dispute, and in 1521 secured Papal dispensation from his monastic vows. He was one of the first priests among the German Reformers to marry (1522). In 1523 he began publicly to preach Lutheranism in Alsace, and was excommunicated by the Bp. of Speyer. During the years which followed, his views developed, and on the subject of the *Eucharist they came nearer to those of H. *Zwingli than to those of Luther, though he attempted to mediate between the two. After the death of Zwingli in 1531 he became the leader of the *Reformed Churches in Switzerland and S. Germany, and took part in the unsuccessful conferences between Catholics and Protestants at *Hagenau (1540), *Worms (1540), and *Ratisbon (1541). He then spent some years assisting *Hermann of Wied in his vain effort to introduce the Reformed doctrines at Cologne. After unavailing opposition to the *Interim of 1548, arranged by the Emp. *Charles V to maintain religious peace in the empire, Bucer came in 1549 to England, where he was received with much honour by *Edward VI and T. *Cranmer, and made Regius professor of divinity at Cambridge. Cranmer is said to have asked his advice on many points, and Bucer had a marked influence on

parts of the Anglican *Ordinal of 1550. He died on 28 Feb. 1551, and was buried in Great St. Mary's church at Cambridge. In 1557 his body was exhumed and publicly burnt on Market Hill.

Scripta Anglicana fere omnia a C. Huberto collecta (Basel, 1577). Collected ed. of his works by R. Stupperich (Paris, 1960 ff.). *Lives* by G. Anrich (Strassburg, 1914) and H. Eells (Yale, 1931). J. W. Baum, *Capito und Butzer* (Strassburg, 1860); A. Lang, *Der Evangelienkommentar Martin Butzers und die Grundzüge seiner Theologie* (Leipzig, 1900); A. E. Harvey, *Martin Bucer in England* (Marburg, 1906); G. Klingenburg, *Das Verhältnis Calvins zu Butzer* (Bonn, 1912); W. Pauck, *Das Reich Gottes auf Erden*. Eine Untersuchung zu Butzers *De Regno Christi* (Berlin, 1928); C. Hopf, *Martin Bucer and the English Reformation* (Oxford, 1946).

BUCHANAN, CLAUDIUS (1766–1815), Bengal chaplain. After conversion and a period spent under the personal influence of the famous Evangelical, J. *Newton, Buchanan entered Queens' College, Cambridge, in 1791 where he made the close acquaintance of C. *Simeon. On being ordained priest in 1796, he accepted a chaplaincy in Bengal, and proceeded to Calcutta shortly afterwards, and was for several years vice-provost of a cultural college which Lord Wellesley had established at Fort William. Though his official position in the East India Company restricted the amount of active mission work he could do, he used his influence to the utmost to further the cause of Christianity in native India; and it was largely through his instrumentality after his return to England (1808) that an Indian episcopate was created, T. F. *Middleton, the first Bp. of Calcutta, being appointed in 1814.

Works (incomplete) in two parts, New York, 1812. H. N. Pearson, *Memoirs of the Life and Writings of the Rev. Claudius Buchanan* (2 vols., 1817).

BUCHMAN, FRANK (1878–1961), founder and director of the *Oxford Group (q.v.). Born of a *Lutheran family of Swiss descent at Pennsburg, Pa., U.S.A., he graduated at Muhlenberg College, studied at Mount Airy Seminary, Philadelphia, and entered the Lutheran ministry. After a year of graduate study abroad he was in charge of a parish in Philadelphia for three years and subsequently of a hostel for poor young men. In 1908 he resigned this work in a spirit of disillusionment and on a visit to England attended the *Keswick Convention where an address on the Atonement in a small church in the neighbourhood convinced him that his previous ministry had been wholly unprofitable and he experienced conversion. On the advice of J. R. *Mott he took up evangelistic work among the students of Pennsylvania State College. In 1915 and 1917–19 he visited *India and the Far East, and in 1920—with introductions from two Anglican missionary bishops whom he met in China—Cambridge, after which some Cambridge undergraduates joined him in a visit to Oxford. Out of this last visit the Group movement grew. In 1929 he visited South Africa as leader of the movement and has since travelled widely, including tours to Canada and U.S.A. in 1932–3 and 1933–4, Scandinavia in 1934–5, Utrecht in 1937, the Near East and Geneva in 1938. In 1938 in London he inaugurated the *Moral Rearmament movement, a phase of the *Group movement which stressed national and social *morale* in place of the largely individual emphasis of the earlier teaching. World Assemblies of this later movement were held at Caux, Switzerland, in 1946 and subsequent years.

See bibl. to *Oxford Group*.

BUCHMANN, THEODOR. See *Bibliander, Theodor*.

BÜCHNER, KARL FRIEDRICH CHRISTIAN LUDWIG (1824–99), German materialist philosopher. While lecturer in medicine at *Tübingen (from 1852), he published in 1855 his celebrated *Kraft und Stoff* in which he defended a purely materialistic doctrine of the natural world, seeking on the bases of the conservation-laws of energy and of matter to reduce everything in the universe, whether mental or physical, to a single nonspiritual source. The book became a sort of Bible for the materialists and aroused such bitter opposition that Büchner was forced to retire. For the rest of his life he lived at Darmstadt, where he published several other widely read treatises. He maintained that his doctrinaire materialism was not incompatible with idealism in practical life.

List of his writings in Überweg, iv, p. 288 f.

BUCKLAND, WILLIAM (1784–1856), Dean of *Westminster from 1845, and geologist. He was elected to a fellowship at Corpus Christi College, Oxford, in 1808, and in 1819 became the first University reader in geology. He saw in the vestiges of the ice age striking proof of the Biblical story of the Flood, defending his views in *Reliquiae Diluvianae, or Observations on the Organic Remains attesting the Action of a Universal Deluge* (1823). In 1836 he issued an ambitious contribution to the *Bridgewater Treatises on *Geology and Mineralogy considered with Reference to Natural Theology*.

Mrs. Gordon [E. O. Buckland, daughter], *The Life and Correspondence of William Buckland* (1894).

BUDDE, KARL (1850–1935), OT scholar. He was professor of OT from 1889 to 1900 at Strassburg and from 1900 to 1921 at Marburg. He did much to further OT criticism on the lines laid down by J. *Wellhausen. Besides many commentaries, his writings include a concise and widely read *Religion of Israel* (1899; Ger. ed., 1900).

Karl Budde's Schrifttum bis zu seinem 80. Geburtstage (Beiheft liv of the *ZATW*, 1930).

BUGENHAGEN, JOHANN (1485–1558), 'Pomeranus', *Lutheran theologian. In early life he was a *Premonstratensian canon of Treptow (in Pomerania) where he was appointed rector of the city school in 1504.

After his marriage in 1522, M. *Luther secured his appointment as pastor in *Wittenberg in 1523, and here he remained till his death, acting as Luther's confessor. He took a leading part in the organization of the Lutheran Church in N. Germany and *Denmark, and the 'Brunswick Church Order' of 1528 was mainly his work. In 1537 Bugenhagen made his way to Denmark, where his presence had been sought by King Christian III, to rearrange ecclesiastical affairs on a Protestant basis, and on 12 Aug. he crowned both King and Queen. He then proceeded to consecrate seven men to be superintendents or 'bishops', and in this way the Danish Church lost the episcopal *Apostolic Succession. He also reorganized the University of Copenhagen, arranging for lectures on St. *Augustine's 'De Spiritu et Littera', Luther's 'Commentary on Galatians', and the 'Loci Communes' of P. *Melanchthon, and he assisted Luther in his translation of the Bible.

Collections of sermons ed. G. Buchwald (Halle, 1885; Leipzig, 1909); Correspondence ed. O. Vogt (Stettin, 1888). Life by H. Hering (Halle, 1888). G. Geisenhof, *Bugenhagiana* (Halle, 1908). W. Leege, *Bugenhagen als Liturgiker* (Diss., Schneidemühl, 1925). G. Kawerau in *P.R.E.* (ed. 3), iii (1897), pp. 525–32; O. Clemen in *R.G.G.* (ed. 2), i (1927), col. 1349 f.

BUGIA (also **scotula, palmatorium**). A portable candlestick containing a lighted candle which is held beside a RC bishop while he performs certain liturgical functions. Its use may be granted to other prelates by special privilege.

BULGAKOV, SERGIUS (1870–1944), Russian theologian. The son of a Russian priest, he was intended for the priesthood but under the influence of G. W. F. *Hegel became a philosophical and religious sceptic and active in Marxist political movements. Disillusioned after the 1905 Revolution, he slowly retraced his steps to the Church. In the Moscow *Sobor* of 1917 which restored the patriarchate, Bulgakov took a prominent part as a layman. He became a priest shortly afterwards. Escaping from Russia, he was Dean of the Orthodox Theological Academy at *Paris from 1923 till his death. He was a man of remarkable personality and intellectual power, well known in W. Europe and America through his participation in the *Oecumenical Movement, of which he was a warm but critical supporter. Theologically he is best known for his contributions to Sophiology, a body of thought claiming descent through V. *Soloviev and P. Florensky from the E. Fathers, which seeks to solve the problems of the relation between God and the world by the concept of the Divine Wisdom or *sophia*. His teaching was condemned, largely it would seem on political grounds, by the Moscow patriarchate in 1935 but without much practical result. His only works translated into English are *The Orthodox Church* (1935) and *The Wisdom of God* (1937). He also published a large work on the Incarnation, *Du Verbe incarné* (1944).

BULL (Lat. *bulla*, 'seal'). A written mandate of the Pope, of a more serious and weighty kind than a 'brief'. Such documents were sealed in earlier times with the Pope's signet-ring, but from the 6th cent. either seal-boxes of lead or signets stamped in wax were used. Since 1878 only the most important bulls ('consistorial bulls') are sealed in this way, others being sealed merely with a red stamp. Consistorial bulls are signed not only by the Pope, but also by the *Cardinals, and are sent out in copy, the original being retained at Rome.

For collections of bulls see *Bullarium*. N. Valois, 'Étude sur le rythme des bulles pontificales' in *Bibliothèque de l'École des Chartes*, xlii (1881), pp. 161–98 and 257–72. R. L. Poole in *D.É.C.H.*, pp. 72–4, s.v. 'Bulls, Papal'; G. Battelli in *E.C.*, ii (1949), cols. 1778–81, s.v. 'Bolla', with bibl.

BULL, GEORGE (1634–1710), Bp. of *St. Davids, and theologian. He was educated at Exeter College, Oxford, and was ordained deacon and priest on the same day in 1655. In 1659 he became Rector of Suddington, in 1686 Archdeacon of *Llandaff, and in 1705 Bp. of St. Davids. In theology he was a staunch High Churchman. His *Harmonia Apostolica* (1669–70) was an attack on the more Protestant theories of *justification, its thesis being that the passages where St. Paul seems to imply human incapacity for moral attainment must be interpreted in the light of St. James' Epistle. In his celebrated treatise, *Defensio Fidei Nicaenae* (1685; he added later several other works by way of postscript), he maintained, largely in criticism of the *Jesuit D. *Petavius, that the teaching of the pre-Nicene Fathers on the Trinity completely agreed with that of orthodox theologians of Nicene and post-Nicene times. The work greatly commended itself to J. B. *Bossuet and other contemporary French theologians, and Bull received the unusual tribute of the formal thanks of the French clergy at their Synod at St. Germain in 1686. In answer to their subsequent inquiries why, in view of so masterly a defence of Catholic doctrine, he did not become a RC, Bull wrote a popular and vigorous work, *The Corruptions of the Church of Rome* (1705). A posthumous work of Bull, popular in later times, was *A Companion for the Candidates of Holy Orders, or the Great Importance of the Priestly Office* (1714). His Life was written by R. *Nelson, who had been a pupil of Bull's at Suddington.

Works, ed. E. Burton (6 vols., Oxford, 1827). R. Nelson, *The Life of Dr. George Bull . . . with the history of* those Controversies in which he was engaged (1713). J. H. Overton in *D.N.B.*, vii (1886), pp. 236–8, s.v.

BULLARIUM. A term said to have been invented by the canonist, Laertius Cherubini (d. 1626), for a collection of Papal *bulls and other similar documents. Such 'bullaria', being the collections of private individuals, have no authority beyond that attaching to their component pieces. Among the best known are those of L. Cherubini (1586); the

'Luxemburg Bullarium' (stated to have been really printed at Geneva) (1727–30); Mainardi's 'Roman Bullarium' (1733–62); and the 'Turin Bullarium' (1857–85).

T. Ortolan in *D.T.C.*, ii (1905), cols. 1243–55, s.v. 'Bullaire', with bibl.; H. *Leclercq, O.S.B., in *D.A.C.L.*, viii (pt. 2; 1929), cols. 2977–82, s.v. 'Lettres des papes'.

BULLINGER, JOHANN HEINRICH (1504–75), Swiss reformer. He was led by the reading of the Bible and the Fathers, the study of the writings of M. *Luther and P. *Melanchthon, and the preaching of H. *Zwingli, to adopt the principles of the Reformation. In 1529 he was made pastor of Bremgarten, and on the death of Zwingli in 1531 appointed to succeed him as chief pastor of Zürich. In 1549 he joined with J. *Calvin in producing the '*Consensus Tigurinus' on the Lord's Supper; and the Second *Helvetic Confession of 1566 was also his work. A voluminous letter-writer, his correspondents included *Henry VIII and *Edward VI of England, as well as many of the leaders of the Edwardian reforms. In the time of *Elizabeth he became something of an oracle among many of the English higher clergy who had enjoyed his hospitality during the reign of *Mary. Elizabeth herself found his prestige a valuable support against the more rigidly Calvinistic Puritans for her settlement of Church affairs; and when, in 1570, *Pius V made the final breach between the Papacy and the English Church, it was to Bullinger that she turned to prepare her reply to the Papal charges.

Autobiography pr. in *Miscellanea Tigurina*, i, Ausg. 2 (Zürich, 1772), pp. 1–103. *The Decades of Henry Bullinger*, tr. and ed. by T. Harding (*Parker Society, 4 vols., 1849–1852), with biogr. notice, vol. iv, pp. vii–xxxi; also modern Eng. tr. of his sermon 'Of the Catholic Church', with introd. notes and bibl. in G. W. Bromiley (ed.), *Zwingli and Bullinger* (Library of Christian Classics, xxiv; 1953), pp. 283–325, 349–52, and 356 f. Four of Bullinger's *Sermons on Sacraments* were also repr., London, 1840. C. Pestalozzi, *Heinrich Bullinger* (1858). A. Bouvier, *Henri Bullinger, le successeur de Zwingli, d'après sa correspondance avec les réformés et les humanistes de langue française* (1940), with bibl. J. Heer–E. Egli in *P.R.E.* (ed. 3), iii (1897), pp. 536–49.

BULTMANN, RUDOLF (1884–   ), NT scholar and theologian. After studying at *Marburg, *Tübingen, and Berlin he became Privatdozent at Marburg in 1912, Extra-ordinary Professor at Breslau in 1916, and professor at Giessen in 1921. From 1921 until 1951 he was professor of NT studies at Marburg.

Bultmann carried the methods of *Form-Criticism, as developed by J. *Weiss and M. *Dibelius, to the point of radical scepticism, notably in an elaborate analysis of the Gospel sources in *Die Geschichte der synoptischen Tradition* (1921, enlarged 1931). In his *Jesus* (1926; Eng. tr. 1934) he discovered the mission of Christ in summoning His followers to decision (*Entscheidung*) to the point of practically ignoring His redemptive work and His moral teaching. With extreme historical scepticism he has combined strong *Barthian sympathies, making a radical hiatus between history and faith. In his later work this has developed into an insistence on the need for a 'demythologization' (*Entmythologisierung*) of the NT. He holds that not merely particular narratives or incidents (e.g. the *Virgin Birth) embody mythological elements, but the whole of the Gospel story is based on a mythical conception of the Universe (e.g. a three-storied heaven, earth, and hell) which cannot be accepted in its *prima facie* meaning. If the mythical element be wholly eliminated the real significance of the Gospel history will be disclosed. See also *Demythologization*.

Bultmann's other works include *Der Stil der paulinischen Predigt und die kynisch-stoische Diatribe* (1910), *Die Erforschung der synoptischen Evangelien* (1925; Eng. trans. 1930), *Das Evangelium des Johannes* (1941), *Offenbarung und Heilsgeschehen* (1941), *Theologie des Neuen Testaments* (3 fascc., 1948–53), and *Das Urchristentum im Rahmen der antiken Religionen* (1949), as well as the art. γνῶσις in G. *Kittel's *Theologisches-Wörterbuch*. His Gifford Lectures for 1955 were published under the title *History and Eschatology* (Edinburgh, 1957).

Festschriften in honour of his 65th birthday, ed. E. Wolf (Stuttgart, 1949), with list of his works, pp. 241–51, and in honour of his 70th birthday, ed. W. Eltester (Berlin, 1954). See also bibl. to *Demythologization*. R. Marlé, S.J., *Bultmann et l'interprétation du Nouveau Testament* (Théologie xxxiii; Paris, 1956). G. Miegge, *L' evangelo e il mito nel pensiero di Rudolf Bultmann* (1956; Eng. tr. 1960).

BUNSEN, CHRISTIAN CARL JOSIAS VON, also known as 'Chevalier Bunsen' (1791–1860), German diplomatist and amateur theologian. From 1823 to 1839 he was minister at the Prussian legation at Rome, where he proved himself a masterly diplomat and settled delicate matters connected with the relations between Germany and the Holy See. After two years as minister at Berne, he was ambassador in London from 1841 to 1854. Here he was regarded as the most distinguished representative of European Protestantism in England and was the chief instrument in the scheme for a joint Lutheran and Anglican Bishopric in *Jerusalem. His voluminous and verbose theological writings, for the most part of little enduring value, include a treatise on the Epp. of St. *Ignatius (1847); *Hippolytus and his Age* (4 vols., 1852); *Christianity and Mankind* (7 vols., 1855, an English version of some earlier writings, then first published as one work); *Gott in der Geschichte* (3 vols., 1857–8); and *Vollständiges Bibelwerk für die Gemeinde* (9 vols., 1858–70).

Memoir by Frances, Baroness Bunsen, widow (2 vols., London, 1868). L. von *Ranke *Aus dem Briefwechsel Friedrich Wilhelms IV mit Bunsen* (1873). B. Baehring, *Bunsen's Bibelwerk nach seiner Bedeutung für die Gegenwart beleuchtet* (1861); id., *Christian Karl Josias Freiherr von Bunsen* (1892).

BUNTING, JABEZ (1779–1858), Wesleyan *Methodist minister. A native of Manchester, he was received on trial into the Methodist ministry in 1799 and admitted into full connexion in 1803 as minister at Oldham Street Chapel, Manchester. He worked in several large towns until in 1833 he was permanently attached to the Methodist headquarters in London. In 1835 he became president of the first Wesleyan Theological College, established at Hoxton. His main work was to transform the Methodist society into a Church, possessed of a sound and consolidated organization independent of the C of E. He was anxious, however, to work in harmony with the Established Church. He also took a keen interest in foreign missions and was for 18 years secretary of the Wesleyan Missionary Society. Despite his love of political and religious freedom, he distrusted the more radical forms of democracy that commended themselves to many Nonconformists of the 19th cent.

Life of Jabez Bunting, D.D., with Notices of Contemporary Persons and Events. By his son, Thomas Percival Bunting (2 vols., 1859, 1887).

BUNYAN, JOHN (1628–88), author of the *Pilgrim's Progress*. Of the external details of his life comparatively little is known. Born at Elstow in Bedfordshire, he was the son of poor parents (his father was a brazier, a trade he himself followed—hence the loose description of him as a 'tinker'), and probably acquired his knowledge and mastery of the English language from reading the Bible. He took part in the Civil War on the Parliamentary side (1644–1646). C. 1649 he married a woman of piety who introduced him to A. Dent's *Plain Man's Pathway to Heaven* and Bp. L. *Bayly's *Practice of Piety*; and these, together with the Bible, the BCP, and J. *Foxe's *Book of Martyrs*, seem to have been his sole reading. In 1653 he was received into an *Independent congregation at Bedford, and after being formally recognized as a preacher in 1657, he soon became well known in that capacity. He suffered much from the repressive measures of the Royalists after the Restoration of 1660, and spent most of the years 1660–72 in Bedford gaol. During and after his imprisonment he wrote extensively, including some verse compositions. Of his prose works, the chief and most famous are his autobiography, *Grace Abounding to the Chief of Sinners* (1666); the *Pilgrim's Progress* (q.v.; 1678 and 1684); and the *Holy War* (1682). For the rest of his life after his release in 1672, he worked among the Independents at Bedford, and took part in evangelistic work in other parts of the country. One of his last writings was a treatise, *Antichrist and her Ruin* (1692, posthumous), against the Church of Rome, whose influence in England under *James II he much feared. If history and biography furnish little aid in understanding the personality of Bunyan, his chief writings demonstrate that to him the world was exclusively the scene of a spiritual warfare and that nothing mattered save the salvation of the soul.

First ed. of collected Works, vol. i (all printed), London, 1692. Later edd. include: 2 vols., London, 1736–7, and 6 vols., Edinburgh, 1769. More recent edd. by G. Offor (3 vols., Edinburgh, 1852–3) and H. Stebbing (4 vols., London, 1859–60). Lives by R. *Southey (London, 1830), J. A. Froude ('English Men of Letters', 1880), J. Brown (London, 1885; new ed. F. M. Harrison, 1928), and W. H. *Hutton (London, [1928]). F. M. Harrison, *A Bibliography of the Works of John Bunyan* (1932). E. Venables in *D.N.B.*, vii (1886), pp. 275–85.

BUONAROTTI. See *Michelangelo*.

BURCHARD (*c.* 965–1025), Bp. of Worms from 1000. He was one of the most influential bishops of his time, and was successful in asserting episcopal authority in the secular affairs of his diocese, in building new churches, in forming new parishes, and in disciplining his clergy. Between *c.* 1008 and 1012 he compiled his *Decretum*, a collection of *canon law, which exercised great influence until it was superseded by the collections of the Hildebrandine Reform.

Decretals [ed. B. Questenburgh] (Cologne, 1548); also pr. Paris, 1549, repr. in J. P. Migne, *PL*, cxl, 537–1058. A Life, approx. contemporary, ed. G. Waitz in *M.G.H.*, Scriptores, iv (1841), pp. 829–46; repr. J. P. Migne, loc. cit., 505–36. Crit. ed. H. Boos, *Monumenta Wormatiensia*. Annalen und Chroniken (Quellen zur Geschichte der Stadt Worms, iii, 1893), pp. 97–126, discussion p. xxvi f. Two later lives ed. O. Holder-Egger in *M.G.H.*, Scriptores, xv (1; 1887), pp. 44–62, of which one has been re-edited by F. J. Bendel (Paderborn, 1912). Studies by H. Grosch (Jena, 1890) and A. M. Koeniger (Veröffentlichungen aus dem kirchenhistorischen Seminar München, II. Reihe, Nr. 6, Munich, 1905), F. Fournier in *Mélanges Paul Fabre* (1902), pp. 189–214, and in *R.H.E.*, xii (1911), pp. 451–73 and 670–701, with bibl. notes. J. Pétrau-Gay in *D.D.C.*, ii (1937), cols. 1141–57.

BURDETT-COUTTS, ANGELA GEORGINA (1814–1906), heiress and philanthropist. She was a granddaughter of Thomas Coutts, the banker, from whom she inherited in 1837 nearly £2,000,000. In 1871 she was raised to the peerage. She included among her many public benefactions some munificent gifts to the C of E, building and endowing the churches of St. Stephen, Rochester Row, *Westminster (1847), St. John, Limehouse (1853), St. James, Hatcham (1854), St. John, Deptford (1855), and St. Stephen, *Carlisle (1865). She was led by her interest in colonial expansion and in religion to endow as dependent sees of the Church at home, the Anglican bishoprics of Cape Town, South Africa (1847), and Adelaide, Australia (1847), and of British Columbia (1857).

Baroness Burdett-Coutts. A Sketch of her Public Life and Work prepared for the Lady Managers of the World's Columbian Exposition by Command of H.R.H., Princess Mary Adelaide, Duchess of Teck (1893). E. Johnson (ed.), *Letters from Charles Dickens to Angela Burdett-Coutts, 1841–1865* (1953). Clara Burdett Patterson (great niece), *Angela Burdett-Coutts and the Victorians* (1953). J. P. Anderson in *D.N.B., 1901–11*, i, pp. 259–66.

BURGHER. A member of the group in the Scottish Secession Church which defended in 1747 the lawfulness of the religious clause in the civil Burgess Oath and thus separated from the '*Antiburghers'.

BURGON, JOHN WILLIAM (1813–88), Dean of *Chichester. Educated at Worcester College, *Oxford, he became a Fellow of Oriel in 1846, Vicar of St. Mary's, Oxford, in 1863, and Dean of Chichester in 1876. He was an old-fashioned High Churchman who was famous for his support of a long series of lost causes. He fiercely denounced the disestablishment of the Irish Church in 1869, the appointment of A. P. *Stanley as a Select Preacher in 1872, and the new BCP lectionary of 1879. He was also a strenuous upholder of the *Textus Receptus of the NT, publishing in 1871 *The Last Twelve Verses of the Gospel according to St. Mark Vindicated*, and in 1883 *The Revision* [i.e. the RV] *Revised*; two further works on the subject were published posthumously. His widely read *Lives of Twelve Good Men* (1888) contained vivid sketches of 19th cent. High Churchmen, often enlivened by Burgon's provocative judgements on his contemporaries.

Life by E. M. *Goulburn (2 vols., London, 1892). A. F. Pollard in *D.N.B.*, Suppl. i (1901), pp. 335–8.

BURIAL ACTS. A series of enactments passed between 1852 and 1900, giving to local authorities powers to deal with the increasing overcrowding of churchyards, and to supervise all burial grounds to secure decency of burial and adequate sanitary precautions. Authority was given for the closing of burial grounds, or their conversion to recreation grounds (in towns), and for the opening of new ones. Various provisions were also made as to the manner of burial, the fees payable, the rights and obligations of the curate of the parish, and disinterment. By the Local Government Act of 1894 permission was given to transfer the powers and duties of the Burial Boards, formerly elected by the vestry, in towns to district councils, and in rural districts to the parish councils. By the Burial Laws Amendment Act of 1880, parishioners who by rubric and canon are forbidden burial acc. to the Prayer Book rite have nevertheless the right to burial in the parish churchyard or cemetery, with or without any form of Christian service.

On the law concerning rights to and duty of burial, see R. Phillimore, *The Ecclesiastical Law of the Church of England*, i (ed. 2, 1895), pp. 650–701; H. W. Cripps, *A Practical Treatise on the Law Relating to the Church and Clergy* (ed. 8 by K. M. MacMorran, 1937), pp. 564–89.

BURIAL SERVICES. Burial is the traditional Christian method of disposing of the dead, and in the 4th cent., which is the earliest period of which we have information, the burials were occasions of joy, and those attending them wore white. But from *c.* the 8th cent., when the prevalence of merely nominal Christianity made such joy not always fitting, the service became 'black', and the prayers petitions for speedy purification and for deliverance from hell. By the later Middle Ages the form had become fixed. The burial itself, at which the rite consisted of the committal prayers, was preceded overnight by *Vespers (or *Placebo), after which *Matins and *Lauds (Dirige or *Dirge) were said in the night, and in the morning *Requiem Mass, with prayers for the absolution of the dead. Requiems were also said on the 3rd, 9th, 30th, and 366th day after death. This order is still used according to the Roman rite. In the BCP the Dirge in a modified form (sentences, psalm, and lesson) is ordered, followed at the graveside by the committal prayers, and is to be used for all except those under (greater) excommunication, the unbaptized, and deliberate suicides. Recent Anglican revisions abroad, and the proposed Book of 1928, make alterations of phrasing, allow other alternative psalms, and shorten the lesson. Special forms are allowed for the burial of a baptized child. (In the Irish BCP a form is given for an unbaptized child of Christian parents, as well as for an adult who had desired but not received baptism.) The S. African BCP (and also the English 1928 Book) recognizes *cremation. Except in modern Protestantism, prayer for the dead, inherited from Judaism, has been a universal Christian custom, and from very early times the Eucharistic Liturgy was offered for the dead as well as the living. See also *Requiem Mass*.

W. Gresswell, *A Commentary on the Order for the Burial of the Dead* (2 vols., 1836).

BURIDAN'S ASS. The famous 'case', traditionally (but wrongly, it appears) ascribed to the Paris philosopher John Buridanus (*c.* 1300–1358), acc. to which an ass, set between two heaps of hay, absolutely equal in respect of quality and quantity, through having no motives to choose one rather than the other, died of starvation. The problem which it poses on the psychology of moral action goes back (with other examples) to *Aristotle.

Buridan's name is also connected, and here too erroneously, with the logical problem known as the *inventio medii* or 'Pons Asinorum', i.e., the bridge by which stupid scholars can find their way from the minor or major to the middle term of a syllogism. In fact the 'Pons Asinorum' is first found in the *Scotist, Peter Tartaretus (rector of Paris university, 1490).

The problem will be found stated in Aristotle, *De Caelo*, II, 13, p. 295 b 32. Überweg, ii, p. 597.

BURKHARDT, GEORG. See *Spalatin, Georg*.

BURKITT, FRANCIS CRAWFORD (1864–1935), NT, Semitic, and Patristic scholar. He was educated at Harrow and at Trinity College, Cambridge, and from 1905 till his death he was Norrisian (from 1934 'Norris Hulse') professor of divinity at Cambridge. He was esp. attracted to some of the more out-of-the-way fields in the history of early Christianity, and did important original work on the *Syriac versions of the NT, putting on a wholly new footing the study of the relation of the *Peshitta to the *Old Syriac Gospels. He also made valuable discoveries in the allied field of Syriac liturgies. Among his more important writings, nearly all of which reflect his brilliant and unconventional mind, are *The Old Latin and the Itala* (1896), *St. *Ephraim's Quotations from the Gospel* (1901), the art. 'Text and Versions' in the *Encyclopaedia Biblica* (vol. 4, 1903), *Evangelion da-Mepharreshe* (2 vols., 1904), *The Gospel History and its Transmission* (1906), *Christian Beginnings* (1924), *The Religion of the Manichees* (1925), *Palestine in General History* (Schweich

Lectures, 1929) and *Church and Gnosis* (1932).

E. C. Ratcliff, 'Francis Crawford Burkitt' in *J.T.S.*, xxxvi (1935), pp. 225–53, with note by G. G. Coulton, ib., p. 253 f., and list of his writings pp. 337–46. J. F. Bethune-Baker in *D.N.B.*, *1931–1940* (1949), p. 124 f., s.v.

BURMA, Christianity in. The kingdoms of Ava and Pegu, subsequently united under British rule as Burma, received their first missionaries from the RC Church, a *Barnabite mission being sent in 1722. This mission, which was transferred to various orders, was abandoned in 1852 but has since been re-started. In 1807 English *Baptists opened a mission, but the first permanent Baptist mission arrived in 1813 from America under Adoniram *Judson. The *SPG has done considerable work (Anglican) among English-speaking Burmese, particularly in education. Wesleyan and Methodist Episcopal missions were also established between 1879 and 1889. Christianity has been most readily welcomed by the Karens (since 1828), a hill tribe with a tradition that they had once possessed and then lost the knowledge of the true God, and that foreigners would help them to find it.

W. C. B. Purser, *Christian Missions in Burma* (S.P.G., 1911). P. A. Bigandet, *An Outline of the History of the Burmese Catholic Mission, 1720–1887* (Rangoon, 1887). H. P. Thompson, *Into All Lands. The History of the Society for the Propagation of the Gospel in Foreign Parts, 1701–1950* (1950), pp. 384–93, with further bibl. p. 732. Latourette, vi (1944), pp. 225–35, and vii (1945), pp. 319–323, both with bibl. reff. G. B. Tragella in *E.C.*, ii (1949), cols. 1669–71, s.v. 'Birmania', with further bibl.

BURNET, GILBERT (1643–1715), Bp. of *Salisbury. He was a native of Edinburgh, educated at Marischal College, Aberdeen, and in 1661 became a *probationer in the ministry of the Church of Scotland. He travelled widely, was the minister of Saltoun 1664–9, and professor of divinity at Glasgow University from 1669 to 1674, when he settled in England. He enjoyed influence at the English and Scottish royal courts, and from 1675 to 1684 was Chaplain to the *Rolls. In 1685 he went abroad after the collapse of the Exclusion agitation had led to the execution and exile of many of his friends. There he was much in the confidence of William of Orange and Mary, sailed with William in 1688 (persuading him at the last moment to land at Torbay instead of Exmouth), and was made Bp. of *Salisbury in 1689. A staunch Whig in politics and a *latitudinarian in theology, he endeavoured to carry through plans which would allow of the incorporation of the Nonconformists into the C of E. His episcopate was a model of zeal and activity, pastoral and administrative. He was also a voluminous author and a determined political controversialist, his most noteworthy writings being his *History of the Reformation in England* (3 vols., 1679–1714), his *Exposition of the XXXIX Articles* (1699), and his *History of My Own Time* (2 vols., 1723–34).

Burnet's *History of My Own Time*, ed., M. J. *Routh (6 vols., Oxford, 1823) and O. Airy (2 vols., reign of *Charles II only; Oxford, 1897–1900; suppl. from unpubld. MSS. by H. C. Foxcroft, ib., 1902). The best study is that of T. E. S. Clarke–H. C. Foxcroft–C. H. Firth (Cambridge, 1907). O. Airy in *D.N.B.*, vii (1886), pp. 394–405.

BURNEY, CHARLES FOX (1868–1925), OT and Semitic scholar. In 1899 he was elected a Fellow of St. John's College, Oxford, and in 1914 Oriel professor of the interpretation of Holy Scripture. He was one of the most original OT scholars of his generation. Among his more important writings are his *Notes on the Hebrew Text of the Book of Kings* (1903), his Schweich Lectures for 1917 on *Israel's Settlement in Canaan* (1918), and his commentary on *Judges* (1918). In his *Aramaic Origin of the Fourth Gospel* (1922) and his *Poetry of Our Lord* (1925), he emphasized the importance of the *Aramaic background of the Gospels for their proper understanding.

BURNING BUSH, The. The scene of *Moses' call, where the Angel of Jehovah appeared to him 'in a flame of fire out of the midst of a bush' (Ex. 3. 2–4 [*J]). The burning bush has frequently been used by Christian writers as a type of the Blessed Virgin.

BURROUGH, EDWARD (1634–63), *Quaker. Having heard G. *Fox preach in Westmorland in 1652, he determined to become a *Friend and began to preach himself, travelling up and down the country. In 1656 or 1657 he defended Quaker doctrines against an attack by J. *Bunyan. In 1660 he took up with *Charles II the cause of the Quakers in New England, who were then being persecuted by the Puritans, but without much success. In 1662 he was arrested in London for holding a meeting illegal under the *Quaker Act and committed to Newgate Prison, where he died. He issued a large number of writings, most of them very brief.

His writings (mainly hortatory treatises and polemical letters) were publd. as *The Memorable Works of a Son of Thunder and Consolation namely, That True Prophet, and Faithful Servant of God, and Sufferer for the Testimony of Jesus* (1672). [F. Howgil, G. Whitehead and others,] *A Testimony concerning the Life, Death, Trials, Travels and Labours of Edward Burroughs, That Worthy Prophet of the Lord* ('1662' [1663]). 'A Memoir of the Life and Religious Labours of that Eminent Servant of Christ and Minister of the Gospel, Edward Burrough' in W. and T. Evans (edd.), *The Friends' Library*, xiv (Philadelphia, 1850), pp. 380–491. E. Brockbank, *Edward Burrough. A Wrestler for Truth, 1634-1662* (1949).

BURSE. A case consisting of two squares of stiffened material in which the *corporal is kept. Its liturgical use in the Eucharist has been general only since the 17th cent. In earlier times the corporal was kept either in the *Missal or in some form of box or bag.

Braun, L. P., pp. 215–17.

BURTON, EDWARD (1794–1836), Regius professor of divinity at Oxford (from 1829). He was a scholar of wide and exact learning, and his writings include *Testimonies of the Ante-Nicene Fathers to the Divinity of Christ* (1826), an edition of the works of Bp. G. *Bull (1827), *Lectures on Ecclesiastical History* (2 vols., 1831, 1833), an edition of Bp. J. *Pearson *On the Creed* (1833), and an edition of

*Eusebius' *Ecclesiastical History* (1838, posthumous).

The Theological Works of Edward Burton, incl. Memoir of the author (5 vols., 1837).

BUSCH, IAN (1399–*c*. 1480). One of the principal members of the *Brethren of the Common Life. He was a native of Zwolle, and from 1420 to 1424 was professor at *Windesheim. In 1424 he was ordained priest at Bödingen, near Cologne, and thereafter filled a variety of offices in the Netherlands and Germany. His ideals were those of the Brotherhood at their best. He took a prominent part in reforming the monasteries in the spirit of the Council of *Basle and for a time worked in close co-operation with *Nicolas of Cusa, who appointed him 'Visitor Apostolic' of the *Augustinian houses of Saxony and Thuringia. He also wrote the history of the Brethren's house at *Windesheim.

His *Chronicon* was first publd. by the *Bollandist, H Rosweyde, S.J., at Antwerp, 1621, while a treatise 'De Reformatione Monasteriorum quorumdam Saxoniae' first appeared in G. W. *Leibniz's *Scriptores Rerum Brunsvicensium*, ii (1710), pp. 476–506 and 806–972. New ed. of both by K. Grube (Halle, 1886). Lives by K. Grube (Freiburg i.Br., 1881) and S. van der Woude (Diss. Edam, 1947). L. Schulze in *P.R.E.* (ed. 3), iii (1897), pp. 577–81.

BUSHNELL, HORACE (1802–76), American *Congregational divine. Born at Bantam, nr. Litchfield, Conn., U.S.A., he graduated at Yale University in 1827 and was assistant editor of the New York *Journal of Commerce* from 1828 to 1829. In 1829 he became a tutor at Yale, at first studying law until, throwing off his religious doubts during a college revival, he entered the theological department of Yale College in 1831. From 1833 to 1859 he was pastor to the North Congregational Church of Hartford, Conn. Owing to ill-health he held no official position in his later years, though he continued active as a writer. In 1856 he assisted in the organization of the College of California at Oakland.

Bushnell was the pioneer of liberal theology in New England. Characteristic was his restatement of the Doctrine of the Trinity. On the ground that language was essentially symbolic and relative to the subject, he held that while this Doctrine might be true for man in that God was experienced under three different aspects, it did not give him real information as to the inner nature of the Godhead nor require the existence of eternal distinctions in His Being. He also stressed the immanence of God in creation, explaining miracles as part of the Divine law of nature, and he interpreted the Atonement in terms of moral influence to the rejection of theories of satisfaction. Among his chief works were *Christian Nurture* (1847), *God in Christ* (1849), *Christ in Theology* (1851), *Nature and the Supernatural* (1858), *Work and Play* (1864), *The Vicarious Sacrifice* (1866), *Sermons on Living Subjects* (1872), and *Forgiveness and Law* (1874).

M. B. Cheney (his daughter), *Life and Letters of H. Bushnell* (New York, 1880); T. T. Munger, *H. Bushnell, Preacher and Theologian* (Boston, 1899; with bibliography).

BUTLER, ALBAN (1710–73), author of the *Lives of the Saints*. Educated at Douai, he was ordained priest in the RC Church in 1735. After long studies and many travels on the Continent, in search of hagiographical material, he published in 1756–9 *The Lives of the Fathers, Martyrs and other principal Saints, compiled from original Monuments and other authentic records, illustrated with the remarks of judicious modern critics and historians.* The *Lives* (over 1,600) are arranged acc. to the Church calendar, and though their chief purpose was edification, and history and legend are not discriminated, they remain a monument of wide research. From 1746 to 1766, Butler was a mission priest in England in the Midland District. From 1766 until his death he was President of the English College at St. Omer, where he was a frequent counsellor of the French clergy.

Drastically revised ed. of *The Lives of the Saints*, by H. Thurston, S.J., Norah Leeson, and D. Attwater (12 vols., 1926–38). *A Dictionary of Saints* to serve also as index to the rev. ed. has been compiled by D. Attwater (London, 1938), and suppl. vol. by id. (ib., 1949). New Revision of *Lives* (abbreviated, but further improved) by D. Attwater, incl. substance of *Dictionary* and of suppl. vol. (5 vols., 1956). [Charles Butler, nephew,] *An Account of the Life and Writings of the Rev. Alban Butler* (1799). E. H. Burton, *The Life and Times of Bishop Challoner*, i (1909), pp. 166 f., 221–4, 321 f., ii (1909), p. 161, incl. extracts from his letters and a portrait. T. Cooper in *D.N.B.*, vii (1886), p. 43 f.

BUTLER, JOSEPH (1692–1752), Bp. of *Durham. A native of Wantage, Berks, and the son of *Presbyterian parents, he studied at the dissenting academy at Tewkesbury where T. *Secker was his fellow-student. At an early age he entered into a correspondence with S. *Clarke on his 'Boyle Lectures' which revealed his remarkable powers of reasoning. Abandoning Presbyterianism he entered Oriel College, Oxford, in 1714, was ordained deacon and, two months later, priest, at *Salisbury in 1718, and from 1718 to 1726 was preacher at the Rolls Chapel. Here he delivered the sermons which won him his reputation. Fifteen were published in 1726, with an important preface, to which six others were added in later editions. In 1722 he had been presented to the rectory of Haughton-le-Skerne, nr. Darlington, and this he exchanged in 1726 for the wealthy benefice of Stanhope, Co. Durham. Here he lived in seclusion, engaged in pastoral duties and preparing his famous *Analogy of Religion* (1736; q.v.). In 1736, through Secker's influence, he was appointed Clerk of the Closet and from now on was constantly in attendance on Queen Caroline till her death (20 Nov. 1737). Commended to George II by the Queen on her death-bed, Butler was rewarded with the poorly endowed see of Bristol in 1738, where he came into hostility with J. *Wesley and G. *Whitefield. To supplement his income, he was preferred in 1740 to the deanery of *St. Paul's *in commendam*, and in 1750 he was translated to the bishopric of Durham. He is said (apocryphally) to have declined the see of *Canterbury in 1747 as he believed it 'too late to try to support a falling Church'.

Butler ranks among the greatest exponents of natural theology and ethics in England since the Reformation. His writings, which were esp. directed against attacks on the Christian conception of the world and the fundamental grounds of morality, stand out by their firm grasp of principle, sustained reasoning, caution, moral force, and, at times, irony. Their elevated tone is in marked contrast with that of the writings which they oppose; and, though his works make considerable demands on the reader, their moral qualities have won for them a permanent place in English literature.

Butler's moral philosophy, developed in his *Fifteen Sermons* and in the 'Dissertation on Virtue', appended to the *Analogy*, is directed esp. against the theories of T. *Hobbes which had risen to popularity in the 18th cent. He maintained that true morality consisted in living in accordance with one's nature and that the primary constituent principles in human nature were self-love, benevolence, and conscience. Actions whose motives lie in the natural passions and instincts do not conform with the interests either of self-love or of benevolence. In criticism of the hedonists of his age, Butler argued that the desire for an object was evoked by the desired object itself, and not by any anticipation of the resulting satisfaction, and that true benevolence or love of one's neighbour was strictly disinterested. To conscience attached a supreme authority which compelled in those who admitted it an obedience which could not consider consequences. The principles of morality were intuitively evident and errors of moral judgement arose only from superstition and self-deception. Belief in Providence, however, convinced Butler that in the end the dictates of conscience and the demands of self-love will be found to have pointed to the same conclusion. (For the argument of the *Analogy of Religion* see s.v.)

The writings of Butler went through a number of editions in the 18th cent., but for a long time did not attract the serious attention which they merited. Throughout the 19th cent. they were widely studied by Anglican candidates for Ordination. J. H. *Newman acknowledged his great debt to the teaching of the *Analogy* on probability and the sacramentalism of nature. More recent students of Butler include H. *Rashdall, A. E. *Taylor and C. D. Broad (b. 1887.)

The best edition of his Works is that by W. E. *Gladstone (2 vols., 1896), with a suppl. vol. of *Subsidiary Studies* (also 1896). T. Bartlett, *Memoirs of Joseph Butler* (1839); R. W. *Church, *Pascal and other Sermons* (1895), pp. 25–51; W. A. Spooner, *Bishop Butler* (1901); C. D. Broad, *Five Types of Ethical Theory* (1930), pp. 53–83; A. E. *Taylor, 'Some Features of Butler's Ethics' in *Philosophical Studies* (1934), pp. 291–329. L. Stephen in *D.N.B.*, viii (1886), pp. 67–72.

BUTLER, JOSEPHINE ELIZABETH (1828–1906), social reformer. She was the daughter of John Grey of Dilston, and in 1852 married George Butler (1819–90), sometime Canon of *Winchester. Her main interest was in the reclamation of prostitutes and the suppression of the 'white slave' trade. To this end she formed in 1869 the 'Ladies' National Association for the Repeal of the Contagious Diseases Acts', and in 1875 called a meeting at Geneva which resulted in the establishment of the International Federation for the Abolition of the State Regulation of Vice. Her inspiring work can best be studied in her *Personal Reminiscences of a Great Crusade* (1896). Behind her activities as a reformer lay a life of almost continuous prayer in which she took as her model St. *Catherine of Siena (whose Life she published in 1878).

G. W. and L. A. Johnson, *Josephine E. Butler. An Autobiographical Memoir* (1909); L. Hay-Cooper, *Josephine Butler* (1922).

BUTLER, WILLIAM JOHN (1818–94), Dean of *Lincoln. Educated at Westminster and at Trinity College, Cambridge, he was ordained in 1841, and in 1846 became vicar of Wantage. Here through a long incumbency he was a model parish priest of the High Church school and trained several curates who later became famous (A. H. *Mackonochie, V. S. S. Coles, W. C. E. Newbolt, H. P. *Liddon, &c.). In 1850 he founded in his parish St. Mary's Sisterhood, which as the Community of St. Mary the Virgin (C.S.M.V.) has grown into one of the largest and most active of the Anglican religious communities. In 1864 he was elected to the bishopric of Natal after J. W. *Colenso's deposition; but owing to Abp. C. T. *Longley's disapproval, declined the invitation. In 1880 he became a canon of *Worcester and in 1885 Dean of Lincoln. He retained the wardenship of the C.S.M.V. till his death.

Life and Letters of William John Butler [ed. by A. J. Butler (son)] (1897); [A. L. Hoare] C.S.M.V., *Butler of Wantage. His Inheritance and His Legacy* [1948].

BUTTERFIELD, WILLIAM (1814–1900), architect. A keen Churchman who had come under the influence of the *Oxford Movement, Butterfield was inspired by the architectural ideals of the *Cambridge Camden Society. His better-known works include: St. Augustine's College, Canterbury (1845); All Saints', Margaret Street, London (1859); St. Alban's, Holborn (1863); the new buildings at Merton College, Oxford (1864) (subsequently much altered); and *Keble College, Oxford (1870–1876). He also built several Anglican cathedrals in the colonies and dominions.

Study by J. Summerson in *Architectural Review*, xcviii (1945), pp. 167–75. P. Waterhouse in *D.N.B.*, Suppl. i (1901), pp. 360–3.

BUTZER, MARTIN. See *Bucer, Martin*.

BYE PLOT, The (1603). Also known as the *Priests' Plot. The lesser of two plots (the 'Main' and the 'Bye' plots) against *James I of England at his accession. William Watson and William Clarke, two RC priests, conspired with George Brooke and Lord Grey of Wilton, two Protestants out of sympathy with the new régime, to kidnap the King's person and extort concessions from him, partly on behalf of the *recusants. The plot was revealed by a Jesuit and another RC priest; Watson, Clarke, and Brooke were executed, and Lord Grey died in prison.

BYRD, WILLIAM (*c.* 1543–1623), English composer, 'Parent of British Music'. Prob. born at *Lincoln and a pupil of T. *Tallis at the *Chapel Royal, he was appointed organist of Lincoln Cathedral in 1563. In 1570 he was sworn as a Gentleman of the Chapel Royal where he became organist with Tallis. In 1575 he and Tallis were jointly granted a monopoly of printing music. He resided at Stondon Place, Essex, from *c.* 1593.

Though he was Catholic in sympathy and involved in frequent litigation for recusancy, Byrd's religion never seems to have prevented him executing his duties in the Chapel Royal. Besides his three superb Masses (prob. publd. 1602), which, although written for the Latin rite, are used in the C of E, and his two books of *Gradualia* (1605 and 1607), he set to music the Preces and Responses and Litany of the English liturgy and composed at least two complete Services ('Short Service' and 'Great Service'). In addition to writing various sacred songs and setting to music Latin motets, he was one of the pioneers of the verse anthem. His many anthems include 'Sing Joyfully', 'Sing Merrily' and 'Bow Thine Ear'. He also wrote a large body of string music, keyboard music and secular choral music esp. madrigals. His publications include *Cantiones Sacrae* (jointly with T. Tallis, 1575), *Psalms, Sonnets and Songs* (1588), *Songs of Sundry Natures* (1589), two further books of *Cantiones Sacrae* (1589 and 1591) and *Psalmes, Songs and Sonnets* (1611).

Complete Works ed. E. H. Fellowes (20 vols., London, 1937–50). The best study is that of id. (Oxford, 1936); earlier lives by id. (Oxford, 1923) and F. Howes ('Masters of Music', London, 1928). W. H. Hadow, 'William Byrd, 1623–1923' in *Proceedings of the British Academy*, x (1921–3), pp. 395–413. W. B. Squire in *D.N.B.*, viii (1886), pp. 123–6; E. H. Fellowes in *Grove's Dictionary of Music and Musicians*, i (ed. 5 by E. Blom; 1954), pp. 1055–60, with bibl. details, pp. 1060–8.

BYZANTINE TEXT OF THE NT, The. The form of the Greek NT text which has become the standard one in the Greek-speaking Church. It is to be found in the great majority of the extant Greek MSS. of the NT, and was closely followed by D. *Erasmus in his 'Greek Testament' (1516) and in the *Textus Receptus. It is probably in essentials the *Syrian text of *Lucian of Antioch, somewhat corrupted, and perhaps also further 'revised', in the course of transmission. See also *Syrian Text*.

BYZANTIUM. See *Constantinople*.

C

CABASILAS, NICHOLAS (b. c. 1322), Byzantine mystical writer. The nephew of the Archbishop of Thessalonica (with whom he has often been confused), he appears to have remained a layman throughout his life. The date of his death is unknown. In the *Hesy-chast controversy he supported the monks of Mount *Athos, though he held the theory of the *Uncreated Light in a moderated form. In his principal work, a set of seven discourses 'Concerning the Life in Christ' (περὶ τῆς ἐν Χριστῷ ζωῆς), he explained how, through the three mysteries of *Baptism, *Confirmation, and the *Eucharist, spiritual union with Christ was to be achieved. He also wrote an 'Interpretation of the Divine Liturgy' (Ἑρμηνεία τῆς θείας λειτουργίας).

His 'Sacrae Liturgicae Interpretatio', his Life of Christ, a Sermon 'Contra Feneratores', and his Life of St. Theodore in J. P. Migne, *PG*, cl, 367–772. Fr. trr. of his Life of Christ by S. Broussaleux, A.A. (Supplement to *Irénikon*, ix, 1932), and of his Interpretation of the Liturgy by S. Salaville, A.A. (*S.C.*, 4, 1943). S. Salaville, A.A., 'Vues sotériologiques chez Nicolas Cabasilas' in *Études Byzantines*, i (1943), pp. 5–57. J. Gouillard in *D.H.G.E.*, xi (1949), pp. 14–21, and S. Salaville, A.A., in *Dict. Sp.* ii (1953), cols. 1–9, both s.v., with bibl. Eng. tr. of his *Interpretation of the Divine Liturgy* by Joan M. Hussey and P. A. McNulty, with introd. by R. M. French (1960).

CABBALA (Rabbinic Heb. קַבָּלָה, *qabbālāh*, 'tradition'). A system of Jewish *theosophy which, by the use of an esoteric method of interpretation of the OT, including cyphers, was believed to reveal to its initiates hidden doctrines, e.g. the creation of the world by means of emanations from the Divine Being. It was a development of tendencies akin to *Gnosticism, and reached the height of its influence in the later Middle Ages and at the Renaissance. A Christian form of it also had considerable vogue in the 15th–16th cents., its Christian exponents such as J. *Reuchlin and *Paracelsus professing to deduce by its means such doctrines as the Trinity, the Atonement, and the Divinity of Christ.

The *Zohar* tr. into Eng. by H. Sperling–M. Simon–P. P. Levertoff (5 vols., 1931–4). G. G. Scholem, *Major Trends in Jewish Mysticism* (Jerusalem, 1941; ed. 2, New York, 1946). C. D. Ginsburg, *The Kabbalah. Its Doctrine, Development and Literature* (1865); J. Abelson, *Jewish Mysticism* (1913). J. L. Blau, *The Christian Interpretation of the Cabala in the Renaissance* (New York, 1944). L. Ginzburg in *J.E.*, iii (1902), pp. 456–79; G. G. Scholem in *E.J.*, ix (1932), cols. 630–732, s.v. 'Kabbala'. Id., *Bibliographia Kabbalistica* (Berlin, 1933; additions in *Kirjath Sepher*, Jerusalem, 1933 ff.). H. Loewe in *H.E.R.E.*, vii (1914), pp. 622–8, s.v. 'Kabbala'.

CABROL, FERNAND (1855–1937), liturgical scholar. In 1877 he was professed a Benedictine monk at *Solesmes, and in 1896 elected prior of the projected monastery at Farnborough in England of which in 1903 he became Abbot. In conjunction with H. *Leclercq he edited the *Dictionnaire d'archéologie chrétienne et de liturgie* (1903–53) and the *Monumenta ecclesiae liturgica* (1900 ff.). His own writings include *Le Livre de la prière*

antique (1900; Eng. trans. *Liturgical Prayer, its History and Spirit*, 1922), *Les Origines liturgiques* (1906), and *L'Angleterre chrétienne avant les Normands* (1909).

L. Gougaud, O.S.B., in *R.H.E.*, xxxiii (1937), pp. 919–22, with reff. to other obituary notices. F. [Philip] Oppenheim, O.S.B., in *E.C.*, iii (1950), col. 265, s.v.

CAECILIAN (d. c. 345), Bp. of *Carthage from 311. His importance lies in his part in the opening stages of the *Donatist controversy. As archdeacon he had supported Mensurius, Bp. of Carthage, in his efforts to suppress the fanatical desire of many Christians for martyrdom and the uncritical veneration for *confessors, and on Mensurius's death in 311 he was elected to succeed him. The opposing rigoristic party at Carthage then consecrated a rival bishop, urging that Caecilian's own consecration was invalid on the ground that he had received his orders from one Felix of Aptunga, a ' *traditor'. He is the only bishop from Latin Africa who is known to have attended the Council of *Nicaea (325).

The chief sources are *Eusebius of Caesarea, St. *Optatus of Milevis, and St. *Augustine. P. Monceaux, *Histoire littéraire de l'Afrique chrétienne*, iv (1913), passim. See also bibl. to *Donatism*. For the Lat. version of the Nicene Canons which goes under his name ('Interpretatio Caeciliani', also 'Vetus Interpretatio'), see Turner, *E.O.M.I.A.* (1899–1939), passim, and F. *Maassen, *Geschichte der Quellen und der Literatur des canonischen Rechts im Abendlande*, i (1870), pp. 8–11; there are no sufficient reasons, however, for the common assumption that Caecilian himself was the author of the version, cf. E. *Schwartz, 'Über die Sammlung des Cod. Veronensis LX', in *Z.N.T.W.*, xxxv (1936), p. 11 f.

CAEDMON (d. c. 680), the earliest English Christian poet. Acc. to *Bede, the source of almost all our knowledge of him, Caedmon was a labourer at the monastery at *Whitby, who received in a vision the gift of composing verses in the praise of God, and as a result became a monk. He was instructed in the Scriptures, which, as Bede also tells us, he turned into verse. He was the first Anglo-Saxon writer of popular religious poetry. Prob. Caedmon's only surviving work is a hymn which he is said to have composed in a dream, and which appears in an 8th cent. hand on a blank leaf in the Moore MS. of Bede. Many other traditional poems are ascribed to him, with doubtful justice. He was venerated as a saint at *Jarrow, and his feast kept on 11 Feb.

The principal source for his life is *Bede, *H.E.*, iv. 22 [24]; notes in ed. C. Plummer (2 vols., Oxford, 1896), vol. i, pp. cxiii and cxxiv, vol. ii, pp. 248–54, and 257 f. Modern edd. of his Hymn, in two versions, in W. J. Sedgefield, *Anglo-Saxon Verse Book* (Publications of the University of Manchester, cliii; 1922), p. 80 f., and in A. H. Smith, *Three Northumbrian Poems* (1933), pp. 38–41. Eng. tr. from Junius MS. by C. W. Kennedy, *The Caedmon Poems* (1916), p. 1. Further bibl., incl. that of Caedmon School and notes of other works attrib. to him, in *C.B.E.L.*, i (1940), pp. 73–5.

CAEREMONIALE EPISCOPORUM. In the RC Church the liturgical book containing the rites and ceremonies for a bishop. A much revised edition was promulgated by

*Clement VIII in 1600, and this has since undergone a number of further changes. In spite of its name, it also deals with much non-episcopal ceremonial, e.g. it orders the cathedral ceremonies celebrated in the absence of the bishop. As it is the official ceremonial handbook in the RC Church, its regulations are of authority in settling matters not covered by the rubrics of the *missal and other service books.

The Caeremoniale which is in three Books (1. The duties of the Bishop at his elevation, on entering his diocese and in his cathedral; the pontifical ornaments; his duties when assisting in choir and at Low Mass. 2. His duties at Pontifical and Solemn Mass and Office. 3. The marks of honour due to the Bishop) has been constantly reprinted. The classical commentary is that of J. Catalani, 2 vols., Rome, 1744. On the constitutive liturgical books, see the fundamental work of M. Andrieu, *Les Ordines Romani du haut moyen-âge* (S.S.L., (1931 ff. [5 vols. to 1958])). -. Le Vavasseur, *Les Fonctions pontificales selon le rit romain* (2 vols., 1865; ed. 3, 'R. P.' Haegy, 1904). F. Mostardi in *E.C.*, iii (1950), cols. 1317–19, s.v. 'Cerimoniale dei vescovi'.

CAEREMONIALE ROMANUM. (1) A Latin service book, compiled *c.* 1275 on the command of *Gregory X, which contains the rite for the investiture of a newly elected Pope. It was first published by J. *Mabillon in 1689 as *Ordo Romanus XIII.

(2) A treatise, also known as the 'Caeremoniale Capellae Pontificiae', which describes the ceremonial of the Papal curia. It was composed in 1488 by P. Piccolomini, Bp. of Pienza (1483–96), on the basis of the *Ordines Romani, and was first published by Christophorus Marcellus, Abp. of Corcyra, in 1516.

On (1) J. Mabillon, O.S.B., *Museum Italicum*, ii (Paris, 1689), pp. 221–41; repr. in J. P. Migne, *PL*, lxxviii, 1105–22.

CAERULARIUS, MICHAEL. See *Michael Cerularius*.

CAESAR. The word, which was virtually a title of the Roman emperors in the 1st–3rd cents. A.D., occurs several times in the NT (e.g. Mk. 12. 14–17, Jn. 19. 12, Acts 25. 8–12). To the inhabitants of Palestine and the provinces, the name denoted the Imperial throne rather than the person occupying it. The emperors contemporary with the NT were: Augustus, 27 B.C.–A.D. 14; Tiberius, A.D. 14–37; Gaius (Caligula), A.D. 37–41; Claudius, A.D. 41–54; Nero, A.D. 54–68; Galba, A.D. 68–9; Otho, A.D. 69; Vitellius, A.D. 69; Vespasian, A.D. 69–79; Titus, A.D. 79–81; and Domitian, A.D. 81–96.

CAESAREA (Palestine). Originally known as 'Straton's Tower', the city on the coast of Palestine north of Jaffa (to be distinguished from the 'Caesarea Philippi' of Mt. 16. 13, Mk. 8. 27, the modern Banias south of Mount Hermon) was rebuilt by *Herod the Great, *c.* 25–13 B.C., prob. as a port for Sebaste (Samaria) and renamed in honour of the Emp. Augustus. It became the capital of Palestine (*c.* 13 B.C.). In the Apostolic Church it was visited by *Philip the Evangelist (Acts 8. 40), who took up his residence here (21. 8), and by

St. *Peter who, in obedience to a vision, made himself known to Cornelius and was the instrument through whom the Holy Spirit was first given to the Gentiles (10. 44 f.). St. *Paul was brought from *Jerusalem to Caesarea after his conversion and sent on thence to Tarsus (9. 30); he landed here on his way from *Ephesus to Jerusalem (18. 22); and he was imprisoned here for two years (23. 23–26. 32), during which period he possibly (so H. E. G. *Paulus, F. *Spitta) wrote his '*Captivity Epistles'. Under *Vespasian it became a colony (A.D. 70). Prob. the scene of a small Council regulating the celebration of *Easter *c.* 196 (*Eusebius, *HE*, v. 25), it became 'Metropolis Provinciae Syriae Palestinae' under Alexander Severus (d. 222). In consequence its Bishop became metropolitan of Palestine (recognized at the Council of Nicaea, can. 7) and held this dignity until the Council of *Chalcedon (451) subordinated him to the Patriarch of Jerusalem.

The home of *Origen from 231, Caesarea became noted as a seat of learning, with its episcopal library which contained many of Origen's works (incl. his *Hexapla*). Its most notable Bishop was Eusebius (Bp., 315–*c.* 340), the most learned man of his age. St. *Jerome also studied here. The city suffered severely in the 7th cent. It was captured by the *Crusaders in 1101, when a chalice was found among the spoil, believed to have been used at the Last Supper. Important during the Crusades, the city was demolished in 1265 and remained in ruins until the 19th cent.

L. Haefeli, *Cäsarea am Meer*. Topographie und Geschichte der Stadt nach Josephus und Apostelgeschichte (1923). F. M. Abel, O.P., *Géographie de la Palestine*, ii (1938), p. 296 f., s.v. 'Césarée de Palestine', with reff. R. Janin, A.A., in *D.H.G.E.*, xii (1953), s.v. 'Cesarée de Palestine', with bibl.

CAESAREA PHILIPPI. The scene of St. *Peter's confession of Christ's Messiahship (Mk. 8. 27, Mt. 16. 13). It was the ancient Paneion, now Banias, at the foot of Mount Hermon. Acc. to *Eusebius (*H.E.*, VII. xviii), it was the home of the woman with the issue of blood (Mt. 9. 20), where a house was shown in his day with statues commemorating the event.

W. Ewing in *H.D.B.*, i (1900), p. 337 f., s.v.; R. Janin in *D.H.G.E.*, xii (1954), cols. 209–11, s.v. 'Césarée de Philippe'.

CAESAREAN TEXT. A form of the Greek text of the NT (analogous, e.g., to the *Neutral and *Western texts) which B. H. *Streeter discovered and described in his *Four Gospels* (1924). It is represented notably in the MSS. Θ (the 'Koridethi MS.', now at Tiflis), and the two families of *minuscules, 13–69–124–346 (the '*Ferrar Group') and 1–118–131–209; but as the text of the MSS. containing it had been very considerably assimilated to the *Lucianic standard, its existence was masked until Streeter isolated it. From a study of the text of Mk. used by *Origen in his Commentary on John, the earlier part of which he is known to have written at *Alexandria and the later part at *Caesarea in Palestine (after 231), Streeter deduced that it was the text in use at Caesarea in the 3rd cent.

More recent study, notably by K. *Lake and his colleagues, has thrown doubt on the existence of the Caesarean Text as a distinct entity. It was certainly not confined to Caesarea, since Origen used a form of the text ('pre-Caesarean') in some of his other writings dating from his Alexandrian period.

B. H. Streeter, *The Four Gospels* (1924), ch. iv, pp. 77–108. McNeile, pp. 387–91. K. *Lake–R. P. Blake–S. New, 'The Caesarean Text of the Gospel of Mark' in *H.T.R.*, xxi (1928), pp. 207–404; T. Ayuso, 'Texto cesariense o pre-cesariense? Su realidad y su trascendencia en la crítica textual del Nuevo Testamento' in *Biblica*, xvi (1935), pp. 369–415; B. M. Metzger, 'The Caesarean Text of the Gospels' in *Journal of Biblical Literature*, lxiv (1945), pp. 457–89.

CAESARIUS, St. (c. 470–542), Abp. of *Arles from 502. In 489 he entered the monastery at *Lerins. He took a prominent part in the ecclesiastical administration of S. Gaul, and with the help of Alaric II and Theodoric the Great succeeded in establishing the claim of Arles to be the primatial see in Gaul. He was largely instrumental in securing the condemnation of *Semi-pelagianism at the Council of *Orange in 529. A large collection of canons, known as the '*Statuta Ecclesiae Antiqua', has been ascribed to him by many modern scholars (e.g. A. Malnory, L. *Duchesne), but probably (so G. *Morin) mistakenly. He was a celebrated preacher, and several of his sermons have survived. His life was written by St. *Cyprian of Toulon in conjunction with some of his other pupils. Feast day, 27 Aug.

Several of his writings ed. J. P. Migne, *PL*, lxvii, xxxix, &c. Crit. ed. G. Morin, O.S.B., 2 vols., Maredsous, 1937–42 (vol. i: Sermones; vol. ii: Concilia a Caesario habita, Regulae Monasticae, Opuscula Theologica, Testamentum, with Vita Caesarii in appendix), which supersedes all earlier texts. Monographs by C. F. Arnold (Leipzig, 1894), A. Malnory (Paris, 1894) and M. Chaillan ('Les Saints', Paris, 1912); also S. Cavallin, *Studien zur Vita Caesarii* (Lund, 1934) and several studies by G. Morin preparatory to his edition. Bardenhewer, v (1932), pp. 345–56; B. Altaner, *Patrologie* (ed. 2, 1950), pp. 426–8. P. Lejay in *D.T.C.*, ii (1905), cols. 2168–85; E. Peterson in *E.C.*, iii (1950), col. 1353 f. See also bibl. to *Statuta Ecclesiae Antiqua*.

CAESARIUS, St., of Nazianzus (d. 369). He held various offices at court, including that of physician. There exists a set of four dialogues attributed to him, but they are much later in date. Our knowledge of him derives mainly from a panegyric delivered at his funeral by his elder brother, St. *Gregory of Nazianzus. Feast day in the W, 25 Feb.; in the E, 9 Mar.

J. P. Migne, *PG*, xxxviii, 851–1190.

CAESARIUS OF HEISTERBACH (c. 1180–1240), ecclesiastical writer. Born in or near *Cologne, in 1199 he entered the *Cistercian Order at the monastery of Heisterbach (near Königswinter, on the Rhine). His best known writings are his 'Dialogus Miraculorum' (c. 1223), a collection of spiritual anecdotes for the edification of novices, full of

supernatural incident, and his eight books (not all extant) 'On Miracles'. The latter throw important light on the events and popular beliefs of his age, as well as on the history of the Cistercian Order. He also wrote a Life of St. Engelbert (murdered at Cologne in 1225).

Dialogus Miraculorum ed. J. Strange (2 vols., Cologne, etc., 1851; Eng. tr., 2 vols., 1929); 'Vita, Passio et Miracula S. Engelberti' ed. A. Poncelet, S.J., in *AA.SS.*, Nov. III (1910), pp. 644–81. A. E. Schönbach, 'Studien zur Erzählungsliteratur des Mittelalters. Teil IV: Ueber Caesarius von Heisterbach' in *Sb.* (Wien), cxliv (1902), Abh. ix; A. Meister, 'Die Fragmente der Libri VIII Miraculorum des Caesarius von Heisterbach' in *R.Q.*, Suppl. xiii (1901); A. Poncelet, S.J., 'Note sur les Libri VIII Miraculorum de Césaire d'Heisterbach' in *Anal. Boll.*, xxi (1902), pp. 45–52. Germ. tr. of Life of St. Engelbert, with useful introd., by K. Langosch (Münster i.W.–Cologne, 1955). Full bibl. in [F. C.] Dahlmann–[G.] Waitz (ed. 9, H. Haering), *Quellenkunde der deutschen Geschichte* (1931), No. 6370, p. 396 f.

CAESAROPAPISM. The system whereby an absolute monarch has supreme control over the Church within his dominions and exercises it even in matters (e.g. doctrine) normally reserved to ecclesiastical authority. The term is most generally used of the authority exercised by the Byzantine emperors over the E. patriarchates, esp. in the centuries immediately preceding the *Great Schism of 1054.

CAIAPHAS. The Jewish *High Priest before whom Christ was tried (Mt. 26. 3, &c.), and at whose instigation He was condemned (Jn. 11. 49 ff.). He was appointed High Priest c. 18 and deposed in 37. He was son-in-law of *Annas.

CAINITES. A *Gnostic sect mentioned by *Irenaeus and other early writers which, regarding the God of the OT as responsible for the evil in the world, exalted those who withstood him, e.g. Cain, Esau, and Korah. They are said to have had an apocryphal Gospel of *Judas Iscariot. The mention of Cain in the NT (1 Jn. 3. 12, Jude 11–19) suggests a very early, perhaps pre-Christian, origin of the sect.

St. *Irenaeus, *Haer.*, i. 31; St. *Hippolytus, *Haer.*, viii. 20; Ps.-*Tertullian, *De Praescr. Haer.*, xxxiii; St. *Epiphanius, *Haer.*, xxxviii. Further reff. in artt. by G. Bareille in *D.T.C.*, ii (1905), cols. 1307–9, and G. Bardy in *D.H.G.E.*, xi (1949), cols. 226–8 s.vv.

CAIRD, EDWARD (1835–1908), Scottish philosopher and theologian. In 1866 he became professor of moral philosophy at Glasgow and in 1893 succeeded B. *Jowett as Master of Balliol College, Oxford. He was one of the chief representatives of the Neo-*Hegelian movement in British philosophy. In *The Evolution of Religion* (1893) and *The Evolution of Theology in the Greek Philosophers* (*Gifford Lectures, 2 vols. 1904) he maintained that the religious principle was a necessary element in consciousness, and that Christianity, in that it overcame the antithesis of the real and the ideal, was the absolute religion. 'In Christianity religion has risen to its own true form.' He also published two important works on I. *Kant, *A Critical Account of the Philosophy of Kant* (1877) and *The Critical Philosophy of Immanuel Kant* (2 vols., 1889, a recasting of the previous book) and a monograph on G. W. F. *Hegel (1883).

H. Jones and J. H. Muirhead, *The Life and Philosophy of Edward Caird* (1921). Obituary note by B. *Bosanquet in *Proceedings of the British Academy* (1907–8), pp. 379–86. *D.N.B.*, *1901–1911*, i, pp. 291–5 (unsigned).

CAIRD, JOHN (1820–98), elder brother of the preceding, divine and philosopher. In 1845 he entered the ministry of the Church of Scotland and in 1862 was elected professor of divinity at Glasgow. In 1873 he became Principal of Glasgow University. Like his brother, he came under the influence of the Neo-Hegelian Movement; but his teaching on the nature of the religious consciousness, was somewhat nearer Christian orthodoxy. His chief writings were an *Introduction to the Philosophy of Religion* (1880) and a posthumously published set of *Gifford Lectures on *The Fundamental Ideas of Christianity* (with a Memoir by E. Caird, 1899).

Memoir by E. Caird (brother) prefixed to *Fundamental Ideas of Christianity*, i (1899), pp. ix–cxli. C. L. Warr, *Principal Caird* (The Scottish Layman's Library, 1926). T. Bayne in *D.N.B.*, Suppl. i (1901), p. 368 f.

CAIUS. See *Gaius*.

CAJETAN, St. (1480–1547), founder of the *Theatine Order. A native of Vicenza, he was ordained priest at Rome in 1516. From the first he exerted himself to spread a fresh spirit of devotion among the clergy and to that end founded in 1524 with Pietro Caraffa (afterwards *Paul IV) and two other priests the congregation known as the *Theatines, for clerics bound by vow and living in common, but engaged in pastoral work. He was beatified in 1629 and canonized in 1671. Feast day, 7 Aug.

Life by Antonio Caraccioli, O. Theat., orig. publ. in Cajetan's *De Vita Pauli IV . . . Collectanea Historica* (Cologne, 1612), pp. 176–260; repr. in *A A.SS.* Aug. II (1735), pp. 282–301. Another early life by G. B. Cataldo, O. Theat. (Rome, 1616). P. Chiminelli, *San Gaetano Thiene* (1948), with full bibl. Other modern lives include those by G. M. Magenis (Venice, 1726; Germ. tr., 1754), M. A. R. Maulde la Clavière ('Les Saints', 1902; Eng. tr., 1902), O. Premoli (Crema, 1910), and P. Chiminelli (Vicenza, 1949). P. Paschini, *S. Gaetano Thiene, Gian Pietro Carafa e le origini dei chierici regolari teatini* (1926). F. Andreu, C.R. (ed.), *Le lettere di San Gaetano da Thiene* (S.T. clxxvii; 1954).

CAJETAN, THOMAS DE VIO (1469–1534), theologian. He was called Gaetano ('Cajetan') from his birthplace, Gaeta. He entered the *Dominican Order in 1484, and taught philosophy and theology at Padua (where contemporary philosophical movements were represented by P. *Pomponazzi and others), Pavia, and Rome. As *General of his order (1508–18), Cardinal (1517), and Bp. of Gaeta (1519) he played an important part in ecclesiastical affairs, urging the cause of reform before the fathers of the *Lateran Council of 1512, reasoning with *Luther in 1518, contributing to the elections of the Emp. *Charles V (1519) and the Pope *Hadrian VI

(1522), and opposing the projected divorce of *Henry VIII (1530). Except for some years during the pontificate of *Clement VII, he was seldom free from onerous duties, but he contrived to study and write continually. In philosophy and theology his acute but conservative Commentary on St. *Thomas's 'Summa theologica' (1507–22) was the first monument of a great revival of *Thomism in the 16th cent., and remains to-day one of the chief classics of scholasticism. Finding that Humanists and Protestants alike were making polemical use of the Scriptures, he subsequently turned to Biblical exegesis, for which he sought the assistance of scholarly philologists; and his commentaries on the Bible contain much enlightened criticism of an unexpectedly 'modern' kind.

Quétif-Échard, ii, pp. 14–21 and 428. A. Cossio, *Il Cardinale Gaetano e la riforma*, i (all publd., Cividale, 1902). J. M. Vosté, O.P., *Thomas de Vio, O.P., Cardinalis Cajetanus, Sacrae Paginae Magister* (Rome, 1935). J. F. Groner, O.P., *Kardinal Cajetan* (Louvain, 1951), with bibl. Nos. 86 and 87 of the *Revue Thomiste*, N.S. xvii (1935), also contain artt. specially devoted to his life and teaching. D. A. Mortier, O.P., *Histoire des maîtres généraux de l'ordre des Frères Prêcheurs*, v (1911), pp. 141–230. P. Mandonnet, O.P., in *D.T.C.*, ii (1905), cols. 1313–29; s.v.; J. R. Volz, O.P., in *C.E.*, iii (1908), pp. 145–8, s.v.; U. degl' Innocenti, O.P., in *E.C.*, iv (1950), cols. 1506–9, s.v. 'De Vio, Tommaso', with further bibl.

CALAMY, EDMUND (1600–66), 'the Elder', English *Presbyterian divine. Of *Huguenot descent, he was educated at Pembroke Hall, Cambridge, where he was excluded from a fellowship on account of his opposition to *Arminian teaching. From 1626 to 1636 he was lecturer at Bury St. Edmunds, and from 1639 *perpetual curate of St. Mary Aldermanbury in London. He took a leading part in the production of the composite work *Smectymnuus directed against J. *Hall's apology for a moderate episcopacy. As an active member of the *Westminster Assembly of 1643, he sought to defend presbyterianism as a middle course between prelacy and congregationalism. During the Commonwealth he worked for the return of *Charles II, and at the Restoration was offered as a reward for his services, but did not accept, the see of Coventry and *Lichfield. At the *Savoy Conference of 1661 he continued to take a moderate line, and hopes were entertained by the Bishops of his conforming; but he refused to yield, and in 1662 he was ejected from his preferments. In 1663 he was committed for a short time to Newgate Prison for disobeying the Act of *Uniformity. Several of his sermons were published.

His Sermon preached on 17 Aug. 1662, is pr. in *Farewell Sermons of Some of the Most Eminent of the Nonconformist Divines, Delivered at the Period of their Ejection by the Act of Uniformity in the Year 1662* (1816), pp. 1–13, with biogr. introd. p. vi f. *Cromwell's Soldiers' Bible . . .* compiled by Edmund Calamy, and issued for the Use of the Commonwealth Army in 1643, was repr. in facsimile (London, 1895). A. Gordon in *D.N.B.*, viii (1886), pp. 227–30.

CALAMY, EDMUND (1671–1732), historian of Nonconformity, the only son of Edmund Calamy 'the Younger' (1635?–85), who was himself the son of Edmund *Calamy 'the Elder' (1600–66). His works threw much light on the history of Nonconformity. Esp. valuable is a chapter (ix, nearly half the first volume) in his *Abridgement of *Baxter's History* (1702; new ed., 2 vols. 1713) entitled 'A Particular Account of the Ministers, Lecturers, Fellows of Colleges, etc., who were silenced and ejected by the Act for Uniformity; with the characters and works of many of them'.

A. G. Matthews, *Calamy Revised*. Being a revision of Edmund Calamy's *Account* of the Ministers and others ejected and silenced, 1660–2 (1934). A. Gordon in *D.N.B.*, viii (1886), pp. 230–5.

CALCED (Lat. *calceatus*, 'shod'). A term applied to some branches of certain religious orders to distinguish them from their '*Discalced' brethren (q.v.). Thus the unreformed *Carmelites, who wear shoes, are called 'calced' as opposed to the Discalced members of the *Teresian reform, who wear sandals; the same applies to the 'calced' Conventual *Franciscans.

CALDERWOOD, HENRY (1830–97), Scottish philosopher. He studied at Edinburgh, and in 1856 was ordained minister of Greyfriars Church at Glasgow. In 1868 he became professor of moral philosophy at Edinburgh. He made it his aim to refute the doctrine of W. *Hamilton (whose pupil he had been) that the human mind cannot know ultimate truth, arguing that a religious faith based on God's unknowableness was little more than a piece of superstition. He held that an important place in religion and ethics must be ascribed to intuition, which puts the soul into immediate contact with God. His writings include *The Philosophy of the Infinite* (1854), published while he was still a student, and some books on the philosophy of the natural sciences.

Life by his son [W. L. Calderwood] and D. Woodside, with account of his philosophical works by A. S. Pringle-*Pattison (London, 1900). T. B. Johnstone in *D.N.B.*, Suppl. i (1901), p. 373 f.

CALDEY ISLAND, off the south coast of Wales, near Tenby, the seat of a monastery as far back as the 5th cent. In 1906 an abbey for Anglican Benedictines was established on the ancient ruins. In 1913 nearly the whole community transferred their allegiance to the RC Church. In 1928 they left Caldey for their present house at Prinknash, near *Gloucester, and the island was taken over by *Trappists from Chimay in Belgium.

The Benedictines of Caldey Island (Caldey, 1907). P. Anson, *The Benedictines of Caldey*. The Story of the Anglican Benedictines of Caldey and their Submission to the Catholic Church (1940). F. L. Cross, *Darwell Stone* (1943), pp. 108–12. A. Zimmermann, O.S.B., in *L.Th.K.*, ii (1931), col. 701 f., s.v., with bibl.

CALEFACTORY (Lat. *calefactorium*, 'warming place'), the room in a medieval monastery provided with a fireplace. Where it existed it was commonly near the refectory.

CALENDAR. The calendar in use at the time when Christianity began was the Julian, devised by Julius Caesar in 46 B.C., in which the length of the years was almost but not quite accurately calculated. By A.D. 325 the error was enough to cause the vernal equinox to fall on 21 instead of 25 Mar., so that the 21st was then fixed as the earliest date for the Paschal full moon. The system was reformed by *Gregory XIII, who in 1582 caused ten days to be omitted from that year to balance the current error, and by altering the leapyear rules prevented its recurrence. The Gregorian Calendar was adopted in England in 1752. The Orthodox Church has not adopted it, and its year now runs 13 days behind the Western.

The beginning of the Christian Era with the date of the Incarnation was suggested at Rome by *Dionysius Exiguus in the 6th cent., and in due course adopted throughout Christendom. Calculation began from 25 Mar. A.D. 1, the supposed date of the *Annunciation, which was taken to be New Year's Day. The Gregorian Calendar restored New Year's Day to 1 Jan.

The observance of commemorations dates from early times. *Easter and *Pentecost were both observed from the very first as Jewish festivals with a new Christian significance, and like the Jewish Passover they were movable according to the moon, the calculations proving at times a source of controversy. Later the fixed festivals grew up, as well as further movable feasts depending for their date upon Easter. Of Saints' Days, those of the Martyrs were the first and most obvious; others followed. So also the periods of fasting were gradually fixed by custom. At a very early stage the Jewish custom of a seven-day week produced regularly recurring fasts on *Wednesdays and *Fridays, an arrangement later modified but in substance preserved; while the observance of *Sunday as a festival dates from the Apostles, though it was only in 321 that an order of *Constantine forbade unnecessary Sunday work. See also *Year*.

The study of chronology was put on a scientific footing for the first time by J. *Scaliger, *De Emendatione Temporum* (Paris, 1583), and D. *Petavius, S.J., *De Doctrina Temporum* (ib., 1627). Important works of more recent date include the Benedictine *L'Art de vérifier les dates de faites historiques, des chartes, des chroniques et autres anciens monuments, depuis la naissance de Notre-Seigneur* [by M. F. Dantine, O.S.B., C. Clémencet, O.S.B., and U. Durand, O.S.B.] (Paris, 1750; ed. 2 [rev. by N. V. de Saint-Allais], 18 vols.+index, 1818–19; further continuation from 1770 to date by J. B. P. J. de Courcelles and F. d'Urban, 4 vols., 1821–38; another complete ed., 18 vols., 1821–44). C. L. Ideler, *Handbuch der mathematischen und technischen Chronologie* (2 vols., 1825–6). B. Krusch, *Studien zur christlich-mittelalterlichen Chronologie* (1880). H. Grotefend, *Zeitrechnung des Mittelalters und der Neuzeit* (2 vols., 1891–8). J. Gerard, S.J., in *C.E.*, iii (1908), pp. 738–42, s.v. 'Chronology (General)', and H. Thurston, S.J., ib., pp. 158–66, s.v. 'Calendar'. P. Harvey, *Oxford Companion to English Literature*, ed. 3 (1946), pp. 907–32, gives calendrical data for England, 1066–1936. See also bibl. to *Chronology* (Biblical), *Year* (Liturgical), and *Gregorian Calendar*.

CALFHILL (or **CALFIELD**), JAMES (*c.* 1530–70), *Calvinistic divine. Educated at Eton and at King's College, Cambridge, in 1548 he became one of the original Students of Christ Church, Oxford. In 1560 he was ordained priest, and in the same year appointed to a canonry at Christ Church. In 1564 he became Lady Margaret professor of divinity at Oxford, in 1565 Dean of Bocking, and in 1570 he was elected to the see of *Worcester, but died before consecration. One of the leading Elizabethan Calvinists, he published in 1565 his principal work, an *Answer to the 'Treatise of the Cross'* [by John Martiall, 1534-97].

His *Answer to John Martiall's Treatise of the Cross* was ed. by R. Gibbings for the *Parker Society, 1846, with biogr. note on Calfhill, p. vii f. Unsigned art. in *D.N.B.*, viii (1886), p. 252 f.

CALIXTINES. The moderate party of the *Hussites of Bohemia and Moravia, also known as the '*Utraquists' (q.v.). They were so named from their contention that the laity should receive Communion in both kinds—i.e. from the chalice ('*calix*') as well as under the species of bread. Both Calixtines and Sub-unites (*sub una specie*) received ecclesiastical recognition at the Prague Compacts of 1433 (confirmed at Iglau, 1436).

G. Constant, *Concession à l'Allemagne de la communion sous les deux espèces.* Étude sur les débuts de la réforme catholique en Allemagne, 1548-1621 (Bibliothèque des Écoles Françaises d'Athènes et de Rome, cxxviii, 2 vols., 1923).

CALIXTUS, GEORG (1586-1656), Protestant theologian. He was educated at the university of Helmstedt, where he became an exponent of eirenic tendencies and conceived a high regard for P. *Melanchthon. He then spent four years (1609-13) travelling in RC and *Calvinist countries. On his return to Helmstedt he was appointed professor of theology (1614), and held the office till his death. He endeavoured to build up a theological system which should lead to reconciliation between *Lutherans, Calvinists, and Catholics. The basis of the proposed reunion was to be the Scriptures, the *Apostles' Creed, and the faith of the first five cents., interpreted in the light of the *Vincentian Canon. He expounded his position (which became known as '*Syncretism') in a long series of writings, of which perhaps the most important was his treatise *Judicium de controversiis theologicis quae inter Lutheranos et Reformatos agitantur, et de mutua partium fraternitate atque tolerantia propter consensum in fundamentis* (1650). He took part at the Colloquy of *Thorn in 1645.

E. L. T. Henke, *Georg Calixtus und seine Zeit* (2 vols., Halle, 1853-60). Shorter life by W. Gass (Breslau, 1846). W. C. Dowding, *German Theology during the Thirty Years' War.* The Life and Correspondence of George Calixtus (1863). E. L. T. Henke – P. Tschackert in *P.R.E.* (ed. 3), iii (1897), pp. 643-7.

CALLING. As a technical theological term the word came into use in Reformation theology for the Divine act whereby those destined for salvation are persuaded to accept the Gospel. It was used in this sense, e.g., in the 'Shorter *Westminster Catechism' of 1647. *Calvinist theologians have commonly held that the Divine Calling is in itself efficacious, whereas *Lutherans have held that it requires a voluntary response. In much Evangelical

Christianity of more recent times the Call of God takes a very important place in the immediate and conscious conversion which is considered normal and necessary in the religious life of every Christian.

CALLISTUS I, St. (d. *c.* 223), Bp. of *Rome from *c.* 217. He was apparently originally a slave. Acc. to *Hippolytus, his first appearance in history was in connexion with some fraudulent banking operations, which finally led to his being sent to the mines of Sardinia. After his release at the request of Marcia, the mistress of the Emp. Commodus, (180-193), he was given a pension by *Victor I. In 217 he succeeded *Zephyrinus, whose chief minister he seems to have been. His pontificate was marked by acute controversy. He was attacked by Hippolytus for countenancing *Sabellianism and for his laxity, esp. in readmitting to communion those guilty of adultery or fornication; but some of the charges against him may be discounted as based solely on the evidence of his adversary. The catacombs of 'San Callisto' on the *Appian Way are named from his having been in charge of them under Zephyrinus. Feast day, 14 Oct.

Hippolytus, *Haer.* IX., xii. *L.P.* (Duchesne) i (1886), p. 141 f. J. J. I. von *Döllinger, *Hippolytus und Callistus* (1853; Eng. tr., 1876). Bardenhewer, ii (ed. 2, 1914), pp. 636-8; Altaner, pp. 130 f., 135 f., 139. That Callistus was the *pontifex maximus quod est episcopus episcoporum* who issued edict on penance (*edictum peremptorium*) attacked by *Tertullian in *De pudicitia*, 81, has been maintained by many modern scholars, incl. O. *Bardenhewer and A. d'Alès, *L'Édit de Calliste* (1914); on the other side, see B. Altaner. C. Cecchelli – E. Josi in *E.C.*, iii (1950), cols. 386-91, s.v. 'Callisto I'.

CALLISTUS II (d. 1124), Pope from 1119. Guido of Burgundy was a descendant of the counts of Burgundy and closely connected with almost all the royal houses of Europe. He was made Abp. of Vienne by Urban II in 1088, became Papal legate in France in 1106, and took part in the *Lateran Council of 1112, which declared null and void the *investiture privileges which Henry V had extorted from *Paschal II. In the same year he himself presided at a Council held at Vienne, which condemned lay investiture as a heresy. Having been elected Pope at *Cluny, he excommunicated Henry at the Council of *Reims in 1119, but the intervention of the German princes, esp. Henry of Bavaria, facilitated a peaceful solution. The long-drawn-out struggle between Pope and Emperor was brought to a conclusion by the Concordat of *Worms (q.v.) in 1122, which was promulgated at the Lateran Council of 1123, where the Pope also issued a series of decrees concerning simony, the marriage of priests, and the election of prelates. In the quarrel between his old see of Vienne and that of Grenoble, Callistus took the side of the former and authenticated a collection of forged privileges of which, however, the larger part dates from earlier times.

U. Robert, *Bullaire du Pape Calixte II* (1119-1124). Essai de restitution (2 vols., Paris, 1891); id., *Histoire du Pape Calixte II* (1891). Studies by M. Maurer (Munich, 2 vols., 1886–9) and G. Ender (Greifswald, 1913). Mann, viii (1910), pp. 139–227. P. F. Palumbo, in *E.C.*, iii (1950), cols. 391–3, s.v. 'Callisto II', with bibl.

CALLISTUS III (1378–1458), Pope from 1455. A native of Valencia, Alfonso de *Borgia enjoyed considerable reputation as a jurist both at the university of Lérida and at the court of Alfonso V of Aragon (King, 1416–58). He originally supported the cause of Benedict XIII (anti-Pope 1394–1417), but eventually induced his successor Clement VIII (anti-Pope 1423–9) to submit to Pope *Martin V in 1429. He was thereupon appointed Bp. of Valencia in the same year and created a *Cardinal in 1444. The main efforts of his papacy were directed to the organization of a crusade against the Turks, to which project he had been esp. devoted since the fall of *Constantinople in 1453. In spite of the victory of St. *Giovanni Capistrano (q.v.) at Belgrade in 1456, his plans met with little success, largely owing to the unsettled state of Europe, which his attempts to arrange peace did little to allay. After the death of Alfonso V (1458), he refused to recognize the claims of his illegitimate son to the throne of Naples, of which Alfonso was overlord. His intervention in the subsequent dynastic disputes lent substance to the charge of nepotism already raised by his elevation to the cardinalate of two of his nephews (incl. the future *Alexander VI) and the appointment of a third as Duke of Spoleto. Prob. the most interesting event of his pontificate was the revision of the trial of *Joan of Arc by the annulment of the sentence and a declaration of her innocence. He was also responsible for the canonization in 1457 of *Osmund, Bp. of *Salisbury.

Vita a Bartholomæo Sacho, printed by L. A. *Muratori, *Rerum Italicarum Scriptores*, iii, pt. 2 (Milan, 1734), cols. 961–66. Pastor, ii (1891), pp. 317–495. E. Vansteenberghe in *D.H.G.E.*, ix, cols. 438–44, s.v., incl. bibl. G. M. Pou y Marti in *E.C.*, iii (1950), cols. 393–5, s.v. 'Callisto III'.

CALOVIUS, ABRAHAM (1612–86), German *Lutheran theologian. In 1650 he was appointed to the chair of theology at *Wittenberg, and in 1652 General-superintendent. A man of great learning, he took part in many controversies, and as a strenuous defender of rigid Lutheran orthodoxy opposed G. *Calixtus's policy of reuniting the Confessions. He also made vigorous attacks on *Socinianism and *Pietism and controverted the liberal views of H. *Grotius on Biblical inspiration. In his doctrine of the 'Unio Mystica', however, he departed (probably far more than he was aware) from the Reformation doctrine of justification. His chief dogmatic work, *Systema locorum theologicorum* (12 vols., 1655–1677), is a monument of Lutheran scholasticism.

J. W. Kunze in *P.R.E.* (ed. 3), iii (1897), pp. 648–54, incl. bibl.

CALOYER (Gk. καλόγηρος, from καλός, 'fine', + γῆρας, 'old age'; i.e. 'venerable'). A designation for Greek monks, esp. of the *Basilian Order.

CALVARY, Mount (Lat. *Calvaria*, Gk. κρανίον, Heb. 'Golgotha', all meaning 'skull'). The place of Christ's crucifixion, just outside *Jerusalem. It may have been originally a place of public execution where the skulls of the executed were to be seen, or the name may have been derived from a neighbouring cemetery or connected with the shape of the ground (traditionally a hill) which may have resembled a skull. Acc. to tradition it was the burial place of *Adam's skull. See also *Holy Sepulchre*.

CALVIN, JOHN (1509–64), French reformer and theologian. Born at Noyon in Picardy, he was intended for an ecclesiastical career, and obtained his first benefice at the age of 12. On this occasion he received the tonsure, the only order ever conferred on him. From 1523 to 1528 he studied theology at *Paris, but from 1527 he seems to have had doubts on his priestly vocation and probably also on matters of faith. From 1528 he studied law at Orléans and later at Bourges, where he came under the influence of Melchior Wolmar and a circle of Protestants. In 1532 he issued a Latin commentary on Seneca's 'De Clementia'. His final break with the RC Church appears to have taken place in 1533 after a religious experience in which he believed he had received a mission to restore the Church to its original purity.

In 1534 he went to Noyon, where he resigned his benefices and seems to have been imprisoned for a short time. Danger from an outbreak of persecution under Francis I led to his flight to Basle in 1535, where he intended to devote his life to study. The first edition of the *Institutes* (in Latin; q.v.), which were to be rewritten and improved throughout his life, followed in March 1536. On a passing visit to *Geneva in July 1536 he reluctantly relinquished his plans for a scholar's life and yielded to G. *Farel's urgent appeals to become his coadjutor in organizing the Reformation at Geneva. He was appointed preacher and professor of theology and in 1536 published his *Articuli de Regimine Ecclesiae*. They contained severe regulations concerning admission to the Lord's supper and required from all Genevan citizens a profession of faith approved by the town council, the refusal of which was to be punished by exile. Despite strong resistance all citizens had accepted the oath by 1538; but his next step, the discipline of excommunication, together with his refusal to conform the usages of the Church at Geneva to those of the more powerful city of Berne, led to the expulsion of both Farel and Calvin later in that year.

For the next three years Calvin was minister of the French congregation and lecturer in the theological school at Strassburg. Here he became a close friend of M. *Bucer, whose influence is visible in the fresh edition, in 1539, of his *Institutes*. He also published a commentary on Romans (1539) and wrote his famous Epistle to Cardinal *Sadoleto, then endeavouring to bring Geneva back to the RC

Church, in which he defended the principles of the Reformation with great vigour. In 1539 he attended the Conference of Frankfurt and in 1540 represented Strassburg at *Hagenau and in 1541 at *Worms. At the Diet of *Ratisbon (1541) he formed a friendship with P. *Melanchthon.

In 1541 Calvin returned to Geneva, where his party had gained the upper hand, and during the next 14 years he devoted himself to establishing a theocratic régime on OT lines. This was effected by a series of 'Ordinances' which placed the government of the new Church in the hands of four classes of men, called pastors, doctors, elders, and deacons. They were assisted by a '*consistory' of ministers and laymen which, under Calvin, was chiefly a tribunal of morals. It wielded the power of excommunication and had far-reaching powers over the private lives of the citizens. These were enforced by new legislation, which inflicted severe punishments even for purely religious offences and prohibited all pleasures such as dancing and games. This régime was resisted by a party incorrectly described as 'Libertines', which Calvin succeeded in overcoming by force. Among the opponents executed after torture were Jacques Gruet (1547), Raoul Monnet (1549), and, best known, Michael *Servetus (1553). By 1555, however, all resistance had ceased and Calvin was the uncontested master of the city. At the same time he also took the lead in the affairs of other Protestant communities. In 1548 he addressed a letter to the Protector *Somerset indicating the changes which he wished to see introduced in England; in 1555 he gave shelter to English Protestant refugees; and he actively supported the French Protestants. All his NT commentaries appeared during this period as well as a number of writings on the Reformation and his treatise on Predestination (1552).

From 1555 to his death he was the unopposed dictator of Geneva, which, through him, had become a city of the strictest morality. He continued his literary activities, commented on most of the OT Books, and in 1559 founded the Academy of Geneva to continue his teaching.

In his revolt from Rome Calvin was more logical and systematic and a greater organizer than Luther, but without the human attractiveness of the German reformer. He was disinterested, simple and austere in his private life, but his vindictiveness and his claim to be the supreme authority to decide what is true Christianity and what is not was resented even by many of his followers. His work as a Church reformer is not to be measured by the part he played in a small republic. During his ministry at Geneva his reputation and influence as an ecclesiastical statesman, as a religious controversialist, educationist, and author was widespread. His theological insight, his exegetical talents, his knowledge of languages, his precision, and his clear and pithy style, made him the most influential writer among the reformers, and his *Institutes* are still of the highest authority in the non-Lutheran Protestant Churches.

The standard ed. of Calvin's works is that by H. W. Baum, E. Cunitz, E. Reuss, P. Lobstein, and A. Erichson (Corpus Reformatorum, xxix-lxxvii; 59 vols., Brunswick, 1863–1900); more modern ed. in Les Textes français, Paris, 1936 ff. *Opera Selecta*, ed. P. Barth (5 vols., Munich, 1926–36). The lives of Calvin by T. *Beza, orig. prefixed to Calvin's Comm. on Joshua (posthumously publd., Geneva, 1564; Eng. tr. of the life, London, 1564), and that prefixed to the ed. of Calvin's letters publd. Geneva, 1575, together with that attributed to Beza (the work of Nicolas Colladon) prefixed to ed. 2 of the Comm. on Joshua (Lyons, 1565), are pr. among his works. E. Doumergue, *Jean Calvin. Les hommes et les choses de son temps* (5 vols., 1899–1917; comprehensive but uncritical). W. Walker, *John Calvin* (New York and London, 1906); H. Y. Reyburn, *John Calvin* (London, 1914). B. B. Warfield, *Calvin and Calvinism* (New York and London, 1931). R. N. Carew Hunt, *Calvin* (London, 1933), with bibl.; J. Mackinnon, *Calvin and the Reformation* (1934). R. Freschi, *Giovanni Calvino*, Vita (Milan, 1934). F. W. Kampschulte (*Old Catholic), *Johann Calvin, seine Kirche und sein Staat in Genf* (2 vols., 1869–99). E. Choisy, *Calvin, éducateur des consciences* (Neuilly [1926]); J. D. Benoît, *Calvin, directeur des âmes* [1949]. H. Olsson, *Calvin och Reformationes Teologi* (Lunds Universitets Årsskrift N.S. Afd. 2, xl, fasc. 1, etc., 1943 ff.). E. A. Dowey, *The Knowledge of God in Calvin's Theology* (New York, 1952). F. Wendel, *Calvin. Sources et évolution de sa pensée religieuse* (Études d'histoire et de philosophie religieuses publiées par la faculté de théologie protestante de l'université de Strasbourg, xli; 1950). W. Niesel, *Die Theologie Calvins* (Munich, 1938; Eng. tr. 1956). A. Erichson, *Bibliographia Calviniana*. Catalogus Chronologicus Operum Calvini (Berlin, 1900). See also bibls. to *Calvinism* and *Institutes*.

CALVINISM. The theological system of J. *Calvin, formulated chiefly in his *Institutes*, and accepted with some modifications by most non-Lutheran reformed Churches. It holds certain of the doctrines characteristic of *Lutheranism, as well as other elements peculiar to itself. Among the former are the doctrine of Scripture as the only rule of faith, the denial of human free-will after the Fall of Adam, and justification by faith without works. To these Calvin added the doctrine of the inamissibility of grace, the certitude of salvation, and absolute predestination. He also modified Luther's teaching on the Church and the Sacraments.

Acc. to Calvin the Bible contains all that is necessary to know God and our duties towards Him and our neighbour. The authority of Scripture is assured by the 'testimonium Spiritus Sancti', an interior persuasion whereby we can also distinguish the canonical Books of Scripture from others. In the state of innocence it was possible for man to attain to beatitude through his own natural powers; but the Fall, which was willed by God, substantially changed human nature so that now all man wills and does is sin. Hence he is no longer free but follows necessarily either the attractions of concupiscence or of grace. All human works outside the Christian faith are sins; and even the good works of Christians are intrinsically evil, though covered and not counted as sins through the imputed merits of Christ. This trust ('faith' in the Protestant sense) extends not only, as in Lutheranism, to the certitude of having obtained justification but to the perfect assurance of eternal salvation, and from this follows the specifically Calvinist doctrine of the inamissibility of grace.

The extreme emphasis on the omnipotence of God, which takes no account of His justice and mercy nor of the freedom which this very omnipotence can leave to His creatures, led

Calvin to formulate his doctrine of absolute predestination. Acc. to him, before the Fall and even before creation, God, in His eternal counsels, predestined some of His creatures to salvation and others to damnation. This entails that God not only wills the reprobation of the damned but also the sin which leads to it, as he who wills the end must will the means. This doctrine was later, however, rejected by the more moderate Calvinists.

Calvin's attitude to the Church differs from that of Luther. He defended a theocratic polity, subjecting the State to the Church, as contrasted with Luther who upheld the supremacy of the State. In the question of the Sacraments, esp. the Lord's Supper, Calvin attempted a compromise between Luther's belief in the *Real Presence, expressed in his doctrine of *consubstantiation, and H. *Zwingli's view of a mere symbolism. His language is at times ambiguous, but his thought seems to tend more in the direction of Zwingli, sometimes regarding the Sacraments as a testimony of God's grace, confirmed by an external sign.

The most influential document of strict Calvinism is the Second *Helvetic Confession of 1566, which was accepted in many reformed countries. The *Huguenots were Calvinists, and in 1622 Calvinism became the State religion in the Netherlands, where there occurred a split over the predestinarian issue which led to the formation of the parties of the *Supralapsarians (*Gomarists) and *Sublapsarians (*Arminians). In England, though Calvinist doctrines infiltrated into the *Thirty-Nine Articles, the spirit of the Episcopalian system was opposed to it, but it gained a firm foothold in the Nonconformist Churches. It found its most congenial soil in Scotland, esp. through J. *Knox, one of its most rigid representatives. From Great Britain it spread to N. America, where many sects profess it in a more or less modified form. In Germany it replaced Lutheranism in several places, e.g. Brandenburg and the Palatinate. Calvinism suffered severe setbacks through the rationalism of the 18th and 19th cents., but recently it has once more come to the fore esp. through the works of K. *Barth, whose influence has been considerable not only in the Protestant Churches on the Continent but also in the C of E. Its attraction for the modern religious mind is probably due to the stress it lays on the omnipotence of God and the nothingness of man as a reaction against the easy humanitarianism of 19th cent. liberal Protestantism.

Dogmatic Confessions in E. F. K. Müller, *Die Bekenntnisschriften der reformierten Kirche* (Leipzig, 1903). A. Kuyper, *Calvinism* (L. P. Stone Lectures [in Eng.], Amsterdam and New York, 1899); W. Hastie, *The Theology of the Reformed Church* (ed. W. Fulton, Croall Lectures for 1892; 1904); T. M. *Lindsay, *A History of the Reformation*, ii (1907); A. Dakin, *Calvinism* (Studies in Theology, 1940). A. Schweizer, *Die Glaubenslehre der evangelisch-reformirten Kirche dargestellt* (2 vols., Zürich, 1844–7); id., *Die protestantischen Centraldogmen in ihrer Entwicklung innerhalb der reformierten Kirche* (2 vols., Zürich, 1854–6). K. Barth, *Die christliche Lehre nach dem Heidelberger Katechismus* (Zürich, 1948). J. T. McNeill, *The History and Character of Calvinism* (New York and London, 1954). A. Baudrillart in *D.T.C.*, ii (1905), cols. 1398–1422. J. Orr in *H.E.R.E.*, iii (1901), pp. 146–55.

CALVINISTIC METHODISM. The Church which was established in Wales through the revivalist preaching of Griffith Jones of Llanddowror (1684–1761), Howell *Harris of Trevecca (1714–73), and Daniel Rowlands of Llangeitho (1713–90). They had contacts with English *Methodists and their first Association was held in 1743 (eighteen months before Wesley's first Conference), but there was no wish to separate from the C of E. At the time of the revival of 1762 Rowlands, whose licence had been suspended by the Bp. of *St. Davids, built a meeting-house at Llangeitho to which his preaching drew great numbers. In 1770 an annotated Welsh Bible was published by Peter Williams. The movement was brought to North Wales by Thomas Charles who joined the Methodists in 1784. Separation from the Establishment began in 1795 as a result of persecution. Since poor preachers, hampered by heavy fines, were obliged to seek the protection of the *Toleration Act, their meeting-houses were registered as Dissenting Chapels. The first ordinations of ministers in the Connexion took place only in 1811. The Confession of Faith (based on the *Westminster Confession) was drawn up in 1823 and the *Constitutional Deed* was formally completed in 1826. The first college for candidates for the ministry was founded at Bala in 1837 with Lewis Edwards as principal, and in 1842 the South Wales Association opened a college at Trevecca, David Charles being principal, which was in 1905 transferred to Aberystwyth. In 1840 a Missionary Society was formed, to work in Brittany and India. By the Calvinistic Methodist or Presbyterian Church of Wales Act of 1933, the autonomy of the Church in spiritual matters was secured and a Properties Board established. In 1935 the bicentenary of the Church was celebrated.

By the constitution local Churches report to the meeting of their district which in turn reports to the monthly meeting of districts whence delegates are appointed to the Quarterly Associations of North and South, which alone have legislative powers. A general meeting of the Quarterly Associations, with purely deliberative functions, was established in 1864. The ministry is no longer itinerant, but preaching is at the invitation of the deacons of a Church and is not rigidly Calvinistic. The Church has considerable strength and the outlook of its members is intensely nationalistic with a keen interest in education, politics, and social service. It is a constituent of the World Presbyterian Alliance. The membership *c.* 1950 was some 250,000.

The *Rules of Discipline* (in Welsh) were first publd. at Caerleon, 1801; the *Confession of Faith* (also in Welsh), preceded by a brief history of the Movement, was publd. at Aberystwyth, 1824; Eng. tr. under the title *The History, Constitution, Rules of Discipline and Confession of the Calvinistic Methodists in Wales* (London, 1827; revised Welsh ed., 1876; Eng. tr., 1877). The *Constitutional Deed* of 1826 is pr. in the *Legal Hand-Book for the Calvinistic Methodist Connexion* (ed. 2, Wrexham [1911]), pp. 57–135. There is a considerable literature in Welsh. Works in English include W. Williams, *Welsh Calvinistic Methodism*. A Historical Sketch of the Presbyterian Church of Wales (London, 1872). M. W. Williams, *Creative Fellowship*. An Outline of the History of Calvinistic Methodism in Wales (Caernarvon, 1935). J. Roberts, 'The Calvinistic Methodism of Wales' in *The Treasury*, xxi (1933), pp. 4 f., 26–8, 38 f., 42, 55–8, 70–2, 86–8, 100 f., 125 f., 155–7, 188–90, xxii (1934), pp. 21 f., 54 f. D. E. Jenkins, *Calvinistic Methodist Holy Orders* (Caernarvon, 1911). A representative picture is given in E. Price, *The History of Penuel Calvinistic Methodist Church, Ebbw Vale* (Wrexham, 1925). F. *Loofs in *P.R.E.* (ed. 3), xii (1903), p. 792 f., with bibl., p. 750, s.v. 'Methodismus', with further reff. See also lives of H. Harris, cited s.v.

CAMALDOLESE. A religious order founded *c.* 1012 by St. *Romuald at Camaldoli (Campus Maldoli) near Arezzo. Its ideal was the barest minimum of communal ties. This primitive severity was gradually relaxed in a number of the daughter hermitages, and in 1102 a monastery was founded at Fontebuono on ordinary *coenobitic lines. St. Romuald left no written rule, and practice in the different congregations has varied considerably to the present day. The habit is a white tunic, with hood and *scapular of the same colour. There is also an order of Camaldolese nuns.

L. Schiaperelli–F. Baldasseroni–E. Lasino (edd.), *Regesto di Camaldoli* (Regesta Chartarum Italiae, ii, v, xiii, xiv, 1907–22). M. Ziegelbauer, O.S.B., *Centifolium camaldulense, sive Notitia Scriptorum Camaldulensium* (Venice, 1750). *Cenni storici del sacro eremo di Camaldoli* (ed. 2, Florence, 1864). Heimbucher, i (ed. 3, 1933), pp. 315–20, and ii (ed. 1934), p. 655, with bibl. reff. A. Des Mazis, O.S.B., in *D.H.G.E.*, xi (1949), cols. 512–36, with bibl.; A. Giabani, O.S.B., in *E.C.*, iii (1950), col. 420 f.

CAMBRIDGE CAMDEN SOCIETY. A society founded in May 1839 by J. M. *Neale and B. *Webb for the study of ecclesiastical art. Its first president was T. Thorp, Archdeacon of Bristol and Webb's tutor at Trinity; and in 1841 it began to issue its monthly periodical, *The Ecclesiologist*. In 1846, when its headquarters removed to London, its name was altered to the 'Ecclesiological Society', under which title it survived till 1863. It greatly stimulated interest in church architecture and traditional Catholic worship, and thus assisted the liturgical and ceremonial revival in the C of E in the later 19th cent.

A *Report* containing Lists of Officers and Members, 'Laws', Lists of Churches Visited, Publications, etc., was publd. annually at Cambridge from 1840 to 1844, at less frequent intervals at London from 1845 to 1864. In all 189 numbers of *The Ecclesiologist* were issued (Nov. 1841–Dec. 1868).

CAMBRIDGE PLATONISTS. They were a group of influential philosophical divines who flourished at Cambridge between 1633 and 1688. They stood between the Puritans and High Anglicans and consistently advocated tolerance and comprehension within the Church, basing their demand on their conception that reason was the arbiter both of natural and of revealed religion. They held that it could judge the data of revelation by virtue of the indwelling of God in the mind, since 'the spirit in man is the candle of the Lord' (B. *Whichcote). This mystical view of

reason was derived principally from *Neoplatonism, though the Cambridge Platonists interpreted it not so much as ecstasy as an abiding direction of will and affection alike. They were in many ways uncritical, discovering, e.g., affinities between *Platonism and the OT. The chief modern influence on their philosophy was R. *Descartes, whose intellectualism appealed to them, though they sought to purge his doctrines from his materialist view of the inanimate world by combining with them belief in an immanent divine soul, and supplementing his mechanism by teleology. They applied their Platonism in the sphere of ethics and epistemology to establish the identity of the Will of God and the '*Summum Bonum' and of the worlds of sense and thought.

The most important of the Cambridge Platonists were B. *Whichcote (1609–83), N. Culverwel (d. 1651?), John Smith (1618–52), R. *Cudworth (1617–88), H. *More (1614–87).

E. T. Campagnac, *The Cambridge Platonists* (selections, 1901); J. Tulloch, *Rational Theology and Christian Philosophy in England in the 17th Century* (2 vols., 1872); F. J. Powicke, *The Cambridge Platonists* (1926).

CAMELAUCUM. The original name of the Papal *tiara (q.v.), found, e.g., in the Life of Pope Constantine (d. 715) in the *Liber Pontificalis*, and in the 'Donation of *Constantine' (mid 8th cent.).

CAMERARIUS, JOACHIM (1500–74), German classical scholar and reformer. In 1530 he sat in the Diet of *Augsburg as deputy for Nuremberg, and took part in drawing up the famous Confession. In 1535 he undertook the reorganization of the University of *Tübingen, and in 1541 that of Leipzig. A personal friend of the eirenic P. *Melanchthon, whose biography he wrote in elegant Latin, he acted as a moderating influence in Lutheranism; and he discussed in 1535 with Francis I and in 1568 with Maximilian II the possibility of reunion between Catholics and Protestants.

T. Kolde in *P.R.E.* (ed. 3), iii (1897), pp. 687–9, s.v., with bibl. Further bibl. in Schottenloher, i (1933), p. 104 (Nos. 2545–62).

CAMERLENGO (Lat. *camerarius*). The chamberlain of the Papal court, who administers the properties and revenues of the Holy See, and during a vacancy in the Papacy those of the whole RC Church. One of his duties is to assemble and direct the *conclave. He is always a *cardinal.

CAMERON, JOHN (d. 1446), Bp. of Glasgow and Chancellor of Scotland. In 1424 he became secretary to James I and in the next year keeper of the Privy Seal. Appointed chancellor *c.* 1426, he supported the King in his attack on the ecclesiastical courts, taking a prominent part in the Council of Perth in 1427 and in drawing up the anti-ecclesiastical Act of Parliament of the same year. In 1428 he was elected Bp. of Glasgow. When *Martin V summoned Cameron to Rome on account of his political activities, the King informed the Pope (1429) that he could not spare his Chancellor. On Cameron's refusal to obey a fresh summons to Rome in 1433, he was excommunicated by *Eugenius IV. He took part, however, in the Council of *Basle as one of the two Scottish representatives. In 1436 he went to Rome, where he obtained the Pope's promise to take steps for the reform of the Church in Scotland. In 1445 he was a member of the commission which had to decide the dispute on the testamentary powers of bishops.

T. A. Archer in *D.N.B.*, viii (1886), pp. 293-5, s.v., with reff.

CAMERON, JOHN (*c.* 1579-1625), Protestant theologian. He was educated at Glasgow university, and in 1600 went to France, where he taught classics at the college of Bergerac and philosophy at the university of Sedan. He later was a private tutor at Paris, Geneva, and Heidelberg, at the same time pursuing his studies. In 1608 he was appointed a minister of the Protestant Church at Bordeaux, and in 1618 he succeeded F. *Gomar as professor of divinity at Saumur. In 1620 religious conditions in France caused him to return to England, and in 1622 he was made principal of the university of Glasgow. He was a supporter of *James (VI and) I and his exalted views on the prerogatives of the royal power, but the unpopularity of these views compelled him to return to Saumur in 1623. In 1624 he became professor of divinity at Montauban, where his doctrine of passive obedience to the secular authorities roused such hostility that he was assaulted in the street and his health severely injured. He died in the following year. Cameron was a very gifted linguist as well as a learned theologian. Among his writings are treatises on Grace and Free-Will (1618) and on the Satisfaction of Christ for sin (1620), in which he upheld that God's action on the will was moral, not physical, and thus was considered by stricter *Calvinists as inclining to *Pelagianism. His doctrines were accepted by a school of contemporary theologians ('Cameronites'), which included S. *Bochart and J. *Daillé.

G. B. Maury, 'John Cameron: A Scottish Protestant Theologian in France (1579-1625)' in *Scottish Historical Review*, vii (1910), pp. 325-45. T. F. Henderson in *D.N.B.*, viii (1886), p. 295 f., s.v.

CAMERON, RICHARD (d. 1680), Scottish *Covenanting leader. In his youth he was a schoolmaster under the episcopal incumbent of Falkland, Fife, but was won by the Covenanting cause and became a field-preacher, influencing thousands by his eloquence. In 1678 he went to Holland, returned in 1680, and shortly afterwards joined with a few other poor men in the 'Sanquhar Declaration', which disowned allegiance to *Charles II, and declared war upon him, attacking strongly all Covenanters who accepted the royal indulgence then offered. He fell in an affray with some royal troops at Airds Moss in Ayrshire on 22 July 1680.

Lives by J. Herkless (London [1896]) and A. Veitch (London, 1948).

CAMERONIANS. A term applied at the end of the 17th cent. to extreme *Covenanters, as the followers of R. *Cameron (q.v.) and esp. of the 'Reformed Presbyterians' who declined the settlement of the Established Church of Scotland made in 1690 under William and Mary, though they themselves repudiated the name.

J. H. Burton, *The History of Scotland from Agricola's Invasion to the Revolution of 1688*, vii (1870), pp. 527-76 passim. F. *Kattenbusch in *P.R.E.*, (ed. 3), iii (1897), pp. 691-3, s.v. 'Cameronianer', with bibl. See also bibl. to *Covenanters*.

CAMILLUS OF LELLIS, St. (1550-1614), founder of the 'Ministers of the Sick'. He was a native of the kingdom of Naples, and early joined the Venetian army against the Turks. His passion for gambling having reduced him to great poverty, he was employed as a labourer by the *Capuchins at Manfredonia in 1574, where, in 1575, he was converted and began to embrace a very penitential life. He tried his vocation with the Capuchins and again with the *Franciscan *Recollects, but an incurable disease in his legs compelled him to leave both and he became a nurse at the hospital of St. Giacomo in Rome. Under the guidance of St. *Philip Neri he grew to great holiness, and resolved to found an order for the care of the sick. He was ordained priest in 1584, and about the same time established a congregation, also called 'Camillians', who take a fourth vow to devote themselves to the service of the sick, esp. the plague-stricken. The congregation was approved by the Pope in 1586 and elevated to an order with the privileges of the *Mendicants by *Gregory XIV in 1591. Despite several painful illnesses Camillus remained its superior-general till 1607, when he resigned the government of his order to devote himself more fully to the care of the sick. His striking reforms in this field envisaged both the spiritual and the material needs of the sick, such as the separation of those afflicted with contagious diseases, well-aired wards, special diet, and, particularly, an effective spiritual assistance to the dying, whence his order is also called 'Fathers of a Good Death' or 'Agonizantes'. He was canonized in 1746, made patron of the sick by *Leo XIII in 1886, and of nurses and nursing associations by *Pius XI in 1930. Feast day, 18 July.

The principal authority is the life by S. Cicatelli, for 26 years his companion and later general of the order, publd. at Viterbo, 1615; Eng. tr. by F. W. *Faber, 2 vols., 1850-51. Further life by G. B. de Rossi, S.J. (Rome, 1644). M. Vanti, *S. Camillo de Lellis 1550-1614*), *apostolo di carità infermiera* (Turin-Rome, 1929). A. C. Oldmeadow, *The First Red Cross, Camillus de Lellis, 1550-1614* (1923; popular). Other lives by T. Blanc (Paris, 1858), W. Baeumker (Frankfurt, 1887), M. Amici (Rome, 1913), and C. C. Martindale, S.J. (London, 1946). M. Vanti, *Lo spirito di S. Camillo de Lellis* (ed. 2, Rome, 1944) and other works by this author. On the Order see also Heimbücher, ii, pp. 114-19 and 664-6.

CAMISARDS. A group of fanatical French Protestants, who rose in revolt in the Cevennes district in 1702 after the rigorous steps taken by *Louis XIV to suppress their religion. They often fell under ecstatic inspiration and fought with a frenzy that neither gave nor expected quarter. Considerable cruelty was shown on both sides, and the revolt was suppressed in 1704. A further outbreak in 1709 was quickly checked. In England, where some of them found sanctuary, the Camisards were known as '*French Prophets'. The word 'Camisard' is of uncertain origin. It may be from *camise* (a 'shirt'—from the fact that they are said to have worn shirts over their clothes as a disguise during night attacks), *camis* (a 'road', from their practice of waylaying people), or *camisade* (a 'nocturnal attack').

C. Tylor, *The Camisards* (1893). C. Bost, *Les Prédicants protestants des Cevennes et du Bas-Languedoc, 1684–1700* (2 vols., 1912). A. Ducasse, *La Guerre des camisards.* La résistance huguenote sous Louis XIV (1946). F. Puaux, 'Origines, causes et conséquences de la guerre des camisards' in *Rev. Hist.*, cxxix (1918), pp. 1–21 and 209–43. R. A. Knox, *Enthusiasm* (1950), pp. 356–71. F. Vernet in *D.T.C.*, ii (1905), cols. 1435–43, s.v.; C. Anderson Scott in *H.E.R.E.*, iii (1910), p. 175 f., s.v.; J. Dedieu in *D.H.G.E.*, xi (1949), cols. 607–14, s.v., with bibl.

CAMPAGUS (Late Lat.). Originally a kind of military boot, the word came into current usage for episcopal *sandals (q.v.).

CAMPANELLA, TOMMASO (baptized Giovanni Domenico) (1568–1639), Italian philosopher. In 1582 he became a *Dominican and in 1590 published his first important work, a defence of the philosopher Bernardino Telesio (d. 1588), called *Philosophia Sensibus Demonstrata.* His open disavowal of the *Aristotelian philosophy aroused the suspicions of his ecclesiastical authorities, while his suspected complicity in anti-Spanish plots provoked the civil authorities of Naples. In 1603 he was sentenced to perpetual imprisonment but he was finally released in 1629. In 1634 he withdrew to France in disguise, and spent the rest of his life at the convent of St.-Honoré in Paris.

His philosophy was in the *Platonist tradition. Anticipating R. *Descartes, he held that individual consciousness was the fundamental fact of experience, and that the existence of God cuold be deduced from the presence of the idea of God in human consciousness. His political philosophy owed much both to *Plato and to St. *Augustine. He advocated a reconstruction of the political order closely modelled on Plato's 'Republic', with society under the control of philosopher-priests who would submit the government of the state to the supreme authority of the Pope. His most important work in this field is the *Civitas Solis* (1623). Campanella was also a poet of some ability.

Lettere ed. by V. Spampanato (Bari, 1926). Eng. tr. of his 'Apologia pro Galileo', by G. McColley in *Smith College Studies in History*, xxii (Northampton, Mass., 1937), Nos. 3 and 4. M. Baldacchini, *Vita di Tommaso Campanella* (Naples, 1847). L. Amabile, *Fra Tommaso Campanella.*

La sua congiura, i suoi processi e la sua pazzia (3 vols., 1882) and other works. L. Firpo (ed.), *Ricerche campanelliane* (Biblioteca Storica Sansoni, N.S., xiii, 1947); G. di Napoli, *Tommaso Campanella* (Problemi d' Oggi. Ser. II, x, 1947). E. G. Gardner, *Tommaso Campanella and his Poetry* (Taylorian Lecture, 1923). L. Firpo, *Bibliografia degli scritti di Tommaso Campanella* (1940). Further bibl. in Überweg, iii, p. 631 f.

CAMPANILE. In general, any bell-tower or bell-steeple; but the name is esp. applied to the detached bell-tower which originated in Italy. The earliest examples of the latter are those of S. Apollinare in Classe and S. Apollinare Nuovo at *Ravenna, both 6th cent. Other famous campaniles are at S. Francesco, Assisi, at S. Front, Périgueux, at S. Marco, *Venice, at S. Zeno Maggiore, *Verona, at Siena Cathedral and the Leaning Tower of Pisa.

CAMPBELL, ALEXANDER (1788–1866), founder of the 'Campbellites'. The son of Thomas Campbell (1763–1854), a *Presbyterian minister of the '*Secession Church', he emigrated in 1809 from Glasgow to the U.S.A., whither his father had gone two years earlier. At first he joined the *Baptist Communion, having become convinced of the necessity for baptism by *immersion; but differences of belief separated him from this body, and in 1827 he founded a congregation known as the '*Disciples of Christ' or Campbellites, who taught, besides baptism by immersion, the imminent *Second Coming of Christ and the rejection of all credal formulas. In 1841 he founded 'Bethany College' as a training college for which the Bible was to be the sole fundamental textbook. He edited, and himself wrote nearly the whole of, *The Christian Baptist* (7 vols., 1835). See also *Disciples of Christ.*

Christianity as it was, being a Selection from the Writings of A. Campbell and others (1867); *The Christian Hymn Book,* compiled from the Writings of A. Campbell and others (1869). Memoirs ed. by R. Richardson (2 vols., Philadelphia, Pa., 1871). G. C. Boase in *D.N.B.*, viii (1886), p. 310 f.

CAMPBELL, JOHN McLEOD (1800–1872), Scottish theologian. Educated at Glasgow and Edinburgh, he was appointed in 1825 to the cure of Row, Dunbartonshire. Here, in 1826, he became convinced of the doctrine of 'assurance of faith', which in conjunction with his belief in the universality of the Atonement, aroused much opposition from his congregation and others as at variance with *Presbyterian principles. In 1831 the *General Assembly found him guilty of heresy and deprived him of his cure. Campbell maintained, however, a successful ministry to an independent congregation at Glasgow from 1833 until 1859, when ill-health forced his retirement. The main thesis of his principal work, *The Nature of the Atonement and its Relation to Remission of Sins and Eternal Life* (1856), was that the spiritual context of the sufferings of Christ, rather than their penal character, made atonement for sin.

J. McL. Campbell, *Reminiscences and Reflections* (ed. by his son, Donald Campbell, 1873). Study by J. McL. Campbell in R. S. Wright (ed.), *Fathers of the Kirk* (1960), pp. 155–67.

CAMPEGGIO, LORENZO (1472–1539), Abp. of *Bologna. After the death of his wife (by whom he had had five children), he was ordained in 1510. He was presented with the Bpric. of Feltre in 1512; and from 1513 to 1517 he was *nuncio at the Imperial court. In 1518 he was sent to England by *Leo X to try to gain *Henry VIII's support for a crusade against the Turks, but without success. He was subsequently made protector of England in the Roman *curia, and in 1524 Henry created him Bp. of *Salisbury, while in 1523 the Pope had made him Abp. of *Bologna. At this time he also contended in behalf of Papal interests in Germany, but with little success. In 1528 he came back to England in the matter of Henry's projected divorce. He was provided with a document which merely defined the relevant ecclesiastical law and asserted that the question of fact must be settled in England by himself and T. *Wolsey, though the Pope had secretly pledged him to refer the matter to Rome before passing final judgement. Failing to satisfy the King, he left England in 1529 and took part in the coronation of *Charles V in the following year. In 1535 he was deprived by Act of Parliament of the see of Salisbury. He was created a cardinal in 1537.

Primary docc. concerning his part in the divorce case ed. S. Ehses, *Römische Dokumente zur Geschichte der Ehescheidung Heinrichs VIII von England, 1527–1534* (Quellen und Forschungen aus dem Gebiete der Geschichte in Verbindung mit ihrem historischen Institut in Rom herausgegeben von der Görres-Gesellschaft, ii, 1893), with introd. on Campeggio's life up to 1528, pp. xvi–xxxi; id., 'Kardinal Lorenzo Campeggio auf dem Reichstage von Augsburg, 1530' in *R.Q.*, xvii (1903), pp. 383–406, xviii (1904), pp. 358–84, and xix (1905), pp. 129–225, with docc. Early life by C. Sigonio (Bologna, 1581). E. V. Cardinal, C.S.V., *Cardinal Lorenzo Campeggio, Legate to the Courts of Henry VIII and Charles V* (Boston, 1935). J. *Gairdner in *D.N.B.*, viii (1886), p. 398 f. T. B. Scannell in *C.E.*, iii (1908), p. 223 f., s.v., with further bibl. See also bibl. to Henry VIII.

CAMPION, EDMUND (1540–81), *Jesuit. The son of a London bookseller, he was educated at the expense of the Grocers' Guild at a London grammar school, Christ's Hospital, and St. John's College, Oxford, where he became a Junior Fellow in 1557. He was distinguished by his powers of leadership and his oratorical ability; in 1566 he was chosen by the university to welcome Queen *Elizabeth to Oxford. Although already Catholic in sympathy, he was ordained deacon in the C of E in 1569, but being troubled in conscience left later in the year for *Dublin, hoping for the revival of the university. Returning to England in disguise in 1571, he joined W. *Allen at *Douai in the same year and was received into the Roman Church. Proceeding to Rome as a pilgrim, he entered the Jesuit Order in 1573 and was ordained in 1578. After a novitiate spent in Brünn, Bohemia, he taught at Prague until in 1580 he joined R. *Parsons in the first Jesuit mission to England. He preached extensively and with considerable effect in London and Lancs. In 1581 he secretly published a pamphlet entitled *Decem Rationes*, defending the RC position. He was arrested later in the year, but appears to have been offered his life if he would return to the C of E. On his refusal he was charged with conspiracy against the Crown, put on the rack and executed at Tyburn (1 Dec. 1581). He was beatified by *Leo XIII in 1886. Feast day, 1 Dec.

[W. *Allen,] *A Brief History of the Glorious Martyrdom of Twelve Reverend Priests* (1582; new ed. by J. H. Pollen, S.J., 1908). R. Simpson, *Edmund Campion* (1867). Modern life by L. I. Guiney ('The St. Nicholas Series', 1908); study by E. Waugh (London, 1935).

CAMP MEETING. A religious revivalist meeting held out of doors and lasting for several days, during which those taking part live in tents or temporary huts. This kind of meeting, first tried in 1799, has on occasion been adopted by several religious bodies, but is most frequently used by *Methodists, esp. in the U.S.A.

CANAAN. The land, later known as Palestine, which the Israelites occupied and conquered by degrees in the latter part of the second millennium B.C. or, acc. to some views, rather earlier. Of the original inhabitants (called Canaanites) some survived, and appear to have had a reactionary influence upon the development and maintenance of Hebrew monotheism.

L. H. Vincent, O.P., *Canaan d'après l'exploration récente* (1907). C. F. Burney, *Israel's Settlement in Canaan* (Schweich Lectures for 1917; 1918); F. Schmidtke, *Die Einwanderung Israels in Kanaan* (1933). A. Barbois, O.P., in *Dict. Bibl.* Suppl. i (1928), cols. 997–1022, s.v., with bibl.; A. Bea, S.J., and E. Josi in *E.C.*, iii (1950), cols. 480–7, s.v. 'Canaan e Cananei', with further bibl.

CANADA, Christianity in. The early settlements of Champlain (Port Royal, Acadia, 1605; Quebec, Canada, 1608) were inspired by two objects: the pursuit of the fur trade and the conversion of the Indians. Though the *Recollects undertook the first organized missionary efforts, leadership passed early to the *Jesuits, whose explorations and martyrdoms form a heroic chapter in Canadian history. They and Bishop Laval (in Canada 1659–88) devoted themselves to curbing the excesses of the fur trade and to building up a purely RC and *ultramontanist colony, free of *Gallicanism and *Jansenism as well as *Huguenots—who were totally excluded from an early date. After the English conquest the continuance of the French-speaking, RC community was assured by the Quebec Act (1774) and the Constitutional Act (1791), which provided a separate province, Upper Canada, for the exercise of British customs. An established Anglican Church was attempted but ultimately abandoned. Today the chief denominations are RC, United Church of Canada, and Anglican, with numerous small churches and sects, reflecting the varied origins of the people. The United Church was formed in 1925 by the union of *Methodists, *Congregationalists, and most *Presbyterians. In the Canadian Council of Churches, formed during the Second World War, most non-Roman churches collaborate to meet the challenges of modern society. RCs and Anglicans are most active in missionary work amongst Indians and Eskimos. Education is controlled by the provinces. In the creation of most provincial systems religion was a crucial issue, with the result that in most provinces education is secular in varying degrees, with the notable exceptions of Quebec and Newfoundland.

A. Gosselin, *La Mission du Canada avant Mgr de Laval, 1615-59* (Évreux, 1909); id., *L'Église du Canada depuis Monseigneur de Laval jusqu'à la conquête* (3 vols., Quebec, 1911-14); id., *L'Église du Canada après la conquete* (2 vols., ib., 1916-17). A. G. Morice, O.M.I., *History of the Catholic Church in Western Canada* (2 vols., Quebec, 1910). C. Lindsey, *Rome in Canada*. The Ultramontane Struggle for Supremacy over the Civil Authority (Toronto, 1877); M. Eastman, *Church and State in Early Canada* (Edinburgh, 1915). R. G. Thwaite (ed.), *The Jesuit Relations and Other Documents*. Travels and Explorations of the Jesuit Missions in New France, 1610-1791 (73 vols., Cleveland, 1896-1901; selections by Edna Kenton, London, 1927). C. de Rochemonteix, S.J., *Les Jésuites et la Nouvelle-France au XVII⁰ siècle* (3 vols., Paris, 1895-6); id., *Les Jésuites et la Nouvelle-France au XVIII⁰ siècle* (2 vols., ib., 1906). C. W. Vernon, *The Old Church in the New Dominion*. The Story of the Anglican Church in Canada (London, 1929), with bibl. C. H. Mockridge, *The Bishops of the Church of England in Canada and Newfoundland* (London, etc., [1896]); O. R. Rowley, *The Anglican Episcopate of Canada and Newfoundland* (Milwaukee, Wisc., and London, 1928). J. Langtry, *History of the Church in Eastern Canada and Newfoundland* (1892); L. N. Tucker, *Western Canada* (Handbooks of English Church Expansion, 1908). H. L. Clarke, *Constitutional Church Government in the Dominions Beyond the Seas* (1924), pp. 206-58. J. C. Roper in C. Jenkins–K. D. Mackenzie (edd.), *Episcopacy Ancient and Modern* (1930), pp. 174-99. H. P. Thompson, *Into All Lands*. The History of the S.P.G., 1701-1950 (1951), pp. 128-55, 242-73, and 502-14, with bibl., p. 726. W. Gregg, *History of the Presbyterian Church in the Dominion of Canada from the Earliest Times to 1834* (Toronto, 1885; ed. 2, 1905); J. T. McNeill, *The Presbyterian Church in Canada, 1875-1925* (ib., 1925). A. Sutherland, *Methodism in Canada*. Its Work and its Story (London, 1903); J. E. Sanderson, *The First Century of Methodism in Canada* (2 vols., Toronto, 1908-10). E. L. Morrow, *Church Union in Canada*. Its History, Motives, Doctrine and Government (ib., 1923); C. E. Silcox, *Church Union in Canada*. Its Causes and Consequences (New York, 1933); G. C. Pidgeon, *The United Church of Canada* (Toronto, 1950). V. J. Eylands, *Lutherans in Canada* (Winnipeg, 1945). A. G. Dorland, *A History of the Society of Friends (Quakers) in Canada* (Toronto, 1927).
S. D. Clark, *Church and Sect in Canada* (Toronto, 1948); H. H. Walsh, *The Christian Church in Canada* (ib, 1956). Latourette, iii, pp. 168-85, with bibl. pp. 458-85 passim, v, pp. 3-45, with bibl. pp. 471-506 passim, and vii, pp. 157-62.

CANDLE. Candles are widely used in Christian worship, both in E. and W., esp. as ornaments of the *altar. They are lighted during liturgical services and at certain other times. The use of candles on the altar seems to have developed out of processional lights which were stood in earlier times beside or on the altar. (See entry *Altar Lights*.) Votive candles are candles lit before statues in church as personal offerings. In the C of E the use of lights is governed by the *Ornaments Rubric, the *Lincoln Judgement (1890), and the *Lambeth Opinion of 1899. The last of these condemned portable lights, but the prohibition is now seldom if ever enforced. See also *Altar Lights, Candlemas, Paschal Candle*.

W. Mühlbauer, *Geschichte und Bedeutung der (Wachs-) Lichter bei den kirchlichen Funktionen* (1874); Rohault, vi (1888), ch. i, pp. 1-33. See also bibl. to *Altar Lights*.

CANDLEMAS. The feast commemorates the purification of the BVM and the presentation of Christ in the *Temple which took place, acc. to Lk. 2. 22-39, forty days after His birth, as the Jewish Law required (Lev. 12. 1-4). It was kept locally at *Jerusalem from c. 350 on 14 Feb. and later on 2 Feb. In 542 the Emp. *Justinian ordered its observance at *Constantinople as a thanksgiving for the cessation of plague, and it thence spread throughout the E., where it was called 'The Meeting' (ὑπαπαντή), i.e. of Christ with *Simeon. Somewhat later it began to be widely kept in the W.

The blessing of candles is now the distinctive rite on this day in the W. Beeswax candles, which are blessed, distributed, and lit whilst the *Nunc Dimittis is sung, are carried in a procession commemorating the entrance of Christ, the 'True Light' (cf. Jn. 1. 9), into the Temple. In the *Liber Pontificalis, the institution of the procession is connected with the pontificate of Pope *Sergius (687-701).

The feast is first described by *Etheria, *Peregrinatio*, 26. Other early reff. are in sermons by St. *Gregory of Nyssa (J. P. Migne, *PG*, xlvi, 1151-82), *Theodotus of Ancyra (J. P. Migne, op. cit., lxxvii, 1389-1412) and Abraham of Ephesus (6th cent.; *P.O.*, xvi, 448-54). It owes its introduction to Rome, with three other feasts of Our Lady, to Pope *Sergius I (d. 701); cf. *L.P.* (Duchesne), i, p. 376. See also L. *Duchesne, *Origines du culte chrétien* (1889), p. 462 (Eng. tr., 1903, p. 479), who prints the description of the Feast in the 'Ordo Romanus of St. Amand'. A. *Baumstark, *Liturgie comparée* (ed. 3, 1953), p. 166 f. D. De Bruyne, O.S.B., 'L'Origine des processions de la chandeleur et des rogations à propos d'un sermon inedit' in *R. Bén.*, xxxiv (1922), pp. 14-26, esp. pp. 18-26. E. de Moreau, S.J., 'L'Orient et Rome dans la fête du 2. février' in *Nouvelle Revue Théologique*, lxii (1935), pp. 5-20. The use of candles is already mentioned in the Life of Abbot Theodosius by *Cyril of Scythopolis (ed. E. *Schwartz, *T.U.*, xlix, Hft. 2, 1939, p. 236). On the blessing of the candles, A. Franz, *Die kirchlichen Benediktionen im Mittelalter*, i (1909), pp. 445-55. H. *Leclercq, O.S.B., in *D.A.C.L.*, iii (pt. 1, i, 1913), cols. 207-10, s.v., 'Chandeleur'. G. Löw, C.S.S.R., in *E.C.*, x (1953), cols. 341-5, s.v. 'Purificazione'.

CANGE, CHARLES DUFRESNE SIEUR DU. See *Ducange, Charles Dufresne Sieur*.

CANISIUS, St. PETER (1521-97), *Jesuit theologian. After studying theology at Cologne and Mainz, where he came under the influence of the Jesuit Pierre Lefèvre, he returned to Cologne. Here he founded a Jesuit colony, and attacked the Protestant views of Abp. *Hermann of Wied. From 1549 onwards he was working in Bavaria, Vienna, and Prague, preaching and lecturing against Protestantism. He secured the patronage of the Archduke, afterwards the Emperor, Ferdinand by whom he was offered the bpric. of Vienna, an offer which the General of his Order commanded him to refuse. A vigorous exponent of the RC, and esp. the Jesuit, position, he compiled a number of catechisms of which the chief was the *Summa Doctrinae Christianae* (or *Catechismus Major*), published in 1554 with 211 questions and answers. Over 130 editions have since been issued. In 1556 he was made *Provincial of Upper Germany and was himself very largely responsible for the foundation of colleges at Augsburg, Munich, and

Innsbruck, and the spread of Jesuit influence to Poland. To him, more than to any other, was due the remarkable success of the *Counter-Reformation in the south German lands. He was canonized in 1925 and at the same time (the first occasion that such an honour had coincided with a canonization) declared to be a *Doctor of the Church. Feast day, 27 April.

Works listed in Sommervogel, ii (1891), cols. 617–87, and viii (1908), cols. 1974–83. O. Braunsberger, S.J. (ed.), *Beati Petri Canisii Societatis Jesu Epistolae et Acta* (8 vols., Freiburg i.Br., 1896–1923); modern ed. of his Catechism by F. Streicher, S.J. (Societatis Jesu Selecti Scriptores, ii, Rome, 1933 ff.). J. Brodrick, S.J., *Saint Peter Canisius, S.J., 1521–1597* (1935). Other lives by L. Michel, S.J. (Lille, 1897), O. Braunsberger, S.J. (Freiburg i.Br., 1917), J. Metzler, S.J. (Münster i.W., 1927) and W. Reany (London, 1931). X. Le Bachelet, S.J., in *D.T.C.*, ii (1905), cols. 1507–37, s.v.

CANO, MELCHIOR (1509–60), Spanish theologian. In 1523 he entered the *Dominican Order at Salamanca, where he studied under F. *Vitoria. In 1533 he began to teach at Valladolid; in 1543 he was appointed to the first theological professorship at Alcalá; and in 1546 he succeeded Vitoria himself at Salamanca. He took an active part in the debates on the *Eucharist and on *Penance at the Council of *Trent. In his later years he became deeply involved in Spanish ecclesiastical politics, zealously opposing the *Jesuits and defending in his *Consultatio theologica* (1556) Philip II's antipapal policy. In 1557 he was elected Provincial of the Dominican Order, but his appointment was not confirmed at Rome; and when re-elected in 1559, confirmation was again refused at first, though eventually granted. As a theologian his reputation rests on his posthumous *De locis theologicis* (Salamanca, 1563), in which he defended the unusual thesis that the consent of the parties is merely the *matter of the sacrament of matrimony, the *form being the sacerdotal blessing (see *Marriage*), a view which gave rise to considerable controversy at the Council of *Trent and later.

Opera publd. Cologne in 1605. Life by F. Caballero (Madrid, 1871). A. Lang, *Die Loci Theologici des Melchior Cano und die Methode des dogmatischen Beweises* (1925). M. Jacquin, O.P., 'Melchior Cano et la théologie moderne' in *Revue des Sciences Philosophiques et Théologiques*, ix (1920), pp. 121–41. F. Marín-Sola, O.P., 'Melchior Cano et la conclusion théologique' in *Revue Thomiste*, Nouvelle Série, iii (1920), pp. 1–13 and 101–15. Quétif–Echard, ii, pp. 176–8. P. Mandonnet, O.P., in *D.T.C.*, ii (1905), cols. 1537–40, s.v.; E. Lamalle, S.J., in *E.C.*, iii (1950), cols. 532–4, s.v., with bibl.

CANON. The Greek word κανών meant a straight rod or bar. Metaphorically the term came to be used of the rules of an art or a trade or to signify a list or catalogue. In Christian language it was adopted to denote the list of inspired books which the Church regarded as composing Holy Scripture (see *Canon of Scripture*), liturgical rules, esp. that part of the Mass which includes the *consecration (see *Canon of the Mass*), and rules concerning the life and discipline of the Church. In law, the word 'canon' was gradually used exclusively of ecclesiastical enactments, and

*Justinian distinguishes (civil) laws from (ecclesiastical) canons. In the Middle Ages the law of the Church came to be known as 'Canon Law' as distinct from 'Civil Law'. In the Councils of the early Church the term was usually reserved for disciplinary decisions; but since the 15th cent. Councils have more often used it for their dogmatic definitions. Generally speaking *Canon Law to-day covers the rules of the Church for her own organization, government, and administration.

H. Oppel, 'ΚΑΝΩΝ. Zur Bedeutungsgeschichte des Wortes und seiner lateinischen Entsprechungen,' *Philologus*, Suppl., xxx (1937), pp. 1–108.

CANON (ecclesiastical title). Though first applied to all clergy on the official staff of a diocese (excluding monks, private chaplains, &c.), the word was gradually limited to those secular clergy belonging to a cathedral or collegiate church. They had a share in the revenues of the Church and were bound to a common life there, though in the early Middle Ages this was not very uniformly interpreted. Before the 11th cent., a canonry was often consistent with the holding of private property and periods of non-residence; but from then onwards those continuing to maintain this mode of life came to be known as 'secular canons' to distinguish them from the *Augustinian or 'regular' canons (q.v.) who lived under a semi-monastic rule.

'Residentiary canons' form the permanent salaried staff of a cathedral and are responsible for the maintenance of its services, fabric, &c. In the C of E they have the right of electing or refusing to elect the Crown's nominee to a vacant episcopal see (but see *Congé d'Élire*). A 'non-residentiary canon' (often 'honorary canon') is one who holds an unsalaried post, which may entail certain privileges and responsibilities. '*Minor canons' are clerics usually chosen for their ability to sing the services in a cathedral, and in general have no say in its government. See also *Prebend and Prebendary*.

J. Molanus, *De Canonicis Libri Tres* (Cologne, 1587). E. Amort, *Vetus Disciplina Canonicorum Regularium et Saecularium* (2 vols., Venice, 1747). The legislation governing the main duties and perogatives of canons in the RC Church is embodied in the *C.I.C.*, cann. 397–421. On canons in the C of E, H. W. Cripps, *A Practical Treatise on the Law Relating to the Church and Clergy* (ed. 8 by K. M. Macmorran, 1937), esp. pp. 137–42. The most readily accessible discussions of the subject are in dictionary artt. D. Dunford in *C.E.*, iii (1908), pp. 252–5, s.v.; H. *Leclercq, O.S.B., in *D.A.C.L.*, iii (pt. 1; 1913), cols. 223–48, s.v. 'Chanoines', with bibl.; K. H. Schäfer in *L.Th.K.*, v (1933), col. 783, s.v. 'Kanoniker'; P. Torquebiau in *D.D.C.*, iii (1942), cols. 471–88, s.v. 'Chanoines'; id., ib., cols. 530–95, s.v. 'Chapitres de chanoines', with bibl.; C. Dereine in *D.H.G.E.*, xii (1953), cols. 355–405, s.v. 'Chanoines' passim (mainly on 'canons regular'). See also bibl. to *Chapter*.

CANON (hymnological). In the E. Church, the series of nine hymns ('*odes'), usually acrostics, used chiefly at the *Orthros. It follows the Biblical Canticle which concludes the office except on Sundays and certain feasts, when all but the last ode precede the Canticle. The nine odes vary through the week to correspond with the theme of the changing Biblical Canticles. The introduction of canons is ascribed to St. *Andrew of Crete. Other famous authors of canons are *Cosmas Melodus, St. *John of Damascus, and St. *Theodore Studites.

Krumbacher, pp. 673-9 (on Andrew of Crete, John of Damascus, and Cosmas of Jerusalem). W. Christ, 'Über die Bedeutung von Hirmos, Troparion und Kanon in der griechischen Poesie des Mittelalters' in *Sb.* (Bayr.), 1870 (ii), pp. 75-108. O. Heiming, O.S.B., *Syrische 'Eniânê und griechische Kanones* (1932). A. Fortescue in *D.A.C.L.*, ii (pt. 2, 1910), cols. 1905-10, with bibl.

CANON EPISCOPALIS. In the Latin Rite, the bishop's liturgical book containing the *Ordinary of the Mass from the '*Aufer a nobis' to the end, and also other prayers and forms used by bishops. It is placed on the altar instead of altar-cards at a pontifical Mass.

CANON LAW. The body of ecclesiastical rules or laws imposed by authority in matters of faith, morals, and discipline.

This *corpus* of law grew up very gradually. Its beginnings are to be traced to the practice of convening Councils to settle matters of uncertainty or dispute and their issue of a considerable number of *ad hoc* pronouncements on matters of doctrine and discipline. Such pronouncements had varying degrees of authority, acc. to the importance of the Council and the area of the Church which it represented. The series of 20 miscellaneous canons promulgated at *Nicaea (325) came to possess a certain primacy in both East and West, owing to the unique authority enjoyed by this Council. To these were added the sets of canons of other Councils. As it happened, in the E. these Councils were often Arianizing assemblies (though this circumstance did not affect the orthodoxy of their canons), while in the W. the canons of the orthodox Council of *Sardica (343) were often attached to those of Nicaea and, owing to a confusion, sometimes supposed to be Nicene. The practice of the African Church of holding plenary Councils with exceptional frequency brought into being a large body of canons from its provinces. Evidence of the existence of canonical collections by the middle of the 5th cent. is provided by the citation at the Council of *Chalcedon (451) of the Antiochene canons of 341 (or possibly 330). Notable private collectors of canons were *John Scholasticus (who arranged the Greek canons known to him under subject-headings) in the E. and *Dionysius Exiguus and the unknown author of the *Hispana Collection in the W.

Side by side with the Councils the decrees of influential Bishops were another source of early ecclesiastical legislation. St. *Dionysius of Alexandria, St. *Gregory Thaumaturgus, St. *Basil of Caesarea, and St. *Amphilochius of Iconium all issued canonical letters. Special authority came to be enjoyed by the letters of the Popes (*Decretals) beginning with that of Pope *Siricius to *Himerius of Tarragona (385). The 4th-5th cents. also saw the ascription of collections of canons to fictitious authors, such as the '*Apostolic Canons' (q.v.) and those attributed to St. *Hippolytus and other names of repute. Under *Charlemagne much standardization took place and by the next generation, as is shown by the *Forged Decretals, a trained body of canonists had come into being.

In the Middle Ages a decisive stage was reached when *Gratian issued his *Decretum* (c. 1140). Though in essence a private collection, the appearance of this work marked an epoch in the history of the subject and students have come to regard Gratian's work as the dividing line between *ius antiquum* and *ius novum*. (The law established later than *Trent has hence come to be termed *ius novissimum*). The authority accorded to Gratian's *Decretum* led to its supplementation by a series of later collections (among them the *Extravagantes), as described in the entry *Corpus Iuris Canonici (q.v.). In the RC Church this last-named Corpus continued to enjoy authority right down to the present century. It was only the issue of a *motu proprio* by *Pius X on 19 Mar. 1904 which led to its being completely overhauled and codified. The standard text is now the *Codex Iuris Canonici* (q.v.), issued in 1917.

Together with laws accepted as universally binding, there have always been others of only local authority. While in general the Roman canon law was binding in England in the Middle Ages, this was supplemented to some extent by the local provincial decrees of Canterbury. In 1433 the Synodal Constitutions of the province from S. *Langton (1222) to H. *Chichele (1416) were issued by W. *Lyndwood in his famous *Provinciale*. In post-Reformation times, these have been modified by the canons of 1603-4 (see *Canons, Book of).

Older works include J. Pignatelli, *Consultationes Canonicae* (3 vols., Rome, 1675; and many later edd.), and the writings of *Benedict XIV (q.v.), the greatest of modern canonists. J. F. von Schulte, *Das katholische Kirchenrecht* (2 vols., 1860, 1856; ed. 4, 1876); R. von Scherer, *Kirchenrecht* (1886). For texts of the Conciliar canons see the *Concilia* of J. *Hardouin, S.J., J. D. *Mansi, E. *Schwartz, and C. H. *Turner (qq.v.); convenient modern ed. of the early collections in F. Lauchert, *Die Kanones der wichtigsten altkirchlichen Concilien* (1896). On the history of early canon law in the West, the standard work is F. *Maassen, *Geschichte der Quellen und der Literatur des kanonischen Rechts im Abendland*, i (1870; all publd.); for the later history, J. F. von Schulte, *Geschichte der Quellen und der Literatur des canonischen Rechts von Gratian bis auf die Gegenwart* (3 vols., 1875-80). P. Fournier-G. Le Bras, *Histoire des collections canoniques en occident depuis les fausses décrétales jusqu'au décret de Gratien* (2 vols., 1931-2). F. Cimetier, P.S.S., *Les Sources du droit ecclésiastique* (Bibliothèque Catholique des Sciences Religieuses, 1930). R. Naz (ed.), *Traité de droit canonique* (4 vols., 1948-9). A. Villien, E. Magnin (A. Amanien, R. Naz) (edd.), *Dictionnaire de droit canonique* (Paris, 1924 ff.; in progress). A. van Hove, *Commentarium Lovaniense in C.I.C.* (Malines, 1928 ff.; ed. 2, 1945), esp. I. i ('Prolegomena'). A. Boudinhon in *C.E.*, ix (1910), pp. 56-66, s.v. 'Law, Canon'.

CANON OF THE MASS (from Gk. κανών, 'measuring rod', 'rule', because fixed and unchanging), the consecratory prayer in the Roman Mass. A prayer of this kind is found in all the Eucharistic liturgies, Gk. and Lat. It always (with the possible exception of the Liturgy of *Addai and Mari) contains the Words of *Institution (q.v.).

Though the Roman Canon must be based

ultimately on Gk. models, it is unlikely (agst. A. *Baumstark) that it was a translation from a Gk. original. It existed as early as the 4th cent. in a nearly related form, which is quoted by St. *Ambrose (d. 397) in his '*De Sacramentis' (q.v.). It received modifications at the hands of St. *Gregory the Great (590–604), by whose period it had assumed virtually its present form. Some early occurrences of it are in the *Gelasian Sacramentary (q.v.), the *Bobbio Missal, and the '*Missale Francorum' (7th cent.). The variations in the text, though they attract the attention of specialists, are of relatively minor importance; the remarkable fact is the universal acceptance of a virtually identical prayer throughout the West.

Its position in the rite is immediately after the *Preface and the *Sanctus, with the former of which it was prob. originally connected, the present Sanctus being an interpolation. But it is now held to begin at the words '*Te Igitur' (q.v.). It is a succession of short prayers, viz. (from their opening words) 'Te Igitur', 'Memento [vivorum]', *Communicantes (intercession, slightly variable at the chief feasts), 'Hanc Igitur', 'Quam Oblationem', 'Qui Pridie' (the actual words of Consecration; accompanied since the Middle Ages by the elevation of the Elements), 'Unde et Memores' (corresponding to the Gk. *Anamnesis, q.v.), 'Supra Quae', 'Supplices Te Rogamus' (possibly the remains of an ancient *Epiclesis, q.v.), 'Memento [defunctorum]', '*Nobis Quoque Peccatoribus', and 'Per Quem Haec Omnia' (concluding Doxology). The want of any clear sequence of thought, the existence of two separate lists of saints, and other considerations suggest that its text was seriously dislocated at an earlier stage in its history; but none of the many modern attempts to reconstruct the original order has won wide acceptance.

Since *c.* A.D. 800 the Canon of the Mass has been recited silently, only the words 'Nobis quoque peccatoribus' and the concluding 'Per omnia secula seculorum' being said aloud. Exceptionally it is recited audibly, but in a subdued voice, by the Celebrant and the concelebrating newly ordained priests at an Ordination Mass.

Crit. text ed. B. Botte, O.S.B., *Le Canon de la messe romain* (Louvain, 1935), with notes. B. Botte, O.S.B., and Christine Mohrmann (edd.), *L'Ordinaire de la messe* (Études Liturgiques, 2, 1953), esp. pp. 74–85. Much the best summary of the contemporary position in Jungmann, ii (1952), pp. 127–340, with full bibl. reff. Older theories on the history of the Roman Canon (some finally disproved by the identification of St. *Hippolytus as author of the *Apostolic Tradition*) summarized in A. *Fortescue, *The Mass* (1912), pp. 138–71. The large literature includes G. *Bickell, *Messe und Pascha* (1872); P. Drews, *Zur Entstehungsgeschichte des Kanons in der römischen Messe* (1902); A. Baumstark, *Liturgia romana e liturgia dell' esarcato. Il rito detto in seguito patriarchino e le origini del *Canon Missae* romano (Rome, 1904); P. Batiffol, *Leçons sur la messe* (1920), pp. 166–275; P. Oppenheim, O.S.B., *Canon Missae Primitivus* (Rome, 1948).

CANON OF SCRIPTURE (from Gk. κανών, 'measuring rod', 'rule'). The term, used also in a larger sense for a list or catalogue, gradually acquired a technical meaning for the Books which were officially received as containing

the rule of the Christian faith. In this sense the words 'canon' and 'canonical', which had already been employed by *Origen, came into general use in the 4th cent. The idea of a Canon of Scripture, however, goes back to OT times.

In Judaism the sacred literature was known as books 'that defile the hands'. Acc. to the legend told in the apocryphal IV *Esdras and preserved in the *Pirqe Aboth, the Hebrew canon was closed by the 'Great Synagogue' starting with Ezra after the return from Exile. Modern scholars, however, agree that it was formed gradually at a later period, and was probably finally closed in the latter part of the 1st cent. A.D. The Jews of the *Dispersion regarded several additional Greek Books as equally inspired, viz. most of the Books printed in the AV and RV among the *Apocrypha. During the first three cents. these were regularly used also in the Church. In the 4th and 5th cents., however, several E. Fathers, e.g. St. *Gregory of Nazianzus and St. *Epiphanius, questioned their canonicity, and in the W. St. *Jerome esp. would admit only the Hebrew books as canonical. Though St. *Ambrose, St. *Augustine, and others placed them on the same footing as the other OT books, through St. Jerome's influence doubts as to their canonicity persisted in the W. throughout the Middle Ages, though they continued to be used in the Liturgy. In the 16th cent. they were rejected by the Reformers, whereas the Council of *Trent in its Fourth Session (8 Apr. 1546) imposed their acceptance as *de fide* on all RCs, a decision confirmed by the *Vatican Council (1870). For the attitude of the Orthodox Churches of the E., see *Bible* (5).

The formation of the NT Canon also had its vicissitudes. Its kernel, the Four Gospels and the 13 Epistles by St. Paul, had come to be accepted *c.* 130 and were placed on the same footing with the OT between 170 and 220. The other NT writings were received later. Doubts persisted, esp. in the case of Heb., Jude, 2 Pet., 2 and 3 Jn. and Rev., as is shown, e.g., by a list drawn up by *Eusebius. On the other hand, certain writings, such as the Ep. of *Barnabas or the 'Shepherd' of *Hermas, were admitted by individual Churches, though rejected by the majority. St. *Athanasius in his *Festal Ep.* for 369 is the earliest exact witness to the present NT Canon. A Council held at *Rome in 382 under St. *Damasus gave a complete list of the canonical books both of the OT and the NT (also known as the '*Gelasian Decree' because it was reproduced by Gelasius in 495), which is identical with the list given at *Trent. In the early stages of this long history an important part was played by the controversy with *Marcion, whose canon consisted of a mutilated Gospel of St. Luke and ten of St. Paul's Epistles (also modified to square with his theology). Other notable early lists of NT Scriptures were the *Muratorian Fragment (q.v.) and can. 60 of the Council of *Laodicea (4th cent.).

The Canon of Scripture thus came to be defined as the collection of inspired writings, made by the tradition and authority of the Church, which contain the rule of Divine Faith. The principle that only the Church has the right to declare a book canonical is recognized by the RC Church, the Orthodox Churches, and the C of E, though the canon of the last-named Communion differs in excluding from the OT those books not contained in the Hebrew Bible. On this last point see also art. *Apocrypha*.

On the OT Canon, W. R. *Smith, *The Old Testament in the Jewish Church* (1881); F. Buhl, *Den gammeltestamentlige Skriftovering* (Copenhagen, 1885), pt. 1 (Eng. tr., 1892, pp. 1–75); G. Wildeboer, *Het Onstaan van den Kanons des Ouden Verbonds* (Groningen, 1889; Eng. tr. by B. W. Bacon, *The Origin of the Canon of the Old Testament*, 1895); H. E. Ryle, *The Canon of the Old Testament* (1892). G. Östborn, *Cult and Canon*. A Study in the Canonization of the Old Testament (Uppsala Universitets Årsskrift, 1950, pt. 10). K. *Budde in *E.Bi.*, i (1899), cols. 647–74 and 681 (bibl.), s.v. 'Canon'; F. H. Woods in *H.D.B.*, iii (1900), pp. 604–16, s.v. 'Old Testament Canon'; H. L. Strack in *P.R.E.* (ed. 3), ix (1901), pp. 741–68, s.v. 'Kanon des Alten Testaments'. On the NT Canon the most ambitious work is T. *Zahn, *Geschichte des neutestamentlichen Kanons* (2 vols. in 3 pts., 1888–92), to be suppl. by the same scholar's *Forschungen zur Geschichte des neutestamentlichen Kanons und der altchristlichen Literatur* (8 pts., 1881–1907). Other treatises include B. F. *Westcott, *A General Survey of the Canon of the New Testament* (1855; ed. 4, 1875). W. *Sanday, *Inspiration* (*Bampton Lectures, 1893); J. Leipoldt, *Geschichte des neutestamentlichen Kanons* (2 pts., 1907–8); E. Jacquier, *Le Nouveau Testament dans l'Église chrétienne*, i (1911); A. *Souter, *The Text and Canon of the New Testament* (1913), pp. 149–204; M. J. Lagrange, *Introduction à l'étude du Nouveau Testament*, i: Histoire ancienne du canon du Nouveau Testament (1933). H. W. Howarth, 'The Influence of St. Jerome on the Canon of the Western Church' in *J.T.S.*, x (1908–9), pp. 481–96; xi (1909–10), pp. 321–47; xii (1911–12), pp. 1–18. McNeile, pp. 310–72. V. H. Stanton in *H.D.B.*, iii (1900), pp. 529–42, s.v. 'New Testament Canon'; T. Zahn in *P.R.E.* (ed. 3), ix (1901), pp. 768–96, s.v. 'Kanon des Neuen Testaments'.

CANONESS. The name was first applied to members of certain communities of women founded in the *Carolingian period. Though they lived in common and took vows of celibacy and obedience, they did not bind themselves to poverty, and thus were bound by less severe restrictions than contemporary nuns. After the 11th cent. many orders of *canons regular had a similar order for women, whose members were known as 'canonesses regular.' As in the case of *regular canons, a number of congregations of these canonesses survive in the RC Church and undertake a variety of functions.

P. Torquebiau in *D.D.C.*, iii (1942), cols. 488–500, s.v. 'Chanoinesses'.

CANONIZATION. In the RC Church the definitive sentence by which the Pope declares a particular member of the faithful departed, previously beatified, to have already entered into eternal glory, and ordains for the new Saint' a public cult throughout the whole Church. In the Russian Church, before the Revolution of 1917–18, canonizations were performed by the *Holy Synod. Canonization is to-day distinguished from *Beatification, which allows only a restricted public veneration of the person beatified, but in the early centuries such a distinction was almost, if not quite, unknown.

In the primitive Church, martyrs were the first to be publicly venerated by the faithful. From the **4th** cent. onwards a *cultus* was extended also to *confessors. Local bishops began to control the various cults in their own dioceses and councils also dealt with the subject. Frequently the veneration of certain saints spread far beyond the limits of their own diocese or country. This raised the problem of the regulation of these cults, and negligence and abuses brought about Papal intervention. The first historically attested canonization is that of *Ulrich of Augsburg by Pope John XV in 993. c. 1170, *Alexander III, in a letter to King Canute of Sweden, asserted that no one should be venerated as a saint without the authority of the Roman Church; and by the inclusion of this passage in the *Decretals of *Gregory IX, it became part of W. canon law. This Papal authority is generally given nowadays only after a long legal process provided for in the *Codex Iuris Canonici (cans. 1999–2141), in which the *Promotor Fidei (q.v.), an official of the *Congregation of Rites, brings forward arguments against the canonization of the person in question. The classical treatise on the whole subject is the *De Servorum Dei Beatificatione et Beatorum Canonizatione* of *Benedict XIV (Prosper Lambertini), first published at Bologna in 1734–8.

Canonization is held to confer a sevenfold honour: (1) the name is inscribed in the catalogue of saints, i.e. public recognition is enjoined; (2) the new saint is invoked in the public prayers of the Church; (3) churches may be dedicated to God in the saint's memory; (4) the Mass and Office are publicly offered to God in the saint's honour; (5) festival days are celebrated in the saint's memory; (6) pictorial representations are made in which the saint is surrounded by a heavenly light of glory; (7) the saint's relics are enclosed in precious vessels and publicly honoured.

L. Hertling, S.J., 'Materiali per la storia del processo di canonizzazione' in *Gregorianum*, xvi (1935), pp. 170–95; T. Klauser, Anhang to 'Die Liturgie der Heiligsprechung' in O. Casel, O.S.B. (ed.), *Heilige Überlieferung* (Suppl. vol. to I. Herwegen, O.S.B. (ed.), Beiträge zur Geschichte des alten Mönchtums und des Benediktinerordens, 1938), pp. 229–33. E. W. Kemp, *Canonization and Authority in the Western Church* (1948). R. Naz in *D.D.C.*, iii (1942), cols. 10–37, s.v. 'Causes de béatification et de canonisation'. G. Löw, C.SS.R., in *E.C.*, iii (1950), cols. 569–607, s.v. 'Canonizzazione', with full bibl.

CANONS, Apostolic. See *Apostolic Canons*.

CANONS, The Book of. In the C of E the collection of 151 canons passed under the influence of Abp. R. *Bancroft by the *Convocation of *Canterbury in 1604 and that of *York in 1606. They are the principal body of canonical legislation made by the C of E since the Reformation. The individual canons are based on a number of sources. Some are a reaffirmation of medieval prescriptions, others depend on M. *Parker's 'Book of *Advertisements' and the *Thirty-Nine Articles. Among the many subjects with which they deal are the conduct of Divine service and administration of the sacraments, the duties and behaviour of clerics, the furniture and care of churches, *churchwardens, the ecclesiastical courts, and marriage regulations; and several of them are directed against the *Puritans, who were endeavouring in the early 17th cent. to achieve a drastic reconstruction of the C of E. They were drawn up in Latin by Bancroft when he was still Bp. of London, and the Latin version alone has authority. A few of them (e.g. can. 37) were modified in the 19th cent., but nearly all of them are still technically binding in their original form.

In 1939, at the request of the Lower House of the Canterbury *Convocation, the Abp. of Canterbury (C. G. *Lang), in conjunction with the Abp. of York (W. *Temple), appointed a 'Canon Law Commission' under the chairmanship of C. F. Garbett, Bp. of *Winchester, to consider the present status of canon law in England. Its terms of reference included both the canons in force before the Reformation and those promulgated since, means of determining which canons should be regarded as obsolete, and the recommendation of proposals for providing the C of E with a body of canons which should be 'certainly operative'. The Commission was also invited, if it deemed it expedient, to prepare a revised body of canons for submission to Convocation. The meetings of the Commission were delayed until 1943. After holding eight full sessions it issued a report, including a proposed set of new canons, in 1947. The revision of the Canons along the lines proposed is still (1955) under consideration by Convocation.

The Lat. text was publd. at London, 1604; Eng. tr., ib. 1604. There have been numerous subsequent edd. of the Eng. tr.; modern ed. of Eng. and Lat. texts by J. V. Bullard (London, 1934). *The Canon Law of the Church of England. Being the Report of the Archbishops' Commission on Canon Law, together with Proposals for a Revised Body of Canons* (1947), with bibl. J. V. Bullard, 'What survives of the Constitutions and Canons of 1604' in id. (ed.), *Standing Orders of the Church of England* (1934), pp. 112-14; id., 'Difficulties in Revision', ib., pp. 18-28.

CANONS REGULAR (Lat. *canonici regulares*). A body of canons living under rule, which originated in the 11th cent. in close connexion with the Reform movement of *Gregory VII. In the 12th cent. they largely adopted the Rule of St. *Augustine and have since come to be known as *Augustinian (Austin) Canons (q.v.).

See bibl. to *Canon* (ecclesiastical title), also to *Augustinian Canons.*

CANOPY, Processional. An awning supported by poles at the corners and carried over the Blessed Sacrament in processions, and also over certain high ecclesiastical dignitaries, in the RC Church.

CANOSSA, near Reggio in N. Italy, the scene of the public humiliation and submission of the Emp. *Henry IV to Pope *Gregory VII (Hildebrand) in 1077. The Emperor is said to have stood for three days in the snow outside the Pope's lodging before absolution from excommunication was granted; but, even if this story be true, the statement by Lambert of Hersfeld that he went as a penance, under the Pope's orders, is contradicted by other sources. The incident may be interpreted as really a victory for Henry, for by it he regained the moral authority over his rebellious subjects which he had lost when excommunicated.

The principal authorities for the event are a letter of Gregory VII (Register IV, 12, pr. J. P. Migne, *PL*, cxlviii, 465-6) and Lambert of Hersfeld, *Annales*, a. 1077 (ed. by O. Holder-Egger in Scriptores Rerum Germanicarum, 1894, pp. 290-8). Studies by O. Holder-Egger in *N.A.*, xix (1894), pp. 537-63; G. Meyer von Knonau in *Deutsche Zeitschrift für Geschichtswissenschaft*, xi (1894), pp. 359-63; W. Sachse, *Canossa.* Historische Untersuchung (1896); H. Otto in *Mittheilungen des Instituts für oesterreichische Geschichtsforschung*, xviii (1897), pp. 615-20; F. Schneider, 'Canossa', in *Z.K.G.*, xlv (1927), pp. 163-75.

CANTATA. A form of musical composition which in its classical period usually consisted of a series of recitatives and arias for solo voices concluding with a *chorale, sung in parts by a choir. Sometimes the cantata opened with a very elaborate chorus-piece. The later *oratorio is a development of the cantata—indeed, the 'Christmas Oratorio' of J. S. *Bach is simply a set of six originally separate cantatas. The age of Bach (early 18th cent.) was the greatest period of the cantata; and his own two hundred 'Church Cantatas', with some by G. F. *Handel such as 'Silete Venti', are among the best examples. Cantatas were at this time used instead of the *gradual in the Lutheran Ante-Communion service.

CANTATE DOMINO (Lat., 'O sing unto the Lord'), Ps. 98, from its first words. In the 1552 and subsequent editions of the BCP it is an alternative to the canticle '*Magnificat' at Evening Prayer. Since 1662 it has been ordered that it shall not be used here on the 19th evening, when it is read among the psalms for the day. In the American Prayer Book of 1789, the 'Magnificat' was entirely omitted and replaced by the 'Cantate'; but in the revision of 1892 the old arrangement of the English book was restored.

CANTERBURY. The history of the present see begins with the arrival of St. *Augustine in 597, who with the assistance of his companions established his first church in the city. Augustine had been ordered to organize England in two ecclesiastical provinces with archbishops at *London and *York. The place of London, however, was from the first taken by Canterbury, which has since then been the see of the archbishop of the southern province, who is *Primate of All England. The northern boundary of the province of Canterbury is now formed by the northern boundaries of the dioceses of *Lincoln, Leicester, Derby, and *Lichfield. In 1920 the Welsh dioceses and Monmouth (which at that time formed part of the diocese of *Llandaff) were taken from Canterbury to form the newly constituted province of the 'Church in *Wales'. From

1375 to 1558 Calais and the surrounding district formed part of the diocese of Canterbury; and the Channel Islands are still in the province, being part of the diocese of *Winchester. From the time of Abp. Stephen *Langton (d. 1228), the archbishops held the title of 'legatus natus', i.e. they were recognized as *ex-officio* permanent Papal legates. The struggle for precedence between the archiepiscopal sees of Canterbury and York ended in the middle of the 14th cent. with a victory for the former. The principal residence of the Abp. of Canterbury is at *Lambeth Palace in London, but he also has a palace at Canterbury. The income of the see is £15,000. See also *Anglican Communion*; and *Cathedrals, Friends of the*.

Acc. to *Bede (*HE*, i, 33) an existing Roman basilica was consecrated by St. Augustine as the Cathedral Church of Christ. Ravaged by the Danes in 1067, the church was rebuilt in Norman style by Abp. *Lanfranc, extended under Abp. *Anselm and consecrated in 1130. After a disastrous fire in 1174 the choir was rebuilt in the transitional style under the guidance of William of Sens and William the Englishman. Under Abp. *Sudbury the nave was pulled down and later rebuilt in perpendicular style. The Chapter House and Cloisters are of the same period. The Chichele Steeple (also Oxford or Dunstan Steeple) was erected by Abp. *Chichele; the central Tower ('Bell Harry Tower') was built between 1495 and 1503. The chief glory of the Cathedral during the Middle Ages was the shrine of St. *Thomas Becket, dedicated on 7 July 1220. The former archiepiscopal throne of Purbeck marble ('St. Augustine's Chair') is perhaps as late as c. 1280. The crypt is mainly Norman with Roman and Saxon fragments. Since 1575 the S. transept of the crypt has been used by Walloon and Huguenot refugees and their descendants.

In c. 598 (acc. to Thorne and Elham) St. Augustine, with King *Ethelbert and his Queen, established a monastery in the east of the city, dedicated to St. Peter and St. Paul, to accommodate the bodies of future Bishops and kings of the region. In 613 the new conventual church was consecrated by Abp. Lawrence (Abp. 604–19), the body of St. Augustine being reinterred in the N. Porch. The first ten Abps. and several kings were buried there before Abp. Cuthbert (Abp. c. 740–58) left instructions that the tradition should be broken. The first outbreak of the chronic enmity between the monks and the Cathedral Chapter ensued. In 978 St. *Dunstan rededicated the conventual church in honour of Sts. Peter and Paul and St. Augustine, it being commonly known by the title of the latter saint. The church was largely rebuilt in the 13th cent.

From its foundation the abbey was richly endowed and seems to have enjoyed a position of favour. It contended that St. Augustine had granted it exemption from the jurisdiction of his successors, but the claim caused friction with the Abps., esp. from the 13th cent. onwards. C. 673 the abbey received, among other gifts from Rome, two MS. copies of the Gospels which may be the oldest books read in England. In 1051 *Leo IX granted the abbots precedence over all others except that of *Monte Cassino; in 1061 *Alexander II made to them the first grant of the right to wear a mitre and other episcopal insignia. Of considerable importance throughout the Middle Ages, in 1538 the monastery, then inhabited by some thirty monks and the Prior, was dissolved. In 1848 a college for the training of missionaries was founded (under the patronage of St. Augustine) on the ruins. In 1952 this was reconstituted as a central house of study for the Anglican Communion.

The archiepiscopal registers are extant from 1278 to 1326 and from 1349 onwards; description in [H. J. Todd] *A Catalogue of the Archiepiscopal Manuscripts in the Library at Lambeth Palace* (1812), p. 266 f. The following have been publd.: that of J. *Peckham ed. C. T. Martin (R.S., 3 vols., 1882–5), more complete ed. by the *Canterbury and York Society (1908 ff.); that of R. *Winchelsea ed. Rose Graham (Canterbury and York Society, 1917 ff.); that of H. Chichele ed. E. F. Jacob (ib., xlii, xlv–xlvii, 1937–47); that of J. Bourgchier ed. F. R. H. Du Boulay (ib., 1953 ff.), and that of M. *Parker ed. E. M. Thompson–W. H. *Frere (ib., xxxv, xxxvi, xxxix, 1907–33). The Acta of S. Langton ed. Kathleen Major (ib., l, 1950). E. H. W. Dunkin–C. Jenkins–E. A. Fry, *Index to the Act Books of the Archbishops of Canterbury, 1663–1859* (Index Library, lv, lxiii, 1929–38). W. F. *Hook, *Lives of the Archbishops of Canterbury* [to Abp. *Juxon] (12 vols., 1860–76). Irene J. Churchill, *Canterbury Administration. The Administrative Machinery of the Archbishopric of Canterbury Illustrated from Original Records* (C.H.S., New Series, xv; 2 vols., 1933). On Christ Church Priory and Cathedral, *The Statutes of the Cathedral and Metropolitical Church of Christ, Canterbury* (Canterbury, 1925). J. B. Sheppard (ed.), *Literae Cantuarienses. The Letter Books of the Monastery of Christ Church, Canterbury* (3 vols., R.S., 1887–9). W. *Dugdale, *Monasticon Anglicanum*, i (ed. 1817), pp. 81–119. R. Willis, *The Architectural History of Canterbury Cathedral* (1845). A. P. *Stanley, *Historical Memorials of Canterbury* (1855). C. E. Woodruff–W. Danks, *Memorials of the Cathedral and Priory of Christ in Canterbury* (1912). S. A. Warner, *Canterbury Cathedral* (1923), with bibl. B. Rackham, *The Ancient Glass of Canterbury Cathedral* (1949). R. A. L. Smith, *Canterbury Cathedral Priory. A Study in Monastic Administration* (Cambridge Studies in Economic History; 1943), with bibl. R. C. Fowler in *V.C.H.*, Kent, ii (1926), pp. 113–21. On St. Augustine's Monastery, W. Dugdale, op. cit., pp. 120–52. R. J. E. Boggis, *A History of St. Augustine's Monastery, Canterbury* (1901). R. C. Fowler in *V.C.H.*, loc. cit., pp. 126–33, with bibl. reff. R. J. E. Boggis, *A History of St. Augustine's College, Canterbury* (1907). W. H. Hutton in *D.E.C.H.*, pp. 90–5, s.v. 'Canterbury, See of'. W. A. Pantin in *D.H.G.E.*, xi (1949), cols. 785–812; s.v. 'Cantorbéry'.

CANTERBURY AND YORK SOCIETY.

A society founded in 1904 for the printing of episcopal registers and other ecclesiastical records.

Lists of the Society's publications are included in its annual reports.

CANTERBURY CAP.

A soft flat cloth cap sometimes worn by English clerical dignitaries and others. Like the college cap and the *biretta, it is simply a later form of the ordinary medieval black cloth head-dress.

CANTICLE (Lat. *canticulum*, dim. of *canticum*, a 'song'.

In the rubrics of the *Breviary, however, the non-diminutive form is used). Song or prayer (other than one of the *psalms) derived from the Bible, which is used in the liturgical worship of the Church. In the Roman *Breviary seven canticles from the OT are used at *Lauds, viz. the *Benedicite; the 'Song of *Isaiah the Prophet' (Is. 12); the 'Song of Hezekiah' (Is. 38. 10–20); the 'Song of Hannah' (1 Sam. 2. 1–10); the two 'Songs of *Moses' (Ex. 15. 1–19 and Dt. 32. 1–43); and the 'Song of *Habakkuk' (Hab. 3. 2–19). Of the NT canticles the *Benedictus is used at Lauds, the *Magnificat at *Vespers, and the *Nunc Dimittis at *Compline. But whereas the OT canticles are of only weekly occurrence, varying from day to day, these three 'evangelical canticles' are sung daily; also, unlike the OT songs, they are placed not among the psalms but in a separated position of great prominence. The Breviary also includes amongst its canticles the *Te Deum and the *Athanasian Creed. In the BCP the word 'canticle' is applied only to the Benedicite, but in common speech it is used of many of the others named above, as well as of the *Jubilate, the *Cantate, and *Deus misereatur.

CANTICLE OF THE SUN, The (Lat. 'canticum solis' or 'laudes creaturarum'). A hymn of St. *Francis in praise of the Divine revelation in nature, traditionally supposed to have been composed in 1225 in the garden of San Damiano at *Assisi. It receives its name from the second stanza, 'Be thou praised, my Lord, with all thy creatures, above all Brother Sun'.

Crit. ed. of text by E. Monaci, Crestomazia italiana dei primi secoli con prospetto delle flessioni grammaticali e glossario, fasc. i (1889), pp. 29–31. Ital. text with Eng. tr. and discussion in H. Goad, Greyfriars. The Story of St. Francis and his Followers (1947), pp. 137–41. J. R. H. Moorman, The Sources for the Life of S. Francis of Assisi (Manchester, 1940), pp. 17–19, incl. reff. to other discussions.

CANTICLES, Book of. See Solomon, Song of.

CANTILUPE, St. THOMAS DE (c. 1218–1282), also St. Thomas of Hereford, Bp. of *Hereford. The descendant of a noble family of Hambleden in Bucks, he was educated at *Oxford, *Paris, and Orléans, and became chancellor of Oxford university in 1262. As chancellor he aided the barons against King Henry III, and in 1264, after the defeat of the King at Lewes, became Chancellor of England. After the collapse of the baronial power in 1265 he retired to Paris as a lecturer, but returned to Oxford in 1272, where he was chancellor a second time. In 1275 he was elected Bp. of Hereford and became the confidential adviser of Edward I. Exercising his influence esp. against simoniacal practices and the vice of nepotism, he firmly suppressed encroachments on the rights of his see by the neighbouring lords. His later years were filled with disputes with John *Peckham, the Franciscan Abp. of Canterbury, on questions of jurisdiction, which led to his excommunication by the Archbishop in 1282. He immediately appealed against the sentence at the Papal court at Orvieto, but

O.D.C.C.–12

died before judgement had been pronounced. Despite the excommunication, the fame of his sanctity and of the miracles that took place at his tomb led to his canonization in 1320. Feast day, originally 2 Oct.; in modern RC calendars, 3 Oct.

The chief source for his life is the Process of Canonization preserved in the Vatican MS 4015, part of which is printed in the A.A.SS., Oct. I (1765), pp. 599–705. Other MS sources are listed in Hardy, iii, pp. 217–20. His Register, transcribed by R. G. Griffiths with introd. by W. W. Capes, was publd. in 1906 by the 'Cantilupe Society' and reissued by the *Canterbury and York Society, ii (1907). T. F. Tout in D.N.B., viii (1886), pp. 448–52.

CANTILUPE, WALTER DE (d. 1266), Bp. of *Worcester, and uncle of St. Thomas de *Cantilupe. He was elected Bishop in 1236, and consecrated by *Gregory IX in person in 1237. He supported many of the actions of R. *Grosseteste, Bp. of *Lincoln; but, despite this, was held to be one of the chief 'friends of the Pope' in England. In the war between King and barons (1258–65) he took the barons' side, and this fact is said to have been the only hindrance to his canonization. He was among the greatest figures of his day both as a diocesan bishop and as a national leader.

The chief sources for his life are the Annales Monastici, ed. H. R. Luard (R.S., 5 vols., 1864–9, esp. i, pp. 101–52, and iv, pp. 428–56); Matthew Paris, Chronica Majora, ed. H. R. Luard (R.S., 1876–82), passim; The Chronicle of William of Rishanger, ed. by J. O. Halliwell (Camden Society, old series xv, 1840), and the letters of R. *Grosseteste, ed. by H. R. Luard (R.S., 1861). H. R. Luard in D.N.B., viii (1886), pp. 452–4.

CANTOR. A singer who pre-intones and leads in the liturgical music of the choir office and in liturgical processions. Acc. to W. usage the number of cantors may be one, two, or four, acc. to the day, and they may be either clerics or laymen. They wear surplices and, on more solemn occasions, copes. See also Precentor and Succentor.

CANTORIS [sc. sedes] (Lat.), 'the place of the cantor'. As the traditional place of the cantor is on the north side of the choir of a cathedral or church, the term (also 'cantorial' or 'cantoral') is used to indicate those who in antiphonal singing sit on that side. The opposite side is known as '*Decani'.

CAPELLE, BERNARD (b. 1884), Abbot of Mont-César. A native of Namur, he was ordained priest in 1906 and professed a *Benedictine monk at *Maredsous in 1919. In 1928 he was elected coadjutor Abbot of Mont-César, Louvain, becoming full Abbot on his predecessor's death in 1942. In 1936 he became Maître de Conférences (History of Liturgy) in the university of Louvain. His many original and important contributions to the history of liturgy, early Christian literature and the Latin Bible, all marked by solidity and sound judgement, include Le Texte du psautier latin en Afrique (Collectanea Biblica Latina, IV, 1913), Pour une meilleure intelligence de la Messe (1946), An Early Euchologium. The *Der-Balizeh Papyrus enlarged and re-edited (with

C. H. Roberts, 1949), and a long series of articles in *Revue Bénédictine*, *Recherches de Théologie Ancienne et Médiévale*, *Questions Liturgiques et Paroissiales*, *Revue d'Histoire Ecclésiastique*, and other periodicals.

Collected *Travaux*, Mont César, Louvain, 1955 ff.

CAPERNAUM. A town near the Sea of Galilee of uncertain site, probably Khân Minyeh or Tell Hûm. It was the headquarters of Christ after His rejection from *Nazareth, and the scene of many of His miracles. The correct form of the name is 'Capharnaum' (Kfar-Nahum, city of Nahum), found in the best Gk. MSS. and the *Vulgate.

W. *Sanday-P. Waterhouse, *Sacred Sites of the Gospels* (1903), pp. 36-48; id., 'The Site of Capernaum' in *J.T.S.*, v (1904), pp. 42-8. B. Meistermann, O.F.M., *Capharnaüm et Bethsaïde* (1921), pp. 1-38 and 104-291. G. Orfali, O.F.M., *Capharnaüm et ses ruines d'après les fouilles accomplies à Tell-Houm par la Custodie Franciscaine de Terre Sainte, 1905-1921* (1922). W. Sanday in *D.C.G.*, i (1906), p. 269 f.; F. M. Abel, O.P., in *Dict. Bibl.*, Suppl. ii (1928), cols. 1045-64, s.v. 'Capharnaüm', with detailed bibl.

CAPITAL PUNISHMENT. The infliction of death by judicial sentence of the State. St. Paul in Rom. 13. (esp. 1-5) appears to recognize its legitimacy, and no religious body as such holds it to be immoral except the Society of *Friends, although individual Christians have sometimes held that it contravenes the 6th commandment. In the C of E the 37th *Article recognizes that it may be inflicted 'for heinous and grave offences'. Its abolition in certain countries, however, and the great diminution since 1800 of the number of crimes punishable by death in others, may legitimately be ascribed to Christian enlightenment.

CAPITILAVIUM (Lat.), 'washing of the head'. A name given to *Palm Sunday in the early Middle Ages, acc. to *Isidore of Seville in reference to the custom of washing the heads of children in preparation for the anointing which took place at baptism on the ensuing *Holy Saturday.

CAPITO, WOLFGANG (1478-1541), Protestant reformer. His real name was Köpfel. He was educated at Freiburg im Breisgau. After ordination he became associated with D. *Erasmus in his projects for ecclesiastical reform, and for a time was an ardent admirer of M. *Luther. In the early stages of the Reformation at Strassburg, before M. *Bucer's rise to influence, Capito was its leading figure in that city, and later he assisted with the compilation of the *Tetrapolitan Confession. He was usually on the side of those who favoured the propagation of Reformation principles by gentle methods and toleration.

J. W. Baum, 'Capito und Butzer von ihrer Geburt bis zu ihrer Ankunft in Strassburg 1478-1522' in K. R. Hagenbach (ed.), *Leben und ausgewählte Schriften der Väter und Begründer der Reformirten Kirche*, iii (1860). P. Kalkoff, *W. Capito im Dienste Erzbischof Albrechts von Mainz* (1907); O. E. Strasser, *Capitos Beziehungen zu Bern* (1927); id., *La Pensée théologique de Wolfgang Capiton dans les dernières années de sa vie* (Mémoires de l'Université de Neuchâtel, xi, 1938). B. Riggenbach in *P.R.E.* (ed. 3), iii (1897),

pp. 715-17, s.v.; Dr. Anrick in *R.G.G.* (ed. 2), i (1927), col. 1450, s.v.

CAPITULAR MASS. The public Mass sung (or occasionally said) daily in RC cathedrals and collegiate churches, and attended by the whole chapter. It is the parallel of the *Conventual Mass in religious communities, and is sometimes itself so described.

CAPITULARY (Lat. *capitulare*). (1) A collection of civil statutes, esp. those made by the Merovingian and Carolingian kings. The first official use of the word in this sense is in an enactment of *Charlemagne of the year 779.

(2) A compilation of previously enacted laws made by the bishops for the practical guidance of the clergy and laity of their dioceses. These 'episcopal capitularies' also date chiefly from Frankish times.

(3) In Biblical MSS. a brief summary of the contents, put at the head of the several books. These capitularies are based on classical models, and date from the 3rd cent. onwards. In some cases a single book is prefaced by several independent capitularies. By the Greeks they were known as κεφάλαια or τίτλοι, by the Latins as *tituli*, *breves*, *breviaria*, *capitula*, or *capitulationes*.

CAPPA MAGNA. In the RC Church, a cloak with a long train and large hood and lined with silk or fur, the use of which is reserved to cardinals, bishops, and certain other dignitaries. Its colour is ordinarily violet, except for cardinals out of Lent, whose *cappa magna* is scarlet; but if the wearer is a member of a religious order, the colour corresponds with that of his religious habit. Its use dates from the end of the Middle Ages.

CAPPADOCIAN FATHERS, The. The three brilliant leaders of philosophical Christian orthodoxy in the later 4th cent., namely St. *Basil the Great, Bp. of Caesarea in Cappadocia, St. *Gregory, Bp. of Nazianzus and St. *Gregory, Bp. of Nyssa (qq.v.). They were the chief influence which led to the final defeat of *Arianism at the Council of *Constantinople of 381. They were all Cappadocians by birth.

Besides general Patrologies, Church Histories and Histories of Doctrine, and works listed in this Dict. under the individual Fathers, see also H. Weiss, *Die grossen Kappadozier Basilius, Gregor von Nazianz und Gregor von Nyssa als Exegeten* (Brunsberg, 1872); id., *Die Erziehungslehre der drei Kappadozier* (1903).

CAPREOLUS, JOHN (*c.* 1380-1444), 'Thomistarum princeps', *Thomist philosopher and theologian. A native of Languedoc, he entered the *Dominican Order at Rodez. From 1408 he lectured on the *Sentences at Paris, where he was granted the licentiate in 1411. Later he was Regent of Studies at Toulouse. His principal work was a defence of St. Thomas's teaching in four books ('Defensiones', 1409-33) against the attacks of

*Henry of Ghent, *Duns Scotus, *Durandus of St.-Pourçain, *William of Occam, and others, which, after more than a century of eclipse, did much to revive the authority of Thomism.

Modern ed. of his Works by C. Paban and T. Pègues, O.P., (7 vols., Tours, 1900–8). Series of articles by T. Pègues, O.P., in *Revue Thomiste*, vii (1899), pp. 63–81, 317–34, 507–29, viii (1900), pp. 50–76, 288–309, 505–30, and xiii (1905), pp. 530–53. J. Ude, *Doctrina Capreoli de Influxu Dei in Actus Voluntatis Humanae secundum Principia Thomismi et Molinismi collata* (1904). U. Degl' Innocenti, O.P., 'Il Capreolo e la questione sulla personalità' in *Divus Thomas*, xliii (xvii, Ser. IIIae, Piacenza, 1940), pp. 27–40. Further bibl. in Überweg, ii, p. 788.

CAPTIVITY EPISTLES, The. The four epistles—Phil., Col., Eph., Philem.—generally believed to have been written by St. Paul towards the end of his life when he was in captivity at *Rome. References to his bondage occur, e.g. at Phil. 1. 7, Col. 4. 18, Eph. 4. 1, Philem. 9. G. S. Duncan has argued that they date from a captivity earlier in his life at *Ephesus. See artt. on the individual epistles.

Besides Commentaries, see G. S. Duncan, *St. Paul's Ephesian Ministry* (1929), whose conclusions, however, have been widely challenged.

CAPUCHINS. An offshoot of the *Franciscan Order, founded by Matteo di Bassi of Urbino (d. 1552), an *Observant Friar, who desired to return to the primitive simplicity of the order. Its members wear a pointed cowl (*capuche*), similar to that of St. *Francis, sandals, and a beard. The Rule, drawn up in 1529, strongly re-emphasized the Franciscan ideals of poverty and austerity. At first the order encountered considerable opposition from the other Franciscans, and the secession in 1541 of the third general, Bernardino *Ochino, to Protestantism nearly led to its suppression. But their enthusiastic preaching and missionary work gained them popular support, and made them one of the most powerful weapons of the *Counter-Reformation. Though the severity of the Rule has been gradually mitigated in practice, the order has remained the stricter of the two Franciscan families. Its members have usually been men of action rather than scholars. The official title of the order is the 'Ordo Fratrum Minorum S. Francisci Capuccinorum' (O.M. Cap.). In England and *Ireland they sign O.S.F.C. ('Ordinis Sancti Francisci Capuccinorum').

Bullarium Ordinis FF. Minorum S.P. Francisci Capuccinorum, ed. M. a Tugio, O.Cap. (7 vols., Rome, 1740–52); contd. by Petrus Damianus of Münster, O.Cap. (3 vols., Innsbruck, 1883–4). Their constitutions were publd. at Paris in 1645. Z. Boverio, O.Cap., *Annales seu Sacrae Historiae Ordinis Minorum S. Francisci qui Capucini nuncupantur* (2 vols., Lyons, 1632–9); contd. by Marcellinus of Pisa, O.Cap. (Lyons, 1676), Silvester Draghetta of Milan, O.Cap. (Milan, 1737), and P. Pellegrino of Forli, O.Cap. (Milan, 4 vols., 1882–5). Other material in Fr. Cuthbert [Hess], O.S.F.C., *The Capuchins* (2 vols., 1928). Heimbucher, i, pp. 724–60 and 824–7, and ii, p. 663 f.; L. v. Ebersberg in *L.Th.K.*, v (1933), cols. 808–17, s.v. 'Kapuziner'; Ilarino da Milano, O.F.M.Cap., in *E.C.*, v (1950), cols. 1738–42, s.v. 'Frati Minori', all with bibl. The *Analecta Ordinis Ordinis Minorum Capuccinorum* has been publd. at Rome, 1884 ff., and the *Monumenta Historica Ordinis Capuccinorum* at Assisi, 1937 ff.

CARAFFA. See *Paul IV*.

CARBONARI (Ital.), 'charcoal-burners'. A secret political society, in some ways resembling the Continental Freemasons (with whom they had friendly relations), which came into existence at the beginning of the 19th cent. They flourished chiefly in France and Italy, and were last heard of *c.* 1840. Their aims were the advancement of liberal ideas in politics and religion. They rejected all forms of Divine revelation, and looked to *natural religion as a sufficient basis for virtue and brotherhood, while in politics their avowed aim was the destruction of absolutism in every form and by any means. In 1820 they and their supporters gained possession of Naples for a brief period. The July Revolution of 1830 in France was also largely inspired by their influence. Many were absorbed in the Young Italy Movement of G. Mazzini (1831).

J. P. Kirsch in *C.E.*, iii (1908), p. 330 f., s.v.; P. Pirri, S.J., in *E.C.*, iii (1950), cols. 765–70, s.v. 'Carboneria', with good bibl.

CARDINAL. (Lat., *cardo*, 'hinge'), a title first applied to any priest permanently attached to a church (in which sense it still survives in the two cardinals among the minor canons at *St. Paul's Cathedral, London) and then restricted to the clergy of *Rome, i.e. the parish priests, the Bishops of the *suburbicarian dioceses, and the seven (later fourteen) district *deacons.

The Cardinals at Rome gradually formed a college, ranked as Roman princes immediately after the Pope, and became (when assembled in *Consistory) his immediate counsellors. They assumed the government of the RC Church during the vacancy of the *Holy See. In the Middle Ages they came to rank with princes of the royal blood.

The three ranks of Cardinals originated at different periods. The Cardinal-Priests were the parish priests of various Roman churches. Cardinal-Deacons had the care of the poor in the seven districts of Rome. Cardinal-Bishops were created *c.* the 8th cent. when the increase of Papal business made it necessary to invoke the help of neighbouring Bishops to act from time to time as the Pope's representatives. The terms 'Cardinal-Subdeacon' and 'Cardinal-Acolyte' were occasionally used of the Subdeacons and Acolytes at Papal ceremonies; but this usage did not persist.

The present functions of Cardinals are chiefly administrative. They are nominated by the Pope, and, since 1586, their number has been fixed at seventy, viz. six Bishops, fifty Priests, and fourteen Deacons. The *Codex (*CIC*, cans. 230–41) requires all Cardinals to be at least in Priests' orders (but in the last century E. *Consalvi and G. *Antonelli were only Deacons), and most are in fact Bishops. Their duties are to reside in Rome, unless excused or Bishops of foreign dioceses, to act as heads of *curial offices and Roman *Congregations, and to preside over ecclesiastical *commissions. They are given the title of 'Eminence' and have various rights in all dioceses, such as the use of a *portable altar everywhere, and they may use all episcopal ornaments in their titular churches. Their insignia include the *red hat, *biretta, and skull-cap, the 'sacred purple', a *ring with a sapphire stone, the *pectoral cross and, on certain occasions, the use of the *ombrellino. Every cardinal resident in Rome has the right to a revenue (*piatto cardinalizio*) if without sufficient private means.

On a vacancy in the Apostolic See (when they wear violet) they meet in secret session to elect a Pope (see *Conclave*), a privilege that has been exclusively theirs since the Third *Lateran Council of 1179 (can. 1).

From time to time the Pope creates a cardinal *in petto*, i.e. privately, but the creation is without effect unless publication follows. The nominee, however, retains his place of seniority.

J. B. Sägmüller (ed.), *Zur Geschichte des Kardinalates*. Ein Traktat des Bischofs von Feltre und Treviso Teodore de' Lelli über das Verhältniss von Primat und Kardinalat (*R.Q.*, Suppl. ii, 1893). Id., *Die Thätigkeit und Stellung der Cardinäle bis Papst Bonifaz VIII* (1896). V. Martin, *Les Cardinaux et la curie, tribunaux et offices, la vacance du siège apostolique* (1930). M. Belardo, *De Juribus S.R.E. Cardinalium in Titulis* (Vatican City, 1939). S. Kuttner, 'Cardinalis: The History of a Canonical Concept' in *Traditio*, iii (New York, 1945), pp. 129–214; M. Andrieu, 'L'Origine du titre de cardinal dans l'Eglise romaine' in *Miscellanea Giovanni Mercati*, v (*S.T.*, cxxv; 1946), pp. 113–44. J. Forget in *Dictionnaire apologétique de la foi catholique*, i (ed. 4 by A. d'Alès, 1911), cols. 851–62, s.v. 'Curie Romaine (Cardinaux)'. N. Hilling in *L.Th.K.*, v (1933), cols. 820–22, s.v. 'Kardinal', with further bibl.; P. Paschini, P. Ciprotti and V. Bartoccetti in *E.C.*, iii (1949), cols. 779–84, s.v. 'Cardinale'.

CARDINAL VIRTUES.

The four 'cardinal virtues' are prudence, temperance, fortitude, and justice. The chief Christian moral theologians, e.g. St. *Ambrose, St. *Augustine, and St. *Thomas Aquinas, took over his classification from *Plato and *Aristotle. In Christian writers the 'cardinal' are contrasted with the '*theological' virtues of *faith, *hope, and *charity.

St. Thomas, *S. Theol. I–II*, qu. 61 ('De Virtutibus Cardinalibus'). F. M. Utz, O.P., *De Connexione Virtutum Moralium inter se secundum Doctrinam S. Thomae Aquinatis* (Vechta, 1937). J. Rickaby, S.J., in *C.E.*, iii (1908), pp. 343–5.

CARDWELL, EDWARD

(1787–1861), ecclesiastical historian. Educated at Brasenose College, Oxford, he became Camden Professor of Ancient History in 1825, and Principal of St. Alban Hall in 1831, in succession to R. *Whately, an office which he held till his death. He issued through the University Press, in the administration of which he took a prominent part, several collections of documents still of great value to the student of English Church history, notably *Documentary Annals of the Reformed Church of England* (2 vols., 1839), *A History of Conferences . . . connected with the Revision of the BCP* (1840), and *Synodalia* (2 vols., 1842).

C. W. Sutton in *D.N.B.*, ix (1887), p. 42 f., s.v.

CAREY, WILLIAM

(1761–1834), *Baptist missionary. Born in humble circumstances in Northamptonshire and baptized an Anglican, he was apprenticed in 1777 to a shoemaker, but, after his conversion (1779), he became convinced of Baptist teaching (1783) and spent part of his time as a preacher. For many years he continued his cobbling by night, whilst running a school by day and acting as pastor of a church. During this time he taught himself Latin, Greek, Hebrew, Dutch, and French. His attention was directed towards the unevangelized tracts of the world, and, at the ministers' meeting at Nottingham in 1792, he promulgated the watchword, 'Expect great things from God and attempt great things for God', which led to the founding of the *Baptist Missionary Society. Sailing for India in 1793 in a Danish vessel, as the East India Company had put a ban on missionaries in British ships, he arrived in Bengal in Nov. 1793, where he was put in charge of an indigo factory at Malda, which became his mission station. In five years he translated the NT into Bengali and itinerated 200 villages. When the factory was closed (1799), he left for Serampore, where he was joined by four new missionaries, with whose assistance he was able to bring his Bengali New Testament into print in 1801. At this time Fort William College was opened at Calcutta, and Carey was appointed professor of Sanskrit, Bengali, and Marathi—a position that he held for 30 years. His many labours included a translation of the whole Bible in Bengali (1809), and its translation, in whole or part, into 24 other languages and dialects. In addition, he published philological works (grammars and dictionaries) in Sanskrit, Marathi, Punjabi, and Telugu. It was his agitation that was largely responsible for the abolition in 1829 of suttee, the ancient custom that had meant the death of every widow at the time of her husband's funeral.

J. Taylor, *Biographical and Literary Notices of William Carey* (1886). Lives also by J. C. Marshman (2 vols., London, 1859), G. Smith (ib., 1885), and S. Pearce Carey (ib., 1923).

CARLILE, WILSON

(1847–1942), Founder of the *Church Army. After a successful business career (1862–78), he entered the London College of Divinity, was ordained in 1880, and served an assistant curacy in Kensington. In 1882 he founded the *Church Army, and combined his work as its honorary Chief Secretary with various parochial appointments. He continued to take part in its administration until a few weeks before his death. In 1949 his grandson, Edward Wilson Carlile (b. 1915), became General Secretary of the Army.

E. Rowan, *Wilson Carlile and the Church Army* (1905; 4th ed., 1933); S. Dark, *Wilson Carlile* (1944); M. Burn, *The Pearl Divers*. Pictures from the Life and Work of Prebendary Carlile (1920); A. E. Reffold, *Seven Stars*. The Story of a Fifty Years' War. A Résumé of the Life and Work of Wilson Carlile and the Church Army (1931; reissued as 'The Audacity to Live', 1938).

CARLISLE. The see was erected in 1133 by Henry I, when he turned the Earldom of Carlisle (founded by William II, and including most of Cumberland and Westmorland) into a bishopric, with Aethelwulf, Prior of the *Augustinian Canons, as first bishop. The church of these Canons, who had been established here since *c.* 1102, became the cathedral, the only one served by this order. A new choir, built *c.* 1250, was burnt down in 1292. Rebuilding was begun *c.* 1300, and in 1392 there was another fire. The N. transept and central tower were rebuilt by Bp. William Strickland (Bp. 1400–1419). The Augustinian priory was dissolved in 1540, and its revenues used to endow the cathedral. After serious damage in the Civil War, the Scots are said to have pulled down most of the nave to repair the castle. In consequence of its partial demolition Carlisle Cathedral is one of the smallest in England. Its chief glory is the great E. window.

The *Register of John de Halton, Bishop of Carlisle A.D. 1292–1324*, transcribed by W. N. Thompson, with an introd. by T. F. Tout (*Canterbury and York Society, xii and xiii; 1913). Extracts from various later Registers in J. Raine (ed.), *Historical Papers and Letters from the Northern Registers* (R.S., 1873), passim. Extant records of the see listed in the *Ninth Report of the Historical Manuscripts Commission*, part i (1863), pp. 177–97. *The Statutes of the Cathedral Church of Carlisle* ed. with introd. by J. E. Prescott (Carlisle, 1879). J. Nicolson–R. Burn, *The History and Antiquities of the Counties of Westmorland and Cumberland*, ii (1777), pp. 243–310. J. Wilson in *V.C.H.*, ii, ed. id. (1905), pp. 131–52. C. K. Eley, *The Cathedral Church of Carlisle* (Bell's Cathedral Series, 1900). J. E. Prescott in *D.E.C.H.* (1912), pp. 95–8, s.v.

CARLOVINGIAN SCHOOLS. See *Carolingian Schools*.

CARLSTADT (*c.* 1480–1541), German reformer. He was so named from his birthplace, his real name being Andreas Bodenstein. After studying at Erfurt and *Cologne, he began to teach in 1505 at the newly founded University of *Wittenberg, where he soon became famous as an upholder of the philosophical doctrines of St. *Thomas Aquinas against the current *nominalism. A visit to Rome in 1515 led to a spiritual crisis, and in 1516, after his return, he repudiated his Thomist beliefs and became a vigorous exponent of the *Augustinian doctrine of the powerlessness of the human will. In answer to J. *Eck's theses, Carlstadt himself published in 1518 a set of theses maintaining 'Protestant' doctrines; and in 1519 he disputed in public with Eck at Leipzig. From that time onwards Carlstadt was recognized as the most extreme of all the Reformers. On Christmas Day, 1521, he celebrated the first Protestant Communion Service, with neither *vestments nor *canon nor *elevation, the laity being communicated under both species. On the day following he carried his attack on clerical celibacy into effect by announcing his engagement to be married. His views became increasingly violent, and he often found himself in very sharp conflict with M. *Luther, who after his release from the Wartburg and return to Wittenberg in

March 1522 directed ecclesiastical affairs there on lines which to Carlstadt savoured of compromise. In 1524 Luther attacked the new 'Judas', as he termed him, in his tract *Wider die himmlischen Propheten*, and Carlstadt was forced to renounce his professorship and flee. Allowed to return in 1525 on condition that he did not lecture, he was again forced to leave in 1528–9, and after many travels eventually reached Zürich. He remained in Switzerland for the rest of his life, from 1534 to his death holding a professorship at Basle.

H. Barge, *Andreas Bodenstein von Karlstadt* (2 vols., 1905); K. Müller, *Luther und Karlstadt* (1907); H. Barge, *Frühprotestantisches Gemeindechristentum in Wittenberg und Orlamünde. Zugleich eine Abwehr gegen Karl Müllers Luther und Karlstadt* (1909). *Corpus Catholicorum*, i (Münster i.W., 1919); J. *Eck, 'Defensio contra Amarulentas D. Andreae Bodenstein Carlostadtini Invectiones (1518)'. H. Barge in *P.R.E.* (ed. 3), x (1901), pp. 73–80, s.v. 'Karlstadt, Andreas', with older bibl.; id. in *R.G.G.* (ed. 2), iii (1929), cols. 632–4.

CARLYLE, THOMAS (1795–1881), Scottish historian, essayist, and moral teacher. Educated at Edinburgh University, he later was elected its rector (1866). His religious influence (which alone can be referred to here) has been widespread, for though he hated creeds, churches, and theologies, he had a profound belief in God and was convinced that 'the Religious Principle lies unseen in the hearts of all good men'. As an idealist who believed that matter exists only spiritually, he was the relentless foe of all materialistic philosophy and, through such works as *Sartor Resartus* (1833–4), *Heroes, Hero-worship, and The Heroic in History* (1841) and *Past and Present* (1843), which exposed worldly pleasure-seeking and money-making, he became the religious teacher of thousands. His independent, critical outlook rejected organized Christianity, but there was as much of the prophet as the poet in him and he consistently preached that the 'Everlasting Yea' is to love God.

Collected Works in 15 vols. (1857–8), in 17 vols. (1885–8), and 'Centenary Edition' by H. D. Traill in 30 vols. (1896–9). Letters, 1814–26, ed. C. E. Norton (2 vols., 1886), and 1826–36 (id., 2 vols., 1888); id., *The Correspondence of Thomas Carlyle and Ralf Waldo *Emerson, 1834–72* (2 vols., 1883), and *Correspondence between Goethe and Carlyle* (1887); A. Carlyle, *New Letters of Thomas Carlyle* (2 vols., 1904) and *Letters of Thomas Carlyle to John Stuart Mill, John Sterling and Robert Browning* (1923). J. A. Froude (ed.), *Reminiscences by Thomas Carlyle* (2 vols., 1881) and *Letters and Memorials of Jane Welsh Carlyle* (3 vols., 1883). Id. *Thomas Carlyle, 1795–1835* (2 vols., 1882); id., *Thomas Carlyle, 1834–1881* (2 vols., 1884). Life by D. A. Wilson (6 vols., 1923–34). S. Sagar, *Round by Repentance Tower*. A Study of Carlyle (1930); J. Symons, *Thomas Carlyle*. The Life and Ideals of a Prophet (London, 1952), with select bibl. F. F. Yandell, *Thomas Carlyle*. Sa métaphysique, sa morale, sa conception religieuse (1906); E. Neff, *Carlyle and Mill*: Mystic and Utilitarian (Columbia Univ. Studies in English and Comparative Literature, New York, 1924). G. McCrie, *The Religion of Our Literature* (1875), ch. i, pp. 2–68.

CARMEL, Mount. The high ridge in N. Palestine, immediately above the modern port of Haifa. It was the scene of the contest described in 1 Kgs. 18 between *Elijah and the prophets of *Baal. *C.* A.D. 500 a church was built there, and a monastery founded by

Greek monks. In the Middle Ages it became famous as the home of the *Carmelite Order. The feast of 'Our Lady of Mount Carmel' is celebrated on 16 July.

CARMELITE ORDER. The 'Order of Our Lady of Mount Carmel' was founded in Palestine c. 1154 by St. Berthold (d. c. 1195; feast day, 29 March), but it has claimed continuity with hermits settled on Mount Carmel in earlier times and even to be a direct descendant of *Elijah and the 'sons of the prophets' (cf. 2 Kgs. 2.). The primitive rule as laid down in 1209 by Albert of Vercelli, Latin Patr. of *Jerusalem, was one of extreme asceticism, prescribing absolute poverty, total abstinence from flesh, and solitude. After the failure of the *Crusades many of its members migrated to Europe, where, under the generalship of the Englishman St. *Simon Stock, the order was reorganized on the lines of the *mendicant friars. An Order of Carmelite Sisters was founded in the Low Countries in 1452, and spread rapidly through France, Italy, and Spain. During the 16th cent. the discipline among friars as well as nuns relaxed considerably until, towards the end of the century, St. *Teresa of Jesus restored in many houses the 'Primitive Rule' with some additions intended to foster the contemplative life. Her disciple, St. *John of the Cross, did the same for the friars, and the so-called 'Teresian Reform' was gradually adopted by the majority of the houses, whose members were called '*Discalced', in contrast to the 'Calced' Carmelites who continued to follow the 'Mitigated Rule'.

The main objects of the order are contemplation, missionary work, and theology (see *Salmanticenses*), the nuns devoting themselves more particularly to intercession (esp. for priests) by prayer and penance. The latter are enclosed and follow the same severe rule as the men, abstaining perpetually from flesh-meat and fasting from the Feast of the *Exaltation of the Cross (14 Sept.) until *Holy Saturday. The order propagates a special devotion to Our Lady and to the Child Jesus, and in the Middle Ages Carmelite theologians were among the earliest defenders of the *Immaculate Conception. The order has produced some of the greatest of Christian mystics, notably, besides St. Teresa and St. John of the Cross, the Calced Carmelite St. *Mary Magdalen of Pazzi (1566–1607; feast day, 29 May [25 May in the order]). The popular saint of our own times, St. *Teresa of Lisieux was also a Sister of the Teresian Reform.

The habit of the order is dark brown with a brown scapular and a white mantle (therefore these religious were popularly called 'Whitefriars'). The nuns wear a black veil.

J. B. de Lezana, O.C.C., *Annales Sacri, Prophetici et Eliani Ordinis Beatae Virginis Mariae de Monte Carmeli* (4 vols., Rome, 1645–56). [C. Villiers de St.-Étienne] *Bibliotheca Carmelitana*. Notis Criticis et Dissertationibus Illustrata (2 vols., Orléans, 1752). B. Zimmerman, O.D.C. (ed.), *Ordinaire de l'ordre de Notre-Dame du Mont-Carmel par Sibert de Beka, vers 1312* (Paris, 1910). L. van den Bossche, *Les Carmes* (1930). R. McCaffrey, O.C.C., *The White Friars.*

An Outline Carmelite History with special reference to the English-Speaking Provinces (Dublin, 1926); L. C. Sheppard, *The English Carmelites* (1943). *Monumenta Historica Carmelitana* (Lirinae, 1905 ff.). *Analecta Ordinis Carmelitarum* (Rome, 1908 ff.). Heimbücher, ii, pp. 54–95, with bibl. B. Zimmerman, O.D.C., in *D.T.C.*, ii (1905), cols. 1776–92, s.v. 'Carmes'; R. Weniger–A. Hofmeister in *L.Th.K.*, v (1933), cols. 839–46, s.v. 'Karmeliten', with bibl.; T. Brandsma, O.C.C., in *Dict. Sp.*, ii (1937–), cols. 156–71, s.v. 'Carmes'.

On the Discalced Carmelites see also *Constitutiones Fratrum Discalceatorum Congregationis S. Eliae Ordinis Beatissimae Virginis Mariae de Monte Carmelo* (Paris, 1638). *Chroniques de l'ordre des Carmélites de la réforme de Sainte-Thérèse depuis leur introduction en France* (5 vols., Troyes, 1846–65; Deuxième Série, 4 vols., Poitiers, 1888–9). *Études carmélitaines* (Paris, 1911 ff.); *Analecta Ordinis Carmelitarum Discalceatorum* (Rome, 1926 ff.). Gabriel de Sainte-Marie-Magdaleine, O.C.D., in *Dict. Sp.*, ii (1937–), cols. 171–209, s.v. 'Carmes Déchaussés', with bibl.

CARNIVAL. Popular etymology derives the word from *caro vale*, i.e. 'good-bye flesh'; but more probable is the derivation from *carnem levare*, 'to put away flesh-meat'. It is the name given in RC countries to the period before *Lent, whether it be the three days immediately previous, or the whole period between 3 Feb. and *Ash Wednesday. Such seasons of feasting and dancing early degenerated into riots, hence the transference of the word to secular festive occasions.

CAROL. A song of joy, originally accompanying a dance; now applied esp. to traditional and popular songs of a religious character. The word is from the Italian *carola*, a 'ring dance' (from *carolare*, 'to sing'). Historically the carol differs from the hymn in being a popular, and often unpolished, reflection on a religious theme, composed for informal singing, whereas the hymn was written by skilled and educated churchmen for formal use in Divine Service. Modern practice in England, where the 19th and 20th cents. have seen a considerable revival of the popularity of carols, has tended to confine the singing of them to Christmastide, and also to break down the distinction between carols and hymns, carols being often sung in church, and hymns outside the liturgy. But there are many traditional carols for other seasons, such as may be found, with Christmas carols, e.g. in *The Oxford Book of Carols* (1928).

CAROLINE BOOKS, The (*Libri Carolini*). A treatise compiled c. 790–92, which purports to have been written by *Charlemagne, but is manifestly the work of a skilled theologian. It was an attack on the *Iconoclastic Council of 754 (for forbidding images altogether) and *Nicaea II of 787 (for allowing excessive reverence to be paid to them). Its true purpose may be explained by Charlemagne's known irritation with the Greek empress, Irene, and his wish, by discrediting Greek authority of whatever kind, to have the more justification for assuming the Imperial title. It is possible that *Alcuin was its real author.

Text in J. P. Migne, *PL*, xcviii, 989–1248; modern ed. by H. Bastgen in *M.G.H.*, Legum Sectio III, Concilia II, Supplement (1924). Id., 'Das Capitulare Karls d. Gr. über die Bilder oder die sogenannten *Libri Carolini*' in *N.A.*, xxxv (1911), pp. 631-66, and xxxvi (1912), pp. 15-51 and 455-533. W. von den Steinen, 'Karl der Grosse und die *Libri Carolini*. Die tironischen Randnoten zum Codex Authenticus', ib., xlix (1931), pp. 207-80. D. de Bruyne, 'La Composition des *Libri Carolini*' in *R. Bén.*, xliv (1932), pp. 227-34. Hefele–Leclercq, iii (pt. 2; 1910), pp. 1061-91. H. Bastgen in *L.Th.K.*, vi (1934), col. 553 f., s.v. 'Libri Carolini', with bibl.

CAROLINE DIVINES, The. The Anglican divines of the 17th cent., esp. when considered as exponents of High Church principles. The term is not ordinarily restricted (as the word would imply) to those who wrote esp. or solely during the reigns of *Charles I (1625–49) and *Charles II (1660–85), but it is taken to include such theologians as L. *Andrewes (d. 1626). See also *Anglicanism*.

Many of their writings are reprinted in the *Library of Anglo-Catholic Theology*, 1841 ff. See also P. E. More–F. L. Cross, *Anglicanism. The Thought and Practice of the C of E illustrated from the Religious Literature of the 17th cent.* (1935).

CAROLINGIAN SCHOOLS. The reign of *Charlemagne (768–814) stimulated an intellectual Renaissance within his domains which continued down to the dark days of the Norsemen invasions and left its mark upon the future history of education. The responsibility for this revival largely rested with Charlemagne himself, and his advisers *Alcuin and *Theodulf of Orléans. By establishing new schools and patronizing scholars he hoped to diminish the illiteracy of the Frankish clergy. In 787 he issued a *capitulary to Baugulf, Abbot of *Fulda, ordering that in all monasteries and bishops' houses there should be study and 'let those who can, teach'. This prescription, which has been termed the 'charter of modern education', was followed in 789 by another capitulary ordering that 'there may be schools for reading-boys; let them learn psalms, notes, chants, the computus and grammar, in every monastery and bishop's house'. Further capitularies (e.g. that of 805) confirmed and elaborated Charlemagne's educational legislation. Through his initiative a Palace School was formed for the cultivation of the *seven liberal arts, which was attended by members of the court as well as the boy lectors of the royal chapel, children of the nobility, and even plebeians. It was probably the first school to give a classical education to members of the laity in any number.

During this period the chief schools were connected with cathedrals and monasteries, the school of Alcuin at Tours being the model for the rest. Of the episcopal schools, those at Orléans (under Theodulf) and at *Reims (later to be under *Hincmar and *Remigius of Auxerre) were the most distinguished. Of the schools more directly connected with monasteries, the schools at *Fulda under *Rabanus Maurus, a breeding-ground for scholars, at *Corbie under Adalhard and *Paschasius Radbertus, at Ferrières under *Lupus Servatus, at St. Wandrille, at St. *Gall, and at St. Riquier, were all notable for their scholarship.

The Carolingian Schools were not outstanding for originality of thought. Alcuin's primers, on orthography, grammar, rhetoric, and dialectic, are by modern standards very crude productions. The main purpose, for instance, why he taught mathematics was to enable pupils to calculate the dates of Church festivals. Even his interpretation of theology was quite elementary. There are many indications (e.g. decrees of the Councils of Paris, 824; of Mainz, 847; of Savonnières, 859) that the educational legislation of Charlemagne was not effectively carried out in the declining years of the Carolingian era. Nevertheless many schools (e.g. St. Gall), thus stimulated by the Carolingian revival, maintained a high reputation through the early Middle Ages as educational centres. Finally the responsibility for restoring Latin to the position of a literary language and the formation of a more accurate orthography largely rests with the scholars of these schools, whilst editions and copies of the classics, both Christian and pagan, were produced which to some extent were to form in a later period the bases of Renaissance scholarship itself.

J. B. Mullinger, *The Schools of Charles the Great and the Restoration of Education in the Ninth Century* (1877); L. Maître, *Les Écoles épiscopales et monastiques de l'occident depuis Charlemagne jusqu'à Philippe-Auguste* (1866), passim. On the Carolingian renaissance in general, the following may be consulted: G. Monod, *Études critiques sur les sources de l'histoire carolingienne* (Bibliothèque de l'École des Hautes Études, cxix; 1898), ch. 2, 'La Renaissance carolingienne', pp. 37–67; E. Patzelt, *Die karolingische Renaissance* (1924). Further, G. Paris, *Histoire poétique de Charlemagne* (1865); K. Strecker, 'Studien zu karolingischen Dichtern' in *N.A.*, xliii (1922), pp. 479–511, and xliv (1922), pp. 209–51; R. Hinks, *Carolingian Art* (1935). M. R. James, 'Learning and Literature till Pope Sylvester II' in *C. Med. H.*, iii (1922), pp. 514–38. M. L. W. Laistner, *Thought and Letters in Western Europe, A.D. 500–900* (1931), pp. 147–325. É. Amann in Fliche–Martin, vi (1947), pp. 71–106. Manitius, i, pp. 243–718. See also bibl. to *Alcuin, Charlemagne,* and *Theodulf of Orléans*.

CARPENTER, JOSEPH ESTLIN (1844–1927), English *Unitarian divine. The grandson of Lant *Carpenter (q.v.), he was educated at University College, London. After some years as Unitarian minister at Clifton, Bristol (1866–9) and Mill Hill, Leeds (1869–75), he became lecturer at *Manchester New College, first at London (1875–89) and then at Oxford (1889–1906). From 1906 to 1915 he was principal of Manchester College. One of the chief figures in modern Unitarianism, he was widely respected for his extensive knowledge in comparative religion, Semitic literature, and other religious subjects. His writings include *The First Three Gospels* (1890), *The Composition of the *Hexateuch* (1902), *Comparative Religion* (in the Home University Library, 1913), and *The Johannine Writings* (1927). He was also the English translator of vols. iii to v of G. H. A. *Ewald's *History of Israel*.

Joseph Estlin Carpenter. A Memorial Volume, ed. by C. H. Herford (1929). J. H. Weatherall in *D.N.B.*, 1922–1930, p. 161 f.

CARPENTER, LANT (1780–1840), *Unitarian minister. Educated at dissenting schools and at Glasgow university (1798–1801), he became a Unitarian minister, and from 1802 to 1805 was librarian of the Liverpool Athenaeum. Afterwards he was head master and pastor at boarding schools, first at *Exeter (1805–17) and then at Bristol (1817–29), where Harriet and James *Martineau were among his pupils. He was drowned near Naples on 5–6 Apr. 1840.

Carpenter did much to foster a more liberal spirit in English Unitarianism. In 1825, on the amalgamation of three older societies into the British and Foreign Unitarian Association, he was instrumental in expunging from the constitution of the new body a preamble branding Trinitarianism idolatrous. He continued, however, to regard baptism as superstitious, substituting a form of dedication of infants. Among his many works were *Unitarianism, the Doctrine of the Gospels* (1809), and *Systematic Education* (2 vols., 1815).

Russell Lant Carpenter (son), *Memoirs of the Life of the Rev. Lant Carpenter, LL.D.* (1842). A. Gordon in *D.N.B.*, ix (1887), pp. 157–9.

CARPENTER, WILLIAM BOYD (1841–1918), Bp. of *Ripon. Educated at St. Catharine's College, Cambridge, he held a succession of parish appointments in which he rapidly gained a great reputation as a preacher. Much liked by Queen *Victoria, he was appointed a Royal Chaplain in 1879, Canon of Windsor in 1882, and Bp. of Ripon in 1884 (resigned, 1911). In 1898 he founded the Ripon Clergy College, which moved in 1919 to Oxford (where it was renamed 'Ripon Hall') and in 1933 to a site just outside Oxford on Boars Hill. From 1911 until his death he was a Canon of *Westminster. His influence in the later 19th cent. was far-reaching, but his prolific writings have little permanent interest.

H. D. A. Major, *The Life and Letters of William Boyd Carpenter* (1925).

CARPOCRATES (2nd cent.), *Gnostic teacher. He was probably a native of *Alexandria. His disciples, the 'Carpocratians', who survived till the 4th cent., preached a licentious ethic, the transmigration of souls, and the doctrine that Jesus was born by natural generation. His son, Epiphanes, wrote a treatise 'On Justice', in which, under the influence of *Plato's 'Republic', he advocated a community of women and goods.

Irenaeus, *Adv. haer.* I. xxv ; *Hippolytus, *Ref.* vii. 32; *Eusebius, *H.E.* IV. vii. 9.

CARPZOV. A family of German theologians and lawyers. Among those most distinguished in ecclesiastical affairs were:

(1) BENEDIKT (1595–1666), who founded the earliest complete system of Protestant ecclesiastical law, in his *Jurisprudentia ecclesiastica seu consistorialis* (1649).

(2) JOHANN BENEDIKT I (1607–57), his brother, who first systematized the *Lutheran creeds in his *Isagoge in libros ecclesiarum Lutheranarum symbolicos* (1665).

(3) JOHANN BENEDIKT II (1639–99) and (4) SAMUEL BENEDIKT (1647–1707),

his sons, who were engaged in the *Pietist controversy, Johann maintaining the traditional position and Samuel supporting the Pietists, until won over by his elder brother.

(5) JOHANN GOTTLOB (1679–1767), son of (4), who was among the foremost orthodox OT scholars of his day in Germany, and attacked the Pietists, the *Moravians, and the first liberal Biblical critics. (See esp. *Introductio in libros Veteris Testamenti* (1714–21) and *Critica sacra* (1728).)

(6) JOHANN BENEDIKT III (1720–1803), grandson of (3). A classical scholar and theologian, he attacked the *rationalism of W. A. Teller (1734–1804) in his *Liber doctrinalis theologiae purioris* (1768); he was also an authority on the NT and on *patristics.

CARROLL, JOHN (1735–1815), Abp. of Baltimore and first bishop of the RC hierarchy in the U.S.A. A native of Upper Marlborough, Maryland, he was educated at *St. Omer in Flanders. He entered the *Jesuit Order in 1753, was ordained priest in 1769, and during the next four years taught philosophy and theology at St.-Omer and Liége. After the suppression of the Jesuits in 1773 he returned to Maryland in 1774, where he led the life of a missionary, and actively supported the movement for political independence. In 1776 he took part in the embassy of B. Franklin to Canada, and, partly through Franklin's influence, was appointed by the Pope in 1784 Superior of the Missions, a step which made the Church in the U.S.A. independent of the *Vicars Apostolic in England. The priests of Maryland having petitioned *Pius VI in 1788 for a bishop for the U.S.A., Carroll was appointed in 1789. In 1790 he was consecrated in the chapel of Lulworth Castle, Dorset, to the see of Baltimore. Here he did a great work in consolidating the RC Church. In 1808 he was made an archbishop, and his enormous diocese was divided into four sees. See also *United States of America, Christianity in.*

P. Guilday, *The Life and Times of John Carroll* (New York, 1922), incl. full bibl. R. J. Purcell in *Dict. Amer. Biog.*, iii (1929), pp. 526–8.

CARSTARES, WILLIAM (1649–1715), statesman and *Presbyterian divine. He was educated at Edinburgh University from 1663 to 1667, and at Utrecht from c. 1669 to 1672, and was probably ordained in the Dutch Reformed Church. While in Holland he was introduced to *William of Orange, who was already looking for agents in Great Britain. From 1674 to 1679 he was imprisoned in the Tower and at Edinburgh without specific charge, and although he was certainly involved in the plots against *Charles II in 1683–4, escaped severe punishment, probably by acting as an informer. He was the principal adviser of William of Orange in Scottish matters, and won a great reputation for wisdom, integrity, and fearlessness. Although completely intolerant of episcopalianism, he showed considerable benevolence to individual episcopalians. In 1703 he was made Principal of Edinburgh University, and he was *Moderator of the Established Church of Scotland in 1705, 1708, 1711, and 1715. He took a prominent part in bringing about the Act of Union in 1707.

R. H. Story, *Character and Career of W. Carstares* (1874). Study by J. B. P. Bulloch in R. S. Wright (ed.), *Fathers of the Kirk* (1960), pp. 94–106. Æ. Mackay in *D.N.B.*, ix (1887), pp. 187–90.

CARTER, THOMAS THELLUSSON (1808–1901), sub-*Tractarian divine. Educated at Eton and Christ Church, Oxford, he left Oxford before the *Oxford Movement began; but when, after a succession of parochial appointments, he became Rector of Clewer, near Windsor, in 1844, he had come deeply under Tractarian influence. In 1849 he founded at Clewer a House of Mercy for the rescue of fallen women, and in 1852 a sisterhood, the Community of St. John the Baptist (C.S.J.B.), to take charge of it. Throughout the rest of his life he continued to take a prominent part in the High Church Movement. He was the author of a long series of spiritual and controversial writings, including the widely used *Treasury of Devotion* (1869).

W. H. Hutchings, *Life and Letters of Thomas Thellusson Carter* (1903).

CARTESIANISM. The set of philosophical principles embodied in the teaching of R. *Descartes (1596–1650).

CARTHAGE, Councils of. The early ecclesiastical Councils held at Carthage fall naturally into four groups:

(1) Those under St. *Cyprian in 251, 252, 254, 255, and 256. At the earlier of these Councils the chief subject was the reconciliation of those who had lapsed during the *Decian Persecution, at the later ones the dispute with Rome about the *rebaptism of heretics.

(2) Those under Gratus c. 348 and Genethlius 390. These are the earliest African Councils of which collections of canons survive.

(3) Those under *Aurelius. There is a long series extending from 393 to 424, the most celebrated being that of May 419 when the claims of Rome to exercise jurisdiction over Africa were strongly contested (see *Apiarius*). To this Council belongs the extended collection of canons (most of them taken over from earlier Councils) known as the '*Codex Canonum Ecclesiae Africanae'.

(4) Those under Boniface, Bp. of Carthage, in 525 and 534. The canons of only the former of these Councils survive.

The texts will be found in the standard collections of J. *Hardouin and J. D. *Mansi. F. *Maassen, *Geschichte der Quellen und der Literatur des canonischen Rechtes in Abendlande bis zum Ausgange des Mittelalters*, i (1870), pp. 149–85.

CARTHUSIAN ORDER. This strictly contemplative order was founded by St. *Bruno, in 1084 at the *Grande Chartreuse (whence its name). At first it had no special Rule, though it demanded perfect mortification and renunciation of the world. The monks were vowed to silence and, by Bruno's orders, each lived in his own cell within the monastery, working and devoting several hours daily to mental prayer and meeting his brethren for the *office, for the conventual *Mass, and for meals only on feast days. In 1127 Guigues de Châtel, Prior of the Grande Chartreuse, compiled as their Rule the 'Consuetudines Carthusiae', which received in 1133 the approbation of Innocent II. This with the resolutions made by the General Chapters since 1127 constituted the 'Statuta Antiqua' (1259). Further additions were made in 1368 ('Statuta Nova'), 1509 ('Tertia Compilatio'), and in 1581 ('Nova Collectio Statutorum'). The elaboration of the Carthusian Rule, however, has hardly modified (except in the number of fasts) the austerity and self-denial characteristic of the order from the beginning. The basis of Carthusian custom was and is a combination of *Benedictine monachism and eremitical *asceticism.

The history of the order has been comparatively uneventful, the most notable incident being a division within the order caused by the *Great Schism (1378–1409), which was healed by the resignation of the two *Generals and the election of a third in their place. The order was one of the least affected by the decline of monasticism in the late Middle Ages. During the Reformation a number of English Carthusians were put to death by *Henry VIII, but the worst persecutions date from more recent times. The Carthusians suffered badly during the French Revolution, and though much of their property was restored in 1816, the *anticlerical legislation of 1901 once again drove them from the Grande Chartreuse. Most of them found refuge in Spain. In 1940 they returned to the Grande Chartreuse. The headquarters of the English Carthusians is now the Charterhouse at Parkminster (est. 1883) in Sussex. Their habit is white, with a white leather belt.

The Carthusians have numbered among their members many mystics and devotional writers. The most famous of English Carthusians is St. *Hugh, the real founder of the first English Charterhouse at Witham in 1175–6, and later Bp. of *Lincoln.

The order also includes a few houses of nuns who live under a similar Rule to the monks. The government of the order rests with the General, who is the Prior of the Grand Chartreuse, elected by the monks of his house, and a General Chapter, consisting of the visitors and priors, which meets every year.

Annales Ordinis Cartusiensis ab anno 1084 ad annum 1429, begun by C. Le Couteulx, Ord. Cart. ('Correrea', 1687), ed. and contd. by Carthusians of Montreuil (8 vols., 1887–91). L. Vasseur, Ord. Cart., *Ephemerides Ordinis Cartusiensis* (ed. by Carthusians of Montreuil, 4 vols., 1890–92). V. M. Doreau, *Les Éphémérides de l'ordre des Chartreux* (4 vols., Montreuil, 1897–1900). C. Bohic, Ord. Cart., *Chronica Ordinis Cartusiensis, ab anno 1084 ad annum 1510* (Parkminster, 1911 ff.). E. Baumann, *Les Chartreux* ('Les Grands Ordres monastiques', 1928). H. Élie, *Les Éditions des statuts de l'ordre chartreux* (Lausanne, 1943). Anon., *Maisons de l'ordre des Chartreux: vues et notices* (4 vols., 1913–19). E. M. Thompson, *The Carthusian Order in England* (C.H.S., N.S., iii, 1930); id., *A History of the Somerset Carthusians*

('Catholic Standard Library', 1895). Heimbücher, i, pp. 376–91, and ii, p. 656. A. Autore, Ord. Cart., in *D.T.C.*, ii (1905), cols. 2274–318, s.v. 'Chartreux', with bibl.; Y. Gourdel, O.S.B., in *Dict. Sp.*, ii (1953), cols. 705–76, s.v. 'Chartreux'.

CARTOUCHE. A type of mural memorial tablet widely introduced into English churches in the 17th and 18th cents. Usually of marble, it is provided with a surface, made to resemble a somewhat bent piece of paper, for the inscription, and surrounded with ornamentation. It is often surmounted with the coat of arms of the deceased.

Katharine A. Esdaile, *English Church Monuments, 1510–1840* (1946), Plates Nos. 25, 28–30.

CARTWRIGHT, THOMAS (1535–1603), *Puritan divine. Elected in 1550 a scholar of St. John's College, Cambridge, which at that date strongly supported Reformation doctrines, he was forced to leave the university on *Mary's accession (1553), and did not return to Cambridge till after her death, when he became a Minor Fellow of Trinity. He took an active part in the theological disputes at the university in the early years of *Elizabeth's reign and, apparently to escape from them, retired to Ireland from 1565 to 1567. In 1569 he was appointed Lady Margaret professor at Cambridge, a triumph for his friends, and then began vigorously to criticize the constitution of the C of E. He was deprived of his professorship in 1570 and of his fellowship in 1571, and made his way to *Geneva, where he established contact with T. *Beza. In Nov. 1572 he returned, but his sympathies with the *Admonition to the Parliament* involved him in a long controversy which ended in his taking flight again and not returning till 1585. From now onwards he took an active part in furthering *Presbyterianism and fostering the Puritan cause. When he was arrested and tried in 1590 by the Court of *High Commission he successfully evaded condemnation and was set free again in 1592. On *James's accession, he drew up the *Millenary Petition (1603), but did not survive till the *Hampton Court Conference, at which it had been intended that he should be the leading Presbyterian spokesman. He was the most gifted, able, and learned of the 16th cent. Puritans.

A. Peel–L. H. Carlson (ed.), *Cartwrightiana* (Elizabethan Nonconformist Texts, i, 1951). B. Hanbury (ed.), *The Ecclesiastical Polity and Other Works of Richard Hooker*, i (1830), 'A Sketch of the Life of Thomas Cartwright', pp. cxxxiv–ccvi. Fuller life by B. Brook (London, 1845). A. F. Scott Pearson, *Thomas Cartwright and Elizabethan Puritanism, 1535–1695* (1925). R. G. Usher in *D.E.C.H.*, p. 101 f., s.v. J. B. Mullinger in *D.N.B.*, ix (1887), pp. 226–30.

CASAUBON, ISAAC (1559–1614), classical scholar. Born and educated at Geneva, he became professor at the university there in 1581. In 1586 he married the daughter of the French scholar-printer H. *Stephanus [II]. In 1596 he was appointed to a professorship at Montpellier, but in 1599 he migrated to Paris, where King *Henry IV gave him a pension and, in 1604, appointed him his sub-librarian. His religious opinions, which were greatly influenced by patristic studies and were

opposed both to RC-ism and extreme *Calvinism, had long been unsettled, and after Henry's death (1610) he decided to leave for England. Appointed to a prebendal stall at *Canterbury and assigned a pension of £300 a year by *James I, he determined to make England his permanent home; but he died a few years later and was buried in Westminster Abbey.

Casaubon's devotion to scholarship, both in classics and theology, was unwearied. His most important classical works were his editions of Suetonius (which first led J. J. *Scaliger to appreciate his merits), Athenaeus, and Polybius. But if he ranks higher as a classical scholar than as a theologian, he was in fact more interested in theology than classical literature. He wrote in defence of *Anglicanism, and in 1614 issued a severe criticism of C. *Baronius' annals. He also published (1587) a translation of the NT.

His son, Méric Casaubon (1599–1671), also an eminent scholar was the editor of *Marcus Aurelius and other classical authors.

Ephemerides (Casaubon's diary, ed. J. Russell, 2 vols., 1850); M. *Pattison, *Isaac Casaubon* (1875; ed. 2, ed. H. Nettleship, 1892). J. H. Overton in *D.N.B.*, ix (1887), pp. 257–61.

CASHEL, Synod of (1171 or 1172). A synod held under Henry II after his invasion of Ireland. It completed the work of bringing the usages of the Celtic Church into conformity with those of the rest of W. Christendom; and in particular revised the rite of *Baptism and introduced an organized system of *tithes. See *Ireland, Christianity in*.

Hardouin, vi, pt. 2, cols. 1627–32; Mansi, xxii (1778), cols. 131–6; Hefele–Leclercq, v (pt. 2; 1913), p. 1053 f., with bibl. note.

CASPARI, CARL PAUL (1814–92), German-Norwegian theologian. Of Jewish descent, he was converted to Christianity in 1838. In 1847 he was appointed lector, and in 1857 professor, at the University of Christiania (Oslo). Here he made some important researches into the history of the early Church, esp. the development of the Baptismal *Creeds, which he published as *Quellen zur Geschichte des Taufsymbols und der Glaubensregel* (vols. 1–3, 1866–75; addit. vol., 1879).

J. Belsheim in *P.R.E.*, iii (ed. 3, 1897), pp. 737–42, s.v.

CASSANDER, GEORG (1513–66), eirenic Catholic theologian. He was born at Pitthem, nr. Bruges, studied at Louvain, taught at Bruges *c.* 1541 and then at Ghent, and from *c.* 1549 lived at *Cologne. In his numerous writings he sought to mediate between the Catholics and the Protestants. His chief work, *De Officio Pii ac Publicae Tranquillitatis vere amantis viri in hoc Religionis Dissidio* (publd. anonymously, Basle, 1561), which took as its basis the Scriptures and the Fathers of the first six centuries, was esp. concerned to show that abuses were no sufficient reason for leaving the Catholic Church, though Cassander did not conceal his dislike of certain exaggerated Papal claims. When submitted to the Colloquy of *Poissy (1561), it gave offence to both sides. In 1564 the Emp. Ferdinand I invoked Cassander's aid in the official attempt at reunion, and to this end Cassander wrote his *Consultatio de Articulis Religionis inter Catholicos et Protestantes Controversis* (posthumously published in 1577), seeking to put a Catholic interpretation on the official Protestant formularies. The work met with strong disapproval from both sides. His other writings include *Hymni Ecclesiastici* (1556), *De Baptismo Infantium* (1563; against the *Anabaptists), and *De Sacra Communione Christiani Populi in utraque Panis et Vini Specie* (1564). A collected edition of his works (incomplete) was issued at Paris in 1616 and put on the *Index in the next year.

Opera Omnia, incl. 117 of Cassander's letters, publ. Paris, 1616. M. Birck, *Georg Cassanders Ideen über die Wiedervereinigung der christlichen Confessionen in Deutschland* (1876); P. Bröder, *Georg Cassanders Vermittlungsversuche zwischen Protestanten und Katholiken* (Diss., Marburg, 1931). C. Weizsäcker in *P.R.E.* (ed. 3), iii (1897), p. 742 f., s.v.

CASSIAN, JOHN (c. 360–435), monk. Though *Gennadius calls him 'natione Scytha', Cassian's birthplace is very uncertain. As a young man he joined a monastery at *Bethlehem, but left soon after (C. 385) to study monasticism in Egypt. We next hear of him as a deacon of the Church of *Constantinople, whence he was sent by St. *Chrysostom on an embassy to Pope *Innocent I. After this he seems to have established himself permanently in the W. C. 415 he founded two monasteries near Marseilles; and there he wrote his two books, the 'Institutes' and the 'Conferences', out of the material collected during his years in the E. The 'Institutes', which sets out the ordinary rules for the monastic life and discusses the eight chief hindrances to a monk's perfection, was taken as the basis of many W. Rules, being drawn on, e.g., by St. *Benedict. The 'Conferences' recount his conversations with the great leaders of E. monasticism. Cassian was apparently the founder of *Semi-pelagianism, (q. v.). He also wrote c. 430 a work in seven books 'De Incarnatione Domini' at the instance of St. *Leo to acquaint the W. with the teachings of *Nestorius. The E. Church treats him as a saint, but in the W. he has never been officially canonized, Marseilles only keeping his feast on 23 July.

Cassian's 'Conferences' were pr. in 1476–8 at Brussels by the *Brethren of the Common Life; other early edd., with the 'Institutes', at Basle, 1485, Venice, 1491, and Basle, 1497. Ed. of his Works by A. Gazaeus (Gazet), 2 vols. in 3, Douai, 1616, repr. J. P. Migne, *PL*, xlix and l. Crit. ed. by M. Petschenig in *C.S.E.L.*, xiii ('Collations', 1886) and xvii ('Institutes', &c., 1888). Eng. tr. with good prolegomena and notes by E. C. S. Gibson in N.P.N.C.F., Ser. 2, xi (1894), pp. 161–641. [W.] O. Chadwick, *John Cassian. A Study in Primitive Monasticism* (1950). E. *Schwartz, *Konzilstudien* (Schriften der wissenschaftlichen Gesellschaft in Strassburg, Hft. xx; 1914), I (pp. 1–17, 'Cassian und Nestorius'). L. Cristiani, *Jean Cassien, ou la spiritualité du désert* (2 vols., 1946). H. I. Marrou, 'Jean Cassien à Marseille' in *Revue du Moyen-Age Latin*, i (1945), pp. 5–26. Bardenhewer, iv, pp. 558–65; Altaner pp. 1950), pp. 401–3. P. Godet in *D.T.C.*, ii (1905), cols. 1823–9; F. *Cabrol, O.S.B., in *D.A.C.L.*, ii (pt. 2; 1910), cols. 2348–57; M. Olphe-Galliard in *Dict. Sp.*, i (1953), cols. 214–76.

CASSINESE CONGREGATION. There exist two *Benedictine Congregations of this name. (1) A Benedictine reform, instituted in 1409 by Ludovico Barbo at the abbey of St. Justina at Padua, to restore the strict *Cluniac observance. It spread to most of the more important Benedictine houses of Italy, including *Subiaco, S. Paulo fuori le Mura at *Rome, and S. Giorgio at *Venice. In 1421 these were formed into a 'Congregation', which was called Cassinese when in 1504 Pope *Julius II united to it the abbey of *Monte Cassino. At one time it numbered some 200 houses in Italy, but to-day there are only a few left, owing to political events and the formation out of it of the following Congregation: (2) The 'Cassinese Congregation of Primitive Observance' or 'Congregatio Sublacensis'. In 1851 the Abbot of Subiaco instituted at Genoa a stricter observance of the Benedictine Rule. In 1872 all those monasteries which desired to embrace this reform, including *Subiaco itself, were made an independent body with the title referred to, and divided into 'provinces' acc. to countries, with the Abbot of Subiaco as Abbot-General. The English province has abbeys at Buckfast in Devon (until 1938 in the French province), Ramsgate in Kent, and Prinknash in Glos.

On (1), Heimbücher, i, pp. 217–19; on (2) ib., p. 267 f.

CASSINO. See *Monte Cassino*.

CASSIODORUS, SENATOR, FLAVIUS MAGNUS AURELIUS (c. 485 – c. 580), Roman author and monk. He was a member of a noble Roman family, and at an early age became legal assessor (*consiliarius*) to his father. He was quaestor in 507, consul in 514, chief of the civil service (*magister officiorum*) by 526, and praetorian prefect in 533. He took a prominent part in reconciling Theodoric, who, like all the Goths, was an Arian, with the Romans, and exercised a beneficial influence on his rule. He founded two monasteries on *Benedictine lines at Vivarium, where he became a monk, when he retired from public affairs in 540. Having tried in vain to establish a theological school in Rome on the model of *Alexandria, he made of his monastery a kind of academy and encouraged secular as well as religious learning and the copying of MSS., and thereby established the monastic tradition of scholarship that preserved the classic culture of Europe during the Dark Ages. The most important of his publications while still a Roman official is the 'Variae' (*sc.* epistolae). They contain twelve books of Imperial edicts and decrees drawn up by himself, and served as a model for the medieval chanceries. His 'De Anima', in which he establishes the spirituality of the soul, not generally recognized in the philosophical writers of his age, forms a link between his secular and religious writings. His 'Institutiones Divinarum et Saecularium Litterarum' was a classic. The work was much influenced by St. *Augustine's

'De Doctrina Christiana' and advocated the union of sacred and profane studies in Christian education. The first part, an introduction to the study of theology, contains a long list of all the books which he recommends for the purpose, whereas the second part is a manual of studies of the Seven Liberal Arts. His 'Complexiones in Psalmos', based on St. Augustine's 'Enarrationes', are remarkable for their extensive use of allegorical exegesis. His 'Historia Ecclesiastica Tripartita', a compilation from *Socrates, *Sozomen, and *Theodoret, whose Church Histories his friend Epiphanius had translated for the purpose into Latin, was designed to continue and supplement *Rufinus's adaptation of *Eusebius. Despite many errors, it was much used throughout the Middle Ages as a manual of Church history. His other writings include a working-over of *Pelagius's Commentaries on the Pauline Epp., a chronicle from Adam to A.D. 519, a history of the Goths, and a treatise 'De Orthographia'.

Opera Omnia ed. by J. Garet (2 vols. bound in 1, Rouen, 1679), repr. in J. P. Migne, PL, lxix, 421–1334, and lxx. Variae ed. by T. *Mommsen in M.G.H. Auctores Antiquissimi, xii (1894); Institutiones, ed. R. A. B. Mynors (Oxford, 1937); Eng. tr. by L. W. Jones, Records of Civilization, No. xl, New York, 1946. Selection of his letters ed. with introd. by T. Hodgkin (London, 1886). Monographs by A. Franz (Breslau, 1872), G. Minasi (Naples, 1895), and A. Van de Vyver in Speculum, vi (1931), pp. 244–92. G. Bardy, 'Cassiodore et la fin du monde ancien' in L'Année Théologique, vi (1945), pp. 383–425. E. Dekkers, Clavis Patrum Latinorum (1951), Nos. 896–911, pp. 156–8.

CASSOCK. The long garment, now usually black (formerly of various colours), worn by the clergy. It originated in *vestis talaris* or ankle-length dress, which was retained by the clergy when, under barbarian influence in the 6th cent., shorter garments became usual for secular use. Its use was already ordered by the Council of Braga (572) and subsequent legislation has continued the tradition. The RC Church normally insists upon its use by clerics both out of church and inside, but in many countries coats of varying length are allowed for outdoor wear. The Anglican Canons of 1604 forbid beneficed clergy to go out in public 'in their doublet and hose, without coats or cassocks' (can. 74). The E. 'rason', the normal dress of clergy and monks, corresponds with the W. cassock. The cassocks of bishops in the W. are violet in colour, those of cardinals red, and that of the Pope white.

CASTEL GANDOLFO. A small town in the Alban Hills, some 18 miles south-east of Rome, not far from the Via Appia Nuova. Since the 17th cent. it has been the site of the Pope's summer residence. Under the *Lateran Treaty of 1929, the Papal palace and gardens were assigned to the extra-territorial (i.e. non-Italian) domains of the Holy See.

CASTELLIO, SEBASTIAN (1515–63), *Calvinist theologian and humanist. A native of Savoy, he went to Strassburg in 1540 where he met J. *Calvin, who converted him to Pro-

testantism and procured him a post as rector at the college at *Geneva. Humanist influences brought him into conflict with Calvin, and in 1544 theological differences, such as the rejection of the Song of *Solomon from the Canon and an unorthodox view of the descent of Christ into hell, caused their separation. Castellio then went to Basle, where, in 1551, he published his principal work, a Latin translation of the Bible, Biblia Sacra Latina, which aimed at classical elegance, though frequently to the detriment of the vigour of the original. It aroused much opposition, esp. on account of its annotations with their unecclesiastical attitude to religious truth and their demand for unrestricted religious toleration. In 1552 he was given the professorship of Greek at Basle. In 1554 he published De Haereticis, a condemnation of the execution of M. *Servetus and a plea for tolerance, which completed his break with Calvin and T. *Beza. In 1555 he brought out a French translation of the Bible, which, however, was less successful than his Latin version. His later writings, Contra Libellum Calvini (1612) and De Praedestinatione (1578), could be published only after his death, owing to the hostile attitude of the Calvinists.

Eng. tr. of De Haereticis (with excerpts from other works of Castellio and David Joris on Religious Liberty) by R. H. Bainton (Records of Civilization, No. xxii, New York, 1935). F. Buisson, Sébastien Castellion, sa vie et son œuvre 1515–1563). Étude sur les origines du protestantisme libéral français (2 vols., 1892). Monographs by É. Broussoux (Strassburg, 1867), E. Giran (Haarlem, 1914), and P. Hemmi (Zürich, [1937]). S. Zweig, Castellio gegen Calvin (1936; Eng. tr., 'The Right to Heresy, Castellio against Calvin', 1936).

CASUISTRY. The art or science of bringing general moral principles to bear upon particular cases. Its exercise is always called for in moral issues, whether the particular decision is made by individual judgement or in accordance with an established code, though the word 'casuistry' is generally restricted to the latter. The introduction of universal private *penance was the natural cause of the rise of formal casuistry in the Church, and by the 7th cent. 'Libri Poenitentiales' were common. Later these were replaced by various 'Summae de Poenitentia' which formed complete legal digests. From the 16th cent. onwards various systems of casuistry, such as *Probabilism, *Probabiliorism, and *Equiprobabilism, developed in the RC Church in competition with each other; the first of these systems, in modified form, eventually won most popularity, largely through the advocacy of St. *Alphonsus Liguori in the 18th cent. Notable Anglican casuists of the 17th cent. were J. *Taylor and R. *Sanderson (qq.v.).

For bibl. see under Moral Theology.

CASWALL, EDWARD (1814–78), hymn-writer. Educated at Brasenose College, Oxford, he was Perpetual Curate of Stratford-sub-Castle, Wilts, from 1840 to 1847. In 1847 he was received into the RC Church, and in 1850 (after the death of his wife) became a

member of the *Oratory at Edgbaston under
J. H. *Newman. Among his many successful
and popular translations of Latin hymns were
'Hark, a thrilling voice is sounding' (A.M. 47,
E.H. 5), 'Bethlehem of noblest cities' (A.M.
40, E.H. 76), and 'Jesu, the very thought of
Thee' (A.M. 178, E.H. 419). He published
Lyra Catholica (1849), besides devotional
writings and other collections of poems.

T. Cooper in *D.N.B.*, ix (1887), p. 276 f., s.v.

CATACOMBS. This term for the subterranean early Christian burial-places is prob.
derived from Gk. κατὰ κύμβας ('at the ravine').
It was applied to the cemetery of San Sebastiano by the *Chronographer of 354 and by
the 9th cent. widely used of similar burial-
places.

Subterranean burial was practised not only
at *Rome, but also in other Italian localities,
Malta, N. Africa, Asia Minor, and some
northern European cities, e.g. *Paris and Trier.
The most famous and extensive catacombs,
however, are those of Rome, where they extend
several hundred miles. Since Roman legislation regarded every burial-place as sacrosanct,
Christians could use the catacombs in the era
of the persecutions and their violation was
extremely rare. In acc. with the law which
required that they should be built outside the
walls, they are esp. found along the great roads
leading from the City. Some forty in all survive, mainly to the N.E. and S. of the capital.
The most important are those named after Sts.
*Callistus (with papal crypt), Praetextatus, and
*Sebastian, all on the Via Appia; after St.
*Domitilla on the Via Ardeatina; after St.
*Agnes, on the Via Nomentana; after St. *Pan-
cras on the Via Aurelia Vetus; and after St.
Commodilla on the Via Ostiensis.

The catacombs consist of labyrinths of galleries and connecting chambers, often arranged
in two to four stories one above the other.
The bodies were placed in niches (*loculi)
hewn in the side-walls, each of which could
hold two or three bodies and was closed by
stone slabs or large tiles. For the more important members of the community, burial
was in spaces hewn out of the wall and surmounted by semicircular recesses (*arcosolia),
the body being sometimes placed in a sarcophagus. The stucco paintings which often
covered the walls, esp. later, are the first
examples of Christian art. The chief services
in the catacombs were the Eucharistic celebrations on the anniversaries of the martyrs.
When in the 4th cent. attendance at these
services increased, shafts (luminaria) were
fitted to let in light and air. Pope *Damasus
(366-84) did much for the embellishment of
the catacombs. During the 5th cent., esp.
after the siege of Rome by Alaric (410), fear of
barbarian invasion caused burials in them to
cease, though the anniversary services continued. In the following centuries, however,
these services were also abandoned and the
relics of the martyrs gradually transferred to
the City churches.

All through the Middle Ages the existence
of the catacombs was completely forgotten
until an accidental discovery in 1578 renewed
interest in them. An important stage was the
publication of A. Bosio's *Roma sotterranea*
(1632). Much damage was done in the 17th
and 18th cents. by the removal of supposed
martyr bones and wall paintings. In the 19th
cent. scientific investigation was resumed, esp.
by G. B. *de Rossi, whose *Roma sotterranea
cristiana* (3 vols., 1864-77) became a classic.
Since then experts, encouraged and assisted by
the ecclesiastical authorities, have continued
to work systematically on the subject. Besides
the exploration of the catacombs themselves,
many paintings, sarcophagi, and other objects
of art have been discovered and published.

Besides older items mentioned in text, M. Armellini, *Gli
antichi cimiteri cristiani di Roma e d' Italia* (1893); O.
Marucchi, *Le catacombe romane secondo gli ultimi studi e le
più recenti scoperte* (1903; ed. 3, 1933, with memoir of author
by E. Josi); J. P. Kirsch, *Le catacombe romane* (1933); P.
Styger, S.J., *Die römischen Katakomben*. Archäologische
Forschungen über den Ursprung und die Bedeutung der
altchristlichen Grabstätten (1933); id., *Römische Märtyrer-
grüfte* (2 vols., 1935); L. Hertling, S.J.-E. Kirschbaum, S.J.,
Le catacombe romane e i loro martiri (1949). J. Wilpert, *Die
Malereien der Katakomben Roms* (2 vols., 1903). N. Müller
in *P.R.E.* (ed. 3), x (1901), pp. 794-877, s.v. 'Koime-
terien, die altchristlichen Begräbnisstätten'; H. *Leclercq,
O.S.B., in *D.A.C.L.*, ii (pt. 2, 1910), cols. 2376-2486, with
bibl., cols. 2447-50; J. Sauer in *L.Th.K.*, v (1933), cols.
867-71, s.v. 'Katakomben'; E. Josi in *E.C.*, iii (1950), cols.
1617-37, s.v. 'Cimiteri cristiani antichi'.

CATAFALQUE. An erection, resembling a
bier and covered with a *pall, which is used at
*Requiem Masses to represent the corpse in
its absence. The derivation of the word is
quite uncertain, but its first syllables prob.
come from the Gk. κατά, 'alongside'.

CATAPHRYGIANS (Gk. Καταφρυγασταί,
Καταφρύγας). An alternative title found in
a few early Christian writers, e.g. St. *Epiphanius, for the *Montanists in reference to
their Phrygian origin.

Epiphanius, *Haer.*, xcviii. i. 3 (*PG*, xli, 856B); cf.
*Jerome, *Comm. in Gal.*, iii (*PL*, xxvi. 356C).

CATECHESIS. Instruction given to Christian *catechumens preparing for *Baptism,
esp. in the primitive Church. The word was
also used of the books containing such instruction, of which the most celebrated is that of
St. *Cyril of Jerusalem.

**CATECHETICAL SCHOOL OF ALEX-
ANDRIA, The.** From the later 2nd cent.
onwards a theological School existed at
*Alexandria, which addressed itself to the
propagation of the Christian faith among the
more cultured classes. Its first known teacher
was *Pantaenus (d. c. 190); but it rose to its
highest influence under his successors *Clement
(c. 190-c. 202) and *Origen (c. 202-31). After
the conflict between Origen and *Demetrius,
his Bishop, and Origen's permanent retirement
to *Caesarea in 231, the School appears to
have come more directly under episcopal control. Among its later heads were Heraclas

(231–c. 233), St. *Dionysius [4] (c. 233–48), *Theognostus (248–82), Pierius (282–c. 290), and *Peter (c. 295–300), and, in the 4th cent., *Didymus the Blind. Side by side with the Christian faith, the profane sciences were taught. The School had great influence on the development of Christian theology alongside the university (*Museum*) of Alexandria and attracted many Christians from distant parts.

H. E. F. Guerike, *De Schola quae Alexandriae floruit Catechetica* (Halle, 1825). W. *Bousset, *Jüdisch-christlicher Schulbetrieb in Alexandria und Rom* (1915). G. Bardy, 'Pour l'histoire de l'école d'Alexandrie' in *Vivre et Penser* [war-time title of *R. Bibl.*], ii (1942), pp. 80–109. A. de La Barre in *D.T.C.*, i (1903), cols. 805–24.

CATECHISM (from Gk. κατηχέω, 'to make hear', hence 'to instruct'). A popular manual of Christian doctrine. Originally the term was applied to the oral instruction on the principal Christian truths given to children and adults before baptism. From this usage the name passed to the book containing such instructions. The term seems first to have been used in the early 16th cent., but the idea is much older. In the Middle Ages prescriptions for catechizing the faithful were frequently issued, e.g. at the Council of *Lambeth (1281), and books were produced containing explanations of the Pater Noster and the Creed, lists of mortal sins, &c., arranged preferably in groups of seven. Thus the seven petitions of the Pater Noster were connected with the *Seven Beatitudes and the *Seven Gifts of the Holy Ghost, and the *Seven Capital Sins were opposed to the Seven Principal Virtues and the *Seven Works of Mercy. One of the most active propagators of catechisms before the Reformation was J. *Gerson, whose 'ABC des simples gens' became very popular at the end of the 15th cent. Other widely used works of the type were the catechism of J. *Colet in England and the 'Christenspiegel' in Germany.

The *Reformation, with its insistence on religious instruction, brought a flood of new catechisms. The most famous is M. *Luther's *Kleiner Katechismus* (1529), which is still the standard book of the *Lutheran Church not only in Germany but also in other Protestant countries. The *Heidelberger Katechismus* (1563) occupies a similar position in the *Calvinist communions. The short catechism of the C of E (see foll. entry) is printed in the BCP as a preparation for *Confirmation, and the *Presbyterian Churches generally follow the 'Humble Advice' of the *Westminster Assembly of 1647. In competition with the Protestants the RC Church, too, produced a number of new catechisms. The most famous of these is St. Peter *Canisius' *Summa Doctrinae Christianae* (1554). The so-called 'Roman Catechism', *Catechismus ex Decreto Concilii Tridentini* (1566), is not a catechism in the ordinary sense, but a doctrinal exposition on the Creed, the Sacraments, the Decalogue, and Prayer for the use of priests. During the following centuries a flood of RC catechisms appeared; in many countries, e.g. in France, there was a different one approved for each

diocese; in England, however, there is only one, *A Catechism of Christian Doctrine*, first issued in 1898, popularly called the 'Penny Catechism'. Catechisms, whether Catholic or Protestant, normally contain the Creed, the Our Father, and the Ten Commandments with explanations; RC ones also add instructions on the *Hail Mary, the three theological virtues, the *Commandments of the Church, the Sacraments, and the Virtues and Vices.

For early Protestant Catechisms see F. Cohrs, *Die evangelischen Katechismusversuche vor Luthers Enchiridion* in *Monumenta Germaniae Paedagogica*, ed. C. Kehrbach, vols. xx–xxiii and xxxix (1900–7); id. in *P.R.E.* (ed. 3), x (1901), pp. 135–64, s.v. 'Katechismen und Katechismusunterricht'.

CATECHISM, The Prayer-Book. The 'instruction', in the form of a series of questions and answers, 'to be learned of every person before he be brought to be confirmed by the bishop'. It consists of an exposition of the Baptismal covenant, including the *Apostles' Creed, the *Decalogue (with a summary), and the *Lord's Prayer (with an explanation), followed by a section on the sacraments of *Baptism and the *Eucharist. A rubric requires the incumbent of the parish to instruct in it such children as are sent to him for the purpose 'upon Sundays and Holydays, after the second lesson at Evening Prayer' (though nowadays such instruction is seldom given in the course of the service). From 1549 to 1662 the Catechism was printed immediately before the *Confirmation rite and not as a separate item. The section on the Sacraments was added in 1604 in response to the *Puritans' request at the *Hampton Court Conference for a fuller exposition of the Christian faith. It is commonly attributed to J. *Overall, though much of it seems to have been the work of A. *Nowell.

G. *Burnet, *An Exposition of the Church Catechism for the Use of the Diocese of Sarum* (1710). W. C. E. Newbolt, *The Church Catechism* (1903). M. Stevenson in *P.B.D.* (1912), pp. 160–3, s.v.

CATECHIST. (1) In the primitive Church, a teacher of *catechumens, or a lecturer in a *catechetical school.

(2) In modern usage, occasionally, a person appointed to give instruction in Christianity, e.g. to children.

(3) In the mission field, a native Christian teacher.

CATECHUMENS (Gr. κατηχούμενοι). In the early Church those undergoing training and instruction preparatory to Christian *Baptism. They were assigned a place in the church, but solemnly dismissed before the *Eucharist proper began. Since F. X. Funk's researches, the older view that they were divided into several grades, corresponding to the well-known stages of those undergoing penance, has been generally abandoned. Only those who had reached the stage of awaiting Baptism at the coming Easter formed a separate group (φωτιζόμενοι). There was an elaborate ritual of preparation, with a succession of scrutinies, in the preceding *Lent, the candidates being finally admitted at the Paschal Mass. Illustrations of early catechetical instruction survive in St. *Cyril of Jerusalem's *Lectures* (348) and St. *Augustine's *De Catechizandis Rudibus* (c 400). In modern times the institution has been revived in the mission-field.

F. X. Funk, *Kirchengeschichtliche Abhandlungen und Untersuchungen*, Bd. i (1897), esp. papers vi, vii, and viii; E. *Schwartz, *Bussstufen und Katechumenatsklassen* (Strassburg, 1911).

CATECHUMENS, Mass of the.
The Ante-Communion, or first part of the *Eucharist. It is so named because in the early Church it was the part of the service which catechumens, who were dismissed before the *Anaphora, were allowed to attend.

CATEGORICAL IMPERATIVE.
In the ethical theory of I. *Kant, the absolute moral law, given in reason, and therefore unconditionally binding upon every rational being. It is contrasted with the 'hypothetical imperative', which being either a counsel of prudence or a rule of skill, implies a hypothesis, or condition under which alone it is operative.

H. J. Paton, *The Categorical Imperative*, A Study in Kant's Moral Philosophy (1947).

CATENA
(Lat.) 'chain' (Gk. σειρά). A word applied to the Biblical commentaries dating from the 5th cent. onwards, in which the successive verses of the Scriptural text were elucidated by 'chains' of passages derived from previous commentators. In a wider sense the word was used of any collection of passages from different authors bearing on a single subject. Among the most celebrated of Biblical catenae was St. *Thomas Aquinas' Catena Aurea' on the Gospels.

J. A. *Cramer, *Catenae Graecorum Patrum in Novum Testamentum* (8 vols., 1838-44); H. *Lietzmann, *Catenen* (1897); M. *Faulhaber, *Hohelied, Proverbien- und Prediger-Catenen* (1902); R. Devreesse, 'Chaînes exégétiques grecques' in *Dict. Bibl.*, Suppl. i (1928), 1084-1233; K. Staab, *Pauluskommentare aus der griechischen Kirche* (1933); J. Reuss, *Matthäus-, Markus- und Johannes-Katenen* (1941).

CATESBY, ROBERT
(1573-1605), English *recusant and conspirator. In 1601 he suffered a heavy fine for his part in the conspiracy of the Earl of Essex, and allied himself with the extreme RC party, who would make no compromise with the state. He was the original mover of the *Gunpowder Plot, which he first devised in the winter of 1603-4, and with which he persevered even after he knew that it had been betrayed. After the failure of the plot he took refuge at Holbeche in Staffordshire, where he was killed on 8 Nov. 1605 while resisting arrest.

M. W. Jones, *The Gunpowder Plot and Life of Robert Catesby* (1909), pp. 1-53. A. Jessop in *D.N.B.*, ix (1887) pp. 281-4.

CATHARI
(Gk. καθαρός, 'pure'). The name has been applied to several sects, e.g. to the *Novatianists by St. *Epiphanius and other

Greek Fathers, and, acc. to St. *Augustine, in the form 'Catharistae' to a group of *Manichaeans. But it is mostly used for a medieval sect, which first came to be so known in Germany in the second half of the 12th cent. It was later applied to this sect also in Italy, whereas its adherents in S. France are commonly called '*Albigenses' (q.v.). It is doubtful whether this medieval sect, despite certain common doctrines, had any historic connexion with the ancient Manichaeans. They probably originated in Bulgaria, where the *Bogomiles were one of their chief branches, and spread to many E. countries. In France they first appeared in the beginning of the 11th cent., where thirteen clerics professing such doctrines were condemned at a Council at Orléans in 1022. From the 11th cent. to the 13th their chief centres were the Milanese district, the S. of France, and the Champagne. *Innocent III and his successors worked hard for their suppression. One of their chief opponents was the Dominican, St. *Peter Martyr, who was murdered by them. The Cathari disappeared in Italy at the end of the 14th cent. In Germany they were less important, and confined to the region of the Rhine.

The principal sources for the 13th cent. Cathari are the work of a Dominican convert from Catharism, Rainer Sacconi, O.P., 'Summa de Catharis et Leonistis' (c. 1250; printed by E. *Martène–U. Durand, *Thesaurus Novus Anecdotorum*, v (Paris, 1717), cols. 1759-76), and the *Liber de Duobus Principiis* ed. A. Dondaine, O.P. (Rome, 1939). Much primary material is also to be found in the records of the *Inquisition, and in the treatise of Moneta of Cremona, a Dominican inquisitor, 'Adversus Catharos et Waldenses' (c. 1250; ed. T. A. Ricchinius, O.P., Rome, 1743). C. Schmidt, *Histoire et doctrine de la secte des Cathares ou Albigeois* (2 vols. bound in one, 1849), with notes on the 'Manuscrits et éditions des ouvrages contre les Cathares', ii, pp. 309-15, for further sources. E. Broeckx, *Le Catharisme* (Louvain Diss., Hoogstraten, 1916). H. Söderberg, *La Religion des Cathares* (Uppsala, 1949). D. Roché, *Études manichéennes et cathares* (Arques, 1952); A. Borst, *Die Katharer* (Schriften des M.G.H., xii, Stuttgart, 1952). R. Nelli, D. Roché, and others, *Spiritualité de l'hérésie. Le catharisme* (1953). S. Runciman, *The Medieval Manichee* (1947), esp. pp. 116-70. See also bibl. to *Albigensians*.

CATHARINUS, AMBROSIUS
(c. 1484-1553), *Dominican theologian. Lancelot Politi, who was born at Siena, studied canon and civil law at his native town and at other Italian universities, and was made doctor in 1500. Influenced by the works of G. *Savonarola, he entered the Dominican convent of San Marco at Florence in 1517, taking the name Ambrosius Catharinus in honour of the two Siennese saints of his order, Bl. Ambrosius Sansedoni and St. Catherine. His superiors soon employed him as a controversialist against the Lutheran doctrines. In 1520 appeared his *Apologia pro Veritate Catholica*, and in 1521 the passionate *Excusatio Disputationis contra Lutherum*. He soon estranged many prominent members of his order, however, esp. T. *Cajetan, by defending the *Immaculate Conception and other opinions opposed to the Dominican tradition. For a time he seems to have lived in a kind of exile in France, where he published his *Opuscula Magna* (1542) which includes treatises on the prescience and providence of God, on Predestination, and on

the Immaculate Conception. His views on predestination esp. earned him the probably undeserved reputation of being a *Molinist before L. de *Molina. He seems to have distinguished between two kinds of men—those predestined by God in a special way, such as our Lady and the Apostles, who, without losing their freedom, received such strong graces from God that they could not resist them, and the majority of men, who receive what may be called 'sufficient grace', which they may either accept or refuse, though in accordance with the Divine decrees 'ante praevisa merita' (before their foreseen merits). He also held that Original Sin was contained directly in the will of every man and that the destiny of unbaptized infants was an abode of bliss where they were consoled by angels.

Catharinus took a prominent part in the Council of *Trent, where his views brought him into conflict with his fellow-Dominicans, B. Carranza, D. *Soto, and B. Spina, and drew him more closely to the *Jesuit theologians, J. *Laynez and A. Salmeron, e.g. on the question of absolute Papal authority. He further defended the opinion that the testimony of the Holy Ghost permits every man to know whether or not he is in a state of grace, against the traditional Thomist view upheld esp. by D. Soto. Despite his doctrinal audacities he was made Bp. of Minori in 1546, and in 1552 his former pupil, *Julius III, appointed him Abp. of Conza.

Quétif–Echard, ii, pp. 144–51, 332, and 825, with list of his works. J. Schweizer, *Ambrosius Catharinus Politus (1484–1553) ein Theologe des Reformationszeitalters* (Reformationsgeschichtliche Studien und Texte. Hftt. 11 and 12; 1910). F. Lauchert, 'Die Polemik des Ambrosius Catharinus gegen Bernadino Ochino' in *Z.K.T.*, xxxi (1907), pp. 23–50; id., *Die italienischen literarischen Gegner Luthers* (1912), pp. 30–133. D. Scaramuzzi, 'Le idee scotiste di un grande teologo domenicano del '500: Ambrogio Catarino' in *Studi Francescani*, Ser. 2, iv (1932), pp. 297–319, and v (1933), pp. 197–217. L. Scarina, O.S.B., *Giustizia primitiva e peccato originale secondo Ambrogio Catarino, O.P.* (Studia Anselmiana, xvii; Rome, 1947). M. M. Gorce, O.P., in *D.T.C.*, xii (pt. 2; 1935), cols. 2418–34, s.v. 'Polito, Lancelot'. See also works cited under *Trent, Council of.*

CATHEDRA. Properly the bishop's chair or throne in his cathedral church, the original position of which was in the centre of the apse behind the *high altar, as still at *Norwich. The phrase 'ex cathedra' (i.e. 'from the throne') is used esp. of the pronouncements uttered by the Pope with the full formal weight of his office as the supposed divinely appointed guardian of Christian faith and morals, and such are held by RCs to be *infallible. No authoritative statement exists as to which particular Papal pronouncements are 'ex cathedra'.

CATHEDRAL. The church which contains the 'throne' (Gk. καθέδρα, Lat. *cathedra*) or official seat (Lat. *sedes*) of the Bishop of the Diocese, and hence, since the throne is one of the most important and oldest of the episcopal *insignia*, its 'mother church' (*matrix ecclesia*). Though not necessarily the largest or most splendid church in the diocese (e.g. at *Rome, where the *Vatican basilica has long outshone

St. John *Lateran, the cathedral church), it is usually of outstanding size and grandeur. In rare instances the Bishop has two thrones and hence two cathedrals (e.g. in the Protestant diocese of *Dublin, q.v.). The original position of the Bishop's chair was at the East end of the church so that he faced West, looking over the high altar. It is now commonly set on the North side of the sanctuary.

Originally the cathedral church, being in the immediate vicinity of the Bishop's residence, was served by the Bishop himself and his household or *familia*. But as the Bishop's pastoral and administrative responsibilities grew and became more exacting and the worship in the cathedral church also became more elaborate, the responsibility for the administration of the cathedral was gradually delegated to a separate body of clergy. The Bishop, who now used his own oratory for his regular private worship, came to visit his cathedral for official worship only on greater occasions, e.g. on the chief ecclesiastical feasts. The result was that those directly responsible for the cathedral came to be a separate ecclesiastical corporation or *chapter with its own privileges and rights.

In medieval England the Cathedrals were of two kinds according as their chapter was a secular or monastic body. The nine secular foundations were *Chichester, *Exeter, *Hereford, *Lichfield, *Lincoln, *London, *Salisbury, *Wells, and *York; the eight religious ones were *Canterbury, *Carlisle, *Durham, *Ely, *Norwich, *Rochester, *Winchester, and *Worcester. These last were all in the custody of *Benedictine monks except Carlisle, which was served by *Augustinian Canons.

With the *Dissolution of the Monasteries under *Henry VIII, the religious foundations naturally came to an end. On these eight cathedrals new constitutions were imposed by the king; they have hence become known as the 'New Foundations' in contrast with the other nine which, retaining their medieval statutes, are known as the 'Old Foundations'. Besides these, five further 'New Foundations' survived out of the six new Bishoprics which Henry VIII created from the monastic spoils, viz. Bristol, *Chester, *Gloucester, *Oxford, and *Peterborough (Henry's sixth creation, that of Westminster (see *Westminster Abbey*), was suppressed again in 1550). Here in every case an earlier (usually monastic) church was constituted the cathedral; and all except Oxford had a body of statutes imposed on them.

The creation of new English dioceses in modern times, beginning with *Ripon in 1836, has brought a corresponding growth of cathedrals. Here again already existing churches have been adapted to use as a cathedral, e.g. collegiate churches at Ripon and Manchester, originally monastic churches at *Southwell and *St. Albans and parish churches at *Southwark and Bradford. New churches, however, have been built at *Truro (here, however, incorporating a small portion of the old parish church of St. Mary) and *Liverpool, and others are in progress at Guildford and Coventry.

English cathedrals are normally governed by a body of clergy consisting of from three to six residentiary canons presided over by a Dean (or, in the case of recent foundations, a Provost). The degree of authority possessed by the Dean in his chapter varies from place to place, in general being considerably greater in the 'New' than in the 'Old' 'Foundations'. Besides the Dean and residentiary canons there is generally also a larger body of non-residentiary canons, sometimes known as *prebendaries or honorary canons. The staff of a cathedral also includes a body of *minor canons whose primary duties are to render the priest's parts of the musical service. Besides there is also a choir to render the daily office, consisting of an organist, choirmen (sometimes known as 'lay clerks'), and choristers. In the older cathedrals there has been a long tradition of high musical performance; and the type of service now general in parish churches was borrowed in the middle of the 19th cent. from the cathedrals and hence at first known as a 'cathedral service'. In most cases the cathedral statutes make provision for all these officials, who sometimes have a considerable degree of independence accorded to them.

A. Barbosa, *Tractatus de Canonicis et Dignitatibus aliisque Inferioribus Beneficiariis Cathedralium* (ed. 3, Lyons, 1640); M. A. Frances, *De Ecclesiis Cathedralibus, eorumque Privilegiis et Praerogativis Tractatus* (Lyons, 1665). J. de Bordenhave, *L'État des églises cathédrales et collégiales* (1643). E. A. Freeman, *History of the Cathedral Church of Wells as Illustrating the History of the Cathedral Churches of the Old Foundation* (1870). E. W. *Benson, *The Cathedral*. Its Necessary Place in the Life and Work of the Church (1878). A. H. Thompson, *The Cathedral Churches of England* (1925), with bibl. Kathleen Edwards, *The English Secular Cathedrals in the Middle Ages* (Publications of the University of Manchester, ccci; 1949). Much information about the cathedrals of England is to be found in W. *Dugdale, *Monasticon Anglicanum* (q.v.). Among modern works dealing with English cathedrals collectively are those of F. Bond (London, 1899), P. H. Ditchfield (ib., 1902), T. F. Bumpus (3 vols., ib., 1905–6; revised ed. 1922), J. Sibree (2 vols., ib., 1911), and T. D. Atkinson (English and Welsh Cathedrals, ib., 1912); photographic studies include those of H. Batsford–C. Fry (Batsford, London, 1934), H. Felton–J. Harvey (ib., 1950), and M. Hürlimann–P. Meyer (London, 1950). E. S. Prior, *The Cathedral Builders in England* (1905). E. H. Fellowes, *English Cathedral Music from Edward VI to Edward VII* (1941).

CATHEDRAL SCHOOLS. Schools established in medieval or later times for the education of the choir-boys of cathedral churches. They sometimes served also the purposes of a grammar-school, providing free education for poor boys living in the cathedral city. Most of these schools have in later times admitted fee-paying pupils, both day boys and boarders, and many of them are now represented on the Headmasters' Conference. The oldest school of this kind is probably that at *York, which claims to have been founded in the 7th cent.

CATHEDRALS, Friends of the. Voluntary organizations designed to support the work and fabric of the English cathedrals. The first such society, the Friends of *Canterbury Cathedral, was founded in 1927 under the auspices of Dr. G. K. A. Bell, then the dean;

its objects were defined as 'to gather round the cathedral in association with the Dean and Chapter a body of supporters who are prepared to take some share in caring for it and in preserving it for posterity'. This precedent has since been followed in the case of many other ancient English (and esp. cathedral) churches.

CATHERINE, St., of Alexandria. Acc. to tradition, she was a virgin martyred at *Alexandria in the early 4th cent.; but though she is among the most widely venerated of women saints, she is not mentioned before the 10th cent. Legend represents her as of a noble family and of exceptional learning, who, as a result of her protest against the persecution of Christians by Maxentius, was tied to a wheel, tortured, and finally beheaded. Her body was said to have been discovered *c.* 800 on Mount *Sinai, whither, acc. to her *acts, it was transported by angels after her death. The monastery on the site, however, goes back to 527, and the earlier pilgrims knew nothing of its connexion with St. Catherine. There was great devotion to her in the Middle Ages, notably in France during the *Crusades. Her symbol is a spiked wheel; and she is patroness of young women, wheelwrights, attorneys, and scholars, and is one of the '*auxiliary saints'. Feast day, 25 Nov.

She has sometimes been identified, but on insufficient grounds, with the unnamed woman mentioned in *Eusebius, *H.E.*, VIII, xiv, 15. There are a number of versions of the legend: four Gk. texts ed. J. Viteau, *Passions des Saints Écaterine et Pierre d'Alexandrie* (1897), pp. 22–65; the legend acc. to Simeon *Metaphrastes is also pr. in J. P. Migne, *PG*, cxvi, 276–301; further texts in H. Kunst, *Geschichte der Legende der h. Katherina von Alexandrien und der h. Maria Aegyptiaca* (1890), pp. 1–109, passim.; two metrical Lat. versions ed. H. Varnhagen (Erlangen, 1891); A. Poncelet, S.J. (ed.), 'Sanctae Catharinae Virginis et Martyris Translatio et Miracula Rotomagensia Saec. XI' in *Anal. Boll.*, xxii (1903), pp. 423–38; full details of edd. of Lat. MSS., to date in *B.H.L.*, i, pp. 250–5 (Nos. 1657–1700), and suppl., p. 70 f. P. Peeters, S.J. (ed.), 'Une Version arabe de la passion de Sainte Catherine d'Alexandrie' in *Anal. Boll.*, xxvii (1907), pp. 5–32, incl. Lat. tr. R. Fawtier, 'Les Reliques rouennaises de Sainte Catherine d'Alexandrie', ib. xli (1922), pp. 357–68. J. A. *Robinson, 'The Passion of Saint Catharine and the Romance of Barlaam and Joasaph' in *J.T.S.*, xxv (1924), pp. 246–53. E. Weigand, 'Zu den ältesten abendländischen Darstellungen der Jungfrau und Märtyrin Katherina von Alexandria' in *Pisciculi. Studien zur Religion und Kultur des Altertums Franz Joseph Dölger . . . dargeboten* (*Antike und Christentum.* Ergänzungsband, i, 1939), pp. 279–90, with reff. A. Zachou, Σινᾶ καὶ ἁγία Αἰκατερίνη (1937). On iconography, H. *Bremond, *Sainte Catherine d'Alexandrie* (L'Art et les saints', 1917). Tito da Ottone, O.M.Cap., *La leggenda di Santa Caterina vergine e matire di Alexandria* (Genoa, 1940), incl. information on the growth of the cult. J. P. Kirsch in *L.Th.K.*, v (1933), col. 890 f., s.v. 'Katharina', with further bibl.

CATHERINE, St., of Genoa (1447–1510), mystic. Caterinetta Fieschi was of a noble Ligurian family, who at the age of 16 married Giuliano Adorno. Ten years later she was suddenly converted; and, though she found continued life with her pleasure-loving husband burdensome, she succeeded in reaching great heights of spirituality. Later he was also converted, and after this assisted her in her selfless care of the sick in a hospital in Genoa.

Eventually Giuliano became a Franciscan *tertiary, but Caterinetta joined no order. She underwent a number of remarkable mental and at times almost pathological experiences, which were the subject of F. *von Hügel's familiar study and evaluation. Her spiritual doctrine is contained in the book published in 1551 as the *Vita e dottrina*, though perhaps she did not herself put this account of her visions and convictions into their present literary form; this is the source of her 'Dialogues on the Soul and the Body' and of her 'Treatise on Purgatory' which have often been issued separately. From 1475 she received communion almost daily, a practice extremely rare except for priests in the later Middle Ages. Feast day, 15 Sept.

Modern Eng. tr. of Catherine's 'Treatise on Purgatory' and 'Dialogue' by C. Balfour and H. D. Irvine (London, 1934). F. von Hügel, *The Mystical Element of Religion as studied in St. Catherine of Genoa and her Friends* (2 vols., 1908). Von Hügel's contention that the *Dialogo tra anima corpo, amor proprio, spirito, humanità e Deo* and the *Trattato del purgatorio* did not receive literary shape until a late date has been severely criticized by Umile [Bonzi] da Genova, O.M. Cap., in an imp. art. in *Dict. Sp.*, ii (1938), s.v. 'Catherine de Gênes', cols. 290–325 (with bibl.). L. Sertorius, *Katherina von Genua* (Munich, 1939). Gabriele da Pantasina, *Vita di Santa Caterina Fieschi adorno con ricordi e documenti* (Genoa, 1929). F. Casolini in *E.C.*, iii (1950), cols. 1145–8. In 1944, St. Catherine was proclaimed by *Pius XII Patroness of the Hospitals in Italy.

CATHERINE, St., dei Ricci (1522–90), Italian visionary. Her baptismal name was Alessandra Lucrezia Romola. She entered the *Dominican Order at Prato in 1535, where she was professed in the following year and remained till her death. She is chiefly remarkable for an ecstasy into which she was rapt for 28 hours every week (from noon Thursday until 4 p.m. Friday) over a period of several years. These extraordinary experiences, combined with her fame for sanctity, brought pilgrims of all ranks to visit her. She was beatified in 1732 and canonized in 1746. Feast day, 13 Feb.

Le lettere spirituali e familiari di S. Caterina de' Ricci ed. C. Guasti (Prato, 1861). *Acta Canonizationis . . . Catharinae de Ricci* was publd. at Rome, 1749; other docc. concerned with the process publd. ib. 1713, 1729, 1731, and 1742. The principal early authorities are the life by S. Razzi, O.P. (Lucca, 1594), and F. Guidi (Florence, 1617). H. Bayonne, *Vie de Sainte Catherine de Ricci de Florence* (2 vols., 1873); F. M. Capes, *St. Catherine de' Ricci. Her Life, Her Letters, Her Community* [1905]; G. Bertini, *Santa Caterina de' Ricci. Con lettere inedite della santa* (1935).

CATHERINE, St., of Siena (1347 [?1333]–1380), *Dominican tertiary. Caterina Benincasa was the daughter of a Sienese dyer. From her earliest years she received visions and lived a life of mortification among many difficulties at home. At the age of 16 she joined the Third Order of St. Dominic, and for three years gave herself to contemplation and the service of the sick and poor and the conversion of sinners. Her extraordinary sanctity won her a large band of followers, including many of noble rank. In 1376 she undertook a journey to *Avignon to plead with *Gregory XI on behalf of Florence, which was in arms against the Pope, and persuaded him to return to Rome.

She then returned to Siena and her former way of life, gathering around her a devoted group of supporters. When the *Great Schism in the Papacy broke out on Gregory's death in 1378, she became active in support of *Urban VI, urging cardinals and monarchs to return to his obedience. Many of her letters are extant as well as the 'Dialogo', a spiritual work of some importance. She was canonized in 1461. Feast day, 30 Apr.

Works ed. G. Gigli (4 vols., Lucca, 1707–21). Modern edd. include those of the *Dialogo* by I. Taurisano, O.P. (Rome, 1947), and of her letters by N. Tommaseo–P. Miscatelli (6 vols., Florence, 1939–47). There have been various Eng. trr. of individual works. The principal sources for her life are the 'Legenda Major' by Raymond of Capua, her confessor, a suppl. to it by Thomas Caffarini, and the 'Legenda Minor' by Thomas Caffarini. An Eng. tr. of the Legenda Major was publd. by W. *Caxton c. 1493; *editio princeps* of the Lat. text by T. Löher (Cologne, 1553), repr. in *AA.SS.* Apr. III (1675), pp. 853–959. The supplement has not yet been publd.; an edition is being prepared for the *Fontes Vitae S. Catharinae Senensis Historici* (vid. inf.). The Legenda Minor was ed. B. Mombritius, *Sanctuarium*, i (Milan, c. 1480), pp. 168–88; also ed. R. Fawtier, 'La Légende mineure de Sainte Catherine de Sienne' in *Mélanges d'Archéologie et d'Histoire*, xxxii (1912), pp. 397–509; and ed. E. Franceschini (*Fontes Vitae*, etc., x, Milan, 1942); an early Italian tr. was ed. F. Grottanelli (Bologna, 1668) and by E. Franceschini (Pubblicazioni dell' Università Cattolica del S. Cuore, Ser. 4, xxxviii, Milan, 1942). H. Laurent, O.P.–F. Valli (edd.), *Fontes Vitae S. Catharinae Senensis Historici* (Florence and Milan, 1936 ff.). R. Fawtier, *Sainte Catherine de Sienne. Essai de critique des sources* (Bibliothèque des Écoles françaises d'Athènes et de Rome, cxxi and cxxxv; 1921–30). Modern lives include those of A. Capecelatro (2 vols., Naples, 1856), Augusta T. Drane (London, 1880; with bibl.), E. G. Gardner (ib., 1907), J. Joergensen (Paris, 1919; Eng. tr., 1938), Alice Curtayne (ib., 1929), A. Lennoyer, O.P. ('Les Saints', 1934), A. Levasti (Turin, 1947; Eng. tr., 1954), M de La Bedoyère (London, 1947; popular), J. Wilbois (Tournai-Paris, 1948), and I. M. Taurisano, O.P. (Rome, 1948). R. Fawtier–L. Canet, *La Double Expérience de Catherine Benincasa* (1948), G. Kaftel, *St. Catherine in Tuscan Painting* (1949). A. Dondaine, O.P., 'Sainte Catherine de Sienne et Niccolò Toldo' in *Archivum Fratrum Praedicatorum*, xix (1949), pp. 169–207 (critique of R. Fawtier). M. M. Gorce, O P., in *Dict. Sp.*, ii (1953), cols. 327–48, s.v., with bibl.

CATHERINE, St., of Sweden (1331–81). The daughter of St. *Bridget, she herself early showed signs of great sanctity. After her mother's death in 1374, she succeeded her as head of the Order of St. Saviour, the so-called *Brigittines. The remainder of her life was largely spent in Italy, obtaining confirmation of the order, and unsuccessfully seeking her mother's canonization. Like St. *Catherine of Siena, she supported the party of *Urban VI during the *Great Schism. Feast day, 22 Mar.

Life by Upho, a monk of Gotland (d. 1433), pr. in *AA.SS.*, Mar. III (1668), pp. 505–17; crit. ed. by C. Annerstedt (Scriptores Rerum Svecicarum Medii Aevi, iii, pt. 2, Upsala, 1871), pp. 244–63. I. Collijn (ed.), *Processus seu Negocium Canonizacionis B. Katerine de Vadstenis* (Corpus Codicum Suecicorum Medii Aevii, ii Copenhagen, 1943). She is also mentioned in the biographies of St. Bridget.

CATHERINE DE' MEDICI (1519–89), Queen-Consort of France from 1547, and Queen-Mother from 1559. A niece of Pope *Clement VII, she was married in 1533 to Henry, son of *Francis I of France, in order that French support might free the Pope from the control of the Emp. *Charles V. Through the reigns of Francis I and her husband (Henry II), she had little influence on politics; but during those of her sons, Francis II (1559–60), Charles IX (1560–74), and Henry III (1574–89), she exercised much power, and for most of Charles's reign was the real ruler of the country. In the wars of religion then raging in France she advocated at first a policy of toleration, since she wished to use the Protestants as a check upon the dominant Catholic party, without allowing them to gain any control of affairs. Between 1567 and 1570, however, she took violent measures in face of a Protestant rebellion, and, after a brief interval of mildness in a vain effort to gain the support of *Elizabeth of England, attempted to re-establish her position, which seemed threatened, by the murder of G. *Coligny, the Protestant leader, and the Massacre of St. *Bartholomew (23 Aug. 1572), for which she must bear the chief responsibility. After 1574 she returned to a policy of compromise, but her influence on affairs grew steadily less.

Letters ed. by les Ctes Hector de la Ferrière and Baguenault de Puchesse (Paris, 10 vols., 1880–1909; Index by A. Lesort, 1943). E. Sichel, *Catherine de' Medici and the French Reformation* (1905); J. H. Mariéjol, *Catherine de Médicis (1519–1589)* (1920); P. Van Dyke, *Catherine de Medicis* (2 vols., 1923). J. E. Neale, *The Age of Catherine de Medici* (1943).

CATHOLIC. A word derived from the Gk. καθολικός, and meaning 'general' or 'universal'. It is first met with in Christian literature in St. *Ignatius of Antioch (*Ep. ad Smyr.* 8. 2). In Christian terminology it has come to have various uses: (1) Of the universal Church as distinct from local Christian communities. It is applied thus to the faith of the whole Church, i.e. the doctrine believed 'everywhere, always, and by all' (see *Vincentian Canon*). (2) In the sense of 'orthodox', as distinct from 'heretical', or (later) from 'schismatical'. (3) In historical writers, of the undivided Church before the final schism of E. and W. in 1054. Thereafter the W. Church usually referred to itself as 'catholic', the E. preferring to describe itself as 'orthodox'. (4) Since the *Reformation RCs have come to use it of themselves exclusively. *Anglicans, and later *Old Catholics, have also adopted it to cover besides themselves and the RC Church also the E. Orthodox in the belief that these Communions together represent the undivided Church of earlier ages. (5) In general, in present-day usage, it is employed of those Christians who claim to be in possession of a historical and continuous tradition of faith and practice, as opposed to Protestants, who tend to find their ultimate standards in the Bible as interpreted on the principles of the Reformation of the 16th cent.

J. H. Maude in *H.E.R.E.*, iii (1910), pp. 258–61, s.v. 'Catholicism, Catholicity'.

CATHOLIC ACTION. Organized religious activity, esp. of a social, educational, or quasi-political kind, on the part of the RC laity, particularly when conceived as an extension of the apostolate of the hierarchy. A powerful impetus was given to such work when *Pius XI, in the encyclical 'Ubi Arcano' (23 Dec. 1922), encouraged the creation of elastic organizations for the purpose, under the direction of the clergy, in many European countries. Among such organizations are the *Jocists (q.v.), begun in Belgium, the 'Legion of Mary', founded in Ireland in 1921, and the 'Grail Movement', founded in Holland in 1929.

The vast literature includes L. Civardi, *Manuale di azione cattolica secundo gli ultimi ordinamenti* (1924; Eng. tr. of vol. i, ed. 17, by C. C. Martindale, S.J., 1935); E. Guerry, *Code de l'action catholique* (1928); J. Fitzsimons, O.P.–P. McGuire, *Restoring All Things* (1939); C. K. Murphy, *The Spirit of Catholic Action* (1943).

CATHOLIC APOSTOLIC CHURCH. A religious body partly inspired in its origins by the teaching of E. *Irving (q.v.), its members also being known as Irvingites. It developed out of a revivalist circle which had gathered round H. *Drummond and counted Irving among its members. They believed in the near approach of the Second Coming of Christ, in preparation for which they resolved to re-establish the primitive offices of the Church, viz., those of Apostles, prophets, evangelists, pastors, and teachers, to which others, e.g. 'angels' (bishops) and deacons, were added later. The first 'Apostle' was formally appointed by Drummond in 1832. In 1835 the full 'College of Apostles', numbering twelve, held its first 'council' in London, and in 1836 addressed memoranda to the bishops of the C of E and to William IV stating their mission. Shortly afterwards they undertook missionary journeys to the Continent and to America, each 'Apostle' being assigned one or more countries for his activities. The effect on them of their travels, perhaps helped by the spread of *Tractarianism in England, was an increasing inclination towards Catholic doctrines and practices. It was expressed in their service book of 1842, a mixture of RC, Greek, and Anglican rites. Their 'priests' wore vestments and used incense; later Anointing of the Sick, a ceremony called 'Sealing' based on Rev. 7. 3 ff., *Reservation in the Tabernacle, and the use of *holy water were also introduced. In 1853 they built their large church in Gordon Square, London. On the Continent they carried on a vigorous though mostly secret propaganda, esp. in *Holland and Germany, where in the beginning they gained the adherence of several Catholic priests. Their chief successes, however, were obtained in the Protestant north, where they were favoured by the Prussian nobility. Their influence in Britain diminished considerably after the death, in 1901, of the last 'Apostle', who had been expected to survive till the *Second Advent. They have still a number of adherents in the U.S.A. and in Germany.

P. *Schaff, *A History of the Creeds of Christendom* (1877), pp. 909–15, with bibl., p. 905. E. Miller, *The History and Doctrines of Irvingism* (2 vols., 1878). W. A. Curtis, *A History of Creeds and Confessions of Faith in Christendom and Beyond* (1911), pp. 377–88. P. E. Shaw, *The Catholic Apostolic Church* (New York, 1946), with bibl. J. G. Simpson in *H.E.R.E.*, vii (1914), pp. 422–8, s.v. 'Irving and the Catholic Apostolic Church'.

CATHOLIC ASSOCIATION, The. An association created by D. *O'Connell for the defence of RC interests in Ireland. It was founded in May 1823, but did not come into effective existence till the following February. Through the exertions of the RC clergy a branch of it was established in nearly every parish in the country, and it greatly encouraged the Irish peasantry. In Feb. 1825 the government suppressed it, but this did not prevent its work being continued under a new name. Its influence largely contributed to the passing of the Catholic Emancipation Act in 1829.

Proceedings of the Catholic Association in Dublin from May 13, 1823, to February 11, 1825 (London, 1825). T. Wyse, Historical Sketch of the late Catholic Association of Ireland (2 vols., ib., 1829). See also lives of D. O'Connell, cited s.v.

CATHOLIC EMANCIPATION ACTS. See *Catholic Relief Acts*.

CATHOLIC EPISTLES, The. A title used properly of the NT Epp. of Jas., 1 and 2 Pet., 1 Jn., and Jude, because they were 'general' (i.e. universal) epistles, and (unlike those of St. *Paul) not addressed to specified Churches or individuals. It is usual, however, to include 2 and 3 Jn. among them, though these are addressed respectively to 'the elect lady and her children' and to Gaius. On this reckoning they thus total seven in all. The word 'catholic' may originally have been applied to some or all of these epistles for a different reason, viz. to indicate that their *canonicity was accepted. See also artt. on separate epistles.

CATHOLIC MAJESTY, His. A traditional title of the Kings of *Spain, said to have been granted by Innocent VIII to *Ferdinand of Aragon in 1492 in recognition of his conquest of Granada. In earlier times it had been borne by certain Kings of France, e.g. *Pepin in 767.

The precise circumstances in which the title arose are obscure. It is the subject of a letter dated 5 Feb. 1495, by Peter Martyr (Ital. historian, 1455–1526), pr. in his *Opus Epistolarum* (Amsterdam and Paris, 1670), p. 88 f. (No. 157). W. H. Prescott, *History of the Reign of Ferdinand and Isabella*, ii (ed. J. F. Kirk, 1902), p. 283 f., for note on the subject; P. de Roo, *Material for a History of Pope Alexander VI*, v (Bruges, 1924), p. 2 f., with reff.

CATHOLIC RECORD SOCIETY. An organization, founded in 1904, to print and circulate records bearing on the history of English RC-ism since the 16th cent. It has issued a long series of publications.

F. A. *Gasquet, Introduction to *Miscellanea*, i (Publications of the C.R.S., i, 1905), pp. vii–xv. Annual reports and lists of members are printed in most vols. of the Society's Publications.

CATHOLIC RELIEF ACTS (also 'Catholic Emancipation Acts').

(1) In 1778 by 17 & 18 Geo. III, c. 49 [Ireland] Catholics were allowed henceforward to own landed property on taking an oath not involving a denial of their religion; priests ceased to be subject to persecution at the denunciation of the common informer; and life-long imprisonment for keeping a Catholic school was abolished. The Act was followed by the *Gordon Riots (q.v.).

(2) In 1791 those who took the prescribed oath were freed from the Statutes of Recusancy and the Oath of Supremacy; Catholic worship and schools were tolerated; and certain posts in the legal and military professions were opened to RCs.

(3) In 1793 Catholics in Ireland were admitted to the franchise, the universities, and the professions.

(4) In 1829, when the Irish situation was critical, the most decisive of the Emancipation measures, the 'Roman Catholic Relief Act' (10 Geo. IV, c. 7), was passed. Almost all disabilities were removed and Catholics were admitted to most public offices. The unrepealed restrictions, some of which were from the first a dead letter, included the prohibition of public religious celebrations and of taking the title of the ancient episcopal sees and the invalidity of marriage before a priest.

(5) Most of these remaining disabilities were removed by an Act of 1926 (16 & 17 Geo. V, c. 55). Among those still retained is the law which restrains either the King or the Queen of England from being a RC. The same applies to the offices of Regent, Lord Chancellor, and Keeper of the Great Seal. The disability of priests sitting in the House of Commons is shared with the clergy of the C of E (but not with ministers of the Free Churches). RCs are also still disabled from presenting or nominating to any benefice, the right passing by 3 & 4 Jas. I, c. 5 to the universities of Oxford and Cambridge acc. to a geographical distribution.

CATHOLIC TRUTH SOCIETY. A RC society formed at the suggestion of Dr. (later Cardinal) Herbert *Vaughan in 1884 for the printing of cheap literature, chiefly leaflets and tracts, of a devotional, educational, or controversial nature.

G. E. Anstruther and P. E. Hallett, *Catholic Truth Society, The First Fifty Years* (1934); C. Collingwood, 'The Catholic Truth Society' in *Clergy Review*, xxxvii (1952), pp. 641–58.

CATHOLIC UNIVERSITY OF AMERICA. The university was founded at Washington, D.C., in 1889, for the education of clergy and laity under RC direction, and as a centre of learning in the U.S.A. It is governed by trustees appointed by the RC hierarchy, and presided over by the Abp. of Washington, who is *ex officio* Chancellor. Many religious communities, particularly teaching orders, are attached or affiliated to it, and it has taken an important part in the reorganization of RC schools and in education generally. Its publications include a series of 'Patristic Studies'.

J. T. Ellis, *The Formative Years of the Catholic University of America* (Washington, 1946); P. H. Ahern, *The Catholic University of America, 1887–1896*. The Rectorship of John J. Keane (Washington, 1948); P. E. Hogan, S.S.J., *The*

Catholic University of America, 1896–1903. The Rectorship of Thomas J. Conaty (Washington, 1949); C. J. Barry, O.S.B., *The Catholic University of America, 1903–1909.* The Rectorship of Denis J. O'Connell (Washington, 1950).

CATHOLICOS (Gk. καθολικός). A title now restricted to the two *Patriarchs of the *Nestorian and *Armenian Churches. In secular usage it was originally applied to certain high financial officials, and then in early Christian usage to the head of a number of monasteries in the same city. At one period it was used of certain bishops of metropolitical rank, in addition to the two patriarchs named.

CATON, WILLIAM (1636–65), one of the early *Quakers. He became a Quaker in 1652 under the influence of G. *Fox and was chosen as a preacher for the Swarthmore district, where he received much harsh treatment. He then became an itinerant missioner, and attempted to plant his doctrines first in France and then in Holland, where he spent some years. He wrote a good deal in a simple style and his *Journal* (ed. by G. Fox himself, 1689) is still much read among Friends.

List of his writings, among them an 'Abridgement' of *Eusebius' Chronologies (n. pl., 1661), in *D.N.B.*, ix (1887), p. 322, s.v.

CAUSSADE, JEAN PIERRE DE (1675–1751), ascetic writer. In 1693 he joined the *Jesuit Order at Toulouse, was professed in 1708, and later travelled widely, being much appreciated as a preacher. From 1729 until 1740 he resided mainly in Lorraine. His last years were passed at Perpignan (1741–1743), Albi (1744–6), and Toulouse (1746–51). His extensive correspondence with the *Visitandines at Nancy is a leading source of our knowledge of his doctrines.

His influence did much to rehabilitate *mysticism at a time when its claims were still suffering from the condemnation of *Quietism. Caussade tried to show that it had justification in the teaching of J. B. *Bossuet, whose authority here was of the highest in view of his part in the Quietist controversy. His principal writings, apart from his letters of spiritual direction, were his *Instructions spirituelles en forme de dialogue sur les divers états d'oraison* (1741; Eng. tr. with introduction by J. *Chapman, 1931) and a treatise on abandonment to God's will, which was first published by H. Ramière as *L'Abandon à la providence divine* (1867; Eng. tr., *Abandonment to Divine Providence*, 1921).

Sommervogel, ii (1891), cols. 900–2. Pourrat, iv, pp. 341–6. M. Olphe-Galliard in *Dict. Sp.*, ii (1953), cols. 354–70, incl. full bibl.

CAUTEL. A rubrical direction for the correct administration of the Sacraments. The word is used esp. of those prefixed to the Roman *Missal to give the celebrant guidance in the case of accidents or defects during the service.

CAVE, WILLIAM (1637–1713), *Patristic scholar. He was incumbent successively of Islington (1662), All Hallows the Great, Thames Street, London (1679), and Isleworth (1690). His principal writings were his *Apostolici* (1677), a history of the chief figures in the first three hundred years of the Church's existence; his *Ecclesiastici* (1682), a continuation of the *Apostolici* for the 4th cent.; and his *Scriptorum Ecclesiasticorum Historia Literaria* (part i, 1688; ii, 1698), a history of ecclesiastical writers down to the 14th cent. His works were all erudite and lucidly arranged.

J. H. Overton in *D.N.B.*, ix (1887), pp. 341–3, s.v.

CAXTON, WILLIAM (c. 1422–91), the first English printer. After spending his early years in commerce in London, Antwerp, and Bruges, where he was Governor of the Merchant Adventurers, he entered the service of Margaret, Duchess of Burgundy. Under the stimulating influence of the Court he translated into English 'The Recuyell of the Histories of Troye'. The popularity of this work caused him to learn the art of printing, and in 1474 it was published in printed form at Bruges (though Caxton had probably learned to print at Cologne). In Sept. 1476 he set up his printing press at the Almonry, Westminster, and before 13 Dec. 1476 he had published an *indulgence of *Sixtus IV (the first of his known works in England). Other works printed by Caxton include *Dictes and Sayings of the Philosophers* (1477), *Ordinale secundum Usum Sarum* [1477], and *Horae ad Usum Sarum* [1477/8], *Boethius's *Consolatio Philosophiae* (before 1479), G. *Chaucer's *Canterbury Tales* [c. 1484], the *Golden Legend* [c. 1483/5] and St. *Bonaventura's *Speculum Vitae Christi* [1486]. He was not only a printer but also a translator, editor, and moralist, and an enthusiast for standardizing the English language.

Good modern reprints exist of several of Caxton's books. The standard study is W. Blades, *The Life and Typography of William Caxton* (2 vols., 1861–3; revised ed., 1877). List of his publications in E. G. Duff, *Fifteenth Century English Books* (1917), pp. 125–7. A. W. Pollard, 'The New Caxton Indulgence' in *The Library*, Ser. 4, ix (1928/9), pp. 86–9.

C.C.C.S. ('Colonial and Continental Church Society'). A society founded in 1838 to enable *Evangelicals of the C of E to take an active part in the work of Church extension in the British colonies. It continues to work in several missionary dioceses, and also provides Anglican chaplains at many places on the Continent.

CEADDA, St. See *Chad, St.*

CECILIA, St. (2nd or 3rd cent.). One of the most venerated martyrs in the early Roman Church. Acc. to her acts, which are apocryphal and date from about the end of the 5th cent., she converted her pagan husband, Valerian, and his brother, Tibertius, both of whom were then martyred before her, and, after herself dying for the Christian faith, was buried in the *catacomb of St. Callistus. When her relics were discovered in the catacomb of Praetextatus by Paschal I (817–24), they were moved to the church which bears her name in Trastevere in the city of Rome. Here her body is said to have been found entire and uncorrupted when the church was being repaired in 1599. She is frequently represented as playing on the organ, and is the patroness of church music. Feast day, 22 Nov.

H. *Delehaye, S.J., *Étude sur le légendier romain*. Les saints de novembre et de décembre (Subsidia Hagiographica, xxiii, 1936), pp. 77–96, incl. full bibl. reff.

CEDD, or CEDDA, St., Bp. of the East Saxons and brother of St. *Chad (q.v.). Two of his other brothers were priests. He was brought up with St. Chad at *Lindisfarne under St. *Aidan and in 653 was one of the four priests sent by Oswy, King of Northumbria, to evangelize the Middle Angles. Shortly afterwards he was recalled for a similar mission to Essex and consecrated Bp. of the East Saxons in 654. Here he founded many churches and established monasteries at West Tilbury and Ythancester (Bradwell-on-Sea, the Roman Othona). On a visit to Northumbria he also founded the abbey of Lastingham, Yorks, of which he became the first Abbot. At the Synod of *Whitby (664) he accepted the Roman Easter. Shortly afterwards he died of the plague at Lastingham (26 Oct. 664). He is reckoned by Florence of Worcester and *William of Malmesbury (on no sufficient grounds) the second Bp. of London. Feast day, 7 Jan.

The primary authority for his life is *Bede, *H.E.*, iii, 21–3, 25, and iv, 3 (see also notes in ed. C. Plummer, esp. ii, pp. 176–81 and 190). T. F. Tout in *D.N.B.*, ix (1887), p. 413 f., with reff.; C. P. S. Clarke in *D.E.C.H.*, p. 102 f.

CEDRON. The valley or gorge on the east of *Jerusalem, between the city and the Mount of *Olives. It was the scene of the burning of an *Asherah by Asa (1 Kgs. 15. 13) and of another by Josiah (2 Kgs. 23. 6). It is mentioned only once in the NT (Jn. 18. 1; RV, 'Kidron'), as the 'brook' crossed by Christ in the night before His Passion. The spelling 'Kidron' is consistently that of the English versions of the OT (AV and RV). Since the 4th cent. A.D. it has been identified with the 'Valley of *Jehoshaphat' (q.v.).

CEILLIER, REMI (1688–1763), ecclesiastical historian. In 1705 he joined the *Benedictine monastery of Moyen-Moutier in the Vosges, in 1718 was elected prior of that of St.-Jacques de Neufchâteau, and, having moved to that of Flavigny-sur-Moselle in 1724, was prior there from 1733 till his death. His *Histoire générale des auteurs sacrés et ecclésiastiques* (23 vols., 1729–63) is a remarkably full record of what is known of Christian writers down to the middle of the 13th cent. (esp. complete for the *Patristic period), though somewhat diffuse in treatment.

A. Beugnet, *Étude biographique et critique sur Dom Remi Ceillier* (Mémoires de la Société des Lettres, Sciences et Arts de Bar-le-Duc, Sér. 2, x, 1891). Id. in *D.T.C.*, ii (1905), cols. 2049–51, s.v.

CELEBRET (Lat.), 'let him celebrate'. In the RC Church a certificate from a competent source, normally the priest's *ordinary, authorizing its possessor to say Mass. Generally it possesses validity only for a certain period. In its absence a priest is not permitted (except in rare circumstances) to celebrate Mass in a church where he is unknown.

CELESTINE I, St. (d. 432), Pope from 422. He continued the theological policy of his predecessor, *Boniface I, by sending *Germanus of Auxerre to Britain in 429 to combat *Pelagianism, and by writing to S. Gaul in 431 against the *Semi-pelagian teaching of John *Cassian. His support of the African presbyter *Apiarius, who had appealed to Rome from the Church authorities in Africa, led a Council of *Carthage of c. 424 to protest against what they held to be an infringement of their rights. At a Roman Synod in Aug. 430, he formally condemned *Nestorius and charged St. *Cyril of Alexandria with carrying through his excommunication and deposition. Feast day, in the E., 8 Apr.; in the W., formerly 6 Apr., but since 1922 27 July.

Letters, mostly dealing with Nestorian conflict, collected in J. P. Migne, *PL*, l, 417–558. Crit. ed. by E. *Schwartz in *A.C.O.*, I, i (pt. 7; 1929), pp. 125–37, and I, ii (1925–6), pp. 5–101. E. Portalié in *D.T.C.*, ii (1905), cols. 2052–61, s.v. For the text of the spurious 'Capitula Caelestini' against *Semi-pelagianism, from the early 6th cent. attributed to this Pope, but prob. the work of *Prosper of Aquitaine, see Denz.-Bann., pp. 61–7 (Nos. 129–42); M. Cappuyns, O.S.B., 'L'Origine des capitula pseudo-célestiniens contre le semi-pélagianisme' in *R. Bén.*, xli (1929), pp. 156–70. On the synod of 430, Hefele–Leclercq, ii (pt. 1; 1908), pp. 260–4. H. Hemmer in *D.T.C.*, ii (1905), col. 2051 f.

CELESTINE III (c. 1106–98), Pope from 1191. Giacinto Bobo was a member of the Roman family of the Orsini. He defended *Abelard at the Council of *Sens (1140–1), and, after becoming a cardinal in 1144, advocated a conciliatory policy towards *Frederick Barbarossa, and urged St. *Thomas Becket to adopt a less intransigent attitude towards Henry II of England. He was elected Pope in his 85th year. His reign was marked by indecision. One of his first Papal acts was the coronation as Emperor of King Henry VI, who, having failed to conquer Sicily, oppressed the Church in Germany, and caused Richard the Lion-hearted to be imprisoned on his return from the Crusade. The aged Pope failing to take prompt action, Henry once more invaded Sicily after the death of King Tancred in 1194. Having blinded his young successor, William III, committed many other cruelties, and united Sicily with the Empire, Henry calmed the Pope with feigned promises of a *Crusade. The Pope was firmer in his dealings with the matrimonial affairs of the European princes. He forced King Alfonso IX of Leon to give up his plan of a marriage with a Portuguese princess within the forbidden degrees, and declared invalid a divorce conceded to King Philip Augustus by his complacent French bishops. He favoured the idea of a *Crusade and approved the orders of the *Knights Templar, the *Hospitallers, and the newly founded *Teutonic Order.

His registers are lost, but 330 of his letters are printed in J. P. Migne, *PL*, ccvi, 867–1240, and a few further documents in *N.A.*, ii (1877), p. 218; xi (1886), p. 398 f., and xii (1887), pp. 411–4. Study by J. Leineweber (Jena, 1905). Mann, x (1914), pp. 383–441. F. X. Seppelt in *L.Th.K.*, ii (1931), col. 1008 s.v.; R. Mols in *D.H.G.E.*, xii [1950], cols. 62–77, incl. further bibl.; L. Spätling, O.F.M., in *E.C.*, iii (1950), cols. 1256–8, s.v.

CELESTINE V, St. (*c.* 1215–96). Founder of the *Celestine Order and, for some months in 1294, Pope. At the age of 17 he became a *Benedictine, but his love of solitude led him to retire to Monte Morrone in the Abruzzi, where the many disciples who collected around him became the nucleus of the *Celestine Order. He became very celebrated as an ascetic and seems to have had some connexions with the widespread religious movement of which the '*Spiritual Franciscans' were a part. When nearly 80 he was elected as Pope on 5 July 1294, through an impasse at a Papal *Conclave. His pontificate was astonishing and disastrous. Naïve and ignorant of all procedure, he became a tool in the hands of Charles II of Naples, and, after alienating his supporters, abdicated on 13 Dec. of the same year. His acts were abrogated by his ambitious successor, *Boniface VIII, who also had him arrested and imprisoned in the castle of Fumone where he died. Partly because of his sanctity, and partly as a political move against Boniface's pontificate, Celestine was canonized by Clement V in 1313. His baptismal name was Peter, whence he is sometimes known as 'St. Peter Celestine'. Feast day, 19 May.

Two versions of a 14th cent. Life in *Anal. Boll.*, ix (1890), pp. 149–200, x (1891), pp. 385–92, and xvi (1897), pp. 393–487, with discussion of sources, xvi, pp. 365–92, and xviii (1899), pp. 34–42. F. X. Seppelt, *Monumenta Coelestiniana* (1921). J. Hollnsteiner, 'Die "Autobiographie" Celestins V' in *R.Q.*, xxxi (1923), pp. 29–40. Mann, xvii (1931), pp. 247–341. R. Mols in *D.H.G.E.*, xii [1950], cols. 79–101, incl. full bibl.; L. Oliger, O.F.M., in *E.C.*, iii (1950), cols. 1258–61, s.v., also with bibl.

CELESTINE ORDER. This branch of the *Benedictine Order, founded by Pope *Celestine V (q.v.) in 1250 on Monte Morrone, rapidly rose to great influence and its founder even imposed their constitutions for a time on the mother Benedictine house of *Monte Cassino. The severity of its discipline did not prevent its numbering at one time as many as 150 monasteries. It came to an end in 1785 when the last surviving house at Calavino, near *Trent, was closed.

C. Gérin, 'Les Bénédictins français avant 1789 [xii: Célestins], in *R.Q.H.*, xix (1876), pp. 509–12. Heimbucher, i, pp. 212–14. The foundation of the Order is also discussed in lives of Pope Celestine V.

CELESTIUS (5th cent.), heretic. A native of Britain, he was practising as an advocate in *Rome when he met *Pelagius, who induced him to turn from secular pursuits. The two men, alarmed by the low morality of their day, became convinced that it could be reformed only by stressing the responsibility of men for their actions, and so began teaching a doctrine of freewill which left no room for *grace. Celestius went so far as to deny that *baptism is for the remission of sins, and indeed that *original sin ever existed. He was condemned in Africa (whither he had migrated *c.* 410) by the Council of *Carthage of 412, and retired to *Ephesus. The condemnation was reaffirmed by the Council of Diospolis (Lydda) in 415, and by two African councils in 416. Pope *Innocent upheld this decision, but his successor, *Zosimus (417), was inclined to favour the two friends, and reversed Innocent's decree, though he was constrained to retract his decision by an Imperial decree of banishment against them. The chief opponents of Celestius and Pelagius were St. *Augustine and St. *Jerome. His teachings were condemned at the Council of Ephesus (431) (cans. 1 and 4).

See bibl. to *Pelagius*.

CELIBACY OF THE CLERGY. In the E., many early councils asserted or implied the right of the higher clergy to be married, and this position was stabilized by the Council of *Trullo of 692 (can. 13). At the Council of *Nicaea (325) a proposal to compel all clergy to give up cohabitation with their wives was rejected, and the legal position in the E. has always been the same—priests and deacons may marry before ordination, but not after. Bishops, on the other hand, must be celibate.

In the W., a legal position was gradually reached by which all the higher clergy must be celibate. The earliest canonical enactment is can. 33 of the Council of Elvira (*c.* 306). In 386 a *decretal of Pope *Siricius ordered celibacy for 'priests and levites'; this was repeated by *Innocent I (402–17). Similar legislation was introduced in Africa, which even extended to *subdeacons. *Leo the Great (440–61) forbade the higher clergy to put away their wives on ordination; they were to go on living with them as brother and sister. This course was open to obvious objections, and it was not long before Gallican councils refused to ordain married men before mutual vows of continence had been exchanged between them and their wives. The wives then retired to a monastery, or were enrolled in the orders of *widows or *deaconesses. This remained the position in the (Latin) RC Church until the new *Codex Iuris Canonici* of 1917 which forbids altogether the ordination of a married man (can. 132).

Practice has not always kept pace with legislation in this matter and there have been periods in the history of the W. Church when clerical concubinage has been rife, e.g. the 10th and 15th cents. It was a matter of debate among the Schoolmen whether celibacy was enjoined on the clergy by the law of God or the law of the Church; and was decided in favour of the latter (St. *Thomas, *Sum. Theol.* II, ii, q. 88, a. 11). The relation of this law of the Church to the vow of perfect chastity required of subdeacons since the 11th cent. is still the subject of dispute among canonists. The importance of the debate lies in the degree of difficulty in granting dispensations which would follow from the answer. In practice dispensations are very rarely given; never for bishops, almost never for priests, occasionally for deacons or subdeacons, who being at the point of death, for conscience' sake desire to have their unions ratified. The Popes have, however, allowed priests to continue in marriage who contracted marriage during schism, e.g. *Pius VII to priests who married in the French Revolution, and *Julius III to English priests who married in the reign of *Henry VIII.

In the C of E the celibacy of the clergy was formally abolished in 1549, and thereby the marriage of Abp. T. *Cranmer was technically legalized.

H. C. Lea, *History of Sacerdotal Celibacy in the Christian Church* (2 vols., 1907; hostile and uncritical in details). F. X. Funk, *Kirchengeschichtliche Abhandlungen und Untersuchungen*, i (1897), pp. 121–55 ('Coelibat und Priesterehe'); E. Vacandard, *Études de critique et d'histoire religieuse* (1905), pp. 69–120 ('Les Origines du célibat ecclésiastique'). E. Vacandard in *D.T.C.*, ii (1905), cols. 2068–88, s.v. 'Célibat ecclésiastique'; H. *Leclercq, O.S.B., in *D.A.C.L.*, ii (pt. 2, 1910), cols. 2802–32, s.v. 'Célibat', with extensive bibl.; E. Jombart–E. Herman, S.J., in *D.D.C.*, iii (1942), cols. 132–56, s.v. 'Célibat des clercs', also with bibls. H. Thurston, S.J., in *C.E.*, iii (1908), pp. 481–8, s.v.; M. Scaduto, S.J., in *E.C.*, iii (1950), cols. 1261–5, s.v. 'Celibato'.

CELL. (1) The private apartment of a *religious of either sex. In monasteries or convents the cell forms part of the community house, but the hermit's cell is naturally a building on its own. The cell usually contains only bare necessities. In some orders the brethren sleep in their cells, in others there is a common dormitory.

(2) A small religious house dependent on a larger one.

(3) In quite recent times the word has come into use for small groups of Christians, mainly lay people, who have pledged themselves to intensive work for the propagation of the Christian faith in the secular surroundings in which their lot is cast. The members of such cells commonly meet together frequently for prayer, study, and mutual counsel and encouragement.

CELLA (also **cella coemeterialis**). A small chapel erected in cemeteries in early Christian times, and intended primarily for commemorating the departed buried there. *Cellae* were often also used as places of ordinary worship.

CELLARER. One of the officials or *obedientiaries in a medieval monastic community. In theory he was responsible for the catering, and his chief duty was to see that there was always sufficient food and drink ready at hand. In practice, however, the cellarer was usually responsible for almost the whole of the monastery's dealings with outside tradesmen. Items such as coal, iron, nails, wood, or wax are frequently found in his accounts. For the performance of his duties he was allowed considerable freedom from the Rule, including non-attendance at the Divine *Office and leave of absence to visit the neighbouring markets and fairs.

CELSUS (2nd cent.), pagan philosopher. His 'True Discourse' (Ἀληθὴς Λόγος) is the oldest literary attack on Christianity of which the details have survived (c. 178). We know of it from *Origen's reply, 'Contra Celsum' in eight books, which dates from the middle of the 3rd cent. and preserves about nine-tenths of the 'Discourse'. Celsus' attitude is that of a detached pagan observer, interested in, but with no strong feelings about, religion. He praised the *Logos Doctrine and the high Christian code of morals, but he objected to the exclusive claims of the Church. Making his own some of the Jewish objections to Christianity, he criticized much in Biblical history for its miracles and absurdities, and expressed his repugnance to the Christian doctrines of the Incarnation and Crucifixion. Objecting that Christians, by refusing to conform to the State, undermined its strength and powers of resistance, he made an impassioned appeal to them to abandon their religious and political intolerance. All extant MSS. of the 'Contra Celsum' go back to a 13th cent. archetype in the *Vatican Library (No. 386).

Editio princeps of the 'Contra Celsum' by D. Hoeschel, Augsburg, 1605. Crit. ed. by P. Koetschau in G.C.S. *Origenes Werke*, i (Leipzig, 1899), pp. 49–374, and ii (ib., 1899). Eng. tr., with valuable introd., by H. Chadwick (Cambridge, 1953); also by F. Crombie in A.N.C.L., vols. x and xxiii. The large bibl. includes T. Keim, *Celsus' Wahres Wort* (Zürich, 1873); E. Pélagaud, *Un Conservateur au second siècle*. Étude sur Celse (1878); A. Miura-Stange, *Celsus und Origenes* (Beihefte zur Z.N.T.W., iv, 1926); W. Völker, *Das Bild vom nichtgnostischen Christentum bei Celsus* (1928). Bardenhewer, ii, pp. 161–6; J. Quasten, *Patrology*, ii (1953), pp. 52–7, both with further bibl.

CELTIC CHURCH, The. The name generally applied to the Church which existed in the British Isles before the mission of St. *Augustine from *Rome in 596–7. It was founded by the 2nd or 3rd cent. at latest by missions from Rome or Gaul. In the 4th cent. it was sufficiently organized and established to send envoys to the Synod of *Arles in 314 and the Council of *Ariminum in 359. It would appear that by the 4th cent. Christianity had extended even beyond the limits of Roman Britain, but from the poverty of the delegates to Ariminum and the fact that there is very little evidence of Christian remains in the rich villas of the period, it seems that it was confined to the poorer people until late in the century, when there are evidences that it spread to the upper classes and the army. A small undated Celtic church has been unearthed at Silchester.

There are few signs that Britain was affected by the heresies of the 4th cent. Although Pelagius was himself a native of the country

*Pelagianism did not gain a footing in Britain till 421, when a number of Pelagians sought refuge there, and began to teach their opinions. St. *Germanus of Auxerre paid two visits to Britain in 429 and 447 to check the growth of this heresy. During this period, in spite of the retirement of the Romans, the Celtic Church was in frequent contact with the Church of the Continent, and immediately adopted the arrangements of *Leo I for keeping Easter (455). Similar Continental influence marked the first missions to *Scotland, *Wales, and *Ireland (for which see individual articles).

The coming of the Saxons in the second half of the 5th cent. submerged Celtic culture, and with it the Celtic Church in England. The towns, where earlier in the cent. Christianity had had strongest footing, were destroyed or abandoned, and the Christian communities that survived in Cornwall, Wales, and elsewhere, were cut off from intercourse with Rome and the Continent. The Celtic Christians therefore found it hard to approve of the Roman Christianity to which St. Augustine summoned them in 603 to submit; and though agreement was effected almost completely at the Synod of *Whitby in 664, an independent Celtic Christianity lingered on in Wales and Ireland for many years.

L. Gougaud, O.S.B., *Les Chrétientés celtiques* (1911; Eng. tr., revised, 1932). F. E. Warren, *Liturgy and Ritual in the Celtic Church* (1881); W. Stokes, *Ireland and the Celtic Church* (1907). W. *Bright, *Early English Church History* (1878); H. Williams, *Christianity in Early Britain* (1912). L. Gougaud in *D.A.C.L.*, ii (pt. 2; 1910), cols. 2969–3032, s.v. 'Celtiques (liturgies)'; H. Jenner in *C.E.*, iii (1908), pp. 493–504, s.v. 'Celtic Rite'. Nora K. Chadwick and others, *Studies in the Early British Church* (Cambridge, 1958). Nora K. Chadwick, *The Age of the Saints in the Early Celtic Church* (1961). See also bibl. to *Wales, Christianity in*.

CEMETERY. A place set apart for the burial of the dead. The Gk. word (κοιμητήριον) means a 'sleeping-place', and seems to have been used exclusively of Christian burial-grounds. RC canon law still insists that, where circumstances allow, the Church should always have its own cemeteries (*CIC, 1206), from which the burial of infidels, apostates, heretics, and schismatics is to be excluded. See also *Burial Acts*.

CENACULUM, The. The 'upper room' or 'cenacle' in *Jerusalem (Mk. 14. 15, Lk. 22. 12, ἀνώγεον; Acts 1. 13, ὑπερῷον) in which the *Last Supper was celebrated and the Holy Ghost descended at *Pentecost. Acc. to St. *Epiphanius, a small Christian church (which appears to have been the only church in Jerusalem until the early 4th cent.) existed on the spot from the time of Hadrian (117–38). A large *basilica on the south-west hill of Jerusalem was erected later on, presumably the same site. After being several times destroyed and rebuilt, it fell into Moslem hands in the middle of the 16th cent., and has since remained their property. The lower part of the present building is now known as 'David's tomb'.

H. Vincent, O.P.–F. M. Abel, O.P., *Jérusalem. Recherches de topographie, d'archéologie et d'histoire*, ii, Jérusalem nouvelle (1926), pp. 421–81. E. Power, S.J., in *Dict. Bibl.*, Suppl. i (1928), cols. 1064–84, s.v. 'Cénacle'.

O.D.C.C.–K

CENOBITES. See *Coenobites*.

CENSER. See *Thurible*.

CENSURES, Ecclesiastical. Punishments imposed upon an offender against the law of the Church for the good of his soul and for the well-being of the community. Some of the most important are (a) deposition from Holy Orders, i.e. the reduction of an offending cleric to the ranks of the laity; (b) deprivation, i.e. removal of a cleric from a particular office in the Church; (c) public *penance; (d) *excommunication. These censures are imposed only by a competent authority in a public tribunal and for open and notorious offences.

A. Bride in *D.D.C.*, iii (1942), cols. 169–233, s.v., with bibl.

CENTRE PARTY (Ger. *Zentrum*). The party founded by the Prussian Catholics in 1870–1 to counteract the anti-Catholic policy of the Conservatives and esp. of the National Liberals. Under the leadership of L. *Windthorst (q.v.) it was the most effective opponent of Bismarck in the '*Kulturkampf'. In the closing phases of the struggle the party had become so strong that the Chancellor could no longer be certain of a majority against it. After the war of 1914–18 the Centre Party became one of the chief bulwarks against the growing numbers of Communists on the left and National Socialists on the right. Under the chancellorship of its member, H. Brüning (1930–2), it made a last effort to stem the rising tides of exaggerated nationalism and open paganism. It was suppressed by A. Hitler together with the other German parties in 1933.

CENTURIATORS OF MAGDEBURG, The. The authors of a Church history from its beginnings down to 1400, divided by 'centuries', which was publd. (in Lat.) as the *Historia Ecclesiae Christi* at Basle, 1559–74. The work, which was dominated by the rigid *Lutheranism and anti-Romanism of M. *Flacius (q.v.), its principal author, depicted the pure Christianity of the NT as coming progressively under the power of the 'Papal Antichrist' until liberated by M. *Luther. In its breadth of conception the work was a landmark in ecclesiastical history; but its inaccuracies, and esp. the liberties it took with the texts of original documents, made it an easy target for C. *Baronius in his *Annales Ecclesiastici*.

P. Polman, O.F.M., 'Flacius Illyricus, historien de l'Église' in *R.H.E.*, xxxvii (1931), pp. 27–73. See also bibl. to *Flacius, Matthias*.

CERDO (2nd cent.), Syrian *Gnostic teacher who taught in *Rome c. 140. He maintained that the Creator God revealed in the Law of Moses and the Hebrew Prophets was to be distinguished from the Father of Jesus Christ, and also that only the soul, and not the body, will share in the resurrection. *Marcion was one of his disciples.

The chief sources include *Irenaeus, *Haer.*, i. 27, and iii. 4, *Hippolytus, *Haer.*, vii. 37, and x. 19, and *Tertullian, *Adv. Marc.*, I, ii. Also (Ps.-)Tertullian, *De praescr. haer.*, li; Epiph., *Haer.*, xli. G. Bareille in *D.T.C.*, ii (1905), col. 2138 f., s.v.

CERE CLOTH (Lat. *cera*, 'wax'). Acc. to W. usage a cloth impregnated or smeared with wax (also known as a 'chrismale'), which is laid on the surface of the altar to prevent the linen cloths above from becoming soiled, e.g. by the holy oils used in the consecration of the *mensa.

CEREMONIAL. In ecclesiastical usage, the performance of Divine worship with pre-scribed and formal actions. Strictly 'cere-monial' is concerned with action only, the term '*ritual' being used of the form of words, but the two are often used interchangeably.

CERINTHUS (*fl. c.* 100), *Gnostic heretic. The source of his opinions is uncertain, but he seems to have had connexions both with the *Ebionites and with Alexandrine *Gnosticism. He taught that the world had been created, not by the supreme God (who, he held, transcended the universe completely), but either by a *Demiurge, a far less exalted being, or by angels, who had produced it out of form-less matter. Jesus, he held, began His earthly life as a mere man, though at His baptism 'the Christ', a higher Divine power, descended upon Him, only to depart from Him again before the crucifixion. His fantastic doctrines created distress among the orthodox. *Poly-carp, e.g., is said to have related that John, 'the disciple of the Lord', on hearing that Cerinthus was in the bath-house at *Ephesus, ran out, fearing that the house would fall on the enemy of truth (Eus. *Hist. Eccl.* III, xxviii, 6). *Irenaeus (*Adv. haer.* III, xi, 1) asserts that St. John wrote his Gospel to refute Cerinthus, while the *Alogi held the curious belief that Cerinthus was himself the author of Jn. and Rev.

The chief source is Irenaeus, *Haer.*, i. 21 and 25; cf. also Hippolytus, *Haer.*, vii. 33. T. *Zahn, *Geschichte des neutestamentlichen Kanons*, i (1888), pp. 220–62; ii (pt. 2; 1892), pp. 973–91. G. Bardy 'Cérinthe' in *R. Bibl.*, xxx (1921), pp. 344–73. J. M. Fuller in *D.C.B.*, i (1877), pp. 447–9, with bibl.; E. Peterson in *E.C.*, iii (1950), col. 1319 f.

CERNE, Book of. A collection of non-liturgical prayers, largely Celtic in origin, dating from *c.* the 8th cent. The MS., which once belonged to Cerne Abbey in Dorset, is now in the Cambridge University Library. (Ll. i. 10.)

The Prayer Book of Aedeluald the Bishop, commonly called the Book of Cerne, ed. by Dom A. B. Kuypers (Camb., 1902).

CERTOSA. The Italian name for a *Car-thusian religious house.

CERULARIUS. See *Michael Cerularius*.

CESARINI, JULIAN (1398–1444), cardinal. A member of a noble Roman family, he studied at Perugia and Padua, where he became a friend of *Nicholas of Cusa. He later entered the service of the *Curia and was employed on several diplomatic missions. In 1419 he accompanied Branda de Castiglione on his mission against the *Hussites, and later repre-sented Papal interests in France (1425) and England (1426). He was created cardinal in 1426, and in 1431 was sent as the legate of *Martin V on a crusade against the Hussites. In the same year he was appointed president of the Council of *Basle, where he at first sought to induce the Pope, *Eugenius IV, to adopt a more conciliatory attitude. After the transfer of the Council to *Ferrara and *Florence he took a prominent part in the negotiations for the union between the Roman and Greek Churches. In 1442 he was sent to Hungary to preach the Crusade against the Turks. Through his influence King Ladislaus repudiated the Peace of Szegedin (July, 1444). The war was then resumed and ended with the total defeat of the Christians at the hands of the Turks at Varna (in Bulgaria) on 10 Nov. 1444, Cesarini being killed in the flight.

Cesarini's correspondence with *Pius II on the Council of Basle is printed among the latter's works (Basle, 1551). E. Hofmann, S.J. (ed.), 'Ein Brief des Kardinals Julian Cesarini an Cosimo von Medici' in *O.C.P.*, v (1939), pp. 233–5. R. C. Jenkins, *The Last Crusader*. The Life and Times of Cardinal Julian (1861). H. Fechner, *Giuliano Cesarino (1398–1444) bis zu seiner Ankunft in Basel am 9. September 1431* (Mar-burg diss., 1907); R. Becker, *Giuliano Cesarini* (Münster diss., Kallmünz, 1935). R. Mols, S.J., in *D.H.G.E.*, xii (1953), cols. 220–49, s.v., with detailed bibl.

CHABURAH (cf. Heb. חָבֵר, 'friend'). In Jewish practice a group of friends formed for religious purposes. The *Talmudic directions suggest that the chief object of such groups was to secure strict observance of the laws of ritual cleanness and of tithe, but there are indications, e.g. in the Berakôth of the *Mishnah and *Tosephta, that they also served a wider social purpose as a common weekly meal, usually on the eves of sabbaths or holy days. It has been argued that our Lord and His disciples formed such a chaburah and that the *Last Supper was a chaburah meal; the thanksgiving or blessing over the bread would then be the Jewish *berakah used when the bread was broken at the beginning of the meal, and that over the cup the berakah at the end. Further support is sought in the Gospel of St. John, which avoids connecting the Last Supper with the Passover meal and asserts that the Crucifixion took place before the feast (18. 28, 19. 14), as well as in the reff. in Acts to weekly (20. 7) or daily (2. 46) Christian assemblies for the breaking of bread; these would be the con-tinuation of the regular chaburah meal of Jesus with His disciples, but with the new significance He had given it at the Last Supper. See also *Kiddush*.

On such Jewish meals, cf. J. Elbogen, *Der jüdische Gottesdienst in seiner geschichtlichen Entwicklung* (1913). Close study of the primary sources, however, leaves it un-certain how far these groups of 'Chaburoth' had any formal organization. Scholars for whom the 'Chaburah' provides the setting of the Last Supper include: W. O. E. Oesterley, *The Jewish Background of the Christian Liturgy* (1925), pp. 156–93; H. *Lietzmann, *Messe und Herrenmahl* (1926), p. 250; R. *Otto, *Reich Gottes und Menschensohn* (1934), p. 235 f. (Eng. tr., 1938, p. 278 f.); and G. *Dix, O.S.B., *The Shape of the Liturgy* (1944), pp. 50–96. For a critique of this view, see J. Jeremias, *Die Abendmahlsworte Jesu* (ed. 2, 1949), p. 25 f.

CHAD, St., also Ceadda (d. 672), Bp. of *Lichfield and brother of St. *Cedd. He was a native of Northumbria and a pupil of St. *Aidan at *Lindisfarne. In 664 on his brother's death he became Abbot of Lastingham, Yorks. Shortly afterwards he was irregularly made Bp. of the Northumbrians, with his see at *York, by King Oswy, the King having become impatient at the absence of St. *Wilfrid who had originally been appointed to the see but had gone to France to receive consecration. On Wilfrid's return Abp. *Theodore denied the legitimacy of Chad's appointment, and he nobly accepted this decision and in 669 retired to Lastingham. In the same year he was sent to be Bp. of the Mercians and fixed his see at Lichfield. He was tireless in spreading the Gospel and journeyed as far afield as N. Lincolnshire where he is said to have founded the monastery of Barrow. Feast day, 2 Mar.

The main source for his life is *Bede, *H.E.*, iii, 23, 28, and iv, 2 f.; ed. C. Plummer, ii (Oxford, 1896), pp. 198 f., 206 f. with reff. *AA.SS.*, Mar. I (1668), pp. 143–5. R. H. Warner, *Life and Legends of St. Chad, Bishop of Lichfield 669–672* [1871]. Short study by H. E. Savage (York Minster Historical Tracts, iv [1928]). W. R. W. Stephens in *D.N.B.*, ix (1887), pp. 391–3, s.v. 'Ceadda'.

CHALCEDON, Council of (A.D. 451). The Fourth *Oecumenical Council, held in the city of Chalcedon in Asia Minor, nearly opposite Byzantium. It was convoked by the Emp. *Marcian to deal with the *Eutychian heresy. At the first meeting, held on 8 Oct. 451, some 500–600 bishops were present, all of them Easterns except two bishops from the province of Africa and the two Papal legates, *Paschasinus and Boniface. The decisions of the *Latrocinium (449) were annulled and Eutyches was condemned. The Council then drew up a statement of faith, the so-called *Chalcedonian Definition, and made a large number of important enactments. All the dogmatic decisions of the Council were accepted by the W. Church, but can. 28, which gave the Bp. of *Constantinople the title of *Patriarch and made his see second only to Rome (a canon which had been opposed by the Roman legates), was rejected in the W., in order (it was stated) to protect the interests of the older E. patriarchates. See also foll. art.

Hardouin, ii, 662–772. Mansi, vi (1761), cols. 529–1230, vii (1762), cols. 1–872. Crit. ed. of *Acta* ed. E. *Schwartz, *A.C.O.*, II (1932–8: 1. Acta Graeca. 2. Versiones Particulares. 3. Versio Antiqua a Rustico Correcta. 4. Leonis Papae I Epistolarum Collectiones. 5. Codex Encyclicus. 6. Indices). Hefele–Leclercq, II (2) (1908), pp. 649–857, with full bibl., p. 650 f. E. Caspar, *Geschichte des Papsttums*, i (1930), pp. 511–31. A. Grillmeier, S.J.–H. Bacht, S.J. (edd.), *Das Konzil von Chalcedon* (3 vols., 1951–54) with many imp. artt. J. Bois in *D.T.C.*, ii (1905), cols. 2190–2208, s.v. 'Chalcédoine (Concile de)'; M. Jugie, A.A., *E.C.*, iii (1950), cols. 324–8.

CHALCEDON, The Definition of. The statement of the Catholic Faith made by the Council of Chalcedon of 451, and eventually accepted in both E. and W., except by the *Monophysite Churches. It reaffirms the definitions of *Nicaea and *Constantinople, asserting them to be a sufficient account of the orthodox faith about the Person of Christ, but declares that the new errors of *Nestorius and *Eutyches must be formally repudiated. It therefore expressly excluded the views (1) of those who deny the title *Theotokos* ('Godbearer') to the Virgin *Mary, thereby implying that the Humanity of Christ is separable from His Divine Person; and (2) of those who confuse the Divine and Human natures in one, and therefore hold that the Divine nature is by this confusion passible. The synodical Epistles of *Cyril to Nestorius and to the Easterns, and the Epistle of *Leo to *Flavian (the *Tome), are reasserted; the duality of Sons, the passibility of the Godhead, any mixture or confusion of the two natures, the thesis that the Human nature in Christ is of a heavenly or any other essence, and the doctrine which holds two natures before the Incarnation, which became one at the Incarnation, are rejected; and the existence of One Person in Two Natures, which are united unconfusedly, unchangeably, indivisibly, inseparably (ἀσυγχύτως, ἀτρέπτως, ἀδιαιρέτως, ἀχωρίστως), is affirmed.

It seems clear that its purpose was to define the limits of legitimate speculation rather than to make an exact and final statement of a theological position. Even so, it did not prove universally acceptable, and for two centuries after the Council Christendom was torn by the *Monophysite and *Monothelite heresies. From the end of the 7th cent., however, it has been generally received both in E. and W., except among the small Monophysite bodies; and its theological standpoint was in the 8th cent. expressed in systematic form by St. *John of Damascus in his 'De Fide Orthodoxa'.

The text is included in all edd. of the Acta (see previous bibl.). Only crit. ed. of Gk. text in *A.C.O.*, II, 1 (2), 1933, pp. 126–30; the early Lat. versions (Versio Antiqua, Versio Rustica) are also printed by E. Schwartz, ib. 2 (3). F. E. *Brightman, 'Six Notes. vi: The Definition of Chalcedon,' in *J.T.S.*, xxix (1927–8), p. 164 f. I. Ortiz de Urbina, S.J., 'Das Glaubenssymbol von Chalcedon. Sein Text, sein Werden, seine dogmatische Bedeutung' in A. Grillmeier, S.J.–H. Bacht, S.J., *Das Konzil von Chalcedon*, i (1951), pp. 389–418. On the theology of the Definition, see, besides Histories of Doctrine and several essays in A. Grillmeier–H. Bacht, op. cit., also J. S. Macarthur, *Chalcedon* (1931), and R. V. Sellers, *The Council of Chalcedon* (1953).

CHALDEAN CHRISTIANS. The convenient, if not very appropriate, title applied to the descendants of the ancient *Nestorian Churches now in communion with the see of Rome. They fall into two main groups, those of Turkey and Persia and those of *Malabar. When in the 13th cent. the Nestorians of Turkey and Persia came into contact with RC missionaries, negotiations for reunion were begun which lasted over centuries, and in 1830 a Chaldean body was established by Pius VIII, with George Hormizd as the first *Uniat

'Patriarch of Babylon'. Their customs and discipline have been increasingly assimilated to those of the Latin rite, and they follow the Gregorian Calendar; but they preserve the use of Syriac as their liturgical language. The total number in this Turco-Persian group is probably less than 75,000. For the Indian group, see *Malabar Christians.*

D. Attwater, *The Catholic Eastern Churches* (Milwaukee, Wisc. [1935]), pp. 227–41. J. Tfinkdji, 'L'Église chaldéenne autrefois et aujourd'hui' in *Annuaire Pontifical Catholique*, xvii (1914), pp. 449–69. G. Beltrami, *La chiesa caldea nel secolo dell' unione* (Orientalia Christiana, xxix, fasc. 83, 1933), with bibl. S. Bello, *La Congrégation de S. Hormisdas et l'Église chaldéenne dans la première moitié du XIXᵉ siècle* (Orientalia Christiana Analecta, fasc. cxxii; 1939). H. W. Codrington, 'The Chaldean Liturgy' in *The Eastern Churches Quarterly*, ii (1937), pp. 79–83, 138–52, 202–9; A. A. King, *The Rites of Eastern Christendom*, ii (Rome, 1948), ch. 8, pp. 251–415, with bibl. J. Labourt in *C.E.*, iii (1908), p. 559 f., s.v.; E. Tisserant in *D.T.C.*, xi (1931), cols. 225–323, s.v. 'Nestorienne (l'Église)'. On Chaldean canon law see J. Dauvillier in *D.D.C.*, iii (1942), cols. 292–388, s.v. 'Chaldéen (droit)'.

CHALDEE. An alternative, but misleading, name for *Aramaic (the language used in a few passages in the OT). The word appears to go back to St. *Jerome and probably owes its origin to an incorrect identification of the languages referred to in Dan. 1. 4 and 2. 4 respectively. In recent times it has practically gone out of currency in this sense.

CHALICE (Lat. *calix*, 'cup'). In eccl. usage, the cup used to contain the wine consecrated in the Eucharist. The earliest Christian chalices were commonly of glass, though other materials were sometimes used. By the 4th cent. the precious metals had become general, and valuable chalices of gold or silver set with precious stones are mentioned by St. *Augustine and St. *Chrysostom. The use of materials other than metal was not forbidden, however, till the 9th cent. The earliest form of chalice, frequently depicted in the catacombs, consists of a bowl with two handles but without stem. In Carolingian times two types were known, ministerial chalices, used for the communion of the people at times of general communion (corresponding to the earlier type), and sacrificial chalices, for the use of the priest. From the 14th cent. the stem was gradually elongated, and the bowl of the chalice made smaller as communion in one kind became universal, though a chalice of unconsecrated wine was often offered to the communicant as he left the altar. In England after the Reformation the restoration of communion under both kinds caused the chalices of the 17th and following cents. to be made considerably larger than before.

Rohault, iv [1887], pp. 45–153, with plates cclxx–cccxiv; Braun, *C.A.* (1932), pp. 17–196, with plates 1–40. H. *Leclercq, O.S.B., in *D.A.C.L.*, ii (pt. 2; 1910), cols. 1595–1645, s.v. 'Chalice' with reff. W. W. Watts, *Catalogue of Chalices and other Communion Vessels* (Victoria and Albert Museum, 1922), pp. 1–38 and 47–70.

CHALICE VEIL. A square of material, usually silk, corresponding in colour to the Eucharistic vestments, used in the W. to cover the *chalice and *paten during those parts of the *Mass when they are not in use, i.e. until the *offertory and after the *ablutions. It is placed over the *pall. It is a comparatively late ornament; even in the 16th cent. the chalice was commonly brought to the altar in a 'sacculum' or small bag. The chalice was previously covered only with a second folded *corporal, which was spread over it after the Communion. The rubric of the BCP, ordering that the chalice be covered with a 'fair linen cloth', may more nearly correspond to this usage. The *Carthusians still use instead a large corporal and draw one end over the vessels. See also *Humeral Veil.*

N. F. Robinson, S.S.J.E., 'Concerning Three Eucharistic Veils of Western Use' in *Transactions of the St. Paul's Ecclesiological Society*, vi (1906–10), pp. 129–60, esp. pp. 140–53. Braun, *L.P.*, pp. 213–15.

CHALLONER, RICHARD (1691–1781), author of the '*Garden of the Soul'. Born at Lewes of *Presbyterian parents, Challoner became a RC while still a boy, and at the age of 14 was sent to *Douai to be trained for the priesthood. Here he was successively student, professor, and vice-president, and did not return to England till 1730. In 1738 he deemed it wise to leave England again for a short time, owing to Conyers *Middleton's resentment at a preface in which Challoner had attacked him. In 1741 he was consecrated at Hammersmith Bishop (*in partibus*) of Debra and coadjutor to the *Vicar Apostolic, Dr. Petre, whom he succeeded in 1758. Challoner was the author of many books, both controversial and devotional, including a new translation of the Bible. His *Garden of the Soul*, first issued in 1740 as a prayer-book for the laity, has remained one of the favourite devotional books of English RCs. His *Meditations for Every Day of the Year* (1753) has also enjoyed great popularity.

Life by J. Barnard (London, 1784). E. H. Burton, *The Life and Times of Bishop Challoner, 1691–1781* (2 vols., 1909). T. Cooper in *D.N.B.*, ix (1887), pp. 440–3.

CHALMERS, JAMES (1841–1901), *Congregational missionary to New Guinea. Born in the Scottish Highlands, he intended to enter the ministry of the *United Presbyterian Church, but, after acceptance by the *L.M.S., he pursued his studies at Cheshunt College. After ordination, he left England in 1866 and, after a long and adventurous voyage, reached Rarotonga in the New Hebrides. There he did much to render the Church indigenous before sailing (in 1877) for New Guinea. In what was then an unknown land, full of savagery and human degradation, he slowly won the confidence of the people so that he was able to facilitate the establishment of British rule in the northern part of the country in 1888. He vigorously opposed any move to westernize the dress or customs of the natives. Like D. *Livingstone, Chalmers stands out as a missionary-explorer, and his two books, *Work and Adventure in New Guinea* (1885) and *Pioneering in New Guinea* (1887), contained much new geographical detail. His sphere of activity was constantly extending, taking in a visit to Samoa, where he made contact with R. L. Stevenson. His last ten years were devoted to the task of establishing peaceful relations with the many wild tribes, and to this end he sailed for Dopima off the south coast of Papua, where he and some of his party were brutally put to death.

R. Lovett, *James Chalmers, his Autobiography and Letters* (1902). A. R. Buckland in *D.N.B.*, *1901–1911*, pp. 343–5.

CHALMERS, THOMAS (1780–1847), theologian, preacher, and philanthropist. In 1823 he became professor of moral philosophy at St. Andrews, and in 1828 of theology at Edinburgh. He was known in his early days as an able evangelical preacher, a formidable intellectual defender of Christianity, a brilliant mathematician, and a pioneer of popular education and modern methods of poor relief. But his chief importance lies in his leadership of the movement for the choice of ministers in the Established Church of Scotland by the people, and of the Free Church schism of 1843 which followed its failure. In that year he left the Established Church with a considerable body of followers, and founded the *Free Church of Scotland, becoming in the same year principal and professor of divinity at New College, Edinburgh. His theology was *Calvinistic, with the stress rather on the needs of man than on the election of God. His many writings include the first of the *Bridgewater Treatises.

W. Hanna, *The Life and Writings of T. Chalmers* (4 vols., 1849–52); H. Watt, *Thomas Chalmers and the Disruption* (1943). W. G. Blaikie in *D.N.B.*, ix (1887), pp. 449–54.

CHAMBERS, JOHN CHARLES (1817–74), author of *The *Priest in Absolution* (q.v.). Educated at Emmanuel College, Cambridge, he was ordained deacon in 1842 to a curacy at Sedbergh, Yorks. On his ordination as priest in 1846 he proceeded to Perth, where he worked till 1855. From 1856 till his death he was incumbent of St. Mary's, Crown Street, and warden of the 'House of Charity', both in Soho. Here he was remarkably successful as a mission priest, working esp. among the ragged children in his cure. Besides various religious writings issued under his own name, he was the anonymous author of the celebrated *Priest in Absolution* (Part i, 1866; Part ii, 1870).

See W. Wroth in *D.N.B.*, x (1887), p. 19 f., where, however, all reference to *The Priest in Absolution* has been avoided. J. Embry, *The Catholic Movement and the Society of the Holy Cross* (1931), ch. v, pp. 97–127.

CHAMBERS, ROBERT (1802–71), Scottish publisher and author. In 1818 he began business with a bookstall in Leith Walk, Edinburgh, and eventually joined his brother, William Chambers (1800–83), in the publishing firm of W. & R. Chambers. He was the part or sole author of a great mass of encyclopaedic works. His most famous production, the *Vestiges of the Natural History of Creation* (1844), was a popular handbook of the natural

sciences (geology, zoology, &c.), defending an evolutionary (essentially Lamarckian) theory of man's origin. The work attracted much controversy; but it helped to prepare the public for the Darwinian theory. Great pains were taken to preserve anonymity—it was ascribed to the Prince Consort, Charles Lyell, and others—but in Chambers' later years his authorship was widely accepted, and publicly avowed by Alexander Ireland in a posthumous edition of 1884. Chambers himself appears to have been a man of sincere piety, and to have regarded the question at issue as purely one of science.

William Chambers (brother), *Memoir of Robert Chambers* (1872). A. Ireland, 'Story of the authorship of the "Vestiges" told for the first time' prefixed to his ed., the twelfth, of Chambers, *Vestiges of the Natural History of Creation* (1884), pp. vii–xxvii. F. Watt in *D.N.B.*, x (1887), pp. 23–5. *C.B.E.L.*, iii, p. 709 f.

CHANCEL (Lat. *cancellus*). Originally the part of the church immediately about the altar, now called the 'sanctuary'. When further space was reserved for clergy and choir westward from the sanctuary, the word was applied to this area as well, and hence is now normally employed for the entire area within the main body of the church east of the nave and transepts. In medieval times a screen often separated chancel and nave, and some modern churches have followed this arrangement. In England, the repair of the chancel, unlike that of the rest of the church, usually falls upon the incumbent, or upon the *lay rector, where such exists, but custom occasionally makes the parishioners responsible. Where a lay rector is responsible, he probably has the right of access to the chancel at all times, but not that of excluding the incumbent.

Francis Bond, *The Chancel of English Churches* (1916).

CHANCELLOR, Diocesan. The chief representative of the *Bishop in the administration of the temporal affairs of his diocese. In particular he is the usual president of the *Consistory Court (q.v.). The office was orig. that of a private secretary; but as the *Archdeacon's responsibilities extended and he lost his personal connexion with the Bishop, many of his former duties passed to the chancellor. In the C of E he nowadays performs the duties of the Bishop's *Official Principal and of his *Vicargeneral (qq.v.). The extent of his jurisdiction varies somewhat acc. to the terms of the Bishop's letters patent appointing him. Normally his chief function is the hearing of applications for and granting of *faculties, *dispensations, etc. He is statutorily responsible for the fixing of tables of fees in new parishes, also for hearing, either alone or with assessors, complaints against clerics for immorality under the Clergy Discipline Act of 1892. Through his surrogates, he also issues *marriage licences. In the C of E the chancellor must be over 26 years of age and 'learned in the civil and ecclesiastical law' (Can. 127 of 1604), but he is not ordinarily in *Holy Orders. If the Bishop fails to appoint a chancellor, it falls to the *Metropolitan to do so.

In the RC Church the Diocesan Chancellor, who is invariably a priest, is responsible for the preservation and arrangement of the diocesan archives (*C.I.C.*, can. 372). In addition he is sometimes the confidential secretary of the Bishop and does much of the work otherwise executed by *vicars general.

In England the title of chancellor is also held by one of the four principal dignitaries of *cathedrals of the Old Foundation. He was responsible for the Cathedral School and also the library. In modern times he is often assigned wider educational functions.

R. *Phillimore, *The Ecclesiastical Law of the Church of England* (ed. by W. G. F. Phillimore), ii (1895), pp. 914, 916 f., 929–33, 938 f.; H. W. Cripps, *A Practical Treatise on the Law Relating to the Church and Clergy* (ed. 8 by K. M. Macmorran, 1937), pp. 62, 143–7, 151, and 153 f.

CHANCELLOR, Papal, head of the Papal chancery. The office dates from the latter part of the 11th cent., when the Papal Chancery became an independent institution responsible only to the Pope. The Chancery has been entrusted to Cardinals except for the period from Honorius III (1216–27) to *Clement V (1305–14). Early in the 13th cent. the head of the Chancery took the title of Vice-Chancellor, and the designation survived until *Pius X's reform of the Curia (1908). During the Middle Ages the office was highly remunerative as the Chancellor was responsible for all Papal bulls and briefs. At the end of the 14th cent. he was given a 'regens' or 'praesidens cancellariae' to assist him, on whom devolved most of the work. In modern times the office has considerably diminished in importance.

R. L. Poole, *Lectures on the History of the Papal Chancery down to the Time of Innocent III* (1915), incl. reff. to earlier work.

CHANNEL ISLANDS, Christianity in the. Christianity was apparently introduced into the Channel Islands about the 5th–6th cent., largely by the saints who are commemorated in many of the place-names of the islands. In 933 the islands became the property of the Dukes of Normandy, but after the Norman Conquest, when England and Normandy were united under the same sovereign, it was doubtful for some time to which part of his dominions they were conceived to belong. After the separation of England and Normandy (1204), they were annexed by *John to England. Between 1482 and 1486 the islands were granted neutrality in the English-French wars; but this neutrality was annulled by *William of Orange in 1689. These changes in political status affected ecclesiastical history. Before the Reformation the islands had formed part of the diocese of Coutances (on the neighbouring mainland), except for a time under King John, when they had belonged to *Exeter, and under *Henry VI (d. 1471), when they had been attached to *Salisbury. In 1568 they were finally annexed to *Winchester. In the 16th cent. Protestant refugees from

France and elsewhere induced the islanders to adopt *Presbyterianism; but Episcopalian polity and canons agreeable to the standards of the C of E were imposed at the end of the reign of *James I and this has been the official creed since that time, though even now *Huguenot Protestantism is strong. The two large islands of Jersey and Guernsey have each a dean, who is also a parochial incumbent.

French trr. of the BCP for use in the Channel Islands were authorized and publd. at London in 1616 and 1667, the latter being a rendering of the 1662 Book by J. Durel. P. Falle, *An Account of the Island of Jersey* (1694), pp. 115–92 (ed. E. Durell, 1837, pp. 175–262); J. Duncan, *The History of Guernsey* (1841), pp. 314–404. On the introd. of Christianity into the Channel Islands, M. Pégot-Orgier, *Histoire des îles de la Manche* (1881), pp. 37–49; E. F. Carey, *The Channel Islands* (1904), pp. 22–32. M. Lelièvre, *Histoire du méthodisme dans les îles de la Manche, precédée de l'histoire de la réformation huguenote dans cet archipel* (1885).

CHANNING, WILLIAM ELLERY (1780–1842), American *Unitarian pastor. He graduated at Harvard in 1798, became regent there in 1802, and in 1803 was appointed pastor of the Congregational Church in Federal Street, Boston. In the schism some time later between conservative and liberal *Congregationalists in America, Channing espoused the liberal or Unitarian cause, and preached against the doctrines of the *Trinity, the *Atonement, and *total depravity. From about 1820, he was considered to be a *Unitarian, and is often reckoned the greatest American Unitarian theologian; but he disapproved of Unitarianism as a sect, and regarded himself as belonging 'not to a sect, but to the community of free minds'. He 'desired to escape the narrow walls of a particular church'.

Works (5 vols., Boston, 1841; 2 vols., London, 1865). *Memoir* by William Henry Channing (3 vols., London, 1848). Other Lives by Elizabeth P. Peabody (Boston, Mass., 1880) and J. W. Chadwick (ib., 1903).

CHANTAL, St. JANE. See *Jane Frances de Chantal, St.*

CHANTRY. A term applied to the office or the benefice maintained to sing or say Mass for the souls of the founder and his friends, and also to the little chapel in which such masses were usually said. The chapel usually took the form either of an altar erected in a space partitioned off for the purpose within the parent building, or of a building constructed as a 'chantry chapel', annexed to the church or detached from it. In the latter case, the chantry chapel, which was often close to the churchyard or at the entrance of a bridge, might have an extra story, designed for the more secular duties of the chantry priest.

The creation of a chantry chapel in the later Middle Ages in England required a monetary endowment for its erection and upkeep, the permission of the ordinary, the consent of the crown for the alienation of lands held in *mortmain, and a guarantee to the priest of the parish that the chantry priest would not interfere with his rights.

Although the erection of chantries and the endowment of chantry priests dates back to the early Middle Ages, it was only in the 14th and 15th cents. that chantries became numerous. In addition to his purely ecclesiastical duties the chantry priest often had to act as schoolmaster, curate, or chaplain. At the Reformation the fate of the chantries was not long in the balance. In 1545, owing to the financial needs of the French war, an Act was passed stating that the possessions of chantries were generally misapplied and vesting them in the King for the term of his life; and commissioners were appointed to inquire into their property. Although some surrendered voluntarily it seems doubtful if any chantries were suppressed before the death of Henry VIII. In 1547 a new Act was passed suppressing some 2374 chantries and guild chapels. Though it was provided that the money should be applied to public and charitable purposes, much of it merely went into the pockets of Edward's advisers. It was laid down, however, that pensions should be paid to the chantry priests. One of the chief losses to religious life was educational. The chantries had frequently been educational centres, and indeed, many of them later evolved into the 'Edwardian' grammar schools.

A. Hamilton Thompson (ed.), 'The Certificates of the Chantry Commissioners for the College of Southwell in 1546 and 1548, with an Introduction and Notes' in *Transactions of the Thoronton Society*, xv (1912), pp. 63–158; id., 'The Chantry Certificate Rolls for the County of Nottingham, ib., xvi (1913), pp. 91–133, xvii (1914), pp. 59–119, xviii (1915), pp. 83–184; J. E. Ray, *Sussex Chantry Records* (Sussex Record Society, xxxvi; 1931); F. R. Raines (ed.), *A History of the Chantries within the County Palatine of Lancaster, being the Reports of the Royal Commissioners of Henry VIII, Edward VI, and Queen Mary* (Chetham Society, lix and lx, 1862). D. *Rock, *The Church of Our Fathers*, iii (pt. 1; 1852); pp. 104–40; K. L. Wood-Legh, *Studies in Church Life under Edward III* (1934), ch. 4, pp. 89–126, with reff. A. Hamilton Thompson, *The Historical Growth of the Parish Church* (1911), ch. 2, pp. 24–50; F. Bond, *An Introduction to English Church Architecture from the Eleventh to the Sixteenth Century*, i (1913), pp. 102–12; G. H. Cook, *Mediaeval Chantries and Chantry Chapels* (1947).

CHAPEL. The word, which is first found in Marculfus (7th cent.), seems to derive from the temporary structure in which the Kings of France housed the 'cape' (late Lat. *cappella*, dim. of *cappa*) of St. *Martin (q.v.) when carrying it on their military campaigns as a sacred relic. By an extension of use it was applied to shrines containing other relics (cf. esp. the '*Sainte-Chapelle' at *Paris, built to receive the *Crown of Thorns), and then to a variety of buildings which in various ways were less than churches. They include the following.

(1) Chapels of a private institution, such as a school, college, or hospital. Such chapels are often of imposing dimensions, e.g. those of some of the colleges at Oxford and Cambridge. (2) RC and dissenting places of worship, in distinction from the English parish churches. Before the 19th cent. the word 'church' was rarely applied to such buildings. Hence 'Church and Chapel' was a common phrase for 'Members of the C of E and Nonconformists'.

In Ireland the term is still current for RC churches, though these are often larger than the Protestant churches in the same town. (3) A part of a large church, or cathedral, with a separate altar. The dedication of such chapels is commonly other than that of the main church. One of them (frequently the most considerable of them) is often dedicated to the BVM and hence known as the '*Lady Chapel' (q.v.). (4) The '*Chapels Royal' (q.v.), which differ from cathedral and parish churches in being under the direct jurisdiction of the Sovereign. (5) A '*Chapel of Ease' (q.v.), a building for the ease of parishioners who are too far from the parish church. (6) A '*Proprietary Chapel' (q.v.), a church in private hands; there are very few, if any, now surviving in England.

On the Continent, the word is often used for the chancel of a church. It has hence come to be applied to a (musical) choir, whether religious or secular, e.g. in *Kapellmeister* ('the master of a choir').

See also *Oratory*, esp. for the RC legislation on chapels, and *Chantry*.

O.E.D., ii (1893), pp. 274–6, s.v.

CHAPEL OF EASE. A chapel subordinate to a mother church, for the ease of parishioners in prayers and preaching. From the 12th cent. such chapels were frequently founded, and many by custom or express licence rose to parochial status and were used for the administration of the Sacraments and for burials. They proved esp. useful in the vast parishes of N. England, where distance and natural obstacles made attendance at the mother church difficult, if not impossible, for many parishioners. Some of these foundations disappeared during or shortly after the Edwardian dissolutions (c. 1548) and many have become independent parish churches. In modern times chapels of ease have usually been served by the parish clergy as opportunity allows, without the appointment of a separate priest-in-charge.

CHAPEL ROYAL. A private chapel attached to a Royal court. In England these chapels are not subject to the jurisdiction of the bishop of the diocese in which they are situated, but to the 'Dean of the Chapels Royal'. They are now regularly served by priests-in-ordinary appointed by the Crown. The present English Chapels Royal are (or are situate at) St. James's Palace; Buckingham Palace; Windsor Castle; Sandringham; Chapel Royal, Windsor Great Park; Hampton Court; Balmoral; The Royal College of St. Katherine by the Tower; the Chapels Royal of St. John the Evangelist and St. Peter *ad vincula* within H.M. Tower of London and The King's Chapel of the Savoy. Several of these have had a distinguished tradition of choral music. The *Sainte-Chapelle at Paris was formerly a Chapel Royal of the French court.

E. F. Rimbault (ed.), *The Old Cheque-Book, or Book of Remembrance, of the Chapel Royal, from 1561 to 1744* (Camden Society, N.S., iii, 1872).

CHAPLAIN. Orig. a priest or minister who has the charge of a *chapel (q.v.). He is ordinarily a cleric who performs non-parochial duties.

Chaplains are often appointed to monarchs, to bishops and other high ecclesiastical dignitaries, and to noblemen; they are also appointed to serve in various institutions, such as schools, colleges, prisons, workhouses, cemeteries, and at embassies, legations, and consulates abroad. The Indian Civil Service used to appoint a number of chaplains. In the armies, navies, and air forces of most Christian countries chaplains are appointed, both permanent and temporary. In Great Britain Army and R.A.F. chaplains are given permanent or temporary commissions, and rank equivalent to captain or above according to seniority; in the Navy they do not hold official rank; and in all the services these chaplains are drawn from all the larger religious bodies. Chaplains appointed by the State are paid by the State, those by private persons by their employers. Since 1905, when Church and State were separated in France, and the clergy became liable for military service, no chaplains have been appointed in the French forces; but in other countries where Church and State are independent of each other, e.g. the U.S.A., chaplains are maintained.

CHAPLET (Fr. *chapelet*, dim. of Old Fr. *chape*, 'headgear'; hence a 'crown' or 'wreath'). The name given to the three parts into which the devotion of the *Rosary is divided, each corresponding to a set of five of the fifteen *Mysteries. It thus consists of five *decades, each concerned with one Mystery, and forms a complete devotion in itself. The word is also used of the string of beads constructed to count the prayers of one complete chaplet of the Rosary devotion and sometimes to denote the devotion as a whole. (*Chapelet* is the word most commonly used in France in this last sense.) The name has also been adopted for a devotion of Rosary type taught in the C of E by Fr. M. W. T. Conran, *S.S.J.E., entitled *A Chaplet of Prayer* and sanctioned by certain bishops for public use in their dioceses. It uses different prayers and Mysteries from the customary ones.

CHAPMAN, JOHN (1865–1933), NT and Patristic scholar. He was educated at Christ Church, Oxford, and ordained deacon in the C of E in 1889. In 1890 he joined the RC Church and in 1892 entered the *Benedictine Order. In 1912 he became Superior of *Caldey Island, in 1922 Prior, and in 1929 Abbot, of *Downside Abbey. In his monograph *John the Presbyter and the Fourth Gospel* (1911) he sought to disprove the existence of a '*John the Elder' distinct from St. John the Apostle, and in *Matthew, Mark, and Luke* (ed. J. M. T. Barton; 1937) to show the priority of St. Matthew's Gospel to the other *Synoptists. He also endeavoured to rehabilitate the supposed interpolations in the text of St.

*Cyprian's 'De Unitate Ecclesiae', which appear to tell in favour of the primacy of the Pope. His other writings include *Notes on the Early History of the Vulgate Gospels* (1908), *St. Benedict and the Sixth Century* (1929), and his valuable *Spiritual Letters* (1935).

The Spiritual Letters of Dom John Chapman, O.S.B., ed. with introd. memoir by R. Hudleston, O.S.B. (1935). Id. in *Dict. Sp.*, ii (1953), cols. 488–92, s.v.

CHAPTER (Lat. *capitulum*). The word is in current use in a variety of ecclesiastical senses:

(1) Orig. it denoted a section of the monastic rule, such as was daily read publicly in religious houses.

(2) The assembly of the members of a religious house to listen to this reading or for similar purposes (receiving the abbot's instructions, transacting the business of the monastery, &c.). (See also *Chapter House*.) By extension the assembly of the monks or their representatives of a whole province or order came to be referred to as a 'provincial chapter' or 'general chapter'.

(3) The members of a religious house in their corporate capacity. Hence

(4) The members of any corporate body responsible for an ecclesiastical institution. In England esp. of the body responsible for the spiritual and temporal concerns of a cathedral church. In some cathedrals two capitular bodies (the Lesser and Greater Chapters) exist with different functions, the smaller body usually consisting of the residentiary members and being included in the larger body (whose members are commonly known as 'Prebendaries' or 'Honorary Canons').

The duties of cathedral chapters in the RC Church are laid down in *C.I.C.*, cann. 391–444. On chapters in the C of E, H. W. Cripps, *A Practical Treatise on the Law Relating to the Church and Clergy* (ed. 8 by K. M. Macmorran, 1937), pp. 127–46. A. H. Thompson in *D.E.C.H.* (ed. 1948), pp. 103–5; L. R. Misserey, O.P., in *D.D.C.*, iii (1942), cols. 595–610. See also bibl. to *Canon*.

CHAPTER, Little. A short lesson, consisting of a verse or two of Scripture, usually taken from the Prophets or the Epistles, which forms part of all the *Day Hours of the *Breviary.

CHAPTER HOUSE. A building used for meetings of a cathedral or monastic chapter. Separate buildings for such purposes appear early in the 9th cent. Their plan varies considerably, the polygonal form being almost confined to certain English cathedrals and the oblong commonest on the Continent.

CHARACTER. In the Catholic theology of the Sacraments, the indelible quality which *Baptism, *Confirmation, and *Ordination are held to imprint on the soul. As this character is indelible and, even after the gravest sins, including apostasy, therefore remains, none of these Sacraments can be received more than once by the same person. The doctrine received explicit formulation, largely under the influence of St. *Augustine, by the Scholastics, but it was foreshadowed from an early date by such expressions as 'the Lord's seal' (σφραγὶς τοῦ Κυρίου) applied by *Clement of Alexandria to Baptism, itself based on such NT passages as Eph. 1. 13.

CHARDON, LOUIS (c. 1596–1651), French mystical author. He entered the *Dominican Order in 1618 at the reformed Convent S. Annuntiationis at *Paris, where most of his life was spent in the offices of novice master and spiritual director. His greatest work, *La Croix de Jésus* (1647), for a long time remained almost forgotten, until the study of H. *Bremond directed the attention of a wider public to it. Drawing from the teaching of Pseudo-*Dionysius and J. *Tauler, as well as from the *Thomist theology of grace, he builds his doctrine of the mystical life on the action of *Sanctifying Grace in the soul and the presence in it of the Three Divine Persons. Like St. *John of the Cross, he lays great emphasis on the salutary effects of spiritual desolation. Among his minor works are *La Vie de St. Samson d'Yore* (1647), *Raccourci de l'art de méditer* (1649), and *Méditations sur la passion de Jésus-Christ* (1650), as well as translations of St. *Catherine of Sienna and J. *Tauler.

Modern ed. of 'La Croix de Jésus' by F. Florand, O.P. (Paris, 1937); review by H. D. Simonin in *Archivum Fratrum Praedicatorum*, vii (1937), pp. 337–40. Bremond, viii (1928), pp. 3–77. Series of articles by F. Florand, O.P., in *La Vie spirituelle*, Suppl., xlii (1935), pp. 15–57, 108–27; xliv (1935), pp. 17–55, 85–96; xlv (1936), pp. 22–35, 100–20; lviii (1939), pp. 33–43, incl. reff. to other works. F. Florand, O.P., in *Dict. Sp.*, ii (1953), cols. 498–503.

CHARGE. An address delivered by a bishop, archdeacon, or other ecclesiastical person at a *visitation of the clergy under his jurisdiction. Charges are also delivered to their ordinands by bishops (and, in the Presbyterian Church, by ministers) immediately before ordination. A charge is usually more of the nature of an admonitory exhortation than a definite command, though the latter could quite properly be conveyed through a charge. See also *Visitation*.

CHARISMATA (Gk. χαρίσματα, plur. of χάρισμα, 'a gift of grace'). The blessings, spiritual and temporal, bestowed on every Christian for the due fulfilment of his vocation. In a narrower sense, the word is used esp. for the supernatural graces which individual Christians need to perform the specific tasks incumbent on them in promoting the spiritual advancement of their fellows. In 1 Cor. 12. 8–11 they are enumerated as comprising the word of wisdom, the word of knowledge, faith, the gift of healings, workings of miracles, prophecy, discernings of spirits, tongues, and the interpretation of tongues, to which are added, in ver. 28, the charismata given to Apostles, prophets, teachers, and those entrusted with the government of the Church.

O.D.C.C.–K 2

CHARITY (Lat. *caritas*). The greatest of the '*theological virtues'. Usually, though not consistently, it is the AV translation of ἀγάπη, the virtue of which the nature and characteristics are described by St. *Paul in 1 Cor. 13. It is directed primarily towards God; but it is also owed to ourselves and our neighbours as the objects of God's love. Its natural opposite is hatred, which may also take the negative form of indifference. See also *Love*.

CHARLEMAGNE (c. 742–814), 'Charles the Great', the first Emperor (from 800) of the 'Holy Roman Empire'. The son of *Pepin III, King of the Franks, and Bertrada, he was anointed with his father and Carloman, his brother, by Pope *Stephen II in 754. On Pepin's death in 768 he and Carloman divided the kingdom between them. The death of Carloman in 771 left Charlemagne sole ruler.

For the next 28 years, Charlemagne was mainly occupied with extending his kingdom in all directions. He first subdued Lombardy, at the behest of *Hadrian I. Having forced the king, Desiderius, to retire to a monastery, Charlemagne assumed the Lombard crown, and was rewarded by the Pope with the title of *patricius*. Next followed (772–85) a long series of arduous campaigns against the Saxons. In 778 Bavaria was conquered, and between 791 and 796 the Avar kingdom and Pannonia fell into his hands. Meanwhile dissensions among the Moslems in Spain had tempted Charlemagne over the Pyrenees. In his first expedition (778), which was a failure, Roland, the Warden of the Breton Marches, was killed; the tradition of his campaign long survived into the Middle Ages in a romantic form through the *Chansons de Roland*. The systematic conquest of Northern Spain began in 785; and eventually in 801, Barcelona was captured and made the centre of the 'March of Spain'.

In addition to his conquests and wars abroad, Charlemagne brought consistency, reform, and uniformity into his government at home. His creation of a strong central administration, his employment of *missi dominici* (itinerant royal legates), and his standardization of laws by means of *capitularies, which he issued for both his hereditary and his newly conquered domains, reflect the vigour of his government. His encouragement of ecclesiastical reform and patronage of letters have rightly earned for his reign the title of the 'Carolingian Renaissance'. He completed the reform of the administration and manners of the Frankish clergy. He himself had real theological interests and he employed *Alcuin to write against the *Adoptianist heretics led by *Felix of Urgel. His patronage of the scholars who formed the Palace School did much to stimulate learning (see *Carolingian Schools*). It was by the King, acting through mixed ecclesiastico-civil councils, rather than from the Pope directly, that the restoration of the hierarchy and of Church discipline, the unity of the liturgy, the definition of doctrine, and the encouragement of education were achieved, and they, rather than his conquests, form his chief title to fame. The culmination of his reign was his coronation as first 'Holy Roman Emperor' by Pope *Leo III on Christmas Day, 800. This constituted a challenge to the E. empire, with whom relations were strained for the rest of his life.

Official docc. ed. E. Mühlbacher in *M.G.H.*, Diplomata Karolina, i (1906), pp. 77-484. The 'Codex Carolinus' (letters from Popes Gregory II, *Zacharias, *Stephen II, Paul I, Constantine II, *Stephen III, and *Hadrian I to Charles Martel, Pepin, and Charlemagne), ed. W. Grundlach in *M.G.H.*, Epistolae, iii (1892), pp. 469-657; the latter also ed., together with various other letters, life by *Eginhard and other primary material, by P. Jaffé, *Monumenta Carolina* (Berlin, 1867). Life by Eginhard ed. H. W. Garrod-R. B. Mowat (Oxford, 1915); also ed., with Fr. tr., by L. Halphen (Paris, 1932); Eng. tr. by W. Glaister, 1877; see also bibl. to *Eginhard*. Other primary material listed in *B.H.L.*, i, pp. 238-45 (Nos. 1577-1618); Suppl., p. 66 f. S. Abel-B. Simson, *Jahrbücher des fränkischen Reiches unter Karl dem Grossen* (Jahrbücher der deutschen Geschichte; 2 vols., 1866-83). Modern studies include those of J. I. Mombert (London, 1888), T. Hodgkin ('Foreign Statesmen', London, 1897), H. W. C. Davis ('Heroes of the Nations', 1900), A. Kleinclausz (Paris, 1934, with good introd. on sources; see also other works of this author), and J. Calmette (ib., 1945); popular studies by G. P. Baker (London, 1932) and [J.] D. Woodruff (ib., 1934). L. Halphen, *Études critiques sur l'histoire de Charlemagne* (1921); id., *Charlemagne et l'empire carolingien* (1947); K. Heldmann, *Das Kaisertum Karls des Grossen* (Quellen und Studien zur Verfassungsgeschichte des deutschen Reiches in Mittelalter und Neuzeit, vi, Hft. 2; 1928). P. Folz, *Études sur le culte liturgique de Charlemagne dans les Églises de l'empire* (Publications de la Faculté des Lettres de l'Université de Strasbourg, fasc. 115, 1951). J. Bryce, *The Holy Roman Empire* (ed. 1904), pp. 50-75. C. Bayet-C. Pfister-A. Kleinclausz in E. Lavisse (ed.), *Histoire de France*, ii (pt. i; 1903), pp. 280-357. G. Seeliger in *C. Med. H.*, ii (1913), pp. 595-629 and 655-84, with bibl. pp. 809 and 813. P. F. Palumbo in *E.C.*, iii (1950), cols. 866-82, s.v. 'Carolomagno', for further bibl.; A. P. Frutaz, ib., cols. 882-6, on the liturgical reform of his reign, with bibl. For works on the Carolingian Renaissance see bibl. to *Carolingian Schools*.

CHARLES I (1600-1649), King of Great Britain and Ireland from 1625. On his accession to the throne, Charles found a considerable party among the clergy disposed to abandon the *Calvinistic views which had been predominant in the previous century, and to welcome a theological position much nearer to traditional Catholicism. The King, who personally favoured the new movement, took arbitrary and repressive steps to silence the controversy, meanwhile promoting High Churchmen to important positions, and in 1633 giving the see of *Canterbury to W. *Laud, their leader. Laud's vigorous policy in enforcing a fixed standard of ceremonial and repressing Calvinism earned him wide unpopularity, while the King, whose administrative, financial and foreign policy had been as disastrous as it had been well-intentioned, suffered with him. The fact that *Henrietta Maria was a RC added to the difficulties, since Charles, torn between her demands for complete toleration for her co-religionists and the violent anti-popery of the mass of his subjects, unsuccessfully compromised; but of this policy the only result was popular indignation at the difference between the half-hearted enforcement of the recusancy laws against RCs and the rigour with which the Star Chamber, under Laud's direction, passed sentence on Puritan Dissenters, even though such sentences were lenient in comparison with what RCs and Puritans alike had suffered under *Elizabeth.

Charles's Scottish policy was equally unfortunate. In Scotland the earlier agitation against episcopacy had died down, but between his coronation in 1633 at Edinburgh and the Prayer Book riot of 1637 Charles did everything to inflame it. His coronation was carried out with the fullest Anglican ceremonial; he insisted that Scotland should adopt the English or a similar Prayer Book, and conform to the Laudian usages in externals; and, worst of all, the government and policy of the Church of Scotland was to be dependent upon Canterbury or upon Scottish bishops controlled by the King and Laud. The *Covenant of 1638, which pledged Scotland to Presbyterianism, was the result.

The Civil War, which broke out in England in 1642, was only in part caused by the ecclesiastical situation, but the defeat of Charles in 1645-6 meant the disestablishment of the C of E and the establishment of Presbyterianism in its place. The failure of Charles to negotiate successfully with his enemies in the following years must be put down in part to the evidence he had earlier given that his word was unreliable, but it was due even more to the fact that his principles refused to let him consent to a permanent sacrifice of episcopacy in order to conciliate the goodwill of the Scots and the moneyed English laity. His execution, an illegal action carried through by fanatical Army leaders, has been justly considered as a martyrdom, since in the end it was conditioned only by his resolution to defend the Church. His personal character, though marred by indecision, imprudence, and faithlessness, was, in his private life, of high moral purity and beauty, and, in his public position, of that religious principle and personal responsibility which appeared to full effect in the dignity of his last hours.

On the day of his death the *Eikon Basilike, a memoir in somewhat hagiographical terms, was published, and the dead King was acclaimed widely as a martyr. From 1662 to 1859 a special service for 30 Jan., the day of his death, was annexed to the *BCP by royal mandate, and the anniversary was required to be kept as a day of national fasting and humiliation. Five churches have been dedicated in his name.

C. Petrie (ed.), *The Letters, Speeches and Proclamations of King Charles I* (1935). S. R. Gardiner, *History of England from the Accession of James I to the Outbreak of the Civil War* (10 vols., 1883-4), esp. vols. vi ff.; id., *History of the Great Civil War, 1642-1649* (3 vols., 1886-91). F. M. G. Higham, *Charles I*. A Study (1932), with notes on authorities. C. W. Coit, *The Royal Martyr* (1942); V. Staley, 'The Commemoration of King Charles the Martyr' in his *Liturgical Studies* (1907), No. 6, pp. 66-83; M. R. Toynbee, 'Charles I and the King's Evil' in *Transactions of the Folk-Lore Society*, lxi (1950), pp. 1-14.

CHARLES II (1630-85), King of Great Britain and Ireland (in exile) from 1649, restored 1660. He adopted *Presbyterianism in 1650 in order to obtain Scottish help, but abandoned it in 1651 on the failure of the attempt at restoration. After the Restoration in 1660 the King's good-nature and religious indifference inclined him to toleration, to which he tried to give effect in the abortive *Declarations of Indulgence of 1662 and 1672, but the opposition of parliament and country to this policy was shown by the *Corporation Act (1661), the Act of *Uniformity (1662), the *Conventicle Act (1664), the *Five Mile Act (1665), and the *Test Act (1673). These measures Charles was too anxious for his own security to oppose, nor did he venture to interfere with the execution of 35 innocent RCs between 1678 and 1681, which followed the denunciations by Titus *Oates. An attempt, however, made by the Commons in 1680–81 to exclude the Duke of York from the succession as being a RC led Charles to govern without a parliament from 1681 to 1685. On his deathbed the King made formal profession of the RC faith, which he is held to have secretly favoured for many years before.

A. Bryant (ed.), *The Letters, Speeches and Declarations of King Charles II* (1935). Lives by C. Airy (London, 1901) and A. Bryant (London, 1931). D. Ogg, *England in the Reign of Charles II* (2 vols., 1935).

CHARLES V (1500–1558), Emperor. The eldest son of Philip of Burgundy and the grandson of *Ferdinand and *Isabella, Charles soon became the most powerful man in Europe. By 1519, when he was elected to the Empire, he held, besides Burgundy, the Netherlands, Spain and the Spanish American Empire, the kingdom of Naples and had a claim to N. Italy and Milan. The very extent of his power was, however, his chief source of weakness; for though in Spain and the Netherlands his centralized administration was absolute, in all his other dominions his position was weakened by enemies within and without— France, the Papacy, the Turks, and the Protestant princes. The most urgent problem that confronted him was the rise and growth of *Lutheranism. The Diet of *Worms (1521) had banned M. *Luther, but for many years Charles's other difficulties only allowed him to pursue an alternating policy of concession and repression. After 1544 he managed at last to break up the *Schmalkaldic League. The Protestants, however, soon reasserted their strength, drove the Emperor out of Germany, and at the Diet of *Augsburg (1555) forced upon him the principle of '*cuius regio, eius religio'. To avoid the anomaly of persecuting Protestants in one part of his dominions and tolerating them in another, Charles abdicated in 1556, and died in retirement at the monastery of Yuste in Estremadura.

Among more substantial works on Charles V are those of W. Robertson–W. H. Prescott (2 vols., London, 1857); E. Armstrong (2 vols., London, 1902), with bibl.; and W. L. McElwee (London, 1936). Also H. Baumgarten (3 vols., Stuttgart, 1885–92); K. Brandi (Munich, 1937; Eng. tr., 1939) and J. Babelon (Paris, 1947.) W. Friedensburg, *Kaiser Karl V und Papst Paul III, 1534–1549* (1932).

CHARLES BORROMEO, St. (1538–84), Abp. of Milan. He was one of the leaders of the *Counter-Reformation. Born of noble parentage at Arona on Lake Maggiore, he was early destined for the priesthood, and received his first benefice at the age of 12. In 1552 he went to Pavia where he studied civil and canon law under Alciati. In 1559 his uncle, the newly elected *Pius IV, summoned him to Rome and in 1560 created him cardinal and Abp. of Milan. In the third and last group of sessions of the Council of *Trent, Borromeo took a prominent part, notably in drafting the *Catechism. On his return to Milan he set about a radical reformation of his see, tightening up the morals and manners of clergy and laity, and making the work of the diocese more effective. Thus he patronized the *Jesuits, established seminaries for the education of the clergy, and founded a Confraternity of Christian Doctrine for instructing children. He took much personal interest in the sick and the poor, notably in the great plague of 1576. His reforms provoked great hostility, but his influence was felt far outside his diocese, and in particular in Switzerland. He was canonized in 1610. Feast day, 4 Nov.

Federico Borromeo (1564–1631), his cousin and successor in the see of Milan from 1595, was the founder of the *Ambrosiana* (q.v.; 1609). Other members of his family held high office in Church and State.

Charles Borromeo's Sermons ed. J. A. Sassi (5 vols., Milan, 1747–8). The primary authorities are the lives by A. Valiero (Verona, 1586), C. Bascapè (Ingolstadt, 1592), and J. P. Giussano (Rome, 1610; Eng. tr., with preface by H. E. *Manning, 2 vols., 1884). A. Sala, *Documenti circa la vita e le gesta di San Carlo Borromeo* (4 vols., 1857–62). Id., *Biographia di San Carlo Borromeo* (1858). Other modern studies by E. H. Thompson (London, 1858), C. Sylvain (3 vols., Lille, 1884), C. Orsenigo (ed. 2, Milan, 1911), L. Celier ('Les Saints', 1912), D. Franceschi (I grandi cardinali italiani nella vita e nella storia, iv; Bologna [1911]), A. Rivolta (Milan, 1938), and M. Yeo (London, 1938; popular). G. Galbiati (ed.), *Echi di San Carlo Borromeo* (Pubblicazione milanese di contributi per la storia della religione e della coltura; 20 fasc., 1937–8; index in id., *Scritti su S. Carlo Borromeo* (1941), pp. 45–90). A. *Butler, *The Lives of the Saints* (ed. H. Thurston, S.J., and D. Attwater), xi (1938), pp. 42–53, with bibl. For further bibl. see accounts by F. Van Ortroy, S.J., in *Anal. Boll.*, xxix (1910), pp. 372–5, xxxi (1912), pp. 119–21, and xxxiv–xxxv for 1915–16 (publd. 1921), pp. 338–45. G. Galbiati in *E.C.*, iii (1950), cols. 853–61, s.v. 'Carlo Borromeo'; R. Mols, S.J., in *D.H.G.E.*, xii (1953), cols. 486–534, s.v. 'Charles Borromée'.

CHARLES MARTEL (*c.* 690–741), Frankish ruler. An illegitimate son of Pepin, Mayor of the Palace to the Merovingian kings, he showed marked vigour and martial ardour from early years. After leading a victorious campaign against the Neustrians in 716, he became himself Mayor of the Palace and brought the Neustrians and Burgundy within the sphere of his rule. He also made himself master of Normandy and compelled Eudo, Duke of Aquitaine, to submit to him. The greatest event of his career was his victory over the *Saracens, who were invading France, at Tours in 732, which, even if its significance has been overestimated, was of decisive importance for the future of Christendom. In his latter years he penetrated into Germany and Frisia, compelling many of the tribes to pay allegiance to him. He corresponded with St. *Boniface and other Anglo-Saxon missionaries, and established friendly relations with the Roman see. Many of Charles's characteristics seem to have been inherited by his grandson, *Charlemagne.

T. Breysig, *Jahrbücher des fränkischen Reiches, 714-741*. Die Zeit Karl Martells (1869), with important excursus on sources, pp. 109-15. G. Waitz, 'Kleine Beiträge zur fränkischen Geschichte. Ueber den Beinamen "der Hammer"' in *Forschungen zur deutschen Geschichte*, iii (1863), pp. 147-9. F. Lot–C. Pfister–F. L. Ganshof, *Les Destinées de l'empire en occident de 395 à 768* (Histoire générale, ed. G. Glotz, Histoire du moyen-âge, i, pt. 1; 1928), pp. 294-402, passim, esp. pp. 394-402, with reff. See also lives of St. Boniface cited s.v.

CHARLES, ROBERT HENRY (1855–1931), Biblical scholar. He was educated at Queen's University, Belfast, and *Trinity College, Dublin. After some years as a parish priest in London and in research at *Oxford, he became professor of Biblical Greek at Dublin in 1898. From 1906 to 1913 he was again in Oxford. In 1913 he became Canon, and in 1919 Archdeacon, of *Westminster. In matters of Jewish eschatology and apocalyptic he was the greatest authority of his day, and produced editions of the *Book of Enoch* (1893; 1912), the *Book of *Jubilees* (1894), *The* (Slavonic) *Secrets of Enoch* (1895), *The Apocalypse of *Baruch* (1896), *The Assumption of *Moses* (1897), *The Ascension of *Isaiah* (1900), and *The *Testaments of the XII Patriarchs* (1908). General summings-up of his researches appeared in *Eschatology* (1899; ed. 2, 1913) and *Between the Old and New Testaments* (1914), as well as in *The Apocrypha and Pseudepigrapha of the OT* (2 vols., 1913)—the last a comprehensive *corpus* in English of late Jewish writings, with introductions and notes. His latest books were *Studies in the Apocalypse* (1913), and editions of *Revelation* (2 vols., 1920) and *Daniel* (1929).

F. C. *Burkitt in *Proceedings of the British Academy*, xvii (1931), pp. 437-45. Brief Memoir by C. F. D'Arcy prefixed to Charles's *Courage, Truth, Purity* (posthumous, 1931), pp. xiii–xxxv. T. W. Manson in *D.N.B.*, *1931-1940*, p. 169 f.

CHARRON, PIERRE (1541-1603), French preacher and philosopher. He was a native of Paris, and after studying law at Orléans, Bourges, and Montpellier, became a priest and soon made a great reputation as a preacher. In 1576 he became a canon at Bordeaux, where he published *Les Trois Vérités* (1593), an apologetic work for the Catholic religion. The book, which included an elaborate attack on the Calvinist, P. *Du Plessis-Mornay, went through many editions. In 1594 Charron became Vicar-General at Cahors, and later Canon of Condom. In 1601 appeared his principal work, *De la sagesse* (3 vols.), largely inspired by G. Du Vair and M. de *Montaigne. Here he distinguished three kinds of wisdom, the evil wisdom of the world, condemned by philosophy and revelation alike; the highest wisdom, which is the theological wisdom produced by reflexion and aided by grace; and, between the two, human wisdom, the principal subject of his work. The treatise was in three books. The first dealt with the knowledge of man and his condition, which is one of weakness, misery, and presumption. The second expounded the preparation for wisdom, which

consists in freedom from the passions and from the prejudices of the mind. In the third book he developed this theme in connexion with the four cardinal virtues. The treatise, which reflected pagan rather than Christian thought, opened the way for the secularization of morals, for *Deism, and for free thought.

Complete edition of Charron's Works publd. at Paris in 1635. J. B. Sabrie, *De l'humanisme au rationalisme. Pierre Charron* (1913); H. Busson, *La Pensée religieuse française de Charron à Pascal* (1933).

CHARTERHOUSE. Eng. version of Fr. *maison chartreuse*, a *Carthusian religious house. The most famous house of that name was established in 1371 just west of Aldersgate, London, and on the site of it a chapel, almshouse, and school were founded by Thomas Sutton in 1611. The school, which in 1872 was removed to near Godalming, in Surrey, is now among the most famous of English public schools.

CHARTRES. Since the 4th cent., with intervals, the town has been the seat of a bishop. In the earlier Middle Ages it was famous for its school, of which *Bernard, *Thierry, and *Gilbert de la Porrée were members. Its magnificent cathedral, one of the finest of French Gothic buildings, was begun in the 11th cent., but was not dedicated until 1260. Particularly celebrated are the fine glass and the rich sculpture on the portals.

L. *Duchesne, *Fastes épiscopaux de l'ancienne Gaule*, ii (ed. 2, 1910), pp. 422-30. J. A. Clerval, *Les Écoles de Chartres au moyen-âge du Ve au XVI siècle* (Chartres, 1895). J. M. Parent, O.P., *La Doctrine de la Création dans l'École de Chartres* (Ottawa, 1938). J. A. Clerval, *Guide chartrain* (Chartres, 1876); Y. Delaporte–E. Houvet, *Les Vitraux de la cathédrale de Chartres* (4 vols., Chartres, 1926); id., *La Cathédrale de Chartres* (collotype plates, 17 vols., Chartres, 1919-21). H. Leclercq, O.S.B., in *D.A.C.L.*, iii (pt. 1, 1914), cols. 1019-45; E. Griffe and B. Degenhart in *E.C.*, iii (1950), cols. 1394-6, with bibl.

CHARTREUSE, La Grande. See *Grande Chartreuse, La*.

CHASIDIM, also HASIDAEANS. The conservative Jews in Palestine (the name means the 'pious' or 'godly') who in the 2nd cent. B.C. endeavoured to maintain the traditional Hebrew Law, with its scribal interpretation, against the prevalent Greek influences. When the *Maccabees revolted under Mattathias in 168 against the Hellenizing party, the Chasidim at first supported him, but once religious freedom had been secured (in 162), they refused to fight for national independence. The Chasidim were probably the immediate ancestors of the party of the *Pharisees. The word was used later in other senses, e.g. as a title for Jewish mystics and as the name of a Jewish sect founded in the 18th cent.

CHASUBLE. The outermost garment worn by bishops and priests in celebrating the *Eucharist, and rarely at other times. It is derived from the 'paenula' or 'planeta', the outdoor cloak of both sexes in the later Greco-

Roman world. In shape it was originally like a tent, with a hole for the head, but gradually it was reduced in size. This took place in the W. by the cutting away of the sides, whereas in the E., where it is known as the 'phelonion', the garment was gathered up or cut away in the front. In the BCP of 1549 the chasuble was retained, with the cope as an alternative; in that of 1552 it was abolished; but it has been widely held that the *Ornaments' Rubric of 1559, re-enacted in 1661, reimposes its use. In practice, however, it seems to have been little used, if at all, in post-Reformation times in the C of E before the ceremonial revival of the 19th cent., when decisions of the civil courts against the use of Eucharistic vestments failed to check its widespread reintroduction. The *Lutheran Church in Germany retained the chasuble for some time after the Reformation, and the Scandinavian Churches still use it.

Rohault, vii (1888), pp. 111–81, with plates dlxi–dci. Braun, L.G., pp. 149–247. On the revival of the use of the chasuble in the C of E in the 19th cent., cf. F. E. *Brightman in D.E.C.H., p. 612, s.v. 'Vestments'.

CHATEAUBRIAND, FRANÇOIS RENÉ VICOMTE DE (1768–1848), French Romantic writer.

He was a native of St.-Malo. In 1791 he crossed to America, but soon returned, and lived from 1793 to 1800 in England. In his later life he had a distinguished career as a politician, becoming a peer, ambassador, and foreign minister. He was buried at his own request in the island of Grand Bé, near St.-Malo.

His fame rests mainly on his *Génie du christianisme, ou beautés de la religion chrétienne*, a brilliant rhetorical defence of Catholic Christianity, which he published in 1802 on the morrow of the *Concordat. He had been converted to a living faith in Christianity by a deep emotional crisis that followed the deaths of his mother and sister (*ma conviction est sortie du cœur; j'ai pleuré et j'ai cru*). In the *Génie* he sought to lift Christianity from the discredit into which the destructive work of the 18th cent. rationalist philosophers had brought it by transferring the debate from the plane of reason to that of feeling. He argued that the study of history proved the Christian faith to have been the main fountain of art and civilization in Europe, by the recurrent stimulus it gave to the intellectual and spiritual aspirations of mankind. His other writings of religious significance include his novel *Les Martyrs, ou le triomphe de la religion chrétienne* (1809) and a Life of De *Rancé (1844).

Several edd. of his 'Œuvres complètes', incl. that in 11 vols. of Brussels, 1852. *Correspondance générale*, ed. L. Thomas (5 vols., Paris, 1912–24). There is much autobiographical material in his *Mémoires d'outre-tombe* (MS. completed 1836; 12 vols., 1848–50; Eng. tr., 6 vols., 1902). C. A. Sainte-Beuve, *Chateaubriand et son groupe littéraire sous l'empire* (1861). The innumerable modern studies include works by G. Bertrin (Paris, 1906), J. Lemaître (Paris, 1912), P. Moreau (Paris, 1927; also Paris, 1933), H. Gillot (Strasbourg, 1934), M. Duchemin (Paris, 1938; with bibl.). G. Bertrin, *La Sincérité religieuse de Chateaubriand* (1889); V. Giraud, *Le Christianisme de Chateaubriand* (2 vols., 1925–8). Popular life by Joan Evans (London, 1939), incl. select bibl.

CHAUCER, GEOFFREY (c. 1340–1400), English poet.

He was the son of a London vintner. As a page to the Lady Elizabeth de Burgh, he served in Edward III's last invasion of France, and was captured at 'Retters'. Ransomed by the King, he afterwards entered his service, and during the next thirty years was employed in various diplomatic missions. Under Richard II he was Clerk of the Works at Windsor and *Westminster; but despite his posts and his pensions he seems usually to have been in a state of penury.

The *Canterbury Tales* were written apparently from 1386 to 1390. They were first printed by W. *Caxton c. 1476–7. Since the time of J. *Foxe, who first advanced the theory that Caxton was an admirer of J. *Wycliffe, many have aimed at proving that Chaucer was an agnostic and an anti-clerical. Yet it seems probable that he was neither one nor the other. Certainly he was not conspicuously pious, but neither was he hostile to the Church. He strove to give a true and fair presentation of 14th cent. life as he saw it. With a character such as the Summoner he is merciless in his satire; for the 'Poor Parson of a Town' he has nothing but praise and respect.

Crit. edd. of his Works by W. W. Skeat (7 vols., London, 1894–7) and F. N. Robinson (Cambridge, Mass., and London, 1933), with notes and bibl. W. D. Selby–F. J. Furnival–E. Bond–R. E. G. Kirk (edd.), *The Life Records of Chaucer* (Chaucer Society, Ser. 2, pts. xii, xiv, xxi, and xxxii, 1875–1900); E. P. Kuhl, 'Index to the Life-Records of Chaucer' in *Modern Philology*, x (1912–13), pp. 527–52. Modern lives by A. W. Ward ('English Men of Letters', 1879) and M. Chute (London, 1951). Studies by T. R. Lounsbury (3 vols., London, 1892), E. [H.] Legouis ('Les Grands Écrivains étrangers', Paris, 1910; Eng. tr., 1913), G. L. Kittredge (Cambridge, Mass., 1915), G. L. Cowling (London, 1929), G. K. *Chesterton (London, 1932), J. Livingstone Lowes (London, 1934) and N. Coghill (H.U.L., 1949). G. G. Coulton, *Chaucer and his England* (1908). H. S. Bennett, *Chaucer and the Fifteenth Century* (Oxford History of English Literature, ii, 1947), esp. pp. 1–95. Further bibl. in R. D. French, *A Chaucer Handbook* (New York, 1927; ed. 2, 1947), and C.B.E.L., i (1940), pp. 208–49.

CHELTENHAM LIST, The. See *Mommsen Catalogue, The*.

CHEMNITZ, MARTIN (1522–86), *Lutheran theologian.

After lecturing for a short time in the philosophical faculty at *Wittenberg, where in 1553 he expounded the *Loci Communes* of P. *Melanchthon, Chemnitz left for Brunswick in 1554. Here he spent the rest of his life in a pastoral capacity, refusing the many important appointments offered him. In his *Repetitio sanae doctrinae de vera praesentia* (1561) he defended the Lutheran doctrine of the real presence of Christ in the Eucharist, including Luther's teaching on ubiquity, though he deprecated further elaboration as to the mode of the presence; and in his *Examen concilii Tridentini* (1565–73) he attacked the Council of *Trent. He was one of the main influences in consolidating Lutheran doctrine and practice in the generation following Luther's death. His *Loci Theologici* (published 1591), based on his lectures, ably defend a mainly Melanchthonian theology.

H. Hachfeld, *Martin Chemnitz* (1867); R. Mumm, *Die Polemik des M. Chemnitz gegen das Konzil von Trient* (1905). Schottenloher, i (1933), p. 116 f. (Nos. 2850–8).

CHERUBICON. Also 'The Cherubic Hymn'. (Gk. χερουβικόν). In the E. Church, a hymn sung during the *Greater Entrance by the choir, as the mystical representatives of the *Cherubim. In the Russian Church it is set to very elaborate music, and is considered the most striking musical item in the Liturgy.

CHERUBIM. The highest of the nine orders of *angels. In the OT they appear as God's attendants, e.g. they guard His presence from profanity (Gen. 3. 24, Ezek. 28. 14, &c.), and representations of them were set up in *Solomon's *Temple at *Jerusalem, overshadowing the *ark (Ex. 25. 18–22). It is possible that Assyrian influences exercised some influence on Jewish conceptions of the cherubim. In Christian angelology they have usually been grouped with the *thrones and the *seraphim, though in the earliest times they were not included in the angelic lists (which were based on Eph. 1. 21 and Col. 1. 16),

J. Petersen, *Cherubim. Kurze Zusammenstellung der wichtigsten Ansichten und Erklärungen seit Luther* (1898). P. Dhorme, O.P.–L. H. Vincent, O.P., 'Les Chérubins' in *R. Bibl.*, xxxv (1926), pp. 328–58 and 481–95. M. Kmoskó, 'Kerub und Kurib' in *Biblische Zeitschrift*, xi (1913), pp. 225–34. On their representation in art, K. Künstle, *Ikonographie der christlichen Kunst*, i (1928), p. 245 f. E. Kirschbaum, S.J., 'L' angelo rosso e l' angelo turchino' in *Rivista di Archeologia Cristiana*, xvii (1940), pp. 209–48.

CHESTER. The city was perhaps the seat of the bishops of the kingdom of Mercia; but in the Middle Ages it ceased to be a bishopric, except between 1075 and *c*. 1100, when the present church of St. John Baptist served as the cathedral. The see was refounded by *Henry VIII in 1541, who made the church of the dissolved abbey of St. *Werburgh the cathedral, under a new dedication to Christ and the BVM, and Chester has remained a bishopric ever since. In 1542, the diocese was transferred from the province of *Canterbury to that of *York.

R. C. Christie (ed.), *Annales Cestrienses*; or, Chronicle of the Abbey of S. Werburg, at Chester (The Record Society for the Publication of Original Documents relating to Lancashire and Cheshire, xiv; 1886). T. Hughes–T. C. Hughes (edd.), *The Registers of Chester Cathedral, 1687–1812* (Parish Record Society, 1904). J. Tait (ed.), *The Chartulary or Register of the Abbey of St. Werburgh, Chester* (Chetham Society, lxxix and lxxxii; 1920–23). W. *Dugdale, *Monasticon Anglicanum* (ed. 1819), pp. 370–401. C. Hiatt, *The Cathedral Church of Chester* (Bell's Cathedral Series, 1897). *A History of Chester Cathedral*: with biographical notices of the Bishops and Deans. By a member of the Chester Archaeological Society [1852]. F. Sanders in *D.E.C.H.* (1912), p. 108 f., s.v.

CHESTER BEATTY PAPYRI. A group of papyrus codices, found near Hermopolis in Egypt, most of which were acquired by Mr. A. Chester Beatty in 1931. Though they are all imperfect, several are of substantial size. They comprise (1) 50 leaves (of an original 66) of Genesis, 4th cent.; (2) 27 leaves (out of 84) of Genesis, 3rd cent.; (3) 50 leaves (out of 108) of Numbers and Deuteronomy, early 2nd cent.; (4) 1½ leaves of Ecclesiasticus, 4th cent.; (5) portions of 33 leaves (out of 104) of Isaiah, 3rd cent.; (6) two small fragments of Jeremiah, 2nd cent.; (7) 50 leaves (out of 118) of Ezekiel, Daniel, and Esther, 3rd cent.; (8) portions of 30 leaves (out of 220) of the Gospels and Acts, early 3rd cent.; (9) 86 leaves (out of 99) of the Pauline epistles, early 3rd cent.; (10) 10 leaves (out of 32) of Revelation, 3rd cent.; (11) 8 leaves containing the last eleven chapters of the apocryphal Bk. of *Enoch, and 6 containing part of a homily on Christ's Passion, by *Melito, Bp. of Sardis, 4th cent. Of the papyri not in Mr. Chester Beatty's possession, most of the Ezekiel is at Princeton University, and 30 leaves of St. Paul, with small fragments of other MSS., at Michigan University. The age of these papyri makes them very valuable evidence for the text of the Greek Bible, since they are a century or more older than the earliest vellum MSS.

Ed. of text by F. G. Kenyon, 8 vols., London, 1933–7 (with a parallel series of facsimile plates). On item (9) above ('P46'), also H. A. Sanders, *A Third-Century Papyrus Codex of the Epistles of St. Paul* (University of Michigan Studies, Hum. Series, No. 38, 1935); on item (7) above ('968'), A. C. Johnson, H. S. Gehman, and E. S. Kase, *The John H. Scheide Biblical Papyri: Ezekiel* (Princeton University Studies in Papyrology, 1938). The large and scattered literature, mainly in periodicals, is summarized by E. Vogt and A. Calderini in *E.C.*, ii (1949), cols. 1113–15, s.v. 'Beatty, Chester, Papyri'.

CHESTERTON, GILBERT KEITH (1874–1936), poet and essayist. After beginning a course of training in art in 1891, he abandoned it for journalism. His defence of orthodoxy and conventionality in an individual and unconventional style soon established his literary reputation. Among those of his early works which were directly or indirectly concerned with religious topics, the best known are *Heretics* (1905) and *Orthodoxy* (1908). His poems include the hymn 'O God of Earth and altar'. In his novels there is less of religious interest, though his appreciation of the RC clergy appears in the 'Father Brown' stories. In 1922 he left the C of E for the RC Church; but the change of allegiance had little effect on his style or outlook. His *Autobiography* (1936) gives an illuminating picture of literary-religious circles from *c*. 1895 to his death.

Maisie Ward, *Gilbert Keith Chesterton* (1944).

CHEYNE, THOMAS KELLY (1841–1915), OT scholar and critic. He was the grandson of T. H. *Horne. Educated at Worcester College, Oxford, he was successively vice-principal of St. Edmund Hall (1864), Fellow of Balliol (1868), rector of Tendring, Essex (1880), and Oriel professor of the interpretation of Scripture at Oxford (1885–1915). In 1884 he became a member of the OT Company engaged on the *Revised Version. Studies at Göttingen under H. G. A. *Ewald in 1862 having led him to a critical view of the OT. he upheld as early as 1871 the now general theory of Pentateuchal sources. His mind, however, went through many phases. His pastoral work at Tendring lent his writings an evangelical and homiletic colour for some years. Later he became highly, and finally recklessly, unconventional in his Biblical criticism and ideas. Among his chief writings are *Prophecies of Isaiah* (1880–1), *Job and Solomon* (1887), *Book of Psalms* (1888), *The Origin and Religious Contents of the Psalter* (1891), *Founders of OT Criticism* (1893), *Introduction to the Book of Isaiah* (1895), and *Jewish Religious Life after the Exile* (1898). The chief production of his last period, the *Encyclopaedia Biblica* (4 vols., 1899–1903), which he edited in conjunction with J. Sutherland Black, reflects the combination of daring and originality which marked his later work.

Much autobiographical matter is to be found in the prefaces to many of his books. R. H. *Charles in *Proceedings of the British Academy* (1915–16), pp. 545–51. A. S. Peake in *D.N.B., 1912–21*, p. 119 f.

CHICAGO-LAMBETH ARTICLES. See *Lambeth Quadrilateral.*

CHICHELE, HENRY (?1362–1443), Abp. of *Canterbury. Educated under the patronage of *William of Wykeham at Winchester and Oxford, he was ordained priest in 1396. His abilities as an administrator and diplomat soon attracted the attention of both the King and the Pope, and he became Bp. of *St. David's in 1408 and Abp. of Canterbury in 1414. In 1409 he was one of the English delegates to the Council of *Pisa. When Henry V left England for the French wars in 1414, Chichele was among those appointed to assist the Duke of Bedford in administering the kingdom. He was severely reprimanded by *Martin V for failing to secure the repeal of the Statutes of *Provisors and *Praemunire, and had to suffer the humiliation of seeing his legatine powers suspended and the Bp. of *Winchester and the Abp. of *York created cardinals and given precedence over him. The traditional view that he encouraged the war with France to divert attention from abuses in the Church is without contemporary support. He was not a great man, but did his best to carry out the duties of his office in the face of great difficulties. His care for learning is attested by his foundation of the college of All Souls at Oxford (1438).

The Register of Henry Chichele Archbishop of Canterbury 1414–1443, ed. by E. F. Jacob–H. C. Johnson (*Canterbury and York Society, xlii, xlv, xlvi, and xlvii, 1937–47; also published separately, 4 vols., 1938–47). A. Duck, *Vita Henrici Chichele* (Oxford, 1617; Eng. tr., 1699). E. F. Jacob, *Two Lives of Archbishop Chichele* (1932).

CHICHESTER. The name is held to be derived from the Saxon, Cissa (A.-S. *Cissaceaster*, i.e. 'Cissa's camp'), younger son of Aella, who is said to have repaired *c.* 490 the Roman city of Regnum, which previously existed on the site. The see, which was founded at Selsey by St. *Wilfrid during his exile from *York, was transferred to Chichester in accordance with a decree of the Council of London of 1075. Its bishops have included St. *Richard (1245–54), L. *Andrewes (1605–9), and John Lake, the non-juror (1685–9). The present diocese is conterminous with the county of Sussex. The cathedral was built in the 12th–13th cents. A Roman inscription, the 'Pudens Stone', which is preserved outside the Town Hall, records the gift of land for a (pagan) temple by a Pudens, son of Pudentinus, whom some have attempted to identify with the Pudens of 2 Tim. 4. 21.

Three surviving medieval episcopal registers, with other primary material, incl. muniments of the Dean and Chapter, are described in *Historical Manuscripts Commission. Report of Manuscripts in Various Collections*, i (1901), pp. 177–204. C. Deedes (ed.), *The Episcopal Register of Robert Rede, O.P., Lord Bishop of Chichester, 1397–1415* (Sussex Record Society, viii and xi, 1908 and 1911); id. (ed.), 'Extracts from the Episcopal Register of Richard Praty, S.T.P., Lord Bishop of Chichester, 1438–1445' in *Sussex Record Society*, iv (1905), pp. 83–236. The episcopal registers from 1478 are continuous. F. G. Bennett–R. H. Codrington–C. Deedes (edd.), *Statutes and Constitutions of the Cathedral Church of Chichester* (Chichester, 1904). W. D. Peckham (ed.), *The Chartulary of the High Church of Chichester* (Sussex Record Society, lxvi; 1944). A. S. Duncan-Jones (ed.), *The Chichester Customary* (modern observances; *Alcuin Club Collections, xxxvi, 1948). T. G. Willis, *Records of Chichester* (1928), pp. 149–220. H. Corlette, *The Cathedral Church of Chichester* (Bell's Cathedral Series, 1911); A. S. Duncan-Jones, *The Story of Chichester Cathedral* [1933]. J. Warrillow in *D.H.G.E.*, xii (1953), cols. 665–74, s.v., with bibl.

CHILDERMAS. An old English name for (1) the Feast of the *Holy Innocents (28 Dec.); (2) the day of the week throughout the year on which that feast fell, widely held to be a day of ill-omen.

CHILDREN, Song of the Three. See *Song of the Three Children.*

CHILDREN'S CRUSADE (1212). A march of children who gathered from France and W. Germany after the disastrous failure of the Fourth *Crusade (1202–4) with the intention of 'recapturing *Jerusalem'. It is difficult to disentangle history and legend from the surviving records, but it seems clear that few of the parties of children ever got as far as disembarking from the S. of France and Italy, and that such as did soon perished. The historical nucleus of the 'Pied Piper of Hamelin' is apparently to be found in this 'Crusade'.

The event is mentioned by most of the chroniclers of the period, esp. those who deal with the Crusades (q.v.). G. Z. Gray, *The Children's Crusade. An Episode of the Thirteenth Century* (New York, 1870). C. de Janssens, *Étienne de Cloyes et les croisades d'enfants au XIIIe siècle* (1890). R. Röhricht, 'Der Kinderkreuzzug, 1212' in *Historische Zeitschrift*, xxxvi (1876), pp. 1–8; D. C. Munro, 'The Children's Crusade' in *American Historical Review*, xix (1914) pp. 516–24. P. Alphandéry, 'Les Croisades d'enfants' in *Revue de l'Histoire des Religions*, lxxiii (1916), pp. 259–82.

CHILE, Christianity in. The Spanish invasion of Chile, which began in 1535, was followed about the end of the 16th cent. by great missionary activity on the part of the *Franciscan and *Jesuit orders, though the complete conversion of the country was not achieved till some 150 years later. In 1810–28 political separation from Spain was secured, but the RC Church continued to be 'protected' and state-subsidized, though other religions were tolerated. The considerable immigration into Chile over many years brought to the country a large non-RC minority, which has consisted chiefly of *Anglicans, *Presbyterians, and German *Lutherans. Education is provided by both state and sectarian schools.

C. S. Cotapos, *Historia eclesiástica de Chile* (Santiago, 1925), with bibl. *La provincia eclesiástica chilena*. Erección de sus obispados y división en parroquias (Freiburg i.Br., 1895). F. Enrich, S.J., *Historia de la Compañía de Jesús en Chile* (2 vols. only, [down to 1822], Barcelona, 1891). R. Lagos, O.F.M., *Historia de las misiones del colegio de Chillán* (Barcelona, 1908). P. Gazulla, *Los primeros mercedarios en Chile, 1536–1600* (Santiago, 1918). J. T. Medina, *La inquisición en Chile* (vol. i only; Santiago, 1890). Latourette, iii (1940), p. 152 f.; v (1943), p. 82 f., 95, 119; vii (1945), p. 170. G. Rommerskirchen and S. Furlani in *E.C.*, iii (1950), cols. 1607–10, s.v. 'Cile', with further bibl.

CHILIASM (Gk. χίλιοι, 'a thousand'). Another name for *Millenarianism, the theory that Christ will return to earth and reign here for a thousand years before the final consummation of all things. The belief is based on an interpretation of Rev. 20. 1–5.

CHILLINGWORTH, WILLIAM (1602–1644), Anglican divine. A scholar (1618) and fellow (1628) of Trinity College, Oxford, he first attracted attention when he engaged a Jesuit, 'John *Fisher', in controversy. As a result of this incident, Chillingworth was converted to the RC Church, and went to *Douai in 1630. In the following year, however, he returned to England, and in 1634 again declared himself a Protestant. His best known work was his *Religion of Protestants, a Safe Way to Salvation* (1638), written as his contribution to a controversy raging between a Jesuit, Knott, and the Provost of Queen's College, Oxford, on the subject of whether Protestants could be saved. On the plea that 'the Bible only is the religion of Protestants', he defended the rights of reason and free inquiry in doctrinal matters, and denied that any Church has the gift of infallibility. He affirmed that he belonged to the C of E, because he considered her doctrine sufficiently pure to ensure salvation, and that adequate grounds were wanting to warrant disturbing the 16th cent. settlement. During the Civil War he was a chaplain in the Royalist army, and was captured in 1643. His death in captivity at *Chichester was said to have been hastened by the efforts of the other side to convert him.

The collected edd. of Chillingworth's Works are numbered acc. to the edd. of *The Religion of Protestants a Safe Way to Salvation*, the first bearing the title *The Works of William Chillingworth* and being 'ed. 7', London, 1719. Life by T. Birch, prefixed to ed. 10, London, 1742, pp. ii–viii. P. Des Maizeaux, *An Historical and Critical Account of the Life and Writings of Wm. Chillingworth* (1725; ed. J. Nichols, 1863). There is also a very brief study of J. D. Hyman (Cambridge, Mass.,1931). M. *Creighton in *D.N.B.*, x (1887), pp. 252–7.

CHIMERE. A silk or satin gown without sleeves, worn by Anglican bishops and by doctors of divinity. It perhaps derives from the tabard, a medieval upper garment. It is frequently worn at liturgical functions, but also constitutes part of episcopal full dress on important civil occasions, and of the full academic dress of those entitled to wear it. It is incorrect to wear a chimere under a vestment or cope.

CHINA, Christianity in. Legend has it that St. *Thomas the Apostle preached in China as well as in India. On the evidence of the tablet, found in 1625 at *Sigan-Fu and of date A.D. 781, it is known that *Nestorian missionaries reached China in the 7th cent., and Nestorianism survived there till the 14th. The first W. and Catholic missionary was John of Monte Corvino, who arrived in 1292. He laboured successfully, at first alone and then with seven assistants, producing Mongol versions of the NT and Psalms, and making thirty thousand converts. The advent of the Ming dynasty, however, in 1368, proved fatal to this mission. In 1582 two *Jesuits, Michele Ruggiere and Matteo *Ricci, arrived and preached with much success. They thought it right to allow to their converts a certain measure of syncretism with traditional pagan rites, and as a result various disputes arose between later emperors and popes. There was also intermittent persecution in the 17th cent. Finally in 1723 Christianity was proscribed, and complete toleration was not restored to RCs until 1858. In the meantime, non-RC missions had begun. The *L.M.S. sent Robert *Morrison, who arrived in 1807, and published the OT and NT in Chinese in 1823. Between 1830 and 1840 various American Episcopalian and Protestant missions landed, and medical missions began in 1835. In the years of external peace between 1842 and 1860 British, American, and German missions entered, and established their position, though few converts were made. After the war of 1860 the missions were given great opportunities by the terms of peace imposed, but their changed status did more harm than good to the Christian cause, since it gave colour to the idea that Christianity was a foreign religion supported by a hostile military power. Nevertheless, the *China Inland Mission, founded in 1865, must be credited with much success, and the existing missions of the foreign concessions made fruitful advances into the interior. Some material assistance was also possible for the victims of famine, floods, and pestilence. In 1900 occurred the Boxer rebellion, only one of many occasions, though the worst, in which thousands of martyrs were killed in wild anti-foreign outbreaks.

K. S. Latourette, *A History of Christian Missions in China* (1929) with full bibl., pp. 847–99. M. Huc, *Le Christianisme en Chine, en Tartarie et au Thibet* (4 vols., bound in 2, 1857–8; Eng. tr., 3 vols., 1857–8); A. Launay, *Histoire des missions de Chine* (3 vols., 1903–8). P. M. D'Elia, S.J., *The Catholic Missions in China* (Shanghai, 1934). J. de Moidrey, S.J., *La Hiérarchie catholique en Chine, en Corée et au Japon* (Variétés sinologiques, xxxviii; ib., 1914), esp. pp. 1–158;

L. Pfister, S.J., *Notices biographiques et bibliographiques sur les Jésuites de l'ancienne mission de Chine, 1552–1773* (ib., lix and lx, 1932–4). J. Richter, *Allgemeine evangelische Missionsgeschichte*, iv, Das Werden der christlichen Kirche in China (1928). Latourette, vi, pp. 253–363, and vii, pp. 238–78, with bibl. H. Cordier in *C.E.*, iii (1908), pp. 669–79, s.v. 'China, Missions'; P. M. D'Elia, S.J., in *E.C.*, iii (1950), cols. 1656–68, s.v. 'Cina, III Evangelizzione della C.', with further bibl.

CHINA INLAND MISSION (C.I.M.). An interdenominational and international mission to the interior of *China founded by J. H. *Taylor in 1865. Its work has from the first been primarily evangelical, though it has a certain number of schools and dispensaries under its care. The Bible, to the inspiration of which in its entirety members of the Mission are committed, is the basis of the work, but individuals are encouraged to remain loyal to the tenets of the particular religious body to which they belong, and there is grouping by denominations in the mission field. The Mission has met with remarkable success and has had associated with it a large body of Chinese workers.

M. Broomhall, *The Jubilee Story of the China Inland Mission* [1915]. P. Thompson, *D. E. Hoste. . . .* Hudson Taylor's Successor as General Director of the China Inland Mission, 1900–1935 [c. 1947]. See also bibliography to *Taylor, Hudson*, esp. studies by H. and G. Taylor.

CHOIR (architectural). A term generally used to describe the part of a church containing the seats of the clergy. In the Roman *basilicas these seats at first were set in a semicircle round the *apse and behind the altar. Later they were placed in a railed-off space within the nave, or body of the church, and at its eastern end. Later still, in various parts of Christendom, *chancels replaced apses; they were much larger, and rectangular in shape, and the choir was included within the chancel, at its W. end. The term 'ritual choir' is sometimes used for the seats of the clergy when these do not occupy the (architectural) choir of the church.

CHOIR (musical). A body of singers assisting at Divine Service. As early as the 4th cent. such bodies existed, made up of clerks in *minor orders and of boys, and, by the time of St. *Gregory the Great (d. 604), the *Schola Cantorum was fully established. In the Middle Ages the choirs of cathedrals and monasteries were almost the only places where music of any kind was taught, and there, until a conventional notation came in *c.* 1100, instruction was given orally. About the 15th cent. harmonized music began to supplement the liturgical plainchant of the Church, and lay singers to augment church choirs. In all sections of W. Christendom this change reached its fullest development *c.* the 18th cent., when church music was at its most elaborate and florid stage, and the singers often skilled professionals. It also became customary in this period to set the singers in a gallery at the west end. The *Oxford Movement in the C of

E and the *Liturgical Movement among RCs have tended to restore the choir to the *chancel, while various efforts have been made in the 20th cent. to give the congregation fuller scope for partaking in the music of the services, and, except where there are expert professional choirs, to discourage the use of music in which the congregation cannot share. The traditional dress of male singers is the *surplice, worn over the *cassock, though ordinary lay clothes are sometimes worn.

CHOIR SISTERS. Nuns who are under obligation to attend all choir *offices, as contrasted with lay sisters, who, though living under rule, attend only certain services. The distinction is most marked in the *Carthusian Order, where the choir sisters receive solemn consecration as virgins by a rite similar to that used in ordinations to the diaconate.

CHOREPISCOPUS (Gk. χωρεπίσκοπος; also ἐπίσκοπος τῶν ἀγρῶν). In the early Church, a bishop of a country district in full episcopal orders. The powers which he could exercise were severely restricted (cf. Conc. *Ancyr. can. 13; Conc. *Antioch. can. 10). He could ordain only to the lower ranks of the clergy and was wholly subject to the authority of his diocesan. Such chorepiscopi were very numerous in the 4th cent., esp. in Asia Minor. At the Council of *Nicaea 15 signed in their own right. But the appointment of further chorepiscopi was forbidden by the Council of *Laodicea (can. 57), which ordered that their place be taken by 'periodeutai', i.e. visiting priests (cf. Conc. *Sard. can. 6, which forbids the appointment of bishops to tiny places so that the name of bishop shall not be cheapened). At the Council of *Chalcedon (451) they signed only as representatives of their diocesans. In the E. their functions were progressively restricted to those of a modern *archdeacon, and by the 13th cent. they had disappeared. As an honorary title the word survives to the present day in the Orthodox and *Uniat Patriarchates of Antioch.

In the W. they are first mentioned in 439 at the Council of Riez. They were numerous in missionary districts in Germany in the 8th cent., but became unpopular in the 9th when they sought to extend their authority, and finally disappeared in the 12th cent. Their administrative authority passed to the archdeacon; their liturgical functions were continued by mitred abbots.

D. *Petavius, 'De Chorepiscopis', append. to *Haer.*, lxix, in his ed. of *Epiphanius, *Opera* (1622, ii, pp. 276–82; *PG*, xlii, 1045–54). H. Bergère, *Étude historique sur les chorévêques* (thesis, Paris; 1905); C. J. *Hefele-H. *Leclercq, O.S.B., *Histoire des conciles*, ii (pt. 2; 1908), pp. 1197–1237 ('La Législation conciliaire relative aux chorévêques'); T. Gottlob, *Der abendländische Chorepiskopat* (Kanonistische Studien und Texte, i; 1928). J. Parisot, O.S.B., 'Les Chorévêques' in *Revue de l'Orient Chrétien*, vi (1901), pp. 157–71 and 419–43. H. Leclercq in *D.A.C.L.*, iii (pt. 1; 1913), cols. 1423–53, s.v. 'Chorévêques', with good bibl., and A. M. Koeniger in *L.Th.K.*, ii (1931), col. 893 f., s.v. 'Chorbischof'.

CHRISM (Gk. χρῖσμα, from χρίω, 'anoint'). A mixture of olive oil and balsam, used in the ritual of the Greek and Latin Churches. The use of special oils for liturgical functions such as the consecration of priests and kings was familiar in the OT. The practice was taken over by the early Church, and its use in *Baptism and *Confirmation is attested by several early Fathers, e.g. *Tertullian, St. *Ambrose, and *Theodoret. St. *Cyril of Jerusalem refers to it as 'the mystic chrism' (τὸ μυστικὸν χρῖσμα), and the Council of *Laodicea as 'holy chrism'. To St. *Augustine Confirmation is the 'Sacrament of the Chrism', to which a special power is attributed, conferred by the Holy Ghost, while the *Apostolic Constitutions name it 'the strength of confessors' and St. *Gregory the Great the 'chrism of salvation'. The strength-giving richness of the oil and the fragrance of the balsam, representing the fullness of sacramental grace and the gifts of the Holy Ghost as well as the sweetness of Christian virtue, made it a favourite subject of allegorical interpretation to *Dionysius the Areopagite and later writers. The early Schoolmen held that the chrism was a purely ecclesiastical institution, but St. *Thomas Aquinas and *Duns Scotus both teach that its liturgical use, though not mentioned in the NT, goes back to Christ Himself. The Council of *Trent followed this view, claiming for it the support of early authorities such as Pope *Fabian (d. 250). The texts adduced, however, have since been recognised as apocryphal, and the supposed institution of the chrism by Christ is still a matter of dispute among RC theologians.

Of the two ingredients required for the Chrism oil is the older element, whereas the first known mention of balsam occurs in the 6th cent. Both are alluded to in the *Gelasian and *Gregorian Sacramentaries. In the E. Churches a large variety of perfumes is used in addition to balsam. From the early Middle Ages chrism is distinguished from the other holy oils, e.g. that used for the unction of the sick, to which balsam is not added. Only bishops have the right to consecrate the chrism, as is already stated by the Second Council of *Carthage (390; can. 3), an injunction repeated by several later Councils. In the E. Churches it became the privilege of the *Patriarchs only. By the end of the 5th cent. the rite of its consecration had developed into a very impressive ceremony. Acc. to the present Latin usage, which dates in its essentials from the 8th cent., it is consecrated by the bishop assisted by 12 priests, 7 deacons, and 7 subdeacons, on *Maundy Thursday at High Mass after the Communion.

Chrism is used in the three Sacraments that confer a *character, viz. at Baptism, Confirmation, and Holy Orders, as well as at the consecration of churches, altars, chalices, and patens, and in the solemn blessing of baptismal water and of church bells.

Current RC legislation in *C.I.C.*, cann. 734 f., 780 f., and 945 f. P. Hofmeister, O.S.B., *Die heiligen Öle in der morgen- und abendländischen Kirche* (Das östliche Christen-

tum, N.F. Hftt. 6–7; Würzburg, 1948). L. Eisenhofer, *Handbuch der katholischen Liturgik*, i (1932), pp. 308–17. P. Morrison in *C.E.*, ii (1908), p. 696 f., s.v.; P. Bernard in *D.T.C.*, ii (1905), cols. 2395–2414, s.v. 'Chrême (saint)'; F. *Cabrol, O.S.B., in *D.A.C.L.*, vi (pt. 2; 1925), cols. 2777–91, s.v. 'Huile'.

CHRISMATORY. A small vessel, in use since the Middle Ages, for keeping the three kinds of holy oils, viz. oil of the catechumens, oil of the sick, and *chrism, from which last the name is derived. Of the vessels used for these oils one set, preserving the supply for the year, is kept in the sacristy of the cathedral. Another set containing oil for parochial use is kept in a locked cupboard in the chancel of the parish church.

CHRISOM. See *Chrysom*.

CHRIST (Gk. χριστός, lit. the 'Anointed One'). The word is the Gk. translation of the Heb. '*Messiah' (q.v. for the development of the conception among the Jews and in the early Church). Orig. a title, it very soon came to be used by the followers of the risen Jesus as a proper name for their Lord (e.g. Gal. 1. 6, Heb. 9. 11), so much so that they themselves came to be known as '*Christians' (q.v.) before long. In early Christian theology, the name was at first employed to emphasise the Lord's position as the fulfilment of the Old Israel, e.g. in St. *Paul's contrast between *Adam and Christ as the 'Old' and the 'New Man'; but here again it soon lost its OT associations and was used purely as a proper name. See also *Jesus Christ*; and for the growth of the doctrine of the Person of Christ see *Christology*.

Editors and G. F. Moore (cf. p. 346 n.) in F. J. Foakes Jackson–K. *Lake, *The Beginnings of Christianity*, I, i (1920), pp. 346–68; E. De W. Burton, *Galatians* (I.C.C., 1921), pp. 392–9. W. Bauer, *Griechisch-deutsches Wörterbuch zu den Schriften des Neuen Testaments und der übrigen urchristlichen Literatur* (ed. 4, 1952), cols. 1609–11, s.v. Ἀριστός'. A. Romeo in *E.C.*, iv (1950), cols. 918–21.

CHRIST, Disciples of. See *Disciples of Christ*.

CHRIST THE KING, Feast of. The Feast observed in the RC Church on the last Sunday of October in celebration of the all-embracing authority of Christ which shall lead mankind to seek the 'peace of Christ' in the 'Kingdom of Christ'. It was instituted by *Pius XI in the encyclical *Quas primas* of 11 Dec. 1925 at the close of the *Jubilee Year. In the RC calendar it ranks as a '*double of the first class'. It is also kept unofficially in some Anglican churches.

Text of *Quas primas*, in *A.A.S.*, xvii (1925), pp. 593–610.

CHRIST CHURCH, OXFORD. This, the largest college in the University of Oxford, was founded in 1525 by T. *Wolsey as 'Cardinal College', and, seven years later, refounded as 'King *Henry the Eighth's

College'. In 1545 the latter was dissolved and in 1546 reconstituted in substantially its present form as Christ Church ('Aedes Christi') by Henry VIII. At the same time the new episcopal see was moved from Oseney Abbey to the adjacent church of St. Frideswide, which thus became both a cathedral and a college chapel, and the whole establishment was placed under a Dean and eight Canons. The number of canonries is now six, of which five are attached to professorships in the faculty of theology.

H. L. Thompson, *Christ Church* (1900); S. A. Warner, *Oxford Cathedral* (1924); E. W. Watson, *The Cathedral Church of Christ in Oxford* (1935); W. G. Hiscock, *A Christ Church Miscellany* (1946).

CHRISTADELPHIANS. A Christian sect. They were originally called 'Thomasites' after John Thomas (1805–71), who founded them in America in 1848. The name 'Christadelphians' ('Christ's brethren') was Thomas's substitute for 'Christian', which term he rejected, teaching that the beliefs and religious development which it connoted constituted an apostasy. He claimed to return to the beliefs and practice of the earliest disciples. Christadelphian doctrines include the acceptance of the Bible as inspired and infallible, and the interpretation of Hebrew prophecy and, e.g. the Book of Revelation in terms of current and future events. The doctrine of the Trinity is rejected. The core of the Gospel is belief in the return of Jesus Christ in power and great glory to set up a visible world-wide theocracy beginning at Jerusalem, and assurance of this is held to be necessary to salvation. Christadelphians also hold no form of Baptism to be valid except immersion, that the wicked will be annihilated, and that the unconverted, the ignorant, and infants will not be raised from the dead. They have no ministers or clergy. The sect publishes no statistics as to its membership.

R. Roberts, *Dr. Thomas*. His Life and Work (1884). F. J. Powicke in *H.E.R.E.*, iii (1910), pp. 569–71, s.v.

CHRISTIAN. The name was orig. applied to followers of Christ by outsiders, being first used, acc. to Acts 11. 26, at *Antioch c. A.D. 40–44. In the NT it occurs in only two other places, in Acts 26. 28 where it is used by King Agrippa speaking to St. *Paul, and in 1 Pet. 4. 16, where its use by enemies or persecutors is envisaged. Acc. to *Tacitus (*Annals*, xv, 44) it was already current among the populace at Rome at the time of the *Neronian persecution (A.D. 64) and it was always the official Roman designation of members of the Church; thus during times of persecution it was often the confession or denial of this name which was crucial, e.g. in the cases reported by *Pliny (q.v.). The form of the word, parallel to, e.g., 'Herodians' (Mk. 12. 13, &c.) and 'Caesarians' (supporters or clients of Caesar), shows that 'Christ' was taken as a proper name, in ignorance of its significance as the title of the Messiah, and has also been thought to indicate

that Christianity was considered as a quasi-political movement. Owing to its pagan origin the word was long avoided by Christian writers, except in reference to conflict with paganism. Thus in 1 Pet. 4. 16 the readers are bidden not to be ashamed of suffering on the charge of being a 'Christian', and St. *Ignatius of Antioch writing of his approaching martyrdom says 'let me not merely be called "Christian" but be found one' (Ign. *Rom.* iii, 2). By pagans the name 'Christus' was often confused with 'chrestus' (χρηστός, good, kind) and hence the form 'Chrestiani' was used. The *Apologists (e.g. *Tertullian, *Apol.* iii and v) retorted that this, though a misunderstanding, was a true indication of the character of Christianity and that the name 'Christian' stood for nothing worthy of punishment. As the name for which the martyrs suffered (cf. Lk. 21. 12) and as containing the name of Christ, the term easily came to fill the obvious need for a proper name by which the Church could designate itself as distinct from Jews and pagans (and later from Moslems, etc.), rather than the earlier terms 'brethren' (Acts 1. 16), 'disciples' (Acts 11. 26), 'believers' (Acts 2. 44), and others found in the NT.

In modern times the name Christian has usually been claimed by every form of belief stemming from historic Christianity, and has tended, in nominally Christian countries, to lose any credal significance and imply only that which is ethically praiseworthy (e.g. 'a Christian action') or socially customary ('Christian name'). It was disclaimed, as too narrow, by some *Unitarians in the 19th cent., though claimed by the main Unitarian tradition. On the other hand, it has been occasionally adopted in a particular sense by sects which claim to practise mere 'New Testament Christianity' and reject denominational labels (e.g. *Bible Christians).

R. A. *Lipsius, *Ueber den Ursprung und den ältesten Gebrauch des Christennamens* (Jena, 1873). J. B. *Lightfoot, *The Apostolic Fathers*, Pt. II, S. Ignatius and S. Polycarp, i (1885), pp. 400–4. E. Peterson, 'Christianus' in *Miscellanea Giovanni Mercati*, i (Studi e Testi, cxxi; 1946), pp. 356–72; E. J. Bickerman, 'The Name of Christians' in *H.T.R.*, xlii (1949), pp. 109–24. S. C. Gayford in *H.D.B.*, i (1898), pp. 384–6, s.vv.; H. *Leclercq, O.S.B., in *D.A.C.L.*, iii (pt. 1; 1913), cols. 1464–78, s.v. 'Chrétien', with bibl.

CHRISTIAN LIBRARY, The. The collection of fifty spiritual books which J. *Wesley selected and reissued in handy form to meet the devotional and intellectual needs of his followers. It was published in 1749–55.

CHRISTIAN MAJESTY, His Most (Lat. *Rex Christianissimus*). A title belonging to the Kings of France, and from 1464 invariably used by the Popes in addressing them.

CHRISTIAN SCIENCE. The tenets of a religious body concerned chiefly with the propagation of faith healing. It was founded by Mrs. Mary Baker Eddy (1821–1910), a native of New Hampshire and of *Calvinistic origin. Having been subject from her youth to various ailments, generally held to have been of a hysterical nature, she believed she was healed by a mesmerist, P. P. Quimby, recommended to her by her second husband. After Quimby's death (1866) she began to develop her own system of faith healing, built on the principle that mind is the only reality and matter an illusion. She maintained that Christ had healed by His spiritual influence, and this art she claimed to have recovered. In her famous *Science and Health* (1875), which had an immense success and went through many editions, she stated her principles and her healing methods. Suffering and death are the effects of false thinking, which consists in a mistaken belief in the existence of matter. Health, therefore, is to be restored not by medical treatment but by opposing right thinking to the illusions of the patient. After her third marriage, in 1877, to Mr. Eddy, an experienced business man, the body began to flourish. In 1879 the 'First Church of Christ Scientist' was opened in Boston, Mass., and in 1881 the 'Metaphysical College' followed. From that time Christian Science spread esp. in the English-speaking countries, and also in Germany. The other writings of Mrs. Eddy include *Unity of Good and Unreality of Evil* (1887) and *Retrospection and Introspection* (1891).

Since the death of the foundress the organization has been in the hands of a board of directors, who hold their office for life and appoint their successors. Their leading publication, the *Christian Science Monitor*, a well-informed newspaper, is one of their principal assets. The 'Christian Science' services are very simple, consisting chiefly in the reading from the Bible and the works of Mary Baker Eddy, the singing of hymns, and accounts of cures by members of the congregation. The principles of 'Christian Science' are not admitted by the Christian Churches and sects. Its teaching on the unreality of matter, sin, and suffering conflicts with the fundamental Biblical doctrines of the Creation, Fall, and Redemption. While its claim to cure disease by spiritual means is justified in certain cases, the universal applicability of its methods is not admitted outside the body of Christian Scientists.

M. C. Sturge, *The Truth and Error of Christian Science* (1903). G. Milmine, *The Life of Mary Baker G. Eddy and the History of Christian Science* (1909). S. Paget, *The Faith and Works of Christian Science* (1909) is a criticism of the system from the medical point of view. H. A. L. Fisher, *Our New Religion* (1933), criticizes both the life and character of the foundress and her work and gives much detailed information.

CHRISTIAN SOCIALISM. A movement for social reform initiated in the 19th cent. by members of the C of E. It arose as a reaction against the hostility of the 18th cent. Established Church towards the discussion of social questions and was directed esp. against the *Utilitarian and laissez-faire doctrines of J. Bentham, J. and J. S. Mill, and their school. The system aimed at a combined reform of

individuals and of society by the application of Christian principles in all social relationships, and came into prominence by the issue of a manifesto to the workmen of England on the morrow of the failure of the Chartist Movement in 1848. Its best-known leaders were J. M. F. *Ludlow, F. D. *Maurice, C. *Kingsley, and Thomas Hughes. Their short-lived periodical, *Politics for the People*, though very moderate in its descriptions of the social injustices of the time, roused much opposition and had soon to be abandoned for lack of support. After the failure of the paper the group of friends, which soon found a wider circle of sympathizers, began to organize evening classes, which gradually developed into their 'Working Men's College', a centre established in Great Ormond Street in 1854. They also engaged in practical relief work and, in 1850, backed by a 'Society of Promoters', opened co-operative workshops for tailoring, building, iron-founding, and other crafts. In the same year they began to publish *Tracts on Christian Socialism*, which, like *Politics for the People*, met with much hostility. The eventual failure of the movement may be attributed not only to the indifference of the official C of E but also to the unresponsiveness of the workers themselves and to the absorption of public interest by the Crimean War. Its work, however, marked the beginning of the modern social movement in the C of E and had much influence in the formation of the trade unions, in early co-operative legislation, and in working-class education.

A. V. Woodworth, *Christian Socialism in England* (1903). C. E. Raven, *Christian Socialism, 1848–1854* (1920). G. C. Binyon, *The Christian Socialist Movement in England* (1931). M. B. Reckitt, *Faith and Society*. A Study of the Structure, Outlook and Opportunity of the Christian Social Movement in Great Britain and America (1932).

CHRISTIAN YEAR, The. The collection of poems for the Sundays and holy days of the year, by J. *Keble, published in 1827. It was very popular throughout the 19th cent., and several well-known hymns have been taken from it (e.g. *Eng. Hym.* Nos. 216, 370).

CHRISTINA (1626–89), Queen of *Sweden. The only surviving child of *Gustavus Adolphus and Maria Eleonora of Brandenburg, she succeeded to the Swedish throne at the age of 6 on her father's death at the Battle of Lützen (1632). Until 1644 the government was in the hands of a Council of Regency, presided over by the chancellor, Axel Oxenstierna, and Christina, who was given a boy's education, received instruction in politics (from Oxenstierna), ancient and modern languages, and philosophy (from Johannes Matthiae, Bp. of Strängnäs). Throughout her life she continued a masterful, but tireless, student. After assuming the direction of affairs on her 18th birthday (8 Dec. 1644), she made it her first aim to end the *Thirty Years War and was largely responsible for the Treaty of *Westphalia (1648). At home she actively promoted education, increasing and improving the schools and colleges founded by Gustavus and bringing into effect the first school ordinance for the whole kingdom (1649). She also sought to encourage learning by the patronage of foreign scholars, artists, and scientists, among them R. *Descartes, H. *Grotius, G. J. *Voss, S. *Pufendorf, Olaus Rudbecks (discoverer of the lymphatic vessels), and J. A. *Comenius, who helped her with her school reforms.

Religious interest in the RC faith, combined with dislike of the monotony of rule and her Council's repeated requests that she should marry, made her suggest abdication as early as 1651. On 6 June 1654, largely through disagreements with her foreign policy (proposed alliances with Spain) and misgivings at her growing extravagance, the Council accepted her resignation. In Nov. 1655, she was received into the RC Church at Innsbruck by L. *Holste and settled in *Rome with her home first at the Palazzo Farnese and from 1668 at the Palazzo Riario. Her allegiance to her new faith, although absolute, was never blind. She made repeated attempts to lessen the penalties imposed by the *Inquisition, and in a letter to Chevalier de Terlon on the Revocation of the Edict of *Nantes, dated 3 Feb. 1686, she criticized the use of force ('military men are strange apostles'). At Rome she became the centre of a group of intellectuals, later known as the 'Arcadia Academy', who aimed at purifying poetry.

After her abdication she twice attempted (1660; 1667) to resume the Swedish crown, intrigued with J. *Mazarin to become ruler of the Spanish kingdom of Naples, and, on the abdication of John Casimir of Vasa (1668), sought the crown of Poland; but her efforts to regain political power were unsuccessful. As she advanced in years she became increasingly eccentric. She died at Rome, leaving Cardinal Azzolini her chief heir. There is a monument to her memory in *St. Peter's.

Christina left, in French highly praised by Descartes, some fragmentary writings of her own (autobiography; reflexions on Alexander the Great and Julius Caesar; some detached aphorisms). Her intellectual gifts were celebrated in verse by Andrew Marvell and J. *Milton, and she endeavoured, through Whitelock, to persuade Milton to visit her court. She made a collection of MSS., consisting of works on theology, Church history, philosophy, civil law, and medicine which are deservedly famous and have been incorporated in the *Vatican Library ('Reginenses').

J. Arckenholtz, *Mémoires concernant Christine, reine de Suède* (4 vols., Amsterdam, 1751–60), incl. some of her works and letters, with her autobiography in vol. iii, pp. 1–69; Eng. tr. of some of her Works (London, 1753), with account of her Life, Character, and Writings by the translator, pp. iii–xx. F. W. Bain, *Christina, Queen of Sweden* (1890 [1889]); I. A. Taylor, *Christina of Sweden* (1909). C. Weibull, *Drottning Christina*. Studier och Forskingar (1934); id., *Drottning Christina och Monaldesco* (1936). J. Castelnau, *Christine, reine de Suède, 1626–1689* (1944). C. N. D. de Bildt, *Christine de Suède et le cardinal Azzolino*

Lettres inédites, 1666–1668, avec introduction et des notes (1899); id. *Christine de Suède et le Conclave de Clement X., 1669–1670* (1906). G. Claretta, *La regina Cristina di Svezia in Italia, 1655–1689* (1892). J. d'Orliac, *Christine de Suède, la reine chaste et folle* [1934]. G. B. *Pitra–H. Stevenson, *Codices Manuscripti Graeci Reginae Suecorum et Pii PP. II* (Bibliothecae Apostolicae Vaticanae Codices Manuscripti Recensiti iubente Leone XIII; Rome, 1888).

CHRISTKATHOLIKEN. The official name of the *Old Catholics of Switzerland. The 'Christkatholische Kirche der Schweiz' was formally founded at a synod at Olten in 1875.

CHRISTMAS. Though speculation as to the time of year of Christ's Birth dates from the early 3rd cent., *Clement of Alexandria, e.g., suggesting 20 May, the celebration of the anniversary does not appear to have been general till the later 4th cent. The earliest mention of the observance on 25 Dec. is in the *Philocalian Calendar, representing Roman practice of the year 336 (25 Dec.: *natus Christus in Betleem Judeae*). This date was prob. chosen to oppose the feast of the *Natalis Solis Invicti* by the celebration of the birth of the 'Sun of Righteousness', and its observance in the W. seems to have spread from Rome. In the E. the closely related Feast of the *Epiphany (6 Jan.), which commemorated also the Baptism of Christ, was at first the more important; but in the later 4th cent. it was connected with the Nativity, esp. in Syria, and by the middle of the 5th cent. most of the E. had adopted 25 Dec., though the Church of *Jerusalem held to 6 Jan. until 549. In the *Armenian Church 6 Jan. is still observed as Christmas Day. The controversies of the 4th to 6 cents. on the Incarnation and the Person of Christ doubtless contributed to the growth in importance of the feast.

The day is celebrated in the W. rite by three Masses, of the night (normally said at midnight), of the dawn, and of the day, which have been held to symbolize the threefold birth of Christ, eternally in the bosom of the Father, from the womb of the Virgin Mary, and mystically in the soul of the faithful. The BCP provides a Proper *Preface.

The popular observance of the feast has always been marked by the joy and merrymaking formerly characteristic of the Roman *Saturnalia* and the other pagan festivals it replaced. It developed considerably in England in the 19th cent. through the importation of German customs by the Prince Consort (e.g. Christmas trees) and the influence of Charles Dickens.

L. *Duchesne, *Origines du culte chrétien* (1889), pp. 247–54 (Eng. tr. of ed. 3, 1903, pp. 257–65). H. Usener, *Das Weihnachtsfest* 1889; ed. 2 by H. *Lietzmann, 1911); B. Botte, O.S.B., *Les Origines de la Noël et de l'Épiphanie* (1932). H. Frank, O.S.B., 'Zur Geschichte von Weihnachten und Epiphanie' in *J.L.W.*, xii ('1932'; publd. 1934), pp. 145–55; xiii ('1933'; 1935), pp. 1–38; id., 'Frühgeschichte und Ursprung des römischen Weihnachtsfestes im Lichte neuerer Forschung' in *Archiv für Liturgiewissenschaft*, ii (1952), pp. 1–24; H. Engberding, O.S.B., 'Der 25. Dezember als Tag der Feier der Geburt des Herrn', ib., pp. 25–43. C. A. Miles, *Christmas in Ritual and Tradition, Christian and Pagan* (1912). G. Rietschel in *P.R.E.* (ed. 3), xxi (1908), pp. 47–54, s.v. 'Weihnachten', with full bibl. to date; C. Martindale, S.J., in *C.E.*, iii (1908), pp. 724–8; K. *Lake in *H.E.R.E.*, iii (1910), pp. 601–8; H. *Leclercq, O.S.B., in *D.A.C.L.*, xii (pt. 1; 1935), cols. 905–58, (esp. 910–34), s.v. 'Nativité de Jésus'.

CHRISTOCENTRIC. (1) A word originally used of systems of theology which maintain that God has never revealed Himself to man except in the Incarnate Christ. Christocentric theology bases itself on a literal interpretation of Mt. 11. 27, to the exclusion of the passages in Scripture which seem to refer to or imply a revelation in nature, and thus precludes the possibility of *natural theology altogether. Among its modern advocates are A. *Ritschl, W. *Herrmann, and K. *Barth.

(2) More generally, of any set of religious beliefs which is focused primarily on the Person of Christ.

CHRISTOLOGY. The study of the Person of Christ, and in particular of the union in Him of the Divine and human natures. The NT presents the facts about His Person rather than any attempted explanations of them, but the Gospels indicate that the historical Christ claimed to be both God and Man, and from the Acts and Epistles it is clear that the earliest Christians regarded Him as such. The task of later Christological speculation was to work out and express in precise terms the theological truth therein implied. St. *Paul and the earliest writers were more concerned to insist on the reality of both the Godhead and the manhood (cf. 1 Cor. 15. 1 ff. with Col. 1. 15–20) than to attempt to interrelate them. It was only when one-sided distortions of the truth had come into being, such as the *Ebionite view which conceived of Christ as the Jewish (human) Messiah, to the neglect of His divinity, and the *Gnostic view that the Incarnation was purely an appearance of God, without real assumption of humanity, that the *Apologists of the 2nd cent. were at pains to begin elaborating the philosophical implications of the Incarnation. In their writings they developed the *Logos doctrine put forth in St. *John (1. 1–18), contending that the Word, Who is the eternal expression of God, appeared on earth in history as Jesus Christ, so that the Incarnation is, at least from one point of view, the expression in time of an eternal relationship which exists within the Godhead. St. *Irenaeus of Lyons worked this conception out, and added the idea of *Recapitulation, that Christ not only expresses God in time, but sums up humanity in Himself.

In the next period the great difference between the orthodox, if sometimes incomplete, expressions of faith and those of the heresiarchs lay in the fact that the orthodox kept within the terms of these data, while their opponents went outside them, either by failing to maintain the unity and distinctness of the Person of the Son, or the reality either of His divinity or His humanity. *Arius (256–336), contending for the unity of the Godhead, denied that the Son is truly God; and striving

to uphold the unity of Christ's historical experience, denied that there are two natures in Christ, asserting instead that the nature of the Son took the place of the human soul in the historical Christ. The Creed which was adopted by the Council of *Nicaea in 325 replied to these views by the phrases, 'Being of one substance with the Father' (ὁμοούσιος τῷ πατρί) and 'became man' (ἐνανθρωπήσας). *Apollinarius (d. *c.* 390), while like Arius he attempted to uphold a single nature in Christ, was esp. concerned to maintain the Godhead of Christ, and so asserted that the Divine nature took the place of His human spirit, or in other words that His humanity consisted in the purely animal elements present in human nature. On the other hand, *Theodore of Mopsuestia (d. 428), and his pupil *Nestorius (d. after 439), as good *Antiochenes, were so concerned to preserve the reality of Christ's purely human experience that they separated the divinity and humanity in Him almost to the point of making Him into two Persons. The Council of *Ephesus in 431 condemned this view, asserting that He who was born of Mary is God. Then *Eutyches (d. after 454) maintained that though in Christ there were two natures 'before the Incarnation', there was only one 'after the Incarnation', thereby developing the view of *Origen that the union of human and Divine took place in a pre-existent state, but adding to this questionable view the theologically unsatisfactory theory of the coalescence of the two natures into one. This and the earlier heresies the Council of *Chalcedon (451) excluded by holding 'one . . . Christ . . . in two natures, without confusion, without change, without division, without separation'. In spite of this definition, the next two centuries saw the wide prevalence of *Monophysitism, as well as of *Monothelitism, teaching which was condemned in the 2nd and 3rd Councils of *Constantinople (553 and 680 respectively). In this period *Leontius of Byzantium (d. *c.* 543) insisted on the *Enhypostasia as expressing the union of two natures in one person, without either dividing the personality or destroying the distinct characteristics of the other.

At the Reformation *Lutheranism tended to emphasize the unity of Christ's Person, and to argue that His assumption of humanity meant simply that He abstained, except on rare occasions, from the use of Divine attributes, a view which might, if logically pressed, have led back to Apollinarianism; the *Reformed theologians, on the other hand, stressed the difference between the Divine and the human, though a return to *Nestorianism was largely prevented by the acceptance of various *Kenotic theories which eventually grew up. Among other modern theories are that of F. D. E. *Schleiermacher (1768–1834), acc. to which the Divinity of Christ lies in the *consciousness* of a unique relation to God, and that of the *Ritschlian school to the effect that the statement that the historical Person, Jesus Christ, is Divine is a value-judgement rather than a judgement of fact. There was also the view of W. *Sanday (1843–1920) that the characteristics of Deity were present in the subconscious mind of Christ in His Incarnate life, and only appeared to the conscious mind by the normal processes of the development of human consciousness. See also *Incarnation*; *Hypostasis*; and *Hypostatic Union*.

Among the more important modern works in English are R. I. *Wilberforce, *The Doctrine of the Incarnation* (1848); *Lux Mundi*, ed. C. Gore (1889); C. Gore, *The Incarnation of the Son of God* (Bampton Lectures, 1891); Id., *Dissertations* (1895); R. L. Ottley, *The Doctrine of the Incarnation* (2 vols., 1896); A. J. Mason, *The Conditions of Our Lord's Life on Earth* (1896); F. *Weston, *The One Christ* (1907); W. *Sanday, *Christologies, Ancient and Modern* (1910); H. R. Mackintosh, *The Person of Jesus Christ* (1912); F. *Loofs, *What is the Truth about Jesus Christ?* (1913); H. M. Relton, *A Study in Christology* (1917); C. Gore, *Belief in Christ* (1922); W. *Temple, *Christus Veritas* (1924); S. Cave, *The Doctrine of the Person of Christ* (1925); *Essays on the Trinity and the Incarnation*, ed. A. E. J. Rawlinson (1928); L. Hodgson, *And Was Made Man* (1928); L. S. Thornton, C.R., *The Incarnate Lord* (1928); H. *Rashdall, *God and Man* (1930); E. *Brunner, *The Mediator* (Eng. trans., 1934); J. K. Mozley, *The Doctrine of the Incarnation* (1936); J. M. Creed, *The Divinity of Jesus Christ* (1938); R. V. Sellers, *Two Ancient Christologies* (1940); E. L. Mascall, *Christ, the Christian and the Church* (1946); D. M. Baillie, *God was in Christ* (1948).

CHRISTOPHER, St. (Gk. Χριστοφόρος, 'one who bore Christ'), one of the 14 *auxiliary saints. Acc. to tradition, he suffered martyrdom in Asia Minor during the 3rd cent. Many legends have gathered round his name. One represents him as a powerful giant who earned his living by carrying travellers across a river, and on one occasion numbered among his passengers a small child who caused him to bow beneath his burden, since the child was none other than the Christ and His weight that of the whole world. It was a common medieval custom to place a large mural painting of the saint opposite the south door of the church, in the belief that the sight of it would safeguard the passer-by from accident that day. St. Christopher is the patron of wayfarers; recently he has been adopted esp. by motorists. Feast day, 25 July.

Various Gk. and Lat. texts of legend in *AA.SS.*, Jul. VI (1729), pp. 125–49, in *Anal. Boll.*, i (1882), pp. 121–48, and x (1891), pp. 393–405, and in H. Usener (ed.), *Acta S. Marinae et S. Christophori* (Bonn, 1886), pp. 54–76. K. Richter, *Der deutsche S. Christoph. Eine historisch-kritische Untersuchung* (1896). F. Mainguet, *Saint Christophe. Sa vie et son culte* (1891). H. F. [C.] Rosenfeld, *Der hl. Christophorus. Seine Verehrung und seine Legende* (Acta Academiae Aboensis, Humaniora, x, No. 3; 1937). E. K. Stahl, *Die Legende vom heil. Riesen Christophorus in der Graphik des 15. und 16. Jahrhunderts* (1920); H. C. Whaite, *St. Christopher in English Mediaeval Wall-painting* (University College (London), Monographs on English Mediaeval Art, i; 1929). C. Johnson, *St. Christopher. The Patron Saint of Travellers* (1936). R. Hindringer in *L.Th.K.*, ii (1931), cols. 934–6, s.v. 'Christophorus', with bibl.

CHRISTOPHERSON, JOHN (d. 1558), Bp. of *Chichester. He was one of the original Fellows of Trinity College by the charter of 1546, and among the first to introduce Greek studies to Cambridge. As an opponent of the Reformation he retired abroad during *Edward VI's reign, but his college continued to support him. When on Mary's accession William Bill, a pronounced

Protestant, was ejected from the Mastership of Trinity, Christopherson was put in to replace him; and he became chaplain and confessor to the Queen. In 1554 he was appointed Dean of Norwich and in 1557 Bp. of Chichester. For preaching a violent sermon on 27 Nov. 1558 after *Elizabeth's accession, against the Reformation, he was imprisoned and died shortly afterwards. He was a learned and enthusiastic Patristic scholar who rendered into Latin the writings of *Philo (*Philonis Judaei Scriptoris eloquentissimi libri iv*, Antwerp, 1553) as well as the Church Histories of *Eusebius, *Socrates, *Sozomen, *Evagrius, and *Theodoret (published posthumously, Louvain, 1570). He also collected a considerable number of MSS. which he bequeathed to Trinity College.

T. Cooper in *D.N.B.*, x (1887), pp. 293–5, s.v., with reff.

CHRISTOPHORIA (Gk.), 'the carrying of Christ.' In the *Ambrosian rite, the title of a Feast observed on 7 Jan., the day following the *Epiphany, and commemorating the Return from Egypt (Mt. 2. 21).

CHRISTOPOLITES. See *Bogomiles*.

CHRODEGANG, St. (d. 766), Bp. of Metz from 742. He was one of the chief ecclesiastical reformers of his time. A relation of King *Pepin, he became private secretary, chancellor, and chief minister to *Charles Martel, offices which he retained after he became Bp. of Metz. In 748 he founded the abbey of Gorze, near Metz, and continued to take a keen part in furthering monasticism throughout his diocese. He also caused the canons of his cathedral to live a community life, drawing up for them the 'rule' which bears his name (c. 755). The picture given by this rule is that of a community consisting essentially of clerics, monastic in their common life and in the performance of the Divine Office, but unmonastic in their close connexion with diocesan officials such as the bishop and archdeacon, and, above all, in their licence to hold private property. He also introduced the Roman chant and liturgy into the diocese of Metz. Feast day, 6 Mar.

'Rule' repr. from L. *d'Achéry in J. P. Migne, *PL*, lxxxix, 1057–96; crit. ed. from Leyden Cod. Voss. Lat 94 by W. Schmitz (Hanover, 1889). Early Eng. tr., together with Lat. text, ed. A. S. Napier in *E.E.T.S.* Original Series, cl (1916), pp. 1–101, with introd., pp. vii–x. A. Werminghoff, 'Die Recensionen der Regula Chrodegangi' in *N.A.*, xxvii (1902), pp. 646–51. Life ascribed to John, Abbot of Gortz (historically valueless), ed. G. H. Pertz in *M.G.H.*, Scriptores, x (1852), pp. 552–72. Of more importance is relevant section of Paul Warnefridi's *Liber de Episcopis Mettensis* ed. G. H. Pertz in *M.G.H.*, Scriptores, ii (1829), p. 267 f. M. Buchner, 'Die "Vita Chrodegangi"—eine kirchenpolitische Tendenzschrift aus der Mitte des 9. Jahrhunderts, zugleich eine Untersuchung zur Entwicklung der Primatial- und Vikariatsidee' in *Zeitschrift der Savigny-Stiftung für Rechtsgeschichte.* Kanonistische Abt., xvi (1927), pp. 1–36, with reff. to earlier studies. A. Sturm in *L.Th.K.*, ii (1931), col. 944, s.v. T. de Morembert in *D.H.G.E.*, xii (1953), cols. 781–4, s.v., with bibl.

CHROMATIUS, St. (d. 407), Bp. of Aquileia, N. Italy. He succeeded Valerian in the see *c.* 388. A learned scholar, he conducted an active correspondence with several illustrious contemporaries, among them St. *Ambrose, St. *Jerome, and *Rufinus. In the *Origenistic dispute he sought to mediate between the two last named. He was a strong supporter of St. John *Chrysostom on whose behalf he interceded, without success, with the Emp. Honorius. Eighteen of his Homilies on Mt. [3. 15–17; 5. 1–6. 24], including a separate treatise on the Eight Beatitudes, have survived. Feast day, 2 Dec.

His Works are repr., mainly from the text ed. P. Braida, Udine, 1816, in J. P. Migne, *PL*, xx, 247–436. Bardenhewer, iii, p. 548 f. P. Paschini in *E.C.*, iv (1950), col. 1001, s.v. 'Cromazio'.

CHRONICLES, Books of. These OT Books record the history of Israel and Judah from the Creation to the return from Exile under Cyrus (536 B.C.). In the Heb. Canon they are a single Book; the division into two goes back to the *Septuagint, where they are called Παραλειπομένων α' β', i.e. 'that which is left over', *sc.* from Sam. and Kgs. The term 'Chronicles' was introduced by St. *Jerome, whence it made its way into the English and German versions. The work, which originally formed one continuous whole with the Books of *Ezra and *Nehemiah, is divided into four parts. 1 Chr. 1–9 are genealogies from *Adam to the death of Saul; 10–29 describe the reign of *David; 2 Chr. 1–9 the reign of *Solomon; and 10–36 give a history of the kings of Judah.

Throughout the Books the interest concentrates on the religious aspects of the history, esp. the *Temple and its worship, to which is assigned a very large place. Thus the story of David is much concerned with his preparations for the building of the Temple, and the reign of Solomon with long descriptions of the Temple itself, its structure, liturgy, and personnel. With the same religious interest in view the less edifying episodes in the lives of David and Solomon are omitted, and the whole subsequent history of the kings of Judah is seen as a series of rewards and punishments acc. to their attitude to religion. The obvious aim of the work is to inculcate respect for the Law and to stress the advantages of its observance.

The sources used in Chr. are the canonical books, esp. Gen., Ex., Num., Josh., and Sam. and Kgs., but also extra-canonical material, among which the author names a 'History of the Kings of Israel and Judah' and a 'Midrash of the Kings of Israel and Judah'. Acc. to the list of high priests the book seems to have been written in the latter half of the 4th cent. B.C., a date which would agree with the fact that it is continued in Ezra and Nehemiah. On its historical value opinions are divided. The older critics, such as W. M. L. *de Wette and J. *Wellhausen, refused it all credibility, whereas recent scholars are more moderate, conceding that it used reliable information at least for the later period. Acc. to conservative

exegetes, it contains valuable material even for the earlier centuries, though all are agreed that the picture it presents of Jewish history is manipulated in the interest of religious edification.

Commentaries by W. E. Barnes (Camb. Bib. AV, 1889), E. L. Curtis–A. A. Madsen (I.C.C., 1910), W. A. L. Elmslie (Camb. Bib. RV, 1916), I. Benzinger (K.H.A.T., xx, 1901), R. Kittel (H.K.A.T., Abt. 1, Bd. vi, Theil i, 1902), N. Schlögel (Vienna, 1911), J. Hänel (2 vols., K.A.T., xviii, 1927). A. C. Welch, *The Work of the Chronicler.* Its Purpose and Date (Schweich Lectures, 1938; 1939). G. von Rad, *Das Geschichtsbild des chronistischen Werkes* (Beiträge zur Wissenschaft vom Alten und Neuen Testament, lix, Folge 4, iii, 1930). A. Noordtzij, *De Boeken der Kronieken* (2 vols., 1937–8). E. Podechard, 'Les Références du chroniqueur' in *R. Bibl.* [xxiv], N.S. xii (1915), pp. 236–247. W. F. Albright, 'The Date and Personality of the Chronicler' in *Journal of Biblical Literature*, xl (1921), pp. 104–24. A. Bea, S.J., 'Neue Arbeiten zum Problem der biblischen Chronikbücher' in *Biblica*, xxii (1941), pp. 46–58.

CHRONICON EDESSENUM (Edessene Chronicle). A Syriac Chronicle extending from 133 B.C. to A.D. 540, the date of its compilation, but with very few entries before the 3rd cent. A.D. Its principal interest lies in the history of *Edessa, but it sometimes supplies important incidental information on general history both E. and W. It appears to have been the work of an Edessene cleric of the orthodox school, but with some *Nestorian sympathies. L. Hallier argued that its principal sources were some early documents from *Antioch, a lost history of the Persians, and the Edessene city archives. It exists only in a single MS. (Cod. Vat. syr. 163), derived from the Convent of Our Lady in the Nitrian desert.

Syr. text first publd. in J. S. *Assemani, *Bibliotheca Orientalis*, i (1719), pp. 387–417. Crit. edd. by L. Hallier, with Germ. tr. and comm., in *T.U.*, ix, 1 (1892), and by I. Guidi, with Lat. tr., in C.S.C.O., 1903. A. *Baumstark, *Geschichte der syrischen Literatur* (1922), p. 99 f.

CHRONICON PASCHALE. A Byzantine chronicle compiled in the first half of the 7th cent., so named from its having been based on the Easter reckoning. It contained a chronological outline of events from the creation of Adam to the 20th year of the Emp. *Heraclius (629); but not all of it has survived. The author used *inter alia* the Easter Tables of *Alexandria, the 'Fasti Consulares', Sextus *Julius Africanus, and the 'Chronicon' of *Eusebius of Caesarea, and for the last 27 years he has the value of a contemporary historian. The principal MS. is the *Vatican cod. gr., 1941 (10th cent.).

The document is sometimes known as the 'Chronicon Alexandrinum'; it owes the name 'Paschal Chronicle' to its first editor, C. D. *Du Cange. Best ed. by L. Dindorf in C.S.H. Byz. (2 vols., 1832); repr. in J. P. Migne, *PG*, xcii, 9–1160. G. *Mercati, 'A Study of the *Paschal Chronicle*' in *J.T.S.*, vii (1906), pp. 397–412; repr. in *S.T.*, lxxvii (1937), pp. 462–79. E. *Schwartz in *P.W.*, iii (1899), cols. 2460–77, s.v.

CHRONOGRAPHER OF A.D. 354, The. The name given by T. *Mommsen to the unknown compiler of an almanac drawn up for the use of Christians at *Rome in the 4th cent. The document, devoid of literary pretensions, remains an invaluable source for the study of early ecclesiastical history. All the extant MSS. are fragments, but by piecing their witness together practically the whole document can be reconstructed. Acc. to Mommsen, these are all dependent on a now lost 'Codex Luxemburgensis'. The compilation contained *inter alia* these items: (1) a calendar of Roman holidays; (2) a list of the consuls (from A.U.C. 245 to A.D. 354); (3) an Easter Table (from A.D. 312 to 354, with an extension to A.D. 410); (4) a list of the city prefects at Rome from A.D. 254 to 354; (5) 'Depositio episcoporum', a list of the dates of death of the Bishops of Rome from A.D. 255 to 352; (6) a sort of primitive Roman *Martyrology; (7) a list of the Roman Bishops from St. *Peter down to Pope *Liberius (see *Liberian Catalogue*); (8) a chronicle based on that of St. *Hippolytus, combined with (9) a chronicle of Roman secular history from early times down to the death of the Emp. Licinius (325); (10) an account of the 14 regions of the city of Rome.

Text pr., with extended comm., in T. Mommsen, 'Über den Chronographen vom Jahre 354' in *Abh.* (Sächs.), i (1850), pp. 547–693; and again in *M.G.H.*, Auctores Antiquissimi, ix (pt. 1; 1892), pp. 13–196. C. Nordenfalk, *Der Kalender vom Jahre 354 und die lateinische Buchmalerei des iv. Jahrhunderts* (Göteborg, 1936); H. Stern, *Le Calendrier de 354*. Étude sur son texte et sur ses illustrations (Institut français d'Archéologie de Beyrout. Bibliothèque Archéologique et Historique, lv; 1953). Bardenhewer, iii, pp. 558–60. O. Seeck in *P.W.*, iii (1899), cols. 2477–81; A. Ferrua, S.J., in *E.C.*, iv (1950), cols. 1007–9, s.v. 'Cronografo dell' a. 354'. See also bibl. to *Liberian Catalogue*.

CHRONOLOGY, Biblical. (1) *Old Testament.* It is very difficult to date accurately the events which are narrated in the OT owing to (a) the absence in the ancient world of any widely recognized chronological era, and (b) the few allusions in the OT to events outside Israel known to us from extraneous sources. The Hebrew records are themselves sometimes inadequate, e.g. while the duration of the sojourn in Egypt is given (Gen. 15. 13, Ex. 12. 40–41), the names of the Pharaohs are not recorded. Among the important chronological data supplied in the OT are the interval between the *Exodus and the building of Solomon's Temple (1 Kgs. 6. 1); the duration of the wandering in the wilderness (Num. 14. 33); and the lengths of the reigns of the Kings of Israel and Judah in the Books of the Kings. But the figures supplied are not always consistent even in the Hebrew text, and there are frequent divergences in the *Septuagint. However, from the 9th cent. B.C. onwards the dates of the events narrated can be roughly discovered by comparing them with the more detailed and accurate Assyrian and Persian chronologies.

(2) *New Testament.* The range here is shorter and the problem simpler, but even so there are many difficulties. Complications are caused by the different methods by which the years of monarchs were reckoned and by the intricacies of the Jewish calendar. Acc. to Mt. 2. 1, Jesus was born 'in the days of *Herod the King' (d. *c.* 4 B.C.), but acc. to Lk. 2. 2 during 'the first enrolment made when Quirinius was governor of Syria' (probably A.D. 6–9). Jesus was baptized in 'the fifteenth year of the reign of Tiberius *Caesar' (Lk. 3. 1), i.e. in A.D. 29 or 28, while acc. to Jn. 2. 15–20 the first *Passover after His Baptism was the forty-sixth year of the building of Herod's Temple (A.D. 27). Jesus would thus be about 30 years old when He began to teach (Lk. 3. 23). The length of Christ's ministry is in the Synoptic Gospels a year, whilst the Fourth Gospel supposes at least a two-years' ministry, and there are difficulties concerning the date of the Crucifixion. However, all are agreed that Jesus 'suffered under Pontius *Pilate', who was procurator of *Judaea from A.D. 26 to 36. With regard to the chronology of the Apostolic Age, the date of St. *Paul's conversion, on which so much depends, is uncertain, in spite of the data which he supplies in Gal. 1. 18, and 2; the earliest date would be just after the Crucifixion. The concluding part of St. Paul's life is also obscure, as his death is not recorded. Nevertheless these uncertainties are of no great theological or religious moment, and if the NT dates could be determined by precision, it would hardly affect the main outlines of our picture of the course of early Christianity.

Among the first attempts to put Biblical Chronology on a sound basis was J. *Ussher, *Annales Veteris et Novi Testamenti* (2 parts, 1650–9); its dates gained wide currency through their frequent printing in the margins of the AV. A modern attempt to deal with the problems of Biblical Chronology as a whole is E. Ruffini, *Chronologia Veteris et Novi Testamenti in Aeram Nostram Collata* (Rome, 1924). On the chronology of the OT, W. *Bousset, 'Das chronologische System der biblischen Geschichtsbücher' in *Z.A.T.W.*, xx (1900), pp. 136–47; O. Fischer, 'Chronologische Studien zum Alten Testament', ib., xxxiv (1914), pp. 45–53. A. T. Richardson, *Bible Chronology* (1930). S. A. *Cook in *C. Anc. H.*, i (1923), pp. 156–66. K. Marti in *E.Bi.*, i (1899), cols. 773–99, s.v. 'Chronology, Old Testament'; L. Curtis in *H.D.B.*, i (1900), pp. 397–403, s.v. 'Chronology in the Old Testament'; S. R. *Driver in *E.B.* (ed. 11), iii (1910), pp. 865–72, s.v. 'Bible, Old Testament Chronology'; L. Pirot–V. Coucke in *Dict. Bibl.*, Suppl. i (1928), cols. 1244–79, s.v. See also bibl. to individual books. On the NT, the classical discussion is that of C. H. *Turner in *H.D.B.*, i (1900), pp. 403–25, s.v. 'Chronology in the New Testament'. U. Holzmeister, S.J., *Chronologia Vitae Christi* (Scripta Pontificii Instituti Biblici, 1936); G. Ogg, *The Chronology of the Public Ministry of Jesus* (1940). J. Lebreton, S.J., in *Dict. Bibl.*, Suppl. iv (1949), cols. 970–5, s.v. 'Jésus-Christ. Chronologie de la vie de Jésus', and F. Prat, ib., i (1928), cols. 1299–1304, s.v. See also lives of Christ and bibl. to Acts and Epp. of St. Paul. For general discussions on chronology, see bibl. to *Calendar*.

CHRYSIPPUS (*c.* 405–79), 'of Jerusalem', ecclesiastical writer. A native of Cappadocia, he accompanied his two brothers, Cosmas and Gabriel, to Jerusalem *c.* 428 and became a monk at the laura of St. *Euthymius. He was ordained priest *c.* 455 and later succeeded Cosmas as guardian of the Holy Cross at the Church of the *Holy Sepulchre ('staurophylax'). His few surviving writings include panegyrics of (1) the BVM, (2) St. Theodore Tiro, (3) St. *Michael the Archangel, and (4) St. *John Baptist.

Interest in Chrysippus is comparatively recent. The chief evidences for his life are the reff. in *Cyril of Scythopolis' 'Life of St. Euthymius'. For text of the four panegyrics mentioned above see: for (1), ed. M. Jugie, A.A., in *P.O.*, xix (1926), pp. 336–43 (a repr., with corrections, of ed.

F. *Ducaeus, 1624); for (2), ed. A. Sigalas (*Byzantinisches Archiv*, vii, 1921); for (3), ed. id. in 'Επετηρὶς 'Εταιρείας Βυζαντινῶν Σπουδῶν, iii (Athens, 1926), pp. 85–93; for (4), ed. id. (*Texte und Forschungen zur byzantinisch-neugriechischen Philologie*, xx; 1937). S. Vailhé, A.A., 'Chrysippe Prêtre de Jérusalem' in *Revue de l'Orient Chrétien*, x (1905), pp. 96–9. Altaner (ed. 1951), p. 190. A. Sigalas in *L.Th.K.*, ii (1931), col. 944; M. Jugie, A.A., in *E.C.*, iv (1950), col. 881, s.v. 'Crisippo di Gerusalemme'.

CHRYSOGONUS, St. Though his cultus
at *Rome dates from the 5th cent. at latest, very little is known of him. Acc. to legend, he was arrested in Rome during *Diocletian's persecution and subsequently slain at Aquileia. From the 6th cent. onwards he was supposed to have been the spiritual director of St. *Anastasia of Rome, with whom he is held to have corresponded on the behaviour of Christians towards their pagan husbands and wives. His name is included in the *Canon of the Roman Mass. Feast day in the E., 22 Dec.; in the W., 24 Nov.

Chief source of the legend is the 'Passio S. Anastasiae', ed. H. *Delehaye, S.J., *Étude sur le Légendier romain* (Subsidia Hagiographica, xxiii, 1936), pp. 221–49; cf. also pp. 151–63. On the theory that Chrysogonus was orig. the owner of a church in Rome (*titulus Chrysogoni*), the name being later misunderstood as a dedication, cf. J. P. Kirsch, *Die römischen Titelkirchen im Altertum* (1918), pp. 108–13. M. Mesnard, *La Basilique de saint Chrysogone à Rome* (Studi di Antichità Cristiana, IX, 1935); V. L. Kennedy, C.S.B., *The Saints of the Canon of the Mass* (id., XIV, 1938), pp. 128–30, with further bibl. reff.

CHRYSOLOGUS, St. PETER (c. 400–
450), Bp. of *Ravenna. He preached his first sermon as bishop in the presence of the Empress *Galla Placidia, and thenceforward received her continuous support for his ambitious building projects. A large collection of sermons attributed to him survives, but almost all his other writings are lost. In a letter to *Eutyches (449) he viewed his case with favour, though in a striking passage he asserted the necessity for adherence in matters of faith to the Roman see. The materials for his life are contained mainly in the 'Liber *Pontificalis Ecclesiae Ravennatis' of Abbot *Agnellus (9th cent.). He was apparently named 'Chrysologus' (Gk. 'golden-worded') to make him a W. counterpart of '*Chrysostom' ('golden-mouthed'). In 1729 he was declared a *doctor ecclesiae*. Feast day, 4 Dec.

Ed. princeps of his Sermons ed. Agapitus Vincentinus, Bologna, 1534. Later edd., Bologna, 1643, and Venice, 1750; latter repr. in J. P. Migne, *PL*, lii, 9–680. No crit. text exists. Monographs by H. Dapper (Cologne, 1867), F. von Stablewski (Posen, 1871), F. J. Peters (Cologne, [1918]), and G. Böhmer (Paderborn, 1919). A. Olivar O.S.B., 'Der hl. Petrus Chrysologus als Verfasser der Pseudo-Augustinischen Predigten Mai 30, 31 und 99 (§ 2–3)' in B. Fischer–U. Fiala (edd.), *Colligere Fragmenta*. Festschrift Alban Dold (1952), pp. 113–23. J. H. Baxter, 'The Homilies of St. Peter Chrysologus' in *J.T.S.*, xxii (1920–1), pp. 250–8; C. Jenkins, 'Aspects of the theology of St. Peter Chrysologus' in *C.Q.R.*, ciii (1927), pp. 233–59. Bardenhewer, iv, pp. 606–10. G. Lucchesi in *E.C.*, ix (1952), cols. 1433–5, s.v. 'Pietro Crisologo'.

CHRYSOM. The 'chrism-robe' put on a child
at baptism, as a symbol of the cleansing of its sin. Originally it may have been a cloth put over the head, to prevent the *chrism from being rubbed off. If the child died within a month of its baptism, the chrysom was used as a shroud; hence the expression 'chrysom child'. The use of the 'whyte vesture, commonly called the Chrysome' was ordered in the BCP of 1549. It was to be put on before the unction, not after it as in the pre-Reformation English rites, and returned to the priest at the mother's *churching. Its use disappeared in 1552, and has not been officially revived, except in the S. African alternative rite.

CHRYSOSTOM, St. JOHN (c. 347–407),
Bp. of *Constantinople, and '*Doctor of the Church'. He was educated for the law under the great pagan orator Libanius at *Antioch, where he studied theology under *Diodore of Tarsus, the leader of the *Antiochene School. He early felt a call to the monastic life. As the care of his widowed mother Anthusa prevented the immediate fulfilment of this desire, he lived for some time under rule at home, and later became a hermit (c. 373–c. 381) following the *Pachomian Rule with austerities which undermined his health. He was made deacon in 381, and served at Antioch under the bishop Flavian, who ordained him priest in 386, and appointed him to devote special attention to the work of preaching (a task in which his ability gained him the name of Chrysostom, 'golden-mouthed'). During the years 386–98, when his great powers of oratory were directed esp. to the instruction and moral reformation of the nominally Christian city of Antioch, he delivered his series of 'Homilies' on Gen., Mt., Jn., Rom., Gal., Cor., Eph., Tim., and Tit., which establish his title as the greatest of Christian expositors. These works combine a great facility for seeing the spiritual meaning of the author with an equal ability for immediate practical application. He was opposed, however, to the *allegorical exegesis of the Scriptures, and insisted that they must be interpreted literally. Against his wish, Chrysostom was made Patr. of Constantinople in 398, and immediately set about the work of reforming the city, where the corruption of court, clergy, and people alike had been encouraged by the complaisance and self-indulgence of his predecessor, St. *Nectarius.

His combination of honesty, asceticism, and tactlessness, when joined with the hatred of *Theophilus, the unworthy Patr. of *Alexandria, his disappointed rival, and of the Empress Eudoxia, who with some reason took all attempts at moral reform as a censure of herself, was sufficient to work his ruin. At the Synod of the *Oak (403), carefully packed by Theophilus, Chrysostom was condemned on 29 charges, the most serious being those of *Origenism (quite unjustified) and improper remarks about the Empress. Chrysostom, removed from his see, was shortly afterwards recalled by the court; but very soon his plain speaking brought the displeasure of the Empress on him again, and his enemies saw their opportunity, and secured his banishment on a charge of unlawfully reassuming the duties of a see from which he had been canonically deposed (404). Even the support of the people of Constantinople, of the Pope (*Innocent I), and of the entire W. Church, failed to save him. He was exiled at first to near Antioch, and when it became clear that in spite of his enfeebled health he would not die there soon enough, he was moved to Pontus, and finally deliberately killed by enforced travelling on foot in severe weather. His chief claim to remembrance, apart from his personal holiness, rests on his preaching, his exegesis, and his liturgical reforms. (See foll. art.) His early work, 'On the Priesthood', is a finely conceived description of the responsibilities of the Christian minister. Feast day, 27 Jan.

A very large number of Chrysostom's sermons has come down to us. It was his practice often to preach several sermons on a single theme, among the most celebrated of his series being those 'On the Statues' (Mar. and Apr., 387) addressed to the turbulent populace of Antioch who had revolted against the Imperial taxes. His great repute as a preacher caused many sermons to be falsely ascribed to him in succeeding generations; the *spuria* of the printed edd. hence offer the student a fruitful field of research. Besides homilies and expositions of Scripture, Chrysostom also wrote some treatises, esp. on practical subjects, and a collection of letters survives.

Collected edd. of his works by F. *Ducaeus, S.J. (12 vols., Paris, 1609–33), H. *Savile (8 vols., Eton, 1612, without Lat. tr.; with important prefaces and notes by I. *Casaubon and others, and generally, except for the portions ed. by F. *Field, still the best ed. of the text), and B. de *Montfaucon, O.S.B. (13 vols., Paris, 1718–38). This last was repr. (the most convenient ed.), with revisions by G. R. L. von Sinner (13 vols., Paris, 'apud fratres Gaume', 1834–40); and, with suppls., in J. P. Migne, *PG*, xlvii–lxiv. Valuable edd. by F. Field of *Homm. on Matt.* (3 vols., Cambridge, 1839) and of *Interpr. Omnium Epp. Paulinarum* (7 vols., Oxford, 1845–62). Other separate edd. include the *De Sacerdotio* ed. J. A. *Bengel (Stuttgart, 1725) and J. A. Nairn (Cambridge Patristic Texts, 1906). Selection of passages ed., with admirable notes, by J. F. D'Alton (London, 1940). Eng. tr. of sets of Homilies in L.F., 16 vols., 1839–52, and N.P.N.C.F., First Series, ix–xiv, 1888–93. Fr. trr., with Gk. text from J. P. Migne, of the *Epistolae ad Olympiadem* by A. M. Malingrey (S.C., xiii; 1947), and of the *De Incomprensibili* by R. Flacelière, with introd. by F. Cavallera, S.J.–J. Daniélou, S.J. (S.C., xxviii; 1951). Life (pr. in edd. of Chrysostom) by *Palladius, entitled 'Dialogus de Vita S. Joannis Chrysostomi' (crit. ed. P. R. Coleman-Norton, Cambridge, 1928). Further biog. material in *Socrates, *H.E.*, vi, 2–23, vii, 25–45, *Sozomen, *H.E.*, viii, 2–28, and *Theodoret, *H.E.*, v, 27–36. Modern lives by G. Hermant (Paris, 1664), J. A. W. *Neander (3 vols., Berlin, 1821–2; Eng. tr. of vol. i, 1838, all publd.), W. R. W. Stephens (London, 1872), R. W. Bush (London, 1885), A. Puech (Paris, 1891), id. ('Les Saints', 1900; Eng. tr., 1902), and A. Moulard (Paris, 1941). Of primary importance, esp. for chronology, L. S. de *Tillemont, *Mémoires pour servir à l'histoire ecclésiastique des six premiers siècles*, ix (1706), pp. 1–405 and 547–626. F. H. *Chase, *Chrysostom. A Study in the History of Biblical Interpretation* (1887). Important work by P. Chrysostomus Baur, O.S.B., *Der heilige Johannes Chrysostomus und seine Zeit* (2 vols., Munich, 1929–30; Eng. tr., 2 vols., 1959–60). A. Naegle, *Die Eucharistielehre des heiligen Johannes Chrysostomus* (1900). L. Meyer, *Saint Jean Chrysostome, maître de perfection chrétienne* (1933). Study by D. Attwater (Milwaukee, 1939; London, 1959). L. *Duchesne, *Histoire ancienne de l'Église*, iii (1910), pp. 72–105; B. J. Kidd, *A History of the Church to 461*, ii (1922), pp. 355–9 and 417–54. Bardenhewer, iii, pp. 324–61; Altaner (ed. 1950), pp. 278–89. E. Venables in *D.C.B.*, i (1877), pp. 518–35; E. Preuschen in *P.R.E.* (ed. 3), iv (1898), pp. 101–11; G. Bardy in *D.T.C.*, viii (pt. 1; 1924), cols. 660–90, s.v. 'Jean Chrysostome'; Q. Cataudella in *E.C.*, vi (1951), cols. 534–43, s.v. 'Giovanni Crisostomo'.

CHRYSOSTOM, Liturgy of St. The Liturgy now in general use in the Orthodox E. Church except on the few days in the year for which the Liturgy of St. *Basil is prescribed.

In its present form it is very much later than the time of St. *Chrysostom, whose name it bears, and the grounds for connecting it with him at all are insecure. It probably owed its great influence to being the liturgy of the Imperial capital, and after the older liturgies of St. James (*Jerusalem and *Antioch) and St. Mark (*Alexandria) had been considerably assimilated to it, finally superseded them in the 13th cent. It is used in several different languages in the Orthodox Churches of the E.

Gk. text in F. E. *Brightman, *Liturgies Eastern and Western*, i (1896), pp. 309–44 (based on MS. Barb., iii, 55) and 353–399 (modern text). Eng. tr. in *The Orthodox Liturgy* (ed. Patrick [J.] Thompson, S.P.C.K., 1939). Oldest Lat. version ed. A. Strittmatter, O.S.B., in *Ephemerides Liturgicae*, lv (1941), pp. 2–73, and *Traditio*, i (New York, 1943), pp. 79–137. Syr. vers. ed. H. W. Codrington (Rome, 1940). On authorship see also P. de Meester, O.S.B., in *D.A.C.L.*, vi (pt. 2; 1925), cols. 1596–1604, s.v. 'Grecques (liturgies)', with bibl.

CHRYSOSTOM, The Prayer of St. The familiar prayer in the BCP was drawn by T. *Cranmer from the Liturgy of St. *Chrysostom (q.v., ed. F. E. *Brightman, p. 367). In the original Book (1549) it is only found in the *Litany, where it owes its presence to the fact that in 'Chrysostom' (on which Cranmer was largely dependent for the English Litany) its place was near the Deacon's Litany. It was first included among the concluding prayers at Mattins and Evensong in 1662. Its authorship is unknown.

J. Dowden, *The Workmanship of the Prayer Book* (1899), pp. 227–9.

CHURCH. (1) *Terminology.* The Eng. 'church', Germ. *Kirche*, Dutch *kerke*. etc., come ultimately from the Gk. κυριακόν, '[thing] belonging to the Lord', which was applied orig. to a church building. The Lat. *ecclesia* and its derivatives (Fr. *église*, Ital. *chiesa*, etc., including Welsh *eglwys*), although used of the building, come from the Gk. ἐκκλησία, which in secular Greek meant an assembly, primarily of citizens in a self-governing city (e.g. that of *Ephesus, Acts 19. 39). In the *Septuagint ἐκκλησία was used of the 'assembly' or 'congregation' of the Israelites (Heb. קָהָל) and esp. of those 'within the covenant' as opposed to 'the stranger in your midst' (Deut. 23. 3, Neh. 13. 1). In Acts 7. 38 the word is used with this OT ref.

In the Gospels, the word ἐκκλησία occurs only twice on the Lord's lips, at Mt. 16. 18 (the words to St. *Peter, 'upon this rock [*petra*] I will build My Church'), and at 18. 17 (when a brother will not heed private remonstrance, the matter is to be told to 'the Church'). In Acts the word is first found, in its Christian sense, in 5. 11, where 'the whole church' is to be identified with 'the church in Jerusalem' at 8. 1. (The best MSS. do not attest the word at 2. 47, where it is found in the AV). It is uncertain whether the Jerusalem Christians applied the equivalent Aramaic word to themselves at this date; but it is clear from St. *Paul's Epp. that among Greek-speaking Christians ἐκκλησία was the regular word from an early date, both for a local Christian community (e.g. 'the churches of Galatia', 'the church of the Thessalonians', Gal. 1. 2, 1 Thess. 1. 1) and for the whole Christian community (e.g. 1 Cor. 12. 28).

(2) *New Testament*. The claim of the primitive Church to be an organic society rests on the belief that it was the inheritor of the promises made to Israel. Such is implied in the Lord's teaching about the *Kingdom, in the choosing of the Apostles as the nucleus of its ministry, and in the institution of the Sacramental rites. F. *Kattenbusch argues that the conception comes from the vision of the saints of the Most High in Dan. 7. St. Paul conceives of the Church as Christ's Body (Col. 1. 24; cf. 1 Cor. 12. 27), as His Bride (2 Cor. 11. 2, cf. Eph. 5. 32), and as His Temple (1 Cor. 3. 16, 2 Cor. 6. 16, Eph. 2. 20–22). The NT also points to the priestly character of the Church (1 Pet. 2. 9). It is the clear teaching of the NT as a whole that the Church was established by Christ as the New Israel and endowed by Him with the Holy Spirit at Pentecost, and is not merely a voluntary association of individual disciples.

(3) *Catholicism and the Church*. This conception of the Church was elaborated as time went on. Increasing stress was laid on the Divine constitution and corporate nature of the Church. Its essence was epitomized in the four traditional 'notes of the Church', viz. unity, holiness, catholicity, and apostolicity. It was held that there could be only one such body founded by Christ; as being of Divine origin it must be holy; as being by Divine intention world-wide, and having in fact spread over most of the known world before it was challenged by particular and local movements, it was in purpose catholic; and as teaching the Apostles' doctrine and historically descended from them it was apostolic. Thus conceived, the Church is essentially a visible body. Its membership (at least as far as the living are concerned), its orders of ministers, and its unity are all constituted by participation in visible sacraments, viz. those of *Baptism and *Confirmation, of *Holy Orders and of *Holy Communion, respectively. In contrast with this visible Church 'Militant here in earth', there exists the invisible Church of the faithful departed, divided into the Church Expectant (undergoing purification in *purgatory) and the Church Triumphant (already enjoying the *beatific vision in heaven). Separation from the Church Militant is the sin of *schism, and rejection of its apostolic doctrine *heresy.

In early times the doctrine of the visible Unity of the Church was accepted on all sides. The schismatic bodies which arose (*Melitians, *Donatists, *Monophysites) all considered themselves the whole Church. But a theology of the Church gradually developed, which gave precision to the status of those in schism. Against rigorist movements such as Donatism, St. *Augustine maintained that the sacraments were everywhere to be regarded as acts of the Church. Their validity was independent of the personal qualities of the minister, provided he had the necessary sacramental status and, later theologians added, intended to do what the Church had always intended. In this way the sacraments of bodies of Christians in heresy or schism could in certain instances be validated through the historical relation of these bodies to the Catholic Church.

Since the schism between the E. and the W., finally consummated in 1054, the RC and Eastern Orthodox Churches each maintain that the other is in schism, and that itself is now the historic manifestation of the visible Church. Anglicans and others who do not accept the exclusive claim of any Church in this matter often maintain that all parts of the Church Militant, including Rome, are now to some extent in schism.

(4) *Protestantism and the Church*. The *Reformation led to a reformulation of the idea of the Church. It sought to proclaim its inner being in terms of the Word of God rather than in sacramental relationships. Two doctrines of the Church received wide acceptance: (a) the more conservative, that the Church is a visible body and in the Divine intention one throughout the world, but that in view of corruptions and errors which had arisen it was justified within a particular nation in reforming itself, even if this involves a breach of visible unity; (b) the more radical, that the true Church is in essence an invisible body, since the essential fact by which a man is saved and made a member of the Church is the inward fact of faith. Thus constituted, the Church is a body whose actual membership is known only to God. Acc. to most holders of this conception of the Church, it was desirable that it should possess an outward and visible organization, membership of which should correspond as closely as possible to the true invisible Church, though identity was impossible. In the view of some the visible organization of the Church should as far as possible be one throughout Christendom, or at least throughout reformed Christendom. In each nation or area of civil government this visible unity was to be secured by an 'established religion', determined by decree of the ruler, and on this basis the national Churches on the *Lutheran or *Calvinist model were organized. But another group of theologians held that unity of organization between Christian congregations in different places was unnecessary. The *Independents maintained that the only essential outward unity was that of each local congregation and that national Churches were undesirable.

(5) *Contemporary Revival*. In recent times renewed interest has been taken in the theology of the Church by Catholics and Protestants alike. The revived understanding of the Bible, the actuality of eschatology, the growth of the *Oecumenical Movement and the desire for reunion, the reaction from individualism in politics, organic doctrines in philosophy, and the increased sense of history have all played their part. The Church as such is being recognized in a new sense as a fundamental fact in the Christian Revelation. As the New Israel she inherits the promises of the OT dispensation. With this renewed sense

of the Church has gone hand in hand a recognition of the Church's transcendence over and separateness from the world. Among its practical results have been the *Liturgical Movement (q.v.), a renewed recognition of the place of the Gospel and the Sacraments in the Christian life, and a more constructive and less polemical approach to differences which have traditionally divided Protestant and Catholic theology. The rediscovery of the Church is reflected in K. *Barth's change in title from *Die christliche Dogmatik* to *Die kirchliche Dogmatik*. Among the leading exponents of this revived ecclesiology are K. Adam, M. J. Congar, L. S. Thornton, D. Jenkins, H. de Lubac, A. M. Ramsey, A. G. Hebert (see Bibliography). In the RC Church some aspects of this new teaching found official expression in the encyclical *Mystici Corporis Christi* (29 June 1943).

K. Adam, *Das Wesen des Katholicismus* (1928; Eng. trans., 1929); W. J. Phythian Adams, *The Fulness of Israel* (1938); M. J. Congar, O.P., *Chrétiens désunis. Principes d'un œcuménisme catholique* (Unam Sanctam I, 1937; Eng. trans., *Divided Christendom*, 1939); id., *Esquisses du mystère de l'Église* (1941); R. Newton Flew, *Jesus and His Church. A Study of the Idea of the Ecclesia in the NT* (1938); G, Gloege, *Reich Gottes und Kirche im Neuen Testament* (1929); H. F. Hamilton, *The People of God* (2 vols., 1912); A. *Harnack, *The Constitution and Law of the Church* (Eng. trans., 1910); A. C. *Headlam, *The Doctrine of the Church and Christian Reunion* (1920); A. G. Hebert, S.S.M., *The Form of the Church* (1944); F. J. A. *Hort, *The Christian Ecclesia* (1897); D. Jenkins, *The Nature of Catholicity* (1942); G. Johnston, *The Doctrine of the Church in the New Testament* (1943); F. *Kattenbusch, 'Der Quellort der Kirchenidee' in *Festgabe für A. von Harnack* (1921), pp. 142–72; T. A. *Lacey, *The One Body and the One Spirit* (1925); H. de Lubac, S.J., *Catholicisme. Les Aspects sociaux du dogme* (1937); E. L. Mascall, *Christ, the Christian and the Church* (1946); F. D. *Maurice, *The Kingdom of Christ* (1838); E. Mersch, S.J., *Le Corps mystique du Christ. Études de théologie historique* (Museum Lessianum, 2 vols., 1933); id., *La Théologie du Corps mystique* (2 vols., 1944); R. C. *Moberly, *Ministerial Priesthood* (1897); W. *Palmer, *Treatise on the Christian Church* (2 vols., 1838); A. M. Ramsey, *The Gospel and the Catholic Church* (1936); K. L. Schmidt, *Die Kirche des Urchristentums* (1932); id., art. 'Ecclesia' in G. Kittel's *Wörterbuch*, iii, 502–39 (1938); D. *Stone, *The Christian Church* (1905); id., *The Notes of the Church* (1910); H. B. *Swete, *The Holy Catholic Church* (1915); L. S. Thornton, C.R., *The Common Life in the Body of Christ* (1943); C. H. *Turner, *Catholic and Apostolic* (ed., H. N. Bate, 1931). B. C. Butler, O.S.B., *The Idea of the Church* (1962).

CHURCH, RICHARD WILLIAM (1815–1890),

Dean of *St. Paul's. He was born at Lisbon and spent his earlier years in Florence. In 1833 he was sent to Wadham College, Oxford, because the college at that time, under B. P. Symons, had a reputation for Evangelicalism. He came under the influence of C. *Marriott of Oriel, who enlisted him in his band of translators of the Fathers, and introduced him to J. H. *Newman, E. B. *Pusey, and J. *Keble. In 1838 he was elected a Fellow of Oriel where he remained until 1852 when he became Rector of Whatley in Somerset. As Junior Proctor he shared with H. P. Guillemard of Trinity in the dramatic vetoing of the condemnation of *Tract 90 in the university convocation (1845). He was one of the prime movers in establishing the *Guardian*, which from the first (1846) espoused High Church principles. After nearly twenty years at Whatley, Church was appointed in 1871 to the Deanery of St. Paul's

where he remained until his death. In his *The Gifts of Civilization* (1870, incorporating earlier work) he developed his beliefs about the relation of the Church to the world; and illustrated the same theme in his lives of *St. *Anselm* (1870), *Spenser* (1879), and *Bacon* (1884). His book *The Oxford Movement, Twelve Years, 1833–1845* (posthumously published in 1891) is a masterpiece, as a judicious and balanced interpretation of the history of the movement.

Life and Letters of Dean Church, edited by his daughter, Mary C. Church (1894). D. C. Lathbury, *Dean Church* (1905). H. C. Beeching in *D.N.B.*, Suppl. ii (1901), pp. 6–9.

CHURCH ARMY.

A voluntary Anglican organization, founded in 1882 in the slums of *Westminster on the model of the *Salvation Army, for evangelistic purposes by Wilson *Carlile. Since 1889 its activities have included social and moral welfare work among the poor in great cities, and missions in prisons and workhouses. In time of war the 'Army' undertakes work for the welfare of the troops, such as recreation huts, clubs, canteens (mobile and stationary), and hostels, besides canteens and hostels for homeless civilians and relatives of men on active service.

See bibl., s.v. *Carlile*.

CHURCH ASSEMBLY.

This body, officially the 'National Assembly of the Church of England', was authorized by the *Enabling Act (q.v.) of 1919 'to deliberate on all matters concerning the Church of England and to make provision in respect thereof'. It is composed of a House of Bishops comprising all the members of the two Upper Houses of *Convocation; a House of Clergy, consisting of all the members of the two Lower Houses of Convocation; and a House of Laity, elected every five years by the representative electors of the Diocesan Conferences. It is debarred from issuing pronouncements on matters of theology, which are reserved to the Convocations. Its most important function is to prepare ecclesiastical measures for transmission to Parliament. Among the measures passed by the Assembly and Parliament have been the Parochial Church Councils Measure (1921) conferring statutory powers on parochial church councils, the Clergy Pensions Measure (1926), and the Cathedrals Measure (1931) setting up the Cathedral commissioners. Although the Revised Prayer Book was twice accepted by the Assembly (1927, 1928), it was in each case subsequently rejected by Parliament. The Assembly exercises great influence, through the Central Board of Finance, on the financial affairs of the C of E and on other administrative bodies such as the Missionary Council, Central Advisory Council of Training for the Ministry, and the *National Society. It normally meets in London about three times a year.

The Reports of the Proceedings are publd. conjointly by the Church Information Board and the *S.P.C.K. *The Church Assembly and the Church. A Book of Essays* (1930). *The Church Assembly News*. The Official Publication of the

Church Assembly (London, 1924 ff., monthly). Much contemporary information is contained in the *The Official Year Book of the National Assembly of the Church of England* (annually).

CHURCH ASSOCIATION, The.

A society formed in 1865 during the ritual controversies by several leading Evangelical Churchmen to maintain the Protestant ideals of faith and worship in the C of E. Previously active in litigation (cf. *Church Discipline Act, *Ritual Commission) it came ultimately to rely rather on publicity. In 1950 it became (with the National Church League) the Church Society.

CHURCH BUILDING SOCIETY, The.

Founded in 1818 and incorporated in 1828, the Society has taken an important and continuous part in furthering the construction and repair of Anglican churches in England and Wales.

CHURCH COMMISSIONERS for England.

The body formed by the fusion of the *Ecclesiastical Commissioners and *Queen Anne's Bounty in 1948 to manage the estates and revenues of the C of E. It consists of the archbishops and bishops of England, three lay 'Church Estates Commissioners', twenty-five persons appointed by the *Church Assembly (five deans, ten other clerks in holy orders, and ten laymen), four laymen appointed by the Crown, four persons appointed by the Abp. of Canterbury, certain officers of state (see the corresponding list of former 'Ecclesiastical Commissioners'), and representatives of the cities of London and York and the universities of Oxford and Cambridge. The Board of Governors is formed of not more than 30 of the Commissioners, and day-to-day business is carried on by a small Estates and Finance Committee, which includes the three Church Estates Commissioners. In addition to their main responsibilities (trusteeship, financial administration, etc.), the Commissioners have certain wider administrative duties such as reorganizing the legal structure of parishes and rural deaneries from time to time, and fixing the statutory fees chargeable for marriages, funerals, and other rites.

The Church Commissioners Measure, 1947, as finally approved by the Asssembly, 21 June 1946, is printed for the Church Assembly, C.A. 794A (1946). P. B. Wilbraham, *The First Five Years*. The Story of the Church Commissioners, 1948–53 (1953).

CHURCH CONGRESSES.

A series of unofficial gatherings of Anglican Churchmen which have been held from 1861 onwards (annually down to 1913, and less regularly since). They assemble for about three days at different provincial centres and discuss problems connected with the life and work of the C of E. The first meeting (1861) was at Cambridge. Owing to other means of contact between different centres of Church life in the provinces, e.g. the erection of the *National Assembly in 1920, the usefulness of the Congresses declined after the War of 1914–18.

Official reports of the Proceedings of the first fifty-nine congresses were issued in uniform vols., 1862–1925; thereafter in the name of the editor.

CHURCH DISCIPLINE ACT (1840).

This Act (3 & 4 Vict. c. 86) empowers the bishop, in cases of an alleged non-criminal offence by a cleric (e.g. irregularities in doctrine or ritual, also *simony), either to issue a Commission of Inquiry which shall institute a preliminary investigation and decide whether or not there is a *prima facie* case or, alternatively, himself to transmit the case by Letters of Request to the provincial Court of Appeal. Conviction may be followed by suspension or deprivation.

For details of procedure under the Act see R. *Phillimore, *The Ecclesiastical Law of the Church of England* (ed. 2, 1895), ii, 1013–25.

CHURCH HISTORICAL SOCIETY.

A society founded in 1894 (under the presidency of Mandell *Creighton, Bp. of London) for the diffusion of historical knowledge esp. in so far as it affected the authority and claims of the C of E. It has issued through the *S.P.C.K. a long series of writings, for the most part of small dimensions, but marked by a high standard of scholarship. More recently it has published larger works on ecclesiastical history. In its early years its publications owed much to the stimulating editorship of W. E. Collins (1867–1911), later (from 1904) Bp. of Gibraltar.

CHURCH HOUSE, WESTMINSTER.

The building in which the *Convocation of Canterbury and the *National Assembly of the C of E generally sit and the headquarters of many Anglican organizations. It replaced a set of buildings erected between 1891 and 1902 on a site fronting on Dean's Yard, *Westminster. It was designed by Sir Herbert Baker, and completed and opened in 1940.

CHURCH HYMNARY, The.

The authorized hymnal of most of the English-speaking Presbyterian Churches. The first edition was issued in 1898, and a much revised form in 1927. In addition to over 700 hymns, it contains certain doxologies and canticles arranged for singing; and there is a 'Supplement', consisting chiefly of metrical psalms, for use in the Presbyterian Churches of England and of Wales.

J. *Moffatt and M. Patrick, *Handbook to the Church Hymnary* (1935).

CHURCH HYMNS.

A hymn-book formerly much used in the C of E, but since *c.* 1910 almost entirely supplanted by other hymnals. Preliminary editions (*Hymns*, 1852; *Psalms and Hymns*, 1855) had been published by the *S.P.C.K., who were responsible for the publication of the standard edition of 1870 (when the name 'Church Hymns' was first used) and also for the entire revision of 1903. Its standpoint was that of 'official *Anglicanism', in contrast to the *Anglo-Catholicism of '*Hymns, Ancient and Modern', and the *Evangelicalism of the '*Hymnal Companion'.

CHURCH MEETING. The regular (usually monthly) assembly of all the members of a *Congregational or *Baptist church for the purposes of Church administration, the admission of members and the election of officers, and the exercise of discipline in that particular congregation. 'The covenanted people of God' meeting in such a local unit have complete autonomy.

CHURCH MISSIONARY SOCIETY. See C.M.S.

CHURCH MISSIONS TO JEWS. Officially known as the 'London Society for Promoting Christianity amongst the Jews', this organization was founded as an Anglican society in 1809 and now works in three continents.

W. T. Gidney, *The History of the London Society for Promoting Christianity among the Jews, from 1809 to 1908* (1908).

CHURCH OF ENGLAND, The. It is impossible to say at what date Christianity was first planted in Great Britain, but the presence of British bishops at the Council of *Arles in 314 is evidence of the existence of an organized Church. With the coming of the Anglo-Saxon invaders, British Christianity and Christians were driven before them into the western parts of Britain and the new faith suffered a temporary eclipse. The conversion of the Teutonic pagan conquerors was effected from two sources, by the labours of *Celtic missionaries from the monasteries of Ireland and Scotland and by the mission headed by St. *Augustine sent from Rome (597). To this mission the British Christians would at first pay neither obedience nor submission. The Christianization of the Heptarchy progressed slowly, and with many set-backs, for the varying fortunes of the various kingdoms involved those of the Christian bishops. Not until the several local kingdoms gave place to a loosely united national kingdom was the Church enabled to settle down to the task of administrative unification of its scattered dioceses. Before this could be attempted, the differences between the Celtic and Roman missions had first of all to be composed. Springing from a fundamental difference of temper, the Celtic monastic tradition lacked the administrative organization of the Roman Church, and the deep divergences between the two found expression in many minor points, such as the date of Easter. At a synod held at *Whitby in 664 the conflict was at length resolved in favour of the Roman customs, and the way thereby opened for the organization of the whole Church in England under one head.

*Theodore of Tarsus, sent from Rome as Abp. of *Canterbury, undertook this vital work of unification by subdivision of dioceses, summoning of ecclesiastical councils, legislative decrees, and encouragement of learning. He was the first of a long line of statesmen-archbishops of the English Church. His work was mainly that of organizing the higher administration of the Church, for the factor of the proprietary church, an institution bequeathed in England, as elsewhere throughout W. Europe, by Teutonic paganism, presented a stubborn and enduring obstacle to the assertion of episcopal control over the secular parish priests. Anglo-Saxon Christianity enjoyed a transient golden age following the vigorous primacy of Theodore, producing both scholars such as *Bede, the author of one of the greatest historical narratives of all ages, and missionaries such as *Boniface of Crediton. England largely through its monasteries both shared in and contributed to the renaissance of the age of *Charlemagne.

Darkness, however, supervened again upon this period of light. The plundering raids of the Northmen fell with especial devastation upon religious houses, and the standard of clerical life and learning declined under these severe blows. The reign of *Alfred provided a temporary barrier against the Danes, and saw the beginnings of a revival of religion and learning, but the confusion of the times was detrimental to the highest developments of both. Under Edgar, Abp. *Dunstan, in addition to his work as a statesman, laboured to reform the monasteries and cathedral chapters by fighting against the evils of clerical marriage and simony in accordance with contemporary European movements. The isolation of England from the main life of the Continent, both in political and ecclesiastical affairs, could not be maintained; and the question whether these islands would pass into the orbit of a N.W. Scandinavian empire or become joined to the main states of W. Europe was finally settled by the Norman Conquest under William I. The last of the old English kings, *Edward the Confessor, had assisted the introduction of Norman culture. He also refounded and rebuilt the famous abbey-church of St. Peter at *Westminster.

With the Norman domination, the English Church entered into the main stream of European religion at a time when the Hildebrandine reforming movement, associated with the pontificate of *Gregory VII, was powerfully affecting the life of the Church. *Lanfranc, the new Norman Abp. of Canterbury, assisted by a body of foreign bishops and abbots, led the way to a revival of religious life in England. The Norman age saw the removal of episcopal sees from remote villages to cities, the beginning of that tremendous outburst of building of which the cathedrals constitute the finest monuments, the restoration of learning and education, and the reorganization of ecclesiastical administration, including the assertion of the supremacy of Canterbury over York. Most important of all, the royal separation of the ecclesiastical and civil courts opened the way for the entrance of the Roman canon law, itself the chief agent of Papal control throughout the W. Church. The English Church henceforth could not escape the ubiquitous influence of the Popes. Under kings less scrupulous than William I, relations between Church and state were not harmonious. The investiture conflict was itself but a symbol of the attempt of the spiritual power to free itself from the control of the temporal, which in the lower orders of the clergy was typified by the proprietary Church and in the episcopate by the contest between Papacy and kings for the right to nominate bishops. *Anselm maintained this struggle on its highest plane of principle in his differences with Henry I, whilst *Thomas Becket's dramatic conflict with Henry II, ending in victory through his martyrdom, was evidence of the personal passions inextricably interlocked with the assertion of principle. Henry II believed himself to be maintaining the ancient customs of the English crown, as asserted by William I, but Becket was representative of the augmented prestige of the Papacy consequent on the Hildebrandine Movement and the separation of the ecclesiastical and civil courts in England by the Conqueror. Behind this foreground of struggle the English Church was influenced by the several monastic revivals of Europe, an Englishman, *Stephen Harding, being the author of the *Carta Caritatis*, the rule of the *Cistercian Order.

The 13th cent. was in many ways the culmination of the Middle Ages. In England, after the combined victory of Church and barons over King *John symbolized in the 'Great Charter', promising freedom to the Church from royal absolutism, the long reign of *Henry III afforded wide opportunities for the Papacy and the Church. Under Henry, himself a king of deep piety and the second refounder of Westminster Abbey, the Papacy came to exercise a marked influence in episcopal appointments, esp. to the see of Canterbury, and sent representatives to England to seek financial aid for the Papal struggle against Frederick II. During his reign, moreover, the *Friars came to England, university life was fostered, the constitutions of Otto and Ottobonus developed ecclesiastical law, and amongst the Henrician episcopate was numbered one of the most famous of all English prelates, *Grosseteste of Lincoln, distinguished alike as scholar, pastor, and administrator. *Innocent III had died before Henry's accession, but the influence of his ecclesiastical reforms, esp. as reflected in the decrees of the Fourth *Lateran Council of 1215, were felt in the English Church during his rule. There followed a period of consolidation of royal power under Edward I and, after the brief misrule of his son, under Edward III, whose reign saw the development of parliamentary institutions in England and the successful struggle of the lower clergy to avoid inclusion of their proctors in the lower parliamentary house.

With the accentuation of national self-consciousness on the one hand, and the Papal scandals of the *Babylonish captivity and *Great Schism on the other, the exactions and policy of the Roman see became the subject of increasing criticism in England. During the Hundred Years' War with France alien priories were suppressed, and their revenues diverted to the crown, whilst the statutes of *Provisors and *Praemunire attempted to curtail in the royal interest the Papal practice of diverting the revenues of English benefices to the support of foreign ecclesiastics and the payment of Papal creditors. The failure of the Conciliar Movement, however, demonstrated the impossibility of a constitutional Papacy, and national kings found their interests better served by concordats with the Papacy through which a financial division of the spoils of the Church and a sharing of ecclesiastical appointments were effected. The chief results of the policy of concordats were to strengthen the hold of the monarchy on the Church in England and to extinguish any corporate sentiment of loyalty towards the Papacy on the part of the episcopate.

When, in the 16th cent., the Tudor sovereigns deemed it expedient to measure their strength against the Papacy, they found many elements in the nation ready to lend their support. Criticism of ecclesiastical wealth, accompanied amongst the lower classes by sporadic heresy, had been prominent since the time of J. *Wycliffe. Merchants cast hungry glances upon the riches of monastic property. Civil lawyers bore the canonists a deep grudge, and many citizens of all ranks resented Papal exactions. More intangible but undeniable were the evidences of religious dissatisfaction, represented amongst the learned by the Renaissance revolt against Scholasticism and its devotion to the study of Hebrew and Greek of which *Erasmus and J. *Colet were typical in England, and expressed amongst the unlettered by vague strivings after a more personal and spiritual religion and by revulsion against the multiplication of *chantries and requiems. The occasion of the Tudor Reformation was the famous 'divorce' of *Henry VIII; but its causes lay deeper. T. *Wolsey had removed the last lingering affection amongst the episcopate for Papal supremacy, whilst pointing the way to a royal supremacy. Under Henry VIII the *Convocations acknowledged the King to be Supreme Head on earth of the Church of England, and a series of laws severed the financial, judicial, and administrative bonds between Rome and England. Despite the influx of *Lutheran books and ideas and the inclusion of men of reforming opinions amongst the episcopate, Henry VIII refused to allow any doctrinal changes. His order for the setting-up of the *Great Bible in all churches was an event of which the full influence and importance were not realized until later. Apart from the overthrow of Papal supremacy and the bringing of Convocation under the control of the crown, the main events of this reign were negative, such as the dissolution of the monasteries and the destruction of shrines. Under *Edward VI, Abp. T. *Cranmer produced the First and Second Books of *Common Prayer in 1549 and 1552, an English *Ordinal, and a statement of doctrine, the *Forty-Two Articles. This advance towards Protestantism was followed by a reaction under *Mary which restored the Papal supremacy and undid all the work of her father. Upon the accession of *Elizabeth the Papal obedience was again repudiated, the Crown assumed the title of 'Supreme Governor', the Second Edwardine Prayer Book with some changes became the service book of the Church of England, the Articles of Religion were reduced to *Thirty-Nine, and the episcopate under the prudent and scholarly leadership of Abp. M. *Parker attempted to achieve national unity and uniformity in religion.

Two bodies of critics opposed the Elizabethan settlement. In 1570 the Papal bull of excommunication ('*Regnans in excelsis') created a stubborn enclave of Popish recusants within the nation. On the other side a considerable volume of *Puritan opinion regarded the Prayer Book, Articles, and episcopacy as only a half-way house to a fuller and better reformation. The majority of divines of this standpoint remained within the Church, striving for changes from within, and controversy ranged over a wide ground from the wearing of the surplice to the reform of the Prayer Book and the supplanting of episcopacy by *presbyterianism. In J. *Jewel and R. *Hooker the C of E found apologists against both Rome and Geneva, who argued for its position in the *Via Media, appealing to Scripture, the Fathers, and human reason. Ecclesiastical controversy, however, drove the episcopate into close dependence upon the crown, working through the Court of *High Commission for the enforcement of uniformity. Under *James I the Convocations, by royal licence and assent, published the *Canons of 1604; but under both him and his son, *Charles I, Puritan opposition was sharpened, and as a result of the ascendancy of Abp. W. *Laud and his endeavours to secure a higher standard of common order in the Church, episcopacy and Anglicanism became a subject of conflict in the Civil Wars. The victory of parliament led first to a presbyterian reform, and then, owing to the influence of the Army, to *Independency. During the Commonwealth and Protectorate the use of the BCP was prohibited, and benefices were held by episcopalian, presbyterian, and independent ministers indifferently. With the restoration of *Charles II, the C of E returned to its position as the established Church. The failure of an attempt at comprehension at the *Savoy Conference was followed by a revision of the Prayer Book, its enforcement by a new Act of *Uniformity in 1662, and by persecuting measures against dissenters. The attempts of Charles II and *James II to use the royal prerogative of indulgence to secure toleration for dissenters and Papists failed, and James II's open attack on the C of E was largely responsible for his downfall. The Protestant succession in the persons of William of Orange and later the House of Hanover

delivered the Church from the dreaded danger of Popery.

After a century of fierce controversy against both Papist and Puritan, the C of E settled down from 1689 to an epoch of quiescence. A limited religious toleration pacified the dissenters, the Convocation, having lost its power of voting clerical taxation, sank into torpor, theological disputes became unpopular, and the alliance of Church and State became a mutually defensive pact against all subversive forces. The *Methodist revival was the parent both of a new Christian body and of the Anglican *Evangelical revival. *Latitudinarianism continued to dominate the intellectual atmosphere of the Georgian age, until the thoroughgoing reforms of the third decade of the 19th cent. awoke the protest of J. *Keble and effected a second administrative reformation of the Church. From this last there sprang new bishoprics and parishes, and a series of financial administrative reforms, followed by the revival of Convocation. From Keble's protest proceeded the *Oxford Movement which laid a new emphasis upon the catholic and apostolic character of the established Church, and upon the order of episcopacy. The Tractarian leaders, esp. J. H. *Newman and E. B. *Pusey, became the storm-centres of much controversy, and this initial period of strife culminated in the secession to Rome of Newman (1845), and at a later date of H. E. *Manning (1851).

When this revival of Church life became involved in ceremonial novelties, with consequent litigation, a generation of acute disputation set in. From another standpoint new problems of Biblical interpretation and of the relation of theology to secular science produced controversies of another kind, which centred in the publication of such composite volumes as *Essays and Reviews and *Lux Mundi. Behind the dismal series of so-called ritualistic lawsuits, the Church was attempting to adjust its beliefs to a revolutionary background of human knowledge. Relations between Church and State were strained, and the 20th cent. opened with much continuation of controversy. These disputes tended to obscure the often growing and deepening activities of the Church in education and pastoral ministration. At the close of World War I in 1919 a readjustment of the relations of Church and state was effected by the passing of the Church of England National Assembly (Powers) Act. By this measure the three houses of the assembly, of bishops, clergy, and laity, were given powers to prepare legislation on ecclesiastical matters for the consideration of parliament. The modification worked well until, in 1927 and 1928, the House of Commons twice rejected a project for the revision of the Prayer Book, and created a deadlock in the relations between the *Church Assembly and parliament. Various suggestions for further legislative change have been made, but none have reached the stage of practical proposals. Between the wars, perhaps the most significant theological event was the publication of the Report of the Archbishops'

Commission on '*Doctrine in the Church of England'. Among the major problems before the C of E since World War II have been pastoral reorganization, the limits of doctrinal latitude, the supply of ordinands and the need for improved standards of clerical education, the evolution of a constitutional episcopate, the revision of *canon law, reunion, and the relations between Church and State as reflected in the position of the Church Assembly relative to that of parliament. See also *Anglican Communion* and *Anglicanism*.

The principal authority for the early history of Christianity in England is Bede, *H.E.* Important collection of docc. for the period to the end of the 12th cent. ed. A. W. Haddan–W. *Stubbs, *Councils and Ecclesiastical Documents Relating to Great Britain and Ireland*, vols. i, ii (pt. 1), and iii (1869–73); see also earlier collections there cited. General collection of docc. in Gee–Hardy. G. G. Perry, *The Student's English Church History* (3 vols., 1878–87; still useful); H. O. Wakeman, *An Introduction to the History of the Church of England from the Earliest Times to the Present Day* (1896; ed. 8 revised by S. L. Ollard, 1914). W. R. W. Stephens–W. Hunt (edd.), *A History of the English Church* (8 vols. in 9, 1899–1910). W. H. *Hutton, *A Short History of the Church in Great Britain* (1900). M. W. Patterson, *A History of the Church of England* (1909). E. W. Watson, *The Church of England* (H.U.L., 1914; ed. 2 with additional ch. by A. [T. P.] Williams, 1944). J. R. H. Moorman, *A History of the Church in England* (1953), with bibl. F. Makower, *Die Verfassung der Kirche von England* (1894; Eng. tr., 1895). S. C. Carpenter, *The Church in England, 597–1688* (1954). H. M. Gwatkin, *Church and State in England to the Death of Queen Anne* (1917). H. Williams, *Christianity in Early Britain* (1912). W. *Bright, *Chapters of Early English History* (1878; ed. 3, 1897). Z. N. Brooke, *The English Church and the Papacy from the Conquest to the Reign of John* (1931). J. R. H. Moorman, *Church Life in England in the Thirteenth Century* (1945). K. L. Wood-Legh, *Studies in Church Life in England under Edward III* (1934). H. M. Smith, *Pre-Reformation England* (1938); id., *Henry VIII and the Reformation* (1948). T. M. Parker, *The English Reformation to 1558* (H.U.L., 1950). G. Constant, *La Réforme en Angleterre* (1930 ff.; Eng. tr., 1934 ff.); P. Hughes, *The Reformation in England* (3 vols., 1950–4). W. A. Shaw, *A History of the English Church During the Civil Wars and under the Commonwealth, 1640–1660* (2 vols., 1900). R. G. Usher, *The Reconstruction of the English Church* (2 vols., 1910). J. W. Legg, *English Church Life from the Restoration to the Tractarian Movement* (1914). N. Sykes, *Church and State in England in the XVIIIth Century* (Birkbeck Lectures for 1931–3; 1934). S. C. Carpenter, *Church and People, 1789–1889* (1933). *D.E.C.H.* For the 15th cent., see also bibl. to *Lollardy* and *Wycliffe, J.*; for the period ot the Reformation, see bibl. to *Cranmer, T., Cromwell, T., Edward VI, Elizabeth I, Henry VIII*, and *Wolsey*; from the beginning of 19th cent. among the most important sources are the biographies of leading churchmen such as F. *Temple, R. T. *Davidson, C. G. *Lang, W. *Temple, A. P. *Stanley, E. B. *Pusey, etc.; for this period see also bibl. to *Oxford Movement*. On the whole subject see also entry *Anglicanism*, and bibl.

CHURCH PASTORAL AID SOCIETY. See *C.P.A.S.*

CHURCH SISTERS. In the Church of Scotland, women specially set apart to assist in parochial work, generally in busy industrial areas, in connexion with the Women's Home Mission. They are appointed by *kirk-sessions and are under the oversight of an Assembly Committee and the minister of the parish in which they labour. They have now been merged in an Order of *Deaconesses.

CHURCH SOCIETY. See *Church Association*.

CHURCH TIMES, The. A weekly religious newspaper, founded to propagate *Anglo-Catholic principles. Its first issue appeared on 7 Feb. 1863. From the outset it was edited with marked ability, and is now the most widely read English Church newspaper.

Much historical information in *Church Times*, vol. cxlvi, no. 5,217; 8 February 1963 ['Centenary Number', pp. 56].

CHURCH UNION, The. An Anglican association which exists 'to uphold the doctrine and discipline of the Church; to extend the knowledge of Catholic Faith and practice at home and beyond the seas; and so to bring everyone to worship the Lord as Saviour and King'. It was formed in 1934 under the presidency of the second Lord *Halifax by the amalgamation of the *English Church Union and the *Anglo-Catholic Congress.

CHURCH UNITY OCTAVE. The *octave of prayer observed annually from 18 Jan. (Feast of St. Peter's Chair at Rome) to 25 Jan. (Conversion of St. Paul) by a group of Anglican High Churchmen and others for the visible reunion of the Church, with Rome as the central see of Christendom. It was first kept in 1908.

CHURCHES OF CHRIST. See *Disciples of Christ*.

CHURCHING OF WOMEN, The. The form of thanksgiving which Christian women make after childbirth. The custom, which is based on the Jewish rite of *Purification (Lev. 12. 6), is mentioned in a letter of St. *Augustine of Canterbury to St. *Gregory the Great. The oldest extant forms of service, however, are medieval. The present BCP office is essentially the same as that of the *Sarum rite except that psalms 116 and 127 replace 121 and 128. It is intended to precede Holy Communion. The Sarum rubric directed that the woman's place shall be 'ante ostium ecclesiae', the 1549 BCP 'nigh unto the quire door', the 1552 book nigh unto the place where the table standeth' and the present book 'in some convenient place as hath been accustomed, or as the *ordinary shall direct'. In many churches a special pew was until recently reserved for the purpose. The wearing of a white veil by the woman was anciently customary and enforced by law in *James I's reign. The woman makes a thank-offering at this service. The RC office is closely similar, but includes a blessing and an aspersion of holy water.

E. *Martène, *De Antiquis Ecclesiae Ritibus*, I, cap. ix, art. v, ordo 11. S. Cheetham in *D.C.A.*, i (1875), p. 390 f., s.v., with primary reff. C. L. Feltoe in *P.B.D.* (1925), p. 203 f., s.v. A. J. Schulte in *C.E.*, iii (1908), p. 761, s.v.

CHURCHMEN'S UNION. See *Modern Churchmen's Union*.

CHURCHWARDENS. By can. 89 of 1604, Churchwardens are to be chosen by the incumbent and the parishioners, or, if they fail to agree, one is to be appointed by the incumbent, the other by the people. The latter practice has become general and is provided for by the Church Building and New Parishes Acts of 1818 to 1884. The election is ordinarily made at the Easter Vestry; but in the case of new parishes, it must take place within two months from the date the parish is formed. The duties of Churchwardens comprise the business and financial side of parochial activity, particularly the collection and apportioning of alms, and the care and preservation of the fabric and furnishings of the church. Acc. to the canon they have also the duty of presenting offenders against ecclesiastical law, a function which they fulfilled until the 19th cent. Until the establishment of *Parochial Church Councils in 1921 they were the sole official representatives of the laity in each parish.

R. *Phillimore, *The Ecclesiastical Law of the Church of England*, ii (ed. 2 by W. G. F. Phillimore, 1895), esp. pp. 1463–91. H. W. Cripps, *A Practical Treatise on the Law Relating to the Church and Clergy* (ed. 8 by K. M. Macmorran, 1937), pp. 158–77.

CHURCHYARD. Properly the ground in which a church stands, though the word is often used as though equivalent to '*cemetery' (which it may or may not be). In the past such enclosures were often used as public meeting-places for the conduct of trials, markets, and other secular business.

CIBORIUM (Gk. κιβώριον). (1) A chalice-shaped vessel, with a lid, used to contain the Sacramental Bread of the Eucharist. It apparently came into general use early in the Middle Ages. (2) The term is also sometimes applied to the canopy ('ciborium magnum') resting on four pillars over the altar of Christian *basilicas and other churches, now more usually termed in the W. the '*baldacchino'.

(1) Braun, *A.G.*, pp. 280–347, with plates 51–9.
(2) Braun, *C.A.*, ii, pp. 185–261, with plates 152–8. H. *Leclercq, O.S.B., in *D.A.C.L.*, iii (pt. 2, 1914), cols. 1588–1612, s.v.

CIMABUE (c. 1240–c. 1302), usual name of 'Cenni di Pepo'. Florentine painter. Little is known of his life. G. Vasari, the 16th-cent. historian of Italian art, makes him the teacher of *Giotto and almost the father of the Italian Renaissance; and his fame is attested by *Dante's mention of him in the 'Divina Commedia' (*Purg.* xi. 94–6). Among the pictures that have been attributed to him, none of which can claim documentary evidence, are the 'Madonna and Child' in the Louvre, the 'Madonna and Child with Angels' in the National Gallery in London, and the paintings in the church of St. *Francis at *Assisi, esp. a monumental 'Virgin with Child' between four angels, a large figure of St. Francis, and an impressive 'Crucifixion'. His mosaics in the cathedral of Pisa, the finest of them being the 'Christ in glory', were executed during the last years of his life. The famous 'Madonna' of the chapel of the Rucellai in S. Maria Novella at Florence, which tradi-

tion has ascribed to him, has in recent times been assigned to the Sienese painter, Duccio di Buoninsegna (c. 1255–1319) and dated at 1285.

A. Nicholson, *Cimabue*. A Critical Study (Princeton Monographs in Art and Archaeology, XVI, 1932) incl. reff. to other works. R. Salvini, *Cimabue* (Rome, 1946).

CINCTURE. See *Girdle*.

CIRCUMCELLIONS. Fanatical bands of predatory peasants who flourished in the north of Africa, esp. Numidia, in the 4th cent. They were so named by their Catholic opponents, from their encircling attacks on their dwellings (*circum cellas*), but they preferred themselves to be known as 'Agonistici', i.e. 'soldiers (of Christ)'. Though they were originally concerned only with the remedy of (probably genuine) social grievances, they became linked up with the *Donatists; and as such they used great violence in behalf of the Donatist cause, taking as their battle-cry the words 'laudes Deo' ('praises be to God'). The civil government tried to subdue them by force and persuasion in turn, but they survived into the 5th cent. E. *Gibbon compared them with the *camisards of Languedoc of the early 18th cent.

The chief Patristic reff. include *Optatus, *De Schismate Donatistarum*, iii, 4, and St. *Augustine, *Contra Gaudentium*, I, xxviii, 32, and *Enarratio in Ps.* cxxxii, 3, 6. Further Patristic reff. in W. H. C. Frend, *The Donatist Church*. A Movement of Protest in Roman North Africa (1952), esp. pp. 172–8, and in art. by G. Bareille in *D.T.C.*, ii (1905), cols. 2315–18, s.v. 'Circoncellions'. D. M. von Nathusius, *Zur Charakteristik der Circumcellionen* (1900).

CIRCUMCISION. Though circumcision had long been in use as a religious rite among the Jews, for whom it was part of the Law of *Moses (e.g. Gen. 17. 12, Ex. 12. 48), it was abandoned at a very early date by nearly the whole Christian Church. The conference at *Jerusalem c. A.D. 50 (cf. Acts 15 and Gal. 1 and 2) determined that it should cease to be obligatory on Gentiles; and St. Paul frequently insisted that even for those who continued to practise it, it was valueless unless accompanied by inward conversion. From a remote date, however, the rite has been in use in the Church of *Ethiopia, where it is performed between the third and eighth day after birth, i.e. before the child is baptized. In St. Paul's Epistles (e.g. Rom. 3. 30, Eph. 2. 11), 'the circumcision' (ἡ περιτομή) is often used substantivally of the Jewish people.

The Jewish Rite of Circumcision, with prayers and laws appertaining thereto. Translated into English, with an introductory essay by A. Asher (1873). Articles by L. H. Gray ('Introductory'), L. Spence ('American'), G. Foucart ('Egyptian'), D. S. Margoliouth ('Muslim'), and G. A. Barton ('Semitic') in *H.E.R.E.*, iii (1910), pp. 659–80.

CIRCUMCISION, Feast of the. The feast kept on 1 Jan., the eighth day after *Christmas, in commemoration of Christ's circumcision (cf. Lk. 2. 21: 'when eight days were accomplished'). The observance goes back to the middle of the 6th cent. It then spread, at first esp. in Gaul, but it did not become established at *Rome till the 9th cent. Its relatively late introduction into the Christian calendar has been connected with the unwillingness of the Church to introduce a festival on New Year's Day which had been kept with great riot and licence by the pagans. Indeed, many early Missals provided a second Mass for use on that day against idolatrous practices (*ad prohibendum ab idolis*). In the *Armenian Church, the feast is observed on 13 Jan. In the RC Church it is a Feast of *Obligation.

F. Bünger, *Geschichte der Neujahrsfeier in der Kirche* (1910). F. *Cabrol, *Les Origines liturgiques* (1906), Appendice C, 'le Premier des Calendes de Janvier et la Messe contre les Idoles', pp. 203–10. Id. in *D.A.C.L.*, iii, pt. 2 (1914), cols. 1717–28, s.v., incl. further bibl.

CIRCUMINCESSION. Also Circumin-session. In Christian theology the technical term for the interpenetration of the Three Persons of the Holy Trinity. The corresponding Gk. word, περιχώρησις (lit. 'a proceeding around'), used by St. *John of Damascus in this connexion, was rendered into Latin 'circumincessio' by Burgundio of Pisa (d. 1194); and this later became changed into 'circuminsessio' through similarity of sound.

CISTERCIAN ORDER. The order of White Monks, so called from the mother house at *Cîteaux, which was founded in 1098 by St. *Robert of Molesme and several other brethren who sought to establish a form of *Benedictinism stricter and more primitive than any then existing. After some precarious years Cîteaux rose rapidly to celebrity through its connexion with its most famous son, *St. Bernard of Clairvaux, who became a novice there in 1112. In the following decades the order spread very rapidly to almost every part of W. Europe. Before the end of the 12th cent. 530 Cistercian abbeys were established and 150 more in the next hundred years. The first notable foundation in England was at Waverley, Surrey (1128–9), soon followed by *Rievaulx (*c.* 1131).

The Cistercian life was to be one of secluded communal intercession and adoration. Houses were to be erected only in remote situations, while its churches were to be plain in character and their ornaments and vestments were not made from precious materials. Strict rules on diet and silence were laid down and manual labour given its primitive prominent position. The Cistercians thus became important agricultural pioneers, playing a notable part in English sheep farming, the care of their estates being for long undertaken by lay brethren who lived under somewhat less severe rules.

The 'Charter of Love' drawn up in 1119 by the English Abbot of Cîteaux, St. *Stephen Harding, laid down the constitution of the order. Each house regulated its own affairs in accordance with the ordinances of the annual General Chapters at Cîteaux, at which

it was represented. The General Chapter saw to the maintenance of discipline, due observance of old customs, and the establishment of necessary new ones. Cistercian observances powerfully influenced those of other medieval orders, notably certain congregations of *regular canons, and after 1215 their scheme of periodic general chapters was made obligatory for other monastic orders. After the 13th cent. the fame of the order waned considerably, but the 17th cent. saw the rise of certain important reformed congregations of which the most notable was that of *La Trappe (see *Trappists*) founded by the abbot, de *Rancé (d. 1700).

J. M. Canivez, Ord. Cist. Ref. (ed.), *Statuta Capitulorum Generalium Ordinis Cisterciensis* (8 vols., Bibliothèque de la Revue d'Histoire Ecclésiastique, fascc., ix–xivB, 1933–41). P. Guiguard (ed.), *Les Monuments primitifs de la règle cistercienne*, publiés d'après les manuscripts de l'abbaye de Cîteaux (1878). B. Tissier, O.S.B. (ed.), *Bibliotheca Patrum Cisterciensium, id est Operum Abbatum et Monachorum Ordinis Cisterciensis qui Saeculo S. Bernardi aut paulo post eius Obitum floruerunt* (8 vols., bound in 3, Bonnefontaine and Paris, 1660–9). P. Le Nain, Ord. Cist., *Essai de l'histoire de l'ordre de Cîteaux* (9 vols., 1695–7). J. B. Mahn, *L'Ordre cistercien et son gouvernement, des origines au milieu du XIIIᵉ siècle, 1098–1265* (Bibliothèque des Écoles Françaises d'Athènes et de Rome, cxvi; 1945). *A Concise History of the Cistercian Order . . . with its Revival in England.* By a Cistercian Monk (1852). J. S. Fletcher, *The Cistercians in Yorkshire* (1919). Heimbücher, i (1933), pp. 330–62, and ii (1934), p. 655 f., with bibl. A Dietrich in *L.Th.K.*, x (1938), cols. 1078–83, s.v. 'Zisterzienser', with bibl.; J. M. Canivez, Ord. Cist. Ref., in *D.H.G.E.*, xii (1953), cols. 874–997, s.v. 'Cîteaux (Ordre)', with full bibl. The *Cistercienser-Chronik* ed. by the Cistercians of Mehrerau (ib., 1889 ff.); *Analecta Sacri Ordinis Cisterciensis* (Rome, 1945 ff.). A. A. King, *Cîteaux and her Elder Daughters* (1954), pp. 1–105. L. Bouyer, Cong. Orat., *La Spiritualité de Cîteaux* (1955; Eng. tr., 1958).

CITATION. A summons to appear before a court of justice, and esp. an ecclesiastical court. In the days when the probate of wills was a matter for these courts, citation was the normal method of opening proceedings. Any person may still be cited, e.g. even a *lay rector not himself a member of the C of E, for offences against ecclesiastical law.

CÎTEAUX (Lat. *Cistercium*). The mother house of the *Cistercian Order (q.v.) in Burgundy, some 16 miles S. of Dijon. The house and property, lost by the Order in 1791, were restored to it in 1898. The abbot, who retains his headship of the order, resides in *Rome, and governs his community through an auxiliary.

J. M. Canivez in *D.H.G.E.*, xii (1953), cols. 852–74, s.v., with bibl. L. M. Cottineau, O.S.B., *Répertoire topo-bibliographique des abbayes et prieurés* (Mâcon, 1935), cols. 787–90, with extensive bibl.

CITIES OF REFUGE, The (Heb. עָרֵי מִקְלָט). In the Mosaic Law the six walled cities, three on each side of *Jordan, which were to be set aside as a protection for those who had committed accidental homicide (Deut. 4. 41–3, 19. 1–13, and Josh. 20). The existence of such places was made necessary by the primitive law which required blood vengeance from the next of kin (*goel*). In the earlier legislation of Exod. 21. 13 f. (the 'Book of the Covenant'), apparently any altar offered such asylum. Acc. to Deut. 19. 1, three were to be appointed when the Hebrews were established W. of Jordan and three more when the whole land was conquered (Deut. 19. 1 f.). In Josh. 20, where the selection of the Cities is attributed to *Joshua (not, as in Deut. 4. 41–3, to *Moses), their names are Kedesh, Shechem, Hebron, Bezer, Ramoth in Gilead, and Golan. Asylum involved trial; and if the verdict was murder, the refuge was withdrawn.

CIVIL CONSTITUTION OF THE CLERGY, The. The legislative measures voted during the French Revolution by the 'Constituante' on 12 July 1790, and sanctioned by Louis XVI, which imposed on the Church of France a schismatic organization. Inspired by an exaggerated *Gallicanism, they were designed to realize the independence of the French Church from the Papacy except in strictly doctrinal matters, and to follow up the preliminary measures of the abolition of tithes (1789) and the withdrawal of the civil sanction of religious vows (1790). This 'Constitution Civile du Clergé' abolished the old dioceses and conformed the ecclesiastical districts to the *départements* of the civil administration. Of the hierarchy only the curés, vicaires, and bishops were retained, but the powers of these last were considerably diminished, being made dependent on an 'episcopal council'. The Pope, though still recognized as the head of the new Church, with whom it was desired to remain in communion, was deprived of all actual power, including the right of the canonical confirmation of bishops, which was transferred to the metropolitans. The salaries of the clergy of all grades were to be regulated by the State, as whose officials they were henceforth to be regarded. Other administrative reforms were introduced.

This Constitution, which was signed by Louis XVI against his will, was immediately opposed by the entire French episcopate, who attacked its provisions as schismatic, on the ground that it separated France from her legitimate bishops and from the Pope, and as heretical, because it denied the doctrines of the Papal primacy of jurisdiction, the hierarchical superiority of bishops over priests, and the right of the Church to govern herself. The legitimate bishops continued to ignore the new laws and to administer their old dioceses. On 24 Nov. 1790 the Constitutional Oath was imposed on the entire clergy under pain of punishment. It was taken by only four of the 130 diocesan bishops and a small percentage of the lower clergy, the others, called the '*réfractaires*', being immediately deprived of their offices. The Civil Constitution was formally condemned by Pius VI in the brief 'Caritas' of 13 Apr. 1791, in which the oath was denounced as sacrilegious, the 'Constitution' pronounced heretical, sacrilegious, and schismatic in several of its articles, and all ordinations made under it declared sacrilegious and null. See also *Constitutional Church.

Text in *Archives parlementaires de 1787 à 1860*. Recueil complet des débats législatifs et politiques des chambres françaises imprimé par ordre du Sénat et de la Chambre des Députés sous la direction de . . . J. Mavidal . . –E. Laurent, Série Iᵉ, xvii (1884), pp. 55–60; Eng. tr. of main clause, with comm., in S. Z. Ehler–J. B. Morrall (edd.), *Church and State Through the Centuries* (1954), pp. 236–49. The brief 'Caritas' is pr. in A. Barléri–R. Segreti, I.C. (edd.), *Bullarii Romani Continuatio . . . Clementis XIII. Clementis XIV. Pii VI. Pii VII. Leonis XII. et Pii VIII.*, ix (Rome, 1845), pp. 11–19. C. Constantin in *D.T.C.*, iii (1908), cols. 1537–1605, s.v. 'Constitution civile du clergé', with bibl. See also bibl. to *Constitutional Church.*

CIVILTÀ CATTOLICA. A periodical published twice monthly by the Italian *Jesuits. At the time of the *Vatican Council (1869–70), it actively attacked *liberalism and supported Papal Infallibility.

CLAIRVAUX (Lat. *Clara Vallis*). The fourth house of the *Cistercian Order, founded in 1115 by St. *Bernard of Clairvaux. It rapidly rose to fame, and in 1143 Alfonso I of Portugal made his kingdom a vassal to it, undertaking to pay a yearly tribute. After a period of decadence, the strictness of the Cistercian Rule was re-established at Clairvaux by Abbot Denis Largentier in 1615. The community was broken up, and the house and property taken over by the state in 1790, during the French Revolution.

A. A. King, *Cîteaux and her Elder Daughters* (1954), pp. 207–328. A. [E.] Prévost, 'Recueil des chartes et bulles de Clairvaux' in *Revue Mabillon*, xiv (1924), pp. 140–56, 233–242, xv (1925), pp. 145–67, 258–71, 308–17, xvi (1926), pp. 49–62, 166–9, 237–48, 369–84, xvii (1927), pp. 62–71, 286–290, 421–8, xviii (1928), pp. 66–76, 158–76, 240–56, 324–37, and xix (1929), pp. 161–72. J. Waquet (ed.), *Recueil des chartes de l'abbaye de Clairvaux* (Troyes, 1950 ff.). J. J. Vernier (ed.), 'Inventaire du trésor de la sacristie de l'abbaye de Clairvaux de 1640' in *Bibliothèque de l'École des Chartes*, lxiii (1902), pp. 599–677. H. M. d'Arbois de Jubainville–M. L. Pigeotte, *Études sur l'état intérieur des abbayes cisterciennes et principalement de Clairvaux au XIIᵉ et au XIIIᵉ siècles* (1858). P. Pietresson de Saint-Aubin (ed.), 'Le Livre des sépultures des abbés de Clairvaux (1114–1647)' in *Revue Mabillon*, xix (1929), pp. 303–23. J. M. Canivez, Ord. Cist. Ref., in *D.H.G.E.*, xii (1953), cols. 1050–61, s.v., with bibl.

CLANDESTINITY. The celebration of marriages without the cognizance of proper authority. The abuse became widespread in the later Middle Ages and in the 16th cent. Protestants and Catholics alike were anxious for reform. In his *Von Ehesachen* (1530) M. *Luther strongly opposed unions contracted without parental knowledge or approval, regarding such marriages (to which he esp. applied the term 'clandestine') as null and void; and he was closely followed by P. *Melanchthon, J. *Brenz, J. *Calvin, and T. *Beza. The RC canonists, though less concerned with parental consent (in which they saw a frequent danger to the liberty of the children), were at least as eager for publicity. But to insist on it as a *sine qua non* seemed to imply that the Church possessed the power of altering the matter of a sacrament. After long discussions it was laid down in Session XXIV of the Council of *Trent that though clandestine marriages were true and proper marriages (*vera et rata matrimonia*), provided that they had not been rendered void by the Church, in future all such marriages in places where the ruling of the decree obtained would be held to be null. Henceforward all marriages were to be *in facie ecclesiae*, i.e. before the parish priest. This ruling has now been embodied in the decree *Tametsi* and its recent modification in *Ne Temere* (qq.v.).

In the C of E publicity is secured by the publication of banns or the issue of a licence, and by the requirement of proper witnesses to the ceremony. Marriages without banns were formally condemned in the 11th Canon of the Synod of *Westminster (1200). Can. 62 of the English *Canons of 1604 also orders that the marriage shall take place 'in time of Divine service'. In 1754, civil legislation was introduced to prevent clandestine marriages by Lord *Harwicke's Act (q.v.), while since the Marriage Act of 1823 (4 Geo. IV, c. 76, s. 28) the law has required as a minimum of publicity two or more credible witnesses, besides the minister. In the C of E clandestinity is commonly held not to void a marriage though the canons provide for the punishment of ministers celebrating such marriages.

CLAPHAM SECT. An informal group of wealthy Anglican *Evangelicals, so named by Sydney Smith (1764–1840), because the majority of its members lived near Clapham and worshipped in its parish church. Among the most outstanding were J. *Venn, Rector of Clapham from 1792 to 1813, Charles Grant (1746–1832), Z. *Macaulay (q.v.), Lord Teignmouth (1751–1834), James Stephen (1758–1832), Henry Thornton (1760–1815), Granville Sharp (1735–1813) and W. *Wilberforce (q.v.). Although at bottom conservative in their attitude to the social order, they shared a keen sense of moral responsibility and the belief that religion must be manifested in good works. Among the most important schemes in which they engaged were the struggle for the abolition of the *slave-trade, the extension of missionary enterprise, esp. in *India, the foundation of the *British and Foreign Bible Society and the establishment of a model colony in Sierra Leone. They also promoted such schemes for the improvement of moral standards at home as the Proclamation Society (founded 1789), the Society for Bettering the Conditions and Increasing the Comforts of the Poor (1794) and the extension of *Sunday Schools. Towards the end of her life H. *More (q.v.) was closely connected with the group. Mainly through the personal position of its members, many of whom were interrelated by marriage, the group was able to exercise on parliament and public opinion an influence out of all proportion to its numbers.

J. Stephen, *Essays in Ecclesiastical Biography*, ii (1849), pp. 287–382 ('The Clapham Sect'). E. M. Howse, *Saints in Politics*. The 'Clapham Sect' and the Growth of Freedom (1953).

CLAPTON SECT. A rather loosely defined group of Anglican High Churchmen at the beginning of the 19th cent., so called because the home of Joshua Watson (1771–1855), the most prominent, was at Clapton (with allusion also to the then much talked of *Clapham Sect of Low Churchmen). They were also known as the 'Hackney Phalanx'.

E. Churton (ed.), *Memoir of Joshua Watson* (2 vols., 1861) passim. Y. Brilioth, *The Anglican Revival*. Studies in the Oxford Movement (1925), p. 25 f.

CLARE, St. (1194–1253), foundress of the '*Poor Clares'. In 1212, moved by the teaching of St. *Francis of *Assisi, she gave up all her possessions and joined him at the *Portiuncula. He placed her at first in a *Benedictine house, but very soon, when other women wished also to live on Franciscan lines, he set up a separate community, with St. Clare as abbess (1215), and she occupied this position for the rest of her life. Several daughter houses were soon founded in Italy, France, and Germany. The austerity of the rule went far beyond any that women had previously undertaken, and, although many of the daughter houses obtained dispensations from the original ban upon communal property, the community of 'San Damiano' at Assisi, with those of Perugia and Florence, obtained at St. Clare's wish the 'privilegium paupertatis' from *Gregory IX, which enabled them to maintain their original state of entire poverty. She was canonized by Alexander IV in 1255. Feast day, 12 Aug.

Contemporary life, attributed to *Thomas of Celano, pr. in *AA.SS.*, Aug. II (1735), pp. 754–67; also ed. from MS. 338 of the Bibl. Comunale of Assisi by F. Pennacchi (Assisi, 1910). Eng. tr. by P. Robinson, O.F.M. (London, 1910), with Eng. tr. of her rule in appendix, pp. 99–123. B. Bughetti, O.F.M. (ed.), 'Legenda Versificata S. Clarae Assisiensis, Saec. XIII' in *A.F.H.*, v (1912), pp. 237–60 and 459–81; 14th cent. metrical life ed. L. Oliger, O.F.M., ib., xii (1919), pp. 110–31. Life, written in 1494, by Ugolino Verino (1442–1505), ed., with introd. and notes, W. Seton (Chelsea, 1921). Z. Lazzeri, O.F.M., 'Il processo di canonizzazione di S. Chiara d'Assisi' in *A.F.H.*, xiii (1920), pp. 403–507. E. Gilliat-Smith, *Saint Clare of Assisi*. Her Life and Legislation (1914). P. Robinson, O.F.M., 'St. Clare' in A. G. Little (ed.), *Franciscan Essays* (1913), No. iii, pp. 31–49. Other studies by L. Moisson (Paris, c. 1913), M. Beaufreton ('Les Saints', 1916), and C. Mauclair (Paris, 1925). L. Oliger, O.F.M., in *E.C.*, iii (1950), cols. 1419–21, s.v. 'Chiara d' Assisi', for further bibl. See also bibl. to *Poor Clares*.

CLARENDON, The Constitutions of. Sixteen enactments, put forward by Henry II of England in the name of English custom to regulate the relations between ecclesiastical and lay jurisdiction and other matters. They were presented at the Council of Clarendon (1164) for the assent of St. Thomas *Becket, Abp. of *Canterbury, who accepted them at the Council, but refused the irrevocable act of affixing his seal. The most important clauses asserted the King's jurisdiction in criminal cases over clerics as well as lay persons; but later Becket withdrew his assent to these clauses, the Pope condemned them, and the claim was never put forward again until the 16th cent. But the King secured other important constitutions, notably the right of lay persons to retain advowsons, the control of churches in the King's fee, and the election of

Bishops in the King's chapel. As an early attempt, partly successful, to define the legal relations between Church and State, the Constitutions were a landmark in English ecclesiastical history.

Text in W. *Stubbs (ed.), *Select Charters* (ed. 9 by H. W. C. Davis, 1913), pp. 163–7, with introd., pp. 161–3. Eng. tr. in Gee–Hardy, pp. 68–73 (No. xxiii). See also bibl. cited under *Becket*, St. Thomas.

CLARKE, SAMUEL (1675–1729), divine. A native of *Norwich, he was educated at Caius College, Cambridge, where he came under I. *Newton's influence. His ability attracted the notice of J. Moore, Bp. of Norwich, who in 1698 appointed him his chaplain. In 1704 and 1705 he delivered two sets of Boyle Lectures in defence of rational theology against the empiricism of J. *Locke. They were later published (1705–6), with the joint title (from 1716) of *A Discourse concerning the Being and Attributes of God, the Obligations of Natural Religion, and the Truth and Certainty of the Christian Revelation*. Though a critic of the *Deists, Clarke did not conceal his sympathy with some aspects of their teaching. In *A Letter to Mr. Dodwell* (1706) he defended against H. *Dodwell the natural immortality and incorporeality of the soul. In 1706 he was appointed Rector of St. Benet's, Paul's Wharf, and in 1709 Rector of St. James's, Piccadilly. In 1712 he aroused the indignation, esp. of High Churchmen, by his *Scripture-Doctrine of the Trinity*, which had marked *Unitarian leanings. He was attacked by R. *Nelson and D. *Waterland; and the Lower House of Convocation sought his condemnation. The Upper House, however, imposed no formal retractation, when Clarke promised to write no further on the subject. In the next years he entered into a correspondence with G. W. *Leibniz on space and time (publd. 1717), defending the Newtonian doctrines, and also on the nature of free-will. On Newton's death (1727) he declined an invitation to succeed him as Master of the Mint. His other writings include *Three Practical Essays, viz. on Baptism, Confirmation, Repentance* (1699), a critique of J. *Toland's *Amyntor* (1699), *Paraphrases on the Gospels of Mt. (1701), Mk. and Lk. (1702), and some collections of *Sermons*.

Collected ed. of his Works (4 vols., London, 1738), with life by B. *Hoadly repr. in vol. i, pp. i–xiv (previously prefixed to ed. of Clarke's Sermons by John Clarke, 10 vols., 1730–1, vol. i, pp. i–l). The principal authority is the life by his friend, W. *Whiston (London, 1730; a brief memoir by T. Emlyn is appended to ed. 3, 1748). R. Zimmermann, 'Samuel Clarke's Leben und Lehre. Ein Beitrag zur Geschichte des Rationalismus in England' in *Denkschriften der k. Akademie der Wissenschaften*. Phil.-hist. Cl., xix (Vienna, 1870), pp. 249–336; J. E. Le Rossignol, *The Ethical Philosophy of Samuel Clarke* (Diss., Leipzig, 1892). L. Stephen in *D.N.B.*, x (1887), pp. 443–6.

CLARKSON, THOMAS (1760–1846), antislave-trade agitator. Educated at St. John's College, Cambridge, he decided to devote his life to the repression of the slave trade, on which he had just written a prize essay. He was ordained deacon but hardly ever exercised his ministry. With some leading *Quakers and with W. *Wilberforce he formed in 1787 a group which pressed in the House of Commons for the abolition of the slave trade. Their vigorous efforts were rewarded by the Act of 1807 ending the traffic, and the emancipation of the slaves in 1833. Clarkson spent some time in France soon after the outbreak of the Revolution, urging here also the abolition of slave trade with other abuses, and after the Peace of Vienna in 1815 propagated his views at the various European congresses. His books include *A Portraiture of Quakerism* (1806); *History of the Rise, Progress, and Accomplishment of the Abolition of the African Slave Trade by the British Parliament* (2 vols., 1808); *Memoirs of the Private and Public Life of William Penn* (2 vols., 1813); and *Researches, Antediluvian, Patriarchal, and Historical concerning the Way in which Men first acquired their Knowledge of God and Religion* (1836).

E. L. Griggs, *Thomas Clarkson. The Friend of Slaves* (1936), incl. complete bibl. G. F. R. Barker in *D.N.B.*, x (1887), pp. 454–6.

CLASS MEETING. A meeting, usually held weekly, of small sections of each congregation of *Methodists, under a class leader appointed by the pastor, at which contributions to the Church funds are paid, and inquiry is made into the conduct and spiritual progress of individual members. This institution, peculiar to Methodism, dates from 1742.

CLAUDEL, PAUL LOUIS CHARLES (1868–1955), French Catholic author and diplomat. He was born at Villeneuve-sur-Fin (Aisne) and, at the age of 18, was converted from worldliness to Christian fervour. He entered the diplomatic service in 1892, and after a distinguished career, which led him to the U.S.A., the Far East, and many cities of Central Europe, became ambassador at Tokio in 1921. His claim to fame rests chiefly on his poetry and a striking series of mystery plays of which the central theme was the consecration of the world to God in Christ. The most beautiful of his plays is the famous *L'Annonce faite à Marie* (1912), a canticle on the religious meaning of voluntary suffering and expiation lived by the leprous woman Violaine, who thus becomes a mediatrix of grace to others. In *Le Soulier de satin* (1929) he resumed the same theme of the sacrificial life, though with less poetic vigour, and with a man as the central figure. His poems, remarkable for their fascinating rhythm as well as for their deep religious insight, have appeared in several collections, among them *Cinq Grandes Odes* (1910), *Deux Poèmes d'été* (ed. 2, 1914), *Feuilles des saints* (1925), and *Un Poète regarde la croix* (1938). Though not always easy to understand, their profound symbolism, powerful Biblical imagery, and stirring realization of the Cross as the centre of the world, rank them with the finest Christian poetry of our time.

Jacques Rivière et Paul Claudel. Correspondance, 1907–1914, ed. I. Rivière (1926), with introd., pp. i–xxi (Eng. tr. as 'Letters to a Doubter', 1929); *Paul Claudel et André Gide*. Correspondance, 1899–1926, ed. R. Mallet (1949; Eng. tr., 1952). J. Rivière, *ludes* (1911), No. 3: 'Paul Claudel, poète chrétien', pp. 61–129. F. Lefèvre, *Les Sources de Paul Claudel* (1927); J. Madaule, *Le Génie de Paul Claudel* (1933); id., *Le Drame de Paul Claudel* (1936); C. Chonez, *Introduction à Paul Claudel* (1947). P. Rywalski, O.F.M. Cap., *Claudel et la Bible*. La Bible dans l'œuvre littéraire de Paul Claudel (1948). K. O'Flaherty, *Paul Claudel and the Tidings Brought to Mary* (1948). M. Ryan, *Introduction to Paul Claudel* (1951), with bibl. p. 110 f.

CLAUDIANUS MAMERTUS (c. 425–c. 474),
Christian philosopher and younger brother of St. *Mamertus, Abp. of Vienne. Born in the vicinity of Lyons, after practising as a rhetorician, he became a monk, probably at Lyons, and was later ordained a presbyter by his brother. He was also a close friend of *Sidonius Apollinarius. His principal work was a treatise 'De Statu Animae' (3 Books, 467–472) in which he defended against *Faustus of Riez, who, following an earlier W. tradition (*Tertullian, *Hilary), held that the soul as a created substance was of a corporeal and extended character, the *Neo-platonist doctrine accepted by St. *Augustine that the soul was immaterial. He also wrote a letter to the rhetorician Sapaudus in which he bemoaned the level of the arts in his age.

Works in J. P. Migne, *PL*, liii, 697–786. Crit. ed. by A. Engelbrecht in *C.S.E.L.*, xi (1885). Id., 'Untersuchungen über die Sprache des Claudianus Mamertus' in *Sb.* (Wien), cx (1886), pp. 423–542. Study by R. de la Broise (Paris, thesis, 1890). P. Courcelle, *Les Lettres grecques en occident* (Bibliothèque des Écoles Françaises d'Athènes et de Rome, clix; 1943), pp. 223–35 (on Claudianus' relation to *Porphyry). Bardenhewer, iv, pp. 591–4. A. Seider in *L.Th.K.*, ii (1931), col. 980 f.

CLAUDIUS (d. c. 830–840), Bp. of Turin.
He was of Spanish birth, and became master of the royal schools of Aquitaine before his promotion to the see of Turin c. 817. He made a series of attacks on image-worship, relics, the adoration of the Cross, and indeed every visible symbol of Christ's life, as well as on *pilgrimages and the intercession of saints. He had scant regard for the authority of the Roman see, and his views, which were regarded as heretical by many, were refuted at the request of *Louis the Pious by Dungal and Jonas of Orléans. He was also famous for his Biblical commentaries which displayed an unusually wide knowledge of the works of St. *Augustine. Some of the older historians of the *Waldenses (J. Leger, A. Muston) claimed him as their founder.

Most of his writings are still in MS.; those publd. are repr. in J. P. Migne, *PL*, civ, 615–928. Crit. ed. of 'Epp.' by E. Dümmler in *M.G.H.*, Epistolae, iv (1895), pp. 586–613. Id., 'Über Leben und Lehre des Bischofs Claudius von Turin' in *Sb.* (Berl.) (1895), pp. 427–43. E. J. Martin, *A History of the Iconoclastic Controversy* (C.H.S. [1930]), esp. pp. 262–6. Manitius, i, pp. 390–6 (with account of MS. material). F. Vernet in *D.T.C.*, iii (1908), cols. 12–19, s.v.

CLAUDIUS APOLLINARIUS. See *Apollinarius, Claudius*.

CLAUSURA ('closure' or, more usually, 'enclosure').
(1) The practice of separating a part of a religious house to the exclusion of those of the opposite sex to the community;

and (2) the portion so enclosed. The clausura is found in all religious orders, both in E. and W., and dates from the earliest monastic rules. Permission, general or particular, is needed for religious to go outside the clausura, or for outsiders to come in, while in some cases even lay persons of the same sex as the community are held to violate the clausura by entrance. In some communities, certain parts of the house or church are neutral ground, which both the community and outsiders may enter without leave. The enclosure is more strict in women's orders than men's, and most strict of all in the enclosed orders.

CLAYTON, JOHN (1709–73),
one of the first '*Methodists'. Educated at Manchester Grammar School and Brasenose College, Oxford, he was a member of the '*Holy Club', founded by the *Wesleys. After ordination in 1732, he was put in charge of the Sacred Trinity Chapel, Salford, where J. Wesley and G. *Whitefield often preached for him. In 1740 he became a chaplain, and in 1760 a Fellow, of the Manchester Collegiate Church. Throughout his life he was a supporter of the Jacobites, giving great offence by his political views to the Whigs of the district. For many years he also conducted an academy at Salford.

Memoir by L. Tyerman, 'The Rev. John Clayton, M.A., the Jacobite Churchman', in *The Oxford Methodists* (1873), pp. 24–56. C. W. Sutton in *D.N.B.*, xi (1887), p. 13 f.

CLEMENS NON PAPA. Jacques Clement
(c. 1500–c. 1556), a Dutch composer of Church music, who was facetiously so called to pretend to distinguish him from the contemporary Pope, Clement VII. He was a forerunner of G. P. da *Palestrina.

CLEMENT OF ALEXANDRIA, St. See
after Pope *Clement XIV*.

CLEMENT OF ROME, St. (fl. c. 96), Bp.
of *Rome. He was probably the third bishop after St. *Peter, though he was often held in primitive times to have been his immediate successor. He may have belonged, e.g. as an ex-slave, to the family of T. Flavius Clemens, cousin of the Emp. *Domitian, which there is reason to associate with Christianity, and it is just possible he is the Clement referred to in Phil. 4. 3 (written from Rome?). Besides the spurious '*Clementine Literature' (q. v.), two 'Epp. to the Corinthians' have been ascribed to him. The former Epistle ('I Clement') is genuine, and is his real title to fame. It was written c. 96 in the name of the Roman Church to deal with fierce strife in the Church at Corinth, where certain presbyters had been deposed. Clement issued a call to repentance, insisting that God required due order in all things and that the deposed presbyters must be reinstated and legitimate superiors obeyed. The Apostles 'appointed bishops and deacons' in every place, and it was they who gave directions how the ministry should perpetuate

itself. Clement calls the higher class of ministers indifferently 'bishops' (ἐπίσκοποι) and 'presbyters' (or elders, πρεσβύτεροι). He refers to 'offering the gifts' (*sc.* of the *Eucharist) as one of their functions, and to some or all of them as 'rulers' of the Church. Here and elsewhere he affords valuable evidence of the state of the ministry in his time, on the history of the Roman Church and (it has been held) the martyrdoms of Sts. Peter and Paul. The epistle, which was highly regarded, was being read in church at Corinth along with the Scriptures *c.* 170. Feast day, 23 Nov.

The so-called 'Second Epistle of Clement', preserved in the *Codex Alexandrinus and in primitive Syriac Biblical MSS., is really a homily, assigned on stylistic grounds to a separate author. The earliest surviving Christian sermon, it sets out in general terms the character of the Christian life and the duty of repentance. It probably belongs to Corinth (so F. X. Funk, G. Krüger), though some scholars have assigned it to Rome (A. *Harnack, who attributed it to Pope *Soter) or Alexandria (J.R. *Harris, J. V. Bartlet, B. H. *Streeter).

In later tradition St. Clement became the subject of a variety of legends. In the 'Clementine Literature' he figures as the intermediary through whom the Apostles transmit their teaching to the Church. Quite another tradition, preserved in some apocryphal *acta* (not earlier than the 4th cent.), describes how he was banished to the Crimea in the reign of Trajan and forced to work in the mines. It is said that his missionary labours in those parts met with remarkable success and that he was bound to an anchor and thrown into the Black Sea. The legend adds that his tomb, which was built by angels, was shown once a year to the inhabitants by the miraculous ebbing of the tide. Feast day, 23 Nov.

Fullest collection of material, Patristic and modern, in J. B. *Lightfoot, *Apostolic Fathers*. Part I (rev. ed., 2 vols., 1890). The two 'Epp.' survive in two MSS., the [Biblical] *Codex Alexandrinus (B. Mus.; text imperfect) and the Cod. Hierosol. of A.D. 1056 (of *Didache fame) discovered by P. *Bryennios. They were first printed by P. *Young ('Junius'), Oxford, 1633 (whence incorporated by J. B. *Cotelier in his *Patres Apostolici*, 1672); crit. ed. by J. B. Lightfoot, op. cit. Text also in J. P. Migne, *PG*, i and ii (incl. *Clementines). Separate edd. of Gk. text by R. Knopf (*T.U.*, xx, 1, 1899) and C. T. Schaefen (Florilegium Patristicum 44, 1941). Ancient Lat. tr. of I Clem. ed. G. *Morin, O.S.B., Maredsous, 1894; ancient Syr. tr. ed. R. L. Bensly–R. H. *Kennett, London, 1899; Copt. frgmts. ed. F. Rösch, Strassburg, 1910; Eng. tr. of 'Epp.' in J. B. Lightfoot, op cit.; also of I Clem. with useful notes, W. K. Lowther Clarke, S.P.C.K., 1937. W. *Wrede, *Untersuchungen zum ersten Klemensbrief* (1891); T. Schermann, *Griechische Zauberpapyri und das Gemeinde- und Dankgebet im I. Klemensbriefe* (*T.U.*, xxxiv, 2b, 1909); F. Gerke, *Die Stellung des I. Clemensbriefes innerhalb der Entwicklung der altchristlichen Gemeindeverfassung und des Kirchenrechts* (*T.U.*, xlvii, 1, 1931); L. Sanders, *Le Hellénisme de St. Clément de Rome et le paulinisme* (Louvain, 1943). Bardenhewer, i, pp. 116–31; Altaner (ed. 1950), pp. 73–7. J. *Chapman, O.S.B., in *C.E.*, iv (1908), pp. 12–17.

CLEMENT V (1264–1314), Pope from 1305. Bertrand de Got, a member of an influential French family, after studying at Toulouse, Orléans, and *Bologna, was appointed Bp. of Cominges in 1295 and Abp. of Bordeaux in

1299. Elected Pope in 1305 as successor to Benedict XI, he was crowned at Lyons in the presence of Philip the Fair, whose powerful influence made Clement's policy henceforward largely subservient to French interests. By fixing his residence at *Avignon in 1309 and thus inaugurating the seventy years' 'Captivity', Clement further increased his dependence on Philip, and the King insisted on a formal condemnation of Clement's predecessor, *Boniface VIII, on charges of heresy and immorality. The process, however, though actually begun in 1310, was, with Philip's assent, abandoned in 1311 when the King substituted a plan for the abolition of the *Templars whose property he coveted. The order was suppressed at the Council of *Vienne (1311) and, though the Knights Hospitallers received from the Pope the title to its property, the French King contrived to lay his hands on most of its possessions. As a vassal of Edward I, Clement was also brought into English affairs. In 1306 he was persuaded to suspend Robert of *Winchelsea, Abp. of *Canterbury, who was accused by the King of treason for his support of Boniface VIII, but in 1308, under Edward II, Robert was reinstalled at the request of the King. In 1306 he excommunicated Robert Bruce of Scotland for his part in the murder of Red Comyn, and soon after deposed two bishops who had been actively in favour of the Scots rebellion. Despite his political difficulties and the discredit he brought on the Papacy by his taxation and sale of offices, Clement V did much to further scholarship, esp. the study of medicine and oriental languages, and founded the universities of Orléans (1306) and Perugia (1308). He also added to Medieval Canon Law by the so-called '*Clementines' (q.v.).

Bulls ed. by the monks of *Monte Cassino, *Regestum Clementis Papae V ex Vaticanis Archetypis . . . nunc primum editum cura et studio Monachorum Ordinis S. Benedicti (9 vols., bound in 7, with appendix, Rome, 1885–92). R. Fawtier–Yvonne Lanhers, *Tables des registres de Clément V publiés par les Bénédictins* (Bibliothèques des Écoles Françaises d'Athènes et de Rome, 3ᵉ Série, 1948). E. *Baluse, *Vitae Paparum Avenionensium*, ed. G. Mollat (4 vols., 1916–27), esp. vol. i, pp. 1–106 and 551–66. E. Berchon, 'L'Histoire du Pape Clément V (1305–1314)' in *Actes de l'Académie Nationale des Sciences, Belles-Lettres et Arts de Bordeaux*, lv (1893), pp. 493–535, and lvi (1894), pp. 5–171. C. Wenck, *Clement V und Heinrich VII* (1882); G. Lizerand, *Clément V et Philippe IV le Bel* (thesis, Paris, 1910). H. G. Richardson, 'Clement V and the See of Canterbury' in *E.H.R.*, lvi (1941), pp. 96–103; C. Perrat, 'Un Diplomate gascon au XIVᵉ siècle, Raymond de Piis, nonce de Clément V en Orient' in *Mélanges d'Archéologie et d'Histoire*, xliv (1927), pp. 35–90. G. Mollat, *Les Papes d'Avignon* (1912), Book I, ch. 1, and passim. L. *Pastor, *The History of the Popes from the Close of the Middle Ages* (Eng. tr.), i (1891), pp. 58–63. H. Hemmer in *D.T.C.*, iii (1908), cols. 61–9, s.v.; G. Mollat in *D.H.G.E.*, xii (1952), cols. 1115–29, s.v., with full bibl.

CLEMENT VI (1291–1352), Pope from 1342. Pierre Roger entered the *Benedictine monastery of La Chaise-Dieu at the age of 10, and later studied and taught at *Paris. He made a rapid career, becoming Abbot of Fécamp in 1326, Bp. of Arras in 1328, Abp. of Sens in 1329, and Abp. of Rouen in 1330. He was created cardinal by *Benedict XII in 1338. On 7 May 1342 he was elected Pope at *Avignon.

He was a devoted adherent of Philip of Valois, and his French sympathies prevented him from restoring peace between England and France except for the short-lived truce of Malestroit in 1343. He carried on the struggle of his predecessors against Louis of Bavaria, to whom he opposed Charles IV (Charles of Moravia) as anti-King, but Louis's death in 1347 resolved the difficulties. Shortly afterwards the Pope received the submission of *William of Occam and the schismatical *Franciscans, who had lost their strongest protector in the Emperor. In 1347 Clement censured Cola di *Rienzo, whom he had first favoured, for encroaching on the temporal power of the Papacy. Despite the danger of Italy slipping more and more from his control, he established himself firmly at Avignon, the sovereignty of which he bought from Joanna of Naples in 1348. He also appointed a large number of French cardinals. He sought to meet the costs of his enterprises against the Turks as well as those of his own luxurious living by reserving to himself an increasing number of appointments to bishoprics and benefices, a measure which caused great hostility, esp. in England. In 1351 Edward III issued the First Statute of *Provisors, by which the King reserved to himself the right of presentation in all Papal appointments to benefices.

Though strongly inclined to nepotism and prodigality, Clement VI was a benefactor of the poor, whom he generously and courageously assisted, esp. during the epidemic of the black death at Avignon in 1348–9. He was a good theologian, and his jubilee bull of 1350 is a valuable document for the doctrine of *Indulgences. He defended the *Mendicant orders against the secular prelates, and was a protector of the Jews, whose position in the Papal States was better than elsewhere in Europe.

E. Déprez (ed.), Clément VI (1342–1352). Lettres closes, patentes et curiales se rapportant à la France (Bibliothèque des Écoles Françaises d'Athènes et de Rome, 3ᵉ Série, No. 3, 1901 ff.); U. Berlière, O.S.B. (ed.), Lettres de Clément VI, 1342–1352 (Analecta Vaticano-Belgica, vi, etc.; 1924 ff.); id. (ed.), Suppliques de Clément VI, 1342–1352 (ib., i; 1906); E. Griffe (ed.), Lettres patentes des évêques de France, recueillies dans les registres du Pape Clément VI, 1342–1352 (Acta Episcoporum Galliae Saeculo XIV, 1933 ff., i, Province de Bourges); L. Klicman (ed.), Acta Clementis VI Pontificis Romani, 1342–1352 (Monumenta Vaticana Res Gestas Bohemicas Illustrantia, i, Prague, 1903). E. *Baluze, Vitae Paparum Avenionensium (ed. G. Mollat, esp. i (1916), pp. 241–308, with notes, ii (1927), pp. 335–433). P. Fournier, 'Pierre Roger (Clément VI)' in Histoire littéraire de la France, xxxvii (1938), pp. 209–38. H. Frank, 'Clemens' VI finanzpolitische Beziehungen zu Deutschland' in R.Q., xxxviii (1930), pp. 209–79. G. Mollat, 'L'Œuvre oratoire de Clément VI' in Archives d'Histoire Doctrinale et Littéraire du Moyen-Âge, iii (1928), pp. 239–74; P. Schmitz, O.S.B., 'Les Sermons et discours de Clément VI, O.S.B.' in R. Bén., li (1929), pp. 15–34. A. Maier, 'Der literarische Nachlass des Petrus Rogerii (Clement VI) in der Borghesiana' in Recherches de Théologie Ancienne et Médiévale, xv (1948), pp. 332–56, and xvi (1949), pp. 72–98. J. Gay, Le Pape Clément VI et les affaires d'orient, 1342–1352 (thesis, Paris, 1904). G. Mollat, Les Papes d'Avignon (1912), esp. Bk. I, ch. 4. Pastor, i (1891), pp. 85–92. H. Hemmer in D.T.C., iii (1908), cols. 69–72, s.v.; G. Mollat in D.H.G.E., xii (1953), cols. 1129–62, s.v., with full bibl.

CLEMENT VII (1478–1534), Pope from 1523. The son of Giuliano de' Medici and a cousin of *Leo X, he rapidly rose to a high position, becoming Abp. of Florence and Cardinal in 1513. In 1523 he succeeded *Hadrian VI. Though Clement was personally of blameless character, his lack of courage led his reign to be marked by shifty diplomacy and intrigue. He attempted to steer a middle path between the conflicting aims of Francis I of France and the Emp. *Charles V, siding first with the former by the League of Cognac (1526), and then, after the sack of Rome (1527) by the Imperial armies, with the latter by the treaty of Barcelona (1529). He pursued the same irresolute policy of procrastination in relation to the divorce of *Henry VIII from Catherine of Aragon. It was his failure to foster the movement for reform within the Church that encouraged the rapid spread of Protestant doctrine during his pontificate. In his ready patronage of scholars and artists, among the latter B. Cellini, *Raphael, and *Michelangelo, he was a true son of the house of Medici.

H. M. Vaughan, The Medici Popes, Leo X and Clement VII (1908), pp. 285–346; E. Rodocanachi, Histoire de Rome. Les pontificats d'Adrien VI et de Clément VII (1933), pp. 87–270, with bibl. pp. 281–4. Among the principal sources for the history of his relations with Henry VIII are the Calendars of the State Papers of the reign (see s.v. 'Henry VIII'); S. Ehses (ed.), Römische Dokumente zur Geschichte der Ehescheidung Heinrichs VIII von England, 1527–1534 (1893). P. Crabitès, Clement VII and Henry VIII (1936). Pastor, ix (1910), pp. 231–67, and x (1910). H. Hemmer in D.T.C., iii (1908), cols. 72–6, s.v., with bibl., R. Mols, S.J., in D.H.G.E., xii (1953), cols. 1175–1224, s.v., with full bibl. (inaccurate).

CLEMENT VIII (c. 1536–1605), Pope from 1592. The son of Salvestro Aldobrandini, a distinguished Italian lawyer, Ippolito Aldobrandini was a man of high personal character. He became a cardinal in 1585 and was elected Pope in 1592. It was his policy to secure the representation of all the conflicting influences in the *curia, and esp. to limit the dominance of Spanish influence. He supported the League against *Henry of Navarre, but this did not prevent his negotiating with Henry, so that in 1595 Henry was received back into the Catholic Church. Clement was also largely responsible for the ensuing Treaty of Vervins (1598) which brought about peace between France and Spain. His hopes of converting King *James I of England and his queen, Anne of Denmark, to Roman Catholicism were not realized, however. In ecclesiastical matters he pursued a policy of reform. He took a keen interest in the revision of the service books, and issued new editions of the *Vulgate, the *Missal, the *Breviary, the '*Caeremoniale Episcoporum', and the *Pontifical.

P. Van Isacker, 'Notes sur l'intervention militaire de Clément VIII en France à la fin du XVIᵉ siècle' in R.H.E., xii (1911), pp. 702–13. A. Louant, 'L'Intervention de Clément VIII dans le traité de Vervins' in Bulletin de l'Institut Historique Belge de Rome, xii (1932), pp. 127–86. A. O. Meyer, 'Clement VIII und Jakob I von England' in Quellen und Forschungen aus italienischen Archiven und Bibliotheken, vii (1904), pp. 268–306; J. Martin, P.S.S., 'Clément VIII et Jacques Stuart' in Revue d'Histoire Diplomatique, xxv (1911), pp. 279–307 and 359–78. Cav. L. F. Mathaus-Voltolini, 'Die Beteiligung des Papstes Clemens VIII an der Bekämpfung der Türken in den Jahren 1592–1595' in R.Q., xv (1901), pp. 303–26 and 410–23. Pastor, xxiii (1933) and xxiv (1933). J. de La Servière, S.J., in D.T.C., iii (1908), cols. 76–86, s.v.; R. Mols, S.J., in D.H.G.E., xii (1953), cols. 1249–97, s.v., with full bibl. (inaccurate).

CLEMENT XI (1649–1721), Pope from 1700. Giovanni Francesco Albani, who was a native of Urbino, was educated at the Roman College, became a doctor of both Laws, and entered on an administrative career in the Papal States. In 1687 he was appointed Secretary of Papal Briefs and in 1690 he was created cardinal. He was an ecclesiastic of austere habits who, accepting election to the Papacy with reluctance, continued to discharge faithfully his pastoral duties. He met with ill success in the political sphere. In 1701 he protested, without effect, against the assumption of the title of King of Prussia by the Elector of Brandenburg. In the War of the Spanish Succession, having previously favoured the candidature of Philip of Anjou (1683–1746), he afterwards tried to remain neutral and procure a peaceful solution, but was forced in 1701 to recognize Philip, and in 1709, when the Imperial troops had invaded the Papal States, to abandon him in favour of the Archduke Charles; consequently in the Treaty of Utrecht (1713) his rights in Sicily, Sardinia, Parma and Piacenza were ignored. In the same year he quarrelled with the Duke of Savoy about his rights of investiture in Sicily; and when he issued an interdict, all the clergy who accepted it were banished until the island was conquered by Philip V of Spain in 1718. On the declaration of war by the Turks on Venice in 1714, he tried, without success, to organize an alliance of princes against them.

During Clement's reign the long-drawn-out *Jansenist controversy continued within the French Church and Jansenism was once more condemned in the bull '*Vineam Domini Sabaoth' (16 July 1705). This was followed by the condemnation of P. *Quesnel's *Abrégé de la morale de l'évangile* in 1708, and, later, by the famous bull '*Unigenitus Dei Filius' (8 Sept. 1713). He also had to decide the dispute between *Dominicans and *Jesuits on the question of the Chinese rites, esp. the cult of ancestors and of Confucius, which the former condemned while the latter tolerated it. The Pope approved the decision of the *Holy Office which censured the opinion of the Jesuits, but the controversy was not finally settled until the reign of *Benedict XIV. Clement XI was a generous protector of arts and scholarship, one of the most important additions to the *Vatican Library being the MSS. collected at his instigation by J. S. *Assemani.

In 1708 he made the Feast of the *Immaculate Conception of the BVM one of obligation throughout the Church.

Works, inc. Bullarium, ed. by his nephew, Card. Albani (7 vols., Rome, 1722–4), with life [by J. C. Battellus] prefixed to Bullarium (1723); later ed. (2 vols., Rome, 1729). [P. Polidori,] *De Vita et Rebus Gestis Clementis Undecimi* (Urbano, 1727). S. Reboulet, *Histoire de Clément XI Pape* (2 vols., Avignon, 1752). F. Pometti, 'Studii sul pontificato di Clemente XI, 1700–1721' in *Archivio della R. Società Romana di Storia Patria*, xxi (1898), pp. 279–457; xxii (1899) pp. 109–179; xxiii (1900), pp. 239–76, 449–515. L. Nina, *Le finanze pontificie sotto Clemente XI* (1928). A. Aldobrandini, *La guerra di successione di Spagna negli stati dell' Alta Italia dal 1702 al 1705 e la politica di Clemente XI dal carteggio di Mons* (1931). L. Just, *Clemens XI und der Code Léopold (1701–10)* (1935). [J.] Schmidlin, 'Der Konflikt der Anima mit Clemens XI' in *R.Q.*, xvii (1903), pp. 141–59 and 301–23.

P. Feret, 'Négociation secrète entre Louis XIV et Clément XI' in *R.Q.H.*, lxxxv (1909), pp. 108–45. Pastor, xxxiii (1941), with bibl. J. de La Servière, S.J., in *D.T.C.*, iii (1908), cols. 98–111, s.v., with bibl.; R. Mols, S.J., in *D.H.G.E.*, xii (1953), cols. 1326–61, s.v., with full bibl.

CLEMENT XIII (1693–1769), Pope from 1758. Carlo della Torre Rezzonico was a native of Venice, studied with the *Jesuits at *Bologna, and became a doctor of law at Padua. Having been appointed Auditor of the *Rota for *Venice in 1725, he was made cardinal in 1737 and Bp. of Padua in 1743, where he endeared himself to his people by his lavish almsgiving. Soon after his election to the Papacy the storm gathered against the Society of Jesus, which came to be the chief preoccupation of his pontificate. It began in *Portugal, where the all-powerful minister, Sebastian Carvalho, afterwards Marquis de Pombal, first imprisoned and then expelled all the members of the Society under pretext of having conspired against the King, and all relations between the country and the Holy See were severed in 1760. In 1761 the Portuguese example was followed by *France, where the Parlement of Paris demanded drastic alterations in the constitutions of the Society, which Clement refused with the famous words: *Sint ut sunt aut non sint* ('They shall be as they are or not be at all'). In 1764 nearly all the French Jesuits had to go into exile, and Louis XV abolished the order by law in his kingdom. The Pope replied by the bull 'Apostolicum pascendi munus' of 9 Jan. 1765, giving warm praise to the Society and all its good works. In 1767 the Jesuits were expelled also from *Spain, and shipped to Civitavecchia, and soon after also from Naples and Parma. At last, in 1769, the three ambassadors of Spain, Naples, and France demanded the complete and irrevocable destruction of the Society, and the secularization of its members throughout the world, a step which is believed to have hastened Clement's death, which occurred a few days afterwards. The suppression of the Society by Papal authority was effected by his successor, *Clement XIV.

Bulls in A. Babèri (ed.), *Bullarii Romani Continuatio . . . Clementis XIII. Clementis XIV. Pii VI. Pii VII. Leonis XII. et Pii VIII*, ed. C. A. Spetia, i–iii (Rome, 1835–8). J. Holzwarth, *Die Verschwörung der katholischen Höfe gegen Clement den Dreizehnten* (1872). P. Dudon, 'De la suppression de la Compagnie de Jésus (1758–73)' in *R.Q.H.*, cxxxii (1938), pp. 75–107. [G. J. X.] de Lacroix de Ravignon, S.J., *Clément XIII et Clément XIV* (2 vols., 1854), vol. i, pp. 1–236, with documents vol. ii, pp. 1–362. A. Theiner, Orat., *Geschichte des Pontificats Clemens' XIV*, i (Fr. tr., 1852, pp. 23–147). Pastor, xxvi (1950), pp. 143–504, and xxvii (1950). J. de La Servière, S.J., in *D.T.C.*, iii (1908), cols. 115–24, s.v., with bibl.; J. Mols, S.J., in *D.H.G.E.*, xii (1953), cols. 1381–1410, s.v., with full bibl.

CLEMENT XIV (1705–74), Pope from 1769. Giovanni Vincenzo Antonio Ganganelli was the son of a surgeon at Sant' Arcangelo, nr. Rimini, who entered the *Franciscan Order in 1723. In 1746 he was appointed Consultor of the *Holy Office by *Benedict XIV, and in 1759 created cardinal by *Clement XIII. In 1769 he was elected Pope after a stormy conclave, the Bourbon courts having decided to recognize only a Pope determined to suppress the *Jesuits, though whether Ganganelli actually made such a promise is uncertain.

As Pope he made it his chief aim to preserve peace with the Catholic princes in order to gain their support against the growing irreligion. He therefore restored good relations with Parma and *Spain, and esp. *Portugal, by creating cardinal the brother of Marquis de Pombal, the Portuguese prime minister. He also suspended (1773) the annual issue of the bull '*In Coena Domini', which contained the censures reserved to the Pope. But all these concessions failed to satisfy the Bourbon courts, bent on the destruction of the Society of Jesus. After hesitating and using half-measures for some time, Clement at last yielded to the pressure of France and Spain, who threatened a schism if the order were not suppressed. In the Brief '*Dominus ac Redemptor' of 21 July 1773 which decreed its suppression, he gave as the only reason for the step the hostility which the Jesuits incurred and the controversies in which they had been implicated. Thus the order was suppressed in all Catholic states, though Catharine II of Russia and Frederic II of Prussia (the latter only until 1780) refused to promulgate the Papal Brief, so that the Society continued to exist in their realms.

The sacrifice of the Society of Jesus did not, however, procure better relations between the Papacy and the European princes. The former Papal possessions of *Avignon and Benevento were, indeed, restored to the Holy See, but in France a royal commission for the reform of the religious orders continued its activities, suppressing religious houses without Papal approval; in Portugal the secular authorities interfered with ecclesiastical affairs and with the education of the young; and in *Poland hostile tendencies made themselves felt even among the clergy, and esp. in the Order of the *Piarists. Clement XIV introduced many measures for the development of trade and industry in the Pontifical States, but with little success, owing to the opposition of the cardinals and the Roman nobility, who could not forgive the suppression of the Jesuits.

Epistolae et Brevia Selectiora, ed. A. Theiner, Orat. (Paris, 1852). A. L. de Caraccioli, *La Vie du Pape Clément XIV* (1775; Eng. tr., 1776). A. Theiner, Orat., *Geschichte des Pontificats Clemens' XIV* (2 vols., 1853; Fr. tr., 1852). A. von Reumont, *Ganganelli. Papst Clement XIV. Seine Briefe und seine Zeit* (1847). C. Uschener, *Klemens XIV. Ein Lebens- und Charakterbild* (1866). J. A. M. Crétineau-Joly, *Clément XIV et les Jésuits* (1847); C. F. J. Goetting, *Ein verrückter Papst? Ganganelli. Eine Streit- und Zeitschrift* (1886). [G. J. X.] de Lacroix de Ravignon, S.J., *Clément XIII et Clément XIV* (2 vols., 1854), vol. i, pp. 237-483, and vol. ii, pp. 363-492. L. *Pastor, *The History of the Popes from the Close of the Middle Ages* (Eng. tr.), xxxviii ('1951' [1952]). J. de La Servière, S.J., in *D.T.C.*, iii (1908), cols. 124-34, s.v., with bibl.; P. Paschini in *E.C.*, iii (1950), cols. 1836-41, s.v. 'Clemente XIV', with bibl., E. Préclin in *D.H.G.E.*, xii (1953), cols. 1411-23, s.v., with bibl.

CLEMENT OF ALEXANDRIA, St. (*c.* 150–*c.* 215), theologian. He was prob. an *Athenian by birth who, after studying Christianity and philosophy in several places, became a pupil of *Pantaenus, the head of the *Catechetical School at *Alexandria, whom he succeeded in 190. In 202 he was forced to flee by persecution. He was succeeded in turn by his pupil *Origen. His chief works are the 'Protrepticus', or 'An Exhortation to the Greeks'; the 'Paedagogus', on Christian life and manners; and the 'Stromateis', or 'Miscellaneous Studies'. It was the age of *Gnosticism, and Clement so far agreed with the Gnostics in holding 'gnosis', religious knowledge or illumination, to be the chief element in Christian perfection. But for him the only true 'gnosis' was that which presupposed the faith of the Church, Apostolic in its foundation and possessing Divine revelation. While thoroughly loyal to this, Clement explained and supplemented it with the ideas of Greek philosophy, which he also regarded as a Divine gift to mankind. Christ, the *Logos, the second Person of the Divine Trinity, was both the source of all human reason and the interpreter of God to mankind. He became man in order to give a supreme revelation, and that through Him men might partake of immortality. In this latter the sacraments of *Baptism and the *Eucharist are instrumental. Clement saw ignorance and error as a more fundamental evil than sin, and, though he held that not all men would attain to the highest level of blessedness, he took an optimistic view of the ultimate destiny of even the most erring. His 'Quis Dives Salvetur?' is a beautiful exposition of Mk. 10. 17–31, finishing with the narrative of the young man who was baptized, lost, and re-won by St. *John the Apostle. His name occurs in the earlier *martyrologies, where it is assigned to 4 Dec., but *Clement VIII excised it on the advice of C. *Baronius on the grounds of the doubtful orthodoxy of some of Clement's writings.

The 'Protrepticus' and 'Paedagogus' survive in the 'Arethas Codex' (Par. gr. 451 of A.D. 914) and some dependent MSS., the 'Stromateis' in the Florence MS. Laur. V. 3 (saec. xi) and a copy. *Edd. principes* by P. Victorius (Florence, 1550) and F. Sylburg (Heidelberg, 1592); good ed. by J. *Potter, 2 vols., Oxford, 1715. J. P. Migne, *PG*, viii and ix. Crit. ed. by O. Stählin in *G.C.S.*, vols. 1-3, text, 1905-9; vol. 4 (very fine) index, 1934-6. *Stromateis* ('Miscellanies'), Bk. VII, ed. F. J. A. *Hort and J. B. Mayor, with notes, &c., London, 1903; *Protrepticus and Quis Dives Salvetur*, with frgmt., ed. G. W. Butterworth, Loeb, with Eng. tr., 1919; for edd. of *Excerpta ex Theodoto*, see s.v. 'Theodotus'. Studies by C. E. Freppel (Paris, 1865), E. de Faye (Paris, 1898), J. Patrick (London, 1914), R. B. Tollinton (2 vols., London, 1914), G. Bardy (Paris, 1926), G. Lazzati (Milan, 1939), and C. Mondésert, S.J. (Paris, 1944). C. *Bigg, *The Christian Platonists of Alexandria* (ed. F. E. *Brightman, 1913), esp. pp. 72-150. C. Merk, *Clemens Alexandrinus in seiner Abhängigkeit von der griechischen Philosophie* (1879); J. Munck, *Untersuchungen über Klemens von Alexandrien* (1933). E. Molland, 'Clement of Alexandria on the Origin of Greek Philosophy' in *Symbolae Osloenses*, xv-xvi (1936); id., *The Conception of the Gospel in the Alexandrian Theology* (Oslo, 1938), pp. 5-84. Bardenhewer, ii, pp. 15-62; Altaner, pp. 159-64. See also A. de la Barre in *D.T.C.*, iii (1908), cols. 137-99, and G. Békés in *E.C.*, iii (1950), cols. 1842-57.

CLEMENT MARY HOFBAUER, St. See *Hofbauer, St. Clement Mary.*

CLEMENT OF ROME, St. See before Pope *Clement V.*

CLEMENTINE LITERATURE. The many apocryphal writings which circulated in the early Church under the name of St. *Clement of Rome include, besides the so-called 'Second Ep. of Clement' (q.v.), (1) the '*Apostolic Constitutions', (2) two 'Epp. to Virgins', (3) and (4) the 'Clementine Homilies' and 'Recognitions', (5) 'Epitomes' of the last named, (6) the 'Apocalypse of Clement', more commonly known as the 'Apocalypse of St. *Peter' (q.v.), (7) an unpublished Arabic Apocalypse akin to the preceding, and (8) spurious letters in the *False Decretals (q.v.). The term 'Clementines' (Κλημέντια) is by convention restricted to (3), (4), and the less important (5).

(1) The CLEMENTINE HOMILIES ('Ομιλίαι) is a religious and philosophical romance, arranged as twenty discourses, which Clement is supposed to have sent from *Rome to *James of Jerusalem, the Lord's brother, and preceded by two letters from Peter and Clement, also addressed to James. They describe Clement's travels in the East when he met St. Peter and witnessed his conflict with *Simon Magus. The work contains much legendary matter, e.g. about Clement's family. Until A. R. M. Dressel published a complete text on the basis of Cod. Ottobon. 443 in 1853, they were only known in a defective Cod. Par. gr. 930.

(2) The CLEMENTINE RECOGNITIONS ('Αναγνώσεις), in ten books, closely resembles the 'Homilies' in historical setting and theological outlook. Their narrative parts go over much the same ground, with additional details of the vicissitudes of several members of Clement's family and their final reunion after their 'recognition' (hence the title) by St. Peter. The original Greek is lost; the work survives in the Lat. of *Rufinus (d. 410), who in a prefatory letter mentions that he had made various curtailments. The 'Recognitions' have been dated between 211 and 231 on the ground that they refer to the extension of the Roman franchise throughout the Empire, which took place under Caracalla, and that the work is already quoted by *Origen in his *Comm. on Genesis.* They also survive in Syriac.

(3) The two Greek EPITOMES ('Επιτομαί) are evidently later. They omit most of the theological discussions of the earlier works and introduce an account of Clement's martyrdom. Two Arabic epitomes also survive.

The literary and theological problems raised by the Clementines are still warmly debated. The fact of a literary connexion between the 'Homilies' and the 'Recognitions' is undisputed, but while A. *Hilgenfeld maintained that the 'Recognitions' were earlier, most later scholars (G. Uhlhorn, C. Schmidt, O. Cullmann) have held that the 'Homilies' came first. The parallels are probably to be explained not from direct borrowing, but from common dependence on a lost document (*Grundschrift*). O. Cullmann assigned this *Grundschrift* to an early 3rd cent. Judaeo-Christian, holding that it was itself dependent on the 'Itinerary of Peter' (Περίοδοι Πέτρου) and a Jewish Apology dating from *c.* 135.

Theologically the Clementines have a Judaistic-Gnostic tendency. In the 'Recognitions' Christ is a Divine Aeon, who had previously been revealed in *Adam and *Moses. Jesus is the True Prophet and special emphasis is laid on the Jerusalem Church. There are also strong ascetic elements. Peter is a strict vegetarian and the use of water alone is allowed in the Eucharist. On the other hand there is a definite repudiation of celibacy (a mark of Jewish influence). The religious standpoint of the 'Homilies' is similar, though here the Judaistic element is less pronounced. *Arian influences have also been upheld by J. *Chapman, who assigned the final edition of the 'Recognitions' to a disciple of *Eunomius.

The documents were given a wholly disproportionate importance by the *Tübingen School, who, putting them very early, saw in the narratives of Simon Magus a reflection of the fierce conflict between 'Petrinism' and 'Paulinism' in pre-Catholic Christianity.

Homilies (1–19a only) first printed from Par. gr. 930 by J. B. *Cotelier in his '*Apostolic Fathers' (1672), i, pp. 546–746. A. R. M. Dressel's complete text (1853; reprinted in J. P. Migne, *PG*, ii, 19–468), was soon superseded by the more satisfactory edition of P. de *Lagarde (*Clementina*, Leipzig, 1865). The *Recognitions* were edited by J. *Faber Stapulensis as early as 1504. Subsequent editions by J. B. Cotelier (1672) and E. G. Gersdorf (1838; reprinted *PG*, i, 1158–1474). New text in preparation (1956) for the *Griechische christliche Schriftsteller* (B. Rehm). The literature is vast. Among the more important is A. *Hilgenfeld, *Die klementinischen Recognitionen und Homilien* (1848); C. *Bigg, 'The Clementine Homilies' in *Studia Biblica et Ecclesiastica*, ii (1890), pp. 157–93; F. J. A. *Hort, *Notes Introductory to the Study of the Clementine Recognitions* (1901); A. C. *Headlam, 'The Clementine Literature' in *J.T.S.*, iii (1901–2), pp. 41–58; H. Waitz, 'Die Pseudoklementinen', *T.U.*, xxv, 4 (1904); J. Chapman, 'On the date of the Clementines', *Z.N.T.W.*, ix (1908), pp. 21–34, 147–59; O. Cullmann, *Le Problème littéraire et historique du roman pseudo-clémentin* (1930); E. *Schwartz, 'Unzeitgemässe Betrachtungen zu den Clementinen', *Z.N.T.W.*, xxxi (1932), pp. 151–99; B. Rehm, 'Zur Entstehung der pseudoclementinischen Schriften', ib., xxxvii (1938), pp. 77–184. For lexical purposes, W. C[hawner], *Index of Noteworthy Words and Phrases found in the Clementine Homilies* (1893).

CLEMENTINES. In canon law, the collection of *Decretals, also known as the **Liber Septimus,** issued by *Clement V. It contains Decretals of *Boniface VIII, *Benedict XI, and Clement himself. Clement promulgated it, together with the decrees of the Council of *Vienne (1311), on 21 Mar. 1314 at Monteux, nr. Carpentras. Its authority being uncertain owing to Clement's having died before its general acceptance, it was promulgated afresh by *John XXII on 25 Oct. 1317. It was the last item officially embodied in the '*Corpus Iuris Canonici'.

G. Mollat in *D.D.C.*, iv (1949), cols. 635–40, s.v. 'Corpus Juris Canonici, IV. Les Clémentines', with reff. to lists of editions and Commentators and also bibl.

CLEOPAS. One of the two disciples to whom the risen Christ appeared on the road to *Emmaus on the day of the Resurrection, and made Himself known in the 'breaking of bread' (Lk. 24. 13–35). He is sometimes identified with the Clopas of Jn. 19. 25 (RV), the husband of a certain Mary, who, on the assumption that the Gk. Κλωπᾶς is the equivalent of the Aramaic חַלְפִי (also 'Alphaeus'), has been identified with Mary, the mother of James (cf. Mk. 3. 18, 15. 40).

CLERGY, BENEFIT OF. See *Benefit of Clergy*.

CLERICAL DISABILITIES ACT, 1870 (33 & 34 Vic. c. 91). The Act which allows a cleric of the C of E after resigning his preferments to execute a Deed of Relinquishment and thereby regain such civil rights as he has lost through being a clergyman (e.g. that of sitting in the House of Commons). By a Measure of the Church Assembly of 1934 (24 & 25 Geo. V, No. 1), a cleric who has availed himself of the Act may in certain circumstances resume his former status.

CLERICAL SUBSCRIPTION ACT (28 & 29 Vic. c. 122). The Act of 1865 amending the 36th *Canon of 1604 by changing the form of declaration made by Anglican clergymen at ordination and on accepting ecclesiastical preferment. The chief points of difference are that an Oath of Allegiance to the King is alone required, and the acknowledgement of the Royal Supremacy is no longer imposed; and that a (general) '*assent' is now demanded to the *Thirty-Nine Articles, instead of the obligation to 'acknowledge *all and every* [Article] to be agreeable to the Word of God'. The Act also provided that every beneficed clergyman, on taking up a new cure of souls, should, on the first Sunday, or on some other day appointed by the bishop, read the Articles to his congregation, and make a formal assent to them and to the BCP.

CLERICALISM. A term, often used in an opprobrious sense, for an excessively professional attitude of outlook, conversation, or conduct on the part of clergymen, or for the imitation of a supposedly clerical manner by lay persons. It is also used to describe undue clerical influence in secular affairs. See also *Anticlericalism*.

CLERICIS LAICOS. The bull issued by *Boniface VIII on 25 Feb. 1296 to protect the clergy of England and France against the exactions of the secular power. It forbade any cleric to pay ecclesiastical revenues to laymen without the authority of the Roman see, and any layman, under threat of excommunication, to receive such payments. The vehemence of its language aroused fierce opposition on the part of Philip the Fair and Edward I, and considerably weakened its effectiveness.

Complete text in A. Thomas, M. Faucon, and G. Digard (edd.), *Les Registres de Boniface VIII*, i (Bibliothèque des Écoles Françaises d'Athènes et de Rome, 1907), No. 1567, p. 584 f.; Operative part of text also in C. Mirbt, No. 369, p. 208 f.; Eng. tr. in H. Bettenson (ed.), *Documents of the Christian Church* (1943), pp. 157–9. S. Vigor, ed. by P. Dupuy, *Histoire du différend entre le Pape Boniface VIII et Philippe le Bel roy de France* (1655); J. Rivière, *Le Problème de l'Église et de l'état au temps de Philippe le Bel* (S.S.L., viii, 1926), esp. pp. 63–70. T. R. S. Boase, *Boniface VIII* (1933), esp. ch. v, pp. 129–56.

CLERICUS. See *Leclerc, Jean*.

CLERK, Parish. See *Parish Clerk*.

CLERK IN HOLY ORDERS. A designation, chiefly legal and formal, for a bishop, priest, or deacon in the C of E, as contrasted with such clerks as 'Lay Clerks', 'Bible Clerks', &c., who execute minor ecclesiastical functions without ordination. Before the *Reformation, the word 'clerk' without qualification was applied to those in *Minor Orders, while the orders of bishop, priest, and deacon (and also the *subdiaconate from the 13th cent.) were specified as *Major, or Holy, Orders.

CLERK OF THE CLOSET. The cleric who presides over the Royal College of Chaplains. When a vacancy occurs in the list of chaplains, he is asked by the Master of the Household to suggest possible names to the King. Among his duties are the presentation of bishops to His Majesty when they do homage after consecration, and the examination of theological books whose authors wish to present copies to the King.

CLERKS REGULAR. A term applied to certain bodies of RC clergy, bound under religious vows, who live in community, and engage esp. in active pastoral work. Such Regular Clerks originated in the 16th cent. through the efforts of various bands of clerics to perfect their pastoral work by the stimulus of ordered discipline. The first communities were largely Italian, and met with striking success at a time when the waning prestige of the Church called for such intensified effort. They included the '*Theatines' (1524), the 'Clerks Regular of the Good Jesus' founded at *Ravenna (1526), and the '*Barnabites' established at Milan in 1532. The largest and most important member of the family is that of the *Jesuits or Society of Jesus (1534). Since the close of the 16th cent. there have been no official additions to the number of orders of regular clerks, but their name has been adopted by other religious congregations. The mode of life of regular clerks has greatly influenced the constitutions of various modern bodies, monastic and non-monastic, living under rule. They may be regarded as the modern counterpart of the *regular canons (q.v.).

CLERMONT, Collège de, also known as the Collège Louis le Grand. The celebrated *Jesuit house at *Paris, at one time the property of G. du Prat, Bp. of Clermont (1529–60). Through the energies of J. *Sirmond and others, it acquired a celebrated collection of

MSS. known to scholars as the 'Claromontani'. In 1764 the College was dissolved and the MSS. dispersed.

G. Dupont-Ferrier, *Du collège de Clermont au collège Louis-le-Grand* (3 vols., 1921-5). H. Fouqueray, S.J., *Histoire de la compagnie de Jésus en France*, i (1910), pp. 363-433.

CLERMONT, The Council of (1095). Summoned by *Urban II to plan the First *Crusade, it met at Clermont on 18 Nov. 1095. It was attended by over 200 bishops. It confirmed the '*Truce of God' and made other regulations for the conduct of the crusades. It issued 32 canons and decreed, *inter alia*, that the pilgrimage to *Jerusalem made every other penance superfluous (can. 2); that no one below the rank of subdeacon should be appointed to bishoprics (can. 5); that no fee should be exacted for burials (can. 8); that no king or prince should grant *investiture (can. 16); that no flesh meat should be eaten between *Ash Wednesday and *Easter (can. 23); that holy orders should be conferred only in *Ember seasons and on the Saturday before the Fourth Sunday (*Laetare) in Lent (can. 24); and that communicants should receive in both kinds separately unless necessity require otherwise (can. 28). The primacy of the see of Lyons was also confirmed.

Hardouin, vi (pt. 2, 1714), cols. 1717-42; Mansi, xx (1725), cols. 815-920. Hefele–Leclercq, v (pt. 1; 1912), pp. 396-444. G. R. Crégut, *Le Concile de Clermont en 1095 et la première croisade* (1895). For further bibl. on *Crusades* see s.v.

CLETUS, St. See *Anacletus, St.*

CLIFFORD, JOHN (1836-1923), *Baptist leader. As a boy he worked in a lace factory. He experienced conversion in 1850 and was baptized in the following year. In 1858 he became the minister of the Baptist Church at Praed Street, Paddington, and when the congregation, attracted by his successful pastorate, grew too large, Westbourne Park Chapel was built for him (opened, 1877). In 1888 he became president of the Baptist Union. He was keenly interested in upholding the cause of working people and also led the movement for 'passive resistance' to A. J. *Balfour's Education Act of 1902, which he believed to be injurious to Nonconformist interests. His influence did much towards bringing about the defeat of the Unionists at the polls in 1906. He held several important offices in the Baptist Church, and from 1905 to 1911 was the first president of the Baptist World Alliance. Theologically he inclined towards a more liberal position than had been traditional in his own communion. His many writings exercised great influence on his generation.

Life and Letters of Dr. John Clifford, ed. J. Marchant (1924).

CLIMACUS, St. JOHN. See *John Climacus, St.*

CLINICI. See under *Baptism* (p. 125, col. 2).

CLITHEROW, MARGARET (*c.* 1556-86), the 'martyr of *York'. The daughter of a Sheriff of York, she was converted to the Roman obedience at the age of 18, and became an ardent friend of the persecuted RCs. In 1586 she was arrested and charged at the York Assizes with harbouring priests. To save her children from being forced to witness against her, she refused to plead, and was barbarously crushed to death. She was beatified by *Pius XI in 1929; feast day, 2 Apr.

Life by John Mush, her confessor (first publd. London, 1849). Later study by Laetitia S. Oliver (London, 1886).

CLOISTER. An enclosed space, usually in the form of a covered arcade, forming a means of communication between different parts of cathedral precincts, monasteries, or other religious buildings. The term is also used in general for a Religious House, or the Religious Life. See also *Clausura*.

CLOSE, FRANCIS (1797-1882), Dean of *Carlisle. He was educated at Merchant Taylors' School and St. John's College, Cambridge, and became incumbent of Cheltenham in 1826. His sermons, modelled on those of C. *Simeon, soon won him a large following, and made him one of the best known of Evangelical preachers. By his opposition to the theatre, horse racing, and esp. 'Sabbath-breaking', he exercised great influence on the public life of Cheltenham. At first a definite Churchman, he gradually reached a position strongly hostile to *Tractarianism and saw in 'Popery', whether Anglican or Roman, one of the chief dangers of the age. From 1856 to 1881 he was Dean of Carlisle. His long series of books (largely sermons) and tracts were of great influence in their day. The Dean Close School was founded at Cheltenham as a public school for boys in his memory.

Close publd. many of his sermons, incl. *Miscellaneous Sermons, preached in the Parish Church of Cheltenham* (2 vols., 1829-34) and *Nine Sermons Illustrative of some of the Typical Persons in the Old Testament* (1838). 'Contem Ignotus' [Richard Glover], *The Golden Decade of a Favoured Town. Being Biographical Sketches and Personal Recollections of the Celebrated Characters who have been connected with Cheltenham from 1843 to 1853* (1884), pp. 10–69; *Memorials of Dean Close*, ed. by one who knew him (Carlisle, 1885). G. Berwick, 'Close of Cheltenham: Parish Pope' in *Theology*, xxxix (1939), pp. 193–201 and 276–85. G. C. Boase in *D.N.B.*, xi (1887), p. 123 f.

CLOTILDE, St. (474-545), Frankish queen. By birth a Burgundian princess, she married *Clovis, King of the Salian Franks, in 492 or 493. She at once endeavoured to convert him to Christianity, and in 496, partly as a result of a great victory over the Alemanni, he and many of his followers were baptized by St. *Remigius, Bp. of Rheims. After her husband's death in 511 her life was saddened by internecine struggles between her sons and the tragic fate of her daughter, and she retired to the abbey of St. *Martin at Tours, where her reputation for piety and good works continued undimmed. In later times the events of her life were much embroidered in the interests of epic. Feast day, 3 June.

Crit. ed. of a Life, prob. 10th cent., by B. Krusch in *M.G.H.*, Scriptores Rerum Merovingicarum, ii (1888), pp. 349–51. G. Kurth, *Sainte Clothilde* ('Les Saints', Paris, 1897; Eng. tr., 1898).

CLOUD OF UNKNOWING, The. An English mystical treatise of the 14th cent. Its authorship has been much debated. It has been attributed to Walter *Hilton, and also to two 16th-cent. *Carthusians, but it seems to have been written before Hilton and after Richard *Rolle. E. *Underhill believed the author to have been a contemplative monk, whereas Dom M. Noetinger and Dom J. McCann favour the view that he was a secular priest. Deeply influenced by the 'negative' mysticism of *Dionysius the Areopagite, the author insists on the impossibility of knowing God by human reason. The 'cloud of unknowing' which lies between God and man is pierced not by the intellect, but only by 'a sharp dart of love'; therefore contemplative prayer takes place in the affective, not in the intellectual, part of the soul, and thus necessarily contains an element of ignorance. The treatise, which develops only certain aspects of mystic prayer, is not meant for beginners in the spiritual life, as the author explains in the 'Prologue', but only for those actually called to contemplation.

Crit. ed. of text by Phyllis Hodgson (E.E.T.S. Orig. Series, ccxviii; 1944, pp. 1–133), with introd. and bibl. Modernized edd. of the text, from an unknown MS. by H. Collins (London, 1871), and from 15th cent. MS. by E. *Underhill (London, 1912) and J. McCann, O.S.B. (ib., 1924), the latter with comm. by A. *Baker (1575–1641), pp. 287–405; completely modernized version (anon.), with introd. by H. H. Brinton (New York and London, 1948). Fr. tr. by M. Noetinger, O.S.B. (Tours, 1925), with introd. Greta Hort, *Sense and Thought* (1936).

CLOVESHO, Councils of. A series of synods representing both the Church and State of all England south of the Humber. Record survives of those which were held in 742, 747, 794, 798, 803, 824, and 825. Those of 747 and 803 are the most important. The former dealt with ecclesiastical discipline and liturgy, ordering in the latter strict adherence to the Roman Rite. The latter was the occasion of the abolition of the archiepiscopal status of *Lichfield, set up in 782, and the restoration of the Mercian sees to the province of *Canterbury. The site of Clovesho is unknown.

Hefele–Leclercq, iii (pt. 2; 1910), pp. 805 f., 903–11, 1113, 1123, and iv (pt. 1; 1911), p. 38 f., with reff. (but there are no sufficient reasons for identifying Clovesho with Abingdon, Berks.).

CLOVIS (*c.* 466–511), King of the Franks. The son of Childeric I, he became King of the Salian Franks in 481 and forthwith began to expand his domain. He attacked and defeated the Roman general, Syagrius, at Soissons, and incorporated into his dominions much of Roman Gaul and other territories, including those of the Ripuarian Franks and the Thuringians. The decisive event in his career was his conversion to Catholic Christianity and baptism in 496 (see *Clotilde*). This step gave him an excuse to attack the *Arian King of the Visigoths, Alaric II, whose forces he overthrew at the battle of Vouillé in 507; and, further, it enabled him to consolidate his dominions, since he gained the aid of the Catholic bishops and Roman officials in governing the country. In 508 the E. Emp. Anastasius I conferred on him the title of 'Proconsul'. Ruthless and cruel, Clovis was a man of consummate ability, and his rule, particularly his codification of the Salic law and his endeavours to fuse the Romans and the Teutons, laid the foundations of the modern French nation.

G. Kurth, *Clovis* (Tours, 1896). A. van de Vyver, 'La Victoire contre les Alamans et la conversion de Clovis' in *Revue Belge de Philologie et d'Histoire*, xv (1936), pp. 859–914, and xvii (1937), pp. 35–94; id., 'Clovis et la politique méditerranéenne' in *Études d'histoire dédiées à la mémoire de Henri Pirenne* [ed. by F. L. Ganshof, E. Sabbe, and F. Vercauteren] (1937), pp. 367–87.

CLUNY, Order of. The influential monastery of Cluny, near Mâcon in Burgundy, was founded by William the Pious, Duke of Aquitaine, in 910. The high standard of monastic observance set by Berno of Baume, its first Abbot (910–27), was adopted before Berno's death in some five or six neighbouring monasteries. The real founder of Cluny's influence, however, was Berno's successor, St.*Odo (927–942), under whose encouragement many monasteries in the S. of France, and even some of the most important Italian houses (*Monte Cassino, Santa Maria on the Aventine, *Subiaco) reformed themselves after the Cluniac model. Under Odo's gifted successors Aymardus (942–948 [perh. 964]), Majolus (948 [perh. 964]–994) and St. *Odilo (994–1048; q.v.) an ever-growing number of houses, old and new, adopted the reform. Its objects included a return to the strict *Benedictine rule, esp. as expounded by St. *Benedict of Aniane, cultivation of the personal spiritual life, stress on the choir office (which tended to grow to excessive length) and the splendour and solemnity of worship generally, with a corresponding reduction in manual labour. Great attention was also paid to sound economic organization and the independence of lay financial control. It now seems clear that in the 10th cent. the Cluniac houses were not yet welded into a system, which only developed under Odilo.

Esp. in the 11th and 12th cents. Cluny exercised decisive influence on the life of the Church. Its leading figures came from noble families who increasingly enjoyed the confidence of sovereigns and popes. Their refusal of high ecclesiastical office (leading bishoprics, cardinalates) added to the respect accorded them. Their ideals were widely admired by the secular clergy and largely inspired the reforms (repression of simony, celibacy of clergy) of *Gregory VII, who had been a monk at Cluny. The new church at Cluny, of which Paschal II consecrated the high altar in person on 25 Oct. 1095 and Innocent II the whole church (except the *narthex) in 1131–2, was then the largest church in Europe (555 ft.).

After Odilo's death the next abbots were *Hugh (1049–1109), Pontius (1109–22), and *Peter the Venerable (1122–57). In the middle of the 12th cent., when the influence of the Order reached its height, the number of Cluniac houses is given as 314. Then the centralization was such that the heads of the subject-houses were ordinarily priors, not abbots. In the later Middle Ages the influence of Cluny greatly declined, but the monastery survived until 1790. The *Hôtel de Cluny* in Paris (since 1833 a museum) was formerly the town-house of the Abbots of Cluny.

The first English Cluniac house was St. Pancras at Lewes, founded by William de Warenne in 1077. Others soon followed at Wenlock (c. 1081), Bermondsey (c. 1085), Castle Acre (1089), and Thetford (1104), and, in Scotland, at Paisley (1163). By the middle of the 12th cent. their number had risen to thirty-six. As alien priories they were frequently sequestered by the Crown during the French Wars. In the later Middle Ages the control from Cluny was in fact slight. At the Dissolution there were eight greater and nearly thirty lesser Cluniac houses.

G. F. Duckett, *Charters and Records among the Archives of the ancient Abbey of Cluni* (2 vols., 1888); E. Sackur, *Die Cluniacenser* (2 vols., 1892–4); L. M. Smith, *The Early History of the Movement of Cluny* (1925); Heimbucher, i (ed. 3, 1933), pp. 183–8; J. Evans, *Monastic Life at Cluny*, 910–1157 (1931); R. Graham, 'The Relation of Cluny to some other Movements of Monastic Reform' in *English Ecclesiastical Studies* (1929); M. D. Knowles, *The Monastic Order in England* (1941), esp. chs. viii, xvi. G. de Valous in *D.H.G.E.*, xiii (['1953']), cols. 35–174, with extensive bibl.

C.M.S. The 'Church Missionary Society', originally called the 'Society for Missions in Africa and the East', was founded in 1799 with John Venn (1759–1813) as president. Though later in date than the *S.P.C.K. and the *S.P.G., it became the first effective organ of the C of E for missions to the heathen. The 19th cent. saw the Society battling against apathy, opposition, and the tremendous difficulties of pioneer work; but its success is measured in the contrast between its sending five missionaries in the first ten years of its existence and an annual expenditure (in 1955) of over half a million pounds, with missionaries at work in Africa, Palestine, Iran, India, Pakistan, Ceylon, and the Far East. Its theology has been consistently *Evangelical. See also *B.C.M.S.*

E. Stock, *The History of the Church Missionary Society. Its Environment, its Men and its Work* (3 vols., 1899; Supplementary vol. iv, *The History of the Church Missionary Society*, 1916). C. Hole, *The Early History of the Church Missionary Society for Africa and the East to the end of A.D. 1814* (1896). *The Jubilee Volume of the Church Missionary Society for Africa and the East* (1849); *The Centenary Volume of the Church Missionary Society for Africa and the East, 1799–1899* (1902); S. M. Johnson, *A History of the Church Missionary Society in Australia and Tasmania* (1925); F. E. Bland, *How the Church Missionary Society Came to Ireland* (1935). E. Headland, *Brief Sketches of C.M.S. Workers* (1897); C. F. Pascoe, *The Finished Course. Brief Notices of Departed Church Missionaries* (1865). There is also a Register of Missionaries and Native Clergy from 1804 to 1904.

COADJUTOR-BISHOP. A bishop appointed to assist a diocesan bishop in his duties, often with the right of succession to the see at the next vacancy. The practice of appointing coadjutor-bishops is much followed in the RC Church, but seldom in the Anglican Communion, except in certain dioceses outside England, and in the *Protestant Episcopal Church of America, where it is a common practice.

COAT OF CHRIST, The Holy. See *Holy Coat*.

COCCEIUS, JOHANNES (1603–69), Johann Koch, dogmatic theologian. A German by birth, he went in 1629 to study at Franeker, Holland, where he was appointed to the chair of Hebrew in 1636, and theological professor in 1643. In 1650 he moved to *Leyden. In his works, which were grounded in considerable knowledge of Oriental languages, he sought to expound dogmatic theology on a purely Biblical basis; but although professedly a *Calvinist, he objected both to the Calvinist spirit and to Calvinist 'orthodoxy'. He interpreted the relation between God and man in terms of a personal covenant and his system thus became known as *Föderaltheologie*. After his death his followers were openly accused of unorthodoxy, and there seems little doubt that his teaching was a factor leading to the later growth of *pietism. His most important treatise was his *Summa doctrinae de Foedere et Testamento Dei* (1648). His *Collected Works* (8 vols.) were published in Amsterdam (1673–5).

His collected works were ed., with a brief life, by his son, J. H. Cocceius (8 vols., Amsterdam, 1673–5). G. Schrenk, *Gottesreich und Bund im älteren Protestantismus, vornehmlich bei Johannes Cocceius* (1923). A. *Ritschl, *Geschichte des Pietismus in der reformierten Kirche*, i (1880), pp. 130–52. E. F. K. Müller in *P.R.E.* (ed. 3), iv (1898), pp. 186–94, s.v.

COCHLAEUS, JOHANNES (1479–1552), RC controversialist. His real name was Dobeneck. He went to *Cologne in 1504, where he developed a distaste for *Scholasticism, and a strong sympathy for the *Platonist and humanist revival of the *Renaissance. In 1521 and the following years he was engaged in writing against M. *Luther, but the bitter tone of his polemic gained little favour even from his own side. In 1526 he accepted a canonry at Mainz, c. 1534 at Meissen, and in 1539 at Breslau. He attended many of the conferences of the period, at which the points of difference between Catholics and Protestants were argued, but on these occasions his services were little used. His best-known works are *Historiae Hussitarum Libri XII* (1549) and *Commentaria de Actis et Scriptis M. Lutheri, 1517–1546* (1549). In 1525 he had made every endeavour to prevent the printing of W. *Tyndale's English New Testament at Cologne.

Lives, C. Otto (Berlin, 1874), F. Gess (Diss., Leipzig, 1886), and M. Spahn (Berlin, 1898; the most substantial work). A. Herte, *Die Lutherkommentare des Johannes Cochläus* (Reformationsgeschichtliche Studien und Texte, Hft. xxxiii, 1935). Further bibl. in Schottenloher, i (1933), p. 123 f. (Nos. 2998–3033). T. Kolde in *P.R.E.* (ed. 3), iv (1898), pp. 194–200, s.v.

CO-CONSECRATOR. A bishop who assists the chief consecrator in the laying-on of hands at the making of a bishop. There should be at least two (cf. Conc. *Nic. [325], can. 4), though the absence of an assistant is not deemed to invalidate the consecration. It is also a widely held belief among dogmatic theologians that all who lay hands are consecrators, so that, even assuming some defect in the chief consecrator, the consecration might still be valid.

CODE OF HOLINESS, The. See *Holiness, Code of.*

CODEX ALEXANDRINUS ('A'). The early 5th cent. MS. of the Greek Bible which Cyril *Lucar, then Patr. of *Constantinople, presented to *James I (1603–25) through the British Ambassador, Sir Thomas Roe (d. 1644). The MS. did not reach England, however, until 1627. In 1757 it passed with the rest of the Royal Library to the newly founded British Museum, which is its present home. Its earlier history is obscure, but there are grounds for supposing that it came from Mt. *Athos and that it was perhaps written in Egypt. In the Gospels, the Codex follows a predominantly *Lucianic text, with a number of *Western readings. With the possible exception of Pap. 47 it probably contains the best extant text of Rev. Besides the NT, it includes the two (so-called) Epp. of *Clement.

The Codex Alexandrinus was one of the earliest of the uncial MSS. to be made available to scholars. The first ep. of Clement was ed. from it by P. *Young (Oxford, 1633). It was used by B. *Walton in the *Biblia Polyglotta* (6 vols., London, 1657). The OT was ed. J. E. *Grabe (2 vols., Oxford, 1707–20) and by H. H. Baber (3 vols., London, 1816–21). NT ed. A. C. Woide (London, 1786). Photographic ed. by E. M. Thompson (4 vols., London, 1878–83), with introd. in vol. i, pp. 3–12; reduced photographic ed. by F. G. Kenyon (London, 1909 ff.), with introd. prefixed to first vol. of NT, pp. 5–11). F. C. *Burkitt, 'Codex "Alexandrinus"' in *J.T.S.*, xi (1910), pp. 603–6. F. H. A. *Scrivener, *A Plain Introduction to the Criticism of the New Testament*, i (ed. 4 by E. Miller, 1894), pp. 97–105; F. G. Kenyon, *Our Bible and the Ancient Manuscripts* (1895), pp. 128–32. J. F. Fenlon in *C.E.*, iv (1908), p. 80 f., s.v.

CODEX AMIATINUS. The oldest extant MS. of the Latin *Vulgate. It contains the whole Bible. It was written for Ceolfrid, Abbot of *Wearmouth, at either Wearmouth or Jarrow, who in 716 set out with it for *Rome, intending to present it to *Gregory II, but he died at Langres on the way. From the 9th to the 10th cent. until 1786 the MS. was in the monastery of Monte Amiata, hence its name. It is now in the Laurentian Library at Florence. Fragments of one of the sister Bibles were discovered in 1909 and 1937 and are now in the British Museum (Add. MSS. 37777 and 45025 respectively).

The MS. was used for the revision of the *Vulgate for the Sixtine ed., publd. Rome, 1590; its readings were noted by F. F. Fleck in his ed. of the Vulgate NT (Leipzig, 1840), and are the basis of the ed. of J. *Wordsworth–H. J. White, &c. (3 vols., Oxford, 1889–1954). The complete text of the NT was publd. by C. *Tischendorf (Leipzig, 1850; reissued, 1854). There is no complete ed. of the OT, but much of it is pr. in T. Heyse–C. Tischendorf (edd.), *Biblia Sacra Latina*

(Leipzig, 1873). Two facsimile plates, with introd., in *The Palaeographical Society. Facsimiles of Manuscripts and Inscriptions*, second series, vol. i, ed. E. A. Bond–E. M. Thompson–G. F. Warner (1884–94), plates 65 f. G. B. *de Rossi, *La Bibbia offerta da Coelfrido abbate al sepolcro di S. Pietro* (1888). P. Corssen, 'Die Bibeln des Cassiodorus und der Codex Amiatinus' in *Jahrbücher für Protestantische Theologie*, ix (1883), pp. 619–33. J. Wordsworth, 'The Date and History of the Great Latin Bible of Monte Amiata' in *The Academy*, xxxi (1887), pp. 111–13; other important correspondence on the subject by W. *Sanday, F. J. A. *Hort, H. J. White, J. Wordsworth, E. M. Thompson, P. Corssen, G. F. Browne and others in this and the two foll. vols. H. J. White, 'The Codex Amiatinus and its Birthplace' in *Studia Biblica et Ecclesiastica*, ii (Oxford, 1890), pp. 273–309. G. Schmid, 'Zur Geschichte des Codex Amiatinus' in *T.Q.*, lxxxix (1907), pp. 577–84; A. Mercati, 'Per la storia del Codice Amiatino' in *Biblica*, iii (1922), pp. 324–8. J. F. Fenlon in *C.E.*, iv (1908), pp. 80–3, s.v. See also bibl. to *Vulgate*.

CODEX BEZAE ('D'). This (prob. 5th cent.) Graeco-Latin MS. of the Gospels (in the order Mt., Jn., Lk., Mk.) and Acts, with a small fragment of the Latin of 3 John (11-15), was presented in 1581 to the University of Cambridge by T. *Beza. In 1546 the codex was taken by the Bp. of Clermont to the Council of *Trent and it was used by H. *Stephanus for his 'editio regia' of the NT published at Paris in 1550; but its earlier history is uncertain. Its bilingual character implies that it was written in a region where both Greek and Latin were in use (hence not in Egypt, as A. C. Clark contended), and thus probably in the W. Among the places suggested are Sicily (J. H. *Ropes), Lyons, N. Africa, and Sardinia. It is the principal representative of the *Western text (q.v.).

The text was first publd. by T. Kipling (2 vols., fol., Cambridge, 1793). Crit. ed., with introd. and notes, by F. H. A. *Scrivener (Cambridge, 1864). Photographic ed. in 2 vols., Cambridge, 1899. The Readings of the Codex Bezae are noted by C. *Tischendorf in his edd. of the NT (Leipzig, 1841, etc.). J. R. *Harris, *A Study of the Codex Bezae* (Texts and Studies, ii, No. 1; Cambridge, 1891). F. H. Chase, *The Old Syriac Elements in the Text of the Codex Bezae* (1893). J. R. Harris, *The Annotators of the Codex Bezae* (1901). K. *Lake, 'On the Italian Origin of Codex Bezae. I, Codex Bezae and Codex 1071' in *J.T.S.*, i (1900), pp. 441–5; F. E. *Brightman, part II, 'The Marginal Use of Lections', pp. 446–54; F. C. *Burkitt, 'The Date of Codex Bezae', ib., iii (1902), pp. 501–13; H. Quentin, O.S.B., 'Le *Codex Bezae* à Lyon au IXᵉ siècle? Les citations du Nouveau Testament dans le martyrologe d'Adon' in R. Bén., xxiii (1906), pp. 1–25; E. A. Loewe, 'The Codex Bezae' in *J.T.S.*, xiv (1913), pp. 385–8; G. *Mercati, 'On the Non-Greek Origin of the *Codex Bezae*', ib., xv (1914), pp. 448–51; E. A. Lowe, 'The Codex Bezae and Lyons', ib., xxv (1924), pp. 270–4; F. C. Burkitt, 'Codex Bezae and the "Sortes Sangallenses"', ib., xxviii (1927), p. 58 f. E. A. Lowe, *Codices Latini Antiquiores*, ii (Oxford, 1935), p. 7 (No. 140).

CODEX CANONUM ECCLESIAE UNIVERSAE. A collection of *canons of certain of the early Greek councils. It was so named by C. Justel (1580–1649), who edited it in 1610, on the erroneous supposition that it received from the Council of *Chalcedon (451), and subsequently from the Emp. *Justinian (d. 565), official authority throughout E. and W. It contained the canons of *Nicaea, *Ancyra, *Neocaesarea, *Gangra, * Antioch, * Laodicaea, * Constantinople, *Ephesus, and *Chalcedon in a continuous sequence (207 items), with a Latin translation. With the exception of the canons of Ephesus,

the whole of the 'collection' was included by
*Dionysius Exiguus in his 'Codex'.

F. *Maassen, *Geschichte der Quellen und der Literatur des
canonischen Rechts im Abendlande* (1870), pp. xxix–xli.

CODEX EPHRAEMI ('C').

A 5th cent.
Greek MS. of the Bible now at *Paris (Bibl.
Nationale, Gk. Reg. 9.). In the 12th cent. it
was converted into a *palimpsest by a covering of some of the writings of St. *Ephraem
Syrus. Only portions of the original MS.
have survived, and the text is not always
decipherable; but every book of the NT except
2 Thess. and 2 Jn. is represented to some
extent. In the Gospels the text is fundamentally *Alexandrian, but it also contains a
*Western element.

Text of NT (as much as could be deciphered) ed., with
introd. by C. *Tischendorf, Leipzig, 1843; of OT, ib., 1845.
F. H. A. *Scrivener, *A Plain Introduction to the Criticism of
the New Testament*, i (ed. 4 by E. Miller, 1894), pp. 121–4;
F. G. Kenyon, *Our Bible and the Ancient Manuscripts* (1895),
pp. 137–9. J. F. Fenlon in *C.E.*, iv (1908), p. 84 f., s.v.

CODEX FULDENSIS.

The Latin MS. of
the NT, written in 541–6 to the order of
*Victor, Bp. of Capua. The four Gospels are
arranged in a harmony, in the manner and
order of *Tatian's '*Diatessaron', though the
text has been revised to agree with that of the
*Vulgate. The MS. at one stage belonged to
St. *Boniface, and since his death (754) has
been at *Fulda.

Text ed. E. Ranke (Marburg and Leipzig, 1868). H. J.
Vogels, *Beiträge zur Geschichte des Diatessaron im Abendland*
(Neutestamentliche Abhandlungen, viii, Hft. 1; 1919), pp.
1–34.

CODEX IURIS CANONICI, ('CIC').

The
code of *canon law in force in the RC Church
at the present day. By the end of the 19th
cent. the material of Roman canon law had
become so unwieldy that in 1904 *Pius X
appointed a commission under the direction
of Cardinal Gasparri to collect and redact the
canon law and produce a new codex. The
result of their labours, a comparatively small
volume divided into five books and 2414
canons, was promulgated by *Benedict XV
on 27 May 1917, and came into force at
*Pentecost in the following year. See also
Canon Law; Corpus Iuris Canonici.

Among the many commentaries, those in English include
Charles Augustine [Bachofen], O.S.B., *A Commentary on the
New Code of Canon Law* (8 vols., St. Louis and London,
1918–22); S. Woywood, *A Practical Commentary on the Code
of Canon Law* (2 vols., New York, [c. 1925]; ed. 2, revised,
1926). H. A. Ayrinhac, *General Legislation in the New Code
of Canon Law.* General Norm (Can. 1–86). Ecclesiastical
Persons in General (Can. 87–214) (New York, 1923; London,
1930); id., *Constitution of the Church in the New Code of
Canon Law* (Lib. II., Can. 215–486) (New York, 1925;
London, 1929); id., *Legislation on the Sacraments in the New
Code of Canon Law* (Lib. III., Can. 726–1011, 1144–53)
(New York and London, 1928); id., *Marriage Legislation in
the New Code of Canon Law* (New York, 1919; revised ed.
New York and London, 1932); id., *Administrative Legislation
in the New Code of Canon Law* (Lib. III., Can. 1154–1551)
(New York and London, 1930). A. Vetulani–R. Naz in
D.D.C., iii (1942), cols. 908–40, s.v., with bibl. D. Staffa in
E.C., iii (1949), cols. 1911–19, s.v., with further bibl.

CODEX SINAITICUS ('ℵ').

The cele-
brated MS. of the Greek Bible, discovered
by C. *Tischendorf in the monastery of St.
Catherine on Mount *Sinai. On a visit in
1844 he found some leaves of the OT books,
but it was not until a later visit in 1859 that
he saw the NT and recognized its great value.
After many intricate but perfectly correct
negotiations, he arranged that the MS. should
be acquired by the Tsar of Russia, and it thus
found its way into the Imperial Library at St.
Petersburg. The Soviet Government sold it
in 1933 for £100,000 to the Trustees of the
British Museum, where it now has the press-
mark 'B. Mus. Addit. MS. 43725'. The British
Government guaranteed half of the sum, while
the rest was raised by public subscription.

Besides the OT, the MS. contains the whole
of the NT as well as the 'Ep. of *Barnabas'
and part of the 'Shepherd' of *Hermas. It is
written in *uncials on vellum, four columns
to a page, and in quires of eight leaves. Several
hands (four acc. to C. Tischendorf and K.
*Lake) took part in the original writing, and
the text has been revised by a number of correctors. Tischendorf's theory that one of its
scribes also wrote most of the NT of *Codex
Vaticanus ('B') is no longer accepted. Most
scholars, however, believe that, like the
Vaticanus, it was written in Egypt, though
there have been recent advocates of *Caesarea
in Palestine, and also of Italy. Its date is
probably the later 4th cent.

The NT text of the codex is closely allied
to that of the Vaticanus, together with which
it is the chief witness to the '*Neutral Text'.
The MS. exercised a decisive influence on the
text of the '*Revised Version' of the NT of
1881.

Text ed. C. *Tischendorf (4 vols., St. Petersburg, 1862);
two further fragments ed. id., *Appendix Codicum Celeberrimorum Sinaitici Vaticani Alexandrini* (Leipzig, 1867),
pp. 3–6; additional fragment ed. H. B. Bey (Leipzig, 1875).
Photographic ed. by Helen and K. *Lake (2 vols., Oxford,
1911–22), with introd. by K. Lake. H. J. M. Milne–T. C.
Skeat, *Scribes and Correctors of the Codex Sinaiticus* (1938).
Idd., *The Codex Sinaiticus and the Codex Alexandrinus*
(1938), pp. 5–27; *The Mount Sinai Manuscript of the Bible*
(publd. by the Trustees of the British Museum, 1934).
B. F. *Westcott–F. J. A. *Hort, *The New Testament in the
Original Greek.* Introduction (1881), pp. 210–30 and 246–71.
F. H. A. *Scrivener, *A Plain Introduction to the Criticism of
the New Testament*, i (ed. 4 by E. Miller, 1894), pp. 90–7;
F. G. Kenyon, *Our Bible and the Ancient Manuscripts* (1895),
pp. 121–8; ed. 4 (1945), pp. 128–35. J. F. Fenlon in *C.E.*,
iv (1908), pp. 84–6, s.v. See also bibl. to *Neutral Text.*

CODEX VATICANUS ('B').

The 4th cent.
MS. of the Greek Bible, now in the *Vatican
Library (Vat. gr. 1209), where its presence is
vouched for, at any rate since the 1481 catalogue, which mentions it ('*Biblia in tribus
columnis ex membranis in rubeo.*' This is probably the same item as the *Biblia ex membranis
in rubeo* of the 1475 catalogue). Its earlier
history is unknown. In the NT all after Heb.
9. 14 has been lost. The sheets are of a fine
vellum, said to be antelopes' skins, each page
being composed of three columns of over forty
lines. The NT is the work of two hands, one
of whom, however, wrote only the first few
chapters of Mt. F. J. A. *Hort thought that

the MS. was probably of Roman provenance; but to-day scholars incline to the opinion that it was written in *Alexandria. Its NT readings, together with those of the *Codex Sinaiticus, are the chief witness to the '*Neutral Text'.

The MS. was the basis of the Sixtine ed. of the *Septuagint publd. at Rome, 1587, and its successors. The complete text was ed. A. *Mai (5 vols., Rome, 1857); also ed., under the auspices of Pope *Pius IX, by C. Vercellone–J. Cozza (6 vols., Rome, 1869–81). The NT was also ed., after Mai, by C. *Tischendorf (Leipzig, 1867, with appendix, 1869). Photographic ed. by J. Cozza-Luzzi (5 vols., Rome, 1889–1890); also in 4 vols., ib., 1904–7. B. F. *Westcott–F. J. A. Hort, *The New Testament in the Original Greek.* Introduction (1881), pp. 210–46 and 250–70. F. H. A. *Scrivener, *A Plain Introduction to the Criticism of the New Testament,* i (ed. 4 by E. Miller, 1894), pp. 105–21; F. G. Kenyon, *Our Bible and the Ancient Manuscripts* (1895), pp. 132–7. U. Benigni in *C.E.,* iv (1908), pp. 86–8, s.v. See also works cited under *Septuagint* and bibl. to *Neutral Text.*

CODRINGTON, CHRISTOPHER (1668–1710), soldier, poet, and colonial administrator. In 1690 he became a probationer-fellow of All Souls, Oxford, and varied his life in Oxford with military expeditions to Flanders. In 1699 he was appointed to succeed his father as Captain-General of the Leeward Islands, but he resigned his post after the failure of an expedition against Guadeloupe in 1703, and lived in retirement in Barbados until his death, studying Church history and metaphysics. In his will he left £10,000 and a large library to All Souls, and also bequeathed two estates, with part of Barbuda, to found in Barbados a college of physic and divinity, where the members were to live under vows of poverty, chastity, and obedience, and do missionary work in the West Indies. The provision for the threefold vow was disregarded, but Codrington Missionary Training College was built in 1714–42, and still continues its work.

V. T. Harlow, *Christopher Codrington 1668–1710* (1928). A. Dobson in *D.N.B.,* xi (1887), p. 203 f.

COELESTIS URBS JERUSALEM. Breviary hymn for the office of the dedication of a church. See *Urbs Beata Hierusalem.*

COEMGEN, St. See *Kevin, St.*

COENACULUM. See *Cenaculum.*

COENOBITE (Gk. κοινόβιος, 'living in a community', from κοινός, 'common' and βίος, 'life', or 'way of life'). A religious in vows who lives in a community (as opposed to a *hermit). The word is also used in a technical sense of *anchorites who occupy separate dwellings and observe a rule of silence, but live otherwise as a community of *monks in a common enclosure. This latter way of life originated in the desert and is now followed in the W. chiefly in the *Carthusian Order.

COFFIN, CHARLES (1676–1749), hymnwriter. In 1712 he became principal of the College Dormans-Beauvais at Paris, and in 1718 rector of the University. In 1727 he published a collection of Latin hymns, many of which were adopted in the *Paris Breviary* of 1736. Several are well known in their English versions, e.g. 'On Jordan's banks the Baptist's cry', 'The Advent of our God', and 'O Holy Spirit, Lord of Grace'.

The majority of Coffin's hymns were publd. in his *Hymni Sacri* (Paris, 1736) and in the *Hymnes du nouveau bréviaire de Paris* (Paris, 1736, to which he was one of the contributors; this was ed. J. H. *Newman, Oxford, 1838). Collected ed. of his works publd. in 2 vols., Paris, 1755.

COGITO ERGO SUM (Lat. 'I think, therefore I am'). The primary datum of truth accepted by R. *Descartes in his method of doubt, on the ground that however much a man doubted, he could never think away himself as the doubting subject.

COLBERTINE BREVIARY, The. A breviary compiled for the household of J. B. Colbert, *Louis XIV's finance minister, and printed between 1675 and 1680. It had close affinities with the breviary of Cardinal F. de *Quiñones. It appears to have been the work of the Abbé J. Gallois (1632–1707).

Edited from the Brit. Mus. copy (C. 35, f. 21) by T. R. Gambier-Parry, H.B.S., 1912 (2 vols.; 1912, 1913).

COLENSO, JOHN WILLIAM (1814–83), Bp. of Natal. Born at St. Austell, Cornwall, he was educated at St. John's College, Cambridge, where he was elected Fellow in 1837. In 1836 he became a mathematics master at Harrow, in 1842 returned to St. John's as a tutor, and in 1846 became vicar of Forncett St. Mary, Norfolk. In 1853 he was appointed the first Bishop of the newly constituted see of Natal, where he soon became keenly interested in the native problem and provoked criticism from the orthodox by his leniency in not insisting on the divorce of the wives of polygamists on their baptism. In 1861 he issued a *Commentary on the Epistle to the Romans* which by its denial of eternal punishment and rejection of much traditional sacramental theology aroused a storm of protest; still greater opposition was provoked by his papers on *The Pentateuch and the Book of Joshua Critically Examined* (in parts, 1862–79), challenging the traditional authorship and historical accuracy of these Books; and in 1863 he was declared deposed by his Metropolitan, Robert Gray of Cape Town (Bp. 1847–72). Colenso, however, denied the Bp. of Cape Town's jurisdiction. He appealed to the *Judicial Committee of the Privy Council which delivered sentence in his favour (20 Mar. 1865) on the ground that the Letters Patent appointing him preceded those appointing Gray. Hence, although solemnly excommunicated in 1866 by Gray, who in 1869 consecrated W. K. Macrorie (b. 1831, d. 1905) as Bp. of Maritzburg and Natal with a jurisdiction conterminous with that of Natal, Colenso maintained his position and by a series of judicial decisions secured the cathedral and endowments of the see. Though his attitude to the native question and some of his practical activities on their behalf (which were carried on after his death by his daughter Harriette, 1847–1932) continued to alienate many, esp. in Great Britain, he retained the affection of his diocese.

On his death his followers, styled 'the Church of England in Natal', applied to the Abps. of *Canterbury and *York for the consecration of a successor. In 1891 Macrorie resigned and after protracted negotiations all parties agreed that the Abp. of Canterbury should appoint a Bishop of Natal; and in 1893 the Archbishop consecrated A. H. Baynes (1854–1942). On his failure to reconcile the Church of St. Paul's, Durban, Baynes resigned (1901) though the Vestry agreed to reunion in the following year. The schism was not finally healed until 1911 when the Bp. of Natal recovered the endowments of which Colenso had been registered proprietor.

Life by G. W. Cox (2 vols., London, 1888). Shorter sketch by Florence Gregg (ib., 1892). H. L. Clarke, *Constitutional Government in the Dominions beyond the Seas and other Parts of the Anglican Communion* (1924), pp. 325–9; C. Lewis–G. E. Edwards (edd.), *Historical Records of the Church of the Province of South Africa* (1934), pp. 310–56. See also bibl. to *South Africa, Christianity in*.

COLERIDGE, JOHN TAYLOR (1790–1876), the biographer of J. *Keble. He was a nephew of S. T. *Coleridge. In 1809 he was elected a scholar of Corpus Christi College, Oxford, and from 1812 to 1818 was a Fellow of Exeter. After leaving Oxford he became a barrister of the Middle Temple. In 1832 he was appointed Recorder of *Exeter and from 1835 to 1858 was a Justice of the King's Bench. A keen Churchman, he published in 1869 his biography of J. Keble (d. 1866), whose lifelong friend he had been.

[B. J. S.] Coleridge, *The Story of a Devonshire House* (1905), esp. chs. x–xix.

COLERIDGE, SAMUEL TAYLOR (1772–1834), poet and thinker. He was born at Ottery St. Mary, Devonshire, where his father was vicar. He was educated at Christ's Hospital and Jesus College, Cambridge, but left the university in 1793 probably on account of debts and a love affair. After a short-lived attempt to join the 15th Dragoons, he returned to Cambridge for a time but took no degree. In 1795 he married Sarah Fricker, and in the same year made the acquaintance of W. *Wordsworth. After some unsuccessful publishing ventures he thought of taking up the career of a *Unitarian minister, with which sect he had come into contact at Cambridge, but gave up the plan when Josiah and Thomas Wedgwood settled an annuity on him. In 1798 he published, in conjunction with Wordsworth, the *Lyrical Ballads*, his most famous contribution being 'The Ancient Mariner'. In the same year he went to Germany to study the *Kantian philosophy. The chief fruit of the journey was his brilliant translation of F. Schiller's *Wallenstein* (1800). During the next years he wrote his last great poems, among

them the second part of 'Christabel' (1800) and the 'Ode to Dejection' (1802). From that time his poetic powers declined, possibly under the influence of his growing addiction to opium. After travelling in Malta (1804) and Italy (1805–6), he lectured in London on Shakespeare and other poets with considerable success (1810–13), and in 1813 had his tragedy 'Remorse' produced at Drury Lane. In 1816 he made a partly successful effort at conquering the opium habit, and in the same year published a volume of poems containing 'Christabel', 'Kubla Khan', and 'Pains of Sleep'. Also in 1816 appeared his *Lay Sermons* and in 1817 *Sibylline Leaves* and *Biographia Literaria*. On *the Constitution of Church and State* (1830) and the popular *Aids to Reflection* (1825) are among his most important religious publications. They were followed by the posthumous *Confessions of an Enquiring Spirit* (1840).

Coleridge's religious development partly reflects the trends of his time. After the rationalistic influences of his school-days and the Unitarian leanings of his early manhood he came under the sway of the *pantheism of J. *Boehme and B. *Spinoza, which had been revived by J. W. Goethe and other German thinkers. It was so congenial to his nature that he never seems to have really abandoned it, even in his avowedly Christian period, dating from c. 1810. He preached the need of man for a spiritual interpretation of life and the universe against a fossilized Protestant orthodoxy as well as against the materialistic and rationalist trends of his time; but his thirst for freedom in every department of life frequently led him beyond the boundaries of the Christian Revelation. His denial of any inherent opposition between the development of modern science and the essence of Christianity showed an insight rare in his time; but he refused to admit metaphysical proofs of religious truth and only conceded the pragmatical test of its beneficent influence on human life. This conviction, that Christianity is primarily ethical, led him to believe in the possibility of a unification of Christendom on a wide basis of common tenets; and earned him the title of 'Father of the Broad Church Movement'.

Complete Works, ed. W. G. T. Shedd (7 vols., New York, 1853). The best edd. of his *Poetical Works* are those of J. D. Campbell (London and New York, 1893) and E. H. Coleridge (grandson, 2 vols., Oxford, 1912). Various hitherto unpubld. pieces ed. H. N. Coleridge, *The Literary Remains of Samuel Taylor Coleridge* (4 vols., 1836–8). *Letters*, ed. E. H. Coleridge (2 vols., London, 1895); *Unpublished Letters*, ed. E. L. Griggs (2 vols., London, 1932). The standard biography is the life by J. D. Campbell (London, 1894). Other lives and studies by J. Gillman (vol. i only publd., London, 1838), H. D. Traill ('English Men of Letters', 1884), A. Brandl (Berlin, 1886; Eng. tr., 1887), H. Caine (London, 1887), J. Aynard (Paris, 1907), H. I'A. Fausset (psychological; London, 1926), J. Charpentier (Paris, 1928; Eng. tr., 1929), S. Potter (London, 1935), E. K. Chambers (Oxford, 1938), L. Hanson (on his early years, London, 1938), and M. Carpenter (London, 1954). R. W. Armour–R. F. Howes (edd.), *Coleridge the Talker*. A Series of Contemporary Descriptions and Comments (Ithaca, New York, and London, 1940). E. Blunden–E. L. Griggs (edd.), *Coleridge*. Studies by Several Hands on the Hundredth Anniversary of his Death (1934). L. Livingston Lowes, *The Road to Xanadu* (1927). A. Snyder, *Coleridge on Logic and Learning* (New Haven and London, 1929). E. Winkelmann, *Coleridge und die Kantische Philosophie* (Palaestra, clxxxiv, 1933). C. R. Sanders, *Coleridge and the Broad Church Movement* (Durham, N.C., 1942), pp. 19–88. J. L. Haney, *A Bibliography of Samuel Taylor Coleridge* (Philadelphia, 1903); T. J. Wise, *A Bibliography of the Writings in Prose and Verse of Samuel Taylor Coleridge* (London, 1913); id., *Coleridgeana*. Being a Supplement to the Bibliography of Coleridge (ib., 1919); Virginia W. Kennedy, *Samuel Taylor Coleridge*. A Selected Bibliography (Baltimore, 1935). T. M. Raysor in *C.B.E.L.*, iii, pp. 172–9. L. Stephen in *D.N.B.*, xi (1887), pp. 302–16.

COLET, JOHN (1466?–1519), Dean of *St. Paul's. The son of Sir Henry Colet, who had been twice Lord Mayor of *London, he studied probably at Magdalen College, *Oxford, and later in Paris and Italy where he learned Greek. In 1497 he returned to Oxford where he delivered a series of lectures on St. Paul's Epistles, notable for their critical spirit and their plea for a return to the discipline of the primitive Church. From this time onwards he constantly inveighed against the worldliness of the higher clergy, pluralities, and non-residence, and, though he never challenged the traditional dogmas of the Church, he was frequently suspected of heresy. His opinions were very sympathetically received by his two famous friends, D. *Erasmus (to whom he later paid an annuity) and Sir Thomas *More. From 1505 till his death he was Dean of St. Paul's. On his father's death he received a large fortune, part of which he spent, in the face of opposition, in founding St. Paul's School where 153 boys, without restriction of nationality, could gain the rudiments of education, be brought up in a sound Christian way, and learn Greek as well as Latin (first High Master of the School, William Lilly).

His *Opus de Sacramentis Ecclesiae* was ed. as 'A Treatise on the Sacraments of the Church' (1867), his *Super Opera Dionysii* as 'Two Treatises on the Hierarchies of Dionysius' (1869), his *Enarratio in Epistolam S. Pauli ad Romanos* as 'An Exposition on St. Paul's Epistle to the Romans' (1873), his *Enarratio in Primam Epistolam S. Pauli ad Corinthios* as 'An Exposition on St. Paul's First Epistle to the Corinthians' (1874), his *Opuscula Quaedam Theologica* as 'Letters to Radulphus on the Mosaic Account of the Creation, together with other Treatises' (1876), all ed. for the first time with Eng. tr., introd., and notes by J. H. Lupton. J. H. Lupton (ed. and tr.), *The Lives of Jehan Vitrier . . . and John Colet . . . written . . . by Erasmus in a Letter to Justus Jonas* (1883). F. *Seebohm, *The Oxford Reformers of 1498* (1867). J. H. Lupton, *A Life of John Colet* (1887); id., *The Influence of Dean Colet upon the Reformation of the English Church* (1893). J. A. R. Marriott, *The Life of John Colet* (1933). S. L. Lee in *D.N.B.*, xi (1887), pp. 321–8. E. W. Hunt, *Dean Colet and his Theology* (C.H.S., 1956).

COLETTINES. A branch of the Poor *Clares founded by St. Colette (1381–1447), a native of *Corbie in Picardy who was canonized in 1807 (Feast day, 6 Mar.). She established seventeen convents in her lifetime. To-day the Colettine Sisters are found mainly in France.

COLIGNY, GASPARD DE (1519–72), *Huguenot leader. A member of one of the greatest families in France, he spent much of his life at court and in the service of the French Army. He was converted to *Calvinism in 1560, and after the death of the Prince de Condé in 1569 became the recognized leader of the Huguenot cause. His influence at court over the young King, Charles IX,

led France to aid the Netherlands in their revolt against the Duke of Alva. The queen-mother, *Catherine de Medici, who was a keen Catholic and also jealous of Coligny's position, tried to have him assassinated on 22 Aug. 1572; and when that had failed, provoked the Massacre of St. *Bartholomew two days later, in which he was killed.

J. Delabore, *Gaspard de Coligny, amiral de France* (3 vols., 1879–82); A. W. Whitehead, *Gaspard de Coligny, Admiral of France* (1904); C. Merki, *L'Amiral de Coligny, la maison de Châtillon et la révolte protestante, 1519–1572* (1909); J. A. G. Binet-Valmer, *Un Grand Français*. Coligny (1927).

COLLATION. The word is used in several senses, secular and ecclesiastical. Among the latter are: (1) the light meal allowed on days of fasting in addition to the one full meal (the 'comestio'). Cf. *CIC*, 1251; (2) the lives of the *Fathers, esp. as arranged for reading in monasteries. This usage perhaps derives from the title of John *Cassian's 'Collationes Patrum', a record of his conversations with the hermits of the Egyptian deserts; and (3) *institution to an ecclesiastical benefice when the *ordinary is himself the patron (i.e. when *presentation and institution are one and the same act).

COLLECT (Lat. *oratio*, also *collecta*). The short form of prayer, constructed (with many varieties of detail) from (1) an invocation, (2) a petition, and (3) a pleading of Christ's name or an ascription of glory to God; and one of the most characteristic items in the W. liturgy. The prayers later known as *Secrets and *Post-communions are structurally indistinguishable, though the term 'collect' is normally confined to the prayer (or prayers) in the Eucharistic rite which immediately precedes the lections. They are already met with in the earliest Latin *Sacramentaries (*Leonine, *Gelasian, *Gregorian). They also secured an established place in the daily offices as well as in the Eucharist. Early collects were always directed to the Father (or the Trinity); but since the Middle Ages collects addressed to the Son have been regularly admitted to the liturgy.

The term 'collect' (*collecta*) was orig. a title in the *Gallican rite. It denoted, as B. *Capelle (after *Walafrid Strabo) has shown, the 'collecting' of the petitions of the several members of the congregation into a single prayer (cf. Synod of *Agde, A.D. 506, can. 30). This sense of the word is thus not connected with the use of *collecta* for the assembly ('collection') of the congregation for worship, as has often been supposed.

Since the Middle Ages it has been the practice on certain days other than the Greater Feasts to recite more than one collect in the Liturgy. In the Latin rite the choice and number of the additional collects follow elaborate rules, e.g. when two feasts of not widely different rank occur on the same day, the inferior feast is normally commemorated by a second collect, while on days of relatively lesser importance, there are usually three collects. The Secrets and Postcommunions always correspond in number and in general content with the collects.

The collects in the BCP mostly derive from the medieval sources, esp. the *Sarum Missal and Breviary. Several, however, were T. *Cranmer's original compositions (e.g. those for Advent I and II), while the wording of many which have a Latin basis was freely modified and adapted, to give a good English rhythm. In 1662, a few further collects were provided (e.g. those for Epiphany VI, for which the earlier forms of the BCP had made no provision, and Advent III). At Mattins and Evensong two unalterable collects are provided for recitation after the collect for the day daily throughout the year.

Jungmann (1949), i, pp. 445–81; Eng. tr. (1951), pp. 359–90 (full discussion with bibl. reff.). B. *Capelle, O.S.B., 'Collecta' in R. Bén., xlii (1930), pp. 197–204; O. Casel, O.S.B., 'Beiträge zu römischen Orationen' in J.L.W., xi (1931), pp. 35–45.

COLLECTAR (Lat. *Collectarium*). A medieval liturgical book containing the collects used in the Divine *offices.

COLLEGIALISM. A term applied (prob. first by J. H. Boehmer of Halle, d. 1745) to the thesis esp. associated with H. *Grotius (1583–1645) and S. *Pufendorf (1632–94) that Church and State are both purely voluntary associations (*collegia*) in which supreme authority rests with the body of the members, and that the civil magistrate has no other relations with the Church than those which he enjoys with every other voluntary association within his territory.

COLLEGIANTS. An obscure offshoot of the *Remonstrants (q.v.), founded in *Holland c. 1619, and so called because they termed their communities 'colleges'. They were also known as 'Rynsburgers' from Rynsburg, near *Leyden, where they held their early meetings. They held that the Church was an invisible society and every externally constituted Church a corruption. Apart from the belief that Christ was the Messiah and the Bible inspired Scripture, they admitted no confession of faith or organized ministry. Their theology in general was very liberal and their ethics pietistic. *Baptism was generally administered by *immersion when each year the whole sect met at Rynsburg for prayer, study and a commemoration of the Last Supper. At the end of the 17th cent. they were influenced by the views of B. *Spinoza (who resided at Rynsburg 1661–4), over whose teaching there were divisions within the sect. The sect seems to have died out towards the end of the 18th cent. when most of its adherents were absorbed in the *Arminians or the *Mennonites.

J. C. Van Slee, De Rijnsburger Collegianten (1895). R. M. *Jones, Spiritual Reformers in the 16th and 17th Centuries (1914), pp. 113–32.

COLLEGIATE CHURCH. In the C of E a church which is endowed for a body of canons and/or prebendaries (the 'chapter'), but is not, like a *cathedral, a bishop's see. Instances are *Westminster Abbey and St. George's Chapel, *Windsor.

COLLIER, JEREMY (1650–1726), English *Nonjuror. In 1685 he was made lecturer of Gray's Inn. Having written in favour of *James II, after the Revolution he was kept at Newgate for some months (1689) without trial, and in 1692 was again imprisoned on suspicion of treason. In 1696 he was outlawed for giving absolution on the scaffold to two attempted assassins of William III, but returned to London in 1697. For some years he wrote frequent attacks on the stage of his day, denouncing its immorality, and thereby provoking angry replies from W. Congreve and others. In 1713 he was consecrated as a 'bishop of the Nonjurors', and joined in their attempt at reunion with the Orthodox Church. He was also largely responsible for the production of the Nonjurors' Communion Office of 1718. This rite, which in some matters followed that of 1549, influenced the Scottish Liturgies of 1764 and 1929. His many writings include An Ecclesiastical History of Great Britain (2 vols., fol. 1708–14).

Life by T. Lathbury in his ed. of An Ecclesiastical History of Great Britain, ix (1852), pp. i–xlviii. R. Anthony, S.C., The Jeremy Collier Stage Controversy, 1698–1726 (Milwaukee, Wisconsin, 1937); K. Ressler, 'Jeremy Collier's Essays' in Seventeenth Century Studies, ed. by R. Shafer, Second Series (Princeton, 1937), pp. 179–285. W. Hunt in D.N.B., xi (1887), pp. 341–7.

COLLINS, ANTHONY (1676–1729), *Deist. He was a native of Heston in Middlesex, and educated at Eton and King's College, Cambridge. He subsequently lived in London until 1715 when he settled in Essex and became deputy-lieutenant. He was greatly influenced by J. *Locke, of whom he was an intimate friend, and his works are an epitome of English freethinking. In his first important publication, an Essay Concerning the Use of Reason (1707), he opposed the traditional distinction between things that are above and those that are against human reason. In Priestcraft in Perfection (1709) he tried to prove that the clause in Art. 20 of the *Thirty-Nine Articles on the power of the Church to decree rites and ceremonies and to decide religious controversies had been inserted by fraud. His principal work, A Discourse of Freethinking (1713), contains bitter attacks on the ministers of all denominations. It argued that free inquiry was the only means of attaining to the truth and was commanded by Scripture. The book, which was designed as a defence of Deism, was attacked by many Churchmen, among them R. *Bentley, B. *Hoadley, J. *Swift, and W. *Whiston. In 1715 he published his Inquiry Concerning Human Liberty, a concise and able statement of *Determinism, which was sharply attacked by S. *Clarke. In his Discourse of the Grounds and Reasons of the Christian Religion (1724) he denied that the OT contains prophecies of Christ. As he held fulfilled prophecies to be the only valid proof of the truth of Christianity, the book was intended as an implied rejection of it. He also denied the canonicity of the NT, as well as the immateriality and immortality of the soul.

L. Stephen in *D.N.B.*, xi (1887), p. 363 f. See also bibl. to *Deism*.

COLLOQUY OF MARBURG. See *Marburg, Colloquy of*.

COLLUTHUS (4th cent.), schismatic priest of *Alexandria. During the episcopate of St. *Alexander (312–28), he assumed the power of conferring orders, though only a presbyter. In 324 he was deposed at the Council convened at Alexandria by St. *Hosius to deal with the *Arian issue (though Colluthus himself does not seem to have supported Arius). Nothing is known of his subsequent history. Some scholars have found in his career support for the view that in its early days ordination in the Alexandrian Church was conferred by presbyters.

The authorities include *Athanasius, *Apol. c. Arianos*, 12 and 75; *Epiphanius, *Haer.*, lxix, 2; *Theodoret, *H.E.*, i, 8; and *Augustine, *Haer.*, lxv. Brief art. by G. *Salmon in *D.C.B.*, i (1877), p. 596, s.v.

COLLYRIDIANS. A 4th-cent. sect, mentioned by St. *Epiphanius (*Haer.* 79). Acc. to him it originated in Thrace and consisted mostly of women, who offered an idolatrous cult to the BVM. They sacrificed cakes (κολλυρίς, hence the name) to her, which they afterwards consumed. The custom may have originated in connexion with the popularization of the title '*Theotokos', and been influenced by the pagan habit of offering cakes to the goddess Ceres.

Brief notice by G. Bareille in *D.T.C.*, iii (1908), col. 369 f., s.v.

COLMAN, St. (d. 676), leader of the *Celtic party in Northumbria. A native of Ireland, he became a monk of *Iona, and later (661) succeeded St. *Finan as Bp. of *Lindisfarne. Here he supported the king, Oswy, in maintaining Celtic customs against the Romanizing party in the court, headed by Eanfleda, Oswy's Kentish queen. To settle the quarrel, Oswy summoned the Synod of *Whitby in 664, at which Colman pleaded for the retention of such customs as the Celtic time of keeping Easter and the Celtic tonsure and appealed to the authority of St. *Columba. St. *Wilfrid, however, who claimed for the Roman practices the authority of St. Peter, finally won the king over to his side. Colman then left Lindisfarne and passed the rest of his life at the monastery of Innisboffin, Co. Mayo. Feast day, 18 Feb.

The primary authority is *Bede, *H.E.*, iii, 25 f., and iv, 4; notes *ad loc.*, ed. C. Plummer, ii (1896), pp. 188–94 and 210. W. Hunt in *D.N.B.*, xi (1887), p. 389 f.

COLOGNE. The see was founded in or before the reign of *Constantine (d. 337), and the city occupied by the Franks at intervals from 330 onwards. In the 11th–12th cents. the Abps. of Cologne became important secular princes and later (1356) were recognized as imperial electors. The see remained politically important until 1801, when its property was secularized, though the archbishopric was restored in 1821. The present cathedral dates from the 13th–15th and the 19th cents., and contains the shrine of the *Magi. Among other famous churches of the town are St. Maria in Kapitol and St. Gereon's, both built in the 11th cent. (both badly damaged in the Second World War).

There is an exceptionally large literature on the subject in its many aspects—topography, archbishopric, cathedral, churches, university, and schools. Good survey of bibl. by J. Greven in *L.Th.K.*, vi (1934), cols. 80–93, s.v. 'Köln'.

COLOMBINI, Bl. GIOVANNI (c. 1300–1367), founder of the *Gesuati. He belonged to an old patrician family of Siena. He was converted by *reading the Life of St. *Mary of Egypt, and from that time devoted himself to the service of the poor and the sick, many of whom he received into his house. After eight years of this life he persuaded his wife to accept a separation, settled an annuity on her, distributed the rest of his property to several religious institutions, and, together with his friend Francisco Mini, led a life of evangelical poverty, prayer, and works of mercy. When his example was imitated by many young men from noble Sienese families, the authorities of the city exiled him. With 25 followers he visited several Italian towns, and by his preaching and example effected a great number of conversions. When soon afterwards an epidemic broke out in Siena, it was regarded as a punishment, and Colombini was called back. In 1367 he and his disciples were formally constituted by *Urban V into the congregation of the Gesuati, and he died shortly after. He was beatified by *Gregory XIII. Feast day, 31 July.

Letters ed. A. Bartoli (Lucca, 1856). Short life by Bl. John Tossigna (d. 1446), printed by J. D. *Mansi (ed.), *Stephani Baluzii . . . Miscellanea*, iv (Lucca, 1764), pp. 566–71. Life by F. Belcari (Florence, [c. 1480]), ed. R. Chiarini (Arezzo, 1904); Eng. tr. from edd. of 1541 and 1832 (London, 1874). Life by J. B. Rossi, S.J. (Rome, 1646), pr. in *A A.SS.*, July VII (1731), pp. 354–98. Modern life by the Comtesse de Rambuteau (ed. 3, Paris, 1893). G. Pardi, 'Della vita e degli scritti di Giovanni Colombini da Siena' in *Bullettino Senese di Storia Patria*, ii (1895), pp. 1–50 and 202–30, with docc.; id., 'Il Beato Colombini da Siena' in *Nuova Rivista Storica*, xi (1927), pp. 287–336.

COLONIAL AND CONTINENTAL CHURCH SOCIETY. See *C.C.C.S.*

COLONIAL CLERGY ACT. The Act of 1874 (37 & 38 Vic. c. 77) which regulates the conditions under which those ordained to the Anglican ministry in the British colonies can receive preferment or officiate in public in Great Britain. The written permission of the archbishop of the English province and a Declaration of *Assent in terms similar to that provided for in the *Clerical Subscription Act of 1865 are required.

COLONNA FAMILY. A distinguished Roman family which has played a considerable part in Papal and European politics, esp. between the 12th and 18th cents. The Colonnas were vassals of the Pope, but their political leanings in the Middle Ages were mostly Ghibelline and pro-Imperial. They were the hereditary adversaries of the Orsini family. The Colonnas gave a number of cardinals to the Church, the first being the Benedictine monk, Giovanni Colonna (d. 1216), who was created cardinal in 1193 by Pope Celestine III. A protector of the *Franciscan Order, he was praised for his virtues by St. *Bonaventure. His nephew, also called Giovanni (d. 1244), was made cardinal in 1212. He took part in the conquest of Damietta (1219) during the Fifth Crusade, and later assisted the Emp. Frederick II against the Pope. His nephew Giacomo (d. 1318) was created cardinal in 1278 by Nicholas III, of the house of Orsini, who hoped by this step to reconcile the two hostile families. Together with his nephew Pietro he bitterly opposed *Boniface VIII, who, in 1297, deprived both cardinals of their dignity, excommunicated the whole family, and seized their property. They were reinstated by *Clement V in 1305. The family, which continued to be given cardinalates by the Popes in the 14th cent., received fresh distinction through the election of one of its members, Odo, to the Papacy (1417), who, as *Martin V, ended the W. schism in 1429. After continued strife with the Orsini in the latter half of the 15th cent., a reconciliation was effected in the 16th, for the perpetuation of which *Sixtus V arranged a marriage between the two houses. The most famous woman of the family was Vittoria Colonna (1490–1547), remarkable alike for her literary talents and for her gift of attracting the finest spirits of her time, among them esp. *Michelangelo. She was deeply interested in the reform of the Church, and probably at one time lent towards the Reformation, but her connexion with Card. R. *Pole kept her faithful to the Catholic Church. Among the later members of the family were Marc Antonio (d. 1584), who took part in the victory of *Lepanto (1571), and his learned namesake (d. 1597) who was appointed head of the Commission of the *Vulgate by Sixtus V and librarian of the Vatican by *Clement VIII.

P. Colonna, *I Colonna dalle origini all' inizio del secolo XIX* (1927).

COLOPHON. The paragraph often found at the end of MSS. and early printed books giving information about authorship, sources, date, and sometimes (in the case of MSS.) the scribe himself. The use of the word in this sense does not seem to be earlier than the 18th cent.

COLOSSEUM, The. The name by which the 'Flavian Amphitheatre' at *Rome has been known since about the 8th cent. The largest arena in the world, it was completed by Titus *c.* 80, and has long been venerated as the scene of many martyrdoms in the early Church, though the truth of this tradition has been questioned by modern scholars, notably H. *Delehaye. Its present imperfect state is due partly to destruction by earthquakes and partly to its use as a quarry for stone until *Benedict XIV forbade its further demolition. The Cross erected in the centre of the arena in the 18th cent. was removed in 1874, but replaced in 1927. Elaborate excavations were begun in 1938.

F. Guadet, *Étude sur la construction et la déposition du Colossée, amphithéâtre flavien* (1878); H. Babucke, *Geschichte des Kolosseums* (1899). H. Delehaye, 'L'Amphithéâtre flavien et ses environs dans les textes hagiographiques' in *Anal. Boll.*, xvi (1897), pp. 209–52. S. B. Platner, *A Topographical Dictionary of Ancient Rome* (ed. by T. Ashby, 1929), pp. 6–11, incl. further general reff.

COLOSSIANS, Epistle to the. St. *Paul wrote this epistle, like *Phil., when he was in prison, probably at *Rome, but possibly at *Ephesus. The church at Colossae, a city on the Lycus (*Churuk Su*), had been founded not by St. Paul in person, but by Epaphras (1. 7), apparently when St. Paul was working at Ephesus. The primary purpose of the epistle is to recall its readers to faith in Christ as their all-sufficient Redeemer and Lord. After a solemn statement of Christ's position in relation to God, creation, and the Church (1. 3 ff.), a warning is given against a certain 'philosophy' which was making converts at Colossae (2. 1 ff.). In the course of the epistle St. Paul refers to certain features of the Hellenistic and Judaic religion of the period, e.g. the 'rudiments' or 'elements' (τὰ στοιχεῖα) of the world, angelic mediators, law-keeping, and asceticism, which later filled a prominent place in *Gnosticism. The epistle has important passages dealing with the Person of Christ (1. 15), the redeemed life (3. 1 ff.), and Christian morals (3. 5–4. 6). There are many close verbal parallels with the Ep. to the *Ephesians (q.v.).

Modern commentaries by J. B. *Lightfoot (London, 1875; with Philemon), T. K. Abbott (I.C.C., 1897; with Eph.), M. *Dibelius (Hb.N.T., 1911; ed. 2, 1927; with Philemon), J. Knabenbauer (in Lat., Paris, 1912), E. Lohmeyer (H. A. W. Meyer Comm., 1930; with Philemon). L. B. Radford (West. Comm., 1931; with Philemon). E. Percy, *Die Probleme der Kolosser- und Epheserbriefe* (Acta Reg. Soc. Human. Litt. Lundensis, xxxix; Lund, 1946). On the heresies condemned in the Epistle, cf. also F. J. A. *Hort, *Judaistic Christianity* (1894), pp. 116–29. McNeile, pp. 158–64. J. O. F. Murray in *H.D.B.*, i (1898), pp. 454–6; Teodorico da Castel S. Pietro in *E.C.*, iv (1950), cols. 24–7, s.v. 'Colossesi, Epistola ai'. C. F. D. Moule, *The Epistles of Paul the Apostle to the Colossians and Philemon* (Cambridge, 1957), pp. 1–137.

COLOURS, Liturgical. A sequence of colours at different seasons of the ecclesiastical year for vestments and other liturgical objects is first found in the use of the *Augustinian Canons at *Jerusalem at the beginning of the 12th cent. But it is not until much more recent times that a standard sequence in general use in the W. Church became established. The colours prescribed by the modern Roman service books are five,—white (*albus*), red (*rubeus*), green (*viridis*), purple (*violaceus*), and black (*niger*). White is used e.g. on *Trinity Sunday, on the Feasts of Christ (so far as they are not memorials of His Passion) and of the BVM, on *Corpus Christi, and on the feasts of virgins and confessors; red, e.g. at *Whitsun and on the feasts of apostles (except St. John) and of martyrs; green on the Sundays and *ferial days between the octave of the *Epiphany and *Septuagesima and between Trinity Sunday and *Advent, both exclusive; purple, e.g. in *Lent and Advent; and black on *Good Friday and in Masses and offices of the dead. In the *Sarum use, red was commonly used on the days for which the Roman books prescribe green, and in a few Anglican churches the Sarum sequence has been introduced in recent times, though the Roman sequence is that usually followed. Of the Eucharistic vestments, the *stole, *maniple, and *chasuble are usually of the appropriate colour, as are also the *chalice veil and *burse, and the *altar hangings. In the E. Church there are no definite rules about colours, though there is a natural tendency to use more sombre colours at penitential seasons, while white is used at all services, including funerals, from Easter to Ascensiontide.

J. W. Legg, *Notes on the History of the Liturgical Colours* (1882); W. St. J. Hope-E. G. C. F. Atchley, *English Liturgical Colours* (S.P.C.K., 1918). Braun, *L.G.*, pp. 728–60.

COLUMBA, St. (c. 521–597), abbot and missionary.

He came of a noble Irish family, and after being trained in Irish monasteries by St. *Finnian and others, himself founded several churches and monasteries in his country. About 563, impelled by missionary zeal, he left his home and established himself with twelve companions on the island of *Iona. There he lived for thirty-four years evangelizing the mainland and establishing monasteries in the neighbouring islands. Although only in priest's orders, he was the chief ecclesiastical authority of the whole of this district. He succeeded in converting Brude, king of the Picts, and in 574 the new king of the Scots of Dal Riada came to Iona to receive his sacring at Columba's hands. Feast day, 9 June.

Crit. ed. of the 'Altus Prosator', the best known of the poems attributed to St. Columba, by C. Blume in *A.H.M.A.*, li (1908), pp. 275–83; other hymns, pp. 283–8 and 325 f. For lit. *re* St. Columba's authorship of various other works, see Kenney, infra. The principal source for his life is the work of St. *Adamnan (q.v.); modern ed. by W. Reeves (Irish Archaeological and Celtic Society; Dublin, 1857); also ed. J. T. Fowler (Oxford, 1894), with introd.; Eng. tr. by id. (London, 1895). Two further lives, with introd., are pr. in *AA.SS.*, Jun. II (1698), pp. 180–97 (the life by Adamnan also here, pp. 197–236). The best modern study is that of W. D. Simpson, *The Historical Saint Columba* (Aberdeen, 1927); but cf. P. Grosjean, S.J., in *Anal. Boll.*, liv (1936), pp. 408–12. Other lives by J. Smith (Edinburgh, 1798), E. A. Cooke (London, 1888), Lucy Menzies (London, 1920), and T. H. Walker (Paisley, 1923). J. F. Kenney, *The Sources for the Early History of Ireland*, i (Records of Civilization, New York, 1929), pp. 263–5 (on the works attributed to St. Columba) and 422–42 (on the lives, legends, and form of his name). C. Hole in *D.C.B.*, i (1877), pp. 602–5, s.v.; N. Moore in *D.N.B.*, xi (1887), pp. 409–13. See also bibl. to *Adamnan*.

COLUMBANUS, St. (c. 550–615), abbot and missionary.

A native of Ireland, he went by way of England to Gaul c. 590, where he set up monasteries with very strict rules at Anegray and *Luxeuil, in the wilderness of the Vosges. He aroused much opposition by his introduction of the usages of the *Celtic Church, but vigorously defended their continuance, both at *Rome and before a Gallican synod (603). His monks, after expulsion from Burgundy in 610 for their outspoken rebukes of the royal court, began missionary work at Bregenz on Lake Constance among the heathen Alemanni; but they were driven out from their new quarters in 612 by an extension of the dominions of the King of Burgundy. They then settled at *Bobbio in N. Italy, where their house became a great centre of learning. The 'Monastic Rule' ascribed to him seems genuine, but the 'Penitential Rule' is almost certainly spurious. Feast day, 23 Nov. See also *Luxeuil*.

Crit. ed. of his Rule by O. Seebass in *Z.K.G.*, xv (1895), pp. 366–86, and xvii (1897), pp. 215–34. Some of his letters ed. W. Gundlach in *M.G.H.*, Epistolae iii (1892), pp. 154–90. The Rule, the Penitential ascribed to him, and a selection of letters also pr. in J. P. Migne, *PL*, lxxx, 209–84. Crit. ed. of Life by Jonas of Susa and other material by B. Krusch in *M.G.H.*, Scriptores Rerum Merovingicarum, iv (1902), pp. 1–156, and vii, pt. 2 (1920), pp. 822–7; also pr. in *Ionae Vitae Sanctorum Columbani, Vedastis, Iohannis* (Scriptores Rerum Germanicarum, 1905), pp. 1–294. Eng. tr. by D. C. Munro (Translations and Reprints from the Original Sources of European History, No. 7, Philadelphia, 1895). 'Miracula Sancti Columbani', ed. by H. Bresslau in *M.G.H.*, Scriptores xxx, pt. 2 (1934), pp. 993–1015. Full bibl. details of sources in J. F. Kenney, *The Sources for the Early History of Ireland*, i (New York, 1929), pp. 186–205. L. E. Martin, *Saint Columban, vers 540-615* (1905); J. J. Laux, *Der hl. Kolumban, sein Leben und seine Schriften* (1919); F. Blanke, *Columban und Gallus* (1940). L. Gougaud, O.S.B., *Les Saints irlandais hors d'Irlande* (Bibliothèque de la *R.H.E.*, fasc. 16, 1936), pp. 51–62. G. Morin, O.S.B., 'Le *Liber S. Columbani* et le MS. Ambros. C 301 Inf' in *R. Bén.*, xxxviii (1926), pp. 164–77. W. Hunt in *D.N.B.*, xi (1887), pp. 413–16. Crit. ed. of Works by G. S. M. Walker (Scriptores Latini Hiberniae ii; Dublin, 1957).

COLVILL, JOHN. See *Covel, John*.

COMBEFIS, FRANÇOIS (1605–79), *Patristic scholar.

A native of Aquitaine, he entered the *Dominican Order in 1624. He published first editions of the Greek text of several of the fathers, among them *Amphilochius of Iconium, *Methodius of Olympus, and *Andrew of Crete (all in one vol., 1644), and also an excellent edition of *Maximus the Confessor (1675). He also produced an edition (1679) of St. *Basil the Great, though this has since been superseded by the still better *Maurist edition (1721–30).

Quétif-Échard, ii, pp. 678–87, incl. list of his works.

COMBER, THOMAS (1645–99). Dean of

*Durham from 1691. He was the author of *A Companion to the Temple and Closet; or a Help to Publick and Private Devotion, in an Essay upon the Daily Offices of the Church* (1672–6), written with the intention of reconciling Protestant dissenters to the services of the C of E. Comber strongly resisted *James II's attempts to fill Anglican benefices with

RCs, and unreservedly welcomed *William and Mary.

C. E. Whiting (ed.), *The Autobiographies and Letters of Thomas Comber* (Surtees Society, clvi–clvii, 1941–2), incl. list of MS. sources for life.

COMENIUS, JOHANNES AMOS (1592–1670), Bohemian educationist. He belonged to the *Bohemian Brethren (Moravian), and studied theology at the *Calvinist universities of Herborn and Heidelberg, where he came under the influence of *millenarianism. From 1618 to 1621 he was a Moravian minister at Fulneck, and later at Lissa in Poland where he wrote his most important educational works, *Didactica Magna* (published 1657) among them. From 1641 onwards he travelled in England, Sweden, and Germany, collecting material for further educational writings. He returned to Lissa in 1648 and became first senior of the Brethren; and from 1650 to 1654 he lived in Hungary, where he founded a school on his principles at Sáros-Patak. After Lissa had been destroyed by the Poles in 1656, Comenius found a refuge in Holland where he finished his last work, the *Unum Necessarium*, in 1668.

His educational ideals were deeply influenced by his personal religious experience. Hoping for a Utopian Church which would unite all religions in Christian love, the 'unum necessarium', he regarded education as the surest way to its fulfilment. In numerous schools men were to be formed into images of Christ by means of the 'pansophia', i.e. an organic development of all elements of Divine wisdom. The methods he advocated were far in advance of the ordinary practice of his time. Coercion was to be avoided; the senses were to be employed wherever possible; and everything to be learnt was first to be properly understood. Not much learning, but the development of the character on Christian lines, was to be the ultimate aim. His ideas had a considerable influence in the 19th cent. In 1890 a 'Comenius Society' was founded for their further propagation.

Facsimile reissue of the 1631 ed. of his *Sapientiae Primae Usus Tertium Catholicum Appelandus* (Prague, 1922). Modern Eng. trr. of *Didactica Magna* (London, 1896; ed. 2 with additions, 1910), *Labirynt Sweta a Lusthawz srdce, to Gest* ('The Labyrinth of Peace and the Paradise of the Heart', London, 1901), *Via Lucis* (London, 1938), and *Angelus Pacis* (New York [1944]). There is also an ed. in Latin, Bohemian, French, English, and German of the *Angelus Pacis* (n.p., 1927). Studies on his educational significance by S. S. Laurie (1881), W. S. Monroe (London, 1900), and A. Heyberger (Travaux publiés par l'Institut d'Études Slaves, viii, Paris, 1928). J. Needham (ed.), *The Teacher of Nations* (1942), incl. bibl.; J. F. Young, *Comenius in England* (1932). M. Spinka, *John Amos Comenius*. That Incomparable Moravian (Chicago, 1943); J. V. Klíma (ed.), *Jan Amos Komensky* (Prague, 1947). *Comenius und die böhmischen Brüder* (Selections and Introd. by F. Eckstein, Leipzig, [1922]).

COMES (Lat. *Liber Comitis, Liber Comicus*), a book containing the passages to be read at *Mass as *Epistles, or as *Gospels, or as both. Originally it was merely a list of the opening words of the lections, i.e. a reference book, but the name 'liber comicus' came later to be applied to books with their complete text. In this connexion the word 'comes' originally meant a book of texts to serve as a 'companion', i.e. a 'vade-mecum'.

W. H. *Frere, *Studies in Early Roman Liturgy*, iii, The Roman Epistle-Lectionary (*Alcuin Club Collections, xxxii; 1935), esp. pp. 1–25 (text of 'Liber Comitis' from Corbie lectionary at Leningrad) and pp. 45 f., 49–61, and 73–84. H. *Leclercq, O.S.B., in *D.A.C.L.*, ix (pt. 1, 1930), cols. 220–43, s.v. 'Liber Comicus'; A. Manser, O.S.B., in *L.Th.K.* iii (1931), col. 7 f., s.v.; G. Löw, C.SS.R., in *E.C.*, iv (1950), col. 44 f., s.v.

COMFORTABLE WORDS, The. Four passages from the NT (Mt. 11. 28, Jn. 3. 16, 1 Tim. 1. 15, 1 Jn. 2. 1 f.) which the celebrant at the Holy Communion in the C of E recites after the Absolution of the people, to confirm the pardon just given. They are based on Abp. *Hermann's 'Consultatio' (1543), where (with the exception of the first, which was added by the Anglican Reformers) they appear between the Confession and Absolution.

A short 'Pastoral and Theological Commentary' by W. W. S. March (London, 1961).

COMFORTER, The. The title of the Holy Ghost found in the AV and RV of Jn. 14. 16 and 26, 15. 26, and 16. 7. The Greek word here (παράκλητος) should probably be translated 'Advocate' or 'Helper', in accord with the earlier Latin versions, which rendered it by *advocatus*. The *Vulgate, however, left it untranslated as *paracletus*. The translation *consolator*, which first appeared in the 7th cent., gave rise through the French to the rendering 'Comforter'.

COMGALL, St. (*c.* 516–*c.* 601), first Abbot of *Bangor (in Ireland). Born in Dalaradia in Ulster, he is said to have served in the army and afterwards studied at Clonard and Clonmacnoise. After returning to Ulster, where he retired for a time to an island in Lough Erne, he was ordained and became a zealous propagator of monasticism, his most famous foundation being Bangor on Belfast Lough (*c.* 555). He seems to have made a missionary expedition to *Iona and other places in Scotland. Among his disciples was St. *Columbanus. Feast day, 10 May.

There are two Latin Lives pr. in *AA.SS.* Mai. II (1680), pp. 580–8; an Irish text of the first, perh. from the 10th cent., ed. with Eng. tr. by J. G. O'Keeffe in *Ériu*, i (Dublin and London, 1904), pp. 43–8; crit. ed. of the second by C. Plummer (ed.), *Vitae Sanctorum Hiberniae* (Oxford, 1910), vol. ii, pp. 3–21, with introd. in vol. i, p. lviii f. P. Grosjean, S.J. (ed.), 'S. Comgalli Vita Latina Accedunt Duae Narrationes Gadelicae' in *Anal. Boll.*, lii (1934), pp. 343–56. The Rule ascribed to him in three MSS. ed. J. Strachan in *Ériu*, i (1904), pp. 191–208; ii (1905), p. 58 f. J. MacCaffrey in *C.E.*, iv (1908), p. 152, s.v.

COMMA JOANNEUM. See *Johannine Comma*.

COMMANDERY. Among the *Hospitallers, an estate or manor in the charge of a member of the order. In 1540 all commanderies which survived in England were seized by the Crown. The corresponding institution among the *Templars was the '*preceptory'.

COMMANDMENTS, The Ten, also called the 'Decalogue' (from Gk. δέκα, 'ten', and λόγος, 'word'), the precepts divinely revealed to *Moses on Mt. *Sinai and engraven on two tables of stone. Acc. to Ex. 32. 19, the tables were broken by Moses on coming down from the mountain because of the idolatry of the people, but later replaced by another pair (Ex. 34. 1) which were deposited in the *Ark. The text of the Commandments is preserved in the OT in two closely similar versions (Ex. 20. 1–17 and Deut. 5. 6–18). The chief differences are that whereas in Ex. the observance of the *Sabbath is motivated by a religious reason, viz. Jehovah's rest on the seventh day of Creation, in Deut. the ground is humanitarian. Also in the prohibition of covetousness, Ex. classes a man's wife with his other domestic property, whereas Deut. treats her separately. These differences comport with the less developed social teaching of the writer of the Ex. account. As regards the origin of the Decalogue, many of the older critical scholars, e.g. F. *Delitzsch, R. *Kittel, and S. R. *Driver, held it to be of the Mosaic age. But J. *Wellhausen, C. H. *Cornill, R. Smend, and other recent historians believe that it legislates for a settled agricultural community, not for wandering nomads, and that its moral teaching reflects the ideals of the 8th and 7th cent. Prophets; they therefore bring it down to the 7th cent. There is another and, acc. to most OT critics, much older version of the 'Ten Words' preserved in Ex. 34. 11–28 where much more emphasis is laid on ritual prescriptions.

The Ten Commandments, as we have them to-day, form an organic body of religious and moral principles, based on the Hebrew monotheistic conception of God. They are clear and succinct; and, apart from the prohibition of images and the precept of observing the Sabbath, they contain only rules of life that are the common property of mankind. Hence they were never abrogated in the New Dispensation, but rather deepened and supplemented by our Lord's teaching in the *Sermon on the Mount, and summed up by Him in the double precept of love towards God and one's neighbour (Mk. 12. 29–31). Acc. to *Tertullian the Divine precepts were engraven on the hearts of men even before being written on the tables of stone, an opinion later found also in St. *Augustine and St.*Gregory the Great. Acc. to St. *Thomas Aquinas, St. *Bonaventure, and other Schoolmen, all precepts of the Old Law belong to the *Natural Law, and hence the Commandments were given only to remind men of their obligations which had been obscured by sin.

By the time of St. Augustine the Ten Commandments had gained a prominent place in the instruction of catechumens. They were esp. used to counteract the moral errors of the *Manicheans, who alleged the Decalogue to be the work of the evil principle. They came to the fore again in the development of the penitential system in the 9th cent., and from the 13th cent. have kept their central place in Christian instruction. They received an esp. prominent place in the popular systems of teaching of the *Reformers, and were fully commented on by M. *Luther in his 'Grosser' and 'Kleiner Katechismus'. There is a difference in the enumeration in the different Churches. In the C of E as well as in the Greek and the Reformed (Calvinist and Zwinglian) Churches the prohibitions relating to false worship are reckoned as two, whereas the RC Church and the Lutherans count them as one. Thus the enumeration of the subsequent Commandments differs, e.g. the fourth (Anglican, etc.) Commandment on the sanctification of the Sabbath is reckoned as the third by those following the RC method. The number ten is made up by the latter splitting up the last Commandment forbidding covetousness into two. In the 1552 BCP the recitation of the Ten Commandments was introduced into the Communion Office, where they are to be regarded as a substitute for the lessons from the OT in ancient liturgies or, more probably, for the *Kyrie Eleison of the Medieval Rite. The rubric requiring their recitation at every Celebration still remains in the BCP, though in modern practice they are often either replaced by the Kyrie Eleison or summed up in our Lord's Two Great Commandments (Mt. 22. 36–40) or left out altogether.

S. Mowinckel, *Le Décalogue* (Études d'Histoire et de Philosophie religieuses publiées par la Faculté de Théologie protestante de l'Université de Strasbourg, xvi; 1927), with bibl. R. M. Grant, 'The Decalogue in Early Christianity' in *H.T.R.*, xl (1947), pp. 1–17. E. Mangenot–E. Dublanchy in *D.T.C.*, iv (1911), cols. 161–76, s.v. 'Décalogue'; A. Eberharter in *Dict. Bibl.*, Suppl. ii (1934), cols. 341–51, s.v. 'Décalogue', F. Spadafora in *E.C.*, iv (1950), cols. 1261–3, s.v. 'Decalogo', each with bibl. See also comm. on *Exodus* and *Deuteronomy*, cited s.vv.

COMMANDMENTS OF THE CHURCH (also **Precepts of the Church**). Certain moral and ecclesiastical precepts, imposed by the RC Church on all her members. They were tabulated in the Middle Ages, and later more strictly classified. Thus St. *Peter Canisius in his *Summa Doctrinae Christianae* (1555) and St. Robert *Bellarmine in his *Doctrina Christiana* (1589) mention five of them, though the catechism *Ad Parochos*, published by order of the Council of *Trent in 1566, does not speak of them. Four of these Commandments of the Church, viz. to hear Mass on all Sundays and Feasts of Obligation, to observe the days of fasting and abstinence, to go to Confession once a year, and to receive Holy Communion during the *Easter season, are now binding on Catholics of all countries. The obligation of contributing to the support of the clergy and of abstaining from the solemnization of marriage at the forbidden times, on the other hand, are formally imposed on RCs only in England and the U.S.A., whereas other precepts are sometimes added in other countries.

There is no formal list in the *C.I.C. J. W. Melody in *C.E.*, iv (1908), p. 154 f., s.v.; E. Dublanchy in *D.T.C.*, iii (1908), cols. 388–93, s.v. 'Commandements de l'Église', both with bibl.

COMMEMORATION. Acc. to W. liturgical custom, when two feasts fall on the same date, that of lesser rank is commonly only 'commemorated'. This is done, e.g. at Mass, by its *collect, *secret, and *postcommunion being read after the corresponding prayers of the feast of greater rank which is being observed. See also *Occurrence, Concurrence*.

COMMENDAM (Med. Lat. *commenda*, a 'trust' or 'custody'). An individual was said to hold an ecclesiastical benefice *in commendam* when its revenues were granted to him temporarily during a vacancy. The person so provided might be a layman, in which case he would *ipso facto* be debarred from performing the duties. Gradually the word came to be restricted, esp. to benefices which a bishop or other dignitary held more or less permanently along with his see. The first reference to the custom is in the writings of St. *Ambrose, who mentions a Milanese church which he had 'commended'. The practice not unnaturally led to great abuses. By an Act of 1836, the holding of benefices *in commendam* was prohibited in England.

COMMENDATIO ANIMAE (Lat. 'Commendation of the soul'). The prayers prescribed in the *Ritual of the W. Church to be said at the bedside of a dying person. They plead that the soul may go forth in the name of God and His saints, and that its sins may be pardoned.

COMMINATION SERVICE. The service drawn up by the compilers of the BCP for use on *Ash Wednesday (as a substitute for earlier penitential discipline) and for other days appointed by the *ordinary. It consists of an exhortation, clearly intended for use by a nonpreaching clergy (during which the Curses are solemnly recited), Psalm 51, suffrages, and prayers. It first appeared in the BCP of 1549, and has been included in all subsequent revisions.

COMMODIAN, Christian Latin poet. He is generally held to have flourished in Africa in the middle of the 3rd cent., but some modern scholars have put him later, e.g. H. Brewer who believed that he wrote in the 5th cent. in S. Gaul. The earlier date is supported by his apparent references to the *Novatianist schism. One passage in his writings may imply a connexion with Gaza in Palestine. He was a convert from heathenism. Two of his poems have survived, 'Instructiones adversus Gentium Deos pro Christiana Disciplina' and 'Carmen Apologeticum adversus Judaeos et Gentes'. Although altogether wanting in literary style, his work is a landmark in the history of Latin verse, as his rhythm is based on accent alone, without attention to quantities. Theologically he was a *Chiliast and *Patripassianist, and

in the *Decretum Gelasianum his works were reckoned as apocryphal.

Ed. princeps of 'Instructiones' by N. Rigaltius, Toul, 1649, repr. in J. P. Migne, *PL*, v, 201–62; of 'Carmen Apologeticum' by J. B. *Pitra in *Spicilegium Solesmense*, i (1852). Crit. edd. of Works by E. Ludwig, Bibl. Teubn., Leipzig, 1877–8, and by B. Dombart, *C.S.E.L.*, xv, 1887. H. Brewer, S.J., *Kommodian von Gaza. Ein Arelatensischer Laiendichter aus der Mitte des fünften Jahrhunderts* (Paderborn, 1906); id., *Die Frage um das Zeitalter Kommodians* (Paderborn, 1910); J. Martin, *Studien und Beiträge zur Erklärung und Zeitbestimmung Commodians* (*T.U.*, xxxix, 4, 1913). G. Boissier, 'Commodien' in *Mélanges Renier* (Bibl. de l'École des Hautes Études, fasc. 73, 1887), pp. 37–63. A. F. van Katrijk, *Lexicon Commodianeum* (Amsterdam, 1934); H. B. Vroom, *De Commodiani Metro et Syntaxi Annotationes* (Utrecht, 1917). P. Courcelle, 'Commodien et les invasions du Ve siècle' in *Revue des Études Latines*, xxiv (1946), pp. 227–46. Bardenhewer, ii, pp. 647–57; Altaner (1950), p. 363 f. A. G. Amatucci in *E.C.*, iii (1950), cols. 63–5, s.v.

COMMON LIFE, Brethren of the. See *Brethren of the Common Life.*

COMMON OF THE SAINTS (Lat. *Commune Sanctorum*). In the W. Church, those parts of the *Missal and *Breviary containing the office for such saints as have not a complete individual office (a '*proper') of their own.

COMMON ORDER, The Book of. (1) The directory of worship drawn up by J. *Knox in 1556 for the English Protestant congregations in *Geneva. It is also known as 'The Order of Geneva' and as 'Knox's Liturgy'. It was appointed for use in Scotland by the General Assembly in 1562; revised and enlarged in 1564; and continued in general use among the *Calvinists of Scotland until 1645, when it was replaced by the *Westminster Directory.

(2) The service-book authorized by the *General Assembly for use in the Church of *Scotland. The present book was prepared, on the instruction of the General Assembly in 1936, by the Committee on Public Worship and Aids to Devotion and issued in 1940. It draws extensively on two earlier authorized Books, viz. *Prayers for Divine Service* (1923; 1929) and the *Book of Common Order, 1928*, of the then *United Free Church. It is expressly stated that the issue of the *Book* does not imply a desire to supersede free prayer. Besides several alternative Orders for the Morning and Evening Services, it contains forms for the Sacraments and Ordinances of the Church (including four Orders for the Lord's Supper) and many prayers for the Christian Year (several drawn from the BCP) and other occasions.

COMMON PRAYER, The Book of. The official service book of the C of E containing the daily offices of Morning and Evening Prayer, the forms for administration of the *Sacraments and other public and private rites, the *Psalter and (since 1552) the *Ordinal. The book was compiled originally through the desire of T. *Cranmer and others to simplify and condense the Latin services of the medieval Church and to produce in English a single, convenient, and comprehensive volume as an authoritative guide for priest and people. A printed edition of the (Latin) Sarum *Breviary (1543) and the issue of the *Litany in English (1544) and of the Order of the *Communion (1548), which was an English supplement to the Latin Mass, paved the way for the complete reform.

In 1548 Cranmer discussed the draft of a new Prayer Book with a conference of scholars, and in 1549 Parliament had the 'First Prayer Book of Edward VI' printed, and by the first Act of *Uniformity enforced it as the national Use. An Ordinal was issued in 1550. In doctrine and ritual this First BCP was a compromise between the old and the new schools, and it failed to please either. The criticisms of the latter, represented by e.g. P. *Martyr and M. *Bucer, were concerned chiefly with *Vestments, Prayers for the Dead, and the Invocation of the Holy Spirit in the Prayer of Consecration. Revision in the light of these criticisms led to the issue by Parliament in 1552 of the 'Second Prayer Book of Edward VI', which added the present introductory portion to Matins and Evening Prayer, recast the Holy Communion office, ordered the use of the surplice instead of other vestments, and omitted all reference to 'Mass' and 'Altar'. The *Black Rubric was added without the sanction of the Act of Uniformity. Before the book was in general use, Mary's Act of Repeal (1553) restored the ancient services. As the 'Elizabethan BCP' (1559) it was reissued with a few slight alterations, and, except for a few minor details, it remained unchanged for the rest of the 16th cent. The part played by Convocation in the issue of these three books is obscure; so also is the origin of the *Ornaments' Rubric which was attached to Elizabeth's book.

Puritan objections to the BCP, which had been accumulating under Elizabeth, were ventilated on the accession of *James I by the *Millenary Petition. Hence 1604 saw the *Hampton Court Conference between bishops and Puritan divines, and a further revision in which the most important change was the addition of the second part of the *Catechism. After the 16 years in which the Book was superseded by the *Directory for Public Worship (1645), the *Savoy Conference (1661) met to consider afresh Puritan grievances. On its proving abortive, Convocation took over the task of yet another revision, and the Act of Uniformity of 1662 authorized the BCP as revised (see *Durham Book*). The re-insertion, with modification, of the Black Rubric, omitted in Elizabeth's BCP, was one of the few concessions to Puritans. The most important change was the introduction of the AV of 1611 for the Epistles and Gospels.

The 1662 BCP has remained practically unchanged ever since, though a Revised *Lectionary was drawn up in 1871 and another for optional use authorized in 1922, while the *Shortened Services Act (1872) allowed a more elastic interpretation of some of the rubrics.

In the face of the persistent ritual controversies a Royal Commission on Ecclesiastical Discipline was appointed on 23 Apr. 1904, with Michael Hicks Beach as chairman. It held 118 meetings and reported on 21 June 1906 recommending the issue of 'Letters of Business' to the Convocations with a view to Prayer Book revision. The Crown issued Letters on 10 Nov. 1906 and the subject was before the Convocations for nearly two decades. After long debates it was decided to retain the 1662 Book and embody all changes in a new Book, the use of which should be wholly permissive. The casting of the new Book into its final form was entrusted to the Bishops who presented it to the Convocations on 7 Feb. 1927.

The new Book represented a compromise. Its (alternative) Eucharistic rite approximated more closely to the medieval service (rearrangement of the *canon, use of the *Kyrie Eleison and *Benedictus qui venit). The rites of Baptism and Matrimony were brought into closer accord with modern sentiment and the Reservation of the Sacrament (in both kinds), under rather narrowly guarded conditions, was permitted. In the Convocations and the Church Assembly the Book passed with large majorities (517 to 133 in the Assembly, where the Bishops' votes were 34 to 4). But Protestant opposition, combined with the sense that it failed to satisfy the more advanced wing of the High Church party, led to its rejection in Parliament. It passed the Lords by 241 votes to 88, but was rejected in the Commons on 15 Dec. 1927 by 238 to 205. In the following year an amended form of the Book was issued, designed to remove some of the Protestant objections. This modified Book went through the same procedure as before, securing large (but reduced) majorities in the Convocations and the Church Assembly (396 to 153). It failed, however, to commend itself even so to the Commons. On 14 June 1928 it was defeated by a slightly larger majority than before (266 to 220).

Though without formal authority, the 1928 Book was issued, and continues to be sold, in a variety of editions designed for liturgical use. It has come to be used in many churches, particularly for *Baptisms, *Marriages, and other occasional offices and for the *Propers of days not provided for in the 1662 BCP.

The privilege of printing the BCP is confined to the Queen's Printer and the University Presses of Oxford and Cambridge, to which an Order in Council from the Privy Council Office is transmitted on the occasion of any necessary change (e.g. of names in the State Prayers). The various edd. of the BCP are set out in parallel columns, with meticulous accuracy, in F. E. *Brightman, *The English Rite* (2 vols., 1915), with important introd. E. C. Ratcliff, *The Booke of Common Prayer of the Churche of England.* Its Making and Revisions M.D.XLIX–M.D.CLXI (with 80 illustrations, 1949). Among the classical commentaries on the BCP are those of A. *Sparrow (1661), R. *Sanderson (1674), and C. *Wheatly (1710). F. Procter, *A History of the Book of Common Prayer* (1855; new ed. by W. H. *Frere, C.R., 1901); L. Pullan, *The History of the Book of Common Prayer* (1900); W. K. Lowther Clarke (ed.), *Liturgy and Worship.* A Companion to the Prayer Books of the

Anglican Communion (1932). F. A. *Gasquet–E. *Bishop, *Edward VI and the Book of Common Prayer* (1890); J. W. Legg, *Some Principles and Services of the Prayer-Book historically considered* (1899); J. Dowden, *The Workmanship of the Prayer Book* (1899); id., *Further Studies in the Prayer Book* (1908). G. Harford–M. Stevenson–J. W. Tyrer (edd.), *Prayer Book Dictionary* (1912; revised ed. 1925). B. [J.] Wigan (ed.), *The Liturgy in English* (1962).

COMMUNICANTES. The section of the *Canon of the Roman Mass, so named from its first word, which comes shortly before the *Words of Institution. Like the 'Hanc igitur' and 'Qui pridie', it is subject to some modification acc. to the ecclesiastical calendar, having variant forms for *Christmas, *Epiphany, *Maundy Thursday, *Easter, *Ascensiontide, and *Pentecost. It consists of a memorial of the saints, mentioning by name the BVM, the eleven Apostles and St. *Paul, eleven Roman martyrs, and one African (St. *Cyprian). In earlier times local saints were sometimes added in particular districts, but since 1570 the prayer has been recited everywhere in the same form as at Rome.

Jungmann (1952), ii, pp. 213–25. V. L. Kennedy, C.S.B., *The Saints of the Canon of the Mass* (Vatican City, 1938); passim. A. *Baumstark, 'Das *Communicantes* und seine Heiligen-liste' in *J.L.W.*, i (1921), pp. 5–33; C. Callewaert, 'S. Léon, le *Communicantes* et le *Nobis quoque peccatoribus*' in *Sacris Erudiri*, i (1948), pp. 123–64. H. Frank, O.S.B., 'Beobachtungen zur Geschichte des Messkanons' in *Archiv für Liturgiewissenschaft*, i (1950), p. 111 f.

COMMUNICATIO IDIOMATUM (Lat. 'communion of the properties'; Gk. ἀντίδοσις τῶν ἰδιωμάτων). The doctrine propounded by several of the Fathers, e.g. *Cyril of Alexandria, that while the human and Divine natures in Christ were separate, the attributes of the one may be predicted of the other in view of their union in the one Person of the Saviour. The doctrine received conciliar authority by its inclusion in the '*Tome' of St. *Leo (449), but in later times it was sometimes understood in a heterodox fashion, esp. in some Lutheran circles.

COMMUNION, Frequency of. On a possible interpretation of Acts 2. 46, the apostolic community communicated daily, and from such passages as Acts 20. 7, and various 2nd cent. writers, it seems that the members of the local churches all communicated at the Sunday Eucharist. But in later times, even though attendance at the Liturgy was general, communion became very infrequent. The Fourth *Lateran Council (1215) (cap. 21) provided that all Christians should communicate at least once a year, and this minimum was the normal later medieval practice. In post-medieval times, nearly all religious revivals, both Catholic and Protestant, have aimed at increasing frequency of communion; the BCP in 1549 and later editions fixed the minimum at three times a year; the *Wesleys communicated two or three times a week; the leaders of the *Oxford Movement urged frequent communion; and in 1905 Pope *Pius X strongly pressed it upon RCs (Decree of 20 Dec. 1905). At present weekly or even daily communion is not uncommon among many of the laity in the RC Church and the C of E, though in the E. Churches and among Protestant non-episcopal bodies it is unusual for communion to be made, even by the devout, more often than once a month, and the majority of RCs and Anglicans adopt less frequent standards.

P. Browe, S.J., *De Frequenti Communione in Ecclesia Occidentali usque ad annum Christi 1000*. Documenta Varia (Rome, 1932); id., *Die häufige Kommunion im Mittelalter* (1938). E. Dublanchy in *D.T.C.*, iii (1908), cols. 515–52, s.v. 'Communion eucharistique (fréquente)', with bibl.; J. Dühr, S.J., in *Dict. Sp.*, ii (1949–53), cols. 1234–92, s.v. 'Communion fréquente'.

COMMUNION, The Order of the (1548). A form for administering Holy Communion, drawn up in English for use in conjunction with the *Sarum (Latin) Mass. It was the first step towards the English Communion Service, and it came into use at *Eastertide, 1548. Its essential parts were an exhortation, a brief address to the intending communicants, the *General Confession followed by the Absolution, the *Comfortable Words, the Prayer of *Humble Access, the Words of Administration (for both kinds), and the Blessing; and it was interpolated into the Latin Mass between the communion of the priest and that of the people. The whole of its contents found a place in the later Anglican BCPs, though the position of its several items has varied. An early copy sent to Frankfurt was translated into German by Miles *Coverdale.

The interpolation of this Order into the rest of the Eucharistic rite in the 1549 BCP bore the title 'The Supper of the Lord and the Holy Communion, commonly called the Mass', which in turn became 'The Order of the Administration of the Lord's Supper, or Holy Communion' in 1552 and later revisions. Hence the origin of the most commonly used title for the Eucharist in the C of E.

A facsimile of the British Museum copy C. 25, f. 15 was edited for the *Henry Bradshaw Society by H. A. Wilson (1908). See also bibl. to *Common Prayer, Book of*.

COMMUNION ANTHEM (Lat. *Communio*). In the Roman Mass the short anthem said by the priest after the *ablutions and, if there is music, also sung by the choir. It is an abbreviated survival of the long chants which were formerly sung during the communion of the people—hence its name. Its present form is probably in origin an *antiphon to a psalm. From the *Apostolic Constitutions (4th cent.) and other sources it would seem that Ps. 34 was commonly chosen in early times, no doubt through the especial appropriateness of verse 8.

Jungmann (1952), ii, pp. 486–96. H. *Leclercq, O.S.B., in *D.A.C.L.*, iii (pt. 2; 1914), cols. 2427–36, s.v. 'Communion (rite et antienne de la)'.

COMMUNION OF SAINTS (Lat. *Communio Sanctorum*). Part of the ninth article of the *Apostles' Creed. It has been interpreted in several senses. (1) The spiritual union existing between each Christian and Christ, and so between each and every Christian, whether in *Heaven (the 'Church *Triumphant'), in *Purgatory (the 'Church *Expectant'), or on earth (the 'Church *Militant'). J.*Pearson (*On the Creed*, s.v.) expounds this communion as the communion of holy persons on earth with the Holy Trinity, with the Angels, with nominal Christians (e.g. in Baptism), with other holy persons, and with the saints in Heaven. He does not mention the Church Expectant. (2) The fellowship of Christians upon earth only. (3) The sharing of holy *things*, i.e. the share which all Christians have in the Sacraments, esp. the *Eucharist, *sanctorum* here being taken as neuter. Of these, (1) is the traditional view.

H. B. *Swete, *The Holy Catholic Church, The Communion of Saints* (1915), pp. 147-69. J. P. Kirsch, *Die Lehre von der Gemeinschaft der Heiligen im christlichen Altertum* (1900; Eng. tr., 1911); G. *Morin, O.S.B., 'Sanctorum Communionem' in *Revue d'Histoire et de Littérature Religieuses*, ix (1904), pp. 209-36; F. J. Badcock, 'Sanctorum Communio as an Article in the Creed' in *J.T.S.*, xxi (1919-20), pp. 106-26. J. F. Sollier in *C.E.*, iv (1908), pp. 171-4; P. Bernard in *D.T.C.*, iii (1908), cols. 429-54, s.v. 'Communion des saints, son aspect dogmatique et historique', with bibl.; R. S. Bour, ib., cols. 454-80, s.v. 'Communion des saints d'après les monuments de l'antiquité chrétienne', with bibl.; H. Leclercq, O.S.B., in *D.A.C.L.*, iii (pt. 2; 1914), cols. 2447-54; F. Bauducco in *E.C.*, iii (1950), cols. 119-25.

COMMUNION PLATE. In the RC Church, a plate of silver or metal gilt held under the chin of the communicant at the reception of Holy Communion. It may be held either by the communicant himself or a server. Its use was directed by an instruction of the *Congregation of the Sacraments (26 Mar. 1929).

COMMUNION SUNDAY. A Sunday on which the Holy Communion is celebrated. The phrase was in common use in England until the general revival in the latter part of the 19th cent. of celebrations in the C of E at least every Sunday.

COMMUNION TABLE. The table at which the Holy Communion is celebrated. In the C of E the word is used esp. by *Low Churchmen, High Churchmen commonly preferring the word 'altar' as better expressive of the Eucharistic sacrifice, which they believe is offered upon it. Since in 'high' churches the altar (for the same doctrinal reason) is often of stone and not of wood, there is a further reason in such cases against its being described as a 'table'. In Latin theology the word *mensa*, however, is of widespread and ancient usage for the 'altar'.

COMMUNION TOKENS. Metal tokens stamped with such devices as texts, initials, chalices, and the *Good Shepherd, which were used as certificates of fitness for admission to the Communion. There is evidence of the employment of '*houselling tokens' in England in 1534. In the Ch. of *Scotland, where they

have been most generally used, they were common from the first and the institution has survived, their place being taken to-day by printed cards on which the communicants' names are written. As these cards are distributed previously by the elders and collected at the service, a check is kept on those who do not communicate. In isolated Presbyterian churches in Scotland and the Dominions, however, the old metal tokens are still retained.

COMMUNION UNDER BOTH KINDS. The custom of receiving Holy Communion under the two species of bread and wine was general until about the 12th cent. There were, however, exceptions. *Tertullian and St. *Cyprian, e.g., attest the widespread African custom of the laity taking the consecrated bread home with them for private Communion. This usage, which had probably sprung up during the persecutions, is attested in the 4th cent. for Egypt and *Alexandria by St. *Basil and for *Rome by St. *Jerome. In the E. it seems to have survived till the 8th cent. Another exception to the rule was the practice of the 3rd cent. anchorites of communicating with the reserved Eucharistic bread alone. The sick and the children seem also to have been habitually communicated under one species only, in the case of infants usually that of wine. The Mass of the *Presanctified, too, presupposed always, for priests and people alike, Communion under the species of bread only. From the 7th cent. the 'intinctio panis', i.e. the dipping of the bread into the consecrated wine, became a widespread usage. Forbidden by the Third Council of Braga (675), the custom again became popular in the 11th cent., chiefly because it prevented the spilling of the Precious Blood. It was again forbidden, e.g. by the Council of *Westminster in 1175. In the E. the 'intinctio' seems to have been unknown during the first nine centuries, but acc. to the testimony of Card. *Humbert (d. 1061), was generally practised before the 11th. By the 13th cent. the practice of communicating under the species of wine had almost universally disappeared in the W., the Synod of *Lambeth of 1281, e.g., restricting in can. 1 the consecrated wine to the celebrant. The legitimacy of this practice was denied by the *Hussites, esp. the party of the *Calixtines, who were condemned by the Council of *Constance in 1415. The chalice was conceded to them, however, by the Council of *Basle (1437), but the decision, which had never been confirmed by the Pope, was revoked in 1462. See also *Intinction, Utraquism*.

The subject again became a matter of acute controversy in the 16th cent. The Reformers insisted that Communion in both kinds alone had Scriptural warrant. In reply the Council of *Trent ruled that there was no Divine precept to communicate under the two species and that existing practice was justified by the doctrine of *concomitance. Hence, in the RC Church, Communion under both kinds is restricted to the celebrating priest. In the E. it is the almost general practice to give Communion from a spoon containing the Eucharistic Bread, sprinkled with a few drops of Wine. The C of E and all the reformed Churches administer Communion under both kinds.

The Tridentine Doctrine was formulated in Session xxi (16 July, 1562); cans. repr. in Mirbt, p. 320 f. Classical discussion by J. B. *Bossuet, *Traité de la communion sous les deux espèces* (1682). E. Dublanchy in *D.T.C.*, iii (1908), cols. 552-72, s.v. 'Communion eucharistique (sous les deux espèces)'. See also bibl. to *Eucharist*.

COMMUNITY OF THE RESURREC-TION. This Anglican community was founded at *Oxford in 1892 by C. *Gore, then principal of Pusey House. Its original members were, besides C. Gore, its first superior, J. O. Nash, J. Carter, M. C. Bickersteth, G. Longridge, and W. H. *Frere. In 1893 the Community moved to Radley, Berks, and five years later to Mirfield, Yorks. From the beginning one of the chief aims of the Community was to adapt the religious life to the changed circumstances of the modern age. Most of the original members continued to combine the scholarly, educational, and evangelistic work in which they had been engaged before profession with common life; but with growing numbers the Community began to develop work of its own, notably the College of the Resurrection for the training of ordinands, and missionary and educational work in S. Africa.

C.R. Diamond Jubilee Book (1952). G. P. H. Pawson, C.R., *Edward Keble Talbot. His Community and his Friends* (1954).

COMNENA, ANNA. See *Anna Comnena*.

COMPANY OF JESUS. See *Jesuits*.

COMPARATIVE RELIGION. A modern name, not (as its form would imply) for a particular kind of religion, but for the branch of study which investigates by scientific and historical methods the religions of the world in their mutual relations. Its development dates from the later 19th cent. under the influence of evolutionary ideas and the greatly increased factual knowledge of other religions through the researches of anthropologists. Its successful pursuit as a science rests on the universality of religion among primitive as well as civilized peoples and the frequent recurrence of certain patterns of religious experience and activity in widely separated ethnological and social groupings. In scope, Comparative Religion studies the conditions under which these various forms of religious behaviour manifest themselves, the processes of their growth and the part which they play in the cultures and traditions to which they belong. On the other hand, questions relating to the ultimate philosophical and theological validity of the various religions are beyond its purview, its avowed purpose being to describe and classify phenomena rather than to evaluate them.

None the less, despite this theoretical exclusion of questions of validity, the discipline

O.D.C.C.—M

has raised various pressing questions for the Christian faith, notably by its recognition that much in the Christian tradition is not, as was long supposed, exclusive to it, but is held in common with other world religions. The recognition of these parallels has acutely raised the question of the 'Absoluteness' of Christianity (E. *Troeltsch). On the other hand, as Christian students of the subject have argued with great cogency, the study has emphatically brought out the distinctiveness of certain elements in the Christian religion which, judged even by purely historical categories, indicate its pre-eminence above all other religions. Among these are its conception of God and of human personality and the high quality of the Christian ethic. On the practical side the study has brought Christian apologists a deeper understanding of the non-Christian religions and exercised a far-reaching influence on missionary methods.

There is a large literature. Popular works include L. R. Farnell, *The Evolution of Religion* (1905); N. *Söderblom, *The Living God* (*Gifford Lectures, 1931); E. O. James, *Comparative Religion* (1938); A. C. Bouquet, *Comparative Religion* (Penguin Books, 1941); N. Micklem, *Religion* (Home University Library, 1948); T. H. Robinson, *A Short Comparative History of Religions* (new ed., 1951); cf. also S. A. Cook in *H.E.R.E.*, x (1918), pp. 662-93, s.v. 'Religion'. More ambitious works are J. G. Frazer, *The Golden Bough. A Study in Comparative Religion* (2 vols., 1890; ed. 3, 12 vols., 1907-15); C. H. Toy, *Introduction to the History of Religions* (1895); S. A. Cook, *The Study of Religions* (1914); H. Pinard de la Boullaye, *L'Étude comparée des religions* (2 vols., 1922-5). Much valuable material in J. *Hastings (ed.), *Encyclopaedia of Religion and Ethics* (12 vols. and index, 1908-26) and H. Gunkel, L. Zscharnack, and others (edd.), *Die Religion in Geschichte und Gegenwart* (ed. 2, 5 vols. and index, 1927-32). On the relation of Christianity to the non-Christian religions, cf. H. Kraemer, *The Christian Message in a Non-Christian World* (1938). See also bibl. to *Animism, Anthropology*, etc.

COMPETENTES (Lat. 'those qualified'). In the early Church *catechumens admitted to the final stage of preparation for *Baptism. They were also known as 'electi', or, in the E., as 'illuminated ones' (φωτιζόμενοι).

COMPLINE (Lat. *Completorium*). The last of the canonical day-hours (see *Office*) in the W. Church, said before retiring for the night. There is evidence that St. *Basil compiled an office approximating to compline, but in the W. it received its liturgical form from St. *Benedict, who included it in his rule, prob. by formalizing prayers which were already customarily said in the evening.. The corresponding service in the E. Church is known as ἀπόδειπνον (Gk. 'after supper'). The W. office consists of psalms appropriate to the time of day (anciently Pss. 4, 31. 1-6, 91, and 134, but in the modern Roman Breviary a more varied selection is used), an evening hymn (usually the *Te lucis ante terminum*), and the canticle '*Nunc dimittis' (added later than the time of St. Benedict and still not used in the monastic office). The details of the service, however, vary greatly in the different W. breviaries. The essential parts of it were incorporated into the *Evensong of the BCP; and a form of it was included in the 1928 revision of the BCP as a separate 'late evening service' to be used 'when Evensong has been previously said'.

N. Gihr, *Prim und Komplet des römischen Breviers, liturgisch und aszetisch erklärt* (Theologische Bibliothek, 1907). J. Pargoire, 'Prime et Complies' in *Revue d'Histoire et de Littérature Religieuses*, iii (1898), pp. 281–8 and 456–67.

COMPLUTENSIAN POLYGLOT. The edition of the Bible undertaken by Card. F. *Ximenes in 1502, to commemorate the birth of *Charles V of Spain, and issued at Alcalá (Lat. 'Complutum'). It contained the OT in Hebrew, Greek, and Latin, and the NT in Greek and Latin. Its text of the Greek NT was the earliest to be printed (1514), though D. *Erasmus' Greek Testament (1516) was the first to be published, as the *Polyglot* was not put into circulation until 1522. The work is ustly admired for its splendid typography.

COMPOSTELA. A city in N.W. Spain, properly Santiago [i.e. 'St. James'] de Compostela, traditionally supposed to be the place of burial of St. *James the Apostle. In or shortly before 1095 the ancient see of Iria was transferred to Compostela, and the city became the centre from that time onwards of the national and Christian movement against the Moslem rulers of the country. The shrine of St. James is a centre for pilgrimages from all over Spain, and from many other parts of the world.

C. G. Hartley, *The Story of Santiago de Compostella* ('Medieval Towns Series', 1912); J. S. Stone, *The Cult of Santiago*. Traditions, Myths and Pilgrimages. A Sympathetic Study (1927), incl. sources.

COMPRECATION. The word is used esp. of the intercession which the saints are believed to make on behalf of the rest of the Church. Some Anglican theologians (e.g. J. *Bramhall) have maintained that though direct *invocation of the saints is an unwarranted practice, it is legitimate to request God for their prayers; and such requests for the saints' intercessions have also been called loosely comprecation.

COMPTON, HENRY (1632–1713), Bp. of *London. He was educated at Queen's College, *Oxford, and in early life served in the army. After ordination in 1662, he held various preferments, was appointed Bp. of Oxford in 1674, and translated to London in 1675. A friend of Danby, he was tutor of the princesses Mary and Anne, and officiated at the marriages of both of them. His stoutly anti-Papist attitude and his friendliness towards Protestant Dissenters failed to commend him to *James II, and he was restrained by the *High Commission Court from the exercise of his spiritual functions, nominally on the ground of his refusal to suspend J. *Sharp, then Rector of St. Giles'-in-the-Fields, for his anti-Roman sermons. Having signed the invitation to *William of Orange and officiated at the Coronation, he strongly supported the project for comprehension and the *Toleration Act. For some not very clearly known reason, he

was twice passed over when the primacy was vacant, in favour of J. *Tillotson and T. *Tension successively; and during the reign of *Anne he became regarded as a High Churchman, if not a Tory, since he voted for the *Occasional Conformity Bill and in favour of the resolution that the Church was in danger. In 1686 he published under the title *Episcopalia* a set of addresses to his clergy.

Anon. life, perh. by Nathaniel Salmon, London, c. 1715. New ed. of his *Episcopalia*, with brief memoir of Compton by S. W. Cornish, Oxford, 1842. E. Carpenter, *The Protestant Bishop* (1956). S. L. Lee in *D.N.B.*, xi (1887), pp. 443–7.

COMTE, AUGUSTE (1798–1857), founder of French *Positivism and of the 'Religion of Humanity'. He was a native of Montpellier and educated at the École Polytechnique, *Paris, where he studied esp. science and mathematics. Having lost his religious faith he came under the influence of H. *Saint-Simon, whose disciple he was from 1816 to 1824. His *Système de politique positive* (1822) contains in germ most of his later ideas. His principal work was his *Cours de la philosophie positive* (6 vols., 1830–42). The foundation of his system is the law of the three stages—the theological, the metaphysical, and the 'positive'—which constitute the phases of development of the human race as a whole as well as of its individual members. Whereas in the theological and metaphysical stages the human mind seeks a cause or essence to explain phenomena, in the third or positive phase explanation is discovered in a law. Comte advocated the organization of mankind in one vast system in which altruism was to conquer egoism. Conceiving this to be possible only on a religious basis, he constructed a new kind of religion, with humanity, the 'great being', in the place of God. He introduced an elaborate cultus, borrowed chiefly from Catholicism, with its priests and sacraments, and even produced a 'Positivist Calendar' in which the names of scientists and scholars replaced those of the saints. His revolutionary ideas lost him his post as examiner in mathematics at the École Polytechnique, which he had held from 1837 to 1844, and from this time he was supported chiefly by the generosity of his disciples, among whom, with reservations, was J. S. *Mill. In 1848 he founded the 'Positive Society' which aimed at applying the principles of Positivism to the reconstruction of society. In his chief sociological work, *Système de politique positive*, he attempted to apply his utilitarian ethical principles to social and political questions.

Several collections of his letters have been publd. The numerous studies include those of J. F. E. Robinet (Paris, 1860), [M. P.] E. Littré (ib., 1863), J. S. *Mill (London, 1865; repr. from the *Westminster Review*), E. *Caird (Glasgow, 1885), L. Lévy-Bruhl (Paris, 1900; Eng. tr., 1903), and F. S. Marvin (London, 1936).

CONCELEBRATION. The joint act of celebration effected by the recitation of the *Canon at the *Eucharist by a number of priests, simultaneously with the principal celebrant. Such was the usual custom in the early Church, when the bishop in each place was normally the chief celebrant; and it still survives as the regular practice of the E. Church. In the W. it has gradually given place to separate celebration, each priest saying the Liturgy at a different time or place. Traces of the earlier custom remain, however, at *Ordinations, at which the newly ordained priests concelebrate with the bishop.

D. Giorgi, *De Liturgia Romani Pontificis in Solemni Celebratione Missarum*, ii (Rome, 1743), Dissertatio I, cap. i, pp. i–xiii, and iii (ib., 1744), Dissertatio I, pp. i–xxiv. P. de Puniet, O.S.B., in *D.A.C.L.*, iii (pt. 2; 1914), cols. 2470–88, s.v., with bibl. L. Beauduin, O.S.B., 'La Concélébration' in *Maison-Dieu*, vii (1946), pp. 7–26. A. *Fortescue in *C.E.*, iv (1908), p. 190, s.v.

CONCEPTION OF THE BVM, The. See *Immaculate Conception of the BVM, The.*

CONCERNING THE SERVICE OF THE CHURCH.' The present title of the preface to the original (1549) edition of the BCP. When the present 'Preface' was added in 1662 (immediately before the 1549 preface) it was necessary to give the original preface a new name, and it then received the above title. Its contents were based on the preface to the reformed Roman *Breviary of F. *Quignon, and it is probably the work of T. *Cranmer. Its object was to explain the merits of the new Book over its Latin predecessors, e.g. continuity in the reading of the Bible, simplicity of ritual, the use of the vernacular, and uniformity of rite.

CONCLAVE (Lat. *cum clave*, 'with a key'). The closed apartment in which the college of *cardinals is shut up during the entire process of electing a new Pope. The custom of keeping the cardinals enclosed was adopted in 1271 to hasten a Papal election which was still not made after nearly three years, and this practice has been followed ever since. The word 'conclave' is also applied to the meeting itself either for this particular occasion or, more loosely, of the cardinals for any purpose.

L. Lector [really Mgr. J. Guthlin], *Le Conclave, origines, histoire, organisation, législation ancienne et moderne* (1894); A. Ceccaroni, *Il conclave*. Storia, costituzioni, cerimonie (1901). E. Ruffini Avondo, 'Le origini del conclave papale' in *Atti della Reale Accademia delle Scienze di Torino*, xxvii (1927), pp. 409–31. Further bibl., with reff. to doc. sources, in F. Cerroti, *Bibliografia di Roma medievale e moderna*, i (1893), esp. pp. 544–52. A. Molien in *D.D.C.*, iii (1942), cols. 1319–42, s.v.

CONCOMITANCE. The doctrine that in the Eucharist the Body and Blood of Christ are present in each of the consecrated species. It implies that the fullness of communion is to be had under either element alone, and it has been held, esp. among RCs, to justify the withdrawal of the chalice from the laity. In a more extended sense, the word is also used for the doctrine that in virtue of the *hypostatic union of God and man in Christ, the Godhead and the human soul of Christ are also present in the Eucharistic elements after their consecration. See also *Communion under both Kinds.*

CONCORD, The Formula (1577) and Book (1580) of. The 'Formula of Concord', the last of the classical *Lutheran formulae of faith, was drawn up in Mar. 1577, by a number of theologians, among them Jakob Andreae (1528–90), M. *Chemnitz, and Nikolaus Selnecker (1530–92). In language it is precise and emphatic, and represents the definitive statement of Lutheran orthodoxy, corresponding to the similar pronouncements on the Catholic side at the Council of *Trent. The *Melanchthonist position was excluded as much as the Romanist and the *Calvinist. The subjects dealt with were the stock topics of contemporary controversy—the sacraments, sin, and salvation, and the relation between the Divine and Human natures in Christ, and between Divine foreknowledge and human freedom. In its positive definitions, the formula occupies a middle position between Trent and *Geneva. Thus Christ's Real Presence in the Eucharist is asserted, but it is represented as in no way a special presence, or different from His general presence in all creation. Again, on the question of *Predestination, man's total depravity after the *Fall is explicitly stated, but its logical outcome, *Double Predestination, is denied.

After much discussion, the Formula, together with the three Creeds (*Apostles', *Nicene, and *Athanasian), the *Augsburg Confession and Apology (1530), the *Schmalkaldic Articles (1537) and M. *Luther's two *Catechisms, as well as the three earlier drafts on which it was based (the 'Swabian and Saxon Formula' [1574–5], the 'Maulbronn Formula' [1575], and the '*Torgau Articles' [1576]), was published in German at Dresden in 1580 as the 'Book of Concord' (*Konkordienbuch*). The first authoritative Latin edition appeared in 1584. It was signed by 86 representatives of the Lutheran state-churches and some 8,000 pastors and teachers. It met, however, with much opposition, esp. outside Germany, and was rejected, e.g. in Denmark, and hence has never possessed the authority of the *Augsburg Confession (1530).

P. Schaff, *The Creeds of Christendom* (1877), i, 258–340; iii, 93–180 (text).

CONCORD OF WITTENBERG. See *Wittenberg, Concord of.*

CONCORDANCE. A book of reference indicating and usually quoting in part all the passages of Scripture in which a given word is found. The most famous (and still the standard) English Concordance is that compiled in 1737 by A. *Cruden (q.v.), which in its later editions is extremely detailed and complete. A Hebrew Concordance, compiled 1437–45 by Rabbi Isaac b. Kalonymus, was publd. at Venice in 1523 and tr. into Lat. 1556; it was revised by M. de Calasio, O.F.M. (Rome, 1621). A *Hebrew Concordance adapted to the English Bible* was publd. by J. *Taylor (2 vols., 1754–7). In 1230 a Latin Concordance to the *Vulgate was compiled by Hugo de Saint-Cher, assisted by 500 *Dominicans; this work merely gave the Biblical reff., though later three English Dominicans added the quotations. The first Concordance to the Vulgate was publd. at Strassburg *c.* 1474; that in common use is based on the work of F. P. Dutripon (Paris, 1838). A Concordance to the *Septuagint was compiled by C. Kircher (3 vols., Frankfurt, 1607); the standard modern work is that of E. *Hatch–H. A. Redpath (3 vols., Oxford, 1892–1900). The pioneer Concordance to the Gk. NT was that of S. Birck, publd. at Basle, 1546; in 1638 it was followed by the ταμεῖον of Erasmus Schmidt (publd. Wittenberg), which was ed. by C. H. Bruder (Leipzig, 1842; rev., with readings of S. P. *Tregelles and B. F. *Westcott–F. J. A. *Hort, Leipzig, 1888). This has now been generally replaced among English scholars by that of W. F. *Moulton–A. S. Geden (Edinburgh, 1897). The most significant work based on Cruden's Concordance was the revision of it by J. Eadie and others (Glasgow, 1840). The chief later Concordance to the English Bible is R. *Young's *Analytical Concordance to the Bible* (Edinburgh, 1879). A Concordance incl. reff. to the RV was publd. in 1894 (ed. J. Strong, London); a Concordance to the translation of J. *Moffatt appeared in London, 1950.

H. E. Bindseil, 'Ueber die Concordanzen' in *Theologische Studien und Kritiken*, xliii (1870), pp. 673–720. A. Kleinhans, O.F.M., 'De Concordantiis Biblicis S. Antonio Patavino aliisque Fratribus Minoribus Saec. XII Attributis' in *Antonianum*, vi (1931), pp. 273–326; id., 'De Prima Editione Catholica Concordantiarum Hebraico-Latinarum Sacrorum Bibliorum' [1621 ed.] in *Biblica*, v (1924), pp. 39–48. E. Mangenot in *Dict. Bibl.*, ii (1899), cols. 892–905, s.v. 'Concordances de la Bible'; D. Macfadyen in *E.B.* (ed. 11), vi (1910), p. 83f f., s.v.; A. Penna, C.R.L., in *E.C.*, iv (1950), col. 185 f., s.v. 'Concordanze bibliche', with further bibl. See also bibl. to *Cruden, A*.

CONCORDAT. An agreement between the civil and ecclesiastical authorities upon some matter of vital concern to both parties. See also, besides the following entry, *Lateran Treaty* (1929).

CONCORDAT OF 1801. The agreement concluded, on 16 July 1801, between *Pius VII and Napoleon Bonaparte, then First Consul, which led to the formal restoration of the Catholic Church in France. By its terms the French government recognized the Catholic religion as that of the great majority of French citizens. All existing bishops were to resign their sees; fresh dioceses were mapped out; and the state was given the right of nominating new bishops—a provision which enabled it to exercise control over the political complexion of the clergy. Alienated Church property was to remain in the hands of those who had acquired it, but the government agreed to ensure a fitting maintenance to the bishops and parish priests. The expected benefits of these terms to the Church were considerably reduced by Napoleon's subsequent publication of the *Organic Articles (q.v.).

Le Cte Boulay de La Meurthe (ed.), *Documents sur la négociation du concordat et sur les autres rapports de la France avec le saint-siège* (6 vols., 1891–1905), with Texte Définitif du Concordat in Lat. and Fr. No. 645, vol. iii, pp. 213–19; the Fr. version, lacking the preamble, also printed in Mirbt, No. 558, p. 419 f. Le Cte Boulay de La Meurthe, *Histoire de la négociation du concordat de 1801* (Tours, 1920). W. M. Sloane, *The French Revolution and Religious Reform* (1901), pp. 245–81, with Fr. text of Concordat, pp. 309–12. A. Debidour, *Histoire des rapports de l'Église et de l'État en France de 1789 à 1870* (1898), ch. 6, pp. 183–227; G. Pariset in E. Lavisse, *Histoire de la France contemporaine depuis la Révolution jusqu'à la paix de 1919*, iii (1921), pp. 78–112, with reff. C. Constantin in *D.T.C.*, iii (1908), cols. 744–79, s.v.; R. Naz in *D.D.C.*, iii (1924), cols. 1404–31, s.v.

CONCORDIA REGULARIS. See *Regularis Concordia*.

CONCUPISCENCE. In moral theology the inordinate desire for temporal ends which has its seat in the senses. The notion of concupiscence has its Biblical foundations esp. in the teaching of St. *Paul (Eph. 2. 3, Rom. 7. 7 ff., etc.) and was developed by St. *Augustine in his struggle against *Pelagianism. Acc. to Augustine the cause of concupiscence is the *Fall of *Adam, who, having lost *Original Righteousness, transmitted to us a nature in which the desires of the flesh are no longer subordinated to reason. St. *Thomas Aquinas, elaborating the Augustinian teaching, regards it as the material (i.e. passive, because residing in the senses) element of Original Sin, the formal (active, residing in the will) element being loss of Original Righteousness. From the moral point of view it is *materia exercendae virtutis* for it provides reason and will with opportunities for resisting the disordered movements of the senses. Orthodox Protestant theology, on the other hand, both in its *Lutheran and in its *Calvinist forms, regards concupiscence itself as sin and its very existence as an offence against God; and the *Jansenists held a similar view. The Council of *Trent (sess. 5) followed St. Thomas's teaching against the Reformers, and in post-Tridentine theology it is usually regarded as a consequence of Original Sin rather than as part of it.

A. Chollet in *D.T.C.*, iii (1908), cols. 803–14, s.v.; P. Parente–C. Testore, S.J., in *E.C.*, iv (1950), cols. 207–9, s.v. 'Concupiscenza'.

CONCURRENCE. The falling on consecutive days of ecclesiastical feasts or other days to be observed, so that Second *Vespers or *Evensong of the first coincides with First Vespers or Evensong of the second. In such cases, in the W. Church, the collect of the more important feast is said first, and, if it is of very high rank, that of the other is omitted. When the two feasts are of equal rank, the one which is about to begin takes precedence of that which is ending. On the evening of 1 Nov., however, Vespers of *All Saints is said without commemoration of All Souls (2 Nov.) and followed at once by Vespers of the Dead without commemoration of All Saints.

CONCURSUS DIVINUS (Lat.) 'Divine concourse'. A technical theological term for the co-operation of the *grace of God with the actions of finite creatures.

Catholic theologians are in general agreement that it is of two forms, viz. (1) *mediate*, such as God's gift of capacities to His creatures appropriate to the performing of certain tasks, and (2) *immediate*, such as the direct dependence of man on God in the actual exercise of these capacities; but the exact manner in which the concursus takes place has been much disputed. *Thomists have held that immediate concursus precedes the action (*praemotio physica*), whereas *Molinists have maintained that the concursus and the action are simultaneous (*concursus simultaneus*). Among Protestant theologians, the fact of the 'Divine concourse' was allowed by *Lutherans and rejected by *Calvinists. The two facts which the several accounts of the 'Divine concourse' have been concerned to maintain are man's own responsibility for his sinful acts and the universality of God's sovereign rule.

CONDIGNITY. In the Scholastic theology of *grace, those actions which fallen man performs as a Christian in conscious reliance on the Holy Spirit are held to merit the grace of God 'by condignity' (*gratia de condigno*), i.e., as from a Debtor. NT support is found in the case of Cornelius, whose prayers and alms are said to have come up for a memorial before God. (Cf. Acts 10. 31, esp. *Vulgate text).

CONDITIONAL BAPTISM. See *Baptism, Conditional*.

CONDITIONAL IMMORTALITY (also known as **Annihilationism**). A theory acc. to which immortality is not a necessary attribute of the immaterial soul but conditional on its behaviour during its life in the body. Though this opinion had a solitary representative in the 4th cent. African Christian author, *Arnobius, it was never held in Christendom until recent times, except in isolated cases of philosophical speculation, and it was formally condemned at the Fifth *Lateran Council in 1513. In the 19th cent., however, it found favour with many thinkers as a possible way of accounting for the fate of the impenitently wicked without accepting either the orthodox doctrine of eternal punishment or the *Origenistic theory of universalism. It was elaborated by Edward White, a *Congregational minister, in his *Life in Christ* (1846; expanded and completely recast, 1875), which attempted to prove from Scripture that 'Immortality is the peculiar privilege of the regenerate', and it found some acceptance among English and American as well as Continental thinkers. It was restated in a milder form by J. *Martineau, acc. to whom the wicked are not annihilated, but lose their personal being, and this belief was admitted to be tolerable by C. *Gore. The

teaching of the mortality of the soul is generally considered to be opposed to the Christian doctrine of man and to the dignity and responsibility of the human soul. Though still used in certain kinds of popular apologetics, it has nowadays but few defenders among serious Christian theologians.

H. W. Fulford in *H.E.R.E.*, iii (1901), pp. 822–5, s.v.; G. C. Joyce, ib., i (1908), pp. 544–9, s.v. 'Annihilation'; both with bibl.

CONDREN, CHARLES DE (1588–1641), French theologian and mystic. Though destined by his father to a military career, he early gave himself to prayer and the study of the Scriptures. In 1613 he entered the *Sorbonne and in 1614 was ordained priest. After some hesitation he entered the Congregation of the *Oratory in 1617, where he was soon charged with the foundation of the houses at Nevers, Langres, and Poitiers. In 1629 he succeeded P. de *Bérulle as Superior-General. A famous director of souls, he was so modest that he refrained from publishing anything during his lifetime, and his doctrine has survived mainly through his letters, collected in 1642 as *Lettres et discours*, and the well-known *L'Idée du sacerdoce et du sacrifice de Jésus-Christ* (1677), actually written by his disciples, but containing his authentic teaching. The two focal points of his doctrine were a strong theocentrism and an intense devotion to the mysteries of the Incarnate Christ. The Sacrifice of the Mass was immediately related to the eternal Sacrifice which the risen and ascended Christ offers in heaven. Despite the fact that he himself wrote hardly anything, de Condren's influence has been considerable, esp. through his devoted disciple, J.-J. *Olier, while in Great Britain his Eucharistic teaching came to be appreciated widely, chiefly through the *Tractarians.

The best collected ed. of his works is that of L. M. Pin (2 vols., Paris, 1857–8); crit. ed. of his Letters by P. Auvray, Cong. Orat.–A. Jouffrey, Cong. Orat. (Paris, 1943). The primary source for his life is the biography by D. Amelote (anon., Paris, 1643). Modern life by L. M. Pin (Paris, 1855). Study in English by M. V. Woodgate (Dublin, 1949), with bibl. Bremond, iii, pp. 283–340; Pourrat, iii, pp. 521–5 and 551–67. A. Molien, Cong. Orat., in *Dict. Sp.*, ii (1953), cols. 1373–88, s.v., with further bibl. See also bibl. to *Oratorians*.

CONDUCT. A name formerly in general use for any priest who was engaged to read the prayers in the chapel of a college of which he was not on the foundation. The chaplains at Eton College are still so described.

CONFESSING CHURCH (*Bekennende Kirche*), formerly more commonly 'Confessional Church' (*Bekenntnis-Kirche*). The group of German Evangelical Christians which most actively opposed the '*German-Christian' Church Movement sponsored by the Nazis between 1933 and 1945 and which claimed, esp. at the outset, to stand fast by the *Augsburg and other Reformation Confessions. It came into being in Nov. 1933 as the 'Pastors' Emergency League' under the leadership of

M. *Niemöller, and at first was largely concerned to resist the policy of Reichsbischof L. *Müller and (later) Hans *Kerrl, the Nazi Minister for Church Affairs. After the Synod at Barmen in May 1934 it set up its own 'Provisional Church Administration' (*Vorläufige Kirchenleitung*), which exercised canonical authority over groups of 'Confessing Christians' in those territorial Churches whose official Administrators were 'German Christians'; and its claims to authority were often upheld in the law courts. Owing to Nazi dominance it was forced increasingly to work underground, and after 1937 its influence declined. Gradually the group was eclipsed by the 'Lutheran Council' (created for a similar purpose in Aug. 1934 with August Marahrens, Bp. of Hanover, Theophil Wurm, Bp. of Württemberg, and Hans Meiser, Bp. of Bavaria, as its chief members), whose opposition to the Nazis was less radical but proved more durable.

After the end of the war (1945), the hope of the leaders of the Confessing Church that they would leaven most of German Protestantism was not realized, and in 1949 Niemöller was not re-elected to the Vice-Presidency of the federal 'Evangelical Church in Germany', set up under his influence in 1948. His 'Confessing Church Group', however, decided to continue in separate existence as a movement within the Church, though ceasing to claim to be the only true Church government. It is led by a 'Council of Brethren' (*Brüderrat*) comprising representatives of each Territorial Church. It takes its stand on the historic creeds and the *Barmen Declaration, but is against undue stress on denominationalism.

In the earlier stages of the conflict the group generally called themselves the 'Confessional Church' to emphasize that their opposition to the Nazis was primarily religious (based on confessions of faith), not political. But the revival of largely forgotten and divergent theological formulae among the different Lutheran and Calvinist Territorial Churches led the term 'Confessional Church' to be discarded as no longer specially appropriate and also as divisive; and Niemöller's group, which sought to minimize these doctrinal divergences in the endeavour to secure Protestant unity, came gradually to prefer the name 'Confessing Church', with the sense of being a Church of confessors for the faith rather than of those who owed allegiance to a formal dogmatic Confession.

H. Hermelink (ed.), *Kirche im Kampf*. Dokumente des Widerstands und des Aufbaus in der Evangelischen Kirche Deutschlands von 1933 bis 1945 (1950). A. Frey, *Cross and Swastika* (1938); A. S. Duncan-Jones, *The Struggle for Religious Freedom in Germany* (1938); M. Niemöller, *Kampf und Zeugnis der Bekennenden Kirche* (1948).

CONFESSIO AUGUSTANA. See *Augsburg Confession.*

CONFESSIO HELVETICA. See *Helvetic Confession.*

CONFESSIO SCOTICA. See *Scottish Confession.*

CONFESSION. (1) A tomb of a *martyr ('*confessor'). The term is used also of the structure built over such a tomb, and of a crypt or shrine under the High *Altar of a church, in which relics are placed. In the Middle Ages the word was further applied to the entire church in which a martyr was buried. The *confessio* of St. Peter in the *Vatican is perhaps the most celebrated of all such tombs.

(2) The profession of faith made by a martyr or confessor (e.g. 1 Tim. 6. 13, 2 Cor. 9. 13), and so in general a declaration of religious belief. In this sense the word has been occasionally applied to the ancient oecumenical *creeds, but it is more generally used of the Protestant professions of faith in the 16th and 17th cents., of which the Confession of *Augsburg (1530) was the earliest. From this sense derives its use for a communion, or religious body.

(3) An acknowledgment of sin, made either in general terms by a congregation in the course of liturgical worship, or specifically by an individual penitent in public confession, or more usually in private or *auricular confession.

CONFESSION, Seal of. See *Seal of Confession.*

CONFESSIONS OF ST. AUGUSTINE, The, written *c.* 400. Its title is to be taken in the Biblical sense of 'confessing', i.e. 'praising', 'God' rather than in its modern meaning of 'avowal', the work being St. Augustine's thanksgiving for his conversion. Its main theme is expressed in the famous sentence 'Thou hast made us for Thyself and our heart is restless until it rests in Thee'. Its purpose is to demonstrate the work of God's grace in his soul whereby he was transformed from a vessel of wrath into a vessel of election. The autobiographical part (Books 1–9) describes his efforts at finding ultimate truth, from his youthful studies at Carthage and disappointment with *Manichaism to his acquaintance with *Plato and his final conversion in the garden near Milan (386). Book 10 deals with the faculty of memory, 11 offers a theory of time, and Books 12 and 13 contain an allegorical exposition of the first verses of Genesis.

Modern edd. by E. B. *Pusey (Oxford, 1838; inaugurating the *Tractarian *Bibliotheca Patrum*), P. Knöll (C.S.E.L., xxxiii, 1896), J. Gibb–W. Montgomery (Cambridge Patristic Texts, 1908), P. de Labriolle (2 vols., Paris, 1925–7), A. C. Vega, O.S.A. (Escurial, 1930), and F. Skutella (Leipzig, 1934). Eng. trr. by Sir Tobie Matthew (St.-Omer, 1620; mod. ed. by R. Huddleston, O.S.B., 1923), W. Watts (1631; repr. in Loeb, 2 vols., 1912), E. B. Pusey (L.F., i, 1838; revision of tr. of W. Watts), and F. J. Sheed (1943).

The intrinsic interest of the work, with the contrast in temper between the *Confessions* (*c.* 400) and the *Dialogues* from the time of St. Augustine's conversion (*c.* 386), has produced an unusually large literature, much of it of a high quality. Among the more important items are A. *Harnack, *Augustins Confessionen* (Giessen, 1888; Eng. tr., 1901); F. Wörter, *Die Geistesentwicklung des hl. Augustins bis zu* seiner Taufe (1892); H. Becker, Augustin. Studien zu seiner geistigen Entwicklung (1908); W. Thimme, Augustins geistige Entwicklung in den ersten Jahren nach seiner Bekehrung, 386–391 (Neue Studien zur Geschichte der Theologie und Kirche, iii, 1908); P. Alfaric, L'Évolution intellectuelle de saint Augustine (thesis, Paris, 1918); R. L. *Ottley, Studies in the Confessions of St. Augustine (1919); C. Boyer, S.J., Christianisme et néo-platonisme dans la formation de saint Augustin (thesis, Paris, 1920); M. Wundt, 'Ein Wendepunkt in Augustins Entwicklung' in Z.T.N.W., xxi (1922), pp. 53–64; K. Holl, Augustins innere Entwicklung (Abh. (Berl.), Jg. 1922, Hft. 4; 1923), repr. in Holl's Gesammelte Aufsätze zur Kirchengeschichte, iii (1928), pp. 54–116; K. Nörregaard, Augustins Bekehrung (1923); M. Zepf, Augustins Confessiones (Heidelberger Abhandlungen zur Philosophie und ihrer Geschichte, ix, 1926), W. J. Sparrow Simpson, St. Augustine's Conversion (1930); K. Adam, Die geistige Entwicklung des heiligen Augustinus (1931); P. Henry, S.J., La Vision d'Ostie. Sa place dans la vie et l'œuvre de saint Augustin (1938). P. Courcelle, Recherches sur les confessions de saint Augustin (1950), with valuable bibl., pp. 259–78. J. M. Le Blond, Les Conversions de saint Augustin (1950). J. O'Meara, The Young Augustine (1954).

CONFESSOR. (1) In the early Church one who suffered for confessing his or her faith, but only to an extent which did not involve martyrdom. Later the term was applied loosely to markedly holy men, and ultimately to those pronounced to be such by the Pope. King *Edward (d. 1066) was declared a Confessor by *Alexander III in 1161.

(2) A priest who hears (esp. private) confessions.

CONFIRMATION. In Sacramental theology, the rite whereby the grace of the Holy Spirit is conveyed in a new or fuller way to those who have already received it in some degree or fashion at *Baptism. Though the rite goes back to very early times, there have been wide differences as to its method of administration, as well as to the theological interpretation put upon it. It has been held, at least among Catholic theologians, to imprint a *character on the recipient, so that the same person cannot be confirmed more than once.

Theologians find early instances of Confirmation in the imposition of hands by the Apostles, e.g. by St. *Peter and St. *John on the converts of Samaria (Acts 8. 14–17) and by St. *Paul on the disciples at *Ephesus (19. 1–7). Other NT passages which may refer to it are the 'laying on of hands', as distinct from the 'teaching of baptisms', in Heb. 6. 2, or again the frequent mention in the NT of the 'sealing with the Spirit' (e.g. 2 Cor. 1. 20 f., Eph. 1. 13, 4. 30), though perhaps these belong with more probability to Baptism. The difficulty of fitting the NT references into a wholly unified pattern becomes clear when we observe that whereas in many places the full impartation of the Holy Ghost is closely linked with the actual Baptism, e.g. in the Baptism of the Lord Himself (Mk. 1. 10) and of the first converts on the Day of *Pentecost (Acts 2. 38), in others the Spirit is given prior to, and seemingly independently of, Baptism (Acts 9. 17 f.).

In the sub-Apostolic age, a similar variety of practice is met with. Washing with water, anointing with oil, and the laying on of hands all came to be associated with initiation into the fullness of Christian life and the aggregate spiritual effect which flowed from these outward observances was held to include the removal of sin, admission to the Church of the Redeemed, 'sealing' to eternal life and the impartation of the Spirit. But there was considerable variety alike of practice and interpretation. While at one place washing, anointing, and imposition of hands might be all considered different parts or aspects of a single rite, elsewhere they could be regarded as connected with two, or possibly even more, stages in the Christian's progress into the fullness of Sacramental life.

'Confirmation' (but not by this name) appears as a rite clearly separate from Baptism in *Tertullian (De Baptismo, 6; De Res. Carnis, 8; Adv. Marc., i. 14). The same clear distinction is made by St. *Cyprian (Epp., 70, 74) and by Pope *Cornelius (ap. *Eusebius, H.E., vi, xliii). By the 4th cent. Confirmation, whether conferred by anointing or laying on of hands, was everywhere a separate rite. The Bishop, who in primitive times was able to take a personal interest in all the candidates for Baptism, now found that the number of those seeking admission into the Church was such that he could no longer baptize all in person, and the functions of parish priest (immersion) and Bishop (anointing), originally usually closely associated, gradually became distinct. What had once often been scarcely distinguishable elements in the single Baptismal-Confirmation rite, were now performed by different ministers.

The practice, however, became stereotyped in different ways in the E. and W. In the E. the primitive custom of conferring 'Confirmation' in immediate relation to Baptism was retained. This was achieved by confining the Bishop's part to the consecration of the oil used for the anointing. This was then conveyed to the parish priest, who performed the actual rite of Confirmation as occasion required. After anointing, it became the regular custom in the E. to dispense Holy Communion at once, so that the infant received all three Sacraments in a single service. Such has remained the practice in the E. down to the present day.

In the W., on the other hand, the Bishop retained his function as the regular minister of the rite (as he had been originally also of Baptism). Confirmation was therefore deferred until an opportunity arose of presenting the candidate to the Bishop in person. One result was that owing to difficulties of communication and the manifold duties apt to claim the attention of the Bishop, Confirmation became very irregular in the Middle Ages and later. But, at least until the 16th cent., the separation was accidental and the ideal of the two rites being conferred together never lost. *Elizabeth I was brought by *Henry VIII to Baptism and Confirmation when but three days old.

The precise theological significance of the rite has been, and still is, disputed. Some regard it as an integral part of, and in its effects indistinguishable from, Baptism. Others regard it as conveying a new gift of the Spirit, esp. the grace necessary to strengthen the candidate in his conflict with evil. The latter view, elaborated in a homily wrongly ascribed to *Eusebius of Emesa (acc. to G. *Morin, the work of *Faustus of Riez), gained wide currency through its incorporation in the *Forged Decretals (where it was mistakenly ascribed to Pope 'Melchiades' [*Miltiades]), and it is still widely held in the W. In the Middle Ages Confirmation came to be accounted one of the *Seven Sacraments. St. *Thomas Aquinas (*Summa Theol.*, III, q. 72) and other *Dominican theologians held that it was immediately instituted by Christ; St. *Bonaventura (for whom it was 'the sacrament of warriors') believed that it was instituted by the Holy Ghost under the 'successors of the Apostles' (*In Sent.*, IV, dist. vii, art. 1); while *Alexander of Hales expressed the curious view that it was constituted a Sacrament by the Council of Meaux of 845 (*Summa*, IV, q. 9). The *Tridentine theologians were remarkably reticent on the subject. In the RC Church there have been wide differences as to wherein the 'matter' of the Sacrament consists. Acc. to some (J. *Sirmond, D. *Petavius), it was the laying on of hands; acc. to others (St. *Thomas, Card. *Bellarmine), anointing with chrism; acc. to still others (J. *Morinus), the two together.

Since the later Middle Ages the practice in the RC Church has been to confer Confirmation as soon as convenient after the seventh birthday. The Bishop anoints the candidate's head with oil administered with the sign of the Cross, gives him a slight tap (*alapa) on the cheek, and extends his hands over the candidates in blessing. In exceptional cases (isolated mission stations) faculties have long been given to priests to administer Confirmation with oil blessed by the Bishop. By the decree 'Spiritus Sancti Munera' of 1 Jan. 1947, the faculty of conferring the rite on those *in articulo mortis* was conceded to parish priests generally, under strict safeguards.

At the Reformation, the C of E continued the medieval practice; but the use of oil ceased in 1549 and the Sign of the Cross in 1552. The 1552 BCP introduced the current formula of administration, recited by the Bishop at the imposition of hands: 'Defend, O Lord, this [Thy] child with Thy heavenly grace, that he may continue Thine for ever; and daily increase in Thy Holy Spirit more and more, until he come unto Thy everlasting kingdom. Amen'. In 1662, a solemn ratification of the Baptismal vows was introduced, serving to emphasize the primitive link between the two rites. Acc. to a rubric in the BCP (taken over from the *Sarum rite) no one is to be admitted to Communion until he is confirmed or 'ready and desirous to be confirmed'. The usual practice is for a course of instruction in Christian faith and practice to precede Confirmation, while the title of the *Catechism states that it shall be learnt of every child before he be brought to Confirmation. Hence in the C of E Confirmation provides a regular opportunity for giving adolescents systematic instruction in the Christian faith. The rite is also in general use, and with similar pastoral purposes, among

*Lutherans and some other Protestant bodies.

In recent times Anglican theologians have much discussed the nature of the gift conveyed by Confirmation. Acc. to one group (A. T. Wirgman, D. *Stone, G. W. H. Lampe), the fullness of the Holy Spirit is imparted to the Christian at Baptism, and Confirmation is of relatively less significance. Another school (F. W. Puller, S.S.J.E., A. J. Mason, A. C. A. Hall, K. E. *Kirk, L. S. Thornton, C.R.) regards the gift of the Spirit in Confirmation to be of such importance that without it Baptism is virtually incomplete. The complexity of the evidence is such as to suggest that a final solution will not be reached by an appeal to history.

For current RC legislation see *C.I.C.*, cans. 780–800 Among the classical RC works are J. *Morin, Cong. Orat., *De Sacramento Confirmationis* (part of his *Opera Posthuma*; Paris, 1703); 'Vitassius', Cong. Orat., *Tractatus de Confirmatione* (Venice, 1738); cf. also L. *Holste, *De Forma Sacramenti Confirmationis apud Graecos* (orig. ed. in Holste's *Annotationes*, Rome, 1666). Anglican works include J. *Hall, Χειροθεσία, *or the Apostolic Institution of Imposition of Hands* (1649); H. *Hammond, *De Confirmatione* (1661); J. *Taylor, Χρῖσις Τελειωτική. *A Discourse of Confirmation* (1663); cf. also R. *Baxter, *Confirmation and Restauration* (1658).

Among modern treatises should be mentioned F. W. Puller, S.S.J.E., *What is the Distinctive Grace of Confirmation?* (1880); M. Heimbücher, *Die heilige Firmung* (Augsburg, 1889); A. J. Mason, *The Relation of Confirmation to Baptism* (1891; ed. 2, 1893); A. T. Wirgman, *The Doctrine of Confirmation considered in Relation to Holy Baptism as a Sacramental Ordinance of the Catholic Church* (1897); A. C. A. Hall, *Confirmation* (Oxford Library of Practical Theology, 1900); F. Dölger, *Das Sakrament der Firmung* (Theologische Studien der Leo-Gesellschaft, xv, 1906); F. H. Chase, *Confirmation in the Apostolic Age* (1909); J. B. Umberg, S.J., *Die Schriftlehre vom Sakrament der Firmung* (1920); J. Coppens, *L'Imposition des mains et les rites connexes dans le Nouveau Testament et l'Église ancienne* (Louvain diss., Wetteren and Paris, 1925); G. *Dix, O.S.B., *Confirmation or the Laying on of Hands?* (Theology Occasional Papers No. 5; 1936); G. C. Richards, *Baptism and Confirmation* (1942); G. Dix, *The Theology of Confirmation in Relation to Baptism* (lecture; 1946); G. W. H. Lampe, *The Seal of the Spirit. A Study of the Doctrine of Baptism and Confirmation in the New Testament and the Fathers* (1951), with bibl.; L. S. Thornton, C.R., *Confirmation. Its Place in the Baptismal Mystery* (1954).

Comprehensive discussions in A. *Tanquerey, *Synopsis Theologiae Dogmaticae*, iii (ed. 25, 1947), pp. 383–412; *Confirmation, or the Laying on of Hands*, vol. 1: Historical and Doctrinal; vol. ii: Practical (S.P.C.K., 1926–7). On its liturgical aspects see E. *Martène, O.S.B., *De Antiquis Ecclesiae Ritibus* (1699), I, i, 2; T. Thompson, *The Offices of Baptism and Confirmation* (Cambridge Handbooks of Liturgical Study, 1914), esp. pt. II; F. Procter–W. H. *Frere, *A New History of the Book of Common Prayer* (1901), esp. pp. 602–7. The text of the current Latin RC rite will be found in the *Pontificale Romanum*. T. Scannell in *C.E.*, iv (1908), pp. 215–22; various writers in *D.T.C.*, iii (1908), cols. 975–1103; H. J. Lawlor–H. Thurston, S.J., in *H.E.R.E.*, iv (1911), pp. 1–10; P. de Puniet, O.S.B.–H. *Leclercq, O.S.B., in *D.A.C.L.*, iii (pt. 2; 1914), cols. 2515–2551; various writers in *E.C.*, iv (1950), cols. 852–66, s.v. 'Cresima'.

CONFITEOR (Lat.) 'I confess'. The form of confession of sins (so named from its first word) which is commonly used in the RC Church, e.g. at *Mass and at the *Offices. In its usual form confession is made to God, to the BVM, to St. *Michael, St. *John the Baptist, St. *Peter, St. *Paul, and 'all the saints'. It has also been widely adopted in the C of E, though it is not contained in the BCP, where there are a number of other forms provided for liturgical use.

CONGÉ D'ÉLIRE (Fr. 'permission to elect', *sc.* a bishop). Acc. to the Chronicle of Ingulphus of Crowland, a contemporary of the Conqueror, the disposal of English sees had already been for some centuries in the hands of the English kings. Disputes with the Popes about this royal prerogative arose under William Rufus. In 1214 King *John agreed that bishops should be elected by the dean and chapter of the cathedral, but that the royal permission to proceed to the election, the *congé d'élire*, was to be first secured, and the election to be confirmed by Royal Assent afterwards. This settlement, later confirmed by Edward I and again by Edward III, remained in force until the Reformation. In 1534, by the *Annates Statute (25 Hen. VIII, c. 20), the appointment of bishops was vested in the crown. When a bishopric fell vacant, a *congé d'élire* was granted to the dean and chapter, who were required to elect the person named by the King in the accompanying 'letter missive'. Failure to elect the royal nominee rendered the dean and chapter subject to the penalties of *praemunire, and the King was then empowered to appoint to the see by letters patent. Under *Edward VI a fresh Act (1547) substituted for the *congé d'élire* nomination by letters patent in all cases, but this Act was repealed under *Mary and never re-enacted. The Act of 1534 was revived by the Act of *Supremacy of 1559 and still remains in force.

H. W. Cripps, *A Practical Treatise on the Law Relating to the Church and Clergy* (ed. 8, by K. M. Macmorran, 1937), p. 74 f. See also bibl. s.v. 'Episcopacy'.

CONGREGATIO DE AUXILIIS. See *De Auxiliis*.

CONGREGATION OF THE LORD, The (also **The Congregation of Christ** or simply **The Congregation**). The title was assumed in *Mary's reign by the Scottish Reformers who supported J. *Knox. It appears to derive from the language of the *National Covenant (1557), where the word 'congregation', in the sense of a religious community, occurs eight times.

CONGREGATIONALISM. Congregationalism is that form of Church polity which rests on the independence and autonomy of each local church. It professes to represent the principle of democracy in Church government, a polity which is held to follow from its fundamental belief in Christ as the sole head of His Church. All the members of the Church, being Christians, are 'priests unto God'. Where two or three such meet in Christ's name He is in their midst guiding their thoughts and inspiring their actions, and each such community is regarded as an outcrop and representative of the Church Universal. It is held that the system is primitive in that it represents the earliest form of Church order. It requires a very high standard of Christian devotion to maintain it, though it is admitted

that in practice it has fallen sometimes sadly below that ideal.

Modern Congregationalism begins with the Reformation. M. *Luther himself taught the priesthood of all believers, though he never carried the doctrine to what Congregationalists consider to be its logical conclusion. As early as 1550 there is evidence of bodies of men and women meeting together to preach the pure Word of God and administer the Sacraments as separatists from the national Church. When it became apparent that *Elizabeth I did not intend any drastic reformation of the Church, the number of these companies greatly increased. When, therefore, R. *Browne, in 1582, wrote *A Book which sheweth the Life and Manners of all true Christians* and *A Treatise of Reformation without tarrying for any and of the Wickedness of those Preachers which will not reform till the Magistrate command or compel them*, the little books found a public prepared to receive them. Browne maintained that 'the Kingdom of God was not to be begun by whole parishes, but rather of the worthiest, were they never so few', and in insisting that these 'gathered Churches', and bound under God by covenant, should be independent of the state and have the right to govern themselves, he laid down the lines of essential Congregationalism. He was followed by the martyrs H. *Barrow, J. *Greenwood, and J. *Penry. In 1589 the two former wrote *A true Description out of the Word of God of the visible Church* which set forth a doctrine of the Church practically identical with that of Browne.

From this time onward we have evidence that Brownists (as they were then called) became numerous all over the country. Separatism was merging into Congregationalism and Churches were formed in *Norwich, *London, and elsewhere. But persecution soon did its work, and the movement was driven underground, but only to break out again in Amsterdam and *Leyden, and ultimately, through emigration, in America. There Congregationalism played a great part in shaping both the religion and the politics of the new country. But in England also the leaven continued to work and the Independents, as they were then called, became leaders in the struggle against *Charles I and W. *Laud, and ultimately formed the backbone of O. *Cromwell's army. At the *Westminster Assembly in 1643, the Five Dissenting Brethren stoutly defended the Congregationalist cause and the *Savoy Declaration (q.v.) of 1658 laid down their polity afresh in the light of experience gained in Holland and America.

The Act of *Uniformity (1662) made Nonconformists of Independents and Presbyterians alike, but the *Toleration Act (1689) restored to them at least the right to exist. Attempts at fusion between these two types of Church were not successful mainly because of theological differences. Independents, in spite of their Calvinism, were the broader in outlook and the more evangelical in tone. They grew in numbers and influence, and being excluded from the ancient universities, set up Dissenting Academies of their own which did fine educational work, and they were ultimately largely responsible for founding London University. As R. W. *Dale pointed out in 1891, 'Congregationalists for many generations were accustomed to assert the claims of the intellect in religion far more earnestly than other evangelical Churches'. At the same time they were evangelistic in practice, as witness their founding of the London Missionary Society (*L.M.S.).

The independency of these Churches did not involve them in complete isolation. From the first they recognized the bond of a common faith and order, and the stronger among them used to help the weaker. In time they came to form County Associations of Churches for mutual intercourse and support. In 1832 these Associations combined in the Congregational Union of England and Wales which now includes all the Congregational Churches, and there are similar Unions in Scotland and Ireland. The basis of this Union was a full recognition of the distinctive principle of Congregationalism, namely, 'the scriptural right of every separate church to maintain perfect independence in the government and administration of its own particular affairs'. The Union has therefore no legislative authority, but serves to advise, encourage, and help the churches and to express their common mind. One of the first acts of the Union was to issue a Declaration of Faith and Order, a long and carefully worded document setting forth the moderate Calvinism which represented the average thought of the Churches at that time. Congregationalists are sometimes described as creedless. But though they regard creeds or confessions as useful declarations of faith, they insist that such formulae are not to be imposed as tests of communion.

R. W. Dale, *Manual of Congregational Principles* (1884). J. Waddington, *Congregational History* (5 vols., 1869–80). H. M. Dexter, *The Congregationalism of the Last Three Hundred Years as seen in its Literature* [1880]. R. W. Dale (ed. A. W. W. Dale), *History of English Congregationalism* (1907), with bibl. A. Mackennal, *Sketches in the Evolution of English Congregationalism* (1901). W. B. Selbie, *Congregationalism* ('The Faiths'; 1927). A Peel, *These Hundred Years*. A History of the Congregational Union of England and Wales, 1831–1931 (1931); id., *The Congregational Two Hundred, 1530–1948* (1948). Id. (ed.), *Essays Congregational and Catholic*. Issued in Commemoration of the Centenary of the Congregational Union of England and Wales (1931). W. Walker, *A History of the Congregational Churches in the United States* (New York, 1894). *Transactions of the Congregational Historical Society* (London, 1901 ff.). R. T. James, *Congregationalism in England 1662–1962* (1962).

CONGREGATIONS, Religious. Religious societies with simple vows, in contradistinction to those with solemn vows (see *Vows*) or orders in the strict sense. The congregations in the RC Church are a modern development, among the first being the *English Ladies (approved in 1703) and the *Passionists (approved in 1741). They are dependent either directly on the Holy See or on a bishop. In the former case they receive a special approbation which, since 1908, has been given by the *Roman Congregation of Religious. Even the congre-

gations under Papal government, however, are not exempt from episcopal jurisdiction, except in a few cases, e.g. the Passionists and the *Redemptorists, and in no case may congregations be introduced into a diocese without permission from the ordinary. The organization of a congregation is the same as that of an order. The individual houses are governed by superiors responsible to a *Provincial. All the provinces are under the authority of the Superior-General, who is elected by the *General Chapter. Those congregations not regulated by the Roman Congregation of Religious, i.e. under episcopal authority only, must be authorized by the Pope before they can be established in a particular diocese. They are not under their own superior but under the bishop, with whom rests all authority.

The term 'congregation' is also applied to groups of monastic houses which have arisen since the close of the Middle Ages, to facilitate discipline and reform. Such groups may be united under an *Abbot-General. Examples in the *Benedictine Order are the *Cassinese Congregation dependent on *Monte Cassino, as well as the various national Congregations, e.g. the English and the Belgian.

Modern RC legislation in *C.I.C.*, cans. 488, n. 2; 492, n. 1; 604. M. Félix, *Congrégations religieuses*. Étude historique et juridique (1908 ff., 4 vols., 1929). Heimbucher, ii, pp. 341–551. J. Creusen, S.J., in *D.D.C.*, iv (1949), cols. 181–94, s.v., with bibl. See also bibll. to separate congregations.

CONGREGATIONS, ROMAN. See *Roman Congregations*.

CONGRUISM. The doctrine that God confers *grace for the performance of good works ('gratia de congruo') in accordance with such human circumstances as He foresees will be most favourable to its use. The doctrine is an attempt to reconcile the dependence of human moral action upon Divine grace with the freedom of the human will. It was strongly advocated *c.* 1580 by certain *Jesuits, esp. the *Molinists, and imposed upon all schools of the Society of Jesus in 1613 by *Acquaviva, then General of the Order. The 13th Anglican *Article of Religion denies that works done before justification 'as the School-authors say, deserve grace of congruity'.

The classical expositions of Congruism are to be found in the writings of F. *Suarez, S.J. (d. 1617), and of St. Robert *Bellarmine (d. 1621). For Aquaviva's decree ('De Observanda Ratione Studiorum, deque Doctrina S. Thomae Sequenda'), issued 14 Dec. 1613, see *Praepositorum Generalium Selectae Epistolae et Documenta ad Superiores* (Besançon, 1877), pp. 54–60. H. Quilliet in *D.T.C.*, iii (1908), cols. 1120–38, s.v.

CONNOLLY, RICHARD HUGH (1873–1948), *Patristic scholar. Born at Carcoar, N.S.W., he was educated at *Downside and at Christ's College, Cambridge. He made his solemn profession at Downside Abbey in 1896, was ordained priest in 1899, and became Head of Benet House, Cambridge (1904–16), where he was closely associated with some outstanding Patristic scholars in the university (J. A.

*Robinson, F. C. *Burkitt, J. F. Bethune-Baker). His main work lay in the field of early Syrian Christianity. He co-operated with J. F. Bethune-Baker in introducing *Nestorius's 'Book of Heracleides' to the notice of European scholars (1908), edited the *Liturgical Homilies of Narsai* (1909; important appendix by E. *Bishop), established the Hippolytan author-ship of the 'Apostolic Tradition' (*The So-called Egyptian Church Order*, 1916), edited (in English) the *Didascalia Apostolorum* (1929), and made out a strong case for the *Ambrosian authorship of the *De Sacramentis* (1942). He also contributed frequent papers to the *Journal of Theological Studies*, among them some important articles on the *Didache.

CONRAD OF GELNHAUSEN (c. 1320–1390), theologian.

CONRAD OF GELNHAUSEN (c. 1320–1390), theologian. In 1359 he became a canon of Mainz and later (c. 1380) Provost of Worms. One of the earliest advocates of the Conciliar Movement, he urged that the circumstances of the *Great Schism provided a sufficient reason for summoning a *General Council without Papal convocation. His view, which largely derived from *Marsiglio of Padua and *William of Ockham, was expounded in his principal work, the *Epistola Concordiae* (1380).

His 'Epistola Concordiae' ed. F. P. Bliemetzrieder, *Literarische Polemik zu Beginn des grossen abendländischen Schismas* (Publikationen des österreichischen historischen Instituts in Rom, i; 1910), pp. 111–40. L. Schmitz, 'Ein Brief von Konrads von Gelnhausen aus dem Jahre 1379' in *Römische Quartalschrift*, ix (1895), pp. 185–9, with text. A. Kneer, *Die Entstehung der Konziliaren Theorie. Zur Geschichte des Schismas und der kirchenpolitischen Schriftsteller Konrad von Gelnhausen (gest. 1390) und Heinrich von Langenstein (gest. 1397)* (*Römische-Quartalschrift* Supp. i; 1893). K. Wenck, 'Konrad von Gelnhausen und die Quellen der Konziliaren Theorie' in *Historische Zeitschrift*, lxxxvi (1896), pp. 6–61. F. P. Bliemetzrieder, *Das Generalkonzil im grossen abendländischen Schisma* (1904), passim. For further bibl. see A. Posch in *L.Th.K.*, vi (1934), col. 144, s.v. 'Konrad von Gelnhausen'.

CONRAD OF MARBURG (c. 1180–1233),

CONRAD OF MARBURG (c. 1180–1233), Papal *Inquisitor. He was prob. a native of *Marburg and his title 'Magister' shows that he studied at one of the universities, perhaps *Paris or *Bologna. A man of strong force of character and much learning and severely ascetic, in 1213 he appeared as an ardent preacher of the *Crusade of *Innocent III. Soon afterwards he was charged with various reforming missions in Germany, including the visitation of certain convents. These tasks won him the confidence of the Landgrave Ludwig IV of Thuringia, who entrusted him with important ecclesiastical appointments in his dominions. In 1225 he became the spiritual director and confessor of St. *Elizabeth (q.v.), Ludwig's wife, whom he treated, esp. in her later years, with excessive severity; and after her death (19 Nov. 1231) he was appointed as one of the witnesses in the cause of her canon-ization. Meanwhile he proved himself a zealous opponent of heresies (*Cathari, *Waldenses) and on 11 Oct. 1231 *Gregory IX (1227–41) nominated him the first Papal Inquisitor in Germany, with absolute authority over heret-ics. He exercised his authority ruthlessly,

often condemning persons on insufficient evidence and handing them over for punish-ment to the secular arm. When he charged Henry II, Count of Sayn, with heresy (1233) he was publicly denounced at a court of bishops and princes at Mainz and murdered on his way back to Marburg on 30 July 1233.

B. Kaltner, *Konrad von Marburg und die Inquisition in Deutschland* (Prague, 1882); A. Hausrath, *Kleine Schriften* (1883), pp. 137–233 ('Der Ketzermeister Konrad von Marburg'). K. Benrath in *P.R.E.* (ed. 3), x (1901), pp. 747–51, s.v. 'Konrad von Marburg'.

CONSALVI, ERCOLE (1757–1824),

CONSALVI, ERCOLE (1757–1824), Italian statesman. He entered the Papal service at an early age, and was thrown into prison as a declared anti-Revolutionary after the French occupation of the Papal States in 1798. On recovering his freedom he joined the new Pope, *Pius VII, and in 1800 was created a cardinal and made Secretary of State. In this office he was chiefly responsible for the negotia-tion of the *Concordat with Napoleon, and for fostering opposition to the *Organic Articles. Though Napoleon managed to secure his dis-missal, Consalvi would not be intimidated, and became the leader of the 'black cardinals' in Paris until he was forcibly retired to *Reims. On Napoleon's abdication (1814) he was immediately reappointed as Secretary, and, after a short visit to England, represented the Pope at the Congress of Vienna (1815). Here he secured the restoration of the Papal States, the reorganization of which occupied his remaining years.

*Mémoires du Cardinal Consalvi. . . . Avec une introduction et des notes par J. Crétineau-Joly (2 vols., Paris, 1864; enlarged ed. by J. E. B. Drochon [c. 1896]); M. N. Rocca di Corneliano (ed.), *Memorie del cardinale Ercole Consalvi* (1950). E. L. Fischer, *Cardinal Consalvi. 'Lebens- und Charakterbild des grossen Ministers Papst Pius VII'* (1899); M. Petrocchi, *La restaurazione, il cardinale Consalvi e la riforma del 1816* (1941). L. von *Ranke, *Historisch-Biographische Studien* (1877), 'Cardinal Consalvi und seine Staatsverwaltung unter dem Pontificat Pius VII', pp. 1–180.

CONSANGUINITY, blood-relationship.

CONSANGUINITY, blood-relationship. By Scripture and *canon law, consanguinity within certain degrees is a *diriment impedi-ment to marriage; that is, it makes the marriage of the persons concerned not only unlawful, but null and void. See also under *Kindred and Affinity, Table of*.

G. Oesterlé in *D.D.C.*, iv (1949), cols. 232–48, s.v., with full bibl.

CONSCIENCE (Lat. conscientia, 'knowledge with another', 'knowledge within oneself').

CONSCIENCE (Lat. *conscientia*, 'knowledge with another', 'knowledge within oneself'). Orig. meaning inward knowledge in a general sense, the word has followed its Lat. predeces-sor in acquiring a moral significance and has come to be applied to the faculty or principle which enables a man to judge the rightness of his actions. Christians agree that it is among the higher faculties of man, to whom it is unique, and that its effectiveness is increased by use and through grace. In an extreme and impressive form the absolute supremacy of conscience was upheld by I. *Kant, whose *Grundlegung zur Metaphysik der Sitten* (1785) opened with the words, 'There is nothing wholly good without qualification either in the world or without it except the good will ' (See *Categorical Imperative*). The Schoolmen differed as to whether its root lay in the affections, as the *Franciscans held, or in the will, as St. *Thomas Aquinas and the *Dominicans taught. It is generally agreed that when a man, after informing himself to the best of his ability on the requirements of the moral law, acts as his conscience dictates, he is to be held guiltless, even if his actions judged by extrinsic theological considerations or by their results be reprehensible. In such a case the imperfection of his action is excused by '*invincible ignorance' (q.v.). What is to be done when the conscience is doubtful is one of the points at issue in the dispute about *probabilism (q.v.).

The inexorable claims of conscience have constantly seemed to point man to a Being higher than himself, who has the power of imposing such obligations on him. On this basis I. Kant deduced the existence of God when he had rejected the *ontological and other arguments. Conscience, thus considered, is the mediator between the Law of God and the will of man, and as such has been called the 'Voice of God'. This divine voice was sometimes termed by the Schoolmen '*synderesis' (q.v.), after a copyist's error for 'syneidesis' in St. *Jerome's Commentary on Ezekiel. But since it is liable to error and, in the case of the hardened criminal and the pathologically scrupulous, even to total disease (moral insanity), Christian moralists refuse to identify its utterances with the Divine Law itself. They regard it rather as an organ whereby fallible man can normally ascertain the Will of God, though with the reservation that, at least since the *Fall, its verdict is liable to distortion by human infirmity.

The subject is treated in all works on moral philosophy, e.g. H. *Rashdall, *The Theory of Good and Evil* (2 vols., 1907), esp. i, pp. 164–8, 175 f. Cf. also id., *Conscience and Christ. Six Lectures on Christian Ethics* (1916). On medieval discussions, H. Simar, *Die Lehre vom Wesen des Gewissens in der Scholastik des 13ten Jahrhunderts* (i: Die Franziscanerschule, 1885; all publd.). J. Rickaby in *C.E.*, iv (1908), pp. 268–73, s.v.; M. Waldmann in *L.Th.K.*, iv (1932), cols. 476–9, s.v. 'Gewissen'.

CONSECRATION. The separation of a thing or person for Divine service. In Christian vocabulary, common uses of the term are: (1) Of the *Eucharist: the act whereby bread and wine become the Body and Blood of Christ. (2) Of *Bishops: the conferment by bishops of the *character which is inherent in their office upon others. (3) Of *altars and churches and of Eucharistic vessels: the solemn rite of setting apart these things exclusively for the service of God. The consecration of a church, an act reserved to the bishop, differs from its blessing or '*dedication' in that it is held to be an irrevocable act, so that the building can never be secularized. See *Dedication*.

CONSECRATION, The Prayer of. The central prayer in the Eucharistic Rite of the

BCP, corresponding to the middle of the *Canon in the Roman Mass and (to a lesser extent) of the *Anaphora in E. rites. In its present form it consists of (1) a 'memorial' of the death of Christ; (2) a prayer that in the reception of the Sacrament the faithful may partake of the Body and Blood of Christ; (3) a recital of the narrative of institution, with a performance of the *manual acts; (4) *Amen*, said by the congregation.

CONSENSUS GENEVENSIS (also known as the **De aeterna Dei Praedestinatione**). J. *Calvin's elaborate reformulation of his teaching on *Predestination to combat that of J. H. *Bolsec. After obtaining the support of the ministers of *Geneva on 18 Dec. 1551, Calvin presented it to the City Council of Geneva on 1 Jan. 1552. Its uncompromising reassertion of Calvin's teaching put an end to the hopes of reunion of the Calvinists with *Lutheranism.

The text is pr. in H. A. Niemeyer (ed.), *Collectio Confessionum in Ecclesiis Reformatis Publicatarum* (Leipzig, 1840), pp. 218–310; part is repr. in Kidd, pp. 643–5 (No. 314). See also bibl. to *Calvinism*.

CONSENSUS TIGURINUS (Lat.) 'the Zürich Agreement'. The formula of faith agreed upon in May 1549 by J. *Calvin and G. *Farel, representing the Protestants of French Switzerland, and H. *Bullinger (H. *Zwingli's successor in the town of Zürich), representing those of German Switzerland. Its 26 arts. were primarily concerned to set forth a doctrine of the Eucharist which conformed with *Calvinist principles and was free from the objections which, in the eyes of the Zwinglians, attached to *Consubstantiation.

The text, besides being pr. among Calvin's works, is pr. in H. A. Niemeyer (ed.), *Collectio Confessionum in Ecclesiis Reformatis Publicatarum* (Leipzig, 1840), pp. 191–217; the principal clauses are repr. in Kidd, pp. 652–6 (No. 319). B. Christ in *P.R.E.* (ed. 3), xxi (1908), pp. 732–4, s.v. 'Züricher Konsens'. See also bibl. to *Calvinism*.

CONSIGNATORIUM (also known as the **Chrismarium** or **Locus Chrismatis**). The room or building sometimes adjoining the *baptistery in which the bishop on *Holy Saturday or the Vigil of *Pentecost (the two days on which baptism was solemnly conferred in the early Church) used to confirm the newly baptized by 'signing' them with the *chrism. Some fine examples of such 'consignatoria' have been discovered in N. Africa.

CONSISTORY (Lat. *consistorium*). Orig. the ante-chamber of the Imperial palace at *Rome where the Emperor administered justice from a seat on a tribunal with the others standing around him (*consistentes*). The word is now used of certain ecclesiastical courts.

In the C of E the Consistory Court is the Bishop's court for the administration of ecclesiastical law within his own diocese, except in the diocese of Canterbury where it is known as 'the Commissary Court'. The judge is styled the '*Chancellor' (in Canterbury, the Commissary-General). Except when the Bishop in his patent appointing the Chancellor reserves to himself the power to try certain cases, the Chancellor is the sole judge and may even try cases to which the Bishop is a party. Appeal normally lies to the Provincial Court and thence to the *Judicial Committee of the Privy Council. These Courts lost much of their former importance when their jurisdiction in matrimonial and testamentary matters was removed by the Court of Probate Act (1857) and the Matrimonial Causes Act (1857).

In the RC Church the Consistory is the assembly of *cardinals convoked by and meeting in the presence of the Pope (*quia simul praesente Papa consistunt cardinales*). Such consistories are of three kinds, 'public', 'semi-public', and 'private'. At the first the Pope receives foreign sovereigns and ambassadors, confers the red hat on new cardinals, and carries forward to a new stage the process of *canonization. Semi-public consistories, attended by bishops residing within a hundred miles of Rome, and certain other Italian prelates, as well as by the cardinals, also have an important function in canonization. The last, at which none but the Pope and cardinals are present, is the ordinary court in which the more important business of the Papacy is transacted.

In many *Presbyterian Churches (Switzerland, Holland, U.S.A.), the Consistory Court is the name given to the court corresponding to the *Kirk-session (q.v.) in *Scotland.

On the C of E Consistory Court, R. *Phillimore, *The Ecclesiastical Law of the Church of England* (ed. 2 by W. G. F. Phillimore, 1895), vol. i, p. 197 f.; vol. ii, pp. 926 f., 999, 1038; H. W. Cripps, *A Practical Treatise on the Law Relating to the Church and Clergy* (ed. 8 by K. M. Macmorran, 1937), pp. 64, 143 f., 156, 174, 288. See also bibl. to *Chancellor (Diocesan)*.
On the RC Consistory, A. Boudinhon in *E.B.* (ed. 11), vi (1910), p. 978 f., s.v.; H. Papi, S.J., in *C.E.*, iv (1908), p. 285 f., s.v.; J. Raffalli in *D.D.C.*, iv (1949), cols. 354–6, s.v. See also bibl. to *Curia*.

CONSTANCE, Council of (1414–18). The Council was convoked in 1413 by Pope *John XXIII at the instigation of the Emp. Sigismund. It was designed to end the Great Schism, to bring about the reform of the Church, and to deal with various heresies. It was opened on 5 Nov. 1414 in the cathedral of Constance, where all the public sessions were held. The soul of the Council was the French cardinal P. *d'Ailly (q.v.), who, in concert with the Emperor, J. *Gerson, chancellor of the university of *Paris, and the majority of the Council, favoured the abdication of all three Popes. They were John XXIII, the successor of the Pope elected by the Council of *Pisa (1409), *Gregory XII, and the antipope, *Benedict XIII (Peter de Luna). Gregory had promised to abdicate if John XXIII also abdicated; but the latter hesitated, and the Council, to break his resistance, changed the usual method of the personal vote, which would have given his Italian supporters a majority, to the vote by

'nations'. These were at first England, Germany, France, and Italy, to which was added Spain after the arrival of its delegates in 1416. In 1415 John promised under oath to resign, but fled soon after to his friend Duke Frederick of Austria. This step, which deprived the Council of its authority, would have led to its dissolution if Sigismund had not enforced its continuance. At the following public session of 29 Mar. 1415 the four famous 'Articles of Constance' were drawn up. Inspired by d'Ailly and supported by Germany, France, and England, they became the charter of *Gallicanism. They proclaimed the present Council to be a *General Council, which derived its authority directly from God, and whose decisions every Christian, even the Pope, was bound to obey under pain of ecclesiastical punishment. They also declared the flight of the Pope scandalous and affirmed that he had enjoyed perfect liberty at the Council. The Italians rejected the articles as injuring the Papal dignity, and, after the cardinals had refused to publish them, they were announced by Andrew, Bp. of Posen.

Several weeks after his flight John XXIII was brought back to Constance as a prisoner, and deposed for simony, abetting of schism, and scandalous life, at the 12th session, 29 May 1415. Gregory XII now resigned and the Council was convoked anew in his name by the *Dominican cardinal, *John of Ragusa [q.v., par. 2]; and from now on it is regarded by many RC theologians as a legitimate General Council. The antipope Benedict XIII, who refused to abdicate, was finally deposed in the 37th session of 26 July 1417. The Council then disagreed on the question whether the reform of the Church or the election of a new Pope should be the next business. The dispute was settled by Henry, Bp. of *Winchester, who suggested that a Pope should be elected first, but that he should give a formal promise to effect serious reforms immediately after his election. Owing to the abnormal circumstances the 23 cardinals had to vote together with 30 other deputies, and after a conclave of three days Odo *Colonna was elected (11 Nov. 1417), who took the name of *Martin V.

Apart from the healing of the schism, the reform of the Church had been demanded from the beginning esp. by the Germans, and two successive commissions had been formed, but no agreement had been reached. Martin V appointed a third, but this achieved no more unanimity than its predecessors. Before its close, however, the Council agreed on several points, demanding, among others, that unions of benefices should be diminished, that all simony should be forbidden, and that the Papal right to impose tithes on the clergy should be restricted. Many of the aspirations of the individual nations were settled by *concordats, a term which seems here to have been used for the first time.

The Council also dealt with contemporary heresies, esp. those of J. *Wycliffe and J. *Hus. It condemned over 200 propositions of the former, and ordered his body to be removed from consecrated ground. The latter, who had taught doctrines similar to those of Wycliffe, came to Constance under safe-conduct from the Emperor. After violating the Papal prohibition to preach and say Mass, he was imprisoned. Refusing to recant, he was condemned as a heretic on 6 July 1415 and handed over to the secular authorities to be burned at the stake. In the next year, *Jerome of Prague, his follower and friend, suffered the same fate. The affairs of the French Franciscan, John Parvus, and the Dominican, John Falkenburg, who had taught the legality of tyrannicide, were also treated at the Council, but not finally decided.

The Council of Constance is usually reckoned by RC theologians as the Sixteenth General Council; but the anti-Papal decrees of the 3rd-5th sessions are considered devoid of authority. The failure of the Council to effect any real reform in the Church was one of the main causes of the Reformation.

Hardouin, viii, cols. 209-944; Mansi, xxvii (1784), cols. 519-1240, and xxviii (1785), cols. 1-958. Crit. ed. of the *Acta Concilii Constantiensis* by H. Finke (4 vols., Munster, 1896-1928). H. von der Hardt, *Magnum Oecumenicum Constantiense Concilium* (6 vols., Frankfurt and Leipzig, 1697-1700; indices, &c., 1742). J. Lenfant, *Histoire du concile de Constance* (2 vols., Amsterdam, 1714; enlarged ed., 2 vols., 1727); L. Tosti, *Storia del concilio di Costanza* (2 vols. bound in one, Naples, 1853); H. Finke, *Forschungen und Quellen zur Geschichte des Konstanzer Konzils* (1889). J. H. Wylie, *The Council of Constance to the Death of Hus* (Ford Lectures for 1900; 1900). Hefele–Leclercq, vii (pt. 1; 1916), pp. 71-584. H. Hollnsteiner, 'Studien zur Geschäftsordnung am Konstanzer Konzil. Ein Beitrag zur Geschichte des Parlamentarismus und der Demokratie' in *Abhandlungen aus dem Gebiete der mittleren und neueren Geschichte und ihrer Hilfswissenschaften*. Eine Festgabe zum siebzigsten Geburtstage . . . Heinrich Finke (1925), pp. 240-56; id., 'Das Konstanzer Konzil in der Geschichte der christlichen Kirche' in *Mitteilungen des österreichischen Instituts für Geschichtsforschung*, Ergänzungsband, xi (1929), pp. 395-420. E. F. Jacob, *Essays in the Conciliar Epoch* (Publications of the University of Manchester, cclxxxiii; Historical Series, lxxx, 1943). M. *Creighton, *A History of the Papacy from the Great Schism to the Sack of Rome* (1882), Bk. II (ed. 1897, i, pp. 299-388, and ii, pp. 3-128). A. Baudrillart in *D.T.C.*, iii (1908), cols. 1200-24, s.v.; L. Cristiani in *D.D.C.*, iv (1949), cols. 390-424. See also bibl. to *D'Ailly, Pierre; Gerson, Jean le Charlier; Hus, John*, and *Wycliffe, John*.

CONSTANCE MISSAL, The (*Missale Speciale Constantiense*). A 15th-cent. printed *Missal, perhaps the earliest printed book known. It is in single type throughout, and exhibits a very primitive technique. O. Hupp and others have claimed it as a very early product of J. G. *Gutenberg, but some authorities attribute it to a press at Basle *c.* 1470. It contains the text of the Masses for the most important feasts of the year and those proper to the diocese of Constance. Three copies are known to exist.

O. Hupp, *Ein Missale Speciale, Vorläufer des Psalteriums von 1457* (1898); id., *Gutenbergs erste Drucke* (1902); id., *Zum Streit um das Missale Speciale Constantiense* (1917). G. Zedler, 'Das vermeintliche Gutenbergsche Missale' in *Centralblatt für Bibliothekswesen*, xx (1903), pp. 32-55; I. Collijn, 'Ein neuaufgefundenes Exemplar des L. Rosenthalschen Missale Speciale' in *Gutenberg Jahrbuch*, i (1926), pp. 32-46; K. Hälber 'Das "Missale Speciale Constantiense"', id., iv (1930), pp. 67-72. W. H. I. Weale–H. Bohatta, *Catalogus Missalium Ritus Latini ab Anno M.CCCC.LXXIV Impressorum* (London, 1927), No. 304, p. 53 f. See also *T.L.S.*, liii (1954), pp. 144 (26 Feb.).

CONSTANTINE THE GREAT (274 or 288-337), Roman emperor. The son of the Emp. Constantius Chlorus and St. *Helena, he was sent in 292 to the court of *Diocletian, the senior emperor, under whose influence he learned the new Byzantine ideas of absolute sovereignty which were rapidly replacing the Roman conception of the principate. In 306, on the death of Constantius, he was proclaimed Emperor at *York, and became senior ruler of the empire in 312, after defeating his rival Maxentius at the *Milvian Bridge. At that battle Constantine adopted the *Labarum standard, as the champion of Christianity, and shortly afterwards toleration and Imperial favour were given to the Christian faith, though whether there was ever a formal and comprehensive proclamation, such as the supposed Edict of *Milan, is a matter of disagreement among historians.

Since Constantine's policy was to unite the Christian Church to the secular state by the closest possible ties, it was natural that even before he formally professed Christianity himself he should be concerned with the internal affairs of the Church. In 313 the *Donatist schismatics in Africa appealed to him to settle their controversy with the Church of that province, and at their request he referred the matter first to a commission of bishops, then to a synod of Gaul and Italy (*Arles, 314), and finally in 316 heard the case himself. In each trial the verdict went against the Donatists, who thereupon attacked not only their ecclesiastical opponents, but also the state, encouraging rioting and brigandage. Constantine was therefore constrained to reinforce his verdict with repressive measures.

A similar appeal from the contending parties led Constantine to summon the Council of *Nicaea (325) to settle the *Arian dispute about the Person of Christ. The Emperor himself presided, though unbaptized, a circumstance which foreshadows the Byzantine theory of the emperors as supreme rulers of Church and State alike. The victory of orthodoxy which the creed of the council symbolized did not prevent Constantine from banishing prominent orthodox leaders in later years (e.g. St. *Athanasius in 336) at the instance of their enemies. Constantine's ecclesiastical advisers included men of various beliefs, esp. *Hosius, Bp. of Cordova, *Eusebius, Bp. of Caesarea, and *Lactantius.

The breach with the old traditions of Rome was complete when, after the victory at Chrysopolis (324) which had made him sole emperor, Constantine fixed his capital at Byzantium (rebuilt and inaugurated as 'Constantinople' in 330). Throughout his reign he did his best to conciliate both pagans and Christians, and it is difficult to say when he first decided to embrace Christianity. He was not baptized until just before his death, but deferment of baptism was common in those days, and his policy and legislation, though not free from grave blemishes, show a strongly Christian tendency from the first. He humanized the criminal law and the law of debt, mitigated the conditions of slavery, made grants to support poor children, thus discouraging the exposure of unwanted babies, freed celibates and unmarried persons from special taxation, legislated against incontinence, and exempted Christian clergy from the burden of the decurionate. In 321 he ordered that *Sunday should become a public holiday. He liberally endowed Christian church building, esp. at the Holy Places in Palestine.

If the centralization of the empire at Constantinople led to an increasing Imperial control of the E. Church, it had also the consequence, perhaps unforeseen, of making the bishops of Rome more prominent than any other figure, lay or ecclesiastical, in the W.; and it is from the 4th cent. that the Papacy begins to assume its secular importance, and the position which it held in the Middle Ages.

Legend has added much to history. A tradition going back to the 5th cent. asserts that he was baptized at the *Lateran by Pope *Sylvester, and his connexions with the Pope are further embellished in the *Donation of Constantine (q.v.). In the E. Church he has been named the 'Thirteenth Apostle' and is venerated as a saint. Feast day, 21 May (with St. *Helena).

The chief primary sources are several official edicts of Constantine; some contemporary panegyrics by pagan orators; *Lactantius, De Mortibus Persecutorum; and *Eusebius, Vita Constantini. A collection of the edicts and other material relating to Constantine is pr. in J. P. Migne, PL, viii. The genuineness of the documents purporting to be by Constantine in the Vita Constantini has been challenged (A. Crivellucci and others) in recent times; but their authenticity has been ably upheld in I. A. Heikel, Kritische Beiträge zu den Constantin-Schriften des Eusebius (T.U., xxxvi, Hft. 4, 1911), and I. Daniele, I documenti constantiniani della Vita Constantini di Eusebio di Cesarea (1938). More recently H. Grégoire, 'Eusèbe n'est pas l'auteur de la "Vita Constantini" dans sa forme actuelle et Constantin n'est pas "converti" en 312', in Byzantion, xiii (1938), pp. 561–83, has denied the genuineness of the whole work: but he also has had little following.

The modern study of Constantine may be said to begin with J. Burckhardt, Die Zeit Konstantins des Grossen (1853). The problem posed here as to the genuineness of Constantine's acceptance of Christianity has been the subject of a large and important literature. Among the chief items are T. Keim, Der Übertritt Constantins des Grossen zum Christenthum (1862); T. *Zahn, Constantin der Grosse und die Kirche (1876); F. J. Dölger (ed.), Konstantin der Grosse und seine Zeit. . . . Festgabe zum Konstantinsjubiläum (R.Q., Suppl. xix, 1913). E. *Schwartz, Kaiser Konstantin und die christliche Kirche (1913; ed. 2, 1936). J. Maurice, Numismatique constantinienne (3 vols., 1906–12); id., Constantin le Grand [1927]. There is a masterly survey of the questions involved in N. H. Baynes' Raleigh Lecture, 'Constantine the Great and the Christian Church' in The Proceedings of the British Academy, xv (1929), pp. 341–442. More recent literature includes A. Piganiol, L'Empereur Constantin (1932); H. Lietzmann, 'Der Glaube Konstantins des Grossen' in Sb. (Berl.), 1937, pp. 263–75. H. Berkhof, Kirche und Kaiser. Eine Untersuchung der Entstehung der byzantinischen und der theokratischen Staatsauffassung im vierten Jahrhundert (Germ. tr., Zürich, 1947; orig. Dutch, 1946). A. Alföldi, The Conversion of Constantine and Pagan Rome (1948). A. H. M. Jones, Constantine and the Conversion of Europe (1948).

Modern summaries, with further bibl., C.Anc.H., xii. H. M. D. Parker, A History of the Roman World from A.D. 138 to 337 (1935), pp. 238–309. L. Hertling and others in E.C., iv (1950), cols. 716–27, s.v. 'Costantino'. On the cult of *Constantine, see esp. H. *Leclercq, O.S.B., in D.A.C.L., iii (pt. 2, 1914), cols. 2622–95, s.v.

CONSTANTINOPLE. In A.D. 330 *Constantine inaugurated Constantinople as his capital on the site of the Greek city of Byzantium. The town, which was later considerably enlarged, remained the capital of the E. Empire until 1453, except from 1204 to 1261 when, after capture by the *Crusaders, it was the capital of a Latin empire. From 1453 it was the Turkish capital until this was transferred to Ankara in 1923.

Byzantium had a Christian community at least from the 2nd cent., and Constantinople was a Christian city from its inauguration. The Bishop was at first subject to the see of Heraclea; but before long, as the Bishop of the 'New Rome', he took his place beside the Bps. of *Alexandria, *Antioch, and *Rome. At the council in the city in 381 he was given honorary pre-eminence after the Bp. of Rome, and in 451, though the Pope objected, patriarchal powers were formally conferred upon him (can. 28). Meanwhile Alexandria had striven with Constantinople for supremacy in the E., and *Theophilus and *Cyril of Alexandria obtained respectively the depositions of *Chrysostom (in 403) and *Nestorius (in 431). Finally Rome and Constantinople were left to struggle for preeminence, and in the end the breach between the Catholic W. and the Orthodox E. came in 1054. Since the 6th cent. the Patr. (as the Bp. was now designated) of Constantinople has been recognized as the *Oecumenical Patriarch of the E.

Since the city has come under Turkish domination, most of its many ancient churches have become mosques, including the celebrated church of *St. Sophia (more recently, converted into a museum). By the Treaty of Lausanne (1918) the Turkish Republic is bound to protect the Greek Christians in Constantinople; but the Patriarch may be chosen only from residents in Turkey.

The classical treatise is C. D. *Du Cange, Constantinopolis Christiana (Paris, fol., 1680; still useful). Modern works include A. van Millingen, Byzantine Constantinople (1899). Id., Byzantine Churches in Constantinople (1912). C. Diehl, Constantinople (Paris, 1912). Valuable study, with full bibl., by S. Vailhé, A.A., in D.T.C., iii (1908), cols. 1307–1519, s.v. 'Constantinople (Église de)'; more recent study by R. Janin, A.A., in D.H.G.E., xiii ('1954'), cols. 626–754.

CONSTANTINOPLE, First Council of (381). It was convened by the Emp. *Theodosius I to unite the E. Church at the end of the long *Arian controversy on the basis of the *Nicene faith. 150 orthodox and 36 heretical bishops took part, under the presidency of *Meletius, Bp. of Antioch (who died during the Council). Although neither W. bishops nor Roman legates were present, its achievement was sufficiently significant for it to come to be regarded as the Second *General Council in both E. and W. The work of the Council of *Nicaea with regard to the doctrine of Christ was ratified, and the humanity of Christ safeguarded by condemning *Apollinarianism. The so-called *Niceno-Constantinopolitan Creed, traditionally ascribed to this Council, was probably not drawn up by it, and it is possible that the Council had no direct connexion with it. In ecclesiastical matters the Council (a) appointed Nectarius as Bp. of Constantinople, in place of St. *Gregory of Nazianzus; (b) granted to Constantinople honorary precedence (τὰ πρεσβεῖα τῆς τιμῆς) over all Churches save Rome; and (c) misguidedly appointed as Bp. of *Antioch Flavian rather than *Paulinus, who, by an agreement of the schismatic parties, should have succeeded *Meletius.

Hardouin, i, cols. 807–26; Mansi, iii (1759), cols. 521–600. Hefele–Leclercq, ii (pt. 1; 1908), pp. 1–48. Text of Canons also in Lauchert, pp. 84–7; crit. ed. of Lat. versions in E.O.M.I.A., II, iii (1929), cols. 401–72. W. *Bright, Notes on the Canons of the First Four General Councils (ed. 2, 1892), pp. 90–128. C. A. Kneller, S.J., 'Zum zweiten allgemeinen Konzil vom Jahre 381' in Z.K.T., xxvii (1903), pp. 789–99. G. Bardy and J. R. Palanque in Fliche–Martin, iii (1936), pp. 285–92. F. A. *Loofs in P.R.E. (ed. 3), ii (1897), p. 43 f., s.v. 'Arianismus'; J. Bois in D.T.C., iii (1908), cols. 1227–31, s.v.

CONSTANTINOPLE, Second Council of

(553). This, the Fifth General Council, was convoked by the Emp. *Justinian to decide the prolonged controversy over the *Three Chapters, and esp. whether *Theodore of Mopsuestia, *Theodoret of Cyrus, and *Ibas of Edessa should be condemned as tainted with *Nestorianism, or whether, following the attitude of the Council of *Chalcedon, they should be spared. The adherents of *Monophysitism, who were anxious to shake the authority of Chalcedon, as well as the Emperor, who wished to reconcile the Monophysites, were opposed to any toleration of Theodore and his associates. After much Monophysite agitation the Emperor issued a decree (c. 551) condemning the Three Chapters. When this was accepted by Askidas, Menas, and other bishops of the Imperial party, Pope *Vigilius excommunicated them (551).

The Council was convened under the presidency of Eutychius, Patr. of *Constantinople, on 5 May 553. The 165 bishops who signed the acts were almost all Easterns. The Three Chapters were condemned and their authors anathematized. During its course Vigilius, who refused to attend for fear of violence as well as in protest against the preponderance of E. bishops present, drew up the so-called 'Constitutum', signed by himself and 16 W. bishops, in which while condemning 60 propositions of Theodore of Mopsuestia, he refused to anathematize his person on the grounds that he had not been condemned at *Ephesus (431) or Chalcedon (451) and that it was not the custom of the Church to condemn the dead. The Council replied by erasing the Pope's name from the diptychs in the 7th session. Vigilius was for a short time exiled, but as the Emperor had nothing to gain from a rupture with the Pope he used every means to bring about a reconciliation. Vigilius finally agreed to accept the Council and annulled his former decisions in favour of the Three Chapters.

Of the 14 anathemas pronounced by the Council the first 12 are directed chiefly against Theodore of Mopsuestia, the 13th against Theodoret of Cyrus, and the 14th against Ibas. In the 11th anathema the name of *Origen

occurs in a list of heretics, but there are grounds for believing this to be an interpolation. Despite the Papal acceptance the Council was not at once recognized as oecumenical in the W. *Milan and Aquileia even broke off communion with Rome, and relations were not restored with Milan until the end of the 6th, and with Aquileia until the end of the 7th cent. The Council, unlike the four preceding General Councils, issued no canons.

Hardouin, iii, cols. 1–328; Mansi, ix (1743), cols. 157–658. H. *Noris, Dissertatio Historica de Synodo Quinta Oecumenica (1673; repr. in Noris's Opera, i, Verona, 1729, cols. 550–820). F. Diekamp, Die origenistischen Streitigkeiten im sechsten Jahrhundert und das fünfte allgemeine Konzil (1899), pp. 77–98. Hefele–Leclercq, iii (pt. 2; 1909), pp. 1–156. L. Bréhier in Fliche–Martin, iv (1937), esp. pp. 472–87. J. Bois in D.T.C., iii (1908), cols. 1231–59, s.v.; R. Janin in D.H.G.E., xiii ('1954'), cols. 757–60, s.v., both with bibl. See also bibl. to Monophysitism, Theodore of Mopsuestia, and Three Chapters.

CONSTANTINOPLE, Third Council of

(680). This, the Sixth General Council, was convoked at the demand of the Emp. Constantine IV (Pogonatus) to settle the prolonged *Monothelite controversy in the E. Church. Pope *Agatho, having held a Synod at *Rome (680) in which the doctrine of the Two Wills in Christ was again affirmed, sent his delegates to the Emperor with a letter expounding this teaching. On their arrival the Emperor called a Council of the bishops of the patriarchates of *Constantinople and *Antioch. The debates of its 18 sessions, conducted chiefly by the Papal envoys, were concerned solely with the Monothelite question. Macarius, the Patr. of Antioch, was condemned as a Monothelite, and in the 13th session the principal leaders of the heresy, among whom the Council included the former Pope *Honorius, were anathematized.

The Dogmatic Decree of the Council is principally a reproduction of the profession of faith drawn up at *Chalcedon, affirming the doctrine of the Two Natures, to which is added, as a necessary consequence, the statement of the reality of the Two Wills (θελήματα) and the Two Operations (ἐνέργειαι). The Council rejected all physical unity of the two wills, but admitted the existence of a moral unity, resulting from the complete harmony between the Divine and the human will in the God-man. The same position was affirmed regarding the duality of operations. The decree concluded with a résumé of the Christological teaching of the various Councils. This Council also issued no canons.

Hardouin, iii, cols. 1043–1644; Mansi, xi (1765), cols. 189–922; Hefele–Leclercq, iii (pt. 1; 1909), pp. 472–538. L. Bréhier in Fliche–Martin, v (1938), pp. 183–91. J. Bois in D.T.C., iii (1908), cols. 1259–73; R. Janin in D.H.G.E., xiii ('1954'), cols. 760–3, s.v. See also bibl. to Monothelitism.

CONSTANTINOPOLITAN CREED. See Nicene Creed.

CONSTITUTIONAL CHURCH, The.

The schismatic Church established in France during the Revolution by the *Civil Constitution of the Clergy (q.v.) of 12 July 1790. It was organized in 1791, under the protection of the National Assembly, whilst beside it the 'legitimate Church', whose priests refused to take the Constitutional Oath, continued to exist. The majority of the faithful sided with the latter, esp. when the schismatics abandoned the old discipline and priests and bishops began to marry and divorces came to be permitted. After the triumph of the Jacobins, who proclaimed the 'cult of reason', the Constitutional Church itself had to endure persecution, and many of its priests apostatized. After the fall of Robespierre (1794) a certain amount of toleration was granted, but the state now refused to pay the Constitutional priests, a measure which hit the schismatic Church particularly hard, as it could count on very little support from its laity. Its reputation, too, had suffered considerable damage by the apostasies within its ranks. When Napoleon concluded the *Concordat of 1801, *Pius VII had little difficulty in obtaining its abolition by the intervention of the secular power, the agency which had created it.

There is an extensive literature on the Catholic Church in France at the time of the Revolution. L. Sciout, *Histoire de la constitution civile du clergé, 1790–1801* (4 vols., 1872–1881). C. S. Phillips, *The Church in France, 1789–1870* (1929), pp. 7–78, with bibl., p. 305 f. A. Debidour, *Histoire des rapports de l'Église et de l'État en France de 1789 à 1870* (1898), pp. 83–223. P. de La Gorce, *Histoire religieuse de la Révolution française* (5 vols., 1909–23), esp. vol. i, pp. 349–506. A. Aulard, *Le Christianisme et la Révolution française* (1925; Eng. tr., 1927). A. Dansette, *Histoire religieuse de la France contemporaine*, i (1948), pp. 76–187. See also bibl. to *Civil Constitution of the Clergy* and *Concordat of 1801*.

CONSTITUTIONS OF CLARENDON.
See *Clarendon, Constitutions of.*

CONSUBSTANTIAL.
Of one and the same substance or being. The word is used esp. of the eternal relationship which subsists between the three Persons of the Holy Trinity. The Latin *consubstantialis* is the W. counterpart of the Greek ὁμοούσιος (see *Homoousios*), the test-word of theological orthodoxy in the *Arian controversy, and may indeed have been its immediate source.

CONSUBSTANTIATION.
In the doctrine of the *Eucharist, the belief, esp. associated with the name of M. *Luther, that, after the consecration, the substances both of the Body and Blood of Christ and of the bread and wine coexist in union with each other. Luther illustrated it by the analogy of the iron put into the fire whereby both fire and iron are united in the red-hot iron and yet each continues unchanged. The doctrine was formulated in opposition to the medieval doctrine of *transubstantiation, acc. to which the substances of the bread and wine were no longer present after consecration, but only their '*accidents' persisted.

K. Algermissen in *L.Th.K.*, vi (1934), col. 179, s.v. 'Konsubstantiation'.

CONSUETUDINARY.
See *Customary.*

CONTAKION
(Gk. κοντάκιον). In the Byzantine Church, the word is used of (1) a vellum roll of liturgical prayers, wound round a piece of wood; (2) a hymn in several strophes (e.g. those of St. *Romanos), sung at an early point in the Liturgy; and (3) the usual modern sense, a rhythmic hymn of a single strophe, sung antiphonally in the Offices, which sets forth the mystery or commemoration of the day. The book containing these hymns throughout the year is known as the 'Contakarion' (κοντακάριον).

CONTARINI, GASPAR
(1483–1542), cardinal. He belonged to one of the foremost families of Venice. After education at the University of Padua, where he was won for the New Learning, he served as Venetian ambassador at the court of *Charles V (attending in this capacity the Diet of *Worms of 1521), in England, in Spain, and at the Papal court. He soon became famous as a theologian. In 1516 he published a treatise defending (against P. *Pomponazzi) the immortality of the soul, and c. 1530 a book against M. *Luther, *Confutatio Articulorum seu Quaestionum Lutheri*. His popularity at Rome led him, though only a layman, to be created a cardinal by *Paul III in 1535. In 1536 he was put on the commission which was to prepare the way for the Council (of *Trent) and in 1536–7 he issued his 'Consilium de emendanda ecclesia', proposing many radical reforms. In 1536 he became Bp. of Belluno. At the Conference of *Ratisbon (1541) he took an active part in this last attempt at reunion with the Lutherans, before the influence of the *Jesuits and of *Counter-Reformation ideals finally closed the possibility of reconciliation. It was while searching at Ratisbon for a common formula on justification that he wrote his 'Epistola de justificatione' (25 May 1541), a profession of faith in which Contarini was believed in many quarters to have compromised the Catholic doctrine.

Opera [ed. by L. Contarini, with a life by G. della Casa] (Paris, 1571). F. Dittrich (ed.), *Regesten und Briefe des Cardinals Gasparo Contarini, 1483–1542* (1881). Id., *Gasparo Contarini, 1483–1542*. Eine Monographie (1885). T. Brieger, *Gasparo Contarini und das Regensburger Concordienwerk des Jahres 1541* (1870); G. Bianchini, *Un magistratocardinale del secolo XVI* (1895); W. Braun, *Kardinal Gasparo Contarini oder der 'Reformkatholizismus' unserer Tage im Lichte der Geschichte* (1903); H. Rückert, *Die theologische Entwicklung Gasparo Contarinis* (1926); H. Hackert, *Die Staatsschrift Gasparo Contarinis und die politischen Verhältnisse Venedigs im sechzehnten Jahrhundert* (Heidelberger Abhandlungen zur mittleren und neueren Geschichte, Hft. lxix, 1940). F. Hünermann, 'Die Rechtfertigungslehre des Kardinals Gasparo Contarini' in *T.Q.*, cxxi (1921), pp. 1–22. H. Jedin in *D.H.G.E.*, xiii ('1955'), cols. 771–84.

CONTEMPLATION.
As used by modern religious writers, non-discursive mental prayer, as distinguished from *meditation (q.v.). In so far as this stage of prayer is held to be reached by the normal development of the natural faculties, it is termed 'acquired contemplation' (also the 'prayer of simplicity'); but when considered as the fruit of supernatural grace, directly acting on the soul, it is known as 'infused contemplation'. Mystical

writers such as St.*Teresa of Avila distinguish between several forms of mystic contemplation.

C. Baumgartner in *Dict. Sp.*, ii (1953), cols. 1645–2193, s.v., with reff

CONTEMPLATIVE LIFE, The. The state of life devoted primarily to prayer. Though a measure of contemplation is demanded of every Christian, whatever his state, in its usual meaning the term 'Contemplative Life' is confined to certain religious living under vows. In the Contemplative Orders much time is spent in prayer, both vocal (the performing of the Divine Office) and mental, though considerable periods are devoted to manual work. The life is normally very austere. Silence is strictly observed for the greater part of the day, and severe fasts and vigils are kept. Among the best-known Contemplative Orders are the *Carthusian monks and nuns, and the *Carmelite, *Poor Clare, *Dominican (second order), and many *Benedictine nuns.

CONTESTATIO (Lat.). In *Gallican service books, the usual name for the *Preface at the *Eucharist.

CONTINGENCY. In metaphysics, the condition of an existent which might have been other than it actually is, or alternatively what is incidental in contrast to what is necessary. St. *Thomas Aquinas defined it as the possibility of being and not being (*contingens est, quod potest esse et non esse*). Acc. to Christian belief, the created world is possessed of contingent being, and thereby stands in utter contrast with the necessary being of God. The argument which professes to demonstrate the necessary existence of God from the contingency of the created world is known as the '*Cosmological Argument' (q.v.).

CONTRA-REMONSTRANTIE. The counter-declaration in which the more rigid *Calvinists stated their objections to the *Arminian '*Remonstrance' (q.v.). It was drawn up for the Conference which met at the Hague on 11 Mar. 1611. Its main points were: (1) Unconditional and absolute predestination of some souls to damnation. (2) Children as well as adults may be among the elect. (3) Election is not acc. to works or belief, but only at God's pleasure. (4) Christ died only for the elect. (5) The Holy Ghost speaks in Scripture only to the elect. (6) The elect can never lose the true belief. (7) This preservation does not lead to carelessness of life, but to positive virtue.

The text is in J. Trigland, *Kerckelijcke Geschiedenissen begrypende de swaere Bekommerlijcke Geschillen in de Vereenigde Nederlanden voor-gefallen* (Leyden, 1650), pp. 544–52 (the seven articles on pp. 549 f.).

CONTRITION (Lat. *contritio*, 'a wearing away of something hard'). Contrition is a form of interior repentance, defined by the Council of *Trent as 'sorrow of heart and detestation of sin committed, with the purpose of not

sinning in future' (sess. xiv, cap. 4). Moral theologians commonly hold that to be real it must have its grounds in the love of God, and hence distinguish it from *attrition (q.v.), an imperfect form of sorrow for sin, inspired by such lower motives as the fear of punishment. The classical utterance of the contrite heart in the OT is the *Miserere (Ps. 51). In the Gospels the need for contrition is taught esp. in the Parables of the Prodigal Son (Lk. 15. 11–32) and of the Pharisee and the Publican (Lk. 18. 9–14).

*Leo X replied to M. *Luther's attack on the medieval notions of contrition in his bull, *Exsurge, Domine* (15 June 1520; list of heresies condemned repr. in Denz.–Bann. (ed. 1952), pp. 275–8, Nos. 741–81). P. de Letter, S.J., 'Perfect Contrition and Perfect Charity' in *Theological Studies*, vii (1946), pp. 507–24. E. J. Hanna in *C.E.*, iv (1908), pp. 337–40; T. Ortolan in *D.T.C.*, iii (1908), cols. 1671–94; F. Carpino in *E.C.*, iv (1950), cols. 474–8, s.v. 'Contrizione'.

CONVENT. The name convent is derived from the Lat. *conventus*, a meeting or association of men for some purpose. In ecclesiastical usage it can refer either to the buildings in which a body of religious live together, or to the religious community itself. Historically it has been applied to the domicile of religious of either sex, though it tends now to be restricted to houses of nuns.

CONVENTICLE ACT (1664). The Act (16 Car. II, c. 4) which declared illegal all meetings in private houses or elsewhere of more than five persons (in addition to the household) for worship other than that prescribed by the BCP. A second Act of 1670 (22 Car. II, c. 1) mitigated the penalties laid down in 1664, but gave wider powers to those employed in suppressing conventicles. The acts were repealed by the *Toleration Act of 1689.

The Second Conventicle Act is pr. in Gee–Hardy, pp. 623–632 (No. cxix).

CONVENTUAL MASS. The public Mass sung (or occasionally said) in religious communities where public *choir office is recited. This Mass is attended by the whole community, and is usually a *High Mass (q.v.). On certain days there are more than one such Mass. In cathedrals and collegiate churches the conventual Mass is properly known as a *capitular Mass, though the more general term 'conventual' is sometimes used.

CONVENTUALS. The branch of the *Franciscan Order which favoured the accumulation and common holding of property and followed a mitigated rule in contrast with the friars of the older tradition ('*Observantists' or 'Observants') who rejected property altogether. Their policy was approved by Pope *John XXII in 1322.

CONVERSI, a name widely used of lay brothers (q.v.) in monasteries. Their exact relation in medieval times to the other members of the community is a matter of considerable obscurity.

CONVERSION OF ST. PAUL, Feast of.
The feast, kept on 25 Jan., is peculiar to the
W. and of *Gallican origin, as contrasted with
that of Sts. Peter and Paul (29 June), which
originated in *Rome. In some early *martyrologies it is called the *translatio* of St. Paul,
a fact which suggests that the date in the
calendar was connected with the *translation
of the relics of the Apostle (to his *basilica
outside Rome?), though this still leaves its non-
Roman origin unexplained.

**CONVOCATIONS OF CANTERBURY
AND YORK.** The two ancient provincial
assemblies of the clergy of the C of E. Traces
of Church assemblies of the nation are already
met with in *Bede, but their history properly
begins with the ecclesiastical reorganization
under Abp. *Theodore (668–90). In 733 began
the separate provincial authority of *York,
which henceforth remained a separate body.

Originally the assemblies consisted only of
prelates, but in 1225 Stephen *Langton summoned in addition Proctors for the cathedral
and monastic chapters. In 1258 Archdeacons
were also convoked with letters of proxy from
their clergy. The future form of the Convocation of Canterbury was finally reached under
Abp. *Peckham in 1283; it consisted of the
Bishops, Abbots, Deans, and Archdeacons,
together with two representatives from the
clergy of each diocese and one representative
from each chapter. At first the Bishops and
lower clergy sat together and the whole body
of clergy still constitute what is properly one
assembly; but since the 15th cent. the convocations have sat as two Houses—the 'Upper' and
'Lower' Houses. The president of the Upper
House and of the whole body when both
Houses are sitting together, is the Abp. of
Canterbury (or York). The Lower House
elects one of its own number as president, who
is known as the '*prolocutor'. The Lower
House can initiate synodical action by means
of *gravamina* or *reformanda* which it presents
to the Upper House through its prolocutor.
Since the Reformation the heads of religious
houses have not sat in Convocation. In modern
times the representation of the parochial
clergy has been increased. One Proctor is
elected for each 70 parochial electors and a
large diocese such as Oxford thus sends up to
as many as nine Proctors. Since 1936 the
universities have also been represented in the
Convocation of Canterbury.

From a very early date these assemblies were
the means through which the clergy taxed
themselves. Edward I's attempt under the
'*praemunientes* clause' (1295) to summon representatives of the clergy to Parliament and thus
compel the clergy to grant their taxes in this
body failed, and it was not until after the
Restoration that Convocation surrendered the
right of making its own grants to the King
(1664).

In the Middle Ages and later the legislative
powers of Convocation varied considerably.
The normal method of legislation was by

Canons. The King was always on the look-out
for any infringement of the Royal prerogative;
and in 1532 *Henry VIII extorted from Convocation the '*Submission of the Clergy (q.v.)',
later embodied in an Act of Parliament (1534).
This Act severely limited the powers of Convocation and had a far-reaching effect on its
subsequent fortunes. It has generally been
held, since the breach with Rome, that Convocation must dissolve with Parliament, and this is
the usual practice, though in 1640 it continued
to sit and passed a famous set of Canons.

After the Revolution of 1688 the Convocations entered upon a stormy period, when they
were drawn into the current disputes about
*Divine Right, Non-Resistance, and Passive
Obedience. But while the majority of the
clergy were High Churchmen and often
Jacobite in sympathy, the Government secured
in the early 18th cent. a Whiggish Bench of
Bishops, so that the Upper House of Convocation was often in disagreement on important
questions with the High Church clergy of the
Lower House. This conflict was brought to
an end with the *Bangorian Controversy in
1717, when, to prevent the condemnation of a
sermon and book by Bp. B. Hoadley, the
Convocations were prorogued by Royal Writ.
For nearly a century and a half the powers of
the Crown under the Act for the Submission
of the Clergy were interpreted as making it
inexpedient for the Convocations to discuss
any business whatever, and its meetings were
purely formal. It was not until 1852, under
the combined influence of the *Evangelical
and *Oxford Movements, that the Convocation
of Canterbury took the bold step of discussing
business again. York followed the example of
Canterbury in 1861.

The Houses of Convocation have always
been, and still are, exclusively clerical assemblies. But since 1885 there has been associated
with Convocation a 'House of Laymen' in
each Province chosen by the Diocesan conferences. At the beginning of the 20th cent.,
the practice of joint sittings of the two Convocations was also initiated, and in 1904 a Representative Council consisting of the members of
both the Convocations together with the two
Houses of Laymen, sitting conjointly, was
begun. This Representative Council, however, had no legal position or authority until
1920, when it was superseded by the present
*Church Assembly (q.v.) whose powers were
defined in 'The Church of England Assembly
(Powers) Act' of 1919, commonly known as the
*Enabling Act.

The Convocations nowadays meet for the
inside of a week two or three times a year.
Each day's meeting is known as a 'session' and
the whole meeting of three or four days as a
'group of sessions'.

E. *Gibson, *Synodus Anglicana*, or the Constitution and
Proceedings of an English Convocation, shown from the
Acts and Registers thereof to be Agreeable to the Principles
of an Episcopal Church (1702; ed. E. *Cardwell, 1854), with
numerous primary docc.; E. *Cardwell (ed.), *Synodalia*. A
Collection of Articles of Religion, Canons, and Proceedings
of Convocations in the Province of Canterbury, from the
Year 1547 to the Year 1717, ii (1842). The proceedings of

the Convocation of Canterbury are publd. in the *Chronicle of Convocation* (London, 1859 ff.); those of the Convocation of York in the *York Journal of Convocation* (London, 1874 ff.). T. Lathbury, *A History of the Convocation of the Church of England* [to 1742] (1842). Dorothy B. Weske, *Convocation of the Clergy*. A Study of its Antecedents and its Rise with special emphasis upon its Growth and Activities in the Thirteenth and Fourteenth Centuries (C.H.S., 1937). On the early development of Convocation, E. Barker, *The Dominican Order and Convocation* (1913), pp. 31–76. T. Twiss–T. A. Ingram in *E.B.* (ed. 11), vi (1910), pp. 64–7, s.v., with selection of controversial 18th cent. works. G. Grosse in *D.E.C.H.* (ed. 1948), pp. 144–50, s.v. N. Sykes, *From Sheldon to Secker* (1959), pp. 36–67. E. W. Kemp, *Counsel and Consent* (*Bampton Lectures for 1960; 1961).

CONVULSIONARIES. Enthusiasts of the party of *Jansenist *Appellants against the bull '*Unigenitus' (1713), who exhibited supposedly miraculous phenomena, akin to those of epilepsy. These 'convulsions' were first observed, together with cures, prophesyings, conversions, &c., in 1731, at the tomb of the Jansenist François de Paris (1690–1727) at Saint-Médard, Paris. Instances continued to be recorded in various parts of France until the end of the 18th cent.

P. Gagnol, *Le Jansénisme convulsionnaire et l'affaire de la planchette d'après les archives de la Bastille* (1911). R. A. Knox, *Enthusiasm* (1950), esp. ch. 16, 'The Convulsionaries of Saint-Médard', pp. 372–88. L. Loevenbruck in *D.T.C.*, iii (1908), cols. 1756–62, s.v. 'Convulsionnaires', with further reff. See also general works on *Jansenism* cited s.v.

CONYBEARE, FREDERICK CORNWALLIS (1856–1924), *Armenian scholar. He was Fellow of University College, Oxford, from 1881 to 1887, and spent much of his life travelling in search of Armenian MSS. Among his works were a *Collation with the Ancient Armenian Versions of the Greek Text of Aristotle's Categories* (1892), and editions of important early documents of the Armenian Church, some of which he published in his *Rituale Armenorum* (1905). His discovery of an Armenian MS. in which the concluding verses of St. Mark's Gospel (16. 9–20) were assigned to the 'Presbyter 'Aristion' attracted much attention. For several years he was a member of the Rationalist Press Association, and his *Myth, Magic and Morals, a Study of Christian Origins* (1909), written as an attack on Christianity, evoked a reply from W. *Sanday under the title *A New Marcion* (1909).

L. Mariès, 'Frederick Cornwallis Conybeare (1856–1924). Notice biographique et bibliographie critique' in *Revue des Études Arméniennes*, vi (1926), pp. 185–332. D. S. Margoliouth in *D.N.B., 1922–1930*, p. 210 f.

CONYBEARE, WILLIAM JOHN (1815–1857), joint author with J. S. *Howson (q.v.) of *The Life and Epistles of St. Paul*. Educated at Westminster and Trinity College, Cambridge, he was from 1842 to 1848 first principal of Liverpool Collegiate Institute, where he was joined in 1845 by his friend Howson. After resigning through poor health, he became vicar of Axminster, Devon (1848–54). *The Life and Epistles of St. Paul* (2 vols., 1852), perhaps the most widely studied work on St. Paul published in the 19th cent., marked the beginning of the modern understanding of St. Paul in the English-speaking world. It embodied the results of wide theological, historical, and geographical studies, but in its method of treatment kept in mind the needs and interests of the general reader. Conybeare was also a frequent contributor to the *Edinburgh Review*.

Unsigned art. (based on information from his son) in *D.N.B.*, xii (1887), p. 62 f.

COOK, STANLEY ARTHUR (1873–1949), Biblical critic and Semitic historian. A native of King's Lynn, he was educated at Wyggeston School, Leicester, and at Gonville and Caius College, Cambridge, where he was afterwards Fellow and lecturer (1904–32). From 1932 to 1938 he was Regius professor of Hebrew. His extensive writings were marked by a wide knowledge, esp. of early Semitic customs and archaeology, which he interpreted with freshness and imagination, though the unconventionality of his conclusions set his work somewhat apart from the main stream of OT discussion. From 1896 to 1903 he was a member of the editorial staff of the *Encyclopaedia Biblica*, and from 1902 to 1932 edited the journal of the *Palestine Exploration Fund. He was also one of the editors of the *Cambridge Ancient History*, to which he himself contributed important chapters (in vols. i, ii, iii, and vi). His writings include *The Study of Religions* (1914), *The Religion of Ancient Palestine in the Light of Archaeology* (Schweich Lectures, 1930), *The Old Testament: a Reinterpretation* (1936), and *The 'Truth' of the Bible* (1938); and he edited W. R. *Smith's *Kinship and Marriage in Early Arabia* (1903) and *Religion of the Semites* (1927) and R. H. Kennett's *Old Testament Essays* (1933).

Select bibl. of his works in D. W. Thomas (ed.), *Essays and Studies Presented to Stanley Arthur Cook . . . in Celebration of his Seventy-fifth Birthday 12 April 1948* (Cambridge Oriental Series, No. 2, 1950), pp. 1–13.

COOPER, THOMAS (*c.* 1520–94), also 'Cowper', Bp. of *Winchester. Educated at Magdalen College, Oxford, he later became a Fellow and Master of the Choir School, where W. Camden was among his pupils. His Protestant beliefs led him to abandon his project of ordination on *Mary's accession (1553), but he fulfilled his intention shortly after her death (1558). He was a man of great learning, and among his works were a Latin Dictionary (1548), a Chronicle ('Cooper's Chronicle', 1549, a continuation of an unpublished chronicle of Thomas Lanquet, d. 1545), and a *Thesaurus Linguae Romanae et Britannicae* (1565). In 1562 he wrote *An Answer in Defence of the Truth against the Apology of Private Mass* directed against an attack on Bp. J. *Jewel's *Apology*. In 1567 he became Dean of *Christ Church, Oxford, in 1569 Dean of *Gloucester, in 1571 Bp. of *Lincoln, and in 1584 Bp. of Winchester. In the latter capacity he wrote against the *Marprelate tracts.

Cooper's *Admonition to the People of England* [against Martin Marprelate] (orig. publd. 1589) was ed. by J. Petheram (London, 1847) and by E. Arber (English Scholar's Library, xv; Birmingham, 1882); his *Answer in Defence of the Truth against the Apology of Private Mass* was ed. W.

Goode (*Parker Society, 1850), with list of Cooper's works, pp. xi–xv. C. W. Foster (ed.), *Lincoln Episcopal Records in he Time of Thomas Cooper* (Publications of the Lincoln Record Society, ii; 1912; repr. by the *Canterbury and York Society, ix; 1913). W. Benham in *D.N.B.*, xii (1887), pp. 149–51.

COORNHEERT, DIRCK VOLCKERTS-ZOON

(1522–90), Dutch theologian. Brought up in Spain, Portugal, and Amsterdam, he settled at Haarlem, where he practised as an engraver in copper, and also published translations of the Latin classics into Dutch. He became one of the leading supporters of William the Silent. He defended liberalism against the strongly *Calvinist doctrines then current in Holland, advocating toleration, opposing capital punishment for heretics, and criticizing the *Heidelberg Catechism. Through the influence of the writings of S. *Castellio, and esp. of the '*Deutsche Theologie', he urged the necessity of interior piety and the inward dominion of the Holy Spirit. He rejected the idea of a visible Church and maintained the sufficiency of a faith inspired by the Bible and the Apostles' Creed. J. *Calvin wrote against him his *Response à un certain Hollandais lequel sous Ombre de faire les Chrétiens tout spirituels, leur permet de polluer leurs Corps en toutes Idolatries* (1562). The *Arminians, and also the *Pietists, owed something to his thought. A Dutch version of the NT on which he was engaged was incomplete at his death.

His Works were published at Amsterdam (3 vols., 1630). Studies by F. D. J. Moorrees (Nijmegen, 1887), Olga Rinck-Wagner (Historische Studien, cxxxviii, 1919), and B. Becker (Rijks Geschiedkundige Publicatiën, Kleine Serie, xxv; 1928).

COPE.

A semicircular cloak worn at liturgical functions when the *chasuble is not used. Both vestments took their origin in the Roman 'paenula' or 'pluviale', the cope gradually reaching its present form by being opened in front. It has been held that it did not become a liturgical vestment until the 9th cent. or later, but H. *Leclercq has collected a large number of examples from primitive frescoes and mosaics which suggest that it was regarded as typical of the clergy at least by the 6th cent. The term 'cappa' first appears in *Gregory of Tours (d. 594). In the Middle Ages it was widely used as a ceremonial choir habit by whole communities on feasts, while the 'cappa nigra', a cloak of thick black material serving the same purpose as the original 'pluviale', was worn in choir as a protection against the cold. The hood of the original garment survives as a triangular-shaped ornament on the back of the cope.

In the BCP of 1549, the Celebrant at the Holy Communion was ordered to wear a cope or vestment (i.e. chasuble), but in 1552 the rubric was withdrawn. The use of a cope by the Celebrant at the Communion in cathedral and collegiate churches was prescribed by can. 24 of 1604. Probably its use never wholly died out in the C of E. It has been extensively revived in England since the middle of the 19th cent.

Braun, *L.G.*, pp. 306–58. E. *Bishop, 'The Origins of the Cope as a Church Vestment' in *Dublin Review*, cxx (1897), pp. 17–37, repr. in *Liturgica Historica* (1918), ch. xi. H. *Leclercq, O.S.B., and E. Mombert in *D.A.C.L.*, iii, pt. i (1913), cols. 365–81, s.v. *Chape*.

COPERNICUS, NICOLAS

(1473–1543), the father of modern astronomy. After studying medicine, philosophy, and mathematics at the University of Cracow, he went to Italy, reading law at *Bologna and lecturing on mathematics and astronomy at *Rome. Returning to Prussia in 1505, he went first to Heilsberg, where he began to formulate the theories which were to make him famous, and then, in 1512, to Frauenburg, of which he had been a canon since 1497, where he was to remain for the rest of his life. Rejecting the generally accepted Ptolemaic system of the universe, he found the centre of the solar system not in the earth but in the sun, on the ground that it was improbable that a large body such as the sun should revolve around a small body like the earth. Despite certain defects in his system, it prepared the way for the work of J. *Kepler, G. *Galileo, and I. *Newton, and provided a valuable explanation of many scientific phenomena, such as the variation of the seasons, the precession of the equinoxes, and the stationary and retrogressive motions of the planets. A brief outline of his theory, the *Commentariolus* (published in 1531), received the approbation of Pope *Clement VII. The full treatise *De revolutionibus orbium coelestium* was not published until 1543, and the first printed copy reached him just before he died, too late, however, for him to disown a preface, written by A. *Osiander, which had been inserted warning its readers that its conclusions were to be regarded as only hypothetical. The *Galileo affair led the work to be put on the *Index in 1616, and it was not removed from it till 1757.

Several edd. of the *De Revolutionibus*, notably Nuremberg, 1543; Basle, 1566; Thorn, 1873. Collected ed. of Works, Munich, vol. i, 1944. *Three Copernican Treatises*. Tr., with introd. and notes, by E. Rosen (New York, 1939). J. Czyński, *Kopernik et ses travaux* (1847); L. Prowe, *Nicolaus Coppernicus* (2 vols., Berlin, 1883–4; also many earlier works by this author). Many works, of varying merit, were issued, esp. in Germany, in 1943 to mark the 4th centenary of his death. Dorothy Stimson, *The Gradual Acceptance of the Copernican Theory of the Universe* (New York, 1917); H. Sandblad, *Det Copernikanska Världssystemet i Sverige* (2 vols., 1944–5).

COPLESTON, EDWARD

(1776–1849), Bp. of *Llandaff. A fine classical scholar, he was elected a Fellow of Oriel College, Oxford, in 1795 and Provost of the college in 1814. In 1826 he became Dean of *Chester, and in 1827 both Bp. of Llandaff and Dean of St. Paul's, holding the offices in plurality. While at Oxford he was largely instrumental in instituting the system of examinations which in essence still survives, and in raising his college to its position of intellectual pre-eminence in the earlier half of the 19th cent., thus providing the setting for the *Oxford Movement. In his theological views Copleston was a '*Noetic', who, despite his scant sympathy with the

Tractarians, counted himself a High Churchman. His writings, which are few, included some brilliant replies to attacks made on Oxford in the *Edinburgh Review*.

Copleston's *Advice to a Young Reviewer with a Specimen of the Art*, orig. publd. Oxford, 1807, was repr. ib., 1926; also ed. G. [S.] Gordon, *Three Oxford Ironies* (1927), pp. 49–73, with introd., pp. 7–17 and 37–44. John W. Ward's letters to Copleston were ed. by Copleston and publd. under the title, *Letters of the Earl of Dudley to the Bishop of Llandaff* (1840). Memoir by William James Copleston (London, 1851), with selections from his diary and correspondence. Further extracts from his works pr. by R. *Whately, *Remains of the late Edward Copleston* (1854), with introd. reminiscences, pp. 1–98. W. Tuckwell, *Pre-Tractarian Oxford* (1909), pp. 17–50. T. E. Kerbel in *D.N.B.*, xii (1887), pp. 174–6.

COPTIC (language). 'Copt' is a European form of the Arabic 'Kibt', which is itself derived from the Gk. Αἰγύπτιοι ['Egyptians']. Coptic was the language usually spoken by the 'Copts', the native populace of Egypt, from about the 3rd to the 10th cents. After the 10th cent. the language was gradually supplanted by Arabic; but it appears to have survived in a few places down to the end of the 17th cent., and is still that of the liturgy of the *Coptic Church. In essence it was the language of ancient Egypt, into which a large number of Greek words had been incorporated, and was written in an alphabet closely akin to that of the Greeks. It occurs in several dialects, among them * Sahidic, * Bohairic, and *Fayumic. The NT was translated into all three, first into the Sahidic, the dialect used in the south of Egypt where the need was greatest as the influence of Greek culture was least. Of the extensive remains of early Christian literature in Coptic, much the greater part consists in translations from the Greek. It includes the Gnostic '*Pistis Sophia', of which the Greek has been lost. Among the few surviving writings originally composed in Coptic are some legends of the saints. See also *Jung Codex*.

Coptic grammars by J. M. Plumley (Sahidic; London, 1948), A. Mallon (in French; Beyrout, 1904; ed. 3, 1926, with valuable bibl., pp. 246–325), G. Steindorff (Berlin, 1894; revised ed., Chicago, 1951). W. Till, *Achmimisch-koptische Grammatik* (1928); id., *Koptische Chrestomathie für den fayumischen Dialekt* (1930). M. Chaine, *Éléments de grammaire dialectale copte* (1933). W. E. Crum, *A Coptic Dictionary* (1929–39). W. Kammerer, *A Coptic Bibliography* (Ann Arbor, 1950).

Crit. edd. of Coptic NT by G. Horner: In Bohairic dialect, 4 vols., Oxford, 1898–1905; in Sahidic dialect, 7 vols., ib., 1911–24. Coptic OT edited very incompletely and in scattered places; cf. A. Vaschalde, 'Ce qui a été publié des versions coptes de la Bible' in *R. Bibl.*, xxviii (1919), pp. 220–43, 513–31; xxix (1920), pp. 91–106, 241–58; xxx (1921), pp. 237–46; xxxi (1922), pp. 81–88 and 234–58; cont. in *Le Muséon*, xliii (1930), pp. 409–31; xlv (1932), pp. 117–58; xlvi (1933), pp. 299–313. Cf. also list of principal items in *E.C.*, iv (1950), col. 513.

COPTIC CHURCH. After the condemnation of *Dioscorus, Patr. of *Alexandria, at the Council of *Chalcedon (451), the Egyptian Church became formally *Monophysite and increasingly isolated from the rest of Christendom. At first its energies were largely dissipated in unedifying disputes with the orthodox (*Melchite) body centred at Alexandria. In Upper Egypt, however, there was a rapid development of monasticism. The activity of the monks, who became large landowners and a leading political force, is attested by the many Coptic 'Lives of the Saints' and 'Sayings of the Fathers' and abundant ruins of their buildings. In 616 the Copts passed for a time under the Persian domination. In 642 they were conquered by the Arabs, whose rule in varying forms has lasted until the present day. Long periods of comparative peace were on occasion suddenly broken by persecution, e.g. under the Caliph el Hakim (996–1021), who is said to have destroyed 3,000 churches and caused large numbers to apostatize. The Copts only obtained real freedom of worship with the British occupation which followed the battle of Tel-el-Kebir (1882).

In the course of centuries their numbers gradually declined. They now number some 800,000 out of a total population in Egypt of over 12,000,000. Their hierarchy consists of the Patriarch, 12 bishops (who elect the Patriarch), and priests and deacons. All speak Arabic, Coptic being found only in their service-books with the Arabic text in a parallel column; but the clergy, who are generally of little education, sometimes cannot read even the Arabic. The liturgy in use is that of *St. Mark (q.v.). They observe five important fasts: (1) The pre-Lenten 'Fast of *Nineveh' (q.v.); (2) The Great Fast of Lent (55 days); (3) The Fast of the Nativity, before Christmas (28 days); (4) The Fast of the Apostles, after the Ascension; and (5) The Fast of the Virgin, before the Assumption (15 days).

There is also a small *Uniat Coptic Church, dating from 1741 when Athanasius, the Coptic Bp. of Jerusalem, joined the RC Church. At the present time it numbers some 4,000.

J. M. Wansleben, *Histoire de l'Église d'Alexandrie, fondée par S. Marc* (1677). A. J. Butler, *The Ancient Coptic Churches of Egypt* (2 vols., 1884); E. L. Butcher, *The Story of the Church of Egypt* (2 vols., 1897). J. Maspero (posthumous), *Histoire des patriarches d'Alexandrie depuis la mort de l'empereur Anastase jusqu'à la réconciliation des Églises jacobites, 515–616* (Bibliothèque de l'École des Hautes Études, fasc. ccxxxvii, 1923); R. Strothmann, *Die koptische Kirche in der Neuzeit* (Beiträge zur historischen Theologie, vii, 1932). S. C. Malan (ed. and tr.), *Original Documents of the Coptic Church* (3 pts., 1872–3); R. M. Woolley (ed. and tr.), *Coptic Offices* (1930); A. A. King, *The Rites of Eastern Christendom*, i (Rome, 1947), ch. 5, pp. 337–495, with bibl. M. Jugie, A.A., *Theologia Dogmatica Christianorum Orientalium ab Ecclesia Catholica Dissidentium*, v (Paris, 1935), pp. 349–787 passim, esp. pp. 458–64. Id., in *D.T.C.*, x (pt. 2; 1929), cols. 2251–306, s.v. 'Monophysite (Église Copte)', with bibl. A. *Fortescue, *The Lesser Eastern Churches* (1913), pp. 163–290; D. Attwater, *The Dissident Eastern Churches* (Milwaukee, Wisc., [1937]); id., *The Catholic Eastern Churches* (ib., [1935]), pp. 135–49, with bibl.

CORBAN ('oblation'). A Heb. word (קָרְבָּן), peculiar to *Ezekiel and the 'P' sections of the *Pentateuch, for altar offerings, either the fixed obligatory dues, or free-will votive gifts. It is probably to this latter kind of gift that Christ refers in Mk. 7. 11, when He objects to the practice of letting 'Corban' take precedence of the duty of maintaining one's parents.

CORBIE. This celebrated monastery, some ten miles to the east of Amiens, was founded from *Luxeuil *c.* 660. It possessed a fine collection of MSS. many of which were transferred in 1624 to the monastery of Saint-Germain-des-Prés at Paris and thence passed at the time of the Revolution (1794) to the Bibliothèque Nationale.

L. Delisle, 'Recherches sur l'ancienne bibliothèque de Corbie' in *Bibliothèque de l'École des Chartes*, Série 5, i (1860), pp. 393-439, 498-515; id., *Le Cabinet des MSS. de la Bibliothèque Nationale*, ii (1874), pp. 104-41, 427-40. W. M. Lindsay, 'The Old Script of Corbie. Its Abbreviation Symbols' in *Revue des Bibliothèques*, xxii (1912), pp. 405-29. A. *Wilmart, O.S.B., in *D.A.C.L.*, iii (pt. 2, 1914), cols. 2913-58, s.v. 'Corbie (Manuscrits liturgiques de)'. H. Peltier in *D.H.G.E.*, xiii ('1955'), cols. 809-24, with bibl.

CORDELIERS. A name sometimes given in France to the Franciscan *Observantines from the knotted cord which they wore round the waist. The word was also assumed by a political club during the French Revolution, as the convent in which it met had once belonged to the Cordeliers.

CORINTH. In NT times, Corinth was the capital of the Roman province of Achaia. It lay on the great trade route between *Rome and the E. and occupied a very important site for the propagation of the Christian Gospel on account of its political and geographical position, its cosmopolitan population, and its commercial supremacy. The Church was established here by St. *Paul *c.* 50, and included many prominent Jewish converts (Acts 18. 4, 8, 1 Cor. 9. 20), but it appears, both from Acts and the two Epp. of Paul to Corinth, that the Christian community consisted mainly of Gentiles, who, on the whole, belonged to the poorer classes (1 Cor. 1. 26), though they contributed generously to the collection for the saints (2 Cor. 9. 2-5). St. Paul was helped by *Silas and *Timothy and, in spite of Jewish opposition, 'he dwelt there a year and six months' (Acts 18. 11). During his stay, the proconsul *Gallio dismissed a charge against Paul of worshipping contrary to the Jewish Law, a decision which in effect amounted to permission to preach in the province. Paul left behind him a flourishing community, but the pagan antecedents of his converts seriously affected the life of the Church, as is seen in the Epp. to the *Corinthians. In fact the city was noted for its profligacy and moral laxity. In later Christian history, Corinth took a relatively less notable part.

Good summary in W. M. *Ramsay in *H.D.B.*, i (1898), pp. 479-83, s.v. On the modern excavations carried out under the direction of the American School of Classical Studies at Athens, see *Corinth* (Cambridge, Mass., 1929) and various reports by O. Broneer, R. Stillwell, Charles H. Morgan II, and others in *American Journal of Archaeology*, esp. xxxvii (1933), pp. 554-72; xxxix (1935), pp. 53-75; xl (1936), pp. 21-45, 466-84; xli (1937), pp. 539-52; xlii (1938), pp. 362-70; xliii (1939), pp. 255-67, 268-77, 592-600; xliv (1940), pp. 297-324, 325-7. H. *Leclercq, O.S.B., in *D.A.C.L.*, iii (pt. 2; 1914), cols. 2959-66, s.v.; T. Lenschau and others in *P.W.*, Suppl. iv (1924), cols. 991-1036, s.v. 'Korinthos'; both with further bibl. reff

CORINTHIANS, Epistles to the. These two Epistles of St. *Paul to his converts were both written from *Ephesus *c.* 52-5.

1 Corinthians was occasioned by news which St. Paul had received from the church at Corinth. The subjects dealt with include party-feeling among the Corinthian Christians, and their tendency to think too highly of a certain kind of human 'wisdom' (1. 10-4. 21); his own position as an apostle (4. 1-13, and 9); the sin of fornication at Corinth and the treatment of a particular offender (5 and 6); the question of litigation between Christians (6. 1-8); and certain points on which they had consulted him in a letter, viz. marriage and celibacy in relation to the Christian gospel (7), problems regarding the relations of Christians with the surrounding paganism (8), behaviour at Christian worship (10; 11), 'spiritual gifts' such as prophecy and speaking with tongues (12), and the *resurrection of the dead (15). The sections on the *Eucharist (10. 16 ff., 11. 20 ff.), on Love (*agape*) as the highest of spiritual gifts (13), and on the Resurrection (15), are among the most important in the NT.

In 2 Corinthians the principal topic is St. Paul's personal position in relation to the Church at Corinth. The Church, as the letter shows, had seriously failed in a matter of morality; and, as concerned himself, his status as an apostle had been challenged and his conduct attacked. In the earlier chapters he defends his conduct, setting out at length the authority and ministry of the Christian Apostle, and the proclamation of man's reconciliation with God by the atoning death of Christ (3. 4-6. 10). He rejoiced that he and the Corinthians are now at one again (7. 9 ff.). (The passage 6. 14-7. 1 seems to be a fragment of an earlier epistle, now lost, which has been accidentally inserted here.) Chs. 8-9 deal with the collection for the Church at *Jerusalem which St. Paul was organizing. In ch. 10, where a new beginning is made, there is a fresh treatment of St. Paul's relations with the Church of Corinth, and a severe condemnation of his opponents (ψευδαπόστολοι, 'false apostles'). The tone is quite different from that of the earlier chapters, and the reconciliation implied in 7. 9 ff. is apparently ignored. It is widely held that chs. 10-13 are part of a different epistle, sent on an earlier occasion than chs. 1-9, or else that these two groups of chapters were addressed to two different groups, or parties, within the Corinthian Church.

Ancient commentators include *Chrysostom (Gk.) and *Theodoret (Gk.), *Ambrosiaster (Lat.) and *Pelagius (Lat.). Modern commentaries on 1 Cor. by G. Heinrici (H. A. W. Meyer's Komm., 1896), H. L. Goudge (West. Comm., 1903), H. *Lietzmann (*Hb.N.T.*, 1907; ed. 2, with 2 Cor., 1923), J. Weiss (H. A. W. Meyer's Komm., 1910), A. *Robertson–A. Plummer (I.C.C., 1911), E. Evans (Clar. Bib., 1930), E. B. Allo (Paris, 1934), J. *Moffatt (Moffatt Comm., 1938) and J. Héring (Neuchâtel, 1949); on 2 Cor. by A. Plummer (I.C.C., 1915), H. Windisch (K.E.K., 1924), H. L. Goudge (West. Comm., 1927), R. H. Strachan (Moffatt Comm., 1935), E. B. Allo (Paris, 1937). J. H. Kennedy, *The Second and Third Epistles to the Corinthians* (1900). K. *Lake, *The Earlier Epistles of St. Paul* (1911), pp. 102-252. T. W. Manson, 'St. Paul in Ephesus. The Corinthian Correspondence' in *Bulletin of the John Rylands Library*, xxvi (1941-1942), pp. 101-20, 327-41. A. *Schlatter, *Die korinthische Theologie* (Beiträge zur Förderungchristlicher Theologie, xviii, Hft. 2; 1914). K. *Barth, *Die Auferstehung der Toten. Eine akademische Vorlesung über I Kor. 15* (1935). McNeile, pp. 132–42. A. Robertson in *H.D.B.*, i (1898), pp. 483–98. Teodorico da Castel Pietro in *E.C.*, iv (1950), cols. 549–56.

CORINTHIANS, Third Epistle to the. An apocryphal letter which is properly part of the 'Acts of *Paul' (*c.* 170). It survives, as a separate entity, in the Biblical *canon of the *Armenian Church as well as in two *Vulgate Latin MSS. (one at Milan, the other at Laon), while St. *Ephraem Syrus (*c.* 360) commented on it as though it were a genuine Pauline document. The author insists on the authority of the OT prophets, the resurrection of the flesh, the birth of Christ from Mary, and the creation of man, facts which show that its purpose was anti-*Gnostic.

Coptic text in C. Schmidt's crit. ed. of the 'Acta Pauli' (1936, q.v.). Armenian recension in Germ. tr. and two Lat. texts in P. Vetter, *Der apokryphe dritte Korintherbrief* (1894). Eng. tr. in M. R. James, *The Apocryphal New Testament* (1924), pp. 288–91; another tr. in K. *Lake, *The Earlier Epistles of St. Paul* (1911), pp. 236–40, with brief discussion. Bardenhewer, i, pp. 601–5; J. Quasten, *Patrology*, i (1950), p. 155, with further bibl. E. Amann in *Dict. Bibl.*, Suppl. i (1928), col. 518 f., s.v. 'Apocryphes du Nouveau Testament, IV, i'; Teodorico da Castel S. Pietro in *E.C.*, iv (1950), col. 556 f., s.v.

CORNELIUS (d. 253), Bp. of *Rome. He was elected Pope in April 251, when, owing to the *Decian persecution and the martyrdom of *Fabian, the see of Rome had been vacant for 14 months. He found himself faced with strong opposition from the *Novatianist schismatics, who objected to his relatively lenient policy towards those who had lapsed during the persecutions; but he had the support of synods at Rome and *Carthage (251–2). Several of his letters, written in a colloquial 'vulgar Latin', have survived, including a correspondence with St. *Cyprian. He died in exile, traditionally as a martyr, at Centum Cellae (Civitavecchia), and was buried at Rome in the crypt of Lucina in the 'Coemeterium Callisti', where his tomb is still to be seen with the Latin inscription 'Cornelius Martyr'. Feast day, 16 Sept.

His Epp. to Cyprian are printed *inter Epp. Cypr.*, Nos. 49 and 50. P. *Constant, *Epistolae Romanorum Pontificum*, i (1721), cols. 123–206; M. J. *Routh, *Reliquiae Sacrae*, iii (ed. 2, 1846), pp. 11–89. G. Mercati, *D' alcuni nuovi sussidii per la critica del testo di S. Cipriano* (1899), pp. 72–86 ('Le lettere di S. Cornelio papa'). Bardenhewer, ii, p. 639 f.

CORNELIUS A LAPIDE (1567–1637), Cornelis Cornelissen van den Steen, Flemish Biblical exegete. He was born at Bocholt nr. Liége, and educated at the *Jesuit colleges of Maastricht and *Cologne. In 1592 he entered the Jesuit Order, and was professor of exegesis at Louvain from 1596. In 1616 he was called to *Rome, where he taught the same subject and finished his celebrated commentaries, comprising all the Canonical Books except Job and the Psalms. In order of appearance they were *Epistolae Divi Pauli* (1614); *Pentateuchus* (1617); *Jeremias*, together with Bar. and Lam. (1621); *Ezechiel* (1621); *Daniel* (1621). Then followed Is. with a new edition of the three preceding works as *Quattuor*

Maiores Prophetae (1622); *Duodecim Minores Prophetae* (1625); *Actus Apostolorum, Epistolae Canonicae, Apocalypsis* (1627); *Ecclesiasticus* (2 vols., 1633–4); *Proverbia* (1635). Posthumous were *Ecclesiastes* (1638); *Cantica Canticorum* (1638); *Liber Sapientiae* (1638); *Evangelia*, i (Mt. and Mk., 1639); *Evangelia*, ii (Lk. and Jn., 1639); *Josue, Iudicum, Ruth, I-IV Regum, I-II Paralipomenon* (1642); *Esdras, Nehemias, Tobias, Iudith, Esther, I-II Machabaei* (1645). His works have owed their enduring popularity, esp. among preachers, to their clarity, deep spirituality, and allegorical and mystical exegesis, buttressed by a wide erudition which enabled the author to draw extensively on the Fathers and medieval theologians.

Complete edd. of his Comm. on the Bible publd. in 10 vols., Amsterdam, 1681; 11 vols., Venice, 1717; 11 vols., Cologne, etc., 1732; 11 vols., Venice, 1740; and several later edd. Eng. tr. by T. W. Mossman of his Comm. on the Gospels (5 vols., 1876–86) and by W. E. Cobb of his Comm. on I Cor. (1896) and on II Cor. and Gal. (1897). S. Pagano, O.M.I., 'Analysis Notionis Inspirationis S. Scripturae apud Cornelium a Lapide' in *Revue de l'Université d'Ottawa*, xv (1945), pp. 65*–85*. Sommervogel, iv (1893), cols. 1511–26, ix (1900), col. 573. G. Heinrici in *P.R.E.* (ed. 3), iv (1898), pp. 289–91, s.v. U. Holzmeister, S.J., in *E.C.*, iv (1905), col. 569, s.v., for further bibl.

CORNILL, CARL (1854–1920), OT scholar. He was professor of OT exegesis at Königsberg (1886), Breslau (1898), and Halle (1910). In the main he was a disciple of J. *Wellhausen. He wrote several books, notably an *Introduction to the Canonical Books of the OT* (1891) (Eng. trans. of ed. 5, 1907) and a *History of the People of Israel* (1898, Eng. trans. also 1898), which through their wide circulation did much to spread Wellhausen's methods of criticism and exegesis.

CORONATION OF OUR LADY, The. The final triumph of the Blessed Virgin in heaven, wherein she was crowned by her Divine Son. It is the subject of the fifth *Glorious Mystery of the *Rosary. It is observed in a few places as a liturgical feast (Calabria, Guatemala).

CORONATION RITE IN ENGLAND. The rite for the coronation of English kings falls into three parts: (1) The promises made by the king and his acclamation by the people; (2) the consecration and anointing of the king; (3) the vesting, coronation, and enthronement of the king (and coronation of the queen consort), followed by the homage and the king's Communion. These three divisions appear throughout the history of the rite.

In the 9th cent. (and perhaps for some time before) a rite was in use, based on that used for the coronation of the Popes. At the coronation of Edgar in 973 this was displaced by a new rite, which was probably a conscious adaptation of the rite then in use for Imperial coronations. Its success was such that it was used for many centuries both in England and in many parts of Europe. In the course of time it underwent various modifications, the most elaborate form of it being that in the *Liber Regalis*, which was used in 1308 for Edward II. For the coronation of *James I in 1603 it was translated into English, and the penitential psalms were omitted, and the Eucharist was conformed, with certain variations, to that in the BCP. A drastic rearrangement and curtailment was made in 1685 by Abp. W. *Sancroft to suit current ideas, and since *James II, being a RC, could not communicate, the Communion Service was omitted. For the coronation of William III in 1689 the Eucharist was reinstated in its central position, and among other changes Parliament caused an oath to be added for the defence of *Protestantism. Since 1689 the only changes have been minor abbreviations.

The most useful collection of documents is L. G. Wickham Legg, *English Coronation Records* (1901). Much interesting material is assembled in A. Taylor, *The Glory of Regality* (1820). Texts of the rite in J. Wickham Legg (ed.), *Three Coronation Orders* (H.B.S., xix, 1900; contains the Order of William III and Mary, an Anglo-French version of the English Coronation Order, and the Consecration of the Anglo-Saxon King); Christopher Wordsworth (later Subdean of Salisbury), *The Manner of the Coronation of King Charles the First* (H.B.S., ii, 1892); F. Sandford, *The History of the Coronation of . . . King James II . . . and Queen Mary* (1687); *The Coronation Service of her Majesty Queen Elizabeth II*. With a short historical Introduction, Explanatory Notes, and an Appendix by E. C. Ratcliff (1953). Modern studies include R. M. Woolley, *Coronation Rites* (Cambridge Handbooks of Liturgical Study, 1915); E. C. Ratcliff, *The English Coronation Service* (1936; with text of Rite used in 1911); R. H. Murray, *The King's Crowning* (1936), with bibl. P. E. Schramm (Eng. tr. from Germ. by L. G. Wickham Legg, *A History of the English Coronation*, 1937). E. Eichmann, *Königs- und Bischofsweihe in Sb.* (Bayr.), 1928, Abh. 6; id., *Der Kaiserkrönung im Abendland* (2 vols., Würzburg, 1942). P. L. Ward, 'The Coronation Ceremony in Mediaeval England' in *Speculum*, xiv (1939), pp. 160–78, with reff. C. Dawson, *Beyond Politics* (1939), pp. 93–115 ('Considerations on the Coronation of an English King').

CORPORAL (from Lat. *corpus*, 'body', since it holds the Body of the Lord). In W. liturgical usage, a square piece of linen on which the bread and wine are placed and consecrated in the *Eucharist. Such a cloth was used in the 4th cent., but there was no distinction between the corporal and the ordinary linen altar cloth now used under the corporal before the 9th cent. Formerly it was large enough to cover the chalice also (as it still is among the *Carthusian monks), but later a second folded corporal (now called the *pall) was introduced for this purpose. See also *Antimension* and *Burse*.

Braun, *L.P.*, pp. 205–9. E. G. C. F. Atchley, 'On Certain Variations from the Rule Concerning the Material of the Altar Linen' in *Transactions of the St. Paul's Ecclesiological Society*, iv (1900), pp. 147–60, esp. pp. 156–60. N. F. Robinson, S.S.J.E., 'Concerning Three Eucharistic Veils of Western Use', ib., vi (1906–10), pp. 129–60, esp. pp. 129–40. H. Thurston, S.J., in *C.E.*, iv (1908), p. 386 f., s.v.

CORPORAL WORKS OF MERCY. There are traditionally seven: (1) feeding the hungry; (2) giving drink to the thirsty; (3) clothing the naked; (4) harbouring the stranger; (5) visiting the sick; (6) ministering to prisoners; (7) burying the dead. Cf. Mt. 25. 35. See also *Spiritual Works of Mercy*.

CORPORATION ACT (1661). The Act of the 'Cavalier Parliament' (13 Car. II, st. ii, c. 1) requiring all members of municipal corporations to take an oath abjuring rebellion against the king, declaring the *Solemn League and Covenant null and unlawful, and affirming that they had received the Sacrament of Communion acc. to the rites of the C of E within the year preceding their election. It was repealed in 1828.

Text repr. in Gee–Hardy, pp. 594–600 (No. cxvi).

CORPUS CATHOLICORUM. The organization formed by RC states in the Holy Roman Empire, to maintain RC interests against the *Corpus Evangelicorum (q.v.). It first assembled at Ratisbon in 1524, and thenceforward existed as an informal body until its organization in 1720. Like the 'Corpus Evangelicorum' it disappeared at the dissolution of the empire in 1806.

E. A. Friedberg in *P.R.E.* (ed. 3), iv (1898), p. 291 f., s.v.

CORPUS CHRISTI, Feast of. The feast commemorating the institution and gift of the Holy *Eucharist, observed in the W. Church on the Thursday after *Trinity Sunday. The natural day in the Christian calendar for this commemoration would be *Maundy Thursday, on which the Eucharist was instituted; but the memory of the Passion on that day made a separate day for the Eucharist desirable, and the Thursday after Trinity Sunday was chosen as the first free Thursday after Eastertide. The institution of the feast was largely due to the influence of Blessed *Juliana (d. 1258), a devout nun of Liége who was led to take action in the matter *c.* 1230 in response to a vision. In 1264 its observance was commanded by the bull 'Transiturus' of *Urban IV, and in the 14th cent. the keeping of the feast became universal in the W. The services of the day were drawn up by St. *Thomas Aquinas, who also himself composed their very fine hymns (incl. '*Lauda Sion' and '*Pange Lingua').

P. Browe, S.J., 'Die Ausbreitung des Fronleichnamsfestes' in *J.L.W.*, viii (1928), pp. 107–44; id., *Textus antiqui de Festo Corporis Christi* (Münster i.W., 1934). E. Dumoutet, *Corpus Domini. Aux sources de la piété eucharistique médiévale* (1942). C. Lambot, O.S.B.–I. Fransen, O.S.B., *L'Office de la Fête-Dieu primitive*. Textes et mélodies retrouvés (Maredsous, 1946). *Studia Eucharistica: DCC Anni de Condito Festo Sanctissimi Corporis Christi 1246–1946* (Antwerp, 1946). F. Oppenheim, O.S.B., in *E.C.*, iii (1950), cols. 611–13.

CORPUS EVANGELICORUM. A body of delegates from the Evangelical states in the *Holy Roman Empire whose aim was to defend the Protestant interests in the Imperial Diet. Its organization developed gradually, and did not finally crystallize until the Diet of Ratisbon (1653) after the end of the *Thirty Years War (1618–48), when 39 Protestant states were represented in the Diet. The Presidency was attached permanently to Saxony, a provision which created an awkward situation when in 1677 the Elector Friedrich August of Saxony became a Catholic. The 'Corpus Evangelicorum' continued to exist until the disappearance of the Holy Roman Empire in 1806. See also *Corpus Catholicorum*.

Resolutions from 1663 to 1752 ed. E. C. W. von Schauroth, *Sammlung aller Conclusorum, Schreiben und and Verhandlungen des Corpus Evangelicorum* (3 vols., Regensburg, 1751–3); continued by N. A. Herrich (ib., 1786). H. W. von Bülow, *Über Geschichte und Verfassung des Corporis Evangelicorum* (1795). A. Frantz, *Das katholische Directorium des Corpus Evangelicorum* (1880).

CORPUS IURIS CANONICI. The chief collection of *canon law in the W. Church before the promulgation of the *Codex Iuris Canonici in 1917. It was composed of (a) the 'Decretum' of *Gratian, a collection of canons of Councils and decrees of Popes put together in the middle of the 12th cent. by Gratian, a Bolognese monk. This collection had no authority other than that of the individual canons which composed it ; (b) the collection of *Decretals of *Gregory IX, composed at the command of that Pope by St. *Raymond of Pennafort, and intended as a supplement to the 'Decretum' of Gratian. It was divided into five books and promulgated between 1230 and 1234. In addition to the authority already possessed by its component parts, it received the further authority of Gregory IX; (c) the *Sext. A sixth book added to the Decretals of Gregory by *Boniface VIII; (d) the '*Clementines', a further collection compiled by *Clement V and promulgated after his death by *John XXII in 1317; (e) the '*Extravagantes' of John XXII, viz. the decrees of that Pope collected by a private person and published in 1325; (f) the 'Extravagantes Communes', the decrees of various Popes between 1261 and 1471. These several items are found in a single collection in printed editions from 1499 onwards, though the name did not come into general use till after Gregory XIII's bull 'Cum pro munere' (1 July, 1580).

Best ed. by E. Friedberg (2 vols., Leipzig, 1879–81). P. Torquebiau and G. Mollat in *D.D.C.*, iv (1949), cols. 610–64, s.v., incl. bibl.

CORRECTORY (Lat. *Correctorium*). In the Middle Ages, a book containing a set of variant readings for 'correcting' the corrupted text of the Latin *Vulgate Bible. The *Dominican and *Franciscan friars took an active part in the compilation and diffusion of such books.

CORRODY. Originally the right possessed by the benefactor of a religious house or his nominee to board and lodging within it. The term came also to be applied to pensions and other similar allowances (mostly in kind) made by the monastery to those who served its various needs or who, by the payment of a lump sum, had secured a corrody as a kind of annuity for life. Their prevalence was one of the causes of monastic impoverishment in the later Middle Ages.

On the etymology of the word see *O.E.D.* s.v. J. R. H. Moorman, *Church Life in England in the Thirteenth Century* (1945), pp. 46 and 269–71; K. L. Wood-Legh, *Studies in Church Life in England under Edward III* (1934), pp. 27–9.

COSIN, JOHN (1594–1672), Bp. of *Durham. He was a member of a wealthy family of *Norwich and educated at Caius College, Cambridge. After holding several other benefices he was collated to a canonry at Durham in 1625 and became rector of Brancepeth in Co. Durham in 1626. He was a personal friend of W. *Laud and R. *Montague, and as such incurred the hostility of the *Puritan party. This was increased when he published, in 1627, his famous *Collection of Private Devotions*, a book of prayers compiled at the instigation of *Charles I for the use of Queen *Henrietta Maria's English maids of honour. In 1635 he was elected master of Peterhouse, whose chapel he decorated acc. to High Church principles, and in 1640 he was appointed Dean of *Peterborough. The Long Parliament deprived him of all his benefices on account of his 'Popish innovations', and in 1642 he also lost the mastership of Peterhouse. In the same year he went to *Paris, where he became chaplain of the C of E members of the Queen's household. He was a friend of the *Huguenots, and engaged in bitter controversy with the RCs, disinheriting his son on his reception into the RC Church. After the Restoration he returned to England and was made Bp. of Durham in 1660. He attended the *Savoy Conference in 1661, trying in vain to bring about a reconciliation between the C of E and the Presbyterians. He was a friend of elaborate ritual, and at the Convocation of 1661 suggested several reforms in that direction, some of which were taken over into the BCP of 1662. A rigid disciplinarian, he used all the legal powers at his command to make both Puritans and RCs conform to the C of E in his diocese. He was also a keen business man who sanctioned the sale of offices in his patronage, and he was one of the three bishops who advocated divorce in cases of adultery. Most of his literary works are of a controversial nature, being directed esp. against RC doctrine. He attacked *Transubstantiation in his *Historia Transubstantionis Papalis* (written 1656, publd. 1675), and the inclusion of the so-called Apocrypha in the RC Canon of the Scriptures in *A Scholastical History of the Canon of Holy Scripture* (1657).

His works were publ. in the *Library of Anglo-Catholic Theology (5 vols., 1843–55), with Life in vol. i, pp. xiii–xx; G. Ornsby (ed.), *The Correspondence of John Cosin* (Surtees Society, lii for 1868, and lv for 1870, 1869–72). Modern life by P. H. Osmond (London, 1913). J. H. Overton in *D.N.B.*, xii (1887), pp. 264–71.

COSMAS AND DAMIAN, Sts. The patron saints of physicians. Nothing precise as to their lives seems discoverable, though it is unnecessary to suppose that their legend has a mythological basis founded on that of the 'Dioscuri'. Acc. to later tradition, the twin brothers practised their profession without claiming reward from their patients, and were hence known as the 'silverless' (ἀνάργυροι). Both are also supposed to have suffered martyrdom. Their Passion, which exists in several forms and languages, is late and historically valueless. Their cultus was firmly established in the E. in the 5th cent., and at

*Rome a church was constructed in their honour on the edge of the Forum out of a temple of Romulus, by Felix IV (526–530), with the saints depicted in mosaics. The two saints are mentioned in the *canon of the Roman Mass. Feast day, in the E., 27 Oct.; in the W., 27 Sept.

The Gk. and Lat. recensions of the Acta and Passio are enumerated in *B.H.G.* (ed. 1909), pp. 54–6, and in *B.H.L.*, i (1898–9), p. 297 f., and Suppl. (1911), p. 83 f. Discussion and extracts in *AA.SS.*, Sept. VII (1760), pp. 430–77. L. Deubner, *Kosmas und Damian*. Texte und Einleitung (1907). Evidence for growth of the cult in *AA.SS.*, Nov. II, pt. ii (1931), p. 528 f.

COSMAS INDICOPLEUSTES (Κοσμᾶς Ἰνδικοπλεύστης, i.e. 'Cosmas, the Indian navigator'; mid. 6th cent.), geographer. He was a merchant of *Alexandria who became in later life a monk. His 'Christian Topography' (Χριστιανικὴ τοπογραφία), in 12 Books *c.* 547, attacks the Ptolemaic system in favour of various fantastic astronomical doctrines intended to harmonize with a literal understanding of the Bible. The chief value of the book lies in its geographical information (esp. on *Ceylon) and its witness to the spread of the Christian Church at his time. His other writings, except for a few fragments on the Pss., have been lost. In exegesis Cosmas follows *Theodore of Mopsuestia; and it is possible that he was a *Nestorian.

Ed. princeps by B. *Montfaucon, O.S.B., *Collectio Nova Patrum*, ii (1707), pp. 113–345, from Vat. gr. 699, the oldest MS. (saec. viii–ix); repr. in J. P. Migne, *PG*, lxxxviii, 9–476. Crit. ed. by E. O. Winstedt, Cambridge, 1909. C. Stornaiolo, *Le miniature della Topografia cristiana di Cosma Indicopleuste Cod. Vat. gr. 699* (Milan, 1908). H. Gelzer, 'Kosmas der Indienfahrer' in *Jahrbücher für protestantische Theologie*, ix (1883), pp. 105–41; E. Peterson, 'Die alexandrinische Liturgie bei Kosmas Indicopleustes' in *Ephemerides Liturgicae*, xlvi (1932), pp. 66–74. Krumbacher, pp. 412–14, with bibl. Bardenhewer, v, pp. 95–8.

COSMAS MELODUS (b. *c.* 700), also 'Cosmas of Jerusalem' and 'Cosmas of Maïuma', author of Greek liturgical hymns. He was adopted by the father of St. *John of Damascus and educated by a monk, also called Cosmas, who also wrote poetry, whence a certain confusion regarding the authenticity of some of the poetry of the younger author. *C.* 732 he entered the *Laura of St. *Sabas nr. *Jerusalem, and in 743 became Bp. of Maïuma nr. Gaza. The most famous of his works are his '*canons' (κανόνες), odes in honour of the great Christian feasts such as *Easter, the *Nativity, and the *Exaltation of the Cross, of which 14 were incorporated in the liturgical books of the E. Church. He also wrote ἰδιόμελα, which are smaller poems, also dealing with religious subjects. His poetry is brilliant in form and metrical design, inspired by the language of the Bible and the doctrine of the Church, though the clarity of thought and expression is frequently impaired by the artificial structure of the verse. Cosmas is also most probably the author of a Commentary on the poems of St. *Gregory of Nazianzus, first publd. by A. *Mai in *Spicilegium Romanum*, ii. 2 (1839), pp. 1–306.

His 14 Canones are pr. in W. Christ–M. Paranikas (edd.), *Anthologia Graeca Carminum Christianorum* (Leipzig, 1871), pp. 161–204. His Comm. on the Carmina of St. Gregory Nazianzen repr. from A. Mai in J. P. Migne, *PG*, xxxviii, 339–680. Comm. on these canons by Theodore Prodromus (early 12th cent.; cf. Krumbacher, pp. 87 f., 749–60), publd. in part by H. M. Stevenson (Rome, 1885). On the canon on the Recovery of the Cross cf. H. J. W. Tillyard, 'A Canon by Saint Cosmas' in *B.Z.*, xxviii (1928), pp. 25–37 (with ed. of music).

COSMOCRATOR (Gk. κοσμοκράτωρ, lit. 'Lord of the World'). The word, taken from pagan religious vocabulary, is used by St. *Paul (Eph. 6. 12) in the plural for the devil and his demons (cf. Jn. 12. 31, 2 Cor. 4. 4). In Hellenistic writers, it was esp. employed of the supposed rule of malignant spirits over the powers of nature, and thus came to be used as a technical term for Satan, e.g. by the *Gnostics and *Marcion. In the system of *Valentinus the Cosmocrator was contrasted with the *Demiurge.

COSMOGONY (Gk. κοσμογονία). A doctrine or myth about the origin of the universe. The word is used esp. of the speculations of the early Greek philosophers and also of the pagan mythologies.

COSMOLOGICAL ARGUMENT (from Gk. κόσμος, 'world'). The argument which defends the existence of God from the existence of the world. Under this name are combined the first four of the *Quinque Viae (q.v.) of St. *Thomas Aquinas, in contradistinction to the fifth, the *Teleological Argument, and to the *Ontological Argument (q.v.) of St. *Anselm. The Argument, which goes back to *Aristotle, is based on the principle of causality. It contends that no satisfactory explanation of the data of experience can be given without assuming the existence of a self-sufficient primary cause responsible for the world of phenomena. It was attacked by D. *Hume, who denied the principle of universal causation, and by I. *Kant, who denied that this principle, which he admitted for the world of phenomena, could be applied to a reality beyond them. Despite these attacks (which are valid only in the context of certain presuppositions) the Cosmological Argument is still held to be among the most cogent of the proofs of the existence of God.

St. Thomas, *Summa Theologica*, part i, qu. 2, art. 3; R. Descartes, *Meditations*, 3; I. Kant, *The Critique of Pure Reason*, 'Transcendental Dialectic', i. 3. 5.

COSMOLOGY (Gk. κόσμος, 'the world'+ λόγος, 'a doctrine'). The part of *metaphysics which deals with the world, considered as a totality of phenomena in time and space. It was one of the accepted divisions of philosophy among thinkers of the *Aufklärung, and the word was adopted thence by I. *Kant, who denied, however, that its conclusions were capable of ultimate justification by the speculative intellect.

COTELIER, JEAN BAPTISTE (1627–86), French *Patristic scholar. In 1667 he was appointed by J. B. Colbert to assist with the cataloguing of the Greek MSS. in the Royal Library at Paris. His writings include a celebrated edition of the *Apostolic Fathers published in 1672, as well as *Ecclesiae Graecae Monumenta* (3 vols., 1677–86).

J. B. Martin in *D.T.C.*, iii (1908), cols. 1922–4.

COTTA. A shortened form of the *surplice reaching to the waist or a little lower, with less ample sleeves, and a square-cut yoke at the neck. In modern times it has virtually ousted the medieval shape of surplice in the RC Church, but the latter is being revived in certain places.

Braun, *L.G.*, pp. 136–46.

COTTONIAN LIBRARY. The large collection of MSS., state papers, and books brought together by Sir Robert (Bruce) Cotton (1571–1631). It was in the possession of his descendants until an Act of Parliament in 1700 (12 & 13 Will. III, c. 7) brought it under public control. In 1731, while housed at Ashburnham House, a large part of the collection was destroyed by fire. When the British Museum was founded in 1753, it was transferred to Bloomsbury, its present home. Among its many MSS. of theological and religious interest are the 'Cottonian Genesis' (Otho B, vi. 5–6; a MS. of the *Septuagint text but now surviving only in fragments) and the 'Lindisfarne Gospels' (Nero D. IV). The curious shelf-marks with the names of the Roman emperors were introduced when the books were arranged under a series of Imperial busts.

A Catalogue of the Manuscripts in the Cottonian Library deposited in the British Museum (1802).

COUNCIL. A formal meeting of bishops and representatives of several churches convened for the purpose of regulating doctrine or discipline. General or *Oecumenical Councils are assemblies of the bishops of the whole Church. The decrees of such General Councils are held to possess the highest authority which the Church can give, and RCs assert that such councils must be summoned, and their decrees confirmed, by the Pope. Local or 'particular' councils represent the various units—e.g. *provinces, *patriarchates, *exarchates—of the Church, but these are now more often called by other names, e.g. 'synods'. The first council of the Church was that described in Acts 15.

Of the many edd. of the Acta of Ecclesiastical Councils, the first was that of J. Merlin (2 vols., Paris, 1524). Later important collections include those of J. *Hardouin, J. D. Mansi, and E. *Schwartz (qq.v.). Fullest ed. of British Councils by D. *Wilkins (q.v.). C. J. *Hefele-H. *Leclercq, O.S.B., *Histoire des conciles* (1907 ff.).

COUNSELS OF PERFECTION, The. Traditionally three, viz. poverty, or complete renunciation of personal property; chastity, or complete abstention from sexual relations; and obedience, or complete submission of the will in all things, sin only excepted, to a superior. They form the basis of the religious life in nearly all its forms.

COUNTER-REFORMATION. The revival of the RC Church in Europe, usually considered as extending from about the middle of the 16th cent. to the period of the Thirty Years War (1618–48). Both the conception and the term itself have their dangers, since, though greatly stimulated by Protestant opposition, reform movements within the RC Church had begun almost simultaneously with the Lutheran schism, and the two reforming movements may be regarded with some justification as streams proceeding in reverse directions but from the same source. F. *Ximenes, G. *Savonarola, and M. *Luther himself, in his early career as a Catholic reformer, represent early stirrings of conscience within the Church against the abuses of the Renaissance age, but the new religious orders of the 1520s (*Capuchins, *Theatines, *Barnabites) should probably be regarded as the first organic signs of the Counter-Reformation. These orders preceded by some years St. *Ignatius Loyola's foundation of the *Jesuit Order, but after its confirmation by *Paul III in 1540 the latter organization rapidly became the spear-head of the movement both within Europe and as a missionary force in America and the East. The definitions of doctrine and minor internal reforms accomplished in the last session of the Council of *Trent (1562–3) sealed the triumph of the Papacy both over those Catholics, like the Emp. Ferdinand I and Charles IX of France, who wished for conciliation with the Protestants, and over those French and Spanish bishops who had opposed Papal claims. The Popes of the later 16th cent., notably *Paul IV, *Pius V, and *Sixtus V, took advantage of the *pax Hispanica* then reigning in Italy to improve discipline and efficiency within the *Curia and amongst the episcopate. With the *Inquisition they extended a Spanish conception of ecclesiastical discipline to Italy and elsewhere, while Spain under *Philip II, the strongest military power of the day, constituted itself the secular arm of the Counter-Reformation throughout Europe. If, however, the movement in its later stages appears increasingly a product of Spanish hegemony and national ideals, there can be no question regarding the apostolic zeal which continued to mark such leaders as St. *Francis de Sales and St. *Charles Borromeo, or regarding the spiritual qualities of the Spanish mystics. The all-pervasive zeal of the Jesuits, the co-operation of the Papal nuncios, the *Index Librorum Prohibitorum*, the skilful manipulation of the constitutional machinery of the Holy Roman Empire, and the conversion of several important princes were but a few of the factors making for success during the late 16th and early 17th cents. Within Europe the greatest triumph of the movement was the reconquest to the Roman obedience of S. Germany and Poland. In Central Europe the position was scarcely stabilized until the Peace of *Westphalia (1648).

M. Philippson, *Les Origines du catholicisme moderne*. La contre-révolution religieuse au XVIe siècle (Brussels, etc., 1884); A. W. Ward, *The Counter Reformation* (1889); B. J. Kidd, *The Counter Reformation, 1550–1600* (1933). R. V. Laurence, 'The Church and Reform' in *C.M.H.*, ii (1903), ch. xviii, pp. 639–89, with bibl., pp. 818–24. Fliche-Martin, xvii (1948) and xviii [when publd.]. There is also much material in the histories of the Popes by L. von *Ranke and L. *Pastor. J. H. Pollen, S.J., in *C.E.*, iv (1905), pp. 437–44, s.v., with bibl. See further bibl. to *Trent, Council of.*

COUNTESS OF HUNTINGDON'S CONNEXION. See *Huntingdon, Selina, Countess of.*

COURAYER, PIERRE FRANÇOIS LE
(1681–1776), French theologian. He became a *canon regular of St.-Geneviève at Paris in 1697, professor of theology in 1706, and librarian of St.-Geneviève in 1711. While at Paris he corresponded with Abp. W. *Wake on the subject of the episcopal succession in the English Church. In 1721 he completed a treatise defending the validity of *Anglican Ordinations, but the censorship caused publication to be delayed till 1723, when it was issued at Nancy, France (with the name of a Brussels bookseller on the title-page), as *Dissertation sur la validité des ordinations des Anglais et sur la succession des évêques de l'église anglicane, avec les preuves justificatives des faits avancés* (Eng. trans. D. Williams, 1725). In 1726 Courayer issued a reply to his many (esp. *Jesuit) critics. His thesis was then formally condemned by the French bishops, and in 1728 he was excommunicated and fled to England. He received for the rest of his life generous hospitality in England, though he never joined the C of E. In his will he professed his continued adherence to the Church of Rome, though dissociating himself from some of her tenets.

Courayer later publd. a new Fr. tr. of P. *Sarpi's *History of the Council of Trent* (2 vols., London, 1736; new ed., Amsterdam, 3 vols., 1751). His *Dissertation on the Validity of the Ordinations of the English* was issued in a revised trans. at Oxford, 1844, with a memoir of the author. *Relation historique et apologétique des sentiments et de la conduite du P. Le Courayer* (2 vols., Amsterdam, 1729). E. Préclin, *L'Union des Églises gallicane et anglicane*. Une tentative au temps de Louis XV. P. F. Le Courayer (de 1681 à 1732) et Guillaume Wake (1928). G. G. Perry in *D.N.B.*, xii (1887), pp. 328–30.

COURT OF DELEGATES. See *Delegates, Court of.*

COURT OF FACULTIES. See *Faculties, Court of.*

COURTENAY, WILLIAM (c. 1342–96),
Abp. of *Canterbury. The fourth son of Hugh, Earl of Devon, and through his mother great-grandson of *Edward I, he rose rapidly to high position in Church and state. In 1367 he was appointed Chancellor of Oxford and proved himself a vigorous upholder of the University's independence. In 1370 he was appointed Bp. of *Hereford, in 1375 Bp. of *London, and in 1381 Abp. of Canterbury. As archbishop he was a strong opponent of J. *Wycliffe and John of Gaunt and a supporter of Papal authority, save when national interests were directly attacked. He was responsible for the calling of the Blackfriars Council of 1382 which condemned Wycliffe's doctrines.

Register of William de Courtenay, Bp. of Hereford (A.D. 1370–5), ed. by W. W. Capes (Cantilupe Society, 1913; also in *Canterbury and York Society, xv, 1914). Short Life by T. S. Holmes in *Typical English Churchmen*, Series II (1909), iii, pp. 83–98. K. B. McFarlane, *John Wycliffe and the Beginnings of English Nonconformity* (1952 [1953]), pp. 70–80, 105–16 and passim. W. Hunt in *D.N.B.*, xii (1887), pp. 342–7.

COUSTANT, PIERRE (1654–1721), French
patristic scholar. He was a native of Compiègne, where he was educated at the *Jesuit College. After entering in 1671 the *Benedictine monastery of the *Maurist congregation of Saint-Rémi at *Reims, he was sent in 1681 to the abbey of *Saint-Germain-des-Prés in *Paris to help T. Blampin with the edition of St. *Augustine. His principal achievement, however, was his edition of the works of St. *Hilary (1693). It contains an elaborate preface, defending the orthodoxy of Hilary's doctrine, followed by a detailed biography of the saint; and the various treatises have separate prefaces giving information on their occasion, aim, and time of writing, and are carefully annotated. After a three-years' term as prior at Nogent-sous-Courcy he returned to Saint-Germain, where he was entrusted with the monumental undertaking of editing a complete collection of Papal letters from St. *Clement of Rome to *Innocent III. After more than twenty years of work the first volume of the *Epistolae Romanorum Pontificum*, covering the period from A.D. 67 to 440, appeared in 1721, with its erudite introductions and notes. The continuation of the work was prevented by his death. Coustant also wrote two treatises, *Vindiciae Manuscriptorum Codicum* (1706) and *Vindiciae Veterum Codicum* (1715), in defence of the *Maurist editions of the Fathers against the *Jesuit, B. Germon, who had questioned the genuineness of several of their sources.

M. Ott in *C.E.*, iv (1908), p. 454 f., s.v.; M. Lalmant, O.S.B., in *D.D.C.*, iv (1949), cols. 729–31, s.v., with bibl. See also works cited under *Maurists*.

COVEL, JOHN (1638–1722), also 'John Colvill' master of Christ's College, Cambridge. Born at Horningsheath, Suffolk, he was educated at Bury St. Edmunds and Christ's College, Cambridge, where he delivered a Latin oration on the return of the Stuarts. Appointed chaplain to the British Embassy at *Constantinople in 1669, he there amassed material for his unpublished diaries and future publications. On his return to England (1679) he was appointed Margaret Preacher of Divinity at

Cambridge, and in 1681 chaplain to the Princess of Orange at the Hague. He was master of Christ's from 1688 till his death, and vice-chancellor of Cambridge University in 1689 and 1708. His chief work on the Greek Church, *Some Account of the present Greek Church, with Reflections on their present Doctrine and Discipline, particularly on the Eucharist and the rest of their seven Pretended Sacraments* (1722), was published after many delays just before his death. Though not widely noticed it was one of the few books that gave information on the Greek Church till the 19th cent. Covel's Diaries and Collections are preserved in the British Museum.

'Extracts from the Diaries of Dr. John Covel, 1670–1679', ed. J. T. Brent, *Early Voyages and Travels in the Levant* (Hakluyt Society, lxxxvii, 1893), pp. 101–287. W. Hunt in *D.N.B.*, xii (1887), p. 355 f.

COVENANT. A bond entered into voluntarily by two parties by which each pledges himself to do something for the other. The idea of the covenant between the God of Israel and His people is fundamental to the religion of the OT. Some scholars hold that the original bond was simply the payment of sacrificial dues by Israel in return for the help of Jehovah in war, the symbol of the *Ark being esp. associated with His presence and covenant. The prophets press the truth that the perfect relation between God and man is based on the inward righteousness of the heart, and *Jeremiah (31. 31 ff.) looks forward to a new and ethical covenant. Christ takes this conception a step further when He shows that in His life and death is the perfect covenant between God and man, wherein men, instead of offering their own imperfect righteousness in exchange for the mercies of God, receive a supernatural gift of Divine grace whereby their righteousness may be made perfect. (The word διαθήκη is, in the NT, sometimes translated as 'covenant', sometimes as 'testament'.) This concept is fully worked out in the Ep. to the *Hebrews.

COVENANT, The National. See *National Covenant, The.*

COVENANTERS. The bodies of *Presbyterians in Scotland who in the 16th and 17th cents. bound themselves by religious and political oaths to maintain the cause of their religion. Various small covenants were signed between 1556 and 1562, leading up to the *King's Confession of 1581, which was signed by Scotsmen of all classes. In the next century, the attempt of *Charles I to introduce the Scottish Prayer Book of 1637 prompted the *National Covenant of 1638, which was very widely signed, and even professed loyalty to the crown. After the outbreak of civil war, the English Parliament made an alliance with the rebel Scots in the terms of a *Solemn League and Covenant (1643; often known simply as 'the Covenant'), which carried with it the attempt to force Presbyterianism on England, but, though temporarily successful, it led in the end to divisions among the Covenanters themselves. The persecution of the Presbyterians in Scotland between 1661 and 1688 gave rise to further new Covenants. When the Covenanting cause triumphed in Scotland on the arrival in England of William of Orange, certain of the more fiery Covenanters objected to the settlement, and formed the sect of the *Cameronians, which was joined to the *Free Church in 1876.

J. K. Hewison, *The Covenanters. A History of the Church in Scotland from the Reformation to the Revolution* (2 vols., 1908). H. D. Fleming, *The Story of the Scottish Covenants in Outline* (1904); J. Dodds, *The Fifty Years' Struggle of the Scottish Covenanters, 1638–88* (1860) and general works on history of Scotland.

COVERDALE, MILES (1488–1568), translator of the Bible. Ordained priest in 1514, he entered the house of the *Augustinian friars at Cambridge, where, under the influence of the prior, Robert Barnes (1495–1540), he became an enthusiast for ecclesiastical reform. After preaching against confession and images, he was forced to reside abroad, and in 1535 he produced on the Continent the first complete English Bible, a translation made from the *Vulgate, M. *Luther's Bible, W. *Tyndale's Pentateuch and NT, and other sources, and probably printed at Zürich. In 1538 he made a translation of the NT based solely on the Vulgate, and in 1539 he issued with R. Grafton the '*Great Bible'. After serving as pastor at Bergzabern, he returned to England, took part in the suppression of the W. Rebellion, and in 1551 became Bp. of *Exeter. He went into exile again in Mary's reign, returning in 1559. He assisted at M. *Parker's consecration, and for the rest of his life was a leader of the Puritan party. See also *Bible* (English Versions).

G. Pearson (ed.), *Writings and Translations of Myles Coverdale, Bishop of Exeter* (*Parker Society, 1844), with introd., pp. vii–xi; id. (ed.), *Remains of Myles Coverdale* (ib., 1846), with biogr. notice, pp. vii–xxiii. *Memorials of Myles Coverdale* (1836). H. Guppy, 'Miles Coverdale and the English Bible, 1488–1568' in the *Bulletin of the John Rylands Library*, xix (1935), pp. 300–38. J. F. Mozley, *Coverdale and his Bibles* (1953).

COWL. A garment with a hood (*vestis caputiata*) worn by monks. By St. *Benedict's time the cowl was composed of the cloak or mantle together with the hood, and this has now become the usual meaning of the word. The *Servites and the *Augustinian Canons, however, wear a cowl which is simply an unattached hood.

On the derivation and history of the word, see *O.E.D.* s.v. 'Cowl, sb.1'.

COWLEY FATHERS, The. A colloquial name for the priests of the Society of St. John the Evangelist (see *S.S.J.E.*), founded in the parish of Cowley, near Oxford.

COWPER, THOMAS. See *Cooper, Thomas.*

COWPER, WILLIAM (1731–1800), poet and hymn-writer. Born at Great Berkhamstead, where his father was rector, he was a pupil at Westminster School from 1741 to 1747. In 1748 he was entered at the Middle Temple and in 1754 called to the Bar. In 1759 he moved to the Inner Temple and was appointed Commissioner of Bankrupts; he was, however, more interested in literature than law. From this period his attacks of depression appear to date. Fear of an examination for a disputed appointment to the clerkship of the House of Lords in 1763 provoked a suicidal mania, prob. aggravated by a frustrated love for his cousin. His delusions began to take a religious colouring, and he was sent to a private lunatic asylum near *St. Albans. His terrors at first increased, but were gradually soothed by Dr. Nathaniel Cotton (1705–88) who was himself something of a poet. In 1765 he moved to Huntingdon to be near his brother, eventually residing with the Rev. Morley Unwin and Mary, his wife. He accompanied the latter to Olney on the death of her husband in 1767. Having become intensely devout since his illness, he worked as a lay assistant to the *Evangelical incumbent, John *Newton, at whose request he began composing hymns. A further attack of insanity (1773–6) prevented his marriage with Mary Unwin, who encouraged him to write secular poetry. In 1786 they moved to Weston, Bucks, and in 1795 to East Dereham. He does not seem entirely to have recovered from an attack of insanity in 1787, and suffered a serious relapse in 1794.

Cowper contributed his finest hymns to the 'Olney Collection', published in conjunction with J. Newton in 1779. They include 'God moves in a mysterious way' (written as a period of madness approached; first publd. 1774), 'Hark my soul! it is the Lord' (first publd. 1768; transl. into Italian by W. E. *Gladstone), 'O for a closer walk with God' (first publd. in 1772), and 'Jesus, where'er Thy people meet' (first publd. in the *Olney Hymns*). His secular poetry, much of which has a religious bent, is marked by a love of nature and a tenderness which foreshadows the romantics. This includes *The Task* (1785), the famous ballad of John Gilpin (publd. 1783) and *The Loss of the Royal George*. He also published a translation of Homer (1791) and began to translate J. *Milton's Latin and Italian poems (posthumously publd. 1808).

Collected Works, ed. J. Newton, 10 vols., London, 1817. Later edd. include those of R. *Southey (15 vols., London, 1835–7, and 8 vols., Bohn's Standard Library, 1853–5) and of W. Hayley and T. S. Grimshawe, 8 vols., London, 1835. Cowper first issued his (collected) Poems in 2 vols., London, 1782–5; many later edd., including those of H. F. Cary (London, 1839), J. Bruce (3 vols., 1865; Aldine ed.), and H. S. Milford ('Oxford Edition', 1905; 3rd ('standard') ed. 1926). Life and posthumous writings ed. W. Hayley (3 vols., Chichester, 1803–4); Life and Letters, ed. id. (4 vols., Chichester, 1809). Modern Lives include those of Goldwin Smith ('English Men of Letters, 1880), T. Wright of Olney (1892), H. I'A. Fausset (1928). Lord David Cecil, *The Stricken Deer* (1929); G. Thomas, *William Cowper and the Eighteenth Century* (1935); M. J. Quinlan, *William Cowper. A Critical Life* (Minneapolis, 1953). Bibl. by H. S. Milford in *C.B.E.L.*, ii (1940), pp. 341–3.

COWPER TEMPLE CLAUSE. The section (No. 14) of the *Education Act of 1870 dealing with the religious teaching to be given in the elementary schools constituted by the Act under public, instead of Church, control. The clause provided that in all such schools 'no religious catechism or religious formulary which is distinctive of any particular denomination shall be taught'. The clause reflects the influence of the National Education League and the *Broad Church Group, of which W. F. Cowper Temple (1811–88) was the chairman.

COX, RICHARD (*c.* 1500–81), Bp. of *Ely. He was educated at Eton and King's College, Cambridge, and held a number of ecclesiastical appointments. He sat on the commission which drew up the *King's Book (1543). On *Edward VI's accession, his reforming zeal came to the front. He helped in compiling the 'Order of the *Communion' of 1548, and the Prayer Books of 1549 and 1552; and he was also on the commission appointed in 1551 for reforming the *canon law. As Chancellor of Oxford (1547–52) and first Dean of Christ Church (1547–53), he was mainly responsible for introducing *Peter Martyr and other foreign divines into the university, and his alteration of statutes, diversion of funds, and destruction of books, ornaments, and MSS. in order to eradicate Popery won him the name of 'Cancellor' of the university. On *Mary's accession he was imprisoned for a time and deprived of preferments, and then went into exile at Frankfurt, where his successful disputes with J. *Knox gave rise to the names 'Coxians' and 'Knoxians'. Under *Elizabeth, he became Bp. of Ely (1559–80), but refused to minister in the Queen's chapel on account of its crucifix and lights. He was an honest but narrow-minded ecclesiastic; he was severe on Romanists, and impatient of *Puritans.

Several of Cox's letters are printed in the *Correspondence of Matthew Parker*, ed. by H. Bruce for the *Parker Society (1853), pp. 151 f. and 281 f.; in *The Zürich Letters*, ed. by H. Robinson for the Parker Society, i (1842), pp. 26–8, 65–7, 112 f., 207 f., 220 f., 234–8, 243–5, 268 f., 279–82, 282–6, 297–300, 306–9, 314–19, 328–30; ii (1845), pp. 41 f., 192–5; and in *Original Letters Relative to the English Reformation written during the Reigns of King Henry VIII, King Edward VI, and Queen Mary, chiefly from the Archives of Zürich*, ed. by id. for the Parker Society, i (1846), pp. 119–24. R. W. Dixon in *D.N.B.*, xii (1887), pp. 412–14.

C.P.A.S. ('Church Pastoral Aid Society'). A society founded in 1836 to assist the home mission work of the Anglican Church by making grants of money for the stipends of curates and men and women lay workers. Its sympathies are markedly Evangelical.

CRAKANTHORPE, RICHARD (1567–1624), *Anglican divine. He was educated at Queen's College, Oxford, where he was elected Fellow in 1598. Here he became a disciple of J. *Rainolds and a learned defender of *Puritan principles. Early in the reign of *James I he accompanied the ambassador, Lord Evers, to the court of the Emp. Rudolph II. In 1605 he was appointed rector of Black Notley, nr. Braintree, Essex, and in 1617 rector of Paglesham. He interested himself esp. in the Romanist controversy. His principal work, *Defensio Ecclesiae Anglicanae* (1625; posthumous), was an answer to the *Sui Reditus ex Anglia Consilium* of M. A. *de Dominis, in which the Abp. of Spalato had defended his recantation. It was a learned work and written in excellent Latin, but its tone was ferocious and the argument too closely dependent on de Dominis's text to allow Crakanthorpe to develop his own views. His other writings include books on metaphysics (1619) and logic (1622) and a *Defence of Constantine with a Treatise of the Pope's Supremacy* (1621).

Modern ed. of his *Defensio Ecclesiae Anglicanae* [by C. Wordsworth] in L.A.C.T. (1847). His treatise 'Of the Pope's Temporal Monarchy' is printed in J. Brogden, *Catholic Safeguards Against the Errors, Corruptions and Novelties of the Church of Rome*, iii (1851), pp. 44–109. G. G. Perry in *D.N.B.*, xiii (1888), p. 2 f.

CRAMER, JOHN ANTONY (1793–1848), Dean of *Carlisle. Educated at Christ Church, he became Principal of New Inn Hall, Oxford, in 1831, Regius professor of modern history in 1842 (in succession to T. *Arnold), and Dean of Carlisle in 1844. Besides several classical writings he published the '*Catenae' of many of the Greek fathers on the NT (8 vols., 1838–1844).

[He is to be distinguished from Johann Andreas Cramer (1723–88), who translated St. *Chrysostom's Homilies into German (1748–1751).]

CRANACH, LUCAS (1472–1553), 'the Elder', German painter. In his youth he was celebrated as a painter of altar-pieces and all his life of portraits. In the very early days of the *Reformation he espoused the *Lutheran cause, and was a friend and admirer of M. *Luther and the other reforming leaders, several of whom he painted. He also produced many woodcuts of religious subjects. His zeal for the new ideas is shown in a picture now at Leipzig, and dated 1518, which shows the soul of a dying man rising to meet the Trinity, in illustration of the doctrine of *justification by faith alone.

M. J. Friedlander and J. Rosenberg (edd.), *Die Gemälde von Lucas Cranach* (1932), and H. Posse, *Lucas Cranach d. A.* (Vienna, 1942).

CRANMER, THOMAS (1489–1556), Abp. of *Canterbury. Born at Aslacton, Notts, he was educated at Jesus College, Cambridge, of which he became a Fellow, and was ordained in 1523. When it seemed likely that the royal divorce proceedings against Catherine of Aragon in 1529 would break down, Cranmer's suggestion to two of the King's advisers that the universities of Europe might be consulted so gratified *Henry VIII that he determined to employ Cranmer in his service. Soon after, while on an embassy to the Emp. *Charles V, he met and secretly married (1532) Margaret

Osiander, the niece of Andreas *Osiander, the *Lutheran reformer.

On his return, Cranmer was appointed in 1532 to the see of Canterbury in succession to W. *Warham. He accepted the office with the greatest reluctance, but it was soon clear that he was to be Henry's chief instrument for overthrowing the Papal supremacy in England. In 1533 he annulled Catherine's marriage with Henry and three years later pronounced a similar judgement on the King's marriage with Anne Boleyn. He also married Henry to and divorced him from Anne of Cleves. But despite this apparent subordination and subservience to the King's will, he acted not only at the behest of Henry but also in conformity with his own opinions. He was partly responsible for the '*Ten Articles' and for the dissemination of the Bible in the vernacular. On the other hand, he took relatively little part in the *dissolution of the monasteries and opposed the '*Six Articles' of 1539, under which, indeed, he had to banish his own wife (whom he had already kept in seclusion).

After Henry's death (1547), Cranmer became one of the most influential counsellors of the young *Edward VI. His ideas more and more developed in a Protestant direction. This is esp. noticeable in his attitude to the Eucharist, on which he had taken up a more or less *Zwinglian standpoint. On his initiative a number of Continental theologians, among them P. *Martyr and M. *Bucer, were invited to England, and Cranmer continued in other ways to push forward his project for union with the reforming Churches of Europe. He was largely responsible for the abolition of the old Church ceremonies, for the destruction of images and other relics, for the BCP of 1549 (the greatest monument of his genius) and that of 1552, as well as for the '*Forty-Two Articles'. He disagreed with Northumberland, Edward's unscrupulous adviser, and with reluctance acknowledged Lady Jane Grey as Edward's successor.

On the accession of *Mary Tudor (1553), Cranmer, who had indeed been partly responsible for the tragedy of her mother's life, was accused of high treason, tried and sentenced, but the Queen spared his life. He was, however, imprisoned and finally tried for heresy. He was sentenced and degraded, but then made several recantations affirming his belief in *transubstantiation and in the Papal supremacy. These were written, as he later asserted, 'for fear of death', but it was only a temporary lapse. He renounced his recantations and died at Oxford at the stake on 21 Mar. 1556, showing great courage.

Cranmer has been frequently accused of inconsistency, weakness, and timidity. But he was a convinced *Erastian, and he held to his Erastianism with great sincerity and tenacity. And if his own views on ecclesiastical matters continued to change in conformity with those of the crown, that was his good fortune. It was his very Erastianism which put him in a curious dilemma in Mary's reign when the sovereign herself accepted Papal supremacy. For one reason, at any rate, his masterly English style, as expressed in the Prayer Books, in his *Homilies* and Litany, Cranmer's greatness will remain assured.

Works ed. H. Jenkyns, *The Remains of Thomas Cranmer* (4 vols., Oxford, 1833). *Miscellaneous Writings and Letters* also ed. E. Cox (*Parker Society, 1846); *Writings and Disputations . . . Relative to the Sacrament of the Lord's Supper,* ed. id. (ib., 1844). Cranmer's *Defence of the True and Catholic Doctrine of the Last Supper* also ed. [C. H. H. Wright] (London, 1907). A MS. showing his early attempts to frame the offices of *Mattins and *Evensong was ed. J. W. Legg, *Cranmer's Liturgical Projects* (H.B.S., vol. l; 1915), with introd. The principal source for his life, apart from the Calendars of the State Papers (see bibl. to *Henry VIII*), is the biography by J. *Strype (London, 1694). The MS. which forms the basis of the account by J. *Foxe is ed. J. G. Nicholas, *Narratives of the Days of the Reformation* (Camden Society [first series], lxxvii; 1859), pp. 218–33. Modern lives by H. J. Todd (2 vols., London, 1831), C. H. Collette (ib., 1887), A. J. Mason (ib., 1898), A. D. Innes (Edinburgh, 1900), A. F. Pollard (New York and London, 1904), C. H. Smyth (Cambridge, 1926), A. C. Deane (London, 1927), and H. *Belloc (ib., 1931). F. E. Hutchinson, *Cranmer and the English Reformation* (1951). J. *Gairdner in *D.N.B.*, xiii (1888), pp. 19–31.

CRASHAW, RICHARD (c. 1613–49), English lyrical and religious poet. The son of a Puritan divine, he was educated at Charterhouse and at Pembroke Hall, Cambridge, where he came under the influence of many High Church friends, esp. N. *Ferrar whom he often visited at *Little Gidding. He was elected to a fellowship at Peterhouse in 1637, but expelled in 1644 owing to his refusal to subscribe to the *National Covenant. He then fled to France where he was received into the RC Church. In 1646 his friend, A. Cowley, found him in great destitution at Paris and persuaded Queen *Henrietta Maria to exert her influence on his behalf. As a result he went to Italy where he became an attendant to Card. Palotta. Owing to his denunciation of some persons of the cardinal's household he had to leave Rome for *Loreto in 1649 where he had obtained a small benefice. He died there soon afterwards. His poetry, collected in *Steps to the Temple* (1646) and *Carmen Deo Nostro* (1652), is filled with a devotion nourished on the Song of Solomon and the mysticism of St. *Teresa. His style, though often somewhat heavy and diffuse, is vivid with unusual imagery as in the famous 'Wishes to his Supposed Mistresse', and expressive of ardent religious feeling as in the fervent 'Hymn to St. Teresa', which inspired S. T. *Coleridge's 'Cristabel'. Crashaw exercised a considerable influence on other later poets such as J. *Milton and A. Pope.

L. C. Martin (ed.), *The Poems English, Latin and Greek of Richard Crashaw* (1927), incl. list of earlier eds.; review by F. E. Hutchinson, 'Richard Crashaw, "Poet and Saint"', in *Church Quarterly Review*, cvi (1928), pp. 140–55. Studies on his poetry by R. C. Wallerstein (University of Wisconsin Studies in Language and Literature No. 7, Madison, 1935), [E.] A. Warren (Louisiana, 1939) and T. Foy (Dublin, 1933). F. E. Hutchinson in *C.B.E.L.*, i, p. 456 f.

CREATION. In theology, the notion that the Universe was brought into being out of nothing by the free act of God, hence termed the Creator.

This doctrine, esp. characteristic of the Hebrew-Christian tradition, is to be contrasted with such theories as *Pantheism and emanationism on the one hand and *Dualism on the other. Since it finds a place at once for Divine Transcendence and Divine Immanence, it is closely linked with the philosophical position known as *Theism (q.v.) with its insistence on Personality in God. Its corollary is belief in the contingency of the world. And since on this view creatures owe their being to God, they partake of His goodness and hence are to be accounted 'very good' (Gen. 1. 31).

When fully elaborated the belief is clearly incompatible with the view that in constructing the universe God made use of pre-existing matter (*Plato). Certain Fathers, however, notably *Justin (*Apol.*, i. 59) and *Clement of Alexandria (*Strom.*, v. 14), accepted this Platonic view, finding support for it in Wisd. Sol. 11. 17. Clement, indeed, held that Plato derived his teaching from *Moses. But it was rejected in favour of the view of creation 'out of nothing', e.g. by *Theophilus of Antioch (*Apol. ad Autolycum*, ii. 4); and it received its death-blow in the conflict with *Gnosticism. Hence from the end of the 2nd cent. the thesis of creation *ex nihilo* was almost universally accepted in the Church. It was dogmatically formulated at the Fourth *Lateran Council of 1215, and reaffirmed by the *Vatican Council of 1870.

Though a doctrine of Creation does not as such require that the world took its beginning in or with time, Christian theologians in general have decisively rejected the eternity of the universe. But they have commonly held its temporal origin is capable of being established only through revelation (cf. Gen. 1). St. *Thomas Aquinas, e.g., asserted that it was incapable of rational proof, being 'credible, but not demonstrable or knowable' (*credibile, non autem demonstrabile vel scibile*, Cont. Gentiles, ii. 38). Similarly in the 18th cent. I. *Kant, in his famous section on the 'Antinomies' in the *Critique of Pure Reason*, upheld the incompetence of reason to prove either the creation of the world in time or the contrary. It should, however, be added that there has been a tendency in modern Christian theology to conceive of creation as a continuous process through time rather than as having been completed by a single Divine *fiat* once in the remote past.

The changes in the traditional picture of creation brought about by increased scientific knowledge (astronomical, geological, palaeontological, biological) since the beginning of the 19th cent. have at times caused much religious unsettlement to orthodox Christians. But though they must radically affect our view of the order, dating, and character of the events (and hence also the degree to which the OT can be conceived as a scientific book), they hardly touch the fundamental philosophical questions which surround the notion of creation. These remain in essentials unaffected. In still more recent times it has often been suggested that the whole question is put into a new light by modern physics (relativity, etc.), on the ground that it is now possible to measure the dimensions of the Universe in both space and time. But even here the philosopher may do well to consider how far scientific observations, which presuppose certain inherited conceptions about the nature of space and time, can themselves overthrow these presuppositions, and may hence doubt whether they can have any real bearing on the metaphysical issues involved.

Classical medieval discussion by St. Thomas Aquinas, *Cont. Gent.*, II, qq. vi–xxxviii, and *Summa Theol.*, I, qq. xliv–xlvi. F. *Suarez, S.J., *De Opere Sex Dierum* (2 vols., Lyons, 1621); D. *Petavius, S.J., *Theologica Dogmatica*, iii (Paris, 1644), pp. 220–585 ('De Opificio Sex Dierum'). Modern RC doctrine was summarized by the Vatican Council of 1870, Sess. III, can. 1 ('De Deo Rerum Omnium Creatore'). A. D. Sertillanges, O.P., *L'Idée de création et ses retentissements en philosophie* (1945). F. P. Siegfried in *C.E.*, iv (1908), pp. 470–5, s.v.; H. Pinard in *D.T.C.*, ii (1908), cols. 2034–201, s.v.; J. Strahan in *H.E.R.E.*, iv (1911), pp. 226–31, s.v.; C. Boyer, S.J., in *E.C.*, iv (1950), cols. 814–25, s.v. 'Creazione I', all with bibl. See also bibls. to *Metaphysics*, *Theism*, and comms. on *Genesis*.

CREATIONISM, also 'Creatianism', the doctrine that God creates *de nihilo* a fresh soul for each human individual at its conception or birth. It is opposed to *Traducianism (q.v.) which maintains that the soul is generated with the body, as well as to any doctrine of the soul's pre-existence (e.g., that in W. *Wordsworth's 'Ode to Immortality'). It was vigorously upheld by St. *Jerome as alone compatible with Catholic theology, though he admitted that the W. tradition (*Tertullian, etc.) was in favour of Traducianism. It was also defended by St. *Hilary and the medieval theologians generally, who accepted *Peter Lombard's formula *catholica ecclesia animas docet in corporibus infundi et infundendo creari* (*Sent.*, lib. ii, d. 18, n. 8); and St. *Thomas Aquinas (*Summa Theol.*, i, q. 118, a. 2) held the contrary doctrine heretical. Among Protestants, *Calvinists have tended to hold Creationism, *Lutherans Traducianism.

The word is occasionally used also for the doctrine that the world was created (as opposed, e.g., to *monism and *pantheism).

F. P. Siegfried in *C.E.*, iv (1908), p. 475 f.

CREDENCE. A small side table, also known as a 'credence table', usually placed permanently in the south of the sanctuary near the altar, to hold the bread, wine, and water to be used at the Eucharist, and other accessories of the service. The name (from Lat. *credo*, I believe, trust) seems to have developed from the use of the word for any side table on which meats were placed for tasting or assaying.

CREDITON. St. *Boniface (Wynfrith) was born here *c.* 680. In 909 it was created the see of a new bishopric covering Devonshire which was carved out of the diocese of *Sherborne. It was united *c.* 1040 with the see of Cornwall; and in 1049 (owing to exposure to pirates) Leofric, Bp. of Crediton from 1046, with the approval of *Leo IX, moved the see to *Exeter. The church of Holy Cross is a fine, mainly perpendicular, medieval building.

CREDO UT INTELLIGAM (Lat.), 'I believe so that I may understand'. A formula in which St. *Anselm summarized his conception of the relations between faith and knowledge (*Proslogion*, ch. 1). In essence it was the teaching of St. *Augustine.

CREED. A creed is a concise, formal, and authorized statement of important points of Christian doctrine, the classical instances being the *Apostles' Creed and the *Nicene Creed. Originally, candidates for baptism accepted a short formula of belief which varied in detail in different localities. By the 4th cent. these baptismal confessions had become more uniform and were everywhere tripartite in structure, following Mt. 28. 19. Finally, the Apostles' Creed in the W. and the Nicene Creed in the E. became, as they remain, the only baptismal confessions in use. The Council of *Nicaea (325) put in a credal form the profession of faith which it promulgated as a general standard of orthodoxy; and the use of creeds for this purpose rapidly spread in the 4th cent. The present practice of reciting the (Nicene) Creed at the Eucharist did not begin until the 5th cent., when it was introduced as a local custom in the E.

Texts in A. Hahn, *Bibliothek der Symbole und Glaubensregeln der alten Kirche* (ed. 3, revised by G. L. Hahn, 1897). The best single handbook on the whole subject is J. N. D. Kelly, *Early Christian Creeds* (1950). Other textbooks by A. E. Burn (London, 1899; also three separate volumes on the several creeds by the same author, 'Oxford Church Text Books', 1906–12), E. C. S. Gibson ('Oxford Library of Practical Theology', 1908), and F. J. Badcock (London, 1930; ed. 2, 1938). P. *Schaff, *The Creeds of Christendom*, with a History and Critical Notes (3 vols., New York, 1877). C. P. *Caspari, *Ungedruckte, unbeachtete, und wenig beachtete Quellen zur Geschichte des Taufsymbols und der Glaubensregel* (3 vols., Christiania, 1866–75); id., *Alte und neue Quellen zur Geschichte des Taufsymbols und der Glaubensregel* (ib., 1879). C. H. *Dodd, *The Apostolic Preaching and its Developments* (1936). D. van den Eynde, *Les Normes de l'enseignement chrétien* (1933). O. Cullmann, *Die ersten christlichen Glaubensbekenntnisse* (1943; Eng. tr., *The Earliest Christian Confessions*, 1949). H. Lietzmann, 'Symbolstudien, I–XIV' in *Z.N.T.W.*, xxi (1922), pp. 1–34, xxii (1923), pp. 257–79, xxiv (1925), pp. 193–202, and xxvi (1927), pp. 75–95. See also bibls. to *Apostles' Creed*; *Athanasian Creed*; *Nicene Creed*.

CREED, The Apostles'. See *Apostles' Creed, The.*

CREED, The Nicene. See *Nicene Creed, The.*

CREED OF PIUS IV. The formula, often called the **Professio fidei Tridentinae**, published by *Pius IV in the bull 'Injunctum nobis' of 13 Nov. 1564, and since that date imposed on every holder of ecclesiastical office in the RC Church. The Creed contains a summary of the doctrines promulgated at the Council of *Trent, among them the Tridentine doctrines of the relation between Scripture and tradition, of original sin and justification, of the Mass and the *seven sacraments, of the saints, of *indulgences, and of the primacy of the Roman see. The form of it was slightly modified in 1877 so as to include subscription also to the decrees of the *Vatican Council.

The Creed, which is pr. in the main collections of conciliar decrees, is repr. in Denz.–Bann (ed. 1946), pp. 346–9 (Nos. 994–1000). Eng. tr. in Bettenson, pp. 372–4.

CREED OF ST. ATHANASIUS. See *Athanasian Creed.*

CREEPING TO THE CROSS. See *Cross, Veneration of the.*

CREIGHTON, MANDELL (1843–1901), Bp. of London. Educated at Merton College, Oxford, of which he became a Fellow and Tutor, he devoted himself to historical work, delivering lectures on ecclesiastical, Italian, and Byzantine history. In 1870 he was ordained to the diaconate and in 1875 was appointed Vicar of Embleton, Northumberland, where he became friendly with the Greys of Howick and Fallodon. In 1884 he was elected to the Dixie professorship of ecclesiastical history at Cambridge and to a fellowship at Emmanuel College. During his tenure of the professorship he continued his great but uncompleted work on the *History of the Papacy* (5 vols., London, 1882–94), a clear, dispassionate, and erudite study, and acted as first editor of the *English Historical Review* on its foundation in 1886. In 1891 he succeeded W. C. Magee as Bp. of *Peterborough and six years later was translated to London. His episcopate was marked by statesmanship, scrupulous efficiency, and tact, esp. in dealing with the conflicts between *Ritualists and *Kensitites.

Mandell Creighton, his Life and Letters, by Mrs. [Louise] Creighton [his wife] (2 vols., 1904). G. W. Prothero in *D.N.B.,* Suppl. ii (1901), pp. 82–8.

CREMATION. Disposal of the dead by reducing the body to ashes. The practice was not common in primitive times, but in the ancient civilized world it was the normal custom except in Egypt, Judaea, and China. Belief in the *resurrection of the body made cremation repugnant to the early Christians, whose use of burial is attested by the evidence of the *catacombs at *Rome. By the 5th cent. Christian influence had caused it to be abandoned throughout the Roman Empire. It was revived in the 19th cent., largely in freethinking circles, though among some Christians it has now come into favour. The RC Church forbids its members to dispose of their dead in this way, mainly on account of the associations of the practice (*CIC* 1203, 1240); but passive assistance at a cremation is tolerated, and the matter is held to be one of ecclesiastical discipline rather than of Divine precept or of natural law. No other Christian body has legislated in the matter.

E. Valton in *D.T.C.,* iii (1908), cols. 2310–23, s.v. 'Crémation'; H. *Leclercq, O.S.B., in *D.A.C.L.,* vii (pt. 1; 1926), cols. 502–8, s.v. 'Incinération'; –. Schian in *R.G.G.* (ed. 2), ii (1928), cols. 572–4, s.v. 'Feuerbestattung'; P. Palazzini in *E.C.,* iii (1950), cols. 838–42, s.v. 'Cremazione', all with bibls.

CREMER, HERMANN (1834–1903), German Protestant theologian. In 1870 he was elected to a professorship at Greifswald (an office he combined with a pastorate in the city until 1890), and held this till his death, refusing further preferment. He strongly resisted the liberalizing movement in theology, and in *Die paulinische Rechtfertigungslehre* (1899) reaffirmed a traditionalist interpretation of St. Paul's teaching about redemption. His best-known work, is his lexicon to the NT (Eng. trans., *Biblico-Theological Lexicon of NT Greek,* 1878), a forerunner of G. *Kittel's *Theologisches Wörterbuch zum Neuen Testament.*

K. M. A. Kaehler, *Wie Hermann Cremer wurde?* Erinnerungen eines Genossen (Beiträge zur Förderung christlicher Theologie, Jahrg. viii, Hft. 1, 1904); E. Cremer, *Hermann Cremer. Ein Lebens- und Charakterbild* (1912).

CRIB, Christmas. By popular custom in the W. Church, a representation of the crib (or manger) in which Jesus was laid at His birth (Lk. 2. 7), containing a model of the Holy Child, is placed on Christmas Eve (24 Dec.) in church, where it remains until the octave day of the *Epiphany (13 Jan.). Figures of the BVM and St. *Joseph, cattle, angels, and shepherds are usually included, and figures of the *Magi are added on the Epiphany (6 Jan.). St. *Francis of Assisi is thought to have made the first model of the crib at Greccio in 1223. The traditional site of Christ's birth is crowned with the Church of the Nativity at *Bethlehem, and the reputed remains of His crib are preserved at *Santa Maria Maggiore in *Rome.

R. Berliner, *Denkmäler und Krippenkunst* (21 Lfgg., 1926–30); E. Guardascione, *Il presepe* (1934). H. *Leclercq, O.S.B., in *D.A.C.L.,* i (pt. 2; 1907), cols. 2047–59, s.v. 'Âne'; ii (pt. 1; 1910), cols. 966–71, s.v. 'Bœuf', and iii (pt. 2; 1914), cols. 3022–9, s.v. 'Crèche'; B. Bagatti, E. Josi, E. Lavagnino, and V. Mariani in *E.C.,* ix [c. 1952], cols. 1970–5, s.v. 'Presepe'.

CRISIS, Theology of. Another name for the *Dialectical Theology of K. *Barth and his disciples, based on a triple set of associations of the Greek word κρίσις, viz. (1) 'separation', i.e. the sharpness of the dialectical distinction between temporal history and God's Eternity; (2) 'judgement', i.e. God's sentence of condemnation on all human effort and achievement; and (3) 'catastrophe', i.e. the suddenness and finality of that Divine verdict.

CRISOM. See *Chrysom.*

CRISPIN and CRISPINIAN, Sts. (c. 285), martyrs. Acc. to the purely legendary account of their martyrdom, they were two Christian brothers who came of a noble Roman family. During the persecution of *Diocletian they fled to Soissons where they set up as shoemakers, taking for their work only such money as was freely offered them, and finally were put to death. They are held to be the patrons of shoemakers, cobblers, and other leather-workers. Another tradition connects them with Faversham in Kent. Feast day, 25 Oct.

Martyrium and other material, with full commentary, in *AA.SS.,* Oct. XI (1864), pp. 495–540. A. *Butler (ed. by

H. Thurston and D. Attwater), *The Lives of the Saints*, x (1936), pp. 331–3.

CRITICAL APPARATUS (Lat. *Apparatus criticus*). In printed editions of texts (e.g. of the Greek NT), a list of MS. readings differing from those in the accepted text. The apparatus is commonly printed at the foot of the page. The first edition of the Greek NT to contain a critical apparatus was that of R. *Stephanus (1550); the fullest is that in the 8th and last edition of C. *Tischendorf (1869–72), though a revision of this is now in progress (Mk., 1935; Mt. 1940; both ed. S. C. E. Legg).

'CRITIQUE OF PURE REASON', The. The treatise in which I. *Kant set out for the first time the principles of the 'Critical Philosophy'. It was published at Riga in 1781. A much-altered 2nd edition appeared in 1787. Its difficulties and apparent contradictions are probably to be largely explained by the fact that its composition was extended over a period of ten or eleven years and that it incorporates drafts representing several stages in the development of the philosopher's beliefs.

The best Eng. tr. is that of N. K. Smith (London, 1929). The standard commentaries are those of H. Vaihinger (2 vols., Stuttgart, 1881–2) and, in English, by N. K. Smith (London, 1918). See also bibl. to *Kant, I*.

CRITOPULOS, Metrophanes. See *Metrophanes Critopulos.*

CROCE, BENEDETTO (1866–1952), Italian philosopher. He came under the influence of *Hegelianism while a law student at Rome and from 1886 onwards devoted himself to philosophical studies at Naples. His philosophy is a form of 'Creative Idealism' which concentrates on the forms taken by the life of the Spirit. Of these forms Croce recognizes four, viz. 'Intuition' (art), 'Concept' (science, philosophy, and history), 'Individuality' (economics), and 'Universality' (ethics). Religion he held to be a sub-form of Intuition, and Theology an illicit application of Concept, and both only transitory manifestations of the Spirit. His principal writings are the series collectively entitled *Filosofia dello spirito*, viz. I, *Estetica come scienza dell' espressione linguistica generale* (1902); II, *Logica come scienza del concetto puro* (1909); III, *Filosofia della practica. Economica ed etica* (1909); IV, *Teoria e storia della storiografia* (1917). Many of his writings have been translated into English.

Cinquant' anni di vita intellettuale italiana, 1896–1946, Scritti in onore di Benedetto Croce (ed. C. Antoni and R. Mattioli, 2 vols., Naples, 1950). The distinguished translators of Croce's works into Eng. include Cecilia M. Ady, D. Ainslie, E. F. Carritt, and R. G. Collingwood. Studies by G. Prezzolini (Naples, 1909), E. Chiocchetti (Milan, 1915), H. Wildon Carr (London, 1917), A. Aliotta (Naples, 1920), R. Piccoli (London, 1922). T. M. Knox in *Chambers's Encyclopaedia* (ed. 1950), iv, p. 255 f., N. Petruzzellis in *E.C.*, v (1950), cols. 1364–7, s.v. 'Filosofia dello spirito'.

CROMWELL, OLIVER (1599–1658), Lord Protector. Born at Huntingdon, he entered Sidney Sussex College, Cambridge, in 1616, married Elizabeth Bourchier, the daughter of a City merchant, in 1620, and was elected M.P. for Huntingdon in 1628.

The turning-point of his career was his election as M.P. for Cambridge in the Short Parliament of 1640, a position which he retained during the ensuing momentous Long Parliament. Henceforth he vehemently asserted the religious and political views of the *Puritan party which he combined with the fervent spirituality of the *Independents. Thus when the Civil War broke out (1642), it appeared to him no less than to *Charles I as a religious struggle. He built up a magnificently trained and disciplined fighting force—the 'New Model Army'—which he used with startling effect on the battlefields of Marston Moor (1644) and Naseby (1645). In politics he exercised his influence on behalf of the Independents against the rigid intolerance of the Presbyterians. After the defeat of the Scots (who had supported the King in the Second Civil War) at Preston (1648), he foresaw that the Puritan cause could not be finally successful without the removal of the King, and accordingly he now urged the necessity for his execution. Cromwell's name stands fourth among the signatures on Charles I's death warrant.

In the ensuing few years Cromwell used his army to repress any attempts at insurrection. The Irish revolt was crushed with a ruthlessness which can be understood only when it is remembered that in Ireland Cromwell saw the embodiment of RC-ism. He defeated the insurgent Scots on 3 Sept. 1650 at Dunbar and a year later to the day at Worcester. He had long been dissatisfied with the inefficiency and oligarchical ways of the Long Parliament, and on 20 Apr. 1653 he forcibly dismissed it.

Henceforward Cromwell, who was installed as 'Lord Protector' on 16 Dec. 1653 under the *Instrument of Government*, ruled England by a series of constitutional experiments—from 'Barebones' Parliament' of 140 'saints' to the Major-Generals—none of which really proved successful. Yet his rule was firm, efficient, and tolerant. The C of E was remodelled to some extent on Puritan lines (though the ecclesiastical organization was chaotic), and a committee of *Triers set up to eject unfit clergy. Attempts were also made to improve the morals and manners of the country, to further education, to reform the law, and to instil 'true godliness'. Yet it is doubtful whether his government could ever be truly called popular, for from the first there were signs of disaffection of one kind or another. Cromwell died on 3 Sept. 1658, the anniversary of the battles of Dunbar and Worcester, and was buried in *Westminster Abbey. At the Restoration his body was disinterred and hung at Tyburn.

Cromwell's character, a combination of rugged mysticism and practical efficiency, is not easy to interpret, nor have historians past or present reached any agreement about it. Perhaps Clarendon best summarizes it in the words 'He was one of those men *quos vituperare ne inimici quidem possunt nisi ut simul laudent'*. He believed that he was the instrument of a Divine providence: 'I have not sought these things; truly I have been called unto them by the Lord'. His conception of government was analogous to that of a 'constable set to keep the peace of the parish'. He was not without ambition, yet his refusal of the *Humble Petition and Advice* (urging him to take the title of king) shows that Mrs. Hutchinson's charge that the 'poison of ambition ulcerated Cromwell's heart' had no basis in fact. At times ruthless and at others magnanimous, he was undoubtedly the genius of the Commonwealth.

Letters and Speeches, ed. T. *Carlyle (2 vols., London, 1845; revised ed. by S. C. Lomas, with introd. by C. H. Firth, 3 vols., ib., 1904); new ed. by W. C. Abbot (4 vols., Cambridge, 1937–47). The best modern studies are those of F. Harrison ('Twelve English Statesmen', London, 1888), S. R. Gardiner (London, 1899), J. Morley (ib., 1900), C. H. Firth (ib., 1901), G. R. S. Taylor (ib., 1928), and M. P. Ashley (ib., 1937). More popular lives by J. Buchan (London, 1934) and H. *Belloc (ib., 1934). H. Kittel, *Oliver Cromwell. Seine Religion und seine Sendung* (Arbeiten zur Kirchengeschichte, ed. H. Lietzmann, ix, 1928). E. Barker, *Oliver Cromwell and the English People* (1937). C. H. Firth in *D.N.B.*, xiii (1888), pp. 155–86.

CROMWELL, THOMAS (c. 1485–1540), Earl of Essex. After an adventurous and probably ill-spent early life, he returned to England from the Continent, where he had served in the French army in Italy, and took up his father's trade as a cloth-dresser. For some time he seems to have combined this with legal work. Through the latter he gained the favour of T. *Wolsey and in 1523 he entered the House of Commons. In 1524 Wolsey made use of him for the suppression of a number of small monasteries to provide the endowment of his two proposed colleges at Ipswich and Oxford. On Wolsey's disgrace (1529), he entered the King's service and became a strong advocate of Protestantism and the royal supremacy in Church and State. His rise was rapid and in 1535 he was appointed Vicar General and became the chief adviser and instrument of the King in all ecclesiastical affairs. It was he who arranged for the visitation, and finally the *dissolution, of the monasteries between 1536 and 1539, and he also acted as the chief intermediary between Henry and the Reformation Parliament in which he sat as the M.P. for Taunton. In 1536 and 1538 he issued *Injunctions, ordering that a Bible should be provided in every church, that the clergy should perform certain definite duties, and that a register of births, marriages, and deaths should be kept. In his foreign policy he endeavoured to bring about the alliance of England with the Protestant princes of Germany, and with this in view he arranged a marriage between Henry VIII and Anne of Cleves. The king's disgust at the marriage and the fact that he now had no further use for Cromwell were the causes of his undoing; for though Cromwell had only recently been created Earl of Essex (7 Apr. 1540) and was the recipient of landed estates confiscated from the monasteries, he was arrested, sentenced for treason, and beheaded on 28 July 1540.

R. B. Merriman, *Life and Letters of Thomas Cromwell* (2 vols., 1902). A. Galton, *The Character and Times of Thomas Cromwell* (1887); P. Van Dyke, *Renascence Portraits* (London, 1906), ch. 3, pp. 138–258, with Appendix, 'Reginald Pole and Thomas Cromwell: An Examination of the Apologia ad Carolum Quintum', pp. 377–418; P. Wilding, *Thomas Cromwell* (1935). J. *Gairdner in *D.N.B.*, xiii (1888), pp. 192–202.

CROSIER. The crook-shaped staff of bishops, sometimes carried also by abbots and abbesses. Its origin has been traced by some to the rod used by Roman augurs in their divinations, by others to the ordinary walking-stick. It is first ordered as a liturgical ornament in the 7th cent. In the E. Church the crosier is surmounted by a cross between two serpents. The familiar W. form resembling a shepherd's crook is due to later symbolism. In the 19th cent., antiquaries often applied the term wrongly to the archiepiscopal cross.

K. Lind, *Über den Krummstab*. Eine archäologische Skizze (1863). C. Robault de Fleury, *La Messe*. Études archéologiques sur ses monuments, viii (1889), pp. 75–110, with plates DCXLI–DCLIII. P. Hofmeister, O.S.B., *Mitra und Stab der wirklichen Prälaten ohne bischöflichen Charakter* (Kirchenrechtliche Abhandlungen, Hft. 104; 1928), passim. R. Fage, 'Les Voiles de crosses' in *Mélanges offerts à M. Gustave Schlumberger*, ii (1924), pp. 477–86. P. Morrisroe in *C.E.*, iv (1906), p. 515 f., s.v.; J. Sauer in *L.Th.K.*, ii (1931), col. 378 f., s.v. 'Bischofsstab', both with bibl. On the Eng. word 'Crosier', cf. *O.E.D.*, ii (1893), p. 1191, s.v.

CROSS, Devotion to the. See *Exaltation of the Cross; Invention of the Cross; Veneration of the Cross.*

CROWLAND ABBEY. This monastery was founded on an island in the fens by King Ethelbald in 716 in honour of St. *Guthlac, who had lived as a hermit on the site. After a fire in 1091 it was rebuilt, and added to in the succeeding centuries. At the *Dissolution (1539), the east part of the church and the transepts were demolished, but the nave and aisles were used as a parish church until the end of the 17th cent. Then the roof and south aisle fell, and since that date the north aisle only has been so used. The Early English west front survives in a ruined state. The form 'Croyland Abbey' is also found.

Ingulfi Croylandensis Historia [ed. W. Fulman] (Rerum Anglicarum Scriptorum Veterum, i (1684), pp. 1–107); *Historiae Croylandensis Continuatio* (ib., pp. 451–593). W. *Dugdale, *Monasticon Anglicanum* [ed. J. Caley–H. Ellis–B. Blandinel, ii, 1819), pp. 90–126). R. Gough, *The History and Antiquities of Croyland Abbey in the County of Lincoln* (1783). F. M. Page, *The Estates of Crowland Abbey* (1934). Rose Graham in *V.C.H.*, Lincoln, ii, ed. W. Page (1906), pp. 105–18.

CROWN OF THORNS. One of the instruments of Christ's Passion (Jn. 19. 2). Its supposed preservation as a relic is first mentioned in the 5th cent., and in the 6th *Cassiodorus refers to it as one of the glories of the earthly *Jerusalem. The *Jerusalem relic is said to have been later moved to *Constantinople, and in the 13th cent. to have come into the possession of St. *Louis IX, King of France, who built the *Sainte-Chapelle at Paris (completed 1248) to house it. Acc. to other traditions it was broken up into smaller relics.

F. De Mély, *Exuviae Sacrae Constantinopolitanae* (Paris, 1904), pp. 165-440. J. E. A. Gosselin, *Notice historique sur la sainte couronne d'épines de Notre-Seigneur Jésus-Christ, et sur les autres instruments de sa passion, qui se conservent dans l'église métropolitaine de Paris* (1828); C. Rohault de Fleury, *Mémoire sur les instruments de la passion de N.-S. J.-C.* (1870), Book ii, ch. 3, pp. 199-224.

CROZIER. See *Crosier*.

CRUCIFIX. A model of the cross, bearing an image of the crucified Lord. Crucifixes are widely used as objects of private and public devotion in the W. In the E. their place is taken by crosses with flat likenesses, i.e. a form of *ikon. In pre-Reformation times the crucifix was common throughout the W. Church, esp. as the central object of the rood-screen, which ran across the entrance to the *chancel of many churches. As the central ornament of the altar it began to come into general use in the 15th cent., though it had occasionally been so used earlier; and this use of it is now almost universal in RC churches. In the C of E it was occasionally used on the altar after the Reformation, e.g. in Queen *Elizabeth I's private chapel, but instances are very rare until the liturgical revival in the 19th cent. Among Protestants, the sole body which habitually uses the crucifix is the *Lutheran Church.

J. Hoppenot. *La Crucifix dans l'histoire et dans l'art, dans l'âme des saints et dans notre vie* (1899). L. Bréhier, *Les Origines du crucifix dans l'art religieux* (1904); G. Schönermark, *Der Kruzifixus in der bildenden Kunst* (Zur Kunstgeschichte des Auslandes, Hft. lxii, 1908); G. de Jerphanion, S.J., *La Voix des monuments*. Notes et études d'archéologie chrétienne (1930), No. vii, 'La Représentation de la croix et du crucifix aux origines de l'art chrétien', pp. 138-64. C. Costantani, *Il crocifisso nell' arte* (1911). L. H. Grondijs, *L'Iconographie byzantine du Crucifié mort sur la croix* (Bibliotheca Byzantina Bruxellensis, i; [1941]). Braun, *A.G.*, pp. 466-92, with plates 88-92. O. *Marucchi, F. *Cabrol, O.S.B., and H. Thurston, S.J., in *C.E.*, iv (1908), pp. 517-39, s.v. 'Cross and Crucifix'; H. *Leclercq, O.S.B., in *D.A.C.L.*, iii (pt. 2; 1914), cols. 3045-3131, s.v. 'Croix et crucifix'; B. Leoni, E. Zocca, K. Rathe, E. Lavagnino and G. Carandente in *E.C.*, iv (1950), cols. 864-80, s.v. 'Croce', with bibl. E. J. Hunt, *English and Welsh Crucifixes 970-1550* (S.P.C.K., 1956).

CRUCIFIXION. Infliction of death by nailing or binding to a cross. It arose in the E., and was also frequently used by the Carthaginians. By the Romans it was much used as the extreme punishment for slaves, but it might also be inflicted upon any person who could not prove Roman citizenship. It was preceded by scourging. From the reign of Galba (A.D. 68-9) the lower orders among Roman citizens might also suffer this penalty. *Constantine abolished crucifixion as a legal punishment, but isolated instances are recorded later in the 4th cent. Some of the Christian martyrs under the Roman Empire suffered in this way; and (acc. to tradition) some, as St. *Peter, were crucified head downwards or, as St. *Andrew, on an X-shaped cross.

The Crucifixion of Jesus Christ between two thieves is recorded by all four Evangelists (Mt. 27. 35-8, Mk. 15. 24-7, Lk. 22. 33, Jn. 19. 18).

He was offered and tasted, but declined to drink, the potion of medicated wine provided by a group of charitable women in Jerusalem for such sufferers. The Ep. of *Barnabas, which compares the cross with the letter T, implies that the Lord's Cross was of the shape known as a 'crux commissa'. But the more general view, held e.g. by St. *Augustine (in Ps. ciii. 14) on the basis of Eph. 3. 18, was that it was a 'crux immissa', with the upright extending above the transom.

D. Smith in *D.C.G.*, i (1917), pp. 397-9, s.v.

CRUDEN, ALEXANDER (1701-70), compiler of the 'Biblical Concordance'. Born in Aberdeen, he was educated on rigid *Presbyterian principles, taking his degree from Marischal College, c. 1720. His subsequent life was marked by eccentricities bordering on insanity, apparently caused by disappointments in love; and he was several times put in confinement. Moving to London c. 1726, he was employed successively as a private tutor, a proof-corrector and French reader to the Earl of Derby. On dismissal from this last post, he established a bookshop in London in 1732 and was appointed bookseller to Queen Caroline in 1735. In 1736 he began to compile his Concordance (OT and NT), a task for which he was pre-eminently qualified by long study of the Scriptures, an ingrained conscientiousness, and esp. a habit of tracing words through the Bible for amusement. He completed the work in some eighteen months and presented a copy to Queen Caroline in Nov. 1737. The work remains the standard concordance for users of the AV. In later life Cruden set himself to reform the morals of the country. Calling himself 'Alexander the Corrector', a title prob. suggested by his work for the press, he even made application to Parliament (1755) for official nomination to the office. He published two further editions of the Concordance (1761 and 1769), as well as a number of religious pamphlets.

E. Olivier, *The Eccentric Life of Alexander Cruden* (1934). The earliest Life is that by A. Chalmers (8 pp.) prefixed to the 6th ed. of the Concordance (1810). W. D. Macray in *D.N.B.*, xiii (1888), pp. 249-51.

CRUETS. Vessels of glass or precious metal in which the wine and water for the *Eucharist are brought to the altar.

Braun, *C.A.*, pp. 414-40, with illustrations, plates 80-6.

CRUSADES. This title originated to describe the military expeditions undertaken by Christians of the 11th, 12th, and 13th cents. for the recovery of the *Holy Land from Islam. The name comes from the cross which the Crusaders bore upon their clothing.

For many centuries after the Mohammedan capture of *Jerusalem (637), pilgrimages thither continued from W. Europe. In the 11th cent. difficulties began to arise owing partly to the schism of E. and W. in 1054, but more because of the capture of Jerusalem by the Seljukian Turks (1071), a fiercer race than the Arabs. Christians had never entirely given up the idea of the recovery of the Holy Places from the heathen, and during the two centuries preceding the first Crusade, the gradual expulsion of the Arabs from Spain and Sicily held out some promise of success for an expedition to the E. The search for new trade routes to the E. was another factor tending to encourage the Crusades.

After the capture of Jerusalem by the Turks, an expedition was immediately undertaken against them by the E. Emperor who was speedily and disastrously defeated in battle, and in the same year (1071) almost the whole of Asia Minor, Europe's last bulwark of defence, passed into the hands of the infidel. An appeal for help was soon made from the E. to Pope *Gregory VII, but with little practical result. After repeatedly renewed appeals from the Emp. Alexius I Comnenus to *Urban II, the Pope on 27 Nov. 1095 delivered a great speech at the Synod of *Clermont which led to the beginning of the First Crusade.

I: 1096–9. Inspired by the Pope's appeal, preachers, the most notable of whom was *Peter the Hermit, travelled all over Europe stirring up the people to help in the recovery of the Holy Land. The First Crusade was predominantly French in character. Its leaders were Raymond of Toulouse, Bohemund of Otranto and his nephew Tancred, Godfrey of Bouillon, and Robert of Normandy. Their scattered and poorly organized followers drifted into *Constantinople where they joined Alexius. There were at once difficulties about the distribution of the spoils of the Crusade, but eventually the armies proceeded southwards into Palestine. In June 1098 *Antioch was captured and the discovery of the Holy *Lance encouraged the Crusaders. Quarrels at once broke out over the possession of the city and this delayed further progress. At last Jerusalem itself was besieged and captured on 15 July 1099. Godfrey of Bouillon was appointed 'Defender of the Holy Sepulchre' and in fact Governor of Jerusalem. On his death in 1100 he was succeeded by his brother, Baldwin, who established the Latin kingdom of Jerusalem and was crowned on Christmas Day, 1100.

II: 1147–9. The Latin kingdom of Jerusalem flourished for some years and extended its borders, but in 1144 *Edessa was captured by the Emir Zengi, and Pope *Eugenius III committed the preaching of a new Crusade to St. *Bernard of Clairvaux in 1146. In spite of the leadership of Louis VII of France and Conrad III of Germany, the expedition was a failure. Many of the Crusaders never reached the Holy Land at all, and Conrad returned to Germany in 1148 and Louis to France in the following year.

III: 1188–92. The years following the Second Crusade saw a gradual consolidation of Mohammedan power and the unification of the various sections under Saladin, who captured Jerusalem in 1187. When the news reached Germany, *Frederick Barbarossa swore, at the Diet of Mainz (1188), to under-

take a new Crusade, and he was joined by Philip Augustus of France and Henry II of England. Frederick was drowned in 1190 and the rivalries of the kings of France and England brought the Crusade little success. Eventually Richard I, who had succeeded his father as King of England, made a three-years peace with Saladin in 1192, and small bodies of Crusaders were allowed to visit the Holy Sepulchre.

IV: 1202–4. The Fourth Crusade was begun under the influence of *Innocent III and was diverted by Philip of Swabia into an expedition against Constantinople where a usurper was on the throne. The son of the dethroned emperor was established in his rightful place (1202), but was unable to reward his benefactors, who stormed the city, and in 1204 Baldwin of Flanders became the first Latin Emperor of Constantinople. Innocent III, dazzled by the apparent *fait accompli* of the reunion of E. and W., was prevailed upon to acquiesce in this affair. The effect, however, was merely to remove the bulwark which the E. Empire had formed against Islam, and to embitter further the relations of E. and W. Christendom.

In 1212 there took place the *Children's Crusade (q.v.).

V: 1217–21. At the Fourth *Lateran Council of 1215, Innocent III proclaimed a fresh Crusade for 1217. The military operations took place mostly in Egypt and resulted in the surrender of the Holy Cross in 1221 to the Christians.

VI: 1228–9. This Crusade took place under the leadership of the Emp. *Frederick II who was at the time excommunicated. In 1229 he secured by treaty possession of *Nazareth, *Bethlehem, and Jerusalem. In Jerusalem he crowned himself king on 18 Mar. 1229. For fifteen years the Holy City was in the possession of the Christians, but in 1244 it was finally lost to the infidel.

VII: 1248–54. In 1245, at the Council of *Lyons, Innocent IV preached a Crusade against the heathen and against Frederick II. In 1248 St. *Louis of France started out on an expedition against Egypt, where he was routed and captured in 1250. On his release he went to the Holy Land, but being unable to do much for the kingdom of Jerusalem he returned home in 1254.

VIII: 1270. The last Crusade was undertaken also by St. Louis with the aid of his brother, Charles of Anjou. An attack was made on Tunis, but St. Louis died there in 1270 and Charles concluded the Crusade by negotiation. Soon the whole of the former kingdom of Jerusalem passed into the hands of the Mohammedans.

The Crusades were a favourite subject for medieval writers; they were much inspired by the ideals of chivalry; and they gave rise to the foundation of the military orders of the *Templars and *Hospitallers.

The term Crusade has also been used in a wider sense for expeditions blessed by ecclesiastical authority against heretics and heathen.

The standard collection is *Recueil des historiens des croisades* publié par les Soins de l'Académie Royale des Inscriptions et Belles-Lettres. Historiens occidentaux (5 vols. bound in 6, 1844–89); Historiens grecs (2 vols., 1875–81); Documents arméniens (2 vols., 1869–1906); Historiens orientaux (5 vols. bound in 6, 1872–1906); Lois (2 vols., 1841–3). F. Wilken, *Geschichte der Kreuzzüge* (7 vols., 1807–32); J. Michaud, *Histoire des croisades* (7 vols., 1817–1822; Eng. tr., 3 vols., 1852). B. Kugler, *Geschichte der Kreuzzüge* (1880); T. A. Archer–C. L. Kingsford, *The Crusades* ('The Story of the Nations'; 1894); W. B. Stevenson, *The Crusaders in the East* (1907); L. Bréhier, *L'Église et l'orient au moyen-âge*. Les Croisades (1907). E. Barker, *The Crusades* (repr. from *E.B.* (ed. 11), s.v.; 1923). H. Pissard, *La Guerre sainte en pays chrétien*. Essai sur l'origine et le développement des théories canoniques (Bibliothèque d'Histoire religieuse, x; 1912); C. Erdmann, *Die Entstehung des Kreuzzugsgedankens* (Forschungen zur Kirchen- und Geistesgeschichte, vi; 1935); M. Villey, *La Croisade*. Essai sur la formation d'une théorie juridique (1942). R. Grousset, *Histoire des croisades* (3 vols., 1934–6); S. Runciman, *A History of the Crusades* (3 vols., 1951-4), with full bibl. for sources and modern works. W. B. Stevenson, C. L. Kingsford, and J. Passant in *C. Med. H.*, v (1929), pp. 265–333, with detailed bibl., pp. 867–71. H. v. Sybel, *Geschichte des ersten Kreuzzugs* (1841). R. Röhricht, *Geschichte des ersten Kreuzzuges* (1901); A. C. Krey, *The First Crusade* (Princeton, &c., 1921); F. Chalandon, *Histoire de la première croisade jusqu'à l'élection de Godefroi de Bouillon* (1925). R. Röhricht, *Geschichte des Königreichs Jerusalem, 1100–1291* (1898). C. Cahen, *La Syrie du Nord à l'époque des croisades et la principauté franque d'Antioche* (1940), A. S. Aiyiya, *The Crusades in the Later Middle Ages* (1938). J. Michaud, *Bibliothèque des croisades* (4 vols., 1829). H. B. Workman in *H.E.R.E.*, iv (1911), pp. 345–51, s.v., with bibl.

CRUSIUS, CHRISTIAN AUGUST (1715–1775), German theologian. He became professor of philosophy at Leipzig in 1744, and of theology 1750. He attacked the philosophies of G. W. *Leibniz and C. *Wolff as anti-Christian, and urged that their determinist doctrines were dangerous to morality. He also objected strongly to the view, which first became common in his time, that the books of the Bible should be studied on the same principles of criticism as other literature. His chief writings were his *Entwurf der notwendigen Vernunftwahrheiten* (1745) and his *Hypomnemata ad theologiam propheticam* (3 vols., 1764–1768). He was held in high regard by I. *Kant, whose ethical doctrines he probably influenced.

A. Marquardt, *Kant und Crusius* (Diss., Kiel, 1885); A. Seitz, *Die Willensfreiheit in der Philosophie des C. A. Crusius* (1899); H. Heimsoeth, *Metaphysik und Kritik bei C. A. Crusius* (1926). E. Schwarz–P. Tschackert in *P.R.E.* (ed. 3), iv (1898), p. 344 f., and H. Hoffmann in *R.G.G.* (ed. 2), i (1927), col. 1749 f.

CRUTCHED FRIARS (*Fratres Cruciferi*). An order of *mendicant friars of uncertain origin. They were established in Italy by 1169, in which year *Alexander III gave them an essentially *Augustinian rule. In 1244 they came to England, and similar orders are known to have existed from the 13th cent. in France and the Low Countries. It is possible that the name 'friars' or 'fratres' was adopted some time after the first foundation of the order, and the word 'crutched' or 'cross-bearing' clearly refers to the cross, which was prominent in the design of their habits. The order was finally suppressed by *Alexander VII in 1656.

C. R. Hermans, *Annales Canonicorum Regularum S. Augustini, Ordinis S. Crucis* (3 vols., 's Hertogenbosch, 1858). Heimbücher, i, pp. 419-22, and ii, p. 656 f.

CRYPT. A cellar or vault beneath a church, such as is often used as a chapel, or a burying-place. These uses no doubt date from the earliest ages of the Church, when Christian assemblies and services took place in the *catacombs or underground burying-places in Rome, the tombs of martyrs often serving as altars, and later as centres for pilgrimages. Sometimes, as at *Rochester Cathedral, the crypt is partly above ground.

CRYPTO-CALVINISM. The doctrine of the Reformer, Philip *Melanchthon (1497–1560), also known as '*Synergism' or 'Philippism'. Melanchthon had always been more moderate in his theology than M. *Luther, and after the latter's death in 1546 he advocated a policy of conciliation both towards the RC Church by accepting *Charles V's 'Interim' in matters that were indifferent, and towards the *Calvinists by softening Luther's dogmatism on the subject of the Eucharistic Presence. The strict Lutherans, led by *Flacius Illyricus, accordingly attacked them as secret ('crypto') Calvinists. The so-called *Adiaphoristic Controversy thus begun introduced those endless disputes among the Lutherans which were to be in the next generations a major cause of their political weakness.

M. A. Landerer and G. Kawerau in *P.R.E.* (ed. 3), xv (1904), pp. 322–31; A. Herte in *L.Th.K.*, vi (1934), col. 284 f.

CUDWORTH, RALPH (1617–88), *Cambridge Platonist. Born at Aller in Somerset, where his father was rector, he became successively Fellow of Emmanuel College, Cambridge (1639), Master of Clare Hall (to which he was appointed by the Parliamentary visitors, 1645), Regius professor of Hebrew (also 1645), and Master of Christ's College (1654). In addition he held the livings of North Cadbury from 1650, of Ashwell from 1662, and a prebendal stall at Gloucester from 1678. Perhaps the most distinguished representative of the *Cambridge Platonists, he was an opponent both of religious dogmatism and of atheism of the T. *Hobbes type. In his chief work, *The True Intellectual System of the Universe* (1678), a cumbrous composition which he never completed, he argued that the only real source of knowledge is the Christian religion. Religious truth was embodied in three great principles: the reality of the supreme Divine intelligence and the spiritual world which that intelligence has created, the eternal reality of moral ideas, and the reality of moral freedom and responsibility. It was in this way that Cudworth, who, as his conception of a 'Plastic Medium' indicates, was very strongly influenced by Platonic ideas, attempted to assert the necessity for a revealed religion against the atheism of his day. His ethical beliefs were worked out in his *Treatise concerning Eternal and Immutable Morality* (not published till 1731).

Cudworth's *True Intellectual System of the Universe* was tr. into Lat. by J. L. *Mosheim (2 vols., Jena, 1733); partly from this Lat. tr. the English was ed. by T. Birch, along with Cudworth's *Discourse concerning the true Notion of the Lord's Supper* (orig. publd. 1642) and two Sermons, as *The Works of Ralph Cudworth* (4 vols., Oxford, 1829), with account of his life and writings in vol. i, pp. 7–37. C. E. Lowrey, *The Philosophy of Ralph Cudworth* (New York, 1884); G. Aspelin, *Ralph Cudworth's Interpretation of Greek Philosophy* (Göteborgs Högskolas Årsskrift, xlix, pt. 1; 1943); J. A. Passmore, *Ralph Cudworth. An Interpretation* (Cambridge, 1951). F. J. Powicke, *The Cambridge Platonists* (1926), pp. 110–29. L. Stephen in *D.N.B.*, xiii (1888), p. 271 f.

CUIUS REGIO, EIUS RELIGIO (Lat.),

'In a [prince's] country, the [prince's] religion'. The formula adopted at the Religious Peace of *Augsburg (1555), by which the princes of the Empire were to be permitted to settle the religion of their own lands.

CULDEES.

This name, given to certain Irish and Scottish monks in the 8th and following cents., is derived more probably from the old Irish (*céle dé*) for 'companion' than from the Latin '*cultores Dei*' ('worshippers of God'). The Culdees appear to have been in origin *anchorites who, gradually banded together, usually into groups of thirteen (on the analogy of Christ and His Apostles). By the 11th cent. they had become indistinguishable from secular canons, and, having become hopelessly corrupt, were gradually superseded by *Canons Regular. In a few places, as at *Armagh, they managed to survive for a time side by side with the newcomers. They should probably be regarded as the last remnant of the old Celtic Christianity before it succumbed finally to the influx of Continental Catholicism. See also *Oengus, St.*

W. Reeves, *The Culdees of the British Isles, as they appear in History* (Dublin, 1864); id., 'On the Céli-Dé, commonly called Culdees' in *The Transactions of the Royal Irish Review*, Antiquities, xxiv (1873), pp. 119–263. J. von Pflugk-Harttung, 'Die Kuldeer' in *Z.K.G.*, xiv (1894), pp. 169–92. An ancient Litany of the Culdees in use in the monastery of Dunkeld is printed in A. W. Haddan–W. *Stubbs (edd.), *Councils and Ecclesiastical Documents Relating to Great Britain and Ireland*, ii (pt. 1; 1873), pp. 278–85. T. Jones Parry in *H.E.R.E.*, iii (1911), p. 357 f., s.v.; L. Gougaud, O.S.B., in *D.A.C.L.*, iii (pt. 2; 1914), cols. 3186–90, s.v., with bibl. J. F. Kenney, *The Sources for the Early History of Ireland*, i ('Records of Civilization, Sources and Studies', New York, 1929), esp. pp. 468–77. See also bibl. to *Oengus, St.*

CUM OCCASIONE.

The constitution of *Innocent X, dated 31 May 1653, condemning five propositions which embodied the dogmatic substance of *Jansenism.

Text in *Bullarum, Diplomatum et Privilegiorum Sanctorum Romanorum Pontificum Taurinensis Editio*, xv (Turin, 1868), p. 720 f. The condemned propositions repr. in Denz.–Bann. (ed. 1952), p. 360 f. (Nos. 1092–6); cf. notes on this text by J. Rivière in *Bulletin de Littérature ecclésiastique*, xliii (1942), p. 231 f. See also bibl. to *Jansenism*.

CUMBERLAND, RICHARD (1632–1718),

Bp. of *Peterborough and moral philosopher. Having turned from the study of medicine and anatomy to that of theology, he became Vicar of Brampton (Northants) in 1658, and of All Hallows, Stamford, *c.* 1667. In 1691, though little known as an ecclesiastic, he was appointed to the see of Peterborough, which he adminis-

tered faithfully, though without special distinction, for the rest of his life. His principal work, *De legibus naturae disquisitio philosophica* (1672), which, through being commended by S. *Pufendorf, established Cumberland's reputation abroad, was designed as a reply to T. *Hobbes. In it Cumberland maintained that the laws of nature are ethical and immutable, and that their root-principle was that of 'Universal Benevolence' (which he opposed deliberately to the 'Egoism' of Hobbes). He was the real founder of English *utilitarianism.

S. Payne, *A Brief Account of the Life, Character and Writings of . . . Richard Cumberland* (1720). E. Sharp, 'The Ethical System of Richard Cumberland and its Place in History of British Ethics' in *Mind*, N.S., xxi (1912), pp. 371–98. L. Stephen in *D.N.B.*, xiii (1888), p. 289 f.

CUNEIFORM (Lat. *cuneus*, 'wedge').

The characters of wedge-shaped or arrow-headed components in which the ancient Assyrian and Persian inscriptions were written. It was probably invented by the Sumerians, who developed it out of what was originally a pictorial form of writing.

The name is said to have been first used by Thomas Hyde, Regius Professor of Hebrew at Oxford (d. 1703). For sign lists see R. Labat, *Manuel d'épigraphie akkadienne. Signes, syllabaire, idéogrammes* (1948). G. R. Driver, *Semitic Writing. From Pictograph to Alphabet* (Schweich Lectures for 1944; 1948), pp. 1–77, with full bibl. reff.; D. Diringer, *The Alphabet. A Key to the History of Mankind* [1948], pp. 41–57, with bibl. Good elementary account by O. R. Gurney in *Chambers's Encyclopaedia* (ed. 1950), p. 297.

CURATE.

Properly, a clergyman who has the charge ('cure') of a parish, i.e. in England a *rector, *vicar, or *perpetual curate. Such a clergyman is also known as the 'incumbent'. He is chosen by the 'patron' (the person having the right to nominate a clergyman for the parish in question), and is admitted to the cure of souls ('instituted' or 'licensed') by the bishop of the diocese. He can be removed only by resignation, exchange of cure, promotion to another benefice involving the cure of souls, or deprivation following a public conviction for some disgraceful offence.

In general speech, however, the word is now used to denote an assistant or unbeneficed clergyman, e.g. one appointed to assist the incumbent in the performance of his duties, or to take charge of a parish temporarily during a vacancy, or while the incumbent is unable to perform his duties. Assistant curates are nominated by the incumbent or the bishop, and licensed by the bishop. This licence may be revoked by the bishop after due notice.

From 1662 to 1688 the episcopalian incumbents of Scottish parishes were styled curates.

CUR DEUS HOMO (Lat., 'Why [did] God [become] man?').

The title of St. *Anselm's famous treatise on the *Atonement (1097–8), in which he rejected the theory that the death of Christ could be explained in terms of a ransom from the devil and interpreted it in the light of the justice and mercy of God. See *Satisfaction*.

For bibl. see s.v. *Anselm*.

CURÉ D'ARS, The, Jean-Baptiste Marie Vianney (1786–1859). He was born at Dardilly, near Lyons, and intended for the priesthood from an early age. His education and training were interrupted by his conscription for the army, from which he deserted, and again considerably lengthened by his inability to learn Latin. After ordination at last in 1815, he was for three years assistant priest at Écully, and then appointed in Feb. 1818 parish priest at Ars. In this remote village he achieved almost world-wide fame. First from the neighbouring parishes, then from all France, finally from other countries too, came men and women, of all sorts and conditions, to seek his counsel. By 1855 the number of his visitors was computed at 20,000 a year, and during his last few years he was forced to spend 16 to 18 hours a day in the confessional. He was beatified in 1905, canonized in 1925, and in 1929 created the patron of parish priests. Feast day, 9 Aug.

Sermons (4 vols., Lyons, 1883). A. Monnin, S.J., *Le Curé d'Ars*. Vie de M. Jean-Baptiste Vianney (2 vols., 1861; Eng. trr., 1907 and 1924); J. Vianey, *Le Saint Curé d'Ars, 1786–1859* ('Les Saints', 1905; Eng. tr., 1906); F. Trochu, *Le Curé d'Ars*. Saint Jean-Marie-Baptiste Vianney (1786–1859) d'après toutes les pièces du procès de canonisation et de nombreux documents inédits (1925; Eng. tr., 1927); id., *L'Admirable Vie du Curé d'Ars* (1932; Eng. tr. as *The Insight of the Curé d'Ars*, 2 vols., 1934). Other lives by J. Darche (Paris, 1865), H. *Ghéon (Paris, 1928; Eng. tr., 1929), and J. Oxenham, *A Saint in the Making* (1931).

CURETON, WILLIAM (1808–64), *Syriac scholar. Educated at Christ Church, Oxford, he was ordained in 1831, became a sublibrarian of the *Bodleian Library in 1834, and from 1837 to 1849 was on the staff of the British Museum. There it was Cureton's task to catalogue the Syriac MSS. brought back from the *Nitrian monasteries by H. *Tattam. Among his discoveries were the Syriac text of three of St. *Ignatius's Epistles (to *Polycarp, to the Eph. and to the Rom.; published 1845), which he argued were the only genuine ones (a position no longer held); the 'Curetonian' *Old Syriac text of the Gospels (published 1858); and the 'Festal Letters' of *Athanasius (published 1848).

His *Ancient Syriac Manuscripts relative to the earliest Establishment of Christianity in Edessa and the neighbouring Countries* was posthumously publ. by W. Wright (1864), with preface, pp. i–ix. S. Lane-Poole in *D.N.B.*, xiii (1888), p. 325 f., s.v.

CURIA. The Papal court and its functionaries, esp. those through whom the government of the RC Church is administered. It includes the *Roman Congregations, Tribunals, and Curial Offices, and also certain permanent commissions, and acts with the delegated authority of the Pope. The term is also used in the RC Church of the court of diocesan officials (esp. legal officials) who act on behalf of an individual diocesan bishop. In medieval times the word was commonly used of any court, ecclesiastical or lay.

There is an extensive specialized literature. More general modern works include: D. Bouix, *Tractatus de Curia Romana* (Paris, 1880); F. M. Cappello, *De Curia Romana iuxta Re-*

formationem a Pio X sapientissime inductam (2 vols., Rome, 1911–'1912' [1913]); A. Monin, *De Curia Romana, eius Historia ac Hodierna Disciplina juxta Reformationem a Pio X inductam* (Louvain, 1912). K. Jordan, 'Die Entstehung der römischen Kurie' in *Zeitschrift der Savigny-Stiftung für Rechtsgeschichte*, lxxii, Kanon. Abt., xxviii (1939), pp. 97–152, with reff. B. Ojetti, S.J., in *C.E.*, xiii (1912), pp. 147–54, s.v. 'Roman Curia'; F. X. Hecht in *L.Th.K.*, vi (1934), cols. 310–15, s.v. 'Kurie'; P. Torquebiau in *D.D.C.*, iv (1939), cols. 971–1008, s.v. 'Curie romaine'. On the diocesan synod see id. ib., cols. 961–71, s.v. 'Curie diocésaine'. See also bibls. to *Roman Congregations* (also under the sep. headings) and *Cardinal*.

CURSIVE SCRIPT. The formal bookhand, properly called 'Greek minuscule', which used small, rounded ('lower-case') letters, joined together for speed of writing. Its letter-forms are first found in Egyptian documentary hands of the 7th and 8th cents. At the beginning of the 9th cent. the fully developed minuscule replaced *uncial (except in large volumes for liturgical use) as the only book-hand for copying Greek literary works. The earliest dated example is the Leningrad Gospels (MS. 219) of A.D. 835. It continued in use, with only minor modifications, until the invention of printing.

CURSOR MUNDI. An early English poem on the history of the world, probably dating from the late 13th cent. It is based on the Bible, but it incorporates much that is legendary. The first four books extend from the Creation to the successors of Solomon, the fifth deals with the early life of Jesus and Mary, the sixth with Christ's later life and the Apostles, and the seventh with the Last Judgement. It is written in a northern dialect and seems to have been written in the neighbourhood of *Durham, but the author is unknown.

There is an edition by R. Morris in four parallel columns from different MSS. (Early English Text Society, 3 vols., 1874–93). J. E. Wells in *C.B.E.L.*, i, p. 182 f.

CUSANUS, NICOLAUS. See *Nicholas of Cusa*.

CUSTOMARY (also known as a **Consuetudinary** or **Liber Ordinarius**). The book containing (1) the rites and ceremonies for the services, and/or (2) the rules and customs of discipline, of a particular monastery, cathedral, or religious order. In the Middle Ages, when local differences were great, they were of considerable practical use; but the greatly increased standardization of worship and discipline in more recent times, e.g. by the Congregation of *Rites (founded in 1588), led to their disappearance. The medieval customaries are of great value as source-books for the historian and the liturgiologist.

CUTHBERT, St. (d. 687), Bp. of *Lindisfarne. In 651 he became a monk at the monastery at Melrose. Somewhat later he moved with the abbot Eata to *Ripon, but returned to Melrose in 661, where he soon became prior. In 664 he again moved with his abbot to Lindisfarne, where they both adopted the Roman usages in the matter of the *tonsure and the date of *Easter. At Lindisfarne, also, Cuthbert was prior and he improved the discipline of the monastery. In 676, feeling the call to a solitary life, he withdrew to the neighbouring island of Farne where he remained as a hermit for eight years. In 684 he was elected Bp. of Hexham, but was unwilling to accept the see. In the following year, however, when Eata had become Bp. of Hexham, Cuthbert allowed himself to be consecrated Bp. of Lindisfarne. His short episcopate of nearly two years was marked by great missionary zeal and energy. He died in 687 and was buried in the church at Lindisfarne, but the Danish invasions did not allow his body to rest in peace and it was not until more than three hundred years had passed that it reached in 999 its final tomb in the cathedral at *Durham. Feast day, 20 Mar.

B. Colgrave, *Two Lives of Saint Cuthbert.* A Life by an anonymous monk of Lindisfarne and Bede's Prose Life. Text, Translation and Notes (1940). W. Jaager, *Bedas metrische Vita Sancti Cuthberti* (Palaestra, cxcviii. Untersuchungen und Texte aus der deutschen und englischen Philologie, 1935). 'Libellus de Nativitate Sancti Cuthberti de Historiis Hybernensium exceptus et translatus' in Surtees Society, vol. viii (1838), pp. 60–87. J. Raine, *Saint Cuthbert.* With an Account of the State in which his Remains were found upon the Opening of his Tomb in Durham Cathedral in the Year MDCCCXXVII (1828). Other Lives by C. Eyre (London, 1849) and H. Colgrave (Durham, 1947). C. F. Battiscombe (ed.), *The Relics of Saint Cuthbert* (1956). W. Hunt in *D.N.B.*, xiii (1888), pp. 359–62.

CYNEWULF (c. 750), Anglo-Saxon poet. His name, spelled out in runic letters, is found in the epilogues of four Anglo-Saxon poems which are therefore certainly his work. They are all religious in content. 'The Christ' celebrates the three mysteries of the Incarnation, Ascension, and Last Judgement; 'Juliana' is the account of the martyrdom of the saint; 'Elene', which many scholars consider his masterpiece, tells the story of the finding of the true Cross by St. *Helena; and 'The Fates of the Apostles' is a fragment of legendary character. The poems, which are obviously inspired by great devotion to the mysteries of the Christian faith and to the saints, have many passages of great beauty and show considerable knowledge. Besides the authentic four, others have been attributed to Cynewulf, among them the beautiful 'Dream of the Rood', some verses of which are carved on the Ruthwell Cross, but all these assignations are conjectural. Of the author himself nothing is known; he has been identified with Cynewulf, Bp. of *Lindisfarne (d. 783), and also with Cynulf, an otherwise unknown priest whose signature is appended to the decrees of the Council of *Clovesho (803). The former view, though resting on doubtful evidence, seems the more probable of the two.

C. W. Kennedy, *The Poems of Cynewulf translated into English Prose* (1910), with important introd., pp. 1–83, and bibl., pp. 335–47. Good crit. edd., with full notes, by A. S. Cook of 'The Christ' (Boston, 1900), of 'Elene', 'Phoenix', and 'Physiologus' (a poem prob. to be assigned to Cynewulf; New Haven, U.S.A., and London, 1919), and of the 'Dream of the Rood' (Oxford, 1905); by W. Strunk of 'Juliana' (Boston and London, 1904), and by G. P. Krapp of 'Andreas' and 'The Fate of the Apostles' (Boston, 1905). C. Shaar, *Critical Studies in the Cynewulf Group* (Lund Studies in English, xvii; 1949), with bibl. K. Sisam, 'Cynewulf and his Poetry' in *Proceedings of the British Academy*, xviii (1932), pp. 303–31. K. Jansen, *Die Cynewulf-Forschung von ihren Anfängen bis zur Gegenwart* (Bonner Beiträge zur Anglistik, xxiv; 1908). M. S. Serjeantson in *C.B.E.L.*, i, pp. 75–8, for further bibl.

CYPRIAN, St. (d. 258), Bp. of Carthage. Thascius Caecilianus Cyprianus was a pagan rhetorician converted to Christianity c. 246. Within two years he was elected Bp. of Carthage, having by that time acquired a profound knowledge of the Scriptures and the writings of *Tertullian. A few months later the *Decian persecution broke out (autumn 249), and he was forced to flee, but continued to rule his Church from exile by letter. He returned in 251. Large numbers of Christians had lapsed from their faith, and many more had secured *libelli pacis. The confessors, i.e. those who had stood firm, were reconciling the lapsed on ridiculously easy terms, by virtue of the merits of the martyrs. Cyprian was strongly opposed to their practice and two councils (251, 252) decided that the lapsed should be reconciled after suitable penance and delay. In 252 there occurred an outbreak of the plague in Carthage, which was ascribed to the crimes of the Christians. In spite of their charitable works, organized by Cyprian, hatred of them and esp. of their leader, increased. Meanwhile the schism of *Novatian, rising out of the question of the lapsed, gave rise to the *Rebaptism controversy. Cyprian received the support of the African bishops in three councils (255–6) in demanding the rebaptism of schismatics, on the ground that no one outside the Church could administer her sacraments. As the Church at Rome held that both schismatics and heretics could validly administer baptism, there followed a violent correspondence between Cyprian and Stephen, Bp. of Rome, which has also acquired significance for later controversy concerning the Papal claims. But for the moment the controversy was cut short by the persecution of the Emp. *Valerian. Cyprian having been banished, an attempt was made in 258 to arrest him. For the time being he hid himself, in order that he might suffer in his own city; but on the second attempt he gave himself up, and was martyred in Carthage on 14 Sept. 258.

Cyprian's writings, mainly short treatises and letters, enjoyed great popularity from the first. He had none of the brilliance of his predecessor, Tertullian, but his sober judgement and pastoral instincts gained him his hearing. Some of his works are also of theological importance, esp. those dealing with the Church, the ministry, and the Sacraments. They include (1) *Ad Quirinum* or *Testimonia* (c. 248), a collection of Biblical proof-texts in three Books, arranged under subjects; (2) *De Habitu Virginum* (c. 249), in praise of virginity; (3) *De Lapsis* (c. 251), dealing with the conditions for reconciling the lapsed; (4) *De Catholicae Ecclesiae Unitate* (251), a treatise held in special esteem, on the nature of true unity in the

Church in its relation to the episcopate ('habere non potest Deum patrem qui ecclesiam non habet matrem', cap. vi). Probably Cyprian issued this work in two recensions, one of them designed for Rome; (5) *De Opere et Eleemosynis* (c. 253), on almsgiving as a means of obtaining grace; and (6) *Ad Fortunatum* (257), against idolatry.

A like importance attaches to his correspondence, some of his letters (e.g. Ep. 63, on the Eucharist) being virtually short treatises. The *corpus* consists of 81 items (65 Cyprian's own and 16 replies). Here again the subjects are practical rather than dogmatic, and we gain a clear picture of his ideals as a bishop.

Though slain on 14 Sept., he is commemorated in the BCP calendar on 26 Sept. (by confusion with a converted magician of Antioch venerated on that day; see foll. entry) and in the Roman Missal on 16 Sept. (to avoid *Holy Cross day and the *Octave of the *Nativity of the BVM). The proposed 1927-8 revision of the BCP had yet another date, 13 Sept. (also to avoid Holy Cross Day).

Ed. princeps of Cyprian's works by J. Andreas (Rome, 1471). Important later edd. by D. *Erasmus (Basle, 1521), J. *Fell-J. *Pearson (Oxford, 1682), and S. *Baluze and P. *Maren (Paris, 1726). This last repr. in J. P. Migne, *PL*, iv (unsatisfactory). Crit. ed. by W. Hartel in C.S.E.L. (3 vols., 1868-71). Eng. tr. by R. E. Wallis in A.N.C.L. (2 vols., 1868-9); also *Select Epistles of St. Cyprian*, ed. T. A. *Lacey (S.P.C.K. [1922]). There survive a contemporary Life (not wholly reliable), acc. to St. *Jerome by Cyprian's deacon *Pontius, and the official description of his martyrdom ('Acta Proconsularia'). Modern Lives by C. F. Freppel (Paris, 1865), E. W. *Benson (London, 1897), and P. Monceaux ('Les Saints', Paris, 1914). Also P. Monceaux, *Histoire littéraire de l'Afrique chrétienne*, ii: St. Cyprien et son temps (1902). On the variant texts of the *De Catholicae Ecclesiae Unitate*, fullest study that of M. Bévenot, S.J., *St. Cyprian's De Unitate, chap. 4, in the Light of the Manuscripts* [1939]. On Cyprian's doctrines, A. d'Alès, *La Théologie de S. Cyprien* (1922). Cf. also H. Koch, *Cyprian und der römische Primat* (*T.U.*, xxxv, 1, 1910); id. *Cyprianische Untersuchungen* (1926); B. Poschmann, *Ecclesia Principalis. Ein kritischer Beitrag zur Frage des Primats bei Cyprian* (1933). I. Schrijnen–C. Mohrmann, *Studien zur Syntax der Briefe des heiligen Cyprian* (2 vols., Nijmegen, 1936-7). Bardenhewer, ii, pp. 442-517; Altaner (ed. 1950), pp. 142-51. M. Pellegrino in *E.C.*, iii (1950), cols. 1685-91, with bibl.

CYPRIAN, St. (*c.* 300), converted magician of *Antioch. Acc. to an apparently worthless legend, Cyprian was a pagan magician and astrologer who, when using his arts to ensnare a Christian virgin, Justina, was converted to her faith. Cyprian eventually became a Bishop and Justina the head of a convent. In the *Diocletianic Persecution both were apprehended, brought to the Imperial residence at Nicomedia, and beheaded. Their reputed relics are in the Baptistery of St. John Lateran at *Rome. Feast day, with St. Justina, 26 Sept. (wrongly allotted to St. *Cyprian of Carthage, q.v., in the BCP).

In an early form the legend was known to St. *Gregory of Nazianzus (d. 381) and *Prudentius (d. *c.* 410). Gk. and Lat. text of Legend, with commentary, in *AA.SS.*, Sept. VII (1750), pp. 195-246. H. *Delehaye, S.J., 'Cyprien d'Antioche et Cyprien de Carthage' in *Anal. Boll.*, xxxix (1921), pp. 314-32. T. *Zahn, *Cyprian von Antiochien und die deutsche Faustsage* (1882). R. Reitzenstein, 'Cyprian der Magier' in *Nachr.* (Gött.), 1917, pp. 38-79. L. Radermacher, *Griechische Quellen zur Faustsage in Sb.* (Wien), ccvi, Abh. 4; 1927, pp. 1-41. ('Der Zauberer Cyprianus').

CYPRIAN, St. (d. 549), Bp. of Toulon. He was the principal author of a Life of his friend, St. *Caesarius of Arles. In 529 at the Council of *Orange he took an active part in combating *Semi-pelagianism. A letter to Maximus of Geneva is extant in which Cyprian shows knowledge of the '*Te Deum', and defends himself against the charge of *Theopaschitism. Feast day, 3 Oct.

His Life of St. Caesarius of Arles in *AA.SS.*, Aug. VI (1743), pp. 64-75, and in J. P. Migne, *PL*, lxvii, 1001-24. Crit. ed. by B. Krusch in *M.G.H.*, Scriptores Rerum Merovingicarum, iii (1896), pp. 433-501. Cyprian's Letter to Maximus ed. by W. Gundlach in *M.G.H.*, Epistolae, iii (1892), pp. 434-6, and with introd. by C. Wawra in *T.Q.*, lxxxv (1903), pp. 576-94. S. Cavallin, *Literarhistorische und text-kritische Studien zur Vita S. Caesarii Arelatensis* (Lunds Universitets Årsskrift, N.F., Avd. 1, Bd. xxx, Nr. 7, 1934). Discussion of material for his life in *AA.SS.*, Oct. II (1768), pp. 164-78.

CYPRUS, Christianity in. Cyprus was evangelized by Sts. *Paul and *Barnabas (Acts 13). The many Cypriot saints mentioned in Byzantine *Synaxaria point to the firm hold Christianity secured in the island at an early date. At the Council of *Nicaea (325), Cyprus was represented by three bishops, including St. *Spiridion, while later in the century St. *Epiphanius (d. 403) was a distinguished Bp. of Salamis. About this time definite claims to independence of the patriarchates, esp. of *Antioch, were made by the Church of Cyprus, and in spite of the adverse view of Pope *Innocent I (402-17), the Council of *Ephesus in 431 formally recognized the claims of the Cypriot bishops in its 7th Session. A subsequent decision by *Acacius, Patr. of *Constantinople, confirmed this independence when it was challenged in 488 by *Peter the Fuller, Patr. of Antioch. Since then the archbishop, or *exarch, has been held to rank immediately after the five patriarchs. Arcadius and Sergius, Abps. of Constantia (Salamis) in the 7th cent., are famous as opponents of the Emp. *Heraclius.

The Cypriots passed under Arab rule, but were set free in the 10th cent., and at this time the great monasteries of the island were built. The Crusaders were welcomed, but soon caused trouble by introducing in 1196 a Latin hierarchy, which with unrelenting cruelty took control of Church affairs, so that the history of the next four centuries contains in Church events nothing but Greco-Latin strife. But the Latin Church was completely extinguished when the Turks took the island in 1571. The Greeks were more fortunate. Though many were massacred, they were permitted eventually to reconstitute their Church in four dioceses. In 1821, at the beginning of the Greek War of Independence, all four Cypriot bishops were executed. Since the establishment of British rule in 1878, the bishops and clergy have occasionally found relations strained with the authorities because they tend to be nationalist leaders. The Church in Cyprus is governed by the Holy Synod of the four dioceses. There are a very few RCs, who are under the spiritual care of *Franciscan friars, and also some *Uniats.

J. Hackett, *A History of the Orthodox Church of Cyprus from the Coming of the Apostles Paul and Barnabas to the Commencement of the British Occupation* (A.D. 45–A.D. 1878) *together with Some Account of the Latin and other Churches existing in the Island* (1901). H. T. F. Duckworth, *The Church of Cyprus* (S.P.C.K., 1900). R. Janin, A.A., in *D.H.G.E.*, xii (1953), cols. 791–820, s.v. 'Chypre', with full bibl.

CYRIL, St. (c. 315–86), Bp. of *Jerusalem from about 349. In 357 *Acacius, the extreme *Arian Bp. of *Caesarea, who claimed ecclesiastical jurisdiction over Jerusalem, had Cyril banished from his see on the ground of his opposition to Arianism, but the Council of *Seleucia recalled him in 359. Two further banishments followed. Meanwhile Cyril's beliefs on the burning question of the Godhead of Christ had been suspect in the opposite quarter, since he disliked the *Homoousios (the watchword of the Nicene faith) as being a man-made term. Accordingly the Council of *Antioch in 379 sent St. *Gregory of Nyssa to Palestine to report on the situation. He brought back word that though the life of the Jerusalem Church was morally corrupt and full of factions, its faith was sound. It has been suggested that Cyril, to prove his orthodoxy, recited the creed traditionally in use at Jerusalem (which like the *Nicene Creed contained the Homoousios) at the Council of *Constantinople in 381, and that its adoption by the Council stereotyped it in its present form.

The 24 'Catecheses', delivered c. 347 as instructions in Lent and Eastertide to the *catechumens who were baptized on *Holy Saturday, are the chief surviving work of Cyril. They give a full and very illuminating picture of the preparation for baptism then in use and much material for reconstructing the Palestinian liturgy of the 4th cent. Cyril does not mention the Words of *Institution in the Eucharist, perhaps because they were too familiar, perhaps because they were too sacred; but it is just possible his rite did not contain them. He speaks of non-communicating attendance at the Eucharistic rite, and stresses the Real Presence. He strongly affirms the value and efficacy of Baptism with its anointing, renunciations, washing-away of sins, and laying-on of hands. Feast day, 18 Mar.

Early edd. by J. Prévot (Paris, 1608) and T. Milles (London, 1703). Much improved ed. by the *Maurists, A. A. Touttée and P. *Maran (Paris, 1720), repr. in J. P. Migne, *PG*, xxxiii. More recent edd. by W. K. Reischl and J. Rupp, 2 vols., Munich, 1848–60, and (of Procatechesis and Mystagogical Lectures only) by F. L. Cross, S.P.C.K., 1951, with bibl. Eng. tr. by R. W. *Church in *L.F.*, with pref. by J. H. *Newman, Oxford, 1838); rev. by E. H. Gifford in N.P.N.C.F., viii (1894), pp. 1–157. Imp. 'Dissertationes' by A. A. Touttée, op. cit. Modern studies by J. T. Plitt (Heidelberg, 1855), G. Delacroix (Paris, 1865), and J. Mader (Einsiedeln, 1891). J. Lebon, 'La Position de St. Cyrille de Jérusalem dans les luttes provoquées par l'arianisme' in *R.H.E.*, xx (1924), pp. 181–210 and 357–86; B. Niederberger, *Die Logoslehre des hl. Cyrillus von Jerusalem* (Paderborn, 1923). The ascription of the Five Mystagogical Catecheses to St. Cyril has been challenged by W. J. Swaans, 'A propos des catéchèses mystagogiques attribuées à St. Cyrille de Jérusalem' in *Le Muséon*, xl (1942), pp. 6–43, who attributes them to his successor, John of Jerusalem, perhaps on insufficient grounds. X. Le Bachelet in *D.T.C.*, iii (1908), cols. 2527–77, and M. Jugie,

A.A., in *E.C.* iii (1950), cols. 1725–9, s.v. 'Cirillo di Gerusalemme'. Altaner (1950), pp. 268–70.

CYRIL, St. (d. 444), Patr. of *Alexandria. In 412 he succeeded his uncle Theophilus in the patriarchal see. He soon opened warfare with impartial vigour upon *Novatianism, *Neoplatonism, the Jews, and the Imperial prefect, Orestes, and if he himself bore no personal responsibility for the death of the distinguished philosopher *Hypatia, her murder was certainly the work of his supporters. The chief contest of his life, however, came c. 430. It arose out of the support given by *Nestorius, Patr. of *Constantinople, to his chaplain, Anastasius, who had preached against the application of the word *Theotokos ('God-bearer') to the Blessed Virgin, saying that she was the mother of only the humanity of Christ. The rivalry of the patriarchal sees, the antipathy of *Alexandrian to *Antiochene theological thought, and a personal love of conflict, made Cyril the obvious champion of the contested word, and he defended it in his Paschal letter for 429. He then persuaded Pope *Celestine to summon a synod at *Rome in 430 and condemn Nestorius, had the condemnation repeated in his own synod at Alexandria, and sent notice of both decrees to Nestorius with a covering letter and 12 anathemas. This letter, which epitomized Cyril's faith, was formally approved by the councils of *Ephesus (431) and *Chalcedon (451; after Cyril's death), but at the latter council his anathemas were omitted. At the Council of Ephesus, Cyril himself assumed control and had Nestorius condemned before the Antiochene bishops had arrived. On their arrival the Antiochenes held a separate council, and Cyril in turn was pronounced deposed. The Emperor at first confirmed both depositions, though that of Cyril was quickly reversed. In 433 an agreement was reached by Cyril and the more moderate Antiochenes.

Whatever may be thought of some of the methods adopted by Cyril in his controversies, his distinction and ability as a theologian are beyond dispute. The most brilliant representative of the *Alexandrian theological tradition, he put into systematic form, on the basis of the teaching of St. *Athanasius and the *Cappadocian Fathers, the classical Greek doctrines of the Trinity and of the Person of Christ. Where, in points of detail, his Christology appears to differ from that of the Council of *Chalcedon, the divergence is partly, if not wholly, terminological. He appears to have used the Greek word φύσις as almost if not quite the equivalent of ὑπόστασις ('person'), and not in its later sense of 'nature'; and it was this use of language which gave a ready handle to those who later sought to claim his authority for *Monophysitism.

His writings reflect Cyril's outstanding qualities as a theologian. They are marked by precision in exposition, accuracy in thought, and skill in reasoning, though they lack elegance in style. They include a large collection of letters (among them, 29 'Paschal homilies'); many exegetical books, e.g. commentaries on Jn. and Lk. and, in his *De adoratione et cultu in spiritu et veritate* with its supplement, the *Glaphura*, on selected passages in the *Pentateuch; several treatises on dogmatic theology; an Apology against *Julian the Apostate; and a rather meagre (in view of Cyril's celebrity as a preacher) collection of sermons. Feast day, 9 Feb.

The only collected ed. of Cyril's *Opera* is due to J. Aubert, Canon of Notre-Dame, Paris (6 vols., Paris, 1638; repr., with additions, J. P. Migne, *PG*, lxviii–lxxvii). Further texts ed. A. *Mai, Rome, various dates. New ed. of certain treatises, mainly commentaries, by P. E. *Pusey (7 vols., Oxford, 1868–77). Crit. text of several of Cyril's Epp. in E. *Schwartz (ed.), *Acta Conciliorum Oecumenicorum*, I. Concilium Ephesinum (Berlin, 1922 ff.). Syr. text of his Comm. on Luke, pt. 1, ed. J. B. Chabot in C.S.C.O., Scriptores Syri, Ser. 4, i (1912). Eng. tr. of selected writings, Oxford, 1872 and 1881. Studies by J. Kopallik (Mainz, 1881) and C. Papadopoulos (Alexandria, 1933). *Kyrilliana*. Études variées à l'occasion du XVᵉ centenaire de St. Cyrille d'Alexandrie (various authors, Cairo, 1947). Cyril also receives much notice in the Church Histories (Le N. *Tillemont, L. *Duchesne, B. J. *Kidd) and Histories of Dogma (L. J. Tixeront, A. *Harnack, R. L. *Ottley) of the times. A. Rehrmann, *Die Christologie des hl. Cyrillus von Alexandrien systematisch dargestellt* (Hildesheim, 1902); E. Weigl, *Die Heilslehre des hl. Cyrill von Alexandrien* (1905); A. Struckmann, *Die Eucharistielehre des hl. Cyrill von Alexandrien* (1910); A. Eberle, *Die Mariologie des hl. Cyrillus von Alexandrien* (1921); H. du Manoir de Juaye, S.J., *Dogme et spiritualité chez S. Cyrille d'Alexandre* (1944). N. Charlier, C.SS.R., 'Le *Thesaurus de Trinitate* de Saint Cyrille d'Alexandrie' in *R.H.E.*, xlv (1950), pp. 25–81. Bardenhewer, iv, pp. 23–74, and Altaner (1950), pp. 243–7, both with bibls. J. Mahé in *D.T.C.*, iii (1908), cols. 2476–2527, s.v., and M. Jugie, A.A., in *E.C.*, iii (1950), cols. 1715–1724, s.v. 'Cirillo d' Alessandria'.

CYRIL, St. (826–69), and **METHODIUS, St.** (*c.* 815–85). The 'Apostles of the Slavs'. They were brothers who came of a Greek, senatorial family of *Thessalonica. The younger brother, originally 'Constantine', did not assume the name of Cyril till he became a monk in 868. The several legends of their lives vary considerably and leave many uncertainties. After being ordained, they went to *Constantinople, where 'Cyril' became librarian of the church of the *Santa Sophia. In 862 the Emp. Michael III sent the two brothers as missionaries to what is now Moravia, where they taught in the vernacular. At once they took a keen interest in the language, and Cyril invented an alphabet called *Glagolithic (see also *Cyrillic*), and thus became the founder of Slavonic literature, adopting Slavonic also for the celebration of the Liturgy and circulating a Slavonic version of the Scriptures. A few years later they journeyed to Rome. Here Cyril died in a monastery shortly after taking his vows and was solemnly buried in the church of San Clemente. Methodius was then consecrated bishop and returned to Moravia. But though he was fortified with full Papal authority, he was opposed by the German bishops and imprisoned for over two years. Pope John VIII secured his release, but he deemed it expedient to withdraw the permission to use Slavonic as the regular language. Acc. to some sources, it was St. Cyril who brought the reputed remains of St. *Clement to Rome from the shores of the Sea of Azov. Feast day, now 7 July (formerly 9 Mar.).

Text of the two principal Slavonic lives pr., with Lat. tr., in F. Pastrnek, *Dějiny Slovanských Apoštolů Cyrilla a Methoda* (Spisův Poctěných Jubilejní Cenou Král. České Společnosti Náuk v Praze, xiv; 1902), pp. 154–238. Gk. text of life of St. Clement, a disciple of Methodius, ascribed to *Theophylact in J. P. Migne, *PG*, cxxvi, 1194–1240. P. Duthilleul, 'Les Sources de l'histoire des saints Cyrille et Méthode' in *Échos d'Orient*, xxxviii (1935), pp. 272–306. F. Grivec, *Die heiligen Slavenapostel Cyrillus und Methodius* (1928). F. Dvorník, *Les Légendes de Constantin et de Méthode vues de Byzance* (Byzantinoslavica, i; 1933), with bibl. F. Grivec, 'Vitae Constantini et Methodii Versio Latina, notis dissertationibusque de Fontis ac de Theologia SS. Cyrilli et Methodii Illustrata' in *Acta Academiae Velehradensis*, xvii (1941), pp. 1–127, with bibl.

CYRIL LUCAR. See *Lucar, Cyril*.

CYRIL OF SCYTHOPOLIS (6th cent.), Greek monk and hagiographer. Born at Scythopolis, the ancient Bethshan, of parents who kept a hospice for travelling monks, Cyril, while still a child, came under the influence of St. *Saba (q.v.; d. 532). In 543 he received the *tonsure and made his way to Jerusalem, where St. John the Hesychast sought to win him for his monastery. Cyril, however, at first determined to live the life of an anchorite on the banks of the *Jordan. Before long (544) he attached himself to the monastery of St. Euthymius (d. 473). The *Origenist controversies having brought this community to an end (555), Cyril entered the neighbouring monastery of St. Saba two years later. He was the author of the Lives of seven Palestinian abbots (St. Euthymius, St. Saba, St. John the Hesychast, St. Cyriacus, St. Theodosius, St. Theognius, St. Abraham). They are among the best of the Gk. hagiographical productions, being remarkable for their accurate detail. Written in popular Gk. they also have considerable philological interest.

His 'Lives' were first issued separately, by J. B. *Cotelier B. de *Montfaucon, O.S.B., and others; repr. in J. P. Migne, *PG*, cxiv, 595–734. Crit. ed. by E. *Schwartz in *T.U.*, xlix (Hft. 2; 1939); for critique of Schwartz's datings in this work cf. E. Stein in *Anal. Boll.*, lxii (1944), pp. 169–86. F. Diekamp, *Die origenistischen Streitigkeiten im sechsten Jahrhundert* (1899), pp. 1–25. T. Hermann, 'Zur Chronologie des Kyrill von Skythopolis' in *Z.K.G.*, xlv (1926), pp. 318–39. Krumbacher, p. 185 f.; Bardenhewer, v, pp. 124–30. S. Vailhé in *D.T.C.*, iii (1908), col. 2581 f.

CYRILLIC. The alphabet used by the Slavonic peoples of the E. Church. It is so named from its attribution to St. *Cyril, one of the two 'Apostles of the Slavs' (9th cent.), though in fact '*Glagolitic' and not 'Cyrillic' is the alphabet St. Cyril devised. Cyrillic dates, however, from almost the same time. It differs from Glagolitic in being based on Greek *uncials, and not on Greek *minuscules.

CZECHOSLOVAK CHURCH, The (*Ceskoslovenská Církev*). A Czech national Church founded in 1920. Its origins go back to an association of Catholic priests in 1890, called 'Jednota', which aimed at the introduction of the Czech language into the Liturgy, the abolition of compulsory celibacy for the priesthood, and the participation of the laity in the government of the Church. In 1919 these demands were submitted to Rome. On their rejection the Jednota, whose main inspiration was nationalist, decided to form an independent religious body in 1920. Within a few months they had won many adherents and were recognized by the government.

The Czechoslovak Church was constituted on Presbyterian lines, though with four bishops. These were elected, but not consecrated, and there is no belief in the *Apostolic Succession. In doctrine the Church was strongly rationalistic, owing to the influence of its first patriarch, Karl Farsky. The Divine Sonship of Christ and the Eucharist were interpreted on modernist lines, and the doctrines of *Original Sin, *Purgatory, and the Veneration of Saints were rejected. Scriptural exegesis rested on the principles of reason, experience, and the results of scholarship. After Farsky's death (1927) the doctrines became more conservative. After the first attraction was past, the numbers of the Czechoslovak Church dwindled, and probably never included more than 5 per cent of the population.

F. M. Hník–A. Spisar–F. Kovář, *The Czechoslovak Church* (Prague, 1937). G. A. Procházka, 'Die tschechoslowakische Nationalkirche' in F. Siegmund-Schultze (ed.), *Ekklesia*, v, Lfg. 20 (1937), pp. 175–85, with bibl.

D

'D'. In Biblical criticism, the symbol for the *Pentateuchal source most characteristically represented by the Bk. of Deut. (nearly all of which belongs to 'D'). In contrast to the legalism of 'P' (q.v.) and the more naïve narrative style of *J and *E (qq.v.), it is predominantly hortatory. One of its author's chief concerns was to safeguard monotheism. He forbade anything savouring of heathenism, e.g. sacrifice except at one central sanctuary (Deut. 12), prob. *Jerusalem. 'D' consequently has close points of contact with the 'Book of the Law' found in the Temple in the reign of Josiah (2 Kgs. 22 f.) which led the king to put down the '*high places' and henceforth confine sacrifice to Jerusalem. Its outlook is in harmony with that of the 8th and 7th cent. Prophets who denounced the idolatry of the high places and with that of the final redactors of the Books of Sam. and Kgs.

D'ACHÉRY, JEAN LUC (1609–85), French patristic scholar. He was professed at the *Maurist (*Benedictine) abbey at Vendôme in 1632. Sent to Paris in 1637, he became librarian of the abbey *St. Germain-des-Prés, where he edited numerous ancient authors, whose MSS. he recovered from oblivion. Among his most important publications are an edition of *Lanfranc, *B. Lanfranci . . . Opera Omnia* (1648), and the 13 vols. of his *Veterum aliquot Scriptorum . . . Spicilegium* (1655–77). One of the chief promoters of scholarship in his order, he became the master of many disciples, among them J. *Mabillon, with whom he shared in the production of the first volume of the *Acta Sanctorum Ordinis S. Benedicti*.

'Quelques Pages supprimées dans le tome cinquième du Spicilège de Luc d'Achéry' are printed in the *Anal. Boll.*, xviii (1899), pp. 43–8. U. Berlière in *D.T.C.*, i (1903), col. 310 f., incl. reff.

DAILLÉ, JEAN (1594–1670), French Reformed theologian and controversialist. He was born at Châtellerault, and after studying at Poitiers and Saumur, became tutor in the house of P. *Duplessis-Mornay in 1612, with whose grandsons he travelled on the Continent, esp. in Italy, and in England. In 1625 he became pastor at Saumur, and from 1626 till his death he was pastor at Charenton, where the Reformed Church of *Paris held its services. Among the French Protestants he had a great reputation as an orator and theologian. In his *Traité de l'employ des saints pères* (1632) he rejected the authority of the Fathers, for which he was attacked not only by RC but later also by Anglican scholars such as J. *Pearson, W. *Beveridge, and W. *Cave. He followed up the controversy in *La Foi fondée sur les saintes écritures* (1634), where he attempted to prove that all the Christian doctrines are either explicitly stated in Scripture or at least directly deducible from it. In his celebrated *De Scriptis Quae sub Dionysii Areopagitae et Ignatii Antiochenii Nominibus circumferuntur* (Geneva, 1666) he compiled no less than 66 objections to the genuineness of the Ignatian literature. Its confusions were exposed and its main contentions successfully refuted by J. Pearson (1672). Among his other works are *De Pseudepigraphis Apostolicis* (1653), *Adversus Latinorum de Cultus Religiosi Objecto Traditionem* (1664), and *De Cultibus Religiosis Latinorum* (1671).

Abbrégé de la vie de Mr Daillé [by Jean Daillé, son] printed with *Les Deux Derniers Sermons de Mr Daillé* (Paris, 1670). Study by E. Mettey (Strasbourg, 1863). List of his publications in E. and E. Haag, *La France protestante*, iii (1852), pp. 182–6; extended in ed. 2, by H. Bordier, v (1886), cols. 28–36. J. de la Servière, S.J., in *D.T.C.*, iv (1911), cols. 3–5.

D'AILLY, PIERRE (1350–1420), French cardinal and theologian. He was a native of Compiègne, and in 1363 entered the College of Navarre in *Paris, then a stronghold of *Nominalism, where he became master of arts in 1368 and doctor of theology in 1381. During this period he commented on the 'Sentences' of *Peter Lombard and wrote several scientific, philosophical, and theological treatises which show the great influence of R.*Bacon and esp. of *William of Occam. Having become canon at Noyon in 1381, he was made rector of the College of Navarre in 1384, chancellor of the university of Paris in 1389, and soon afterwards confessor and almoner to Charles VI. In 1391 he obtained the archdeaconry of Cambrai in addition to many other benefices which he held in plurality. After the death of *Clement VII he became a favourite with his successor *Benedict XIII, who appointed him Bp. of Puy in 1395. He never entered his diocese, and in 1397 was translated to the more important see of Cambrai. The chief concern of his life was to find a means of healing the Western Schism. With this end in view he broke with Benedict XIII in 1408 and in 1409 attended the Council of *Pisa, where he supported the newly elected third Pope, *Alexander V. In 1411 he assisted at the Council of Rome, convoked by Alexander's successor, *John XXIII, for which he outlined a programme of reforms entitled 'Capita Agendorum'. In 1412 John XXIII created him cardinal in the hope of retaining his support, and shortly afterwards he was made Papal Legate to the German Emperor Sigismund. In 1414 he took part in the Council of *Constance, where he supported the theory of the supremacy of the General Council over the Pope, without, however, entirely approving the famous 'Decrees of Constance'. In 1416 he published his 'Tractatus super Reformatione Ecclesiae', the third part of an elaborate work 'De Materia Concilii Generalis'. Its first part was published among the works of his friend and disciple, J. *Gerson, the second is still in MS. Several of its suggestions for ecclesiastical reforms were later adopted by the Council of *Trent. The 'Tractatus' had a great influence esp. in England and Germany.

In his doctrinal teaching he most frequently accepted the views of Occam. He held that the existence of God was not a rationally demonstrable truth, and that sin was not as such inherently evil but sinful only because God wills it to be so. He maintained that bishops and priests received their jurisdiction directly from Christ and not mediately through the Pope, and that neither Pope nor Council was infallible. These and other of his opinions were later adopted and developed by M. *Luther and the other Reformers; and his teaching on the Church exercised a decisive influence on *Gallicanism. D'Ailly is also remarkable for his studies in astrology and geography; his *Imago Mundi*, in which he suggested that the Indies could be reached from the W., was known to Columbus.

Most of his sermons were printed by the *Brethren of the Common Life under the title *Tractatus et Sermones* (Brussels, c. 1484). Modern ed., with Fr. tr., of *Imago Mundi* by E. Buron (3 vols., Paris, 1930), with valuable introd. in vol. i, pp. 5–113, and bibl., pp. 113–24. Studies by A. Dinaux (Cambrai, 1824), L. Salembrier (Lille, 1886; also other works by this author) and P. Tschackert (Gotha, 1877); also a brief sketch by R. Pontvianne (Le Puy, 1896). Agnes E. Roberts, 'Pierre d'Ailly and the Council of Constance. A Study in "Ockhamite" Theory and Practice' in *Transactions of the Royal Historical Society*, Fourth Series, xviii (1935), pp. 123–142. L. Salembrier in *D.H.G.E.*, i (1912), cols. 1154–65, s.v. 'Ailly, Pierre de'. See also bibl. to *Constance, Council of*, and *Gerson, Jean le Charlier de*.

DAIR BALAIZAH FRAGMENTS. See *Der Balyzeh Fragments*.

DALE, ROBERT WILLIAM (1829–95), *Congregationalist preacher, theologian, and educational reformer. From 1853 until his death he was pastor (co-pastor 1853–9) of Carr's Lane Chapel, Birmingham. He came to take a leading part in municipal affairs in Birmingham, co-operating closely with Joseph Chamberlain, and in 1870 he keenly supported W. E. Forster's Education Bill. In 1891 he was president of the International Congregational Council. He stood for progressive, but in fundamentals orthodox, Evangelicalism. In *The Atonement* (1875), his most influential work, he strongly maintained a penal doctrine against the liberal views of such men as B. *Jowett and H. *Bushnell. But his orthodoxy here differed from that of traditional *Protestantism. He sought to put the emphasis on the ethical rather than the forensic, and in some respects his teaching on the Atonement has points of contact with that of H. *Grotius. His other writings include sets of lectures on *Preaching* (1877) and on *Ephesians* (1882).

Biography by his son, A. W. W. Dale (London, 1898). A. Gordon in *D.N.B.*, Suppl. ii (1901), pp. 104–6.

D'ALEMBERT, JEAN LE ROND (1717–1783), French mathematician, philosopher, and *Encyclopaedist. A foundling discovered near

the church of St. Jean le Rond, *Paris (hence his name), he was educated by the *Jansenists at the Mazarin College. He soon showed remarkable mathematical talents and, after short-lived attempts to train as a lawyer and a physician, resolved to devote himself wholly to mathematics. In 1741 he was admitted a member of the Academy of Sciences. In 1743 in his *Traité de dynamique* he developed the mechanical principle henceforward known as 'D'Alembert's Principle'. Several important other works and papers on mathematics followed. He was drawn into various religious disputes by his extensive collaboration for some years in *Diderot's *Encyclopédie* and his association with the 'philosophic' circle of freethinkers that produced it. D'Alembert contributed the *Discours préliminaire*, which dealt, along lines laid down by F. *Bacon and J. *Locke, with the rise, progress, and affinities of the several sciences, as well as many articles on literary, and esp. mathematical, subjects. His article on '*Geneva' provoked the *Calvinists to a lively controversy. Among his other writings were an attack on the *Jesuits (1765) and a collection of biographies of members of the Academy who died between 1700 and 1772.

Collected Works, 18 vols., Paris, 1805. Unpublished items ed. M. C. Henry (Paris, 1887). Eng. tr. of 'Miscellaneous Pieces' (London, 1764). Study by J. Bertrand (Paris, 1889). M. Muller, *Essai sur la philosophie de Jean d'Alembert* (1926). Überweg, iii, pp. 429, 435 f., 700. See also bibl. to *Encyclopaedists*.

DALGAIRNS, BERNARD (baptismal names John Dobree) (1818–76), priest of the *Oratory. He was a supporter of the *Oxford Movement in its earliest days, but in 1845, after spending some time in retirement with J. H. *Newman at Littlemore, was, like him, received into the RC Church. After some months in France and Italy he attached himself to the Oratory in London in 1849, and wrote here some widely used devotional and theological works, including *The Devotion to the Sacred Heart of Jesus* (1853), *The German Mystics of the 14th Century* (1858), *The Holy Communion, its Philosophy, Theology, and Practice* (1861).

Good character sketch in R. W. *Church, *The Oxford Movement* (1891), p. 206. T. Cooper in *D.N.B.*, xiii (1888), p. 388 f.; S. Bowden in *C.E.*, iv (1908), p. 604 f., s.v.

DALLÆUS, JOHANNES. See *Daillé, Jean*.

DALMAN, GUSTAF HERMANN (1855–1941), Biblical scholar. In 1895 he was appointed professor of the Institutum Delitzschianum (see *Delitzsch, Franz*) at Leipzig. From 1902 to 1917 he was director of the German Evangelical Institute for Archaeology in Palestine, and afterwards professor at Greifswald. In 1925 he went out again to Palestine as director of the Gustaf Dalman-Institut für Palästinawissenschaft. He conducted many important researches into the language, ideas, and customs of 1st cent. *Judaism, and his work may be said to have established that Christ spoke ordinarily in

Aramaic and not in Greek. His writings include *Grammatik des jüdisch-palästinischen Aramäisch* (1894); *Christentum und Judentum* (1898; Eng. trans., 1901); *Die Worte Jesu* (1898; Eng. trans., 1902); *Orte und Wege Jesu* (1919; Eng. trans., 1935); *Jesus-Jeschua* (1922; Eng. trans., 1929).

A. Alt in *Palästinajahrbuch des deutschen evangelischen Instituts für Altertumswissenschaft des heiligen Landes zu Jerusalem*, Jahrg. xxxvii (1941), pp. 5–18.

DALMATIC. An over-tunic reaching to the knees worn in the W. Church at *High Mass by *deacons, and on certain occasions also by bishops. The Eastern bishop's 'sakkos' is almost identical. Perhaps of Dalmatian origin, it became a popular garment among the upper classes in Rome in the 2nd cent. Till the 10th cent. it was invariably white and made of linen or wool; later it was coloured and of silk. It is ornamented with two *clavi* or coloured strips running from front to back over the shoulders, which at one time were invariably red. The dalmatic is bestowed upon the deacon at his ordination in the Latin Rite. It is considered a festal vestment and hence is not worn in penitential seasons. In England, the sovereign wears a dalmatic at his coronation. See also *Tunicle*.

Braun, L. G., ch. xii, 'Dalmatik und Tunicella', pp. 247–305.

DAMASCUS. The ancient capital of Syria. Mentioned as far back as the 16th cent. B.C. by the Egyptian king, Thutmoses III, it is frequently referred to in the OT, owing to the conflicts and alliances between Syria, Israel, and Judah in the earlier days of the Hebrew monarchy. After its fall in 732 B.C. to the Assyrian king, Tiglath Pileser III, it lost most of its importance for several centuries. In the Seleucid period it was overshadowed by the new Syrian capital of *Antioch. It was on the road from *Jerusalem to Damascus that St. Paul was converted to the Christian faith (Acts 9). A Christian community has existed here continuously from Apostolic times.

J. L. Porter, *Five Years in Damascus*, with travels and researches in Palmyra, Lebanon and the Hauran (2 vols., 1855). A. Kremer, *Mittelsyrien und Damascus*. Geschichtliche ethnografische und geografische Studien (1853); H. Sauvaire, 'Description de Damas' in *Journal Asiatique*, Ser. 9, iii (1894), pp. 251–318; iv (1894), pp. 242–331; v (1895), pp. 269–315; vi (1895), pp. 221–313, and vii (1896), pp. 185–285. C. Watzinger–K. Wulzinger, *Damascus* (2 vols., 'Die Antike Stadt' and 'Die Islamische Stadt', Wissenschaftliche Veröffentlichungen des Deutsch-Türkischen Denkmalschutz-Kommandos, Hft. iv–v, 1921–24). L. Jalabert in *D.A.C.L.*, iv (pt. i, 1920), cols. 119–45, s.v. 'Damas', with bibl.

DAMASCUS FRAGMENTS. Portions of an ancient Hebrew work discovered in 1896 by S. Schechter in the *Geniza of the synagogue at Cairo. They are the work of a Jewish sect, held by Schechter to be the 'Zadokites' (7th cent. A.D.), but the fragments are now generally considered much earlier (170 B.C., Eduard Meyer). They have points of contact with the '*Testaments of the XII Patriarchs',

the 'Book of *Jubilees', and parts of the 'Book of *Enoch'. Their contents are partly admonition, partly in the form of a law-book; the latter throw much light on the growth of the *Halacha.

The sect (the 'Sons of Zadok' or the 'New Covenant') appears to have been led by its rigorism to secede from orthodox Judaism and to have settled at *Damascus. Great stress is laid on ceremonial purity (avoidance of unclean foods, dealings with the Gentiles, fornication), monogamy, love of one's neighbour, confession of sin and *Sabbath observance. There is special condemnation of marriage between uncle and niece. In matters of doctrine, emphasis is laid on Divine election, angels, and the expectation of a *Messiah. In the life of the community the priest is assigned a less important part than a lay president.

Nothing certain is known of the later history of the sect. R. H. *Charles suggests that many of them joined the Christian Church (cf. Acts 6. 7). The MSS. are now preserved in the University Library, Cambridge (T.-S. 10 K.6 and T.-S. 16.311). See also *Dead Sea Scrolls*.

Text first pr. by S. Schechter (Documents of Jewish Sectaries, i; Cambridge, 1910); also ed. L. Rost (Kleine Texte für Vorlesungen und Übungen ed. H. *Lietzmann clxvii; 1933), with full bibl. to date; crit. ed. with Eng. tr. by C. Rabin, *The Zadokite Documents* (Oxford, 1954). Photographs of the MS., with introd., by S. Zeitlin (*J.Q.R.* Monograph Series, i; Philadelphia, 1952). Eng. tr. and comm. in R. H. Charles, *The Apocrypha and Pseudepigrapha of the Old Testament*, ii (1913), pp. 785–834. E. Meyer, *Die Gemeinde des neuen Bundes im Lande Damaskus*. Eine jüdische Schrift aus der Seleukidenzeit (*Abh.* (Berl.), 1919, Hft. 9); L. Ginzberg, *Eine unbekannte jüdische Sekte*, i (all publd., New York, 1922); W. Staerk, *Die jüdische Gemeinde des neuen Bundes in Damaskus* (1922); G. F. Moore, *Judaism in the First Three Centuries of the Christian Era*, i (Cambridge, Mass., 1927), pp. 200–204. B. Reicke, *The Jewish 'Damascus Documents' and the New Testament* (Symbolae Biblicae Upsalienses. Supplementhäften till Svensk Exegetisk Årsbok; 1946). H. H. Rowley, *The Zadokite Documents and the Dead Sea Scrolls* (1952), with detailed bibl.

DAMASUS, St. (*c.* 304–84), Pope from 366. Of Spanish descent, he entered the service of his predecessor, Pope *Liberius, who appointed him a deacon. On Liberius' death (24 Sept. 366), a fierce conflict broke out between the supporters of Damasus and those of his rival, Ursinus (or Ursicinus). Ursinus was elected Pope in the basilica of Julius (S. Maria in Trastevere), while Damasus was chosen by the great majority of the clergy and people of *Rome in S. Lorenzo in Lucina. In the ensuing struggle, during which the supporters of Ursinus gained possession of the Liberian Basilica (S. Maria Maggiore), acc. to Ammianus Marcellinus 137 persons (acc. to the *Gesta inter Liberium et Felicem*, 160) were killed. The Emp. Valentinian I intervened in support of Damasus and banished Ursinus for a time to *Cologne, though it was not until *c.* 381 that the troubles ceased.

Damasus was very active, by Synods and with the help of the Imperial power, in suppressing heresy (*Arianism, *Donatism, *Macedonianism, *Luciferians). From 371 he was engaged in protracted dealings with St. *Basil of Caesarea with a view to the overthrow of

Arianism; and at Antioch he supported the party of *Paulinus. Damasus did much to strengthen the position of the see of Rome (Decree of Gratian, 378), made provision for the proper housing of the Papal archives and was keenly interested in the monuments of the martyrs, adorning their tombs with the series of famous marble inscriptions engraved by *Filocalus. He also erected the titular church of S. Lorenzo in Damaso, and a church on the Via Ardeatina at the catacombs of Sts. Marcus and Marcellianus. He commissioned St. *Jerome, who had been his secretary, to prepare the *Vulgate version of the Bible; and at the Council of Rome of 382 (or perh. 374), under Jerome's influence, promulgated a Canon of Scriptural Books. In the Middle Ages he was erroneously held to be the author of the *Liber Pontificalis. See also Fides Damasi. Feast day, 11 Dec.

Works in J. P. Migne, PL, xiii, 109–424. Crit. ed. of the docs. on the Ursinian schism in C.S.E.L., 35 ('Collectio Avellana'), pp. 48–58. L.P. (Duchesne), i, pp. 212–15. M. Ihm (ed.), Damasi Epigrammata (Leipzig, 1895); A. Ferrua, S.I., Epigrammata Damasiana (Sussidi allo studio delle antichità cristiane, ii, 1942; 59 Epigrams are here recognized as genuine). Study by M. Rade (Freiburg i.Br., 1882). J. Wittig, 'Papst Damasus I' in R.Q. Suppl., xiv (1902); E. [B. D.] Schäfer, Die Bedeutung der Epigramme Damasus I für die Geschichte der Heiligenverehrung (Rome, 1932). C. H. *Turner, 'Latin Lists of the Canonical Books, I: The Roman Council under Damasus, A.D. 382' in J.T.S., i (1899–1900), pp. 554–60. A. Ferrua, in E.C., iv (1950), cols. 1136–9, with bibl.

DAMIAN, St. See Cosmas and Damian, Sts.

DAMIAN, St. PETER. See Peter Damian, St.

DAMIEN, Father (1840–89), leper missionary. Joseph Deveuster, the son of a small farmer, became a member of the Picpus Society (Fathers of the Sacred Heart of Jesus and Mary) in 1859, taking the religious name 'Damien'. Sent to the Sandwich Islands in 1863, he was ordained priest at Honolulu in the following year, and later put in charge of several districts in the islands of Hawaii and Molokai, where he converted the natives and built them chapels. In 1873 he was sent at his own request to a settlement of lepers at Molokai who were without any attendance. Here he ministered single-handed to the spiritual and physical needs of 600 lepers, dressing their wounds, building them houses, and digging their graves. Even after he had caught the disease himself he continued his work, now assisted by other members of his order and Sisters of Charity, until he became helpless.

Letters ed. by his brother, Father Pamphile [A. P. de Veuster] (London, 1889), with introd. There are many lives, among them (in English) those by E. Clifford (London, 1889), Irene Caudwell (ib., 1901), May Quinlan (ib., 1909), P. Compton (ib., 1933), C. J. Dutton (ib., 1934), and J. V. Farrow (ib., 1937).

DAMNATION. In general, 'condemnation', but esp. to eternal loss (damnum) in hell. Some theologians have distinguished the loss of the *Beatific Vision, the attainment of which constitutes the joy of heaven, from positive retributive punishment for the sins done on earth, and asserted that both are present in the sufferings of the damned; others have held that the deprivation and conscious loss of heaven and of God is itself the natural and sufficient consequence of persistence in sin. The eternity of damnation for those who finally reject the will of God appears to follow from various sayings of Christ, e.g. Mt. 25. 46.

DANCE OF DEATH, The. An allegorical subject in European art, in which the figure of Death, often represented as a skeleton, is shown meeting various characters in different states of life and leading them all in a dance to the grave. It was often painted on the walls of cloisters and graveyards in the later Middle Ages, but examples survive chiefly in engravings, e.g. the series by H. Holbein (the younger). It was called in German Totentanz and in French Danse macabre.

Modern facsimile ed. of The Dance of Death by Hans Holbein (1497–1543), with introd. and notes by J. M. Clark (London, 1947). F. Douce, The Dance of Death exhibited in Elegant Engravings on Wood, with a dissertation on the several representations of that subject (1833). Hans Holbein's Celebrated Dance of Death, illustrated by a series of photo-lithographic facsimiles from the copy of the first edition now in the British Museum, with explanatory description by H. N. H[umphreys] (1868). J. G. Kaster, Les Danses des morts. Dissertation et recherches historiques, philosophiques, littéraires et musicales, sur les divers monuments de ce genre qui existent ou qui ont existé tant en France qu'à l'étranger (1852). G. Buchheit, Der Totentanz. Seine Entstehung und Entwicklung (1926). W. Stammler, Die Totentänze des Mittelalters (1922); id., Der Totentanz. Entstehung und Deutung (1948), with bibl. L. P. Kurtz, The Dance of Death and the Macabre Spirit in European Literature (Publications of the Institute of French Studies, Columbia University, New York, 1934). J. M. Clark, The Dance of Death in the Middle Ages and Renaissance (Glasgow, 1950), with bibl. Ethel C. Williams, 'The Dance of Death in Painting and Sculpture in the Middle Ages' in The Journal of the British Archaeological Association, Series 3, i (1937), pp. 229-57.

DANIEL, Book of. The Book falls into two main divisions:

I. A narrative section describing the experiences of Daniel and his three companions under Nebuchadnezzar (1–4) and Belshazzar (5), kings of Babylon, and Darius the Mede (6). These include their refusal to eat unclean meats (1), Daniel's successful interpretation of Nebuchadnezzar's dream (2), the miraculous release of the three companions from the fiery furnace (3), Nebuchadnezzar's madness (4), the supernatural writing on the wall ('Mene, Mene, Tekel, Upharsin') at Belshazzar's feast (5), and Daniel's preservation in the lions' den (6).

II. A series of visions granted to Daniel in the reigns of Belshazzar (7, 8), Darius the Mede (9), and Cyrus (10–12), which reveal the future destinies of the Jewish people. Several of the passages in these later chapters bear all the characteristics of *Apocalyptic literature.

The traditional belief that the Book was written in the 6th cent. B.C. by Daniel, one of the Jewish exiles in Babylon, is now almost universally regarded as untenable. A number of historical errors make it next to impossible to believe that it dated from the period of the Exile, and a much later date is borne out also by its doctrinal standpoint, its language (even Greek words occur), and its position in the *Canon of Scripture. All these considerations point to a much later date, and the consensus of critical opinion is that it was written between 168 and 165 B.C. On this hypothesis the purpose of the Book was to encourage the reader during the persecutions of the Jews at the hands of *Antiochus Epiphanes (175–163 B.C.). The section 2. 4–7. 28 is written in *Aramaic (not Hebrew).

There is only one passage where Daniel is directly quoted in the NT, namely, the reference to the 'abomination of desolation' in Mk. 13. 14 and parallels. But there are many points where its teaching has been taken up and developed, e.g. the use of the figure of the *Son of Man (7. 13), the conception of angels mediating between a transcendent God and man, and above all the doctrine of the *resurrection of the dead in 12. 2.

In the *Apocrypha of the OT there appear three 'books' which are explained as additions to Daniel, viz. 'The Song of the Three Holy Children', 'The History of Susanna', and 'The History of the Destruction of Bel and the Dragon'. All of these are Greek writings, later than the Book itself, and found their way into the *Septuagint. On these, see the separate entries.

Commentaries by S. R. *Driver (Camb. Bib., AV, 1900), C. H. H. Wright (London, 1906), J. A. Montgomery (I.C.C., 1927), with bibl. pp. xv–xxvi, R. H. *Charles (Oxford, 1927), K. Marti. (K.H.C., xviii, 1901), G. Behrmann (H.K.A.T., Abt. 3, Bd. iii, Theil 2, 1894), and A. Bentzen (H.A.T., Reihe 1, Bd. ix; 1937). Among the older writers, upholding the conservative view, the best known is E. B. *Pusey, Daniel the Prophet. Nine Lectures (1864). C. H. H. Wright, Daniel and His Prophecies (1906). H. H. Rowley, Darius the Mede and the Four World Empires in the Book of Daniel (1935). R. H. Charles–C. C. Torrey in E.B. (ed. 14), vii (1929), pp. 27–30, s.v.

DANIEL, St. (d. 493), *Stylite. He was the most famous of the disciples of St. *Simeon Stylites, whose cowl he received. After spending his early years at Samosata and other monasteries in the E., at the age of 47 he took up his position on a pillar four miles from *Constantinople, on which he was ordained priest by St. *Gennadius and lived for thirty-three years. Generally regarded as an oracle, he only once left his pillar (c. 476), to rebuke the Emp. Basiliscus for supporting *Monophysitism. Feast day, 11 Dec.

Early Gk. life, ed. H. *Delehaye, S.J., in Anal. Boll., xxxii (1913), pp. 121–229; repr. in id. (ed.), Les Saints stylites (Brussels, 1923), pp. 1–94. Eng. tr. in Elizabeth [A. S.] Dawes–N. H. Baynes, Three Byzantine Saints (1948), pp. 1–77, with notes, pp. 72–84. On this Vita cf. N. H. Baynes in E.H.R., xl (1925), pp. 397–402. Other lives listed in B.H.G., p. 69. J. P. Kirsch in L.Th.K., iii (1931), col. 148 f.

DANTE (1265–1321), Italian poet. Little is known about his youth except that he lost his parents as a boy and made his philosophical studies under the guidance of the *Dominicans.

His early love for Beatrice, probably the daughter of a Florentine citizen Portinari, was celebrated in his first work, Vita nuova (1294), four years after her death; it accompanied him as a semi-religious longing through the vicissitudes of his subsequent life and found its mature expression in the mysterious figure of Beatrice in the Divina commedia. In 1301 Dante became involved in the dissensions that split Florence in two parties. Having been an ardent supporter of the anti-Papal faction which was defeated, he was accused of corrupt practices and hostility to the Pope; his property was confiscated and he himself exiled. He now began to lead the restless life of a wanderer from one Italian city to another, *Verona, *Bologna, and Padua among them. The Emp. Henry VII's visit to Italy in 1310 raised in him a short-lived hope for betterment of the state of things in Italy and for his own return; but his prospects were shattered by the death of Henry, whom he had induced to besiege the rebellious Florence. In 1315 his native city renewed her sentence against him, and two years later he finally settled at *Ravenna. His political views are laid down in his De Monarchia (c. 1313), a Latin treatise advocating a universal monarchy in which all temporal power was to be vested and which was to exercise its authority independently of, but side by side with, the Pope who was the supreme spiritual authority, in accordance with the twofold end of man, temporal happiness in this world and eternal blessedness in the next. The last years of his life were devoted to the completion of his greatest work, the Divina commedia (q.v.), which established him as one of the few poets who belong to all times and to all nations.

Best collected ed. of Opere by the Società Dantesca Italiana, ed. M. Barbi, E. G. Parodi, and others, Florence, 1921–2. Good earlier ed. by E. Moore (Oxford, 1894; ed. 3, 1904; reissue, Chelsea, 1909). Crit. edd. of Vita nuova by M. Barbi (Florence, Edizione Nazionale, vol. i, 1932), of the Convivio by M. Barbi (Florence, 1935, with comm.), of the Monarchia by L. Bertalot (Friedrichsdorf, 1918), of the Letters by P. Toynbee (Oxford, 1920), of the Eclogue by P. H. Wicksteed and E. G. Gardner (London, 1902). For Eng. trr. of Divina commedia, see bibl. to that entry; Eng. trr. of other works in Temple Classics. There is a vast literature in all modern languages. Introductions include E. G. Gardner, Dante (London, 1923); C. Foligno, Dante (Benn's Sixpenny Library, 1929), M. Barbi, Dante (Florence, 1933), F. Maggini, Introduzione allo studio di Dante (Bari, 1936), and U. Cosmo, Guida a Dante (Maestri e Compagni, v; 1947; Eng. tr., A Handbook to Dante Studies, Oxford, 1950), with full bibl. reff. Among more substantial works are P. Toynbee, Dante Alighieri (1900; ed. 4, 1910) and N. Zingarelli, La vita, i tempi e le opere di Dante ('ed. 3', in Storia letteraria d' Italia, 2 vols., 1931; based on work orig. publd. 1903); P. Toynbee, Dante Studies and Researches (1902); id., Dante in English Literature from Chaucer to Cary (2 vols., 1909; with anthology of allusions); id., The Oxford Dante Society (1920). B. *Croce, La Poesia di Dante (1921). E. *Gilson, Dante et la philosophie (1939; Eng. tr. 1949). Dorothy L. Sayers, Introductory Papers on Dante (1954). C. [W. S.] *Williams, The Figure of Beatrice (1943). L. Pietrobono in E.C., iv (1950), cols. 1169–1212.

DARBOY, GEORGES (1813–71), Abp. of *Paris. He was ordained priest in 1836, and after holding some teaching and other appointments became Bp. of Nancy in 1859 and Abp. of *Paris in 1863. In his first year at Paris he consecrated the newly restored cathedral of

*Notre-Dame. His *Gallican sympathies and claims to episcopal independence brought him into conflict with Rome, and both before and during the *Vatican Council he was one of the chief opponents of the definition of Papal infallibility, although he eventually subscribed to it. During the siege of Paris in 1870–1, he devoted himself wholeheartedly to the care of the destitute and helpless. When in 1871 the Commune secured control of the city, he was seized and shot in cold blood on 24 May 1871, blessing his executioners. His writings include a Life of St. Thomas *Becket (2 vols., 1858).

Œuvres pastorales de Mgr Darboy, comprenant ses mandements et ses allocutions, depuis son élévation au siège de Nancy jusqu'à sa mort (2 vols., 1876). 'Monseigneur Darboy et le saint-siège. Documents inédits' in Revue d'Histoire et de Littérature religieuses, xii (1907), pp. 240–81. J. A. Foulon, Histoire de la vie et des œuvres de Mgr Darboy, archevêque de Paris (1889). Further Life by J. A. Guillermin (Paris, 1888). P. A. Pierron, Mgr. Darboy. Esquisses familières (1872); L. C. Price, Archbishop Darboy and Some French Tragedies, 1813–1871 [c. 1915].

DARBY, JOHN NELSON (1800–1882), *Plymouth Brother and founder of the 'Darbyites'. He was ordained to a title in Wicklow c. 1826, but resigned in 1827, and shortly after joined a sect called the 'Brethren', then newly founded by A. N. Groves, which rejected all Church order and outward forms. In 1845 a quarrel within this body caused a local schism at Plymouth, and in 1847 at Bristol; and Darby became the leader of the stricter Brethren, which were organized as a separate body ('Darbyites'). Both before and after this time Darby made many tours abroad to lecture and preach, visiting France, Switzerland, Germany, Canada, the U.S.A., the West Indies, and New Zealand between 1830 and his death. Darby wrote countless controversial, doctrinal, and devotional works. He was also a hymn-writer, and edited the hymn-book generally used by the Plymouth Brethren.

Collected Writings ed. by W. Kelly (London, 32 vols. and index, [1867–83]). There is much autobiographical material in his Personal Recollections of many Prominent People whom I have Known, and of Events—especially those Relating to the History of St. Louis—during the First Half of the Present Century (St. Louis, 1880). Modern Life by W. G. Turner (London, 1926). A. Reese, The Approaching Advent of Christ. An Examination of the Teaching of J. N. Darby and his Followers [1937].

D'ARCY, MARTIN CYRIL (1888–   ), *Jesuit philosophical theologian. Educated at Stonyhurst, Oxford, and the *Gregorian University at *Rome, he entered the Jesuit Order and was ordained priest in 1921. From 1933 to 1945 he was Master of Campion Hall, Oxford. He has expounded Catholic principles and philosophy to a public with less narrowly theological interests. Among his larger works are St. Thomas Aquinas (1930); The Nature of Belief (1931), an analysis of faith which, following J. H. *Newman's Grammar of Assent, emphasizes its affective and non-logical elements; and The Mind and Heart of Love (1945), an assessment of the Christian conception of love (Agape, as contrasted with Eros and Philia), strongly influenced by D. Saurat and A. *Nygren. Among his other writings are Catholicism (1927), Mirage and Truth (1935), and The Pain of this World and the Providence of God (1935); but much of his most characteristic writing is in essays, articles, and contributions to collected works. From 1945 to 1950, Fr. D'Arcy was Provincial of the English Province of the Jesuits.

DARK AGES, The. A term in current use for the period in W. Europe extending from the decay of classical culture c. the 5th cent. to the beginning of medieval culture c. the 11th cent. It was formerly in common usage to cover also the medieval period down to the *Renaissance.

DARWINISM. The form of the theory of evolution put forward by Charles Darwin (1809–82), esp. in his works The Origin of Species (1859) and The Descent of Man (1871). He held that species of living beings evolve by natural selection, the fittest for their biological purpose in each generation alone surviving. In his later years Darwin modified his theory in some measure, and was prepared to take more account of the influence of environment upon evolution. Darwin himself became gradually more and more of an agnostic in religion.

Gertrude Himmelfarb, Darwin and the Darwinian Revolution (1959), with bibl.

D'AUBIGNÉ, JEAN HENRI MERLE. See Merle d'Aubigné, Jean Henri.

DAVENPORT, CHRISTOPHER (in religion **Franciscus a Sancta Clara**) (1598–1680), English RC theologian. After studying at *Dublin and *Oxford, he was converted to the RC faith and in 1615 went to *Douai. He entered the *Franciscan Order at Ypres in 1617, and later returned to England where he became chaplain successively to Queens *Henrietta Maria and Catherine of Braganza. He was on good terms with many of the Anglican clergy, and in his Paraphrastica Expositio Articulorum Confessionis Anglicanae (published separately in 1634, afterwards as an appendix to his Deus, natura, gratia) he endeavoured to show that the *Thirty-Nine Articles could be interpreted in conformity with Catholic tradition.

Collected ed. of his works (corrected), Douai, 2 vols.,1665–7. Paraphrastica Expositio Articulorum Confessionis Anglicanae was repr. from the Lat. ed. of 1646, with Eng. tr., ed. F. G. *Lee (London, 1865), with sketch of the author's life, pp. xix–xxx. G. G. Perry in D.N.B., xiv (1888), p. 108 f.; E. Burton in C.E., iv (1908), p. 639 f., s.v.

DAVENPORT, JOHN (1597–1670), *Puritan divine. Educated at Oxford, first at Merton, together with his brother Christopher (see preceding entry), and afterwards at Magdalen, he became Vicar of St. Stephen's, Coleman Street, in 1624. He incurred the hostility of W. *Laud, who nevertheless called him 'a most religious man', through a 'feoffment scheme' for the purchase of lay impropriations and his efforts to raise money for distressed ministers in the Palatinate. In 1633 he resigned his living and became co-pastor of the English church in Amsterdam. In 1637 he sailed to Boston with other well-known refugees, and in 1638 founded at Quinnipiac the colony of New Haven. In the colony, which was governed by 'The Seven Pillars of the State' (of which he was one), church membership was obligatory for electors and civil officers, until in 1665 the colony was absorbed in Connecticut. In 1662 he became involved in a controversy over Baptism, connected with the ''*Half-Way Covenant'. In 1668 he was ordained a minister, and set over the first church at Boston. He was the author of many works, including *A Catechism containing the chief Heads of the Christian Religion* (1659) and *The Power of Congregational Churches Asserted and Vindicated* (1672). In 1642 there appeared *The Profession of the Faith of the Reverend and Worthy Divine, Mr. John Davenport*.

Letters ed. I. McB. Calder (New Haven, Conn., 1937), with short biographical sketch, pp. 1–12. J. T. Adams in *Dict. Amer. Biog.*, v (1930), pp. 85–7.

DAVID (prob. d. *c.* 970 B.C.), first king of the Judaean dynasty. His reign is recounted in 1 Sam. 16–1 Kgs. 2 and in the idealized description of 1 Chron. 2 f., 10–29. He is hardly mentioned in any source outside the Bible.

David, the youngest son of Jesse, a Judaean of *Bethlehem, first appears when under Divine guidance he was anointed by *Samuel to the future kingship (1 Sam. 16. 13). Acc. to one tradition (1 Sam. 16. 14–23) he was summoned to the court of *Saul as a skilful player upon the harp and eventually appointed the king's armour bearer. Acc. to another, he appears to have first attracted Saul's attention when as an untried youth he gained his victory over Goliath, the Philistine giant (1 Sam. 17. 12–18. 4). After having been promoted by Saul, won the affection of Jonathan, Saul's son, and married Michal, Saul's daughter, he excited the king's jealousy and came in danger of his life. He fled to Nob (1 Sam. 21. 1) and thence prob. to western Judaea. Here he gathered a band of supporters. After defeating a body of the Philistines near Keilah, south of Adullam (1 Sam. 23. 1–5), he established himself at Ziklag as a vassal of Achish, King of Gath (1 Sam. 27. 6). He was saved from taking part in a campaign against the Israelites only by the distrust of the Philistine lords (1 Sam. 29).

On the death of Saul on Mt. Gilboa (*c.* 1010 B.C.), David, prob. still under Philistine patronage, set himself up at Hebron as king of the Judaean tribes (2 Sam. 2. 1–4). Seven and a half years later, when Ishbosheth, Saul's son, had been murdered he was accepted also by the Israelites (2 Sam. 4 f.). As soon as he had captured *Jerusalem, he established it as his capital (2 Sam. 5), where he reigned for thirty-three years. He restored the *Ark to the city (2 Sam. 6) and also seems to have planned the building of the *Temple (carried out in the next reign). In a series of battles he broke the supremacy of the Philistines and secured ascendancy over the neighbouring tribes (2 Sam. 8). Concerning his long reign in Jerusalem relatively little information survives, however, beyond the accounts of the quarrels of his sons (Absalom, *Solomon, &c.) which embittered the last years of his life.

Our portrait of David, one of the most life-like in the OT, is that of a ruler who both gave and inspired deep affection, not least through the magnanimity which he frequently showed to his personal enemies. If on occasion he fell into what to later ages seemed grievous sins (adultery with Bathsheba, murder of Uriah; 2 Sam. 11 f.), we should not forget the standards of his age nor (more significant) the depth and simple sincerity of his repentance. Throughout his life he was a consistent defender of the prophetic Hebrew faith.

David has traditionally been regarded as the author of the *Psalms (q.v.), many of which have been associated in later times with particular incidents in his life, e.g. the *Miserere (Ps. 51) with his repentance after the Uriah incident. But the tendency of modern OT scholarship is against assigning to David more than a small fraction of the Psalter. There is little reason, however, to doubt that he composed the dirges over Saul and Jonathan (2 Sam. 1. 19–27) and Abner (2 Sam. 3. 34).

In Hebrew tradition, the name of David came to occupy a central position. He was the king whose house and dominion were to stand for ever (2 Sam. 7. 12–16). But though his dynasty continued to reign in Judah, it lost the allegiance of the northern tribes (Israel) on the death of Solomon, and after frequent misfortunes and attacks fell to the Babylonians in 586 B.C. These calamities led the Prophets to look to the re-establishment of the full sovereignty of 'David' (i.e. of the house of David) as part of the deliverance of the nation (e.g. Amos 9. 11, Hos. 3. 5, Is. 16. 5, Jer. 30. 9, Ezek. 37. 24) to be achieved through a future prince of the house (Is. 9. 6 f.), a 'Branch' from the stock of Jesse (Is. 11. 1–10, Jer. 33. 15–22). As the hope of the *Messiah grew, the Deliverer was awaited from among the descendants of David, while David himself was conceived as a *type of the expected Messiah on the basis e.g. of such references as Ps. 110.

In the NT the Evangelists assume the Davidic descent of the Messiah (see *Genealogies of Christ*). It is as the 'Son of David' (Mt. 21. 9) that the Lord is welcomed to Jerusalem before His Passion. His Davidic ancestry is also stressed by St. *Paul (Rom. 1. 3, 2 Tim. 2. 8) and in the Book of Rev. (5. 5, 22. 16).

In the Fathers the idea of David as the type of Christ is a commonplace. St. *Augustine draws a parallel between David's victory over Goliath and that of the Lord over Satan; St. *Cyril of Alexandria explains that David's sling foreshadows the Cross of Christ; while in both St. Augustine and St. *Gregory the Great the victory of David in his weakness foreshadows that of the Church and the Christian martyrs. In Christian art he is regularly depicted with a crown and harp. His role as the ancestor of Christ is graphically represented in the *Jesse Windows (q.v.).

L. Desnoyers, *Histoire du peuple hébreu des juges à la captivité*, ii (1930), pp. 71–327, iii (1930), esp. pp. 184–8. T. H. Robinson in W. O. E. Oesterley–T. H. Robinson, *A History of Israel*, i (1932), pp. 200–238. Popular sketch by [A.] Duff Cooper (London, 1945). H. A. White in *H.D.B.*, i (1900), pp. 560–73, s.v., with reff. to older literature; L. Pirot in *Dict. Bibl.* Suppl., ii (1934), cols. 287–330, s.v., with reff. See also commentaries to Sam. and Kings, cited s.vv., and histories of Israel.

DAVID, St. (d. *c.* 601), patron saint of *Wales. Though he is one of the most famous British saints, there is no reliable biography of him. His earliest Life, that by Bp. Rhygyfarch or Ricimas, which dates from the second half of the 11th cent., was written with a view to supporting the claims of the Welsh bishops to independence of *Canterbury. Acc. to the legend, he belonged to a noble family; after having become a priest, lived for a time in retirement; later became the founder of 12 monasteries; and finally settled at Mynyw or Menevia, where he established an abbey whose religious led a life of extreme asceticism modelled on that of the Egyptian monks. *C.* 560 he is said to have attended the Synod of Brefi (the modern Llanddewi Brefi), apparently one of the few historically established facts of his life; but the story that he spoke there with such eloquence that he was chosen primate of the Cambrian Church seems to be legendary, as well as the assertion that he transferred the episcopal see from Caerleon to Menevia, now *St. Davids. He is related to have called in 569 a Council, generally styled the 'Synod of Victory', because held at a place the Latin name of which is given as 'Lucus Victoriae' (Caerleon). Other features of St. David's life, such as his pilgrimage to *Jerusalem and his consecration as archbishop by its patriarch, are mere inventions. St. David's cult seems to have been approved by Pope *Callistus II *c.* 1120; in 1398 Abp. *Arundel ordered his feast to be kept throughout the province of Canterbury. Feast day, 1 Mar.

St. David is first mentioned in the 'Catalogue of the Saints of Ireland' (*c.* 730) and in the 'Martyrology of Oengus' (*c.* 800), but without giving any details of his life. The text of Rhygyfarch's Life ed. by A. W. Wade-Evans in *Y Cymmrodor*, xxiv (1913), pp. 4–28. The same author published an Eng. trans. with copious notes, *The Life of St. David* (1923). See also E. Rhys, *The Life of Saint David* (1927), and S. M. Harris, *Saint David in the Liturgy* (Cardiff, 1940).

DAVID OF AUGSBURG (*c.* 1200–72), German preacher and mystic. A native of Augsburg, he entered the *Franciscan Order at Regensburg, where he soon became novice-master. In 1243 he was transferred to the newly founded convent at Augsburg, where with his friend, Berthold of Regensburg (d. 1272), also a great preacher, he carried on an active evangelism. His principal Latin writings, which have frequently been ascribed to St. *Bernard and to St. *Bonaventure, are 'De Compositione Hominis Exterioris', 'De Reformatione Hominis Interioris', 'De Septem

Processibus Religiosorum', and two letters to novices. The authenticity of 'De Inquisitione Haereticorum' (ed. 1879) has been doubted. He also was the first author to publish spiritual treatises in German. 'Die sieben Vorregeln der Tugend' and 'Der Spiegel der Tugend' are certainly genuine, whereas 'Die vier Fittiche geistlicher Betrachtung', 'Von der Anschauung Gottes', and others are doubtful. His teaching was eminently practical. He inculcated perfect obedience and humility, warned against illusions, and though enlarging more on the active than on the contemplative life, kept in view the mystic union of the soul and its three faculties of memory, understanding, and will with God.

David's 'De Compositione Hominis Exterioris' and other Lat. works for novices ed. Quaracchi, 1899; his German works in F. Pfeiffer (ed.), *Deutsche Mystiker des vierzehnten Jahrhunderts*, i (1845), pp. 309–405. Eng. tr. of various Lat. works by Dominic Devas, O.F.M., under the title *Spiritual Life and Progress* (2 vols., 1937), with introd. D. Stöckerl, *Bruder David von Augsburg* (Veröffentlichungen aus dem kirchenhistorischen Seminar München, iv, Hft. 4; 1914). G. Bareille in *D.T.C.*, iv (1911), cols. 153–7, s.v.; H. Lang, O.S.B. in *L.Th.K.*, iii (1931), col. 166, s.v.

DAVID OF DINANT (d. after 1210), *pantheistic philosopher. Practically nothing is known of his life except that he taught in Paris; it is even doubtful whether he is to be connected with Dinant in Belgium or Dinan in Brittany. His chief work was his treatise *De Tomis, hoc est De Divisionibus* (cf. *Erigena's *De Divisione Naturae*), which is prob. to be identified with his 'Quaternuli', condemned by a Council of the province of Sens held at *Paris in 1210 and at *Rome in 1215. From considerable extracts in St. *Albertus Magnus we gather that David taught that all distinctions in real being (*ens in actu*) are to be explained by a primal possible being (*ens in potentia, materia prima*), which David identified with the Divine Being. All things, material, intellectual, and spiritual, have one and the same essence, viz. God. Earlier students saw the main source of David's teaching in *Neoplatonism (Erigena, *Liber de Causis*); but G. Théry has maintained that he is primarily dependent on Aristotelian Physics and Metaphysics. He was probably closely connected with *Amalric of Bena, who was also (posthumously) condemned at Paris in 1210 for pantheistic teaching.

The primary authorities for his teaching include St. *Albert the Great, *Summa Theologica*, I, tract iv, qu. 20, m. 2; St. *Thomas Aquinas, *In Sent.*, I, Dist. xvii, qu. 1, a. 1; id., *Cont. Gent.*, i, 17; id., *Summa Theologica*, Ia, qu. iii, art. 8. C. Jourdain, 'Mémoire sur les sources philosophiques des hérésies d'Amaury de Chartres et de David de Dinan' in *Mémoires de l'Institut Impérial de France*, Académie des Inscriptions et de Belles-Lettres, xxvi (1867), pp. 467–98, esp. pp. 479–98; M. Hauréau, 'Mémoire sur la vraie source des erreurs attribuées à David de Dinan', ib., xxix (1877), pp. 319–30. G. Théry, O.P., *Autour du Décret de 1210:* I. David de Dinant (Bibliothèque Thomiste, vi; 1925). Überweg, ii, pp. 251 f., 706 f. M. *Grabmann in *L.Th.K.*, iii (1931), col. 167, s.v., with further bibl.

DAVIDSON, ANDREW BRUCE (1831–1902), Scottish OT scholar. He belonged to the Free Church of Scotland, and was educated at Marischal College, Aberdeen, and at New College, Edinburgh. At the latter he became assistant professor of Hebrew in 1858 and professor of Hebrew and Oriental languages in 1863. He was one of the first to introduce historical methods of OT exegesis into Scotland, and though his own dogmatic orthodoxy was seldom challenged, that of several of his pupils, who carried his principles a stage further, notably W. R. *Smith, was fiercely contested. His writings include *An Introductory Hebrew Grammar* (1874); commentaries on *Job* (1884), *Ezekiel* (1892), and *Nahum, Habakkuk, Zephaniah* (1896), in the 'Cambridge Bible'; *The Theology of the Old Testament*, ed. S. D. F. Salmond (1904); and a large number of articles in J. *Hastings' *Dictionary of the Bible*. He was also a member of the OT Revision Committee.

J. Strahan, *Andrew Bruce Davidson* (1917). Also biographical introduction by A. T. Innes to A. B. Davidson, *The Called of God*, ed. by J. A. Paterson (1902), pp. 3–58. Complete list of his works in *The Expository Times*, xv (1904), p. 453. S. R. *Driver in *D.N.B.*, *1901–1911*, i, p. 471 f.

DAVIDSON, RANDALL THOMAS (1848–1930), Abp. of *Canterbury. The son of Scottish Presbyterian parents, he was educated at Harrow (where also he was confirmed) and at Trinity College, Oxford, and then trained for holy orders by C. J. *Vaughan. He was ordained deacon in 1874 to the curacy of Dartford, Kent, where he remained until in 1878 he became resident chaplain to the Abp. of Canterbury, A. C. *Tait, whose second daughter he married. An interview with Queen *Victoria, on the occasion of Tait's death in 1882, greatly impressed her with his personality, and in 1883 he was appointed Dean of Windsor. In 1891 he became Bp. of *Rochester, in 1895 of *Winchester, and in 1903 Abp. of Canterbury. He resigned in 1928.

As the confidential adviser of Queen Victoria, and afterwards as Primate, Davidson exercised an exceptional influence upon the life of Church and nation. He endeavoured esp. to maintain the comprehensiveness of the C of E and to strengthen the Church as a spiritual and moral witness in national life. His Primacy was a period of special difficulty, requiring him to take action with regard to such varied questions as the disestablishment of the Church in *Wales, the *Kikuyu Controversy, the *Enabling Act, the *Malines Conversations, the Coal Strike (1926), and *Prayer Book Revision. Though suffering from lifelong ill-health owing to an accident in boyhood, he was an indefatigable worker. He possessed the courage necessary in a leader, even if he more often preferred to exercise the caution of a chairman. His elevation to the peerage as 'Baron Davidson of Lambeth', after his resignation of the Primacy, was the recognition of one whose service to the Church was also, in a high degree, service to the nation.

G. K. A. Bell, *Randall Davidson* (2 vols., 1935). Id. in *D.N.B.*, *1922–1930*, pp. 240–8.

DAWES HICKS, GEORGE. See *Hicks, George Dawes*.

DAY HOURS. The services of the *Breviary other than *Matins, the 'night office'; that is, *Lauds, *Prime, *Terce, *Sext, *None, *Vespers, and *Compline. The office-book which contains these services is known as the *Diurnal.

DAY OF ATONEMENT; JUDGEMENT. See *Atonement*; *Judgement, Day of*.

DAY'S PSALTER. A popular name (which does not appear on any title page) for the metrical edition of the Psalms by Thomas *Sternhold (d. 1549) and John Hopkins (d. 1570). It applies to the early complete editions of this Psalter, which were printed by John Day (1552–84) from 1562 onwards. More commonly called the *Old Version*, it had been in use, in incomplete form, since 1549. Reissued by other printers, it continued to circulate widely for over a hundred years.

DEACON (Gk. διάκονος, 'servant', 'minister'; cf. διακονέω, 'I serve'), the rank in the Christian ministry next below the presbyter (priest) and bishop. The institution of the diaconate is traditionally seen in the ordination of the Seven, among them *Stephen and *Philip, by imposition of hands for the service of the poor and the distribution of alms (Acts 6. 1–6), though the word διάκονος is not found here. Where it occurs in the NT in a technical sense (Phil. 1. 1, 1 Tim. 3. 8) it is of ministers who serve under the presbyter-bishops. In the *Pastoral Epp. the deacons are a separate class of Church officers, charged chiefly with material duties.

In post-NT times deacons continued to exercise similar functions. They are mentioned in *Clement of Rome's Ep. to the Corinthians, and also several times in the Epp. of *Ignatius together with bishops and priests, always in the third place. In the Patristic age, when the office was normally held for life, their functions varied from place to place. They commonly read or chanted the *Epistle and *Gospel at the Eucharist, received the offerings of the faithful, and inscribed the names of the donors in the *diptychs, assisted the priest in the distribution of Holy Communion or distributed it themselves, directed the prayers of the laity during the service, and gave the signal for penitents and catechumens to leave the church before the beginning of the *Canon. These liturgical functions were considerably curtailed when, in 595, St. *Gregory the Great transferred many of their musical duties to the *cantors.

Their original office of collecting and distributing the alms gave them considerable importance and the *archdeacon, the chief deacon of a given place, became the bishop's principal administrative officer. In Rome their influence was esp. marked through their association with the Pope, where their number was long restricted to seven, a tradition which has survived in the seven *Cardinal Deacons. It gave rise, however, to abuses. Already at *Nicaea (325; can. 18) their powers were curbed and the Council of *Toledo in 633 and the *Trullan Synod in 692 had to stress their hierarchical inferiority to the priesthood. Their influence diminished considerably during the Middle Ages, and in episcopal Churches in modern times the diaconate has become merely a stage (in the C of E the first) in preparation for the priesthood.

In the C of E a cleric begins his ministerial work on becoming a deacon. He is debarred from celebrating the Eucharist, from giving private Absolution, and from pronouncing the General Absolution or the Blessing. Before entering the diaconate the candidate must provide the bishop with evidence of moral and intellectual suitability, and must have been accepted for some ecclesiastical preferment ('title'). Unless he has a *faculty, he may not enter the diaconate before he is 23 years old. He generally remains in the order for a year.

Similar rules bind the diaconate in the RC Church. The deacon now has hardly any functions beyond his ministrations at High Mass and at Benediction. He is no longer allowed to preach and to administer Solemn Baptism except with special permission from his superiors. But he retains the right to chant the Gospel, to present the sacrificial offerings to the celebrant, to invite the congregation to pray, and to chant the 'Ite Missa est' at Mass and to expose the Bl. Sacrament and put it back into the Tabernacle at Benediction. He also sings the *Exultet on Holy Saturday. But owing to the short time spent in the diaconate and hence the fewness of deacons, the liturgical functions proper to a deacon are now usually performed by a priest. The characteristic vestments of the deacon are the dalmatic, and stole worn over the left shoulder. It is disputed whether or not ordination to the diaconate conveys '*character'. It is held, however, that the diaconate is indelible and that the deacon is bound to celibacy.

In many of the Protestant Churches the name is applied to the holders of an office in the ministry. In the *Lutheran Church the word deacon is applied to assistant parochial ministers, even though they are in full Lutheran orders. J. *Calvin's Institutes (IV, iii, 9) recognized two classes of deacons, those who administered the alms and those who cared for the poor and sick. Such remain the functions of deacons in Presbyterianism where there is also provision for a deacons' court, directly responsible to the presbytery and concerned with the proper distribution of Church goods. Where such a court does not exist, the deacons' functions are performed by elders. In the *Baptist and *Congregational Churches more definitely spiritual functions are assigned to the deacons, who assist the pastor and also distribute the elements at the Communion.

J. N. Seidl, Der Diakonat in der katholischen Kirche (Ratisbon, 1884). O. Zöckler, Diakonen und Evangelisten (1893). J. Viteau, 'L'Institution des diacres et des veuves' in R.H.E., xxii (1926), pp. 513-37. H. W. Beyer in T.W.B., ii (1935), pp. 88-93, s.v. διάκονος. S. Cheetham in D.C.A.,

i (1875), pp. 526-32, s.v.; H. M. *Gwatkin in H.D.B., i (1898), p. 574 f., s.v.; H. Thurston, S.J., in C.E., iv (1908), pp. 647-651, s.v.; J. Forget in D.T.C., iv (1911), cols. 703-31, s.v. 'Diacres'; H. *Leclercq, O.S.B., in D.A.C.L., iv (pt. 1; 1920), cols. 738-46, s.v. 'Diacre'; F. Claeys-Bouuaert in D.D.C., iv (1949), cols. 1198-1206, s.v. 'Diacre'; P. Palazzini in E.C., iv (1950), cols. 1535-44, s.v. 'Diacono e archidiacono'.

DEACONESS. In the early Church the term designated a woman officially charged with certain functions in the Church. The institution, though not the designation, apparently goes back to the Apostolic age. St. *Paul's mention of Phoebe, 'deaconess (οὖσαν διάκονον) of the Church that is at Cenchreae' (Rom. 16. 1), as well as 1 Tim. 3. 11, are usually held to refer to a special office; and *Pliny, in his letter to Trajan, speaks of two 'ancillae quae ministrae dicebantur'. The term διακόνισσα (Lat. diaconissa) did not, however, come into use until the 4th cent. Earlier documents use 'diacona', 'vidua', or 'virgo canonica', and the distinction between widows and deaconesses is rather obscure.

The office, which developed greatly in the 3rd and 4th cents., is described in the '*Didascalia' and the '*Apostolic Constitutions'. The age of entry, fixed at 60 by St. Paul and at 50 by the 'Didascalia', was reduced to 40 by the Council of *Chalcedon. The deaconess devoted herself to the care of the sick and the poor of her sex; she was present at interviews of women with bishops, priests, or deacons; instructed women catechumens, and kept order in the women's part of the church. Her most important function was the assistance at the baptism of women, at which, for reasons of propriety, many of the ceremonies could not be performed by the deacons. When, therefore, adult baptism became rare, the office of deaconess declined in importance. This process was helped by abuses which had crept in, when deaconesses arrogated to themselves ministerial functions, e.g. in the *Monophysite and *Nestorian communities, where they administered Holy Communion to women, read the Scriptures in public, &c. The Councils of Epaon (517) and of Orléans (533) abrogated the office, but it is found in other places till the 11th cent. In the E., where the prerogatives of deaconesses were more marked, including the investiture with the stole and the distribution of the chalice, the process was somewhat slower. The reception of stole and maniple by the *Carthusian nuns at their profession would seem to be a survival of the ancient office.

In the 19th cent. the office was revived in a modified form. The first Protestant community of deaconesses was that established by the German pastor, T. Fliedner, at *Kaiserswerth (q.v.) in 1836. From there it spread to other countries, notably England and the U.S.A. At the ceremony of dedication the deaconess promises to be obedient and faithful to her calling as long as God will keep her in it. In the C of E the order is described as 'the one existing ordained ministry for women' to which they are 'admitted by episcopal imposition of hands' conferring lifelong status.

The first deaconess in the C of E (Miss Elizabeth Ferard) was dedicated to her work in 1861 by A. C. *Tait, Bp. of London. Diocesan institutes on the model of Kaiserswerth were founded in many parts of the country, and rules drawn up for them in 1871. The example was followed by the *Methodists in 1888, and in the same year deaconesses were established in the Church of Scotland.

J. Pien, 'Tractatus... de Ecclesiae Diaconissis' in *A A.SS.*, Sept., I (1746), pp. i–xxviii. J. Mayer (ed.), *Monumenta de Viduis, Diaconissis, Virginibusque Tractantia* (Florilegium Patristicum, xlii; Bonn, 1938), with reff. T. Schäfer, *Die weibliche Diakonie in ihrem ganzen Umfang* (3 vols., ed. 2, 1887–94). H. Seesemann–N. Bonwetsch, *Das Amt der Diakonissen in der alten Kirche* (1891); A. Kalsbach, *Die altkirchliche Einrichtung der Diakonissen bis zu ihrem Erlöschen* (Römische Quartalschrift, Supplementheft, xxii; 1926). C. H. *Turner, 'Ministries of Women in the Primitive Church. Widow, Deaconess and Virgin in the First Four Christian Centuries' in *The Constructive Quarterly*, vii (1919), repr. in *Catholic and Apostolic*, ed. H. N. Bate (1931), No. xi, pp. 316–51, esp. pp. 328–43. C. Robinson, *The Ministry of Deaconesses* (1898). *The Ministry of Women*. A Report by a Committee Appointed by the Abp. of Canterbury (S.P.C.K., 1919).

DEAD, Prayers for the. The practice of offering prayers on behalf of the dead is closely connected with the doctrine of *Purgatory (q.v.). The warrant for it is the belief that those in purgatory are still part of the Church and, as members of the Mystical Body of Christ who have not yet arrived at the beatific vision, can be helped by the intercessions of those still alive. Explicit scriptural justification for the practice has been found in 2 Macc. 12. 40–6. There is ample evidence for its use in the inscriptions of the *Catacombs, with their constant prayers for the peace and refreshment of the souls of the departed, and the early liturgies also commonly contain commemorations of the dead. Of the early Fathers, *Tertullian, *Cyprian, and others are witnesses of the regular practice of private prayers for the dead, and in the 4th cent. one of the counts against the heretic, *Aerius, was that he denied its efficacy and legitimacy. On the other hand, the early Church never prayed for the martyrs, because they were believed to be in full possession of beatitude immediately after death, a refusal extended later to all canonized saints. Nor, it is held, can the damned, i.e. those who have died in unrepented mortal sin, be assisted by our prayers, though who they are is known to God alone. Acc. to the teaching of Catholic theologians, private prayers and Masses for the Dead may be said also for those outside the Church, but the public offering of Mass and other liturgical offices for them is forbidden.

At first the Protestant Reformers continued the traditional custom of praying for the dead. But before long they came to denounce it, partly on the ground that it was not expressly ordered in the Bible (2 Macc. 12. 40–6 was dismissed, since the 'Apocrypha' no longer ranked as Scripture), partly through their rejection of the doctrine of purgatory. In the C of E express prayers for the dead have been absent from the BCP since 1552 and the practice is denounced as unprofitable in the

*Homily 'On Prayer' (Part iii) on the ground that it is useless to intercede for the dead who are already either in heaven or hell. Since the middle of the 19th cent., however, the practice had been increasingly adopted in the C of E. Prayers for the Dead were included in an authorized 'Form of Intercession' put out in 1900 on behalf of the forces serving in South Africa and since then in other official forms of service. In a somewhat veiled form they were inserted in the proposed revision of the BCP in 1927–8; and their use is now very common except among Churchmen of pronounced Evangelical beliefs.

The traditional Catholic teaching was reasserted at the Council of *Trent, sessions XXII (cf. can. 3) and XXV (for both, cf. Denz.-Bann., ed. 18–20, 1932, Nos. 940, 950, 983), as well as in the Decree of Union subscribed at the Council of *Florence of 1439 (ib., No. 693). See also art. *Purgatory*.

DEAD SEA, The. The inland sea to the SE of Palestine into which the *Jordan flows. It is much the lowest lake in the world, being nearly 1,300 feet below sea-level. Acc. to Hebrew tradition, it was formed when the cities of the plain, Sodom and Gomorrah, were overthrown for their wickedness (Gen. 13). There are several refs. to it in the OT (e.g. Ezek. 47. 18, Zech. 14. 8), though never as the 'Dead Sea' by name. In the NT there is no mention of it. The designation 'Dead Sea' (θάλασσα νεκρά) is first found in Pausanias and Galen.

G. A. *Smith, *The Historical Geography of the Holy Land* (ed. 25; 1931), ch. xxiii, pp. 497–530, with bibl. reff. F. M. Abel, O.P., *Géographie de la Palestine*, i (1933), pp. 167–9. L. Gautier in *E. Bi.*, i (1899), cols. 1042–7, s.v., with bibl.

DEAD SEA SCROLLS, The. The name popularly given to the remains of a once considerable collection of *Hebrew and *Aramaic MSS., written for the most part in an early form of the square (or 'Assyrian') script, and discovered in caves in the neighbourhood of Qumran, at the north-western end of the Dead Sea, between 1947 and 1956. No one manuscript has been preserved without damage, and of the great majority there survive only tiny fragments. Nearly all the books of the canonical OT are represented (some of them by several copies), together with many *apocryphal and pseudepigraphal books (known hitherto only from translations), and a number of other works not previously known at all. Esp. interesting in this last class are: (1) a series of OT Commentaries which interpret the Biblical text as prophecy fulfilled in events of the commentators' own times; (2) a collection of 'Psalms of Thanksgiving', very much on the lines of the Biblical Psalms and largely composed of phrases derived from them; (3) a strange work, to which the name 'The War of the Sons of Light against the Sons of Darkness' has been given, possibly apocalyptic in character; (4) a hand-book, somewhat analogous to the *Didache and called variously 'The Manual of Discipline' or 'The Sectarian Document', containing the rules governing the life of the religious community to which the compiler obviously belonged; and (5) the so-called '*Damascus Fragments' or 'Zadokite Documents'.

About the origin and date of the Scrolls all that can safely be said is that they once belonged to the library of the Jewish community (some would say 'sect') which was centred on a large building (or monastery) at Qumran about the beginning of the Christian era, and that in all probability most of them were written there. Excavation of the building has shown that it was first occupied about 135 B.C. and continued in occupation, with a break of some thirty or forty years during the lifetime of *Herod the Great, down to the time of the First Jewish Revolt (A.D. 66–70). From this and certain other considerations deriving from the study of the Scrolls and the circumstances in which they were found, it is generally agreed that they are to be dated within the limits 20 B.C. and A.D. 70; and their finding in the caves is best explained on the hypothesis that they were hidden there for safe-keeping when the destruction of the centre seemed imminent.

In view of the fact that practically no other MS. material in Hebrew and Aramaic has survived from this period, the Scrolls are of great importance palaeographically. Equally important is their bearing upon our knowledge of the history of the OT text. They show clearly both that the *Massoretic text was no new creation of the Christian era, and also that the critical view that other types of text were current in the pre-Christian era is abundantly justified. Furthermore, they provide significant first-hand evidence for Jewish life and thought (albeit 'sectarian') at the time that Christianity was born. Hence they are a source of information which no student of Christian origins can afford to ignore.

M. Burrows (ed.), *The Dead Sea Scrolls of St. Mark's Monastery* (2 vols., New Haven, 1950–5); D. Barthélemy, O.P.–J. T. Milik (edd.), *Discoveries in the Judaean Desert* (Oxford, 1955 ff.); E. L. Sukenik (ed.), *Dead Sea Scrolls of the Hebrew University* (Jerusalem, with comm. in Hebrew, 1954; in English, 1955); Y. Yadin (ed.), *The Scroll of the War of the Sons of Light with the Sons of Darkness* (Jerusalem, 1956; in Hebrew; Eng. tr. in preparation, 1957). T. H. Gaster (ed.), *The Scriptures of the Dead Sea Sect in English Translation* (New York, 1956; texts). M. Burrows, *The Dead Sea Scrolls* (New York, 1955), incl. Eng. tr. of extracts. J. T. Milik, *Dix Ans de découvertes dans le désert de Juda* (1957). C. Rabin, *Qumran Studies* (1957); M. Black, *The Scrolls and Christian Origins* (1961).

DEADLY SINS, Seven. See *Seven Deadly Sins*.

DE ALEATORIBUS (or Adversus Aleatores). A short homily, written in somewhat uncouth Latin, which vigorously denounces dice-players and all games of chance. Its authorship has been much disputed. At one time it was believed to be a work of *Cyprian (d. 258), but this view has now been almost universally abandoned. In 1888 A. *Harnack ascribed it to Pope *Victor I (189–99), thus making it the earliest piece of Christian Latin literature. Subsequent study has made it probable, however, that it drew upon Cyprian's writings, and that the work is thus not earlier than the middle of the 3rd cent. Harnack

himself came later to believe it was the work of a *Novatianist antipope at Rome.

Crit. ed of text in Cyprian's *Opera*, ed. W. Hartel, C.S.E.L., iii (1), pp. 92–104; text also in J. P. Migne, *PL*, iv, 827–36. A. Harnack, *Der pseudocyprianische Tractat De Aleatoribus, die älteste lateinische Schrift, ein Werk des römischen Bischofs Victor I (saec. II)* (*T.U.* v, Hft. 1; 1888); id., 'Zu Pseudocyprian. *Adv. Aleat.* 1 (p. 93, 1f., ed. Hartel)' in *T.U.*, xx, Hft. 3 (1900), pp. 112–16. H. Koch, 'Zur Schrift adversus aleatores' in *Festgabe für K. Müller* (1922), pp. 58–67. Bardenhewer, ii, p. 498 f.

DEAN (Lat. *decanus*, from *decem*, 'ten'). The title of various, originally minor, officials, e.g. a monk supervising ten novices.

(1) *Rural deans assist the *bishop in administering a subdivision of an *archdeaconry. In the 9th cent. this office replaced the archpresbyterate.

(2) The dean of a *cathedral (also formerly an archpresbyter) controls its services and, with the *chapter, supervises its fabric and property. He ranks next to the bishop, of whom in the Anglican, but not the Roman, Church he is considerably independent. In recent foundations, however, the bishop is also dean, and decanal functions are largely discharged by a *provost under his authority. In the C of E deans are appointed by the crown.

(3) The heads of the *collegiate churches of *Westminster, *Windsor, and other peculiars which are governed by Deans (and chapters) are independent of episcopal authority.

(4) The 'Dean of the Province of *Canterbury' is the Bp. of London *ex officio*. He summons the Bishops of the Southern Province to meet in *Convocation under a mandate from the Abp. of Canterbury.

(5) For *Dean of the Arches, see foll. entry.

(6) In the RC Church, the Dean of the Sacred College is the *Cardinal Bishop senior by consecration, who also holds the see of *Ostia.

(7) The *Lutheran superintendent and *Calvinist overseer are sometimes styled dean.

The title of dean of a college or a university faculty, very often held by a layman, should not be confused with the ecclesiastical title; but the Dean of *Christ Church, Oxford, is both head of the college and dean of the cathedral.

DEAN OF THE ARCHES. The lay judge in the Court of *Arches. Formerly *Bow Church ('Sta. Maria de Arcubus'), from which he derived his title, was, with twelve other parishes, exempt from the jurisdiction of the Bp. of *London, and the Dean exercised '*peculiar jurisdiction' over the thirteen parishes. The original office is now extinct, owing to the incorporation of the parishes into the see of London, but the legal functions that gradually came to be attached to it are still performed by a judge who retains the title. He is the only judge capable of passing sentence of deprivation against a *clerk in holy orders. See also *Arches, Court of*.

Irene J. Churchill, *Canterbury Administration* (2 vols., 1933), esp. i, pp. 436–46, and ii, pp. 186–92, with list of Deans, pp. 238–40. R. Phillimore, *The Ecclesiastical Law of the Church of England*, i (ed. 2, 1895), p. 214.

DEARMER, PERCY (1867-1936), writer on ceremonial subjects and religious music. He was educated at Westminster and at *Christ Church, Oxford, where he was much influenced by James Adderley and C. *Gore and became one of the first members of the *Christian Social Union. Ordained deacon in 1891, he set himself to popularize the adaptation of medieval English ceremonial to the Prayer Book rite, setting out his ideals in *The Parson's Handbook* (1899), a widely used manual, and putting them into practice as Vicar of St. Mary's, Primrose Hill, Hampstead (1901-15), where he attracted the interest of many leading artists. From 1919 to 1936 he was Professor of ecclesiastical art at *King's College, London, and in 1931 he became a Canon of Westminster. He was co-editor of the *English Hymnal* (1906), **Songs of Praise* (1925), and the *Oxford Book of Carols* (1928); to these hymnals he contributed several hymns and translations. His many books on ecclesiastical, topographical, and other subjects include *Oxford: The Cathedral and See* (1897) and *Wells: The Cathedral and See* (1898), both in 'Bell's Cathedral Series', *Highways and Byways in Normandy* (1900), G. van der Goude's *Dat Boexken vander Missen* (*Alcuin Club, 1903), *Body and Soul* (1909; on spiritual healing), *Everyman's History of the English Church* (1909), *Everyman's History of the Prayer Book* (1912), *The Art of Public Worship* (1919), *Art and Religion* (1924), *The Truth about Fasting* (1928), and *Songs of Praise Discussed* (1933).

Life by his wife, Nan Dearmer (1940, with bibl.)

DE AUXILIIS. In 1597 *Clement VIII appointed the 'Congregatio de Auxiliis' to deal with the contemporary disputes on the manner in which Divine *grace operated. Though Reformation controversies had forced the subject on the attention of RC theologians, the Council of *Trent (1546-63) had left many of the issues unsettled, and towards the end of the 16th cent. division of opinion had become very acute. A fresh stage was reached when the *Jesuit theologian, L. de *Molina, published his *De Concordia liberi arbitrii cum gratiae donis* (1598), and the *Dominican theologian, D. *Bañez vigorously controverted his teaching. The 'Congregatio' reported for the first time on 19 Mar. 1598, advising that the circulation of Molina's book be forbidden and 90 propositions extracted from it condemned; but the Pope declined to ratify the decision. A second attempt to secure Papal confirmation when the number of offending propositions had been reduced to 20 was equally unsuccessful. Yet a further attempt, under *Paul V, to achieve the same object failed. Finally, on 5 Sept. 1607, in an attempt to satisfy both sides, the Pope decreed that the *Dominicans could not justly be accused of *Calvinism nor the *Jesuits of *Pelagianism, and that neither side should pronounce the contrary teaching heretical.

DE BRUYS, PIERRE. See *Peter of Bruys*.

DECADARY CULT. The system of worship instituted during the French Revolution on the basis of a 10-day 'week' (ending with 'Décadi', the day of rest) to supplant that associated with the Christian calendar.

DECADE (Lat. *decem*, 'ten'). The name technically used for each of the five divisions into which each *chaplet of the Rosary is subdivided, because each contains *ten* *Hail Marys, together with an *Our Father and (in general practice) a *Gloria Patri. As each decade is associated with one of the fifteen *Mysteries of the Rosary, they form unities in themselves and are sometimes recited as such, without the whole chaplet being said.

DECALOGUE. See *Commandments, The Ten*.

DECANI [sc. *sedes*], (Lat.) 'the place of the dean' (*decani*). As the dean's stall is on the south side of the cathedral, the term 'decani' is used to indicate those who in antiphonal singing sit on the decanal side of the choir. It is now in common usage for other churches, besides cathedrals. The opposite side is known as the '*cantoris'.

DE CANTILUPE, St. THOMAS and **WALTER.** See *Cantilupe, St. Thomas de* and *Walter*.

DECAPOLIS, The. A region consisting of ten allied cities E. of the *Jordan in N. Palestine. It included the towns of *Damascus, Gerasa, and Gadara, and contained a Greek-speaking population. Cf. Mt. 4. 25, Mk. 5. 20 and 7. 31.

G. A. *Smith, *The Historical Geography of the Holy Land* (ed. 25, 1931), ch. xxix, pp. 621-38; F. M. Abel, O.P., *Géographie de la Palestine*, ii, p. 145 f. J. van Kasteren, S.J., in *Dict. Bibl.*, ii (1899), cols. 1333-6, s.v. 'Décapole'.

DE CAUSSADE, JEAN PIERRE. See *Caussade, Jean Pierre De*.

DECEASED WIFE'S SISTER'S MARRIAGE ACT (1907). The provisions of this Act (7 Edw. VII, c. 47), though it has full civil sanction, are in conflict with traditional ecclesiastical law, which disallows the marriage of a widower with his wife's sister or of a widow with her husband's brother. A corresponding Deceased Brother's Widow's Marriage Act (11 & 12 Geo. V, c. 24) was passed in 1921. Both classes of marriages were forbidden in M. *Parker's 'Table of *Kindred and Affinity' (q.v.). An incumbent of the C of E who has scruples is not compelled to solemnize any such marriage, but he is not entitled to repel from the altar those who have married under the provisions of the Acts as 'open and notorious evil livers'. See also *Affinity*.

DECIUS (d. 251), Roman Emperor from 249. C. Messius Quintus Decius was appointed by the Emp. Philip the Arabian in 248 to take command on the Danube against the Goths. By temporarily checking their invasion, he won the confidence of the troops who proclaimed him Emperor in 249. After Philip's defeat and death near *Verona, Decius was accepted by the Senate. In the next year he undertook the first systematic persecution of the Christians, beginning with the execution of *Fabian, Bp. of *Rome, in Jan. 250. In June all citizens were required to furnish proof of having offered sacrifice to the Emperor; and, though many gave way or escaped through bribery, thousands were put to death. The defections raised in an acute form the question whether penance was possible for the *lapsed (q.v.) and led to the conflict between St. *Cyprian and *Novatianists over their treatment. The persecution, which was probably initiated to combat the allegedly fissiparous influence of Christianity, was ended by the death of Decius in June 251, when he was trapped and killed by the Goths near Abrittus in the Dobrudja. See also *Libellatici*.

See St. *Cyprian's works *passim*, and *Eusebius, *HE.*, vi–vii.

DECLARATION AGAINST TRANSUBSTANTIATION. The Declaration imposed by the *Test Act of 1673 on all persons holding civil or military office. It ran as follows: 'I, A. B., do declare that I do believe that there is not any transubstantiation in the Sacrament of the Lord's Supper, or in the elements of bread and wine, at or after the consecration thereof by any person whatsoever'.

DECLARATION OF ASSENT. See *Assent, Declaration of.*

DECLARATIONS OF INDULGENCE, The. Four royal declarations are so named.

(1) On 25 Oct. 1660 *Charles II issued a Declaration in which he announced his purpose of calling a Conference which should implement the Declaration of *Breda (q.v.) giving 'a liberty to tender consciences', and granting indulgence in certain mainly ceremonial matters (Cross in Baptism, bowing at the Holy Name, use of surplice) at least until after the projected (*Savoy) Conference (15 Apr.–24 July 1661).

(2) On 26 Dec. 1662 Charles II issued a further Declaration, proclaiming his continued intention of honouring his promises at Breda and of placing before Parliament a bill allowing him to exercise more freely the power of suspending the penal laws against religious dissentients. But in Feb. 1663 the Commons petitioned for the stern enforcement of the Act of *Uniformity and the bill for toleration was defeated in the Lords. The legal force of this Declaration is obscure, since Charles appeared at once to claim the dispensing power

as involved in the royal prerogative of mercy and to acknowledge the supremacy of Parliament.

(3) On 15 Mar. 1672 Charles II issued a 'Declaration of Indulgence for Tender Consciences', suspending the execution of the penal laws in matters ecclesiastical against all nonconformists and recusants. In 1673 Parliament resolved that 'Penal Statutes in matters ecclesiastical cannot be suspended but by Act of Parliament' and the Declaration was withdrawn.

(4) On 4 April 1687 *James II issued a Declaration of Indulgence proclaiming full liberty of worship. It suspended the execution of the penal laws, allowed peaceable meetings of nonconformists provided that the Justices of the Peace were notified, ordained that the *Oaths of Supremacy and Allegiance and all the tests prescribed by the *Test Act should not be required of those employed in the royal service and remitted all penalties pending for ecclesiastical offences. The Declaration was republished, with some changes, a year later (27 Apr. 1688) and in the following week (4 May) an Order in Council required it to be read on two successive Sundays in all Anglican churches in the Kingdom (20 and 27 May in London, 3 and 10 June elsewhere). The opposition of the London clergy provoked the arrest (8 June) and trial of the *Seven Bishops.

For the 1662 Declaration see P. Bayne, *Documents Relating to the Settlement of the Church of England by the Act of Uniformity of 1662* (1862), pp. 460–8; for those of 1672 and 1687, W. C. Costin and J. S. Watson, *The Law and Working of the Constitution*, i (1952), p. 324 f. and 343–5; for that of 1688, Gee-Hardy, No. cxxi, pp. 641–4, and in H. Bettenson, *Documents of the Christian Church* (1943), pp. 407–10. F. Bate, *The Declaration of Indulgence 1672* (1908).

DECLARATION OF THE FRENCH CLERGY. See *Gallican Articles.*

DECLARATION OF THE SOVEREIGN. Also known as the 'Royal Declaration'. The Declaration repudiating the RC faith which was imposed on William III and Mary by Parliament (1 W. & M., Sess. 2, c. 2) when they came to the throne. It has been taken by all subsequent sovereigns. In its original form it was based on the *Declaration against Transubstantiation contained in the *Test Act of 1673, but included also a repudiation of the Roman doctrines of the *Invocation of Saints and of the *Sacrifice of the Mass, and a 'long rigmarole' wherein the sovereign affirmed that he was not being dispensed by the Pope from taking the Oath in its plain meaning. The Oath survived the repeal of the Test Act in 1829; but to remove offence it was altered in 1910 to 'I, N., do solemnly and sincerely in the presence of God profess, testify, and declare that I am a faithful Protestant, and that I will, according to the true intent of the enactments to secure the Protestant Succession to the throne of my realm, uphold and maintain such enactments to the best of my powers according to law'.

DECLARATORY ACTS. In the [Presbyterian] Church of *Scotland, two Acts relieving ministers from their obligation to subscribe to every item of the subordinate standards of faith, esp. the *Westminster Confession. (1) The Declaratory Act of 1879, passed in its synod in the *United Presbyterian Church, dealt with certain of the harsher *Calvinist doctrines, and affirmed *inter alia* that the damnation of infants and heathen is not necessarily involved in election and that total depravity and fore-ordination to death must allow for human responsibility. It also upheld liberty of opinion on such matters as the six days in the Genesis account of creation, disapproved of anything in the standards supposed to over-exalt the civil magistrate and to teach intolerance, and asserted the Church's obligation to maintain *voluntaryism. (2) The Declaratory Act of the *Free Church of Scotland of 1892 followed similar lines, but refrained from reference to voluntaryism and any implied attack on a State Church as such. This latter Act was rejected by a small conservative body, chiefly Highland, which formed themselves into the 'Free Presbyterian Church'.

Texts in J. R. Fleming, *A History of the Church in Scotland, 1875–1929* (1933), pp. 306–8; cf. also p. 22 f.

DECOLLATION OF ST. JOHN THE BAPTIST, The. The feast celebrated on 29 Aug. in commemoration of the martyrdom of St. *John the Baptist at the hands of *Herod Antipas, as related in Mt. 14. 3–12 and Mk. 6. 14–30. It is already mentioned in the **Martyrologium Hieronymianum* and the *Gelasian Sacramentary. It has been observed in England at least since 668.

*Augustine, *Sermones*, cccvii and cccviii (ed. Ben.). Reff. in the Martyrology of *Ado and elsewhere indicate that the Feast orig. commemorated the translation of the head of St. John Baptist from a monastery near *Emesa known as the Spelaion to the church in the city. Cf. H. *Leclercq, O.S.B., in *D.A.C.L.*, vii (pt. 2; 1927), cols. 2167–84, esp. 2170 f.

DE CONDREN, CHARLES. See *Condren, Charles de.*

DECRETALS. Papal letters, strictly those in response to a question. They have the force of law within the Pope's jurisdiction. The first decretal was that sent in 385 by Pope *Siricius to Himerius, Bp. of Tarragona. The earliest influential collection was that made by *Dionysius Exiguus (*c.* 520). About 850 appeared the '*False Decretals' (q.v.), containing many forged letters of popes before Siricius. After *Gratian had systematized existing *canon law in his 'Decretum' (*c.* 1140), authoritative collections of later decretals were published by *Gregory IX (1234), *Boniface VIII (1298), and *Clement V (1317).

H. Grisar, S.J., 'Über Sammlungen ältester Papstbriefe und deren theologische Verwerthung' in *Z.K.T.*, xii (1888), pp. 487–532; K. Silva-Tarouca, S.J., 'Beiträge zur Uberlieferungsgeschichte der Papstbriefe des iv., v., und vi. Jahrhunderts', ib., xliii (1919), pp. 467–81 and 657–92. A. Van Hove in *C.E.*, iv (1908), pp. 670–3, s.v.; A. Villien in *D.T.C.*, iv (1911), cols. 206–12, s.v. 'Décrétales'. See also bibl. to *False Decretals*.

DECRETALS, False. See *False Decretals*.

DECRETUM GELASIANUM. An early Latin document, handed down most frequently under the name of Pope *Gelasius (492–96), but in some MSS. as the work of *Damasus (366–84) or *Hormisdas (514–23), containing *inter alia* a Latin list of the Books of the Bible. Acc. to E. von Dobschütz, it is not a Papal work at all, but a private compilation which was composed in Italy (but not at *Rome) in the early 6th cent. The document is in five parts, dealing with (1) Christ and the Holy Ghost; (2) the Canonical Scriptures; (3) the Roman Church and its dependent sees; (4) the Orthodox Councils and Fathers; (5) the 'Books to be Received' (works of the Fathers) and the *Apocryphal writings (Biblical and Patristic). The last item (*De libris recipiendis et non recipiendis*) gives the usual title to the whole work.

Text in part in J. P. Migne, *PL*, lix, 157–61. Crit. ed. by E. von Dobschütz in *T.U.*, xxxviii, Hft. 4 (1912). J. *Chapman, O.S.B., 'On the *Decretum Gelasianum* De Libris recipiendis et non recipiendis' in *R. Bén.*, xxx (1913), pp. 187–207 and 315–33. E. *Schwartz, 'Zum *Decretum Gelasianum*, in *Z.N.T.W.*, xxix (1930), pp. 161–8. Bardenhewer, iv, p. 626 f. H. *Leclercq, O.S.B., in *D.A.C.L.*, vi (pt. 1; 1924), cols. 722 47, s.v. 'Gélasien (Décret)', with extensive bibl.

DEDICATION, The Jewish Feast of the. The feast instituted by *Judas Maccabaeus in 165 B.C., to commemorate the purification of the Temple and its altar after their defilement by *Antiochus Epiphanes (1 Macc. 4. 59; 2 Macc. 10. 6). It was ordered to be observed on the 25th day of Chislev each year and kept for 8 days. A special feature of the feast, apart from the fact that it could be celebrated outside Jerusalem, was the lighting of lamps; hence it was sometimes called the 'Feast of the Lights'. Modern Jews observe the feast as 'Hanukkah'. The only reference to it in the NT is at Jn. 10. 22.

O. S. Rankin, *Origins of the Festival of Hanukkah* (1930); review by L. Finkelstein in *The Jewish Quarterly Review*, N.S., xxii (1931), pp. 169–73. S. Zeitlin, 'Hanukkah, its Origin and Significance' in *The Jewish Quarterly Review*, N.S., xxix (1938), pp. 1–36; J. Morgenstern, 'The Chanukkah Festival and the Calendar of Ancient Israel' in *Hebrew Union College Annual*, xx (1947), pp. 1–136, and xxi (1948), pp. 365–496.

DEDICATION OF CHURCHES. The earliest recorded instance of the dedication of a Christian church is that of the cathedral at Tyre in 314, described in the 'oratio panegyrica' of *Eusebius (*HE*, 10. 3 f.). The *Gelasian Sacramentary (7th cent.) contains a rite consisting of prayers, blessings, and sprinklings with holy water. In the following cents. the ceremonies increased in number, and by the 13th cent. the ritual had reached in essentials its present state, as is witnessed by the '*Pontifical' of *Durandus. It contains already the six principal parts, the blessing outside, the blessing in the middle of the church, the preparation for the consecration of the altar, the actual consecration of the altar, the procession of the relics, and the blessing of the altar vessels, ornaments, etc., followed finally by the Mass.

Acc. to modern W. practice, a church may be dedicated either by solemn consecration or by simple blessing. The former may be performed only by the bishop and is confined to churches designed for permanent ecclesiastical use; the latter, which is intended for temporary churches and those built of wood or metal, may be performed also by a priest (cf. *CIC*, 1147, §1; 1165, §1). The distinction had its beginnings in the 4th–6th cents., when only churches containing relics were solemnly consecrated, as may be seen from a letter of Pope *Vigilius (*c.* 538; J. P. Migne, *PL*, lxix, 18) in which he stated that the celebration of Masses was in itself sufficient blessing for a church without relics. Later, however, solemn consecration was more widely used, irrespective of the presence of relics. In its later forms, the blessing is a short ceremony consisting of prayers and sprinkling with holy water, followed by Mass. Desecrated churches must be reconciled by a special rite.

The Feast of the Dedication is the annual celebration of the day of the dedication of the church, and is to be kept, strictly speaking, only by consecrated churches. It is to be distinguished, of course, from the Patronal Feast. The first recorded observance of such a feast is that of the Dedication of the Church of the *Anastasis (see *Holy Sepulchre*) in *Jerusalem, described by *Etheria. In 1536 the English Convocations ordered that the Feast of Dedication 'throughout this realm' should be kept on the first Sunday in October, and this practice is commonly followed in England where the date of consecration is not known, though no such feast is contained in the calendar of the BCP. The Revised Book of 1928, however, proposed the first Sunday in October, 'if the day of consecration be not known'. In the RC Church the dedication festivals of the four principal Roman *basilicas, the *Lateran (9 Nov.), those of Sts. Peter and Paul (S. Pietro in Vaticano and S. Paolo fuori le mura; 18 Nov.), and *Santa Maria Maggiore (5 Aug.), are celebrated as feasts of the universal Church.

E. *Martène, *De Antiquis Ecclesiae Ritibus*, iii (1702), pp. 232–327, Lib. II, cap. xiii. R. W. Muncey, *A History of the Consecration of Churches and Churchyards* (1930). D. Stiefenhofer, *Die Geschichte der Kirchweihe vom 1.–7. Jahrhundert* (Veröffentlichungen aus dem kirchenhistorischen Seminar München, III. Reihe No. 8; 1909). J. Baudot, O.S.B., *La Dédicace des églises* (1909). W. H. *Frere, *Pontifical Services Illustrated from Miniatures of the XVth and XVIth Centuries* (*Alcuin Club Collections, iii and iv; 1901), 'Pontifical Services not included in the Book of Common Prayer. I. The Consecration of Churches', vol. i, pp. 1–54, and vol. ii, Pll. vii and xi, Figg. 33 and 34. J. Wickham Legg (ed.), *English Orders for Consecrating Churches in the Seventeenth Century, together with Forms for the Consecration of Churchyards, the First Stone of a Church, the Reconciliation of a Church and the Consecration of Altar Plate* (*Henry Bradshaw Society, xli; 1911). J. *Wordsworth, *On the Rite of Consecration of Churches, especially in the Church of England . . . together with the Form of Prayer and Order of Ceremonies in use in the Diocese of Salisbury* (Church Historical Society Tract lii; 1899). L. Eisenhofer, *Handbuch der katholischen Liturgik*, i (1932), pp. 589–91, and ii (1933), pp. 447–74. P. de Puniet in *D.A.C.L.*, iv (1921), cols. 374–404, s.v. 'Dédicace des églises', with reff. J. E. Swallow in G. Harford–M. Stevenson–J. W. Tyrer (edd.), *The Prayer Book Dictionary* (1912), pp. 241–4, s.v. 'Consecration of Churches and Churchyards'. Frances Arnold-Forster, *Studies in Church Dedications or England's Patron Saints* (3 vols., 1899); F. Bond, *Dedications and Patron Saints of English Churches* (1914).

DE DOMINIS, MARCO ANTONIO (1566–1624), 'Spalatrensis', Abp. of Spalato. He entered the *Jesuit Order as a youth, became famous as a professor of mathematics at Padua and of rhetoric and logic at Brescia, left the Order in 1596, and was Abp. of Spalato and Primate of Dalmatia from 1602 to 1616. Political conflicts between Rome and *Venice, to whose territory his see belonged, and personal difficulties with his clergy led him to resign his office and go to England. On his way there he wrote a bitter pamphlet against Rome, *Scogli del cristiano naufragio*. He was warmly welcomed by *James I, received as a member of the C of E, and made Dean of Windsor and Master of the Savoy in 1617. In the same year he assisted at the consecration of G. Montaigne (d. 1628) as Bp. of *Lincoln and published the first part of his main work *De Republica Ecclesiastica*, an attack on the monarchical government of Rome and a defence of national Churches. In 1619 he edited without authority Fr. Paul *Sarpi's (Italian) history of the Council of Trent, which he dedicated to James I. But his pride and avarice soon lost him his English friends, and fearing for his security when negotiations began for the Spanish marriage of Prince *Charles, he sought reconciliation with Rome. He left England in 1622, and now attacked the C of E as violently as formerly the Church of Rome, in *Sui Reditus ex Anglia Consilium* (1623; Anglican reply by R. *Crakanthorpe, 1625). After the death of Gregory XV, however, he came into conflict with the *Inquisition and was confined to the castle of Sant' Angelo at Rome as a relapsed heretic, where he died soon after.

H. Newland, *The Life and Contemporaneous Church History of Antonio de Dominis* (1859). G. G. Perry in *D.N.B.*, xv (1888), pp. 201-3, s.v. 'Dominis, M. A. de'.

DEDUCTION. In Logic, the process of reasoning whereby a conclusion is reached from an already known or accepted premiss. The opposite process is termed '*Induction'.

DEER, Book of. A 9th–10th-cent. MS. which formerly belonged to the monastery of Deer in Buchan (Aberdeen). It contains a corrupt text of St. John's Gospel, with portions of the other Gospels, the *Apostles' Creed, a fragment of a service for the *Visitation of the Sick (with Gaelic rubrics), and a series of grants to the monastery, the last being in a later hand. The Visitation of the Sick agrees in character with the Irish Books of Dimma and Mulling, while the grants throw important light on the social structure of *Scotland at the time. The MS., which was formerly in the library of John Moore, successively Bp. of *Norwich and *Ely (d. 1714), is now in Cambridge University Library (I. i. b. 32).

Ed. by J. Stuart for the Spalding Club (Edinburgh, 1869).

DEFENDER OF THE FAITH (Lat. *Fidei Defensor*). A title conferred at his own request on *Henry VIII in 1521 by Pope *Leo X in recognition of his treatise *Assertio Septem Sacramentorum*, in which, with the assistance of J. *Fisher, he had defended the doctrine of the *seven sacraments against M. *Luther. In 1544 Parliament recognized the style as an official title of the English monarch and it has been borne since that date by all British sovereigns. It may be compared with the titles 'Christianissimus' and 'Catholicus' formerly taken by the kings of France and Spain respectively.

Text of bull conferring title in T. Rymer, *Foedera*, xiii 1712), pp. 756–8, with facsimile.

DEFENDER OF THE MATRIMONIAL TIE (Lat. *Defensor Matrimonii*). A person whose duty is to uphold the marriage tie when cases in which the validity or nullity of particular marriages is in dispute are heard in the RC ecclesiastical courts. The office was constituted by Pope *Benedict XIV in his *bull 'Dei Miseratione' (3 Nov. 1741). The chief *raison d'être* of such an official is to prevent annulments by collusion between the parties concerned.

DEFENESTRATION OF PRAGUE. The incident which precipitated the *Thirty Years War. On 23 May 1618 the Bohemian Protestant insurgents broke up a meeting of the Imperial Commissioners in the Hradschin Palace at Prague by throwing two of the Catholic councillors, Wilhelm von Slawata and Jaroslav von Martinitz, and their secretary out of the window.

Cecily V. Wedgwood, *The Thirty Years War* (1938), pp. 78–80, with reff. to sources. See also other works cited s.v. *Thirty Years War*.

DE FIDE. In Catholic theology, a proposition is said to be *de fide* (or *de fide catholica*) if it has been expressly declared and defined by the Church to be true and to contradict it would be heretical. The expression is used, e.g., by *Suarez and John de *Lugo, and constantly by modern Catholic apologists.

DE FOUCAULD, CHARLES EUGÈNE (1858–1916), French explorer and 'Hermit of the Sahara'. After an easy and dissipated life as a lieutenant of cavalry, he became seized with a passion for Africa and in 1883–4 undertook a dangerous expedition through Morocco, the results of which he published in the fundamental work, *Reconnaissance au Maroc* (1888). A period of spiritual unrest followed this expedition, but he was brought back to the Catholic Faith under the experienced direction of the Abbé Huvelin (1887). In 1888–9 he made a pilgrimage to the Holy Land, and in 1890 entered the *Trappist monastery of Notre-Dame-des-Neiges. Desirous of a life of even greater solitude and austerity, he left the order in 1897, lived as a servant of the *Poor

Clares at *Nazareth and *Jerusalem until 1900, and returned to France to be ordained priest in 1901. A few months later he went to Algeria where he led a hermit's life, first in the oasis of Beni Abbès and, from 1905, in the still more remote Hoggar Mountains and at the oasis of Tamanrasset. Here, besides studying the language of the Tuaregs and composing dictionaries and translations, he made his chief occupation prayer, penance, and works of charity which won him the admiration and love of the French soldiers as well as of the Mohammedan desert tribes, though he did not obtain conversions. In 1916 he was assassinated by the Tuaregs for reasons which remain obscure, but probably in connexion with the Holy War of the Senoussi. Two French missionary associations, the Association Charles de Foucauld and the Mission de Foucauld, carry on his work. The cause of his beatification was introduced at Rome in 1927.

Les *Écrits spirituels de Charles de Foucauld*, ed. by R. Bazin (1923; Eng. tr., 'Meditations of a Hermit', 1930). R. Bazin, *Charles de Foucauld, explorateur du Maroc, ermite au Sahara* (1921, Eng. tr. 1923). D. Hull, *The Priest of the Legion* (1947); T. Lloyd, *Desert Call*. The Story of Charles de Foucauld, Explorer of Morocco and Hermit of Sahara (1948). A. Fremantle, *Desert Calling* (New York, 1949), incl. bibliographical details of his other published works, and other reff.

DE GROOT, HUGO. See *Grotius, Hugo*.

DE HAERETICO COMBURENDO. The Act of 1401 (2 Hen. IV, c. 15) which was the first step taken by Parliament to suppress *Lollardy. By it persons holding heretical views were to be arrested and tried by canon law. If the diocesan pronounced sentence of heresy, they were to be handed over to the secular courts, who would 'cause [them] to be burnt that such punishment may strike fear to the minds of others'. Its provisions were not altogether new. Under earlier legislation the state could be compelled by the Church to carry out the penalty of burning prescribed by canon law, and the execution of the Lollard, William Sawtre, was hurried through before the passing of this act to maintain the principle. The act was repealed by *Henry VIII, revived by *Mary, and finally repealed by *Elizabeth.

Eng. tr. of text in Gee–Hardy, No. xlii, pp. 133–7; repr. in H. Bettenson (ed.), *Documents of the Christian Church* (1943), pp. 251–5. K. B. McFarlane, *John Wycliffe and the Beginnings of English Nonconformity* [1953], pp. 149–56.

DE HAURANNE, DUVERGIER. See *Saint-Cyran, Abbé de*.

DEIFICATION. See *Apotheosis*

DEINIOL, St. (c. 584), Welsh saint. He was probably the founder of the monastery of *Bangor Is-Coed and is alleged to have been consecrated first Bp. of Bangor by St. *Dubritius in 516; but very little is really known of him. Among the Welsh churches dedicated to him is that at Hawarden in Flintshire. St. Deiniol's Library, Hawarden, a residential library for students in the arts, was founded by W. E. *Gladstone in 1896, and of the 60,000 books, some 30,000 are from Gladstone's own collection. Feast day, 11 Sept.

Brief note, with reff., by C. Hole in *D.C.B.*, i (1877), p. 802, s.v., T. F. Tout in *D.N.B.*, xiv (1888), p. 18 f., s.v. 'Daniel'.

DEIR BALYZEH FRAGMENTS. See *Der Balyzeh Fragments.*

DEISM (from Lat. *Deus*, 'God'). The term, orig. interchangeable with *Theism (q.v.), i.e., belief in one Supreme Being as opposed to *Atheism and *Polytheism, is now generally restricted to the system of natural religion which was first developed in England in the late 17th and 18th cents. Among its precursors are P. *Charron, J. Bodin (c. 1530–96), and esp. Lord *Herbert of Cherbury (q.v.), who in his *De Veritate* (1624) set out five truths common to all religions. J. *Locke, though himself objecting to the title of 'Deist', also profoundly influenced subsequent developments through his *Reasonableness of Christianity* (1695). The classical exposition of Deism is J. *Toland's *Christianity not Mysterious* (1696), which argues against revelation and the supernatural altogether. S. *Clarke, in his *Demonstration of the Being and Attributes of God* (1704–6), distinguished four classes of Deists. For the first, God is only the Creator with no further interest in the world; the second group admit a Divine Providence, but only in the material, not in the moral and spiritual order; the third believe in certain moral attributes of God, but not in a future life; and the fourth accept all the truths of natural religion including belief in a life to come, but reject revelation. A. *Collins' *Discourse on Freethinking* (1713) argued that freedom of thought was sufficient for the discovery of truth, while the authority of the Biblical records was doubtful. M. *Tindal in *Christianity as Old as Creation* (1730) maintained that the religion of nature is the common element of all creeds. As it developed, the negative elements in Deism received greater emphasis. Belief in Divine Providence, as well as in rewards and punishments, was gradually abandoned. The chief mark of later Deism was belief in a Creator God whose further Divine intervention in His creation was rejected as derogatory to His omnipotence and unchangeableness.

Deism, which was never widely accepted in this country, had a great influence in *France, where *Voltaire, J.-J. *Rousseau, and the *Encyclopaedists were its chief exponents. In Germany the movement became widespread during the reign of Frederick II of Prussia; Tindal's work, which was translated by J. L. Schmidt in 1741, was drawn upon by H. S. *Reimarus, whose fragments were published by G. E. *Lessing (1773–8); I. *Kant's *Die Religion innerhalb der Grenzen der blossen Vernunft* (1793) states the Deist position from the point of view of transcendental *Idealism.

Deism, which by its separation of the Creator from His creatures undermined all personal religion, soon found vigorous critics. Among its most influential refutations was Bp. J. *Butler's *Analogy of Religion* (1736) which argued that the difficulties in the way of accepting Revealed Religion are no more formidable than those confronting the advocate of the Natural Religion proposed by Deism.

J. Leland, *A View of the Principal Deistical Writers* (2 vols., 1754–6); G. V. Lechler, *Geschichte des englischen Deismus* (2 vols., 1841); A. S. Farrar, *A Critical History of Free|Thought* (*Bampton Lectures, 1862); L. Stephen, *History of English Thought in the Eighteenth Century*, i (1876), chs. ii–iv, pp. 74–277, with bibl., p. 276 f.

DEISSMANN, ADOLF (1866–1937), Protestant theologian. In 1897 he became professor of the NT at Heidelberg, and in 1908 at Berlin. He did distinguished pioneer work in Biblical philology, making full use of the material from the recently discovered *papyri. His many writings include two series as *Bibel Studien* (1895, 1897; Eng. trans. as *Bible Studies*, 1901), *Licht vom Osten* (1908; Eng. trans. as *Light from the Ancient East*, 1910), and *The Religion of Jesus and the Faith of Paul* (1923). In 1930 he edited (in conjunction with G. K. A. Bell) *Mysterium Christi*, a collection of papers on Christology by British and German theologians. He also took a prominent part in the *Oecumenical Movement.

To mark his 60th birthday, there appeared a *Festgabe für Adolf Deissmann* (Tübingen, 1927), with a portrait.

DE LA BIGNE, MARGUERIN (c. 1546–1589), French Patristic scholar. His chief work was *Sacra Bibliotheca Sanctorum Patrum* (8 vols. 1575; index vol. 1579), in which a vast number of Patristic works were published, some of them for the first time.

J. P. Migne, *PL*, lxxxi, 209–12 ('Epistola Dedicatoria').

DE LAGARDE, PAUL ANTON. See *Lagarde, Paul Anton De.*

DE LA TAILLE, MAURICE (1872–1933), French theologian. A native of Semblançay, he was educated at St. Mary's College, Canterbury, where he entered the *Jesuit Order in 1890. From 1905 to 1916 he taught theology at the Catholic university of Angers, and from 1916 to 1918 was military chaplain to the Canadian army. From 1919 onwards he taught dogmatic theology at the *Gregorian university at Rome. His principal work, *Mysterium Fidei* (1921), is an original and comprehensive study of the Mass. Divided into three books, dealing with the Sacrifice once offered by Christ Himself, with the Mass as the Sacrifice of the Church, and with the Eucharist as a Sacrament, its dominating thought is the unity of the Redeemer's sacrifice begun in the oblation of the Last Supper, consummated in the Passion, and continued in the Mass. Acc. to de la Taille there is only one real immolation, that on Calvary, to which the Supper looks forward and on which the Mass looks back. He uses a wealth of material, chiefly patristic and scholastic, to support his thesis, and to defend his doctrine against theologians who hold that there must be a real immolation in the Mass. In several minor writings occasioned by this controversy, among them *The Last Supper and Calvary* (1924) and *The Mystery of Faith and Human Opinion* (1930), the author has defended himself against his critics.

J. Lebreton, S.J., 'Le Père Maurice de la Taille', in *Recherches de Science Religieuse*, xxiv (1934), pp. 5–11. M. Lepin, *L'Idée du sacrifice de la messe d'après les théologiens depuis l'origine jusqu'à nos jours* (1926), pp. 659–720. A. Piolanti in *E.C.*, vii (1951), col. 931 f., s.v. 'La Taille, M. de'.

DELEGATES, Court of. In England the court erected in 1534 by 25 Hen. VIII, c. 19, to hear and pronounce final sentence upon appeals from the archbishops' courts, which had hitherto gone to *Rome. A commission consisting usually of three puisne judges and three or four civilians was appointed for each separate case. The court was abolished in 1832 and in 1833 its place taken by the *Judicial Committee of the Privy Council.

H. C. Rothery (ed.), 'Introduction with Appendix to the Return of all Appeals in Causes of Doctrine and Discipline made to the High Court of Delegates' as Hist. App. IX to the *Report of the Commissioners appointed to inquire into the Constitution and Working of the Ecclesiastical Courts* [Cd. 3760], pp. 253–66 of the MS. pagination. The best historical account of the court is that drawn up by W. *Stubbs for the Hist. App. I, ib., pp. 46–9 (pr. among the Parliamentary Papers, 1883, xxiv, pp. 120–3 of the MS. pagination). Further information in the Report, pp. xl–xliv (pp. 40–4 of the MS. pagination in the same vol. of the Parliamentary Papers).

DELEHAYE, HIPPOLYTE (1859–1941), *Bollandist. A native of Antwerp, he entered the *Jesuit Order in 1879. After studying philosophy at Louvain (1879–82), teaching mathematics for a time at the Collège St.-Barbe at Ghent (1882–6), and studying theology at Innsbruck (1886–7), he settled in Brussels in 1887. He was ordained priest in 1890. In 1891 he joined the Bollandists and for the rest of his life was actively engaged in hagiographical studies. In 1912 he became President of the Bollandists.

Delehaye contributed regularly to the *Acta Sanctorum* [AA.SS.] from 1894 until his death. For AA.SS. Nov. II (1) (1894) he wrote the life of St. *Wolfgang (pp. 527–97); he was also joint editor and among the principal contributors to the *Propylaeum ad AA.SS. Novembris* (1902), of the AA.SS., Nov. III (1910), Nov. IV (1928), and Nov. II (2) (1931), and of the *Propylaeum ad AA.SS. Decembris* (1940); and for Nov. II (2) he prepared (with H. *Quentin) the important text and study of the *Hieronymian Martyrology. Under the influence of C. Smedt he undertook the cataloguing of scattered hagiographical MSS. (*Bibliotheca Hagiographica Graeca*, 1895). He also assisted in the preparation of the catalogues of the hagiographical MSS. in the Bibliothèque Nationale at Paris (1896) and the Vatican (1899), and of the *Catalogus Codicum Hagiographicorum Germaniae Belgii Angliae* (1913). His books, all based on wide erudition but many of them directed to a non-specialized public,

include *Les Légendes hagiographiques* (1905; Eng. trans. 1907), *Les Légendes grecques des saints militaires* (1909), *Les Origines du culte des martyrs* (1912), *Les Passions des martyrs et les genres littéraires* (1921), *Deux Typica byzantins de l'époque des paléologues* (1921), *Saint Jean Berchmans* (1921; Eng. trans., 1921), *Les Saints Stylites* (1923), *Sanctus* (1927), and *Étude sur le Légendier Roman* (1936). He was also a constant contributor to the *Analecta Bollandiana*.

'Le R. P. Hippolyte Delehaye' in *Anal. Boll.*, lx (1942), pp. i–lii, incl. list of works (239 items) and reff. to other notices.

DE LISLE, AMBROSE LISLE MARCH PHILLIPPS (1809–78), English RC writer. Born of Anglican parents, he was converted to Roman Catholicism in 1824. In 1835 he gave 230 acres of Charnwood Forest to the *Trappist Order for the building of the monastery of Mount St. Bernard and in 1838 founded the 'Association of Universal Prayer for the Conversion of England'. Over much of his life he was active in furthering reunion between the C of E and Rome, and was on friendly terms with the leaders of the *Oxford Movement. In 1857 he joined in founding the 'Association for Promoting the Unity of Christendom' (*A.P.U.C.), which included Anglicans and Orthodox as well as RCs, withdrawing, however, when it was condemned by Rome in 1864. In 1862 he assumed the name of De Lisle (signing prior to that date Ambrose Lisle Phillipps).

E. S. Purcell, *Life and Letters of Ambrose Phillipps de Lisle* (2 vols., 1900).

DELITZSCH, FRANZ JULIUS (1813–90), OT scholar and orientalist. A native of Leipzig, where he taught for some years, he later held professorships at Rostock (1846–50), Erlangen (1850–67), and Leipzig (1867–90). Of a pietistic *Lutheran background and Jewish descent, he esp. sought to combat anti-Semitism and foster the conversion of the Jews, editing a periodical *Saat auf Hoffnung* from 1863, founding a Jewish missionary college, establishing at Leipzig an 'Institutum Judaicum' (1886; later 'Institutum Delitzschianum') and translating the NT into Hebrew (publd. 1877). He published a long series of Commentaries on the OT, conservative and practical in tendency, but displaying increasing understanding of the critical view of the OT. In 1857 he issued a commentary on Heb. (Eng. trans., 2 vols., 1868–70). He also wrote extensively on Rabbinic subjects, edited in conjunction with S. Baer the Heb. text of the OT (except Ex.–Deut.; 1861–97), and published some devotional works. As a final apology he issued *Der tiefe Graben zwischen alter und moderner Theologie. Ein Bekenntnis* (1888).

D. W. Volck (ed.), *Theologische Briefe der Professoren Delitzsch und von Hofmann* (1891). 'Memorial Tribute' by S. I. Curtiss (Edinburgh, 1891), with bibl. A. Köhler in *P.R.E.* (ed. 3), iv (1898), pp. 565–70; F. Vigouroux in *Dict. Bibl.*, ii (1899), cols. 1341 f., with complete list of Delitzsch's writings; H. *Gunkel in *R.G.G.* (ed. 2), i (1927), col. 1822.

DELITZSCH, FRIEDRICH (1850–1922), German Assyriologist. He was the son of F. J. *Delitzsch, and held professorships at Leipzig (1878), Breslau (1893), and Berlin (1899). He published various works on Oriental subjects, among them *Prolegomena eines neuen hebr.-aram. Wörterbuchs zum AT* (1886), *Assyriche Grammatik* (1889), *Geschichte Babyloniens und Assyriens* (1891), and *Summerische Grammatik* (1914). His most celebrated book, however, was his *Babel und Bibel* (2 parts, 1902–3; Eng. trans., 1903), based on lectures delivered before the Emp. Wilhelm II which claimed that several OT narratives were of Babylonian origin and that Judaism was essentially dependent on Babylonian culture.

The author reviewed the controversy aroused by his book in *Babel und Bibel. Ein Rückblick und Ausblick* (1904). Among his later writings, all hostile to Christian orthodoxy, were *Mehr Licht* (1907), *Zur Weiterbildung der Religion* (two lectures; 1908), and *Die grosse Täuschung* (2 vols., 1920–1). In conjunction with P. Haupt, he edited the *Assyriologische Bibliothek* (1881–1927) and *Beiträge zur Assyriologie und semitischen Sprachwissenschaft* (10 vols., 1889–1927). H. *Gunkel in *R.G.G.* (ed. 2), i (1927), cols. 1822 f.

DELLA ROBBIA, Florentine family of artists. The two most celebrated are:

(1) **Luca della Robbia** (1399–1482). His early works were sculptures, of which the singing and dancing boys (1431–8), done in marble, for the organ gallery of the cathedral of Florence, is the most famous (now in the Museo del Duomo). His principal work in bronze is the sacristy door of the cathedral, which is divided into several panels representing the Madonna, St. John the Baptist, and other saints. From c. 1440 he began to work chiefly in glazed terracotta (majolica), a technique which he greatly improved. These reliefs show most often white figures on a pale-blue ground, framed by brilliantly coloured borders of fruits and flowers. His Madonnas of the Roses and of the Apple in the Bargello at Florence are of exquisite charm and real dignity, and the Crucifix at San Miniato, the Tabernacle at Impruneta, and other decorative works, belong to the finest specimens of Italian majolica.

(2) **Andrea della Robbia** (1431–1528), nephew of Luca. He continued the tradition of his uncle, whose works cannot always be distinguished from his. He did the fine series of medallions with infants for the front of the Foundling Hospital at Florence and a large number of Madonnas. Most of them are of great charm, expressing the love between Mother and Child. The best known is the Madonna adoring the Child in the National Museum at Florence.

A. Marquand, *Luca della Robbia* (Princeton Monographs in Art and Archaeology, iii; 1913); id., *Andrea della Robbia* (2 vols., ib., xi; 1922). On other members of the family, see id., *Giovanni della Robbia* (ib., viii; 1920); id., *The Brothers of Giovanni della Robbia* (ib., xiii; 1928), all with illustrations and detailed bibl. M. Reymond, *Les della Robbia* (1897); Maud Cruttwell, *Luca and Andrea della Robbia and their Successors* (1902). I. B. Supino in *Allgemeines Lexikon der bildenden Künstler von der Antike bis zur Gegenwart*, ed. U. Thieme–F. Becker, &c., xxviii (1934), pp. 413–17, s.v. 'Robbia', with full bibl.

DELUGE, The. See *Flood, The.*

DE LUGO, JOHN. See *Lugo, John de.*

DE MAISTRE, JOSEPH (1753–1821), French *Ultramontane writer. He was born at Chambéry in Savoy and educated by the *Jesuits. At first influenced by the 18th-cent. rationalists, after the Revolution of 1789 he became a reactionary, who saw in the Church the safeguard of political stability. In 1802 he was appointed Sardinian minister at St. Petersburg, where he remained until 1817, when he returned to Savoy. In his principal work, *Du pape* (1819), he argued that the only true basis of society lay in authority which took the double form of spiritual authority vested in the Papacy and temporal authority committed to human kings. The religious basis of history, which was to be understood as throughout under the direction of Divine Providence, was manifested in the redemptive power of suffering and blood. His other writings include *De l'Église gallicane* (1821) and *Soirées de St.-Pétersbourg, ou Entretiens sur le gouvernement temporel de la Providence* (1821). De Maistre has been called the 'Prophet of the Past' (P. S. Ballanche, 1776–1847), but his ideas did much to further the overthrow of *Gallicanism and assist the rise of *Ultramontanism (F. R. de *Lamennais, C. R. F. *Montalembert, *Vatican Council) in the later 19th cent.

Œuvres (7 vols., Brussels, 1838); *Œuvres complètes* (14 vols., Lyons, 1884–7), incl. his posthumous works and unpublished correspondence, with 'Notice biographique' by his son, Rudolphe de Maistre, in vol. i, pp. v–xliii, orig. publ. in the latter's ed. of his father's *Lettres et opuscules inédits* (2 vols., 1851), vol. i, pp. v–xxvi. J. Morley, *Critical Miscellanies* (1871), 'Joseph De Maistre', pp. 115–92. F. Vermale, *Notes sur de Maistre inconnu* (1921); id., *Joseph de Maistre émigré* (Société Savoisienne d'Histoire et d'Archéologie, lxiv; 1927); R. Johannet, *Joseph de Maistre* (Paris, 1932). G. Goyau, *La Pensée religieuse de Joseph de Maistre* (1921); E. Dermenghem, *Joseph de Maistre mystique* (1923). C. Latreille, *Joseph de Maistre et la papauté* (1906); G. Breton, '*Du pape' de Joseph de Maistre*. Étude critique (1931). M. Jugie, A.A., *Joseph de Maistre et l'Église gréco-russe* [1922]. F. Bayle, *Les Idées politiques de Joseph de Maistre* (1945). C. S. Phillips, *The Church in France, 1789–1848* (1927), pp. 207–13, with bibl., p. 307.

DE MARCA, PIERRE. See *Marca, Pierre de.*

DEMETRIUS. The name of two persons in the NT. (1) A silversmith of *Ephesus, who led an unsuccessful riot against St. *Paul, on the ground that the Apostle's preaching would endanger the trade in silver images (Acts 19. 24 ff.). (2) A disciple commended by St. *John, of whom nothing else is known (3 Jn. ver. 12).

DEMETRIUS, St. (d. 231 or 232), Bp. of *Alexandria from 189. The interest in him centres in his relations to *Origen. As Bp. of Alexandria he began by supporting Origen, whom he appointed to the headship of the famous Catechetical School in his city c. 203. Later, however, when the Bps. of *Jerusalem and *Caesarea allowed him to preach in spite of his being a layman, Demetrius recalled him to Alexandria and censured his conduct. At a synod in 231 he finally banished him for having been ordained priest irregularly at Caesarea, and shortly afterwards deprived him of the priesthood. Demetrius took a leading part in the controversies with the *Gnostics of his day. He is greatly venerated in the Coptic Church. Feast day, 9 Oct.

*Eusebius, *H.E.*, VI. iii, viii, xix, and xxvi. *Bardenhewer, ii, p. 194 f.; L. *Duchesne, *Histoire ancienne de l'Église*, i (1906), pp. 341–6. Brief note, with reff., by B. F. *Westcott in *D.C.B.*, i (1877), p. 803, s.v.

DEMIURGE. This, the English form of a Greek word (δημιουργός) meaning 'craftsman', was used of the Divine Being by *Plato in his account of the formation of the visible world, and so by Greek Christian writers simply of God as the Creator of all things. The *Gnostics used the word disparagingly of the inferior deity to whom they ascribed the origin of the material universe, distinguishing him from the supreme God. In its English form the word is commonly used in reference to this Gnostic doctrine.

DEMYTHOLOGIZATION (Germ. *Entmythologisierung*). A term employed by R. *Bultmann (q.v.) for a method of interpreting the Scriptures in the categories of modern man by eliminating the elements of 'myth' (e.g. belief in a three-storied universe) taken for granted by the Biblical writers.

R. Bultmann, 'Neues Testament und Mythologie', incl. in his *Offenbarung und Heilsgeschehen* (Beiträge zur evangelischen Theologie, Bd. vii, 1941). H. W. Bartsch (ed.). *Kerygma und Mythos* (3 vols., 1948 ff.), with repr. of Bultmann's paper, i, pp. 15–53; Eng. tr. (selections; Bultmann's paper, pp. 1–44), by R. H. Fuller (1953), with bibl. pp. 224–8. I. Henderson, *Myth in the New Testament* (Studies in Biblical Theology, vii; 1952). R. Prenter, 'Mythe et évangile' in *Revue de Théologie et de Philosophie*, xxxv (1947), pp. 49–67. F. *Gogarten, *Entmythologisierung und die Kirche* (1953; Eng. tr. 1955). J. Macquarrie, *The Scope of Demythologizing* (1960).

DENIFLE, HEINRICH SEUSE (1844–1905), Church historian. Born at Imst in the Tyrol, he entered the *Dominican Order in 1861, was ordained priest in 1866, and taught philosophy and theology at Graz from 1870 to 1880. Called to Rome in 1880 as associate to the General of the Order, he became a collaborator in the projected new edition of the works of St. *Thomas Aquinas, travelling all over Europe in search of MSS. In 1883 he was appointed sub-archivist at the *Vatican. In 1885 he founded, with F. *Ehrle, the *Archiv für Litteratur und Kirchengeschichte des Mittelalters*, and in 1887 he was appointed editor of the records of Paris University.

His writings include his monumental *Chartularium Universitatis Parisiensis*, written in conjunction with É. Châtelain (Paris, 4 vols., 1889–97); several works on the German mystics of the 14th cent., Meister *Eckhart, J. *Tauler, and H. *Suso; and an unfinished work on M. *Luther and Lutheranism. This last is a brilliant, but wholly unsympathetic, exposition of Luther's teaching and methods, based on a

wide study and acute analysis of contemporary sources.

J. P. Kirsch, *Le P. Henri Suso Denifle, O.P.* (Louvain, 1905). O. Spiess, O.P., in *Dict. Sp.*, iii (1954), cols. 238–41.

DENISON, GEORGE ANTHONY (1805–1896), Archdeacon of Taunton from 1851. Ordained deacon and priest in 1832, he was Vicar of East Brent from 1845 till his death. He was throughout his life a vigorous defender of rigid High Church principles. Between 1854 and 1858 he was unsuccessfully prosecuted in the civil courts for teaching the doctrine of the *Real Presence in the *Eucharist. From 1839 to 1870 he strongly supported the cause of Church education against the movement for universal and compulsory education in state schools, a cause which was largely lost when the *Education Act of 1870 was passed.

L. E. Denison (his niece), *Fifty Years at East Brent* (1902). J. M. Rigg in *D.N.B.*, Suppl. ii (1901), pp. 127–9.

DENMARK, Christianity in. After one or two unsuccessful missions to Denmark, the Christian faith gained a firm footing in the 9th cent., when the Danish chief, Harold, was baptized on a visit to Louis the Pious, the Frankish king, and on his return brought with him St. *Anskar. Under Sven I (985–1014) and Cnut the Great (1014–35) Christianity became generally accepted. In 1104 the Church in Denmark was separated from the metropolitan see of Hamburg-Bremen, to which it had been united since the time of St. Anskar, and its seven bishops placed under the primacy of the Bp. of Lund. During the later Middle Ages the bishops acquired considerable temporal power and became correspondingly unpopular.

The Reformation in Denmark took place between 1520 and 1540. The chief events were the formal proclamation of religious freedom at the Diet of Odense in 1527, the adoption of a *Lutheran symbol (the *Confessio Hafnica*) in 1530, the expropriation of the hierarchy and the monasteries in the following years, and the visit of J. *Bugenhagen to set up a Lutheran episcopate and introduce a new liturgy in 1537. The Danish Bible appeared in 1550. Restrictions upon RC's were milder than in other Protestant countries, but in 1624 the death penalty was imposed by royal rescript upon any RC priests found performing their official duties, while the *Danske Lov* of 1683 ordered that converts to Romanism should lose all their property.

The country suffered greatly from the deadness and rationalism which beset esp. Lutheranism in the 18th cent. A revival of orthodox Lutheranism, in which the *Libri Symbolici*, or ecclesiastical creeds, were restored to honour, was largely due to N. F. S. *Grundtvig (1783–1872), whose view of Scripture and tradition inclined towards the Catholic standpoint. To him also was due the idea of the *Folk High Schools (*Folkehöjskoler*) which have since proved a strong Christian influence. In contrast to him was S. *Kierkegaard (1813–55), who opposed both the State Church and what passed for orthodox theology. By laws of 1849 and 1852, which gave complete religious liberty to Denmark, the Evangelical Lutheran Church was officially disestablished, but continued to receive state grants, and remained entirely subordinate to the state in all matters of legislation. At present practically all Danes are nominally Lutherans, though there is a very small RC minority. The Lutheran primate, who ordains the other bishops, is the Bp. of Zealand; he resides at Copenhagen, but his cathedral church is at Roskilde. In 1934–5 the Danish Church was strongly influenced by a campaign of the *Oxford Group Movement. Danish missions abroad began in 1814, and have been established in various parts of the world; their most extensive and successful work had been done in Greenland.

A. Krarup (ed.), *Bullarium Danicum.* Pavelige Aktstykker Vedrørende Danmark, 1198–1316 (2 halvbind, Copenhagen, 1931–2); *Acta Pontificum Danica.* Pavelige Aktstykker Vedrørende Danmark, 1316–1536, ed. L. Moltesen and other (7 vols., ib., 1904–43). A. Krarup–W. Norvin (edd.), *Acta Processus Litium inter Regem Danorum et Archiepiscopum Lundensem* (ib., 1932). M. C. Gertz (ed.), *Vitae Sanctorum Danorum* (ib., 1908–12). L. N. Helveg, *Den danske Kirkes Historie* (5 vols., 1870); L. P. Fabricius, *Danmarks Kirkehistorie* (2 vols., 1934–5). F. Siegmund-Schultze (ed.), *Ekklesia,* II, iii (Lfg. vii, pt. 1, Die Kirche in Dänemark; 1937), with detailed bibl. E. H. Dunkley, *The Reformation in Denmark* (*Church Historical Society; 1948), with bibl. J. O. Andersen, *Der Reformkatholizismus und die dänische Reformation* (1954); M. Neiiendam, *1536. Den Danske Reformations Historie folkelig genfortalt* (1936). J. Schnell, *Die dänische Kirchenordnung von 1542 und der Einfluss von Wittenberg* (1927), [A. J. Mason,] 'The Loss of the Succession in Denmark' in *The Church Quarterly Review,* xxxii (1891), pp. 149–87. A. T. Jörgensen, 'Die evangelisch-lutherische Volkskirche Dänemarks' in *Neue kirchliche Zeitschrift,* xxxvi (1925), pp. 687–714. W. J. Karup, *Geschichte der katholischen Kirche in Dänemark vom Beginn bis zur Gegenwart* (1863). E. A. F. Jessen, *Die Hauptströmungen des religiösen Lebens der Jetztzeit in Dänemark* (1895).

DENNEY, JAMES (1856–1917), Scottish *Free Church theologian. Educated at Glasgow University and Glasgow Free Church College, he was made minister of East Free Church, Broughty Ferry, in 1886. From 1897 till his death he taught theology at the Glasgow Free Church College. In his later years he became actively involved in the administration of the *United Free Church, becoming in 1913 convener of its Central Fund. He also took a prominent part in the movement for reunion with the Established Church of *Scotland. As a theologian he moved doctrinally from a liberal to an evangelical position, which was that of his mature life. In his *Christology he asserted firmly the traditional doctrine of the Person of Christ. He held the Atonement to have a purely substitutionary character. His main works were *The Death of Christ* (1902), *Jesus and the Gospel* (1908), *The Christian Doctrine of Reconciliation* (1917), and editions of *I and II Thessalonians* (1892), *II Corinthians* (1894), and of the Greek text of *Romans* (1900).

Letters of Principal James Denney to W. Robertson Nicoll, 1893–1917 [1920], with 'Appreciation' by W. R. Nicoll (pp. xiii–xxvii) and 'Memoirs of a Student', by J. A. Robertson (pp. xxxi–xliii). J. *Moffatt (ed.), *Letters of Principal James Denney to his Family and Friends* [1922]. T. H. Walker, *Principal James Denney, D.D.* A Memoir and a Tribute (1918). A. S. *Peake in *D.N.B., 1912–1921,* p. 153 f.

DE NOAILLES, LOUIS ANTOINE (1651–1729), Abp. of *Paris. Born at the Château of Teyssière in the Auvergne, he was educated at the Collège du Plessis, Paris. In 1679 he was consecrated Bp. of Cahors, in 1680 translated to Châlons-sur-Marne, and in 1695, through the influence of Mme de Maintenon, became Abp. of Paris. He was created a Cardinal by Innocent XII in 1700, and made head of the *Sorbonne in 1710. He was a zealous and devoted pastor and an ardent reformer of clerical practice (obligation of residence in seminaries before Ordination; annual retreats; courses on moral theology). He fostered the use of the traditional French liturgical books (Breviary, Missal, Rituale, Caeremoniale), and also in other ways upheld *Gallican ideals. His commendation (1695) of P. *Quesnel's *Réflexions morales* and his disapproval of *Probabilism made him suspect of *Jansenism, and though he condemned certain fundamental Jansenist doctrines (1698), he had to face much opposition from the *Jesuits. He opposed the bull '*Unigenitus' (1713) and formally appealed against it in Sept. 1718; and though he eventually accepted it in 1728, he signed a private recantation before his death. He became involved in most of the controversies of his age, notably with F. Fénelon over his *Maximes des Saints.* His writings include his *Mandement à l'occasion du miracle opéré dans la paroisse de Sainte-Marguerite, le 31 mai, jour du Saint Sacrement* (1727) and a large number of pastoral institutions.

E. De. Barthélemy, *Le Cardinal de Noailles, évêque de Châlons, archevêque de Paris, d'après sa correspondance inédite, 1651–1728* (1886). M. Fosseyeux, 'Le Cardinal de Noailles et l'administration du diocèse de Paris (1695–1729)' in *Revue Historique,* cxiv (1913), pp. 261–84, and ib., cxv (1914), pp. 34–54. J. Carreyre in *D.T.C.,* xi (pt. 1; 1931), cols. 678–81, s.v. 'Noailles', with notes on sources.

DE NOBILI, ROBERT (1577–1656), *Jesuit missionary. He was a native of Tuscany, entered the order in 1597, and was sent on the Indian mission in 1604. In his eagerness to convert esp. the Brahmins, he adopted the mode of life of the Indian penitents and avoided public intercourse with the Pariahs. When his methods aroused the opposition of his fellow-missionaries, he had to interrupt his work and justify himself before the Abp. of Goa, but he was allowed by the Holy See to continue his mode of life. He proposed the appointment of special missionaries for the different Indian castes, and the gradual removal of the prejudice against Christianity among certain members of the higher castes was largely due to his labours. He was an eminent linguist and wrote more than twenty books in Sanskrit, Tamil, and Telugu, including many hymns, two catechisms, a treatise on Christian doctrine, and a Life of our Lady in Sanskrit verse. It is estimated that his converts numbered some 100,000.

Lat. text of his *Première Apologie* (orig. publ. 1610), ed. with Fr. tr. and notes by P. Dahmen, S.J. (Paris, 1931). P. Dahmen, S.J., *R. de Nobili.* Ein Beitrag zur Geschichte der Missionsmethode (1924), with bibl.; id., *Un Jésuite brahme.* Robert de Nobili ('Museum Lessianum'; 1924); M. de Crisenoy, *Robert de Nobili, apôtre des Brahmes* [1939]. Sommervogel, v (1894), col. 1779 f.

DENYS. See *Dionysius*.

DEODAND (Lat. *Deo dandum*, 'to be given to God'). In old English law, a personal chattel or thing which had been the cause of the death of a person, and as such was forfeit to the crown to be applied to pious uses, e.g. given in alms. The law regulating deodands was formally abolished in 1846.

DEO GRATIAS (Lat.), 'thanks be to God'. A liturgical formula in constant use in the services of the W. Church. In the Roman Mass it is ordered to be said by the server at the conclusion of the *Epistle and of the *Last Gospel. The Rule of St. *Benedict requires its use by the doorkeeper in receiving a stranger or a beggar (cap. 66). During the *Donatist controversy in *Africa it was a mark of orthodoxy as contrasted with the 'Deo laudes' used by the schismatics. Instances are met with of 'Deogratias' as a Christian proper name.

DEONTOLOGY. A term used first by J. *Bentham in 1826 for the science of ethics or moral obligation, esp. as distinct from jurisprudence.

DEOSCULATORIUM (Lat. from *deosculor*, 'to kiss feelingly'). Another name for the object known as the *Pax, sometimes used in the *Mass.

DEPRECATIO GELASII (Lat., 'intercession of Gelasius'). The Latin litany included by *Alcuin in his 'Officia per Ferias' under feria V (Friday). Although both form and much of the content are of E. origin, it was probably compiled at Rome in the time of Pope *Gelasius (492–6) and is thus the earliest extant Latin litany. There is no evidence as to the purpose for which it was originally composed. By the time of Alcuin it was probably already being superseded by the more popular *Litany of the Saints.

Text in J. P. Migne, *PL.*, ci, 560–2. Crit. text by W. Meyer in *Nachr.* (Gött.), 1912, pp. 87–108. W. *Bousset, 'Zur sog. *Deprecatio Gelasii*', ib., 1916, pp. 135–62. B. *Capelle, O.S.B., 'Le Kyrie de la messe et le Pape Gélase' in *Rev. Bén.*, xlvi (1934), pp. 126–144, also with crit. text; C. Callewaert, 'Les Étapes de l'histoire du kyrie' in *R.H.E.*, xxxviii (1942), pp. 20–45. Jungmann (1952), i, pp. 433–5.

DE PROFUNDIS (Lat.), 'out of the deep'. A title of Ps. 130, from its opening words. The psalm is one of the fifteen '*Gradual Psalms', as well as one of the seven '*Penitential Psalms'. Its appeal for help from the misery of sin, and its expression of trust in deliverance, have led to its traditional use in the W. Church, esp. in the Office for the Departed. In *Ireland it is regularly recited at Mass after the *Last Gospel for the victims of former religious persecution.

H. Thurston, S.J., 'The *De Profundis*' in *The Month*, cxxxii (1918), pp. 358–68; repr. in *Familiar Prayers*, ed. P. Grosjean, S.J. (1953), No. X, pp. 164–77.

DE RANCÉ, ARMAND JEAN LE BOUTHILLIER. See *Rancé, Armand Jean le Bouthillier de*.

DER BALYZEH FRAGMENTS. A few Gk. papyrus fragments of liturgical prayers and a Creed (*c.* 6th cent.), discovered by W. Flinders Petrie and W. Crum at Der Balyzeh (Dair Balaizah), south of Assiout, in 1907. They throw important light on the history of Christian worship in Egypt, e.g. the existence (cf. the liturgies of St. *Serapion and of St. Mark, also Egyptian) of a Eucharistic *Epiclesis before the Words of *Institution. The compilation of the prayers has been variously dated (T. Schermann and P. Drews, *c.* 225; F. E. *Brightman, *c.* 350; B. *Capelle, *c.* 575). The Creed has affinities with the short Creed in the *Apostolic Tradition of St. *Hippolytus. The papyrus is preserved in the *Bodleian Library (MS. Gr. Lit. d.2–4 [P]).

Edd. of text, with Commentaries, by P. de Puniet (*Report of the 19th Eucharistic Congress held at Westminster, 9–13 Sept., 1908*, 1909); T. Schermann (*T.U.*, xxxvi, 1b, 1910), C. Wessely (*P.O.*, xvii, 1924) and J. Quasten (Flor. Patr., vii (1), ed. 2, 1936); all now superseded by C. H. Roberts (text)–B. Capelle (commentary) in *Bibliothèque du Muséon*, vol. 23, Louvain, 1949 (based on fresh reconstruction of the MS). P. E. Kahle, jun. (ed.), *Bala'izah*. Coptic texts from Deir Bala'izah in Upper Egypt (2 vols., 1954).

DE' RICCI, SCIPIO. See *Ricci, Scipio de'*.

DE ROSSI, GIOVANNI BATTISTA (1822–94), archaeologist. Born in Rome, after studying philosophy at the Collegio Romano from 1838 to 1840 and jurisprudence at the Sapienza from 1840 to 1844, he was appointed a Scriptor of the Vatican Library in 1844. In 1841 he met Giuseppe Marchi, S.J. (d. 1860), who fired his interest in the Roman *catacombs, to the excavation and study of which he devoted the rest of his life. He recognized, as none of his predecessors had done, the value of a thorough knowledge of literary sources (calendars, *Patristic allusions, etc.) for the interpretation of archaeological data; he considerably widened the scope of the investigations by examining the later materials and the contents of rubble as well as the original galleries and their monuments; and he recognized the contribution to be made by geology (here being helped by his brother, Michele Stefano de Rossi, a geologist, d. 1898).

The range of his publications was immense. Among those of primary importance were *Inscriptiones Christianae Urbis Romae septimo saeculo antiquiores* (I, 1861; II, i, 1888), *Imagines selectae Deiparae Virginis in Coemeteriis udo depictae* (1863), *La Roma sotterranea cristiana* (3 vols., 1864–77), *Sur les catacombes de Rome* (1867), *Mosaici cristiani e saggi dei pavimenti delle chiese di Roma anteriori al secolo XV* (25 fasc., 1872–92), *Inscriptiones Urbis Romae Latinae*, colleg. G. Henzen and J. B. de Rossi (1876; appeared in *Corpus Inscriptionum Latinarum*, vi), and *Piante iconografiche e prospettiche di Roma anteriori al secolo XVI* (1879). He also edited with L. *Duchesne the *Martyrologium Hieronymianum for the *Acta Sanctorum (Nov. II. i, 1894). In 1863 he founded the Bullettino di Archeologia Cristiana which he edited for thirty years.

There is a complete list of his works up to 1892 in the Mélanges de G. B. Rossi (Supplément aux Mélanges d'Archéologie et d'Histoire publiés par l'École français de Rome, xii, 1892). P. M. Baumgarten (ed.), Giovanni Battista de Rossi, der Begründer der christlich-archäologischen Wissenschaft (Festschrift zum 71. Geburtstage, 1892; It. tr., 1892). O. *Marucchi, Giovanni Battista de Rossi. Cenni biografici (1903).

DE SACRAMENTIS. A short liturgical treatise on the Sacraments, almost certainly the work of St. *Ambrose (d. 397). Its six addresses ('Books'), addressed to the newly baptized in Easter week, treat of *Baptism, *Confirmation, and the *Eucharist. Its special interest is that it is the earliest witness to the Roman *Canon of the Mass in substantially its present form; also, granted its Milanese provenance, it attests the influence of Roman usage in N. Italy. The author insists that it is the word of Christ which consecrates (conficit) the Eucharist; and in his canon he refers to the species as an unbloody offering (incruentem hostiam) and a figure (figura) of the Body and Blood of Christ (cf. *Serapion's ὁμοίωμα). The doubts expressed by the Benedictine editors of St. Ambrose (1690) as to its authorship were widely shared by subsequent scholars, some, e.g. Le N. *Tillemont and T. Schermann, ascribing it to *Maximus of Turin (c. 451–65) and a date in the 5th or 6th cent. being commonly assumed. Recently R. H. *Connolly, following hints in F. *Probst and G. *Morin, has put its Ambrosian authorship virtually beyond question.

J. P. Migne, PL, xvi, 409–62. Crit. ed. by B. Botte, O.S.B., in Sources Chrétiennes, 25 (1950; ed. 2, 1961), with important introd. Eng. tr. by T. Thompson, London, S.P.C.K., 1919, with introd. by J. H. Srawley; new and extensively revised ed., 1950. G. *Morin, O.S.B., 'Pour l'authenticité du De Sacramentis et de l'Explanatio Symboli de S. Ambroise' in J.L.W., viii (1928), pp. 86–106; R. H. Connolly, O.S.B., The De Sacramentis a Work of Ambrose. Two Papers (*Downside Abbey, 1942). Further bibl. in Altaner (ed. 1951), p. 336.

DESCARTES, RENÉ (1596–1650), philosopher and scientist. Educated at the *Jesuit college of La Flèche, in 1613 he went to Paris. In 1619 he decided to devote himself to philosophy, and after travelling for some years returned to Paris in 1625. Finding there no opportunity for his studies, in spite of the encouragement of Cardinal *Bérulle, he settled in Holland in 1629, and there wrote his most important works. At Queen *Christina's invitation he went in 1649 to Sweden, where he died.

The significance of Descartes as a philosopher lies chiefly in his originality of method. He based philosophical reasoning upon the principles and methods of mathematics, thereby refusing (as he believed) to make any initial metaphysical assumptions. The beginning of his philosophy was his own self-consciousness —'Cogito, ergo sum'. He next turned to the ideas of his own mind, and concluded that in experience as in mathematics whatever is clearly and distinctly conceived—that is, whatever can be conceived as part of a logical and coherent whole—is true. The first 'clear and distinct idea' which a thinking ego finds outside itself is the idea of God, and this idea is unaccountable except on the assumption that God exists; the veracity of our other ideas is guaranteed in turn by God's existence and goodness (implied in the conception of a perfect being). Descartes' arguments for God's existence were in effect three in number: an a priori argument based on the *ontological argument of *Anselm; an argument from causation—that God must be held to exist as the cause of our idea of Him; and a third, akin to the *cosmological argument in St. *Thomas Aquinas. In his reasoning about the world of experience he had difficulty in determining the relations of mind and matter. His basing of reason upon sense-experience led to the subjective idealism of J. *Locke, G. *Berkeley, and D. *Hume, and to the difficulty that if experience is our only source of information and if we have no reason to suppose that anything in objective reality corresponds with the evidence of our senses, we can know nothing.

Descartes's principal works are the Discours de la méthode (1637), Meditationes de prima philosophia (1641), Principia philosophiae (1644), and Les Passions de l'âme (1649).

The best edition is that of C. Adam and P. Tannery (12 vols., 1897–1910). His more important philosophical works have been translated into English by E. S. Haldane and G. R. T. Ross (Cambridge, 2 vols., 1911). A. Boyce Gibson, The Philosophy of Descartes (1932); J. Maritain, Trois Réformateurs, Luther–Descartes–Rousseau (1925; Eng. trans., 1928); E. Gilson, Index Scholastico-cartésien (1913).

DESCENT OF CHRIST INTO HELL, The. This belief is based on such Biblical passages as Mt. 27. 52 f., Lk. 23. 43, 1 Pet. 3. 18–20, though various opinions have been held as to their exact meaning. Some have thought that the descent into hell refers to the victory over the powers of evil, others have connected it with the Dereliction on the Cross and the full bearing by Christ of the fruits of sin in our stead. Most Christian theologians, however, believe that it refers to the visit of our Lord after His death to the realm of existence, which is neither heaven nor hell (qq.v.) in the ultimate sense, but a place or state where the souls of pre-Christian people waited for the message of the Gospel, and whither the penitent thief passed after his death on the cross (Lk. 23. 43).

The earliest known occurrences of the article in the Creeds are in 4th cent. *Arian formularies, viz. the Fourth Creed of *Sirmium of 359 and those of Nike and Constantinople of 360. Thence it found its way into the Aquileian Creed of *Rufinus (it is not found in the *Old Roman Creed), gradually spread over the W., and found a place in the *Apostles' Creed. It also occurs in the *Athanasian Creed and is the subject of Art. III of the *Thirty-Nine

Articles, but is absent from the *Niceno-Constantinopolitan formula. See also *Hell*.

The large literature includes E. H. Plumptre, '*The Spirits in Prison*'. A Sermon (1871); J. M. Usteri, '*Hinabgefahren zur Hölle*' [on 1 Pet. 3. 18–22 and 4. 6] (1885); F. *Spitta, *Christi Predigt an Geister* [1 Petr. 3. 19 ff.] (1890); C. Clemen, '*Niedergefahren zu den Toten*'. Ein Beitrag zur Würdigung des Apostolikums (1900); J. Kroll, *Gott und Hölle*. Der Mythos vom Descensus Kampf (Studien der Bibliothek Warburg, xx, 1932). See also Comms. on 1 Pet. 3. 18–20 (esp. E. G. Selwyn, pp. 314–62), on the Apostles' Creed (among older works, esp. J. *Pearson), and on the Thirty-Nine Articles. Good collection of material by F. *Loofs in *H.E.R.E.*, iv (1911), pp. 654–63, s.v. 'Descent into Hades (Christ's)'. Cf. also A. E. Burn in *D.C.G.*, i (1906), pp. 713–16 s.v. 'Hell (Descent into)' and J. H. *Bernard in *D.A.C.*, i (1915), pp. 289–92, s.v. 'Descent into Hades'.

DETERMINISM. A name popularized esp. by J. S. Mill, for systems of philosophy which hold that the entire universe, including all human activity, is subject to a rigid law of cause and effect which leaves no room for the exercise of free will. As it tolerates no first and undetermined principle outside the universe, Determinism is essentially bound up with a doctrine of immanence. In antiquity such doctrines were upheld by Democritus, and in recent philosophy they have come to the fore esp. through the influence of such thinkers as T. *Hobbes and B. *Spinoza and the materialistic systems of the 19th cent. The chief argument urged on its behalf is that free and undetermined phenomena in the world would make the universe unintelligible and all science and philosophy impossible. This line of argument is most commonly rebutted by an appeal to the facts of the moral consciousness. The fact that in making a decision man experiences awareness of choosing freely between different possible courses of action would seem to preclude universal determinism. Indeed in a completely determined world there would be neither vice nor virtue in the accepted sense of these terms, and therefore no place for morality. Determinism with its opposition to human freedom is a feature of all materialistic systems. Its attraction for many minds is to be explained by its correspondence with the need of the intellect for unification. But the fact that it is possible intelligently to debate its claims at all would seem to be its refutation.

DE THOU, JACQUES AUGUSTE (1553–1617), historian and book-collector. Coming from a family of magistrates, De Thou ('Thuanus') held high legal office, and helped to enact the Edict of *Nantes (1598). His Latin history of contemporary France, *Historiae sui temporis* (5 vols., 1604–20) describes the religious wars in detail. It was placed on the *Index, though its author remained a (very *Gallican) Catholic. The library was doubled in size by his son, JACQUES AUGUSTE DE THOU (1609–77). The MSS. from it came eventually to the Bibliothèque Royale in 1732 and 1754; the printed books were dispersed at the De Soubise sale in 1789.

For editions of his works see H. Hauser, *Les Sources de 'histoire de France*. XVIᵉ siècle (1494–1610), ii (1909),

P. 35, No. 775. *Catalogus Bibliothecae Thuanae* (Paris, 1679). H. Harrisse, 'Les De Thou et leur célèbre Bibliothèque 1573–1680–1789' in *Bulletin du Bibliophile*, 1903 and 1904. Further study by J. Collinson (London, 1807).

DEUSDEDIT, St. (before consecration known as **Frithona**) (d. 664), Abp. of *Canterbury. He was the first Anglo-Saxon to hold this position, to which he was consecrated in 655. Hardly anything is known of the events of his primacy. Feast day, 14 July.

The principal authority is *Bede, *H.E.*, iii, 20, 28, and iv, 1; notes to ed. by C. Plummer, ii (Oxford, 1896), p. 174 f. The Life by *Goscelin (extracts in *AA.SS.*, Jul. IV (1725), pp. 48–50) adds nothing of historical value. C. Hole in *D.C.B.*, i (1877), p. 821 f., s.v.; T. A. Archer in *D.N.B.*, xiv (1888), p. 422, s.v., with reff.

DEUS MISEREATUR. The Psalm (67) provided in the BCP of 1552 and later editions as an optional alternative to the *Nunc Dimittis at *Evensong, except on the 12th day of the month. In the Roman *Breviary office it is said on Tuesdays at *Lauds.

DEUTEROCANONICAL BOOKS, The. An alternative name for the Books contained in the Greek (*Septuagint) version of the OT, but not in the Hebrew. They are more commonly known as the *Apocrypha.

DEUTERO-ISAIAH. The name commonly given to the unknown author of most or all of the later chapters of the Book of Is. Older OT critics, e.g. S. R. *Driver, G. A. *Smith, in the belief that Is. 40–66 was a unity, applied the term to the author of all these chapters; it is now usually restricted to the author of 40–55 (56–66 being probably of later date). Deutero-Isaiah wrote in the later years of the Babylonian Exile (549–538 B.C.). See also *Isaiah* and *Trito-Isaiah*; and, esp. for bibl., *Servant Songs*.

DEUTERONOMY, Book of. The fifth and last Book of the *Pentateuch. Its English title comes via the Lat. *Deuteronomium* from the Gk. Δευτερονόμιον ('repetition of the law'), a *Septuagint mis-rendering of Deut. 17. 18 where the Heb. means 'a copy of the law'. In Heb. tradition the Book is commonly referred to by its two opening words אֵלֶּה הַדְּבָרִים ('These are the words').

The Book, which contains *Moses' final utterances on the east side of the *Jordan before his death, consists essentially of seven mainly legislatory and hortatory addresses (1. 6–4. 40; 5–11; 12–28; 29. 1–30. 20; 31. 1–13; 32. 1–47; 33), as follows: (1) After a brief introduction (1. 1–5), a survey of the journey from Mount Sinai to the Promised Land with its lessons (1. 6–4. 40). (2) Exhortations to serve Jehovah as the only true God, with certain laws interspersed (4. 45–11. 32); 5. 6–21 contains the Ten *Commandments in their Deuteronomic form and 6. 4–9 the principal section of the *Shema. (3) The central core of the legislation in the Book, the so-called 'Deuteronomic

Code' (12.1–28.68). 12–16 deal mainly with religious duties (Law of the One Sanctuary; *Tithes; Feasts of *Passover, of *Unleavened Bread, and of Weeks, etc.); 17–20 with civil enactments (Monarchy; *Cities of Refuge; Laws of War; etc.); and 21–25 with social and domestic regulations (aliens, usuries, vows, etc.). (4) Exhortations to keep the Covenant with Jehovah, with the threat of punishment for disobedience and the promise of restoration for repentance (29 f.). (5) The appointment of *Joshua as Moses' successor and the giving of the custody of the 'Book of the Law' to the *Levites (31. 1–29). (6) The 'Song of Moses', with an appendix (31. 30–32. 52). (7) The 'Blessing of Moses' (33), followed by an account of Moses' death (34).

The distinctive style and diction of Deut. mark it off from the other Pentateuchal Books. Throughout, emphasis is laid on the fact that Jehovah is the only true God, that His love for His peculiar people Israel is unbounded, and that Israel must love Him in return.

Acc. to the view traditional in the Church, the Book was written by Moses. Most modern critics, however, have sought to bring it to a much later date. The view most widely held assigns it to the 7th cent B.C. Stress is laid on the close contact with, and apparent dependence of its theology on, the teaching of the Eighth Century Prophets, e.g. its emphasis on the love of God (esp. characteristic of *Hosea), its monotheism and its humane modifications of the supposedly earlier laws of the 'Book of the Covenant' (Ex. 20. 22–23. 33). On the other hand its apparent identification of 'the sons of Aaron' with 'the Levites' (two classes later distinguished) and the absence of ref. to the Day of *Atonement and the Levitical system in general, indicate a date earlier than the 'Priestly Code' (6th cent. or later). It has hence commonly been supposed that the Book of the Law found in the Temple which was the basis of Josiah's Reformation (621 B.C.; cf. 2 Kgs. 22 f.) was none other than the central section of Deuteronomy. If so, it was not improbably compiled shortly before this date, perhaps in the reign of Manasseh (698–43) or even in the early part of that of Josiah himself (640–609 B.C.). Some recent critics, however, have argued for a date in the 8th cent.

Commentaries by S. R. *Driver (I.C.C., 1895), G. A. *Smith (Camb. Bib., RV, 1918), C. Steuernagel (K.H.A.T. Abt. 1, Bd., iii; 1898), A. Bertholet (K.H.C. Abt.v; 1899). A. C. Welch, The Code of Deuteronomy. A New Theory of its Origin [1924]; id., Deuteronomy. The Framework of the Code (1932). G. von Rad, Das Gottesvolk im Deuteronomium (Beiträge zur Wissenschaft von Alten und Neuen Testament, xlvii (3. Folge, xi) 1929); id., Deuteronomium-Studien (1947). A. R. Siebens, L'Origine du code deutéronomique (thesis, Paris, 1929). J. Skinner, Prophecy and Religion (1922), ch. vi, 'Jeremiah and Deuteronomy', pp. 89–107. W. Baumgartner, 'Der Kampf um das Deuteronomium' in Theologische Rundschau, N.F., i (1929), pp. 7–25. G. F. Moore in E.Bi., i (1899), cols. 1079–94, s.v.

DEUTSCHE CHRISTEN. See German-Christians.

DEUTSCHORDEN. See Teutonic Order.

DE VEUSTER, JOSEPH. See Damien, Father.

DEVIL. (Gk. διάβολος, 'calumniator', 'accuser'). In theological terminology the chief of the fallen angels. In the older books of the OT he is mentioned very rarely. In the narrative of the *Fall (Gen. 3) the serpent, which seduces *Eve and is thus the cause of man's first sin, has traditionally been considered an embodiment of the devil, through whom, acc. to the Book of *Wisdom (2. 24), 'death entered into the world'. The evil spirit tormenting Saul (1 Sam. 18. 10) has also been regarded as a devil, as also the lying spirits that deceive the prophets of Ahab (1 Kgs. 22. 21–3). In the Book of Job, Satan acts as a tempter and tormentor, always in submission to the will of Jehovah. In 1 Chr. 21. 1 *David's decision to number Israel is attributed to Satan, and in the vision of *Zechariah he acts as the accuser of the high priest Joshua (Zech. 3. 1–2). In the pseud-epigraphical Jewish literature there is a much more developed demonology with many traces of pagan influence. The Book of *Enoch interprets the narrative of Gen. 6. 1–4 about the 'sons of God' whose intercourse with women produced a race of giants, of fallen angels, and says that they were condemned to eternal punishment. Similar stories are reported in the Book of *Jubilees, the *Testaments of the Twelve Patriarchs, and other late Jewish writings.

The NT embodies and develops the later Jewish teaching on the devil. He tempts the Lord at the beginning of His public ministry (Mk. 1. 13, Mt. 4. 1–11, Lk. 4. 1–13), presenting himself as the master of the world (Mt. 4. 8–9), and Christ shows by His teaching and example his powerlessness over those who resist him. Later Satan renews his attacks in the persons of the demoniacs, thus manifesting the enmity between his kingdom and the kingdom of God, which is also taught in several parables, e.g. that of the tares among the wheat (Mt. 13. 24–30). He has wanted the disciples, esp. St. Peter, but our Lord has prayed for them, that their faith might not fail (Lk. 22. 31–2); for the power of Satan, whom Jesus saw 'fallen as lightning from heaven' (Lk. 10. 18), is already broken. Being 'a murderer from the beginning' (Jn. 8. 44), he is the 'prince of the world' but has no power over Christ (Jn. 14. 30), for he is already judged (Jn. 16. 11), and at the Last Judgement he and all those who belong to him will depart into eternal fire (Mt. 25. 41). St. *Paul and the other Apostles follow this teaching. St. *Peter recommends sobriety and vigilance as the chief means of resisting him (1 Pet. 5. 8–9), and in St. *Jude we find a brief allusion to the fall of the angels (1. 6; cf. 2 Pet. 2. 4). A fuller account of the angels' fall is given in Rev. 12. 7–9, which chapter also contains a detailed description of the devil's persecution of the Church under the figure of the Woman clothed with the sun.

In *patristic times there was no fixed teaching on the subject. Great influence was exercised by the apocryphal literature, esp. by the Book of Enoch. The view that demons are the sons of the fallen angels and human mothers is reproduced by many early Fathers, e.g. St. *Justin Martyr, and similar opinions were held by *Tertullian and St. *Cyprian. Others, e.g. St. *Irenaeus and *Clement of Alexandria, distinguish between the serpent, the seducer of Eve, and the other fallen angels, and most of them hold that the fall of the angels was caused by their envy of man. *Origen, however, rejects the tales of the Book of Enoch about the carnal intercourse between angels and women and attributes the fall of the former not to envy but to pride. His view was accepted first in the E., e.g. by St. *Athanasius and also by St. *Basil, who affirms that the devil is a spiritual being fallen from heaven through pride, and later also in the W., though the idea of angelic marriage was not at once rejected. St. *Augustine held that the devil fell through pride, because he would not submit to God, and that his envy of man was only a later consequence of his first sin. Though refusing to explain the fall of the angels by concupiscence, he assumed that they have bodies. He rejected the opinion advanced by Origen that the devils may finally be reconciled to God (ἀποκατάστασις).

In the Middle Ages there was much speculation on the subject, represented esp. by the *Dominican and the *Franciscan schools. Acc. to the former, following St. *Albert the Great and St. *Thomas Aquinas, all angels were created in a state of grace, though not of beatitude. The initial sin of the devil, which fixed him in evil, was committed after the first instant of his creation had passed. It consisted in pride, manifesting itself in the desire not for equality with God, which the angelic intellect knows to be impossible, but for a natural beatitude obtained by his own powers. The fall of the other angels was caused by their consent to his sin. The Franciscans, on the other hand, following *Duns Scotus, held that the devils committed various kinds of sin before becoming obstinate in evil, that Lucifer, their chief, desired equality with God, and that his sin consisted in an immoderate love of his own excellence. From the 15th cent. Latin theologians have in general followed either the Thomist or the Scotist view. A compromise was attempted by F. *Suarez, who advanced the novel opinion that the sin of the devil consisted in the desire of being himself hypostatically united to the Word. Since the 16th cent. the traditional teaching in its main outlines has been accepted by nearly all Christians, but there has been a marked reaction against the speculative elaborations of the Middle Ages.

There have been very few doctrinal decisions on the subject. The Council of *Braga (561) defined against the *Priscillianists that the devil was created good and could not himself create; and the 4th *Lateran Council (1215) affirmed that he became evil by his own will.

L'Abbé Lecanu, Histoire de Satan, sa chute, son culte, ses manifestations, ses œuvres, etc. (1861); J. M. Cayla, Le Diable, sa grandeur et sa décadence (1864); M. Hagen, S.J., Der Teufel im Lichte der Glaubensquellen (1899). P. Carus, The History of the Devil and the Idea of Evil from the Earliest Times to the Present Day (1900). L. Coulange [pseud. for J. Turmel], The Life of the Devil (1929; Eng. tr. of work publ. under his own name, Histoire du diable, 1931). H. Colleye, Histoire du diable (1945). G. Bazin and others, Satan (Études carmélitaines, 1948), with full bibl. Eng. tr. of part, with additional essays and introd. by C. Moeller, Satan (1951). E. Mangenot–T.Ortolan in D.T.C., iv (1911), cols. 321–409, s.v. 'Démon', with bibl.; E. Krebs in L.Th.K., x (1938), cols. 10–17, s.v. 'Teufel', also with bibl.

DEVIL'S ADVOCATE, The. See Promotor Fidei.

DEVOTIO MODERNA (Lat., 'Modern Devotion'). The term is applied to the revival and deepening of the spiritual life which, from the end of the 14th cent., spread from Holland to parts of Germany, France, and Italy. It originated in the circle round G. de *Groote, and found its classical expression in *Thomas à Kempis' *'Imitation of Christ'. It laid great stress on the inner life of the individual and encouraged methodical meditation, esp. on the Life and Passion of Christ. St. *Augustine, St. *Bernard, and St. *Bonaventure were among its acknowledged spiritual guides. The Modern Devotion made its way among the people chiefly through free associations of secular priests and lay people, called '*Brethren of the Common Life' (q.v.), whereas among the religious the *Windesheim Canons were its principal representatives.

The lives of G. Groote, Florentius Radewin, and their followers by Thomas à Kempis are tr. into Eng. by J. P. Arthur (London, 1905). C. Ullmann, Reformatoren vor der Reformation, ii (1842; Eng. tr. in Clark's Foreign Theological Library, New Series, viii; 1885). M. Schoengen, Die Schule von Zwolle von ihren Anfängen bis zur Einführung der Reformation, i (1898), A. Hyma, The Christian Renaissance. History of the 'Devotio Moderna' (New York, 1925). M. S. Muller, 'De Moderne Devotie te Utrecht' in Nederlandsch Archief voor Kerkgeschiedenis, N.S., xii (1916), pp. 16–19. E. F. Jacob, 'Gerard Groote and the Beginnings of the "New Devotion" in the Low Countries' in J.E.H., iii (1952), pp. 40–57.

DEVOUT LIFE, Introduction to the. The celebrated treatise on the spiritual life by St. *Francis de Sales. It grew out of a small manual compiled by Francis for the private use of his cousin's wife, Mme de Charmoisy. Its purpose is to show the possibility of and to foster a life of Christian devotion amid worldly distractions. It was addressed in the first instance to those living in the secular atmosphere of the French royal court, but its teaching is of very general application. The first edition appeared at Lyons at 1609, but Francis frequently revised it down to 1619, the date of the definitive edition.

In addition to the numerous popular editions there is a good critical edition by C. Florisoone in the 'Collection Guillaume Budé' (1930).

DE WETTE, WILHELM MARTIN LEBERECHT (1780–1849), German theologian. He was born at Ulla, near Weimar, studied at Jena, and held theological chairs at Heidelberg (1809) and Berlin (1810). From 1806 he published works on Biblical criticism and from 1813 on systematic theology. His radical rationalism raised a storm of opposition and, nominally because he had supported the murderer of A. F. F. von Kotzebue, he was deprived of his professorship and had to leave Berlin (1819). After a short stay at Weimar he accepted the theological chair at Basle (1822). In his later years he became more conservative. Under the influence of J. F. Fries and F. D. E. *Schleiermacher, he sought to do justice to the transcendent by faith and to the finite by scientific knowledge, to emphasize the importance of religious experience, to spiritualize dogma, and to construct a theology without a metaphysical basis. But his condemnation of cold reason displeased the rationalists, and his doubts regarding Biblical miracles and his reduction of the stories of the Birth, Resurrection, and Ascension of Christ to myths offended the *Pietists. His numerous writings include *Kommentar über die Psalmen* (1811), *Lehrbuch der historisch-kritischen Einleitung in die kanonischen und apokryphischen Bücher des AT* (1817), *Christliche Sittenlehre* (1819–23), *Einleitung ins NT* (1826; Eng. trans., 1858), and *Das Wesen des christlichen Glaubens* (1846).

Obituary oration by K. R. Hagenbach (Leipzig, 1850), with list of de Wette's writings, pp. 117–20. A. F. J. Wiegand, *W. M. L. de Wette, 1780–1849* (1879). G. Frank-F. *Kattenbusch in *P.R.E.* (ed. 3), xxi (1908), pp. 189–98, with full bibl.

D'HULST, MAURICE (1841–96), French scholar and priest. He played a prominent part in founding the Catholic University of Paris (1875), and in 1880 he became first rector of the newly constituted *Institut Catholique. Throughout his life he laboured for the higher education of the French clergy. In his first years at the Institut Catholique he was closely associated with many of those who later became *Modernists, but after the encyclical '*Providentissimus Deus' (18 Nov. 1893), he became more conservative. His *Question biblique* (1893) represented his earlier attitude. D'Hulst was also much esteemed as a preacher and spiritual director.

A. Baudrillart, *Vie de Mgr d'Hulst* (2 vols., 1912–14).

DIACONICON (Gk., 'appertaining to the deacon'). The area to the south of the sanctuary in a Byzantine church, so-called because it is in the charge of the deacons. In it the sacred vessels are kept and cleansed, and the vestments, service books, and other necessaries of Divine service are stored. It thus corresponds with the *sacristy in the W. Through the door piercing the *iconostasis the deacon passes to and fro between the diaconicon, the sanctuary, and the nave, during the Liturgy. The corresponding area to the north of the sanctuary is termed the *Prothesis. The word is also used of the book containing the deacon's part in the Liturgy.

DIADOCHUS (mid-5th cent.), Bp. of Photike after 451. Hardly anything is known of his life. He was the author of 100 'Capita Gnostica' (κεφάλαια γνωστικά) on the means of attaining spiritual perfection, which enjoyed great popularity in succeeding generations and were cited by St. *Maximus the Confessor, in the *Doctrina Patrum, and by *Photius. He finds the basis of all spiritual contemplation in the three *theological virtues, esp. love. A homily on the Ascension also survives.

His writings are in J. P. Migne, *PG*, lxv, 1141–1212. The 'Capita Gnostica' are printed here only in a Latin text. The Greek is to be found in ib. clxii (very rare), 713–54. There is a critical edition by J. E. Weis-Liebersdorf (Leipzig, 1912). F. Dörr, *Diadochus von Photike und die Messalianer. Ein Kampf zwischen wahrer und falscher Mystik im fünften Jahrhundert* (1937). Bardenhewer, iv, pp. 186–8; Altaner (ed. 1950), p. 292. *Œuvres spirituelles*, ed., with Fr. tr., by E. des Places, S.J. (*S.C.* v bis, 1955).

DIALECTICAL THEOLOGY. A title applied to the theological principles of K. *Barth (q.v.) and his school on the ground that, in distinction from the dogmatic method of ecclesiastical orthodoxy, which treats of God as a concrete Object (*via dogmatica*), and the negative principles of many mystics, which forbid all positive affirmations about God (*via negativa*), it finds the truth in a dialectic apprehension of God which transcends the 'Yes' and the 'No' of the other methods (*via dialectica*). Its object is to preserve the Absolute of faith from every formulation in cut-and-dried expressions.

After the publication of Barth's *Römerbrief* in 1918 the Dialectical Theology rapidly spread, at first esp. in Continental Protestantism. Rejecting the whole liberal tradition in modern theology, whose spirit it saw classically embodied in F. D. E. *Schleiermacher, it sought to go back to the principles of Reformers, esp. J. *Calvin, and drew its inspiration from thinkers in revolt against the humanist ideal, notably S. *Kierkegaard, F. M. *Dostoievsky, and the *Blumhardts. Its principal exponents (with varying degrees of emphasis) include E. *Brunner, F. *Gogarten, and E. *Thurneysen (qq.v.). Before long its stress on the Divine transcendence commended it also to many theologians of other traditions. In Great Britain its influence has been greatest in the Church of *Scotland; but it has also been considerable in the C of E, esp. since E. C. *Hoskyns' translation of the *Römerbrief* in 1935. The rise of *Existentialism (q.v.) in the RC Church also owed much to its influence.

For bibl., *see Barth, K.*

DIAMPER, Synod of (1599). A diocesan Synod of the native (St. Thomas) Church of *India, held under Alexis Menezez, Abp. of Goa, at Diamper (now Udayamperūr, some twelve miles south-east of Cochin). It brought the *Malabar Uniat Church (q.v.) into being. *Nestorianism was renounced, complete submission to Rome imposed, and many much needed reforms were made. Continuity of worship and practice was preserved, including the use of the (Syriac) Liturgy of *Addai and

Mari. For a long time Portuguese authority enforced the decisions of the synod, but as its influence waned the Church began to disintegrate and there were many secessions, notably in 1653.

[C. J. *Hefele–H. *Leclercq,] *Histoire des conciles d'après les documents originaux*, xi: C. de Clercq, 'Conciles des orientaux catholiques', pt. i (1949), pp. 36–67. Id. in *D.D.C.*, iv (1949), cols. 1207–10, s.v.

DIARIO ROMANO ('The Roman Daybook'). An official annual publication giving particulars of all feasts and fasts to be observed, of the special ceremonies celebrated in particular churches, and of the days on which they are celebrated, in the diocese of Rome.

DIASPORA, Jewish. The Dispersion (διασπορά) of the Jews had its beginnings in the Assyrian and Babylonian deportations (722 and 597 B.C.). Originally confined to parts of Asia, esp. Armenia and Iran, it later spread throughout the Roman Empire to Egypt, Asia Minor, Greece, and Italy. By NT times, acc. to *Philo, there were not less than a million Jews in *Alexandria. The Jews of the Diaspora remained in close touch with their home country, paying the *Temple taxes and keeping their religion and the restrictions of the Law, though Hellenic culture penetrated into their thought, as is evident from *Philo and *Josephus. The Jewish synagogues in Asia and Asia Minor were the first scenes of Christian preaching (cf. Acts). On the other hand, the missionary activities of the Jews in the Roman Empire, hampered from the first by their exclusiveness, were soon eliminated by the growing power of Christianity. Henceforth the Jews of the Dispersion became more and more cut off from the surrounding Gentile civilization, and under the influence of the Palestinian rabbis the religion of Moses developed into the Talmudic Judaism that has subsisted through the Middle Ages into modern times.

In Germany the word 'diaspora' is used of members of any religious body living as a minority among those of other beliefs, and esp. of Protestants living in Catholic parts and vice versa.

E. *Schürer, *Geschichte des jüdischen Volkes im Zeitalter Jesu Christi*, iii (ed. 4, 1909), pp. 1–188. Editors in F. J. Foakes Jackson–K. *Lake (edd.), *The Beginnings of Christianity*, I. i (1920), pp. 137–68. H. *Lietzmann, *Geschichte der Alten Kirche*, i (1932), pp. 68–101 (Eng. tr., 1937, pp. 95–134). R. H. Pfeiffer, *History of New Testament Times* (New York, 1949; London, 1954), pp. 166–96. On the word, J. H. Ropes, *James* (I.C.C.; 1916), pp. 120–3. H. Guthe in *E.Bi.*, i (1899), cols. 1106–17, s.v. 'Dispersion'; T. Reinach in *J.E.*, iv (1903), pp. 559–74, s.v.; E. Schürer in *H.D.B.*, v (extra vol., 1904), pp. 91–109, s.v.; all with bibl. A. Causse, *Les Dispersés d'Israël. Les Origines de la Diaspora et son Rôle dans la Formation du Judaïsme* (1929).

DIATESSARON. The edition of the four Gospels in a continuous narrative, compiled by the Gnostic *Tatian *c.* 150. From an early date it circulated widely in *Syriac-speaking Churches, where it became the standard text of the Gospels down to the 5th cent., when it gave way to the four separate Gospels. Its original language may have been Syriac, Greek, or (so

F. C. *Burkitt) even Latin. Its publication in the 2nd cent. is a notable witness to the authority already enjoyed by the Four Gospels.

Our knowledge of its structure and contents is derived principally from five sources: (1) The 'Commentary' on it made by St. *Ephraim Syrus in the 4th cent. This survives only in an *Armenian version, first published by the *Mechitarist Fathers at Venice in 1836. (2) Two late MSS. of an Arabic translation of the work. (3) The Latin *Codex Fuldensis, where the order of the Diatessaron has been preserved, though the text has been assimilated to that of the *Vulgate. (4) A medieval Dutch Harmony of the Scriptures, dependent on the text of the Diatessaron, which was discovered by Dr. D. Plooij at Liége in 1923. (5) A short Greek papyrus fragment of 14 imperfect lines, containing the account of the request for the body of Christ made by *Joseph of Arimathaea. This fragment, which was found at *Dura Europos and identified at Yale in 1933, has strengthened the case for the Diatessaron having been originally compiled in Greek.

Arab. text ed. P. A. Ciasca, Rome, 1888 (ed. 2, 1934); also by A. S. Marmardji, O.P., Beyrout, 1935. Eng. tr. of Arab. text publ. by J. H. Hill as *The Earliest Life of Christ ever compiled from the Four Gospels* (1894). Med. Dutch version ed. D. Plooij, C. A. Phillips, A. J. Barnouw, etc., Amsterdam, 1929 ff.; 13th–14th cent. Ital. version ed. V. Todesco, A. Vacari, S.J., and M. Vattasso (S.T., lxxxi; 1938). C. H. Kraeling, *A Greek Fragment of Tatian's Diatessaron from Dura* (Studies and Documents, 3, 1935). F. C. *Burkitt (ed.), *Evangelion Da-Mepharresche*. The Curetonian Version of the Four Gospels, with the readings of the Sinai Palimpsest and the early Syriac Patristic Evidence, ii (1904), esp. pp. 173–212. J. F. Stenning in *H.D.B.*, extra vol. (1904), pp. 451–61; H. *Leclercq, O.S.B., in *D.A.C.L.*, iv (1921), cols. 747–70, s.v. Full bibl. of recent lit. in J. Quasten, *Patrology*, i (1950), pp. 225–8. See also bibl. to *Codex Fuldensis*.

DIBELIUS, MARTIN (1883–1947), NT scholar. A native of Dresden, he was educated at Neufchâtel, Leipzig, Tübingen, and Berlin. From 1910 to 1915 he was a Privatdozent at Berlin. In 1915 he succeeded J. *Weiss as Prof. of NT Exegesis and Criticism at Heidelberg, holding office until his death. He was an active supporter of the *Oecumenical Movement and a leader of the *Faith and Order Commission.

At first interested esp. in the study of Semitic languages and of comparative religion, he concentrated increasingly on the NT. Here he was a pioneer of the *Formgeschichtliche Method (q.v.), the technique of which he handled with imagination but also with restraint and a due sense of its limitations. Working on the foundations of Weiss, he laid great emphasis on preaching as a medium of transmission of the Lord's words; and in general his attitude to the Gospel traditions was more conservative than that of most members of the school. His most considerable work in this field was *Die Formgeschichte des Evangeliums* (1919; ed. 2, 1933; Eng. trans., *From Tradition to Gospel*, 1934).

Dibelius's other publications include *Die Geisterwelt im Glauben des Paulus* (1909), *Die Isisweihe bei Apuleius und verwandte Initiations-Riten* (1917), *Geschichtliche und übergeschichtliche*

Religion im Christentum (1925), *Geschichte der urchristlichen Literatur* (1926; Eng. trans. 1936), *Die Botschaft von Jesus Christus* (1935; Eng. trans. 1939), *Gospel Criticism and Christology* (1935), *Jesus* (Sämmlung Göschen, 1939). He also contributed to the *Handbuch zum Neuen Testament* (ed. H. *Lietzmann) commentaries on 1 and 2 Thess. and Phil. (1911), Col., Eph., and Philem. (1911), 1 and 2 Tim. and Tit. (1913) and *Hermas (1923), and to the H. A. W. Meyer series (*Kritisch-Exegetischer Kommentar über das N.T.*) that on James (1921).

His cousin, OTTO DIBELIUS (1880–), born at Berlin, after several other pastoral cures in the Lutheran Church, was appointed to the church 'Zum Heilsbronnen' in Berlin in 1915. In 1925 he became *General Superintendent of the Kurmark. Owing to his support of the *Confessing Church, he was put under restraint during much of the Nazi period. In 1945 he became Bishop of Berlin and in 1949 Presiding Bishop of the Evangelical Church in Germany, in which capacity he has vigorously upheld religious freedom in the face of Communistic atheism. His works include *Das Vaterunser. Umrisse zu einer Geschichte des Gebets in der alten und mittleren Kirche* (1903), *Das Jahrhundert der Kirche*. *Geschichte, Betrachtung, Umschau und Ziele* (1927), *Friede auf Erden?* Frage, Erwägungen, Antwort (1930) and *Grenzen des Staates* (1949).

List of M. Dibelius's works in 'Bibliographia Dibeliana atque Bultmanniana' in *Coniectanea Neotestamentica*, ed. A. Fridrichsen, viii (1944), pp. 1–22. M. Dibelius, *Gesammelte Aufsätze zur Apostelgeschichte* (ed. H. Greeven, 1951). Further collected papers, *Botschaft und Geschichte*, ed. G. Bornkamm, Bd. i (1953).

DIDACHE (Gk. διδαχή, 'teaching'). The elements in primitive Christian apologetic of an instructional kind, as contrasted with *Kerygma or 'preaching'.

DIDACHE, The. (Διδαχὴ Κυρίου διὰ τῶν δώδεκα ἀποστόλων). A short early Christian manual on morals and Church practice. Of its 16 brief chapters, chs. 1–6 describe the 'Two Ways', the 'Way of Life' and the 'Way of Death', and are probably based on a Jewish source; they include quotations from the *Sermon on the Mount. Chs. 7–15 contain instructions on *baptism, *fasting, *prayer, the *Eucharist, and how to treat *prophets, *bishops, and *deacons. Ch. 16 is a prophecy of the *Antichrist and the Second *Advent. The treatise contains much of interest to the student of early Christian liturgy. The Lord's Prayer is given in full. Baptism is by *immersion if possible, otherwise by threefold *affusion. Fasting on Wednesdays and Fridays is ordered. Two eucharistic prayers, of an unusual and primitive kind, are given. The ecclesiastical organization described is undeveloped. In addition to bishops and deacons (the presbyterate is not separately mentioned), the travelling prophets fill a role of great importance ('they are your chief priests'), and may celebrate the Eucharist.

The author, date, and place of origin are unknown. It is, however, the earliest of the series of 'Church Orders', and forms the basis of the 7th Book of the '*Apostolical Constitutions'. Many have assigned the Didache to the 1st cent.; L. *Duchesne put it under Trajan (d. 117); but the trend of recent opinion (J. A. *Robinson, J. Muilenburg, R. H. *Connolly) has been to put it later. It seems to describe the life of an isolated Christian community, probably in Syria (not Egypt). The author knew the Gospels of Mt., Lk., and probably Jn.; and there is certainly some literary connexion between the Didache and the Ep. of *Barnabas and also *Hermas, the exact nature of which (important in connexion with dating the Didache) is much disputed.

The only known MS. (written in 1056) was discovered by P. *Bryennios at the 'Jerusalem Monastery of the Holy Sepulchre' at *Constantinople in 1875 and published by him in 1883. For part of it a Latin version also exists.

The publication of the 'Didache' in 1883 evoked a vast literature. Ed., with facsimile, by J. R. *Harris (Baltimore and London, 1887). Other edd. by A. *Harnack (*T.U.* ii, Hfft. 1–2; 1884), P. *Schaff (New York and London, 1885), T. W. Crafer (London, 1920), H. *Lietzmann (Berlin, Kleine Texte 6, 1936), T. Klauser (Florilegium Patristicum, i; Bonn, 1940), as well as in the edd. of the *Apostolic Fathers (q.v.) by F. X. Funk (1887), J. B. *Lightfoot–J. R. Harmer (1891), K. *Lake (Loeb, 1912–13), and K. Bihlmeyer (1924). Eng. tr. by C. *Bigg (1898; rev. by A. J. Maclean, 1922), and by J. B. Lightfoot and K. Lake (opp. citt.). Early Lat. tr. ed. J. Schlecht from Cod. Monac. 6264 (11th cent.) at Freiburg, i. Br., 1900; cf. L. Wohleb, *Die lateinische Übersetzung der Didache* (Studien zur Geschichte und Kultur des Altertums, vii, Hft. 1; 1913). Coptic frag. in B.Mus. (MS. Or. 9271), ed. G. Horner in *J.T.S.*, xxv (1923–4), pp. 225–31; cf. C. Schmidt in *Z.N.T.W.*, xxiv (1925), pp. 81–99. J. A. Robinson, *Barnabas, Hermas and the Didache* (Donnellan Lectures for 1920; 1920); J. Muilenburg, *The Literary Relation of the Epistle of Barnabas and the Teaching of the Twelve Apostles* (Yale Univ. Diss. of 1926; Marburg, 1929); R. H. Connolly, O.S.B., 'The Didache in Relation to the Epistle of Barnabas' in *J.T.S.*, xxxiii (1932), pp. 237–53. F. E. Vokes, *The Riddle of the Didache* (1938), with bibl. E. Peterson, 'Ueber einige Probleme der Didache-Ueberlieferung' in *Riv. A.C.*, xxvii (1951), pp. 37–60. On the Eucharistic prayers, Jungmann, i (ed. 1948), pp. 17–19, and lit. cited. Bardenhewer, i, pp. 90–113; Altaner (1950), pp. 37–40; J. Quasten, *Patrology*, i (1950), pp. 29–39, all with extensive bibl. J. P. Audet, O.P., *La Didaché* (Études Bibliques, 1958).

DIDASCALIA APOSTOLORUM, an early *Church Order, professedly 'the Catholic Teaching of the Twelve Apostles and holy Disciples of our Redeemer' (Syriac title). Its author, prob. a physician who had been converted from Judaism, seems to have composed it in N. Syria in the earlier half of the 3rd cent. The work is addressed to readers in various states of life, esp. married persons (chs. 2–3), and deals with such subjects as the Bishop's duties, penance, liturgical worship, behaviour during persecution, widows and deaconesses, the settlement of disputes and the administration of offerings; but the arrangement is unmethodical and disorderly. It is esp. directed against Christians who regard the Jewish ceremonial law as still binding. The author is far more lenient than his W. contemporaries (*Tertullian, *Cyprian) in allowing repentant sinners back to Communion. A six-days' fast before Easter is enjoined.

The work, orig. in Gk., survives complete

only in a Syriac version, with some fragments in Latin. As it was worked over and embodied in the *Apostolic Constitutions, much of the Greek text can be reconstructed with tolerable certainty. Among the sources used are the '*Pericope Adulterae' (Jn. 7. 53–8. 11), the *Didache, the *Ignatian Epp., St. *Justin's 'Dialogue with Trypho' and the *Sibylline Oracles (Book IV).

Syr. text ed. P. de *Lagarde, Leipzig, 1854. Lat. text, partly constructed by Funk, in F. X. Funk (ed.), *Didascalia et Constitutiones Apostolorum*, i (Paderborn, 1905), pp. 2–384, with introd., pp. iii–xiv. R. H. *Connolly, O.S.B., *Didascalia Apostolorum*. The Syriac Version translated and accompanied by the Verona Latin Fragments (Oxford, 1929). Gk. fragments, ed. J. V. Bartlet, 'Fragments of the Didascalia Apostolorum' in *J.T.S.*, xviii (1916–17), pp. 301–9. P. Galtier, S.J., 'La Date de la Didascalie des Apôtres' in *R.H.E.*, xlii (1947), pp. 315–51. J. Quasten, *Patrology*, ii (1953), pp. 147–52, with full bibl.

DIDEROT, DENIS (1713–84), French *encyclopaedist. A native of Langres, he studied at *Paris where he became a publisher's hack. In 1746 he published *Pensées philosophiques*, a defence of the sufficiency of natural religion. In 1749 followed his *Lettres sur les aveugles* which attracted wide notice by their materialistic doctrines and led to a short imprisonment. Meanwhile Diderot's intellectual powers, esp. his gifts as a conversationalist, brought him into the circle of advanced thinkers in Paris which centred in Baron P. H. D. d'Holbach (1723–89). A request from a bookseller for a translation of Ephraim Chambers's *Cyclopaedia* had suggested the idea of a new encyclopaedia; and J. le R. *d'Alembert having promised his aid, he embarked on the task which was to occupy him for most of his life. The first volume appeared in 1751; but its advocacy of toleration and democracy was resented by the Church and the work formally suppressed in 1759. The Encyclopaedia continued to be issued clandestinely, however, and the main body (28 vols.) was completed by 1772. (See *Encyclopaedists*.) Among the articles by Diderot himself were 'Christianisme', 'Foi', 'Liberté', and 'Providence'; but, much to Diderot's chagrin, the publisher excised many of his more challenging passages. As the Encyclopaedia and his various lesser writings brought their author little financial reward, Diderot would have been in serious straits had not the Empress Catherine of Russia (whom he visited to thank her in 1773–4) bought his library and appointed him its librarian. His other writings include *Le Rêve de d'Alembert* (written 1769; publd. 1830), *Regrets sur ma vieille robe de chambre* (1772), *Jacques le fataliste* (1773; publd. 1796), and *Éloge de Richardson* (1761). Diderot had a fertile imagination and keen sensibility, but he can hardly be reckoned a considerable constructive thinker.

The best ed. of his collected works is that of J. Assézat [–M. Tourneux] (20 vols., Paris, 1875–77). J. A. Naigeon, *Mémoires historiques et politiques sur la vie et les ouvrages de D. Diderot* (1821). Later studies by J. Rosenkranz (2 vols., Leipzig, 1866), J. Morley (2 vols., London, 1878), L. Ducros (Paris, 1894), J. Reinach (ib., 1894), A. Collignon (ib., 1895), A. Billy (ib., 1932), and D. Mornet (ib., 1941). M. Tourneux, *Diderot et Catherine II* (1899). Ueberweg, iii, pp. 430–2,

with bibl., p. 698. J. Morley in *E.B.* (ed. 11), viii (1910), pp. 204–6, s.v. See also bibl. to *Encyclopaedists*.

DIDYMUS (the Gk. form of the Heb. 'Thomas', i.e. 'twin'). An alternative name in Jn. 11. 16, 20. 24, 21. 2 for the Apostle Thomas.

DIDYMUS THE BLIND (*c.* 313–98), *Alexandrian theologian. He was blind from his infancy. Erudite, though not creative, he was entrusted by St. *Athanasius with the direction of the *Catechetical School' at Alexandria, where he numbered among his pupils *Gregory of Nazianzus, *Jerome, and *Rufinus. Of his numerous writings, most of which have perished, there survive his works 'On the Holy Spirit', 'On the Trinity', 'Against the Manichaeans', and fragments of exegesis. The tract 'Against Arius and Sabellius', preserved under the name of *Gregory of Nyssa, is probably also his work. In trinitarian theology he was a staunch *Nicene; but he was condemned as an *Origenist at the Council of *Constantinople in 553.

Editio princeps of *De Trinitate*, by J. A. Mingarelli, Bologna, 1769; repr., with other writings of Didymus, in J. P. Migne, *PG*, xxxix, 131–1818 (the only collected ed.). Many exegetical fragments in a crit. ed. by K. Staab, *Pauluskommentare aus der griechischen Kirche* (Neutestamentliche Abhandlungen, xv; 1933), pp. 1–45. J. Leipoldt, *Didymus der Blinde von Alexandrien* (T.U., xxix, Hft. 3; 1905); G. Bardy, *Didyme l'Aveugle* (1910). J. Lebon, 'Le Ps. Basile (Adv. Eunom., iv–v) est bien Didyme d'Alexandrie' in *Muséon*, l (1937), pp. 61–83. Bardenhewer, iii, pp. 104–15; Altaner (ed. 1951), p. 239 f. W. *Bright in *D.C.B.*, i (1877), pp. 827–9, s.v.; F. Zoepfl in *L.Th.K.*, iii (1931), col. 305 f., s.v.; M. Pellegrino in *E.C.*, iv (1950), col. 1567 f., s.v. 'Didimo il Cieco'.

DIES IRAE (Lat., 'Day of Wrath'), the opening words, and hence the name, of the *sequence in the Mass for the Dead in the W. Church. Its author is almost certainly a 13th cent. *Franciscan, but prob. not *Thomas of Celano. It was not originally intended for liturgical use as it is written in the 1st person sing. The first printed Missal containing it as the sequence for Requiem Masses is that of Venice, 1493. In the present Roman rite it is to be said in the Masses on *All Souls' Day, on the day of decease or burial of the person for whom the Mass is offered, and on the anniversary of the death, but may be omitted on other days. Many translations into English have been made (e.g. E.H. 351), but the vigour of the concise Latin original is usually lost.

F. Ermini, *Il Dies Irae e l' innologia ascetica nel secolo decimoterzo*. Studi sulla litteratura latina del medio evo (1903). Raby, pp. 443–50, incl. orig. text, p. 448, and note of trr., p. 449, with bibl., p. 485.

DIETRICH OF NIEHEIM (or of 'Niem') (*c.* 1340–1418), Papal notary and historical writer. Entering the service of the curia he became Abbreviator and Scriptor, and published two treatises on curial administration. He was appointed Bp. of Verden by Boniface IX in 1395 without, however, receiving consecration, and was deprived of the office four years later.

After the election of Gregory XII he took a prominent part in the efforts to end the Great Schism. He was present at the Council of *Constance (1415), where he renounced John XXIII and upheld the conciliar standpoint vigorously. His historical works, though one-sided, are an invaluable source for contemporary events, esp. 'Nemus Unionis' (1408) and 'De Schismate' (1410). Of his writings advocating reform the most important is 'Avisamenta edita in Concilio Constanciensi' (1414), in which he asserted the plenary powers of a General Council including its right to depose the Pope, attacked clerical abuses, and put forward schemes for ecclesiastical reform.

Crit. text of his 'Stilus Palatii Abbreviatus' (Leipzig, 1888); of his 'De Schismate', ed. G. Erler (Leipzig, 1890). H. Heimpel, 'Eine unbekannte Schrift Dietrichs v. Niem über die Berufung der Generalkonzilien (1413/1414)', in *Sb.* (Heid.), 1929/30, Abh. 1. G. Erler, *Dietrich von Nieheim* (Leipzig, 1887); W. J. M. Mulder, *Dietrich von Nieheim, zijne Opvatting van het Concilie en zijne Kroniek* (with text, 1907); H. Heimpel, *Dietrich von Niem* (Westfälische Biographien, Bd. 2, 1932); E. F. Jacob, 'Dietrich of Niem. His Place in the Conciliar Movement' in the *Bulletin of the John Rylands Library, Manchester*, xix (1935), pp. 388–410; repr. in *Essays in the Conciliar Epoch* (Manchester, 1943), pp. 24–43.

DIGAMY. In the early Church, second marriages were generally looked upon with disfavour (cf. 1 Cor. 7. 39 f.). *Athenagoras went so far as to regard them as 'a specious adultery' (*Legat.* 33), and this view became part of the official teaching of certain heretical bodies (*Montanists, *Novatianists). Even the orthodox Council of *Neocaesarea (314) presupposed the imposition of a slight penance on digamists (can. 7). The Council of *Nicaea (325), however, in providing for the reconciliation of Novatianists, insisted (can. 8) that those who had married twice should not be excluded from Christian fellowship.

The Eastern Church has always been more severe in this matter than the W. Second marriages were often held not to be marriages at all, and even now the nuptial blessing is not given in the same form as for a first marriage. Even more suspect were third marriages, and since the 10th cent. fourth marriages have been forbidden altogether.

St. Paul's words that a bishop must be the husband of one wife (1 Tim. 3. 2: μιᾶς γυναικὸς ἄνδρα) were widely held, e.g. by *Innocent I and St. *Augustine, to make digamy a dis-qualification for Ordination, though St. *Jerome held the contrary view (*Ep.* 69). In modern RC canon law (C.I.C., can. 984. 4) the impediment persists.

DIGGERS. See *Fossors*.

DIGGERS (17th cent.). A section of the *Levellers, founded in 1649 by Gerrard Winstanley. Its adherents held that Christian principles required a communistic mode of life and the cultivation of crown property and common land with the spade. Work was started in April 1649 at St. George's Hill, Oatlands, Surrey, where some 50 men began digging up waste land. Winstanley expounded his principles and schemes in several pamphlets, but the movement soon collapsed.

G. H. Sabine (ed.), *The Works of Gerrard Winstanley*, with appendix of docc. relating to the Digger Movement (New York, 1941); L. Hamilton (ed.), *Gerrard Winstanley*. Selections from his Works, with an introduction by C. Hill (London, 1944). L. H. Berens, *The Digger Movement in the Days of the Commonwealth as Revealed in the Writings of Gerrard Winstanley, the Digger* (1906); D. W. Petegorsky, *Left-Wing Democracy in the English Civil War*. A Study of the Social Philosophy of Gerrard Winstanley (1940).

DILLMANN, CHRISTIAN FRIEDRICH AUGUST (1823–94), German Biblical scholar and orientalist. He studied at Tübingen under H. *Ewald and F. C. *Baur, and later worked on Ethiopic MSS. in Paris, London, and Oxford, producing catalogues of the Ethiopic MSS. in the British Museum and the Bodleian Library (1847–8). In 1848 he returned to Tübingen, where in 1853 he obtained a professorship, and later he held chairs at Kiel (1854), Giessen (1864), and Berlin (1869). To him more than any other scholar is due the revival of Ethiopic studies in the 19th cent. He was also a capable OT critic. Among his works were a grammar (1857) and lexicon (1865) of Ethiopic, and editions of Ethiopic texts of the OT down to Kings, of the Apocrypha, and of some non-canonical books, while late in life he produced commentaries on the *Hexateuch (1875–86; Eng. trans. of Genesis by W. B. Stevenson, 1897) and on Isaiah (1890).

Dillmann's *Handbuch der alttestamentlichen Theologie* was posthumously ed. by R. *Kittel (1895). There is a portrait and very brief life prefixed to vol. v. of Dillmann's ed. of the Ethiopic OT (*Libri Apocryphi*, Berlin, 1894; no pagination). W. Baudissin in *P.R.E.* (ed. 3), iv (1898), pp. 662–9, s.v., with list of obituary notices.

DILTHEY, WILHELM (1833–1911), German philosopher of history and culture. Born at Biebrich, nr. Wiesbaden, he was professor successively at Basle (1866), Kiel (1868), Breslau (1871), and Berlin (1882, in succession to H. Lotze). He was also a leading member of the Prussian Academy and entrusted with its edition of I. *Kant (1902 ff.). In the front rank of historians of modern culture and ideas and also the virtual creator of the philosophy of history in its present form, Dilthey stressed the fundamental differences between the methods of the 'Human Sciences' (*Geisteswissenschaften*), employed in the study of culture, art, religion, etc., and those adapted to the Natural Sciences (*Naturwissenschaften*). He worked out his position in his *Einleitung in die Geisteswissenschaften*: Versuch einer Grundlegung für das Studium der Gesellschaft und der Geschichte (vol. i, 1883) which, like many of Dilthey's other works, was never completed. His belief that the current methods of empirical psychology failed to reach the real spiritual life of persons as studied in the Human Sciences issued in his *Ideen über eine beschreibende und zergliedernde Psychologie* (1894), in which he elaborated the ideal of a 'descriptive and analytic' psychology. Other important works were *Das Erlebnis und die Dichtung* (1905), *Der Aufbau der geschichtlichen Welt in den Geisteswissenschaften* (Part i, 1910) and *Die Typen der Weltanschauungen* (1911). Dilthey continued critical, however, of the possibility of a philosophy of history in the traditional sense, as well as of a systematic sociology, holding that the spiritual life was too complex to be comprehended in formulae. Dilthey's own studies in religion were esp. directed to it as an element in human culture. The religious *Weltanschauung*, unlike the philosophical, was restricted in that it did not aim at universality. His doctrines on history have exercised influence on Christian thought, esp. through E. *Troeltsch. His extended studies in hermeneutics, which, however, take the word in a very wide sense, are very relevant to the problem of Biblical exegesis.

Dilthey's works, most of which were orig. publd. in the *Abh.* (Berl.), were collected and ed. by Georg Misch and others (Berlin, 1914 ff.); among those not so far publd. in this collection is *Das Leben Schleiermachers*, i (all publd., 1870). Diary and letters for the period 1852–70 ed. Clara Misch (Leipzig-Berlin, 1933); further collections of correspondence ed. S. von der Schulenburg (Halle, 1923) and E. Weniger (*Abh.* (Berl.), 1936, No. 9). H. A. Hodges, *Wilhelm Dilthey. An Introduction* (1944); id., *The Philosophy of Wilhelm Dilthey* (1952), both with detailed bibl. J. Stenzel, *Dilthey und die deutsche Philosophie der Gegenwart* (Philosophische Vorträge, xxxiii; 1934). Ueberweg, iv, pp. 551–5, with bibl., p. 720.

DING-AN-SICH (Germ.), 'thing-in-itself'. A philosophical term for real objects in so far as their structure and being are held to stand out of relation to any subject which apprehends them. The concept occupied a central position in the philosophy of I. *Kant (1724–1804), who denied that any knowledge of things-in-themselves was possible.

DIOCESE. In ecclesiastical use, the territorial unit of administration in the Church. It is governed by a bishop, with the assistance of the inferior clergy, and sometimes one or more other bishops, and it is usually divided into parishes, which are frequently grouped in *rural deaneries and *archdeaconries. Dioceses are commonly associated to form a *province over which one of the diocesan bishops presides with varying powers of intervention in the affairs of other dioceses. Traditionally the bishop is supreme in his diocese and possesses *ordinary jurisdiction. In the RC Church, however, there has been an ever increasing tendency in modern times to make the jurisdiction of the diocesan bishop dependent upon delegation from the Pope.

In the early days of the Church, when Christianity was chiefly an urban religion, dioceses covered only the principal towns and cities. As the new religion spread, the limits of the various dioceses were extended, and new rural dioceses were created until now there is hardly any part of the world which is not within the jurisdiction of some diocesan bishop.

The word 'diocese' (Gk. διοίκησις) only gradually established itself in its current Christian sense. The original word for a local group of Christians was simply a 'church' (ἐκκλησία). Later, e.g. in the *Apostolic (cans. 14, 15) and *Nicene (can. 16) Canons, it was 'parish' (παροικία), and in the E. Church this word is still retained for the territory subject to a bishop, διοίκησις being used for the *patriarch's area of control. In the W., however, the word was in use in Africa in its modern sense at the end of the 4th cent., though *parochia* continued to be employed down to the 9th cent. and even later. The word also had a long secular history for the larger administrative units of the later Roman Empire.

The word διοίκησις, primarily 'administration', was first used in Cicero's time of a territorial area over which supervision was exercised, viz. of the three regions of Cibyra, Apamea, and Synnada added to Cilicia (Cicero, *Ep. ad Fam.*, iii, 8, 4; xiii, 67, 1). Under *Diocletian it was adopted for the twelve new regions into which the Empire was divided for the purposes of civil government, the largest of these Dioceses being 'Oriens' (sixteen provinces) and the smallest Britain (four provinces). Its ecclesiastical use was of slow growth. As late as *Anastasius Bibliothecarius it was applied to the ecclesiastical province, as distinct from the area governed by a single bishop. On the history of the word, see C. D. *Ducange, *Glossarium*, s.v.; J. *Bingham, *Origines Ecclesiasticae*, ix, esp. cap 2, sect. 2; W. *Bright, *The Canons of the First Four General Councils* (ed. 2, 1892), pp. 101–5. See also G. Hill, *English Dioceses. A History of their Limits* (1900).

DIOCLETIAN, VALERIUS DIOCLETIANUS (245–313), Roman Emperor from 284 to 305. Diocles, who was born of humble parents at Salona in Dalmatia, took up a military career, serving with distinction under Probus and Aurelian. On 17 Sept. 284, on the murder of Numerian, the army proclaimed him Emperor at Chalcedon. He was defeated in the ensuing hostilities against Carinus, Numerian's joint-Emperor; but as Carinus was promptly slain by his own officers, Diocletian (as he now chose to call himself) became undisputed master. Endowed with immense energy, great gifts of organization, and a mind dominated by logic, he made it his main purpose to stabilize and reform the Empire. To this end, he created an absolute monarchy, centring all power in himself as the semi-Divine ruler, and making his palace the *domus divina* and his own person sacred; and henceforth the Senate was to be permanently in a subordinate position. In 286 he associated Maximian in the government as co-Augustus, taking the Eastern Empire for himself and giving Maximian the West. In 292 he further divided the Empire by the creation of two 'Caesars', Constantius Chlorus and Galerius. Of the four areas (the 'tetrarchy'), Diocletian now ruled the East, Maximian Italy and Africa, Constantius Britain, Gaul, and Spain, and Galerius Illyricum and the Danube basin, with Nicomedia, *Milan, Trier, and Sirmium as their respective capitals. With this strong organization, parts of the Empire which had been lost (Britain, Persia) were restored and the Marcomanni defeated. Diocletian also introduced far-reaching military, administrative, fiscal, and economic reforms, including the celebrated Edict on Maximum Prices ('De pretiis rerum venalium') of 301. On 1 May 305 he formally abdicated at Nicomedia, compelling his reluctant colleague Maximian to take a like step. He lived his last years in retirement at his large palace at Spalato (Split).

For the greater part of his reign the Christians seem to have enjoyed the tranquillity which had been theirs since the Rescript of Gallienus (260). Only the *Manichees were repressed, by an edict dated 31 March 296, as a sect lately originating in Persia. It was in 303 that the Great Persecution broke out. Diocletian seems to have been instigated to it mainly through pressure from Galerius. An edict issued at Nicomedia on 23 Feb. enjoined the demolition of churches and the burning of Christian books. Some incidents which followed (fires in the palace at Nicomedia, reports of unrest at Melitene and in Syria) led to further edicts. The next two were directed solely against the clergy. The punishment inflicted for resistance was imprisonment, torture, and, in some cases, death. A fourth edict issued early in 304 extended these penalties to the laity as well. The persecution brought a very large number of martyrs. Its severity varied in different parts of the Empire acc. to the changing fortunes of the Imperial rulers in the next decades. Its final collapse was due to *Constantine's defeat of Maxentius at the *Milvian Bridge on 28 Oct. 312 and the 'Edict of Milan' (q.v.) early in the next year.

Good discussion, with first-class bibls., in *C.A.H.*, xii (1939), esp. chs. ix (by H. Mattingly), x, and xi (by W. Ensslin); and, for the Persecution, ch. xix (by N. H. Baynes). Two recent studies are W. Ensslin, *Zur Ostpolitik des Kaisers Diokletian*, Sb. (Bayr.), 1942, Hft. 1, and W. Seston, *Dioclétien et la tétrarchie*. I. Guerres et réformes, 284–30 (Bibliothèque des Écoles Françaises d'Athènes et de Rome, clxii; 1946), the latter with full bibl. reff. C. Cecchelli, *Studi e scoperte italiane sull' archeologia et l' arte del tardo impero* (1938). G. Niemann, *Der Palast Diokletians in Spalato* (1910). Cf. also H. M. D. Parker, *A History of the Roman World from A.D. 138 to 337* (1935), pp. 223–39 and 262–90. For the Persecution, the chief ancient authorities are, besides the *Acta of the Martyrs (useful list in *C.A.H.*, xii, pp. 790-3), *Eusebius, *H.E.*, VIII and IX, and *De Martyribus Palestinae*, and Lactantius, *De Mortibus Persecutorum*. A. J. Mason, *The Persecution of Diocletian* (1876); J. E. Belser, *Zur diokletianische Christenverfolgung* (1891); K. Stade, *Der Politiker Diokletian und die letzte grosse Christenverfolgung* (Frankfurt a.M., Diss., 1926). L. *Duchesne, *Histoire ancienne de l'Église*, ii (ed. 2, 1907), ch. i, pp. 1–55; B. J. Kidd, *A History of the Church to A.D. 461*, i (1922), pp. 510–45. See also bibl. to *Constantine*.

DIOCLETIANIC ERA. The reckoning of time from the year of *Diocletian's accession (A.D. 284). It is also known as the **Era of the Martyrs** (though in fact the *persecution of the Christians did not break out till 303; see previous entry). It is still followed by the *Abyssinians and *Copts.

DIODORE (d. *c.* 390), Bp. of Tarsus. A native of *Antioch, Diodore studied at *Athens and then ruled a monastery near Antioch until the strength of *Arianism drew him into the city to combat it. He also opposed *Julian the Apostate. Banished to Armenia in 372, he later returned and became Bp. of Tarsus in 378. In 381 he was named by *Theodosius I

one of the bishops communion with whom was a test of orthodoxy.

As a teacher, he followed the *Antiochene tradition in theology, insisting on literal and historical exegesis and, against *Apollinarius, on the complete humanity of Christ. His pupils included St. *Chrysostom and *Theodore of Mopsuestia. Only fragments of his very extensive writings (largely Biblical commentaries) survive. Many were destroyed by Arians, while others perished when the condemnation of his pupil, Theodore, made Diodore himself suspect of Christological heresy.

Considerable fgmts. of his 'De Fato' are preserved in *Photius, *Bibl. cod.* 223; cf. ib. 102 and also 18, where Photius asserts, apparently by an error, that Diodore was condemned by the Fifth General Council of 553. Frgmts. ed. by B. Corderius (Antwerp, 1643–6) and by A. *Mai; repr. in J. P. Migne, *PG*, xxxiii, 1545–1628. L. Mariès, S.J., *Études préliminaires à l'édition de Diodore de Tarse sur les psaumes* (1933). A. *Harnack, *Diodor von Tarsus*. Vier pseudojustinische Schriften als Eigentum Diodors nachgewiesen (*T.U.*, xxi, 4, 1901). Bardenhewer, iii, pp. 304–11, and Altaner (ed. 1950), p. 275 f. P. Godet in *D.T.C.*, iv (1911), cols. 1363–6; P. Sherwood, O.S.B., in *E.C.*, iv (1950), cols. 1657–60, with good bibl.

DIOGNETUS, The Epistle to. A letter written by an unknown Christian to an otherwise unknown inquirer. It probably dates from the 2nd, or perhaps the 3rd, cent. Answering three questions (ch. 1), the author explains why paganism and Judaism cannot be tolerated (2–4), describes Christians as the soul of the world (5–6), and insists that Christianity is the unique revelation of God, whose love works man's salvation (7–10). Chs. 11 f., which contain a *Logos-doctrine and a comparison of the Church to Paradise, are widely regarded as a fragment of another work. The letter survived antiquity in a single 13th–14th cent. MS. (which was destroyed at Strassburg in 1870), in which it followed certain treatises wrongly ascribed to St. *Justin Martyr.

Ed. princeps, by H. *Stephanus (Paris, 1592). The Epistle is commonly included in edd. of *Apostolic Fathers (*e.g.* J. B. *Lightfoot; O. von Gebhardt and A. *Harnack; F. X. Funk; K. *Lake); also repr. in J. P. Migne, *PG*, ii. 1167–86. Good modern edd., with introd. and notes by H. G. Meecham (Manchester, 1949) and by H. I. Marrou (in *Sources Chrétiennes*, 33, 1951). Eng. trr. by L. B. Radford (S.P.C.K., 1908) and in collected trr. of Apostolic Fathers. G. N. Bonwetsch and E. *Schwartz have argued that chs. 11 f. are to be ascribed to *Hippolytus. Bardenhewer, i, pp. 316–25; Altaner (ed. 1950), p. 102 f. P. Godet in *D.T.C.*, iv (1911), cols. 1366–9, s.v.

DIONYSIUS (1) THE AREOPAGITE. His conversion by St. Paul at Athens is recorded in Acts 17. 34. Dionysius (2) of Corinth calls him the first bishop of the Church at Athens. Later, confusion was caused by the attempt to identify Dionysius (3) of Paris with him, and to assign to him the writings on mystical theology described below (6).

DIONYSIUS (2) (*c.* 170), Bp. of *Corinth. He wrote several letters briefly described by Eusebius (*HE.* IV., xxiii), in one of which he thanks the Roman Church for assisting Corinth and mentions that *Clement's letter was habitually read in their Church. Feast day in the E., 8 Apr.

Four fgmts. of Dionysius' Ep. to Rome are preserved in Eusebius (*H.E.*, IV, xxiii, 10–12, and II, xxv, 8), who also records that Dionysius wrote an Ep. to the Nicomedians directed against *Marcion (IV, xxiii, 4). Fgmts. collected in M. J. *Routh, *Reliquiae Sacrae*, i (ed. 2, 1846), pp. 175–201. W. Bauer, *Rechtgläubigkeit und Ketzerei im ältesten Christentum* (1934), esp. pp. 110–12 and 128–31. Bardenhewer, i, pp. 439–42; Altaner (ed. 1950), p. 109.

DIONYSIUS (3) St., of Paris (c. 250), also

St. Denys, patron saint of France. Acc. to *Gregory of Tours (6th cent.), he was one of seven 'bishops' sent to convert Gaul and, after becoming Bp. of Paris, suffered martyrdom. In 626 his remains were translated to King Dagobert's foundation at *St.-Denis, near Paris. In the 8th cent. it was believed that he had been sent by *Clement of Rome, c. A.D. 90; and in the 9th-cent. Life by Hilduin, Abbot of St. Denys (d. 840), he was further identified with Dionysius the Areopagite (1), and consequently believed to be the author of the Pseudo-Dionysian writings (6). Feast day, 9 Oct.

He is commemorated with Sts. Rusticus and Eleutherius. Gregory of Tours, *Hist. Franc.*, i, 31. *AA.SS.*, Oct. IV (1780), pp. 865–987. *B.H.L.*, i (1898–9), Nos. 2171–89. J. Stiglmayr, S.J., in *L.Th.K.*, iii (1931), col. 339 f.

DIONYSIUS (4) 'THE GREAT' (d. c. 264),

Bp. of *Alexandria. A pupil of *Origen, Dionysius was in turn head of the Catechetical School (from c. 233) and Bp. of Alexandria (from 247). During the *Decian persecution (250) he fled from the city, was captured, escaped, and lived in hiding. He returned (? 251), but was banished during the persecution of Valerian (257). Again he returned to face civil war, famine, and plague, and died an old man c. 264. Feast day, 17 Nov.

His importance as a theologian rests on the writings evoked by the many controversies in which he was engaged. He decided to readmit the lapsed to the Church (see *Cyprian*) and, with Pope *Stephen, not to rebaptize heretics and schismatics, though he refused to break with the Churches which did so. Being *Origen's pupil, he attacked *Sabellianism, but he was himself accused of tritheism by *Dionysius of Rome (5, below), who, however, accepted his defence. Later, *Athanasius defended, but *Basil rejected, his orthodoxy. He also opposed *Paul of Samosata. He shewed notable independence as a Biblical critic, setting out strong arguments for denying the common authorship of the Fourth Gospel and Rev.

His writings have survived mainly in extracts preserved by *Eusebius, *Athanasius, and others.

Fgmts. ed. S. de Magistris (Rome, 1796); also in J. P. Migne, *PG.*, x, 1233–1344, 1575–1602. Crit. ed., with introd. and notes, by C. L. Feltoe, 'Cambridge Patristic Texts', 1904. Eng. tr., also by C. L. Feltoe, S.P.C.K., 1918. —. Dittrich, *Dionysius der Grosse von Alexandrien* (1867). Bardenhewer, ii, pp. 203–27; Altaner (ed. 1950), p. 175. B. F. *Westcott in *D.C.B.*, i (1877), pp. 850–2; M. Pellegrino in *E.C.*, iv (1950), col. 1661–2, s.v. 'Dionigi d' Alessandria'.

DIONYSIUS (5) (d. 268), Bp. of *Rome from

259. Little is known of him except his controversy on *Subordinationism with *Dionysius (4) of Alexandria. *Basil of Caesarea (Ep. 70) records that he sent help to the Church of Caesarea when it was invaded by barbarians (perh. 264). Feast day, 26 Dec.

Genuine and spurious writings in J. P. Migne, *PL*, v. 99–136. The chief authorities are scattered reff. in Eusebius, *H.E.*, VII, and in *Athanasius, *De Decretis*, xxv and xxvi, and *De Sententiis Dionysii*, passim. Bardenhewer, ii, p. 644 f.

DIONYSIUS (6), the Pseudo-Areopagite

(c. 500), mystical theologian. The name given to the author of a *corpus* of theological writings to which the *Monophysites appealed at a colloquy at Constantinople in 533, attributing them to Dionysius (1) of Athens. Though at an early date Hypatius, Bp. of Ephesus (c. 520–40) rejected the attribution, it was generally accepted until, and even after, the 16th cent. Since the author draws on Proclus (411–85) and is first cited by *Severus, Patr. of Antioch (c. 513), he is believed to have written about 500, probably in Syria.

His extant writings, which combine *Neo-Platonism with Christianity, are the following: (1) The 'Celestial Hierarchy' (περὶ τῆς οὐρανίας ἱεραρχίας), which explains how the nine orders of angels mediate God to man. (2) The 'EcclesiasticalHierarchy' (περὶ τῆς ἐκκλησιαστικῆς ἱεραρχίας), which deals with the Sacraments and the three 'ways' of spiritual life—purgation, illumination, and union. These are explained as the three means by which human nature is deified. (3) The 'Divine Names' (περὶ θείων ὀνομάτων), which examines the being and attributes of God. (4) The 'Mystical Theology' (περὶ μυστικῆς θεολογίας), which describes the ascent of the soul to union with God. There also survive ten letters, and Dionysius mentions other parts of an elaborate theological system, probably never achieved.

The Pseudo-Dionysian writings aim at achieving a synthesis between Christian dogma and *Neo-Platonist thought. Their leading idea, which has made them the charter of Christian mysticism, is the intimate union (ἕνωσις) between God and the soul, and the progressive deification (θείωσις) of man. This is to be obtained by a process of 'unknowing', in which the soul leaves behind the perceptions of the senses as well as the reasoning of the intellect. The soul will then enter an obscurity in which it will be increasingly illuminated by the 'Ray of Divine Darkness' and brought ultimately to the knowledge of the ineffable Being that transcends affirmation and negation alike. The relations between God and the world are established by a hierarchically graded series of beings, the nine choirs of angels. They are divided into three orders, to which, on the terrestrial plane, corresponds the threefold hierarchy of bishops, priests, and deacons, both, together with the Sacraments, ordained to lead man to 'deification'. There are three stages in the spiritual life by which this goal is reached, the purgative, the illuminative, and the unitive way, a division which has become the groundwork of subsequent treatises on the mystic life.

The supposed apostolic authority of these writings, added to their intrinsic value, caused the 'Pseudo-Dionysius' to exercise a profound influence on medieval theology both in the E. and in the W. In the E. Churches his works were regarded almost as a 'Summa Theologica', commented on by, among others, St. *Maximus the Confessor, *Andrew of Crete, and George Pachymeres. In the W. the approval of St. *Gregory the Great and *Martin I, and esp. that of the *Lateran Council of 649 which quoted them against the *Monothelites, established the Pseudo-Dionysian writings as an uncontested doctrinal authority. They became generally known in the W. through the translation of John Scotus *Erigena, and despite their obscurity of style soon came to be one of the bases of medieval theology. They were commented on by such doctors as *Hugh of St.-Victor, St. *Albert the Great, St. *Thomas Aquinas, and St. *Bonaventure; and the medieval mystics, e.g. Master *Eckhart, John *Tauler, 'The *Cloud of Unknowing', and Richard *Rolle, are deeply indebted to them. A great change in the earlier estimate of them took place in the 16th cent., when not only the Reformers but also Catholic scholars such as T. *Cajetan, J. *Sirmond, and D. *Petavius contested their authenticity, which was warmly defended by C. *Baronius, St. Robert *Bellarmine, L. *Lessius, and others. Only the researches of modern scholars, esp. J. Stiglmayr and H. Koch, have definitely established their late 5th cent. date and the relations of the author with moderate *Monophysitism.

A critical ed. of the Gk. text is a great desideratum. There is none later than that of B. Corderius, S.J. (2 vols. fol., Antwerp, 1634), which has frequently been repr., e.g. in J. P. Migne, *PG*, iii and iv (incl. Lat. tr. and commentaries on Dionysius). Erigena's translation is repr. from the Cologne ed. of 1556 and other sources in J. P. Migne, *PL*, cxxii, 1023–1194. For other Lat. versions see P. Chevalier, O.S.B. (ed.), *Dionysiaca. Recueil donnant l'ensemble des traductions latines des ouvrages attribués au Denys de l'Aréopage* (2 vols., Paris, 1937–50). Eng. tr. of his works by J. Parker (2 vols., London-Oxford, 1897–99); further tr. of the 'Divine Names' and 'Mystical Theology', by C. E. Rolt (Translations of Christian Literature. Series 1, Greek Texts, S.P.C.K., 1920), with introd., pp. 1–47, and bibl., pp. 47–9. Fr. tr. of his works, with introd. and bibl. by M. de Gandillac (Bibliothèque Philosophique, 1945). J. Stiglmayr, S.J., 'Der Neuplatoniker Proclus als Vorlage des sog. Dionysius Areopagita in der Lehre vom Übel' in *Hist. J.*, xvi (1895), pp. 253–73 and 721–48. H. Koch, *Pseudo-Dionysius Areopagita in seinen Beziehungen zum Neuplatonismus und Mysterienwesen* (Forschungen zur christlichen Litteratur- und Dogmengeschichte, i, Hftt. 2–3; 1900). B. Honigmann, *Pierre l'Ibérien et les écrits du Pseudo-Denys l'Aréopagite* (Académie Royal de Belgique. Classe des Lettres et des Sciences Morales et Politiques. Mémoires, xlvii, 3; 1932). G. Théry, *Études dionysiennes* (Études de Philosophie Médiévales, xvi and xix; 1932–7). R. Roques, *L'Univers dionysien. Structure hiérarchique du monde selon le Pseudo-Denys* (Théologie. Études publiées sous la direction de la Faculté de Théologie S.J. de Lyon Fourvière 29, 1954). Stiglmayr's later attempt in 'Der sog. Dionysius Areopagitica und Severus von Antiochien' in *Scholastik*, iii (1928), pp. 1–27 and 161–89, to identify Dionysius with *Severus of Antioch has been generally rejected. A. van Daele, S.J., *Indices Pseudo-Dionysiani* (Louvain, 1941). Ueberweg, ii, pp. 119 and 126–8, with bibl., p. 667 f. Bardenhewer, iv, pp. 282–99. Altaner (ed. 1951), p. 453–7. J. Stiglmayr, S.J., in *L.Th.K.*, iii (1931),

cols. 334–6, s.v. E. Beck, O.S.B.–C. Fabro, C.P.S., in *E.C.*, iv (1950), cols. 1662–8, s.v. 'Dionigi l' Areopagita'.

DIONYSIUS (7) EXIGUUS, a Scythian monk who lived in Rome *c.* 500–550. Acc. to *Cassiodorus, he dubbed himself 'Exiguus' owing to his humility. Very little is known of his life. He is famous for his contributions to ecclesiastical chronology and canon law. When called upon to construct a new Easter cycle, he abandoned the era of *Diocletian, and (wrongly) accepting 753 A.U.C. as the year of the Incarnation, introduced the system still in use. This 'Christian Era' was adopted in England at the Synod of *Whitby, 664, and later became widespread on the Continent. His *corpus* of canon law was the first collection to gain wide influence. In its second edition, which was its classic form, it contained the *Apostolic Canons; the canons of the Councils of *Nicaea, *Ancyra, *Neocaesarea, *Gangra, *Antioch, *Laodicaea, *Constantinople, *Chalcedon and *Sardica, and of *Carthage, 419; and forty-one Papal decretals from *Siricius (384–98) to Anastasius II (496–8). This collection was in general use in the 6th and 7th cents., and, somewhat augmented, was sent by Pope *Hadrian to *Charlemagne, 774. It was accepted by the Frankish Church at Aachen, 802. Dionysius also translated many important Greek patristic writings into Latin.

Works in J. P. Migne, *P.L.*, lxvii, 9–520. The Dionysian Canons are printed in all early canonical collections; most accessible in J. P. Migne, loc. cit., 139–316. Crit. text in *E.O.M.I.A.* (under each council). 'First Recension' of Canons ed. A. Strewe, *Die Canonensammlung des Dionysius Exiguus in der ersten Redaktion* (1931). F. *Maassen, *Geschichte der Quellen und der Literatur des canonischen Rechts*, i (1870), pp. 132–6, 422–40, 960–5. H. Wurm, *Studien und Texte sur Dekretalensammlung des Dionysius Exiguus* (1939). B. Krusch, *Studien zur christlich-mittelalterlichen Chronologie*, pt. ii: Dionysius Exiguus, der Begründer der christlichen Ära (*Abh.* (Berl.), 1938, No. 8), pp. 59–87. Good survey in Bardenhewer, v, pp. 224–8; Altaner (1950), p. 431 f., also p. 213.

DIONYSIUS (8) THE CARTHUSIAN (Denys van Leeuwen, Denys Ryckel) (1402–71), theologian and mystic. He was educated at the University of *Cologne and entered the Charterhouse of Roermund in 1423. He compiled a series of very extensive commentaries on the OT and NT, edited or commented on the works of *Boethius, *Peter Lombard, *John Climacus, and those attributed to *Dionysius the Areopagite (by whom he was much influenced), and also wrote books on moral theology, ecclesiastical discipline, homilies, and a tract against the Mohammedans. His writings became very popular in the centuries succeeding his death, though Dionysius has little real claim to be considered an original writer. His mystical experiences gained for him the title of 'Doctor Ecstaticus'. In 1451 he accompanied Cardinal *Nicholas of Cusa to Germany in the cause of Church reform and to preach a crusade against the Turks.

Earliest complete ed. by D. Loer, with the aid of J. Host von Romberg (2 vols., Cologne, 1534–40). New ed. by the Carthusians, Montreuil-sur-Mer and (later) Tournai, 42 vols. and additional index vol., 1896–1913 [Vols. 1–14, Comm.

on whole Bible; 15 f., on Dionysius the Areopagite; 17 f. 'Summa Fidei' and 'Dialogion'; 19–25, Comm. on *Sentences; 26–28 on Boethius, *Cassian and John Climacus; 29–32, Sermons; 33–42, 'Opera Minora'. Vol. I also contains a Life by D. Loer (orig. publd. 1532) and a list by Dionysius of his 187 writings and of the writers he had studied]. Studies by H. Welters (Roermonde, 1882), A. Mougel (Montreuil-sur-Mer, 1896) and P. Albers (Utrecht, 1897). K. Krogh Tonnig, *Der letzte Scholastiker* (Freiburg i.Br., 1904). P. Teeuwen, *Dionysius de Karthuizer en de philosophisch-theologische Stroomingen aan de Keulsche Universiteit* (Brussels, 1938). S. Autore in *D.T.C.*, iv (1911), cols. 436–48, s.v. 'Denys le Chartreux'; A. Combes in *E.C.*, iv (1950), cols. 1671–4, s.v. 'Dionigi Certosino'.

DIOSCORUS (d. 454), Patr. of *Alexandria. During St. *Cyril's patriarchate he became Archdeacon of Alexandria, and on his death in 444 succeeded to the see. When *c.* 448 *Eutyches began to attract attention by his Christological doctrines Dioscorus gave him his support, and in 449 presided over the '*Latrocinium' at *Ephesus. Here he deposed *Flavian, Bp. of Constantinople. His fortunes changed with the reversal of theological policy on the death of the Emp. *Theodosius II in 450. At the Third Session of the Council of *Chalcedon in 451, when Eutychianism was condemned, he was deposed and excommunicated, and banished by the civil authorities to Gangra in Paphlagonia. A few of his letters, and a legendary panegyric of his life by the deacon Theopistus, have survived in Syriac.

Our most reliable source on Dioscorus is the 'Acta' of the Council of Chalcedon (q.v.). Syr. text of 'Life' by Theopistus, with Fr. tr., ed. F. Nau in *Journal Asiatique*, Sér. 10, i (1903), pp. 5–108 and 241–310. F. Haase, 'Patriarch Dioskur I von Alexandrien nach monophysitischen Quellen' in M. Sdralek (ed.), *Kirchengeschichtliche Abhandlungen*, vi (1908), pp. 141–233. J. Lebon, *Le Monophysisme sévérien* (1909), pp. 84–93 ('Les Écrits de Dioscore I d'Alexandrie'). Bardenhewer, iv, p. 78 f. W. *Bright in *D.C.B.*, i (1877), pp. 854–62.

DIPPEL, JOHANN KONRAD (1673–1734), German *Pietist and alchemist. The son of a *Lutheran pastor, he was educated at Giessen university, became a private tutor, and in the controversy between Lutheran orthodoxy and Pietism at first upheld the former, but later, under G. *Arnold's influence, became himself a Pietist. He wrote many controversial works in defence of his new convictions, the best known being *Orthodoxia Orthodoxorum* (1697) and *Papismus Protestantium Vapulans* (1698). They emphasized the alleged contrast between Christianity and the Church, between ethics and dogma, and between right living and right doctrine, maintaining that the development of Christianity from *Constantine onwards was a gradual declension from the high ideals of primitive times. His opposition to Protestant orthodoxy roused the hostility of the Lutheran ecclesiastical authorities, who forbade him to issue further theological publications. He now turned to chemistry, becoming the inventor of the Prussian Blue, and also occupied himself with alchemy. In 1704 he came to Berlin, but he had to leave it in 1707 because of continued Pietist activities and found refuge in Holland. Here he took his medical degree at *Leyden

(1711), but he was again expelled for his theological views. In 1714 he went to Altona, which at that time belonged to Denmark, but becoming embroiled with the government he was condemned in 1719 to lifelong captivity on the island of Bornholm. Having been freed and expelled from Denmark in 1726, he went to Sweden, where, through his influence, Pietism began to gain ground, so that the orthodox Lutheran clergy brought about his expulsion. He now went back to Germany, where he finally found a refuge at Berleburg. The main inspiration of his life was his belief that the Christian religion consisted not in a dogmatic creed but in the practice of charity and self-sacrifice.

His Works were edited (3 vols.) at Berleburg in 1747. Life by W. Bender (Bonn, 1882).

DIPTYCHS. The lists of names of living and departed Christians for whom special prayer is made in the Greek and Latin Eucharistic Liturgies. Though now read secretly, the diptychs were formerly recited publicly, and the inclusion or exclusion of a name was held to be a sign of communion or of excommunication. The term is derived from the two-leaved folder (Gk. δίπτυχον) within which the lists were written. See also *Book of Life.*

A. F. Gori, *Thesaurus Veterum Diptychorum Consularium et Ecclesiasticorum* (3 vols., Florence, 1759; with full discussion and reproducton of 'Consular Diptychs', *i.e.*, diptychs usually with elaborately incised covers, which were distributed by consuls on taking office and became the artistic model for ecclesiastical diptychs). R. Delbrück, *Die Consulardiptychen und verwandte Denkmäler* (1929; plates 1926–9). F. *Cabrol, O.S.B., in *D.A.C.L.*, iv (pt. 1; 1920), cols. 1045–94, s.v. 'Diptyques (Liturgie)', and H. *Leclercq, O.S.B., in ib., cols. 1094–1170, s.v. 'Diptyques (Archéologie)'; J. Sauer in *L.Th.K.*, iii (1931), col. 344 f.; and G. Bovini and F. Oppenheim in *E.C.*, iv (1950), cols. 1759–63.

DIRECTORY OF CHURCH GOVERNMENT, The (1644). An English translation of a Book of *Discipline compiled by W. *Travers in Latin *c.* 1586 (not, as is sometimes said, of his *Full and Plain Declaration of Ecclesiastical Discipline* of 1574). The Book was divided into 'Disciplina Sacra' and 'Disciplina Synodica'. The work circulated in manuscript among the Elizabethan Puritans, many of whom formally subscribed its articles. It was issued in 1644 in the interests of the projected introduction of the Presbyterian system into England.

A facsimile edition of the 1644 translation was published in 1872 (ed. P. Lorimer). F. *Paget, *Introduction to the Fifth Book of Hooker's Ecclesiastical Polity* (1907), Appendices III and IV. A. F. Scott Pearson, *Thomas Cartwright and Elizabethan Puritanism* (1925), pp. 257–9, and passim.

DIRGE (Lat. *Dirige*). A traditional name for the *Office for the Dead. The office, which dates from the Middle Ages, is contained in the ancient *breviaries and in the early English *primers. The name, which derives from the antiphon, 'Dirige Domine Deus meus in conspectu tuo viam meam' (Ps. 5. 8), was originally confined to the morning office; but it later came to include the *Vespers (the '*Placebo') sung on the evening before. It has often been set to music, one of its most famous settings being the *Mattutino di Morti* of David Perez of Lisbon (1752). The term has for some time been obsolete except in figurative use.

DIRIMENT IMPEDIMENT. In *canon law, a fact or circumstance relating to a person that makes him or her incapable of contracting a valid marriage. It is to be distinguished from a 'prohibitive impediment', which only renders a marriage unlawful, but not null and void. Acc. to present RC canon law, the existing diriment impediments include insufficient age, impotency, an already existing marriage, abduction, solemn religious vows, holy orders, disparity of religion, affinity, and consanguinity; but such of the impediments as are not of Divine Law may be dispensed by the ecclesiastical authorities for good reason.

F. Freisen, *Geschichte des canonischen Eherechts bis zum Verfall der Glossenlitteratur* (1888), esp. 221-7. O. D. Watkins, *Holy Marriage* [1924], pp. 68-71. G. H. Joyce, S.J., *Christian Marriage* (1933), passim. E. Valton in *D.T.C.*, iv (1911), cols. 2440-99, s.v. 'Empêchements de mariage'; G. Micheli in *E.C.*, vi (1951), cols. 1703-7, s.v. 'Impedimenti, II. matrimoniali', with bibl.

DISCALCED (from Lat. *discalceare*, 'to make unshod'). The term is applied to certain religious orders and congregations whose members wear sandals, e.g. the Discalced *Carmelites, *Trinitarians, and *Passionists. The custom was followed by the primitive E. monks, who went barefooted, after Mt. 10. 10. It was introduced into the W. by St. *Francis of Assisi, and was followed in its most rigorous form, i.e. without any kind of footwear, by the Discalced *Franciscans, founded by St. *Peter of Alcantara. To-day sandals are always worn, either with or without stockings, though in the latter case exceptions are usually made in particularly severe climates.

DISCIPLES OF CHRIST. The religious body which originated in the U.S.A. in 1811 through the work of Alexander *Campbell (q.v.) as a group within *Presbyterianism and was organized as a separate religious communion in 1827. Its members were largely influenced in doctrine and practice by the work of John *Glas, who seceded from the Church of Scotland in 1728, and Robert Sandeman (1718–71), who propagated Glas's views in New England. They have been variously known as 'Campbellites', 'Disciples of Christ', and 'Churches of Christ'. The Scriptures are the exclusive basis of faith and all credal formulae are rejected. The churches are congregationally organized, practice believers' baptism and celebrate the Lord's Supper as the chief act of worship every Sunday. They have always taken a prominent part in education and founded a number of universities in the U.S.A. and elsewhere; and they have been keenly alert to the problem of the Christian unity.

Their membership *c.* 1950 was somewhere over a million. In Great Britain where, as in

Australia, New Zealand, and South Africa, they are generally known as 'Churches of Christ', the community numbered about 15,000; it has a College at Overdale, Birmingham.

E. Gates, *The Disciples of Christ* (New York, 1905); T. [W.] Philips, *The Church of Christ* (New York and London, 1905). W. E. Garrison, *Religion Follows the Frontier.* A History of the Disciples of Christ (New York, 1931). B. B. Tyler, 'A History of the Disciples of Christ' in *The American Church History Series*, xii (New York, 1894), pp. 1–162. W. Robinson, *What the Churches of Christ Stand for.* The Origin, Growth, and Message of a Nineteenth-Century Religious Movement (Birmingham, 1926), with bibl. H. L. Willett in *H.E.R.E.*, iv (1911), p. 713 f., s.v., with bibl. See also bibl. to *Campbell, A.*

DISCIPLINA ARCANI (Lat., 'Discipline of the Secret'). The practice ascribed to the early Church of concealing certain theological doctrines and religious usages from *catechumens and pagans. The term is said to have been coined by the Calvinist, J. *Daillé (d. 1670); but in 1614 I. *Casaubon had already explained certain silences of the early Fathers on the supposition that they imitated the secrecy of the mystery religions. Daillé himself held that the practice was mainly educational, to give catechumens a greater desire and reverence for the Sacraments. A third explanation was put forward by E. *Schelstrate who held that it was of Dominical institution and practised by the Apostles, and that its application extended not only to *Baptism and the *Eucharist, but also explained the scarcity or absence of early Christian evidences on such subjects as the *Trinity, the *Mass, the number of the *Sacraments, *Transubstantiation and the cult of the *Saints. The discussion continued through the 18th and 19th cents., RC theologians generally defending Schelstrate's theory, whereas most Protestant scholars (E. *Hatch, N. Bonwetsch, and others) followed Casaubon in tracing the practice to a pagan model.

In recent times the traditional theories have been generally abandoned. Acceptance of theological development makes them largely superfluous. Borrowing from the mysteries is most unlikely in view of the early Christian abhorrence of such rites. But the existence of the practice in a restricted degree seems attested. It was adopted partly through the reticence necessary in an age of persecution, partly through the natural human instinct to withdraw the most intimate and sacred elements of faith from the knowledge of outsiders; and it was reflected in the custom of not admitting catechumens to the central part of the Eucharist. Allusions to it are found in *Tertullian, St. *Cyprian, and *Origen, and more definitely in 4th and 5th cent. writers, among them St. *Cyril of Jerusalem, *Etheria and *St. Chrysostom for the E., and St. *Ambrose, *Innocent I, and St. *Augustine for the W. By the 6th cent. the practice seems to have disappeared.

I. Casaubon, *De Rebus Sacris et Ecclesiasticis* (London, 1614), Exercitio XVI, pars xliii, 'Mysterium' (pp. 541-67). E. A. Schelstrate, *De Disciplina Arcani* (Rome, 1685). P. *Batiffol, *Études d'histoire et de théologie positive* (1902) pp. 3–41; F. X. Funk, 'Das Alter der Arkandisziplin', repr. in his *Kirchengeschichtliche Abhandlungen und Untersuchungen*, iii (1907), pp. 42–57. G. Mensching, *Das heilige Schweigen* (Religionsgeschichtliche Versuche und Vorarbeiten, xx, Hft. 2; 1926), pp. 125–33. N. Bonwetsch in *P.R.E.* (ed. 3), ii (1897), pp. 51–5, s.v. 'Arkandisciplin'; P. Batiffol in *D.T.C.*, i (1903), cols. 1738–58, s.v. 'Arcane'; E. Vacandard in *D.H.G.E.*, iii (1924), cols. 1497–1513, s.v. 'Arcane'; F. Oppenheim, O.S.B., in *E.C.*, i (1949), cols. 1793–7, s.v. 'Arcano, Disciplina dell' '; O. Perler in *R.A.C.*, i (1950), cols. 667–76, s.v. 'Arkandisziplin', all with bibl.

DISCIPLINE. The word has several religious connotations.

(1) The totality of ecclesiastical laws and customs regulating the religious and moral life of the Church. In this sense it comprises all Church activities not regulated by Divine law, such as the administration of the Sacraments, offices, feasts, devotions, etc.

(2) In a more restricted sense, a system of mortification, e.g. that involved in the religious life (monastic discipline).

(3) A scourge of knotted cords for use as an instrument of penance.

(4) As a technical term, the word is applied esp. to the *Calvinist polity, which, in contrast with that of M. *Luther, was built up on rigid principles. Its object is the good of the offender, the purity of the Church, and the glory of God. It is the duty of the consistories, formed by elders and pastors, to fix penalties for neglect of religious duties, culminating in excommunication. In grave cases, offenders were formerly handed over to the state. This practice was taken up by the *Presbyterians who laid down their principles in the *Book of *Common Order* and the *First Book of *Discipline* (qq.v.). In the past disciplinary measures were frequently in the face of the congregation. Nowadays cases are generally dealt with by the minister. Processes against a minister are begun before his presbytery and appeal can be made to the *General Assembly.

DISCIPLINE, Books of. The 'First Book of Discipline' (1560), drawn up at Edinburgh at the government's request by J. *Knox and five of his fellow-Reformers as a plan for the ordering and maintenance of the new Scottish Church, was an adaptation of the Genevan 'Ordonnances' to the needs of a nation. Its nine heads were: (1) Doctrine; (2) Sacraments; (3) Abolishing of Idolatry; (4) Ministers and their Lawful Election; (5) Provision for the Ministers; (6) Rents and Patrimony of the Kirk; (7) Ecclesiastical Discipline; (8) Election of Elders, Deacons, etc.; and (9) The Policy of the Church. Knox's more ardent supporters welcomed its rigid discipline, but parts of the Book were obnoxious to the nobility, esp. the proposed system of national education, which threatened the newly possessed landlords with the loss of their revenues. Hence, civil authority being needed for its enforcement, the Book remained a dead-letter.

The so-called 'Second Book of Discipline' (1578), chiefly the work of A. *Melville, was prepared as a manifesto of the stricter Presbyterians against efforts to restore a modified episcopacy. It was endorsed by the General Assembly in 1581, though this Book also never obtained complete civil recognition.

The text of the First and Second Books of Discipline is pr. in D. Calderwood, *The History of the Kirk of Scotland* (8 vols. 1842–49), ii, pp. 51–120, and iii, pp. 529–55, respectively.

DISCUS (Gk. δίσκος, δισκάριον). In the E. Church, the plate on which the bread of the Eucharist is offered and consecrated, corresponding to the *paten in the W. It is commonly somewhat larger and more concave and, esp. in *Russia, stands on a central foot. It is never placed on the chalice. The *Last Supper is sometimes represented on its inner surface.

DISMAS. The traditional name of the Good Thief (Lk. 23. 39–43) crucified with Christ. The name of the other is said to have been Gestas.

The name, from the Gk. δυσμή, 'dying', is found in the 'Gospel of *Nicodemus', ch. 10; cf. C. *Tischendorf, *Evangelia Apocrypha* (ed. 2, 1876), pp. 192 f., 362. H. Lesêtre in *Dict. Bibl.*, iv (1908), cols. 94–6, s.v. 'Larron'; H. *Leclercq, O.S.B., in *D.A.C.L.*, viii (pt. 1; 1928), cols. 1402–4, s.v. 'Larrons (Les Deux)'; E. Eisentraut in *L.Th.K.*, iii (1931), col. 346 f., s.v.

DISPENSATIONS. Licences granted by ecclesiastical authority to do some act otherwise canonically illegal, or for the remittance of a penalty for breaking such a rule. The practice of granting dispensations began very early. By the 5th cent. the bishops of Rome were employing the dispensing power, and a similar power was also used on occasion by other bishops, councils, and even (in minor matters) parish priests. By the later Middle Ages the dispensation had become more or less a prerogative of the Pope, and this position, with the elimination of minor abuses, was maintained by the Council of *Trent. The *canon law, by the revision of 1917 (esp. cans. 80–86), holds that a dispensation is a relaxation of the law in a special case, which may be granted by the lawgiver or by an authorized power, and that no authority below the Pope can dispense with the general laws of the Church without pontifical permission. Bishops, however, are regularly granted certain powers, including those conferred by the Pope every five years (*facultates quinquennales*).

All writers on the subject are agreed that there must be an adequate reason for the use of the dispensing power. Thus St. *Basil urges that the needs of the time and the advantages of the Church are the two main requisites for a just dispensation and this has been the consistent teaching of later canonists. The chief objects of the dispensing power are in relation to the ordination of clergy, the translation of bishops, vows, marriage, and divorce. The Church can suspend or abrogate, however, only laws of its own making, and not such as are natural (*ius naturale*) or Divine (*ius divinum*).

In England the dispensing power of the Pope was eliminated in 1534 by the legislation of *Henry VIII, but it was bestowed in a restricted form on the Abp. of Canterbury. It has been rarely used and was further limited in 1838 by the Pluralities Act.

Early treatment of subject by *Ivo of Chartres, 'Prologue in *Decretum*' (*PL*, clxi, 47–60). Classical discussions by F. *Suarez, S.J., *Tractatus de Legibus* (Antwerp, 1613), pp. 449–95 (lib. vi, capp. 10–24), and P. de *Marca, *De Concordia Sacerdotii et Imperii* (Paris, 1641), pp. 512–56 (lib., iii, 13–15). W. J. Sparrow Simpson, *Dispensations* (1933), with bibl. M. A. Stiegler, *Dispensation, Dispensationswesen und Dispensationsrecht im Kirchenrecht*, i (all publd., 1901). J. Brys, *De Dispensatione in Iure Canonico praesertim apud Decretistas et Decretalistas usque ad Medium Sacculum Decimum Quartum* (Louvain thesis, 1925). J. Besson in *C.E.*, v (1909), pp. 41–6, s.v.; A. Villien in *D.T.C.*, iv (1911), cols. 1428–40, s.v. 'Dispenses'; R. Naz in *D.D.C.*, iv (1949), cols. 1284–96, s.v. 'Dispense'; G. Miceli in *E.C.*, vii (1951), cols. 1048–51, s.v. 'Legge'.

DISPERSION, The. See *Diaspora.*

DISRUPTION, The (1843). The great split in the Established Church of *Scotland, when the *Free Church of Scotland (at first, 'Free Protesting Church of Scotland') was formed by the secession of 474 (out of 1203) ministers on 18 May 1843. The dispute centred in the demand of the presbyteries for a voice ('veto') in matters of patronage. In 1833 legislation (the 'Veto Act') had been introduced into the *General Assembly to secure the right to object to a presentee to a benefice on reasonable grounds. After being thrown out in that year, in 1834, largely through the exertions of T. *Chalmers (q.v.), the Act passed. The consequence was a succession of conflicts in the next decade between the General Assembly and the civil court ('Court of Session'), culminating in the Disruption. At first the destinies of the Free Church were in the hands of T. Chalmers, who was elected the first moderator and organized the Church with great ability. He created a Sustentation Fund for the support of the clergy by imposing a subscription of one penny a week from every member of the Church. The schism was not finally healed until 1929.

DISSENTERS' MARRIAGE ACT. The Act of 1836 (6 & 7 Will. IV, c. 85) which relieved Nonconformists of the necessity of marriage in an Anglican church, and allowed it to be solemnized in any registered place of religious worship. It provided that marriage could also take place in a registrar's office, or acc. to the usages of *Jews and *Quakers. By a further Act of 1898, the presence of the registrar at the chapel, required by the Act of 1836, was no longer demanded.

DISSOLUTION OF THE MONASTERIES, The. The wealth of the English monasteries, a certain moral laxity, and what many regarded as their undue stress on the contemplative aspect of the religious life, had made them in the later Middle Ages an object of criticism. Spasmodic attempts at reform had met with little success and various small suppressions had taken place. It was, however, from personal motives that *Henry VIII effected the complete abolition of the system. To replenish his treasury and to facilitate the establishment of the royal supremacy in ecclesiastical affairs, he decided first on the suppression of the smaller monasteries. A biased report (based on a hurried visitation of a fraction of the monasteries involved) declared the evil condition of the houses, and in 1536 the Act for the Dissolution of Smaller Monasteries (27 Hen. VIII, c. 28) was passed. It suppressed all religious houses having an annual value of less than £200, some 200 being involved. The popularity of monasticism in the north coupled with certain important economic grievances led to the popular rising known as the *Pilgrimage of Grace, which broke out in Yorkshire and Lincolnshire in Oct. 1536. It was quickly put down, however, by cajolery and force. Unscrupulous royal agents vigorously pushed on individual suppressions of the greater religious houses, and in 1539 the Act for the Dissolution of the Greater Monasteries (31 Hen. VIII, c. 13) completed the process of dissolution, the last houses surrendering in the spring of 1540. The King's principal adviser throughout was his Vicar General, Thomas *Cromwell (q.v.).

Effected in a highly unscrupulous manner, the Dissolution of the Monasteries met with small resistance. Care was taken to observe the letter of the law, and the subsequent economic and social dislocation is now known to have been considerably less than used to be thought. The religious, with the exception of the friars, were pensioned, and a considerable number in due course obtained benefices as secular clergy. Nuns, debarred from ecclesiastical office and, until the reign of *Edward VI, marriage, had mostly to subsist on very meagre pensions. The incidental losses to charity, art, and learning were considerable, many precious MSS. and church furnishings perishing through destruction and decay.

Most of the spoils of the Dissolution sooner or later passed from the crown to the rising Tudor squirearchy, but part of the proceeds went to the foundation of the six new sees of Bristol, *Chester, *Gloucester, *Oxford, *Peterborough, and *Westminster (the last soon suppressed).

The *Valor Ecclesiasticus (q.v.) is an important source for the financial state of the monasteries immediately prior to the dissolution. The principal authority for the actual dissolution is the Calendar of State Papers for the reign of Henry VIII (details in bibl. to Henry VIII). T. Wright (ed.), Three Chapters of Letters Relating to the Suppression of the Monasteries (Camden Society, xxvi; 1843). F. A. *Gasquet, Henry VIII and the English Monasteries (2 vols., 1888–9); G. Baskerville, English Monks and the Suppression of the Monasteries (1937). A. Savine, English Monasteries on the Eve of the Dissolution (Oxford Studies in Social and Legal History, i; 1909). E. J. Davis, 'The Beginning of the Dissolution: Christ Church, Aldgate, 1532' in Transactions of the Royal Historical Society, Ser. 4, viii (1925), pp. 127–50; G. S. Thomson, 'Woburn Abbey and the Dissolution of the Monasteries', ib., xvi (1933), pp. 129–60. A. G. Dickens, 'The Edwardian Arrears in Augmentation Payments and the Problem of the Ex-Religious' in E.H.R., lv (1940), pp. 384–418, with reff. List of monasteries dissolved in

J. Gairdner, *The English Church in the Sixteenth Century from the Accession of Henry VIII to the Death of Mary* (1902), pp. 419-30. See also *Henry VIII.*

DITTOGRAPHY (Gk. διττός, 'double', and γράφω, 'write'). The repetition by a copyist, through carelessness, of the same letter(s) or word(s), e.g. in the text of Acts 2. 4 in the Codex Laudianus (*et repleti sunt et repleti sunt omnes spiritu sancto*). It is a frequent source of corruption in the transmission of MSS.

DIURNAL. The service-book containing the 'Day *Hours' (*horae diurnae*), i.e. all the canonical hours except *Matins.

DIVES (Lat.), 'rich'. A word which has become a convenient, almost a proper, name for the unnamed rich man in the parable, Lk. 16. 19-31. He was condemned not for his wealth but for his selfish enjoyment of it.

DIVINA COMMEDIA, La. *Dante's great work is a trilogy whose parts correspond to the three realms of the next world—*Inferno*, *Purgatorio*, and *Paradiso*. In the form of a vision the poem describes the soul's journey from the state of separation from God to the ultimate goal of the *Beatific Vision. Under the guidance of Virgil, who represents natural reason, Dante descends into the deepest regions of hell. The torments of the damned are described in realistic visions which give him opportunity to denounce the vices of his time, esp. ecclesiastical ambition and corruption. From hell Virgil takes the poet up the seven terraces of the mountain of Purgatorio where the souls are purified from their disordered love, and which leads into the Earthly Paradise. Here Virgil leaves him, entrusting him to Beatrice, who represents reason enlightened by Divine Revelation. She leads Dante through the nine heavens peopled by saints and angels in hierarchical order up to the threshold of the empyrean where she cedes her place to St. *Bernard, the representative of mystic contemplation. He introduces the poet to the Blessed Virgin, at whose intercession he at last obtains a glimpse of the Beatific Vision. The whole is a grand poetic version of the scholastic system of Theology, closely interwoven with scenes alive with human emotion and sublime thought. Though sometimes marred by excessive personal bitterness, *La Divina Commedia* never questions the spiritual authority of the Church. How much the work was appreciated by Dante's contemporaries is shown by the fact that more than 500 MSS. have been preserved. The poem has been translated into all civilized languages. In the 19th cent. it exercised a deep influence on English literature, particularly on the Romantics and the Pre-Raphaelites.

For editions, see bibl. to *Dante.* The classical Eng. tr. is that of H. F. Cary (3 vols., London, 1814). More recent trr. by L. Binyon of *Inferno* (London, 1933), and of *Purgatorio* (ib., 1938), and of *Paradiso* (ib., 1943); and by Dorothy L. Sayers of *Inferno* (Penguin Books, 1947) and of *Purgatorio* (ib., 1955).

DIVINE PRAISES, The. A series of praises, beginning with the words 'Blessed be God, Blessed be His Holy Name', commonly said after *Benediction of the Blessed Sacrament (usually in the vernacular) before the Host is replaced in the tabernacle. They are thought to have been compiled *c.* 1797 by Louis Felici, S.J., to be used in reparation for blasphemy and profanity. In 1801 they were indulgenced by *Pius VII. Praise of the *Immaculate Conception was added to the original Praises *c.* 1856-7, praise of the *Sacred Heart in 1897, and praise of St. *Joseph in recent years.

H. T[hurston, S.J.], 'The Divine Praises' in *The Month*, cxxxi (1918), pp. 510-13, incl. reff. to earlier discussions.

DIVINE RIGHT OF KINGS. The doctrine that a monarch in the hereditary line of succession has a divine and indefeasible right to his kingship and authority, and that for a subject to rebel against him is the worst of political crimes. Where active obedience to an evil ruler is morally impossible, it is held that passive obedience (i.e., the willing acceptance of any penalty imposed for non-compliance) is demanded. In England the doctrine was already clearly enunciated in the first part of the *Homily against Wilful Rebellion* (1569), in which the goodness or badness of rulers is affirmed to be God's reward or punishment of a nation, and rebellion always a sin against God. Under the Stuarts the doctrine was upheld by almost all the leading Anglican divines. It was in obedience to this principle that many of the *Nonjurors found it impossible to accept William III's claim to the throne, though here there was the independent objection that change of allegiance meant breaking the oaths previously taken to *James II. It is doubtful, however, how genuinely the doctrine was really held, for many who, like J. *Tillotson, G. *Burnet, and E. *Stillingfleet, had strenuously upheld it under the Stuarts found no difficulty in accommodating themselves to the Revolution.

J. N. *Figgis, *The Theory of the Divine Right of Kings* (Cambridge Historical Essays, ix, 1896; ed. 2 with additional essays, 1914).

DIVINE SERVICE. A title which, like the Lat. *servitium divinum* from which it is derived, would seem properly to belong only to the *choir office, and hence to Matins and Evensong, and not to be applicable, e.g. to the Holy Communion. Cf. the preface to the BCP which since 1661 has been headed '*Concerning the *Service* of the Church' and refers only to the choir offices. It was customary for English church notice-boards in the 19th cent. to distinguish between the times for Divine service and those for Holy Communion. The expression is, however, often used more loosely for any form of religious service.

F. E. *Brightman, 'Common Prayer', in *J.T.S.*, x (1908-9), pp. 515-18.

DIVINO AFFLATU (Lat.), 'by God's Inspiration'. The constitution of Pope *Pius X, issued on 1 Nov. 1911, which introduced important reforms into the manner of reciting the Divine office and celebrating Mass. Among many other changes, it provided for the regular recitation of a much greater portion of the Psalter than had hitherto been used, and also laid down revised rules for the office when two or more feasts occur on the same day.

Text in *A.A.S.*, iii (1911), pp. 633–8, with 'Rubricae in Recitatione Divini Officii et in Missarum Celebratione Servandae ad Normam Constitutionis Apostolicae "Divino Afflatu"', pp. 639–51. E. Burton–E. Myers, *The New Psalter and its Use* (1912), incl. text of constitution, pp. 2–8, and Eng. tr., pp. 8–14.

DIVORCE. The word is used in two senses, (1) *a vinculo*, i.e. as a dissolution of the marriage bond, and (2) *a mensa et thoro*, i.e. legal separation. Since Western *canon law has always insisted upon the principle of indissolubility, divorce in sense (1) is not permitted by the RC Church and is contrary to the canons and formularies of the C of E. But the Popes have claimed and practised the right to dissolve unconsummated marriages for grave reasons. In the E. Church, the civil legislation begun by the Emp. *Justinian has been tolerated, if not approved, and divorce is allowed on a wide number of grounds. Civil legislation in England, by a series of Acts of Parliament culminating in the Act of 1937, has extended the grounds on which a decree of divorce may be obtained. In the second sense of the word, W. canon law permits divorce for grave causes, the chief of which is adultery. In this case the separation granted is permanent. In all other cases the right to live apart holds good only for so long as the cause remains.

For bibl. see that to *Matrimony*, esp. the works of G. H. Joyce, S.J., K. E. *Kirk, T. A. *Lacey–R. C. Mortimer, and O. D. Watkins. A. Villien in *D.T.C.*, iv (1911), cols. 1455–1478, s.v.; R. Naz in *D.D.C.*, iv (1949), cols. 1315–25, s.v., with bibl.

DIX, GREGORY (1901–52), Anglican *Benedictine monk and liturgical scholar. Educated at Westminster School and Merton College, Oxford, from 1924 to 1926 he was a lecturer in modern history at Keble College, Oxford. He was ordained priest in 1925, entered Nashdom Abbey, Bucks, in the following year, and took his final vows in 1940. In 1946 he was appointed Select Preacher in the university of Cambridge and proctor in *Convocation for the diocese of Oxford. In 1948 he was elected Prior of Nashdom.

Dix, who became in his later years one of the best-known figures in the C of E, owed his influence to his brilliance, unconventionality and good humour as a controversialist. These qualities largely contributed to the success of *The Shape of the Liturgy* (1945), his most considerable work; it did much to revive and popularize liturgical studies in the C of E. His other writings include *The Treatise on the Apostolic Tradition of St. Hippolytus of Rome*

(Church Historical Society, vol. i [all publd.], 1937), *A Detection of Aumbries* (notes on the history of *Reservation, 1942) and *The Question of Anglican Orders*. Letters to a Layman (1944), besides contributions to *The Parish Communion* (1937), to *The Apostolic Ministry* (ed. K. E. *Kirk, 1946) and to *Laudate* and other periodicals.

DOBENECK, JOHANN. See *Cochlaeus, Johannes*.

DOCETISM. Gk. δοκέω, 'I seem'). In the early Church, a tendency, rather than a formulated and unified doctrine, which considered the humanity and sufferings of the earthly Christ as apparent rather than real. Evidence for its existence is to be found in the NT (1 Jn. 4. 1–3; 2 Jn. 7; cf. Col. 2. 8 f.), but it reached its zenith in the next generation, esp. among the *Gnostics. In some forms it held that Christ miraculously escaped the ignominy of death, e.g. by *Judas Iscariot or *Simon of Cyrene changing places with Him just before the Crucifixion. Docetic doctrines were vigorously attacked by St. *Ignatius and all the leading anti-Gnostic writers. Among those esp. charged with Docetism was *Cerinthus. *Serapion, Bp. of Antioch (190–203), who is the first to use the name 'Docetists' (Δοκηταί), and some others wrote of them as a distinct body.

G. *Salmon in *D.C.B.*, i (1877), pp. 867–70, s.v.; A. *Fortescue in *H.E.R.E.*, iv (1911), pp. 832–5, s.v.; G. Bareille in *D.T.C.*, iv (1911), cols. 1484–1501, s.v. 'Docétisme', all with patristic reff. See also bibl. to *Gnosticism*.

DOCTORS, Scholastic. In later medieval times, the outstanding Scholastic teachers and others were given distinguishing epithets, of which the following are among the better known:

Doctor acutus	*Gregory of Rimini
Doctor angelicus (or *communis* or *sanctus*)	St. *Thomas Aquinas
Doctor christianissimus	John *Gerson
Doctor ecstaticus	John *Ruysbroek (also of *Dionysius the Carthusian)
Doctor irrefragabilis (or *doctorum*)	*Alexander of Hales
Doctor invincibilis (or *singularis*)	*William of Ockham
Doctor mellifluus	St. *Bernard of Clairvaux
Doctor mirabilis (or *admirabilis*)	Roger *Bacon
Doctor profundus	Thomas *Bradwardine (also of Jacobus de Esculo)
Doctor seraphicus (or *devotus*)	St. *Bonaventura
Doctor solidus (or *copiosus*)	*Richard of Middleton
Doctor subtilis	*Duns Scotus
Doctor universalis (or *venerabilis* or *expertus*)	St. *Albertus Magnus

DOCTORS' COMMONS. An association of ecclesiastical lawyers founded in 1511 by Richard Bodewell (or Blodwell), then *Dean of the Arches. It served as a college of advocates for those practising in the ecclesiastical courts, as also in the Admiralty Court. The judges of the Archbishops' Courts were always selected from this college. From 1565 until 1857, when the college was dissolved by the Court of Probate Act, its headquarters were in Knightrider Street, near *St. Paul's Cathedral.

DOCTORS OF THE CHURCH (Lat. *Doctores Ecclesiae*). A title regularly given since the Middle Ages to certain Christian theologians of outstanding merit and acknowledged saintliness. Originally the W. theologians, *Gregory the Great, *Ambrose, *Augustine, and *Jerome, were held to be the 'four doctors' *par excellence*; but in later times the list has been gradually increased to over 20.

*Benedict XIV, *De Servorum Dei Beatificatione*, iv (Bonn, 1738), pt. 2, cap. xi, No. 8–cap. xii, No. 9, pp. 96–107. Bardenhewer, i, pp. 42–6; J. de Ghellinck, S.J., 'Les Premières Listes des "Docteurs de l'Église" en Occident' in *Bulletin d'ancienne Littérature et d'Archéologie chrétienne*, ii (1912), pp. 132–4. V. Pugliese–G. Löwe, C.S.S.R.–G. Carandente in *E.C.*, iv (1950), cols. 1901–7, s.v. 'Dottori della chiesa', with list of doctors and bibl.

'DOCTRINE IN THE CHURCH OF ENGLAND' (1938). The Report of the Commission on Doctrine set up in 1922 by the Abps. of *Canterbury and *York. The Commission consisted of Anglican theologians of moderate *Catholic, *Evangelical, and *Modernist beliefs under the chairmanship first of H. M. Burge, Bp. of *Oxford, and, after his death in 1925, of W. *Temple, then Bp. of Manchester. The Commission's terms of reference were 'to consider the nature and grounds of Christian doctrine with a view to demonstrating the extent of existing agreement within the C of E and with a view to investigating how far it is possible to remove or diminish existing differences'. Among its members were F. R. Barry, E. J. Bicknell, J. M. Creed, L. W. Grensted, W. L. Knox, W. R. Matthews, W. H. Moberly, J. K. Mozley, O. C. *Quick, A. E. J. Rawlinson, E. G. Selwyn, W. Spens, V. F. Storr, B. H. *Streeter, A. E. *Taylor, L. S. Thornton (C.R.), C. C. J. *Webb and H. A. Wilson.

The body of the Report, after Prolegomena on 'the Sources and Authority of Christian Doctrine', is in three parts. The first, on 'the Doctrines of God and of Redemption', contains a summary statement of some of the chief elements in the Christian doctrine of God and the world. There follow discussions in some detail of the fact of sin and of the Person and Work of Christ, esp. His Birth and Resurrection. It concludes with two brief sections on the Holy Spirit and the Trinity. In the second and largest part, which deals with the Church and Sacraments, the Ministry and the Eucharist are the chief subjects of discussion; the section on the Eucharist expounds the Biblical teaching on sacrifice and priesthood

at length; the Church, Baptism, and 'those five commonly called sacraments' are more briefly treated. The third part on Eschatology was added through the widespread confusion arising from the tendency to interpret literally the apocalyptic symbolism of the NT. The Report concluded with four unsigned appendices on the psychological aspects of sin, on finitude and original sin, on the meaning of the terms 'body' and 'blood' in Eucharistic theology, and on the relation of sacraments to grace. The approach throughout is theological and, in the main, Biblical.

On its presentation to the *Convocations, the Report met with much hostile criticism, perhaps partly through a misunderstanding of its character and purpose. Certainly it did not claim to be an authoritative epitome of the doctrine of the C of E, or even of the limits within which doctrinal variation was permissible, but simply an examination of beliefs actually held. Moreover, the Report tended to reflect the trends of Anglican theological thought at the time of the appointment of the Commission. The theological perspective had already changed before it was completed.

DODD, CHARLES HAROLD (1884–), NT scholar and theologian. Educated at University College, Oxford, and at Berlin, he was ordained minister of Warwick *Congregational Church in 1912. In 1915 he was appointed NT lecturer at Mansfield College, Oxford, in 1930 Rylands professor at Manchester, in 1935 Norris-Hulse professor of divinity at Cambridge, and in 1950 General Director of the New Translation of the Bible (see *Bible*, English Versions, 5). Dodd's earlier works include *The Authority of the Bible* (1928), *The Epistle to the Romans* (*Moffatt NT Comm., 1932) and *The Bible and the Greeks* (1935). In *The Parables of the Kingdom* (1935), *The Apostolic Preaching and its Developments* (1936) and *History and the Gospel* (1938) he put forward his much discussed conceptions of 'realized eschatology', viz. that the OT promises of, and Christ's authentic words on, the coming of the *Kingdom of God (q.v.) received their realization in the Incarnation and its consequences for mankind, and of the 'kerygma', viz. the existence of a primitive and constant element in the NT presentation of Christianity consisting in the proclamation of the saving acts of God in history and esp. the passion and resurrection of Christ (cf. 1 Cor. 15. 3 ff.). He has since published an important study on *The Interpretation of the Fourth Gospel* (1953). In 1954–5 he delivered the first course of Sarum Lectures at Oxford on *The Historical Tradition in the Fourth Gospel*.

The Background of the New Testament and its Eschatology, ed. W. D. Davies–D. Daube. In Honour of C. H. Dodd (1956), with bibl. of Dodd's works, pp. xiii–xviii.

DODDRIDGE, PHILIP (1702–51), *Nonconformist divine and hymn-writer. He was the twentieth child of a prosperous London merchant of nonconformist ancestry, and was educated mainly by nonconformists, falling particularly under the influence of Samuel Clarke (1684–1750; not to be confused with the metaphysician of the same name, q.v.). After the death of his father he refused the offer of a university training for the C of E made by the Duke of Bedford, and against the advice of E. *Calamy sought entrance to the nonconformist ministry. With the assistance of Clarke, he was enabled to enter the liberal theological Academy in Leicestershire, directed by John Jennings (d. 1723), an Independent, whom he was to succeed as Principal in 1729. In 1723 he became Minister at Kibworth, Leics., moving in 1725 to Market Harborough but continuing his former ministry. After declining several appointments, mainly because he did not wish to commit himself to any particular sect, he moved (1729) to Northampton on accepting the invitation to continue the Academy of Jennings, where he also had charge of a large Independent Congregation. In 1730 he was 'ordained a presbyter' by eight ministers of whom five were *Presbyterians. In 1736 he was awarded a D.D. by the university of Aberdeen. At Nottingham in 1737 he followed the example of Clarke in establishing a Charity School, and in 1743 was among the founders of the County Infirmary. His scheme for the distribution of Bibles at home and abroad puts him among the pioneers of nonconformist missionary enterprise. On the breakdown of his health in 1751 he sailed to Lisbon, where he died soon after his arrival.

Doddridge laboured throughout his ministry to obliterate the old party lines and to unite the nonconformists. He was strongly opposed to the rigidity of some of the Calvinists. In 1748 he approached Abp. T. *Herring with a scheme for the interchange of pulpits of the established and dissenting clergy. He also wrote a large number of hymns which were widely circulated in MS. during his life; they are largely modelled on those of I. *Watts. Those in common use among Anglicans as well as nonconformists include 'Hark my soul, the Saviour comes', 'My God and is Thy Table spread', 'O God of Bethel, by Whose Hand' and 'Ye servants of the Lord'. His prose works include *Free Thoughts on the Most Probable Means of Reviving the Dissenting Interest* (anon. 1730) and *On the Rise and Progress of Religion in the Soul* (1745), besides various sermons, Scriptural commentaries and discourses on technical subjects.

Works, incl. Memoir by [J.] Orton, in 10 vols. (1802–5) and in 5 vols. (1803–4). J. D. Humphreys (grandson, ed.), *The Correspondence and Diary of Philip Doddridge* (5 vols. bound in 4, 1829–31). J. Orton, *Memoirs of the Life, Character and Writings of the late Reverend Philip Doddridge* (1766; ed. by D. Russell, 1825). C. Stanford, *Philip Doddridge* (1880). Other lives by J. Stoughton (London, 1852) and D. A. Harsha (Albany, 1865). A. Gordon in *D.N.B.*, xv (1888), pp. 158–64.

DODWELL, HENRY (1641–1711), 'the elder', English theologian. Educated at Trinity College, Dublin, of which he became a Fellow, he resigned his fellowship in 1666 from reluctance to take holy orders. He then settled in London where he soon acquired a great reputation for learning and in 1688 was appointed Camden praelector of ancient history at Oxford. He defended the *Nonjuring bishops, and in 1691 was deprived for refusing to take the Oath of Allegiance. Later, he retired to Shottesbrooke, near Maidenhead, where he spent the rest of his life, and the antiquary, T. *Hearne, was for a time his pupil. In 1710 he rejoined the established Church. His voluminous writings were for the most part very learned, but their cumbrous and often eccentric judgements did little to commend them. They include an edition of St. *Francis de Sales's *Introduction to the Devout Life* (1673), *Two Short Discourses against the Romanists* (1676), *De Sacerdotio Laicorum* (1685; against H. *Grotius), *Dissertationes in Irenaeum* (1689), *De nupero schismate Anglicano paraenesis* (1704), *Occasional Communion fundamentally destructive of the Discipline of the Primitive Catholic Church* (1705), *A Discourse concerning the Use of Incense in Divine Offices* (1761), and many works on classical subjects.

His son, HENRY DODWELL 'the younger' (d. 1784), was a *Deist, who secured some notoriety from his *Christianity not founded on Argument* (1742).

F. Brokesby, *The Life of Henry Dodwell, with an Account of his Works* (1715). J. H. Overton in *D.N.B.*, xv (1888), pp. 179–82 (on both Dodwells).

DOGMA (Gk. δόγμα, 'opinion', from δοκεῖν). The original meaning of the word was 'that which seems good', and hence it was applied by classical authors as a technical term either to the distinctive tenets of the various philosophical schools or to the decrees of public authorities. In this second sense it is used in the *Septuagint and the NT, e.g. Dan. 2. 13, Acts 16. 4, Eph. 2. 15, &c., whereas the Patristic use developed from the first. 'Dogma', in the Christian sense as opposed to the teachings of the philosophers, soon acquired a definite theological significance. In the accepted Christian meaning the term signifies a religious truth established by Divine Revelation and defined by the Church.

DOLLING, ROBERT WILLIAM RAD-CLYFFE, Father (1851–1902), *Anglo-Catholic missioner. An Irishman by birth, though not by descent, Dolling was educated at Trinity College, Cambridge. In 1878 he came to London, where he soon fell under the influence of Fr. A. H. *Stanton at St. Alban's, Holborn. His work as a warden of a fellowship for postmen (the 'St. Martin's Postmen's League') earned him the name of 'Brother Bob'. In 1885, two years after his ordination, he was put in charge of St. Agatha's, Landport, the Winchester College Mission, where for ten years he fought very successfully against the evils of slum life. The remarkable transformation that was achieved in the parish under his influence is vividly set out in his *Ten Years in a Portsmouth Slum* (1896). Though without any intrinsic interest in ceremonial, he refused to modify his practice where change might seem to imply concession in matters of faith, and consequently he was led in 1896, through opposition from R. T. *Davidson, then Bp. of Winchester, to resign from Landport. From 1898 till his death he was Vicar of St. Saviour's, Poplar.

Life by C. E. Osborne (London, 1903); shorter memoir by J. Clayton (ib., 1902). W. B. Owen in *D.N.B., 1901–1911*, i, p. 512 f.

DÖLLINGER, JOHN JOSEPH IGNATIUS VON (1799–1890), Bavarian Church historian. Ordained priest in 1822, he was from 1823 to 1826 professor of Church history at Aschaffenburg and from 1826 until 1873 at Munich. At first he held strong *Ultramontane opinions, and his early writings show few signs of the independence which characterized his later work. Contact with the newer tendencies of Church history in other countries, and his friendship with such men as J. H. *Newman and Lord *Acton, gradually aroused his critical sense. Before 1840 he had developed his notion of a German Church free from state control, but in full communion with Rome, and this project he defended in the National Parliament of Frankfurt, as well as in several of his writings, notably his *Reformation* (3 vols., 1845–8) and *Luther* (1851).

In the fifties he wrote several important works on Church history, among them *Hippolitus und Callistus* (1853), *Heidenthum und Judenthum* (1857), and *Christentum und Kirche* (1860). He gradually came to be distrustful of Roman influence, and in 1861, in two published lectures, he attacked the temporal power of the Pope, and aroused the hostility esp. of the *Jesuits. In 1863 he took the leading part at the Congress of Munich where a liberal form of Catholicism was defended. The publication of the '*Syllabus' in 1864 and the calling of the *Vatican Council with the avowed intention of suppressing Liberalism further increased his disagreement with Roman policy. The *Letters of* *'*Janus* (in conjunction with others; 1869) and *Letters of* *Quirinus* (1869–1870) revealed him as a formidable critic of the Council and of the doctrine of *infallibility. After refusing to submit to the Conciliar decisions, he was excommunicated in 1871 by Abp. G. v. Scherr of Munich. In his later years he largely identified himself with the *Old Catholic Churches, and worked for reunion (see *Bonn Reunion Conferences*). As a mark of general esteem, he was appointed in 1873 president of the Bavarian Royal Academy of Sciences in succession to J. von Liebig.

Döllinger's other writings included *Die Papstfabeln des Mittelalters* (1863), *Die Geschichte der Moralstreitigkeiten in der römisch-katholischen Kirche seit dem 16. Jahrhundert* (2 vols., 1889; with F. H. Reusch) and *Briefe und Erklärungen über die vatikanischen Dekrete* (1890). His publications showed that a background of dogmatic orthodoxy could produce work of no less brilliance and calibre than the destructive criticism of the *Tübingen School. His capacity for work was almost limitless and

his personal life simple. He was also a great teacher.

Many of his works have been tr. into Eng. H. Schörs (ed.), *Ignaz von Döllinger's Briefe an eine junge Freundin* (1914). J. *Friedrich, *Ignaz von Döllinger. Sein Leben auf Grund seines schriftlichen Nachlasses* (3 vols., 1899–1901). E. Michael, S.J., 'Döllinger. Ein Charakterbild' in *Z.K.T.*, xv (1891), pp. 401–76, 577–666, xvi (1892), pp. 1–81, 193–230, 385–427, rev. and reissued as *Ignaz von Döllinger. Eine Charakteristik* (ed. 2, 1892). L. von Kobell, *Ignaz von Döllinger. Erinnerungen* (1891; Eng. tr., 1892). S. Lösch, *Döllinger und Frankreich* (1955).

D.O.M., i.e. **Deo Optimo Maximo** (Lat.), 'to God, the Best and Greatest'. Originally a pagan formula addressed to Jupiter, it came to be widely used with a Christian application over the doors of churches and on sepulchral monuments. The celebrated temple of Jupiter on the Capitol at *Rome was pre-eminently that to Jupiter 'Optimus Maximus', and this was no doubt the immediate source of the Christian application of the phrase.

DOM (abbreviation of *Dominus*, 'Master'). A title given to professed monks of the *Benedictine, *Cistercian, and *Carthusian orders, as well as to certain *canons regular. In the *Cassinese congregation of the Benedictines it is also given to novices. The corresponding Italian 'Don' is used in a wider sense, e.g. of Don *Bosco.

DOM. See *Duomo.*

DOME OF THE ROCK, The (Arab. *Kubbet es-Sakhra*). The Moslem shrine in *Jerusalem, built in the area of the Jewish *Temple. It dates from about the end of the 7th cent. The rock from which it takes its name is supposed by *Mohammedans to be that from which Mohammed ascended to heaven, and by Jews to be that on which *Abraham prepared to sacrifice *Isaac. Both are also held to be on the site of Araunah the Jebusite's threshing floor (2 Sam. 24. 18) and of the altar of burnt sacrifice of *Solomon's Temple. The shrine is also known as the 'Mosque of Omar', a name given to it in the belief that it was the work of the second Caliph, Omar (581–644).

R. Hartmann, *Der Felsendom in Jerusalem und seine Geschichte* (Zur Kunstgeschichte des Auslandes, Hft. 69; 1909). K. A. C. Creswell, *The Origin and Plan of the Dome of the Rock* (British School of Archaeology in Jerusalem, Supplementary Papers, 2; 1924), with full reff.

DOMINE QUO VADIS? (Lat., 'Lord, whither goest thou?'). Acc. to the apocryphal *Acta Petri* (see *Peter, Acts of*), St. *Peter was persuaded by the Church towards the end of his life to flee from Rome to escape persecution. Meeting the Lord on the way, he addressed to Him the question 'Domine quo vadis?' and received the answer, 'I go to Rome to be crucified,' whereupon St. Peter turned back and gave himself up for crucifixion. Legend connects the incident with the site of the 'Quo Vadis Chapel' on the *Appian Way, a half-mile from the Porta San Sebastiano.

DOMINIC, St. (1170–1221), founder of the Order of Friars Preachers. A native of Calaruega in Old Castile, Spain, probably of the ancient family of the Guzman, he began his studies at Palencia at the age of 14. During a famine in 1191 he is said to have sold all his possessions, including his books, in order to help the poor. In 1199 he became a canon of Osma, his native diocese, where Martin de Bazan, Bp. of Osma (1190–1201) had established a strict discipline among his canons, following the Rule of St. *Augustine. Dominic soon became head of this community where he remained until, in 1203, he accompanied Diego on a preaching tour against the *Albigensian heretics in Languedoc. In 1206 they opened an institute for women in danger of the heresy at Prouille, within Albigensian territory, and attached to it a number of missionary friars. Two years later, after the murder of the Papal legate Peter of Castelnau, *Innocent III started a crusade against the Albigensians, and during the seven years of war that ensued, Dominic laboured to win the heretics back to the Church, often in danger of his life, but with comparatively little success. When in 1214 the castle of Casseneuil was put at his disposal by Count Simon IV of Montfort, his plan to found a special order for the conversion of the Albigensians took definite shape. Several volunteers joined him, and in 1215 these were recognized by the Bp. of Toulouse, and a few months later approved by the Pope on condition that they would follow one of the established rules. In 1216 Dominic went to Rome, where he obtained the formal sanction of the Pope by two bulls granting several privileges to the order. His subsequent years were spent in ceaseless journeys all over Italy, to Spain (1218), and to Paris (1219), establishing friaries and organizing the order. In 1220 he attended the first General Chapter at *Bologna. A year later he set out to preach to pagans in Hungary, but fell ill and had to return to Bologna, where he died on 6 Aug. 1221. He was canonized in 1234. Feast day, 4 Aug.

Though the austere Spaniard, Dominic, is a less popular figure than his contemporary, *Francis of Assisi, he was a man of heroic sanctity, ever zealous to win souls from error by the preaching of pure doctrine. His humility—he refused a bishopric three times—was as great as his courage and his capacity as ruler and organizer. He is traditionally, but wrongly, held to have instituted the devotion of the *Rosary.

F. Balme and P. Lelaidier, O.P., *Cartulaire ou histoire diplomatique de St. Dominique* (3 vols., 1891–1901); M. H. Laurent, O.P. (ed.), *Monumenta Historica S.P.N. Dominici* (Monumenta Ordinis Fratrum Praedicatorum Historica, xv [1933] and xvi [1935]. P. Mandonnet, O.P., *St. Dominique*. L'idée, l'homme, et l'œuvre (posthumous, notes by M. H. Vicaire and R. Ladner, 2 vols., 1937; Eng. tr., St. Louis, 1944), incl. bibl. Bede Jarrett, O.P., *Life of St. Dominic* (1924).

DOMINICA IN ALBIS. In the W. Church, the name given to *Low Sunday as that on which those newly baptized at *Easter put aside their white robes. The expression is an abbreviation of 'Dominica in Albis deponendis' or 'depositis'. The previous Saturday is correspondingly known as 'Sabbatum in albis'.

DOMINICAL LETTER. See *Sunday Letter*.

DOMINICAN ORDER (Ordo Praedicatorum, O.P.). The Dominicans are also known as **Friars Preachers** or, in England, **Black Friars** (from the black mantle worn over a white habit) or, in France, **Jacobins** (from their first house in *Paris which was under the patronage of St. *James, i.e. St. Jacobus). They are an order specially devoted to preaching and study, and were the first religious to abandon manual labour and put intellectual work in the forefront. Under the direction of St. *Dominic the order took definite shape at two General Chapters at *Bologna in 1220 and 1221. At the saint's suggestion it was decided that the new order, like that of St. *Francis, should practise not merely individual but corporate poverty, i.e. that it should have no possessions except its actual houses and churches, and live by begging. The order spread rapidly throughout Europe and soon extended into Asia. In the 14th and 15th cents. it was agitated by constitutional and disciplinary controversies, and there was considerable relaxation of discipline. After the Black Death the abuse arose of farming out 'limites', i.e. the exclusive rights of preaching and hearing confessions, to individual friars, who kept any surplus revenue from the resulting emoluments. Such friars lived in luxury and rarely came to their convents. In 1465 Pope *Sixtus IV revoked the law of corporate poverty and allowed the order to hold property and have permanent sources of income. In contrast with the Franciscan reaction to a similar move, the change caused no troubles, as it was felt that it did not touch St. Dominic's fundamental idea.

The chief interest of the Dominicans was, and is, educational. Every friary is a centre of teaching activity, primarily for the members of the order. There is a carefully organized teaching system culminating in the 'Studia Generalia' usually located in connexion with a university. During the Middle Ages the Dominicans established houses in most university towns and supplied many of the leaders of European thought. The adaptation of *Aristotle to Christian philosophy was the work esp. of the Dominicans, chiefly of St. *Albertus Magnus and St. *Thomas Aquinas.

The Dominicans, who excelled as organizers, sent from every convent representatives (the prior and one chosen by election) to the annual provincial chapters; and the provinces in turn sent representatives to the Chapter General, the supreme legislative authority in the order which, among its other functions, chose the 'Master General'. There are grounds for believing that the representative system of the Dominican elections influenced the development in England of *Convocation and perhaps even of Parliament.

The Popes used the Dominicans esp. for such missions as the preaching of Crusades, the collecting of monetary levies, and the carrying-out of diplomatic missions. The *Inquisition

was habitually staffed by members of the order
—a task for which their position as 'watch-
dogs of orthodoxy' (*Domini canes*) gave them a
certain suitability, but one not calculated to
increase their popularity. In the great age of
exploration, the Dominicans bent on missionary activity followed close upon the
Portuguese and Spanish explorers in both the
E. and W. hemispheres. With the rise of new
orders in the *Counter-Reformation period,
and esp. of the *Jesuits, often their rivals and
supplanters, the Dominicans fell somewhat
into the background; but they remain one of
the most influential of the Religious Orders,
and retain their original characteristics as the
champions of learning and orthodoxy.

The Dominicans, like the Franciscans, have
attached to them a Second and a Third Order.
The Second Order consists of nuns who live
under a rule similar to that of the friars but are
strictly enclosed and purely contemplative.
The majority of the Sisters of the Third Order,
on the other hand, live the active life without
strict enclosure. In 1852 H. *Lacordaire
founded a Third Order for priests with simple
vows, which was destroyed by the French anticlerical laws of 1901. Apart from these the
Dominicans, like the other Mendicant Orders,
have *Tertiaries (q.v.) attached to them, among
whom were Sts. *Catherine of Siena and *Rose
of Lima and Bl. *Grignion of Montfort.

Works of individual Dominican writers in J. Quétif-
J. Échard, O.P., *Scriptores Ordinis Praedicatorum* (2 vols.,
1719–21). T. M. Mamachi, O.P., and others, *Annales Ordinis
Praedicatorum* (Rome, 1756); P. T. Masetti, S.J., *Monumenta et Antiquitates Veteris Disciplinae Ordinis Praedica-
torum ab anno 1216 ad 1348* (Rome, 2 vols., 1864). G. R.
Galbraith, *The Constitution of the Dominican Order, 1216–
1360* (University of Manchester Historical Series, No. xliv,
1925). A. Walz, *Compendium Historiae Ordinis Praedicatorum* (Rome, 1930); id., *Studi Domenicani* (1939). A.
Puccetti, *L' ordine domenicano* (1927). Bede Jarrett, O.P.,
The English Dominicans (1921); W. A. Hinnebusch, *The
Early English Friars Preachers* (Rome, 1951). *Monumenta
Ordinis Praedicatorum* (Rome, 1897 ff.; 23 vols. to 1952);
Archivum Fratrum Praedicatorum (Rome, 1931 ff.; 22 vols.
to 1952). Artt. by P. Mandonnet, O.P., in *C.E.*, xii (1911),
pp. 354–70, s.v. 'Preachers, Order of', and in *D.T.C.*, vi
(1920), cols. 863–924, s.v. 'Frères Prêcheurs', incl. extensive
bibl. reff.

DOMINIS, MARCO ANTONIO DE. See
De Dominis, Marco Antonio.

DOMINUS AC REDEMPTOR. The
brief of *Clement XIV of 21 July 1773, which
suppressed the *Jesuit Order. It was issued
mainly at the instigation of Joseph Moniño, the
Spanish ambassador, to whom it probably owes
most of its provisions. As its execution was left
mainly to the local bishops, the treatment
meted out to the Jesuits varied widely in
different localities.

Text in A. Barbèri–A. Spetia (edd.), *Bullarii Romani Continuatio*, iv (Rome, 1841), pp. 607–18; the main clauses are
repr. in Mirbt, pp. 404–11 (No. 546), with reff. See also
works cited under *Jesuits*.

DOMINUS VOBISCUM. A Latin liturgical salutation, meaning 'The Lord be with
you', to which the response is *Et cum spiritu
tuo*, 'And with thy spirit'. Both formulae are
probably as old as Latin Christianity. The
salutation occurs in Ruth 2. 4. The response

is a Semitism for 'And with thee' (cf. 2 Tim.
4. 22). Salutation and response are both
found in the *Apostolic Tradition of St.
*Hippolytus.

It was the subject of a short treatise by St. *Peter
Damian, pr. in J. P. Migne, *PL*, cxlv, 231–52. A. Manser,
O.S.B., in *L.Th.K.*, iii (1931), col. 398.

DOMITIAN, TITUS FLAVIUS (A.D. 51–
96), Roman emperor. The son of Vespasian,
he succeeded his brother Titus in A.D. 81. He
gradually assumed to himself despotic powers
and demanded that public worship should be
given to him as *Dominus et Deus*. At the end
of his reign a *persecution of the Christians and
Jews broke out. Acc. to a very widespread
tradition it was during this persecution that the
Apostle John, in exile at *Patmos, received the
revelations recorded in the Apocalypse. See
also foll. entry.

The principal authorities incl. Suetonius, 'Domitianus' in
De Vita Caesarum, viii (ed., with Eng. tr., by G. W. Mooney,
London, 1930, pp. 156–87), Dio Cassius, *Hist. Rom.*, lxvii
(ed., with Eng. tr. by E. Cary, Loeb ed., viii, 1925, pp.
316–59), and *Eusebius, *H.E.*, III, xiii–xx. S. Gsell, *Essai
sur le règne de l'empereur Domitien* (1893). D. McFayden,
'The Occasion of the Domitianic Persecution' in *The
American Journal of Theology*, xiv (1920), pp. 46–66. D. W.
Riddle, 'Hebrews, First Clement, and the Persecution of
Domitian' in *Journal of Biblical Literature*, xliii (1924),
pp. 329–48. R. B. Weynand in *P.W.*, vi (1909), cols. 2541–
96, s.v. 'Flavius'; H. *Leclercq, O.S.B., in *D.A.C.L.*, iv
(1921), cols. 1388–1401, s.v.

DOMITILLA, FLAVIA (c. A.D. 100). A
Roman matron of the Imperial family who
became a Christian. Her grandmother and
mother, who both bore the same name, were
the wife and daughter of the Emp. Vespasian.
(reigned, 70–79). She was further connected
with the Imperial family through having
married Titus Flavius Clemens, a first cousin
to *Domitian. Whether or not her husband
was a Christian, as Suetonius and others may
imply, she herself certainly was. Clemens was
put to death and Flavia Domitilla banished to
the island of Pandateria, probably in both cases
for professing Christianity. The 'Coemeterium
Domitillae', on the Via Ardeatina outside
Rome, which had been her property, was used
as a Christian place of burial as early as the
1st cent. See also *Glabrio* and *Nereus and
Achilleus*, Sts.

Artt. by H. *Leclercq in *D.A.C.L.*, iv (2) (1921), cols.
1401–42, s.v. 'Domitille (Flavie)' and 'Domitille (Cimetière)',
incl. reff.

DONATION OF CONSTANTINE (*Constitutum* or *Donatio Constantini*). A document which was fabricated probably in the
Frankish Empire in the 8th–9th cent., to
strengthen the power of the Church and in
particular of the Roman see. It had great
influence in the Middle Ages. In it the Emp.
*Constantine purported to confer on Pope
*Sylvester I (314–35) the primacy over
*Antioch, *Constantinople, *Alexandria, and
*Jerusalem, and dominion over all Italy,
including Rome and the 'provinces, places, and
civitates of the Western regions'. The Pope
was also made supreme judge of the clergy,
the chief of whom were to have the rank of

Senators, and he was even offered the Imperial crown (which, however, he refused). The document, which was embodied in the *False Decretals and the collections of *canons, came to be treated as authoritative even by the opponents of the Papacy. It was first used to support Papal claims in a letter written in 1054 by *Leo IX to *Michael Cerularius, and consistently employed by his successors for the purpose. In the 15th cent. its genuineness was challenged and its falsity demonstrated by *Nicholas of Cusa, Bp. R. *Pecock, and L. *Valla.

Text in Mirbt (ed.), No. 228, pp. 107–12, with reff. Eng. tr., omitting capp. 3–5 (on Christian doctrine), in S.Z. Ehler–J. B. Morrall (edd.), *Church and State Through the Centuries* (1954), pp. 16–22. J. Friedrich, *Die constantinische Schenkung* (1889). G. Laehr, *Die konstantinische Schenkung in der abendländischen Literatur des Mittelalters bis zur Mitte des 14. Jahrhunderts* (Historische Studien Hft. clxvi; 1926). H. Grauert, 'Die konstantinische Schenkung' in *Historisches Jahrbuch*, iii (1882), pp. 3–30, with text, pp. 15–29, iv (1883), pp. 45–95, 525–617, 674–80, and v (1884), pp. 117–20. L. Weiland, 'Die constantinische Schenkung' in *Zeitschrift für Kirchenrecht*, xxii (1889), pp. 137–60. E. Loening, 'Die Entstehung der konstantinischen Schenkungsurkunde' in *Historische Zeitschrift*, lxv (1890), pp. 193–239. Dr. Sägmüller, 'Die konstantinische Schenkung in Investiturstreit' in *T.Q.*, Jahrg. lxxxiv (1902), pp. 89–110. A. Schönegger, S.J., 'Die kirchenpolitische Bedeutung des "Constitutum Constantini" im frühern Mittelalter (bis zum Decretum Gratiani)' in *Z.K.T.*, xlii (1918), pp. 327–71 and 541–90. J. Kirsch, 'Die Heimat der konstantinischen Schenkung' in *R.Q.*, xxiii (1909), pp. 110–14; M. Buchner, 'Rom oder Reims die Heimat des *Constitutum Constantini*' in *Historisches Jahrbuch*, liii (1933), pp. 137–68, with reff. H. Böhmer in *P.R.E.* (ed. 3), xi (1902), pp. 1–7, s.v. 'Konstantinische Schenkung'; M. Buchner in *L.Th.K.*, vi (1934), cols. 166–8, s.v. 'Konstantinische Schenkung', with further bibl.

DONATISM. The Donatists were a schismatic body in the African Church who became divided from the Catholics through their refusal to accept *Caecilian, Bp. of Carthage (consecrated 311), on the ground that his consecrator, Felix of Aptunga, had been a *traditor during the *Diocletianic Persecution. The Numidian bishops, supporting the objectors, consecrated Majorinus as a rival to Caecilian, and he was soon afterwards succeeded by Donatus, from whom the schism is named.

A commission, under *Miltiades, Bp. of Rome, investigated the dispute in 313. It decided against the Donatists, who thereupon appealed unsuccessfully first to the Synod of *Arles (314), and then to the Emperor (316). But the schism prospered, for theologically (with doubtful justification) it claimed St. *Cyprian's authority, while politically it drew upon African nationalist feeling, since the Catholics were supported by Rome. It also relied upon Numidian jealousy of Carthage and on economic unrest. The Emperor began coercion in 316, but abandoned it in 321. When, later, the Donatist leaders associated themselves with violent bands of marauders, called *circumcelliones, state repression began again (347) under Constans, but was relaxed under *Julian (361–3).

The theological attack on the Donatists was led first by St. *Optatus, and later by St. *Augustine. The efforts of their own more moderate supporters, such as the orator Tyconius, probably did more harm than good to their cause. In 405 the state again intervened against them, and at a large conference at Carthage in 411 the Imperial commissioner pronounced finally against Donatism. The schism, though greatly weakened, persisted until the African Church was destroyed by the Saracens in the 7th–8th cent.

Theologically the Donatists were rigorists, holding that the Church of the saints must remain 'holy' (cf. *Novatianism), and that sacraments conferred by *traditores were invalid. Apart from their denial that Felix of Aptunga was in fact a *traditor, the Church maintained that the unworthiness of the minister did not affect the validity of sacraments, since, as Augustine insisted, their true minister was Christ. The Donatists, on the other hand, went so far as to assert that all those who communicated with *traditores were infected, and that, since the Church is one and holy, the Donatists alone formed the Church. Converts to Donatism were rebaptized, a proceeding repeatedly condemned by orthodox synods.

The chief sources are Optatus, *De Schismate Donatistarum* (*c.* 368), and the anti-Donatist writings of Augustine (ed. Ben., vol. ix). D. Völter, *Der Ursprung des Donatismus* (1883); W. J. Sparrow Simpson, *St. Augustine and African Church Divisions* (1910); P. Monceaux, *Histoire littéraire de l'Afrique chrétienne*, iv (1912)–vi (1922). W. H. C. Frend, *The Donatist Church. A Movement of Protest in Roman North Africa* (1952). J. P. Brisson, *Autonomisme et christianisme dans l'Afrique romaine de Septime Sévère à l'invasion vandale* (1958).

DONNE, JOHN (1571/2–1631), *Metaphysical poet and Dean of *St. Paul's. He was a member of a RC family, his mother being the sister of the *Jesuit missionary priest Jasper Heywood, and a granddaughter of a sister of Thomas *More. He entered Hart Hall, Oxford, in 1584, left in 1587 to study at Trinity College, Cambridge, and in 1592 began to study law at Lincoln's Inn. Some time afterwards he renounced the RC faith and became a member of the C of E, a step which, though not consciously insincere, left his soul troubled, as is borne out by the stirring sonnet written as late as 1617, 'Show me, dear Christ, thy spouse'. During the following years Donne led a worldly and rather reckless life. In 1596 he accompanied Essex and Raleigh to Cadiz, and in 1597 to the Azores; and much of his secular poetry belongs to this period. In 1598 he became private secretary to Sir Thomas Egerton, a post from which he was dismissed four years later owing to his secret marriage to Ann More, his master's wife's niece, in 1601. During the next years he and his growing family lived in poverty and dependence on the charity of friends. In 1610 he wrote the *Pseudo-Martyr*, a controversial treatise against the persecuted RCs, and in the next year the *Conclave Ignati*, a bitter attack on the Jesuits. About the same time he composed the *Biathanatos* (publd. 1644), a casuistic defence of suicide in certain circumstances. After long struggles of conscience and repeated failure to embrace a secular career, he complied with the wish of the King and was ordained in 1615. He was appointed a royal chaplain and given the living of Keyston, Hunts, in 1616, and soon after became rector of Sevenoaks and reader in divinity at Lincoln's Inn. The death of his wife in 1617 increased the intensity of his religious fervour. In 1621 he became Dean of St. Paul's, where he preached most of his celebrated sermons. During a serious illness in 1623 he wrote his *Devotions upon Emergent Occasions* (1624), meditations and prayers issuing from a profound trust in, and familiarity with, God. In 1624 he was made prolocutor of the Lower House of Convocation, and a fortnight later vicar of St. Dunstan's in the West. To his last years, which were chiefly spent in preaching and study, belong some of the finest of his *Divine Poems*, e.g. the famous 'Hymn to God the Father'. The dating of the *Holy Sonnets* is disputed.

John Donne was one of the most remarkable poets as well as preachers of the 17th cent. His character, a strange mixture of sensual passion and intellectual austerity, worldly ambition and fervent devotion, is mirrored in his poetry, and makes him the finest poet of the so-called 'metaphysical' school. Though not easily accessible on account of their subtlety of thought and their unusual imagery, his poems are of rare spiritual power, enhanced by his firm grasp of dogma which frequently betrays the strong faith of his early years, as e.g. in several poems on the BVM ('that she-Cherubin which unlocked Paradise'), in the powerful description of an almost Dantesque hierarchically graded heaven in 'The Progresse of the Soul', and in 'The Litanie' with its choirs of angels, patriarchs, prophets, apostles, &c. Penetrated by a deep sense of sin and death sometimes bordering on the morbid, his religious poetry centres in the Passion, which it ever pleases him to present in its setting between the Annunciation and the Ascension. Though both language and rhythm are often too rugged to be called beautiful, they are extraordinarily impressive, and reflect the troubled soul of their author, torn between earthly desires and heavenly aspirations. His sermons, which attracted vast audiences, are packed with patristic learning and make full use of the exaggerated allegorical interpretation of Scripture and rhetorical conceits common in the 17th cent., but abound also in passages of striking beauty, esp. when he turns to exhortation and gives scope to fervent meditations on the sinfulness of man, the mercy of God, and the Four Last Things. Long almost forgotten as a poet, Donne has only recently been rediscovered. He has exercised a profound influence on some modern writers, notably T. S. *Eliot.

'Collected Works' [Sermons, Devotions, Poems and Letters only] ed. H. *Alford (6 vols., London, 1839); sermons also ed. G. R. Potter–Evelyn M. Simpson (10 vols., Berkeley, Conn., 1953 ff.); Selected Passages ed. with essay by L. P. Smith (Oxford, 1919). Modern edd. of his Poems by A. B. Grosart (2 vols., 'The Fuller Worthies' Library', privately pr., 1896) and H. J. C. Grierson (2 vols., Oxford, 1912). *Complete Poetry and Selected Prose* ed. J. Hayward (London, 1929). *Devotions upon Emergent Occasions* ed. J. Sparrow (Cambridge, 1923); *Divine Poems* ed. Helen Gardner (Oxford, 1952); *Essays in Divinity* ed. Evelyn M. Simpson (ibid., 1952). Life by I. *Walton (1640; q.v.). E. Gosse, *The Life and Letters of John Donne* (2 vols., 1899). M. P. Ramsey, *Les Doctrines Médiévales chez Donne* (London, 1917).

Evelyn M. Simpson, *A Study of the Prose Works of John Donne* (1924; ed. 2, 1948). C. M. Coffin, *John Donne and the New Philosophy* (New York, 1937). J. B. Leishman, *The Monarchy of Wit* (1951). H. C. Combs–Z. R. Sullens, *A Concordance to the English Poems of John Donne* (Chicago, 1940). G. [L.] Keynes, *A Bibliography of Dr. John Donne* (Publications of the Baskerville Club ii; 1914); W. White, *John Donne since 1900. A Bibliography of Periodical Articles* (Bulletin of Bibliography Pamphlets xxxvii; 1942). G. L. Keynes in *C.B.E.L.*, i, pp. 441–4.

DOORKEEPER. The doorkeepers, or *ostiarii*, constitute the lowest of the *Minor Orders of the W. Church. Their functions, as stated in the *Pontifical, are similar to those of the modern verger; in antiquity they were particularly responsible for excluding unauthorized persons from attending the Eucharist. The order, which was probably established at Rome during the first half of the 3rd cent., is first attested in a letter of Pope *Cornelius written in 251. It is no longer recognized in the E. Churches, though doorkeepers (θυρωροί) are mentioned in the canons of *Laodicea (can. 24).

A. Michel in *D.T.C.*, xii (pt. 2; 1935), cols. 2600–2, s.v. 'Portier', with bibl.; H. *Leclercq, O.S.B., in *D.A.C.L.*, xiv (pt. 2; 1948), cols. 1525–33, s.v. 'Portier'; A. Piolanti in *E.C.*, ix (1952), cols. 435–7, s.v. 'Ostiariato'.

DORCHESTER, Oxon. Originally a Roman station, it was conquered by the West Saxons *c.* 560. In 635 St. *Oswald, King of Northumbria, and Cynegils, King of the West Saxons, concurred in establishing it as a see, with St. *Birinus as bishop. The diocese covered an area stretching from Dorset to Bucks and from Surrey to the Severn, territory which for centuries was disputed between the kingdoms of Wessex and Mercia. In later pre-Conquest times the diocese extended north to the Humber. In 1086, when the importance of the place had declined, Bp. Remigius, formerly a monk of Fécamp (consecrated 1067, d. 1090), transferred the see to *Lincoln. In 1140 Alexander, Bp. of Lincoln, founded an abbey of *Augustinian Canons which was suppressed in 1536. By the 16th cent. the abbey church was the only notable feature of the village. In 1939 the Bishopric of Dorchester was re-created suffragan to *Oxford. Until 1956 it was held in conjunction with the Archdeaconry of Oxford.

J. H. Parker (ed.), *The History of Dorchester, Oxfordshire British Earthworks—Roman Camp—Bishopric, and the Architectural History of the Church* (Oxford, 1882). On the Augustinian house, H. E. Salter in *V.C.H., Oxford*, ii, ed. W. Page (1907), pp. 87–90.

DORDRECHT, Synod of. See *Dort*.

DORNER, ISAAC AUGUST (1809–84), German *Lutheran theologian. The son of a Lutheran pastor, he was educated at *Tübingen, where he was a pupil of F. C. *Baur. In 1838 he became professor of theology at Tübingen, in 1839 at Kiel, in 1843 at Königsberg, in 1847 at Bonn, in 1853 at Göttingen, and finally in 1862 at Berlin. In theology he sought to interpret the *Kantian and post-Kantian systems in terms of the traditional Lutheran faith. He also took a prominent part in the ecclesiastical life of his time. The best known of his many writings was his treatise on the history of the doctrine of the Person of Christ, first published in 1839 (Eng. trans. in 5 vols., 1861–6). In 1867 he issued his *Geschichte der protestantischen Theologie* (Eng. trans., 2 vols., 1871). He was the founder, and for many years the editor, of the *Jahrbücher für deutsche Theologie* (1856 ff.).

His son, AUGUST DORNER (1846–1920), later became a distinguished theologian, holding professorial chairs at *Wittenberg and Königsberg.

I. A. Dorner's *System der christlichen Sittenlehre* was publd. posthumously by August Dorner (1885; Eng. tr. C. M. Mead –R. T. Cunningham, 1887, with introd. on I. A. Dorner, pp. v–xii). Correspondence between H. L. *Martensen, Bp. of Zealand, and I. A. Dorner, 2 vols., Berlin, 1888. I. Bobertag, *Isaak August Dorner* (Gütersloh, 1906). O. Kirn in *P.R.E.* (ed. 3), iv (1898), pp. 802–7.

DOROTHEUS, St. (6th cent.), ascetical writer. He entered a Palestinian monastery near Gaza when he came under the influence of Barsanuphius, the author of a work against the errors of *Origen and *Evagrius, and *c.* 540 founded a monastery of his own, also near Gaza, of which he became *archimandrite. For the use of its members he wrote a series of 'Instructions' (Διδασκαλίαι Ψυχωφελεῖς) on the ascetic life, though not all the 24 items in the standard edition which was made in the 9th cent. are from Dorotheus himself. In his spiritual doctrine he gives an exceptionally high place to humility, not only maintaining that it was the cement of all the other virtues but even putting it above love. His 'Instructions' are an important source for earlier ascetic writers ('fathers'), on whose doctrines he frequently drew. Eight of his Letters also survive. His writings were highly esteemed by A. J. de *Rancé, who translated them into French for use by his *Trappists.

'Instructions' ed. J. Grynaeus, *Orthodoxographia*, i (Basle, 1569), pp. 195–361; cf. also J. P. Migne, *PG*, lxxxviii, 1611–1842. Bardenhewer, v, p. 69 f.; Altaner (ed. 1950), p. 469. S. Vailhé, A.A., in *D.T.C.*, iv (1911), col. 1785 f., s.v. 'Dorothée de Gaza'.

DOROTHY, St., also Dorothea, Virgin and martyr, prob. in the Persecution of *Diocletian (d. 313). The earliest historical source mentioning her is the '*Hieronymian Martyrology,' where her name appears together with a 'Theophilus'. Acc. to the later legendary *Acta* she was martyred at Caesarea in Cappadocia; on her way to martyrdom a young lawyer, Theophilus, mocked her, asking her to send him fruits from the garden to which she was going. At the place of execution she knelt to pray, when an angel appeared with a basket of apples and roses, which she sent to Theophilus. When he had tasted of the fruit he, too, became a Christian and a martyr. Her martyrdom was made the subject of one of the charming *Sieben Legenden* of Gottfried Keller, the Swiss novelist. Feast day, 6 Feb.

Discussion and text of 'Acta ex tribus MSS codibus' in *AA.SS.*, Feb. I (1658), pp. 772–6. Further recensions listed in *B.H.L.*, i (1898–99), p. 349 f, Nos. 2321–5, and Suppl. (revised ed., 1911), p. 99. A certain Christian lady (Χριστιανή) mentioned in *Eusebius, *H.E.*, VIII, xiv, 15, acc. to *Rufinus called Dorothea, is sometimes taken to refer to her. G. Keller, *Sieben Legenden* (1872), pp. 123–35.

DORSAL, also Dossal. A piece of cloth, often embroidered, which is sometimes hung at the back of an altar in place of a *reredos. It is apparently a survival of the curtains which in earlier times were hung between the four columns of the *ciborium.

DORT, Synod of (1618–19). The assembly of the Dutch Reformed Church, convened at Dort (Dordrecht) by the States-General to deal with the *Arminian Controversy. Although primarily a national gathering of Dutch theologians, several foreign delegates from Switzerland, the Palatinate, Scotland, England, and other states took part, the British representatives including G. Carleton (Bp. of *Llandaff), J. *Hall, J. Davenant, S. Ward (Archdeacon of Taunton), and W. Balcanquall. The Synod, which met in 154 formal sessions, sat from 13 Nov. 1618 to 9 May 1619, though the Arminians ('*Remonstrants'), led by S. *Episcopius, were not introduced till 6 Dec. 1618. John Bogerman of Leeuwarden, a strict *Calvinist, was elected president. The Synod, supported by Prince Maurice of Orange, was biased against *Arminianism from the start and its decisions were a foregone conclusion. Five sets of articles passed on 23 Apr. 1619 asserted (1) unconditional election, (2) a limited atonement, (3) the total depravity of man, (4) the irresistibility of grace, and (5) the final perseverance of the saints. At a final session on 9 May 1619 the Synod drew up 93 canonical rules and confirmed the authority of the *Belgic Confession* and the *Heidelberg Catechism*. This victory for Calvinist principles led to some 200 Arminian clergy being deprived, H. *Grotius being sentenced by the States-General to perpetual imprisonment, and J. van Oldenbarneveldt being beheaded on a false charge of high treason.

Lat. text of canons, orig. publ. 6 May 1619, printed in P. *Schaff, *The Creeds of Christendom*, iii (1877), pp. 550–80, with abridged Eng. tr., pp. 581–97; introd. in vol. i (1877), pp. 512–15. M. Graf, *Beyträge zur Kenntniss der Geschichte der Synode von Dordrecht* (Basel, 1825). B. Glasius, *Geschiedenis der Nationale Synode in 1618 en 1619 gehouden te Dordrecht* (2 vols., Leyden, 1860–1). A. W. Harrison, *The Beginnings of Arminianism to the Synod of Dort* (1926), pp. 300–83.

DORTER. A dormitory, esp. in a monastery. It was sometimes of great length, e.g. that at *Durham (1398–1404) 194 ft. long (now a library and museum). They often gave direct access to the church for the night office.

DOSITHEUS (2nd cent.), Judaeo-*Gnostic heretic. He belonged to *Samaria, but very little is known of him. Acc. to *Hegesippus (*Eusebius, *HE*, iv, 22), he was one of five original founders of sects in Palestine. *Origen, who mentions him several times, states (*Cont. Celsum*, vi, 2) that he set himself up as the Messiah foretold in Deut. 18. 18 and insisted on strict observance of the Sabbath. Acc. to the *Clementine Recognitions (2. 8), Dositheus was first a disciple, and afterwards the teacher of *Simon Magus. His followers (Dositheans) never seem to have been more than a very small body (Origen, *Cont. Cels.* vi, 11, mentions 'scarcely thirty' as surviving in his day), but they survived down to the 10th cent.

A. *Hilgenfeld, *Die Ketzergeschichte des Urchristentums* (1884), pp. 155-61. S. Krauss, 'Dosithée et les Dosithéens' in *Revue des Études juives*, xlii (1901), pp. 27-42; A. Buechler, 'Les Dosithéens dans le Midrasch', ib., pp. 220-31. Bardenhewer, i, pp. 345-7. G. *Salmon in *D.C.B.*, i (1877), p. 902 f.; A. *Jülicher in *P.W.*, x (1905), col. 1608 f.

DOSITHEUS (1641-1707), Patr. of *Jerusalem from 1669. A native of the Peloponnese, prob. of humble family, on the death of his father, at the age of eight he was placed by the Abp. of *Corinth in a neighbouring monastery. He was ordained deacon three years later, and prob. educated at Athens under N. Keramevs (d. 1663). Before 1657 he entered the service of the Patr. of Jerusalem and in 1661 became Archdeacon of Jerusalem and in 1666 Abp. of *Caesarea. On the resignation of Nectar Pelopides (1661-69) he was appointed Patr. of Jerusalem by a synod held at *Constantinople. His best-known achievement was the Synod of Jerusalem (q.v.) held in 1672 and intended to combat the influence of Protestantism in the Greek Church; Dositheus was the principal author of its decrees and confession. His patriarchate was also marked by the inauguration of various monastic and financial reforms, and more esp. by his vigorous defence of the Greeks against the Latins, as in the dispute with the *Franciscans over their rights to Holy Places. He tried to extend the influence of Hellenism in Russia by adroit intervention in the disputes aroused by the patriarchate of *Nikon, by joining with Callixtus II (Patr. of Constantinople 1689-93) in condemning the *Calvinistic teaching of J. Karophyllis on the *Eucharist in 1691 and by opposition to the *Uniat Churches in his writings against L. *Allatius and R. *Bellarmine. To combat western influence in theology he established a printing press at Jassy in 1680. His many theological works, characterized by wide erudition rather than original thought, include an Ἐγχειρίδιον against Calvinism (Bucharest, 1690) and a Τόμος Καταλλαγῆς (Jassy, 1692). He also compiled a history of the Patriarchate of Jerusalem in 13 books (ed. anonymously by P. Keramevs; posthumously published, Bucharest, 2 vols., 1715).

Dositheus published many other writings, most of them at Jassy. Chrysanthos Notaras, his nephew, inserted a Life of his uncle into Dositheus's posthumous 'History of the Jerusalem Patriarchate' ('Ἱστορία περὶ τῶν ἐν Ἱεροσολύμοις Πατριαρευσάντων; also, from its division into twelve books, known as the Δωδεκάβιβλος; Bucharest, 1715). A. Palmieri, O.S.A., *Dositeo, patriarca greco di Gerusalemme* (Florence, 1909). A. Palmieri, O.S.A., in *D.T.C.*, iv (1911), cols. 1788-1800, with full bibl.; M. Jugie, A.A., in *E.C.*, iv (1950), col. 1890 f., s.v. 'Dositeo'.

DOSTOIEVSKY, FEODOR MICHAELOVITCH (1821-81), Russian novelist. He was the son of a retired military Russian surgeon of *Orthodox or *Uniat priestly ancestry, born at Moscow where he was educated at a private boarding-school. From 1838 to 1843 he attended the Military Engineering College at St. Petersburg, but resigned his commission after three years. In 1849 he was arrested for revolutionary activities and eight months later condemned to death. Although the sentence was reprieved, this imminence of death made a deep impression on him. During four years' forced labour in Siberia, he gained an intimate knowledge and deep affection for the ordinary Russian people. In 1854 he was transferred as a private in an infantry battalion to Semipalatinsk, where he was able to resume his writing. In 1856 he formed an unhappy marriage terminated by the death of his wife in 1863. He returned to St. Petersburg in 1859, and with his elder brother in 1861 founded the review *Vremya* (suppressed 1863), in which he defended Slavophil democratic ideas. Deeply in debt through gambling and general mismanagement, in 1867 he married his secretary, who later became his publisher. In 1873 he was invited by Prince Meshchersky to edit the newspaper *Grazhdanin*, to which he contributed his *Author's Diary* (published separately, 1876). Although known chiefly as a journalist in his life-time, his more enduring works were the novels in which he penetrated the deep recesses of the human mind. They include (all written in Russian) *Memoirs from the Underworld* (1864), *Crime and Punishment* (1865-66), *The Idiot* (1869), *The Possessed* (1871), and *The Brothers Karamazov* (1880). The centre of Dostoievsky's religious experience which has made him, together with S. *Kierkegaard, one of the forerunners of modern *Dialectical Theology, is the consciousness of salvation as the free gift of God to the weak and miserable and the refusal to admit any co-operation between God and man. There is no way from man to God, only one from God to man, who is united to his fellows by the common bond of sin. The result is a complete absence from religion of reason and will, and the moral effort that flows from them. The heroes and heroines of Dostoievsky's novels live entirely by their emotions, of which the foremost is boundless and irrational compassion. In the short story 'The Grand Inquisitor', incorporated in *The Brothers Karamazov*, the institutional Church is represented as the great tyrant and falsifier of Christ whom she would crucify again if He came back to earth. Dostoievsky's ideas have had a profound influence on the Continent, where they found a fertile soil in the distrust of reason and the worship of irrational forces which has marked much 20th cent. thought.

The standard English translation of Dostoievsky's novels is that by Constance Garnett (12 vols., 1912-20). There is a very extensive literature, mainly in Russian. More substantial studies available in English include works by J. M. Murray (London, 1916), A. Gide (Paris, 1923; abridged Eng. tr., 1925), J. Meier-Graefe (Berlin, 1926; Eng. tr., 1928), E. H. Carr (London, 1931), A. Yarmolinsky (New York, 1934), H. Troyat (Paris, 1940; Eng. tr., New York, 1946), and E. J. Simmons (New York, 1940). There is also a brief interpretation by N. *Berdyaev (in Russian, Prague, 1923; Eng. tr. from Fr. version, 1934).

DOUAI, in Flanders. Formerly a university, it was the seat of several colleges founded for the benefit of English RC scholars in exile under *Elizabeth I, of which the most important was that established by W. *Allen in 1568. This was originally intended to ensure a learned clergy in England when the RC faith should be re-established, but it soon became a seminary for the training of mission priests to work in England. Many of its *alumni* suffered death either for their faith or as political conspirators, and members of the college were responsible for the production of the *Douai-Reims Bible. At the French Revolution the college was suppressed and the work transferred to England, where it was carried on at Crook Hall, near Ushaw, and at St. Edmund's Old Hall, Ware. The Benedictine Community of St. Gregory, founded at Douai in 1605, has been established in England since 1795 (at *Downside Abbey, in Somerset, since 1814).

The First and Second Diaries of the English College, Douay, ed. by the Fathers of the Congregation of the London Oratory with hist. Introd. by T. F. Knox, Cong. Orat. (Records of the English Catholics under the Penal Laws, i, 1876); E. H. Burton and T. L. Williams (ed.), *The Douay Diaries, Third, Fourth and Fifth, with the Rheims Report, 1579–80* (*Catholic Record Society, x and xi, 1911); E. H. Burton, *The Douay College Diaries*. The Seventh Diary, 1715–1778, preceded by a Summary of Events, 1691–1715 (ib., xxviii, 1928). P. Guilday, *The English Catholic Refugees on the Continent, 1558–1795*, i (1914), chs. iv and ix, 'The English College at Douai', pp. 63–120 and 307–45, incl. full bibliographical notes to date. J. H. Baxter, 'The Scots College at Douai' in *The Scottish Historical Review*, xxiv (1927), pp. 251–7.

DOUAI-REIMS BIBLE. The traditional version of the Bible in use among English-speaking RCs. It was the work of members of the English College at *Douai, of whom the chief were G. *Martin (d. 1582), Thomas Worthington, Richard Bristowe, and William *Allen, all of them formerly from Oxford. It claimed to provide a version free from the heretical renderings in the earlier English Bibles. The work was begun at Douai, but owing to the migration of the college to Reims in 1578, the NT was completed in that city and published there in 1582. The OT, which did not appear till 1609, was published at Douai, whither the college had returned in the meantime. The translation, which was made not from the original languages but from the Latin *Vulgate, was painstaking and reached a high standard of consistency, but was often too literal to be suitable for use in public worship or private devotional reading. There was also a strong tendency to retain technical words (e.g. 'pasch', 'parasceve', 'azymes') without alteration, and many passages are more an anglicization than a translation of the Latin, e.g. Phil. 2. 7 (8): 'He exinanited Himself'. The dogmatic intentions of its authors found expression in the prologue and in the notes that accompany the text. Its language exercised considerable influence on the text of the *Authorized Version. Modern editions of this translation are based on the revision made by R. *Challoner in 1749–50. The Reims NT was vigorously attacked in 1589 by W. *Fulke.

J. G. Carleton, *The Part of Rheims in the Making of the English Bible* (1902). B. F. *Westcott, *A General View of the History of the English Bible* (ed. 3 by W. A. Wright; 1905); pp. 102–6, 245–55; A. W. Pollard, *Records of the English Bible* (1911), pp. 33–7, with documents pp. 298–313;

J. Isaacs in H. Wheeler Robinson (ed.), *The Bible in its Ancient and English Versions* (1940), pp. 190–5. Darlow-Moule, i (1903), pp. 97 f., 129 f. For background, see also Douai diaries and other works cited s.v. *Douai*, and Letters and Memorials of W. Allen s.v. *Allen*.

DOUBLE MONASTERY. A religious house for both men and women. The two sexes dwelt in separate but contiguous establishments, worshipped in distinct parts of a common church, and were ruled by a common superior. Such monasteries are first found in the E. in the last generations of the Roman Empire, whence they spread to W. Europe where they became numerous and influential in the Dark Ages. To this type belonged the famous abbey of *Whitby ruled in the 7th cent. by St. *Hilda. Most of them disappeared in the disorders of the 9th and 10th cents., but were revived (generally only for a short time) by certain of the smaller monastic orders of the 12th cent., including the Order of *Sempringham.

Mary Bateson, 'Origin and Early History of Double Monasteries' in *Transactions of the Royal Historical Society*, New Series, xiii (1899), pp. 137–98. U. Berlière, O.S.B., *Les Monastères doubles au XIIᵉ et XIIIᵉ siècles* (Académie Royale de Belgique. Classe des Lettres et des Sciences Morales et Politiques. Mémoires, Sér. 2, xviii; 1923).

DOUBLE PROCESSION OF THE HOLY GHOST, the doctrine of the W. Church acc. to which the Holy Ghost proceeds from the Father and the Son. Support for it is found in several NT passages, notably Jn. 16. 13–15, where Christ says of the Holy Ghost 'He shall take (λήψεται) of Mine and shall declare it unto you'. It is urged that in the Inner-Trinitarian relations one Person cannot 'take' or 'receive' (λήψεται) anything from either of the others except by way of Procession. Among other texts adduced for the doctrine are Gal. 4. 6, where the Holy Ghost is called 'the Spirit of the Son', Rom. 8. 9 'the Spirit of Christ', Phil. 1. 19 'the Spirit of Jesus Christ', and the Johannine texts on the sending of the Holy Ghost by Jesus (14. 16, 15. 26, 16. 7).

Among the Greek Fathers St. *Cyril of Alexandria is usually considered one of the most important witnesses to the doctrine. He develops it in his struggle against *Nestorianism, calling the Holy Spirit the property of the Son, τὸ ἴδιον τοῦ Υἱοῦ. He also uses several times the characteristic Latin formula 'and the Son' side by side with the Greek phrase 'through the Son', the former indicating the equality of principle, the latter the order of origin. The doctrine was expressly denied, on the other hand, by *Theodore of Mopsuestia and *Theodoret. Among the Latin Fathers, St. *Jerome, St. *Ambrose, and esp. St. *Augustine are representatives of the teaching summed up in the '*Filioque' (q.v.). But the doctrine did not become a matter of controversy until the time of *Photius (864), who asserted it to be contrary to the teaching of the Fathers and even suspected the relevant passages as interpolations. At the Council of *Florence (1439), Mark of Ephesus repeated this theory; but to-day most theologians of the

E. Church recognize that St. Augustine and other Latin Fathers taught the Double Procession, but only as a private opinion. The objection urged by E. theologians against the doctrine is that there must be a single Fount of Divinity (πηγὴ θεότητος) in the Godhead. The consideration urged by W. theologians in its support is that, as both Latins and Greeks attribute everything as common to the Father and the Son except the relation of Paternity and Filiation, the Spiration of the Holy Ghost, in which this relation is not involved, must also be common to both.

H. B. *Swete, *On the History of the Doctrine of the Procession of the Holy Spirit from the Apostolic Age to the Death of Charlemagne* (1876). M. Jugie, A.A., *Theologia Dogmatica Christianorum Orientalium a Ecclesia Catholica Dissentium*, i (Rome, 1926), esp. pp. 286–311, and ii (1933), pp. 296–535. Id., *De Processione Spiritus Sancti ex Fontibus Revelationis et secundum Orientales Dissidentes* (Lateranum, N.S., ii, N. 3–4; 1936), with reff. See fuller bibl. s.v. *Filioque*.

DOUBLE FEASTS. In the Roman *Missal and *Breviary, the more important feasts. They are distinguished as (ordinary) Doubles, Greater Doubles, Doubles of the Second Class, and Doubles of the First Class. The use of the term is of uncertain origin.

DOUKHOBORS (Russ.), 'Spirit-fighters'. A Russian sect of unknown origin. It seems to have arisen among Russian peasants in the district of Kharkov *c.* 1740, and spread rapidly. Under Paul I (d. 1801) the Doukhobors came into conflict with the government and were banished to Siberia; under Alexander I (d. 1825) they settled in Taurida as an agricultural community run on communist lines. Owing to the intolerance of the Orthodox clergy and their own growing moral laxity, they were again banished and sent to Transcaucasia in 1841. In 1895, having come under the influence of L. *Tolstoy, they refused to serve in the army and burned their weapons. Being once more expelled they found themselves reduced to starvation, when the assistance of Tolstoy and the *Quakers enabled most of them to emigrate to Cyprus and Canada. Here they became a nuisance to the government because they refused to own land as individuals and to register births, deaths, and marriages. Those still in Russia are said to have established relations with the Communist government in 1921. The Doukhobors believe in one God manifested in the human soul as memory (Father), reason (Son), and will (Holy Ghost). Jesus Christ is not God but a man possessing Divine reason in the highest degree. The Bible and all Christian dogmas are interpreted allegorically, while the human soul is eternal and suffers *metempsychosis.

J. Elkington, *The Doukhobors. Their History in Russia. Their Migration to Canada* (Philadelphia, 1903); A. Maude, *A Peculiar People. The Doukhobors* (London, 1904). A. Palmieri in *D.T.C.*, iv (1908), cols. 1802–11, incl. full bibl. (mainly Russian). F. C. *Conybeare, *Russian Dissenters* (Harvard Theological Studies, x, 1921), pp. 266–87. A. A. Stamouli in *H.E.R.E.*, iv (1911), pp. 865–7.

DOVE. As a Christian symbol, the dove has many meanings. (1) From the dove with the olive branch in its beak in the story of the Flood (Gen. 8. 11), it is a sign of peace and reconciliation. (2) In the primitive Church, from the ref. to His descent upon Christ at His baptism under the form of a dove (Mk. 1. 10), it was esp. a type of the Holy Ghost. This symbol is found esp. in the vaults of early churches and frequently in conjunction with pictorial representations of the other two Persons of the Trinity. (3) From the Song of Solomon, where the Bride is called a dove (e.g. 2. 14, 5. 2), the symbol has been applied either to the Church, e.g. by *Tertullian, St. *Ambrose, and St. *Augustine, or to the individual soul regenerated by baptism, e.g. by St. *Hilary of Poitiers. (4) Other meanings of the dove are to denote inspired theological knowledge in the case of many saints, e.g. St. *Gregory the Great, St. *Dominic, St. *Thomas Aquinas, and St. *Teresa; and (5) to represent certain Christian virtues, notably purity and humility.

The 'Eucharistic Dove' is a hollow receptacle in the shape of a dove to contain the Blessed Sacrament. Its use was formerly believed, apparently wrongly, to go back to Tertullian. It is attested by a Martyrology of Auxerre of *c.* 1000, and in the 'Consuetudines Cluniacenses' of Udalricus. Two such receptacles dating from the 12th cent. are still extant. To-day their use survives only in very few churches, e.g. in the cathedral of Amiens and in the Greek college of Sant' Atanasio in Rome.

F. Sühling, *Die Taube als religiöses Symbol im christlichen Altertum* (Römische Quartalschrift Suppl., xxiv; 1930), with full reff. Id., 'Taube und Orante. Ein Beitrag zum Orantenproblem' in *R.Q.*, xxxix (1931), pp. 333–54. W. Stegel, *Das Taubensymbol des Heiligen Geistes* (1904). J. P. Kirsch in *D.A.C.L.*, iii (pt. 2; 1914), cols. 2198–231, s.v. 'Colombe'. On the Eucharistic Dove, F. Raible, *Der Tabernakel einst und jetzt* (1908), pp. 131–52; Braun, *C.A.*, ii (1924), pp. 608–616, with plates, 353–5; id., *A.G.*, pp. 319–23.

DOWNSIDE ABBEY. St. Gregory's Abbey, Downside, near Bath, is the premier house of the English *Benedictine Congregation. It traces its origin to a small settlement of English monks founded by Bl. John Roberts at *Douai in 1605, for which a monastery was built in 1611 with a school attached for the education of English RC boys. Expelled from Douai in the French Revolution, the monks found refuge in England where Sir Edward Smythe put his Shropshire country seat at their disposal. In 1814 the community moved to Downside. In 1899 it was raised from the status of a priory to that of an abbey. It is to-day one of the centres of RC life in England, maintaining in its own buildings its large and important school. The Abbey church, finished in 1925, is one of the finest examples of modern Gothic in England. The monks, who carry on the Benedictine liturgical tradition, edit a quarterly periodical, *The Downside Review*, chiefly devoted to Church history, esp. monastic interests and philosophy. Scholars of distinction at Downside in recent times include F. A. *Gasquet, E. C[uthbert] Butler (1858–1934),

R. H. *Connolly, and B. C[hristopher] Butler (b. 1902).

H. N. Birt, O.S.B., *Downside*. The History of St. Gregory's School from its Commencement at Douay to the Present Time (1902). H. van Zeller, O.S.B., *Downside By and Large* (1954). Artt. in *The Downside Review*, xxxiii (1914). *Downside Abbey*. Church Guide (1905 and subsequent edd.).

DOWSING, WILLIAM (? 1596–? 1679), Puritan iconoclast. He is remembered for his energy in carrying out the order of Parliament of 1643 for the destruction of the ornaments in churches. He was employed on this work under the Earl of Manchester in Cambridgeshire (1643–4) and in Suffolk (6 Jan.–1 Oct. 1644), and his journal testifies to the zeal and completeness of his work. At the Restoration he was left unpunished, and died in obscurity.

The original MS. of the *Suffolk Journal* is lost. The *Journal* was first printed by R. Loder (1786) from a transcript made in 1704 when the original MS. was sold. Loder's text was reprinted in 1840 and 1844. The original MS. of the *Cambridge Journal* is also lost, but a transcript survives in the Baker MSS., vol. 38 (c. 1738), pp. 455–8 and 471–3, in the Cambridge University Library. It was first published by Z. Grey in 1739, apparently from a different MS. There is a modern edition by A. C. Moule (Cambridge, 1926).

DOXOLOGY. An ascription of glory (Gk. δόξα) to the Persons of the Holy Trinity. (1) The Greater Doxology is the *Gloria in Excelsis*. (2) The Lesser Doxology is the *Gloria Patri*. (3) Metrical versions of the Lesser Doxology, in some cases with special reference to a particular mystery of Christ or season of the Church, were appended to the hymns of the *Breviary, and in later times to other hymns also. Among the most familiar of these in English is the verse which begins 'Praise God from Whom all blessings flow,' written by T. *Ken.

DRAGONNADES (1683–6). The fierce attacks, so named from their being carried out by mounted troops ('dragoons'), which were made on the *Huguenots under the direction of Louis XIV with a view to crushing their independence and forcing them to accept the Catholic religion. Their alleged success in inducing the great majority of the Huguenots to accept the faith was made a pretext for revoking the Edict of *Nantes on 18 Oct. 1685.

E. Lavisse, *Histoire de France depuis les origines jusqu'à la Révolution*, vii (pt. i; 1905), pp. 64–6 and 72–5; A. J. Grant in *C.M.H.*, v (1908), p. 24, with bibl. p. 766. See also works cited under *Nantes, Edict of*.

DRAMA, Christian. In the first centuries of the Christian era, drama existed only in the form of *spectacula* which necessarily incurred the deep hostility of the Church. All plays, in the remote historical origins of the dramatic art, were acts of religious worship; and even the sterilizing degeneration of Classical and post-Classical polytheism had not destroyed the superficially liturgical character of the public shows. To take part, even as a spectator, in such a performance was to make an overt act of paganism, whether or not any definitely idolatrous ceremony was involved in it. This is the chief foundation of *Tertullian's invective in his *De Spectaculis* (c. 200). Besides, the moral tendency of the pagan shows was wholly inconsistent with the Christian character, as two examples — the gladiatorial combats and the obscene comedies — sufficiently prove. Tertullian used this argument, but it was more thoroughly developed by *Cyprian (3rd cent.) and *Chrysostom (4th cent.). The pagans themselves acknowledged the demoralizing effect of their spectacles; the Emp. *Julian forbade pagan priests to go to the theatre (363); and *Augustine's friend, Alypius, though a heathen, abhorred all such 'deadly amusements' in his first youth (c. 370). A third cause of the antagonism of the early Church towards *spectacula* in general lay in the supposed opposition between that asceticism implicit in the Christian profession and the pursuit of secular pleasures.

The destruction of the Roman Empire and of the Imperial religion involved the disappearance of the traditional pagan shows, and although plays of a kind were certainly performed in various places throughout the Dark Ages, the drama ceased to present an important problem for the Christian conscience. In the 9th cent. two significant documents indicate a new development. The Saxon nun, *Hrosvit, wrote a number of edifying 'comedies' in imitation of Terence, and the English monk, *Ethelwold, described the 'praiseworthy custom' of celebrating the death and resurrection of Christ by a representation, with mime and dialogue, to be performed in church during or after the liturgical rites. Hrosvit was doubtless wholly ignorant of the conditions of dramatic performance, and the inventors of the earliest Resurrection 'play', using the *trope *Quem quaeritis*, were only developing a representational or dramatic tendency implicit in all liturgical worship, and esp. marked in the *Gallican Rite. In the later Middle Ages the composition and presentation of Latin 'comedies' became a normal exercise in scholastic establishments, and prepared the way for the Classical drama of the Renaissance, while the liturgical drama developed into the *Mystery (or Miracle) Plays (q.v.). Already in the 11th cent. a robustly comic element had found its way, in the characters of Balaam and Herod, into plays actually performed in Church: the *Mystère d'Adam* (12th cent.) has stage directions which show that it was performed outside the church, and mark the final elimination of all liturgical spirit by a deliberately naturalistic technique of *décor* and production.

Side by side with the elaboration of the mysteries and miracle plays, there took place a great development of purely secular drama in all parts of Christendom. The attitude of the medieval Church towards stage plays in general was not wholly consistent, and individual instances of intolerance can be found: but since most of the plays were at least ostensibly edifying, and the players organized in ostensibly pious confraternities, the traditional hostility of the early Fathers to the *spectacula* had no longer any direct relevance to the changed situation. Since the 16th cent. the drama has been once more released from the ecclesiastical connexion. The more puritanical of the Reformers and their followers, e.g. W. *Prynne, tended to repudiate the stage altogether, though T. *Beza wrote mystery plays for a Protestant public. But on the whole, Christian people, while exhibiting a certain mistrust of the moral effects of play-going and esp. of acting, have acquiesced in the establishment of the drama as a normal part of social life. The traditional religious plays have survived in various parts of the world (see *Oberammergau*), while in quite recent times there has been a considerable revival of expressly religious drama in England, e.g. such plays as T. S. *Eliot's *Murder in the Cathedral* (1935). This movement is fostered by the 'Religious Drama Society'.

G. Crosse, *The Religious Drama* ('The Arts of the Church', 1913). K. Hase, *Das geistliche Schauspiel* (1858; Eng. tr., 1880); M. Sepet, *Le Drame chrétien au moyen-âge* (1878). E. K. Chambers, *The Medieval Stage* (2 vols., 1903); K. Young, *The Drama of the Medieval Church* (2 vols., 1933), with bibl. O. Cargill, *Drama and Liturgy* (New York, 1930). E. de Coussemaker, *Drames liturgiques du moyen-âge*. Texte et musique (1861). A. W. Pollard (ed.), *English Miracle Plays, Moralities and Interludes*. Specimens of the Pre-Elizabethan Drama, ed., with introd., notes, and glossary (1870). H. Craig, *The English Religious Drama of the Middle Ages* (1955). M. J. Rudwin, *A Historical and Bibliographical Survey of the German Religious Drama* (University of Pittsburgh Studies in Language and Literature; 1924). G. Cohen, *Le Théâtre en France du moyen-âge* (Bibliothèque Générale Illustrée, vi), i, 'Le Théâtre religieuse' (1928). M. Sepet, *Origines catholiques du théâtre moderne* [1901].

DREWS, ARTHUR (1865–1935), German anti-Christian apologist. A disciple of E. von *Hartmann (q.v.), he taught from 1896 onwards at the Technical High School at Karlsruhe. Identifying God and world in a 'concrete monism', he held that religion consisted in a man's consciousness of himself as a supraindividual being and that true religion was based solely on reason, not on history. Hence he explained Christianity as a form of *Gnosticism and challenged the historical existence of the Person of Christ. Among his writings were *Das Ich als Grundprinzip der Metaphysik* (1897), *Die Religion als Selbst-Bewusstsein Gottes* (1906), *Der Monismus* (1908), *Die Christusmythe* (2 vols., 1909–11), *Die Petruslegende* (1910), *Freie Religion* (1921), *Die Entstehung des Christentums aus dem Gnosticismus* (1924), and *Die Bestreitung der Geschichtlichkeit Jesu* (1926).

A. Drews also edited the collective work *Der Monismus* (2 vols., Jena, 1908). List of his writings in W. Ziegenfuss (ed.), *Philosophen-Lexikon*, i (1949), p. 256.

DREXELIUS, i.e. Jeremias Drexel [not 'Drechsel'] (1581–1638), spiritual writer. In 1598 he entered the *Jesuit Order, and for many years was professor of the humanities at Augsburg. He is remembered chiefly as the author of a long series of devotional treatises which went through numerous editions and translations and circulated equally among Protestants and Catholics. Among the most popular of them were his *Heliotropium; seu*

conformatio humanae voluntatis cum divina (1627) and his *Noe architectus arcae, in diluvio navarchus, descriptus et morali doctrina illustratus* (1642).

His works are enumerated in Sommervogel, iii (1892) cols. 181–205, and ix (1900), cols. 243–5.

DRIVER, SAMUEL ROLLES (1846–1914), OT and Hebrew scholar. Of *Quaker descent, he was educated at Winchester and New College, Oxford, and in 1870 elected a Fellow of New College. From 1883 until his death he was Regius professor of Hebrew and Canon of *Christ Church (in succession to E. B. *Pusey). His wide and exact knowledge of the OT, combined with sound judgement, caution and a strong Christian faith, did much to foster the spread of the critical view of the OT in Britain. His *Treatise on the Use of the Tenses in Hebrew* (1874) established his reputation as a Semitic scholar; and his *Introduction to the Literature of the Old Testament* (1897) remained a standard work for some fifty years. Before his death he had issued commentaries of one kind or another on about half of the OT, the more notable being those on *Deuteronomy (1895), *Joel and *Amos (1897), *Daniel (1900), and *Genesis (1904). His other writings included *Notes on the Hebrew Text . . . of the Books of Samuel* (1890), *The Parallel Psalter* (1904), *Modern Research as illustrating the Bible* (Schweich Lectures, 1909), and *Ideals of the Prophets* (ed. by G. A. Cooke, 1915). He also collaborated with F. Brown and C. A. Briggs in the preparation of the Oxford Hebrew Lexicon (1891–1905) and contributed extensively to J. *Hastings' *Dictionary of the Bible* and other reference works.

His son, GODFREY ROLLES DRIVER (b. 1892), is also a distinguished Semitic philologist. His writings include *Grammar of the Colloquial Arabic of Syria and Palestine* (1925), *Nestorius: The Bazaar of Heraclides* (with L. Hodgson, 1925), *Assyrian Laws* (with J. C. Miles, 1935), and *Semitic Writing* (Schweich Lectures for 1944, 1948).

W. *Sanday, *The Life-Work of Samuel Rolles Driver*. A Sermon Preached in Christ Church on March 8, 1914 (1914); G. A. Cooke, 'Driver and Wellhausen' in *H.T.R.*, ix (1914), pp. 249–57. Bibl. of his published works in Driver's *Ideals of the Prophets* (ed. by G. A. C[ooke], 1915), Appendix A, pp. 213–34.

DROSTE-VISCHERING, CLEMENS AUGUST VON (1773–1845), Abp. of *Cologne. A native of Münster i.W., he was the descendant of a devout Catholic family of the Westphalian nobility. In 1827 he became Auxiliary Bp. of Münster, and in 1835 he was elected Abp. of Cologne at the suggestion of the Prussian government, who hoped by this step to reconcile the Catholic nobility of Westphalia and the Rhineland as well as the clergy and laity to their policy. Soon, however, he came into conflict with the government through refusing his approbation to theological lectures and publications propagating the doctrines of G. *Hermes, which had been condemned by *Gregory XVI in 1835. The final break occurred over mixed marriages, which led to the Archbishop's imprisonment in the fortress of Minden in 1837 under pretext of treasonable activities. Gregory XVI protested; but the most powerful defence of the Archbishop was J. J. von *Görres' *Athanasius* (1838), which roused the support even of hitherto lukewarm Catholics. The effect of the conflict was a considerable increase in the vigour of Catholic life in Germany. Droste-Vischering was freed in 1839 and retired to Münster. After the accession of Frederick William IV in 1841 the struggle ended in a compromise, the Archbishop retaining his dignity but leaving the government of his diocese to a coadjutor more acceptable to Prussia. His writings included *Über die Religionsfreiheit der Katholiken* (1817), written on the occasion of the tercentenary of M. *Luther's Ninety-Five Theses, and *Über den Frieden unter der Kirche und den Staaten* (1843).

H. J. Kappen, *Clemens August, Erzbischof von Köln. Ein Lebensbild* (1897). Short study by H. Kipper (Frankfurter Zeitgemässe Broschüren, N.F., xxvii, Hft. 2, 1907). J. Will, 'Die achtzehn Thesen des Erzbischofs Klemens August von Köln in ihrer dogmatischen Berechtigung' in *Theologie und Glaube*, xxi (1929), pp. 316–28. F. Lauchert in *L.Th.K*, iii (1931), cols. 462–4.

DRUMMOND, HENRY (1786–1860), politician and *Irvingite leader. After some years in business he entered Parliament in 1810, and although ostensibly a Tory, voted throughout his life independently on the merits of individual measures, giving esp. support to those directed against RCs and Jews, but also taking a vigorous part in secular debates. In 1817 he went to *Geneva, and there carried on a campaign against *Socinianism which split the local Protestant Church. From 1826 onwards he took a leading part in founding the Irvingite body (*Catholic Apostolic Church), in which he held the rank of apostle, evangelist, and prophet, and which he helped greatly to finance. In 1834 he was ordained 'angel for Scotland' by the Irvingites, and continued to preach until 1856.

Short Introductory Notice by Lord Lovaine to his ed. of H. Drummond's *Speeches in Parliament and Some Miscellaneous Pamphlets*, i (1860), pp. iii–ix. J. A. Hamilton in *D.N.B.*, xvi (1888), p. 28 f.

DRUMMOND, HENRY (1851–97), theological writer and revivalist. Brought up in the Free Church of Scotland, he was educated at New College, Edinburgh, and at *Tübingen. In 1874–5 he assisted D. L. *Moody and I. D. Sankey in their mission in Ireland and England and worked with Moody on a similar undertaking in 1882. In 1883 he published his *Natural Law in the Spiritual World*, a work which sought to interpret the spiritual in terms of the principle of continuity evident in the natural order. In his later years Drummond conducted successful missions to several universities of Great Britain. He was also well known as a geologist and explorer in N. America and Central Africa. His other writings include *Tropical Africa* (1888) and *The Ascent of Man* (1894).

Lives by G. A. *Smith (London, 1899) and C. Lennox (ib., 1901). Anthology ed. J. W. Kennedy (New York, 1953), with biog. introd., pp. 19–62. Brief sketches by J. Y. Simpson ('Famous Scots Series', London, 1901) and A. H. Walker (London, 1913). T. Seccombe in *D.N.B.* Suppl. ii (1901), p. 157 f.

DRUMMOND, JAMES (1835–1918), *Unitarian divine. Educated at Trinity College, Dublin, and at *Manchester New College, London, he became in 1860 assistant pastor of Cross Street Chapel, Manchester. From 1885 to 1906 he was principal of Manchester New College, first in London and later (from 1889) at Oxford. In his books he attempted to write without bias either for or against orthodoxy, and valued *Unitarianism rather for its encouragement of theological freedom than for its own particular dogmatic negations. This outlook led sometimes to unexpected and unconventional conclusions. Thus he maintained that the Resurrection and the nature miracles of the Gospels were not *a priori* impossible, though the evidence for affirming them was insufficient, and that, though the Apostle *John was the author of the Fourth Gospel, the gospel was of only very limited historical value. Among his works were: *The Jewish Messiah* (1877), *Philo-Judaeus* (2 vols., 1888), *Via, Veritas, Vita* (*Hibbert Lectures for 1894; 1894), *The Character and Authorship of the Fourth Gospel* (1903), and *Studies in Christian Doctrine* (1908).

A Memorial Introduction by E. Drummond (daughter) and G. D. *Hicks is prefixed to his *Pauline Meditations* (1919), pp. vii–lxii. A. S. *Peake in *D.N.B., 1912–1921*, p. 163 f.

DRY MASS (*Missa sicca*). An abbreviated form of Mass which became customary esp. in the later Middle Ages. It was not properly a Mass at all since the *Offertory, *Canon and Communion were omitted, but it was used on a variety of occasions, e.g. when the priest wished to say a second Mass on a particular day (the prescriptions against *bination prohibiting a proper Mass); on the occasion of pilgrimages, when a priest who had not broken his fast was not available; in rough sea on board ship (then called a *missa nautica* or *missa navalis*); or on hunting expeditions (*missa venatoria, missa venatica*). The celebration of Dry Masses was particularly widespread in France, and made its way even to Rome. It survives among the *Carthusians, who say a Dry Mass of Our Lady in their cells after *Prime. In the Roman rite the Blessing of Palms on Palm Sunday, and in the C of E the *Ante-Communion service when ended with the 'Prayer for the Church Militant', may be regarded as forms of it.

J. Pinsk, 'Die *Missa sicca*' in *J.L.W.*, iv (1924), pp. 90–118.

DRYDEN, JOHN (1631–1700), poet, dramatist, and critic. His first work, *Heroic Stanzas* (1659), which was a tribute to the memory of O. *Cromwell, was followed shortly afterwards by *Astraea Redux*, written to celebrate the return of *Charles II. His verse reached its maturity in his brilliant political satire *Absalom and Achitophel (1681) directed against Shaftesbury. In 1682 he expressed his Anglican convictions in his *Religio Laici*; but, on the accession of *James II he announced his conversion to RC-ism, in 1686, and wrote the *Hind and Panther* (1687), in which Nonconformity and the C of E fall under his lash, while the Church of Rome is the milk-white hind. He has been unjustly charged with time-serving in his changes of faith. He persisted a RC after the Revolution.

The standard ed. of his Works is that of W. *Scott (18 vols., London, 1808), with life as vol. i; revised ed. by G. Saintsbury (18 vols., Edinburgh, 1882–93). Dramatic Works also, ed. M. Summers (6 vols., London, 1931–2); Letters ed. C. E. Ward (Duke University Press, 1942) and Poetical Works ed. G. R. Noyes (Cambridge, Mass., 1950). G. Saintsbury, *Dryden* (1881); A. Verrall ed. M. de G. Verrall, *Lectures on Dryden* (1914). M. van Doren, *The Poetry of John Dryden* (New York, 1920); C. Hollis, *Dryden* (1933); J. M. Osborn, *John Dryden. Some Biographical Facts and Problems* (New York, 1940). H. Macdonald, *John Dryden. A Bibliography of Early Editions and Drydeniana* (1939). L. I. Bredvold–H. Macdonald in F. W. Bateson (ed.), *The Cambridge Bibliography of English Literature*, ii (1940), pp. 262–75.

DUALISM. (1) A philosophical doctrine which holds that mind and matter are distinct, equally real, and not essentially related, as opposed to *monism, which asserts that all that exists has a single ultimate nature.

(2) A metaphysical system which holds that good and evil are the outcome or product of separate and equally ultimate first causes.

(3) The view, attributed to the *Nestorians by their enemies, but repudiated by themselves, that in the Incarnate Christ there were not merely two natures, but two persons, a human and a Divine.

DUBLIN (*Dubh-linn*, 'the black pool'). Christianity was introduced by *Palladius and St. *Patrick, but the present see was not established till 1038, when the Danish king, Sitric II, founded the Cathedral of the Holy Trinity and appointed Donatus its first bishop, who was consecrated by, and subject to, the Abp. of *Canterbury. This dependence came to an end at the Synod of Kells, in 1152, when Dublin was made an archbishopric. In 1162 St. Lawrence O'Toole was consecrated Archbishop, who made his cathedral chapter into a community of canons regular. During his archiepiscopate the invasion of Ireland by the English took place, and after his death (1181) the see was ruled exclusively by English bishops, nominated by the English kings, down to the Reformation. John Comyn (Abp. 1182–1212), St. Lawrence's successor, carried through a strongly pro-English policy. He also laid the foundations of St. Patrick's cathedral and secured new privileges for his see at the expense of *Armagh. In 1536 *Henry VIII appointed George *Browne to the see, who, under *Edward VI, introduced the BCP and was deposed under *Mary. During the next two centuries Dublin had only a few resident RC bishops, most of whom were imprisoned, and the RC see was frequently governed by *vicars-general who,

however, mostly suffered the same fate. Normal Catholic life was resumed at the end of the 18th cent., when, under the *Dominican, Abp. Thomas Troy (1786–1823), *Maynooth College was founded, the pro-cathedral, dedicated to our Lady, was built, and many schools and religious houses established. The old Cathedral of the Holy Trinity, now Christ Church, as well as the Cathedral of St. Patrick, passed to the Church of Ireland during the Reformation. *Trinity College, founded under Queen *Elizabeth in 1591, contains among the books in its famous library the 'Book of *Kells' and the 'Book of *Armagh'. Notable Protestant Archbishops in modern times include R. *Whately (1831), R. C. *Trench (1864), J. H. *Bernard (1915), and C. F. D'Arcy (1919; translated to Armagh in 1920), a considerable philosopher. Since 1929 Dublin has been the seat of a Papal nuntius.

J. T. Gilbert, *A History of the City of Dublin* (3 vols., 1854–9); D. A. Chart, *The Story of Dublin* (Medieval Towns Series, 1907). W. Butler, *The Cathedral of Holy Trinity, Dublin. Christ Church* (1901); J. H. Bernard, *The Cathedral Church of St. Patrick* (Bell's Cathedral Series, 1903). N. Donnelly, *Short History of Some Dublin Parishes* (1906). For ecclesiastical history see also bibl. s.v. *Ireland, Christianity in*.

DUBLIN REVIEW, The. This quarterly RC review owes its origin to M. J. Quin (1796–1843), an Irishman who practised at the English bar. The first issue appeared in May 1836. It has exercised from the first a great influence both within and outside the RC Church. For its success in its earliest years, N. *Wiseman and D. *O'Connell were largely responsible; and it was a quotation from St. *Augustine—*securus iudicat orbis terrarum*—in an article by N. Wiseman in the issue for Aug. 1839, that encouraged J. H. *Newman's first serious doubts about the Catholicity of the C of E. From 1863 to 1878, under the editorship of W. G. *Ward, it strongly supported the cause of Papal Infallibility and attacked theological liberalism. Since 1961 it has been renamed the *Wiseman Review*.

Artt. in *Dublin Review*, cxcviii (1936), pp. 187–321.

DUBOURG, ANNE (c. 1520–59), French Protestant martyr. In 1547 he became professor of civil law in the University of Orléans, and in 1557 *conseiller clerc* to the Parliament of *Paris. Intercourse with French Protestants and the study of the Scriptures and early Church history convinced him of Reformation principles, and at Easter, 1559, he made his communion with the *Huguenots. He now began to defend the Protestants in the Parliament against the frequent attacks of the Catholic party, and a provocative speech in the presence of Henry II led to his arrest. After unsuccessful appeals to various prelates and statesmen, he was burnt at the stake in Paris on 23 Dec. 1559.

La Vraye Histoire contenant l'unique jugement et fausse procédure faite contre Anne Dubourg . . ., publ. Anvers, 1561, repr. in *Mémoires de Condé*, i (ed. 1743), pp. 217–304. J. Viénot, *Histoire de la réforme française des origines à l'édit de Nantes* (1926), pp. 251 f. and 296–9. T. Schott in *P.R.E.* (ed. 3), v (1898), pp. 50–3, s.v., with further reff.

DUBRICIUS, St. (6th cent.), also 'Dyfrig', reputed Bp. of *Llandaff. None of the traditions about him seems to merit credence. He is said to have been a pupil of St. *Germanus of Auxerre (chronologically impossible); to have had his headquarters at Henllan near Ross and at Moccas, whence he established many other monastic settlements; and to have spent his last years as a hermit on the island of Bardsey (Ynys Enlli). He was the subject of many medieval legends, *Geoffrey of Monmouth making him Abp. of Caerleon and asserting that he crowned King Arthur. Tradition also makes him the consecrator of St. *Samson of Dol and of St. *Deiniol. Feast day, 14 Nov.

The sources for his life are all late: *The Liber Landavensis* (Book of *Llandaff; ed. J. G. Evans J. Rhys, 'Old Welsh Texts', iv, Oxford, 1893, pp. 68–86); Geoffrey of Monmouth, *Historia Regum Britanniae*, viii, 12, ix, 4, 12, and 15 (ed. A. Griscom, New York and London, 1929, pp. 413, 432, 437, 453, and 458); late 12th cent. life by Benedict of Gloucester pr. in H. Wharton, *Anglia Sacra*, ii (London, 1691), pp. 654–61. Hardy, i, pp. 40–4. S. Baring-Gould–J. Fisher, *The Lives of British Saints*, ii (1908), pp. 359–82. T. F. Tout in *D.N.B.*, xvi (1888), p. 82 f.

DUCAEUS, FRONTO (1558–1624), Fronton du Duc, *Patristic scholar. He became a *Jesuit in 1577 and was librarian at the College of Clermont at Paris from 1604. He edited many Greek Patristic writings, including those of *Chrysostom (12 vols., 1609–36), *Gregory of Nyssa (2 vols., 1615), and *Basil the Great (3 vols., 1618–38). He also issued an extended reply to *Du Plessis-Mornay's book on the Eucharist.

Sommervogel, iii (1892), cols. 233–49, and ix (1900), col. 254. P. Lejay in *C.E.*, v (1909), p. 181, s.v. 'Duc, Fronton du'; P. Bernard in *D.T.C.*, vi (1920), cols. 930–3, s.v. 'Fronton du Duc'.

DU CANGE, CHARLES DUFRESNE (1610–88), French historian and philologist. He was educated as a lawyer, but becoming dissatisfied with that profession, purchased in 1645 the position of Treasurer of France. His interest in history led him to a special study of Byzantine Greek and Low Latin, of which languages he soon became master. In 1678 he published his *Glossarium ad scriptores mediae et infimae latinitatis* (3 vols., fol.) which remains the principal complete dictionary of late Latin. It is a work of immense erudition based on a great variety of sources. This was followed in 1688 by a similar work on Low Greek (2 vols., fol.). Du Cange is also the author of important works on Byzantine and French history.

The Lat. 'Glossary' has frequently been edited and much expanded. An ed. in 6 vols. was issued by the *Maurists, Paris, 1733–6; standard ed. by L. Favre (10 vols., Niort, 1883–7), with 'Notice sur la vie et les ouvrages de Charles Dufresne Du Cange' appended to vol. ix (separate pagination; it is followed by a detailed list of his works, publd. and unpubld.). A photographic repr. of the Gk. 'Glossary' was issued at Paris, 1943. M. Esposito in *D.A.C.L.*, iv (1921), cols. 1654–60, s.v., with detailed bibl.

DUCHESNE, LOUIS (1843–1922), French Church historian. After being ordained priest in 1867, he continued his theological studies in Rome and subsequently travelled in Greece

and Asia Minor. In 1877 he was appointed professor of Church history at the *Institut Catholique at Paris, a position he temporarily resigned in 1885 owing to the opposition aroused by his lectures on the history of doctrine. From 1895 to his death he was director of the French school at Rome; in 1910 he became a member of the French Academy. He was eminent esp. in the field of Christian archaeology and the history of the early Church, and was often attacked for his bitter criticisms and negative attitude to traditional legends. His works include an edition of the *Liber Pontificalis* (2 vols., 1886–92), *Origines du culte chrétien* (1889; Eng. trans. by M. L. McClure under the title *Christian Worship*, S.P.C.K., 1903), *Fastes épiscopaux de l'ancienne Gaule* (3 vols., 1894–1915), *L'Histoire ancienne de l'Église chrétienne* (3 vols., 1906–10, put on the *Index in 1912; Eng. trans., 3 vols., 1909–1924), *L'Église au sixième siècle* (1925).

E. Dupont, *Mgr Duchesne chez lui en Bretagne* (1923). C. d'Habloville, *Grandes Figures de l'Église contemporaine* (1925), pp. 1–177. F. *Cabrol, O.S.B., 'Monseigneur Louis Duchesne. Son œuvre historique' in *J.T.S.*, xxiv (1922–3), pp. 253–82. A. P. Frutaz in *E.C.*, iv (1950), cols. 1960–5, s.v.

DU DUC, FRONTON. See *Ducaeus, Fronto*.

DUELLING, Christian Attitude to. Despite the protest of the Church, the recognition of the judicial duel by civil law continued till the later Middle Ages; and until the early 19th cent. in England, and much later abroad, the duel, though forbidden by law, was a recognized court of appeal in questions of 'honour' among the upper classes. By C.I.C., can. 2351, participants, spectators, and those in any way concerned in a duel, incur excommunication *ipso facto*. Duellants who die without sign of repentance are excluded from ecclesiastical burial.

V. Cathrein, S.J., in *C.E.*, x (1909), pp. 184–7, s.v.; P. Fourneret in *D.T.C.*, iv (1911), cols. 1845–56, s.v. 'Duel'; A. Scharnagl in *L.Th.K.*, x (1938), cols. 1109–11, s.v. 'Zweikampf'; P. Palazzini–R. Danieli–P. Ciprotti in *E.C.*, iv (1950), cols. 1966–70, s.v. 'Duello'; L. Falletti in *D.D.C.*, v (1953), cols. 3–40, s.v. 'Duel', all with bibl. On the general history of the duel, G. Neilson–L. H. Gray in *H.E.R.E.*, v (1912), pp. 114–17, s.v. 'Duelling', with bibl.

DUFF, ALEXANDER (1806–78), Scottish *Presbyterian missionary. The first missionary of the Established Church of Scotland to India, he arrived at Calcutta in 1830, after twice being shipwrecked. At once he opened a school there, which later developed into a college that became a centre of W. education in India. From 1834 till 1840 he was engaged in stirring up the Church of Scotland to support his work; but shortly after his return to India in 1840 came the Schism of 1843, and Duff, joining the Free Church, lost all his mission property. He nevertheless continued his work, until in 1849 he had to return home. In 1851 (and again in 1873) he was elected chairman of the General Assembly of the Free Church. During his last stay in India (1856–1864) he was largely occupied with the foundation of the University of Calcutta. In 1864 he visited S. Africa, and on his return to Scotland spent much of the rest of his life working for the missionary cause.

Life by G. Smith (2 vols., 1879). *Memorials of Alexander Duff* (1890) by his son. W. Paton, *Alexander Duff* (S.C.M., 1923).

DUFRESNE, CHARLES, SIEUR DU CANGE. See *Ducange, Charles Dufresne.*

DUGDALE, WILLIAM (1605–86), author of the **Monasticon Anglicanum* (q.v.). He spent nearly all his life in antiquarian research. His share in the *Monasticon Anglicanum* began with his meeting in 1638 with Roger Dodsworth, then engaged in collecting documents illustrating the history of Yorkshire and the foundation of monasteries in the N. of England. A little later, in view of the dreaded war, he was commissioned by Sir Christopher Hatton to make exact drafts and records of monuments in the principal churches of England. During the Civil War he was employed by *Charles I in the delivery of royal warrants demanding the surrender of castles held by rebel garrisons. Besides the *Monasticon*, of which the first volume appeared in 1655, his writings included *Antiquities of Warwickshire* (1656), *History of St. Paul's Cathedral* (1658), and *Baronage of England* (1675–6). In 1677 Dugdale was created Garter Principal King-at-arms.

His Visitation of the County of Yorks was pr. in *The Surtees Society*, xxxvi (1859), with index by G. J. Armytage (London, 1872), and ed. J. W. Clay (3 vols., Exeter, 1894–1917); that of Lancs ed. F. R. Raines (Chetham Society lxxxiv, lxxxv, and lxxxviii, 1872–3); that of Staffs ed. H. S. Grazebrook in *The William Salt Archaeological Society*, ii (pt. 2; 1881), pp. 23–65, and by G. J. Armytage–W. H. Rylands (The Publications of the Harleian Society, lxiv; 1912); that of Derby publ. London, 1879; that of Durham ed. J. Foster (London, 1887) and pr. in *The Newcastle upon Tyne Record Series*, v (1925), pp. 1–84; that of Cumberland and Westmorland ed. J. Foster (Carlisle, 1891); that of Northumberland ed. id. (Newcastle upon Tyne, 1891) and pr. in *The Newcastle upon Tyne Record Series*, iv (1924), pp. 1–102. W. Hamper (ed.), *The Life, Diary and Correspondence of Sir William Dugdale* (1827). Short anon. life (London, 1713); life in *Heraldic Miscellanies* (London [1793]), pp. 1–24; W. F. S. Dugdale, 'Sir William Dugdale' in A. Dryden (ed.), *Memorials of Old Warwickshire* (1908), pp. 219–30. D. C. Douglas, *English Scholars* (1939), pp. 31–59.

DUKHOBORS. See *Doukhobors.*

DULIA (Latinized form of Greek δουλεία, 'service'). The reverence which, acc. to Orthodox and RC theology, may be paid to the saints, as contrasted with *hyperdulia* (ὑπερδουλεία), which may be paid only to the BVM, and *latria* (λατρεία), which is reserved for God alone. In classical as contrasted with ecclesiastical usage δουλεία is a stronger term than λατρεία.

DU MOULIN, PIERRE (1568–1658), 'Molinaeus', French Reformed theologian. The son of a Protestant preacher, Joachim du Moulin, whose family had settled at Sedan, Pierre became tutor in 1588 to the young Duke of Rutland. In 1592 he returned from England to the Continent and was appointed professor of philosophy and Greek in the University of *Leyden. From 1599 to 1620 he was minister of the Reformed Congregation at Charenton, and from 1620 till his death minister and professor at Sedan. He took a prominent part in religious controversy, upholding a mediating position which irritated Catholics and Calvinists alike; and more than 80 writings flowed from his pen. Over a long period he kept up relations with many Anglican divines, including *James I. P. *Jurieu (1637–1713) was his grandson.

His Autobiography was publd. in the *Bulletin de l'Histoire du Protestantisme français*, vii (1858). Eng. tr. of his *Nouveauté du papisme, opposée à l'antiquité du vray christianisme* by his son, Peter Du Moulin (London, 1662), with life by id. (no pagination). G. Gory, *Pierre Du Moulin. Essai sur sa vie, sa controverse et sa polémique* (thesis, Paris, 1888); J. Massip, *Un Vieux Prédicateur huguenot. Essai sur les sermons de Pierre Du Moulin* (thesis, Montauban, 1888). G. Bonet Maury in *P.R.E.* (ed. 3), v (1898), pp. 56–60, s.v.

DUNKARDS, DUNCKERS. See *Tunkers.*

DUNS SCOTUS, JOHANNES (c. 1264–1308), 'Doctor Subtilis' or 'Doctor Marianus', medieval philosopher. Very little is known of his life. He was born at Maxton, near Roxburgh, and took the *Franciscan habit, possibly at *Oxford, where he studied theology under William de Ware and later taught himself. C. 1302 he went to *Paris, and five years afterwards to *Cologne, where he died suddenly in 1308.

His teaching combines with the *Aristotelianism prevalent in his time certain elements from the older *Augustinianism. The root difference between him and St. *Thomas (d. 1274) is that in the Thomist system knowledge and reason hold the first place, whereas Duns Scotus gives the primacy to love and the will. Thus he holds that the natural law depends wholly on the will of God and not, as St. Thomas teaches, on His mind, and that it is therefore not absolutely immutable; also that the beatitude of the souls in heaven does not formally consist in the intellectual vision, but in the act of love for God. He is, however, at one with St. Thomas in asserting that revelation does not contradict reason, and has many affinities with him in his theory of knowledge and his psychology, opposing strongly the doctrine of innate ideas which he denies even in *angels. His conception of *form and *matter, on the other hand, differed considerably from the teaching of St. Thomas. Duns Scotus held that 'prime matter' (*prima materia*) was common to all creatures whether heavenly spirits, souls, or bodies, but that there was a plurality of forms, so that in man, e.g., being body as well as soul, there is a spiritual and a corporeal form. The 'principle of individuation' is not inherent in matter but is a third principle (which he calls *haecceitas*), superimposed on matter and form. Duns Scotus has become famous not only for the subtlety of his thought, but as the first great theologian to defend the *Immaculate Conception, which he based on the perfect mediatorship of Christ. He also held, in common with other Franciscan theologians, as against the Thomists, that the Incarnation would have taken place irrespectively of the Fall.

The Scotist system, which was accepted by the Franciscans as their doctrinal basis, exercised a profound influence during the Middle Ages. The word 'dunce', used by humanists and the Reformers to ridicule the subtleties of the Schools, is a curious testimony to its popularity.

Collected edd. of his works [by L. *Wadding, O.F.M., F. Pitigiano, O.F.M., Mauricius a Portu, O.F.M., H. Cavello, O.F.M., F. Lycheto, O.F.M., J. Poncio, O.F.M., and A. Higuaeus, O.F.M.] (12 vols., Lyons, 1639; with repr. of his Life by Wadding from the *Annales*), and F. Vivès (26 vols., Paris, 1891–5); crit. ed. studio et cura Commissionis Scotisticae ad fidem codicum editum, praeside C. Balić (Rome, 1950 ff.). *De Primo Principio*, ed. with Eng. tr. by E. Roche, O.F.M. (Franciscan Institute Publications, Philosophy Series, v; New York and Louvain, 1949). N. Landry, *La Philosophie de Duns Scot* (Paris thesis, 1922); E. Longpré, *La Philosophie de B. Duns Scot* (1924; repr. from *Études franciscaines*); C. R. S. Harris, *Duns Scotus* (2 vols., Oxford, 1927, with full bibl.; erroneously ascribes certain *spuria* to Scotus); P. Minges, O.F.M., *Ioannis Duns Scoti Doctrina Philosophica et Theologica quoad res praecipuas proposita et exposita* (posthumous; 2 vols., Quaracchi, 1930); E. *Gilson, *Jean Duns Scotus*. Introduction à ses positions fondamentales (Études de Philosophie médiévale, xlii; 1952). R. Seeberg, *Die Theologie des Johannes Duns Scotus* (Studien zur Geschichte der Theologie und der Kirche, v; 1900). M. Heidegger, *Die Kategorien- und Bedeutungslehre des Duns Scotus* (1916). [C. Balić,] *Les Commentaires de Jean Duns Scotus sur les quatres livres des sentences*. Étude historique et critique (Bibliothèque de la *R.H.E.*, i; 1927). M. Fernández García, O.F.M., *Lexicon Scholasticum Philosophico-Theologicum* [to Scotus] (Quaracchi, 1910). Überweg, ii, pp. 504–17, with bibl. pp. 765–8. P. Raymond, O.F.M.Cap., in *D.T.C.*, iv (1911), cols. 1865–1947; C. Balić in *E.C.*, iv (1950), cols. 1982–90.

DUNSTAN, St. (c. 909–88), Abp. of *Canterbury. After being attached for some time to the court of King Athelstan, he made his profession as a monk at *Glastonbury (where he had earlier received the tonsure) and c. 943 became abbot. He was a strict ascetic who completely reformed the monastery, insisting on the full observance of the *Benedictine Rule, and under him the monastery became famous for its learning. He became a minister and treasurer under King Edred (946–55), but during the next reign had to migrate to Flanders. After his recall in 957 by Edgar, King of Mercia and Northumbria, he was made Bp. of *Worcester, of London, and, in 959, when Edgar also became King of Wessex, Abp. of Canterbury. The King and the Archbishop together planned and carried out a thorough reform of Church and state. After the death of Edgar, Dunstan and his friend St. *Oswald secured the election of King *Edward the Martyr who continued his predecessor's policy. Edward, however, ruled for only a short time, and under his successor Dunstan's influence began to decrease. The restoration of monastic life, which seems to have been virtually extinct in England by the middle of the 10th cent., was almost wholly Dunstan's work. Among the foundations which he established were those of *Peterborough (966), *Ely (970), and Thorney (972). He zealously supported the cause of learning and himself achieved fame as musician, illuminator, and metal-worker. In the political field his most important work was his support of King Edgar. Feast day, 19 May.

W. *Stubbs (ed.), *Memorials of Saint Dunstan, Archbishop of Canterbury* (Rolls Series, 1874). F. A. *Gasquet and E. *Bishop, *The Bosworth Psalter* (1908), Appendix by L. A. St. L. Toke, 'Some Notes on the Accepted Date of St. Dunstan's Birth', pp. 131–43. J. A. *Robinson, *The Times of St. Dunstan* (Ford Lectures, 1922; 1923), esp. No. iv, pp. 81–103. D. Pontifex, O.S.B., 'St. Dunstan in his First Biography' in *Downside Review*, li (1933), pp. 20–40 and 309–25. Study by Eleanor S. Duckett (London, 1955).

DUOMO (cf. Lat. *domus*, 'a house'). The Italian name for a cathedral, as pre-eminently the House of God's people in the diocese.

DUPANLOUP, FÉLIX ANTOINE PHILIBERT (1802–78), Bp. of Orléans from 1849. A native of Savoy, he was educated in *Paris, and, on being ordained priest in 1825, was appointed *vicaire* of the *Madeleine, whence he was transferred to the church of St.-Roch in 1834. He instituted the method of teaching children known as the 'Catechism of *St.-Sulpice', and became one of the foremost Catholic educationists of France. As superior of the seminary of St.-Nicolas-du-Chardonnet (1837–45) he tried his new educational methods with the greatest success. As Bp. of Orléans, Dupanloup exerted strong pressure on public policy, esp. in education, and was active in securing for the Church the right, conceded by the 'Loi Falloux' of 1850, to conduct voluntary schools. Later he was an ardent advocate of the Pope's claims against the House of Savoy. At the *Vatican Council of 1870 he strongly advised the minority, of whom he was one, to abstain from voting and to withdraw, but he loyally accepted the decision of the Council when promulgated. His published works included *La Haute Education intellectuelle* (1850), *La Femme studieuse* (1869) and several panegyrics and pastoral letters.

Selected Letters ed. F. Lagrange (2 vols., Paris, 1888). Standard life by id. (3 vols., ib., 1883–4; Eng. tr., 2 vols., 1885); cf. [M.] U. Maynard, *Monseigneur Dupanloup et M. Lagrange son historien* (1884). Other lives by M. M. F. Trench (anon., London, 1890) and E. Faguet (Paris, 1914). J. F. Sollier in *C.E.*, v (1909), p. 202 f.; A. Largent in *D.T.C.*, iv (1911), cols. 1949–53, s.v. For works dealing with his relations with the Vatican Council, see bibl. to the latter.

DUPERRON, JACQUES DAVY (1556–1618), French cardinal and statesman. He was the son of a *Calvinist minister at St.-Lô. In 1573 he came to the court of Paris, and under the influence of his studies of the Fathers and the Schoolmen as well as later RC theologians, esp. St. Robert *Bellarmine, was received into the RC Church by the *Jesuits in 1577 or 1578. He became a close friend of Henry III, and after his death (1589) supported *Henry IV, who made him Bp. of Évreux in 1591, and whose conversion he brought about in 1593. In 1595 he went to Rome where he obtained the King's absolution from heresy. He now devoted himself esp. to religious controversy, and in 1600 defeated P. *Du Plessis-Mornay, the 'Pope of the *Huguenots', in a public dispute. He was created cardinal in 1604, and soon afterwards was sent to Rome as chargé d'affaires. He was elected Abp. of Sens in 1606, in 1607 brought about the reconciliation between the Pope and *Venice, and in the same year returned to France. From 1610 he was involved in the conflicts between *Gallicans and *Ultramontanists. In 1611 he attacked E. Richer's *De Ecclesiastica et Politica Potestate*, a defence of Gallican principles, and in 1611–1612 also carried on a correspondence with *James I on the question of the true Church. In the famous 'Harangue' of 1615 he again upheld the Ultramontanes against the *tiers état*. Among his works are the *Réplique à la réponse du sérénissime roy de la Grande-Bretagne* (publd. 1620), in which he defended the identity of the early Church with the modern Church of Rome by quotations from the Fathers, and the *Traité de l'eucharistie* (publd. 1622), in which is incorporated a refutation of Du Plessis.

Collected Works ed. by his nephew, Jacques Duperron, under the title *Les Diverses Œuvres de l'illustrissime cardinal Du Perron* (Paris, 1622), with life, pp. 1–36. Fuller biographies by [J. L.] de Burigny (Paris, 1768) and P. Ferret (ib., 1877). G. Grente, *Quae Fuerit in Cardinali Davy Du Perron Vis Oratoria* (Paris thesis, 1903). C. Constantin in *D.T.C.*, iv (1911), cols. 1953–60, s.v.

DUPIN, LOUIS ELLIES (1657–1719), a theologian of *Gallican sympathies. Though he had connexions with *Port-Royal, he is hardly to be considered a *Jansenist himself. His vast *Nouvelle Bibliothèque des auteurs ecclésiastiques* (some 60 vols., 1686–1719) aroused much opposition, notably from J. B. *Bossuet, through its unconventional treatment of early Church history; but though his views were officially condemned, the book was not put on the *Index till 1757. His other writings include a *Traité de la puissance ecclésiastique et temporelle* (1707) (which, being a defence of the four *Gallican Articles, was immediately attacked), and an excellent edition of the works of St. *Optatus (1700). Shortly before his death he entered into friendly relations (Feb. 1718) with Abp. W. *Wake in an unsuccessful attempt to achieve reunion between the Anglican and Roman Churches.

J. Carreyre in *D.T.C.*, xii (1935), cols. 2111–15, s.v. *Pin*, incl. reff. See also, J. H. Lupton, *Archbishop Wake and the Project of Union, 1717–1720* (1896).

DU PLESSIS-MORNAY, PHILIPP (1549–1623), French statesman and *Huguenot leader. He was a native of Normandy. After the death of his father (1559), his family became Protestants. He studied at *Paris, where P. *Ramus was one of his teachers, and served for a time with Condé. After escaping from the St. *Bartholomew Massacre (1572) he fled to England, and for the next ten years acted as a military leader in the Huguenot cause and as diplomatic agent to William of Orange and *Henry of Navarre. In 1578 he published at London his *Traité de l'Église* and in 1579 completed his *Traité de la vérité de la religion chrétienne*. He actively furthered the proceedings of the general synods of the French Reformed Church and cherished the ideal of

the union of all Protestant Churches. In 1589 he became governor of Saumur where he built a Protestant church and founded (1593) a Protestant university. The conversion of Henry IV (1593), whose trusted counsellor he had been, came as a great blow; but he continued to work hard for the toleration of the Huguenots and secured in 1598 the Edict of *Nantes. In 1598 he issued a treatise on the Eucharist, *De l'institution, usage et doctrine du saint sacrement de l'eucharistie en l'Église ancienne*, the fruit of many years' study. J. D. *Duperron charged its author with several hundred misquotations from the Fathers, and at a public disputation before Henry IV, at Fontainebleau, 4 May 1600, du Plessis Mornay was defeated. His *Mysterium Iniquitatis sive Historia Papatus* (Saumur, 1611; also in French) was an attack on C. *Baronius and R. *Bellarmine. In 1621, after the renewal of persecution under Louis XIII and the occupation of Saumur by royal troops, he retired to his castle, La Fôret-sur-Sèvre, where he died.

Suite des lettres et mémoires de Messire Philippes de Mornay (4 vols.; vol. i, n. pl., vol. ii, La Forest, and vols. iii, iv, Amsterdam, 1624–52; also ed. 12 vols., bound in 7, Paris, 1824–5, with memoir of Mme de Mornay on his life, vol. i, pp. 5–503). Mme de Witt (ed.), *Mémoires de Madame de Mornay*. Édition . . . accompagnée de lettres inédites de Mr et de Mme Du Plessis Mornay et leurs enfants (Société de l'Histoire de France, 2 vols., 1886–7). [David de Liques, and others], *Histoire de la vie de Messire Philippes de Mornay* (Leyden, 1647). T. Schott in *P.R.E.* (ed. 3), v (1898), pp. 80–92, s.v., with reff.

DUPLEX. The Latin name for ecclesiastical feasts known as *Doubles.

DUPLEX QUERELA. In the C of E the form of action open to a cleric whom the bishop refuses to institute to a benefice to which he has been presented. Unlike the patron's corresponding action, *Quare Impedit* (q.v.), it takes place in an ecclesiastical court, viz. the Court of *Arches. Appeal lies to the archbishop of the province. Where the cleric is himself the patron he may sue the bishop either under *Duplex Querela* or *Quare Impedit* but not in both actions at the same time.

DUPLICATION. See *Bination*.

DUPPA, BRIAN (1588–1662), Bp. of *Winchester. In 1629 he became Dean of *Christ Church. A High Churchman, he was in favour with the court. On W. *Laud's recommendation he was appointed tutor to the Prince of Wales (later *Charles II) and the Duke of Gloucester, with the former of whom he retained much influence all his life. In 1638 he became Bp. of *Chichester, and in 1641 of *Salisbury. From 1645 to 1660 Duppa was one of the leaders of the persecuted Church. He remained in close touch with *Charles I till his death, and during the Commonwealth did his utmost to keep the extruded clergy together and held private ordinations as opportunity offered. From 1653 to 1660 he was making plans to preserve the episcopal succession, but no new consecrations in fact took place until the Restoration. In 1660 he was translated to Winchester.

A spiritual manual by Duppa, *Holy Rules and Helps to Devotion, both in Prayer and Practice* (1673), was ed. by B. Parry (1675); it was frequently repr. in the 19th cent. N. Pocock in *D.N.B.*, xvi (1888), p. 242 f.

DURA EUROPOS. This ancient city (the 'Pompeii of the Syrian desert') on the right bank of the Euphrates, half way between Aleppo and Baghdad, first attracted attention in 1921 through the accidental discovery of some paintings here by a British army officer. A preliminary survey was made by J. H. Breasted (1921), and the site systematically excavated by F. Cumont (1922–3) and later jointly by Yale University and the French Academy of Inscriptions (1928–37). The city, which was earlier a Seleucid fortress and then a Parthian caravan city, came into Roman hands *c.* A.D. 165, when it was again made a fortress. It was held until *c.* 256, when it was abandoned. It has yielded a rich harvest of discoveries, among them: (1) a 3rd cent. Gk. fragment of *Tatian's *Diatessaron; (2) the earliest known Jewish synagogue, A.D. 245, with notable paintings of events from OT history; and (3) the earliest known Christian church, *c.* A.D. 232. This last was constructed from two rooms of a private house by removing the partition wall. It had a raised platform, doubtless for the altar, at the E. end, while a third room of the house was converted into the *baptistery.

F. Cumont, *Fouilles de Doura-Europos, 1922–1923* (Paris, 1926). P. V. C. Baur, M. I. Rostovtzeff and others, *The Excavations at Dura-Europos* (preliminary reports of excavations undertaken Oct. 1928–36 in annual sessions issued in 10 vols., New Haven, Conn., 1929–52; final report publd. ib., 1943 ff.). General survey in M. I. Rostovtzeff, *Dura Europos and its Art* (1938), with bibl. to date. G. Bovini in *E.C.*,'iv (1950), cols. 1998–2004, with bibl. (incl. discussion on the Christian church).

DURANDUS OF SAINT-POURÇAIN (*c.* 1270–1332), scholastic philosopher, 'Doctor Modernus', also (by later writers) 'Doctor Resolutissimus'. He became a *Dominican and taught at *Paris, where he lectured on the *Sentences and in 1312 became 'magister in theologia'. In 1313 he was summoned to the Papal Court at *Avignon. Later he became Bp. successively of Limoux (1317), Le Puy-en-Velay (1318), and Meaux (1326). He was one of the earliest exponents of *Nominalism, which he developed in avowed opposition to the teaching of St. *Thomas Aquinas. Rejecting the current doctrine on intelligible and sensible species, he held that the only real entities were individuals, and that the search for a principle of individuation was meaningless. In theology he stood for a sharp contrast between faith and reason, holding, e.g., that rational argument could not disprove that the doctrine of the Trinity did not contain impossibilities. He also held that the presence of Christ in the Eucharist did not preclude the continuing existence of the bread and wine. His principal work, a 'Commentary on the

Sentences', survives in the recensions, (1) before 1308, (2) 1310–12, (3) 1317–27. The objections of his superiors to certain strongly anti-Thomistic theses led him to make certain omissions in the later recensions. His other writings include *De paupertate Christi et Apostolorum* (1322), *De Origine Potestatum et Jurisdictionum* (1329), and a treatise on the condition of human souls after their separation from the body (1333). Eleven articles in the last-named work were censured by a Papal Commission (6 Sept. 1333).

Comm. on the Sentences (third recension) publd. at Paris, 1508; several other edd. in the 16th cent.; crit. ed. of the *Quaestio de Natura Cognitionis* (II Sent. (A) d. 3., qu. 5) by J. Koch (Opuscula et Textus Historiam Ecclesiae eiusque Vitam atque Doctrinam illustrantia, vi; Münster, 1929). *De Origine Potestatum et Jurisdictionum*, publd. at Paris, 1506. *Tractatus de Habilibus* ed. J. Koch (Opuscula et Textus Historiam Ecclesiae eiusque Vitam atque Doctrinam illustrantia, viii; Münster, 1930). *De Visione Dei quam habent Animae Sanctorum ante Iudicium Generale*, pr. in part in O. Raynaldus, *Annales Ecclesiastici*, xv (Cologne, 1652), under the year 1333, Nos 49–57; brief extract from *De Paupertate Christi et Apostolorum*, ib., under the year 1322, Nos. 59–61. J. Koch, *Durandus de S. Porciano, O.P.* Forschungen zum Streit um Thomas von Aquin zu Beginn des 14. Jahrhunderts, Teil 1, Literargeschichtliche Grundlegung (*B.G.P.M.*, xxvi, Hft. 1; 1927). P. Fournier, 'Durand de Saint-Pourçain, théologien' in *Histoire littéraire de la France*, xxxvii (1938), pp. 1–38, with reff. Quétif–Échard, i, p. 586 f. Ueberweg, ii, pp. 518–24, with bibl. p. 768 f. P. Godet in *D.T.C.*, iv (1911), cols. 1964–6, s.v. A. d' Amato, O.P., in *E.C.*, iv (1950), col. 2006, s.v., for further bibl.

DURANDUS OF TROARN (*c.* 1010–88), Abbot of Troarn in Normandy from 1059. His 'Liber de Corpore et Sanguine Domini' was one of the earliest medieval treatments of Eucharistic doctrine. In it Durandus made a vigorous attack on *Berengar of Tours, whom he regarded as holding a purely figurative doctrine of the presence of Christ in the Eucharist. Like *Paschasius Radbertus and his contemporary, *Lanfranc, he upheld the conversion of the elements into the identical body and blood of Christ, but emphasized the spiritual nature of the change; and he was one of the earliest writers to speak of the presence of Christ in the Eucharist as a 'substantial' presence.

His 'Liber de Corpore et Sanguine Domini', orig. pr. by J. L. *D'Achery in an appendix to his ed. of Lanfranc (1648), is repr. in J. P. Migne, *PL*, cxlix, 1375–1424. R. Heutevent, *Durandus de Troarn et les origines de l'hérésie bérengarienne* ('Études de Théologie historique', v; 1912), with bibl.

DURANDUS, WILLIAM (1230–96), Bp. of Mende (hence known as **Mimatensis**) from 1285. He was one of the principal canonists of his day. A legal official of the Roman Curia, he attended Pope *Gregory X at the second Council of *Lyons (1274), the decrees of which he drafted. Some of his writings on canon law, e.g. his *Speculum judiciale*, were very widely studied. His best-known work, however, is his *Rationale divinorum officiorum*, a compendium of liturgical knowledge with mystical interpretation. His *Pontifical was taken, for contents and arrangement, as a model, and is the direct ancestor of the modern *Pontificale Romanum*.

He is to be distinguished from his nephew and successor in the bishopric of Mende of the same name (d. 1330), to whom the authorship of the *Pontificale* is sometimes accredited.

Crit. ed. of his Pontifical by M. Andrieu, *Le Pontifical romain du moyen-âge*, iii (*S.T.*, lxxxviii; 1940), with important introd. J. Berthelé–M. Valmary (edd.), 'Les Instructions et Constitutions de Guillaume Durand, le Spéculateur, d'après le manuscrit de Cessenon' in *Académie des Sciences et Lettres de Montpellier. Mémoires de la Section des Lettres*, 2ᵉ Série, iii (1900), pp. 1–148. Eng. trr., with notes, of the first book of his *Rationale*, with introd. by J. M. *Neale-B.*Webb, *The Symbolism of Churches and Church Ornaments* (1843), and of the third book by T. H. Passmore, *The Sacred Vestments* (1899). V. Le Clerc, 'Guillaume Duranti, évêque de Mende, surnommé le Spéculateur' in *Histoire littéraire de la France*, xx (1842), pp. 411–97, with notes of edd. of his works to date. M. R. von Heckel, 'Eine Kanzleianweisung über die schriftmässige Ausstattung der Papsturkunden aus dem 13. Jahrhundert in Durantis Speculum Iudiciale' in *Festschrift für Georg Leidinger* (1930), pp. 109–18, with note on the name Durandus, p. 110, note 4. L. Falletti in *D.D.C.*, v (1953), cols. 1014–75, s.v. 'Guillaume Durand', with bibl. On William Durandus, his nephew, also Bp. of Mende, with whom he has constantly been confused since the 15th cent., see P. Viollet, 'Guillaume Durnat le Jeune, évêque de Mende' in *Histoire littéraire de la France*, xxxv (1921), pp. 1–139.

DÜRER, ALBRECHT (1471–1528), German painter and engraver. A native of Nuremberg, at first he entered his father's goldsmith business, but in 1486 began the study of wood engraving under Michael Wohlgemuth. After travelling abroad he settled down at Nuremberg. Of his religious paintings, the best known are the Baumgartner altar-piece (the 'Adoration of the Christ Child'; before 1505) and the 'Four Apostles' (1526), both at Munich, and the 'Adoration of the Magi' (1504) at Florence; of his woodcuts, the series known as the 'Great Passion', the 'Little Passion', and the 'Mass of St. Gregory' (all 1511); and of his copperplate work (which is characterized by highly wrought landscape backgrounds), 'St. Eustace with the Stag' (an early product), the 'Virgin with the Monkey' (c. 1500), and 'St. Jerome in his Study' (1514).

Dürer was supreme among the exponents of the late Gothic style. His work is marked by rugged strength and vital action, tempered by classical severity. Although he never renounced his Catholic faith, he felt sympathetic towards the *Reformation, and after his death he was eulogized by M. *Luther. He enjoyed the friendship of the Emp. Maximilian, D. *Erasmus, and many of the chief statesmen, humanists, and reformers of his day.

The three best collections of Dürer's drawings are in the Albertina at Vienna, the Kupferstichkabinett at Berlin, and the British Museum. Editions of his works of art by F. Lippmann–F. Winkler (7 vols., Berlin, 1883–1929; drawings), F. F. Leitschuh (Nuremberg, 1892; engravings), C. Dodgson (London, 1928; drawings from Albertina Coll. at Vienna), and several others. Many of his works ed. for the Dürer Society by C. Dodgson, G. Pauli, and S. M. Peartree (12 vols., 1898–1911). Letters, Diaries, etc., ed. E. Heidrich (Berlin, 1908). Monographs (innumerable) include those by M. Thausing (Leipzig, 1876; ed. 2, 1884; Eng. tr., 2 vols., 1882), [G.] A. Weber (Ratisbon, 1894; ed. 3, ib., 1903), H. Wölfflin (Munich, 1905), E. Panofsky (Berlin, 1915), M. J. Friedländer (Leipzig, 1921), E. Panofsky (Princeton, 2 vols. 1943; ed. 3, 1948; with full list of Dürer's works and useful select bibl., i, pp. 287–96). Bibliography to date of publication by H. W. Singer (Strassburg, 1903; ed. 2, 1928). S. Colvin in *E.B.* (ed. 11), viii (1910), pp. 699–703, s.v.

DURHAM. At the end of the 10th cent. the see of *Lindisfarne was removed to Durham, and a cathedral was begun as a shrine for the relics of St. *Cuthbert. Bp. Carilef began to build the present cathedral in place of the older one in 1093, and replaced the secular clergy by a *Benedictine community, which lasted till the suppression in 1540. The Galilee chapel, projecting from the W. end, was built at the end of the Norman era, and the celebrated Chapel of Nine Altars, with its rose windows and elaborate carving, is Early English. The medieval bishops held immense civil jurisdiction, ranking as Counts Palatine; this dignity, which became less important at the Reformation period, was attached to the see down to the time of W. *van Mildert, bishop from 1826 to 1836. In his episcopate the University of Durham was founded (1832). The see of Durham still shares with those of *London and *Winchester a rank inferior only to *Canterbury and *York, and superior to all others in the two provinces; and the bishop is entitled to sit in the House of Lords immediately he takes possession of his see, irrespectively of his seniority of consecration. A hall at Oxford for students from Durham, established c. 1300 by Prior Richard de Hoton and refounded in 1380 by Bp. Hatfield as 'Durham College', was re-established in 1555 as Trinity College, Oxford.

T. D. Hardy (ed.), *Registrum Palatinum Dunelmense*. The Register of Robert de Kellawe, Lord Palatine and Bishop of Durham 1311–1316 (4 vols., Rolls Series, 1873–8); G. W. Kitchin (ed.), *Richard d'Aungerville of Bury*. Fragments of his *Register and other Documents* (Surtees Society, cxix; 1910); Marjorie P. Howden (ed.), *The Register of Richard Fox, Lord Bishop of Durham, 1491–1501* (ib. cxlvii; 1932). J. Raine (ed.), *Historiae Dunelmensis Scriptores Tres.* Gaufridus de Coldingham, Robertus de Graystanes, et Willielmus de Chambre (ib., ix; 1839). *Sanctuarium Dunelmense* printed in *The Publications of the Surtees Society*, v (1837), pp. 1–90. J. Stevenson (ed.), *Liber Vitae Ecclesiae Dunelmensis* (ib., xiii; 1841). J. Raine (ed.), *The Durham Household Book*: or The Accounts of the Bursar of the Monastery of Durham from Pentecost 1530 to Pentecost 1534 (ib., xviii; 1844). Id., *Depositions and other Ecclesiastical Proceedings from the Courts of Durham extending from 1311 to the Reign of Elizabeth* (ib., xxi; 1845). Id., *The Obituary Roll of William Ebchester and John Burnby, Priors of Durham* (ib., xxxi; 1856). W. Greenwell (ed.), *Bishop Hatfield's Survey.* A Record of the Possessions of the See of Durham, made by order of Thomas de Hatfield, Bishop of Durham (ib., xxxii; 1856). J. T. Fowler (ed.), *Extracts from the Account Rolls of the Abbey of Durham* (ib., xcix, c, ciii; 1898–1901). Id., *The Rites of Durham.* Being a Description or Brief Declaration of all the Ancient Monuments, Rites and Customs belonging or being within the Monastical Church of Durham before the Suppression. Written 1593 (ib., cvii; 1903). J. M. Falkner–A. H. Thompson (ed.), *The Statutes of the Cathedral Church of Durham* (ib., cxliii; 1929). F. Barlow (ed.), *Durham Annals and other Documents of the Thirteenth Century* (ib., clv; 1945). R. A. B. Mynors, *Durham Cathedral Manuscripts to the End of the Twelfth Century* (1939); W. A. Pantin, *Report on the Muniments of the Dean and Chapter of Durham* (privately pr., 1939). W. Dugdale, *Monasticon Anglicanum*, i (ed. 1817), pp. 219–52. B. Willis, *A Survey of the Cathedrals of York, Durham, Carlisle*, etc., i (1727), pp. 221–83. [H. C. Englefield], *Some Account of the Cathedral Church of Durham*, Illustrative of the Plans, Elevations and Sections of that Building [drawn by J. Carter] (1801). R. W. Billings, *Architectural Illustrations and Description of the Cathedral Church at Durham* (1843). J. E. Bygate, *The Cathedral Church of Durham* (Bell's Cathedral Series; 1899); J. Wall, *Durham Cathedral* (Cathedrals, Abbey and Famous Churches; 1930); J. E. C. Welldon–J. Wall, *The Story of Durham Cathedral* [c. 1933]. C. R. Peers, J. Queckett, and F. H. Cheetham in *V.C.H. Durham*, iii, ed. W. Page (1928), pp. 93–114. J. Bilson, 'On the Recent Discoveries at the

East End of the Cathedral Church of Durham' in *The Archaeological Journal*, liii (1896), pp. 1–18; id., 'Durham Cathedral. The Chronology of its Vaults', ib., lxxix (1922), pp. 101–60.

DURHAM BOOK, The. One of the primary documents lying behind the 1662 Book of *Common Prayer. It is a folio copy of the BCP printed in 1619 with MS. annotations in the margin and between the lines. These MS. notes, by J. *Cosin (q.v.) and his chaplain, W. *Sancroft, were designed as a first draft for the revision of 1662. They appear to have been begun *c.* 1626/7, but for the most part they belong to the summer of 1661; and they included the proposals of the *Savoy Conference (Apr.–July 1661). The Book is preserved in the Cosin Library, Durham (formerly D. 3. 5, now in a special safe). A fair copy was made by W. Sancroft later in 1661 in another copy of the BCP (printed in 1634); this now exists in the Bodleian Library (Auct. v. 3. 16). Most of the proposals in Sancroft's 'Fair Copy' were taken over into the 'Convocation Book' and the '*Annexed Book' (q.v.) and thus found their way into the 1662 BCP.

Text, with full introd., notes, and bibl., ed. by G. J. Cuming (London, 1961).

DURIE, JOHN (1596–1680), Protestant Scottish divine. Appointed in 1628 minister to the English Company of Merchants at Elbing in Prussia, he devised plans for the reunion of the non-RC Churches, esp. the *Lutherans and *Calvinists, and between 1630, when his appointment ceased, and 1633 visited various dignitaries in England and on the Continent on behalf of his designs. In 1634 he was ordained priest in the C of E, and made a chaplain to the King, and down to 1641 he again travelled widely in the cause of religious unity. In the Civil War he was at first a royalist, and tutor at The Hague to Princess Mary of Orange, but in 1643 he took up a chaplaincy at Rotterdam, and in 1645 returned to London to take part in drawing up the *Westminster Confession and Catechisms. From 1645 to 1654 he was in England, but made another tour for negotiation from 1654 to 1657, meeting with nothing but acrimony from the Lutherans. His bases of reunion were too vague to win enthusiasm. Being out of favour at the Restoration, he left England again in 1662, and settled at Cassel, where he died.

Durie's pamphlet, *A Case of Conscience*: whether it be lawful to admit Jews into a Christian Commonwealth (orig. publd. *c.* 1650), is repr. from the ed. of 1656 in *The Harleian Miscellany*, vii (1811), pp. 251–5; *The Reformed Librarie-Keeper* (1650) was ed. by Ruth S. Grannis (Chicago, 1906), with biographical sketch, pp. 9–36. Study by J. M. Batten (Chicago, 1944), with list of his works. G. Westin, *Negotiations about Church Unity, 1628–1634* (Uppsala Universitets Årsskrift, 1932, Teologi 3). J. Westby-Gibson in *D.N.B.*, xvi (1888), pp. 261–3.

DUVERGIER DE HAURANNE. See *Saint Cyran, Abbé de.*

DYFRIG, St. See *Dubricius, St.*

DYKES, JOHN BACCHUS (1823–76), writer of hymn tunes. He was educated at St. Catherine's College, Cambridge, where he was a noted amateur musician. Ordained deacon in 1847, he became a minor canon at *Durham cathedral in 1849 and vicar of St. Oswald's, Durham, in 1862, where his High Church sympathies led to a long and unhappy conflict with his Bishop (Charles Baring). His melodic hymn-tunes, of which many were included in *Hymns Ancient and Modern*, became very popular. Among them were those to 'Jesu, Lover of my soul', 'The King of Love my Shepherd is', 'Holy, Holy, Holy!' and 'Saviour, again to Thy dear Name we raise'.

J. T. Fowler (ed.), *Life and Letters of John Bacchus Dykes* (1897).

DYOPHYSITES (Gk. δυοφυσῖται, from δύο, 'two', and φύσις 'nature'; the form διφυσῖται is also found). A title used by the *Monophysites for the Catholics in reference to the orthodox belief that in the Person of Christ there coexist the two separate natures of God and man, and not one composite nature. In modern times it has been used by F. *Loofs as a distinguishing mark of the Christology of the *Antiochene school of theologians.

DYOTHELETES (Gk. δύο, 'two', θέλημα, 'will'). Those who, as against the *Monothelites, hold the orthodox doctrine that in the Person of Christ there are two separate wills, the one human and the other Divine.

DYSTELEOLOGY. A term introduced by E. Häckel to denote 'purposelessness of nature' (the opposite of 'teleology'). It is also used of the study of certain rudimentary organs, thought by some to be purposeless in the evolution of species.

E

'E.' The name given (since the work of J. *Wellhausen) to the Elohistic (Heb. *'elohim*, 'God') source held to be embodied in the *Pentateuch. It consists largely of narrative, and together with 'J' (q.v.) comprises most of the famous stories of the Patriarchs and Exodus; it is distinguished from 'J' by its regular use of '*elohim*' ('God') where 'J' uses the divine name Yahweh (Jahveh or Jehovah). It is commonly dated somewhat later than 'J' (perh. 8th cent. B.C.) but, as with 'J,' it is increasingly recognized that precise dating is from the nature of the source impossible.

EADMER (*c.* 1055–*c.* 1124), historian and theologian. He was brought up from childhood at the monastery of Christ Church, *Canterbury, where he eventually became precentor. In 1121 he was offered the Bishopric of St. Andrews, but he was never consecrated. His writings include a valuable Life of St. *Anselm, to whom he was greatly devoted at Canterbury; the Lives of some of the early English saints (including *Wilfrid and *Dunstan); and a *Historia Novorum in Anglia* covering the period from *c.* 1066 to *c.* 1120, an important source for the history of its times. The *Tractatus de conceptione S. Mariae*, formerly attributed to St. Anselm, and one of the earliest systematic treatises on the doctrine of the *Immaculate Conception of the BVM, which it defends, is probably also his work.

Collected ed. of his works appended to those of St. Anselm ed. G. Gerberon, O.S.B. (Paris, 1675; sep. pagination); repr. from the Paris ed. of 1721 in J. P. Migne, *PL*, clix, 345–808, with reff.; life of Anselm, ib., clviii, 49–118. Eadmer's *Historia Novorum in Anglia* and *Vita Sancti Anselmi*, also ed. M. Rule (R.S., 1884, with introd.); his life of St. Dunstan, ed. W. *Stubbs, *Memorials of Saint Dunstan* (R.S., 1874), pp. 162–249; his life of St. Wilfrid, ed. J. Raine, *The Historians of the Church of York and its Archbishops* (2 vols., R.S., 1879–86), vol. i, pp. 161–226, together with a 'Breviloquium Vitae Sancti Wilfridi', perhaps by Eadmer, pp. 227–37; his life of St. *Oswald, ed. id., ib., ii, pp. 1–59. *Tractatus de Conceptione Sanctae Mariae*, ed. H. Thurston, S.J.–T. Slater, S.J. (Freiburg i.Br., 1904). 'Nova Opuscula de Sanctorum Veneratione et Obsecratione', ed. A. *Wilmart, O.S.B., in *Rev. S.R.*, xv (1935), pp. 184–219 and 354–79. A. W. Burridge, *White Father, 'L'Immaculée Conception dans la théologie de l'Angleterre médiévale' in *R.H.E.*, xxxii (1936), pp. 570–97, esp. pp. 581–8, with reff. to earlier discussions on the chronology of Eadmer's life. A. J. Macdonald, 'Eadmer and the Canterbury Privileges' in *J.T.S.*, xxxii (1931), pp. 39–55. See also bibl. to *Anselm*.

EADMUND, St. See *Edmund, St.*

EARLE, JOHN (*c.* 1601–65), Bp. of *Salisbury. He was born at *York, educated at *Christ Church and Merton College, Oxford, and early secured literary fame by his *Microcosmography, or A Piece of the World* (1628), a pleasing and popular collection of character studies modelled on those of Theophrastus. He attracted royal favour by his pleasing manners

and was appointed tutor to Charles, Prince of Wales. In 1643 he became Chancellor of Salisbury Cathedral, but was soon deprived by the *Puritans. He accompanied *Charles II in his exile, and at the Restoration was appointed in quick succession Dean of *Westminster (1660), Bp. of *Worcester (1662), and Bp. of Salisbury (1663). In the administration of his diocese he showed himself tolerant towards Nonconformists and a critic of the *Conventicle and *Five Mile Acts.

Modern edd. of Earle's *Microcosmography* by P. Bliss (London, 1811) and by A. S. West (Cambridge, 1897); also later edd. List of edd. in *C.B.E.L.*, i, p. 722 f. G. G. Perry in *D.N.B.*, xvi (1888), p. 320 f.

EARTHQUAKE SYNOD, The. The Synod held at Blackfriars, London, under Abp. W. *Courtenay on 21 May 1382, during which the city was shaken by an earthquake. It condemned as heretical 24 theses from the writings of J. *Wycliffe, some of them identical with those condemned in *St. Paul's Cathedral on 19 Feb. 1377 with new articles against the begging friars, *transubstantiation, etc.

Hardouin, vi, cols. 1889–1900; Mansi, xxvi (1784), cols. 695–706. The twenty-four propositions condemned and the list of members of the Council are also pr. in W. W. Shirley (ed.), *Fasciculi Zizaniorum* (R.S., 1858), as appendices iv and v, pp. 493–7 and 498–500 respectively; account of synod, ib., p. 272 f. Hefele–Leclercq, vi (pt. 2; 1915), pp. 1406–16 (on synods of 1377 and 1382). See also bibl. to *Wycliffe, John*.

EASTER. The Feast of the Resurrection of Christ, being the greatest and oldest feast of the Christian Church. Its importance is emphasized liturgically by the long preparation of *Lent and *Passion-tide, by the special ceremonies of *Holy Week, and by the following *Paschal-tide (till the Saturday before *Trinity Sunday), characterized both in E. and W. by the frequent reiteration of *Alleluia at the *Mass and in the Divine *Office, as the expression of Easter joy. In the ancient Church the *catechumens, after watching all Saturday night, were baptized early on Easter Day and received Holy Communion. The night before Easter was celebrated by the illumination of the churches and even whole cities. In the E. Church the original night vigil has been kept unaltered, but in the W. it was put back to the afternoon in the 10th cent., and to the morning of *Holy Saturday in the 14th, so that in the RC Church the first Easter Mass came to be celebrated on Saturday. Since 1950, the early custom of offering the first Mass of Easter at midnight on the Saturday-Sunday has been gradually restored. The BCP provides special anthems for use on Easter Day in place of the *Venite.

The derivation of the name 'Easter' is uncertain. Acc. to *Bede, it is connected with an Anglo-Saxon spring goddess 'Eostre'. At any rate it seems clear that, as in the case of Christmas (q.v.), the Christian feast of Easter has superseded an old pagan festival. The popular custom of exchanging 'Easter eggs' is of very ancient origin.

The date of the Easter feast is determined by the Paschal Full Moon, its extreme limits being 21 Mar. and 25 Apr. In the early Church, the two principal methods of computation were those of *Alexandria (owing to its astronomical resources) and *Rome. For the various disputes on the subject see *Paschal Controversies*.

There seems to be no satisfactory single treatment of the whole subject. On the early history of the feast, cf. H. Schürmann, 'Die Anfänge christlicher Osterfeier' in *T.Q.*, cxxx (1951), pp. 414–25; O. Casel, O.S.B., 'Art und Sinn der ältesten christlichen Osterfeier' in *J.L.W.*, xiv (1938), pp. 1–78; Christine Mohrmann, 'Pascha, Passio, Transitus' in *E.L.*, lxvi (1952), pp. 37–52. On the religious and theological significance of the observance, L. Bouyer, Cong. Orat., *Le Mystère pascal* (Lex Orandi, vi; 1945; Eng. tr., 1951). F. L. Cross, *1 Peter*. A Paschal Liturgy (1954). F. G. Holweck–H. Thurston, S.J., in *C.E.*, v (1909), pp. 224–30; H. *Leclercq, O.S.B., in *D.A.C.L.*, xiii (pt. 2; 1938), cols. 1521–74, s.v. 'Pâques'; J. B. Lehner–G. Kieffer in *L.Th.K.*, vii (1935), cols. 809–15, s.v. 'Ostern'; P. Siffrin, O.S.B., in *E.C.*, ix (1952), cols. 898–901, s.v. 'Pasqua, II: la pasqua cristiana'. See also bibl. to *Paschal Controversies*.

EASTER LITANY. The principal confession of faith of the *Bohemian Brethren. It takes the form of the *Apostles' Creed with considerable expansions, mainly from Scripture, though it is conceived more as an act of worship than as a dogmatic formulary and is designed primarily for use in church on Easter morning. It dates from 1749.

The text (German and English) is printed in P. Schaff, *The Creeds of Christendom*, iii (1877), pp. 799–806.

EASTWARD POSITION. The practice of the celebrant of the Eucharist standing on the west side of the altar and facing east, which was introduced at *Rome in the 8th or 9th cent. (previously the celebrant had faced west), had probably been customary in other places much earlier. The authority for its use in the C of E depends on the interpretation of three rubrics in the BCP, viz. the fourth rubric at the beginning of the service, the rubric before the absolution, and the rubric before the prayer of consecration. The first of these, which dates from 1552, legislated for the time when the altar-table was placed, at the time of a celebration of the Communion, in the body of the church or chancel. Since the traditional altar-wise position came back in the 17th cent., the rubric, although retained in the 1662 BCP, has strictly ceased to be applicable, though in 1890 Abp. E. W. *Benson pronounced the Eastward Position to be a legitimate interpretation of this rubric. The second rubric is less precise. The third rubric has been interpreted legally as permitting either position, provided the 'manual acts' are visible to the congregation. In practice, the Eastward Position is now almost universally adopted in the C of E, except in extreme Evangelical churches, where the '*north end' is taken.

EBEDJESUS (Abdh-isho bar Berikha) (d. 1318). The last important *Nestorian theological writer. He became Bp. of Sigar and Bêt Arabâjê in 1284/5, and a little later Metropolitan of Armenia. His (Syriac) writings (some of them lost, as is shown by a catalogue he drew up) included treatises on philosophy and science, a commentary on the Bible, and a work against all forms of heresy. Those which survive include his *Margaritha* ('the Pearl'), a theological work, his *Nomocanon*, a collection of ecclesiastical *canons, and his *Paradisus-Eden*, a series of 50 poems, as well as others which are still unpublished.

His Collection of Canons and his 'Epitome Canonum Apostolicorum', with a Lat. tr. by [J.] A. *Assemani, are printed by A. *Mai, *S.V.N.C.*, x (Rome, 1838), pp. 1–331. A. *Baumstark, *Geschichte der syrischen Literatur* (1922), pp. 323–5, incl. full reff.

EBERLIN, JOHANN (1470–1533), Reformation controversial writer. He was born at Günzburg-on-the-Danube (Bavaria), and became a *Franciscan. He gave his support to M. *Luther almost from the outset, and in 1521 published a series of 15 pamphlets (the *Bundsgenossen*), with such titles as 'Of the forty days fast before Easter and others which pitifully oppress Christian folk', 'How very dangerous it is that priests have not wives', 'Against the false clergy, barefooted monks, and Franciscans'. In other early writings he sought to foster radical social changes. The extremities of the *Anabaptists and others, and the failure of the Reforming Movement in Germany to sustain the moral standards of its opening years, led him to take a more moderate line in his later writings. As a diversion he produced a German translation of Tacitus's *Germania*.

Ausgewählte [sämtliche] Schriften, ed. by L. Enders (3 vols., Neudrucke deutscher Litteraturwerke des xvi. und xvii. Jahrhunderts, Nos. 139–41, 170–2, and 183 and 188. Flugschriften aus der Reformationszeit, xi, xv, and xviii, 1896–1902). B. Riggenbach, *Johann Eberlin von Günzburg und sein Reform-Programm*. Ein Beitrag zur Geschichte des sechszehnten Jahrhundert (1874); M. Radlkofer, *Johann Eberlin von Günzburg und sein Vetter Hans Jakob Wehe von Leipheim* (1887). Studies on his *Bundsgenossen* by J. H. Schmidt (Leipzig, 1900) and W. Lucke (Halle, 1902). Full bibl. in Schottenloher, i (1933), p. 205 f, Nos. 5144–67. T. Kolde in *P.R.E.* (ed. 3), v (1898), pp. 122–5.

EBIONITES (Heb. אֶבְיוֹנִים, 'poor men'). A sect of Jewish Christians which flourished in the early cents. of the Christian era. The several scattered sources from which our knowledge of them is derived cannot easily be harmonized and related. It seems clear, however, that the sect flourished esp. on the E. of the *Jordan and that two of their principal tenets were (1) a 'reduced' doctrine of the Person of Christ, to the effect, e.g., that Jesus was the human son of Joseph and Mary and that the Holy Spirit in the form of a dove lighted on Him at His baptism, and (2) over-emphasis on the binding character of the Mosaic Law. They are said to have used only the 'Gospel of St. Matthew' (? 'the Gospel of the Ebionites'; see following entry) and to have rejected the Pauline Epistles. A poor community, they appear to have adopted a severely ascetic mode of life and to have remained outside the main stream of Christian development. It is difficult to state exactly what their relation was to such sects as the *Nazarenes; A. *Harnack and F. J. A. *Hort identified the two bodies, while J. B. *Lightfoot and T. *Zahn distinguished them.

The sources are scattered. They include *Justin, *Dial. c. Tryph.*, 47; *Irenaeus, *Haer.* I. xxvi, 2; III. xxi. 1; V. i. 3; *Tertullian, *De Praescr.*, 33; *Hippolytus, *Haer.* vii, 34, and ix, 13–17; *Epiphanius, *Haer.* xxx. V. Ermoni, 'L'Ébionisme dans l'Église naissante' in *R.Q.H.*, lxvi (1899), pp. 481–91. M. *Dibelius, *Der Brief des Jacobus* (1921), pp. 37–44. J. M. Fuller in *D.C.B.*, ii (1880), pp. 24–8; G. Bareille in *D.T.C.*, iv (1911), cols. 1987–95; W. Beveridge in *H.E.R.E.*, v (1912), pp. 139–45, with bibl.; H. *Leclercq, O.S.B., in *D.A.C.L.*, iv (pt. 2; 1921), cols. 1703–9.

EBIONITES, Gospel of the.

This apocryphal gospel appears to have been written in Greek on the E. of the *Jordan in the latter half of the 2nd cent. The quotations in *Epiphanius (*Haer.* xxx), from which nearly all that is known of it is derived, show it to have been modelled on the canonical Gospel of Mt. Its *Ebionite affinities are indicated by its vegetarian sympathies (*John the Baptist eats not locusts, but honey) and its *adoptionist Christology. Acc. to Epiphanius, the Ebionites referred to it as the 'Gospel according to the Hebrews' (though it is clearly different from the book described in the entry with that title [q.v.]), and it seems to have been identical with the 'Gospel of the Twelve Apostles' referred to by *Origen (*Hom.* on Lk. 1. 1 ff.). The title 'Gospel of the Ebionites' is modern.

A. *Hilgenfeld, *Novum Testamentum extra Canonem Receptum*, fasc. iv (1866), pp. 32–8. M. R. James, *The Apocryphal New Testament* (1924), pp. 8–10. A. Meyer, 'Ebionitenevangelium (Evangelium der zwölf Apostel)' in E. Hennecke (ed.), *Neutestamentliche Apokryphen* (1904), pp. 24–7. A. Schmidtke, 'Zum Hebräerevangelium' in *Z.N.T.W.*, xxxv (1936), pp. 24–44; H. Waitz, 'Neue Untersuchungen über die sogen. judenchristlichen Evangelien', ib. xxxvi (1937), pp. 60–81.

ECCE HOMO

(Lat., 'Behold the Man!'). The title of the Life of Christ, published (orig. anonymously) by Sir John *Seeley in 1865. It was a typical expression of the phase in 19th-cent. liberal thought which was more interested in the 'historic' Jesus than in the 'metaphysical Christ of the Creeds'. In it Seeley presented in an easy style an attractive picture of Christ as a moral reformer. So much, however, that belonged to the traditional conception of Christ was passed over in silence that the orthodoxy of its author was widely challenged, among others by J. H. *Newman, A. P. *Stanley, and W. E. *Gladstone. The work secured an immense circulation.

There is an edition in the 'Everyman Library', with an introduction by Sir Oliver Lodge.

ECCHELLENSIS. See *Abraham Ecchellensis*.

ECCLESIA DOCENS

(Lat.), 'the teaching Church'. A term used by some Catholic writers of the clergy, who are commissioned to teach the Christian faith, as distinguished from the laity, who are called *ecclesia discens*, 'the learning Church'.

ECCLESIASTES, Book of.

The main theme of the Book, traditionally ascribed to *Solomon, is the worthlessness and vanity of human life. The title 'Ecclesiastes' found in the Greek and Latin versions is an attempted rendering of the Hebrew title 'Qoheleth', which in the AV and RV is translated not quite satisfactorily as 'the Preacher', the probable meaning of the Hebrew word being 'a speaker in an assembly'. In the Hebrew Bible it was the last of the five '*Megilloth' or Rolls, and was read publicly in the Jewish Church on the Feast of *Tabernacles. It belongs to the so-called *Wisdom Literature, a fact which explains its association with the name of Solomon, who is no longer seriously held to be the author. Considerations of subject-matter and linguistic style make it clear that the book is the product of a late age in OT history, and it is known that it was one of the latest books to be admitted to the Hebrew canon. The occasional passages which are out of harmony with its general pessimism are treated by many scholars, e.g. A. H. McNeile, as later interpolations in the interests of orthodoxy and canonicity, although many scholars remain satisfied with the unity of the Book. There have been many attempts, both Jewish and Christian, to interpret the Book so as to bring its teaching into accord with orthodox ethical principles. No direct quotations of it occur in the NT.

Commentaries by G. A. Barton (I.C.C., 1908), G. C. Martin (Cent. Bib. on Prov., Eccles, and Song of Sol., 1908, pp. 211–83), A. L. Williams (Camb. Bib., RV, 1922), H. Odeberg (Uppsala, 1929; in Eng.), F. *Delitzsch (Biblischer Commentar über das Alte Testament, Theil 4, Bd. iv, on Song of Sol. and Eccles., 1875, pp. 191–436), F. Hitzig (ed. 4 by W. Nowack, Kurzgefasstes exegetisches Handbuch zum Alten Testament, vii, on Prov. and Eccles., 1883, pp. 185–314), G. Wildeboer (K.H.C., xvii, on Song of Sol., Ruth, Lam., Eccles., and Est., 1898, pp. 109–68), G. Siegfried (H.K.A.T., Abt. 2, Bd. iii, Theil 2 on Eccles. and Song of Sol., 1898, pp. 1–77), E. Podechard (Études bibliques, 1912), H. W. Hertzberg (K.A.T., xvi, 4; 1932) and K. Galling (H.A.T., Reihe 1, Bd., xviii, on Ruth, Song of Sol., Eccles., Lam., and Esther, 1940, pp. 47–90). C. H. H. Wright, *The Book of Koheleth, commonly called Ecclesiastes, considered in relation to Modern Criticism* (1883). A. H. McNeile, *An Introduction to Ecclesiastes* (1904). G. Kuhn, *Erklärung des Buches Koheleth* (Beihefte zur *Z.A.T.W.*, xliii; 1926). A. Lamorte, *Le Livre de Qohéleth. Étude critique et philosophique de l'Ecclésiastique* (1932). M. Jastrow, *The Gentle Cynic* (1919). J. Pedersen, 'Scepticisme israélite' in *R.H.P.R.*, x (1930), pp. 317–70 (repr. as Cahiers de la *R.H.P.R.* [No. 22], 1931).

ECCLESIASTICAL COMMISSIONERS.

The body which from 1835 to 1948 managed the estates and revenues of the C of E. In 1835 two commissions were appointed to consider reforms in the allotment of Church revenues; and in the following year an Act of Parliament (6 & 7 Will. IV, c. 77) was passed, establishing a permanent body of Ecclesiastical Commissioners, who were constituted a corporation with power to hold and purchase lands and to prepare schemes for the alteration and redistribution of ecclesiastical revenues. Its constitution was several times amended. In 1948 it consisted of the archbishops and bishops of England, the deans of *St. Paul's, *Westminster, and *Canterbury, the Lord

Chancellor, the Lord President of the Council, the First Lord of the Treasury, the Chancellor of the Exchequer, one of the principal Secretaries of State, the Lord Chief Justice, the Master of the Rolls, and certain lay members of the C of E appointed by the crown and the Abp. of Canterbury. The joint treasurers were three lay 'Church Estates Commissioners', two of them appointed by the crown and the third by the Abp. of Canterbury. The Commission presented an annual report to Parliament. In 1948 the Ecclesiastical Commissioners and *Queen Anne's Bounty united in a new body, the *Church Commissioners for England (q.v.).

R. *Phillimore, *The Ecclesiastical Law of the Church of England* (ed. 2, by W. G. F. Phillimore), ii (1895), pp. 1658–1675; H. W. Cripps, *A Practical Treatise on the Law Relating to the Church and Clergy* (ed. 8, by K. M. Macmorran, 1937), pp. 365–72. G. F. A. Best, *Temporal Pillars*. Queen Anne's Bounty, the Ecclesiastical Commissions, and the Church of England, 1704–1948 (1963).

ECCLESIASTICAL COURTS COMMISSIONS.
There were two Parliamentary Commissions on the English Church courts in the 19th cent.

(1) That set up under the influence of Lord Brougham, orig. appointed on 28 Jan. 1830 and reappointed with additional members on 5 July 1830. It included Abp. W. *Howley and five Bishops. Under pressure from Brougham, it recommended (25 Jan. 1831) the replacement of the Court of *Delegates by the Privy Council as the final court of appeal in ecclesiastical matters. The full report, issued in Feb. 1832, advocated many drastic changes, incl. trial by jury in ecclesiastical cases and the abolition of the provincial courts of *York. Some of its less revolutionary recommendations were adopted later in the 19th cent.

(2) That appointed by the Prime Minister (W. E. *Gladstone) and Lord Chancellor (Selborne), at the request of the Abp. of *Canterbury (A. C. *Tait), on 16 May 1881 'to enquire into the constitution and working of the Ecclesiastical Courts as created or modified under the Reformation Statutes of the 24th and 25th years of King Henry VIII and any subsequent Acts'. Its immediate object was to find some new and better way of dealing with the ritual controversies. It consisted of 25 members, among them both Archbishops (Tait and W. Thomson), Bp. E. W. *Benson, Lord Penzance, R. *Phillimore, E. A. Freeman and W. *Stubbs. It recommended in its report (July 1883) a radical revision of the courts, the final court to consist of five lay judges appointed by the Crown, who had formally affirmed that they belonged to the C of E. Only nine of the commissioners signed the report without qualification and Convocation objected to the constitution proposed for the final court. No legislation followed. Several of the appendices to the report, esp. those of Stubbs, are of great historical value.

(1) *The Special and General Reports made to his Majesty by the Commissioners appointed to Inquire into the Practice and Jurisdiction of the Ecclesiastical Courts in England and Wales* (Parliamentary Papers, 1831–2, xxiv [C. 199]). (2) *Report of the Commissioners Appointed to Inquire into the Constitution and Working of the Ecclesiastical Courts* (2 vols.; Parliamentary Papers, 1883, xxiv [C. 3760 and 3761]).

ECCLESIASTICAL DISCIPLINE, The Royal Commission on.
The Commission, appointed in 1904 to inquire into 'breaches or neglect of the Law relating to the conduct of Divine Service in the Church of England and to the ornaments and fittings of Churches' and to devise remedies. Its members included Viscount St. Aldwyn (Michael Hicks Beach, Chairman), the Abp. of *Canterbury (R. T. *Davidson), the Bp. of *Oxford (F. *Paget), E. C. S. Gibson (appointed Bp. of *Gloucester in 1905), the Lord Chief Justice (Lord Alverstone), and the *Dean of the Arches (Sir Lewis Dibdin). Evidence was taken from 164 witnesses, mainly hostile to High Church practice, though its accuracy was not open to serious challenge. This was sent to the Bishops of the respective dioceses concerned for their comment, together with a list of questions relating chiefly to the use of vestments and the obedience paid to the *Lincoln Judgement and the *Lambeth Opinion (qq.v.). The Commissioners reported unanimously on 21 June 1906 that the law of public worship in the C of E was too narrow, and that the machinery for discipline had broken down. They recommended that practices significant of teaching repugnant to the doctrine of the C of E should be made to cease, if necessary by force of law; that Letters of Business should be issued to the *Convocations to regularize the vestments of the minister, and to provide greater elasticity in public worship; that the recommendations of the *Ecclesiastical Courts Commission of 1883 should in the main be carried out; that the *Public Worship Regulation Act should be repealed; and that dioceses should be divided, to secure greater supervision. The Letters of Business envisaged were duly issued on 10 Nov. 1906, thus initiating the long project of Prayer Book Revision (defeated in Parliament in 1927 and 1928): see *Common Prayer, Book of*.

The *Report of the Royal Commission on Ecclesiastical Discipline* [Cd. 3040] and the *Minutes of Evidence taken before the Royal Commission on Ecclesiastical Discipline* [Cd. 3069 and Cd. 3070] are pr. among the Parliamentary Papers, 1906, vol. xxxiii. G. K. A. Bell, *Randall Davidson* (1935), ch. xxv, pp. 454–73.

ECCLESIASTICAL TEXT OF THE NT.
A name occasionally given to the *Byzantine text on the ground that it was the text which established itself for official use in the Greek-speaking Church.

ECCLESIASTICAL TITLES ACT (1851).
The Act (14 & 15 Vict. cap. 60) passed at the time of the '*Papal Agression' forbidding the assumption by RCs of territorial titles within the United Kingdom under penalty of a fine, and rendering void all bequests or donations made to persons under such titles. It was introduced as a counter-measure to the restitution of the RC hierarchy in 1850, but, being a dead letter from the first, was repealed by the Ecclesiastical Titles Act, 1871 (34 & 35 Vict. cap. 53).

ECCLESIASTICISM. A word, commonly used in a depreciatory sense, for (1) over-attention to the external details of ecclesiastical practice and administration, or (2) the point of view which is formed and guided solely by the interests of the Church as an organization.

ECCLESIASTICUS. Book of the *Apocrypha, orig. 'the Wisdom (or 'Proverbs') of Jesus the son of Sirach', also known as 'Ben-Sira' or 'Sirach'. The name 'Ecclesiasticus' is found already in *Cyprian; it is referred by *Rufinus to the Book's pre-eminence among the *deuterocanonical writings as a 'Church Book' (*liber ecclesiasticus*) for the purposes of moral instruction; but this explanation is doubtful since (1) the name is earlier than the distinction between the deuterocanonical ('Apocryphal') Books and the rest of the OT, and (2) other evidence is wanting that the Book occupied this position in the Patristic period, the Apocryphal Book most quoted by the Fathers being Wisd. Sol. The origin of the name therefore remains uncertain.

Ecclus. is one of the *Wisdom writings and was written or compiled by Jesus (i.e. Joshua) the son of Sira of *Jerusalem (prologue, cf. 50. 27). The translator's prologue ('Whereas many', AV and RV) states that the translation was made by the author's grandson in Egypt after 132 B.C. (The first prologue printed in the AV is spurious.) The historical catalogue of famous men (44–50) ends with Simon the son of Onias the High Priest, who appears to be the High Priest of this name who held office *c.* 225–200 B.C. (not his earlier namesake, *c.* 300–270 B.C.). The author also apparently knew nothing of the conflict between faithful Jews and Hellenists which dominates the literature of the *Maccabaean period (*c.* 170 B.C. onwards). Internal evidence thus confirms a date about two generations before 132 B.C. for the original writing. It was presumably composed wholly or mainly in Palestine, though the author was aware of the larger Hellenistic world (cf. 10. 8) and his ideal scribe is represented as travelling abroad and appearing before rulers (39. 4).

The Book was known until recent times only in its Greek translations. A Hebrew text, however, was known to *Jerome and was quoted in the *Talmud. Since 1896 extensive fragments of the Book in Hebrew have been discovered by S. Schechter and others in the *geniza of an ancient synagogue in Cairo. These form parts of two versions, one of them held to be the original of Ben-Sira and the other a recension under *Pharisaic influence; to these correspond two Greek versions, the *textus receptus* and a different recension represented by some MSS. The text represented by the RV (1895) is thus capable of considerable improvement.

Hebrew text ed., with Fr. tr. and comm., by I. Levi (Bibliothèque de l'École des Hautes Sciences, Sciences religieuses, x; 2 vols., 1898–1901); also ed., with Germ. tr., by R. Smend (Berlin, 1906). Separate Eng. tr. of revised text by W. O. E. Oesterley (Translations of Early Documents, Series 1, Palestinian Jewish Texts (Pre-Rabbinic),

ii; 1916). Commentaries by R. Smend (Berlin, 1906), W. O. E. Oesterley (Camb. Bib. RV, 1912), by G. H. Box-W. O. E. Oesterley in R. H. *Charles (ed.), *The Apocrypha and Pseudepigrapha of the Old Testament,* i (1913), pp. 268–517. N. Peters (Exegetisches Handbuch zum Alten Testament, ed. J. Nickel, xxv; 1913) and A. Eberharter (Die heilige Schrift des Alten Testaments, ed. F. Feldmann-H. Herkenne, Bd., vi, Abt. 5; 1925). R. Smend, *Griechisch-syrisch-hebräischer Index zur Weisheit des Jesus Sirach* (1907). R. H. Pfeiffer, *History of New Testament Times with an Introduction to the Apocrypha* (New York, 1949; London, 1954), pp. 352–408.

ECCLESIOLOGY (Gk. ἐκκλησία, a 'church'). The science of the building and decoration of churches. The word was first used in the 19th cent. when interest in ecclesiastical buildings was much increased by such groups as the *Cambridge Camden Society. This Society published *The Ecclesiologist*, until it was later taken over by the Ecclesiological Society, 29 vols. in all (1841–68).

ECK, JOHANN (1486–1543), **Johann Maier 'of Eck'** (his birthplace, Egg an der Günz), hence **Eckius**, German theologian. From 1510 till his death he was professor of theology at Ingolstadt. He came under humanist influences, and his early writings, which included commentaries on *Aristotle and Petrus Hispanus, were almost anti-Scholastic in their theology. In 1514 he attacked the medieval prohibition of interest, defending a return on capital up to 5 per cent, and won support for his thesis at *Bologna and Vienna. Until the controversy over *indulgences broke out, he was on good terms with M. *Luther; but, in the public debate at Leipzig in 1519 he opposed *Carlstadt and Luther, and was largely responsible for procuring the latter's excommunication by the bull '*Exsurge Domine' at Rome in 1520. About this time he wrote an extended defence of the Papal position in *De primatu Petri adv. Ludderum libri III* (Paris, 1521), besides shorter works against Luther; and for the rest of his life he took a prominent part in organizing Catholic opposition to German Protestantism. In 1530 he was the champion of the Catholic attack on the *Augsburg Confession. In 1537 he published a German-dialect version of the Bible for Catholic use.

T. Wiedemann, *Dr. Johann Eck* (Ratisbon, 1865). J. Greving, *Johann Eck als junger Gelehrter*. Eine literar- und dogmengeschichtliche Untersuchung über seinen *Chrysopassus Praedestinationis* aus dem Jahre 1514 (Reformationsgeschichtliche Studien und Texte, i; 1906); id., *Johann Ecks Pfarrbuch für U. L. Frau in Ingolstadt* (ib., iv and v; 1908), with text; A. Brandt, *Johann Ecks Predigttätigkeit an U.L. Frau zu Ingolstadt, 1525–42* (ib., xxvii and xxviii; 1914), with text; H. Schauerte, *Die Busslehre des Johannes Eck* (ib., xxxviii and xxxix; 1919); E. Iserloh, *Die Eucharistie in der Stellung des Johannes Eck*. Ein Beitrag zur vortridentinischen Kontroverstheologie über das Messopfer (ib., lxxiii and lxxiv; 1950). J. P. Kirsch in *C.E.*, v (1909), pp. 271–3, s.v.; J. Metzler in *L.Th.K.*, iii (1931), cols. 523–6, s.v., incl. list of works with notes of modern edd.

ECKHART (*c.* 1260–1327), 'Meister Eckhart', German *Dominican mystic. Born at Hochheim in Thuringia of a noble family, he entered the Dominican convent at Erfurt as a youth, completed his studies at Paris with the degree of master in 1302, became Provincial of the Saxon province of his order in 1304, and was entrusted with the reform of the Bohemian houses in 1307. In 1311 he was sent as a teacher to *Paris. He returned to Germany *c.* 1313, living first at Strasburg and afterwards at *Cologne, where he became one of the most famous preachers of his time. Accused of heretical teaching, he was tried before the court of the Abp. of Cologne in 1326, but appealed to the Pope, and died during the proceedings. In 1329 *John XXII condemned 28 of his sentences as heretical or dangerous. This censure by the Church, though it did not lessen the veneration of his disciples, among whom were J. *Tauler and H. *Suso, seriously affected the circulation of his works, so that to-day the larger part is still lost and the others are only partially or uncritically edited.

The ambiguities arising out of Eckhart's attempt to express the inexpressible and the fact that he was first rediscovered by romantic poets and philosophers out of sympathy with, and often ignorant of, the theological tradition in which he stood, have led to many widely divergent interpretations of Eckhart's teaching. He has been acclaimed as the forerunner of M. *Luther's emphasis on faith, of I. *Kant's Critical Idealism, of G. W. F. *Hegel's *Pantheism, and of the Nazi 'Deutschreligion' (A. Rosenberg). Against these arbitrary assignments, which are agreed for the most part in regarding Eckhart unquestioningly as a pantheist, there has been a steady reaction since his works have become better known, beginning with the researches of H. *Denifle, and Eckhart is now more generally seen in his historical setting as a Dominican, and as dependent for the substance of his teaching on the Schoolmen.

Eckhart wrote in both German and Latin. His German writings, which include Sermons, Treatises, and Fragments, were ed. by F. Pfeiffer (Leipzig, 1857; repr. 1924); several partial edd. have appeared more recently. New collected ed. of *Opera Latina*, ed. Institutum S. Sabinae [by G. Théry, O.P., and R. Klibansky] (Leipzig, 1934 ff.); another ed. (partly under Nazi auspices) by J. Quint for the 'Deutsche Forschungsgemeinschaft', Stuttgart-Berlin, 1936 ff. Eng. tr. of Pfeiffer's ed., with some omissions and additions, by C. de B. Evans (2 vols., London, 1924–31); new translation of selected works by R. B. Blakney (New York and London, 1941). Lives by O. Karrer (Munich, 1926) and A. Dempf (Leipzig, 1934). J. M. Clark, *The Great German Mystics* (1949), ch. ii, pp. 7–35, with bibl. pp. 110–14. Überweg, iv, pp. 553, 651–71, and 779 f. (full bibl.). S. M. Deutsch in *P.R.E.* (ed. 3), v (1898), pp. 142–54, s.v. F. Vernet in *D.T.C.*, iv (1911), cols. 2057–81, s.v. M. Schmaus in *L.Th.K.*, iii (1931), cols. 527–30, s.v. A. Walz in *E.C.*, v (1951), cols. 28–32, s.v., all with bibl. Selected extracts of his sermons, with introd., by J. M. Clark (London, 1957).

ECLECTICISM. Any system of theology or philosophy which, rather than adhere to one school or tradition, selects such elements as seem the best in several systems, and combines them.

ECPHONESIS (Gk. ἐκφώνησις). Esp. in the E. Church, the concluding words, uttered in an audible voice, of a prayer the rest of which has been recited silently (μυστικῶς).

ECSTASY. The term has come to be applied to several preter- or supernatural states which, however, are in no way related to each other.

In the OT many cases of ecstasy are recorded, esp. among the prophets. Here ecstasy usually consists in a sudden seizure of the prophet by the Divine power which spoke through his mouth or showed him the future in visions. These ecstasies, however, were mostly isolated phenomena which were induced *ad hoc* for such purposes as teaching and exhortation.

Mystic ecstasy in the Christian sense is one of the normal stages of the mystic life. St. *Teresa places it between the 'Prayer of Union' and the 'Mystic Marriage'; but as ecstasies have frequently occurred in the case of children (e.g. St. *Hildegard, St. *Catherine of Siena, St. *Peter of Alcántara), this sequence, though corresponding to the normal development, is not a *conditio sine qua non*. The chief characteristic of the ecstatic state is the alienation of the senses, caused by the violence of the Divine action on the soul. The body, unable to bear the strain, becomes usually immovable, and sight, hearing, &c., cease to function. In contrast to the pathological 'case', the mystic remembers what has taken place during the ecstasy, which is usually an intuitive knowledge of some mystery of religion accompanied by a distinct consciousness of the Divine Presence. Moreover, whereas pathological ecstasies lead to a state of increasing enervation, mystic ecstasy, though it may produce temporary physical fatigue, increases not only the sanctity of the ecstatic, but also his powers of reason and will, and frequently prepares him for more vigorous action, as is evident in the case of St. Teresa. Certain physical phenomena, such as levitation and *stigmatization, sometimes accompany the ecstasy, but they are never more than concomitants and do not belong to its essence, which consists in the union of the human will with the Divine.

ECTENE (Gk. ἐκτένεια, 'earnest prayer'; cf. Acts 12. 5, προσευχὴ δὲ ἦν ἐκτενῶς γινομένη, 'prayer was made without ceasing'). In the E. Church, a prayer constructed like a *Litany for use in the Liturgy. It consists of short petitions said by the *deacon to which choir or congregation respond with *Kyrie Eleison.

ECTHESIS, The (Gk. ἔκθεσις, 'a statement of faith'). The formula issued in 638 by the Emp. *Heraclius forbidding the mention of 'energies' (ἐνέργειαι), whether one or two, in the Person of Christ and asserting that the two Natures were united in a single Will (*Monothelitism, q.v.). It had been drafted earlier in the year by *Sergius, Patr. of *Constantinople after consultation with Pope *Honorius (q.v.). It was accepted by Councils held at Constantinople in 638 and 639, but soon disowned by Heraclius as well as by Honorius' two successors in the Roman see (Severinus, 638–40; John IV, 640–2).

The text is preserved among the acts of the Lateran Council of 649, sess. 3; pr., with Lat. tr., in Hardouin, iii, cols. 791–6, and Mansi, x (1764), cols. 991–8. The condemnation in can. 18 of this council is repr. in Denz.–Bann. (ed. 28, 1952), p. 124 f. (No. 271). Hefele–Leclercq, iii (pt. 1; 1909), pp. 387–99, with full reff. L. Bréhier in Fliche–Martin, v (1938), pp. 131–4. See also bibl. to *Heraclius* and *Monothelitism*.

ECUMENICAL COUNCILS, &c. See *Oecumenical Councils, &c.*

EDEN, The Garden of. In the OT, the site of *Paradise, where *Adam and *Eve were created (Gen. 2. 8–17). From it issued the four rivers Pishon, Gihon, Hiddekel, and Euphrates (ib.). The name is prob. connected with the Babylonian *édinu*, 'a plain' (such as would be made very fertile by irrigation), but would suggest in Heb. 'delight'. The writer of the Gen. narrative may have had in mind the well-watered country of Mesopotamia (cf. ver. 14), but the geographical ideas implied are very primitive or even mythological, for Cush (ver. 13) normally means *Ethiopia and hence Gihon was traditionally identified with the Nile. In Is. 51. 3, Ezek. 28. 13 and 31. 9, and Joel 2. 3 Eden is mentioned as a place of extreme fertility and magnificent trees. Older Biblical scholars frequently made attempts to identify the site, e.g. Friedrich *Delitzsch put it some 100 miles north of Bagdad and Fritz Hommel (1854–1936) and A. H. *Sayce at Eridu, a sacred city of Babylonia near the Persian Gulf.

F. Delitzsch, *Wo lag das Paradies?* (1881). J. Skinner, *Genesis* (I.C.C., 1910), pp. 62–6 ('The Site of Eden'); H. E. Ryle, *Genesis* (Cambridge Bible, 1914), p. 47 f. ('Note on the Rivers of Paradise').

EDERSHEIM, ALFRED (1825–89), Biblical scholar. An Austrian of Jewish parentage and upbringing, he was converted at Pest to Christianity by a Scottish *Presbyterian, John Duncan, and accompanied him to Edinburgh. After studying theology at Edinburgh and Berlin, he entered the Presbyterian ministry in 1846, but later joined the C of E (1875), and from 1876 to 1882 was Vicar of Loders in Dorsetshire. He made an intensive study of the doctrines, practices, and conditions of *Judaism in the centuries preceding and following the beginning of the Christian era. Of his writings the most widely read was his *Life and Times of Jesus the Messiah* (2 vols., 1883), a work of great erudition written in an easy style, but somewhat lacking in critical judgement.

Tohu-Va-Vohu [*'Without Form and Void'*]. A Collection of Fragmentary Thoughts and Criticisms ed. with a memoir by Ella Edersheim [daughter] (1890; memoir, pp. vii–xxxii). S. R. *Driver in *D.N.B.* Suppl., ii (1901), p. 175 f.

EDESSA. The site has probably been inhabited from remote times but the present city (now Urfa) was founded by Seleucus I in 304 B.C. After the fall of Seleucid power it was the centre of an independent kingdom from *c.* 132 B.C. until A.D. 216, and then tributary to Rome. It

was from a very early date the centre of Syriac-speaking Christianity. The church there, destroyed in 201 after a flood, is the oldest known Christian edifice. It is probably the home both of the *Old Syriac and *Peshitta versions of the NT, and possibly also of the *Diatessaron. Its fame was enhanced by its claim to possess from A.D. 394 onwards the relics of the Apostle St. *Thomas. For a time it was one of the headquarters of both *Nestorianism and *Monophysitism. In 641 it fell into the hands of the Arabs. See also *Abgar, Legend of* and *Chronicon Edessenum.*

W. *Cureton (ed.), *Ancient Syriac Documents relative to the Earliest Establishment of Christianity in Edessa and the Neighbouring Countries, from the Year After Our Lord's Ascension to the Beginning of the Fourth Century* (1864). L. J. Tixeront, *Les Origines de l'église d'Édesse et la légende d'Abgar.* Étude critique suivie de deux textes orientaux inédits (1888). R. Duval, 'Histoire politique, religieuse et littéraire d'Édesse jusqu'à la première croisade' in *Journal asiatique*, 8e Série, xviii (1891), pp. 87–133, 201–78, 381–439, and xix (1892), pp. 5–102. A. *Baumstark, 'Vorjustinianische kirchliche Bauten in Edessa' in *Oriens Christianus*, iv (1904), pp. 164–83. W. Bauer, *Rechtgläubigkeit und Ketzerei im ältesten Christentum* (1934), pp. 6–48.

EDICT OF MILAN. See *Milan, Edict of.*

EDICT OF NANTES. See *Nantes, Edict of.*

EDINBURGH CONFERENCE (1910), World Missionary Conference. Convened as a consultative gathering to study missionary endeavour in the light of the circumstances of the day, the Conference was significant esp. for its presentation of the ideal of world-evangelization and as a forerunner of the *Oecumenical Movement. Through the creation of the International Missionary Council and the opening of *Edinburgh House, it also led to much greater co-operation among Missionary Societies. Some 1,200 delegates, representative of many Christian bodies and some 160 Missionary Boards or Societies, took part. J. R. *Mott was chairman of the Committee and J. H. Oldham general secretary of the Conference.

World Missionary Conference, 1910 (Report, 9 vols., [1910]). W. H. T. *Gairdner, *Edinburgh 1910.* An Account and Interpretation of the World Missionary Conference (1910).

EDINBURGH CONFERENCE (1937). The second World Conference on *Faith and Order, which continued the work of *Lausanne (q.v.). Its subjects were Grace, the Word of God, the Communion of Saints, the Ministry and Sacraments, and the Church's Unity in Life and Worship. The Report issued by the Conference stated the agreements as well as the differences. Grace, equated with the manifestation of God's love in the creation and redemption of man, is given in the Church through the Word and the Sacraments. Scripture is the principal rule of Christian doctrine and worship, but there was dissension as to the authority of the Church to interpret it, on the place assigned to Tradition, and on the nature, visibility, and membership of the Church. The Communion of Saints was interpreted in various ways as synonymous with the Holy Catholic Church, as the way of life of Christians in the state of grace, or, esp. by the Orthodox, as including also the angels and the Saints in heaven. There was considerable division on the number and efficacy of the Sacraments and on the ministry, the Presbyterians and other Protestants rejecting episcopacy as taught in the Orthodox Church and in the C of E. The union visualized by the Conference was largely one of co-operative action, confederation, and intercommunion, founded on essential unity in faith. The principal obstacle in the way of its achievement was the opposition between two main types of the conception of the Church as 'authoritarian' and 'personal' respectively. The Conference approved the proposal of a '*World Council of Churches' (q.v.), which has since come into being.

The Second World Conference on Faith and Order, held at Edinburgh, August 3–18, 1937, ed. L. Hodgson (1938).

EDINBURGH HOUSE. The institution set up in London (2 Eaton Gate, S.W.1) as a result of the *Edinburgh Conference (1910, q.v.). It houses the office of the Conference of British Missionary Societies, and also the London headquarters of the International Missionary Council (founded 1921), which has its parallel office in New York.

EDMUND, St., of Abingdon (also **Edmund Rich**) (*c.* 1180–1240), Abp. of *Canterbury. Born at Abingdon, Berks, of pious parents, Edmund early obtained a reputation for austerity and sanctity. *c.* 1222 he became Treasurer of *Salisbury Cathedral, and in 1233 Abp. of Canterbury. During his short tenure of the primacy he boldly, though ineffectually, attempted to check royal mismanagement and Papal exactions. When the legate, Cardinal Otto, whom Henry III had induced the Pope to appoint, arrived, Edmund protested against the infringement of his archiepiscopal rights; but he failed to stop the exploitation of ecclesiastical wealth and patronage, and retired to Pontigny in self-imposed exile. In his earlier years he had taught the new logic at Oxford, and his association with the University is commemorated in St. Edmund Hall, the one surviving medieval Hall in Oxford, which is traditionally supposed to have been built on the site of his residence. He was canonized by *Innocent IV in 1247. Feast day, 16 Nov.

The chief authorities are the Monastic Chroniclers, esp. *Matthew Paris, and several early biographies. Modern lives by W. Wallace (London, 1893), Frances de Paravicini (ib., 1898), B. Ward (ib., 1903), and M. R. Newbolt (ib., 1928). A. B. Emden, *An Oxford Hall in Medieval Times* (1927). T. A. Archer in *D.N.B.*, xvi (1888), pp. 405–10; H. W. C. Davis in *D.E.C.H.*, p. 191.

EDMUND CAMPION. See *Campion, Edmund.*

EDMUND THE MARTYR, St. (*c.* 840–70), King of East Anglia. The son of a king of 'Saxony' (perhaps Kent), who was adopted

as their king by the East Angles, Edmund succeeded his father in 855. His equitable rule was cut short in 870 by the invasion of the Danes under Inguar and Hubba. After the defeat of his army, he was captured; but though the invaders promised him his life if he would share his kingdom with Inguar, he refused as a Christian to associate himself thus with a pagan, and was condemned to be made the target of the Danes' archery practice, and finally beheaded. The cult of the martyr started almost immediately, and his body was translated in the 10th cent. to the present Bury St. Edmunds, where the abbey rapidly became a great place of pilgrimage. Feast day, 20 Nov.

T. Arnold (ed.), *Memorials of St. Edmund's Abbey,* i (R.S., 1890), includes 'Passio Sancti Edmundi' of *Abbo of Fleury (pp. 3–25), 'De Infantia Sancti Edmundi' of Gaufridus de Fontibus (pp. 93–103), and other material on the miracles attributed to Edmund. *Corolla Sancti Edmundi.* The Garland of Saint Edmund, King and Martyr, ed. with a preface by Lord Francis Hervey (1907; with Eng. tr. of chief sources). Id., *The Story of King Edward the Martyr and the Early Years of his Abbey.* Corpus Christi College, Oxford MS 197 (1927). *La Vie de Seint Edmund le Rei,* an Anglo-Norman poem of the Twelfth Century by Denis Piramus ed. by F. L. Ravenel (Philadelphia, 1906). Less critical modern lives by J. R. Thompson (London, 1890) and J. B. Mackinlay, O.S.B. (London, 1893).

EDWARD, St. (*c.* 963–78), king and martyr. He was the eldest son of Edgar the Peaceful, King of England, whom, contrary to the wishes of his stepmother, Queen Elfrida, but with the support of Abp. *Dunstan, he succeeded on his death in 975. Three years later he was murdered. Acc. to the details in *William of Malmesbury, this took place near Corfe in Dorset at the instigation of Elfrida, who had him stabbed while drinking by one of her attendants. His body was buried in the church of Wareham and later (980) translated to Shaftesbury. In 1001 he was officially styled a martyr and miracles were reported at his tomb. Feast day, 18 Mar.; of his translation, 20 June.

The chief authorities are *William of Malmesbury, Florence of Worcester and the Anglo-Saxon Chronicle, and the *Vita S. Oswaldi.* See also *Memorials of St. Dunstan* (ed. W. *Stubbs, R.S., 1874). W. Hunt in *D.N.B.*, xvii (1889), p. 5 f.

EDWARD THE CONFESSOR, St. (1003–1066), English king. The son of Ethelred II and Emma, the daughter of Duke Richard I of Normandy, he was sent to Normandy in 1013 and educated there in Norman ways. On the death of his half-brother, Hardicanute, in 1042, he was acclaimed King. He owed the throne largely to the support of the powerful Earl Godwin, whose daughter, Eadgyth (or Edith), he married later in 1045. Although his reign was outwardly peaceful, internally it was marked by struggles between Earl Godwin and his Saxon supporters and the Norman advisers and barons, including *Robert of Jumièges, Abp. of Canterbury, whom Edward, more a Norman than a Saxon, had brought over with him. In 1051 Earl Godwin was banished but the next year was restored through a counter-revolution. At the King's death the disputed succession, as well as the administrative disunity of the kingdom, plunged the nation into hostilities. Edward himself was mainly occupied with religious matters, and in particular with the building of the great abbey of St. Peter at *Westminster, which was consecrated late in 1065. He died on 5 Jan. 1066. His reputation for piety continued after his death and he was canonized in 1161. Feast day, 13 Oct.

H. R. Luard (ed.), *Lives of Edward the Confessor* (R.S., 1858), includes text of earliest (anon.) life (pp. 389–435) and other material. M. Bloch, 'La Vie de S. Édouard le Confesseur par Osbert de Clare' in *Anal. Boll.*, xli (1923), pp. 5–131, incl. text, pp. 64–131. Some information about Edward also in *The History of Westminster Abbey by John Flete* [fl. 1421–65], ed. by J. A. *Robinson (1906).

EDWARD VI (1537–53), King of England. The son of *Henry VIII and Jane Seymour, an ailing, precocious, and studious boy, he succeeded his father in 1547, at a critical moment for the C of E. Having delegated his royal authority to the Privy Council, dominated first by the Protector, *Somerset, and then by the Earl of Northumberland, he was himself of little account politically. His reign, however, is outstanding ecclesiastically for the numerous alterations in a *Calvinist direction often forced on the Church by an *Erastian civil government. It was marked by the publication (1547) of a Book of *Homilies, drawn up by T. *Cranmer; by the *Injunctions (1547) condemning pictures and all lights except the two before the Blessed Sacrament, providing a copy of the *Great Bible and of the paraphrase of D. *Erasmus in every parish church, and enforcing the reading in English of the Epistle and Gospel at *High Mass; by the Acts of Parliament (1547) imposing penalties on those who spoke irreverently of the Sacrament of the Altar, and enjoining that Communion be given in both kinds, abolishing the *congé d'élire and repealing the *Lollard heresy laws and the Act of *Six Articles; by the Privy Council's Proclamations (1548) enumerating ceremonies no longer to be enforced, abolishing all images, and enforcing the use of the newly drawn-up order in English for the giving of Communion in both kinds; by the recognition (1548) of clerical marriages; by the Act of *Uniformity (1549) imposing by penal legislation the use of the First BCP; by the new *Ordinal (1550); by the destruction of altars (1550), instigated by N. *Ridley, Bp. of London, and the substitution of wooden tables; by the attack on the doctrine of the Real Presence; by the Second and more Calvinist BCP (1552); the *Forty-Two Articles of Religion (1553), and the *Catechism and *Primer of 1553.

J. G. Nichols (ed.), *Literary Remains of King Edward the Sixth* (Roxburghe Club, 2 vols., 1857). R. H. Brodie (ed.), *The Calendar of the Patent Rolls preserved in the Public Record Office. Edward VI, 1547–1553* (6 vols., 1924–9); other calendars of the papers of his reign issued by the Master of the Rolls in their respective series. P. F. Tytler, *England under the Reigns of Edward VI and Mary* (2 vols., 1839), vol. i, and vol. ii, pp. 1–187. F. G. *Lee, *King Edward the Sixth, Supreme Head* (1886). C. R. Markham, *King Edward VI. An Appreciation* (1907). The portion of J. A. Froude, *History of England from Fall of Wolsey to Defeat of Spanish Armada* (12 vols., 1856–70), dealing with

his reign, ed. W. L. Williams in Everyman's Library [1909]. A. F. Pollard, 'The Reformation under Edward VI' in *C.M.H.*, ii (1903), pp. 474–511, with bibl. pp. 795–801. J. D. Mackie, *The Earlier Tudors, 1485–1558* (Oxford History of England, vii; 1952), pp. 478–525.

EDWARDS, JONATHAN (1703–58), American *Calvinist and philosopher. From a very early age he showed an interest in philosophy, in which he was much influenced by a study of J. *Locke's *Essay* in 1717. In 1727, after an experience of conversion, fully described in his diary, he was ordained to the ministry of the *Congregational church at Northampton, Massachusetts, where he struggled hard to stem the drift towards *Arminianism. His labours led to a religious revival, which Edwards minutely analysed in his *Faithful Narrative of the Surprising Works of God* (1737). His extreme Calvinism, displayed in his wish to exclude all 'unconverted' from the Communion, led to his removal from Northampton in 1749. In the following year he embarked on missionary work at Stockbridge. It was there that he wrote his most important works —his essay on *Original Sin* (posthumous), his *Dissertation concerning the Nature of True Virtue* (also posthumous), and, most famous of all, his *Inquiry into the Modern Prevailing Notions respecting that Freedom of the Will which is supposed to be essential to Moral Agency* (1754). Freedom, as popularly understood, he rejected, maintaining that self-determination was 'unphilosophical, self-contradictory, and absurd', and that the essence of virtue and vice lay 'not in their cause but in their nature'. In theology, he was an orthodox Calvinist of mystical inclination, and it was indubitably his desire to defend the extreme position of 'election' that inspired his metaphysical account of freedom. After his death a 'New England Party' of philosophical Calvinists carried on his teaching, but these disciples did little except to expound their master. Among them was his son, JONATHAN EDWARDS 'the younger' (1745–1801), chiefly remembered for his 'New England Theory of the Atonement', which he expounded in *The Necessity of the Atonement and its Consistency with Free Grace in Forgiveness* (1785).

See also *Great Awakening*.

Works ed. by E. Williams and E. Parsons (8 vols., Leeds, 1806–11; 2 Supp. vols., Edinburgh, 1847); by S. Austin (8 vols., Worcester, Mass., 1808–9; repr. Boston, 1843); and by S. E. Dwight, incl. Memoir (10 vols., New York, 1830). A. V. G. Allen, *Life and Writings of Jonathan Edwards* (1889). Other Lives by H. B. Parkes (New York, 1930), A. C. McGiffert ('Creative Lives', 1932) and O. E. Winslow (New York, 1940), incl. bibliographical reff. to scattered artt. on specific aspects. H. T. Johnson, *The Printed Writings of Jonathan Edwards, 1703–1758*. A Bibliography (Princeton University Library Publication, 1940). D. J. Elwood, *The Philosophical Theology of Jonathan Edwards* (New York, 1961).

EDWIN (c. 585–633), Northumbrian king. The son of Ælla, King of Deira (i.e. S. Northumbria), Edwin was banished by the King of Bernicia (N. Northumbria) who had seized his father's kingdom. After taking refuge, first in N. Wales, then in Mercia, and finally with Redwald, King of E. Anglia, he was restored to the throne through Redwald's victory over the Bernician king, Ethelfrid, in 617. He proved an able ruler, and in 625 married Ethelburga, the sister of the Kentish king, Eadbald, and daughter of King *Ethelbert, a Christian woman who was accompanied to Northumbria by her chaplain, *Paulinus. Edwin's victory over the West Saxons which made him the most powerful monarch in England, was followed by his baptism at Paulinus' hands (627). He then appointed Paulinus Bp. of *York and set about building a stone church there, but his plans were foiled by the invasion of his kingdom by Penda, the heathen King of Mercia, and his ally, Cadwallon of N. Wales. His defeat and death at the battle of Heathfield, 12 Oct. 633, was followed by the break-up of his kingdom. He was long venerated as a saint, his festival being kept on 12 Oct.

The primary authority is *Bede, *H.E.*, ii, 9–20. Notes to *Baedae Opera Historica*, ed. by C. Plummer, ii (1896), pp. 93–117; further reff. in index, s.v. *Aeduini*, p. 401 f.

EFFETA. See *Ephphatha*.

EFFICACIOUS GRACE. In the RC theology of *grace, grace to which free consent is given by the will so that it always produces its effect (*effectum*). In the controversy between the *Dominicans (D. *Báñez) and the *Jesuits (L. *Molina), the former held the efficacy of such grace to be dependent on the character of the grace itself, while the latter on the fact that it is given under circumstances which God foresees to be congruous with the dispositions of the recipient. Both parties were agreed that although the result was inevitable, the grace did not necessitate the will and destroy freedom. Both sufficient and efficacious grace are regarded as different forms of 'actual grace'.

EGBERT (d. 766), Abp. of *York. A member of the Northumbrian royal house, he was educated in a monastery, ordained deacon at *Rome, and appointed Bp. of York *c.* 732. In 735, on the advice of the Ven. *Bede (in a letter still surviving), he applied for the *pallium from Pope Gregory III. Owing to this increase of dignity and the harmonious relations with the king which ensued when his brother ascended the Northumbrian throne in 738, he was able to carry out many reforms. His most important work was the foundation of the cathedral school, where he himself taught theology and numbered *Alcuin among his pupils. Of the literary works connected with his name the best known is the compilation of canons known as the 'Excerptiones e dictis et canonibus SS. Patrum' (the *Excerptiones Egberti*) or in some MSS. as the 'De Jure Sacerdotali'; in its present form, however, this cannot be earlier than the 11th cent. The 'Dialogus Ecclesiasticae Institutionis', a treatise on various points of Church discipline, and the 'Poenitentiale' (or 'Confessionale') which exists in Latin and the vernacular, have been much added to from later sources. The

'Pontificale', which also bears his name, is of great value as an early source for the history of the liturgy and of the English *Coronation Rite. A letter from St. *Boniface to Egbert has also survived.

The 'Excerptiones', 'Dialogus Ecclesiasticae Institutionis', and 'Poenitentiale' repr. from G. B. *Mansi, with introd., in J. P. Migne, *PL*, lxxxix, 377–451; better text of the 'Poenitentiale', which more probably represents the genuine work of Egbert, repr. from F. W. H. Wasserschleben, *Die Bussordnungen der abendländischen Kirche* (1851), pp. 231–247, in A. W. Haddan–W. *Stubbs (edd.), *Councils and Ecclesiastical Documents Relating to Great Britain and Ireland*, iii (1871), pp. 416–31, with important note on Egbert's works, pp. 413–16. Anglo-Saxon text of the 'Poenitentiale' ed. J. Raith (Bibliothek der angelsächsischen Prosa, xiii; 1933) and R. Spindler (Leipzig, 1934). 'Pontificale' ed. W. Greenwell (Surtees Society, xxvii; 1853). The letter of Bede is pr. among his *Opera Historica* ed. C. Plummer, i (Oxford, 1896), pp. 405–23, with notes, ii (1896), pp. 378–88; also in A. W. Haddan–W. Stubbs, op. cit., pp. 314–26; Eng. tr. in Dorothy Whitelock (ed.), *English Historical Documents c. 500–1042* (English Historical Documents, ed. D. C. Douglas, i; 1955), pp. 735–45 (No. 170). The letter from St. Boniface is pr. in A. W. Haddan–W. Stubbs, op. cit., p. 757 f. On the Excerptiones, P. Fournier–G. Le Bras, *Histoire des collections canoniques en occident*, i (1931), pp. 316–20. On the Pontifical, F. *Cabrol, O.S.B., in *D.A.C.L.*, iv (1921), cols. 2211–20, s.v. 'Egbert (Pontifical de)', with full bibl. J. Raine in *D.C.B.*, ii (1880), pp. 50–2, s.v. 'Egbert (6)'.

EGBERT, St. (d. 729), Northumbrian hermit. He was a monk of *Lindisfarne who crossed to *Ireland in search of learning and sanctity, where during a plague he vowed that if his life were spared he would never go back to his native land. He was largely instrumental in organizing the evangelization of Germany and arranged the mission of St. *Willibrord and others. From 716 till his death he lived a life of great devotion at *Iona, where he persuaded the monks to observe the Roman method of calculating the date of Easter (see *Paschal Controversy*). He died on the very day that the feast was being so observed for the first time. Feast day, 24 Apr.

The principal authority is *Bede, *H.E.*, iii, 4, 27; iv, 3, 26; v, 9 f., 22–4; notes in ed. by C. Plummer (2 vols., Oxford, 1896), esp., ii, pp. 258, 335–7. T. F. Tout in *D.N.B.*, xvii (1889), p. 146 f., s.v., with reff. W. Levison, *England and the Continent in the Eighth Century* (Ford Lectures for 1943; 1946), pp. 52 f., 271.

EGEDE, HANS (1686–1758), *Lutheran missionary from Norway to Greenland, the 'Apostle of the Eskimos'. From 1707 to 1717 he ministered at Vaagen, in the Lofoten Islands. In 1717 went to Bergen to get support for a scheme for a mission to Greenland and in 1721 he set out. After many difficulties, but much success, he returned to Copenhagen in 1736, where he founded a seminary for missionaries to Greenland. His work among the Eskimos was carried on after 1736 by his son, Paul Egede (1708–89).

H. M. Fenger, *Bidrag til Hans Egedes og dem grønlandske Missions Historie 1720–60* (1879). F. Belsheim in *P.R.E.* (ed. 3), v (1898), pp. 177–80, s.v., with bibl.

EGERTON PAPYRUS. Two imperfect leaves and a scrap of papyrus in the British Museum (numbered 'Egerton Papyrus 2') containing passages from a Gk. writing akin to, but distinct from, the canonical Gospels. On palaeographical grounds the papyrus, which was part of a codex (not a roll), must be dated not later than *c.* 150 A.D., perhaps considerably earlier. It is thus the oldest known specimen of Christian writing. The surviving leaves contain four incomplete narratives, all relating to the period of Christ's Ministry. Their closeness to the canonical Gospels may imply that the author was acquainted with them; on the other hand, it seems likely that he had access to independent historical material derived from genuine tradition. The actual date of the 'unknown Gospel' is presumably considerably earlier than that of the codex, as there is no reason to suppose it is an autograph.

The text was first publd., with Eng. tr., by H. I. Bell–T. C. Skeat as *Fragments of an Unknown Gospel and other early Christian Papyri* (1935), with facsimiles. Idd., *The New Gospel Fragments* (more popular, with revised text, 1935). Eng. tr. also in M. R. James, *The Apocryphal New Testament* ('1924' ['corrected repr.', 1953]), p. 567 f. 'Fr. Gr.' [i.e. G. *Dix, O.S.B.], 'Gospels in the Second Century' in *Laudate*, xiii (1935), pp. 97–109. C. H. *Dodd, 'A New Gospel' in *Bulletin of the John Rylands Library*, xx (1936), pp. 56–92. G. Mayeda, *Das Leben Jesu-Fragment Papyrus Egerton 2 und seine Stellung in der urchristlichen Literaturgeschichte* (1946). H. I. Bell, 'The Gospel Fragments P., Egerton 2', in *H.T.R.*, xlii (1949), pp. 53–63.

EGINHARD (*c.* 770–840), also 'Einhard', Frankish historian. He was educated at the school of *Fulda, and later became a member of *Charlemagne's palace school at Aachen and one of the Emperor's most trusted friends. On Charlemagne's death Einhard continued in the favour of his successor, Louis I, and was presented by him with the estates of Michelstadt and Mulinheim (Seligenstadt), whither he retired about 830. He was the author of several works, of which the chief, the 'Life of Charlemagne', was one of the most remarkable biographies of the Middle Ages. It is modelled on the *Vitae* of Suetonius, and thereby freed from the cramped annalistic methods of its contemporaries, and distinguished for its fresh and accurate presentation of the Emperor's character and rule. G. H. Pertz also assigns to him the authorship of the so-called 'Annales Einhardi', but this ascription is doubtful.

Annales ed. G. H. Pertz in *M.G.H.*, Scriptores, i (1826), pp. 174–218, with introd. pp. 124–33. *Vita Caroli*, first crit. ed. id., ib., ii (1829), pp. 426–63; ed., with notes on previous edd., H. W. Garrod–R. B. Mowat (Oxford, 1915); also ed., with Fr. tr., by L. Halphen (Les Classiques d'histoire de France au moyen-âge; 1923); Eng. tr., A. J. Grant, *Early Lives of Charlemagne* (The King's Classics, xxii; 1905), pp. 4–56. *Translatio et Miracula Sanctorum Marcelli et Petri* ed. G. Waitz in *M.G.H.*, Scriptores, xv (pt. 1; 1887), pp. 238–64; Eng. tr. by B. Wendell (Cambridge, Mass., 1926). *Epistolae* ed. K. Hampe in *M.G.H.*, Epistolae v (1899), pp. 105–45. H. Wibel, *Beiträge zur Kritik der Annales Regni Francorum und der Annales q.d. Einhardi* (1902). O. Holder-Egger, 'Zur Ueberlieferung von Einhards *Vita Karoli Magni*' in *N.A.*, xxxvii (1912), pp. 395–414; F. L. Ganshof, 'Notes critiques sur Éginhard, biographe de Charlemagne' in *Revue belge de Philologie et d'Histoire*, iii (1924), pp. 725–58. J. Cahour, *Petit Lexique pour l'étude de la "Vita Karoli" d'Éginhard* (1928). M. Boudois, *La Translation des saints Marcellin et Pierre*. Étude sur Einhard et sa vie politique de 827 à 834 (Bibliothèque des Écoles des Hautes Études, clx; 1907). F. Kurze, *Einhard* (1899). A. Kleinclausz, *Éginhard* (Annales de l'Université de Lyon, Sér. 3, fasc. 12; 1942), with full reff.

EGYPT, Christianity in. See *Coptic Church*.

EGYPTIAN CHURCH ORDER, The. The early liturgical treatise which, as a result of the researches of Dom Hugh *Connolly and E. *Schwartz, is now commonly identified as the '*Apostolic Tradition' of St. *Hippolytus (q.v.). It was so described by H. Achelis (1891), when it was known to exist in *Ethiopic, *Coptic, and Arabic versions, 'merely to give it a name, which so far it lacks'.

EGYPTIANS, Gospel according to the. An apocryphal gospel, probably written in Egypt in the first half of the 2nd cent., which seems to have circulated widely since it was known to *Clement of Alexandria, *Theodotus (his *Gnostic adversary), and *Origen. Its standpoint is markedly ascetic (apparently *Encratite). Only a few quotations from it survive.

*Clement Al., Strom., iii. 9 (63–6); iii. 13 (92); *Hippolytus, Ref., v. 7; *Epiphanius, Haer., lxii. 2. M. R. James, *The Apocryphal New Testament* (1924), pp. 10–12. Bardenhewer, pp. 521–4.

EGYPTIAN VERSIONS OF THE BIBLE. See *Boharic, Fayumic, Sahidic*.

EHRLE, FRANZ (1845–1934), medievalist. A native of Isny in Württemberg, he was educated by the *Jesuits of Feldkirch and entered their novitiate at Gorheim in 1861. Driven from Germany by the *Kulturkampf, he lived from 1873 to 1877 at Ditton Hall, Cambs., where he was ordained priest in 1876. After travelling on the Continent for some years and examining a great number of medieval MSS., he went to *Rome in 1880, where he remained till his death, except during the war years of 1915–19, which he spent at Feldkirch and later at Munich. In 1885 he started, in conjunction with H. *Denifle, the *Archiv für Litteratur- und Kirchengeschichte des Mittelalters*, and in 1890 published the first volume of his *Historia Bibliothecae Romanorum Pontificorum*. From 1895 to 1914 he was prefect of the *Vatican Library, which he reorganized on modern lines, attaching to it a reference library and a department for the restoration of MSS. He was created cardinal in 1922. In 1924, on the occasion of his 80th birthday, he was presented with the 5 vols. of *Miscellanea Francesco Ehrle*, containing essays by many scholars of European reputation on a large variety of subjects. His *Der Sentenzenkommentar Peters von Candia* (1924) was an important study in 14th cent. Scholasticism and his *I più antichi statuti della facoltà teologica dell' Università di *Bologna* (1934). With Denifle, Ehrle was the founder of the scientific study of the history of Scholasticism.

The 'Album' appended to the *Miscellanea Francesco Ehrle* (S.T., xxxvii–xlii, 1924) includes 'Cenni biografici' (pp. 12–16) and list of his publications to date. A. Pelzer in *R.H.E.*, xxxi (1935), p. 636 f., gives reff. to main obituary appreciations and other works concerning his life.

EICHHORN, JOHANN GOTTFRIED (1752–1827), Biblical scholar and orientalist. He studied at Göttingen (1770), and became professor of oriental languages at Jena in 1775. From 1788 he was professor of philosophy at Göttingen. He was one of the first commentators to make a scientific comparison between the Biblical books and other Semitic writings. He was also among the earliest critics to divide *Genesis between the 'Jehovist' and 'Elohist' sources, and to distinguish the priestly law in *Exodus–*Leviticus–*Numbers from the popular code in *Deuteronomy. His most important works include his *Einleitung ins Alte Testament* (3 vols., 1780–3); *Einleitung in die apokryphischen Bücher des AT* (1795); *Einleitung in das NT* (2 vols., 1804–12). His work, though inaccurate, was popular and did much to encourage Biblical study and criticism.

H. C. A. Eichstaedt, *Oratio de Jo. Godofredo Eichhornio* (Jena [1827]). E. Bertheau–C. Bertheau in *P.R.E.* (ed. 3), v (1898), pp. 234–7.

EIGHTEEN BENEDICTIONS, The (Heb. *Shemoneh 'Esreh*, 'eighteen'; also *Tephillah*, 'prayer', or *Amidah*, 'standing'). A group of prayers, now 19, largely made up of Biblical phrases, which are recited on week-days at each of the three services of the Jewish synagogue. The first three, which are benedictions, and the last three, which are thanksgivings, are used also on *Sabbaths, festivals, and the Day of *Atonement, but the middle group consisting of petitions is then replaced by other prayers. Acc. to the *Talmud, they go back to 'the first wise men' or (acc. to another passage) to '120 elders, among these a number of prophets'. They were revised, apparently to preclude their use by Jewish-Christians and *Gnostics, by Simeon ha-Pakoli in the time of Gamaliel II (c. 80–120). Their contents date mainly from pre-Christian times; but apparently they were for long not written down and varied in number and wording esp. in the middle section.

The current text is in the 'Morning Service' in S. Singer, *The Authorised Daily Prayer Book of the United Hebrew Congregations of the British Empire*. They are printed also, with the Talmudic text, in C. W. Dugmore, *The Influence of the Synagogue upon the Divine Office* (1944), pp. 114–25.

EIKON BASILIKE, 'The Portraiture of His Sacred Majesty in His Solitudes and Sufferings'. An anonymous work published shortly after the death of *Charles I in 1649, and attributed by some to the King himself, but by many to John *Gauden, later Bp. of Exeter. It provoked a reply in John *Milton's *Eikonoklastes* (1649).

C. Wordsworth, *Who Wrote* ΕΙΚΩΝ ΒΑΣΙΛΙΚΗ? (1824), and later writings by the same author; H. J. Todd, *Bishop Gauden, the Author of* Εἰκὼν βασιλική (1829). E. Almack, *A Bibliography of the King's Book, or Eikon Basilike* (1896). 'New Bibliography' by F. F. Madan (Oxford Bibliographical Society, N.S., iii, for 1949, 1950).

EILETON (Gk. εἰλητόν; lit. 'something wrapped' or 'wound'). In the E. Church, a silk cloth spread on the altar during the Liturgy. It is the real counterpart of the W.

*corporal, though the functions of the latter are now partly filled by the *antiminsion. It is interpreted as symbolizing the linen cloth wrapped around Christ's head during His entombment.

EINHARD. See *Eginhard*.

EINSIEDELN. *Benedictine abbey and pilgrimage in Switzerland. Previously the dwelling-place of the hermit, St. *Meinrad (q.v.), the abbey was founded by St. Benno, Bp. of Metz, and Eberhard in 937. Since 1350 it has been the recognized National Sanctuary of the Swiss Confederation. The present church is a fine baroque building of enormous dimensions, and in the abbey library is a large collection of valuable MSS.

'Annales Einsidlenses' ed. G. H. Pertz in *MGH*, Scriptores, iii (1839), pp. 137–49. Calendar of docc. by G. Morel, O.S.B., *Die Regesten der Benedictiner-Abtei Einsiedeln* (Regesten der Archive in der schweizerischen Eidgenossenschaft ed. T. v. Mohr, i; Chur, 1848). Profession book ed. R. Henggeler, O.S.B. (Einsiedeln, 1934). G. Meier, O.S.B., *Catalogus Codicum Manuscriptorum qui in Bibliotheca Monasterii Einsidlensis O.S.B. servantur* (1899). O. Ringholz, O.S.B., *Geschichte des fürstlichen Benediktinerstiftes U.L.F. von Einsiedeln, seiner Wallfahrt, Propsteien, Pfarreien und übrigen Besitzungen*, vol. i (no more published, Einsiedeln, 1904). Id., *Die Kultarbeit des Stiftes Einsiedeln* (ib., 1913). R. Henggeler, O.S.B., *Das Stift Einsiedeln und die französische Revolution. Ein Beitrag zur Einsiedler Klostergeschichte von 1730–1808* (ib., 1924). F. Segmüller, O.S.B., in *L.Th.K.*, iii (1931), col. 603 f., s.v.; T. Schwegler, O.S.B., in *E.C.*, x (1953), cols. 1866–8, s.v. 'Santissima Vergine Maria di Einsiedeln', both with further bibl. L. H. Cottineau, O.S.B., *Répertoire topo-bibliographique des abbayes et prieurés* (Mâcon, 1935), cols. 1034–9.

EKPHONESIS. See *Ecphonesis*.

EKTHESIS. See *Ecthesis*.

ELDAD AND MODAD, Book of. An apocryphal book, forged on the basis of Num. 11. 26–9. Though it no longer survives, it was quoted by *Hermas (*Vis.* 2. 3) and perhaps (J. B. *Lightfoot) also by *Clement of Rome (1 Clem. 23. 3 f.; cf. also '2 Clem.' 11. 2 f.).

See comm. to Numbers, cited s.v., esp. L. E. Binns (West. Comm., 1927), p. 71. J. B. Lightfoot (ed.), *S. Clement of Rome. The Two Epistles to the Corinthians* (1869), notes on pp. 91 f. and 205 f. J. T. Marshall in *H.D.B.*, i (1898), p. 676, s.v.

ELDER. A Church officer in the *Presbyterian Church. Elders are of two kinds: (1) 'Teaching elders', whose function is pastoral; (2) 'Ruling elders', i.e. laymen set apart by ordination who assist the pastor in the administration and government of the Church. Biblical support for the distinction was found by J. *Calvin and others in 1 Tim. 5. 17. When the word is used without further specification, the latter class is commonly meant.

For the history of the office in the early Church, see *Presbyter*.

ELECTION (Gk. ἐκλογή, 'choice'). In the vocabulary of theology, an act of the Divine Will exercising itself on creatures, among which it chooses some in preference to others. In the

OT the Divine election bears esp. on Israel, the 'Chosen People', and among them in particular on those who do the will of God and remain faithful in time of trial. In the NT the place of the Old Israel is taken by the members of the new Christian community. The number of the elect is small (Mt. 22. 14), but Satan cannot prevail against them and they will be gathered together 'from the uttermost part of the earth' (Mk. 13. 22 and 27) on the Last Day. In St. Paul the term 'election' usually signifies vocation acc. to the Divine predilection, e.g. in Rom. 9. 11 and 11. 5, 7, 28, and 1 Thess. 1. 4. In the teaching of the Fathers and Schoolmen the term plays an important part in connexion with *Predestination (q.v.). St. *Augustine expounds at length the belief that gratuitous predestination to eternal salvation presupposes an act of election on the part of God. Though the Fathers frequently use the terms 'election' and 'predestination' without distinction, some later theologians, e.g. St. *Thomas Aquinas, give 'election', as an act of the will, a logical priority over predestination, as an act of the intelligence, because God must first will the end, viz. salvation, for a creature, i.e. elect it, before ordaining it towards this end, i.e. predestining it. Most *Jesuit theologians, however, reject the Thomist distinction and use the terms election and predestination indifferently, as was done by the Fathers.

The doctrine of election filled a central place in the *Institutes of J. *Calvin, who affirmed that certain persons are elected by God wholly without relation to faith or works. This belief was everywhere held by Calvinist theologians till questioned by the school of *Arminius, for whom election was God's choice of those who believe and persevere by grace in faith and works. An even wider interpretation was given to it in the works of F. D. E. *Schleiermacher, who maintained that election includes all humanity, but that, on earth, only certain men and women are, through historical circumstances, elect.

It is to be observed that, while a natural consequence of belief in election might be expected to be to weaken or destroy moral effort, history in fact does not bear out this deduction, even in the case of those holding an extreme form of the doctrine.

ELEPHANTINE PAPYRI, The. A collection of *Aramaic documents from the reigns of Xerxes, Artaxerxes I, and Darius II (485–404 B.C.), found in 1904–8 on the site of an ancient Jewish military colony which had settled at Elephantine in the far south of Upper Egypt some time before the conquest of Egypt by the Persians. The papyri throw valuable light on the organization, law, and religious beliefs and practices of the colony, and indirectly of the Jewish *Diaspora in the 5th cent. B.C. They provide evidence for the existence of a syncretistic form of Judaism which is in sharp contrast with the orthodox Judaism of *Ezra and *Nehemiah.

Plates, with Eng. tr. and notes, ed. A. H. Sayce–A. E. Cowley, *Aramaic Papyri Discovered at Assuan* (1906). Crit. edd. of the text by E. Sachau, *Aramäische Papyrus und Ostraka aus einer jüdischen Militär-Kolonie zu Elephantine* (1911, with Germ. tr. and notes), and, with Eng. tr. and full notes, by A. [E.] Cowley, *Aramaic Papyri of the Fifth Century B.C.* (1923). Separate Eng. tr. by A. [E.] Cowley, *Jewish Documents of the Time of Ezra* (Translations of Early Documents, Series I, Palestinian Jewish Texts (Pre-Rabbinic), 1919). N. Peters, *Die jüdische Gemeinde von Elephantine-Syene und ihr Tempel im 5. Jahrhundert vor Christi Geburt* (1910); E. Meyer, *Der Papyrusfund von Elephantine* (1912); A. van Hoonacker, *Communauté judéo-araméenne à Eléphantine, en Égypte, aux VIe et Ve siècles* (Schweich Lectures for 1914; 1915). A. Vincent, *La Religion des Judéo-Araméens d'Éléphantine* (1937).

ELEVATION, The. At the Eucharist, the lifting of the sacred elements in turn by the celebrant immediately after each species has been consecrated. Its purpose is both to symbolize their offering to the Father and to exhibit them for adoration. The practice seems to have been first adopted in France towards the end of the 12th cent., apparently in order to rebut the teaching of certain theologians that the consecration of the bread did not take place until after the words of consecration had also been pronounced over the wine. In the *Roman, *Ambrosian, and *Mozarabic rites there is a second elevation (the so-called 'lesser elevation') at the end of the *Canon.

E. Dumoutet, *Le Désir de voir l'hostie et les origines de la dévotion au saint sacrement* (1926). P. Browe (S.J.), 'Die Elevation in der Messe' in *Jahrbuch für Liturgiewissenschaft*, ix (1929), pp. 20–66; id., *Die Verehrung der Eucharistie im Mittelalter* (1933), ch. 2, pp. 26–69.

ELEVEN THOUSAND VIRGINS. See *Ursula, St.*

ELGAR, EDWARD (1857–1934), musician. Succeeding his father as organist of St. George's RC church, Worcester, he rose to fame as a composer of choral-orchestral music. He was professor of music at Birmingham university from 1905 to 1908, and in 1929 became Master of the King's Music. Among his chief works of a religious kind are his setting of J. H. *Newman's *'Dream of Gerontius' (1900), and his oratorios, 'The Apostles' (1903) and 'The Kingdom' (1906).

B. Maine, *Elgar, his Life and Works* (2 vols., 1933). Other Studies by E. Newman (London, 1906), J. F. Porte (London, 1921 and 1933), R. J. Buckley (London, 1935), W. H. Reed (London, 1936 and 1939), Mrs. R. Powell (London, 1937), and T. F. Dunhill (London, 1938). L. B. M. Dyer, *Music by British Composers*. A Series of Complete Catalogues, No. 2, Sir Edward Elgar [1931].

ELIAS. See *Elijah*.

ELIAS OF CORTONA (c. 1180–1253), General of the *Franciscan Order. A native of *Assisi and one of the earliest of the companions of St. *Francis, he soon rose to prominence. In 1219 he became first Provincial of Syria, and in 1221 Vicar-General of the order. On Francis's death (1226) he was mainly instrumental in the erection of the basilica at Assisi as a burial-place for the saint. In 1232 he became the third General of the order, but his government was marked by repeated crises, as he acted in a despotic manner towards all those, and esp. the '*Spiritual Franciscans', who opposed his princely way of life. In 1239 he was deposed from his office by Pope *Gregory IX. Thenceforth he supported the Emp. *Frederick II in his anti-Papal policy, and later was excommunicated and expelled from the order. For the small body of friars who followed him, he erected a monastery at Cortona. On his deathbed he is said to have made his submission to the Pope. A man of remarkable gifts, he was possessed of a character which was a strange combination of piety and pride.

His 'Epistola Encyclica de Transitu S. Francisci . . . ad omnes Provincias Ordinis Missa', pr. in *Analecta Franciscana*, x (1941), pp. 525–8. I. Affò, O.F.M., *Vita di Frate Elia, ministro generale de' Francescani* (Parma, 1783). E. Lempp, *Frère Élie de Cortone*. Étude biographique (1901). P. *Sabatier, *Examen de la vie de Frère Élie du* Speculum Vitae, *suivi de trois fragments inédits* (Opuscules de Critique historique, xi; 1904). D. Sparacio, *Fra Elia compagno, vicario e successore di S. Francesco Serafico* (ed. 2, 1923). S. Attal, *Frate Elias compagno di Francesco* (1936). L. Mirri, 'Frate Elia da Cortona' in *Miscellanea Francescana*, xxxi (1931), pp. 89–95, 175–87, and 233–43. P. Robinson, O.F.M., in *C.E.*, v (1909), pp. 382–5, and R. Pratesi, O.F.M., in *E.C.*, v (1950), cols. 235–7, both with reff. to primary sources.

ELIGIUS, St. (c. 590–c. 660), Fr. 'Éloi', Bp. of Noyon and patron saint of metal workers. He was born at Chaptelat near Limoges. Through his skill in working in precious metals, he was given positions at the courts of the Frankish kings, Clothaire II (d. 629), who made him Master of the Mint at Marseilles, and his son, Dagobert I (d. 639), whose chief councillor he became. Under Dagobert he was instrumental in ransoming captives, founding monasteries, and building churches. In 641 he was consecrated Bp. of Noyon (on the same day as his close friend St. *Ouen was consecrated Abp. of Rouen) and became a zealous pastor, evangelizing Flanders, esp. the territories round Antwerp, Ghent, and Courtrai. Two genuine homilies of St. Eligius survive, one attacking superstition and the other on the Last Judgement. The fourteen other homilies attributed to him are of doubtful authenticity. Feast day, 1 Dec.

'Vita Eligii Episcopi Noviomagensis', pr. in J. P. Migne, *PL.*, lxxxvii, 481–594; crit. ed. by B. Krusch in *M.G.H.*, Scriptores Rerum Merovingicarum, iv (1902), pp. 634–761. His letter to Pope Desiderius in J. P. Migne, op. cit., 259; also ed. by W. Arndt in *M.G.H.*, Epistolae, iii (1892), p. 206. The Homilies attributed to him are printed in J. P. Migne, op. cit., 593–654. E. Vacandard, 'Les Homélies attribuées à saint Éloi' in *R.Q.H.*, lxiv (1898), pp. 471–80; F. Plaine, O.S.B., 'Nouvelles Remarques sur les homélies attribuées à saint Éloi', ib., lxv (1899), pp. 235–42; E. Vacandard, 'Réponse aux remarques de Dom Plaine', ib., pp. 243–55. P. Parsy, *Saint Éloi, 590–659* ('Les Saints', 1907). E. Vacandard in *D.T.C.*, iv (1908), cols. 340–9, incl. further bibl.

ELIJAH (Gk. form, 'Elias') (9th cent. B.C.). Traditionally held to be the greatest Hebrew prophet. He maintained the ascendancy of the worship of Jehovah in the face of Canaanite and Phoenician cults (1 Kgs. 18) and upheld the claims of moral uprightness and social justice (1 Kgs. 21). With *Enoch he shared the glory of not seeing death but of translation

into heaven (2 Kgs. 2. 1–18); and such was the impression which he made on his people that his return was held to be a necessary prelude to the deliverance and restoration of Israel (Mal. 3. 5f.). In the NT (e.g. Mk. 9. 4) he appears as the typical representative of the OT prophets.

ELIOT, THOMAS STEARNS (1888–   ), poet and critic. Born in St. Louis, Missouri, he was educated at the Smith Academy, St. Louis, Harvard (1906–9 and again 1911–13), the *Sorbonne (1910–11) and Merton College, Oxford (1913–15). Marrying in 1915 (his wife died in 1947), he taught for a short time in Highgate Grammar School, London, and worked for Lloyds Bank; and from this period his main interests appear to have been literary. Assistant editor of *The Egoist* from 1917 to 1919 and a frequent contributor to *The Athenaeum*, in 1923 he became editor of *The Criterion*, which he made a leading organ of literary expression until it ceased in 1939. He was appointed Clark lecturer at Trinity College, Cambridge, for 1926, and Charles Norton Professor of Poetry at Harvard from 1933 to 1936. He was elected President of the Classical Association in 1943 and in 1948 invested with the Order of Merit and awarded the Nobel Prize for literature.

Brought up in the American *Congregationalist tradition, Eliot passed through a period of agnosticism reflected in his earlier poetry, e.g. *Prufrock* (1917) and *Poems 1920* (1920). The expression of his sense of the emptiness of life reached its climax in *The Waste Land* (1922) and is also seen in *The Hollow Men* (1925). Shortly afterwards he adopted an *Anglo-Catholic position apparent in *Ash Wednesday* (1930) and such religious verse as *Murder in the Cathedral* (1935; written for the *Canterbury Festival of 1935). In all his poetry, incl. his inquiry into the nature of time and experience in *Four Quartets* (1944), Eliot has broken with tradition and employed a complicated poetic technique characterized by an extreme form of compression by means of allusion, the juxtaposition of contrasting ideas and the indirect communication of meaning by suggestion. His work is marked by a strong sense of tradition in thought and is esp. influenced by the works of the great mystics, such as St. *John of the Cross, by *Dante, the 17th cent. *Metaphysical Poets and the 19th cent. French symbolists. His specifically religious prose works include *The Idea of a Christian Society* (1939) and *Reunion by Destruction* (1944).

H. R. Williamson, *The Poetry of T. S. Eliot* (1932); F. O. Matthiesen, *The Achievement of T. S. Eliot.* An Essay on the Nature of Poetry (1935); B. Rajan (ed.), *T. S. Eliot.* A Study of his Writings by Several Hands (1947); R. March and Tambimuttu (compilers), *T. S. Eliot.* A Symposium (1948); H. Gardner, *The Art of T. S. Eliot* (1949); E. Drew, *T. S. Eliot.* The Design of his Poetry (1950); D. E. S. Maxwell, *The Poetry of T. S. Eliot* (1952). Further Studies by T. McGreevy (London, 1931), A. Orans (Acta et Commentationes Universitatis Tartuensis (Dorpatensis), B, Humaniora, xxviii, 3, 1932), E. M. Stephenson (London, 1944) and V. H. Brombert (Yale and London, 1949). D. Gallup, *T. S. Eliot.* A Bibliography (1952).

ELIPANDUS (*c.* 718–802), Abp. of *Toledo. He was the originator and chief exponent of the *Adoptianist heresy in Spain, though his capacities as a theologian were much inferior to those of his supporter, *Felix of Urgel. He seems to have been led to his theological position by opposition to a form of *Sabellianism which in the person of *Migetius had condemned at a council at Seville in 782. Though his doctrines were proscribed as heretical in synods at Ratisbon (792), Frankfurt (794), Rome (798), and Aachen (800), the Arab domination enabled him to retain possession of his see till his death. A few of his letters survive.

The chief sources of Elipandus's doctrine are his letters, pr. in J. P. Migne, *PL*, xcvi, 859–82, and the attacks of Beatus of Liebana and Etherius of Osma, whose letter to Elipandus is pr. ib., 893–1030. J. F. Rivera, *Elipando de Toledo. Nueva aportación a los estudios mozárabes* (Toledo, 1940), with full bibl. F. Vernet in *D.T.C.*, iv (1911), cols. 2333–40.

ELISHA (Gk. form, 'Eliseus') (9th cent. B.C.), Hebrew prophet and the successor of *Elijah. Various stories of his life are told in 1 Kgs. 19 –2 Kgs. 13, but he had not the individuality or strength of character of his predecessor. He appears as the head of a band of enthusiasts called the 'sons of the prophets'.

ELIZABETH, St. The mother of *John the Baptist and 'cousin' (Lk. 1. 36) of the BVM. The visit of the Blessed Virgin to her shortly before the birth of Christ is commemorated in the Feast of the *Visitation (2 July). Acc. to a few MSS. of the NT, it was she, and not Mary, who spoke the words called the '*Magnificat'. Feast day in the W., 5 Nov.; in the E., 8 Nov.

ELIZABETH, St., of Hungary (also known as **Elizabeth of Thuringia**) (1207–31). She is to be distinguished from Elizabeth of Hungary, the *Dominican nun (1293–1337). The daughter of King Andrew II of Hungary, she was born at Pressburg. In 1211, with a view to a future marriage for political purposes, she was sent to Thuringia and did not again leave Germany; and in 1221 she married Louis IV, the Landgrave of Thuringia. From an early age she showed a desire for the ascetic life, and, esp. in the first years after her early marriage, came under the influence of the *Franciscans who had recently arrived in Germany. On her husband's death on the *Crusade in 1227, she was driven from the court by his brother, Henry Raspe, on the pretext that her charities were exhausting the state finances, and this determined her to renounce the world completely. In 1228 she settled at Marburg, where she came under the absolute rule of *Conrad of Marburg who had been her spiritual director since 1225. Under his orders, which seem to have been quite unsuited to Elizabeth's devout and delicate nature, she gave up her children, submitted to physical chastisement at his hands, and amid

a life of great austerity, spent all her energies in visiting and caring for the sick and poor. She was canonized in 1235. The fine Gothic Elizabethskirche at Marburg was built to enshrine her relics, where they remained till removed by the reforming *Philip of Hesse in 1539. Feast day, 19 Nov.

Early lives by Theodoric of Apolda, O.P. (b. 1228), ed. by H. Canisius, *Antiquae Lectiones*, v (Ingolstadt, 1604), pp. 147–217; by *Caesarius of Heisterbach in a letter to Gregory XI, ed. by A. Huyskens in *Annalen des historischen Vereins für den Niederrhein*, lxxxvi (1908), pp. 1–59; by Conrad of Marburg, ed. by id., *Quellenschriften zur Geschichte der hl. Elisabeth Landgräfin von Thüringen* (1908), pp. 110–40; this last work includes a full discussion of sources. Id. (ed.), *Der sog. Libellus de dictis Quattuor Ancillarum S. Elisabeth Confectus* (1911). Further anonymous life ed. by D. Henniges, O.F.M., in *A.F.H.*, ii (1909), pp. 240–68. K. Wenck, 'Quellenuntersuchungen und Texte zur Geschichte der heiligen Elisabeth: I. Über die Dicta Quattuor Ancillarum Sanctae Elisabeth' in *N.A.*, xxxiv (1908), pp. 427–502. P. Braun, *Der Beichtvater der heiligen Elisabeth und deutsche Inquisitor Konrad von Marburg* (1909). Further short studies by H. Mielke (Rostock, 1888) and C. Boerner in *N.A.*, xiii (1888), pp. 433–515. F. Schmoll, *Zur Ikonographie der heiligen Elisabeth im 13. bis 16. Jahrhundert* (1914). Modern lives by C. R. F. *Montalembert (Paris, 1836; Eng. tr., 1904), C. A. Jones (London, [1873]), E. Horn (Paris, 1902), W. Canton (London [1913]), and E. Busse-Wilson (Munich, 1931). There is also an uncritical life by F. J. Weinrich (Munich, 1930; Eng. tr., 1933).

ELIZABETH I (1533–1603), Queen of England from 1558. She was the daughter of *Henry VIII and Anne Boleyn. Though apparently illegitimate through the invalidity of the King's marriage both by canon and civil law, she was placed next in succession after *Edward and *Mary by Act of Parliament. Together with Prince Edward she was given a careful education at Hatfield House. When Edward became king (1547) she was left under the care of Catherine Parr and was involved in an unpleasant affair with Catherine's second husband, Lord Seymour, in which she behaved with great prudence. During the reign of Mary (1553–8) she conformed outwardly to Catholicism. Though suffering imprisonment after the plot of Thomas Wyatt in 1554, she succeeded in clearing herself of suspicion and was readmitted to court at the end of the year. Until Mary's death she lived mostly in retirement at Hatfield, continuing her studies with great success under the guidance of the accomplished Roger Ascham.

On her accession one of her main difficulties was the religious question. Devoid of strong convictions, she sought to solve it acc. to political expediency. The country as a whole was still predominantly Catholic, though with a strong *Calvinistic undercurrent. Elizabeth disliked the former because it denied her legitimacy, and the latter because it abolished episcopacy which she held to be essential for the safety of kings. She therefore distrusted both Calvinists and Catholics and aimed at a compromise between the *Lutheran political theory with its emphasis on the prerogatives of the temporal ruler, and the episcopal organization of Catholicism, many of whose institutions, such as the celibacy of the clergy and the use of crucifixes and statues, she wished to retain. All the bishops, however, refused to take the

Oath of Allegiance and declined to take part in the coronation, a ceremony which was eventually performed by the Bp. of *Carlisle, Owen Oglethorpe. But in the country changes were made slowly, much of the old ritual was retained, the doctrine of the *Real Presence was not actually denied, and, as the majority of parish priests were still Catholic, the old and the new rites were often celebrated side by side. The Second (1552) Prayer Book of Edward VI was reissued (1559) with some significant minor changes designed to remove offence to RCs. Owing to the many changes since the reign of Henry VIII Church life in general had become chaotic, but after M. *Parker's appointment as Abp. of Canterbury (1559) uniformity began gradually to be restored. Parker's policy, which both in doctrinal and liturgical questions sought to steer a middle course, resulted in the *Thirty-Nine Articles and the '*Advertisements'. Though these documents were more Calvinistic than Elizabeth would have wished, the situation could hardly have been otherwise, as the government had to rely for support more and more on the Protestant party. The climax was reached when, in 1570, *Pius V excommunicated Elizabeth and released her subjects from their allegiance. This step was followed by the restoration of Article 29 (withdrawn in 1563 at the last moment), the proscription of the Mass, and the increasing persecution of Catholics. In 1587, under the menace of the Spanish invasion, the Queen ordered the execution of her cousin, *Mary Stuart, after 19 years of imprisonment, fearing that she might become a rallying centre for her disaffected RC subjects. The defeat of the Armada (1588) removed the Spanish peril, and at the same time gave a powerful impetus to the new nationalism. It is largely through her genius that England became the foremost Protestant power in Europe to which Continental Protestantism was to look for support during the centuries to come.

The principal primary material for the reign is to be found in the Calendars of the State Papers, Domestic and Foreign. Useful collections of docc. repr. in G. W. Prothero (ed.), *Select Statutes and other Constitutional Documents Illustrative of the Reigns of Elizabeth and James I* (1894; ed. 4, 1913, pp. 1–249), and J. R. Tanner (ed.), *Tudor Constitutional Documents, A.D. 1485–1603* (1922). G. B. Harrison (ed.), *The Letters of Queen Elizabeth* (1935, with reff. to earlier collections). The most important modern studies are those by E. S. Beesley ('Twelve English Statesmen', London, 1892), M. *Creighton (London, 1896), and J. E. Neale (1934). Other studies by M. Wilson (London, 1932), E. Thane (ib., 1933), T. Maynard (ib., 1943), and M. Waldman (ib., 1952). F. Chamberlin, *The Private Character of Queen Elizabeth* (1921). J. B. Black, *The Reign of Queen Elizabeth, 1558–1603* (Oxford History of England, viii; 1936), with bibl. A. L. Rowse, *The England of Elizabeth* (1950).

ELKESAITES. A Jewish Christian sect which arose c. A.D. 100 in the country E. of the *Jordan. They took their name from their sacred writing, the 'Book of Elkesai', which professed to contain the revelation given to Elkesai ('sacred power') by an angel 96 miles high. They held beliefs similar to those of the *Ebionites, insisting on a very strict observance of the rites and teaching of the Mosaic Law,

rejecting sacrifices and certain Biblical books, esp. the Pauline Epistles, maintaining a *Docetic view of the Person of Christ, and placing great emphasis on the redemptive nature of Baptism. Their ethical and social teaching was ascetic in character. Almost all our knowledge of them derives from references in St. *Hippolytus' *Philosophumena* (ix, 13–17; x, 29) and St. *Epiphanius's *Haereses* (xix; xxx, 17; liii).

Fragg. of 'Book of Elkesai' collected by A. *Hilgenfeld in *Novum Testamentum extra Canonem Receptum*, fasc., iii (Leipzig, 1866), pp. 153–67. W. Brandt, *Elchasai*. Ein Religionsstifter und sein Werk (1912). G. *Salmon in *D.C.B.*, ii (1880), pp. 95–8; G. Bareille in *D.T.C.*, iv (1911), cols. 2233–9, s.v. 'Elcésaïtes'.

ELLERTON, JOHN (1826–93), English hymn-writer. Educated at Trinity College, Cambridge, he was ordained in 1850 and held a succession of parochial appointments. He is esp. remembered for his many hymns, both original compositions and translations, among them being 'The day Thou gavest, Lord, is ended', 'Saviour, again to Thy dear Name we raise', and 'O Strength and Stay, upholding all creation'.

H. Housman, *John Ellerton*. Being a Collection of his Writings on Hymnology together with a sketch of his Life and Works (1896; life, pp. 15–181).

ELLICOTT, CHARLES JOHN (1819–1905), English divine. Educated at St. John's College, Cambridge, of which he became a Fellow (1845), he subsequently occupied the chair of divinity at King's College, London (1858–61) and the Hulsean professorship at Cambridge (1860–1). In 1861 he became Dean of *Exeter and two years later Bp. of *Gloucester and Bristol. On the division of the see into two parts in 1897, he became Bp. of Gloucester, resigning in 1904. He sat on many commissions, being chairman of the British New Testament Revision Company 1870–81, of which he missed only 2 out of the 407 sittings. He edited a considerable number of the Pauline Epistles (Gal., 1854; others 1855–8; 1 Cor. 1887), and wrote several other theological and religious books.

His *Addresses on the Revised Version of Holy Scripture* (1901), forming the Charge to the Archdeaconry of Cirencester at the Visitation in Oct. 1901, were repr. in 1933. R. Bayne in *D.N.B., 1901–1911*, i, p. 618 f.

ELMO, St. The popular name for St. Peter González (c. 1190–1246). After accompanying *Ferdinand III on his expedition against the Moors, this famous *Dominican preacher devoted the rest of his life to work amongst the seafaring folk of the coasts of Spain. After his death he was canonized as the patron saint of seamen; and the electrical discharge often seen at the mast-heads and yard-arms of ships was interpreted as a sign of his protection, just as the ancients regarded it as a sign of the presence of Castor and Pollux. Feast day, 14 Apr.

There is considerable confusion between him and St. Erasmus, one of the 14 *Auxiliary Saints and a martyr in the *Diocletianic persecution, who is also known as St. Ermo or St. Elmo; (apparently corruptions of 'St. Erasmus'); the feast of this saint is on 2 June.

On the former, see 'Legenda b. Petri', together with account of his miracles, decree for his canonization, and other material, in H. Florez, O.S.A., *España sagrada*, xxiii (Madrid, 1767), pp. 245–89. 16th cent. life by Stephanus Sampayo, O.P., in *AA.SS.*, Apr. II (1675), pp. 391–9. Gerard de Fracheto, O.P., *Vitae Ordinis Praedicatorum* (ed. B. M. Peichert, Monumenta Ordinis Fratrum Praedicatorum Historica, i; 1897, pp. 296–8). On the latter, *AA.SS.*, Jun. I (1695), pp. 211–19.

ELOHIM (Heb. אֱלֹהִים, lit. 'gods'). Used occasionally in the OT of heathen gods, supernatural beings, or earthly judges, but generally of the God of Israel, for whom it is a very frequent term, esp. in what is commonly reckoned the second oldest Pentateuchal source (the supposed writer of which is therefore referred to by critics as 'the Elohist'). The use of the plural form to describe the one God is frequently explained as a 'plural of majesty'. The singular form, 'Eloah', is at any rate rare and late.

ÉLOI, St. See *Eligius, St.*

ELPHEGE, St. See *Alphege, St.*

ELVIRA, Council of. A Spanish council held about 306, just after a period of persecution. It passed 81 canons whose interest lies in the severe disciplinary penalties enforced for apostasy and adultery. It also required continence of all the clergy under pain of deposition (can. 33). Several of the canons order lifelong excommunication without reconciliation even at death.

Hardouin, i (1715), cols. 247–58; Mansi, ii (1759), cols. 1–406. Canons also in Lauchert, pp. 13–26. Hefele-Leclercq, i (1; 1907), pp. 212–64. A. W. W. Dale, *The Synod of Elvira and Christian Life in the Fourth Century*. A Historical Essay (1882). L. *Duchesne, 'Le Concile d'Elvire et les Flamines chrétiens' in *Mélanges Renier* (1886), pp. 159–74; H. Koch, 'Die Zeit des Konzils von Elvira' in *Z.N.T.W.*, xvii (1916), pp. 61–7; L. von Sybel, 'Zur Synode von Elvira' in *Z.K.G.*, xlii (1923), pp. 243–7. E. Göller, 'Analekten zur Bussgeschichte des 4. Jahrhunderts: I. Die Synode von Elvira und das öffentliche Busswesen nach der Lehre Pacians' in *R.Q.*, xxxvi (1928), pp. 236–61. E. Hennecke in *P.R.E.* (ed. 3), v (1898), pp. 325–7; G. Bareille in *D.T.C.*, iv (1911), cols. 2378–97, s.v.

ELY. In 673 St. *Etheldreda (Audrey) founded a *double monastery here for monks and nuns, endowing it with the principality of the Isle. After her death in 679, her shrine became a place of pilgrimage and the importance of Ely grew. In 870 the monastery was destroyed by the Danes, but in 970 it was restored, for monks only, by King Edgar and *Ethelwold, Bp. of *Winchester, and about a hundred years later a new church, now the cathedral, was begun by Abbot Simeon (1082–1093). In 1109 Henry I and Abp. *Anselm formed the see of Ely out of the large diocese of *Lincoln, and the prior and monks became the cathedral chapter. At the *Dissolution the prior became the dean, and eight canonries

were founded (1541). The cathedral, which contains every style of architecture from early Norman to late Perpendicular, is famous for its Galilee Porch (1198–1215) and its central octagon (1322–8), the roof of which (known as the 'Lantern') is the only Gothic dome in the world. The Grammar School was founded in 1541, and the Theological College in 1876 (opened in 1881).

Extracts from the *Liber Eliensis* in H. *Wharton, *Anglia Sacra*, i (1691), pp. 593–677; modern ed. of books i and ii by D. J. Stewart (Anglia Christiana Society, iii; London, 1848). E. Chapman (ed.), *The Sacrist Rolls of Ely* (2 vols., Cambridge, 1907). S. J. A. Evans (ed.), *Ely Chapter Ordinances and Visitation Records, 1241–1515* (Camden Miscellany, xvii, 1940). A. Jessopp, 'The Manuscripts of the Bishop of Ely' in the *Twelfth Report of the Historical Manuscripts Commission*, Appendix, Part ix (1891), pp. 375–88; id., 'The Manuscripts of the Dean and Chapter of Ely', ib., pp. 389–96. W. *Dugdale, *Monasticon Anglicanum*, i (ed. 1817), pp. 457–500. B. Willis, *A Survey of the Cathedrals of Lincoln, Ely, Oxford and Peterborough* (1730), pp. 331–401. J. Bentham, *The History and Antiquities of the Conventual and Cathedral Church of Ely from the Foundation of the Monastery, A.D. 673, To the Year 1771* (Cambridge, 1771; ed. 2, 1812, with suppl. by W. Stevenson, Norwich, 1817); id., *A Catalogue of the Principal Members of the Conventual and Cathedral Church of Ely* (1756). D. J. Stewart, *On the Architectural History of Ely Cathedral* (1868). C. W. Stubbs, *Historical Memorials of Ely Cathedral In Two Lectures*: i, The Shrine of St. Awdrey, ii, Alan de Walsingham (1897). W. D. Sweeting, *The Cathedral Church of Ely* (Bell's Cathedral Series, 1901); B. E. Dorman, *The Story of Ely and its Cathedral* (Ely, 1945). T. D. Atkinson, *An Architectural History of the Benedictine Monastery of Saint Etheldreda at Ely* (Cambridge, 1932, with a vol. of plates). E. Miller, *The Abbey and Bishopric of Ely. The Social History of an Ecclesiastical Estate from the tenth to the early fourteenth century* (Cambridge Studies in Medieval Life and Thought, N.S., i; 1951). M. D. Ellis–L. F. Salzman in *V.C.H., Cambridge and the Isle of Ely*, ii, ed. L. F. Salzman (1948), pp. 199–210. W. Hunt in *D.E.C.H.*, (1912), pp. 202–206, s.v.

ELZEVIR. 16th–17th cent. Dutch family of printers at *Leyden, celebrated for their book production. In 1624 they issued their first edition of the Greek NT, which, though it was little more than a reprint of T. *Beza's text of 1565, at once won favour and was accepted for some two centuries as the *Textus Receptus.

A. C. J. Willems, *Les Elzévier* (1880); G. Berghman, *Études* (1885) and *Nouvelles Études* (1897) *sur la bibliographie elzévirienne*; H. B. Copinger, *The Elzevier Press* (1927); D. W. Davies, *The Work of the Elzeviers, 1580–1712* (The Hague, 1954).

EMBER DAYS. Four groups each of three days, in the Church year, viz., the Wednesday, Friday, and Saturday after St. *Lucy (13 Dec.), *Ash Wednesday, *Whitsunday, and *Holy Cross Day (14 Sept.) respectively, which are observed as days of fasting and abstinence in the Churches of the W. The name is perhaps a corruption of *quatuor tempora* (Lat.), 'four seasons'. Their early history and original purpose is obscure. At first there were apparently only three groups, perhaps taken over from the pagan religious observances connected with seed-time, harvest, and autumn vintage; and in this form they traditionally date back to the time of Pope *Callistus (c. 220). They were certainly well established at Rome in the time of Pope *Leo (440–61), who preached a series of Embertide sermons. From Rome their observance spread outwards through W. Christendom. The connexion of the days with the crops has now been largely lost, and they are associated to-day almost entirely with the ordination of the Church's ministers, which, in the C of E, usually takes place on the ensuing Sunday.

M. W. Quadt, *Die Liturgie der Quatembertage erklärt* (1869). G. *Morin, O.S.B., 'L'Origine des Quatre Temps' in *Rev. Bén.*, xiv (1897), pp. 337–46. L. Fischer, *Die kirchlichen Quatember.* Ihre Entstehung, Entwicklung und Bedeutung (Veröffentlichungen aus dem Kirchenhistorischen Seminar München, IV, 3, 1914). K. Holl, *Gesammelte Aufsätze zur Kirchengeschichte*, ii (1928), Nr. 9, 'Die Entstehung der vier Fastenzeiten in der griechischen Kirche' [1923], pp. 155–203. A. Molien in *D.T.C.*, xiii (pt. 2; 1937), cols. 1447–55, s.v. 'Quatre-Temps'.

EMBOLISM (Gk. ἐμβολισμός, 'intercalation'). In the Roman *Mass, the name given to the prayer in the *Canon which begins 'Libera nos quaesumus, Domine, ab omnibus malis', inserted between the Lord's Prayer and the *Fraction of the Bread. Its opening words take up the final words of the Lord's Prayer ('Libera nos a malo') which has just preceded it. Many E. liturgies have a similar prayer at this point. The word is also used (not in a specifically religious sense) to denote the difference of days in the calendar between the lunar year of 354 days and the solar year of $365\frac{1}{4}$ days, also known as the '*epact'.

Jungmann (1949), pp. 343–55, with full reff.

EMBURY, PHILIP (1728–75). The first *Methodist preacher in America. A native of Ireland, he was converted by J. *Wesley in 1752, and began to preach soon afterwards. In 1760 he emigrated to America, but did not begin to preach there till 1766. In 1768 he built the first Methodist church in America, in New York, but in 1770 he removed to Camden, where he founded a Methodist society.

H. E. Starr in *Dict. Amer. Biog.*, vi (1931), p. 125 f., with reff.

EMERSON, RALPH WALDO (1803–82), American essayist, philosopher and poet. The son of a *Unitarian minister of Boston, Mass., he was educated at Boston Latin School and Harvard College, and trained for the Unitarian ministry at the Divinity School, Cambridge, Mass. He was 'approbated to preach' in 1826 and ministered at Boston from 1829 to 1832, when he resigned owing to his extremely unconventional views on the *Eucharist; he continued to preach until 1847. On a visit to Europe in 1833 he met T. *Carlyle, S. T. *Coleridge and W. *Wordsworth, with the first of whom he formed a close friendship. Returning to America the same year, he settled at Concord, Mass., where, with the exception of the period of a second visit to Great Britain in 1847–8, he remained for the rest of his life as a lecturer on literature and philosophy.

Emerson's philosophy was founded on a combination of rationalism and mysticism. Although he disowned the name, it appears that he fundamentally believed in 'Transcendentalism', viz. the doctrine that 'the highest revelation is that God is in every man'. It

follows that man contains all that is needful in himself and that everything that happens to him has its origin within him. In his lecture on *The Defects of Historical Christianity* (delivered 1835) he went so far as to maintain that even redemption was to be sought within the soul. In spite, however, of the exalted position which he accorded to man philosophically, he had little liking for democracy and was only reluctantly led (by 1856) to support the cause of the abolition of slavery. At least from the 1840's he enjoyed a wide influence and popularity enhanced by the freshness and imagination of his style. From 1840 to 1844 Emerson was editor of *The Dial*, a Transcendentalist periodical in which some of his poetry was published. His prose works, of which the majority were based on his lectures, include *Nature* (1838), two series of *Essays* (1841, 1844), *Representative Man* (1850), *English Traits* (1856), *Conduct of Life* (1860), *Society and Solitude* (1870) and *Letters and Social Aims* (1876). They are mainly ethical in purpose, but are possessed of an underlying religious tone. His poetry, though attractive in its inspiration, lacks the polish of his prose.

Complete Works, ed. by E. W. Emerson (Centenary Edition, 12 vols., c. 1903–4); *Journals*, ed. by E. W. Emerson and W. E. Forbes (10 vols., 1909–14); *Letters*, ed. by R. L. Rusk (6 vols., 1939). F. I. Carpenter, *Ralph Waldo Emerson. Representative Selections*, with introduction, bibl. and notes (New York, 1934); *Young Emerson Speaks*, ed. by A. C. McGiffert (Boston, 1938; early sermons). J. E. Cabot, *A Memoir of Ralph Waldo Emerson* (2 vols., 1887). J. Benton, *Emerson as a Poet* (New York, 1883); O. W. Holmes, *Ralph Waldo Emerson* (1885); G. E. Woodberry, *Ralph Waldo Emerson* (New York, 1907); J. S. Harrison, *The Teachers of Emerson* (1910); B. Perry, *Emerson Today* (Princeton, 1931); K. W. Cameron, *Emerson the Essayist* (2 vols., Raleigh, N.C., 1945). G. W. Cooke, *A Bibliography of Ralph Waldo Emerson* (New York, 1908; only 530 copies printed).

EMINENCE. A title of honour given to a *cardinal of the RC Church. Until a decree of *Urban VIII in 1630 confined its use to the cardinals, the Imperial electors and the Grand Master of the Hospital of St. John of Jerusalem (who still retains it), it had been more widely used. Before that date cardinals were entitled 'Illustrissimi' or 'Reverendissimi'.

EMMANUEL. See *Immanuel.*

EMMAUS. The village in which our Lord made His Resurrection appearance to two of the disciples (Lk. 24. 13–35). It was 60 furlongs from *Jerusalem (Lk. 24. 13; but acc. to a variant reading 160, perhaps an accommodation to the ancient identification of this Emmaus with that mentioned in 1 Macc. 3. 40, &c.). Among suggested sites are Kuloniyeh ('Colony') to the W. and Khamasah to the SW of Jerusalem.

L. H. Vincent, O.P., and F. M. Abel, O.P., *Emmaüs.* Sa basilique et son histoire (1932).

EMMERICK, ANNA KATHARINA (1774–1824), ecstatic. She entered an *Augustinian house at Agnetenberg, Dülmen, Westph., in 1802, where she aroused the dislike of some of the laxer members by the fervour of her spiritual life. In 1812 the house was closed by order of the civil authorities, and she took refuge in a private house, where she had a serious illness. At about this time she received the *Stigmata of the Passion on her body. Her 'Meditations on the Passion' (*Das bittere Leiden unseres Herrn und Heilandes Jesus Christ*) were taken down by Clemens Brentano (1778–1842) and published in 1833.

The most recent crit. edd. of *Das bittere Leiden*, both based on Brentano's notes, are those of A. Michelitsch (Graz, 1935) and D. K. Bücher (Munich, 1937). W. Hümpfner, *Clemens Brentanos Glaubwürdigkeit in seinen Emmerick-Aufzeichnungen* (Würzburg, 1923). Biogr. by K. E. Schmöger (2 vols., Freiburg i.Br., 1867–70), and many others. Best modern life is H. J. Seller, *Im Banne des Kreuzes. Lebensbild der stigmatisierten Augustinerin Anna Katharina Emmerik* (Würzburg, 1940). Full bibl. to date by W. Hümpfner in *Theologie und Glaube*, xvi (1924), pp. 455–82. W. Hümpfner in *L.Th.K.*, iii (1931), col. 660 f., and C. Baus in *E.C.*, v (1950), cols. 313–15.

EMMONS, NATHANAEL (1745 – 1840), American *Congregationalist divine. He graduated at Yale in 1767, was admitted preacher in 1769, and from 1772 to 1827 was pastor at Franklin, Mass., where he also trained theological students for the Congregationalist ministry. In his sermons he developed a system of 'consistent *Calvinism', largely based on the doctrines of Samuel Hopkins (1721–1803), a disciple of Jonathan *Edwards. Though avowedly opposed to all forms of *Arminianism, *Universalism, and *Unitarianism, he was a less extreme Calvinist than Hopkins, from whom he differed in asserting that man's part in regeneration is active, not passive. He was also politically interested, being a keen patriot during the War of Independence.

Works, with a Memoir by E. A. Park, ed. by J. Ide (6 vols., Boston, 1861–3). B. W. Bacon in *Dict. Amer. Biog.*, vi (1931), p. 150 f.

EMS, Congress of. A conference attended by representatives of the four archbishops of Mainz, Trier, *Cologne, and Salzburg, which was held at Bad Ems in Hesse-Nassau in 1786. Its object was to carry into effect the teachings of 'Justinus Febronius' (J. N. von *Hontheim), which repudiated Papal interference in all but purely spiritual matters. It issued on 25 Aug. the 'Punctation of Ems' (*Emser Punktation*), proposing, *inter alia*, that in future appeals to Rome in Germany should be restrained, the bishops should have the control of matrimonial dispensations, and Papal bulls and other official Roman decisions should not be binding until accepted by the German episcopate. The project failed to secure the support of the German bishops, who interpreted the plan as a device of the archbishops to aggrandize their own position.

L. *Pastor, *The History of the Popes from the Close of the Middle Ages* (Eng. tr.), xl (1953), pp. 43–65. M. Höhler (ed.), *Des kurtrierischen Geistlichen Rats Heinrich Aloys Arnoldi Tagbuch über die zu Ems gehaltene Zusammenkunft der vier Erzbischöflichen . . . Deputierten, 1786* (Mainz, 1915). C. Mirbt in *P.R.E.* (ed. 3), v (1898), pp. 342–50, and M. Braubach in *L.Th.K.*, iii (1931), cols. 669 f., both with bibl.

EMSER, HIERONYMUS (1478–1527), editor of earlier writers, secular essayist, and controversialist. From about 1504 he was secretary to Duke George of Saxony. He is chiefly remembered for his controversy with M. *Luther, which lasted from 1519 till his death, and was popular and scurrilous in character. He disliked Luther's 'December Bible' of 1522, and published a counter-edition in 1527, made to resemble it as much as possible, with introduction and notes added. In 1530 the *Brethren of the Common Life settled at Rostock issued it in a Low German translation. Emser's Bible went into over 100 editions in the 16th, 17th, and 18th cents.

His first writings against Luther were edited by F. Thurnhofer in the *Corpus Catholicorum*, 4 (1921). G. E. Waldau, *Nachricht von Hieronymus Emsers Leben und Schriften* (Anspach, 1783). Life by G. Kawerau (1898); id. in *P.R.E.* (ed. 3), v (1898), pp. 339–42.

ENABLING ACT, The. This Act, officially 'the Church of England Assembly (Powers) Act,' 1919, removed certain legal disabilities from the C of E. Its provisions closely followed recommendations in the *Report on the Relations of Church and State* (1916). Its chief effect was to confer legislative powers on the *Church Assembly, notably the preparation and modelling of ecclesiastical measures and their presentation to Parliament. It also established an Ecclesiastical Committee consisting of 15 members of each of the Houses of Parliament, nominated by the Lord Chancellor and the Speaker respectively, to which its measures were to be submitted before proceeding to Parliament. It provided that while Parliament can accept or reject measures (as happened in the case of the Prayer Book Measures of 1927 and 1928), it cannot amend a measure passed by the Assembly.

ENARXIS (Gk. Ἔναρξις, lit. 'beginning'). In the Byzantine liturgy, the section between the *Prothesis and the *Little Entrance. It consists of three Diaconal Litanies, each followed by a variable antiphon sung by the choir. The celebrant meanwhile silently recites the prayers known as the 'Prayers of the Antiphon' (Εὐχαὶ Ἀντιφώνου). It was prob. first introduced into the Liturgy in the 9th cent.

Text in Brightman, *L.E.W.*, pp. 310–12.

ENCLOSURE. See *Clausura.*

ENCRATITES. A title applied to several groups of early Christians who carried their ascetic practice and doctrine to extremes which were in most cases considered heretical. They are referred to by *Irenaeus, *Clement of Alexandria, and *Hippolytus, who respectively call them ἐγκρατεῖς, ἐγκρατηταί, and ἐγκρατῖται. The name, however, seems never to have been used very precisely, but to have been applied in a general sense to many of the *Gnostic, *Ebionite and *Docetic sects. They commonly rejected the use of wine and flesh-meat, and often also of marriage. It was largely in encratite circles that the *Apocryphal Gospels and Acts were produced.

Irenaeus, *Adv. Haer.*, i, 28; Clement Al., *Strom.*, vii, 17 (108. 2), etc.; Hippolytus, *Philos.*, viii 20; cf. also *Epiphanius, *Haer.*, xlvi, xlvii. A certain Julius Cassian, the author of a book Περὶ Εὐνουχίας, was reckoned a leading exponent of Encratite doctrines, while St. *Jerome (*Ep.* 48. 2) names *Tatian as the *princeps encratitarum*. C. Bareille in *D.T.C.*, v (1913), cols. 4-14, s.v., with bibl.

ENCYCLICAL. A circular letter sent to all the churches of a given area. In early times the word might be used of a letter sent out by any bishop, but in modern RC usage the term is restricted to such letters as are sent out by the Pope. It has also been used from the first (1867) of the letters issued by the Anglican bishops at the end of the *Lambeth Conferences.

ENCYCLOPAEDISTS. The name given to the contributors to the *Encyclopédie*, published between 1751 and 1780 in 35 volumes (vols. 1–28 at Paris, the remaining 7 as a supplement at Amsterdam). It was to be a complete review of the arts and sciences of the day. The editor, D. *Diderot, and many of the contributors, were supporters of an exclusively natural religion; and though the censorship exercised by Church and state preserved impartiality in the principal articles, some of the smaller articles proved useful media for anti-Catholic and anti-aristocratic views. The influence of this group of writers, which became known as the 'philosophic' party, was among the principal disruptive intellectual elements which assisted the French Revolution.

J. Lough (ed.), *The Encyclopédie of Diderot and D'Alembert. Selected Articles* (1954). J. Morley, *Diderot and the Encyclopaedists* (2 vols., 1878); L. Ducros, *Les Encyclopédistes* (1900). F. Venturi, *L' origini dell' Enciclopedia* (1946); N. N. Schargo, *History of the Encyclopedie* (New York, 1947). Überweg, iii, pp. 427–39, 698–700. E. S. Haldane in *H.E.R.E.*, v (1912), pp. 302–6, s.v.; E. Passerin in *E.C.*, v (1951), cols. 337–40, s.v. 'Encyclopédie' for further bibl. See also bibl. to Diderot, D'Alembert, etc.

ENERGUMEN (Gk. ἐνεργούμενος). In ancient Christian literature a term used of demoniacs and others possessed of abnormal mental and physical states, esp. insanity. Following the example of the Lord, the Church treated them with special pity and care. They received the ministrations of *exorcists. At the Eucharist they were normally dismissed at the end of the *Missa Catechumenorum with prayer and blessing, though if not violent they might be admitted to communion. They were debarred from ordination, even after cure.

E. *Martène, O.S.B., *De Antiquis Ecclesiae Ritibus*, iii (1702), cap. 9, pp. 497–530. H. *Leclercq, O.S.B., in *D.A.C.L.*, v (pt. 1, 1922), cols. 964–78, s.v. 'Exorcisme', 'Exorciste'; J. Sauer in *L.Th.K.*, iii (1931), cols. 671 f., s.v. 'Energumenen'.

ENGLAND, CHURCH OF. See *Church of England* (for history); *Anglicanism* (for theological outlook).

ENGLISH CHURCH MUSIC, School of. See *Royal School of Church Music.*

ENGLISH CHURCH UNION. A society formed in 1859 as the 'Church of England Protection Society', and renamed in 1860 the 'English Church Union', when it incorporated various local Church societies. Its object was to defend, and further the spread of, High Church principles in the C of E. The Union championed many priests during the ritual prosecutions, and frustrated many attacks upon Catholic practices. In 1934 the E.C.U. was united with the *Anglo-Catholic Congress to form the 'Church Union'. In 1868 Charles Lindley Wood, afterwards Viscount *Halifax, was elected president and was for many years its dominating personality.

G. Bayfield Roberts, *The History of the English Church Union, 1859–1894* (1895).

ENGLISH COLLEGE, The. The seminary at *Rome for English candidates for the RC priesthood. It was founded in 1362 as a hospice for English pilgrims. In 1578 *Gregory XIII converted it into a seminary whose students had to take an oath to go to England when it should seem good to their superiors. Soon afterwards its direction was entrusted to the *Jesuits, who were in charge of it until the suppression of the Society in 1773. It then passed into the hands of Italian secular priests, under whose direction it remained till it was closed during the invasion of the French. In 1818 it was restored by *Pius VII, and since then its rectors have always been members of the English secular clergy, the most famous of them being N. P. S. *Wiseman, afterwards cardinal.

Liber Ruber Venerabilis Collegii Anglorum de Urbe, ed. by W. Kelly, assisted by O. Littledale, S. Roxburgh, and I. Vaughan. I. (1) Annales Collegii; Nomina Alumnorum (*Catholic Record Society, xxxvii and xl, 1940–3), incl. bibl., i, p. xiv, note i. Incomplete Eng. tr. by H. Foley, S.J., *Records of the English Province of the Society of Jesus*, vi (1880), pp. 1–540, with other material from the College archives. F. A. *Gasquet, *A History of the Venerable English College, Rome. An Account of its Origins and Work from the Earliest Times to the Present Day* (1920). See also Lives of W. *Allen, R. *Parsons, and N. P. S. Wiseman.

ENGLISH HYMNAL, The. This Anglican hymnal, publd. in 1906, was the result of a considered attempt by a group, mainly of Anglo-Catholic sympathies, to eradicate banalities and generally to raise the quality of English hymnody, in the matter both of words and music. The editorial committee responsible for the words included W. J. *Birkbeck, P. *Dearmer, and T. A. *Lacey, while the musical editor was R. Vaughan Williams (b. 1872). It included *Office Hymns and *Propers for the Sung Eucharist, both taken mainly from the *Sarum books. The Hymnal has been, and is, very widely used, esp. in cathedrals and Anglo-Catholic churches, but also in many ordinary parishes. A new edition, with extensive revision of the plainchant music by J. H. Arnold, was issued in 1933.

ENGLISH LADIES (Germ. *Englische Fräulein*). A popular name for the 'Institute of the Blessed Virgin Mary', an active body of religious founded in 1609 at St.-Omer by Mary *Ward (1585–1645) which was designed as an order for women similar to the *Jesuit Order for men. The foundation's independence of ecclesiastical authority led *Urban VIII to promulgate a bull suppressing it in 1631; but the suppression was soon withdrawn and Urban himself encouraged the founding of a house shortly afterwards on the Esquiline in Rome under a slightly changed rule and stricter ecclesiastical control. The rules of the order did not receive formal Papal approval, however, till 1703. In 1749 each house of the order was placed under the jurisdiction of its diocesan bishop. The congregation includes 'ladies' and lay sisters, both taking simple vows, dispensable by the Pope; and houses exist in Germany, England, Ireland, and elsewhere.

M. Philip, I.B.V.M., *Companions of Mary Ward* (1939). J. Leitner, *Geschichte der englischen Fräulein und ihre Institute seit ihrer Gründung bis auf unsere Zeit* (1869). J. Grisar, S.J., 'Das erste Verbot der Ordensgründung Maria Wards, 1628' in *Stimmen der Zeit*, cxiii (1927), pp. 34–51; id., 'Der Endkampf um Maria Wards erste Ordensgründung', ib., pp. 131–50. M. G. F. von Pechmann, I.B.V.M., *Geschichte des Englischen Institutes Beatae Mariae Virginis in Bayern* (1907). Heimbucher, ii, pp. 454–61 and 668, with bibl. p. 454. See also bibl. to *Ward, Mary*.

ENHYPOSTASIA (Gk. ἐν 'in', and ὑπόστασις 'person'). The doctrine advanced by *Leontius of Byzantium and St. *John of Damascus that in the Incarnate Christ the personal humanity of Christ was not lost, but included within the *hypostasis of the Godhead, and that thereby He included within Himself all the attributes of perfect humanity. It was believed to give a fuller place to the human side of Christ's work than was done by the doctrine of the 'Anhypostatic Manhood' taught by theologians under the influence of St. *Cyril of Alexandria. In recent times the doctrine has been defended by H. M. Relton (*A Study in Christology*, 1917). The noun ἐνυποστασία is apparently not found in the ancient writers, though the theologians mentioned make abundant use of its cognates.

ENLIGHTENMENT. See *Aufklärung*.

ENNODIUS, ST. MAGNUS FELIX (c. 473–521), Christian rhetorician and Bp. of Pavia. Born at Arles, he was brought up probably at Pavia (possibly at *Milan). After ordination as deacon c. 493 by St. Epiphanius, Bp. of Pavia, he went to Milan where he taught rhetoric until consecrated Bp. of Pavia c. 514. In the dispute about the succession to Pope Anastasius II (d. 496), he defended Symmachus and wrote a *libellus* against those who challenged the synod of 502, maintaining that the Papal office was *de jure* exempt from all interference from the secular power. He was twice sent by Pope *Hormisdas on missions to Anastasius, Patr. of *Constantinople, to effect a reconciliation with the E. His abundant writings suffer from a turgid style, but are valuable through the incidental light they throw on the happenings and cultural ideals of his age. They include an account of his own religious experiences ('Eucharisticon de Vita Sua'), a long panegyric on the Arian King Theodoric (507), a Life of St. Epiphanius of Pavia, several discourses ('Dictiones'), many epitaphs and epigrams, and a considerable collection of hymns, modelled on those of St. *Ambrose. His work is probably the last serious attempt to combine a fundamentally pagan culture with the profession of the Christian creed. His epitaph survives in the church of S. Michele in Pavia. Feast day, 17 July.

His writings, edited by J. *Sirmond (Paris, 1611), are reprinted in J. P. Migne, *PL*, lxiii, 13–364. There are good critical editions by W. Hartel (C.S.E.L., 1882) and F. Vogel (*M.G.H.*, 1884, with full *prolegomena*). M. Fertig, *Ennodius und seine Zeit* (3 vols., 1855–60); S. L'Église, *St. Ennodius et la suprématie pontificale au sixième siècle* (1890); A. Dubois, *La Latinité d'Ennodius* (1903).

ENOCH. OT patriarch. The OT records nothing of Enoch except that he was the father of Methuselah and that 'he walked with God and he was not; for God took him' (Gen. 5. 24). In Jewish tradition many legends became attached to him and in the NT his translation is referred to at Heb. 11. 5. For the pseudepigraphical books ascribed to Enoch, see the foll. entry.

ENOCH, Books of. (1) The 'Ethiopic Book of Enoch' is the longest of the surviving Jewish pseudepigraphical writings. Properly it is not a single Book, but a heterogeneous collection of writings which have much in common, and all appear to date from the last two cents. B.C. It embodies a series of revelations, of which Enoch is the professed recipient, on such matters as the origin of evil, the angels and their destinies, and the nature of *Gehenna and *Paradise. R. H. *Charles divides the Book as follows into five sections composed at different dates. Section 1 (chs. 1–36) incorporates fragments of the 'Book of Noah'; 2 (chs. 37–71) contains the 'Parables' or 'Similitudes', c. 105–64 B.C.; 3 (chs. 72–82), the 'Book of the Heavenly Luminaries', was written before 110 B.C.; 4 (chs. 83–90), the 'Dream Visions', is *Maccabean (165–161 B.C.); and 5 (chs. 91–104), incorporating an 'Apocalypse of Weeks', contains materials of various dates. Apart from a few Greek and still fewer Latin fragments, this Book survives only in an Ethiopic Version. Its original language, however, seems to have been Hebrew or Aramaic.

The passages on the 'Son of Man' in the 'Parables' or 'Similitudes' (chs. 37–71) have been widely held to have influenced the NT writings. Other NT titles, such as the 'Righteous One' (1 En. 38. 2, 53. 6; cf. Acts 3. 14, 7. 52, 22. 14) and the 'Elect One' (1 En. 40. 5, 49. 2, 4, &c.; cf. Lk. 9. 35, 23. 35), first appear in Enoch as Messianic designations.

Attention has also been drawn to the important part played by the spiritual world of evil powers in Enoch and in the NT; and a passage from 1 Enoch seems actually to be quoted in Jude (vv. 4 and 14; cf. 1 En. 1. 1, 9). Among the patristic writers who are influenced by, or quote, 1 Enoch are the Ep. of *Barnabas, St. *Justin Martyr, St. *Irenaeus, *Tertullian (who regards it as Scripture), *Origen, and *Lactantius.

(2) The so-called 'Slavonic Enoch', also known as 'The Book of the Secrets of Enoch', which has many points of contact with the preceding, first came to the knowledge of W. scholars in the last years of the 19th cent. Originally written in Greek, it is extant only in two Slavonic versions. The first part (1–23) describes Enoch's assumption into heaven and his visions there; the second (24–38) contains an account of creation and Enoch's visit to his family on earth; the third part (39–54) gives an account of the secrets of the created universe and contains a set of moral exhortations to his sons; and the fourth (54–67) contains Enoch's address to his family and his final translation into heaven. The Book appears to be of various dates near the beginning of the Christian era, and of Egyptian *provenance*. Among Christian writers who used it are the author of the Ep. of Barnabas (xv. 4) and Origen (*De Princ.* I, iii, 2).

(3) Yet another treatise, 'Third Enoch', of post-Christian date, has gradually come to light, mainly in fragments, from *c.* 1870 onwards. The continuous Hebrew text was first publd. by H. Odeberg in 1928 from a Bodleian MS. of *c.* 1511 A.D. Its subjects include the destinies of 'Metatron', i.e. the Divine servant who is identified with Enoch; many descriptions of angels and their operations; and an account of *Sheol. The work appears to betray traces of an anti-Christian polemic.

Ethiopic text ed. A. *Dillmann (Leipzig, 1851), J. Flemming (T.U., xxii; 1902), and R. H. Charles (Anecdota Oxoniensia. Semitic Series, pt. xi; 1906); Eng. tr. of Dillmann's text by R. H. Charles (Oxford, 1893) and of his own ed. (ib., 1912). German trr. of Slavonic text, with introd. by G. N. Bonwetsch (*Abh.* (Gött.), i, Hft. 3; 1897, and T.U., xliv; 1922). Eng. tr. by W. R. Morfill, with introd. by R. H. Charles (Oxford, 1896). Hebrew text ('3 Enoch') ed., with Eng. tr. and notes, by H. Odeberg (Cambridge, 1937). C. Bonner (ed.), *The Last Chapters of Enoch in Greek* (Studies and Documents, ed. K. *Lake–S. Lake, viii; 1937). R. H. Charles, *The Apocrypha and Pseudepigrapha of the Old Testament*, ii (1913), pp. 163–277 (on Enoch (1) above) and 425–69 (on Enoch (2) above). G. Kuhn, 'Beiträge zur Erklärung des Buches Henoch' in *Z.A.T.W.*, xxxix (1921), pp. 240–75; N. Messel, *Der Menschensohn in den Bilderreden des Henoch* (Beihefte zur *Z.A.T.W.*, xxxv; 1922); H. L. Jansen, *Die Henochgestalt.* Eine vergleichende religionsgeschichtliche Untersuchung (Skrifter utgitt av det Norske Videnskaps-Akademi i Oslo, II, Hist.-Filos. Klasse, 1939, No. 1). R. H. Pfeiffer, *History of New Testament Times with an Introduction to the Apocrypha* (New York, 1949; London, 1954), pp. 75–9.

ENTHRONIZATION. The rite by which a newly consecrated Archbishop, Bishop or Sovereign is put into possession of his throne. It is normally performed by ceremonially leading him to it and seating him thereon; in the case of a Sovereign it forms part of the rite

of *Coronation (q.v.). Since a Bishop's throne was the earliest emblem of his office, his enthronement prob. orig. signified his assumption of power to govern the Church; it would seem to have been performed in silence by the consecrating Bishop immediately after the candidate's consecration and before the Celebration of the Mass. By the time of the earliest English Pontificals (10th cent.) enthronization was accompanied by the recitation of a prayer (prob. of *Gallican origin) and a blessing of the new Bishop, prob. by the consecrator. In the late 12th cent., owing to the growing custom of consecrating Bishops outside their cathedral churches, it became a separate rite, which was accompanied by prayers and performed by a third Bishop appointed by the Metropolitan. In the 13th cent. various changes in the wording of the rite gave ground to the legal interpretation of the ceremony as parallel to the *induction of a clerk, i.e. it was understood as the formal assumption (*possessio*) of the see; at the same time Metropolitans began to assign the task to their *Archdeacons. In the later Middle Ages the increase in the practice of translation gave the ceremony an added importance; a new and more precise formula became customary; and, as the legal aspects were emphasized, cathedral Chapters used the occasion to demand from the new Bishop, who needed access to the cathedral for the purpose, an oath of loyalty to the church and pledges to preserve its rights. Until the *Reformation the ceremony was performed at *Canterbury by the Prior and at *York by the Dean. In the C of E it is now usually undertaken by the Archdeacon of the metropolitical diocese of the province. In the RC Church enthronization is usually performed by the consecrating Bishop if the candidate is consecrated in his own cathedral church; but it is no longer of any juridical significance. The enthronement of the Pope in the Church of St. Peter, *Rome, was formerly a ceremony of considerable importance, because, until 1059, it was deemed to confer on him the power of administering the Church.

The term is also applied to the sealing up of relics in a new altar and in the E. Church to induction to a cure of souls.

E. C. Ratcliff, 'On the Rite of the Inthronization of Bishops and Archbishops' in *Theology*, xlv (1942), pp. 71–82.

ENTHUSIASM (Gk. ἐνθουσιασμός). The original meaning of the word, the 'being possessed by a god', was current in the 17th cent. Later it took on the sense of fancied inspiration, S. *Johnson defining it as 'a vain confidence of Divine favour or communication'; and in the 18th cent. it was widely used for extravagance in religious devotion.

R. A. Knox, *Enthusiasm.* A Chapter in the History of Religion (1950).

ENTRANCE, Great; Little. See *Great Entrance; Little Entrance.*

ENURCHUS, St. (4th cent.), Bp. of Orléans. Hardly anything is known with certainty of him. Feast day, 7 Sept. In 1604 a mention of the feast was included, probably (via the *Preces Privatae* of 1564) from the Calendar of the *York Breviary, in that of the BCP, to mark Queen Elizabeth's birthday. The form 'Evurtius' found in modern Prayer Books appears to be a printer's alteration to correspond with the form in the 1524 edition of the York Breviary, which reads 'Euurcius'.

A highly legendary 'Vita' by Lucifer the Subdeacon, prob. 11th cent., is pr. in the *AA.SS.*, Sept. III (1750), pp. 52–8, with discussion by J. Stilting, S.J., pp. 44–52; revised text in *Catalogus Codicum Hagiographicorum Latinorum Antiquorum Saeculo XVI qui asservantur in Bibliotheca Nationali Parisiensi*, ii (1890), pp. 312–19. L. S. Le Nain de *Tillemont, Mémoires pour servir à l'histoire ecclésiastique des six premiers siècles*, viii (ed. 2, 1713), p. 555 f. On the commemoration in Anglican calendars, see V. Staley, *The Liturgical Year* (1907), pp. 43–5.

EPACT (Gk. ἐπακτός, 'brought in'). (1) The excess of days in the solar year over the lunar year of twelve months. (2) The age in days of the moon on 1 Jan. of a given year. In the latter sense the Epact is used in ecclesiastical calculations of the date of Easter.

EPAPHRODITUS. A 'brother, and fellow-worker, and fellow-soldier' of St. *Paul, mentioned only in Phil. (2. 25 and 4. 18; and perhaps also 4. 3). He carried a gift from Philippi to Paul and returned, probably bearing the Ep. to the Philippians. There is no reason to identify Epaphroditus with the Epaphras of Col. 4. 12.

EPARCHY (Gk. ἐπαρχία). In the E. Church, the name for an ecclesiastical *province. It is a subdivision of the civil diocese or 'exarchate'. The word is of frequent occurrence in the canons of E. councils, e.g. in those of *Nicaea (325) and *Chalcedon (451). Its ecclesiastical head is the 'eparch', often called the 'metropolitan', who has a veto on the election of the bishops of the dioceses in his eparchy. In the Council of Chalcedon (can. 17), however, the phrase 'eparch of the [civil] diocese' (ἔπαρχος τῆς διοικήσεως) is used to describe what is more commonly and accurately called the '*exarch' (ἔξαρχος).

EPHESIANS, Epistle to the. The Epistle opens with an exposition of God's eternal purpose to redeem Jews and Gentiles alike in Christ, and their common destiny of being built up into the Church 'upon the foundation of the apostles and prophets, Jesus Christ Himself being the chief corner-stone' (1. 3–2. 22). These promised glories for the Church are echoed through the whole epistle. The author then proceeds to speak of his own position as Apostle of the Gentiles (3. 1–13), and to dwell on the spiritual (3. 14–21) and moral (4. 1–6. 9) implications of conversion, with particular instructions on the duties of the married life (5. 22–33), of children and parents (6. 1–4), and of slaves and their masters (6. 5–9). There is a concluding section exhorting his readers to 'put on the whole armour of God' in their spiritual struggle (6. 10–20).

The Epistle raises many critical questions. It was apparently written when the author was in prison. Considerations of style, as compared with that of the other epistles of St. Paul, and the difficulty of fitting it in with the *Pastorals, have led some modern scholars to question its genuineness, but the problems have not received any agreed solution. The original destination of the Epistle is uncertain. The words 'in Ephesus' in 1. 1 are wanting in some early MSS. (ℵ P⁴⁵), a circumstance which, combined with the absence of all personal references, has led some scholars to suppose it was a circular letter addressed largely to Christians whom the author had not met (cf. 1. 15; 3. 2), and that the place was inserted differently in the copies sent to different churches. There are close literary parallels with Col., which are almost certainly to be explained by direct connexion between the two; and it has sometimes been held that Eph. is a working up of Col. into a more systematic doctrinal treatise.

Commentaries by T. K. Abbott (I.C.C. on Eph. and Col., 1897, pp. 1–191, with introd., pp. i–xlv), C. *Gore (London, 1898), J. A. *Robinson (London, 1903), M. *Dibelius (*Hb.N.T.*, xii, on Col., Eph., Philem., 1911; ed. 2, 1927, pp. 42–77), J. Schmid (Biblische Studien begründet von O. *Bardenhewer, xxii, Hftt. 3–4, 1928), W. *Lock (West Comm., 1929). F. J. A. *Hort, *Prolegomena to St. Paul's Epistles to the Romans and the Ephesians* (1895), pp. 63–192. E. J. Goodspeed, *The Meaning of Ephesians* (Chicago, 1933). E. Percy, *Die Probleme der Kolosser- und Epheserbriefe* (Skrifter utgivna av kungl. Humanistika Vetenskapssamfundet i Lund, xxxix; 1946), pp. 179–474. C. L. Mitton, *The Epistle to the Ephesians*. Its Authorship, Origin and Purpose (1951). F. L. Cross (ed.), *Studies in Ephesians* (1956). W. Lock in *H.D.B.*, i (1898), pp. 714–20, s.v.; A. *Jülicher in *E.Bi.*, i (1890), cols. 860–9, s.v. 'Colossians and Ephesians'. E. J. Goodspeed, *The Key to Ephesians* (Chicago, 1956).

EPHESUS. In NT times, Ephesus, one of the largest cities of the Roman world, was the capital of the Proconsular Province of Asia and, although its harbour was then silting up, was still a great port and commercial centre. Its fame was due largely to its great temple, dedicated to Artemis, or 'Diana' as the Romans called her. This, the fifth on the site, had been erected c. 330 B.C. and counted as one of the 'Seven Wonders of the World'; and Ephesus's proudest title was that of 'temple warden' (νεωκόρος), lit. 'temple-sweeper' to the goddess (Acts 19. 35).

In early Christian times Ephesus was the scene of important labours of St. Paul (see esp. Acts 18 and 19), the traditional home of the aged St. *John, and the scene of the Third General Council of the Church in A.D. 431. During St. Paul's three years' residence in the city, the great riot took place in the theatre so graphically described in Acts 19. 21–41. The belief that St. John the Apostle lived in Ephesus in his old age is widespread, though disputed. An ancient tradition makes the city the scene of his encounter with the heretic *Cerinthus, and the ruins of a large Byzantine church built by *Justinian mark his traditional burial-place. Ephesus was one of the 'Seven

Churches' addressed by the Seer in the Apocalypse (Rev. 2. 1–7), the Ephesians being commended for their hatred of the works of the *Nicolaitans (2. 6). The ruins of a double church near the theatre are almost certainly those of the church in which the Council met in A.D. 431. About a mile from the theatre is a cave where the *Seven Sleepers of Ephesus are reputed to have taken refuge during the *Diocletianic persecution. See also *Ephesians, Epistle to the; Polycrates, St.

J. T. Wood, *Discoveries at Ephesus, including the Site and Remains of the Great Temple of Diana* (1877 [1876]; popular). D. G. Hogarth, with others, *Excavations at Ephesus*. The Archaic Artemisia (British Museum Publication, 1908; atlas in separate vol., 1908). *Forschungen in Ephesos* veröffentlicht vom Österreichischen archäologischen Institute (Vienna, 1906 ff.). C. Picard, *Éphèse et Claros*. Recherches sur les sanctuaires et les cultes de l'Ionie du nord (Bibliothèque des Écoles Françaises d'Athènes et de Rome, cxxiii; 1922). W. M. *Ramsay, *The Letters to the Seven Churches in Asia and their Place in the Plan of the Apocalypse* (1904), pp. 210–50. R. Tonneau, O.P., 'Éphèse au temps de saint Paul' in *R.Bibl.*, xxxviii (1929), pp. 5–34 and 321–63. [L.] Bürchner in *P.W.*, v (1904), cols. 2773–822, s.v. 'Éphesos'; S. Vailhé, A.A., in *C.E.*, v (1909), p. 490 f., s.v.; H. Hörmann–G. Graf in *L.Th.K.*, iii (1931), cols. 708–13, s.v. 'Ephesus I–III', with bibls.; P. Antoine in *Dict. Bibl.* Suppl., ii (1934), cols. 1076–1104, s.v.

EPHESUS, Council of (431). The third General Council, summoned by *Theodosius II in the hope of settling the *Nestorian controversy. With the support of Memnon, Bp. of Ephesus, St. *Cyril of Alexandria, who was the chief opponent of *Nestorius, opened the council on 22 June 431, without waiting for the arrival either of the Syrian bishops, headed by *John of Antioch, who formed the party most likely to take a sympathetic view of Nestorius, or of the legates of the Pope, *Celestine. Nestorius was deposed from his see of *Constantinople and excommunicated, his doctrines condemned, and the Creed of *Nicaea reaffirmed. When they had arrived, the Syrian bishops, joined by *Theodoret and a considerable group who had protested against Cyril's action, held a rival meeting at which Cyril and Memnon were excommunicated. A reconciliation between John and Cyril was finally effected in 433. The council passed eight canons, the first seven dealing with matters arising out of the doctrinal question and the eighth with the jurisdictional rights of *Cyprus. In its rejection of Nestorianism, the council gave formal approval to the *Theotokos (q.v.).

Earlier texts of 'Acta' pr. in Hardouin, i, cols. 1271–1722; Mansi, iv (1760), cols. 567–1424; v (1761), cols. 7–1022. These are now superseded by the crit. ed. of E. *Schwartz, *A.C.O.* I (5 parts, 1922–30). Coptic Acts (of little historical value), ed. W. Kraatz (T.U., xxvi, Hft. 2; 1904). I. Rucker, *Ephesinische Konzilsakten in armenisch-georgischer Überlieferung* (Sb. (Bayr.) 1930, Hft. 3). A. d'Alès, *Le Dogme d'Éphèse* (1931). I. Rucker, *Studien zum Concilium Ephesinum zur 1500-Jahrfeier des dritten ökumenischen Konzils* (5 Hfte, privately publd., Oxenbronn über Günzburg a.D., 1930–5). Hefele–Leclercq, ii (pt. 1; 1908), pp. 287–377. Fliche–Martin, iv (1939), pp. 163–96. M. Jugie, A.A., in *D.T.C.*, v (1913), cols. 137–63, s.v. 'Éphèse (Concile de)'; id. in *E.C.*, v (1950), cols. 114–19, s.v. 'Efeso II, Concilio di ', with reff. to series of artt. in *Échos d'orient* and other bibl.

EPHESUS, Robber Council of 449. See *Latrocinium*.

EPHESUS, Seven Sleepers. See *Seven Sleepers of Ephesus*.

EPHOD. A Jewish ecclesiastical vestment of linen and beaten gold, most probably in the form of a waist-cloth with shoulder-straps. It is described in Ex. 28. 6 and 39. 2. It was worn apparently only by the high priest, but a similar garment entirely of linen was worn by other persons, as by Samuel when serving before the tabernacle at Shiloh (1 Sam. 2. 18), and by David when performing a prophetic dance (2 Sam. 6. 14). Originally the same word was applied to a certain kind of image (frequently in Jgs., e.g. 17. 5).

W. R. Arnold, *Ephod and Ark*. A Study in the Records and Religion of the Ancient Hebrews (Harvard Theological Studies, iii, 1917), esp. pp. 7–23 and 122–32. K. Budde, 'Ephod und Lade' in *Z.A.T.W.*, xxxix (1921), pp. 1–42. G. F. Moore in *E.Bi.*, ii (1901), cols. 1306–9.

EPHOR (Gk. ἔφορος). In the E. Church, a lay guardian or protector in whose charge monastic property was often vested from the 10th cent. onwards. The practice was much abused, as such property was apt to be diverted to secular purposes, e.g. the enrichment of the ephor himself. The word is used also of the holders of various ecclesiastical offices.

EPHPHATHA. The ceremony in the Roman Baptismal rite in which the priest in pronouncing the words 'Ephphatha, that is, Be opened' (Mk. 7. 34) moistens the ears and nose of the candidate with saliva. It is found from an early date in the Baptismal service for Easter Eve at Rome and Milan.

EPHRAEM SYRUS, St. (c. 306–73), Syrian Biblical exegete and ecclesiastical writer. Acc. to Syriac sources he was the son of a pagan priest at Nisibis, his native town; but from indications in his own writings most modern scholars believe that his parents were Christians. It is not impossible that he accompanied St. *James of Nisibis to the Council of *Nicaea (325). Syriac authors ascribe to his prayers the miraculous deliverance of Nisibis from the Persians in 338. After the cession of Nisibis to Persia in 363, Ephraem withdrew into the Roman Empire and settled at *Edessa, where most of his extant works were written. Later very unreliable legends report journeys to Egypt, where he is said to have spent eight years and confuted the *Arians, and to the Cappadocian Caesarea, where he is stated to have visited St. *Basil. He became famous for the austerity and sanctity of his life as well as for his learning.

Ephraem's voluminous exegetical, dogmatic, controversial, and ascetical writings are mostly in verse. Their inspiration is Scriptural throughout, but their style, characterized by repetitions and the accumulation of metaphors, is repellent to modern readers, though it was much appreciated by his Syrian contemporaries. Among his very varied literary productions are cycles of hymns on the great feasts of the Church and on the Last Things, funeral hymns, and refutations of heretics, esp. *Marcion, *Bardesanes, and *Manes, as well as the 'sceptics', i.e. *Arians and *Anomoeans. One of his favourite subjects was the Last Judgement, which he described in terrifying colours. He enjoined devotion to the saints, esp. to the BVM, whose perfect sinlessness he stated in such absolute terms that he has often been invoked as a witness to the Immaculate Conception. He seems to have written exclusively in Syriac, but his works were translated into Armenian and Gk. at a very early date, and via the latter into Lat. and Slavonic. Feast day in the E., 28 Jan.; in the W., formerly 1 Feb., but since 1920, when he was declared by the Pope a Doctor of the Church, 18 June.

There is no satisfactory ed. of Ephraem's works. The standard collection is that of J. S. and S. E. *Assemani and P. B. Mobarek, S.J., ed. Rome, 3 vols. of Syriac texts (1737–46) and 3 vols. of Greek texts (1732–46). Incomplete ed. of Syr. works by J. J. Overbeck (Oxford, 1865; intended Lat. tr. never publd.). Edd. of Hymns by G. Bickell (Leipzig, 1866) and T. J. Lamy (4 vols., Malines, 1882–1902). Crit. ed. of Gk. text begun by S. J. Mercati (I, fasc., i, Rome, 1915; all publd.). Eng. trr. of 'Metrical Hymns and Homilies' by H. Burgess (2 vols., 1835), of 'Select Works' by J. B. Morris in *L.F.*, 1847, and of Selections by J. Gwynn in N.P.N.C.F., Ser. II, vol. xiii, pt. 2 (1898), with useful introductory Dissertation. C. W. Mitchell (ed.), *St. Ephrem's Prose Refutations of Mani, Marcion and Bardaisan* (Text and Translation Society, 2 vols., 1912–21). C. Émereau, *Saint Éphrem le Syrien: son œuvre littéraire grecque* (Paris thesis; 1919). Bardenhewer, iv, pp. 343–75. Altaner (ed. 1951), pp. 299–301. A. Rücker in *L.Th.K.*, iii (1931), cols. 715–18; F. Nau in *D.T.C.*, v (1913), cols. 188–93, s.v.; I. Ortiz de Urbina, S.J., in *E.C.*, v (1950), cols. 126–9, s.v. 'Efrem'.

EPICLESIS (Gk. ἐπίκλησις). Though in Christian writings the term meant originally 'an invocation by name' and subsequently 'a prayer' in general, it is now generally used for the petition in the E. *Eucharistic anaphora invoking the Father to send the Holy Spirit upon the bread and wine to change them into the Body and Blood of Christ. The history and theological significance of this type of petition is highly controversial. A primitive date is sometimes assigned to its introduction, but the earliest certain evidence for it is in the Catechetical Lectures of St. *Cyril of Jerusalem (c. 347). The Anaphora in the *Apostolic Tradition of St. *Hippolytus, written c. 215, contains (in its Latin form) a petition for the illapse of the Spirit upon the bread and wine, but here apparently the purpose of the illapse is not so much to consecrate the Eucharistic elements as to charge them with 'holy spirit', conceived as a Divine δύναμις or impersonal power, in order that by reception the communicants may be filled with 'holy spirit'. There is also evidence which suggests that at one time the Holy Spirit was invoked upon the communicants that they might enjoy the benefits of communion. In several E. Liturgies this form of invocation has been conflated with the consecratory type. In the Egyptian Anaphora of *Serapion, the *Logos (or Word) is regarded as the agent of consecration, and the Epiclesis is framed accordingly.

Though there is no passage in the *Canon of the Roman Mass which is a clear Epiclesis, T. *Cranmer introduced such a prayer ('With Thy Holy Spirit and Word vouchsafe to bless and sanctify these Thy gifts and creatures of Bread and Wine') before the Words of Institution into the BCP of 1549. It was removed in 1552 and not reintroduced in 1662. In the proposed BCP of 1927–8, an Epiclesis, but here after the Words of Institution ('With Thy Holy and Life-giving Spirit vouchsafe to bless and sanctify both us and these Thy gifts of Bread and Wine), found a place in the Alternative Order for the Communion.

L. A. Hoppe, *Die Epiklesis der griechischen und orientalischen Liturgien und der römische Consekrationskanon* (Schaffhausen, 1864). J. T. Franz, *Der eucharistische Konsekrationsmoment* (1875); R. Buchwald, *Weidenauer Studien* (1906), pp. 21–56 ('Die Epiklese in der römischen Messe'); J. Brinktrine, *De Epiclesis Eucharisticae Origine* (Rome, 1923). A. Fortescue in *C.E.*, v (1905), p. 502 f.; S. Salaville, A.A., in *D.T.C.*, v (1913), cols. 194–300, s.v. 'Épiclèse Eucharistique'; F. *Cabrol, O.S.B., in *D.A.C.L.*, v (pt. 1, 1922), cols. 142–84; J. Brinktrine in *L.Th.K.*, iii (1931), cols. 723 f.; M. Jugie, A.A., in *E.C.*, v (1951), cols. 409–13.

EPICTETUS (c. 50–c. 130), *Stoic philosopher. He was probably born at Hierapolis in Phrygia. A slave in the household of Nero, he attended the lectures of the Stoic Musonius Rufus and later became a freedman. He taught in Rome till expelled by Domitian c. 90, when he settled at Nicopolis in Epirus. Though he wrote nothing, his discourses were taken down by his disciple, Flavius Arrianus, and issued in two treatises, the longer 'Discourses of Epictetus' (Ἐπικτήτου Διατριβαί), of which four Books survive, and a shorter and more popular 'Encheiridion'. They reveal him as a religious thinker earnestly seeking for truth and concerned to uphold moral righteousness. His conception of God as the Father of men is more in keeping with belief in a personal and transcendent God than with the Stoic pantheism which he inherited. He stressed the kinship of God and man, the brotherhood of men, and the obligation of moral perfection, to be attained by resignation and renunciation (ἀνέχου καὶ ἀπέχου). The influence of Christian ideas on Epictetus or vice versa has often been discussed, but the resemblances hardly go beyond a striking similarity of moral temper. Only once are the Christians ('Galileans') mentioned in his writings, and then contemptuously.

Best edd. of the Discourses are those of J. Schweighäuser (5 vols., Leipzig, 1799–1800) and H. Schenkl (Teubner ed., 1894; ed. 2, 1916); ed. based on Schenkl, with Eng. tr., by W. A. Oldfather (Loeb, 2 vols., 1926–8); Enchiridion, ed. J. Schweighäuser (Leipzig, 1798). Epictetus's relation to Christianity is discussed by F. W. *Farrar, *Seekers after God* (1868), pp. 186–256; T. *Zahn, *Der Stoiker Epiktet und sein Verhältnis zum Christentum* (1894); K. Kuiper, *Epictetus en de christlijke Moraal* (1906); A. Bonhoeffer, *Epiktet und das Neue Testament* (Religionsgeschichtliche Versuche und Vorarbeiten, x; 1911). D. S. Sharp, *Epictetus and the New Testament* (1914). H. von Arnim in *P.W.*, vi (1909), cols. 123–31, s.v. 'Epiktetos (3)'; E. V. Arnold in *H.E.R.E.*, v (1912), p. 323 f., s.v.

EPICUREANISM. The system of philosophical ethics founded by the Greek thinker, Epicurus (342–270 B.C.). Epicurus held that the senses, as the one and only source of all our ideas, provided the sole criterion of all truth. On this basis he reasserted the materialistic atomism of Democritus and denied immortality. He did not reject the existence of gods, but refused to concede their interference in human affairs. The goal of human conduct he sought in pleasure, maintaining that prudence was the chief virtue, as the surest means of attaining happiness. During and after his lifetime his doctrines proved very attractive. Among later Epicureans were Apollodorus, Zeno of Sidon, and (the most famous) the Roman Lucretius. In the NT, Epicureans are referred to in Acts 17, 18. Fragments of many of Epicurus's writings have been recovered from the charred papyri of Herculaneum.

Fragments of Epicurus ed. H. Usener (Leipzig, 1887), P. von der Mühll (Teubner ed., 1922), and, with Eng. tr., by C. Bailey (Oxford, 1926). 'Ethica', ed. by W. Schmid from Pap. Herc. 1251 (Studia Herculanensia, i, 1939) and by C. Diano (Florence, 1946); Letters, also by C. Diano (Florence, 1946). A. Vogliano, *Epicuri et Epicureorum Scripta in Herculanensibus Papyris Servata* (Berlin, 1928). See also id., *I resti dell' xi libro del* Περὶ φύσεως *di Epicuro* (Publications de la Société Fouad I de Papyrologie, Textes et Documents, iv, Cairo, 1940). C. Jensen, 'Ein neuer Brief Epikurs wiederhergestellt und erklärt' in *Abh.* (Gött.), 3. Folge, Nr. 5 (1933). Diogenes Laertius, *Lives and Opinions of Eminent Philosophers*, x (ed. with Eng. tr. by R. D. Hicks, Loeb, 1925, ii, pp. 528–677). [J.] M. Guyau, *La Morale d'Épicure et ses rapports avec les doctrines contemporaines* (1878). W. Wallace, *Epicureanism* ('Chief Ancient Philosophies', 1880); R. D. Hicks, *Stoic and Epicurean* ('Epochs of Philosophy', 1910), pp. 151–311; A. E. *Taylor, Epicurus* ('Philosophies Ancient and Modern', 1910). C. Bailey, *The Greek Atomists and Epicurus*. A Study (1928); E. Bignone, *L'Aristotele perduto e la formazione filosophica di Epicuro* [1936]. R. D. Hicks in *H.E.R.E.*, v (1912), pp. 324–30, s.v. 'Epicureans'.

EPIGONATION (Gk. ἐπιγονάτιον; from ἐπιγουνίς, 'thigh'). In the E. Church, the lozenge-shaped vestment worn depending from the girdle on the right side. Its use was originally confined to bishops, but in more recent times it has also been worn by *archimandrites, and is sometimes granted to individual priests as a mark of distinction.

EPIKLESIS. See *Epiclesis*.

EPIMANIKION (Gk. ἐπί, 'on'; Lat. *manica*, 'sleeve'). The epimanikia are cuffs, usually of embroidered silk, worn over the ends of the sleeves of the *sticharion by bishops, priests, and occasionally deacons in the E. Church. Their use, which dates at least from the 11th cent., was in the 12th cent. still confined to bishops, and hence they may be a development of the cuffs of the bishop's sticharion itself. They seem to have a W. counterpart in the 'manica' referred to in the description of the *Gallican Rite in the Letters attributed to St. *Germanus of Paris.

EPIPHANIUS, St. (c. 315–403), Bp. of Salamis. A native of Palestine, he became an enthusiastic supporter of the monastic movement and founded c. 335 a monastery near Eleutheropolis in Judaea. His repute for

earnestness and organization was such that in 367 he was elected by the bishops of Cyprus to become their metropolitan, as Bp. of Salamis. He continued throughout his life an ardent upholder of the faith of *Nicaea, and intolerant of all suspicion of heresy. Of his writings in defence of orthodox belief, the most important was his 'Panarion', commonly known as the 'Refutation of all the Heresies', in which he described and attacked every heresy known to him from the beginning of the Church. Though, like all his works, it is badly constructed and far too receptive of facts and legends which support his position, it preserves much invaluable historical material. In his later life he took an active part in the *Apollinarian and *Meletian controversies, and after meeting St. *Jerome in Rome in 392, joined forces with him in his attack on *Origenism. A visit to *Jerusalem for the purpose in 394 led to serious friction with the bishop, John, in which Jerome also became involved. In 400 he travelled to *Constantinople on behalf of *Theophilus, Bp. of Alexandria, who had expelled the Origenist monks; but, seeing that he was being used as a tool against John *Chrysostom, he set out again for Salamis and died at sea on the way back. Besides the 'Panarion' he also wrote a doctrinal treatise, the 'Ancoratus' (Ἀγκυρωτός), in the MSS. of which the *Nicene-Constantinopolitan creed perhaps appears for the first time, and treatises 'On Measures and Weights' and 'On Gems'. His unbending rigidity, his want of judgement, and his complete inability to understand any who differed from him, were reflected in his writings no less than in his life. Feast day, 12 May.

Editio princeps of Epiphanius' chief works by J. Oporinus, Basle, 1544. Much improved text ed. D. *Petavius, S.J., 2 vols., Paris, 1622; repr. in J. P. Migne, *PG*, xli–xliii. More recent text by W. Dindorf, 5 vols., Leipzig, 1859–62. Crit. text of 'Ancoratus' and 'Haereses', ed. K. Holl, in *G.C.S.*, 3 vols., 1915–33 (Index vol. to follow). Syr. text of 'De Mensuris et Ponderibus', ed. J. E. Dean (Chicago, 1935); Georg. text of 'De Gemmis', by R. P. Blake and H. de Vis (*Studies and Documents*, ed. K. *Lake, ii, London, 1934). Bardenhewer, iii (1912), pp. 293–302; Altaner (ed. 1950), pp. 271–4; both with bibl.

EPIPHANY (Gk. ἐπιφάνεια, 'manifestation'; later τὰ Ἐπιφάνια is used of the feast). Feast of the Church on 6 Jan. It originated in the E. where it was celebrated in honour of our Lord's Baptism (sometimes also in connexion with the Nativity) from the 3rd cent. onwards. Its observance is attested for the *Gnostic sect of the *Basilidians by *Clement of Alexandria (d. c. 217; *Strom.* I. 21). From the 4th cent. there is ample evidence for it, when it ranked with *Easter and *Pentecost as one of the three principal feasts of the Church. One of its main features in the E. is the solemn blessing of the baptismal water.

It was introduced into the W. Church in the 4th cent. but here lost its character as a feast of the Baptism of Christ, which it has retained in the E. Church down to the present day. Instead it became associated with the manifestation of Christ to the Gentiles in the person of the *Magi, as is borne out by the

Homilies of St. *Leo on the 'Theophania' (an alternative name of the feast). The blessing of the water was consequently dropped in the W. (where it came to be part of the ceremonies of *Holy Saturday), and in the Mass and Office of the Feast the Magi were given the chief place though the original connexion with the Baptism was emphasized in the liturgy of the *Octave. Further secondary associations are the Miracle of *Cana and the Finding of the Child Jesus in the Temple. In England the sovereign makes offerings of gold, frankincense, and myrrh in the *Chapel Royal on the feast.

John, Marquess of Bute–E. A. W. Budge, *The Blessing of the Waters on the Eve of the Epiphany.* The Greek, Latin, Syriac, Coptic, and Russian Versions edited or translated from the Original Texts (1901). H. Usener, *Das Weihnachtsfest* (Religionsgeschichtliche Untersuchungen, i, 1889; ed. 2 by H. *Lietzmann, 1911). K. Holl, 'Der Ursprung des Epiphanienfestes' in *Sb.* (Berl.), 1917, pp. 402–38, repr. in Holl's *Gesammelte Aufsätze zur Kirchengeschichte*, ii (1928), pp. 123–54. B. Botte, O.S.B., *Les Origines de la Noël et de l'Epiphanie* (Louvain, 1932). H. Frank, 'Zur Geschichte von Weihnachten und Epiphanie' in *J.L.W.*, xii (1934), pp. 145–56; xiii (1935), pp. 1–39. C. C. Martindale, S.J., in *C.E.*, v (1909), pp. 504–6. K. *Lake in *H.E.R.E.*, v (1912), pp. 330–2. W. A. A. N. Caspari in *P.R.E.* (ed. 3), v (1898), pp. 414–17.

EPISCOPACY (Gk. ἐπίσκοπος, lit. 'overseer'), the system of Church Government by Bishops. Where it prevails it is commonly held to be the continuation of the institution of the *Apostolate by Christ. In the NT the word ἐπίσκοπος (AV, 'bishop') appears to be used of the same office as πρεσβύτερος ('presbyter'). See *Bishop*.

EPISCOPALIAN. Properly a member of any Church ruled by bishops (*episcopi*), but esp. of the Anglican Church as opposed to non-episcopal bodies, e.g. the Church of *Scotland.

EPISCOPI VAGANTES (Lat.), 'wandering bishops'. The name given to persons who have been consecrated bishop in an irregular or clandestine manner or who, having been regularly consecrated, have been excommunicated by the Church that consecrated them and are in communion with no recognized see. A man is also included in this group when the number in communion with him is so small that his sect appears to exist solely for his own sake. W., but not E., theology is generally ready to admit that such consecrations are *valid. In recent times the main streams of succession deriving from 'episcopi vagantes' are those founded by A. H. *Mathew, J. R. *Vilatte, and an Armenian, Leon Chechemian; and the principal sects founded and governed by them are the 'American Catholic Church' (Vilatte), the 'Old Roman Catholic Church' (Mathew), the 'Negro Orthodox Church' (Vilatte), and the 'Free Protestant Church of England' (Armenian). In addition to these are smaller sects and stray bishops whose orders have been obtained by dubious means or come from doubtful sources,

as well as certain *Theosophist bishops who trace their orders to Mathew.

A. J. Macdonald, *Episcopi Vagantes in Church History* (1945); H. R. T. Brandeth, *Episcopi Vagantes and the Anglican Church* (1947).

EPISCOPIUS. The assumed name of Simon Bischop (1583–1643), who systematized the typical tenets of *Arminianism. Born at Amsterdam, he studied at *Leyden (1600–1606), where he came under the influence of *Arminius. In 1612 he succeeded S. *Gomar as professor of theology at Leyden. In 1619 he and twelve other *Remonstrants were condemned by the Synod of *Dort and expelled from the country. Episcopius then went to the Spanish Netherlands where he wrote an Arminian confession of faith (published 1622). After a few years in France (1621–6), where he continued the exposition of his views, he became minister of the Arminian Church in Rotterdam and ultimately (1634) was appointed Rector and Prof. of Theology in the Arminian College, Amsterdam. He emphasized the practical nature of Christianity, affirmed that the Church is based upon a minimum of speculative beliefs, remonstrated against current Calvinist dogmas of *predestination and *original sin, stressed the responsibility of man, not God, for sin, and taught a reduced view of the divinity of Christ and a *subordinationist doctrine of the Trinity.

Opera Theologica, ed. posthumously by S. Curcellaeus and P. van Limborch (2 vols., Amsterdam, 1650–65). Life by P. van Limborch (Amsterdam, 1701). F. Calder, *Memoirs of Simon Episcopius* (1835). A. H. Haentjens, *Simon Episcopius als Apologeet van het Remonstratisme* (Leyden, 1899). H. C. Rogge in *P.R.E* (ed. 3), v (1898), pp. 422–4; J. Dutilleul in *D.T.C.*, v (1913), cols. 367–9.

EPISTEMOLOGY (Gk. ἐπιστήμη, 'knowledge'), also known as **Theory of Knowledge**. The philosophical discipline which examines the nature and validity of human cognition.

EPISTLE. In Christian worship, the former of the two passages of Scripture always read or sung at the Eucharist. Ordinarily it is taken from the NT Epistles, less commonly from the OT, Acts, or Rev. Formerly, both in E. and W., several lessons preceded the Gospel, of which the Epistle was the last, but in the Roman rite, except on a few penitential days, e.g. in the *Ember Weeks, the Epistle alone survives. At *High Mass it is now read by the *subdeacon, but down to the 8th cent. it was assigned to the *lector; and it was formerly read from the *ambo or from the *rood-screen where such existed. In early times the selection of the Epistles was made to provide continuity from Sunday to Sunday, and traces of this 'lectio continua' can still be seen. The series of Epistles in the BCP was taken over from the *Sarum Missal. In the C of E the reader or chanter of the Epistle has sometimes been known as the 'Epistoler'; in the *Canons of 1603 (can. 24), the form 'Epistler' occurs. The 'Epistolary' was the medieval name for the book containing the Epistles.

Jungmann (1949), pp. 483–519 (Eng. tr., i, New York, 1951, pp. 391–421), with reff. W. H. *Frere, *Studies in Early Roman Liturgy*, iii, The Roman Epistle-Lectionary (*Alcuin Club Collections, xxxii; 1935). G. Godu in *D.A.C.L.*, v (pt. 1; 1922), cols. 245–344, s.v. 'Épîtres'. F. E. *Brightman, *The English Rite* (2 vols., 1915), passim.

EPISTLE OF THE APOSTLES, The.
See *Testament of Our Lord in Galilee*.

EPISTOLAE OBSCURORUM VIRORUM.
The famous pamphlet in the dispute between J. *Reuchlin and the *Dominicans of Cologne. It appeared in two parts (1515 and 1517), the first written chiefly by Crotus Rubianus (1486–1540), the second almost entirely by Ulrich von *Hutten (1488–1523). Most of the letters are addressed to Ortwin Gratius, who, though a humanist, belonged to the party of the Dominicans. Written in a style parodying the most monkish Latin, they are a witty and bitter satire on the methods of later Scholasticism, on the religious practices of their age, and on many ecclesiastical institutions and doctrines. Their great popularity contributed much to discredit the old theological learning and its representatives.

Epistolae Obscurorum Virorum. The Latin Text with an English Rendering, Notes and an historical Introduction by F. G. Stokes (1909).

EPITRACHELION
(Gk. ἐπιτραχήλιον; from τράχηλος, 'neck'), also **Peritrachelion**. The form of the stole worn by the priest in the E. Church. It is a long strip of silk, fastened in front and decorated with crosses and a fringe. It is to be distinguished from the *orarion which is the liturgical garment of the deacon.

EQUIPROBABILISM.
The moral system defended by St. *Alphonsus Liguori (q.v.). It sought to steer a mid-course between *Probabiliorism and *Probabilism, holding that the stricter course should be followed if the question concerns the cessation of the law, while the laxer course may be pursued if the question is as to the law having ever existed.

ERA OF THE MARTYRS.
See *Diocletianic Era*.

ERASMUS, St.
See *Elmo, St.*

ERASMUS, DESIDERIUS
(c. 1466–1536), 'Roterodammensis' or 'Roterodamus', humanist. He was probably the (illegitimate) son of Rogerius Gerardus. Christened 'Herasmus', he took in adult life the name of 'Desiderius' as a Latinized form of 'Erasmus', itself a supposed Greek equivalent of his baptismal name. He went to school first at Gouda and then to the '*Brethren of the Common Life' at Deventer, where the humanist, Alexander Hegius, was one of his masters. Despite considerable reluctance, he became an *Augustinian canon at St. Gregory's, Steyn, nr. Gouda, in 1486, and eagerly began to read the Classics and the

Fathers. In 1492 he was ordained priest. Finding about this time a protector in Henry of Bergen, Bp. of Cambrai, with the agreement of his superiors he left his monastery. In 1495 he began to study at Paris, residing at the College of Montaigu. In 1499 he accompanied his pupil, William Blount, 4th Baron Mountjoy (d. 1534), who afterwards became his patron, to England. Here he was received with enthusiasm by J. *Colet, who encouraged his dislike of Scholasticism and directed him to the study of the NT. Having returned to the Continent in 1500, he went to Paris and Louvain, where he refused a professorship, and after another visit to England made his way to Italy in 1506. He did not, however, find the hoped-for intellectual stimulus in Italy. On the accession of *Henry VIII (1509), Mountjoy induced him to return to England and Erasmus stayed for a time in T. *More's house, where he wrote his witty Ἐγκώμιον Μωρίας. The universities of Oxford and Cambridge conferred degrees on him, and John *Fisher gave him the newly created Lady Margaret professorship of Greek and theology at Cambridge. While in England he completed his translation of the NT. In 1516 he accepted an invitation to Brussels to the court of the future *Charles V, who made him a royal councillor. Having been freed from all his obligations to his monastery by a Papal brief in 1517, he resumed his wanderings, but in 1521 made his permanent abode at *Basle, in the house of the famous printer, J. *Froben. In order to keep his freedom he refused many brilliant offers, including one from Francis I at Paris, another from the Archduke Ferdinand at Vienna, and a third from Henry VIII to return to England. When, in 1529, the Reformation was introduced at Basle, he fled to Freiburg im Breisgau, where he lived till 1535, continually advocating religious peace. He died at Basle, whither he had gone to supervise the printing of his edition of *Origen.

Among Erasmus's earliest works are the *Adagia* (1500), a collection of Greek and Latin proverbs, later followed by several enlarged editions, and the *Enchiridion Militis Christiani* (1504), in which he shows the usefulness of scholarship for the formation of the Christian. His well-known Ἐγκώμιον Μωρίας, *seu Laus Stultitiae* (1509), is a bitter satire on monasticism and the corruptions of the Church and helped to prepare the way for the Reformation. In 1516 appeared his celebrated edition of the Greek NT with his new translation into classical Latin. Though based on insufficient MS. material and not without bias, it exercised a profound influence on theological studies and was several times revised during Erasmus's lifetime. In 1524 he entered the Reformation controversy by his *Diatribe de Libero Arbitrio*, in which he emphasized the importance of human free-will against M. *Luther. Luther replied in his *De Servo Arbitrio* (1525), which Erasmus answered in its turn by his *Hyperaspistes* (1526). He also edited a large number of Fathers, among them his favourite St. *Jerome (9 vols., 1516–18), St. *Irenaeus

(1526), St. *Ambrose (1527), St. *Augustine (1526), St. *Epiphanius (1524), and St. *Chrysostom (1530), all published by Froben. In some of these Erasmus's own share probably did not go much further than writing the prefaces.

During his lifetime the most famous scholar in Europe, Erasmus was a man of vast if not always deep erudition, of uncommon intellectual powers, but averse to metaphysical speculation, esp. in its medieval and Scholastic forms. Though he had himself paved the way for the Reformation by his merciless satires on the doctrines and institutions of the Church, his scholarly character, which abhorred violence and sought tranquillity, prevented him from joining the Protestants, and threw him back on the tradition of the Church as the safeguard of stability. In the later years of his life he became suspect to both parties. Luther inveighed against him as a sceptic and Epicurean, and on the other side, though the Popes, esp. *Leo X, had been favourable to him, the university of Paris censured his teaching in 1527. After his death his writings were forbidden by *Paul IV in 1559 and by *Sixtus V in 1590.

The *editio princeps* of his Works was made by his friend and disciple, Beatus *Rhenanus (9 vols., Basle, 1540–1). Another was issued by Jean *Leclerc (10 vols, Leyden, 1703–1706). Of his over 2,200 letters those of the last 18 years of his life were edited by F. M. Nichols (3 vols., 1901–19); but this has now been superseded by the complete collection, excellently edited by P. S. Allen (1906–47). There are modern Lives by J. A. *Froude (1894), P. Smith (1923), and J. Huizinga (1924). His attitude to the Reformation has been studied by R. H. Murray, *Erasmus and Luther* (1920), and L. E. Binns, *Erasmus the Reformer* (1928).

ERASTIANISM. The ascendancy of the State over the Church in ecclesiastical matters, so named from the Swiss theologian, Thomas Erastus (Germ. Lieber or Lüber; 1524–83).

Born at Baden in Switzerland, Erastus studied philosophy and medicine and was appointed professor of medicine at Heidelberg in 1558. When the extreme *Calvinists endeavoured to introduce their 'Holy Discipline' in the Palatinate, Erastus wrote against them his *Explicatio Gravissimae Quaestionis*, which, however, was not published until 1589 in London. In Erastus's view, the civil authorities in a state which professes but one religion have the right and the duty to exercise jurisdiction in all matters whether civil or ecclesiastical, and to punish all offences; and even such purely ecclesiastical sanctions as *excommunication are subject to their approval.

The book was translated into English under the title, *The Nullity of Church Censures* in 1659, but its ideas had begun to take root in this country from the end of the 16th cent. Among the earliest representatives of Erastian tenets is R. *Hooker, who defends the supremacy of the secular power in his *Ecclesiastical Polity* (1594). Erastian ideas came to the fore in the '*Westminster Assembly' in opposition to the Independents, who attempted to make themselves completely free from the state. They were somewhat modified when applied

to the modern secularized state as visualized, e.g., by T. *Hobbes. In this case the representatives of the state, though themselves professing any or no religion, assert their right to legislate on religious matters concerning the Established Church, e.g., when, in 1928, the revised Prayer Book was rejected by Parliament. In this modified sense the term is now generally understood.

J. N. *Figgis, 'Erastus and Erastianism' in *J.T.S.*, ii (1901), pp. 66–101. A. Bonnard, *Thomas Éraste, 1524–1583, et la discipline ecclésiastique* (thesis, Lausanne, 1894). J. N. Figgis in *D.E.C.H.*, p. 206 f., s.v.

ERCONWALD (d. *c.* 693), Bp. of *London. Born of a princely family, he devoted his fortune to the founding of two religious houses, over one of which, that at Barking, he placed his sister, St. *Ethelburga, and over the other at Chertsey he himself acted as abbot. In 675 he succeeded Wini as Bp. of London and proved himself a pious and able prelate. He was buried in *St. Paul's Cathedral where his tomb soon became a centre of veneration. Feast day, 30 Apr.

The principal authority is Bede, *H.E.*, iv, 6.

ERIC OF AUXERRE. See *Heiric of Auxerre*.

ERIGENA, JOHN SCOTUS (*c.* 810–*c.* 877), philosopher. An Irishman, he went abroad and gained the patronage of Charles the Bald, by whom he was made head of the palace school at Paris. He took a notable part in two theological disputes—the controversy on *predestination centring in *Gottschalk, and that on the *Eucharist, initiated by *Paschasius Radbertus. The latter years of his life are very obscure. A doubtful tradition affirms that he was invited to England by King *Alfred and taught at the abbey of *Malmesbury.

His philosophy, which was suspected of heterodoxy only at a much later date, is an attempted reconciliation of the *Neo-Platonist idea of emanation with the Christian idea of creation. In his greatest work, *De Divisione Naturae*, Erigena urged that Nature should be divided into four categories. First, Nature which creates and is not created, i.e. God; secondly, Nature which is created and which creates, i.e. the world of primordial causes or Platonic ideas; thirdly, Nature which is created and which does not create, i.e. things perceived through the senses; and lastly, Nature which neither creates nor is created, i.e. God, to whom all things must in the end return. Thus the world was held to begin and end with God. There is a strong savour of pantheism about his teaching; and the treatise was condemned at *Paris in 1210 and again by *Honorius III at Sens in 1225. In his *De Predestinatione*, written against *Gottschalk, he argued that in reality, i.e. for God, evil is nonexistent, and in consequence sin and its punishment are corollaries, the sin bearing the punishment in itself.

A solitary luminary, Scotus was a deeply original thinker and a great scholar. He did an important work in translating the writings of *Dionysius the Areopagite into Latin and bringing them to the notice of his successors. He also translated the *Ambigua* of St. *Maximus the Confessor and the *De hominis opificio* of St. *Gregory of Nyssa; and wrote a number of exegetical works.

Collected Works, ed. H. J. Floss for J. P. Migne, *PL*, cxxii, 125–1244. Crit. ed. of his poetry by L. Traube in *M.G.H.*, Poetae, iii (1896), pp. 158–53, with appendix, p. 554 f.; of his commentary on the *Opuscula Sacra* of *Boethius by E. K. Rand (Quellen und Untersuchungen zur lateinischen Philologie des Mittelalters, i, Hft. 2; 1906); two letters, ed. E. Dümmler in *M.G.H.*, Epistolae, vi (1925), pp. 158–62; full text of his *Expositiones super Ierarchiam Caelestem*, ed. H. F. Dondaine, O.P., in *Archives Doctrinale et Littéraire du Moyen-Age*, xvii and xviii (1951), pp. 245–302, with reff. H. Silvestre, 'Le Commentaire inédit de Jean Scot Érigène au mètre ix du livre III du "De Consolatione Philosophiae" de Boèce' in *R.H.E.*, xlvii (1952), pp. 44–122. E. K. Rand, 'The Supposed Autograph of John the Scot' in *University of California Publications in Classical Philology*, v (1920), pp. 135–41, with plates [fasc. 8]. T. Christlieb, *Leben und Lehre des Johannes Scotus Erigena* (1860); J. Huber, *Johannes Scotus Erigena* (Munich, 1861); Alice Gardner, *Studies in John the Scot* (1900); H. Bett, *Johannes Scotus Erigena* (1925). M. Cappuyns, O.S.B., *Jean Scot Érigène. Sa vie, son œuvre, sa pensée* (Universitas Catholica Lovaniensis. Dissertationes . . . Ser. II, xxvi; 1933), with bibl. M. dal Pra, *Scoto Eriugena ed il neoplatonismo medievale* (Storia Universale della Filosofia, xxi; 1941). J. Dräseke, *Johannes Scotus Erigena und dessen Gewährsmänner in seinem Werke De Divisione Naturae Libri V* (Studien zur Geschichte der Theologie und der Kirche, ix, Hft. 2; 1902). Überweg, ii, pp. 166–77, with bibl. p. 693 f. F. Vernet in *D.T.C.*, v (1913), cols. 401–34, s.v. 'Érigène', with bibl. B. Nardi in *E.C.*, xi (1953), cols. 162–6, s.v. 'Scoto Eriugena, Giovanni'.

ERNESTI, JOHANN AUGUST (1707–81), German *Lutheran theologian. For the first part of his career he was chiefly engaged in classical teaching, and brought out several famous editions of ancient authors. After holding professorships in Leipzig in non-religious subjects, he became in 1759 a theological professor there. His chief importance lies in his attempt to reconcile the theological tradition of his Church with historical criticism of the Bible, in opposition alike to uncritical rationalism and to mystical and allegorical interpretation. He insisted that the meaning of Scripture must be determined by philological and grammatical considerations and not by dogmatic presuppositions. His most important work was his *Institutio interpretis Novi Testamenti* (1761).

Collected works in *Opuscula Oratoria, Orationes, Prolusiones et Elogia* (Leipzig, 1762), *Opuscula Philologica Critica* (Leipzig, 1764; ed. 2, 1776), *Opuscula Theologica* (Leipzig, 1773) and *Opuscula Varii Argumenti* (Leipzig, 1794). Eulogy by A. W. Ernesti is appended to the *Opusculorum Oratoriorum Novum Volumen* (Leipzig, 1791), pp. 253–72. J. E. Sandys, *A History of Classical Scholarship*, iii (1908), pp. 11–13. G. Heinrici in *P.R.E.*, v (ed. 3, 1898), pp. 469–74.

ERRINGTON, GEORGE (1804–86), titular RC Abp. of Trebizond. A native of Yorkshire, he was educated from 1814 to 1821 at St. Cuthbert's College, Ushaw. In 1821 he entered the *English College in *Rome, and in 1827 was made doctor of theology and ordained priest. He was appointed vice-rector of the English College in 1832, but had to resign this post on account of a breakdown in his health. During the next eight years he travelled, mainly in France and Spain. In 1840 he returned to England with N. P. S. *Wiseman, and from 1843 to 1847 was president of St. Mary's College, Oscott. In 1848 he was sent as a missionary priest to Liverpool, and in 1849 to Salford. After the re-establishment of the RC hierarchy (1850) he was made Bp. of Plymouth in 1851, but left his diocese in 1855 when he was appointed coadjutor to Wiseman and titular Abp. of Trebizond, with the right of succession to the see of *Westminster. During the following years his relations with Wiseman became strained owing to his coolness towards the converts from the *Oxford Movement, and esp. to H. E. *Manning and his Community of the Oblates of St. Charles. In 1860 the cardinals, acting, it has been supposed under Manning's influence, advised Errington's removal. After rejecting a proposal of *Pius IX that he should resign, his connexion with Westminster was severed by the Pope in 1862. Though twice offered important sees elsewhere, Errington refused to leave England, still hoping to secure succession to Westminster after Wiseman's death. In 1869–1870 he took part in the *Vatican Council, where he was one of the signatories of the Anti-Infallibility Petition. After his return from Rome in 1870 he went to Prior Park, where he spent his remaining years as tutor of the theological students of St. Paul's College.

C. Kent in *D.N.B.*, xvii (1889), p. 398.

ERSKINE, EBENEZER (1680–1754), founder of the Scottish Secession Church. From 1703 to 1731 he was minister of Portmoak. Here he refused to take the Oath of Abjuration of the Pretender imposed by the Act of 1712, declining to do so, however, on the ground of its *Erastian form rather than through personal allegiance to the Stuart cause. In 1731 he was made minister of the third charge of Stirling, and elected moderator of the Synod of Stirling and Perth. A dispute in which he unsuccessfully maintained the rights of the laity in Church patronage led him to secede in 1733 and form an 'associate presbytery'. In 1736 he issued a 'judicial testimony' against the Established Church, and in 1740 he was formally deposed from his charge. He thereupon founded the Secession Church, which, however, as a separate body was soon itself hampered by schisms, in the course of one of which Erskine was 'deposed from the ministry' by his opponents (1748). He continued to minister at Stirling till his death.

Sermons and Discourses (4 vols., 1762). J. Ker and J. L. Watson, *The Erskines* (1880). Study by H. Watt in R. S. Wright (ed.), *Fathers of the Kirk* (1960), pp. 106–18. A. Gordon in *D.N.B.*, xvii (1889), pp. 404–7.

ERSKINE, THOMAS (1788–1870), Scottish religious thinker. Erskine was born and lived at Linlathen, Angus. He was brought up by his maternal grandmother, Mrs. Graham of Airth Castle, a strict Episcopalian, and educated at Edinburgh university. In 1810 he was admitted a member of the Faculty of

Advocates. On succeeding to the family estates at Linlathen in 1816 he gave up the bar and devoted himself to the study of theology, making personal contacts with religious and philosophical thinkers of diverse views in many countries. He developed very liberal opinions, finding the true meaning of Christianity mainly in its conformity with man's spiritual and ethical needs. In 1831 he warmly took up the cause of J. McLeod *Campbell after his deposition by the General Assembly for teaching the universal atonement. In England he was attracted to the teaching of F. D. *Maurice. Erskine never severed formal connexion with the Church of Scotland, though he used to read the service of the BCP. His writings included *Remarks on the Internal Evidence for the Truth of Revealed Religion* (1820), an *Essay on Faith* (1822), *The Unconditional Freeness of the Gospel* (1828), and *The Brazen Serpent* (1831). His letters were of unusual grace and distinction.

W. Hanna, *Letters of Thomas Erskine of Linlathen* (2 vols., 1877). W. Benham in *D.N.B.*, xvii (1889), p. 444 f.

ESCHATOLOGY (from Gk. ἔσχατος, 'last', and λόγος, 'discourse'). The doctrine of the last things. The term, which does not seem to have been used in England before the 19th cent., connotes the part of systematic theology which deals with the final destiny both of the individual soul and of mankind in general. In the OT eschatological teaching is closely bound up with the Messianic hope. It is contained mostly in the later books, esp. in *Daniel, but also in many of the prophets, e.g. *Isaiah, *Ezekiel, *Zechariah, some of the *Psalms (e.g. 49 and 73), and the latter parts of *Job. It plays a far more important part in the apocryphal books such as the Bk. of *Jubilees and the Bk. of *Enoch. In the NT it is the subject of many of our Lord's Parables, e.g. those of the Tares among the Wheat and of the Drag Net, and in Mk. 13 and Mt. 24 it is the dominant theme. St. *Paul often treats of it, esp. in 1 and 2 Thess., and it is the main subject of the vividly depicted apocalypses in the Bk. of Rev.

In modern Protestant theology eschatology has been given a new meaning, esp. through the studies of A. *Schweitzer, who attempted to interpret the whole of our Lord's teaching on the assumption that He expected the end of the world in the immediate future. Acc. to him, primitive Christianity was exclusively an eschatological preaching of judgement and salvation. Eschatological considerations are also a dominant factor of the teaching of K. *Barth and his school of '*Dialectical Theology', which sees the life of the individual Christian and of the Church as a series of 'decisions' invested with an eschatological character, which will be consummated in the final cataclysm at the end of time. Recently many attempts have been made to draw out the present and abiding significance of future eschatological happenings, e.g. by C. H. *Dodd

in his conception of 'realized eschatology', and by the studies of O. Cullmann and J. Marsh.

Of the innumerable studies on the subject generally may be mentioned S. D. F. Salmond, *The Christian Doctrine of Immortality* (1895); F. *von Hügel, *Eternal Life* (1912); J. Baillie, *And the Life Everlasting* (1934); A. E. *Taylor, *The Christian Hope of Immortality* (1938). Cf. also F. Holmström, *Das eschatologische Denken der Gegenwart* (Germ. tr., 1936; orig. in Swedish).
On the Biblical teaching besides the works of A. Schweitzer and K. Barth (qq.v.), important studies include J. *Weiss, *Die Predigt Jesu vom Reiche Gottes* (1892; ed. 2, 1900). R. H. *Charles, *A Critical History of the Doctrine of a Future Life in Israel, in Judaism and in Christianity* (Jowett Lectures for 1898–9; 1899; ed. 2, 1913); H. A. A. Kennedy, *St. Paul's Conceptions of the Last Things* (1904). W. O. E. Oesterley, *The Doctrine of the Last Things, Jewish and Christian* (1908). P. Volz, *Jüdische Eschatologie von Daniel bis Akiba* (1903; new ed. as *Die Eschatologie der jüdischen Gemeinde im neutestamentlichen Zeitalter*, 1934). O. Cullmann, *Christus und die Zeit* (Zürich, 1946; Eng. tr., 1951); J. Marsh, *The Fulness of Time* (1952).
A. B. *Davidson in *H.D.B.*, i (1898), pp. 734–41, s.v.; R. H. Charles in *E.Bi.*, ii (1901), cols. 1335–92, s.v.; J. A. MacCulloch in *H.E.R.E.*, v (1912), pp. 373–91, s.v.

ESDRAS, Books of. 'Esdras' is the Greek and Latin form of *Ezra. In the *Septuagint there are two books of this title,—I Esdras (Esdras A), a Greek book based on parts of 2 Chr., Ez. and Neh., with an interpolated story not extant in Hebrew; and II Esdras (Esdras B), a straightforward rendering of the Hebrew Ezra-Neh. (treated as one book). In the current form of the *Vulgate these are increased to four, viz.: I and II Esdras, i.e. St. *Jerome's rendering of Ezra and Neh., treated as separate books; III Esdras, the *Old Latin version of Esdras A; and IV Esdras, another book not extant in Greek (see below). For the original Vulgate Jerome deliberately confined himself to the first two of these, rejecting the other two as uncanonical (*Praef. in Esd.*, c. Vigil. 7); but all four books are commonly included (with some confusion in the numbering) in Latin biblical MSS. In 1546 the Council of *Trent (sess. iv) finally rejected III and IV Esdras from the RC Canon, and in subsequent editions of the Vulgate they appear (with the Prayer of *Manasses) as an Appendix following the NT. In the *Geneva Bible (1560) and subsequent English Versions, I and II Esdras of the Vulgate are entitled 'Ezra' and 'Nehemiah', while III and IV Esdras are the '1' and '2' Esdras of the Apocrypha.

1 ESDRAS (i.e. Esdras A of the LXX, III Esdras of the Vulgate, or *The Greek Ezra*) is mainly composed of matter taken from the Heb. canonical books, viz.:

(a) 1–2: a brief account of Josiah and the last Kings of Judah, the decree of Cyrus permitting the return of the first Jewish exiles (537 B.C.), the beginning of the rebuilding of the *Temple and the complaints made by enemies of the Jews to 'Artaxerxes', by which the work was stopped 'until the second year of Darius'. This is taken from 2 Chr. 35 and 36, Ez. 1 and 4. 7–24, and contains nothing original.

(b) 3. 1 – 5. 6: a story of the competition of three young men of the bodyguard of Darius in solving the riddle 'What thing is strongest?'.

The victory is found to rest with neither 'wine' nor 'the king' nor 'women', but with 'truth.' This leads on to a speech by Zerubbabel (see *Zechariah*), in favour of monotheism as the worship of the God of Truth. Adjudged the winner, Zerubbabel receives as his prize from Darius royal assistance for the Jews in their rebuilding of the Temple.

(c) 5. 7–9. 55: a list of the returning exiles (Ez. 2) and subsequent narrative concerning Ezra, taken from Ez. 3. 1–4. 5 and 5–10, Neh. 7.73–8.13.

It was formerly held that the 'Greek Ezra' was a re-editing of Esdras B found in the Septuagint, i.e. the straightforward Greek version of Ezra-Neh. (E. *Schürer), or of some other Greek translation (H. *Ewald); but it is now recognized that it was derived independently from the Heb. (H. St. J. Thackeray). From the Lat. of 4. 41 comes the often cited sentence *Magna est veritas et praevalet* (frequently misquoted as *praevalebit*), 'Great is truth and it prevails' (or 'will prevail'). The book is generally dated between *c.* 200 and *c.* 50 B.C.

2 ESDRAS (IV Esdras of the Vulgate, or *The Ezra Apocalypse*) is composite, viz.:

(a) 1–2: an introductory section beginning *Liber Esdrae Prophetae Secundus*, extant only in Latin. This is a denunciation of the sins of Israel, largely following in phraseology and content the OT prophets. Part of it (esp. 2. 10–48) is also based on the NT and Christian belief, e.g. the vision of the multitude of the redeemed and of the Son of God in 2. 42–8 (the only definitely Christian passage in the Apocrypha).

(b) 3–14: the 'Ezra-Apocalypse' proper, in which the writer, speaking in the name of Salathiel ('Who am also Ezra'), relates his visions and discourses with an angel. Ch. 13 contains a vision of the Messiah described as a *Son of Man, seen rising from the depths of the sea (i.e. from somewhere inaccessible to human knowledge, 13. 51–2), who destroys a hostile multitude by the breath of his mouth (cf. 2 Thess. 2. 8) and gathers to himself a peaceable multitude (explained as the *ten tribes, 13. 39 f.).

This central section of the book (3–14) was certainly written in Hebrew (J. *Wellhausen). It is extant in Syriac, Ethiopic and Arabic versions as well as in Latin; a Greek version (not recovered) is quoted by *Clement of Alexandria (*Strom.* iii, 16) and in the *Apostolic Constitutions* (viii, 7). The visions of the Eagle (chs. 11–12) and of the Son of Man, and the story of Ezra and the canon (ch. 14), were believed by G. H. Box to be of different authorship from the rest of the 'Ezra-Apocalypse'. The Apocalypse proper is dated by most scholars after the fall of Jerusalem (70) and reasons are advanced for placing it not later than the reign of Hadrian (117–38).

(c) 15–16. These chapters, which are no part of the Ezra-Apocalypse, were apparently written as an appendix to 2 Esdras (IV Esdras) and in some MSS. are separately reckoned as 'V Esdras', but they appear never to have been separately current.

On I Esdras, S. A. *Cook in R. H. *Charles (ed.), *The Apocrypha and Pseudepigrapha of the Old Testament*, i (1913), pp. 1–58. C. C. Torrey, *Ezra Studies* (Chicago, 1910). E. Bayer, *Das dritte Buch Esdras, und sein Verhältnis zu den Büchern Esra-Nehemiah* (Biblische Studien, ed. O. *Bardenhewer, xvi, Hft. 1; 1911).

On II Esdras, Lat. text ed. R. L. Bensley, with introd. by M. R. James (Texts and Studies, iii, No. 2; Cambridge, 1895); Eng. tr. with commentary and Lat. text in appendix, by G. H. Box, *The Ezra-Apocalypse*, Being Chapters 3–14 of the Book commonly known as 4 Ezra, or II Esdras (1912); further Eng. tr. and comm. by G. H. Box in R. H. Charles (ed.), *The Apocrypha and Pseudepigrapha of the Old Testament*, ii (1913), pp. 542–624. B. Violet (ed.), *Die Esra-Apokalypse (IV. Esra)*. Erster Teil, Die Überlieferung (G.C.S., xviii; 1910); id., *Die Apokalypsen des Esra und des Baruch in deutscher Gestalt* (ib., xxxii; 1924), pp. 1–202 (with comm.), introd., pp. xiii-lv. Eng. tr. and comm. by W. O. E. Oesterley, *II Esdras* (West. Comm., 1933). Lat. text, with Fr. trr. of Syriac and Ethiopic versions, and comm. by L. Gry (2 vols., Paris, 1938).

See also bibl. to *Ezra and Nehemiah, Books of.*

ESPEN, ZEGER BERNHARD VAN. See *Van Espen, Zeger Bernhard.*

ESPOUSALS OF THE BLESSED VIRGIN MARY (*Desponsatio BMV*). A feast of the Latin Church. Its institution in honour of St. *Joseph was advocated by P. *D'Ailly and J. *Gerson, but its existence as a feast of Mary is first attested in 1517 when *Leo X permitted its celebration to the Nuns of the Annunciation. Since then it has spread to several countries, notably Germany and Spain, but its observance has never been extended to the Universal Church. It is usually kept on 23 Jan.

ESSAYS AND REVIEWS (1860). A collection of essays by seven authors who believed in the necessity of free inquiry in religious matters. Among them were M. *Pattison's 'Tendencies of Religious Thought in England, 1688–1750', B. *Jowett's 'The Interpretation of Scripture', and F. *Temple's 'The Education of the World'. The volume at first attracted little notice and the *Guardian* reviewed it in a temperate although hostile manner, but when Bp. S. *Wilberforce denounced its liberalism in violent terms in the *Quarterly*, general interest was aroused. A meeting of the bishops at Fulham, urged on by Wilberforce, condemned the book in Feb. 1861, and the archbishop issued this condemnation as an encyclical. The Lower House of *Convocation proposed a synodical condemnation, and legal action was taken against two of the essayists (H. B. Wilson and R. Williams), who were condemned to deprivation for a year, although they secured the reversal of this verdict by the *Judicial Committee of the Privy Council. As a protest against the minimizing spirit of the volume, 11,000 of the clergy declared their belief in the inspiration of the Scriptures, and the eternity of punishment, and the book was at length synodically condemned in 1864.

H. P. *Liddon, *Life of Edward Bouverie Pusey*, esp. iv (1897), pp. 38–62 and 68–81; S. C. Carpenter, *Church and People, 1789–1889* (1933), pp. 505–12. V. F. Storr, *The Development of English Theology in the Nineteenth Century, 1800–1860* (1913), pp. 429–54.

ESSAYS CATHOLIC AND CRITICAL
(1926). An influential volume of fifteen essays by a group of Anglo-Catholic scholars on leading themes of Christian belief, with special attention to the issues raised by recent Biblical studies and philosophy. The editor was E. G. Selwyn (b. 1885, later Dean of *Winchester), the other contributors E. O. James, A. E. *Taylor, A. E. J. Rawlinson, W. L. Knox, L. S. Thornton, E. C. *Hoskyns, J. K. Mozley, E. J. Bicknell, K. E. *Kirk, E. Milner-White, A. H. Thompson, N. P. *Williams, and W. Spens. The essayists maintained that the terms 'catholic' and 'critical' were not antithetical, but stood for two moments which in union led to a deeper understanding of historic Christianity. Typical of the book are essays seeking to reconcile religion with primitive anthropology and the fact of the *Fall with psychological theories of human nature, and to reinterpret the Person and Work of Christ in the light of contemporary criticism of the *Synoptic Gospels.

ESSENES.
A Jewish ascetic sect, mentioned neither in the Bible nor the *Talmud, but referred to by *Philo, *Josephus, and the elder Pliny. The name probably means 'the pious ones'. They seem to have originated in the 2nd cent. B.C. and come to an end in the 2nd cent. A.D., and never to have passed beyond the limits of Palestine. At the beginning of the Christian era they numbered about 4,000. Their manner of life was highly organized and communistic; they imposed on candidates for membership a three-year novitiate, with oaths of obedience and secrecy; and they abstained from all but the simplest forms of earning their livelihood. Their piety was akin to that preached by orthodox *Judaism of a *Pharisaic type, though it is possible that details of their worship and teaching came from non-Jewish sources. The suggestions, occasionally made, that St. *John the Baptist and even Christ Himself had Essene connexions are most improbable. See also *Dead Sea Scrolls*.

The chief sources are Josephus, *Jewish Antiquities*, XIII, v, 9; XV, x, 4 f.; XVIII, i, 5; id., *Jewish War*, II, viii, 2–13; Philo in *Eusebius, *Praeparatio Evangelica*, viii, 11, and Pliny, *Natural History*, v, 17. J. B. *Lightfoot, *St. Paul's Epistles to the Colossians and to Philemon* (1875), pp. 83–95 and 114–79. A. Dupont-Sommer, *Nouveaux Aperçus sur les manuscrits de la mer Morte* (1953; Eng. tr. as *The Jewish Sect of Qumran and the Essenes*, 1954), passim. C. D. Ginsburg in *D.C.B.*, ii (1880), pp. 198–208, s.v.; F. C. Conybeare in *H.D.B.*, i (1898), pp. 767–72, s.v.; A.*Jülicher in *E.Bi.*, i (1901), cols. 1396–1400, s.v.; all with bibl. to date. L. Marchal in *Dict. Bibl.* Suppl., ii (1934), cols. 1109–1133, s.v.

ESTHER, Book of.
This Book relates an episode in the reign of Xerxes I (here called 'Ahasuerus'), King of Persia from 486 to 465 B.C. It tells how Esther, a kinswoman of the Jew, Mordecai, attained a position of influence and honour as the royal consort, and used it to save her fellow-countrymen when they were in danger of extirpation by the grand-vizier, Haman. Although there may be an historical basis for the story, in its present form it seems to be a popular romance; it contains indeed very little of a directly religious purport, and it is noticeable that no mention is made in the Book of the name of God. The probable reason for its inclusion in the *canon of the OT was that it described the institution of *Purim (q.v.), a feast still kept as one of the annual commemorations of the Jewish year. Nothing is known of the author. The Greek Bible preserves certain additional chapters, which appear in the English Bible in the *Apocrypha and supply information left out of the Hebrew version as we have it to-day. There are no quotations from Esther in the NT.

Commentaries by A. V. Streane (Camb. Bibl., RV, 1907), L. B. Paton (I.C.C., 1908), G. Wildeboer (K.H.C., xvii, on Song of Songs, Ruth, Lam., Eccles., Est., 1898, pp. 169–97), and C. Siegfried (K.K.A.T., Abt. i, Bd. vi, Teil 2, on Esr., Neh., and Est., 1901, pp. 134–75). S. Jampel, 'Esther. Eine historisch-kritische Untersuchung' in *Monatschrift für Geschichte und Wissenschaft des Judentums*, xlix (1905), pp. 405–26, 513–33; id., 'Studien zum Buche Esther', ib., I (1906), pp. 152–68, 289–315; id., 'Das Buch Esther in geschichtlicher Beleuchtung', ib., pp. 513–38, 641–63. A. E. Morris, 'The Purpose of the Book of Esther' in *The Expository Times*, xlii (1930–1), pp. 124–8. H. Striedl, 'Untersuchung zur Syntax und Stilistik des hebräischen Buches Esther' in *Z.A.T.W.*, lv (1937), pp. 73–108. See also bibl. to *Purim*.

ESTIENNE, HENRI; ROBERT. See *Stephanus*.

ESTIUS (1542–1613), Latinized name of
Willem Hessels van Est, exegete and hagiographer. He was a native of Gorcum in S. Holland and studied at Louvain, where one of his masters was M. *Baius. He became a doctor of theology in 1580, and professor at *Douai in 1582. In 1595 he was made chancellor of the university of Douai, the theological faculty of which at that time ranked among the foremost in Europe. His *Historia Martyrum Gorcomiensium* (1603) was a well-documented history of the *Gorcum martyrs, to one of whom his family was related, and considered the most important piece in the process of their beatification. His principal work, the *Commentarii in Omnes Divi Pauli et Catholicas Epistolas* (1614–16), is valuable esp. for its careful exegesis of the literal sense and its judicious choice of *patristic material, following the *Antiochene rather than the *Alexandrian school. It was frequently reprinted down to the end of the 19th cent. Estius, who was considered a saint by his friends and pupils, took part in the controversies of his time, esp. in that on *Molinism, in which he opposed the *Jesuits. He also left extensive notes for a new edition of St. *Augustine. He was called 'Doctor Fundatissimus' by *Benedict XIV.

All Estius's publications except the *Historia Martyrum Gorcomiensium*, were posthumous. Collected ed. of his Biblical works, 3 vols., Venice, 1659. L. Salembier in *D.T.C.*, v (1913), cols. 871–8, with bibl.

ETERNAL CITY, The (Lat. *Urbs Aeterna*).
A designation of *Rome found in classical writers such as Ovid and Tibullus, as well as in official documents of the period of the Empire. As applied to Christian Rome, it

emphasizes the continuous and pervasive influence of the see in the history of (esp. W.) Christendom.

ETERNAL LIFE. In Christianity, not only a life of endless duration but the fullness of life of which the believer becomes possessed here and now through participation in God's eternal being. It unites the strong sense of historical process characteristic of Hebrew thought with elements from the Greek (*Platonic) belief that man's true life lies in a timeless world in which he is freed from the impediments of material and temporal existence. The modern appreciation of its implications owes much to F. D. *Maurice for whom eternal life was sharing in the life of God and eternal death refusal to share in that life ('Eternity has nothing to do with time or duration'), and also to F. von *Hügel, notably his book *Eternal Life* (1912). In the NT its conditions are esp. emphasized in St. John's Gospel.

J. Baillie, *And the Life Everlasting* (1934). F. D. Maurice, *Theological Essays* (1853), p. 436 f.

ETHELBERT, St. (*c.* 560–616), King of Kent. A descendant of Hengist, the legendary ancestor of the Jutish royal House of Kent, he became king in 560 and is stated by *Bede to have extended his power to all England south of the Humber. His marriage with Bertha, daughter of Charibert, the Frankish king, marks the first introduction of Christianity into Anglo-Saxon England, since Charibert insisted that she should be free to practise her Christian faith (Bede, *H.E.*, i, 25). Probably through Bertha's influence, he welcomed St. *Augustine and the Roman mission in 597, was himself converted in the same year, and thenceforward gave his full support to the cause of Christianity in his realm. He was thus the first Christian English king. Feast day, 24 Feb.; in modern calendars, 25 Feb.

Almost the sole authority is *Bede, *H.E.*, i, 25 f and 32 f, and ii, 3–5; the reff. in the Anglo-Saxon Chronicle, s. 565 and 568, introduce chronological difficulties. The best ed. of his 'Dooms', with German tr., by F. Liebermann, *Die Gesetze der Angelsachsen*, i (ed. Savigny-Stiftung, 1903), pp. 3–8. Lat. version pr. in J. P. Migne, *PL*, lxxx. 345–54; 'Donationes ad Diversas Ecclesias', ib. 431–6.

ETHELBERT, St. (d. *c.* 793), King of the East Angles and martyr. He is said to have been treacherously killed by Offa of Mercia or his wife, Cynethryth, to whose daughter he was to have been betrothed. He was buried at *Hereford, where the cathedral is placed under his patronage, jointly with that of the BVM. Feast day, 20 May.

An unreliable life, abridged from that in the *Speculum Historiale de Gestis Regum Angliae* of Richard of Cirencester (ed. by J. E. B. Mayor, R.S., i, 1863, pp. 262–94), is repr. from J. Brompton, *Historiae Anglicanae Scriptores Decem* (1652), cols. 748–54, in the *AA.SS.*, Mai. V (1685), pp. 241*–246*, with certain miracles from a life by Giraldus (Cotton MS Vitell. E. VII, destroyed 1731), p. 246* f. Summary, with other MS lives, in Hardy, i, pt. 2 (1862), pp. 494–6. Giraldus's Life ed. M. R. James in *E.H.R.*, xxxii (1917), pp. 214–44. Ethelbert is also mentioned in the Anglo-Saxon Chronicle, s. 792, and other histories of the period.

ETHELBURGA, St. (d. *c.* 676), Abbess of Barking. She was the sister of St. *Erconwald, Bp. of London, and the first abbess of his *double monastery at Barking in Essex. The dedication of the church at Bishopsgate is perhaps to be ascribed to her, but there were a number of other prominent women of the same name in Anglo-Saxon Christianity. Feast day, 11 Oct.

The chief authority is *Bede, *H.E.*, iv, 6–9; notes in ed. C. Plummer, ii (1896), pp. 217–19. 'Acta' by J. Capgrave pr. in *AA.SS.*, Oct. V (1786), pp. 649–52.

ETHELDREDA, St. (d. 679), founder of the *double monastery at *Ely. The daughter of Anna, a Christian king of the East Angles, she was married at an early age to the Prince of the Gyrvii, but retained her virginity. On his death, three years later, she withdrew to the Isle of Ely for a life of prayer. After five years, at the request of her relatives, she returned to the world to marry Egfrid of Northumbria, but refused to consummate this marriage also. After another twelve years, she obtained Egfrid's consent to become a nun and *c.* 672 received the veil from St. *Wilfrid at Coldingham where her aunt, Ebbe, was abbess. About a year later she founded the double monastery of Ely, of which she was abbess until her death. From another form of her name, 'St. Audry', the word 'tawdry' is derived through the cheap finery exposed for sale at St. Audry's fair. Feast day, 23 June; of her translation, 17 Oct.

The chief authority is *Bede, *H.E.*, iv, 3, 19 f.; notes in ed. C. Plummer, ii (1896), pp. 234–42. *Liber Eliensis*, esp. chs. i–xiv; ed. D. J. Stewart for the Anglia Christiana Society, i (1848), pp. 12–64. *William of Malmesbury, *Gesta Pontificum*, ed. by N. E. S. A. Hamilton (R.S., 1870), pp. 323 ff. Short modern life by J. L. Low (Newcastle, 1886). C. W. Stubbs, *Historical Memorials of Ely Cathedral*. Two Lectures (1897), Lecture I, with Notes, 'The Shrine of St. Audrey', pp. 1–94.

ETHELHARD (d. 805), Abp. of *Canterbury. (He is to be distinguished from Ethelhard, Bp. of *Winchester, d. 759.) He was prob. Abbot of 'Hlud' (? 'Lydd' or 'Louth'), when, in 791, he was elected to the archbishopric, apparently as Offa's nominee. He was not consecrated until two years later. The opposition of the Kentish people to a Mercian archbishop, which probably caused this delay, broke out openly in 796 when Eadbert Praen, a cleric and member of the royal House of Kent, headed the rebellion of the Kentish nobility and forced the Archbishop to flee. After Eadbert's capture, in 798, Ethelhard recovered his see, and now strove to restore it to its old power which it had lost when Offa had obtained archiepiscopal status for *Lichfield from *Hadrian I. This was abolished in 802 after a visit of Ethelhard to *Leo III at Rome, and the Papal decision in favour of Canterbury was acknowledged by the Council of *Clovesho in 803, which marked an important step towards national unity. Throughout his life Ethelhard enjoyed the friendship of *Alcuin, who gave him active support in his difficulties.

Documents relating to his episcopate in A. W. Haddan and W. *Stubbs (edd.), *Councils and Ecclesiastical Documents Relating to Great Britain and Ireland*, iii (1871), pp. 467–535. Two of Alcuin's letters to him, with other information, are given by *William of Malmesbury, *Gesta Pontificum*, ed. by N. E. S. A. Hamilton (R.S., 1870), pp. 17–19. He is also mentioned in the Anglo-Saxon Chronicle, s. 791 and 799, and in most other chroniclers of the period.

ETHELWOLD, St. (c. 908–84), Bp. of *Winchester. Like St. *Dunstan, with whom he was closely associated all his life, he was one of the leaders of the reform movement in the English Church in the late 10th cent. He was first a monk at *Glastonbury, then Abbot of Abingdon, and from 963 Bp. of Winchester. Together with St. *Oswald of Worcester he effected the revival of English monasticism, which had fallen on evil days during the anarchy and confusion of the Danish invasions, taking as his model the usages of the abbey of *Fleury. The *Regularis Concordia* was partly, perhaps mainly, his work. Feast day, 1 Aug.

Several early Vitae, incl. that of Ælfric, pr. in the *Chronicon Monasterii de Abingdon*, ed. J. Stevenson, R.S., ii (1858), pp. 255–66. J. A. *Robinson, *The Life and Times of St. Dunstan* (1923), pp. 104–22. D. J. V. Fisher, 'The Early Biographies of St. Ethelwold' in *E.H.R.*, lxvii (1952), pp. 381–91.

ETHERIA, Pilgrimage of. A treatise narrating the journey of a (prob.) Spanish abbess or nun to Egypt, the *Holy Land, *Edessa, Asia Minor, and *Constantinople, at the end of the 4th cent. It is the work of a pilgrim of considerable intelligence and powers of observation. In the first part, she records her identifications of various places and scenes *en route* with the sites of Biblical events, e.g. *Moses' brook, the place where the Golden Calf was made, the city of *Melchizedek ('Sedima'). In the latter part the descriptions are mainly of liturgical matters, esp. the services at *Jerusalem and the neighbourhood. They include accounts of the daily and Sunday offices, *Epiphany (including the Night Station at *Bethlehem), *Holy Week and *Easter (including the procession with palms to the Mount of *Olives and the *Veneration of the Cross), and *Whitsuntide, in all of which Etheria had evidently taken part. It becomes clear that in her day in Egypt and at Jerusalem the Feast of the Nativity was kept on 6 Jan. She is also the earliest writer to mention the Feast of the *Purification (here 14 Feb.).

The text is preserved (apart from a few fragments also contained in a Madrid MS.) in a single 11th cent. MS. which was discovered by F. Gamurrini at Arezzo in 1884. Gamurrini held the writer to be St. Silvia, the sister of the Roman prefect, Rufinus, and hence the document came to be known as the 'Peregrinatio Silviae'. In 1903, however, Dom M. Férotin argued that she was very probably to be identified with one Etheria (perhaps, 'Egeria' or 'Aiheria'), referred to by a 7th cent. abbot, and this identification is now very widely accepted. The 'Peregrinatio' is written in a curious Latin dialect, though how far this is a local form is disputed.

Edd. by J. F. Gamurrini (1887), J. H. *Bernard (1891), P. Geyer (C.S.E.L., 1898), W. Heraeus (1908), H. Pétré (1948). Eng. tr. by M. L. McClure–C. L. Feltoe (1919). F. *Cabrol, *Étude sur la Peregrinatio Silviae* (1895); M. Férotin, 'Le Véritable Auteur de la *Peregrinatio Silviae*. La vierge espagnole Éthéria' in *R.Q.H.*, lxxiv (1903), ii, pp. 367–397); A. Bludau, *Die Pilgerreise der Aetheria* (1927); A. Lambert, 'Egeria' in *Revue Mabillon*, xxvi (1936), pp. 71–94, xxvii (1937), pp. 1–24, xxxviii (1938), pp. 49–69. E. Löfstedt, *Philologischer Kommentar zur Peregrinatio Aetheriae* (Upsala, 1911),

ETHICAL MOVEMENT. In 1876 an association, the 'Society for Ethical Culture', was founded in the U.S.A. by Felix Adler, to unite those who hold that morality is the fundamental element in religion. It is, in Adler's own words, 'based upon three tacit assumptions, sex purity, the principle of devoting the surplus of one's income beyond that required for one's own genuine needs to the elevation of the working classes, and, finally, continued intellectual development'. Adler originally professed the Jewish faith, but the movement quickly broke off relations both with Judaism and Christianity. A corresponding movement for Great Britain, begun in 1887 by Stanton Coit, has not met here with corresponding support, though certain prominent British philosophers (e.g. J. H. Muirhead, B. *Bosanquet, S. Alexander, and J. S. Mackenzie) have expressed sympathy with it.

Ethics and Religion. A Collection of Essays by Sir John Seeley, Dr. Felix Adler, Mr. W. M. Salter, Prof. Henry Sidgwick, Prof. G. von Gizycki, Dr. Bernard Bosanquet, Mr. Leslie Stephen, Dr. Stanton Coit, and Prof. J. H. Muirhead (1900). F. Adler, *The Religion of Duty* (1905); id., *An Ethical Philosophy of Life* (1918). W. M. Salter, *Ethical Religion* (Boston, 1889); W. L. Sheldon, *An Ethical Movement* (1896). S. Coit (ed.), *Ethical Democracy*. Essays in Social Dynamics (1900). H. J. Bridges (ed.), *Aspects of Ethical Religion*. Essays in honour of Felix Adler on the Fiftieth Anniversary of his Founding of the Ethical Movement, 1876, by his colleagues (New York, 1926). G. Spiller in *H.E.R.E.*, v (1912), pp. 412–14, s.v., with further bibl.

ETHIOPIAN CHURCH. Christianity was introduced into Ethiopia in the 4th cent. by St. *Frumentius and Edesius of Tyre. Acc. to the account of *Rufinus (*Hist. Eccl.* I, ix), the two missionaries were taken to Abyssinia as prisoners, but gained the favour of the Emperor and were set free. Frumentius went to St. *Athanasius, from whom he received episcopal consecration (c. 350), and returned to Abyssinia to convert it. At the end of the 5th cent. and the beginning of the 6th the arrival of the 'Nine Roman [i.e. Byzantine] Saints', probably from Syria, strengthened its Christian faith; it is doubtful whether these 'Saints' were *Monophysites or *Chalcedonians. After a brief period of prosperity, when a cathedral was built at Axum, the religious capital, the Abyssinian Church declined as Mohammedanism began to spread in Africa.

When c. 640 the old patriarchate of *Alexandria was transferred to Cairo, the Abyssinian Church was made entirely dependent on it and its Monophysite patriarch. Little is known of its history during the next centuries. A Jewess apparently seized power c. 920 and the Christians were persecuted; but c. 960 another Christian dynasty was established which lasted till 1268. The Church was frequently left without a patriarch ('*Abuna'), owing to the hostility of the neighbouring Mohammedans; subjection to pagan and Jewish influences, which had for long been strong, continued; polygamy remained rife esp. among the ruling classes; and the Abunas themselves were given to greed and immorality.

When, in 1268, the old dynasty was restored, the Church entered upon another period of vitality, owing to the influence of the abuna, Takla Hâymanôt, who combined great austerity of life with energy and ambition. After his death the abbots of the Convent of 'Mount Lebanon', erected in his honour, were made 'assistants to the throne' and enjoyed great power and prestige. At the end of the 13th cent. repeated efforts were made to restore the country to communion with Rome. Many popes, among them *Innocent IV (1254), *Urban IV (1261), *Benedict XI (1303), and *Clement V (1305), sent letters and missionaries for this purpose; but the success of the *Dominican mission which arrived at the end of the 13th cent. was short-lived, owing to the hostility of the Negus, and the religious were martyred.

In the centuries that followed, the Abyssinian Convent in *Jerusalem became a centre from which relations with the W. were fostered. In 1441-2 Abyssinian delegates took part in the Council of *Florence, where they accepted the act of union, which, however, came to nothing because they had acted without authority from the Emp. Zara Jacob. This sovereign played an important part in the history of the Church, esp. as a reformer of its cult, feasts, and chants. He supported monasteries and schools, but himself tolerated and practised polygamy. During the Mohammedan invasions (1520-51) there were renewed attempts at reunion as the price of military help given by the Portuguese. Under *Julius III *Jesuit missionaries were sent into the country, who met with some success, and conversions on a large scale were effected by the Jesuit P. Paez. When in 1614 belief in the two natures of Christ was imposed under pain of death, the Monophysite party rebelled, but it was defeated in the field in 1621 and the Emperor Susenyos renounced polygamy, abrogated the divorce laws, and became a Catholic. In 1625 a Catholic patriarch, Alphonsus Mendez, was sent from Rome, and in 1626 Catholicism was declared the official religion. It was, however, enforced by violence, the heir to the throne was opposed to it, and with Susenyos's abdication in 1632, the union came to an end and the Jesuit missionaries were banished. After their expulsion Franciscans were frequently sent by the Congregation of *Propaganda, most of whom were martyred. From 1838 more sustained missionary efforts were made, esp. by the *Lazarists and (from 1846) the *Capuchins. When in 1936 the country was opened again to the W. by the Italian conquest, the Monophysite patriarch was confirmed in his office, but compelled to break with the Coptic Church in Egypt.

The Canon of the Scriptures of the Abyssinian Church contains a number of apocryphal books such as the Bk. of *Enoch, the 'Shepherd' of *Hermas, and the 'Ascension of *Isaiah'. The literary language, Ge'ez, has for centuries been used in public worship, though it is not popularly understood. The Abyssinians observe several Jewish practices, esp. the keeping of the Sabbath, circumcision, and the distinction between clean and unclean meats. During the last three centuries there have been violent controversies on the 'Unction of Christ', which have split it into two parties. Acc. to the one, Christ, as man, has become the natural Son of God by the unction of the Holy Ghost which has divinized His human nature so as to absorb it completely; acc. to the other, the union of the two natures does not result from the unction, but is made perfect by it. Both parties, however, profess the unity of natures.

The Abyssinian Church has two kinds of clergy: the rather ignorant priests, who administer the Sacraments, and the more learned lay clerks (*dabtaras*), who are entrusted with the chant of the Church offices and the teaching in the schools. The priests may be either secular, in which case they are married, or regular. The regulars belong to a monastery, but community life is little developed.

There is a small number of *Uniat Abyssinians, most of whom live in Eritrea. They are governed by a Vicar Apostolic and observe the rites and canon law of the old Church of Abyssinia.

M. *Lequien, *Oriens Christianus, ii (Paris, 1750), cols. 641-60. H. M. Hyatt, The Church of Abyssinia (Oriental Research Series, 1928). De L. [E.] O'Leary, The Ethiopian Church, Historical Notes on the Church of Abyssinia (1936); J. S. Trimingham, The Christian Church and Missions in Ethiopia (1950). S. A. B. Mercer, The Ethiopic Liturgy (Hale Lectures for 1914-15; Milwaukee, 1915). J. B. Coulbeaux (ed. J. Bateman), Histoire politique et religieuse d'Abyssinie (3 vols. [1929]), with extensive bibl. E. A. W. Budge, A History of Ethiopia, Nubia and Abyssinia (2 vols., 1928), passim, also with bibl. E. Littmann, 'Geschichte der äthiopischen Litteratur' in C. Brockelmann, Geschichte der christlichen Litteraturen des Orients (1907), pp. 185-269; J. M. Harden, An Introduction to Ethiopic Christian Literature (1926). M. Chaîne, La Chronologie des temps chrétiens de l'Égypte et de l'Éthiopie (1925). A. *Fortescue, The Lesser Eastern Churches (1911), pp. 293-322; B. J. Kidd, The Churches of Eastern Christendom [1927], pp. 447-53; D. Attwater, The Catholic Eastern Churches (Milwaukee; revised ed., 1937), pp. 150-60. J. B. Piolet in C.E., i (1907), pp. 76-9, s.v. 'Abyssinia'; I. Guidi in D.H.G.E., i (1912), cols. 210-27, s.v. 'Abyssinie (Église d')'; M. Froidevaux, ib., cols. 227-35, s.v. 'Abyssinie (Missions au XIXᵉ siècle)'; E. Coulbeaux in D.T.C., v (1913), cols. 922-69, s.v. 'Éthiopie (Église d')'; C. Santi, O.F.M., E. Cerulli, M. Gordillo, S.J., A. Raes, S.J., U. Monneret de Villard in E.C., v (1951), cols. 684-708, s.v. 'Etiopia'; all with bibl.

ETHIOPIC BOOK OF ENOCH. See Enoch, Books of.

ETHIOPIC VERSIONS OF THE BIBLE. The Scriptures were translated into Ethiopic (Ge'ez), prob. from the Greek, in the 4th–5th cent. Both OT and NT exist entire, but the surviving texts are all late (oldest 13th cent.) and show strong influence of the *Coptic and medieval *Arabic versions; those of the *Maccabees are prob. much later translations from the Latin. The Ethiopic OT contains, in addition to the *Septuagintal books, *Jubilees, the Ethiopic *Enoch, IV *Esdras, the Rest of the Words of *Baruch and other items. The Ep. of *Eusebius to Carpianus and the *Eusebian Canons are included in some MSS. of the NT. There is no satisfactory complete edition, though most books of the OT have for some time been published and the NT edited entire by P. Gualterius and M. Victorius (Rome, 1548–9). More scholarly editions include texts of the Psalms by J. *Ludolf (Frankfurt, 1701); of Gen.–2 Kgs. and part of the Apocrypha (2 vols., bound in 3, Leipzig, 1853–94), of Jubilees (Göttingen, 1859), and the *Ascension of Isaiah (Leipzig, 1877), all by A. *Dillmann; and of Mal. (Halle, 1892), Lam. (ib., 1893), and Is. (Berlin, 1893), all by P. J. Bachmann. Portions of the Apocrypha, notably Enoch (1893), Jubilees (1895), and the Asc. of Is. (1900), were also edited by R. H. *Charles. An edition of the OT with the Apocrypha, ed. by F. da Bassano, appeared at Asmara in 4 vols., in '1915–8' (Eth. dating), and of the NT ('ed. 2') in '1926'.

R. H. *Charles in *H.D.B.*, i (1898), pp. 791–3, s.v., with reff.; L. Méchineau, S.J., in *Dict. Bibl.*, ii (1899), cols. 2020–2033, s.v. 'Éthiopienne (Version) de la Bible'.

EUCHARIST. (1) *Name.* The title 'Eucharist' (Gk. εὐχαριστία, 'thanksgiving') for the central act of Christian worship is to be explained either by the fact that at its institution Christ 'gave thanks' (1 Cor. 11. 24, Mt. 26. 27, &c.) or by the fact that the service is the supreme act of Christian thanksgiving. Early instances of its occurrence are in the *Didache (9. 1), in St. *Ignatius (*Philad.* 4, &c.), and in St. *Justin (*Apol.* 1. 66). Other names for the service are the 'Holy Communion', the '*Lord's Supper', and the '*Mass' (qq.v.).

(2) *Origin.* In the NT there are four accounts of its institution, one by St. Paul in 1 Cor. 11. 23–5, and three in the *Synoptic Gospels (Mt. 26. 26–8, Mk. 14. 22–4, Lk. 22. 17–20). It is recorded to have been celebrated by the early Christian community at *Jerusalem (Acts 2. 42, 46) and by St. *Paul on his visit to Troas (Acts 20. 7). These passages show that from a very early date the service was a regular part of Christian worship, and was held to have been instituted by Christ. There is no record of the institution in the Fourth Gospel, but its existence is suggested in Jn. 6. 32–58. Traditionally it has been held that there was preparation for it in the OT, e.g. in the presentation of bread and wine by *Melchizedek, King of Salem (Gen. 14. 18), in the offerings of fine flour and wine (e.g. Lev. 2, 23. 13), in the descriptions of the meal to which Wisdom invites in Prov. (9. 1–5) and Ecclus. (24. 19–21), in the *Passover, and in the '*Kiddush'; and it has sometimes been held that the Divine preparation for it included some pagan sacramental rites as well. The main background in the NT, however, is Jewish and not pagan.

(3) *Doctrine.* The development of Eucharistic doctrine was gradual. In the *Patristic period there was remarkably little in the way of controversy on the subject, but the emphases were different in different parts of the Church.

(a) That the Eucharist conveyed to the believer the Body and Blood of Christ was universally accepted from the first, and language was very commonly used which referred to the Eucharistic elements as themselves the Body and Blood. Even where the elements were spoken of as 'symbols' or 'antitypes' there was no intention to deny the reality of the Presence in the gifts. From the 4th cent., language about the transformation of the elements began to become general; but both before and after this, while some theologians wrote as if they believed in the persistence of the bread and wine after consecration, others wrote as though they held them to be no longer there. In the later part of the Patristic period, the same lines of thought are continued uncontroversially, though there is a tendency towards a division between the precursors of *Transubstantiation on the one side and those who emphasized the continued reality of the bread and wine (as well as the presence of the Body and Blood) in the consecrated sacrament on the other. Later, as the earlier conception of a 'symbol' as that which conveys and is what it represents gave way to the understanding of it as being other than what it represents, the description of the bread and wine as symbols dropped out or was denied. But hardly anywhere is there any attempt at precise formulation. The fathers who made important contributions to the early development of Eucharistic doctrine include St. *Cyril of Jerusalem, St. *Chrysostom, St. *Gregory of Nyssa, St. *Cyril of Alexandria, *Theodoret, St. *Ambrose, St. *Augustine, and St. *John of Damascus.

The first controversies on the nature of the Eucharistic Presence date from the earlier Middle Ages. In the 9th cent. *Paschasius Radbertus raised doubts as to the identity of Christ's Eucharistic Body with His Body in heaven, but won practically no support. Considerably greater stir was provoked by the teaching of *Berengarius in the 11th cent., who opposed the doctrine of the Real Presence. He retracted his opinion, however, before his death in 1088. These controversies had the effect of making some more precise definition desirable, and at the Fourth *Lateran Council (1215) the transubstantiation of the elements was affirmed. Later in the century this teaching was worked out in much detail, with the assistance of the newly recovered philosophy of *Aristotle, notably by St. *Thomas Aquinas. It was maintained that consecration effected a change in the 'substance' of the Bread and Wine, whereas the 'accidents' (i.e. the outward appearance) remained. Concurrently with this development went a great increase in Eucharistic devotion and the institution by Urban IV (1261–4) of the Feast of *Corpus Christi (1264).

At the Reformation, great controversies on the subject took place. M. *Luther defended a doctrine of *consubstantiation, acc. to which after the consecration both the bread and wine and the Body and Blood of Christ coexisted. H. *Zwingli, on the other hand, affirmed that the Lord's Supper was primarily a memorial rite, and that there was no change in the elements whatever. It was this deep-rooted divergence of Eucharistic belief that prevented the union of the forces of the German and Swiss Reformers, despite the attempt to heal the breach at the Colloquy of *Marburg (1529). J. *Calvin and his followers held a view of the Eucharist intermediate between these two. They denied that any change in the elements took place, but maintained that the faithful received the power or virtue of the Body and Blood of Christ, a doctrine which thus became known as *Virtualism; and this or a very similar doctrine was held by some of the chief Anglican Reformers. At the Council of *Trent (sess. xiii, 11 Oct. 1551), where recent disputes had made some formulation desirable, the doctrine of Transubstantiation was reaffirmed in language more explicit than in 1215, but care was taken to avoid any formal definition of it in terms of accidents and substance, despite the general acceptance of this explanation among the leading RC theologians of the time.

Since the 16th cent. great attention has continued to be paid to Eucharistic doctrine in all parts of W. Christendom. It has been the subject of many refinements in the RC Church, e.g. in the writings of M. *Cano, F. *Suarez, J. de *Lugo, J. B. *Franzelin. Apart from Transubstantiation, which on the *prima facie* reading of the 28th *Article of Religion is excluded, a large variety of doctrines have been held in the C of E. The ambiguous, if not actually divergent, language of the BCP has encouraged the coexistence of these doctrines. It has been maintained that the consecrated elements are the Body and Blood of Christ, or that they possess the virtue of the Body and Blood, or that the faithful communicant receives with them the Body and Blood, or that they are merely symbols in the modern sense of the word. There has also been considerable variety of teaching in the Nonconformist Churches.

(b) It was also widely held from the first that the Eucharist is in some sense a sacrifice, though here again definition was gradual. The suggestion of sacrifice is contained in much of the NT language. In Judaism bread and wine were sacrificial elements, and the words at the institution, 'covenant' (διαθήκη), 'memorial' (ἀνάμνησις), 'poured out' (ἐκχυννόμενον), all have sacrificial associations. In early post-NT times the constant repudiation of carnal sacrifice and emphasis on life and prayer at Christian worship did not hinder the Eucharist from being described as a sacrifice from the first. It was long, however, before any attempt was made to define the nature of the sacrifice, though from the 14th cent. onwards

a vast literature on the subject developed. Among the Reformation theologians there arose a strong tendency either to deny the sacrifice or to explain it in an unreal sense. The Council of Trent, on the other hand, dealt fully with the doctrine of the Sacrifice of the Mass. It affirmed that the Sacrifice of the Mass was propitiatory (*propitiatorium*), that it availed for the living and the dead, that it did not detract from the sufficiency of the Sacrifice of *Calvary. It embodied its teaching on the sacrifice in nine canons (sess. xxii; 17 Sept. 1562).

In recent times a good deal of attention has been paid to the nature of the Eucharistic Sacrifice. Many modern writers have stressed the close relation between what takes place at the earthly altar and the perpetual Sacrifice of Christ in Heaven. In this connexion F. C. N. Hicks and others have urged that the purpose of all sacrifice is life, the victim being slain not for its death as such but to liberate its blood, which is pre-eminently its life. M. *de La Taille (q.v.) elaborated the parallelism between the Oblation at the Last Supper and that on the Christian altar, holding that both were integrally related to the one immolation on Calvary. Another development (A. Vonier, O.S.B.; E. Masure) has been to interpret the Eucharistic Sacrifice in terms of Sacrament, setting out from the conviction that it is of the essence of a sacrament to be meaningful and significant. In a less theoretical direction the *Liturgical Movement has assisted these developments by its emphasis on the fundamental relation of the Eucharist to the whole corporate life of the Church, on the essential function of the laity in the Church's Eucharistic life, and on the sociological significance of Eucharistic worship.

Introductory: T. B. *Strong, *The Doctrine of the Real Presence* (1899); C. *Gore, *The Body of Christ* (1901); D. *Stone, *The Holy Communion* (1904); J. C. Hedley, *The Holy Eucharist* (1907; RC); *Report of the Anglo-Catholic Congress,* 1927 (Subject: The Holy Eucharist); Y. Brilioth, *Eucharistic Faith and Practice, Evangelical and Catholic* (Eng. trans. by A. G. Hebert, 1930); W. K. Lowther Clarke (ed.), *Liturgy and Worship* (1932); G. Dix, O.S.B., *The Shape of the Liturgy* (1945). On the History of Eucharistic doctrine, P. *Batiffol, *Études d'histoire et de théologie positive,* Sér. 2: L'Eucharistie (1905); D. Stone, *A History of the Doctrine of the Holy Eucharist* (2 vols., 1909); E. B. *Pusey *The Doctrine of the Real Presence as contained in the Fathers* (1855); C. Gore, *Dissertations on Subjects connected with the Incarnation,* Diss. III: 'Transubstantiation and Nihilianism' (1895); B. J. Kidd, *The Later Medieval Doctrine of the Eucharistic Sacrifice* (1898). On the theology of the Eucharist, R. I. *Wilberforce, *The Doctrine of the Holy Eucharist* (1853); J. B. Franzelin, *Tractatus de SS. Eucharistiae Sacramento et Sacrificio* 1868); W. *Sanday (ed.), *Different Conceptions of Priesthood and Sacrifice* (1900); M. de La Taille, *Mysterium Fidei* (1921); A. Vonier, O.S.B., *A Key to the Doctrine of the Eucharist* (1925); F. C. N. Hicks, *The Fullness of Sacrifice* (1930); E. Masure, *The Christian Sacrifice* (Eng. trans., 1944). On special points and aspects, P. Gardner, *The Origin of the Lord's Supper* (1893); A. *Schweitzer, *Das Abendmahl in Zusammenhang mit dem Leben Jesu und der Geschichte des Urchristenthums* (1901); W. Heitmüller, *Taufe und Abendmahl bei Paulus* (1903); M. Goguel, *L'Eucharistie, des origines à Justin Martyr* (1909); H. *Lietzmann, *Messe und Herrenmahl* (1926); C. W. Dugmore, *Eucharistic Doctrine in England from Hooker to Waterland* (1941); F. S. Renz, *Geschichte des Messopferbegriffes* (1901); É. Dumoutet, *Le Désir de voir l'Hostie et les origines de la dévotion au saint sacrement* (1926); J. Jeremias, *Die Abendmahlsworte Jesu* (1935; ed. 2, 1949; Eng. tr., 1955).

EUCHARISTIC CONGRESSES.

EUCHARISTIC CONGRESSES. International congresses organized by the RC Church for promoting devotion to the Blessed Sacrament. Their ancestor, a local gathering arranged through the exertions and enthusiasm of Mgr Gaston de Ségur, met at Lille in 1881. In succeeding years the Congresses have gradually developed to their present international character. That of 1908 which met in London was the first occasion on which a Papal *Legate had entered England since Cardinal R. *Pole (d. 1558).

Reports of some of the Congresses have been publd. shortly afterwards. J. Vaudon, *L'Œuvre des congrès eucharistiques, ses origines* (1911); M. L. Paladini, *Die eucharistischen Kongresse*. Ursprung und Geschichte (1912). T. F. Meeham in *C.E.*, v (1909), pp. 592–4, s.v.; J. Sauren in *L.Th.K.*, iii (1931), col. 831 f., s.v. 'Eucharistische Kongresse'; B. Spini, S.S.S., in *E.C.*, iv (1950), cols. 350–2, s.v. Congressi eucharistici', with bibl.

EUCHARISTIC FAST, The.

EUCHARISTIC FAST, The. As traditionally understood, complete abstinence from food and drink between the preceding midnight and the reception of Holy Communion. It differs from other forms of fasting in that it is designed less as a form of asceticism than to do honour to the Eucharistic Gifts.

The practice appears to have developed gradually. The earliest express legislation on the subject is in the Council of *Hippo of 393 (can. 28), which allowed, however, an exception on *Maundy Thursday; this decree was re-enacted at Carthage in 397 (can. 29). St. *Augustine (ep. 54, ad Januarium; *c.* 400 A.D.) advocates it, believing it to be of universal observance and dating back to Apostolic times. Throughout the Middle Ages, its observance was virtually universal. It was also taken over by the Reformers who tended to stress esp. its disciplinary value. Among Protestants, however, it gradually died out; in England it also seems to have almost disappeared in the 18th cent. In the 19th cent. the observance was assiduously encouraged by the *Tractarians and their followers. It led to the institution of the early morning Celebration and the discouragement of communicating at the mid-morning High Celebration, except by the (still fasting) Celebrant. Another consequence was that *Evening Communions (q.v.) were strongly deprecated by High Churchmen. By the end of the 19th cent. the practice had become widespread in the C of E and was a strong devotional influence. The proposed BCP of 1928 (not, however, that of 1927) contained the rubric: 'It is an ancient and laudable custom of the Church to receive this Holy Sacrament fasting. Yet for the avoidance of all scruple it is hereby declared that such preparation may be used or not used, according to every man's conscience in the sight of God'.

Since the beginning of the 20th cent. the RC Church has shown an increasing tendency to relax the discipline in certain circumstances. Influences in this direction have been the encouragement of more frequent Communion (see *Communion, Frequency of*) and the disorganization of social habits by two World Wars. Special relaxations have been gradually introduced for those in sickness and on active service, and for others for whom a rigid fast would be burdensome. More recently the practice of Evening Masses has been allowed. In *Pius XII's Apostolic Constitution *Christus Dominus* (16 Jan. 1953) and the accompanying Instruction of the *Holy Office of the same date, these dispensations were standardized. The infirm, even when not confined to bed, are allowed, with the consent of a confessor, to take non-alcoholic liquids, and also solid medicines, before Communion. Priests celebrating at a late hour, or after hard pastoral labour or a long journey, may drink non-alcoholic liquids up to an hour before Mass; and similar concessions were granted in like circumstances to the laity provided they have the 'prudent advice of a confessor' (*de prudenti confessarii consilio*). Another new ruling with important practical consequences is to the effect that water may be consumed at liberty without breaking the natural fast.

H. T. Kingdon, *Fasting Communion* (1873; ed. 2, 1875, much extended); F. W. Puller, S.S.J.E., *Concerning the Fast before Communion* (1903); J. Wickham Legg (ed.), *Papal Faculties allowing Food before Communion* (C.H.S., No. 87; 1905). P. *Dearmer, *The Truth about Fasting, with special Reference to Fasting Communion* (1928). J. M. Frochisse, S.J., 'À propos des origines du jeûne eucharistique' in *R.H.E.*, xxviii (1932), pp. 594–609; G. R. Dunstan, 'The Fast before Communion' in *Theology*, liii (1950), pp. 11–19 and 57–64. The Ap. Const. 'Christus Dominus' is pr. in *A.A.S.*, xlv (1953), pp. 15–24, with the accompanying Instruction, ib., pp. 47–51. Both are repr., with Eng. tr. and comm., in W. Conway, *The New Law on the Eucharistic Fast* (Dublin, 1954). A. Bride in *D.D.C.*, fasc., xxxi (1954), cols. 142–81, s.v. 'Jeûne eucharistique'.

EUCHARISTIC VESTMENTS.

EUCHARISTIC VESTMENTS. In the W. the traditional vestments of the priest celebrating Mass are the *amice, *alb, *girdle, *maniple, *stole, and *chasuble. They derive from the ordinary secular clothing of Roman citizens in the 2nd cent., the alb being a development of the *tunica*, the chasuble of the *paenula*, and the maniple of the *mappula*. In the E. Church the vestments are fundamentally the same but differ in shape. In the RC Church the celebration of Mass without vestments is forbidden. In the Anglican Church since the *Reformation their history is complex. The BCP of 1549 ordered a 'white alb plain, with a vestment or cope', but in the Book of 1552 they were abolished. The *Ornaments Rubric in the present (1662) Book, however, at least on a *prima facie* interpretation, orders their use. After falling into complete disuse for over two centuries, they were restored on the authority of the Rubric in the 19th cent., being first worn at Wilmcote in Warwickshire in 1845. From that date controversy on the subject raged violently. In 1908 a sub-committee of five bishops reported to the Upper House of Convocation that their use was permitted, if not commanded, by the Ornaments Rubric; and they were also tolerated by the rubrics of the proposed Prayer Book of 1927–8.

For bibl., see under separate vestments and also under *Vestments* and *Ornaments Rubric*.

EUCHELAION (Gk. εὐχέλαιον). In the Greek Church, the regular term for the Sacrament of Holy *Unction.

EUCHERIUS, St. (d. c. 449), Bp. of Lyons. Although married and a father, he entered the famous monastery of *Lérins and became a keen exponent of the ascetic way of life. C. 434 he was elected to the see of Lyons, but of his administration we know very little. Together with *Hilary of Arles he presided over the Synod of *Orange (441). His writings comprise two exegetical works (*Formulae Spiritalis Intelligentiae* and *Instructiones ad Salonium*), a *Passio Agaunensium Martyrum* (on the *Theban Legion) and two small ascetic treatises (*De Laude Heremi* and *De Contemptu Mundi*). Feast day, 16 Nov.

Editio princeps by J. A. Brassicanus, Basle, 1531. J. P. Migne, *PL*, l. 685–1214 (with account of earlier edd., cols. 687–98). Crit. ed. (unfinished) by K. Wotke in *C.S.E.L.*, xxxi (1894). *Gennadius, *De Viris Ill.*, lxiii. Bardenhewer, iv, pp. 567–70; Altaner (ed. 1950), p. 404 f., both with bibl.

EUCHITES (Gk. εὐχῆται or εὐχῖται). The heretical sect also known as the *Messalians (q.v.). The Greek, like the Syriac, title means 'those who pray'.

EUCHOLOGION (Gk. εὐχολόγιον). In the E. Church, the liturgical book containing the text and rubrics of the three Eucharistic rites in current use (of St. *Chrysostom, of St. *Basil, and the Liturgy of the *Presanctified), the invariable parts of the Divine *Office, and the prayers required for the administration of the *Sacraments and *Sacramentals. It thus combines the essential parts of what in the W. is contained in the *Missal, *Pontifical, and *Ritual.

Among the earliest MSS of the Euchologion are the 'Barberini Codex S. Marci III. 55 (77)', now Vat. gr. 366; the Cod. Porphyr., formerly of the Imperial Library at St. Petersburg; and the Cod. Sin. 957; all 8th–9th cent. The earliest printed texts come from Venice (1526, 1544, 1550, etc.). A collection of texts, with crit. discussion, in J. *Goar, O.P., Εὐχολόγιον, *sive Rituale Graecorum* (Paris, 1647; ed. 2, Venice, 1750). L. Eisenhofer in *L.Th.K.*, v (1931), col. 834 f., and P. de Meester, O.S.B., in *E.C.*, v (1951), col. 784–6.

EUDEMONISM. The ethical theory which defines the end of right action as εὐδαιμονία, 'well-being'. The classical exponent of this system is *Aristotle. St. *Thomas Aquinas, who uses *Augustine's term *beatitudo* ('blessedness') for εὐδαιμονία, found a place for it in Christian moral philosophy; but in his account the 'well-being' of man is discovered in the vision of God. This Christian eudemonism has been criticized, especially by the *Quietists, on the ground that it leaves no room for the pure disinterested love of God, which should be the foundation of Christian morals. Among Anglican moral philosophers, H. *Rashdall defended a form of eudemonism.

EUDES, St. JOHN (1601–80), French missioner. Born at Ri in Normandy and educated at the *Jesuit college at Caen, he was accepted by the Superior General of the *Oratory in 1623 and priested in 1625. After heroic service in plagues in 1627 and 1631, he spent ten years in conducting missions. In 1641 he founded the 'Order of our Lady of Charity', dedicated to the heart of Mary, to care for fallen women, which in 1644 was entrusted to the *Visitandines of Caen. In 1643 he withdrew from the Oratory and founded at Caen the 'Congregation of Jesus and Mary', dedicated to the Hearts of Jesus and Mary, an association of priests whose object was to conduct seminaries. In 1657 the Caen sisters set up an independent community ('Sisters of our Lady of Charity of the Refuge'), with a fourth vow, to care for fallen women.

St. John Eudes shares with St. *Margaret Mary Alacoque the claim to have initiated devotion to the *Sacred Heart of Jesus. He sought to give it a theological foundation and wrote several offices of the feast. He also fostered devotion to the heart of Mary, introducing in his congregation a feast in its honour in 1648, and publishing in 1670 *Le Cœur admirable de la Mère de Dieu*. The best known of his other writings is *La Vie et le royaume de Jésus* (1637). He was beatified in 1909, and canonized in 1925. Feast day, 19 Aug.

The 'Congregation of Jesus and Mary,' whose members are commonly known as 'Eudists', was almost extinguished by the Revolution. It was reconstituted in 1826 and is now chiefly concerned with secondary education. In recent times it has been active in South America, the *West Indies, and esp. *Canada. In 1835 a separate congregation, the Sisters of our Lady of Charity of the Good Shepherd, was formed to establish reformatories.

Œuvres complètes publ. with introd. and notes, 12 vols., Paris, 1905–9. Lives by Père Hérambourg, de la Cong. de Jésus et Marie, ed. A. Le Doré (Paris, 1869), C. de Montzey (London, 1874), D. Boulay (4 vols., Paris, 1905–8), M. Russell, S.J. (London, 1910), H. Joly ('Les Saints', 1907; Eng. tr., 1932), E. Georges (Paris, 1925). H. *Bremond, *Histoire littéraire du sentiment religieux en France*, iii (1921), pp. 583–671. C. Lebrun, C.J.M., *La Spiritualité de S. Jean Eudes* (1933; Eng. tr., 1934).

EUDISTS. See previous entry.

EUDOXIUS (300–370), *Anomoean leader. A native of Cappadocia, he was appointed by the *Arians Bp. of Germanicia and took part in many of the Arian councils of the 4th cent. In 358 he secured possession of the see of *Antioch; and though soon forced to withdraw, he became Bp. of *Constantinople in 360. Of his writings only a few fragments of his treatise on the Incarnation (Λόγος περὶ σαρκώσεως) survive.

On the treatise mentioned, see C. P. *Caspari, *Alte und neue Quellen zur Geschichte des Taufsymbols und der Glaubensregel* (Christiania, 1877), pp. 176–85 ('Das christologische Bekenntniss des Eudoxius von Constantinopel'). F. *Loofs in *P.R.E.* (ed. 3), v (1898), pp. 577–80; M. Jugie, A.A., in *D.T.C.*, v (1913), cols. 1484–7; id. in *E.C.*, v (1951), col. 788.

EUGENIUS III (d. 1153), *Cistercian, Pope from 1145. Bernardo Pignatelli of Pisa entered the Cistercian abbey of *Clairvaux under St. *Bernard in 1135 and was subsequently made Abbot of St. Anastasio at Rome. Elected Pope in 1145 he had to flee before his consecration, owing to his refusal to recognize the sovereignty of the Roman Senate. He went to Farfa where he was consecrated, and from there to Viterbo, and in 1147 to France where he worked for the Second *Crusade which he commissioned St. Bernard to preach. He held synods at *Paris (1147), Trier (1147), *Reims (1148) dealing chiefly with matters of doctrine, esp. the heresy of *Gilbert de la Porrée and the visions of St. *Hildegard, and at Cremona (1148), where he excommunicated *Arnold of Brescia who had become the leader of the rebellious Roman Senate. In 1149 he returned to Rome but had to leave it again. In 1153 he concluded the Treaty of Constance with *Frederick I (Barbarossa), who guaranteed the rights of the Church. Early in the same year Eugenius had re-entered Rome where he died seven months later. An ardent reformer of the morals of the clergy and of monastic observance, he had formed his life on the spiritual counsels of St. Bernard, who had written for him his famous ascetical treatise 'De Consideratione'. His cult was approved by *Pius IX in 1872. Feast day, 8 July.

592 of Eugenius' letters in J. P. Migne, *PL*, clxxx, 1013-1614, with reff. Jaffé, ii (ed. 2, 1888), pp. 20-89. The principal sources are the Life by Card. Boso in *L.P.* (Duchesne, ii, 1892, p. 386 f.) and the account of *John of Salisbury, *Historia Pontificalis* (ed. R. L. Poole, 1927, pp. 5-90 passim), M. Jocham, *Geschichte des Lebens und der Verehrung des seligen Papstes Eugenius III* (1873); H. Gleber, *Papst Eugen III., 1145-1153, unter besondere Berücksichtigung seiner politischen Tätigkeit* (Beiträge zur mittelalterlichen und neueren Geschichte, ed. F. Schneider, vi; 1936). E. Caspar, 'Die Kreuzzugsbullen Eugens III' in *N.A.*, xlv (1924), pp. 285-305, with text. Mann, ix (1914), pp. 127-220. A. Clerval in *D.T.C.*, v (1913), cols. 1490-2.

EUGENIUS IV (1383-1447), Pope from 1431. Gabriele Condulmaro was born of a wealthy Venetian family, and at an early age entered an *Augustinian monastery. In 1408 he was appointed Cardinal-Priest of *San Clemente by his uncle, Gregory XII. He was elected Pope in 1431, one of his first acts being to dismiss the Council of *Basle (q.v.) which had met in spring of the same year. The Council refused to dissolve, however, and reasserted the *Gallican theory of conciliar supremacy, which had been defended at *Constance. In 1433 Eugenius gave way and recognized the Council as canonical. A year later a revolt in Rome forced the Pope to flee to Florence, where he remained until 1443. Meanwhile relations with the Council, which tried to destroy Papal authority completely, grew steadily worse and ended in the election of an antipope, Felix V (Amadeus VII, Duke of Savoy), in 1439. Eugenius, however, had called a council at Ferrara (1438), and in 1439 concluded the union of the Greek and Roman Churches at Florence which, though not permanent, greatly increased his authority.

In 1443 he returned to Rome. In the following year the *Crusade against the Turks in which he was deeply concerned ended with the defeat of the Christians at Varna. With France relations had become strained owing to the semi-schismatic *Pragmatic Sanction of Bourges (1438), but through the skill of his envoy, Aeneas Sylvius Piccolomini (later *Pius II), the Pope secured a diplomatic success which brought the Empire over to his side (1447). See also *Florence, Council of.*

Eugenius was a Pope of austere piety, a vehement opponent of nepotism, but often imprudent in his policy. His residence at Florence brought him into contact with the Italian Renaissance, and he showed himself a patron of art and literature.

F. P. Abert, *Papst Eugen der Vierte* (1884). E. v. Ottenthal, 'Die Bullenregister Martins V und Eugens IV' in *Mittheilungen des Instituts für oesterreichische Geschichtsforschung.* Ergänzungsband i (1885), pp. 401-589. P. Paschino, *Roma nel rinascimento* (Storia di Roma, xii; 1940), pp. 120-65. Pastor, i (1891), pp. 281-361. P. Moncelle in *D.T.C.*, v (1913), cols. 1492-6, s.v. 'Eugène IV', with bibl. P. Paschini in *E.C.*, v (1950), cols. 802-4, s.v. 'Eugenio IV'.

EUGIPPIUS (c. 455-535), Abbot of Lucullanum, near Naples. In 511 he wrote the Life of St. *Severinus of Noricum. He also compiled a collection of extracts from the writings of St. *Augustine which was much read in the Middle Ages.

Works pr. J. P. Migne, *PL*, lxii, 549-1200. Crit. ed. by P. Knoell (C.S.E.L., ix, 2 pts., 1895-6). 'Vita Sancti Severini', also ed. by H. Sauppe in *M.G.H.*, Auctores Antiquissimi, i, pt. 1 (1877), and by T. *Mommsen in *Scriptores Rerum Germanicarum* (1898). P. Knöll, 'Das Handschriftenverhältniss der Vita S. Severini des Eugippius' in *Sb.* (Wien), xcv (1880), pp. 445-98; T. Mommsen, 'Eugippiana. Sauppe Contra Knöll' in *Hermes*, xxxiv (1897), pp. 454-68. C. C. Mierow, 'Eugippius and the Closing Years of the Province of Noricum Ripense' in *Classical Philology*, x (1915), pp. 166-187. Bardenhewer, v, pp. 220-4. For further works on the life of St. Severinus see s.v. *Severinus, St.*

EUHEMERISM. The theory that the ancient beliefs about the gods originated from the elaboration of traditions of actual historical persons. The name is derived from Euhemerus, a Sicilian writer (c. 315 B.C.), who developed this thesis in a book, Ἱερὰ Ἀναγραφή. Christian apologists, like *Lactantius, saw in this theory the true explanation of the origins of the Greek gods.

EULOGIA (Gk. εὐλογία, 'a blessing'). The word was used in early times both actively for a 'benediction' and passively for 'something blessed'. In the latter sense it was applied to the blessed bread which was distributed to *catechumens and others after the Mass was ended, for consumption either before leaving the church or at home later. See also *Pain Bénit.*

EUNAN, St. See *Adamnan, St.*

EUNOMIUS (d. c. 395), *Arian Bp. of Cyzicus in Mysia. He came from a peasant family of Cappadocia and went to *Alexandria

where he became a disciple of *Aetius (q.v.) c.
356. With Aetius he attended the Arian Synod
of Antioch in 358 and was ordained deacon.
After the Council of *Seleucia (359) Eunomius
followed the *Homoean bishops to *Constantinople and was appointed Bp. of Cyzicus.
Shortly afterwards he compromised himself
by openly professing *Anomean doctrines, had
to resign his see, and retired to Cappadocia.
He later reappeared at Constantinople and elsewhere in the E. Empire, agitating for his party,
of which he was the sole head after the death of
Aetius. He spent his last years at Dakora, continuing to write against the faith of *Nicaea.

Eunomius's principal work, an ’Απολογητικός,
was composed c. 360. It was answered by St.
*Basil, whose reply survives. Eunomius issued
a counter-reply, Ὑπὲρ τῆς ’Απολογίας ’Απολογία,
probably in 378. St. *Gregory of Nyssa's
Contra Eunomium (c. 382) was an elaborate
attack on his whole system. Eunomius was
also the author of a Commentary on Rom. and
of a collection of Epistles, both now lost.

Eunomius taught a single supreme Substance whose simplicity is opposed to all, even
virtual, distinction whether of properties or
attributes. This Substance, which he called
ἀγεννησία ('ungenerated Being'), he held to be
absolutely intelligible. He denied that the
generation of the Son took place within the
Divine Nature, but regarded Him as a being
immediately produced by the Father, from
whom He received the creative power which
caused Him to resemble the Father. Among
the beings created by the Son the Holy Ghost
held the first place. He is the Son's instrument
for the sanctification of souls. He taught that
piety does not consist in the invocation of holy
names or in the use of rites and symbols,
but in exactitude of doctrine, teaching which
necessarily led to the disregard of the Sacraments and of ascetical practices. His views
met with no lasting success and were soon
forgotten.

Part of Eunomius's Apology was first pr. (with Lat. tr. by
H. *Wharton) by W. *Cave (Scriptorum Ecclesiasticorum
Historia Literaria, i, ed. 1740, pp. 220–3); complete text
in J. A. *Fabricius, Bibliotheca Graeca, viii (Hamburg, 1717),
pp. 262–305, and in J. P. Migne, PG, xxx, 835–68; Basil's
reply, ib., xxix, 497–774. Ancient sources incl. *Socrates,
H.E., iv, 7, *Philostorgius, x, 6, and *Photius, Cod. 138.
M. Albertz, Untersuchungen über die Schriften des Eunomius
(Diss., 1908). E. Vandenbussche, S.J., 'La Part de la
dialectique dans la théologie d'Eunomius "le Technologue" '
in R.H.E., xl (1944–5), pp. 47–72. F. Diekamp, 'Literar-
geschichtliches zu der eunomianischen Kontroverse' in B.Z.,
xviii (1909), pp. 1–13. E. Venables in D.C.B., ii (1880),
pp. 286–90, s.v. Bardenhewer, iii (1912), pp. 137–40, with
bibl.

EUPHEMIA, St. (perh. 4th cent.), Virgin
and Martyr. She was greatly venerated in the
E., esp. as patroness of the church where the
Council met at *Chalcedon in 451; but the
legends are all late and unreliable. There is a
church dedicated to her in *Rome which was
restored by Pope Sergius (687–701). Her
name occurs in the *Ambrosian Canon of the
Mass. Feast day, 16 Sept.

AA.SS., Sept. V (1755), pp. 255–86. A. M. Schneider,
'Sankt Euphemia und das Konzil von Chalkedon' in A.

Grillmeier, S.J.–H. Bacht, S.J. (edd.), Das Konzil von
Chalkedon, i (1951), pp. 291–302. H. *Leclercq, O.S.B., in
D.A.C.L., v (pt. 1; 1922), col. 745 f., s.v., with bibl. notes.

EUSEBIAN CANONS, The. The system
of tables (κανόνες) devised by *Eusebius of
Caesarea on the basis of the *Ammonian
Sections (q.v.) to enable the reader of the
Gospels to turn up the passages in the other
Gospels parallel to the one before him. These
tables are often prefixed or appended to the
Gospels in Greek and Latin MSS., esp. down
to the 13th cent., with the corresponding
numbers inserted in red ink in the margins.
Sometimes the table was elaborately illuminated. Eusebius himself explained the system
in his epistle to Carpianus.

J. P. Migne, PG, xxii, 1275–92. E. *Nestle, 'Die
eusebianische Evangelien-Synopse' in Neue Kirchliche
Zeitschrift, xix (1908), pp. 40–51, 93–114, 219–32. See also
bibliogr. to Ammonian Sections.

EUSEBIUS (c. 260–c. 340), Bp. of *Caesarea,
the 'Father of Church History'. He was a
pupil of the scholar and martyr, *Pamphilus,
who trained him in the tradition of *Origen
and imbued him with a hatred of *Sabellianism,
which remained with him all his life. After
Pamphilus's death (309), he fled from the
persecution to Tyre, and then into Egypt,
where he spent some months in prison. C. 315
he became Bp. of Caesarea. During the
*Arian controversy he was the leader of the
moderate party. At the Council of *Nicaea
(325), where he seems to have been on trial for
orthodoxy, he produced the baptismal creed of
Caesarea as a proposed compromise. But the
absence of the crucial word 'homoousios' led to
its rejection in favour of the *Nicene Creed
(q.v.) which Eusebius, now allowing that
*Arius, whom he had hitherto upheld, was
really heretical, ultimately accepted. His fear
of Sabellianism remained, and he never gave
*Athanasius his full support. In 331 he was
offered the bishopric of Antioch, but refused
it. In 335 he attended the Council of Tyre
and the dedication of the Church of the Resurrection at *Jerusalem, and was afterwards
summoned by *Constantine to advise on the
case of Athanasius. He continued active until
his death.

Of Eusebius's many writings the most celebrated is his 'Ecclesiastical History', the principal source for the history of Christianity from
the Apostolic Age till his own day. As with
all Eusebius's writings, its literary style is poor.
But it contains an immense range of material
on the E. Church (he has little to say about
the W.), largely in the form of long extracts
taken over bodily from earlier writers. If
Eusebius's interpretation of these documents
was sometimes in error, this is to be explained
by his want of critical judgement and not
by conscious perversion of the facts. The
'History' consists of ten Books, of which the
last three deal in great detail with the events
of his own time. Indeed, it seems that the
'History' had originally ended before 303 with
Book VII, and that the later Books were added

in successive editions, the final edition with Book X being issued in A.D. 323. Besides the original Greek, it survives in Latin, *Syriac, and *Armenian versions.

Among his other historical writings are: 'The Martyrs of Palestine', an account of the *Diocletianic Persecution between 303 and 310, of which he was an eye-witness; a 'Chronicle' in two books, i.e. a summary of universal history with a table of dates; and a 'Life of Constantine', a panegyric which, though excessive in its flattery, contains invaluable historical matter. His apologetic writings include a defence of Christianity 'Against Hierocles' (a pagan governor of Bithynia), and a pair of treatises, the 'Preparation for the Gospel' and the 'Demonstration of the Gospel'. The former of these (in 15 books) shows why Christians accept the Hebrew and reject the Greek tradition, while the latter (in 20 books, only partly extant) attempts to prove Christianity by the OT. The 'Preparation' contains many quotations from classical authors now lost. His other extant writings are a work on the Incarnation called 'The Theophany', two books against *Marcellus of Ancyra, a collection of OT passages foretelling the coming of Christ, commentaries on the Psalms and Isaiah (which employ the allegorical methods of Origen), a book on Problems of the Gospels, a treatise on 'Easter' (*De solemnitate Paschali*) in which he expounds the *Eucharistic Sacrifice, and a valuable work on Biblical topography called the *Onomasticon*.

Editio princeps of 'Eccl. Hist.' by R. *Stephanus (Paris, 1544); much improved text by H. *Valesius (Paris, 1659); crit. text, with Rufinus's version, by E. *Schwartz–T. *Mommsen in *G.C.S.* (Leipzig, 2 vols., text, 1903–8; vol. iii, introd., 1909). Eng. trr. by A. C. McGiffert (London, 1890), K. *Lake (2 vols., Loeb, 1912–13), and H. J. Lawlor–J. E. L. Oulton (2 vols., S.P.C.K., 1927–8). Other writings pr. from various sources in J. P. Migne, *PG*, xix–xxiv. Much of Eusebius, in excellent crit. texts, in *G.C.S.*, ed. H. Gressmann, J. A. Heikel, R. Helm, J. Karst, E. Schwartz, and others.
H. J. Lawlor, *Eusebiana* (1912); J. Stevenson, *Studies in Eusebius* (1929). M. Weis, *Die Stellung des Eusebius von Caesarea im arianischen Streit* (1920); H. G. Opitz, 'Euseb von Caesarea als Theolog' in *Z.N.T.W.*, xxxiv (1935), pp. 1–19; H. Berkhof, *Die Theologie des Eusebius von Caesarea* (Amsterdam, 1939). On the genuineness of the documents included in the 'Vita Constantini', cf. A. Crivellucci, *Della fede storica di Eusebio nella vita di Costantino* (Leghorn, 1888); N. H. Baynes, *Constantine the Great and the Christian Church* (1930), pp. 40–50; I. Daniele, *I documenti costantiniani della Vita Constantini di Eusebio di Cesarea* (1938); H. Grégoire, 'Eusèbe n'est pas l'auteur de la *Vita Constantini* dans sa forme actuelle et Constantin ne s'est pas converti en 312' in *Byzantion*, xiii (1938), pp. 561–83; J. Vogt, 'Berichte über Kreuzeserscheinungen aus dem 4. Jahrhundert n. Chr.' in *Mélanges Henri Grégoire*, i (Annuaire de l'Institut de Philologie et d'Histoire Orientales et Slaves, ix, Brussels, 1949), pp. 593–606. Bardenhewer, iii (1912), pp. 240–62; Altaner (ed. 1950), pp. 195–201. J. B. *Lightfoot in *D.C.B.*, ii (1880), pp. 308–48; E. Schwartz in *P.W.*, vi (pt. i; 1907), cols. 1370–1439; A. P. Frutaz and A. Penna in *E.C.*, v (1951), cols. 841–54. D. S. Wallace-Hadrill, *Eusebius of Caesarea* (1960).

EUSEBIUS (d. *c.* 359), Bp. of Emesa (Homs) in Syria. He was a native of *Edessa, a Biblical exegete and writer on doctrinal subjects, of *Semi-Arian sympathies, and prob. a disciple of *Eusebius of Caesarea. Having declined to fill the see of *Alexandria when Athanasius was deposed in 339, he

became Bp. of Emesa shortly afterwards. Until recently, apart from a conjectural restoration to him of some 14 homilies of his Caesarean namesake, only fragments of his writings (mainly in exegetical catenae) have been known. Now a collection of 17 homilies (in Lat. tr.) in the MS. Troyes 523 (formerly belonging to *Clairvaux) has been ascribed to him with great probability by A. *Wilmart, O.S.B. Collections of Lat. sermons of Gallican provenance have long gone under his name.

Part of an encomium on Eusebius of Emesa by *George of Laodicea is preserved in *Socrates, *H.E.*, ii, 9, and *Sozomen, *H.E.*, iii, 6. The chief older study on Eusebius is J. C. Thilo, *Über die Schriften des Eusebius von Alexandrien und des Eusebius von Emisa* (Halle, 1832). New ed. of texts by E. M. Buytaert, O.F.M., in S.S.L., fasc., xxvi (i, La Collection de Troyes; Discours I–XVII), 1953 [another fasc. in preparation, ii, La Collection de Sirmond; Discours XVIII–XXIX]. A. Wilmart, O.S.B., 'Le Souvenir d'Eusèbe d'Émèse' in *Anal. Boll.*, xxxviii (1920), pp. 241–84 (text, pp. 263–84). G. *Morin, O.S.B., 'La Collection gallicane dite d'Eusèbe d'Émèse et les problèmes qui s'y rattachent' in *Z.N.T.W.*, xxxiv (1935), pp. 92–115; E. M. Buytaert, O.F.M., 'L'Authenticité des dix-sept opuscules contenus dans le MS. T.523 sous le nom d'Eusèbe d'Émèse' in *R.H.E.*, xliii (1948), pp. 1–89; id., *L'Héritage littéraire d'Eusèbe d'Émèse*. Étude critique et historique (Bibliothèque du Muséon, xxiv; 1949). Further lit. in Altaner (1950), p. 201.

EUSEBIUS (d. *c.* 342), Bp. of Nicomedia. He was the leader of the Arian party in the first half of the 4th cent. In early life he had been a disciple of *Lucian of Antioch, with *Arius as his fellow-pupil, and after Arius's deposition by *Alexander, the Patr. of Alexandria, *c.* 320, Eusebius espoused his cause. By his influence with the Imperial family, Eusebius transformed what might have remained an Egyptian dispute into an oecumenical controversy; and his ascendancy over *Constantine (d. 337), whom he baptized in his last illness, and *Constantius (d. 361) enabled him to organize the forces of the State and of the Church against *Athanasius and his supporters. At the Council of *Nicaea (325), however, he signed the Creed. In 339 he secured his translation from Nicomedia to Constantinople. His followers were commonly known by his name (οἱ περὶ Εὐσέβιον).

A. Lichtenstein, *Eusebius von Nikomedien*. Versuch einer Darstellung seiner Persönlichkeit und seines Lebens unter besonderer Berücksicht seiner Führerschaft im arianischen Streite (1903).

EUSEBIUS, St. (d. 371), Bp. of Vercelli from 340. He was born in Sardinia. A strong supporter of orthodoxy in the *Arian conflict, at the request of Pope *Liberius he accompanied St. *Lucifer of Cagliari on his embassy to *Constantius in 354. After the Synod of *Milan (355) he was exiled to the E., whence he did not return until the reign of *Julian (362). He lived with his clergy at Vercelli under rule and has hence been sometimes regarded by the *canons regular as one of their founders (with St. *Augustine of Hippo). Three of his letters have survived, and the ancient *Old Latin Gospel Codex in the cathedral library of Vercelli (cod. *a*) is ascribed, somewhat doubtfully, to Eusebius's own hand. He also made a Lat. trans. of *Eusebius of Caesarea's 'Commentary on the Pss.', now lost; and various other works which have come down under the names of other authors (among them the *Athanasian Creed, so C. H. *Turner) have been attributed to him in modern times. Feast day, 16 Dec.

J. P. Migne, *PL*, xii, 9–972 (on the Codex, 9–948; text of Epistolae, 947–54). St. Ferrerius, *S. Eusebii Vercellensis ejusque Successorum Vita* (Turin, 1609). C. H. Turner, 'On Eusebius of Vercelli' in *J.T.S.*, i (1899–1900), pp. 126–8.

EUSEBIUS, St. (d. 380), Bp. of Samosata from 361. He belonged theologically to the group led by *Basil of Ancyra which was strongly opposed to *Arianism. Later he became closely associated with St. *Basil of Caesarea, from whom he was the recipient of several letters, and St. *Gregory of Nazianzus. In 374 he was exiled for his orthodoxy to Thrace, but four years later recalled by the Emp. *Gratian. He was killed by an Arian woman who threw a brick at his head. Feast day, 21 June.

Theodoret, *H.E.*, V. iv. 8. *AA.SS.*, Jan. IV (1707), pp. 235–42. Syr. Life, perh. based on Gr. sources, in P. Bedjan (ed.), *Acta Martyrum et Sanctorum*, vi (1896), pp. 335–77.

EUSEBIUS (mid. 5th cent.), Bp. of Dorylaeum. He was an ardent advocate of theological orthodoxy. In 429, at that time a lawyer of *Constantinople, he made a public protest against the teaching of *Nestorius in a 'Contestatio' (Διαμαρτυρία), addressed to the clergy of Constantinople. By 448 he had become Bp. of Dorylaeum in Phrygia Salutaris, in which year he led the attack on the heresy of *Eutyches at the 'Home Synod' at Constantinople. In 449 he was deposed and exiled by the '*Latrocinium' of *Ephesus. His position changed after the reversal of theological policy at court by the accession of Marcian (450), and he took a prominent part at the Council of *Chalcedon (451), where, after being reinstated in his see, he assisted in drafting its Definition of the Faith.

His *Contestatio* in Mansi, iv, 1007–12. Early Lat. version in J. P. Migne, *PG*, lxxxiv, 581–3. Crit. ed. of Gk. in E. *Schwartz, *A.C.O.*, I, i, 1 (1927), p. 101 f. G. Bareille in *D.T.C.*, v (1913), cols. 1532–7, s.v., with bibl.

EUSTACE, St., also 'Eustachius', early Christian martyr. His very existence is doubtful. Acc. to 7th-cent. legends he was a Roman general under Hadrian and converted by a vision of a stag with a crucifix between its antlers, which occurred at Guadagnolo near Praeneste (Palestrina). (Details from the story were later incorporated in the legend of St. *Hubert, q.v.). He and his family are said to have been later roasted to death in a brazen bull. Some of his relics appeared in the 12th cent. in *Paris where they were destroyed by the *Huguenots in 1567. He is one of the Fourteen so-called *Auxiliary Saints and is the patron of hunters and of the city of Madrid. Feast day in the E., 2 Nov.; in the W., 20 Sept.

Legends of St. Eustace and his family in *AA.SS.*, Sept. VI (1757), pp. 106–37. A. Monteverdi, *La leggenda di S. Eustachio* (Bergamo, 1909); id., *I testi della leggenda di S. Eustachio* (ib., 1910). H. *Delehaye, S.J., 'La Légende de St. Eustache' in *Académie Royale de Belgique. Bulletins de la Classe des Lettres et des Sciences Morales et Politiques*, Brussels, 1919, pp. 175–210, with full bibl. reff. A. P. Frutaz in *E.C.*, v (1951), cols. 859–61, with bibl.

EUSTATHIUS, St., Bp. of *Antioch from c. 324 to 330. At the Council of *Nicaea (325) he was given a position of honour, and on his return to his diocese banished many of his clergy suspected of *Arianism. His uncompromising orthodoxy brought him into conflict with *Eusebius of Caesarea, whom he denounced as favouring the Arians, Eustathius in turn being charged with *Sabellianism. When feeling at the court had swung in favour of Arianism, Eusebius succeeded in securing the support of *Constantine for his deposition at a council at *Antioch in 330, and Eustathius was forthwith banished to Thrace, where he remained till his death (see *Meletian Schism*). He was famed for his eloquence. Of his writings there survives only 'de Engastrimutho' (against *Origen), but there are several fragments of, and references to, Eustathius's other works. His Christology was characteristically '*Antiochene', and in many respects foreshadowed the later (heretical) teaching of *Nestorius. E. *Schwartz has ascribed to him the pseudo-*Athanasian 'Sermo Major de Fide'. Feast day, 16 July.

Collection of texts and fragments in J. P. Migne, *PG*, xvii, 609–1066. The sermon pr. in F. Cavallera, *S. Eustathii Episcopi Antiochensis in Lazarum, Mariam et Martham Homilia Christologica* (Paris, 1905; with useful collections of fragments), is prob. not the work of Eustathius. More recent ed. of fragments, with discussion, in M. Spanneut, *Recherches sur les écrits d'Eustathe d'Antioche, avec une édition nouvelle des fragments dogmatiques et exégétiques* (Mémoires et Travaux publiés par des Facultés Catholiques de Lille, No. 55; 1948). Crit. ed. of 'De Engastrimutho' in E. Klostermann, *Origenes, Eustathius und Gregor von Nyssa über die Hexe von Endor* (Lietzmann's *Kl. Texte*, No. 83, 1912), pp. 16–62. Crit. reconstruction of his Ep. to *Alexander of Alexandria on the subject of *Melchisedek in B. Altaner, 'Die Schrift Περὶ τοῦ Μελχισεδέκ des Eustathios von Antiocheia' in *B.Z.*, xl (1940), pp. 30–47. E. Schwartz, 'Der sog. *Sermo Maior de Fide* des Athanasius' in *Sb* (Bayr.), 1925, No. 6. On his theology, R. V. Sellers, *Eustathius of Antioch and his Place in the Early History of Christian Doctrine* (1928). Bardenhewer, iii, pp. 230–7; Altaner (ed. 1950), p. 267. E. Peterson in *E.C.*, v (1951), col. 862 f., s.v.

EUSTATHIUS (c. 300–c. 377), Bp. of Sebaste in Pontus from c. 357. In his youth he was a pupil of *Arius at *Alexandria, and throughout his life vacillated in his attitude to the *Nicene cause. At the synods of *Ancyra (358) and Lampsacus (365) he defended *homoiousian doctrines. His main interests, however, esp. in his earlier years, were in the *monastic movement, in the organization of which he took a prominent part. In this connexion he seems to have greatly influenced St. *Basil the Great, with whom for a time he was on terms of close friendship, in the foundation of his rule. In his later years he became the leading spirit in Asia Minor in furthering the *Macedonian heresy.

F. *Loofs, *Eustathius von Sebaste und die Chronologie der Basilius-Briefe*. Eine patristische Studie (1898); id. in

P.R.E. (ed. 3), v (1898), pp. 627–30, s.v. H. M. Gwatkin, *Studies of Arianism* (1882), Note O, p. 269 f. S. Salaville, A.A., in *D.T.C.*, v (1913), cols. 1565–71, s.v., with bibl.

EUSTOCHIUM, St. JULIA (370–*c.* 419).

A Roman virgin of noble descent. With her mother, Paula, she came under the influence of St. *Jerome, who counselled them in an attempt to lead the life of the Egyptian hermits in the midst of Rome. A letter (Jerome, *Ep.* 22) which he addressed to her on the subject of virginity created such a stir that they were obliged to leave the city (385). After visiting Syria and Egypt on the way, they settled in *Bethlehem, where they built four monasteries, of which Eustochium assumed the direction on her mother's death in 404. Feast day, 28 Sept.

In addition to *Ep.* 22 (*PL*, xxii, 394–425), St. Jerome addressed to Eustochium Epp. 31 (ib., 445 f.) and 108 (ib. 878–906); a letter from Paula and Eustochium is pr. among Jerome's Epp. (No. 46; ib., 483–92); further reff. include those in Epp. 54 (ib., 550–60) and 66 (ib. 639–47). *AA.SS.*, Sept. VII (1760), pp. 630–45. W. H. Fremantle in *D.C.B.*, ii (1880), p. 392, s.v., with further reff.

EUTHALIUS.

The reputed author of a collection of editorial material found in many MSS. of the Greek NT. The editor's work, which consisted of (1) an arrangement of the text in short lines as an aid to reading it aloud, (2) a system of references to quotations from other parts of the Bible, and (3) a division of the Books into chapters, with summary headings of their contents, extended over the Pauline Epp., the Acts, and the Catholic Epp. Attached to the Euthalian prologue to the Pauline Epp. is a 'Martyrium Pauli' which appears to date from either 458 (L. A. Zacagni) or 396 (F. C. Conybeare); but the reasons for identifying the author of this item with that of the rest of the Euthalian material now seem insufficient, and J. A. *Robinson has argued that Euthalius is to be dated in the middle of the 4th cent. Virtually nothing further is known of him beyond the fact that he is described as 'a deacon'. Adequate grounds for identifying him with the author of a long confession of faith (7th cent.), ascribed to 'Euthalius, Bp. of Sulce', are wanting. It seems probable that the Euthalian Biblical material is of Syrian or Egyptian origin.

L. A. Zacagni, *Collectanea Monumentorum Veteris Ecclesiae Graecae et Latinae*, i (Rome, 1698), pp. 401–708, mostly reprinted in J. P. Migne, *PG*, lxxxv, 619–790. J. A. Robinson, 'Euthaliana' in *Texts and Studies*, III, iii (Cambridge, 1895).

EUTHYMIUS ZIGABENUS (early 12th

cent.), Byzantine theologian. He was a monk of the Περιβλέπτου convent at *Constantinople, whom the Emp. Alexis Comnenus ordered to write a work against all heresies. In this work, the Πανοπλία Δογματική, the old heresies are refuted by an array of patristic texts; the new ones, comprising the last 6 of the 28 chapters, are treated more independently. The most interesting is the section (27) on the *Bogomiles, our knowledge of whom rests almost entirely on this description. The work was supplemented later by the Θησαυρὸς Ὀρθοδοξίας of *Nicetas Akominatos (d. *c.* 1215). Euthymius's other important works are his extensive commentaries on the Psalms, the Four Gospels, and the Epp. of St. Paul, in which he utilizes mainly patristic sources, esp. St. *Chrysostom. His works are remarkable esp. for the account they take of the literal sense of the Bible, an achievement unusual among the later Greek exegetes.

The Gk. text of his 'Panoplia Dogmatica' was first publd. by Metrophanes Gregoras (Tergovist, 1710); of his Comm. on Pss. by A. Bongiovanni (Venice, 1763); of his Comm. on Gospels by C. F. Mathaei (3 vols. bound in 4, Leipzig, 1792); and of his Comm. on Pauline Epp. by N. Kalogeras, Abp. of Patras (2 vols., Athens, 1887). Collected ed. in J. P. Migne, *PG*, cxxviii–cxxxi. J. Wickert, 'Die Panoplia Dogmatica des Euthymios Zigabenos' in *O.C.*, viii (1911), pp. 278–388. Krumbacher, pp. 82–4. W. Gass–P. Meyer in *P.R.E.* (ed. 3), v (1898), pp. 633–5; M. Jugie, A.A., in *D.T.C.*, v (1913), cols. 1577–82.

EUTYCHES (*c.* 378–454), heresiarch. He

was *archimandrite of a large monastery at *Constantinople, with great influence at court through the eunuch, Chrysaphius. His keen opposition to *Nestorianism led him to be accused in 448 by *Eusebius of Dorylaeum of the opposite heresy of confounding the two natures in Christ (see *Christology*). Deposed by *Flavian, Abp. of Constantinople, after synodical action, he then appealed to Pope *Leo for support, and by court influence secured a re-trial and acquittal at the *Latrocinium at Ephesus in 449. Meanwhile Leo repudiated his doctrines in his '*Tome'. A change of emperor in 450 turned the scales against him, and at the Council of *Chalcedon in 451 he was deposed and exiled. Eutyches denied that the manhood of Christ was consubstantial with ours, a view which went far towards rendering our redemption through Him impossible. He also maintained that there were 'two natures before, but only one after, the Union' in the Incarnate Christ and was thus the real founder of Monophysitism (q.v.).

E. *Schwartz, 'Der Prozess des Eutyches' in *Sitz.-ber. Bayerischen Akad. der Wissenschaften*, Phil.-hist. Abt., Jhrg. 1929, Hft. 5 [Texts with notes and commentary]. M. Jugie in *D.T.C.*, v (1913), cols. 1582–1609, s.v. 'Eutychès et eutychianisme', with full bibl. For further bibl., see s.v. *Monophysitism*.

EUTYCHIANISM. See *Monophysitism*.

EVAGRIUS PONTICUS (346–99), spiritual

writer. A native of Pontus, he was ordained deacon by St. *Gregory of Nazianzus and became a noted preacher at *Constantinople. In 382 he departed to the *Nitrian desert to cultivate his soul among the monks, where he became a friend and disciple of St. *Macarius of Egypt. Here he spent the rest of his life. From 553 onwards he was condemned several times for *Origenistic views.

Recent studies show that he occupied a central place in the history of Christian spirituality. The first monk to write extensively, he deeply influenced *Palladius,

*Cassian, *Dionysius the Areopagite, and *Maximus the Confessor, to all of whom he transmitted many of Origen's central ideas. His writings (largely lost or extant only in Lat. or Syr. translations) include his 'Monachos' (on the active and spiritual life of the monk), collections of Apophthegms, and a treatise 'On the Eight Evil Thoughts'. Certain works hitherto assigned to *Nilus of Ancyra (e.g. 'On Prayer') prob. belong to Evagrius. He also wrote Commentaries on Pss. and Prov. (only fragments survive).

Works (incomplete) in J. P. Migne, *PG*, xl, 1213–86; also ib., lxxix, 1165–1200 (*De Oratione* of 'Nilus'). W. Frankenberg, *Evagrius Ponticus* in *Abh.* (Gött.), N.F., 13.2, 1912, pp. 49–635 (Syr. texts, with Gk. retransl.). R. Melcher, *Der 8. Brief des hl. Basilius ein Werk des Evagrius Ponticus* (1923). Imp. studies by J. Muyldermans, I. Hausherr, S.J., J. Urs von Balthasar, S.J., K. Rahner, S.J., A. *Wilmart, O.S.B., E. Peterson and others listed in Altaner (ed. 1950), p. 227 f., and J. de Ghellinck, S.J., *Patristique et moyen-âge*, iii (1948), pp. 215–17, note.

EVAGRIUS, 'SCHOLASTICUS' (c. 536–600), Church historian.

A native of Coele-Syria, he was a lawyer by profession. His 'History', which is in six books, extends from the Council of *Ephesus (431) to 594, and thus continues the Histories of *Eusebius and his successors. Though a poor theologian and a credulous gatherer of legends, he made use of several excellent sources and, like *Eusebius, of Caesarea, incorporated extracts from them.

'Ecclesiastica Historica' with Lat. tr., ed. by H. *Valesius and W. Reading in *Historiae Ecclesiasticae*, iii (Cambridge, 1720), pp. 249–473; repr. in J. P. Migne, *PG*, lxxxvi (2), 2415–906. Crit. ed., J. Bidez and L. Parmentier ('Byzantine Texts', ed. J. B. Bury, London, 1898). Eng. tr., with short account of Evagrius and his writings, together with *Theodoret, in Bohn's Ecclesiastical Library (1854), pp. 251–467. C. de Boor, 'Die handschriftliche Überlieferung der Kirchengeschichte des Evagrius' in *Z.K.G.*, v (1882), pp. 315–22. L. Thurmayr, *Sprachliche Studien zu dem Kirchenhistoriker Evagrios* (1910); E. Cernousov, 'Des Euagrios Scholastikos Kirchengeschichte als eine Quelle für die Zeit Anastasios I. Dikoros' in *B.Z.*, xxvii (1927), pp. 29–34. Bardenhewer, v (1932), p. 119 f., incl. further bibl.

EVANGELIARY.

(1) A book containing the complete text of the Four Gospels. (2) The liturgical book containing the portions of the Four Gospels which are read as the 'Gospel' at the *Eucharist, arranged acc. to their place in the ecclesiastical calendar. When in the 10th cent. the practice of incorporating the text of the 'Gospel' into the *Sacramentaries began to become general, the Evangeliaria lost much of their importance.

EVANGELICALISM.

(1) In a wider sense the term 'Evangelical' has been applied since the Reformation to the Protestant churches by reason of their claim to base their teaching pre-eminently on the 'Gospel'. The Church created in Prussia in 1817 by the union of *Lutheran and *Reformed was officially known as the 'Evangelical Church' (*Evangelische Kirche*). A more recent instance is the inclusive designation of all the Protestant Churches of Germany as the 'Evangelische Kirche Deutschlands' (constituted 1948).

(2) In Germany and Switzerland, the word 'Evangelical' (*evangelisch*) was long in use, esp. of the Lutheran group of Protestant Churches as contrasted with the *Calvinist ('Reformed') bodies.

(3) In the C of E the term is currently applied to the school which lays special stress on personal conversion and salvation by faith in the atoning death of Christ. The group originated in the 18th cent. to bring reality into religion when a low tone pervaded English life and the clergy were negligent and worldly. It had several points of contact with the *Methodist movement, esp. in the more Calvinistic form of G. *Whitefield; but it sought to work on the basis of the parochial system and never contemplated separation from the C of E. Among its early leaders were John *Fletcher (1729–85) of Madeley in Shropshire, Henry *Venn (1725–95) of Huddersfield, William *Romaine (1745–95) of London, and John *Newton (1725–1807) of Olney. To a rather later date belonged Charles *Simeon (1759–1836), who made Evangelicalism a powerful force at Cambridge and indirectly later at the other universities, Henry Martyn (1781–1812), the missionary to India, and the influential *Clapham Sect (q.v.). Dislike of their religious earnestness led to much opposition, and in 1768 six students were expelled from St. Edmund Hall, Oxford, for 'too much religion'. But their piety and humanity gradually won them a large following and in the 19th cent. they took a leading part in missionary work and social reform (abolition of slavery, factory laws). The *Church Missionary Society and the *Colonial and Continental Church Society both owed their origin to the Evangelicals. From 1827 Churchmen of Evangelical sympathies have met annually in the 'Islington Conference'.

Theologically Evangelicals have commonly upheld the verbal inspiration and sole authority of Scripture (denying that the Church has power to impose its interpretation upon the individual); belief in the near return of Christ to redeem His elect; the supreme importance of preaching, with a relative minimizing of liturgical worship; rejection of the doctrines of Baptismal regeneration and the Eucharistic sacrifice; and, in general, a strong suspicion of the RC Church and hostility to characteristic *Tractarian and *High Church doctrines. For some recent developments see *Liberal Evangelicalism* and *Anglican Evangelical Group Movement*.

J. H. Overton, *The Evangelical Revival in the Eighteenth Century* (1886); H. C. G. *Moule, *The Evangelical School in the Church of England* (1901); G. R. Balleine, *A History of the Evangelical Party in the Church of England* (1908).

EVANGELICAL ALLIANCE.

An interdenominational body, formed in London in 1846, to 'associate and concentrate the strength of an enlightened *Protestantism against the encroachments of *Popery and *Puseyism, and to promote the interests of a Scriptural Christianity'. Its dogmatic basis included belief in the inspiration and authority of the

Bible, in the *Trinity, in the depravity of man, in the mediation of the Incarnate Son of God, in *justification by faith alone, in conversion and sanctification by the Holy Ghost, in the traditional *eschatology, in the Divine institution of the ministry, and in the obligation of Baptism and the Lord's Supper. It received support in varying degrees from almost the whole of the Protestant world, though the keen controversy on *slavery at its first meeting delayed the institution of a branch in the U.S.A. till 1867. Friedrich Wilhelm IV, who strongly favoured it, summoned a large meeting to Berlin in Sept. 1857; but it never gained a real hold in Germany, where its place was taken by the '*Evangelische Bund' (q.v.). Much work was done by the alliance in the 19th cent. for oppressed religious minorities in Europe. In the present century its influence has greatly declined. It is now known as the 'World's Evangelical Alliance'. From the first it has observed a week early in January as an annual week of prayer.

J. A. Arnold, 'These Fifty Years. A Brief Epitome of the History of the Evangelical Alliance' in *Jubilee of the Evangelical Alliance.* Proceedings of the Tenth International Conference held in London June–July 1896 (1897), pp. 43–64. J. W. Ewing, *Goodly Fellowship.* A Centenary Tribute to the Life and Work of the World's Evangelical Alliance, 1846–1946 [1946]; J. E. Orr, *The Second Evangelical Awakening in Britain* (1949). Reports of the General Conferences were usually issued under the title *The Religious Condition of Christendom.*

EVANGELICAL ASSOCIATION, The. See following entry.

EVANGELICAL CHURCH, The. A small Protestant religious body, sometimes known as the **Albright Brethren** from their founder Jacob Albright (1759–1808), a native of Pennsylvania and a member of the *Lutheran Church. After an experience of conversion in 1791, Albright associated himself with the Methodist Episcopal Church and in 1796 began to preach among the Germans living in his state. Failing to win the support of his Methodist leaders, he created for his followers an independent organization. At a conference in 1809, his followers agreed to be known as the 'So-called Albright People', and from 1816 as the 'Evangelical Association'. C. 1890 internal controversies led to a schism, but this was healed in 1922, and since that date the reunited body has called itself the 'Evangelical Church'. Its activities have always been confined principally to the U.S.A., but it has long ceased to work exclusively among those of German descent. Its total membership is over 200,000.

W. W. Orwig, *History of the Evangelical Association*, i (all publd., Cleveland, Ohio, 1858); R. Yaekel, *Albright and his Co-Labourers* (ib., 1883); id., *History of the Evangelical Association* (2 vols., ib., 1892–5). S. P. Spreng, 'History of the Evangelical Association' in *The American Church History Series*, xii (New York, 1894), pp. 383–439. A. Stapleton, *Annals of the Evangelical Association of North America and History of the United Evangelical Church* (Harrison, Pa., 1900). R. Kücklich, *Die evangelische Gemeinschaft in Europa.* Ill. Festschrift zum 75-jähr. Jubiläum ihres Bestehens, 1850–1925 (1925). F. *Loofs in *P.R.E.* (ed. 3), v (1898), pp. 667–72, s.v. 'Evangelische Gemeinschaft', with further bibl.

EVANGELICAL COUNSELS. See *Counsels of Perfection.*

EVANGELICAL UNION, The. A religious denomination formed in Scotland in 1843. In 1841 James *Morison (1816–93), minister of a United Secession congregation in Kilmarnock and a close Biblical student, was suspended by his presbytery for his anti-Calvinistic views. He affirmed that Christ made atonement for all and condemned the doctrine of unconditional election. In 1843, along with three other ministers, he founded the 'Evangelical Union', which was soon joined by a number of Scottish Congregationalists. The Union was an association of independent churches over which it exercised no jurisdiction. Its members were commonly called 'Morisonians'. In 1897 most of the churches in the Union joined with the Congregational Union of Scotland.

J. R. Fleming, *A History of the Church in Scotland, 1843–1874* (1927), esp. pp. 10 f., 48 f., 109, and 248 f.; id., *A History of the Church in Scotland, 1875–1929* (1933), pp. 51 f. and 155 f.

EVANGELISCHE BUND, The (Germ., 'Evangelical League'). An alliance of German Protestants founded in 1886–7 by Prof. W. *Beyschlag and others for the defence of Protestant interests against the growing power of Catholicism. It furthered its purposes by contacts with the secular press and through the issue of literature of its own, as well as by other methods. The movement, which took on a strongly nationalistic colour in the years immediately preceding the War of 1914–18, had gained by 1914 a membership of 540,000. Since then its influence has considerably declined.

H. Hüttenrauch, *Der evangelische Bund. Sein Werden, Wachsen und Wirken* (1911). G. Warneck, *Der evangelische Bund und seine Gegner* (1889); F. Nippold, *Ziele und Vorgeschichte des evangelischen Bundes* (1890). A. Wächtler, *Der evangelische Bund nach 25 Jahren* (1912). W. Beyschlag, *Zur Entstehungsgeschichte des evangelischen Bundes* (1926). Id. in *P.R.E.* (ed. 3), iii (1897), pp. 549–53, s.v. 'Bund, Evangelischer'; D. Mirbt in *R.G.G.* (ed. 2), ii (1928), cols. 447–51, s.v.

EVANGELIST (Gk. εὐαγγελιστής, 'a proclaimer of the εὐαγγέλιον or Gospel').

(1) In the NT the word is thrice used of a travelling missionary (Acts 21. 8; Eph. 4. 11; 2 Tim. 4. 5). Probably no special office is designated, but the evangelist ordinarily combined his duty of proclaiming the Gospel with such offices as those of *bishop or *deacon. *Philip, e.g., was both a 'deacon' and an 'evangelist' and the Apostles are also said to have 'evangelized'. In modern usage the word is applied to certain laymen in Protestant Churches who do home missionary work.

(2) In a more technical sense, the author of one of the canonical Gospels, i.e. exclusively St. *Matthew, St. *Mark, St. *Luke, and St. *John. This usage established itself in the 3rd cent. Traditionally the four evangelists are symbolized respectively by a man, a lion, an ox, and an eagle, on the basis of Rev. 4. 6–10.

EVANGELISTARIUM (Gk. εὐαγγελιστάριον). In the Orthodox Church, a book of tables indicating the Gospel lections for each year in accordance with the varying date of *Easter.

EVANSON, EDWARD (1731–1805), divine. After becoming Vicar of *Tewkesbury in 1769, and of Longdon in Worcestershire in 1770, he developed views with *Unitarian affinities, advocating the removal of the *Nicene and *Athanasian creeds from the BCP. A prosecution instituted against him in 1775 before the Bp. of *Gloucester failed on a technical point, but in 1778 he resigned his living and became a schoolmaster at Mitcham. Here he held occasional services and administrations of the Lord's Supper, which he considered the only Sacrament. Besides some controversial writings against J. *Priestley, he published *The Dissonance of the Four Generally Received Evangelists* (Ipswich, 1792) in which he accepted only the Gospel of Luke. His book was the earliest formal attack on the traditional authorship of St. John's Gospel.

His Sermons were issued in 2 vols in 1807, prefixed by a Life. T. Falconer replied to his book on the Gospels in his *Bampton Lectures for 1810 (publd. 1811). *D.N.B.*, xviii (1889), p. 78 f. (unsigned).

EVE. The first woman, the wife of *Adam. Acc. to Gen. 3. 20 she was so named because she was the mother of all living beings; but the Hebrew word (חַוָּה) for Eve may have meant 'serpent', and her name thus been associated with the primitive myth that all life originated in a primeval serpent. Eve is tempted by the serpent to eat of the fruit of the tree of knowledge; she and Adam disobey, '*fall' and are driven out from *Eden; and Eve is punished with the pain of childbirth. In the NT (1 Cor. 11. 9 f., 1 Tim. 2. 13 ff.) the relationship of Adam and Eve is used by St. *Paul to support his teaching about the relative status of man and woman in Christian worship. It was a common medieval conceit that the Latin form of her name ('Eva'), spelled backwards, was the first word of the angel's address to the BVM ('*Ave') and symbolized the reversal of Eve's fall through the Incarnation.

W. H. Bennett in *H.E.R.E.*, v (1912), p. 607 f.; E. Mangenot in *D.T.C.*, v (1915), cols. 1640–55, with bibl.; J. Goettsberger in *L.Th.K.*, iii (1931), col. 874 f. For the decree of the *Biblical Commission issued 30 June 1909 requiring express belief in the creation of Eve from the ribs of Adam (*formatio primae mulieris ex primo homine*; cf. Gen. 2.7), cf. *A.A.S.*, i (1909), p. 568 (ad iii).

EVELYN, JOHN (1620–1706), Anglican diarist. Born at Wotton in Surrey, he was educated at Southover free school, near Lewes, and at Balliol College, Oxford, which he left without taking a degree. In 1641 he visited Holland and in 1642 for a short period served in the King's army. From 1643 to 1645 he travelled extensively in France and Italy making many acquaintances and recording, with full descriptions, his experiences. In 1647 he married at Paris Mary, the daughter of

Sir Richard Browne (1605–83), a girl of not more than twelve years. In 1649, after the King's execution, he went abroad again. After his final return (Feb. 1652), he settled at Sayes Court, a large estate near Deptford. Here he interested himself in gardening and other rural pursuits until the *Restoration, carrying on a friendly correspondence with John *Wilkins (1614–72), then Warden of Wadham, and Robert *Boyle, with both of whom he was closely associated in the creation of the Royal Society. He also became connected with Jeremy *Taylor, whom, among other dispossessed clergy, he befriended under the Commonwealth. He enjoyed the favour of *Charles II and *James II and was on intimate terms with many leading personalities at Court and elsewhere. He held several royal appointments, nobly remaining at his post when one of these required his residence in London during the Great Plague. He played a prominent part in Church affairs, esp. in the rebuilding of *St. Paul's Cathedral, and continued to take an active interest in the Royal Society. After the Revolution he lived in comparative retirement.

Evelyn's wide interests made him a very prolific writer. The *Diary*, if it lacks the liveliness of that of Pepys (1633–1703), is a true reflection of his character and an important document for social history. It reveals him a representative of much that was best in 17th cent. lay Anglicanism. He was a man of scholarly temperament and wide culture, which he combined with a firm devotion, and a strong loyalty to the royalist cause even though he disapproved of much of the life of the Court. His best known works include *Fumifugium* (1661), *Sculptura* (1662) and *Sylva* (1664). Of more specifically religious interest are his *Mystery of Jesuitism* (1664), *The Pernicious Consequences of the New Heresie of the Jesuites Against the King and the State* (anon., 1666) and his translation of *The Golden Book of St. John Chrysostom concerning the Education of Children* (1659); and two posthumous publications, *The Life of Mrs. [Margaret] Godolphin* (ed. by S. *Wilberforce, 1847) and *The History of Religion* (ed. by R. M. Evanson, 2 vols., 1850).

EVENING COMMUNION. In the C of E the practice of Evening Celebrations, encouraged esp. nowadays by *Low Churchmen appears to date from the middle of the 19th cent. In 1852, W. F. *Hook, not himself a Low Churchman, introduced it at Leeds to meet the needs of his industrial parish. It met with much opposition from the first (notably from H. P. *Liddon) as in conflict with the traditional rule of fasting from the preceding midnight. In the RC Church, with the relaxation of rules about Fasting Communion since the Second World War, Evening Masses have been increasingly allowed under special conditions (standardized in 1953 in the encyclical 'Christus Dominus'). See also *Eucharistic Fast*.

The practice was deprecated in many episcopal charges in the 19th cent., notably by S. *Wilberforce, Bp. of *Oxford. [H. P. Liddon], 'Evening Communion' in *The Christian Remembrancer*, xl (1861 for 1860), pp. 191–214; repr., with additions and notes [by W. *Bright; also anon.], as *Evening Communion Contrary to the Teaching and Practice of the Church in all Ages* (1872); J. Hughes-Games, *Evening Communion*. The Argument for the Practice Stated and the Objections against it Answered (1894). E. Dekkers, O.S.B., 'L'Église ancienne a-t-elle connu la messe du soir?' in *Miscellanea Liturgica in Honorem L. Cuniberti Mohlberg*, i (Bibliotheca 'Ephemerides Liturgicae', Sect. Hist., xxii, 1948), pp. 231–57, with reff. See also bibl. to *Eucharistic Fast*.

EVENING PRAYER. See *Evensong*.

EVENSONG. The name given in medieval England to the canonical hour of *Vespers. It is now in common use for the BCP service of Evening Prayer. The structure of this latter is closely related to the traditional type of Divine service. After preparatory prayers the service proper opens with the versicles and responses, 'O Lord, open thou, &c.', and the Lord's Prayer. This is followed by certain psalms varying acc. to the day of the month, a reading from the OT, the *Magnificat, a further reading from the NT, and the *Nunc Dimittis. After the recitation of the *Apostles' Creed follow the *Kyrie Eleison, the Lord's Prayer, versicles and responses, the Collect for the day, two invariable collects, 'in quires and places where they sing' the *anthem, and further prayers. In substance it is a conflation of the *Sarum services of Vespers and *Compline. The name 'Evensong', found in the 1549 BCP, was replaced by 'Evening Prayer' in 1552, but came back again (in the Table of Proper Lessons) in 1662.

EVURTIUS, St. (4th cent.), Bp. of Orléans. Another form of **St. *Enurchus.** (qv.).

EWALD, HEINRICH GEORG AUGUST (1803–75), OT theologian and orientalist. He was educated at the University of Göttingen, where he taught from 1827 to 1837. In 1838 he went to *Tübingen and joined in the attack on F. C. *Baur and the Tübingen School. From 1847 to 1867 he was back in Göttingen. He was the author of a long series of books. His 'Hebrew Grammar' (1827) was a landmark in the history of OT philology, but of even greater influence was his *Geschichte des Volkes Israel* (5 vols., 1843–55; to ed. 2 two further vols. on the Apostolic Age were added in 1858–9). In its English translation (vol. 5, 1865; the rest, 1867–86), it much influenced British scholarship. Ewald exercised a healthy restraining influence on the negative tendencies of much OT criticism in his day.

Life by T. Witton Davies (London, 1903). T. K. *Cheyne, *Founders of Old Testament Criticism* (1893), pp. 66–118. E. Bertheau–C. Bertheau in *P.R.E.* (ed. 3), v (1898), pp. 682–7.

EXALTATION OF THE CROSS, The. The feast in honour of the Cross of Christ, observed on 14 Sept. It is also known as 'Holy Cross Day'. In the W. Church, the *Martyrology and *Offices commemorate on this day the exposition of the supposed true Cross at *Jerusalem in 629 by the Emp. *Heraclius, after his recovery of it from the Persians into whose hands it had fallen in 614. Actually this event in Jerusalem took place in the spring, and the date, 14 Sept., has become attached to it through confusion with a much earlier commemoration kept in Jerusalem on that day, viz. of the dedication in 335 of the basilica built by the Emp. *Constantine on the site of the *Holy Sepulchre. It seems likely that the '*Invention' of the Cross, now observed on 3 May, was commemorated on this day before the celebration of the incident of 629.

The first clear mention of the Feast in the W. is in the notice of Pope *Sergius (687–701) in the *L.P.* (ed. Duchesne), i, p. 374; cf. Duchesne's note, p. 378 f. There is an early ref. to the adoration of the Cross at Jerusalem in the *Pilgrimage of *Etheria* (ch. 48 f.); but Etheria does not record its date of observance in the calendar. Cf. A. Bludau, *Die Pilgerreise der Aetheria* (Studien zur Geschichte und Kultur des Altertums, xv, Hitt. 1/2; 1927), pp. 185–90. I. de Combes, *Études sur les souvenirs de la Passion*. La Vraie Croix perdue et retrouvée (1902; Eng. tr., 1907). H. Thurston, S.J., 'Relics, Authentic and Spurious' [The Cross and Title] in *The Month*, clv (1930), pp. 420–9. H. *Leclercq, O.S.B., in *D.A.C.L.*, iii (pt. 2; 1914), cols. 3131–9, s.v. 'Croix (Invention et exaltation de la vraie)'; A. Bugnini in *E.C.*, iv (1950), cols. 960–3, s.v. 'Croce VII'. See also bibl. to *Invention of the Cross*.

EXAMINING CHAPLAINS. The duty of examining candidates for holy orders belongs properly to the *archdeacon, as the BCP Ordinal shows. But canon 35 (1604) requires further that either the bishop or certain priests appointed by him should diligently examine such persons as to their fitness for ordination. The canon further specifies that such examining chaplains should be at least three in number; should be members of his cathedral church, if possible, or at any rate of his diocese; and should assist at the laying-on of hands.

S. C. Gayford in *P.B.D.* (1912), p. 326 f., s.v. 'Examination'.

EXARCH. The title of (1) certain civil governors in the later Roman Empire, notably the Exarch of *Ravenna; (2) certain bishops lower in rank than *patriarchs but having rights over the *metropolitans of one civil diocese (though the title was sometimes given to patriarchs and metropolitans themselves); (3) the primate of certain autocephalous Orthodox Churches, e.g. of *Bulgaria and *Cyprus.

EXCARDINATION. (Lat. *cardo*, 'hinge'; hence *excardinare*, 'to unhinge'). In W. canon law, the liberation of a cleric from his present *Ordinary with a view to fresh enlistment ('incardination') under a new superior. For details see *Incardination*.

EX CATHEDRA. See *Cathedra*.

EXCEPTIONS, The. The long list of objections made by the *Puritans at the *Savoy Conference (1661) to the existing

Prayer Book (of 1604) with a view to its revision. They were directed against certain of the Book's doctrinal affirmations and ceremonial prescriptions, as well as minor matters where no question of principle was involved. The Puritans pressed for such changes as the omission of *Lent and of saints' days with their vigils, the use of the AV instead of the text of the *Great Bible (1539) for all Scriptural passages in the Book, the substitution of the word 'minister' for 'priest' and 'curate', and of 'Lord's Day' for 'Sunday'. Of a few of these 'Exceptions' account was taken in the revised Book of 1662 (the present one), but for the most part they were disallowed.

Text in E. *Cardwell, *A History of Conferences . . . connected with . . . the Book of Common Prayer* (1840), ch. vii, § S.

EXCLUSION, Right of (Lat. *Ius Exclusionis* or *Ius Exclusivae*). The right formerly claimed by the heads of certain Catholic states to name a particular candidate whom they desired to exclude from being elected Pope. The claim goes back to the 16th cent., and the last occasion on which it was exercised was by the Austrians in 1903 (against Cardinal Rampolla). The right was finally annulled by *Pius X by *Commissum Nobis* (20 Jan. 1904) and *Vacante Sede Apostolica* (25 Dec. 1904).

EXCOMMUNICATION. An ecclesiastical censure imposed by competent authority which excludes those subjected to it from the communion of the faithful and imposes on them other deprivations and disabilities. It does not profess to extend to the union of the soul with God, since that union is held to depend on the immediate effect of sanctifying grace and to be unaffected by any act of the Church. Hence it is not impossible for a man to be excommunicated and yet to be and remain in a state of grace.

In earlier times excommunication could be either 'greater' or 'less'. The greater deprived a man of the right to administer or receive the Sacraments and of all intercourse, public or private, with his fellow-Christians, and of all rights and privileges in the Church of any kind whatsoever, save only the last rites. The lesser deprived him only of the right to administer or receive the Sacraments. In the RC Church the lesser excommunication now scarcely exists. But a new distinction has been introduced between the excommunications 'vitandus' and 'toleratus'. The 'vitandus' corresponds closely to a man under the greater excommunication. He may not attend any form of public Divine worship, he loses any and every ecclesiastical office, rank, stipend, or dignity which he may possess, and the faithful are warned to have as little social intercourse with him as it is possible or convenient. No one is 'excommunicatus vitandus' unless he has offered physical violence to the Pope, or been explicitly and by name pronounced 'vitandus' by the Holy See. All other excommunicated persons are 'tolerati'. Such persons may not lawfully administer or receive the Sacraments, but though legally debarred from attending any public worship except sermons, they need not be expelled if they do attend. And though they may not legitimately exercise any ecclesiastical rights, e.g. of patronage or election, if they do, their acts are valid. If they had been 'vitandi', such acts would have been invalid. Current RC practice is outlined in the 1917 *Codex Iuris Canonici (cans. 2257–67), where it is distinguished from two other forms of censure, viz. *interdictum* and *suspensio* (can. 2255).

Though the use of excommunication is implied in the rubrics of the BCP and is openly threatened in the canons of 1604, it has in fact been very rare in the C of E. It is, however, more common in the Anglican Churches overseas, esp. in missionary dioceses. Except in the case of heathen converts, it is usually confined to 'minor excommunication'.

É. Jombart in *D.D.C.*, v (1953), cols. 915–27, s.v. See also commentaries to *Codex Juris Canonici*, cited s.v.

EXEGESIS (from Gk. ἐξηγέομαι, 'I narrate', 'explain'). In theology the explanation of Biblical texts. Its rules are governed by the science of *Hermeneutics (q.v.), the practical application of which is the concern of exegesis. On account of the obscurities in Scripture, Biblical exegesis has been practised from early times, both by the Jewish *Rabbis and by the Christian *Fathers. A chiefly allegorical mode of interpretation was fostered esp. in the *Alexandrian school, whose principal exponents were St. *Clement and *Origen. By contrast the school of *Antioch, represented, among others, by St. John *Chrysostom and *Theodore of Mopsuestia, cultivated the explanation of the literal sense of the Bible. The most important exegetes among the W. Fathers were St. *Jerome and St. *Augustine, who sought to combine the two kinds of exegesis, though the former emphasized the literal, the latter the allegorical sense. Among the later Greek Fathers the science of exegesis was represented esp. by *Hesychius of Jerusalem, St. *John of Damascus, and *Euthymius Zigabenus. In the W. many of the Schoolmen were actively concerned with the methods of exegesis, notably *Peter Lombard, *Alexander of Hales, and St. *Thomas Aquinas. They favoured the fourfold method of literal, figurative, moral, and anagogical exegesis; their chief contribution was an increase in the systematization of materials and in logical order.

The *Reformation introduced a new principle into the science of exegesis. Whereas hitherto the dogma of the Church had guided the exegetes in their determination of the sense of Scripture, it was now Scripture as interpreted by the various schools of thought that was to determine dogma. Thus Protestant exegesis, after a period of exaggerated dogmatism which regarded even the Hebrew vowel signs as inspired, tended increasingly towards great liberty of Biblical interpretation. From the 18th cent., under the influence of B. *Spinoza and others, Protestant exegesis, esp. in Germany, came to give up the doctrine of inspiration and developed on mainly rationalistic lines. J. S. *Semler, J. J. *Wetstein, and J. A. *Ernesti are among the principal exponents of this school. In England, after a short period of criticism in the early 18th cent., exegesis, under the influence of *Methodism in the 18th and of the *Oxford Movement in the 19th cent., developed along mainly conservative lines, e.g. in E. B. *Pusey. J. B. *Lightfoot's Commentaries on the Pauline Epistles and B. F. *Westcott's on the Fourth Gospel and Hebrews took into account the results of modern criticism, but remained out of sympathy with the destructive tendencies of German exegetes. They combined with wide sympathies and deep scholarship an essentially constructive interest and also drew largely on the Fathers. A more receptive attitude to modern critical theories was adopted by W. Robertson *Smith, T. K. *Cheyne, and other more recent scholars, which is reflected, e.g., in many volumes in the International Critical Commentary and the *Moffatt Commentary. Among recent prominent German exegetes are J. *Wellhausen, R. Kittel, B. Duhm, T. *Zahn, and B. *Weiss, whereas K. *Barth is the chief representative of a return to a more dogmatic and conservative method. All recent exegetes make extensive use of the findings of secular sciences, the study of comparative religion, &c. RC scholars, among whom M. J. *Lagrange, O.P., is pre-eminent, have also become more ready to accept these, though in the RC Church exegesis remains subject to the doctrine of the Church and, in recent times, has been guided by the decisions of the *Biblical Commission.

F. W. *Farrar, *History of Interpretation* (*Bampton Lectures for 1885; 1886); W. *Sanday, *Inspiration* (Bampton Lectures for 1893; 1893). R. *Simon, *Histoire critique des principaux commentatateurs du Nouveau Testament* (Rotterdam, 1693). J. G. Rosenmüller, *Historia Interpretationis Librorum Sacrorum in Ecclesia Christiana* (5 parts, Heidelberg and Leipzig, 1795–1814). J. Bonsirven, S.J., *Exégèse rabbinique et exégèse paulinienne* (1939). G. Heinrici in *P.R.E.* (ed. 3), vii (1899), pp. 718–50, s.v. 'Hermeneutik'; P. Cruveilhier in *Dict. Bibl.* Suppl., iii (1938), cols. 1482–1524, s.v. 'Herméneutique sacrée'; G. Bardy, ib., ii (1934), cols. 73–103, s.v. 'Commentaires patristiques de la Bible'. A. Penna, C.R.L., in *E.C.*, vii (1951), cols. 100–108, s.v. 'Interpretazione biblica'. Beryl Smalley, *The Study of the Bible in the Middle Ages* (1941; ed. 2, 1952).

EXEMPLARISM. The view of the *Atonement (sometimes also known as the 'moral' or 'subjective' theory) which holds that the value of the Death of Christ for us lies purely in the moral example which it sets us of complete love and self-surrender, thus moving our imagination and will to repentance and holiness. Those who object to this view criticize it rather as inadequate than as erroneous. One of its chief supporters in recent times was H. *Rashdall, in *The Idea of Atonement* (1919), but the origin of the theory lies as far back as the works of P. *Abelard (d. 1142), if not much earlier.

EXEMPTION. In an ecclesiastical sense, freedom from control by one's normal superior (usually the Bishop of the diocese) and hence in general immediate subjection either to the superior of one's religious house or order, or to the Pope. The term 'exempt' is also applied to dioceses which are not subject to a metropolitan but directly under the Holy See. The earliest known instance of monastic exemption is that granted by Pope *Honorius I in 628 to the Abbey of *Bobbio. Such exemptions, which from the 11th cent. became common and from the 12th cent. the normal rule, were the cause of much friction between the Bishops and the religious orders in the Middle Ages. Other corporations (e.g. cathedral chapters) or private persons were also increasingly granted exemptions, and by the 16th cent. the practice had been carried to an extreme. One of the chief reforms effected by the Council of *Trent was the restoration to the Bishop of his proper ordinary jurisdiction.

EXEQUATUR (Lat. 'he may perform'). The right, also known as the 'Regium Placet', claimed by certain governments to prevent ecclesiastical enactments of the Roman see from taking automatic effect in their territories. In the 17th and 18th cents. the *Jansenists and the *Gallicanists, e.g. Z. B. *van Espen in his *De Promulgatione Legum Ecclesiasticarum* (1712), were the chief supporters of these claims from the ecclesiastical standpoint. The attempts of the Papacy in recent times to restrain it, e.g. that of *Pius IX in his *Syllabus* of 1864, have met with varying success, and certain modern governments have continued to exercise some controlling power of this kind.

H. Papius, 'Zur Geschichte des Placets' in *Archiv für katholisches Kirchenrecht*, xviii (1867), pp. 161–237. S. Luzio in *C.E.*, v (1909), p. 707 f., s.v.; A. Bertola in *E.C.*, v (1950), cols. 917–19, s.v., both with further bibl.

EXETER. (In Roman times, Isca Dumnoniorum.) The see owes its existence to the subdivision of the diocese of *Sherborne by Abp. Plegmund in 909 into the three dioceses of Somerset, Devon, and Cornwall. Originally the see was at *Crediton (q.v.). On the death of Burwold, Bp. of Cornwall (c. 1040), the two W. dioceses were united, with Crediton still the see, until c. 1049 when *Leofric removed it to Exeter. The boundaries of the diocese remained practically unchanged until the foundation of the diocese of *Truro in 1876. It is now almost conterminous with the county of Devonshire.

In 932 Aethelstan established a monastery at Exeter which was refounded by Canute in 1019. It was destroyed by William Warelwast (Bp., 1107–35), who began to erect a Norman cathedral, of which only the towers remain. The present structure was begun by Walter Bronescombe (Bp., 1258–80). Peter Quivil (Bp., 1280–91) introduced the decorated style in which most of the cathedral is built and transformed the towers into transepts. The building was dedicated by John Grandison

(1328–69) and completed by Thomas Branting-
ham (1370–94). Under the Commonwealth it
was temporarily divided by a brick wall and
used as two dissenting chapels. The interior
was restored under the direction of Gilbert
Scott between 1870 and 1877. Notable are its
*miserere seats dating from the episcopate of
William Bruere (1224–44), a clock made at
*Glastonbury in 1285 and brought to Exeter
in 1314, the Bishop's throne installed by
Walter de *Stapeldon (1308–26), and the West
front (1370–94). In the cathedral library are
preserved the deed signed by St. *Edward the
Confessor, Earl Godwin, and Tostig, installing
Leofric as first bishop; the 9th cent. *Codex
Exoniensis* presented by Leofric; and the Exon
Domesday. Edmund Lacey (Bp., 1419–55)
was honoured as a popular saint. Other
famous bishops include R. *Fox (1487–92),
M. *Coverdale (1551–3), J. *Hall (1627–41),
H. *Phillpotts (1831–69), and F. *Temple
(1869–85).

The University of Exeter received its charter
in 1955.

The fullest account is to be found in the learned works of
George Oliver (1781–1861), the chief of which are *The
History of Exeter* (1821; ed. 2, 1861); *Ecclesiastical Antiqui-
ties of Devon* (1828; '2nd ed.', really a new work, 3 vols.,
1839–42); *Monasticon Diœcesis Exoniensis* (1846); and *Lives
of the Bishops of Exeter and a History of the Cathedral* (1861).
Selection of Episcopal Registers, ed. by F. C. Hingeston-
Randolph (9 vols., 1886–1909); the second part of that of
Edmund Lacey (Bp. of Exeter, 1420–55) ed. by O. J. Reichel
(Devon and Cornwall Record Society, 1915). E. A. Freeman,
Exeter (Historic Towns, 1887). E. C. Mortimer in *D.E.C.H.*
(ed. 3, 1948), pp. 220–3.

EXETER HALL. A building in the Strand,
London, which was erected *c.* 1830 and used
for religious and philanthropic assemblies, esp.
by those of Evangelical sympathies, down to
1907. 'Exeter Hall' thus came to be used
allusively as a title for a certain type of
*Evangelicalism.

EXISTENTIALISM. The term, which
derives from S. *Kierkegaard (d. 1855; q.v.),
has been recently applied to several philosophical doctrines which share in common a
radical concern for the individual existing
person. Such teaching came into much
prominence in France during the Second
World War. Negatively, it is a critique of
western science and philosophy from Greek
antiquity onwards, on the ground that it has
confined its interests to universal 'essences'
(*Plato) to the virtual exclusion of individual
'existence'. The first positive task of the
Existentialist, on the other hand, is to recover
real personal being.

Though its exponents point to Existentialist
thinkers in all ages (e.g. St. *Augustine, B.
*Pascal), the contemporary movement looks
back mainly to S. Kierkegaard, who had convinced himself that modern philosophy and culture could not satisfy his spiritual and religious
needs. It dates esp. from 1918 onwards, when
the writings of Kierkegaard, who was practically unheeded by his own generation, began
to be known outside Denmark and his critique
of scientific liberalism welcomed esp. in Ger-

man speaking countries, and above all by K.
*Barth and the other upholders of *Dialecti-
cal Theology (F. *Gogarten). Existentialist
doctrines thus made their first appearance in
European thought in a theological dress.
Rather later Kierkegaard's leading doctrines
were re-thought, on less theological lines, by
the German philosopher K. *Jaspers (q.v.).

In its next stage Existentialist teaching was
linked (somewhat oddly) with the *Phenomenological Movement (q.v.) in Germany. In his
earlier work Edmund Husserl had emphatically excluded all metaphysical questions from
Phenomenology. But already in Husserl's
Ideen (1913) a metaphysics, at least implicit,
had revealed itself; and this became more pronounced as his thought developed (e.g. in his
art. 'Phenomenology' in *E.B.*, ed. 14). In his
disciple Martin Heidegger (b. 1883), who later
succeeded him at Freiburg i.Br., phenomenology was wholly recast in an Existentialist
form. In an obscure language, consciously
opposed to the intellectual vocabulary of the
scientific Greek tradition, Heidegger elaborated his metaphysic of the human person. His
chief writings are *Sein und Zeit* (1927), *Vom
Wesen des Grundes* (1929), *Was ist Metaphysik?*
(1930), and *Vom Wesen der Wahrheit* (1943).
Here Existentialism, so far from being theologically motivated, was avowedly atheistic.

Associated with M. Heidegger is the most
influential of the modern French Existential-
ists, Jean Paul Sartre (b. 1905). He too had
studied under Husserl at Freiburg and is
openly atheistic, holding that the problems of
life and morality belong not to the world of
intellectual theorizing but to concrete human
experience; hence the best vehicles for conveying existentialist principles are not philosophical treatises, but the drama, the novel
and personal diaries. Sartre expounded his
doctrines in *L'Être et le néant*. Essai d'ontologie
phénoménologique (1943) and in various
shorter writings, among them *L'Imagination*
(1936), *L'Imaginaire* (1940), *L'Existentialisme
est un humanisme* (1946), and *Esquisse d'une
théorie des émotions* (1948), as well as in several
novels and plays (which did much to popularize
them), incl. *La Naussée* (1938), *Huis-Clos*
(1945), *La Putain respecteuse* (1946), *Les Mains
sales* (1948). Other French exponents of
Existentialism on these lines are Madame
Simone de Beauvoir (*Pyrrhus et Cinéas*, 1943;
Le Sang des autres, 1945) and George Bataille
(*L'Expérience intérieure*, 1943).

The most prominent exponent of a Christian
Existentialism in France is Gabriel Marcel
(b. 1889; baptized 1929). Originally an idealist, he went through an intellectual struggle
recorded in his *Journal métaphysique* (from
1914 onwards; publd. 1930). After twenty
years he came to the 'melancholy assurance'
that he could never reach a philosophy which
was metaphysically satisfying. No intellectual
system is adequate to deal with the problems
of personal existence, for religious faith consists not in adhesion to a dogmatic formula but
in trust in a Person. The genesis of religion
he sought, however, not (like Kierkegaard) in

despair, but in hope. The primary task to which the ego is called is to create not other things but itself; hence its vocation is to 'be' rather than to 'have'. Among his principal writings are *Être et avoir* (1935; Eng. tr. by Katherine Farrer, 1949), *Du refus à l'invocation* (1942) and *Homo Viator* (1944). He is also the author of many plays.

Throughout, the movement has been fostered by the pessimism of the 20th cent., engendered by two World Wars. With Christianity it shares a supreme interest in the human person, as well as a distrust of philosophical idealism. On these grounds E. *Gilson claimed that St. *Thomas Aquinas was fundamentally an Existentialist (*Le Thomisme*, ed. 3, 1941; cf. E. L. Mascall, *Existence and Analogy*, 1949, ch. iii). But since the condemnation of the Movement by *Pius XII in *Humani Generis* (1950), it has been less sympathetically studied by Catholic apologists.

J. Wahl, *Études kierkegaardiennes* (1938); id., *Existence humaine et transcendance* (1944); P. Foulquier, *L'Existentialisme* (1946); E. Mounier, *Introduction aux existentialismes* (1947); J. Hessen, *Existenzphilosophie* (Essen, 1948); F. H. Heinemann, *Existentialism and the Modern Predicament* (1953). C. Fabro in *E.C.*, v (1951), cols. 586–91, s.v. 'Esistenzialismo'.

EXODUS, Book of.

This Book, the second in the *Pentateuch, records the events attending the 'Exodus', i.e. the release of the Israelites under *Moses from their Egyptian bondage, and Jehovah's subsequent giving of the Law on Mount *Sinai. It describes the oppression of the Israelites, who had settled in Egypt in the time of *Joseph, at the hands of a new king (1); the birth and preservation of Moses from slaughter, and his Divine commission to deliver his fellow-slaves (2–4); the refusal of the *Pharaoh to release the Israelites, even in the face of the 'plagues' (the waters turned to blood, frogs, swarms of flies, murrain of beasts, hail, locusts, &c.), until the loss of his firstborn made him relent, and the institution of the *Passover (5.1–12.36); the escape of the Israelites through the miraculous parting of the *Red Sea and the destruction of their Egyptian pursuers in its returning waters (12.37–18.27); the encampment of the Israelites at Mount *Sinai and Moses' ascent to the summit of the mount, where he received from Jehovah the Ten *Commandments and a large body of other legislation, moral, ceremonial, and religious (19–40).

The authorship of the Book has traditionally been ascribed to Moses, but modern Biblical scholars believe it, like the other Books of the Pentateuch, to be a composite work of a much later age, most of its strata having been written at varying dates from the 9th to the 4th cents. B.C. Perhaps the earliest item is the 'Song of Moses' (15.1–18), which is certainly one of the oldest fragments of the OT. Critical scholarship has been much exercised, esp. in quite recent times, about the date of the Exodus, the evidence for which is partly Biblical, partly archaeological. The extreme limits seem to be 1580 B.C. and 1215 B.C., and at present the most favoured date is perhaps the beginning of the 15th cent. B.C.

Elsewhere in the Bible, frequent and fervent references to the Exodus occur (e.g. Ps. 78. 43–53, Heb. 11.27–29). Indeed the deliverance was throughout Jewish history regarded as the outstanding instance of God's favour to His chosen people. Christian writers from NT times have used the imagery of the *Passover in ch. 12 with reference to the sacrifice of Christ on Calvary and mediately to the Christian sacrifice of the *Eucharist. On the Decalogue, see *Commandments, The Ten*.

Commentaries by A. H. McNeile (West. Comm., 1908), S. R. *Driver (Camb. Bib., RV, 1911), H. Holzinger (K.H.C., Abt. ii, 1900), B. Baentsch (H.K.A.T., Abt. 1, Bd. ii, on Ex., Lev., Num., 1903, pp. 1–305), J. *Weiss (Graz-Vienna, 1911), and G. Beer (H.A.T., Reihe 1, Abt. 3, 1939). On the Exodus, C. F. *Burney, *Israel's Settlement in Canaan*. The Biblical Tradition and its Historical Background (Schweich Lectures for 1917, 1918). J. W. Jack, *The Date of the Exodus in the Light of External Evidence* (1925). A. Lucas, *The Route of the Exodus of the Israelites from Egypt* (1938). H. H. Rowley, *From Joseph to Joshua*. Biblical Tradition in the Light of Archaeology (Schweich Lectures for 1948; 1950).

EXOKAMELAUKION (Gk. ἐξωκαμηλαύκιον).

The veil that hangs down at the back from the head-dress worn by monks and the higher clergy in the E. Church.

EXOMOLOGESIS (Gk. ἐξομολόγησις).

Properly a full or public *Confession of sin. In the early Church the word was applied to the whole process of confession, satisfaction, and forgiveness by which a penitent sinner was reconciled to the Church.

EX OPERE OPERATO.

A term in use among theologians at least since the early 13th cent. to express the essentially objective mode of operation of the sacraments, and its independence of the subjective attitudes of either the minister or the recipient. The 'opus operatum' ('act done') is contrasted with the doing of the act, whether the 'opus operans' ('act doing') or the 'opus operantis' ('act of the doer'). To say, therefore, that a sacrament confers grace 'ex opere operato' is to assert in effect that the sacrament itself is an instrument of God, and that so long as the conditions of its institution are validly fulfilled, irrespective of the qualities or merits of the persons administering or receiving it, grace is conferred. It is this property of being effective 'ex opere operato' which Catholic theologians hold to differentiate the sacraments from other channels of Divine grace. The doctrine, which does not deny that right dispositions are necessary on the part of the recipient if grace is to be really effectual, was formally approved at the Council of *Trent (sess. 7, *de sacramentis in genere*, can. 8).

EXORCISM.

The practice of expelling evil spirits by means of prayer or set formulas was common among the Jews and pagans, and was taken over by the Christian Church after the example of Christ and His Apostles (cf. Mt. 10. 1 ff., Lk. 11. 14 ff., Acts 16. 18, 19. 13 ff., &c.). Exorcism has been practised on persons possessed with an evil spirit from NT times onwards. It has always been applied to catechumens; the BCP of 1549 preserved one such prayer in the Baptismal Office; in the Latin rite three exorcisms are administered before the actual baptism. These, as well as the lesser exorcisms used in the blessings of water, oil, sacred vessels, &c., do not presuppose a state of possession, but are prayers asking for the restraint of the powers of evil. There is an elaborate rite for the exorcism of evil spirits, the use of which is restricted to priests who have episcopal permission, contained in the '*Rituale Romanum'.

J. *Martène, O.S.B., *De Antiquis Ecclesiae Ritibus* (3 vols., Rouen, 1700–2), vol. i, pp. 32 f., 52 f., 81, 159–61; ii, 259, 302 f., 307 f., 347, 359, 371, 390, 394, 400, 427, 431 f., 446, 451, 465, 474, 488 f.; iii, 498 and 517–20. F. *Probst, *Sakramente und Sakramentalien in den drei ersten christlichen Jahrhunderten* (1872), pp. 16–62. F. J. Dölger, *Der Exorzismus im altchristlichen Taufritual* (Studien zur Geschichte und Kultur des Altertums, iii, Hftt. 1–2; 1909. R. M. Woolley, *Exorcism and the Healing of the Sick* (C.H.S., 1932). J. Forget in *D.T.C.*, v (1913), cols. 1762–80, s.v. 'Exorcisme'; H. *Leclercq, O.S.B., in *D.A.C.L.*, v (1922), cols. 964–78, s.v. 'Exorcisme, exorciste'. See also bibl. s.v. 'Exorcist'.

EXORCIST.

EXORCIST. The second of the *Minor Orders. The power of exorcizing evil spirits, however, was never confined to the members of a particular order (cf. preceding entry). Bishops and priests from the earliest times assumed the primary responsibility for the sick and possessed, and even laymen are known to have exercised the gift of healing. The office of 'exorcist' is first mentioned in a letter of Pope *Cornelius (d. 253). Its duties came to include the imposition of hands on '*energumens', the exorcizing of *catechumens, and the pouring-out of the water at Mass. In the RC Church to-day these functions of the exorcist are practically extinct, and the office constitutes only a step to the priesthood. In the E. Church, where there exists no separate order of exorcists, exorcism is regarded, as in the primitive Church, as a charismatic gift not attached to an office.

T. Bischofberger, *Die Verwaltung des Exorcistats nach Massgabe des römischen Benediktionale* (1884; rev. ed. by C. Wehrmeister, 1927). F. Wieland, *Die genetische Entwicklung der sog. Ordines Minores in den drei ersten Jahrhunderten* (R.Q., Suppl. vii; 1897), pp. 114–32 and 172–4. See also bibl. to previous entry.

EXOUCONTIANS.

EXOUCONTIANS. The extreme *Arians of the 4th cent., so called from their doctrine that the Son was created out of non-being (ἐξ οὐκ ὄντων). Their leader was *Aetius. They were also known as 'Aetians' and '*Anomoeans'.

EXPECTANT.

EXPECTANT. A name formerly used of a candidate for the *Presbyterian ministry in *Scotland before he had received a licence to preach the Gospel.

EXPECTANT, The Church.

EXPECTANT, The Church. The body of Christians waiting between earth and heaven, in what is traditionally called *Purgatory, and thus distinguished from the Church in *heaven (*triumphant) and that still on earth (*militant).

EXPECTATION SUNDAY.

EXPECTATION SUNDAY. A title occasionally given to the Sunday between *Ascension Day and *Whitsunday. The name is in reference to the Apostles' 'expectation' of the Descent of the Holy Spirit after Christ's ascension (Acts 1. 4 f.).

EXPIATION.

EXPIATION. The atoning or making up for an offence committed against God or one's neighbour. Christianity claims that the only sufficient expiation of human sin is the offering made by Jesus Christ of His earthly life and death, and that of this offering the merits are infinite. Acc. to Catholic theology, its effects are applied to the soul in baptism and (for sins thereafter committed) in absolution. In virtue of its all-sufficiency the performance by Christians of good or pious works, done as penance, has value only through their being effected in union with the perfect expiation offered by Christ. See also *Atonement*.

EXPIATION, Day of.

EXPIATION, Day of. An alternative name for the Jewish feast usually known as the Day of *Atonement (Tisri 10).

EXPOSITION OF THE BLESSED SACRAMENT.

EXPOSITION OF THE BLESSED SACRAMENT. The exhibition of the consecrated Eucharistic *Host for the purpose of devotion. Such exhibition may be private (*expositio privata*), when, e.g., only the doors of the *tabernacle, where the Host is reserved, are opened, or public (*expositio publica*), when the Host is exhibited on a throne in a *monstrance. In the RC Church, public exposition is allowed only at the Feast of *Corpus Christi, or on some important ground with the consent of the bishop. The form of service which accompanies Exposition is similar to that of *Benediction. The devotion became current in the 14th cent., and in various forms has been in use in the RC Church ever since. In the C of E it went out of use at the *Reformation, but in recent times it has been reintroduced, often under the name of 'Devotions'.

J. B. Thiers, *Traité de l'exposition du St. Sacrament de l'autel* (Paris, 1673). F. Raible, *Das Tabernakel einst und jetzt*. Eine historische und liturgische Darstellung der Andacht zur aufbewahrten Eucharistie (1908), pp. 150–316 passim. H. Thurston, S.J., 'Our Popular Devotions', No. iv, 'Benediction of the Blessed Sacrament: Part II, Exposition', in the *Month*, xcviii (1901), pp. 58–69; id., 'Exposition of the Blessed Sacrament', ib., xcix (1902), pp. 537–40. Id. in *C.E.*, v (1909), p. 713 f., s.v., with bibl. E. Dumoutet, *Le Désir de voir l'Hostie et les origines de la dévotion au Saint Sacrement* (1927), pp. 75–98.

EXSURGE, DOMINE.

EXSURGE, DOMINE. The bull issued by *Leo X on 15 June 1520 excommunicating M. *Luther, the 'new *Porphyry' (*novus*

Porphyrius). It listed 41 propositions, attributed to Luther, which it condemned as 'heretical or scandalous or false or offensive to pious ears, or seducing to simple minds and standing in the way of the Catholic faith'. They dealt with such matters as *indulgences, *penance, *purgatory, sacramental *grace, and the Pope's teaching authority. Its promulgation in Germany was entrusted to J. *Eck, whose unpopular and provocative methods met with fierce opposition both at Leipzig (29 Sept.) and at *Wittenberg (3 Oct.). After an unsuccessful appeal for a *General Council on 17 Nov., Luther finally broke with the Papacy by publicly burning the bull at Wittenberg on 10 Dec. 1520.

For the text (somewhat abbreviated), see B. J. Kidd, *Documents Illustrative of the Continental Reformation* (1911), No. 38. The propositions are also in H. Denzinger–C. Bannwart, *Enchiridion Symbolorum*, Nos. 741–81.

EXTRA-LITURGICAL SERVICES. Services for which no fixed form is provided in the authorized liturgical formularies. For the form of such functions the person conducting them is responsible, subject to the directions of the bishop and parish priest.

EXTRAVAGANTES. The term, at one time applied to certain officially recognized Papal *decretals which had 'wandered outside', i.e. were not included in, the 'Decretum' of *Gratian ('extra decretum vagantes'), is now used almost exclusively of the two concluding sections of the *Corpus Iuris Canonici, viz. the 'Extravagantes Ioannis XXII' and the 'Extravagantes Communes'. The latter is a collection of decretals of various Popes from *Boniface VIII (d. 1303) to Sixtus IV (d. 1484). Down to 1917, when the new *Codex Iuris Canonici was issued, the official authority of many items in the Extravagantes was allowed, though it belonged to them only as individual documents, and not because of any authority attaching to these two collections as a whole.

Crit. text by E. Friedberg in his ed. of *Corpus Iuris Canonici*, ii (1881), cols. 1201–1312; cf. also Friedberg's Prolegomena, ib., cols. lxiv–lxviii.   J. W. Bickell, *Über die Entstehung und den heutigen Gebrauch der beiden Extravagantensammlungen des* Corpus Juris Canonici (1825). K. Guggenberger in *L.Th.K.*, iii (1931), col. 920, s.v.

EXTREME UNCTION. See *Unction.*

EXULTET. In the W. liturgy, the 'Paschal Proclamation' (*praeconium paschale*) or 'Paschal Praise' (*laus paschalis*) sung by the deacon at the blessing of the *Paschal Candle on *Holy Saturday, and so named from its opening word, 'exultet'. It seems that originally it was the practice for the deacon to compose his own *praeconium*; but the form now in use can be traced back to the 7th cent. and had completely displaced other forms by the 9th. The chant to which it is sung is one of the finest in the Latin liturgy.

In S. Italy, from the early 10th cent. to the 13th cent., it was customary to write out this prose, with appropriate musical directions, on rolls known as 'Exultet Rolls'. The text, finely written in Beneventan script, was divided into sections interspersed with illuminated pictures disposed in the reverse way from the text, so that the pictures might be the right way up for the congregation when the section of the roll which had been read had been slipped over the back of the *ambo. About thirty such rolls are known to survive.

L. *Duchesne, *Les Origines du culte chrétien* (1889), pp. 242–6; Eng. tr. of ed. 3 (1903), pp. 252–6. H. M. Bannister, 'The *Vetus Itala* Text of the *Exultet*' in *J.T.S.*, xi (1910), pp. 43–54. A. Franz, *Die kirchlichen Benediktionen im Mittelalter*, i (1909), pp. 519–53, with bibl. B. *Capelle, O.S.B., 'L' "Exultet" pascal, œuvre de Saint Ambroise' in *Miscellanea Giovanni Mercati*, i (Studi e Testi, cxxi, 1946), pp. 219–46, with reff.
On the Exultet Rolls, A. M. Latil, O.S.B. (ed.), *Le miniature nel rotoli dell' Exultet* (Monte Cassino, 1899; coloured plates); M. Avery, *The Exultet Rolls of South Italy*, vol. ii (plates; all publd.; Princeton, 1936). There is also a facsimile ed. of an 11th cent. Exultet Roll from Monte Cassino (of great artistic merit) from B.M. MS. (Add. MS, 30337), with introd. by J. P. Gilson (London, 1929). E. Bertaux, *L'Art dans l'Italie méridionale de la fin de l'empire romain à la conquête de Charles d'Anjou*, ii (1903), pp. 216–40, with supplement on 'Iconographie comparée des rouleaux de l'Exultet. Tableaux synoptiques' (1903).

EXUPERIUS, St. (d. after 410), Bp. of Toulouse. He was renowned for his liberality to the poor and also to monks, and for having finished the basilica of St. Saturninus at Toulouse. St. *Jerome dedicated to him his Commentary on Zech. Feast day, 28 Sept.

For the text of St. *Innocent I's Ep. to Exuperius (Ep. vi; 20 Feb. A.D. 405), with its important list of the Canonical Books of Scripture, prescriptions on clerical celibacy, etc., see J. P. Migne, *PL*, xx, 495–502. *AA.SS.*, Sept. VII (1760), pp. 623–30. G. Bareille in *D.T.C.*, v (1913), cols. 2022–7.

EYCK, HUBERT and JAN VAN. See *Van Eyck, Hubert* and *Jan.*

EZEKIEL, Book of. Ezekiel was the third and last of the 'Greater' OT Prophets, the successor of *Isaiah and *Jeremiah. The Book of Ezekiel falls into four divisions: (1) Chs. 1–24. Here the message is denunciation and the main theme the forthcoming destruction of *Jerusalem and the Jewish nation. These chapters contain Ezekiel's characteristic teaching on individual responsibility, that 'the soul that sinneth, it shall die' (18). (2) Chs. 25–32. A series of prophecies directed against foreign nations, viz. Ammon (25. 1–7), Moab (25. 8–11), Edom (25. 12–14), Philistia (25. 15–17), Tyre and Sidon (26–28), Egypt (29–32). (3) Chs. 33–39. Prophecies relating to the redemption and reconstitution of the Jewish people. Their resurrection is described in ch. 37 under the image of the Valley of Dry Bones. (4) Chs. 40–48. A detailed vision of the ideal theocracy and esp. the form and worship of the reconstructed *Temple.

Ezekiel's prophecies were prob. all written in Babylon, whither he had been carried captive by Nebuchadnezzar in 597 B.C. The contrast in tone between chs. 1 to 24 and chs. 25 to 48 is most easily to be explained by the change in circumstances through the Fall of *Jerusalem in 586 B.C.; but some recent scholars have argued that the contrast demands a theory of dual authorship. The possibility that the whole Book was revised by an editor subsequently is compatible, of course, with either view. It is clear that the Book was issued from the first as a written document, and not (as some of the earlier prophetical writings) delivered orally and then recorded. In many places the text is very corrupt.

The prophet wrote as one overawed with the majesty and holiness of God. His own experience, shared by his fellow-exiles, had convinced him of the universality of God's rule, Who can and must be worshipped in Babylon as in Palestine. Like Jeremiah, he stressed the responsibility of the individual soul in the sight of God, but he also had a firm belief in the corporate nature of the religious community, as is shown by his careful provisions for the future well-being of the restored state. Though there are no direct quotations from Ezekiel in the NT, the combination of priestly and prophetic religion in the Book paved the way for the later Judaism in which the Gospel was planted.

Commentaries by A. B. *Davidson (Camb. Bib., AV, 1892; revised for RV text by A. W. Streane, 1916), W. F. Lofthouse (Cent. Bibl., 1907), H. A. Redpath (West. Comm., 1907), G. A. *Cooke (I.C.C., 1936), I. G. Matthews (An American Commentary on the Old Testament, Philadelphia, 1939), C. H. *Cornill (Heb. text, Germ. tr. and Comm., Leipzig, 1886), A. Bertholet (K.H.C., Abt. xii, 1897), R. Kraetzschmar (H.K.A.T., Abt. 3, Bd. iii, Theil 1, 1900), J. Herrmann (K.A.T., xi, 1924), and A. Bertholet–R. Galling (H.A.T., Reihe 1, Bd. xiii, 1936). J. Smith, The Book of the Prophet Ezekiel. A New Interpretation (S.P.C.K., 1931). J. Herrmann, Ezechielstudien (Beiträge zur Wissenschaft vom Alten Testament, ii; 1908); G. Hölscher, Hesekiel. Der Dichter und das Buch (Beihefte zur Z.A.T.W., xxxix; 1924); V. Herntrich, Ezechielprobleme (ib., lxi; 1932). J. B. Harford, Studies in the Book of Ezekiel (1935); W. A. Irwin, The Problem of Ezekiel. An Inductive Study (Chicago, 1943).

EZNIK (5th cent.), Bp. of Bagrevand in *Armenia. A native of Kolb and a disciple of St. *Mesrob, he was one of the most polished and learned of early Christian Armenian writers. His principal surviving work is a treatise, The Confutation of the Sects (c. 441–448), in four books, directed respectively against (1) the pagans, (2) the religion of the Persians, (3) the Greek philosophers, and (4) the *Marcionites. He also took part in translating the Armenian version of the Bible, and, acc. to native tradition, wrote some homilies which have perished.

The Confutation of the Sects has been published (in Armenian) at Smyrna (1762) and Venice (1826, 1863). German version by J. M. Schmid (1900). L. Mariès, S.J., Le De Deo d'Esnik de Kolb, connu sous le nom de Contre les sectes (1925). Bardenhewer, v, pp. 209–16; Altaner (ed. 1950), p. 306.

EZRA. The Jewish priest and scribe, who played a central part in the reform of *Judaism in the 5th or 4th cent. B.C. His activities are recorded in the Books of *Ezra and Nehemiah, and of 1 *Esdras. On his arrival in *Jerusalem from Persia 'in the seventh year of Artaxerxes the king' (Ez. 7. 7), he set about his purposes on the basis of a royal warrant. His work marks the stage in the history of Judaism at which the distinction between the universalist and exclusivist attitudes to the Gentiles became clearly defined, and as a champion of the latter Ezra took strict measures to secure the racial purity of the Jews and the development of Judaism along the straight and narrow way laid down by *Ezekiel. After his establishment in Jerusalem, he solemnly promulgated a code of laws (see Pentateuch), one of the first responses to which was a solemn observance of the Feast of *Tabernacles. The chronology of the period is obscure and there is apparently considerable confusion in the OT record; but there is an increasing consensus of opinion that the 'Artaxerxes the king' of Ez. 7. 7 is the second Persian monarch of that name (404–359 B.C.) and that Ezra's arrival is thus to be dated in 397 B.C. If so, he belonged to a later generation than *Nehemiah. The very existence of Ezra has been questioned by C. C. Torrey, who supposes him to be the idealized creation of the *Chronicler's imagination, but this drastic critical hypothesis has received little support.

For bibl. see foll. entry.

EZRA and NEHEMIAH, Books of. These Books continue the history of the Hebrew people begun in the Books of *Chronicles, and are evidently the work of the same compiler. The narrative extends from the end of the Babylonian Exile (537 B.C.) down to the latter half of the 5th cent. B.C., the greater part of it being concerned with the work of Ezra and Nehemiah. Ez. 1–6 relates the return of the exiles from Babylon, the efforts made to rebuild the Temple at *Jerusalem and the encouragement given to the project by the prophets *Haggai and *Zechariah; 7–10 deals with Ezra's mission to Jerusalem and the reforms he introduced, notably in the matter of mixed marriages. Neh. 1–7 contains Nehemiah's plans for the restoration of Jerusalem; 8–10 record the reading and acceptance of the Law; 11 and 12 describe his arrangements for the occupation of the city; and 13 narrates a further series of Nehemiah's reforms.

It is generally supposed by modern scholars that the compiler of the books ('the Chronicler', i.e. the author also of the Books of Chronicles) wrote at a date considerably later even than the time of Nehemiah. There are a number of historical inaccuracies in the Books, e.g. in the chronological details of the Persian kings, the foundation of the *Temple, and the arrival of Ezra and Nehemiah in Jerusalem, most easily accounted for by the insufficient data and the preconceived ideas of a compiler of much later date. He clearly drew his matter from several sources. Large sections appear to be derived from the 'Memoirs of Ezra' and the 'Memoirs of Nehemiah'. Ez. 4. 8–6. 18 and 7. 12–26 are written in *Aramaic, not Hebrew, and may therefore have been taken from a collection of official Aramaic documents. No doubt the source from which the various catalogues of names are drawn was also a set of official lists. See also *Esdras, Books of.*

Commentaries by H. E. Ryle (Camb. Bib., RV, 1893), L. W. Batten (I.C.C., 1913), C. Siegfried (H.K.A.T., Abt. 1, Bd. vi, Theil 2, on Ezr., Neh., and Esther, 1901, pp. 1–133),

A. Bertholet (K.H.C., xix, 1902) and W. Rudolph (H.A.T., Reihe 1, Bd. xx, 1949). C. C. Torrey, *The Composition and Historical Value of Ezra-Nehemiah* (Beihefte zur Z.A.T.W., ii; 1896). Id., *Ezra Studies* (Chicago, 1910). H. H. Schaeder, *Esra der Schreiber* (1930), M. Kegel, *Die Kultusreformation des Esra.* Aussagen moderner Kritik über Neh. 8–10 (1921). A. van Hoonacker, *Nouvelles Études sur la restauration juive après l'exil de Babylone* (1896), pp. 151–310. L. E. Browne, *Early Judaism* (1920).

F

FABER, FREDERICK WILLIAM (1814–1863), *Oratorian and hymn writer. Born at Calverley in the W. Riding of Yorkshire, he was educated at Shrewsbury and Harrow and at Balliol and University Colleges, Oxford. In 1837 he was elected to a Fellowship at the latter college. His upbringing was *Calvinist; but at Oxford he came under the influence of J. H. *Newman and collaborated in the work on the *Library of the Fathers*. In 1837 he was ordained deacon and in 1839 priest. He was an enthusiastic and observant traveller, publishing in 1842 *Sights and Thoughts in Foreign Churches and among Foreign Peoples*, dedicated to W. *Wordsworth. In the same year he was appointed Rector of Elton, Hunts. In 1844 he published a short *Life of St. Wilfrid* which created a sensation from its RC sympathies. On 17 Nov. 1845 he was received into the RC Church, a few weeks after Newman. With other converts he formed a small community, the 'Brothers of the Will of God', at Birmingham; in 1847 he was ordained priest; and in 1848, with his companions, joined the Oratory of St. *Philip Neri, recently introduced into England by Newman. In 1849 Faber became the head of the London branch, at first established in King William Street, Strand, and from 1854 on its present site in the Brompton Road.

Faber was the author of many hymns and devotional books. His writings owed their popularity to their fervent spirituality and their lucid style, in which profound truths were made accessible to the simplest minds. They have been translated into many languages. Among the better known are *All for Jesus* (1853), *Growth in Holiness* (1854), *The Blessed Sacrament* (1855), *The Creator and the Creature* (1858), and *Bethlehem* (1860). Many of his hymns have remained favourites, e.g. 'Hark! hark, my soul', 'My God, how wonderful Thou art', and 'Sweet Saviour, bless us ere we go'.

Life and Letters, ed. J. E. Bowden (1869; new ed., 1888). F. A. Faber (brother), *A Brief Sketch of the Early Life of F. W. Faber* (1869). Life by R. [G.] Chapman (London, 1961). T. Cooper in *D.N.B.*, xviii (1889), pp. 108–11.

FABER, JACOBUS (c. 1455–1536), also known as Lefèvre d'Étaples or Stapulensis, early French humanist. A native of Étaples, after ordination to the priesthood he devoted himself to the study of the classics at *Paris, where he made the acquaintance of some of the leading humanists. In 1492 he went to Italy and there became keenly interested in the ancient philosophers, esp. *Aristotle. In 1507 the abbot at the monastery of St. *Germain-des-Prés, who was one of his former pupils, appointed him librarian. Exchanging his secular for religious studies, he published in 1512 a Latin commentary on St. Paul's Epistles. Two critical essays on St. *Mary Magdalene

(1517 and 1518) were followed by his formal condemnation by the *Sorbonne for heresy in 1521. As he showed sympathies with the Reformation, the government was also led to condemn him, and in 1525 he was forced to flee to Strassburg. Later he was taken under the protection of the Queen of Navarre. He never accepted the Reformation doctrines on grace, justification, and predestination, and his attitude to the Reformation has been compared with that of *Erasmus. His other writings include the first printed text of the (Lat.) *Ignatian Epp. (Paris, 1498) and a transl. of the NT into French (1523; from the *Vulgate), followed by the Pss. in 1525 and the OT complete in 1528.

Studies by C. H. Graf (Strassburg, 1842) and J. Barnaud (Paris, 1900). H. Doerries, 'Calvin und Lefèvre' in *Z.K.G.*, xliv (1925), pp. 544–81. É. Amann in *D.T.C.*, ix (pt. 1; 1926), cols. 132–59, s.v. 'Lefèvre d'Étaples'.

FABER, JOHANN (1478–1541), German theologian. A native of Leutkirch in Württemberg, he studied at *Tübingen and Freiburg, and in 1530 became Bp. of Vienna. Ferdinand I employed him on several important missions, including a visit to England to engage *Henry VIII's help against the Turks. His lifelong friendship with D. *Erasmus led him at first to sympathize with P. *Melanchthon and H. *Zwingli in their desire to reform the Church; but as the underlying doctrinal cleavage manifested itself, he withdrew his support from the Reformation programme and became a zealous defender of Catholic orthodoxy, earning the title 'the hammer of the heretics'. His works consist chiefly of controversial treatises and a few collections of sermons.

Faber's *Malleus in Haeresim Lutheranam* was first publd. Cologne, 1524; 'Opuscula', ed. J. *Cochläus, Leipzig, 1537; 'Opera' (mostly sermons, letters, and diaries), ed. Cologne, 3 vols., fol., 1537–41. A. Horawitz, 'Joh. Heigerlin (genannt Faber), Bischof von Wien, bis zum Regensburger Convent' in *Sb.* (Wien), cvii (1884), pp. 83–220. Further study by L. Helbling (*Reformationsgeschichtliche Studien und Texte*, Hftt. lxvii–lxviii, Münster i.W., 1941). E. Tomek in *L.Th.K.*, iii (1931), col. 934 f., s.v. 'Fabri, Johannes', with further bibl. Modern ed. of his *Malleus in Haeresim Lutheranam* by A. Naegele (Corpus Catholicorum xxiii–xxvi, Münster i.W., 1941–52).

FABIAN, St. (d. 250), Bp. of Rome from 236. Little is known of his pontificate beyond the fact that when the *Decian Persecution broke out early in 250, he was the first to suffer martyrdom. Acc. to the *Liber Pontificalis, it was he who divided the city of Rome into seven ecclesiastical regions, each of them in charge of a deacon. His body was buried in the *catacomb of San Callisto and later moved to the church of San Sebastiano, where it was discovered in 1915. Feast day, 20 Jan.

*Cyprian, *Ep.* ix; *L.P.* (Duchesne), i (1885), p. 148 f.; P. Styger, 'Scavi a San Sebastiano' in *R.Q.,* xxix (1915), pp. 73–110 (esp. 'La scoperta del corpo di S. Fabiano', pp. 100–5); F. Grossi-Gondi, S.J., *S. Fabiano, papa e martire dopo le scoperte sull' Appia* (1916).

FABIOLA, St. (d. 399), Roman matron. She belonged to the patrician *gens Fabia*. Having divorced her first husband for his vicious life, she remarried (contrary to the Church canons). After the death of her second 'husband', she did public penance before the *Lateran and entered on a life of great austerity, distributing her immense wealth to the poor and tending the sick. In 395 she went to *Bethlehem, where she stayed with St. *Paula and St. *Eusto-chium and put herself under the direction of St. *Jerome. The tensions created by the *Origenistic controversy, her personal distaste for the isolated convent life at Bethlehem, and finally the incursion of the Huns into Palestine, led her to return to Rome, where she continued her charitable works until her death. Feast day, 27 Dec.

To St. Fabiola St. Jerome addressed two letters: Epp. 64 (J. P. Migne, *PL*, xxii, 607–22) and 78 (ib., 698–724); the principal source is the letter which Jerome wrote on her death, Ep. 77 (ib., 690–98). W. H. Fremantle in *D.C.B.*, ii (1880), p. 442 f., with reff. See also bibl. to *Jerome*.

FABRI, FELIX (1442–1520). A learned *Dominican friar of Ulm who in his *Evaga-torium in Terrae Sanctae, Arabiae et Egypti peregrinationem* has left a vivid record of a pilgrimage to *Jerusalem in 1483.

Evagatorium, &c., ed. G. D. Hassler (Stuttgart, 1843–9); Eng. tr. by A. Stewart (Palestine Pilgrims' Text Society, vii–x; 1892–3). P. S. Allen, *The Age of Erasmus* (1914), pp. 238-51.

FABRI, JOHANNES. See *Faber, Johann*.

FABRICIUS, JOHANN ALBERT (1668–1736), *Lutheran classical scholar and biblio-grapher. Born at Leipzig and educated there and at Quedlinburg, in 1693 he settled in Hamburg as a private librarian. From 1699 until his death he taught rhetoric and ethics and was rector of the Johanneum from 1708 to 1711.

Fabricius was an indefatigable student whose monumental bibliographical work, if lacking in scientific accuracy, laid the foundations for all subsequent histories of literature. His *Bibliotheca Graeca* (14 vols., 1705–28; revised and continued by G. C. Harles, 1790–1812) covered the period from Homer to the fall of *Constantinople (1453). His other compila-tions include the *Bibliotheca Latina* (1697; revised and enlarged 3 vols., 1721–2), *Bibliotheca Latina Mediae et Infimae Aetatis* (5 vols., 1734–6; vol. vi, in collaboration with C. Schoettgen, 1746). He also did important work on the Apocrypha, publishing an edition of the *Liber Tobiae, Judith, Oratio Manassae, Sapientia et Ecclesiasticus, gr. et lat., cum pro-legomenis* (1691), followed by the *Codex Apocryphus Novi Testamenti* (2 vols., 1703, enlarged with 3rd vol. 1719) and the *Codex Pseudepigraphus Veteris Testamenti* (1713). He also produced the first collected edition of the works of St. *Hippolytus (2 vols., 1716–18), which has not been superseded, and editions of Sextus Empiricus (1718), St. *Philaster of

Brescia (1721) and Dion Cassius (completed by H. S. *Reimarus, 1750–1).

H. S. Reimarus (son-in-law), *De Vita et Scriptis Joannis Alberti Fabricii Commentarius* (Hamburg, 1737). There is also a brief introd. on Fabricius's life and works prefixed to the ed. of his *Bibliotheca Latina* (6 vols. bound in 3, Florence, 1858), vol. i, pp. xx–xxiv. G. Uhlhorn in *P.R.E.* (ed. 3), v (1898), pp. 730–2, s.v.; B. Heurtebize in *D.T.C.*, v (1913), cols. 2063–5, s.v.

FACULTIES, Court of. The court of the Abp. of *Canterbury which grants *faculties. Its judge, who is called the 'Master of the Faculties', is usually the same person as the Dean of *Arches. When in 1534 it was enacted that *dispensations, licences, and faculties which had previously been granted by the Pope were to be henceforth granted by the Abp. of Canterbury in the provinces both of Canterbury and of *York, the Court of Faculties took over this jurisdiction.

See bibl. to foll. entry.

FACULTY. A dispensation or licence from an ecclesiastical superior permitting someone to perform an action or occupy a position which without it he could not lawfully do or hold. Thus the Preface to the *Ordinal in the BCP forbids anyone to be admitted a deacon under twenty-three years of age 'unless he have a faculty'. Under 25 Henry VIII, c. 21, the 'Court of *Faculties' (q.v.) was created to restrain persons from suing for dispensations from Rome. As in every diocese the conse-crated buildings and lands and their contents are in the ultimate guardianship of the Bishop, faculties are necessary for additions or altera-tions to churches and churchyards. In such cases they are normally issued by the Bishop's *Chancellor or the *Archdeacon, and without the faculty the erection of, e.g., an altar, a statue, or a memorial tablet in a church is illegal. When once erected (whether with or without a faculty), a fresh faculty is needed for the removal of such objects, even temporarily.

In the academic world a Faculty is the organization for the teaching of a particular subject, so called because it can grant a faculty to receive or to sue for a degree. The tradi-tional Faculties are those of Theology, Canon and Civil Law, Medicine, and Arts.

H. W. Cripps, *A Practical Treatise on the Law Relating to the Church and Clergy* (ed. 8 by K. M. Macmorran, 1937), esp. pp. 147–57.

FACUNDUS (6th cent.), Bp. of Hermiane in the province of Byzacena in Africa. In the *Monophysite controversy he was one of the chief supporters of the *Three Chapters. In view of the dispute he made his way to *Con-stantinople, and in 547–8 completed there an apology for the accused in his treatise 'Pro Defensione Trium Capitulorum', in which he upheld the orthodoxy of each of the three theologians concerned—*Ibas, *Theodore of Mopsuestia (in this case with some reserves), and *Theodoret—and argued forcibly that to condemn the Three Chapters meant to reject the Christology of *Chalcedon (451). After his return to Africa, and the anathematization of the Three Chapters at the Second Council of Constantinople (553), he and his supporters were excommunicated for a time by Pope *Vigilius. He defended himself in two further writings, both of them dating from c. 571— 'Contra Mocianum Scholasticum' and 'Epistola fidei catholicae in defensione trium capitulorum'.

Works ed. J. *Sirmond, S.J., Paris, 1629; repr. in J. P. Migne, *PL*, lxvii, 527–878. Study (in Russian) by A. Dobroklonskij (Moscow, 1880; discussed by A. *Harnack in *T.L.Z.*, 1880, cols. 632–5). Bardenhewer, v, pp. 320–4; M. Pellegrino in *E.C.*, v (1950), col. 954 f., s.v. 'Facondo di Ermiana'.

FAIRBAIRN, ANDREW MARTIN (1838–1912), *Congregational theologian. Of Covenanting ancestry, Fairbairn was born at Inverkeithing in Fife and studied at Edinburgh university. He was successively minister of the Evangelical Union church at Bathgate (1860–72) and of St. Paul's Congregational church in Aberdeen (1872–7), principal of the Airedale Theological College at Bradford (1877–86), and principal of Mansfield College, Oxford (1886–1909). Through visits to Germany he came under the influence of I. A. *Dorner, F. A. G. *Tholuck, and E. W. *Hengstenberg, and warmly advocated theological liberalism. His eloquence, learning, and personal character won him a unique position among Congregational divines in his generation. His writings include *Studies in the Philosophy of Religion and History* (1876), *Catholicism, Roman and Anglican* (1899), and *The Philosophy of the Christian Religion* (1902). He also took an active part in religious and political controversy, notably in connexion with the Education Act of 1902.

W. B. Selbie, *Life of Andrew Martin Fairbairn* (1914). Id. in *D.N.B., 1912–1921*, p. 179 f.

FAITH. The term is used in at least two quite distinct senses in a Christian context.

(1) It is applied objectively to the body of truth ('the Christian faith') to be found in the *Creeds, in the definitions of accredited *Councils, in the teachings of doctors and saints, and, above all, in the revelation contained in the Bible. This complex of doctrine is held to embody or else follow from the teaching of Christ Himself, and as God's supreme revelation to mankind to be wilfully rejected by man only at the peril of his salvation. Technically it is known as 'the faith believed in' (*fides quae creditur*).

(2) To this objective faith is opposed 'subjective' faith. Faith thus understood is the first of the three '*Theological virtues', set by St. *Paul side by side with 'hope' and 'love' (1 Cor. 13. 13). It is the human response to Divine truth, inculcated in the Gospels as the childlike and trusting acceptance of the *Kingdom and its demands, and known as the 'faith whereby belief is reached' (*fides qua creditur*).

Acc. to orthodox theologians, faith in this latter sense is a supernatural, not a natural, act.

The Christian can make an act of faith only in virtue of God's action in his soul. The widespread modern notion that the faith of a Christian believer in, say, the truth of the Incarnation (as a doctrine which cannot be proved) is of a piece with the scientist's 'faith' in atoms and electrons reflects a conception of faith radically different from that of Christian orthodoxy. Faith, so far from being a mere readiness to go beyond the *data* of established fact where the evidence ceases (as does the scientist in the case just instanced), is held to be made effective by the immediate operation of the grace of God in the Christian soul, which carries with it complete conviction. It is possible only in the context of the Christian revelation.

Moreover, faith demands an act of the will, and is thus more than purely intellectual. St. *Augustine defined it as 'thinking with the giving of assent' (*cum assentione cogitare*). This voluntaristic moment in the act of faith accounts for the moral quality which it is held to possess and the conviction that wilful unbelief, as a misdirection of the will, merits the censure of God. To express this twofold element in the full act of faith, *Peter Lombard distinguished between (*a*) 'unformed faith' (*fides informis*), i.e. pure intellectual assent to a proposition, and (*b*) 'faith formed by love' (*fides formata caritate*), i.e., the developed faith, e.g. of St. Paul in Gal. 5. 6. It is in the light of this distinction that the apparent opposition between the teaching of St. *James and that of St. *Paul about faith has been held to be capable of reconciliation.

As a supernatural act, faith is a higher faculty than reason. In the developed teaching of the Middle Ages, a distinction was drawn between those truths accessible to the human intellect by the light of natural reason, e.g. the existence of God, and those which could be appropriated only by faith, e.g. belief in the Trinity. There was difference of opinion as to whether there were any conclusions which could in a full sense be the objects of both faith and reason; ín so far as any overlap was conceded, it was held by the most reputable theologians that the conclusions of reason and of faith were coincident. Only in the later and decadent Scholasticism was it maintained that one and the same proposition could be proved untrue by reason and accepted as true by faith.

At the Reformation, the part of faith in the Christian religion received a new emphasis. M. *Luther's teaching on *justification by 'faith only' stressed the voluntaristic side of faith, in so far as faith was allowed to be a human act at all. The chief moment in it was trust (*fiducia*), and supremely personal trust and confidence in the atoning work of Christ. The Lutheran theologians of the next generation analysed the act of faith into its three components of knowledge (*notitia*), assent (*assensus*), and trust (*fiducia*), though they held that the two former were subordinate to *fiducia*. The Anglican *Thirty-Nine Articles, while by referring favourably to Justification by Faith only (Art. XI) and denying merit to works done before justification (Art. XIII) they guard against ascribing virtue to human effort apart from divine grace, assert, nevertheless, that works which are the fruit of faith are pleasing to God (Art. XII). Here, too, faith is held to be an essentially supernatural act. It was only later, e.g. in I. *Kant, with his use of the word for the moral consciousness ('I had to remove knowledge [*Wissen*] to make room for faith [*Glaube*]'), that it was used outside a theological context.

Classical discussion in St. Thomas Aquinas, *Summa Theologica*, II (2), qq. 1-7. J. *Butler, *The *Analogy of Religion* (1736); J. H. *Newman, *An Essay in Aid of a Grammar of Assent* (1870). From the vast modern literature, the foll. may be mentioned: A. J. *Balfour, *Foundations of Belief* (1895); J. V. Bainvel, *La Foi et l'acte de foi* (1898; Eng. tr., St. Louis and London, 1926); W. R. *Inge, *Faith* (Studies in Theology, 1909); W. Spens, *Belief and Practice* (1915); F. H. Brabant–P. Hartill, *Faith and Truth* (1926); M. C. *D'Arcy, S.J., *The Nature of Belief* (1931); J. *Oman, *The Natural and the Supernatural* (1931); Dorothy M. Emmet, *Philosophy and Faith* (1936). H. Pope, O.P., in *C.E.*, v (1909), pp. 752-9, s.v.; S. Harent in *D.T.C.*, vi (1920), cols. 55-514, s.v. 'Foi'.

FAITH, Defender of the. See *Defender of the Faith*.

FAITH, Promoter of. See *Promotor Fidei*.

FAITH, St. (d. *c.* 287), virgin and martyr. Acc. to the legend which dates from the 8th or 9th cent., she suffered for the faith at Agen in Aquitaine, under Maximian Hercules and the procurator Dacian, together with St. Caprasius. Dulcidus, Bp. of Agen (5th cent.), translated her relics to a basilica which he built in honour of St. Faith and St. Caprasius, and many miracles are believed to have taken place at her shrine. Her relics were brought *c.* 855 to the abbey of Conques, which became a famous place of pilgrimage, visited e.g. by the Emp. *Frederick Barbarossa. Her cult was very popular in the Middle Ages, and many churches were dedicated to her, among them that of Farringdon Ward Within, London. It was pulled down in 1240 to make room for the choir of *St. Paul's Cathedral, a chapel of which was then dedicated to St. Faith. This dedication survives in the 'St. Faith's Chapel' in the crypt of the present cathedral. Feast day, 6 Oct.

AA.SS., Oct. III (1770), pp. 263-329, incl. text of Acta, p. 288 f.; other versions of the Acta listed in *B.H.L.*, i (1898-1899), pp. 441-4 (Nos. 2928-65), and Suppl. (1911), p. 123 f. The *Liber Miraculorum Sancte Fidis*, ed. A. Bouillet (Paris, 1897). On the 11th cent. *Chanson de Sainte Foi* (ed., with modern Fr. tr., by A. Thomas, Paris, 1925), see E. Hoepffner–P. Alfaric, *La Chanson de Sainte Foy* (Publications de la Faculté des Lettres de l'Université de Strasbourg, xxxii and xxxiii; 1926). A. Bouillet–L. Servières, *Sainte Foy, vierge et martyre* (1900). L. *Duchesne, *Fastes épiscopaux de l'ancienne Gaule*, ii (ed. 2, 1910), pp. 144-6.

FAITH AND ORDER. The branch of the *Oecumenical Movement of which the chief object has been to bring about the reunion of the Christian Churches, and by which the Conferences at *Lausanne in 1927 and *Edinburgh in 1937 were organized. It is now absorbed in the *World Council of Churches.

FAITHFUL, Mass of the (Lat. *Missa Fidelium*). The part of the *Mass which extends from the *Offertory to the end. It contains all the most essential parts of the service. It is so named because in early times the (unbaptized) *catechumens were dismissed before the Offertory and only the baptized (the 'fideles') remained to join in the Eucharistic offering.

FALDA. A white vestment worn over the cassock and reaching from the hips to the ground. Its use is confined to the Pope, who wears it only on solemn occasions.

E. Dante in *E.C.*, v (1950), col. 962, s.v., with ill., col. 961.

FALDSTOOL (Lat. *faldistorium*). In the RC Church the folding stool used in the *sanctuary by bishops and other prelates when they do not occupy the throne. The absence of a back enables it to be used both for sitting on and as a *prie-dieu. Unlike the throne, it may be used not only by the bishop of the diocese, but also by prelates who have no *ordinary jurisdiction in the place.

FALK, PAUL LUDWIG ADALBERT (1827–1900), German Liberal politician. In 1872 he was appointed Minister of Public Worship and Education by Bismarck with explicit instructions to defend the rights of the state against the Church in the *Kulturkampf. In this he succeeded only in two points, viz. in excluding the Church from the supervision of schools and from civil marriage. His *May-Laws, designed to put the relations between Church and state on an entirely new basis, were a failure owing to the uncompromising resistance not only of the Catholic Church but also of orthodox Protestantism to a measure destructive of all positive Christian education. Bismarck's consequent change of policy in 1879 caused Falk's resignation and also marked the end of the Kulturkampf.

Short study by H. R. Fischer (Hamm, 1901); full life by E. Foerster (Gotha, 1927). Id. in *R.G.G.* (ed. 2), ii (1928), cols. 503-5, s.v.

FALL, The. The first act of disobedience of *Adam and *Eve whereby man lost his primal innocence and happiness and entered upon his actual condition of sin and toil. As described in Gen. 2 f., Eve, tempted by the serpent, ate of the forbidden fruit of the 'tree of the knowledge of good and evil' in the Garden of *Eden, and then induced Adam to follow her example. The punishment was expulsion from Paradise, the imposition of toilsome work on Adam and the pains of childbirth on Eve, and the decree of perpetual enmity between the serpent, which would 'bruise [man's] heel', and the man, who would 'bruise [the serpent's] head' (Gen. 3. 15). Acc. to traditions as old as the *Apocrypha, the Divine words to Adam, 'Dust thou art and unto dust shalt thou return' (3. 19), were understood to mean the loss of immortality, and the serpent was identified with the *Devil (cf. Wisd. 2. 23 f. and Ecclus. 25. 24). But these consequences are not drawn elsewhere in the OT. The story itself suggests rather that Adam and Eve were not originally possessed of immortality (though they might have obtained it; cf. Gen. 3. 22 f.). What the Biblical narrative teaches positively is that sin arose by free human choice, and that all human life has been thereby radically altered for the worse, so that its actual state is very different from that purposed for it by the Creator. The doctrine of evil which it inculcates is, as against every form of dualism (which makes evil as well as good of Divine origin), pantheism (which denies the distinction between Creator and creation), or determinism (which denies human free will), that sin arose through free human agency; and this belief is integral to Christianity and Judaism alike.

Other questions often more prominent in theological debate, but really subordinate to this fundamental doctrine, concern (1) the ultimate origin of the evil manifested in Eve's and Adam's sin, (2) the historicity of the story of Gen. 2 f., and (3) the nature and extent of the consequences of the Fall for mankind. These issues are closely intertwined.

The common Christian belief down to modern times considered the Fall of Adam and Eve as an historical event. The serpent, which is represented in the Gen. narrative quite naïvely as a talking animal, was identified with the Devil or Satan, a spiritual being, who must have been created good and himself previously fallen, and hence the original Fall was inferred to be that of Satan rather than that of Adam and Eve. Adam and Eve being considered as historical persons and all subsequent humanity as their descendants, the consequences of the Fall were held to affect all mankind by inheritance, or even by a theory of 'seminal identity' by which an ancestor's act may involve all his descendants also (cf. Heb. 7. 9 f.). Acc. to the view expressed in Wisd. and Ecclus. (cf. above) and strongly endorsed by St. *Paul (Rom. 5. 12 ff., 1 Cor. 15. 22), it was Adam's sin that 'brought death into the world' because 'in Adam all sinned' and therefore became liable to death. It is noteworthy that as St. Paul appeals to this belief as a premiss accepted by his readers, it appears to have been generally accepted in the Early Church, at least among Gentile Christians, and the Fall thus to have been, from the first, part of the background against which the Christian doctrine of Redemption was expounded. Until the rise of *Pelagianism it was not a subject of controversy. The Gk. Fathers (esp. *Theodore of Mopsuestia), however, tended to minimize the evil done to man by the sin of Adam, laying more stress on the responsibility of each individual, while the Latins (esp. St. *Augustine), emphasizing the enormity of Adam's transgression and the magnitude of its consequences for mankind, developed the doctrine of *Original Sin (q.v.), which Pelagius opposed by denying the reality of any evil consequences from the Fall to subsequent mankind. *Origen (q.v.), alone among the Fathers, found the ultimate source of evil in a pre-mundane Fall or falls of equal created spirits who by voluntarily declining to a greater or less degree from the goodness in which they were created, became respectively demons, men, or angels. For him the human fall took place in a spiritual pre-natal existence (*De Princ.*, ii, 8 f.) and the story of Eden was to be interpreted allegorically (*De Princ.*, iv, 3).

In modern times the Biblical story of the Fall, and often the whole conception, have been widely rejected as inconsistent with the facts of man's development known to science, esp. with evolution. Most modern students of the Gen. narrative recognize that it is told with much anthropomorphic and metaphorical detail. Orthodox Christian apologists insist, however, that man possesses a power of moral choice not shared with the animals; that at some stage in human development this God-given power began to be misused; and that once begun, such wrong use has necessarily affected subsequent generations and given rise to the vast accumulated power of sin in the world. They would say that it was this fact which necessitated the redemption of the world by Christ. And since it was in close connexion with the doctrine of Redemption that Christian thought about the Fall developed, the Church has seen in the story of Gen. 2 f. a fundamental truth about man in his relation to God, even if the truth is held to be there conveyed in legendary form.

Belief in the fall of Adam is defined as *de fide* by the Council of *Trent, Sess. V, Can. 1 (A.D. 1546). F. R. Tennant, *The Sources of the Doctrines of the Fall and Original Sin* (1903); id., *The Origin and Propagation of Sin* (Hulsean Lectures, 1902). N. P. *Williams, *The Ideas of the Fall and of Original Sin* (Bampton Lectures for 1924, 1927). J. Denney, J. A. MacCulloch, and D. S. Margoliouth in *H.E.R.E.*, v (1912), pp. 701–15, s.v. See also Comms. on Gen. and bibl. to *Original Sin*.

FALSE DECRETALS, The. A collection of documents, attributed to St. *Isidore of Seville (d. 636), but really compiled somewhere in France (perhaps at Le Mans or Tours) *c.* 850. It contains (1) letters of ante-Nicene Popes, all of them forgeries; (2) a collection of canons of councils, for the most part genuine; and (3) a large collection of letters of Popes from *Silvester I (d. 335) to *Gregory II (d. 731), 35 of which are spurious. They were drawn up to defend the rights of diocesan bishops against their metropolitans and, to a lesser extent, to claim early authority for Papal supremacy; and their compiler, who had access to an enormous collection of historical matter, put them together with astonishing skill and precision. Pope *Nicholas I used them in 865, apparently knowing them to be forgeries; but in the Middle Ages they were generally assumed to be historical, and both T. *More and J. *Fisher, unaware of their true character, used them to defend the Papacy. Their genuineness was virtually disproved in 1558 by the Magdeburg *Centuriators, and it is now universally rejected. The (mainly genuine) canons were one of the chief sources of the collections of canon law in the Middle Ages.

Editio princeps in J. Merlin, *Concilia* (Paris, 1524 ['1523']). They have been regularly repr. in subsequent edd. of the *Concilia*. Text also in J. P. Migne, *PL*, cxxx. The only crit. ed. is that of P. Hinschius, *Decretales Pseudo-Isidorianae et Capitula Angilramni* (Leipzig, 1863), with valuable Preface. P. Fournier, 'Étude sur les "Fausses Décrétales" ' in *R.H.E.*, vii (1906), pp. 33–51, 301–16, 543–64, 761–84, and viii (1907), pp. 19–56. P. Fournier–G. Le Bras, *Histoire des collections canoniques en occident*, i (1931), pp. 127–233. J. Haller, *Nikolaus I und Pseudoisidor* (1936). Important artt. by E. Seckel in *P.R.E.* (ed. 3), xvi (1905), pp. 265–307, s.v. 'Pseudoisidor' (with full bibl. to date), and by L. Saltet in *C.E.*, v (1909), pp. 773–80, s.v. 'False Decretals'. Cf. also A. Villien in *D.T.C.*, iv (1911), cols. 212–22, s.v. 'Décrétales (Les Fausses)'; E. Stolz in *L.Th.K.*, viii (1936), cols. 549–51, s.v. 'Pseudo-Isidor'; R. Naz in *D.D.C.*, iv (1949), cols. 1062–1064, s.v. 'Décrétales (Fausses)'.

FAMILISTS. The members of a sect, called the 'Family of Love', founded by H. *Nicholas (q.v.). They propagated a vague philanthropism of pantheistic hue and antinomian tendencies. Though founded in *Holland, their main field of activity was in Britain. In 1580 Queen *Elizabeth's 'Proclamation against the Sectaries of the Family of Love' ordered their books to be burned and themselves to be imprisoned, but they continued nevertheless to spread. In 1645 J. Etherington attacked them; and though under O. *Cromwell many of Nicholas's books were reprinted, the sect disappeared at the end of the 17th cent., amalgamating with the *Quakers and other bodies.

F. A. *Loofs in *P.R.E.* (ed. 3), v (1898), pp. 750–5, s.v. 'Familisten'; G. Bareille in *D.T.C.*, v (1913), col. 2070 f., s.v. 'Famille d'Amour'. See also bibl. to *Nicholas, H.*

FAN, Liturgical (Lat. *flabellum*). From the 4th cent. at latest, fans were sometimes used at the Eucharist for keeping flies and other insects away from the oblations, and the practice continued in the W. down to the 14th cent. Their use survives at Pontifical Masses in the *Greek and *Armenian Rites, though their significance now is purely symbolical. As a mark of honour, two fans are used whenever the Pope is carried in procession on the '*sedia gestatoria'.

Braun, *A.G.*, pp. 624–60, with plates 140–2. H. *Leclercq, O.S.B., in *D.A.C.L.*, v (pt. 2; 1923), cols. 1610–1625, s.v. 'Flabellum', with extensive bibl. to date.

FANAR, The. See *Phanar, The.*

FANON. Of uncertain derivation, the word has been applied to several accessories of religious worship, apparently common to all being the fact that they are made from an embroidered piece of stuff. Among them are the *maniple; the white linen cloth in which the congregation formerly brought their Eucharistic offerings; the strings of the *mitre; the *humeral veil of the *subdeacon; and processional *banners. In current usage the word is confined to what is now a collar-shaped liturgical garment (Ital. *fanone*) worn by the Pope over his *amice when celebrating a solemn pontifical Mass. This garment was formerly known as the 'orale'.

Braun, *L.G.*, pp. 52–7.

FAREL, GUILLAUME (1489–1565), Reformer of French Switzerland. While studying at the University of Paris, he came under the influence of J. *Faber (Stapulensis), and on becoming suspect of discipleship to M. *Luther he retired in 1524 to Basle, where he disputed with the opponents of the Reformation despite an interdict from the bishop and the University. He was soon afterwards banished from the city, possibly at the suggestion of *Erasmus, whom he had called 'a new Baalam'. In 1530 he introduced the Reformation at Neuchâtel with some iconoclastic violence, and in 1535 he and Peter *Viret led a triumphant struggle which established the Reformation at Geneva. In the following year he detained J. *Calvin, who was passing through Geneva, persuaded him to stay, and declared him called to be a preacher and teacher of theology. For the rest of his life his fortunes were largely bound up with those of Calvin, though Calvin disapproved of his marriage at the age of 69 with a young refugee widow from Rouen. He was a powerful preacher. His writings, though voluminous, were too hastily composed to be of much permanent value.

Much of his correspondence is pr. by A. L. Herminjard (ed.), *Correspondance des réformateurs dans les pays de langue française* (8 vols., 1866–97). Modern lives by M. Kirchhofer (2 vols., Zürich, 1831–4; Eng. tr., 1837), S. Delattre (Paris, 1931), and the monumental composite vol., *Guillaume Farel, 1489–1565*. Biographie nouvelle écrite d'après les documents originaux par un groupe d'historiens, professeurs et pasteurs de Suisse, de France et d'Italie (by C. Schnetzler and others), ed. by the Comité Farel (Neuchâtel-Paris, 1930). In Eng. there is a briefer sketch by [E.] F. Bevan (London, 1880). J. J. *Herzog–R. Staehelin in *P.R.E.* (ed. 3), v (1898), pp. 762–7, s.v.; J. Dutilleul, S.J., in *D.T.C.*, v (1913), cols. 2081–90, s.v.

FARMERY, also 'fermery', another form of 'infirmary', esp. of a monastery. It was usually a separate building in charge of the *infirmarian (q.v.). In it the normal monastic discipline as to food and other matters was greatly relaxed.

FARRAR, FREDERIC WILLIAM (1831–1903), Dean of *Canterbury. He was educated at *King's College, London, where he was influenced by F. D. *Maurice, and at Trinity College, Cambridge, and became in turn house master at Harrow (1855), headmaster of Marlborough (1871), Canon of Westminster and Rector of St. Margaret's (1876), and Dean of Canterbury (1895). A 'Broad Church Evangelical', he had great influence on the religious feeling and culture of the Victorian middle classes, esp. through his *Life of Christ* (1874), which went through twelve editions in a year, and his *Life and Works of St. Paul* (1879). In these he expressed devout faith interpreted by wide scholarship and set out in a popular style. His *Eternal Hope* (1877), a collection of sermons in which he questioned the doctrine of eternal punishment for the wicked, provoked great controversy. Besides other theological works, Farrar wrote fiction. *Eric; or Little by Little* (1858), a school tale partly autobiographical, was long popular. It was followed by *Julian Home* (1859) and *St. Winifred's; or the World of School* (1862).

Life by Reginald Farrar, son (London, 1904), with list of his works, pp. xiii–xxii. R. Bayne in *D.N.B., 1901–1911*, ii (1912), pp. 9–12.

FASTIDIUS (early 5th cent.), British ecclesiastical writer. *Gennadius (*De viris ill.* 56) terms him 'Britannorum episcopus', but nothing further is known of his life. He is the probable author of a 'Corpus Pelagianum' and of a pseudo-Augustinian writing, 'De vita christiana', which from early times has also been ascribed to *Pelagius.

'Corpus Pelagianum', ed. C. P. *Caspari, *Briefe, Abhandlungen und Predigten aus den zwei letzten Jahrhunderten des kirchlichen Alterthums und dem Anfang des Mittelalters* (Christiania, 1850), pp. 352–75. His 'De Vita Christiana' is pr. among the works of St. *Augustine (ed. Ben., vi, 1685, appendix, cols. 183–92; repr. J. P. Migne, *PL*, xl, 1031–46). R. S. T. Haslehurst, *The Works of Fastidius* (text and Eng. tr., 1927; inaccurate). G. *Morin, O.S.B., 'Pelagius ou Fastidius' in *R.H.E.*, v (1904), pp. 258–64, with reff. to earlier discussion. I. Kirmer, O.S.B., *Das Eigentum des Fastidius im pelagianischen Schrifttum* (Diss., Würzburg, 1937; critique of G. de Plinval's assignment of many of Fastidius' works to Pelagius). Bardenhewer, iv, pp. 518–520, with further bibl. See also bibl. to *Pelagius.

FASTS and FASTING. Fasting, which was rigorously practised in Judaism and by the disciples of St. *John the Baptist, was recommended by Christ both by example and teaching (Mt. 6. 16, Mk. 2. 20 and 9. 29, AV). It was observed by the Apostles (Acts 13. 2, 14. 23, 2 Cor. 11. 27), and in the early Church regular weekly fast days soon developed, *Wednesday and *Friday being mentioned in the *Didache. In the W. *Saturday was later substituted for Wednesday (*c.* 400), but again abolished in more recent times. The fast of *Lent (q.v.), which was from the beginning connected with the feast of *Easter, lasted originally only two days, but it had been extended at least in many places to forty by the 4th cent. (*Athanasius, *Festal Epp.*). The E. Church added three further periods of fasting, *Advent (from 15 Nov.), from *Trinity Sunday to Sts. *Peter and Paul, and the fortnight before the *Assumption. The W. only developed the *Vigil fasts before the great feasts and the fasts of the *Ember Days.

In early times fasting meant entire abstention from food for the whole or part of the fast day. The only complete fast still retained is the Eucharistic fast lasting from the previous midnight. In modern RC practice fasting generally means one chief meal at midday and a small 'collation' in the morning and in the evening, and also demands abstention from fleshmeat; days of *Abstinence have been distinguished from Fast Days proper since 1781. The rules for fasting vary in the different countries and leave ample freedom of application. The C of E in the BCP contains a 'Table of the Vigils, Fasts and Days of Abstinence' to be observed in the year, but no specific directions are given as to their mode of observance; they were generally kept in the 16th and 17th cents. and their observance was re-vived in the 19th cent. under the influence of the *Oxford movement.

As a penitential practice, fasting is designed to strengthen the spiritual life by weakening the attractions of sensible pleasures. Our Lord Himself coupled it with prayer, and in the lives of the saints the two almost always go together. More or less rigorous fasts are practised in all the austerer religious orders, e.g. by the *Carthusians, *Cistercians, and *Carmelites. See also *Abstinence*.

A. Linsenmayr, *Entwicklung der kirchlichen Fastendisziplin bis zum Konzil von Nicäa* (1877); J. Schümmer, *Die altchristliche Fastenpraxis. Mit besonderer Berücksichtigung der Schriften Tertullians* (Liturgiegeschichtliche Quellen und Forschungen, Hft. xxvii; 1933). V. Staley, *The Fasting Days Appointed to be Observed in the English Church* (ed. 2, 1899). A. J. Maclean, 'Fasting and Abstinence' in W. K. L. Clarke (ed.), *Liturgy and Worship* (1932), pp. 245–56, with bibl. Id.–A. R. Whitman in *P.B.D.* (1912), p. 333 f., s.v. F. *Cabrol, O.S.B., in *D.A.C.L.*, vii (pt. 2; 1927), cols. 2481–2501, s.v. 'Jeûnes'; M. Waldmann in *L.Th.K.*, iii (1931), cols. 963–8, s.v. 'Fasten'; P. Palazzini, G. Sirna, O.F.M., A. Galieti and E. Remotti in *E.C.*, iv (1950), cols. 1589–99, s.v. 'Digiuno'. See also bibl. to *Abstinence, Lent, Ember Days, Vigils,* and *Eucharistic Fast.*

FATHER (Lat. *Pater*). Originally the title of bishops (cf. the BCP *Ordinal, where the bishop is addressed as 'Reverend Father in God'), it was later applied esp. to confessors, called in medieval English 'ghostly fathers'. As a title of religious the term properly belongs only to *Mendicant Friars whereas monks and *canons regular are called *Dom (Lat. *Domnus* or *Dominus*). In England, however, all RC priests, whether regular or secular, are now called 'Father', a custom introduced apparently from Ireland in the latter half of the 19th cent. and favoured by H. E. *Manning and others. It has also come into widespread currency among Anglo-Catholics. On the Continent other terms are used for the secular clergy, e.g. 'Monsieur le Curé' (or 'Monsieur le Vicaire') in French, 'Signore' or 'Don' in Italian. 'The Holy Father' is a popular title of the Pope.

FATHERS, Apostolic. See *Apostolic Fathers.*

FATHERS, White. See *White Fathers.*

FATHERS OF THE CHURCH. From an early date the title (πατήρ) was applied to bishops as witnesses to the Christian tradition, but from the end of the 4th cent. it was used in a more restricted sense of a more or less clearly defined group of ecclesiastical authors of the past whose authority on doctrinal matters carried special weight. St. *Basil and St. *Gregory of Nazianzen are among the first to prove the orthodoxy of their teaching by appealing to the agreement of series of patristic texts, later known by the technical term 'consensus Patrum'. In the great Christological controversies of the 5th cent. all parties claimed the authority of the Fathers for their teaching, e.g. St. *Cyril of Alexandria and the Council of *Ephesus (431) as well as *Theodoret. By the end of the 5th cent. the term had come to be applied also to teachers who were not bishops, e.g. to St. *Jerome. The so-called '*Gelasian Decree' gives a list of works of the 'Holy Fathers' which include even those of the layman *Prosper of Aquitaine. Acc. to the commonly accepted teaching, the Fathers of the Church were characterized by orthodoxy of doctrine, holiness of life, the approval of the Church, and antiquity. This last condition was variously interpreted till the 18th cent. From that time the patristic period is generally held to be closed with St. *Isidore of Seville in the W. and St. *John of Damascus in the E.

The authority of the Fathers was held by the older Catholic theologians to be infallible only when they taught a doctrine unanimously. The teaching of individual Fathers, on the other hand, though not lightly to be set aside, was admittedly liable to error. In modern usage *Tertullian, *Origen, and a few other ancient authors, though not of unimpeachable orthodoxy, are usually numbered among the Fathers of the Church. In any case, it is a popular rather than an exact title and, unlike '*Doctor of the Church', not formally conferred.

Bardenhewer, i, pp. 37–50 ('Kirchenvater, Kirchen-schriftsteller und Kirchenlehrer'). É. Amann in *D.T.C.*, xii (pt. 1; 1933), cols. 1192–1215, s.v. 'Pères de l'Église'.

FATIMA. A small town in the middle of Portugal, famous as a place of pilgrimage to the Basilica and Shrine of Our Lady of Fatima.

On 13 May 1917 three illiterate children, between the ages of 10 and 13 saw a vision of a lady, who reappeared on five subsequent occasions. On the last she declared herself to be 'Our Lady of the Rosary', told them to recite the Rosary daily, and asked for a chapel to be built in her honour. Two of the children died in 1919, but the third, Lucia Santos (still alive in 1957), became a *Carmelite nun at Coimbra. She wrote two accounts of the visions, in 1936–7 and 1941–2, and by permission of authority she was allowed to reveal a part of the 'secret'. It is thus that we learn the 'Threefold Message of Fatima', namely the practice of Penance, the recitation of the Rosary, and Devotion to the Immaculate Heart of Mary. But the complete story of Fatima cannot be written until after 1960, when the full account of the 'secret' may be unsealed.

There is a vast literature; the more important works include L. Fischer, *Fátima. Das portugiesische Lourdes* (1930), and other works of this author; L. Gonzaga da Fonseca, S.J., *Le meraviglie di Fatima* (ed. 2, 1932; many subsequent edd.); W. T. Walsh, *Our Lady of Fátima* (1949). There is also a popular account by F. Ryan, O.P., *Our Lady of Fatima* (Dublin, 1939), and an attractive record of a pilgrimage to Fatima by C. C. Martindale, S.J., *Portuguese Pilgrimage* (1949), with bibl., p. 148. E. Dhanis, S.J., 'À propos de "Fatima et la critique"' in *Nouvelle Revue Théologique*, lxxiv (1952), pp. 580–606.

FAULHABER, MICHAEL VON (1869–1952), German cardinal. A native of Franconia, he was ordained priest in 1892, spent the years from 1895 to 1898 in Rome, taught theology at Würzburg university from 1899 to 1903, and was appointed professor of OT theology at Strassburg in 1903. In 1910 he became Bp. of Speyer, and in 1917 Abp. of Munich; he was created cardinal in 1921. In his earlier years Faulhaber made some important contributions to *patristics, notably in his edition in *Die Prophetenkatenen nach römischen Handschriften* (1889), and in assigning to St. *Hesychius of Jerusalem a commentary on the Psalms formerly attributed to St. *Athanasius (1901). Later he became the leader of the right-wing German Catholics, and after the accession of A. Hitler to power (1933) was one of the most courageous and outspoken critics of the Nazis. He has also published several books dealing with contemporary problems, e.g. the emancipation of women.

Episcopus. Studien uber das Bischofsamt . . . zum 80. Geburtstag dargebracht (1949); *Festschrift Kardinal Faulhaber zum achtzigsten Geburtstag dargebracht* [1949].

FAUSTINUS AND JOVITA, Sts. (2nd cent.), martyrs of Brescia. Acc. to the legend, they were brothers of noble birth whose faith excited the wrath of their fellow-townsmen of Brescia. They were taken prisoner under Trajan, and then tortured and transported to Milan, Rome, and Naples, making innumerable converts on the way. Owing to their persistence Hadrian, who happened to pass through Brescia, ordered their execution. Several cities (incl. Brescia, Rome, and *Bologna) claim to possess their relics. It is very doubtful if any of the incidents in the legend are historical, and no mention of them is made by the two best-known early ecclesiastical writers of Brescia, *Philaster and *Gaudentius. Feast day, 15 Feb.

'Acta' with discussion in *AA.SS.*, Feb. II (1658), pp. 805–821. Further discussion and texts ed. F. Savia, S.J., 'La Légende des SS. Faustin et Jovite' in *Anal. Boll.* xv (1896), pp. 5–72, 113–59, and 377–99.

FAUSTUS OF MILEVIS (late 4th cent.), *Manichaean propagandist. A native of Melevis, he won fame as a rhetorician at Rome. When Faustus visited Carthage in 383, *Augustine, himself still a Manichee, put himself under his direction; but he found Faustus a fraud, and thus the way was prepared for his acceptance of the Catholic faith. Faustus's teachings can be partly reconstructed from Augustine's *Contra Faustum Manichaeum* (c. 400).

For bibl., see *Augustine, St*.

FAUSTUS OF RIEZ, St. (c. 408–c. 490), *Semi-Pelagian teacher. Probably of British or Breton origin, he entered the monastery of *Lérins and in 433 succeeded Maximus as abbot. About 459 he became Bp. of Riez (Rhegium in Provence), but was later driven from his see for a time by the Visigothic king, Euric, on account of his opposition to Euric's Arianizing policy. Requested by Leontius, Abp. of Arles, to refute the *predestinarian doctrines of a certain Lucidus, he wrote his 'De Gratia', a book which was approved by the Council of Arles (472 or 473). Here he adopted a semi-Pelagian position, insisting even more emphatically than J. *Cassian on the necessity of human co-operation with Divine grace, and on the initial free will of men, even when in sin, for the acceptance of that grace. Though his teachings were condemned at the Second Council of *Orange in 529, he is revered as a saint in the S. of France. Feast day, 28 Sept.

Opera, ed. A. G. Engelbrecht, *C.S.E.L.* xxi (1891). J. P. Migne, *P.L.*, lviii, 783–870 and liii, 681–890. Studies by A. Engelbrecht, Vienna, 1889), A. Koch (Stuttgart, 1895), F. Wörter (Münster i.W., 1900), A. G. Elg (Upsala, 1937) and G. Weigel (Philadelphia, 1938).

FAWKES, GUY (1570–1606). The most famous member of the *Gunpowder Plot conspiracy. Born in Yorkshire, he was brought up a Protestant, but becoming a Papist he sold his English property and joined the Spanish Army in 1593. In 1604 he was brought into the Plot by R. *Catesby and given the task of firing the gunpowder. While keeping watch on the cellar he was arrested (5 Nov. 1605), but disclosed the conspiracy only under torture. In company with his fellow-conspirators, T. Winter, A. Rokewood, and R. Keyes, he was executed on 31 Jan. 1606.

[R. Davies], *The Fawkes's of York in the Sixteenth Century*: including notices of the Early History of Guye Fawkes, the Gunpowder Plot Conspirator (1850), esp. pp. 27–47. D. Carswell (ed.), *The Trial of Guy Fawkes and Others*. The Gunpowder Plot ('Notable British Trials', 1934). See also bibl. to *Gunpowder Plot*.

FAYÛM GOSPEL FRAGMENT. A brief papyrus fragment, discovered in Egypt in 1882, which contains an imperfect account of the prediction of St. *Peter's denial, closely akin to Mk. 14. 27–30. It may be either an extract from a lost gospel or (perhaps more probably) a fragment of some early ecclesiastical writer who was making a free quotation from the canonical gospels. It is preserved at Vienna among the Rainer Papyri.

The text was publd. by G. *Bickell in *Z.K.T.*, ix (1885), pp. 498–504. A. *Harnack, 'Das Evangelienfragment von Fajjum' appended to A. Resch, *Agrapha* (T.U., v, Hft. 4; 1889), pp. 481–97.

FAYUMIC. A dialect of *Coptic spoken in early Christian times in Middle Egypt. The NT was translated into it, probably from *Sahidic, but only a few fragments of the version exist. It was formerly known (incorrectly) as 'Bashmuric', from a province in the Delta.

FEASTS, Ecclesiastical. These come under three chief headings: (1) *Sundays*. The weekly commemoration of the Resurrection, which falls on the first day of every week. Sundays have been kept by Christians from Apostolic times as days of worship, and in 321 the Emp. *Constantine proclaimed that Sunday should be a general holiday.

(2) *Movable Feasts*. Of these the most important are (i) *Easter, the annual commemoration of the Resurrection, and (ii) *Pentecost or Whitsunday, the 7th Sunday after Easter, the commemoration of the descent of the Holy Ghost upon the Church. Both are of Apostolic origin, and replace respectively the Jewish *Passover and Feast of *Weeks, like which they vary with the Paschal full moon. Certain other feasts, and also the fast of *Lent, vary with the date of Easter; these came into use later.

(3) *Immovable Feasts*. Of these the earliest were probably the anniversaries of martyrs, which were kept at Rome from the 3rd cent., and in Asia Minor as early as the 2nd. Later, other saints were commemorated either on their death-day or the day of translation of their relics, or occasionally on other days. By the 4th cent. various fixed festivals of our Lord, esp. *Christmas and the *Epiphany, became generally observed, and later various feasts of the BVM, with other feasts of our Lord, were added.

Ecclesiastical feasts are observed by a '*proper' in the Eucharist and *Offices. The fullest calendars in present use are those of the RC and Orthodox bodies; the C of E provides a list of days to be observed, and a further list without specific instructions that they must be kept. Both together are of modest dimensions, but various Anglican provinces outside England have enlarged their calendar.

See bibl. to *Year, Liturgical*.

FEASTS OF OBLIGATION. In the RC Church, feast days of outstanding importance which the laity as well as the clergy are obliged to observe by hearing Mass and abstaining from *servile work. The list of such feasts varies somewhat from country to country, but everywhere all Sundays in the year are 'Days of Obligation'. In England and Wales they are at present: the *Circumcision (1 Jan.), the *Epiphany (6 Jan.), *Ascension Day, *Corpus Christi, Sts. Peter and Paul (29 June), the *Assumption of BVM (15 Aug.), *All Saints (1 Nov.), and *Christmas Day (25 Dec.). Scotland and Ireland both add the *Immaculate Conception of BVM (8 Dec.), Scotland also St. Joseph (19 Mar.), and Ireland also St. Patrick (17 Mar.). For details see *Codex Iuris Canonici* (cans. 1247–9: 'De diebus festis').

FEATHERS TAVERN PETITION (1772). A petition to Parliament signed at the Feathers Tavern, Strand, London, by *c.* 200 liberal Christians for the abolition of subscription to the *Thirty-Nine Articles, and its replacement by a simple declaration of belief in the Bible. Among its principal sponsors were Francis Blackburne, Archdeacon of Cleveland (1705–87), Theophilus *Lindsey, and John Jebb (1736–86). The petition was presented to the Commons by Sir William Meredith and debated on 6 February 1772. Largely through the influence of a speech of E. Burke it was defeated on a division by 217 votes to 71.

The text of the petition is pr. among *The Works . . . of Francis Blackburne*, ed. by his son, Francis Blackburne, vol. vii (1805), pp. 15–19, with various associated docc. in the same volume. The greater part of Burke's speech on the subject, which he preserved with a view to possible publication, is in his *Works*, ed. 1, vol. v (1812), pp. 323–36 (ed. F. H. Willis–F. W. Raffety, 6 vols. World's Classics, vol. iii (1906), pp. 291–303).

FEBRONIANISM. The movement in the RC Church in Germany in the 18th cent. against the claims of the Papacy, esp. in the temporal sphere. It may be considered from some points of view as the German counterpart of *Gallicanism. In 1742 the three Archbishop-Electors invited N. von *Hontheim (q.v.), suffragan Bp. of Trier, to investigate their existing grievances against Rome, and in 1763 he published his findings in *De statu ecclesiae et legitima potestate Romani pontificis*, under the pen-name of 'Justinus Febronius'. The book, while recognizing that the Pope was the head of the Church and the supervisor of Church administration and (subject to the Universal Church or a General Council) of faith and morals, attacked the medieval accretions of temporal power. It advocated that Church affairs should be kept as far as possible in episcopal and civil hands, and that all Papal claims based on the *False Decretals should be annulled. In 1764 it was put on the *Index, but in 1769 it received the approval of the Archbishop-Electors, who drew up a list of thirty objections against the Papal claims. The Archbishop-Electors attempted to assert their claims at Bad *Ems (q.v.) in 1786, but without success. The outbreak of the French Revolution and lack of support from other German bishops caused the movement to collapse. See also *Wessenberg, I. H. von*.

O. Meyer, *Febronius, Weihbischof Johann Nicolaus von Hontheim und sein Widerruf* (Tübingen, 1880); J. Küntziger, *Fébronius et le fébronianisme* (Mémoires couronnés et autres mémoires publiés par l'Académie Royale des Sciences, des Lettres et des Beaux-Arts de Belgique. Collection en 8º; xliv; 1891; présenté à la Classe des Lettres dans la séance du 6 mai, 1889). F. Lauchert in *C.E.*, vi (1909), pp. 23–5, s.v.; A. *Fortescue in *H.E.R.E.*, v (1912), pp. 807–9, s.v.; T. Ortolan in *D.T.C.*, v (1913), cols. 2115–24, s.v. 'Febronius'; M. Braunach in *L.Th.K.*, iii (1931), cols. 974–6, s.v., all with bibl.

FECHNER, GUSTAV THEODOR (1801–1887), psychologist and spiritualistic philosopher. He spent nearly all his life at Leipzig, where he held a professorship from 1834 to 1839. He became well known as a psychologist by his law ('Fechner's Law') of the mathematical relation between the intensity of a sensation and the corresponding stimulus. In philosophy he expounded an extreme form of '*animism' contending that all existents in the universe were endowed with consciousness, and that everything was enclosed by the all-pervasive Being of God. His writings include *Elemente der Psychophysik* (2 vols., 1860) and *Die Tagesansicht gegenüber der Nachtansicht* (1879).

There is an Eng. tr. of Fechner's *Das Büchlein vom Leben nach dem Tode* (orig. publ. under name of Dr. Mises; 1836) by H. Wernekke (London, 1882). Selections of his Works in Eng. tr. by W. Lowrie, *Religion of a Scientist* (New York and London, 1946), with bibl. Life by J. F. Kuntze (nephew; Leipzig, 1892). K. Lasswitz, *Gustav Theodor Fechner* (1896). Überweg, iv, pp. 292–8, with further bibl., p. 708.

FELICITY, St. (2nd cent.), Roman martyr. She is one of the seven Roman martyrs named in the *Depositio Martyrum* of the '*Liberian Catalogue' for 10 July. Acc. to the *acta* (not later than 6th cent.), she was martyred with her seven sons. Acc. to F. C. *Burkitt and V. L. Kennedy, she is the Felicity referred to in the *canon of the Roman Mass. Feast day, 23 Nov. She has also been commemorated with her sons ('The Seven Brothers') on 10 July.

Acta in T. *Ruinart, *Acta Primorum Martyrum Sincera et Selecta* (Paris, 1689), pp. 21–3. Further sources listed in *B.H.L.*, p. 429 f. (Nos. 2853–5), and suppl. p. 119 f. F. C. Burkitt, 'St. Felicity in the Roman Mass' in *J.T.S.*, xxxii (1930–1), pp. 279–87; V. L. Kennedy, C.S.B., *The Saints of the Canon of the Mass* (Studi di antichità cristiana, xiv, 1938), pp. 164–8. H. *Leclercq, O.S.B., in *D.A.C.L.*, v (pt. 1; 1922), cols. 1259–98, s.v. 'Félicité (Passion et cimetière de)'. J. P. Kirsch in *L.Th.K.*, iii (1931), col. 989, s.v.

FELICITY, St. (d. 203), African martyr. She was one of the companions of St. *Perpetua (q.v.), with whom she was martyred. Feast day, 6 Mar. (formerly 7 Mar.).

For the contemporary *acta*, see art. *Perpetua*.

FELIX, St. (d. c. 648), Bp. of Dunwich. He was a native of Burgundy. After converting the East Anglian prince, Sigeberht, then in exile, to Christianity, he made his way to England where, under the direction of Honorius, Abp. of *Canterbury, he successfully preached the Gospel to the heathen in East Anglia. He fixed his episcopal see at the seaport town of Dunwich in Suffolk (now mainly submerged) and acc. to *Bede (*HE* ii. 15) ruled his diocese for seventeen years. His name survives in Felixstowe in Suffolk and Feliskirk in Yorkshire. His relics were preserved at Ramsey Abbey. Feast day, 8 Mar.

The chief authority is Bede, *H.E.*, ii, 15; iii, 18, 20, 25. See also notes, ed. C. Plummer, ii (1896), pp. 106–8, 168, 174. Short account also in *William of Malmesbury, *De Gestis Pontificum Anglorum*, ii, 74 (ed. N. E. S. A. Hamilton, R.S., 1870, p. 147). M. *Creighton in *D.N.B.*, xviii (1889), p. 291 f.

FELIX (d. 818), Bp. of Urgel in Spain. With *Elipandus, Bp. of Toledo, he was one of the leaders of the *Adoptianist heresy. He was charged as a heretic at the Council of Ratisbon (792) in the presence of *Charlemagne, but, on being vanquished in debate, solemnly recanted and a little later publicly renounced his error before *Hadrian I at Rome. Shortly afterwards, however, he became convinced of his heresy again. He professed to be unconvinced by a criticism that *Alcuin wrote of his doctrines and, on his refusal to give way, he was formally accused at the Councils of *Frankfurt (794) and Aachen (798). At the latter Alcuin apparently persuaded him that his teaching was at variance with Christian tradition, notably as expressed in St. *Cyril of Alexandria and St. *Leo, and he recanted a second time. But his orthodoxy was not considered altogether irreproachable, and he remained until his death under the supervision of the Abp. of Lyons.

Confessio repr. in J. P. Migne, *PL*, xcvi, 881–8. The *Liber de Variis Quaestionibus adversus Judaeos seu ceteros Infideles vel plerosque Haereticos*, ed. A. C. Vega–A. E. Anspach (Escurial, 1940), who ascribed it to St. *Isidore of Seville, has been claimed as the work of Felix, by J. Madoz, S.J., 'Una obra de Félix de Urgel, falsamente adjudicada a San Isidoro de Sevilla' in *Estudios eclesiásticos*, xxiii (1949), pp. 147–68. Id. in *E.C.*, v (1951), col. 1137.

FELL, JOHN (1625–86), Bp. of *Oxford. He was educated at *Christ Church, Oxford, where he became a student at the early age of 11. His loyalty to the crown caused his ejection in 1648, but he contrived with a small group of friends to maintain the C of E service in a private house, and at the Restoration he was rewarded with a canonry at Christ Church, and, in Nov. 1660, with the deanery. He took the keenest interest in the spiritual and intellectual life of the college, and himself regularly went to service four times daily. In 1676 he became Bp. of Oxford, retaining the deanery. His own writings include Lives of H. *Hammond (1661) and R. *Allestree (1684) and a valuable critical edition (the so-called 'Oxford text') of the writings of St. *Cyprian (1682). He is the subject of the well-known epigram beginning 'I do not love thee, Dr. Fell' (a transl. by Thomas Brown, a Christ Church undergraduate, of Martial, *Epigrams*, 1. 32).

His father, SAMUEL FELL (1584–1649), was Dean of Christ Church from 1638 to 1647, when he was deprived by the parliamentary visitors.

H. L. Thompson, *Christ Church* ('University of Oxford, College Histories', 1900), pp. 82–104. List of reff. by J. E. B. Mayor in *Notes and Queries*, 5th series, vi (1876), p. 251. *A Specimen of the Several Sorts of Letter given to the University by Dr. John Fell, late Bishop of Oxford* (1693; facsimile repr. with introd., 1928). G. G. Perry in *D.N.B.*, xviii (1889), pp. 293–5.

FÉNELON, FRANÇOIS DE SALIGNAC DE LA MOTHE (1651–1715), Abp. of Cambrai. After studying at the seminary of *St.-Sulpice he was ordained priest in 1675 and made superior of the Catholiques Nouvelles, a house of recent converts from Protestantism, for whom he wrote his *Traité de l'éducation des filles* (1681, published 1687). From 1686 to 1688 he undertook a mission to the *Huguenots. A year later he was appointed tutor to Louis XIV's grandson, the Duke of Burgundy, for whom he wrote his famous educational novel, *Télémaque* (1693; publd. 1699, but not in its complete form till 1717). In the autumn of 1688 he became acquainted with Mme *Guyon whose *Quietist tendencies won his warm sympathy. He defended her for a long time, though in 1696 he signed the Thirty-four Articles of *Issy which condemned Quietism. In 1695 he had become Abp. of Cambrai. In 1697 he published his *Explication des maximes des saints*, forty-five articles setting forth true and false mysticism. Its issue was the beginning of his long and bitter controversy with J. B. *Bossuet which ended with the condemnation of his book by the Holy See (Brief of 12 Mar. 1699) and Fénelon's submission. Soon after this the *Jansenist controversy broke out again and Fénelon vigorously defended the

infallibility of the Church in several pastorals. In his diocese his charitable generosity did much to mitigate the sufferings caused by the Spanish-French Succession war, while his eloquent sermons contributed much to the religious education of his contemporaries. Many of his Letters of spiritual counsel were published after his death.

Œuvres complètes publ. in 10 vols., Paris, 1810, with 'Essai historique sur la personne et les écrits de Fénelon' from life by P. Querbeuf (vol. i); in 23 vols., Versailles and Paris, 1820–30, and 10 vols., Paris, 1848–52. X. Barbier de Montault (ed.), *Lettres inédites de Fénelon* [1863]; much of his correspondence with Mme Guyon, ed. M. Masson, *Fénelon et Mme Guyon*. Documents nouveaux et inédits (1907). A. M. Ramsay, *Histoire de la vie de F. de Salignac de la Mothe-Fénelon* (La Haye, 1723; ed. 2, Amsterdam, 1727; Eng. tr., 1723; modern Eng. tr., 1897). L. F. Bausset, *Histoire de Fénelon* (3 vols., 1808; Eng. tr., 1810). P. Janet, *Fénelon* (Les Grands Écrivains français; 1892; Eng. tr., 1914). A. Delplanque, *Fénelon et la doctrine de l'amour pur, d'après sa correspondance avec ses principaux amis* (1907; excerpts as *Fénelon et ses amis*, 1910). H. *Bremond, *Apologie pour Fénelon* (1910). M. Cagnac, *Fénelon*. Études critiques (1910); E. Griselle, *Fénelon*. Études historiques (1911). E. Jovy, *Fénelon inédit, d'après les documents de Pistoia* (1917), with texts. G. Joppin, *Fénelon et la mystique du pur amour* (1938). J. L. May, *Fénelon*. A Study (1938); E. Carcassonne, *Fénelon*. L'Homme et l'œuvre [1946]; K. D. Little, *Francis de Fénelon*. Study of a Personality (New York, 1951). P. Pourrat, P.S.S., *La Spiritualité chrétienne*, iv (ed. 2, 1928), pp. 253–305. *Revue Fénelon* (Paris, 1911 ff.).

FERDINAND V (1452–1516), 'the Catholic', King of Aragon. The son of John II of Aragon, he married in 1469 his cousin *Isabella, the heiress of Castile, and by thereby uniting the two Kingdoms when he succeeded his father in 1479, laid the foundations of modern Spain. While Isabella lived, however, she retained control of her own patrimony. Ferdinand exhibited all the marks of the Renaissance prince, among them unblushing perfidy and unwearied ambition for dominion and power. His treatment of Columbus after his initial support, and his relations with Louis XII of France, whom he boasted of having tricked twelve times, were characteristic. For his expulsion of the Moors from Granada in 1492 and his zeal for the *Inquisition he earned the title of 'the Catholic'.

W. H. Prescott, *History of the Reign of Ferdinand and Isabella* (3 vols., '1838' [1837], and many later edd.); R. B. Merriman, *The Rise of the Spanish Empire in the Old World and the New*, ii (New York, 1918); J. M. Doussinagne, *La política internacional de Fernando el Católico* (1944).

FERDINAND II (1578–1637), Holy Roman Emperor. Brought up by the *Jesuits at Ingolstadt University, Ferdinand was one of the chief upholders of the *Counter-Reformation. Before he became emperor in 1619, he had already re-established Catholicism in his own domains; and on succeeding to the other Hapsburg estates he set himself to exterminate Protestantism by a rigid application of the principle '*cuius regio, eius religio'. His success, both political and religious, induced the Protestant princes to rebel; but his generals, Wallenstein and Tilly, forced the Protestant leader, Christian of Denmark, to agree to the Treaty of Lübeck (1629). Emboldened by this success, Ferdinand published the 'Edict of Restitution', ordering Protestants to restore to the Catholics all appropriated ecclesiastical property within their dominions. Once again the Protestants rebelled, and for a time under Gustavus Adolphus they almost overthrew the Emperor. Gustavus's death in battle (1632) saved Ferdinand, and for the rest of his reign the *Thirty Years' War pursued its desultory and disastrous course.

F. C. Khevenhiller, *Annales Ferdinandei* (9 vols., Regensburg, 1640–6). F. Hurter, *Geschichte Kaiser Ferdinands II und seiner Eltern* (Schaffhausen, 11 vols., 1850–64); R. de Cesare, *La fine di un regno*. Napoli e Sicilia (2 vols., 1900). J. Loserth (ed.), 'Akten und Korrespondenzen zur Geschichte der Gegenreformation in Innerösterreich, unter Ferdinand II' in *Fontes Rerum Austriacarum. Österreichische Geschichts-Quellen*. Abt. 2, Diplomataria et Acta, lviii (1906) and lx (1907).

FERETORY (Lat. *feretrum*, from Gk. φέρειν, 'to bear'). Another name for a *Shrine (q.v.), in which a saint's relics were deposited and venerated.

FERIA. While in classical Latin the word means 'feast day' or 'holiday', in ecclesiastical language it is applied to such days (other than Saturdays and Sundays) on which no feast falls. The history of this change of meaning is involved and somewhat obscure. 'Greater Ferias' are certain privileged days in the year, when the service of the week-day takes precedence of feasts of low rank falling on the same day, e.g. the week-days in *Lent. Acc. to W. use, on ferias which have no office of their own either the Mass of the previous Sunday is repeated or *Votive Masses may be substituted. The BCP provides that 'the Collect, Epistle and Gospel appointed for the Sunday shall serve all the week after, where it is not in this book otherwise ordered'.

'Feria' is applied to week-days already in *Tertullian (*De jejunio*, 2). For some suggestions as to how the word changed its meaning, see art. by R. Sinker in *D.C.A.*, i (1875), p. 667 f., s.v.

FERMENTUM (Lat. 'leaven'). In *Rome (5th cent.), the fragments of the Bread of the Eucharist sent on Sundays from the Papal Mass to the presbyters in the parish churches (*tituli*) to typify the unity of the faithful in Christ. The practice is attested by Pope *Innocent (*Ep. xxv ad Decentium*, 5). In a modified form it survived on *Maundy Thursday down to the 8th cent.

There is a useful note in *L.P.* (Duchesne), i (1886), p. 169, note 4. Jungmann, ii (ed. 1949), pp. 379–81. F. *Cabrol, O.S.B., in *D.A.C.L.*, v (1922), cols. 1371–4, with patristic reff. J. A. Jungmann, S.J., '*Fermentum*. Ein Symbol kirchlicher Einheit und sein Nachleben im Mittelalter' in *Colligere Fragmenta* (Festschrift A. Dold, Beuron, 1952.)

FERRANDUS (Fulgentius Ferrandus), deacon of the Church of Carthage from 520 to 547. His 'Breviatio canonum' is an important epitome, systematically arranged, of canons of the early councils, Greek and African. There survive also his Life of St. *Fulgentius, and some letters.

Works ed. P. F. Chifflet, Dijon, 1649; repr. in J. P. Migne, *PL*, lxvii, 877–962, and ('Vita Fulgentii') ib., lxv, 117–50. Bardenhewer, v, pp. 316–19; Altaner (ed. 1951), p. 442, both with bibl. See also bibl. to *Fulgentius*.

FERRAR, NICHOLAS (1592–1637), founder of *Little Gidding. A native of London, in 1605 he entered Clare Hall, Cambridge, where he was one of the most brilliant of his generation, and in 1610 was elected a Fellow. In 1613 he had to leave Cambridge on account of his health and during the next five years travelled on the Continent, chiefly in Germany, Italy, and Spain. Having returned to England in 1618 he was employed by the Virginia Company, of which he became Deputy-Treasurer in 1622. Shortly before the dissolution of the Company, in 1624, he was returned to Parliament, but the sombre political prospect as well as his religious aspirations determined him to give up the brilliant career which was opening before him. In 1625 he settled at Little Gidding in Huntingdonshire, an estate bought by his mother in the preceding year. There he was joined by his brother and brother-in-law with their families in order to establish a kind of community life in accordance with the principles of the C of E. In 1626 he was ordained deacon by W. *Laud, and under his direction this household of some 30 persons lived a life of prayer and work under a strict rule. At the beginning of every hour, from 6 A.M. to 8 P.M., there was an office of a quarter of an hour, in which several groups of the community took their turn. It consisted of a hymn and portions from the Psalms and the Gospels, the whole of the Psalter being thus recited every day and the Gospels once a month. In addition to this two or more members watched every night from 9 P.M. to 1 A.M. while reciting once more the whole of the Psalter. Ferrar himself kept this watch two, later even three, times a week, on the other nights allowing himself only four hours' sleep. His great austerity in other directions was exemplified in a very sparing diet and an almost complete absence of recreation. His piety and ideals, essentially Biblical and founded on the BCP, were warmly approved by the Bp. of Lincoln, J. *Williams. In 1633 *Charles I visited Little Gidding and was greatly impressed by their life. The community incurred, however, the hostility of the Puritans, and after Ferrar's death was denounced in a pamphlet entitled *The Arminian Nunnery* (1646) as an attempt to introduce RC practices in the country. Most of Ferrar's manuscripts were destroyed in a Puritan raid in 1646, which also brought the community to an end. His only publications are translations of J. *Valdez' *Divine Considerations* and L. *Lessius' treatise *On Temperance*.

Ferrar's community, which was dispersed in 1646, had been an active centre of charitable works for the whole neighbourhood. Its members visited and relieved the poor and the sick and taught the children the Psalms. They were skilled in the art of bookbinding, and the famous 'Harmonies', now in the British Museum, were arranged, illustrated, and bound by them under Ferrar's direction. The community also had a study circle called the Little Academy, which met frequently to tell and discuss stories illustrating events in the Church's Year and Christian virtues.

Interest in Ferrar and his community was reawakened by the publication of J. H. *Shorthouse's famous novel, *John Inglesant* (1881), with its vivid and, except for the romance of Mary Collett, historically accurate picture of life at Little Gidding.

The two contemporary Lives, one by his brother John Ferrar, the other by Dr. Jebb, both ed. J. E. B. Mayor, 1855; crit. ed. of former in B. Blackstone, *The Ferrar Papers* (1938), pp. 9–94, with introd., pp. xvii–xxi, and 'A Selection of Family Letters', pp. 223–312. P. Peckard, *Memoirs of the Life of Mr. Nicholas Ferrar* (1790); T. T. *Carter (ed.), *Nicholas Ferrar*. His Household and his Friends (1892); H. P. K. Skipton, *The Life and Times of Nicholas Ferrar* (1907); A. L. Maycock, *Nicholas Ferrar of Little Gidding* (1938). M. *Creighton in *D.N.B.*, xviii (1889), pp. 377–80. See also bibl. to *Little Gidding*.

FERRAR MSS. A group of NT *minuscule MSS. (Nos. 13, 69, 124, 346, 543, 788. 826, 828, 980), the common origin of which was established in 1868 by W. H. Ferrar, Trinity College, Dublin. They are also known as 'Family 13'. With the exception of 69, they were all written between the 11th and 13th cents. in Calabria; 69 is later. They are one of the principal witnesses to the *Caesarean text of the NT. A peculiarity of them is the transference of the '*pericope adulterae' (Jn. 7.53–8.11) to follow Lk. 21. 38.

K. *Lake–S. Lake, *Family 13*. The Ferrar Group (Studies and Documents, No. xi, 1941).

FERRARA-FLORENCE, Council of. See *Florence, Council of*.

FESTIVALS, Ecclesiastical. See *Feasts, Ecclesiastical*.

FÊTE-DIEU ('Feast of God'). The French title for the Feast of *Corpus Christi.

FETTER DIENSTAG (Ger.), 'Fat-Tuesday'. An old German name for *Shrove-Tuesday, now *Fastendienstag* or *Fastenabend*, from the practice of consuming on that day the eggs and fat prohibited during Lent. (Fr. *mardi gras*.)

FETTER DONNERSTAG. (Ger.), 'Fat-Thursday'. The Thursday preceding *Ash Wednesday, traditionally observed, like the following Monday and (Shrove-) Tuesday, as a day of feasting. (Fr. *jeudi gras*.)

FEUARDENT, FRANÇOIS (1539–1610), French *patristic scholar and controversialist. A native of Coutances, he studied at Bayeux and *Paris, and after becoming a *Franciscan was ordained priest in 1561. For some years he devoted himself wholeheartedly to the cause of the Catholic League, preaching extensively in Paris and the Low Countries. The chief of his numerous writings against Calvinism is his *Theomachia Calvinistica* (1604), in which he claimed to refute 1,400 errors of his Calvinist

adversaries. His patristic writings, the most valuable part of his work, include editions of St. *Ildefonsus of Toledo (1576), St. *Irenaeus (1576; reissued, Cologne, 1596), Michael *Psellus (1597), St. *Ephraem Syrus (1579), *Arnobius (1596), and *Lactantius (never published). He also commented on several Biblical Books and produced a new edition of the *Postils of *Nicholas of Lyra.

Édouard, O.F.M.Cap., in *D.T.C.*, v (1913), cols. 2262–5.

FEUERBACH, LUDWIG ANDREAS (1804–72), German philosopher. He began as a student of theology at Heidelberg. In 1824 he went to Berlin, where he came under the personal influence of G. W. F. *Hegel and decided to exchange theology for philosophy. In 1828 he began teaching at Erlangen, but for the greater part of his life held no public office. He sought to recast Hegel's teaching in a positivistic sense openly hostile to Christianity. Rejecting all belief in transcendence, he held that theology and philosophy were properly concerned only with the nature of man, who was the true *ens realissimum*. Christianity was but an illusion, in Hegelian language the 'dominance of subjectivity' (*die Allmacht der Subjektivität*). Of his many writings the most celebrated was his *Wesen des Christentums* (1841; Engl. trans. by George Eliot as *The Essence of Christianity*, 1854). He exercised a far wider influence than the intrinsic merits of his writings deserved, notably on F. *Nietzsche and R. Wagner, and esp. on K. Marx and the whole Communist school in Germany.

Feuerbach's other writings include *Grundsätze der Philosophie der Zukunft* (Zürich, 1843), *Das Wesen der Religion* (1845), *Theogonie* (1857), *Gottheit, Freiheit und Unsterblichkeit* (1866; vol. x of Sämmtl. Werke). Collected Works in 10 vols., Leipzig, 1846–66; new ed. by W. Bolin and F. Jodl, 10 vols., Stuttgart, 1903–11. Selected Letters, ed. W. Bolin (2 vols., Leipzig, 1904). F. Engels, *Ludwig Feuerbach und der Ausgang der klassischen deutschen Philosophie* (1888; Eng. trr., Chicago, 1903, and London [1934]). W. B. Chamberlain, *Heaven wasn't his Destination*. The Philosophy of Ludwig Feuerbach (1941), with bibl. K. Grün, *Ludwig Feuerbach* (2 vols., 1874). Überweg, iv, pp. 223–6, 697. J. Engert in *L.Th.K.*, iii (1931), col. 1025 f.

FEUILLANTS. The reformed *Cistercians of Les-Feuillans (formerly Fulium) in the neighbourhood of Toulouse, founded in 1577 by Abbot J. de la Barrière (1544–1600). After expelling from his house, which had grown lax and corrupt, those who would not accept his reform, the Abbot established a new rule stricter than the original. *Gregory XIII approved his action in 1581 and in 1589 *Sixtus V established the independence of the order. In 1588 a similar order for women, the 'Feuillantines', was begun. The Feuillants spread to Italy, where they were called 'Bernardines', and both the French and Italian branches produced some distinguished men, among them Cardinal J. Bona (d. 1674). In the 17th cent. the rigours of the original rule were somewhat relaxed. The order came to an end during the Napoleonic wars. Some *martyrologies describe de la Barrière as 'Venerable', and keep his feast on 25 Apr.

C. J. Morotius, O. Cist., *Cistercii Reflorescentis seu Cong. cistercio-monasticarum B. Mariae Fuliensis in Gallia et reformatorum in Italia Chronologica Historica* (Turin, 1690). [P. Helyot,] *Histoire des ordres monastiques, religieux et militaires, et des congrégations séculières*, v (1718), pp. 401–20; Heimbucher, i, pp. 374–6. Life of Jean de la Barrière by A. Bazy (Toulouse, 1885). E. M. Obrecht, O.C.R., in *C.E.*, vi (1909), p. 64 f., s.v.; J. Besse, O.S.B., in *D.T.C.*, v (1913), cols. 2265–8, s.v.

FICHTE, JOHANN GOTTLIEB (1762–1814), German Idealist philosopher. He was educated at Schulpforta and at the universities of Jena and Leipzig, where he studied Protestant theology. In 1790 he became acquainted with I. *Kant's philosophical system. His 'attempt at a critique of all revelation' (*Versuch einer Kritik aller Offenbarung*, 1792) showed his great powers, and he was appointed professor of philosophy at Jena in 1794, but dismissed in 1799 for atheism. In 1807–8 he delivered his famous *Reden an die deutsche Nation* which had great influence on the development of German nationalism and the overthrow of Napoleon. From 1809 till his death he was professor at the newly founded university of Berlin.

Fichte claimed that his philosophical doctrines were implicit in those of I. Kant, which he sought to develop on the lines of 'spontaneity' and 'autonomy'. Acc. to him the objects of our knowledge are the products of the consciousness of the ego as regards both their matter and form. This ego, however, is not the individual 'I', but the Absolute Ego, which can be known only by philosophical intuition. It develops in three phases. In the first it posits itself, in the second it posits a non-ego against itself, and in the last it posits itself as limited by the non-ego. Acc. to Fichte God is the absolute Ego, 'the living operative moral order'; but He is not to be conceived as personal. True religion consists in 'joyously doing right'. When society will have reached a condition in which morality is the norm, the existence of the Church will be unnecessary.

Fichte expounded his doctrines, which have been summed up as 'ethical pantheism', in a long series of works. Among the more important were *Grundlage der gesamten Wissenschaftslehre* (1794–5), *Grundlage des Naturrechts* (1796), *Erste* and *Zweite Einleitung in die Wissenschaftslehre* (both 1897), *System der Sittenlehre* (1798), *Der geschlossene Handelsstaat* (1800), *Die Bestimmung des Menschen* (1800), *Grundzüge des gegenwärtigen Zeitalters* (1806), and *Anweisung zum seligen Leben* (1805), the last his chief contribution to the philosophy of religion.

Sämtliche Werke (ed. I. H. Fichte, son), 8 vols., Berlin, 1845–6. *Nachgelassene Werke*, ed. id., 3 vols., Bonn, 1834–5. *Nachgelassene Schriften*, Berlin, 1937 ff. Crit. ed. of his Correspondence by H. Schulz (2 vols., Leipzig, 1925–30). Eng. tr. of 'Popular Works', 2 vols., London, 1848–9. Lives by I. H. Fichte (2 Thle., Sulzbach, 1830–31), K. Fischer (*Geschichte der neueren Philosophie*, v, Heidelberg, 1869; ed. 4, vol. vi, ib., 1914), R. Adamson (Knight's Philosophical Classics, 1881), F. Medicus (Leipzig, 1914). C. C. Everett, *Fichte's Science of Knowledge*. A Critical Exposition (Chicago, 1884). X. Léon, *La Philosophie de Fichte*

(1902); id., *Fichte et son temps* (3 vols., 1922–7). E. Lask, *Fichtes Idealismus und die Geschichte* (1902). G. H. Turnbull, *The Educational Theory of J. G. Fichte* (Liverpool, 1926; with translations). M. Wundt, *Fichte-Forschungen* (1929). Überweg, iv, pp. 11–35, 670–2. R. Adamson in *E.B.* (ed. 11), x (1910), pp. 313–16, s.v.

FICINO, MARSILIO (1433–99), Italian humanist and philosopher. Born at Figline near Florence, he was orig. intended by his father to be a physician. His early promise commended him to Cosimo de' Medici (1389–1464) who, under the influence of *Gemistus Plethon, who had come to Florence for the Council (1439), had conceived the idea of founding a Platonic Academy; and before Ficino was twenty, Cosimo had received him into his household and appointed him its head. In 1459 Ficino became the pupil of John Argyropoulos, then lecturing on Greek literature and language at Florence, and before long had made himself a competent Greek scholar. He undertook a complete fresh translation of Plato, a task which, by leading him to consult many of the chief scholars of the day, did much to promote the study of Plato and philosophy generally. By the death of Cosimo (1464) ten of the Dialogues were finished and the whole in 1477. The translation was printed at Florence in 1483–4.

Meanwhile, Ficino's original mind, with its love of nature and its bent towards mysticism, gained him a wide influence. In 1473, after some hesitations, he sought ordination to the priesthood and became exemplary in his new duties. He continued to defend his 'Platonic philosophy', which meant for him not only the teachings of the *Neo-Platonists, but all the nobler elements in Greek thought. This synthesis of Christianity and Greek mysticism he expounded in *De Religione Christiana* (1477; dedicated to Lorenzo de' Medici, d. 1492), in immediate intention directed esp. against the critics of Christianity among the contemporary *Averroists. In 1484 he was appointed a Canon of Florence, where his expositions of the Gospels and Epistles formed the basis of his 'Commentaries'. His principal philosophical work, *Theologica Platonica de Immortalitate Animae* (written in 1474), largely based on Plato's *Phaedo*, appeared in 1487. In his later years he translated into Latin *Plotinus, *Porphyry, and *Dionysius the Areopagite. Shortly before his death he was charged with magic, on the grounds of his belief in planetary influences, but he succeeded in purging himself.

Though he lacked critical judgement and had little sense of history, his erudition, wide sympathies, and enthusiasm gave him a far-reaching influence. He was sought out by scholars from all over Europe, among them J. *Colet and J. *Reuchlin, and kept up a large correspondence. His Florentine 'Academy' did not survive him, but his version of Plato remained the standard Lat. text for the next hundred years.

Letters publd. Venice, 1495. Collected Works publd. in 2 vols., Basle, 1561, 1576, and Paris, 1641. *Supplementum Ficinianum*. Marsilii Ficini Florentini Philosophi Platonici

Opuscula Inedita et Dispersa, ed. P. O. Kristeller (2 vols., Florence, 1937). Modern ed. of his Commentary on Plato's Symposium, with Eng. tr., by S. R. Joyce (Univ. of Missouri Studies, xix, No. 1; Columbia, 1944). L. Galeotti, 'Saggio intorno alla vita ed agli scritti di Marsilio Ficino' in *Archivio storico italiano*, N.S., ix (pt. 2; 1859), pp. 25–91, and x (pt. 1; 1859), pp. 3–55. W. Dress, *Die Mystik des Marsilio Ficino* (Arbeiten zur Kirchengeschichte, xiv; 1929). [A. M.] J. Festugière, *La Philosophie de l'amour de Marsile Ficin et son influence sur la littérature française au XVI*e *siècle* (Études de Philosophie Médiévale, xxxi, 3; 1941). P. O. Kristeller, *The Philosophy of Marsilio Ficino* (New York, 1943), with bibl., pp. 413–17. Überweg, iii, pp. 16 and 18–20, with bibl., p. 629. F. Vernet in *D.T.C.*, v (1913), cols. 2277–2291, s.v. 'Ficin, Marsile'; B. Nardi in *E.C.*, v (1950), cols. 1239–43, s.v.

FIDEI DEFENSOR. See *Defender of the Faith*.

FIDEISM. A term applied to a variety of doctrines which hold in common belief in the incapacity of the intellect to attain to knowledge of divine matters and correspondingly put an excessive emphasis on faith. The word was apparently coined (for their own doctrines) by the Paris Protestant theologians, A. *Sabatier and E. Ménégoz (1838–1921), whose irrationalism derived from I. *Kant and F. D. E. *Schleiermacher. Later it came to be used much more widely and for the most part in a hostile sense. Scholastic theologians regularly charged the *Modernists with 'Fideism' in their theories of knowledge.

FIDELIUM, Missa. See *Faithful, Mass of the*.

FIDES DAMASI (or Tome of St. Damasus). The Confession of Faith ('Post Concilium Nicaenum') drawn up by Pope *Damasus at a Roman synod, probably early in 380. It consists of a Creed (a Latin rendering of *Nicaea, 325) to which are appended 24 anathemas against various heretics and schismatics, among them the *Sabellians, the *Eunomians, the *Macedonians, *Melitius of *Antioch, and the *Apollinarians. It is an important witness to the orthodoxy of the Roman Church at this date. Shortly after its compilation, it was included by Damasus in his Epistle 'Per filium' to *Paulinus, Bp. of Antioch.

The text was printed by P. *Quesnel (ii, c. 55) and the *Ballerini (iii, 400–5) in their editions of St. *Leo. It is also printed in A. Hahn, *Bibliothek der Symbole und Glaubensregeln der alten Kirche* (ed. 3, 1897), § 199, pp. 271–5. There is a Greek version in *Theodoret, *HE*, v, xi. The Latin and Greek texts are critically edited by C. H. *Turner, *Ecclesiae Occidentalis Monumenta Iuris Antiquissima*, 1, ii. (1), 1913, pp. 281–96. P. Galtier, 'Le "Tome de Damase": Date et Origine', in *Recherches de Science religieuse*, xxvi (1936), pp. 385–418, 563–78.

FIDES HIERONYMI. An early form of the *Apostles' Creed, prob. late 4th cent. and perhaps the work of St. *Jerome. Attention was drawn to its existence in several MSS. (St. Mihiel 28; Oxford, Bod. 147; Cambridge, Trinity College, O. 5. 5; London, B.Mus.Royal 6. B. XIII) by Dom G. *Morin. It is one of the earliest Latin Creeds with the words 'de-

scended into hell' ('descendit ad inferna') and 'the *communion of saints' ('sanctorum communionem').

G. Morin, 'Un Symbole inédit attribué à saint Jérôme' in *R. Bén.*, xxi (1904), pp. 1–9.

FIELD, FREDERICK (1801 - 85), Biblical and patristic scholar. Educated at Christ's Hospital and Trinity College, Cambridge, he was elected a Fellow of his college in 1824, and from 1842 to 1863 was rector of Reepham in Norfolk. In the latter year he resigned his living and moved to *Norwich in order to devote his entire time to scholarship. In 1870 he became a member of the OT Revision Company. Field was one of the most learned and accurate patristic scholars of the 19th cent. His editions of St. *Chrysostom's 'Homilies on St. Matthew' (3 vols., 1839) and 'on St. Paul's Epistles' (1849–62) marked the first attempt at establishing a critical text since the time of H. *Savile and B. *Montfaucon. His splendid edition of *Origen's *Hexapla (2 vols., 1875) embodied the results of many years' research. He was also a keen student of the Greek text of the OT and NT, which he sought to understand in the light of a wide knowledge of classical literature; and many of his results in this field were contained in his *Otium Norvicense* (3 parts, 1864–81; part 3 republished posthumously, with additions by the author, 1897).

W. A. Greenhill in *D.N.B.*, xviii (1889), pp. 402–4, s.v.

FIELD, RICHARD (1561–1616), Dean of *Gloucester. He was educated at Magdalen College, Oxford, and became Divinity Reader at *Winchester Cathedral in 1592, Rector of Burghclere c. 1595, chaplain in ordinary to Queen *Elizabeth in 1598, and Prebendary of Windsor in 1604. In 1603 he took part in the *Hampton Court Conference and in 1609 he was appointed Dean of Gloucester (where, however, he rarely resided). His principal work, his treatise *Of the Church* (Bks. I–IV, 1606; Bk. V, 1610), was primarily conceived as an apology for the C of E against Rome, though controversy was subordinated to the exposition of principles. The notes of the true Church were (1) Antiquity, (2) Succession, (3) Unity, (4) Universality, and (5) the name 'Catholic'; and Field argued that the counterpart of the modern RC Church was to be found in early times in the *Donatists with their claims to exclusiveness and purity. Field held that the Protestant bodies on the Continent were also part of the Church of Christ. The intimate friend of R. *Hooker, H. *Savile, and other noted scholars, Field was one of the most learned and acute theologians of his age.

There is a modern repr. of his treatise *Of the Church*, publd. by the Eccl. Hist. Soc., 4 vols., 1847–52. *Some Short Memorials concerning the Life of . . . Richard Field . . . by his son Nathaniel Field . . . published by John Le Neve* (1717). R. Hooper in *D.N.B.*, xviii (1889), pp. 410–12.

FIFTH MONARCHY MEN. A fanatical sect of the middle of the 17th cent. whose members aimed at bringing in the 'Fifth Monarchy' (Dan. 2. 44) which should succeed the four empires of Assyria, Persia, Greece, and Rome. During it, Christ was to reign with His saints for a thousand years (Rev. 20. 4). For a time they supported O. *Cromwell, in the belief that the Commonwealth was a preparation for the Fifth Monarchy, but when they found their theocratic hopes unlikely to be realized they turned against him. After an unsuccessful rising in Jan. 1661, its leaders were beheaded and the sect died out.

L. F. Brown, *The Political Activities of the Baptists and Fifth Monarchy Men in England During the Interregnum* (American Historical Association. Herbert Baxter Adams Prize in European History for 1911; Washington and London, 1912); E. Rogers, *Some Account of the Life and Opinions of a Fifth-Monarchy-Man.* Chiefly extracted from the Writings of John Rogers, Preacher (1867); C. H. Firth, *The Life of Thomas Harrison* (from Proceedings of the American Antiquarian Society, at the Semi-Annual Meeting, April 26, 1893; Worcester, Mass., 1893).

FIGGIS, JOHN NEVILLE (1866–1919), Anglican historian and theologian. The son of a Brighton minister of 'Lady *Huntingdon's Connexion', he was educated at St. Catharine's College, Cambridge, where he studied mathematics and, later, history, and came under the influence of F. W. *Maitland and M. *Creighton. After being received into the C of E he went to *Wells Theological College in 1894, and was ordained in the same year to a curacy at Kettering. In 1896 he published *The Divine Right of Kings*, an original attempt to exhibit the permanent religious significance of the doctrine from a study of its development. From 1896 to 1902 he was lecturer at St. Catharine's and chaplain to Pembroke College, and from 1902 to 1907, rector of Marnhull in Dorset. In the meantime he had become an ardent disciple and correspondent of Lord *Acton, some of whose writings he later edited. In 1907 appeared *From *Gerson to *Grotius*, a useful contribution to the history of political thought. In the same year he entered the *Community of the Resurrection at Mirfield. In 1908–9 he delivered the *Hulsean Lectures on *The Gospel and Human Needs* (1909). In 1914 appeared *The Fellowship of the Mystery* (Paddock Lectures, 1913), a defence of Christianity against modern unbelief with much pungent criticism of contemporary religion. His other writings include *Civilisation at the Cross Roads* (1912), *Churches in the Modern State* (1913), *Some Defects in English Religion* (1917), *The Political Aspects of St. Augustine's 'City of God'* (1921; posthumous), and contributions to the *Cambridge Modern History*. Figgis's brilliance and depth of thought, clothed in an easy style, made him an unusually effective apologist. In his conception of the Christian State, the subject which above others specially attracted him, he was a resolute opponent of the idea of absolute sovereignty and was among the first Christian thinkers alive to the dangers to religion and human freedom of the modern omnicompetent state.

M. G. Tucker, *John Neville Figgis. A Study* (1950).

FILARET. See *Philaret*.

FILASTER. See *Philaster*.

FILIOQUE (Lat. 'And the Son'). The dogmatic formula expressing the *Double Procession of the Holy Ghost (q.v.), added by the W. Church to the Nicene-Constantinopolitan *Creed immediately after the words 'the Holy Ghost Who proceedeth from the Father'. It is no part of the original Creed, but is first met with as an interpolation (acc. to the usual texts) at the Third Council of *Toledo (589). In 796 its use was defended by *Paulinus of Aquileia at the Synod of Friuli and from *c.* 800, when the Creed began to be generally chanted at the Mass throughout the Frankish Empire, the words became widely familiar. Its introduction by Frankish monks in 847 into their monastery at *Jerusalem on the Mount of *Olives aroused strong but easily understandable opposition from the Eastern monks of St. *Sabas, and when the matter was referred to *Leo III he tried to suppress the addition to the formula while approving the doctrine. He caused the Creed in its original form to be engraven on two silver tables deposited at the tomb of St. *Peter. The 'Filioque', however, continued to be sung, and, soon after 1000, had been adopted also at *Rome. Since the time of *Photius, who violently denounced it, the 'Filioque' has been made the chief ground of attack by the Orthodox Church on the Church of Rome. At the Reunion Councils of *Lyons (1274) and *Florence (1439), the acceptance of the doctrine, though not of the addition to the Creed, was imposed on the Greeks as a condition of the short-lived union. English theologians, following the *Thirty-Nine Articles, have generally accepted the W. tradition, e.g. R. *Hooker, J. *Pearson, and E. H. *Browne, and it was vigorously upheld by E. B. *Pusey in *On the Clause 'And the Son'* (1876). Discussions on the formula took place between Anglicans, *Old Catholics, and the E. Church at *Bonn in 1874 and 1875, and again at St. Petersburg in 1912 in the conversations between F. W. Puller, S.S.J.E., and Russian Orthodox theologians, but in both cases without positive results. See also *Double Procession*.

The history of the phrase is discussed in all works on the Creed, its doctrinal significance in treatises on the Holy Ghost. J. N. D. Kelly, *Early Christian Creeds* (1950), pp. 358–67. P. de Meester, O.S.B., 'Études sur la théologie orthodoxe', iv, 'Le *Filioque*' in R. *Bén.*, xxiv (1907), pp. 86–103. A. E. Burn, 'Some Spanish MSS. of the Constantinopolitan Creed' in *J.T.S.*, ix (1908), pp. 301–3. M. Jugie, A.A., 'Origine de la controverse sur l'addition du *Filioque* au symbole' in *Revue des Sciences Philosophiques et Théologiques*, xxviii (1939), pp. 369–85. A. J. Maas, S.J., in *C.E.*, vi (1909), p. 73 f., s.v.; A. Palmieri in *D.T.C.*, v (1913), cols. 2309–43, s.v., with full bibl.; E. Candal, S.J., in *E.C.*, v (1950), col. 1298 f. See also bibl. to *Double Procession*.

FINAN, St. (d. 661). The successor of St. *Aidan as Bp. of *Lindisfarne. He was an Irishman by birth, and in his earlier life a monk of *Iona. He vigorously and consistently upheld the Celtic ecclesiastical traditions against the successors of St. *Augustine of Canterbury, who, coming from the South, strove to bring English customs into closer conformity with those of Rome. He was a keen missionary and baptized Peada, Prince of the Middle English, and Sigebert, King of the East Angles. Feast day, 9 or 17 Feb.

The principal authority is *Bede, H.E., iii 17, 21 f., and 25-7; notes ad loc., ed. C. Plummer, ii (1896), pp. 176-8 and 188 f.

FINDING OF THE CROSS. See *Invention of the Cross*.

FINLAND, Christianity in. The origins of Christianity in Finland are obscure. The monastery of Valamo claims to have been founded as early as 992. It seems clear, at any rate, that Finland had received Christianity by the 12th cent. from *Sweden and *Russia, and that in 1220 an independent Church organization was established under Thomas, Bp. of Räntemäkia (an Englishman). In the 15th cent. the Church of Finland had sufficient eminence for its divines to hold prominent positions in the world of learning, the best known being Olaus Magni, Bp. of Åbo from 1450 to 1460, who was twice rector of the *Sorbonne.

*Lutheranism was introduced into Finland in 1523 by Peter Särkilax (d. 1530); and Michael Agricola (1512-57) was later prominent in the Reform Movement. The latter gained a ready hearing through his issue of popular Finnish religious writings, while his translation of the NT (1548) virtually created the Finnish written language. Severe measures were taken for the extermination of RCism. In Karelia (E. Finland), however, the population remained Orthodox, though it suffered persecution when the land fell to Sweden in 1617. In 1809 Finland came under Russian rule, and the Greek Orthodox Church of Finland rapidly increased in numbers and influence. By the Acts of 1869 and 1889 RCism was tolerated for the first time since 1523, but the RCs form an inconsiderable minority. The National Church of Finland is the Lutheran body, in which episcopal succession was maintained until 1884, when it was lost through all its three sees becoming vacant simultaneously and their successors being consecrated by the (non-episcopal) Dean of Åbo. Since then it has gradually been recovered with the help of the Church of Sweden. The independence gained by Finland in 1917-18 did not materially alter the religious position in the inter-war period. In 1934 a measure of intercommunion between the Church of Finland and the C of E was established.

F. Siegmund-Schultze, *Ekklesia*, II, 4 (Lieferung 8, Die Kirche in Finland; 1938), with bibl.; A. Lehtonen, 'The Church of Finland' in *C.Q.R.*, cv (1928), pp. 314-47, with bibl. G. Sentzte, *Die Kirche Finlands* (Göttingen, 1935). F. Collan, *De Reformationis initiis Dissertatio Academica* (Helsingfors [1843]). A. Malin, *Der Heiligenkalendar Finnlands. Seine Zusammensetzung und Entwicklung* (Suomen Kirkkohistoriallisen Seuran, xx; Helsingfors, 1925). U. Holmberg-Harva in *R.G.G.* (ed. 2), v (1928), col. 600 f., s.v. 'Finnische Religion'; Pfarrer Israel, ib., cols. 601-5, s.v. 'Finnland'. *The Church of England and the Church of Finland*. A Summary of the Proceedings at the Conferences held at Lambeth Palace, London, on October 5 and 6, 1933, and at Brändö, Helsingfors, on July 17 and 18, 1934 (1935). G. K. A. Bell (ed.), *Documents on Christian Unity*, Third Series, 1930-48 (1948), Nos. 188-92, pp. 146-53.

FINNIAN, St. (c. 495-579). The chief patron of Ulster. A pupil of St. *Colman, he made a pilgrimage to Rome and, having brought back thence a copy of the *Vulgate NT and Pentateuch, established a famous monastery at Moville. Many legends were later attached to his name. Feast day, 10 Sept. (He is not to be confounded with St. Finnian of Clonard, d. 549 or 522; feast day, 12 Dec.)

Life by John of Tynemouth, written between 1325 and 1350, based on sources now lost, pr. in J. Capgrave, *Nova Legenda Angliae* (London, 1516), pp. cxlvii (reverse)-cxlix (ed. C. Horstman, Oxford, 1901, i, pp. 444-7). J. F. Kenney, *The Sources for the Early History of Ireland*, i (New York, 1929), p. 390 f. (On St. Finnian of Clonard, cf. Kenney, ib., pp. 374-6; also T. Olden in *D.N.B.*, xix (1889), pp. 39-41; I. Cecchetti in *E.C.*, v (1950), col. 1395, s.v.)

FIORETTI, The. See *Little Flowers of St. Francis, The*.

FIRMAMENT (lit. 'something made solid'). In the OT (Gen. 1. 6, Ezek. 1. 26, &c.), the word commonly refers to the dome or canopy of heaven, which was supposed by the Hebrews to be a solid vault dividing the upper or celestial from the lower or terrestrial waters. It was conceived that the upper waters came down as rain through opened sluices, and that above these waters Jehovah sat enthroned (cf. Ps. 29. 9, BCP version). In the *Song of the Three Children, 33, it denotes heaven itself.

FIRMICUS MATERNUS, JULIUS (d. after 360), rhetorician. Little is known of him beyond the facts that he was prob. of Sicilian origin and converted to Christianity in adult life. While still a pagan, he wrote his *Mathesis* in eight books, a compendium of astrology interwoven with moral reflections. His most important work, the *De errore profanarum religionum* (written at Rome c. 347), is an appeal to the emperors Constantius and Constans to destroy the pagan idols by force. A treatise in three books, *Consultationes Zacchaei et Apollonii*, has been ascribed to him, perhaps mistakenly, by Dom G. *Morin.

The *Consultationes* and *De Errore*, pr. in J. P. Migne, *PL*, xx, 1071-1166, and xii, 971-1050. Critical edd. of *Mathesis* by W. Kroll, F. Skutsch and K. Ziegler (2 vols., Teubner, 1898-1913), *De Errore* by K. Ziegler (Teubner, 1907) and G. Heuten with commentary (Travaux de la Faculté de Philosophie et Lettres de l'Université de Bruxelles, viii, 1938) and of the Consultationes by G. *Morin, O.S.B. (Florilegium Patristicum, xxxix, 1935). Studies and articles by G. Morin, O.S.B. (*Hist. J.*, xxxvii, 1916, pp. 229-66), T. Wickström (Upsala, 1935), B. Axelson (Lund, 1937), and A. C. Lawson (*R. Bén.*, lvii, 1947, pp. 187-95). Bardenhewer, iii, pp. 456-60; Altaner (ed. 1950), p. 314 f.

FIRMILIAN, St. (d. 268), Bp. of Caesarea in Cappadocia from c. 230. A great admirer of *Origen, Firmilian once summoned him to the Cappadocian Caesarea for instruction and later went himself to Origen's *Caesarea (in

Palestine) to sit at his feet. He supported St. *Cyprian against Pope Stephen I in his doctrine that baptism could be validly performed only within the confines of the Church, and that heretics on joining the Church must therefore be 'rebaptized'. His only extant writing is a letter on the subject addressed to Cyprian (Cyp. *Ep.* 75 [ed. Hartel]). In 264 he was president of the first of the synods of Antioch held to consider the case of *Paul of Samosata, and died on his way to the second. Feast day in the E., 28 Oct.

Our chief source of information about Firmilian is *Eusebius, *H.E.*, VI, xxvii; xlvi, 3; VII, v, 1; xiv; xxviii, 1; xxx, 4 f. *Opera Cypriani*, ed. W. Hartel (C.S.E.L., iii (2), 1871), pp. 810–27 (the Lat. tr. is apparently the work of Cyprian himself; there are no sufficient grounds for holding it to be interpolated). B. Bossue, S.J., 'De Firmiliano . . . Commentarius Historicus' in *AA.SS.*, Oct. XII (1867), pp. 470–510. Bardenhewer, ii, pp. 312–14.

FIRST FRIDAYS. The special observance of the first Friday in each month in the RC Church is based on the promise which Christ is supposed to have made to St. *Margaret Mary Alacoque (1647–90) that unusual graces and favours would be given to all who received Holy Communion on the first Friday of nine consecutive months. Those who fulfilled this obligation could rest in the assurance that they would have the grace of full repentance, that they would not die in sin or without the sacraments, and that the *Sacred Heart would be their refuge at the hour of death.

J. O'Connell, *The Nine First Fridays*. The 'Great Promise' of the Sacred Heart of Jesus to Saint Margaret Mary. Its Origin, Authenticity and Meaning (1934), incl. bibl.

FIRST-FRUITS. See *Annates*.

FISH (Gk. ἰχθύς). In Christian art and literature the fish is a symbol of Christ, also sometimes of the newly baptized and of the Eucharist. It came into use in the 2nd cent., but neither its origin nor its meaning have so far been completely elucidated. It occurs in *Tertullian's 'De Baptismo', where the writer compares the neophytes to little fishes, following the Fish, in connexion with the ideal of the second birth in the waters of Baptism. This image is found also in the 'Shepherd' of *Hermas, in the Inscription of *Abercius, in *Clement of Alexandria, and in many other old Christian documents; but it is doubtful whether the symbol is exclusively Christian or influenced by Babylonian and Indian mythology. Opinions are also divided as to whether the symbol is derived from the acrostic ΙΧΘΥΣ = 'Ἰησοῦς Χριστός, Θεοῦ Υἱὸς Σωτήρ (' Jesus Christ, Son of God, Saviour '), or the acrostic from the symbol. The acrostic is frequently held to have originated in *Gnostic circles, since it is found in the '*Sibylline Oracles'. In the 4th and 5th cents. the fish became an emblem also of the Eucharist, and is frequently found in the paintings of the *catacombs in combination with bread and wine.

From early times fish, esp. in a dried condition, has taken the place of meat on days of fasting and abstinence. See *Fast*.

J. B. *Pitra, O.S.B., *Spicilegium Solesmense*, iii (Paris, 1855), pp. 499–543 ('ΙΧΘΥΣ, sive de Pisce Allegorico et Symbolico'); J. B. *de Rossi, ib., pp. 545–84 ('De Christianis Monumentis ΙΧΘΥΝ exhibentibus'); H. Achelis, *Das Symbol des Fisches und die Fischdenkmäler der römischen Katakomben* (Marburg, 1888); R. Pischel, 'Der Ursprung des christlichen Fischsymbol' in *Sb.* (Berl.), 1905 (1), pp. 506–32; C. R. Morley, 'The Origin of the Fish-Symbol' in *Princeton Theological Review*, viii (1910), pp. 93–106, 231–46, and 401–32; I. Scheftelowitz, 'Das Fisch-Symbol im Judentum und Christentum' in *Archiv für Religionswissenschaft*, xiv (1911), pp. 1–53. F. J. Doelger, ΙΧΘΥΣ (vol. i, *R.Q.*, Supplementheft, xvii; 1910; vols. ii-v, Münster i.W., 1922–40). V. Schultze, ΙΧΘΥΣ (Vortrag, Greifswald, 1912). R. St. J. Tyrwhitt in *D.C.A.*, i (1880), p. 673 f., s.v., and pp. 625–8, s.v. 'Eucharist (in Christian Art)'; F. Cumont in *P.W.*, ix (pt. 1; 1914), cols. 844–50, s.v. 'Ichthys'; H. *Leclercq, O.S.B., in *D.A.C.L.*, vii (pt. 2; 1927), cols. 1990–2086, s.v. ΙΧΘΥΜ

FISHER, St. JOHN (1469–1535), Bp. of *Rochester. Educated at Michaelhouse, Cambridge, he was appointed master in 1497. In 1501 he became vice-chancellor and in 1504 chancellor of the University, on whose destinies he left a permanent mark. As chaplain of the Lady *Margaret Beaufort he had her generous support for his efforts at raising the standard of the University, which also profited much by his appreciation of D. *Erasmus, whose work at Cambridge he greatly encouraged. In 1503 he was appointed the first Lady Margaret professor of divinity, and a year later Bp. of Rochester. He enjoyed a great reputation as a preacher, and was chosen to preach the funeral orations of Henry VII and, a little later, of the Lady Margaret. When in the 'twenties of the 16th cent. Protestant tendencies began to make themselves felt in the English universities, Fisher strongly upheld the doctrines of the *Real Presence and the Eucharistic Sacrifice (*De Veritate Corporis et Sanguinis Christi in Eucharistia*, 1527), but he was probably not, as is sometimes asserted, the author of *Henry VIII's *Assertio Septem Sacramentorum*. When the King began to contemplate divorce the Bp. of Rochester, who was confessor to the Queen, strongly protested, and from that time his relations with Henry VIII steadily deteriorated. In 1531 he had been able to secure the insertion into the Act acknowledging Henry as the head of the English Church of the words 'as far as the Law of God allows it', but in 1534 he had his property confiscated and was condemned to perpetual imprisonment, though in view of his poor health the sentence was commuted into a fine. After his refusal to accept the Act of Succession, however, he was again arrested and confined in the Tower, where he wrote a treatise on prayer as 'a spiritual consolation to his sister Elizabeth' (published 1577). Though T. *Cromwell himself entreated him to recognize the King as supreme head of the English Church, he remained firm, and on the trumped-up charge of concealing treasonable statements of Elizabeth *Barton, Parliament condemned him to death. The fact that the Pope in recognition of his merits created him a cardinal only increased the fury of the King, who had him executed on 22 June 1535. Fisher was not only one of the greatest scholars of his day—he possessed one of the finest libraries in Europe—but devoted to the cares of his diocese as much as to the learning of his university. He was canonized by *Pius XI in 1936. Feast day, 22 June.

The English Works of John Fisher, ed. by J. E. B. Mayor (E.E.T.S., Extra Series, xxvii, 1876); modern ed. of his Sacri Sacerdotii Defensio Contra Lutherum (1525), by H. K. Schmeink (Corpus Catholicorum, ix, Münster i.W., 1925); Eng. tr. by P. E. Hallett (London, 1935). The most reliable authority for his life is the State Papers of King Henry VIII, i (1830), vi (1849), vii (1849), and viii (1849); index in xi (1852), p. 551 f. A contemporary life (prob. by John Young, Vice-Chancellor of Cambridge), ed. by T. Bailey, The Life and Death of John Fisher (1655); a more accurate ed. by F. van Ortroy, S.J., in Anal. Boll., x (1891), pp. 121–365, and xii (1893), pp. 97–281. One MS. (B.M. Harleian MS. 6382), ed. by R. Bayne (E.E.T.S., Extra Series, cxvii, 1921). Modernized ed. by P. Hughes (London, 1935). T. E. Bridgett, C.SS.R., Life of Blessed John Fisher (1888). Other lives by J. Lewis (2 vols., London, 1855), V. McNabb, O.P. (London, 1935), and with that of T. More, by R. L. Smith. (London, 1935) and by H. E. G. Rope (London, 1935). P. McCann, A Valiant Bishop Against a Ruthless King. The Life of St. John Fisher (1938). E. E. Reynolds, St. John Fisher (1955). J. B. Mullinger in D.N.B, xix (1889), pp. 58–63.

FISHER THE JESUIT (1569–1641), i.e. **John Fisher**, RC controversialist. His real surname was Percy. A native of Co. Durham, he was converted to the RC faith as a young man and later succeeded in winning W. *Chillingworth to the same faith. He entered the *Jesuit Order in 1594. Having returned to England after some years in exile, he was chosen to represent the Roman side in the disputations held before the Countess of Buckingham, with Bps. F. *White and (later) W. *Laud as the principal Anglican protagonists. An extensive controversial literature followed, in which Fisher wrote under the initials 'A. C.' [? 'A Catholic'], but the level of much of it did not rise above that of one of the titles, The Fisher catched in his own Net. Laud himself published a Relation of his controversy with Fisher in 1639.

Modern ed. of W. Laud, A Relation of the Conference between William Laud, late Archbishop of Canterbury, and Mr. Fisher the Jesuit, with introd. and notes, by C. H. Simpkinson ('The English Theological Library', 1901). T. Cooper in D.N.B., xix (1889), p. 63 f.

FISTULA. A tube, usually of gold or silver, through which the laity in the Middle Ages used to receive communion from the chalice at the Eucharist. Its use is now confined to solemn Papal Masses, when the Pope and his deacon receive communion in this way.

Braun, C.A., p. 250 f. H. J. Hotham in D.C.A., i (1875), p. 675, s.v.; W. Henry in D.A.C.L., ii (pt. 2; 1910), col. 1583, s.v. 'Calamus', with bibl.

FITZRALPH, RICHARD (c. 1295–1360), Abp. of *Armagh. He became Chancellor of *Oxford University in 1332 and of *Lincoln Cathedral in 1334, Canon of *Lichfield in 1335, Archdeacon of *Chester and Dean of Lichfield in 1337, and Abp. of Armagh in 1347. He was a celebrated preacher, deeply imbued with scholasticism, and an eager promoter of learning among his clergy. In 1350, while on a visit to *Avignon, he presented the complaints of the secular priests against the privileges of the Mendicant Orders. He formulated his opinions in the treatise 'De Pauperie Salvatoris', in which he dealt with the question of evangelical poverty and the connexion of dominion, possession, and use, with the state of grace; it later greatly influenced J. *Wycliffe. At about the same time he was engaged in a controversy with emissaries of the *Armenian Church which culminated in his learned attack on the Greek and Armenian standpoint entitled 'Summa in Quaestionibus Armenorum' (published 1511). In 1357 he was again called to Avignon in the matter of the Mendicant Orders, where he maintained that voluntary begging was against the teaching of Christ. His position was not officially condemned, and he died three years later at Avignon.

Modern ed. of his 'De Pauperie Salvatoris' appended to R. L. Poole's ed. of Wycliffe's De Dominio Divino (Wyclif Society, 1890), pp. 273–476. L. L. Hammerich, The Beginning of the Strife between Richard FitzRalph and the Mendicants, with an edition of his autobiographical Prayer and his Proposition Unusquisque (Copenhagen, 1938). G. Meersseman, O.P. (ed.), 'La Défense des ordres mendicants contre Richard Fitz Ralph, par Barthélemy de Bolsenheim O.P. (1357)' in Archivum Fratrum Praedicatorum, v (1935), pp. 124–73. A. Gwynn, S.J., 'The Sermon Diary of Richard FitzRalph, Archbishop of Armagh' in Proceedings of the Royal Irish Academy, xliv (1937–8), Section C, pp. 1–57; id., The Austin Friars in the Time of Wyclif (1940), ch. 2, pp. 80–9, with reff. R. L. Poole in D.N.B., xix (1889), pp. 194–198.

FIVE MILE ACT, The. One of the statutes (17 Car. II, c. 2) passed in 1665, as part of the Clarendon Code, to secure the position of the C of E at the Restoration. It prohibited any clergyman from teaching or from coming within five miles of a city or corporate town unless he took the non-resistance oath, declaring that he would not 'at any time endeavour any alteration of Government either in Church or State'. Its effects were severely felt by the Dissenters as their congregations were chiefly situated in the towns.

Documents Illustrative of English Church History (ed. H. Gee–W. J. Hardy, 1896), No. cxviii.

FLABELLUM. See Fan, Liturgical.

FLACIUS, MATTHIAS (1520–75), from his birthplace also known as **Illyricus**, *Lutheran theologian. As he wished in his youth to become a monk, his uncle, who was a supporter of the Reformation and hoped to win him from his intention, sent him to study in Protestant parts. From Basle and *Tübingen he passed in 1541 to *Wittenberg, where he was received by P. *Melanchthon and M. *Luther, and in 1544 appointed professor of Hebrew. Here he became a convinced antihumanist and as a strict dogmatist strongly opposed the *Augsburg Interim and the *Adiaphorists, and was forced by Melanchthon to leave Wittenberg. After some other academic appointments, he became professor of NT at Jena in 1557. Here his insistence on a view of human nature verging on *Manicheism made him the subject of attack by V. *Strigel and others who were defending *synergistic doctrines, and in 1562 he left Jena. His subsequent attempt to found a Lutheran academy at Ratisbon failed. In the later years of his life he found himself compelled by the unpopularity of his doctrines to travel from place to place. He was a theologian of great erudition and the leading spirit among the *Centuriators of Magdeburg. His other writings include *Catalogus Testium Veritatis* (1556), *Clavis Scripturae Sacrae* (1567) and *Glossa Compendiaria in NT* (1570). See also *Missa Illyrica*.

Lives by J. B. Ritter (Frankfurt, 1725), A. D. C. Twesten (Berlin, 1844), and W. Preger (Erlangen, 2 parts, 1859-61). J. Haussleiter, 'Matthias Flacius als Herausgeber von Luthers Koburger Briefen und Trostsprüchen (1530)' in *Neue Kirchliche Zeitschrift*, xxviii (1917), pp. 149-87; P. Polman, O.F.M., 'Flacius Illyricus, historien de l'Église' in *R.H.E.*, xxvii (1931), pp. 27-73.

FLAGELLANTS. The bands of men who in medieval times scourged themselves in public procession, often to the accompaniment of psalms, in a penance for the sins of the world. Such organized exhibitions of penance date from the 13th cent. The anarchy and famine caused by war in North and Central Italy and the prophecies of *Joachim of Flora combined to produce a conviction of the Divine displeasure, and in 1260 there was an outbreak of such penitential processions throughout Italy. In the next year they were condemned by ecclesiastical authority. Little more is heard of them till 1348-9, when the Black Death created a recrudescence of similar sentiments and a belief that the end of the world was near, and bands of flagellants, calling people to repentance, soon appeared all over Europe. In Germany they rapidly became an organized sect and, falling into heresy, were condemned. In Italy processions of flagellants, orthodox in belief, continued to be held at intervals through the succeeding centuries, one being seen in Rome as late as 1870. Similar practices exist to-day in distant RC missionary countries, e.g. the Philippine Islands, restrained and regulated to some extent by ecclesiastical authority.

For the main sources see Haupt, cited below. P. Runge (ed.), *Die Lieder und Melodien der Geister des Jahres 1349 nach der Auszeichnung Hugo's von Reutlingen* (1900); U. Berlière, O.S.B., 'Trois Traités inédits sur les flagellants de 1349' in *R. Bén.*, xxv (1908), pp. 334-57. L. A. *Muratori, *Antiquitates Italicae Medii Aevi*, vi (Milan, 1742), pp. 446-82, Diss. lxxv, 'De Piis Laicorum Confraternitatibus earumque Origine, Flagellantibus, et Sacris Missionibus'. P. Fredericq, *De Secten der Geeselaars en der Dansers in de Nederlanden Tijdens de 14de Eeuw* (Mémoires de l'Académie Royale des Sciences, des Lettres et des Beaux-Arts de Belgique, liii, 1895-1898; separate pagination; repr 12 Oct. 1896). A. Hübner, *Die deutschen Geisslerlieder* (1931). K. Lechner, 'Die grosse Geisselfahrt des Jahres 1349' in *Hist. J.*, v (1884), pp. 437-62. H. Haupt in *P.R.E.* (ed. 3), vi (1899), pp. 432-444, s.v. 'Geisselung (kirchliche) und Geisslerbruderschaften', with bibl.; L. A. St. L. Toke in *C.E.*, vi (1909), pp. 89-92, s.v.

FLAGS ON CHURCH TOWERS. Acc. to a ruling given in 1938 by the Earl Marshal, the proper flag to fly on a church tower in England is the red Cross of St. *George, with an escutcheon of the Arms of the See in which the church is ecclesiastically situate in the first quarter;

but, where this flag cannot be obtained, custom sanctions the use of the plain St. George's Cross. No rules have been laid down as to the occasions on which the flag is to be flown, but it is usual for this to be done on important Church festivals, on special occasions of rejoicing, and sometimes on days of national observance.

FLAVIA DOMITILLA. See *Domitilla, Flavia*.

FLAVIAN, St. (d. 449), Patr. of *Constantinople from 446. He is remembered for the important part which he took in the *Monophysite struggle. In 448 he had excommunicated *Eutyches at a synod at Constantinople (the so-called σύνοδος ἐνδημοῦσα) for heretical teaching about the Person of Christ. In the following year Imperial pressure secured the reversal of this decision at the *Latrocinium at Ephesus, and the maltreatment that Flavian suffered here is said to have caused his death a few days later. His remains were subsequently brought solemnly to Constantinople by the Empress *Pulcheria. Feast day, 18 Feb.

Flavian's *libellus appellationis*, written immediately after the Latrocinium and directed to Pope *Leo, was found in 1874 by G. Amelli, the librarian of the *Ambrosiana, in the Novara Capitular MS. 30 and first published by Amelli in *S. Leone Magno e l' Oriente* (1882). It was reissued by T. *Mommsen, *Neues Archiv*, xi (1886), pp. 362-4. A subsequent edition, with an important introduction, was published by T. A. *Lacey, *Appellatio Flaviani*. The Letters of Appeal from the Council of Ephesus, A.D. 449, addressed by Flavian and Eusebius to St. Leo of Rome (Church Historical Society, lxx, 1903). P. *Batiffol, *Le Siège apostolique* (1924), pp. 513-19.

FLÉCHIER, ESPRIT (1632-1710), French preacher. After studying at Tarascon, he was ordained and went to *Paris (1660), where he gained royal favour for a poem on Louis XIV and was appointed tutor to the Dauphin. His greatly admired sermons soon made him famous. He was at his best in his funeral panegyrics (outstanding being that on Turenne), but his oratory, despite its formal elegance, was artificial and pretentious. In 1673 he was elected a member of the French Academy. In 1685 he became Bp. of Lavaur and in 1687 of Nîmes, where his conciliatory and tolerant disposition did much to quiet the passions aroused by the revocation of the Edict of *Nantes (1685) and also to win over many *Huguenots to Catholicism.

Œuvres complètes, ed. by G. M. Ducreux (10 vols., Nîmes, 1782) and by J. P. *Migne (2 vols., Paris, 1856). A. E. Delacroix, *Histoire de Fléchier d'après les documents originaux* (1865). Further life by L. Ménard (Nîmes, 1872). A[ntonin] Fabre, *La Jeunesse de Fléchier* (2 vols., 1882); id., *De la correspondance de Fléchier avec Mme Deshoulières* (1872); id., *Fléchier, orateur* (1872). Notice by C. A. Sainte-Beuve prefixed to M. Chéruel (ed.), *Les Mémoires de Fléchier sur les Grands-Jours d'Auvergne* (1856), pp. iii-xxxix.

FLEMING, RICHARD (d. 1431), Bp. of *Lincoln and founder of Lincoln College, Oxford. Educated at University College,

Oxford, he became a Prebendary of *York in 1406. In 1407 he was Junior Proctor at Oxford. At this period he had *Wycliffite sympathies, which brought him into conflict with T. *Arundel, Abp. of *Canterbury, then attempting to eradicate *Lollard doctrine from the university. Not later than 1415 he became rector of Boston, Lincs., and in 1420 Bp. of Lincoln. In 1423 Fleming represented the English nation at the Councils of Pavia and *Siena, where he made an eloquent speech before *Martin V championing the Papacy. In 1424 Martin V promoted him to the see of York, but the Chapter having already elected the Bp. of *Worcester, the King's ministers refused to confirm the appointment. In 1427 Fleming founded Lincoln College, Oxford, primarily as a school for opponents of Wycliffite teaching (which he himself had long since forsworn).

Preface to Statutes of Lincoln College in *Statutes of the Colleges of Oxford*, i (1853), pp. 7-8. For his supposed Lollard sympathies, *Snappe's Formulary and Other Records*, ed. by H. E. Salter (Oxford Historical Society, lxxx, 1924), pp. 95-100 and 121-8. R. L. Poole in *D.N.B.*, xix (1889), pp. 282-4.

FLETCHER, JOHN WILLIAM (1729-85), Vicar of Madeley in Shropshire from 1760. (His original name was de la Fléchère.) A Swiss by birth and education, he settled in England c. 1750 and shortly afterwards joined the *Methodist Movement in the C of E. In 1757 he was ordained deacon and priest on two successive Sundays, and in 1760 he accepted the living of Madeley as a benefice providing more work and less income than another which he had been offered and declined. From 1768 to 1771 he also exercised, so far as his parochial duties allowed, a general supervision over Lady *Huntingdon's college at Trevecca for the training of ministers. Although he took no prominent part in leading or organizing the Methodist Movement, his outstanding sanctity and the devotedness of his work among the Shropshire colliers issued from its influence. His theological works included *Checks to Antinomianism* (1771), which was occasioned by the disputes between the '*Arminians' and the '*Calvinists'. He also controverted the *Unitarian doctrines of J. *Priestley.

Collected works, 9 vols., London, 1800-4; 7 vols., ib., 1826; and 2 vols., Shebbear, Devon-London, 1835. L. Tyerman, *Wesley's Designated Successor* (1882). Other lives by J. *Wesley (1786), R. Cox (1822), F. W. Macdonald (1885), and J. Marrat (1902), all London. J. H. Overton in *D.N.B.*, xix (1889), pp. 312-14.

FLEURY (Lat. *Floriacum*). The place owed its celebrity to the (real or supposed) transference hither in the 7th cent. of the remains of Sts. *Benedict and *Scholastica from *Monte Cassino after the Lombards had ravaged Italy, and the large monastery that was erected to house them. Of the abbey buildings, the enormous church, a magnificent Romanesque basilica, alone survives. The place, known as Saint-Benoît-sur-Loire, is now little more than a hamlet.

G. Chenesseau, *L'Abbaye de Fleury à Saint-Benoît-sur-Loire. Son histoire, ses institutions, ses édifices* (Paris 1931). L. H. Cottineau, O.S.B., *Répertoire topo-bibliographique des abbayes et prieurés* (Mâcon, 1935), cols. 2610-13, s.v. 'St-Benoît-sur-Loire', with extensive bibl.

FLEURY, CLAUDE (1640-1725), ecclesiastical historian. Born at *Paris, he was educated by the *Jesuits at the Collège de Clermont and in 1658 called to the bar. Here his talents brought him into contact with many of the leading personalities of France, among them J. B. *Bossuet and L. *Bourdaloue, under whose influence he was led to offer himself for ordination (c. 1672). In 1672, he was appointed by Louis XIV tutor to the young Princes de Conti; in 1684 Abbot of the *Cistercian monastery of Loc-Dieu in Brittany; in 1689 tutor to the grandsons of Louis XIV; and in 1696 he was elected to the Academy. Having come under the patronage of Fénelon, he found his position endangered at court in the *Quietistic controversy over the *Maximes des saints*, but he was generously saved by Bossuet. In 1706 he became Prior of Notre-Dame-d'Argenteuil, near Paris. After Louis XIV's death (1715), he was chosen confessor to the young Louis XV, as one who was 'neither *Jansenist nor *Molinist nor *Ultramontane, but Catholic'.

Fleury is known to posterity chiefly through his eloquent *Histoire ecclésiastique* (20 vols., 1691-1720), the first large-scale history of the Church, which is deservedly held in repute for its learning and judgement. Before his death Fleury had carried it down to 1414; later it was continued to 1778 by J. C. Fabre and others. Among his other writings were *Histoire du droit français* (1674) and *Institution au droit ecclésiastique* (anon., 1677; new ed., with Fleury's name, 1687), *Les Mœurs des Israélites* (1681), *Les Mœurs des chrétiens* (1682), and *Grand Catéchisme historique* (1683). Several of these, incl. the *Histoire ecclésiastique*, were put on the *Index for their *Gallican views. In 1687 he issued a Lat. tr. of Bossuet's famous *Exposition de la foi catholique*.

Several collections of Fleury's sermons and treatises were issued posthumously, incl. Discours (2 vols., Paris, 1752) and Opuscules (5 vols., Nîmes, 1780). J. *Wesley incorporated extracts from Fleury's *Les Mœurs des chrétiens* (Brussels, 1682) with the title *The Manners of the Antient Christians* in his 'Christian Library' (ed. 3, 1767). Eng. tr. of portions of the *Histoire ecclésiastique*, by J. H. *Newman (3 vols., 1842-1844). F. Gaquère, *La Vie et les œuvres de Claude Fleury, 1640-1723* (Paris, 1925).

FLIGHT INTO EGYPT, The. The journey from *Bethlehem into Egypt of St. *Joseph, accompanied by the BVM and the infant Jesus, after the visit of the *Magi. It was undertaken in obedience to an angelic message to enable the Child to escape the hostility of *Herod the Great. After the death of Herod, the Holy Family returned to *Nazareth (Mt. 2. 13-23).

FLOOD, The. The 'flood of waters' which, acc. to Gen. 6. 5-9. 17, God brought upon the earth 'to destroy all flesh' (Gen. 6. 17) because of the wickedness of the whole human race, who thus perished, only Noah and his family, with specimens of each species of animal life, being preserved in the *Ark to repeople the earth. In the Biblical text there appears to be a conflation of two accounts, which critics have assigned to the two Pentateuchal sources 'J' and 'P'. Parallel flood stories are found in Babylonian sources, e.g. on the clay tablets discovered in the library of Assurbanipal (see *Gilgamesh*), which date the flood *c.* 3000 B.C., and in a history of Babylon by Berossus, a Babylonian who wrote *c.* 300 B.C. The excavations of Sir Leonard Woolley at Ur (Tell-el-Mukkayar) in 1929 seemed to indicate a historic foundation for the Babylonian tradition of a very widespread flood.

J. Skinner, 'Genesis' (I.C.C.; 1910), pp. 174–81 ('The Deluge Tradition'). J. G. Frazer, *Folk-lore in the Old Testament* (1918), i, ch. 4 (pp. 104–361). Large collection of Flood stories in R. Andree, *Die Flutsagen* (1891). F. H. Woods in *H.E.R.E.*, iv (1911), pp. 545–55, s.v. 'Deluge'.

FLORENCE, Council of (1438–45). It is counted by the RC Church as either the 16th or the 17th Oecumenical Council, the numbering depending on the refusal or admission of oecumenicity to the Council of *Basle (1431, q.v.). The Council was held successively in three cities, at Ferrara (1438–9), at Florence (1439–42), and at Rome (1442–5). Its chief object was reunion with the Greek Church, which sought support from the W. against the Turks, who were nearing *Constantinople. After the majority of the members assembled at Basle had refused to move to a place more convenient to the Greeks, Pope *Eugenius IV transferred the Council to Ferrara, where it opened on 8 Jan. 1438. Among its most distinguished members were the Greek Emperor, John VIII Palaeologus, and Joseph, Patr. of Constantinople. Its leading theologians included, on the Latin side, Card. J. *Cesarini and the *Dominican, John of *Torquemada; on the Greek the unionist *Bessarion, Abp. of *Nicaea and later cardinal, and the anti-unionist Mark, Bp. of *Ephesus. During the Council delaying tactics of the anti-unionist party led to the formation of commissions, consisting of Latins and Greeks in equal numbers, who were to discuss the principal controversial points. These were the *Double Procession of the Holy Ghost, the use of *unleavened bread for the *Eucharist, the doctrine of *Purgatory and the primacy of the Pope. The chief obstacle to an agreement was the *Filioque clause, the Greeks objecting that any addition to the Creeds, however doctrinally correct, was unlawful. When the costs of the Council became too heavy for the Pope, the Florentines offered to bear them, and on 26 Feb. 1439 the Council was consequently transferred to Florence. The Greeks now wishing to conclude it as soon as possible, the Emperor intervened frequently and even suspended the votes of the anti-unionists. Having dropped the discussions on the Filioque, the commissions discussed for three months the question whether the Holy Ghost proceeds from the Father alone, acc. to the Greeks, or from the Father and the Son, acc. to the

Latins. During the discussions Bessarion pronounced the famous discourse (printed as 'Discursus Dogmaticus', in J. P. *Migne, *PG*, clxi, 543–614) in which he endeavoured to prove that the Double Procession is taught more or less explicitly by both Greek and Latin Fathers, and that the Greek Church has never denied that the Holy Ghost proceeds from the Son. This was followed by more discussions, until the promise of help against the Turks at last induced the Greeks to admit the Latin teaching. The questions of Purgatory and of unleavened bread were settled quickly acc. to the views of the Latins, but the primacy of the Pope roused fresh difficulties. The Latins adduced the Petrine texts as well as the honourable reception which the Councils had always accorded to Papal documents, and the Greeks at last accepted the supremacy of the Pope, though in vaguer terms than originally intended. The Decree of Union, beginning with the words '*Laetentur Coeli' (q.v.), was finally signed on 5 July 1439. Mark of Ephesus was the only bishop to refuse his signature.

After the departure of the Greeks the Council continued in session to deal with the schismatic Council of Basle and the union with other E. Churches. All members of the Council of Basle were declared heretics and excommunicated, and the superiority of the Pope over the Councils affirmed in the famous bull 'Etsi non dubitemus' of 20 Apr. 1441. In 1442 union was established with the *Jacobites, and in 1443 the Council was transferred to Rome. Little is known of its further activities, except that several other E. Churches, such as the Mesopotamians (1444), the *Chaldaeans, and the *Maronites (1445), were also reconciled. The Orthodox synods, however, refused to ratify the union between Latins and Greeks, and the other unions proved equally ephemeral.

Hardouin, ix cols. 1–1080; Mansi, xxxi (1798), cols. 459–1120, and in suppl. to vol. xxxi (1801), cols. 1121–1998. Crit. ed. of the surviving Gk. acta by J. Gill, S.J., with Lat. tr. (Concilium Florentinum. Documenta et Scriptores. Editum consilio et impensis Pontificii Instituti Orientalium Studiorum, Series B, vol. v, Fascc. 1 and 2, 1953). G. Hofmann, S.J. (ed.), *Epistolae Pontificiae ad Concilium Florentinum Spectantes* (ib., Series A., 3 partes, 1940–6); id., *Acta Camerae Apostolicae et Civitatum Venetiarum, Ferrariae, Florentiae, Ianuae de Concilio Florentino* (ib., vol. iii, 1950 ff.); id., *Documenta Concilii Florentini de Unione Orientalium* (Pontificia Universitas Gregoriana. Textus et Documenta, Series Theologica, xviii, xix, xxii; 1935–6). L. Petit (ed.), 'Documents relatifs au concile de Florence. I, La Question du purgatoire à Ferrare' in *P.O.*, xv (1927), pp. 1–169 (fasc. i); II, 'Œuvres anticonciliaires de Marc d'Éphèse', ib. xvii (1933), pp. 309–524 (fasc. ii). Further documents ed. G. Hofmann, S.J., *Concilium Florentinum* (Orientalia Christiana, xvi, 3 (No. 57), xvi, 2 (No. 59), and xxii, 1 (No. 68); 1929–31). Contemporary account by a Greek, hostile to the Union, Sylvester Sguropulus, *Vera Historia Unionis non Verae inter Graecos et Latinos* (ed., with Lat. tr., by R. Creyghton, The Hague, 1660). E. Cecconi, *Studi storici sul concilio di Firenze* (pt. 1 only publd., Naples, 1869, with docc.). G. Hofmann, S.J., *Papato, conciliarismo, patriarcato, 1438–1439*. Teologi e deliberazioni del Concilio di Firenze (Miscellanea Historiae Pontificiae edita a Facultate Historiae Ecclesiasticae in Pontificia Universitate Gregoriana, ii (pt. 1; collectionis totius N.2; 1940). J. Gill, S.J., 'The Sources of the "Acta" of the Council of Florence' in *O.C.P.*, xiv (1948), pp. 43–79; id., 'The "Acta" and the Memoirs of Sgyropoulos as History', ib., pp. 303–55, with reff. to earlier discussions. Hefele–Leclercq, vii (pt. 2; 1916), pp. 951–1106. G. Hofmann, S.J., in *E.C.*, v (1951), cols. 1417–23, s.v. 'Firenze, II', with bibl. J. Gill, S.J., *The Council of Florence* (1959). See also bibl. to Basle, Council of.

FLORENTIUS RADEWYNS (1350-1400).

One of the earliest members of the *Brethren of the Common Life. He belonged to the group which had come under the influence of G. *Groote, and on Groote's death in 1384 became the head of the community which he had founded at Deventer in Holland. His house here was the first settled establishment of the Brethren, who seem previously not to have lived under a common roof. Under his influence the monastery at *Windesheim was founded in 1387.

The principal authority is the life by *Thomas à Kempis, pr. among the latter's works (Nuremberg, 1494, fol. xxxviii (reverse)-fol. xliv (reverse), and in all later edd.); Eng. tr. by J. P. Arthur, *The Founders of the New Devotion* (1905), pp. 81-162. S. Kettlewell, *Thomas à Kempis and the Brothers of the Common Life*, i (1882), pp. 209-62; A. Hyma, *The 'Devotio Moderna' or Christian Renaissance* (Grand Rapids, Michigan [1925]), esp. pp. 49-58, virtually repr. in his *The Brethren of the Common Life* (ib., 1950), pp. 55-63. L. Schultze in *P.R.E.* (ed. 3), vi (1899), pp. 111-14, s.v. See also other works cited under *Brethren of the Common Life*; *Devotio Moderna*; *Groote, Gerard*; and *Windesheim*.

FLORILEGIA

(Lat. *flos*, 'a flower', and *lego*, 'I gather'). Collections of selected passages from the writings of previous authors. Special interest attaches to the *Patristic florilegia. Besides those composed of excerpts from commentaries on the Bible and known as *catenae, a considerable number of dogmatic florilegia compiled from the 5th cent. onwards have survived. Such collections of passages (χρήσεις) were often drawn up to establish the orthodoxy or heterodoxy of individual theologians, and many became incorporated into the *Acta* of the ecclesiastical councils. For the historian they are often of much value, esp. when they preserve passages from works of which the bulk has been lost. A Patristic florilegium of a non-dogmatic kind is the collection of extracts made by *Gregory of Nyssa and *Basil of Caesarea from the writings of *Origen and known as the 'Philocalia' (c. 362).

Among the more important dogmatic florilegia are the 'Doctrina Patrum de Incarnatione Verbi' (preserved in MSS. Vat. gr. 2200, Bodl. Misc. 184, etc.; ed. F. Diekamp, Münster i.W., 1907) and the 'Anti-Chalcedonian Collection in Vat. gr. 1431' (ed. E. *Schwartz, *Abh.* (Bayr.), xxxii, Hft. 6, 1927; with valuable discussion of florilegia generally). Convenient ed. of Origen's 'Philocalia', by J. A. *Robinson (Cambridge, 1895). Krumbacher, pp. 206-18. F. Diekamp in *L.Th.K.*, iv (1932), col. 44 f., s.v., with further bibl.

FLORUS

(d. c. 860), Deacon of Lyons. His writings were concerned with the ecclesiastical, theological, and liturgical controversies of his time, in which he took a prominent part. After the deposition of *Agobard, Bp. of Lyons, by the civil power at the Synod of Diedenhofen in 835, he defended the rights of the Church in a treatise 'De iniusta vexatione ecclesiae Lugdunensis'. His other writings include a sermon 'De praedestinatione', in which he attacked *Gottschalk, three treatises against *Amalarius of Metz who attempted to make changes in the ancient Lyons liturgy, commentaries on the Epp. of St. Paul, a collection of poems, and some additions to the *Martyrology of *Bede.

Works collected in J. P. Migne, *PL*, cxix, 11-424. Three letters ed. E. Duemmler in *M.G.H.*, Epistolae, v (1899), pp. 206-10, 267-74, and 340-3. Crit. ed. of his verse by id. in *M.G.H.*, Poetae, ii (1884), pp. 509-66. Dom C. Charlier, O.S.B., who has shown the MS. Lyons 484 to be mainly an autograph of Florus, has also restored to him several writings which were later issued under other names, e.g. a work 'Adversum Scotum', all the writings of Remigius of Lyons, the 'Liber contra Iudaeos' of Amolon, and the 'De Imaginibus Sanctorum' of Agobard. Cf. C. Charlier, O.S.B., 'Les Manuscrits personnels de Florus de Lyon et son activité littéraire' in *Mélanges E. Podechard* (Lyons, 1945), pp. 71-84. Manitius, i, pp. 560-8. A critical ed. from C. Charlier is awaited.

FLUE, NIKOLAUS VON. See *Nicholas of Flue*.

FOGAZZARO, ANTONIO

(1842-1911), Italian RC writer, poet, and philosopher. In 1906 the Vatican put his most famous novel, *Il Santo* (1905), on the *Index. All his writings are marked by a liberalism characteristic of his age, but his attachment to Catholicism was as sincere as his liberalism. He also strove to reconcile the theory of evolution with Church teaching. His early poetical romance, *Miranda*, has Wordsworthian simplicity and pathos.

Tutte le opere, ed. P. Nardi (14 vols., Milan, 1931-41); *Lettere scelte*, ed. T. Gallarati-Scotti (Milan, etc., 1940). Lives by S. Rumor (Milan, 1912) and T. Gallarati-Scotti (ib., 1920; Eng. tr., 1922). L. Portier, *Antonio Fogazzaro* (Paris thesis, 1937, with discussion of earlier works on Fogazzaro, p. ix f.; Fr. tr. of his poetry as suppl. vol., 1937). F. Montanari in *E.C.*, v (1950), cols. 1459-62.

FOLDED CHASUBLE.

A form of the *chasuble pinned up in front (*planeta plicata*) which is worn in the W. Church by the *deacon and *subdeacon at *High Mass in penitential seasons. It is a survival from the time when the chasuble was not a specifically priestly vestment. The so-called *broad stole worn by the deacon at the reading of the Gospel is in origin also a 'folded chasuble', but folded in another way.

Braun, *L.G.*, pp. 166-9 ('Anlegungsweise der Kasel bei den Diakonen, Subdiakonen und Akolythen. Die Planeta Plicata).

FOLIOT, GILBERT

(d. 1188), Bp. of London. Of a Norman family, he made his profession at *Cluny, where he rose to be Prior. Respect for his learning, eloquence, and austerity brought its reward and he became Abbot of Abbeville, Abbot of *Gloucester (1139), and Bp. of *Hereford (1148). Gradually he came to play a leading part in ecclesiastical and political affairs. He supported Matilda, acted as confidential adviser to *Theobald, Abp. of *Canterbury, and in 1162 opposed the election of *Becket to the see of Canterbury as one who had persecuted the Church and destroyed her goods. When translated to the see of London in 1163, he objected to taking the customary vow of canonical obedience to Canterbury on the ground that he had already done so on becoming Bp. of Hereford. He then made the claim that London by early history and political eminence was a metropolitical city independent of Canterbury. He supported the King in his struggle with the primate, notably at Clarendon and Northampton, and acted as one of Henry's envoys to *Alexander III. On Palm Sunday, 1169, Becket, then at *Clairvaux, formally excommunicated him; but on Foliot's appeal to Rome, the Pope empowered the Bp. of *Exeter (Bartholomew) and the Abp. of Rouen to absolve him (Easter, 1170). On 14 June, in defiance of the rights of Canterbury, he joined with the Abp. of *York in crowning Henry's son and was forthwith excommunicated again by Becket. He crossed to Normandy to seek Henry's protection on the same day that Becket returned to England (1 Dec. 1170). Though in no way responsible, he was popularly associated with Becket's murder, and not absolved until May 1172. He continued to take a prominent part in ecclesiastical affairs until his death, e.g. in connexion with the elections of Richard of Dover and *Baldwin. A treatise on the Song of Songs is ascribed to him.

Letters ed. by J. A. Giles ('Patres Ecclesiae Anglicanae', 2 vols., Oxford, 1845), repr. in J. P. Migne, *PL.*, cxc, 739–1068, index, 1500–6. 'Expositio in Cantica Canticorum', ed. by P. Young (London, 1638), repr. in J. P. Migne, *PL.*, ccii, 1147–1304. *Materials for the History of Thomas Becket*, ed. by J. C. Robertson, v–vii (R.S., 1881–5), passim. [M.] D. Knowles, *The Episcopal Colleagues of Archbishop Thomas Becket* (Ford Lectures for 1949, 1951), esp. pp. 37–49. G. G. Perry in *D.N.B.*, xix (1889), pp. 358–60.

FOLKESTONE RITUAL CASE. See *Ridsdale Judgement*.

FONT (Lat. *fons*, 'spring of water'). Receptacle for baptismal water, normally made of stone, more rarely of metal. In early times, when adult baptism by immersion was the rule, it was a large basin below ground-level in which the neophyte stood while the water was poured over him. When infant baptism came to be the norm, the font, still rather large, was raised slightly above the ground so that the child could conveniently be immersed by the minister. Later still, when *affusion became the prevalent form of baptism, fonts became smaller and higher, being frequently richly ornamented, and gradually took on their present cup shape. They also came to be covered by a lid that was sometimes locked to preserve the purity of the baptismal water and to guard it from profanation. In some churches the font stands either in a separate chapel (*baptistery) or is railed off in a locked enclosure.

F. Simpson, *A Series of Ancient Baptismal Fonts Chronologically Arranged* (1828); [T. Combe,] *Illustrations of Baptismal Fonts* (1844) with an introduction by F. A. Paley. F. Bond, *Fonts and Font Covers* (1908), incl. bibl. C. J. Wall, *Porches and Fonts* (1912), pp. 175–338. E. Tyrrell-Green, *Baptismal Fonts* (1928). J. G. Davies, *The Architectural Setting of Baptism* (1962). H. *Leclercq, O.S.B., in *D.A.C.L.*, xiv (pt. 1, 1939), cols. 1080–1119, s.v. 'Piscine'.

FONTEVRAULT, Order of. A 'double order' of monks and nuns, living under the rule of *one abbess, though in separate convents. In 1100 Bl. Robert d'Arbrissel (d.

1117) founded an abbey at Fontevrault, in the south of France, on the basis of the *Benedictine Rule, with certain more rigorous additions, and in *c.* 1115 gave it a constitution with Petronilla as its first abbess. Dependent houses were soon established in many parts of France, and a few in England and Spain. In the 13th cent. the Order was very poor, but considerably prospered in the 14th, and after a period of decadence in the 15th was reformed by successive abbesses between 1475 and 1502. It disappeared in the Revolution of 1789, but was revived as an order for women only by Mme Rose in 1806, certain modifications being then made to the original Rule.

[H. Nicquet, S.J.,] *Histoire de l'ordre de Fontevrault* (Angers, 1586; Paris, 1642). Édouard [pseudonym of A. Biron], *Fontevrault et ses monuments* ou histoire de cette royale abbaye depuis sa fondation jusqu'à sa suppression, 1100–1793 (2 vols., 1873–4); L. F. Bossebœuf, *Fontevrault. Son histoire et ses monuments* (Tours, [1890]). *Histoire de l'ordre de Fontevrault, 1100–1908*, by the Religious of Sainte-Marie-de-Fontevrault-de-Boulaur now located in Vera in Navarre (3 vols., Auch, 1911–15). E. *Bishop, 'Bishop Giffard and the Reform of Fontevrault' in *Downside Review*, v (1886), pp. 51–7. Heimbucher, i, pp. 327–9.

FOOLS, Feast of. A mock religious festival which was widely celebrated in the Middle Ages on or about 1 Jan., esp. in France. It may have grown out of a 'festival of the *subdeacons', sometimes kept on 1 Jan. The feast was an occasion of much buffoonery and extravagance, often approaching the blasphemous, and several ecclesiastical reformers (e.g. R. *Grosseteste, Bp. of Lincoln) made attempts to suppress it. In 1435 very severe penalties were imposed by the Council of *Basle for its observance, and it seems to have finally disappeared in the middle of the 16th cent. See also *Misrule, Lord of*; *Boy Bishop*; *Asses, Feast of*.

E. K. Chambers, *The Medieval Stage* (1903), i, pp. 274–335. G. M. Dreves, S.J., 'Zur Geschichte der *Fête des Fous* in *Stimmen aus Maria Laach*, xlvii (1894), pp. 571–87. H. Thurston, S.J., in *C.E.*, vi (1909), p. 132 f., s.v.

FOOT-PACE. See *Predella*.

FOOT-WASHING. See *Pedilavium*.

FORBES, ALEXANDER PENROSE (1817–1875), Bp. of Brechin, the 'Scottish Pusey'. Originally in the East India Company, he entered Brasenose College, Oxford, in 1840. Here he came under the influence of the *Oxford Movement, gave up his intention of returning to India and decided to be ordained. On the nomination of E. B. *Pusey, he became Vicar of St. Saviour's, Leeds, in 1847, but a few months later he was elected Bp. of Brechin, where he remained for the rest of his life and laboured hard to further Tractarian principles in Scotland. His defence of the doctrine of the Real Presence in his primary charge, delivered on 5 Aug. 1857, led to his censure in 1860 by the college of bishops. Later he became keenly interested in the cause of the *Old Catholics. His writings, mainly

practical, but with a sound scholarly (esp. *Patristic) basis, included a *Commentary on the Seven Penitential Psalms* (1847), *A Short Explanation of the *Nicene Creed* (1852; ed. 2, much enlarged, 1866), a translation of Part I of Claude Arvisenet's *Memoriale Vitae Sacerdotalis* (1853), and *An Explanation of the Thirty-Nine Articles* (2 vols., 1867 – 8; written at Pusey's suggestion). He also published, partly in conjunction with his brother (see foll. entry), several liturgical and hagiographical texts and contributed extensively to reviews.

D. J. Mackey, *Bishop Forbes: A Memoir* (1888); W. Perry, *A. P. Forbes* (1939). A. Vian in *D.N.B.*, xix (1889), p. 378 f.

FORBES, GEORGE HAY (1821 – 75), *Patristic scholar. Brother of the preceding, he was hampered throughout his life by acute paralysis of the legs. At an early age he developed keen liturgical interests, becoming a strong advocate of the Scottish Liturgy against the party in the Episcopalian Church which favoured the English BCP. His High Church beliefs, in which he was permanently confirmed by the study of J.*Johnson's *Unbloody Sacrifice*, brought him into relation with the *Tractarians. In 1848, despite his infirmity, he was ordained deacon by Patrick Torry, Bp. of St. Andrews (1844–52), and in the same year started an Episcopal mission at Burntisland, where he worked as a model parish priest, building a church and setting up his own printing press. In 1849 he was ordained priest. In 1850 he issued a new Prayer Book (dated 1849) which, though authorized by Torry for use in his diocese, met with great opposition, notably from Charles Wordsworth, Warden of Glenalmond, and later Torry's successor at St. Andrews. Among the many works he edited, some of them unfinished and mostly from his own press, were W. *Forbes, *Considerationes Modestae* (2 vols., 1850–6); certain works of St. *Gregory of Nyssa (1855 ff.); *Ancient Liturgies of the Gallican Church* (with J. M. *Neale, 2 parts, 1855–7); the *Arbuthnott Missal (with A. P. *Forbes, 1864); the *Missale Drummondiense* (posthumous, 1882). All his publications reflected his meticulous accuracy. He also issued some periodicals from his press, notably the *Panoply* (1858–74).

W. Perry, *George Hay Forbes, A Romance in Scholarship* (1927).

FORBES, WILLIAM (1585–1634), first Bp. of Edinburgh. A native of Aberdeen, he was educated at Marischal College in the town, where he was for a time professor of logic. After holding various offices, he was appointed by *Charles I Bp. of Edinburgh in 1634, but died two months later. He is remembered esp. for his erudite *Considerationes modestae et pacificae controversarium de Justificatione, Purgatorio, Invocatione Sanctorum, Christo Mediatore et Eucharistia*, published posthumously in 1658. It shows Forbes as a strong High Churchman, keen on reconciliation with Rome and zealous for episcopacy. In his treatment of the *Eucharist he defended

O.D.C.C.–S

a doctrine of the Real Presence; and though he criticized the doctrine of *Transubstantiation, he denied that it was heretical. He also held that the Eucharist was a propitiatory sacrifice.

The *Considerationes Modestae* were reissued, with an Eng. trans., by G. H. *Forbes in the Lib. of Ang.-Cath. Theol., 2 vols., 1850–6.

FORGED DECRETALS. See *False Decretals*.

FORM (Gk. μορφή). The concept of form played an important part in Greek philosophy. In *Aristotle it was the unchanging element in an object, considered apart from the changing manifestations of the things of sense-experience. The notion of form was transmitted to the Middle Ages by St. *Augustine. In Scholastic philosophy it was the intrinsic determining principle of things, that is, the 'nature' of things by which they are what they are.

Medieval thinkers distinguished several kinds of 'forms', the more important being (1) 'substantial forms', which are the principles determining prime matter to a particular nature, e.g. man or horse; (2) 'accidental forms,' which determine substances to some accidental mode of being, e.g. whiteness or greatness; (3) 'separated forms', which exist apart from matter, thus the angels and human souls after death. Acc. to St. *Thomas Aquinas there can be only one substantial form for every being, whereas the Franciscan school admits several. The concept of the substantial form was used in the question of the relations between soul and body. Acc. to the Thomist teaching, approved by the Council of *Vienne in 1312 and the Fifth *Lateran Council in 1513, the rational soul is the form of the human body which gives it its human condition. The notions of form and matter were also employed in connexion with the theology of the Sacraments. The form was held to consist of the words which give significance to the sacramental use to which the matter was being put. Thus in Baptism the matter of the Sacrament was water, whereas its form consisted of the Trinitarian formula employed.

In modern philosophy the conception of form is esp. applied to the order of thought, in so far as it is held to rest on the subjective structure of the human mind. I. *Kant distinguishes between the two forms of perception (*Anschauungsformen*), viz. space and time, and the forms of thought (*Verstandesformen*) arranged in 12 'categories' of unity, plurality, totality, &c., which are valid *a priori*. See also foll. entry.

FORMALISM. The word is used in religious contexts in at least three senses. (1) Undue insistence on the outward observances of religion or the prescriptions of a moral code, with a corresponding neglect of the inner spirit or significance which the 'forms' were designed to safeguard.

(2) In the 17th cent. the word was used of readiness to support the religious body or party in power at the moment, i.e. for religious time-serving. This sense is now obsolete.

(3) Of theories of ethics which look for the ground of moral action in the form of the moral law alone (e.g. in the '*Categorical Imperative' of I. *Kant), without reference to any specific purposes or values which it is desired through the action to achieve or realize. An elaborate criticism of the Kantian form of this doctrine is contained in Max Scheler's *Der Formalismus in der Ethik und die materiale Wertethik* (1913–16).

FORMAL SIN. A sinful act which is both in itself wrong and known by the person committing it to be wrong. See also *Material Sin*.

FORM-CRITICISM (Germ. *Formgeschichte*). As applied esp. to the Bible, the attempt to trace the *provenance* and assess the historicity of particular passages by a close analysis of their structural forms. The success of the method depends largely on the assumption that the same forms recur in non-Biblical literature, e.g. in the *Rabbinic traditions and in Hellenistic folklore. The method was first applied by H. *Gunkel to the OT narratives of Gen., but its most notable use has been upon the oral traditions behind the *Synoptic Gospels. J. *Weiss pointed the way in his article in *Religion in Geschichte und Gegenwart* (ed. 1, 1912), and in 1919 M. *Dibelius published his analysis of the Gospels into various literary forms, assigning them to preachers, teachers, and narrators, and assuming that the earliest original form to which we can get back is the short sermon, such as we find it in Acts. A little later, R. *Bultmann (1921) produced a still more sceptical analysis, while M. Albertz (1921) argued that the Gospel discourses were in part modified by early 'community debates', and G. Bertram (1922) that the form even of the narratives of Christ's Passion (which most of the Form-critics regard as much more primitive than the rest of the Gospels) was influenced by the liturgical needs and practices of the early Church.

Form-criticism entails three distinct processes: (1) the analysis of the Gospel material into the separate units, of each of which the form is held to have been gradually fixed in the process of transmission from mouth to mouth; (2) the recovery of the earlier history of these forms; and (3) the ascertainment of the historical setting which determined the various forms. The main classes of form which emerge are: (i) *Pronouncement Stories* (called by M. Dibelius '*Paradigms', i.e. models for preachers). Short stories culminating in an Apophthegm or Logion of Jesus, such as the Tribute Money (Mk. 12. 13–17). (ii) *Miracle Stories* or *Novellen*. These contain more elaborate descriptions of the circumstances, the actual miracle, and its effects. (iii) *Sayings*. Bultmann divides these (more acc. to their content than acc. to their form) into Logia or Maxims,

Prophetic and Apocalyptic Sayings, Legalistic Dicta, Sayings in the First Person (a crossdivision), and *Parables. (iv) *Myths* and *Legends*, such as the *Baptism and *Transfiguration of Christ. Bultmann even includes among these the Entry into Jerusalem and the Passion and Resurrection Narratives.

C. F. *Burney, *The Poetry of our Lord* (1925); B. S. Easton, *The Gospel before the Gospels* (1928); T. W. Manson, *The Teaching of Jesus*, ch. 3 (1931); V. Taylor, *The Formation of the Gospel Tradition* (1933); M. Dibelius, *From Tradition to Gospel* (Eng. trans., 1934); R. H. Lightfoot, *History and Interpretation in the Gospels* (1935); C. H. *Dodd, *The Parables of the Kingdom* (1935); id., *History and the Gospel* (1938); H. Riesenfeld, *The Gospel Tradition and its Beginnings* (lecture; 1957).

FORMOSUS (*c.* 816–96), Pope from 891. He became Cardinal-Bp. of Porto in 864, and was employed by successive Popes on several diplomatic missions. As Pope he showed great intransigence towards the E. Church, refusing, e.g., to accept as priests those ordained by the Patr. *Photius. After his death the party opposed to him in Imperial politics charged him with usurpation of the Holy See, and a synod convened by Pope Stephen VI (896–7) in Jan. 897 exhumed, stripped, and mutilated his body, and declared him deposed. Succeeding Popes, however, reversed the decisions of this synod.

His Letters (8) in J. P. Migne, *PL*, cxxix, 837–48; crit. ed. of four letters by G. Laehr in *M.G.H.*, Epistulae VII (1928), pp. 366–70. Hefele–Leclercq, iv (2; 1911), pp. 708–719, with bibl. Fliche–Martin, vii (1940), pp. 20–6, 113 f. F. Vernet in *D.T.C.*, vi (1920), cols. 594–9, also with bibl.

FORMULA MISSAE ET COMMUNIONIS. The reformed Communion Service, prepared for N. Hausmann, Pastor of Zwickau, which M. *Luther put out in Dec. 1523. The Latin language was kept, and up to the Creed the traditional form of the Roman Mass was scarcely altered. The 'Mass of the *Faithful', however, underwent drastic revision. The *Offertory was made into a mere preparation of the elements, without any prayers; the Words of *Institution were included in the *Preface; then followed immediately the singing of the *Sanctus and the '*Benedictus qui venit', during which the *Elevation took place; and the rest of the *Canon was omitted altogether. During the giving of Communion, which was to be in both kinds, the *Agnus Dei was sung. The purpose of this unprecedented arrangement was to avoid any suggestion of the doctrine of the Eucharistic sacrifice. The form of service, moreover, was intended only to give general guidance to the celebrant, who was left free to modify it as he wished. It was upon this rite that Luther's 'German Mass' of 1526 and the majority of the later Lutheran liturgies were modelled.

Text ed. H. *Lietzmann in his Kleine Texte für theologische und philologische Vorlesungen und Übungen, No. 36 (Bonn, 1909). A. L. Richter, *Die evangelischen Kirchenordnungen des sechszehnten Jahrhunderts*, i (1846), pp. 1–17, incl. text, pp. 2–7. Text and further reff. in E. Sehling, *Die evangelischen Kirchenordnungen des XVI. Jahrhunderts*, i (pt. 1; 1902), pp. 3–9. Extracts in Kidd, pp. 127–32 (No. 66). F. E. *Brightman, *The English Rite*, i (1915), pp. xxxi f.

FORMULA OF CONCORD. See *Concord, Formula of.*

FORSYTH, PETER TAYLOR (1848–1921), British *Congregationalist divine. After holding pastorates in five towns, he became principal of Hackney College, Hampstead, in 1901. In early life he was a liberal in theology, largely through the influence of G. W. F. *Hegel and A. *Ritschl; but he later radically modified his attitude to liberalism through a deep sense of need of Atonement through the Cross. By the freshness of his approach to the fact of Redemption, combined with a study of all recent work on the subject, he gave a new significance to such words as 'substitution', 'penalty', and 'satisfaction'. If his many published writings did not pretend to scholarship in the narrower sense, they were full of penetrating discussions. They include *The Cruciality of the Cross* (1909); *The Person and Place of Jesus Christ* (1909), in which a form of *kenoticism is linked with a doctrine of progressive Incarnation; *The Work of Christ* (1910), where it is argued that, in the Atonement, God is both reconciler and reconciled; *The Christian Ethic of War* (1916); *The Justification of God* (1916); and *The Soul of Prayer* (1916).

Selections from his practical writings, ed. H. Escott, *Peter Taylor Forsyth (1848–1921), Director of Souls* (1948), with biog. and bibl. notes, pp. xvii–xx, and 'An Appraisement', pp. 3–33. Memoir by Jessie Forsyth Andrews (daughter) prefixed to ed. 2 of his *Work of Christ* (1938), pp. vii–xxviii. G. O. Griffith, *The Theology of P. T. Forsyth* (1948); W. L. Bradley, *P. T. Forsyth. The Man and his Work* (1925).

FORTESCUE, ADRIAN (1874–1923), writer on liturgical and historical subjects. Educated at the Scots College at Rome (1891–4) and at Innsbruck university (1894–9), he was ordained priest in 1898. After serving several parishes and missions in England he became the RC parish priest at Letchworth in 1907, where he built a church which he made a centre of liturgical life. Apart from his pastoral work he devoted himself to writing on a variety of subjects, esp. on Liturgy and on the E. Churches. *The Orthodox Eastern Church* (1907), *The Lesser Eastern Churches* (1913), and *The Uniate Eastern Churches* (1923) all cover a wide range of historical material. *The Mass* (1912) is a useful summary of modern studies in the Roman rite. *The Ceremonies of the Roman Rite* (1918; ed. 3, revised by J. B. O'Connell, 1930) is a serviceable and widely used directory of modern ceremonial practice.

J. G. Vance–J. W. Fortescue (distant cousin), *Adrian Fortescue. A Memoir* (1924), with list of main works, p. 61 f. H. *Leclercq, O.S.B., in *D.A.C.L.*, ix (pt. ii; 1930), col. 1739, s.v. 'Liturgistes' (critical).

FORTUNATUS, VENANTIUS. See *Venantius Fortunatus.*

FORTY HOURS' DEVOTION (also known as the **Quarant' Ore** or **Quarantore**). A modern Catholic devotion in which the Blessed Sacrament is exposed (see *Exposition*) for a period of *c.* forty hours, and the faithful pray before it by turns throughout this time. A solemn High Mass, with Procession of the Sacrament, opens and closes the devotion, and a solemn Mass for peace is sung on the intervening day. In its present form this devotion began in Italy in the 16th cent. The period of forty hours was probably fixed as that during which Christ's body rested in the tomb. The *Codex Iuris Canonici* (can. 1275) orders the devotion to be held annually in all RC churches where the Blessed Sacrament is habitually reserved.

H. Thurston, S.J., *Lent and Holy Week.* Chapters on Catholic Observance and Ritual (1904), pp. 114–48, incl. bibl. notes.

FORTY MARTYRS OF SEBASTE. See *Sebaste, Forty Martyrs of.*

FORTY-TWO ARTICLES. The collection of Anglican doctrinal formulae which were issued in 1553. They were accompanied by a Royal Mandate, dated 19 June 1553, requiring all clergy, schoolmasters, and members of the universities on taking their degrees, to subscribe to them. They were, for the most part, drafted by T. *Cranmer, and not later than the spring of 1552. It is very doubtful, despite the assertion on their title that they had been 'agreed on by the bishops and other learned men in the Synod at London, in the year of our Lord God MDLII', whether they ever received the authority of *Convocation. Owing to the restoration of the RC faith under Mary (1553–8), they were never enforced, but they formed the basis of the later *Thirty-Nine Articles.

The text (both Latin and English) is printed in E. C. S. Gibson, *The Thirty-Nine Articles of the Church of England* (1896–7), at the end of the 'Introduction'.

FORUM (Lat. 'place of public assembly', hence 'judicial tribunal'). In *moral theology the term is applied to the exercise by the Church of her judicial power. A distinction is made between the 'internal forum', where, esp. in the Sacrament of *Penance, judgement is given on matters which relate to the spiritual good of the individual, and the 'external forum', e.g. the ecclesiastical courts, where the public good of the Church and her members is in question. The term 'forum of conscience' (*forum conscientiae*) is also used of the decisive authority of conscience over every individual soul.

FOSDICK, HARRY EMERSON (1878–), American divine. He was ordained to the *Baptist ministry in 1903. From 1904 to 1915 he was pastor at Montclair, N.J., and from 1908 also taught homiletics at the *Union Theological Seminary, New York. In 1918 he was called to a *Presbyterian pulpit, but owing to *fundamentalist pressure requiring his acceptance of traditional Presbyterian standards of doctrine, he withdrew in 1925. From 1926 to 1946 he was minister of the Riverside Baptist Church, New York. Latterly his approach to dogma has been more positive. He has written many books from the evangelical liberal point of view, among them *The Manhood of the Master* (1913), *The Meaning of Prayer* (1915), *The Modern Use of the Bible* (1924), *A Pilgrimage to Palestine* (1928), *Successful Christian Living* (1937), *Living under Tension* (1941), and *A Faith for Tough Times* (1952).

Autobiography (London, 1957).

FOSSORS (Lat. *fossores* or *fossarii*, from *fodere*, 'to dig'), grave-diggers. In very early Christian times they were regarded as inferior clergy, and in the latter part of the 4th and earlier part of the 5th cents. became powerful corporations, with the management of the *catacombs in their hands. They had power to sell grave-spaces, and numerous inscriptions survive in which such sales are recorded. Included in their corporations were the artists who adorned Christian tombs. Burial in the catacombs at Rome becoming impossible after the fall of the city in 410, the inscriptions of the *fossores* virtually cease, but a chronicle as late as the 6th cent. includes them among the *clerici*. They were also called *lecticarii* from their habit of carrying the corpse on a *lectica* ('bier'), as well as *copiatae* (probably from the Gk. κόπος, 'labour').

F. Wieland, *Die genetische Entwicklung der sog. Ordines Minores in den drei ersten Jahrhunderten* (*R.Q.*, Supplementheft vii; 1897), pp. 57–60 and 163–5. J. Wilpert, *Malereien der Katakomben Roms* (1903), pp. 520–3, with reff. to plates. H. *Leclercq, O.S.B., in *D.A.C.L.*, v (pt. 2; 1923), cols. 2065–92, s.v. 'Fossoyeurs', with reff.

FOUCAULD, CHARLES DE. See *De Foucauld, Charles*.

'FOUNDATIONS'. A theological symposium, published in 1912. It professed to be a 'statement of Christian belief in terms of modern thought', and consisted of nine essays, with an introduction by B. H. *Streeter. The contributors, who were all Oxford men, were, in addition to Streeter, N. S. Talbot, R. Brook, A. E. J. Rawlinson, R. G. Parsons, W. *Temple, and W. H. Moberly. The book marked a definite stage in current theological debate and it exercised much immediate influence, but its optimistic liberalism and immanentist standpoint proved increasingly unacceptable in succeeding decades. On its publication the book created much controversy, notably over some of Streeter's conclusions in his essay on the Historic Christ.

See the contemporary religious journals. R. A. Knox, *Absolute and Abitofhell* (1912; reprinted in *Essays in Satire*. 1928), is a brilliant satire 'in the manner of Mr. John Dryden'. Cf. also R. A. Knox, *Some Loose Stones* (1913). F. A. Iremonger, *William Temple* (1948), ch. ix. (pp. 155–66).

FOUNTAINS ABBEY. A *Cistercian abbey, three miles southwest of Ripon, which was founded from *York in 1132. The numbers

of the community increased so rapidly that within twenty years they were able to found eight daughter-houses. At the Reformation the monastery was surrendered to the crown by Abbot M. Bradley, on 26 Nov. 1539. Of the present ruins the most conspicuous structure is the great tower, built by Abbot Huby *c.* 1500, a splendid example of Perpendicular work.

Main primary material in J. R. Walbran (ed.), *Memorials of the Abbey of St. Mary of Fountains* (Surtees Society, xlii and lxvii, 1863–78). W. H. St. John Hope, 'Fountains Abbey', in *The Yorkshire Archaeological Journal*, xv (1900), pp. 269–402. G. Hodges, *Fountains Abbey*. The Story of a Medieval Monastery (1904). J. Solloway in *The Victoria History of the County of York*, iii (1913), pp. 134–8.

FOUR CAUSES, The. Acc. to *Aristotle, there are four kinds of cause, viz. 'material' (that of which a thing is made), 'formal' (what a thing is, i.e. the genus, species, &c., which distinguishes it from other things), 'efficient' (the effective or motive force which brings it into being), and 'final' (the end or purpose of its existence). St. *Thomas Aquinas, who attempted to set the Aristotelian philosophy in a Christian context, refers the second, third, and fourth causes directly to God, Who is at once the origin of the separate and individual being of everything, the effective creative force, and the reason and end of the being of all that exists (*Summa Th.* 1. 44).

FOUR CROWNED MARTYRS. See *Quattro Coronati*.

FOUR GALLICAN ARTICLES. See *Gallican Articles*.

FOURTEEN HELPERS IN NEED, The. See *Auxiliary Saints, The*.

FOX, GEORGE (1624–91), founder of the Society of *Friends (q.v.). He was born at Fenny Drayton in Leicestershire, where his father was a weaver, and apprenticed to a shoemaker. In 1643 he felt the call to give up all ties of family and friendship and spent the next years travelling in search of enlightenment. In 1646, after long interior struggles, he won moral victory in reliance on the *Inner Light of the living Christ. Henceforward he abandoned attendance at church and in 1647 he began to preach, teaching that truth is to be found in the inner voice of God speaking to the soul. He was frequently imprisoned, first at Nottingham in 1649, but his enthusiasm and moral earnestness soon attracted followers ('Friends of the Truth') whom he formed into a stable organization. In 1652 he made his home at Swarthmore Hall, near Ulverstone, which was the house of Thomas Fell, Vice-Chancellor of the Duchy of Lancaster, whose widow Margaret (1614–1702) he married in 1669. In 1656 he was confined for eight months in Launceston gaol. To promote the growth of the Society of Friends he undertook frequent missionary journeys—to Ireland in 1669, to the West Indies and N. America 1671–2, and to Holland in 1677 and 1684. He was a magnetic personality of great spiritual power, selfless devotion, and patience in persecution, and of remarkable organizing abilities. He died on 13 Jan. 1691. His famous *Journal* was first published posthumously in 1694.

Complete ed. of *Journal* by Norman Penney (1911); *Short Journal and Itinerary of George Fox*, also by N. Penney (1925). A collected edition of his writings (incomplete) was issued at Philadelphia, 1852. T. Hodgkin, *George Fox* (1896); A. N. Brayshaw, *The Personality of George Fox* (1919); H. J. Cadbury, *George Fox's Book of Miracles* (1948). Good ed. of his *Journal* for general readers by J. L. Nickalls (Cambridge, 1952). A. Gordon in *D.N.B.*, xix (1889), pp. 117–22.

FOXE, JOHN (1516–87), martyrologist. He went to *Oxford at an early age, and was Fellow of Magdalen from 1539 to 1545. On the accession of Queen *Mary he fled to the Continent, and stayed successively at Strassburg, Frankfurt, and Basle, where he met other Protestant refugees, notably J. *Knox and E. *Grindal. At this period he wrote a history of the Christian persecutions, first issued in Latin at Strassburg in 1554. An expanded English edition appeared in 1563 as the *Acts and Monuments of matters happening in the Church*, commonly known as 'Foxe's Book of Martyrs'. The book, which was approved and officially publicized by the bishops, went through four editions in Foxe's lifetime. Its chief object was to extol the heroism and endurance of the Protestant martyrs of Mary's reign. Its homely style, combined with its vivid descriptions of the sufferings imposed on the victims of Papist tyranny, gained it great popularity. As a work of history, its value is impaired by its author's credulity and bitterness. In 1559 Foxe had returned to England, and in 1560 was ordained by Grindal, Bp. of London. Though he subsequently received a prebendal stall at both *Salisbury and *Durham, he lived mainly in London. His rigidly *Calvinist views probably stood between him and higher preferment.

Earliest Life, pr. in English and Latin in vol. ii of the 1641 ed. of his *Acts and Monuments* (no pagination); it professes to be the work of his son. *Acts and Monuments*, ed. by G. Townsend (8 vols., 1843–9), contains a further life (i, pp. 1–160) and a defence of the veracity of the work (pp. 161–236). A more accurate Memoir, by J. Pratt (The Church Historians of England, Reformation Period, i, 1870). J. F. Mozley, *John Foxe and his Book* (1940). S. L. Lee in *D.N.B.*, xix (1889), pp. 141–50.

FOXE, RICHARD (?1448–1528), Bp. of *Winchester and founder of Corpus Christi College, *Oxford. He appears to have been educated at Magdalen College, Oxford. After Henry VII's accession (1485), as a reward for earlier services, he was appointed bishop successively of *Exeter (1487), *Bath and Wells (1492), *Durham (1494), and Winchester (1501), preferments intended primarily to provide him with financial means while engaged in important diplomatic work. Under *Henry VIII (1509–47) he at first retained his ascendancy but from 1511 onwards was gradually superseded by T. *Wolsey. Only in the later years of his life did he seriously

concern himself with his episcopal duties. His sympathies for the New Learning found expression in his foundation of Corpus Christi College, at Oxford, in 1515–16.

The Register of Richard Fox while Bishop of Bath and Wells, A.D. MCCCCXCII–MCCCCXCIV, ed. by E. C. Batten (1889), incl. life (pp. 1–142); part of this Register is ed. with that of Robert Stillington by H. C. Maxwell-Lyte (Somerset Record Society, lii, 1937), pp. 174–200; *The Register of Richard Fox Lord Bishop of Durham 1494–1501*, ed. by M. P. Howden (Surtees Society, cxlvii, 1932). *Letters of Richard Fox, 1486–1527*, ed. by P. S. and H. M. Allen (1929). T. Fowler in *D.N.B.*, xix (1889), pp. 150–6.

FRA ANGELICO, FRA BARTOLOMMEO. See *Angelico* (Fra), *Bartolommeo* (Fra).

FRACTION. The formal breaking of the bread which in all Eucharistic liturgies takes place before the Communion. It goes back to Christ's action at the original institution (Mt. 26. 26 and par.) and was a sufficiently striking element in the primitive rite to make the 'breaking of bread' (Acts 2. 42; cf. 20. 7) a regular name for the Eucharist.

The precise moment of the Fraction varies. In the Roman rite it takes place after the Lord's Prayer in the *Canon, where the rubrics require the Host to be divided into three parts and one of them to be dropped into the chalice (the 'commixture'). In other rites the Fraction is much more elaborate. Thus in the *Mozarabic Rite the Host is divided into nine portions, seven of which are then arranged in the form of a cross. A rubric in the 1662 BCP orders the breaking of the bread immediately before it is consecrated. At the time of the Fraction, the Koinonikon is sung in the Byzantine Liturgy, the Confractorium in the Ambrosian, and the *Agnus Dei in the Roman rite.

'Fractio Panis' as a title is used of the early 2nd cent. fresco which perhaps depicts an early Eucharist in the Capella Greca in the *Catacomb of St. Priscilla, uncovered by J. Wilpert in 1893.

L. *Duchesne, *Origines du culte chrétien* (1889), pp. 62, 79 f., 175–7, 208–12 (Eng. tr., 1903, pp. 63, 85, 184–6, 218–22). T. Schermann, 'Das "Brotbrechen" im Urchristentum' in *Biblische Zeitschrift*, viii (1910), pp. 33–52 and 162–83. B. *Capelle, O.S.B., 'Le Rite de la fraction dans la messe romaine' in *R. Bén.*, liii (1941), pp. 5–40. W. E. Scudmore in *D.C.A.*, i (1875), pp. 686–9, s.v.; F. *Cabrol, O.S.B., in *D.A.C.L.*, v (pt. 2; 1923), cols. 2103–16, s.v. 'Fractio Panis'.

On the fresco mentioned above, cf. J. Wilpert, *Fractio Panis. Die älteste Darstellung des Eucharistischen Opfers in der 'Cappella Greca'* (1895).

FRANCE, Christianity in. It is uncertain when Christianity first reached Roman Gaul, but in 177 there was a Christian community at Lyons, which in that year suffered persecution and the loss of its bishop, Pothinus, who had been a disciple of St. *Polycarp. This fact, in conjunction with Gallic differences from Roman usage in later times, suggests that Gallic Christianity may have come from Asia Minor. The name of *Irenaeus of Lyons (*c.* 130–*c.* 200), apologist and theologian, was famous all over Christendom. The synod of the W. Church held at *Arles in 314 marks the importance of Christian Gaul at that time. Gaul was much troubled in turn by the heresies of *Novatianism, *Arianism, *Priscillianism, and *Semi-Pelagianism. From the end of the 4th cent. the country produced some of the most illustrious of the saints. Such were St. *Martin (c. 330–97), famous as a missionary and as the first organizer of Gallic monasticism, which he adapted from the Egyptian model; St. *Hilary of Poitiers (c. 315–c. 367), the great anti-Arian theologian; St. *Paulinus of Nola (353–431), a native of Bordeaux, scholar and poet; and St. *Germanus of Auxerre (c. 380–448), who reorganized the British Church. The christianization of the rural districts was still incomplete when the country was overrun first by the Visigoths, who were Arians, and then by the Franks, who were pagans, but whose king, *Clovis, was baptized as a Catholic Christian in 496. In the times of invasion, the bishops of Gaul were intermediaries between the old order and the new, and made the change easier for the people. The Church of Gaul was in those days individual in its usages, and looked to Milan rather than Rome for direction, and even later to Rome by way of Milan. A famous convert to Christianity in this period was *Sidonius Apollinaris (c. 430–c. 480), the last poet and writer in the dying classical tradition.

By c. 500 Gaul had been entirely divided up into dioceses. The first missions, in the 2nd cent., had centred in Lyons, which has retained the rank of the primatial see of France. But by 250 there appear to have been seven sees in existence, while at the Synod of Arles fourteen Gallic bishops attended. From the 4th to the 7th cents. frequent councils were held in Gaul, the canons of which were embodied in the later classical collections.

Under Frankish rule the country was troubled by perpetual dynastic quarrels, and the history of the Church is obscure. Individual names stand out, like that of the historian *Gregory of Tours (d. 594), and there is evidence of missionary activity beyond the borders of the Frankish kingdoms. Liturgical developments during this period suggest gradual assimilation, though never complete, to Roman usage. In 751 the Pope gave consent to the formal assumption by the Carolingian house of the throne they had virtually occupied for generations, and *Pepin the Short (d. 768) was crowned by the Papal envoy in 752, and by the Pope himself in 754. Pepin and his son, *Charlemagne (d. 814), built up the Holy Roman Empire, and Charlemagne was crowned unexpectedly by the Pope in 800. Disliking the suggestion that his power depended on the Papacy, he crowned his son Louis himself. Charlemagne, perhaps consciously, set out to bring St. *Augustine's 'City of God' into being, and looked upon his empire as the means for doing God's Will on earth, and with this spiritual conception would allow no higher administrative authority in the Papacy. But by 843 the empire was divided

into three parts, and this date may be taken as the beginning of the modern kingdom of France. It was the ecclesiastic, *Hincmar (806–82), Abp. of Reims, who was largely responsible for the settlement. By the 11th cent. there were no less than 55 virtually independent feudal provinces in the old Frankish kingdom; but among these the dukes of Francia had soon taken the lead, and, supported by the Church, Hugh Capet was in 987 enthroned to replace the ineffective Carolingians.

Under the new dynasty the influence of the Church upon the affairs of state was such as it has never attained either before or since. The German ideal of knighthood was transformed and christianized, and in France during this period is seen at its best. Several of the reforming Popes, including *Gregory VII himself, were Frenchmen. The new religious orders, which were to reform and revive monasticism, had their beginning in the Congregation of *Cluny, founded in 910. In the 12th cent. Louis VI and VII, while avoiding the royal absolutism of Henry II of England, joined with the Church to break the power of the feudal lords, and to assure to the towns their charters of freedom. This was the age of the great writers and theologians St. *Anselm (c. 1033–1109), Peter *Abelard (1079–1142), and St. *Bernard of Clairvaux (1090–1153). It was largely through the great part that France played under St. Bernard's influence in the early Crusades that the Latin Westerns were always known in the Near East as Franks, and the Christians of those lands still look to France as their protector. The alliance of Church and state reached its highest point in the reign of St. *Louis IX (reigned 1226–70). In the 13th cent. Gothic art was born in France and spread all over the W. world, while the foundation of the University of *Paris between 1208 and 1213 made France the centre of the rebirth of learning in the *Scholastic Movement.

Philip the Fair (reigned 1285–1314) continued the policy of reducing the power of the feudal lords, but in virtue of his theory of *Divine right of kings claimed also to override the Papal power. The election to the Papacy in 1305 of *Clement V, who was his nominee, together with the removal of the Papal court to *Avignon, within French dominion, was a significant reply to the unprecedented claims made for the Papal power by *Boniface VIII in 1300. The Hundred Years War, however, marked a rapid decline of French power, and from the Treaty of Troyes (1420) the whole of France was under English rule. But sudden and almost miraculous deliverance began in 1429 with the victories of St. *Joan of Arc (1412–31). In popular sentiment French nationalism again seemed almost identified with the cause of Christianity, and the custom of addressing French kings as *Rex Christianissimus*, which began about a hundred years earlier, became the fixed practice of the Popes from 1464. The Conciliar Movement of the 15th cent., which upheld the rights of bishops and councils against the Papacy, was strongly supported in France, but opposed by Charles VII (reigned 1422–61).

The growing power of France about 1500 was skilfully diverted from troubling the Papacy (at a time when France might easily have headed the *Reformation Movement) by the wise concessions of *Leo X in the Concordat of 1516, when he admitted the right of the King to nominate to all benefices in France, and by thus surrendering Church temporalities removed any financial interest Francis I might have had in a change of religion, even though military necessities forced him into Protestant alliances. It is remarkable, however, that the decrees of the Council of *Trent were not accepted or published in France.

*Lutheranism was the first Protestant faith to appear in France, but its supporters were few, and it was almost tolerated. *Calvinism, however, became much more widely spread, and ruthless persecution of its adherents began in 1547. In spite of this, by 1561 there were 2,000 Calvinist churches in France, and the Calvinists had already become a political faction and seemed a danger to the state. In the ensuing war both sides had help from abroad. In the adoption of the RC faith by *Henry IV in 1593, the Catholic faction secured its final triumph, but it is significant that toleration was given to their opponents by the Edict of *Nantes in 1598, a toleration which they employed to form a virtual *imperium in imperio*. Under Louis XIV (reigned 1643–1715) all restrictions consistent with the letter of the Edict of Nantes were reimposed, and finally in 1685 the Edict itself was repealed. See also *Huguenots*.

Louis XIV had absolutist conceptions of his own power, and his desire to remove the French Church from the immediate control of Rome and make it dependent upon himself took effect in his inducing the French clergy to publish the four *Gallican Articles of 1682. By this time the *Counter-Reformation had made itself felt in France, especially in the lives of such men as St. *Francis de Sales (1567–1622) and St. *Vincent de Paul (c. 1580–1660). The 17th cent. is also famous for the great theologians and teachers J. B. *Bossuet (1627–1704) and F. de *Fénelon (1651–1715). But there was also a very widespread trend towards *Quietism and *Jansenism. The measures of repression brought to bear upon Jansenism by the Papacy were supported by Louis at the end of his reign, and even more strongly by the regents for Louis XV (reigned 1715–74), although the Jansenists were strongly *Gallican, esp. after the bull '*Unigenitus' (1713) which condemned them. This bull was largely the work of *Jesuit influence, for the Jesuits had flourished in France in the 17th cent. and were at the height of their power under Louis XV. Meanwhile the French Empire was rapidly growing, and missionary work on a great scale was being undertaken both within French territory and far beyond it, especially in the Near and Far East.

France had a part in the moral decadence and religious unbelief of the 18th cent., and the Church had no one of equal brilliance to oppose to such men as *Voltaire and *Rousseau. Nor was French Protestantism more than a shattered remnant; the revocation of the Edict of Nantes and the suppression of the *Camisard rebellion of 1703–5 had crushed what little life remained, so that the granting of toleration to Protestants in 1787 made little difference to the nation at large.

No direct attack was made upon Christianity or the Church in the first outbreak of the Revolution of 1789, though disendowment of Church property was considered a necessary part of the suppression of feudalism, and a state grant to the Church was substituted. The *Civil Constitution of the Clergy (1790) aimed at reducing Papal control of the clergy and increasing that of metropolitans, and at giving the civil electorate the chief voice in the appointment of bishops and parish clergy. Most of the clergy obeyed the order of *Pius VI to refuse the oath to this constitution, and they suffered a measure of repression through the period of the Revolution and the Directory; but the rest of the clergy, who were known as the 'Constitutionalists', remained secure in their benefices throughout, though not always safe from mob violence or from the attentions of the avowedly atheistic section of the Revolutionary Government. Under the Directory of 1795–9 the clergy were required to swear hatred of royalty and anarchy, but were otherwise unmolested.

The *Concordat of 1801 between Napoleon and *Pius VII replaced the Constitutionalists by the exiles, and virtually restored the powers of the RC Church, though Napoleon acted on the assumption that the Concordat included the *Gallican Articles of 1682, an assumption denied by the Pope. The tyranny of Napoleon in ecclesiastical matters and his personal conduct towards Pius VII, however, were the most effective guarantee of popular reaction against *Gallicanism in France, and the temper of the country at the Bourbon restoration was ready for the growth of that *Ultramontanism which achieved at least a partial triumph at the *Vatican Council of 1870. Meanwhile the years following 1801 saw the founding of numerous fresh religious orders at home, and the intensification of missionary activity to all parts of the world. The names of '*Lourdes' and the '*Curé d'Ars' (qq.v.) are indicative of a widespread growth in personal piety.

The various political changes in France during the 19th cent. did not disturb the position of the RC Church; but meanwhile French Calvinism revived in some measure, though in 1872 there came a threefold split between orthodox, moderates, and liberals which weakened it considerably.

Towards the end of the century various acts were passed to weaken the influence of the Church, the most significant being the Education Act of 1882 which completely secularized primary education, and subsequent acts which placed restrictions on religious teaching in secondary education. In 1904 a series of quarrels between the French Government and the Holy See, combined with a growing anti-religious feeling in the country, prompted the entire severance of Church and state which took place in 1905. The state grant to the Church ceased, and all recognition of the Church as an institution ceased with it. No distinction was now made between clergy and others in liability to military service; and no pious bequests, except to individuals, were legally valid, because the Church no longer had a legal personality. On the other hand, Catholics and Protestants alike had their rights of assembly as private persons guaranteed by the state.

In recent times the Church in France has shown abundance of life and spiritual power which disestablishment has increased rather than weakened. In devotion, popular fervour is great; in theology and philosophy, and in social, political, and economic theory and practice, the ecclesiastics and thinkers of the French Church are pre-eminent in Christendom. On the other hand, the masses of the French people have been largely alienated from the Church, and Communist teaching has led to active hostility in many parts. The various youth movements and gallant attempts such as the institution of 'priest-workmen' have sought to deal with this situation and met with undoubted success where they have been able to make their influence felt. But a great problem confronts the Church of which as yet only the fringe has been touched.

A large mass of documentary material is contained in *Gallia Christiana (q.v.). Much information on the history of the Church will be found in all histories of France, e.g. E. Lavisse, Histoire de France depuis les origines jusqu'à la Révolution (9 vols., 1900–11); id., Histoire de France contemporaine, depuis la Révolution jusqu'à la paix de 1919 (10 vols., 1920–22),both with detailed bibll. [R. F. W.] Guettée, Histoire de l'Église de France (12 vols., 1847–56). R. T. Smith, The Church in France [1894]. G. Goyau, Histoire religieuse de la France (1922; new ed., with continuation by G. Hanotaux, 1942). C. Poulet, O.S.B., Histoire de l'Église de France (3 vols., 1944), with good bibl. E. Le Blant, Inscriptions chrétiennes de la Gaule antérieures au VIIIe siècle (2 vols., 1856–65). L. *Duchesne, Fastes épiscopaux de l'ancienne France (3 vols., 1894–1915). T. Scott Holmes, The Origin and Development of the Christian Church in Gaul during the First Six Centuries of the Christian Era (Birkbeck Lectures for 1907 and 1908; 1911). R. Génestal, Le Privilegium Fori en France du décret de Gratien à la fin du XIVe siècle (Bibliothèque des Écoles des Hautes Études. Sciences Religieuses, xxxv and xxxix; 1921–4). J. Rivière, Le Problème de l'Église et de l'état au temps de Philippe le Bel (S.S.L., viii; 1926). N. Valois, La France et le grand schisme d'occident (4 vols., 1896–1902). W. H. Jervis, The Gallican Church. A History of the Church of France from the Concordat of Bologna, A.D. 1516, to the Revolution (1872). [P. G. J. M.] Imbart de La Tour, Les Origines de la réforme (4 vols., 1905–35). A. A. Tilley, 'The Reformation in France' in C.M.H., ii (1903), pp. 280–304. F. Roquain, La France et Rome pendant les guerres de religion (1924). L. N. Prunel, La Renaissance catholique en France au XVIIe siècle (1921). Viscount St. Cyres, 'The Gallican Church' in C.M.H., v (1908), pp. 72–91, with bibl., pp. 780–5. W. H. Jervis, The Gallican Church and the Revolution (1882). C. S. Phillips, The Church in France, 1789–1848. A Study in Revival (1929); id., The Church in France, 1848–1907 (C.H.S. publications, N.S., No. 19; 1936); W. J. Sparrow Simpson, French Catholics in the Nineteenth Century (1918). A. Debidour, Histoire des rapports de l'Église et de l'état en France de 1789 à 1870 (1898); id., L'Église catholique et l'état sous la Troisième République (2 vols., 1906–9). P. de la Gorce, Histoire religieuse de la Révolution française (5 vols., 1909–23). A. Dansette, Histoire religieuse de la France contemporaine (2 vols., 1948–51). A. Aulard, Le Christianisme et la Révolution française (1925; Eng. tr., 1927). A. Sicard, L'Ancien Clergé de France (3 vols., 1893–1903). G. Constant, L'Église de France sous le consulat et l'empire, 1800–1814 (1928). E. Lecanuet, Cong. Orat., L'Église de France sous la Troisième République (2 vols., 1907–10). E. Barbier, Histoire du catholicisme libéral et du catholicisme social en France, 1870–1914 (6 vols., Bordeaux, 1924). E. Mâle, L'Art religieux du 12e siècle en France (1922); id., L'Art religieux du 13e siècle en France (1898; Eng. tr., 1913); id., L'Art religieux de la fin du moyen-âge en France (1908). Bremond. G. Goyau, La France missionnaire dans les cinq parties du monde (2 vols., 1948). G. Goyau in C.E., vi (1909), pp. 167–90, s.v.; G. Allemang, O.M.I., in L.Th.K., iv (1932), cols. 94–106, s.v. 'Frankreich', with good bibl. Various authors in E.C., v (1950), cols. 1623–88. See also bibll. to Concordat, Constitutional Church, Gallicanism, Huguenots, Jansenism, Modernism, and Quietism.

FRANCES OF ROME, St. (1384–1440), St. Francesca Romana, foundress of the *Oblates of St. Benedict of Tor de' Specchi. Born at Rome, she was married in 1397 to Lorenzo de' Ponziani, although she desired to enter religion. She was an exemplary wife and mother, at the same time living a life under rule with her husband's brother's wife, Vannozza. She and her family suffered much when Ladislas of Naples took Rome in 1408. In 1425 she realized her long-cherished plan of founding a society of pious women, not under strict vows, to help the poor. At first called the Oblates of Mary, they later became known as the Oblates of Tor de' Specchi from the house in which they lived. After Lorenzo's death (1436) Francesca entered the community and became Superior. During her later years she is said to have enjoyed the continuous vision of her guardian angel. She was canonized in 1608 and *Pius XI declared her a patroness of motorists. Feast day, 9 Mar.

Lat. recension of life by Giovanni Mattiotti, her confessor, pr. in AA.SS., Mar. II (1668), pp. *92–*176; It. recension (prob. the earlier) ed. M. Armellini (Rome, 1882); modern It tr. by M. Scarpini (Florence, 1923). Life by M. M. Anguillaria (Rome, 1641) adds little; Lat. tr. in AA.SS., loc. cit., pp. *176–*211. Account of canonization, ib., pp. *212–*216; introd., pp. *88–*92. P. T. Lugano (ed.), I processi inediti per Francesca Bussa dei Ponziani (Santa Francesca Romana), 1440–1453 (S.T., cxx; 1945), with reff. to earlier works, esp. p. xxxiv; see esp. artt. in Rivista storica benedettina. Modern lives by Georgiana Fullerton (London, 1855), J. Rabory (Paris, 1884), Ctesse. de Rambuteau (ib. 1900), Berthem-Bontoux (ib., 1931), Irene Hernaman (London, 1931; slight) and C. Albergotti (Rome, 1940).

FRANCIS OF ASSISI (1181/2–1226), founder of the *Franciscan Order. The son of Pietro Bernardone, a rich cloth merchant of Assisi, and his wife, Pica, Francis assisted his father in his business until he reached the age of twenty. Gallant, high spirited, and generous, he lived as a youth the life usual for one of his station. In 1202, during a border dispute between Perugia and Assisi, he was taken prisoner and held captive for some months. After his release he returned to Assisi, but, becoming dissatisfied with his worldly life during a serious illness, after much inner conflict determined to devote himself to prayer and the service of the poor. On a pilgrimage to Rome he was moved by compassion for the beggars before St. Peter's and, exchanging his clothes with one of them, spent a day himself begging for alms. This experience of being penniless deeply affected him; he discovered both the joys and hardships of poverty; and on his return to Assisi, after being disowned by his father, devoted himself to ministering to lepers and employing his time in repairing the ruined church of S. Damiano. One morning c. 1208, while worshipping in the church of the *Portiuncula some two miles below Assisi, he heard the Lord's words read, bidding His disciples to leave all (Mt. 10. 7–19), and at once understood them as a personal call. He discarded staff and shoes, put on a long dark garment girded with a cord and set out to save souls. Before long he gathered round him a little band of like-minded followers.

Francis now drew up a simple rule of life for himself and his associates ('Regula Primitiva'), based on sayings from the Gospels, and on a visit to Rome in 1209–10 secured approval for it from *Innocent III. On his return he spent some time at Rivo Torto in the neighbourhood of Assisi, and from now on his associates, who took the name of 'friars minor' (fratres minores), rapidly increased and went on ever wider missions. In 1212 his ideals were accepted by St. *Clare (q.v.), a noble lady of Assisi, who founded a similar society for women centred at the church of S. Damiano. In 1214–15 Francis made his way through the S. of France and Spain with a view to converting the Moors, but illness prevented his reaching Africa. It was the tradition that after his return to Assisi in 1216 *Honorius III granted him the 'Portiuncula Indulgence' (q.v.). At the Chapter at Assisi at Pentecost, 1217, the Order was organized by provinces, with ministers appointed to supervise them. In 1219 he made a preaching tour with eleven companions to Eastern Europe and Egypt; he was present at the siege and capture of Damietta (Nov. 1219).

During this absence in the East, Francis's personal relation to the Order underwent a great change. Its direction passed into the hands of other friars (*Elias of Cortona; Petrus Cataneo, d. 1221) and Francis, realizing that he lacked the qualities for supervising and administering what had now become a vast enterprise, never sought to resume the leadership. In 1221 he founded his *Tertiaries, i.e. a band of those living in the world who wished to adopt his ideals as far as was compatible with a normal mode of life. A more definite and settled rule for the friars (the 'Regula Prima') was drawn up in 1221, and after further revision received formal authorization by Honorius III on 29 Nov. 1223 (the 'Regula Bullata'). In his later years he became a close friend of Cardinal Ugolino of Ostia, whom he first met at Florence in 1217, and this friendship served his Order well when in 1227 the Cardinal became Pope as *Gregory IX. In Sept. 1224 Francis received on Mt. Alvernia, a retreat in the Apennines which had been granted to Francis and his followers by the Lord of Chiusi, the gift of the *Stigmata. He died in the chapel of the Portiuncula on 3 Oct. 1226. On 16 July 1228, less than two years

later, he was canonized by Gregory IX. Feast day, 4 Oct. (of the Stigmata, 17 Sept.).

Francis's generosity, his simple and unaffected faith, his passionate devotion to God and man, his love of nature and his deep humility have made him one of the most cherished saints in modern times. The revival of interest in him among the more educated owes much to the study of P. *Sabatier, the Calvinist pastor at Strassburg, who combined original research into the early Franciscan documents with warm sympathy for and a fascinating presentation of his ideals.

See also Franciscan Order, Canticle of the Sun, and Little Flowers of St. Francis.

The authentic writings of St. Francis are all quite short. They include his Testament, a set of 28 Admonitions, 'De Reverentia Corporis Domini', 'De Religiosa Habitatione in Eremis', the '*Canticle of the Sun', a collection of seven letters, 'Laudes Domini' (a paraphrase of the Lord's Prayer), and the prayer 'Absorbeat'. There also survive a series of valuable early lives, notably two by *Thomas of Celano, the Life by the 'Three Companions' ('Vita Trium Sociorum', viz. Leo, Angelo, and Rufino). Genuine traditions about St. Francis are prob. also incorporated in the 'Little Flowers' (q.v.); acc. to P. Sabatier, in the 'Speculum Perfectionis' (which Sabatier believed to be the work of Brother Leo); and possibly also in other early Franciscan sources. In the later Middle Ages, the most important work was Bartholomew of Pisa's 'Liber de Conformitate Vitae b. Patris Francisci ad Vitam Domini Nostri Jesu Christi', presented by its author to the Chapter General of the Franciscans in 1399.
The earliest collected ed. of his works is that of L. *Wadding, O.F.M., Antwerp, 1623 (often repr.). Eng. trr. of his works include those by 'A Religious of the Order' (London, 1882) and Paschal Robinson, O.F.M. (ib., 1906). Celano's 'Prima Vita', though known to Wadding, was first pr. in the AA.SS., Oct. II (1768), pp. 683–723; his 'Vita Secunda' was not publd. until the 19th cent., by S. Rinaldi, Seraphici Viri s. Francisci Assisiati Vitae duae auct. B. Thoma de Celano (Rome, 1806), pp. 137–273; crit. ed. of both by Eduardus d'Alençon, O.F.M.Cap. (London, 1906). The 'Vita Trium Sociorum' was first pr. in AA.SS., loc. cit., pp. 723–42; first crit. ed. by M. Faloci-Pulignani, Foligno, 1898. In 1266, the Order gave official authority to the 'Legenda Major' of St. *Bonaventura, a life designed to mediate between the *Spirituals and the less austere members of the Order; best ed. in the works of St. Bonaventura, ed. Quaracchi, viii (1898), pp. 504–64. Convenient collection of texts in H. Boehmer (ed.), Analekten zur Geschichte des Franciscus von Assisi (1904). See also B.H.L., i, pp. 463–71 (Nos. 3095–3136), and Suppl., pp. 129–36.
Among the large number of modern lives, special importance attaches to that of P. Sabatier (Paris, 1893; Eng. tr., 1894), which inaugurated modern Franciscan studies. Others include those of K. Hase (Leipzig, 1856), Mrs. [Margaret O. W.] Oliphant (London, [c. 1870]), W. J. Knox Little (London, 1897), J. Jörgensen (Copenhagen, 1907; Eng. tr., 1912), Fr. Cuthbert [Hess], O.S.F.C. (London, 1912), and L. Salvatorelli (Bari, 1926; Eng. tr., 1929). Good popular studies by G. K. *Chesterton (London, [1923]) and T. S. R. Boase ('Great Lives', London, 1936). W. Seton (ed.), St. Francis of Assisi: 1226–1926. Essays in Commemoration (London, 1926). On the sources and their literary relations W. Goetz, Die Quellen zur Geschichte des hl. Franz von Assisi (1904). J. R. H. Moorman, The Sources for the Life of S. Francis of Assisi (Publications of the University of Manchester, cclxxiv, Historical Series, lxxix; 1940). E. C. *Butler in E.B. (ed. 11), x (1910), pp. 937–9. Eng. tr. of Works and early records by L. [D.] Sherley-Price (London, 1959).

FRANCIS BORGIA, St. See Borgia, St. Francis.

FRANCIS OF PAOLA, St. (1416–1507), founder of the Order of *Minims. Born of a poor family, he spent a year with the *Franciscans as a boy in fulfilment of a vow of his parents. Here he developed a great love of austerity, and in 1431 began to lead a strictly ascetic life as a hermit in the cave of a rock near the Tyrrhenian Sea. In 1436, the date held to be the foundation of his order, he was joined by two companions. Before long the number of his followers increased and in 1453 a church and a house were built for them; and other foundations followed later. He became renowned for his holiness throughout Italy and beyond its frontiers, and many miraculous cures were attributed to him. His fame was such that Louis XI of France, in terror of death after an apoplectic fit, sent for him; while his son, Charles VIII, kept him near him as his spiritual director and built him two monasteries. The last three months of his life St. Francis spent preparing himself for death in his cell in complete solitude. He was canonized in 1519. His emblem is the word *CARITAS* in a circle of rays. Feast day, 2 Apr.

AA.SS., Apr. I (1685), pp. 103–234. The 'anonymous life' [by L. Clavense] also ed. G. M. Perrimezzi (2 vols., Rome, 1707). Modern lives by l'Abbé Rolland (Paris, 1874) and J. N. Dabert (ed. l'Abbé Pradier, Tours, 1892). The apostolic letter of Pope *Pius XII appointing him patron of Italian seafarers is pr. in *A.S.S.*, xxxv (1943), p. 163 f. See also bibl. to *Minims*.

FRANCIS OF SALES, St. (1567–1622), Bp.
of Geneva from 1602, and one of the leaders of the *Counter-Reformation. Born at the castle of Sales in Savoy, he was educated at Annecy, Paris (1581–8) and Padua (1588–92), and gave up brilliant secular prospects in response to an overmastering vocation to holy orders. In 1593 he was ordained priest, and was made Provost of Geneva. In 1593 he started on a mission to win the Chablais from *Calvinism to Catholicism, and in the face of great personal sufferings and dangers, succeeded. In 1599 he was nominated Coadjutor-Bp. of Geneva, with the title of Bp. of Nicopolis, but not consecrated till he succeeded to the see in 1602. In addition to the administration of the diocese, he continued regularly to preach, to minister as confessor and director, and to organize the teaching of the Catechism. In 1603 he met St. *Jane Frances de Chantal, whose spiritual director he soon became; and in 1610, through their combined inspiration and labours, the *Visitandines were founded. His most famous writings, the *Introduction to the *Devout Life* (1608; q.v.) and the *Treatise on the Love of God* (1616), were adapted for publication from instructions given to individuals. He was beatified in 1661, canonized in 1665, and declared a '*Doctor of the Church' in 1877 and 'Patron of the Catholic Press' in 1923. Feast day, 29 Jan. See also *Bosco, St. John*, and *Salesians*.

The best ed. of his works is that publ. by the Visitandines of Annecy (26 vols., Annecy, 1892–1932); Eng. tr. by H. B. Mackey, O.S.B., and others, under the direction of J. C. Hedley, O.S.B. (6 vols., 1883–1908). The primary contemporary authority is Charles-Auguste de Sales (nephew), *De Vita et Rebus Gestis . . . Francisci Salesii* (Lyons, 1634; mod. Fr. tr., 2 vols., 1857). J. P. Camus, *L'Esprit du bienheureux François de Sales* (6 vols., 1639–41; numerous Fr. edd.; mod. Eng. abridged trr., 1872, 1910, and New York, 1952). A. J. M. Hamon, *Vie de Saint François de*

Sales (2 vols., 1854; Eng. tr., 2 vols., 1925–9); F. Trochu, *Saint François de Sales* (2 vols., Paris, 1946), with full reff. to sources. Other modern studies include those of [H. L. S. Lear,] the author of 'A Dominican Artist' (London, 1871), F. Strowski (Paris, 1898), A. de Margerie ('Les Saints', 1899; Eng. tr., 1900), Mary M. Maxwell-Scott (London, 1913), H. Vincent (Paris, 1923), Ella K. Sanders (London, 1928), and M. Müller (ib., 1936). Bremond, i (1916), pp. 68–127; Eng. tr., i (1928), pp. 55–100; Pourrat, iii (1925), esp. pp. 406–81; Eng. tr., iii (1927), pp. 272–321. R. Pernin in *D.T.C.*, vi (1920), cols. 736–62. Popular Life by M. de la Bedoyere (London, 1960).

FRANCIS OF VITORIA. See *Vitoria, Francis of*.

FRANCIS XAVIER, St. (1506–52), 'Apostle
of the Indies' and 'of Japan'. He was one of the greatest of Christian missionaries, and an original member of the *Jesuits. The son of an aristocratic Spanish-Basque family, he was born in Navarre. While at the University of Paris he met St. *Ignatius Loyola, and on 15 Aug. 1534, with Ignatius and five others, took vows to follow Christ in poverty and chastity, and to evangelize the heathen. All seven were ordained priests in Venice on Midsummer Day, 1537. On 7 Apr. 1541, at the invitation of John III of Portugal, Francis left Lisbon to evangelize the East Indies, and in May 1542 he reached Goa, which he made his headquarters. From there he went on to Travancore, Malacca, the Molucca Islands, and *Ceylon. In 1549 he landed in Japan, the language of which he studied, and founded there a Church which endured through great persecutions. He returned to Goa in 1552, but left in the same year for a mission to China. On the way, at the island of Chang-Chuen-Shan (St. John's Island) he fell ill and died before he could enter the country. His body was brought to the church of the Good Jesus at Goa, where it lies magnificently enshrined. His work is remarkable for the extent of his journeys (in spite of his invariable seasickness), and the large number of his converts. The Jesuits have attributed to him more than 700,000 conversions. Wherever he preached he left organized Christian communities. His methods have sometimes been attacked, e.g. he has been criticized for not attempting to understand the oriental religions, for invoking the help of the *Inquisition, for approving the persecution of *Nestorians, and for using the government at Goa as a means of proselytizing. The well-known hymn, 'O Deus, ego amo Te' ('My God, I love Thee, not because', tr. E. *Caswall), long ascribed to Xavier, appears to be a Lat. rendering of a Spanish sonnet. He was canonized in 1622, and *Pius X named him 'Patron of Foreign Missions'. Feast day 3 Dec.

Monumenta Xaveriana (Monumenta Historica Societatis Jesu, 2 vols., Madrid, 1899–1912); letters also ed. G. Schurhammer, S.J.–I. Wicki, S.J. (ib., vols. lxvii and lxviii, Rome, 1944–5). H. Tursellini, S.J., *De Vita Francisci Xaverii* (Rome, 1594; Eng. tr., Paris, 1632). Other lives by D. Bouhours, S.J. (Paris, 1682; Eng. tr. by J. *Dryden, 1688), H. Venn (London, 1862), H. J. Coleridge, S.J. ('Quarterly Series', 2 vols., 1872), L. J. M. Cros, S.J. (2 vols., Toulouse, 1894), M. H. McClean (London, 1895), A. Brou (2 vols., Paris, 1912), A. Bellessort in *Revue des Deux Mondes*, xxxi (1916), pp. 797–841, xxxii (1916), pp. 315–45, xxxiii (1916), pp. 92–123, xxxiv (1916), pp. 352–78, xxxv (1916), pp. 339–81, E. A. Stewart (London, 1917), with tr. of letters by D. Macdonald, E. A. Robertson (ib., 1920), G. Brou (2 vols., Paris, 1922), M. Yeo (London, 1931), C. J. Stranks (ib., 1933), T. Maynard (New York, 1936), and J. Brodrick, S.J. (London, 1952). A. Astrain, S.J., in *C.E.*, vi (1909), p. 233 f.; C. Testore, S.J.–E. Lavagnino in *E.C.*, v (1950), cols. 1616–20.

FRANCISCAN ORDER. The Order of Friars Minor was founded by St. *Francis of Assisi (q.v.) in 1209, when he gave his followers their first rule, now lost. This rule was recast in 1221 and brought into its final form in 1223 when *Honorius III confirmed it by bull, whence it is known as 'Regula bullata'. Its distinguishing mark is the insistence on complete poverty not only for individual friars but corporately for the whole order. The friars were to live by the work of their hands or, if need be, by begging, but were forbidden to own any property or to accept money. With the rapid spread of the order and the need for settled houses, this ideal soon proved unworkable if taken literally. Thus two schools of thought developed in the order. The one, whose members were called '*Spirituals', insisted on interpretation acc. to the letter; the other, followed by the majority, preferred a more moderate view in accordance with the requirements of the times. From 1245 onwards the discussion grew violent and endangered the unity of the order, though it temporarily abated under the conciliatory influence of St. *Bonaventure, who was General from 1257 to 1274. From 1310 to 1312 the question was debated before the Pope, and in 1317–8 decided against the stricter party by two bulls of *John XXII which permitted the order corporate ownership. Many of the Spirituals fled and became schismatics under the name of 'Fraticelli'. In 1321 the problem of poverty arose again, this time in the theoretical form as to whether Christ and the Apostles had owned property, and a heated scholastic discussion between Franciscans and *Dominicans developed. These futile disputes, together with the Black Death (1348–1352) and the Great Schism (1378–1417), led to a general decline of the order in the 14th cent. Laxity also increased as their material prosperity grew. But during this period many efforts at reform were made, and a return to poverty was brought about by the so-called 'Observants', who opposed the lax 'Conventualists'. The 'Observants' gained ecclesiastical recognition when in 1415 the Council of *Constance granted their French province special provincials, and in 1443 *Eugenius IV provided them with a separate Vicar General. In 1517 they were finally separated from the Conventuals and declared the true Order of St. Francis. Early in the 16th cent. another reform, introduced by Matteo di Bassi (1495–1552), led to the establishment of the *Capuchins (q.v.), whose rule was drawn up in 1529. During the 17th and 18th cents. reform parties sprang up again. Of these the chief were the 'Reformati', the Recollects and the Discalced, who lived after their own statutes, though remaining under the same General.

Besides these internal differences, the political events of the 18th and 19th cents., esp. the French Revolution, the secularization of *Joseph II, the revolutions in Spain (1834), Poland (1831), Italy, and the *Kulturkampf in Prussia, did great harm to the order. At the end of the last century, however, the order regained new vigour by the reunion of its different branches, which was confirmed by *Leo XIII in 1897.

The Order which has always cultivated popular preaching and missionary activities, has given a great number of saints to the Church, the best known being St. *Anthony of Padua, popular as a miracle-worker. Though not primarily instituted as a learned order, it has produced many celebrated scholars, among them St. *Bonaventure, *Duns Scotus, and *William of Ockham. Among the popular devotions they promote are esp. the *Angelus, the *Crib, and the *Stations of the Cross. Franciscans were among the chief defenders of the *Immaculate Conception in the Middle Ages.

To the Franciscan friars is attached their organization of Tertiaries (q.v.) living in the world. Their Second Order of contemplative nuns are the Poor Clares (q.v.), whereas their Third Order communities of women are devoted to works of charity and have no strict enclosure.

In 1224 the first Franciscans to establish themselves in England arrived under Agnellus of Pisa and settled at once at *Canterbury, London, and *Oxford. Their piety and learning won them a ready hearing, and by the middle of the century there were some 50 friaries and over 1200 friars in England. Their early history (down to c. 1258) was vividly described by Thomas of Eccleston ('De Adventu Fratrum Minorum in Angliam'). John *Peckham, one of their number, held the see of Canterbury from 1279 to 1292. In the 14th cent., when they no longer possessed the same moral and intellectual qualities, they became the object of J. *Wycliffe's attacks. The *Observants were introduced by Henry VII and acted as confessors to *Henry VIII and Catherine of Aragon; but they were scattered before the *Dissolution. Since the middle of the 19th cent., many Franciscan houses have been re-established.

In the C of E a group inspired by Franciscan ideals settled near Batcombe (Cerne Abbas) in Dorset in 1921, to minister in the first place to the unemployed who tramped the roads. In 1931 they took vows and were constituted a religious community. They have grown considerably in numbers and influence and have been active in evangelistic work, esp. in the universities. A small Anglican community for women has also been started with its headquarters at Freeland, Oxon.

The most important source for the Order as a whole, apart from its official docc., is L. *Wadding, O.F.M. (q.v.), *Annales Minorum* (8 vols., Lyons, 1625–54; later edd. much extended); id., *Scriptores Ordinis Minorum* (Rome, 1650; suppl., with corrections, by J. H. Sbaralea, O.F.M., 1806). *Bullarium Franciscanum* (4 vols., ed. J. H. Sbaralea, O.F.M., Rome, 1759–68; 3 further vols. ed. C. Eubel, O.F.M., ib.,

1898–1904, + Epitome et Supplementum by id., Quaracchi, 1908). *Analecta Franciscana*, sive Chronica aliaque varia Documenta ad Historiam Fratrum Minorum Spectantia, ed. by the Franciscans of Quaracchi (10 vols. to date, Quaracchi, 1885–1941). Useful collection of sources for the history of the Order in England ed. J. S. Brewer–R. Howlett, *Monumenta Franciscana* (2 vols., R.S., 1858–82). For details of edd. of early constitutions and other sources see A. G. Little, *A Guide to Franciscan Studies* (Helps for Students of History, xxiii; 1920). H. Holzapfel, O.F.M., *Handbuch der Geschichte des Franziskanerordens* (1909). A. Masseron, *Les Franciscains* ('Les Grands Ordres monastiques et instituts religieux', 1931; Eng. tr., 1931). A. G. Little, *Franciscan Papers, Lists and Documents* (Publications of the University of Manchester, cclxxiv, Historical Series, lxxxi; 1943). A. Gemelli, O.F.M., *Il francescanesimo* (ed. 2, Vita e pensiero, 1932; Eng. tr., 1934). [M. Badin in religion,] Père Gratien de Paris, O.F.M.Cap., *Histoire de la fondation et de l'évolution de l'ordre des Frères Mineurs au XIIIᵉ siècle* (1928). V. D. Scudder, *The Franciscan Adventure*. A Study in the First Hundred Years of the Order of St. Francis of Assisi (1931). F. de Sessevalle, of the Third Order, *Histoire générale de l'ordre de Saint François*, la première partie, le moyen-âge, 1209–1517 (2 vols., 1935–7). R. M. Huber, O.F.M., *A Documented History of the Franciscan Order, 1182–1517* (Milwaukee, Wisc., and Washington, D.C., 1944). A. G. Little, *Studies in English Franciscan History* (Ford Lectures for 1916; Publications of the University of Manchester, cxiii, Historical Series, xxix; 1917) and other works; E. Hutton, *The Franciscans in England, 1224–1538* (1926). [M.] D. Knowles, O.S.B., *The Religious Orders in England* (1950), pp. 114–45, 171–93, 205–52. A. Jessop, *The Coming of the Friars and Other Historical Essays* (1889), pp. 2–52; Father Cuthbert [Hess], O.F.M.Cap., *The Friars and How They Came to England* (1903; Eng. tr. of Thomas of Eccleston's 'De Adventu FF. Minorum in Angliam', with pref. essay, 'On the Spirit and Genius of the Franciscan Friars', pp. 1–128). L. Lemmens, O.F.M., *Geschichte der Franziskaner-missionen* (Missionswissenschaftliche Abhandlungen und Texte, ed. J. Schmidlin, xii; 1929). The many collections of studies and periodicals devoted to the affairs of the Order include the publications of the British Society of Franciscan Studies (19 vols., Aberdeen, 1908–37), *Études franciscaines* (Paris, 1899 ff.), *Archivum Franciscanum Historicum* (Quaracchi, 1908 ff.), *Franziskanische Studien* (Münster i.W., 1914 ff.), *Revue d'Histoire Franciscaine* (Paris, 1924 ff.), and *Franciscan Studies* (New York, 1941 ff.). Heimbucher, i, pp. 656–814, with detailed bibl. M. Bihl, O.F.M.–Z. Engelhardt, O.F.M., in *C.E.*, vi (1909), pp. 281–302, s.v. 'Friars Minor, Order of'; Édouard d'Alençon, O.F.M.Cap., in *D.T.C.*, vi (1920), cols. 809–863, s.v. 'Frères Mineurs'; M. Bihl, O.F.M., in *L.Th.K.*, iv (1932), cols. 125–32, s.v. 'Franziskaner'; R. Pratesi, O.F.M.–L. di Fonzo, O.F.M.Conv., in *E.C.*, v (1950), cols. 1722–38, s.v. 'Frati Minori', all with bibl. See also bibll. to *Capuchins, Observants, Recollects,* and *Spiritual Franciscans*.

FRANCISCUS A SANCTA CLARA. See *Davenport, Christopher*.

FRANCK, SEBASTIAN (*c.* 1499–*c.* 1542),

German humanist. After studying at Ingolstadt and Heidelberg, he was ordained priest. *c.* 1525 he became a *Lutheran and held pastoral appointments at Nuremberg and Strassburg. Later, however, he advocated complete freedom of thought and defended a form of undogmatic Christianity for which he was persecuted by Catholics and Reformers alike. He spent his later years at Basle. His varied writings are largely of secular purpose; but in the historical compilation issued as *Chronica* (3 vols., 1531), he gave full expression to his liberal attitude to religious questions. His more specifically theological books include a German edition of A. Althamer's *Diallage* (1528; a treatise against the *Anabaptists) and an index to the Bible (1539). In 1534 he published a German translation of *Erasmus' *Encomium Moriae*.

Life by C. A. Hase (Leipzig, 1869). A. Hegler, *Geist und Schrift bei Sebastian Franck* (1892); A. Reimann, *Sebastian Franck als Geschichtsphilosoph* (Comenius-Schriften zur Geistesgeschichte, Hft. i; 1921). A. Hegler in *P.R.E.* (ed. 3), vi (1899), pp. 142–50.

FRANCKE, AUGUST HERMANN (1663–1727).

German *Pietist and educationist. He was born at Lübeck, and after studying philosophy and theology at Erfurt and Kiel became a lecturer at Leipzig in 1685. Under the influence of P. J. *Spener he was attracted to Pietism and held 'Collegia Philobiblica' in which the Bible was expounded on devotional lines. In 1692 he was appointed professor at the newly founded university of Halle and pastor of Glauchau, nr. Halle, where his sermons and pastoral activities soon attracted a large congregation. In 1695 he laid the foundation of his famous Institutes, later known as 'Francke-sche Stiftungen', by opening a poor-school in his house. In 1696 he founded his 'Paedago-gium' and his orphanage. Both grew rapidly, and during the next years other institutions such as a publishing house and a dispensary were added. His great success, chiefly due to his eminently practical sense, combined with his stress on the personal nature of Christianity, made him many enemies among the clergy of Halle; but the opposition against him diminished after a visit in 1713 from the Prussian king, Frederick William I, whose subsequent educational legislation shows the influence of Francke's work.

His writings were mainly of a devotional and practical character. There is no complete ed., though some collections of his works were made during his lifetime. The two chief lives are those by H. E. F. Guerike (Halle, 1827; Eng. tr., 1837) and G. Kramer (2 vols., Halle a.S., 1880–2); also a large number of popular lives. A. Nebe, *Neue Quellen zu August Hermann Francke* (1927). T. Förster-Halle in *P.R.E.* (ed. 3), vi (1899), pp. 150–8, s.v.; H. Leube in *R.G.G.* (ed. 2), ii (1928), col. 651 f. See also bibl. to *Pietism*.

FRANKFURT, Councils of.

Frankfurt on Main was the scene of some sixteen Imperial councils during the Carolingian epoch. The best known of them was called by *Charlemagne in 794 to condemn the *Adoptianist heresy. It was attended by bishops from all over the Frankish kingdom, from Aquitaine, Italy, and even from England. Besides repudiating Adoptianism it condemned the decree of the Second Council of *Nicaea (787) on the worship of *ikons, probably through a misunderstanding of the distinction made between λατρεία and προσκύνησις.

On the Council of 794, Hardouin, iv, cols. 865–912; Mansi, xiii (1767), cols. 829–56. Hefele-Leclercq, iii (pt. 2; 1910), pp. 1045–60, with bibl. to date, p. 1045; Appendice vii, pp. 1240–6. H. Barion, 'Der kirchenrechtliche Charakter des Konzils von Frankfurt 794' in *Zeitschrift der Savigny-Stiftung für Rechtsgeschichte*, l, Kan. Abt., xix (1930), pp. 139–70. B. Dolhagaray in *D.T.C.*, vi (1920), cols. 712–20, s.v. 'Francfort, Concile de', with bibl. M. Buchner in *L.Th.K.*, iv (1932), col. 91 f., s.v. 'Frankfurt a.M. IV', with bibl.

FRANZELIN, JOHANN BAPTIST, (1816–1886),

Austrian cardinal and theologian. He entered the Society of Jesus in 1834, and in 1857 was appointed professor of dogmatic theology at the Roman College. He took a prominent part in preparing the *Vatican Council, where he acted as one of the leading theologians. In 1876 he was raised to the cardinalate. A theologian of great learning and accuracy of mind, he wrote a long series of dogmatic works of which the chief was his *De Divina Traditione et Scriptura* (1870). In his treatise on the Eucharistic Sacrifice (1868) he followed J. de *Lugo in teaching that the immolation in the Sacrifice consisted in the reduction to a lower state of Christ's human nature by being clothed in the species of bread and wine. Franzelin took an active part in the controversy with Greek Orthodox and Protestant scholars on the procession of the Holy Spirit, setting forth the traditional W. doctrine in his *Examen doctrinae Macarii Bulgakov* (1876).

'Commentarius de Vita Eminentissimi Auctoris' prefixed to his posthumous *Theses De Ecclesia Christi* (1887), pp. v–xxxi. N. Walsh, S.J., *John Baptist Franzelin, S.J.* . . . A Sketch and a Study (Dublin, 1895). P. Bernard in *D.T.C.* vi (1920), cols. 765–7.

FRASER, ALEXANDER CAMPBELL (1819–1914), idealist philosopher. He was a pupil of Sir William Hamilton at Edinburgh, and in 1844 was ordained in the *Free Church of Scotland, which had been created by the schism in the previous year, to the charge of Cramond, nr. Edinburgh. On Hamilton's death in 1856, he succeeded to his professorship at the University and held the chair till 1891. His main philosophical interest was the study of G. *Berkeley, whose writings he twice edited for the Clarendon Press (1871, 1901). The earlier was accompanied by a volume of Berkeley's *Life and Letters* incorporating much new material, and in 1881 he contributed the volume *Berkeley* to Blackwood's Philosophical Classics. He also published a set of *Gifford Lectures on *The Philosophy of Theism* (1895–6). Though his own philosophical position was greatly influenced by the doctrines of Berkeley, Fraser did not follow him slavishly; and his success as a teacher owed more to his ability to stimulate interest in the issues of philosophy than to the inculcation of any particular conclusions. He described the course of his philosophical development in his *Biographia Philosophica* (1904).

J. Kellie, *Alexander Campbell Fraser*. A Sketch of his Life and Philosophical Position (1909). A. S. Pringle-*Pattison, 'Alexander Campbell Fraser, 1819–1914' in *Mind*, xxiv (1915), pp. 289–325; id. in *D.N.B., 1912–1921* (1927), pp. 195–7.

FRATER, the hall of a monastery or friary used for meals or refreshment. The word is in origin related to 'refectory' (*refectorium*) through the Old French *refraitour*.

FRATICELLI. A name originally applied to all members of the *Mendicant Orders, but since the condemnation of the followers of Angelo Clareno (d. 1337) by Pope *John XXII in the bull 'Sancta Romana' (1317), esp. to the *Spiritual Franciscans (q.v.). It was also

in common use for the disciples of Michael of Casena (the so-called 'Michaelites') and several other minor groups.

FREDERICK I (Barbarossa) (*c.* 1123–90), Holy Roman Emperor. On the death of Conrad III in 1152, Frederick of Swabia was elected to the German throne. He soon showed his intention to be a *Charlemagne *redivivus*. Internally his popularity and statesmanship, together with his descent from both Ghibelline and Guelph stock, gave Germany a unity which it had not enjoyed for many years. In his relations with the Church he looked back to the time when the Papacy was the puppet of the emperor, and the German bishops were Imperial servants; and, despite the Concordat of *Worms, it was his intention to restore that relationship. To secure Papal subservience one thing was necessary, the control of N. Italy. Hence the history of Frederick's reign is that of a series of expeditions across the Alps against the Italian communes; and it was the resistance of the Lombard League rather than Papal intransigence that eventually proved his undoing, ending with his total defeat at Legnano (1176). In return for recovering Rome from the party of *Arnold of Brescia, he had been crowned emperor by *Hadrian IV in 1155; but three years later he was indignantly repudiating the Pope's ambiguous claim to have bestowed 'beneficia' (kindness or fiefs). At the Synod of Pavia (1160) he recognized Victor IV as Pope in opposition to *Alexander III, thus creating a schism in the Church and considerably embarrassing the Papacy. His excommunication, however, and his long absences in Italy, weakened his position in Germany, and enabled Henry of Bavaria to rebel and revive the old Guelph-Hohenstaufen feud. The marriage (1186) of his son and heir, Henry, to Constance, the heiress of the Norman kingdom of Sicily, made the Empire at his death a greater threat than ever before to the Papacy. After the fall of Jerusalem (1187), he took the cross and led the Third *Crusade, on which he perished in the Cilician river Saleph (1190).

'Constitutiones', ed. by L. Weiland in *M.G.H.*, Constitutiones et Acta Publica Imperatorum et Regum, i (1893), pp. 191–463. The main chronicle sources are *Otto of Freising's *Chronicon* and *Ottonis et Rahewini Gesta Friderici I Imperatoris*, ed. 3, by G. Waitz (Scriptores Rerum Germanicarum, 1912). A. Chroust (ed.), *Quellen zur Geschichte des Kreuzzuges Kaiser Friedrichs I (M.G.H., Scriptores Rerum Germanicarum, N.S., v, 1928). A. L. Poole, 'Frederick Barbarossa and Germany' in *C. Med. H.*, v (1939), ch. xii, pp. 381–412, and U. Balzani, 'Frederick Barbarossa and the Lombard League', ib., ch. xiii, pp. 413–53; bibls., pp. 878–84. R. Wahl, *Kaiser Friedrich Barbarossa* (1941).

FREDERICK II (1194–1250), Holy Roman Emperor. The son of Henry VI and Constance, he succeeded to the Sicilian kingdom at the age of four. During his minority *Innocent III acted as his guardian, and received in return from Frederick, when he came of age (1216), recognition of the Papal overlordship in Sicily. As the price of his coronation as emperor (1220) Frederick further had to promise to go on Crusade. But though starting under such heavy obligations to the Papacy, he was quite as determined as his predecessors to maintain his independence. Both by character and by upbringing he was a Sicilian Norman. His only interest in Germany was as a source of the men and money necessary for the control of N. Italy; and for the most part he left it to regents to govern, ensuring the loyalty of the princes, ecclesiastical and temporal, by the grant of considerable privileges. Rome, however, looked on this union of the North and South as a threat to Papal independence, and strained every nerve to break it. For failure to keep his crusading vow Frederick was excommunicated (1227). His subsequent highly successful Crusade (1229), made while he was still excommunicate, ended in his crowning himself King of Jerusalem, and *Gregory IX was forced to accept it as a *fait accompli* by the Peace of San Germano (1230). The rebellion of his son, Henry, compelled his return to Germany where he held the Diet of Mainz (1235), at which the famous Laws of the Empire were promulgated. He next marched against the Lombards, and promptly found the Papacy against him; and for attacking the Papal states he was again excommunicated (1239). For the rest of his reign he was pursued by the implacable hatred of the Papacy. He died at Fiorentino in Apulia (13 Dec. 1250) and was buried in the cathedral at Palermo.

Principal official docc. pr. in J. L. A. Huillard-Bréholles (ed.), *Historia Diplomatica Friderici Secundi* (6 vols. in 11, Paris, 1852–61, with important introd. in prefatory vol., ib., 1859). E. Winkelmann, *Kaiser Friedrich II* (Jahrbücher der deutschen Geschichte, 2 vols. [1218–33]; 1889–1897). The standard modern work, in spite of being somewhat panegyrical, is the life by E. Kantorowicz (Berlin, 1927; suppl. vol., 1931; Eng. tr., 1931). In Eng. there is also the classical life by T. L. Kington (2 vols., London, 1862), and lives by L. Allshorn, *Stupor Mundi* (London, 1912) and R. Oke, *The Boy from Apulia* (1936; popular). Other studies by W. Schirrmacher (4 vols. in 2, Göttingen, 1859–65), E. Winkelmann (Berlin, 1863; suppl. vol., 1865), F. J. Biehringer (Historische Studien, cii; 1928), K. Pfister (Munich, 1942; with bibl., pp. 391–408) and R. Wahl (ib., 1947; also with bibl.). A. L. Poole in *C. Med. H.*, vi (1929), pp. 80–109; M. Schipa, ib., pp. 131–65, with bibl., pp. 863–74. See also bibl. to *Crusades*.

FREDERICK III (1463–1525), Elector of Saxony, surnamed 'the Wise'. (He is not to be confused with Frederick II (1482–1556), Elector of the Palatinate, also known as 'the Wise'.) He succeeded his father, Ernst, as Elector in 1486. In 1500 he became president of the Council of Regency (Reichsregiment). From the outset he showed himself interested in the New Learning and in the reform of the Church. In 1502 he founded the university of *Wittenberg and later invited M. *Luther and P. *Melanchthon to teach there. When in 1518 Luther was cited to Rome, Frederick intervened, secured his trial on German soil, and led the Pope to choose C. von *Miltitz, a Saxon nobleman, to act as his nuncio. In 1520 he refused to put into execution the bull '*Exsurge Domine' (15 June 1520) against the Reformer, and after the Diet of *Worms (1521)

had imposed the Imperial ban, he procured him a hiding-place at the *Wartburg. His natural caution and reputation for justice earned him the title of 'the Wise'. How far he himself accepted Lutheran ideas is disputed. He certainly protested against the iconoclastic tendencies of Luther's followers. See also *Spalatin*, Georg.

G. *Spalatin's historischer Nachlass und Briefe*. Aus dem Originalhandschriften hrg. von C. G. Neudecker–L. Preller: i, Friedrichs des Weisen Leben und Zeitgeschichte (1851). M. M. Tutzschmann, *Friedrich der Weise, Kurfürst von Sachsen, ein Lebensbild aus dem Zeitalter der Reformation* (1848); T. Kolde, *Friedrich der Weise und die Anfänge der Reformation* (1881); P. Kirn, *Friedrich der Weise und die Kirche* [1926]. R. Bruck, *Friedrich der Weise als Förderer der Kunst* (Studien zur deutschen Kunstgeschichte, Hft. xlv, 1903). T. Kolde in *P.R.E.* (ed. 3), vi (1899), pp. 279–83, s.v. 'Friedrich der Weise'; F. Lauchert in *L.Th.K.*, iv (1932), col. 199 f., s.v. 'Friedrich der Weise', with further bibl.

FREDERICK III (1515–76), Elector Palatine of the Rhine, surnamed 'the Pious'. Through his wife Maria (d. 1567), the daughter of Casimir of Bayreuth, whom he married in 1537, Frederick became well disposed towards the *Calvinists. In 1557 he succeeded to the Palatine Electorate. At first he suppressed his personal leanings to Calvinism and sought to foster in his dominions unity between Calvinists and *Lutherans; but, meeting with little success, he came out openly on the side of Calvinism and in 1563 caused the *Heidelberg Catechism (q.v.) to be drawn up and imposed on Catholics and Lutherans alike. To further the Calvinist cause, he sent aid in men and money both to the *Huguenots of France and the rebels in the Netherlands; and also supported Calvinism in many parts of Germany beyond his own territories. He was constantly intriguing against the Catholic Electors in the Diet to secure the abrogation of the 'ecclesiastical reservation' of 1555. His son, Louis VI (d. 1583), who succeeded him in the Electorate, abandoned Calvinism for Lutheranism.

Letters ed. A. Kluckhohn (2 vols. in 3, Brunswick, 1868–1872); id., *Friedrich der Fromme, Kurfürst von der Pfalz, der Schützer der reformirten Kirche, 1559–1576* (Nördlingen, 1879). T. J. Ney in *P.R.E.* (ed. 3), vi (1899), pp. 275–8, s.v. 'Friedrich III'. Further bibl. in Schottenloher, iii (1936), pp. 376–8 (Nos. 32124–48).

FREE CHURCH FEDERAL COUNCIL. The Council formed in 1940 by the union of the National Free Church Council and the Federal Council of the Evangelical Free Churches. See foll. entry.

FREE CHURCH FEDERATION. Following a congress in Manchester in 1892 a National Free Church Council was formed to which was affiliated a loose network of local councils. Membership was not grounded on any representative principle and the annual assembly dealt with a wide range of public questions as well as theological and ecclesiastical matters. Hugh Price *Hughes, a *Methodist, and John *Clifford, a *Baptist, played notable parts in the movement. In 1919, under the leadership of J. H. *Shakespeare, of the Baptist Union, the Federal Council of Evangelical Free Churches was organized. There was a declaratory statement of common faith and practice, which excluded *Unitarians, and membership was put on an officially approved representative basis. In 1940 the National Free Church Council united with the Federal Council in the *Free Church Federal Council. The new body provides the machinery for joint representation and action by the Free Churches, and for the possible further development of federal relationships between them.

E. K. H. Jordan, *Free Church Unity.* History of the Free Church Council Movement, 1896–1941 (1956).

FREE CHURCH OF ENGLAND. A small Protestant body which traces its beginnings to a dispute in 1843 between H. *Phillpotts, Bp. of *Exeter, and one of his clergy, James Shore, in charge of Bridgetown chapel-of-ease, Totnes. Shore's cause was taken up by T. E. Thoresby (d. 1883), a Minister of the Countess of *Huntingdon's Connexion, and eventually in 1863 the Free Church of England received definite shape in association with the latter. It accepted the *Thirty-Nine Articles, and recognized the legitimacy of episcopacy though its ministry at first was presbyterian. Later in the century it became affiliated to a similar group which had separated in 1873 from the Protestant Episcopal (Anglican) Church in U.S.A. under G. D. Cummins, formerly Assistant Bp. of Kentucky, and known as the 'Reformed Episcopal Church'. This association enabled the English body to obtain episcopal orders. In 1927 the two bodies were legally united.

F. Vaughan [Bishop Primus], *A History of the Free Church of England, otherwise called the Reformed Episcopal Church* [1938]. G. H. Jones in *H.E.R.E.*, x (1918), pp. 629–31, with bibl., p. 632, s.v. 'Reformed Episcopal Church'.

FREE CHURCH OF SCOTLAND, The. The religious body formed at the *Disruption (1843) by the separation of nearly a third of the ministers and members of the established Church of *Scotland. In 1900 it united with the *United Presbyterian Church to form the *United Free Church (q.v.).

FREE CHURCHES. See *Nonconformity*.

FREE FROM ROME MOVEMENT. See *Los von Rom.*

FREE SPIRIT, Brethren of the. See *Brethren of the Free Spirit.*

FREEMASONRY, Christianity and. The origins of the Freemasons go back probably to the 12th cent., when the English masons established a religious fraternity under the protection of St. *John the Baptist, to guard the secrets of their craft. In the later Middle Ages this brotherhood came to be concerned almost exclusively with the moral and religious education of its members. It was abolished by *Edward VI in 1547, but later reorganized for social and educational purposes, and in the 18th cent. became a stronghold of *Deism. Freemasonry spread from England to many other countries. In France, Italy, and the other Latin countries the Masonic Lodges were openly hostile to the Church and to religion in general, whereas in England, Germany, and the Germanic countries they professed for the most part an undoctrinal Christianity. The hostility of Latin Freemasonry to religion led to its repeated condemnation by the Church and the prohibition of membership for Catholics under pain of excommunication. The subject was dealt with by many Popes, among them Clement XII (1738), *Benedict XIV (1751), and *Pius VII (1814). *Pius IX attacked Freemasonry in several pastorals and allocutions, and esp. in the '*Syllabus' of 1864, and *Leo XIII in the encyclical 'Humanum Genus' of 20 Apr. 1884. Acc. to the CIC can. 2335 Freemasons incur excommunication *ipso facto* reserved to the Holy See. In Great Britain as well as in the U.S.A. Freemasonry, though undogmatic, demands belief in God from its members and is not hostile to religion as such. It is concerned chiefly with philanthropic and social activities and has the support of royalty and the nobility, many of whom it counts among its members.

FREER LOGION, The. The saying attributed to Christ in a remarkable passage added to the text of Mk. 16. 14 in the 5th cent. Greek Codex 'W', now in the Freer Museum at Washington. It runs: 'The limit of the years of the power of Satan is fulfilled; but other fearful things draw near even upon them for whom, because they had sinned, I was delivered unto death that they may return unto the truth and sin no more; that they may inherit the spiritual and incorruptible glory of righteousness in heaven. But go ye into all the world', &c. [as in Mk. 16. 15]. Though the passage forms no part of the original text, as the whole of Mk. 16. 9–20 is a later addition to the gospel, its language is in agreement with its context, and the fragment may well be of the same *provenance* and date. It appears to have been known to St. *Jerome.

Text in H. A. Sanders, *The Washington Manuscript of the Four Gospels* (University of Michigan Studies, Humanistic Series, ix; 1912), p. 246; repr. in V. Taylor, *The Gospel According to St. Mark* (1952), with Eng. tr., p. 614 f. C. R. Gregory, *Das Freer Logion* (Versuche und Entwürfe, i; 1908). A. E. J. Rawlinson, *St. Mark* (West. Comm., 1925), p. 248 f.

FREEWILL OFFERINGS. In the Hebrew sacrificial system, one of the three forms of peace offering (Lev. 7. 11–16), was so named because it went beyond what legal demands required. It resembled the 'votive offering' in being made in connexion with a prayer for particular blessings, but differed in being offered whether the blessing was granted or not. The feast of harvest was customarily accompanied by such a freewill offering (Deut. 16. 10). In recent years the term has been applied to a method of Church finance whereby members of the congregation agree to pay regular contributions to a 'freewill offering fund' over and above, or in place of, the usual collections made in times of Divine service.

FRENCH PROTESTANTS. See *Huguenots.*

FREQUENCY OF COMMUNION. See *Communion, Frequency of.*

FRERE, WALTER HOWARD (1863–1938), Bp. of *Truro. Educated at Trinity College, Cambridge, and Wells Theological College, he was ordained in 1887. He was a High Churchman, and in 1892 joined the *Community of the Resurrection, Mirfield, in which he was Superior from 1902 to 1913, and again from 1916 to 1922. In 1923 he became Bp. of Truro. He was a leading authority on liturgical matters, and, in matters of practice, an advocate of 'English' rather than 'Roman' forms of ceremonial. His writings in this field include *The Use of Sarum* (2 vols., 1898, 1901); *A New History of the Book of Common Prayer* (based on F. Procter's earlier work; 1901); and *The Principles of Religious Ceremonial* (1906). He was also actively interested in promoting the reunion of Christendom, esp. between the Anglican and E. Orthodox Churches; and he took part in the *Malines Conversations. In 1935 he resigned the see of Truro and ended his life at Mirfield.

J. H. Arnold–E. G. P. Wyatt (edd.), *Walter Howard Frere.* A Collection of his Papers on Liturgical and Historical Subjects (*Alcuin Club Collections, xxxv; 1940); R. C. D. Jasper (ed.), *Walter Howard Frere.* His Correspondence on Liturgical Revision and Reconstruction (ib., xxxix; 1954). Memoir ed. C. S. Phillips (London, 1947).

FRIAR. The distinctive title of a brother (*frater*) or member of one of the Mendicant Orders founded during the Middle Ages. In England these orders were chiefly distinguished by the colours of their mantles, the four chief being the 'Grey Friars' (*Franciscans), the 'Black Friars' (*Dominicans), the 'White Friars' (*Carmelites), and the '*Austin Friars'. Among others were the 'Trinity' or 'Red Friars', and the 'Crutched' or 'Crossed Friars'.

FRIDAY (Old Engl. *frigedæg*, day of [the goddess] Frig', the wife of Odin). In the Christian Church, Friday is widely kept as a weekly commemoration of the Passion of Christ, being frequently observed by *abstinence from meat (*Christmas Day, if it falls on a Friday, is excepted by the rubrics of the BCP, and, in the RC Church, certain other great festivals also). The *Wednesday and Friday fasts were probably derived from the Jewish bi-weekly fast. The primitive practice was to keep a complete fast until 3 p.m., when a service took place, which in some places was the *Eucharist, and elsewhere in essentials an *Ante-Communion. Friday is the Moslem sabbath, in commemoration of the creation of

*Adam on this day (Gen. 1. 24–31). See also *First Fridays.*

Early reff. to the observance of Friday in *Didache, viii, 1, and *Hermas, Simil., v, 1. For the Friday abstinence, see *C.I.C., can. 1252.

FRIDAYS, First. See *First Fridays.*

FRIDESWIDE, St. (d. *c.* 735), patron saint of the city and university of *Oxford. The little that is known of her depends on much embellished 12th cent. and later sources. Acc. to these she was the daughter of Didanus, a Mercian prince, and, after taking a vow of virginity, fled to Oxford to avoid marriage with a neighbouring prince, King Algar. Here, after taking refuge for three years in a village near by named Benton (perh. Binsey), she founded a nunnery over which she became abbess. A monastery bearing her name and occupied by secular canons is known to have existed in Oxford before the Conquest. Its occupants were succeeded by *Augustinian Canons early in the 12th cent. Her shrine, translated on 12 Feb. 1180 and again in 1289, became a place of pilgrimage until its spoliation in 1538. Twice a year the shrine was solemnly visited by the university and in 1434 Abp. H. *Chichele ordered her feast (19 Oct.) to be observed as that of the patroness of the university. In 1525 St. Frideswide's monastery was suppressed by T. *Wolsey as part of his plan for Cardinal College; and in 1546 the monastic church became the cathedral of the new diocese of Oxford. In 1561 the relics of St. Frideswide were mixed by J. *Calfhill with the remains of the wife of *Peter Martyr (Vermigli) which had been buried in the cathedral under *Edward VI. Her festival was abolished in 1549, but it appears in the Latin BCP of 1560 and in the Oxford University Calendar.

AA.SS., Oct. VIII (1853), pp. 533–90. F. M. Stenton, 'St. Frideswide and her Times' in *Oxoniensia,* i (1936), pp. 103–12 (revised and issued separately as St. Frideswide Papers, ii, privately pr. at Oxford, 1953); E. F. Jacob, *St. Frideswide the Patron Saint of Oxford* (St. Frideswide Papers, i, privately pr. at Oxford, 1953). The *Cartulary of the Monastery of St. Frideswide at Oxford* was ed. S. R. Wigram (Oxford Historical Society, xxviii and xxxi, 1895–6).

FRIEDRICH. See also *Frederick.*

FRIEDRICH, JOHANNES (1836–1917), Church historian. Born at Poxdorf in Upper Franconia, he was educated at Bamberg and Munich, and taught at Munich from 1862. He soon gained a great reputation for sound historical judgement and in 1869 J. A. Hohenlohe (1823–96), Abp. of Ephesus (*in partibus*) and afterwards (1876) Cardinal, a leading German prelate, took him as his secretary to *Rome for the *Vatican Council. He joined J. J. I. von *Döllinger (to whom he sent much of the material for *Quirinus's *Letters from Rome*) and others in resisting the definition of Papal Infallibility, believing it to be historically indefensible. He left Rome before the Council ended, but he refused to accept the decrees and in April 1871 he was excommunicated.

The Bavarian Government offered him protection and in 1872 he was nominated professor of church history at Munich. He was at first a leading member of the *Old Catholic communion in Germany, but withdrew when it ceased to uphold clerical celibacy. His writings, which were many, include *Johann Wessel* (1862); *Die Kirchengeschichte Deutschlands* (2 vols., 1867–9); *Tagebuch während des vatikanischen Concils* (1871), followed by a *Verteidigung* (1872); a large scale *Geschichte des vatikanischen Konzils* (3 vols., 1877–87); *Beiträge zur Geschichte des Jesuitenordens* (1881); *Johann Adam Möhler* (1894); and *Ignaz von Döllinger* (3 vols., 1899–1901).

F. Hacker, 'Johannes Friedrich als Führer der altkatholischen Bewegung' in *Internationale kirchliche Zeitschrift*, viii (1918), pp. 252–74.

FRIENDS, Society of (i.e. of Friends of the Truth), the body of Christians founded by G. *Fox (q.v.), also called *Quakers. (The title 'Society of Friends' is not earlier than 1800.)

The Friends were organized as a distinctive Christian group in 1668 when Fox drew up his 'Rule for the Management of Meetings'. They soon engaged in missionary work and in 1682 W. *Penn founded Pennsylvania on a Quaker basis. Until the *Toleration Act of 1689 they suffered constant persecution, esp. as, unlike other Nonconformist bodies, they refused to meet in secret. During the 18th cent. they came to regard themselves more and more as a 'peculiar people', laying great stress on outward observances in speech (use of 'thou' and 'thee') and dress, cutting themselves off from the cultural life of the nation and rejecting art and music as frivolous. Their main activities were trade and philanthropic pursuits (J. *Woolman) for which they became famous.

In the 19th cent. a split occurred in the Quaker community in the U.S.A., owing to the teaching of Elias *Hicks (q.v.) whose emphasis on the 'Christ within' seemed to set aside the authority of Scripture and the historical Person of our Lord. Repercussions of the split were felt in the 'Beacon controversy' in England, so named from the *Beacon to the Society of Friends* (1835) by Isaac Crewdson (1780–1844), which strongly criticized Hicks's views. Considerable numbers of Friends joined other Protestant bodies, whilst the remainder endeavoured to imbue the sect with a more Evangelical spirit. Gradually the removal of the disabilities of dissent led to an almost complete exterior adaptation of the Friends to the habits of their contemporaries in dress, speech, and other external matters.

The religious tenets of the Friends are set forth in the classic work of R. *Barclay (q.v.), *Theologiae Verae Christianae Apologia* (1676). Their central doctrine is the 'Inner Light', which is superior to the Scriptures and the Church. Its possession consists chiefly in the sense of the Divine and the direct working of God in the soul, by which man is freed from sin, united to Christ, and enabled to perform good works. Its visible effects are mostly of a moral character, viz. simplicity, purity, and truthfulness. From the paramount importance given to the Inner Light derives the rejection of the Sacraments, the ministry and all set forms of worship. Their 'meetings' are held in bare rooms and begin in silence, in 'holy expectation before the Lord' until some member of the congregation, whether man or woman, feels stirred to speak. Their organization is democratic. Its lowest unit, the 'Preparative Meeting', consists of a single congregation; the 'Monthly Meeting' comprises representatives of several 'Preparative Meetings'; above it are the 'Quarterly Meetings', and at the top the 'Yearly Meeting', comprising in this country Great Britain without Ireland. The Yearly Meeting has legislative powers and deals with questions of policy, social work, etc. Apart from these there is also a permanent Meeting, first established in the time of persecution (1675), which deals with cases of hardship all over the world and therefore called 'Meeting for Sufferings'. There is no formal ministry, but the Society recognizes certain officers with specific duties. Among these there are 'elders' who are responsible for the holding and due conduct of meetings for worship, and 'overseers' whose chief task is the pastoral supervision of the congregation. As baptism is not administered, Quaker parentage automatically confers membership.

The Quaker refusal of military service and oaths has often brought them into conflict with the civil authorities. But their devotion to social and educational work (and also, esp. in the 20th cent., international relief), as well as their high standards of personal integrity, has won popular opinion to their side, and in most countries they are free to live as their consciences direct, without serious interference. Noted Quakers, besides those already mentioned, include Elizabeth *Fry, the prison reformer; Joseph Lancaster (1778–1838), the pioneer of elementary education; Joseph *Rowntree and George Cadbury (1839–1922), the cocoa manufacturers, the latter of whom gave his home at Woodbrooke, Selly Oak, as a social and religious centre; and J. R. *Harris, the student of early Christian origins.

Beside Barclay's *Apology* (see above) the old classical work on the Society of Friends is W. Sewel's *History of the Rise, Increase, and Progress of the People called Quakers* (1717). W. C. Braithwaite, *The Beginnings of Quakerism* (1912); id., *The Second Period of Quakerism* (1919); A. N. Brayshaw, *The Quakers* (1921); E. Grubb, *Quaker Thought and History* (1925); R. M. Jones, *The Faith and Practice of the Quakers* (1927); H. Brinton, *Friends for 300 Years*. Beliefs and Practice of the Society of Friends since George Fox started the Quaker Movement (1953).

FRIENDS OF CATHEDRALS. See *Cathedrals, Friends of.*

FRIENDS OF GOD. See *Gottesfreunde.*

FRITH, JOHN (c. 1503–33), Protestant martyr. He was educated at Eton and King's College, Cambridge. In 1525 T. *Wolsey made him a junior canon of his newly founded 'Cardinal College' (Christ Church), Oxford. In 1528 he was imprisoned for heresy, but escaped to Marburg, where he assisted W. *Tyndale with his work on the Bible. On his return in 1532 he was arrested, and after a book of his on the sacraments (written for a friend and not intended for publication) had come into the hands of T. *More, he was condemned to death for denying that *purgatory and *transubstantiation were necessary dogmas, and burned at Smithfield on 4 July 1533. While at Marburg he had published *A Pistle to the Christen Reader; Antithesis wherein are compared together Christ's Acts and our Holy Father the Pope's* (1529), and *A Disputation of Purgatory* (1531).

The Whole Works of W. Tyndall, John Frith and Doct. Barnes, ed. by J. *Foxe ('1572'), incl. short life (separately paginated). Life from J. Foxe, Acts and Monuments of the Christian Martyrs, with extracts from his collected works, pr. in [L. Richmond (ed.)] The Fathers of the English Church: or A Selection from the Writings of the Reformers and Early Protestant Divines of the Church of England, i (1807), pp. 341–474. D. Alcock, John Frith, Scholar, Reformer and Martyr ('Lives of Great Men' [1904]; pamphlet. A. C. Bickley in D.N.B., xx (1889), pp. 278–80.

FROBEN, JOHN (c. 1460–1527), 'Frobenius', printer and scholar. A native of Hammelburg, Bavaria, Froben studied at Basle and in 1491 started in the city a press whose high standards of scholarship and accuracy soon made his name famous throughout Europe. In his earlier years he worked in close association with Johannes Amerbach (1443–1513). From *c.* 1513 onwards *Erasmus, whose friendship Froben had had the good fortune to make, prepared or supervised a long series of editions for Froben's press, the most famous being Erasmus' *editio princeps* of the Greek Testament (1516). Among the Church Fathers which Erasmus edited through Froben were *Jerome (1516), *Cyprian (1520), *Hilary of Poitiers (1523), *Ambrose (1527), and *Augustine (1528). A generous patron of scholarship, he died poor. After his death his press was carried on by his son, Jerome Froben, and his son-in-law, Nicolaus Episcopius.

Two of his letters are printed among the Erasmi Epistolae ed. by P. S. Allen, No. 419, ii (Oxford, 1910), p. 250 f., with notes, and No. 801, iii (1913), p. 255. Those of Erasmus to him, ib., No. 602, iii, p. 12 f.; No. 629, p. 53; No. 635, p. 56 f.; No. 795, p. 250 f.; No. 885, p. 421 f. I. Stockmeyer and B. Reber, Beiträge zur Basler Buchdruckergeschichte (1840), pp. 85–115, incl. list of books publ. by him.

FROISSART, JEAN (c. 1335–c. 1405), French chronicler. He was a native of Valenciennes, and at an early age visited the English court, whither he returned in 1361. The consort of Edward III, Philippa of Hainault, became his benefactress, at whose suggestion he went to Scotland in search of material for his chronicles. He returned to France in 1367. From 1373 to 1382 he was parish priest at Les Estinnes, nr. Thuin, and from 1383 till his death canon at Chimay. These offices, however, did not prevent him from undertaking lengthy journeys over much of Europe collecting first-hand information for his work. These famous 'Chroniques' relate in four books the history of the more considerable European countries between 1325 and 1400, most of it being based on eye-witness accounts. The work presents a remarkably lively picture of the times of the Hundred Years War, though it is unreliable in chronological and geographical details. Much of it is derived from a similar work by Jean le Bel, a canon of Liége. Froissart also wrote poems of love and adventure in the style of his time.

Œuvres de Froissart. Chroniques ed. le Baron Kervyn de Lettenhove (28 vols., Brussels, 1867–77), with revised ed. of id., Froissart. Étude littéraire sur le XIVᵉ siècle (2 vols. bound in one, 1857) in vol. i; Poésies ed. A. Scheler (3 vols., ib., 1870–2). Best ed. of Chroniques, publ. by La Société de l'Histoire de France, ed. S. Luce–F. Raynaud–L. Mirot (1899 ff., 12 vols. (up to 1385) in 1931). Eng. tr. by Sir John Berners (London, 1523), ed. W. P. Ker (6 vols., 1903); abridged ed. by G. C. Macaulay (London, 1895); condensed version of Chronicles, in Eng. tr., in Everyman's Library, lvii; 1906. M. Darmesteter, Froissart (Paris, 1894; Eng. tr., 1895). F. S. Sheares, Froissart, Chronicler and Poet (1930); G. G. Coulton, The Chronicler of European Chivalry (1930).

FRONTAL (Lat. *antependium, pallium altaris*). The panel of embroidered cloth, or in some cases of wood or metal, ornamented with carving or enamel, placed in front of the altar. It is most usual for the frontal to be changeable, and its colour to agree with the liturgical colour of the season or day; and a *rubric in the Roman *Missal orders this practice to be followed 'where possible' (*quoad fieri potest*; Rubr. Gen. xx). The Anglican Canons of 1603 order that the Lord's Table should be 'covered, in time of Divine Service, with a carpet of silk or other decent stuff, thought meet by the Ordinary of the place' (can. 82).

FROUDE, RICHARD HURRELL (1803–36), *Tractarian. The elder brother of James Anthony Froude, the historian, he was educated at Eton and Oriel College, Oxford, where he became a Fellow (1826) and shortly afterwards (1827) a tutor, of his college. Intimacy with his colleague, J. H. *Newman, greatly influenced both. After travels with Newman in the Mediterranean in the winter of 1832–3, he took part in the conference on Church reform at Hadleigh Rectory (July 1833), and collaborated closely with Newman and J. *Keble in the early stages of the Tractarian Movement, though symptoms of consumption caused him to spend much of his remaining years out of England. His *Remains*, which were edited posthumously, with a preface by Newman (part i, 2 vols., 1838; part ii, 2 vols., 1839), and which were largely extracts from his private diary, provoked a storm. His strictures on the Reformers, the more exaggerated of them written half jestingly, were thought by those who had not known Froude personally, disloyal, while the records of his spiritual and ascetic practices, which even his close friends had not suspected to lie behind his handsome appearance and lively manner, and his praise of clerical celibacy and devotion to the BVM, startled his readers.

The primary source is his *Remains* referred to above. J. H. Newman, *Apologia pro Vita Sua*, pt. iii (ed. Oxford, 1913, pp. 125–7). R. W. *Church, *The Oxford Movement* (1891), ch. iii (with some recollections by Lord Blachford appended). Louise I. Guiney, *Hurrell Froude. Memorials and Comments* (1904).

FRUCTUOSUS, St. (d. 259), Bp. of Tarragona. With two deacons, Augurius and Eulogius, he was arrested in the persecution under Valerian and burnt at the stake in the amphitheatre. The *acta* of his passion seem certainly authentic. His martyrdom is referred to by *Prudentius (*Peristephanon*, hymn 6) and St. *Augustine (*serm.* 273). Feast day, 21 Jan.

AA.SS., Jan. II (1643), pp. 339–42. His *Acta* are also pr. in T. *Ruinart, *Acta Primorum Martyrum Sincera et Selecta* (Paris, 1689), pp. 220–3. P. F. de' Cavalieri, *Note agiografiche*, viii (S.T., lxv; 1935), 'Gli atti di S. Fruttuoso di Tarragona', pp. 127–99, incl. text, pp. 183–94. Bardenhewer, ii, p. 691.

FRUITS OF THE HOLY GHOST. These, based on Gal. 5. 22 f. (AV, RV), are 'love, joy, peace, long-suffering, gentleness, goodness, faith, meekness, temperance', to which the *Vulgate text adds 'modesty, continence, chastity', making twelve in all. That the correct number of the fruits is twelve is defended on theological grounds by St. *Thomas Aquinas, *Summa Theol.* II, i, q. 70, a. 3.

A. Gardeil, O.P., in *D.T.C.*, vi (1920), cols. 944–9, s.v. 'Fruits du Saint-Esprit'.

FRUMENTIUS, St. (*c.* 300–*c.* 380), 'Apostle of the Abyssinians'. Acc. to *Rufinus (*HE*, i, 9 f.), Aedesius and Frumentius were the two young companions of a Tyrian merchant, Meropius. After all three were captured on the way back from a voyage to 'India' by the Ethiopians, Meropius was executed, but the two others, who were both Christians, were taken before the King at *Axum, whom they later assisted in the government of his country. Frumentius took advantage of the opportunity to carry on mission work, and on reporting the fruits of his work at *Alexandria was consecrated bishop by St. *Athanasius *c.* 340. He received the title '*Abuna', i.e. 'Our Father', which was henceforward assumed by the holders of the primacy of the Abyssinian Church. Frumentius appears to have been a strong opponent of *Arianism. Feast day, by the Greeks, 30 Nov., by the Copts, 18 Dec.; in the W., 27 Oct.

Frumentius is also mentioned in the 5th-cent. Histories of *Socrates (I, 19), *Sozomen (II, 24), and *Theodoret (I, 22); cf. also Athanasius, *Apol. ad Const.*, 31. *AA.SS.*, Oct. XII (1867), pp. 257–70, with discussion of chronology. L. *Duchesne, *Histoire ancienne de l'Église*, iii (1910), pp. 576–8.

FRY, ELIZABETH (1780–1845), *Quaker prison reformer. Born at Norwich, the third daughter of John Gurney, banker, in 1800 she married Joseph Fry, a London merchant and a strict Quaker, by whom she had a large family. In 1808 she established a girls' school at Plashet, nr. East Ham. In 1811 she was admitted a 'minister' in the Society of Friends and became a noted speaker. In 1813 her interest was aroused in the appalling state of the prisons and, at the instigation of William Forster (1784–1854), she devoted herself to the welfare of female prisoners in Newgate. Here her Bible readings made a deep impression. In 1817 she formed an association to supply clothes for the destitute and began a campaign for prison reform which aimed at the separation of the sexes, classification of criminals, female supervision of women and adequate provision of secular and religious instruction; and in 1818 she gave evidence on the state of the prisons to a committee of the House of Commons. From now on she devoted herself increasingly to other classes of the helpless, took part in the formation of a 'Nightly Shelter for the Homeless' in London (1820), and instituted visiting societies in Brighton and elsewhere to deal with mendicancy. In her later years she travelled extensively in Europe, fostering prison reform. Under her influence libraries were provided in all coastguard stations in 1836, and in the naval hospitals at Plymouth and Haslar, Portsmouth. Behind all her philanthropic work there was a strong Christian impulse and she never ceased to combine it with active evangelization.

Her writings include *Texts for Every Day in the Year* (1831) and a report, issued jointly with her brother, J. J. Gurney, on Irish social conditions (1827). In 1846 an asylum was founded in her memory in Mare Street, Hackney, for women discharged from prison under the name of the 'Elizabeth Fry Refuge'.

Memoir, with extracts from her journal and letters, ed. by two of her daughters (2 vols., 1847; revised and enlarged ed. 1848; abridged ed. by Mrs F. Cresswell, daughter, 1856). R. B. Johnson (ed.), *Elizabeth Fry's Journeys on the Continent 1840–1841*, from a Diary kept by her Niece, Elizabeth Gurney (1931). Other lives by T. Timpson (1847), S. Corder (1853), G. K. Lewis (1910), and Janet P. Whitney (1937), all publd. at London. W. G. Blaikie in *D.N.B.*, xx (1889), pp. 294–6.

FULBERT, St. (*c.* 960–1028), Bp. of *Chartres. Born in Italy, prob. near *Rome, where he met *Gerbert of Aurillac (later Pope Sylvester II), he studied under Gerbert at *Reims and *Chartres. In 990 Odo, Bp. of Chartres (968–1004), appointed him chancellor of his cathedral school. By his genius in drawing men to himself, Fulbert made the school of Chartres the most vigorous in Europe, and its distinctive tradition persisted long after his death. His range of knowledge included all the sciences studied in his day. In 1007 he became Bp. of Chartres. His extant writings comprise sermons; many poems and hymns, including the 'Chorus Novae Jerusalem' ('Ye choirs of New Jerusalem'); and letters. He was also a distinguished statesman, enjoying the confidence of the Duke of Aquitaine and the King of France, and a notable builder, though of his new cathedral only the crypt now remains. Feast day, 10 Apr.

Opera Varia ed. C. de Villiers (Paris, 1608); works repr. mainly from the 'Magna Bibliotheca Patrum' with additions and introd. notices in J. P. Migne, *PL*, cxli, 163–374. C. Pfister, *De Fulberti Carnotensis Vita et Operibus* (Paris thesis; Nancy, 1885). A. Clerval, *Les Écoles de Chartres au moyen-âge* (Paris thesis; Paris, 1895), pp. 30–42 and 58–142. J. A. Enders, *Forschungen zur Geschichte der frühmittelalterlichen Philosophie* (B.G.P.M., xvii; 1915), pp. 21–5 ('Fulbert von Chartres als Freund der freien Künste'). Hilda Johnstone, 'Fulbert of Chartres' in *C.Q.R.*, cii (1926), pp. 45–67, Manitius, ii, pp. 682–94. Raby, pp. 258–63, with bibl., p, 478. M. Ott, in *C.E.*, vi (1909), p. 312 f.; A. Clerval in *D.T.C.*, vi (1920), cols. 964–7; J. Geiselmann in *L.Th.K.*, iv (1932), col. 224 f., for further bibl.; all s.v.

FULDA. The *Benedictine abbey of Fulda in Hesse Nassau was founded in 744 by St. Sturmius, a disciple of St. *Boniface, to assist missionary work among the Saxons. Boniface's tomb made it a great pilgrimage centre, and it became a rich and powerful corporation with lands all over Germany. Under *Rabanus Maurus (abbot, 822–42), it was one of the foremost centres of Christian culture in Europe, and from the latter half of the 10th cent. its abbot possessed certain rights over all German Benedictine houses. In the 16th cent. the *Lutherans gained control for a time, but mainly through the work of the *Jesuits the abbey was again firmly established in Catholic hands shortly after the beginning of the 17th cent. In 1802 the abbey was finally secularized; but from 1829 Fulda has been an episcopal see.

Annales Fuldenses, 680–901, ed. G. H.|Pertz in *M.G.H.*, Scriptores, i (1826), pp. 337–415. *Annales Necrologi Fuldenses, 779–1065*, ed. G. Waitz, ib. xiii (1881), pp. 161–218. J. F. Schannat, *Historia Fuldensis* (Frankfurt, 1719). P. Lehmann, *Fuldaer Studien* (*Sb.* (Bayr.), 1925, Abh. 3, and 1927, Abh. 3). L. H. Cottineau, O.S.B., *Répertoire topo-bibliographique des abbayes et prieurés* (Mâcon, 1935), cols. 1229–1232, s.v., with full bibl. H. *Leclercq, O.S.B., in *D.A.C.L.*, v (pt. 2; 1923), cols. 2684–92, s.v. 'Fulda (Manuscrits liturgiques de)', with bibl.

FULGENTIUS, St. (468–533), Bp. of Ruspe in N. Africa. He abandoned the Roman civil service for the monastic life, and suffered constant persecution from the *Arian king, Thrasamund. Soon after becoming Bp. of Ruspe *c.* 507, he was banished to Sardinia with 60 other Catholic bishops, returned to Africa in 515 for a public discussion with the Arian clergy, was banished again *c.* 517, and finally allowed by King Hilderic to return in 523. Scholarly and acquainted with Greek, Fulgentius was a thoroughgoing follower of St. *Augustine. He wrote many treatises, of little originality, against *Arianism and *Pelagianism. A few letters survive, but of the many sermons ascribed to him, only eight are certainly authentic. His life was written by his friend, *Ferrandus of Carthage. Feast day, 1 Jan.

Works ed. by the Maurist L. Mangeant (Paris, 1684) repr. in J. P. Migne, *PL.*, lxv, 103–1020. Two newly recovered sermons ed. J. Leclercq, O.S.B., 'Deux Sermons inédits de S. Fulgence' in *R. Bén.*, lvi (1945–6), pp. 93–107. New tr. of Ferrandus's Life of Fulgentius ed. G. G. Lapeyre (1932). G. G. Lapeyre, *Saint Fulgence de Ruspe* (1929), with bibl. G. Ficker, 'Zur Würdigung der *Vita Fulgentii*', in *Z.K.G.*, xxi (1900), pp. 9–42; J. Stiglmayr, S.J., 'Das *Quicunque* und Fulgentius' in *Z.K.T.*, xlix (1924), pp. 341–357 (ascribes *Athanasian Creed to Fulgentius). Bardenhewer, v (1932), pp. 303–16.

FULGENTIUS FERRANDUS. See *Ferrandus.*

FULKE, WILLIAM (1538–89), *Puritan theologian. He was educated at St. John's College, Cambridge, where he was elected Fellow in 1564. He soon became involved in the *Vestiarian Controversy; indeed his zeal in persuading nearly 300 members of his college to abandon the use of the surplice in chapel led to his expulsion for a time. In 1578 he was elected Master of Pembroke Hall. He continued to take a prominent part in the Puritan cause and in 1581 disputed with the *Jesuit, E. *Campion. His many treatises in defence of extreme Protestant principles were learned and effective, though their language was often coarse and virulent. By a strange irony, it was largely his polemical attack on the *Reims version of the NT (the text of which Fulke printed side by side with that of the '*Bishops' Bible') that led to its becoming widely known in England and opened the way for its influence on the language of the AV. He was succeeded as Master of Pembroke Hall by L. *Andrewes.

Modern edd. of his *Stapleton's Fortress Overthrown.* A Rejoinder to Martiall's Reply. A Discovery of the Dangerous Rock of the Popish Church Commended by Sanders (1580), by R. Gibbings (*Parker Society, 1848), and of *A Defence of the Sincere and True Translations of the Holy Scriptures against the Cavils of Gregory Martin* (1583), by C. H. Hartshorne (ib., 1843). E. Venables in *D.N.B.*, xx (1889), pp. 305–8.

FULLER, ANDREW (1754–1815), *Baptist divine. A native of Cambridgeshire, he was ordained pastor of the Baptist congregation at Soham in 1775, and in 1782 became minister at Kettering. While at Soham he published *The Gospel worthy of all Acceptance* [*c.* 1785], a book directed against the extreme form of *Calvinism which allowed 'nothing spiritually good to be the duty of the unregenerate'. The book greatly impressed W. *Carey, and when in 1792 the Baptist Missionary Society was founded with Fuller as its first secretary, Carey spoke of him as 'holding the rope' while he 'went down into the mine'. In 1793 he published a defence of Calvinistic Baptist teaching against some *Socinian charges that free grace implies moral relaxation, and against *Deism he wrote *The Gospel its own Witness* (1799). He also published collections of expository and other sermons.

Complete Works, with a Memoir of his life by A. G. Fuller (son), in 23 parts (London [*c.* 1831–] 1846). J. Ryland, *The Work of Faith, the Labour of Love, and the Patience of Hope illustrated; in the Life and Death of the Reverend Andrew Fuller* (1816). Further Memoirs of his Life and Writings by J. W. Morris (London, 1815) and T. E. Fuller, grandson (London, 1863). G. Laws, *Andrew Fuller. Pastor, Theologian, Ropeholder* (1942). W. G. Blaikie in *D.N.B.*, xx (1889), p. 309 f.

FULLER, THOMAS (1608–61), Anglican historian. Educated at Queens' College, Cambridge, he was later Curate of St. Benet's, Cambridge (1630–3), Rector of Broadwindsor, Dorset (1634–41), Curate of Waltham Abbey (from *c.* 1649; where he was summoned before O. *Cromwell's *Tryers, though he managed to escape deprivation), and Rector of Cranford (1658–61). His witty and popular style won him a wide reputation. Of his historical writings, the most renowned are his *Church History of Britain* (1655) and his *Worthies of England* (posthumous, 1662), on both of which Fuller worked for a great part of his life, collecting some of his material during his campaigns with the royalist forces in the Civil War. Of a more popular kind was *The Holy State and the Profane State* (1642), a series of 'characters' illustrating the Christian moral ideal. He also wrote a *History of the Holy War* (1639), on the *Crusades, besides other works.

Full Life, with bibliography, by J. E. Bailey (1874). *Collected Sermons*, ed. J. E. Bailey and W. E. A. Axon (1891); *Selections*, ed. E. K. Broadus (1928). D. B. Lyman, *The Great Tom Fuller* (1935).

FULLO, PETRUS. See *Peter the Fuller*.

FUNDAMENTALISM. A movement in various Protestant bodies which developed after the War of 1914–18, esp. in the U.S.A. It rigidly upheld what it believed to be traditional orthodox Christian doctrines and esp. the literal inerrancy of Scripture. It attracted widespread public attention in 1925 when William Jennings Bryan (1860–1925), the American Democrat leader, assisted in the prosecution of J. T. Scopes, a school teacher of Dayton, Tennessee, who was convicted on the charge of violating the state law by teaching the doctrine of biological evolution. In a wider sense the term is applied to all profession of strict adherence to (esp. Protestant) orthodoxy in the matter of Biblical interpretation.

N. F. Furniss, *The Fundamentalist Controversy, 1918–1931* (Yale Historical Publications, Miscellany, lix; 1954).

FUNERAL SERVICES. See *Burial Service*.

G

GABBATHA. Acc. to Jn. 19. 13, the place in *Jerusalem where *Pilate sat down in judgement on Christ. The 'Hebrew' (more accurately, the *Aramaic) word is stated in the Gospel to be the equivalent of the Greek λιθόστρωτος, 'Pavement'. Modern archaeological opinion inclines to the view that Pilate's residence was in what is now called the Citadel of Jerusalem. If that is so, the Gabbatha from which Pilate sought to negotiate with the people (Jn. 18. 29) and where he exposed Christ (Jn. 19. 5) would be in front of the so-called Tower of David.

Le Père Barnabè, d'Alsace, O.F.M., *Le Prétoire de Pilate et la Fortresse Antonia* (1902). L. H. Vincent, O.P.–F. M. Abel, O.P., *Jérusalem*, ii (1922), pp. 562–86. L. H. Vincent, O.P., 'L'Antonia et le prétoire' in *R. Bibl.*, xlii (1933), pp. 83–113; id., 'Autour du prétoire', ib., xlvi (1937), pp. 563–70; id., 'Le Lithostrotos évangélique', ib., lix (1952), pp. 513–30; P. Benoît, O.P., 'Prétoire, Lithostroton et Gabbatha', ib., pp. 531–50.

GABIROL, SALOMON BEN. See *Avicebron*.

GABRIEL (Heb.), 'man of God'. One of the seven *archangels. He is mentioned in Dan. 8. 15 f. and 9. 21 f., where he assists Daniel in the understanding of his visions. In the NT he foretells the birth of St. John the Baptist to his father, Zacharias, and announces the conception of our Lord to the BVM (Lk. 1. 11 f., 1. 26). As the messenger of Divine comfort, he is accorded in Jewish theology the place of highest rank after *Michael. Feast day, 24 Mar. (i.e. the day before the *Annunciation).

E. B. *Pusey, *Daniel the Prophet* (1864), p. 520 f. O. *Bardenhewer, *Mariä Verkündigung*. Ein Kommentar zu Lk. 1, 26–38 (Biblische Studien, x, Hft. 5, 1905), pp. 48–59. See also general commentaries on St. Luke's Gospel (s.v.).

GABRIEL SEVERUS (1541–1616), theologian. A native of the Morea, Gabriel was consecrated Metropolitan of Philadelphia, now Ala-Shehr, in Asia Minor, in 1577. The see being in Turkish hands and its duties slight, Gabriel migrated to Venice to act as bishop for the Greek Christians in the Venetian Republic. There he acquired a reputation as a theologian and anti-Latin controversialist. His best known work is a defence of the Greek practice of venerating the eucharistic elements at the *Great Entrance on the ground that, being dedicated for consecration, they are no longer common bread and wine, but have become 'holy' and 'honourable' by participation (μετοχικῶς), and therefore deserve a reverence only second in order to the adoration due to the consecrated Eucharist. Some of his writings were translated into Latin by R. *Simon and published by him at Paris in 1671 as *Fides Ecclesiae Orientalis seu Gabrielis Metropolitae Philadelphiensis Opuscula*.

M. Jugie, A.A., 'Un Théologien grec du XVIe siècle, Gabriel Sévère et les divergences entre les deux Églises' in *É.O.*, xvi (1913), pp. 97–108, with bibl. D. *Stone, *A History of the Doctrine of the Holy Eucharist*, i (1909), pp. 173–5. M. Jugie, A.A., in *D.T.C.*, vi (1920), cols. 977–83, s.v., also with bibl.

GAETANO DA TIENE. See *Cajetan, St.*

GAIRDNER, JAMES (1828–1912), English historian. In 1846 he entered the Public Record Office. His many writings include editions of the *Calendar of Letters and Papers of the reign of *Henry VIII* (London, 1862–1905), and of the *Paston Letters* (1872–5), as well as *Henry VII* (1889), *The English Church in the Sixteenth Century* (1902), and *Lollardy and the Reformation in England* (4 vols., 1908–1913). A diligent and accurate historian, he wrote particularly on the period of the *Reformation in England, where he believed that modern historians had commonly done less than justice to the Catholic case.

Preface by W. Hunt in his ed. of Gairdner's *Lollardy and the Reformation*, iv (posthumous, 1913), pp. v–xii. R. H. Brodie in *D.N.B., 1912–1921*, p. 206.

GAIRDNER, WILLIAM HENRY TEMPLE (1873–1928), Anglican missionary. Educated at Rossall and Trinity College, Oxford, he went to Cairo as a *C.M.S. missionary in 1898, was ordained priest in 1901, and worked in co-operation with his friend Douglas Thornton, whose biography he wrote (1908), until the latter's death in 1907. After prolonged study of Arabic and Islamics, he threw himself into the reorganization of the Arabic Anglican Church, with the determination to make it a living spiritual home for converted Moslems. He became the apostle of Arabic Christian scholarship and a pioneer teacher of the colloquial language, producing a Conversation Grammar of *Egyptian Colloquial Arabic* (1917), *The Phonetics of Arabic* (1925), besides hymns and versified Gospel stories in the vernacular. He also published many other works, devotional, exegetic, doctrinal, musical, and linguistic, in Arabic and in English, the *Reproach of Islam* (1909) being the best known.

C. E. Padwick, *Temple Gairdner of Cairo* (1929). M. D. Gairdner (widow; ed.), *W. H. T. G. to his Friends*. Some Letters and Informal Writings of Canon W. H. Temple Gairdner of Cairo, 1873–1928 [1930].

GAISFORD, THOMAS (1779–1855), Dean of Christ Church, Oxford, from 1831. Educated at Christ Church, he became Regius professor of Greek in 1812. In 1829 he was offered the bishopric of Oxford on the death of C. Lloyd, but refused it. His reputation rests chiefly on his contributions to the study of the Greek classics (e.g. Hephaestion, Herodotus, Stobaeus). In the field of *Patristics, he prepared critical editions of *Eusebius of Caesarea's *Praeparatio* (1843) and *Demonstratio Evangelica* (1852), as well as of the Byzantine lexicographer, *Suidas (1834).

H. R. Luard in *D.N.B.*, xx (1889), pp. 370–2, s.v. H. L. Thompson, *Christ Church* (1900), pp. 193–202.

GAIUS, also Caius (early 3rd cent.), Roman presbyter. Acc. to *Eusebius (*HE*, 2. 25. 6; cf. 6. 20. 3), he was an orthodox Churchman (ἐκκλησιαστικὸς ἀνήρ). Under *Zephyrinus (198–217) he held a debate with a Montanist, Proclus. He accepted the thirteen Epp. of St. Paul, but rejected the Gospel and Rev. of St. John, holding them to be the work of *Cerinthus. *Photius describes him as 'Bishop of the Gentiles' (ἐθνῶν ἐπίσκοπος), but this is probably due to confusion with *Hippolytus, with whom, as we learn from a Commentary of the Jacobite, Dionysius Bar-Salibi (12th cent.), Gaius also had a controversy.

G. Bareille in *D.T.C.*, ii (1905), cols. 1309–11, s.v. 'Caius', with bibl.

GALATIANS, Epistle to the. St. *Paul wrote this letter to his Galatian converts on receiving news of a counter-mission requiring them to keep all the commands of the Jewish Law, and thereby (as he thought) imperilling the whole value of their faith in Christ.

The Epistle opens with an account of his career from his conversion onwards, intended to show (a) that he had received his commission directly from God; (b) that no human teacher had authority to change the Gospel that he, Paul, had preached; and (c) that the original *Apostles at *Jerusalem, *Peter, *James, and *John, had recognized the rightfulness of his mission to the Gentiles. He then emphasizes the futility of trying to live by 'law', i.e. a prescribed code of conduct, and maintains that the way in which a man is justified in the sight of God is not that of 'law' but of 'faith'. This is illustrated by the case of Abraham as the most striking example of one who was justified by belief in God's promises. As these promises to Abraham were fulfilled in Christ, all external considerations, such as whether a man is a Jew or a Greek, are transcended in the Christian Church. Those who receive them are rewarded with the gift of the Spirit, and it is the possession of the Spirit which is the condition of the Christian life and the source of its fruits, 'love, joy, peace, long-suffering, kindness, goodness, faithfulness, meekness, temperance' (5. 22). The epistle ends with another warning to his readers not to put their trust in Jewish observances.

The epistle, which was written with a passionate intensity of feeling, is universally recognized as genuine. Traditionally it has been held that it was addressed to Christians in the country of Galatia in the interior of Asia Minor, which had been peopled by Gauls in the 3rd cent. B.C. An objection raised against this supposition is that there is no independent evidence that St. Paul ever preached the Gospel in these parts, and hence many modern scholars,

e.g. W. M. *Ramsay, K. *Lake, C. W. Emmet, have argued that 'Galatia' must be taken to mean the Roman province of Galatia, which covered a much wider area in Asia Minor, and included the cities of Pisidian Antioch, Iconium, Derbe, and Lystra, mentioned in Acts 13 f. Among recent scholars, however, there has been a certain tendency to revert from the 'South Galatian theory' to the older view. On either theory there are complex problems as to how to relate the events of St. Paul's life as recorded in Gal. 1 f. with those in Acts. Older scholars were almost unanimous in identifying the journey to Jerusalem in Gal. 2. 1–10 with that in Acts 15. But some Biblical students, among them J. *Calvin, but esp. exponents of the 'S. Galatian theory', e.g. W. M. Ramsay, have equated the journey recorded in Gal. 2. 1–10 with that in Acts 11. 29 f. and thereby explained the absence of reference to the 'decrees' of Acts 15. 20 on the assumption that the epistle was written before the Council had taken place. On this hypothesis Gal. could be dated in A.D. 50 or a little earlier, and thus be the earliest of all the NT epistles. Exponents of the N. Galatian theory tend to date it at *c.* A.D. 57–58.

Modern commentaries by J. B. *Lightfoot (Cambridge and London, 1865), W. M. Ramsay (London, 1899), H. *Lietzmann (Hb.N.T., iii, *Die Briefe des Apostels Paulus*, 1910, pp. 225–64; ed. 2, as separate vol. x; 1923; ed. 3, 1932), C. W. Emmet (London, 1912), M. J. *Lagrange, O.P. (Études Bibliques, 1918; ed. 4, 1942), E. de W. Burton (I.C.C., 1921), A. W. F. Blunt (Clar. Bib., 1925), G. S. Duncan (Moff. Comm., 1934), F. Amiot (Verbum Salutis, xiv; Paris, 1946; with Thess., pp. 11–241), H. Schlier (H.K.N.T., Siebente Abteilung, ed. 10; 1949). E. H. Askwith, *The Epistle to the Galatians*. An Essay on its Destination and Date (1899); D. Round, *The Date of St. Paul's Epistle to the Galatians* (1906). K. Lake, *The Earlier Epistles of St. Paul* (1911), pp. 253–323. J. H. *Ropes, *The Singular Problem of the Epistle to the Galatians* (Harvard Theological Studies, xiv; 1929). McNeile, pp. 143–50. W. J. Woodhouse and P. W. *Schmiedel in *E.Bi.*, ii (1901), cols. 1589–1626, s.vv. 'Galatia' and 'Galatians (The Epistle)'; F. S. Marsh in *D.A.C.*, i (1915), pp. 430–7.

GALE, THOMAS (*c.* 1635–1702), antiquary. After studying at Trinity College, Cambridge, he became successively Regius professor of Greek at Cambridge (1666), high master of St. Paul's School (1672), and Dean of *York (1697). A versatile scholar of European reputation and a correspondent of J. *Mabillon, he was the editor of *Historiae Anglicanae Scriptores Quinque* (1687) and *Historiae Britannicae Scriptores* (1691), the latter of which contained as its first three items the texts of Gildas, Nennius, and Eddi. The *Rerum Anglicarum Scriptores* (1684), often attributed to Gale, was in fact the work of William Fulman, who collaborated with Gale in some of his other writings. These three folios, which were all published anonymously at Oxford, contained the monastic chronicles of several of the lesser houses such as Burton and Margam, and are a valuable source, not only for local history, but also for the study of the history of medieval England in general. He was also the author of several other works, including an unpublished edition of *Origen's 'Philocalia'.

J. E. B. Mayor, *Cambridge in the Time of Queen Anne* (1911), pp. 448–50, incl. sources and list of MSS. G. Goodwin in *D.N.B.*, xx (1889), pp. 378–80.

GALERIUS (d. 311), Roman Emperor. An Illyrian of humble birth, he was appointed by *Diocletian in 293 to be co-regent ('Caesar') of the E. He won victories first over the Germans on the Danube (between 293 and 295) and later over the Persians. His fierce hatred of the Christians led him to persuade *Diocletian to issue (303) the edicts inaugurating the eight years' persecution. On Diocletian's abdication (305), Galerius succeeded to the throne. Only under the threat of the alliance of *Constantine and Maxentius did he issue in 311 his 'Edict of Toleration'. He died shortly afterwards of a horrible disease, the details of which are described, not without considerable relish, by *Lactantius (*De Mortibus Persecutorum*, 33).

The chief sources are Lactantius, *De Mortibus Persecutorum*, 9–35, and *Eusebius, *H.E.*, VIII, xvi f. H. M. D. Parker, *A History of the Roman World from A.D. 138 to 337* (1935), pp. 229–52. H. Mattingly in *C. Anc. H.*, xii (1939), esp. pp. 328–51. E. Stein, *Geschichte des spätrömischen Reiches*, i (1928), pp. 98–138. W. Ensslin in *P.W.*, xiv (1930), cols. 2516–28, s.v. 'Maximus (Galerius)'.

GALGANI, St. GEMMA (1878–1903), Italian *stigmatic. She was born of poor parents at Camigliano in Tuscany and lived most of her life at Lucca. Ill-health frustrated her desire of becoming a *Passionist nun, though she took the three vows privately and, in addition, a vow of perfection. She enjoyed frequent ecstasies, and received the *stigmata and marks of scourging intermittently between 1899 and 1901. Apart from her conviction of occasional diabolical possession, her spiritual life was normally peaceful. She was beatified in 1933 and canonized in 1940. Feast day, 11 Apr.

Lettere ed. by the Passionists, with preface by E. Pellegrinetti (Isola del Liri, 1941); *Estasi, diario, autobiografia*, ed. idd., also with preface by E. Pellegrinetti (ib., 1943). The principal secondary authority is the life by her confessor, Germano di S. Stanislao (Rome, 1907; many subsequent edd.). There are also a large number of lesser lives, mainly in Italian, among them those of G. Casali (Lucca, 1933) and Suor Gesualda dello Spirito Santo (Rome, 1941); in Eng. there is a short sketch by B. Williamson (London [1932]).

GALILEE (Heb. הַגָּלִיל). (1) Originally the term was applied only to part of the tribe of Naphtali, but in NT times it was given to all the district in N. Palestine extending from the Mediterranean to the *Jordan and the word is now generally used in this sense. It constituted one of the four Roman divisions of Palestine. Its position on the main trade routes between Egypt and Syria had made it from early times a cosmopolitan province. It was the scene of almost all the Lord's earlier Life and of a great part of His Ministry and included such places as *Nazareth, *Capernaum, *Bethsaida, and Magdala. Many of its chief towns were situated on the 'Sea of Galilee', a lake some 680 ft. below the level of the Mediterranean through which the R. Jordan flows.

(2) In medieval cathedrals, an outer porch or chapel to which penitents are said to have been admitted on *Ash Wednesday, before being brought into church to do their *penance.

S. Klein, *Beiträge zur Geographie und Geschichte Galiläas* (1909); id., *Neue Beiträge zur Geschichte und Geographie Galiläas* (Palästina-Studien, Hft. 1; 1923). E. Huntingdon, *Palestine and its Transformation* (1911), ch. viii, pp. 163–79; G. A. *Smith, *The Historical Geography of the Holy Land* (ed. 25; 1931), pp. 413–63. S. Merrill in *H.D.B.*, ii (1899), pp. 98–102, s.v.; T. K. Cheyne in *E.Bi.*, i (1901), cols. 1628–32, s.v., both with bibl.

GALILEE, Testament of our Lord in. See *Testament of our Lord in Galilee*.

GALILEI, GALILEO (1564–1642), popularly 'Galileo', Italian astronomer and mathematician. He was a native of Pisa and educated at the monastery of *Vallombrosa, near Florence, where for a time he hoped to enter the monastic life. After studying medicine and mathematics at Pisa for four years, he was forced by poverty to leave in 1585 without taking his degree. A little later he attracted attention by his invention of the hydrostatic balance and in 1589 he was appointed mathematical lecturer at Pisa. Here from the study of falling bodies he discovered the laws of dynamics. The success of his new methods, based on empirical observation in place of deduction from abstract principles, earned him the permanent hostility of the *Aristotelians; and in 1591 he withdrew to Florence. In 1592 he was given the mathematical chair at Padua, which he held for 18 years. Here his discovery of the four satellites of Jupiter (7 Jan. 1610) by the aid of his newly invented telescope revolutionized the study of astronomy and led him to indicate in the *Sidereus Nuntius* (1610) his belief in the *Copernican theory of the solar system; and his name became famous throughout Europe. In the autumn of 1610 he was appointed philosopher and mathematician extraordinary to the Duke of Tuscany at Florence. His *Historia e dimostrazioni intorno alle macchie solari* (1613), which boldly asserted the Copernican theory, brought him into conflict with the *Holy Office, which still maintained the Ptolemaic belief. In 1616 the Copernican theory was condemned at Rome and Galileo forbidden 'to hold, teach or defend' it. At the same time the Congregation of the *Index issued a decree suspending *Copernicus' *De Revolutionibus Orbium Coelestium* (1543) 'until it was corrected' (*usque corrigatur*). Nevertheless, in 1632 Galileo broke silence and published the *Dialogo dei due massimi sistemi del mondo*, a sharp attack on Ptolemaic astronomy. The work was handed over to the *Inquisition; and in the following year Galileo was summoned to Rome, forced to recant under threat of torture, and condemned to imprisonment as 'vehemently suspected of heresy'. His famous words *Eppur si muove* ('None the less it does move') seem, however, to be legendary. After a few months of confinement, he was allowed to return to Florence, where he died on 15 Feb. 1642. He is buried in the church of Sta. Croce.

The primary documents relating to the heresy charge are in two series, viz. the registers of the Trial and the registers of the Decrees, both belonging to the *Holy Office. The former were taken to France by Napoleon in 1811 and returned to Rome in 1845 only on condition of publication. Editions, all incomplete, were issued by M. Marini (Rome, 1850), Henri de l'Épinois in *R.Q.H.*, iii (1867), pp. 68-145; and, with corrections, with 'Avant-propos', Paris, 1877, and D. Berti (Rome, 1876). Complete ed. by C. von Gebler (2 vols., Stuttgart, 1876-7). New and more accurate ed., which also includes the first crit. ed. of Decrees, by A. Favaro (Florence, 1907). Complete Works of Galileo, ed. E. Alberi (16 vols., Florence, 1842-56); improved ed. ('Edizione Nazionale') by A. Favaro and others (20 vols., Florence, 1890-1909). There is a vast literature, listed to date in A. Carli-A. Favaro, *Bibliografia galileiana (1568-1895)* (Rome, 1896). A. Favaro has also written *Galileo e lo studio di Padova* (1883) and many other studies. Works in Eng. include J. J. Fahie, *Galileo, His Life and Work* (1903); F. R. Wegg Prosser, *Galileo and his Judges* (1889); and F. S. Taylor, *Galileo and the Freedom of Thought* (1938). Agnes M. Clerke in *E.B.* (ed. 11), xi (1910), pp. 406-11; E. Vacandard in *D.T.C.*, vi (1920), cols. 1058-94; P. Paschini in *E.C.*, v (1950), cols. 1871-80, all s.v.

GALL, St. (*c.* 550-645), missionary. An Irishman, he was one of the twelve disciples who accompanied St. *Columbanus from (the Irish) *Bangor to Gaul and established themselves with him at *Luxeuil. He separated from Columbanus in 612, when the latter went to Italy, and remained in the part of Swabia which is now Switzerland, living mostly as a hermit. He is symbolically represented in art by a bear. Feast day, 16 Oct.

The famous Benedictine monastery at St. Gallen dates from about a hundred years later, though tradition traces it back to St. Gall's time. From the end of the 9th cent. its '*scriptorium' and collection of MSS. were for long among the most famous in Europe. The monastery seems to be unique in still housing a library which made it celebrated over a thousand years ago.

(1) SAINT. Contemporary reff. in Jonas, 'Vita S. Columbani'. The oldest Life of St. Gall ('Vita Vetustissima') dates from *c.* 750; surviving fragments ed. by E. Egli in *Neues Archiv*, xxi (1895), pp. 361-71, and B. Krusch in *M.G.H.*, Scriptores Rerum Merovingicarum, IV (1902), pp. 251-6. Life by *Walafrid Strabo in *Acta Sanctorum O.S.B.*, II (1669), pp. 228-68; modern ed. by B. Krusch, loc. cit., 280-337, Eng. tr. by Maud Joynt (Translations of Christian Literature, Ser. V, S.P.C.K., 1927). Fragments of metrical life by *Notker in *M.G.H.*, Poetae Latinae, IV, ii (1923), pp. 1093-1108. On St. Gall's life see also B. Krusch, *loc. cit.*, pp. 229-41.

(2) ABBEY. H. Wartmann [contd. by P. Bütler, T. Schiess, and J. Müller], *Urkundenbuch der Abtei St. Gallen* (6 vols., 1863 ff., latest fasc. to date, 1941); G. Meyer von Knonau (ed.), 'St. Gallische Geschichtsquellen' in *Mittheilungen zur vaterländischen Geschichte*, xii (N.F., ii; 1870), pp. 1-150, xiii (N.F., iii; 1872), and xv (N.F., v)-xviii (N.F., viii; 1877-81). J. von Watt (ed. by E. Götzinger), *Chronik der Aebte des Klosters St. Gallen* (Deutsche historische Schriften, 2 vols., 1875-77). J. M. Clark, *The Abbey of St. Gall as a Centre of Literature and Art* (1925), with bibl. A. Merton, *Die Buchmalerei in St. Gallen vom neunten bis zum elften Jahrhundert* (1912); K. Löffler, 'Die Sankt Galler Schreibschule in der 2. Hälfte des 8. Jahrhunderts' in W. M. Lindsay (ed.), *Palaeographia Latina*, vi (St. Andrews University Publications, xxviii; 1929), pp. 5-66.

GALLA PLACIDIA (*c.* 390-450), Roman Empress. The daughter of *Theodosius I, she was carried off by Alaric the Goth, when he captured *Rome in 410, and in 414 married his successor, King Ataulf. After his murder in 415, she rejoined Honorius, her brother, and on the accession of her son, Valentinian III, in 425 she acted as regent. An important influence in the religious struggles of the time, she was an uncompromising Catholic and gave her support to Pope *Leo I, in the *Eutychian controversy. She built several famous churches at *Ravenna, among them her own mausoleum, which is adorned with splendid mosaics.

T. Hodgkin, *Italy and her Invaders*, I, ii (1892), pp. 817-88. C. Ricci, *Il mausoleo di Galla Placidia in Ravenna* (1914). Also H. *Leclercq, O.S.B., in *D.A.C.L.*, vi (pt. 1; 1924), cols. 248-75; C. Cecchelli in *Enciclopedia Italiana*, xvi (1932), pp. 286-8; and M. Mazzotti in *E.C.*, v (1950), cols. 1883 f., with full bibl.

GALLANDI, ANDREA (1709-79), *Patristic scholar. An *Oratorian priest who lived at Venice, he is best known for his *Bibliotheca veterum patrum antiquorumque scriptorum ecclesiasticorum Graecorum* (14 vols., 1765-81), a collection of treatises drawn from 380 writers of the first seven cents. of the Christian era, in which special attention was paid to the less-known authors. It is still a work of great service to students of the Fathers. He also published *De vetustis canonum collectionibus sylloge* (1778), an important collection of writings on the history of canon law.

P. Godet in *D.T.C.*, vi (1914), col. 1095, with bibl.

'GALLIA CHRISTIANA'. A documentary account of the bishoprics, bishops, abbeys, and abbots of France. It derives from a work under this title first published by Claude Robert in 1626. A later edition issued in 1656 was approved by the Assembly of the French Clergy, but only after a passage suspected of *Jansenism had been removed. Since the beginning of the 18th cent., when a thorough revision was undertaken by the *Maurist, Denys de Sainte-Marthe (1650-1725), the work has been continued chiefly by Benedictine scholars, among them, Felix Hodin, Étienne Brice and Jacques Taschereau. For students of the detailed history of France, it remains indispensable.

Work partly repr., with some minor changes, by P. Piolin, O.S.B. (Paris, 1870-77). A not very satisfactory revision was begun as *Gallia Christiana Novissima* by U. Chevalier (Montbéliard, 7 vols., 1899-1920). V. Fouque, *Du Gallia Christiana et de ses auteurs*. Étude bibliographique (1857). A. Degert, 'Pour refaire la *Gallia Christiana*' in *Revue d'Histoire de l'Église de France*, viii (1922), pp. 281-301. H. *Leclercq, O.S.B., in *D.A.C.L.*, vi (1924), cols. 277-310.

GALLICAN ARTICLES, The Four (1682). The rights and privileges claimed by the French clergy at an assembly of 36 bishops and 34 deputies held at Paris on 19 March 1682. The demands arose from the dispute between Louis XIV and *Innocent XI over the appointment of bishops and the revenues of vacant sees. The document was drawn up by J. B. *Bossuet (q.v.).

The first denied that the Pope had dominion (*puissance*) over things temporal, and affirmed that kings are not subject to the authority of the Church in temporal and civil matters or to deposition by the ecclesiastical power, and that their subjects could not be dispensed by the Pope from their allegiance. The second upheld the decrees of the Council of *Constance (1414–18), and thus reaffirmed the authority of General Councils over the Pope. The third insisted that the ancient liberties of the Gallican Church were inviolable. The fourth asserted that pending the consent of the Church (i.e. until a General Council was convened), the judgement of the Pope is not irreformable. The Articles were quashed by the constitution 'Inter multiplices' of Alexander VIII of 4 Aug. 1690, and by Louis XIV in 1693, but for over a decade they were taught in the French theological schools and made a test for admission to academic degrees and public office.

C. Gérin, *Recherches historiques sur l'assemblée du clergé de 1682* (1869; ed. 2, revised, 1870), with text of articles, p. 317 f. of ed. 2. The constitution 'Inter Multiplices' is pr. in the *Bullarum, Diplomatum et Privilegiorum Sanctorum Romanorum Pontificum Taurinensis Editio*, xx (Naples, 1883), pp. 67–70, with reff. to earlier papal declarations. The main clause of the constitution, together with the text of the articles, is repr. in Denz.–Bann. (ed. 1952), pp. 385–7 (Nos. 1322–6). See also bibl. to *Gallicanism*.

GALLICAN CONFESSION. The *Confessio de foi* or *Confessio Gallicana*, adopted in the First National Synod of Protestants at Paris in 1559. The first draft was the work of J. *Calvin, but it was revised, chiefly by his pupil, Antoine de la Roche Chandieu (1534–1591), before its formal acceptance. It was written in French and contained 35 articles, and in substance was an epitome of Calvin's central doctrines. A modified form of it, with 40 articles, was ratified at the Synod of La Rochelle in 1571. The Confession has often been attached to editions of the French Bible.

P. Schaff, *Creeds of Christendom* (1877), i, 490–8; iii, 356–82 (text).

GALLICAN PSALTER. The second of St. *Jerome's three revisions of the Latin *Psalter. It was a working-over of the corrupted Latin texts which were current in the 4th cent., with the aid not only of the *Septuagint (the Greek version which Jerome perh. used for his earlier '*Roman Psalter'), but also of *Theodotion's translation and, through *Origen's 'Hexapla', of the Hebrew. This version soon became very popular esp. in Gaul (probably through the influence of *Gregory of Tours), and was ultimately accepted as the official version for recitation in the W. Church. In Italy, however, it did not displace the Roman Psalter (which still survives at St. Peter's, Rome) till the time of *Pius V (1566–72).

GALLICAN RITE. This term is used with three meanings: (1) for the liturgical forms in use in Gaul before the imposition of the Roman Rite by *Charlemagne; (2) loosely, for all the non-Roman rites of the early W. Church; (3) for the 'Neo-Gallican' liturgies of the 17th and 18th cents. What follows relates only to (1).

There was no single form of service imposed upon Merovingian Gaul, for it was neither a political nor an ecclesiastical unity. It is possible, nevertheless, to distinguish liturgical forms of Gallican type from those of Rome by certain well-defined characteristics, many of which are shared by the *Mozarabic, *Celtic, and even *Ambrosian rites. Not only are Gallican forms more prolix and oratorical than the austere forms of the Roman *Sacramentaries, but the structure of the services is in certain respects remarkably different. And, although the extant Mass books (with the exception of F. J. *Mone's fragments) have been 'Romanized', several points of contrast can be pointed out. (1) THE *MASS. (a) The *Trisagion was regularly sung in Greek and Latin before the *Kyries (which were in threefold form) and before and after the *Gospel. (b) The *Benedictus Dominus followed the Kyries, and the *Benedicite was sung after the OT Lesson. (c) The *Diptychs and the *Kiss of Peace occurred before the *Canon. (d) The Canon, with the exception of the *Institution, varied with the season. (e) The Institution, in many extant Masses, was followed by a prayer *post pridie*, which was sometimes a form of *Epiclesis. (f) The *Fraction took place, accompanied by its own *antiphon, *before* the *Paternoster. (g) A Trinitarian hymn (the *Trecanum) was sung during the *Communion. (2) *BAPTISM. The most notable points of contrast with the Roman Rite are the placing of the profession of faith before the actual baptism and the addition of the rite of '*pedilavium'. (3) *ORDINATION. The Gallican Rite seems to have included a public ceremony for the minor orders which has been borrowed by Rome. And in many ways the Gallican Ordination services have influenced the Roman. See *Statuta Ecclesiae Antiqua.

It is not known why in early times the rites of N. Italy, Gaul, Spain, and the *Celtic Church differed from that of Rome, nor are scholars agreed as to their *provenance*. The two problems are closely linked. Of the explanations put forward: (1) The older theory was that the non-Roman rites could be traced back to Apostolic origin in *Ephesus, whence they spread to the W. via *Lyons (see *Irenaeus*). But the archetype of these rites does not seem to have become generally current till the late 4th cent. when the influence of Lyons was small; and in the 5th cent. Lyons was a centre of liturgical 'Romanization'. (2) Others, e.g. Dom. P. Cagin, have held that this 'non-Roman' type of rite represents the primitive Roman Rite; but this theory assumes somewhat gratuitously that the Roman Rite was revised into its present form under Pope *Damasus (c. 384). (3) Another widely accepted view, e.g. of L. *Duchesne, was that the liturgies came from Milan, which at the turn of the 4th and 5th cents. was very influential. (4) Perhaps the least unsatisfactory view, that it was indigenous to Gaul. Recently discussion has been radically affected by A. *Wilmart's contention that the Letters ascribed to St. *Germanus of Paris are really much later and R. H. *Connolly's vindication of the *Ambrosian authorship of De Sacramentis. It is evident that the last word has not been said on these problems, and even those who accept the Milanese origin of the dissemination of the non-Roman rites are not agreed whether their earlier ancestry is to be sought at Rome or in the East.

The Gallican Rite, which was already being conflated with the Roman in certain places, was formally 'abolished' by Charlemagne; but his order was not exactly carried out. The present Roman Rite still bears marks of its conflation with that of Gaul.

For the Mass the chief texts are the *Bobbio Missal, the *Missale Gothicum, the Missale Gallicanum Vetus, and the Masses publd. by F. J. Mone (Frankfurt, 1850). The chief authority for the ceremonial is the set of Epp. ascribed to St. Germanus of Paris. See also J. *Mabillon, O.S.B., De Liturgia Gallicana (Paris, 1685; repr. in J. P. Migne, PL, lxxii. 101–448; M. Gerbert, O.S.B., Monumenta Veteris Liturgiae Alemannicae (St. Blasien, 1777); J. M. *Neale and G. H. *Forbes, The Ancient Liturgies of the Gallican Church Burntisland, 1855); F. E. Warren, Liturgy and Ritual of the Celtic Church (1881); L. Duchesne, Christian Worship (Eng. tr., 1903), esp. ch. vii; P. Cagin, O.S.B., 'Avant-propos à l'antiphonaire ambrosien' in Paléographie Musicale, vol. v (1896), pp. 70–97.

GALLICANISM. The collective name for the body of doctrine which asserted the more or less complete freedom of the RC Church, esp. in France, from the ecclesiastical authority of the *Papacy. During the *Great Schism, such theologians as J. *Gerson and P. *D'Ailly had ably represented a primitive form of Gallican doctrine which had been taught in the *Sorbonne almost from the time of its foundation (1257). At this period the chief question at issue was the claim of the French Church to a privileged position in relation to the Papacy, these libertés de l'Église gallicane (whence the name Gallicanism) being based upon supposed prerogatives of the French Crown (prerogatives which a sober view of history scarcely warranted). In 1516 the *Pragmatic Sanction of Bourges (1438) was superseded by a *concordat in which the French king's right of nomination to bishoprics and other high ecclesiastical offices was conceded. The constitutional decisions of the Council of *Trent (1545–63) were not received in France, and such writers as P. *Pithou, Edmond Richer (1559–1631), and P. de *Marca popularized a theory of Church government which minimized in various ways the authority claimed by the Papacy over the national churches ('royal Gallicanism'), and over the individual bishops ('episcopal Gallicanism'). In 1663 the Sorbonne published a declaration the substance of which was reaffirmed by the Assembly of the French clergy in 1682 in the formula known as the Four *Gallican Articles (q.v.). This declaration, though solemnly withdrawn by king and clergy in 1693, remained the typical Gallican manifesto. Gallican principles were preached throughout the 18th cent. by the opponents of the bull '*Unigenitus', and once more officially codified and proclaimed at the synod of *Pistoia in 1786. The *Organic Articles added to *Napoleon's concordat of

1801 included Gallican provisions, and Napoleon himself favoured the Gallican party among his clergy. After the Restoration, however, the work of the *Jesuits, and of such writers as J. *de Maistre and F. *Lamennais, bore fruit in a renascence of *ultramontanism in France, so that F. *Dupanloup and A. J. A. *Gratry found little support for their Gallican positions at the time of the *Vatican Council (1869–70). The definition of Papal *infallibility by the Council has had the effect of making the Gallican principles incompatible with the profession of *Roman Catholicism, so that henceforward Gallicanism has preserved only an historical importance, unless such small organizations as the *Old Catholics may be held to exhibit its persistence to-day. See also Febronianism.

V. Martin, Les Origines du gallicanisme (2 vols., 1939). N. Valois, La France et le grand schisme en occident (4 vols., 1896–1902), passim. V. Martin, Le Gallicanisme et la réforme catholique. Essai historique sur l'introduction en France des décrets du concile de Trente, 1563–1615 (1919); id., Le Gallicanisme politique et le clergé de France (Université de Strasbourg. Bibliothèque de l'Institut de Droit Canonique, iii, 1929). L. Mention (ed.), Documents relatifs aux rapports du clergé avec la royauté de 1682 à 1705 (Collection de Textes pour servir à l'Étude et à l'Enseignement de l'Histoire, 1893). F. C. Gérin, Recherches historiques sur l'assemblée du clergé de France de 1682 (1868); id., Louis XIV et le saint-siège (2 vols., 1894). H. Dubruel–H. X. Arquillière in A. d'Alès, S.J. (ed.), Dictionnaire apologétique de la foi catholique, ii (1911), cols. 193–273, with full bibl. reff.; M. Dubruel in D.T.C., vi (1920), cols. 1096–1137, s.v. A. Degert in C.E., vi (1909), pp. 351–6, s.v.; J. Turmel in H.E.R.E., vi (1913), pp. 156–63, s.v. See also bibl. to Pragmatic Sanction of Bourges.

GALLIO, LUCIUS JUNIUS. The brother of the philosopher, *Seneca (q.v.). He was the Proconsul of Achaia before whom St. *Paul was accused at *Corinth (Acts 18. 12). He held office c. A.D. 52. His name occurs in an inscription found at Delphi in 1905.

The Delphic inscription is an important fixed date for NT Chronology. Cf. summary in L. Hennequin in Dict. de la Bible, suppl. (ed. L. Pirot), ii (1934), cols. 355–73, s.v. 'Delphes (Inscription de)', with full bibl. W. Larfeld, 'Die delphische Gallioinschrift und die paulinische Chronologie' in Neue kirchliche Zeitschrift, xxxiv (1923), pp. 638–47. J. E. Roberts in D.A.C., i (1915), p. 439 f., s.v. 'Gallio', and (esp.) A. C. Zenos, ib., p. 275 f., s.v. Dates, 'III. 3', with useful bibl. F. Spadaforza in E.C., v (1951), col. 1904 f., s.v. 'Gallione'.

GAMALIEL. The great Jewish rabbi, 'had in reputation among all the people' (Acts 5. 34), who was the teacher of St. *Paul in his pre-Christian days (Acts 22. 3). He was a grandson of the liberal *Hillel, and his broad, tolerant views were well exemplified in his attitude to St. *Peter and St. *John (Acts 5. 34–40). It has been doubted, but on insufficient grounds, whether so fiery and intolerant a character as St. Paul could have sat at the feet of such a tolerant master. Acc. to a late and prob. worthless tradition in the *Clementine Recognitions (1. 65), Gamaliel afterwards became a Christian.

A. Büchler, Das Synedrion in Jerusalem und das grosse Beth-Din in der Quaderkammer des Jerusalemischen Tempels (1902), pp. 115–31. H. Graetz, Geschichte der Juden, iii (ed. 3, 1878), pp. 373–5; Eng. tr., ii (1891), pp. 193–5; ed. 5 by M. Brann, iii (pt. i; 1905), pp. 348–50; E. *Schürer,

Geschichte des jüdischen Volkes, ii (ed. 4; 1907), pp. 429–31; Eng. tr., ii (pt. 1; 1885), pp. 363–5. A. M. Hyman, *Toledoth Tanna'im we-'Amora'im* [in Hebr.], i (London, 1910), pp. 305–10, with sources; J. Klausner, *History of the Second Temple* (Hebr.), iv (ed. 2, Jerusalem, 1950), pp. 294–7, and v (1951), p. 92 f. H. L. Strack-P. Billerbeck, *Kommentar zum Neuen Testament aus Talmud und Midrasch*, ii (1924), pp. 636–9; H. L. Strack, *Einleitung in Talmud und Midrasch* (ed. 5, 1930), p. 120 f., with bibl. (Eng. tr., Philadelphia, 1945), pp. 109 f. and 304.

GAMBLING. See *Betting and Gambling*.

GAMS, PIUS BONIFATIUS (1816–92), Church historian. A native of Württemberg, he became professor at Hildesheim in 1847, and in 1855 a Benedictine at St. Boniface's monastery at Munich. His two chief works are a history of the Church of Spain (*Kirchengeschichte von Spanien*, 3 vols., 1862–79), a massive compilation, but somewhat uncritical in its treatment of sources; and an invaluable *Series Episcoporum* (1873; supplement, 1886), which contains, arranged acc. to their sees, the names of all the known bishops in communion with Rome down to that date.

F. Lauchert, 'Die kirchengeschichtlichen und zeitgeschichtlichen Arbeiten von P. B. Gams in Zusammenhang gewürdigt' in *Studien und Mitteilungen aus dem Benediktiner- und dem Cistercienser-Orden*, xxvii (1906), pp. 634–49, xxviii (1907), pp. 53–71, 299–305, with list of his works, pp. 305–15.

GANDOLPHY, PETER (1779–1821), *Jesuit preacher. Born in London and educated abroad, he attained fame as a preacher at the Spanish Chapel in Manchester Square, London, where he made many converts. In 1812 he issued *A Liturgy, or Book of Common Prayers and Administration of Sacraments . . . for the Use of all Christians in the United Kingdom of Great Britain and Ireland*, which was modelled upon the Anglican Prayer Book. This publication, together with his sermons, caused him to be accused by his ordinary, Bp. W. Poynter (d. 1827), of heresy. Although vindicated by the Congregation of *Propaganda in Rome (1817), he gave up his work in London (1818) and retired to his family home at East Sheen.

Sommervogel, iii (1892), col. 1181 f., s.v.; T. Cooper in *D.N.B.*, xx (1889), p. 400 f., s.v., with further reff.

GANG-DAYS. An obsolete title of the three *Rogation Days (the Monday, Tuesday, and Wednesday before *Ascension Day) from the ancient practice of perambulating the parish bounds on those days. The forms 'Gang-Monday', 'Gang-Week', are also met with.

GANGRA, Council of. A Council held at Gangra in Paphlagonia *c.* 345. It passed 20 canons, directed against a false asceticism (led by *Eustathius, Bp. of Sebaste) which condemned marriage and avoided the ordinary services of the Church. To these canons are added an epilogue, often called 'canon 21', explaining the true nature of asceticism. The canons are not in themselves important; but, as they were included in the first Greek *corpus*

translated into Latin, they attained a very wide circulation.

Hardouin, i, cols. 529–40; Mansi, ii (1759), cols. 1095–1122. Canons also in Lauchert, pp. 79–83; crit. ed. of Lat. texts in *E.O.M.I.A.*, II, ii (1913), pp. 145–214. Hefele–Leclercq, i (pt. 2; 1907), pp. 1029–45. H. M. Gwatkin, *Studies of Arianism* (1882), pp. 185–8 (Note E: 'Date of the Council of Gangra'); O. Braun, 'Die Abhaltung der Synode von Gangra' in *Hist. J.*, xvi (1895), p. 586 f.

GANSFORT, WESSEL HARMENUS. See *Wessel*.

GARDEN OF EDEN. See *Eden, Garden of*.

GARDEN OF GETHSEMANE. See *Gethsemane, Garden of*.

'GARDEN OF THE SOUL', The. The 'Manual of Spiritual Exercises and Instructions for Christians who, living in the world, aspire to Devotion' compiled by R. *Challoner and first published in 1740. It at once became a favourite with English RCs and has remained in continuous use ever since, though in the course of 200 years parts of it have been modified almost out of recognition. The influence exercised by the earlier editions in moulding the deep but sober piety of English RCs, before more Italian forms of devotion became popular, led the older school to be often known as 'Garden-of-the-Soul Catholics'.

A well-produced repr. of the 1741 impression for practical use, with some minor alterations, was issued by the 'Society of St. Peter and St. Paul' (London) in 1916. See also bibl. to *Challoner, R.*

GARDINER, STEPHEN (*c.* 1490–1555), Bp. of *Winchester. From 1525 to 1549 he was master of Trinity Hall, Cambridge, and took an active interest in promoting Greek studies in the university. He was employed by *Henry VIII and T. *Wolsey on diplomatic business, notably in the negotiations with Rome for annulling the marriage with Catharine of Aragon, and in 1533 acted as an assessor in the court which finally declared the marriage null and void. In 1531 he had been given the see of Winchester. He accepted, at least for a time, the royal supremacy over the Church, arguing in his *De Vera Obedientia* (1535) that the Pope had no legitimate power over national Churches. He strongly opposed, however, the Protestant influences of T. *Cromwell, was probably very largely responsible for the *Six Articles, and by the end of Henry's reign he was regarded as the chief opponent in England of the Reformation doctrines. In *Edward VI's reign he was imprisoned in the Tower (1548) and deprived of his bishopric (1551), but was restored to his see by *Mary, and became Lord High Chancellor. He approved of the submission of England to Rome, but was instrumental in securing the retention of the property of the dissolved monasteries by their lay owners. The mediating course which he followed in the reign of Henry VIII has led his character to be variously judged.

H. Chitty–H. E. Maldon (edd.), *Registra Stephani Gardiner et Johannis Poynet, Episcoporum Wintoniensium* (*Canterbury and York Society, xxxvii, 1930), pp. 1–91; J. A. Muller (ed.), *Letters of Stephen Gardiner* (1933). P. Janelle (ed.), *Obedience in Church and State.* Three Political Tracts by Stephen Gardiner (1930). J. S. Brewer (ed.), *State Papers*, vii–xi (1849–52), passim; J. Brewer–J. *Gairdner (ed.), *Letters and Papers, Domestic and Foreign, of the Reign of Henry VIII*, iv–xxi (1870–1910), and Addenda, pts. i and ii, ed. by A. E. Sharp (1929–32), passim. J. A. Muller, *Stephen Gardiner and the Tudor Reaction* (S.P.C.K., 1926).

GARNET or GARNETT, HENRY (1555–1606), English *Jesuit. He became a RC while a boy, went to Rome, and studied under R. *Bellarmine. In 1586 he set out to work on the English Mission, of which he became Superior in 1587. He was arrested and executed, some months after the *Gunpowder Plot, for complicity in it. Though he certainly had some knowledge of it beforehand, it is disputed whether his information was entirely gained through a confessional case, referred to him under the *seal, or whether he had independent evidence. In support of the latter view is the fact that, although English law gave no protection to the confessional, the prosecution apparently preferred not to use evidence based upon it. In any case, it was not suggested that Garnet personally took part in the plot; he was condemned and executed for not having revealed his knowledge of it.

Life in H. Foley, S.J., *Records of the English Province of the Society of Jesus*, iv (1878), pp. 35–192. Artt. by J. H. Pollen, S.J., in *The Month*, lxi (1887), pp. 305–20; lxiii (1888), pp. 58–73 and 382–97; lxiv (1888), pp. 41–59; also by J. Gerrard, S.J., in ib., xci (1898), pp. 6–21 and 144–52. R. *Challoner–J. H. Pollen, S.J., *Memoirs of Missionary Priests* (1924), pp. 282–8.

GARNIER, JEAN (1612–81), S.J., *Patristic scholar. He was a native of *Paris, who entered the *Jesuit Order at Rouen in 1628 and taught theology at the Collège de *Clermont at Paris from 1653 to 1679. In 1673 he published his edition of *Marius Mercator (in J. P. *Migne, *PL*, xlviii) with valuable treatises on *Pelagianism and *Nestorianism which were the basis of all subsequent research on both subjects. In 1680 he edited the 'Liber Diurnus' of the Roman pontiffs, adding historical, doctrinal, and critical notes esp. on the ordinations and professions of faith of the Popes, and a treatise on the orthodoxy of Pope *Honorius (also reproduced in Migne, *PL*, cv, but without the treatise on Honorius). He also completed J. *Sirmond's edition of *Theodoret (1684; posthumous), with critical essays on his works and doctrine. He published, besides, several works on Scholastic philosophy and on moral and doctrinal theology.

He is not to be confounded with Julien Garnier (1670–1725), O.S.B., the *Maurist editor of St. *Basil.

Sommervogel, iii (1892), cols. 1228–32. P. Bernard in *D.C.T.*, vi (1920), cols. 1160–3.

GASCOIGNE, THOMAS (1403–58), English scholar and theologian. He was born at Hunslet, nr. Leeds, and educated at *Oxford,

probably at Oriel, where he continued to live for the rest of his life. He was frequently either chancellor or vice-chancellor of the university. Ordained priest in 1427, he held the rectory of Kirk Deighton for a short time; but with the exception of a prebendal stall in *Wells Cathedral, he declined all other ecclesiastical offices, including the chancellorship of *York Minster, to devote himself to scholarly pursuits. He was also very active as a preacher and, though hostile to *Wycliffite influences, severe in his denunciations of pluralities, appropriations, and other ecclesiastical and monastic abuses. His principal work was the 'Liber Veritatum' or 'Dictionarium Theologicum' (written between 1431 and 1457), a theological dictionary which is both an important guide to the political and religious history of the time and an interesting revelation of Gascoigne's own views. He also wrote Lives of St. *Jerome and of St. *Bridget.

'Collectanea Historica' from Gascoigne's *Dictionarium Theologicum* are printed in T. *Hearne's ed. of Walter Hemingford (*fl.* 1300), *Historia de Rebus Gestis Edwardi I, Edwardi II et Edwardi III*, ii (1731), pp. 509–50, with life, pp. 504–8; J. E. T. Rogers (ed.), *Loci e Libro Veritatum.* Passages Selected from Gascoigne's Theological Dictionary Illustrating the Condition of the Church and State, 1403–1453 (1881). R. L. Poole in *D.N.B.*, xxi (1890), pp. 41–4.

GASQUET, FRANCIS AIDAN (1846–1929), cardinal and historian. Born in London of an old Provençal family, he was educated at *Downside and entered the *Benedictine Order in 1866. Elected Prior of Downside in 1878, he raised the standard both of priory and school and considerably enlarged their scope. From 1885 he carried on research at the British Museum and Record Office. In 1896 he went to Rome where he played an important part as a member of the Commission on *Anglican Ordinations. On his return he became chairman of the commission for the reform of the English Benedictine Congregation, whose abbot-president he was from 1900 to 1914. In 1907 *Pius X made him president of the International Commission for the Revision of the *Vulgate. In 1914 he was created cardinal, and henceforward resided in Rome. On the death of Pius X he took part in the conclave, countering anti-British propaganda, and negotiated for the appointment of a British minister to the Vatican. He became Prefect of the Archives of the Holy See in 1917, and two years later *Vatican Librarian. Card. Gasquet was a fertile writer whose books largely increased the knowledge of medieval English monasticism. Though not always critical in the use of his material, his views on the Reformation in England and the spoliation of the monasteries have come to be widely accepted. Among his best-known works are *Henry VIII and the English Monasteries* (2 vols., 1888–9), which caused a great stir, *Religio Religiosi* (1918), and *Monastic Life in the Middle Ages* (1922). He is buried at Downside.

Notes by J. C. Fowler, O.S.B., B. Kuypers, O.S.B., and U. Butler, O.S.B., in *The Downside Review*, xlvii (1929), pp. 123–56, incl. bibl. of his works, pp. 147–9. S. Leslie, *Cardinal Gasquet.* A Memoir (1953).

GAUDEN, JOHN (1605-62), Bp. of *Worcester. He was educated at St. John's College, Cambridge, studied later also at Wadham College, Oxford, and in 1640 became Vicar of Chippenham. In the early days of the Civil War his sympathies were with Parliament, and for a short time in 1643 he was a member of the *Westminster Assembly. After *Charles I's death (1649) he began to change his opinions, but was able none the less to retain his living throughout the Commonwealth period. At the Restoration in 1660 he was made Bp. of *Exeter, and in 1662 was translated, not, as he had hoped, to *Winchester, but to Worcester. He published several controversial works against the Puritans, including his monumental *Ecclesiae Anglicanae Suspiria* (1659), and defences of the Anglican ministry and liturgy. He was probably the author of the *Eikon Basilike (q.v.), alleged to have been written by Charles I in prison.

See bibl. s.v. 'Eikon Basilike'. R. Hooper in *D.N.B.*, xxi (1890), pp. 69-72.

GAUDENTIUS, St. (4th-5th cent.), Bp. of Brescia. A friend of St. *Ambrose, he succeeded *Philaster in the see of Brescia before 397. In 404-5 he journeyed to Constantinople to plead with the Emperor on behalf of St. *Chrysostom, but without avail. Several of his sermons have survived. Feast day, 25 Oct.

Of his 21 surviving sermons, a set of 10 delivered in the Easter week have many reff. to the Eucharist; Serm. 21 is on *Philaster of Brescia. J. P. Migne, *PL*, xx, 827-1002; crit. ed. by A. Glueck in *C.S.E.L.*, lxviii (1936). J. Wittig, *Filaster, Gaudentius und Ambrosiaster* (Kirchengeschichtliche Abhandlungen, No. 8, Breslau, 1909), pp. 1-56. C. R. Norcock, 'St. Gaudentius of Brescia and the *Tome* of St. Leo' in *J.T.S.*, xv (1913-14), pp. 593-6. Bardenhewer, iii, p. 485 f. E. Peterson in *E.C.*, v (1951), col. 1962.

GAUDETE SUNDAY. The Third in *Advent, from the opening words of the *Introit. As on Mid-Lent Sunday (*Laetare) rose-coloured vestments are tolerated.

GAUME, JEAN JOSEPH (1802-79), theological writer. Ordained priest in 1825, he spent his earlier years in teaching and pastoral work at Nevers. Later he was Vicar-general successively of *Reims and Montauban. He came to notice through his advocacy of excluding the pagan classics from all Christian schools and substituting Patristic texts; he was supported by L. *Veuillot but controverted by F. *Dupanloup among others. His extensive writings (of unequal value) include *Le Manuel des confesseurs* (1837; ed. 11, 1880), *Catéchisme de persévérance* (8 vols., 1838), *L'Europe en 1848* (1848), *Lettres à Monseigneur Dupanloup, évêque d'Orléans, sur le paganisme dans l'éducation* (1852), *Bibliothèque des classiques chrétiens* (30 vols., 1852-5), *La Révolution* (12 vols., 1856-9), and *Pie IX et les études classiques* (1875). The first named, publd. in an adapted Eng. tr. for the use of Anglican confessors by E. B. *Pusey (1877), was also widely used in England.

A. Ricard, *Étude sur Mgr Gaume. Ses œuvres, son influence, ses polémiques* (1872). H. P. Liddon, *Life of E. B. Pusey*, iv (1897), pp. 303-6. E. Mangenot in *D.T.C.*, vi (1920), cols. 1168-71.

GAUNILO, Count. The 11th cent. Benedictine monk of Marmoutiers, near Tours, who, in the guise of the 'fool' (cf. Ps. 14. 1) criticized in his *Liber pro insipiente* the validity of the *Ontological Argument for the existence of God which St. *Anselm had formulated in his *Proslogion*. Anselm replied with his *Liber apologeticus adversus respondentem pro insipiente*.

GAVANTI, BARTOLOMMEO (1569-1638), *Barnabite liturgical scholar. He took an important part in the reform of the *Breviary and *Missal under Popes *Clement VIII and *Urban VIII. In his *Thesaurus sacrorum rituum, Seu Commentaria in rubricas Missalis et Breviarii Romani* (Rome, 1628), his most considerable work, he brings together much historical information on the origin and mystical significance of W. liturgical practice.

Opera Theologico-Canonica (2 vols., bound in 1, Venice, 1760). O. Premoli, Barnabite, *Storia dei Barnabiti nel seicento* (1922), pp. 178-82; G. Boffito, Barnabite, *Scrittori barnabiti*, ii (1933), pp. 132-48, with bibl.

GEBIROL, SALOMON IBN. See *Avicebron*.

GEDDES, JENNY. Acc. to tradition, the name of a vegetable-seller who, on Sunday 23 July 1637, threw her folding stool at the head of David Lindsay, Bp. of Edinburgh, in St. Giles' Cathedral when the new and hated Scottish Prayer Book was used for the first time.

The occurrence of a tumult on the introduction of the Scottish BCP is recorded in the contemporary annals. The name of 'Jane or Janot Gaddis (yet living at the time of this relation)' is apparently first mentioned in Richard Baker, *A Chronicle of the Kings of England from the Time of the Romans Government unto the Death of King James*. Continuation [by E. Phillips], 5th impression (1670), p. 478.

GEHENNA (Gk. γέεννα). Lit. 'the Valley of Hinnom' (Heb. הִנֹּם גֵּי); the meaning of Hinnom is unknown. It was orig. used purely topographically, prob. for the Wady er-Rabâbi to the S.W. and S. of Jerusalem, which joined at the S.E. of the city with the valley of the *Cedron, though it has sometimes (e.g. by Sir Charles Warren) been identified with the Cedron. In this sense the 'Valley of Hinnom' is mentioned at Jos. 15. 8 and 18. 16. From early times it was a place of human sacrifices, esp. to Moloch at Topheth (cf. 2 Kgs. 16. 3, 21. 6), and as such was polluted by Josiah (2 Kgs. 23. 10-12); it was foreshadowed by *Jeremiah as the 'Valley of Slaughter' (Jer. 7. 32, 19. 6). In later Jewish thought it was increasingly looked upon as a Divinely appointed place of punishment for apostates and other great sinners (e.g. Eth. *Enoch, 27. 2 f., 90. 26 f.; 2 *Esdras 7. 36-8). Hence in the NT the word is used for the final place of torment for the wicked after the Last Judgement (Mt. 5. 29, 10. 28, 18. 9; Jas. 3. 6; EVV 'hell'). The statement of Kimchi (c. A.D. 1200) that fires were continually kept burning in the

Valley of Hinnom has commonly been accepted by modern commentators; but it seems to be without earlier authority.

H. Vincent, O.P., *Jérusalem*, i (1912), pp. 123–34. H. L. Strack–P. Billerbeck, *Kommentar zum N.T. aus Talmud und Midrasch*, iv (1928), pp. 1029–1118. R. H. *Charles in H.D.B.*, ii (1899), p. 121 f., s.v. J. Chaine in *Dict. Bibl.*, Suppl. iii (1938), cols. 563–79, s.v. J. Jeremias in *T.W.B.*, i (1933), p. 655 f., s.v. 'γέεννα', with bibl. reff.

GEILER VON KAISERSBERG, JOHANN

(1445 – 1510), 'the German *Savonarola*', preacher. Born at Schaffhausen on the Rhine Geiler (also 'Geyler') was educated at Ammersweiher, nr. Kaisersberg in Alsace, and Freiburg University. From 1465 to 1471 he lectured on *Aristotle at Freiburg and from 1471 to 1476 on theology at Basle, where he also preached in the cathedral. In 1476 he returned to Freiburg as professor, becoming rector of the university in the same year. But his reforming interests soon led him to abandon academic work; and after declining an invitation to a pulpit at Würzburg on grounds of patriotism he accepted a special office of preacher created for him in the Cathedral of the neighbouring Strassburg in 1478. Except for a short interval he remained here for the rest of his life.

Geiler seems to have been an uncommonly forceful and impressive preacher. In spite of his austere moral ideals and his denunciation of the vices of all classes, his freshness, vivacity, apt illustration and knowledge of the human heart won and held his hearers. If his satire is not always to our taste, it appears to have been highly acceptable to his age. Although he demanded reform, he never seems to have contemplated abandoning the Church. Personally something of a mystic, he is said to have enjoyed preaching but been haunted by fears arising from his work in the confessional. Many of his sermons have been published in a text which is prob. not verbally accurate. His other published works include an edition of the works of J. *Gerson (4 vols., 1488–1502).

Ausgewählte Schriften, ed. P. de Lorenzi (4 vols., Trier, 1881–4); *Älteste Schriften*, ed. L. Dacheux (Freiburg i.Br., 1882). Modern edd. of his *Ars Moriendi* by A. Hoch (ib., 1901) and of his *Seelenparadies* by F. X. Zacher (M. Gladbach, 1923). C. Schmidt, *Histoire littéraire de l'Alsace à la fin du XVe et au commencement du XVIe*, siècle, ii (1879), pp. 373–90 for details of the early edd. of his works. L. Dacheux, *Un Réformateur catholique à la fin du XVe siècle* (1876). C. Schmidt, *op. cit.*, i (1879), pp. 337–461. N. Scheid in *C.E.*, vi (1909), pp. 403–5, s.v.

GEISSHÄUSSLER, OSWALD. See *Myconius*.

GELASIAN DECREE, The. See *Decretum Gelasianum*.

GELASIAN SACRAMENTARY, The. An

early Roman Sacramentary (Vat. Reg. 316, saec. viii), first printed by G. M. *Tommasi in 1680. It is the oldest known Roman Missal with the Feasts arranged acc. to the ecclesiastical year and certainly of pre-Gregorian origin; but its common (purely conjectural) ascription

to Pope *Gelasius (492–6) is now known to be mistaken (B. *Capelle). It contains the Roman *Canon of the Mass in practically its present form. The text in the Vatican MS. embodies some Gallican elements (e.g. mention of *Francorum imperium* in the *Good Friday Prayers) and the copy perhaps comes from St.-Denis, near Paris. In a later form ('Frankish Gelasianum'), which embodied other Roman material as well as Gallican elements, it circulated widely in Gaul in the 8th cent.

Early edd., after that of G. M. Tommasi, by L. A. *Muratori (Venice, 1748) and J. A. Assemani (Rome, 1751). Crit. ed. by H. A. Wilson (Oxford, 1894). E. *Bishop, *Liturgica Historica* (1918), pp. 39–61 ('The Earliest Roman Mass Book'). B. Capelle, O.S.B., 'L'Œuvre liturgique de S. Gélase' in *J.T.S.*, N.S., ii (1951), pp. 129–44. F. *Cabrol, O.S.B., in *D.A.C.L.*, vi (pt. 1, 1924), cols. 747–77, s.v. 'Gélasien (le Sacramentaire)'; A. Bugnini in *E.C.*, ix (1953), cols. 1564–6, s.v. 'Sacramentario III'.

GELASIUS, St. (d. 496), Pope from 492.

Acc. to his own account he was 'Romanus natus', but the *Liber Pontificalis* asserts that he was 'natione Afer'. On his accession to the Papacy he continued the policy of his predecessor, Felix III, in tenaciously upholding the primacy of the Roman See against *Constantinople during the *Acacian Schism. His genuine writings include a treatise on the Two Natures in Christ (*Adversus Eutychen et Nestorium*), other works on the Acacian conflict, and a large collection of *Letters* on practical matters arising out of *Arianism, *Pelagianism, and *Manichaeism, and various disciplinary subjects. To rebut the Manichean abhorrence of wine, he insisted on the Eucharist being received in both kinds. He also laid down (*Ep.* 15) the now established rule that ordinations should be at the *Ember Seasons. Wrongly ascribed to him are the *Decretum Gelasianum* and the *Gelasian Sacramentary (qq.v.). Feast day, 21 Nov.

His Epp. (many, esp. in relation to his brief pontificate) are listed in Jaffé-Wattenbach, pp. 83–95; in Ep. 12 (ad Imp. Anastasium) a famous passage on the superiority of the ecclesiastical to the civil power anticipates much medieval political doctrine. Text of his letters, and other docc., in J. P. Migne, *PL*, lix, 13–190. *L.P.* (Duchesne), i, pp. 255–7. Study by A. Roux (Paris, 1880). E. Michaud, 'Le Pape St. Gélase et le monophysisme eucharistique' in *Revue Internationale de Théologie*, vii (1899), pp. 303–9; id., 'La Papauté romaine d'après le Pape Gélase (492–496)', ib., xvi (1908), pp. 38–58. H. Koch, *Gelasius im kirchenpolitischen Dienste seiner Vorgänger der Päpste Simplicius, 468–483, und Felix III, 483–492* (*Sb.* (Bayr.), 1935, Hft. 6). On his liturgical work, see B. *Capelle, O.S.B., 'L'Œuvre liturgique de S. Gélase' in *J.T.S.*, N.S., ii (1951), pp. 129–44; C. Coebergh, O.S.B., 'Le Pape Saint Gélase Ier auteur de plusieurs messes et préfaces du soi-disant Sacramentaire léonien' in *Sacris Erudiri*, iv (1952), pp. 46–102. Bardenhewer, iv, pp. 625–9; Altaner (ed. 1951), pp. 413–15. L. Spätling, O.F.M., in *E.C.*, v (1950), cols. 1980–3, s.v.

GELASIUS (d. 395), Bp. of *Caesarea in

Palestine from c. 367. He was the son of St. *Cyril of Jerusalem's sister. A convinced *Nicene, Gelasius was ousted from his see during the reign of *Valens (when Euzoïus was intruded), returning on the accession of *Theodosius in 379. He wrote (1) a continuation of *Eusebius's 'Ecclesiastical History'.

Possibly (so A. Glas, P. Heseler) this was the basis of *Rufinus' last two books, but more probably (P. van den Veen, P. Peeters, S.J.) the latter was an original work; (2) A treatise against the *Anomoeans; (3) An 'Expositio Symboli', a work prob. akin to Cyril's Catechetical Lectures, of which fragments survive.

He is praised by *Jerome, *De Vir. Ill.*, 130, and *Theodoret, *H.E.*, v, 8. Coll. of fragments, with introd., by F. Diekamp, *Analecta Patristica* (Orientalia Christiana Analecta, cxvii; 1938), pp. 16–49 (fragments, pp. 44–9). A. Glas, *Die Kirchengeschichte des Gelasios von Kaisareia* (Byzantinisches Archiv, vi; 1914). Bardenhewer, iii, p. 282; Altaner (ed. 1950), p. 202, with full bibl.

GELASIUS OF CYZICUS (*fl.* 475), ecclesiastical historian. He wrote a 'Syntagma', or collection of the *Acta* of the *Nicene Council (325), to refute the *Monophysite claim that their faith was identical with that professed by the Nicene Fathers. It has been proved recently that Gelasius made use of good sources such as *Eusebius, *Rufinus, *Socrates, and *Theodoret; but his book has little, if any, independent historical value. Its existence has sometimes been supposed (prob. wrongly) to lend support to the view that an official record of the *Acta* of Nicaea was current in the early Church.

J. P. Migne, *PG*, lxxxv, 1191–1360. Crit. ed. by G. Loeschcke–M. Heinemann (G.C.S., 1918). G. Loeschcke, 'Das Syntagma des Gelasius Cyzicenus' in *Rheinisches Museum*, lx (1905), pp. 594–613, and lxi (1906), pp. 34–77. C. H. Turner, 'On Gelasius of Cyzicus' in *J.T.S.*, i (1899), p. 125 f. O. *Bardenhewer, *Geschichte der altkirchlichen Literatur*, iv (1924), pp. 145–8.

GELLERT, CHRISTIAN FÜRCHTEGOTT (1715–69), German poet. He spent most of his life at Leipzig, where he became a teacher at the university. He wrote, besides fables on the model of La Fontaine, many Church hymns which became very popular among both Lutherans and Catholics. They include the familiar Easter hymn, 'Jesus Lives! thy terrors now'. Some of them were set to music by L. van Beethoven.

Sämtliche Schriften, ed. J. A. Schlegel–G. L. Heyer (10 vols., Leipzig, 1769–74), with life by J. A. Cramer as vol. x. Eng. life in Mrs. Douglas's tr. of Gellert's *Moral Lessons delivered . . . in the University of Leipzig* (3 vols., 1805), vol. i. K. R. Hagenbach–C. Bertheau in *P.R.E.* (ed. 3), vi (1899), pp. 482–5, s.v., with bibl. E. Werth, *Untersuchungen zu Chr. F. Gellerts geistlichen Oden und Liedern* (Diss., Breslau, 1936), with further reff.

GELLONE, Sacramentary of. An early Sacramentary of the *Gelasian ('of the 8th cent.') type, written *c.* 772–95, and a primary authority for the history of the early Roman liturgy. It formerly belonged to the *Benedictine abbey of Gellone, near Aniane, whence it passed in the 17th cent. to St.-Germain-des-Prés and in 1795 to the Bibliothèque Nationale, where it is now Par.lat.12048.

Text ed., with comm., by P. de Puniet, O.S.B., in *E.L.*, xlviii (1934), pp. 3–65, 157–97, 357–81, 517–33, xlix (1935), pp. 109–25, 209–29, 305–47, l (1936), pp. 3–33, 261–95, li (1937), pp. 13–63, 93–135, 269–309, and lii (1938), pp. 3–27. P. Cagin, O.S.B., 'Note sur le sacramentaire de Gellone' in *Mélanges de littérature et d'histoire religieuses publiés à*

l'occasion du jubilé épiscopal de Mgr de Cabrières, i (1899), pp. 231–91. H. *Leclercq, O.S.B., in *D.A.C.L.*, vi (pt. 1; 1924), cols. 777–94, s.v.

GEMARA. A name used of the second part of the *Talmud, which consists of a Rabbinic commentary on the first part (the *Mishnah). The Gemara of the Babylonian Talmud is written in E. Aramaic (a language closely allied to *Syriac), that of the Palestinian Talmud in W. Aramaic.

GEMATRIA. A method of interpretation employed by the Rabbis to extract hidden meanings from words. The name 'Gematria', which is Hebrew, is perhaps a corruption of the Greek word γεωμετρία ('geometry'). As in Hebrew every letter possessed a numerical value, it was possible, by counting up the values of the letters in a Hebrew word, to assign to it a numerical value; and on this basis the method operated. Thus the Rabbis argued that Eliezer, the steward of *Abraham (Gen 15. 2), must be worth all the servants of Abraham put together, on the ground that Abraham had 318 servants (Gen. 14. 14), and 318 is the numerical equivalent of the word Eliezer.

Use was occasionally made of this strange method of interpretation by early Christians. In Rev. 13. 18 the number of the Beast is given as 666, and this is the numerical equivalent for the two Hebrew words for 'Nero Caesar'. In the Ep. of Barnabas (c. 9) gematria is applied on the basis of the corresponding number of the Greek numerals, to give a mystical significance to the number of Abraham's servants. 300=τ=the Cross, and 18=ιη the first two letters of the name Jesus. Therefore the number of servants typifies Jesus and the Cross.

S. Waldberg, *Darkhe ha-shinnuyim* [in Hebr.] (Lwów, 1870). C. Taylor, *Sayings of the Jewish Fathers* (1877), p. 76, Note 46. F. Dornseiff, *Das Alphabet in Mystik und Magie* (Στοιχεῖα, vii; 1922), pp. 91–118. Very competent summary by C. Levias in *J.E.*, v (1903), pp. 589–92, s.v. See also bibl. to *Cabbala*.

GEMISTUS PLETHON, GEORGIUS (*c.* 1355–*c.* 1450), Renaissance scholar. A native of *Constantinople, he visited W. Europe when about 15 years old in the train of the Emp. John Paleologus; and on his return to the E. he settled at Mistra in the Peloponnese. He conceived a great veneration for the doctrines of *Plato, and exchanged his original name for that of 'Plethon', apparently through its similar sound with that of his master. In 1438–9, when, as one of the E. spokesmen, he attended the Council of *Florence, he was welcomed with enthusiasm by some of the Italian humanists, notably Cosimo de' Medici, and did much to overthrow the previous dominance of *Aristotle in the W. He set forth his philosophical doctrines in his 'Laws' (Νόμοι), a work (of which only fragments survive) written on the model of the 'Laws' of Plato. He was less interested in theology than in philosophical speculation; but he wrote in defence of the E. doctrine of the *Procession of the Holy Spirit.

Works collected in J. P. Migne, *PG*, clx, 805–1020. Fragments of the Laws, ed. C. Alexandre, with Fr. tr. by A. Pellissier (Paris, 1858). W. Gass, *Gennadius und Pletho. Aristotelismus und Platonismus in der griechischen Kirche, nebst einer Abhandlung über die Bestreitung des Islam im Mittelalter* (2 vols., 1844), vol. i, pp. 24–58, with Gk. text of his 'Liber contra Gennadii Scripta pro Aristotele', vol. ii, pp. 54–116. J. Wilson Taylor, *G. Gemistos Pletho's Criticism of Plato and Aristotle* (Diss., Menasha, Wisc., 1921); I. P. Mamalakis (Texte und Forschungen zur byzantinisch-neugriechischen Philologie, xxxii, Athens, 1939). M. V. Anastos, 'Pletho's Calendar and Liturgy' in *Dumbarton Oaks Papers*, Number Four (Cambridge, Mass., 1948), pp. 183–305. B. Tatakis, *La Philosophie byzantine* (Suppl. to E. Bréhier, *Histoire de la philosophie*, fasc. 2; 1949), pp. 281–93, 299–305. F. Masai, *Pléthon et le platonisme de Mistra* (1956). E. Stéphanou in *D.T.C.*, xii (1933), cols. 2393–404, s.v. 'Pléthon', with further bibl.

GEMMA GALGANI, St. See *Galgani, St. Gemma*.

GENEALOGIES OF CHRIST, The. The gospels of Mt. and Lk. both contain a Genealogy of Christ, the former (1. 2–17) tracing His descent from *Abraham and the latter (3. 23–38) carrying it back to '*Adam, the son of God'. The Genealogies are intended in both cases to emphasize that Christ belonged to the House of *David. The differences between them are probably to be explained by the 'Jewish' and 'Gentile' interests of the respective Evangelists.

GENERAL. The usual name for the head of a religious order or congregation. The necessity for the office arose out of the centralized government required by the *Mendicant orders and the later congregations. The term is usually combined with a noun. Thus, the *Franciscans and *Capuchins have a 'Minister General', the *Dominicans a 'Master General', the *Carmelites a 'Prior General', and the *Jesuits, *Redemptorists, and others a 'Superior General'. Since 1893 the *Benedictine congregations, too, have a General in the 'Abbot Primate', whose rights, however, are restricted by the independence of the individual monasteries prescribed by the rule. The General is normally elected by the 'General Chapter' for a term of three or six years, but in the case of the Jesuits for life. Heads of orders and sometimes also of congregations approved by the Pope reside in Rome.

GENERAL ASSEMBLY. The highest court in *Presbyterianism. It consists of ministers and elders elected to represent the whole Church, over which it exercises supreme jurisdiction.

GENERAL BAPTISTS. As contrasted with the *Particular Baptists (q.v.), those *Baptists whose theology was *Arminian and whose polity allied with that of the *Presbyterians. To this group belonged the earliest English Baptists, led by T. *Helwys. After many General Baptist Churches had moved

O.D.C.C.–T

towards *Unitarianism, a New Connexion was formed in 1770 under the influence of the Evangelical revival. This group united with the *Particular Baptists in 1891.

GENERAL CHAPTER. A canonical meeting of the heads and representatives of a religious order or congregation esp. for the purpose of electing new superiors and dealing with business concerning the whole order. They were introduced in the *Cistercian Order in 1119 and made compulsory for all orders by the Fourth *Lateran Council in 1215. Their frequency varies, but to-day they are normally held every three or four years. Apart from the Pope they constitute the highest authority for their respective religious.

GENERAL CONFESSION. (1) In the BCP the Confession at the beginning of *Matins and *Evensong 'to be said of the whole congregation after the minister, all kneeling'. It is in three parts—a confession of sin, a supplication for forgiveness of past misdeeds, and a prayer for grace to live righteously in the future. It was first added to the BCP in 1552 and has remained virtually unchanged.

(2) The term is also applied to a private confession where the penitent (exceptionally) resolves to confess, so far as he is able, all his past sins and not only those since his last confession. General confessions are often recommended when the penitent is entering on a new state of life, e.g. marriage, Holy Orders, or the religious life, or leaving for a foreign land.

GENERAL COUNCILS. See *Oecumenical Councils*.

GENERAL JUDGEMENT, The. Also the Last Judgement. In Christian theology, the final judgement on mankind after the Resurrection of the Dead. In contrast with the so-called *Particular Judgement (q.v.) on souls only immediately after death, the General Judgement is held to be the occasion of God's final sentence on humanity as a whole, as well as His verdict on both the soul and body of each individual.

GENERAL SUPERINTENDENT. Formerly the highest ecclesiastical office in many of the German Protestant Churches. The General Superintendent exercised his authority in conjunction with the provincial consistory and synod. The number varied in the different provinces, e.g. there were four in Brandenburg, three in Saxony, two in Pomerania. In recent times the title has been replaced, often after much controversy, in the Western provinces by that of Präses; and in the Eastern provinces there has now been set up a Bishop of Berlin over the General Superintendents. The appointment is purely ecclesiastical and does not receive confirmation from the State.

GENERAL THANKSGIVING, The. In the BCP the first of the Thanksgivings 'to be used before the two final prayers of the Litany or of Morning and Evening Prayer', so named to distinguish it from the *particular* thanksgivings ('for rain', &c.) which follow. It was composed in 1661 by Bp. E.*Reynolds.

GENERAL THEOLOGICAL SEMINARY, New York City. The largest training centre for clergy of the Protestant Episcopal Church of U.S.A. It was founded in 1817 in answer to a demand within the Church for a more thorough, systematic, and disciplined training for the ministry, and it seeks to cater for the needs of the Church in all parts of the country. Assisted by bequests, the seminary has been able to erect several fine buildings. Training is now given to over a hundred students in both academic and practical subjects by a large and scholarly faculty. The 'Paddock Lectures' are delivered regularly by noted visitors.

Special number of the *Historical Magazine of the Protestant Episcopal Church*, v (1936), No. 3, pp. 145–264, incl. E. R. Hardy, 'The Organization and Early Years of the General Theological Seminary', pp. 147–76; E. C. Chorley, 'The Oxford Movement in the Seminary', pp. 177–201; W. W. Manross, 'Growth and Progress since 1860', pp. 202–24; M. H. Gates, 'Deans and Professors', pp. 238–64.

GENESIS, Book of. The opening Book of the OT, and the first of the five Books of the *Pentateuch. The English title follows that of the *Septuagint (Greek) version, the Hebrew title (בְּרֵאשִׁית, 'Bereshith', i.e. 'in the beginning') being the first word of the text. The Book contains the story of the Creation of the universe and of the early history of man, including accounts of the *Fall and the *Flood (chs. 1–11), and the story of the *Patriarchs, *Abraham (12–25. 18), *Isaac (25. 19–26), *Jacob (27–36) and Joseph (37–50). Its purpose is not so much to offer exact science and accurate history as to record the progressive character of the Divine revelation and to indicate the spiritual mission of the Israelite people. For the Christian theologian it is of value as containing the Biblical basis of much Christian doctrine, e.g. of the *Creation and the *Fall. Upon the promise made to Abraham and his seed (22. 15–18) depends the covenant relationship between God and the chosen nation of Israel, a conception fundamental to the OT as a whole, although the relationship was extended in later times to all peoples. Both in Jewish and Christian tradition the Book has long been held to be the work of *Moses, but nearly all modern Biblical critics are agreed that the Book is not the work of a single hand, but a composite structure made up of varying material from sources which can also be traced in other Books of the Pentateuch.

Commentaries by S. R. *Driver (West. Comm., 1904; ed. 12, with appendix by G. R. Driver, 1926), J. Skinner (I.C.C., 1910), H. E. *Ryle (Camb. Bib., RV; 1914), A. *Dillmann (K.E.H., ed. 4; 1882; Eng. tr., 2 vols., 1897), H. Holzinger (K.H.C., Abt. i, 1898), H. Gunkel (K.H.A.T., i; 1901), O. Procksch (K.A.T., i; 1913). G. J. Spurrell, *Notes*

on the Text of the Book of Genesis (1887); H. E. Ryle, *The Early Narratives of Genesis* (1892). W. Eichrodt, *Die Quellen der Genesis von neuem untersucht* (Beihefte zur Z.A.T.W., xxxi; 1916); M. Löhr, *Untersuchungen zum Hexateuchproblem*, I, Der Priesterkodex in der Genesis (ib., xxxviii; 1924). P. Humbert, 'Die neuere Genesis-Forschung' in *Theologische Rundschau*, N.F., vi (1934), pp. 147–60, 207–28, with full bibl., p. 147 f. J. Chaine, *Le Livre de la Genèse* (1949). G. F. Moore in *E.Bi.*, ii (1901), cols. 1669–78, s.v. More recent commentary by G. von Rad (Göttingen, 1956; Eng. tr. 1961).

GENEVA BIBLE. This translation of the Bible, popularly known as the 'Breeches Bible' from its rendering of Gen. 3. 7 ('they … made themselves *breeches*'; AV '*aprons*'), was first published as a whole at Geneva in 1560. It was the first English edition to introduce verse enumeration. Issued in a handy form, instead of in folio, with compendious notes of a *Calvinist flavour, it was the Bible most widely read in private use in England for fifty years. For further details, see *Bible, English Versions*.

C. Easson, *The Geneva Bible*. Notes on its Production and Distribution (1937). A. W. Pollard, *Records of the English Bible* (1911), pp. 24–8, 43–5, with docc., pp. 279–86. J. Isaacs in H. Wheeler Robinson (ed.), *The Bible in its Ancient and English Versions* (1940), pp. 181–9. Darlow-Moule, i, p. 61 f.; for further edd. of Geneva Bible, see pp. 65, 73 f., and 81–151 passim.

GENEVA GOWN. The black preaching-gown worn by the early *Reformed ministers, loose fitting, with full sleeves. It was almost universally replaced by a surplice for Anglican preachers in the 19th cent. after some controversy, and is now worn by *Presbyterians and other Calvinist Dissenters. Its use was held to emphasize the ministry of the Word, over against belief in a sacrificing priesthood.

GENEVAN ACADEMY. This celebrated school was founded in 1559 by J. *Calvin with the support of the City Council and under the guidance of the Compagnie des Pasteurs, primarily for the education of theologians. Students were attracted in large numbers from all over Europe, and Geneva soon became the centre of international Protestantism. The first Rector was T. *Beza, and among early members were T. *Cartwright, who lectured in theology in 1571, J. *Arminius, and J. Uytenbogaert (1557–1644), the leader of the Dutch Arminians. The scope of studies, at first purely theological, was gradually widened. In 1872 a Faculty of Medicine was created and the Academy transformed into the modern university.

C. Borgeaud, *Histoire de l'Université de Genève* (4 vols., 1900–32).

GENEVAN CATECHISM, The. A name applied to two quite distinct formulae of J. *Calvin:

(1) *Catechismus Genevensis Prior.* A compendium of doctrine (*Instruction et confession de foi dont on use en l'Église de Genève*), based on the *Institutes. It was issued early in 1537 and followed on 27 Apr. by a formal Confession, compiled either by Calvin himself or

by G. *Farel. The documents were forthwith imposed on the inhabitants of Geneva. As yet the Trinity was not made a doctrine of faith.

(2) *Catechismus Genevensis.* A catechism in the form of question and answer, first published in French in 1542 and formally reissued in a Latin version in 1545. It became one of the basic documents of the Genevan ecclesiastical state. Its five sections are on Faith, the Law, Prayer, the Word of God, and the Sacraments.

Text of (1) is pr. among Calvin's works, ed. H. W. Baum–E. Cunitz–E. Reuss, xxii (Brunswick, 1880), cols. 33–96; Lat. tr., ib., v (1866), cols. 317–62; Fr. text repr., with notes by R. Rilliet–T. Dufour (Geneva, 1878). Text of (2), Lat. and Fr. in columns, with appendices, pr. among Calvin's works, ed. cit., vi (1867), cols. 1–160; Lat. version also pr. in H. A. Niemeyer (ed.), *Collectio Confessionum in Ecclesiis Reformatis Publicatarum* (Leipzig, 1840), pp. 123–190. An Eng. tr. was publd. at Geneva, 1556; also in [W. Dunlop (ed.),] *A Collection of Confessions of Faith, Catechisms, Directories, Books of Discipline, etc., of Public Authority in the Church of Scotland*, ii (1722), pp. 141–251. Extracts from the Confession of 27 April, 1537, and of (2), in Kidd, pp. 568–72 (No. 286) and pp. 604–15 (No. 304) respectively. M. Boegner, *Les Catéchismes de Calvin* (Paris thesis, Pamiers, 1905). P. *Schaff, *A History of the Creeds of Christendom*, i (1877), pp. 467–71. See also works cited under *Calvin*.

GENEVIÈVE, St., or Genovefa (c. 422–c. 500), Virgin and chief Patroness of the city of *Paris. Acc. to the ancient Life, she consecrated herself to God at the age of 7, and was specially blessed by St. *Germanus of Auxerre. At 15 she took the veil, and from then onwards devoted herself to a life of mortification. The great power attributed to her intercession was seen in her influence with the Frankish conquerors of Paris, and in the diversion from the city in 451 of the hordes of Huns under Attila II. After her death, her intercession continued to be invoked, and to it was attributed the cessation of a fierce pestilence in 1129. The trustworthiness of her Life, which exists in three main recensions, has been contested in recent times; but some competent scholars continue to defend the traditional account. Feast day, 3 Jan.

Of the three recensions of the Life: 'Text A' ed. by B. Krusch in *M.G.H.*, Scriptores Rerum Merovingicarum, iii (1896), pp. 204–38; 'Text B' by C. Kohler, *Étude critique sur le texte de la vie latine de Sainte Geneviève* (Bibliothèque de l'École des Hautes Études, xlviii, 1881), pp. 5–47; and 'Text C' by C. Künstle, *Vita Sanctae Genovefae* (Teubner ed., 1910). G. Kurth, *Études Franques*, ii (1919), No. xii, 'Étude critique sur la vie de Sainte Geneviève', pp. 1–96, with good bibl. Modern lives by C. H. Lesêtre ('Les Saints', 1900), A. D. Sertillanges (Paris, 1917), and Mme Reynès-Monlaur (Paris, 1924). H. *Leclerq, O.S.B., in *D.A.C.L.*, vi (pt. 1; 1924), cols. 960–90, s.v. 'Geneviève (Vie de Sainte)'.

GENIZA (from Heb. גנז, 'to hide'). The chamber attached to a *synagogue used to house MS. books unfit for use in worship, e.g worn-out copies of the Scriptures and also heretical books. Valuable fragments of Biblical and other Jewish MSS. were discovered in 1896–8 by S. Schechter in the geniza of an ancient synagogue at Cairo, dating from A.D. 882, among them portions of the Hebrew text of *Ecclesiasticus and the text published as *Fragments of a Zadokite Work.* They now

constitute the Taylor-Schechter Collection in Cambridge University Library. See also *Damascus Fragments.*

P. Kahle, *The Cairo Geniza* (1947); R. H. *Charles (ed.), *Apocrypha and Pseudepigrapha of the OT*, ii (1913), pp. 785–834.

GENNADIUS I (d. 471), Patr. of *Constantinople. In his earlier years he vigorously opposed the Christological teaching of St. *Cyril of Alexandria (d. 444). In 458 he succeeded Anatolius (449–58) as Patriarch and in 460 he received a letter from St. *Leo (*ep.* 170), warning him against *Timothy Aelurus. Gennadius was the author of many Commentaries, notably on Gen., Dan., and the Pauline Epp.; considerable sections of these have survived, mainly in *catenae.* A few fragments of his dogmatic writings have also been preserved, among them extracts from a work against Cyril's 'Twelve Anathemas' and of a treatise 'Ad Parthenium'. He also wrote an encomium on the *Tome of St. Leo and an encyclical against *simony (from a Synod at Constantinople, prob. 459). Feast day, in the E. 25 Aug. (also in Roman martyrology) and also 17 Nov.

Fragg. collected in J. P. Migne, *PG*, lxxxv (2), 1613–1734; others in K. Staab, *Pauluskommentare aus der griechischen Kirche* (1933), pp. 352–418. F. Diekamp, *Analecta Patristica* (Orientalia Christiana Analecta, cxvii, 1938), sect. vi, 'Gennadius von Konstantinopel', pp. 54–108. R. Devreesse, 'Anciens Commentateurs grecs de l'Octateuque', sect. xvii, in *R. Bibl.*, xlv (1936), p. 384. C. H. *Turner in *H.D.B.*, v (extra vol., 1904), pp. 517–19, s.v. 'Patristic Commentaries'. Basic material for his life in *AA.SS.*, Aug. VI (1743), pp. 106–16.

GENNADIUS II. See *George Scholarius.*

GENNADIUS OF MARSEILLES (fl. 470), presbyter and ecclesiastical historian. His chief surviving work, the 'De Viris Illustribus', is a continuation of *Jerome's book of the same name. Completed about 480, it contains 101 notices (10 of them added by a later hand) of ecclesiastical writers, E. and W., mostly of the 5th cent. While biographical detail is slight, the bibliographical information is invaluable. The account of Gennadius himself (No. 100 [101]) mentions several dogmatic works of which only fragments remain. He was a *Semi-pelagian.

J. P. Migne, *PL*, lviii, 1059–1120. Modern edd. of *De Vir. Illust.* by C. A. Bernoulli (Samml. ausgew. kirchen- und dogmengesch. Quellenschr., xi, 1895) and E. C. Richardson (T.U., xiv (1), 1896). Text of *Liber Ecclesiasticorum Dogmatum*, ed. C. H. *Turner in *J.T.S.*, vii (1905–6), pp. 78–99, viii (1906–7), pp. 103–14. Important studies by A. Feder, S.J., in *Scholastik*, ii (1927), pp. 481–514, iii (1928), pp. 238–43, and viii (1933), pp. 217–32 and 380–99. G. *Morin, O.S.B., 'Le *Liber Dogmatum* de Gennade de Marseille et problèmes qui s'y rattachent' in *R. Bén.*, xxiv (1907), pp. 445–55. H. Koch, *Vincenz von Lerin und Gennadius* (T.U., xxxi (2b), 1907). Bardenhewer, iv, pp 595–9.

GENNESARET. A district on the western shore of the Sea of *Galilee, which is hence called also the Lake of Gennesaret (Lk. 5. 1). Christ landed there after the Feeding of the Five Thousand (Mk. 6. 53).

GENTILE, GIOVANNI (1875–1944), Italian philosopher and educationist. He was born at Castelvetrano and studied philosophy and literature at Palermo. After teaching philosophy at Naples from 1898 to 1906, he was professor of the history of philosophy at Palermo (1906–14), Pisa (1914–17), and Rome from 1917. Shortly after this last appointment he was made a senator. He was one of the earliest supporters of Fascism, which he regarded as the incarnation of Idealism, and on B. Mussolini's accession to power became Minister of Education (1922–4). As such, he carried out important paedagogic reforms and reintroduced the teaching of the Catholic religion into the schools.

Gentile developed his idealist philosophy in conjunction with B. *Croce (from whom he later parted on political grounds) under the influence of G. B. *Vico, I. *Kant, and G. W. F. *Hegel. Reality, which was fundamentally historical, was the idea as realized in the human mind, so that philosophy was the supreme form of self-consciousness, in which the process of self-formation culminated. God was the 'transcendent pure thinking', which overcomes all mental differences and antagonisms. The significance of religion was that it promoted the awareness of objective ideas, and in particular of the reality to which all others were subordinate. It was a complete intuition of life, and the Catholic form of it was esp. suited to the needs of the Italian people.

His works include *La filosofia di Marx* (1898), *Storia della filosofia italiana* (1902 ff.), *Il modernismo* (1909), *I problemi della scolastica* (1913), *Sommario di pedagogia come scienza filosofica* (2 vols., 1913–14), *Teoria generale dello spirito* (1916; Eng. trans., 1922), *Le origini della filosofia contemporanea in Italia* (4 vols., 1917–23), *La riforma dell' educazione* (1920; Eng. trans., 1923), *Scritti politici* (1925), *La filosofia dell'arte* (1931). He was assassinated by anti-Fascists at Florence on 15 April 1944.

Opere complete (partly Milan, partly Florence, 1928 ff.; 16 vols. to 1946). E. Chiocchetti, *La filosofia di G. Gentile* (1922); V. la Via, *L' idealismo attuale di G. Gentile* (1925); R. W. Holmes, *The Idealism of G. Gentile* (1937); B. Bianchi, *Il problema religioso Giovanni Gentile* (Problemi filosofici, v. 1940). *Giovanni Gentile. La vita é il pensiero* (4 vols., 1948–51).

GENTILES. A Biblical term (Heb. םיוֹגּ, 'nations'; Gk. ἔθνη, 'nations', or Ἕλληνες, 'Greeks') usually applied to non-Jews. The meaning of the corresponding Lat. word, *gentiles*, used in the *Vulgate to translate the Heb. and Greek, has changed during the centuries. In post-Augustan Latin it meant 'fellow-countrymen' and in still later Latin more generally 'foreigners'.

GENUFLECTENTES (*Lat.*, 'those who kneel'). In the ancient Church a class of *Penitents who were permitted to be present at the first part of the liturgy, kneeling at the west end of the nave. They were dismissed, together with the *catechumens and *energumens, before the Mass of the *Faithful.

GENUFLEXION. A momentary kneeling on the right knee, with the body erect, used in the W. Church as a ceremonial reverence when passing before the Blessed Sacrament, or before the unveiled cross on *Good Friday, at the *incarnatus* in the *Nicene Creed, and on certain other occasions. A double genuflection, made by kneeling on both knees and bowing the head, is used only before the Blessed Sacrament exposed.

H. *Leclercq, O.S.B., in *D.A.C.L.*, vi (pt. 1; 1924), cols. 1017–21.

GEOFFREY OF MONMOUTH (*c.* 1100–1154), Bp. of *St. Asaph and chronicler. He was educated under the supervision of his uncle, Uchtryd, Archdeacon, and later Bp., of *Llandaff, and prob. became a *Benedictine monk. In 1129 he was one of the witnesses of the foundation charter of Oseney Abbey. He was made Archdeacon of St. Teilo's *c.* 1140 and Bp. of *St. Asaph in 1152, but he died before entering his diocese.

The first version of his famous 'Historia Britonum' was completed by 1139; but the text which survives seems to date from 1147. It purports to be a translation from an old Celtic book brought to England by Walter the Archdeacon, but the truth of this statement has been questioned. Its historical value is very slight, it abounds in chronological impossibilities, and it is largely the work of Geoffrey's own imagination; but it soon acquired a great reputation which no historical criticism could diminish. It became a potent factor in the unification of England through its emphasis on the common origin of Britons, Saxons, and Normans, as well as a rich source for chroniclers and poets. It was drawn upon by Geoffrey Gaimar for his 'Estorie des Engles' (*c.* 1147–53) and by Wace for the 'Roman de Brut' (1153), and in the 13th cent. by Layamon's 'Brut' (1205) and Robert of Gloucester's rhymed chronicle. Among later authors R. Holinshed, M. Drayton, J. *Milton, and others used it extensively, and the *Gorboduc* and W. Shakespeare's *King Lear* derived their inspiration from it. Above all, it was the principal source of the stories of Arthur and the Knights of the Round Table, which, based on Nennius, were much elaborated in Geoffrey's 'Historia', whence they were derived in Chrétien de Troyes, Robert de Borron's 'Roman du saint graal' and 'Roman de Merlin', the medieval stories of Lancelot and Tristan, and Thomas Malory's 'Morte d'Arthur'. Among other legends popularized by Geoffrey are the stories of the giant Goëmagot, Merlin, and Vortigern and Rowena. A 'Vita Merlini' has also been attributed to him, but its authenticity has been contested.

Editio princeps of 'Historia Britonum', Paris, 1508. Other edd. by J. A. Giles (London, 1844), A. Schulz (Halle, 1854), and A. Griscom (London, 1929). Eng. trr. by A. Thompson (London, 1718), J. A. Giles (ib., 1842), and S. Evans (ib., 1904). Modern ed. of the 'Vita Merlini', with Eng. tr., by J. J. Parry (University of Illinois Studies in Language and Literature, x, No. 3; 1925), with reff. to earlier it. E. Faral, *La Légende arthurienne*, I, ii (Bibliothèque de l'École des Hautes Études, cclvi; 1929). J. S. P. Tatlock, *The Legendary History of Britain* (Berkeley, Cal., 1950). H. R. Tedder in *D.N.B.*, xxi (1890), pp. 133–5.

GEORGE, St., Patron Saint of England and Martyr. Very little is known of his life, or even of his martyrdom; but his historical existence, though still sometimes disputed, is now generally accepted. Despite E. *Reynold's and E. *Gibbon's identification of the two, he seems to have nothing to do with *George of Cappadocia. A not improbable view is that he suffered at or near Lydda before the time of *Constantine (d. 337). He is perhaps referred to (though not by name) in *Eusebius (*H.E.*, VIII, v); but not until the 6th cent. did his cultus become popular and the legends of his exploits receive elaboration. The slaying of the dragon is first credited to him in the latter part of the 12th cent. and the belief became popular from its appearance in the 13th cent. '*Golden Legend'. It may have derived from the myth of Perseus's slaying of the sea monster at Arsuf or Joppa, both cities in the neighbourhood of Lydda. In the E. he is distinguished as the great martyr (μεγαλόμαρτυς). Feast day, 23 Apr. He is reckoned one of the *Auxiliary Saints.

The circumstances in which St. George became the patron saint of England, where he appears to have been known at least from the 8th cent., are obscure. His *acta* were translated into Anglo-Saxon and pre-Conquest churches (e.g. one at Doncaster, 1061) are dedicated to him. In 1222, St. George's Day was made a lesser holiday at the Synod of Oxford. From the 14th cent. the red cross on a white background ('St. George's arms') became a kind of uniform for soldiers and sailors. His rank as patron of England (in place of St. *Edward the Confessor) prob. dates from the reign of Edward III, who founded the Order of the Garter under St. George's patronage (c. 1347). In 1415 the Constitution of Abp. H. *Chichele made his feast one of the chief holy days of the year. W. *Caxton's translation and printing of the 'Golden Legend' did much to popularize the story.

AA.SS., Apr. III (1675), pp. 100–63. Widely variant Acts of St. George exist in many recensions (Gk., Lat., Syriac, Coptic, Ethiopic, Armenian, etc.). Gk. Acts ed., with discussion, by K. Krumbacher–A. Ehrhard (*Abh.* (Bayr.) xxv, Hft. 3; 1911); crit. ed. of Ethiopic Acts by V. Arras, O.F.M. (C.S.C.O., cxxxviii, 1953; Lat. trans. C.S.C.O., cxxxix, 1953). M. Huber, O.S.B., 'Zur Georgslegende' in *Festschrift zum XII. Allgemeinen Deutschen Neuphilologentage in München, Pfingsten 1906* (Erlangen, 1906), pp. 175–235 (with Lat. texts, pp. 194–235). H. *Delehaye, S.J., *Les Légendes grecques des saints militaires* (1909), pp. 45–76. Popular account in G. J. Marcus, *Saint George of England* (1939). A. Amore, O.F.M.–V. Wehr–P. Toschi in *E.C.*, vi (1951), cols. 441–5, s.v. 'Giorgio, santo, martire' incl. Iconography and Folklore).

GEORGE (c. 640–724), 'Bp. of the Arabians'. He was born in the neighbourhood of *Antioch and in 686 became bishop of the Arabian nomads in Mesopotamia, with his see at Akula. His writings are one of the principal authorities for the history of *Syriac Christianity and literature. They include a translation of parts of *Aristotle's 'Organon', scholia to the Homilies of St. *Gregory Nazianzen, additions to the 'Hexaemeron' of *James of Edessa, and a long series of letters on matters of doctrine, liturgy, and ascetic practice.

His verse treatises on the consecration of *chrism and the lives of the hermits ed. V. Ryssel in *Atti della R. Accademia dei Lincei*, Cl. di Scienze morali, storiche e filologiche, ix (1892), pp. 45–93. Selected works tr. into Germ. by id., *Georgs des Araberbischofs Gedichte und Briefe* (1891). 'An Exposition on the Rites of Baptism, the Eucharist and the Consecration of the Chrism' ed. R. H. *Connolly–H. W. Codrington, Text and Translation Society, 1913, pp. 3–14 (of the Syriac), with Eng. tr. pp. 11–23. W. Wright, *A Short History of Syriac Literature* (1894), pp. 156–9; A. *Baumstark, *Geschichte der syrischen Literatur* (1922), p. 257 f.

GEORGE OF CAPPADOCIA (4th cent.). *Arian bishop who was intruded into the see of *Alexandria. Our knowledge of him, though derived almost exclusively from hostile sources, leaves little doubt of his grasping and violent character. He took possession of the see of Alexandria in the Lent of 357, i.e. about a year after Athanasius's retirement in Feb. 356, and held it till he was murdered by the rabble on 24 Dec. 361. As a member of the extreme Arian party, he was opposed by the *Semi-Arians no less than the orthodox. E. *Gibbon and others have argued that he is the historical character underlying the legendary story of St. *George, but this view now finds little acceptance.

W. *Bright in *D.C.B.*, ii (1880), pp. 638–40, s.v. 'Georgius (4)'.

GEORGE HAMARTOLOS (9th cent.), 'George the Sinner', also 'George the Monk', Byzantine chronicler. He flourished under Michael III (842–67). He wrote a 'Chronicon Syntomon' in four Books, extending from the Creation down to A.D. 842. Though coloured by its bitter hatred of *Iconoclasm, it is an important source for the period immediately preceding *Photius. Its main interests are those of the more educated members of a Byzantine monastery. In the MSS. it is carried on to 948 by 'The Logothete' (prob. *Simeon Metaphrastes), and to the 12th cent. by other writers. It was translated at an early date into Old Church Slavonic and Georgian.

Editio princeps of complete chronicle by E. de Muralt (St. Petersburg, 1857, unsatisfactory; repr. in J. P. Migne, *PG*, cx). Crit. ed. by C. de Boor (2 vols., Teub., 1904). [The 'Vitae Recentiorum Imperatorum' in *PG*, cix, 823–984, is only an extract from the Chronicon, repeated from cx, 979–1194.] K. Praechter in *B.Z.*, xv (1906), pp. 307–30 (review of C. de Boor's ed.). Slavonic text ed. V. M. Istrin (3 vols., Leningrad, 1920–30); Georgian text ed. S. Kauchtschischwili (Tiflis, 1910–16). Krumbacher, pp. 352–8.

GEORGE OF LAODICEA (4th cent.), *Semi-Arian bishop. A native of Alexandria, he became a strong supporter of the Arian party which followed *Eusebius of Nicomedia, and c. 335 was appointed Bp. of Laodicea in Syria. In doctrine, however, he took up a less extreme position than Eusebius, and became one of the chief exponents of the *Homoiousian theology. In defence of his position he composed in 359, in conjunction with *Basil of Ancyra and others, a statement of his faith which is preserved by *Epiphanius (*Haer.* 73, 12–22). He appears to have died shortly after 360.

F. *Loofs in *P.R.E.* (ed. 3), vi (1899), pp. 539–41. Bardenhewer, ii, p. 264 f.

GEORGE SCHOLARIUS (c. 1400–c. 1468), Patr. of *Constantinople. In early life he seems to have been first a teacher of philosophy and then a civil court judge in Constantinople. He attended the Council of *Florence (1439), where he supported the scheme for reunion in opposition to his fellow-Greek, *Gemistus Plethon. On returning to the East,'however, he very soon became the enemy of all projects of union. A little later he entered a monastery and took the name of 'Gennadius'. After the capture of the city he was made Patriarch as 'Gennadius II' in 1454 by the Sultan Mohammed II, who himself invested him with his crozier and mantle, and established with him the *concordat which in effect governed the relations between the Orthodox Church and the Moslem power until 1923. After two (or possibly five) years in office he resigned, and ended his days in a monastery. He was a prolific writer on a variety of subjects, and many of his works survive in the (sometimes not very legible) autographs.

Crit. ed. of his Works by L. Petit, A.A.–X. A. Siderides –M. Jugie, A.A. (8 vols., Paris-Athens, 1928–36), with full introd. Older edd. repr. in J. P. Migne, *PG*, clx, 319–774. The only satisfactory study of George Scholarios is by M. Jugie, A.A., in *D.T.C.*, xiv (pt. 2; 1941), cols. 1521–70, with bibl. Older studies by E. *Renaudot, *Gennadii ... Homiliae de Sacramento Eucharistiae* (Paris, 1709; repr. J. P. Migne, loc. cit., cols. 249–312), and L. *Allatius, *De Georgiis et eorum Scriptis* (Paris, 1651). Cf. also J. Dräseke, 'Zu Georgios Scholarios' in *B.Z.*, iv (1895), pp. 561–80. Krumbacher, pp. 119–21. M. Jugie in *L.Th.K.*, iv (1932), cols. 380–2 (with useful analysis of new crit. ed. in bibl.).

GEORGE SYNCELLUS (*fl. c.* 800), Byzantine historian. Little is known of him beyond the facts that he lived for some time in Palestine and was later the '*Syncellus' of Tarasius, Patr. of *Constantinople (784–806). He wrote an important 'Chronicle' from the Creation to the time of *Diocletian, which after his death was brought down by his friend, Theophanes the Confessor, to A.D. 813. The treatment of Biblical times is much fuller than that of the later period. His sources included (either directly or indirectly) *Eusebius, *Julius Africanus, Anianus of Alexandria (5th cent.), Panodorus (c. 400), and other writers. He possessed some critical insight into the value of his material and preserves some important fragments, but his use of his sources is dull and unimaginative.

Chronicle ed. W. Dindorf (C.S.H. Byz., 1828). Krumbacher, pp. 339–42. R. A. Laqueur in *P.W.*, iv (2. Reihe; 1932), cols. 1388–1410, s.v. 'Synkellos'.

GEORGIAN VERSION. The earliest version of the New Testament in the Georgian language, which like *Armenian probably owes its alphabet to St. *Mesrob (5th cent.), dates from the 6th cent. The translation was apparently made from the Armenian, though from better texts than any now surviving Armenian MS. R. P. Blake has observed that certain MSS. of the Georgian Gospels represent a type of the *Caesarean text, which in the Adysh MS. of the Gospels (897) has been preserved in relative purity, though in most MSS. it has been more or less completely 'corrected' to the *Lucianic type. The Gospels and the Pauline Epp. were always written until modern times in distinct MSS., so that their textual traditions are independent.

Ed. princeps of OT by Prince Vakhusht, Moscow, 1742–3. Modern edd. of Matt. and Mk. by B. V. Beneševič (St. Petersburg, 1909–11), of Mk. and Matt. by R. P. Blake in *P.O.*, xx, fasc. 3 [pp. 437–574] (1928), and xxiv, fasc. 1 [pp. 1–168] (1933). K. *Lake–R. P. Blake, 'The Caesarean Text of the Gospel of Mark' in *H.T.R.*, xxi (1928), pp. 207–404, esp. pp. 286–307. L. J. M. Bebb in *H.D.B.*, iv (1902), p. 861, s.v. 'Versions'; M. Tarchnišvili in *E.C.*, vi (1951), col. 75 f., s.v. 'Georgia V, versione della Bibbia', with bibl. On Georgian theological literature generally see K. Kekelidze, *History of Georgian Literature* (in Georgian, Tiflis, 1923); R. P. Blake in *J.T.S.*, xxvi (1924–5), pp. 50–64 (discussion of Kekelidze's work); and J. Karst, *Littérature georgienne chrétienne* (1934). M. Tarchnišvili, *Geschichte der kirchlichen georgischen Literatur* (S.T., clxxxv, 1955).

GERALD DE BARRI. See *Giraldus Cambrensis.*

GERALD OF WALES. See *Giraldus Cambrensis.*

GERBERT OF AURILLAC. See *Sylvester II.*

GERHARD, JOHANN (1582–1637), *Lutheran theologian. From 1616 he was professor at Jena where, with Johann Major and Johann Himmel, he formed the so-called 'Trias Johannea'. In his *Loci communes theologici* (1610–22), he issued a systematized and detailed exposition of Lutheran theology which for long remained a standard work. He also wrote a very popular devotional book, *Meditationes Sacrae ad veram pietatem excitandam* (1606), the English translation of which by R. Winterton (1631) went through a large number of editions.

New ed. of Gerhard's *Loci Communes Theologici* by F. J. Cotta (20 vols., bound in 7, Tübingen, 1762–81), with index by G. H. Müller (2 pts., ib., 1787–9), and by E. Preuss (9 vols., bound in 5, Berlin, 1863–75). Life by E. R. Fischer, together with some of his letters (Leipzig, 1723). E. *Troeltsch, *Vernunft und Offenbarung bei Johann Gerhard und Melanchthon* (Göttingen Diss., 1891). R. Hupfeld, *Die Ethik Johann Gerhards* (1908). J. Kunze in *P.R.E.* (ed. 3), vi (1899), pp. 554–61, s.v.

GERHARD OF ZUTPHEN (1367–98) (Gerhard Zerbolt), member of the *Brethren of the Common Life. After studying at various places he became a priest and librarian of the Brethren of the Common Life at Deventer. He became a close friend of *Florentius Radewyns. He was remarkable for his learning esp. in moral theology and canon law as well as in ascetic and mystic theology, and an excellent director of souls. Of his writings the best known are 'De reformatione virium animae' and 'De spiritualibus ascensionibus' which influenced the '*Spiritual Exercises' of *Ignatius of Loyola. His authorship of two treatises on prayer and the reading of Scripture in the vernacular is uncertain.

His 'Scriptum pro quadam Inordinate Gradus Ecclesiasticos et Praedicationis Officium Affectante', ed. A. Hyma in *Nederlandsch Archief voor Kerkgeschiedenis*, N.S., xx

(1927), pp. 179–232. Life by *Thomas à Kempis in *Opera et Libri Vite Fratris Thomae de Kempis* [Nuremberg, 1494], fo. xxix–xxxviii. G. H. J. W. Geesink, *Gerhard Zerbolt von Zutphen* (Amsterdam, 1879). F. Jostes, 'Die Schriften des Gerhard Zerbolt von Zutphen "De Libris Teutonicalibus"' in *Hist. J.*, xi (1890), pp. 1–22 and 709–17; A. Hyma, 'Is Gerard of Zutphen the author of the "Super Modo Vivendi"?' in *Nederlandsch Archief voor Kerkgeschiedenis*, N.S., xvi (1921), pp. 107–28. S. D. van Veen in *P.R.E.* (ed. 3), xxi (1908), pp. 735–7, s.v. Zütphen, Gerhard Zerbolt van'.

GERHARDT, PAUL (c. 1607–76), German *Lutheran hymn - writer. After studying theology at *Wittenberg and spending some years as a private tutor at Berlin he became provost at Mittelwalde in 1651 and pastor at the St. Nikolaikirche at Berlin in 1657. He resigned this post in 1666 through unwillingness to sign a declaration submitting to the *Syncretist edicts of the Elector of Brandenburg. In 1668 he was appointed archdeacon at Luebben, where he remained to his death. Though in his theology he was an uncompromising Lutheran, he was susceptible to the influence of Catholic mysticism, esp. that of St. *Bernard, and one of his most beautiful hymns, 'O sacred head, sore wounded', is based on the 'Salve caput cruentatum' attributed to the saint. Combining a deep personal piety and filial trust in God with the love of nature of the true poet, as expressed, e.g., in the fine verses of 'The duteous day now closeth' (Eng. tr., R. *Bridges), his hymns have become widely known, esp. in Germany. He ranks as one of the greatest hymn-writers of German Protestantism.

P. Wackernagel (anon. ed.), *Paulus Gerhardts geistliche Lieder* [1843]. E. G. Roth, *Paul Gerhardt*. Nach seinem Leben und Wirken aus zum Theil ungedruckten Nachrichten dargestellt (1829). E. Kochs, *Paul Gerhardt*. Sein Leben und seine Lieder (1907). H. Petrich, *Paul Gerhardt* (1914). R. Eckart, *Paul Gerhardt*. Urkunden und Aktenstücke zu seinem Leben und Kämpfen (1919). T. B. Hewitt, *Paul Gerhardt as a Hymnwriter and his Influence on English Hymnology* (New Haven and London, 1919), with bibl. R. Eckart, *Paul Gerhardt-Bibliographie* (1909). C. Palmer–C. Bertheau in *P.R.E.* (ed. 3), vi (1899), pp. 561–5, s.v., with bibl.

GERHOH OF REICHERSBERG (1093–1169). One of the principal agents of the Gregorian (see *Gregory VII*) reforms in Germany. After studying at Moosburg, Freising, and Hildesheim, he became 'scholasticus' of the cathedral school at Augsburg in 1119, which post he had to leave two years later owing to his opposition to his simoniacal bishop, Hermann of Augsburg. After their reconciliation in 1123 he accompanied him to the First *Lateran Council, where he submitted his plans for reforming the clergy by means of the introduction of the communal life. As his proposals were rejected he entered the monastery of *Augustinian Canons at Rottenbuch on his return to Germany in 1124, and introduced a reform of the rule. His ideas on Church discipline were laid down about the same time in his 'Liber de aedificio Dei' (c. 1130). In 1132 he was appointed provost of the Canons Regular of St. Augustine at Reichersberg, to the great spiritual and material advantage of the community. He was often sent on embassies to Rome, where he came into contact with St. *Bernard of Clairvaux; but his zeal for reform gained him much hostility. He was even accused of heresy, though he had always defended the orthodox teaching, esp. against the *Christological errors of *Abelard and *Gilbert de la Porrée. In 1166 he was banned by the Emp. *Frederick I and forced to flee from his monastery because he refused to support the Imperialist antipope. His ideas on the schism were laid down in his famous work 'De Investigatione Antichristi' (c. 1161) in which he advocates a clearer definition of the spheres of Papal and Imperial power.

Opera Omnia in J. P. Migne, *PL*, cxciii, 461–1814, and cxciv, 9–1490; F. Scheibelberger (ed.), *Gerhohi . . . Opera Hactenus Inedita* (Lincii, 1875); much of his work also ed. E. Sackur in *M.G.H.*, Libelli de Lite Imperatorum et Pontificum Saeculis XI. et XII., iii (1897), pp. 131–525, with bibl. to date, p. 135 f. Continuation of the *Annales Reicherspergenses* by Magnus (d. 1195), ed. W. Wattenbach, ib., Scriptores, xvii (1861), pp. 490–5 being relevant. H. F. A. Nobbe, *Gerhoh von Reichersberg* (1881). H. H. Jacobs, 'Studien über Gerhoh von Reichersberg. Zur Geistesgeschichte des 12. Jahrhunderts' in *Z.K.G.*, l (1931), pp. 315–77; H. von Fichtenau, 'Studien zu Gerhoh von Reichersberg' in *Mitteilungen des Österreichischen Instituts für Geschichtsforschung*, lii (1938), pp. 1–56. J. Günster, *Die Christologie des Gerhoh von Reichersberg. Eine dogmengeschichtliche Studie zu seiner Auffassung von der hypostatischen Union* (1940). V. Zollini in *E.C.*, vi (1951), col. 112 f., for further bibl. *Opera Inedita*, edd. D. and O. Van den Eynde (Rome, 1955 ff.).

GERMAIN, St. See *Germanus, St.*

GERMAIN-DES-PRÉS, St.- See *Saint-Germain-des-Prés.*

GERMAN BAPTISTS. See *Tunkers.*

GERMAN-CHRISTIANS (Deutsche Christen). The Protestants who, during the Hitler régime, tried to bring about a synthesis between Nazism and Christianity. Their more extreme adherents wished to eliminate the OT, St. *Paul ('the Rabbi'), and the doctrines of St. *Augustine (with their 'Jewish' sense of sin), and to eradicate from the Gospels everything Jewish or 'servile'. Finding their Holy Land not in Palestine, but in Germany, they held that the law of God was embodied in Hitler. It was their professed purpose to 'complete' M. *Luther's Reformation. Concealment of their more extreme aims, coupled with a broadcast by Hitler urging all Nazis to vote, gained them a large majority at the Church elections in July 1933; and L. *Müller (q.v.), the most influential figure in the group, was elected *Reichsbischof. Müller's extreme measures, notably his incorporation of the Evangelical Youth into the 'Hitler Jugend', wholly alienated the embryonic '*Confessing Church' and he was virtually superseded by the appointment of Hans Kerrl as Minister for Church Affairs in 1935. None the less, the 'German-Christians' dominated more than half the German *Landeskirchen* during the Second World War. After it the more extreme members disappeared from public view, while others seceded from the official *Landeskirchen* to join in a free Church.

GERMANUS, St. (*c.* 378–448), Bp. of Auxerre. Trained as a Roman advocate, Germanus ruled part of Gaul before his election to the see of Auxerre in 418. The chief events of his life can be distinguished from legendary accretions. In 429 he came to Britain (with Lupus of Troyes) to combat *Pelagianism and silenced the heretics at Verulamium. In 447 he revisited Britain, when he led British troops to victory over the Picts and Saxons, teaching them, it is said, the war-cry 'Alleluia'. In 448 he was at *Ravenna, pleading for the rebellious Armoricans. There he died. *Patrick of Ireland and Illtud of Wales were probably his pupils, and he is said to have encouraged the early religious life of St. *Geneviève. Feast day, 31 July.

A 'Vita', with good historical basis but many miraculous details, was written *c.* 480 by Constantius, a presbyter of Lyons. It is printed, with many 9th cent. interpolations, in *A.A.SS.*, Jul. VII (1731), pp. 200–20. The original form was first printed in B. Mombritius, *Sanctuarium seu Vitae Sanctorum*, i (Milan, 1480), pp. 319–25; crit. ed. by W. Levison in *M.G.H.*, Scriptores Rerum Merovingicarum, vii (i; 1919), pp. 225–83. Metrical version, dating from *c.* 875, ed. L. Traube in *M.G.H.*, Poetae Latinae, iii (1896), pp. 428–517. W. Levison, 'Bischof German von Auxerre und die Quellen zu seiner Geschichte' in *N.A.*, xxix (1904), pp. 97–175. Modern Life by L. Prunel (Paris, 1929), with bibl. See also bibl. to *Heiric of Auxerre*.

GERMANUS, St. (*c.* 496–576), Bp. of *Paris. A native of Autun (Augustodunum), he was ordained priest in 530 and rose to become abbot of the monastery of St. Symphorian in his own city, where he exercised great generosity to the poor. In 555 he became Bp. of *Paris. Here he sought to check the licence of the Frankish kings and stop the perpetual civil wars; and he won considerable influence over Childebert, son of Clovis. He took part in several Councils, among them Paris III (557), Tours II (566), and Paris IV (573). His prophecy that death would overtake Sigebert if he did not desist from invoking the trans-Rhenish barbarians against his brother, Chilperic, was fulfilled when Sigebert was murdered by assassins. The church of St.-Germain-des-Prés stands on the site of an elaborate 7th cent. tomb over his remains (destroyed, 1793). His Life, written by *Venantius Fortunatus, abounds in miraculous legends. Feast day, 28 May; of his translation, 25 July.

Two Letters attributed to him are of great importance for the history of the *Gallican Liturgy. Older scholars, accepting their genuineness, used them in the reconstruction of the Gallican Rite; but A. *Wilmart, following up doubts expressed by H. Koch and E. *Bishop, has made out a strong case against their authenticity. Wilmart maintains that they were written in the S. of France *c.* 700, and represent a rite as much Spanish as French, which had already absorbed a number of foreign elements.

Crit. ed., with introd., of the 'Vita' by Venantius Fortunatus, by B. Krusch in *M.G.H.*, Scriptores Rerum Merovingicarum, vii (1919), pp. 337–418; another brief life, together with the account of the translation of his relics, ib., pp. 419–28. These three items also pr. in *A.A.SS.*, Mai. VI (1688), pp. 774–806; the life by Venantius Fortunatus, also J. P. Migne, *PL*, lxxii, 55–78. Bardenhewer, v, p. 377.

The two letters mentioned above are preserved in an 8th cent. MS. at Autun. They were first pr. by E. *Martène, O.S.B., in his *Thesaurus Novus Anecdotorum*, v (Paris, 1717), pp. 91–100; repr. in J. P. Migne, *PL*, lxxii, 89–98. On their authenticity, see P. *Batiffol, *Études de liturgie et d'archéologie chrétienne* (1919), pp. 245–90 ('L'Expositio Liturgiae Gallicanae attribuée à St Germain de Paris'), and A. *Wilmart, O.S.B., in *D.A.C.L.*, vi (pt. 1; 1924), cols. 1049–102, s.v.

GERMANUS, St. (*c.* 634–*c.* 733), Patriarch of *Constantinople. Descended from a noble Byzantine family, Germanus received a careful education and became one of the clergy of *Santa Sophia in 668, of which he was later made the head. He was among the chief promoters of the *Quinisext Council (692) and he seems to have been appointed to the metropolitan see of Cyzicus in return for services rendered shortly afterwards, though acc. to his 9th cent. 'Vita' not until *c.* 705–6. It seems that at the synod convoked by the Emp. Philippicus in 712 to restore the *Monothelite heresy he ceded to the threats of the Emperor and signed the declaration against the Sixth Oecumenical Council. If he actually did so, a fact which has been contested, he soon returned to orthodoxy. He was elected patriarch in 715 and at a synod called shortly afterwards officially proclaimed the Catholic faith and anathematized the Monothelites. In 725 the Emp. *Leo III, the Isaurian, issued his first edict against the veneration of icons (see *Iconoclastic Controversy), and during the four subsequent years of his patriarchate Germanus was the soul of resistance against Iconoclasm. He was forced to resign in 730 and retired to Platonium, where he probably wrote his treatise 'De haeresibus et synodis', his only extant historical work. Among his other writings, many of which perished at the hands of the Iconoclastic Emperors, there survive four dogmatic letters, three of them bearing on the Iconoclastic Controversy, and seven homilies on the BVM, of whose cult he was one of the most ardent promoters. Mary's incomparable purity, foreshadowing the doctrine of the *Immaculate Conception, and her universal mediation in the distribution of supernatural blessings, are his two frequently recurring themes. He is probably also the author of the 'Historia mystica ecclesiae catholicae', an interpretation of the contemporary Byzantine Liturgy, as well as of several fine liturgical poems. Feast day, 12 May.

Life from various sources pr. in *A.A.SS.* Mai. III (1680), pp. 155–61. Works in J. P. Migne, *PG*, xcviii, 9–454. His *Historia Mystica*, ed. S. Pétrides in *Revue de l'Orient Chrétien*, x (1905), pp. 287–309 and 350–64; the Lat. vers. by *Anastasius Bibliothecarius by J. Cozza-Luzi in Mai, *N.P.B.*, x (2; 1905), pp. 9–28; on this work, see F. E. *Brightman, 'The *Historia Mystagogica* and other Greek Commentaries on the Byzantine Liturgy' in *J.T.S.*, ix (1907–8), pp. 248–67 and 387–98. See also F. Cayré in *D.T.C.*, vi (1920), cols. 1300–9, s.v., and Bardenhewer, v, pp. 48–51, both with full bibl.

GERONTIUS, The Dream of. This celebrated poem by J. H. *Newman was first published in the periodical, the *Month*, for April and May 1865, and in book form in 1866. It is a vision of a just soul leaving a body at death and of its subsequent intercourse with the angels. It has been set to music by E. *Elgar, and two of the poems in it are well known as hymns—'Firmly I believe and truly' and 'Praise to the Holiest in the height'.

GERSON, JEAN LE CHARLIER DE (1363–1429), French Churchman and spiritual writer, the 'doctor christianissimus'. He was born nr. Rethel in the Ardennes. In 1377 he entered the College of Navarre at *Paris, then the centre of *Nominalism, where he studied under Pierre *d'Ailly, who remained his lifelong friend. He was made doctor of theology c. 1394, and in 1395 succeeded d'Ailly as Chancellor of Notre-Dame and of the University. From the beginning of his career he worked for the reform of the Church from within, which he endeavoured to bring about chiefly by a renewal of the spirit of prayer and sacrifice, and for the abolition of the Great Western Schism. In 1397 he fled from the strain of the life in Paris to Bruges, where he held the benefice of Dean of the Church of St. Donatian. While there he wrote his famous treatise 'On the Manner of Conducting oneself in a Time of Schism', exhorting clergy and laity of both obediences to recognize each other's Sacraments and urging charity in their judgements. In 1398 he did not vote for the refusal of obedience to the *Avignon Pope, and the later return of France to the obedience of *Benedict XIII was largely his work, due esp. to his treatise 'De Restitutione Obedientiae'. After his return to Paris (1401) he resumed his office as chancellor and was instrumental in bringing back the *Dominicans (1403), who had been expelled from the University for their teaching on the *Immaculate Conception. He approved the decisions of the Councils of *Pisa (1409) and Rome (1412–13), though not taking part in them himself. In 1415 he attended the Council of *Constance, which he encouraged to continue its sessions after the flight of *John XXIII. He asserted the superiority of a General Council over the Pope and demanded that the doctors of theology should have a deliberative and definitive voice in it together with the bishops. He also took an important part in the drawing-up of the famous Four Articles of Constance, the future Charter of *Gallicanism. He had a share in the condemnation of J. *Hus, and denounced the propositions advanced by Jean Petit in favour of tyrannicide. This earned him the hostility of the Duke of Burgundy, Jean sans Peur, who had had the Duke of Orléans assassinated, and in whose defence Jean Petit had drawn up his theses. The hatred of Burgundy prevented Gerson from returning to Paris after the conclusion of the Council, and he went to the Benedictine abbey of Melk, nr. Vienna, where he wrote his treatise 'De Consolatione Theologiae', modelled on *Boethius. After the death of Jean sans Peur he returned to France (1419), where he spent the last ten years of his life in seclusion at Lyons,

devoting himself entirely to the practice of the spiritual life and pastoral work.

Among his writings dealing with the position of the Church are 'De Unitate Ecclesiae', 'De Auferibilitate Papae ab Ecclesia', and 'De Potestate Ecclesiae' (1417), in which he developed the Conciliar theory but without rejecting the Primacy of the Pope. In moral theology he accepted the extreme Nominalist doctrine, then generally taught in the schools, acc. to which nothing was sinful in itself but the sinfulness or goodness of an act depended solely on the Will of God. Among the large number of his treatises devoted to the spiritual life are 'The Mountain of Contemplation' (1397, his principal work), 'Mystical Theology', 'Perfection of the Heart', and Commentaries on the *Magnificat and on the *Song of Solomon. His mystical teaching, which has marked *Augustinian tendencies, is a synthesis of much that is best in Catholic mysticism from *Dionysius the Areopagite to J. *Ruysbroeck, his particular sympathies being with St. *Bernard, the *Victorines and St. *Bonaventure. He consciously opposed this spiritual teaching of the 'antiqui' to the dry intellectualist activities of the Nominalist 'moderni', who threatened to convert theology into mere dialectics. Gerson was also a zealous advocate of frequent *Communion.

Gerson's influence has been deep and lasting mainly in two directions; his Conciliar views found an echo in Gallicanism, of which he is sometimes called the father, and his mystic teaching was admired by *Nicholas of Cusa and by the *Brethren of the Common Life as well as by St. *Ignatius Loyola, St. Robert *Bellarmine, and St. *Francis of Sales. His writings were also greatly valued by M. *Luther in his early years. The '*Imitation of Christ' has sometimes been ascribed to him, esp. by French scholars, but it is now generally admitted that both internal and external evidence are against this attribution.

Editio princeps of his collected works, 4 vols., Cologne, 1483–4; the best ed. is that of L. E. *Dupin (5 vols., Antwerp, 1706, with life). *Notulae super quaedam verba Dionysii de Caelesti Hierachia*, ed. A. Combes (Études de philosophie médiévale, xxx, 1940, with full introd. on proposed ascription to Gerson); six sermons in the vernacular, ed. L. Mourin (Études de théologie et d'histoire de la spiritualité, viii; 1946); Fr. text of the sermon on the Passion ('Ad Deum Vadit'), ed. G. Frénaud, O.S.B. (Paris, 1947; Lat. in Works, ed. Dupin, iii, pp. 1134–42). J. B. Schwab, *Johannes Gerson* (Würzburg, 1858); J. L. Connolly, *John Gerson, Reformer and Mystic* (Louvain, 1928). J. Stelzenberger, *Die Mystik des Johannes Gerson* (Breslauer Studien zur historischen Theologie, x; 1928); M. J. Pinet, *La Vie ardente de Gerson* (1929); W. Dress, *Die Theologie Gersons* (1931). A. Combes, *Jean de Montreuil et le Chancellier Gerson* (Études de Philosophie Médiévale, xxxii; 1942); id., *Essai sur la critique de Ruysbroeck par Gerson* (Études de théologie et d'histoire de la spiritualité, iv and v (1); 1945–8), with reff. to other studies by this author. L. Salembier in *D.T.C.*, vi (1920), cols. 1312–30, s.v.; A. Combes–L. Mourin–F. Simone in *E.C.*, vi (1952), cols. 185–91, s.v. with detailed bibl. T. M. *Lindsay in *E.B.* (ed. 11), xi (1910), pp. 904–6.

GERTRUDE, St. (1) (626–59), abbess. She was the daughter of Pepin the Elder (d. 640). On her father's death, her mother, Blessed Ida, founded a convent at Nivelles in Belgium, and on Ida's death Gertrude became its first abbess. She ruled the convent well, but her personal austerities so weakened her that *c.* 656 she resigned her office and gave herself wholly up to devotion until her death three years later. She is widely venerated in Holland and Belgium, and is invoked as patroness of travellers. Her symbol is the mouse, though the reason is unknown. Feast day, 17 Mar.

A contemporary Vita is printed in *A A.SS.*, Mar. II (1668), pp. 592–99; critical ed. of two recensions by B. Krusch in *M.G.H.*, Scriptores Rerum Merovingicarum, ii (1888), pp. 447–74. *B.H.L.* (1898–1901), Nos. 3490–504, pp. 520–22.

GERTRUDE, St. (2), 'The Great' (1256–*c.* 1302), German mystic. She is to be distinguished from the Abbess Gertrude of Hackeborn (1232-92), with whom she is confused in older works and in the Breviary. At the age of five she was entrusted to the *Benedictine (or *Cistercian) convent of Helfta in Thuringia, where she received a sound education. She experienced a conversion at the age of twenty-five, and from that time led a life of contemplation. Her 'Legatus Divinae Pietatis', of which only the Second Book was written by herself (the other four being based on her notes), is one of the finest literary products of Christian mysticism. Most of her mystic experiences took place during the liturgical offices of the Church which were the mainspring of her spirituality. St. Gertrude was one of the first exponents of devotion to the *Sacred Heart, which she believed was revealed to her in several visions, described in her book with great beauty and simplicity. She also wrote a collection of prayers, 'Exercitia Spiritualia', some of which have become very popular in RC piety. She was never formally canonized, but her cult was first authorized in 1606 and extended to the entire RC Church by *Clement XIII in 1738, and since 1677 she has been included in the *Roman Martyrology. Feast day (since 1932), 16 Nov.; in the Benedictine Order, 17 Nov. She is the patroness of the West Indies.

St. Gertrude's Revelations were first publd. in the vernacular, along with those of St. *Mechtild of Magdeburg, by Marcus von Weida, O.P., Leipzig, 1503; Lat. ed. by J. Lansperge-T. Loher, Cologne, 1536. The best ed. of her works is that of the Benedictines of Solesmes, Poitiers, and Paris, 1875, with important introd. Numerous Eng. trr. Modern studies by G. Ledos ('Les Saints', 1901), M. Molenaar (Amsterdam, [*c.* 1925]) and W. Lampen, O.F.M. (Hilversum, 1939). *St. Gertrude the Great* (anon., London, 1912; often, but apparently wrongly, ascribed to G. Dolan, O.S.B.). Pourrat, ii, pp. 126–36. F. Vernet in *D.T.C.*, vi (1920), cols. 1332–8, s.v., with detailed bibl.

GERVASIUS and PROTASIUS, Sts., the protomartyrs of Milan. When, in 386, St. *Ambrose was about to dedicate his new church at Milan, the predecessor of the present S. Ambrogio, he obeyed 'a presentiment' (*cuiusdam ardor praesagii*) and dug in the church of Sts. Felix and Nabor in search of relics. Two large skeletons were discovered, perfect except that the heads had been severed. These were recognized as the remains of two early martyrs, Gervasius and Protasius, and were transferred to the new church, whereat,

it is recorded, miraculous healings took place, to the discomfiture of the *Arians and the edification of the orthodox. Of Gervasius and Protasius nothing certain is known, though later tradition declared that they had been martyred in the latter half of the 2nd cent. It has even been sought (J. R. *Harris) to identify them with the pagan deities, Castor and Pollux. Feast day, 19 June.

Ambrose, *ep.* 22 (*PL*, xvi, 1019–26). *A A.SS.*, Jun. III (1701), pp. 817–46. J. R. Harris, *The Dioscori in the Christian Legends* (1903); crit. by H. *Delehaye, S.J., 'Castor et Pollux dans les légendes hagiographiques' in *Anal. Boll.*, xxiii (1904), pp. 427–32. H. Delehaye, *Les Origines du culte des martyrs* (1912), passim. See also H. *Leclercq, O.S.B., in *D.A.C.L.*, vi (pt. 1; 1924), cols. 1232–9, and J. P. Kirsch in *L.Th.K.*, iv (1932), col. 447, s.v.

GESENIUS, HEINRICH FRIEDRICH WILHELM (1786–1842), orientalist and Biblical scholar. From 1811 till his death he was professor of theology at Halle, where he concentrated his attention on problems of Semitic philology and became the most outstanding Hebraist of his generation. In 1810–1812 he issued the earliest edition of his celebrated *Hebräisches und chaldäisches Handwörterbuch*, which went through many revisions, and formed the basis of the Hebrew Lexicon (1906) of C. A. *Briggs, S. R. *Driver, and F. Brown. This was followed in 1813 by the 1st edition of his 'Hebrew Grammar', and in 1820–1 by his commentary on Isaiah.

T. K. *Cheyne, *Founders of Old Testament Criticism* (1893), pp. 53–65. E. F. Miller, *The Influence of Gesenius on Hebrew Lexicography* (Contributions to Oriental History and Philology, No. 11, New York, 1927). E. *Reuss-R. Kraetzschmar in *P.R.E.* (ed. 3), vi (1899), pp. 624–7, s.v.

GESS, WOLFGANG FRIEDRICH (1819–1891), German theologian. From his earliest years he possessed a deep faith, built up on an intensive study of the Bible. In 1850 he became professor at the Protestant 'Missionshaus' at Basle, in 1864 ordinary professor of systematic theology at Göttingen, and in 1871, professor at Breslau. From 1880 to 1885 he was *General superintendent of the province of Posen. He was among the earliest defenders of a *Kenotic doctrine of the Incarnation, which he expounded in *Die Lehre von der Person Christi* (1856), his most important work. He claimed to base this teaching (as, indeed, all his theology) on the Bible alone, without reference to the Creeds or other post-Biblical authority.

Gess elaborated his views on the Person of Christ further in *Christi Selbstzeugnis* (Basle, 1870) and several later works. W. Schmidt in *P.R.E.* (ed. 3), vi (1899), pp. 642–6.

GESTAS. See *Dismas*.

GESUATI (or, officially, **Clerici apostolici S. Hieronymi**). A congregation of laymen, founded *c.* 1360 by Bl. John *Colombini (*c.*1300–1367). They devoted themselves esp. to prayer, mortification, and works of charity, and followed at first the *Benedictine, later the *Augustinian Rule. Their popular name derived from their frequent use of the ejaculations 'Praised be Jesus', or 'Hail Jesus', esp. at the beginning and end of their sermons. Originally a very loosely knit group, they received Papal approbation from *Urban V in 1367 on condition that they established proper monasteries. At the same time they adopted a uniform habit, consisting of a white tunic with a square hood and a greyish-brown cloak. They only took *minor orders till 1606, when they were allowed to have one or two priests in each of their convents. After Colombini's death (1367) they spread throughout Italy, and in 1425 founded houses also in Toulouse. They were dissolved by Clement IX in 1668 because they had lost the spirit of their order.

They also had a female institute of contemplative nuns, the 'Jesuatesses' or 'Sisters of the Visitation of Mary', founded c. 1367 by Colombini's cousin, Catherine Colombini (d. 1367). They led a very austere life and existed as a congregation till 1872.

P. Helyot (anon.), *Histoire des ordres monastiques, religieuses et militaires*, iii (1715), pp. 407–22. Heimbucher, i (ed. 3, 1933), pp. 596–8.

GETHSEMANE, The Garden of. The garden to which our Lord retired with His disciples after the Last Supper and which was the scene of His agony and betrayal (Mt. 26. 36, &c.). It is in the valley between *Jerusalem and the Mount of *Olives, just across the brook *Cedron. The traditional site is now in *Franciscan hands.

G. Orfali, O.F.M., *Gethsémani, ou Notice sur l'Église de l'Agonie de la Prière, d'après les fouilles récentes accomplies par la custodie franciscaine de Terre Sainte, 1909 et 1920* (1924); [L.] H. Vincent, O.P.–F. M. Abel, O.P., *Jérusalem*, ii (1914–26), pp. 301–27, with appendix on 'L'Église primitive de Gethsémani', pp. 1007–13.

GEULINCX, ARNOLD (1624–69), Belgian philosopher. A native of Antwerp, he studied philosophy and theology at Louvain (1641–6), where he became professor of philosophy in 1646. In 1658 he was deprived of his chair on account of his attacks on Scholasticism and monasticism. In the same year he went to *Leyden where he became a *Calvinist. In 1662 he was made a lecturer on logic, and professor of philosophy in 1665. Among the works that appeared during his lifetime are *Quaestiones Quodlibeticae* (1653), *Logica* (1662 and 1668), *Methodus* (1663), and *Ethica* (1666). His more important works, however, viz. the Γνῶθι σεαυτόν, *sive Ethica* (1675), and the *Metaphysica Vera* (1691), were posthumous.

Starting from R. *Descartes's distinction between body and thought, Geulincx was led to develop the theory known as '*Occasionalism', denying any action of bodies on bodies or bodies on spirits or spirits on bodies, and consequently all movements produced by our will. God is the sole Cause of all movement and of all thought, all secondary causes, acc. to Geulincx, being illusory. As man is incapable of exercising any activity whatever on the outside world or on his own body, on each 'occasion' of a bodily event God causes the corresponding feeling in the soul and vice versa, and thereby everything is immediately subjected to God. The human will, which is capable of making a voluntary effort towards the good, has only an appearance of freedom, for the resulting activity, whether it be success or failure, depends on God alone. Man can thus in fact achieve nothing of himself. He is a spectator of what God works in him, the greatest virtue being a resigned and humble submission to all that happens. God himself, however, is wholly inaccessible to man, and in order to lead the moral life man must turn to the Divine in himself, i.e. the human reason by which he participates in the Divine nature. This combination of a rigorous determinism with an almost pantheistic exaltation of reason, which was one of the main features of Geulincx's thought, was later developed by N. *Malebranche and B. *Spinoza.

Complete Works, ed. J. P. N. Land (3 vols., The Hague, 1891–3). V. van der Haeghen, *Geulincx. Étude sur sa vie, sa philosophie et ses œuvres* (Ghent, 1886); J. P. N. Land, 'Arnold Geulincx and his Works' in *Mind*, xvi (1891), pp. 223–42; id., *Arnold Geulincx und seine Philosophie* (1895). E. Pfleiderer, *Arnold Geulin als Hauptvertreter der okkasionalistischen Metaphysik und Ethik* (1882); E. Terraillon, *La Morale de Geulincx dans ses rapports avec la philosophie de Descartes* (1912). Überweg, iii, pp. 262–5, 663.

GEYLER VON KAISERSBERG. See *Geiler von Kaisersberg.*

GHÉON, HENRI, pseudonym of Henri Léon Vangeon (1875–1944), French Catholic writer. The son of a chemist, he was born at Bray-sur-Seine, educated at Sens and Paris and became a doctor by profession. He was brought up as a Catholic by his mother, but at the age of c. 15 appears to have lost all faith, until the death of his niece and other friends precipitated his reconciliation (1914). From early childhood his primary interest was in poetry and drama. In 1897 he published his first collection of verse, *Chansons d'aube*, followed by *Solitude de l'été* (1898) and other works. In 1909 he was among the founders of the *Nouvelle Revue Française*. A friend of P. *Claudel, in 1910 he also became acquainted with C. *Péguy. His first play, *Le Fils de M. Sage:—Le Pain* (performed in 1912), was a popular tragedy written in verse. His first two specifically Christian dramas, *Trois Miracles de sainte Cécile* and *Le Pauvre sous l'escalier*, both 1921, were failures, a fact which convinced him of the need to appeal to a wider Catholic public. He soon devoted himself to the task of building up a Christian theatre, producing his own plays and working with a company of young Catholics founded by himself in 1924 under the title 'Les Compagnons de Notre-Dame' and from 1931 with their successors 'Les Compagnons de Jeux'. Many of his works had kinship with the 15th cent. miracle plays. Their subject was the lives of the Saints and other sacred themes and their deliberate *naïveté* of tone was an attempt to reproduce the atmosphere of medieval hagiography. They include *La Vie profonde* de S. François d'Assise (written 1925), Le Mystère du Roi S. Louis (1931), Le Mystère de l'invention de la Croix (1932), Mystère des prodiges de Notre-Dame de Verdun (1937), and Le Jeu de S. Laurent de Fleuve (1938). Henri Ghéon's biographies, which combined the freshness of his plays with a higher standard of authenticity, appealed to a wide public; they included lives of the *Curé d'Ars (1928; Eng. trans. 1929), of St. *Theresa of Lisieux (1934; Eng. trans. 1935), of St. John *Bosco (1935; Eng. trans. 1935), of St. *Vincent Ferrer (1939; Eng. trans. 1939), and of St. *Martin (1941; Eng. trans. 1946). He also wrote the script for a film on John Bosco (1936), four novels and a considerable body of literary criticism.

GHETTO. In former times the street or quarter of a city in which the Jewish population customarily lived. The word is perhaps a shortened form of the Ital. diminutive borghetto, 'small borough'. The earliest ghettoes were found in the Italian cities of the 11th cent. but they became common in the later Middle Ages, and in 1556 *Paul IV established a ghetto in Rome which was not finally abolished until 1870. As a general rule the Jews were not allowed to leave the ghetto, which was commonly surrounded by walls and gates, at night or on Christian holy days. The ghettoes were often self-governing. Ghettoes of great importance existed at *Venice, Frankfurt, Prague, and Trieste.

GIBBON, EDWARD (1737–94), historian of the later Roman Empire. He was born at Putney. His weak constitution prevented a normal school career, but he was an omnivorous reader, esp. on historical subjects. He was educated at Westminster and in 1752, at the early age of 15, sent to Magdalen College, Oxford, where he was converted to the RC Church (1753). Though of short duration, his conversion was sincere. To detach him from Catholicism, his father placed him with M. Pavilliard, a *Calvinist minister at Lausanne, where by wide and systematic reading of French literature and the Latin classics he laid the foundations of his vast erudition. In 1754 he returned to Protestantism; in 1758 he was back in England; and in 1761 published an Essai sur l'étude de la littérature in defence of the study of ancient literature. From 1763 to 1765 he again travelled on the Continent, visiting France, Switzerland, and Italy. On 15 Oct. 1764, at Rome, as he 'sat musing amidst the ruins of the Capitol, while the barefooted friars were singing vespers in the temple of Jupiter', he conceived the plan of the Decline and Fall of the Roman Empire, which was to occupy him for nearly all the rest of his life. Vol. i, which was published in 1776, had an immediate success, vols. ii and iii followed in 1781. For a time he was M.P. for Liskeard (1774–80) and Lymington (1781–1783). In 1783 he went to Lausanne, where between 1782 and 1787 he finished the last

three volumes (publd. 1788). They were followed by his Memoirs, written in 1789. He returned to England in 1793, and died in the following year. He was a typical representative of cultured 18th-cent. society, widely read, elegant, temperate, and content.

The Decline and Fall remains unchallenged as a history on the grand scale of the later Roman Empire. It is based on a very wide study of original material, supplemented by the researches of such French and Italian historians as *Tillemont, J. *Mabillon, B. *Montfaucon, and L. A. *Muratori. Its breadth of treatment, large perspectives, and meticulous accuracy are among its principal merits; and its author's mastery of style, despite its pomposity, adds to its fascination. In the famous chs. 15 and 16 of vol. i, the rapid growth of early Christianity is ascribed to five causes, viz. the intolerant zeal of its followers, the doctrine of a future life, the miraculous powers ascribed to the early Church, the pure morals of its members, and the discipline it enforced; and the violent controversy provoked by Gibbon's hostile attitude is even to-day not wholly extinct. The history of the Byzantine Empire is a medley of superstition and crimes and the Middle Ages are the 'triumph of barbarism and religion'. All supernatural considerations are treated with bitter irony and ridicule; but the author's indirect method escaped the prosecution to which an open attack on Christianity would have exposed him.

The best ed. of The Decline and Fall is that of J. B. Bury (7 vols., 1896–1900). Miscellaneous Works of Edward Gibbon with Memoirs of his Life and Writings (3 vols., 1796–1815). Autobiography, repr. from ed. 2, with introd. by J. B. Bury ('The World's Classics', 1907); J. Murray (ed.), The Autobiographies of Edward Gibbon printed verbatim from the hitherto unpublished MSS (1896); R. E. Prothero (ed.), Private Letters of Edward Gibbon, 1753–1774 (2 vols., 1896). Studies by H. H. *Milman (London, 1839), J. M. Robertson ('Life-Stories of Famous Men', 1925), G. M. Young (London, 1932), R. B. Mowat (London, 1936), D. M. Low (London, 1937), and P. Fughum (Oslo Studies in English, Oslo and Oxford, 1953). S. T. McCloy, Gibbon's Antagonism to Christianity (1933). G. [L.] Keynes, The Library of Edward Gibbon. A Catalogue of his Books (1940), with introd., pp. 11–36. L. Stephen in D.N.B., xxi (1890), pp. 250–6.

GIBERTI, GIAN MATTEO (1495–1543), Bp. of *Verona. He was one of the leading advocates in Italy of ecclesiastical reform who prepared the way for the Council of *Trent. Patronized by Cardinal Giulio de Medici, whose secretary he became, in 1521 he was sent as envoy to *Charles V and in 1524 became Bp. of Verona. He was a trusted counsellor of *Clement VII and *Paul III, and in 1536 was appointed to sit on the reforming commission known as the 'consilium de emendenda ecclesia'. He also produced some good editions of various patristic writings (e.g. of *Chrysostom and *John of Damascus).

Works (Constitutiones Gibertinae, Costituzioni per le monache, Monitiones generales, Edita selecta, Lettere scelte, &c.), ed. P. and H. *Ballerini (Verona, 1733). Life by G. B. Pighi (Verona, 1900; ed. 2, 1924). M. A. Tucker, 'Gian Matteo Giberti. Papal Politician and Catholic Reformer' in E.H.R., xviii (1903), pp. 24–51, 266–86, 439–69. T. Pandolfi, 'G. M. Giberti e l' ultima difesa della libertà d' Italia negli anni 1521–25' in Archivio della R. Società Romana di Storia Patria, xxxiv (1911), pp. 131–237.

GIBSON, EDMUND (1669–1748), Bp. of London. A native of Westmorland, he was educated at Queen's College, Oxford, where he was elected a taberdar in 1690. His early publications included editions of the Anglo-Saxon Chronicle (1692), of Quintilian's *De Institutione Oratoria* (1693), and of W. Camden's *Britannia* (1695). In 1696 he was appointed by T. *Tenison *Lambeth Librarian, and in 1697 ordained priest. He entered the lists against F. *Atterbury in the *Convocation controversy, upholding the archbishop's prerogatives over both Houses. A fruit of the controversy was his standard manual *Synodus Anglicana; or the Constitution and Proceedings of an English Convocation* (1702; new ed. by E. *Cardwell, 1854). In 1703 he became Canon of *Chichester and rector of Lambeth. After prolonged studies he issued in 1713 his *magnum opus*, the *Codex Iuris Ecclesiastici Anglicani* (ed. 2, 1761), still the most complete collection of English ecclesiastical statutes. Soon after the accession of George I, Gibson was elected Bp. of *Lincoln (1716) and began to play an important part in ecclesiastical politics. Himself a High Church Whig, he made it his chief object to reconcile the clergy, nearly all Tories, to the House of Hanover. He also furthered many schemes of ecclesiastical reform and was constantly consulted by Robert Walpole about appointments. Theologically he upheld orthodoxy, writing against the *Latitudinarians and the *Deists. On the other hand, he was relatively tolerant towards the *Methodists, personally befriended I. *Watts, and strenuously opposed Walpole in the *Quakers' Relief Bill (1736). He was the driving force behind the foundation of the Regius Professorships of Modern History at Oxford and Cambridge. In 1723 he became Bp. of London, ruling his diocese energetically and conscientiously, and actively promoting the religious welfare of the American plantations, still under the jurisdiction of the see of London. Among his later writings were *A Preservative against Popery* (3 vols., 1738), a collection of controversial treatises, mainly from the time of *James II.

N. Sykes, *Edmund Gibson*. A Study in Politics and Religion in the Eighteenth Century (1926). G. G. Perry in *D.N.B.*, xxi (1890), p. 274 f.

GICHTEL, JOHANN GEORG (1638–1710), German sectarian. A native of Ratisbon in Bavaria and of Protestant upbringing, he came under the influence of Dutch visionaries and, exiled from Ratisbon, spent most of his life in Amsterdam. Here he read the writings of J. *Boehme, which he esteemed as highly as the Bible and of which he made the first complete edition in 1682. He himself became the founder of a small sect which condemned marriage and Church services, and which had followers in Holland and Germany until recent times.

G. C. A. von Harless, *Jakob Böhme und die Alchymisten. Ein Beitrag zum Verständniss J. Böhme's* (1870), Anhang, 'J. G. Gichtel's Leben und Irrthümer', pp. 117–85. A. W. Hegler in *P.R.E.* (ed. 3), vi (1899), pp. 657–60, s.v.

GIDDING, Little. See *Little Gidding*.

GIESELER, JOHANN KARL LUDWIG (1792–1854), German Protestant Church historian. Of a Westphalian family, he was educated at Halle, and after holding various scholastic appointments became professor of theology at Bonn in 1819. In 1831 he accepted a chair at Göttingen, where he lectured on Church history and doctrine and also took an important part in the administrative work of the university. His earliest work, *Historisch-kritischer Versuch über die Entstehung der Evangelien* (1818), was a minute examination of the oral tradition behind the Gospel narratives. His main publications, however, lay in the field of Church history, the chief of them being his *Lehrbuch der Kirchengeschichte* (5 vols., 1824–57; Eng. trans., *A Compendium of Ecclesiastical History*, also 5 vols., by S. Davidson and J. W. Hull, 1846–55), which was long a standard book in Great Britain, esp. valued for its selection of original documents. He also wrote several monographs on the early heretics.

A supplementary vol. to his *Lehrbuch der Kirchengeschichte* was issued in 1855. Note by E. R. Redepenning on 'Gieseler's Leben und Wirken' in vol. v (1857), pp. xliii–lvi. N. Bonwetsch in *P.R.E.* (ed. 3), vi (1899), p. 663 f., s.v. F. C. *Baur, *Die Epochen der kirchlichen Geschichtschreibung* (1852), pp. 232–6.

GIFFORD LECTURES. The series of lectures delivered in the Scottish universities under the foundation of Adam Gifford, Lord Gifford (1820–87), 'for promoting, advancing, teaching, and diffusing the study of natural theology, in the widest sense of that term, in other words, the knowledge of God' and 'of the foundation of ethics'. The first course was delivered in 1888. Notable Gifford Lecturers (with their years of tenure) include J. Ward (1896–8), R. B. Haldane, B. *Bosanquet (1911–1912), A. S. Pringle-*Pattison (1912–13), A. J. *Balfour (1914 and 1922–3), S. Alexander (1916–18), W. R. *Inge (1917–18), C. C. J. *Webb (1918–20), F. *von Hügel (1924–6), E. W. Barnes (1927–9), E. *Gilson (1931–1932), E. R. Bevan (1932–4), W. *Temple (1932–4), K. *Barth (1937–8), R. *Niebuhr (1939), C. Dawson (1947–8), G. Marcel (1949–1950), L. Hodgson (1955–7) and V. A. Demant (1956–8).

GILBERT FOLIOT. See *Foliot, Gilbert*.

GILBERT DE LA PORRÉE (1076–1154), 'Porretanus', Scholastic theologian. He came from the school of *Bernard of Chartres, and from 1142 till his death was Bp. of Poitiers. In his doctrine of '*universals', he was anxious to avoid the pantheism involved in taking them to be crudely real. He therefore distinguished between the 'class essence' (*subsistentia*), which is only conceptually one and the same in many things, and the real 'substance' (*substantia*), which makes a thing exist as an individual. Applying this distinction to the Divine Being, he held that the Divine Nature could be regarded as a concept of the human mind (like 'unity', as opposed to the individual which is 'one'), and that only the Persons were real. He was charged with tritheism, and attacked by St. *Bernard of Clairvaux at the Synod of *Reims (1148). The 'Liber Sex Principiorum', commonly attributed to him, is a metaphysical interpretation of *Aristotle; it became a standard textbook in scholastic education. Gilbert also wrote commentaries on *Boethius's tractates.

Gilbert's commentaries on four of Boethius's *Opuscula Sacra* first pr. among Boethius's works, Basle, 1570, pp. 1119–1273; repr. J. P. Migne, *PL*, lxiv, 1255–412; crit. edd. by N. M. Haring of Comm. on Boethius's 'De Hebdomadibus' in *Traditio*, ix (1953), pp. 177–211; on 'Contra Eutychem et Nestorium' in *Archives d'histoire doctrinale et littéraire du Moyen Âge*, xxi (for 1954; 1955), pp. 241–357; and on the two Opuscula on the Trinity in *Nine Mediaeval Thinkers*, ed. J. R. O'Donnell, C.S.B. (Toronto, 1955), pp. 23–98. The 'Liber Sex Principiorum' pr. in J. P. Migne, *PL*, clxxxviii, 1257–70; crit. ed. by A. Heysse, O.F.M. (Opuscula et Textus, vii; 1929). Studies by A. Berthaud (Poitiers, 1892), and on his theology by R. M. Martin in *R.H.E.*, xiii (1912), pp. 647–91; A. Landgraf in *Z.K.T.*, liv (1930), pp. 180–213; and M. E. Williams (Analecta Gregoriana, lvi; 1951). N. M. Haring, 'The Case of Gilbert de la Porrée' in *Mediaeval Studies*, xiii (1951), pp. 1–40. P. Vernet in *D.T.C.*, vi (1920), cols. 1350–8, s.v.

GILBERT OF SEMPRINGHAM, St. (c. 1083–1189), founder of the Gilbertine Order. While parish priest of his native *Sempringham, he encouraged seven women of his flock to adopt a rule of life on a *Cistercian model, and about a year later, with the support of Alexander, Bp. of *Lincoln, received their profession. He soon associated with them companies of lay sisters and lay brothers to assist with the manual work of the community. Their numbers grew; in 1139 a second foundation was established; and further foundations followed. In 1148 Gilbert journeyed to Cîteaux, seeking the incorporation of his nuns in the Cistercian Order; but when the chapter declined to govern communities of women, Gilbert returned and arranged for the spiritual direction of his communities by *Canons Regular who followed the *Augustinian Rule. Henceforward his communities took the form of a double order. In 1148 Gilbert had received papal approbation of his work. The only purely English order, it rapidly grew, and at the time of Gilbert's death numbered nine double monasteries and four of canons only. It was generously treated by several of the English kings, notably Henry II and *Henry VI. At the Dissolution they possessed some 25 houses, which were surrendered to the Crown without resistance. Feast day, 4 Feb.

The principal source is a 'Vita S. Gilberti Confessoris' by an unknown canon of the Order, pr. ('ex Cod. MS. in bibl. Cotton. (sub. effigie Cleopatrae B 1) f 37 b') by W. *Dugdale, *Monasticon Anglicanum*, vi (pt. 2; ed. 1830), pp. *v–*xxix (between p. 946 and p. 947); early Eng. tr. in J. J. Munro, *John Capgrave's Lives of Saint Augustine and Saint Gilbert of Sempringham . . .* (E.E.T.S., Original Series, cxl, 1910), pp. 61–142. Life based on Capgrave in *AA.SS.*, Feb. I (1658), p. 572 f. [J. B. *Dalgairns after W. Lockhart], 'St. Gilbert, Prior of Sempringham' in *Lives of the English Saints*, ed. J. H. *Newman (1844), in ed. 2, iv (1901), pp. 3–155. Rose Graham, *S. Gilbert of Sempringham and the Gilbertines* (1901), esp. pp. 1–28. R. Foreville, *Un Procès de canonisation à l'aube du XIIIᵉ siècle (1201–1202). *Le Livre de Saint Gilbert de Sempringham* (1943), with text. T. A. Archer in *D.N.B.*, xxi (1890), pp. 315–17.

GILDAS, St. (c. 500–c. 570), monk and first British historian. The facts of his life are very uncertain. Acc. to the oldest life (11th cent.), the work of a monk from the Abbey of St.-Gildas-de-Ruys in Brittany (acc. to F. Lot, Abbot Vitalis of Ruys, 1060–7), which perhaps draws on some genuine traditions, Gildas was born at Arecluta (Strathclyde), was forced to flee to Wales, where he married, and, after the death of his wife, became a pupil of St. *Illtyd. He then spent some time in *Ireland, went on a pilgrimage to Rome c. 520, founded a religious house at Ruys in Brittany on the way back, reached Wales again in 527, later visited Ruys and also Ireland once more, and died at Ruys on 29 Jan. 570. It has been questioned whether the sections of the 'Vita' connecting him with Ruys deserve credence; and indeed whether Gildas ever visited Brittany at all. There are two later lives, but these are of even less value.

His famous history, 'De Excidio et Conquestu Brittaniae ac flebili Castigatione in Reges, Principes et Sacerdotes' (prob. written between 516 and 547), is the only history of the Celts. Written in a cumbrous and verbose style, it covers the period from the coming of the Romans to Gildas's own time; but the amount of real history in it is strictly limited and, its whole purpose being hortatory, it may safely be presumed to take an exaggerated view of the evils of its times. Among other writings attributed to him are some penitential canons. Feast day, 29 Jan.

Crit. ed. of Gildas's 'De Excidio' by T. *Mommsen in *M.G.H.*, Auctores Antiquissimi, xiii [=Chronica Minora, iii] (1896), pp. 25–85; other works, pp. 86–90. The life by the monk of Ruys ed. id., ib., pp. 91–106; 12th cent. life by Caradoc of Lancarvan also ed. id., ib., pp. 107–110; introd., pp. 3–24. Gildas's 'De Excidio' was also ed. for the English Historical Society by J. Stevenson (London, 1838); an older ed. (here erroneously divided into two works) is repr. in J. P. Migne, *PL*, lxix, 329–92. Eng. tr. of Stevenson's ed. by J. A. Giles, *Six Old English Chroniclers* (1885), pp. 295–380. A. de La Borderie, 'La Date de la naissance de Gildas' in *Revue Celtique*, vi (1883–5), pp. 1–13. F. Lot, 'De la valeur du *De Excidio* . . . de Gildas' in *Medieval Studies in Memory of Gertrude Schoepperle Loomis* (Paris and New York, 1927), pp. 229–64; C. E. Stevens, 'Gildas Sapiens' in *E.H.R.*, lvi (1941), pp. 353–73. Hardy, i (pt. 1; 1862), pp. 151–6. Bardenhewer, v, pp. 399–401. T. F. Tout in *D.N.B.*, xxi (1890), pp. 344–6, s.v. C. Testore, S.J., in *E.C.*, vi (1951), col. 394 f.

GILES, St. (? 8th cent.), Lat. *Aegidius*. One of the Fourteen *Auxiliary Saints. Acc. to a 10th cent. biography, St. Giles was an Athenian who fled to France from the admiration of his countrymen and made himself a hermitage in a forest near the mouth of the Rhône, where he lived on herbs and the milk of a hind. Once when Flavius Wamba, king of the Visigoths, was hunting in the forest, the monarch chased the hind to the abode of the hermit and was so impressed by Giles's holiness that he built him a monastery. Though the medieval account, which makes him an Athenian and connects him with persons as far apart in time as St. *Caesarius of Arles (d. 542) and *Charlemagne (d. 814), is clearly unhistorical, it may contain a basis of real fact. A 9th cent. Papal bull mentions Wamba as having founded an abbey for him, to which a charter was given by Benedict II (684–5). Later on, the town of St. Gilles, which grew up near his grave, became a famous place of pilgrimage. He was one of the most popular medieval saints, and in England alone 160 churches were dedicated to him. He was invoked as their patron by cripples, beggars, and blacksmiths. Feast day, 1 Sept.

The principal authority is an anonymous Lat. life pr. in *A.A.SS.*, Sept. I (1746), pp. 299–304, with introd. and brief extracts of his miracles (see below), pp. 284–99; another recension of the life is pr., with introd., in *Anal. Boll.*, viii (1889), pp. 102–20. The *Liber Miraculorum Sancti Aegidii*, written before 1124, ed. in full by P. Jaffé in *M.G.H.*, Scriptores, xii (1861), pp. 316–23; also pr. in *Anal. Boll.*, ix (1890), pp. 393–422. *B.H.L.*, i, p. 17 f. (Nos. 93–8); suppl., p. 6 f. E. Rembry, *Saint Gilles. Sa vie, ses reliques, son culte en Belgique et dans le nord de la France* (2 vols. bound in 1, Bruges, 1881–2); E. C. Jones, *Saint Gilles. Essai d'histoire littéraire* (Paris thesis, 1914). F. Brittain, *Saint Giles* (Cambridge, 1928).

GILES OF ROME (*c.* 1247–1316), otherwise 'Aegidius Romanus', medieval philosopher. He was born at Rome, perhaps descended from the *Colonna family. At an early age he became an *Augustinian hermit at *Paris and attracted attention by his intellectual gifts which later won him the surname of 'doctor fundatissimus'. From 1269 to 1271 he had as his teacher St. *Thomas Aquinas. In 1292 he was elected *General of his order, which he strove to extend by the foundation of many convents. In 1295 *Boniface VIII made him Abp. of Bourges.

Giles was a very fertile author whose writings include commentaries on *Aristotle's 'Physics', the 'De Anima', and the '*Liber de Causis', and on *Peter Lombard's 'Sentences'; treatises against the *Averroists, on *Angels, and on *Original Sin; and exegetical writings on several Pauline Epp. and on St. John's Gospel. His most popular work, which was translated into many languages, was the 'De Regimine Principum' written *c.* 1285 for his pupil, the future King Philip the Fair. His treatise 'De Summi Pontificis Potestate' was the foundation of Boniface VIII's famous bull '*Unam Sanctam' (q.v.). In his teaching Giles of Rome followed St. Thomas on such points as the unity of the substantial form and the real distinction between essence and existence in creatures, but against him he maintained the primacy of will over reason and denied that before the Fall Adam possessed sanctifying grace. His teaching, both past and future (*sententias scriptas et scribendas*), was prescribed to be followed in the schools of the Augustinian Order in 1287.

His writings were widely printed in the 15th and 16th cents. For bibl. details, see G. Boffito, *Saggio di bibliografia egidiana* (Florence, 1911), and G. Bruni, *Le opere di Egidio Romano* (1936). Crit. ed. of Giles's 'De Erroribus Philosophorum' by J. Koch (Milwaukee, 1944). Überweg, ii, pp. 532 f., 543–6, 774. N. Merlin in *D.T.C.*, vi (1920), cols. 1358–65, s.v. 'Gilles de Rome'; A. Trape in *E.C.*, v (1951), cols. 138–41, s.v. 'Egidio Romano', with good bibl.

GILGAMESH, The Epic of. A long Babylonian epic poem, dating, at least in part, from *c.* 1198 B.C. and chiefly known from twelve tablets of the 7th cent. B.C., discovered at Nineveh by George Smith (1840–76) in 1872. It depicts the hero, Gilgamesh, an historical ruler of the first dynasty of Uruk, as a demi-god who rules tyrannically. In an account of the Flood elaborated by the immortal Utnapishtim for the edification of Gilgamesh (*c.* 200 lines of Tablet XI) there are several close parallels to the Biblical narrative in Gen. 6–9 (plan of ark; use of bitumen to make it water-tight; grounding of ark on mountain; only very few saved; gods smelling goodly savour of sacrifice). It has been very widely supposed (C. F. A. *Dillmann, S. R. *Driver, H. *Gunkel, and F. *Delitzsch) that the Biblical narrative is partly dependent on this epic or, alternatively, that the similarities derive from the common stock of ancient oriental mythology.

Best ed. of the cuneiform text, with transliteration and notes, by R. Campbell Thompson (Oxford, 1930); Eng. tr. into hexameters by id. (ib., 1928). [E. A. Wallis Budge–R. H. Hall], *The Babylonian Story of the Deluge and the Epic of Gilgamesh* (British Museum, 1920). A. Heidel, *The Gilgamesh Epic and Old Testament Parallels* (Chicago, 1946), with bibl. reff. L. W. King, *Legends of Babylon and Egypt in Relation to Hebrew Tradition* (Schweich Lects., 1918), esp. pp. 41–3 and 132–5.

GILL, ERIC (1882–1940), sculptor, letterist, and wood-engraver. The son of a minister in the Countess of *Huntingdon's Connexion who became an Anglican priest, he joined the RC Church in 1913 and became a *Dominican tertiary. After training in an architect's office, he studied lettering under Edward Johnston. His best-known works are the *Stations of the Cross in *Westminster Cathedral (finished 1918), ten panels in the New Museum, Jerusalem (1934–7), and the bas-reliefs of 'The Re-creation of Adam' with the words of G. M. *Hopkins, 'Thou mastering me God', inscribed above it (1935–8) in the League of Nations Council Hall at Geneva. A Christian craftsman with a love for the liturgy, he was also a social philosopher, a pacifist, and a writer. As a stone-carver who revived the art of working directly upon the stone, he excelled as a carver of inscriptions, and a maker of small stone objects such as crucifixes and holy-water stoups.

Eric Gill, *Autobiography* (1940); W. Shewring (ed.), *Letters of Eric Gill* (1947). J. Thorp, with critical monograph by C. Marriott, *Eric Gill* (1929), with plates. Further studies by J. K. M. Rothenstein (anon.; 1927) and D. Attwater ('Modern Christian Revolutionaries' [1945]). Evan R. Gill, *Bibliography of Eric Gill* (1953).

GILPIN, BERNARD (1517–83), 'Apostle of the North'. He was a great-nephew of C. *Tunstall, Bp. of *Durham. A native of Westmorland, he was educated at Queen's College, Oxford, where he came under the spell of D. *Erasmus's writings. After *Henry VIII's refoundation of Cardinal College as *Christ Church, Gilpin was elected one of its first students. Disapproving of the doctrinal changes and disgusted by the robbery of Church property, he had serious scruples about giving his support to the Reforming Movement and in 1552 preached before *Edward VI at Greenwich on sacrilege. He found the persecution under *Mary hateful and became more outspoken in advocating a reformation of clerical scandals. He was protected by Tunstall, who even granted him the important benefice of Houghton-le-Spring. On the accession of *Elizabeth I, he was offered, but declined, both the Bishopric of *Carlisle (1559) and the Provostship of Queen's (1560). His scruples about the doctrinal changes soon revived and, horrified by E. *Sandys's views on the Eucharist, he accepted the new order with some reluctance. In the next years he made many long and successful missionary journeys in the N. of England during which his unbounded liberality and unsparing denunciation of abuses brought him a very large following, including some of the *Puritans.

The sermon preached before Edward VI in 1552 was pr. in ed. 4 of Carleton's life, 1636 (see below), and in 1752 with W. Gilpin's life. The primary authority is the life by George Carleton, Bp. of *Chichester (London, 1628, in Lat.; Eng. version, ib., 1629); more substantial life by William Gilpin, a collateral descendant (London, 1752). G. G. Perry in *D.N.B.*, xxi (1890), pp. 378–80.

GILSON, ÉTIENNE (b. 1884), French *Thomist philosopher. He was educated at the *Sorbonne where he came under the influence of H. *Bergson and L. Lévy-Bruhl. At the latter's suggestion he embarked on a study of the Scholastic influences on the philosophy of R. *Descartes and thus became conversant with medieval thought. In 1913 he was appointed professor at Lille, in 1919 at Strassburg, in 1921 professor of medieval philosophy at the *Sorbonne, and in 1932 at the Collège de France. From 1929 he also held the post of Director of the Pontifical Institute of Medieval Studies at Toronto.

The first-fruits of the studies suggested by Lévy-Bruhl were the *Index scolastico-cartésien* (1912) and *La Liberté chez Descartes et la théologie* (1913). *Études de philosophie médiévale*, a collection of miscellaneous studies, followed in 1921, and in 1922 *La Philosophie au moyen-âge* (Collection Payot, 2 vols.), a popular manual tracing the development of philosophy from the age of *Charlemagne and *Erigena to the end of the Middle Ages. One of the lesser purposes of the last-named, as indeed of many of Gilson's other writings, was to exhibit the systems of the Middle Ages as achievements in their own right. In *Le Thomisme* (1919, Eng. trans., 1924) he gave an outline of St. Thomas's metaphysics. *La Philosophie de St. Bonaventure* (1924; Eng. trans., 1938) was an elaborate analysis of St. *Bonaventure's conception of philosophical and mystical experience, and in close relation to this study of the *Augustinian tradition in Scholasticism came *Introduction à l'Étude de Saint Augustin* (1928). His *Gifford Lectures, *L'Esprit de la philosophie médiévale* (1932; Eng. trans., 1936), represent medieval philosophy in its bearing on such subjects as knowledge, love, free-will, and morality. *La Théologie mystique de Saint Bernard* (1934; Eng. trans., 1940) is a study of the special character-

istics of *Cistercian mysticism. His other writings include *Christianisme et philosophie* (1936), an analysis of the relations between theology and philosophy which arose out of lectures given to Protestant students; *The Unity of Philosophical Experience* (1938), an attempt to show that the philosophy of history does not necessarily lead to historical relativism; *Héloïse et Abélard* (1938), an account of the romance against the background of its times; and *Reason and Revelation in the Middle Ages* (1939), a study of the various Christian 'spiritual families' such as Augustinians, Thomists *Averroists, &c. In 1952 he published *Les Métamorphoses de la Cité de Dieu*.

J. *Maritain and others, *Étienne Gilson*. Philosophie de la chrétienté (Rencontres, xxx, 1949), with brief life and list of works to date, pp. 13–21.

GIOBERTI, VINCENZO (1801–52), Italian politician and religious philosopher. He was born and educated at Turin and ordained priest in 1825. Under the influence of Giuseppe Mazzini (1805–72), he made it his chief ambition to free Italy from foreign political and intellectual domination. On resigning a chaplaincy which he held at court (1833), he was arrested on suspicion of political intrigue and banished from Italy (1834). For the next eleven years he taught at Brussels where he published most of his philosophical works. Returning to Italy in 1847, he became President of the Chamber of Deputies and in 1849 a member of the Cabinet of Victor Emmanuel II (1820–78). After unsuccessful negotiations in Paris, he relinquished his political position shortly afterwards and lived in France for the rest of his life.

Gioberti's philosophical ideas were in substance *Ontologistic. He held that there was an exact correspondence between the orders of being and knowing and that the human mind directly perceived the absolute necessary Being, God, the creative cause of all existence and the source of human knowledge. The Pantheistic character of some of his later teaching, in which he came to regard creation as the essential function of thought, caused some of his treatises to be put on the *Index. Despite the affinities of his doctrines with those of A. *Rosmini, the two philosophers wrote against each other.

His principal writings were *Teoria del sovrannaturale* (Brussels, 1838), *Introduzione allo studio della filosofia* (ib., 1840), *Considerazioni sulle dottrine religiose di V. Cousin* (ib., 1840), *Lettre sur les doctrines philosophiques et politiques de M. de Lamennais* (ib., 1841), *Del bello* (Venice, 1841), *Degli errori filosofici di Antonio Rosmini* (3 vols., Brussels, 1841–4), *Del buono* (id., 1843), *Del primato morale e civile degli Italiani* (2 vols., ib., 1843), and *Prolegomeni del primato* (ib., 1845).

Among Gioberti's posthumous writings were *Meditazioni filosofiche inedite di Vincenzo Gioberti* (ed. E. Solmi, Florence, 1909), *Epistolario* (ed. G. *Gentile and G. Balsamo-Crivelli, 11 vols., Turin, 1927–37), and *Cours de philosophie, 1841–42* (ed. G. Calò and M. Battistini, Milan, 1947). Anthology by G. Gentile entitled *Nuova protologia* (Bari, 1912). 'National Edition' of his complete works (unfinished)

Milan, 1938–42. Gioberti has received much attention in Italy, esp. in the Fascist period; works on him by B. Spaventa (Naples, 1863), D. Berti (Florence, 1881), A. Anzilotti (Florence, 1922 and 1923), V. Piccolo (Rome, 1923), V. Padovani (Milan, 1927), S. Caramella (Genoa, 1927), F. Palhoriès (Paris, 1929), J. Rivieri (Genoa, 1931), A. Bruni (Turin, 1937), L. Stefanini (Milan, 1947), and G. Bonafede (Palermo, 1950). L. Stefanini in *E.C.*, vi (1951), cols. 414–22.

GIOVANNI CAPISTRANO, St.

GIOVANNI CAPISTRANO, St. (1386–1456), *Franciscan friar. He was born at Capistrano in the Abruzzi and studied law at Perugia, where in 1412 he was made governor by King Ladislaus of Naples and married. Taken prisoner in a war with the family of the Malatestas, he experienced a vision of St. *Francis while in captivity, which fired him with a desire to enter religion. On his release he obtained a dispensation from the impediment of matrimony and in 1416 sought admission to the novitiate of the Friars Minor. He was professed in 1417, priested in 1420, and immediately undertook a series of missions throughout Italy. In 1429, with other *Observant Friars, he was charged at Rome with heretical teaching on the poverty of Christ but acquitted. He took part in the General Chapter of the Order which met at *Assisi in 1430 to secure the union of the Conventuals and the Observants, and assisted his old master, St. *Bernadino of Siena (d. 1444), in the reform of the order. On several occasions he was vicar-general of the order. In 1451 he was sent by Pope Nicholas V to Austria in response to an appeal by the Emp. Frederick III for help against the *Hussites. His successful labours all over Eastern Europe were ended by the advance of the Turks after the capture of *Constantinople (1453). After failing to arouse Bavaria and Austria to the danger, he went to Hungary, where early in 1456 the Turks were preparing to attack Belgrade. Together with Hunyady he raised an army which completely defeated the Turks on 22 July, but died of plague on 23 Oct. of the same year. He was beatified in 1694, canonized in 1724; the feast was made of general observance in 1890, when it was transferred to 28 Mar.

The primary authorities, besides his own writings, are the contemporary lives by his companions in the order, viz. (arranged chronologically) Jerome of Utino, pr. in *A A.SS.*, Oct. X (1861), pp. 483–91; Nicholas of Fara, pr. ib., pp. 439–83, with variant MS. of the preface ed. E. Hocedez, S.J., in *Anal. Boll.*, xxiii (1904), pp. 320–4; Christopher of Varèse, pr. in *A A.SS.*, loc. cit., pp. 491–545; the Hungarian, Peter of Oedenburg (completed by 1489), publd. Vienna, 1523. Seven of his letters are pr. in *A A.SS.*, loc. cit., pp. 546–52, with important introd. by J. van Hecke, S.J., pp. 269–439. Considerable material also in the works of L. *Wadding (q.v.). A. Hermann, *Capistranus Triumphans* (Cologne, 1700). Other modern lives by L. de Kerval (Bordeaux, 1887) and E. Jacob (2 vols., Breslau, 1903–5). J. Hofer, *Johannes von Capistrano* (Innsbruck, [1936]; the best modern work). H. Lippens, O.F.M., 'S. Jean de Capistrano en mission aux états bourguignons, 1442–1443' in *A.F.H.*, xxxv (1942), pp. 113–32 and 254–95, with docc. In English there is a brief life by Vincent Fitzgerald, O.F.M. (London, 1911). Édouard d'Alençon, O.F.M., in *D.T.C.*, ii (1905), cols. 1686–8, s.v. 'Capistran (Saint Jean de)' for list of his works.

GIRALDUS CAMBRENSIS

GIRALDUS CAMBRENSIS (1147–c. 1223), **Gerald de Barri**, historian. A native of Pembrokeshire, he studied at Paris, and from 1175 to 1203 was Archdeacon of Brecon. He was elected Bp. of St. *David's in 1176 and again in 1198, but on each occasion failed to obtain consecration to the see, as the English feared that a Welshman would seek to make his Church independent again of *Canterbury. He filled, however, several other important offices, and in 1188 preached the Third *Crusade in Wales, on which he would have gone himself had not Henry II dissuaded him. Among his more important writings are 'Topographia Hibernica', 'Expugnatio Hibernica', 'Vita S. Remigii', 'Itinerarium Cambriae' and 'De iure Menevensis Ecclesiae'. They are amusing and vivid, though at times much influenced by personal and party feeling and their facts exaggerated.

Works ed. J. S. Brewer (R.S., 8 vols., 1861–91). Crit. ed. of *De Invectionibus* by W. S. Davies (Y Commrodor, xxx; 1920). Eng. tr. of Historical Works by T. Forester-R. C. Hoare-T. Wright (Bohn's Antiquarian Library, 1863); of his Autobiography by H. E. Butler (London, 1937), with introd. by C. H. Williams, pp. 9–21; of the first version of 'Topographia Hibernica' by J. J. O'Meara (Dundalk, 1951). H. Owen, *Gerald the Welshman* (1889; enlarged ed., 1904). F. M. Powicke, 'Gerald of Wales' in *Bulletin of the John Rylands Library*, xii (1928), pp. 389–410, repr. in his *Christian Life in the Midd.e Ages and other Essays* (1935), pp. 107–29. H. R. Luard in *D.N.B.*, xxi (1890), pp. 389–93.

GIRDLE

GIRDLE (Lat. *cingulum*). As an article of liturgical attire, an essential accompaniment of the *alb, and hence one of the six Eucharistic vestments. It is held to typify sacerdotal chastity and, in ref. to Lk. 12. 35–8, spiritual watchfulness. In the E. Church its use is confined to bishops and priests, the deacon's alb being worn ungirdled.

Braun, *L.G.*, pp. 101–17.

GLABRIO, MANIUS ACILIUS

GLABRIO, MANIUS ACILIUS, consul in A.D. 91. Ordered by the Emp. *Domitian to fight with the wild beasts in the amphitheatre at Albano, he was banished after a successful contest, and finally executed with Flavius Clemens, Flavia *Domitilla, and others *c.* 96. It is probable he was a Christian and there are some grounds for supposing he was martyred for his creed.

The authorities are Dio Cassius, *Hist.*, lxvii, 13 f., and *Suetonius, *Domitianus*, 10. The family grave of the Christians of the *Gens Acilia*, discovered by G. B. *de Rossi in 1888, is described by de Rossi, 'L 'ipogeo degli Acilii Glabrioni nel cimitero di Priscilla', in *Bullettino di Archeologia Cristiana*, Ser. IV, vi (1888–9), pp. 15–66 and 103–33. See also H. *Leclercq, O.S.B., in *D.A.C.L.*, vi (1924), cols. 1259–74. s.v.

GLADSTONE, WILLIAM EWART

GLADSTONE, WILLIAM EWART (1809–1898), English statesman. Under the influence of his ardently evangelical mother he early showed religious inclination. He was educated at Eton and Christ Church, Oxford, but his desire to take holy orders was frustrated by his father, who had destined him for a political career, and he entered Parliament in 1832. Though he left Oxford before the beginning of the *Oxford Movement, he was brought into contact with it by his friends James Robert Hope [-Scott] (1812–73) and H. E. *Manning.

His study of R. *Hooker and other 16th- and 17th-cent. English divines and of the 'Occasional Offices' of the BCP convinced him of the soundness of the High Church doctrines, which he succeeded in combining with the tenets of his Evangelical education, and for the defence of which he frequently used his political position. In 1838 he published *The State in its Relations with the Church*, written from the point of view of the politician and in favour of the establishment of the Church, not without pungent criticisms of the RC position. In *Church Principles considered in their Results* (1840) he upheld the visibility of the Church, the certainty of the Apostolic Succession, and the efficacy of the Sacraments as well as the Divine Institution of the C of E. In 1845 he defended the grant made to the RC college of *Maynooth. His High Church views led him to address an Open Letter to the Bp. of London (C. J.* Blomfield) after the *Gorham case, in which he maintained the compatibility of the royal supremacy with the intrinsic jurisdiction of the Church. In 1854 he supported Archdeacon G. A. *Denison, who was prosecuted for teaching the *Real Presence, a doctrine to which Gladstone was deeply attached. Owing to these convictions he was sometimes suspected of sympathy with the RC Church, which, however, he strongly repudiated mainly on the grounds that it was a régime of tyranny. After having been several times Chancellor of the Exchequer he became in 1865 for the first time leader of the House of Commons, and in 1867, despite his convinced Anglicanism, leader of the Liberal Party, which then was esp. representative of Nonconformist interests. As such he was responsible for the law abolishing compulsory Church rates and fought the next election on the issue whether the Irish Church was to be disestablished. Having abandoned his earlier view, and defended disestablishment in his *Chapter of Autobiography* (1868) and carried it through as Prime Minister in 1869. In 1873 he brought in a bill proposing a combined Catholic and Protestant university for Ireland, which was defeated. In the next year he opposed Abp. A. C. *Tait's *Public Worship Bill in the interests of the liberty of the C of E, and in the same year published several bitter attacks on the Church of Rome, esp. on the *Vatican decrees, which were answered by J. H. *Newman and H. E. Manning. In 1896 he pleaded in a letter to Card. M. Rampolla for the recognition of *Anglican Ordinations. Though he kept close to Tractarian principles throughout his life, he adopted the doctrine of *Conditional Immortality in his *Studies Subsidiary to the Works of Bishop Butler* (1896). Gladstone in his private life lived up to the tenets of his religion; he was a weekly communicant, lavish in almsgiving and frugal in his habits, esp. in matters of sleep and food. He was responsible for the founding of many new sees in the growing British Empire, and his keen and sympathetic interest in all theological and ecclesiastical questions was a valuable support for the C of E in general and Tractarianism in particular throughout the 19th cent.

J. Morley, *The Life of W. E. Gladstone* (3 vols., 1903); G. W. E. Russell, *W. E. Gladstone* (1891); *Correspondence on Church and Religion of W. E. Gladstone*, ed. by D. C. Lathbury (2 vols., 1910). A. R. Vidler, *The Orb and the Cross. A Normative Study in the Relations of Church and State with Reference to Gladstone's Early Writings* (1945).

GLAGOLITIC. The ancient Slavonic alphabet, still used in the liturgical books of the *Uniats in Dalmatia, &c. It was devised by St. *Cyril, the Apostle of the Slavs, in the 9th cent. Other surviving literature in the alphabet includes translations of the Gospels and collections of Homilies. In modern Glagolitic *Missals (since 1927), only the *canon is printed in Glagolitic letters, the rest being in Latin type. See also *Cyrillic*.

GLANVILL, JOSEPH (1636–80), religious writer. Educated at Exeter and Lincoln Colleges, Oxford, he became rector of the Abbey Church, Bath, in 1666. Throughout his life he took a keen interest in natural phenomena, esp. in their bearing on religion, and he became one of the original members of the Royal Society. In several of his many treatises he endeavoured to prove that the evidence derived from the most varied physical phenomena lent support to religious belief. Like most of his scientific contemporaries, he was an ardent believer in the *Cartesian philosophy. In his *Sadducismus Triumphatus* (1681) he defended belief in witchcraft. A passage in his *Vanity of Dogmatizing* (1661) suggested to Matthew *Arnold his poem the 'Scholar Gipsy'.

Life prefixed to *Sadducismus Triumphatus*, ed. 4, 1726. F. Greenslet, *Joseph Glanvill. A Study in English Thought and Letters* (Columbia University Studies in English, i, 1900); H. Habicht, *Joseph Glanvill. Ein spekulativer Denker im England des XVII. Jahrhunderts* (Zürich, Diss., [1936]). J. *Tulloch, *Rational Theology and Christian Philosophy in England in the Seventeenth Century*, ii (1872), pp. 443–55; B. Willey, *The Seventeenth Century Background* (1934), ch. ix, pp. 170–204. H. S. and I. M. L. Redgrove, *Joseph Glanvill and Psychical Research in the Seventeenth Century* (1921). L. Stephen in *D.N.B.*, xxi (1890), p. 408 f.

GLASITES (also **Sandemanians**), a small Scottish sect named after John Glas (1695–1773) and his son-in-law, Robert Sandeman (1718–71). Their founder, John Glas, the son of the (*Presbyterian) minister at Auchtermuchty, Fife, was ordained in 1719 as minister of Tealing, near Dundee. Having come to doubt the Scriptural basis of the *Presbyterian civil polity and holding that secular and political weapons were unlawful instruments of reformation and that a National Church was unscriptural, he gave public expression to his views in *The Testimony of the King of Martyrs concerning His Kingdom* (1727). He was accordingly suspended from his ministerial work in 1728 and deposed in 1730. His followers ('Glasites') organized communities on a *Congregational basis at Dundee, Edinburgh, and elsewhere. They introduced several peculiar customs, including the celebration of the *Agape with broth.

Gradually the leadership of the movement passed into the hands of his son-in-law, then minister at Perth. Sandeman, whose name was soon applied to the whole body, laid great stress on the sole sufficiency of faith (which provoked a charge of antinomianism) and also adopted a number of unusual practices and rites (e.g. the custom of members washing one another's feet). His followers never had more than a small following but here and there communities were established outside Scotland, and for a time Michael Faraday, the physicist and natural philosopher, was a member of the London Sandemanians.

The *Works* of Glas, who was a man of considerable erudition, were published at Edinburgh (4 vols., 1761) and again at Perth (5 vols., 1872). A. Gordon in *D.N.B.*, xxi (1890), p. 417 f. and (1897), p. 255 f.

GLASTONBURY ABBEY. Probably the oldest and one of the most influential English monasteries. Orig. a *Celtic foundation believed to date from the 7th cent., it was turned into a Saxon monastery by King Ina *c.* 708. It was destroyed in the 9th cent. by the Danes. Later it seems to have been served by a small group of clerks until, in 943 or 944, King *Edmund made St. *Dunstan its abbot. From his time dates the great revival of the monastery, which was organized acc. to the *Benedictine Rule, and soon became one of the main educational and religious centres in the country. *C.* 970 it adopted the '*Regularis Concordia', designed to unify English monastic life. It continued to flourish under the Normans, and became a famous place of pilgrimage, owing to the tombs of King Arthur and St. Dunstan, which it was believed to contain. *C.* 1135 *William of Malmesbury wrote its history, 'De Antiquitate Glastoniensis Ecclesiae' (J. P. Migne, *PL*, clxix, 1681–1734), in which are recorded the legends which associate it with *Joseph of Arimathaea (q.v.), King Arthur, and St. *Patrick. Under Richard I a long drawn-out dispute arose between the abbey and the Bp. of *Bath and Wells, who claimed its revenues. It was eventually settled by the Pope in favour of the monks. The monastery was suppressed in 1539 and its last abbot, Bl. Richard Whiting, executed. Since 1908 the ruins have been the property of Diocesan Trustees; and adjoining is an Anglican Retreat House.

Around the 'Glastonbury Thorn', a kind of Levantine hawthorn which flowered twice a year, about Christmas and in May, several legends collected. It was cut down by one of O. *Cromwell's soldiers, but descendants of it remain till the present day.

C. I. Elton (ed.), *Rentalia et Custumaria Michaelis de Ambresbury, 1233–1252, et Rogeri de Ford, 1252–1261*; *Abbatum Monasterii Beatae Mariae Glastoniae* (Somersetshire Record Society, v, 1891); F. W. Weaver (ed.), *A Feodary of Glastonbury Abbey* (ib., xxvi, 1910); A. Watkin, O.S.B. (ed.), *The Great Cartulary of Glastonbury* (ib., lix and lxiii, 1947–52). W. *Dugdale, *Monasticon Anglicanum*, i (ed. 1817), pp. 1–79. W. Robinson, *Glastonbury Abbey* [Tottenham, 1844]; J. Parker, 'Glastonbury: the Abbey Ruins' in *Somersetshire Archaeological and Natural History Society*, xxvi (1881), pp. 25–106; the excavations under the direction of C. R. Peers–A. W. Clapham–E. Horne, O.S.B., begun in 1929, are reported ib., lxxv (1930), and foll. vols. J. A. *Robinson, *Two Glastonbury Legends*. King Arthur and St. Joseph of Arimathea (1926).

GLEBE. In English and Scots ecclesiastical law, the land devoted to the maintenance of the incumbent of the parish. Every church was at first entitled to a house and glebe, but the term now excludes the parsonage house and the land on which it is built. It can be cultivated either by the incumbent himself or by tenants to whom he leases it; and recent legislation permits of its being alienated altogether from the benefice in certain circumstances. By an Act of 1925, all the glebe in Scotland will ultimately be vested in the General Trustees of the Church.

GLORIA IN EXCELSIS. The initial words in Latin, and hence the common designation, of the hymn 'Glory be to God on high', &c. It is also known as the 'Greater *Doxology' and the 'Angelic Hymn'. A Greek Christian 'private psalm', i.e. a hymn composed upon the model of the canonical Psalms, its authorship and age are alike unknown. In the 4th cent. it formed part of morning prayers, and is still recited in the Byzantine *Orthros. In the Roman Mass it is sung after the *Kyries on Sundays (except those of *Advent and from *Septuagesima to *Palm Sunday) and on certain feast days, a usage the beginning of which appears in the *Gregorian Sacramentary. In the English BCP of 1549 the hymn followed the Kyries as in the Roman Mass. In later editions of the BCP it has been moved to the conclusion of the service, where it immediately precedes the Blessing. The American Prayer Book permits its use at the end of the Psalms for the day in Evening Prayer.

C. Blume, 'Der Engelhymnus *Gloria in Excelsis Deo*' in *Stimmen aus Maria Laach*, lxxiii (1907), pp. 43–62; A. *Baumstark, 'Die Textüberlieferung des Hymnus Angelicus', in *Hundert Jahre Marcus-und-Weber Verlag* (Bonn, 1909), pp. 83–7; J. Brinktrine, 'Zur Entstehung und Erklärung des *Gloria in Excelsis*' in *R.Q.*, xxxv (1927), pp. 303–15; Jungmann (1949), i, pp. 429–45; B. *Capelle, O.S.B., 'Le Texte du *Gloria in excelsis*' in *R.H.E.*, xliv (1949), pp. 439–57.

GLORIA PATRI. The first words of the Lesser *Doxology ('Glory be to the Father', &c.), an ascription of praise to the Holy Trinity. It probably originated as an adaptation of the Jewish 'blessings' addressed to God, early Christian examples being Rom. 16. 27, Phil. 4. 20, Rev. 5. 13, but its form was no doubt influenced by the Trinitarian Baptismal Formula of Mt. 28. 19. The use of the Gloria Patri at the end of Psalms dates from the 4th cent., and it is found quite early in metrical form at the end of hymns in the Offices. Acc. to the Roman *Missal and *Breviary it is omitted from the Mass in *Passiontide and at *Requiems, from the Psalms of the Offices on the last three days of *Holy Week and in the *Office of the Dead, and from the *Venite in Passiontide. The English Puritans forbade its use as unscriptural, but it was restored with the BCP at the Restoration.

H. Thurston, S.J., 'Notes on Familiar Prayers: ix, The "Gloria Patri"' in *The Month*, cxxxi (1918), pp. 406–17;

repr. in Thurston's *Familiar Prayers*, ed. P, Grosjean, S.J. (1953), pp. 178–92. J. A. Jungmann, S.J., 'Die Stellung Christi im liturgischen Gebet' in *Liturgiegeschichtliche Forschungen*, Hft. 7/8 (1925), pp. 151–77. Jungmann, i (ed. 1949), p, 404 f.

GLORIOUS MYSTERIES, The Five.

The third *chaplet of the *Rosary (q.v.), consisting of (1) the Resurrection; (2) the Ascension; (3) the Descent of the Holy Ghost at Pentecost; (4) the *Assumption of our Lady; and (5) the *Coronation of our Lady.

GLOSSOLALIA (Gk. γλῶσσα, 'tongue', and λαλία, 'talking'). The faculty of speaking with 'tongues'. It was a common phenomenon in NT times. Thus Acts 2. 4 records how on the Day of *Pentecost the Apostles 'were all filled with the Holy Ghost and began to speak with other tongues as the Spirit gave them utterance'; and St. *Paul attests that the custom was widespread at *Corinth, though here the inability of those possessing the faculty to disclose their meaning led him to regard it with suspicion and to contrast it with 'prophecy' (1 Cor. 14. 1 ff.). Similar phenomena are constantly met with in religious revivals. In all cases their healthiness or otherwise is best judged by their effect on the character and moral resolution of the person under possession. The word 'Glossolalia' is a 19th cent. coinage, without ancient authority.

GLOUCESTER. Until 1541, Gloucester was in the diocese of *Worcester. The abbey-church of St. *Peter, the present cathedral, is on the site of an earlier religious house, established in 681 and converted into a college of secular priests in 823. This college, refounded by St. *Wulfstan, Bp. of Worcester, in 1022 as a Benedictine monastery, was rebuilt in 1059 by Aldred, Bp. of Worcester. In 1088 Aldred's buildings were destroyed and in 1089 Serlo, the first Norman Abbot (1072–1104), began the present church. This Norman structure was constantly added to and embellished in the Middle Ages. Specially notable are the early perpendicular tracery superimposed on the Norman pillars in the choir (c. 1330); the large East window, a war-memorial to those slain at Crécy (1346) and the siege of Calais (1347); and the ornate cloisters with the earliest example of fan tracery. In the N. ambulatory is the tomb of Edward II, whose body was brought here after his murder at Berkeley Castle, 21 Sept. 1327; it soon became an important place of pilgrimage and its wealth greatly increased.

In 1539 the monastery was suppressed and in 1541 John Wakeman, the last Abbot of *Tewkesbury, became the first Bishop of the newly founded see of Gloucester. The diocese covered most of Gloucestershire, with parts of Herefordshire and Worcestershire. In 1836 it was united with the see of Bristol, but separated again in 1897. From 1713 to 1937 one of the canonries was attached to the Mastership

of Pembroke College, Oxford. Notable Bps. of Gloucester have been J. *Hooper (1551–4), burnt in St. Mary's Square outside the Abbey gates; W. *Warburton (1760–79); C. J. *Ellicott (1863–1905); E. C. S. Gibson (1905–1924), a competent historian, who published notable works on the *Articles and the *Creeds; and A. C. *Headlam (1923–45). Every third year the *Three Choirs Festival is held at Gloucester.

W. H. Hart (ed.), *Historia et Cartularium Monasterii Sancti Petri Gloucestriae* (3 vols., R.S., 1863–7). H. G[ee] (ed.), *The Statutes of Gloucester Cathedral* (1918). 'The Records of the Dean and Chapter of Gloucester' are described by W. H. Stevenson in the *Twelfth Report of the Historical Manuscripts Commission*, Appendix, Part ix (1891), pp. 397–9. B. Willis, *A Survey of the Cathedrals of York, Durham, Carlisle, Chester, Man, Lichfield, Hereford, Worcester, Gloucester and Bristol*, ii (1727), pp. 691–757. W. *Dugdale, *Monasticon Anglicanum*, i (ed. 1817), pp. 531–66. W. H. St. J. Hope, 'Notes on the Benedictine Abbey of St. Peter at Gloucester' in *The Archaeological Journal*, liv (1897), pp. 77–119. H. J. L. J. Massé, *The Cathedral Church of Gloucester* (Bell's Cathedral Series, 1898). Rose Graham, 'The Abbey of St. Peter at Gloucester' in *V.C.H., Gloucester*, ii, ed. W. Page (1907), pp. 53–61. E. Foord, *Gloucester, Tewkesbury and District* (Cathedrals, Abbeys and Famous Churches; 1925), pp. 25–88. C. W. C. Oman in *D.E.C.H.*, pp. 244–7, s.v.

GLOVES, Liturgical (Lat. *chirothecae*). In the W. Church, the privilege of wearing liturgical gloves belongs ordinarily to the Pope, the cardinals, and the bishops, though it is sometimes conferred on abbots and others by the Holy See. They are worn during a *Pontifical Mass and are of the colour of the day (never black, however, as they are not worn at *Requiems or on *Good Friday). Apparently first used in France at about the end of the 9th cent., they made their way thence to Rome a little later. In the E. Church, the *Epimanikia* (ἐπιμανίκια), or liturgical cuffs, are their counterpart.

X. Barbier de Montault, *Les Gants pontificaux* (Tours, 1877). Braun, *L.G.*, pp. 359–84; id., *L.P.*, pp. 154–7.

GNOSTICISM. The name, derived from the Greek word γνῶσις ('knowledge'), given to a complex religious movement which in its Christian form comes into clear prominence in the 2nd cent. It is now generally held that Christian Gnosticism had its origins in trends of thought already present in pagan religious circles. In Christianity, the movement appeared at first as a school (or schools) of thought within the Church; it soon established itself in all the principal centres of Christianity; and by the end of the 2nd cent. the Gnostics had mostly become separate sects. In some of the later books of the NT, e.g. 1 John and the *Pastoral Epistles, forms of false teaching are denounced which appear to be similar to, though less developed than, the Gnostic systems of teaching referred to by 2nd cent. writers.

Gnosticism took many different forms, commonly associated with the names of particular teachers, e.g. *Valentinus, *Basilides, and *Marcion (qq.v.). But though Marcion and his community stand somewhat apart, certain features are common to the movement as a whole. A central importance was attached to 'gnosis', the supposedly revealed knowledge of God and of the origin and destiny of mankind, by means of which the spiritual element in man could receive redemption. The source of this special 'gnosis' was held to be either the Apostles, from whom it was derived by a secret tradition, or a direct revelation given to the founder of the sect. The systems of teaching range from those which embody much genuine philosophical speculation to those which are wild amalgams of mythology and magical rites drawn from all quarters, with the most slender admixture of Christian elements. The OT Books and many of the NT Books were used and expounded by the greater sects, and a central place was assigned to the figure of Jesus, but on a number of fundamental points the interpretation of these Christian features differed widely from that of orthodox Christianity.

Characteristic of Gnostic teaching was the distinction between the *Demiurge or 'creator god' and the supreme remote and unknowable Divine Being. From the latter the Demiurge was derived by a longer or shorter series of emanations or 'aeons'. He it was who, through some mischance or fall among the higher aeons, was the immediate source of creation and ruled the world, which was therefore imperfect and antagonistic to what was truly spiritual. But into the constitution of some men there had entered a seed or spark of Divine spiritual substance, and through 'gnosis' and the rites associated with it this spiritual element might be rescued from its evil material environment and assured of a return to its home in the Divine Being. Such men were designated the 'spiritual' (πνευματικοί), while others were merely 'fleshly' or 'material' (σαρκικοί or ὑλικοί), though some Gnostics added a third intermediate class, the 'psychic' (ψυχικοί). The function of Christ was to come as the emissary of the supreme God, bringing 'gnosis'. As a Divine Being He neither assumed a properly human body nor died, but either temporarily inhabited a human being, Jesus, or assumed a merely phantasmal human appearance.

The principal anti-Gnostic writers, such as *Irenaeus, *Tertullian, and *Hippolytus, emphasized the pagan features of Gnosticism, and appealed to the plain sense of the Scriptures as interpreted by the tradition of the Church, which had been publicly handed down by a chain of teachers reaching back to the Apostles. They insisted on the identity of the Creator and the supreme God, on the goodness of the material creation, and on the reality of the earthly life of Jesus, esp. of the Crucifixion and the Resurrection. Man needed redemption from an evil will rather than an evil environment. The sect of the *Manichees, founded by Mani the Persian in the 3rd cent. and widely influential for over a century in the Roman Empire, closely resembled the earlier Gnostic sects, as do some of the modern forms of

*Theosophy. See also *Docetism*; *Mystery Religions*; *Jung Codex*.

The principal items in the small *corpus* of Gnostic literature known until recently (apart from the specifically *Manichaean texts, q.v.) were the Ep. of Ptolemy to Flora (new ed. by G. Quispel in S.C., xxiv; 1949), the '*Pistis Sophia', and the 'Book of *Jeû' (qq.v.). The chief sources for Gnostic doctrines and practice were (and in 1957 still are) the anti-heretical writings of the Church fathers, notably Irenaeus, *Adversus Haereses*, *Clement of Alexandria, *Excerpta ex Theodoto*, Tertullian, *De Praescriptione*, Hippolytus, *Philosophoumena*, and *Epiphanius, *Panarion*. Useful collection of Gnostic texts in W. Völker, *Quellen zur Geschichte der christlichen Gnosis* (1932). In 1946 a large collection of Gnostic texts in Coptic (apparently mainly, if not all, translations from the Greek) was discovered at Nag Hammadi in Upper Egypt. Most of these have been acquired by the Coptic Museum at Cairo and await publication; summary description of their contents by H. C. Puech, 'Les Nouveaux Écrits gnostiques découverts en Haute-Égypte' in *Coptic Studies in Honor of Walter Ewing Crum* (Boston, Mass., 1950), pp. 91–154; on the codex now at Zürich, see *Jung Codex*.
There is no comprehensive modern study of Gnosticism in English. The more important literature includes F. C. *Baur, *Die christliche Gnosis oder die christliche Religionsphilosophie in ihrer geschichtlichen Entwicklung* (1835); R. A. *Lipsius, *Die Quellen der ältesten Ketzergeschichte neu untersucht* (1875; on the literary relations between the early anti-Gnostic writers); H. L. *Mansel, *The Gnostic Heresies of the First and Second Centuries* (1875); A. *Hilgenfeld, *Ketzergeschichte des Urchristenthums, urkundlich dargestellt* (1884; with text of chief fragments); W. Anz, *Zur Frage nach dem Ursprung des Gnosticismus* (1897); E. de Faye, *Introduction à l'étude du gnosticisme* (1903); id., *Gnostiques et gnosticisme* (1925); W. *Bousset, *Hauptprobleme der Gnosi* (1907); W. Köhler, *Die Gnosis* (1911); H. Leisegang, *Die Gnosis* (1924; ed. 2, 1936). F. C. *Burkitt, *Church and Gnosis* (1932); H. Jonas, *Gnosis und spätantiker Geist* (1934 ff.); R. P. Casey, 'The Study of Gnosticism' in *J.T.S.*, xxxvi (1935), pp. 45–60; G. Scholem, *Major Trends in Jewish Mysticism* (Hilda Stich Stroock Lectures for 1938; New York, 1941). G. Quispel, *Gnosis als Weltreligion* (Zürich, 1951). Bardenhewer, i, pp. 343–76; Altaner (ed. 1950), pp. 105–8. W. Bousset in *E.B.* (ed. 11); xii (1910), pp. 152–9; E. F. Scott in *H.E.R.E.*, vi (1913), pp. 231–42; G. Bareille in *D.T.C.*, vi (1920), cols. 1434–67; J. F. Steffes in *L.Th.K.*, iv (1932), cols. 554–7; E. Peterson in *E.C.*, vi (1951), cols. 876–82, s.v. 'Gnosi'. R. McL. Wilson, *The Gnostic Problem* (1958). R. M. Grant, *Gnosticism and Early Christianity* (1959). See also bibls. to individual Gnostic teachers.

GOAR, JACQUES (1601–54), French liturgiologist. He was a native of Paris, and after studying Greek and Latin entered the *Dominican Order in 1619. Having been lecturer at the convent at Toul, he went to Greece in 1631 as prior of the convent of St. Sebastian in Chios in order to perfect himself in the language and to study the rites of the Greek Church. In 1637 he went to Rome as prior of San Sisto, and in 1644 settled at Paris, where he brought out a series of works, the most important being his celebrated Εὐχολόγιον sive *Rituale Graecorum* (Paris, 1647; ed. 2, much improved, Venice, 1730). It contains the rites of the Greek Liturgy, Offices, Sacramentaries, &c., based on MSS. as well as on printed sources, and gives Latin translations and valuable notes. It is still the classical work for Greek liturgical studies, which has served as a basis for all subsequent research on the subject. Among his other works are editions of the *Compendium Historiarum* of George Cedrenus (1647), the *De Officiis Magnae Ecclesiae* of the so-called Codinus Curopalata (1648), and of the *Chronographia* of George Monachus and the Patr. Tarasius (1652).

Quétif-Échard, ii, pp. 574 f. R. Coulon, O.P., in *D.T.C.*, vi (1920), cols. 1467–9.

GOD. The Greek word for God (θεός) is used both as a common noun, e.g. in polytheism, where a number of supposed existences claim belief, worship, and service, and as a proper name, e.g. in monotheism, where there is and can be but one such existence. As contrasted with Jewish and Moslem monotheism which tend to separate God completely from the world (*deism), Christian monotheism combines God's presence and activity in the world (*immanence) with His eternal and infinite reality beyond the world of time and space (transcendence). Christianity also affirms that God is a trinity in unity, a 'Trinity', consisting of 'three persons in one substance', the Father being the Source of all existence, the Son the Eternal Object of the Father's love and the Mediator of that love in creation and redemption, and the Holy Ghost (the Spirit of God) the Bond of Union between Father and Son.

In the OT revelation to *Moses on Sinai (Ex. 3. 2–15 and 6. 2–8) God makes Himself known in the Divine name '*Yahweh' ('I am who I am') as the unique God (Ex. 20. 3, 5), who tolerates no rival, and is alone Lord of the earth (Ex. 9. 29), omnipotent and holy (Ex. 15. 3–15), merciful and faithful to His word (Ex. 34. 6 f.) and demanding obedience to His commandments (Ex. 20. 1–17). This exalted conception of the Creator-God came to be affirmed by all the greatest religious leaders of Israel. The prophets esp. developed the different aspects of God acc. to their character and special mission. *Amos preached the righteousness of God, limited by no national barriers, while *Hosea was the first to proclaim His fatherhood in regard to Israel and His gentleness which desires 'mercy, not sacrifice' (Hos. 6. 6). *Isaiah, and later *Ezekiel, exalt His incomparable holiness and transcendence, a conception which finally triumphed in the Exile. With *Jonah the idea of God as the saviour of Gentiles as well as Jews makes its first appearance. This universality is esp. reflected in some of the Psalms, in which Book all the strands of Jewish monotheistic piety are gathered. Yet the full development of the revelation of the One God could not be completely achieved while in popular Jewish teaching He remained pre-eminently the God of a single nation, whose chief function it was to fulfil the earthly hope of temporal blessings.

It was to make patent the fullness of truth about God that (acc. to Christian belief) a new revelation was given. This was made through the Incarnate Son, who revealed God as the Father of all men, whose infinite goodness has no need to manifest itself in material recompenses. It was in the light of this new knowledge that St. John conceived God as light, life, and love; but no epitome can convey the richness and extent of the several aspects of the revelation contained in the NT. Above all, it was a revelation of God through the facts of history. Certain events of an historic order were perceived to possess a unique status and significance for those to whom the truth was committed. There resulted a conception of

God which, while safeguarding the legitimacy of natural theology (cf. Rom. 1. 18 ff.) within certain limits, recognized His character as *sui generis*.

In the Patristic age three principal factors determined the development of the doctrine of God: (1) the *data* of Scripture, (2) the controversies with pagans, Jews, and heretics, and (3) the Greek philosophy which was the foundation of the education of most of the Fathers. Whereas the *Apostolic Fathers confined themselves to the Scriptural teaching, the exigencies of controversy led the *Apologists of the 2nd and 3rd cents. to a greater preoccupation with reason and philosophy. Thus St. *Justin Martyr, who was much influenced by *Platonist teaching, stressed the ineffability, omnipotence and impassibility of God. This attitude was shared by *Tatian and many others, whereas *Athenagoras and *Theophilus elaborated His simplicity, indivisibility and universal Providence. St. *Irenaeus developed his doctrine esp. against the *Gnostics, to whose dualism and emanationism he opposed the absolute self-sufficiency and perfection of God. The theology of the early Alexandrian Fathers, *Clement and *Origen, is characterized by their vigorous affirmation of the Divine transcendence, incomprehensibility, and ineffability. Despite this emphasis, however, they upheld the natural knowability of God through creation. This is also stressed by *Tertullian, who adds to it the testimony of the human soul and deduces from the conception of God as the First Cause His possession of all perfections. Thus by the time of *Nicaea (325) the great lines of Christian thought were fixed, and such Divine attributes as eternity, immutability, omniscience, and omnipotence had become the undisputed belief of all Christians.

The doctrine of the pre-Nicene age was deepened by the great speculative theologians of Alexandria, esp. St. *Athanasius, St. *Didymus, and St. *Cyril. They insist that God, though incomprehensible in His inner Being, can be known through the human soul, made in His image, and through the visible creation. St. *Cyril of Jerusalem deals with the subject implicitly in his 'Catecheses', esp. with the unity, sovereign dominion, and creative action of God. The *Cappadocians were led to an explicit examination of the Divine nature and our knowledge of it in their call to reply to *Eunomius, who had asserted that the full Being of God is adequately expressed by the word 'Unoriginate' (ἀγέννητος), to which all other designations can be reduced. Against him St. *Gregory of Nazianzus maintained that negative attributes are not enough, and that such positive names as love, wisdom, justice, &c., should be added, the most suitable, however, being God and Being.

The speculations of the Fathers were gathered up into a powerful synthesis in the various works of St. *Augustine. He gives several proofs for the existence of God, e.g. from contingency, from the order and beauty of the world, from the eternal principles of human reason, and the moral argument from conscience. These proofs, however, were not yet elaborated with the systematic methods of the Middle Ages. The influence of Plato shows itself in Augustine's idea of God as the First Principle, cause of all truth and of all goodness. Though God is above all human thought and language, He is not abstract and indeterminate being, but concrete and actual, 'above whom, outside whom, and without whom nothing exists' (*Soliloq.* I. i. 4). In his theology the three ways of conceiving God by affirmation, negation, and eminence are combined. Thus while His goodness (way of affirmation) is asserted, He may also be called 'not good', i.e. not good in the way a man is called good (way of negation), and 'super-good', i.e. above all human ideas of goodness (way of eminence). Those last two methods of conceiving the Divine Being were esp. favoured by the Greek theologian known as *Dionysius the Areopagite in his treatises 'De Divinis Nominibus' and 'De Mystica Theologia'. Though stressing the Divine transcendence more than any other Father, he avoids agnosticism by recognizing that man may elevate himself to the Supreme Being by considering Him as the cause of all creatures. This Cause, however, is so infinitely superior to all created things that it is more fitting to the Divine Majesty to deny Him all the perfections predicated to creatures than to affirm them of Him, unless by way of eminence. This latter leads the author to a whole series of almost untranslatable superlatives such as 'super-essential', 'essential super-goodness', &c.

The ideas of Dionysius were taken over, with some modifications, by his translator John Scotus *Erigena. Acc. to Erigena God is known by reason as the cause of things, but not as what He is. A higher knowledge of Him is possible by contemplation, but even here and in the *Beatific Vision He is not seen Himself but only through theophanies, which he produces in the angels and the elect; all affirmations of Scripture and the Fathers are but metaphors devised for the ignorant. This fundamental agnosticism led to reiterated condemnations of his doctrine; but the stress he laid on philosophy constitutes a link between the Patristic age and the Scholasticism that was to follow.

One of the principal concerns of the Schoolmen was to investigate the Divine Nature by the method of rational proof, without direct appeal to revelation. St. *Anselm of Canterbury was the author of the *Ontological Argument (q.v.) for His Being. Under the influence of the newly discovered *Aristotle, St. *Thomas Aquinas introduced some radical changes and developments. He rejected the Ontological Argument; but on the principle that only something itself in the state of 'act' can move anything from the state of 'potentiality' to the state of 'act', he elaborated his famous fivefold proof for the existence of God (*Quinque Viae). Starting with creation, he argued from its visible effects to the conception of God as the First Immovable Mover, the First Efficient Cause, the necessary Being, the most perfect

Being, and the Ordainer of the universe. He endeavoured to hold the balance between an anthropomorphic conception of God and an exaggerated transcendence. In God, as self-subsistent Being, essence was identical with existence, and as 'Actus purus' without any admixture of potentiality He was Himself all perfections. Though St. Thomas was not immediately followed in his rejection of the Ontological Argument, which continued to be upheld by theologians of the *Franciscan school, e.g. St. *Bonaventure and *Duns Scotus, his doctrine of God became the officially accepted basis of the teaching of *Tridentine Catholic theology.

The shattering personal experiences of the Reformers were reflected in their intensely personal conceptions of God. M. *Luther directed a fierce tirade against the speculative theology of the Schools. J. *Calvin esp. emphasized the Divine Majesty and transcendence. And even in Catholic quarters the *nominalism of the late Middle Ages contributed to the disintegration of the Thomistic synthesis. One of the first Christian thinkers to abandon belief in a knowable God, distinct from the world, had been *Nicholas of Cusa (d. 1464), who maintained that God is necessarily unknowable and immanent in the world. The fundamental unity of God and the world was stated even more clearly in the next century by G. *Bruno, for whom God was the world-soul. In contrast to these pantheistic conceptions, R. *Descartes endeavoured to uphold the transcendence of the Divine Being. In his former argument in his *Meditations* for the Being of God, he urged that the human mind can conceive an infinite and perfect Being only because the idea of the other exists in our minds and this idea has a proportionate cause. His other argument was essentially a reformulation of the Ontological Argument. The pantheistic trend of modern philosophy was resumed by B. *Spinoza, who elaborated the threefold notion of God as thought, as substance, and nature. There are no two separate terms of Creator and creature, but a complex series of stages from God to the universe, so that the exact transition from the Divine to the finite is incapable of definition. Descartes's ontological argument for the existence of God was reasserted, with an attempt at greater stringency, by G. W. *Leibniz. If a perfect and necessary Being is not a contradictory and fictitious object, such a Being must exist, because existence is one of its attributes.

A decisive attack on natural theology was made in the 18th cent. by I. *Kant, who, in his *Critique of Pure Reason* (1781), attempted to prove the impossibility of any rational proof of the existence of God. This was a consequence of his attack on speculative metaphysics in all its forms. He also urged that in any case the arguments from causality and teleology would be insufficient to prove what Christian Theism means by God without the assistance of the Ontological Argument. The only valid proof of the existence of God is that from morality. 'I had to remove knowledge (*Wissen*) to make way for faith (*Glauben*)'. The reality of moral obligation implied the existence of a wise, holy, and omnipotent Being, Who would ensure the future harmony between the accomplishment of duty and happiness. The step from the refusal of any metaphysical basis for the belief in God to resting the belief on feeling ('*Anschauung und Gefühl*') was made by F. D. E. *Schleiermacher. All religious statements must be derived not from deductive logic but from personal experience, and the origin of belief in God be sought in the feeling of dependence, common to human beings. Among British thinkers of the 19th cent. Sir W. Hamilton and H. L. *Mansel sought to uphold the traditional conception of God on a basis of agnosticism which had affinities with the teaching of Kant.

But the 19th cent. also witnessed under the stimulus of G. W. F. *Hegel a powerful movement in speculative theology. In a grandiose system, Hegel fused evolutionary conceptions with the pantheism of Spinoza and thereby, while doing violence to the Christian doctrine of creation, put philosophical theology into relationship with modern physical, biological, and historic conceptions. His work exercised great influence in England through its presentation, in a much modified form, in T. H. *Green, F. H. *Bradley, and B. *Bosanquet, as well as in more recent times, with much greater reserve, in A. S. Pringle-*Pattison, C. C. J. *Webb and W. *Temple.

The main trend in the present century has been against immanentism, with a reaffirmation of the Divine transcendence. The beginnings of the movement are probably to be sought in the Anti-Intellectualism of such movements as *Pragmatism (W. *James, H. *Bergson, F. C. S. Schiller's 'Humanism') and also RC *Modernism (M. *Blondel, A. *Loisy). Since 1914 the movement has been esp. associated in Protestant theology with the names of K. *Barth and, in a less extreme form, E. *Brunner. In Catholic theology this movement has had its counterpart in a revival of the Scholastic teaching about a Divine Being at once rigidly traditional in its fundamental principles and yet anxious to take full account of the changed position of secular thought. This Scholastic movement, which may be said to take its origin with the constitution 'Dei Filius' of the *Vatican Council (1870), was fostered by *Leo XIII and the Louvain School (D. J. *Mercier). Among its more recent exponents are E. *Gilson, R. Garrigou-Lagrange, J. *Maritain, and M. C. *D'Arcy. All these groups have been widely represented in England, where the most notable of recent exponents of theism, besides those already mentioned, include A. E. *Taylor, F. *von Hügel, A. M. Farrer, and E. L. Mascall.

From the vast modern literature may be mentioned: J. Baillie, *Our Knowledge of God* (1939); K. Barth, *The Knowledge of God and the Service of God according to the Teaching of the Reformation* (1938); F. H. Bradley, *Appearance and Reality* (1893); A. Caldecott–H. R. Mackintosh, *Selections from the Literature of Theism* (1904); R. Garrigou-Lagrange, O.P., *Dieu, son existence et sa nature* (1915); E. Gilson, *The Spirit of Medieval Philosophy* (1936); F. J. Hall, *The Being and Attributes of God* (1909); F. von Hügel, *Essays and Addresses on the Philosophy of Religion* (2 Series, 1921, 1926);

J. Maritain, *Distinguer pour unir. Les degrés du savoir* (1932; Eng. trans., *The Degrees of Knowledge*, 1937); E. L. Mascall, *He Who Is* (1943); A. S. Pringle-Pattison, *The Idea of God in the Light of Recent Philosophy* (1917); A. E. Taylor, art. 'Theism' in Hastings' *ERE*, xii, pp. 261–87; id., *The Faith of a Moralist* (2 vols., 1930); id., *Does God Exist?* (1943), W. Temple, *Nature, Man and God* (1934); C. C. J. Webb, *Studies in the History of Natural Theology* (1915); id., *God and Personality* (1918).

GOD SAVE THE KING, British National Anthem. The origins of both words and tune are obscure; and as regards the words it is also uncertain whether the Eng. or Lat. version is the older. The opening words of the Lat. are 'O Deus optime, salvum nunc facito, Regem nostrum'.

The phrase 'God save the King' occurs in the Eng. Bible at 1 Sam. 10. 24, 2 Sam. 16. 16, and 2 Kgs. 11. 12, both in the *Coverdale version (1535) and in the AV of 1611, while as early as 1545 'God save the King' was a watchword in the Navy, with 'Long to reign over us' as a counter-sign. It seems probable that the anthem arose from a series of common loyal phrases being gradually combined into one national hymn; and there is some evidence that the words were put into substantially their present form for use in the RC chapel of *James II. Among individuals of later date to whom the authorship of the Anthem has sometimes (prob. wrongly) been attributed are Henry Carey (c. 1685–1743), author of 'Sally in our Alley', and James Oswald (c. 1710–1769), a Scotsman settled in London. It was certainly much used in its present form in London theatres in 1745 (the year of the landing of the Young Pretender); the three stanzas were printed in the *Gentleman's Magazine* for Oct. of the same year; and its general popularity dates from that time.

In a similar way the tune seems to be a 17th cent. recasting of earlier phrases. We find the earliest elements in the medieval plainsong notation to the antiphon to the *Magnificat for the Saturday before the Seventh Sunday after Pentecost ('Unxerunt Salamonem '). The same rhythm occurs in a 16th-cent. Genevan folk-song. In the tune of a Christmas carol, dated 1611, and attributed to John Bull (c. 1562–1628), it begins to take the familiar form. In the U.S.A., where the tune goes by the name of 'America', it is sung to the words 'My country, 'tis of thee'.

W. H. Cummings, *God Save the King*. The Origin and History of the Music and Words of the National Anthem (1902); P. A. Scholes, '*God Save the King!*' Its History and its Romance (1942). Id., *God Save the Queen!* The History and Romance of the World's First National Anthem (1954; the most substantial work on the subject).

GODCHILDREN. See *Godparents*.

GODESCALC. See *Gottschalk*.

GODET, FRÉDÉRIC LOUIS (1812–1900), Swiss Protestant theologian and NT scholar. He was a native of Neuchâtel. From 1838 to 1844 he was tutor to the Crown Prince Friedrich Wilhelm of Prussia; from 1850 to

1873 professor of NT exegesis in the Swiss Academy (now the university) at Neuchâtel; and from 1873 to 1887 professor in the new faculty of the Free Church of Neuchâtel, which he helped to found. Besides interpreting German thought to French-speaking Protestants, he was himself a considerable exegete whose influence extended far beyond Switzerland. He published Commentaries on Jn. (1863–5), Lk. (1871), Rom. (1880), and Cor. (1886), as well as other Biblical treatises. In the main his influence was in a conservative direction.

Philippe E. Godet, *Frédéric Godet (1812–1900), d'après sa correspondance et d'autres documents inédits (1913)*.

GODFREY OF BOUILLON (*c.* 1060–1100).

One of the leaders in the First *Crusade. He was a French noble who had fought under the Emp. *Henry IV. In 1096 he led a German contingent on the First Crusade, and in 1099, after forcing Raymond of Toulouse to march on *Jerusalem, himself took a prominent part in the siege and capture of the city. After Raymond had declined the honour, Godfrey was chosen ruler of Jerusalem under the title of 'Advocate [i.e. protector] of the Holy Sepulchre'. He seems to have contemplated a theocracy as the future government of Jerusalem, but died in 1100 and was succeeded by his brother Baldwin I as king. See also *Assizes of Jerusalem*.

The primary authorities for his career include the *Liber Christianae Expeditionis pro Ereptione, Emundatione et Restitutione Sanctae Hierosolymitanae Ecclesiae* of Albert of Aix (Lotharingian; pr. in *Recueil des historiens des croisades* publié par les Soins de l'Académie des Inscriptions et Belles-Lettres, Historiens occidentaux, iv (1879), pp. 265–713) and, from the opposite angle, the *Historia Francorum qui ceperunt Jerusalem* of Raymond of Aquilers (Provençal; ib., iii (1866), pp. 231–309); there is also much information in the work of *William of Tyre (q.v.). In later legend Godfrey of Bouillon appears as the type of the ideal Christian knight. His career is discussed in all works dealing with the Crusades and the Latin Kingdom of Jerusalem. For main bibl. see works cited under *Crusades*. Modern works specifically devoted to him include T. Breysig, 'Gottfried von Bouillon vor dem Kreuzzuge' in *Westdeutsche Zeitschrift für Geschichte und Kunst*, xvii (1898), pp. 169–201, with reff.; C. Moeller, 'Godefroy de Bouillon et l'avouerie du saint-sépulchre' in *Mélanges Godefroy Kurth*, i (1908), pp. 73–83; M. Lobet, *Godefroid de Bouillon. Essai de biographie antilégendaire* (Brussels, 1943); H. Dorchy, 'Godefroid de Bouillon, Duc de Bas-Lotharingie' in *Revue Belge de Philologie et d'Histoire*, xxvi (1948), pp. 961–99 (mainly on his earlier life). E. Barker in *E.B.* (ed. 11), xi (1910), p. 172, s.v.

GODPARENTS, also Sponsors.

Witnesses, in person or by proxy, to a Christian baptism, who take on themselves special responsibilities for the Christian upbringing of the newly baptized. These responsibilities are most serious in the case of infant baptism, at which the godparents also make the promises of renunciation, faith, and obedience in the child's name. The BCP requires every candidate for baptism to have at least three godparents, of which two are to be of its own sex.

GOERRES, J. J. VON. See *Görres, J. J. von.*

GOG AND MAGOG.

In Rev. 20. 8 Gog and Magog are two powers under the dominion of Satan. In the OT they are mentioned together in Ezek. 38. 2, where, however, Gog is a people (apparently the Scythians who ravaged W. Asia about 630 B.C.) and Magog a land. In the later *apocalyptic and *rabbinic literature they are conventional figures for those opposed to the people of God. Acc. to an almost independent medieval legend, formerly embodied in the well-known wooden statues of Gog and Magog at the Guildhall, London (destroyed in the fire, 29 Dec. 1940), they were two giants who were made porters at 'Troynovant' (London) by 'Brutus the Trojan'.

S. H. Hooke, 'Gog and Magog' in *The Expository Times*, xxvi (1914–15), pp. 317–19. J. Halévy in *Revue Sémitique*, xii (1904), pp. 370–5. A. H. Sayce in *H.D.B.*, ii (1899), p. 224, s.v. 'Gog', and iii (1900), p. 212, s.v. 'Magog'. F. Spadafora in *E.C.*, vi (1951), col. 900 f., s.v. See also commentaries to Ezekiel, &c., cited s.vv.

GOGARTEN, FRIEDRICH (1887–   ),

Protestant theologian. A native of Dortmund, he became pastor at Stelzendorf in Thuringia in 1917 and at Dorndorf in 1925. From 1927 he taught Systematic Theology at Jena. In reaction from E. *Troeltsch's historicism, Gogarten formulated a fresh interpretation of culture and civilization in the spirit of K. *Barth's *Dialectical Theology, but (unlike the other leading theologians of the school) from a *Lutheran, as opposed to a *Calvinist, background. Real historical happenings take place only in the obedience of faith when the Ego accepts the unconditional claims of a concrete 'Thou'. His writings include *Fichte als religiöser Denker* (1914), *Religion und Volkstum* (1915), *Von Glauben und Offenbarung* (1923), *Ich glaube an den dreieinigen Gott* (1926), and *Entmythologisierung und die Kirche* (1953; Eng. tr., 1955). He also contributed extensively to the Barthian periodical *Zwischen den Zeiten* (1923 onwards).

GOLDEN CALF (עֵגֶל, the Heb. word

translated 'calf', would be more properly rendered 'young bull'). An object of worship set up (a) by the Israelites in the wilderness (Ex. 32); (b) by King Jeroboam I (937–915 B.C.) at Bethel and Dan for the worship of the Ten Tribes (1 Kgs. 12. 28).

GOLDEN LEGEND, The.

This manual, also known as the 'Lombardica Historia', which consists mainly of lives of the saints and short treatises about the Christian festivals, was drawn up by *Jacob of Voragine (q.v.) between 1255 and 1266. Its 177 (or, acc. to other enumerations, 182) chapters are disposed acc. to the Church's year. The purpose of its engagingly written narrative, full of anecdotes and curious etymologies, is to foster piety; and it soon became exceedingly popular. In the 14th cent. it was translated into French by Jean Belet de Vigny; and it was issued constantly in a variety of languages from the earliest printing presses. Its real literary merits tended to be lost sight of in the 16th cent., when it was condemned on considerations purely of its historicity by such scholars as L.*Vives and M. *Cano.

Editio princeps by J. Zainer (printer), Ulm, c. 1469; crit. ed. by T. Graesse, Dresden and Leipzig, 1846. Caxton's translation was repr. by W. Morris and F. S. Ellis, 3 vols., London, 1892; also ed., in modern Eng., by F. S. Ellis in The Temple Classics, 7 vols., 1900. Modern Eng. tr. from the Lat. by G. Ryman–H. Ripperger, New York and London, 1941. P. Butler, *Legenda Aurea—Légende dorée—Golden Legend*. A Study of Caxton's Golden Legend with Special Reference to its Relation to the Earlier English Prose Translation (thesis; Baltimore, 1899). Sister Mary Jeremy, 'Caxton's *Golden Legend* and Voragine's *Legenda Aurea*' in *Speculum*, xxi (1946), pp. 212–21; R. E. Seybolt, 'Fifteenth Century Editions of the *Legenda Aurea*', ib., pp. 327–38 [with bibl.]; id., 'The *Legenda Aurea*, Bible and *Historia Scholastica*', ib., pp. 339–42. J. Baudot in *D.T.C.*, viii (part 1; 1924), cols. 310–13, s.v. 'Jacques de Voragine', with reff.

GOLDEN NUMBER, The. The number of any year in the Metonic cycle (devised in 432 B.C. by the Athenian astronomer Meton) and adopted in the ecclesiastical calendar since the time of St. *Hippolytus. The calculation rests on the assumption (very nearly correct) that 235 lunations ('lunar months') correspond with 19 solar years. As stated in the tables at the beginning of the BCP, the Golden Number of any given year is found by adding 1 to the number of the year of Our Lord, and then dividing by 19; the remainder is the Golden Number of the year in question (or, if there is no remainder, it is 19). It was the value of the number for computing the date of *Easter that led it to be termed in the Middle Ages the Golden Number (*aureus numerus*). The view sometimes found that it was so named because it was printed in calendars in letters of gold is without authority.

GOLDEN ROSE. An ornament of wrought gold and gems in the form of a rose which is blessed by the Pope on the Fourth Sunday in *Lent ('Rose Sunday') and afterwards presented as a mark of special favour to some distinguished individual or community. In recent times it has often been sent to the queens of Catholic countries. If there is no worthy recipient, the rose is laid up in the *Vatican, where it is blessed every year until distribution is made. The origin of the custom is obscure; but as early as 1049 *Leo IX speaks of it as an ancient institution. That sent by *Clement V to the city of Basle is preserved in the Musée de Cluny at Paris.

C. Cartari, *La rosa d' oro pontificia* (Rome, 1681); A. Baldassarri, S.J., *La rosa d' oro. Che si benedice nella quarta dominica di quaresima dal sommo pontifice* (Venice, 1709). A. Shield, 'The Golden Rose' in *The Month*, xcv (1900), pp. 294–304. P. M. J. Rock in *C.E.*, vi (1909), p. 629 f., s.v.; N. Del Re in *E.C.*, x (1953), cols. 1344–6, s.v. 'Rosa d' oro', with further bibl.

GOLDEN RULE. A (modern) name for the precept in the Sermon on the Mount: 'All things whatsoever ye would that men should do to you, do ye even so to them' (Mt. 7. 12; cf. Lk. 6. 31). In a negative form it is found in the *Western text of Acts 15. 29, and in the *Didache (1, 2).

GOLDEN SEQUENCE, The. The *Sequence for *Whitsunday, '*Veni, Sancte Spiritus' (q.v.).

GOLGOTHA. See *Calvary, Mount*.

GOMAR, FRANCIS (1563–1641), Dutch *Calvinist leader. A native of Bruges, he studied at Strassburg, Neustadt, *Oxford, Cambridge, and Heidelberg. In 1587 he became pastor of the Dutch community at Frankfurt, and in 1594 was appointed professor of theology at *Leyden. Here he became an upholder of rigid Calvinist principles, and engaged in a prolonged controversy with J. *Arminius, esp. after he became his fellow-professor in 1603. After Arminius's death (1609) the bitterness of the controversy was further increased through the appointment of the liberal C. *Vorstius as Arminius's successor. Accordingly in 1611 Gomar resigned and became preacher of the Reformed congregation at Middleburg. From 1614 to 1618 he taught at Saumur, and from 1618 till his death held a professorship at Groningen. At the Synod of *Dort (1618–19) he was among the principal opponents of Arminianism. In his later years he took part in the revision of the Dutch OT. His extreme Calvinism is shown by his rejection on theological grounds of a plea for the toleration of heretics.

Works publd. in 3 vols. fol., Amsterdam, 1644. Full study by G. P. van Itterzon (The Hague, 1929). C. Sudhoff–S. D. van Veen in *P.R.E.* (ed. 3), vi (1899), p. 763 f., s.v.; J. Forget in *D.T.C.*, vi (1920), cols. 1477–86, s.v. See also works cited under *Dort, Synod of*.

GONZALES, St. PETER. See *Elmo, St.*

GOOD FRIDAY ('Feria sexta in Parasceve'). The Friday before Easter on which the anniversary of the Crucifixion is kept. It is a day of fast, abstinence, and penance, and in the RC Church Good Friday, together with (since 1954) *Holy Saturday, are the only days in the year on which no Celebration of the Mass takes place.

The present Latin Rite goes back to the early days of Christianity. It consists of three parts: (1) the lessons and prayers, which are virtually the old 'Mass of the *Catechumens', with the singing of the Passion acc. to St. John; (2) the ceremonial *Veneration of the Cross, described already in the 'Peregrinatio *Etheriae' with the chanting of the *Reproaches and the *Trisagion; and (3) the Mass of the *Presanctified (q.v.). The evening service is the *Tenebrae (q.v.) of Holy Saturday. The liturgical colour of the day is black, no bells are rung, the organ is silent, and after the Mass of the Presanctified the altars are stripped and in some churches washed, and the empty Tabernacle is left open.

Most of these practices were abolished by the Churches of the Reformation. The C of E provides for the normal celebration of the

Eucharist, but it now rarely happens. In some Nonconformist Churches the day is kept as a feast rather than a fast; in Continental Protestantism it is customary to have the usual services with sermons, and often Good Friday is a special day for the administration of the Lord's Supper. In the RC Church popular devotions have developed beside the liturgical services. The best known are the *Three Hours Service from noon to 3 P.M., a post-Reformation devotion propagated by the *Jesuits and now widely taken over in the C of E; the *Stations of the Cross, usually made at 3 P.M.; and the 'Desolation of Mary', an evening service with sermon. In the Greek Church it is known as the 'Great Friday' (ἡ μεγάλη παρασκευή).

H. Thurston, S.J., *Lent and Holy Week* (1904), pp. 326–403. L. Eisenhofer, *Handbuch der katholischen Liturgik*, i (1932), pp. 524–32. T. P. Gilmartin in *C.E.*, vi (1909), pp. 643–5, s.v.

GOOD SAMARITAN, The.
The Samaritan of the Parable in Lk. 10. 30–37 who, in contrast to the priest and levite who 'passed by on the other side', tended the traveller who had fallen among thieves on his way from *Jerusalem to *Jericho and provided hospitality for him at an inn. His action illustrates the Christian response to the question: 'Who is my neighbour?' (Lk. 10. 29).

GOOD SHEPHERD, The.
The title of Christ, based esp. on His discourse in Jn. 10. 7–18 and the Parable of the Good Shepherd in Lk. 15. 3–7 (cf. Mt. 18. 12–14). The theme is taken up later in the NT, e.g. in Heb. 13. 20 and 1 Pet. 2. 25 and 5. 4. In early Christian art Christ was frequently represented (e.g. in the *catacombs) as the Good Shepherd with a lamb upon His shoulders. The Second Sunday after *Easter is known as 'Good Shepherd Sunday', on account of the Gospel for the day.

GORCUM MARTYRS, The.
A group of nineteen religious and secular priests who were put to death by *Calvinists at Briel on 9 July 1572, after the capture of Gorcum (S. Holland) by the Gueux (26 June 1572). Eleven of the martyrs were friars of the *Franciscan convent at Gorcum. They were beatified by Clement X in 1675 and canonized by *Pius IX on 29 June 1867. Feast day, 9 July.

W. *Estius, *Historia Martyrum Gorcomiensium* (Douai, 1603), repr. in *AA.SS.*, Jul. II (1721), pp. 736–847. J. Meerbergen, *Die HH. Martelaren van Gorcum* (Tongerloo, 1928). G. Hesse, 'De oudere Historiografie der HH. Martelaren van Gorcum' in *Collectanea Franciscana Neerlandica*, ii (1931), pp. 447–98.

GORDON RIOTS (also No Popery Riots).
The riots that broke out on 2 June 1780 when a mob, headed by Lord George Gordon, an eccentric and fanatic, marched to Parliament with a petition for the repeal of the *Catholic Relief Act of 1778. The huge procession of demonstrators carried flags with the legend 'No Popery', and, after pillaging the houses of Catholics, the rioters became completely out of hand and held the City of London until, at the personal command of George III, they were dispersed by the military. 210 persons were killed in the streets and another 75 died of wounds. Lord George Gordon, after being acquitted on a charge of high treason (1781), became a Jew and finally (1793) died insane in Newgate prison.

J. P. de Castro, *The Gordon Riots* (1928), with bibl. The proceedings of the trial of Gordon for high treason on 5th and 6th Feb. 1781, taken in shorthand by S. Gurney, are repr. in *A Complete Collection of State Trials and Proceedings for High Treason and other Misdemeanours*, ed. T. R. Howell, xxi (1814), cols. 485–652; the trial of H. J. Maskell, also connected with the riot, is pr. ib., cols. 653–88. *The Life of Lord George Gordon* by his friend and admirer, Robert Watson (London, 1795). Modern life by P. Colson, *The Strange History of Lord George Gordon* (London, 1937). L. Stephen in *D.N.B.*, xxii (1890), p. 197 f., s.v. 'Gordon, Lord George'.

GORDON'S CALVARY.
The site outside the Damascus Gate in the north wall of *Jerusalem which is held by some modern archaeologists to be the place of Christ's Crucifixion. As against the traditional site of the *Holy Sepulchre, this place was first proposed by O. Thenius in 1849. It derives its usual name from General C. G. Gordon, a strong advocate of it. It is a cliff with weathermarks which have a certain likeness to the features of a human countenance (cf. Jn. 19. 17: 'the place of a skull'), and in its favour is also the fact that it was indisputably outside Jerusalem, whereas the traditional site may have been within the city, even in A.D. 30. Near by is a tomb, known as the 'Garden Tomb', which advocates of Gordon's Calvary hold to have been the site of Christ's burial.

C. G. Gordon, *Reflections in Palestine 1883* (1884), pp. 1–3. See further general works, s.v. *Calvary* and *Jerusalem*.

GORE, CHARLES (1853–1932), Bp. of *Oxford.
Educated at Harrow and Balliol College, Oxford, he was elected a Fellow of Trinity College, Oxford, in 1875. From his schooldays he had been a High Churchman, and in 1884, on H. P. *Liddon's recommendation, was appointed first principal of Pusey House, Oxford. His independent mind, combined with an almost prophetic strength of character, brought a new strand into the Anglo-Catholic Movement. In his concern to bring Catholic principles to bear on social problems and to come to terms with OT criticism, he exercised great influence on the younger generation at Oxford. When in 1889 *Lux Mundi (q.v.) appeared under Gore's editorship, his own essay on 'The Holy Spirit and Inspiration' caused disquiet among many of the older and more conservative school of High Church theologians. In *The Ministry of the Christian Church* (1888; new ed., 1919, by C. H. *Turner) he upheld Catholic teaching about episcopacy, largely in criticism of E. *Hatch's *Bampton Lectures. His own Bampton Lectures (1891) on 'The Incarnation of the Son of

God' were a popular exposition of the *Chalce-donian Doctrine of the Person of Christ. They were supplemented by his *Dissertations* on allied subjects in 1895.

Meanwhile Gore had been actively con-cerned with the foundation of the *Community of the Resurrection (now at Mirfield), and, in 1893, he became vicar of Radley, Berks, settling the community in the vicarage. From 1894 to 1902 he was Canon of *Westminster. Here he became widely known as a preacher and exe-gete, and several series of his NT expositions were afterwards issued as books. In his *Body of Christ* (1901), a work on the Eucharist, he set out the place of the Sacrament in the Christian life and also sought to re-formulate the doctrine of the Real Presence without *transubstantiation.

In 1902 he was consecrated Bp. of *Wor-cester and when, largely through his initiative, the diocese of Birmingham was established in 1905 he became its first bishop. Here in the civic life of Birmingham he was highly success-ful. In 1911 he was translated to Oxford. He was far less happy in this large rural diocese and became increasingly conscious of isolation through the trend of various theological con-troversies (*Foundations, *Reservation, &c.) and the absence of Catholic support in the Con-vocations. In 1919 he resigned his see. In his later years he continued to write in defence of the Christian faith. His trilogy, *Belief in God* (1921), *Belief in Christ* (1922), and *The Holy Spirit and the Church* (1924)—the three works being subsequently reissued in a single volume as *The Reconstruction of Belief*—was very widely read and appreciated. After 1920 his attitude towards certain developments in Anglo-Catholicism became increasingly criti-cal, and in 1925 he summarized his position in *The Anglo-Catholic Movement To-day*; but he remained a fervid apologist for High Church principles until his death. His other writ-ings include *The Question of Divorce* (1911), *The Religion of the Church* (1916), and *Jesus of Nazareth* (Home University Library, 1929).

G. L. Prestige, *The Life of Charles Gore*. A Great English-man (1935). G. Crosse, *Charles Gore* (1932); A. Mansbridge, *Edward Stuart Talbot and Charles Gore* (1935). W. R. *Inge, 'Bishop Gore and the Church of England' (anon.), in *Edinburgh Review*, ccvii (1908), pp. 79–104; repr. in Inge's *Outspoken Essays*, i (1919), pp. 106–36. Alwyn Dunelm [A. T. P. Williams] in *D.N.B., 1931–1940*, pp. 349–53. J. Carpenter, *Gore. A Study in Liberal Catholic Thought* (1960).

GORGONIA, St. (d. *c*. 370), sister of St. *Gregory Nazianzen (q.v.) and St. *Caesarius. She is known almost exclusively through St. Gregory's panegyric (*orat.* 8) which represents her as of a pious and generous disposition. An incident in her life has sometimes (but probably wrongly) been taken as an early in-stance of devotion to the Reserved Sacrament. In acc. with contemporary custom she was not baptized until the end of her life. Feast day, 9 Dec.

Gregory's *Oratio* is repr. in J. P. Migne, *PG*, xxxv, 787–818. H. Thurston, S.J., 'The Early Cultus of the Reserved Eucharist' in *J.T.S.*, xi (1909–10), pp. 275–9.

GORHAM CASE. In 1847 the Rev. G. C. Gorham was presented by the Lord Chancellor to the vicarage of Brampford Speke in the diocese of *Exeter. The Bp. of Exeter, H. *Phillpotts, who suspected his orthodoxy, examined him, found him unsound on the doctrine of *baptismal regeneration, and refused to institute him to the living. After a complicated lawsuit, Gorham appealed to the recently formed *Judicial Committee of the Privy Council, which, attributing to him a view which he did not hold, declared it to be not contrary to the doctrine of the C of E. The decision gave great offence to High Church-men and aroused a storm of controversy. Over 60 books and pamphlets were published, and many seceded to Rome, including H. E. *Manning and R. I. *Wilberforce. As the Bp. of Exeter still refused to institute, Gorham was eventually instituted by Abp. J. B. *Sumner. The case had the result of drawing attention to the limitations of the Privy Council as an ecclesiastical court of appeal.

J. C. S. Nias, *Gorham and the Bishop of Exeter* (1951), with full bibl. details of pamphlets and other contemporary literature.

GÖRRES, JOHANN JOSEPH VON (1776–1848), German Catholic author. A native of Coblenz, he was educated under the deep influence of the rationalism of the 18th cent. As a youth he was an enthusiastic supporter of the French Revolution, but a stay at Paris in 1799–1800 disillusioned him. In 1800–6 he taught natural science at Coblenz. The study of J. G. *Herder and F. W. J. *Schelling awakened his religious interests, which found expression in his *Glaube und Wissen* (1805), a work of largely pantheistic character. In 1806–7 he lectured at Heidelberg university, mainly on historical and literary subjects. Here he came into contact with the leaders of German Romanticism, whose love of the religious history of the past inspired his *Mythengeschichte der asiatischen Welt* (2 vols., 1810). During the Napoleonic wars he took up the cause of German independence and was for a time an immensely popular figure. In 1814 he started the first great German newspaper, the *Rheinischer Merkur*. After the Peace of Paris (1815) he met with increasing hostility from the reactionary Prussian government and his paper was suppressed in 1816. In *Teutsch-land und die Revolution* (1819) he demanded liberty and a fuller place for the Catholic Church in public life. An order of arrest followed, but Görres escaped by flight to Strassburg. In 1824 he formally returned to the faith of the RC Church. In 1827 Ludwig I of Bavaria offered him a professorship at Munich university, where he became the centre of a circle of famous Catholic scholars, among whom were J. J. I. *Döllinger and J. A. *Möhler. From 1828 to 1832 they pub-lished the influential periodical *Eos*, which opposed Catholic ideals to the contemporary rationalism. There followed his *Christliche Mystik* (4 vols., 1836–42), which, though un-critical in the use of sources and sometimes fanciful, gave a strong impulse to the study of the mystics. When, in 1837, the Abp. of Cologne, Clemens August von *Droste-Vischering, was deposed and imprisoned by the Prussian government, Görres took up his cause in his tract *Athanasius* (1837), which brought all Catholic Germany to the defence of the Church. Another treatise, *Die Triarier* (1838), directed against the defenders of the government, received special Papal approval. His last years were darkened by the scandal round Lola Montez which resulted in the deposition of several professors belonging to his circle. A brilliant writer, he devoted himself unstintingly to the cause he had at heart. His work contributed considerably to the spread of Catholic ideas in modern Germany.

The 'Görres-Gesellschaft zur Pflege der Wissenschaft im katholischen Deutschland' was founded at Coblenz on the centenary of Görres' birth (25 Jan. 1876) to promote scientific and historical studies on Catholic principles. Suppressed by the Nazis in 1941, when its property was confiscated, it was reconstituted in 1948. It has published, *inter alia*, two important periodicals, the *Historisches Jahrbuch* and *Oriens Christianus*. Collected ed. of Görres' writings, Munich, 9 vols., 1854–74; crit. ed. by W. Schellberg under auspices of the Görres-Gesellschaft (Cologne, 1926 ff.). Lives by J. Galland (Freiburg i.Br., 1876), J. N. Sepp (Nördlingen, 1877; ed. 2, Dresden, 1896), W. Schellberg (Cologne, 1926), and others. Selection from the large German literature on Görres cited in J. Grisar, S.J., in *L.Th.K.*, iv (1932), cols. 582–5.

GORTON, SAMUEL (*c.* 1592–1677), founder of the 'Gortonites'. Born in Lancashire, he worked as a clothier in London for some time before he sailed *c.* 1636 for Boston, Mass., in the hope of enjoying complete religious freedom. Of a fiery and difficult temperament, he found himself engaged in continual conflict with the civil authorities in America. He gradually came to hold many unorthodox doctrines, e.g. he denied that of the Trinity and professed faith in *conditional immortality. Further difficulties with the civil powers led him to return to England in 1644, where he published an attack on what he held to be the repressive policy of the Massachusetts government, *Simplicitie's Defence against Seven-Headed Policy* (1646). He died in America. His followers survived as a sect till the middle of the 18th cent.

His *Simplicitie's Defence* and a letter to Nathaniel Morton are repr. in P. Force (ed.), *Tracts and Other Papers Relating Principally to the Origin, Settlement and Progress of the Colonies in North America*, iv (1846); further letters in *Collections of the Massachusetts Historical Society*, Ser. 4, vii (1865), pp. 601–31. Lives by J. M. Mackie ('The Library of American Biography', ed. J. Sparks, Ser. 2, v, 1845) and Adelphos Gorton (Philadelphia, 1907). C. Goodwin in *D.N.B.*, xxii (1890), pp. 251–3.

GOSCELIN (d. *c.* 1099), English *hagiographer. He is believed to have been born at or near Terouanne, in France, and entered the *Benedictine monastery of St. Bertin's at *St. Omer. Acc. to his own account he accompanied Bp. Hermann of *Salisbury (d. 1078) to Rome before the Council of *Reims in 1049 and went with him to England, probably in 1053. Here he visited a number of abbeys and cathedrals where he collected material for Lives of the saints, e.g. those of St. *Etheldreda at *Ely,

now lost, of St. *Ivo at Ramsey, and the important biography of St. *Swithun. His chief works were written at the monastery of St. *Augustine of *Canterbury, where he composed two Lives of the saint and a description of the translation of his relics in the year 1091, dedicated to St. *Anselm, as well as a biography of St. *Mildred. His works are normally based on older sources, but his habit of embellishing them with the products of his own imagination lessens their historical value.

One of Goscelin's lives of St. Augustine (the *Historia Maior*) is repr. from J. *Mabillon in *A.A.SS.*, Mai. VI (1688), pp. 375–95, also in J. P. Migne, *PL*, lxxx, 43–94; the other (the *Historia Minor*) is repr. from the appendix to J. L. *d'Achéry's ed. of the works of Lanfranc in J. P. Migne, op. cit. cl, 743–64; the account of the translation of St. Augustine's relics is pr. in *A.A.SS.*, loc. cit., pp. 411–30 and 432–43; repr. in J. P. Migne, op. cit., clv, 13–46. Other lives repr. from the various entries in *A.A.SS.* in J. P. Migne, op. cit., clv, 47–116. *Histoire littéraire de la France*, viii (1747), pp. 660–77, with detailed list of his works. 'Liber Confortatorius' ed. C. H. Talbot, *Studia Anselmiana*, 37 (Rome, 1955), pp. 1–117. T. A. Archer in *D.N.B.*, xxii (1890), p. 253 f., s.v.

GOSPEL (Gk. εὐαγγέλιον, Old Eng. *godspel*, 'good news'). (1) The central content of the Christian revelation, the glad tidings of redemption. Hence Christ's own preaching is a 'Gospel' (Mk. 1. 14 f.). The use of the word in Christian vocabulary probably comes from the OT, and perhaps Christ Himself quoted Is. 61. 1, where the *Septuagint has the verb εὐαγγελίζομαι. For a pre-Christian pagan use of the word, cf. an inscription from Priene (9 B.C.), where Augustus's birthday is said to have been 'for the world the beginning of things which owing to him are *glad tidings*'. (2) Somewhat later the word came to be used as a title for the written books in which the Christian Gospel was set forth. The usage probably originated from the occurrence of the word in the opening sentence of Mk. (1. 1). As there was but one single Good News, the separate Gospels were distinguished as 'the Gospel *according* to Matthew' (τὸ εὐαγγέλιον κατὰ Ματθαῖον), etc. The unique authority belonging to the four Gospels of Mt., Mk., Lk., and Jn. was fully established by the middle of the 2nd cent. (e.g. *Tatian's *Diatessaron, *Irenaeus). The so-called '*Apocryphal Gospels' (q.v.), which mostly arose in heretical circles, are wholly inferior works of later date and virtually devoid of historical value. They never seriously challenged the authority of the canonical Gospels. See also entries on separate Gospels; also *Synoptic Problem* and *Form-criticism*.

General works on the Gospels include B. F. *Westcott, *An Introduction to the Study of the Gospels* (1851; ed. 8, 1895); R. C. *Trench, *Studies in the Gospels* (1867); J. C. Hawkins, *Horae Synopticae* (1899); F. C. *Burkitt, *Two Lectures on the Gospels* (1901); V. H. Stanton, *The Gospels as Historical Documents* (3 vols., 1903–20); J. *Wellhausen, *Einleitung in die drei ersten Evangelien* (1905); F. C. Burkitt, *The Gospel History and its Transmission* (1906); G. *Salmon, *The Human Element in the Gospels* (1907); B. H. *Streeter, *The Four Gospels. A Study of Origins* (1924); B. S. Easton, *The Gospel before the Gospels* (1928); V. Taylor, *The Gospels. A Short Introduction* (1930); id., *Formation of the Gospel Tradition* (1933); R. H. Lightfoot, *History and Interpretation in the Gospels* (1934); C. C. Torrey, *The Four Gospels. A New Translation* [1934]; M. *Dibelius, *Gospel Criticism and Christology* (1935); R. H. *Lightfoot, *Locality and Doctrine in the Gospels* (1938).

GOSPEL (in the Liturgy). In the Eucharistic rite, the lection from the Gospels proper to each Mass. It varies greatly in length, from one or two verses to a whole chapter or more. It always occupies the last place (i.e. after the Epistle and other lections, if any) as the position of honour. Traditionally it is the privilege of the Deacon to read it, though at one time it was read at *Constantinople on Easter Day by the Bishop and at *Alexandria by the Archdeacon (*Sozomen, *H.E.*, VII. xix). It was formerly read from the *ambo on the north side of the nave, the deacon facing south, nowadays at High Mass acc. to the Roman rite at a point outside, but near to, the sanctuary, with the reader facing north.

In the W. rite, the deacon, bearing the book, goes to the appointed place accompanied by *subdeacon,*thurifer, and *acolytes, and before beginning to read sings 'Dominus vobiscum', announces the place, makes the *sign of the cross on the book and on himself and censes the book. The Gospel is then read in its proper tone and at the end the deacon himself is censed. The use of lights at the Gospel is already mentioned by St. *Jerome (*Bethlehem, A.D. 378). From the earliest times it has been the custom for the congregation to stand at the Gospel; cf. the rubric in the BCP (inserted by J. *Cosin in 1661). See also *Last Gospel*.

Jungmann (ed. 1949), i, pp. 545–62; Eng. tr. (New York, etc., 1951), pp. 442–55), with reff.

GOSPELLER. The person who reads or sings the Gospel at the *Eucharist. The word is used esp. of the deacon who is selected by the Bishop from among the newly ordained to perform this function at an Ordination Mass.

GOTHER, JOHN (d. 1704), RC controversialist. A native of Southampton, he came from a *Presbyterian family and was converted to the RC faith at an early age. In 1668 he entered the English College at Lisbon, where he was ordained priest and later became prefect and supervisor of studies. Being sent to England in 1682, he defended the RC cause during the controversies under *James II. In 1685 he published the first part of his famous work, *A Papist Misrepresented and Represented*, the second and third parts following in 1687. It evoked a long line of answers from E. *Stillingfleet and other Anglican divines. After the Revolution of 1689 Gother became chaplain at Warkworth Castle, where he received R. *Challoner into the RC Church. There he also wrote several treatises on doctrinal subjects such as *Transubstantiation and the use of *images, as well as devotional books on hearing Mass, Confession, and other religious duties.

His writings were edited by W. Crathorne, *Spiritual Works* (16 vols., 1718–36).

GOTHIC VERSION. Acc. to *Philostorgius (*H.E.*, ii, 5), *Socrates (*H.E.*, iv, 33), and *Sozomen (*H.E.*, vi, 37), the Greek Bible was translated into the Gothic language by the *Arian bishop *Ulphilas (d. 383). Of the NT only 2 Cor. and considerable portions of the four Gospels and the other Pauline Epp. survive. Of the OT only three short fragments of Ezra and Neh. exist. These MSS. all date from the period of Ostrogothic rule in Italy (489–555). Among the NT MSS. is the celebrated 'Codex Argenteus', written in gold and silver letters upon purple vellum, and now at Uppsala; it contains more than half of the text of the Gospels.

The Gospels were publd. from the 'Codex Argenteus' by A. Uppström (Uppsala, 1854); photographic facsimile ed. of this codex issued by order of the Senate of University of Uppsala, with introd. by O. von Friesen, Uppsala [1928]. Full text ed. W. Streitberg (Heidelberg, 1908–10). G. W. [S.] Friedrichsen, *The Gothic Version of the Gospels. A Study of its Style and Textual History* (1926); id., *The Gothic Version of the Epistles. A Study of its Style and Textual History* (1939). E. *Nestle in *P.R.E.* (ed. 3), iii (1897), pp. 59–61, s.v. 'Bibelübersetzungen, 3a. Die gothische Bibelübersetzung des Ulfila'. A. Kleinhans, O.F.M., in *E.C.*, vi (1951), cols. 960 f., s.v. 'Gothica, Versione della Bibbia'. G. W. S. Friedrichsen, *Gothic Studies* (Oxford, 1961). See also bibl. to *Ulphilas.

GOTHIC VESTMENTS. The name popularly given to Eucharistic *vestments of medieval shape and pattern, the *stole and *maniple being long and narrow, and the *chasuble circular, or nearly so, when laid out flat. The name is applied by contrast with the (esp. post-*Tridentine) Roman pattern, in which the stole and maniple are broad and short, and the chasuble approximately rectangular. The older shape was that generally used, at any rate at first, when vestments were revived in the C of E in the 19th cent. In recent years Gothic vestments, which never became entirely obsolete, have reappeared in many places in the RC Church, esp. in churches and religious communities influenced by the *Liturgical Movement.

GOTTESFREUNDE. A group of 14th cent. mystics in the Rhineland and Switzerland who conceived of themselves as the 'friends of God', probably on the basis of such passages as Jas. 2. 23 and Jn. 15. 14. Over against the seeming externality of certain aspects of ecclesiastical life, they stressed the transforming personal union of their souls with God. For the most part they remained within the Church, though some of the more extreme became organized into separate societies with a *pantheistic theology. The '*Theologia Germanica' came from these circles. Their chief sources of inspiration were *Eckhart, J. *Tauler, and H. *Suso, and the movement had connexions with the '*Brethren of the Common Life' in the Netherlands.

Works by R. Merswin and Sieben ed. P. Strauch, *Schriften aus der Gottesfreund-Literatur* (Altdeutsche Textbibliothek, xxii, xxiii, and xxvii; 1927–9). Id. in *P.R.E.* (ed. 3), xvii (1906), pp. 203–27, s.v. 'Rulman Merswin und die Gottesfreunde', with bibl. to date. A. Jundt, *Les Amis de Dieu au quatorzième siècle* (1879). K. Rieder, *Der Gottesfreund vom Oberland. Eine Erfindung des Strassburger Johanniter Bruders Nikolaus von Löwen* (1905); important critique by P. Strauch in *Zeitschrift für deutsche Philologie*, xxxix (1907), pp. 101–36. J. B. Schoemann, S.J., *Die Rede von den 15 Graden. Rheinische Gottesfreunde-Mystik* (Germanische

Studien, Hft. lxxx; 1930). On the name, E. Peterson, 'Der Gottesfreund. Beiträge zur Geschichte eines religiösen Terminus' in *Z.K.G.*, xlii (1923), pp. 161–202.

GOTTHARD, St. (d. 1038), also Godehard, Bp. of Hildesheim.

A native of Reichersdorf in Bavaria, he received the monastic habit at Nieder-Altaich in 990 where he rose to be prior and later abbot. His success as a ruler attracted the attention of the Emp. Henry I (who when Duke of Bavaria had been present at Gotthard's installation), who later commissioned him to reform many of the monasteries in Upper Germany. In 1022 he became Bp. of Hildesheim, where he was an ardent and successful ruler. It is said that the famous St. Gotthard Pass in the Alps takes its name from a former chapel dedicated to him on the summit. Feast day, 4 May.

Two lives by his disciple, Wolfher, the one written shortly after his death, the other *c.* thirty years later, ed. G. Pertz, in *M.G.H.*, Scriptores, xi (1854), pp. 167–218, with introd., pp. 162–5. Some letters addressed to him are ed. by K. Strecker, ib., Epistolae Selectae, iii (1925), pp. 59–71 and 108–110. Modern lives by F. X. Sulzbeck (Ratisbon, 1863) and O. J. Blecher (Hildesheim, 1931). J. Machens in *L.Th.K.*, iv (1932), col. 563, s.v. 'Godehard'.

GOTTSCHALK (*c.* 805–*c.* 868),

heterodox monk and theologian. A son of the Saxon count Bruno, he was compelled by his parents to enter the *Benedictine abbey of *Fulda as an oblate. Having fled from the monastery before receiving major orders, he was absolved by the Synod of Mainz (829) of his monastic profession. But owing to the objection of the newly elected abbot, *Rabanus Maurus, the dispensation was cancelled, and on his enforced return to the religious life he was assigned to the monastery of Orbais in the diocese of Soissons. Here he devoted himself to the study of theology and elaborated an extreme doctrine of Divine predestination. Basing himself on the teaching of St. *Augustine and St. *Fulgentius, he seems to have taught a double predestination, acc. to which not only are the good predestined to blessedness but the wicked also to damnation. His opponent, *Hincmar of *Reims (q.v.), whose 'De una et non trina Deitate' and 'De Praedestinatione' are directed against him, also accused him of teaching *supralapsarianism, and of having denied the universal saving will of God as well as human free-will. Although Gottschalk found defenders in *Walafrid Strabo, St. *Prudentius of Troyes, Servatus *Lupus, *Ratramnus, and others, his teaching was condemned at the Synod of Mainz of 848 and again at *Quiercy in 849. He was deprived of the priesthood, which he had obtained uncanonically, and imprisoned for the rest of his life in the monastery of Hautvillers. From there he carried on his feud with Hincmar, whom he accused of *Sabellianism for having altered the words 'Trina Deitas' of the Vespers hymn of the Common of Many Martyrs to 'Una Deitas'. He died unreconciled in a state bordering on insanity, broken by his privations. His pronounced Augustinianism attracted the sympathetic notice of the *Jansenists in the 17th cent.

Very few of Gottschalk's writings were known until the discovery of a collection in the Berne MS. (Bibl. de la Ville 83) by G. *Morin, O.S.B., in 1930; cf. G. Morin, 'Gottschalk retrouvé' in *R. Bén.*, xliii (1931), pp. 302–12. Crit. ed. of texts in C. Lambot, O.S.B. (ed.), *Œuvres théologiques et grammaticales de Godescalc d'Orbais* (S.S.L., fasc. xx; 1945); id., *Godescalc*. Sa vie, ses œuvres, ses doctrines (ib., in preparation). The Schedula Gothescaldi, 'Quod Trina Deitate dici Possit', is pr. in the ed. of Hincmar in J. P. Migne, *PL*, cxxv, 475–9; Poems ed. L. Traube in *M.G.H.*, Poetae III (1896), pp. 707–38. N. Fickermann, 'Wiedererkannte Dichtungen Gottschalks' in *R. Bén.*, xliv (1932), pp. 314–21.

GOULBURN, EDWARD MEYRICK (1818–97), Dean of *Norwich.

Educated at Eton and Balliol College, Oxford, he was a Fellow of Merton from 1841 to 1846. In 1847 he became chaplain to S. *Wilberforce and in 1849 headmaster of Rugby. In 1850 he preached the *Bampton Lectures on the Resurrection of the Body (publd. 1851). His dislike of the liberal tradition upheld by his predecessors at Rugby, T. *Arnold and A. C. *Tait, led to a decline in numbers and in 1857 he felt obliged to resign. In 1859 he became vicar of St. John's, Paddington, and in 1866 Dean of Norwich. Here he upheld a strict but moderate ecclesiastical orthodoxy and published his *Thoughts on Personal Religion* (1862) and *The Pursuit of Holiness* (1869), both very popular in their day. He was also the author of the Life of J. W. *Burgon (2 vols., 1892), *Reminiscences of C. P. Golightly* (1886), and of several other works.

B. Compton, *Edward Meyrick Goulburn* (1899).

GRABE, JOHANNES ERNST (1666–1711),

Anglican divine of German birth. Born and educated at Königsberg, where he was appointed Privatdozent in 1685, he was led to question the validity of Lutheran orders and contemplated becoming a RC. On the recommendation of P. J. *Spener, however, he made his way to England in 1697 in the belief that here he would find a Church possessing the *Apostolic succession. He was ordained to the priesthood and entered into close relations with the *Nonjurors, but without losing his esteem for the Establishment. A royal pension having been soon settled on him, Grabe gave himself up to researches into the texts of the Bible and the early Fathers. His published writings included *Spicilegium SS. Patrum ut et haereticorum seculi post Christum natum I, II, et III* (2 vols., 1698–9), editions of the *First Apology* of St. *Justin (1700) and of St. *Irenaeus (1702), and an edition of a considerable portion of the *Septuagint based on the *Codex Alexandrinus (1707–9).

R. Hooper in *D.N.B.*, xx (1890), p. 306 f., s.v.; J. Erdmann in *P.R.E.* (ed. 3), vii (1899), p. 56 f., s.v. On his ed. of the Septuagint, H. B. *Swete, *An Introduction to the Old Testament in Greek* (1900), pp. 182–4.

GRABMANN, MARTIN (1875–1949),

historian of medieval philosophy. He was born at Winterzhofen, ordained priest in 1898, and appointed professor of theology and philosophy at Eichstätt in 1906. In 1913 he became professor of Christian philosophy at Vienna university and in 1918 professor of theology at

Munich. His works deal chiefly with the history of medieval philosophy and theology. Among them are *Die Lehre des heiligen Thomas von Aquin von der Kirche* (1903), *Die Geschichte der scholastischen Methode* (1909–11), *Mittelalterliches Geistesleben* (3 vols., 1926–56), *Der lateinische Averroismus* (1931), *Die Werke des heiligen Thomas von Aquin* (1931), *Die Geschichte der katholischen Theologie* (1933), and *Methoden und Hilfsmittel des Aristoteles-Studiums im Mittelalter* (1939). Accessible in English is *Thomas Aquinas* (1928), a brief compendious exposition.

Festschrift for Grabmann's 60th birthday, entitled *Aus der Geisteswelt des Mittelalters* (B.G.P.M., Supplementband iii, 2 Hftt., 1935), with bibl. to date [i, pp. xxiii–xxxv]. Autobiographical introduction appended to Grabmann's *Mittelalterliches Geistesleben*, iii (1956), pp. 1–9, and bibl. by L. Ott, pp. 10–35.

GRACE. In Christian theology, the supernatural assistance of God bestowed upon a rational being with a view to his sanctification. While the necessity of this aid is generally admitted, the manner of it has been a subject of discussion among Christians since the 4th cent.

The Scriptural doctrine, though fragmentary, is historically of the utmost importance because of the way in which isolated texts have been handled in controversy. *Adam before the Fall was righteous, possessed of free-will, and under probation (Gen. 1. 31, 2. 16 f.). By the Fall he became sinful in God's sight (Gen. 3. 8–24) and involved all men in the consequences of his act (Rom. 5. 12, 14, 1 Cor. 15. 22). God desires the salvation of all men (Mt. 18. 14, 1 Tim. 2. 4), and Christ died for all men (Rom. 5. 18 f., 1 Tim. 2. 6, Heb. 2. 9). Man, being free, is responsible for his acts (Deut. 30. 15–20, Ezek. 18, Jn. 12. 47), but requires God's aid to do what is good (Jn. 6. 44, 65; 15. 4 f.; 1 Cor. 15. 10). Predestination is by the will of God (Rom. 9. 11–26), without regard to merit.

The first attempt at formulating a doctrine of grace is found in *Tertullian, whose original contribution was the idea of grace as the Divine energy working in the soul. Although at times he represented it as coercive, he elsewhere emphasized strongly man's responsibility (e.g. *Adv. Marc.* ii. 9). But the theology of Grace first emerged clearly in the controversy between St. *Augustine and *Pelagius, the complete divergence between whose doctrines was caused by their opposing views of human nature. To the former fallen man was 'one mass of sin' (*De div. quaest. ad Simplicianum* I. 2, 16); to the latter sin was only the following of an evil example. Logically, therefore, Augustine held that all deserved damnation (*De nat. et grat.* 5), from which, however, God's mercy reserved a fixed number of souls (*De corrept. et grat.* 39). The logical inference from this, though Augustine never taught it, was predestination to damnation. Grace was at all times necessary, since man by himself, in consequence of the Fall, could only sin (*De spir. et litt.* 5). In Baptism was received remission of sins and the grace of justification

(*De pecc. mer. et remiss.* III. 6, 9). Such grace was essential to the Christian for the performance of good works, and existed in an attenuated form in Jews and heretics. The apparent virtues of the heathen were only vices (*C. duas Epist. Pelag.* 3. 14). Against this teaching *Pelagianism held that grace was not needed for the performance of good actions, but was given in order that the commands of God might be more easily fulfilled (*De grat. Christi et de pecc. orig.* I., 26). Augustine at times called such Divine grace the gift of the Spirit. At other times he equated it with the Spirit Himself. It was not indefectible since for salvation the gift of perseverance was needed (*De corrept. et grat.* 10), but it is not unfair to say it was irresistible, for he stated that it unfailingly attained its object (ib. 38, 45).

Augustine endeavoured to preserve man's free-will by distinguishing between prevenient grace (i.e. grace antecedent to conversion) which is the free gift of God, and subsequent grace, in which the Divine energy co-operates with man after his conversion, and also by distinguishing sufficient from efficacious grace. The former, though adequate, is not in fact followed by its proper result, while the latter is so followed. The effect depends on the congruity or appropriateness of the grace, and that is of God's choice. In practice, though controversy led him to emphasize the influence of God's grace at the expense of man's free-will, he strongly emphasized man's responsibility (e.g. *De grat. et lib. arb.* 2, 5).

*Semi-Pelagianism endeavoured to mediate between the doctrines of Augustine and Pelagius. Its chief exponent, John *Cassian, while accepting Augustine's teaching on original sin, rejected total depravity, irresistible grace, and unconditional predestination (i.e. *ante praevisa merita*). Though grace was universally necessary, the will remained free at all stages.

The Second Council of *Orange (529) attempted to settle the question on an Augustinian basis, but with important modifications. Prevenient grace was taught, being rendered necessary by the Fall, but emphasis was laid on human co-operation after conversion. Reprobation (i.e. predestination to damnation) was anathematized. When in the 9th cent. *Gottschalk attempted to teach a sharpened Augustinianism, embodying double predestination and denying that Christ died for all, he was condemned by the Council of Mainz in 848.

Controversy revived in the 13th cent. St. *Thomas Aquinas in general followed the teaching of St. Augustine, though he differentiated more clearly between predestination to grace and that to glory and laid more stress on free-will. He was the first to distinguish accurately between 'habitual' and 'actual' grace (v. inf.). The teaching of *Duns Scotus, *Alexander of Hales, and St. *Bonaventure is of considerable interest. In general they are in sympathy with the teaching of Cassian, himself largely dependent on St. John *Chrysostom. Original sin was reduced to a 'loss of 'original righteousness', owing to the 'deprivation of supernatural gifts' that Adam suffered at the Fall, so that even the unbaptized could, by initiating some movement towards virtue, merit '*congruous grace'. Other striking medieval doctrines are Alexander's identification of prevenient grace with the 'general assistance' (*assistentia generalis*) of God and *Scotus's teaching on the timelessness of God in relation to the theology of grace.

Later controversies are in essence contained in the above. The Reformers returned to Augustinianism. M. *Luther, at any rate in his earlier period, and the followers of J. *Calvin taught absolute predestination, to which the latter added the indefectibility of grace. In Holland the followers of Jacobus Arminius (d. 1604) taught a doctrine (see *Arminianism*) closely resembling that of Cassian, which had affinities with Caroline thought on the subject in England.

The Church of England in the *Thirty-Nine Articles and the Church of Rome in the Council of *Trent substantially followed the Council of Orange. An attempt to introduce Calvinist teaching in the *Lambeth Articles of 1595 was unsuccessful. In the Roman Church there have been two serious controversies. The teaching of the later scholastics reappeared in the doctrines upheld by L. de *Molina, S.J. and the resultant controversy dragged on until 1607, when it was shelved by *Paul V. The Jansenist controversy arose from the posthumous publication in 1640 of the *Augustinus* by C. O. *Jansen, Bp. of Ypres (d. 1638). Two propositions allegedly contained in it, and embodying an exaggerated Augustinianism, were condemned by *Innocent X in 1653. It is disputed how far they accurately represent Jansen's position.

The relation between grace and the Sacraments has produced similar difficulties. There are four main lines of approach. (1) The Sacraments are symbols, which produce feelings in the recipients which enable them to receive grace. This denies a unique status to the Sacraments. (2) They are God's instruments for the direct causation of grace. This does not account for the difficulties that arise in the reception of, e.g., baptism in bad faith. (3) The theory of moral causation, i.e. the Church impetrates for the recipient the particular grace implied. The Sacrament becomes an acted prayer of the Church, and therefore of Christ. (4) The Sacraments convey a title exigent of grace. The title can only be appropriated if a right disposition is attained.

In the theology of grace, the following distinctions have been currently drawn:

(1) *Habitual or sanctifying grace*. The gift of God inhering in the soul, by which men are enabled to perform righteous acts. It is held to be normally conveyed in the Sacraments.

(2) *Actual grace*. A certain motion of the soul, bestowed by God *ad hoc* for the production of some good act. It may exist in the unbaptized.

(3) *Prevenient grace*. That form of actual

grace which leads men to sanctification before the reception of the Sacraments. It is the free gift of God ('gratuitous'), and entirely unmerited.

See also *Efficacious Grace, Sufficient Grace*.

The subject is treated at length in the standard textbooks of Dogmatic Theology. The Tridentine teaching is stated in full in D. *Soto, O.P., *Ad Sanctum Concilium Tridentinum de Natura et Gratia* (Venice, 1547). The Jesuit doctrine had its classical exponent in various works of F. Suarez, S.J. (q.v.). Cf. also D. *Petavius, S.J., 'De Lege et Gratia', pr. in his *Opus de Doctrina Temporum*, iii (new ed., Antwerp, 1703), pp. 212-55. G. H. Joyce, S.J., *The Catholic Doctrine of Grace* (1920; ed. 2, 1930). Studies by Anglicans include E. Jauncey, *The Doctrine of Grace up to the End of the Pelagian Controversy* (1925); N. P. *Williams, *The Grace of God* (1930); and A. G. Hebert, S.S.M., *Grace and Nature* (1937). J. Pohle in *C.E.*, vi (1909), pp. 689-710, s.v. 'Grace', and pp. 710-14, s.v. 'Grace, Controversies on', both with full bibl. H. R. Mackintosh in *H.E.R.E.*, vi (1913), pp. 364-7, s.v.; E. L. van Becelaere, ib., pp. 367-72, s.v. 'Grace, Doctrine of (Roman Catholic)', with valuable bibl. J. Van der Meersch in *D.T.C.*, vi (1920), cols. 1554-1687, s.v.; various writers, incl. E. *Brunner, in *R.G.G.* (ed. 2), ii (1928), cols. 1253-68, s.v. 'Gnade Gottes'.

GRACE AT MEALS (in earlier English, Graces). The custom of giving thanks before and after food is natural and not exclusively Christian. It was followed by Christ (Jn. 6. 11) and the Apostles (e.g. Acts 27. 35). In religious houses, and later in schools and colleges, fixed forms were provided, and are recited audibly at the principal meals. The *Breviarium Romanum* provides a form with the title *Benedictio Mensae*. Many other forms of grace are traditional among both RCs and other Christians.

E. von der Goltz, *Tischgebete und Abendmahlsgebete in der altchristlichen und in der griechischen Kirche* (T.U., xxix (2b), 1905). L. Gougaud, O.S.B., 'Notes sur les prières chrétiennes de la table' in *Rassegna Gregoriana*, viii (1909), col. 524-7. W. E. Scudamore in *D.A.C.*, i (1875), p. 745 f., s.v.; J. Baudot in *D.A.C.L.*, i (1910), cols. 713-16, s.v. 'Bénédiction de la table ou des aliments'. T. Barnes in *H.E.R.E.*, vi (1913), pp. 372-4 (with many examples of liturgical graces).

GRACE, Pilgrimage of. See *Pilgrimage of Grace*.

GRADINE (a word of French origin). A ledge above and behind the altar upon which the cross, candlesticks, and other ornaments may be placed. Such ledges became common from the 16th cent. Since the altar is properly a table, gradines are now very generally held to be the mark of a debased use, on the ground that the correct place for the ornaments is on the altar itself. See also *Retable*.

GRADUAL (Lat. *gradus*, 'step'). In the W. Church, the set of *antiphons, usually from the Psalms, sung immediately after the *Epistle. The name, which is found as far back as *Rabanus Maurus, derives from the practice of singing it either on the altar steps or while the *deacon was ascending the steps of the *ambo. Originally it was chanted only by the cantors or choir, and not till the later Middle Ages did the present practice of its recitation also by the priest become established. From the First Sunday after *Easter to the Saturday before *Whitsun the gradual is omitted. The word is also applied to the book containing such antiphons. The older Eng. form of the word is 'Grail'.

Jungmann (ed. 1949), i, 519-36; Eng. tr. (New York, 1951), pp. 421-35, with reff.

GRADUAL PSALMS, The. The group of Psalms, Pss. 120-34, each of which bears a title in Hebrew rendered by St. *Jerome 'canticum graduum', and in the AV 'A Song of Degrees' (RV, 'ascents'). Various explanations of the title have been offered, referring it (1) to the supposed literary character of the Psalms, as containing instances of a step-like progression, or (2) to the 'lifting-up' of the heart in praise, or (3) to the 'going up' of the Jews from Babylon to Jerusalem after the Exile, or most probably (4) to the 'going up' of pilgrims to Jerusalem for annual festivals.

In addition to comm. on Psalms (q.v.), see also W. Riedel, 'Die Stufenpsalmen' in *Neue Kirchliche Zeitschrift*, xvii (1906), pp. 43-56 and 83-105; J. Calès, 'Le Psautier des montées' in *Rech. S.R.*, xvii (1927), pp. 288-313, 434-44, 532-7, and xviii (1928), pp. 326-44 and 489-99.

GRAFFITI (*Ital.*). The name given to ancient inscriptions which are merely roughly or casually scratched and not properly carved. Christian graffiti are numerous, esp. in the *catacombs of Rome and at other ancient holy places. They generally take the form of memorials of the dead and prayers to God or the saints commemorated there, scratched by mourners, worshippers, or visitors.

G. B. *de Rossi, *La Roma sotterranea cristiana*, ii (1867), pp. 13-20. H. *Leclercq, O.S.B., in *D.A.C.L.*, vi (pt. 2; 1925), cols. 1453-1542, s.v. 'Graffites', with reff.

GRAFTON, RICHARD (d. *c.* 1572), printer of *Matthew's Bible and English Prayer Books. A London merchant, who had become an ardent supporter of the Reformation, he arranged *c.* 1536 with a fellow-merchant, Edward *Whitchurch, for the printing at Antwerp of the modified form of M. *Coverdale's translation known as Matthew's Bible. A copy was dispatched to T. *Cranmer on 13 Aug. 1537 and six more to T. *Cromwell on 28 Aug. Their enthusiastic reception led Grafton to arrange for a large edition at Paris, then noted for its paper and founts, from the press of François Regnault, and in Nov. 1538 copies of the NT, with the Latin text against the English, were put on sale in London. The printing of the whole Bible (the '*Great Bible') was completed in 1539; but shortly afterwards it was suspended by the *Inquisition. Grafton escaped to England and later the types were also rescued and brought over. Other works bearing the imprint of Grafton (mostly in conjunction with Whitchurch) were *The *Prymer* (q.v., 1540), the proclamation directing the Great Bible to be read in churches (6 May 1541), the English Gospels and Epistles (8 May 1546), the *First Book of *Homilies* (1547), and the First (1549) and Second (1552) *Books of Common Prayer*. Under *Mary he

lost his position as King's Printer, and for a time suffered imprisonment. In 1554 and again in 1557 he was elected M.P. for London and in 1563 for Coventry.

His Chronicle (2 vols., 1568) was repr. in 2 vols., London' 1809. J. A. Kingdon, *Incidents in the Lives of T. Poyntz and R. Grafton* (1895); id., *Richard Grafton, Citizen and Grocer of London and one time Master of his Company, Servant and Printer to Edward, Prince and King and First Treasurer General of Christ's Hospital* (1901). S. L. Lee in *D.N.B.*, xxii (1890), pp. 310-13.

GRAHAM, 'BILLY' (William Franklin Graham, 1918-), American evangelist. Born in North Carolina, he experienced conversion at the age of sixteen and began to preach while still at high school, and later as a student, first at the Bible Institute, Florida, then in Tennessee, and then at Wheaton College, Illinois, where he graduated. Having entered the Southern *Baptist ministry, in 1943 he took a leading part in the American 'Youth For Christ' movement. In 1948 he became President of Northwestern Schools, Minneapolis, and in 1949 began his first great evangelistic campaign at Los Angeles. Thereafter he toured U.S.A., making full use of radio and television. He first visited Great Britain in 1954 where he made a deep impression on large gatherings at Harringay and elsewhere.

GRAIL. An older form of the word **Gradual** (q.v.), derived through the Old French *grael* from the same root.

GRAIL, The Holy. In Medieval Romances, a vessel possessing spiritual powers and qualities, and affording, under certain conditions, mystical benefits to its beholders. The legend first appears in the *Perceval* of Chrestien de Troyes (? 1180-90), and, in a Christianized version, in the *Estoire dou Graal* (or *Joseph d'Arimatie*) of Robert de Boron (*c.* 1190). In the *Cistercian *Queste del Saint Graal* and in the *Parzifal* of Wolfram von Eschenbach (*c.* 1200) the legend of the Grail is incorporated with the stories of Arthur and the Round Table, and made to bear an exalted moral interpretation. The origins of the legend, which appears to contain elements of the most diverse provenance, are obscure. In the extant versions, the Grail itself is sometimes identified with the cup used by Christ in the *Last Supper, which later belonged to *Joseph of Arimathea, and its effects upon those who see it are made to correspond closely with the effects of Holy Communion upon communicants. The whole legend, however, remained within the field of secular literature, and was never recognized by any ecclesiastical authority.

The *Perceval* was ed. from a MS. of the Dukes of Burgundy at Brussels (MS. 11145) by C. Polvin, Brussels, 1866; Eng. tr. of this text by S. Evans, *The High History of the Holy Graal* (2 vols., Temple Classics, 1898; repr. in Everyman's Library [1910]). Further Eng. tr. of *The Quest of the Holy Grail* by W. W. Comfort, London, 1926. There is a very wide literature on the subject. Studies in English include A. Nutt, *Studies on the Legend of the Holy Grail*, with special reference to the Hypothesis of its Celtic Origin (Folk-Lore Society, xxiii; 1888); S. Evans, *In Quest of the Holy Grail*.

An Introduction to the Study of the Legend (1898); Dorothy Kempe, *The Legend of the Holy Grail, its Sources, Character and Development* (E.E.T.S., Extra Series, xcv, 1905), with reff. to edd. of Early English versions; Jessie L. Weston, *The Legend of Sir Percival* (Grimm Library, xvii and xix; 1906–9). Id., *From Ritual to Romance* (1920), pp. 130–54; R. S. Loomis, *Celtic Myth and Arthurian Legend* (New York, 1927), pp. 139–270; id., *Arthurian Tradition and Chrétien de Troyes* (New York, 1949), pp. 335–459. Jessie L. Weston in *E.B.* (ed. 11), xii (1911), p. 320 f., s.v. Further bibl. in *Chambers's Encyclopaedia*, vi (ed. 1950), p. 466.

GRANDE CHARTREUSE, La. The mother house of the *Carthusian Order, situated in the Dauphiné Alps, some 15 miles north of Grenoble. A primitive monastery on the site was built by St. *Bruno in 1084. It was many times destroyed by fire and rebuilt before the present monastery was begun in 1676. In 1904 the monks were forcibly ejected under the 'Association Laws' of 1901, and the building secularized. The famous liqueur was thereafter made by the expelled monks at Tarragona in Spain. In 1940 Carthusians were permitted to return to La Grande Chartreuse.

[C. M. Boutrais, O.S.B.,] *La Grande Chartreuse* (Grenoble, 1881, and numerous subsequent editions; abridged Eng. tr., 1893). L. H. Cottineau, O.S.B., *Répertoire topo-biblio-graphique des abbayes et prieurés* (Mâcon, 1935), cols. 1322–1324, s.v., for full reff.

GRANDMONT, Order of. French religious order, now extinct. It was founded by St. Stephen of Muret (*c.* 1054–1124). Its early history is uncertain, and its rule was not drawn up until 1143. The order established their mother house at Grandmont in Normandy under a prior. The discipline was severe, strict poverty and silence were observed, and the monks were popularly known as 'Bons Hommes'. From *c.* 1184 disputes arose between monks and lay brothers, and though these were temporarily allayed, discipline began to relax more and more. In 1643 a Strict Observance branch was formed, but it was short-lived, and the order came to an end in the French Revolution. There had been three houses in England (*c.* 1222–1464): Alberbury, Creswell, and Grosmont.

Rose Graham–A. W. Clapham, 'The Order of Grandmont and its Houses in England' in *Archaeologia*, lxxv (1926), pp. 159–210, with reff. Heimbucher, i, p. 326 f., with bibl.

GRATIAN (12th cent.; d. not later than 1179), author of the 'Concordantia Discordantium Canonum', better known as the 'Decretum Gratiani', and virtually the father of canon law. Next to nothing is known with any certainty about his life. He appears to have been a *Camaldolese (or possibly a Benedictine) monk and to have taught at *Bologna. His 'Decretum', which incorporates decisions of the Second *Lateran Council of 1139 and hence cannot be earlier than that year, prob. appeared *c.* 1150. It contains a vast collection of Patristic texts, conciliar decrees, and Papal pronouncements, arranged systematically and accompanied by comment. Though success was not immediate, it gradually grew in esteem and later received official recognition

as the first part of the *Corpus Iuris Canonici (q.v.). It was regularly glossed and commented on. *Dante (*Paradiso*, x, 103–5) assigns Gratian a place in paradise.

Crit. ed. of Decretum by J. H. Boehmer (Halle, 1747), revised by A. L. Richter (Leipzig, 1836), repr. in J. P. Migne, *PL*, clxxxvii. *Commemoratio Decreti Gratiani Octavo Recurrente Saeculo ab eius Editione* (Pontificum Institutum Utriusque Iuris, Rome, 1948; repr. from *Apollinaris*, xxi). J. F. R. von Schulte, 'Zur Geschichte der Literatur über das Dekret Gratians' in *Sb.* (Wien), lxiii (1870), pp. 299–352, lxiv (1870), pp. 93–142, and lxv (1870), pp. 21–76. A. Villien, S.J., and J. de Ghellinck, S.J., in *D.T.C.*, vi (1920), cols. 1727–2511; K. Guggenberger in *L.Th.K.*, iv (1932), col. 651, both s.v. *Studia Gratiana post Octava Decreti Saecularia* (Bonn, 1953 ff.; important). See also bibl. to *Canon Law* and *Corpus Iuris Canonici*.

GRATRY, AUGUSTE JOSEPH ALPHONSE (1805–72), French Catholic apologist. After a severe mental conflict, described in *Souvenirs de ma jeunesse* (published 1874 by A. Perraud), he was ordained priest in 1832. He was successively professor of the Petit Séminaire of Strasbourg (1828), director of the Collège Stanislas (1840), and chaplain of the École Normale Supérieure (1846). In 1861 he became Vicar-general of Orléans and in 1867 was elected a member of the French Academy. He was deeply concerned for the revival of Church life in France and took a principal part in the restoration of the *Oratory (under the title of the Immaculate Conception). He was among the *Inopportunists in opposing the definition of Papal Infallibility, but, after the *Vatican Council, submitted to the decrees. His many books, which sought to present the Christian faith to educated opinion and had a large circulation, include *De la connaissance de Dieu* (2 vols., 1853), *La Logique* (1855), *Les Sources, conseils pour la direction de l'esprit* (1861–2), *La Morale et la loi de l'histoire* (1868), and *Lettres sur la religion* (1869). His somewhat independent approach to theology, which included a proof of the existence of God by induction with the aid of the infinitesimal calculus, brought him into conflict with some of the authorities during his lifetime. His teaching had some affinities with *ontologism; but Gratry certainly rejected ontological doctrines in the form given them by N. *Malebranche.

Souvenirs de ma jeunesse (1874; autobiographical). A. Perraud, *Le Père Gratry. Ses derniers jours, son testament spirituel* (1872; Eng. tr., 1872); id., *Le Père Gratry, sa vie et ses œuvres* (1900); A. Chauvin, *Le Père Gratry d'après des documents inédits* (1901); J. Vaudon, *Une Âme de lumière, le Père Gratry* (1914). A. Largent in *D.T.C.*, vi (1920), cols. 1754–63, s.v.

GRAVAMEN (Med. Lat., a 'grievance'). A memorial sent from the Lower to the Upper House of *Convocation with a view to securing the remedy of disorders or grievances in the Church.

GRAVE-DIGGERS. See *Fossors*.

GRAY, GEORGE BUCHANAN (1865–1922), OT and Semitic scholar. In 1893 he was ordained to the *Congregational ministry, and from 1900 until his sudden death was professor of Hebrew and OT exegesis at Mansfield College, Oxford. He combined original and sound judgement with great knowledge of detail, and became one of the most respected OT scholars and teachers of his generation. Of outstanding merit were his volumes in the 'International Critical Commentaries'—*Numbers* (1903), *Isaiah I–XXVII* (1912), and *Job* (with S. R. *Driver, 1921). In his *Sacrifice in the Old Testament* (1925, posthumous) he made a notable contribution to OT Theology.

List of G. B. Gray's publd. writings in the last-named work, pp. ix–xi. G. R. Driver in *D.N.B., 1922–1930*, pp. 356–8.

GREAT AWAKENING, The. A name applied to a widespread religious revival which centred in New England in 1740–43. It was largely the outcome of the preaching of Jonathan *Edwards and G. *Whitefield, though both preachers discouraged the excessive emotionalism (dramatic preaching, abnormal bodily excitement, groanings, etc.) which marked the revival. Stress was laid on visible evidences of conversion and those who did not manifest such tokens of inward grace, whether clergy or laymen, were openly denounced as unregenerate. The general unsettlement led the General Court of Massachusetts in 1742 to forbid itinerant preaching, except with the consent of the resident clergyman. In the later 40's the Awakening spread to other parts of the U.S.A. J. Edwards's *Treatise concerning Religious Affections* (1746) was designed to discriminate between the healthy and morbid elements in the revival. Several separatist churches were the result, some of which later became the nucleus of the American *Baptists.

J. Tracy, *The Great Awakening* (Boston, 1842); W. M. Gewehr, *The Great Awakening in Virginia, 1740–90* (Durham, N.C., 1930); M. W. Armstrong, *The Great Awakening in Nova Scotia, 1776–1809* (Studies in Church History, vii; Chicago, 1948).

GREAT BIBLE, The. The edition of the English Bible which T. *Cromwell had ordered in Sept. 1538 to be set up in every parish church. It was not issued till the early summer of 1539 and was the work of M. *Coverdale, who had used as his basis *Matthew's Bible. The printing was begun in Paris, but owing to the hostility of the *Inquisition, Coverdale was forced to transfer such of the sheets as he could rescue and the type to London. Its handsome title-page, which represents God blessing the King, who is handing out copies of the Bible to T. *Cranmer and T. Cromwell, is usually held to be the work of Hans Holbein. In Apr. 1540, after extensive revision by Coverdale, the 'Great Bible' was reissued with an important preface by Cranmer; in this version it is sometimes known as 'Cranmer's Bible'. From its rendering of Jer. 8. 22 the Great Bible was also popularly known as the *Treacle Bible. It was printed by R. *Grafton (q.v.).

Darlow–Moule, i (1903), pp. 21–6; later edd., pp. 27–33, and passim. A. W. Pollard, *Records of the English Bible* (1911), pp. 17–24, with Documents, pp. 223–74, passim. J. Isaacs in H. Wheeler Robinson (ed.), *The Bible in its Ancient and English Versions* (1940), pp. 175–181. See also bibl. to Bible (*English Versions*).

GREATER ANTIPHONS, The. See *O-Antiphons*.

GREATER ENTRANCE, The (Gk. ἡ μεγάλη εἴσοδος). In the E. Church, the solemn procession just before the *Offertory at which the Eucharistic bread and wine are carried from the *prothesis to the *altar. See also *Lesser Entrance*.

GREECE, Christianity in. Christianity was first preached in Greece in the 1st cent., principally by St. *Paul, whose main centre was *Corinth. Under the Christian Empire the Greek clergy won favour with their people by their general support of the popular cause, often against the Byzantine court and patriarchate. In the *Iconoclastic Controversy the Greeks always stood firm in the cause of the images against the iconoclastic emperors. Meanwhile, during the 8th to 10th cents., Slavonic invaders from the north were hellenized and converted, chiefly by the exertions of the Greek clergy. During the Frankish occupation, from 1204 onwards, the Church, though subject to a RC archbishop, retained its E. character and its hold upon the affections of its people. When the Turks became masters of Greece in 1503, the Greek clergy were favoured; they were given positions as minor officials and also acted as the representatives of their own nation in dealing with the Turks. In the War of Independence it was Abp. Germanos of Patras who raised the standard of revolt in Morea (Peloponnese) in 1821.

The Greek Church is in communion with *Constantinople, though it repudiated hierarchical connexion with it in 1833. It is governed by the 'Holy Synod' of the nation, subject in several respects to state control. The clergy are practically unpaid, and as a rule combine some form of lay work with the exercise of their priesthood. The Metropolitan of Athens has a primacy of honour. There is a relatively small community of RCs (mainly of the Latin Rite), with Abps. of Athens, Corfu, and Naxos, and a very few Protestants.

Maximilian, Prince of Saxony, *Das christliche Hellas* (Leipzig, 1918). C. Papadopoulos, Ἱστορία τῆς Ἐκκλησίας τῆς Ἑλλάδος (Athens, 1920 [19th cent.]). A. Fortescue in *C.E.*, vi (1909), pp. 737–44; s.v.; H. Alivisatos in *R.G.G.* (ed. 2), ii (1928), cols. 1455–9, s.v. 'Griechenland'; J. Lippl in *L.Th.K.*, iv (1932), col. 696 f., s.v. 'Griechenland'.

GREEK (Biblical and Patristic). The basis of the Greek of both the *Septuagint and the NT is the Hellenistic Greek (known as the Κοινή or 'Common' dialect) which spread over the Near East as the result of the conquests of Alexander the Great (d. 323 B.C.). This was a simplified form of Attic Greek, with some contributions from other dialects, the more delicate refinements in the use of particles, prepositions, participial constructions, and use of moods being smoothed away. Hellenistic Greek in its literary form appears in such writers as Polybius (d. 122 B.C.), *Philo, and *Josephus. Until recently it was generally supposed that the differences between the common Hellenistic and Biblical Greek were due to the influence on the latter of Hebrew and Aramaic; but the papyrus documents discovered in thousands in Egypt in the last fifty years have shown that very many of the usages and phrases supposed to be Biblical are in fact part of the vernacular language of the time. Some Hebrew influence remains, esp. in the Septuagint (which in turn influenced the NT), but often this means no more than that, of two forms of phrase employed in the vernacular, that one is chosen which comes nearest to the Hebrew phraseology.

Subject to these general considerations, there are differences between different writers. In the Septuagint, the *Pentateuch and Is. are in good Hellenistic Greek; the other Prophets, the Pss., Chron. and most of Sam. and Kgs., are in inferior Greek, nearer to the vernacular. On the other hand, some of the later books (Dan., 1 Esdr., Est., Job, Prov., Wisd.) are more literary and deliberately artistic in style. In the NT, Luke is the most literary writer, then comes St. Paul and the author of Heb. St. Paul's style is educated Hellenistic Greek, but without deliberate literary refinements, while Heb. shows some conscious rhetoric. At the other end of the scale, Rev. is in an uneducated vernacular Greek, being frequently quite ungrammatical, though not more so than some of the papyri (the want of grammar, of course, disappears in the AV translation).

Apart from the general loss of the finer shades of Attic idiom, Hellenistic Greek is marked by such changes as the disappearance of the dual, a diminished use of the dative, interchange of the prepositions ἐν and εἰς, a tendency to amalgamate the perfect and aorist (leading in Patristic Greek to the gradual disuse of the perfect), an almost complete disuse of the optative, and modifications, too many to describe, in the use of many words. Just as in pronunciation the differentiation of vowels, and esp. of diphthongs, tends to become obliterated, so the whole system becomes that of a simple language for general utility, in place of the delicate sensitiveness of Attic Greek.

For the first three cents., Christian writers remained generally free from the influence of pagan literature. But when Christianity had become the religion of the Empire, Christians shared the education of the Greek world, and were moulded by the prevailing literary tendencies. These tendencies were preeminently a deliberate cultivation of Attic models, and a conscious elaboration of style fostered by the schools of rhetoric. *Patristic Greek is coloured by both these influences, found in varying degree in all the principal writers. Of the two most celebrated for their style, *Chrysostom, with his unselfconscious zeal for moral instruction, comes nearest to true Attic, while *Gregory of Nazianzus shows

the elaborate rhetoric of the schools in all its intentional artistry. The Fathers in general —*Basil the Great, the *Cyrils, *Athanasius, and others of less note—show the current manner of Byzantine Greek on a lower plane of achievement. In all, however, the language is progressively affected by modifications in the meanings of words necessitated by the requirements of Christian theology and philosophy. These can be followed only in a detailed Patristic lexicon. In general, however, it may be said that Biblical Greek is the common Hellenistic Greek of the people, somewhat modified by Hebrew or Aramaic influence, while Patristic Greek is the Byzantine Greek of the rhetoricians and literary artists, somewhat modified to suit the needs of Christian thought and terminology.

The standard Greek-English Dictionary for general purposes is that of H. G. Liddell and R. Scott (ed. 1, Oxford, 1843), constantly revised and extended by the orig. editors until the last ed. of 1897 (often reissued). In the present century a complete overhaul of the work was undertaken by H. S. Jones and R. Mackenzie with the help of a large team of scholars and issued in 10 parts [2 vols., 1925–40] as the 'New Edition'. From this 'New Edition', however, words and usages found only in Patristic and Byzantine authors were excluded, in view of the projected 'Lexicon of Patristic Greek' (successive editors H. B. *Swete, 1906–15; D. *Stone, 1915–41; F. L. Cross, 1941–8; G. W. H. Lampe, 1948–); fascc. i, 1961; ii, 1962. Of older lexicons, the most ambitious was that of H. *Stephanus (4 vols., Paris, 1572; new ed. in 10 vols., London, 1816–28; revised in 8 vols., Paris, 1831–65). Of lexicons for the vocabulary of the NT only, the best of the older dictionaries was C. L. W. Grimm–J. H. Thayer (Edinburgh, 1886). More recent are the successive edd. of E. Preuschen (Giessen, 1910; ed. 2 by W. Bauer, ib., 1928; since ed. 3, 1936, with Bauer's name only; ed. 4, 1952; adapted Eng. tr. of ed. 4 by W. F. Arndt and F. W. Gingrich (Cambridge, 1957); this admirable work takes full account of the new knowledge of Hellenistic Greek and has full bibliographies. On the theological aspects of NT vocabulary, there is the important *Theologisches Wörterbuch zum Neuen Testament*, ed. G. Kittel (1933 ff.). Good concise dictionary by A. *Souter, *A Pocket Lexicon to the Greek New Testament* (1916; often repr.).

Of NT Greek grammars, the most elaborate is A. Debrunner, *Friedrich Blass' Grammatik des neutestamentlichen Griechisch* (ed. 6, 1931). More modern in method is the illuminating work of J. H. Moulton, *A Grammar of New Testament Greek* (vol. i, Prolegomena, 1906; vol. ii, Accidence and Word-Formation, ed. W. F. Howard, 1919–29; esp. notable is Moulton's introd. in vol. i). L. Radermacher, *Neutestamentliche Grammatik. Das Griechisch des Neuen Testaments im Zusammenhang mit der Volkssprache* (Hb. N.T., I (1), 1911; ed. 2, 1925). A. T. Robertson, *A Grammar of the Greek New Testament in the Light of Historical Research* (1914). H. E. Dana–J. R. Mantey, *A Manual Grammar of the Greek New Testament* (1927). C. F. D. Moule, *An Idiom Book of New Testament Greek* (1953).

For Patristic Greek, in addition to the above, E. A. Sophocles, *Greek Lexicon of the Roman and Byzantine Periods, B.C. 146–A.D. 1100* (Boston, Mass., 1870). Much useful material of a lexical and factual kind also in J. C. *Suicer (q.v.), *Thesaurus Ecclesiasticus e Patribus Graecis* (2 vols., Amsterdam, 1682). For OT Greek, H. St. J. Thackeray, *A Grammar of the Old Testament in Greek*, vol. i (all publd., 1909), and R. Helbing, *Grammatik der Septuaginta* (2 vols., 1907–28). Cf. also F. M. Abel, O.P., *Grammaire du grec biblique* (1927).

Further important works include E. Hatch, *Essays in Biblical Greek* (1889); A. Thumb, *Die griechische Sprache im Zeitalter des Hellenismus* (1901); A. *Deissmann, *Licht vom Osten* (1908; ed. 4, 1923; Eng. tr. as *Light from the Ancient East*, 1910; revised from the 4th Germ. ed., 1927).

J. Vergote in *Dict. Bibl.*, Suppl. iii (1938), cols. 1320–69, s.v. 'Grec biblique', with good bibl. See also bibl. to *Papyrology*.

GREEN, THOMAS HILL (1836–82), philosopher. Educated at Rugby under E. M. *Goulburn and at Balliol College, Oxford, under B. *Jowett, he was elected a Fellow of Balliol in 1860 and, after a period of unsettlement, eventually (1866) became a tutor at Balliol, where his unaffected sincerity exercised a deep and permanent influence over many of his pupils. From 1878 until his early death he was Whyte Professor of moral philosophy at Oxford. In his later years he took an active part in projects for educational and social reform.

Green's main endeavour was to re-think and propagate in the English world the idealistic philosophical doctrines of I. *Kant and G. W. F. *Hegel. His position was largely worked out in polemic against the empirical views of D. *Hume and the then influential J. S. Mill. Theologically he owed much to F. D. *Maurice. He held that the analysis of consciousness proved that reality was an organic whole, a 'world of thought relations' and not a mere aggregate; that the evidence of art, morality, and religion all pointed to the spiritual nature of reality; that God, the eternal consciousness, was realized in each individual person; and that since personality alone gave meaning to the evolutionary process, the permanence and immortality of the individual were assured. The basis of the State was not an externally imposed coercive authority, but a desire for the common good (a 'general will').

Green's teaching exercised a great influence on the *Lux Mundi school, which rejected, however, its extreme *immanentism. His chief published works were his Introduction to an edition of Hume's Treatise of Human Nature (1875), Prolegomena to Ethics (ed. by A. C. Bradley, 1883), and his Lectures on the Principles of Political Obligation (1895; ed. B. *Bosanquet).

Most of Green's writings were collected by R. L. Nettle ship (3 vols., 1885–8). The 'Introduction to Hume' is in Vol. i; and a Memoir is prefaced to Vol. iii. W. H. Fair brother, The Philosophy of T. H. Green (1896). L. Stephen in D.N.B., xxiii (1890), p. 55 f.

GREEN THURSDAY (Lat. dies viridium; Germ. Gründonnerstag). The usual name in Germany, also occasionally found elsewhere, for *Maundy Thursday. Its origin is perhaps connected with a custom of providing penitents, who had made their confession on *Ash Wednesday, with green branches on that day as tokens that their *penance was completed and that they were thereby received back into full ecclesiastical communion.

GREENWOOD, JOHN (d. 1593), a leader among the early English separatists. As a young man he was chaplain to Lord Rich, a *Puritan, and conducted unauthorized services in his house. When these were suppressed he moved to London, where he either found or created the 'Ancient Church' in a house in St. Paul's Churchyard. For this he was imprisoned in 1586; and he remained in prison for seven years with a short interval in 1592. He was constantly examined before the *High Commission and other courts, but stood firm, and along with his fellow prisoner, H. *Barrow,

wrote many pamphlets defending the separatist cause. Both Barrow and Greenwood were hanged in 1593.

His own account of his examination, written in 1586 and publ. with that of H. Barrow and J. Penry (London, c. 1593), is repr. in The Harleian Miscellany, iv, c. 1745, pp. 338–40; 'A Pastoral Letter from Prison', prob. written c. the end of 1586, is pr. in Relics of the Puritan Martyrs, 1593 (Congregational Historical Society; 1906), pp. 17–23. B. Brook, The Lives of the Puritans, ii (1813), pp. 23–44, with account of examination. F. J. Powicke, Henry Barrow, Separatist (1550?–1593) and the Exiled Church of Amsterdam (1592–1622) (1900), esp. pp. 31–79 passim. C. L. Kingsford in D.N.B., xxiii (1890), p. 84 f.

GREGORIAN CALENDAR. The calendar as reformed in 1582 by *Gregory XIII, and now in use throughout most of the Christian world. As the Julian Calendar, devised by Julius Caesar (B.C. 46), did not correspond with sufficient accuracy to the period taken by the earth to go round the sun (just under 365¼ days), an error of ten days had accumulated by the 16th cent. Gregory in his bull 'Inter gravissimas' of 24 Feb. 1582 ordered that matters should be remedied by reckoning the day after 4 Oct. of that year as 15 Oct. To prevent a recurrence of the situation it was decided that the century years were only to be leap years when divisible by 400 (e.g. 1600, 2000). Protestant countries were reluctant to introduce it, and it was not adopted in England until 1752. In a few RC Churches of E. rites it had been accepted before the beginning of the 19th cent., but even now most of their individual members follow the Julian Calendar. The Orthodox Churches only began to accept it in 1924. In the Julian Calendar fixed feasts now fall thirteen days later than in the Gregorian, but the two Easters, and feasts depending thereon, coincide about once every three years.

The classical early work on the subject is C. Clavius, S.J., Romani Calendarii a Gregorio XIII P.M. Restituti Explicatio (Rome, 1603). F. Kaltenbrunner, 'Die Vorgeschichte der gregorianischen Kalenderreform' in Sb. (Wien), lxxxii (1876), pp. 289–414; id., 'Die Polemik über die gregorianische Kalenderreform', ib., lxxxvii (1877), pp. 485–586; id., 'Beiträge zur Geschichte der gregorianischen Kalenderreform', ib., xcvii (1881), pp. 7–54. C. Trasselli in E.C., iii (1950), col. 357 f., s.v. 'Calendario', with bibl., col. 364. Further bibl. in Schottenloher, iv (1938), pp. 255–7 (Nos. 37544a–37571). See also works cited under Calendar.

GREGORIAN SACRAMENTARY. One of the early forms of the Roman Liturgy. The *Sacramentary was sent, c. 790, by Pope *Hadrian I to the Emp. *Charlemagne at Aachen, and through its wide circulation in the Frankish Empire, became the accepted liturgical standard in Charlemagne's dominions. It was probably based on a book which goes back to the year 595 (i.e. to the pontificate of Pope *Gregory I) and reached substantially the form in which it has come down to us at about the end of the 7th cent. The oldest MS. is preserved in the Chapter Library at Padua (cod. D47; 9th cent.). In the forms which circulated in the Frankish Empire, it contained a considerable section of *Gallican additions, derived from pre-Carolingian usage in France as well as a preface (Hucusque) provided (it is widely held) by *Alcuin (d. 804).

The Sacramentary was first publd. by G. Pamelius (Cologne, 1571). Later edd. by H. Ménard, O.S.B. (Paris, 1642), and L. A. *Muratori (Venice, 1748). Crit. ed. by H. A. Wilson in *Henry Bradshaw Society series (1915). H. *Lietzmann claimed to present text orig. sent by Hadrian to Charlemagne in *Das Sacramentarium Gregorianum nach dem Aachener Urexemplar* (1921), on basis of MS. Cambrai 164 (saec. ix). Pre-Hadrianic text ed. K. Mohlberg, O.S.B.–A. *Baumstark, *Die älteste erreichbare Gestalt des Liber Sacramentorum, Cod. Pad. D. 47* (1927). H. Lietzmann, 'Auf dem Wege zum Urgregorianum' in *J.L.W.*, ix (1929), pp. 132–8. F. *Cabrol, O.S.B., in *D.A.C.L.*, vi (pt. 2, 1925), s.v. 'Grégorien (le Sacramentaire)', cols. 1776–96 with bibl.; A. Bugnini in *E.C.*, ix (1953), cols. 1566–9, s.v. 'Sacramentario IV', also with bibl.

GREGORIAN WATER.

Acc. to W. usage, solemnly blessed water used in the consecration of churches and altars with which not only salt (as in ordinary *Holy Water), but also ashes and wine, have been mixed. The beginnings of its ceremonial use go back to the *Gelasian Sacramentary, and it has an established place in the 9th cent. *Pontificals. It is so named from the formula used in blessing it being attributed to *Gregory the Great.

L. Eisenhofer, *Handbuch der katholischen Liturgik*, ii (1933), pp. 455–68 passim.

GREGORIANA.

The Jesuit university (Pontificia Università Gregoriana) at Rome. It was founded in 1551 as the 'Collegium Romanum' by St. *Ignatius Loyola, and in 1582–4 provided by Pope *Gregory XIII with adequate buildings and resources and constituted a university. Since 1920 it has published a quarterly periodical entitled *Gregorianum*.

P. Tacchi-Venturi, S.J., 'L' inaugurazione della Pontificia Università Gregoriana' in *Gregorianum*, xxxiv (1953), pp. 333–40.

GREGOROVIUS, FERDINAND

(1821–1891), German historian. After studying at Königsberg and some time spent as a schoolmaster, he went to Italy in 1852, where he stayed for more than twenty years. He afterwards took up his residence at Munich. During his sojourn in Rome he wrote his *Geschichte der Stadt Rom im Mittelalter* (1859–1872; Eng. trans. as *History of Rome in the Middle Ages*, 13 vols., 1894–1900), covering the period from A.D. 400 to 1534. It was a monumental work and brilliantly written, though often somewhat subjective in its judgements. His other writings include *Geschichte des Kaisers Hadrian und seiner Zeit* (1851), *Wanderjahre in Italien* (3 vols., 1864), *Lucrezia Borgia* (1874), *Die Grabdenkmäler der Päpste* (1881), and *Geschichte der Stadt Athen im Mittelalter* (1889). His poetical attempts, among which was a play *Der Tod des Tiberius* (1851), were less successful. An English translation of his 'Roman Journals' (1892), was published in 1907.

J. Hönig, *Ferdinand Gregorovius als Dichter* (Breslauer Beiträge zur Literaturgeschichte, xxxix; 1914); id., *Ferdinand Gregorovius der Geschichtsschreiber der Stadt Rom* (1921; with correspondence, pp. 183–528); enlarged ed., without the letters, as *Ferdinand Gregoroviu Eine Biographie* (1944), with bibl. reff.

GREGORY I., St.

(c. 540–604) (Gregory the Great), Pope from 590. He was the fourth and last of the traditional Latin '*Doctors of the Church' and the father of the medieval Papacy. The son of a senator, he became prefect of the city (Praefectus Urbi) in 573, but, like many of the finer men of the age, he sold his vast property and devoted the proceeds to the relief of the poor. He founded seven monasteries, six in Sicily and one in *Rome, which last he himself entered as a monk c. 574. After a few years of a very austere life, the Pope compelled him to leave the cloister, creating him 'regionarius', i.e. one of the seven deacons of Rome. Soon afterwards (c. 578) *Pelagius II made him 'apocrisiarius' at the Imperial court of *Constantinople. His experiences there, which convinced him that no help was to be expected from the decaying E. Empire, largely influenced his future course of action as Pope. C. 585 he returned to Rome and became abbot of his former monastery (St. Andrew's). To this period probably belongs the famous story, told by St. *Bede, of his encounter with the fair Saxon slaves in the market ('Non Angli, sed angeli').

On his accession to the Papacy, accepted only after a severe interior struggle, Gregory found Italy in an alarming state. The land was devastated by inundations, famine, pestilence, and the invasion of the Lombards, and the position of the Church threatened by the claims of the Imperial power at Constantinople. It was owing to Gregory, in whom firmness and strength of character were tempered by gentleness and charity, that many of these evils were conquered. Of particular significance were his relations with the Lombards, with whom he concluded, in 592–3, what amounted to a separate peace. By this unprecedented step he set aside the authority of the exarch of *Ravenna, the Emperor's representative. Throughout this period of unrest, aggravated by the weakness and treachery of the Byzantine authorities, he followed a course of independent action, appointing governors to the Italian cities and providing war materials, and thus establishing the temporal power of the Papacy. In his administration of the vast estates of the Church, in which he spent great sums on works of charity, he showed conspicuous ability. In his frequently strained relations with the E. he upheld the supremacy of the Roman see and refused to recognize the title of '*Oecumenical Patriarch', adopted by the Patr. of Constantinople. One of the greatest successes of his Pontificate was the conversion of England, for which task he selected St. *Augustine, later of *Canterbury, with about 40 missionaries from his own monastery. He also intervened with great effect in strengthening the Church in Spain, Gaul, and N. Italy.

Gregory was a very fertile author, of a practical rather than speculative bent of mind. His 'Liber Regulae Pastoralis' (c. 591) sets out the directives for the pastoral life of a bishop, whom he regards first as a shepherd of souls. The book, which was translated by King *Alfred, became the textbook of the medieval episcopate.

The 'Dialogues' (c. 593), which told the lives and miracles of St. *Benedict and other early Latin saints, reflect the uncritical credulity of the age; they served as a model to most medieval hagiographers. His 'Expositio in Librum Iob, sive Moralium Libri XXV' is an exegesis of the Book of Job in the threefold literal, mystical, and moral sense, with special emphasis on the last. The 'Homilies on the Gospels' were sermons preached on texts from the Gospels; they were much drawn on as lessons for the third *Nocturn in the *Breviary. There is also a collection of 854 of Gregory's letters, which are of extreme interest for the information they supply on the Pope's character and multifarious activities.

St. Gregory was an ardent promoter of Benedictine monasticism. By granting the monks 'privilegia', which partly restricted episcopal jurisdiction, he laid the foundations of the later *exemption of religious orders that brought them under direct Papal control. In his theology he did not aim at originality, but followed the teaching of St. *Augustine of Hippo, whose ideas he accommodated to the minds of his contemporaries. He developed esp. the doctrine of *Purgatory, teaching that the pains of the souls detained there may be relieved by the Sacrifice of the Mass, and popularized St. *Dionysius the Areopagite, esp. his angelology. He fostered the veneration of relics if authentic. In the liturgy he made some important changes and was the author of the original form of the *Gregorian Sacramentary (q.v.). To Gregory is also due the so-called 'Gregorian Chant', and he gave to the Roman 'schola cantorum' its definite form. His pontificate and personality did much to establish the idea in men's minds that the Papacy was the supreme authority in the Church, and his achievement was the more impressive in that (as is reflected in the title 'servus servorum Dei', which he applied to himself) he had great personal humility. He was canonized by popular acclamation immediately after his death. Feast day, 12 Mar.

The best ed. of his collected Works is that of the *Maurist, D. de Sainte-Marthe (4 vols., Paris, 1704), supplemented by J. B. Galliccioli (16 vols., Venice, 1768–76), repr. in J. P. Migne, PL, lxxv–lxxviii. Crit. ed. of his 'Registrum Epistolarum' by P. Ewald–L. M. Hartmann in M.G.H., Epistolae i and ii (1891–99). The earliest life is the brief one in L.P. (Duchesne), i, 312, with notes, pp. 312–14. Other early lives by an unnamed monk of *Whitby (c. 713), first ed. by F. A. *Gasquet (London, 1904); by *Paul the Deacon, a late 8th cent. *Cassinese monk, ed. in its original form by H. Grisar, S.J., in Z.K.T., xi (1887), pp. 158–73, and in an expanded form in the older edd. of Gregory's Works (PL, lxxv, 41–60); and by John the Deacon (9th cent.; PL, lxxv, 59–242). Two important modern lives are F. H. Dudden, Gregory the Great. His Place in History and Thought (2 vols., 1905), and by P. *Batiffol (Paris, 1928; Eng. tr., 1929). Gregory's life and work are also discussed in all histories of the Papacy and of the Middle Ages. E. Spearing, The Patrimony of the Roman Church in the Time of Gregory the Great (1918). [E.] C. *Butler, O.S.B., Western Mysticism (1922), pp. 89–133 and 211–41. Mann, i (1902), pp. 1–250. Bardenhewer, v, pp. 284–302; Altaner (ed. 1951), pp. 417–24. J. Barmby in D.C.B., ii (1880), pp. 779–91, s.v. 'Gregorius (51)'; G. R. Huddleston, O.S.B., in C.E., vi (1909), pp. 780–7, s.v.; H. *Leclercq, O.S.B., in D.A.C.L., vi (pt. 2; 1925), cols. 1753–76, s.v. 'Grégoire le Grand', and viii (pt. 2; 1929), cols. 2861–70, s.v. 'Lettres chrétiennes'; B. Pesci–K. Rathe–P. Toschi in E.C., vi (1951), cols. 1112–16, s.v.

GREGORY II, St. (669–731), Pope from 715. As a deacon he accompanied Pope Constantine I to *Constantinople in 710, where he distinguished himself by his lucid answers in the discussions on the canons of the Council of *Trullo. Having succeeded to the Papacy in 715, he was at once confronted with the Saracen danger, against which he had the walls of Rome repaired, and the paganism of the German tribes, esp. in Bavaria, Thuringia, and Hesse. In 719 he sent there St. *Boniface, aided by British monks and nuns. In his instructions to the missionaries he advocated a lenient view in the question of marriage among the newly converted, authorizing separation in certain cases and exceptions in the matter of forbidden degrees. In 726 *Leo III, the Isaurian, inaugurated the *Iconoclast controversy, in the course of which Gregory severely rebuked the Emperor at the synod of Rome in 727 without, however, countenancing the planned revolt of Italy against Byzantium and the election of another Emperor. His relations with the Lombards who tried to conquer Italy under *Liutprand were for the most part friendly owing to his personal influence with their king. The *Benedictine Order enjoyed Gregory's special protection and during his reign King Ine of Wessex entered a Roman monastery. Feast day, 13th Feb.

The chief authorities are L.P. (Duchesne), i (1886), pp. 396–414), *Bede, *Paul the Deacon and *Theophanes Confessor. A. Schäfer, Die Bedeutung der Päpste Gregor II (715–731) und Gregor III (731–741) für die Gründung des Kirchenstaates (Diss. Münster i.W.; 1913), esp. pp. 14–33. Mann, i (pt. 2; 1902), pp. 141–202. P. Moncelle in D.T.C., vi (1920), cols. 1781–5, s.v. 'Grégoire II'.

GREGORY VII, St. (c. 1021–85), Pope from 1073. Hildebrand was a native of Tuscany, born of poor parents, who came to Rome at an early age. He was educated at the monastery of St. Mary on the Aventine, but probably did not become a monk. He was chosen by Pope Gregory VI as his chaplain, and went into exile with him to Germany in 1046. On the Pope's death, in 1047, he retired to a monastery, probably *Cluny, where he was confirmed in his austere views of the obligations of clerical life. He returned to Rome in 1049 with the newly elected Pope St. *Leo IX, who appointed him administrator of the patrimony of St. Peter. Under him and his successors, on whose elections he exercised great influence, Hildebrand was the virtual guide of the Papacy. Under Victor II he had a large share in the decree which assigned the election of the Popes to the cardinals, in 1059 he became Archdeacon of the Roman Church, and under *Alexander II he was made chancellor of the Apostolic See.

After his unanimous election to the Papacy Hildebrand (1073) began his work for the reform and moral revival of the Church by issuing decrees against the simony and incontinence of the clergy in the Lenten synod of 1074. In the following year he forbade lay *investiture, which had made the Church dependent on the secular power and led to the bestowal of ecclesiastical offices on entirely unqualified persons. This measure, which was enforced by Papal legates who deposed simoniacal and immoral clerics, was violently opposed esp. in Germany, France, and England. In England, however, William the Conqueror refused to comply in the matter of lay investiture, though he escaped excommunication, as he carried out the other Papal decrees with zeal. In France nearly the whole episcopate was renewed despite Philip I's opposition. In Germany, *Henry IV, threatened with ban and deposition, held two synods at Worms and at Piacenza (1076) which declared the Pope deposed. Gregory replied by deposing and banning Henry, and freeing his subjects from their oath of allegiance at the Lenten synod of 1076. The Emperor, whose situation soon became desperate, submitted to the Pope at *Canossa in 1077, did penance, and was absolved from his censures. In spite of this the German princes elected Rudolf of Swabia in the same year. The Pope did not recognize him until 1080, when he once more excommunicated Henry, who had not fulfilled the promises given at Canossa. The latter now set up Wibert, the excommunicated Abp. of *Ravenna, as antipope and marched against Rome, which he took after a two years' siege. Gregory was freed by Robert Guiscard, whose Norman troops, however, exasperated the Roman population, so that they turned against Gregory, who had called them in. The Pope had to flee first to *Monte Cassino and later to Salerno, where he died.

Gregory virtually achieved his aim and procured spiritual liberty and regeneration for the Church, which had become deeply involved in the feudal organization of Europe. He may be regarded as the virtual author of the Concordat of *Worms (1122) which in great measure removed the abuses of lay investiture. He reconciled *Berengar of Tours, who had denied the real change of the Bread and Wine into the Body and Blood of Christ in the Mass. His efforts at reuniting the E. Church to the W. failed, and his struggle against Henry IV prevented him from carrying out the plan of a crusade against the Turks, suggested by the E. Emperor, Michael VII. Though Gregory was once regarded as an ambitious tyrant, most modern historians have revised this judgement and are agreed on his purity of intention and his desire for justice. He was canonized in 1606. Feast Day, 25 May.

Epistolae et Diplomata Pontificia in J. P. Migne, *PL*, cxlviii, incl. Register (repr. from G. D. *Mansi, cols. 283–645, and works doubtfully attributed to him as 'Monumenta Gregoriana', cols. 847–1448. Crit. edd. of his *Registrum* by E. Caspar in *M.G.H.*, Epistolae Selectae, ii (pts. 1 and 2; 1920–3); Eng. tr. of selections by E. Emerton (Records of Civilisation, Sources and Studies, xiv, New York, 1932); for letters not in *Registrum* see ed. by P. Jaffé, *Monumenta Gregoriana* (Bibliotheca rerum Germanicarum, 1865). Life by Paul Bernried, completed 1128, in J. P. Migne, op. cit., 39–104. A. F. Gfrörer, *Papst Gregorius VII und sein Zeitalter* (7 vols., 1859–61); O. Delarc, *Saint Grégoire VII et la réforme de l'Église au XIe siècle* (3 vols., 1889–90); W. Martens, *Gregor VII*. Sein Leben und Wirken (2 vols. bound in one, 1894). A. Fliche, *La Réforme grégorienne* (S.S.L., vi, ix, and xvi, 1924–37), with full bibl. H. X. Arquillière, *Saint Grégoire VII*. Essai sur sa conception du pouvoir pontifical (1934). G. B. Borino (ed.), *Studi gregoriani per la storia di Gregorio VII e della riforma gregoriana* (1947 ff.). W. R. W. Stephens, *Hildebrand and his Times*

(1888); A. Fliche, *Saint Grégoire VII* ('Les Saints'; 1920); A. J. Macdonald, *Hildebrand* (1932); J. P. Whitney, *Hildebrandine Essays* (1932), I and II, pp. 1–94. Z. N. Brooke in *The Cambridge Medieval History*, v (1929), pp. 51–85; A. Fliche in Fliche–Martin, viii (1944), pp. 55–198, with bibl. Mann, vii (1910), pp. 1–217. P. Moncelle in *D.T.C.*, vi (1920), cols. 1791–1804, s.v., with bibl.; L. Spälting, O.F.M., in *E.C.*, vi (1951), cols. 1130–4, s.v. 'Gregorio VII', with bibl.

GREGORY IX (c. 1148–1241), Pope from 1227. Count Ugolino of Segni, a nephew of *Innocent III, studied at *Paris and *Bologna. He was created Cardinal Deacon on the accession of his uncle in 1198, Cardinal Bp. of Ostia in 1206, and was employed as Papal Legate on a series of diplomatic missions to Germany. In 1217 he was commissioned to preach a *Crusade in northern, and later in central, Italy; from him the Emp. *Frederick II took the Cross at his coronation (1220). Insisting on the immediate fulfilment of the vow as soon as he became Pope, he forced the Emperor to embark in 1227, excommunicated him (29 Sept.) when he returned a few days later, and refused his overtures for peace. When Frederick II sailed unreconciled (1228) he proclaimed an interdict over his lands and wherever he should go. After conducting an unsuccessful campaign against Sicily, he agreed in 1230 to the Treaty of San Germano with the Emperor, loosing him from the ban. In 1239, however, he again excommunicated Frederick for invading Lombardy and usurping the rights of the Church in Sicily, tried to secure the election of an anti-king and in 1241 summoned a General Council to Rome which Frederick II, however, prevented from meeting. He died while the Emperor was besieging Rome (22 Aug. 1241).

A personal friend of St. *Francis of Assisi, he was appointed Protector of the *Franciscan Order as early as 1220 and assisted in the development of the *Third Order. To the *Dominicans he entrusted the *Inquisition in 1232. He canonized St. Francis in 1228, St. *Antony of Padua in 1232 and St. *Dominic in 1234. In 1230 he commissioned *Raymond of Penafort to collect the papal decretals (published in 1234) and in 1231 instructed William of Beauvais to examine the works of *Aristotle and prepare an orthodox edition to supersede the old Latin translation, the use of which had been forbidden in 1210 ('Physics') and 1215 ('Metaphysics'). Throughout his pontificate he laboured unsuccessfully to effect a union with the Eastern Church.

L. Auvray (ed.), *Les Registres de Grégoire IX* (Bibliothèque des Écoles Françaises d'Athènes et de Rome, Sér. 2, ix, 1896–1910; index still wanting). G. Levi (ed.), *Registri dei Cardinali Ugolino d' Ostia ed Ottaviano* (Fonti per la storia d' Italia, viii, 1890). There is a contemporary life, prob. by John of Ferentino; best ed. by P. Fabre–L. *Duchesne (ed.), *Liber Censuum*, ii (Bibliothèque des Écoles Françaises d'Athènes et de Rome, Sér. 2, vi, 1910), pp. 18–36. P. Balan, *Storia di Gregorio IX e dei suoi tempi* (3 vols., Modena, 1872–3); J. Felten, *Papst Gregor IX* (1886). C. Thouzellier, 'La Légation en Lombardie du Cardinal Hugolin (1221). Un épisode de la cinquième croisade' in *R.H.E.*, xlv (1950), pp. 508–42, with reff. to earlier litt. Mann, xiii (1925), pp. 165–441, with bibl. details. Fliche–Martin, x [1950], pp. 225–38. A. Clerval in *D.T.C.*, vi (1920), col. 1805 f., s.v. 'Grégoire IX'; O. Bonmann, O.F.M., in *E.C.*, vi (1951), cols. 1134–40, s.v. 'Gregorio IX', with further bibl. See also bibl. to the Emperor *Frederick II*.

GREGORY X (1210–76), Pope from 1271. Teobaldo Visconti was elected Pope at Viterbo after the Holy See had been vacant for three years, though he was neither cardinal nor even priest. He was forthwith summoned to Italy from Acre, whither he had accompanied Prince Edward of England on his pilgrimage to the Holy Land. The deliverance of *Jerusalem, the reform of the Church, the reunion with the Greeks, and the pacification of the German Empire, were the leading ideas of his short pontificate. He solved the German question by recognizing Rudolf of Habsburg as Emperor and inducing Alfonso of Castile to resign his claims to the German throne. At the Council of *Lyons (1274–5), which Gregory had summoned immediately on his accession, the Greek Emp. Michael Paleologus made his submission to the Pope for purely political reasons, but the reunion was short-lived. The plan of a Crusade was discussed at the Council, but, though financial preparations were made, it came to nothing. One of the most important ecclesiastical innovations of Gregory's reign was the introduction of the *Conclave at the election of the Pope by the Constitution 'Ubi periculum' of 1274. After his death, which took place on his way back from the Council, he received a local cult in several dioceses, e.g. Arezzo and Piacenza; *Benedict XIV added his name to the Roman *Martyrology. Feast day, 10 Jan.

Les Registres de Grégoire X, 1272–1276, ed. J. Guiraud–L. Cadier (Bibliothèque de l'École Française d'Athènes et de Rome, 2ᵉ Serie, xii; 4 fascc.; still lacks index; 1892–1906). A. Zisterer, *Gregor X. und Rudolf von Habsburg in ihren beiderseitigen Beziehungen* (1891); H. Otto, *Die Beziehungen Rudolfs von Habsburg zu Papst Gregor X* (1895). O. Joelson, *Die Papstwahlen des 13. Jahrhunderts bis zur Einführung der Conclaveordnung Gregors X* (Historische Studien, Hft. clxxviii; 1928). Mann, xv (1929), pp. 347–501, with discussion of sources. A. Clerval in *D.T.C.*, vi (1920), col. 1806 f., s.v. 'Grégoire X', with further bibl.; P. Brezzi in *E.C.*, vi (1951), col. 1140, s.v. 'Gregorio X', with bibl.

GREGORY XI (1329–78), Pope from 1370. Pierre Roger de Beaufort was the last French Pope. After being created cardinal by his uncle, *Clement VI, at the age of 18, he studied at Perugia. A skilled canonist, he was elected Pope at *Avignon in 1370. His chief efforts were directed towards pacifying the Papal states which were then revolting against the foreign officials under the leadership of Florence. Gregory finally excommunicated the city and sent against it the ruthless cardinal, Robert of Geneva (Antipope *Clement VII). The Florentines having thereupon persuaded St. *Catherine of Siena to negotiate for them, the Pope yielded to the entreaties of the saint, and decided to return to Italy to restore order, despite the protests of the King of France and most of the cardinals. He solemnly entered Rome on 17 Jan. 1377. Unable to put an end to the disturbances, he contemplated returning to Avignon, but the plan was prevented by his death in the following year. While in Rome, Gregory condemned the teachings of J. *Wycliffe (May 1377). After his death began the 'Great Schism'.

Five lives in S. *Baluze, *Vitae Paparum Avenionensium* (ed. G. Mollat, i, 1914, pp. 415–67; other material in vol. iv, 1922 passim). J. P. Kirsch, *Die Rückkehr der Päpste Urban V und Gregor XI von Avignon nach Rom* (Quellen und Forschungen aus dem Gebiete der Geschichte, iv; 1898), pp. 169–262. Pastor, i (1891), pp. 100–16, with reff.; G. Mollat, *Les Papes d'Avignon* (ed. 9, 1950), pp. 122–33 and passim. A. Clerval in *D.T.C.*, vi (1920), col. 1807 f., s.v. 'Grégoire XI'; R. Paolucci in *E.C.*, vi (1951), col. 1140 f., s.v. 'Gregorio XI', both with bibl.

GREGORY XIII (1502–85), Pope from 1572. Ugo Buoncompagni studied and later taught law at *Bologna. In 1539 he was called to Rome by *Paul III, where he was appointed judge of the Capitol, and some years later he was sent to *Trent as one of the Pope's jurists. In 1564 he was made Cardinal-Priest of San Sisto. Elected Pope in 1572, his main endeavour was the reform of the Church and the restoration of the Catholic faith. Though he failed in his efforts at winning back *Sweden and at obtaining religious freedom for RCs in England, he furthered the cause of the *Counter-Reformation by carrying into effect the decrees of the Council of *Trent wherever possible. He erected numerous seminaries and colleges in Rome and elsewhere, mostly under the direction of the *Jesuits, who enjoyed his special favour. He approved the Congregation of the *Oratory (1574) and the Discalced *Carmelites (1580), and was esp. interested in the missions to the Far East. One of the chief events of his reign was his institution in 1582 of the *Gregorian Calendar (q.v.). He also issued an improved edition of the '*Corpus Iuris Canonici' (1582). Towards the end of his life the Papal finances became increasingly bad, owing to the vast sums spent on education and architecture, and the menace of the *banditti* which had developed in the Papal states was not conquered till after his death. In 1579 he founded the English College at Rome as a seminary for training missionaries for England.

M. A. Ciappi, *Compendio delle heroiche et gloriose attioni et santa vita di Papa Gregorio XIII* (1591); G. P. Maffei, S.J., *Degli annali di Gregorio XIII*, publd. by C. Cocquelines (2 vols., 1742). I. Bompiano, *Historia Pontificatus Gregorii XIII* (Rome, 1655). L. Karttunen, *Grégoire XIII comme politicien et souverain* (Annales Academiae Scientiae Fennicae, Ser. B., vol. ii, Helsinki, 1911). K. Schellhass, 'Wissenschaftliche Forschungen unter Gregor XIII für die Neuausgabe des Gratianischen Dekrets' in *Papsttum und Kaisertum. Forschungen zur politischen Geschichte und Geisteskultur des Mittelalters Paul Kehr zum 65. Geburtstage dargebracht*, ed. A. Brackmann (1926), pp. 674–90. G. Levi della Vida, *Documenti intorno alle relazioni delle chiese orientali con la s. sede durante il pontificato di Gregorio XIII* (S.T., cxliii, 1948). Pastor, xix and xx (1930), with full bibl. P. Moncelle in *D.T.C.*, vi (1920), cols. 1809–15, s.v. 'Grégoire XIII'; M. E. Viora in *E.C.*, vi (1951), col. 1143 f., s.v. 'Gregorio XIII'. See also bibl. to *Gregorian Calendar*.

GREGORY XVI (1765–1846), Pope from 1831. Bartolomeo Cappellari entered the *Camaldolese monastery of San Michele di Murano in 1783. In 1799 he published *Il trionfo della Santa Sede* in which he treated of the sovereignty of the Pope and developed the doctrine of Papal Infallibility. In 1807 he was made Abbot of San Gregorio, but had to leave Rome in the following year, owing to the

Napoleonic suppression of the religious orders. He returned in 1814, was created Cardinal and Prefect of the *Propaganda in 1826, and elected Pope in 1831 by the party of the Zelanti after a conclave lasting over fifty days. Soon after, revolution broke out in the Papal states and was quelled only by the intervention of Austria, a fact which caused the five great powers—Austria, Russia, England, France, and Prussia—to demand reforms in their administration. As these were only partly carried out, the revolt began again, and in 1832 Austrian troops were recalled, whereupon the French occupied Ancona and did not withdraw till 1838. But the troubles continued, and on Gregory's death, in 1846, dissatisfaction was rife and the finances of the Holy See in disorder, owing to the heavy expenditure involved by the upkeep of a strong military force. Gregory's relations with the foreign powers remained strained during the greater part of his reign. He condemned Liberalism in the person of H. F. R. de *Lamennais (encyclical *Singulari nos, 1834) and its application to theology in the German scholar, G. *Hermes (Dum acerbissimas, 1835). Despite the political difficulties in which he was involved, Gregory XVI did much for the missions, erecting many new bishoprics and vicariates. He also favoured science and art. The Etruscan and Egyptian museums at the Vatican and the Christian museum at the *Lateran were founded by him.

Acta Gregorii Papae XVI, ed. A. M. Bernasconi (Rome, 1901–4). N. *Wiseman, Recollections of the Last Four Popes and of Rome in their Times (1858), part iv (pp. 415–532). J. Leflon, 'La Crise révolutionnaire 1789–1846' in Fliche-Martin, xx (1949), pp. 426–71, and P. dalla Torre in E.C., vi (1951), cols. 1148–56, both with bibl.

GREGORY, St. (d. c. 638), Bp. of Agrigentum (Girgenti) in Sicily. Born near Agrigentum, he made a pilgrimage to Palestine, where he was ordained deacon by the Patr. of *Jerusalem. Later he visited other parts of the East and also Rome. Here he was ordained Bp. of Agrigentum and is related to have been the victim of a plot against his character. His (Greek) Commentary on Ecclesiastes survives. There is a long Greek life by a certain Leontius, who is said to have been prior of the monastery of St. Saba at Rome. Feast day, 23 Nov.

Ed. princeps of Gregory's 'Comm. on Eccl.' by S. A. Morcelli (Venice, 1791), repr. with other works in J. P. Migne, PG, xcviii, 525–1228 (Life by Leontius, 549–716). C. Mercurelli, Agrigento paleocristiana. Memorie storiche e monumentali, in Atti della Pont. Accad. Romana di Archeologia, Serie III. Memorie VIII (Rome, 1948), passim. Bardenhewer, v, pp. 105–7. C. Hole in D.C.B., ii (1880), p. 776 f.

GREGORY DIALOGOS, St. The title commonly given to St. *Gregory the Great in the MSS. and editions of the Greek 'Liturgy of the *Presanctified' which baselessly presuppose that he was its author.

GREGORY OF ELVIRA, St. (d. after 392), Bp. of Elvira ('Illiberis'), near Granada. One of the most intransigent opponents of *Arian-

ism, he supported the refusal of *Lucifer of Cagliari to pardon those who 'Arianized' at the Council of Ariminum (359), and after Lucifer's death became the leader of the 'Luciferians'. Controversy continues over the extent of his written work, but it probably includes (1) 'Homilies on Canticles' (ed. by A. *Wilmart, Bulletin de littérature ecclésiastique, 1906, pp. 233–9); (2) the '*Tractatus Origenis' (ed. P. *Batiffol, 1900); (3) the 'De Arca Noe' (Revue Bénédictine, xxvi (1909), 1–12); (4) the 'De Fide' (J. P. *Migne, PL, xx, 31–50). His exegesis of Scripture was highly allegorical.

Besides works quoted, see P. Lejay, 'L'Héritage de Grégoire d'Elvire' in R. Bén., xxv (1908), pp. 435–57, and H. Koch, 'Zu Gregors von Elvira Schrifttum und Quellen' in Z.K.G., li (1932), pp. 238–72. Cf. also Giuseppe Madoz, S.J., in E.C., vi (1951), col. 1085 f.

GREGORY THE ILLUMINATOR, St. (c. 240–332), the 'Apostle of *Armenia'. He appears to have been of royal descent and to have been brought up as a Christian while an exile in Cappadocia. After returning to Armenia, he eventually (c. 280) succeeded in converting the King, Tiridates (c. 238–314), to the Christian Faith, which forthwith became the official religion of the country. He was consecrated Bishop (*Catholicos) by the Metropolitan of Caesarea in Cappadocia and the episcopate remained for some generations in his family. His son, Aristakes, whom Gregory had consecrated to succeed him, attended the Council of *Nicaea (325). The homilies and epistles ascribed to him are probably not genuine. There is a 'Life' by *Agathangelos. Feast day, 30 Sept.

G. Garitte, Documents pour l'étude du livre d'Agathange (S.T., cxxvii; 1946), esp. ch. x. H. Gelzer, 'Die Anfänge der armenischen Kirche' in Ber. (Sächs.), xlvii (1895), pp. 109–74. S. Weber, Die katholische Kirche in Armenien (1903), esp. pp. 115–231. P. Peeters, S.J., 'S. Grégoire l'Illuminateur dans le calendrier lapidaire de Naples' in Anal. Boll., lx (1942), pp. 91–130. Bardenhewer, v, pp. 182–5. G. Amaduni in E.C., vi (1951), col. 1086 f. See also bibl. to Armenia.

GREGORY OF NAZIANZUS, St. (329–389), 'the Theologian', one of the '*Cappadocian Fathers'. He was the son of the Bp. of Nazianzus in Cappadocia (also 'Gregory') and studied at the university of Athens, where he was a contemporary of St. *Basil. Soon afterwards he adopted the monastic life, which he found very congenial to his contemplative and retiring spirit. Under pressure and against his will he was ordained priest (? c. 362), and c. 372 was consecrated to the see of Sasima, a small village in Cappadocia (which he never visited, however). Until his father's death in 374 he remained at Nazianzus to help his father as suffragan, and soon afterwards retired for some years to Seleucia in Isauria. In 379 he was summoned to Constantinople, where his eloquent preaching in the Church of the Anastasis was a great influence in restoring the *Nicene Faith and leading to its final establishment at the Council of *Constantinople in 381. During the Council he was appointed Bp. of Constantinople, but he resigned the see before the end of the year, retiring first to Nazianzus and later to his own estate, where he died.

His more important writings include his 'Five Theological Orations' which date from his Constantinopolitan period and contain an elaborate treatment of the doctrine of the Holy Spirit; the 'Philocalia', a selection from the writings of *Origen which he compiled in conjunction with St. Basil; several important letters against *Apollinarianism; and a large collection of poems. Feast day in the E., 25 and 30 Jan.; in the W., 9 May.

Early edd. of his Works were publd. at Basle (1550) and Paris (1609 and 1630). Much improved *Maurist ed. by C. Clémencet, O.S.B., and A. B. Caillau (Paris, vol. i, 1778; vol. ii, 1840); repr. in J. P. Migne, PG, xxxv–xxxviii. Crit. ed. of Five Theological Orations by A. J. Mason (Cambridge Patristic Texts, 1899). The nine Orations hastily tr. by *Rufinus into Lat. (Nos. 2, 6, 16, 17, 26, 27, 38, 39, 40), ed. by A. Engelbrecht (C.S.E.L., xlvi; 1910). Eng. tr. of Select Orations and Letters, with introd., by C. G. Browne–J. E. Swallow in N.P.N.C.F., Ser. II, vol. vii (1894), pp. 185–498. The main sources for his Life are his own writings, esp. his poem 'De vita sua' (PG, xxxvii, 1029–1166). Biog. of ample dimensions by a 7th cent. presbyter named Gregory (pr. PG, xxxv, 243–304). Modern lives by C. Clémencet (PG, xxxv, 147–242), C. Ullmann (Darmstadt, 1825; ed. 2, Gotha, 1866), A. Benoît (2 vols., Paris, 1876; ed. 2, 1884) and P. Gallay (Lyons, 1943). M. Guignet, St. Grégoire de Nazianze et la rhétorique (1911). M. Pellegrino, La poesia di S. Gregorio Nazianzeno (1932). P. Gallay, Langue et style de S. Grégoire de Nazianze dans sa correspondance (1943). J. Plagnieux, Saint Grégoire de Nazianze théologien (Strasbourg thesis; Paris, 1952). J. Dräseke, 'Neuplatonisches in des Gregorios von Nazianz Trinitätslehre' in B.Z., xv (1906), pp. 141–60. Bardenhewer, iii, pp. 162–88; Altaner (ed. 1951), pp. 256–60. F. *Loofs in P.R.E. (ed. 3), vii (1899), pp. 138–46; Q. Cataudella in E.C., vi (1951), cols. 1088–96.

GREGORY OF NYSSA, St.

(c. 330–c. 395), Bp. of Nyssa, *Cappadocian Father. He was a younger brother of St.*Basil. Though early destined for an ecclesiastical career he temporarily became a rhetorician, but returned to his first vocation and entered a monastery founded by his brother. He was consecrated Bp. of Nyssa, c. 371. A warm supporter of the faith of *Nicaea, he was deposed by the *Arians in 376 and remained in exile until the death of *Valens in 378, when he regained his see. In 379 he attended the Council of Antioch, and in the next year was elected Bp. of Sebaste, but protested against the election. At the Council of *Constantinople in 381 he eloquently championed the Nicene cause. In his later life he travelled considerably and was much in demand as a preacher. In 394 he took part in the Council of Constantinople convoked by the Patr. *Nectarius; he seems to have died soon afterwards.

St. Gregory of Nyssa was a thinker and theologian of great originality and knowledge, acquainted esp. with *Platonist and *Neo-Platonist speculation, as well as an outstanding exegete, orator, and ascetical author. His principal theological works are polemical treatises against *Eunomius, *Apollinaris, and the *Tritheistic teaching of a certain Abladius. In his famous 'Catechetical Orations' he expounded the doctrines of the Trinity, Incarnation, and Redemption, and the Sacraments of Baptism and the Eucharist for those whose duty it was to instruct the catechumens. Among his exegetical works, which are influenced by *Origen and deal esp. with the mystical sense of Scripture, are a 'Life of Moses', 'On the Pythonissa', and homilies on Ecclesiastes, the Song of Songs, the *Lord's Prayer, and the *Beatitudes. His ascetical works include treatises on virginity, in which he develops the thought that by virginity the soul becomes a spouse of Christ, and on Christian perfection, as well as the attractive Life of his sister, St. *Macrina. Many of his sermons, funeral orations, and letters have also survived.

He was an ardent defender of the Nicene dogma of the Trinity, and distinguished carefully between the generation of the Son and the procession of the Holy Ghost. The Second Person of the Trinity was incarnate in the womb of Mary, who therefore is truly θεοτόκος, for Christ is one Person in two natures. In his eschatology he is influenced by Origen, with whom he holds that ultimately both the souls in hell and the devils will return to God. In his account of the Atonement he employs, prob. for the first time, the simile of the fish-hook by which the devil was baited. Feast day, 9 Mar.

Works ed. F. *Ducaeus, S.J., 2 vols., Paris, 1615; rev., with additions by J. Gretser, S.J., 3 vols., ib., 1638 (repr. J. P. Migne, PG, xliv–xlvi); the text of this, the last complete ed., remains very unsatisfactory. Crit. ed. of De Anima et Resurrectione by J. G. Krabinger (Leipzig, 1837) and of De Oratione Dominica by id. (Landshut, 1840); of Apol. in Hexaemeron, etc., by G. H. *Forbes (2 pts., Burnt-island, 1855–61); of Catechetical Oration by J. H. Srawley (Cambridge Patristic Texts, 1903). Crit. text of his whole works by W. Jaeger in preparation; so far, the Contra Eunomium ed. W. Jaeger (2 vols., Berlin, 1921), Epistulae ed. G. Pasquali (Berlin, 1925), and Opera Ascetica, pt. i, ed. W. Jaeger and others (Leiden, 1952). Syr. version of Gregory's Commentary on Song of Songs, ed. C. van den Eynde, O.P. (Bibliothèque du Muséon, x; Louvain, 1939). Eng. tr. of 'Select Writings' in N.P.N.C.F., Ser. 2, vol. v (1890); of 'Life of St. Macrina' ed., W. K. L. Clarke (S.P.C.K., 1916), and of 'The Lord's Prayer' and 'The Beatitudes' by Hilda C. Graef (Ancient Christian Writers, xvii; 1954). Fr. tr. of Vita Moysis and De Hominis Opificio, ed. J. Daniélou, S.J. (S.C., i and vi [1942–3]). Crit. ed. of his works now in progress by W. Jaeger [and H. Langerbeck] (Leiden, [1959], 1960 ff.).

F. Diekamp, Die Gotteslehre des hl. Gregor von Nyssa (1896). J. B. Aufhauser, Die Heilslehre des hl. Gregors von Nyssa (1910). H. F. Cherniss, 'The Platonism of Gregory of Nyssa' in University of California Publications in Classical Philology, xi, for 1930–3 (1934), pp. 1–92. G. González, La fórmula μία οὐσία τρεῖς ὑποστάσεις en S. Gregorio de Nisa (Analecta Gregoriana, xxi; 1939). H. U. von Balthasar, S.J., Présence et pensée. Essai sur la philosophie religieuse de Grégoire de Nysse (1942). J. Daniélou, S.J., Platonisme et théologie mystique. Essai sur la doctrine spirituelle de St. Grégoire de Nysse (1944). A. Lieske, S.J., 'Die Theologie der Christusmystik Gregors von Nyssa' in Z.K.T., lxx (1948), pp. 49–93, 129–68, 315–40. R. Leys, S.J., L'Image de Dieu chez Saint Grégoire de Nyssa (Museum Lessianum, xlix; 1951). Bardenhewer, iii, pp. 188–220; Altaner (ed. 1951), pp. 261–5. P. Godet in D.T.C., vi (1920), cols. 1847–1852, s.v.; also R. Arnou, S.J., in D.T.C., xii (pt. 2; 1935), cols. 2343–8, s.v. 'Platonisme des pères'. Valuable art. by 'G.' [Giovanni] Daniélou, S.J., in E.C., vi (1951), cols. 1096–1111.

GREGORY PALAMAS

(c. 1296–1359), Greek theologian and chief exponent of *Hesychasm (q.v.). He was born probably at *Constantinople of a noble Anatolian family. His brothers and sisters as well as his widowed mother all embraced the religious life. In 1318 Gregory himself went to Mt. *Athos, where he made rapid progress in the life of prayer as taught by the Hesychasts. On the invasion of the Turks he fled to *Thessalonica, where he was ordained priest in 1326 and subsequently retired as a hermit to a mountain near Beroea, whence he returned to Athos in 1331. In 1333 he became involved in a controversy with the Calabrian monk, Barlaam, whom he reproached for his W. methods of theological reasoning. When Barlaam retorted with a satire on the contemplative practices of the Hesychasts, Palamas wrote a violent defence, Ὑπὲρ τῶν ἱερῶς ἡσυχαζόντων (1338). In a second work he attempted to outline his theory of the Divine Light and the real distinction between the essence and the operations of God. In a third work he went so far as to mention several Divinities, θεότητες, distinguishing between the superior invisible Divine Essence and the inferior and visible Divine 'energy'. When Barlaam accused him of heresy he called a kind of synod at Mt. Athos and had his doctrine approved in a document drawn up by the monks and known as the Ἁγιορειτικὸς Τόμος ('Hagioritic Tome'). The backing of the powerful monks so impressed the Patr. of Constantinople that a synod convoked there in 1341 declined to make a doctrinal decision and imposed silence on both parties. When, in spite of this, Palamas continued to propagate his views he was interned in a monastery in 1342, his writings were condemned by two synods, and he himself excommunicated c. 1344. In 1347, however, when John Canta-cuzenus usurped the throne of Constantinople, Palamas was set free and appointed Bp. of Thessalonica, though he was not accepted by the citizens until Cantacuzenus occupied the city in 1350. In 1351 the so-called 'Blacherna Synod' solemnly recognized the orthodoxy of his teaching. In 1368 another synod of Con-stantinople canonized Palamas as a 'Father and Doctor of the Church', thus placing him on a level with such Doctors as St.*Athanasius and St.*Cyril of Alexandria. His feast is kept on the Second Sunday of Lent as well as on 14 Nov.

The bulk of his writings are still in MS. Most of those which have been publd., which include a treatise against the W. doctrine of the Holy Ghost and 43 Homilies, together with a life of Palamas by Philotheos Kokkinos, Patr. of Constantinople (1353–4 and 1364–76; d. 1379), are repr. in J. P. Migne, PG, cl, 771–1372, and cli, 9–678. New ed. of Prosopopoeia animae accusantis corpus et corporis se defendentis by A. Jahn (Halle, 1884); but it now appears that this writing really belongs to Michael Akominatos. Full and important study by A. Jugie, A.A., in D.T.C., xi (pt. 2; 1932), cols. 1735–76.

GREGORY OF RIMINI (d. 1358), 'Doctor authenticus', medieval philosopher. He joined the *Augustinian Hermits, studied in *Paris from 1322 to 1329, and subsequently taught at *Bologna, Padua, and Perugia. In 1340 he returned to Paris, where he lectured on the *Sentences and in 1345 was made doctor of the *Sorbonne by *Clement VI. Elected *General of his order in 1357, he began at once to intro-duce reforms, but his work was cut short by his death in the following year. His philosophical doctrines carried further the *nominalist teaching of *William of Occam. His theology

was thoroughly Augustinian. He taught that works done without grace are sinful and that unbaptized infants incur eternal damnation, an opinion which, though held by St. Augustine, earned him the title 'tortor infantium'. He also wrote a treatise on Usury. His influence was great and can be traced in the works of M.*Luther.

His work on the Sentences was publd. at Paris in 1482 (later edd. 1487, 1642) and Venice (1532), his De Usuris at Rimini (1622). J. Würsdörfer, Erkennen und Wissen nach Gregor von Rimini. Ein Beitrag zur Geschichte der Erkennt-nistheorie des Nominalismus (B.G.P.M., xx, Hft. 1, 1917); M. Schüler, Prädestination, Sünde und Freiheit bei Gregor von Rimini (Forschungen zur Kirchen- und Geistesge-schichte 3, 1934). Überweg, ii, pp. 587–90, 783. N. Merlin in D.T.C., vi (1920), cols. 1852–4, s.v. 'Grégoire de Rimini'. G. Leff, Gregory of Rimini (Manchester, 1961).

GREGORY THAUMATURGUS, St. (c. 213–c. 270), Greek Church Father. He came from a noble family of Neocaesarea in Pontus, and studied law and rhetoric. C. 233 he went to *Caesarea in Palestine, where he became a disciple of *Origen, who converted him to the Christian faith and with whom he remained for five years. Soon after his return to his native city he was made its bishop, and during his episcopate converted its pagan population. The wealth of legends and miracles which were attributed to him in later times and to which he owes his surname of Thaumaturgus or wonder-worker, such as the moving of a mountain and the drying-up of a swamp, testify to his uncommon strength of character as well as to his popularity. In 253–4 he witnessed the Goths devastating Pontus, as described in his so-called 'Canonical Letter'. In 264–5 he took part in the first Synod of *Antioch against *Paul of Samosata; he also fought *Sabellian-ism and *Tritheism. Acc. to *Suidas he died in the reign of the Emp. Aurelian (270–5).

St. Gregory was a practical Churchman rather than a speculative theologian. He based his teaching on Origen, but his terminology is still undeveloped and often equivocal. His name has been affixed to a number of treatises, only a few of which are authentic. His first extant work is his panegyric on Origen, Εἰς Ὠριγένην . . . Προσφωνητικός, delivered when he took leave of his master. It contains much autobiographical material as well as an account of Origen's teaching methods. His Ἔκθεσις τῆς Πίστεως is a Trinitarian exposition of belief, the basis of his instructions to catechumens. Acc. to St.*Gregory of Nyssa, whose grand-mother St.*Macrina had been instructed by Gregory Thaumaturgus, it was given to him in a vision by St.*John the Evangelist at the command of our Lady, the first known instance of a record of a Marian apparition. His Ἐπιστολὴ Κανονική contains much information on the penitential discipline of the early Church. His Μετάφρασις εἰς τὸν Ἐκκλησιαστήν is a paraphrase of Ecclesiastes, and his letter to Theopompus, extant only in a Syriac transla-tion, is a philosophical colloquy on the im-passibility of God. Feast day, 17 Nov.

Life, by Greg. of Nyssa, in J. P. Migne, PG, xlvi, 893–958. There also exist Syr., Armen., and Lat. lives, all of little value. Works (incl. several dubia and spuria) publd. by

G. Voss (Mainz, 1604) and others; repr. from A. *Gallandi in J. P. Migne, *PG*, x, 963–1232. Crit. text of Gregory's address to Origen ed. P. Koetschau (Sammlung ausgewählter Quellenschriften, No. 9, 1894). V. Ryssel, *Gregorius Thaumaturgus. Sein Leben und seine Schriften* (1880). M. Jugie, A.A., 'Les Homélies mariales attribuées à S. Grégoire le Thaumaturge' in *Anal. Boll.*, xliii (1925), pp. 86–95. On his Creed, cf. L. Froidevaux, 'Le Symbole de Saint Grégoire le Thaumaturge', in *Rech. S.R.*, xix (1929), pp. 193–247. A. Poncelet, S.J., 'La Vie latine de Saint Grégoire le Thaumaturge', ib., i (1910), pp. 132–60. W. Telfer, 'The Cultus of St. Gregory Thaumaturgus' in *H.T.R.*, xxix (1936), pp. 225–344. See also P. Godet in *D.T.C.*, vi (1920), cols. 1844–7, and Erik Peterson in *E.C.*, vi (1951), cols. 1158 f., s.v.

GREGORY OF TOURS, St. (*c.* 540–94), Bp. of Tours and historian of the Franks. He came of a Gallo-Roman senatorial family which had already produced several bishops, and was elected Bp. of Tours in 573. Though he had at first to oppose King Chilperic, he readily supported the 'good king', Guntram, against the turbulent aristocracy, thus gaining royal favour for the Church. *C.* 576 he began his *Historia Francorum*. Book I runs quickly from the Creation to 397; Books II to IV, based on valuable sources, relate early Frankish history to 575; and Books V to IX cover the years 575 to 591 in detail. The important position Gregory filled in Church and state and the access he thus obtained to original documents made him a well-informed historian, without whose work the early history of France could hardly be written. But his History, though honest and vivid, was untidy and unreflective; and his knowledge of events outside France was slight. His chief hagiographical work is his eight *Miraculorum Libri*: (1) *In Gloriam Martyrum*, on the miracles of Our Lord, the Apostles, and esp. Gallic martyrs; (2) *De Virtutibus S. Juliani*, on miracles at the tomb of St. Julian, put to death at Clermont-Ferrand in 304; (3–6) *De Virtutibus S. Martini*, on miracles at the tomb of St. *Martin*; (7) *De Vita Patrum*, lives of 23 Gallic saints; (8) *In Gloriam Confessorum*, miracles of (esp. Gallic) saints not martyrs. Here he often displays extreme credulity, so that the work is of altogether less historical value than his *Historia Francorum*. Feast day, 17 Nov.

Editio princeps of the *Historia Francorum*, with a few other works (Paris, 1522). Improved ed. of his works by T. *Ruinart, O.S.B. (Paris, 1699), repr. in J. P. Migne, *PL*, lxxi. Crit. ed. by W. Arndt–B. Krusch in *M.G.H.*, Scriptores rerum Merovingicarum, i (2 pts., 1884–5), which prints the author's orig. text with all its asperities before its 'revision' to conform it with the Carolingian standards of elegance; the *Historia Francorum* from this ed. was rev. by B. Krusch–W. Levison (ib., 1951); Gregory's Lat. tr. of the 'Passio Septem Dormientium apud Ephesum' was ed. B. Krusch in *M.G.H.*, loc. cit., vii (pt. 2; 1920), pp. 757–69. Eng. trr. of *Historia Francorum*, with valuable introd. and notes, by O. M. Dalton (2 vols., Oxford, 1927; vol. i, introduction, vol. ii, tr.), and of selections of his Minor Works by W. C. McDermott (Philadelphia, etc., 1949). G. Kurth, *Études francques* (2 vols., 1919), esp. i, pp. 1–65, and ii, pp. 117–271. Bardenhewer, v, pp. 357–67; Altaner (ed. 1951), p. 428 f., both with bibl. H. *Leclercq, O.S.B., in *D.A.C.L.*, vi (pt. 2; 1925), cols. 1711–53. A. Ghinato in *E.C.*, vi (1951), col. 1158 f., with further bibl.

GREGORY, ROBERT (1819–1911), Dean of *St. Paul's. He came from a Nottingham Methodist family, and, influenced by the *Tractarian Movement, studied at Corpus Christi College, *Oxford (1840–3), and was ordained priest of the C of E in 1844. After serving several curacies he was vicar of St. Mary-the-Less, Lambeth, from 1853 to 1873, interesting himself esp. in elementary education. In 1868 he was appointed Canon of St. Paul's, where he collaborated with H. P. *Liddon and R. W. *Church in making the cathedral a centre of active religious life in London. The introduction of more elaborate ritual and decorations led to considerable hostility against him, esp. after he had been appointed Dean in 1890. He was succeeded as Dean by W. R. *Inge.

W. H. *Hutton, *Robert Gregory, 1819–1911, being the Autobiography of Robert Gregory, D.D., Dean of St. Paul's* (1912). A. R. Buckland in *D.N.B., 1901–1911*, Suppl. ii (1912), p. 163 f.

GREMIAL. Acc. to W. liturgical usage, a cloth spread by the bishop upon his lap when he is seated during the singing of the *Kyries, *Gloria in excelsis*, and *Creed in the Mass, and on certain other occasions, to prevent the soiling of his vestments by his hands. Its use, originally not confined to bishops, first appears in the late 13th cent. The word 'gremiale', however, is first met with in the 15th cent.

Braun, *L.P.*, p. 231 f. J. Braun, S.J., in *C.E.*, vii (1910), p. 26.

GREY FRIARS. Friars of the *Franciscan Order (q.v.), so named from the colour of their habit (now brown), to distinguish them from the Black Friars (*Dominicans) and White Friars (*Carmelites).

GREY NUNS. A name given to Sisters of Charity in various countries. The best known are the Grey Nuns of Charity in N. America. They were founded by Madame d'Youville (Ven. Marie-Marguerite Dufrost de Lajemmerais) at Montreal in 1737 as a small community of ladies who devoted themselves to the care of the sick. Eight years later they adopted a Rule which was sanctioned by episcopal authority in 1754 and approved by *Leo XIII in 1880. Besides the three religious vows, the Sisters promise to devote their lives to the relief of human suffering. From Montreal the Sisters spread to other parts of N. America, and separate congregations were formed in different cities, one of the most notable being the Grey Nuns of the Cross founded at Ottawa in 1845. Apart from the American Grey Nuns, the name is given to Sisters of Charity in France and in Germany ('Grey Sisters of St. Elisabeth').

On the Grey Nuns of N. America and the Grey Nuns of the Cross, see Sisters M. E. Ward and V. O'Leary in *C.E.*, vii (1910), p. 31 f., s.vv. respectively. Also life of Mère d'Youville by A. Ferland-Angers (Montreal, 1945). On the Grey Sisters of St. Elizabeth there are commemorative volumes to mark the 50th anniversary of their foundation by J. Jungnitz (Breslau, 1892) and to mark the 80th anniversary by O. Cohausz (ib., 1922). Heimbücher, ii, pp. 481–3. H. C. Wendlandt in *L.Th.K.*, iv (1932), col. 654 f., s.v. 'Graue Schwestern'.

GRIESBACH, JOHANN JAKOB (1745–1812), NT scholar. A pupil of J. S. *Semler, he was professor of the NT at Jena from 1775 until his death. The first critic to make a systematic application of literary analysis to the Gospels, he maintained that St. *Mark was the latest of the three Synoptics and based his work on Mt. and Lk. (the 'dependence theory'). His most valuable work, however, was in the field of *textual criticism. After travels in England and France to work at MSS., he published an edition of the Greek NT in which, for the first time in Germany, the '*Textus Receptus' was abandoned (2 vols., 1775–7), and thereby laid the foundations of all subsequent work on the Greek text.

Griesbach's writings included *Symbolae Criticae ad supplendas et corrigendas Variarum N.T. Lectionum Collectiones* (Halle, 2 vols., 1785–93) and *Commentarius Criticus in Textum Graecum Novi Testamenti* (Jena, 1793–1811). A collection of his *Opuscula Academica* was issued by his pupil, J. P. Gabler (Jena, 2 vols., 1824–5). J. C. W. Augusti, *Über J. J. Griesbachs Verdienste* (Berslau, 1812). E. Reuss in *P.R.E.* (ed. 3), vii (1899), pp. 170–2.

GRIGNION DE MONTFORT, LOUIS MARIE, St. (1673–1716), popular missionary. Educated at the *Jesuit College at Rennes, he devoted himself early to a life of poverty and prayer, and was ordained priest in 1700. From 1701 to 1703 he was chaplain at a hospital at Poitiers where he founded the 'Daughters of Wisdom', a congregation for nursing the sick and educating poor children. In 1704 he began to realize his true vocation, the giving of missions throughout W. France, where he suffered from persecutions from the *Jansenists, who grudged his influence. *C.* 1712 he founded the 'Company of Mary', a congregation of missionaries. Both his foundations were almost extinct at his death, but they have subsequently revived. His *Traité de la vraie dévotion à la Sainte Vierge*, after having long been lost was recovered in 1842 and has exercised a powerful influence on Catholic devotion. He was beatified in 1888, and canonized by *Pius XII on 20 July 1947. Feast day, 28 Apr.

There is an Eng. tr. of his *Traité de la vrai dévotion à la Sainte Vierge* by F. W. *Faber (London, 1863). There is much documentary material in the report of the inquiries leading up to his canonization, publ. by the Sacra Rituum Congregatio, Sectio Historica, Nos. 66 and 67; Rome, 1947. Lives and studies include those of P. Grandet (Nantes, 1724), P. Picot de Clorivière, S.J. (Paris, Saint-Malo, and Rennes, 1785), J. M. Quérard (4 vols., Rennes, 1887), 'A Secular Priest' ([Dr. Cruikshank], *Blessed Louis Marie Grignon de Montfort and his Devotion*, 2 vols., London, 1892, with bibl.), A. Lhoumeau (Paris, 1902), J. M. Texier (ib., 1902), E. Jac ('Les Saints', 1903), A. Laveille, Cong. Orat. (Paris, 1907), G. Rigault (Marseilles, 1930; Eng. tr., 1932), E. Tisserant (Rome, 1943; incl. text of his Testament), G. Bernoville (Paris, 1946) and P. Eyckeler (Maastricht, etc., 1947). Id., *Le Testament de S. Louis-Marie Grignon de Montfort*. Étude historique (Maastricht, etc., 1953). E. Tisserant, 'Le Testament de S. Louis-Marie Grignon de Montfort' in *Anal. Boll.*, lxviii (1950), pp. 464–74.

GRIMSHAW, WILLIAM (1708–63), perpetual curate of Haworth. Educated at Christ's College, Cambridge, he was ordained deacon in 1731 and for some years was chaplain at Todmorden, where he emerged from a long spiritual crisis a fervent missionary. Becoming perpetual curate of Haworth, Yorks, in 1742, by his devoted zeal and consistency he gained a remarkable influence in his own and the surrounding parishes. He welcomed to his pulpit *Methodists and *Evangelicals, among them J. *Wesley, G. *Whitefield, and H. *Venn, and later himself engaged in itinerant preaching. When troubles arose from incumbents in the parishes where Grimshaw preached uninvited, his evident sincerity led his diocesan, the Abp. of *York (Matthew Hutton, 1747–57), to give him a measure of support. Grimshaw was himself a strong *Calvinist, though not intolerant of *Arminians and others with whom he disagreed.

R. Spence Hardy, *William Grimshaw, Incumbent of Haworth, 1742–1763* (1860). J. H. Overton in *D.N.B.*, xxiii (1890), p. 254 f.

GRINDAL, EDMUND (1519?–83), Abp. of *Canterbury. The son of a Cumberland farmer, he was educated at Cambridge, and became a fellow of Pembroke Hall in 1538, and later, chaplain to *Edward VI and prebendary of *Westminster. He went into exile under *Mary to Frankfurt, where he sought to reconcile the party of J. *Knox and the defenders of the 1552 BCP. In 1559 he was made Bp. of London and one of the revisers of the BCP, in 1570 Abp. of *York, and in 1575 Abp. of Canterbury. On his refusal to suppress the Puritan 'prophesyings' he was suspended in 1577 from his jurisdictional, but not from his spiritual, functions; these were restored to him in 1582. His theology was moderately *Calvinist, and he had considerable sympathy even with the Puritan critics of episcopacy.

J. *Strype, *History of the Life and Acts of Edmund Grindal* (1710; new ed., 1821). W. Nicholson (ed.), *The Remains of Archbishop Grindal* (*Parker Society, 1843), with preface by the editor. H. Robinson (ed.), *The Zürich Letters* (2 vols., Parker Society, 1842–5), passim. M. *Creighton in *D.N.B.*, xxiii (1890), pp. 261–4.

GRINFIELD, EDWARD WILLIAM (1785–1864), Biblical scholar. Educated at Lincoln College, Oxford, he was ordained in 1808, and wrote a large number of pamphlets and articles in defence of a rigid theological orthodoxy. He is remembered esp. by the lectureship at Oxford which he founded in 1859 to promote the study of the *Septuagint.

N. D. F. Pearce in *D.N.B.*, xxiii (1890), p. 265.

GROCYN, WILLIAM (1446?–1519), English Renaissance scholar. He was educated at New College, Oxford, and later taught at Magdalen and Exeter Colleges. After studying Greek and Latin in Italy under famous teachers from *c.* 1489 to 1491, he was recognized on his return to Oxford as the foremost English scholar and teacher of his time. J. *Colet, T. *More, and D. *Erasmus all sought his guidance. His influence in the university made it unnecessary for the future to go to Italy for Greek learning. In his religious attitude he was more conservative than most of those who had come under similar influences, e.g. he preferred *Aristotle to *Plato and did not cease to study the *Schoolmen. In his later life he denied, however, the traditional attribution of the 'Ecclesiastical Hierarchy' to *Dionysius, the companion of St. Paul, though he had earlier defended it.

The best account is the memoir by M. Burrows appended to his ed. of 'Linacre's Catalogue of Books belonging to William Grocyn in 1520 together with his Accounts as Executor', pr. in O.H.S. *Collectanea*, ii (O.H.S., xvi; 1890), pp. 317–31, the memoir being pr. pp. 332–80. S. Lee in *D.N.B.*, xxiii (1890), pp. 266–9.

GROOTE, GEERT DE (1340–84), **Gerardus Magnus**, the mystic who founded the ''*Brethren of the Common Life'. A native of Deventer, he was educated at *Paris, where he had a brilliantly successful career. For a time he taught at *Cologne and elsewhere, living (as his means easily allowed) in great luxury and self-indulgence. In 1374 he was converted and began to live a devout and simple life. After three years spent in the monastery of Munnikhuizen, he followed the advice of Jan van *Ruysbroeck and became (1379) missionary preacher in the diocese of Utrecht, though he was never ordained priest. Here his outspoken condemnation of the abuses of the time led his licence to be withdrawn in 1383; but his appeal against the sentence was never answered as he died soon after. Groote gathered round him a few friends who lived a quasi-monastic life at Deventer and became the nucleus of the Brethren of the Common Life. Some years earlier he had started a community for women on similar lines in the town. Groote succeeded in giving mysticism a note at once less unworldly and less self-centred than it commonly assumed. His Life was written by *Thomas à Kempis.

Epistolae ed. W. Mulders, S.J. (Tekstuitgaven van Ons Geestelijk Erf, iii; Antwerp, 1933). Life by Thomas à Kempis pr. among the latter's works (Nuremberg, 1494, fol. xxix–xxxviii); Eng. tr. by J. P. Arthur, *The Founders of the New Devotion* (1905), pp. 1–78. G. Bonet-Maury, *Gérard de Groote* (Paris, 1878); C. L. Grube, *Gerhard Groot und seine Stiftungen* (1883). R. R. Post, *De Moderne Devotie*. Geert Groote en zijn Stichtingen (Amsterdam, 1940), esp. pp. 9–44. J. van Ginneken, S.J., *Geert Groote's Levensbeeld naar de Oudste Gegevens bewerkt* (Verhandelingen der Nederlandsche Akademie van Wetenschappen, Afd. Letterkunde, Nieuwe Reeks, Deel xlvii, No. 2; 1942). K. C. L. M. De Beer, *Studie over de Spiritualiteit van Geert Groote* (Brussels-Nijmegen, 1938), with bibl. E. F. Jacob, 'Gerard Groote and the Beginnings of the "New Devotion" in the Low Countries' in *J.E.H.*, iii (1952), pp. 40–57. Unsigned art. in *Enciclopedia Ecclesiastica*, ed. A. Bernareggi, iv (1950), cols. 270–3, s.v., with detailed bibl. See also bibl. to *Brethren of the Common Life, Devotio Moderna, Imitation of Christ*, and *Windesheim*.

GROPPER, JOHANN (1503–59), theologian. He studied jurisprudence and theology at *Cologne university, where he became known as 'Os cleri Coloniensis', and in 1532 he was appointed a Canon of Xanten. After attending a Synod at Cologne (1536), called by the Abp. *Hermann to combat the teaching of the Reformers, he drew up an *Enchiridion* in which he included an exposition of the *Creed, the *Seven Sacraments, the Lord's Prayer, and the *Decalogue. This, though later (1596) placed on the *Index, was well received by the

theologians of Cologne, and by Cardinals G. *Contarini, R.*Pole, and G. *Morone, who regarded it as a suitable basis for a reconciliation between the Protestants and Rome. In the cause of reunion Gropper negotiated with M. *Bucer in 1540, but, though some agreement was reached on grace and justification, none was attempted on authority and the Eucharist. When the Abp. of Cologne himself became a Protestant, Gropper secured his deposition, and restored the Catholic religion, for which services he was made Provost of Bonn in 1547, and in 1556 *Paul IV offered him a cardinal's hat.

Lives by W. van Gulik (Freiburg i.Br., 1906) and W. Lipgens (Münster i.W., 1951; with portrait and bibl.). L. Pastor, *Die kirchlichen Reunionsbestrebungen während der Regierung Karls V* (1879). S. Ehses, 'Johannes Groppers Rechtfertigungslehre auf dem Konzil von Trient' in *R.Q.*, xx (1906, II), pp. 175–88. A. Humbert in *D.T.C.*, vi (1920), cols. 1880–5.

GROSSTESTE, ROBERT (c. 1175–1253), Bp. of *Lincoln. He was the descendant of a poor family of Stradbroke in Suffolk. Little is known of his early life except that he studied at *Oxford and possibly at *Paris. Early in the 13th cent. he came to Oxford as a teacher, and became the most famous master of the time. He was given many preferments and sinecures, among them the Archdeaconry of Leicester, but after a grave illness he resigned all in 1232 except a prebend at Lincoln. From 1224 to 1235 he taught at the newly founded *Franciscan house of studies at Oxford; he was a close personal friend of *Adam Marsh and a great admirer of the order, the English branch of which mainly owed to him its position in Oxford as well as its interest in scholarship. In 1235 he was elected Bp. of Lincoln, then the largest diocese in England, and at once began a thorough visitation, in the course of which he deposed many abbots and priors. He saw their chief fault in neglecting to staff adequately the parish churches in their care. In 1236 he witnessed the confirmation of Magna Charta. From 1239 to 1245 he was at variance with his dean and chapter, who claimed exemption from episcopal visitation, and in the course of the conflict suspended and deprived the dean. The affair was settled when *Innocent IV by a bull of 25 Aug. 1245 gave the bishop full power over the chapter. In 1245 Grosseteste also attended the Council of *Lyons, and in 1250 visited Rome, where he made his famous speech 'De corruptelis Ecclesiae', directed esp. against the custom of appointing Italians, ignorant of the language and country, to rich English benefices. The last years of his life were troubled by the appointment of one of the Pope's nephews to a canonry of Lincoln, which he refused to recognize. Several attempts to secure Grosseteste's canonization came to nothing.

Grosseteste's interests covered a very wide range of learned studies, including astronomy, mathematics, optics, and other scientific subjects. His experiments in natural science were commended by, and probably inspired, Roger

*Bacon. His translations from the Greek include *Aristotle's 'Nicomachean Ethics' and 'De Virtute', works of St. *John of Damascus and of Pseudo-*Dionysius with the *scholia* of *Maximus Confessor, the Epp. of St. *Ignatius of Antioch, and the '*Testaments of the Twelve Patriarchs' in collaboration with John of Basingstoke, all of them very literal. He also commented on Book VIII of Aristotle's 'Physics' and the 'Nicomachean Ethics', the works of Pseudo-Dionysius and several Biblical books, among them Psalms 1–100 and St. *Paul's Epp. to the Romans and to the Galatians. His philosophico-theological works include treatises 'De Anima', 'De Libero Arbitrio', 'De Forma Prima Omnium', 'De Veritate', 'De Potentia et Actu', and 'Quaestiones Theologicae'. In his philosophy of nature he follows St. *Augustine and the Arab *Neoplatonists rather than Aristotle, taking over esp. the Augustinian doctrine of light, on which he builds a complete system of metaphysics in his treatise 'De Luce'. He held that light was a very subtle corporeal substance and the first form to be created in prime matter, from which all else develops acc. to immanent laws. He also taught that God was the exemplary cause of all things and that His existence was immediately known but could also be proved from the argument of motion. He was with the Franciscan school in teaching the primacy of will over intellect. In addition he wrote a number of pastoral and devotional works, including treatises on confession, on the *Eucharist, and on the pains of *Purgatory, as well as Sermons and Letters.

A number of his works were printed in the 16th cent., but many still remain unpublished. *Epistolae* ed. H. R. Luard (R.S., 1861); these are the chief source for his life. *Rotuli*, ed. F. N. Davis (*Canterbury and York Society, x, 1913; Lincoln Record Society, xi, 1914). Other texts in L. Baur, *Die philosophischen Werke des Robert Grosseteste* (B.G.P.M., ix; 1912). Lives by S. Pegge (London, 1793), G. G. Perry (ib., 1871), and F. S. Stevenson (ib., 1899). E. Franceschini, 'Roberto Grossatesta, vescovo di Lincoln, e le sue traduzioni latini' in *Atti del Reale Instituto Veneto di Scienze, Lettere ed Arti*, xciii, Parte Seconda (1934), pp. 1–138. A. C. Crombie, *Robert Grosseteste and the Origins of Experimental Science* (1953). D. A. Callus, O.P. (ed.), *Robert Grosseteste, Scholar and Bishop*. Essays in Commemoration of the Seventh Centenary of his Death (1955). S. H. Thomson, *The Writings of Robert Grosseteste* (1940; bibliography). H. R. Luard in *D.N.B.*, xxiii (1890), pp. 275–8.

GROTIUS, HUGO (1583–1645), Huig van Groot, Dutch jurist and theologian. He was the descendant of an influential family of Delft. A very precocious boy, he went to *Leyden university at the age of twelve, where he was deeply influenced by humanism (J. J. *Scaliger). At the age of fifteen he accompanied J. van Oldenbarnevelt on a visit to France, and at eighteen he was appointed Historian of the States General and in 1607 Advocate Fiscal of Holland, Zeeland, and W. Friesland. He now began to take a keen interest in theological questions, siding with the *Arminians. In 1613 he was sent on a diplomatic mission to England, where he acquainted *James I with the religious situation in the Netherlands, but without being able to gain him to his opinions. On his return (1613) he was made Pensionary of Rotterdam. By his support of moderation in his *Ordinum Pietas* (1613) he incurred the hostility of Prince Maurice of Nassau, the leader of the Calvinists. In 1614 he drafted a *Resolution for Peace in the Church*. His eirenical sympathies, combined with his friendship for Oldenbarnevelt, led to a sentence of lifelong imprisonment in 1618. His wife having contrived to arrange his escape in a box of books, he settled at *Paris in 1621, where Louis XIII awarded him a pension. But though in sympathy with many Catholic doctrines, Grotius refused the advantages which conversion would have brought him and remained outside the RC Church. In 1622 he wrote his treatise *De Veritate Religionis Christianae*, and in 1623 began the work that established his permanent fame as a jurist, *De Jure Belli ac Pacis* (Paris, 1625). Having returned to Holland in 1631, he was banished and went a little later to Germany. In 1635 he returned to Paris as ambassador of Queen *Christina of Sweden. In these later years his literary energies were mainly devoted to the cause of reunion, among his writings being *Via ad Pacem Ecclesiasticam* and *Votum pro Pace Ecclesiastica* (both 1642). He died at Rostock on his way back from Sweden to France from the consequences of a shipwreck.

Grotius's principal religious work was the *De Veritate Religionis Christianae*. Designed as a practical handbook for missionaries, it sought to uphold the evidences of natural theology and to establish the superiority of the Christian faith to all other creeds. It found the essentials of the Gospel in a perfect trust in Divine Providence and in the ordering of human life acc. to the principles laid down by Christ. The book contained much that was valued by Christians of all denominations and became a standard work. In his teaching on the Atonement, Grotius anticipated some of the more liberal doctrines of the 19th–20th cents.

Of his other theological writings, his *Annotationes in Vetus et Novum Testamentum* (1642) marked a new departure in the science of exegesis. Discarding the current belief in Biblical inspiration, Grotius here adopted the method of philological criticism. At the same time he stressed the necessity of ecclesiastical tradition for the right understanding of Scripture, tradition, acc. to him, holding the same place in this domain as custom interpreting the written law holds in jurisprudence.

His great work, *De Jure Belli ac Pacis*, also rests its theses to a large extent on tradition. Though it finally severed law from theology, fixing the principle of justice in the unalterable Law of Nature which has its source in man as a social being, it utilized medieval and modern theologians, and, by its comprehensive systematization, earned him the title of 'Father of International Law'.

Grotius's *Opera Theologica*, ed. 3 vols. fol. at Amsterdam, 1644–6 (repr. London, 1660). Letters first ed. Leiden, 1648; fuller collection ed. Amsterdam, 1687. Eng. tr. of *De Iure Belli* (abridged) by W. Whewell (3 vols., Cambridge, 1853). J. ter Meulen–P J. J. Diermanse, *Bibliographie des écrits imprimés de Hugo Grotius* (The Hague, 1950). Early bibl.

in P. A. Lehmann, *Hugonis Grotii Manes Vindicati* (Delft, 1727); modern bibl. by J. Ter Meulen, *Concise Bibliography of Hugo Grotius* (Leiden, 1925). Lives by P. A. Lehmann (in op. cit.), C. van Brandt–C. van Cattenbuch (2 vols., Dordrecht, 1727), C. Butler (London, 1826). W. S. M. Knight, *The Life and Works of Hugo Grotius* (Grotius Society Publications, iv; London, 1925). R. S. Franks, *A History of the Doctrine of the Work of Christ in its Ecclesiastical Development*, ii [1918], pp. 48–73. M. *Pattison in *E.B.* (ed. 11), xii (1910), pp. 621–4.

GROTTAFERRATA (Lat. *Crypta ferrata*). The site of a *Basilian monastery on the lower slopes of the Alban hills, near Rome, founded in 1004 by St. Nilus the Younger. It has remained a centre of Greek learning in Italy, though in the Middle Ages it came largely under Latinizing influences. In the Renaissance period its (*commendatory) abbots included many distinguished scholars, notably Cardinals *Bessarion, Giulio della Rovere (afterwards Pope *Julius II), and *Consalvi. In 1881 *Leo XIII re-established here a purely Byzantine Rite. The monastery contains a fine collection of Greek MSS.

A. Rocchi, *Codices Cryptenses* (Rome, 1884); id., *La badia di S. Maria di Grottaferrata* (Rome, 1884); P. *Batiffol, *L'Abbaye de Rossano* (Paris, 1891); A. Muñoz, *L'Art byzantin à l'exposition de Grottaferrata* (Rome, 1906); O. Marucchi, 'Grottaferrata. Scoperta di un antico cimitero cristiano' in *Nuovo Bullettino di Archeologia Cristiana*, xix (1913), pp. 230–7.

GROU, JEAN NICOLAS (1731–1803), French *Jesuit. From 1751 to 1755 he was professor at the Jesuit college of La Flèche. Later he lived at Pont-à-Mousson, at Paris, and (from 1792 till his death) in England. He published several works on *Plato as well as a vigorous defence of the Jesuit Order. 'Père Grou' is best known, however, for his fine spiritual writings, some of which have circulated very widely both in French and in translations, —among them his *Caractères de la vraie dévotion* (1778), *Maximes spirituelles* (1789), *Méditations en forme de retraite sur l'amour de Dieu* (1796), besides several posthumous books, notably *L'École de Jésus-Christ* (2 vols., 1855).

A. Cadrès, S.J., *Notice sur la vie et les œuvres du Père Jean-Nicolas Grou* (1862; repr. in J. N. Grou, *L'Intérieur de Jésus et de Marie*, posthumous, 1862, pp. xiii–cii). Sommervogel, iii (1892), cols. 1868–82, and ix (1900), 442 f. P. Bernard in *D.T.C.*, vi (1920), cols. 1888–90, s.v.

GROUP MOVEMENT. See *Oxford Group*.

GRUNDTVIG, NIKOLAI FREDRIK SEVERIN (1783–1872), Danish religious teacher. From 1839 till his death he was preacher at the Vartov Hospital at Copenhagen, and in 1861 was given the title and rank of a 'Bishop'. In 1824, after some deep religious experiences, he started a reforming movement in Danish Lutheranism, attacking the rationalism and state domination of religion, and seeking to restore dogmatic orthodoxy with the *Apostles' Creed as the standard. With the movement thus begun ('Grundtvigianism') came a renewed understanding of the Church and the Sacraments in Danish theology. He

was also active in founding the Folk High Schools in Denmark. He was an authority on Anglo-Saxon and Norse literature. He and S. *Kierkegaard together are the most notable figures in Danish theology in the 19th cent.

Grundtvig's extensive MSS. are housed in the Royal Library at Copenhagen. No complete edition of his writings exists. The fullest is that ed. H. Begtrup (10 vols., Copenhagen, 1904–9). Correspondence ed. G. Christensen and Stener Grundtvig (2 vols., ib., 1924–6). His poetry was ed. by Svend Grundtvig (7 vols., ib., 1880–9). Grundtvig's correspondence with Ingemann between 1821 and 1850 also ed. Svend Grundtvig (ib., 1882). Germ. tr. of collection of his writings by J. Tiedje (2 vols., Jena, 1927). Danish Life, setting Grundtvig in relation to the history of Denmark in 19th cent., by F. Rönning (8 vols., Copenhagen, 1907–14). Shorter lives in Danish by H. Brun (2 vols., Kolding, 1879–82) and in German by J. *Kaftan (Basle, 1876). J. P. Bang, *Grundtvig og England* (1932). H. Begtrup, *N. F. S. Grundtvigs danske Kristendom*. Historisk Fremstillet (2 vols., 1936); also several other writings by the same author. P. G. Lindhardt, *Grundtvig. An Introduction* (S.P.C.K., 1951), with useful bibl., pp. 137–9. L. Schröder in *P.R.E.* (ed. 3), vii (1899), pp. 206–17; H. de Boor in *R.G.G.* (ed. 2), ii (1928), cols. 1519–21.

GRÜNEWALD, MATTHIAS (c. 1475–1528), German painter. Very little is known of his life. The most famous work attributed to him is the altar-piece of Isenheim, near Colmar, a polyptych of eleven panels completed before 1516, and now in the Colmar Museum. The Crucifixion is portrayed with cruel realism, with St. *John the Baptist directing an exceptionally long index finger to the Cross, with the inscription: 'He must increase and I must decrease' (Jn. 4. 30). K. *Barth sees in the Baptist the true type of the Christian witness, pointing away from himself and his experience to the objective Word of God.

Paintings and drawings ed. H. A. Schmid (2 parts and suppl., Strasbourg, 1908–11). Collection of drawings also ed. M. I. Friedländer (Berlin, 1927). A. Burckhard, *Matthias Grünewald*. Personality and Accomplishment (Cambridge, Mass., 1936), with detailed bibl. Other general studies by F. Bock (Strasbourg, 1904), O. Hagen (Munich, 1923), and H. Feurstein (Bonn, 1930), all with copious illustrations. W. Fraenger, *Matthias Grünewald in seinem Werke*. Ein physiognomischer Versuch (1936). H. A. Schmid in *Allgemeines Lexikon der bildenden Künstler*, ed. U. Thieme–F. Becker and others, xv (1922), pp. 134–7, s.v., with bibl.

GUALBERT, St. JOHN. See *John Gualbert, St.*

GUARANTEES, The Law of. The law passed on 13 May 1871 to regulate the relations between the first government of the new Kingdom of Italy and the Papacy. The Pope's person was declared sacred and inviolable; he was to receive an annual sum of 3,225,000 lire, free of taxation, for certain specified expenses; the *Vatican, the *Lateran Palace, and the Papal villa at *Castel Gandolfo were to remain in the Pope's possession; the freedom of *conclaves and of *General Councils was guaranteed; the diplomatic immunity of foreign envoys to the Holy See was recognized; and the seminaries in Rome and in the six *Suburbicarian sees were to be under the sole authority of the Pope. The relations between the Vatican and the Italian government were regulated by it until the *Lateran Treaty of 1929.

Text (Italian) ed. H. v. Kremer-Auenrode–P. Hirsch in *Das Staatsarchiv*, Erster Supplementband zu Band xxiii, xxiv (1877), pp. 63–6; operative clauses of Germ. tr. repr. in Mirbt, No. 608, pp. 466–8. F. Olgiati, *La questione romana e la sua soluzione* (1929), pp. 75–91, also with operative clauses of (Ital.) text, pp. 77–81. G. Amabile, *La legge delle guarentigie*. Studi giuridico-politico (Catania, 1897). U. Benigni in *C.E.*, vii (1910), p. 48 f., s.v.; C. Corsanego in *E.C.*, vii (1951), cols. 1060–2, s.v. 'Legge delle guarentigie'.

GUARDIA NOBILE. See *Noble Guard*.

GUARDIA PALATINA D' ONORE. See *Palatine Guard*.

GUARDIAN. The superior of a *Franciscan friary. He normally holds office for three years.

GUARDIAN, The. A weekly Anglican religious newspaper, founded in 1846, by R. W. *Church, Frederic Rogers, and others, to uphold *Tractarian principles, and to show their relevance to the best secular thought of the day. The *Guardian* always claimed to be the offspring of the Tractarian movement, and to provide independent comment upon theological, political, and social issues. It ceased publication in 1951.

GUARDIAN ANGELS. The belief that God assigns to every man an angel to guard him in body and soul was common to the pagan (e.g. *Plato, *Phaedo*, 108 B) and the Jewish world, though it is not clearly formulated in the OT. It is expressed in *Enoch (100. 5), where the author states that the just have protecting spirits. In the NT the popular belief is reflected in Acts 12. 15 and confirmed, in the case of children, by the Lord (Mt. 18. 10). Though the *Shepherd* of *Hermas (*c.* 140–55) says that every man has an angel to guide him (Mand. VI. ii. 1–3), there is much variety of opinion among the Fathers in general. St. *Ambrose (*In Ps.* 37. 43) believed that the righteous were deprived of guardian spirits in order that, having a harder struggle against evil, they might attain to greater glory, while St. *Jerome (*In Jerem.* 30. 12) and St. *Basil (*Hom. in Ps.* 33. 5) state that sin drives them away. *Honorius of Autun (d. 1151), who was followed by subsequent teachers, first defined the belief clearly. He held that each soul, at the moment that it was introduced into the body, was entrusted to an angel (*Unaquaeque etiam anima, dum in corpus mittitur, angelo committitur, Elucidarium* ii, 31). St. *Thomas Aquinas (*S. Theol.* I, q. 113, a. 4) held that only angels of the lowest order fulfilled this function, whereas *Duns Scotus and others maintained that the mission might be committed to any member of the angelic host.

The function of the Guardian Angels is the protection of body and soul and the presentation of prayers to God (Rev. 8. 3 f.). They were originally commemorated with St. *Michael, but an independent feast, first found in *Portugal in 1513, was extended to the whole RC Church by Clement X in 1670, and assigned to 2 Oct.

J. Duhr in *Dict. Sp.*, i (1937), cols. 586–98, s.v. 'Anges gardiens', with reff.; further bibl., col. 624 f. H. Pope in *C.E.*, vii (1910), p. 49 f., s.v. A. Wilmart, O.S.B., *Auteurs spirituels et textes dévots du moyen-âge latin* (1932), ch. xiv, 'Prières à l'ange gardien', pp. 537–58.

GUDULE, St. (d. ?712), Patroness of Brussels. She is said to have belonged to a noble family of Brabant, but since the oldest surviving Life dates from the 11th cent., little is known of her with any certainty. Since 1047, the principal church of Brussels, whither her remains were translated in that year, has been dedicated to her. She is often depicted with a lantern, in reference to the legend that when the devil had one morning blown out the taper by which she regularly discovered her way to church, it was miraculously rekindled. Feast day, 8 Jan.

AA.SS., Jan. I (1643), pp. 513–30 which includes (pp. 514–24) the Life by Hubert of Brabant (11th cent.; mainly apocryphal). J. *Bollandus, 'De S. Gudila Virgine Commentarius Praevius' in *Acta Sanctorum Belgii*, v (1798), pp. 667–89. R. Podevyn, O.S.B., 'Étude critique sur la *Vita Gudulae*' in *Revue Belge de Philologie et d'Histoire*, ii (1923), pp. 619–41.

GUÉRANGER, PROSPER LOUIS PASCAL (1805–75), French *Benedictine monk. He was ordained to the priesthood in 1827. With a view to the re-establishment of the Benedictine Order in France, he bought the priory of *Solesmes in 1832, opened it in 1833, and in 1837 made his profession at Rome and was appointed by *Gregory XVI the first Abbot of Solesmes, where he spent the rest of his life. He was keenly interested in liturgical matters, and as a zealous *ultramontane led the movement in France for replacing the existing local diocesan uses by the one rite of Rome. He was a voluminous writer, whose popular style led some of his books to circulate very widely. Among the best known were his *Institutions liturgiques* (3 vols., 1840–51) and *L'Année liturgique* (a devotional commentary on the ecclesiastical year; 9 vols., 1841–66).

For his writings (126 items) see F. *Cabrol, *Bibliographie des bénédictins de la congrégation de France* (Solesmes, 1889), pp. 3–33. [P. Delatte, O.S.B.,] *Dom Guéranger, abbé de Solesmes* (2 vols., 1909); E. Sevrin, *Dom Guéranger et Lamennais* (1933); B. *Capelle, O.S.B., 'Dom Guéranger et l'esprit liturgique' in *Questions liturgiques et paroissiales*, xxii (1937), pp. 131–46. H. Heurtebize in *D.T.C.*, vi (1920), cols. 1894–8.

GUEST, EDMUND (1518–77), Bp. of *Salisbury. He was educated at Eton and King's College, Cambridge, of which he became a Fellow and vice-president. In 1548 he published *A Treatise against the Privy Mass* in which he repudiated the Eucharistic Sacrifice and the adoration of the consecrated elements. In 1549 he spoke against the dogma of

*Transubstantiation in discussions held at Cambridge before the Commissioners. During the reign of *Mary he remained in hiding. On the accession of *Elizabeth he became a domestic chaplain to M. *Parker (1559) and in the same year Archdeacon of *Canterbury. In 1560 he was appointed Bp. of *Rochester, and in 1564 he took part in the disputes concerning the *Real Presence, which he defended. In 1571 he subscribed the *Thirty-Nine Articles despite some difficulties about their Eucharistic doctrine. In the same year the Queen, one of whose favourites he was, appointed him to the see of Salisbury.

H. G. Dugdale, *The Life and Character of Edmund Geste* (1840). For his Eucharistic teaching, see also G. F. Hodges, *Bishop Guest: Articles Twenty-eight and Twenty-nine* (1894). E. T. Bradley in *D.N.B.*, xxiii (1890), pp. 316–18.

GUEUX (Fr. 'ragamuffins'). A title given (originally in contempt) to the Protestants who in 1566 petitioned Margaret of Parma, the regent of the Netherlands, against the *Inquisition. It was later adopted by other bodies of Protestants who opposed the Spaniards in the Low Countries.

GUNKEL, HERMANN (1862–1932), Protestant theologian. After holding teaching appointments at Göttingen (1888), Halle (1889), and Berlin (1894), he became Prof. of OT Theology at Giessen in 1907 and at Halle (succeeding C. H. *Cornill) in 1920. He was a leading member of the *Religionsgeschichtliche Schule and one of the first to develop the method of *Form-criticism (esp. in relation to the OT). His writings include *Die Wirkungen des heiligen Geistes nach der populären Anschauung des apostolischen Zeit* (1888), *Schöpfung und Chaos in Urzeit und Endzeit* (1895), Commentaries on Gen. (1901) and 1 Pet. (1907), and a series of important studies on the Psalms (seeking to date and interpret them, on the basis of classification acc. to their literary forms). He also contributed several important articles to *R.G.G.*

Eng. tr. of various short works by A. K. Dallas as *What Remains of the Old Testament and other Essays* (1928). On his work on the Psalms, see A. R. Johnson in H. H. Rowley (ed.), *The Old Testament and Modern Study* (1951), pp. 162–81. L. Hennequin in *Dict. Bibl.*, Suppl. iii (1938), cols. 1374–7, s.v., with reff. to obituary notices.

GUNNING, PETER (1614–84), Bp. of *Ely. From 1633 to 1646 he was a fellow of Clare College, Cambridge. He was a staunch Churchman, opposed to both Romanism and Puritanism, who continued during the Commonwealth to minister to Anglican congregations and held the C of E service at Exeter House in the Strand. At the *Restoration he was rewarded with rapid promotion. In 1660 he became Lady Margaret professor, and in 1661 Regius professor of divinity at Cambridge, in 1669 Bp. of *Chichester, and in 1674 Bp. of Ely. He took a leading part at the *Savoy Conference, where as 'the incomparable hammer of the schismatics' he argued against

R. *Baxter. He probably wrote the original draft of the prayer for 'All Sorts and Conditions of Men' in the BCP, though the prayer has also been ascribed to Bp. R. *Sanderson.

Modern ed. of his treatise *The Paschal or Lent Fast* (1662) by C. P. Eden in L.A.C.T. (1845). J. H. Overton in *D.N.B.*, xxiii (1890), pp. 345–8.

GUNPOWDER PLOT, The (1605). The attempt to blow up the Houses of Parliament and destroy the King, Lords, and Commons together, in the hope that the RCs would then be enabled to seize the government. A small band headed by R. *Catesby hired a cellar under the Houses of Parliament in 1604, stored it with gunpowder, and arranged for Guy *Fawkes to start the explosion. The plot was revealed to Lord Salisbury by Lord Monteagle, and the leading conspirators were executed. It resulted in the greater unpopularity of Popery and an increased severity in the Penal Code. A form of service in commemoration of the frustration of the Plot was added by Royal Proclamation to the BCP in 1605, and appointed to be used annually on 5 Nov. Its use was revoked in 1859.

The Trial of Guy Fawkes and Others (The Gunpowder Plot), ed. D. Carswell (London, 1934). D. Jardine (ed.), *Criminal Trials*, ii, *The Gunpowder Plot* (1835), with full introd. Id., *A Narrative of the Gunpowder Plot* (1857). J. Gerard, S.J., *What was the Gunpowder Plot? The Traditional Story Tested by the Original Evidence* (1897); S. R. Gardiner, *What Gunpowder Plot was* (1897). P. Sidney, *A History of the Gunpowder Plot. Its Conspiracy and its Agents* (1904). G. B. Morgan, *The Great English Treason known as the Gunpowder Plot and its (faked) Miraculous Discovery with its hitherto unknown greater Betrayal in the Year 1605* (2 vols., privately printed, Oxford, 1931–2). H. R. Williamson, *The Gunpowder Plot* (1941), with further bibl.

GÜNTHER, ANTON (1783–1863), religious philosopher. He was ordained priest in 1820, spent two years in a *Jesuit novitiate, and settled down for the rest of his life at Vienna without official position, where he actively propagated in lectures and books a system of philosophy and speculative theology. He made it his aim to interpret Catholic sacramentalism in terms of modern pantheistic idealism, esp. that of F. W. J. *Schelling and G. W. F. *Hegel. He held that the human reason could prove scientifically the mysteries of the Trinity and the Incarnation, and that there was no real cleavage between natural and supernatural truth. By a form of the *ontological argument, he maintained that the existence of God could be deduced from the analysis of self-consciousness. All the dogmas of the Church, he held, were liable to revision and improvement in the light of fuller knowledge. In spite of influential friends, all his works were condemned by the *Index in 1857, and Günther submitted to the decision. After the *Vatican Council, most of those who still adhered to his philosophy joined the *Old Catholics.

Günther's writings include (titles abbreviated): *Vorschule zur spekulativen Theologie* (1828–9), *Peregrins Gastmahl* (1830), *Süd- und Nordlichter* (1832), *Der letzte Symboliker*

(1834; on the controversy between J. A. *Möhler and F. C. *Baur), *Thomas a Scrupulis* (1835; against *Hegelianism), *Die Juste-Milieus in der deutschen Philosophie gegenwärtiger Zeit* (1838; against Baur), *Eurystheus und Herakles* (1843), and *Antisavarese* (posthumous, 1883). Collected works ed. in 9 vols., Vienna, 1882. P. Knoodt, *Anton Günther* (2 vols., Vienna, 1881). Überweg, iv, pp. 259–62, 699 f. F. Lauchert in *C.E.*, vii (1910), pp. 85–8, with full bibl.; P. Godet in *D.T.C.*, vi (1920), col. 1992 f.; A. Piolanti in *E.C.*, vi (1951), cols. 1307–9.

GUSTAV-ADOLF-VEREIN. A German Protestant society to aid the weaker sister Churches in the '*diaspora'. It was founded in 1832 by the Leipzig professor C. G. L. Grossmann, to commemorate the bicentenary of the death of King Gustavus Adolphus of Sweden, but did not gain importance until, in 1842, the court preacher, Karl Zimmermann of Darmstadt, amalgamated it with a similar society of his own. The activities of the Gustav-Adolf-Verein are extended to all the Protestant Churches irrespective of denomination, and though mainly devoted to the needs of German Protestants, do not exclude members of other nations. The help it gives takes various forms, esp. the building of churches and schools and provision for pastors and teachers. The society, which once formed a strong bond of union between the various Protestant Churches on the Continent and in N. America, and to a lesser degree also in England, has been accused of systematically fighting Rome on the one hand and trying to Germanize other countries on the other.

K. Zimmermann, *Der Gustav-Adolf-Verein nach seiner Geschichte, seiner Verfassung und seinen Werken*, ed. W. Zimmermann (son; 1878) and other works of K. Zimmermann. H. F. von Criegern, *Der Gustav Adolf-Verein in den ersten 50 Jahren seines Bestehens* (1882); id., *Geschichte des Gustav-Adolf-Vereins* (Schloessmann's Bücherei für das christliche Haus, iv; 1903). P. Lutze, *Das Buch vom Gustav Adolf-Verein* (1932); F. Blanckmeister, *Ehrenbuch des Gustav Adolf-Vereins*. Gustav Adolf-Stunden (1932). H. Drescher, *Der Gustav Adolf-Verein . . .* Festschrift zum Jahrhundert-Jubiläum (1932). W. Zimmermann in *P.R.E.* (ed. 3), vii (1899), pp. 252–7; F. Rendtorff in *R.G.G.* (ed. 2), ii (1928), cols. 1539–43; and K. Algermissen in *L.Th.K.*, iv (1932), cols. 756 f., all s.v., and with bibl.

GUSTAVUS II ADOLPHUS (1594–1632), King of *Sweden. He was the son of Charles IX, received a careful Protestant upbringing, and succeeded his father in 1611, making Axel Oxenstjerna his chancellor. In 1613 he brought the war with Denmark to an end, and in 1617 successfully concluded that with Russia by the Peace of Stolbova. In 1621 he began a war against the Catholic Vasas in Poland, to uphold the Protestant cause and make Sweden the principal power in the Baltic. In 1626 he transferred the war to the Prussian provinces, occupying Pillau, Ermland, and the delta of the Vistula. After repeated defeats by the Poles in 1627 and 1628, he concluded in 1629 the six years' truce of Altmark. In 1630 his fear of the increasing Imperial power in the Baltic led him to intervene in the *Thirty Years War. He landed a large army in Pomerania, and by the Treaty of Bärwalde obtained help from France for the promise of maintaining Catholic worship in the Catholic places he should conquer. After opposition even from the Protestant

German princes, the majority of them finally joined him after his victory over Tilly at Breitenfeld (1631). Acclaimed everywhere as the hero of Protestantism, he penetrated deeply into W. and S. Germany, wintered at Mainz, and in the spring of 1632 took the field against Tilly, whom he defeated in the battle of Rain on the Lech. After devastating Bavaria he turned against Wallenstein, whom he confronted for two months near Nuremberg. At last he offered battle at Lützen, where he was killed.

Though Gustavus Adolphus saved German Protestantism by his intervention, his premature death probably alone secured the survival of Germany. His powerful personality and his strategic gifts are generally praised; but the traditional notion that he took up arms in defence of the Gospel rather than for political reasons has been widely challenged in modern times.

Skrifter [ed. C. G. Styffe] (Stockholm, 1861). Studies by W. Harte (2 vols., London, 1759), F. F. von Soden (3 vols., Erlangen, 1865–9), G. Droysen (2 vols., Leipzig, 1869–70), J. L. Stevens (London, 1885), C. R. L. Fletcher (New York and London, 1892), N. Ahnlund (Stockholm, 1918; Eng. tr., Princeton, 1940), G. Wittrock (Stockholm, 1927), G. Mac-Munn (London, [1930]), J. Paul (Leipzig, 1932), and M. Roberts (London, 1953 ff.). *Gustaf II Adolf*. Minnesskrift på 300-Årsdagen av Slaget vid Lützen utarbetad inom Generalstabens Krigshistoriska Avdelning (Stockholm, 1932). See also bibl. to *Thirty Years War*.

GUTENBERG, JOHANN (*c.* 1396–1468), inventor of printing. Born at Mainz and trained as a goldsmith, Gutenberg went to Strassburg *c.* 1430. By 1448, when he returned to Mainz, he had begun to use movable type cast in separate letters and had probably invented a typecasting machine. At Mainz he received financial aid from Johann Fust, but became insolvent and surrendered most of his property to Fust in 1455. By 1456 the 42-line (*Mazarin) Bible had appeared. Peter Schoeffer, who probably cut the type for it, became Fust's partner and the firm produced in 1457 the first dated book, a beautiful Psalter. Gutenberg, separated from the firm, printed the 36-line Bible and probably the *Catholicon* (a vocabulary) of 1460. In his last years he was pensioned by the Abp. of Mainz. Schoeffer continued to print until 1502.

The best general study is the life by A. Ruppel (Berlin, 1939; rev. ed. 1947; with bibl.). D. C. McMurtie (ed.), *The Gutenberg Documents, with Translations of the Texts into English* (New York, 1941). Festschriften for the fifth centenary of his birth ed. O. Hartwig (Mainz, 1900), and for the twenty-fifth anniversary of the foundation of the Gutenbergmuseum at Mainz ed. A. Ruppel (ib., 1925), with important items by K. Schorbach in each. G. P. Winship, *John Gutenberg*. A Lecture at the University of Pennsylvania delivered on February 14, 1940 (Chicago, 1940). P. Butler, *The Origin of Printing in Europe* (Chicago, 1940), esp. pp. 114–37. Popular account of his work in H. G. Aldis, *The Printed Book* (1916), pp. 7–12, ed. 3 by J. Carter –B. Crutchley (1951), pp. 3–8.

GUTHLAC, St. (? 673–714), early English hermit. He was related by blood to the royal house of Mercia. Originally a monk at the *double monastery at Repton, he later migrated to an island in the marshes around the site of the present *Crowland Abbey, where for 15 to 20 years he lived a life of severe asceticism. Feast day, 11 Apr. (in some calendars, 12 Apr.).

The Guthlac Roll, now in the British Museum (Harley Roll Y 6), is a vellum roll consisting of seventeen-and-a-half drawings depicting the life of St. Guthlac. It was probably executed in the later half of the 12th cent. for the Abbot of Crowland.

The primary authority is the life (not later than 749) by Felix, prob. a monk of Jarrow, pr. in *A A.SS.*, Apr. II (1675), pp. 38–50; also ed. W. de G. Birch, *Memorials of Saint Guthlac* (Wisbech, 1881), pp. 1–64; Eng. tr. in C. W. Jones, *Saints' Lives and Chronicles in Early England* (New York, 1947), pp. 123–60. An Anglo-Saxon prose version of this life was ed., with Eng. tr., by C. W. Goodwin (London, 1848); on this life see P. Gosner, *Das angelsächsiche Prosa-Leben des hl. Guthlac* (Anglistische Forschungen, xxvii; 1909), and B. P. Kurtz, 'From St. Antony to St. Guthlac. A Study in Biography' in *University of California Publications in Modern Philology*, xii (1925–6), pp. 133–46, with reff. On the early English poem derived from the same source in the Codex Exoniensis (10th cent.), see F. Olivero, 'Sul poemetto anglosassone "Guthlac"' in *Memorie della Reale Accademia delle Scienze di Torino*, Ser. 2, lxx (1942), pp. 223–65, with full reff. On the early lives see Hardy, i, 404–10 (Nos. 920–32), and *B.H.L.*, i, 555 f. (Nos. 3723–32), and Suppl., p. 153. Facsimile ed. of the Guthlac Roll, with useful introd. by G. F. Warner (Roxburghe Club, Oxford, 1928). C. Hole in *D.C.B.*, ii (1880), pp. 823–6, s.v. [Crit. text of Felix's Life ed. B. Colgrave, Cambridge, 1956.]

GUTHRIE, JAMES (c. 1612–61), Scottish *Presbyterian. He was educated at St. Leonard's College, St. Andrews. At first an Episcopalian, he became a Presbyterian under the influence of S. *Rutherford and was ordained a minister in 1642. From 1644 to 1651 he was a member of the *General Assembly. In 1650 he excommunicated General J. Middleton as an enemy of the *Covenant and forced him to do public penance. In 1651 he became one of the 'Protesters' (or 'Remonstrants') against the ecclesiastical jurisdiction of the King and was deposed by the Assembly, which favoured a less rigid policy. In 1654 the English Privy Council appointed him one of the *Triers and a visitor for the universities. After the Restoration he attempted to prove his loyalty to the King, but his efforts were unsuccessful. In 1661 he was arraigned for high treason and tried by a commission presided over by Middleton, who had never forgiven the insult of compelling him to do public penance. He was hanged at the cross of Edinburgh after making a long speech from the scaffold.

T. McCrie and T. Thomson, *Lives of Alexander Henderson and James Guthrie* (1846), pp. 141–284 (by T. Thomson). D. P. Thomson, *James Guthrie, the Covenanting Minister of Lauder and Stirling* (1946). A. Gordon in *D.N.B.*, xxiii (1890), pp. 377–9.

GUTHRIE, THOMAS (1803–73), Scottish divine and social reformer. After ten years at Edinburgh university he was licensed as a preacher by the presbytery of Brechin in 1825, and in 1830, after a period of study abroad, inducted to the charge of Arbirlot, Angus, where he revealed his remarkable pastoral gifts. In 1837 he moved to Edinburgh to assist John Sym in the pastorate of Old Greyfriars; and in 1840 he became minister of St.

John's Church, Victoria Street, Edinburgh. At the *Disruption (1843), he came out as a strong supporter of the Free Church, and soon gained recognition by his outstanding success in collecting funds for manses for the disestablished ministers. From 1847 onwards he was engaged in establishing his celebrated 'Ragged Schools', where the poor could be given a sound education on a Protestant basis. From 1844 onwards he also identified himself with the cause of total abstinence. He was the author of many popular tracts, his most substantial work being *The Gospel in Ezekiel* (1856).

Autobiography [to 1843] ed. with a Memoir by David K. Guthrie–Charles J. Guthrie, sons (2 vols., London, 1874–5). Shorter studies by T. Muller (Geneva, 1890) and O. Smeaton (Edinburgh–London, 1900). C. J. Guthrie in *D.N.B.*, xxiii (1890), pp. 380–2. Study by A. L. Drummond in R. S. Wright (ed.), *Fathers of the Kirk* (1960), pp. 167–81.

GUYARD, MARIE (1599–1672), Ven. Marie de l'Incarnation, first Superior of the *Ursulines at Quebec. A native of Tours, she was early drawn to the religious life, but in 1617, in obedience to her parents, married Claude Joseph Martin (d. 1620), by whom she had a son, later Dom Claude Martin, O.S.B. (1619–1696). In 1631 she entered the Ursuline convent at Tours where she was appointed novice-mistress in 1633. Inspired by visions which she had received since her childhood, with the blessing of the Abp. of Tours, she joined Mme de la Peltrie (1603–71) and two other sisters in accepting an invitation of the *Jesuit mission to form a convent in Quebec in 1639. The community, of which she was appointed superior, settled first in Lower Quebec and in 1641 moved to its present site. It engaged in educational work among French and Indians, and despite hardships of climate, fire and attacks of the natives, prospered, largely owing to her leadership. She was the recipient of religious experiences which she recorded in obedience to her directors (1633 and 1654). Her works, published posthumously, include her letters (1681), *Retraites* (1682) and *L'École sainte, ou Explication familière des mystères de la foi* (1684). In 1911 she was pronounced Venerable by *Pius X.

Letters ed. Claude Martin, O.S.B., son (Paris, 1681); enlarged ed. by P. F. Richaudeau (2 vols., Tournai, 1876); supplement by E. Griselle (Paris, 1909). Claude Martin, O.S.B., *La Vie de la vénérable Mère Marie de l'Incarnation* (Paris, 1677). Other lives by F. X. Charlevoix (Paris, 1724), H. R. Casgrain (Quebec, 1864), P. F. Richaudeau (Paris, 1874), and L. Chapot (2 vols., ib., 1892). P. Renaudin, *Une Grande Mystique française au XVIIe siècle: Marie de l'Incarnation. . . .* Essai de psychologie religieuse (1935); J. Klein, *L'Itinéraire mystique de la vén. Mère Marie de l'Incarnation* (1938). Bremond, vi (1922), pp. 3–176.

GUYON, Madame (1648–1717), French *Quietist author. Jeanne Marie Bouvier de la Mothe was born at Montargis, where after a neurotic youth she came under the influence of the Duchesse de Béthune. Her unhappy marriage in 1664 to Jacques Guyon, an invalid 22 years older than herself, increased her leaning towards mysticism, and after his death (1676) she entered on a life of religious devotion. She soon fell under the spell of the Quietist works of M. de *Molinos, and in 1681 she began, in company with an imprudent *Barnabite friar, F. Lacombe (1643–1715), her spiritual director, a five years' journey through France, endeavouring to propagate her mystical beliefs. Suspected of heresy and immorality, they were arrested in 1687. Lacombe remained in prison until 1699 (he eventually died of insanity), but Mme Guyon was freed by the efforts of Mme de Maintenon. She now became prominent in the royal circle and often lectured in Mme de Maintenon's girls' school at St.-Cyr. Her greatest follower was F. *Fénelon (q.v.), with whom she corresponded from 1688. J. B. *Bossuet, who distrusted her illuminism, though he judged her sincere, wrote her a doctrinal letter in 1694. In the following year she demanded a theological commission to clear her. The resulting Conference of *Issy (1695), in which Fénelon took part, condemned her, and she was again arrested. She was finally released in 1702 on her submission, and spent the remainder of her life in Blois. Meanwhile her cause was vigorously defended by Fénelon against Bossuet. Mme Guyon's chief mystical writings include *Moyen court et très facile de faire oraison* (1685) and *Le Cantique des cantiques* (1688). She taught complete indifference, even to eternal salvation, and that in contemplation all distinct ideas should be repulsed, even of the attributes of God and the mysteries of the life of Christ.

Works ed. by her disciple, P. *Poiret (39 vols., 'Cologne', 1713–32). Eng. tr. of her autobiography in 2 vols., London, 1897. Many of her other works have also been translated into English, incl. a tr. of her Poems by W. *Cowper (Newport Pagnell, 1801). Modern studies by T. C. Upham (London, 1854; revised ed. [1905]), L. Guerrier (Paris, 1881), and E. Aegerter (ib., 1941). [P.] M. Masson, *Fénelon et Mme Guyon.* Documents nouveaux et inédits (1907). E. Seillière, *Mme Guyon et Fénelon, précurseurs de J.-J. Rousseau* (1918). Dorothy L. Gilbert–R. Pope, 'The Abbé and the Lady: The Correspondence of Fénelon and Mme Guyon' in *Journal of Religion*, xxi (1941), pp. 147–72. H. Bremond, *Apologie pour Fénelon* (1910), pp. 3–150. R. A. Knox, *Enthusiasm* (1950), pp. 319–52. Pourrat, iv, pp. 231–66. A. Largent in *D.T.C.*, vi (1920), cols. 1997–2006. See also bibl. to *Fénelon* and *Quietism*.

H

HABAKKUK, Book of. The eighth of the *Minor Prophets. Its date has been variously fixed between the last years of the reign of Manasseh (698–643) and the invasion of Judah by the Chaldeans in 600, which it predicts. Many recent critics, however, attribute the greater part of it to the Exile, or even later. B. Duhm argued that it belonged to the Greek period, the 'Chaldeans' (*Chasdim*) being an error for Greeks ('Kittim'; from Cyprus). All modern scholars are agreed that ch. 3 is an independent addition. E. Sellin, e.g., takes this chapter to be a liturgical piece concerning the Chaldean dangers, whereas B. Duhm and C. C. Torrey believe it to be directed against Alexander the Great (336–323 B.C.).

The Book opens with Habakkuk's complaint at the reign of oppression and lawlessness and God's answer that punishment is imminent in the invasion of the Chaldeans. The Prophet, terrified lest God should abandon His people, is instructed that the Chaldeans, too, will eventually fall through pride and idolatry. Ch. 3, a poem (or psalm) describes a sublime vision of the Holy God coming from Mount Paran to work the deliverance of His people and expresses the writer's unshakable confidence in Him.

Chs. 1-2 are written in the form of a dialogue of great power and beauty between Jehovah and His prophet. Their central message is that while the Chaldean is filled with pride, 'the just shall live by his faith' (2. 4) which will sustain the innocent who is involved in the sufferings of the guilty. This passage has played an important part in Christian thought through its use in Rom. 1. 17 and in Gal. 3. 11, and also in Heb. 10. 38, as the starting point of the theological concept of faith.

Commentaries by A. B. *Davidson (Camb. Bib., AV, on Nah., Hab., Zeph., 1896, pp. 45–94), W. H. Ward (I.C.C. on Mic., Zeph., Nah., Hab., Obad., Joel, 1912; sep.) and G. W. Wade (West. Comm. on Zeph., Nah., Hab., 1929, pp. 141–215)· also by B. Duhm (Tübingen, 1908). G. G. V. Stonehouse, *The Book of Habakkuk*. Introduction, Translation and Notes on the Hebrew Text (1911). P. Humbert, *Problèmes du livre d'Habaccuc* (Neuchâtel, 1944). C. C. Torrey, 'The Prophecy of Habakkuk' in *Jewish Studies in Honour of George A. Kohut*, ed. S. W. Baron–A. Marx (New York, 1935), pp. 565–82. W. A. Irwin, 'The Psalm of Habakkuk' in *Journal of Near Eastern Studies*, i (1942), pp. 10–40. S. R. *Driver in H.D.B., ii (1899), pp. 269–72, s.v.; K. *Budde in E.Bi., ii (1901), cols. 1921–8, s.v. Further commentaries under *Minor Prophets*.

HABIT (Religious dress). The distinctive outward sign of the religious state. A habit is worn by all members of the old orders (monks, friars, and nuns), and normally consists of a tunic, belt or girdle, scapular, hood for men and veil for women, and a mantle for use in choir and out of doors. The colours are, as a rule, white, brown, or black. Some modern orders and Congregations dispense with a habit in the case of men (e.g. the *Jesuits).

HABITUAL GRACE. See *Grace*.

HABURAH. See *Chaburah*.

HADES (Gk. ᾅδης). The place or state of departed spirits. The word is used in the *Septuagint as a translation for the Hebrew '*Sheol' (e.g. Is. 38. 18). In later Judaism the term took on a more definite meaning, of a place of reward for the pious dead, or alternatively, and later, of a place of waiting before judgement. In English usage it first appears *c*. 1600, as a term used to explain the article in the Creed, 'He descended into hell', where the place of waiting (the place of 'the souls in prison', 1 Pet. 3. 19) into which our Lord is there affirmed to have gone after the Crucifixion needed to be distinguished from that more usually called 'hell', i.e. the place or state of those finally damned. See also *Hell* and *Descent of Christ into Hell*.

G. Beer, 'Der biblische Hades' in *Theologische Abhandlungen. Festgabe zum 17. Mai 1902 für H. J. Holtzmann*, ed. W. Nowack and others (1902), pp. 2–29. On the passage in 1 Peter 3. 19, Bo Reicke, *The Disobedient Spirits and Christian Baptism* (Acta Seminarii Neotestamentici Upsaliensis, xiii; Copenhagen, 1946). J. Jeremias in *T.W.B.*, i (1933), pp. 146–50, s.v. 'ᾅδης' with reff.; W. Bauer, *Griechisch-Deutsches Wörterbuch* (ed. 4, 1952), cols. 21 f., s.v. 'ᾅδης'. See also bibl. to *Descent into Hell*.

HADRIAN I (d. 795), Pope from 772. He was a Roman of noble birth. During his long pontificate he continued the policy of *Stephen III of maintaining close relations with *Charlemagne. By persuading Charlemagne to conquer Lombardy (774) and depose its king, Desiderius, he freed the Papacy from a longstanding menace. But Charlemagne's increased power meant a corresponding limitation of the Church's freedom, though Hadrian's personal relations with Charlemagne continued for the most part amicable. Charlemagne occasionally intervened in purely ecclesiastical matters, e.g. in defending the claims of the Abp. of *Ravenna against the Pope. The Pope also enlisted the King's help in suppressing *Adoptianism and in his efforts for uniformity in liturgy and canon law. In the *Iconoclastic controversy, however, Emperor and Pope differed, and Charlemagne, refusing to sanction the decisions of the Synod of *Nicaea of 787, formally condemned them at Frankfurt in 794. Hadrian was a notable administrator, restoring aqueducts, walls, and towers, and fortifying the city of Rome.

His epp. are printed in J. P. Migne, *PL*, xcvi, 1203–44, and xcviii, 261–438. *L.P.* (Duchesne), i. (1886), pp. 486–523 (also in *PL*, xcvi, 1167–1204); id., *Les Premiers Temps de l'état pontificale* (1911), pp. 134–48. Also H. Hemmer in *D.T.C.*, i (1903), cols. 448–52, and M. Jugie, A.A., in *D.H.G.E.*, i (1912), cols. 614–19. On the collection of canons which goes under his name (the so-called 'Hadriana'), cf. F. *Maassen, *Geschichte der Quellen und der Literatur des canonischen Rechts im Abendlande*, i (1870), pp. 441–71. M. Jugie, A.A., in *E.C.*, i (1949), cols. 338–41, s.v. 'Adriano I'.

HADRIAN IV (*c.* 1100–59), Nicholas Break-spear, Pope from 1154. He is the only English-man who has occupied the See of Peter. Prob. the son of a clerk attached to *St. Albans, he studied in France, and having entered the *Augustinian monastery of St. Rufus near *Avignon became Abbot in 1137. When on a mission to Rome he was retained by *Eugenius III (1145–53), who appointed him Cardinal Bp. of Albano at some date before 1150. Soon afterwards he was sent as papal legate on a mission to Scandinavia where he reorganized the Churches of *Sweden and *Norway, made Trondhjem (Nidaros) an in-dependent archbishopric (1152) and did much to reform abuses. In 1154 he was unanimously elected Pope. He forthwith forced the expul-sion of *Arnold of Brescia (q.v.) and finally secured his execution (1155). In 1155 he exacted full homage from *Frederick I (Bar-barossa) before consenting to crown him. He at first refused to recognize William I (d. 1166) as King of Sicily, but after a disastrous military campaign agreed to invest him with the terri-tory he held in return for an oath of homage and annual tribute. His claim that the Emperor held his crown as a *beneficium* from the Pope precipitated a quarrel with Barbarossa which outlasted his pontificate and became acute under *Alexander III. Hadrian IV also intervened in France, where he confirmed a royal sentence against the Duke of Burgundy. He is said to have granted to Henry II of England, possibly at the suggestion of *John of Salisbury, the overlordship of *Ireland, but the facts are uncertain and the bull in question ('Laudabiliter') is prob. a forgery.

Surviving 'Epistolae et Privilegia' printed in J. P. Migne, *PL*, clxxxviii, 989–1088; further docc. calendared in P. Jaffé (ed.), *Regesta Pontificum Romanorum*, ii (ed. 2 by G. Watten-bach, Leipzig, 1888), pp. 102–45. Life by Boso, his English disciple (d. *c.* 1178), in *L.P.* (Duchesne), ii (1892), pp. 388–97. H. K. Mann, *Nicholas Breakspear (Hadrian IV)*, *A.D. 1154–1159, the Only English Pope* (1914). Edith M. Almedingen, *The English Pope. Adrian IV* (1925). H. Schroers, *Untersuchungen zu dem Streite Kaiser Friedrichs I mit Papst Hadrian IV, 1157–1158* (1916); A. Eggers, *Die Urkunde Papst Hadrians IV für König Heinrich II von England über die Besetzung Irlands* (Historische Studien Hft. 151; 1922). H. K. Mann, *The Lives of the Popes in the Middle Ages*, ix (1914), pp. 231–340. M. * Creighton in *D.N.B.*, i (1885), pp. 143–6; A. U. Clerich in *C.E.*, i (1907), pp. 156–9, s.v. 'Adrian IV'; P. Brezzi in *E.C.*, i (1948), s.v. 'Adriano IV'.

HADRIAN VI (1459–1523), Pope from 1522. Adrian Dedel was a native of Utrecht. He studied under the *Brethren of the Common Life at Deventer or Zwolle, and later at Louvain, where he became a doctor of theology in 1492. In 1507 he was chosen as tutor to the future *Charles V, and from 1516 he was the virtual ruler of Spain. In the same year he became Bp. of Tortosa, and in 1517 he was made *Inquisitor of Aragon and Navarre and created cardinal. He was unanimously elected Pope in 1522 on the death of *Leo X. The principal aims of his pontificate were the re-form of the Roman Curia, the reconciliation of the European princes, the check of the spread of Protestantism, and the deliverance of Europe from the menace of the Turks. But the times were against him, and Hadrian found himself compelled to struggle almost single-handed against the depravity, luxury and restlessness of his age. His efforts after reform met with frustration on all sides. Nor was he more successful in arousing the princes of Christendom to defend Rhodes, which fell on 24 Oct. 1522. He died a premature death, worn out with the burdens of his office, after a pontificate of little over a year. He was the author of a number of theological writings, only two of which, the *Commentarii in IV libros Sententiarum* (1516) and the *Quaestiones Quodlibeticae* (1515), were published. Except Marcellus II, he is the only Pope of modern times who has retained his baptismal name.

M. Gachard (ed.), *Correspondance de Charles-Quint et d'Adrien VI* (1859). C. Burmann (ed.), *Hadrianus VI, sive Analecta Historica de Hadriano VI* (Utrecht, 1727). E. H. J. Reusens (ed.), *Anecdota Adriani Sexti ... partim ex codice ipsius Adriani autographo, partim ex autographis* (Louvain, 1862). C. von Höfler, *Papst Adrian VI, 1522–1523* (1880); A. Lepitre, *Adrien VI* (Dijon thesis, Paris, 1880); G. Pasolini, *Adriano VI* (1913); E. Hocks, *Der letzte deutsche Papst* (1939), with further bibl. E. H. J. Reusens, *Syntagma Doctrinae Theologicae Adriani Sexti P.M. ... una cum Apparatu de Vita et Scriptis Adriani* (Louvain, 1862). E. Rodocanachi, *Les Pontificats d'Adrien VI et de Clément VII* (1933), pp. 7–86 and 273–9, with bibl. pp. 281–4. Pastor, ix (1910), pp. 1–230. J. F. Loughlin in *C.E.*, i (1907), p. 159 f., s.v. 'Adrian VI'; J. Forget in *D.T.C.*, i (1903), cols. 459–61, s.v. 'Adrien VI'; P. Richard in *D.H.G.E.*, i (1912), cols. 628–30, s.v. 'Adrien VI'; P. Maarschalkerweerd, O.F.M., in *É.C.*, i (1949), col. 348 f., s.v. 'Adriano VI'.

HADRIAN THE AFRICAN, St. (d. 709), monk. An African by birth, he became head of a monastery near Naples and a great friend of Pope *Vitalian. Having declined the Pope's offer of the see of *Canterbury for him-self, he was instrumental in securing the appointment for *Theodore of Tarsus, and set out with him for England in 668. He was detained in France on the way, but arrived at Canterbury two years later, where he became abbot of the monastery of Sts. Peter and Paul and master of the school. For forty years he furthered the movement for conforming the religious customs and practices of England to those of Rome. A man of great learning, he keenly furthered education, and established a large number of schools in different parts of England. Feast day, 9 Jan.

*Bede, *H.E.*, iv. 1 f.; v. 20, 23; notes to *Baedae Opera Historica* ed. by C. Plummer, ii (1896), pp. 202–5, 233, and 329. The passages from Bede and the legend as given by J. Capgrave in *Acta Sanctorum*, Jan. 1 (1643), pp. 595–7. T. D. Hardy, *Descriptive Catalogue of Materials relating to the History of Great Britain and Ireland to the End of the Reign of Henry VII*, i, pt. 1 (Rolls Series, 1862), p. 403 f.

HAECKEL, ERNST HEINRICH (1834–1919), German scientist. He was born at Potsdam, and after studying medicine and science at the universities of Würzburg, Berlin, and Vienna, became director of the Zoological Institute at Jena in 1862 and professor of biology in 1865. He remained at Jena till his death. A keen naturalist, he popularized C. *Darwin's theory of evolution in a treatise on General Morphology (1866) and in *Natürliche Schöpfungsgeschichte* (1867; Eng. trans., 1892). In his most widely read book, *Die Welträtsel*

(1899; Eng. trans. *The Riddle of the Universe*, 1901), he attempted to apply Darwin's theories to philosophical and religious questions. He upheld the essential unity of organic and inorganic nature and derived all the phenomena of life, physical, intellectual, and spiritual, from natural causes, denying all doctrines of a personal God, of human free-will, and of the immortality of the soul. The *Welträtsel* was followed in 1904 by the supplementary work *Lebenswunder*. His literary output was immense. In 1906 he became honorary president of the Deutscher Monistenbund, a society founded at his instigation for the spread of a monistic interpretation of the world. Though Haeckel's theories attracted wide attention, they were never of real philosophical consequence and were rejected by many of his fellow-scientists. They are now chiefly of historical interest.

Was wir Ernst Haeckel verdanken. Ein Buch der Verehrung und Dankbarkeit, ed. H. Schmidt (2 vols., 1914). Überweg, iv, 321-5 (incl. list of Haeckel's writings) and 705-7 (long bibl.).

HAERETICO COMBURENDO, De. See *De Haeretico Comburendo*.

HAGENAU, Conference of. The gathering convened in June–July 1540 by the Emp. *Charles V to discuss the points of dispute between the Catholics and Protestants of Germany. Unable to agree upon the essential nature of the Church, and therefore to proceed to the discussion of particular doctrines, the conference broke up without achieving any result. It was arranged that there should later be another gathering at Worms. See *Worms, The Disputation of*.

L. *Pastor, *Die kirchlichen Reunionsbestrebungen während der Regierung Karls V* (1879), pp. 184-98. L. Cardauns, *Zur Geschichte der kirchlichen Unions- und Reformsbestrebungen von 1538 bis 1542* (Bibliothek des kgl. Preussischen historischen Instituts in Rom, v; 1910), pp. 33-7, with various relevant docc., pp. 131-57. Pastor, xi (1912), pp. 391-6, with reff. Further bibl. in Schottenloher, iv (1938), p. 531 f. (Nos. 41323a-28). G. Kawerau in *P.R.E.*, vii (1899), pp. 333-5, s.v. 'Hagenauer Religionsgespräch'. See also bibl. to *Charles V* and *Worms, Disputation of*.

HAGGADAH (Heb. הַגָּדָה, 'narrative'). The portions of the Jewish tradition which are of a non-prescriptive kind, i.e. such as do not belong to the *Halacha. The Haggadah thus includes legend, folk-lore, homiletics, astrology, magic, and other subjects.

HAGGAI, Book of, the tenth of the *Minor Prophets. The Book, which was written in the second year of Darius, i.e. 520–519 B.C., consists of four separate discourses concerned to promote the rebuilding of the *Temple. It is addressed esp. to the two leaders of the people, Zerubbabel, the governor of Judah, and Joshua, the son of Josedech, the high priest. Though the foundations of the Temple had been laid, the work had been interrupted chiefly owing to the opposition of the *Samaritans and other neighbours of the Jews. The first discourse

(1. 4–11) attributes the prevalent drought and famine to the people's neglect of rebuilding the Temple; in the second (2. 2–9) the prophet consoles the Jews for the inferiority of the present building and prophesies a glorious future in the Messianic age, when all the nations will come to Jerusalem; the third prophecy (2. 11–19) predicts a return of fertility to the land; and the fourth (2. 21–24) promises Zerubbabel victory over his enemies. This last prophecy has been frequently regarded as referring to the Messiah.

Commentaries by H. G. Mitchell (I.C.C. on Haggai, Zech., Mal., and Jonah, 1912, pp. 3–79) and W. E. Barnes (Camb. Bib. on Hag. and Zech., RV, 1917, pp. 1–20). P. F. Bloomhardt, 'The Poems of Haggai' in *Hebrew Union College Annual*, v (1928), pp. 153–95. G. A. Cooke in *H.D.B.*, ii (1899), pp. 279–81; W. R. *Smith–T. K. *Cheyne in *E.Bi.*, ii (1901), cols. 1935–7, s.v. Further comm. under *Minor Prophets*.

HAGIOGRAPHA (Heb. כְּתֻבִים, i.e. 'Kethubim'; Gk. ἁγιόγραφα, 'writings'). A title applied to the third division of the OT canonical Scriptures, i.e. all Books not belonging to the 'Law' or the 'Prophets'. The Books comprised are Pss., Prov., Job; the five *Megilloth, i.e. Ruth, Lam., Song of Songs, Eccles., and Esther; and Dan., 1 and 2 Chron., Ezra, Neh. They were the latest Books in the Hebrew OT to achieve canonicity.

HAGIOGRAPHY. The writing of the lives of the saints. It involves a study and comparison of the extant sources, the assessment of their historical importance, and the relating of them to contemporary secular history. The primary sources include *martyrologies, *passions, calendars, biographies, prose and verse compositions, and liturgical texts. The earliest collection of such material, now unhappily lost, was that compiled by *Eusebius (c. 260–340). The critical examination of these writings, which dates from the 17th cent., has been esp. fostered by the *Bollandists. See also *Acta Sanctorum; Delehaye, Hippolyte.

The principal collections of sources, besides the *Acta Sanctorum* (q.v.), are listed under the various countries and religious orders (qq.v.); many also in *E.C.* (see below). Socii Bollandiani, *Bibliotheca Hagiographica Graeca* (1895; ed. 2, 1909); idd., *Bibliotheca Hagiographica Latina Antiquae et Mediae Aetatis* (2 vols., Brussels, 1898–1901; suppl., 1911). A. *Butler, *The Lives of the Fathers, Martyrs and other Principal Saints* (homiletic; 4 vols., 1756–9; rev. by H. Thurston–D. Attwater, 12 vols., 1926–38, with suppl. vol. by D. Attwater, 1949); D. Attwater, *A Dictionary of Saints*, being also an index to the revised edition of Alban Butler's 'Lives of the Saints' (1938). *The Book of Saints*, compiled by the Benedictine Monks of St. Augustine's Abbey, Ramsgate (1921); F. G. Holweck, *A Biographical Dictionary of Saints* (1924). F. von S. Doyé, *Heilige und Selige der römischen Kirche* (2 vols., 1929). P. F. de' Cavalieri, *Note agiografiche* (Studi e Testi, viii, ix, xxii, xxiv, xxvii, xxxiii, xlix, lxv; 1902 ff.); id., *Hagiographica* (ib., xix; 1908). H. Delehaye, S.J., *Les Légendes hagiographiques* (1905: Eng. tr., 1907) and other works cited, s.v. J. Minischthaler, *Heiligenlegenden* (2 vols., 1911–13). F. Grossi-Gondi, *Principi e problemi di critica agiografica* (1919). R. Aigrain, *L'Hagiographie, ses sources, ses méthodes, son histoire* (1953). *Analecta Bollandiana* (Brussels, 1882 ff.). L. Oliger, O.F.M., in *E.C.*, i (1948), cols. 449–54, s.v. 'Agiografia', for further bibl.

HAGIOLOGY (fr. Gk. ἅγιος, 'holy' and λογία, 'discourse', i.e. the science of holiness). The literature dealing with the lives and legends of the saints and their cultus. See *Hagiography*.

HAGIOS O THEOS. See *Agios O Theos*.

HAGIOSCOPE, also 'squint'. An opening in the chancel walls of ancient churches, to permit worshippers in the transepts, side aisles, or other parts of the church from which the altar is not otherwise visible to see the elevation of the *Host at Mass. Such openings were also known as **squints**.

HAIL, HOLY QUEEN. See *Salve Regina*.

HAIL MARY (Lat. *Ave Maria*; also known as **The Angelic Salutation**). The form of prayer to the BVM, based on the greetings of *Gabriel (Lk. 1. 28) and *Elizabeth (Lk. 1. 42). In its modern form it is as follows: '(a) Hail Mary full of grace, the Lord is with thee: Blessed art thou among women and blessed is the fruit of thy womb, Jesus. (b) Holy Mary, Mother of God; pray for us sinners now and in the hour of our death.' The devotional use of (a) goes back to the 11th cent., and first became common in the 12th, whereas the complete Hail Mary, with (b) added, did not come into general use until the 16th cent. In this later form it received official recognition from its inclusion by Pope *Pius V in the new Roman Breviary (1568).

T. Esser, O.P., 'Geschichte des englischen Grusses' in *Hist. J.*, v (1884), pp. 88–116. S. Beissel, S.J., *Geschichte der Verehrung Marias in Deutschland während des Mittelalters* (1909), ch. 13, 'Das "Gegrüsset seist du, Maria" und der Rosenkranz bis zum 15. Jahrhundert', pp. 228–50; id., *Geschichte der Verehrung Marias im 16. und 17. Jahrhundert* (1910), pp. 5–16 and passim; H. *Leclercq, O.S.B., 'Prière à la Vierge Marie sur un ostrakon de Lougsor' in *Bulletin d'ancienne Littérature et d'Archéologie chrétiennes*, ii (1912), pp. 3–32, repr. Hefele–Leclercq, v (ii; 1913), App. IV, pp. 1734–59; E. Vacandard, L'Histoire de l'Ave Maria' in *Revue du Clergé français*, lxxi (1912), pp. 315–19; H. Thurston, S.J., 'The Origins of the Hail Mary' in *The Month*, cxxi (1913), pp. 162–76 and 379–84; repr. in Thurston's *Familiar Prayers*, ed. P. Grosjean, S.J. (1953), pp. 90–114. E. Campana, *Maria nel culto cattolico*, i (1933), pp. 519–64; G. M. Roschini, O.S.M., 'L'Ave Maria. Note storiche' in *Marianum*, v (1943), pp. 177–85. Good introductory discussion by H. Thurston, S.J., in *C.E.*, vii (1910), pp. 110–12, s.v. H. Leclerq in *D.A.C.L.*, x (pt. 2; 1932), cols. 2043–62, s.v. 'Marie (Je vous salue)'.

HAIR-SHIRT. A shirt made of cloth woven from hair, and worn at all periods in the history of the Church as a means of discipline by penitents and ascetics.

HALACHA (Heb. הֲלָכָה, 'that by which one walks'). In the Jewish schools, the body of legal decisions not directly enacted in the *Mosaic law. It arose from the pious wish to make the law apply to even the most trivial and unexpected situations in daily life. At first handed down by word of mouth, it was later collected and written down, and thus gave rise to such treatises as the *Mishnah. It forms the bulk of the *Talmud, the non-Halachic remainder being known as the *Haggadah. In the course of time, elaborate rules of exegesis were devised to enable 'halachoth' to be discovered out of the Biblical text.

M, Guttmann–S. Bialoblocki in *E.J.*, vii (1931), cols. 836–848, s.v., with bibl. See also bibl. to *Talmud* and *Midrash*

HALES, ALEXANDER OF. See *Alexander of Hales*.

HALES, JOHN (1584–1656), Anglican divine, known as the 'ever-memorable'. He was a native of Bath, and educated at the Bath grammar school and at Corpus Christi College, *Oxford, where he took his degree in 1603. In 1605 he was elected Fellow of Merton, and in 1612 he became public lecturer in Greek at the university. He probably had a large share in H. *Savile's edition of St. *Chrysostom (1610–1613). In 1613 he pronounced the funeral oration on Sir T. *Bodley, and in the same year became Fellow of Eton. In 1616 he went to Holland as chaplain to the English ambassador, Sir Dudley Carleton, in which capacity he was present at the Synod of *Dort (1618). In 1619 he returned to Eton. In 1639 he became chaplain to Abp. W. *Laud and canon of *Windsor. He was dispossessed of his canonry by the parliamentary committee in 1642, and of his Fellowship at Eton in 1649. He then became tutor to a nephew of the Bp. of *Salisbury. He died in retirement at Eton. Perhaps the best known of his works is his tract *Schism and Schismatics* (written 1636, first publd. 1642) which reflects his broad-minded and eirenical position. The *Golden Remains* was published posthumously.

Collected Works [ed. by David Dalrymple, Lord Hailes] (3 vols., Glasgow, 1765). Life by J. H. Elson (New York, 1948, with detailed bibl.). A. Gordon in *D.N.B.*, xxiv (1890), pp. 30–2.

HALF-WAY COVENANT, The. A doctrine current in American *Congregationalism in the 17th and 18th cents. expressive of the relationship in which those (esp. baptized) members of the community who were devoid of personal religious faith were held to be bound to God. Its purpose was by giving such persons a definite status to prevent the Church from being reduced to an assemblage of individuals and Baptism from losing all significance for those who professed no change of heart. Its Scriptural basis was found in Jehovah's Covenant with *Abraham (Gen. 17. 7). The doctrine has now been generally rejected as incompatible with the principles of Congregationalism acc. to which the only true basis of relationship of man to God must be personal faith.

HALIFAX, CHARLES LINDLEY WOOD (1839–1934), Second Viscount Halifax. He was the son of Sir Charles Wood, First Viscount Halifax (1800–85) and Mary, d. of Earl Grey, and educated at Eton and at Christ Church, Oxford, where under the influence of E. B. *Pusey's sermons, J. M. *Neale's writings, H. P. *Liddon's friendship, and R. I. *Wilberforce's *Doctrine of the Incarnation* he became a strong and devoted High Churchman. In 1865 he was associated with the foundation of the *S.S.J.E. and himself had thoughts of joining the Society, but was dissuaded by R. M. *Benson. He continued, however, to take a keen interest in its work and made his annual retreat at Cowley until 1931. Acceptance in 1868 of the Presidency of the *English Church Union, vacant by Colin Lindsay's impending secession to Rome, brought him into most of the ecclesiastical controversies of his lifetime (*Athanasian Creed; *Public Worship Regulation Act; W. J. E. *Bennett and A. H. *Mackonochie cases; Trial of Bp. E. *King; *Lambeth Opinions; *Deceased Wife's Sister bill; *Modernism; projects for *Prayer Book Revision), in many of which he took a leading part. He held the office continuously until 1919 and again from 1927 until his death. A friendship with E. F. Portal which began at Madeira in 1890 led him to interest himself in promoting reunion between the C of E and the Holy See. With Portal he was responsible for initiating the conversations at Rome in 1894–6 and the publication of the *Revue Anglo - Romaine*; and their abortive termination by *Apostolicae Curae* (13 Sept. 1896), largely, as he thought, through the influence of the English RC Hierarchy under Cardinal H. *Vaughan, caused him profound disappointment. He later published a fully documented account of the negotiations in *Leo XIII and Anglican Orders* (1912). After the *Lambeth Appeal of 1920 he reopened the matter with Cardinal D. J. *Mercier with whom he arranged the *Malines Conversations (q.v.); but soon after Mercier's death in Jan. 1926 they were terminated. In Jan. 1928, impatient with the caution and delay of the Anglican authorities, he issued the Report himself and, soon after, his *Notes on the Conversations at Malines*. This was followed in 1930 by *The Conversations at Malines. Original Documents* (printed in France). In 1930 he also published *The Good Estate of the Catholic Church*, summing up many of his ecclesiastical ideals and expressing his long-held high regard for the BCP of 1549.

His son, EDWARD FREDERICK LINDLEY WOOD (1881–   ), Baron Irwin (1925), 1st Earl of Halifax (1944), President of the Board of Education (1922–4 and 1932–5), Viceroy of India (1926–31), Chancellor of Oxford University (from 1933), Foreign Secretary (1938–40), is also a devoted High Churchman. He is the author of a *Life* of John Keble (1909).

J. G. Lockhart, *Charles Lindley Viscount Halifax*. Part I, 1839–85 (1935); Part II, 1885–1934 (1936). Id. in *D.N.B.*, 1931–1940, pp. 919–21.

HALL, JOSEPH (1574–1656), Bp. of *Norwich. He was educated at Emmanuel College, Cambridge, and soon became keenly interested in the Roman controversy. He won favour with *James I, who in 1616 made him Dean of *Worcester and in 1618 sent him as his representative to the Synod of *Dort. In 1627

he became Bp. of *Exeter, but he was held suspect by W. *Laud as being too favourable to *Calvinism and *Puritanism, though he maintained conformity in his diocese. When the bishops were attacked by the Parliament of 1640, Hall came forward to defend his order, and pleaded for an unprelatical episcopacy in his *Episcopacy by Divine Right* (1640). His *Humble Remonstrance to the High Court of Parliament* (1640–1) evoked the reply of '*Smectymnuus'. In 1641 he was translated to Norwich, but before he could reach his see was sent to the Tower with the rest of the bishops. After release, his income was impounded by Parliament, and in 1647 he was ejected from his palace and lived in poverty until his death. Hall represented the moderating influence among the bishops. Of his voluminous writings the earlier ones were verse satires, the later ones controversial and devotional. His *Heaven upon Earth* (1606) was reprinted by J. *Wesley in his '*Christian Library'. His *Hard Measure* is autobiographical and narrates the persecution of the bishops by Parliament.

His writings were three times issued in collected editions in the last century—by Josiah Pratt (1808), by Peter Hall (1837), and by Philip Wynter (1863). G. G. Perry in *D.N.B.*, xxiv (1890), pp. 75–80.

HALL, ROBERT (1764–1831), *Baptist preacher. Born at Arnesby, Leicestershire, he was trained at the Baptist Academy at Bristol and King's College, Aberdeen. Later he became an influential preacher in Bristol (1785–1790 and 1826–31), Cambridge (1791–1806) and Leicester (1807–25). He was of commanding presence and eloquence; and his discourse on *Modern Infidelity* (1800), his sermon on the death of Princess Charlotte (1817), and his championship of the Leicestershire laceworkers brought him a wide following. His writings include *Christianity consistent with a Love of Freedom* (1791; defending J. *Priestley), *Reflections on War* (1802), *On Terms of Communion* (1815) and *Memoir of Thomas Toller* (1821).

Works, with Memoir by O. G. Gregory (6 vols., 1832). A. Gordon in *D.N.B.*, xxiv (1890), pp. 85–7.

HALLEL (Heb. הלל, 'praise'). A name given by the Jews to Pss. 113–18, and less frequently to other groups of Pss. between 104 and 150. Pss. 113–18 were also sometimes called the 'Egyptian Hallel', from the tradition that they were sung during the killing of the *Passover lambs. They were recited at all the principal Jewish festivals, and may have been the hymn sung by Christ and the Apostles after the *Last Supper (Mt. 26. 30). The title, the 'Great Hallel', was used esp. of Ps. 136.

HALLELUJAH. See *Alleluia*.

HALLER, BERCHTOLD (1492–1536), Reformer of Berne. After studying theology at *Cologne he became chaplain of the bakers' guild at Berne in 1513 and, in 1520, was given the canonry formerly held by his friend, T. *Wyttenbach, who had imbued him with the reformatory ideas of H. *Zwingli. Though he had become suspect by his preaching activities he was acquitted of heresy in 1523, but he ceased to say Mass two years later. He took part in the Conferences of Baden (1526) and *Berne (1528), and collaborated with F. Kolb in the composition of a Protestant liturgy and the reformatory edict of 1528. After most members of the Council of Berne had accepted the Reformation, he became the acknowledged religious leader of the town, being actively engaged in preaching, visitations, and catechetical instructions, but he failed in his efforts at establishing Protestantism at Solothurn. His last years were filled with controversies against the *Anabaptist movement. He has left no writings except a few letters.

M. Kirchhofer, *Bertold Haller, oder die Reformation von Bern* (1828). F. Trechsel–E. Blösch in *P.R.E.* (ed. 3), vii (1899), pp. 366–70, with bibl.

HALO (or **NIMBUS**). A circle or disc of light round the head or, more rarely, round the whole body. It was used in the religious symbolism of the Hellenistic period as a distinguishing mark in the representation of gods and demi-gods, later also of the Roman Emperors. Christian art adopted it only gradually. In the 3rd and 4th cents. its use was restricted to Christ and the Lamb, from the 5th cent. it was extended to the BVM, the angels and the saints, and soon also to other important personages. In the Middle Ages the round halo was used only for angels and saints, in the case of Christ being usually distinguished by a cross or the monogram A and Ω, whereas at the same period a rectangular form was sometimes employed for the representation of living people, esp. Popes and bishops, as in the famous picture of St. *Gregory the Great in the monastery of Clivus Scauri at Rome. The colour of the halo seems originally to have been blue, but from the 5th and 6th cents. gold, yellow, or rainbow colours were preferred. In modern RC practice a halo is permitted only for persons canonized or beatified or whose cultus has been otherwise approved by the Latin Church.

A. Krücke, *Der Nimbus und verwandte Attribute in der frühchristlichen Kunst* (Strassburg, 1905); J. Wilpert, *Die römischen Mosaiken und Malereien der kirchlichen Bauten vom 4. bis 13. Jahrhundert*, i (ed. 2, 1917), pp. 97–113; ii (ed. 2, 1917), pp. 1193–5; K. Künstle, *Ikonographie der christlichen Kunst*, i (1928), pp. 25–9, with reff. H. *Leclercq in *D.A.C.L.*, xii (pt. 1; 1935), cols. 1272–1312, s.v. 'Nimbe' and J. Sauer in *L.Th.K.*, vii (1935), cols. 595 f., s.v. 'Nimbus'.

HAMANN, JOHANN GEORG (1730–88), German religious thinker. He was born at Königsberg. After having followed a rather irregular course of studies at the university from 1746, he became a private tutor in 1752. In 1758 he entered the service of a merchant of Riga, who sent him to London on a business enterprise which proved a failure. The disappointment was accompanied by an interior crisis, resulting in a conversion experience.

Having returned to Königsberg in 1759, he nursed his ailing father until his death in 1766. He then accepted a subaltern post at an excise office, which left him sufficient time for his literary pursuits.

Hamann was one of the fathers of the German 'Storm and Stress' period. A prophet of religious 'immediacy', he proclaimed the rights of the individual personality and attacked the rationalism of the *Aufklärung*. His works are written in an aphoristic and somewhat obscure style, which earned him the title of 'The Magus in the North'. The best known are *Sokratische Denkwürdigkeiten* (1759), *Aesthetica in nuce* (1761), and *Golgatha und Scheblimini* (1784). In the last of these, his most important contribution to religious thought, he upholds Christianity as the historical revelation of the Triune God, of Atonement and of Redemption, against the rationalistic popular philosophy of Moses Mendelssohn. Though a personal friend of I. *Kant, he opposed his philosophy and insisted on the importance of inner experience, esp. in matters of religion. He regarded himself as the rejuvenator of Lutheranism, and was in some respects a precursor of F. D. E.*Schleiermacher and A. *Ritschl.

Works ed. by F. Roth and G. A. Wiener (8 Theile in 9 vols., Augsburg, 1821–43). Later ed., incl. his correspondence with F. H. Jacobi, by C. H. Gildemeister (6 vols., Gotha, 1857–73). F. Thoms, *Hamanns Bekehrung* (Beiträge zur Förderung christlicher Theologie, xxxvii, Hft. 3; 1933); J. Nadler, *Johann Georg Hamann, 1730–1788. Der Zeuge des Corpus Mysticum* (Salzburg [1949]). Überweg, iii, pp. 607 f., 614, 751. F. C. Arnold in *P.R.E.* (ed. 3), vii (1899), pp. 370–5; H. Stephan in *R.G.G.* (ed. 2), ii (1928), cols. 1595–7.

HAMARTOLOS, GEORGE. See *George Hamartolos*.

HAMILTON, JOHN (1511–71), Abp. of St. Andrews. The natural son of James Hamilton, first earl of Arran, he entered the *Benedictine monastery of Kilwinning as a boy but probably never became a monk. In 1525 he was appointed Abbot of Paisley, and retained the office till his death. In 1540 he took a three-years course of studies at *Paris. On his return to Scotland he was appointed keeper of the privy seal and two years later Bp. of Dunkeld. On the assassination of D. *Beaton in 1546 he was made Abp. of St. Andrews and Primate of Scotland. From this time until his death he was one of the most influential opponents of Protestantism. He called a succession of synods (1548, 1549, 1552, and 1559) with the view to a reform of the morals of the clergy and the religious education of the laity, the chief result of which was the compilation of a valuable catechism in the vernacular, known as *Archbishop Hamilton's Catechism* (1552). In 1560 he protested against the acceptance by Parliament of J. *Knox's new confession of faith. Three years later he was imprisoned for saying Mass and hearing confessions, but was released at the intervention of Queen *Mary, whose son, later *James VI, he baptized in 1566. In her subsequent troubles he became her faithful supporter, advising her, though in vain, to remain in Scotland. After her flight he was pronounced a traitor and captured at Dumbarton Castle, where he had sought safety. Three days later he was hanged at Stirling in his pontifical vestments.

A man of political prudence and moderation and an intrepid defender of his religion, Hamilton was not blameless in his personal life. He had several illegitimate children, and his annulment of Bothwell's marriage which enabled him to marry the Queen was gravely irregular. On the other hand, his complicity in the assassinations of Darnley and Moray, of which he was accused, is doubtful.

His *Catechism* and *The Two-Penny Faith*, ed. together, with introd. by A. F. Mitchell; the *Catechism* also ed. by T. G. Law (1884). J. Robertson, *Concilia Scotiae* (Bannatyne Club, 1866), i, 147–82. T. G. Law in *D.N.B.*, xxiv (1890), pp. 190–2.

HAMILTON, PATRICK (*c.* 1504–28), Scottish Protestant proto-Martyr. While still a boy, in 1517, he was made Abbot of Fern. He studied at Paris, where M. *Luther's writings attracted his attention, and afterwards at St. Andrews. From 1526 he began to show open sympathy with Lutheran ideas and in 1527 he visited both *Wittenberg, where he met Luther and P. *Melanchthon, and *Marburg with its newly founded Protestant university. Here he wrote his only work, a set of *Loci Communes* ('Patrick's Pleas'). Towards the end of 1527 he returned to Scotland. A. *Alesius, who was deputed to convince him of his errors, was himself converted to the Protestant creed. Early in the following year he was formally charged with heresy by Abp. James Beaton and burnt at the stake on 29 Feb.

P. Lorimer, *Patrick Hamilton*. An Historical Biography (1857); D. M. Kay, *Patrick Hamilton, Scottish Martyr, 1528* (1929); A. Cameron (ed.), *Patrick Hamilton, First Scottish Martyr of the Reformation* (1929). Æ. Mackay in *D.N.B.*, xxiv (1890), pp. 201–3.

HAMILTON, WALTER KERR (1808–69), Bp. of *Salisbury. He was the first of the *Tractarians to become a diocesan bishop in England. Educated at *Christ Church, Oxford, he was for a time a Fellow and tutor of Merton College and from 1837 to 1841 Vicar of St. Peter's-in-the-East, Oxford; and from *c.* 1838 he came under the influence of the *Oxford Movement. In 1841 he became a canon of Salisbury and in 1854 Bishop. Here he did much to stimulate the spiritual life of his diocese, e.g. by instituting Diocesan *Retreats; and in 1860 he founded Salisbury Theological College. In 1861–4 he prosecuted Rowland *Williams (1817–70), one of the contributors to *Essays and Reviews*, who was beneficed in his diocese. In his Charge for 1867 he defended the Eucharistic Sacrifice, the Real Presence, and Sacramental Confession; and he was attacked by Lord Portman in the House of Lords. He was devoted to his work at Salisbury cathedral and in 1853 issued *Cathedral Reform*.

H. P. *Liddon, *W. K. Hamilton*. A Sketch, repr. with Additions and Corrections, from *The Guardian* (1869); id., *Life in Death*. A Sermon preached in Salisbury Cathedral on 8 Aug. 1869. W. A. Greenhill in *D.N.B.*, xxiv (1890), p. 216 f.

HAMMOND, HENRY (1605–60), Anglican divine. Born at Chertsey, Surrey, he was educated at Eton and from 1619 at Magdalen College, Oxford, where he became a fellow in 1625. He was ordained in 1629. In 1633 he was presented to the living of Penshurst, Kent, where he worked with great energy, instituting daily services in church and monthly celebrations of the Holy Communion. In 1643 he was appointed Archdeacon of *Chichester and also nominated as a member of the *Westminster Assembly, but never sat. Forced to leave Penshurst during the Civil War, he returned to Oxford and composed, among other things, his *Practical Catechism* (publd. anon. 1645), which rapidly became very popular. As chaplain to the royal commissioners at the conference at Uxbridge in 1645, he was called upon to defend *Episcopacy. In 1645 he was presented to a Canonry at *Christ Church, Oxford, and became Chaplain in Ordinary to the King. After visiting Penshurst in 1646, he attended the king until his imprisonment at Carisbrooke in Dec. 1647. On his return to Christ Church he was deprived and confined first in Oxford and then under light restraint at Clapham, Bedfordshire. In 1649 he moved to Westwood, Worcs. He suffered personally from the decree (1655) forbidding the clergy of the C of E to exercise their ministry and devoted himself to relieving the deprived clergy and to raising funds to train a succession of future ordinands. Throughout his life he maintained a high standard of personal devotion and a discipline bordering on asceticism.

Besides innumerable topical pamphlets and pastoral treatises, Hammond compiled *A Paraphrase and Annotations upon all the Books of the New Testament* (1653), a pioneer work of English Biblical criticism. He also assisted Brian *Walton in the compilation of his *Polyglott* (1657) and wrote a prefatory letter for the *Whole Duty of Man*.

Works ed. W. Fulham (4 vols., London, 1674–84); repr. by N. Pocock as *The Miscellaneous Theological Works of Henry Hammond* (L.A.C.T., 3 vols. in 4, 1847–50). The admirable life by Bp. J. *Fell, orig. publd. London, 1661, is repr. among his works. Short life by G. G. Perry (London, [1864]). R. Hooper in *D.N.B.*, xxiv (1890), pp. 242–6.

HAMPDEN, RENN DICKSON (1793–1868), Bp. of *Hereford. After a brilliant university career he was elected a Fellow of Oriel College, Oxford, in 1814, and made friends with T. *Arnold and R. *Whately, both *Broad Churchmen like himself. In 1832 he expounded in his *Bampton Lectures on *The Scholastic Philosophy, considered in its relations to Christian Theology* a view of Christianity in which its dogmatic elements were greatly reduced. In 1833 he was appointed Principal of St. Mary's Hall,

Oxford. His name came into much prominence in 1836 when the *Tractarians, suspicious of his theology, unsuccessfully attempted to prevent his becoming Regius professor of divinity. In 1837, however, his suspension from the board which nominated Select Preachers was achieved. In 1847 Lord John Russell offered him the see of Hereford, and, despite violent High Church opposition, he was consecrated bishop in the following March. He administered his see conscientiously till his death, displaying tolerance and charity. His *Essay on the Philosophical Evidence of Christianity* (1827) and other writings illustrate a phase in liberal thought, but have little permanent value.

Henrietta Hampden (daughter), *Some Memorials of Renn Dickson Hampden* (1871). G. C. Boase in *D.N.B.*, xxiv (1890), pp. 264–6.

HAMPTON COURT CONFERENCE.

The conference held at Hampton Court in January 1604, between the English bishops and the Puritan leaders and presided over by *James I. Its purpose was to consider the Puritan demands for reform in the Church, set out in the *Millenary Petition. The Puritans were led by John *Rainolds, Dean of Lincoln, and the bishops by R.*Bancroft and T. Bilson. When Rainolds demanded the modification of Episcopacy, James declared that he had learnt in Scotland 'No bishop, no king', and so gave the bishops his support. The only concessions to the Puritans were slight changes in the BCP. The most substantial result of the Conference was a new translation of the Bible issued as the *Authorized Version 1611.

E. *Cardwell, *A History of the Conferences and other Proceedings Connected with the Revision of the Book of Common Prayer from 1558 to 1690* (1840), pp. 121–228. R. G. Usher in *D.E.C.H.*, p. 258 f., s.v.

HANDEL, GEORGE FREDERICK (1685–1759),

musical composer. The original form of his name was Händel. He was born in Saxony, and, after spending some years in Italy, came in 1710 to England, which he afterwards left for only very short periods, becoming a naturalized British subject in 1726. Of his religious compositions, the most famous are the *oratorios, among them 'Esther' (complete version, 1733); 'Deborah' (1733); 'Athaliah' (1733); 'Saul' (1738); 'Israel in Egypt' (1738); 'Messiah' (1741; it was first produced in 1742); 'Samson' (1743); 'Belshazzar' (1745); 'Judas Maccabaeus' (1747); 'Joshua' (1748); 'Alexander Balus' (1748); 'Solomon' (1749); 'Susanna' (1749); 'Theodora' (1750); 'Jephtha' (1751, first produced 1752). Of these works, the 'Messiah', 'Israel in Egypt', and 'Judas Maccabaeus' are the only ones frequently performed in modern times, though several of the others (e.g. 'Samson') are of considerable merit. In many places, esp. in the north of England, the annual performance of the 'Messiah' by local amateur choral societies is one of the principal religious and musical events of the winter.

Selection of his Works published by the English Handel Society (London, 13 vols., 1843–57). Complete ed. by [F. Chrysander for] the Händel-Gesellschaft (Leipzig, 96 vols., pt. 49 not yet published, 1859–1902). E. H. Müller (ed.), *The Letters and Writings of George Frideric Handel* (1935). J. Mainwaring, *Memoirs of the Life of George Frederic Handel* (1760). Later lives and studies by V. Schoelcher (London, 1857), F. Chrysander (3 vols., Leipzig, 1858–67), and W. N. Flower (London, 1923). S. Goddard in *Grove's Dictionary of Music and Musicians*, iv (ed. 5; 1954), pp. 37–60.

HANDS, Imposition of.

A manner of blessing used in the OT (e.g. Gen. 48), and followed by Christ, who used it in working miracles, and by the Church. The Apostles and the primitive Church employed it in *Confirmation (Acts 8 and 19) and in *Ordination (Acts 13. 3, 1 Tim. 4, 14), if such be the Christian use of χειροτονεῖν and the proper interpretation of these passages, as is commonly held; and it has certainly been traditionally used by the Church in these rites. Acc. to the Latin Rite it is also used in *Baptism and *Unction. It also has a place in the rite of Unction authorized by the Convocations of Canterbury in 1935. In private blessings of individuals, the hands may be placed on the heads of men and the shoulders of women, e.g. by a newly ordained priest after his first Mass.

J. Behm, *Die Handauflegung im Urchristentum* (1911); J. Coppens, *L'Imposition des mains et les rites connexes dans le N.T. et dans l'Église primitive* (1925). C. H. *Turner, 'Χειροτονία, χειροθεσία, ἐπίθεσις χειρῶν (and the accompanying verbs)' in *J.T.S.*, xxiv (1922–3), pp. 496–504. H. B. *Swete, in *E. Bi.*, ii (1901), col. 1956, s.v. 'Laying on of Hands'; P. Galtier, S.J., in *D.T.C.*, vii (pt. 2; 1923), cols. 1302–1425; F. *Cabrol, O.S.B., in *D.A.C.L.*, vii (pt. 1; 1926), cols. 391–413.

HANNINGTON, JAMES (1847–85), Bp. of

E. Equatorial Africa. After offering himself to the *C.M.S., he landed in Zanzibar in June 1882 at the head of six missionaries, but fever and dysentery compelled him to return to England in the following May. On recovering, he again offered himself for the work, was consecrated the first Bp. of Eastern Equatorial Africa in June 1884, and was back in Mombasa in Jan. 1885. In Oct. 1885 he was murdered by the natives of Uganda when leading a hazardous expedition to open up a shorter route to Lake Victoria Nyanza.

E. C. Dawson, *James Hannington* (1887); id., *The Last Journals of Bishop Hannington* (1888).

HAPLOGRAPHY.

In the copying of manuscripts, the writing of any letter(s) or word(s) only once where it ought to be repeated. The opposite error is known as '*dittography'.

HARDENBERG, ALBERT (c. 1510–74),

Reformer. Educated by the *Brethren of the Common Life at Groningen in Holland, he entered the monastery at Aduard c. 1527, studied at Louvain university, and took his doctor's degree in 1537 or 1539 at Mainz where he came into contact with John *Laski. On his return to Louvain he was opposed by the university authorities for teaching the doctrine of *Justification by faith. Retiring to Aduard, he cultivated relations with the

Reformers, esp. Abp. *Hermann of Wied, P. *Melanchthon, and J. Laski, and was finally persuaded to join them openly. In 1542 he went to *Wittenberg, and from there to Cologne to help Hermann of Wied establish the Reformation. He also took part in the Diets of *Speyer (1544) and *Worms (1545). After Hermann's resignation (1547), Hardenberg was appointed cathedral preacher at Bremen; but in 1561 he was expelled from this post for his denial of the *Lutheran doctrine of the Lord's Supper, and for the next four years he lived quietly under the protection of the Count of Oldenburg. In 1565 he became pastor at Sengwarden, and from 1567 to his death he was preacher at Emden.

Life by B. Spiegel (Bremen, 1869); lesser study by W. Schweckendieck (Emden, 1859). Schottenloher, i (1933), p. 325 (Nos. 7938–54). C. Bertheau in *P.R.E.* (ed. 3), vii (1899), pp. 408–16, s.v., with bibl.

HARDENBERG, FRIEDRICH LEOPOLD FREIHERR VON. See *Novalis.*

HARDING, St. STEPHEN. See *Stephen Harding, St.*

HARDOUIN, JEAN (1646–1729), French scholar. A native of Brittany, he became a *Jesuit at about the age of 16 and for most of his life (from 1683) was Librarian of the Jesuit Collège Louis le Grand at Paris. He published many excellent editions of the classics and other ancient writings. He took great delight in defending paradoxical and fantastic theories, maintaining, e.g., that the NT was originally written in Latin, that the great majority of the ancient classics were really the product of 13th cent. monks, and that all the councils commonly supposed to have preceded that of *Trent (1546–63) were fabrications. The last of these theories did not prevent him from producing a valuable edition of the texts of the ecclesiastical councils from NT times onwards (*Conciliorum Collectio Regia Maxima*, Paris, '1715', but for some years the French government withheld it from circulation owing to its ultramontane notes); it was largely drawn on by J. D. *Mansi and has not yet been superseded. Hardouin was also a great authority on numismatics, his works in the field including *Chronologia Veteris Testamenti ad vulgatam versionem exacta et unmmis illustrata* (1696).

H. *Quentin, O.S.B., *J. D. Mansi et les grandes collections conciliaires* (1900), pp. 38–54; E. Galletier, 'Un Breton du XVIIe siècle à l'avant-garde de la critique. Le père Jean Hardouin de Quimper', in *Annales de Bretagne*, xxxvi (1925), pp. 462–83, and xxxviii (1928), pp. 171–87. Sommervogel, iv (1893), cols. 84–111. P. Bernard in *D.T.C.*, vi (1920), cols. 2042–6, s.v.

HARDWICKE, Act of Lord (1754) (26 Geo. II, c. 33). This Act, 'for the Better Prevention of Clandestine Marriages', for the first time made clandestine marriages, which had previously been regulated by canon law, subject to statute. All marriages in England and Wales (except those of members of the Royal family, Jews and *Quakers) were required to be celebrated in the parish church of one of the parties and after banns, save that the Archbishop could grant a special licence for the marriage to be celebrated in some other church and without the delay entailed by banns and that the Bishop had the right to dispense from banns. All other unions were declared invalid. The Act also invalidated the marriage of infants without consent of parents or guardians. The Act initiated modern English statute law on *matrimony (q.v.).

HARE, JULIUS CHARLES (1795–1855), Archdeacon of Lewes. Having entered Trinity College, Cambridge, in 1812, he was elected a Fellow in 1818, and intended at first to enter the legal profession. In 1826, however, he was ordained, and in 1832 appointed Rector of Hurstmonceaux. Through travel in Germany, he came much under the influence of German theologians and men of letters and introduced many German ideas to English theology. He was a *Broad Churchman. His writings, some of which secured great popularity, included *Guesses at Truth* (1827; it was written in conjunction with his brother, Augustus), a collection of observations on philosophy, religion, literature, and other subjects, *The Victory of Faith* (1840; ed. 3, 1874) and *Sermons preacht on Particular Occasions* (1858). He also issued, in conjuction with C. *Thirlwall, a translation of B. G. Niebuhr's *History of Rome* (2 vols., 1828-32). In 1840 he was appointed Archdeacon of Lewes.

Anon. Introd. (by F. D. *Maurice) to *Charges to the Clergy of the Archdeaconry of Lewis, delivered at the Ordinary Visitations in the Years 1843, 1845, 1846* (1856), pp. i–lxiii, and anon. study (by A. P. *Stanley) in the *Quarterly Review*, xcvii (1855), pp. 1–27, both repr. in Hare's *The Victory of Faith* (ed. 3, by E. H. Plumptre, 1874), pp. xvii–cxxxii. A. J. C. Hare (nephew), *Memorials of a Quiet Life* (2 vols., 1872). A. J. C. Hare in *D.N.B.*, xxiv (1890), pp. 369–72.

HARKLEAN VERSION. A revision of the *Philoxenian Syriac Version of the NT made by Thomas of Harkel ('Heraclea') in 616, on the basis of readings derived from Greek MSS. in the library of the Enaton, near Alexandria. In the margin Thomas recorded many variants which are textually of great interest and value, mostly akin to those of *Codex Bezae. About 50 MSS. of this version have survived, the oldest dating from *c.* the 7th cent. It is this version of the text of Rev. which is printed in the current ('*Peshitta') Syriac New Testaments. The Harklean revision is the counterpart of the contemporary version of the OT made by Paul of Tella.

Only ed. is that of Joseph White with the inappropriate title 'Versio Philoxeniana': Gospels, Oxford, 1788; Acts and Epp., ib., 1799–1803. Later (partial) edd. of Gospel of Jn. by G. H. Bernstein (Leipzig, 1853) and of Heb. 11. 28–13. 25 by R. L. Bensly (Cambridge, 1889). List of MSS. in C. R. Gregory, *Textkritik des Neuen Testaments*, ii (1902), pp. 524–8. G. Zuntz, *The Ancestry of the Harklean New Testament* (British Academy Supplemental Papers, No. vii [1945]). P. E. Kahle, 'The Chester Beatty Manuscript of the Harklean Gospels' in *Miscellanea Giovanni Mercati*, vi (S.T., cxxvi; 1946), pp. 208–33. G. Zuntz, 'Études harkléennes' in *R. Bibl.*, lvii (1950), pp. 550–82.

HARLESS, GOTTLIEB CHRISTOPH ADOLPH VON (1806–79), German *Lutheran theologian. When a student at Halle university he was converted under the influence of F. A. G. *Tholuck to an ardent belief in the doctrine of justification by faith. From 1829 to 1845 he was Prof. of NT exegesis at Erlangen, where he considerably raised the standard of the theological faculty and founded the *Zeitschrift für Protestantismus und Kirche* (1838–76). From 1845 to 1850 he was professor at Leipzig. Appointed court preacher at Dresden in 1850, he was called to Munich two years later and made president of the supreme consistory of Bavaria. Here he reorganized the Lutheran State Church, to which he gave a new hymn-book and a new Order of Services. He was one of the most influential representatives of Lutheran orthodoxy of his generation.

W. Langsdorff, *Adolf von Harless*. Ein kirchliches Charakterbild (1898). D. Bachmann, 'Adolf von Harless. . . . Eine Studie zur Geschichte der neueren Theologie' in *Neue kirchliche Zeitschrift*, xvii (1906), pp. 860–91, 944–72, incl. list of his works. A. von Stählin in *P.R.E.* (ed. 3) vii (1899), pp. 421–32, s.v., with further bibl.

HARMONY, Pre-established. See *Pre-established Harmony*.

HARMONY SOCIETY. A communist sect, also known as the 'Harmonists', founded by J. G. Rapp (1757–1847). Rapp first established his sect in Württemberg; but in 1803–4 he emigrated to the U.S.A., and there settled his community on a site of some 5,000 acres in Butler County (Pa.), giving it the name of 'Harmony'. In 1814 his followers transferred themselves to a much larger estate in Posey County (Ind.). The Harmonists held many eccentric ideas. Rapp himself believed that Napoleon was God's ambassador, that attendance at school was wicked, and that Baptism and the Lord's Supper were the work of the devil. By the middle of the 19th cent. the Harmonists had almost died out.

A. Williams, *The Harmony Society at Economy, Penn'a* (Pittsburgh, 1866); J. A. Bole, *The Harmony Society*. A Chapter in German American Culture History (Americana Germania, New Series, Philadelphia, 1904). M. Holloway, *Heavens on Earth*. Utopian Communities in America 1680–1880 (1951), pp. 88–95, with chapter on The New Harmony, pp. 101–15. R. B. Taylor in *H.E.R.E.*, iii (1910), p. 780 f., s.v. 'Communistic Societies of America: I, The Harmony Society'.

HARMS, CLAUS (1778–1855), German *Lutheran theologian. A native of Holstein, after helping his father in his corn mill he went to the university of Kiel in 1799 where the study of F. D. E. *Schleiermacher's writings made him a zealous Evangelical. In 1806 he was elected deacon at Lunden nr. Norder Ditmarsch (Holstein), where he became popular as a preacher. Ten years later he was appointed archdeacon at St. Nicolai at Kiel, and in 1835 provost. In 1834 he had declined an offer to succeed Schleiermacher at the Dreifaltigkeits church at Berlin. He is chiefly remembered for his defence of *Lutheran theology at a time

when its distinctive elements were threatened by the movement for reuniting the two Protestant confessions in Prussia. On the third centenary of the outbreak of the Reformation (1817) he published, together with M. *Luther's 95 theses, 95 theses of his own directed to the quickening of Lutheran piety. They stressed the necessity of the forgiveness of sins and the importance of the Sacraments, and won the approval of Schleiermacher. His other writings include a *Pastoraltheologie* (1830) and numerous collections of sermons.

Lebensbeschreibung verfasset von ihm selber ('Zweite Auflage', Kiel, 1851). Studies (mostly brief) by K. Schneider (Bielefeld, 1861), J. *Kaftan (Basle, 1875), C. Lüdemann (Kiel, 1878), J. Lorentzen (Erlangen, 1937), and others. H. C. Carstens in *P.R.E.* (ed. 3), vii (1899), pp. 433–9, with full bibl., and H. Hermelink in *R.G.G.* (ed. 2), ii (1928), col. 1632 f.

HARNACK, ADOLF (1851–1930), German Church historian and theologian. He was the son of Theodosius Harnack (1817–89), professor of pastoral theology at Dorpat and the author of *Luthers Theologie* (2 vols., 1862–6). He studied at Dorpat and then at Leipzig, where he became Privatdozent (1874) and Extraordinary Prof. (1876). He later held full professorships at Giessen (1879–86), Marburg (1886–9), and Berlin (1889–1921). From 1905 to 1921 he was also Director of the Prussian Staatsbibliothek and in 1910 he became President of the 'Kaiser Wilhelm Gesellschaft' for furthering learning and science.

In the range of his achievements Harnack was prob. the most outstanding *Patristic scholar of his generation. He made himself complete master of the early Christian literature, esp. of the pre-Nicene period, and published innumerable contributions to its history. In conjunction with O. von Gebhardt, he founded the important series *Texte und Untersuchungen zur Geschichte der altchristlichen Literatur* (1882 ff.), very many of its papers being his own compositions or owing their inspiration to his enthusiasm. These extended historical studies formed the basis of his *Lehrbuch der Dogmengeschichte* (3 vols., 1886–9; Eng. trans. as *History of Dogma*, 7 vols., 1894–9), which traced the history of Christian doctrine down to the Reformation, with esp. attention to the earlier period. The work reflected throughout Harnack's theological standpoint (a form of *Ritschlianism) which regarded the metaphysics which came into Christian theology as an alien intrusion from Greek sources ('Hellenization'). This critical attitude to traditional Christian dogma evoked strong opposition from conservative theologians, who resisted, but without success, his call to Berlin. Here he became involved in a long controversy on the *Apostles' Creed, embodying his views in *Das apostolische Glaubensbekenntnis* (1892). In the winter of 1899–1900 he delivered a celebrated course of lectures stressing the moral side of Christianity, esp. the claims of human brotherhood, to the exclusion of all that was doctrinal. They were subsequently published as *Das Wesen des*

Christenthums (1900; Eng. trans. 1901) and attracted very wide attention. Meanwhile, Harnack pursued his historical studies with sustained energy, issuing, *inter alia*, *Die Geschichte der altchristlichen Literatur bis Eusebius* (3 vols., 1893–1904). Later he published a series of notable studies on the *Synoptic Problem, in which (to the surprise of friends and foes alike) he upheld very early dates for the Synoptic Gospels and *Acts, holding e.g. that Acts was written by St. *Luke when St. *Paul was still in his (first) Roman Captivity and assigning a very early date to '*Q'. These studies were embodied in *Beiträge zur Einleitung in das Neue Testament* (4 parts, 1906–11; Eng. trans. under separate titles, e.g. *Luke the Physician*, 1907; *The Sayings of Jesus*, 1908; *The Acts of the Apostles*, 1909). His other writings included *Die Mission und Ausbreitung des Christentums in den ersten drei Jahrhunderten* (1902; ed. 4, much enlarged, 1924; Eng. trans. by J. *Moffatt, from ed. 1 only, 2 vols., 1904–5), *Entstehung und Entwickelung der Kirchenverfassung* (1910; Eng. trans. 1910), *Marcion* (1921; ed. 2, 1924), and *Briefsammlung des Apostels Paulus* (1926). With E. *Schürer he also founded the *Theologische Literaturzeitung* (1876 ff.).

Life by Agnes von Zahn-Harnack (Berlin, 1936). J. de Ghellinck, S.J., *Patristique et Moyen-âge*, iii (1948), Étude III, pp. 1–102.

HARRIS, HOWEL (1714–73), founder of Welsh *Calvinistic Methodism. Born at Trevecca, Breconshire, he was intended for Ordination in the Anglican Church. In 1735 he was converted to a life of great religious seriousness, and later in the year went up to St. Mary Hall, Oxford; but after a term's residence he returned to Wales where he became an ardent mission preacher and rapidly gathered large crowds. Owing to the resistance encountered from orthodox Anglicans and the refusal of Ordination, he was driven to separation from the C of E. For several years his cause was helped by Daniel Rowlands (1713–1790) of Llangeitho, Cards., but some obscure misunderstanding led to a violent conflict in 1751. Shortly afterwards he established a religious community at Trevecca where, towards the end of his life, he gained the warm support of Selina, Countess of *Huntingdon. He published some books in Welsh.

A *Brief Account of the Life of Howell Harris, Esq.*, Extracted from Papers written by himself, To which is added a concise Collection of his Letters from the Year 1738 to 1772 [ed. B. La Trobe–E. Moses] (Trevecca, 1791). Lives in Eng. by J. Bulmer (Haverfordwest, 1824), E. Morgan (Holywell, 1852), H. J. Hughes (London, 1892), H. E. Lewis (ib. [1912]), and G. T. Roberts (Wesley Historical Lecture No. 17; London, 1951). R. J. Jones in *D.N.B.*, xxv (1891), p. 6 f.

HARRIS, JAMES RENDEL (1852–1941), Biblical scholar and orientalist. He was brought up as a *Congregationalist, but later became a *Quaker. Educated at Plymouth Grammar School and Clare College, Cambridge, he taught in the U.S.A. (1882–92), at Cambridge (1893–1903), and at Woodbrooke

Settlement, Birmingham (1903–18), and from 1918 to 1925 was Curator of MSS. at the John Rylands Library, Manchester. Harris was the author of many studies on Biblical and early Christian texts and on the Mediterranean cults. In 1889 he discovered at the St. Catherine's Monastery on Mount *Sinai the Syriac text of the 'Apology' of *Aristides (published 1891); and in 1910 issued the Syriac text of the 'Odes of *Solomon'. His numerous other works include *Biblical Fragments from Mount Sinai* (1890), *The *Diatessaron* (1890), *Lectures on the Western Text of the NT* (1894), *The Teaching of the Apostles and the *Sibylline Books* (1885), *Testimonies* (1917; 1920). In collaboration with R. L. Bensley and F. C. *Burkitt he edited *The Four Gospels from the Syriac Palimpsest* (1894). His writings reflect his unconventional and speculative mind, and immense, if at times somewhat unbalanced, erudition.

C. A. Phillips, 'Rendel Harris' in *Expository Times*, lii (1941), pp. 349–52.

HARRISON, FREDERIC (1831–1923), English *Positivist. Educated at Wadham College, Oxford, where he was elected a Fellow in 1854, he began to practise as a barrister-at-law in 1858. In his earlier years he was a member of the C of E, influenced by the school of F. D. *Maurice and also by H. P. *Liddon, a school friend with whom he kept up a friendship till Liddon's death; but he came gradually under the influence of A. *Comte, and embraced Positivism in 1870. From 1880 to 1905 he was president of the 'English Positivist Committee', and the recognized leader in England of that school of thought. Among his writings were *The Creed of a Layman* (1907), *The Philosophy of Common Sense* (1907), and *The Positive Evolution of Religion* (1912).

Autobiographic Memoirs (2 vols., London, 1911); Austin Harrison (son), *Frederic Harrison. Thoughts and Memories* (1926). A. Cochrane in *D.N.B.*, *1922–1930*, pp. 406–8.

HARROWING OF HELL, The. The medieval English term for the defeat of the powers of evil at the *Descent of Christ into Hell after His death. It was a favourite theme of art and drama in the Middle Ages.

HARTMANN, EDUARD VON (1842–1906), German philosopher. Born at Berlin, in 1858 he became an artillery officer in the Prussian Guards, but owing to an affection of the knee he was forced to resign in 1865, and resided at Berlin for the rest of his life.

The main outlines of his system, which owed much to the influence of G. W. F. *Hegel, A. *Schopenhauer and F. W. J. *Schelling, were already contained in his early treatise on the 'Philosophy of the Unconscious' (*Die Philosophie des Unbewussten*, '1869', really Nov. 1868; Eng. trans. by W. C. Coupland, 1884). He saw in the 'Unconscious' an all-pervasive monistic principle which was at once will (*Wille*) and presentation (*Vorstellung*), and the ground of evolutionary development.

Rejecting mechanism in favour of a teleological vitalism, he became a robust champion of progress, enlightenment and practical activity, uniting his disciples in the service of 'Concrete Monism'. Christianity, which was only a stage along the way to the religion of Absolute Spirit, was now at length dead and its gravedigger was modern Protestantism.

Among von Hartmann's other writings were *Das religiöse Bewusstsein der Menschheit im Stufengang seiner Entwickelung* (1882), *Die Religion des Geistes* (1882), *Die deutsche Aesthetik seit Kant* (1886), and *Die Philosophie des Schönen* (1887). Of specifically religious import were *Die Selbstzersetzung des Christentums und die Religion der Zukunft* (1874) and *Die Krisis des Christentums und die moderne Theologie* (1880).

Von Hartmann found an enthusiastic disciple in A. *Drews (q.v.).

There is a large literature, mainly in German. Überweg v, pp. 331–9, also p. 707 f. with list of his writings and full bibl. to date. Later bibl. items in W. Ziegenfuss (ed.), *Philosophen-Lexikon*, i (1949), pp. 449–54, s.v.

HARVEST THANKSGIVING. In Gt. Britain an unofficial religious festival of thanksgiving for the fruits of the earth, usually observed on a Sunday in Sept. or Oct. after the ingathering of the harvest. In the C of E and Free Churches it is customary to decorate the church with fruit, flowers, and vegetables which are later devoted to charity; special hymns are sung; and there is frequently a visiting preacher. In medieval England *Lammas Day (1 Aug.) was prob. recognized as a thanksgiving for the first fruits of the harvest, bread made with the new wheat being offered at Mass and solemnly blessed. This last custom was revived by R. S. Hawker (1804–75) at Morwenstow, Cornwall, in 1843. Although no provision is made for any such observance in the BCP, special forms of thanksgiving for abundant harvests were occasionally authorized from the end of the 18th cent. By the mid 19th cent. an annual festival was common and a parochial thanksgiving replaced the traditional Harvest Home. In 1862 the Convocation of Canterbury issued a form of service. The proposed Revised Prayer Book of 1927–8 provided a Collect, to follow that of the day, and an Epistle and Gospel; and other Anglican Revisions (e.g. the *Scottish and *South African Prayer Books) have made similar provision. The American Prayer Book of 1789 contains a form of thanksgiving for the first fruits of the earth, which is usually employed on the last Thursday in November when a general holiday ('Thanksgiving Day') is observed.

H. C. Batterbury in *P.B.D.* (1912), p. 377 f., s.v. 'Harvest Festival'.

HASE, KARL AUGUST VON (1800–90), German Church historian. After teaching for a short time at Tübingen and Leipzig, he held a professorship at Jena from 1830 till 1883. In 1829 he published a Life of Christ in which

the supernatural elements in the Gospels were rationalized. His *Kirchengeschichte* (ed. 1, 1834) long remained a standard work. He also wrote *Evangelisch-protestantische Dogmatik* (1826), *Gnosis oder protestantisch-evangelische Glaubenslehre* (3 vols., 1827–9) and *Handbuch der protestantischen Polemik gegen die römisch-katholische Kirche* (1862; ed. 7, 1900; Eng. trans. *Handbook to the Controversy with Rome* [2 vols., 1906]).

Gesammelte Werke, ed. G. Krüger and others (Leipzig, 1890–6). R. Bürkner, *Karl von Hase* (1900). G. Krüger in *P.R.E.* (ed. 3), vii (1899), pp. 453–61, s.v.

HASIDAEANS. The Greek form ('Ασιδαῖοι) of the Heb. '*Chasidim' (q.v.), found e.g. in 1 Macc. 2. 42.

HASMONAEANS. The family name of the *Maccabees, apparently derived from one of their ancestors.

HASTINGS, JAMES (1852–1922), *Presbyterian divine and editor of religious encyclopaedic works. Educated at the grammar school, the university, and the Free Church Divinity College at Aberdeen, he was ordained a Presbyterian minister in 1884, and appointed pastor of Kinneff, Kincardineshire, Free Church. From 1897 to 1901 he was pastor of Willison Church, Dundee, and from 1901 to 1911 of the United Free Church, St. Cyrus, Kincardineshire, after which he retired to Aberdeen. In 1889 he founded the monthly *Expository Times*, which he edited until his death. He is famous as the editor of the *Dictionary of the Bible* (5 vols., 1898–1904; 1-vol. edition, 1909), the *Encyclopaedia of Religion and Ethics* (12 vols., 1908–21; Index vol., 1926), the *Dictionary of Christ and the Gospels* (2 vols., 1906–8), and the *Dictionary of the Apostolic Church* (2 vols., 1915–18).

Artt. by H. E. *Ryle, W. A. Curtis, and H. R. *Mackintosh in *Expository Times*, xxxiv (1922–3), pp. 102–6. E. R. Micklem in *D.N.B., 1922–1930*, p. 409 f.

HAT, Cardinal's. See *Red Hat*.

HATCH, EDWIN (1835–89), Anglican divine. Educated at Pembroke College, Oxford, he was successively professor of classics at Toronto (1859), rector of Quebec High School (1862), vice-principal of St. Mary Hall, Oxford (1867), rector of Purleigh, Essex (1883), and reader in ecclesiastical history at Oxford (1884). In 1880 he preached a series of *Bampton Lectures on *The Organization of the Early Christian Churches* (1881) in which he maintained that the origin of the Christian episcopate lay in the ἐπίσκοποι or financial administrators of Greek religious associations. His other writings included *The Growth of Church Institutions* (1887), his *Hibbert Lectures for 1888 on *The Influence of Greek Ideas and Usages on the Christian Church* (1890), and his *Essays in Biblical Greek* (1889). He was engaged on a *Concordance to the*

Septuagint (subsequently completed by H. A. Redpath, 1897) at the time of his death.

S. C. Hatch (ed.), *Memorials of E. Hatch* (1890). W. *Sanday, 'In Memoriam Dr. Edwin Hatch' in *The Expositor*, 4th Series, i (1890), pp. 93–111. W. *Sanday in *D.N.B.*, xxv (1891), p. 149 f.

HATFIELD, Council of (680). The Council arose out of the wish of Pope *Agatho to sound the English Church on the subject of *Monothelitism. As his intermediary the Pope chose John, Precentor of St. Peter's, whom St. *Benedict Biscop had brought back with him from Rome to instruct his monks at *Wearmouth in singing. The Council, which met under the presidency of Abp. *Theodore at Hatfield (or ? Heathfield), repudiated Monothelitism, accepted the decrees of the first five General Councils, and affirmed its belief in the *Double Procession of the Holy Spirit.

*Bede, *H.E.*, iv, 17 f. Hardouin, iii, col. 1037 f.; Mansi, xi (1765), cols. 175–80; A. W. Haddan–W. *Stubbs (ed.), *Councils and Ecclesiastical Documents Relating to Great Britain and Ireland*, iii (1871), pp. 141–60. W. *Bright, *Chapters of Early English Church History* (1878), pp. 316–22. Hefele–Leclercq, iii (pt. 1; 1909), pp. 475–84.

HAUCK, ALBERT (1845–1918), German *Lutheran historian. He held professorships at Erlangen from 1878 to 1889 and at Leipzig from 1889. Of his writings, the most considerable was his *Kirchengeschichte Deutschlands* (5 vols., 1887–1920). He was at first joint editor (1880), and from the death of J. J. *Herzog in 1882 sole editor of the 2nd edition of the Herzog-Plitt *Realencyklopädie* (completed 1888); and he also edited the 3rd edition (1896–1913), cited as *P.R.E.* in this Dictionary.

Geschichtliche Studien A. Hauck zum 70. Geburtstage dargebracht (1916). K. Bauer in *R.G.G.* (ed. 2), ii (1928), col. 1647, with list of Hauck's writings.

HAURANNE, JEAN DUVERGIER DE. See *Saint Cyran*.

HAVERGAL, FRANCES RIDLEY (1836–1879), hymn-writer. She was the daughter of William Henry Havergal (1793–1870), the writer of much sacred music. Endowed with remarkable ability for composing verse, she contributed many poems and hymns to *Good Words* and other religious periodicals. Some of these have found their way into most hymnals, e.g. 'Take my life and let it be'.

Memorials of F. R. H., by her sister M. V. G. Havergal (1880).

HAWKINS, EDWARD (1789–1882), Provost of Oriel College, Oxford. Elected a Fellow of Oriel in 1813, he became Vicar of St. Mary's, Oxford, in 1823, and Provost of Oriel in 1828. From 1847 to 1861 he was also (the first) Dean *Ireland professor of the interpretation of Holy Scripture. His sermon on Tradition (1818), urging that Scripture was intended to *prove* doctrine, not to *teach* it, had a profound influence on J. H. *Newman, then an undergraduate of Trinity. Later he developed the same subject in his *Bampton Lectures (1840).

Though a High Churchman, he became involved in an embittered struggle with the *Tractarians, chiefly in connexion with *Tract No. 90*, which he and others maintained interpreted the *Thirty-Nine Articles in a way incompatible with membership of the C of E. In 1874 he withdrew to *Rochester, where he continued to hold the canonry hitherto attached to the provostship of Oriel.

J. W. *Burgon, *Lives of Twelve Good Men*, i (1888), 'iv, The Great Provost', pp. 374–465. W. A. Greenhill in *D.N.B.*, xxv (1891), p. 208 f.

HAYMO OF FAVERSHAM (d. 1244), English *Franciscan friar. Born at Faversham in Kent, he became a Master of Divinity at Paris and in 1224 entered the Order of Friars Minor. Soon afterwards he returned to England and lectured at *Oxford prob. before 1229. In 1230 the General Chapter at *Assisi sent him as one of the deputies to *Gregory IX to seek an official explanation of the rule. In 1233 he was sent on a mission to *Constantinople to negotiate a reunion with the E. Church. He took a leading part in the deposition of Brother *Elias, which finally took place at the General Chapter of the Order at Rome in 1239. At that Chapter he became Provincial of the English Province; in 1240 he was elected General of the Order. At his request the 'Expositio Regulae Quatuor Magistrorum' was written by the Four Masters of Paris (1241–2). He died at Anagni. Among his surviving works are an order for private and conventual Mass on ferias ('Indutus planeta'), presented at the Chapter of *Bologna in 1243, and notes for a ceremonial ('Ordinationes Divini Officii'; 'Ad Omnes Horas'). At the behest of *Innocent IV in 1243–4, he revised the *ordinals for the Roman Breviary, Missal, and grace before and after meals.

The 'Indutus Planeta' is pr. in the *Monumenta Ordinis Minorum* (ed. prob. Leipzig, c. 1509 [in Brit. Mus.], pp. fo. cclxviii–fo. cclxx). The 'Ordinationes Divini Officii' is pr. in the *Analecta Ordinis Minorum Capuccinorum*, xxii (1906), pp. 91–5, 116–22, and 183–6. Full ed. of his works, with introd. by S. J. van Dijk [O.F.M.], is in preparation. C. L. Kingsford in *D.N.B.*, xxv (1891), p. 299. Antoine de Sérent, O.F.M., in *D.H.G.E.*, i (1912), cols. 1192–4, s.v. 'Aimon (14) de Faversham', with bibl.

HEADLAM, ARTHUR CAYLEY (1862–1947), Bp. of *Gloucester. He was born at Whorlton, Durham, and educated at *Winchester and New College, *Oxford. Ordained priest in 1889, he was successively Fellow of All Souls (1885), rector of Welwyn (1896), professor of dogmatic theology at *King's College, London (1903), Regius professor of divinity at Oxford (1918), and Bp. of Gloucester (1923–45). A Central Churchman who disliked all ecclesiastical parties (*Anglo-Catholics, *Evangelicals, and *Modernists), he was one of the most influential of English prelates in the inter-war period. In his early years he devoted his attention esp. to NT problems, collaborating with W. *Sanday in his fine Commentary on *Romans (1895) and contributing extensively to J. *Hastings' *Dictionary of the Bible* (4 vols., 1898–1902). His *Bampton Lectures, *The

Doctrine of the Church and Christian Reunion (1920), written with the forthcoming *Lambeth Conference in view, endeavoured to provide an ecclesiological basis for reunion between the C of E and other religious bodies. His other writings include *St. Paul and Christianity* (1913), *The Life and Teaching of Jesus the Christ* (1923), *Christian Theology* (1934) and *The Fourth Gospel as History* (1948, posthumous; with biographical essay by Agnes Headlam-Morley).

Life and Letters by R. C. D. Jasper (London, 1960). A. T. P. Williams in *D.N.B., 1941–1950* (1959), pp. 369–71.

HEARNE, THOMAS (1678–1735), English antiquary. The son of a humble parish clerk, he was born at Littlefield Green, Berks, and educated in *Nonjuring principles by Francis Cherry and H. *Dodwell. In 1695 he entered St. Edmund Hall, Oxford. Here his close scholarly habits attracted the attention of the principal, John *Mills (d. 1707), and for some years Hearne collated MSS. and held appointments in the *Bodleian Library. Refusing to take the oath to George I in 1716, he was deprived of his post in the Bodleian, and, though denied access to libraries, continued his medieval studies in Oxford, intransigent politically until his death. He produced over 40 learned volumes, including several editions of classical writers (Pliny, Eutropius, Livy, &c.) and esp. medieval authors (Chronicles, works on *Glastonbury, &c.). He also left 140 MS. notebooks, now preserved in the Bodleian. Though at times uncritical, his meticulous accuracy in transcribing authorities make his works valuable for reference. His diaries, published posthumously, contain intimate and often malicious comment on contemporary life in Oxford.

The Life of Mr. Thomas Hearne . . . from his own MS. Copy (Oxford, 1772). P. Bliss (ed.), *Reliquiae Hearnianae* (2 vols., 1867). *Remains and Collections of Thomas Hearne*, ed. C. E. Double, D. W. Rannie, H. E. Salter, and others (Oxford Historical Society, ii, vii, xiii, xxxiv, xlii, xliii, xlviii, l, lxv, lxvii, and lxxii; 1885–1921). P. Ouvry (ed.), *Letters Addressed to Thomas Hearne* (1874). *Impartial Memorials of the Life and Writings of Thomas Hearne. . . . By Several Hands* (1736). W. D. Macray, *Annals of the Bodleian Library, Oxford* (1868), passim; D. C. Douglas, *English Scholars* (1939), ch. 9, 'Portrait of Hearne', pp. 226–48. H. R. Luard in *D.N.B.*, xxv (1891), pp. 335–8.

HEARSE. (1) Formerly **Herse** (Med. Lat. *hercia*). A triangular frame on a stand, holding 15 candles, and used at *Tenebrae in Holy Week, the candles being extinguished one by one during the service. There is also an obsolete use of the word for the triple candlestick used in the *Holy Saturday rite.

(2) Various funeral furnishings. The current use of the word is for the carriage bearing the coffin, but it is also found for a *catafalque, or framework (permanent or temporary) bearing lighted tapers about a coffin.

HEART (Heb. בֵּל, Gk. καρδία). In the Bible it usually designates the whole personality, though, in contrast to modern usage, the emphasis is on the activities of reason and will rather than the emotions. Both in the OT and

NT it is the seat of wisdom (1 Kgs. 3. 12), and of thought and reflection (e.g. Jer. 24. 7, Lk. 2. 19), the instrument of belief (Rom. 10. 10) and of will, the principle of action (Ex. 35. 21) which may be hardened so that it resists God (Deut. 15. 7; Mk. 16. 14). It is the principle both of virtues and vices, of humility (Mt. 11. 29) and pride (Deut. 17. 20), of good thoughts (Lk. 6. 45) and of evil thoughts (Mt. 15. 19). Hence in Scripture the heart is the centre of the human person, in which the physical and the spiritual life are concentrated, and therefore in the NT the dwelling-place of Christ (Eph. 3. 17) in which reigns the peace of God (Col. 3. 15). In this sense it is used in the language of Christian spirituality, which regards the human heart as the special organ of the love of God; and it is here that is to be found the inspiration of the modern devotion to the *Sacred Heart of Jesus (q.v.).

J. Baumgärtel and J. Behm, Καρδία in *T.W.B.*, iii (1938), pp. 609–16.

HEART OF JESUS. See *Sacred Heart*.

HEAVEN. In Christian theology the dwelling-place of God and the angels, and ultimately of all the redeemed, wherein they receive their eternal reward.

In OT language the word 'heaven' or 'heavens' denotes the visible sky and also the abode of God, conceived as in or beyond the physical heavens, where, for example, Jacob saw Him in a dream (Gen. 28. 12 f.) and whence He could 'come down' upon the top of Mt. Sinai (Exod. 19. 18–20, cf. 20. 22); but it was also acknowledged that 'the heaven and heaven of heavens cannot contain' God (1 Kgs. 8. 27), who is omnipresent (Ps. 139. 8–10). In the NT heaven as God's dwelling-place is still conceived as high above the earth: thus Christ raised His eyes 'to heaven' in prayer (Mk. 6. 41, Jn. 17. 1), and at His *Ascension seemed to the disciples to pass away from them upwards to heaven. In the Apostolic Church the Hellenistic conception of a series of heavens was widely accepted (cf. 2 Cor. 12. 2–4), together with that of angelic and demonic powers existing in the heavens (e.g. Eph. 6. 12, RV; cf. Rom. 8. 38 f.) over whom Christ since His Resurrection and Ascension reigns supreme with the Father 'far above all heavens' (Eph. 4. 10).

Whereas in Hebrew thought only exceptional human beings (esp. *Enoch and *Elijah) were conceived as being raised to heaven after this life, for Christians it was the distinctive Christian hope and belief that the faithful disciple, through Christ's victory over death, would eventually reign with Him in glory. This might be thought of as attained in the *Kingdom of God at the end of history when Christ would descend from heaven and the dead would either be raised and caught up to meet Him (1 Thess. 4. 15–17), or enjoy a new life on earth (see *Millenarianism); but, as St. Paul implies when he says that for him to die is to be with Christ (Phil. 1. 23), it was also believed that even before the general resurrection some at least of the redeemed would be with Christ, i.e. in heaven. Acc. to Catholic doctrine, these are the souls who, having died in a state of grace and been purged of their stains in *Purgatory, have passed to heaven, where they enjoy perfect bliss; but, except for the Bl. Virgin *Mary (see *Assumption*), these souls still await reunion with their bodies at the general *resurrection of the dead, after which both body and soul together will enjoy the life of heaven eternally. Catholic theology regards heaven as 'a place' but claims no knowledge of its spatial characteristics or its relation to the physical universe, stressing rather the essential quality of the life of heaven which consists in the enjoyment of the *Beatific Vision (q.v.). Virtually all Christians, while making greater or lesser reservations in regard to details, would agree that heaven is essentially the fulfilment, to a degree impossible on earth, of what is, acc. to the Shorter Catechism of the *Westminster Confession, the 'chief end of man', viz. 'to serve God and to enjoy Him for ever'.

HEBDOMADARIAN (Gk. ἑβδομάς, 'a period of seven days'). In cathedral churches and monasteries, the priest responsible for the performance of the more important religious offices, e.g. the singing of the *High Mass and the giving of the blessings. He was so named because he held office for a week.

HEBER, REGINALD (1783–1826), Bp. of Calcutta. He was educated at Brasenose College, Oxford, and in 1805 elected a Fellow of All Souls. In 1807, on his return from a long tour in Europe, he was ordained and at once became vicar of Hodnet in Shropshire. In 1815 he delivered a course of *Bampton Lectures on *The Personality and Office of the Christian Comforter*. In 1823 he accepted the bishopric of Calcutta. In his short episcopate he laboured hard for the spread of Christianity in his large diocese and beyond. He is best remembered for his hymns which include 'Brightest and best of the sons of the morning', 'Holy, holy, holy, Lord God Almighty', and 'From Greenland's icy mountains', while his prose works include a Life and edition of the writings of Jeremy *Taylor (1822).

Some Account of the Life of Reginald Heber (anon., 1829). A. Heber (widow), The Life of Reginald Heber (2 vols., 1830), incl. selections of correspondence and unpublished works. Later lives by A. Montefiore (London, 1894) and G. Smith (ib., 1895). J. H. Overton in D.N.B., xxv (1891), pp. 355-7.

HEBREW (people). The Hebrews, the inhabitants of Palestine, who entered the land with the *Patriarchs and *Moses, generally spoke of themselves as the Israelites (בְּנֵי יִשְׂרָאֵל, bᵉne Yisrael, 'the Sons of Israel', Gen. 32. 28, 35. 10). The term 'Hebrew' was largely used of them by other peoples, often with a shade of contempt (cf. esp. Gen. 43. 32, 1 Sam. 13. 19 f.). It disappeared with the rise of the monarchy.

The word 'Hebrew' (עִבְרִי, 'ibhrî') was derived by popular Hebrew etymology from the root עבר, 'br, 'to go over', 'to cross', with the meaning that *Abraham came from the other side of the Euphrates (cf. Josh. 24. 2 f.), but the real etymology of the word is uncertain. Similar words in the related languages seem to indicate at first an ethnic group and later a menial social class. It was only in Israel that the ethnic significance continued under the impulse of the new religious nationalism begun by Moses.

HEBREW (tongue). One of the closely related group of languages, known as Semitic, which includes among others Arabic, *Aramaic, and *Syriac. It was the classical language in Israel, in which the OT, except for certain chapters in the Books of *Ezra and *Daniel, was written. So long as it continued in common use only the consonants were transcribed. It ceased to be a spoken language about the 4th century B.C., and as time went on the need for preserving the traditional pronunciation led to the invention of different systems of points, placed above and/or below the consonants to indicate what vowels were to be used.

In our Lord's time Aramaic was the language of Palestine, and this is what is referred to when the 'Hebrew tongue' is mentioned in the NT (e.g. Acts 21. 40).

The standard Eng. Dict. is that of F. Brown–S. R. *Driver–C. A. *Briggs, Oxford, 1906 (corrected repr., 1952); this was based on the classical work of W. *Gesenius (q.v.), esp. ed. 12 by F. Buhl (Leipzig, 1895). More recent dicts. by F. Zorell–L. Semkowski (Rome, 1940 ff.), and L. Koehler–W. Baumgartner (Leyden, 1953). The basic work on Hebrew grammar is W. Gesenius, Hebräische Grammatik (Halle, 1813; ed. 22 by E. Kautzsch, 1878; Eng. tr. of ed. 28 by A. E. Cowley, 1910). Other grammars by A. B. Davidson (Edinburgh, 1874 and 1894), E. König (Leipzig, 1881 and 1897), G. Bergsträsser (ib. 1918), P. Joüon (Rome, 1923 [in French]), M. Laubert (Paris, 1938), J. Weingreen (Oxford, 1939), H. S. Nyberg (Upsala, 1952), and R. Meyer (2 vols., Berlin, 1952–5). On the comparative grammar of Hebr. and other Semitic languages, W. Wright, Lectures on the Comparative Grammar of the Semitic Languages (1890; still useful), and C. Brockelmann, Grundriss der vergleichenden Grammatik der semitischen Sprachen (2 vols., 1907–13). Studies in Hebrew tense system by S. R. Driver (Oxford, 1874), R. H.*Kennett (Cambridge, 1901), and F. R. Blake (Rome, 1951 [in English]). G. R. Driver, Problems of the Hebrew Verbal System (Old Testament Studies published under the Auspices of the Society for Old Testament Study, ii; 1936). General introductions by G. R. Driver, 'The Modern Study of the Hebrew Language' in A. S.*Peake (ed.), The People and the Book (1925), pp. 73–120, with bibl., p. 481 f.; D. W. Thomas, 'The Language of the Old Testament' in H. W. *Robinson (ed.), Record and Revelation (1938), pp. 374–407, with bibl. p. 490 f. Other studies in the Heb. language include E. Brønno, Studien über hebräische Morphologie und Vokalismus (Leipzig, 1943; important for attention to Gk. transliterations of Heb. words) and F. M. Cross–D. N. Freedman, Early Hebrew Orthography (New Haven, Conn., 1952). Grammar by J. Weingreen, cit. sup., ed. 2, 1959.

HEBREWS, Epistle to the. Traditionally included among the letters of St. *Paul, this Ep., unlike most others in the NT, does not contain the name of the writer nor of those addressed. In content it resembles a homily, though it has an epistolary close (13. 18–25). The traditional title (πρὸς Ἑβραίους), though found in the earliest MSS., is prob. an inference from its contents.

The Ep. asserts with emphasis the finality of the Christian dispensation and its superiority to that of the Old Covenant, as a dissuasive from any return to Judaism. Christ is God's Son, the 'effulgence of his glory' (1. 3, RV), the unique and supreme messenger from God to mankind (chs. 1, 2), and hence the Gospel demands unhesitating acceptance (3. 1-4. 13). Christ, moreover, is our High Priest, whose priesthood, unlike that of the Levitical (Aaronic) priests, is eternal (4. 14-6. 20). It is a priesthood 'after the order of *Melchizedek' (Pss. 2. 7, 110. 4), who was greater than *Abraham (Gen. 14. 18 ff.) and was thus *a fortiori* greater than the Levitical priests. In contrast to the repeated sacrifices of the Old Covenant, the Atonement in Christ is eternal. This new covenant, which, as foretold by Jer. 31. 31-4, was to supersede the temporary covenant of the Old Dispensation, was made, acc. to Ps. 40. 6-8, by the perfect obedience offered by Christ to God (7. 1-10. 18). With these facts before them, the readers are encouraged to steadfastness, perseverance, watchfulness for the Coming of Christ, and greater faith. Of the last a long roll of historic examples is cited (10. 19-11. 40). The Ep. concludes with particular ethical instructions and messages (chs. 12 f.).

From an early date the Ep. was received at *Alexandria as Pauline, whether considered as a translation by St. *Luke from St. Paul's Hebrew (*Clement of Alexandria, ap. *Eusebius, *H.E.*, vi, 14), or as St. Paul's in substance, but committed to writing by someone else (*Origen ap. Eusebius, *H.E.*, vi, 24); while in the E. generally, e.g. by the Council of *Antioch (264) and the later E. Fathers, it was regularly quoted as St. Paul's own composition. In the W. it was known to *Clement of Rome (*Ad Cor.*, xxxvi, 1-5; cf. Heb. 1. 1-13), but it was not quoted as Pauline or as certainly canonical before the 4th-5th cent. M. *Luther ascribed it to *Apollos; the Council of *Trent (sess. iv, 1546) affirmed its canonicity but not its Pauline authorship; but the RC *Biblical Commission ruled (1914) that it was in substance St. Paul's. Modern scholars, however, almost unanimously consider that the internal evidence marks it as non-Pauline, while its style shows that it is unlikely to be a translation. Clearly both the author and his intended readers were thoroughly familiar with Jewish worship and the latter were prob. converts from Judaism. But there are indications that this familiarity came through the Biblical ordinances (e.g. those concerning the *Tabernacle) rather than through direct knowledge of the *Temple itself (destroyed A.D. 70), and it has been argued (on the basis of 6. 1 f.) that the recipients of the Ep. were Gentiles. We learn that the author was a contemporary of *Timothy (13. 23), temporarily absent from those whom he was addressing, and expecting to return to them (13. 19). His identification with, e.g. *Silvanus, *Aquila (H. *Alford and others), or *Priscilla (A. *Harnack) cannot be more than conjectural. The use of the Ep. by Clement of Rome and the delay in the W. (as compared with the E.) in accepting it into the

*Canon (supposedly because there was here a genuine tradition of its non-Pauline authorship; so A. *Loisy, followed by A. H. McNeile), together with the ref. to Italy in 13. 24, have suggested to some scholars that the Ep. was originally connected with Rome. In that case 10. 32-4 might allude to the *Neronian persecution. On the other hand, on the ground of the relevance of its ideas to those combated in Col., the recipients have been identified by T. W. Manson with the *Colossians and their neighbours; he would date the Ep. before the writing of Col. and tentatively ascribe it to Apollos. On general grounds, a date before A.D. 70 has been supported by several other scholars, e.g. B. F. *Westcott; some, however, argue for a date under *Domitian. Its theological teaching, notably on the Person of Christ (1. 1-14, etc.), His real Humanity and sinlessness (4. 14 f.), His heavenly Priesthood and the Sacrifice of Calvary (7. 24 ff., etc.), as well as its literary capacity and expository power, reach a level unsurpassed in the NT. But the circumstances of its composition and its authorship remain obscure.

Recent commentaries include those by B. *Weiss (K.E.K., xiii, ed. 5; 1888), B. F. Westcott (London, 1889), A. S. *Peake (Cent. Bib., 1902), E. G. Wickham (West. Comm., 1910), H. Windisch (Hb. N.T., iv, Th. 3; 1913), A. Nairne (C.G.T., 1918), J. *Moffatt (I.C.C., 1924), F. D. V. Narborough (Clar. Bib., 1930), T. H. Robinson (Moff. Com., 1933), O. Michel (K.E.K., xiii, ed. 7, 1936), and C. Spicq, O.P. (Études Bibliques, 1952-3). Modern studies on the theology of the Epistle by E. Ménégoz (Paris, 1894), G. Milligan (Edinburgh, 1899), A. B. Bruce (ib., 1899), E. F. Scott (ib., 1922), and W. Manson (Baird Lecture for 1949; 1950). W. P. Du Bose, *High Priesthood and Sacrifice* (Bishop Paddock Lectures for 1907-8, 1908); J. A. Nairne, *The Epistle of Priesthood* (1913). A. Harnack, 'Probabilia über die Adresse und den Verfasser des Hebräerbriefs' in *Z.N.T.W.*, i (1900), pp. 16-41. C. Spicq, O.P., 'Le Philonisme de l'Épître aux Hébreux' in *R. Bibl.*, lvi (1949), pp. 542-72, lvii (1950), pp. 212-42. T. W. Manson, 'The Problem of the Epistle to the Hebrews' in *Bulletin of the John Rylands Library*, xxxii (1950), pp. 1-17 (argues for very early date). McNeile, pp. 224-39. T. *Zahn in *P.R.E.* (ed. 3), vii (1899), pp. 492-506, s.v. 'Hebräerbrief'; A. B. Bruce in *H.D.B.*, ii (1899), pp. 327-38, s.v. W. R. *Smith-H. von Soden in *E.Bi.*, ii (1901), cols. 1990-2001, s.v.; F. S. Marsh in *D.A.C.*, i (1915), pp. 534-42, s.v.

HEBREWS, Gospel according to the.

An apocryphal Gospel written in W. Aramaic. St. *Jerome, who regarded it as probably the original of the canonical Gospel of Mt., asserted that he had himself translated it into Latin and Greek (*De vir. illust.* 2). The surviving fragments suggest that the work was written from a Jewish-Christian standpoint, but that in its theology it was on the whole orthodox. It contained, besides much that is closely paralleled in the canonical Gospels, esp. Mt., sayings of Christ not recorded elsewhere (e.g. 'Never be glad, except when ye look upon your brother in love', 'He that wonders shall reach the kingdom, and having reached the kingdom shall rest'). Modern scholars have held the most divergent views as to its relation to the canonical Gospels; but the present tendency is to believe that in some places at least it is based on independent traditions of historical value. It has sometimes been termed by modern scholars the 'Gospel of the *Nazarenes'.

The work is mentioned by St. *Clement of Alexandria (*Strom.*, II, ix, 45) and cited several times by *Origen. Acc. to *Eusebius (*H.E.*, IV, xxii, 8), it was already known to *Hegesippus, while Jerome states that he had found a copy in the Library at Caesarea. Fragments collected in M. J. *Lagrange, O.P., 'L'Évangile selon les Hébreux' in *R. Bibl.*, xxxi (1922), pp. 161–81 and 321–49, with crit. discussion. Eng. tr. in M. R. James, *The Apocryphal New Testament* (1924), pp. 1–8. R. Handmann, *Das Hebräer-Evangelium* (T.U., v, Hft. 3; 1888). G. Bardy, 'Saint Jérôme et l'Évangile selon les Hébreux' in *Mélanges de Science religieuse*, iii (1946), pp. 5–36 (denies the trustworthiness of Jerome). Bardenhewer, i, pp. 513–18. A. F. Findlay in *D.C.G.*, i (1906), pp. 675–7, s.v. 'Gospels (Apocryphal), A.1'. E. Amann in *Dict. Bibl.* Suppl., i (1928), col. 471 f., s.v. 'Apocryphes du Nouveau Testament 1 (a)'.

HEBRON, the modern *El-Hâlil*, some 23 miles S.S.W. of *Jerusalem. It is believed to be one of the oldest cities in the world. It was chosen by *Abraham as his nomadic home when he arrived in Palestine (Gen. 13. 18), and he acquired here the Cave of Machpelah as the burying place for his family (Gen. 23). *Joshua made it one of the *Cities of Refuge (Josh. 20. 7). After the death of *Saul, *David made it his headquarters (2 Sam. 2. 1–4) and ruled the kingdom from Hebron for seven years and six months (ib. 2. 11) until he had secured possession of Jerusalem. Absalom in turn, on his revolt from David, made it his capital (2 Sam. 15. 7–11). It has sometimes been identified by Christian writers with the scene of the Visitation of the BVM.

L. H. Vincent, O.P.–E. J. H. Mackay–F. M. Abel, O.P., *Hébron*. Le Ḥaram el-Khalîl, sépulture des patriarches (1923, with sep. vol. of plates). F. M. Abel, O.P., *Géographie de la Palestine*, ii (1938), pp. 345–7, with further reff. C. Warren in *H.D.B.*, ii (1899), pp. 338–40.

HECKER, ISAAC THOMAS (1819–88), founder of the *Paulists. A native of New York, he was at first a keen *Methodist and as a youth took an active interest in the social conditions of the industrial classes. In 1844 he became a RC and, after spending some years in Europe, returned to New York in 1851. Meanwhile he had entered the novitiate of the *Redemptorists in Belgium in 1845 and been ordained priest by N. P. S. *Wiseman in 1849. In the early 'fifties he devoted himself wholeheartedly to the many RC immigrants then entering the U.S.A. Difficulties having arisen with his Redemptorist superiors in 1857 through his independent actions in New York, he was dispensed from his vows by *Pius IX, and founded a new congregation for missionary work in the States which was known as the 'Paulists'. After his death it was frequently suggested, but perhaps mistakenly, that the condemnation of *Americanism by *Leo XIII in his *Testem benevolentiae* (1899) had Hecker in mind.

W. Elliott, *The Life of Father Hecker* (New York, 1891; Fr. tr., with preface by l'Abbé Felix Klein, 1897). C. Maignen, *Étude sur l'américanisme. Le Père Hecker, est-il un saint?* (1898). List of writings with full bibl. in M. de Meulemeester, C.SS.R., *Bibliographie génerale des Écrivains rédemptoristes*, ii (1935), p. 185 f., and iii (1939), p. 316. See also bibl. s.v. 'Americanism'.

HEDONISM. The ethical doctrine which maintains that the proper end of all moral action is pleasure (Gk. ἡδονή, 'pleasure'). It thus closely resembles *Utilitarianism (q.v.). It is also known, esp. by Continental moral philosophers, as 'Eudaemonism' (Gk. εὐδαιμονία, 'true well-being'). The title 'psychological hedonism' is applied to the doctrine which holds that man is so constituted psychologically that he cannot avoid making 'pleasure' the end of his actions, i.e. that even though he may persuade himself that he is doing acts of great sacrifice, it is really his own pleasure that he is seeking all the time. Such a doctrine, of course, by ruling out freedom, precludes the possibility of moral action altogether.

HEFELE, KARL JOSEPH (1809–93), Church historian. Appointed Privatdozent in Church history at Tübingen in 1836 and professor in 1840, he soon won fame both as teacher and scholar. In 1869 he was elected Bp. of Rottenburg. He spent the winter of 1868–9 at Rome, where he took a prominent part as consultor in the preparations for the *Vatican Council of 1870, and was entrusted, owing to his unrivalled historical knowledge in the field, with drawing up the procedure. At the Council itself he was among the most influential of those opposed to the definition of Papal *Infallibility; but after some initial hesitations, he decided (10 Apr. 1871) to publish the Vatican Decrees in his diocese. His most important work was his History of the ecclesiastical Councils (9 vols., 1855–90, the last two by J. *Hergenröther; the earlier vols. exist in an Eng. trans., and the whole is in a French trans. with important additions by H. *Leclercq and others, 1907 ff.).

Hefele's other writings include *Geschichte der Einführung des Christenthums im südwestlichen Deutschland* (1837), *Der Kardinal Ximenes* (1844; Eng. tr., 1860), and *Beiträge zur Kirchengeschichte, Archäologie und Liturgik* (2 vols., 1864). He also contributed regularly to the *Theologische Quartalschrift*. F. X. Funk in id., lxxvi (1894), pp. 1–14. J. B. Sägmüller in *C.E.*, vii (1910), p. 191 f.

HEGEL, GEORG WILHELM FRIEDRICH (1770–1831), German Idealist philosopher. Born at Stuttgart, he entered the Tübingen Stift in 1788, nominally as a student of theology, where J. C. F. *Hölderlin and F. W. J. *Schelling were his contemporaries. Here Hegel devoted himself to classical subjects, without apparent interests in theology or philosophy. He first became interested in Christian origins during a three years' tutorship in Switzerland (1793–6) and worked at a philosophically conceived 'Life of Christ' (unfinished; first publd. in 1906). Ignoring the miraculous, he found the significance of Christ not in His moral teaching but in His proclamation that the contrasts of virtue and vice are transcended in a Life in which our finitude is embraced by the infinite, and that the meaning of life lay not in abstract speculation but in the concrete history of the human race. This early work contained the germs of the whole of Hegel's subsequent system, though later the theological elements receded into the background.

In 1797 Hölderlin procured for him a tutorship at Frankfurt, where he became a keen student of political science, but still holding that all forms of philosophy were subordinate to religion. In 1801 he moved to Jena. At first he found himself in close agreement with Schelling, then supreme among philosophers at Jena. To this period belongs his essay *Die Differenz des Fichteschen und Schellingschen Systems* (1801) and also the *Kritische Journal der Philosophie*, in which he and Schelling collaborated. His *De Orbitis Planetarum* (1801) qualified him for the post of Privatdozent and in 1801-2 he lectured to an audience of some eleven students on Logic and Metaphysics. After Schelling's departure for Würzburg (1803), Hegel set to work to develop his own system. He expounded it in *Die Phänomenologie des Geistes*, proof-sheets of which were circulated among his logic class in 1806. The Battle of Jena (14 Oct. 1806) terminated his career at the university, and for some 18 months (1807-8) he edited a newspaper (the *Bamberger Zeitung*).

In 1808 Hegel became a schoolmaster in Bavaria and in 1816 he accepted a professorship at Heidelberg. His *Wissenschaft der Logik* (vols. i-ii, 1812; iii, 1816) was his first presentation of what was in essentials the final form of his system. It was followed in 1817 by *Die Encyclopaedie der philosophischen Wissenschaften im Grundrisse* (2nd much enlarged ed., 1827; 3rd ed., 1830).

A new stage in his life was reached in 1818 when Hegel succeeded J. G. *Fichte as professor of philosophy of Berlin. He arrived at a time of great political unrest (assassination of Kotzebue, 1819) and sought to lay the theoretical foundations of a stable social order. In its fundamental teaching his *Grundlinien der Philosophie des Rechts* (1821), though standing above contemporary issues and in points of detail diverging from official policy, endorsed the aims of the Government. His influence as a lecturer steadily rose and to this period belong the courses on *Aesthetics*, *Philosophy of Religion*, *Philosophy of History*, *History of Philosophy* which were subsequently published as the well-known books. He was strongly critical of the teaching of F. D. E. *Schleiermacher, a rival influence at Berlin, with its emphasis on feeling in religion. In 1830 he was rector of the university. He died of cholera on 14 Nov. 1831.

Hegel's system, proverbially difficult to apprehend, grew out of the Critical Idealism of I. *Kant, which, carried forward by Fichte and Schelling, reached its ultimate development in his 'Absolute Idealism'. Despite its elaborate speculations, it professed to be severely realistic (as opposed to the romanticism of Schelling) and through and through rational, but only because 'the real is the rational and the rational is the real'. In the form of a 'logic', it claimed to do for the whole of human knowledge what *Aristotle's logic had accomplished for the demonstrative reason. It was a logic not of mere being, but of becoming, and the logical idea fell under

the three heads of being (*Sein*), essence (*Wesen*), and notion (*Begriff*). Development followed through a dialectical process in which a *thesis* was succeeded by an *antithesis*; through the ensuing conflict the two were brought together again at a higher level as a *synthesis*. In this way Hegel expounded an essentially evolutionary view of the universe and brought within the purview of his system not only the natural sciences but also such disciplines as history, law, aesthetics and religion. Truth lay not in individual truths or in individual disciplines, but in the whole ('*Die Wahrheit ist das Ganze*').

Hegel's influence has been immense. The modern study of ecclesiastical history begins with the *Tübingen School (F. C. *Baur, D. F. *Strauss, A. *Hilgenfeld) which drew its inspiration directly from Hegel. On the wider philosophical and religious issues, his followers were divided into two camps. On the one hand his doctrines were developed in a materialist direction by such thinkers as L. *Feuerbach and K. *Marx. On the other hand were those who developed the more spiritualistic aspects of his teaching. Among his leading English disciples were T. H. *Green, W. Wallace (1844-97), F. H. *Bradley, and B. *Bosanquet. Through such exponents, Absolute Idealism exercised a profound influence on English religious philosophy in the years between 1885 and 1914, and provided the philosophical background for the groups which produced *Lux Mundi* (1889) and *Foundations* (1914).

Collected ed. of *Werke*, 19 vols., 1832–1887. Editions of separate treatises, with introductions, by G. Lasson (1905 ff.). Among English versions, the *Logic* (from the *Encyclopaedie*; W. Wallace, 2 vols., 2nd ed., 1893), *Philosophy of Mind* (from the *Encyclopaedie*; W. Wallace, 1894), *Science of Logic* (i.e. the *Wissenschaft der Logik*; 2 vols., 1929), *Philosophy of History* (1858), *Philosophy of Right* (T. M. Knox, 1942), *Early Theological Writings*, ed. T. M. Knox (University of Chicago Press, 1949). J. H. Stirling, *The Secret of Hegel* (1865); E. *Caird, *Hegel* (1883); A. *Seth, *Hegelianism and Personality* (1887); J. M. Sterrett, *Studies in Hegel's Philosophy of Religion* (1891); J. E. McTaggart, *Studies in the Hegelian Dialectic* (1896); id., *Studies in Hegelian Cosmology* (1901); B. *Croce, *Cio che è vivo e cio che è morto della filosofia di Hegel* (1907); G. R. G. Mure, *Hegel* (1940); id., *A Study of Hegel's Logic* (1950). German Studies by K. Rosenkranz (various works; 1840, 1844, 1858, 1870), R. Haym (1857), J. E. Erdmann (1880), K. Fischer (2 vols., 1901)., H. Falkenheim (1911), N. Hartmann (1929). Also W. *Dilthey, *Die Jugendgeschichte Hegels* (1905), and R. Kroner, *Von Kant bis Hegel* (Bd. ii, 1924).

HEGESIPPUS, St. (2nd cent.), Church historian. A converted Jew and probably a native of Palestine, he wrote five Books of 'Memoirs' (ὑπομνήματα) against the *Gnostics. Though they now survive, as far as is known, only in fragments (nearly all preserved in *Eusebius's *Hist. Eccl.*), the work is said to have existed entire in some libraries as late as the 16th–17th cents. The surviving portions deal for the most part with the early history of the Church at *Jerusalem. It appears (Euseb., *H.E.* IV, xxii, 1–3) that he drew up a 'succession-list' (διαδοχή) of the early bishops of the Church at Rome; and it has been argued that the list in *Epiphanius (*Haer.* 27. 6) is a reproduction of this list. If so, it is the earliest witness to the names of the first Roman bishops. Feast day, 7 Apr.

Fragg. collected in M. J. *Routh, *Reliquiae Sacrae*, i (ed. 2, 1846), pp. 207–19 (annott. 220–84), and T. *Zahn, *Forschungen zur Geschichte des neutestamentlichen Kanons*, vi (1900), pp. 228–73. On his 'Papal List' see C. H. *Turner in H. B. *Swete, *Essays on the Early History of the Church and the Ministry* (1918), pp. 115–20 and 207; and T. Klauser in *Bonner Zeitschrift für Theologie und Seelsorge* (1931), pp. 193–213. Further bibl. in Altaner (ed. 1950), p. 110.

HEGIRA. The flight of *Mahomet from Mecca to Medina, the traditional date for which is 16 July 622. From this event begins the Moslem era, though, as its (lunar) years consist of only 354 or 355 days, it is not possible to relate it to the Christian era by simple addition or subtraction.

HEGUMENOS (Gk. ἡγούμενος, lit. 'leader'). A title in the E. for the ruler of a monastery. He is usually elected by the monks of the monastery, though confirmation is required from the patriarch, the diocesan bishop, or the patron (acc. to the status of the monastery).

HEIDELBERG CATECHISM. The Protestant confession of faith compiled in 1562 by Z. Ursinus and K. Olevian, two Heidelberg theologians, and others, at the instance of the Elector, *Frederick III, and accepted in the following year as the standard of doctrine in the Palatinate. In fundamentals its theology is *Calvinist, though the specific doctrines of J. *Calvin have sometimes been modified under the influence of J. H. *Bullinger, and others of even stronger Lutheran sympathies. Its spirit has been said to combine the intimacy of M. *Luther, the charity of P. *Melanchthon, and the fire of J. Calvin.

An Eng. tr. was publ. in 1572. A. Wolters, *Heidelberger Katechismus in seiner ursprünglichen Gestalt, herausgegeben nebst der Geschichte seines Textes im Jahre 1563* (1864). Text from ed. 3 in H. A. Niemeyer, *Collectio Confessionum in Ecclesiis Reformatis Publicatarum* (Leipzig, 1840), pp. 390–461, with introd. pp. lvii–lxiii. P. Schaff, *A History of the Creeds of Christendom*, i (1877), pp. 529–54, with bibl., incl. reff. to modern Eng. trr. A. Lang, *Der Heidelberger Katechismus* (Schriften des Vereins für Reformationsgeschichte, xxxi, 1, 1913). K. *Barth, *Die christliche Lehre nach dem Heidelberger Katechismus* (1948). M. Lauterburg in *P.R.E.* (ed. 3), x (1901), pp. 164–73, s.v. 'Katechismus, Heidelberger', with bibl. Full bibl. in Schottenloher, iv, pp. 329–31 (Nos. 38532–38574).

HEILER, FRIEDRICH (b. 1892), German religious writer. Originally a RC, he studied Catholic theology, philosophy, and oriental languages at Munich, but soon came under the influence of Protestantism, esp. of the Swedish theologian, N. *Söderblom. In 1919 he became a member of the Lutheran Church at *Upsala. In 1922 he was appointed professor of the comparative history of religions at *Marburg. Influenced by the writings of F. von *Hügel, his later development took a more Catholic line. He became the organizer of a German High Church movement, and even founded an Evangelical order of Franciscan *Tertiaries. His first and most important work is *Das Gebet* (1918), a comprehensive historical

analysis of prayer from its most primitive forms in the inarticulate shouts of the savage to the heights of mystic contemplation, the description of the latter being largely based on F. von Hügel, W. R. *Inge, and E. *Underhill. His work on Catholicism, *Der Katholizismus* (1923), is remarkable for its appreciative understanding of it in its earlier expansion, but almost entirely negative on post-Tridentine developments. Among his other works are *Evangelische Katholizität* (1926), *The Spirit of Worship* (1926), and *Die Wahrheit Sundar Singha* (1927).

Eng. tr. of *Das Gebet* (abridged) by S. McComb (New York, 1932). *In Deo Omnia Unum*. Eine Sammlung von Aufsätzen F. Heiler zum 50. Geburtstage dargebracht (ed. C. M. Schröder and others, Munich, 1942 [issue of periodical *Eine Heilige Kirche*]).

HEIM, KARL (b. 1874), *Lutheran theologian. A native of Frauenzimmern in Württemberg, he studied at *Tübingen and was for some years a pastor and schoolmaster. In 1907 he became a Privatdozent at Halle, in 1914 professor of theology at Münster i.W., and in 1920 at Tübingen. For several years he was one of the leading opponents of the (pagan) German Faith Movement. His theology, which developed out of a *Pietistic background, stressed the *Ritschlian contrast of faith and reason and, while fully conscious of the achievements of modern secular culture and science, emphasized the transcendence of faith. He was esp. concerned to analyse the conditions governing the valid apprehension of supernatural truth. In his personalism (the 'I-Thou' relationship; cf. M. *Buber) and his doctrine of 'perspectives', his teaching had affinities with certain *existentialist doctrines. Among his writings are *Das Weltbild der Zukunft* (1904), *Glaubensgewissheit* (1916; ed. 2, 1923), *Das Wesen des evangelischen Christentums* (1926), *Glauben und Denken* (1931; ed. 3, 1934; Eng. trans. as *God Transcendent*, 1935), *Glaube und Leben*, Gesammelte Aufsätze und Vorträge (1925; ed. 3, 1928).

Many of Heim's works have been translated into English. Brief studies on various aspects of his theology by W. Ruttenbeck (Leipzig, 1925), H. E. Eisenhuth (Göttingen, 1928), and F. Spemann (Tübingen, 1932). In English, popular introduction by E. L. Allen, *Jesus Our Leader*. A Guide to the Thought of Karl Heim [1950]. Dr. Winkler in *R.G.G.* (ed. 2), ii (1928), col. 1763 f., s.v.

HEIRIC OF AUXERRE (c. 840–c. 876), hagiographer. When only about 7 years old he entered the monastery of St. *Germanus at Auxerre as an oblate, and later studied under *Lupus Servatus at Ferrières and under Irish scholars at Laon and at Soissons. He then returned to his monastery at Auxerre where he taught until his death. He appears to have been well acquainted with classical authors (quoting e.g. Persius, *Suetonius, and Juvenal) and even to have known some Greek. His chief work was a metrical life of St. Germanus, one of the best hagiographical poems of the times, which he dedicated c. 876 to Charles the Bald. His other writings include a prose writing, 'Miracula S. Germani', and a set of notes on the astronomical writings of *Bede. Many of his pupils, among them *Remigius and Hucbald, became leading teachers in France.

The best text of his metrical life of St. Germanus is that of L. Traube, with important introd., in *M.G.H.*, Poetae, iii (1896), pp. 421–517; it is also pr. in *AA.SS.*, Jul. VII (1731), pp. 221–55. *Miracula S. Germani*, ib., pp. 255–83. On his astronomical commentary see L. Traube, 'Computus Helperici' in *N.A.*, xviii (1893), pp. 71–105, esp. pp. 103–5. Manitius, i, 499–504, with full reff. Überweg, ii, 177 f., with bibl. p. 694 f.

HELENA, St. (*c.* 255–*c.* 330), also Helen, mother of the Emp. *Constantine. Born at Drepanum (later 'Helenopolis' after her) in Bithynia of humble parentage, she became the wife of the Emp. Constantius Chlorus, by whom she bore Constantine in 274. She was abandoned by her husband in 292 when political reasons led him to marry the stepdaughter of the Emp. Maximian. When Constantine became Emperor in 306, Helena was immediately raised to a position of great honour and zealously supported the Christian cause. In 326, at a great age, she made a visit to the Holy Land, where she founded the basilicas on the Mount of *Olives and at *Bethlehem, and (acc. to later tradition; *Sulpicius Severus, *Ambrose, *Rufinus, all *c.* 395–400) discovered the Cross on which our Lord was crucified.

The medieval belief that St. Helena was a native of England derives from the chroniclers who appear to have confounded her with another Helen, the wife of Magnus Clemens Maximus, Emp. in Britain, Gaul, and Spain from 383 to 388, by whom she had several sons, one of them named Constantine. *Geoffrey of Monmouth and later legends described St. Helena as the daughter of Coel ('Old King Cole') of Colchester. From the 9th cent. the abbey of Hautvillers, near *Reims, claimed to possess her body. Feast day, 18 Aug.; in the E., 21 May (with St. Constantine, Emp.).

The chief early sources are *Eusebius, *Vita Constantini*, *Zosimus, *Historia*, ii. 8, and Eutropius, *Breviarium*, x. 2. R. Couzard, *Sainte Hélène d'après l'histoire et la tradition* (1911). On her Palestinian churches, F. Nau, 'Les Constructions Palestiniennes dues à Ste Hélène' in *Revue de l'Orient chrétien*, x (1905), pp. 162–88. A. Heisenberg, *Grabeskirche und Apostelkirche*. Zwei Basiliken Konstantins, ii (1908). H. *Leclercq, O.S.B., in *D.A.C.L.*, vi (pt. 2; 1925), cols. 2126–45, s.v. 'Hélène, Impératrice'. For the legend, see *B.H.L.*, i (1899), Nos. 3772–90. Life by Almannus of Hautvillers in *Acta Sanctorum*, Aug. III (1737), pp. 580–99. J. Maurice, *Ste Hélène* ('L'Art et les saints', illustr.; 1929); A. M. Rouillon, *Sainte Hélène* ('Les Saints', 1908).

HELIAND ('Saviour'; O. Eng. *haeland*, Ger. *Heiland*). An Old Saxon Biblical poem of the 9th cent. It owes its title to its first editor, A. Schmeller (1830), though the work had been discovered in the 17th cent. by F. Junius (d. 1671). It is based on *Tatian's harmony of the Gospels and is written in alliterative verse. The Latin 'Praefatio', now generally considered genuine, states that the Heliand was written by a well-known Saxon bard at the order of King *Louis the Pious for the benefit of his Saxon

subjects recently converted to Christianity. The poem, which shows the influence of the contemporary Anglo-Saxon religious poetry, represents Christ as a liege-lord and the Apostles as His faithful vassals, and inculcates the virtues of humility and love of one's enemies.

The work survives complete in a 10th cent. MS. in the British Museum (Cotton Caligula A. VII); a 9th cent. MS. at Munich has two lacunae; there are also 9th cent. fragments at Prague and the Vatican, the latter also containing a fragment of a *Genesis* in the same style but by a later poet. *Editio princeps* by J. A. Schmeller at Munich, 1830, with crit. apparatus as 'Lieferung 2', ib., 1840. Other edd. by E. Sievers (Halle, 1878), O. Behaghel (ib., 1882; ed. 6, 1948, with bibl.), and P. Piper (Stuttgart, 1897); with Gen. fragments). There is a considerable lit., mainly in German, on the poem from a linguistic angle; recent items listed by G. Cordes in S. H. Steinberg (ed.), *Cassell's Encyclopaedia of Literature*, i (1953), p. 276, s.v. Study of the British Museum MS. by P. Priebsch (Oxford, 1925).

HELKESAITES. See *Elkesaites.*

HELL. Traditionally the place or state of punishment after death. In the AV the word often translates the Heb. *Sheol (q.v.), i.e. the place of all the dead (RV, also 'the grave', 'the pit'). As Ps. 16, 10 indicates, there arose a hope in Judaism that the righteous would not be 'left' there, and, acc. to Acts 2. 27–31, Christ, after passing like all men through death, entered this realm but, by His *Resurrection, fulfilled Ps. 16. 10 in His own person and, becoming 'the firstfruits of them that slept', made possible its fulfilment for all who are 'in Christ' (1 Cor. 15. 20–23, cf. Rom. 6. 5–9).

In Christian theology, however, 'Hell', with few exceptions (see *Descent of Christ into Hell*), denotes the place or state to which unrepentant sinners are held to pass after this life, whereas the redeemed pass either to *Purgatory (q.v.) or direct to *Heaven (q.v.). Its character is inferred from Biblical teaching, esp. Christ's words in the Gospels about the fate of those who refuse the opportunity of entering the Kingdom of Heaven, and so are cast into 'outer darkness' with 'weeping and gnashing of teeth' (Matt. 25. 30, cf. 13. 42), or into 'everlasting fire prepared for the devil and his angels' (Matt. 25. 41), or 'into hell (lit. *Gehenna, q.v.), into unquenchable fire' (Mark 9. 43, cf. RV). To this also Is. 66. 24 is applied, with its suggestion of the destruction of what is already corrupt and useless; cf. the statement (Matt. 10. 28) that God is able 'to destroy both soul and body in hell' (lit. Gehenna). In the Pauline Epp. the ultimate fate of the unredeemed is said to be 'death' (Rom. 6. 21, 23), the encounter with God's 'wrath' bringing 'tribulation and anguish' (Rom. 2. 5, 8 f.), or simply 'destruction' (2 Thess. 1. 9, Phil. 3. 19). In the Gospel and Epp. of St. John those who are not redeemed by Christ will 'perish' (Jn. 3. 16) even their present state being 'condemnation' (Jn. 3. 18) and 'death' (1 Jn. 3. 14). In Heb. 10. 27 a quasi-metaphorical mention of 'fire' recurs, and in Rev. the 'second death' (2. 11) is depicted symbolically as the fate of being cast into a 'lake which burneth with fire and brimstone' (21. 8, cf. 19. 20, 20. 10). From such texts as these last, often understood overliterally, the popular idea of hell was derived.

It is clear that in the NT Hell in this sense is an ultimate state or destiny into which souls pass only by God's final and irrevocable judgement, whether that is conceived as the *Particular Judgement at death or the *General Judgement on the last day. Acc. to the traditional Scholastic theology, souls experience in Hell both the *poena damni*, i.e. the exclusion from God's presence and loss of all contact with Him, and a certain *poena sensus*, denoted in the Bible by fire, which is usually interpreted as an external agent tormenting them. Modern theology tends rather to stress the fact that Hell is but the logical consequence of ultimate adherence to the soul's own will, and rejection of the will of God, which (since God cannot take away free will) necessarily separates the soul from God, and hence from all possibility of happiness. This exclusion from Heaven (in which the unrepentant person would from his very character be both unable and unwilling to share) is held to be contrary neither to God's justice nor to His love, since He will not force response to the good from any creature against his will.

HELVETIC CONFESSIONS, The. Two

important Reformation Confessions of Faith.

(1) *First Helvetic Confession* (also known as the 'Second Confession of *Basle'). It was compiled at Basle in 1536 by J. H. *Bullinger of Zürich, *Myconius and Grynaeus of Basle, and others, after much dissension, esp. on the Eucharist, as a uniform confession of faith for the whole of Switzerland. Its basis was *Zwinglian, but it contained a considerable *Lutheran element. It was accepted by all the Protestant Swiss cantons but rejected by Strassburg and Constance.

(2) *Second Helvetic Confession*. This was the work of J. H. *Bullinger, who made an early draft of it in 1562. It was issued in 1566 in response to a request from the Elector-Palatine, *Frederick III ('the Pious'), who had announced his definite adhesion to *Calvinism. It is among the longest of the Reformation Confessions, in places taking on the character of a theological treatise. Its teaching is mainly Calvinist, with some Zwinglian elements. It soon won acceptance not only in all the Swiss Protestant Churches, but also among the 'Reformed' (i.e. Calvinists) outside Switzerland.

(1) Latin and German text in P. *Schaff, *Creeds of Christendom*, iii, 211–31.

(2) Latin text in P. Schaff, *Creeds of Christendom*, iii, 233–306.

HELVIDIUS (4th cent.). A Latin theologian

who was attacked by St. *Jerome for his denial of the perpetual virginity of the BVM. His underlying motive was the defence of marriage against the prevalent exaltation of virginity. Helvidius declared that the *Brethren

of the Lord were the natural sons of Joseph and Mary. Jerome replied in his *De perpetua virginitate B. Mariae adversus Helvidium* that they were the sons of another Mary, the wife of Alphaeus and the sister of the Virgin. Acc. to St. *Augustine (*De haer.* 84), he won disciples who were known as 'Helvidians'.

Helvidius's tract has not survived. Jerome's reply is repr. in J. P. Migne, *PL*, xxiii, 185–206. Bardenhewer, iii, p. 631. W. Koch in *L.Th.K.*, iv (1932), col. 955.

HELWYS, THOMAS (*c.* 1550–*c.* 1616), Eng-

lish *Baptist divine. Of a Nottinghamshire family, he studied at Gray's Inn. In 1608 he emigrated to Holland with J. *Smyth and became a member of the *Brownist Church at Amsterdam. Here, like Smith, he became convinced that 'Infant Baptism' was not baptism at all, and accordingly received baptism at Smyth's hands. In consequence when he and Smyth were excommunicated (1609), he joined Smyth's separate community at Amsterdam, the first Baptist Church to come into being. In 1612, feeling it his duty no longer to absent himself from the dangers of persecution, he returned to London, where he founded the first *General Baptist congregation in England at Pinners' Hall, London, and met with remarkable success as a preacher. Opposition was aroused, however, when he began to put into circulation his *Declaration of the Mystery of Iniquity*, which, written and printed in Holland (1611–12), contained the first sustained plea by an English divine for universal religious toleration and a denial of the right of the State to legislate on matters which concern a man's relation to God. There seems to be no record of the circumstances of Helwys's death.

A facsimile ed. of *The Mistery of Iniquity* was publd. for the Baptist Historical Society (London, 1935), with introd. by H. Wheeler *Robinson, pp. iii–xv. W. H. Burgess, *John Smith, the Se-Baptist, Thomas Helwys and the First Baptist Church in England* (1911), pp. 107–296 passim. A. C. Bickley in *D.N.B.*, xxv (1891), p. 375 f., with further reff. See also works cited under *Baptists*.

HEMEROBAPTISTS. (Gk. ἡμέρα 'day',

and βαπτιστής, 'baptist'), a Jewish sect for which daily ablution was an essential part of religion. Acc. to *Epiphanius (*Haer.* i. 17) their doctrines were similar to those of the *Pharisees, except that they denied the resurrection. The sect is mentioned by *Hegesippus (Eus., *HE*, IV, xxii) and *Justin Martyr (*Dial. c. Tryph.* 80). The *Clementine Recognitions* (ii, 23) state that *John the Baptist was a Hemerobaptist. J. B. *Lightfoot (*Col.*, p. 402) identified them with the Hebrew sect of Toble-shacharith ('morning bathers').

HEMMERLIN, FELIX, also 'Hemerli' (*c.*

1388–*c.* 1460), also 'Malleolus', reformer. A native of Zürich, he studied canon law at Erfurt (1406–8 and 1413–18) and *Bologna (1408–12 and 1423–4) and states that he was present at the Council of *Constance (1415). In 1421 he became provost at St. Ursus at Solothurn, where he revised the statutes of his collegiate clergy and defended their rights against the municipality. From now on he loudly advocated reforms of all kinds, e.g. suppression of concubinage and simony and reduction of feast-days; and he also attacked the *Mendicant Orders and the *Lollards. He appears to have been a man of small stature, quarrelsome, and in some matters extremely superstitious (defence of cultus of relics). In 1428 he was made Cantor of the Stift at Zürich, and from 1429 onwards he appears as a canon of St. Moritz at Zofingen. In his later years he took a prominent part in politics, supporting the alliance of Zürich with Austria against the Swiss Confederation, which he attacked violently in *Dialogus de Nobilitate et Rusticitate* (*c.* 1452). On the reconciliation of Zürich with the Swiss in 1456 he was condemned to the loss of his ecclesiastical offices and perpetual imprisonment. He spent his last years in mild captivity with the *Franciscans at Lucerne. He was the author of over thirty polemical works.

A collection of his writings was publd. by S. Brandt at Basle *c.* 1497. A. Schneider in *P.R.E.* (ed. 3), vii (1899), pp. 656–9, s.v. 'Hemerli', with bibl. E. F. J. Müller in *L.Th.K.*, iv (1932), col. 956 f., s.v., with further detailed reff.

HENDERSON, ALEXANDER (*c.* 1583–1646), Scottish Covenanting leader. As an Episcopalian he obtained a professorship at St. Andrews, and in 1611 or 1612 was appointed to the parish of Leuchars in Fifeshire. By 1618 he was sufficiently in sympathy with *Presbyterianism to oppose the Articles of *Perth, and later offered strong resistance to the Prayer Book of 1637. He was mainly responsible for drafting the *National Covenant of 1638, became Moderator of the Assembly which met at Glasgow in Nov. 1638, and in Jan. 1639 was inducted to Greyfriars, Edinburgh. During the *Bishops' Wars of 1639–1640 he was the recognized leader of the Scottish Presbyterians, and even *Charles I, on his visit to Scotland in 1641, was forced to accept him as his chaplain and Dean of the Chapel Royal. In 1643 he went to Oxford in a vain attempt at mediation between King and Parliament, while in the following months he prepared the draft of the *Solemn League and Covenant for both Scotland and England (1643) and of the Directory for Public *Worship (1644). In 1646 he spent the last months of his life debating the presbyterian and episcopal systems of Church government with the King.

J. Aiton, *The Life and Times of Alexander Henderson* (1836); T. McCrie and T. Thomson, *Lives of Alexander Henderson and James Guthrie* (1846), pp. 1–140; G. W. Thomson, *Alexander Henderson. A Biography* (1883).

HENGSTENBERG, ERNST WILHELM (1802–69). Biblical exegete. From 1828 till his death he was professor of theology at Berlin. He was brought up in a rationalist atmosphere, then fell under *Pietist influences in 1823–4, and from *c.* 1840 accounted himself an orthodox Lutheran. As editor from 1827 to 1869 of the *Evangelische Kirchenzeitung*, which he had himself founded, he possessed an influential organ in which he attacked the theology of F. D. E. *Schleiermacher and other unorthodox systems. His works include many commentaries on OT and NT books, some of which were translated into English.

J. Bachmann–T. Schmalenbach, *E. W. Hengstenberg. Sein Leben und Wirken nach gedruckten und ungedruckten Quellen* (3 vols., 1876–92). J. Bachmann in *P.R.E.* (ed. 3), vii (1899), pp. 670–4, s.v.

HENOTHEISM. (Gk. εἷς, ἑνός, 'one', and θεός, 'god'). A term first employed by F. *Max Müller in 1860 for a primitive form of faith which, as distinct from *monotheism (belief in the existence of a single god) and monolatry (restriction of worship to a single god) recognizes the existence of several gods, but regards one particular god as the deity of the family or tribe; makes him the centre of its worship; and in its relations with him neglects for practical purposes the existence of others. It thus stands mid-way between 'polytheism' and monotheism. Modern scholars commonly hold that the early Hebrew faith in *Yahweh (down to 8th cent. B.C. or later) took this form.

HENOTICON (Gk. ἑνωτικόν). The theological formula put forward in 482 to secure union between the *Monophysites and the Orthodox and sponsored by the Emp. *Zeno. It was apparently the work chiefly of Acacius, Patr. of *Constantinople, and *Peter Mongo, Patr. of *Alexandria. Though it condemned both *Nestorius and *Eutyches, by its assertion that the orthodox faith was epitomized in the *Nicene-Constantinople Creed together with the Twelve Anathemas of St. *Cyril of Alexandria, and by its omission of all reference to the burning question as to the number of 'natures' in Christ, it really made important concessions to Monophysitism. It was widely accepted in the East, but never countenanced at Rome.

Text in *Evagrius, *H.E.*, iii. 14 (*PG*. lxxxvi, 2620–25). Crit. ed. by E. *Schwartz in *Codex Vaticanus gr. 1431. Eine antichalkedonische Sammlung aus der Zeit Kaiser Zenos* (*Abh.* (Bayr.), xxxii, Hft. 6 [1927], pp. 52–4); Lat. tr. in Liberatus's *Breviarium*, pr. ib., pp. 54–6. E. Schwartz, *Publizistische Sammlungen zum acacianischen Schisma* (*Abh.* (Bayr.) N.F., Hft. 10, 1934), esp. pp. 182–218. S. Salaville, A.A., 'L'Affaire de l'hénotique ou le premier schisme byzantine au Vᵉ siècle' in *É.O.*, xviii (1918), pp. 255–66, 389–97; xix (1920), pp. 49–68. Further bibl. in A. Grillmeier, S.J.–H. Bacht, S.J. (edd.), *Das Konzil von Chalkedon*, ii (1953), p. 120, note 14. 'L.' Salaville, A.A., in *D.T.C.*, vi (1920), cols. 2153–78, s.v. 'Hénotique', with bibl.

HENRICIANS. A medieval heretical sect which arose at Tours in the 12th cent. under the inspiration of *Henry of Lausanne (q.v.). They seem to have been closely connected with the followers of *Peter de Bruys (q.v.).

HENRIETTA MARIA (1609–66). The Queen of *Charles I and daughter of *Henry IV of France. She married Charles in 1625, on condition that the penal laws against

RCs were suspended and that the Queen be allowed free exercise of her religion. After the assassination of Buckingham in 1628, the Queen acquired great influence over Charles. She irritated the country by allowing her court to become the focus of RC intrigues, and it was probably her advice that led Charles to his more despotic acts, e.g. his attempt to arrest the Five Members in 1640. During the Civil War she increased her unpopularity by attempting to raise money and forces for the King from France. She finally left Charles for France in Apr. 1644, where she remained until after the Restoration, when Somerset House was given her for a residence.

Mary A. E. Green (ed.), *Letters of Queen Henrietta Maria* (1857); le Comte [C.] de Baillon, *Henriette-Marie de France, reine d'Angleterre*. Étude historique . . . suivie de ses lettres inédites (1877); H. Ferrero (ed.), *Lettres de Henriette-Marie de France, reine d'Angleterre, à sa sœur Christine, duchesse de Savoie* (Estratto dalla Miscellanea di Storia italiana, Ser. ii, v; 1881). C. Cotolendi, *La Vie de très-haute et très-puissante Princesse Henriette-Marie de France, reine de la Grand' Bretagne* (1690). I[da] A. Taylor, *The Life of Queen Henrietta Maria* (2 vols., 1905); Henrietta Haynes, *Henrietta Maria* (1912); Carola Oman, *Henrietta Maria* (1936). S. R. Gardiner in *D.N.B.*, xxv (1891), pp. 429–36.

HENRY II, St. (972–1024), German king and Roman Emperor. The son of Henry, Duke of Bavaria ('the Quarrelsome'), he succeeded his cousin Otto III as Emperor in 1002, intent on consolidating the political unity of Germany. In his earlier years he was involved in constant warfare first against attacks from the East and then in Lombardy, where he defeated Arduin of Ivrea. In 1006 he created and richly endowed the new see of Bamberg, largely to effect the Germanization of the Wends. He was crowned by Benedict VIII on 14 Feb. 1014 during an expedition to Rome. His frequent and often high-handed interference in Church affairs issued in many disputes with the ecclesiastical leaders in his domains, though he commonly had the political support of Rome. In his later years he became an active supporter of the *Cluniac reform. In 1021, on a last journey to Rome, he assisted in preparations for ending the Greek supremacy in Italy. Later legends saw in him a monarch of outstanding piety and asceticism. He was canonized in 1146. Feast day, 15 July. (His wife, Cunegund, was canonized in 1200; feast day, 3 Mar.).

H. Bresslau–H. Bloch–M. Meyer–R. Holtzmann (edd.), *Die Urkunden Heinrichs II und Arduins* (*M.G.H.*, Diplomata Regum et Imperatorum Germaniae, iii, 1900–3, with 'Nachträgen zu den Urkunden Heinrichs II' in iv (1909), pp. 419–32 and 552). *AA.SS.*, Jul. III (1723), pp. 711–93; crit. text of life by Adalbold, O.S.B., Bp. of Utrecht, 1010–27, ed. G. Waitz, *M.G.H.*, Scriptores iv (1841), pp. 679–95, and of mid. 12th cent. life by Adalbert, deacon of Bamberg, ib. pp. 789–816, with 'Additamentum', pp. 816–820, and of Vita Sanctae Cunegundis, with miracles, pp. 821–8. S. Hirsch, *Jahrbücher des deutschen Reiches unter Heinrich II* (Jahrbücher der deutschen Geschichte, 3 vols. in 2, 1862–75). H. Lesêtre, *Saint Henri* ('Les Saints'; 1899); H. Günter, *Der heilige Kaiser Heinrich II* (Sammlung illustrierter Heiligenleben, i; 1904). H. L. Mikoletzky, *Kaiser Heinrich II und die Kirche* (Veröffentlichungen des Instituts für Österreichische Geschichtsforschung, viii; 1951), with bibl. H. Bloch, 'Die Urkunden Kaiser Heinrichs II für Kloster Michelsberg zu Bamberg' in *N.A.*, xix (1894), pp. 603–49.

HENRY IV (1050–1106), German King and Roman Emperor. He succeeded to the throne in 1056 and was declared of age in 1065. His reign was beset with difficulties owing to the rebellious Saxon princes on the one hand and the reforms of Pope *Gregory VII on the other. Gregory prohibited *simony and lay *investiture which had hitherto enabled the Emperors to appoint to the highest ecclesiastical posts men devoted to the Imperial interests. Henry, having conquered the Saxons in 1075, refused obedience to the Pope and answered the threat of excommunication by declaring Gregory deposed. Thereupon Gregory carried out his threat and released Henry's subjects from their oath of allegiance. The King's position having become desperate when the Saxons rose again and the princes refused obedience unless he was reconciled to the Pope, Henry submitted at *Canossa in 1077 and, having done solemn penance, was freed from excommunication and returned to Germany. The peace between Pope and King was, however, short-lived. Three years later Henry was again excommunicated, but set up an *antipope, Clement III, who crowned him Roman Emperor in 1084. Gregory died the next year, but his successor *Urban II carried on the struggle. The last years of Henry's reign were filled with revolts, two of his sons became rebels, and only his premature death saved Germany from civil war. Under his successor, Henry V (1098–1125), the investiture conflict ended, for the time being, in the compromise of the Concordat of *Worms (1122).

Constitutiones ed. G. H. Pertz in *M.G.H.*, Leges, ii (1837), pp. 44–62; mostly repr. in J. P. Migne, *PL*, cli, 1125–66; D. v. Gladiss (ed.), *Die Urkunden Heinrichs IV* (*M.G.H.*, Diplomata Regum et Imperatorum Germaniae, vi; 1952 ff.). C. Erdmann (ed.), *Die Briefe Heinrichs IV* (Deutsches Mittelalter, i; 1937). 'Vita Henrici IV Imperatoris', ed. W. Wattenbach in *M.G.H.*, xii (1856), pp. 268–83. S. Hellmann, 'Die Vita Henrici IV und die kaiserliche Kanzlei' in *Historische Vierteljahrschrift*, xxviii (1934), pp. 273–334. G. Meyer von Knonau, *Jahrbücher des deutschen Reiches unter Heinrich IV und Heinrich V*, vols. i–v (1890–1904). E. Höhne, *Kaiser Heinrich IV. Sein Leben und seine Kämpfe* (1056–1106) nach dem Urteile seiner deutschen Zeitgenossen (1906). B. Schmeidler, *Kaiser Heinrich IV und seine Helfer im Investiturstreit* (1927). H. Dachs in *L.Th.K.*, iv (1932), cols. 913–15, s.v. 'Heinrich IV' with bibl.

HENRY IV (1553–1610), King of France. Brought up as a Protestant, he became King of Navarre in 1572. He took part in the wars of religion on the Protestant side, and, on the assassination of Henry III in 1589, inherited the crown of France. But his Protestantism made him unacceptable to the Catholic League, which was supported by *Philip II of Spain and the Pope; and though he defeated the Guise party in the field he was not recognized as king until his conversion to Catholicism in 1593. Opinion is now decidedly against the popular legend that this was a merely political move ('Paris vaut bien une messe'). His lengthy discussions with theologians previous to his submission, together with his protestations that 'Religion is not changed as easily as a shirt', are considered sufficient proof of his sincerity. It was not until 1595, however, after many difficulties, that the Pope solemnly absolved Henry from the crime of heresy. In 1598 the King promulgated the Edict of *Nantes which gave freedom of worship to the Protestants in recognized places and permitted them to garrison certain towns as a security for its maintenance. By extending the powers of the crown Henry tried to restore prosperity to his country. The lines of his domestic and foreign policy were later continued by A. J. *Richelieu. He was assassinated by the fanatic Ravaillac on 14 May 1610.

M. Berger de Xivrey–J. Guadet (edd.), *Receuil des lettres missives de Henri IV* (Collection de documents inédits sur l'histoire de France, publiés par ordre du Roi et par les soins du Ministre de l'Instruction Publique, 9 vols., 1843–76). There is also a small modern collection of his letters and speeches publ. in the series 'Les Cahiers de l'Unité française' ed. by J. and R. Wittmann, xii (1941). There is a vast literature on Henry IV. Eng. works include G. P. R. James, *The Life of Henry the Fourth, King of France and Navarre* (3 vols., 1847); Martha W. Freer, *History of the Reign of Henry IV, King of France and Navarre* (3 pts., 6 vols., 1860–3); Catherine C. Jackson, *The First of the Bourbons* (2 vols., 1890); P. F. Willert, *Henry of Navarre and the Huguenots in France* ('Heroes of the Nations'; 1893). J. H. Mariéjol in E. Lavisse, *Histoire de France*, vi (pt. 1; 1904), pp. 303–423 and (pt. 2; 1904) pp. 1–140, with full bibl. reff.; S. Leathes in *C.M.H.*, iii (1904), ch. xx, 'Henry IV of France', pp. 657–95, with full bibl. to date, pp. 860–6. More recent works include P. de Vaissière, *Henri IV* (1925); G. Slocombe, *Henry of Navarre. A Passionate History* (1931); M. Vioux, *Le Vert Galant* (1935; Eng. tr. 1936); Q. Hurst, *Henry of Navarre* (1937); M. Reinhard, *Henri IV ou la France sauvée* (1943); R. Ritter, *Henri IV lui-même.* L'Homme (1944). P. Feret, *Henri IV et l'Église catholique* (1875); M. Brouard, 'Sixte-Quint, Henri IV et la Ligue. La Légation du Cardinal Caetani en France (1589–1590)' in *R.Q.H.*, cxvi (1932), pp. 59–140, with docc.

HENRY VI (1421–71), King of England. He succeeded his father, Henry V, in 1422. During his minority England was ruled by a Council, the King's protector being John Duke of Bedford, and his first spiritual guide the *Carmelite theologian, Thomas *Netter. He was crowned King of England in 1429 and King of France in 1431. Throughout his reign the difficulties in France increased, and the situation in England was unsettled, chiefly through differences between the Duke of Gloucester and Richard of York and popular opposition to Card. H. *Beaufort's peace policy. After Beaufort's death (1447) Suffolk became the chief power, but he was supplanted by Richard of York in 1450. The birth of a son to Henry, in 1453, excluded Richard from the succession. About the same time the King was seized with an attack of mental derangement, during which Richard governed. After his recovery war broke out between York and Henry Beaufort, Duke of Somerset (1436-64), ending with the latter's defeat in 1455. It was resumed in 1459, and in 1460 Henry was taken prisoner and compelled to declare York his heir. After Richard's death (1460) he was freed, but Edward of York made himself king and Henry lived as an exile in Scotland. In 1465 he was captured and imprisoned in the Tower, until, in 1470, Warwick restored him to the throne. After six months, however, he was once more confined to the Tower, where he was murdered, probably by the future Richard III.

Henry VI was a deeply religious man, but too generous and trusting to be a successful ruler in his troubled age. He often sought refreshment in religious houses and gave much time to prayer and pious works. He was passionately devoted to the encouragment of learning, and was the founder of Eton and of King's College, Cambridge (1440 and 1441). The report of many miracles at his tomb at the *Benedictine monastery of Chertsey in Surrey soon made it a place of pilgrimage; and though Richard III had his body removed to St. George's Chapel, *Windsor, he was unable to put a stop to the popular devotion. Henry VII petitioned *Innocent VIII and *Alexander VI for his canonization, and in recent times renewed efforts have been made to this end.

J. Stevenson (ed.), *Letters and Papers Illustrative of the Wars of the English in France during the Reign of Henry the Sixth* (Rolls Series, 2 vols. bound in 3; 1861–4). Memoir of Henry VI by John Blacman, his confessor, orig. publ. London, 1510, repr. mainly from text of T. *Hearne, 1732, by M. R. James (Cambridge, 1919). The Lat. account of his miracles in Brit. Mus. Royal MS. 13 c, viii, written *c.* 1500, ed. R. [A] Knox–S. Leslie, with introd. and Eng. tr. (Cambridge, 1923); crit. ed. by P. Grosjean, S.J. (Subsidia Hagiographica, xxii; 1935). M. E. Christie, *Henry VI* ('Kings and Queens of England'; 1922). F. A. *Gasquet, *The Religious Life of King Henry VI* (1923). T. F. Tout in *D.N.B.*, xxvi (1891), pp. 56–69.

HENRY VIII (1491–1547), King of England from 22 Apr. 1509. The second son of Henry VII, he was born at Greenwich, where he was baptized by R. *Fox in the Church of the Friars *Observants. He was precocious as a child, readily susceptible to the cultural influence of the Renaissance, and learned to speak Latin, French, and Spanish easily. He was also an accomplished musician, even if not (as traditionally supposed) the author of the anthem 'O Lord, Maker of all Things'. The story, first met with in P. *Sarpi and repeated by Lord *Herbert of Cherbury, that Henry was originally destined for an ecclesiastical career is without foundation. Nevertheless he had great theological interests. From an early date he opposed the Reforming Movement and his *Assertio Septem Sacramentorum* (1521), directed against M. *Luther, won for him from *Leo X on 11 Oct. 1521 the title of '*Defender of the Faith'. Throughout his life he showed zeal in the outward practices of religion.

In the opening years of Henry's reign, England under T. *Wolsey's able management played a prominent, if expensive, part in European affairs. In 1525 the balance of power was lost when *Charles V captured Francis I at Pavia. Two years later Henry took the first steps to dissolve his marriage with Catherine of Aragon (b. Dec. 1485), the widow of his elder brother, Arthur, which had taken place by papal dispensation on 11 June 1509. The only one of Catherine's children to survive infancy was a daughter, *Mary, and Henry became increasingly anxious about the Tudor succession. He had already conceived a strong passion for Anne Boleyn, who was determined to become his acknowledged queen. A collusive inquiry, held by Wolsey as Legate and W. *Warham as assessor, on the grounds of supposed doubts as to Mary's legitimacy, resulted only in eliciting from Catherine a solemn statement that her first marriage had never been consummated. Henry next sent his secretary, William Knight, to Rome to sue from *Clement VII for a decree of nullity and the removal of any impediments to marriage with Anne arising from Henry's unlawful connexions with her elder sister. The Pope being at that time the prisoner of Charles V, Catherine's nephew, Knight succeeded only in obtaining a conditional dispensation for a new marriage. Proceedings continued in England before Wolsey and L. *Campeggio as papal commissioners until in July 1529 Clement revoked the cause to Rome, partly to give Catherine facilities lacking in England. The fall of Wolsey followed inevitably and Henry, unprepared to answer a citation outside his own realm, turned to the repudiation of papal authority.

In the autumn of 1529 T. *Cranmer, then a Fellow of Jesus College, Cambridge, suggested that the universities of Europe should be consulted on the divorce; and favourable opinions were soon obtained from seats of learning outside Charles V's dominions. Henry's statesmanship prompted him to associate his people with himself in establishing the new order by summoning Parliament to pass Acts designed to put pressure on the Pope and ultimately to transfer the headship of the Church in England to himself. But the clergy were subjected to repressive measures. In 1530 they were involved in Wolsey's *praemunire for having acquiesced in his legatine authority, and secured pardon only by the payment of a large fine and Convocation's recognition of the Royal Supremacy. In 1532 followed the Commons' Petition to the King against the Clergy, the answer of the Ordinaries, the acceptance by Convocation on 15 May of the '*Submission of the Clergy' and the passing of the Act in restraint of *Annates and *first-fruits. Shortly after Warham's death (August, 1532), Cranmer was appointed his successor. The necessary bulls having been obtained from the Pope in return for withholding the royal assent to the Act against Annates, consecration took place in April, 1533. An Act forbidding appeals to Rome having been passed, Henry agreed that the Archbishop should summon Catherine and himself to Dunstable, where (in the absence of Catherine, who was pronounced contumacious for her non-appearance) Cranmer gave judgement on 23 May that the marriage was invalid. Five days later, at Lambeth, Henry was pronounced to be lawfully married to Anne Boleyn, who was crowned Queen on 1 June. By a Bull of 11 July Clement VII excommunicated Henry and declared his divorce and remarriage null. In the following year Parliament passed Acts for the Submission of the Clergy, for the regulation of ecclesiastical appointments, for the absolute restraint of appeals, as well as forbidding the payment of *Peter's Pence and transferring dispensing

powers to the see of Canterbury. The first Act of Succession entailed the Crown on Anne Boleyn's children, imposing an oath which men of the stamp of T. *More and J. *Fisher could not take. Their execution in 1535 was universally mourned.

The *Dissolution of the Monasteries (1536 and 1539) and the transfer of their wealth won for the monarchy the support of the beneficiaries and brought some replenishment to the royal coffers. Six new bishoprics (*Westminster, *Gloucester, *Peterborough, *Oxford, *Chester, Bristol) were founded and education and the navy derived some benefit. Considerable opposition was aroused among the people by the suppression; the *Pilgrimage of Grace in the North in 1536 was a formidable rising, suppressed only by trickery.

By countenancing the *Ten Articles (1536) and the order that the English Bible should be set up in churches (1538) Henry seems for a brief space to have shown a measure of tolerance for Protestantism. His readiness to make overtures to *Lutheranism, admittedly under political necessity, were reflected in the events which led to his marriage to Anne of Cleves (6 Jan. 1540). But a halt was soon called. The *Six Articles (June 1539) reaffirmed Catholic Doctrine under the threat of severe penalties (H. *Latimer and N. *Shaxton resigned their bishoprics), and Henry's repudiation of Protestantism was symbolized by his marriage to Catharine Howard (8 Aug. 1540). The last years of his reign were marked by some attempts at promoting religious reforms, while maintaining the substance of traditional Catholicism. 1543 saw the formal authorization of the *Sarum use throughout the kingdom and also the issue of the *King's Book (q.v.). In 1544 the *Litany (in English) was issued and in 1545 an Act passed suppressing chantries and other similar foundations. In 1546 Anne *Askew suffered for holding a Protestant view of the Eucharist. It was not until after the death of Henry VIII on 28 Jan. 1547 that in the next reign doctrinal Protestantism became the official ecclesiastical policy.

Documentary evidence in *Letters and Papers, Foreign and Domestic, of the Reign of Henry VIII*, vols. i–iv ed. J. S. Brewer (1862–75); vols. v–xxi ed. J. *Gairdner and R. H. Brodie (1880–1907). Relevant section of Edward Hall's *Chronicle* (1548), ed. C. Whibley (2 vols., 1904). J. S. Brewer (ed. J. Gairdner), *The Reign of Henry VIII from his Accession to the Death of Wolsey* (2 vols., 1884). A. F. Pollard, *Henry VIII* (1902). F. Hackett, *Henry VIII* (1929; a psychological study). C. Fatta, *Il regno di Enrico VIII d' Inghilterra* (1936; esp. for diplomacy). R. W. Dixon, *History of the Church of England from the Abolition of the Roman Jurisdiction to 1570* (6 vols., 1878–1902), vols. i and ii. H. Maynard Smith, *Henry VIII and the Reformation* (1948). F. A. *Gasquet, *Henry VIII and the English Monasteries* (2 vols., 1888–9); G. Baskerville, *English Monks and the Suppression of the Monasteries* (1937). E. Doernberg, *Henry VIII and Luther* (1961). J. Gairdner in *D.N.B.*, xxvi (1891), pp. 76–94.

HENRY BEAUFORT. See *Beaufort, Henry*.

HENRY OF BLOIS (d. 1171), Bp. of *Winchester. The grandson of William the Conqueror and brother of King Stephen, he was brought up at *Cluny, which imbued him with high ideals of religious discipline and of the rights of the Church. In 1126 Henry I made him Abbot of *Glastonbury, which he ruled impeccably for forty-five years, and in 1129 Bp. of Winchester; by a Papal dispensation, he held both offices together. In 1135 he crowned Stephen. After the death of Abp. William of Corbeil (1136), he hoped for the see of *Canterbury; but it was granted to *Theobald (1139). In the same year, however, Innocent II granted Henry of Blois a legatine commission which made him in some matters the Archbishop's superior. In the Chronicles he is termed 'lord of England'. After Stephen's capture at the Battle of *Lincoln (1141), Henry deserted Stephen's cause and declared for Matilda, accompanying her to London for the coronation (which never took place); but finding his assistance unwanted, he returned to Stephen's side and made formal profession of loyalty at a Council at London (Dec. 1141). Until his legatine powers terminated on Innocent's death (1143) he continued to oppose Abp. Theobald, one of his chief endeavours being the elevation of Winchester to an archiepiscopal see (with the seven suffragan sees of *Salisbury, *Exeter, *Wells, *Chichester, *Hereford and *Worcester and a newly created see of Hyde Abbey). After Stephen's death (Oct. 1154) he gave Henry II his support and in the *Becket controversy sought to mediate between King and Archbishop.

Henry was a great builder. He much extended the fabric at Glastonbury; built several castles, including Farnham and Wolvesey; and founded the monastery of St. Cross at Winchester (enlarged by Card. Henry *Beaufort). He was also a munificent benefactor to Cluny. His high character won the esteem of such men as *Peter the Venerable, Becket, and *John of Salisbury.

L. Voss, *Heinrich von Blois, Bischof von Winchester, 1129–71* (Historische Studien, Hft. ccx; 1932), with bibl. M D. Knowles, *The Episcopal Colleagues of Thomas Becket* (Ford Lectures for 1949; 1951), pp. 34–7 and passim. H. W. C. Davis in *D.E.C.H.* (1912), p. 264 f., s.v.

HENRY BRADSHAW SOCIETY. The Society founded in 1890 in memory of Henry Bradshaw (1831–86), librarian of the university of Cambridge, 'for the purpose of printing liturgical MSS. and rare editions of service books and illustrative documents, on an historical and scientific basis, preference being given to those which bear upon the history of the Book of Common Prayer or of the Church of England.' Its publications include many important works, among them *The Manner of the *Coronation of King *Charles I*, 1626 (for 1892), the *Bangor Antiphonarium* (for 1892, 1895), the *Gregorian Sacramentary* (for 1915), and the *Bobbio Missal* (for 1917, 1918, 1923).

'Eleven Letters from Henry Bradshaw to S. W. Lawley', ed. F. Jenkinson in *Fasciculus Ioanni Willis Clark Dicatus* (Cambridge, 1909), pp. 115–34. G. W. Prothero, *A Memoir of Henry Bradshaw* (1888). J. S. Crone, *Henry Bradshaw. His Life and Work* (Lecture; Dublin [1931]).

HENRY OF GHENT (d. 1293), 'De Gandavo' 'Doctor solemnis', theologian. He became a canon at Tournai (1267), and later archdeacon successively of Bruges (1276) and Tournai (1278); but little is known of his life. He was one of the chief representatives among the secular clergy of *Augustinianism, which he defended in his disputations at *Paris university. In 1282 he took part in the fight against the privileges of the Mendicant Orders. In his two most important works, the 'Quodlibeta' and the unfinished 'Summa theologica', he treated of most of the theological and philosophical questions discussed in the Schools, often attacking both St. *Thomas Aquinas and *Duns Scotus in his attempt to combine the old Augustinianism with the new Aristotelian teaching. As against St. Thomas, he held that the 'principle of individuation' was not 'matter', but 'negation'. His rejection of the *species intelligibilis* was destined to exercise great influence on later epistemological theory.

F. Ehrle, S.J., 'Beiträge zu den Biographien berühmter Scholastiker: Heinrich von Gent' in *Archiv für Litteratur- und Kirchengeschichte*, i (1885), pp. 365–410. H. *Delehaye, S.J., 'Nouvelles Recherches sur Henri de Gand' in *Messager des sciences historiques ou Archives des arts et de la bibliographie de Belgique*, lx (1886), pp. 328–55, 438–55, lxi (1887), pp. 59–85; id., 'Notes sur Henri de Gand' ib., lxii (1888), pp. 421–56. M. de Wulf, *Histoire de la philosophie scolastique dans les Pays-Bas et dans la principauté de Liège* (Mémoires couronnés et autres mémoires publiés par l'Académie Royale des Sciences, des Lettres et des Beaux-Arts de Belgique, li; 1895), pp. 46–272. E. Hocedez, S.J., 'Gilles de Rome et Henri de Gand sur la Distinction Réelle (1276–87)' in *Gregorianum*, viii (1927), pp. 358–84; id., 'Le Premier Quodlibet d'Henri de Gand (1276)', ib., ix (1928), pp. 92–117. J. Paulus, *Henri de Gand*. Essai sur les tendances de sa métaphysique (Études de Philosophie médiévale, xxv; 1938), with bibl. J. Forget in *D.T.C.*, vi (1920), cols. 2191–4.

HENRY OF LAUSANNE (d. after 1145), medieval sectarian. Little is known of his life. He was probably a French monk who had left his monastery and may have been connected with *Cluny. He became an itinerant preacher and gave the Lenten sermons at Le Mans in 1101 by permission of the bishop, *Hildebert of Lavardin. His invectives against the worldliness of the clergy and his insistence on the ideal of absolute poverty made him very popular. But he was expelled from the diocese on account of heretical teaching and continued his activities in the south of France. Acc. to St. *Bernard, he denied the objective efficacy of the Sacraments and made it dependent on the worthy character of the priest. In 1135 he was arrested and forced to recant at the Synod of Pisa, but soon resumed his anti-clerical preaching, strongly opposed by St. Bernard. He was arrested a second time c. 1145 and probably died soon after. He was in some respects a precursor of the *Waldensians.

St. Bernard, *Ep.* ccxli (J. P. Migne, *PL*, clxxxii, 434–6). E. Vacandard, *Vie de Saint Bernard*, ii (ed. 1927), pp. 224–242. C. J. *Hefele – H. *Leclercq, O.S.B., *Histoire des conciles*, v (pt. 1; 1912), pp. 710–13 and 731 f. H. C. Lea, *A History of the Inquisition in the Middle Ages*, i (1888), pp. 69–71. J. J. I. von *Döllinger, *Beiträge zur Sektengeschichte des Mittelalters*, i (1890), pp. 75–97. M. Esposito, 'Sur quelques écrits concernant les hérésies et les hérétiques aux XII⁰ et XIII⁰ siècles', I, 'Traité contre Henri l'Hérésiarque' in *R.H.E.*, xxxvi (1940), p. 143 f. F. Vernet in

D.T.C., vi (1920), cols. 2178–83, s.v. 'Henri, hérésiarque', with bibl.; Ilarino da Milano, O.F.M., Cap., in *E.C.*, v (1950). col. 388 f., s.v. 'Enrico di Losanna'.

HENRY SUSO (*c.* 1295–1366), German mystic. Heinrich Seuse entered a *Dominican convent at Constance at the age of 13 and from 1324 to 1328 was a pupil of J. *Eckhart in Cologne. His life as a mystic began at the age of 18, when he made himself 'Servant of the Eternal Wisdom', devotion to Whom dominated and controlled his thoughts for the rest of his life. He was a valued spiritual director in many women's convents, notably in those of the Dominican Order. In the 14th and 15th cents., his work *Das Büchlein der ewigen Weisheit* (1328) became the most widely read meditation book. Among his readers and admirers was *Thomas à Kempis. *Gregory XVI confirmed his beatification in 1831. Feast day, 2 Mar.

Collected ed. of original German Works publ. Augsburg, 1482; crit. ed. by K. Bihlmeyer (Stuttgart, 1907). Edd. in mod. German by M. Diepenbrock (Regensburg, 1829) and H. S. Denifle, O.P. (Munich, vol. i only publd. 1876–1880). Lat. tr. by L. Surius (Cologne, 1555). Mod. Fr. trr. from the German by J. Ancelet-Hustache (Paris, 1943) and by B. Lavaud, O.P. (5 vols., ib., 1946–8). Eng. trr. of his autobiography by T. F. Knox, Cong. Orat. (London, 1865) and J. M. Clark (ib., 1952), and of the *Little Book of Eternal Wisdom* by C. H. McKenna, O.P. (ib., 1910) and, together with the *Little Book of Truth*, with introd. and notes by J. M. Clark (ib., 1953). C. Gröber, *Der Mystiker Heinrich Seuse. Die Geschichte seines Lebens. Die Entstehung und Echtheit seiner Werke* (1941). J. M. Clark, *The Great German Mystics* (1949), pp. 54–74, with bibl. pp. 114–17. K. Bihlmeyer in *L.Th.K.*, iv (1932), cols. 934–6, s.v. 'Heinrich Seuse', with good bibl. É. Amann in *D.T.C.*, xiv (pt. 2; 1941), cols. 2859–64, s.v. 'Suso (Henri)'.

HENRY, MATTHEW (1662–1714), Nonconformist Biblical exegete. The son of Philip Henry, who was ejected in 1662 by the Act of *Uniformity, he began to study for the legal profession, but soon decided to devote himself to theology and resided at the Islington Academy under Thomas Doolittle from 1680 to 1682. From 1687 to 1712 he was Presbyterian Minister at *Chester, where a meeting-house was opened for him in Crook Lane (now Crook St.) in 1700. His *Exposition of the Old and New Testaments* (1708–10), a devotional commentary on the whole of the OT and the Gospels and Acts, is notable esp. for its good sense, pregnant thought, and felicitous expression. He was also the author of many devotional works and sermons.

Works, with a sermon preached at his funeral and Life by W. Tong (see below), publd. at London, fol. 1726; additional matter was included in *The Miscellaneous Works of Matthew Henry*, ed. S. Palmer (ib., 1809); re-edited with further additions, with preface by J. B. Williams (ib., 1830). Lives by W. Tong (London, 1716), J. B. Williams (ib., 1828), and C. Chapman (ib., 1859). A. Gordon in *D.N.B.*, xxvi (1891), p. 123 f.

HENSON, HERBERT HENSLEY (1863–1947), Bp. of *Durham. Educated at Oxford, he was elected a Fellow of All Souls in 1884. He was successively vicar of Barking (1888), Chaplain of St. Mary's Hospital, Ilford (1895), rector of St. Margaret's, Westminster (1900),

Dean of Durham (1912), Bp. of *Hereford (1918), and Bp. of Durham (1920–39). Not long after ordination he abandoned his earlier High Church sympathies for a latitudinarian conception of the C of E, which he defended in several published collections of sermons and other writings, among them *Cross Bench Views of Current Church Questions* (1902), *Sincerity and Subscription* (1903), *The National Church* (1908), *The Liberty of Prophesying* (1909), *The Creed in the Pulpit* (1912), *Anglicanism* (1921), and *Quo Tendimus?* (1924). His doctrinal position, esp. his attitude to the Virgin Birth and the Gospel miracles, provoked strong protests when D. Lloyd George nominated him to Hereford late in 1917, and a serious crisis was averted only when the Abp. of Canterbury (R. T. *Davidson), who had had grave misgivings about consecrating him, and Henson issued a joint statement in which Henson appeared to retract his earlier views. Until his later years Henson was a strong advocate of the Establishment in which he saw the ideal of a nation-wide Church, which should ultimately include all Nonconformists, and a safeguard of theological freedom. But the rejection of the revised Prayer Books in Parliament (1927–8) convinced him the Establishment was incompatible with the Church's freedom and in his *Disestablishment* (1929) he pleaded for liberty for the Church from state control. His other writings include *Notes on Spiritual Healing* (1925); *The Oxford Groups* (1933), a pungent criticism; *Christian Morality* (1936), based on *Gifford Lectures; and *The Church of England* (1939).

Henson publd. his autobiography, *Retrospect of an Unimportant Life* (3 vols., 1942–50); also a collection of papers repr. from *The Bishoprick* under the title *Bishoprick Papers* (1946). Collections of his *Letters* ed. E. F. Braley (S.P.C.K., 1950); *More Letters* (ib., 1954).

HEORTOLOGY (Gk. ἑορτή, 'festival'). The study of the origin, history, and meaning of the festivals and seasons of the Ecclesiastical *Year, and thus a branch of *Liturgiology.

HEPTATEUCH (Gk. ἑπτά, 'seven'+τεῦχος, 'book'). A name sometimes used of the first seven books of the OT, i.e. the five Books of Moses together with Jos. and Jgs., on account of their supposed unity. The word is formed on the analogy of '*Pentateuch'.

HERACLEAN VERSION. See *Harklean Version.*

HERACLEON (*fl. c.* 145–80), *Gnostic teacher. He was a disciple of *Valentinus. He wrote a highly allegorizing commentary (Ὑπομνήματα) on St. John's Gospel; but only fragments have survived, mainly in quotations in *Origen's Commentary on that Gospel.

A. E. Brooke, 'The Fragments of Heracleon', *Texts and Studies*, vol. i, No. 4 (Cambridge, 1891).

HERACLIUS (575–641), Byzantine Emperor. A native of Cappadocia, he secured the throne in 610–11 in place of the usurper Phocas, and then founded a new dynasty which continued until 717. During his reign the Empire was repeatedly attacked. The Visigoths gained complete possession of Spain, and the Persians and later the Arabs invaded the E. On 21 Mar. 629, Heraclius solemnly brought back to *Golgotha the Cross which the Persians had removed from *Jerusalem in 614. In an attempt to secure doctrinal unity in his dominions he issued the *Ecthesis (q.v.) in 638. See also *Exaltation of the Cross*.

A. Pernice, *L' imperatore Eraclio* (1905). E. Gerland, 'Die persischen Feldzüge des Kaisers Herakleios' in *B.Z.*, iii (1894), pp. 330–73. J. B. Bury, *The Later Roman Empire*, ii (1889), pp. 197–398; N. H. Baynes in *C. Med. H.*, ii (1913), ch. ix, pp. 263–301 passim; Fliche–Martin, v (1947), pp. 79–150.

HERBERT, EDWARD (1583–1648), first Lord Herbert of Cherbury; philosopher, deist, and poet. He was appointed ambassador at Paris in 1619, after a youth spent in study, much travel, and many duels. In 1624 he published at Paris his famous philosophical treatise, *De Veritate prout distinguitur a revelatione, a verisimili, a possibili, et a falso*, an original attack on empiricism. The first work of its kind to be written by an Englishman, it greatly influenced J. *Locke. His more specifically religious writings included *Religio Laici* (1645), *Ad Sacerdotes de Religione Laici* (1645), and *De Religione Gentilium* (1663). He maintained that common to all religions were five innate ideas: (1) that there is a God; (2) that He ought to be worshipped; (3) that virtue is the chief element in this worship; (4) that repentance for sin is a duty; and (5) that there is another life of rewards and punishments. His conviction that in these five innate ideas lay the essence of religion, combined with his denial of revelation, made him a forerunner of English *Deism.

His *Autobiography*, extending to 1624, existed in two MS. copies in the 18th cent., but both have now disappeared; one was ed. by H. Walpole (1764); crit. edd., based on Walpole's text, by S. Lee (1886) and C. H. Herford (1928). *The Poems, English and Latin, of Edward, Lord Herbert of Cherbury*, ed. by G. C. Moore Smith (1923). C. de Rémusat, *Lord Herbert de Cherbury, sa vie et ses œuvres* (1874). W. R. Sorley, 'The Philosophy of Herbert of Cherbury' in *Mind*, N.S., iii (1894), pp. 491–508. S. L. Lee in *D.N.B.*, xxvi (1891), pp. 173–81.

HERBERT, GEORGE (1593–1633), poet and divine. A younger brother of Edward, Lord *Herbert of Cherbury, he was educated at Westminster School and Trinity College, Cambridge, where his classical scholarship and musical ability (he played the lute and viol, and sang) secured him a fellowship in 1614. He became Public Orator of the university in 1620, and his success seemed to mark him out for the career of a courtier. The death of *James I, however, and the influence of his friend, N. *Ferrar, led him to study divinity, and in 1626 he was presented to a prebend in Huntingdonshire. In 1630 he was ordained priest, and persuaded by W. *Laud to accept the rectory of Fugglestone with Bemerton, near *Salisbury, where in piety and humble devotion to duty he spent his last years.

Herbert's most famous prose work, *A Priest to the Temple; or the Country Parson* (1652), outlines a sober and well-balanced ideal of the English clergyman. In simple and homely language Herbert shows him as a well-read divine, temperate in all things, a man of duty and prayer, devoted to his flock, who has come to be the model of future generations. His collection of poems entitled *The Temple* was entrusted to N. Ferrar on his deathbed and first published in 1633. An author of sincere religious conviction and considerable poetic gifts, skilful in handling both rhyme and rhythm, Herbert is among the first devotional poets of the C of E of whose spirit and teaching he is an authentic representative. His poems, rather less heavily laden with quaint imagery and 'conceits' than those of many of his contemporaries, breathe a gentle piety and a sincere love of Christian virtue. They also exercised a widespread influence on later poets such as H. *Vaughan and S. T. *Coleridge. Among those in current use as hymns are 'The God of love my Shepherd is' (Ps. 23), 'Teach me my God and King' and 'Let all the world in every corner sing'.

Collected ed. of his Works publ. London, 2 vols. bound in one, 1835–6; modern edd. include *The English Works of George Herbert*, ed. G. H. Palmer (3 vols., 1905), with introd. in vol. i, pp. 17–167, and F. E. Hutchinson (ed.), *The Works of George Herbert* (Oxford, 1941). Poems ed. by A. Waugh (The World's Classics, cxix; [1907]), with introd. pp. v–xviii. I. *Walton, *The Life of Mr. George Herbert* (1670). [J. Daniell], *The Life of George Herbert of Bemerton* (1893); A. G. Hyde, *George Herbert and his Times* (1906); Margaret Bottrall, *George Herbert* (1954); J. H. Summers, *George Herbert. His Religion and Art* (1954). G. H. Palmer, *A Herbert Bibliography* (Cambridge, 1911); further bibl. by F. E. Hutchinson in *C.B.E.L.*, i (1940), pp. 451–3. S. L. Lee in *D.N.B.*, xxvi (1891), pp. 185–8. See also bibl. to *Metaphysical Poets*.

HERDER, JOHANN GOTTFRIED (1744–1803), German critic. With G. E. *Lessing he was a leader of the poetical movement, which saved the *Aufklärung from a dry intellectualism. After various temporary posts, he became *Generalsuperintendent and court preacher at Weimar (1776) where he spent the rest of his life. An early disciple of I. *Kant, he influenced J. W. Goethe in turn, and has been regarded as anticipating C. Darwin in treating human history as a natural science. His interests were as wide as the culture of his age, and his researches and writings dealt with poetry, art, language, and religion; but his most important contribution to the ideas of his time was in the philosophy of history. In his *Ideen zur Philosophie der Geschichte der Menschheit* (1784–91; Eng. trans., 1800) he discovered in the developments of the different nations the stages of an ascending process in the course of which the essence of 'Humanity' comes to progressively fuller expression. Of more exclusively religious interest was his book *Vom Geist der hebräischen Poesie* (1782–3) in which he urged the study of the Bible in a 'human' way. His mediating position in theology, in which he advocated critical principles and conservative findings, brought him the enmity of the orthodox and the suspicions of the rationalists.

Crit. ed. of Herder's Works by B. Suphan (33 vols., Berlin, 1877–99; 1913); later ed. by F. Schultz (Potsdam, 1939 ff.). *Ausgewählte Werke*, ed. B. Suphan (5 vols., 1884–1901). Memoirs, 2 vols., Stuttgart, 1820. Life and Letters, 3 vols., Erlangen, 1846–8. Lives by J. M. H. Döring (Leipzig, 1823). R. Haym (2 vols., Leipzig, 1880–5), H. W. Nevinson (London, 1884), E. Kühnemann (Munich, 1895), R. Buerkner (Geisteshelden 45, 1904), F. MacEachran (Oxford Studies in Modern Language and Literature, Oxford, 1939), A. Gillies (Oxford, 1945; with useful bibl.). A. Werner, *Herder als Theolog* (1871). Überweg, iii (ed. 12, 1924), pp. 614 f., 751–3.

HEREFORD. The see was founded in 676 by Putta, Bp. of *Rochester (669–86), who had fled from the heathen invaders of his diocese. St. *Ethelbert, King of the E. Angles (killed *c.* 793), was buried in the cathedral, and with the BVM designated its joint patron soon afterwards. The original cathedral was damaged by the Welsh in 1055. The main part of the present edifice dates from 1079–1110, though there are considerable later additions. The 'Use of Hereford', a variant of the Roman Rite, with less individuality than that of *Sarum, was displaced by the latter only in the reign of *Henry VIII. The most famous medieval bishop was St. Thomas of Hereford (Thomas de *Cantilupe), 1275–82, whose shrine, after his canonization in 1320, was a centre of pilgrimage from all over England. In 1786 the west end of the cathedral suddenly collapsed, carrying some of the nave with it, and the later restoration was poorly done, though the west front (early 20th cent.) is well in harmony with the building as a whole. The buildings of the College of Vicars-Choral remain intact, and the cathedral school, though its buildings are mostly of the 19th cent., has a continuous history from the 14th cent. The diocese includes Herefordshire, S. Shropshire, and a few parishes in other counties.

The Episcopal Registers are exceptionally nearly complete; the following have been publd. concurrently in the series of the Cantilupe Society [publicn. dates in this series are added here] and of the *Canterbury and York Society: that of Thomas de Cantilupe (1275–82), ed. R. G. Griffiths-W. W. Capes (1906); of Richard de Swinfield (1282–1317), ed. W. W. Capes (1909); of Adam de Orleton (1317–27), ed. A. T. Bannister (1907); of Thomas de Charlton (1327–44), ed. W. W. Capes (1912); of John de Trillek (1344–61), ed. J. H. Parry (1910); of Lewis de Charlton (1361–69), ed. id. (1913); of William de Courtenay (1370–5), ed. W. W. Capes (1913); of John Gilbert (1375–89), ed. J. H. Parry (1913); of John Trefnant (1389–1404), ed. W. W. Capes (1914); Robert Mascall (1404–16), ed. J. H. Parry (1916); Edmund Lacy (1417–20), ed. id.-A. T. Bannister (1917); Thomas Poltone (1420–2), ed. W. W. Capes (1916); Thomas Stofford (1422–1448), ed. A. T. Bannister (1917); Richard Beauchamp (1449–50), ed. id. (1917); Reginald Boulers (1451–3; register of first year only), ed. id. (1917); John Stanbury (1453–74), ed. J. H. Parry-A. T. Bannister (1918); Thomas Mylling (1474–92), ed. A. T. Bannister (1919); Richard Mayew (1504–16), ed. id. (1919); Charles Bothe (1516–35), with extracts from registers of Edmund Foxe and Edmund Bonner, ed. id. (1921). W. W. Capes (ed.), *Charters and Records of Hereford Cathedral* (Cantilupe Society, 1908). Eng. tr. of *Extracts from the Cathedral Registers*, A.D. 1275–1535, by E. N. Dew (Hereford, 1932). The 'Missal according to the Use of Herford' was repr. from the Rouen ed. of 1502 by W. G. Henderson (London, 1874); the 'Breviary', orig. pr. Rouen, 1505, was ed. by W. H. *Frere-L. E. G. Brown (*Henry Bradshaw Society, xxvi, xl and xlvi; 1904–15). A. T. Bannister, *The Cathedral Church of Hereford*. Its

History and Constitution (Studies in Church History, S.P.C.K., 1924). On the cathedral see also W. *Dugdale, *Monasticon Anglicanum, vi (pt. 3; ed. 1830), pp. 1210–17. B. Willis, *A Survey of the Cathedrals of York, Durham, Carlisle, Chester, Man, Lichfield, Hereford, Worcester, Gloucester and Bristol*, ii (1727), pp. 499–622. H. W. Phillott, *Hereford* (Diocesan Histories, 1888); A. H. Fisher, *The Cathedral Church of Hereford* (Bell's Cathedral Series, 1898). E. [A.] Foord, *Hereford and Tintern* (Cathedrals, Abbeys and Famous Churches, 1925), pp. 11–110. Royal Commission on Historical Monuments, England, *An Inventory of Historical Monuments in Herefordshire*, i, South-West (1931), pp. 90–120. A. T. Bannister, *A Descriptive Catalogue of the Manuscripts in the Hereford Cathedral Library* (Hereford, 1927); B. H. *Streeter, *The Chained Library* (1931), pp. 77–119, 311–39. W. W. Capes in *D.E.C.H.*, 266–70, s.v.

HEREFORD, NICHOLAS. See *Nicholas of Hereford.*

HERESIARCH (Gk. αἱρεσιάρχης ; late Lat. *haeresiarcha*). The originator of a heresy, or founder of an heretical sect.

HERESY. The formal denial or doubt of any defined doctrine of the Catholic faith. In antiquity the Greek word αἵρεσις, denoting 'choice' or 'thing chosen', from which the term is derived, was applied to the tenets of particular philosophical schools. In this sense it appears occasionally in Scripture (e.g. Acts 5. 17) and the early Fathers. But it was employed also in a disparaging sense (e.g. 1 Cor. 11. 19) and from St. *Ignatius (Trall. 6, Eph. 6) onwards it came more and more to be used of theological error. From the earliest days the Church has claimed teaching authority and consequently condemned heresy, following Christ's command: 'If he refuse to hear the Church, let him be unto thee as the Gentile and the publican' (Mt. 18. 17). On the other hand the need to rebut heresy has sometimes stimulated the formulation of Orthodox Christian doctrine.

Present RC teaching makes a distinction between 'formal' and 'material' heresy. The former, which is heresy properly so called, consists in the wilful and persistent adherence to an error in matters of faith on the part of a baptized person; as such it is a grave sin involving *ipso facto* excommunication. 'Material heresy', on the other hand, means holding heretical doctrines through no fault of one's own, 'in good faith', as is the case, e.g., with most persons brought up in heretical surroundings. This constitutes neither crime nor sin, nor is such a person strictly speaking a heretic, since, having never accepted certain doctrines, he cannot reject or doubt them. Heresy is to be distinguished from *apostasy and *schism (qq.v.). See also *Inquisition* and *De Haeretico Comburendo.*

C. W. F. Walch, *Entwurf einer vollständigen Historie der Ketzereien, Spaltungen, und Religionsstreitigkeiten bis auf die Zeiten der Reformation* (11 pts., 1762–85). [J. J.] I. von *Döllinger, *Beiträge zur Sektengeschichte des Mittelalters* (2 vols., 1890). J. H. Blunt (ed.), *Dictionary of Sects, Heresies, Ecclesiastical Parties and Schools of Religious Thought* (1874). H. Schlier in *T.W.B.*, i (1933), cols. 179–84, s.v. 'αἱρέομαι'. A. Michel in *D.T.C.*, vi (1920), cols. 2208–57, s.v. 'Hérésie, Hérétique', with bibl.; G. Zannoni in *E.C.*, v (1950), cols. 487–92, s.v. 'Eresia', with bibl.

HERGENROTHER, JOSEPH (1824–90), ecclesiastical historian. He was a native of Würzburg, where he taught from 1852 onwards. In 1857 he published *Photius's 'Liber de Spiritus Sancti mystagogia'*, and in 1867–9 an elaborate work on Photius himself. He represented the more conservative element in German Catholicism, attacking J. J. I. von *Döllinger in 1861 with his *Der Zeitgeist und die Souveranität des Papstes*. Called to Rome in 1868 to act as a consultor for the forthcoming *Vatican Council, he defended the definition of Papal Infallibility, directing against Döllinger *Anti-Janus* (1869; see *Janus*) and other pamphlets. His later writings include a treatise on Church history (*Handbuch der allgemeinen Kirchengeschichte*, 3 vols., 1876–80), which in its successive revisions long remained a standard work. In 1879 he was created a *cardinal. In his later years he devoted himself to continuing K. J. *Hefele's *Konziliengeschichte*.

E. Mangenot in *D.T.C.*, vi (1920), cols. 2257–9, s.v.; C. Testore, S.J., in *E.C.*, vi (1951), col. 1415 f., s.v.

HERIC OF AUXERRE. See *Heiric of Auxerre*.

HERIMANNUS CONTRACTUS (1013–1054), **Hermann the Lame**, Christian poet and chronicler. He was educated in the monastery at *Reichenau, where he later took his vows. Despite great physical infirmities, he possessed one of the most gifted minds of his age, and wrote extensively on a wide range of subjects including mathematics, astronomy, and chronography. His writings included a didactic poem 'De octo vitiis principalibus', based on classical models, and many hymns and antiphons. The widespread attribution to him of the '*Salve Regina' and the 'Alma Redemptoris Mater' rests in each case, however, on insufficient evidence. His 'Chronicon Augiense', which stretches from the beginning of the Christian era to 1054, is based, directly or indirectly, on a large variety of important sources and is of esp. value for its record of contemporary history.

His writings are pr. in J. P. Migne, *PL*, cxliii, 9–458; crit. ed. of his 'Chronicon' by G. H. Pertz in *M.G.H.*, Scriptores, v (1844), pp. 67–133. H. Hansjakob, *Hermann der Lahme von der Reichenau. Sein Leben und seine Wissenschaft* (1875). H. Bresslau, 'Beiträge zur Kritik deutscher Geschichtsquellen des 11. Jahrhunderts. Neue Folge I, Hermann von Reichenau und das Chronicon Suevicum Universale' in *N.A.*, xxvii (1902), pp. 127–69, with reff. to other artt. M. Seidlmayer in *L.Th.K.*, iv (1932), col. 982 f., s.v. 'Hermann', with detailed bibl. See also works cited under *Salve Regina*.

HERITOR. In *Scotland, heritors were the owners of heritable property in a parish to whom descended the ancient obligation to pay the *teinds or tithes to the minister and to keep the parish church and manse in repair. By an Act of Parliament, 1925, with a view to union between the Established and the *United Free Churches, provision was made for the termination of their rights and duties and the transfer of these responsibilities to the Church of Scotland itself.

HERMAN, EMMA, Mrs. (1874–1923), writer on *Mysticism and spiritual subjects. The wife of a *Presbyterian minister, she spent much of her early married life in *Constantinople and Sydney. In 1908, she began regular work as a journalist at Sydney, soon becoming widely known through her brilliant and penetrating writing. In 1913 she was appointed editor of the *Presbyterian* and later held posts in the *Challenge* and the *Church Times*. Towards the end of her life she joined the C of E, where she became warmly sympathetic to *Anglo-Catholicism. Her two chief books—*The Meaning and Value of Mysticism* (1915) and *Creative Prayer* (1921)—are notable for their understanding and interpretation of Christian spiritual values. She was also the author of *Eucken and Bergson* (1912), *Voices of Today* (1912; on contemporary preachers; published under the pseudonym of 'Hugh Sinclair'), and three posthumous collections, *The Finding of the Cross* (1924), *The Secret Garden of the Soul* (1924; with memoir of Mrs. Herman by D. C. Macgregor), and *The Touch of God* (1926).

HERMANN OF REICHENAU. See *Herimannus Contractus*.

HERMANN OF WIED (1477–1552), German reformer. In 1515, while still a *subdeacon, he became Abp.-Elector of *Cologne. He governed his principality with marked efficiency, taking strong measures against the *Anabaptists and at a council at Cologne (1536) tightening up discipline and introducing some liturgical reforms. Throughout his earlier years he was hostile to the Protestant Movement; but *c.* 1539 he set out to create a parallel movement within the Catholic Church, making a start with his own archdiocese and inviting the assistance of M. *Bucer and P. *Melanchthon. He embodied many proposals for a moderate reform of the Church in his *Einfaltigs Bedencken einer christlichen Reformation* (1543), also known as the *'Didagma'*, an English translation of which (*A Simple and Religious Consultation of us, Herman, by the grace of God, Archbishop of Cologne*, 1548) was considerably drawn on by the compilers of the Anglican BCP. In 1544 J. *Gropper published an '*Antididagma' (q.v.) as a reply. Hermann's increasing adhesion to the Protestant cause was an important accession to its strength, but his policy met with hostility from most of his own subjects, from the Emp. *Charles V, and from Pope *Paul III, who excommunicated and deposed him in 1546. He died a Lutheran.

C. Varrentrapp, *Hermann von Wied und sein Reformationsversuch* (1878); id. in *P.R.E.* (ed. 3), vii (1899), pp. 712–14. For his influence on the BCP, see F. E. *Brightman, *The English Rite* (1915), Introd., passim (cf. index, p. 1063).

HERMAS (2nd cent.), author of the 'Shepherd'. He is accounted one of the '*Apostolic Fathers'. Of his life nothing certain is known except what he himself says in his work. We learn that he was a Christian slave, sold in Rome to a woman called Rhoda, who set him free. He married, became a merchant, and enriched himself by means that were not always lawful. In a persecution he lost all his property, was denounced by his own children, and finally he and his whole family did penance.

His book, the 'Shepherd' (ὁ Ποιμήν), purports to have been written in consequence of a series of visions. It is divided into three parts, viz. five 'Visions', twelve 'Mandates', and ten 'Similitudes'. In the 'Visions' a matron appears to him who represents the Church, which is pictured as a tower. In the fifth Vision appears the Angel of Penance in the guise of a shepherd, whence the name of the treatise. In the following 'Mandates' Hermas gives us his teaching on Christian behaviour and virtues, such as faith in one God, truthfulness, chastity, &c. The third section, the 'Similitudes', represent various Christian principles under a series of sometimes very forceful images.

The person of the author of the work has given rise to much speculation. Hermas himself says that he is a contemporary of St. *Clement of Rome (d. c. 96; if he is the Clement mentioned at *Vis.* II, iv, 3); but the *Muratorian Canon (c. 180) attributes the work to a brother of Pope *Pius (d. c. 154), while *Origen believes the Hermas mentioned in Rom. 16. 14 to be its author. A great number of modern scholars, including A. *Harnack, O. *Bardenhewer, and P. *Batiffol, accept the view of the Muratorian Canon, which would suggest a date between 140 and 155. This would also fit the internal evidence, which seems to suggest that the work was written after a considerable period of peace. In the Greek Church of the 2nd and 3rd cents. the work was widely regarded as Scripture, e.g. by St. *Irenaeus, *Clement of Alexandria, also by *Tertullian in his pre-Montanist days, though there was no unanimity on the subject. It was, however, greatly esteemed for its moral value and served as a textbook for catechumens, as is testified by St. *Athanasius. In the *Codex Sinaiticus it comes after the NT, together with the Pseudo-*Barnabas. In the Latin Church it was valued far less highly; the Muratorian Canon denies its inspiration and *Jerome asserts that it was almost unknown in the West (*De vir. illust.* 10). From the 4th cent. it came to be also more and more neglected in the East.

The principal aim of the book is the inculcation of the necessity of penance and of the possibility of the forgiveness of sins at least once after baptism, a doctrine which caused Tertullian, in his Montanist period, to call it the 'Shepherd of the adulterers'. The author seems to identify the Holy Spirit with the Son of God before the Incarnation, and to hold that the Trinity came into existence only after the humanity of Christ had been taken up into heaven.

The Gk. original of the 'Shepherd' is incomplete. In the *Codex Sinaiticus the Gk. text is to be found up to Mand. iv, and in the MS. of Mt. *Athos, ed. by C. *Tischendorf, Leipzig, 1856, as far as Sim. ix. The rest of the text is known from two Lat. versions, one of which, the 'Versio Vulgata', was first publd. by J. *Faber Stapulensis, Paris, 1513, the other ,

known as the 'Versio Palatina', by A. R. M. Dressel, Leipzig, 1857. Further additions to Gk. text from papyrus fragments ed. C. Wessely in *P.O.*, iv (1908), pp. 195–9, and xviii (1924), pp. 468–81. C. Bonner, *A Papyrus Codex of the Shepherd of Hermas (Simil. 2–9), with a Fragment of the Mandates* (University of Michigan, Humanistic Series, xxii; 1934). The Gk. text is pr. in all edd. of the Apostolic Fathers, e.g. O. Gebhardt-A. *Harnack, J. B. *Lightfoot, K. *Lake. J. A. *Robinson, *Barnabas, Hermas and the Didache* (Donnellan Lectures for 1920; 1920). R. van Deemter, *Der Hirt des Hermas. Apokalypse oder Allegorie?* (Delft, 1929); E. Peterson, 'Beiträge zur Interpretation der Visionen im *Pastor Hermae*' in *O.C.P.*, xiii (1947), pp. 625–35. Bardenhewer, i, pp. 465–87; Altaner (ed. 1951), pp. 63–5. G. Bareille in *D.T.C.*, vi (1920), cols. 2268–88, s.v., with bibl. H. *Leclercq, O.S.B., in *D.A.C.L.*, vi (pt. 2; 1925), cols. 2265–90, s.v., also with bibl. [Crit. text forthcoming in *G.C.S.*, ed. Molly Whittaker (due 1957)].

HERMENEUTICS (from Gk. ἑρμηνεύω, 'to interpret'). The science of the methods of the right interpretation of Scripture. It is a preliminary to *Exegesis (q.v.), which applies the rules found by hermeneutics. Its first object is to establish the way by which the reader arrives at the true meaning expressed in the words of the Bible. Acc. to one traditional scheme there is a fundamental distinction between the literal and the typical sense, esp. in the OT, where persons, objects, and events are used as types of Christ and His Church, set forth in the NT. For the finding of the true sense there exist many natural aids to interpretation, such as textual, linguistic, cultural, historical, and psychological studies. The older orthodox exegetes, both Catholic and Protestant, considered themselves bound in the application of these means by a strict doctrine of Scriptural inspiration, which was held to imply that no statement made by an inspired author could contain a falsehood, while Catholic hermeneutics was, and is, further controlled by the consent of the Fathers and the analogy of faith, acc. to which no Biblical statement can contradict a doctrine of the Church. In Christian antiquity the science of hermeneutics hardly existed, though rules for the interpretation of Scripture were framed during the controversy between the *Alexandrian and *Antiochene Schools, esp. by *Origen, and elaborated by *Tychonius and in St. *Augustine's 'De Doctrina Christiana'.

HERMESIANISM. The system of philosophical and theological doctrines taught by Georg Hermes (1775–1831), Prof. of Theology at Münster i. W. It was an attempt to adjust the principles of RC theology to the supposed requirements of the philosophy of I. *Kant. Holding that our only certain knowledge was of ideas and notions actually present in the mind, it taught that the criterion of objective truth must be found in our subjective beliefs. Hermes believed that, starting from this principle, it was possible (as against the contentions of Kant) to prove the existence of God by the theoretical reason; and that when this fact had been established, the possibility of supernatural revelation could then be demonstrated. For a time Hermesian doctrines became very popular, esp. in the Rhineland, where many of the chief theological professorships were filled by Hermes' disciples. Soon after his death, Rome pronounced against them, however, and in 1835 *Gregory XVI put a number of Hermes' writings on the *Index.

Hermes' writings include *Untersuchung über die Wahrheit des Christentums* (1805), *Studierplan der Theologie* (1819), *Einleitung in die christkatholische Theologie* (1819–29), *Positive Einleitung* (1829), and *Christkatholische Dogmatik* (3 vols., 1834–5; posthumous, ed. J. H. Achterfeldt). His doctrines were condemned in the encyclical 'Dum Acerbissimas' (26 Sept. 1835); cf. Denz.–Bann. (ed. 1928), Nos. 1618–21. *Acta Romana*, ed. W. J. Braun and P. J. Elvenich (Hanover, 1838; pro-Hermesian). S. Merkle, 'Der hermesische Streit im Lichte neuer Quellen' in *Hist. J.*, lx (1940), pp. 179–200. Full bibl. to date in D. Gla, *Repertorium der katholisch-theologischen Literatur*, I, ii (1904), 355–70. J. Schulte in *C.E.*, vii (1910), pp. 276–9, s.v. 'Hermes', and A. Thouvenin in *D.T.C.*, vi (1920), cols. 2288–2303, s.v. 'Hermes', with bibl.

HERMETIC BOOKS. A collection of Greek and Latin religious and philosophical writings ascribed to Hermes Trismegistus ('Hermes the Thrice-Greatest'), a later designation of the Egyptian God, Thoth, who was believed to be the father and protector of, all knowledge. Dating probably from between the middle of the 1st and the end of the 3rd cents. A.D., these writings represent a fusion of *Platonic, *Stoic, Neo-Pythagorean, and Eastern religious elements, in the form of the Platonic dialogues. The aim of their mystic teaching was the deification of man through the 'Gnosis', i.e. the knowledge of God. The most important of the writings, '*Poimandres', contains much cosmological and astronomical teaching and describes the ascent of the soul to God through the seven spheres of the planets.

Corpus Hermeticum, ed. A. D. Nock, with Fr. tr. by A. J. Festugière, O.P. (Collection Budé, Paris, 4 vols., 1945–54). Older edd. by F. Patrizi (Venice, 1593) and G. Parthey (Berlin, 1854). Elaborate edition by W. Scott, *Hermetica* (4 vols., Oxford, 1924–36), with Eng. introd. and notes, but it suffers from the editor's over-drastic emendation of the text. The 'Poimandres' ed., with discussion, by R. *Reitzenstein, *Poimandres*. Studien zur griechisch-ägyptischen und frühchristlichen Literatur (1904). A. J. Festugière, O.P., *La Révélation d'Hermès Trismégiste* (Études bibliques, 1944 ff.). C. H. *Dodd, *The Bible and the Greeks* (1935), Part II (pp. 97–248, 'Hellenistic Judaism and the Hermetica'); id., *The Interpretation of the Fourth Gospel* (1953), pp. 10–53.

HERMIAS (date uncertain), Christian philosophical writer. He is known only as the author of a small treatise, the 'Irrisio' or 'Mockery of the Heathen Philosophers' (Διασυρμὸς τῶν ἔξω Φιλοσόφων), which satirizes the conflicting opinions of pagan writers on the human soul (cc. 1–2) and the fundamental principles of the universe (cc. 3–10). The apology is clearly the work of a writer of very mediocre attainments. Some points of literary contact between the 'Irrisio' and the pseudo-Justin's 'Cohortatio ad Gentiles' have been observed, but they are probably not sufficiently close to throw light on their relative dates, esp. in view of the possible use of common sources. Modern authors have assigned various dates to the 'Irrisio' from the 2nd to the 6th cents.

The *editio princeps* was issued by J. Oporinus (Basle, 1553). More recent editions are in J. C. T. de Otto, *Corpus Apologetarum Christianorum*, ix, pp. 1–31, and H. Diels, *Doxographia Graeci* (Berlin, 1879), pp. 649–56. A. Freiherr v. Di Pauli, *Die Irrisio des Hermias* (1907).

HERMIT (Gk. ἐρημίτης, from ἐρημία, 'desert'). One who from religious motives has retired into a solitary life, esp. one of the early Christian recluses.

Christian hermits first began to abound in Egypt and surrounding regions towards the close of the 3rd cent., and from that date the eremitical life quickly gained in popularity, being esp. cultivated in the cents. which witnessed the disintegration of the Roman Empire. In the W. hermits finally died out after the *Counter-Reformation, though much of their tradition is retained in an organized form in certain monastic orders, notably the *Carthusians and *Carmelites. In the E. Church hermits still exist. The hermits observed no uniform rule of life. While some lived in isolation, others were united in loosely organized communities which sometimes formed the nucleus of a new monastery or order (see also *Augustinian Hermits*).

HEROD FAMILY. *Herod the Great* was appointed King of the Jews by the Romans in 40 B.C., and ruled from 37 to 4 B.C. He was of an Idumaean (Edomite) family, and married a granddaughter of Hyrcanus, the last legal *Hasmonaean ruler. By ruthlessness and genuine ability he kept the peace for 37 years in a country very hard to rule. During his reign Christ was born, and the story of the Massacre of the Innocents (Mt. 2. 16) fits his reputation. On his death his territory was divided between his sons: *Archelaus*, as ethnarch of *Judaea, Idumaea, and *Samaria; *Antipas*, as *tetrarch of *Galilee and Peraea; and *Philip*, as tetrarch of the remaining territory to the northeast (Lk. 3. 1). Archelaus was deposed in A.D. 6 and his territory put under Roman procurators, of whom *Pontius Pilate was the fifth or sixth. Antipas, the 'Herod the tetrarch' of the Gospels (4 B.C.–A.D. 39), who married Herodias and beheaded *John the Baptist, and Philip (4 B.C.–A.D. 34) were ruling at the time of Christ's ministry. In 37–41 all these territories were successively conferred on *Agrippa I*, a grandson of Herod the Great, who ruled till A.D. 44 with the title of King. It was he (called 'Herod' in Acts) who put St. *James the Apostle to death and died 'eaten of worms' (Acts 12). In A.D. 50 *Agrippa II*, his son, was made king of various territories in N. Palestine and ruled till *c*. 93. He was the 'king Agrippa' before whom St. *Paul appeared (Acts 25. 13 ff.).

Much the most important authority is *Josephus (q.v.), who for the careers of Antipas and Herod the Great was mainly dependent on the 'Universal History' of Nicolaus of Damascus, Herod the Great's court historiographer. A. H. M. Jones, *The Herods of Judaea* (1938; by a first-class scholar, but without bibl. reff.). H. Willrich, *Das Haus des Herodes zwischen Jerusalem und Rom* (Bibliothek der klassischen Altertumswissenschaften, vi, 1929; a defence of the Herods and their policies). S. Perowne, *The Life and Times of Herod the Great* (1956). A. C. *Headlam in *H.B.D.*, ii (1899), pp. 353–62, with useful 'Index of Herod Family'. W. Otto in *P.W.*, Suppl. ii (1913), cols. 1–200; F. Schühlein in *L.Th.K.*, iv (1932), cols. 995–1000; both s.v. 'Herodes'.

HERODIANS. A party twice mentioned in the Gospels (Mk. 3. 6, in Galilee; Mk. 12. 3, cf.

Mt. 22. 16, in Jerusalem) as a group hostile to Our Lord. They were presumably partisans or retainers of the *Herod family, which was ruling at the time of Christ's ministry in Galilee and Iturea, but no longer in Judaea. The view of Ps. *Tertullian (*De praescr.* 45 fin.), *Philaster (*Haer.* 28), and others that they held Herod to be the Messiah was doubtless a mere (mistaken) conjecture.

W. Otto in *P.W.*, Suppl. ii (1913), cols. 200-2, s.v. 'Herodiani'.

HERRING, THOMAS (1693–1757), Abp. of *Canterbury. A native of Wisbech, he was educated at Jesus and Corpus Christi Colleges, Cambridge, where he early won fame as a preacher. After holding many ecclesiastical appointments he was promoted to the see of *Bangor in 1737. In 1743 he was translated to *York, where he was energetic in defence of the government during the 1745 revolt. In 1747 he was rewarded with the archbishopric of Canterbury but did little of note there. In his religious outlook he is a *Latitudinarian without theological interests. His chief claim to fame are his episcopal Visitation Returns for 1743, which is an important document for the religious history of his times.

Seven Sermons (1763), with pref. life [by W. Duncombe], pp. i–xli; *Letters* [1728–57] . . . *to William Duncombe* (1777). *Visitation Returns* ed. S. L. Ollard–P. C. Walker (Yorkshire Archaeological Society, Record Series, lxxi, lxxii, lxxv, lxxvii, and lxxix; 1928–31), with life by S. L. Ollard as Appendix D, vol. v, pp. 1–30. A. W. Rowden, *The Primates of the First Four Georges* (1916), pp. 167–229. R. Hooper in *D.N.B.*, xxvi (1891), p. 259 f.

HERRMANN, WILHELM (1846–1922), theologian. After an appointment at Halle in 1875, he became professor of systematic theology at *Marburg in 1879. He was a follower of I. *Kant in philosophy, of A. *Ritschl in theology. While, like the latter, he looked upon the Gospels as in some sense the record of a historical personality, he insisted that the Church should teach only those facts about Christ which will act upon man, e.g. His moral teaching as distinguished from His Virgin Birth or Resurrection. He held, too, that the aspects of Christ's Person which had value for the disciples are not necessarily those important for us. He went beyond Ritschl in excluding both mysticism (or personal religious experience) and metaphysics (or intellectual reasoning about ultimate reality) from religion, contending that religion is centred entirely in 'the historical Christ', whose life, however, is relevant to us only in so far as it possesses ethical value. The book in which these views are most fully expounded is *Der Verkehr des Christen mit Gott* (1886; Eng. trans. *The Communion of the Christian with God*).

Herrmann's other writings include *Die Religion im Verhältnis zum Welterkennen und zur Sittlichkeit* (1879), *Ethik* (1901), and *Christlich-protestantische Dogmatik* (in *Die Kultur der Gegenwart*, IV, 1 (2), 1906). His 'Vorlesungsdiktate' on *Dogmatik* were ed. by M. Rade (1925; Eng. tr., *Systematic Theology*, by N. Micklem and K. A. Saunders, 1927). Several of his minor writings in *Gesammelte Aufsätze* (ed. F. W. Schmidt, 1923), with bibl. of his works. See also W. de Boor in *R.G.G.* (ed. 2), ii (1928), cols. 1836–8, with bibl.

HERRNHUT. The village in Saxony, some 40 miles east of Dresden, built and settled in 1722 by a group of *Moravian Brethren (hence known on the Continent as 'Herrnhuter') under Christian David, an artisan, on a site presented by Count N. L. *Zinzendorf. Institutions exist here for the brethren and sisters of the community, though since 1789 the directorate of the community has been centred at Berthelsdorf, about a mile distant. In 1738 J. *Wesley made a pilgrimage here and for some weeks actively took part in the life of the community.

HERSE. See *Hearse*.

HERTFORD, Council of (673). A Council of bishops held on 24 Sept. 673, under *Theodore, Abp. of Canterbury, to promote the reorganization of the English Church. It issued 10 canons, concerned esp. with the rights and duties of clerics and monks. Bishops were not to intrude on the diocese ('parochia') of a neighbouring bishop (can. 2); precedence among bishops was to be determined by their dates of consecration (can. 8); and monks were not to leave their monasteries without their abbot's permission (can. 4). Synods were to be held twice annually, or, if that proved impossible, at least once a year on 1 Aug., at *Clovesho (can. 7). Divorce was forbidden except for fornication, and a man divorced from his wife was not to re-marry (can. 10). The date for the keeping of Easter was settled (can. 1). The Council was the first occasion on which the English Church deliberated and acted as a unity.

*Bede, *H.E.*, iv. 5; notes to ed. C. Plummer, ii (Oxford, 1896), pp. 211–14. Hardouin, iii, cols. 1015–18; Mansi, xi (1765), cols. 127–30; A. W. Haddan–W. *Stubbs (ed.), *Councils and Ecclesiastical Documents Relating to Great Britain and Ireland*, iii (1871), pp. 118–22. W. *Bright, *Chapters of Early English Church History* (1878), pp. 240–9 and 441–4. Hefele–Leclercq, iii (pt. 1; 1909), p. 310.

HERVETUS, GENTIAN (1499–1584), French theologian, translator, and controversialist. He was a native of Olivet, nr. Orleans, where he studied. He then became a private tutor, counting R. *Pole among his pupils, and for a short time *c.* 1534 professor of Greek at Orléans university. He translated several Greek writings into Latin, among them *Aristotle's *De Anima* (1544) and Alexander of Aphrodisias's *De Fato* (1544). He then went to Rome, where he lived in the house of Cardinal Pole, whom he accompanied to *Trent in 1545. In his service he made more translations, esp. of the Greek Fathers, e.g. *Zacharias Scholasticus (1548). He also took an active part in the discussions preceding the decrees of the Council. In 1549 he entered the service of Card. M. Cervini, later Pope Marcellus II, for whom he translated works by *Theodoret (1549), St. *Chrysostom (1549), and St. *Clement of Alexandria (1551). In 1556 he was ordained priest, and shortly afterwards became Vicar General of Noyon. In 1561 he published a treatise *De Reparanda Ecclesiasticorum Disciplina* in which he recommended the enforcing of episcopal residence as the chief means for the reform of the Church. In 1561 he joined the group of theologians formed by Card. Charles of Lorraine for fighting Protestantism and published a number of controversial pamphlets against it. From 1562 he was Canon of *Reims. In 1562 he again went to Trent, in the company of Charles of Lorraine. In 1564 he published a complete French translation of the decrees of the Council entitled *Le Saint, Sacré, Universel et Général Concile de Trente*. In his later years he wrote chiefly pamphlets, and in 1572 published a French translation of St. *Augustine's *Civitas Dei*.

A. Humbert in *D.T.C.*, vi (1920), cols. 2315–20, s.v. 'Hervet'.

HERZOG, JOHANN JAKOB (1805–82), German Reformed theologian. A pupil of F. D. *Schleiermacher and J. A. W. *Neander, he began to teach at Lausanne in 1835, where he was professor of historical theology from 1838 to 1846. Later he held professorships at Halle (from 1847) and Erlangen (from 1854). In 1848 he published *De origine et pristino statu Waldensium*, a study embodying much original research. The greatest of his labours, however, was the editing of the *Realencyklopädie für protestantische Theologie und Kirche* (22 vols., 1853–68), a standard work of reference which was adapted and condensed into an American version by P. *Schaff (3 vols., 1882–4). Both the German and American versions have been rewritten and expanded in more recent editions (see *Hauck, A.*).

Herzog also issued a 2nd ed. of the *Realencyclopädie* (18 vols., 1877–88) in conjunction with G. L. Plitt. F. Sieffert in *P.R.E.* (ed. 3), vii (1899), pp. 782–7.

HESYCHASM (from Gk. ἥσυχος, 'quiet'). In the E Church, the system of mysticism propagated by the monks of Mount *Athos in the 14th cent. Its chief tenet was that man was able, by an elaborate system of ascetic practices, involving esp. perfect quiet of body and mind, to arrive at the vision of the *Uncreated Light of the Godhead. *Symeon of *Studion, the 'New Theologian', is claimed as the father of the movement. Subsequent authors began to invent easy methods for procuring the vision of the Divine Light. These became more and more mechanical, including breathing exercises, the pressing of the chin against the chest, and the indefinite repetition of the ejaculation 'Lord Jesus Christ, son of God, have mercy on me'. The result of these practices was alleged to be an ineffable joy and the seeing of the Divine Light, which was identified with the Godhead and with the light surrounding our Lord on Mount *Tabor. It was held that this Light was not God's Essence, which is unapproachable, but His 'energy', which, though also uncreated and divine, can be perceived by the senses; that it was this Light, and not, as W. theologians hold, God's Essence, which is the object of the Beatific Vision; and that for

the knowledge of God by reason and authentic tradition should be substituted a knowledge by interior illumination. In the 'Hagioritic Tome', drawn up by Philotheus Kokkinus at Mount Athos *c.* 1339, the doctrine is represented as a manifestation of mysteries implicit in the Gospels and experimentally revealed to the contemplatives of the Holy Mountain.

These tenets became an object of theological controversy through the writings of the Calabrian monk, Barlaam, who had been trained in W. theology and denounced the practices of Mt. Athos as superstitious (esp. from 1339). His chief objection was his denial of the possibility of an uncreated light that was not God's essence, on the ground that any distinction in God would destroy His unity and simplicity. Barlaam's principal opponent, *Gregory Palamas (q.v.), passionately defended Hesychasm, and with the support of other Athos monks, prevented its condemnation at the synod held at *Constantinople in 1341. In 1342, however, the writings of Palamas were condemned by two synods, and Hesychasm was in abeyance till the usurpation of power by John Cantacuzenus (1347). From Cantacuzenus's adherence to Hesychasm the hitherto purely religious controversy took on a mainly political aspect. He appointed the Athonite monk, Isidore, patriarch, and a large number of Hesychasts bishops, among them Palamas himself. In 1351 the 'Blacherna Synod' excommunicated all opponents of Hesychasm, and in the next year solemn anathemas against Barlaam and his followers and acclamations of Palamas were introduced into the liturgy of the 'Feast of *Orthodoxy'. In the second half of the 14th cent. Hesychasm was accepted throughout the Greek Church, its adherents being also generally known as 'Palamites'. The fact that the Hesychast theology, which conceives of God as a compound of essence and activity, substance and accident, is radically opposed to Latin doctrine, furthered its success in the E., and Hesychasm came to be identified with Orthodoxy. In the 16th and 17th cents., however, the influence of W. theology made itself felt, esp. in the Russian Church, and the Hesychast doctrine was officially dropped by removing the names of Palamas and Barlaam from the Liturgy of the 'Sunday of Orthodoxy', though the feasts of the former have been retained in its calendar.

The fullest account is that of M. Jugie, A.A., in *D.T.C.*, xi (pt. 2; 1932), cols. 1777–1818, s.v. 'Palamite (Controverse)', with bibl., based largely on unpublished MS. material. The older lit. includes J. Bois, 'Les Hésychastes avant le XIVᵉ siècle' in *É.O.*, v (1901–2), pp. 1–11; id., 'Grégoire le Sinaïte et l'hésychasme à l'Athos au XIVᵉ siècle', ib., pp. 65–73; id., 'Les Débuts de la controverse hésychaste', ib., pp. 353–363. I. Hausherr, S.J., *La Méthode d'oraison des hésychastes* (Orientalia Christiana, ix, pt. 2; fasc. 36 of the series; 1927, paginated pp. 97–209). W. Gass–P. Meyer in *P.R.E.* (ed. 3), viii (1900), pp. 14–8; A. *Fortescue in *C.E.*, vii (1910), p. 301 f., s.v. See also bibl. to *Gregory Palamas*.

HESYCHIUS (*fl. c.* 300), Biblical textual critic. Acc. to St. *Jerome (*in praef. ad Paralipp.*) he made a revision of the text of the *Septuagint at *Alexandria, which he corrected acc. to the Hebrew. He is perhaps to be identified with an

Egyptian bishop, martyred in the *Diocletianic persecution (*Eusebius, *H.E.*, VIII, xiii.), who in conjunction with his colleagues, Pachomius, Theodore, and Phileas, sent a letter to *Melitius of Lycopolis which has survived in a Latin translation.

Lat. tr. of the letter sent to Melitius in J. P. Migne, *PG*, x, 1565–8. H. *Lietzmann in *P.W.*, viii (1913), cols. 1327 f., s.v. 'Hesychios (12)', with bibl. F. G. Kenyon, 'Hesychius and the Text of the New Testament' in *Mémorial Lagrange* (1940), pp. 245–50, with reff. to older lit.

HESYCHIUS OF ALEXANDRIA (prob. 5th cent.), lexicographer. Nothing is known of his life. His elaborate lexicon (Συναγωγὴ πασῶν λέξεων κατὰ στοιχεῖον) is an important authority for the Greek dialects and the vocabulary of some of the Fathers. Based on the lexicon of Diogenianus of Heraclea (2nd cent. A.D.), it also drew on the compilations of Aristarchus, Heliodorus, Apion and others; and appears to have made extensive use of a glossary illustrating the vocabulary of St. *Cyril of Alexandria. It survives in a single 15th cent. MS. (Venice 622), extensively interpolated and disfigured, from which the reff. to the sources of the words have been excised.

Editions by J. Alberti (2 vols., Leyden, 1746–66) and M. Schmidt (5 vols., Jena, 1858–68). A. von Blumenthal, *Hesych-Studien*. Untersuchungen zur Vorgeschichte der griechischen Sprache nebst lexicographischen Beiträgen (1930). H. Schultz in *P.W.* viii (pt. 2, 1913), cols. 1317–22, s.v. 'Hesychios (9)'.

HESYCHIUS OF JERUSALEM, St. (d. after 451), Greek ecclesiastical writer and exegete. In early life he was a monk, and in 412, acc. to *Theophanes Confessor, presbyter at *Jerusalem. Little, however, is known of him beyond the fact that he was held in high repute by his contemporaries. He is said to have commented on the whole Bible. The surviving portions of his commentaries, glosses, and sermons show that he generally followed the *Alexandrian method of exegesis. He defended orthodoxy against the *Manichees, *Arians, *Apollinarians, and other heretics. It seems probable that the bulk of the long Commentary on the Psalms, ascribed by N. Antonelli, its first editor (1746), to St. *Athanasius, is his work. He was also the author of a lost Church History. Feast day in the Greek Church, 28 Mar.

For his Life, cf. *Cyril of Scythopolis, *Vita S. Euthymii*, 31 f. Works, incl. a 6th cent. Lat. version of his Comm. on Lev. and other exegetical remains, in J. P. Migne, *PG*, xciii, 781–1560; Comm. on Pss. in ib., xxvii, 849–1344 (inter Opp. S. Athanasii). On this last see M. *Faulhaber, 'Eine wertvolle Oxforder Handschrift' in *T.Q.*, lxxxiii (1901), pp. 218–32. M. Faulhaber also edited Hesychius's Comm. on Is. (Freiburg i.Br., 1900). K. Jüssen, *Die dogmatischen Anschauungen des Hesychius von Jerusalem* (2 vols., 1931–4). Bardenhewer, iv, pp. 257–61; Altaner (ed. 1950), p. 290 f. A. Vaccari, S.J., in *E.C.*, v (1951), col. 581 f., s.v. 'Esichio di Gerusalemme'.

HEXAEMERON (Gk. ἐξαήμερον, '[a work] of six days'). The account of the creation of the universe in six days, as set forth in Gen. 1. The name is also used of the *patristic commentaries on this narrative, notably those of St. *Basil and St. *Ambrose.

HEXAPLA (Gk. ἐξαπλᾶ, 'sixfold'). The elaborate edition of the OT produced by *Origen, in which the Hebrew text, in Hebrew and Greek characters, and the four Greek versions of *Aquila, *Symmachus, the *Septuagint, and *Theodotion were arranged in six parallel columns. For certain sections of the OT, up to three further Greek versions were used, making a total of nine columns. The complete work was of such enormous dimensions that it was probably never copied in its entirety, and St. *Jerome expressly states he had used the original copy preserved in Origen's library at Caesarea. Considerable portions of it, however, circulated in the early Church, and MSS. of several parts have come down to modern times.

The work, begun before Origen left Alexandria for Caesarea in 231, was not finished until *c*. 245. In 616–17 a very literal rendering into Syriac of its Septuagintal text (i.e. its 5th column), most of which has survived, was made by Paul, Jacobite Bp. of Tella (in Mesopotamia). The most extensive (but not quite complete) coll. of fragments in F. *Field, *Origenis Hexaplorum Quae Supersunt* (2 vols., 1867–75). C. Taylor in *D.C.B.*, iii (1882), pp. 14–23; H. B. *Swete, *An Introduction to the Old Testament in Greek* (ed. 2, 1902), pp. 59–76. Bardenhewer, ii, pp. 112–17. A. Vaccari, S.J., in *E.C.*, v (1951), col. 536 f., s.v. 'Esaple'.

HEXATEUCH (Gk. ἕξ, 'six' + τεῦχος, 'book'). A name given by J. *Wellhausen (1876), and after him by many other modern Biblical scholars, to the first six books of the Hebrew Bible (Genesis to Joshua), in the belief that like the *Pentateuch all are compiled from a single set of literary sources.

HEXHAM, in Northumberland. The site of an abbey founded by St. *Wilfrid of York in 674. In 678 the new see of Bernicia was set up here, which survived until 821, when it was united with the bishopric of *Lindisfarne. The abbey church of St. Andrew is chiefly Early English and Transitional, and since the *Dissolution in 1536 has been used as the parish church. Only fragments of other parts of the monastery remain.

J. Raine (ed.), *The Priory of Hexham, its Chronicles, Endowments and Annals* (Surtees Society, xliv and xlvi 1864–5). W. *Dugdale, *Monasticon Anglicanum*, vi (pt. 1; ed. 1830), pp. 179–85. C. C. Hodges, *The Abbey of St. Andrew, Hexham* (1888). Id.–J. Gibson, *Hexham and its Abbey* (1919), pp. 24–122. *A History of Northumberland*, iii, by A. B. Hinds (1896), pp. 105–200.

HEYLYN, PETER (1600–62), Anglican controversialist and historian. Educated at Burford and at Hart Hall and Magdalen College, *Oxford, he became a Fellow of Magdalen in 1618. In 1627 at a public disputation he defended against H. *Prideaux, the Regius professor of divinity, the visibility of the Church and soon attracted the attention of W. *Laud by his championship of *High Church views. In 1630 he was appointed by *Charles I a royal chaplain and also rector of Hemingford, Hunts. When J. *Williams, Bp. of Lincoln, declined to institute him at Hemingford, Charles made him a prebendary of *Westminster (1631), where he began a long feud with

Williams which ended with Williams's suspension by the Star Chamber in 1637. Other preferments followed in the next years. His rising fame as a controversialist led him to be called in to help W. Noy (1633) to prepare the case against W. *Prynne for his *Histriomastix*. In 1636, at the King's command, he wrote a *History of the Sabbath* against the *Puritans. After 1640 his fortunes altered with the decline in the King's power. His issue during the Civil War of *Mercurius Aulicus*, a royalist newssheet, caused his property at Alresford to be plundered and his library dispersed. Under the Commonwealth he lived quietly at first, but later renewed his controversial writings, one of which, *Ecclesia Vindicata, or the Church of England justified* (1657), again brought upon him the indignation of the government. This was followed in 1659 with an attack on T. *Fuller. As a writer, Heylyn was learned, trenchant, and critical, but he was above all a partisan. Among his principal works are *Historia Quinquarticularis, or a Historical Declaration of the Five Controverted Points reproached in the Name of Arminianism* (1660); *Ecclesia Restaurata, or the History of the Reformation* (1661); *Cyprianus Anglicus* (1668), a defence of Laud; and *Aerius Redivivus, or the History of Presbyterianism* (1670).

G. Vernon, *The Life of the Learned and Reverend Doctor Peter Heylyn* (1682). G. Barnard, *Theologico-Historicus, or True Life of the Most Reverend Divine and Excellent Historian, Peter Heylyn, D.D.* (1683), repr., with additional information from Vernon, in Heylin's *Ecclesia Restaurata*, ed. J. C. Robertson (1849). M. *Creighton in *D.N.B.*, xxvi (1891), pp. 319–23.

HIBBERT, ROBERT (1770–1849), founder of the Hibbert Trust. He was born in Jamaica, was a pupil of Gilbert Wakefield at Nottingham, and studied at Emmanuel College, Cambridge, from 1788 to 1791. On his estate in Jamaica he kept slaves, for whose conversion he employed a *Unitarian minister. In 1847 he founded the Hibbert Trust for 'the spread of Christianity in its most simple and intelligible form' and of 'the unfettered exercise of the right of private judgement in matters of religion'. Its aims were anti-Trinitarian and its recipients must be 'heterodox'. The Trust provides for scholarships and fellowships. Its best-known activities are the Hibbert Lectures (1878 onwards), and the publication of the *Hibbert Journal*, a quarterly founded in 1902 which treats philosophical and religious subjects from a liberal point of view.

J. Murch, *Memoir of R. Hibbert, Esquire, Founder of the Hibbert Trust, with a Sketch of its History* (1874). On the Hibbert Trust see also *The Christian Reformer*, N.S., ix (1853), pp. 246–9. A. Gordon in *D.N.B.*, xxvi (1891), p. 344.

HICKES, GEORGE (1642–1715), *Nonjuring bishop. Educated at Oxford, Hickes became Vicar of All Hallows, Barking, in 1680, and Dean of *Worcester in 1683. He opposed the pro-RC measures of *James II, but in 1689 he refused to take the oaths to William and Mary, and in 1690 he was deprived of his deanery. In his retirement, he remained firm in his principles. In 1694 he was consecrated

titular Bp. of Thetford by the *Nonjurors; and after the death in 1709 of W. Lloyd (formerly Bp. of *Norwich), he was their acknowledged head. Being anxious, in opposition to T. *Ken, to continue the Nonjuring succession, he consecrated three bishops in 1713, viz. J. *Collier, S. Hawes, and N. *Spinckes. Hickes was a man of great piety and wide scholarship. Besides his very learned *Linguarum veterum Septentrionalium Thesaurus* (1703–5), his writings included *The Case of Infant Baptism* (1683); *Speculum Beatae Virginis* (1686); *Institutiones Grammaticae Anglo-Saxonicae et Moeso-Gothicae* (1689); *Of the Christian Priesthood* (1707); and *Of the Dignity of the Episcopal Order* (1707). The posthumous publication of Hickes's *Constitution of the Catholic Church and the Nature and Consequences of Schism* (1716) was the immediate occasion of the *Bangorian Controversy.

His *Two Treatises on the Christian Priesthood and on the Dignity of the Episcopal Order* were ed. by I. B[arrow] in L.A.C.T. (3 vols., 1847–8). There are frequent reff. to him in T. *Hearne's *Remarks and Collections*. J. H. Overton, *The Nonjurors* (1902), pp. 91–113 and passim; D. C. Douglas, *English Scholars, 1660–1730* (1939), No. iv, pp. 93–119. W. D. Macray in *D.N.B.*, xxvi (1891), pp. 350–4.

HICKS, ELIAS (1748–1830), American *Quaker. He was born of Quaker parents at Hempstead, Long Island. After taking little interest in religion as a young man, he gradually came to feel a call to preaching and from 1779 onwards made evangelistic tours, becoming a commanding influence. He also took up the cause of the negroes, esp. in *Observations on the Slavery of the Africans and their Descendants* (1811). He strongly opposed the creation of any credal basis for Quakerism, notably in his *Doctrinal Epistle* (1824), where he protested against insistence on the orthodox doctrines of the Person of Christ and the Atonement. A schism ensued (1827–8) at Philadelphia and elsewhere between his followers (the 'Liberal Branch', called by their opponents 'Hicksites') and the Orthodox, which had repercussions in England (see *Friends, Society of*).

Some of his discourses, taken down in shorthand by M. T. C. Gould, were publ. at Philadelphia in 1825. [V. Hicks–R. Seaman (edd.)], *Journal of the Life and Religious Labours of E. Hicks*, written by himself (ed. 3, New York, 1832). H. W. Wilbur, *The Life and Labours of Elias Hicks* (Philadelphia, 1910) with discussion of sources. E. Russell, *The Separation after a Century* (ib., 1928). R. M. *Jones in *Dict. Amer. Biog.*, ix (1932), p. 6 f.

HICKS, GEORGE DAWES (1862–1941), philosopher. Educated at Owens College, Manchester, at Manchester College, Oxford, and under W. Wundt at Leipzig, he was a *Unitarian minister at Islington from 1897 to 1903 and professor of philosophy at University College, London, from 1904 to 1928. From an intensive interest in I. *Kant, he became a lifelong student of the theory of knowledge. In his *Hibbert Lectures on *The Philosophical Bases of Theism* (1937) he defended the traditional Christian position, arguing that besides the strictly intellectual grounds of theistic belief there was a legitimate place for the argument from religious experience. His other writings mainly took the form of contributions to periodicals, esp. the *Hibbert Journal* (with which he was closely associated from 1902 until his death) and the *Proceedings of the Aristotelian Society*; but he published in 1932 a study of *Berkeley* and in 1937 *Critical Realism*.

HICKSITES. See *Hicks, Elias*.

HIERARCHY. The word has been in use for the ordered body of the Christian clergy since patristic times. RC theologians distinguish the hierarchy of order and that of jurisdiction. The former is subdivided into the three grades of Divine institution (bishops, priests, and deacons) on the one hand and the subdiaconate and minor orders, instituted by the Church, on the other. In the hierarchy of jurisdiction, only the Papacy and the episcopate are held to be of Divine institution. All other grades are of ecclesiastical origin. The latter are divided into two classes, viz. those exercising an authority derived directly from the Pope, e.g. cardinals, legates, and vicars apostolic (C.I.C., cans. 230–328), and those whose authority derives from the bishop, e.g. coadjutors, auxiliary bishops, and cathedral chapters (cans. 350–486). The threefold hierarchical order of bishops, priests, and deacons has been retained by the C of E in common with the RC and E. Churches.

HIEROME, HIERONYMUS. See *Jerome*.

HIERONYMIAN MARTYROLOGY (Lat. *Hieronymianum*). A famous martyrology, based on an earlier Greek martyrology of Asia Minor, which was composed in Italy in the middle of the 5th cent. It gives, after the calendar date in the year, the names of the saints commemorated on that day, the places of their tombs (or alternatively where they were venerated), and other details connected with their cultus. It is so named from a statement in an apocryphal correspondence preceding the text that its compilation was the work of St. *Jerome.

Ed. princeps by F. Fiorentini (Lucca, 1668). Text also in D. *Vallarsi's ed. of Jerome, xi (Verona, 1742), cols. 475–524; repr. in J. P. Migne, *PL*, xxx, 433–86. Crit. ed., with magisterial discussion, by G. B. *de Rossi–L. *Duchesne in *AA.SS.*, Nov. II (pt. 1; 1894), pp. [1]–[195] with text of 'Bernensis', 'Epternacensis', and 'Wisseburgensis' in three columns, with the further text of the 'Laureshamensis' for 38 days, and with prolegomena, pp. [i]–[lxxxii]; 'Commentarius Perpetuus', by H. *Quentin, O.S.B.–H. *Delehaye, S.J., as Nov. II (pt. 2; 1931). A. Bugnini, C.M., in *E.C.*, viii (1952), cols. 249–52, s.v. 'Martirologio, III, 2'.

HIERUSALEM. A Latinized form of the word *Jerusalem (Gk. Ἱερουσαλήμ).

HIGH ALTAR. The main altar of a church, standing in the centre of the east end. In ancient English Gothic churches the length was commonly the same as that of the splay of the east window, which formed the *reredos. Acc. to RC practice, it should be of stone, clear of the wall, not less than 8 ft. long, approached by at least three steps, and provided with a crucifix in the centre, with three large candlesticks, with candles, on either side. Its dedication is that of the church itself.

HIGH CHURCHMEN. The group in the C of E which esp. stresses her historical continuity with Catholic Christianity, and hence upholds a 'high' conception of the authority of the Church, of the claims of the episcopate and of the nature of the Sacraments. Though the existence of the school can be traced back to the Elizabethan age, when such men as R. *Bancroft and R. *Hooker resisted the attacks of the Puritan Reformers, the actual title is not found till the end of the 17th cent. In the 17th cent. the tradition was maintained by L. *Andrewes, W. *Laud, and a host of others. Their doctrine of the *Divine Right of Kings brought a close alliance with the Stuarts, and thus, finding their position compromised when William III became king, the High Churchmen who were more eminent in piety and learning mostly went into schism as '*Non-Jurors.' Those who remained in the Established Church were excluded from ecclesiastical preferment as tainted with Jacobitism and for the most part fell into obscurity. The continuance of High Church opinions is evidenced, however, by such men as J. *Butler and S. *Johnson, and in the next century by the success of the *Tracts for the Times among the older generation. It was the *Oxford Movement which reasserted their position in the Church, though only after the bitterest struggle.

G. W. O. Addleshaw, *The High Church Tradition* (1941).

HIGH COMMISSION, Court of. From 1549 ecclesiastical commissions to check heresy and enforce the forms of worship prescribed by public authority were frequently appointed in England. From 1559 the power of the Crown to create such bodies was expressly recognized by the Elizabethan Act of *Supremacy. The actual term 'High Commission' begins to appear *c.* 1570 and is employed normally after 1580, a development corresponding with the elevation of an *ad hoc* commission into a permanent court. At this stage the visitatorial function of the commission declined by comparison with the multiplication of suits between party and party, while professional lawyers played an increasing part and rigid procedure developed. The High Commission also became the normal court of appeal from the ancient ecclesiastical *courts in doctrinal and disciplinary suits. Together with the other conciliar courts, it incurred the dislike and fear of the common lawyers, even Lord Burghley, Elizabeth's first minister, denouncing the procedure by the oath *ex officio* as savouring of the *Inquisition. Abolished by the Star Chamber Act of 1641, it was revived in a much modified form from 1686 to 1688 by *James II. Apart from the central High Commission, there existed certain regional commissions, e.g., that appointed for the two dioceses of Bristol and *Gloucester in 1574, and that for the Northern Province, which, closely associated with the Council in the North, took a leading part in the repression of *recusancy.

The greater part of the Act Books and other papers belonging to the Registry of the Commission at London seems to have been lost, having probably been destroyed by order of Parliament during the Civil War; some records, however, survive among the State Papers. A large part of the papers of the Commission at Durham has survived; ed., in part, by W. H. D. Longstaffe, *The Acts of the High Commission Court within the Diocese of Durham* (Surtees Society, xxxiv; 1858); and an Act Book of the Commission at Gloucester is extant among the diocesan records. R. G. Usher, *The Rise and Fall of the High Commission* (1913). The only other works of significance on the Court of High Commission in general are J. S. Burn, *The High Commission.* Notices of the Court, and its Proceedings (1865) and W. *Stubbs in *Report of the Commissioners Appointed to Inquire into the Constitution and Working of the Ecclesiastical Courts,* i (Parliamentary Papers, 1883, xxiv), Historical Appendix I, p. 49 f. (p. 123 of MS. pagination). On the Court of High Commission in the North, R. R. Reid, *The King's Council in the North* (1921), passim. F. D. Price, 'The Commission for Ecclesiastical Causes for the Dioceses of Bristol and Gloucester, 1574' in *Transactions of the Bristol and Gloucester Archaeological Society* for 1937 (1938), pp. 61–184. R. G. Usher in *D.E.C.H.*, pp. 275–8, s.v.

HIGH MASS (*Missa solemnis*). In the W. Church, the normal, though not the most usual, form of the Mass. Its essential feature is the presence of *deacon and *subdeacon assisting the celebrant; they are accompanied by the choir, the *thurifer, and a number of *servers or *acolytes. Their respective functions are carefully regulated, the chief office of the deacon being the chanting of the *Gospel and the *Ite Missa Est, and that of the subdeacon the chanting of the *Epistle; whereas choir or people sing the *common and the *proper of the Mass. Other distinctive features are the use of incense and the giving of the *Pax or kiss of peace. The celebration of High Mass is prescribed for parish churches on Sundays and the greater feasts wherever possible; where not practicable a Sung Mass ('*Missa Cantata') is recommended. The daily Conventual and Collegiate Masses should also properly be High Masses.

Jungmann (ed. 1949), i, pp. 248–63; Eng. tr. (New York, 1951), pp. 195–207.

'HIGH PLACES', The. (Heb. במות). In the OT the local sanctuaries other than *Jerusalem at which Jehovah was worshipped with sacrifice in early times. Among the most renowned were *Bethel and Dan. The cultus, which had heathen affinities and was often accompanied by immoral rites, was denounced by many of the Prophets (*Amos, *Hosea, &c.). It was finally abolished by Josiah, under the influence of the legislation of *Deuteronomy (12. 13 f. and passim), in 621 B.C.

HIGH PRAYERS. A title for service in certain college chapels in Oxford on great festivals.

HIGH PRIEST. In the OT the head of the *Levitical priesthood whose institution and vestments are described in Exod. 28. Acc. to this (*P) account, *Aaron, the brother of *Moses, was appointed the first high priest by Jehovah. The chief function of the high priest was the superintendence of the Temple worship, and his special prerogatives the offering of the Liturgy on the Day of *Atonement, when he alone was allowed to enter the Holy of Holies, and the consulting of '*Urim and Thummim'. His exalted office required an unusually high degree of ritual purity, which forbade him to 'defile himself' with the dead even in the case of his nearest relations. His vestments, more precious than those of the other priests, included a violet robe adorned with bells and tassels, a special mitre with a golden plate in front bearing the inscription 'Holy to the Lord', and a breastplate with the names of the twelve tribes of Israel.

Acc. to critical theories of the OT, the institution of the High Priesthood was of post-Exilic origin. At first the office may have been for life and hereditary; but under *Antiochus Epiphanes the appointment and deposition of high priests passed more and more into the authority of the secular powers. In the time of the *Herods and the Roman occupation the high priests were usually taken from the most influential families; they seem to have professed a materialistic creed, believing neither in an immortal soul nor in a future life, and, acc. to the *Talmud, they lived in worldliness and luxury.

Christian theology holds that the Saviour, by His death on the Cross, abolished for the redeemed the high-priestly office and sacrifices, perfecting them in His own Person. This teaching is developed in the NT in the Ep. to the Hebrews, which sets forth the Christ as the perfect High priest, unique and immortal, of whom the long series of imperfect high priests under the old dispensation had been but types and shadows.

E. *Schürer, *Geschichte des jüdischen Volkes im Zeitalter Jesu Christi,* ii (ed. 4, 1907), pp. 267–77, with bibl. W. Graf Baudissin, *Die Geschichte des alttestamentlichen Priesterthums* (1889), esp. pp. 26–8, 88 f., 127–30, 140–2, 251–3. On the High Priest's vesture, see J. Gabriel, *Untersuchungen über das alttestamentliche Hohepriestertum, mit besonderer Berücksichtigung des hohepriesterlichen Ornates* (Theologische Studien der Österreichischen Leo-Gesellschaft, xxxiii; 1933). F. Buhl in *P.R.E.* (ed. 3), viii (1900), pp. 251–6, s.v. 'Hoher Priester'; W. Baudissin in *H.D.B.*, iv (1902), pp. 67–97, s.v. 'Priests and Levites', esp. p. 83 f. N. Schlögl, O. Cist., in *L.Th.K.*, v (1933), col. 107 f., s.v. 'Hohepriester'; G. Schrenk in *T.W.B.*, iii (1938), pp. 265–84, s.v. ἱερεύς [ἀρχιερεύς]. For the conception of Christ as the High Priest, see bibl. to *Hebrews, Ep. to the.*

HIGHER CRITICISM. The critical study of the literary methods and sources used by the authors of (esp.) the Books of the OT and NT, in distinction from Textual ('Lower') Criticism which is concerned solely with the recovery from extant MSS. and other evidence of the text of the Books as it left their authors' hands. The word came into currency from its use ('Higher or Historical Criticism') by W. R. *Smith in *The Old Testament in the Jewish Church* (1881; p. 105).

HILARION, St. (*c.* 291–371). The founder of the *anchoritic life in Palestine. A native of Palestine and the son of pagan parents, he was converted to Christianity at *Alexandria, and under the influence of St. *Antony retired for a short time to the Egyptian desert as a hermit. In 306 he returned to his own land, where he settled in the wilderness south of Majuma, near Gaza, to live a life of extreme asceticism. As his fame and miraculous gifts became increasingly known, enormous crowds visited him, to escape from whom he returned *c.* 353 to Egypt. Later, he went to Libya, Sicily, and Cyprus, where he died. He was well known to St. *Epiphanius, to whom St. *Jerome, the chief authority for his life, was doubtless mainly indebted for his knowledge of him. Feast day, 21 Oct.

Jerome's *Vita* (*c.* A.D. 386–91) is repr. in J. P. Migne, *PL*, xxiii, 29–54; cf. *Sozomen, *H.E.*, III, xiv, V., x, and VI, xxxii. The letter of Epiphanius, mentioned by Jerome as his source, is lost. The attempt of W. Israel, 'Die Vita S. Hilarionis des Hieronymus' in *Zeitschr. für wiss. Theologie*, xxiii (1880), 129–65, to deny all historicity to Hilarion has been generally rejected; cf. O. Zöckler, 'Hilarion von Gaza. Eine Rettung' in *Neue Jahrbücher für deutsche Theologie*, iii (1894), pp. 147–78. G. Grützmacher, *Hieronymus*, ii (1906), pp. 87–91. J. P. Kirsch in *C.E.*, vii (1910), p. 347 f.; A. Amore in *E.C.*, vi (1951), col. 1616 f., s.v. 'Ilarione'.

HILARY OF ARLES, St. (403–49), Abp. of Arles and leader of the *Semi-Pelagian party. He became a monk at *Lérins, under the influence of his kinsman, St. *Honoratus, and in 428–9 succeeded him as Abp. of *Arles. In this capacity he presided over several councils, among them the First Council of *Orange (441) and that of *Vaison (442). In 444, by deposing a bishop, Chelidonius, Hilary appears to have exceeded his rights as *metropolitan, and on the dethroned bishop's appeal to *Leo I, the Pope deprived Arles of its metropolitical jurisdiction and obtained from *Valentinian III a decree granting Rome supreme authority over the Church in Gaul. Hilary wrote a Life of Honoratus which is still extant. Feast day, 5 May.

Fragments of Hilary's works collected in edd. of Leo's *Opera* by P. *Quesnel (1675) and P. and H. *Ballerini (1753–7; qq.v.). Repr. from the latter in J. P. Migne, *PL*, l, 1213–92, with additions. B. Kolon, O.F.M., *Die Vita S. Hilarii Arelatensis* (1925), argues that the Vita (repr. in J. P. Migne, l.c., 1219–46) ascribed by Ps.–*Gennadius to an otherwise unknown Honoratus, Bp. of Marseille, is really the work of a certain Reverentius and historically almost valueless. Crit. texts of *Vitae* ed. S. Cavallin (Skrifter utgivna av Vetenskaps-Societen i Lund, xl; 1952). Bardenhewer, iv, p. 571 f. Altaner (ed. 1951), p. 405 f.

HILARY OF POITIERS, St. (*c.* 315–67). The '*Athanasius of the West'. A convert from *Neo-Platonism, he was elected Bp. of Poitiers *c.* 353 and became at once involved in the *Arian disputes. His defence of orthodoxy led to his condemnation at the Synod of Biterrae (356) and to a 4-years exile to Phrygia by the Emp. *Constantius. In 359 he defended the cause of orthodoxy at the Council of *Seleucia. He became the leading and most respected Latin theologian of his age. His chief works were a treatise 'De Trinitate' (against the Arians), in twelve books; 'De

Synodis', very valuable for the history of the period; and the so-called 'Opus Historicum'. His other writings include commentaries on the Pss. and Mt., in which he closely followed *Origen. His style is difficult and obscure. In matters of detail his doctrinal position deviated at points from later orthodoxy, e.g. he held an almost *Monophysite Christology. In 1851 he was proclaimed by *Pius IX a '*Doctor of the Church'. His feast day (in BCP, 13 Jan.; in the RC Calendar, 14 Jan.) gives its name to the spring term at the Law Courts, and at Oxford and Durham universities.

Editio princeps, by D. *Erasmus (Basle, 1523). Greatly improved text by P. *Coustant, O.S.B. (Paris, 1693), one of the best of the *Maurist editions; further improved by F. S. *Maffei (2 vols., Verona, 1730). This last is repr. in J. P. Migne, *PL*, ix and x. Crit. text in course of publication in C.S.E.L., ed. A. Zingerle–A. Feder, 1891 ff. Eng. tr., with valuable introds. ed. W. *Sanday, in N.P.N.C.F., Ser. 2, vol. ix, 1899. Hilary's *Tractatus Mysteriorum* (or 'De Mysteriis'), which treats of NT types in the OT, first publd. from fragments in the Arezzo MS, which contains the 'Peregrinatio *Etheriae', by J. F. Gamurrini (Rome, 1887); new ed. by J. P. Brisson in *S.C.*, xix (Paris, 1947). Three certainly genuine Hymns of Hilary, who was the first known hymn-writer of the W. Church, also ed. J. F. Gamurrini from the Arezzo MS. (1887); cf. A. J. Mason, 'The First Latin Christian Poet', in *J.T.S.*, v (1904), pp. 413–32 and 636. A. L. Feder, S.J., *Studien zu Hilarius von Poitiers* (*Sb.* (Wien), clxii, Abh. 4, 1909; clxvi, Abh. 5, 1910; clxix, Abh. 5, 1913). P. Smulders, S.J., *La Doctrine trinitaire de S. Hilaire de Poitiers* (Analecta Gregoriana, xxxii; Rome, 1944). Modern lives by J. G. Cazenove (London, 1883), A. Largent ('Les Saints', 1902), and others. Bardenhewer, iii, pp. 365–93; Altaner (ed. 1951), pp. 315–19. J. G. Cazenove in *D.C.B.*, iii (1882), pp. 54–66; X. Le Bachelet in *D.T.C.*, vi (1920), cols. 2388–2462, with bibl.; E. Rapisarda in *E.C.*, vi (1951), cols. 1614–16, s.v. 'Ilario di Poitiers'.

HILDA, St. (614–80), Abbess of *Whitby. Descended from the Northumbrian royal line, she was baptized at Easter, 627, by *Paulinus, Abp. of *York. When her sister, Hereswid, had been professed as a nun at Chelles, near Paris, Hilda sought to join her; but having reached East Anglia she was recalled by St. *Aidan, who in 649 made her abbess of a religious house at Hartlepool. In 659 she founded a monastery for both men and women at 'Streaneshalch', later named Whitby by the Danes, which rapidly grew in fame and influence. At the celebrated Synod of *Whitby (664), Hilda sided with St. Aidan in his defence of the Celtic customs against St. *Wilfrid, though after the decision had gone in favour of the Romanizing party, she loyally accepted it. Feast day, 17 Nov.

The principal authority is *Bede, *H.E.*, iii, 24 f., and iv, 23; notes ine d. by C. Plummer, ii (Oxford, 1896), p. 189 f., 244–8. E. Venables in *D.C.B.*, xxvi (1891), p. 381 f.

HILDEBERT OF LAVARDIN (1056–1133), Abp. of Tours, poet and canonist. He was born at Lavardin near Montoire and educated at the cathedral school of Le Mans, where he became Archdeacon in 1091. In 1096 he was elected Bp. of Le Mans. He had a powerful opponent in William Rufus, who alleging that Hildebert had attacked the royal castle from the towers of his cathedral, forced him to follow him to England in 1099. On regaining his freedom (1100) he went to Rome where *Paschal II confirmed him in his office.

After his return to Le Mans he continued the building of his cathedral and made a reputation as a powerful preacher. He was an ardent defender of the freedom of the Church and of sound doctrine; he expelled *Henry of Lausanne (q.v.) from his diocese, consecrated his cathedral on its completion in 1120, and probably took part in the First *Lateran Council of 1123. In 1125 he became Abp. of Tours. He was involved in a dispute with King Louis VI and presided over the important provincial Synod of Nantes (1127).

Hildebert is famous chiefly for his literary works. He had studied the best classical authors, and his Latin, far superior to that of most of his contemporaries, was looked to as the model of elegant style in the Middle Ages. The modern collections of his works contain much spurious material. Certainly genuine are most of the Letters, the 'Vitae' of St. *Radegunde and St. *Hugh of Cluny, the 'Liber de Querimonia' and a number of poems, among them 'De Sacrificio Missae', 'Vita Mariae Aegyptiacae', and several of the 'Carmina Miscellanea.'

Collected ed. of his Works by A. Beaugendre, O.S.B. (Paris, 1708); repr. with certain alterations by J. J. Bourassé in J. P. Migne, *PL*, clxxi, 45–1458. *Histoire littéraire de la France*, xi (1759), pp. 250–412. M. Hauréau, 'Notice sur les mélanges poétiques d'Hildebert de Lavardin' in *Notices et Extraits des Manuscrits de la Bibliothèque Nationale et autres Bibliothèques*, xxviii (pt. 2; 1878), pp. 289–448; id., 'Notice sur les sermons attribués à Hildebert de Lavardin', ib., xxxii (pt. 2; 1888), pp. 107–55. A. Dieudonné, *Hildebert de Lavardin, évêque du Mans, archevêque de Tours (1056–1133), sa vie, ses lettres* (Paris, 1898; repr. from *Revue historique et archéologique du Maine*). F. X. Barth, *Hildebert von Lavardin(1056–1133) und das kirchliche Stellenbesetzungsrecht* (Kirchenrechtliche Abhandlungen ed. U. Stutz, xxxiv–xxxvi; 1906). Raby, pp. 265–73. Manitius, iii, pp. 853–65. A. *Wilmart, O.S.B., 'Le *Tractatus Theologicus* attribué à Hildebert' in *R. Bén.*, xlv (1933), p. 163 f.; id., 'Les Sermons d'Hildebert', ib., xlvii (1935), pp. 12–51. H. Böhmer in *P.R.E.* (ed. 3), viii (1900), pp. 67–71, s.v. ; J. Besse in *D.T.C.*, vi (1920), cols. 2466–8, s.v.

HILDEBRAND. See *Gregory VII.*

HILDEFONSUS, St., of Toledo. See *Ildefonsus, St., of Toledo.*

HILDEGARD, St. (1098–1179), Abbess of Rupertsberg, near Bingen, the 'Sibyl of the Rhine'. Born of noble family at Böckelheim on the R. Nahe and subject to supernatural religious experiences from early childhood, she was brought up by Bl. Jutta, a recluse in a cell on the adjacent Diessenberg, and *c.* 1116 received into the *Benedictine community which had gathered round Jutta. In 1136 she succeeded Jutta as Abbess. Under the direction of her confessor, she began to record some of her visions. Having won the approval of the Abp. of Mainz, between 1141 and 1151 she dictated her *Scivias* (prob. an abbreviation of 'sciens vias'). Meanwhile *Eugenius III, under the influence of St. *Bernard of Clairvaux, gave his guarded approbation of her visions (1147). Sometime between 1147 and 1152 she moved her community to Rupertsberg, near Bingen, where a large convent was built. Thence she undertook many journeys

in the Rhineland and, prob. in 1165, founded a daughter house at Eibingen, near Rüdesheim. Towards the end of her life she had difficulty with the Chapter of Mainz concerning an excommunicate man who had been buried near her church; and for a short time the convent was placed under an interdict.

Hildegard seems to have exerted a wide influence, numbering the Emp. *Frederick Barbarossa and various kings, prelates, and saints among her correspondents. Her *Scivias*, divided into three books containing 26 visions, contain *inter alia* denunciations of the vices of the world and enigmatic prophecies of disaster. Many of her letters and reported speeches are in the same strain. Her *Physicae Elementorum, Fluminum aliquot Germaniae, Metallorum, Leguminum, Fructuum et Herbarum, Arborum et Arbustorum, Piscium denique Volatilium et Animantium Terrae Natura et Operationes* and her *Liber Compositae Medicinae* reflect a degree of scientific observation unusual in medieval times. Her theological works include an *Explicatio Symboli S. Athanasii*, an *Expositio Evangeliorum*, and an *Expositio Regulae S. Benedicti*, as well as the answers to questions put by the *Cistercians of Villars in Brabant. She also compiled a *Liber Vitae Meritorum* and composed various *carmina* for her nuns. Miracles, already reported during her life, multiplied at her tomb after her death. Various efforts to secure her canonization during the 13th and 14th cents. were unsuccessful; but from the 15th cent. she is called a saint in the *Roman Martyrology. Feast day, 17 Sept. (observed in several German dioceses).

A number of her works are collected in J. P. Migne, *PL*, cxcvii (the text of the 'Scivias' is particularly defective); further works ed. J. B. *Pitra, *Analecta Sacra*, viii (Monte-Cassino, 1882). Modern ed. of her 'Liber de Causis et Curis' by P. Kaiser (Teub., 1903) and of her 'Carmina' by G. M. Dreves in *A.H.M.A.* 1 (1907), pp. 483–92. Collection of works tr. into modern German by J. Bühler (Leipzig, 1922). *AA.SS.*, Sept. V (1755), pp. 629–701, inc. Lat. text of contemporary life by the monk Godefridus, pp. 679–82, cont. by Theodoricus, pp. 683–97 (repr. in J. P. Migne, loc. cit., cols. 91–150); modern Fr. tr. of this life publd. at Paris, 1907. 'Acta Inquisitionis de Virtutibus et Miraculis S. Hildegardis', ed. P. Bruder in *Anal. Boll.*, ii (1883), pp. 116–29. Modern lives of St. Hildegard by J. P. Schmelzeis (Freiburg i.Br., 1879), P. Franche ('Les Saints'; 1903), J. May (Kempten–Munich, 1911), and Francesca M. Steel (London [1914]). C. [J.] Singer, 'The Scientific Views and Visions of Saint Hildegard' in id. (ed.), *Studies in the History and Method of Science*, i (1917), pp. 1–55; H. Fischer, *Die heilige Hildegard von Bingen. Die erste deutsche Naturforscherin und Ärztin* (Münchener Beiträge zur Geschichte und Literatur der Naturwissenschaften und Medizin, Hftt. vii–viii; 1927). L. Bronarski, *Die Lieder der hl. Hildegard* (Veröffentlichungen der Gregorianischen Akademie zu Freiburg (Schweiz), ix; 1922). H. Liebeschütz, *Das allegorische Weltbild der heiligen Hildegard von Bingen* (Studien der Bibliothek Warburg, xvi; 1930). L. Baillet, O.S.B., 'Les Minatures du "Scivias" de Sainte Hildegarde conservé à la Bibliothèque de Wiesbaden' in *Fondation Eugène Piot. Monuments et mémoires publiés par l'Académie des Inscriptions et Belles-Lettres*, xix (1911), pp. 49–149, with plates. F. Vernet in *D.T.C.*, vi (1920), cols. 2468–80, s.v., with detailed bibl. I. Herwegen, O.S.B., in *L.Th.K.*, v (1933), cols. 30–2, s.v., with further bibl.

HILGENFELD, ADOLF (1823–1907), German Protestant theologian. He taught in the university of Jena from 1847 till his death, and was editor of the *Zeitschrift für wissenschaftliche Theologie* from 1858. He adopted the principles of F. C. *Baur and the *Tübingen School, but gave them a somewhat less radical cast, e.g. he defended the genuineness of 1 Thess., Phil., Philem. He wrote extensively on later Judaism, Biblical criticism, and Patristics, and was the author of an important edition of the extra-canonical NT books, *Novum Testamentum extra Canonem receptum* (4 vols., 1866).

List of his works, with brief life by Heinrich Hilgenfeld, son (Leipzig, 1906); additional material in *Zeitschrift für wissenschaftliche Theologie*, 1 (1908), pp. 14–24. Obituary notice by F. Nippold, ib., pp. 154–75. [The *Zeitschrift* finally came to an end in 1914].

HILLEL, School of. The followers of Hillel, an influential rabbinical teacher of the time of Christ. In opposition to the school of *Shammai, the Hillelites upheld a liberal and lenient interpretation of the *Law, and their attitude in controversy, whether religious or political, towards Jew and Gentile alike, was tolerant and conciliatory. The influence of the Hillelites was at its greatest after the destruction of the Temple (A.D. 70). The *Talmud records the many differences of opinion between the two schools.

A. Schwarz, *Die Controversen der Schammaiten und Hilleliten*, i (1893). I. Sonne, 'The Schools of Shammai and Hillel seen from Within' in *Louis Ginsberg Jubilee Volume, on the Occasion of his Seventieth Birthday*. English Section (New York, 1945), pp. 275–91, with reff. G. F. Moore, *Judaism in the First Three Centuries of the Christian Era*, i (Cambridge, Mass., and London, 1927), pp. 72–82, with notes in vol. iii (1930), pp. 29–31. H. Graetz, *Geschichte der Juden*, iii (ed. 5 by M. Brann, 1905), pt. i, pp. 206–11, and pt. ii, pp. 713–15; E. *Schürer, *Geschichte des jüdischen Volkes*, ii (ed. 4, 1907), esp. pp. 424–8. H. L. Strack, *Einleitung in Talmud und Midrasch* (ed. 5, 1930), pp. 118–22 (Eng. tr., Philadelphia, 1931), pp. 108–10, with notes, pp. 301–6. F. J. *Delitzsch, *Jesus und Hillel*. Mit Rücksicht auf Renan und Geiger verglichen (1866); P. Rieger, *Hillel und Jesus*. Ein Wort zur Versöhnung (1904). J. Klausner, *Jesus of Nazareth*. His Life, Times and Teaching (Eng. tr. from Heb. by H. Danby, 1925), esp. pp. 223–7.

HILTON, WALTER (d. 1396), English mystic. Of his life nothing is known except that he was an *Augustinian canon and at one time head of the Augustinian Priory at Thurgarton, Notts. His spiritual writings were widely read in England in the 15th cent. The most famous of them, the *Scala Perfectionis* (first printed 1494), describes the journey of the soul to the Spiritual Jerusalem. The two stages of purification 'in faith' and 'in feeling' are separated by the mystical 'dark night' in which the soul is detached from earthly things and directed towards the things of the spirit. The work is lucid and practical and shows the influence of Richard *Rolle and the *Cloud of Unknowing*. His *Epistle to a Devout Man in Temporal Estate* was printed in 1506 and his *The Song of the Angels* in 1521. Hilton's works were written in a lucid and vigorous English style. A curious tradition of the 15th cent. attributes to him the first three books of the *Imitation of Christ* generally assigned to *Thomas à Kempis.

Crit. ed. of the *Scala Perfectionis* by E. *Underhill (London, 1923); ed. based on the 1659 ed. of S. Cressy, O.S.B., by R. E. Guy, O.S.B. (ib., 1869), with introd. and full description of previous edd.; repr. of 1659 ed., with

introd. by J. B. *Dalgairns, Cong. Orat. (ib., 1870); modernized version of 1494 ed. with introd. by M. Noetinger, O.S.B., tr. from French (The Orchard Books, xiii; 1927). Dorothy Jones (ed.), *Minor Works of Walter Hilton* (ib., xvii; 1929). W. R. *Inge, *Studies of English Mystics* (1906), Lecture III, pp. 80–123; [M.] D. Knowles, O.S.B., *The English Mystics* (1927), pp. 107–27; T. W. Coleman, *English Mystics of the Fourteenth Century* (1938), ch. VI, pp. 106–30. Further bibl. in *C.B.E.L.*, i (1940), p. 194 f.

HINCMAR (c. 806–82), Abp. of *Reims. He was educated at the abbey of *St.-Denis, and in 822 accompanied his teacher, Abbot Hilduin, to the court of Louis the Pious. In 834 he officially entered the King's service, and after Louis's death attached himself to Charles the Bald, whose loyal supporter he became, thereby incurring the hostility of the Emp. Lothair I. Through Charles's influence he was elected Abp. of Reims in 845 and at once began to reorganize his diocese. Persistent friction with Lothair led the Emperor to seek his deposition under the pretext of Hincmar's having unjustly nullified the ordinations of his predecessor. A synod at Soissons in 853, however, came out in his favour, and its decision was confirmed by Benedict III in 855. Hincmar strongly opposed Lothair, King of Lorraine (the second son of Lothair I) when he wished to divorce his wife, Teutberga. In 863 he deposed Rothad, Bp. of Soissons, who had attacked his privileges as metropolitan, but his action was not upheld by *Nicholas I. He succeeded, however, in procuring the condemnation of his own nephew, Hincmar, Bp. of Laon, who had refused to recognize his authority. After King Lothair's death (869) he secured the succession of Charles the Bald, whom he crowned himself, despite the objection of the Pope. In 876 he again opposed the Pope, whose appointment of a *Vicar Apostolic for Germany and Gaul he regarded as an interference with his metropolitan rights. He died at Épernay when fleeing from the Normans.

Though not a speculative theologian, Hincmar took a prominent part in the controversy with the monk *Gottschalk on predestination. He wrote against him 'Ad Reclusos et Simplices', which elicited a sharp reply from *Ratramnus of *Corbie. Hincmar, after vainly seeking defenders among his friends, finally asked John Scotus *Erigena for help. The latter's work, 'De Divina Praedestinatione', roused a storm of indignation both against its author and against Hincmar. The controversy was continued at the Synods of *Quiercy (853), which gave a decision favourable to the archbishop, and *Valence (855), which was against him. Hincmar wrote in his defence 'De Praedestinatione Dei et Libero Arbitrio', a rather disorderly compilation of Scriptural and patristic texts, in which he argued that, if God predestines the wicked to hell, He must be accounted the author of sin. A reconciliation of both parties, largely through weariness with the conflict, was reached at the Synod of Tuzey in 860. Another dispute with Gottschalk and Ratramnus arose from Hincmar's changing the words 'Trina Deitas' from the *Vespers Hymn of the Common of Many

Martyrs into 'Summa Deitas', because he suspected the former version of *Tritheism. He defended his view in the treatise 'De Una et Non Trina Deitate' (c. 865), chiefly by quotations from authorities.

In his practical works, esp. 'De Divortio Lotharii et Teutbergae' (860), he displayed a vast knowledge of canon law, while in 'Opusculum LV Capitulorum', directed against Hincmar of Laon, he ably defended the rights of the metropolitan over his bishops. He was among the first writers to know of the *False Decretals, which were a product of the early years of his archiepiscopate.

Hincmar was also the author of a Life, without historical value, of St. *Remigius and of several poems. Opera, ed. J. *Sirmond, S.J. (2 vols., Paris, 1645), repr. in J. P. Migne, PL, cxxv and cxxvi. Epp. ed. in M.G.H., Epist. VIII (1939). Modern Lives by C. von Noorden (Bonn, 1863) and H. Schroers (Freiburg i.Br., 1884). J. P. Kirsch in C.E., vii (1910), p. 356 f.; H. Netzer in D.T.C., vi (1920), cols. 2482–6; J. Beckmann in L.Th.K., v (1933), col. 64 f.; L. Spätling in E.C., vi (1951), col. 1769 f., s.v. 'Incmaro', all with bibl.

HINNOM, Valley of. See Gehenna.

HINSLEY, ARTHUR (1865–1943), Abp. of *Westminster and cardinal. He was educated at Ushaw and the *English College at *Rome. After being head master of St. Bede's grammar school at Bradford from 1899 to 1904, he was pastor of several parishes and from 1917 to 1928 rector of the English College. In 1930 he was made Titular Abp. of Sardis and *Apostolic Delegate in Africa, and in 1935 Abp. of Westminster. He was created cardinal in 1937. He became known to wide circles through his foundation, in 1940, of the '*Sword of the Spirit', and through the vigorous spiritual and national leadership he gave to English RCs during the first years of the second World War.

J. C. Heenan, Cardinal Hinsley (1944).

HIPPO, Council of. A council of the Catholic (i.e. non-*Donatist) Church in Latin Africa held on 8 Oct. 393. A breviarium of its canons was read at the Council of *Carthage (397) and their substance, then re-enacted, passed, via the *Hispana and the *Quinisext Council, into general canon law.

Text of the breviarium pr. among the works of *Leo I, ed. P.-H. *Ballerini, iii (Venice, 1757), cols. 90–104; repr. in J. P. Migne, PL, lvi, 420–33. Hefele–Leclercq, ii (pt. 1; 1908), pp. 82–91.

HIPPOLYTUS, St. (c. 170–c. 236), ecclesiastical writer and doctor. Though the most important 3rd cent. theologian of the Roman Church, the facts of his life as well as his writings were soon forgotten in the W., perhaps by reason of his schismatic activities and of the fact that he wrote in Greek. Of his early life nothing is known. The assertion of *Photius that he was a disciple of St. *Irenaeus is doubtful. During the first decades of the 3rd cent. he must have been an important personality among the Roman presbyters; when *Origen came to Rome (c. 212) he attended one of his

sermons. Soon afterwards Hippolytus took an active part in attacking the doctrines of *Sabellius. He refused to accept the teaching of Pope *Zephyrinus (198–217), and under his successor, *Callistus (217–222), whom he rejected as a heretic, he seems to have set himself up as an anti-Pope. He continued to attack Callistus' successors, Urban (222–30) and Pontianus (230–5). In the persecution of the Emp. Maximin (235–8), however, he and Pontianus were exiled together to Sardinia, and it is very probable that before his death he was reconciled to the other party at Rome; for under Pope *Fabian (236–50) his body with that of Pontianus was brought to Rome (236). The *Liberian Catalogue (q.v., in the part dated c. 255) already considers him a Catholic martyr and gives him the rank of a priest, not of a bishop. When these facts had been forgotten in Rome, many legends grew up round his person. Pope *Damasus (366–84) makes him a priest of the *Novatianist Schism, a view later accepted by *Prudentius in his 'Passion of St. Hippolytus'. In the Roman Passionals of the 7th and 8th cents. he is represented as a soldier converted by St. *Lawrence, a legend which still survives in the Roman *Breviary. He has also been confused with a martyr of the same name who was buried at Portus, of which city he was believed to have been a bishop. Feast day, 13 Aug.

A list of Hippolytus's writings as well as his Easter tables were discovered on a statue of him, made probably during his lifetime and found in Rome in 1551. Hippolytus's principal work is his 'Refutation of all Heresies', of which books 4–10 were found in a MS. of Mount *Athos and published under the title 'Philosophoumena' in 1851 at *Oxford by E. Miller, who attributed it to Origen; but J. J. I. von *Döllinger argued that its author was Hippolytus. Its main object is to show that the philosophical systems described in books 1–4 are responsible for the heresies dealt with in the latter books. His other works include commentaries on Daniel and the Song of Songs, fragments from a treatise on the nature of the universe against *Noetus and *Plato, and the important treatise on the '*Apostolic Tradition' (q.v.). The 'Little Labyrinth', which Photius attributed to *Gaius of Rome, has also often been ascribed to Hippolytus. See also foll. entry.

The most interesting element in Hippolytus's teaching is his *Logos doctrine. Resuming the speculations of St. *Justin Martyr, he distinguished two states of the Word, the one immanent and eternal (λόγος ἐνδιάθετος) and the other exterior and temporal (λόγος προφορικός). Whether this Logos is really a Divine Person remains vague; Hippolytus seems to regard Him rather as an instrument of creation whose personality is completed only in the Incarnation when He receives the title of Son. This teaching implies a development in the Word which involves a change in the relations between Him and the Father and must ultimately lead to Ditheism, for which he was rebuked by Zephyrinus and Callistus. This charge gains force from his defective teaching on the Holy Ghost, to whom he refuses the title of 'Person'. The other important divergence between his teaching and that of the Roman bishops was his strenuous opposition to the mitigation of the penitential system necessitated by the influx of pagan converts in large numbers. This attitude is an instance among many others of the conservatism and harshness of his character, both of which reveal themselves esp. in his relentless hostility towards Callistus.

The first collected edition was that of J. A. *Fabricius (2 vols., Hamburg, 1716–18; repr. with additions in J. P. Migne, *PG*, x. 261–962). P. A. de *Lagarde, *Hippolyti Romani quae feruntur omnia graece* (London, 1858). Crit. ed. by H. Achelis, G. Bonwetsch, and others in *G.C.S.* (1897 ff.). E. Miller, *Origenis Philosophumena* (Oxford, 1851). *Comm. on Daniel*, ed. by M. Lefèvre and G. Bardy, with Fr. tr., in *Sources chrétiennes* (1947). Eng. trr. of many of his writings in A.N.C.L. (vols. vi and ix, pt. 2); of the *Philosophumena* by F. Legge (2 vols., S.P.C.K., 1921). For edd. of the 'Apostolic Tradition', see bibl. s.v. J. J. I. von *Dollinger, *Hippolytus und Kallistus* (1853; Eng. tr. 1876); C. *Wordsworth, *Hippolytus and the Church of Rome* (1853); J. B. Lightfoot, *The Apostolic Fathers*, I (2) (1890), pp. 317–477 ('Hippolytus of Portus'); G. Ficker, *Studien zur Hippolytfrage* (1893); H. Achelis, *Hippolytstudien* (T.U.), xvi, Hft. 4, 1897; several other items in this series are devoted to Hippolytus); A. D'Alès, *La Théologie de Saint Hippolyte* (1906); G. Bovini, *Sant' Ippolito della Via Tiburtina* (1942); P. Nautin, *Hippolyte et Josippe* (1947). Nautin's bold thesis that a certain Josippus and not Hippolytus was the author of the *Philosophumena* has met with little acceptance; its critics include B. *Capelle, B. Botte, M. Richard. See also bibl. to *Apostolic Tradition* for further items.

HIPPOLYTUS, Canons of St. A collection of canons, mainly on disciplinary and liturgical subjects, which were compiled in Greek prob. *c*. A.D. 500. They are dependent on the '*Apostolic Tradition' of St. *Hippolytus, to whom they are wrongly attributed, as well as on the *Apostolic Constitutions* (late 4th cent.). The Greek text is lost; but they survive in Arabic and Ethiopic versions of a Coptic trans. The extant MSS. are not earlier than the 13th cent. In the later 19th cent. they were generally held, notably by H. Achelis, to be prior to the 'Apostolic Tradition' (then dated in the 4th cent. or later) and St. Hippolytus often held to be the real author, at least of most of the work; and hence they received disproportionate attention in liturgical studies, e.g. large excerpts from them were printed in some editions of L. *Duchesne's *Origines du culte chrétien*. Since the researches of E. *Schwartz and R. H. *Connolly on the 'Apostolic Tradition', they have lost most of their importance.

Arab. text ed. by D. B. von Haneberg, Bp. of Speyer (Munich, 1870, with Lat. tr.); improved ed. (but with many doubtful conjectures) by H. Achelis in T.U., vi., Hft. 4 (1891). W. Riedel, *Die Kirchenrechtsquellen des Patriarchats Alexandrien* (1900), pp. 193–230, with revised (Germ.) tr. See also bibl. to *Apostolic Tradition*.

HISPANA CANONS. The name given to a collection of canons and decretals apparently compiled in Spain in the 6th–7th cents. They are arranged geographically by the parts of the Church in which they originated. The collection is also known as the *Isidoriana*, it having been (wrongly) attributed from the 9th cent.

onwards to St. *Isidore of Seville (d. 636). They formed one of the chief sources of the genuine historical material embodied in the '*False Decretals' (q.v.).

The text as found in the *False Decretals is pr. in all the principal edd. of the *Concilia* from J. Merlin (Paris, 1524 ['1523']) onwards. Only ed. based on early MSS. is that of F. A. Gonzalez (Madrid, 1808), repr. in J. P. Migne, *PL*, lxxxiv. F. Maassen, *Geschichte der Quellen und der Literatur des canonischen Rechts im Abendlande bis zum Ausgange des Mittelalters*, i (1870), pp. 667–716. Altaner (ed. 1951), p. 213, with recent bibl.

HOADLY, BENJAMIN (1676–1761), Bp. in succession of *Bangor, *Hereford, *Salisbury and *Winchester. He was educated at Catherine Hall, Cambridge, where he was elected a Fellow in 1697 and was a tutor from 1699 to 1701. Ordained priest in 1701, he was lecturer at St. Mildred's, Poultry, from 1701 to 1711 and Rector of St. Peter-le-Poor, London, from 1704 to 1724. At the beginning of his public life he advocated conformity for the sake of union; he soon won the leadership of the Low Church divines favoured by the Whigs through his controversy with F. *Atterbury and O. Blackall, Bp. of *Exeter (1708–16), on passive obedience and non-resistance. Recommended to the Queen by the House of Commons in 1709, he became rector of Streatham in 1710 and Chaplain to the Duke of Bedford. On the accession of George I he became chaplain to the King, and was consecrated Bp. of Bangor in 1716. His sermon of 31 Mar. 1717 on the 'Nature of the Kingdom or Church of Christ' provoked the *Bangorian controversy (q.v.). Translated to Hereford in 1721 and to Salisbury in 1723, when he resigned the rectory of Streatham, he was translated to Winchester in 1734. He excited stiff opposition by maintaining that the Lord's Supper was purely commemorative and in upholding *Latitudinarian views generally.

He spent very little time in his dioceses, never visiting Bangor, but living mainly in London, where he engaged in political and theological controversy. His many publications include *A Defence of the Reasonableness of Conformity* (1707; against E. *Calamy the younger), *A Preservative against the Principles and Practices of Non-Jurors both in Church and State* (1716), *A Plain Account of the Nature and End of the Sacrament of the Lord's Supper* (1735) and *The Repeal of the Corporation and Test Acts* (1736; a plea for toleration).

J. Hoadly (son [1711–76], ed.), *The Works of Benjamin Hoadly* (3 vols., 1773), with acct. of author, i, pp. v–xxv. N. Sykes, 'Benjamin Hoadly, Bishop of Bangor', in F. J. C. Hearnshaw (ed.), *The Social and Political Ideals of some English Thinkers of the Augustan Age* (1928), pp. 112–57; id., *Church and State in England in the XVIIIth Century* (1934), esp. pp. 332–62. G. G. Perry in *D.N.B.*, xxviii (1891), pp. 16–21.

HOBBES, THOMAS (1588–1679), philosopher. In early life he travelled much abroad as tutor to the Cavendish family, and met and was influenced by F. *Bacon, G. *Galileo, and M. *Mersenne, the philosopher friend of R. *Descartes. He displeased both Royalists and Parliamentarians by holding that, although sovereignty is ultimately derived from the people, it is transferred to the monarch by implicit contract, so that while the power of the sovereign is absolute, it is not of *Divine right. From 1640 to 1651 Hobbes was in exile, for the most part in Paris, where from 1646 to 1648 he was tutor to the Prince of Wales (later *Charles II). In 1651 he returned and submitted to the *Commonwealth, and in the same year published his greatest work, the *Leviathan, which, though it has been called a reaction against the 'liberty' of the Renaissance and Reformation, is really a philosophical exposition of the system of political absolutism which replaced the supremacy of the medieval Church. In his *Questions Concerning Liberty, Necessity, and Chance* (1656) he expounded a doctrine of psychological *determinism in opposition to Bp. J. *Bramhall's defence of free will. In 1666 the *Leviathan*, which from the first was considered to be atheistic, was censured by name by the House of Commons, and thereafter its author was not allowed to publish ethical writings in England. Hobbes was perhaps the first philosopher to attempt seriously to base a theory of human conduct upon natural science; he was a pioneer in psychology; and his early work *De cive* (1642; Eng. trans., 1651) gives him some claim to be considered the founder of modern social science. His doctrine of political absolutism cut at the root of ethics, however, as it left no room for any genuine moral distinction between good and bad.

Collected ed. of Hobbes's *Opera Philosophica* (Amsterdam, 1668; suppl., London, 1675); of his *Moral and Political Works* (London, 1720), incl. his autobiography, pp. ix–xxviii. Complete ed. of his *English Works* (11 vols., London, 1839–45) and his *Opera Philosophica* (5 vols., ib., 5 vols., 1839–45), both by Sir W. Molesworth. Reprint of the 1651 ed. of the *Leviathan* (Oxford, 1909), with introd. by W. G. Pogson Smith. The extensive literature on Hobbes includes studies by G. Croom Robertson (London, 1886), L. Stephen ('English Men of Letters', 1904), A. E. *Taylor (London, 1908), B. Landry (Paris, 1930), and J. Laird (London, 1934). L. Strauss, *The Political Philosophy of Hobbes* (Oxford, 1936). J. Souilhé and others, *La Pensée et l'influence de Th. Hobbes* (Archives de Philosophie, xii. 2, 1936). H. Macdonald–Mary Hargreaves, *Thomas Hobbes.* A Bibliography (1952). Überweg, iii, pp. 249–59, with bibl., p. 661 f. F. J. E. Woodbridge in *H.E.R.E.*, vi (1913), pp. 728–30, s.v.; C. Constantin in *D.T.C.*, vii (pt. 1; 1922), cols. 1–11, s.v.

HOCKTIDE (also 'Hock Monday' and 'Hock Tuesday'). The second Monday and Tuesday after Easter, on which in medieval times money was collected for church and parish uses, and various sports and amusements took place. The merrymaking at this season survived in some places until the 19th cent. The origin of the name is unknown.

HODGE, CHARLES (1797–1878), American *Presbyterian theologian. He was ordained in 1821, and taught at Princeton for nearly his whole life. His most important works are his commentaries on Rom. (1835), Eph. (1856), 1 Cor. (1857), 2 Cor. (1859), as well as *Constitutional History of the Presbyterian Church in the United States* (2 vols., 1839–40), *Systematic Theology* (3 vols., 1871–3), and *What is Darwinism?* (1874). If less an original thinker than a systematizer and defender of

traditional *Calvinism, Hodge has a real claim to be considered one of the greatest of American theologians, and he had a great influence and following. He took a broader and more tolerant view of other forms of Christianity than many of those in general sympathy with his position.

A. A. Hodge (son), *The Life of C. Hodge, D.D.* (1881); C. A. Salmond, *Princetonia: Charles and A. A. Hodge* (1888). R. H. Nichols in *Dict. Amer. Biog.* ix (1932, p. 98. f)

HODY, HUMPHREY (1659–1707), Anglican divine. Having entered Wadham College, Oxford, in 1676, he was elected Fellow in 1685. In his *Contra historiam Aristeae de LXX interpretibus Dissertatio* (1684) he proved that the 'Letter of *Aristeas' was a forgery. His support of the Established Church against the *Nonjurors brought him to the notice of Abp. J. *Tillotson, who made him his chaplain; and in 1698 he was made Regius professor of Greek at Oxford. His researches into the text of the *Septuagint are embodied in his *De Bibliorum Textis Originalibus* (4 vols., 1703). By his will a number of exhibitions for the study of Hebrew and Greek, which still bear his name, were established at Wadham College.

Study (in Latin) of his life and writings by S. Jebb prefixed to his edition of Hody's *De Graecis Illustribus, Linguae Graecae, Literarumque Humaniorum Instauratoribus, eorum Vitis, Scriptis et Elogiis* (posthumous, 1742), pp. v–xxix. G. Goodwin in *D.N.B.*, xxvii (1891), p. 77 f.

HOFBAUER, St. CLEMENT MARY (1751–1820), the 'Apostle of Vienna'. He was a native of Tasswitz in Moravia and the son of a grazier and butcher; and at the age of 15 he became a baker's apprentice. Led by his religious aspirations to become a hermit, and later a student for the priesthood (1780–4) in Vienna and Rome, he entered the congregation of the *Redemptorists at Rome in 1784 and was professed and ordained in 1785. In the same year he returned to Vienna, but unable to found a house there because of the anti-religious *Josephinist legislation, he went on to Warsaw, where he laboured from 1787 to 1808, chiefly among the German-speaking population. Here he met with remarkable success, devoting himself esp. to the cure of souls and to educational and charitable activities. Appointed Vicar-General for the houses of his congregation N. of the Alps in 1793, he founded several establishments in Poland and one at Jestetten, nr. Schaffhausen (1802). In 1808 he was driven from Warsaw by Napoleon and went back to Vienna. At first he worked mainly at the Italian church, but from 1813 onwards he was confessor to the *Ursulines. His influence in the capital, which spread from the highest to the lowest, powerfully counteracted the effects of *Josephinism and the *Aufklärung. The Redemptorists, however, could not be established in Austria till shortly after his death. He was canonized in 1909. Feast day, 15 Mar.

Monumenta Hofbaueriana (1915 ff.; 12 vols. to 1949, Cracow and Thorn). Lives by S. Brunner (Vienna, 1858), M. Haringer (Vienna, 1877), M. Bauchinger (Vienna, 1888), A. Innerkofler (Ratisbon, 1910), J. Hofer (Freiburg i.Br.

1920; Eng. tr., New York, 1926), G. Hünermann (Innsbruck, 1936), and J. Carr, C.SS.R. (London, 1939). M. B. Schweitzer, 'Die Einwirkung des hl. Clemens Maria Hofbauer auf das Geistesleben in Wien' in *Hist. J.*, xlviii (1928), pp. 389–460.

HÖFFDING, HARALD (1843–1931), Danish philosopher. From 1883 to 1915 he was professor at Copenhagen. In his earlier years he was much under the influence of S. *Kierkegaard, but almost completely abandoned his teaching later. He sought at once to do full justice to the claims of the natural sciences and to show that all knowledge received meaning only in relation to the realm of value. But while he upheld a spiritual interpretation of the universe, he denied that there were sufficient theoretical grounds for applying the notions of 'cause' and 'personality' to the Absolute or for affirming (or denying) belief in personal immortality. He described his position as 'critical monism'. His many writings included a widely-used history of philosophy, *Den nyere Filosofis Historie* (1894; Eng. trans., 2 vols., 1900) and a *Religionsfilosofi* (1901; Eng. trans., 1906).

H. Höffding, *Udvalgte Skrifter* (7 vols., 1902–6); id., *Erindringer* [with portrait] (1928). *Correspondance entre Harald Höffding et Emile Meyerson*, ed. F. Brandt, Hans Höffding, and others (Copenhagen, 1939). G. Schott, *Harald Höffding als Religionsphilosoph* (1913); V. Hansen, *Harald Höffding som Religionsfilosof* (Copenhagen, 1923).

HOFFMANN, MELCHIOR (c. 1500–c. 1543), German *Anabaptist. A leather-dresser by profession, he joined the *Lutherans and became a lay-preacher in Livonia in 1523. Having come into conflict with the authorities he left for Stockholm in 1526, where he became more and more imbued with eschatological ideas and prophesied the approaching end of the world. After a short stay in Holstein he had a disputation with J. *Bugenhagen at Flensburg in 1529 in which he denied the Lutheran doctrine of the Lord's Supper, holding it to be a mere sign. He was consequently banished from Denmark, and went to Strassburg, where he joined the Anabaptists. Between 1530 and 1533 he preached there, in E. Friesland, and in Holland. In 1533 he returned to Strassburg, which was to be the New Jerusalem, to await the Last Day. He was arrested and sentenced to imprisonment for life, but remained unshaken in his eschatological beliefs till his death. His influence on his contemporaries was considerable, and the 'Melchiorites' survived him as a distinct party among the Anabaptists.

F. O. Zur Linden, *Melchior Hoffmann, Ein Prophet der Wiedertäufer* (1885). A. Hegler in *P.R.E.* (ed. 3), viii (1900), pp. 222–7, and W. Koehler in *R.G.G.* (ed. 2), ii (1928), cols. 1982 f., with bibl.

HOFFMEISTER, JOHANNES (c. 1509–1547), *Augustinian hermit. He entered the Augustinian monastery at Colmar as a youth, studied at several German universities, and was made prior in 1533. His life was devoted to the defence of his order against *Lutheran teaching and to the inner reform of the

Church by preaching and writing. In 1543 he became provincial of the Rhenish-Swabian province which had been severely affected by Protestantism. His powerful sermons soon made him widely known and he was frequently called upon to preach on important occasions, e.g. at the Diet of *Worms (1545) and the (second) Colloquy of *Ratisbon (1546). In 1546 he was made vicar-general of the Augustinian hermits in Germany, but his work was cut short by his death in 1547. His writings, which are occasionally marred by their polemical extravagance, include two books of Dialogues (1538) and his *Loci Communes* (Mainz, 1545; often repr.), a collection of Patristic extracts.

N. Paulus, *Der Augustinermönch J. Hoffmeister*. Ein Lebensbild aus der Reformationszeit (Freiburg i.Br., 1891). A. von Druffel, 'Der Elsässer Augustinermönch J Johannes H offmeister und seine Korrespondenz mit dem Ordensgeneral Hieronymus Seripando' in *Abh.* (Bayr.), hist. Kl., xiv, Abt. i (1879), pp. 135–96.

HOFMANN, JOHANN CHRISTIAN KONRAD VON (1810–77), German *Lutheran theologian. A native of Nuremberg, he studied at Erlangen and Berlin, and became lecturer at Erlangen university in 1838. In 1842 he was called to Rostock as professor of theology, and returned to Erlangen in the same capacity in 1845, where he remained till the end of his life. His most important works were *Weissagung und Erfüllung im Alten und Neuen Testament* (2 parts, 1841–4), a study of the theology of prophecy; *Der Schriftbeweis* (3 pts., 1852–6), a treatise in the course of which the vicarious Atonement was denied; *Schutzschriften für eine neue Weise, alte Wahrheit zu lehren* (1856–1859), written in defence of the preceding; and *Die hl. Schriften des Neuen Testaments* (8 parts, 1862–78), an unfinished commentary on the NT. Hofmann aimed at being an uncompromising exponent of Lutheran doctrines. His disciples became known as the 'Erlangen School'.

Theologische Briefe d r Professoren [F.] Delitzsch und von Hofmann (ed. W. Volck, 1891). Life by P. Wapler (Leipzig, 1914). P. Bachmann, *J. C. K. Hofmanns Versöhnungslehre und der über sie geführte Streit* (1910); M. Schellbach, *Theologie und Philosophie bei von Hofmann* (1935). A. Hauck in *P.R.E.* (ed. 3), viii (1900), pp. 234–41.

HOHENHEIM. See *Paracelsus, Theophrastus*.

HOLCOT, ROBERT (d. 1349), medieval theologian. A native of Northamptonshire, he entered the *Dominican Order and studied and taught first at Cambridge, and later at the Dominican house in *Oxford. He is said to have died while nursing the sick at Northampton during the plague. 26 treatises attributed to him are extant, dealing with various subjects of philosophy and theology, but their genuineness is much disputed. He appears frequently to leave the *Thomist tradition of his order and to take up *nominalist positions, e.g. in setting faith and reason in direct opposition and hence doubting the validity of the Aristotelian logic in matters of revelation. In his teaching on merit and the freedom of the will, he largely followed St. *Augustine; but in his voluntarism he went even beyond *William of Occam, holding that God was the primal cause of sin. The well-known 'Philobiblon seu de amore librorum' has often been attributed to him, but should probably be ascribed to Richard de Bury, Bp. of Durham (d. 1345).

Holcot's works were pr. in the 15th and 16th cent. (no modern edd.). 'Philobiblon' publd. Cologne, 1473; modern ed. by A. Altramura, Naples, 1954; Eng. tr. by J. B. Inglis (anon.), London, 1832. B. Smalley, 'Robert Holcot' in *Archivum Fratrum Praedicatorum*, xxvi (1956), pp. 5–97. Quétif–Échard, i, pp. 629–32. Überweg, ii, p. 588 f., with bibl. p. 783. R. Coulon in *D.T.C.*, vii (pt. 1; 1922), col. 30 f., s.v.

HOLGATE, ROBERT (c. 1481–1555), Abp. of *York. He was probably educated at the *Gilbertine house of studies in Cambridge, where he was university preacher in 1524. He became Master of the Order of *Sempringham, and, on the eve of its dissolution (1537), Bp. of Llandaff. He proved an active member of the King's Council in the North, and in 1538 he succeeded C. *Tunstall as Lord President. In 1545 he was translated to York. His marriage and strong support of the Edwardian reforming measures brought about his deprivation by the Marians in 1554. Holgate founded three grammar schools and an almshouse, all in Yorkshire.

A. G. Dickens, 'The Marriage and Character of Archbishop Holgate' in *E.H.R.*, lii (1937), pp. 428–42. W. Hunt in *D.N.B.*, xxvii (1891), pp. 128–30.

HOLIDAYS OF OBLIGATION. See *Feasts of Obligation*.

HOLINESS, The Code of, also 'Law of Holiness'. The collection of Mosaic legislation in Lev. 17–26, so named by A. Klostermann in 1877, and designated 'H'. The subjects dealt with are animal sacrifice and the prohibition of eating blood (17), laws of marriage and chastity (18), miscellaneous religious and ethical precepts (19), penalties for violation of the ritual laws (20), the priesthood (21 f.), the sacred calendar, incl. *Sabbath, *Passover, *Weeks, and the Day of *Atonement (23), the sacred lamp and the *Shewbread (24. 1–9), punishment for blasphemy and the *Lex Talionis* (24. 10–25), the *Sabbatical Year and *Jubilee (25) and final exhortation (26). The recurrence of certain phrases ('I am the Lord'; 'for I, the Lord, am holy'; 'to observe and to do', etc.) supports the view that the section is a unity. Acc. to critical views of the OT, it is post-*Deuteronomic, having been drawn up after the Fall of Jerusalem in 586 B.C. (allusions to the Exile, 26. 34–44; influence of Jer. and perh. Ezek., though some critics hold that the Code influenced Ezek.); and prob. left its compiler's hands c. 550 B.C. It may be supposed to have been united with the rest of *P (q.v.) some 75–100 years later.

K. H. Graf, *Die geschichtlichen Bücher des Alten Testaments* (1866), pp. 66–83, with suggestion that these chapters in their present form were the work of Ezekiel. A. Klostermann, 'Beiträge zur Entstehungsgeschichte des Pentateuchs' in *Zeitschrift für die gesammte lutherische Theologie*

und Kirche, xxxviii (1877), pp. 401–445; id., *Der Pentateuch* (1893), pp. 386–418. L. Horst, *Leviticus XVII–XXVI und Hezekiel* (1881); B. Baentsch, *Das Heiligkeits-Gesetz* (1893). See also works cited under *Pentateuch* and comm. to *Leviticus*, cited s.v.

HOLINESS, His. A title which in the early Church was regularly used of all bishops. Since c. 600 it has been restricted to *patriarchs, a use still followed in the E. Church. In the W., since the 14th cent., it has been used only of the Pope. The title was also occasionally given to the Byzantine Emperors, and there is an instance of its use by *John of Salisbury of Henry II of England.

HOLLAND, Christianity in. The territory now known as Holland was reached by Christian missionaries as early as c. 630. Its effective conversion was mainly the work of St. *Willibrord (q.v.), Bp. of Utrecht from 695 to 739, who at one stage had the support of St. *Boniface. The range and success of Willibrord's activities brought the whole country under the influence of the see of Utrecht, which was the only bishopric until modern times, and its Prince Bishop exerted a dominating influence on the subsequent history of the Church. In the course of the later Middle Ages the see lost much of its political power to the Counts of Holland and Guelders, the Bishop finally surrendering his temporal claims to *Charles V in 1526.

Before the country threw off the Spanish yoke, the Reformation had made its influence felt. *Lutheranism was never popular; but *Calvinism formed a rallying creed for the revolt and found an early exponent in Philip von *Marnix (q.v.). In 1574 the University of *Leyden was established in the Calvinist interest. A conflict between orthodoxy and liberalism raged in the early years of the 17th cent., represented by the two Leyden theologians, S. *Gomarus and J. *Arminius. After the definitive condemnation of the latter group ('*Remonstrants') at the Synod of *Dort (1618–1619), its leaders were executed or exiled and for some two hundred years strict Calvinism was the official creed. The introduction of a more liberal form of Church government under William I in 1816 led some of the stricter Protestants to separate and organize themselves as the 'Christian Reformed Church'. In 1848 the Church was disestablished; in 1857 denominational religious instruction ceased in the schools; and in 1876 'theology' gave place to 'comparative religion' at the universities.

In an endeavour to find favour with the Catholics, *Philip II secured the creation of five new sees under Utrecht, which was now raised to an Archbishopric (1560). But the experiment was a failure, and from 1580 to 1853 the RC Church was without territorial Bishops, being governed by *Vicars Apostolic or Papal Legates. From 1583 to 1795 it was subjected by the government to severe penal restrictions. In 1697 accusations of *Jansenism were launched from Rome against the RCs of Holland, notably against Petrus Codde (1648–1710), then Vicar-General and titular Abp. of Philippi. In 1702 he was officially censured and a schism began. Codde's followers upheld the continuity of their communion with the national Catholic Church of the past. The support of the French Jansenists, who refused to accept the bull '*Unigenitus' (1713), secured for these '*Old Catholics', as they came to be called, the maintenance of the *Apostolic Succession; and the group still survives as a branch of the Old Catholic Church. The main body of Dutch Catholics, however, accepted the condemnation of Jansenism. They looked largely to external (esp. *Jesuit) influence for guidance and protection until the Archiepiscopal see of Utrecht was restored in 1853. In modern Holland (c. 1950) they are a vigorous body, being esp. strong in the provinces of Limburg (c. 93 per cent) and North Brabant (c. 89 per cent).

The Protestants (c. 1950) form c. 47 per cent of the total population (of which c. 36 per cent belong to the 'Dutch Reformed Church', the remainder to other Churches, also mainly Calvinist), the Roman Catholics c. 39 per cent, and those of no confession c. 15 per cent. The Old Catholics are now not more than a few thousand.

The principal works are in Dutch. In English there is a general introduction by P. H. Ditchfield, *The Church in the Netherlands* (1892; dealing with Belgium and Holland). Also D. Nobbs, *Theocracy and Toleration*. A Study of the Disputes in Dutch Calvinism from 1600 to 1650 (1938); J. H. Mackay, *Religious Thought in Holland during the Nineteenth Century* (Hastie Lectures, 1909–1911; 1911) and E. C. Vanderlaan, *Protestant Modernism in Holland* (1924).
W. Moll, *Kerkgeschiedenis van Nederland voor de Hervorming* [1871]; Germ. tr. as *Die vorreformatorische Kirchengeschichte der Niederlande* (1895). J. J. Altmeyer, *Précurseurs de la réforme aux Pays-Bas* (posthumous; 2 vols., 1886; on Belgium and Holland). L. J. Rogier, *Geschiedenis van het Katholicisme in Noord-Nederland in de 16e en de 17e Eeuw* (3 vols., 1945–7). F. Siegmund-Schultze (ed.), *Ekklesia*, iii, Lieferung 1 (Lieferung 9 des Gesamtwerkes), *Die evangelischen Kirchen der Niederlande* (1934), with bibl. E. Lagerwey, 'Die Niederländische Altkatholische Kirche' in F. Siegmund-Schultze (ed.), *Ekklesia*, iii, Lieferung 3 (Lieferung 11 des Gesamtwerkes), pp. 54–64 (484–94 of vol. 3). *Archief voor Nederlandsche Kerkgeschiedenis* (The Hague, 1885–99), cont. as *Nederlandsch Archief voor Kerkgeschiedenis* (ib., 1900 ff.). J. A. Gerth van Wijk in *P.R.E* (ed. 3), viii (1900), pp. 263–79, s.v. 'Holland, Kirchliche Statistik'; Dr. Brouwer in *R.G.G.* (ed. 2), iv (1930), cols. 538–47, s.v. 'Niederland', with bibl. See also bibl. to *Arminianism, Calvinism, Devotio Moderna* and *Old Catholics*.

HOLLAND, HENRY SCOTT (1847–1918), theologian and preacher. Educated at Eton and at Balliol College, *Oxford, where he was influenced by T. H. *Green, he was a Senior Student at Christ Church from 1870 to 1884, canon of St. Paul's Cathedral from 1884 to 1910, and Regius professor of divinity at Oxford from 1910 until his death. He shared the outlook of *Lux Mundi, to which he contributed the first essay (on 'Faith'). He was a robust and independent philosopher and theologian, keenly interested in relating Christian principles to the social and economic problems of human living. The *Christian Social Union found in him its most brilliant spokesman, and he was editor of the *Commonwealth* from 1895 to 1912. His writings, mainly collections of

sermons, include *Logic and Life* (1882), *Creed and Character* (1887), and *God's City* (1894). He was also the author of the hymn 'Judge Eternal, throned in splendour' (E.H., 423).

Stephen Paget, *Henry Scott Holland*, Memoir and Letters (1921); E. Lyttelton, *The Mind and Character of Henry Scott Holland* (1926). T. B. *Strong in *D.N.B.*, 1912–1921, pp. 260–2.

HOLOCAUST (Gk. ὁλόκαυστον, 'something entirely burnt up'). A sacrifice completely consumed by fire ('burnt-offering'), and thus a perfect sacrifice. Less accurately, the word is also used of a sacrifice with many victims.

HOLSTE, LUCAS (1596–1661) (**Holstenius**), *Vatican librarian. A native of Hamburg, he went to *Leyden for his studies, where he was converted in 1625–6 to the RC Church. He became secretary, and later librarian (1636), to Cardinal Francesco *Barberini, and subsequently librarian of the Vatican. In 1665 he received Queen *Christina of Sweden's public abjuration of Protestantism at Innsbruck. He was a scholar of enormous erudition, whose writings included *Codex Regularum Monasticarum et Canonicarum* (3 vols., 1661), studies in many classical and ecclesiastical writings (*Porphyry; *Eusebius, *Contra Hieroclem*; the later Pythagoreans) and an edition of the *Liber Diurnus* (1660).

His correspondence (*Epistolae ad Diversos*) was ed. by J. F. Boissonade (Paris, 1817). [N. Wilckens], *Leben des gelehrten Lucae Holstenii* (Hamburg, 1723). L. G. Pélissier, 'Les Amis d'Holstenius' in *Mélanges d'Archéologie et d'Histoire de l'École française de Rome*, vi (1886), pp. 554–87, vii (1887), pp. 62–128, and viii (1888), pp. 323–402 and 521–608. R. Almagià, *L' opera geografica di Luca Holstenio* (Studi e Testi, 102; 1942).

HOLTZMANN, HEINRICH JULIUS (1832–1910), Protestant theologian and Biblical critic. After study at Berlin university and a pastorate at Baden (1854–57), he taught at Heidelberg (1858–74) and Strassburg (1874–1904). He was a moderate liberal in his beliefs. In *Die synoptischen Evangelien* (1863) he strongly defended the *Marcan hypothesis, at that date rarely accepted. In his later writings he argued for a psychological development in our Lord's self-consciousness, maintaining that there were two principal periods in His earthly life, that of 'success' which reached its climax at *Caesarea Philippi, and a subsequent period of 'failure', when the new conception of a suffering Messiah supervened. His books include an *Einleitung in das NT* (1885); commentaries on the Synoptic Gospels (1889), the Johannine books (1890), and Acts (1901); a *Lehrbuch der NT Theologie* (2 vols., 1896–7); and *Richard *Rothe's Speculatives System* (1899).

Theologische Abhandlungen. Eine Festgabe zum 17. Mai 1902 für H. J. Holtzmann (1902). A. *Jülicher, 'Heinrich Holtzmanns Bedeutung für die neutestamentliche Wissenschaft' in *Protestantische Monatshefte*, vi (1902), pp. 165–72.

HOLY ALLIANCE, The. The declaration signed by Alexander I of Russia, Francis I of Austria, and Friedrich Wilhelm III of Prussia on 26 Sept. 1815, and eventually by all the sovereigns of Europe except the Prince Regent of England, the Pope, and the Sultan. It laid down that the relations of the powers would henceforth be based on 'the sublime truths which the Holy Religion of our Saviour teaches'; that the actions of princes would be guided by justice, charity, and peace; and that the signatories would regard each other as brothers and 'on all occasions and in all places lend each other aid and assistance'. The project originated with the Czar, under the inspiration of Barbara J. von *Krüdener, and appears to have been conceived in sincerity, though Metternich called it a 'loud-sounding nothing', and Castlereagh 'a piece of sublime mysticism and nonsense'. It soon became synonymous, however, with the combined interests of the Great Powers by whom Europe was ruled after 1815 and their policy of reaction. As a diplomatic instrument it was never effective, though it inspired Nicholas II to summon the first international peace conference at the Hague in 1899.

Text in E. Reich (ed.), *Select Documents Illustrating Mediaeval and Modern History* (1905), pp. 119–21, with reff. J. H. Pirenne, *La Sainte Alliance. Organisation européenne de la paix mondiale* (2 vols., [1946–9]). E. Muhlenbeck, *Étude sur les origines de la Sainte Alliance* [1887]. W. P. Cresson, *The Holy Alliance. The European Background of the Monroe Doctrine* (New York and London, 1922). On the circumstances leading up to and following the making of the alliance, see also C. K. Webster, *The Congress of Vienna, 1814–1815* [1919]; id., *The European Alliance, 1813–1825* (Calcutta, 1929). H. G. Schenk, *The Aftermath of the Napoleonic Wars* (1947).

HOLY CITY, The. *Jerusalem (Mt. 27. 53). Among the Arabs the city is now commonly known as *el-Kuds*, *i.e.* 'the Holy'.

HOLY CLUB, The. The nickname given to the group of '*methodists' which Charles and John *Wesley formed at Oxford in 1729 for the deepening of personal religion. At first it met weekly on Sundays, but later every evening. The Greek Testament and the classics were read, and its members received Holy Communion very frequently and fasted on Wednesdays and Fridays. Its members also undertook pastoral work, e.g. among those in the Oxford gaol.

HOLY COAT, The. Both the cathedral of Trier and the parish church at Argenteuil claim the possession of Christ's 'coat without seam' (Jn. 19. 23). Dating alike from about the 12th cent. the two traditions agree both in admitting the other's relic to be a genuine garment of Christ's, and in insisting that their own is that mentioned in Scripture. The Trier tradition would seem to hold the advantage in Papal utterances and popular devotion. Over two million pilgrims visited the Trier relic when it was exposed in 1933. At other places, e.g. Mantua, where an alleged garment of Christ is shown, there is a less-developed cultus.

O. Zöckler in *P.R.E.* (ed. 3), xvii (1906), pp. 58–61; F. Lauchert in *C.E.*, vii (1910), pp. 400–2; L. Kosters in *L.Th.K.*, viii (1936), cols. 928–32, all with extensive bibls.

HOLY CROSS DAY. The name given in the BCP calendar to 14 Sept., also known as the Feast of the '*Exaltation of the Holy Cross' (q.v.).

HOLY DAYS OF OBLIGATION. See *Feasts of Obligation*.

HOLY DOOR, The (*Porta Santa*). The door in the façade of St. Peter's, Rome, which is nearest the *Vatican Palace. The Holy Door is normally sealed with brickwork, except during the *Holy Year, when it is opened for the passage of those wishing to gain the *Indulgence of the Holy Year. The opening and closing of the Holy Door at the beginning and end of the Holy Year are ceremonially performed by the Pope assisted by the Cardinal Penitentiary.

H. Thurston, S.J., *The Holy Year of Jubilee* (1900), ch. ii, 'The Porta Sancta', pp. 28–54, with reff.; Appendix C, 'The Porta Sancta and the Golden Gate of Jerusalem', pp. 405–11.

HOLY FAMILY, The. The Infant Jesus, His Mother (St. *Mary), and His foster-father (St. *Joseph). The cult of the Holy Family as such became widely popular in the RC Church in the 17th cent., and since that time several religious congregations have been founded under this title. A feast of the Holy Family was instituted by the Congregation of *Rites on 26 Oct. 1921, and is kept on the First Sunday after the *Epiphany. Of the innumerable paintings of the Holy Family one of the most celebrated is that by B. E. *Murillo (1670), now in the Louvre.

Institution of Feast in *A.A.S.*, xiii (1921), p. 543 f. G. Löw, C.SS.R., and W. Wehr in *E.C.*, xi (1953), cols. 1551–5, s.v. 'Sacra Famiglia', with bibl.

HOLY FATHER, The Most (*Beatissimus Pater*). A title of the Pope (in common usage abbreviated to 'Holy Father'), which is first quoted in English *c.* 1380.

HOLY GHOST, The. An alternative title of the *Holy Spirit (q.v.), esp. in liturgical usage.

HOLY HELPERS. See *Auxiliary Saints*.

HOLY INNOCENTS. The children of *Bethlehem, 'from two years old and under', massacred by order of *Herod the Great, in a vain attempt to destroy the Infant Jesus (Mt. 2. 16–18). The event is commemorated in the calendar on 28 Dec. Acc. to the Roman Rite, this feast, should it fall on a Sunday, is kept with the full privileges of a martyrs' day (red vestments, and the recital of the *Gloria in Excelsis); but, falling on a week-day, it is celebrated in purple with a penitential rite.

V. Ermoni in *Dict. Bibl.*, iii (1903), cols. 879–81, s.v. 'Innocents (Saints)'; H. *Leclercq, O.S.B., in *D.A.C.L.*, vii (pt. 1; 1926), cols. 608–16, s.v. 'Innocents (Massacre des)'.

HOLY ISLAND. See *Lindisfarne.*

HOLY LANCE, The. See *Lance, The Holy.*

HOLY LAND, The. A name given to Palestine since the Middle Ages with reference both to its having been the scene of the Incarnation and also to the existing sacred sites there, esp. the Holy Sepulchre at Jerusalem.

HOLY MOUNTAIN, The. A designation of Mount *Athos from the large collection of monasteries which covers it.

HOLY NAME OF JESUS. See *Name of Jesus.*

HOLY OFFICE, The. The Roman *Congregation established in connexion with the *Inquisition (q.v.) by *Paul III in 1542 under the title of 'Sacra Congregatio Romanae et Universalis Inquisitionis seu Sancti Officii' as the final court of appeal in trials of heresy. Originally composed of six cardinals, it was reorganized, and the number raised to 13, by *Sixtus V in 1587. On all important occasions the Pope presides in person. In 1908 it was affected by *Pius X's general reorganization of the Roman Congregations (q.v.), and its title changed to 'Congregatio Sancti Officii'. It is now the court to which all final decisions concerning faith and morals are reserved.

H. Bangen, *Die römische Curie, ihre gegenwärtige Zusammensetzung und ihr Geschäftsgang* (1854), pp. 91–124. J. Simor, 'De Sacris Congregationibus Romanis S. Officii et Concilii. I: De Sacra Cong. Officii' in *Archiv für katholisches Kirchenrecht*, xv (1866), pp. 133–6. B. Ojetti, S.J., in *C.E.*, xiii, 1912), pp. 137–9, s.v. 'Roman Congregations'; A. De Jorio in *E.C.*, iv (1950), cols. 313–15, s.v. 'Congregazioni Romane', both with bibl. See also works cited under *Inquisition* and *Roman Congregations.*

HOLY OILS. See *Chrism.*

HOLY ORDERS. The higher grades (*sacri ordines*) of the Christian Ministry, i.e. those of *Bishop, *Priest, and *Deacon (qq.v.). In the RC Church the *Sub-diaconate is also reckoned among the 'Major Orders' (q.v.).

HOLY PLACES, The. The places in Palestine to which pilgrimage is made on account of their traditional association with many of the principal Biblical events.

HOLY ROMAN EMPIRE, The. The Empire of the W. set up by the coronation of *Charlemagne as Emperor on Christmas Day, 800. It was finally brought to an end by Napoleon in 1806, though the later Austrian Empire, which fell in 1918, was in a sense its successor.

J. Bryce, *The Holy Roman Empire* (1864; enlarged and revised ed., 1904); H. [A. L.] Fisher, *The Medieval Empire* (2 vols., 1898). A. Dempf, *Sacrum Imperium*. Geschichtsund Staatsphilosophie des Mittelalters und der politischen Renaissance (1929).

HOLY SATURDAY. The day before *Easter Sunday, also known as Easter Even (as in the BCP). It commemorates the resting of Christ's body in the tomb. In early times there were no special services. The BCP provides a special Collect, Epistle, and Gospel for the day; these are commonly used at the *Ante-Communion service, without a Celebration. In the RC Church the practice of anticipating the first Mass of Easter on the morning of Holy Saturday, current since the Middle Ages, has (since 1956) been abandoned, and the liturgy with the traditional ceremonies, restored to the Saturday-Sunday night (the 'Paschal Vigil').

HOLY SEE, The. The see of the Bishop of Rome. As commonly used, it denotes the Papacy esp. in reference to the authority, jurisdiction, and functions of government which attach to it.

HOLY SEPULCHRE, The. The rock cave in *Jerusalem where, acc. to an early tradition, Christ was buried and rose from the dead. The tomb is said to have been 'discovered' by St. *Helena, mother of the Emperor *Constantine, and the first 'Church of the Holy Sepulchre' (more correctly, that of the 'Anastasis', or Resurrection) was dedicated *c.* 335. In 626 a new church was completed, after the Persians had destroyed the first in 614, but this building was so much damaged in the 10th and 11th cents. that a third building was set up *c.* 1050. In place of this church, the Crusaders built one much larger, *c.* 1130, to cover all the neighbouring holy places, including the site of *Calvary. This in turn, after having been rebuilt in 1310, was partly destroyed by fire in 1808. The present church largely dates from 1810, though some of the earlier bell tower (1160–80) remains, in a poor state of repair.

The main structure of the church consists of two halves: on the west the domed building which covers the Holy Sepulchre itself, and on the east the church proper. There are also several chapels and shrines in which many of the ancient Christian bodies have rights. The scene on Sunday mornings, when the various rites, all with music, are proceeding simultaneously, is unique in Christendom. Here also the Holy Week rites of the different Churches are carried out, each with its peculiar ceremonies and on the dates fixed by its own calendar. Anglicans, with the permission of the Orthodox authorities, have been allowed since the end of the 19th cent. to celebrate the *Eucharist in the 'Chapel of Abraham', which stands above the site of Calvary. The fact that the Holy Sepulchre lies within the city itself (contrast Heb. 13. 12) is attributed to the fact that the modern city occupies a slightly different position from that of NT times. See also *Gordon's Calvary.*

H. Vincent, O.P.–F. M. Abel, O.P., *Jérusalem*, ii (1914–1926), pp. 89–300, with plates 12–29. A. Heisenberg, *Grabeskirche und Apostelkirche*. Zwei Basiliken Konstantins, i (1908); A. *Baumstark, *Die Modestianischen und die Konstantinischen Bauten am heiligen Grabe zu Jerusalem*

(Studien zur Geschichte und Kultur des Altertums, vii, Hftt. 3 and 4; 1915). E. Wistrand, *Konstantins Kirche am heiligen Grab in Jerusalem nach den ältesten literarischen Zeugnissen* (Acta Universitatis Gotoburgensis, lviii; 1952, I). W. Harvey, *Church of the Holy Sepulchre, Jerusalem. Structural Survey. Final Report* (1935). F. Stummer in *L.Th.K.*, iv (1932), cols. 631–3, s.v. 'Grab, Heiliges', with bibl.; B. Bagatti, O.F.M., in *E.C.*, xi (1953), cols. 358–63, s.v. 'Sepolcro santo', with bibl.

HOLY SHROUD, The.

A relic, preserved at Turin since 1578, and venerated as the winding-sheet in which Christ's body was wrapped for burial (Mt. 27. 59, &c.). The shroud bears the imprint of the front and back of a human body marked with the traditional stigmata. Its history cannot be traced beyond the mid-14th cent.

C. U. J. Chevalier, 'Le Saint Suaire de Turin est-il l'original ou une copie?' in *Mémoires et Documents publiés par la Société savoisienne d'Histoire et d'Archéologie*, xxxviii (1899), pp. 105–33, also publd. separately; id., 'Le Saint Suaire de Lirey–Chambéry–Turin et les défenseurs de son authenticité' in *Bulletin d'Histoire et d'Archéologie du Diocèse de Valence*, xxi (1901), pp. 1–41, also publd. separately. Supporters of the genuineness of the relic, basing their conclusions on the photographic evidence obtained after the Exposition of 1898, include P. Vignon, *Le Linceul du Christ. Étude scientifique* (1902; Eng. tr., 1902); id., *Le Saint Suaire de Turin devant la science, l'archéologie, l'histoire, l'iconographie, la logique* (1938); A. S. Barnes, *The Holy Shroud of Turin* (1934); R. W. Hynek, *La passione di Cristo e la scienza medica* (Milan, 1937, tr. from Czech original publd. Prague, 1935; Eng. tr. from Italian, 1951). P. Scotti–A. Vaccari, S.J., in *E.C.*, xi (1953), cols. 692–7, s.v. 'Sindone' with detailed bibl.

HOLY SPIRIT.

In Christian theology, the Third Person of the Holy *Trinity, distinct from, but consubstantial, coequal and co-eternal with, the Father and the Son, and in the fullest sense God. It is held that the mode of the Spirit's procession in the Godhead is by way of 'spiration' (not 'generation') and that this procession takes place as from a single principle.

Christian theologians point to a gradual unfolding of the doctrine in the OT, where the notion of the 'Spirit' (*ruach*) plays a large part as an instrument of Divine Action, both in nature and in the human heart. The Spirit of God is already operative at the Creation, brooding on the face of the waters (Gen. 1. 2). In early times, the Hebrews saw evidence of the Spirit's action in deeds of valour and prowess. The Divine Spirit inspired the artistic skill of Bezaleel (Exod. 36. 1 f.), the successes of *Joshua (Deut. 34. 9), and the strength of *Samson (Jgs. 14. 6). In particular the Spirit was bestowed on those appointed to communicate Divine truth and esp. on the Prophets (Is. 61. 1 f.). He is also the chief power making for moral purity and holiness (Ps. 51. 11). Above all, the Spirit was to be the possession of the Coming Davidic King (Is. 11. 2) and of the Servant of the Lord (Is. 42. 1); and in the future Messianic Age there would be a large extension of the Spirit's activities and power (Jer. 31. 31 ff.; Ezek. 36. 26 f.). In the later OT writings the Spirit was increasingly seen as the Bestower of intellectual capacities. It is the Spirit of understanding which fills the devout man (Ecclus.

39. 6) and conveys to him wisdom and religious knowledge (Wisd. 7. 7, 9. 17).

In the NT, the OT teaching on the Spirit finds further development. It was through the overshadowing of the Spirit that the BVM conceived the Saviour (Lk. 1. 35; cf. Mt. 1. 18–20). The Spirit descended upon Christ at His Baptism (Mk. 1. 10), was His support in the wilderness in His conflict with Satan (1. 12), and was an operative power throughout His Ministry, not least in His miracles. 'Blasphemy against the Holy Ghost' was the sin for which there was no forgiveness (Mk. 3. 19). Teaching on the Spirit receives an esp. characteristic form in St. *John's Gospel, where He is 'another *Paraclete' (Jn. 14. 26, 15. 26). His full mission will lie in the future, after Jesus has been glorified; and it was after the Resurrection that the Apostles received the bestowal of the Spirit in the Upper Room with the power esp. to remit sins.

At *Pentecost the illapse of the Holy Spirit in His fullness on the Church is described in Acts 2. 1–13. It was marked with the gift of tongues, and St. Peter saw in this outpouring of the Spirit the new dispensation prophesied by *Joel (Acts 2. 16 f.; cf. Joel 2. 28–32). Lk. emphasises the extent to which the early Church was possessed by the belief of the Spirit's operation. Deception of the Apostles was deception of the Holy Spirit and lying to God (Acts 5. 3–9). Moreover, the Apostles were conscious of receiving direct communications from the Spirit (Acts 11. 12, 16. 6 f.) and the Holy Spirit shared in the deliberations of the Apostles on the question of the law (Acts 15. 25). And the gift of the Spirit was so far entrusted to the Apostles that it was conveyed to others through the imposition of their hands (Acts 8. 15 f., 19. 6). See *Hands, Imposition of*; *Confirmation*.

In the theology of St. *Paul, the thought of the Spirit occupies a central place. Indeed he associates the exalted Christ so closely with the Spirit that Christ and the Spirit often seem almost identified. The Christian life as life 'in the Spirit' (alternatively life 'in Christ') is sharply contrasted with life 'in the flesh', and it is the presence of the Holy Ghost which makes the Christian's body the temple of God (1 Cor. 3. 16, 6. 17). The Spirit is our Intercessor with the Father (Rom. 8. 26 f.). He divides His gifts to men severally as He will (1 Cor. 12. 11) and the fruits and gifts of the Spirit are described (Gal. 5. 22 f.). Hereafter He will raise up our bodies as 'spiritual bodies' in the likeness of Christ's Resurrection (1 Cor. 15. 42–44, cf. Rom. 8. 11).

The doctrine of the Spirit in a theologically elaborated form, though implicit in the NT, was not reached for some centuries. An important stage was reached in *Tertullian. The *Montanists (q.v.) showed the need to distinguish between true and false operations of the Holy Ghost; but despite the insistence of the Montanists on the Spirit's activities, their strange conceptions of the operation of the Spirit do not seem to have left any permanent mark on the development of the doctrine.

*Origen emphasised that the characteristic sphere of the Spirit's operation was the Church, as contrasted with the whole of Creation which was that of the Word. From A.D. 360 onwards the Doctrine of the Spirit became a matter of acute controversy. A group of theologians known as the '*Macedonians', while maintaining against the *Arians the full Divinity of the Son, denied that of the Spirit. The most considerable work which these discussions provoked was St. *Basil's *De Spiritu Sancto*. At the Council of *Constantinople of 381 Macedonianism was finally repudiated and the full doctrine of the Spirit received authoritative acceptance in the Church. In the West, this doctrine was elaborated by St. *Augustine in his *De Trinitate*, notably by his conception of the Spirit as the Bond of Union in the Holy Trinity.

On the difference between the Eastern and Western doctrines of the Spirit, see also *Double Procession; Filioque*.

Important Patristic discussions of the doctrine include St. *Athanasius, *Epp. ad Serapionem*; St. *Cyril of Jerusalem, *Catech. Lect.*, xvi; St. *Basil, *De Spiritu Sancto*; and St. *Ambrose, *De Spiritu Sancto*. The doctrine also has a prominent place in St. *Augustine, *De Trinitate*. The subject is discussed in all systematic expositions of Christian doctrine, e.g. the works of St. *John of Damascus and of St. *Thomas Aquinas (*S. Theol.* I, i, qq. 36–43), as well as in the modern treatises of D. *Petavius, J. B. *Franzelin, A. *Tanquerey. Modern works dealing expressly with the doctrine include: H. B. *Swete, *The Holy Spirit in the New Testament* (1909); id., *The Holy Spirit in the Ancient Church* (1912), and other works; H. Watkin-Jones, *The Holy Spirit in the Mediaeval Church* (1922); id., *The Holy Spirit from Arminius to Wesley* [1929]. W. H. G. Thomas, *The Holy Spirit of God* (1913). T. Rees, *The Holy Spirit in Thought and Experience* (1915). B. H. *Streeter (ed.), *The Spirit. God and His Relation to Man considered from the standpoint of Philosophy, Psychology and Art* (1919). F. Büchsel, *Der Geist Gottes im Neuen Testament* (1926). H. W. *Robinson, *The Christian Experience of the Holy Spirit* (1928). C. K. Barrett, *The Holy Spirit and the Gospel Tradition* (S.P.C.K., 1947). M. H. Lavocat, O.P., *L'Esprit d'amour*. Essai de synthèse de la doctrine catholique sur le Saint-Esprit (1952 ff.). H. B. Swete in *D.C.B.*, iii (1882), pp. 113–33, s.v.; A. Palmieri in *D.T.C.*, v (1913), cols. 676–829, s.v. 'Esprit-Saint'; and R. Birch Hoyle in *H.E.R.E.*, xi (1920), pp. 784–803, s.v. 'Spirit (Holy)'.

HOLY SYNOD.

From 1721 to 1917, the supreme organ of government in the *Russian Orthodox Church. It was not a real synod, but an ecclesiastical committee composed of bishops, originally established by Peter the Great to replace the earlier government of the Church by the Russian *Patriarch. The lay procurator attended as the Emperor's representative, but was not a member. In 1917, after the first Revolution, it was abolished and the patriarchate restored.

HOLY WATER.

Water which has been blessed for certain specific religious purposes. Acc. to W. usage, it is exorcized and blessed by a priest acting in the name of the Church, who adds to it a small quantity of exorcized and blessed *salt. By a natural symbolism it is used for blessings, dedications, and exorcisms, also at burials, and for ceremonial washing on entering a church as well as at the *Asperges at the beginning of Mass. The Christian use of water for religious purposes other than Baptism can be traced back to the 4th cent. in the E. From the 5th in the W. The use of 'Holy Water stoups' at the entrance of churches had become general at any rate by Norman times. See also *Stoups*.

A. Gastoué, *L'Eau bénite*. Ses origines, son histoire, son usage (1908); A. Franz, *Die kirchlichen Benediktionen im Mittelalter* (1909), pp. 43–220; A. A. King, *Holy Water*. The Use of Water for Ceremonial and Purificatory Purposes in Pagan, Jewish and Christian Times (1926).

HOLY WEEK.

The week preceding *Easter, observed throughout Catholic Christendom both in E. and W. as a period of devotion to the Passion of Christ. The various traditional rites of the week, of which each day has its own, probably began to develop at *Jerusalem in the 4th cent., when pilgrimages became easily possible, and Christians could indulge a natural desire to re-enact the last scenes of the life of Christ in liturgical drama. The Pilgrimage of *Etheria, a document variously dated in the 4th–6th cent., gives a detailed account of the contemporary observance of Holy Week in Jerusalem. For the ceremonies proper to each day in more recent E. and W. liturgical practice, see *Palm Sunday, Maundy Thursday, Good Friday, Holy Saturday, Easter*. A characteristic of the observances throughout is anticipation, i.e. the commemoration of events some hours before the time of their historical occurrence, a practice due chiefly to the desire to commemorate the events of each day at the (early morning) Liturgy.

J. W. Tyrer, *Historical Survey of Holy Week, its Services and Ceremonial* (*Alcuin Club Collections, No. xxix; 1932). H. Thurston, S.J., *Lent and Holy Week* (1904), pp. 149–440. L. Eisenhofer, *Handbuch der katholischen Liturgik*, i (1932), pp. 504–50.

HOLY YEAR.

A year during which the Pope grants a special *Indulgence, the so-called *Jubilee, to all those who visit Rome, on certain conditions. It was instituted in 1300 by *Boniface VIII, who had meant it to be celebrated every 100 years. *Clement VI, in 1343, however, changed the period to 50; *Urban VI, in 1389, to 33 in honour of the years of our Lord's life; and Paul II, in 1470, finally settled on 25, the regular interval that has been kept ever since. The conditions and special benefits are laid down each time by a special bull, issued on the preceding Feast of the *Ascension. The chief conditions are normally worthy reception of the Sacraments and visits to the four *basilicas during a specified time. The benefits include 'plenary indulgence' and exceptional powers for the confessors, who may absolve from most sins ordinarily reserved to higher authority, and commute all vows except those reserved to the Pope. One of the most important ceremonies of the Holy Year is the opening of the *Holy Door (q.v.) by the Pope before the First Christmas Vespers, and its walling up again at the same time a year later. Originally the Jubilee Indulgence was to be gained only at

Rome, but since 1500 it has been extended to all churches throughout the world, to which it is granted for the six months following the Roman year on similar conditions, among them visits to local shrines and works of penance and charity. A Holy Year was last celebrated in 1950.

H. Thurston, S.J., *The Holy Year of Jubilee.* An Account of the History and Ceremony of the Roman Jubilee (1900), with bibl. reff.

HOMBERG, Synod of. A synod which *Philip, Landgraf of Hesse, convoked at Homberg, 20 miles south-west of Cassel, on 21 Oct. 1526 to establish a constitution on Protestant principles for the Church of his domains. A set of 158 articles (*paradoxa*), which had been circulated in advance by F. *Lambert, a former *Franciscan friar, was taken as a basis of the proceedings, while the opponent of the reforming doctrines was Nicolas Ferber. The one important outcome of the synod was the appointment of a committee to draw up a Church Order for Hesse, which issued the 'Reformatio Ecclesiarum Hassiae', a set of regulations on a Protestant basis covering the whole area of Church life. By insisting on the independence of each Christian community, responsible for the maintenance of its own discipline, the 'Reformatio' upheld a congregationalism which went far beyond Luther's teachings. Largely through Luther's influence, Philip of Hesse refrained from allowing it to be promulgated, and in consequence it was never enforced.

The *Reformatio Ecclesiarum Hassiae* was first publd. in F. C. Schmincke (ed.), *Monimenta Hassiaca*, ii (Cassel, 1748), pp. 588–666. Also ed. K. A. Credner (Giessen, 1852). More important clauses in Kidd, pp. 222–30 (No. 98). W. Schmitt, *Die Synode zu Homberg und ihre Vorgeschichte.* Festschrift zur vierhundert-Jahrfeier der Homberger Synode (Homberg, 1926). C. Mirbt in *P.R.E.* (ed. 3), viii (1900), pp. 288–94, s.v. 'Homberger Synode und Kirchenordnung', with bibl. Further bibl. in Schottenloher, iv (1938), p. 640 f. (Nos. 43042–55). See also bibl. to *Lambert, F.*, and *Philip, Landgraf of Hesse*.

HOMILIARY (Lat. *homiliarium*). A collection of homilies arranged acc. to the ecclesiastical calendar for reading at the office of *Matins. Homiliaria were compiled esp. in the earlier Middle Ages, and among surviving examples are those of *Paul the Deacon (c. A.D. 790), made at the command of *Charlemagne, and of Alain of Farfa (d. 770).

HOMILIES, The Books of. The plan of issuing prescribed homilies for the use of disaffected and illiterate clergy was agreed to in the Convocation which met on 20 Jan. 1542. A collection was duly produced twelve months later, but, prob. because *Henry VIII refused to authorize it, not formally issued until early in *Edward VI's reign, when it appeared with the authority of the Council on 31 July 1547. The subjects of its twelve homilies were: (1) A fruitful Exhortation to the Reading of Holy Scripture (T. *Cranmer); (2) Of the Misery of all Mankind (Archdeacon John Harpsfield, 1516–78); (3) Of the Salvation of all Mankind (Cranmer); (4) Of the true and lively Faith (Cranmer); (5) Of Good Works (Cranmer); (6) Of Christian Love and Charity (E. *Bonner); (7) Against Swearing and Perjury; (8) Of the Declining from God; (9) An Exhortation against the Fear of Death (prob. Cranmer); (10) An Exhortation to Obedience; (11) Against Whoredom and Adultery; (12) Against Strife and Contention.

A 'Second Book', with 21 further homilies, was issued under *Elizabeth I. It was prob. completed by the beginning of 1563, but was not published in its final form until 1571. Their titles are listed in Art. 35 of the *Thirty-Nine Articles. The majority are the work of J. *Jewel; but E. *Grindal wrote No. 5 and M. *Parker (prob.) No. 17. No. 21 ('Against Rebellion') was added in 1571 in view of the Northern Rebellion of 1569.

Though unsuitable for modern use, these Homilies retain a measure of authority in view of Art. 35, while Art. 11 refers to the 'Homily of Justification' (presumably No. 3 of the First Book) for a fuller account of the 'most wholesome doctrine' 'that we are justified by faith only'.

HOMILIES, CLEMENTINE. See *Clementine Literature*.

HOMOEANS. The Arian party which came into existence c. 355 under the leadership of *Acacius, Bp. of Caesarea. Repudiating both the *Homoousios and the *Homoiousios, they sought to confine theological discussion about the Person of the Son to the assertion that He was like (Gk. ὅμοιος, 'like') the Father. For a brief interval they were closely associated with the much more orthodox *Semi-arians.

HOMOIOTELEUTON (Gk. ὅμοιος, 'like', and τελευτή, 'ending'). In MSS., the repetition of the same sequence of letters or words in two neighbouring places, considered as a source of error in copying. Where the repeated sequence occurs at the beginning of a word or phrase, the alternative expression 'homoioarcton' is occasionally used.

HOMOOUSION (Gk. ὁμοούσιον, 'of one substance'). The term used in the *Nicene Creed to express the relations of the Father and the Son within the Godhead and originally designed to exclude *Arianism. Its earlier associations with the *Gnostics and *Paul of Samosata at first made it suspect, and many *Origenists, who had no sympathy with Arianism, preferred the term 'Homoiousion', (ὁμοιούσιον, i.e. 'of like substance with the Father'), which was held to leave more room for distinctions in the Godhead. It is possible that the introduction of the word for anti-Arian purposes is to be ascribed to *Hosius of Cordova, who used it to express in Greek the Latin *consubstantialis*.

J. F. Bethune-Baker, *The Meaning of Homoousios in the Constantinopolitan' Creed* (Texts and Studies, vii, No. 1;

Cambridge, 1901). G. L. Prestige, *God in Patristic Thought* (1936), ch. x f., pp. 197–241. C. Hauret, *Comment le défenseur de Nicée a-t-il compris le dogme de Nicée?* ("Gregoriana University thesis; Bruges, 1936). I. Ortiz de Urbina, S.J., 'L' "Homousios" preniceno' in *O.C.P.*, viii (1942), pp. 194–209.

HONORATUS, St. (*c.* 350–429), Abp. of *Arles. Of a consular family, he was converted to Christianity and set out with his brother, Venantius, on a pilgrimage to the holy places in Syria and Egypt; but on his brother's death in Achaia, he returned through *Rome and with the encouragement of Leontius, Bp. of Fréjus, settled in the island of *Lérins, where he founded (*c.* 410) the celebrated monastery. In 426 he became Abp. of Arles, where he was active in establishing orthodoxy and continued to direct his monastery. St. *Hilary of Arles, his successor in the see and biographer, was probably a relative. His writings have been lost. The authorship of the *Athanasian Creed was at one time (1896) ascribed to him by A. E. *Burn. Feast day, 16 Jan.

St. Hilary's 'Sermo de Vita S. Honorati' pr. in *AA.SS.*, Jan. II (1643), pp. 17–24 and, from MSS, in J. P. Migne, *PL*, l. 1249–72. B. Munke (ed.), *Die Vita S. Honorati nach drei Handschriften* (Zeitschrift für Romanische Philologie, Beiheft xxxii, 1911), new ed. by S. Cavallin (Lund, 1952). A. E. Burn, *The Athanasian Creed and its Early Commentaries* (Cambridge Texts and Studies, iv, 1, 1896), esp. ch. iii.

HONORIUS I (d. 638), Pope from 625. He came from a noble family of the Campagna, but little is known of his life before his election to the Papacy. Like his predecessor, St.*Gregory the Great (d. 604), he interested himself in the christianization of the Anglo-Saxons, and sent his congratulations to King Edwin of Northumbria on the occasion of his baptism in 627. He also sent St. *Birinus to preach in Wessex, and gave the pallium to Honorius of Canterbury and *Paulinus of York. He gained considerable influence over the government of Italy by his wise administration of the patrimony of Peter, and despite heavy expenditure on churches and other buildings collected a considerable Papal treasure. One of his principal achievements was the ending of the schism of the patriarchs of Aquileia-Grado, which had been renewed by Fortunatus, whom he deposed, probably with the help of the Exarch of *Ravenna. Gratitude for this assistance may have influenced his attitude towards the Emp. *Heraclius in the matter of the *Monothelite heresy, which has been among the chief historical arguments against Papal Infallibility. *c.* 634 *Sergius, the Patr. of *Constantinople, addressed a letter to the Pope interrogating him on the question of the 'one energy' (μία ἐνέργεια) of Christ. This formula, which, while confessing the two natures, attributed only one mode of activity, viz. that of the Divine Word, to the Incarnate Christ, had been found useful in the E. for reconciling the Monophysites. It was strenuously opposed, however, by *Sophronius of Jerusalem, and Sergius, in his diplomatical letter to Honorius, stressed the unity of the Person of Christ safe-

guarded by the new formula, while disregarding the duality of natures. Without further inquiries, Honorius sent back a favourable reply in which he used the unfortunate formula of 'one will' in Christ. When his injunction of silence on both parties was disobeyed, he wrote a second letter rejecting the expression 'two wills' as giving rise to contentions, though insisting strongly on the two natures. He died in 638, the year of the publication of the"Εκθεσις, the charter of Monothelitism, which utilized Honorius' formula of the 'one will'.

His successors repeatedly condemned the heresy, and at the Council of *Constantinople (681) Honorius himself was formally anathematized. This condemnation, which was forgotten in the W. during the Middle Ages, was discussed in the 15th cent. at the negotiations for reunion between the Catholic and Orthodox Churches, and again in the *Gallican controversies of the 17th and 18th cents., and before the definition of Papal Infallibility in 1870. The authenticity of the letter of Honorius as well as of the Acts of the Council of Constantinople, once rejected by some RC scholars, e.g. C. *Baronius, is now generally admitted. The common argument in defence of Honorius is that the letters do not contain heretical teaching, but only gravely imprudent expressions, and that, in these circumstances, condemnation of a Pope's carelessness by a General Council was justified.

J. P. Migne, *PL*, lxxx. 463–94. J. J. I. von *Döllinger, *Die Papstfabeln des Mittelalters* (1863), pp. 131–53; C. J. *Hefele, *Causa Honorii Papae* (Naples, 1870); J. *Chapman, O.S.B., *The Condemnation of Pope Honorius* (1907). Hefele-Leclerq, iii (pt. i; 1909), pp. 347–538. Mann, i (pt. i; 1902), pp. 304–45. É. Amann in *D.T.C.*, vii (pt. i; 1922), cols. 93–131.

HONORIUS III (d. 1227), Pope from 1216. Cencio Savelli was a native of Rome. Well educated and of a strong religious character, he became successively canon of Sta Maria Maggiore, papal chamberlain (1188), cardinal-deacon (1193), tutor to the Emp. *Frederick II (1197) and cardinal priest (before 1201). On 18 July 1216 he was elected to succeed *Innocent III and consecrated at Perugia on 24 July. In general he continued the policy of his predecessor. On 22 Nov. 1220 he crowned the Emp. Frederick in St. Peter's on promises that he would uphold the rights of the Church and promote a crusade. He took a prominent part in political affairs throughout Europe, acting as arbitrator between Philip II of France and James of Aragon, supporting Henry III of England (which he virtually ruled during the King's minority) against the barons, crowning Peter of Courtenay Emp. of Byzantium (1217), and defending the privileges of the Church in Bohemia (1223). He also approved the *Dominican, *Franciscan and *Carmelite Orders and fostered the growth of their *Tertiary orders. Among his many writings are a large collection of *Decretals ('Compilatio Quinta'), a Life of *Gregory VII, an *Ordo Romanus which included a Coronation Order and an important *Liber Censuum Romanae Ecclesiae* (1192); the last is a valuable record of the secular relations of the Papacy in his day. Several of his Letters and Sermons have also survived. He also wrote a continuation of the *Liber Pontificalis.

Opera Omnia, ed. C. A. Horoy, Medii Aevi Bibliotheca Patristica (5 vols., Paris, 1879–83); Selected Letters, ed. C. Rodenberg in M.G.H., Ep. Saec. XIII, i (1883), pp. 1–260; Regesta Honorii Papae III, ed. P. Pressutti, 2 vols., Rome, 1888–95; Liber Censuum Romanae Ecclesiae, ed. with preface and commentary by P. Fabre and L. *Duchesne ([1889–]1910). J. Clausen, Papst Honorius III (1895). F. Caillemer, Le Pape Honorius III et le droit civile (1881); F. Vernet, Étude sur les sermons d'Honorius III (Thèse, Lyons, 1888); N. Mengozzi, Onorio III e le sue relazioni col regno di Inghilterra (Siena, 1911); A. Keutner, Papsttum und Krieg unter dem Pontificat des Papstes Honorius III (1935). U. Berlière, O.S.B., 'Honorius III et les monastères bénédictins, 1216–1227' in Revue belge de Philologie et d'Histoire, ii (1923), pp. 237–65 and 461–84. H. X. Arquillière in D.T.C., vii (pt. 1; 1922), cols. 135–8, s.v.; and Fliche-Martin, x (1950), pp. 291–304, both with bibl. Also H. *Leclercq, O.S.B., in D.A.C.L.; ix (pt. 1; 1930), cols. 180–220, s.v. 'Liber Censuum', and G. Mollat in E.C., ix (1952), cols. 141–3, s.v. 'Onorio III'.

HONORIUS OF AUTUN (early 12th cent.), (Augustodunensis), Scholastic philosopher. Despite the popularity of his writings in medieval times, nothing certain is known about his life, though the internal evidence of his works makes it very unlikely that he had connexions with Autun in Burgundy. He was perhaps a hermit who lived in the neighbourhood of Regensburg. His many treatises on history, natural science, and theology consist for the most part of extracts from earlier works. Thus, about half his (still unprinted) Clavis physica is derived from *Erigena's De Divisione Naturae. In his own philosophical doctrines he was a follower in the main of the Christianized Platonism of St. *Augustine, being immediately influenced esp. by *Anselm of Laon, *William of Champeaux and *Anselm of Canterbury. His other works include treatises De Cognitione Vitae, De Luminaribus Ecclesiae, the Inevitabile (on free will and grace), a collection of sermons known as the Speculum Ecclesiae and the encyclopaedic Imago Mundi. The widely circulated Elucidarium sive Dialogus de Summa Totius Christianae Theologiae is also the work of Honorius.

Of the works collected and pr. under the name of Honorius, with prolegomena, in J. P. Migne, PL, clxxii, 9–1270, the De Philosophia (cols. 39–102) is the work of *William of Conches, the De Solis Effectibus (cols. 101–16) is of doubtful authorship, and the Quaestiones et ad easdem Responsiones in . . . Proverbia et Ecclesiasten (cols. 311–48) is the work of Salonius of Geneva. His Cognitio Vitae is pr. among the works of St. *Augustine in J. P. Migne, op. cit., xl, 1005–32; further sections of his commentary on the Psalms are pr. among the works of *Gerhoh of Reichersberg in J. P. Migne, op. cit., cxciii, 1315–72 (on Pss. 31–7), and cxciv, 485–730 (on Pss. 78–117); further 'Libelli' ed. I. Dieterich in M.G.H., Libelli de Lite Imperatorum et Pontificum Saeculis XI et XII, iii (1897), pp. 29–80, with bibl. reff. J. A. Enders, Honorius Augustodunensis (Kempten-Munich, 1906). F. Baeumker, Das Inevitabile des Honorius Augustodunensis und dessen Lehre über das Zusammenwirken von Wille und Gnade (B.G.P.M., xiii, Hft. 6; 1914). C. Daux, 'Un Scolastique du XIIᵉ siècle trop oublié' in Revue des Sciences ecclésiastiques et Science catholique (1907), pp. 737–58, 858–84, 974–1002, and 1071–80. F. Bliemetzrieder, 'L'Œuvre d'Anselme de Laon et la littérature théologique contemporaine. I, Honorius d'Autun' in R.T.A.M., v (1933), pp. 275–91. E. Rooth, 'Kleine Beiträge zur Kenntnis des sog. Honorius Augustodunensis' in Studia Neophilologica, xii (1939/40), pp. 120–35. M. *Grabmann,

'Eine stark erweiterte und kommentierte Redaktion des Elucidarium des Honorius von Augustodunum' in Miscellanea Giovanni Mercati, ii (S.T., cxxxii; 1946), pp. 220–58. Eva M. Sanford, 'Honorius, Presbyter and Scholasticus' in Speculum, xxiii (1948), pp. 397–425. Marie Thérèse d'Alverny, 'Le Cosmos symbolique du XIIᵉ siècle', in Archives d'Histoire doctrinale et littéraire du Moyen-Âge, Année xxviii (for 1953; 1954), pp. 31–81. Y. Lefèvre, L'Elucidarium et les Lucidaires. Contribution par l'histoire d'un texte, à l'histoire des croyances religieuses en France au moyen-âge (Bibliothèque des Écoles françaises d'Athènes et de Rome, clxxx; 1954). Überweg, ii, pp. 203–5, with bibl. p. 700 f. É Amann in D.T.C., vii (pt. 1; 1922), cols. 139–58, s.v. 'Honorius Augustodunensis', with reff. to earlier litt.

HONTHEIM, JOHANN NIKOLAUS VON (1701–90), founder of *Febronianism. He was a native of Trier, where he spent the greater part of his life. While a student at Louvain, he came under the influence of the *Gallican canonist, Z. B. *van Espen. In 1728 he was ordained priest and in 1748 became suffragan Bp. of Trier. In 1742 he began an investigation, on behalf of the German Archbishop-Electors, of the historical position of the Papacy, and in 1763, under the pseudonym of 'Justinus Febronius', published his conclusions in his principal work, De statu ecclesiae et legitima potestate Romani Pontificis (see Febronianism). Owing to its Gallican doctrines the book was put on the *Index in 1764; but though for several years Hontheim was involved in controversy, he was not compelled to make a formal retractation until 1778. In 1781 he published Justini Febroni Commentarius in suam retractationem Pio VI, a work which, despite its conciliatory spirit, showed little real change of view. His other writings include two valuable historical works on the city of Trier, Historia Trevirensis Diplomatica (3 vols., 1750) and Prodromus Historiae Trevirensis (2 vols., 1757). His integrity, devotion to truth, and learning were admired even by his enemies.

See bibl. to Febronianism.

HOOK, WALTER FARQUHAR (1798–1875), Dean of *Chichester. Educated at *Winchester and *Oxford, he spent some years after his ordination in parochial work at Coventry and Leeds. As vicar of Leeds (1837–1859), although sympathetic with the *Tractarian Movement, he became involved in a controversy with E. B. *Pusey over the alleged Romish practices at St. Saviour's, Leeds. Differences in their interpretation of the effects of the Reformation on the Anglican Church led to an increasingly heated correspondence until finally their friendship was formally terminated by Hook, who declared himself an enemy of 'Romanism' and 'Puseyism'. In 1859 he became Dean of Chichester. He was the author of many historical and theological works, including a Church Dictionary (1842; often reprinted), a Dictionary of Ecclesiastical Biography (8 vols., 1845–52), and the Lives of the Archbishops of Canterbury (12 vols., 1860–76).

W. R. W. Stephens, The Life and Letters of Walter Farquhar Hook (2 vols., 1878). C. J. Stranks, Dean Hook (1954). W. R. W. Stephens in D.N.B., xxvii (1891), pp. 276–9.

HOOKER, RICHARD (*c.* 1554–1600), Anglican divine. Born at Heavitree near Exeter, he was admitted through the influence of J. *Jewel at Corpus Christi College, Oxford, of which he became a Fellow in 1577. In 1579 he was appointed deputy professor of Hebrew. Vacating his fellowship on his marriage to Joan Churchman 'who brought him neither beauty nor portion' (I. *Walton), in 1584 he was appointed rector of Drayton Beauchamp and in 1585 Master of the Temple, where he controverted the *Calvinistic views of the Reader, W. *Travers. Later (1591) he became rector of Boscombe, Wilts, and finally (1595) of Bishopsbourne, near Canterbury, where he died.

Hooker was *par excellence* the apologist of the Elizabethan Settlement of 1559 and perhaps the most accomplished advocate that Anglicanism has ever had. He developed his doctrines in his *Treatise on the Laws of Ecclesiastical Polity.* Of the five Books which appeared in Hooker's lifetime, I–IV were published in 1594 and V in 1597. Books VI (certainly spurious in its present form) and VIII did not appear until 1648 and Book VII until 1662. In conception the *Treatise* was a *livre de circonstance,* designed to justify episcopacy, but it embodied a broadly conceived philosophical theology. His opposition to the *Puritans, who held to the literal following of the Scriptures as an absolute in the sense that whatever was not expressly commanded in Scripture was unlawful, led him to elaborate a whole theory of law, based on the 'absolute' fundamental of natural law whose 'seat is the bosom of God, her voice the harmony of the world' (*EP,* I, xvi, 8). This natural law, which governs the universe and to which both ecclesiastical and civil polity are subservient, is the expression of God's supreme reason, and everything, including the Scriptures, must be interpreted in the light of it. 'Laws human must be made according to the general laws of nature, and without contradiction unto any positive law in Scripture. Otherwise they are ill made' (*EP,* III, ix, 2). The Puritans were wholly mistaken in regarding the Bible as a mechanical code of rules; for not everything that is rightful finds precise direction in the Scriptures. In a similar way the permanence of law does not preclude development of detail. The Church is an organic, not a static institution, and the method of Church government and ecclesiastical administration will change acc. to circumstances. Hence the C of E, though reformed, possesses continuity with the medieval Church. Further, the visible organized Church is a political society, 'a court not temporal merely', yet able to control its own legislation in a way analogous to that in which the civil state through parliament makes its laws. Hooker developed an essentially contractual theory of political government which influenced future political writers, esp. J. *Locke.

In particular matters, Hooker has been less universally acceptable to Anglicans. In his unreadiness to condemn the orders of Continental Protestants, he denied the necessity of episcopal ordination. His doctrine of the Eucharist, not wholly consistent, closely approximates in many places to *Receptionism. His argument on points of detail is not infrequently difficult to grasp and not wholly clear. But Hooker remains one of the greatest theologians that the English Church has ever possessed; and he conveyed his beliefs in a masterly English prose.

Works ed. by J. *Keble (3 vols., 1836). Life by I. Walton (1665; reprinted in Keble's edition of *Works*). F. *Paget, *An Introduction to the Fifth Book of Hooker's Treatise of the Laws of Ecclesiastical Polity* (1899). L. S. Thornton, C.R., *Richard Hooker* (1924); A. P. d'Entrèves, *The Medieval Contribution to Political Thought.* Thomas Aquinas, Marsilius of Padua, Richard Hooker (1939); C. J. Sisson, *The Judicious Marriage of Mr. Hooker and the Birth of the Laws of Ecclesiastical Polity* (1940); F. J. Shirley, *Richard Hooker and Contemporary Political Ideas* (1949). P. Munz, *The Place of Hooker in the History of Thought* (1952). S. Lee in *D.N.B.,* xxvii (1891), pp. 289–95.

HOOPER, JOHN (d. 1555), Bp. of *Gloucester and *Worcester, and Protestant martyr. A native of Somerset, he was educated at Oxford and probably entered a *Cistercian monastery. On the dissolution of the religious houses he went to London and began to interest himself in the Continental Reformers, esp. H. *Zwingli and J. H. *Bullinger, and returned to Oxford to propagate their views. After a disputation with S. *Gardiner, Bp. of *Winchester he was exiled for heresy and spent the next years travelling in Europe. From 1547 to 1549 he lived at Zürich, where he became a friend of Bullinger, M. *Bucer, and J. *Laski. In 1549 he came back to England and was made chaplain to the Protector *Somerset. In 1550 he was nominated to the see of Gloucester, which he accepted only after the reference to angels and saints had been omitted from the Oath of Supremacy and after further prolonged hesitation on the lawfulness of episcopal vestments, which led to a short term of imprisonment. In 1552, when Gloucester was reduced to an archdeaconry, he was given the see of Worcester. He governed his diocese with exemplary zeal and vigour, introducing, however, many Continental customs. He was also very liberal to the poor. On the accession of *Mary he was imprisoned in the Fleet in 1553. In 1555 he was tried for heresy, and having refused to recant was excommunicated and burned at the stake (9 Feb. 1555). One of the chief English exponents of extreme Continental Protestantism, he exercised a considerable influence on the later Puritans through his writings, which include *A Godly Confession and Protestation of the Christian Faith* (1551), and *A brief and clear Confession of the Christian Faith, containing an hundred Articles acc. to the Order of the Creed of the Apostles* (1581).

S. Carr (ed.), *The Early Writings of John Hooper* (*Parker Society, 1843); C. Nevinson (ed.), *Later Writings of Bishop Hooper* (ib., 1852), with biographical sketch pp. vii–xxx. H. Robinson (ed.), *Original Letters Relating to the English Reformaion, 1537–1558* (ib., 2 vols., 1846–7). Short life by J. C. *Ryle (London, [1868]). G. G. Perry in *D.N.B.,* xxvii (1891), pp. 304–6.

HOPE. One of the three *theological virtues. In its widest sense it may be defined as the desire and search for a future good, difficult but not impossible of attainment. In the course of OT history hope played an important part, often in the form of merely earthly desires, in the preparation of Israel for the Incarnation. By the resurrection of Christ, mankind was 'begotten again into a living hope' (1 Pet. 1. 3). As a Christian virtue its primary end, its motive, and its author, is God Himself, and like faith it may continue even when charity has been lost by mortal sin. It is confined to this life and to purgatory, and has no place either in heaven (where its object, the *Beatific Vision, is already attained) or in hell. Hope, being confidence in God's goodness tempered by fear of His justice, is opposed to both despair and presumption.

R. L. *Ottley in *H.E.R.E.*, iv (1913), p. 779 f., s.v. 'Hope (Christian)'; R. *Bultmann–K. H. Rengstorf in *T.W.B.*, ii (1935), cols. 515–31, s.v '𝜖λπίς', with reff.

HOPKINS, GERARD MANLEY (1844–89),

poet. He was educated at Balliol College, Oxford, where he was the pupil of B. *Jowett and W. Pater, and the friend of R. *Bridges and D. M. Dolben. At this time he came under the religious influence of E. B. *Pusey and H. P. *Liddon. In 1866 Hopkins joined the RC Church, in 1868 he entered the *Jesuit novitiate, and in 1877 he was ordained priest. In 1884 he was appointed professor of Greek at the Royal university, Dublin, a position which he held till his death. He was unknown as a poet during his life, except to two or three friends, and the preservation of his MSS. is due to R. Bridges who first edited them in 1918. His poems, the most ambitious of which is *The Wreck of the Deutschland* and perhaps the most representative *The Windhover: to Christ our Lord*, are marked by their great intensity of feeling, freedom in rhythm, and individual use of words, and have exerted much influence on more recent poets. They show a priest's pastoral care for souls, and conceive the fundamental personal relationship between the soul and its Redeemer as sacrificial. The opening words of *The Wreck of the Deutschland*, 'Thou mastering me God', were carved over the sculpture of the Re-creation of Man by E. *Gill at Geneva.

Poems, ed. with notes by Robert Bridges (1918); 2nd and enlarged edition, with an introduction by Charles *Williams (1930); 3rd and further enlarged ed. with notes and biographical introduction by W. H. Gardner (1948). C. C. Abbott, *The Letters of Gerard Manley Hopkins to Robert Bridges* (1935); id. *The Correspondence of Gerard Manley Hopkins and Richard Watson Dixon* (1935); id. *Further Letters of Gerard Manley Hopkins* (1938; ed. 2 with additional letters, 1956); H. House, *Note-books and Papers of G. M. Hopkins* (1937); G. F. Lahey, S.J., *G. M. Hopkins. A Biography* (1938); J. Pick, *Gerard Manley Hopkins, Priest and Poet* (1942). B. I. Evans in *C.B.E.L.*, iii, p. 325 f.

HORMISDAS, St. (d. 523), Pope from 514.

His chief importance lies in his success in healing the *Acacian Schism which since 484 had divided the E. from the W. After an attempt at union in 515 had come to grief through the obstinacy of the Emp. Anastasius I, Hormisdas secured in 519, under the new Emp. Justin I, the signature of John, the Patr.

of Constantinople, and afterwards of some 250 E. bishops, to a dogmatic formula (the 'Formula Hormisdae') in which the *Chalcedonian Definition and Leo's *Tome were accepted, Acacius and other heretics were expressly condemned, and the authority of the Roman see (on the basis of Mt. 16. 18) was strongly emphasized. He also took a notable part in negotiating with the (*Arian) Goths matters of ecclesiastical concern to the W. Church, and maintained good relations with *Theodoric. It was under his direction that *Dionysius Exiguus made his second version of the Greek ecclesiastical canons. Feast day, 6 Aug.

Some ninety of Hormisdas' genuine letters survive; repr. in J. P. Migne, *PL*, lxiii, 367–534; crit. texts in the so-called 'Collectio Avellana' ed. O. Guenther (C.S.E.L., xxxv, pt. 2; 1898). Life in *L.P.* (Duchesne), i, 269–74. L. *Duchesne, *L'Église au VIᵉ siècle* (1925), pp. 37–40, 48–65. Bardenhewer, v, 279 f. J. P. Kirsch in *C.E.*, vii (1910), p. 470 f., s.v.; É. Amann in *D.T.C.*, vii (pt. 1; 1922), cols. 161–76, s.v.; F. Diekamp in *L.Th.K.*, v (1933), col. 144 f., s.v.

HORNE, GEORGE (1730–92), Bp. of

*Norwich. Born at Otham, nr. Maidstone, he was educated at University College, *Oxford, where he became a friend of W. *Jones ('of Nayland'), his future biographer, and J. Moore, later Abp. of *Canterbury. In 1750 he was elected Fellow of Magdalen College, Oxford, of which he became president in 1768. He was appointed vice-chancellor of the university in 1776 and Dean of Canterbury in 1781. In 1790 he became Bp. of Norwich. Horne was a disciple of J. *Hutchinson, but rejected his more fanciful speculations on Hebrew etymology. Though an adherent of High Church principles, he was in sympathy with the spiritual earnestness of the *Methodists and refused to forbid J. *Wesley to preach in his diocese. He also supported the Scottish bishops' petition to Parliament in 1789. Among his writings are many pamphlets directed in various ways against the views of I. *Newton, D. *Hume, W. *Law, and others, whose importance he seems not always to have understood. Horne was above all a preacher, and his sermons were frequently reprinted. His most important work is his *Commentary on the Psalms* (1771); in it he maintained that the greater number of the Psalms were Messianic.

Collected ed., 6 vols., London, 1809 (incomplete). W. Jones, *Memoirs of the Life, Studies and Writings of the Right Reverend George Horne* (1795; with list of Horne's writings, pp. 414–18). A. C. Bickley in *D.N.B.*, xxvii (1891), pp. 356–8.

HORNE, THOMAS HARTWELL (1780–

1862), Biblical commentator and bibliographer. He was the grandfather of T. K. *Cheyne. Educated at Christ's Hospital, where S. T. *Coleridge was his contemporary, he began as a barrister's clerk. To supplement his income he took up literary work and wrote on a great variety of subjects. For many years he was a *Wesleyan Methodist. In 1808 he was invited to catalogue the Harleian MSS. in the British Museum, and from now on was engaged in several bibliographical undertakings. In 1818 appeared the first edition of his *Introduction to the Critical Study and Knowledge of the Holy Scriptures* (3 vols.), which at once established itself by its completeness as a standard work, though it was without originality. A supplementary volume appeared in 1821, and it went through a large number of editions both in Great Britain and the U.S.A. down to 1860. Among those who helped in the revision of its later editions were S. *Davidson and S. P. *Tregelles. In 1819 Horne was ordained by W. *Howley to the curacy of Christ Church, Newgate Street, and held various ecclesiastical offices in the London diocese till his death. His many other writings include an *Introduction to the Study of Bibliography* (2 vols., 1814), *Deism Refuted* (1819), *The Scripture Doctrine of the Trinity briefly stated and defended* (1820), and *A Compendious Introduction to the Study of the Bible* (1827).

Reminiscences Personal and Bibliographical of Thomas Hartwell Horne, with notes by his daughter, S. A. Cheyne (1862); incl. list of Horne's writings (pp. 199–208). T. Cooper in D.N.B., xxvii (1891), p. 363 f.

HORNECK, ANTHONY (1641–97), Anglican divine. He was a native of Bacharach on the Rhine, of Protestant parentage, who studied theology at Heidelberg and came to England *c.* 1661. In 1663 he was made a member of Queen's College, Oxford, and in 1664 vicar of All Saints, Oxford. He became prebendary of *Exeter Cathedral in 1670, and in the following year preacher at the Savoy, where he enjoyed great popularity. In 1689 he was appointed chaplain to William III, and in 1693 prebendary of *Westminster. He wrote a number of devotional books which were widely used at the time, dealing esp. with Holy Communion. Among them are *The Happy Ascetic* (1681), *The Fire of the Altar* (1683), and *The Crucified Jesus* (1686).

Collected ed. of Several Sermons upon the Fifth of St. Matthew; Being Part of Christ's Sermon on the Mount (2 vols., 1696), with life by Richard Kidder, Bp. of Bath and Wells, vol. i, pp. 3–58, and list of his works, p. 61 f.; also publ. separately (London, 1696). Four Tracts by Horneck were ed. by W. Edwards (London, 1697); The Crucified Jesus was also ed. by W. F. *Hook (Leeds and London, 1848); extracts from The Happy Ascetic were ed. by J. Wesley, The Christian Library, xvi (1823), pp. 291–432; short extract from The Fire of the Altar pr. in P. E. More–F. L. Cross (edd.), Anglicanism (1935), No. 359, p. 777. L. Stephen in D.N.B., xxvii (1891), p. 367 f.

HOROLOGION (Gk. ὡρολόγιον). In the E. Church, the liturgical book which contains the recurrent portions of the ecclesiastical *office extending through the whole year.

HORSIESI, St. See *Orsisius, St.*

HORSLEY, SAMUEL (1733–1806), Bp. of *St. Asaph. He was born in London and educated at Trinity Hall, Cambridge. In 1759 he succeeded his father as rector of Newington Butts in Surrey. His interests in science led him to become a Fellow of the Royal Society in 1767, and its Secretary from 1773 to 1784. In 1771 he was appointed domestic chaplain to the Bp. of London, who made him Archdeacon of *St. Albans in 1781. In 1788 he was consecrated Bp. of *St. David's. He proved an energetic bishop, both in his diocese and in the House of Lords. In 1793 he was translated to *Rochester, and in 1802 once more translated to St. Asaph. He is chiefly famous for his controversy with J. *Priestley over the doctrines of the Trinity and Christ's Divinity in which he defended the traditional view that the pre-Nicene Church was unanimous in its theology of the Lord's Consubstantiality with the Father. His many writings, largely on scientific and philological subjects, include *Providence and Free Agency* (1778) *The Analogy between the Light of Inspiration and the Light of Learning* (1787), *Tracts in controversy with Dr. Priestley* (1789), *An Apology for the Liturgy and Clergy* (1790), *Hosea translated . . . with Notes* (1801), and *The Book of Psalms translated* (1815; posthumous). He also published many separate Sermons.

Sermons [ed. H. Horsley] (2 vols., Dublin, 1810) and later edd.; The Speeches in Parliament of Samuel Horsley [ed. id.] (ib., 1813); The Charges of Samuel Horsley . . . delivered at his Several Visitations of the Dioceses of St. David's, Rochester, and St. Asaph (ib., 1813). His Sermon on 'The Death of Louis XVI', delivered on 30 Jan., 1793, was reissued in D. Macleane, Famous Sermons by English Preachers (1911), pp. 180–92. Heneage Horsley Jebb, A Great Bishop of One Hundred Years Ago, being a Sketch of the Life of Samuel Horsley (1909). A. Gordon in D.N.B., xxvii (1891), pp. 383–6.

HORT, FENTON JOHN ANTHONY (1828–92), NT scholar. Educated at Rugby under T. *Arnold and A. C. *Tait, and at Trinity College, Cambridge, he was from 1852 to 1857 a Fellow of his college, from 1857 to 1872 incumbent of a parish near Hitchin, and from 1872 till his death back at Cambridge, where he held various lectureships. In his early years at Cambridge he became a lifelong friend and fellow-worker with E. W. *Benson, J. B. *Lightfoot, and B. F. *Westcott, and also came under the influence of F. D. *Maurice, C. *Kingsley, Tom Hughes, and others, with whose social endeavours he was in sympathy. His original intention was to publish large-scale commentaries on the Gospels, Acts, and some of the *Catholic Epistles; but most of his energies were in fact diverted to the Greek text of the NT, at which he worked, in conjunction with Westcott, almost continuously from 1852 till its publication in 1881. His work in this field, summarized in his fine 'Introduction' to the Westcott-Hort NT, was remarkable for the accuracy and sobriety of his judgements. Its somewhat difficult style, combined with a modesty which often conceals the range of its writer's learning, can still disguise its distinction and erudition from those who handle it for the first time. Of the first importance also were his *Two Dissertations* (1876) on Μονογενὴς Θεὸς and the *Nicene-Constantinopolitan Creed; and very characteristic his (posthumous) *Judaistic Christianity* (1894) and *The Christian Ecclesia* (1897). Hort had also wide and constructive interests in theology, esp. in its relations with the natural sciences, but these found little expression in writing. His *Hulsean Lectures for 1871, *The Way, the Truth, and the Life* (publd. posthumously, 1893), were an impressive essay in philosophical theology.

Life and Letters, ed. Arthur Fenton Hort, son (2 vols., London and New York, 1896); full review of this work, with appreciation of Hort, by W. *Sanday in *American Journal of Theology*, i (1897), pp. 95–117; further appreciation of Hort by T. B. *Strong in *J.T.S.*, i (1900), pp. 370–86. H. E. Ryle in *D.N.B.*, Suppl. ii (1901), pp. 443–7.

HOSANNA (Gk. ὡσαννά). The Greek form of the Hebrew petition הושׁיעה־נא ('Save, we beseech Thee'). It was used by the multitude when they proclaimed Jesus to be the Messiah on His triumphal entry into Jerusalem on *Palm Sunday (Mt. 21. 9, 15, Mk. 11. 9 f., Jn. 12. 13); and was thence introduced into the Christian liturgies at a very early date (e.g. *Didache 10. 6). The words 'Glory be to thee, O Lord, most High' in the *Sanctus of the Anglican BCP are a rendering of the *Hosanna in excelsis* ('Hosanna in the highest') in the medieval and modern Latin rite.

HOSEA, Book of. The first of the Twelve *Minor Prophets. Its author, Hosea (Vulg. Osee), the son of Beeri, was a younger contemporary of *Amos (q.v.), and apparently a native of the Northern Hebrew Kingdom. He prophesied during the years of its decline, some time before the fall of *Samaria in 722 B.C. The opening chapters (1–3) narrate the story of the prophet's tragic home life, in which he interpreted his experiences with Gomer, his unfaithful wife, as a parable of what had taken place between Israel and God. The remainder of the Book (chs. 4–14) is a development of the theme of Israel's apostasy and unfaithfulness in spite of the enduring love of God. Hosea is the first Biblical writer to use the family tie as an illustration of the relation between God and man (cf. St. Paul's description of the Church as the 'bride of Christ'). His realization of God's character of love also paved the way for the Christian teaching on the Fatherhood of God. Like Amos, he denounced the corrupt and shallow sacrificial worship of his day, but perhaps sought not so much its abolition as its spiritualization.

Commentaries by T. K. *Cheyne (Camb. Bib., AV, 1884), W. R. Harper (I.C.C. on Amos and Hosea, 1905, pp. 201–417), S. L. Brown (West. Comm., 1932). N. Peters, *Osee und die Geschichte* (1924). H. S. Nyberg, *Studien zum Hoseabuche*, zugleich ein Beitrag zur Klärung des Problems der Alttestamentlichen Textkritik (Uppsala Universitets Årsskrift, 1935, pt. 6; 1935). P. Cruveilhier, 'De l'interprétation historique des événements de la vie familiale du prophète Osée' in *R. Bibl.* [xxv], N.S., xiii (1916), pp. 342–62. A. Heermann, 'Ehe und Kinder des Propheten Hosea. Eine exegetische Studie zu Hos. 1. 2–9' in *Z.A.T.W.*, xl (1922), pp. 287–312; H. Schmidt, 'Die Ehe des Hosea', ib., xlii (1924), pp. 245–72; L. W. Batten, 'Hosea's Message and Marriage' in *Journal of Biblical Literature*, xlviii (1929), pp. 257–73. Further commentaries under *Minor Prophets*.

HOSIUS, or OSSIUS (c. 257–357), Bp. of Cordova. He was consecrated Bp. of Cordova c. 296, and suffered in the persecution under Maximian. He took part in the Council of *Elvira (c. 306) and from 313 to the Council of *Nicaea seems to have acted as ecclesiastical adviser to the Emp. *Constantine. In the early stages of the Arian controversy he was sent to *Alexandria to investigate the dispute between *Alexander and *Arius, and it was apparently in consequence of his report that the Emperor summoned the Nicene Council. There are some grounds for believing that here he presided, and also introduced the *Homoousion. He certainly presided at the anti-Arian Council of *Sardica in 343. In 355 he was banished to *Sirmium for his support of St. *Athanasius, and from his exile addressed to *Constantius a letter, which is his only surviving writing. At the Synod of Sirmium (357) he succumbed to pressure to the extent that he signed the 'Blasphemy' which involved communicating with the Arians and was allowed in consequence to return to his diocese. He repudiated his action at Sirmium, however, before his death in his hundredth year.

Primary sources (scattered) incl. Athanasius, *Hist. Ar.*, 42–45; id., *Apol. c. Ar.*, 89; id., *De Fuga*, 5; *Hilary, *Fragmenta*, 2 and 6; id., *De Synodis*, 10 f.; *Socrates, *H.E.*, ii. 31. V. C. De Clercq, C.I.C.M., *Ossius of Cordova. A Contribution to the History of the Constantinian Period* (Catholic University of America Studies in Christian Antiquity, xiii; 1954). For the spelling 'Ossius' see C. H. *Turner in *J.T.S.*, xii (1910–1911), pd. 275–7. See also T. D. C. Morse in *D.C.B.*, iii (1882), pp. 162–74, and Bardenhewer, iii (1912), pp. 393–5, with bibl.

HOSIUS, STANISLAUS (1504–79), Polish cardinal. He was a native of Cracow, of German origin, and studied law at Cracow, at *Bologna, where he came into touch with R. *Pole, and at Padua. He was ordained priest in 1543, and after holding several benefices, he was appointed Bp. of Kulm in 1549. In 1551 he was translated to the diocese of Ermland, where one of his chief tasks was the fight against Protestantism. Here he preached extensively in Latin, Polish, and German. In 1552–3 he published his chief work, the *Confessio Catholicae Fidei Christiana*, in which he contrasted the Catholic dogmas with the opposing beliefs of the Reformers and endeavoured to prove from Scripture and tradition that Catholicism and Christianity were identical. The work had a great success, over 30 editions and many translations appearing in the author's lifetime. Among other controversial writings that followed were his *Confutatio Prolegomenorum Brentii* (1558) against the Württembergian *Lutheran theologian, J. *Brenz, which had a preface by St. Peter *Canisius, and *De Expresso Dei Verbo* (1558), in which he claimed to demonstrate the necessity of an authoritative interpretation of Scripture. In 1558 *Paul IV called him to Rome as his adviser on the religious affairs of Poland and Prussia, and in 1560 *Pius IV appointed him nuncio to Ferdinand I. In this capacity he prepared the reopening of the Council of *Trent and brought back to the RC Church the Emperor's son, Maximilian, who had come under the influence of Protestant preachers. In 1561 he was created cardinal and appointed Papal legate at Trent, where he was entrusted esp. with the leadership in the doctrinal discussions. At the Council he vigorously upheld the primacy of the Pope. After returning to his diocese in 1564, he published the decrees of Trent at the Synod of Parczow (1564) and invited the *Jesuit Order to open a college, the later 'Lyceum Hosianum', at Braunsberg. In 1566 he was nominated legate *a latere* by *Pius V, and from 1569 resided in Rome as the permanent Polish representative. He upheld the use of violence against heretics, but in private life he was a man of a simple and unworldly faith.

Editio princeps of his collected works, Paris, 1562; the best ed. (still incomplete) is that publd. in 2 vols. fol., Cologne, 1584. Modern edd. of selections of his correspondence by F. Hipler-V. Zakrzewski [up to 1558] (Acta Historica Res Gestas Poloniae Illustrantia ab 1507 ad Annum 1795, iv, ix, parts 1 and 2; Editionum Collegii Historici Academiae Litterarum Cracoviensis, xv, xxxiv, xl; Cracow, 1879–88) and S. Steinherz (Nuntiaturberichte aus Deutschland, 1560–1572, nebst ergänzenden Actenstücken, Zweite Abt., Bd. i; Vienna, 1897). Early life (in Lat.) by S. Rescius (his secretary, Rome, 1587; repr. in ed. of his letters by F. Hipler-V. Zakrzewski, cited above, vol. i, pp. ii-cxxiv). Modern studies by A. Eichhorn (2 vols., Kirchheim, 1854–5), B. Elsner (Königsberg, 1911), and J. Lortz (Braunsberg, 1931). S. Frankl, *Doctrina Hosii de Notis Ecclesiae, in luce s. XVI considerata* (Rome, 1934); L. Bernacki, *La Doctrine de l'Église chez le Cardinal Hosius* (1936). G. Grabka, 'Cardinal Hosius and the Council of Trent' in *Theological Studies*, vii (1946), pp. 558–76. A. Humbert in *D.T.C.*, vii (pt. 1; 1922), cols. 178–90; s.v.; J. Lortz in *L.Th.K.*, v (1933), cols. 150–2, s.v.; I. Rogger in *E.C.*, vi (1951), cols. 1483–5, s.v.

HOSKYNS, Sir EDWYN CLEMENT (1884–1937), Anglican Biblical scholar. He was educated at Jesus College, Cambridge, and on the Continent, where he heard A. *Harnack and became a friend of A. *Schweitzer. Having been ordained in 1908, he was successively curate of St. Ignatius, Sunderland (1908–1912), and warden of Stephenson Hall, Sheffield (1912–15). In 1915 he became an army chaplain, and from 1919 till his death he was Dean of Chapel of Corpus Christi College, Cambridge. He made a name by his essay 'The Christ of the Synoptic Gospels' in *Essays Catholic and Critical* (1926), in which he argued that the so-called 'historical Jesus' of Liberal Protestantism was unhistorical, and that the teaching behind the Synoptic Gospels was much more complex and 'Catholic' than was generally supposed by liberal NT critics. His influential *The Riddle of the New Testament* (1931), written in collaboration with F. N. Davey, deals with the principles underlying the critical and historical study of the NT. In these studies Hoskyns passed from a *Modernist position, influenced by A. Schweitzer and A. *Loisy, to an objective and dogmatic attitude. Later he took over much from K. *Barth, whose *Commentary on Romans* he translated (1933). He also adopted the methods of G. *Kittel's *Wörterbuch*, as is shown esp. in his Sermons on the vocabulary of the NT. His great unfinished work, *The Fourth Gospel* (ed. F. N. Davey, 1940), had occupied him since 1923. Against many modern critics he insisted on the unity of St. John's Gospel. In it he was concerned esp. to bring out the theological meaning of the whole, making full use both of patristic and modern exegetical works. Though Hoskyns's literary output was small, his personal influence on generations of theological students at Cambridge has left deep traces in modern Anglican theology.

His sermons were edited with a memoir by C. H. Smyth, *Cambridge Sermons* (1938). J. O. Cobham in *D.N.B.*, *1931–1940*, p. 448 f., s.v.

HOSMER, FREDERICK LUCIAN (1840–1929), American hymn writer. Born at Framingham, Mass., he was educated at Harvard, and, after two years' school teaching (1866–68), was ordained in the *Unitarian ministry in 1869. After holding charges at Quincey, Ill., from 1872 to 1877, at Cleveland, Ohio, from 1878 to 1892, at St. Louis from 1894 to 1899 and at Berkeley, Cal., from 1899 to 1904, he delivered a series of lectures on Church hymnody in 1908 at Harvard Divinity School of which he was president for the year 1920–1. His hymns had a wide appeal esp. among adherents of the emancipated liberal theology of the late 19th cent. They include 'Not always on the Mount may we', 'O beautiful my country', 'O Name all other names above', and 'Thy Kingdom come, On bended knee'. They were mainly published in three series of *The Thought of God in Hymns and Poems*, which he edited in conjunction with W. C. Gannett (1885, 1894, and 1918). He also issued *Way of Life* (1877) for use in Sunday schools and, with W. C. Gannett and J. V. Blake, edited *Unity Hymns and Carols* (1880, enlarged 1911).

H. E. Starr in *Dict. Amer. Biog.*, ix (1932), p. 241 f.

HOSPITALLERS, also 'Knights Hospitaller'. At the end of the 11th cent. the headquarters of the order were a hospital at *Jerusalem under the patronage of St. *John Baptist; hence its members were more fully described as 'Knights of the Order of the Hospital of St. John of Jerusalem'. After 1310 they were also known as the **Knights of Rhodes,** and from 1530 as the **Knights of Malta.**

The beginnings of the order are uncertain; they may have been connected with the old *Benedictine Abbey of Sta Maria Latina in Jerusalem or alternatively with a separate foundation in the city made by merchants of Amalfi *c.* 1050. Its first historical personage is Master Gerard, under whom, after the successes of the *Crusaders in 1099, the order greatly developed and obtained Papal sanction. Under his successor, Raymond of Provence (1120–60), the order added the care of the sick to its original duties of providing hospitality for pilgrims and Crusaders. It also established an armed guard of knights for the defence of pilgrims which soon developed into a regular army. All members of the order were bound by the three religious vows and divided into two classes, the 'military brothers' and the 'brothers infirmarians'. To the latter were added the 'brothers chaplains', responsible for Divine worship and the spiritual needs of the community. During the 12th cent. the order spread to Europe, where it created foundations in Italy, France, Germany, and other countries. Its knights shared both the successes and the defeats of the Crusaders; and after the fall of Acre (1291) they escaped to Cyprus and subsequently conquered Rhodes (1309), which became the centre of their activities for the next 200 years. Here their character became predominantly military, and their power and wealth increased greatly after the suppression of the Knights *Templars (1312; q.v.), whose possessions were assigned to the Hospitallers by the Pope. Their principal achievements during this period were their exploits against the Turks, notably the victorious defence of Rhodes by the Grand Master Pierre d'Aubusson in 1480 and that of 1522 against Soliman II which ended in honourable defeat. After being without a home for seven years, the order received the sovereignty of Malta from *Charles V in 1530, where it regained its old importance for some time. The knights continued fighting the Turks in many battles and in 1571 took a decisive part in the battle of *Lepanto. The 17th and 18th cents. saw the decline of the order in morals and discipline, culminating in the treacherous surrender of Malta to Napoleon in 1798. Since then it has led a somewhat precarious existence. It now devotes itself to the maintenance of hospitals and still has knights under obedience to a Grand Master and several commanders. Its distinctive sign is the eight-pointed Maltese cross worn on a black cloak.

The term 'Hospitallers' is sometimes used in a wider sense, e.g. to include the *Brothers Hospitallers (q.v.) founded by St. *John of God.

J. Delaville le Roulx, *Cartulaire général de l'ordre de S. Jean de Jérusalem, 1100–1310* (4 vols., 1894–1906). Id., *Les Hospitaliers en Terre Sainte et à Chypre, 1100–1310* (1904); id., *Les Hospitaliers à Rhodes jusqu'à la mort de Philibert de Naillac, 1310–1421* (1913); id., *Mélanges sur l'ordre de S. Jean de Jérusalem* (1910). Id., 'Les Statuts de l'ordre de l'hôpital de Saint-Jean de Jérusalem' in *Bibliothèque de l'École des Chartes*, xlviii (1887), pp. 342–56, and other works by the same author. [R. Aubert de] Vertot [d'Aubeuf], *Histoire des chevaliers hospitaliers de S. Jean de Jérusalem appellez depuis les chevaliers de Rhodes et aujourd'hui les chevaliers de Malte* (4 vols., 1726; Eng. tr., 2 vols., 1728). A. v. Winterfeld, *Geschichte des ritterlichen Ordens St. Johannis vom Spital zu Jerusalem* (1859). H. Prutz, 'Die exemte Stellung des Hospitaliter-Ordens. Ihre Entwicklung, ihr Wesen und ihre Wirkungen' in *Sb.* (Bayr.), Jg. 1904, pp. 95–187; id., 'Die Anfänge der Hospitaler auf Rhodos, 1310–1355' (ib., Jg. 1908, I. Abh.). G. Bottarelli, *Storia politica e militare del sovrano ordine di S. Giovanni di Gerusalemme detto di Malta* (2 vols., Milan, 1940). Heimbucher i, pp. 615–17, with further bibl. W. A. Phillips, 'St. John of Jerusalem, Knights of the Order of the Hospital of', in *E.B.* (ed. 11), xxiv (1911), pp. 12–19.

HOSPITALS. Christian hospitals were founded throughout E. Christendom from the 4th cent. onwards, and became exceedingly numerous in W. Europe during the earlier Middle Ages, when they were commonly associated with the monastic orders. From the earliest times different types were instituted to meet different problems, e.g. those of orphans, the sick, the aged, and the impotent poor. With some notable exceptions, e.g. St. Bartholomew's Hospital, London (begun 1123), the medieval hospitals of England were for the most part almshouses for the aged. By the close of the 15th cent. a large proportion

of these had been allowed to perish or to survive only in decadent forms. The secularization of the Reformation period interfered only temporarily with the hospitals of Europe, and numbers of important foundations by rulers, municipalities, and Christian societies took place in the 17th and 18th cents.

R. M. Clay, *The Medieval Hospitals of England* (1909). The *Catholic Encyclopedia*, s.v., has an excellent brief general account.

HOST (Lat. *hostia*). A sacrificial victim, and so the consecrated Bread in the *Eucharist, regarded as the Sacrifice of the Body of Christ.

HOURS, Canonical. The times of daily prayer laid down in the *Breviary, and esp. the services appointed to be recited at these times. In the W. Church, the seven commonly recognized Hours are *Mattins and *Lauds (reckoned as a single hour), *Prime, *Terce, Sext, None, *Vespers, and *Compline (qq.v.).

HOUSEL. A medieval English name for the Eucharist, perhaps descended from a Teutonic stem meaning 'holy'. In *Ulphilas' rendering of Mt. 10. 13, a similar word (*hunsl*) is used for 'sacrifice'.

The 'houselling cloth' was the (late Medieval) long white linen cloth spread before, or held by, the communicants at the time of receiving the Sacrament. It has survived continuously at St. Mary the Virgin's, Oxford, at Wimborne Minster, and perhaps in a few other places. It has been restored in some other Anglican churches in modern times. In the RC Church the use of such a cloth is ordered by the '*Rituale Romanum ' (IV, ii, 1).

Artt. 'Housel' and 'Houseling' in *O.E.D.*, v (1901), p. 423.

HOWARD, JOHN (*c.* 1726–90), English philanthropist and prison reformer. He was a man of Evangelical piety, firmly convinced of the truth of the *Calvinistic creed in which he had been brought up, and though his second wife was a Churchwoman and he accompanied her to the local parish church, he remained a dissenter throughout his life. In 1773 he became High Sheriff of Bedford, where what he saw of the terrible afflictions of both tried and untried in the county gaol inspired him to his work of prison reform. His first step (1774) was to secure official salaries for gaolers, who had hitherto depended on fees extorted from the prisoners. He then visited numerous prisons and hospitals in England and throughout Europe, regardless of the dangers of entering infectious dwellings and noxious cells. His writings included the *State of the Prisons* (1777), which led to the Reform Act of the same year, and an *Account of the Principal Lazarettos in Europe* (1789).

His *State of the Prisons* was ed. by K. Ruck for Everyman's Library, No. 835 (1929). J. Aikin, *A View of the Character and Public Services of the late John Howard*

(1792); J. B. Brown, *Memoirs of the Public and Private Life of John Howard the Philanthropist* (1818). H. Dixon, *John Howard and the Prison-World of Europe* (1849). J. Field, *The Life of John Howard* (1850); id., *Correspondence of John Howard* with memoir and notes (1855). J. Stoughton, *Howard the Philanthropist and his Friends* (1884). L. O. Cooper, *John Howard. The Prisoner's Friend* [c. 1904]. E. C. S. Gibson, *John Howard* (1901). J. F. Rowe, *John Howard. Prison Reformer and Philanthropist* (1927). G. F. R. Barker in *D.N.B.*, xxviii (1891), pp. 44–8.

HOWE, JOHN (1630–1705), *Puritan divine and writer. In 1650 he became chaplain (though apparently unordained), and a little later Fellow, of Magdalen College, Oxford. In 1652 he was ordained by the Puritan rector of Winwick, whom he looked up to as a 'primitive bishop'. *C.* 1654 he became incumbent of Great Torrington, Devon, and in 1657 O. *Cromwell made him his domestic chaplain, an office which he continued to hold under Richard Cromwell. On the latter's resignation he returned to Great Torrington, from which he was ejected in 1662 on the passing of the Act of *Uniformity. Unlike most of his contemporary fellow-*Nonconformists, his standpoint inclined to *latitudinarianism. After some years of wandering he published in 1668 *The Blessedness of Righteousness*, which brought him to the notice of Lord Massarene, and he became his chaplain at Antrim Castle with the approval of the bishop of the diocese. In 1676 he was appointed co-pastor of the Presbyterian congregation at Haberdashers' Hall, where he continued his publications and lived on friendly terms with eminent Anglicans. In 1686, owing to the increasing severity of measures against the Nonconformists, he settled for a while at Utrecht, but in 1687 he returned to England. He headed the deputation of Nonconformist ministers who congratulated William III in 1688. He continued to work for mutual forbearance among Christians of differing denominations, and unsuccessfully sought to unite the *Presbyterians and *Congregationalists.

Works (2 vols., London, 1724), with Memoir by E. *Calamy, vol. i, pp. 1–88; new ed., 3 vols., ib., 1848. Works also ed. J. Hunt (8 vols., London, 1810–22); Posthumous Works, ed. id. (4 vols., ib., 1832); also publ., with general introd. by H. Rogers, by *Religious Tract Society (6 vols., 1862–3). H. Rogers, *The Life and Character of John Howe with an Analysis of his Writings* (1836); R. F. Horton, *John Howe* (1895). A. Gordon in *D.N.B.*, xxviii (1891), pp. 85–8.

HOWLEY, WILLIAM (1766–1848), Abp. of *Canterbury. He was the last 'Prince-Archbishop', the revenues of the archiepiscopal see coming under the control of the *Ecclesiastical Commissioners at his death. Educated at Winchester and at New College, Oxford, he was appointed Regius prof. of divinity at Oxford in 1809, Bp. of London in 1813, and Abp. of Canterbury in 1828. An 18th cent. High Churchman and an extreme Tory, he was opposed to political reform and relief for RCs and Jews, and it was largely his influence that secured the rejection of Lord John Russell's moderate Education scheme in 1839. On the death of William IV (1837), whom he had attended on his sick bed, it fell to him to announce to the Princess Victoria (whom he had baptized when he was Bp. of London) her accession to the crown.

B. Harrison, *The Remembrance of a departed Guide and Ruler in the Church of God*. A Charge delivered to the Clergy of the Archdeaconry of Maidstone (1848). G. F. R. Barker in *D.N.B.*, xxviii (1891), p. 128 f.

HOWSON, JOHN SAUL (1816–85), Dean of *Chester. He was educated at Giggleswick School and Trinity College, Cambridge. After ordination as deacon (1845; priest, 1846), he taught at Liverpool Collegiate Institute, where W. J. *Conybeare was head master. On Conybeare's resignation in 1849, Howson succeeded him. In 1866 Howson was presented to the vicarage of Wisbech. From 1867 till his death he was Dean of Chester, where he laboured for the restoration of the fabric of the cathedral and for schools in the city. He is best known for his *Life and Epistles of St. Paul* (2 vols., 1852), in which he collaborated with Conybeare. The work, based on extensive geographical, archaeological, and historical studies, was an impressive work of scholarship for its time, learned yet not beyond the general reader, and is still worthy of study. Most of the descriptive passages were done by Howson. He also wrote other Pauline studies, among them *The Character of St. Paul* (1862), *Metaphors of St. Paul* (1868), and *The Companions of St. Paul* (1874), as well as other works on NT subjects. An article on 'Deaconesses in the Church of England' in the *Quarterly Review* (1861), reissued in 1862 as a pamphlet, did much to promote the systematized ministry of women in England.

E. Venables in *D.N.B.*, xxviii (1891), pp. 130–2.

HRABANUS MAURUS. See *Rabanus Maurus*.

HROSVIT (10th cent.), German Christian poetess. Of a noble Saxon family, she became a nun of the *Benedictine abbey of Gandersheim in Saxony. She was very learned and well versed not only in Scripture and the Fathers but also in classical literature, Horace, Virgil, Ovid, Plautus, and esp. Terence whom, acc. to her own admission, she took as her model. The MS. of her writings, in Latin, was discovered by the humanist, Conrad Celtes, at Ratisbon and printed for the first time in 1501. Originally her works were divided into three parts containing 8 poems on saints, 6 plays, and a long panegyric on the Ottos which was left unfinished. Among the poems on saints the 'Passio Sancti Pelagii' is esp. interesting, since she claims to have derived her facts from an eye-witness of the martyrdom. It is printed in full by the *Bollandists in the '*Acta Sanctorum'. Other poems treat of our Lady, St. *Basil, St. *Dionysius, and St. *Agnes. The main object of her plays was to oppose to Terence's representations of the frailty of women the chastity of Christian virgins and penitents. 'Gallicanus', 'Dulcitius', and 'Sapientia' describe the steadfastness of martyrs, whereas 'Callimachus', 'Abraham', and 'Paphnutius' deal with the struggle between the spirit and the flesh; and many of them reveal a remarkable sense of the dramatic. She was greatly encouraged by the scholars of her time, but soon after her death almost completely forgotten. In recent times she has once more aroused much interest, esp. in Britain, where modern translations of several of her plays have been made.

Editio princeps by C. Celte (Nuremberg, 1501); also ed. H. L. Schurzfleischius (Wittenberg, 1707), P. de Winterfeld ([M.G.H.] Scriptores Rerum Germanicarum, 1902), and K. Strecker (Teub., ed. 2, 1930). Poems also ed. G. H. Pertz in M.G.H., Scriptores, iv (1841), pp. 302–35. Works repr. from edd. of Schurzfleischius and Pertz in J. P. Migne, PL, cxxxvii, 941–1168. Eng. trr. of her plays by H. J. W. Tillyard (London, 1923, with general introd. and bibl.) and C. St. John (ib., 1923), and of her non-dramatic works by Sister M. Gonsalva Wiegand (St. Louis, Mo., 1936). J. Aschbach, Roswita und Conrad Celtes (1867; ed. 2, much enlarged, 1868). Other studies by R. Köpke (Ottonische Studien, ii; Berlin, 1869) and J. Schneiderhan (Paderborn, 1912). Manitius, i, pp. 619–32. A. Mayer-Pfannholz in L.Th.K., v (1933), col. 162 f., s.v.

HUBER, SAMUEL (c. 1547–1624), Protestant controversialist. A native of Burgdorf, near Berne, he took an active part in a series of religious disputes, generally defending *Lutheran doctrines against the *Calvinism of the Swiss Reformed Church. He caused special offence by his assertion of Christ's universal atonement ('Christum Jesum esse mortuum pro peccatis totius generis humani'), and was banished from Switzerland on 28 June 1588. Shortly afterwards he signed the 'Formula of *Concord' (1580) and for a time held offices in the Lutheran Church in Germany. The title 'Huberianism' was widely given to doctrines of the Atonement identical with or similar to those which Huber advocated.

J. A. Schmid, De Samuelis Huberi Vita Fatis et Doctrina (Helmstedt, 1708), with full list of his works. K. R. Hagenbach and G. Müller in P.R.E. (ed. 3), viii (1900), pp. 409–12, with bibl.

HUBERT, St. (d. 727), 'Apostle of the Ardennes'. C. 705 he succeeded St. *Lambert as Bp. of Tongeren (or Maestricht) and later transferred the see to Liége. The well-known traditions about him are of much later date. Acc. to one story, his conversion from a very worldly life took place on a *Good Friday morning when he was out hunting, and met a stag with a crucifix between its horns. In astonishment, he cast himself to the ground, and on asking for guidance was told to seek instruction from St. Lambert, the bishop, by whom he was converted. He shares with St. *Eustace (of whom a similar story is told) the patronage of huntsmen. He was also invoked against hydrophobia. Feast day, 3 Nov.

AA.SS., Nov. I (1887), pp. 759–930, with seven Lives; crit. ed. of the first by W. Levison in M.G.H., Scriptores Rerum Merovingicarum, vi (1913), pp. 471–96. M. Coens, S.J., 'Notes sur la légende de S. Hubert' in Anal. Boll., xlv (1927), pp. 345–62 (with review of recent lit.). J. Fohl in L.Th.K., v (1933), col. 165 f., with bibl.

HUBERT WALTER (d. 1205), Abp. of *Canterbury. Orig. one of the chaplains of Ranulf de Glanville, he became Dean of *York

in 1186 and Bp. of *Salisbury in 1189. In 1190 he accompanied Richard I on the Third *Crusade, where his efficiency and care for the oppressed won him respect and gratitude from all classes. On his way back to England he visited the imprisoned King at Dürenstein and after his return raised the ransom for the King's release. In 1193 he was elected Abp. of Canterbury. In 1194, when Richard finally left England for his French wars, Hubert Walter was appointed justiciar during the King's absence, and in this capacity governed England for the next four years. He became unpopular through the King's constant demands for money and the consequent heavy taxation; and also came into ill odour by executing William Fitz Osbert, the leader of an insurrection who had sought sanctuary in *Bow Church. These troubles, increased by difficulties with the monks of Christ Church, Canterbury, in which *Innocent III finally decided in favour of the monks, led him to resign his justiciarship in 1198. In the next year, however, he resumed the office, probably because he knew himself to be the only person able to deal with the new king, *John. In 1201 and 1203 he was employed on unsuccessful missions to Philip of France. He died on a journey from Canterbury to Boxley, undertaken to reconcile the *Rochester monks to their bishop. Hubert has been accused of sacrificing his pastoral duties to his political position. He ably administered, however, the temporalities of his see, and did much for his cathedral, to which he made valuable bequests at his death.

Various letters addressed to him or written by him are pr. in W. *Stubbs (ed.), Chronicles and Memorials of the Reign of Richard I, ii, Epistolae Cantuarienses (R.S., 1865), pp. 366–72, 391–3, 394–7, 429 f., 439 f., 445 f., 459–68, 473 f., 479 f., 482 f., 494, 508, and 520. Good account of his political activities, with reff., in H. W. C. Davis, England under the Normans and Angevins (1905), pp. 323–9. W. F. *Hook, Lives of the Archbishops of Canterbury, ii (1862), pp. 584–656. C. R. Cheney, From Becket to Langton (1956), pp. 31–41. Kate Norgate in D.N.B., xxvii (1891), pp. 137–40. H. W. C. Davis in D.E.C.H., p. 615 f., s.v. 'Walter, Hubert'. See also histories of the reign of John, cited s.v.

HÜBMAIER, BALTHASAR (1485?–1528), German *Anabaptist. He studied under J. *Eck at Freiburg (Breisgau) and Ingolstadt, at the latter place becoming professor and parish priest. In 1516 he was appointed preacher at Regensburg cathedral, and in 1521 parish priest at Waldshut. Here he came into contact with the Swiss Reformers, allied himself with H. *Zwingli openly in 1523, and forthwith introduced the Reformation. Soon, however, he abandoned Zwinglian doctrines for those of the Anabaptists, and in his Von dem Tauf der Gläubigen, published in May 1525, asserted the necessity of personal faith for baptism and condemned infant baptism as idolatry. Soon afterwards he became entangled in the *Peasants' War and may have been the author of the *Twelve Articles. When in the night of 5–6 Dec. 1525 Waldshut was occupied by government troops, Hübmaier fled to Zürich, where he was forced by Zwingli to abjure his Baptist views. But early in the next year he left Zürich, renounced his recantation, and in

July 1526 settled at Nikolsburg in Moravia where he worked for the Anabaptist cause esp. by writing pamphlets on theological questions, e.g. on the Lord's Supper and in defence of free-will. In 1527 the Austrian authorities demanded his extradition, and he was taken to Vienna where he was burnt on 10 Mar. 1528.

Modern Lives by J. Loserth (Brünn, 1893), H. C. Vedder (Heroes of the Reformation, London, 1905), W. Mau (Abhandlungen zur mittleren und neueren Geschichte, Hft. xl, Berlin, 1912), and C. Sachsse (Neue Studien zur Geschichte der Theologie und der Kirche, Stk. 20, Berlin, 1914). A. W. Hegler, in *P.R.E.* (ed. 3), viii (1900), pp. 418–424; W. Koehler in *R.G.G.* (ed. 2), ii (1928), col. 2032 f.

HUCK, ALBERT (b. 1867), NT scholar. He has held several pastoral appointments in Germany. He compiled a very widely used 'Synopsis' of the first three Gospels, presenting their Greek text with the parallel passages in adjacent columns. The 1st edition appeared in 1892 and the 9th, much revised by H. *Lietzmann, in 1936. Its existence has greatly assisted modern researches (esp. in the years 1895–1925) into the *Synoptic Problem.

There is an English adaptation of the 9th German edition by F. L. Cross (Tübingen, 1936; Oxford, 1949).

HUET, PIERRE DANIEL (1630–1721), French scholar. In 1652 an invitation from Queen *Christina to his friend, Samuel Bochart (1599–1667), to the court of Sweden, led Huet to accompany him to Stockholm, where, having discovered in the Royal Library some fragments of *Origen's *Comm. on Matt.*, Huet was stimulated to produce an edition of Origen, which he published in 1668. He then edited, in conjunction with Anne Lefèvre, the famous 'Delphin Classics' in some 60 volumes for the Dauphin, whose tutor (with J. B. *Bossuet) he was. His *Demonstratio evangelica* (1679) was an apology for Christianity. Having been ordained in 1676, he became Bp. of Avranches in 1689. After having been at first sympathetic to *Descartes's philosophy, he later abandoned it, for reasons which he outlined in his *Censura philosophiae Cartesianae* (1689). His valuable collection of MSS., which he bequeathed to the Jesuits of the rue St.-Antoine at Paris, passed, after the order was suppressed, for the most part into the Royal Library, and have thus found their way into the Bibliothèque Nationale at Paris.

C. Bartholmèss, *Huet, évêque d'Avranches, ou le scepticisme théologique* (Paris, 1850); J. B. M. Flottes, *Étude sur Daniel Huet* (Montpellier, 1857); A. Dupront, *P. D. Huet et l'exégèse comparatiste du XVIIe siècle* (1930). C. Urbain, 'La Bibliothèque de P. D. Huet' in *Bulletin du Bibliophile et du Bibliothécaire*, 1910, pp. 133–46. B. Heurtebize in in *D.T.C.*, vii (pt. 1; 1922), cols. 199–201, with bibl.

HUG, JOHANN LEONHARD (1765–1846), Catholic NT scholar. From 1791 he was professor at the university of Freiburg (Breisgau). He directed his vast erudition against the rationalistic Biblical criticism of his time. His researches also stimulated the growth of the *textual criticism of the NT, though his ingenious attempt to connect three recensions of the *Septuagint (whose places of origin he

believed assured) with three types of NT text failed. His most important Biblical work was his *Einleitung in die Schriften des NT* (2 vols., 1808–9; Eng. tr., 2 vols., 1827).

A. Maier, *Gedächtnisrede auf Joh. Leonh. Hug, . . .* bei dessen akademischer Todtenfeier in der Universitäts-Kirche zu Freiburg (1847).

HÜGEL, BARON FRIEDRICH VON. See *Von Hügel, Friedrich.*

HUGH, St. (1024–1109), Abbot of *Cluny. Of a noble Burgundian family, he was brought up by his great-uncle, Hugh, Bp. of Auxerre. At the age of 14 he entered the monastery of Cluny under St.*Odilo and owing to outstanding piety was allowed to take his vows only a year later. Before the age of 21 he was Prior and on Odilo's death (1 Jan. 1049) was unanimously chosen Abbot, being installed by the Abp. of Besançon on 22 Feb. 1049. *Leo IX, formerly Bp. of Toul and a warm supporter of Cluniac principles, took him into his confidence, and henceforward Hugh, as adviser to nine Popes, came to exercise a dominating influence in ecclesiastical and political affairs. He took part in securing the condemnation of *Berengar of Tours (1150); assisted Nicholas II in the decree on Papal elections (Council of Rome, 1059); and upheld the privileges of his order against the attacks of his fellow-countrymen (Council of Rome, 1063). He warmly encouraged *Gregory VII's efforts for reform and did his best to mediate in the bitter feud between the Pope and *Henry IV. Despite his constant absence, the monastery suffered no relaxation in discipline and, indeed, reached under Hugh a position never surpassed. In 1068 he settled the usages for the whole Cluniac order. He induced Pope *Urban II (d. 1099) to consecrate in person the high altar of the new basilica at Cluny (25 Oct. 1095), then the largest church in Christendom. During his rule, the first Cluniac house in England, the priory of St. Pancras at Lewes, was founded. At the Council of *Clermont (1095) he took a leading part in the organization of the First *Crusade. Among his liturgical reforms was the introduction of the singing of the *Veni Creator* at terce during Pentecost. He wrote a 'Life of the Blessed Virgin', but this, with most of his letters, has been lost. He was canonized by *Callistus III in 1120. Feast day, 29 April.

Surviving correspondence in J. P. Migne, *PL*, clix, 927–946, with various statutes and other docc. bearing his name, ib., 945–84. M. Férotin, O.S.B., 'Une Lettre inédite de Saint Hugues, abbé de Cluny, à Bernard d'Agen, archevêque de Tolède' in *Bibliothèque de l'École des Chartes*, lxi (1900), pp. 339–45, and lxiii (1902), pp. 682–6, incl. text. Early lives include that of Gilo, first publd. in full by A. L'Huillier, *Vie de Saint Hugues* (Solesmes, 1888), pp. 574–618; extract ed. L. von Heinemann in *M.G.H.*, Scriptores, xv (pt. 2; 1888), pp. 935–40; life, identified by editor with that of Ezelo, mentioned by Rainaud (see below), ed. L. M. Smith in *E.H.R.*, xxvii (1912), pp. 96–101; life by Rainaud, abbot of Vézelay, pr. in *AA.SS.*, Apr. III (1675), pp. 648–53; that by *Hildebert of Lavardin, pr. ib., pp. 634–48; other material, pp. 654–62, with introd. pp. 628–34; the whole entry in *AA.SS.* is repr. in J. P. Migne, loc. cit., 840–928. T. Schieffer, 'Notice sur les vies de Saint Hugues, abbé de

Cluny' in *Le Moyen-Âge*, xlvi (3e Sér., vii; 1936), pp. 81–103. On the development of Cluny under his rule, A. Fliche in Fliche–Martin, viii (1944), pp. 427–44, with bibl. See also bibl. to *Cluny*.

HUGH, St. (1052–1132), Bp. of Grenoble. Born at Châteauneuf, near *Valence, he became (when still a layman) a Canon of Valence. In 1080 he was elected Bp. of Grenoble to reform the disorders in the diocese, where in a long episcopate he successfully redressed abuses and fostered devotions. He welcomed St. *Bruno and his monks to his diocese, granting them La *Grande Chartreuse (1084). He was canonized by Innocent II in 1134, two years after his death. Feast day, 1 Apr.

The primary authority is the Lat. life by his friend Guigo, Prior of the *Grande Chartreuse, pr., with introd., in *AA.SS.*, Apr. I (1675), pp. 36–46; repr. in J. P. Migne, *PL*, cliii, 759–84; also ed. C. Bellet (Montreuil, 1889). Modern life by A. Du Boys (Grenoble, 1837).

HUGH, St. (c. 1140–1200), Bp. of *Lincoln. He was the son of the lord of Avalon in Burgundy. Brought up to be a member of an order of *canons regular near Grenoble, he was early attracted by the much more severe nd secluded life of the newly founded *Carthusian Order, and took vows at the *Grande Chartreuse in 1160. His character and talents became known to Henry II, who was attempting to establish at Witham in Somerset the first Carthusian house in England, and in 1175 he secured the services of Hugh as its prior. This was the beginning of a frequent intercourse between Hugh and the King. In 1186 he became, at Henry's earnest wish, Bp. of Lincoln. As bishop he administered his huge diocese well and showed a courageous independence of the King, e.g. as champion of the people against the royal foresters. He later took the lead, with the Bp. of Salisbury, in refusing a demand of Richard I for money for the King's wars, an event of significance in constitutional history. He never forgot that he was a monk, and every year retired for a time to the priory of Witham. Already in his own lifetime he was greatly revered for his holiness and devotion, e.g. his Christian love towards lepers, and in 1220 he was canonized. His tomb at Lincoln became second to that of St. *Thomas of Canterbury as a place of popular devotion until it was spoiled by *Henry VIII. Feast day, 17 Nov.

Magna Vita, by Adam, monk of Eynsham and chaplain to St. Hugh, ed. F. J. Dimock (Rolls Series, 1864); *Vita*, by *Giraldus Cambrensis in *Opera*, ed. id., vii (ib., 1877), pp. 83–147, with 'Legenda . . . to be Read . . . on the Day of his Obit' in Appendix D, pp. 172–92; metrical life written prob. shortly after his Canonization (1220–35), ed. id. (London, 1860). Modern lives by 'Un Religieux de la Grande Chartreuse' (Montreuil, 1890; Eng. tr. with additions by H. Thurston, S.J., 'Quarterly Series', xcix; 1898); G. G. Perry (London, 1879), C. L. Marson (ib., 1901), F. A. Forbes (ib., 1917), R. M. Woolley (ib., 1927), and J. Clayton (ib., 1931). E. M. Thompson, *The Carthusian Order in England* (The Church Historical Society, New Series, iii, 1930), pp. 54–70.

HUGH OF ST.-VICTOR (c. 1096–1141), *Victorine theologian and mystic. He was probably born at Hartingham in Saxony and belonged to the family of the Counts of Blankenburg. Educated by the *canons regular of St. *Augustine at Hammersleben, nr. Halberstadt, he took their habit, and went to the monastery of St.-Victor at Paris in 1115, which had become famous for its learning under *William of Champeaux. In 1133 he was charged with the direction of studies and made prior. As a philosopher and theologian he was deeply influenced by the Platonic tradition transmitted through St. Augustine (he was called 'Alter Augustinus') and *Dionysius the Areopagite, on whose 'Celestial Hierarchy' he wrote a commentary. His principal theological work is the 'De Sacramentis Christianae Fidei' in which is worked out his symbolist conception of the universe, acc. to which every creature is the sensible expression of a Divine thought. The mystic way leads from natural thought (*cogitatio*) through the intuitive meditation by which the soul tries to discover the Divine thoughts hidden under the veil of both creatures and the Scriptures (*meditatio*), to purity of life, and thence to loving contemplation (*contemplatio*). Accordingly reason plays an important part in his system, faith being at once above reason (*supra rationem*) yet acc. to reason (*secundum rationem*), and therefore patient of rational investigation. He thus rescued the dialectic method from the discredit brought on it by *Abelard and prepared the way for the great Schoolmen of the 13th cent.

Collected ed. of his works first publd. at Paris, 1518; also ed. by the Canons of St.-Victor, 3 vols., Rotterdam, 1648, virtually repr. in J. P. Migne, *PL*, clxxv–clxxvii. Two further works, 'Epitome in Philosophiam' and 'De Contemplatione et eius Speciebus', first publd. by [J.] B. Hauréau, *Hughes de Saint-Victor. Nouvel examen de l'édition de ses œuvres* (1859), pp. 161–75 and 177–210 respectively; 'De Tribus Maximis Circumstantiis Gestorum' first publd. by W. M. Green in *Speculum*, xviii (1943), pp. 484–93; 'De Grammatica', first publd. by J. Leclercq, O.S.B., in *Archives d'Histoire doctrinale et littéraire du Moyen-Âge*, xviii (1943), pp. 263–322. There are also modern edd. of 'Soliloquium de Arrha Animae' and 'De Vanitate Mundi' by K. Müller (Kleine Texte für Vorlesungen und Übungen, cxxiii; 1913); and of 'Didascalion de Studio Legendi' by C. H. Buttimer (Catholic University of America Studies in Medieval and Renaissance Latin, x; 1939). Eng. trr. of 'De Arrha Animae' by F. S. Taylor (London, 1945) and of 'De Sacramentis' by R. J. Deferrari (Medieval Academy of America Publication, No. lviii; 1951). The Explanation of the Rule of St. *Augustine usually attributed to Hugh of St.-Victor, but prob. the work of Lietbert of St. Ruf, was tr. into Eng. by A. Smith, O.S.B. (London, 1911). J. B. Hauréau, *Les Œuvres de Hughes de Saint-Viktor* (1886). A. Mignon, *Les Origines de !1 scolastique et Hughes de Saint-Victor* (2 vols., [1895]). H. Ostler, *Die Psychologie des Hugo von St. Viktor* (B.G.P.M., vi, Hft. 1; 1906). H. Weisweiler, S.J., *Die Wirksamkeit der Sakramente nach Hugo von St.-Viktor* (1932), and numerous articles by this author listed in J. Châtillon, cited below. F. E. Croydon, 'Notes on the Life of Hugh of St.-Victor' in *J.T.S.*, xl (1939), pp. 232–53. J. Châtillon, 'De Guillaume de Champeaux à Thomas Gallus. Chronique d'histoire littéraire et doctrinale de l'école de Saint-Victor', section II, 'Hughes de Saint-Victor', in *Revue du Moyen-Âge latin*, viii (1952), pp. 147–62. Überweg, ii, pp. 261–7, with bibl. p. 709. F. Vernet in *D.T.C.*, vii (pt. 1; 1922), cols. 240–308, s.v. 'Hughes de Saint-Victor', with bibl.; A. Piolanti in *E.C.*, xii (1954), cols. 711–13, s.v. 'Ugo di San Vittore', with more modern bibl.

HUGHES, HUGH PRICE (1847–1902), *Methodist divine. A native of Carmarthen and son of a minister, he began preaching at the age of 14 and, after entering the Wesleyan ministry, became a great preacher, who concerned himself esp. with such social problems as the housing of the poor, sweating, and gambling. In 1885 he started the *Methodist Times*, a weekly which soon became one of the leading organs of Nonconformist opinion. He worked hard to secure co-operation among the various Nonconformist bodies, and in 1896 he became the first president of the National Council of the Evangelical Free Churches. He also took a prominent part in the Education Acts controversy, in which, though supporting the Nonconformist policy, he on one occasion expressed his willingness to accept the *Apostles' Creed as a basis of teaching in the schools.

[Dorothea Price Hughes, daughter], *The Life of Hugh Price Hughes* (1904). J. G. Mantle, *Hugh Price Hughes* ('New Century Leaders Series', 1901). Katherine Price Hughes (wife), *The Story of My Life* (1945).

HUGUENOTS, the *Calvinist French Protestants. The name, which is explained by Henri Estienne (*Stephanus) in his *Apologie d'Hérodote* (1566) as a nickname based on a medieval romance about a King Hugo, came to be applied to the French Protestants *c.* 1560. (The formerly accepted derivation from *Eidgenossen* (Ger. 'confederates'), i.e. those admitted to the Swiss Confederation, is untenable). The movement has been traced back to the publication of J. *Faber's *Sancti Pauli Epistolae xiv . . . cum commentariis* (1512), which upheld a doctrine of *justification by faith alone. But its real originator was J. *Calvin who, though he had to flee from France in 1534, dedicated his *Institutes* (1536) to Francis I. At the Synod of Paris (1559), the French Protestant Church formally organized itself on a Calvinist basis. The movement was fiercely resisted by the family of the Guises, who came into power with the accession of Francis II only a few weeks after the Synod, but by 1561 it had grown to a formidable national minority and was consolidated by the Colloquy of *Poissy (q.v.). For over thirty years (1562–94) there was almost continuous civil war with the Catholic majority in which the Massacre of St. *Bartholomew (1572, q.v.) was the most terrible incident. The increasing influence of the *Politiques (q.v.) led to full freedom of worship by the Edict of *Nantes (13 Apr. 1598). Nevertheless the Huguenots continued to be a disruptive element in the state until their fortress of La Rochelle was reduced in 1628. Under Louis XIV, continual attempts were made to nullify the concessions of the Edict of Nantes, and it was finally revoked on 18 Oct. 1685. Many Huguenots were forced by *dragonnades and similar methods to apostatize, and some 300,000 sought refuge in Holland, Switzerland, America, England and Prussia. In 1702–5 Huguenot extremists raised the rebellion of the *Camisards. But it failed and their influence was negligible for the rest of the century. Marriages celebrated before Huguenot ministers were not recognized by the state until 1787, and only in 1802 was the legal standing of the Huguenot Church

established. From then on, except for a short period of repression after the Bourbon restoration of 1815, they suffered no further restriction, and increased considerably in numbers. From the period 1819–29 date the more important Protestant Church societies of France, for education, missions, and the circulation of the Bible. In the middle of the century dissension between the liberal and traditionalist sections led to a schism in 1872. A step towards reunion was the creation of the 'National Union of the Reformed [i.e. Calvinist] Churches of France' in 1907, a body which combines with non-Calvinistic bodies to form the Protestant Federation of France. See also *France, Christianity in; Du Plessis-Mornay, Philipp; Henry IV*.

M. H. Baird, *History of the Rise of the Huguenots* (2 vols., 1880); id., *The Huguenots and Henry of Navarre* (2 vols., 1886); id., *The Huguenots and the Revocation of the Edict of Nantes* (2 vols., 1895). R. Lane Poole, *A History of the Huguenots of the Dispersion* (1880); A. J. Grant, *The Huguenots* (H.U.L., 1934). J. Viénot, *Histoire de la réforme française des origines à l'édit de Nantes* (1926); id., *Histoire de la réforme française de l'édit de Nantes à sa révocation* (1934). G. H. Dodge, *The Political Theory of the Huguenots of the Dispersion with special Reference to the Thought and Influence of Pierre Jurieu* (New York, 1947). See also bibl. to *France, Christianity in; Camisards; Nantes, Edict of; Henry IV* of France; and *Richelieu*.

HULSEAN LECTURES. The course of lectures delivered annually at Cambridge in acc. with the bequest of the Rev. John Hulse (1708–90). The original distribution of the bequest provided: (1) two divinity scholarships at St. John's College, (2) a prize for a dissertation, (3) a 'Christian Advocate', and (4) a preacher or lecturer. By a revision of the statutes in 1860, a divinity professorship was substituted for (3) and the status of (4) considerably altered. By a further revision in 1934, the Hulsean and Norrissian professorships were united to form the Norris-Hulse Professorship, the first holder of the joint professorship being F. C. *Burkitt.

HULST, MAURICE D'. See *D'Hulst, Maurice*.

HUMANI GENERIS. The encyclical of *Pius XII (12 Aug. 1950) condemning several modern intellectual movements and tendencies of the RC Church. They included *Existentialism; excessive emphasis on the Word of God to the detraction of reason; distrust of theological dogmatism as incompatible with the language of Scripture and the Fathers; contempt for the authority of the Church and unwillingness to identify the Mystical Body of Christ with the Catholic Church in communion with the see of Rome; distrust of *Scholastic philosophy (esp. of St. *Thomas Aquinas); the denial that *Adam existed as a historical person and that *original sin has reached us by direct descent from him; and undue freedom in the interpretation of the Books of the OT.

Text in *A.A.S.*, xlii (1950), pp. 561–78. Eng. tr. by R. A. Knox in *The Tablet*, 2 Sept. 1950. P. Parente in *É.C.*, vi (1951), cols. 1502 f., s.v., with bibl.

HUMBERT OF SILVA CANDIDA (d. 1061), ecclesiastical reformer and statesman. A monk of the Lotharingian monastery of Moyenmoutier, where he became an enthusiastic scholar and reformer, he was created in 1050 Cardinal-Bishop of Silva Candida by *Leo IX and became one of the principal advisers of the Pope in his programme of ecclesiastical reform. His work *Adversus Simoniacos* was a vigorous denunciation of one of the chief evils of the Church; indeed, he refused (unlike *Peter Damian) to admit that Ordination by a simoniac was valid. He was also put in charge of the mission to *Constantinople at the time of the schism (1054). He engaged in controversies with Leo of Bulgaria and Nicetas of Studium over the use of unleavened bread in the Eucharist.

Collection of his works in J. P. Migne, *PL*, cxliii, 929–1218; crit. ed. of his *Adversus Simoniacos* by F. Thaner in *M.G.H.*, Libelli de Lite Imperatorum et Pontificum Saeculis XI et XII, i (1891), pp. 95–253. A. Michel, *Die Sentenzen des Kardinals Humbert, das erste Rechtsbuch der päpstlichen Reform* (Schriften des Reichsinstituts für ältere deutsche Geschichtskunde, vii; 1943), incl. reff. to edd. of this work. Id., *Humbert und Kerullarios* (Quellen und Forschungen aus dem Gebiete der Geschichte, xxi and xxiii; 1925–30). A. Fliche, *La Réforme grégorienne*, i (S.S.L., vi; 1924), pp. 265–308; J. P. Whitney, 'Peter Damiani and Humbert' in *The Cambridge Historical Journal*, i (1925), pp. 225–48, esp. pp. 237–41; repr., with revisions, in Whitney's *Hildebrandine Essays* (1932), pp. 95–142, esp. pp. 120–6. W. Ullmann, 'Cardinal Humbert and the *Ecclesia Romana*' in G. B. Borino (ed.), *Studi gregoriani*, iv (1952), pp. 111–27, with reff.; also H. Trutz, C.S.S.R., ib., pp. 236–72.

HUMBLE ACCESS, The Prayer of. The prayer in the Order of Holy Communion in the present BCP which immediately precedes the Prayer of Consecration. Its name derives from the Scottish Liturgy of 1637, where it is entitled 'Collect of Humble Access to the Holy Communion'. The prayer was composed for the new 'Order of *Communion' of 1548 and thus stood originally between the Communion of the priest and that of the people. In the Book of 1549, it was moved with most of the items in the 'Order of Communion' to a place immediately before the Communion of both priest and people. In the Book of 1552, however, the Prayer of Humble Access was separated altogether from the other items of the 'Order of Communion' and (with slight alterations in the wording) inserted in the position which it has since occupied. Some revisions of the BCP have restored this prayer to its original place, to bring it into closer connexion with the rest of the Communion Devotions, e.g. the Scottish Liturgy since 1637, the South African Book, and the American (1929) Book.

J. Dowden, 'A Contribution towards the Study of the Prayer of Humble Access' in *The Irish Church Quarterly*, i (1908), pp. 8–24, reprinted in id., *Further Studies in the Prayer Book*, Appendix, pp. 317–43.

HUME, DAVID (1711–76), Scottish philosopher and historian. He was a native of Edinburgh, where he was educated, and at an early age resolved to become a philosopher. From 1734 to 1737 he lived in France, where he elaborated his sceptical principles and wrote the *Treatise of Human Nature* (3 vols., 1739–1740), the success of which fell far short of his expectations. In 1741–2 appeared *Essays Moral and Political* (2 vols.) which was favourably received and much appreciated by Bp. J. *Butler. During the following years he held several secretarial and administrative posts in England and abroad. In 1748 he published *Philosophical Essays Concerning Human Understanding* which contained his famous 'Essay upon Miracles', followed, in 1751, by *An Enquiry Concerning the Principles of Morals*. By this time he had also completed his *Dialogues Concerning Natural Religion*, which was published only posthumously (1779). During the latter part of his life his interests turned to history; in 1752 he published his *Political Discourses*, the first of his works to attract general attention, and from 1754 to 1761 his famous *History of England* (6 vols.), written from the Tory standpoint, which long remained a standard work. In 1763 he accompanied Lord Hertford to France, where he was much admired and became the friend of J. Le R. *d'Alembert and A. R. J. Turgot. In 1766 he found for J.-J. *Rousseau a refuge in England. In his last years he almost ceased to write.

Hume's philosophy is based on the experimental method of J. *Locke and G. *Berkeley. By reducing reason to a product of experience he destroyed its claim to sole validity, which had been put forward by the thinkers of the *Aufklärung. All perceptions of the human mind are either impressions of experience or ideas, i.e. faded copies of these impressions. But whereas the relations between ideas can be known with certainty, the facts of reality cannot be established beyond an appearance of probability. Causality is not a concept of logic, but a result of habit and association, impressed on our imagination, and the human soul itself is but a sum of perceptions connected by association. Hence there is no such science as metaphysics; and belief in the existence of God and of the physical world, though a practical necessity, cannot be proved by reason. *Theism is neither the original nor the highest form of religion. The immortality of the soul is doubtful, and suicide is permissible. Our moral life is dominated by the passions, which determine our will and our actions.

Hume was aware that by reducing all cognition to single perceptions and by ruling out any purely intellectual faculty for recording and sifting them, he destroyed all real knowledge and taught pure scepticism. This scepticism is particularly evident in his 'Essay on Miracles'. Basing himself on the assumption that it had never been observed in any place or age that a dead man should come to life again, he brushed aside the historical evidence for miracles with the assertion that the possibility of an event being a miracle is inevitably counterbalanced by the possibility of its being a deception by the witnesses or the writers reporting it. For 'it is contrary to experience that a miracle should be true, but not contrary to experience that testimony should be false'.

Hume's influence has been widespread.

Among the thinkers indebted to him are I. *Kant, J. Bentham, and A. *Comte; and he has received much attention from recent philosophical empiricists.

Hume's autobiography appeared in 1777. His *Life and Correspondence* were edited by J. H. Burton in 1846; W. Knight, *Hume* (1886); J. Y. T. Greig, *David Hume* (1931). Separate studies: A. E. *Taylor, *David Hume and the Miraculous* (1927); R. W. Church, *Hume's Theory of the Understanding* (1935); N. K. Smith, *The Philosophy of David Hume* (1941). For a full bibliography see T. E. Jessop, *A Bibliography of David Hume* (1938). L. Stephen in *D.N.B.*, xxviii (1891), pp. 215–26.

HUMERAL VEIL. In the W. Church, a silk shawl laid round the shoulders serving to cover the hands. Its liturgical use is confined to *High Mass, when the subdeacon holds the *paten with it, from after the *Offertory till after the *Pater Noster. The humeral veil is already mentioned in the Roman '*Ordines' of the 8th and 9th cents., where it is worn by an *acolyte who then held the paten. When *c.* the 11th cent. the *subdeacon became paten-bearer he used the *pall in place of the humeral veil and the latter did not come into use again for this purpose until the 15th cent. Its adoption became universal only in the 19th cent. In extra-liturgical worship it is worn by the priest in processions of the Blessed Sacrament, at the service of *Benediction, and (in some countries) when the *Viaticum is taken to the sick.

Braun, *L.P.*, pp. 228–31. N. F. Robinson, S.S.J.E., 'Concerning Three Eucharistic Veils of Western Use' in *Transactions of the St. Paul's Ecclesiological Society*, vi (1906–10), pp. 129–60, esp. pp. 129 f. and 153–8. J. Braun, S.J., in *C.E.*, vii (1910), p. 542 f., s.v.

HUMILIATI. An order of penitents, founded in the 12th cent., which followed the *Benedictine Rule. They devoted themselves to a life of mortification and care for the poor, and for a time took a prominent part in combating the *Cathari. The discipline of the order became much relaxed in later times; and when in 1571 St. *Charles Borromeo, after trying in vain to reform it, was assaulted by one of its monks, it was finally suppressed.

The principal authority is H. Tiraboschius, S.J., *Vetera Humiliatorum Monumenta* (3 vols., Milan, 1766–8). L. Zanoni, *Gli Umiliati nei loro rapporti con l' eresia, l' industria della lana ed i comuni nei secoli XII e XIII* (Milan, 1911). P. Guerrini, 'Gli Umiliati a Brescia' in *Miscellanea Pio Paschini*, i (Lateranum, N.S., xiv; 1948), pp. 187–214. Heimbucher, i, p. 200, with bibl. F. Vernet in *D.T.C.*, vii (pt. 1; 1922), cols. 312–21, s.v. 'Humiliés', with detailed bibl. Ilarino da Milano, O.F.M., in *E.C.*, xii (1954), cols. 754–6, with later bibl.

HUMILITY. Acc. to St. *Thomas Aquinas, humility is a moral virtue which consists 'in keeping oneself within one's own bounds, not reaching out to things above one' (*Contra Gent.* iv, 55). Catholic theology regards it as part of the cardinal virtue of temperance in that it represses inordinate ambition and self-esteem without allowing man to fall into the opposite error of exaggerated or hypocritical self-abjection. Hence humility is considered the foundation and *conditio sine qua non* of the spiritual life, because it subjects reason and will to God.

It was enjoined by Christ in His teaching (e.g. Lk. 14. 11, Mt. 18. 4) and esp. by His example (Mt. 11. 29; Phil. 2. 7 ff.), and after Him by many of the saints, so that St. *Augustine could write: *Tota Christiana religio humilitas est* ('The whole of the Christian religion is humility'). St. *Benedict in his 'Rule' set forth 12 degrees of humility, and since then spiritual writers have systematically studied it and arrived at various enumerations, esp. with regard to its development both in the life of the religious in general (e.g. St. *Ignatius Loyola in his 'Exercises') and that of the mystics in particular (St. *Bernard and J. *Tauler). By Protestant theologians humility has been variously defined. M. *Luther regarded it as the joyful acceptance of God's will, and modern Protestant moralists (e.g. A. *Ritschl) identify it as complete resignation to our unconditional dependence on God.

R. L. *Ottley in *H.E.R.E.*, vi (1913), pp. 880–2, s.v., with useful reff.

HUNGARY, Christianity in. Christianity was first preached in what is now Hungary in the 4th cent., but made no permanent impression. In the 9th and 10th cents. more successful missions arrived, probably from the W. A formal constitution was laid down for the Church by King *Stephen I in 1001. Since 1279 Esztergom (Gran) has been the primatial see, and there are now three other RC archbishoprics. State control of Church affairs has always been very strong. Joseph II, king from 1780 to 1790, sought to create a nationalist movement among the RCs, similar to but going beyond *Gallicanism (see *Josephinism); but though he succeeded in dissolving over a third of the monasteries, the movement failed. Since the 16th cent. there has been a considerable Protestant minority, confined to certain parts and cities of Hungary, the two principal bodies being the *Calvinists (c. 21 per cent.) and the *Lutherans (c. 6 per cent.).

A. Theiner (ed.), *Vetera Monumenta Historica Hungariam Sacram Illustrantia* (2 vols., Rome, 1859–60). *Monumenta Vaticana Historiam Regni Hungariae Illustrantia* (Budapest; series i, 6 vols., 1884–91; series ii, 3 vols., 1884–1909). P. Bod (1712–69), *Historia Hungarorum Ecclesiastica inde ab Exordio Novi Testamenti ad Nostra usque Tempora*, ed. L. W. E. Rauwenhoff–C. Szalay (3 vols., Leyden, 1888–90). E. Horn, *Le Christianisme en Hongrie* (1906); id., *Organisation religieuse de la Hongrie* (1906). J. R. Borbis, *Die evangelisch-lutherische Kirche Ungarns in ihrer geschichtlichen Entwicklung*, nebst einem Anhange über die Geschichte der protestantischen Kirchen in den deutsch-slavischen Ländern und in Siebenbürgen (1861). E. Horn in *D.T.C.*, viii (pt. 1; 1922), cols. 41–61, s.v. 'Hongrie', and ix (pt. 2; 1927), cols. 1566–71, s.v. 'Magyaire'; O. Székeley, O. Cist., in *L.Th.K.*, x (1938), cols. 383–9, s.v. 'Ungarn', with full bibl. A. Aldásy in *C.E.*, vii (1910), pp. 547–60, s.v.

HUNT, WILLIAM HOLMAN (1827–1910), Pre-Raphaelite painter. A native of London, he was destined by his father for a business career, but began to study art in 1843 and was admitted to the Royal Academy in 1844. Here he began his lifelong friendship with J. E. Millais, and later he also formed a close connexion with D. G. *Rossetti. In 1848 they founded the Pre-Raphaelite Brotherhood, in which Hunt was the guiding spirit. In the following year he painted his first truly Pre-Raphaelite picture, *Rienzi*. Though much attacked by the press, he and his school were warmly defended by J. *Ruskin. In 1852 he completed *The Hireling Shepherd*, and in 1854 the famous *Light of the World*, one of the most popular pictures of modern times, representing our Lord knocking at the door of the soul. From 1854 to 1856 he travelled, mostly in Palestine, which he revisited several times. Here he made studies for *The Finding of the Saviour in the Temple*, completed in 1860, and, in 1869, for *The Shadow of the Cross*. In 1875 he began his great work, *The Triumph of the Innocents*, which was finished in two versions in 1885. In 1904 he re-painted *The Light of the World*, which is now in *St. Paul's, the original being in Keble College, Oxford. In 1905 he published a largely autobiographical work, *Pre-Raphaelitism and the Pre-Raphaelite Brotherhood* (2 vols.). Most of Hunt's works were executed very slowly, and with great love of detail, in which he excelled, though sometimes to the detriment of composition and colouring. His art is imbued throughout with strong religious feeling.

[F. G. Stephens,] *William Holman Hunt and his Works* (1860); A. *Meynell and F. W. *Farrar, *William Holman Hunt. His Life and Work* (1893). W. Armstrong in *D.N.B.*, *1901–1911*, ii, pp. 323–8.

HUNTING. Though this has been generally held to be lawful for the laity, it was forbidden to the clergy by a series of *Gallic councils beginning with a canon (55) of the Council of *Agde (506) which reappears in the '*Corpus Iuris Canonici'. In the Scholastic period a distinction was made between 'quiet' and 'noisy' hunting (*quieta* and *clamorosa*), and there was a division of opinion whether both kinds or only the noisy were forbidden to the clergy. The common opinion was that only the noisy was illicit. By 'noisy' was meant the hunting of large or dangerous animals by a crowd of people accompanied by a numerous pack of hounds. 'Quiet hunting' meant the use of snares, nets, or small packs of hounds for the destruction of hares, foxes, and other small animals.

In modern times, hunting, for laity and clergy alike, has occasionally been condemned altogether by Christian moralists on humanitarian grounds. In the RC Church the stricter view forbidding hunting of either kind to the clergy was taken by *Benedict XIV. The *Codex of 1917 (C.I.C.), can. 138 : 'venationi ne [clerici] indulgeant, clamorosam autem nunquam exerceant'), while disallowing altogether noisy hunting to the clergy, perhaps tolerates the other sort, if by *indulgere* may be understood 'to practise immoderately' or 'at the expense of one's duties'.

HUNTINGDON, SELINA, COUNTESS OF (1707–91). Selina Hastings, foundress of the body of *Calvinistic Methodists known as 'the Countess of Huntingdon's Connexion'. She joined the *Wesleys' Methodist society in 1739, and on her husband's death in 1746 gave herself wholly up to social and religious work, making herself the chief medium for introducing Methodism to the upper classes. In 1768 she opened Trevecca House, Talgarth, as a Methodist seminary. Her chief method of supporting Methodist ministers was by constituting them her *chaplains; but her opinion that she could, as a peeress, appoint to the rank of chaplain as many priests of the established C of E as she wished, and employ them publicly, was disallowed by the consistory court of London in 1779. In consequence of this decision she registered her chapels as dissenting places of worship under the *Toleration Act. In the disputes between J. Wesley and G. *Whitefield she took the side of the latter, at whose death she became trustee of his foundations in America. Before her own death she formed her chapels into an association (1790).

The *Life and Times of Selina Countess of Huntingdon* by a Member of the Houses of Shirley and Hastings [i.e., A. C. H. Seymour] (2 vols., 1839); index compiled by F. M. Jackson printed in *The Wesley Historical Society*, v (1905), following page 256. A. H. New, *The Coronet and the Cross*, or Memorials of the Right Hon: Selina, Countess of Huntingdon (1857); J. B. Figgis, *The Countess of Huntingdon and her Connexion* [c. 1892]. Sarah Tytler [pseud. of H. Keddie], *The Countess of Huntingdon and her Circle* (1907). F. F. Bretherton, *The Countess of Huntingdon* (Wesley Historical Society Lecture, No. 6; 1940); K. M. Davies, 'Lady Huntingdon a Threfecca' in *Journal of the Historical Society of the Presbyterian Church of Wales*, xxvii (1942), pp. 66–75. J. H. Overton in *D.N.B.*, xxv (1891), pp. 133–5, s.v. 'Hastings, Selina'.

HUPFELD, HERMANN (1796–1866), German OT scholar. He was educated at *Marburg and (under W. *Gesenius) at Halle, and for most of his life taught in these two universities. In the history of *Pentateuchal Criticism he occupies an important place through having in his *Die Quellen der Genesis und die Art ihrer Zusammensetzung* (1853) distinguished for the first time between the two sources *P and *E, both of which in Gen. use the same word *Elohim as the Divine Name. He also wrote a commentary on the Pss. (4 vols., 1855–61) and works dealing with Semitic grammar and philology.

Life by E. Riehm (Halle, 1867). A. Kamphausen in *P.R.E.* (ed. 3), viii (1900), pp. 462–7.

HUSS, JOHN (c. 1369–1415), Bohemian Reformer. Born of a peasant family at Husinec (whence 'Huss') he entered Prague university c. 1390 and took his Master's degree in 1396. In 1401 he was elected Dean of the Philosophical Faculty and in 1409 Rector of the university. Having been ordained priest in 1400, he soon became a well-known preacher in Czech at the 'Bethlehem Chapel' at Prague. This was at the time when knowledge of J. *Wycliffe's writings had recently reached Bohemia through the closer relations with England that followed the marriage (1398) of Anne, sister of King Wenceslaus IV (d. 1419), to Richard II; and Huss was esp. attracted to his political doctrines (rejection of the right to property and of the hierarchical organization of society), which had been independently advocated by *Jerome of Prague, and was also sympathetic to his teachings on *Predestination and the Church of the elect. At first he received considerable encouragement from the new Abp. of Prague, Sbinko von Hasenburg, who made him preacher of the synod in 1403, and supported his attack on the pilgrimage of *Wilsnack in 'De Omni Sanguine Christi Glorificato' (1404); and, despite the university's condemnation of 45 of Wycliffe's propositions in 1403, Huss translated Wycliffe's 'Trialogus' into Czech. But before long his violent sermons on the morals of the clergy provoked hostility. They were denounced at Rome in 1407 and the Abp., at *Innocent VII's orders, forbade Huss to preach. Huss replied by 'De Arguendo Clero pro Concione'. When the country became divided over the two claimants to the Papal see (*Alexander V and *Gregory XII), Huss with Wenceslaus and the Czech 'nation' at the University upheld Alexander, while Sbinko and the other three 'nations' (Bavarians, Saxons, and Poles) supported Gregory. His influence was temporarily much increased by a royal decree (18 Jan. 1409) giving control of the university to the Czech nation, which became a stronghold of Wycliffite doctrines, with Huss as Rector. In his isolation Abp. Sbinko transferred his allegiance to Alexander V, who rewarded him with a bull (9 Mar. 1410) ordering the destruction of all Wycliffite books, the retractation of Wycliffite doctrines, and, to stop Huss's influence at the Bethlehem Chapel, the cessation of preaching in private chapels; and in Feb. 1411 Huss was excommunicated by the new Pope, *John XXIII. Opinion now moved against him and in 1412 the Pope imposed on Huss the great excommunication and placed his followers under an interdict. To restore peace Wenceslaus forthwith removed Huss from Prague and he found refuge with his supporters among the Czech nobility. Two conferences in 1412 and 1413 having failed to achieve peace, Huss devoted himself to writing his chief work 'De Ecclesia' (1413), the first ten chapters of which are taken over bodily from Wycliffe. Having appealed from the decision of the papal curia to a general Council, he left Bohemia in 1414 for the Council of *Constance, with a safe-conduct of the Emp. Sigismund. Arriving on 3 November 1414, he soon found his liberty threatened. When the trial opened he was confined in the conventual prison of the *Dominicans, later in a castle of the Bp. of Constance, and in the end in the convent of the *Franciscans, the Emperor's endeavour to free him being of no avail. He suffered death at the stake with great fortitude on 6 July 1415.

By his death he became a national hero. The university of Prague declared him a martyr and fixed his feast on the day of his execution. The schism which he introduced into the nation was perpetuated by the Hussite wars, and the present '*Czechoslovak Church' (q.v.) claims to continue his tradition.

Opera Omnia, ed. by V. Flajshaus (3 vols., Prague, 1903-1908). His Letters were translated into English by H. B. Workman and R. M. Pope (1904), the De Ecclesia by D. S. Schaff (New York, 1915). J. Loserth, Hus und Wiclif. Zur Genesis der husitischen Lehre (1884; Eng. trans., 1884; ed. 2 of German, 1925); F. Lützow, The Life and Times of Master John Hus (1909); J. Herben, Hus and his Followers (1926). M. Spinka, John Hus and the Czech Reform (Chicago, Ill., 1941). J. Loserth in P.R.E. (ed. 3), viii (1900), pp. 472-88.

HUTCHINSON, JOHN (1674-1737), author. He was a native of Yorkshire, and, after being steward to the Earl of Scarborough and the Duke of Somerset, planned a work on the Mosaic account of the Flood. In his chief work, Moses's Principia (1724), he expounds a system of Biblical philosophy, maintaining that Hebrew was the primitive language of mankind which, if rightly interpreted, gave the key to all knowledge whether secular or religious. The book was written in opposition to I. *Newton's Principia and had a considerable success. Its theories were developed by a circle called the 'Hutchinsonians', to which belonged, among others, G. *Horne and W. *Jones of Nayland.

The Philosophical and Theological Works . . . of John Hutchinson, ed. R. Spearman-J. Bate (12 vols., London, 1748-9). An Abstract of the Works of J. Hutchinson (1753). J. P[arkhurst] (ed.), A Supplement to the Works of John Hutchinson . . . being an Index and Explanation of the Hebrew Words cited in the Second Part of his Moses's Principia, with additional Remarks, by R. Spearman (1765), and life by R. Spearman, pp. i-xiv. L. Stephen, History of English Thought in the Eighteenth Century, i (1876), pp. 389-91. L. Stephen in D.N.B., xxviii (1891), p. 342 f.

HUTTEN, ULRICH VON (1488-1523), German humanist and controversialist. He belonged to the lower nobility and was born at the castle of Steckelberg, nr. *Fulda. In 1499 he was placed in the monastery of Fulda by his parents, who designed him for the religious life, probably on account of his weak health. In 1505, however, he fled, and during the next years led an unsettled life, visiting many of the German universities, among them *Cologne, *Wittenberg, and Vienna. In 1512-1513 he took part in the wars of the Emp. Maximilian in Italy as a Landsknecht. In 1515 he began to write a series of attacks (publd. 1519) against Duke Ulrich of Württemberg, who had murdered a member of his family. About the same time he became a contributor to the famous Humanistic satire *Epistolae Obscurorum Virorum. In 1517 he received the laurel crown of the poet from the Emperor and entered the service of the Elector of Mainz, Abp. *Albert of Brandenburg. In 1518 he edited L. *Valla's treatise on the '*Donation of Constantine' with a sarcastic dedication to the Pope and wrote an exhortation to the German princes to take up arms against the Turks. From 1519 he dedicated his life to the propagation of M. *Luther's reformation, in which he saw the instrument for the deliverance of Germany from the power of Rome. A series of Latin and German treatises, among them Febris Secunda, Vadiscus Dialogus (both 1520), and the famous Gesprächbüchlein (1521) served this purpose. Having failed to gain the Archduke Ferdinand for the Reformation, he was dismissed from the service of the Abp. of Mainz and, being under an order of arrest from Rome, fled to Franz von *Sickingen.

After the latter's defeat he sought the protection of D. *Erasmus (1522), who refused to receive him, and at last went to H. *Zwingli, who provided him, broken by disease and misfortune, with a refuge on the island of Ufenau in the Lake of Zürich.

Works ed. E. Böcking, 5 vols. and 2 suppl. vols., Leipzig, 1859–70. German writings ed. S. Szamatólski, Strassburg, 1891. Several modern lives, among them those of D. F. *Strauss (Leipzig, 1858; new ed. by O. Clemen, 1914; Eng. tr., 1874), G. Wolf (Berlin, 1906), K. Jordan (Berlin, 1908), O. Flake (Berlin, 1929), and H. Holborn (Leipzig, 1929; Eng. tr., Yale Historical Publications, No. 11, 1937). P. Kalkoff, *Ulrich von Hutten und die Reformation* (1920), and other works. G. W. Kitchin in *E.B.* (ed. 11), xiv (1910), p. 14 f.; O. Clemen in *R.G.G.* (ed. 2), ii (1928), col. 2058 f.; F. Zoepfl in *L.Th.K.*, v (1933), col. 212 f.; M. Petrocchi in *E.C.*, vi (1951), col. 1517 f., with further bibl.

HUTTERITES. See *Anabaptists*.

HUTTON, RICHARD HOLT (1826–97), lay religious writer. The son of Joseph Hutton (1790–1860), *Unitarian minister at Mill Hill Chapel, Leeds, he was educated at University College, London, where he became a lifelong friend of Walter Bagehot (1826–77). In 1847 he entered Manchester New College to prepare for the Unitarian ministry and came under the influence of J. *Martineau; but failing to secure a permanent ministerial charge, he accepted in 1851 the editorship of *Inquirer*, a Unitarian weekly. His tolerant outlook soon caused offence to conservative Unitarians and before long he had to give up the *Inquirer*. From 1855 to 1864 he edited with Bagehot the *National Review*. Under the influence of F. W. *Robertson and F. D. *Maurice he was increasingly drawn to the C of E of which he became a member. In 1861 he was offered by Meredith W. Townsend (1831–1911) the joint-editorship and proprietorship of the *Spectator*. He made the utmost of this opportunity, using the journal as a pulpit from which to challenge, on Christian principles, the regnant agnosticism (J. S. *Mill, T. H. *Huxley) and to present the case for many worth-while causes; and he held his editorship until his death. He was one of the original members of the *Metaphysical Society (founded 1869) and in his later years became intimate with many leading High Churchmen (R. W. *Church, H. P. *Liddon) and RCs (W. G. *Ward). In 1891 he wrote a Life of J. H. *Newman. His *Essays Theological and Literary* (2 vols., 1871) went through several editions.

J. Hogben, *Richard Holt Hutton of 'The Spectator'*. A Monograph (1899). *D.N.B.*, Suppl. iii (1901), pp. 19–22 [anon.].

HUTTON, WILLIAM HOLDEN (1860–1930), Dean of *Winchester. Educated at Magdalen College, Oxford, he became in 1884 a Fellow of St. John's, where he remained a history tutor for 25 years. From 1911 to 1919 he was Canon of *Peterborough, and from 1919 till his death Dean of Winchester. He was a devoted and influential sponsor of the conservative High Church tradition in *Anglicanism. His writings include Lives of *Sir Thomas *More* (1895) and of *William *Laud*

(1895), a set of *Bampton Lectures on *The Lives of the English Saints* (1903), and a history of *The English Church from the Accession of *Charles I to the Death of Anne, 1625–1714* (1903).

C. W. C. Oman in *D.N.B.*, *1922–1930*, p. 442 f., s.v.

HUXLEY, THOMAS HENRY (1825–95), biologist. A native of Ealing, after a precocious boyhood he studied medicine at Charing Cross Hospital from 1842 to 1845 and in 1846 secured an appointment in the Navy which enabled him to pursue scientific investigations in the *Rattlesnake* (1846–50) in southern tropical waters. Here he carried through some remarkable biological researches. Recognition quickly followed and in 1851 he was elected a F.R.S. In 1854 he left the Navy and accepted a post as lecturer at the Royal School of Mines. From the publication of *Collected Essays* (1854) he became prominent as an advocate of scientific training as the surest remedy for man's intellectual, social, and moral needs. His campaign on behalf of science was greatly stimulated by the controversy aroused in 1859 by C. *Darwin's *Origin of Species*. At the meeting of the British Association at *Oxford in 1860 he had a memorable passage of words with the Bp. of Oxford (S. *Wilberforce) on the subject of evolution. In 1863 there appeared his *Zoological Evidences as to Man's Place in Nature*, a defence of man's descent from the lower animal world, and in 1868 he delivered a lecture on 'The Physical Basis of Life' in which he expounded '*agnosticism' (a term of his own coining a year or two later). Man, he argued, cannot know the nature of either spirit or matter; metaphysics is impossible; and man's primary duty in life is the relief of misery and ignorance. From *c.* 1870 he filled several important administrative offices in some of which he exercised great influence. As a member of the London School Board from 1870 to 1872 he laid stress on the merits of physical, moral, and esp. scientific education, but he held that such education should be supplemented by the study of the Bible as the only means by which religious feeling, the basis of moral conduct, could be sustained. In 1879 he published a study of D. *Hume with a special chapter on *miracles. He would not reject miracles out of hand because 'nobody can presume to say what the order of nature must be', but he explicitly abandoned the theological conception of a Personal God, substituting 'the passionless impersonality of the unknown and unknowable'. Compelled in 1885 to retire from public work for reasons of health, he continued active in writing. His attacks on Christian orthodoxy became more persistent and he carried his agnosticism into the field of NT study, holding that certain knowledge as to the teaching and convictions of Christ was impossible. He summarized his final views in his Romanes Lecture on 'Ethics and Evolution', delivered at Oxford on 18 May 1893. Huxley had few claims to be considered an exact thinker, but his obvious sincerity won him a wide hearing and influence.

Collected Essays (9 vols., 1893–4). Leonard Huxley, *The Life and Letters of Thomas Henry Huxley* (2 vols., 1900). His scientific achievements are treated in P. C. Mitchell, *Thomas Henry Huxley* (1900). W. T. Thiselton-Dyer in *E.B.* (ed. 11), xiv (1910), pp. 17–20; W. F. R. Weldon in *D.N.B.*, Suppl. iii (1901), pp. 22–31.

HUYSMANS, JORIS KARL (1848–1907), French Catholic novelist. Of Dutch descent, he was for thirty years a member of the French Ministry of the Interior, but his main claim to fame lay in his literary work. His early novels, *Marthe* (1876), *À rebours* (1884), and *Là-bas* (1891), reveal his association with the Goncourt-Zola school of literary realism, many of their characters being decadent types. He was converted to a living Christian faith by a visit to the *Trappist monastery of Igny. It found expression in *En route* (1895), *La Cathédrale* (1898), *Sainte Lydwine de Schiedam* (1901, a study in the value of suffering), *L'Oblat* (1903) and other books. His writings generally reflected his deep interest in religious art, ritual, and mysticism.

Œuvres complètes, ed. L. Descaves (18 vols., Paris, 1928–1934). K. Bosch, *J. K. Huysmans' religiöser Entwicklungsgang* (Constance, 1920); H. Bachelin, *J. K. Huysmans. Du naturalisme littéraire au naturalisme mystique* (1926). Life by R. Baldick (Oxford, 1955). L. Deffoux, *J. K. Huysmans sous divers aspects* (1927), with bibl.; E. Seilière, *J. K. Huysmans* (1931); H. Trudigan, *L'Éthique de J. K. Huysmans* (1934). L. Daudet, *A propos de J. K. Huysmans* (1947).

HY. See *Iona*.

HYACINTH, St. (1185–1257), 'Apostle of the North', known to the Poles at St. Iaccho. Acc. to the traditional account, he came of a noble Polish family, and studied at Cracow, Prague, and *Bologna. On a visit to Rome with his uncle, Ivo of Konski, Bp. of Cracow, he met St. *Dominic and in 1220 received the habit from him at Santa Sabina. Becoming the superior of a small band of Dominicans, he set out for Poland in the same year and engaged in missionary work first in his own and the adjacent countries, and then in *Denmark, *Sweden, and *Norway. His later activities are reputed to have extended as far as the Black Sea. There is considerable uncertainty as to the historical truth of some of these details. He was canonized by *Clement VIII in 1594. Feast day, 17 Aug.

L. Cwiklinski, 'De Vita et Miraculis S. Iacchonis (Hyacinthi) Ordinis Fratrum Praedicatorum, auctore Stanislao Lectore Cracoviensi eiusdem Ordinis' and other items in *Monumenta Poloniae Historica* (Lemberg), IV (1884), pp. 818–903. B. Altaner, *Die Dominikanermissionen des 13. Jahrhunderts* (1924), pp. 196–214.

HYDROPARASTATAE (Gk. Ὑδροπαράσται, 'those who advocate water'). A name used from the 4th cent. of the *Aquarians.

HYLOMORPHISM. A metaphysical doctrine derived from *Aristotle, acc. to which the actual specific reality of a physical thing is the

μορφή (*forma*), while the ὕλη (*materia*) contributes to its being only potentiality and limitation. It had a fundamental place in the systems of St. *Albertus Magnus and St. *Thomas Aquinas.

HYLOZOISM. The doctrine that all matter is endowed with life. In a crude form it was taught by the ancient Greek philosophers (Thales, Anaximenes, Heracleitus) and the *Stoics ('world soul') and in a more spiritual form by many of the Renaissance thinkers (B. *Telesio, G. *Bruno), by some of the *Cambridge Platonists (H. *More, R. *Cudworth), and by G. T. *Fechner. A materialistic form of the doctrine was revived by E. H. *Haeckel.

HYMNARY (Lat. *Hymnarium*). The medieval liturgical book of the W. Rite which contained the metrical hymns of the Divine Office arranged acc. to the Liturgical Year. It was often appended to the *Psaltery and sometimes to the *Antiphonary. Its contents were later incorporated into the *Breviary.

HYMNS. Sacred poetry set to music and sung in the course of public worship has always formed part of Christian worship. At first the hymns of the Jewish Church, esp. the Psalms, were in use, and there is the record of the hymn in the Upper Room (Mk. 14. 26), probably the *Hallel. At an early date distinctively Christian compositions, e.g. *Magnificat, *Benedictus, and *Nunc Dimittis, appeared. What seem to be quotations from early Christian hymns also occur in Eph. 5. 14, 1 Tim. 3. 16, 1 Tim. 6. 15 f. The rhythmical prose in use in the early Church (1 *Clement 59–61, Ep. to *Diognetus, *Didache, *Melito's *Homily on the Passion*) furthered the development of hymnody. A 3rd-cent. writer (perhaps *Hippolytus) refers to 'psalms and odes such as from the beginning were written by believers, hymns to the Christ, the Word of God, calling Him God' (Eusebius, *H.E.*, V, xxviii, 5).

The earliest complete Christian hymn that survives, 'Bridle of colts untamed', is a hymn to Christ preserved by *Clement of Alexandria. Other hymns of pre-Nicene date are 'Up Maidens', included by *Methodius of Olympus in his *Symposium*, and (probably) the Φῶς ἱλαρόν 'Hail, gladdening Light' (A.M. 18, E.H. 269), which is still part of the Evening Office of the Eastern Church. The *Gnostics (*Valentinus, *Bardesanes, *Marcion) made extensive use of hymns, but, except for the 'Odes of *Solomon' (q.v.), most of these have been lost.

From the 4th cent. the use of hymns became more general. Two types arose, those designed to express the emotion of the worshipper and those intended to impart doctrine. In the far East St. *Ephraem Syrus (d. 378) wrote *Syriac hymns to counter the heresy of Bardesanes. Early Greek hymn writers include St. *Gregory Nazianzen (d. 390) and *Synesius (d. c. 414), both of whom used classical models.

From the 5th cent. the belief obtained in some quarters that no words other than those of Scripture should be allowed in the Liturgy and as late as 563 the Council of Braga forbade the singing of non-Biblical poetical compositions in church (can. 12). From the 5th cent. *troparia (single stanza hymns), later joined together to form stichera and *contakia, are found in the Eastern service books. The classical Greek hymn writers include *Romanos (6th cent.), *Sergius, Patr. of Constantinople (author of the *Acathistos; d. 641), St. *Andrew of Crete (d. c. 730), *Cosmas Melodus (d. c. 760), St. *John of Damascus (d. c. 750) and St. *Joseph the Hymnographer (c. 810–886). Characteristic of Greek hymns are their dogmatic emphasis and faculty of sustained praise, often offset by monotony of thought and repetition of diction.

Latin hymns appear later than Greek. St. *Hilary (d. 367) wrote hymns, prob. under Eastern influences, when in exile. But the real impetus came from St. *Ambrose (d. 397). His compositions laid down the line of development of Latin hymnody as simple, doctrinal and direct, and it was through his influence that hymns became a recognized and integral part of the public worship of the W. Church. The development was towards an ordered sequence for use at different times and seasons, established through the Hour Services of the monastic orders, with hymns designed to express not the feelings of the individual worshipper but the meaning of the feast or Office. Latin hymn writers include, besides Ambrose, *Prudentius (d. c. 410), (Caelius) Sedulius (d. c. 450), *Venantius Fortunatus (d. 609), St. *Gregory the Great (d. 604), St. *Bede (d. 735), *Theodolph of Orléans (d. 821), *Notker of St. Gall (the populariser of *Sequences, the first hymns introduced into the Mass), *Adam of St.-Victor (d. c. 1172; 'the greatest of the sacred Latin poets of the Middle Ages', R. C. *Trench), *Bernard of Cluny (d. c. 1145), and St. *Thomas Aquinas (d. 1274). The Counter-Reformation led to the composition of new *Breviary hymns in a more classical diction, esp. in France. Among their authors were the brothers Claude (d. 1684) and Jean Baptiste de Santeuil (d. 1697) and Charles Coffin (d. 1769). Two well-known modern Latin hymns are '*Veni, veni, Emmanuel' (A.M. 49, E.H. 8) and '*Adeste Fideles' (A.M. 59, E.H. 28), both of obscure origin.

In England hymns first appear in the vernacular with *Caedmon (Bede, HE, IV, 24), *Aldhelm (d. 709) and King *Alfred (d. 899). Towards the close of the Middle Ages hymns to Christ as Redeemer and to His Holy Mother, together with translations of Latin hymns, became popular. Among the leading medieval English hymn-writers was Richard *Rolle of Hampole (d. 1349).

The Reformation had a deep but varied effect on the development of hymnody. *Lutheranism was marked by a wealth of new hymns written by M. *Luther himself (d. 1546), by M. Weisse (d. 1534), and later by

P. *Gerhardt (d. 1676). The first Protestant hymn book was M. Weisse's Ein New Geseng Buchlen (1531). *Calvinism, on the other hand, would tolerate nothing but the words of Scripture in its services. Hence the Psalms were put into metrical versions, at first in French by C. *Marot (d. 1544) and T. *Beza (d. 1605); these were collected in the 'Genevan Psalter' (1563). Hymns (with the exception of *Veni Creator in the *Ordinal) disappeared also from the English service books, but less, it would seem, on grounds of principle than because T. *Cranmer's literary powers lay in other directions. Metrical versions of the Psalter were made and widely used in England from an early date; they continued in current use until the early 19th cent. The 'Old Version' of the Psalter of T. *Sternhold (q.v.) and J. Hopkins appeared in 1557 and the 'New Version' of N. *Tate and N. *Brady in 1696. In 1623 Hymns and Songs of the Church was published by George Wither (d. 1667), but attained little popularity. Hymns, however, continued to be written for private and local use, e.g. by G. *Herbert (d. 1633) and T. *Ken (d. 1711).

Modern hymn writing and hymn singing was mainly the creation of the 18th cent. A prominent place is filled by Isaac *Watts (d. 1748), the *Congregationalist, whose hymns were written to express the spiritual experience of the singer. In 1737 appeared John *Wesley's Collection of Psalms and Hymns, the first hymn book of modern type, followed in 1739 by Hymns and Sacred Poems by John and Charles Wesley. The latter was the most prolific, and probably the most gifted, of all English hymn writers. The practice of hymn singing was much encouraged and developed by the *Methodists. It soon spread among the *Evangelical party of the C of E, though it was long frowned upon by authority. Other hymn writers of this period were P. *Doddridge (d. 1751) and A. *Toplady (Psalms and Hymns for Public and Private Worship, 1776). In 1779 J. *Newton and W. *Cowper published Olney Hymns, a collection of hymns of the subjective and emotional type characteristic of the Evangelical school.

By the beginning of the 19th cent. prejudice against the use of hymns in the C of E was dying and the time was ripe for a hymn book which should be integrated with the Prayer Book scheme of worship. R. *Heber (d. 1826), who both wrote and collected hymns, intended his (posthumous) Hymns written and adapted to the Weekly Church Services of the Year (1827) to be both 'literary' and 'liturgical'. Though never widely used, it did much to break down the remaining hostility to hymns outside Evangelical circles. A further important influence in fostering the use of hymns came from the *Oxford Movement. The hymns of the ancient and medieval Church were employed to emphasize the antiquity and catholicity of the Church. Translations were made by I. *Williams (d. 1865), J. M. *Neale (d. 1865), F. *Oakeley (d. 1880), E. *Caswall (d. 1878), and W. J. Copeland (d. 1885).

Original compositions came from J. *Keble (d. 1866; *Christian Year*, 1827) and J. H. *Newman (d. 1890; *Dream of Gerontius*, 1865).

By the middle of the 19th cent., hymn singing was firmly established in the Church, and hymn books were published which combined the ancient hymns with those of recent composition. The *Hymnal Noted* appeared in 1852 (Part I) and 1854 (II). This was followed by *Hymns Ancient and Modern* (1861, q.v.), which set the pattern for Anglican Hymn Books with hymns for the liturgical calendar as well as those of personal emotion. It went through a large number of editions and is still probably the most widely used hymn book of the C of E. In the present century the *English Hymnal* (1906) has gained a wide circulation, esp. in churches of the *Anglo-Catholic movement. More recent still is a new type of hymn book, *Songs of Praise* (1925; 2nd ed., 1931), which combines both Christian and humanitarian hymns, intended for use both at gatherings for worship and on other occasions.

W. Christ–M. Paranikas (edd.), *Anthologia Graeca Carminum Christianorum* (Leipzig, 1871). J. B. *Pitra, *Hymnologie de l'Église grecque* (1867). H. A. Daniel (ed.), *Thesaurus Hymnologicus* (5 vols. bound in 2, Leipzig and Halle, 1841–56); F. J. *Mone, *Lateinische Hymnen des Mittelalters* (3 vols. bound in 2, 1853–5); G. M. Dreves, S.J.–C. Blume, S.J. (edd.), *Analecta Hymnica Medii Aevi* (55 vols., Leipzig, 1886–1922); A. S. Walpole–A. J. Mason, *Early Latin Hymns* (1922). U. Chevalier (ed.), *Repertorium Hymnologicum*. Catalogue des chants, hymnes, proses, séquences, tropes en usage dans l'Église latine depuis ses origines jusqu'à nos jours (6 vols. 1892–1921). F. J. E. Raby, *A History of Christian-Latin Poetry from the Beginnings to the Close of the Middle Ages* (1927) [cited as 'Raby']. L. Benson, *The English Hymn* (New York, 1915). C. S. Phillips, *Hymnody Past and Present* (1937). W. T. Whitley, *Congregational Hymn-Singing* (1933); H. A. L. Jefferson, *Hymns in Christian Worship* (1950); E. Routley, *Hymns and Human Life* (1952); M. Frost, *English and Scottish Psalm and Hymn Tunes, c. 1543–1677* (S.P.C.K., 1953). J. Julian, *A Dictionary of Hymnology* (1892; revised ed., 1907) [cited as 'Julian']. A. *Baumstark, A. J. Maclean, D. S. Margoliouth, G. M. Dreves, S.J., E. Hull, and T. G. Crippen in *H.E.R.E.*, vii (1914), pp. 5–38, s.v. E. [R.] Routley, *The Music of Christian Hymnography* (1957), and other works by the same author.

'HYMNS, ANCIENT AND MODERN'.

This famous hymnal (publd. 1861), edited by H. W. *Baker (q.v.), was a product of the *Oxford Movement. It drew freely on ancient, medieval and modern sources and also incorporated many of the traditional *office hymns (often in the translation of J. M. *Neale). The music, expressive and tuneful, which greatly assisted its popularity, was edited by William Henry Monk (1823–89). In 1868 a supplement was added. In 1875 the whole work was completely revised; further supplements were added in 1889 and 1916; and from 1922 onwards these were issued as a single book ('Standard Edition'). A more drastic revision ('New Edition'), issued in 1904, never became popular.

In 1950 a completely new edition ('*Hymns Ancient and Modern. Revised, 1950*') appeared. A few new hymns were added, but many more excised, so that the total number was reduced to 636. More provision was made for processions and special occasions and the arrangement of the book much improved. The music was edited by Sydney H. Nicholson (1875–1947), assisted by G. H. Knight (b. 1908) and J. Dykes Bower (b. 1905).

In its various forms the book has familiarized many generations of Church people with the fundamentals of Anglican doctrine and practice. The Chairmen of the Proprietors, who control the hymnal, have included H. W. Baker, W. H. *Frere, S. H. Nicholson and W. K. Lowther Clarke (b. 1879).

A 'Historical Edition', incl. notes on the words and tune of each hymn and the orig. texts in the case of translations, was publd. by the Proprietors (William Clowes and Sons) in 1909; it is prefaced (pp. ix–cxi) with valuable introd. by W. H. *Frere. M. Frost (ed.), *Historical Companion to Hymns Ancient & Modern* (1962).

HYPAPANTE (Gk. ὑπαπαντή, 'meeting').

The name used in the E. Church for the feast of *Candlemas, in reference to the meeting of *Simeon and Anna with the BVM and the Infant Christ at the *Presentation in the Temple. In the Middle Ages the title ('Occursus Domini') was also frequently used in the W

HYPATIA (c. 375–415), *Neoplatonist

philosopher. The daughter of Theon, the mathematician and philosopher, she was the glory of the Neoplatonic School of Alexandria, where *Synesius, Bp. of Ptolemais, was one of her pupils. On the suspicion that she had set the pagan prefect of Alexandria against the Christians, she was attacked by a Christian mob under Peter the Reader and put to death. The archbishop, *Cyril, was suspected of complicity, but his responsibility was never proved. She was the authoress of works on philosophy and mathematics.

The chief sources are *Socrates, *H.E.*, VII. 15 and *Suidas, s.v. W. A. Meyer, *Hypatia von Alexandria. Ein Beitrag zur Geschichte des Neuplatonismus* (1885). F. Schaefer, 'Cyril of Alexandria and the Murder of Hypatia' in *Catholic University Bulletin* [Washington], viii (1902), pp. 441–53; H. von Schubert, 'Hypatia von Alexandrien in Wahrheit und Dichtung' in *Preussische Jahrbücher*, cxxiv (1906), pp. 42–60. K. Praechter in Pauly-Wissowa, *R.E.*, IX (1916), cols. 242–9. Her story was the basis of C. *Kingsley's novel, *Hypatia* (1853).

HYPERDULIA. (Gk. ὑπέρ, 'more than';

δουλεία, 'servitude', 'veneration'.) The special veneration paid to the BVM on account of her eminent dignity as Mother of God. It is of a more limited kind than '*latria,' the worship due only to God, but higher than '*dulia,' the honour paid to angels and saints.

HYPOCRISY (from Gk. ὑποκρίνομαι, 'to play

a part', 'pretend'). The hiding of interior wickedness under the appearance of virtue. Our Lord denounced it esp. in the case of the *Pharisees (Mt. 23. 1–36) as the vice of those who do their good deeds only in order to be seen by men and not for the glory of God. Not all hiding of one's own sins, however, is to be regarded as hypocrisy, for there is no obligation as such to make them public, and in certain cases to do so might even cause grave scandal. Acc. to moral theologians hypocrisy is the fruit of pride. It is a sin against truthfulness, being a lie expressed by external actions with the intention of deceiving.

HYPOSTASIS (Gk. ὑπόστασις, lit. 'substance'). The Gk. word has had a variety of meanings. In popular language it was used orig. for 'objective reality' as opposed to illusion (so also in *Aristotle and esp. the *Neo-Platonists). In the NT this seems to be roughly its meaning at Heb. 1. 3. Allied to this was its use for 'basis' or 'foundation' and hence also 'confidence', e.g. in Heb. 3. 14 and 11. 1 and 2 Cor. 9. 4 and 11. 17. It often came to be almost identical with οὐσία, i.e. to denote 'being' or 'substantial reality'; it was so used in *Tatian and *Origen, and also in the anathemas appended to the *Nicene Creed of 325.

But side by side with this usage the term also came to mean 'individual reality' and, from the middle of the 4th cent. onwards esp. in Christological contexts, a 'person'. Its employment for this purpose led to great confusion in the minds of Western theologians who naturally translated ὑπόστασις by 'sub'-'stantia' ('substance') and understood the Easterns when speaking of three 'Hypostaseis' in the Godhead to mean three 'Substances', i.e. they suspected them of tritheism. It was mainly under the influence of the *Cappadocian Fathers that the terminology was clarified and standardized, and the theological ambiguities removed. From the Council of *Constantinople of 381 onwards the formula 'Three Hypostaseis in one Ousia' came to be everywhere accepted as an epitome of the orthodox doctrine of the Holy Trinity.

G. L. Prestige, *God in Patristic Thought* (1936), pp. 162–190. J. Tixeront, 'Des concepts de "Nature" et de "Personne" dans les pères et les écrivains ecclésiastiques des V et VIe siècles' in *Revue d'Histoire et de Littérature religieuses* viii (1903), pp. 582–92; repr. in id., *Mélanges de patrologie et d'histoire des dogmes* (1921), pp. 210–27. M. Richard, 'L'Introduction du mot "Hypostase" dans la théologie de l'Incarnation' in *Mélanges de Science religieuse*, ii (1945), pp. 5–32, 243–70. F. Erdin, *Das Wort Hypostasis*. Seine bedeutungsgeschichtliche Entwicklung (1939; Erdin's conclusions generally rejected). A. Michel in *D.T.C.*, vii (pt. 1; 1922), cols. 369–437, s.v. 'Hypostase', with bibl.

HYPOSTATIC UNION, The. The substantial union of the Divine and human natures in the One Person ('Hypostasis') of Jesus Christ. The doctrine was elaborated by St. *Cyril of Alexandria and formally accepted by the Church in the Definition of *Chalcedon (451). See also preceding entry.

A. Michel in *D.T.C.*, vii (pt. 1; 1922), cols. 437–568; E. Krebs in *L.Th.K.*, v (1933), cols. 235–7. See also bibl. to *Christology*.

HYPSISTARIANS (Gk. ὕψιστος, 'highest'). A 4th cent. sect, probably confined to Cappadocia, which is mentioned by *Gregory of Nazianzum (*Orat.* 18. 5, where he says that his father had formerly belonged to it) and by *Gregory of Nyssa. It was so named because its members, refusing to worship God as 'Father' (πατήρ), revered Him only as the 'All Ruler and Highest' (παντοκράτωρ καὶ ὕψιστος). They incorporated into their system many oriental and Jewish elements.

C. Ullmann, *De Hypsistariis* (Heidelberg, 1825). G. T. Stokes in *D.C.B.*, iii (1882), p. 188 f.; G. Bareille in *D.T.C.*, vii (pt. 1, 1922), col. 572; L. Spätling in *E.C.*, vii (1951), col. 181 f.

I

IAMBLICHUS (*c.* 250–*c.* 330). The chief *Neo-Platonist of the Syrian school. He was a native of Chalcis in Coele-Syria, studied under Anatolius and *Porphyry, and later taught in Syria, surrounded by many disciples. He held a very elaborate theory of mediation between the spiritual and physical worlds, modifying the doctrine of *Plotinus by arranging the various emanations in subordinated triads. Above the Plotinian ἕν (One) he placed another still higher ἕν, which is even above the Good, being devoid of all qualities. Below the Good is the world of ideas, below that the world of thinking beings, and lowest of all in the cosmos the world of sense. No soul can remain indefinitely either in the supra-sensible world or in Tartarus, but has to ascend and descend periodically.

Iamblichus incorporated in his system many Greek and Oriental pagan mythologies, whose Deities he amalgamated with his orders of hypostases. He also carried a stage further the development of the number-symbolism cherished by the later Neo-Platonists, e.g. *Proclus. Most of his surviving works are parts of a comprehensive exposition of the Pythagorean philosophy, entitled Συναγωγὴ τῶν Πυθαγορείων Δογμάτων. They include a treatise 'On the Pythagorean Life' (Περὶ τοῦ Πυθαγορικοῦ βίου), an 'Exhortation to Philosophy' (Λόγος προτρεπτικὸς εἰς Φιλοσοφίαν), and various treatises of a speculative kind on mathematics. The 'Liber de Mysteriis' attributed to him by Proclus is apparently not his work, though probably a product of the same school. Iamblichus made no claim to experiences of ecstasy and absorption in the Godhead which were commonly sought by the Neo-Platonists. There are apparently no direct references to Christianity in his writings.

Summary account of Iamblicus' doctrines, with edd. of his writings, in Überweg, i, 612–17, with full bibl., p. 191 f. Eng. tr. of 'Vita Pythagorica' by T. Taylor (London, 1818); of 'De Mysteriis' by id. (Chiswick, 1821; ed. 2, London, 1895). W. Whittaker, *The Neo-Platonists* (1901), pp. 122–32. G. Mau–W. Kroll in *P.W.*, xvii (1914), cols. 645–51. E. R. Dodds in *O.C.D.*, p. 447 f.

IBAS, Bp. of *Edessa from 435 to 457. In the contemporary Christological controversies, he took a mediating position between the dualistic teaching of the *Nestorians and the *Alexandrine position of St. *Cyril, and was closely associated in doctrine and policy with *Theodoret. On account of his views, summarized in his famous letter addressed in 433 to Bp. Mari of Hardascir (in Persia), he was deposed at the *Latrocinium at Ephesus in 449. Though he was vindicated at the Council of *Chalcedon (451), his epistle was condemned by *Justinian and anathematized by the Fifth General Council (553). None of his writings, apart from the Epistle to Mari in a Greek translation from the original Syriac, has survived. See also *Three Chapters*.

Text of Ep. to Mari in *acta* of Councils, e.g. Mansi, vii. 241–50. A. d'Alès, S.J., 'La Lettre d'Ibas à Marès le Persan' in *Rech. S.R.*, xxii (1932), pp. 5–25. Bardenhewer, iv (1924), p. 410 f. E. Venables in *D.C.B.*, iii (1882), pp. 192–6.

ICELAND, Christianity in. Christianity reached Iceland from *Norway *c.* 980. The medieval Church had two bishoprics, Skálholt and Hólar, and was at first under the administrative jurisdiction of Bremen, then of Lund, and finally of Trondhjem (Nidaros). Questions of the jurisdiction of the clergy brought about a civil war in the 13th cent. which ended in her subjection to Norway in 1262. *Benedictine and *Augustinian communities were established in the island for several centuries. At the Reformation Iceland followed *Denmark, to whose rule she had been subject since *c.* 1380, in adopting *Lutheranism. In modern times there has been a revival of Church life. The ecclesiastical government is in the hands of the Lutheran bishop, with deanery and parish councils; and the civil governor-general has also some voice in ecclesiastical appointments.

F. Jónsson, *Historia Ecclesiastica Islandiae* (4 vols., Copenhagen, 1772–8; cont. by P. Pétursson, ib., 1841). J. Helgason, *Islands Kirke fra dens Grundlaeggsle til Reformationen* (ib., 1925); id., *Islands Kirke fra Reformationem til vore Dage* (ib., 1922). J. C. F. Hood, *Icelandic Church Saga* (1946). F. Siegmund-Schultze (ed.), *Ekklesia*, ii, Lieferung vii, pt. 2, 'Die Kirche in Island' (1937), with bibl.

I.C.F. See *Industrial Christian Fellowship.*

ICHABOD, the son of Phinehas and grandson of the priest Eli, the tragic circumstances of whose birth are described in 1 Sam. 4. 19–22. The name, acc. to 1 Sam. 4. 21, means 'The glory has departed' (lit. 'no glory'); hence the use of 'Ichabod' as an exclamation.

ICHTHUS. See *Fish.*

ICON (Gk. εἰκών). Icons are flat pictures, usually painted in oil on wood, but also wrought in mosaic, ivory, and other materials, to represent our Lord, the BVM, or another saint, which are used and venerated in the Greek Church. The likenesses are depicted in the traditional rather stiff Byzantine manner. For protection they are frequently, esp. in Russia, covered with a metal shield on which the outlines of the clothes are carved, but which leave free the face and hands belonging to the painting underneath. Icons became numerous in the E. from the 5th cent., and the effect of the *Iconoclastic Controversy of the 8th and 9th cents. was to increase devotion to them among the people. Since then they have always played an essential part in the public as well as in the private worship of the Greek Church, and they are accorded all the external marks of veneration common in the E. such as kisses, genuflexions, incense, &c. As it is believed that through them the saints exercise their beneficent powers, they preside at all important events of human life and are held to be effective remedies against illness, to drive away devils, to procure both spiritual and temporal blessings, and generally to be powerful channels of Divine grace. Many icons have been famous for their miracles, esp. that of Christ of *Edessa, believed not to have been made by hands (ἀχειροποίητος), and that of the *Theotokos, also 'acheiropoietos', in the monastery of the Abramites at *Constantinople. In modern times perhaps the best-known icon is that of Our Lady of Perpetual Succour at *Rome. See also *Iconostasis* and *Images*.

O. Wulff–M. Alpatoff, *Denkmäler der Ikonenmalerei in kunstgeschichtlicher Folge* (1925). I. Dirks, O.S.B., *Les Saintes Icones* (ed. 2, Amay-sur-Meuse, 1939). W. P. Theunissen, *Ikonen*. Historisch, Aesthetisch en Theologisch Belicht (1948), with bibl. K. P. Kondakóv (Eng. tr. by E. H. Minns from larger Russian work), *The Russian Icon* (Oxford, 1927). P. Muratov, *Les Icones russes* (1928). D. T. Rice, *Russian Icons* (King Penguin Book, 1947); id., *The Beginnings of Russian Icon Painting* (Ilchester Lecture for 1937; 1938).

ICONOCLASTIC CONTROVERSY (from εἰκονοκλάστης, 'iconoclast', 'image-breaker'). The controversy on the veneration of *icons (q.v.) agitated the Greek Church from *c.* 725 to 842. At the end of the 7th and the beginning of the 8th cents. several influences hostile to the veneration of icons had made themselves felt in the E. Empire, notably the *Monophysite heresy which minimized the human side of the Incarnation, the *Manichean tendencies of the *Paulicians, who held that all matter was evil, and possibly also Mohammedanism. The open outbreak of this hostility was due to the Emp. *Leo III, the Isaurian (717–40). Brought up under Paulician influence, he thought the use of icons, which had admittedly become excessive, to be the chief obstacle to the conversion of Jews and Moslems. His intervention was also largely political, as he aimed at a general reorganization of the Church on lines which should give increased influence to the state. In 726 he published an edict declaring all images idols and ordering their destruction. Very soon serious disturbances throughout the Empire followed. The patriarch *Germanus, who appealed to the Pope, was deposed in 730, and a systematic persecution unleashed, esp. against the monks, who were the most ardent defenders of the icons. At the same time St. *John of Damascus wrote his famous apologies against the iconoclasts and Pope *Gregory III held two synods at Rome condemning Leo's supporters (731).

In 741 Leo was succeeded by his son Constantine V (Copronymus), who, after a quickly suppressed revolt of his brother-in-law, Artabasdus, in favour of the icons, continued his father's policy. In 753 he called the Synod of Hieria, which neither the patriarchs of *Antioch, *Jerusalem, and *Alexandria nor the Pope attended. The synod alleged that, by representing only the humanity of Christ, the icon worshippers either divided His unity as the *Nestorians or confounded the two Natures as the *Monophysites; and it further declared that the icons of the BVM and of the saints were idols and decreed the destruction of all of them. The persecution now raged more fiercely than ever, many of the secular clergy giving way, but a great number of monks became martyrs in the cause of the icons.

Under Constantine's son, Leo IV (775–80), the persecution abated, and after his death his wife, the Empress Irene, regent for her young son Constantine, reversed the policy of her predecessors despite the iconoclastic leanings of the army. In 784 *Tarasius became Patr. of Constantinople and, in concert with Irene, opened negotiations with Pope *Hadrian I, who sent legates to the Seventh General Council which met at *Nicaea in 787. This Council completely undid the work of the Synod of Hieria, defined the degree of veneration to be paid to icons, and decreed their restoration throughout the country.

Though the decrees of the Council were officially received, Iconoclasm retained a strong following esp. in the army. In 814 the outbreak of the 'Second Iconoclastic Controversy' took place under Leo V the Armenian, a general elected Emperor by the army. Leo again began to remove icons from churches and public buildings; the Patr. *Nicephorus was deposed (815); St. *Theodore of Studium, the foremost defender of images among the monks, sent into exile; and many others imprisoned and martyred. After Leo's assassination in 820 his successor, Michael II, continued his iconoclastic policy though in a milder form, whereas his son Theophilus, who succeeded him in 829, returned to the violence of Leo, esp. after the enthronization of the iconoclast patriarch John Hylilos in 832. The persecution ended only with Theophilus' death in 842. His widow, Theodora, like Irene, regent for her son, caused the monk Methodius to be elected patriarch in 843, and on the first Sunday of Lent a great feast was celebrated in honour of the icons, since then solemnly kept in the E. Church as the 'Feast of *Orthodoxy'.

The repercussions which the controversy had in the W. were slight and mainly caused by the misunderstanding of certain passages from the Acts of the Second Council of Nicaea. A faulty translation of the Acts, sent to *Charlemagne by Hadrian I, together with a general dislike of the Greeks and political friction, led to a manifesto against the Council by the Frankish bishops in 790, later expanded and issued as the 'Libri Carolini' (*Caroline Books). It was reiterated by the Synod of Frankfurt in 794 which formally condemned the Second Council of Nicaea, misunderstanding it to enjoin an adoration of images equal to that due to the Divine Trinity. A similar attitude was taken up by the bishops who met at Paris in 828, who would tolerate pictures only as ornaments. Owing to the authority of the Popes, however, and the influence of theologians such as *Walafrid Strabo and *Hincmar of Reims, the Frankish bishops gradually accepted the

Nicene decrees, opposition to them having virtually ceased in the 10th cent.

The Iconoclastic Controversy, more important for its practical than for its theological results, is usually considered the last step towards the great schism between E. and W. before the actual breach. The Caesaro-Papism which showed itself with increasing clarity during the struggle encountered less and less resistance in the Greek Church esp. among the secular clergy, while it was viewed by the Popes with growing apprehension. The unity achieved by Imperial decree in 787 and again in 843 proved artificial, and with the restoration of the Empire by the Franks and the development of the temporal power of the Papacy the ground was prepared for the final separation between the independent Church of the W. and the Church of the Byzantine Empire.

K. Schwarzlose, *Der Bilderstreit* (1890); L. Bréhier, *La Querelle des images, VIIIe–IXe siècles* (1904). E. J. Martin, *A History of the Iconoclastic Controversy* (C.H.S. [1930]). Fliche–Martin, v (1938), pp. 431–70 (L. Bréhier) and vi (1937), pp. 107–27 and 229–46 (É. Amann), each with bibl. C. Émereau in *D.T.C.*, vi (pt. 1; 1922), cols. 575–95, s.v. 'Iconoclasme'; H. *Leclercq, O.S.B., in *D.A.C.L.*, vi (pt. 1; 1926), cols. 214–302, s.v. 'Images'; M. Jugie, A.A., in *E.C.*, vi (1951), cols. 1541–6, s.v. 'Iconoclastia'. P. J. Alexander, *The Patriarch Nicephorus of Constantinople* (1958).

ICONOGRAPHY, Christian. The subject of Christian iconography is the pictorial or symbolical representation of Christian ideas, persons, and history. It is not a form of aesthetic criticism, but, like *archaeology, an auxiliary to historical and theological studies.

The earliest Christian art was mainly symbolical. Christ was represented by a *fish (Ichthus) or a young shepherd, a ship symbolized the Church, an anchor hope or salvation, a peacock immortality. Pictorial scenes, drawn from the Bible or the *Apocryphal literature, were also typical, not merely illustrative, e.g. Jonah's story symbolized death and resurrection.

From the time of *Constantine, Christian art could display Christianity triumphant, while Syrian influence brought more realism to counteract the early idealism. Thus Christ appears no longer as a Greek youth, but bearded and in E. dress, and the Crucifixion begins to be portrayed with pathos. The chief descriptive monuments of this period are catacomb paintings, church mosaics, and sarcophagi. Soon reaction from realism set in, due perhaps to influences from further E. Byzantine churches often exhibit a planned system of stylized and didactic decoration, covering the whole interior. After the *Iconoclastic Controversy, this plan was adapted more precisely to the Liturgy and stereotyped for centuries.

W. art also was predominantly didactic, though the artist was freer and his subject matter more comprehensive. Gothic cathedrals, by their sculpture, glass, paintings, and textiles, were encyclopaedias of theology, history, hagiography, natural history (moralized, after the Bestiaries), learning (the seven arts), morality (following *Prudentius' 'Combat of Virtues and Vices'), and the trades and crafts. All activity, this indicated, is religious. While individualism had some play and not all art was didactic, art commonly conformed to a pattern determined by the Church. This was partly based on, partly explained by, the encyclopaedic writings of *Honorius of Autun, Bartholomaeus Anglicus (*c.* 1250), and, above all, *Vincent of Beauvais, which developed the work of *Isidore of Seville and *Rabanus Maurus. Such a cathedral as *Chartres demonstrates a highly organized scheme of decoration.

In the 14th cent. art grew less intellectual and more emotional or mystical. In the next century it became frankly realistic and picturesque. Didactic schemes were already dissolving when the Renaissance killed medieval methods. Since then there have been many experiments in both realism and symbolism, but, while religious art still abounds, it is impossible to discern any dominant tradition or system in Christian art and symbolism.

L. Bréhier, *L'Art chrétien. Son développement iconographique des origines à nos jours* (1918); K. Künstle, *Ikonographie der christlichen Kunst* (2 vols., 1926–8), with bibl. G. de Jerphanion, S.J., *La Voix des monuments.* Notes et études d'archéologie chrétienne (1930), esp. No. 2, 'Le Développement iconographique de l'art chrétien', pp. 30–54. É. Mâle, *L'Art religieux du XIIe siècle en France* (1922); id., *L'Art religieux du XIIIe siècle en France* (1898; Eng. tr., 1913); id., *L'Art religieux de la fin du moyen-âge en France* (1908); id., *L'Art religieux de la fin du XVIe siècle, du XVIIe siècle et du XVIIIe siècle* (1932); Eng. tr. of selected passages from these works issued as *Religious Art from the Twelfth to the Eighteenth Century* (1949). Less scientific are Mrs. [A. B.] Jameson's series of works on the subject (6 vols., London, 1848–64). D. Talbot Rice, *The Beginnings of Christian Art* (1957). L. Réau, *Iconographie de l'art chrétien* (3 vols. in 6, 1955–8). H. Aurenhammer, *Lexikon der christlichen Ikonographie* (1959 ff.).

ICONOSTASIS. The screen which, in Byzantine churches, separates the sanctuary from the nave. Originally a lattice consisting of columns joined by a decorated parapet and coping, since the 14th to 15th cents. the screen has presented the form of a wall of wood or stone, covered with *icons, from which it derives its name. It is pierced by three doors, the central or Royal Door admitting to the altar, and those on the right and left respectively to the *Diaconicon and the *Prothesis.

C. Rohault de Fleury, *La Messe.* Études archéologiques sur ses monuments, iii (1883), pp. 105–34. K. Holl, 'Die Entstehung der Bilderwand in der griechischen Kirche' in *Archiv für Religionswissenschaft*, ix (1906), pp. 365–84; B. Pace, 'Nuova ipotesi sull' origine dell' iconostasio' in *Byzantion*, xix (1949), pp. 195–205. H. *Leclercq, O.S.B., in *D.A.C.L.*, vii (pt. 1; 1926), cols. 31–48, s.v. 'Iconostase'.

IDIORRHYTHMIC. A term applied to certain monasteries on Mount *Athos, which, in contradistinction to the *coenobitic houses, allow considerable freedom to their monks, including the right to possess personal property.

IGNATIUS, St. (*c.* 35–*c.* 107), Bp. of *Antioch. Ignatius describes himself as also called 'Theophoros' (Θεοφόρος, 'bearer of God', or perhaps Θεόφορος, 'borne by God'). He was probably of Syrian origin, and J. B. *Lightfoot, basing himself on a passage from his *Ep. ad Romanos*, believes that he was a pagan and a persecutor of Christians before his conversion. Acc. to *Origen, he was the second Bp. of Antioch, the successor of St. *Peter; acc. to *Eusebius he was the third, following St. Peter's successor, Euodius, c. 69. Nothing is known of his life beyond his journey to martyrdom from Antioch to *Rome under a guard of ten soldiers. He was received en route at *Smyrna with great honour by St. *Polycarp, and visited by many members of neighbouring Christian communities, and wrote thence to the Churches of *Ephesus, Magnesia, and Tralles letters of encouragement, and a fourth to the Church at Rome, begging them not to deprive him of martyrdom by intervention with the pagan authorities. He was then taken to Troas, where he wrote three further letters to the Churches of *Philadelphia and Smyrna and to St. Polycarp, and thence through Macedonia and Illyria to Dyrrhachium, where he was embarked for Italy. That the martyrdom to which Ignatius looked forward in his letters actually took place is already asserted by Polycarp and Origen, the latter of whom expressly mentions Rome as its place (traditionally the *Colosseum). The statement of *John Malalas (6th cent.) that Ignatius was martyred at Antioch is wholly without warrant. There survive five different accounts of his death ('Acta'), none of them meriting much credence.

The high esteem in which Ignatius's letters were held is proved both by patristic quotations, e.g. in *Eusebius and *Theodoret, and also by interpolations and the circulation of spurious letters under his name. A Latin version of the seven genuine but interpolated letters, together with four spurious epistles, was first publd. by J. *Faber (Stapulensis) in 1498. The genuineness of this collection (the 'Long Recension') was a matter of prolonged dispute. It was accepted as authentic in toto by older RC scholars, but rejected equally in toto esp. by anti-episcopalian Protestant divines. The whole matter appeared in a new light when J. *Ussher, who observed that Ignatian quotations in medieval English authors differed from Faber's text but agreed with those in the Fathers, deduced both that the current text was interpolated and that the original text was probably to be found in England. He subsequently discovered a Latin translation which agreed with the old quotations. His Polycarpi et Ignatii Epistolae (1644) was a work of remarkable critical genius and erudition, its only serious error being the rejection of the letter to Polycarp. In 1646 Isaak *Voss edited the corresponding Greek text which Ussher had traced to a Florentine MS. (Laur. Plut. lvii. 7). For a long time, however, many Protestant scholars continued to reject all the letters owing to their strong emphasis on episcopacy. The controversy was virtually settled in favour of the authenticity of the seven letters by J. *Pearson's Vindiciae Ignatianae (1672).

In the 19th cent. the dispute arose afresh through W. *Cureton's publication (1845) of a *Syriac MS. containing a recension of only the three genuine letters to the Ephesians, to the Romans, and to Polycarp. He maintained that this 'Short Recension' was the only authentic one. Lightfoot's learned defence of the authenticity of the seven letters in his monumental edition of the Apostolic Fathers (1885) has, however, won general acceptance. He maintained further that the six apocryphal letters and the interpolations of the 'Long Recension' are by the same 4th cent. hand; but whether the forger held *Arian or *Apollinarian views is still disputed.

The authentic epistles, and esp. that to the Romans, reveal a man passionately devoted to Christ. His consuming desire for martyrdom comes out esp. in the Ep. to the Romans. In the other epistles he warns the recipients against a Judaizing heresy with *Docetic elements. He insists on the reality both of the Divinity and the Humanity of our Lord, whom he calls ὁ θεὸς ἡμῶν Ἰησοῦς Χριστός ('our God Jesus Christ'). His Birth, Passion, and Death were not appearances but realities. The life of Christ is continued in the Eucharist, which he calls 'the bread that is the flesh of Jesus Christ, this flesh which has suffered for our sins'. The best safeguard of the unity of the Christian faith is the bishop, who is pre-eminent because he is 'as the Lord', and without whose authority neither the Eucharist nor marriage may be celebrated. The Church of Rome is referred to with special reverence as 'presiding in the region of the Romans' (ἥτις προκάθηται ἐν τόπῳ χωρίου Ῥωμαίων). There is, however, no reference to the Bp. of Rome.

Feast day, in the Roman Calendar, 1 Feb.; in the (1928) BCP, 17 Dec. (that of his translation in *Roman Martyrology); in the Greek Church, 20 Dec.; and at Antioch, 17 Oct.

The history of Ignatian criticism, with full survey of the MS. material and modern discussions, is fully described in J. B. *Lightfoot, The Apostolic Fathers, Part II (3 vols., 1885), with crit. text and Eng. tr. Gk. text and Eng. trr. also readily accessible in editions of the 'Apostolic Fathers'. Convenient Eng. tr., with notes, by J. H. Srawley (Early English Church Classics, 2 vols., London, 1900); more recent ed., with Fr. tr. and useful commentary, by P. T. Camelot, O.P. (S.C., x; 1944; ed. 2, 1951). T. *Zahn, Ignatius von Antiochien (Gotha, 1873); E. v. der Goltz, Ignatius von Antiochien als Christ und Theologe (T.U., xii, Hft. 3, 1894). H. Schlier, Religionsgeschichtliche Untersuchungen zu den Ignatiusbriefen (Beihefte zur Z.N.T.W., viii; 1929). C. C. Richardson, The Christianity of Ignatius of Antioch (New York, 1935); H. W. Bartsch, Gnostisches Gut und Gemeindetradition bei Ignatius von Antiochien (1940). B. H. *Streeter, The Primitive Church (1929), pp. 163–78. Bardenhewer, i, pp. 131–58; Altaner (ed. 1951), pp. 78–81. G. Bareille in D.T.C., vii (pt. 1; 1922), cols. 685–713.

IGNATIUS LOYOLA, St. (1491 or 1495–1556), founder of the *Jesuits. Born of a noble family at the castle of Loyola not far south of the Pyrenees, he entered on a military career, taking service with the Duke of Nagera. A wound in the right leg which he received during the siege of Pampeluna (1521) reduced him to a prolonged state of inactivity, during which the reading of the Life of Christ and the biographies of the saints led him to change his life and decide to become a soldier of Christ. After his recovery he went to *Montserrat, where he made a general confession, hung up his sword at our Lady's altar, and exchanged clothes with a beggar. From there he went to Manresa, where he stayed a year (1522–3) in retirement, giving himself up to a life of prayer and extreme mortification. From his mystic experiences in Manresa he derived the profound spiritual insight which marks the *Spiritual Exercises* (q.v.), the bulk of which was probably written there. From Manresa Ignatius went first to *Rome and then to *Jerusalem, subsisting on alms and trusting entirely to Divine Providence. On his return to Spain he studied at Barcelona, Alcalá, and Salamanca (1524–8), where he made a deep impression on his fellow-students.

From Salamanca Ignatius went to Paris, where he continued his studies with short interruptions for seven years (1528–35). He laid the foundations of the Society of Jesus in 1534, when he and six companions, among them St. *Francis Xavier and Bl. Peter Faber, made a vow of poverty, chastity, and of a pilgrimage to Jerusalem if possible, which was to be followed by a life devoted to apostolic labours. In 1537 they went to Italy, where Ignatius and several others were ordained priests. Their pilgrimage being prevented by a set of adverse circumstances, they offered their services to the Pope. On their way to Rome Ignatius had the famous vision of La Storta, where he saw Christ promising him to be propitious to them in the City. In 1540 the Society was solemnly sanctioned by *Paul III in the bull '*Regimini militantis Ecclesiae', and Ignatius became its first *general. His remaining years were filled with the organization of his rapidly spreading order. He drew up the constitutions of the Society between 1547 and 1550, continuing to improve them until the end of his life.

Ignatius's three chief endeavours had been the reform of the Church from within, principally by education and the more frequent use of the Sacraments, the preaching of the Gospel to the newly discovered pagan world, and the fight against heresy. He was canonized in 1622. Feast day, 31 July.

Critical edd. in *Monumenta Ignatiana*, Series I, S. Ignatii de Loyola. . . . Epistolae et Instructiones (12 vols., Madrid, 1903–14); Series II, Exercitia Spiritualia Sancti Ignatii de Loyola (Madrid, 1919); Series III, Constitutiones Societatis Jesu (4 vols., Rome, 1934–48); Series IV, Scripta de Sancto Ignatio de Loyola (2 vols., Madrid, 1904–18). Contemporary life by P. Ribadeneira, S.J. (Naples, 1572; Eng. tr., 1616). Other lives by J. A. Polanco, S.J. (6 vols., Madrid, 1894–8), H. Joly ('Les Saints', 1899; Eng. tr., 1899), F. *Thompson–J. H. Pollen, S.J. (London, 1909), H. D. Sedgwick (New York, 1923), P. Van Dyke (New York and London, 1926), P. Dudon, S.J. (Paris, 1934), and C. Hollis (London, 1931).

IGNATIUS, Father. The Rev. Joseph Leycester Lyne (1837–1908), mission preacher. In 1860 he was ordained deacon to the title of a curacy at St. Peter's, Plymouth, under G. R. Prynne. Shortly afterwards he left Plymouth and worked for some months with Rev. C. F. *Lowder at St. George's-in-the-East, London. He made it his chief aim to revive the *Benedictine Order in the Anglican Church, and after various abortive steps eventually acquired in 1869 a site for his monastery at Capel-y-ffin, some four miles from Llanthony. A striking

preacher with great gifts of popular oratory, he carried out successful missions in many parts of England, mainly in secular buildings. He remained a deacon until 1898 when he was ordained priest by J. R. *Vilatte. On Ignatius's death, the buildings at Capel-y-ffin passed into the possession of the Anglican Benedictines at *Caldey Island.

Baroness de Bertouch, *The Life of Father Ignatius, O.S.B.* (1904); D. Attwater, *Father Ignatius of Llanthony* (1931).

IGNORANCE, Invincible. See *Invincible Ignorance*.

IHS. A monogram for the name Jesus, formed by abbreviating the corresponding Greek word which in *uncials is written IHΣΟΥΣ. It is found, e.g., in the Latin text of Lk. 6. 5 in the *Codex Bezae. That the second symbol, H, was really a Greek η and not a Latin h was soon forgotten, and the abbreviation 'ihs' was thus often wrongly expanded to 'Ihesus'. Other attempts to explain the three letters as initials of separate words became very common. Thus they were held to denote *Iesus Hominum Salvator* (i.e. 'Jesus, Saviour of Men') or *In Hoc Signo* [*vinces*] (i.e. 'in this sign [ye shall conquer]'). In the Middle Ages the IHS was widely used among the *Dominicans and later it became popular among the *Jesuits, who sometimes interpreted it as *Jesum Habemus Socium* (i.e. 'We have Jesus as our companion').

F. Victorius, *De Vetustate et Forma Monogrammatis*. . . . *Nominis Jesu* (Rome, 1747). L. Traube, *Nomina Sacra* (1907), pp. 156–9; F. J. Dölger, ΙΧΘΥΣ. Das Fischsymbol in frühchristlicher Zeit, i (R.Q., Suppl. xvii, 1910), pp. 355–61.

ILDEFONSUS, St. (*c.* 607–67), Abp. of *Toledo. He came from a noble family, and is traditionally believed to have been a pupil of St. *Isidore of Seville. While still young, he entered the *Benedictine monastery of Agalia, nr. Toledo, and later became its abbot. As such he attended the Councils of Toledo in 653 and 655. He was appointed Abp. of Toledo in 657. Acc. to St. Julian of Toledo, he was the author of a long list of works, but only four have survived. His 'De Virginitate S. Mariae', in praise of our Lady, towards whom he showed great devotion, was an ardent defence of the privileges of the Mother of God, directed esp. against the Spanish Jews. His 'Annotationes de Cognitione Baptismi' uses skilfully the works of older writers on the subject, esp. St. *Augustine, St. *Gregory the Great, and St. *Isidore of Seville, and contains much valuable information on the discipline of *catechumens. His 'De Itinere Deserti quo Pergitur post Baptismum' completes the 'Annotationes' by a mystical application of the wanderings of the Israelites in the wilderness to the spiritual journey of the soul after baptism. The fourth of his extant works, 'De Viris Illustribus', is an important document of the history of the Spanish Church during the first two-thirds of the 7th cent. St. Ildefonsus was a favourite subject for medieval artists, esp. the legend of the apparition of our Lady presenting him with a chasuble. Feast day, 23 Jan.

Works ed. Card. F. de Lorenzana, Abp. of Toledo, in *Sanctorum Patrum Toletanorum quotquot extant Opera*, i (Madrid, 1782), pp. 94–290; repr. in J. P. Migne, *PL*, xcvi, 9–330. Crit. text of 'De Virginitate Beatae Mariae', with discussion, by V. B. García (Textos latinos de la edad medina española, Madrid, 1937). Spanish tr. of Life by A. Martínez de Toledo (Clásicos castellanos, No. 134, Madrid, 1952). Bardenhewer, i, 7 f., and v, 388 f. (treatment inadequate). Mrs. Humphry Ward in *D.C.B.*, iii (1882), pp. 223–5; G. Bareille in *D.T.C.*, vii (pt. 1; 1922), cols. 740–44; J. Madoz, S.J., in *E.C.*, vi (1951), col. 1620 f., s.v.

ILLINGWORTH, JOHN RICHARDSON
(1848–1915), English divine. Educated at Christ Church, Oxford, he was elected a Fellow of Jesus College in 1872, and ordained in 1875. In 1883 he became Rector of Longworth, Berks, where he remained till his death. A philosopher rather than a theologian, who had come under the influence of the school of T. H. *Green, he applied some of the principles of *Idealistic philosophy to the exposition of the Christian faith. His rectory became the centre of the '*Lux Mundi' group, and Illingworth himself contributed two essays to the volume. His books include *Personality, Human and Divine* (*Bampton Lectures, 1894), *Divine Immanence* (1898), *Reason and Revelation* (1902), and *The Doctrine of the Trinity* (1907).

The Life and Work of J. R. Illingworth, by his wife (1917).

ILLTYD, St. (450–535). Welsh saint. It is difficult to disentangle fact and legend from the records of his life; but it would seem that he was a native of Brittany who came to Britain c. 470, was converted to Christianity in 476, and founded a famous monastery, later named after him 'Llantwit' or 'Llanilltyd' (i.e. 'Church of Illtyd'; probably the modern Llantwit Major, but perhaps *Caldey), and a centre of missionary activity in Wales. A late and unhistorical tradition makes him a cousin of King Arthur. Feast day, 6 Nov.

AA.SS., Nov. III (1910), pp. 219–36, incl. text of anonymous 12th-cent. life, which is the principal source, pp. 225–34. On this life see J. S. P. Tatlock, 'The Dates of the Arthurian Saints' Legends', in *Speculum*, xiv (1939), pp. 345–365, esp. pp. 353–6. H. Williams, *Christianity in Early Britain* (1912), pp. 316–31. D. L. Thomas in *D.N.B.*, xxviii (1891), p. 416 f., s.v.

ILLUMINATI. A name applied to several bodies of religious enthusiasts, among them:
(1) The Alumbrados (q.v.).
(2) The Rosicrucians (q.v.).
(3) A masonic sect founded in Bavaria in 1778 by Adam Weishaupt (1748–1830), who had been trained in a *Jesuit school and become a professor of *canon law at Ingolstadt. Its object was to diffuse knowledge and to stimulate humanistic ideals and brotherly fellowship among its members. Those who belonged to it took names of the ancients and called Munich 'Athens' and Vienna 'Rome'. They aimed at forming a classless society and at bringing about the 'restoration' of the patriarchal state. Repudiating the claims of all existing religious bodies, they professed themselves to be those in whom the 'illuminating' grace of Christ (hence their name; cf. Heb. 6. 4: τοὺς ἅπαξ φωτισθέντας) alone resided, and organized themselves on a new and very elaborate system, which required absolute obedience (largely modelled on *Jesuit ideals) to the unknown superiors. In 1784 they were banished from Bavaria, but they continued to survive elsewhere, e.g. in France. They were also known as Perfectibilists. In quite recent times (1896, and again in 1925) they have been revived in Germany in a modified form.

ILLUMINATION MOVEMENT. See *Aufklärung*.

ILLUMINATIVE WAY (*Via illuminativa*). The intermediary stage of the mystic way between the *purgative and the *unitive ways (qq.v.), also called the 'Way of Proficients.' It is held that the soul is therein cleansed from attachment to creatures and 'enlightened' (illuminated) concerning the things of the spirit.

ILLYRICUS. See *Flacius, Matthias*.

IMAGES. The use of any representations of men, animals, and plants whether carved or painted was prohibited in the Mosaic Law (Exod. 20. 4), by reason of the danger of idolatry. In other parts of the OT, however, images are mentioned, such as the *brazen serpent made by *Moses himself (Num. 21. 9), the *Cherubim standing over the *ark of the covenant (Exod. 25. 18–22), and the carvings in *Solomon's temple (1 Kgs. 6. 18–35). There is no mention of imagery in the NT, as at least from the time of the *Maccabees the Palestinian Jews had observed the Second Commandment rigorously. It was only when the theological significance of the Incarnation came to be more fully grasped, and what was involved in the fact that God had become visible by taking human nature better understood, that, to many, there seemed to be no further obstacle to the use of images and other products of the artistic gifts of mankind in the service of the true religion.

The paintings of the Catacombs, some of which date from the 2nd cent., are the earliest Christian pictures, and after the period of the *Persecutions sacred images came to play an increasing part in the cultus, esp. in the E., where they received a special veneration and called forth the *Iconoclastic Controversy (q.v.) of the 8th and 9th cents. After the final settlement in favour of *icons, which remain the only form of representation legitimate in the Greek Church, they have continued to be an integral element of Orthodox religion, whether public or private, in which they are given a much more important place than in the W. Church.

In the West, the veneration of images, which at an early age began to comprise also statues, made much slower progress. It was given a doctrinal basis by the Schoolmen, esp. St. *Thomas Aquinas, who developed its theoretical justification on the lines laid down by the E. theologians, applying St. *Basil's principle that the honour paid to the image passes on to its prototype.

In the 16th cent. the abuses which had grown up around the use of images in the later Middle Ages led the practice to be violently opposed by the majority of the Reformers, esp. H. *Zwingli and J. *Calvin, who were followed by the *Puritans. The *Lutherans were more tolerant of the practice, and to this day the crucifix is retained in the Lutheran churches. The Anglican Article XXII confines itself to condemning the 'Romish doctrine' on the subject. The Council of *Trent defined that due honour should be paid to images of our Lord, the BVM, and the other saints, on the ground not of any virtue inherent in the image, but because in it the person represented is venerated. This veneration is allowed only to images of actual human persons, not to such symbolical representations as that of God the Father as a venerable old man or the Holy Ghost as a dove, and similar devices.

St. Thomas Aquinas, *In Sent.*, lib. III, dist. ix, a. 2, qu. 2; id., *S. Theol.*, III, i, qu. xxv, a. 3. The Tridentine ruling promulgated in sess. xxv, sect. 'De Invocatione, Veneratione et reliquiis Sanctorum et Sacris Imaginibus', is repr. in Denz.–Bann. (ed. 28, 1952), p. 343 f. (Nos. 986–8). E. Bevan, *Holy Images* (*Gifford Lectures for 1933; 1940). A. *Fortescue in *C.E.*, vii (1910), pp. 664–72, s.v., with bibl. V. Grumel, A.A., in *D.T.C.*, vii (pt. 1; 1922), cols. 766–84, s.v., with full reff. to classical lit. See also bibl. to *Iconoclastic Controversy* and to *Iconography*.

IMAGO DEI, Lat., 'image of God', in which, acc. to Gen. 1. 26 f. and elsewhere, man was created. Acc. to Catholic theologians this image was obscured, but not lost, in the *Fall, in contrast to the *similitudo Dei*, which was destroyed by *Original Sin but is restored by *Baptism. Many theories have been advanced to explain in what the *Imago* consists. Several Gk. Fathers, including St. *Gregory of Nyssa, the author of the 'Spiritual Homilies' attributed to *Macarius of Egypt, and St. *John of Damascus, identify it with human free-will; others seek it in man's superiority to the rest of creation, or in a quality of his soul such as simplicity and immortality, or in his reason. Acc. to St. *Augustine, the Image of the Trinity is to be found in the intellectual nature of the soul and its three powers, Memory (the Father), Intellect (the Son), and Will (the Holy Ghost). In the mystical theology of the E. as well as of the W. Church the *Imago* has played an important part as the point in which the soul is *capax Dei* and hence can enter into union with God.

In Protestant theology the vitiating effect of the Fall on the *Imago Dei* has been strongly emphasized. K. *Barth and E. *Brunner both stress this in different ways, though the latter accuses Barth of exaggerating the principle of *sola gratia* to the extent of destroying the *Imago* completely, and with it all moral responsibility. Acc. to Brunner there is a 'formal image', that which constitutes man as human

and responsible and is the 'point of contact' (*Anknüpfungspunkt*) for grace, which was not destroyed by the Fall, and the 'material image', which has been lost. Barth, on the other hand, rejects the formal image, and holds man to be utterly corrupted by sin and incapable of discovering any kind of truth about God or himself apart from Revelation.

E. Brunner, *Der Mittler* (1927; Eng. trans., 1934); id., *Natur und Gnade* (1934); K. Barth, *Nein!* (1934).

'IMITATION OF CHRIST', The. The purpose of this famous manual of spiritual devotion is to instruct the Christian how to seek perfection by following Christ as his model. The book is divided into four parts. The first two contain general counsel for the spiritual life, the third deals with the interior dispositions of the soul, and the fourth with the sacrament of the Holy Communion. It was first put into circulation (anon.) in 1418, and has traditionally been assigned to *Thomas à Kempis (c. 1380–1471). Indeed a MS. still exists at Brussels (Bibl. Roy., 5855–61) with his signature. Attempts have been made since the 17th cent. to assign it to an earlier writer, among those suggested being J. *Gerson, St. *Bonaventura, and *Innocent III; but the grounds for overthrowing the traditional ascription have failed to win general assent.

Facsimile reprod. of the *editio princeps*, which was printed at Augsburg 1471–2, ed. with introd. by W. J. Knox-Little (London, 1893). Crit. ed. by C. Hirsche (Berlin, 1874); also ed., with important introd., among the works of Thomas à Kempis by M. J. Pohl, vol. ii (Freiburg i.Br., 1904). First Eng. tr. (mid 15th cent.) ed. J. K. Ingram (E.E.T.S., extra series, lxiii; 1892); modern ed. of Eng. tr. made by R. Whitford *c.* 1530 by E. J. Klein with full introd. and notes prepared for E.E.T.S. (New York and London, 1941). There have been a large number of Eng. trr., including that with introd. by J. *Wesley (London, 1735); convenient trr. by C. *Bigg ('The Library of Devotion'; 1898, with useful introd., pp. 1–42), by A. Hyma (New York, 1927), and L. Sherley-Price (Penguin Classics, 1952). Modern discussions on the authorship by C. Hirsche (2 vols., Berlin, 1873–83), S. Kettlewell (London, 1877), O. A. Spitzen (Utrecht, 1881), L. A. Wheatley (London, 1891), F. R. Cruise (ib., 1896), J. E. G. de Montmorency (ib., 1906), and E. F. Jacob in the *Bulletin of the John Rylands Library*, xxii (1938), pp. 493–509; all attributing it to Thomas à Kempis (as do most edd. of the work). G. Bonet-Maury (Paris, 1878), K. C. L. M. De Beer (Brussels-Nijmegen, 1938), J. van Ginneken, S.J. (2 vols., Amsterdam, 1940–41), J. Tiecke (Nijmegen, 1941), and F. Kern (Olten, 1947) all attribute the work to G. *Groote, mainly on the basis of certain 'pre-Kemptistes' texts, ed. by J. van Ginneken, *op. cit.* It was attributed by P. E. Puyol (2 vols., Paris, 1899–1900) to a certain John Gersen of Canabaco, a Benedictine Abbot of Vercelli (an unlikely theory, first suggested by the discovery of a MS. by B. Rossignoli in the 17th cent. describing it as the work of 'Abbatis Johannis Gersen'). The theory of the authorship of J. C. de Gerson has recently been championed by D. G. Barron, *Jean Charlier de Gerson.* The author of the *De Imitatione Christi* (1936), who gives a full discussion of the classical attempts at assigning the authorship. P. E. Puyol, *Descriptions bibliographiques des manuscrits et des principales éditions du livre* De Imitatione Christi (1898). See also works cited under *Devotio Moderna* and *Thomas à Kempis*.

IMMACULATE CONCEPTION OF THE BVM. The dogma that 'from the first moment of her conception the Blessed Virgin Mary was, by the singular grace and privilege of Almighty God, and in view of the merits of Jesus Christ, Saviour of mankind, kept free from all stain of original sin' (Bull '*Ineffabilis Deus' of *Pius IX, 8 Dec. 1854). The belief has had a long and varied history, largely bound up with the observance of a feast of the Conception of the BVM. Biblical support has been found for the doctrine in Gen. 3. 15 and Lk. 1. 28. The argument from tradition is taken from the teaching of the Fathers, who as early as *Justin Martyr and *Irenaeus regarded Mary as the 'new Eve' corresponding to Christ as the 'new Adam'. In the East where *Andrew of Crete and *John of Damascus, without going into theological details, had extolled the perfect sinlessness of Mary as implicit in the title '*Theotokos', the feast of her Conception was known from the 7th cent., and its observance spread to the West where it is attested for Naples and probably *Ireland in the 9th, and for England in the first half of the 11th cent. On its introduction into France (c. 1130–40) St. *Bernard opposed it and a controversy went on for several centuries. Most of the great schoolmen, St. *Albert, St. *Bonaventure, and St. *Thomas among them, declared against the belief on the grounds that in every natural conception the stain of original sin is transmitted and that, as Mary was conceived in the natural way, she was not exempt from this law. In opposition to the Paris theologians the contrary opinion was defended by *Duns Scotus at Oxford and later in Paris, and in his wake the *Franciscans became its protagonists as the *Dominicans, following St. Thomas, its opponents. The 15th cent. brought decisive developments. The Council of *Basle affirmed (1439) the belief as a pious opinion in accordance with Catholic faith, reason, and Scripture; ten years later the *Sorbonne required an oath of all its candidates to defend it, and other universities followed. In 1476 Sixtus IV approved the feast with its own Mass and Office, and in 1708 *Clement XI extended it to the Universal Church and even imposed its observance as a *Feast of Obligation. The Council of *Trent had explicitly declared that its decree on original sin did not include the BVM, and from the 16th cent. belief in the Immaculate Conception became general and was defended not only by the Franciscans but also by the *Carmelites, by many Dominicans, and esp. by the *Jesuits. Of this development the definition of 1854 was the natural result. The Feast of the Immaculate Conception is kept on 8 Dec.

C. Passaglia, S.J., *De Immaculato Deiparae Semper Virginis Conceptu Commentarius* (3 parts, Rome, 1854–5); A. Ballerini, S.J., *Sylloge Monumentorum ad Mysterium Conceptionis Immaculatae Virginis Deiparae Illustrandum* (2 vols., Rome, 1854–6). W. B. *Ullathorne, *The Immaculate Conception of the Mother of God* (1855). E. *Bishop, *Liturgica Historica* (1918), ch. x ('On the Origins of the Feast of the Conception of the Blessed Virgin Mary'). X. Le Bachelet in *D.T.C.*, vii (pt. 1; 1922), cols. 845–1218, s.v. 'Immaculée Conception', with bibl.; P. Bonnetain, P.S.S., in *Dict. Bibl.*, Suppl. iv (1949), cols. 233–98, s.v. 'Immaculée Conception', with bibl.; G. Roschini, O.S.M.–A. Raes, S.J.–G. Löw, C.SS.R.–E. Lavagnino in *E.C.*, vi (1951), cols. 1651–63, with bibl. E. D. O'Connor (ed.), *The Dogma of the Immaculate Conception* (Notre Dame, Indiana, 1958).

IMMANENCE, Divine. The omnipresence of God in His universe. The doctrine is a necessary constituent of the Christian conception of God, but, when held without the parallel doctrine of Divine transcendence, it is commonly indistinguishable from *pantheism (q.v.).

J. R. *Illingworth, *Divine Immanence* (1898).

IMMANUEL, or EMMANUEL (Heb. עִמָּנוּאֵל, 'With us [is] God'). In the OT the word is used only in Is. 7. 14 and 8. 8. There are several interpretations. The prophet may here have meant by the expression (1) Hezekiah, the son of Ahaz; or (2) a son of his own; or (3) the *Messiah. It has also been suggested that no individual is referred to, but only future Divine deliverance. In Mt. 1. 23 the prophecy is interpreted with reference to the Birth of Jesus Christ.

Besides Commentaries on Is. and Matt., see A. S. *Peake in *D.C.G.*, i (1906), pp. 782–4, s.v., with bibl.

IMMERSION. A method of *baptism, employed at least from the 2nd cent., whereby part of the candidate's body was submerged in the baptismal water which was poured over the remainder. The rite is still found in the E. Church. In the W. it began to be replaced from c. the 8th cent. by the method of *affusion, though instances are still found as late as the 16th cent.; it is still permitted in the RC Church. The term is occasionally loosely used to include *submersion, from which it is strictly to be distinguished.

IMMOLATION (Lat. *immolatio*, lit. 'the sprinkling of a sacrificial victim with meal' as required by the pagan ritual), an act of sacrificial offering. In early Christian usage the word was applied esp. to the actual slaughter of the victim, in the *Vulgate being often interchangeable with *mactatio* ('slaying'). In modern Eucharistic theology it has occupied an important place in view of the various doctrines held of the Immolation in the Mass, esp. since the publication of M. *de La Taille's *Mysterium Fidei* (1921).

IMMORTALITY. Though in no sense a specifically Christian doctrine, the hope of immortality is an integral element in Christian belief, where it receives emphatic insistence and a characteristic shape. In pre-Christian times, the Greeks esp. developed a reasoned doctrine on the subject. The rationality of the human intellect seemed to imply an essential kinship of the soul with the principles of reason, so that it partook of their eternity. From this kinship *Plato inferred the existence of the soul before birth as well as its survival of death and saw in the process of learning the reminiscence (ἀνάμνησις) of knowledge possessed in a previous life. The striving of the virtuous man after the eternally valid principles of morality also pointed to the same belief. Plato and other Greeks insisted on the limitations which matter imposed on the soul. The body was an impediment, even a prison-house, from which death brought to the soul release into a fuller existence.

Such philosophical conceptions of immortality have commonly been confined to the few. In early times Hebrew thought about the next world hardly exceeded the conception of a very shadowy existence in *Sheol (q.v.). In later pre-Christian Judaism a greater sense of the reality of the future life developed, partly through reflection on the problem of suffering, partly from the ardent desire for abiding communion with God, partly through the recasting of the Messianic expectation. In this way the Jewish hope was given a fundamentally religious colouring, which looked forward to the Christian teaching on the next life. It also became increasingly bound up with belief in the resurrection of the body, esp. in the *Apocalyptic writers. Outside Palestine later Judaism borrowed extensively from Greek thought; in the Book of *Wisdom, e.g., the doctrine of immortality has a strong Platonic colouring.

The essential shape which the doctrine assumed in Christianity arose from the fact of Christ's Resurrection. Man's highest destiny was more than the survival of an immortal soul. It was a life of abiding union with the risen Christ which reached its completion only by the reunion of body and soul. The teaching of St. *Paul, embodied in 1 Cor. 15 and elsewhere, admirably expresses the essence of the Christian belief. Consequently, in Christian philosophy the defence of immortality after the manner of the Greek philosophers, i.e. apart from the resurrection, has always been an *argumentum ad hominem*.

The Fathers interpret the hope of immortality in close connexion with the redemptive work of Christ. The *Fall of *Adam had brought death and it was through the *Second Adam that life was restored (*Irenaeus, *Athanasius, *Gregory of Nyssa). Most of the Fathers and the earlier Scholastics, however, were liable under Platonist influences to consider the relation of the soul to the body as extrinsic; and it was not until the 13th cent. that a fully elaborated defence of the specifically Christian doctrine appeared. Then the acceptance of the *Aristotelian tenet that the soul was the 'form' of the body gave philosophical justification for the beliefs that a disembodied soul was no true being and that the resurrection of the body was necessary for a full human life in the world to come.

The Scholastic arguments for the future life have been taken over since the later Middle Ages into popular apologetics. They were repeated, without substantial additions, by professional philosophers down to the end of the 18th cent. In *Descartes, with his sharp separation of mind and matter, they reappeared in a Platonic form. In G. W. *Leibniz they received a new emphasis through his belief that the human soul was the primary monad in man. The famous onslaught on the traditional arguments made by I. *Kant rested on his view of the limits of metaphysics. As the structure of the soul was outside the range of

possible experience, it was beyond the competence of the 'theoretical reason' to establish its immortality or the contrary. Nevertheless Kant, who had no doubt about the fact of the future life, maintained that the soul's immortality could be established on the ground of moral experience, i.e. through the 'practical reason'. The abiding character of the moral law and the manifest injustices in this present life were a sure index that there was a purer and fuller life in which these injustices would be remedied. Since Kant's time philosophers have increasingly stressed the moral aspects of the problem of eternal life, and it has been esp. on these lines that immortality has been defended by such thinkers as W. R. Sorley, A. S. Pringle-*Pattison and C. C. J. *Webb. See also *Conditional Immortality; Resurrection of the Dead.

J. *Martineau, A Study of Religion (2 vols., 1888); R. H. *Charles, Eschatology (1899; ed. 2, 1913); F. von *Hügel, Eternal Life. A Study of its Implications and Applications (1912); W. O. E. Oesterley, Immortality and the Unseen World (1921); A. S. Pringle-Pattison, The Idea of Immortality (1922); J. Baillie, And the Life Everlasting (1934).

IMPANATION. A term applied to certain doctrines of the *Eucharist. The first known occurrence of the word is in Guitmund of Aversa (d. c. 1090) who says that while the followers of *Berengar all hold that in the Eucharist the Bread and the Wine are not essentially changed, some, poss. incl. Berengar himself, think that the Body and Blood of the Lord are 'truly present, but hidden, in such a way that they can in a certain manner be received, that is to say, that they are impanated' (revera sed latenter contineri, et ut sumi possint quodammodo, ut ita dixerim, impanari, J. P. *Migne, PL, cxlix, 1430 D). The reason why this word was used is indicated by a passage in Alger of Liége (d. 1131) where certain unnamed heretics are stated to assert that 'Christ is in person impanated in the bread just as God was in person incarnate in human flesh' (ita personaliter in pane impanatum Christum, sicut in carne humana personaliter incarnatum Deum, ib., PL, clxxx, 754 B). In the later Middle Ages, and esp. during and after the Reformation, the term was applied to various Eucharistic doctrines which endeavoured to safeguard a belief in the *Real Presence while denying the destruction of the substance of the natural elements.

IMPASSIBILITY OF GOD, The. There are three respects in which orthodox theology has traditionally denied God's subjection to 'passibility', namely (1) external passibility or the capacity to be acted upon from without, (2) internal passibility or the capacity for changing the emotions from within, and (3) sensational passibility or the liability to feelings of pleasure and pain caused by the action of another being. The doctrine was a regular tenet of philosophical theology among the Greeks, and its foundation in Christian sources is probably due to direct Greek influences. The human and Divine natures of Christ were often distinguished (e.g. at *Chalcedon, 451) as possible and impassible. On the other hand, Hebrew religion, esp. in its early stages, freely ascribed emotions to God.

In Christianity there is an acute tension between the Greek and the Hebrew conceptions. On the one side there is the immutability, perfection, and all-sufficiency of God which would seem to exclude all passion, and this has been the basis of the traditional emphasis among theologians. But on the other side there is the central Christian conviction that God in His essence is love, that His nature is revealed in the Incarnate Christ and not least in His Passion, and that He 'sympathizes' with His Creatures. Recognition of this second aspect has led some modern theologians to doubt whether it is legitimate to speak unreservedly of God's impassibility. Among the earliest writers to challenge the traditional view was James Hinton (*The Mystery of Pain*, 1866). In the present century the same view has been upheld partly on the purely theological ground of belief in a limited God (H. G. Wells, W. *Temple, W. H. Moberly), partly to give meaning to the tragic sufferings esp. of war (G. A. *Studdert-Kennedy). Nevertheless the traditional view has had its staunch defenders, e.g. F. *von Hügel (on the ground that God is 'Unmixed Joy, Entire Delectation') and J. K. Mozley. Perhaps the problem is akin to that of the admitted coexistence of justice and mercy in God and truth lies in the recognition that both aspects must be preserved in a way that it is beyond the competence of human reason to exhibit.

F. von Hügel, *Essays and Addresses*, Second Series (1926), ch. vii; J. K. Mozley, *The Impassibility of God* (1926); B. R. Brasnett, *The Suffering of the Impassible God* (1928).

IMPEDIMENT. In canon law, an obstacle, such as *consanguinity or *clandestinity, standing in the way of a properly constituted marriage. Impediments may be either 'impedient', i.e. non-prohibitive, e.g. the ecclesiastical law against marriage in Lent, or 'diriment', i.e. destructive of the marriage altogether. The latter may be either 'irremovable' (e.g. close blood-relationship or the insanity of either party at the time of marriage) or 'removable' by dispensation, e.g. marriage with a deceased wife's sister. When a diriment impediment is removed by a *post factum* dispensation, the marriage is normally validated only from the moment at which the dispensation is granted. Canon law (but not English statutory law), however, provides for retrospective validation by the process termed *sanatio in radice* (q.v.). See also *Diriment Impediment*.

IMPOSITION OF HANDS. See *Hands, Laying on of*.

IMPRECATORY PSALMS, The. A term apparently first used by W. Robertson *Smith (1881) for the Psalms which, in whole or in part, invoke the Divine vengeance (e.g. Pss.

58, 68. 21–3, 69. 23–9, 109. 5–19, 137. 7–9). The proposed revision of the BCP in 1928 permitted the omission of such portions of the Psalter from public recitation as were considered incompatible with the spirit of Christianity.

IMPRIMATUR (Lat. 'let it be printed'). The certification that a book has been passed for publication by the appropriate authority.

(1) Acc. to the Licensing Act of 1662 (14 Car. II, c. xxxiii) prohibiting the printing or importing of books contrary to the Christian faith or the doctrine and discipline of the C of E, or tending to the scandal of the government, all books were to be entered at the Stationers' Hall and licensed according to their subject by the Lord Chancellor, the Earl Marshal, one of the principal Secretaries of State or the Abp. of Canterbury or the Bp. of London. Such licence was known as the royal imprimatur. The Act remained in force until 1679, was renewed in 1685 and expired in 1695.

(2) In the RC Church certification by a 'censor' normally appointed by the Bishop of the diocese is required before writings on theological or moral subjects are published. When it has been obtained the word 'imprimatur' is printed at the beginning or end of the work together with the censor's name. Many religious orders require in addition approval of their own authorities which is commonly attested by the additional words 'Imprimi potest' ('It may be printed'). The modern rules on licensing of books are contained in the *Codex Iuris Canonici (*CIC*, cans. 1384–1405).

IMPROPERIA. See *Reproaches*.

IMPROPRIATION. The assignment or annexation of an ecclesiastical benefice to a lay proprietor or corporation. It has come to be distinguished from 'appropriation', which was used of benefices assigned to a monastic house. When at the *Dissolution many appropriated monastic benefices passed into the hands of '*lay rectors' (q.v.), it became necessary for such rectors to appoint *perpetual curates (q.v.) to execute the spiritual duties of impropriated benefices.

IMPUTATION (from Lat. *imputare*, Gk. λογίζεσθαι). In theology the ascription to a person, by deliberate substitution, of the righteousness or guilt of another. The idea plays an important part in the *Lutheran doctrine of *Justification by Faith, which asserts that a man is formally justified by the imputation of the obedience and righteousness of Christ, without becoming possessed of any personal righteousness of his own. By a legal fiction God is thus held to regard the sinner's misdeeds as covered by the imputation of the sanctity of Christ. This doctrine seeks support in certain passages of St. *Paul (notably Rom. 3.

21–30, 5. 1 f.; Gal. 3. 21 f.) and also from St. *Augustine. It is opposed both to the traditional Catholic teaching, acc. to which the merits of Christ are not imputed but imparted to man and produce a real change from the state of sin to the state of grace, and to the doctrine of Liberal theologians to the effect that our highest vocation consists in the following of Christ who is our supreme example.

IN COENA DOMINI (Lat. 'On the Lord's Supper'). A series of excommunications of specified offenders against faith and morals which was issued regularly in the form of a Papal bull at *Rome. In later times publication was confined to *Maundy Thursday (hence its name), but originally it was read also on *Ascension Day and the feast of the Chair of St. Peter (18 Jan.); and from the 15th cent. onwards it was also read outside Rome. The practice, which dates from at least the time of *Honorius III (1216–27), was constantly attacked by the civil authorities, who objected to its exalted claims for the Papacy, and in 1522 M. *Luther wrote a tirade against it (*Die Bulle vom Abendfressen des allerheiligsten Herrn*). The issue of the bull was suspended by *Clement XIV in 1773 and the practice finally abrogated by *Pius IX's bull 'Apostolicae Sedis' (12 Oct. 1869), which incorporated many of its censures. Some of these have since found their way into the new *Codex Iuris Canonici.

The text of the bull issued by Pope Urban VIII 'in die Coenae Domini' 1627, after which its form remained practically unchanged until its abrogation, is pr. in *Bullarum, Diplomatum et Privilegiorum Sanctorum Romanorum Pontificum Tauriniensis Editio*, xiii (Turin, 1868), pp. 530–7; principal clauses repr. in Mirbt, pp. 369–71 (No. 513), with reff. to other lit. The text of 'Apostolicae Sedis' is pr. in the *Acta Sanctae Sedis*, v (1869), pp. 287–312, with notes and reff.; also in the *Acta Pii IX*, I, v (Rome [1871]), pp. 55–72. J. F. Le Bret, *Pragmatische Geschichte der soberufenen Bulla Coena Domini* (Ulm, 1769). E. Göller, *Die päpstliche Pönitentiarie von ihrem Ursprung bis zu ihrer Umgestaltung unter Pius V*, i (pt. 1; Bibliothek des Kgl. Preussischen Historischen Instituts in Rom. iii; 1907), pp. 242–76, and ii (pt. 1; ib., vii; 1911), pp. 190–208. G. Friedberg in *P.R.E.* (ed. 3), iii (1897), p. 535 f., s.v. 'Bulla in Coena Domini'; J. Prior in *C.E.*, vii (1910), p. 717 f., s.v.

IN COMMENDAM. See *Commendam*.

IN HOC SIGNO VINCES (Lat. 'by this sign thou shalt conquer'). Acc. to tradition, the words which the Emp. *Constantine saw inscribed across the sun (312). They are first mentioned in *Eusebius' *Life of Constantine* (i, c. 28), where they have the form 'by this, conquer' (τούτῳ νίκα).

INCARDINATION (Lat. *cardo*, 'hinge'; hence *incardinare*, 'to hang on a hinge'). In W. canon law, the permanent enlistment of a cleric under the jurisdiction of a new ordinary. From early times (cf. *Chalcedon, can. 6), all ordinands were ordered to be subject to an ecclesiastical superior; and the primitive rule (*Ap. Can. 15; *Nicaea, can. 16; *Antioch, can. 3; Chalcedon, can. 5) bound a cleric for life to the diocese in which he had been ordained. The process of incardination, with its correlative, *excardination (q.v.), was designed to avoid the inconveniences of the latter rule, while upholding its general principle. In the RC Church such transferences are permitted only for some 'just cause' and always subject to strict regulation. The current RC legislation is in *CIC*, cans. 111–17.

INCARNATION, The. The Christian doctrine of the Incarnation affirms that the eternal Son of God took human flesh from His human mother and that the historical Christ is at once fully God and fully man. It is opposed to all theories of a mere theophany or transitory appearance of God in human form, frequently met with in other religions. By contrast, it asserts an abiding union in the Person of Christ of Godhead and Manhood without the integrity or permanence of either being impaired. It also assigns the beginnings of this union to a definite and known date in human history.

The doctrine, which took classical shape under the influence of the controversies of the 4th–5th cents. (for history, see *Christology*), was formally defined at the Council of *Chalcedon of 451 (q.v.). It was largely moulded by the diversity of tradition in the schools of *Antioch and *Alexandria, the one stressing esp. the human aspects of the Incarnate Christ, the other, under the influence of a *Platonizing philosophy, esp. His Divinity. By its emphasis on the complete manhood of the Incarnate Christ, the Antiochene theology sometimes tended to approximate Incarnation to Inspiration. In Alexandrine circles, on the other hand, insistence on the full continuity between the Divinity of Christ and the Second Person of the Trinity could lead in careless hands to a view of the Incarnation approximating to a theophany. It was these two opposite tendencies which the Chalcedonian formula sought to hold in proper balance.

Yet the Definition was scarcely a solution; it only determined the limits to orthodoxy. Within these limits further refinements were added in the later Patristic and Medieval periods. Orthodox theologians held that the duality of natures entailed a duality of wills. They also emphasized that the Incarnation was an act of the whole Godhead, not of one Person acting independently. In the Middle Ages a much disputed (but never formally settled) matter was whether the Incarnation would have taken place had the Fall not occurred; while *Thomist theologians identified themselves with the belief that it was contingent on *Adam's transgression, *Scotists maintained the opposing doctrine. But in substance the Chalcedonian teaching has been accepted by Christian theologians of all schools down to modern times. It has further provided the dogmatic basis for the theology of Grace and of the Sacraments ('the extension of the Incarnation', a phrase popularized by C. *Gore). On this last ground appeal was made, in Patristic times, to Eucharistic belief in confirmation of Christological doctrines. In modern times, the application of the historical method of study to the Gospels has raised anew the question of the limits of Our Lord's knowledge and its bearing on belief in His Divinity. In this connexion various doctrines of *kenosis have been put forward.

In a wider setting the Incarnation is a special exemplification of the general problem of the relation of Time and Eternity, of Finitude and Infinity. More recently the doctrine has been revalued in terms of philosophy. The post-Kantian *Idealists saw in it the religious expression of the principle of immanence, i.e. the essential relatedness of man and God; and with this immanental re-interpretation the liberalizing movement in theology of the later 19th and early 20th cents. was in sympathy (see *Foundations). Among the more orthodox, the same tendency was reflected in a theological emphasis on the significance of culture and civilization in the purposes of God (R. W. *Church, *Christian Socialism). In both these schools stress was laid on the Incarnation rather than the Atonement as the fundamental Christian verity (*Lux Mundi). Other modern theologians, under Kantian influence distrustful of metaphysics, have sought to interpret the Incarnation in terms of morality and seen the essence of the Lord's Divinity in the complete conformity of His human Will with that of God. More recently, partly under the impact of catastrophic external events, the immanental revaluation of the doctrine popular at the beginning of the present century has been generally abandoned, and the traditional conception of transcendence reaffirmed. Catholic theology, with the help of the doctrine of *analogy, has stressed the essential distinctness of the Lord's divine and human natures, while Neo-Protestant theology, under the influence esp. of K. *Barth and his school, has sometimes been so emphatic in its denial of immanence as almost to imperil belief in a real Incarnation altogether.

In addition to the items on the history and development of the doctrine cited under *Christology*, the following works may be mentioned: Modern RC treatises on the Theology of the Incarnation include those of F. Stentrup, S.J. (2 vols., Innsbruck, 1882–9), J. B. *Franzelin (Turin, 1870), and L. Billot (Rome, 1892). H. P. *Liddon, *The Divinity of Christ* (*Bampton Lectures for 1866, 1867); A. B. *Bruce, *The Humiliation of Christ* (Cunningham Lectures for 1875; 1876); C. Gore, *The Incarnation of the Son of God* (Bampton Lectures for 1891; 1891); A. M. *Fairbairn, *The Place of Christ in Modern Theology* (1893); C. Gore, *Dissertations on Subjects connected with the Incarnation* (1895). P. T. Forsyth, *The Person and Place of Jesus Christ* (1909); W. *Sanday, *Christologies, Ancient and Modern* (1910); H. R. *Mackintosh, *The Doctrine of the Person of Jesus Christ* (1912); W. R. Matthews, *The Problem of Christ in the Twentieth Century*. An Essay on the Incarnation (Maurice Lectures, 1949; 1950). W. D. Mackenzie in *H.E.R.E.*, vii (1914), pp. 505–51, esp. 539–51, s.v. 'Jesus Christ'; A. Michel in *D.T.C.*, vii (pt. 2; 1923), cols. 1445–1539, s.v.; P. Parente in *E.C.*, vi (1951), cols. 1745–53, s.v. For studies on the historical Christ, see under *Jesus Christ*.

INCENSE. Incense is used in many religious rites, the smoke being considered symbolical of prayer. It was used in the worship of the Jewish *Temple, at least in later times, while

Rev. 8. 3–5 has been held to imply that it was used in sub-Apostolic Christian worship. There is, however, no clear evidence of its Christian use until *c.* 500 A.D. Censers or *thuribles may at first have been fixed, both in the E. and W., and the portable thurible have originated, at least in the W., in imitation of that carried before Roman magistrates. The incensing of the altar, church, people, &c., is first recorded in the 9th cent. In the W. incense is only used at solemn sung services, in the E. much more frequently.

The use of incense appears occasionally in the C of E between the 16th and 19th cents., but it only became common in the ceremonial revival which followed the *Oxford Movement. It has been argued that it is required by the *Ornaments Rubric, though Abps. F. *Temple and W. D. Maclagan, in the Lambeth Opinion of 1899, gave it as their personal belief that it was not allowed.

The standard work on the subject is E. G. C. F. Atchley, *A History of the Use of Incense in Divine Worship* (*Alcuin Club Collections, xiii; 1909). *The Case for Incense submitted to his Grace the Archbishop of Canterbury on behalf of he Rev. H. Westall on Monday, May 8, 1899, together with a legal argument and Appendices of the Experts* (London, 1899; includes appendices by W. H. *Frere, W. J. Birkbeck H. R. Percival, D. *Stone, E. Geldart, T. A. *Lacey, and W. H. St. J. Hope). P. Connolly, 'The Use of Incense in the Roman Liturgy' in *E.L.*, xliii (1929), pp. 171–8. On the use of incense in Biblical times, E. Levesque in *Dict. Bibl.*, ii (1899), cols. 1768–77, s.v. 'Encens'; on the use in the early Church, E. Fehrenbach in *D.A.C.L.*, v (pt. 1; 1922), cols. 2–21, s.v. 'Encens'. M. F. Bond in *D.E.C.H.* (ed. 3, 1948), pp. 302–4, s.v.

INCORPORATED CHURCH BUILDING SOCIETY, The. See *Church Building Society, The.*

INCUBATION. The term is used of the practice of sleeping in churches or their precincts in expectation of visions, revelations, and healing from disease. Of pagan origin, the custom was introduced into Christianity after the fall of paganism. Certain saints at definite places were believed in particular to perform the healing miracles formerly attributed to Asclepius, notably St. *Michael in the church of Anaplous near *Constantinople, Sts. *Cosmas and Damian (who had been physicians in their lifetime) also at Constantinople, St. *Andrew at Patras, and our Lady at Athens and in *Notre-Dame de Paris. The practice and the beliefs associated with it are not wholly extinct.

L. Deubner, *De Incubatione* (Teubner, 1900). Mary Hamilton, *Incubation, or the Cure of Disease in Pagan Temples and Christian Churches* (St. Andrews, 1906). R. Herzog, *Die Wunderheilungen von Epidauros* (Philologus, Suppl.band xxii, Hft. 3; 1931). J. Gessler, 'Notes sur l'incubation et ses survivances' in *Le Muséon*, lix (1946), pp. 661–70. G. G. Dawson, *Healing Pagan and Christian* (S.P.C.K., 1935). L. H. Gray in *H.E.R.E.*, vii (1914), p. 206 f., s.v., with bibl.; H. *Leclercq, O.S.B., in *D.A.C.L.*, vii (pt. 1; 1926), cols. 511–17, s.v.

INCUMBENT. In the C of E the holder of a parochial charge. An incumbent may therefore be a *rector, a *vicar, or a *curate-in-charge. In Scotland the word is used only of those holding ecclesiastical office in the Episcopal Church. The term, which in this oenae is peculiar to English, is apparently derived from the medieval Latin *incumbero* in the sense of obtaining possession (*obtinere*, *possidere*) of a benefice.

INCUNABULA (Lat. *incunabula*, 'swaddling clothes', hence 'cradle'). Books produced in the first stages of the art of printing, and esp. those printed before 1500, of which a very large proportion were religious. The earliest known book printed with movable type is the *Mazarin Bible (q.v.). The first known book with a date is the Mainz Psalter of 1457.

Gesamtkatalog ed. Kommission für den Gesamtkatalog der Wiegendrucke (Leipzig, 1925 ff.). K. Haebler, *Handbuch der Inkunabelkunde* (1925; Eng. tr., New York, 1933). H. G. Aldis, *The Printed Book* (ed. 3 by J. Carter–B. Crutchley, 1951), pp. 1–21.

INDEPENDENTS. Another name for the *Congregationalists (q.v.), as upholders of the independence or autonomy of each local congregation. It was in very general use in Britain (but not in the U.S.A., where it was much disliked) down to the end of the 18th cent.

INDEX, Congregation of the. See following entry.

INDEX LIBRORUM PROHIBITORUM (Lat., 'List of prohibited books'), in short, just 'the Index', the official list of books issued by the RC Church which its members are forbidden, except in special circumstances, to read or possess. The first Index was issued by the Congregation of the *Inquisition under *Paul IV in 1557. In 1571 *Pius V established a special 'Congregation of the Index' to be in charge of the list and revise it as needed; and this Congregation survived until 1917 when *Benedict XV transferred its duties to the *Holy Office. In modern times the control of literature likely to be contrary to faith or morals rests much more than formerly with the diocesan Bishops, whose duties were laid down by *Leo XIII in 'Officiorum ac Munerum' (25 Jan. 1897), whence they have passed into the *Codex (cans. 1384–1405). Hence the Index now fills a less prominent place than formerly in the life of the RC Church and in fact many widely circulating books contrary to faith or morals never find their way to it. Besides the Index proper, the Holy Office also issues an 'Index Expurgatorius' of books which may be freely read after certain passages have been deleted from them.

J. Hilgers, S.J., *Der Index der verbotenen Bücher.* In seiner neuen Fassung dargelegt und rechtlich-historisch gewürdigt (1904); id., *Die Bücherverbote in Papstbriefen.* Kanonistisch-bibliographische Studie (1907). F. H. *Reusch, *Der Index der verbotenen Bücher* (2 vols., Bonn, 1883–5); id., *Die Indices Librorum Prohibitorum des sechzehnten Jahrhunderts* (Tübingen, 1886). A. Boudinhon, *La Nouvelle Législation de l'Index.* Texte et commentaire de la constitution *Officiorum ac Munerum* du 25 janvier 1897 [1899]. J. Hilgers in *C.E.*, vii (1910), p. 721 f., s.v.; A. Thouvenin in *D.T.C.*, vii (pt. 2; 1923), cols. 1570–80, s.v.; K. Hilgenreiner–J. B. Haring in *L.Th.K.*, v (1933),

cols. 380–2, s.v. A. de Iorio in *E.C.*, vi (1951), cols. 1825–9, s.v. 'Indice dei libri proibiti'; H. Wagnon–R. Naz in *D.D.C.*, v ('1953'), cols. 1318–30, s.v.

INDIA, Christianity in. A Christian Church, known as 'Syrian', has existed in S. India since at latest the 5th cent. It claims to have been founded by St. *Thomas the Apostle and derives its rite and other traditions from the *Jacobite church of Syria. Part is now a RC *Uniat body and the remainder is divided between the Orthodox Syrian Church and the Mar Thoma Syrian Church. It is practically confined to Indians of Malabar, Travancore, and Cochin and has no missionary activity. See *Malabar Christians*.

European Christianity reached India *c.* 1500 with the coming of the Portuguese to Goa, and missionary work was done by St. *Francis Xavier, who arrived at Goa in 1542. Considerable pressure was exercised in favour of Christianity by the Portuguese civil power, though conversion was never actually enforced. Outside the Portuguese dominions, Robert *de Nobili, who landed at Goa in 1605, founded the 'Madura Mission' of the *Jesuits (1606). He and his followers attempted to commend their preaching by 'conforming to the ways in vogue among the Brahmans' and presenting Christianity as a religion superior to Hinduism, in which converts could retain much that they valued including Christianized versions of Hindu customs and even caste privileges. In this period the primacy of Goa, which became a Bishopric in 1534 and an Archbishopric in 1557, under Portuguese royal patronage (the *padroado*), was unquestioned. In 1637, however, missions under the *Propaganda, independent of Goa, were begun with the appointment of a *Vicar Apostolic of the Great Mogul's dominions. The cession of Bombay to England by Portugal in 1661 led to the expulsion of the clergy of the *padroado* and their replacement by clergy of the Propaganda, and, as the former to some extent returned, a dual jurisdiction, and many occasions of conflict, remained until the 19th cent.

Protestant missions began in 1706, when a mission, staffed mainly by German (in a few cases Danish) *Lutherans, was founded by King Frederick IV of Denmark in the Danish territory of Tranquebar in S. India. Bartholomäus Ziegenbalg (1683–1719), the pioneer missionary, translated the NT and part of the OT into Tamil, and received considerable encouragement, and some material help, from England. When the work was extended into territory under British rule, the *S.P.C.K. took over the support of the missionaries concerned, including the station at Fort St. George (Madras). The greatest of these Lutheran missionaries, C. F. Schwartz (1726–98), who worked continuously in India from 1750 until his death, first at Tranquebar and after 1762 at Trichinopoly, gained the respect of both Indian and British rulers, and made many converts, although his work largely failed to survive his death.

Anglican clergy had served in India as

chaplains under the East India Company since 1614. In the early days occasional converts were made, but the policy of the Company was opposed to missionary activities. The growth of the missionary spirit at the time of the *Evangelical movement (leading to the founding of the *C.M.S. in 1799) was met by a hardening of official opposition to missionary enterprise in India on the ground that it would inflame opinion against Europeans. The first English missionary, W. *Carey, a *Baptist, landed at Calcutta in 1793, but until 1801 he was prevented from working except in the Danish territory of Serampore, where he and five other Baptists established a mission. At the revision of the Company's charter in 1813 Evangelical opinion secured the insertion of provisions for a Bishopric of Calcutta and three archdeaconries, and for freedom of missionary enterprise. T. F. *Middleton became the first bishop (1814–22), but with undoubted jurisdiction only over chaplains and European congregations. At the same time the C.M.S. began to send missionaries, and in 1820 a college for training Indians as Christian teachers was opened, somewhat prematurely, in Calcutta. R. *Heber, the second Bishop (1823–6), licensed the missionaries, including some supported by S.P.C.K. who were Lutherans, but laid down that the missions concerned should for the future be solely Anglican. He ordained some Lutherans, and also the first Indian to receive Anglican orders. In course of time the Lutherans and ex-Lutherans were replaced by Anglican clergy from England, who now came forward in increasing numbers. The dioceses of Madras (1835) and Bombay (1837) were then set up, and the Bp. of Calcutta became Metropolitan, but without the title of Archbishop. Legally the Anglican Church in India was part of the Church of England, under the supremacy of the Crown, exercised through Parliament, and of the Abp. of Canterbury. The episcopate of Daniel Wilson (1832–58), the first Metropolitan, was esp. notable for the growth of the Church.

Meanwhile the Baptist missionaries were reinforced from America in 1813, and other Protestant missions were founded, which, unlike the Lutheran, remained distinct from the C of E. Among the first were missionaries from Basle in 1815, and Scottish Presbyterian missions in 1823 in W. India, and in 1836 in Madras. Between the *Disruption in 1843 and the Reunion in 1929 many of the Scottish Presbyterian missions in India were supported by the *Free Church. India in 1948 contained six out of the sixteen overseas presbyteries of the Church of Scotland. Other Protestant missions were founded from Berlin (1841), America (1842), Denmark (1867), and Canada (1877).

The decline of Portuguese political power led to the lessening of the influence of the padroado compared with that of the Propaganda in the RC Church, and the suppression of the Jesuits in 1773 also furthered this process, their missions in the Madura and the Carnatic being transferred to Vicars Apostolic. In the 19th cent. the see of Goa was at one time deprived of most of its jurisdiction outside Portuguese territory, while the missions of the Propaganda, staffed by various European orders, extended in E. and N. India. In 1886, however, the conflict was resolved by the Bull *Humanae Salutis Auctor* which restored jurisdiction over neighbouring parts of British India to Goa, and set up a regular hierarchy for the rest of the country. In 1938 there were eight archbishoprics, with 28 suffragan sees (excluding Ceylon). The Archbishop of Goa has the honorary titles of Patriarch of the East Indies and Primate of the East.

All European missions under the British Raj after 1813 received freedom but no active help from the Government, which was officially neutral as between all religions which did not offend against civil law. It put down, however, the heathen practices of suttee (burning of widows) and thuggee (murder of strangers practised by a certain sect) and introduced English as the common language of administration, and of all higher education, instead of the variety of Indian languages. The great development of communications in the 19th and early 20th cents. facilitated the spread of Christianity, as of other movements, and educational and medical work under Christian auspices, of which non-Christians freely availed themselves, gained prestige for Christianity. On the other hand, the rise of Indian nationalism and of Hindu and Moslem communal self-consciousness stimulated hostility to Christianity regarded as a European religion. The RC Church in the old padroado districts had long had an Indian and Eurasian clergy, and in all Christian bodies arising from missionary work there has been a gradual transference of responsibility to Indian leaders. In 1930 the Anglican Church (hitherto 'the C of E in India') became 'the Church of India, Burma, and Ceylon', a separate legal entity freed from all State control, and a self-governing part of the Anglican Communion; but state-appointed civil chaplaincies continued in existence until 1948. The Indian Independence Act of 1947 transferred civil power to entirely non-European governments in India and Pakistan. Assurances were given by the new governments that freedom of religion for Christians as well as non-Christians would be preserved, and the attitude of Pandit Nehru, the first Prime Minister of India, was not unfriendly.

By 1947 Christians were found in all parts of India and Pakistan, but Christianity was much stronger in the S. than in the N. In Sept. 1947 the Church of *South India (q.v.) was formally inaugurated after discussions lasting since 1919. In 1954 (figures based on 1951 census) the communicant membership, and the total community (figures in parentheses) for the main non-RC denominations in the Republic of India were given as follows: Church of South India 331,372 (community 960,170); Orthodox Syrian Church, about 350,000 (450,000); Mar Thoma Syrian Church, about 140,000 (257,000); Lutherans, about 283,000 (588,000); Methodists including the 'Methodist Church in Southern Asia', which is strong in N. India and is connected with American missions, about 123,200 (554,150); Methodists of the North India Provincial Synod, 100,586 (400,538); Baptists, about 192,800 (315,600); Anglicans, about 107,000 (250,000); giving a total 'community' figure of about three and three-quarter million. In the official census figures of 1951 the total number of Christians was given as 8,166,255, the main classifications being RCs, 3,673,255, and 'non-RCs' 4,374,847. Of the total population of about 362 million, Christians thus formed some 2¼ per cent, compared with nearly 83 per cent Hindus and nearly 10 per cent Moslems, but they are more numerous than any of the other religious groups, e.g. Sikhs, Parsees, etc. For Pakistan, out of a total population of just over 70 million, RCs numbered about 263,000 or under ½ per cent, the number of other Christians not being stated.

J. Hough, *The History of Christianity in India from the Commencement of the Christian Era* (5 vols., 1839–60; vol. v is ed. by his son, T. G. P. Hough); J. W. Kaye, *Christianity in India* (1859). P. Thomas, *Christians and Christianity in India and Pakistan.* A General Survey of the Progress of Christianity in India from Apostolic Times to the Present Day (1954). A. Lillie, *India in Primitive Christianity* (1909). M. F. X. D'Sa, *History of the Catholic Church in India* (2 vols., Bombay, 1925). E. D. Maclagan, *The Jesuits and the Great Mogul* (1932). M. A. Sherring, *The History of Protestant Missions in India from their Commencement in 1706 to 1871* (1875); J. Richter, *Indische Missionsgeschichte* (Allgemeine evangelische Missionsgeschichte; 1906; Eng. tr. [1908]). E. M. Wherry, *Our Missions in India* (Boston, Mass., 1926; on U.S. Presbyterian Church). E. Chatterton, *A History of the Church of England in India since the Early Days of the East India Company* (S.P.C.K.). 1924). C. J. Grimes, *Towards an Indian Church.* The Growth of the Church of India in Constitution and Life (S.P.C.K., 1946). F. Penny, *The Church in Madras,* being the History of the Ecclesiastical and Missionary Action of the East India Company in the Presidency of Madras in the Seventeenth and Eighteenth Centuries (3 vols., 1904–22). J. A. Sharrock, *South Indian Missions* (S.P.G., 1909). C. F. Andrews, *North India* (Handbooks of English Church Expansion [vi]; 1908). H. L. Clarke, *Constitutional Church Government in the Dominions Beyond the Seas and in other Parts of the Anglican Communion* (S.P.C.K., 1924), pp. 418–25. A. Mayhew, *Christianity and the Government of India.* An Examination of the Christian Forces at Work in the Administration of India and of the Mutual Relations of the British Government and Christian Missions, 1600–1900 (1929). J. W. Pickett, *Christian Mass Movements in India* (New York, 1933). Latourette, iii (1940), pp. 247–84, with bibl. pp. 458–85 passim; vi [1944], pp. 65–214, with bibl. pp. 457–84 passim; vii (1945), pp. 274–315, with bibl. pp. 507–31 passim. E. R. Hull, S.J., in *C.E.,* vii (1910), pp. 728–38. See also bibl. to *Malabar Christians* and *South India, Church of.*

INDICOPLEUSTES. See *Cosmas Indicopleustes.*

INDUCTION (in Logic). The process of reasoning whereby a general law or principle is reached from the observance of particular instances. The word, which in its Lat. form (*inductio*) occurs in Cicero, is a rendering of *Aristotle's ἐπαγωγή.* The opposite process is termed '*deduction*'.

INDUCTION (to a benefice). The term used to denote the final stage, after nomination and

*institution, in the appointment of a new *incumbent. The effect is to place the priest in legal possession of the *temporalities of the *benefice, and in control of his parish. The Bishop after institution issues a mandate to the *archdeacon or other person having the power to induct, who lays the hand of the person to be inducted on the key of the church door and causes him to toll the bell. The induction is also commonly accompanied by other ceremonial acts.

INDULGENCE, Declarations of. See *Declarations of Indulgence.*

INDULGENCES. The remission by the Church of the temporal penalty due to forgiven sin, in virtue of the merits of Christ and the saints. In the RC Church the granting of indulgences is now ordinarily confined to the Pope. The practice presupposes (1) a retributive basis for Divine justice, i.e. that sin must have a penalty either on earth or in purgatory, even after the sinner has been reconciled with God by penitence and absolution; (2) the existence of the 'treasury of merits', i.e. the infinite merits of Christ, together with the merits of the BVM and the saints which the Church possesses in virtue of the Communion of Saints; (3) the belief that the Church, by her power of jurisdiction, has the right of administering the benefit of these merits in consideration of prayers or other pious works undertaken by the faithful.

In the early Church, esp. from the 3rd cent., the intercession of confessors and those awaiting martyrdom was allowed by the ecclesiastical authorities to shorten the canonical discipline of those under penance; and when canonical penance came to be considered a substitute for temporal punishment in purgatory, the transition was easy to the belief that the prayers and merits of the saints availed to shorten such punishment itself, even for sins which did not require canonical penance. Later, with the relaxation of the penitential discipline, alternative works were permitted instead of the prescribed penances, and the merits of Christ and the saints applied to make up the deficiency. For general indulgences, however, there is no certain evidence before the 11th cent. In the 12th cent., however, the practice of granting indulgences became more common. Plenary indulgences were offered to those who took part in the *Crusades, and bishops were authorized to give limited indulgences at the dedication of churches and their anniversaries, one of the most famous of these being the *Portiuncula Indulgence granted to St. *Francis in 1221. The later Middle Ages saw the growth of considerable abuses, such as the unrestricted sale of indulgences by professional 'pardoners', whose false doctrine and scandalous conduct were an immediate occasion of the Reformation, and whose activities were finally prohibited by *Pius V in 1567. Modern RC practice is to encourage piety and good works among the faithful by very liberal grants of indulgences, generally by the Pope himself, but also, within certain limits, by metropolitans and bishops. Indulgences are either 'plenary' (i.e. a remission of all temporal punishment due to sin) or partial, counted by so many days or years (i.e. of so much punishment as would have been worked off by canonical penance for the given time). The number of days attached to the partial indulgences is not held to correspond exactly to the time as reckoned in purgatory. How the proportion works out is known only to God, and the Church has never pronounced on it. It is, however, *de fide* among RCs that the Church has the right to grant indulgences and that they are salutary for the faithful.

Indulgences are usually granted to all those who, in a state of grace and with the intention of gaining the indulgence, visit a certain holy place, or say certain prayers, or do certain good works. They are frequently attached to crucifixes, rosaries, and medals ('real' indulgences), blessed by a priest who has the necessary faculties. Indulgences can also be gained by the living for the souls in purgatory, but only *per modum suffragii*, i.e. by an act of intercession, since the Church on earth has no jurisdiction beyond the grave. See also *Merit, Plenary Indulgence,* and *Raccolta.*

Enchiridion Indulgentiarum. Preces et Pia Opera in Personarum Indulgentiis Ditata et Opportune Recognita Favorem Omnium Christifidelium vel quorumdam Coetum (Rome, 1950), with useful introd. E. Amort, *De Origine, Progressu, Valore ac Fructu Indulgentiarum* (2 pts., Augsburg, 1735; ed. 2 with additions, Venice, 1738). F. Beringer, S.J., *Die Ablässe, ihr Wesen und Gebrauch* (1860; ed. P. A. Steiner, S.J., 2 vols., 1921–30; Fr. tr., 1890). A. H. M. Lépicier, *Indulgences.* Their Origin, Nature and Development (1895; revised ed., 1928). H. C. Lea, *A History of Auricular Confession and Indulgences in the Latin Church,* iii (Philadelphia, 1896; polemical and hostile). J. Hilgers, S.J., *Die katholische Lehre von den Ablässen und deren geschichtliche Entwicklung* (1914). N. Paulus, *Geschichte des Ablasses im Mittelalter, vom Ursprunge bis zur Mitte des 14. Jahrhunderts* (3 vols., 1922–3). B. Poschmann, *Der Ablass im Lichte der Bussegeschichte* (1948).

L. Fanfani, *De Indulgentiis.* Manuale theoretico-practicum ad normam Codicis Iuris Canonici (Rome, 1919; ed. 2, Turin and Rome, 1926).

E. Magnin in *D.T.C.,* vii (1922), cols. 1594–1636, s.v., with bibl.; N. Paulus in *L.Th.K.,* i (1928), cols. 32–6, s.v. 'Ablass'; G. Löw, C.SS.R.–S. De Angelis in *E.C.,* vi (1951), cols. 1901–10, s.v. 'Indulgenze', with bibl.

INDULT (Lat. *indultum,* 'a permission'). A faculty granted by the *Apostolic See to deviate from the common law of the Church. It is generally given for a specific case and for a specific period, and is commonly personal in reference, i.e. it cannot be communicated to others unless special permission be given.

INDUSTRIAL CHRISTIAN FELLOW-SHIP (I.C.F.). An Anglican organization which endeavours to present the Christian faith to the world of industry both by missions to industrial workers and by relating the theory and practice of Christianity to modern industry. It was formed in 1918 by the fusion of two earlier bodies, the Navvy Mission and the Christian Social Union, with the Rev. P. T. R. Kirk as its first General Director.

It was responsible for the convening of the *Malvern Conference in Jan. 1941, and for the meeting in the Albert Hall, London, on 26 Sept. 1942 when Abp. W. *Temple made a strong plea for the application of Christian principles to business and economics. The aims of the Fellowship have similarities with those of *Catholic Action in some RC countries.

INEFFABILIS DEUS. The constitution of *Pius IX, issued 8 Dec. 1854, defining the dogma of the *Immaculate Conception. It asserted that the BVM 'in the first instant of her conception was, by a singular privilege and grace granted by God, in view of the merits of Jesus Christ, the Saviour of the human race, preserved exempt from all stain of original sin'. During the octave of the Feast (8–15 Dec.) it is read in the second *nocturn at *Mattins.

Text in *Acta et Decreta Sacrorum Conciliorum Recentiorum.* Collectio Lacensis. Auctoribus Presbyteris S.J. e Domo B.V.M. sine Labe Conceptae ad Lacum, vi (Freiburg i.Br., 1882), cols. 836–43. Extract in Denz.–Bann. (ed. 1952), p. 458 f. (No. 1641). See also bibl. to *Immaculate Conception.*

INFALLIBILITY. Inability to err in teaching revealed truth. It is a negative condition, complementary to the positive quality of 'inspiration'. While many Christians maintain that the Church is infallible, upon the basis of such texts as Jn. 16. 13, Acts 15. 28, various beliefs have been held as to the seat where such infallibility resides. It has sometimes been sought in those doctrines and truths of revelation which have been accepted by all the historic branches of the Church; at other times in the definitions of such councils of the Church as have been generally accepted as *Oecumenical; while at the *Vatican Council of 1870 the RC Church declared that infallibility attached to the definitions of the Pope in matters of faith and morals, apart from the consent of the Church. In Catholic Christianity it is commonly held that there is more than one such organ through which the faith receives infallible expression.

INFANCY GOSPELS, The. The apocryphal stories about the Birth and Childhood of Christ which were put into circulation in early Christian times. They are all of poor literary quality and devoid of historical value. The two most important are the 'Book of *James' (the '*Protevangelium') and the 'Gospel of *Thomas' (qq.v.).

INFANT BAPTISM. Although from the first *Baptism was the universal means of entry into the Christian community, the NT contains no specific authority for its administration to infants. But by a tradition at least as old as the 3rd cent., and virtually universal until the *Reformation, children born to Christian parents have been baptized in infancy. In the 16th cent. this practice ('paedobaptism') was rejected by the *Anabaptists and since the early 17th cent. also by the *Baptists (and later by the *Disciples of Christ).

In the period of the NT, positive hints of Infant Baptism have been found in the facts that the children of Christian parents are said to be 'holy' whereas they might be 'unclean' (1 Cor. 7. 14), and that they are exhorted to obey their parents 'in the Lord' (Col. 3. 20, Eph. 6. 1); and never is there a suggestion that they will have to seek baptism on reaching years of discretion. St. *Paul also speaks of Baptism as a spiritual counterpart of circumcision, the rite whereby Jews were admitted as infants to the benefits of the Covenant and membership of the religious community (cf. Col. 2. 11 f.). Further, in the households whose baptism is mentioned in Acts 16. 15 and 33 (cf. 18. 8) and 1 Cor. 1. 16, children may well have been baptized together with adults, as were the children of *proselytes to Judaism. Beyond this, evidence is lacking. But since the NT documents are concerned mainly with the expansion of Christianity in the non-Christian world, and hardly at all with the natural recruitment of the Church from persons of Christian parentage and upbringing, this lack of evidence is not surprising. This should be borne in mind in relation to the claim of certain antipaedobaptists that Christ's command to 'make disciples of (μαθητεύσατε) all nations, baptizing them . . .' (Matt. 28. 19) forbids baptism without conscious discipleship.

In post-Apostolic times the evidence becomes more definite. *Justin Martyr (Apol. i. 15) speaks of Christians then of sixty or seventy years of age who had 'from childhood been made disciples' (ἐμαθητεύθησαν, cf. Matt. 28. 19). *Polycarp at his martyrdom (prob. A.D. 155 or 156) claimed to have been 'Christ's servant' for 86 years (Mart. Polyc. 9). *Irenaeus (Haer. ii. 39) speaks of Christ as 'giving salvation to those of every age' (omnem aetatem) who are 'regenerated' (renascentur) through Him, and expressly includes 'infants and little children' (infantes et parvulos) among these. Explicit statements concerning infant baptism are made by *Origen, who refers to it as an established custom, which the Church has received from the Apostles (Hom. in Lev., viii. 4, Comm. in Rom., v. 9). In both passages he finds the practice justified by the need which infants, no less than adults, have for liberation from *original sin. Opposition to infant baptism (implying the prior existence of the practice) is voiced by *Tertullian, who urges (De Bapt., 18) that the baptism of children be deferred (despite Matt. 19. 14) until they can 'know Christ'. This advocacy of delaying baptism for infants, as well as spiritually immature adults, appears to spring from Tertullian's ideas of the impossibility or great difficulty of the remission of post-baptismal sin. Such considerations led to a widespread deferment of baptism in the 4th cent., e.g. in the cases of *Constantine and of St. *Augustine (Conf., I., xi). On the other hand, by the middle of the 3rd cent. infant baptism was regularly performed, as is attested by *Cyprian (Ep. 64), where it is stated to con-

vey remission not only of actual sins but also of original sin. From now onwards evidence for the practice is ample, and even *Pelagius, despite his denial of original sin, did not oppose the established practice. In the Middle Ages it was rejected by a few small sects and movements which were heretical in other ways also.

In the E. Church, infant baptism is followed at once by the administration of *chrism and also of Holy Communion, while in the W. both these are deferred till the age of conscious participation, after instruction (see Confirmation). Except in cases of emergency, sponsors (*godparents) are required for every baptized infant, whose duty it is to see that the child receives Christian instruction and is brought for Confirmation at the appropriate age. Acc. to Catholic doctrine (set forth, e.g., in the service of Infant Baptism in the BCP), the rite conveys the essential gift of regeneration so that 'children which are baptized, dying before they commit sin, are undoubtedly saved'. The Baptists and other Protestants who reject infant baptism do so traditionally on the double ground that it is without warrant in the NT and that as a mere ceremony or ordinance (not a sacrament) it could convey no spiritual benefit to the unconscious recipient. Among those who retain it, e.g. *Lutheran, *Reformed (Presbyterian), *Methodist, and *Congregational bodies, many regard it as a dedication of the child and a declaration of the universal availability of the salvation wrought by Christ, which is prior to any individual response, holding that full Church membership is granted later in response to profession of faith.

In most Churches which practice Infant Baptism there has in recent times been much reconsideration of the traditional practice by individuals and unofficial groups, esp. in view of the fact that many who bring their children for baptism are now only nominally Christian, and reasonable expectation of a Christian upbringing is lacking. In such cases the refusal of baptism, or its deferment on condition of the parents accepting instruction, has been advocated. On theological grounds this deferment has been defended by K. *Barth. Against this it is urged that such a rebuff to those who voluntarily, if ignorantly, seek baptism for their children is inconsistent with the Church's duty to them and that a valuable pastoral opportunity is lost.

The classical English defence of the practice is W. *Wall, The History of Infant Baptism (2 pts., London, 1705). K. Barth, Die kirchliche Lehre der Taufe (ed. 2, Theologische Studien, ed. K. Barth, xiv; Zürich, 1943; Eng. tr. by E. A. Payne, 1948), a vigorous attack on the practice. O. Cullmann, Die Tauflehre des Neuen Testaments (Abhandlungen zur Theologie des Alten und Neuen Testaments, pd. W. Eichrodt–O. Cullmann, xii; Zürich, 1948; Eng. tr. by J. K. S. Reid, Studies in Biblical Theology, i; 1950). Other modern discussions include D. *Stone, Holy Baptism (1899), pp. 96–109 and 254–8. W. F. Flemington, The New Testament Doctrine of Baptism (1953), pp. 130–47. J. Jeremias, Hat die Urkirche die Kindertaufe geübt? J. C. Didier, 'La Pédobaptisme au IVe siècle' in Mélanges de Science religieuse, vi (1949), pp. 233–46; J. Héring, 'Un Texte oublié: Matthieu 18. 10. A propos des controverses récentes sur le pédobaptisme' in Aux sources de la tradition chrétienne. Mélanges offerts à M. Maurice Goguel [1950], pp. 95–102. See also bibl. to Baptism.

INFIDEL. A person who has a positive disbelief in every form of the Christian faith. In medieval times the word (Lat. *infidelis*) was employed esp. of the Mohammedans and also, though less often, of Jews and pagans; but the distinction 'Jews, Turks, Infidels, and Hereticks' in the third *Good Friday *collect of the BCP points to its use in a narrower sense.

INFIRMARIAN. In a monastery or religious house, the person in charge of the sick-quarters.

INFRALAPSARIANS. See *Sublapsarians.*

INFUSION. See *Affusion.*

INGE, WILLIAM RALPH (1860–1954), Dean of *St. Paul's. He was born at Crayke, Yorks, educated at Eton and King's College, Cambridge, and successively Fellow of Hertford College, Oxford (1889–1905), vicar of All Saints', Knightsbridge (1905–7), Lady Margaret Professor of Divinity at Cambridge (1907–11) and Dean of St. Paul's (1911–34). His sympathies with *Platonic spirituality found their expression in a long series of theological and devotional writings, among them *Christian Mysticism* (*Bampton Lectures, 1899), *Personal Idealism and Mysticism* (1907), an essay on 'The Theology of the Fourth Gospel' in *Cambridge Biblical Essays* (ed. H. B. *Swete; 1909), *Faith and its Psychology* (1909), and *The Philosophy of Plotinus* (*Gifford Lectures, 2 vols., 1918). This last was an attempt to assess the positive value of Plotinus's system for the modern world. There followed two widely read series of *Outspoken Essays* (1919; 1922); they included a notable 'Confessio Fidei', which upheld a philosophy of value in which God was the 'supreme value' and true faith 'belief in the reality of absolute value'. Inge's grasp of the tastes and prejudices of the English mind, his provocative and epigrammatic manner of writing and his pure English style made him one of the best-known Churchmen of his generation ('The gloomy Dean'). His later books include *The Platonic Tradition in English Religious Thought* (*Hulsean Lectures, 1926), *Christian Ethics and Modern Problems* (1930), and *God and the Astronomers* (1933).

C. C. J. *Webb, 'William Ralph Inge', in *J.T.S.*, N.S., v ' (1954), pp. 188–94. Life by Adam Fox (London, 1960).

INHIBITION. An episcopal order suspending from the performance of his office an incumbent whose conduct makes such action advisable either for the avoidance of scandal or for some other reason in the interests of the parish. It is the duty of the inhibiting bishop to arrange and provide for the services during the suspension. Such orders are governed by procedure under the Church Discipline Act, 1840, and the Clergy Discipline Act, 1892, and, except temporarily, can be made only after due judicial inquiry.

INJUNCTIONS, Royal. A series of Tudor royal proclamations on ecclesiastical affairs.

(1) By *Henry VIII, 1536. These required the clergy to observe the anti-papal laws and the abrogation of certain holy days and ceremonies, not to extol images, relics, or miracles, to discourage pilgrimages, and to teach their people the Paternoster, the articles of the faith and the Ten Commandments in English. The clergy were also ordered to teach and to administer the Sacraments more regularly and not to frequent taverns. A fortieth part of their income was to go to the poor and a fifth part to the repair of their own churches and parsonages.

(2) By Henry VIII, 1538. This order, after confirming the previous injunctions, provided for the setting up of R. *Grafton's *Great Bible in all churches, for the regular instruction of the people in the Scriptures, and for the checking of certain superstitions. Only duly licensed preachers were permitted to officiate. A register of all marriages, births, and burials was to be kept and stored in the parish chest. The use of *ora pro nobis* in processions was strongly discouraged.

(3) By *Edward VI, 1547. These Injunctions, issued from Grafton's press on 31 July, required regular sermons against superstition and the Pope's authority, and in favour of the royal supremacy. Church services were to be performed regularly, tithes to be paid, an alms-chest to be kept near the high altar, and church registers to be kept. The clergy are to study and teach the Scriptures. Rogationtide processions are to be kept up, and Sunday to be better observed. A pulpit is to be provided in each church. The Litany is in future to be said or sung in English kneeling, and not in procession.

(4) By *Mary I, 1554. These Injunctions abolished the Oath of *Supremacy and required all canons not contrary to statute law to be enforced, married priests to be either removed or divorced, the neglect of baptism and confirmation to cease, heresy to be repressed, holy days and ceremonies to be restored as at the end of Henry VIII's reign, and clerics ordained 'after the new sort' to have 'that thing which wanted in them before' supplied.

(5) By *Elizabeth I, 1559. The first 28 of this series are substantially a re-enactment of those of 1547, with their extreme anti-Romanism somewhat toned down, perhaps in the interests of comprehension. They are followed by 25 new orders. Of these No. 29, without forbidding, sought to discourage the marriage of clergy, but from the first it proved a dead letter. No. 49 was designed to encourage music (apparently plain-chant) in collegiate and parish churches, and permitted the use of hymns before or after service. No 52 enjoined bowing at the Holy Name; No. 53 slow and distinct reading of the service. Others prescribed the proper habiting of the clergy (No. 30), the use of the *Primer (No. 39), and the observance of holy days and fast-days (Nos. 46, 48).

Text in H. Gee and W. J. Hardy, *Documents Illustrative of English Church History* (1896), (1) pp. 269–74; (2) pp. 275–281; (4) pp. 380–83; (3) and (5) pp. 417–42.

INNER LIGHT. The principle of Christian certitude, consisting of inward knowledge or experience of salvation, which is upheld by the Society of *Friends (q.v.).

INNERE MISSION. The term covers all voluntary religious, charitable, and social work organized within the Protestant Churches in Germany apart from the actual parish work. It was first employed by J. H. *Wichern (q.v.) in connexion with his foundation at Hamburg, but he soon came to use it for all 'works of saving love'. The chief object of the Innere Mission is to reclaim those who have strayed, a task carried out by preaching, distributing of religious literature (Bible and Tract societies), and charitable works, such as nursing the sick and assisting the poor. The years of its early enthusiasm (1848–c. 1860) produced a number of new associations and revived old ones for nursing, prison reform, care of the homeless and the mentally deficient, and the institution of deaconesses on the model of the early Church. From 1890 down to 1918 the social question played a paramount part and theoretical discussions on the attitude of the Protestant Churches to socialism, the emancipation of women, and other topical problems, were in the foreground. After 1918 the work was resumed with special stress on education and the winning back of the paganized youth of the cities to Christianity.

F. Mahling in *R.G.G.* (ed. 2), iii (1929), cols. 271–80, s.v., with bibl.; also Rühle in ib., col. 1853 f., s.v. 'Mahling, F.', with list of Mahling's own writings. See also bibl. to *J. H. Wichern.*

INNOCENT I, St. (d. 417), Pope from 402. A man of great ability, firm resolution, and high moral character, he made more substantial claims for the Papacy than any of his predecessors at *Rome. He insisted that major cases of dispute should be brought to the judgement of the Apostolic See. His determination to exercise authority in the E. as well as the W. is reflected in his support of St. *Chrysostom against his adversaries and of St. *Jerome against John, Bp. of *Jerusalem, while nearer home he succeeded with the assistance of the Bp. of *Thessalonica in bringing E. Illyricum, which since 388 had been part of the E. Empire, under the ecclesiastical authority of the W. The civil power also found in Innocent a force to be reckoned with, and it was through his instrumentality that the Emp. Honorius in 404 issued his decree against the *Donatists. Feast day, 28 July.

For his correspondence see J. P. Migne, *PL*, xx, 457–636; also 'Collectio Avellana' (C.S.E.L., xxxv), pp. 92–8. *L.P.* (Duchesne), i, 220–4. H. Gebhardt, *Die Bedeutung Innocenz I für die Entwickelung der päpstlichen Gewalt* (Diss., Leipzig, 1901). E. Caspar, *Geschichte des Papsttums*, i (1930), pp. 296–343. J. Barnaby in *D.C.B.*, iii (1882), pp. 243–9, s.v.; É. Amann in *D.T.C.*, vii (1922), cols. 1940–50, s.v.

INNOCENT III (1160–1216), Pope from 1198. Of a noble family, the Scotti, Lotario de' Conti di Segni was educated at *Paris where he studied theology under Peter of Corbeil, and at *Bologna where he learned canon law under Uguccio of Ferrara. Rising rapidly in the Papal service, he became cardinal in 1190, and in 1198, when not yet in priest's orders, was elected Pope in succession to the aged *Celestine III (1191–8).

In method, Innocent was businesslike and legally minded. He was wholly sincere, diplomatic but opportunist, liable to fits of depression, and above all determined to enforce, extend, and define the 'plenitudo potestatis' of the Roman see. In making the right of the Papacy to interfere in secular affairs depend upon its duty to control the moral conduct of rulers and upon the theory of Papal feudal overlordship, Innocent was enabled by the circumstances of his age and his own will-power and personality to make theory and practice correspond to an extent without parallel, either before or afterwards.

With a view to establishing his authority in Rome and Italy, Innocent began by expelling the German mercenaries from Sicily and elsewhere. The Emp. Henry VI having died in 1197, Innocent used the opportunity for arbitrating between the rival claimants to the Imperial throne. In the bull 'Venerabilem' he laid down that, though the right of electing an emperor lay with the Imperial electors, the Pope must have 'the right and authority of examining the person elected' (*jus et auctoritas examinandi personam electam*), and that the appointment of an emperor came within the sphere of the Papal authority 'principaliter' and 'finaliter',—*principaliter* since the translation of the Empire from the Greeks to the Romans took place through the Pope, and *finaliter* because the blessing, coronation, and investiture of the Emperor lay with the Pope. He supported first Otto IV, then Philip of Swabia, and then, after Philip's murder in 1208 (when Otto, who was left without a rival, became as anti-Papal as his predecessors), *Frederick II, another son of Henry VI, who was elected on condition that he did homage to the Pope for Sicily.

Outside the Empire Innocent was equally successful in enforcing his authority. In France he compelled Philip Augustus to be reconciled to his wife, Ingeborg of Denmark; his consequent support of the French king issued in his victory over the discarded Emp. Otto at Bouvines in 1214. The quarrel over the appointment of Stephen *Langton to the see of *Canterbury led to the submission of King *John of England, who agreed to recognize Innocent as his feudal overlord. The Pope also made his authority felt in *Scandinavia, the *Spanish peninsula, the Balkans, and even as far east as *Cyprus and *Armenia. Like most of the medieval Popes, he wished to preach a *Crusade for the recovery of the Holy Land, but the Fourth Crusade, of 1204, was diverted from its true objective to operate against the Byzantine Empire and he was thereby enabled to nominate a Latin patriarch of *Constantinople in the person of Thomas Morosini, a Venetian. Innocent's patronage of the new orders of Friars, the *Franciscans, and *Dominicans, was yet a further proof of his genius.

The *Lateran Council of 1215 (q.v.) was the culminating event of his reign. Heresies, of which that of the *Albigensians, against whom Innocent had preached a crusade, was the most prominent, were condemned and doctrine clearly formulated. In addition reform decrees were passed, encouraging the foundation of schools and a higher standard of conduct for the clergy.

His pontificate may be considered as marking the climax of the medieval Papacy. He thought of his office in a semi-Divine light, 'set in the midst between God and man, below God but above man'. The vast extent of his ecclesiastical jurisdiction is seen in the number of cases which came up before him for decision from distant parts of the earth. He was the first to employ the title 'Vicar of Christ'. 'No king can reign rightly unless he devoutly serve Christ's vicar.' 'Princes have power in earth, priests over the soul. As much as the soul is worthier than the body, so much worthier is the priesthood than the monarchy.' He was, so he affirmed, *Melchisedech, the priest-king, who would bring a centralized Christian society into being, and, such was his genius, that alone of all the Popes he was able to convert theory into shortlived but nevertheless active reality.

Collected ed. of his *Opera* in J. P. Migne, *PL*, ccxiv–ccxvii; crit. edd. of his *Regestum super Negotio Romani Imperii* by W. Holtzmann (2 vols., Bonn, 1947–8) and F. Kempf, S.J. (Miscellanea Historiae Pontificiae edita a Facultate Historiae Ecclesiasticae in Pontificia Universitate Gregoriana, xii; Rome, 1947). C. R. Cheney–W. H. Semple (edd.), *Selected Letters of Pope Innocent III concerning England, 1198–1216* (Lat. text with Eng. tr., 1953). 'De Miseria Humanae Conditionis', ed. M. Maccarrone (Lugano, 1955). F. Hurter, *Geschichte Papst Innocens des Dritten und seiner Zeitgenossen* (4 vols., 1834–42); J. N. Brischar, *Papst Innocenz III und seine Zeit* (1883); A. Luchaire, *Innocent III* (6 vols., Paris, 1904–8). C. H. C. Pirie-Gordon, *Innocent the Great*. An Essay on his Life and Times (1907); L. E. Binns, *Innocent III* ('Great Medieval Churchmen', 1931). E. W. Meyer, *Staatstheorien Papst Innocenz' III* (Jenaer historische Arbeiten, Hft. ix; 1919); M. Maccarrone, *Chiesa e stato nella dottrina di Papa Innocenzo III* (Lateranum, N.S., vi, Nos. 3–4; 1940). E. F. Jacob in *C. Med. H.*, vi (1929), pp. 1–43. Mann, xi and xii (1915); Fliche–Martin, x (1950), pp. 11–213, with bibl. É. Amann in *D.T.C.*, vii (pt. 2; 1923), cols. 1961–81, s.v.; M. Maccarrone in *E.C.*, vii (1951), cols. 10–12, s.v. 'Innocenzo III'.

INNOCENT IV (d. 1254), Pope from 1243. He was a native of Genoa, who rose to fame as a teacher of *canon law at *Bologna. In 1227 he became *Cardinal and in 1243 Pope after the see had been vacant for some 18 months. He at once tried to compose the Papal dispute with the Emp. *Frederick II, but without success, and in 1245 at the Council of *Lyons declared Frederick to be deposed and proclaimed a crusade against him. Under Frederick's successors he interfered with the affairs of the Empire, until agreement was reached between Pope and Empire after the death of Conrad IV in 1254. In English matters Innocent took the side of Henry III against the barons, encouraged the nomination of foreigners to English ecclesiastical preferment, and extorted heavy taxes from the

country. In his bull 'Ad extirpanda' (1252) he permitted the use of torture by the *Inquisition. He was the author of a commentary ('Apparatus') on the *Decretals, which secured considerable authority.

É. Berger (ed.), *Les Registres d'Innocent IV* (Bibliothèque des Écoles françaises d'Athènes et de Rome, Ser. 2; 4 vols., 1884–1919; full text of docc. not given in all cases); further important docc. are preserved by *Matthew Paris in his *Chronica Majora*. A. Potthast (ed.), *Regesta Pontificum Romanorum*, ii (Berlin, 1875), pp. 943–1286. Contemporary life by his chaplain, Nicolao de Carbio (or Calvi), pr. in L. A. *Muratori, *Rerum Italicarum Scriptores*, iii (pt. i; Milan, 1723), pp. 592 ff.; crit. ed., with introd. and other docc., by F. Pignotti in *Archivio della R. Società Romana di Storia Patria*, xxi (1898), pp. 7–120. É. Berger, *Saint Louis et Innocent IV* (1893). H. Weber, *Der Kampf zwischen Papst Innocenz IV und Kaiser Friedrich II zur Flucht des Papstes nach Lyon* (Historische Studien, xx; 1900); A. Folz, *Kaiser Friedrich II und Papst Innocenz IV. Ihr Kampf in den Jahren 1244 und 1245* (1905); P. Deslandres, *Innocent IV et la chute des Hohenstaufen* (1907). C. Rodenberg, *Innocenz IV und das Königreich Sicilien, 1245–1249* (1892); K. Hampe, *Papst Innocenz IV und die sizilische Verschwörung von 1246* (Sitzungsber. der Heidelberger Akad. der Wiss., Jahrgang 1923, Abh. 8; 1923). G. von Puttkamer, *Papst Innocenz IV*. Versuch einer Gesamtcharakteristik aus seiner Wirkung (1930). Mann, xiv (1928), with detailed bibl., incl. reff. to publ. of docc. not pr. by E. Berger, *op. cit.*). É. Amann in *D.T.C.*, vii (pt. 2; 1923), cols. 1981–95, s.v.; P. Brezzi in *E.C.*, vii (1951), cols. 12–4, s.v. 'Innocenzo IV'.

INNOCENT X, BL. (1574–1655), Pope from 1644. Giambattista Pamfili was a native of Rome. He became consistorial advocate in 1601, Auditor of the *Rota in 1604, nuntius at Naples in 1621, and at Madrid in 1626. He was created cardinal *in petto* in 1627, the appointment being published in 1629. On the death of *Urban VIII he was elected Pope despite the opposition of the French court, which resented his pro-Spanish views. He at once broke the power of the *Barberini, the hated relatives of his predecessor, who were supported by J. *Mazarin. In the bull 'Zelo domus Dei' (26 Nov. 1648) he confirmed the protest of the Papal legate, Fabio Chigi, against the Peace of *Westphalia (1648), on the ground that it violated the laws of the Church; but the protest was ignored. His most important doctrinal decision was the condemnation of the five propositions from the *Augustinus* of C. *Jansenius by the bull 'Cum occasione' (31 May 1653). A much resented feature of his pontificate was the influence of Olimpia Maidalchini, the widow of his brother. He is the subject of the famous portrait by D. Velazquez in the Galleria Doria at Rome.

W. Friedensburg (ed.), 'Regesten zur deutschen Geschichte aus der Zeit des Pontifikats Innocenz X' in *Quellen und Forschungen aus italienischen Archiven und Bibliotheken* herausgegeben vom koenigl. preussischen historischen Institut in Rom, v (1903), pp. 60–124 and 207–22, and vi (1904), pp. 146–73. I. Ciampi, *Innocenzo X Pamfili e la sua corte*. Storia di Roma dal 1644 al 1655, da nuovi Documenti (Imola, 1878). L. *Pastor, *Lives of the Popes from the Close of the Middle Ages* (Eng. tr.), xxx (1940). G. B. Picotti in *E.C.*, vii (1951), cols. 19–22, s.v. 'Innocenzo X'.

INNOCENT XI (1611–1689), Pope from 1676. He became *Cardinal in 1645, and Bp. of Novara in 1650, and in both offices was greatly loved for his piety and generosity. In 1669 his candidature for the Papacy was defeated through the influence of Louis XIV of France, but the latter's interference was unavailing in 1676. By careful economy he much improved the finances of the curia. He struggled continuously against the absolutism of Louis XIV in Church affairs, disapproving of Louis's revocation in 1685 of the Edict of *Nantes; and he also opposed *Gallicanism, which reached its climax in the *Gallican Articles of 1682. Similar motives led him to disapprove of the measures taken by *James II of England to restore RC-ism, and esp. of the *Declaration of Indulgence (1687). His piety and zeal inspired him to bring about several reforms within the Church, and he encouraged daily communion. In the bull 'Sanctissimus Dominus' (1679) he condemned 65 *laxist propositions in moral theology; while in 1687 the bull 'Coelestis Pastor' condemned 68 *Quietist propositions. Innocent is thought, however, to have shown some favour to the *Jansenists, and for this reason his beatification, though begun in the next century, was long delayed. He was finally beatified in 1956.

I. I. Berthier, O.P. (ed.), *Innocentii P.P. XI Epistolae ad Principes* (2 vols., Rome, 1891–5); F. de Bojani (ed.), *Innocent XI. Sa correspondance avec ses nonces* (unfinished; up to 1684, 3 vols., 1910–12). G. B. P[ittoni], *Vita d' Innocenzo Undecimo* (Venice, 1691); F. Caccia, O.F.M., *Innocentia Apostolica* (1697). M. Immich, *Papst Innocenz XI, 1676–1689*. Beiträge zur Geschichte seiner Politik und zur Charakteristik seiner Persönlichkeit (1900). E. Michaud, *Louis XIV et Innocent XI* (4 vols., 1882–3). L. O'Brien, *Innocent XI and the Revocation of the Edict of Nantes* (thesis, Berkeley, Cal.; 1930); J. Orcibal, *Louis XIV contre Innocent XI. Les appels au futur concile de 1688 et l'opinion française* (Bibliothèque de la Société d'Histoire Ecclésiastique de la France; 1949). L. *Pastor, *The History of the Popes from the Close of the Middle Ages* (Eng. tr.), xxxii (1940), pp. 1–524, with Appendix on the Biographies of Pope Innocent XI in vol. xxx (1940), pp. 449–51. J. Paquier in *D.T.C.*, vii (1922), cols. 2006–13, s.v., with bibl.; G. B. Picotti in *E.C.*, vii (1951), cols. 22–5, s.v. 'Innocenzo XI'.

INNOCENTS, Holy. See *Holy Innocents*.

INOPPORTUNISTS. Those at the *Vatican Council of 1869–70 who were opposed to defining Papal Infallibility on the ground not that they positively disbelieved in it, but that they considered the moment for its promulgation 'not opportune'. This position was adopted by the great majority of the opponents of the dogma.

INQUISITION, The. 'Inquisition' denotes the juridical persecution of heresy by special ecclesiastical courts. In early times, the usual punishment for heresy was *excommunication. Physical penalties were generally disapproved of by the Fathers, though after Christianity had become the official religion of the Empire, secular princes tended to regard heresy as a kind of *lèse-majesté* for which confiscation or even death could be inflicted, as e.g. in the case of *Donatism and *Priscillianism in the 4th and 5th cents. The Church, on the whole, kept to her original attitude as late as the 12th cent. when St. *Bernard laid down the principle 'Fides suadenda, non imponenda'. In the latter half of the 12th and the early 13th cents., however, when the *Catharist heresy which threatened not only religion but all the institutions of contemporary society began to spread rapidly, the attitude of the Church changed in favour of securing the help of the secular power.

The Inquisition properly so called came into being when in 1232 the Emp. *Frederick II issued an edict for the whole Empire entrusting the hunting-out of heretics to state officials. Thereupon *Gregory IX, fearing Frederick's political ambitions, claimed this office for the Church and appointed Papal inquisitors. These were selected, not from the bishops or their representatives who had hitherto dealt with heresy, but from members of the mendicant orders, chiefly *Dominicans and *Franciscans, who from their theological learning and the absence of worldly motives seemed esp. fitted for the work. The inquisitors went round the country, admonishing those guilty of heresy to confess voluntarily. If they confessed, an ordinary penance such as fasting or a pilgrimage would be imposed: but after a time of 'grace' of about a month the actual trials began. The inquisitor was normally assisted by a kind of jury, composed of both clerics and laymen, and the suspect persons were summoned by the parish priest. The evidence was established on the testimony of at least two witnesses whose names were at first kept secret, but this custom was abrogated by Pope *Boniface VIII in his 'Ut commissi vobis officii'. The accused was allowed a counsel, whose main interest, however, was not the defence of his client but that justice should be done. If, in face of many proofs, the accused remained obstinate he was frequently imprisoned under severe conditions (*carcer durus*). In 1252 *Innocent IV allowed the use of torture by his bull 'Ad extirpanda', to break the resistance of the accused. The sentence was pronounced at the *sermo generalis* or *auto da fé*, after consultation with the jury. The penalties, in grave cases, were confiscation of goods, imprisonment of various degrees, either temporary or perpetual, and surrender to the secular arm, which meant death at the stake. In 1542 *Paul III established the 'Congregation of the Inquisition' as the final court of appeal in trials for heresy (see *Holy Office*).

The so-called *Spanish Inquisition* which was instituted as late as the end of the 15th cent. bears a somewhat different character, as it is closely bound up with the state. Set up with Papal approval by *Ferdinand V and *Isabella in 1479, it was originally directed against the Marranos and Moriscos, converts from Judaism and Islam respectively, but later served also against Protestantism. Its organization was highly centralized. At the head stood the Grand Inquisitor, who, after consultation with the King, nominated the members of the High Council who assisted him. The procedure established elsewhere was normally followed. The number of persons burnt under its first inquisitor, T. *Torquemada, have been variously estimated. Perhaps 2,000

is a fair estimate. After the Spanish Inquisition had been abolished by Joseph Bonaparte
in 1808 it was reintroduced in 1814 but finally
suppressed in 1820.

H. C. Lea, *History of the Inquisition in the Middle Ages*
(3 vols., 1888; polemical and hostile); A. S. Turberville,
Medieval Heresy and the Inquisition (1920); A. L. Maycock,
The Inquisition (1926). C. Douais, *L'Inquisition*. Ses
origines, sa procédure (1906); J. [H.] Guiraud, *Histoire de
l'inquisition au moyen-âge* (2 vols., 1935–8). See also bibl.
under individual heresies, e.g., *Albigensians*.

I.N.R.I. The initial letters of the Latin
words over the Cross of Christ, viz. 'Iesus
Nazarenus Rex Iudaeorum' ('Jesus of Nazareth, the King of the Jews'). The super-
scription 'was written in Hebrew and in Latin
and in Greek' (Jn. 19. 19 f.).

INSCRIPTIONS, Early Christian. Inscriptions on stone and other materials are a
valuable supplement to other sources of
Christian history. Though they abound at all
periods, esp. in churches and cemeteries,
Christian epigraphy is conventionally limited
to texts of the first six cents. For practical
purposes, inscriptions are 'Christian' if they
bear evidence of Christianity, though others
were doubtless set up by Christians.

Many Christian inscriptions are dated, by
consular years, provincial eras, or indictions,
but usually their date needs to be inferred
from knowledge of either the site or building
in which they are found or from the internal
evidence of each inscription — its content,
style of lettering or accompanying symbols
(e.g. the anchor is early and the forms of the
Chi-Rho monogram (☧) can be dated). If
certain much-discussed scribblings at Pompeii
(destroyed in 79) are Christian, they must be
the earliest extant Christian inscriptions. 2nd
cent. inscriptions are fairly common in the
Roman catacombs. By the 4th cent. they are
very common, esp. in *Rome, N. Africa, Syria,
and Asia Minor. Some of these are heretical,
*Montanist in Phrygia or *Donatist in Africa.
Thousands of original inscriptions exist, mostly
in Greek or Latin, and the text of others
survives in copies.

In contrast to pagan custom, Christian
inscriptions give little personal detail; epitaphs
normally mention only the name, age, and date
of death, occasionally adding the profession of
the deceased. Prominent names occur, particularly in the memorials set up by Pope
*Damasus in the catacombs, but the inscrip-
tions are more valuable *en masse* as evidence of
the texture of a community and the expansion
of the Church. Specially important are those
which record the foundation of churches and
witness to the cult of martyrs. Doctrine is
illustrated vividly, but less fully and precisely
than in the literary sources.

O. *Marucchi, *Epigrafia cristiana* (1910); R. Aigrain,
Manuel d'épigraphie chrétienne (2 vols., 1912, 1913); C. M.
Kaufmann, *Handbuch der altchristlichen Epigraphik* (1917).
Selections in E. Diehl, *Lateinische altchristliche Inschriften*
(2te Aufl., 1913, short); id., *Inscriptiones Latinae Christianae
Veteres* (3 vols., 1925–31). General collections: *Corpus In-
scriptionum Latinarum*, passim; *Corpus Inscriptionum
Graecarum*, esp. t. IV. There are many regional collections,

notably G. B. *De Rossi, *Inscriptiones christianae urbis
Romae*, 1861, continued first by I. Gatti and now by A.
Silvagni. For the rest see F. *Cabrol–H. *Leclercq, *Dictionnaire d'archéologie chrétienne et de liturgie* (1903 ff.), s.v.
'Inscriptions'. This dictionary is rich throughout in discussion and illustration of inscriptions. The progress of
Christian epigraphy may be followed in *L'Année épi-
graphique* (1888 ff.) and *Rivista di Archeologia cristiana*
(1924 ff.).

INSTALLATION. The formal induction
by the Dean or his representative of a canon
or prebendary to a seat or stall in a cathedral
or collegiate church, symbolizing his admission to the chapter and right to perform the
duties and enjoy the privileges of his office.
In the case of canons appointed by the Crown,
it appears that installation is not strictly
necessary. The term is also used of the ceremonies of admission in certain orders of
chivalry, and incorrectly to include both the
*enthronement of a bishop and *induction to a
rectory or vicarage.

INSTANTIUS (late 4th cent.). A Spanish
bishop of unknown see. He was one of the
chief supporters of *Priscillian, whom he
accompanied to Italy (381–2) in a fruitless
endeavour to secure the favour of St. *Ambrose
and Pope *Damasus. In 384 he was deposed
by the Council of Bordeaux. He is the probable author of eleven treatises attributed by
G. Schepps (who first published them from a
Würzburg MS. in 1886) to Priscillian.

The eleven tractates were publd. by G. Schepps in
C.S.E.L., vol. xviii (1889). G. *Morin, O.S.B., '*Pro
Instantio*. Contre l'attribution à Priscillien des opuscules
du manuscrit de Würzburg' in *R. Bén.*, xxx (1913), pp. 153–
73. Critique of Morin by J. Martin, 'Priscillianus oder
Instantius' in *Hist. J.*, xlvii (1927), pp. 237–251. A. D'Alès,
Priscillien et l'Espagne chrétienne à la fin du quatrième siècle
(1936). See also bibl. to *Priscillian*.

INSTITUTE OF CHARITY. See *Rosminians*.

INSTITUTES, The. The abbreviated English title of J. *Calvin's *Christianae Religionis
Institutio*. The first edition, publd. in Latin
in 1536, was a small volume of six chapters,
with a prefatory letter to Francis I, King of
France. Its double purpose was to be a
theological introduction to the Bible and a
vindication of Reformation principles. It was
arranged as an exposition of the Decalogue,
the Apostles' Creed, the Lord's Prayer, the
Sacraments and Church government. In 1539
appeared an enlarged edition with seventeen
chapters and in 1541 a French translation by
Calvin himself. The final edition, comprising
80 chapters, was published in Latin in 1559
and in French in 1560. This last edition consisted of four parts dealing with (1) God the
Creator, (2) God the Redeemer, (3) the Holy
Spirit, and (4) the means of grace and the
Church. Although the arrangements of topics
was altered, the fundamental doctrines remained unchanged throughout.

The treatise is a clear and systematic exposition of Calvin's fundamental beliefs. It soon
became the text-book of Reformed theology,

its central doctrines being the absolute sovereignty of God, the basis of all Christian faith in the Word of God revealed in the Holy Scriptures, and the inability of man to find pardon or salvation apart from the working of the free grace of God. It went far to prevent the Reformation movement, in its revolt against the authority of the visible Church, from becoming individualist or antinomian by its emphatic insistence upon the absolute authority of God.

The earliest Eng. trans. (from the Lat.) was made by T. Norton (1561). Later transs. from the Lat., collated with the French, by J. Allen (3 vols., 1813; reissued, 2 vols., 1838) and H. Beveridge (2 vols., 1845; reissued 1949). B. B. Warfield, *The Literary History of the Institutes* (1909; reprinted in *Calvin and Calvinism*, 1931, pp. 373–428); A. Austin, *L'Institution chrétienne de Calvin* (1919); J. W. Marmelstein, *Étude comparative des textes latin et français de l'Institution de la religion chrétienne* (1921); H. T. Kerr, *A Compend of the Institutes of the Christian Religion* (Philadelphia, 1939; London, 1945).

INSTITUTION. The term used to denote the admission of a new *incumbent into the spiritual care of the parish. It is contrasted with the (subsequent) *induction, which admits him into the temporalities of the cure. The Institution is performed by the bishop of the diocese and (unlike the induction) may take place anywhere.

INSTITUTION, The Words of. The words 'This is My Body' and 'This is My Blood', used by our Lord in instituting the *Eucharist. They appear in the central prayer of the Liturgy in all its forms, with one or two possible exceptions in very early times, and in the W. it has been commonly held that these words alone effect the consecration of the elements. This view clearly underlies the rubric in the BCP that if a second consecration of either species is necessary during the communion of the people, only that section of the Prayer of Consecration which contains the relevant words for that species is to be repeated. See also *Epiclesis*.

Jungmann (ed. 1949), ii, 236–45. A. Raes, S.J., 'Le Récit de l'institution eucharistique dans l'anaphore chaldéenne et malabare des apôtres' in *O.C.P.*, x (1944), pp. 216–26.

INSTITUTS CATHOLIQUES. The five 'free' Catholic institutions for higher studies at *Paris, Angers, Lille, Lyons, and Toulouse. These Institutes were founded on the basis of a French legal enactment of 1875 as Christian counterparts to the secularized state universities, though a later law of 1880 denied them the right of describing themselves as universities. In the concluding years of the 19th cent., the Institut Catholique at Paris was the chief centre of the *Modernist Movement. Its professors have included M. *d'Hulst, L. *Duchesne, and A. *Loisy, and, more recently, L. Bouyer, Cong. Orat., J. Daniélou, S.J., and P. Henry, S.J.

INSTRUMENTS, Tradition of the (Lat. *Traditio* or *Porrectio Instrumentorum*). The solemn delivery to those being ordained of the instruments characteristic of their ministry. This ceremony, which now forms part of the Latin rites of Ordination, belonged originally to the *Minor Orders. At *Rome the ceremony was at first merely symbolical as there was originally no formal ordination to these Orders, but in the *Gallican rites it was accompanied by a charge and formed part of a solemn ordination. During the Middle Ages it was extended to the diaconate and priesthood. Deacons received the Gospel Book and priests the *Paten with the breads and chalice, the delivery being accompanied in each case by an appropriate charge. In his 'Decretum de Unione Armeniorum' (1439) *Eugenius IV gave formal expression to the doctrine already asserted by St. *Thomas Aquinas that this ceremony formed the essential 'matter' of the Sacrament, and this view was widely accepted by Latin theologians until the 17th cent. when J. *Morin, by his research into E. and early W. Ordination rites, showed it to be a comparatively late and entirely W. innovation and hence not an essential for Ordination. In the first Anglican Ordinal (1550) the New Testament was delivered to deacons and the Bible and chalice with the bread to priests, each with a corresponding charge, but in the Ordinal attached to the Second BCP (1552) the chalice with the bread was omitted, at the Ordination of priests, although the accompanying charge remained unchanged.

St. Thomas, *Summa Theologica*, Suppl., qu. xxxv, art. 5 [but a different view is perhaps implied in qu. xxxvii, art. 5]. Relevant section of Eugenius IV's decree is pr. in Denz.–Bann. (ed. 1952), p. 258 f. (No. 701), with useful note. J. *Morin, *Commentarius de Sacris Ecclesiae Ordinationibus* (Paris, 1655), esp. pt. III, Exercitatio, vii (pp. 129–57, 'De Presbyteratus Materia et Forma'). F. Dalbus (pseud. of F. Portal), *Les Ordinations anglicaines* (Arras, 1894; orig. pr. in *La Science catholique* for 15 Dec. 1893, 15 Jan. 1894, and 15 April 1894) [by a *tour de force* argues that the suppression of the *porrectio instrumentorum* at the Reformation is the sole ground against the validity of Anglican Ordinations]. The power of the Church to adapt the matter of Ordination to changing conditions is conceded by *Pius XII in his Apostolic Constitution *Sacramentum Ordinis* of 30 Nov. 1947 (*A.A.S.*, xl (1948), pp. 5–7).

INSUFFLATION. The action of blowing or breathing upon a person or thing to symbolize the influence of the Holy Spirit. The *Vulgate uses the term of the Lord's breathing on the disciples (*haec cum dixisset insufflavit*, Jn. 20. 22). Its purpose is the expulsion of evil spirits. The RC Church has a special rite of insufflation in connexion with the consecration of baptismal water, chrism and the oil used for catechumens on *Maundy Thursday, as well as in the baptism of adults. In some E. rites an insufflation is still found in all baptisms, infant and adult, e.g. among the *Maronites.

INTENTION. The word is used in religious contexts in several senses.

(1) In moral theology, for an act of free will directed to the attainment of an end. Such intention may be 'actual', if one wills with conscious attention; 'virtual', if one continues to will in virtue of an antecedent decision,

though at the moment not consciously aware of it; 'habitual', if all voluntary action has ceased but without the original decision being revoked; and 'interpretative', if a certain intention is ascribed to a person who has no opportunity to confirm or deny the imputation. The intention influences the morality of an action. A good intention makes a morally indifferent action good and increases the worth of an action good in itself, but does not make a bad action good. A bad intention, on the other hand, whilst making an indifferent action bad and worsening an action bad in itself, ruins even a good action.

(2) In the administration of the Sacraments, the purpose of doing what the Church does (*quod facit ecclesia*). If the right *form and the right *matter were alone needed, apart from any intention, Sacraments might occasionally be conferred by accident, e.g. in religious drama or in demonstrations or rehearsals. The requirement of such intention was laid down by the Council of *Trent (Sess. 7, can. 11). In the 16th and 17th cents. it was held by some RC theologians, e.g. by Catharinus in his *De Intentione Ministri* (Rome, 1552), that the required intention existed if the minister intended to perform the customary rites, though not to confer the Sacraments of the Church, i.e. if he possessed the so-called 'exterior intention'. This opinion has also been defended by some Anglican scholars. Most modern theologians, however, agree in requiring the 'interior intention' of the minister for the validity of the Sacrament. It was esp. on the grounds of defect of intention that *Leo XIII condemned *Anglican Ordinations (q.v.) by the bull '*Apostolicae Curae' (1896). The nature of the intention required from the recipient (as opposed to the minister) varies with the particular Sacrament. In the case of children under the age of reason and mentally deficient persons, clearly no intention can be necessary for the validity of such Sacraments as they are capable of receiving.

(3) The special object, spiritual or material, for which a prayer of intercession is made. Thus a 'Mass intention' is the particular end to which the celebrant prays that the fruits of the sacrifice may be applied, e.g. the repose of the soul of one lately dead.

(4) In the Scholastic theories of knowledge, the term was sometimes used of the objects of knowledge in so far as they are present to the knowing consciousness. Thus as contrasted with the real tree, which is the object of external perception, there was held to be an 'intentional tree' in the mind of the knower, and the conceptual tree was thus said to have an 'intentional existence' (*ens* or *esse intentionale*). This doctrine, taken up in the 19th cent. by F. *Brentano, was developed by E. Husserl, who maintained that every mental act was directed towards some entity, and that thus intentionality was the characteristic mark of consciousness.

A. Thouvenin in *D.T.C.*, vii (pt. 2; 1923 cols. 2267–80. S. da Romallo and G. Rambaldi in *E.C.*, vii (1951), cols. 66–73, s.v. 'Intenzione'.

INTERCESSION. Petitionary prayer on behalf of others. Such prayer, implicit or explicit, forms part of almost all Christian worship, and in particular of all the traditional forms of the Liturgy of the *Eucharist. Intercession may be made (1) in words of definite petition, (2) in mental prayer, by direction of thought, (3) by offering a service or action for a specified *intention.

INTERDICT. Acc. to *CIC* can. 2268, an ecclesiastical punishment in the RC Church excluding the faithful from participation in spiritual things, but without loss of the Communion of the Church. Interdicts are of several kinds. The 'personal' interdict is attached only to particular persons; the 'local' forbids sacred actions in particular places; the 'general' refers to a whole district or its population; and the 'partial' visualizes only certain parts or inhabitants of a district. The new (1917) canon law no longer mentions 'cessatio a divinis', which prohibited all cultual actions in certain places.

An interdict can be imposed only by the Pope, except in cases of single persons, groups of persons, or parishes, when it falls within the competence of the bishop. Acc. to present legislation the chief effects of a general local interdict are the cessation of the administration of the Sacraments and of all solemn services. Exceptions are made, however, for the Last Sacraments; for clerics not personally responsible for the interdict, who are allowed to perform all religious rites privately with doors locked and in a low voice; for one Mass which may be said in the cathedral or parish church; and for certain high Feasts, viz. *Christmas, *Easter, *Pentecost, *Corpus Christi, and the *Assumption. The lifting of the interdict follows the expression of repentance.

Cases of interdicts are attested from the 6th cent. At first they were imposed only on the churches of a single city, but from the 9th cent. they were extended to dioceses, and from the 12th to whole countries. *Alexander III placed Scotland under an interdict for the expulsion of the Bp. of St. Andrews, and *Innocent III used this powerful weapon with great effect in his struggles with Philip Augustus of France (1200) and *John of England (1208). With the decline of Papal influence in the later Middle Ages the interdict lost most of its force, and in modern times it is used very rarely. Recent examples are those imposed on the Convent of Marienthal near Strassburg in 1921 and on the parish church of Barbentane in Provence in 1929.

A. Haas, *Das Interdikt nach geltendem Recht mit einem geschichtlichen Ueberblick* (1923). E. J. Coran, *The Interdict* (Washington, 1930). W. Richter, S.J., *De Origine et Evolutione Interdicti usque ad aetatem Ivonis Carnotensis et Paschalis II* (Textus et Documenta in usum Exercitationum et Praelectionum Academicarum, Series Theologica 12 and 13; Pontificia Universitas *Gregoriana, 1934). A. Auer, O.S.B., 'Eine verschollene Denkschrift über das grosse Interdikt des 14. Jahrhunderts' in *Historisches Jahrbuch*, xlvi (1926), pp. 532–49. A. Boudinhon in *C.E.*, viii (1910), pp. 73–5, s.v.; Zaccaria da San Mauro, O.F.M., in *E.C.*, vii (1951), cols. 78–80, s.v. 'Interdetto', with further bibl.

INTERIM OF AUGSBURG. See *Augsburg Interim.*

INTERNATIONAL BIBLE STUDENTS' ASSOCIATION. See *Jehovah's Witnesses.*

INTERSTICES. The spaces of time which, by canon law, must elapse between the conferment of different *orders in the Christian ministry upon the same person. The RC law is that the intervals between *minor orders are at the bishop's discretion, though it is forbidden to confer all four orders on the same day; between the order of *acolyte and that of *subdeacon a year is to elapse, between subdeacon and *deacon three months, and between deacon and *priest three months. These rules are in practice dispensable, but it is strictly laid down that two *major orders may not be received on the same day. The C of E has no independent rule on the subject, but the 32nd canon of 1604 reaffirms the prohibition against conferring the diaconate and priesthood upon the same man on the same day.

For the RC ruling, see C.I.C., can. 978.

INTHRONIZATION. See *Enthronization.*

INTINCTION. In liturgical usage, the practice of dipping the Eucharistic bread into consecrated or unconsecrated wine prior to Holy Communion. Its first use seems to have been in clinical Communion (cf. *Dionysius of Alexandria in *Eusebius, *HE*, VI, xliv); the consecrated bread was moistened with unconsecrated wine to make consumption easier for the sick person. Later it became a regular method of Communion with the two consecrated species both in E. and W. In the E. the Hosts to be reserved for the Mass of the *Presanctified and for *viaticum were intincted by means of the communion spoon (λαβίς). The method in use in the W. is less certain. Intinction was forbidden by the Council of *Braga of 675, but it was reintroduced and is attested for *Cluny in the 10th cent. A third form of intinction, resting on the belief that the consecrated Host itself exercised a consecratory effect on the unconsecrated wine, is described in the *Ordines Romani. In all forms it had virtually disappeared in the Latin West by *c.* 1200. In recent times it has been revived sporadically in the Anglican Communion as a method of giving Holy Communion to the sick.

W. H. Freestone, *The Sacrament Reserved* (1917; Alcuin Club Collections, XXI), ch. x. M. Andrieu, *Immixtio et Consecratio. La consécration par contact dans les documents liturgiques du moyen-âge* (1924).

INTROIT. In the W. Church, the opening act of worship in the Mass. It consists of a psalm-verse proper to the day, with an *antiphon and (except in *Passiontide and at *Requiems) *Gloria Patri. When the choir is present it is sung while the priest says the *Preparation, the priest himself reciting it silently at the altar later. Originally it consisted of a whole psalm, varying on different occasions, which was sung as the celebrant entered the church, but it may always have been the custom, as is provided in the First *Ordo Romanus* (6th–7th cent.), for the celebrant to stop the singing after the first few verses, as soon as he was ready to begin the Mass. By the time of the Tenth *Ordo Romanus* (12th cent.), the present practice of singing a single verse was established. The 1549 BCP provided for an entire psalm, with Gloria Patri, but without antiphon, to be sung as an Introit. In subsequent revisions of the Prayer Book the introits have been omitted, though their use has been widely revived unofficially in the C of E since the middle of the 19th cent.

The Introit is thought to be of later origin than the *Gradual, from which it differs in not being an integral part of the service; it was introduced to fill a gap with singing. In *Gallican rites the Introit was called 'Antiphona ad praelegendum'; in the *Ambrosian, 'Ingressa'; in the *Mozarabic and others, 'Officium'.

Eng. tr. of *Sarum Introits in *E.H.*, Nos. 657–733. H. Leclercq, O.S.B., in *D.A.C.L.*, vii (pt. 1; 1926), cols. 1212–20. Jungmann (ed. 1949), i, 397–412.

INVENTION OF THE CROSS, The. Acc. to legend the three crosses on *Golgotha (of Christ and the two robbers) were found (Lat. *inventae*) by St. *Helena, the mother of *Constantine, the true one being identified by a miracle. St. *Ambrose, whose 'Oratio de Obitu Theodosii' (395) is the first work to connect the event with St. Helena, is followed by many other Fathers such as St. John *Chrysostom and *Paulinus of Nola. St. *Jerome, however, who lived quite near the place, is silent on the matter. St. *Cyril of Jerusalem, without mentioning St. Helena, states that the Cross was found at Jerusalem in the time of Constantine (d. 337), and it has been suggested that this occurred during the excavations for the Emperor's basilica of the *Holy Sepulchre. The relic was preserved in that church in a silver receptacle, after a large part of the wood had been distributed among the churches throughout the world. The veneration of the Cross at Jerusalem is first described in the Pilgrimage of *Etheria. In the Greek Church the Feast of the Finding of the Cross was originally commemorated on 14 Sept., now the Feast of the *Exaltation of the Cross (q.v.), together with the consecration of Constantine's two *Jerusalem basilicas. The present commemoration on 3 May, which seems to go back to the apocryphal treatise 'De Inventione Crucis Dominicae', is not found in the *Gregorian Sacramentary. It was probably first observed on this day in Gaul in the 7th cent. and thence came to Rome *c.* 800. See also *Exaltation of the Cross.*

J. Straubinger, *Die Kreuzauffindungslegende. Untersuchungen über ihre altchristlichen Fassungen mit besonderer Berücksichtigung der syrischen Texte (Forschungen zur christlichen Literatur- und Dogmengeschichte, xi, Hft. 3; 1912). H. *Leclercq, O.S.B., in *D.A.C.L.*, iii (pt. 2; 1914), cols. 3131–9, s.v. 'Croix (Invention et exaltation de la vraie)'; E. Romanelli in *E.C.*, vii (1951), cols. 130–2, s.v. 'Invenzione delle Santa Croce'. On the Feast, cf. A. Bugnini in *E.C.*, iv (1950), cols. 960–3, s.v. 'Croce VII'. See also bibl. to *Exaltation of the Cross*.

INVESTITURE CONTROVERSY, The.

The famous dispute dating from the late 11th–12th cent. over the claim of the Emperor and other lay princes to invest an Abbot- or Bishop-elect with the ring and staff and to receive homage before consecration. The custom, which was closely linked with lay-patronage, was condemned by Pope Nicholas II in 1059; and in 1075 all lay investiture was expressly forbidden by *Gregory VII. Serious attempts were now made to enforce the anti-investiture legislation enacted during the previous forty years; the prohibition was repeated by Gregory in 1076, 1078, and 1080, and by subsequent Popes; and in the ensuing controversy between the Papacy and the Emps. Henry *IV and V, wide political issues became involved. A formal settlement was reached at last by the Concordat of *Worms (1122; q.v.), the provisions of which were reasserted by the Second *Lateran Council (1123; cans. 8 and 9), the Emperor relinquishing the right to invest with ring and staff but continuing to bestow the temporalities, and in Germany receiving homage before consecration and in other parts of the Empire after six months' delay. In Germany he was also allowed some influence in elections.

In England the matter became esp. acute under St. *Anselm who tried to enforce a decree of a Council of Rome (1099) excommunicating all who gave or received lay investiture. He himself refused to do homage to Henry I (1100) or to consecrate Bishops who had received lay investiture. In 1106 a compromise was reached, ratified in the Council of London of 1107, acc. to which Henry was allowed to receive homage and grant investiture of the temporalities before consecration in return for a promise of freedom of election.

For text of the official documents, see bibl. to Popes (Gregory VII, *Urban II, *Paschal II, and *Callistus II), Emperors (Henry IV), and contemporary monarchs concerned. Convenient Eng. tr., with introd., of a selection of the relevant docc. in E. F. Henderson (ed.), *Select Historical Documents of the Middle Ages* (Bohn's Classical Library, 1892), pp. 351–409. Much contemporary information is pr. in *M.G.H.*, Libelli de Lite Imperatorum et Pontificum Saeculis XI et XII (3 vols., 1891–7). E. Bernheim, *Quellen zur Geschichte des Investiturstreits* (Quellensammlung zur deutschen Geschichte; 2 Hfft., 1907); A. Scharnagl, *Der Begriff der Investitur in den Quellen und der Literatur des Investiturstreits* (Kirchenrechtliche Abhandlungen, lvi; 1908). P. Schmid, *Der Begriff der kanonischen Wahl in den Anfängen des Investiturstreits* (1926). A. Fliche, *La Querelle des investitures* (1946), with bibl. Id. in Fliche–Martin, viii (1946), pp. 351–409. K. Löffler in *C.E.*, viii (1910), pp. 84–9, s.v. 'Investitures, Conflict of'. For the controversy in England, H. W. C. Davis in *D.E.C.H.*, p. 296 f., s.v.; see also works cited under *Anselm*.

INVINCIBLE IGNORANCE. A term in

*moral theology denoting ignorance of a kind that cannot be removed by serious moral effort. It totally excuses from sin because, being involuntary, it can involve no intention of breaking the law of God. It is to be distinguished from 'vincible ignorance', which, though partly excusing from sin, is culpable in itself, apart from the action to which it leads, as it involves neglect to acquire information necessary to avoid the transgression. The term 'invincible ignorance' is frequently used esp. by RC theologians, with reference to those who, because of their upbringing and environment, are unable to accept the teachings of the Church.

K. E. *Kirk, *Ignorance, Faith and Conformity* (1925). E. Mangenot in *D.T.C.*, vii (pt. 1; 1922), cols. 731–40, s.v. 'Ignorance'; L. Simeone in *E.C.*, vi (1951), cols. 1606–12, s.v. 'Ignoranza', both with bibl.

INVITATORY. In the Lat. *Breviary, the

Psalm *Venite* (AV, Ps. 95; Vulg., Ps. 94), with its corresponding *Antiphon, which stand at the outset of *Mattins and invite to prayer. The Antiphon (also itself alone sometimes termed the 'Invitatory') varies acc. to the season and is repeated several times in the course of the Psalm. The recitation of the Ps. at the Night Office was already ordered in the Rule of St. *Benedict (ch. 9). For long confined to Sunday, it is now used daily through the year except on the last three days of *Holy Week and *Epiphany. In the BCP it is retained at Morning Prayer, with the Antiphon discarded ('without any Invitatory', 1549). See also *Venite*.

H. *Leclercq, O.S.B., in *C.E.*, viii (1910), p. 89 f.; F. *Cabrol, O.S.B., in *D.A.C.L.*, vii (pt. 1; 1926), cols. 1419–22, with bibl.

INVOCATION OF THE SAINTS. See

Saints, Devotion to the.

I.O.D.G. See *U.I.O.D.G.*

IONA (or Hy). A small island of the Inner

Hebrides; the present form of the name is said to derive from an error in copying 'Ioua insula' (as in *Adamnan's Life of St. *Columba). From another early name of the island, it appears that it was already sacred when St. Columba landed in 563 and founded a monastery which rapidly became the centre of *Celtic Christianity. From this monastery missionaries were sent to *Scotland and N. England and numerous daughter houses were established. After his death, until the removal of his relics in the 9th cent., the island was a popular centre of pilgrimages; and the monastery became famous for its learning. Although many times plundered by Norsemen, it was repeatedly rebuilt and survived until the Reformation. The *Benedictine rule was adopted c. 1203. A nunnery (prob. *Augustinian) was also established in association with the monastery. In 1561 the buildings were dismantled by order of the Convention of Estates.

A bishopric for the Western Isles was established in Iona in 838, but merged with that of *Man in 1098. It was re-established from *c.* 1507 until the time of the Reformation in Scotland. Of the 13th cent. Cathedral Church of St. Mary, a considerable part of the walls and tower remain; the choir and nave have been roofed, and various repairs were undertaken at the end of the 19th cent. The extant conventual buildings, incl. a portion of Norman arcade, appear to be of an earlier date. The ruins of the chapel of St. Oran, built by St. *Margaret of Scotland on the supposed site of St. Columba's cell, are the oldest in Iona. Of the Benedictine nunnery only the chancel and nave of the Norman Chapel remain. The cemetery, supposed to contain the remains of 46 Scottish kings, is said to have had at the time of the Reformation 360 crosses, most of which were thrown into the sea. Those that remain include Maclean's Cross and that of St. Martin, both in good condition, with Runic inscriptions and elaborate scroll work.

The Iona Community was founded in 1938 by the Rev. George MacLeod (b. 1895) for the general purpose of expressing in social terms the theology of the *Incarnation and using as the symbol of its purpose the cooperative rebuilding of the Benedictine abbey. Its members are ministers and laymen of the Church of Scotland who live together in Iona for three months in preparation for work in Scottish industrial areas and in the mission field. It lays special stress on political activity, the discipline of devotional and economic witness and spiritual healing. It was officially recognized by the General Assembly in 1951.

E. C. Trenholme, S.S.J.E., *The Story of Iona* (1909), with bibl.; T. Hannan, *Iona and Some of its Satellites* (1928). J. Drummond, *Sculptured Monuments in Iona and the West Highlands* (Archaeologia Scotia, 1881), pp. 3–6 and pll. I–XLIV. L. H. Cottineau, O.S.B., *Répertoire topo-bibliographique des abbayes et prieurés* (Mâcon, 1935), col. 1461 f., s.v., for further reff. G. [F.] MacLeod, *We Shall Rebuild. The Work of the Iona Community on Mainland and Island* [1944].

IOTA. The Greek letter ι (corresponding to the Hebrew *yod* both in sound and as being the smallest letter of the alphabet), mentioned in Christ's saying that 'one jot or one tittle shall in no wise pass away from the law' (Mt. 5. 18). The English 'jot', a transliteration of this Greek word (ἰῶτα), derives its meaning from this text.

IRELAND, Christianity in. Intercourse with Britain probably brought Christianity to Ireland by the 4th cent., so that perhaps the work to which St. *Germanus of Auxerre sent *Palladius in 431, and to which St. *Patrick went in 432, was primarily the organization of a Church already existing, and only secondarily further evangelization. The chief monument of St. Patrick is the see of *Armagh, founded *c.* 444. After the break-up of Roman civilization Ireland, cut off from the rest of Christendom, developed her Church life alone. The hermit remained the normal type of religious; and there arose a curious type of feudalism, based on property and carrying spiritual authority, whereby heads of land-

owning communities such as abbots and abbesses, and even laymen, exercised a considerable authority over bishops, who were consecrated in large numbers without dioceses. Learning, however, flourished in the Irish monasteries, which were also centres of missionary activity. Notable examples were the mission of St. *Columba to Scotland (563) and of St. *Columbanus to the Continent (590). Under influences from S. Wales the communities were brought into closer alignment with contemporary practice elsewhere. The division in the 7th cent. caused by the dispute between the *Celtic church and St. *Augustine's mission was healed first in southern Ireland, and eventually in the north also. In 795 when the invasions of the Northmen began, Irish scholars and ecclesiastics went abroad in large numbers, among them many non-diocesan bishops, whose irregular ministrations proved a considerable nuisance. Best known among the emigrant scholars were *Sedulius Scottus and Johannes Scotus *Erigena.

The rise of the see of *Dublin in the 11th cent. was linked with a movement for closer contact with Norman England and with the W. Church as a whole. Celsus, Bp. of Armagh (d. 1129), was won over by the reformers, and various steps were taken by the synods of Rathbressil (1118), Kells (1152), and *Cashel (*c.* 1172), of which the most important was the establishment everywhere of fixed dioceses. The English conquest of 1172 completed the ecclesiastical process. In the following centuries there was a tendency to appoint Englishmen to Irish sees; yet the Irish Church always retained a strong individuality, and was never fully amenable to papal authority. The *Cistercian and *Augustinian communities which came from abroad did valuable work in education.

The *Reformation was less thorough in Ireland than elsewhere. The monasteries were suppressed, but the friars continued to live a vagrant life, only suffering a temporary check under the Commonwealth. The *Jesuits arrived in Ireland *c.* 1545. The preaching of Edward Staples, Bp. of Meath, in favour of the Reformation under *Edward VI failed to win popular support. Officially the Church was reformed on the same lines as in England, and, by the enactments of the Irish Parliament of 1560, made, if anything, more dependent on the State. The translation of the Prayer Book into Irish was forbidden (Latin was permitted where English was unknown), but the old service books continued in use in many places. The one solid result of *Elizabeth I's vacillating Irish policy was the foundation of the university of Dublin (*Trinity College).

The plantation of English and Scots settlers at the beginning of the 17th cent. provided a stronghold of militant Protestantism in Ulster. In 1615 the *Irish Articles, slightly more Calvinistic than the *Thirty-nine, were promulgated, but Strafford as governor secured in 1634 the acceptance of the latter. The RC rebellion of 1641 led O. *Cromwell to set up a Protestant economic superiority a few years later, which *Charles II only partially mitigated. Meanwhile, the Church of Ireland lost the adherence of the majority to Rome, and a general spiritual decline set in, though the 17th and 18th cents. had such Bishops as John *Bramhall (1591–1663), Jeremy *Taylor (1613–67), and William King (1650–1729). Disestablishment, foreshadowed by the Church Temporalities Bill of 1833, which reduced the archbishoprics by two, and the other sees by eight, was provided for by the Act of 1869, and came into force in 1871. Since then the government of the Church has been in the hands of the General and Diocesan Synods, subject in certain matters to episcopal veto; the Diocesan Synods elect the bishops. The Prayer Book and Canons were revised in 1870–8, though the dominant Evangelical party failed to make such sweeping changes in the former as they wished.

After the Reformation, which never secured the allegiance of more than a minority of the Irish people, Catholicism retained its hold on the masses outside the pale. The repressive measures of the 17th and 18th cents. helped to consolidate its strength. The toleration promised by William III in the Treaty of Limerick (1691) was not realized. Freedom of worship was at last granted in 1791 and freedom of education in 1793; and *Maynooth College (q.v.) was founded in 1795. Finally, through the efforts of D. *O'Connell and the *Catholic Association (qq.v.), Catholic Emancipation was achieved on 13 Apr. 1829. This was followed by rapid expansion. Churches, still known as 'chapels' despite their often large proportions, were built all over the land. Since the creation of the Irish Free State in 1922, the RC Church in Southern Ireland has received strong governmental support and its rights were given further recognition in the constitution of 1937. There are now four provinces and 28 sees. The vitality of Irish Catholicism as a power in daily life is unsurpassed.

In the island as a whole (c. 1955), c. 75 per cent. of the population professes the RC faith (c. 93 per cent. of the population in the Republic and c. 33 per cent. in Northern Ireland). The main strength of Anglicanism and Presbyterianism is in Northern Ireland, where they form respectively 27 per cent. and 31 per cent. of the population. Of other Christian bodies, the most considerable are the *Methodists.

For further details see entries Dublin, Armagh; also Plunkett.

W. D. Killen, The Ecclesiastical History of Ireland from the Earliest Period to the Present Times (2 vols., 1875). H. Seddall, The Church of Ireland. A Historical Sketch (Dublin, 1886). A. Bellesheim, Geschichte der katholischen Kirche in Irland (3 vols., 1890–91; there appears to be no satisfactory history of the Church in Ireland by a RC written in English). T. Olden, The Church of Ireland [to the Disestablishment] (National Churches, 1892). W. A. Phillips (ed.), History of the Church of Ireland from the Earliest Times to the Present Day (3 vols., 1933), with detailed bibl. T. J. Johnston–J. L. Robinson–R. W. Jackson, A History of the Church of Ireland (Dublin, 1953). G. T. Stokes, Ireland and the Celtic Church. A History of Ireland from St. Patrick to the English Conquest in 1172 (1886; ed. 6 by H. J. Lawlor, 1907). J. Healy, The Ancient Irish Church (1892).

J. Heron, The Celtic Church in Ireland. The Story of Ireland and Irish Christianity from before the Time of St. Patrick to the Reformation (1892). G. T. Stokes, Ireland and the Anglo-Norman Church. A History of Ireland and Irish Christianity from the Anglo-Norman Conquest to the Dawn of the Reformation (1899). J. Ryan, Irish Monasticism. Origins and Development (1931). E. B. Fitzmaurice–A. G. Little (edd.), Materials for the History of the Franciscan Province of Ireland, A.D. 1230–1450 (British Society of Franciscan Studies, ix; 1920). C. de Smedt, S.J.–J. de Backer, S.J. (edd.), Acta Sanctorum Hiberniae ex Codice Salmanticensi (Edinburgh-London, 1888). C. Plummer (ed.), Miscellanea Hagiographica Hibernica (Subsidia Hagiographica, xv; 1925). J. F. Kenney, The Sources for the Early History of Ireland. An Introduction and a Guide, i, Ecclesiastical (Records of Civilization, New York, 1929). J. T. Ball, The Reformed Church of Ireland (1886). H. Holloway, The Reformation in Ireland. A Study of Ecclesiastical Legislation (S.P.C.K., 1919). M. V. Ronan, The Reformation in Ireland under Elizabeth, 1558–1580 (1930). A. L. Evans, The Disestablishment of the Church of Ireland in 1869 (Lancaster, Pa., 1929). H. E. Patton, Fifty Years of Disestablishment (Dublin, 1922). R. D. Edwards, Church and State in Tudor Ireland. A History of the Penal Laws against Irish Roman Catholics, 1534–1603 (1935), with bibl. J. S. Reid, History of the Presbyterian Church in Ireland . . . [to 1735] continued to the Present Time, by W. D. Killen (3 vols., Edinburgh, 1834–53; new ed. revised by D. W. Killen, 3 vols., Belfast, 1867). J. C. Beckett, Protestant Dissent in Ireland, 1687–1780 (1948). I. Grubb, Quakers in Ireland, 1654–1900 (1927). E. A. D'Alton in C.E., viii (1910), pp. 98–116, s.v. See also bibl. to Celtic Church.

IRELAND, JOHN (1761–1842), Dean of *Westminster. Having entered Oriel College, Oxford, as a Bible clerk in 1779, he became Vicar of Croydon in 1793, and succeeded W. *Vincent as Dean of Westminster in 1816. He gave large sums to the university of Oxford for classical scholarships, and in his will he founded the chair of Exegesis of the Holy Scriptures (since 1947 confined to the NT) which goes by his name, and some exhibitions at Oriel College.

E. *Hawkins, An Inaugural Lecture upon the Foundation of Dean Ireland's Professorship, read before the University of Oxford, Nov. 2, 1847, with brief notices of the Founder (1848), esp. pp. 9–12, and Appendix, pp. 45–59, with reff. to obituary notices.

IRENAEUS, St. (c. 130–c. 200), Bp. of Lyons. Relatively little is known of his life, but as he heard *Polycarp as a boy, it is generally supposed that he was a native of Smyrna. He studied at *Rome, and later became a presbyter of Lyons, in which capacity he was commissioned to take letters to Pope Eleutherus at Rome, requesting toleration for the *Montanists of Asia Minor. There is no evidence, however, to show that Irenaeus himself sympathized with the sect. During his absence fierce persecution took place at Lyons (c. 177), in which Pothinus, the bishop, was among the martyrs; and on his return (c. 178) Irenaeus succeeded to the see. In 190 he wrote to Pope *Victor on behalf of the *Quartodecimans of Asia Minor. Whether or not he met a martyr's death is uncertain. Feast-day, 28 June.

Irenaeus forms in thought and action an important link between E. and W. His chief work, the 'Adversus omnes Haereses' (Ἔλεγχος καὶ Ἀνατροπὴ τῆς Ψευδωνύμου Γνώσεως), is a detailed attack upon *Gnosticism, esp. the system of *Valentinus, and the *millenarianism popular in *Montanist circles. Part of it is preserved in Greek, but the whole text survives in a literal Latin version and sections of it are also extant in *Syriac and *Armenian. As sources Irenaeus appears to have drawn upon *Justin and *Theophilus of Antioch, and he was himself drawn upon regularly by subsequent heresiologists. Recently a second work, 'The Demonstration of the Apostolic Preaching' (Εἰς Ἐπίδειξιν τοῦ Ἀποστολικοῦ Κηρύγματος) has been discovered in an Armenian translation. It is an apologetic work, notable for its lavish use of the OT.

St. Irenaeus is the first great Catholic theologian. Unlike *Clement of Alexandria he opposed Gnosticism, not by setting up a rival Christian Gnosis, but by emphasizing the traditional elements in the Church, esp. the Episcopate, the Canon of Scripture, and, so far as such already existed, the religious and theological tradition. In his insistence on Christian Monotheism, on the unity of Father and Son in the work of Revelation and the Redemption, and on the fullness of the Incarnation of Christ he goes behind the *Apologists of the middle of the 2nd cent. to *Ignatius at its beginning. He developed a doctrine of the 'recapitulation' (ἀνακεφαλαίωσις; Lat. recapitulatio), or summary, of human evolution in the humanity of the Incarnate Christ, and thereby gave a positive value of its own to our Lord's full manhood. He also laid great stress on the co-ordinate authority of all four Gospels. See also Pfaff Fragments.

Early edd. of Adv. Haer. by D. *Erasmus (Basle, 1526), F. *Feuardent (Cologne, 1596), J. E. *Grabe (Oxford, 1702), and R. Massuet, O.S.B. (Paris, 1710). Later edd. by A. Stieren (Leipzig, 1848–53) and W. W. Harvey (Cambridge, 1857). Crit. text by F. M. M. Sagnard, O.P., in course of publication (S.C., 1952 ff.). The 'Demonstration' was first publd. by K. Ter-Mekerttschian and E. Ter-Minassiantz in T.U., Bd. 31 (i) (1907). Eng. tr. of Adv. Haer. by J. *Keble in L.F. (posthumous, 1872) and by A. Roberts and W. H. Rambaut in A.N.C.L. (2 vols., 1868–9); of chief passages in Adv. Haer. by F. M. R. Hitchcock in S.P.C.K. 'Early Christian Classics' (2 vols., 1916); of 'Demonstration' by J. A. *Robinson, with good notes, in S.P.C.K. 'Translations of Christian Literature' (1920). There is an immense modern literature. Recent studies in English include F. R. M. Hitchcock, Irenaeus of Lugdunum (1914), and J. Lawson, The Biblical Theology of St. Irenaeus (1948). Good art. by F. Vernet in D.T.C., vii (1923), cols. 2394–2533, s.v., with full bibliographies to date (esp. cols. 2407–10). For later items see Altaner (ed. 1950), pp. 111–16. On Irenaeus's Biblical text, W. *Sanday and C. H. *Turner, Novum Testamentum Sancti Irenaei (Oxford, 1923). On the Lat. vers. of Adv. Haer., S. Lundström, Studien zur lateinischen Irenäusübersetzung (Lund, 1943); id., Neue Studien zur lateinischen Irenäusübersetzung (Lund, 1948). F. M. M. Sagnard, O.P., La Gnose valentinienne et le témoignage de Saint Irénée (1947).

IRISH ARTICLES. The 104 articles of faith adopted by the Irish Episcopal Church in 1615 at its first Convocation. More definitely *Calvinistic than the *Thirty-Nine Articles of the C of E (1562), which had never been accepted in Ireland, they were apparently compiled by J. *Ussher, then head of the faculty of theology at Dublin. They teach absolute predestination and perseverance, affirm that the Pope is antichrist, and make no mention of the threefold ministry nor of the necessity of Episcopal Ordination. They remained the official statement of faith in the Church of Ireland down to 1635, when at a Convocation held under Strafford and his chaplain, J. *Bramhall, the Anglican Thirty-Nine Articles were adopted, apparently with the intention that they should replace those of 1615. Ussher, however, continued for a time to require subscription to both series, though ultimately the earlier ones became a dead letter. They seem to have exercised considerable influence on the text of the *Westminster Confession.

The text is in P. *Schaff, The Creeds of Christendom, iii, 526–44. Cf. also ib. i, § 85, pp. 662–5.

IRON CROWN, of Lombardy. A crown made for Theodelinda, widow of Authoris, King of Lombardy, and presented in 594 to the Duke of Turin, from whom it passed eventually to the recent royal house of Italy. It is of gold with an inner circlet of iron which is said to have been made from a nail of the true *Cross. It is preserved in the cathedral church of Monza.

IRVING, EDWARD (1792–1834), Scottish minister associated with the origins of the '*Catholic Apostolic Church' (q.v.). He was a native of Annan, Dumfriesshire, and educated at Edinburgh university. He was appointed master of a school at Haddington in 1810 and at Kirkcaldy in 1812. Having been licensed to preach in the Church of Scotland in 1815, he became the assistant of T. *Chalmers at Glasgow in 1819, where he had a great influence among the poorer population. In 1822 he was appointed minister of the Caledonian chapel in Hatton Garden, London, where his magnetic personality soon drew large congregations. But his merciless criticism of society and personalities later lost its attraction, and Irving then turned to *millenarian ideas. He was greatly impressed by a work of the Spanish *Jesuit, Lacunza (1816), which he translated under the title The Coming of the Messiah in Glory and Majesty (1827). This work brought Irving into contact with the circle of H. *Drummond who was devoted to eschatological speculations. In 1828 he lectured at Edinburgh on the Book of Revelation. In 1830 he was excommunicated by the London presbytery for his tract on The Orthodox and Catholic Doctrine of our Lord's Human Nature, in which he declared Christ's human nature to be sinful; but he rejected their decision and continued to minister. In 1831 disturbances of a revivalist character began to occur at the services in his church at Regent Square, from which he was finally removed in 1832. His followers now constituted themselves the 'Catholic Apostolic Church'. In 1833 he was expelled from the ministry of the Church of Scotland. After travelling for some time in Dumfriesshire he returned to London, but, surprisingly, was accorded only an inferior rank in the sect which he had helped to found and died soon afterwards.

His Collected Writings appeared in 5 vols. in 1864-5. Life by M. O. W. Oliphant (2 vols., 1862). A. L. Drummond, Edward Irving and his Circle (1938).

ISAAC, OT patriarch. His story is told in Gen. 21–8. The Divinely promised son of *Abraham and Sarah after a long childless marriage, he became the heir of the Messianic blessings (Gen. 17. 19, 21). To try Abraham's faith Jehovah asked him in sacrifice, but, satisfied with the perfect obedience of both father and son, accepted at the last moment a ram instead (Gen. 22). After Sarah's death Abraham procured a wife for Isaac from his own family, Rebecca, who became the mother of Esau and *Jacob (Gen. 24, 25). During a famine Isaac sought Abimelech, the King of the Philistines, at Gerar, where he became very rich and powerful (Gen. 26). Shortly before his death, when he wished to give Esau, his firstborn and favourite son, his paternal blessing, Rebecca frustrated his intention by a ruse and substituted Jacob (Gen. 27).

In the NT Isaac appears in Gal. 3. 16 and 4. 21–31 as a type of Christ and of the Church. He is both the son of the promise and the father of the faithful. In Heb. the sacrifice of Isaac is brought into connexion with the sacrifice of Christ (11. 17–19). This theme was developed in the Fathers, who regard his intended immolation as a type of the sacrifice of *Golgotha. Thus *Tertullian sees in Isaac carrying the wood the type of Christ carrying His Cross. St. *Cyril of Alexandria elaborates in detail the similarities between the two sacrifices, and St. *Augustine compares the ram substituted for Isaac with Christ crucified. In the Middle Ages the sacrifice of Isaac as a prefiguration of the Passion was a favourite topic of theologians. The important part which this conception has played in Christian art is shown by the paintings of the Catacombs where the representation of the scene is used as a figure of the Eucharist. See also *Abraham*.

ISAAC THE GREAT, St. (c. 350–440), 10th *Catholicos of the *Armenian Church. He was the son of St. *Nerses and a lineal descendant of St. *Gregory the Illuminator. After studying at *Constantinople he married, and then, after the early death of his wife, became a monk. He was appointed Catholicos of Armenia in 390. By gaining from Constantinople the recognition of the metropolitical rights of the Armenian Church, he terminated its long dependence on Caesarea in Cappadocia. He was also very active in fostering a national Armenian literature, translating in conjunction with St. *Mesrob much of the Bible and many other Greek works. Tradition also ascribes to him the authorship of many Armenian hymns, as well as (apparently erroneously) the Armenian Liturgy. In 425 he was deposed from his office by the Persians, but allowed later, in view of strong popular support, to regain his see. Feast days ('St. Sahak') in the Armenian Church, 9 Sept. and 25 Nov.

Three of Isaac's letters are preserved by *Moses of Chorene in his 'History of Armenia Major' (iii. 57); further letters ed. J. Izmiveantz in his 'Book of Letters' (Tiflis, 1901; in Armenian). Bardenhewer, v, pp. 195–7; Altaner (ed. 1951), p. 305. S. Vailhé in *C.E.*, viii (1910), p. 175 f., s.v.; A. Merk, S.J., in *L.Th.K.*, v (1933), col. 612, s.v.;

I. Ortiz de Urbina, S.J., in *E.C.*, x (1953), col. 1616, s.v. 'Sahak (Isaac) I'; unsigned art. in *Enciclopedia ecclesiastica*, ed. A. Bernareggi–L. Cortesi, v (1952), p. 102, s.v. 'Isaaco (Saak) I'.

ISAAC OF NINEVEH (d. *c.* 700), also 'Isaac Syrus', *Nestorian Bp. of Nineveh. He was originally a monk of Bethabe in Kurdistan who after a brief episcopate retired to a monastery at Rabban Shapur. In his later years his teaching was under a cloud, owing to its divergence from Nestorian orthodoxy. His extensive writings, mainly on ascetic subjects and all in Syriac, were translated at an early date into Arabic, Ethiopic, and Greek. Extracts from the Greek version, the work of two monks of St. *Saba, Patrick and Abraham, were publd. by Nicephorus Theotokios (Leipzig, 1770) under the title τοῦ ὁσίου πατρὸς ἡμῶν Ἰσαὰκ . . . τὰ εὑρεθέντα ἀσκητικά.

Isaac of Nineveh is often confounded with a 4th cent. Syriac writer, Isaac of Antioch (also 'Isaac the Great', but to be distinguished again from subject of previous entry), extracts from whose writings have been publd. by G. *Bickell (2 vols., 1873–7) and P. Bedjan (1903).

The Syriac text of Isaac of Nineveh is nearly all unpubld. Latin versions in J. P. Migne, *PG*, lxxxvi (1), 811–86 ('De Contemptu Mundi'). A. J. Wensinck, *Mystic Treatises of Isaac of Nineveh translated* (Amsterdam, 1923). J. B. Chabot, *De Isaaci Ninevitae Scriptis et Doctrina* (1892). A. *Baumstark, *Geschichte der syrischen Literatur* (1922), pp. 223–5.

ISABELLA OF CASTILE (1451–1504) ('la Católica'), Queen of Spain. The daughter of John II, King of Castile and Leon, she married *Ferdinand, heir to the Aragonese throne, in 1469, and on the death of Henry IV in 1474 ascended the Castilian throne. The reign of the 'Catholic Sovereigns', as she and her husband are called, laid the foundations of Spanish power and greatness. Under their aegis C. Columbus (d. 1506) made his discoveries, Granada was conquered from the Moors (1492), culture was patronized, the army modernized, and through a series of clever political moves and marriages Spain made one of the focal points of European diplomacy. A woman of strong religious principles and deep personal piety, she exercised a bracing influence at the Castilian court. She greatly assisted the efforts of Cardinal F. *Ximenes to raise the standard of the Spanish clergy, and of B. de *Las Casas to convert the American Indians. She was succeeded on the throne of Castile by her daughter, Juana la Loca ('the Insane'), but Ferdinand virtually ruled the country.

W. H. Prescott, *History of the Reign of Ferdinand and Isabella* (3 vols., '1838' [1837] and many later edd.); Lives by G. de Nervo (1874; Eng. tr. 1897) and W. T. Walsh (1931). See also bibl. to *Ferdinand V*.

ISAIAH. The Hebrew prophet of the 8th cent. B.C., the son of Amoz. He rose to great influence at the court of the kings of Judah, and took a prominent part esp. in foreign politics. Called to the prophetic office in the year of King Uzziah's death (739; Is. 6. 1), he continued his prophetic work till the Assyrian invasion of Judah in 701 B.C. Tradition relates his death by martyrdom in the reign of Manasseh (692–638).

In his teaching Isaiah followed *Amos and *Hosea in asserting the supremacy of *Jehovah, the God of Israel, and in emphasizing His moral demands on His worshippers. He laid special stress on the Divine holiness (ch. 6), giving to this conception for the first time an ethical content. From these beliefs much of his teaching on particular matters followed, e.g. his political counsels, urging Judah to keep out of foreign alliances and trust only in God; his confidence in the inviolability of *Jerusalem; and his insistence that sacrificial worship must be accompanied by spiritual effort in the participants. The names of his sons were symbolic (7. 3; 8. 3), indicating his conviction that a 'remnant' of Judah would be saved from the downfall which was awaiting those who relied on human assistance. His expectations for the future were chiefly centred in the *Messiah, and around his portrait of Him gathered the fervent hopes of successive generations of Jews. From NT times onwards the Messianic passages of Isaiah's prophecies (esp. 7. 14, 9. 6) have been consistently referred by Christian writers to the historic Christ. If Isaiah himself cannot be accredited with having foreseen the exact fulfilment of his predictions in Jesus Christ, he at least pointed the way to belief in a coming Saviour whose person and office should transcend those of any earthly ruler of the house of David. See also foll. entries.

ISAIAH, Ascension of.

A 2nd cent. composite Jewish-Christian writing. It was compiled out of earlier books, viz. the 'Martyrdom of Isaiah' (Jewish), the 'Vision of Isaiah' (Christian), and the 'Testament of Hezekiah' (Christian), and written in Greek, though in its original form it survives only in Ethiopic and (in part) in Latin. It describes the martyrdom of the prophet by being 'sawn asunder' (to which a reference is commonly seen in Heb. 11. 37), and a journey through the seven heavens during which he is shown many mysteries relating to Christ and His Church. The writing throws important light on the beliefs of a group of 2nd cent. Christians on the Trinity, the Incarnation, and the Resurrection, and is the oldest document which refers explicitly to the martyrdom of St. *Peter at Rome (iv. 3). Early reff. to the treatise occur in *Origen (*Comm. on Mt. 13. 57*), the *Apostolic Constitutions (6. 16), and *Epiphanius (*Haer.* 40. 2).

Edd. of Eth. text by A. *Dillmann (Leipzig, 1877), of Gk. fragment and Lat. texts by R. H. *Charles (London, 1900; also with Eng. tr. of Eth. and Lat. tr. of Slavonic), and of Coptic by P. Lacau in *Le Muséon*, lix (1946), pp. 453–67. Eng. tr. of 'Martyrdom of Isaiah' with introd. and notes by R. H. Charles, also in R. H. Charles (ed.), *The Apocrypha and Pseudepigrapha of the Old Testament* (1913), ii, pp. 155–62; also in S.P.C.K. series (London, 1917). L. T. Lefort, 'Coptica Lovaniensia' in *Le Muséon*, li (1938), pp. 24–32, and 'Fragments d'apocryphes en copte-akhmîmique' in ib., lii (1939), pp. 7–10. J. A. *Robinson in *H.D.B.*, ii (1899), pp. 499–501; G. Rinaldi in *E.C.*, vii (1951), col. 244, s.v. 'Isaia, V'.

ISAIAH, Book of.

Traditionally the whole Book is ascribed to *Isaiah, the son of Amoz (q.v.), but critics are now generally agreed that everything after ch. 36, as well as considerable portions of the earlier chapters, have no real claim to be his.

The Book falls naturally into four divisions: (1) Chs. 1–35. The sections which can be ascribed to Isaiah with most assurance are the greater part of chs. 1–12, 16–22, and 28–32. Apart from the Prophet's inaugural vision (6), these prophecies are chiefly bound up either with the Syro-Ephraimite War (735 B.C.) or the threatened invasion of Judah by Sennacherib of Assyria (701 B.C.). The Prophet's concern with the former was the occasion of the famous *Immanuel Prophecy (cf. Matt. 1. 22 f.). The authorship of the Messianic passages in 9. 2–7 and 11. 1–9 is open to some uncertainty. The definitely non-Isaianic items in this part of the Book include the Ode against Babylon (13. 1–14. 23), the Pronouncement of World Judgement (24–27), and the Prophecies on the Downfall of Edom and the Blessedness of God's People (34 f.). All of these would seem to be of considerably later date than the age of Isaiah.

(2) Chs. 36–39. A section taken over from 2 Kgs. 18. 13–20. 19, with the addition of the 'Song of Hezekiah' (Is. 38. 10–20).

(3) Chs. 40–55, '*Deutero-Isaiah'. The main theme is Israel's Redemption and her Mission to the World. Their purpose is to encourage the Jewish exiles in Babylon and their date is immediately prior to the release of the Jews by Cyrus in 537 B.C. This section contains the four famous '*Servant Songs' (q.v.), viz. 42. 1–4, 49. 1–6, 50. 4–9, and 52. 13–53. 12. In their lofty conception of Jehovah and the high vocation which they assign to Israel among the Gentiles, these chapters are among the most sublime in the OT.

(4) Chs. 56–66, '*Trito-Isaiah'. The chapters appear to presuppose that the *Temple had been rebuilt and hence are later than 520 B.C. While they have much in common with (3), they hardly sustain the same level of teaching, notably in their attitude towards the Gentiles, who are conceived less as summoned to join in the common worship of Jehovah than as contributing to Israel's glory and physical needs. The concluding section of the Book (63. 7–66. 24) stands apart from the rest, and is perhaps from yet another hand.

The chief Patristic Commentaries on Isaiah come from *Origen, St. *Basil, St. *Cyril of Alexandria and St. *Jerome. Of the older English works the principal is that of R. *Lowth (London, 1778). More modern commentaries include those of F. J. *Delitzsch (Biblischer Commentar über das Alte Testament, Th.3, Bd. i; 1866; Eng. tr., 2 vols., 1867), T. K. *Cheyne (2 vols., London, 1880–1), G. A. *Smith (Expositor's Bible, 2 vols., 1889–90), A. *Dillmann (Kurzgefasstes exegetisches Handbuch zum Alten Testament, v, ed. 5; 1890; rev. by R. Kittel, 1898), B. Duhm (K.H.A.T., Abteilung 3, Bd. i; 1892; ed. 3, 1922), J. Skinner (Camb. Bib., 2 vols., AV, 1896–8; RV, 1915–17), K. Marti (K.H.C., x; 1900), A. Condamin, S.J. (Études Bibliques, 1905), O. C. Whitehouse (Cent. Bib., 2 vols., 1905–8), G. H. Box (London, 1908), G. W. Wade (West. Comm., 1911), G. B. *Gray (on chs. 1–27; I.C.C., 1912), E. König (Gütersloh, 1926), and E. J. Kissane (2 vols., Dublin, 1941–3). S. R. *Driver, *Isaiah. His Life and Times* [1888]. T. K. Cheyne, *Introduction to the Book of Isaiah* (1895); id., *The Mines of*

Isaiah Re-Explored (1912). R. H. *Kennett, *The Composition of the Book of Isaiah in the Light of History and Archaeology* (Schweich Lectures for 1909; 1910). J. Lindblom, *Die Jesaja Apokalypse, Jes. 24–27* (Lunds Universitats Årsskrift, N.F., Avd. I, Bd. xxxiv, No. 3; 1938). J. A. Bruno, *Jesaja. Eine rhythmische und textkritische Untersuchung* (Stockholm, 1953). H. W. *Robinson, *The Cross of the Servant.* A Study in Deutero-Isaiah (1926). C. C. Torrey, *The Second Isaiah.* A New Interpretation (1928). K. Elliger, *Die Einheit des Tritojesaia (Jesaia 56–66)* (Beiträge zur Wissenschaft vom Alten und Neuen Testament, Folge 3, ix; 1928); id., *Deuterojesaja in seinem Verhältnis zur Tritojesaja* (ib., Folge 4, xiii; 1933). S. Smith, *Isaiah Chapters xl–lv.* Literary Criticism and History (Schweich Lectures for 1940; 1944). C. R. North, *The Suffering Servant in Deutero-Isaiah.* An Historical and Critical Study (1948). A. Neubauer–S. R. Driver, *The Fifty-Third Chapter of Isaiah according to the Jewish Interpreters* (2 vols., 1876–77; text and Eng. tr.). G. A. Smith in *H.D.B.*, ii (1899), pp. 485–99, s.v. A. Feuillet in *Dict. Bibl.*, Suppl. iv (1949), cols. 647–729, s.v. 'Isaie', with bibl. See also bibl. to *Servant Songs*.

ISCARIOT. See *Judas Iscariot*.

ISHO'DAD OF MERV (9th cent.), *Nestorian Bp. of Hedatta. He wrote commentaries on parts, at least, of the OT and on the whole of the NT, packed with quotations from earlier exegetes, e.g. *Theodore of Mopsuestia, *Ephraem Syrus ('Commentary on the *Diatessaron'), and many little-known Syriac authors. His works (all in Syriac) throw valuable light on the history of Biblical interpretation.

Comm. on Hosea, Joel, Jonah, Zach. 9–14, and, in an appendix, Pss. 16, 22, 68, 69, 72, and 45, ed., with Germ. tr., by G. Diettrich (Beihefte zur *Z.A.T.W.*, vi; 1902); Comm. on Job, ed., with Germ. tr., by J. Schliebitz (ib. xi; 1907). NT Commentaries, ed., with Eng. tr., by Margaret D. Gibson, with introd. by J. R. *Harris (Horae Semiticae, v–vii, Cambridge, 1911 [Gospels]; and x and xi, 1913–16 [Acts and three Catholic Epistles, and Epistles of St. Paul, respectively]). Comm. on Song of Sol. ed., with Germ. tr., by S. Euringen in *Oriens Christianus*, xxix (3rd Ser., vii; 1932), pp. 49–74. Commentary on OT (C.S.C.O., Scriptores Syrici, 1950 ff.) Bk. of Gen. ed. J. M. Vosté–C. van den Eynde, vol. lxvii; 1950, with full reff.). A. *Baumstark, *Geschichte der syrischen Literatur* (1922), p. 234.

ISIDORE, St. (d. *c.* 450), of Pelusium, ascetic and exegete. He early took monastic vows and was for some forty years abbot of a monastery on a hill near Pelusium on the eastern estuary of the Nile. He intervened with *Cyril of Alexandria on behalf of the memory of *Chrysostom, whose exegesis he chiefly followed, and also opposed *Nestorius. His writings also show his opposition to *Eutyches, though he seems to have died before the latter's condemnation at *Chalcedon. Of his large correspondence, which contains much of doctrinal, exegetical, and moral interest, some 2,000 items have survived.

Ed. *princeps* by J. Billius (Paris, 1585). Later edd. by C. Rittershaus (Heidelberg, 1605) and A. Schott (Antwerp, 1623; Paris, 1638). J. P. Migne, *PG.*, lxxviii. 9–1674 (repr. of text of P. Possinus, 1680). On the editions, C. H. *Turner in *J.T.S.*, vi (1904–5), pp. 70–85, and K. *Lake, ib., pp. 270–82. R. Aigrain, *Quarante-Neuf Lettres de St. Isidore de Péluse* (1911). H. A. Niemeyer, *De Isidori Pelusiotae Vita, Scriptis et Doctrina Commentatio Historico-theologica* (Halle, 1825; repr. in *PG*, lxxviii, 9–102). A. Schmid, O.S.B., *Die Christologie Isidors von Pelusium* (Paradosis 2, Fribourg, 1948). Bardenhewer, iv, pp. 100–7. G. Bareille in *D.T.C.*, viii (pt. 1; 1924), cols. 84–98.

O.D.C.C.–2 A

ISIDORE, St. (*c.* 560–636), 'Hispalensis', Abp. of Seville. Little is known of his earlier life. He belonged to a noble family of Cartagena; when the city was destroyed by the Arian Goths, his father fled to Seville where Isidore was born. After the death of his parents he was educated at a monastery under the supervision of his brother, St. *Leander, who was a monk before becoming Isidore's predecessor in the see of Seville. During these years he laid the foundations of his encyclopaedic knowledge, with the double aim of checking barbarism in Spain and defending the Catholic faith against *Arianism. He entered a monastery *c.* 589 either as a clerk or a monk, where he continued his studies. He succeeded his brother as Abp. of Seville *c.* 600. As such he devoted all his energies to the spread of Catholicism by founding schools and convents and working for the conversion of the Jews. He presided over several important Spanish Councils, notably *Toledo IV (633), the canons of which reflect his organizing abilities. He was famous for his learning, sanctity, and lavish almsgiving. He was canonized in 1598, and in 1722 was formally given the title of '*Doctor of the Church', which he had already virtually received (*nostri saeculi doctor egregius*) at the Eighth Council of Toledo (653). Feast day, 4 Apr.

His works, which have all been preserved, became a storehouse of knowledge freely utilized by innumerable medieval authors. The most important of them, the 'Etymologiae', is an encyclopaedia of the knowledge of his time, containing information on subjects such as grammar, rhetoric, mathematics, medicine, and history, as well as on the books and offices of the Church and other theological matters. The work received its name from the (frequently quite fanciful) etymological explanations of the words signifying the different subjects. The 'Sententiarum Libri Tres' is a manual of Christian doctrine and practice which draws freely on St. *Augustine and St. *Gregory the Great and became the predecessor of many similar works. 'De Ecclesiasticis Officiis' is a valuable source for the *Mozarabic liturgy as well as for the duties and rights of the various orders in the Church, from the archbishop down to lay men and women. The 'Synonyma' is a curious mixture of linguistic and doctrinal items, in which reason exhorts the soul of the sinner to be converted and aim at perfection. The 'Chronica Majora', extending from the Creation to A.D. 615, contains material borrowed from *Julius Africanus, *Eusebius, St. *Jerome, and other Fathers, and also original information on the history of Spain. The 'Historia de Regibus Gothorum, Vandalorum et Suevorum' is the principal source for the history of these peoples, esp. that of the Visigoths. His 'De Scriptoribus Ecclesiasticis' is a continuation of the similar works of Jerome and *Gennadius. For his supposed authorship of the *False Decretals, see s.v.

Editio *princeps* (incomplete and inadequate) by M. de La Bigne, in his 'Bibliotheca SS. Patrum', Paris, 1580. Of later edd. the best is that of F. Arevalo, S.J., 7 vols., Rome, 1797–1803; repr. in J. P. Migne, *PL*, lxxxi–lxxxiv. Crit. ed. of his 'Etymologiae' by W. M. Lindsay in O.C.T. (2 vols., 1911); of 'Historia Gothorum' and 'Chronica Maiora' by E. Wartz in *M.G.H.*, Auctores Antiquissimi, xi (1894), pp. 241–506; of 'De Haeresibus' by A. C. Vega, O.S.A. (Scriptores Ecclesiastici Hispano-Latini Veteris et Medii Aevi, fasc. v, The Escurial, 1935); of 'De Variis Quaestionibus', ed. id.–A. E. Anspach (ib., vi–viii; 1940). E. Bréhaut, *An Encyclopaedist of the Dark Ages, Isidore of Seville* (Columbia University Studies in History, Economics and Public Law, xlviii, No. 1; New York, 1912); C. H. Beeson, *Isidor-Studien* (Quellen und Untersuchungen zur lateinischen Philologie des Mittelalters, iv, Hft. 2; 1913); P. Séjourné, O.S.B., *Le Dernier Père de l'Église, Saint Isidore de Séville* (1929). *Miscellanea Isidoriana.* Homenaje a S. Isidoro de Sevilla en el XIII: centenario de su muerte . . . Lo edita la provincia de Andalucía S.I. (Rome, 1936). Bardenhewer, v, 401–16; Altaner (ed. 1951), pp. 446–9. Manitius, i, 52–70. G. Bareille in *D.T.C.*, viii (pt. 1; 1924), cols. 98–111, s.v.; A. Anwander in *L.Th.K.*, v (1933), cols. 626–8, s.v.; J. Madoz, S.J., in *E.C.*, vii (1951), cols. 254–8, s.v. 'Isidoro di Siviglia'; R. Naz in *D.D.C.*, vi ('1954'), cols. 66–74, s.v., all with bibl. J. Fontaine, *Isidore de Séville et la culture classique dans l'Espagne wisigothique* (2 vols., 1959). M. C. Díaz y Díaz (ed.), *Isidoriana.* Estudios sobre san Isidoro de Sevilla en el XIV centenario de su nacimiento (1961).

ISIDORE MERCATOR. The pseudonym adopted by the author of the *False Decretals (q.v.), doubtless to suggest a connexion (if not an identity) with St. *Isidore of Seville.

ISLAM (i.e. 'resignation', viz. to the Will of God), the religion founded by Mohammed (c. 570–629). Its doctrine, which is laid down in the *Koran (q.v.) and the 'Sunna', i.e. the 'customs' of the Prophet and of his immediate successors, contains Arabic, Jewish, Christian, and Gnostic elements. Its central dogma is the absolute unity of God (Allah), who has predestined all things. At several periods of history God has sent prophets, one of whom was Jesus who, acc. to Mohammedan teaching, was not the Son of God and whose crucifixion was only apparent. The last of the prophets is Mohammed. The chief of Mohammedan religious practices are confession of faith in Allah and in Mohammed, his prophet, ritual prayer, which is practised five times a day, almsgiving, fasting during the month of Ramadan, and the pilgrimage to Mecca. Islam is split up into various sects, the chief of which are the Sunnites, i.e. the orthodox Arabs and Turks who follow the teaching of the Sunna, and the Shiites, whose chief characteristic is an allegorical interpretation of the Koran, and who are restricted mainly to Persia. The spiritual aspirations of Islam have found expression chiefly in Sufism, a movement aspiring to union with God by renouncing one's personality and practising an ascetic technique.

In the beginnings of Islam Christian ideas exercised a certain influence. Its expansion in the Middle Ages and its contact with Christianity during the Crusades necessitated its theological discussion in the W., where it was dealt with e.g. by *Peter the Venerable and Raymond *Lull. Missionary activities among the Mohammedans were undertaken chiefly by the *Mendicant Orders, but with little success. In modern times they were resumed by many Protestant missionary societies as well as by the *White Fathers, esp. in N. Africa.

H. A. R. Gibb, *Mohammedanism*. An Historical Survey (1949); W. Muir, *The Life of Mahomet* (4 vols., 1858–61; abridged ed. 1923); F. Buhl, *Das Leben Mohammeds* (1930); T. W. Arnold, *The Caliphate* (1924); *The Legacy of Islam*, ed. T. W. Arnold and A. Guillaume (1931); T. W. Arnold, *The Preaching of Islam* (ed. 2., 1913); R. Levy, *An Introduction to the Sociology of Islam* (2 vols., 1933); R. A. Nicholson, *The Mystics of Islam* (1914); id., *Studies in Islamic Mysticism* (1921); H. A. R. Gibb, *Modern Trends in Islam* (Chicago, 1947); *The Encyclopaedia of Islam*, ed. M. T. Houtsma, etc. (4 vols. and suppl., 1913–38).

ISNIK. The modern name of the ancient *Nicaea, now little more than a village.

ISRAEL. The Hebrew nation, because of its descent from the Patriarch Israel (*Jacob), whose twelve sons became the heads of the twelve Israelite tribes (Gen. 49). Acc. to Gen. 32. 28, the name Israel was divinely bestowed on Jacob by an angel; and in the *J narrative of Gen. it is regularly used of Jacob from this point forward. In their history of the period of the Monarchy the Biblical writers normally applied the word (esp. in contrast to 'Judah') to the Ten Northern Tribes, i.e. those which attached themselves to Jeroboam on the death of *Solomon (933 B.C.) and were carried away to Assyria two centuries later (721 B.C.). The name is already found on the *Moabite Stone (c. 850 B.C.).

In a theological sense, the word was used of the nation, esp. in its covenant-relation to Jehovah. In the NT it was transferred to the Christian Church, considered as the new 'Israel of God' (Gal. 6. 16) which now inherits the privileges of ancient Israel.

ISSY, Articles of. The 34 articles drawn up at Issy, near Paris, in 1695 by the ecclesiastical commission charged with the examination of Mme *Guyon's works. Signed by J. B. *Bossuet, F. *Fénelon, and Mme Guyon herself, they condemn theses of the last named and implicitly certain opinions of Fénelon. They are principally directed against the *Quietist teaching on the desirability of suppressing all explicit acts of faith, e.g. in the Trinity and the Incarnation, on the uselessness of petitionary prayer, on the continuous act of contemplation in which all other religious practices are contained, on the depreciation of the exercise of the virtues and mortifications in the state of perfection, and on the idea that every Christian should aim at extraordinary states of passive prayer. On other points, e.g. the nature of passive prayer and disinterested charity, the articles are somewhat ambiguous, owing to the differences between Fénelon and Bossuet. Their publication led to a literary feud between Bossuet and Fénelon, which ended in the condemnation of 23 propositions of the latter in 1699.

Text pr. among J. B. Bossuet's *Œuvres*, xxvii (Versailles, 1817), pp. 12–22. Pourrat, iv, 257–66. R. A. Knox, *Enthusiasm* (1950), p. 341 f. A. Largent in *D.T.C.*, vi (1913), cols. 2146–50, s.v. 'Fénelon', with text of articles repr., cols. 2146–9; P. Pourrat, P.S.S., ib., xiii (pt. 1; 1936), cols. 1576–8, s.v. 'Quiétisme', with further reff. See also bibl. to *Bossuet*, *Fénelon*, *Guyon*, and *Quietism*.

ISTANBUL. See *Constantinople.*

ITALA, The (Lat. 'Italian (version)'). A name sometimes given, esp. by German scholars, to the *Old Latin (pre-*Vulgate) text of the Bible (q.v.). The term derives from a passage in St. *Augustine (*Doctr. Christ.*, ii. 22) where he commends the 'Itala' as the best 'interpretation' (i.e. version or recension) among those current in his day. In this its original context the name has been variously explained as referring to (a) the Italian branch of the Old Latin text generally as distinct from the African (e.g. by B. F. *Westcott, J. *Wordsworth); (b) the recension popular in North Italy (known regularly as 'Italia' at this period), which St. Augustine is held to have adopted under the influence of St. *Ambrose at Milan (e.g. by F. J. A. *Hort); and (c) St. *Jerome's Vulgate, of which the Gospels at least were published in Italy (F. C. *Burkitt).

F. C. Burkitt, *The Old Latin and the Itala* (Texts and Studies, ed. J. A. *Robinson, IV, No. 3; 1896), pp. 55–78; id., 'St. Augustine's Bible and the *Itala*' in *J.T.S.*, xi (1910), pp. 258–68 and 447–58. L. Ziegler, *Die lateinischen Bibelübersetzungen vor Hieronymus und die Itala des Augustinus* (1879).

ITALO-GREEKS. The extant Greek communities descended from (1) Greek settlements in Sicily and S. Italy in Byzantine times, (2) later Greek colonies established in Italian seaports, and (3) Greek and Albanian refugees from the Moslem invasion. Their ecclesiastical status is *Uniat, their rite and usages being *Byzantine with some Roman modifications. The abbey of Grottaferrata is an Italo-Greek monastery.

ITE, MISSA EST. The formula of dismissal, and original conclusion, of the Roman Mass. The word *missa* is the low Latin form of *missio*, 'dismissal', and the meaning of the formula is 'Go, you are dismissed.' This dismissal is now used only in Masses at which the *Gloria in excelsis is recited. See also *Mass.*

T. Michels, O.S.B., *Ite Missa Est. Deo Gratias* (Per Hanc Lucis Viam, viii, Salzburg, 1929). F. Dölger, 'Zu den Zeremonien der Messliturgie. III. *Ite missa est* in kulturund sprachgeschichtlicher Beleuchtung' in *Antike und Christentum*, vi (1940), pp. 81–132. J. A. Jungmann, S.J., *Missarum Sollemnia*, ii (ed. 2, Vienna, 1949), pp. 524–9, with reff.

ITINERARIUM. A brief office now included in the *Breviary and prescribed for recitation by clerics about to set out on a journey. The prayers and the use of the *Benedictus (Lk. 1. 68–79) suggest that it originated in a blessing of pilgrims setting out for the Holy Places in Palestine.

IVES, St. (? 7th cent.). Traditionally, a British bishop of Persian birth. Acc. to the legend of *Goscelin, he came to Great Britain from Persia via Rome, and with three companions preached Christianity in Huntingdonshire. His alleged bones were discovered at St. Ives in that county in 1001. He is commemorated on 24 Apr. and 10 June. The town of St. Ives in Cornwall seems to be named after another saint (a maiden, also known as St. Ia, Hia, or Iva) of whom the extant legends seem equally unhistorical. Her feast day is 1 Feb.

The account by Goscelin is pr. in *AA.SS.*, Jun. II (1698), pp. 288–92. Hardy, i (pt. 1; 1862), pp. 184–6, for further sources. G. H. Doble, 'St. Ivo, Bishop and Confessor, Patron of the Town of St. Ives', in *Laudate*, xii (1934), pp. 149–56. C. Hole in *D.C.B.*, iii (1882), p. 324 f., s.v. 'Ivo, St.' On the Saint after whom St. Ives in Cornwall is named, see *AA.SS.*, Oct. XII (1867), pp. 293–6, with reff.; G. H. Doble, *Saint Euny . . . with St. Ya and St. Erc* (Cornish Saints Series 2; c. 1924), pp. 18–23; L. Gougaud, O.S.B., *Les Saints irlandais hors d'Irlande* (Bibliothèque de la Revue d'Histoire ecclésiastique, xvi; 1934), p. 83 f. C. W. Boase in *D.C.B.*, iii (1882), p. 23, s.v. 'Hia'.

IVO, St. (c. 1040–1116), Bp. of *Chartres (hence **Carnotensis**). Educated at Paris and (under *Lanfranc) at *Bec, he became prior of the *canons regular of St.-Quentin at Beauvais c. 1078 and Bp. of Chartres in 1090. His courageous opposition to the adulterous intentions of King Philip I led to his imprisonment in 1092. The most learned canonist of his age, his three treatises, the *Collectio Tripartita*, the *Decretum* (in 17 books), and esp. the *Panormia* (in 8 books), exercised a determining influence on the development of canon law. Special importance attaches to the principles of the interpretation of canon law, laid down in the 'Prologus' to the *Decretum*, and to his teaching on dispensation. A large collection of his letters has survived which throws much light on the ecclesiastical and religious issues of his age, as well as 24 of his sermons. In the *Investiture struggle, in which he took a prominent part, he advocated moderation. Feast day, 20 or 23 May.

The *Panormia* was first pr. [ed. S. Brant] at Basle, 1499; the *Decretum*, ed. J. Molin, at Louvain, 1561; the *Collectio Tripartita* has not been publd.; cf. A. Theiner repr. in J. P. Migne, *PL*, clxi, li–lxxxviii. Collected ed. of his other works by J. Fronteau, with brief life (no pagination), Paris, 1647; repr., with further notes, in J. P. Migne, *PL*, clxi and clxii. Crit. ed. of his correspondence, with Fr. tr., by J. Leclercq, O.S.B. (Les Classiques de l'histoire de France en moyen-âge publiés sous la direction de Louis Halphen et sous les auspices de l'Association Guillaume Budé; Paris, 1949 ff.). [A.] Esmein, 'La Question des investitures dans les lettres d'Yves de Chartres' in *Bibliothèque de l'École des Hautes Études. Sciences religieuses*, i (1889), pp. 139–78. P. Fournier, 'Les Collections canoniques attribuées à Yves de Chartres' in *Bibliothèque de l'École des Chartes*, lvii (1896), pp. 645–98, lviii (1897), pp. 26–77, 410–44, 624–76; id., 'Yves de Chartres et le droit canonique' in *R.Q.H.*, lxiii (1898), pp. 51–98, 384–405; L. Schmidt, *Der hl. Ivo, Bischof von Chartres* (Studien und Mitteilungen aus dem kirchengeschichtlichen Seminar der theologischen Fakultät der k.k. Universität in Wien, vii; 1911); P. Fournier-G. Le Bras, *Histoire des collections canoniques en occident*, ii (1932), pp. 55–114. F. P. Bliemetzrieder, *Zu den Schriften Ivos von Chartres. Ein literargeschichtlicher Beitrag* (*Sb.* (Wien), lxxxii, Abt. 6; 1917). G. *Morin, O.S.B., 'Rainauld l'Érémite et Ives de Chartres. Un épisode de la crise du cénobitisme au XIe–XIIe siècle' in *R. Bén.*, xl (1928), pp. 99–115. É. Amann–L. Guizard in *D.T.C.*, xv (pt. 2; 1950), cols. 3625–40, s.v. 'Yves de Chartres', with full reff. (but confuses with the later Master Ivo of Chartres, the author of the gloss on the Psalms; cf. Beryl Smalley in *E.H.R.*, l (1935), pp. 680–6).

J

J. The name given (since the work of J. *Wellhausen) to the Jahvistic (Yahwistic or Jehovistic) source held to be embodied in the *Pentateuch. It consists largely of narrative, beginning with the story of *Adam and *Eve (Gen. 2. 4 ff.) and including, in conjunction with 'E' (q.v.), most of the famous stories of the Patriarchs and the Exodus. It is distinguished from the later sources, 'D' and 'P' (qq.v.), by its simple narrative style and relatively primitive ideas (e.g. Gen. 3. 8), and from 'E' (and also from 'P') by its use of the divine name *Jehovah (Yahweh; 'the LORD' in AV and RV) from the first, even before its revelation to Moses in Ex. 3. 14 f. Where this criterion is absent, 'J' cannot always be certainly distinguished from 'E', with which it was probably combined in one cycle of stories before the date of 'D' (7th cent. B.C.). It is commonly dated under the early monarchy (9th cent. B.C.) but it is increasingly recognized that as a cycle of traditional stories it cannot be dated precisely, as can a document by a single author.

JABNEH, Synod of. See *Jamnia, Synod of.*

JACKSON, THOMAS (1579–1640), *Anglican theologian. He was educated at Queen's and Corpus Christi Colleges, Oxford, and resided at Oxford for several years studying and teaching theology. Presentation to the living of St. Nicholas, Newcastle-on-Tyne, in 1623 did not seriously interrupt his work at Oxford. In 1630 he became president of Corpus, largely through W. *Laud's influence, and in 1639 Dean of *Peterborough. Originally of *Puritan sympathies, he later became a member of the *High Church school, and his great learning and theological ability made him one of the most widely esteemed of Caroline divines down to the middle of the 19th cent. His principal work, *Commentaries upon the Apostles' Creed*, was arranged in twelve Books, of which nine had appeared before his death (1613–38). The first complete edition of all 12 books was in his *Collected Works* (3 vols., 1672–3). Jackson was also the author of several volumes of sermons and of a tract against the Puritans.

The last collected edition of Jackson's works was issued at Oxford (12 vols., 1844). E. T. Bradley in *D.N.B.*, xxix (1892), p. 107 f.

JACOB, Hebrew patriarch. He was the son of *Isaac and the grandson of *Abraham (Gen. 25–49 passim). After depriving his brother Esau of his birthright, Jacob fled to his kinsman Laban, whose two daughters, Leah and Rachel, he took to wife. His twelve sons were the ancestors of the twelve tribes of the Hebrew people. At *Bethel he received a

vision and blessing which was one of the outstanding events in early Hebrew history, and at Peniel wrestled with a mysterious Divine stranger and received the Divinely given name '*Israel'. Acc. to tradition, the stone of *Scone beneath the sovereign's coronation chair in *Westminster Abbey is that which served as Jacob's pillow at Bethel (Gen. 28. 11, 18).

JACOB BARADAEUS (*c.* 500–578) (Βαραδαῖος), reputed founder of the *Jacobites. A native of Tella, he was educated in the monastery of Phesilta, near Nisibis. *C.* 528 he went to *Constantinople with a fellow-monk, Sergius, to plead the cause of *Monophysitism with the Empress, and remained here in a monastery for fifteen years until he was consecrated Bp. of *Edessa *c.* 542. Disguised as a beggar to prevent arrest (hence his nickname Baradai or 'ragged'), he wandered about for the rest of his life from Egypt to the Euphrates, preaching and founding independent Monophysite churches. A Life of him has come down, attributed (apparently wrongly) to John of Ephesus (d. 586). See also *Jacobites.*

The Syriac 'Vita Baradaei' ascribed to John of Ephesus was ed. by J. P. N. Land, *Anecdota Syriaca*, ii (Leyden, 1862–75), pp. 364–83. For a 7th cent. revision and expansion of the text, with mention of the removal of the bones of Jacob in A.D. 622, see M. A. Kugener in *Revue de l'Orient chrétien*, vii (1902), pp. 196–217 (with tr.). E. Venables in *D.C.B.*, iii (1882), pp. 328–32, s.v. 'Jacobus (15)'.

JACOB OF EDESSA (*c.* 640–708), *Monophysite Syrian scholar and exegete. *C.* 684 he became Bp. of *Edessa, but after less than five years he withdrew from his see on account of practical difficulties and lived mainly in monasteries at Kaisûm and Tell-Adda. For his range and depth of learning, he has been described as the '*Jerome' of the Syrian Monophysites. He knew Greek and Hebrew and undertook the revision of the *Peshitta text of the OT on the basis of the *Hexapla. His own writings include a treatise on grammar, a continuation of *Eusebius' Chronicle down to A.D. 692, a 'Hexaemeron' (completed by *George, Bp. of the Arabians), and many scholia on the Bible. He also translated and annotated some of the works of *Severus of Antioch, including his hymns and his Ὁμιλίαι ἐπιθρόνιοι. Of his many letters on liturgical and other subjects, only a small proportion have survived.

His principal writings (many still unpubld.) are listed in A. *Baumstark, *Geschichte der syrischen Literatur* (1922), pp. 248–56, with notes of edd. to date. Crit. ed. of his 'Hexaemeron' by I. B. Chabot–A. Vaschalde (C.S.C.O., A. Vaschalde, ib., 1932); also of his tr. of the hymns of Scriptores Syri, Series Secunda, lvi; 1928; with Lat. tr. by Severus of Antioch and others, with Eng. tr., by E. W. Brooks in *P.O.*, vi (1911), pp. 5–179 (fasc. 1); vii (1911), pp. 592–805 (fasc. 5); for edd. of his tr. of Severus's Ὁμιλίαι ἐπιθρόνιοι, see s.v. *Severus of Antioch.* C. J. Ball in *D.C.B.*, iii (1882), pp. 332–5, s.v. 'Jacobus (24) Edessenus'; F. E. Gigot in *C.E.*, viii (1910), p. 277 f., s.v. 'James of Edessa', with bibl.; E. Tisserant in *D.T.C.*, viii (pt. 1; 1924), cols. 286–91, s.v.; A. Rücker in *Th.L.K.*, v (1933), cols. 257–9, s.v., with useful collection of reff. and bibl.

JACOB OF NISIBIS, St. (early 4th cent.),

the 'Moses of Mesopotamia', Bp. of Nisibis. He was always a prominent figure in Syriac Church tradition, and in later times acquired a reputation for great learning, ability, and holiness; but beyond his presence at the Council of *Nicaea (325), where acc. to *Theodoret he took a leading part in the debates, little about him is beyond dispute. He is said to have suffered in the persecution under *Maximin and to have been a keen champion of orthodoxy against *Arius, so that (acc. to an interpolated passage in Theodoret's *Religiosa Historia*) when *Constantine ordered Alexander, Bp. of *Constantinople, to receive Arius back to communion in 336, Jacob persuaded the people to seven days' fast and prayer which was answered by the sudden death of the heresiarch. He is also said to have intervened in the deliverance of Nisibis from the Persians under Sapor II in 338 and again, this time by the miraculous circumvention of the Persian stratagem of a dam across the Mygdon, in 350. He is still honoured, esp. as a theological doctor, by both *Syrians and *Armenians. His relics, saved from the oncoming Persians, finally reached Constantinople *c.* 970. The belief of many older scholars, following N. Antonelli, that Jacob was the author of certain writings traditionally ascribed to *Aphraates has been abandoned. *Abraham Ecchellensis wrongly ascribes to him 84 spurious Arabic Nicene canons. Feast day, 15 July.

*Gennadius, *De Viris Illustribus*, i [*PL*, lviii, 1060 f.; ascribing to Jacob certain works of Aphraates]. P. Peeters, S.J., 'La Légende de saint Jacques de Nisibe' in *Anal. Boll.*, xxxviii (1920), pp. 285–373. Bardenhewer, iv, p. 327 f. (on Aphraates). E. Venables in *D.C.B.*, iii (1882), pp. 325–7, s.v. 'Jacobus (4)'; E. Tisserant in *D.T.C.*, viii (pt. 1; 1924), pp. 292–5, s.v. 'Jacques de Nisibe'.

JACOB OF SARUG (451–521), Syriac

ecclesiastical writer. After education at *Edessa, he was ordained to the priesthood, and during the severe sufferings of his countrymen at the hands of the Persians, did much to encourage his people. In 519 he became Bp. of Batnae, the chief town of Sarug in Osrhoene, but died shortly afterwards. His principal writing was a long series of metrical homilies, most of them on Biblical themes and written in a dodecasyllabic metre, which earned him the title of 'The Flute of the Holy Ghost'. He was also the author of hymns and a large correspondence. His contemporaries considered him orthodox, but his letters to the monks of the monastery of Mar-Bassus, near Apamea, indicate that he was a *Monophysite. Most of his works are rather inaccessible, and many of them still unpublished.

Homiliae Selectae Mar Iacobi Sarugensis, ed. P. Bedjan (5 vols., Paris, 1905–10; Syr. text only). *Epp.* ed. G. Olinder in *C.S.C.O.* (1937). S. Euringer, *Die äthiopischen Anaphoren . . . des hl. Jacobus von Sarug (Orientalia Christiana,*

xxxiii, No. 1 (1934), pp. 79–122). P. Peeters, S.J., 'Jacques de Saroug, appartient-il à la secte monophysite? [No!]' in *Anal. Boll.*, lxvi (1948), pp. 134–98. A. *Baumstark, *Geschichte der syrischen Literatur* (1922), pp. 148–58, with full bibl. and acct. of unpubld. material. C. J. Ball in *D.C.B.*, iii (1882), p. 327 f., s.v. 'Jacobus Sarugensis'. E. Tisserant in *D.T.C.*, viii (pt. 1; 1924), s.v. 'Jacques de Saroug', cols. 300–5, with bibl.

JACOB OF VORAGINE (*c.* 1230–*c.* 1298),

Abp. of Genoa and author of the '*Golden Legend' (q.v.). Born at the village of Varazze, nr. Genoa, he entered the *Dominican Order in 1244, and devoted himself assiduously to preaching and teaching. From 1267 to 1285 he was Provincial of Lombardy. In 1288 he was commissioned by Nicholas IV (Pope, 1288–92) to free the Genoese from the ban imposed on his compatriots for aiding the Sicilians against Charles II of Naples. In 1292 he was persuaded, with much difficulty, to accept the Archbishopric of Genoa. After his death a cultus grew up, which was ratified by *Pius VII in 1816.

Jacob was also the author of (1) *Chronicon Genuense*, a chronicle of the history of Genoa (said to have been founded by Janus, the first King of Italy) down to 1296, part of which is of great value for local history; (2) Sermons for the ecclesiastical year; (3) *Defensorium contra Impugnantes Fratres Praedicatores*; and (4) *Summa Virtutum et Vitiorum Guillelmi Peraldi*, a Dominican who died *c.* 1250.

Early pr. edd. of his Sermons include 'Sermones Quadragesimales', Brixen, 1483; 'Sermones Dominicales', no place, 1484; 'Sermones de Sanctis', no place, 1484, and Augsburg, 1484; 'Sermones de Tempore', Brixen, 1491; and 'Mariale', Venice, 1497; frequent later edd. 'Chronicon Genuense', pr. by L. A. *Muratori, *Rerum Italicarum Scriptores*, ix (Milan, 1726), cols. 2–56; modern ed., with full introd. and notes, by G. Monleone (R. Instituto Storico Italiano per il Medio Evo. Fonti per la storia d' Italia [lxxxiv–lxxxvi]; 1941). M. de Waresquiel, *Le Bienheureux Jacques de Voragine* (1902). E. C. Richardson, *Materials for a Life of Jacopo da Varagine* (New York, 1935). Quétif-Echard, i, 454–9. J. Baudot in *D.T.C.*, viii (pt. 1; 1924), cols. 310–13, s.v. 'Jacques de Voragine'; A. Zimmermann, O.S.B., in *L.Th.K.*, v (1933), col. 265; Maria Sticco in *E.C.*, vi (1951), col. 332 f., s.v. 'Giacomo da Varazze'. See also bibl. to *Golden Legend*.

JACOBINS.

A name given originally to the *Dominican friars in France, from the fact that their first house in the north of France was established at Paris in 1218 in the rue St.-Jacques. In 1789 this house was acquired by the revolutionary political club which thence assumed the name Jacobins.

JACOBITES.

The body of Syrian *Monophysites who rejected the teaching of the Council of *Chalcedon (451) on the Person of Christ. They take their name from *Jacob Baradaeus (q.v.), through whose labours they became the national Church of Syria, though the title 'Jacobites' is not met with till the synodal decree of the Second Council of *Nicaea in 787. Imperial persecution could not repress Jacob's work and bring them back to Orthodoxy and they were encouraged by the vigorous enthusiasm of their monks. After the conquest of Syria by the Arabs (c. A.D. 640), however, many Jacobites became Moslems, and in later times internal divisions caused their numbers to diminish. Still more recently many have seceded to the RC Church, which was established in Syria in 1662. The highest estimate of their present numbers puts them at under 200,000, their chief ecclesiastical official, who is entitled the Patriarch of Antioch, living at Homs. (anc. Emesa) in Syria. Their liturgy, the 'Syriac St. James', is of an Antiochene type. One of their customs is to make the sign of the Cross with one finger to express their belief in the one nature of Christ. The term 'Jacobites' is also used in a wider sense to cover the Monophysite Christians in Egypt.

A. *Fortescue, The Lesser Eastern Churches (1913), pp. 323-52; D. Attwater, The Dissident Eastern Churches (Milwaukee, Wisc. [1937], pp. 269-90. J. Lebon, Le Monophysisme sévérien (1909). A. *Baumstark, Geschichte der syrischen Literatur (1922), pp. 139-93. W. de Vries in E.C., vi (1951), cols. 313-16, s.v. 'Giacobiti'.

JACOBSON, WILLIAM (1803-84), Bp. of *Chester. After being brought up a Nonconformist, he was elected a scholar of Lincoln College, Oxford, in 1825 and held various other appointments in Oxford, until he became Regius professor of divinity in 1848. In 1865 he was appointed Bp. of Chester. One of the more learned patristic scholars of his day, he issued a scholarly edition of the Apostolic Fathers (Patres Apostolici, 2 vols., 1838, and later edns.) based on a study of the MSS., in which against W. *Cureton he upheld the genuineness of the now generally acknowledged seven Epistles of St. *Ignatius. He also published an edition of the writings of R. *Sanderson, Bp. of *Lincoln (6 vols., 1854). Theologically, from his undergraduate days onwards, he was a moderate High Churchman.

For a good sketch of him as 'The Single-Minded Bishop' see J. W. *Burgon, Lives of Twelve Good Men (1888), ii, 238-303. W. Hunt in D.N.B., xxix (1892), p. 124 f.

JACOBUS. See Jacob, and also James.

JACOPONE DA TODI (Jacopo Benedetti) (c. 1230-1306), *Franciscan poet. The relatively late date of the records raises some uncertainty about the facts of his life, but the following account seems probable. After studying law, perhaps at *Bologna, and living for some years a worldly life, he was converted on the death of his wife in 1268 and scandalized his friends by becoming a 'Christian Diogenes'. C. 1278 he became a Franciscan lay-brother and in 1294 he and some of his brethren were granted permission by *Celestine V to live in a separate community, in order to observe the rule of the order in its original strictness. This decision, however, was reversed by *Boniface VIII on his accession in 1298, and Jacopone as one of the *Spirituals was imprisoned till 1303. He wrote many exquisite and deeply devotional poems (Laude) in Latin and in the Umbrian dialect, which became widely popular, among them (probably) the *Stabat Mater. His outstanding austerities and the fame of his

mystical poems would probably have induced his canonization but for his satirical attacks upon Boniface VIII. There is a local cultus at Todi. Feast day, 25 Dec.

Editio princeps of the 'Laude' by F. Bonaccorsi (Florence, 1490); crit. modern ed. by B. Brugnoli (Florence, 1914); first ed. repr., with introd., by G. Ferri (Rome, 1910; also, without the introd., in the series 'Scrittori d' Italia', Bari, 1915) and G. *Papini ('Il Libri della fede', vi; Florence [c. 1923]). Italian text with Eng. tr. of a selection by Mrs Theodore Beck appended to E. *Underhill, Jacopone da Todi, Poet and Mystic (1919), pp. 249-501. A 15th cent. MS. of his life has been publd. by A. Tobler in the Zeitschrift für romanische Philologie, ii (1878), pp. 25-39; for details in the chronicle of J. Oddi (d. 1488) and other sources, see bibl. to article by L. Oliger, O.F.M., cited below. In English, besides the admirable study of E. Underhill, cited above, there is an essay by E. G. Gardner, 'The Poet of the Franciscan Movement. Fra Jacopone da Todi', in The Constructive Quarterly, ii (1914), pp. 446-60. The many other studies include A. d' Ancona, Jacopone de Todi, il Giullare di Dio del secolo XIII (Todi, 1914), and J. Pacheu, Jacopone de Todi (Paris, 1914), with Fr. tr. of selection of 'Laude'. Raby, pp. 429-39 and 484 (bibl.). L. Oliger, O.F.M., in C.E., viii (1910), pp. 263-5, s.v.

JAHWEH. See Yahweh and Jehovah.

JAIRUS. A Galilaean 'ruler of the synagogue' (ἀρχισυνάγωγος) whose young daughter Christ restored to life (Mk. 5. 21-43).

JAMES. The Eng. form (cf. Ital. Giacomo, etc.) of Lat. Jacobus, Gk. Ἰάκωβος, representing the Heb. name which is transliterated directly into Eng. as 'Jacob'. 'James' in the English NT thus represents the same Heb. or Aramaic name as 'Jacob' in OT and elsewhere.

JAMES, St., 'the Lord's brother' (Mk. 6. 3, &c., 1 Cor. 15. 7; cf. Acts 1. 14). He was a leader, with St. *Peter, of the Church at *Jerusalem from a very early date, and continued to be its president and 'bishop' (cf. Gal. 1. 19-2. 12, Acts 12. 17, 15. 13, &c.) until put to death by the Sanhedrin in 62. The NT permits the supposition that he was the son of the BVM and *Joseph (but see Brethren of the Lord). Tradition identifies him with the son of Alphaeus known as St. *James 'the Less'. Among Judaistic Christians, he was held in high repute, and *Hegesippus tells stories of his sanctity. The (fictitious) '*Clementine Homilies' and 'Recognitions', probably 3rd cent. Judaistic writings, purport to be addressed to him, while he is represented also as the author of the apocryphal Infancy Gospel known as the Book of *James. See also James, Epistle of St.; James, Liturgy of St.; Jung Codex.

W. Patrick, James, the Lord's Brother (1906). See also bibl. to Brethren of the Lord.

JAMES, St., 'the Great', Apostle. He was a son of Zebedee, elder brother of St. *John, and with St. *Peter and St. John belonged to the privileged group of disciples who were present at the *Transfiguration and the Agony in *Gethsemane. Because of their ardent zeal (cf. Lk. 9. 49 and 54 and Mk. 10. 37) James and John were named 'Boanerges', i.e. 'sons of thunder' (Mk. 3. 17) by the Lord. St.

James was the first of the Twelve to suffer martyrdom, being beheaded by *Herod Agrippa I in A.D. 44 (Acts 12. 2). Since the 7th cent. it has been alleged that before his martyrdom he preached in *Spain, but the tradition of the early Church, acc. to which the Apostles did not leave Jerusalem till after his death, as well as Rom. 15. 20 and 24, are against the authenticity of this story which is now almost universally abandoned. Acc. to an old Spanish tradition the body of St. James was translated to Santiago de *Compostela (q.v.). In the Middle Ages St. James was one of the most popular Spanish saints, whose patronage was invoked esp. against the Mohammedans. Feast day, 25 July.

AA.SS., Jul. VI (1729), 5–124. Gk. text of his acta (prob. 8th cent.) ed. J. Ebersolt (Paris, 1902). J. B. Mayor in H.D.B., ii (1899), p. 540 f., s.v.; H. *Leclercq, O.S.B., in D.A.C.L., vii (pt. 2; 1927), cols. 2089–109), s.v. 'Jacques le Majeur'; also id., v (pt. 1; 1922), cols. 412–17, s.v. 'Espagne, v; La Légende de Jacques'; A. Wikenhauser in L.Th.K., v (1933), col. 268 f., s.v. 'Jakobus der Ältere'.

JAMES, St., 'the Less', one of the Twelve Apostles and the son of Alphaeus (Mk. 3. 18 &c.). Unless (as is unlikely) the tradition which identifies him with '*James, the Lord's brother' is correct, nothing further is known of him. There are no sufficient reasons for supposing him to be the 'James the less (Gk. ὁ μικρός) referred to in Mk. 15. 40. Feast day, with the Apostle St. *Philip, 1 May.

JAMES, Book of. An apocryphal *Infancy Gospel, apparently compiled by a Jewish Christian from a variety of sources, including the canonical Gospels of Mk. and Lk. Since the 16th cent. it has also been known as the '*Protevangelium'. It consists in the main of a highly embellished version of the account of the events connected with Christ's birth as related in Lk. 1 f. The Book, which professes to be by *James (the Apostle), was probably known to *Justin Martyr, still more probably to *Clement of Alexandria, and certainly to *Origen; and seems to date from the middle of the 2nd cent. It survives in its original Greek, and in several oriental translations incl. Syriac, and in Lat. adaptations. In the Middle Ages its legends about the BVM became popular subjects with artists. It is here that the names of the BVM's parents, *Joachim and *Anna, occur for the first time.

Gk. text in C. *Tischendorf, Evangelia Apocrypha (ed. 2, 1876), pp. 1–50. É. Amann, Le Protévangile de Jacques et ses remaniements latins. Introduction, textes, traductions et commentaires (1910). Eng. tr. in M. R. James, The Apocryphal New Testament (1924), pp. 38–49. On the Lat. workings over of the text, see also M. R. James, Latin Infancy Gospels (1927), who prints those found in MSS Hereford O.3.9, and Brit. Mus., Arundel 404. Bardenhewer, i, 533–7; Altaner (ed. 1951), p. 50 f. P. de Ambroggi in E.C., vi (1951), col. 321 f., s.v. 'Giacomo, IV'.

JAMES, Epistle of St. This NT Book, in the form of an Ep. of 'James, a servant of God and of the Lord Jesus Christ, to the twelve tribes of the Diaspora' (1. 1), stands first among the '*Catholic Epistles'. In a bold paradox the writer opens by insisting on the joy which temptation brings, since by enduring it with prayer a man 'shall receive the crown of life' (1. 2–12); the sins into which he falls, however, are not to be imputed to God (1. 13–15), Who is the author of all good gifts (1. 17 f.). We must, as His creatures, be rightly disposed to receive the Word, not being mere hearers (1. 22 f.); the test of religion is its practical manifestations (1. 27). Subservience to the rich and despising the poor are fundamentally opposed to the Christian ethic (2. 1–13). To make profession of faith which does not issue in works is valueless (2. 14–25). Wisdom requires strict control of the tongue, which, though of divine origin, may issue in great evil (3. 1–12); when wisdom comes from God it manifests itself in peaceableness (3. 13–18). The lustful, the proud, those who do not resist the devil, the censorious, and the presumptuous are never close to God (4. 1–17). The rich are warned of their fate (5. 1–6); patience, as exemplified in *Job, is commended (5. 7–11); oaths are disallowed (5. 12); and *Unction is recommended for the sick (5. 13–18), together with mutual confession of sins (5. 16). Finally, to convert a man from error is to save one's own soul (5. 18 f.).

The Epistle, written in a clear forceful style, using good Greek, is almost entirely moral in content; it seeks to encourage its recipients to endure their trials patiently and to inculcate the primary duties of a righteous life. Its expressions are striking and the writer passes from one thought to another so rapidly as to defy attempts to summarize his argument. Apart from two verses (1. 1 and 2. 11) there is nothing uncontestably Christian in it and it has been argued by F. *Spitta that the work is a revision of a Jewish writing; but the close parallels to the *Sermon on the Mount and other of the Lord's teachings make this theory unlikely. J. H. *Moulton's suggestion that the absence of Christian reference was due to its being addressed to unconverted Jews seems equally improbable. It is, however, unlikely that it was addressed to any particular community.

The traditional view that the author was St. James the Lord's brother has to face the difficulty that the Epistle presupposes a good Greek culture; the suggestion that it is a translation from an original Aramaic is unlikely on stylistic grounds. Also, if (as seems prob.) the passage in 2. 14–26 is directed against a misuse of St. *Paul's doctrine of justification by faith, the Epistle must have been written after A.D. 60 and St. James died in 62. Other arguments urged against the traditional authorship are the absence of reference in the *Muratorian fragment and any other 2nd-cent. writing, the doubts of *Origen and *Eusebius, and the fact that it stands apart from the Judaizing controversy in the 1st cent. in which St. James was the central figure. None of these objections, however, is quite conclusive. There remain the close parallels with the speech of St. James recorded in Acts 15; and the most natural interpretation of 'James' (alone) is the Lord's

Brother, though this may have been a later ascription. Even if the Epistle is not the work of St. James, it seems likely that it was composed before A.D. 95. Some scholars (e.g. J. B. Mayor), impressed by its primitive nature, argue for a date c. A.D. 40. At any rate it is not later than 150. It is first mentioned by Origen and its canonicity seems to have been accepted in the East soon afterwards. In the West it was known in the mid-4th cent. and recognized at the Council of *Hippo of 393. It was translated into Syriac as part of the *Peshitta in the early 5th cent. In modern times the Epistle was disliked by M. *Luther ('a right strawy epistle') and has generally been little valued by orthodox *Protestants.

Modern commentaries by J. B. Mayor (London, 1892; with full bibl.), R. J. Knowling (West. Comm., 1904), W. O. E. Oesterley (Expositor's Gk. Test., 1910), H. Windisch (Hb. N.T., iv, Hft. 2, 1911; on the Catholic Epistles, ed. 2, xv, 1930, pp. 1-36), J. Moffatt (Moff. Comm., with other General Epistles, 1928; pp. 6-83), J. Chaîne (Études Bibliques, 1927). F. J. A. *Hort (as far as Jas. 4. 7, posthumous, London, 1909). R. St. J. Parry, *A Discussion of the General Epistle of St. James* (1903). H. M. Smith, *The Epistle of St. James* (1914). G. H. Rendall, *The Epistle of James and Judaic Christianity* (1927). A. Meyer, *Das Rätsel des Jacobusbriefes* (Beihefte zur Z.N.T.W., x; 1930). A. T. Cadoux, *The Thought of St. James* (1944). G. Kittel, 'Der geschichtliche Ort des Jakobusbriefes' in *Z.N.T.W.*, xli (1942), pp. 71-105. J. B. Mayor in *H.D.B.*, ii (1899), pp. 543-8; W. Montgomery in *D.A.C.* i (1915), pp. 629-33. J. Bonsirven, S.J., in *Dict. Bibl.*, Suppl. iv (1949), cols. 783-95.

JAMES, Liturgy of St. This ancient liturgy, extant in a Greek and a Syriac form, is traditionally ascribed to St. *James, the Lord's brother and the first Bp. of *Jerusalem. It has many points of contact with the liturgy known to St. *Cyril, Bp. of Jerusalem (d. 386) and contains an apparent reference to the discovery of the true cross at Jerusalem in A.D. 326. It came to be much used in the *Syriac, *Armenian, and *Georgian speaking parts of the Church. Its use by the Syrian *Jacobites (who separated from Orthodoxy in 451), after the Council of *Chalcedon as well as by the Orthodox themselves, proves that it cannot be later than the middle of the 5th cent. By the latter it is now celebrated at Žante on 23 Oct. (acc. to the E. Church, the day of St. James' death) and at Jerusalem on the Sunday after Christmas.

Text in Brightman, *L.E.W.*, pp. 31-68 [Gk. text]; 69-110 [Syr. text]. Crit. text with Lat. tr., ed. B. C. Mercier, O.S.B., in *P.O.*, xxvi ('1946'), pp. 119-256. Cf. also O. Heiming, O.S.B., 'Palimpsestbruchstücke der syrischen Version der Jakobusanaphora aus dem 8. Jahrhundert' in *O.C.P.*, xvi (1950), pp. 190-200; A. Rücker, *Die syrische Jakobusanaphora nach der Rezension der Je'qob(h) von Edessa* (Liturgiegeschichtliche Quellen, iv; 1913). Eng. tr. in J. M. *Neale, *The Liturgies of S. Mark, S. James, S. Clement, S. Chrysostom and the Church of Malabar* (1859), pp. 31-65. Classical commentaries by (1) Moses bar Kêphā (813-903), ed., with Eng. tr., by R. H. *Connolly-H. W. Codrington, *Two Commentaries on the Jacobite Liturgy* (1913), pp. 16-66 (in Syriac script); Eng. tr., pp. 24-90, and (2) Dionysius bar Salibi (d. 1171), ed., with Lat. tr., by H. Labourt (C.S.C.O., Scriptores Syrici, xciii; 1903). L. *Allatius, Συμμικτά ('Coloniae Agrippinae' [Amsterdam?] 1653), i, 176-203 ('Ep. i ad Bartodum Nihusium de Liturgia S. Iacobi'), an attempt to prove the Liturgy to be the work of St. James the Apostle. G. *Dix, O.S.B., *The Shape of the Liturgy* [1944], esp. pp. 175-207. A. *Baumstark, *Liturgie comparée* (ed. 3 by B. Botte, O.S.B., 1953), esp. pp. 242-5 (bibl.). A. *Fortescue in *C.E.*, i (1907), pp. 571-4, s.v. 'Antiochene Liturgy'; H. *Leclercq, O.S.B. in *D.A.C.L.*, vii (pt. 2; 1927), cols. 2116-21.

JAMES I (1566-1625), King of England and VI of Scotland. The only son of Henry Stuart, Lord Darnley and *Mary, Queen of Scots, on the abdication of his mother he became King of Scotland in 1567. He was educated mainly by George Buchanan (1506-1582), who endeavoured to inculcate doctrines of constitutional monarchy. Undertaking the direction of government in 1575, he tried to build up the royal power amid strong rival factions of the Scottish nobility by pursuing a middle course in foreign and domestic policy. In 1586 he entered an alliance with England, raising few objections to the execution of his mother. In 1589 he married Anne of Denmark (1574-1619). From that time he generally supported the clergy against the nobility, but heartily resented the political influence of the Kirk. From 1598 he sought the restoration of episcopacy, in 1600 appointing three representatives of the Church in Parliament under the title of Bishops.

On the death of *Elizabeth I (1603), he succeeded to the English throne by right of his mother's descent from Henry VII, under the new style of King of Great Britain. Travelling immediately to London, he was met by the *Puritans who presented the *Millenary Petition in 1603. Although personally prepared to accept the desired changes, he at first adopted a position of mediation at the *Hampton Court Conference. When, however, the name of Presbyter was mentioned, confusing the English Puritans with the Scottish Presbyterians, he scolded the assembly and decided to harry dissenters out of the land. Henceforth he upheld the connexion between *Divine Right of Kings and *Apostolic Succession. At the same time he authorized a new translation of the Bible (the '*Authorized Version' of 1611). He favoured lenient treatment of RCs, and concluded peace with Spain in 1604. The discrepancy, however, between his promises and the policy of his government in 1605 provoked the *Gunpowder Plot, which was followed by stricter laws against *Recusants. He refused to ratify the canons prepared by *Convocation in 1606 because they advocated non-resistance to the king in possession, whereas he believed in the sanctity of hereditary right and denied that tyranny could exist by the appointment of God. In 1610 he persuaded the Assembly of the Scottish Church to agree to the introduction of episcopacy. Three bishops were consecrated in England and he prob. hoped to extend the English rite to Scotland. In 1614 and 1615 he ordered that all persons in Scotland should receive the Holy Communion on Easter Day, and in 1616 called upon the Assembly of Aberdeen to pass the Five Articles finally accepted at *Perth in 1618. On his return he issued the 'Book of *Sports' (1618) approving lawful sport on Sundays.

James's attempts to negotiate a marriage treaty with Spain were frustrated by the refusal of Parliament to repeal the laws against RCs. His efforts to mediate in Bohemia were equally unsuccessful, and he failed to agree with

Parliament on the size of a subsidy for war in 1624. He finally negotiated an alliance with France (1624) but was unable to disclose the terms of a treaty which promised relief to Catholics. Throughout his reign he continually quarrelled with his Parliaments in which a strong Puritan influence, supported by economic interests, advocated war with Spain, while James personally wanted peace abroad and toleration at home, and, having an exalted idea of monarchy, could not see that parliamentary control over finance made compromise necessary. Although renowned for his erudition, he failed to win sympathy through his obstinate pedantry and his high opinion of his own ability. In England he never adapted himself to conditions different from those in Scotland, but, by his tortuous methods and tactlessness, made himself unacceptable to subjects who had already become suspicious of the monarchy and disliked him as a foreigner. His published works include *Essays of a Prentice in the Divine Art of Poetry* (1584), *Poetical Exercises* [1591], *Daemonology* (1597; reprinted 1924), *Basilikon Doron* (1599; modern edition, 2 vols. 1944–50), *The True Law of Free Monarchies* (anon. 1598; 1603), *A Counter Blast to Tobacco* (anon. 1604), *Triplici Nodo, Triplex Cuneus; or an Apology for the Oath of Allegiance* (anon. 1607), *Declaratio pro Iure Regio* (1615), *The Peacemaker* (anon. 1618) and Meditations on the Lord's Prayer (1619) and on Mt. 27. 27–29 (1620).

Collected ed. of his prose Works to date publd. by James [Montague], Bp. of Winchester, in 1616. Repr. of his political works by C. H. MacIlwain, 1918. S. R. Gardiner, *History of England from the Accession of James I to the Outbreak of the Civil War*, vols. i–v, 1883–4. C. and H. Steeholm, *James I of England* (1938). S. R. Gardiner in *D.N.B.*, xxix (1892), pp. 161–81, s.v. 'James VI'.

JAMES II (1633–1701), King of England, 1685–8. The second son of *Charles I, James fought in the Civil War as Duke of York, but after being captured escaped abroad, where he served with the French army. At the Restoration he was made Lord High Admiral (1660) and in 1662 issued 'Instructions' to the Navy which remained in force until the 19th cent. About 1670 he was received into the RC Church and thereafter was in no great favour at Court or with Parliament which tried to pass an Exclusion Bill to keep him from the succession. The Lords having refused to pass the Bill, James ascended the throne in 1685. At first his policy was one of conciliation towards the Established Church, but he publicly professed his Roman allegiance and soon sought to find ways of easing the position of his co-religionists. After the quelling of the rebellion led by the Duke of Monmouth with some Anglican and Protestant support, he began to take repressive measures against Churchmen who opposed his policy, and created a Court of *High Commission in ecclesiastical affairs which suspended H. *Compton, Bp. of London. James claimed power to dispense from the provisions of the *Test Act of 1673 and appointed many Romanists to office in the state and the armed

forces. He also intruded RC dons to University College and Christ Church, Oxford, and overthrew the election of J. Hough as president of Magdalen in favour of his own nominee. Matters were brought to a head by his commanding to be read in all churches the *Declaration of Liberty of Conscience*, which, though allowing liberty to all who dissented from the C of E, was designed to favour the Papists. When W. *Sancroft, Abp. of *Canterbury, and seven other bishops refused to carry out the order and presented a petition to the King, they were committed to the Tower and charged with publishing a seditious libel. Their acquittal by the King's Bench was received with great rejoicing. Alarmed by the rumour of invasion by *William, Prince of Orange, James reversed some of his measures and promised once more to uphold the rights of the C of E, but William landed and James fled to France in Dec. 1688. He attempted to recover Ireland in 1689 and called a Parliament in Dublin which allotted tithes to Romanists, but he was defeated at the Boyne in 1690 and returned to France, to die in 1701 after spending the last four years of his life in religious observance.

The principal authority, apart from the State Papers, is *The Life of James the Second . . . Collected out of Memoirs Writ with his own Hand* [compiled at his son's command shortly after his death] ed. J. S. Clarke, at the command of the Prince Regent (2 vols., London, 1816). On this life cf. L. von *Ranke, *Englische Geschichte vornehmlich im sechszehnten und siebzehnten Jahrhundert*, vii (1868), pp. 137–54; Eng. tr., vi (1875), pp. 29–45. More modern lives by F. M. G. Higham (London, 1934), M. V. Hay (ib., 1938), J. Lane (ib., 1942), F. C. Turner (ib., 1948); also by H. *Belloc (London, 1928). A. W. Ward in *D.N.B.*, xxix (1892), pp. 181–99, s.v. 'James II of England'.

JAMES BARADAEUS. See *Jacob Baradaeus*.

JAMES THE DEACON (7th cent.), companion of St. *Paulinus, Bp. of *York. When Paulinus returned to Kent in 633, James was apparently the sole member of the mission to the N. left behind. Acc. to *Bede (*HE*, ii, 16 and 20), he resided chiefly at a village near Catterick. On the restoration of Christianity in Northumbria, James took an active and successful part in spreading the Gospel and, skilful in music, he taught his converts the Gregorian Chant. In 664 he was present, on St. *Wilfrid's side, at the Synod of *Whitby. He survived until Bede's time.

JAMES OF EDESSA. See *Jacob of Edessa*.

JAMES OF NISIBIS, St. See *Jacob of Nisibis, St.*

JAMES OF SARUG. See *Jacob of Sarug*.

JAMES OF VORAGINE. See *Jacob of Voragine*.

JAMES, WILLIAM (1842–1910), American *Pragmatist philosopher. The son of a *Swedenborgian theologian and brother of the novelist Henry James, he was professor successively of psychology (1889–97) and philosophy (1897–1907) at Harvard university. He held that we have a 'right to believe in' the existence of God (because it makes us 'better off'), but no scientific certainty of the validity of that belief. In his *Gifford Lectures, The Varieties of Religious Experience (1902), he drew the now familiar distinction between 'once-born' and 'twice-born' religious types, and made a scientific analysis of conversion. The cases he quotes have been widely criticized on the ground that they are too predominantly morbid, irrational, and Protestant, but the book remains a classic, and has stimulated much fruitful study of the psychology of religion. His other writings include his Principles of Psychology (2 vols., 1890), an epoch-making contribution to its subject; The Will to Believe and Other Essays (1897); and Pragmatism (1907).

Collected Essays and Reviews ed. R. B. Perry (1920); Letters ed. Henry James, son (1920). R. B. Perry, The Thought and Character of William James (2 vols. [1936]). Commemorative volume (New York, 1942). R. B. Perry in Dict. Amer. Biog., ix (1932), pp. 590–600.

JAMNIA or JABNEH, Synod of. A meeting of *Rabbis held in this city (13 miles south of Jaffa) c. A.D. 100 at which the content of the OT was discussed and, as the *Mishnah may suggest, the extent of the OT Canon finally settled. Since the destruction of the *Temple at *Jerusalem in A.D. 70, the city had been a seat of the 'Great *Sanhedrin' and an important centre of Jewish learning.

On the place, C. Warren in H.D.B., ii (1899), p. 524 f., s.v. 'Jabneel'; A. Legendre in Dict. Bibl., iii (1903), cols. 1115–19, s.v.; M. Seligsohn in J.E., vii (1904), p. 18, s.v. 'Jabneh or Jamnia'. The notion that the Synod of Jamnia settled the OT Canon, often found in English books, was orig. a conjecture put forward in H. E. Ryle, The Canon of the Old Testament (1892), p. 171 f.

JANE FRANCES DE CHANTAL, St. (1572–1641). Foundress of the Order of the *Visitation. The daughter of a noble family, she was married to the Baron Christophe de Chantal in 1592, and on his death in 1601 took a vow of chastity. Her friendship with St. *Francis de Sales, who became her spiritual director in 1604, resulted in the establishment at Annecy in 1610 of the Congregation of the Visitation for young girls and widows unable to endure the severe ascetic life of the ordinary religious house but none the less eager to enter religion. She spent the remainder of her life in the cloister, visiting the sick and poor and fostering her foundation with such success that by her death there were 86 houses in existence. She was beatified in 1751 and canonized in 1767. Feast day, 21 Aug.

Sainte J. F. Frémyot de Chantal. Sa vie et ses œuvres Mémoires sur la vie et les vertus de sainte Jeanne-Françoise Frémyot de Chantal . . . par la mère Françoise-Madeleine de Chaugy (8 vols., 1874–9), with life forming vol. i; Eng. tr. of vol. ii as Exhortations, Conferences, Instructions, and Retreat (Clifton, 1888). L. V. E. Bougaud, Histoire de Sainte Chantal et des origines de la Visitation (2 vols., 1861; Eng. tr. from 11th Fr. ed., 1895). A. Gazier, Jeanne de Chantal et Angélique Arnauld d'après leur correspondance, 1620–1641 (1915). Other lives by W. H. Coombes (2 vols.

bound in 1, London, 1830), Emily Bowles ('Quarterly Series', No. 2; 1872), C. A. Jones (London [1874]), H. *Bremond ('Les Saints', 1912), and Ella K. Sanders (London, 1918). There is also a brief sketch by Janet M. Scott (London, 1948). Bremond, ii (1916), esp. pp. 555–76.

JANNES AND JAMBRES. Two reputed Egyptian magicians who imitated the miracles performed by *Moses before Pharaoh (Ex. 7 ff.). They are mentioned in the NT at 2 Tim. 3. 8. There are many references to them in other literature of the early Christian period, Jewish as well as Christian, while *Origen (Comm. in Mt. 27. 9) refers to an apocryphal 'Book of Jannes and Jambres', which, however, has not been recovered.

J. A. *Fabricius, Codex Pseudepigraphus Veteris Testamenti, i (Hamburg and Leipzig, 1713), pp. 813–25, and ii (Hamburg, 1723), pp. 105–11. E. *Schürer, Geschichte des jüdischen Volkes, ii (ed. 3, 1898), pp. 292–4, with bibl. L. E. Iselin, 'Zwei Bemerkungen zu Schürer's "Geschichte des jüdischen Volkes im Zeitalter Jesu Christi". I. Jannes und Jambres' in Zeitschrift für wissenschaftliche Theologie, xxxvii (1894), pp. 321–6. M. R. James, 'A Fragment of the "Penitence of Jannes and Jambres"' in J.T.S., ii (1901), pp. 572–7, with text p. 573 f. J. T. Marshall in H.D.B., ii (1899), p. 548 f., s.v.

JANSEN, CORNELIUS OTTO (1585–1638) (Jansenius), the author of the *Augustinus (q.v.). He is to be distinguished from his uncle, Cornelius Jansen the Elder (1510–76), who was Bp. of Ghent from 1564 (confirmed by *Pius V, 1568). After two years in the Collège du Faucon at Louvain, he migrated in 1604 to Paris. Here he met *Saint-Cyran, with whom, at Bayonne and Champré, he spent the years 1612–17 in unremitting study. In these years, as his later correspondence with Saint-Cyran reveals, he conceived an elaborate plan of concerted action against the theologians of the *Counter-Reformation. In 1617 he became the director of a newly founded college at Louvain, and in 1626–7 defended at Madrid the cause of the university of Louvain against the aspersions of the *Jesuits. In 1628 he began to write the Augustinus, for which purpose he read the whole of St. *Augustine's writings ten times and the anti-Pelagian writings thirty; but it was not published till 1640, after his death. In 1636 he was consecrated Bp. of Ypres. See also foll. entry.

J. Orcibal, Correspondance de Jansénius ('Les Origines du jansénisme', i, in Bibliothèque de the R.H.E., xxv; 1947). Pastor, xxix (1938), pp. 62–102. J. Forget in C.E., viii (1910), pp. 285–8, s.v. 'Jansenius and Jansenism: I and II'; J. Carreyre in D.T.C., viii (pt. 1; 1924), cols. 319–30 (life, with bibl.) and 330–448 (full analysis of the Augustinus). See also bibls. to Augustinus and Jansenism.

JANSENISM. Technically, Jansenism is summed up in five propositions, extracted (the first two textually, the others by compression) from the *Augustinus (1640) of C. *Jansen, and condemned as heretical by the *Sorbonne (1649) and *Innocent X (1653). The sense of these propositions is (1) that without a special *grace from God, the performance of His commandments is impossible to men, and (2) that the operation of grace is irresistible; and hence, that man is the victim of either a natural or a supernatural determinism, limited only by not being violently coercive. This theological pessimism was expressed in the general harshness and moral rigorism of the movement.

The first generation of French Jansenists were all disciples of *Saint-Cyran (Du Vergier), Jansen's friend and collaborator. This party of 'Cyranists', which included the convent of *Port-Royal, was already in existence in 1638. After Saint-Cyran's death in 1643, Antoine *Arnauld succeeded him as its leader, and in *De la fréquente communion* (1643), *La Théologie morale des Jésuites* (1643), and two *Apologies pour M. Jansénius* (1644–5) defined the directions of the movement. These were (1) the defence of St. *Augustine's theology of grace, as interpreted by Jansen's, against *Molinism; (2) a rigorist tendency in all matters of ecclesiastical discipline; (3) hostility to *Probabilism. The unifying characteristic of the movement was antagonism to the *Jesuits. (2) and (3) remained unchanged throughout the whole history of Jansenism, and were exhibited in all its principal monuments, from the *Lettres provinciales* (1656–7) of *Pascal onwards.

In 1653 five propositions were condemned by *Innocent X in the bull '*Cum Occasione' as summarizing the Jansenist position. The supporters of the movement sought to evade the condemnation by their distinction of 'fact' (*fait*) and 'law' (*droit*). The five propositions were admitted to be heretical, but in 'fact' they were declared unrepresentative of Jansen's doctrine, which the Jansenists professed to uphold. After this distinction had been disallowed by *Alexander VII (1656), attempts were made to compel the Jansenists to sign a formulary embodying the Papal anathema. In 1668 they were persuaded into a qualified submission, but the movement continued to gain sympathisers, particularly among the *Oratorians and *Maurists. P. *Quesnel's *Réflexions morales* (1693), in which all the substantive tenets of Jansenism were reaffirmed, was condemned in the bull '*Unigenitus' (1713). The bull, however, was not accepted by the Jansenists, who consequently suffered persecution in France during most of the 18th cent. In the Netherlands, where many French Jansenists took refuge, Jansenism was tolerated or encouraged by successive *Vicars Apostolic, and in 1723 the Dutch Jansenists nominated for themselves a schismatic Bishop of Utrecht (see *Old Catholics*). In Tuscany, chiefly owing to the anti-Papal policy of the Grand Duke Leopold, Jansenism became so strong that the local synod of *Pistoia (1786) promulgated one of the most comprehensive statements of Jansenist positions that exists. After Napoleon's *Concordat of 1801, French Jansenism survived only as the secret conviction of a few Catholics, and as the guiding spirit of a few pious institutions.

The 'Five Propositions' will be found in Denz.–Bann. (ed. 1952), p. 360 f. (Nos. 1092–6). There has been an immense literature, nearly all polemical, from the outbreak of the controversy onwards. Earlier studies include [G. Gerberon, O.S.B., *Maurist], *Histoire générale du jansénisme, contenant ce qui s'est passé en France, en Espagne, en Italie, dans les Païs-Bas, etc., au sujet du livre intitulé Augustinus*

Cornelii Jansenii (3 vols., Amsterdam, 1700; sympathetic to Jansenist cause). Important modern studies are J. Paquier, *Le Jansénisme.* Étude doctrinale d'après les sources (1909); A. Gazier, *Histoire générale du mouvement janséniste* (2 vols., 1922). E. Préclin, *Les Jansénistes du XVIIIᵉ siècle et la constitution civile du clergé* (1928). L. Ceyssens, O.F.M., *Jansenistica.* Studien in verband met Geschiedenis van het Jansenisme (2 vols., Malines, 1950). P. de Leturia, S.J., and others, *Nuove ricerche storiche sul giansenismo* (Analecta Gregoriana, lxxi; 1954). J. Orcibal, *Les Origines du jansénisme* (Bibliothèque de la *R.H.E.*, xxv, xxvi, 3 vols., 1947–8; 2 further vols to come). On the theological aspects of the movement, N. J. Abercrombie, *The Origins of Jansenism* (1936). A. C. Jemolo, *Il giansenismo in Italia prima della rivoluzione* (Bari, 1928). J. Carreyre, *Le Jansénisme durant la régence, 1715–23* (Bibliothèque de la *R.H.E.*, ii–iv, 1929–33). List of Jansenist works in L. Patouillet (ed.), *Dictionnaire des livres jansénistes* (4 vols., Antwerp, 1752). J. Forget in *C.E.*, viii (1910), pp. 285–94, s.v. 'Jansenius and Jansenism'; J. Carreyre in *D.T.C.*, viii (pt. 1; 1924), cols. 318–529, s.v. 'Jansénisme', with full bibl. B. Matteucci in *E.C.*, vi (1951), cols. 350–60, s.v. 'Giansenio, Cornelio, e giansenismo'. See also bibl. to *Port-Royal*.

JANUARIUS, St., Bp. of Benevento, patron saint of Naples. Several late and historically worthless accounts of his martyrdom survive, but beyond the fact of his death in the neighbourhood of Naples, perhaps at Pozzuoli in the *Diocletianic persecution, nothing is really known of him. His fame rests on the alleged 'liquefaction' of his blood, preserved in a small glass phial, which is believed to take place on some eighteen occasions every year. A vast crowd gathers in the cathedral at Naples to witness the ceremony, headed by a body of poor and aged women, the *zie di San Gennaro* ('aunts of St. Januarius'), who occupy a privileged position in the church. Feast day, 19 Sept.

List of 'Acta' in *B.H.L.*, i (1898–9), Nos. 4115–40. P. Franchi de' Cavalieri, 'San Gennaro, vescovo e martire' in *Note agiografiche*, fasc. 4 (S.T., xxiv; 1912), pp. 79–102 (with ed. of Gk. text, pp. 105–14). Discussion of evidence for liquefaction, H. Thurston, S.J., in *C.E.*, viii (1910), pp. 295–7, with bibl.; cf. also id., 'The Blood-Miracles of Naples' in *The Month*, cxlix (1927, I), pp. 44–55, 123–35, 236–47, and id., 'The "Miracle" of St. Januarius' in ib., clv (1930, I), pp. 119–29. E. Josi, C. Testore, and P. Toschi in *E.C.*, vi (1951), cols. 9–16, s.v. 'Gennaro', with bibls.

JANUS. The pseudonym over which J. J. I. von *Döllinger, with J. N. Huber and J. *Friedrich, issued a series of letters in the Augsburg *Allgemeine Zeitung* early in 1869, attacking the Papal *Syllabus Errorum of 1864 as tending to obscurantism and tyranny. The purpose of the letters was to promote anti-*Ultramontane tendencies in view of the forthcoming *Vatican Council. See also *Quirinus*.

The letters were issued in book form in the same year, both in the original and in an Eng. Trans.

JAPAN, Christianity in. St. *Francis Xavier first brought Christianity to Japan in 1549, and he and his successors gained many converts. In 1587, under the suspicion that the missions were merely preparing the way for a coming conquest of the country, Christianity was proscribed, but still made progress down to 1596. From 1596 to 1598 persecution raged and in 1597 claimed 26 Japanese converts, who suffered martyrdom by crucifixion at Nagasaki (canonized in 1862; feast day, 5 Feb.). It broke out again in 1613, and by 1640 many thousands, both Japanese and foreigners, had suffered for their faith. Then all foreigners were excluded from Japan under pain of death. Their exclusion continued in force, together with the proscription of Christianity, down to 1859, when a treaty between the Japanese Government and France partially removed the former restriction, allowing also liberty of worship to foreigners, though complete toleration for all was not conceded till 1890. In 1859 RC missions re-entered the country and shortly afterwards (1865) discovered that thousands of Christians, in small local communities, had, though without priests or education, secretly kept and handed on their faith through the two centuries of persecution.

In 1859 some American (Anglican) missionaries had arrived; in 1861–3 the Presbyterians. In 1861 came a mission, sent by the Russian Orthodox Church, under Fr. Nicolai (afterwards archbishop), a Basilian monk and second only to Xavier as the apostle of Japan, who founded a communion whose numbers were exceeded only by that of the Roman obedience. Missions of other denominations followed. Though temporarily hindered by the persecution of 1867–73, in which many thousands of Christians were exiled, work went steadily forward in the later years of the 19th cent. The RCs set up a Vicariate-Apostolic in 1866, for which an archbishopric and three suffragan sees were substituted in 1891. In 1877 the various Presbyterian bodies at work in Japan began an amalgamation which was completed in 1891, while the American Episcopalian missions united with missions from the Churches of England and Canada to form the 'Nippon Sei Ko Kwai' (Holy Catholic Church of Japan) (1887), to some of the dioceses of which Japanese bishops came to be appointed. At first conversions were aided not only by the thirst of younger Japanese for W. education, but through desire to enter the civilization of the W. But by 1890 reaction to national self-reliance had set in. This was confirmed by the defeat of Russia (1905), and events from 1931 onwards intensified the nationalist spirit, reinforcing the state religion of Shinto.

The outbreak of war with U.S.A. and Great Britain (Dec. 1941) led to the removal of all European bishops (some of whom suffered harsh imprisonment) and clergy, and the government endeavoured to force all non-RC Christians into a united and national protestant Church, which some Anglicans joined under duress while others consistently stood out. After the war the 'Nippon Sei Ko Kwai' was reconstituted, under an entirely Japanese episcopate, while the government was obliged to grant freedom of religion and decree the 'abolition' of Shintoism.

O. Cary, A History of Christianity in Japan (2 vols., 1909). T. Nagayama, Collection of Historical Material Connected with the Roman Catholic Religion in Japan (Nagasaki, c. 1926), with texts in Japanese and English. L. Pagés, Histoire de la religion chrétienne au Japon depuis 1598 jusqu'à 1651 (2 vols., 1869–70); H. Haas, Geschichte des Christentums in Japan (2 vols., Tokyo, 1902–4 [up to 1570]); L. Delplace, S.J., Le Catholicisme au Japon (2 vols., 1909–10 [1540–1660]); C. R. Boxer, The Christian Century in Japan, 1549–1650 (1951). H. Thurston, S.J., 'Japan and Christianity' in The Month, cv (1905), pp. 157–74, 288–304, and 388–404. H. St. G. Tucker, The History of the Episcopal Church in Japan (Hale Lectures, 1937; 1938 [Anglican]), with bibl. Latourette, iii, 322–35, vi, 370–411, and vii, 379–400, with bibl. reff.

JARROW. See Wearmouth and Jarrow.

JASPERS, KARL (b. 1883), German philosopher. His early interests were in medicine and psychiatry. In 1913 he became Privatdozent, and in 1920 Prof., in Philosophy at Heidelberg. Under the influence of S. *Kierkegaard, F. W. *Nietzsche and Protestant theology he developed a Christian *Existentialism, akin to (but not directly influenced by) the teaching of G. Marcel, in an endeavour to interpret the crisis in post-1918 Germany in secular philosophy and culture. Jaspers put religion and philosophy in contrast, and stressed the limits of science, notably its inability to reach the self. This self is the ground of all existence and esp. characterized by the need for self-communication (a problem evaded, so Jaspers holds, by Kierkegaard). Among his writings are Strindberg und Van Gogh (1922); Die geistige Situation der Zeit (1931; Eng. trans. Man in the Modern Age, 1933); Philosophie (3 vols., 1932); Vernunft und Existenz (1935); Nietzsche. Einführung in das Verständnis seines Philosophierens (1936); Die Schuldfrage (1946); Nietzsche und das Christentum (1946); Der philosophische Glaube (1948); Vom Ursprung und Ziel der Geschichte (1949), and Rechenschaft und Ausblick (1951).

Offener Horizont. Festschrift für Karl Jaspers (1953), with full bibl., pp. 449–59. E. L. Allen, The Self and its Hazards. A Guide to the Thought of Karl Jaspers (slight [1950]). J. Pfeiffer, Existenzphilosophie. Eine Einführung in Heidegger und Jaspers (1933). J. de Tonquédec, L'Existence d'après Karl Jaspers (1945); M. Dufrenne and P. Ricœur, Karl Jaspers et la philosophie de l'existence (1947); P. Ricœur, Gabriel Marcel et Karl Jaspers. Philosophie du mystère et philosophie du paradoxe (1947).

JEAN-BAPTISTE MARIE VIANNEY, St. See Curé d'Ars, The.

JEANNE D'ARC, St. See Joan of Arc, St.

JEANNE FRANÇOISE FRÉMYOT DE CHANTAL. See Jane Frances de Chantal, St.

JEBB, JOHN (1775–1833), Bp. of Limerick. A native of Drogheda, he entered Trinity College, *Dublin, in 1791. After ordination as deacon in 1799 he held curacies in *Ireland and became Rector of Abington, Co. Limerick, in 1809. In 1820 he published his Essay on Sacred Literature which made his name as an author. In 1822 he was appointed Bp. of Limerick.

A lifelong friend of Alexander *Knox, a *Thirty Years' Correspondence* (2 vols.) with whom was published in 1836, he anticipated certain of the leading doctrinal emphases of the *Oxford Movement, e.g. he laid stress on the unbroken continuity of the Church; but. though he was highly spoken of by J. H. *Newman, there is no clear evidence that the course of the movement was directly influenced by Jebb's teaching.

He is to be distinguished from JOHN JEBB (1736–86), a Fellow of Peterhouse, Cambridge, who in 1771 advocated the abolition of clerical subscription at graduation to the *Thirty-Nine Articles and in his later life gave up his ecclesiastical preferments and practised as a physician.

Life by C. Forster, incl. selection of his letters (2 vols., London, 1836). A. Gordon in *D.N.B.*, xxix (1892), pp. 259–61.

JEHOSHAPHAT, The Valley of. On the basis of Joel 3. 2 and 12 (the only OT refs.), the traditional scene of the Lord's Coming Judgement. The name is perh. to be connected with King Jehoshaphat (1 Kgs. 15. 24, 22. 50) or some other historic person, but is prob. artificial since 'Jehoshaphat' means etymologically 'Jehovah judges'. Since the 4th cent. A.D. (*Eusebius, *Bordeaux Pilgrim, *Jerome) the name has been in current use among Jews, Christians and Moslems for the valley separating *Jerusalem on the East from the Mount of *Olives and traversed by the brook *Cedron, though the valley is not so described in the Bible or *Josephus.

C. Warren in *H.D.B.*, iii (1899), p. 561 f.; F. Vigouroux, 'Josaphat (Vallée de)' in *Dict. de la Bible*, iii (1903), cols. 1651–5; H. Vincent, O.P.–F. M. Abel, O.P., *Jérusalem. Recherches de topographie, d'archéologie et d'histoire*, ii, Jérusalem nouvelle (1926), pp. 849–52. G. M. Perrella, C.M., 'La valle di Giosafat e il giudizio universale' in *Divus Thomas* (Piacenza), xxxvi (1933), pp. 45–50.

JEHOVAH. A modern form of the Hebrew Divine Name, more properly '*Yahweh' (q.v.), which arose from a medieval misformation, popularized at the Renaissance. As considerations of reverence led the Jews seldom to utter the word from c. 300 B.C. onwards, and not at all after A.D. 70, the original pronunciation of the Name was lost. In reading the Scriptures, 'Adonai' ('Lord') was substituted, whence the renderings ὁ κύριος of the *Septuagint, *Dominus* of the *Vulgate and 'the LORD' of the English Versions. The substitution was indicated to the reader by the addition of the vowel points of 'Adonai' to the Heb. consonantal text; the form 'Jehovah' was merely a conflation of the consonants of the one word with the vowels of the other.

There is an extensive, but scattered, bibl., much of which is important. Valuable list of more modern items appended to art. by F. Spadafora in *E.C.*, vii (1951), col. 552 f., s.v. E. Kautzsch in *E.Bi.*, iii (1902), cols. 3320–23, s.v. 'Names', para. 109–13; F. Prat in *Dict. Bibl.*, iii (1903), cols. 1220–44, s.v.; G. Quell in *T.W.B.*, iii (1938), s.v. 'Κύριος (C: Der alttestamentliche Gottesname)', pp. 1056–80.

JEHOVAH'S WITNESSES. A sect of American origin, founded by C. T. *Russell (q.v.) under the name of 'International Bible Students'. The centre of Russell's message was his belief in the near end of the world for all save his own adherents, the 'elect of Jehovah', who would be the sole members of the Messianic Kingdom. This Adventist teaching was developed by his successor, J. F. *Rutherford (q.v.), on lines professedly subversive of civil authority. He held the theory of a 'theocratic Kingdom', membership of which prevented allegiance to any country, and in his periodicals *The Watchtower* and *Consolation* carried on a vigorous propaganda against the British Empire as well as against all institutional religion. The RC Church, the C of E, and the Free Churches are the constant butt of abuse in these publications, which deny most of the fundamental Christian doctrines.

Jehovah's Witnesses is an organization with printing establishments all over the world. They carry on an effective propaganda among an uncritical public and attract esp. the dissatisfied elements of society by preaching hatred of all existing institutions. During the war of 1939 to 1945 they were suppressed in several countries, e.g. *Australia and *New Zealand, as a subversive organization. They can hardly be regarded as a religious society, since, acc. to Rutherford's own statement, they hold that 'religion is against God'. From their headquarters in Great Britain (in 1955 at Craven Terrace, London, W.2) they operate under the name of the 'Watch Tower Bible and Tract Society'.

M. S. Czatt, *The International Bible Students: Jehovah's Witnesses* (1933); H. H. Stroup, *The Jehovah's Witnesses* (1945); R. Pike, *Jehovah's Witnesses* (1954); M. Cole, *Jehovah's Witnesses* (New York, 1955; London, 1956).

JELF, RICHARD WILLIAM (1798–1871), Anglican divine. Educated at Eton and at *Christ Church, Oxford, he became a canon of Christ Church in 1830. From 1844 to 1868 he was principal of *King's College, London. During the *Tractarian controversies Jelf was one of the few theologians who gained the confidence of both sides. In 1841, as soon as the attack on *Tract No. 90* was opened, J. H. *Newman addressed an Open Letter to Jelf in explanation of his position, and later in the same year E. B. *Pusey also addressed a *Letter* to Jelf in Newman's defence; and in 1843 he sat on the tribunal which examined Pusey's delated sermon on the Holy Eucharist. In 1844 he delivered a course of *Bampton Lectures on *An Inquiry into the Means of Grace*. While at King's College, he strongly disapproved of the teaching of his colleague, F. D. *Maurice. His lectures on the Thirty-Nine Articles were published posthumously (1873).

W. A. Greenhill in *D.N.B.*, xxix (1892), p. 291 f., s.v. Scattered reff. in H. P. *Liddon, *Life of Edward Bouverie Pusey*, i and ii (1893).

JEREMIAH (7th cent. B.C.), prophet of Judah. He was a native of Anathoth, nr. *Jerusalem, and probably belonged to the family of Abiathar, the high priest whom King *Solomon had deprived of his priestly functions. He was born c. 650, and received his vocation to the prophetic office in 626. His description of this event (Jer. 1. 4–19) is much simpler than those of *Isaiah and *Ezekiel, and his response shows humble distrust of himself. Later, however, this distrust gave way to bold confidence and courageous fulfilment of his mission, which entailed the renunciation of marriage and all personal happiness. Though he played no prominent part during the first years of his ministry, he probably approved Josiah's reform (2 Kgs. 22. 1–23. 30), but without taking part in it. The death of Josiah at Megiddo (608) caused a change in the people and its rulers, who fell back into idolatry under Jehoiakim (607–597), and from now on Jeremiah proclaimed the destruction of Jerusalem and the *Temple. When his prophecies were read before the king, he had them torn up and thrown into the fire. But, by the command of Jehovah, Jeremiah dictated a second roll, adding fresh threats of disaster that were to come unless the people repented. After the fall of Nineveh (606) the prophet counselled submission to Nebuchadnezzar, but the king resisted, and Judah did not give in until the reign of Zedekiah, in 598. Soon, however, Judah sided with Egypt against Babylon, despising the warnings of the prophet, who, during the siege of Jerusalem, was first imprisoned and then thrown into a pit from which he was rescued by the Ethiopian eunuch Ebed-melech (38. 7–13). After the destruction of the city (586) Jeremiah was left free to live in Judah, but after the assassination of the governor, Gedaliah, the Jews forced him to flee with them into Egypt, where he continued to reproach his countrymen for their idolatry (ch. 44). There is no record of his death in Scripture; acc. to a tradition first mentioned by *Tertullian he was stoned to death by the Jews in Egypt (cf. Heb. 11. 37).

Jeremiah is the most personal and sensitive of the OT prophets, conscious throughout of a close union with God and of the value and responsibility of the individual soul. His prophetic office, which entailed the denunciation of the sins of Judah and the proclamation of their punishment, was in tragic conflict with his love for his people, which led him to intercede repeatedly on his nation's behalf. His social teaching shows clear dependence on the ideals of the *Deuteronomist, who has also in places moulded his style.

The Prophet's sufferings, caused by the ingratitude and misunderstanding of his people, his prophecy of the destruction of Jerusalem and his weeping over the doomed city, have traditionally been interpreted as figures of the life of Christ, and the Church has used the Book, together with the Book of *Lamentations ascribed to him, in her Offices for Passiontide.

For Bibliography, see foll. entry.

JEREMIAH, Book of. This is the second of the great prophetic Books, and follows *Isaiah. The Jewish tradition, which ascribes it to *Jeremiah (q.v.), is ancient and unanimous,

and is supported by frequent NT quotations. Modern critics, however, refuse large sections of it to the prophet, though not all go as far as B. *Duhm, who would reject half the Book. Many scholars ascribe a great part of it to editors, esp. to Jeremiah's amanuensis *Baruch, and frequently attribute the splendid *Messianic chapters, 30 and 31, to an author living at the time of the return of the exiles to *Jerusalem (537), because of their resemblances to *Deutero-Isaiah. The so-called Oracles to the Nations are also often denied to Jeremiah, esp. the prophecy against Babylon (chs. 50 and 51), which contradicts the policy of submission consistently advocated by the prophet in other parts of the book. The greatest critical problem raised by the Book, however, is the striking difference between the *Septuagint and the *Massoretic texts. The former is about one-eighth shorter than the latter, and in the Septuagint the Oracles against the Nations do not come at the end, but follow ch. 25. This divergence has been explained in many different ways; but most modern critics believe that the order of the Greek is original. The different order of the two texts may, however, arise from the amalgamation of two collections of prophecies, which were combined in two different ways, a theory which would also explain the chronological confusion noticeable throughout the book. In ch. 36, the prophet himself tells us something of its origin. The prophecies, he says, were written down in the fourth year of Jehoiakim by Baruch, read to the king and burned by him, and then written again with additional material. These prophecies are usually believed to form the kernel of the Book, to which other material was added later either by Jeremiah himself or by his disciples.

The prophecies generally held to be authentic relate to the ruin of Judah and Jerusalem, to the victories of Nebuchadnezzar, and to the captivity; and the prophet's chief object was the preparation of the Jewish people for receiving the lesson of the Exile. Emphatic in his scorn of idols (e.g. 2. 27 f.; 10. 1–5; 11. 10–13), he extols the transcendence of Jehovah, the ruler of the nations (10. 10; 25. 15 ff.), who are to Him as clay to the potter (18. 5–10). He is the God of justice and goodness, who condemns His people because they have abandoned righteousness (e.g. 7. 4–15). This sense of Divine justice causes Jeremiah's astonishment at seeing the wicked prosper (12. 1 f.), and here is raised for the first time in the OT the problem of the good fortune of sinners and the sufferings of the just. In face of the hostility of the official representatives of the Jewish religion, Jeremiah emphasizes the interior cult of the righteousness of the heart and of the observance of the moral law (22. 3), and has hard words for a purely external cult (6. 20; 7. 21 f.), though he assigns a place to a true ritual worship in Messianic times (17. 26; 31. 14) and insists on the importance of the Sabbath (17. 19–27). He denounces the universality of sin, which reigns in Judah from the highest to the lowest among young and old, men and women (2. 29–37; 5. 1), and destroys almost all hope of salvation (5. 20–29). But in the midst of this world of despair the prophet proclaims the Messianic hope (chs. 30 and 31). The most striking characteristic of Jer. is the New Covenant (31. 31–4) which God will make with His people, writing His Law in their hearts, and in which the Gentiles, too, will participate (16. 19–21) under the rule of the Messianic King, of the seed of David (23. 5; 30. 21). The Book of Jeremiah has had a great influence on the formation of exilic and post-exilic Jewish piety, and is one of the most striking adumbrations of the religion of the NT.

Modern commentaries include those of B. Duhm (K.H.C., xi; 1901), A. S. *Peake (Jer. and Lam., 2 vols., Cent. Bibl. [1911], vol. i, and vol. ii, pp. 3–286), S. R. *Driver (London, 1906), A. W. Streane (Camb. Bibl., RV, 1913), L. Elliott Binns (West. Comm., 1919), and A. Condamin, S.J. (Études bibliques, 1920; ed. 3, 1936). T. K. *Cheyne, *Jeremiah. His Life and Times* [1888]. J. Skinner, *Prophecy and Religion.* Studies in the Life of Jeremiah (1922). G. A. *Smith, *Jeremiah* (Baird Lecture for 1922; [1923]). W. F. Lofthouse, *Jeremiah and the New Covenant* (1925). A. C. Welch, *Jeremiah.* His Time and his Work (1928). R. Calkins, *Jeremiah the Prophet.* A Study in Personal Religion (New York, 1930). V. Herntrich, *Jeremia der Prophet und sein Volk* (1938). S. Mowinckel, *Zur Komposition des Buches Jeremia* (Skrifter utvig av Videnskapsselskapet i Kristiania, ii, historisk-filosofisk Klasse, 1913, No. 5). P. Volz, *Studien zum Text des Jeremia* (Beiträge zur Wissenschaft vom Alten Testament, xxv; 1920). E. Podechard, 'Le Livre de Jérémie. Structure et formation' in *R. Bibl.,* xxxvii (1928), pp. 181–97. J. P. Hyatt, 'Jeremiah and Deuteronomy' in *Journal of Near Eastern Studies,* i (1942), pp. 156–73. A. B. *Davidson in *H.B.D.,* ii (1899), pp. 567–78, s.v.; A. Gelin, P.S.S., in *Dict. Bibl.,* Suppl. iv (1949), cols. 857–89, s.v.

JEREMIAH, Lamentations of. See *Lamentations of Jeremiah.*

JEREMY, Epistle of. A short item in the OT *Apocrypha. In what is now in its outward form a letter, the Prophet *Jeremiah (q.v.) declaims to the exiles whom Nebuchadnezzar had brought to Babylon (597 and 586 B.C.) against the folly of idol-worship. The traditional view that it was written in Heb. has had its modern defenders (C. J. Ball, O. Eissfeldt); but more probably the Book was composed in Gk., in which alone it survives. It prob. dates from the 2nd cent. B.C. In most Gk. MSS. it is a separate item; but in a few, as well as in the Vulg. (and in the English Bible, AV and RV), it appears as the conclusion of the Book of *Baruch (Bar. 6).

E. *Schürer, *Geschichte des jüdischen Volkes im Zeitalter Jesu Christi,* iii (ed. 4; 1909), p. 467 f., with reff. to earlier litt. C. J. Ball in R. H. *Charles (ed.), *The Apocrypha and Pseudepigrapha of the Old Testament,* i (1913), pp. 596–611. W. Naumann, *Untersuchungen über den apokryphen Jeremiasbrief* (Beihefte zur Z.A.T.W., xxv; 1913). H. St. J. Thackeray, *Some Aspects of the Greek Old Testament* (Arthur Davis Memorial Lecture, 1927), pp. 54–64. O. Eissfeldt, *Einleitung in das Alte Testament unter Einschluss der Apokryphen und Pseudepigraphen* (1934), p. 651 f. R. H. Pfeiffer, *History of New Testament Times with an Introduction to the Apocrypha* (New York, 1949; London, 1954), pp. 426–32, with bibl. p. 536. A. Robert in *Dict. Bibl.,* Suppl. iv (1949), cols. 849–57, s.v. See also bibl. to *Baruch, Book of.*

JERICHO. A town of Palestine, near the Jordan, north-east of *Jerusalem. Its miraculous capture by Joshua is narrated in Josh. 6.

A later city on the site, in a very fertile valley, was favoured by *Herod the Great, and visited by Christ (Mk. 10. 46, Lk. 19. 1, &c.).

J. Garstang–J. B. E. Garstang, *The Story of Jericho* (1940). E. Sellin–C. Watzinger, *Jericho.* Die Ergebnisse der Ausgrabungen (Wissenschaftliche Veröffentlichung der Deutschen Orient-Gesellschaft, Hft. xxii, 1913). L. H. Vincent, 'La Chronologie des ruines de Jéricho' in *R. Bibl.,* xxxiv (1930), pp. 403–33. Kathleen M. Kenyon, *Digging up Jericho* (1957).

JEROME. Eng. form (cf. Ital. Geronimo) of Lat. 'Hieronymus'. The form 'Hierome' is sometimes found in older (e.g. 17th cent.) English.

JEROME, St. (c. 342–420), Eusebius Hieronymus, Biblical scholar. Born at Strido near Aquileia, Jerome studied at *Rome, where he was baptized, and then travelled in Gaul before devoting himself to an ascetic life with friends at Aquileia. C. 374 he set out for Palestine. He delayed in *Antioch, where he heard the lectures of *Apollinarius of Laodicea until self-accused in a dream of preferring literature to religion ('Ciceronianus es, non Christianus'). He then settled as a hermit at Chalcis in the Syrian desert for four or five years, and while there learnt Hebrew. On his return to Antioch he was ordained priest by *Paulinus, next spent some time in *Constantinople, and from 382 to 385 was back in Rome, where he acted as secretary to Pope *Damasus and successfully preached asceticism (see *Melania; Paula*). After Damasus's death he visited Antioch, Egypt, and Palestine, and in 386 finally settled at *Bethlehem, where he ruled the men's monastery and devoted the rest of his life to study.

Jerome's writings issued from a scholarship unsurpassed in the early Church. His greatest achievement was his translation of the Bible into Latin from the original tongues (see *Vulgate*), to which he had been orig. prompted by Damasus. Jerome's work passed through several stages. Thus he issued no less than three revisions of the Psalter—the '*Roman', the '*Gallican', and the 'Hebrew' (*Psalterium iuxta Hebraeos*). He also wrote many Biblical commentaries, in which he brought a wide range of linguistic and topographical material to bear on the interpretation of the sacred text. Further, he was almost the first of the Christian fathers to understand the relation of the *Apocrypha to the books in the Hebrew *Canon. In addition to his Biblical work, he translated and continued *Eusebius's 'Chronicle'; compiled a 'De Viris Illustribus', a bibliography of ecclesiastical writers; and translated into Latin works by *Origen and *Didymus. His correspondence is of great interest and historical importance. His passionate nature also led him to throw himself into many controversies and to attack *Arianism, *Pelagianism, and *Origenism (the last of which had been championed by his friend *Rufinus of Aquileia). In some of his letters to friends and in his tracts against *Helvidius and *Jovinian, he advocated extreme asceticism.

Since the 13th cent. he has often been depicted in art with a red hat, on the supposition that Damasus created him a cardinal. Other artists have represented him as an ascetic, generally with a lion at his feet. Feast day, 30 Sept.

Jerome himself gives a list of his writings prior to 392 A.D. in his *De Viris Illustribus*, 135. Earliest collected ed. by D. *Erasmus (9 vols., Basle, 1516). Later edd. by Marianus Victorius, Bp. of Rieti (9 vols., Rome, 1565–72) and the *Maurists (mainly J. Martanay, O.S.B., 5 vols., Paris, 1693–1706). Best collected ed. that of D. *Vallarsi (11 vols., Verona, 1734–42), repr. in J. P. Migne, *PL*, xxii–xxx. Several separate works ed. in *C.S.E.L.* Eng. tr. of *De Viris Illustribus* by E. C. Richardson (N.P.N.C.F., Ser. 2, iii, 1892, pp. 359–84) and of letters and other select works by W. H. Fremantle and others (ib., vi, 1893). 'Select Letters' ed., with Eng. tr., by F. A. Wright (Loeb, 1933). Extended studies by G. Grützmacher (3 vols., Leipzig, 1901–8) and F. Cavallera, S.J. (S.S.L., i and ii, 1922; all published). Earlier studies by O. Zöckler (Gotha, 1865), A. Thierry (Paris, 1867), Mrs. C. Martin (London, 1888; popular), and A. Largent ('Les Saints', 1898; Eng. tr., 1900); also P. Monceaux (Paris, 1932; Eng. tr. of pt. i, 1933). *Miscellanea Geronimiana*. Scritti varii pubblicati nel XV centenario dalla morte di San Girolamo (Rome, 1930). L. Hughes, *The Christian Church in the Epistles of St. Jerome* (1923). Bardenhewer, iii, pp. 605–54; Altaner (ed. 1951), pp. 345–56. W. H. Fremantle in *D.C.B.*, iii (1882), pp. 29–50, s.v. 'Hieronymus (4)'; J. Forget in *D.T.C.*, viii (pt. 1; 1924), cols. 894–983; F. Cavallera, S.J., in *Dict. Bibl.*, Suppl. iv (1949), cols. 889–97, s.v.; id. and others in *E.C.*, vi (1951), cols. 652–64, s.v. 'Girolamo'. See also bibl. to *Vulgate*.

JEROME EMILIANI, St. (1481–1537). The founder of the *Somaschi. A native of *Venice, after service in the army he was ordained priest in 1518, and devoted himself for the rest of his life to work among the poor and afflicted, establishing orphanages, hospitals, and houses for fallen women. To foster this work he founded in 1532 a society, with its mother-house at the village of Somasca, between Milan and Bergamo. He was canonized in 1767 and made the patron saint of orphans and abandoned children by *Pius XI in 1928. Feast day, 20 July.

Life by A. Tortora (Milan, 1620), repr. in *AA.SS.*, Feb. II (1658), pp. 220–74. G. Landini, *S. Girolamo Miani dalle testimonianze processuali, dai biografi, dai documenti editi e inediti fino ad oggi* (1947). S. Raviolo, *San Girolamo Emiliani* (1947). See also bibl. to *Somaschi*.

JEROME OF PRAGUE (c. 1370–1416), Bohemian Reformer and friend of J. *Huss. Very little is known of his early life. He was a native of Prague, where he studied and came under the influence of Huss and of the *Wycliffite philosophy. Encouraged by Huss to visit the European centres of learning, after taking his degree at Prague he made his way (1398) to *Oxford. Here he studied the theological writings of Wycliffe, esp. his 'Dialogus' and 'Trialogus', and brought them back to *Paris and Prague (c. 1402). Acc. to his own testimony he was in *Jerusalem in 1403, in Paris again in 1404, and at Heidelberg and Cologne in 1406. In all these universities his exaggerated *Realism aroused much opposition. On his return to Prague in 1407 he took an active part in the religious controversies and became a leader of the nationalist university students. Wishing to gain also the neighbouring countries to Wycliffe's ideas, he had a discussion with King Sigismund of Hungary

at Ofen in 1410 on the vices of the clergy. Being declared suspect of heresy, he fled to Moravia, but in 1412 he was back at Prague where he violently attacked the bull of *John XXIII proclaiming an Indulgence for the crusade against Ladislaus of Naples. In 1413 he accompanied Grand-Duke Witold of Cracow to Russia and Lithuania, and aroused suspicion by showing himself favourable to heterodox rites. In 1415 he followed Huss to *Constance. He escaped when he realized his danger, but was brought back to the Council in chains. After Huss's death (6 July), which led to a schism in Bohemia, the Council wished to avoid a second execution and applied pressure to obtain a retractation from Jerome. On 11 Sept. 1415 he consented to read a document anathematizing the teaching of Wycliffe and Huss and accepting the authority of the Papacy and the Council. The sincerity of this abjuration, however, soon became suspect, and the trial was resumed in May 1416. Jerome defended himself with great eloquence, but in the last part of his speech he took back his abjuration, proclaimed the innocence and sanctity of Huss, and his own adherence to the teaching of Wycliffe on all points except *Transubstantiation, which he accepted. After a last attempt to obtain his submission he was condemned to the stake, where he died with great courage, reciting hymns to the BVM.

The principal sources are the acts of the Council of Constance, and works dealing with Huss, q.v. R. R. Betts, 'Jerome of Prague' in *University of Birmingham Historical Journal*, i (1947), pp. 51–91.

JERUSALEM. Referred to as 'Urusalem' in Egyptian texts c. 1900 B.C. and again in the *Tell-el-Amarna Letters (15th–14th cent. B.C.; it was then subject to Egypt), the city became the capital of Judah, the site of its religious sanctuary (the *Temple, q.v.), and as such the 'Holy City'. The town, which stands on a plateau at its highest some 2680 ft. above sealevel, is a strong natural fortress. It lies apart from the main traffic-routes between Egypt and the East. On the E. it is divided from the Mt. of *Olives by the *Cedron Valley, while to the W. and S. it is protected by the Valley of Hinnom (see *Gehenna*).

Archaeological evidence indicates the existence of habitation on the eastern portion of the site (Ophel) as early as c. 3000 B.C. In pre-Israelite times the inhabitants of the township seem to have been of mixed race. Acc. to Ezek. 16. 3, they included Amorites and Hittites, while elsewhere (e.g. Josh. 15. 63) they are called 'Jebusites'. C. 1000 B.C. the stronghold known as 'Zion' was captured from the Jebusites by *David, who built himself a fortress there (the 'City of David'), while under *Solomon, his successor, the city was enlarged and the first Temple built. Under Hezekiah the water-supply was much improved by a cutting (the 'Siloam Tunnel', c. 720 B.C.), some 1700 ft. long, through the solid rock (2 Kgs. 20. 20). In 701 B.C., Jerusalem was threatened with a siege by Sennacherib of Assyria, but suddenly relieved (2 Kgs. 18 f.). In 598 B.C., and again in 586 B.C., it was captured and devastated by Nebuchadnezzar, and all except the lower classes were deported to Babylon (2 Kgs. 24 f.).

After the Exile it was not refounded till the end of the 6th cent., with the building of the Second Temple. From now on the Jews were an ecclesiastically governed state under the suzerainty first of Persia and then of the Seleucids. This period ended with the *Maccabaean wars of the 2nd cent. B.C., during which the Temple was profaned under *Antiochus Epiphanes (167 B.C.). There followed the revival of Jewish national glory under a short dynasty of priest-kings, ended by the Roman conquest by Pompey (64 B.C.), after which the country was ruled directly or indirectly by Rome. The Third Temple was the work of *Herod the Great, who ruled as a vassal of Rome from 37 to 4 B.C. The turbulence of the people and the misgovernment of Roman procurators and native dynasts combined to produce the rebellion of A.D. 66, which was followed by a four-years siege, and, on its fall in 70, the extermination or removal of most of the population and the destruction of the city. A small and scattered population survived, however, until Hadrian, after the Jewish revolt in his reign, refounded the place as a Gentile city under the name of *Aelia Capitolina (A.D. 135).

The Christian history of the city begins with the short ministry of the Lord, culminating in His Crucifixion and Resurrection. There the Apostles lived and taught for some time after *Pentecost, and after they had scattered farther afield they met in Jerusalem with the 'elders' of the Church for the first Christian council (Acts 15; c. A.D. 49). St. *James, 'the Lord's brother', presided over the local Church after the dispersion of the Twelve, and it seems likely that the kinsmen of the Lord exercised some measure of leadership among the neighbouring Christian community until the foundation of Aelia Capitolina and the banishment at that time of all Jews from the region. From that date the local Church was purely Gentile in composition.

It was not until the visit of St. *Helena (c. A.D. 326), the mother of *Constantine, and the beginning of the fashion of venerating the holy places set by her visit, that the Christian see became of any importance. Until the 5th cent. the see was suffragan to Caesarea. But at the Council of *Chalcedon (451) the bishopric (see *Juvenal*) was granted patriarchal dignity. The see never attained, however, to the prestige of the other patriarchates, and when the Crusaders held the city in the 12th cent., the patriarch lived in *Constantinople. Though for some periods afterwards the patriarchs came back to Jerusalem, they have been permanently settled there only since 1845; and for some time the tendency has been to appoint Greeks instead of Arabs to the see. A Latin (RC) patriarchate was in existence from 1099 till 1291, and nominally till 1374, and was again constituted in 1847. There is also a (Gregorian) *Armenian patriarchate, and

the *Melchite Patr. of Antioch adds the title of Jerusalem to his others.

The Christian centre of Jerusalem is the Church of the Resurrection, commonly known outside the country as the Church of the *Holy Sepulchre. The site of the Temple is now in Mohammedan hands, and is occupied mostly by the *Dome of the Rock. There are numerous other holy places within and outside the city. Where both Orthodox and Latins claim that their particular site is the genuine scene of the mystery commemorated, the Easterns have usually the more ancient tradition, the Latin sites generally having been established at earliest in Crusading times.

The present city does not cover exactly the same site as that of NT times; it is farther to the north by about half a mile, so that some of the sacred places lie outside and to the south of the present walls, whereas the traditional site of Calvary and the Holy Sepulchre is now inside the city (see, however, *Gordon's Calvary*). The walls of the present city date from the 16th cent., though much of the work done in the Frankish rebuilding (c. 1230) still remains.

L. H. Vincent, O.P. – F. M. Abel, O.P., *Jérusalem*. Recherches de topographie, d'archéologie et d'histoire (2 vols., bound in 4, 1912–26); L. H. Vincent, *Jérusalem de l'Ancien Testament*. Recherches d'archéologie et d'histoire, i (1954). C. Mommert, *Topographie des alten Jerusalem* (4 vols., 1901–7). G. A. *Smith, *Jerusalem*. The Topography, Economics and History from the Earliest Times to A.D. 70 (2 vols., 1907–8). H. V. Morton, *In the Steps of the Master* (1934; popular). F. *Cabrol, O.S.B., *Étude sur la 'Peregrinatio Silvae'*. Les églises de Jérusalem. La discipline et la liturgie au IVᵉ siècle (1895). On the Greek Patriarchate, M. *Le Quien, O.P., *Oriens Christianus*, iii (1740), pp. 101–528; C. Papadopoulos, Ἱστορία τῆς Ἐκκλησίας Ἱεροσολύμων (1910); T. Dowling, *The Orthodox Greek Patriarchate of Jerusalem* (S.P.C.K., 1913). L. H. Vincent in *Dict. Bibl.*, Suppl. iv (1949), cols. 898–966, s.v.

JERUSALEM, Anglican Bishopric in.

In 1841 a bishopric was set up in *Jerusalem by the joint efforts of England and Prussia to serve the Anglicans and Protestants of Syria, Chaldaea, Egypt, and Abyssinia. The scheme, which provided that the bishop was to be nominated by England and Prussia alternately, excited opposition both among *Lutherans, who disliked any semblance of episcopal order, and High Church Anglicans, who objected to a virtual union with a Protestant body, without guarantees for the preservation of Church order or doctrine. The first holder of the see was M. S. *Alexander (q.v.), a Christian convert from orthodox Judaism. Estrangement between the two communities increased as the numbers of Germans living in Palestine grew, and the scheme finally collapsed in 1886, when the Anglicans required that the bishop should always be consecrated acc. to the Anglican rite, and should assent to the *Thirty-Nine Articles. Since that date the see has been maintained by the Anglicans alone. Besides serving the spiritual needs of Anglicans in and near Palestine, it does missionary work and is a valued point of contact for Anglicanism with the E. Churches and, to a less degree, with the Latin Churches in the E.

[H. Abeken, anon.], *Das evangelische Bisthum in Jerusalem*. Geschichtliche Darlegung mit Urkunden (Berlin,

1842). Eng. tr. of this work, with additions, in W. H. Hechler (ed.), *The Jerusalem Bishopric* (1883). H. Abeken, *A Letter to the Rev. E. B. Pusey, D.D.*, *in Reference to certain Charges against the German Church* (1842). H. P. Liddon, *Life of E. B. Pusey*, ii (1893), pp. 248–60.

JERUSALEM, Knights of St. John in.
See *Hospitallers of St. John in Jerusalem.*

JERUSALEM, Synod of (1672).
The most important modern Council in the Eastern Church, held in the Basilica of the Nativity at *Bethlehem (hence sometimes known as the 'Synod of Bethlehem'). It was convened by *Dositheus (q.v.), Patr. of Jerusalem, and sought to repudiate the movement fostered by Cyril *Lucar towards accommodation with *Calvinism. In effect it marked the closest approximation of E. Orthodoxy, of which it desired to be fully representative, to *Tridentine Catholicism. It decreed, *inter alia*, that the Church is equally infallible with Scripture; that predestination depends on foreknowledge, and takes account of works; that God cannot be the cause of evil; that the Church has a part in the mediatorial office of Christ; that justification is through faith working by love; that natural virtue is to be distinguished from that of the regenerate; that souls which have fallen from grace may be purified in Hades after death, so as to be fit for the final vision of God; that there are seven sacraments; that *Receptionism, or the doctrine that the beneficial operation of the sacrament depends upon the faith of the recipient, is to be condemned; that Baptism is an effectual sign of grace; that in the Eucharist the elements are transubstantiated (though doubt has been sometimes expressed as to whether the philosophical implications of μετουσιοῦσθαι are the same as those of *transubstantiari*); and that the Books of Tobit, Judith, Ecclus., and Wisdom are to be regarded as canonical.

Acta first pr. by the *Maurist, M. Foucqueret, O.S.B., *Synodus Bethleemitica adversus Calvinistas Haereticos* (Paris, 1676); repr. in Hardouin, ix, cols. 179–274; also in E. J. Kimmel (ed.), *Monumenta Fidei Ecclesiae Orientalis* (Jena, 1850), i, 325–487. Eng. tr., with tr. of Cyril Lucar's Confession of 1631 in an appendix, by J. N. W. B. Robertson, *The Acts and Decrees of the Synod of Jerusalem* (1899). Further bibl. in *D.T.C.*, iv (1911), col. 1793, s.v. 'Dosithée'.

JESSE WINDOW.
A window whose design is based on the descent of Jesus from the royal line of *David, in most cases taking the form of a tree springing from Jesse, the father of David, and ending in Jesus or the Virgin and Holy Child, with the intermediary descendants placed on scrolls of foliage branching out of each other. Examples of the window are to be seen at the cathedrals of *Wells and *Chartres, St. George's, Hanover Square (a 16th cent. window from *Malines), and in *Dorchester Abbey, near Oxford, where the tree forms the central mullion.

A. Watson, *The Early Iconography of the Tree of Jesse* (1934); C. Woodforde, 'A Group of Fourteenth Century Windows showing the Tree of Jesse' in the *Journal of the British Society of Master Glass Painters*, vi (1937), pp. 184–190.

JESU, DULCIS MEMORIA.
The celebrated 11th cent. poem, very familiar through the translations of sections of it in the English hymns 'Jesu, the very thought of Thee, With sweetness fills my breast' (by E. *Caswall) and 'Jesu! the very thought is sweet! In that dear name all heart-joys meet' (by J. M. *Neale). The intense mysticism and honeyed beauty of its language are unsurpassed in medieval devotional literature, though the complete poem (168 lines) suffers from a certain monotony in ideas. It has traditionally (but almost certainly wrongly) been ascribed to St. *Bernard of Clairvaux. Sections of it have been used as a *sequence and an *office-hymn for the Feast of the Holy *Name. It is sometimes known as the 'Rosy Sequence' or as the 'Joyful' (or 'Jubilee') 'Rhythm'.

Lat. text pr. in *Oxford Book of Medieval Latin Verse* (ed. S. Gaselee, 1928), No. 62, pp. 111–17. W. Bremme, *Der Hymnus* Jesu Dulcis Memoria (1899). E. Vacandard, 'Les Poèmes latins attribués à S. Bernard' in *R.Q.H.*, xlix (1891), pp. 218–31. Raby, pp. 329–31.

JESUITS.
The Society of Jesus, founded by St. *Ignatius Loyola (q.v.), was formally approved by *Paul III in 1540 in the bull '*Regimini militantis ecclesiae', but had in fact begun six years earlier when Ignatius and six companions took vows in the Church of Montmartre at Paris. The aim of the order was twofold, to support the Papacy and Catholic truth against prevalent heresy and to undertake missionary work among the heathen. To the normal three vows of religious was added a fourth, that of going, without question or delay, wherever the Pope might order for the salvation of souls. The constitution of the society was military and autocratic, its head being an elected '*General' with absolute authority subject only to the Pope. The work of the Society was performed at first chiefly in teaching, conducting catechisms, and giving '*spiritual exercises'. No Jesuit might take any ecclesiastical dignity unless constrained by the Pope to fill the office on pain of mortal sin.

By 1556, when St. Ignatius died, the order was firmly established in Europe and conducting successful missions in America, Africa, and Asia (see *Francis Xavier*), while the value of its scholarship and learning for the Church was exemplified in the Jesuit theologians who attended the Council of *Trent. St. Ignatius was succeeded as General in 1558 by James *Laynez (after two years as vicar-general), and he in turn was followed by St. *Francis Borgia in 1565. Among the great names of the first hundred years of the Society are those of R. *Bellarmine, F. de *Suarez, *Peter Canisius, and *Aloysius Gonzaga. In England, where the Jesuits first arrived in 1578, they were feared as the most redoubtable advocates of the Papacy and held in abhorrence as teaching that the end justified the means, that the Pope had the right to excommunicate and depose sovereigns, and that excommunicated sovereigns might be assassinated. Before the end of the 16th cent. their elaborate system of education, based on the '*Ratio Studiorum' (q.v.) had been firmly established.

During the 17th and 18th cents. Jesuit missions were esp. active in *India, *China, *Japan, and North America. In *Belgium the Jesuit Scholar, J. *Bollandus, published the first volume of the *Acta Sanctorum in 1643. In *France where they were attacked by B. *Pascal for their lax casuistry, they became the principal opponents of *Jansenism. The French always regarded them with considerable suspicion, as a foreign influence, and in 1764 a combination of their enemies brought about their expulsion from France. In 1759, under the influence of the Marquis de Pombal, the order was banished from *Portugal, and in 1767 by order of Count de Aranda, chief minister of Charles III, 6000 Jesuits were deported from *Spain. In 1773 *Clement XIV gave way to the demands of France, Spain, Portugal and many of the Italian states, and issued the bull '*Dominus ac Redemptor' suppressing the Society.

The suppression did not mean that the Jesuits were wiped out. In Austria and Germany they were allowed to teach, and they were protected by both Frederick II of Prussia and the Empress Catherine of Russia. In White Russia, indeed, a novitiate was opened in 1780. Gradually the Jesuits managed to re-establish themselves, and in 1814 the Society was formally restored by *Pius VII in the bull 'Sollicitudo omnium ecclesiarum'.

At the present day the Jesuits are to be found in most countries of the world. They are responsible for the 'Gregorian University' (the '*Gregoriana') in Rome and have nine Universities among their Eastern Missions. In addition they support and control many schools and academies in all parts of the world and also edit several important periodicals, among them Gregorianum, *Analecta Bollandiana, Biblica, Études, Recherches de Science Religieuse, and The Month.

T. J. Campbell, S.J., The Jesuits, 1534–1921 [1921]; J. Brodrick, S.J., The Origin of the Jesuits (1940); id., The Progress of the Jesuits. 1556–79 (1946). D. Bartoli, S.J., Dell' istoria della Compagnia de Giesu (5 vols., Genoa–Rome, 1656–73). J. Cretineau–Joly, S.J., Histoire religieuse, politique et littéraire de la Compagnie de Jésus (6 vols., 1844–6). M. Meschler, S.J., Die Gesellschaft Jesu. Ihre Satzung und ihre Erfolge (1911); J. Brucker, S.J., La Compagnie de Jésus. Esquisse de son institut et de son histoire, 1521–1773 (ed. 2, 1919); L. Koch, S.J., Jesuiten-Lexikon. Die Gesellschaft Jesu einst und jetzt (1934); H. Becker, Die Jesuiten. Gestalt und Geschichte des Ordens (1951).
Augustin de Backer, S.J.–Aloys de Backer, S.J.–A. Carayon, S.J., Bibliothèque de la Compagnie de Jésus (ed. C. Sommervogel, S.J., 10 vols., 1890–99, with 2 supplementary vols. by E. M. Rivière, S.J., 1911–13). Monumenta Historica Societatis Jesu (Madrid, 1894 ff., and Rome, 1925 ff.); Archivum Historicum Societatis Jesu (Rome, 1932 ff.). M. Heimbucher, Die Orden und Kongregationen der katholischen Kirche, ii (ed. 3, 1934), pp. 130–340 and 666 f.
H. Foley, S.J., Records of the English Province of the Society of Jesus (7 vols. bound in 8, 1877–83). T. Hughes, S.J., The History of the Society of Jesus in North America (3 vols. bound in 4, 1907–17). H. Fouqueray, S.J., Histoire de la Compagnie de Jésus en France des origines à la suppression, 1528–1762 (5 vols., 1910–25). A. Astrain, S.J., Historia de la Compañía de Jesús en la asistencia de España (7 vols., 1902–25). F. Rodrigues, S.J., História da Companhia de Jesus na Assistência de Portugal (1931 ff.). P. Tacchi Venturi, S.J., Storia della Compagnia di Gesù in Italia (2 vols., 1910–22). B. Duhr, S.J., Geschichte der Jesuiten in den Ländern deutscher Zunge (4 vols. bound in 5, 1907–28). J. A. Otto, Gründung der neuen Jesuitenmission durch General Pater Johann Philipp Roothaan (1939). See also bibliographies under separate countries.

JESUS. The Gk. form ('Ιησοῦς) of the Heb. *Joshua (lit. 'Jehovah saves'), who is thus referred to in the NT at Heb. 4. 8 (AV). By Divine command (Lk. 1. 31, Mt. 1. 21) the name was bestowed on the Infant Christ, the Saviour of mankind.

JESUS CHRIST. This article touches on the main aspects of the earthly life and teaching of Jesus as set out in the *Gospels, with a view to understanding the faith in His person and work which the Church has professed from the beginning. The four Gospels embody the accounts of Jesus' words and acts which were at first handed on and repeated orally in the earliest Christian community. The Gospels contain what it was held important for a Christian to know about His earthly life and therefore often fail to satisfy a purely biographical curiosity. Moreover, being written for and by believers, they interpret as well as record, but their aim is to make plain what actually happened, i.e. they are concerned with historical truth as well as with theological interpretation.

(1) *The Birth of Jesus.* Jesus was born before the death of King *Herod the Great (4 B.C.), but probably not more than three or four years before. His mother *Mary and her spouse *Joseph, of *Nazareth in *Galilee, were pious Jews, not identified with any particular party. Jesus is once called 'the carpenter', or stone-mason, but the family though manual workers were not necessarily ill-educated. For comment on stories of the virginal conception of Jesus, see art. *Virgin Birth*; the estimate of these stories will largely depend on the estimate of the other contents of the Gospels.

(2) *The Beginning of Jesus' Public Ministry.* Between A.D. 27 and 29, *John the Baptist began to preach repentance and to baptize those who came to him in preparation for a coming Divine judgement. The public work of Jesus began just before or just after John had been imprisoned by King Herod Antipas. Jesus came to be baptized by John, thereby accepting John as divinely sent and his work as preparatory to His own. At His baptism Jesus received the sign to begin His mission in the form of the access of the Spirit and the assurance of His unique Sonship ('my beloved', i.e. only, 'Son', Mk. 1. 11, &c.). The story of the Temptations which follows expresses (perhaps in a generalized form) His initial and persistent choice of the way of self-abnegation and dependence on the Father's will. The main scene of Jesus' activity was in Galilee and the neighbouring districts of N. Palestine. The first three Gospels record only the one visit to Jerusalem which ended in the crucifixion, but they contain evidence supporting the statement of St. John's Gospel that there were earlier visits to the holy city during the ministry.

(3) *Jesus and the Kingdom of God.* The central and unifying theme of the preaching of Jesus was the imminent approach of the *Kingdom of God. By the Kingdom Jewish teachers meant that visible manifestation of the sovereign power of God which was to usher in 'the last days', bringing judgement on evil and a golden age of Divine blessing for His faithful people. In the teaching of Jesus, the Kingdom 'comes', is 'given', 'received', or 'entered'; it is not a creation of human activity but an irruption of Divine judging and saving power. Thus the parables of growth (the Mustard Seed, the Leaven) emphasize not the gradualness of the development of the Kingdom, but the wonder of its great results. Other parables (e.g. the Marriage Supper, the Wheat and the Tares) portray the urgency of decision, the tragedy of the rejection of the Gospel message, and the certainty of Judgement. Jesus speaks of the coming of the Kingdom and of its accompanying events sometimes as definitely in the future, when the '*Son of Man' will come in glory to judge and the whole present order of things will be brought to a catastrophic end; sometimes it is said that the present generation will see the Kingdom coming in power; sometimes again it is implied that the Kingdom has already arrived or begun to arrive. We may gather that Jesus envisaged the arrival of the Kingdom as an extended series of events in which His own coming and teaching were the decisive beginning. Thus He affirms that His mastery over the evil spirits of disease and madness by the finger or Spirit of God shows that the Kingdom of God has come; and His own miracles are a first sign of the new manifestation of God's sovereign power conquering evil and providing the promise of final triumph. Other sayings indicate the claim of Jesus that with His coming a new dispensation has begun; the old dispensation (the Law and the Prophets) had lasted until John; something greater than Solomon is here; the disciples are seeing what many prophets and kings had looked for. Above all, the mysterious title 'Son of Man' (cf. Dan. 7) used by Jesus of Himself, indicates that He is the accredited agent of God in final judgement and redemption; in the coming and the consummation of the Kingdom His own work is central and decisive. Those who acknowledge Him He will acknowledge before the Father. In the name of the Kingdom and in His own name Jesus made demands on His disciples which knew no limits.

(4) *Jesus and the Fatherhood of God.* The utterances of Jesus concerning the Fatherhood of God must be understood in harmony with the message of the Kingdom. God is Father, Judge, and King, uniting generosity and love with sovereign and holy power. Men can enter into Sonship with Him through faith in His providential power, through repentance and forgiveness, and through obedience to His commandments. God as Father is the supreme giver not only of bodily life and sustenance but of all spiritual blessing, and that not in accordance with man's deserts

(Parables of the Prodigal Son, of the Labourers in the Vineyard) but according to His own limitless goodness which goes out to meet the sinner more than half-way. Jesus Himself not only taught but manifested the true nature both of man's sonship to God and of the Divine Fatherhood, the former by His own faithful obedience to the point of death, the latter in His self-sacrificing concern for the weak and sinful.

(5) *Jesus and Judaism.* The mission of Jesus was confined almost exclusively to the Jewish people. With the authority of the OT Scriptures, to which He constantly appealed, He accepted Israel's privileged position. The Kingdom must be preached to God's people who had been taught by prophets to expect it. But His message by its newness and finality presented the Jewish Church with a critical choice. Thus He called current Judaism to account by an appeal to the OT which in its freedom, insight, and authority attracted the attention and opposition of the Jewish legal experts. His interpretation of the precepts of the Law (e.g. on anger, impurity, divorce) was at once more free and more exacting than any known to Judaism; ceremonial observance was not rejected, but placed in subordination to fundamental principles of charity, sincerity, and humility (e.g. prayer, fasting, almsgiving, sacrifice). The *Pharisees were criticized as having cultivated an elaborate system of ceremonial obedience to the Law, thus obscuring its weightier precepts and generating self-righteous contempt for the less precise. Many parables and sayings imply that Jesus expected His message to be accepted by those who in the eyes of official Judaism were religiously outcast or ignorant ('publicans and sinners'), since they more easily responded to the appeal for humility and repentance. In cleansing the *Temple (Mk. 11. 15–19), Jesus attacked the conduct of Israel's central shrine by the worldly Sadducean priesthood. In all this the Jewish rulers detected the assumption of an authority which was as Divine as that of the Mosaic Law itself. Together with the pronouncement of the forgiveness of the sins of individuals there was the hint that He spoke not merely as a prophet, but as *Messiah and Judge, revealing, proclaiming, and manifesting the sovereignty of God as Father and King and thereby presenting the Jewish Church with an inescapable challenge (cf. the parable of the Wicked Husbandmen). Jesus was in fact claiming that Judaism would be judged by its reaction to Him and His message.

(6) *Jesus and the Disciples.* Jesus selected an intimate band of twelve disciples (see *Apostles*) to be with Him in His mission. On at least one occasion He sent them out to teach and to preach. His claims and authority became apparent to the Jewish authorities in a general way, but He spoke of them turning explicitly only to the disciples. The turning point of the Gospel story (esp. clear in St. Mark) is the incident of St. *Peter's confession at *Caesarea Philippi (Mk. 8. 27–33). When St. Peter acknowledged that He was the Christ,

i.e. the expected Messiah, Jesus proceeded to transform the traditional idea by insisting that the Son of Man must suffer before entering into His glory. His followers must be prepared to accept this way of humility and suffering for themselves. At this stage of His mission, if not from the beginning, it was clear to Him that His challenge to Judaism must end in His death and that His death (a 'ransom for many') was part of the Divine purpose in the establishment of the Kingdom. It is probable that He saw in the passages of *Isaiah describing God's Suffering Servant (esp. Is. 52. 13–53. 12) a prophecy of His own mission. After the days of final conflict with the Jewish authorities in *Jerusalem, Jesus on the night before the Crucifixion interpreted His death to His disciples at the Last Supper. He took bread, and having blessed it, gave it to them to eat, describing it as His body given for them; and He took a cup of wine, and having similarly blessed it, gave it to them to drink, calling it the new covenant in His blood. Apart from any question of the institution of a permanent rite to be repeated, His action had a twofold meaning. First, His death was interpreted as a covenant sacrifice; the shedding of His blood was to found a new covenant relation of forgiveness and fellowship between man and God. Secondly, the new covenant implied a new community with whom the Divine covenant was made: just as the people of Israel had been brought into the old covenant with God by the sacrificial shedding of blood (cf Ex. 24. 1–11). The people of Israel having decided to reject Him, Jesus founded through His sacrifice a new people or Church, of which the nucleus was the Twelve, to be the heir of the blessings of the Kingdom. By His action at the Last Supper Jesus stamped His death in its creative and redeeming results as an essential and indeed the most significant act of His mission.

(7) *The Crucifixion and Resurrection* (see also art. *Resurrection of Christ*). The Jewish authorities, after a preliminary investigation, presented Jesus to the Roman governor, Pontius *Pilate, as worthy of capital punishment, and He suffered crucifixion (a criminal's death) as a claimant to Messianic dignity. For the date of this event the years A.D. 29, 30, or 33 are thought the most probable. The Gospels (in harmony with the mind of Jesus as already indicated) do not portray the Crucifixion as a tragedy or the martyrdom of a human hero deserving of pity or admiration, but as an event which, though brought about by human sin, fulfilled the Divine purpose, and is therefore to be regarded with awe and faith. At the time, the death of their Master seemed to the disciples (in spite of His warnings) the end of all their hopes. It is intelligible that this was so, since the whole idea of a suffering Messiah was entirely new to Jewish minds. It is equally intelligible that in the light of the Resurrection much that He had said returned to their minds with new meaning: the Gospels constantly emphasize the slowness of the disciples in understanding the teaching of Jesus as He

gave it to them. On the third day (i.e. the next day but one) after the Crucifixion, the tomb in which the body of Jesus had been laid was found empty and, during a short period that followed, Jesus presented Himself alive in a glorified but recognizable form to individual disciples and to groups of them. In their details of time and place the stories of the resurrection-appearances raise difficulties, but they testify to an intimate contact with a living person which was not the product of the disciples' imagination. The subsequent confident preaching of the early Church is a strong proof of this. They were convinced that God had raised Him from the state of death, victorious over every evil that could oppose God and beset man. Jesus had entered on His glory through His passion and thus not only vindicated and illuminated much that the disciples remembered Him to have said, but also pointed to much more that remained to be understood. The outpouring of the Holy Spirit subsequently experienced by the community of disciples in Jerusalem indicated that through the work of Jesus the promised blessings of the Kingdom were already being enjoyed by the Church. The new covenant of forgiveness, sonship, and grace was in operation in the community brought into being by Jesus.

(8) *The Person of Jesus*. Official Judaism had crucified Jesus as a troublesome impostor; His disciples in the light of all that had happened believed in Him as Christ and Lord. In the light of the OT faith in God this fairly represented the issue. Those who knew Jesus, disciples and opponents alike, found it impossible to select a few points of His teaching for acceptance and avoid the question of the ultimate authority and nature of His person. To the first Jewish disciples their new faith involved a complete readjustment of established ideas. Jesus was the promised Jewish Messiah, but the manner and magnitude of His claims and His achievement could not be fitted into the traditional picture inherited by Judaism. The disciples found themselves in an attitude of religious dependence on Jesus, risen and exalted, which was nothing else than worship. He had done what God alone can do, namely created a new relation between man and God and brought redemption from evil. Their whole religious life now passed to God through Him. Two fundamental points became clearer to the mind of the early Church as it pondered on the facts presented to it. First, Jesus was more than an inspired prophet; He was the fulfilment of all that the prophets had pointed to. He had not merely brought a new message about God; in Him God had acted to save as well as spoken to illuminate mankind. Jesus thus occupied a place which was inconceivable for an ordinary human individual. Though He had lived as man, He had come into human history from beyond, from the heart of the Godhead itself. St. John accordingly declared that He was the eternal Word, who was in the beginning with God and through whom all things were originally created, as now by His

coming in the flesh they have been redeemed (Jn. 1. 1–18). The doctrine of the deity of Jesus Christ rests on a much broader basis than a few of His own utterances. Secondly, in the light of the whole fact of Jesus the OT revelation of the nature of God and of man was enriched. A new order began. Christians were baptized into the threefold Divine Name of the Father and of Jesus Christ and of the Holy Spirit; man was revealed as alienated from God by sin and in need of the drastic redemption provided by God through the coming and suffering of Jesus. The foundations of this new Christian theology were laid in the NT; the task of understanding the full implications of the life and work of Jesus Christ still rightly claims the attention of the Christian intellect.

Among the innumerable introductory studies may be mentioned the *Life* of F. W. *Farrer (q.v.); also W. *Sanday, *Outlines of the Life of Christ* (1905), and C. *Gore, *Jesus of Nazareth* (1929). Popular treatment, with vivid topographical descriptions, in H. V. Morton, *In the Steps of the Master* (1934). Other works from many different standpoints are: D. F. *Strauss, *Leben Jesu* (2 vols, 1835–6). E. *Renan, *La Vie de Jésus* (1863). [J. *Seeley], *Ecce Homo* (London, 1866). H. P. *Liddon, *The Divinity of Christ* (Bampton Lectures for 1866; 1867). H. Latham, *Pastor Pastorum* (Cambridge, 1890). G. *Dalman, *Die Worte Jesu* (1898; Eng. tr., 1902). P. Wernle, *Die Quellen des Lebens Jesu* (1904; Eng. tr., *Sources of our Knowledge of the Life of Jesus*, 1907). A. *Schweitzer, *Von Reimarus zu Wrede* (1906; Eng. tr., *The Quest of the Historical Jesus*, 1910). W. Sanday, *The Life of Christ in Recent Research* (1907). J. Denney, *Jesus and the Gospel* (1908). F. C. *Burkitt, *The Earliest Sources for the Life of Jesus* (Boston, Mass., 1910; ed. 2, London, 1922). E. F. Scott, *The Kingdom and the Messiah* (1911). H. *Rashdall, *Conscience and Christ* (1916). T. R. Glover, *Jesus of History* (1917). G. Dalman, *Jesus-Jeschua* (1922; Eng. tr., 1929). A. C. *Headlam, *The Life and Teaching of Jesus the Christ* (1923). J. Klausner, *Jesus of Nazareth* (1925). R. *Bultmann, *Jesus* (Berlin [1926]; Eng. tr., 1934). A. E. J. Rawlinson, *The New Testament Doctrine of the Christ* (1926). L. de Grandmaison, S.J., *Jésus Christ. Sa personne, ses messages, ses preuves* (2 vols., posthumous, 1928; Eng. tr., 1935). T. W. Manson, *The Teaching of Jesus* (1931). M. Goguel, *La Vie de Jésus* (Bibliothèque historique, 1932; Eng. tr., 1933). C. Guignebert, *Jésus* (L'Évolution de l'Humanité, 1933; rationalistic). R. *Otto, *Reich Gottes und Menschensohn. Ein religionsgeschichtlicher Versuch* (1934; Eng. tr. entitled *The Kingdom of God and the Son of Man*, 1938). H. D. A. Major–T. W. Manson–C. J. Wright, *The Mission and Message of Jesus* (1937). V. Taylor, *Jesus and His Sacrifice* (1939). W. Manson, *Jesus the Messiah* (1943). G. S. Duncan, *Jesus, Son of Man*. Studies contributary to a modern Portrait (1947). See also bibliography to artt. *Christology* (esp. for works on the Person of Christ); *Gospels*; *Messiah*.

JESUS, Name of. See *Name of Jesus*.

JESUS, Sayings of. See *Sayings of Jesus*.

JEU, Books of. The title of two *Gnostic treatises mentioned in the *Pistis Sophia which are ascribed to *Enoch.

JEUNESSE OUVRIÈRE CHRÉTIENNE. See *Jocists*.

JEW, The Wandering. See *Wandering Jew, The*.

JEWEL, JOHN (1522–71), Bp. of *Salisbury. Educated at Merton and Corpus Christi colleges, Oxford, he was elected in 1542 a Fellow of Corpus. After 1547, largely through the influence of *Peter Martyr, he became one of the intellectual leaders of the Reforming party. Under *Mary, Jewel signed a set of anti-Protestant articles (1554), but notwithstanding he was forced to flee to Frankfurt (1555), where he opposed J. *Knox and the advanced *Calvinists. A little later he joined Martyr at Strassburg and travelled with him to Zürich. On the accession of *Elizabeth he returned to England, and in 1560 was consecrated Bp. of Salisbury. From now onwards he became a strong supporter of the Anglican settlement, opposing both RCs and Puritans, and taking his stand on the Fathers of the first six centuries. In 1562 he published his celebrated treatise in defence of the C of E, the *Apologia Ecclesiae Anglicanae*, which established itself at once as the best defence of the Anglican claims. It endeavoured to prove that a general Reformation had been necessary, that reform by such a body as the Council of *Trent was impossible, and that local Churches had the right to legislate through provincial synods. In the prolonged and bitter controversy that followed with Thomas Harding (1516–72), who defended the Papacy, the lines which the Roman controversy was to take in the 17th cent. were mainly determined; and under *James I, Abp. R. *Bancroft gave official approval to Jewel's teaching. Jewel, who administered his diocese with a vigour unusual in the Elizabethan Church, made several visitations, preached frequently, and built the library of Salisbury Cathedral. Among a number of poor boys whom Jewel maintained and prepared for the university was R. *Hooker, whose *Ecclesiastical Polity* owed much to his patron's teaching.

Collected Works ed. under the direction of R. *Bancroft, London, fol., 1609, with memoir [by D. Featly] (no pagination; ed. 2, 1611). Modern edd. by J. Ayre (*Parker Society, 4 vols., 1845–50), with memoir in vol. iv, pp. v–xxx; and R. W. *Jelf (8 vols., Oxford, 1848). The principal authority is the official biography, sponsored by Abp. M. *Parker, by Jewel's friend, Laurence Humphrey (in Latin; London, 1573); it is the basis of all subsequent memoirs. An anonymous life is prefixed to the Eng. tr. of Jewel's *Apologia Ecclesiae Anglicanae* by 'A Person of Quality' (London, 1685), pp. 1–52. More modern life by C. W. Le Bas (London, 1835). M. *Creighton in *D.N.B.*, xxix (1892), pp. 378–82; C. Wordsworth in *D.E.C.H.*, p. 299 f. W. M. Southgate, *John Jewel and the Problem of Doctrinal Authority* (Cambridge, Mass., 1962).

JEWISH PEOPLE. See *Judaism*.

JEWS, Missions to the. Despite the fact that Christianity found its earliest converts among the Jews, mutual hostility soon impeded missionary enterprise. Legal enactments (e.g. by *Constantine and the Merovingian kings) encouraged, and in some cases compelled, conversion, but a few voices (e.g. that of St. *Bernard of Clairvaux) were raised against the long prevalent policy of persecution. In the 16th cent. this policy was carried to an unsurpassed intensity by the Spanish *Inquisition. In *Rome of the *Counter-Reformation era missionary activity was encouraged from time to time (e.g. by the *Jesuits and St. *Philip Neri), so that between 1634 and 1790 some 2,430 Jews were baptized in the city. But except for the notable work of Ezra Edzard (1629–1708), J. H. Callenberg (1694–1760, under whose auspices, with the support of A. H. *Francke, the *Institutum Judaicum* was founded at Halle in 1728), and some of the *Moravians, little progress was made until the 19th cent. The impulse for creating missionary societies came from Christian Jews. Thus J. S. C. F. Frey (1771–1851) and Ridley Haim Herschell (1807–64) were responsible respectively for the foundation of the 'London Society' and the 'British Society' for 'Promoting Christianity among the Jews'. The former, established in 1809 and known now also as Church Missions to Jews, is still the largest of its kind and has a wide sphere of influence. Other societies include Hebrew Christian Testimony to Israel (estd. 1893), the Barbican Mission to the Jews (estd. 1889), and the Parochial Missions to the Jews. The missions resulted in some very talented converts, among them the scholars C. P. *Caspari, A. *Edersheim, C. D. Ginsburg, and J. A. W. *Neander; Bishops M. S. *Alexander, I. Hellmuth, and S. I. J. Schereschewsky; and the missionaries, H. Stern and J. Wolff. Conversion also resulted in the evolution of a Jewish Christian Church closely associated with the work of the Hebrew-Christian Alliance, and in particular of Joseph Rabinowitz (1837–99).

W. T. Gidney, *The History of the London Society for Promoting Christianity amongst the Jews from 1809 to 1908* (1908).

JIMENEZ DE CISNEROS, FRANCISCO.
See *Ximenez de Cisneros, Francisco.*

JOACHIM, St.
The husband of St. *Anne and the father of the BVM. He is first mentioned in the '*Protevangelium of James' (2nd cent.), where the birth of the Virgin, promised by an angel to her aged and childless parents, is recorded. Apart from this passage, he is rarely referred to in Christian tradition till much later times—in the E. seldom before the 7th cent., and in the W. not till the Middle Ages. In later medieval times he became a frequent subject for the religious artist. He has been commemorated on many different dates; since 1913 his feast day in the RC Church has been assigned to 16 Aug.

É. Amann, *Le Protévangile de Jacques et ses remaniements latins* (1910), pp. 45–51. On his reputed tomb at Jerusalem, see L. Cré, 'Tombeau de St. Joachim et de Ste Anne' in *R. Bibl.*, ii (1893), pp. 245–74, and H. Vincent, O.P., 'La Crypte de sainte Anne à Jérusalem', ib., xiii (1904), pp. 228–41. Further lit. in *L.Th.K.*, v (1933), 447, by B. Kraft, s.v.

JOACHIM OF FIORE (*c.* 1132–1202), or of 'Flora', mystic.
Little is known of his life, which has been richly embellished with legends. He made a pilgrimage to the Holy Land as a young man and during it he is said to have experienced a conversion to the interior life. He subsequently entered the *Cistercian Order, being elected Abbot of Corazzo against his will in 1177. He resigned his office a few years later to devote himself to the writing of his apocalyptic works and resided first at the abbey of Casamari and later at Fiore in Calabria, where the founded a monastery of his own which received Papal sanction in 1196 and developed into a separate order of some local significance. He died before being able to obtain the approval of the Holy See for his works, but in his will he required his successors in the order to seek this and to abide by the decision. The sanctity of his life is unquestioned —he is described by *Dante as *di spirito profetico dotato*,—but some of his views were condemned by the *Lateran Council in 1215, and by Alexander IV in 1256.

The central doctrine of his three chief works, 'Liber Concordiae Novi ac Veteris Testamenti', 'Expositio in Apocalysim', and 'Psalterium Decem Cordarum', is a Trinitarian conception of the whole of history which views it in three great periods ('status'). The first, characterized by the 'Ordo conjugatorum', is the age of the Father in which mankind lived under the Law until the end of the OT dispensation; the second, characterized by the 'Ordo clericorum', is that of the Son which is lived under grace and covers the NT dispensation which Joachim thought would last for forty-two generations of *c.* thirty years each; the third, belonging to the 'Ordo monachorum' or 'contemplantium', is the age of the Spirit which will be lived in the liberty of the 'Spiritualis Intellectus' proceeding from the Old and New Testaments and be inaugurated *c.* 1260. This last age would see the rise of new religious orders destined to convert the whole world and to usher in the 'Ecclesia Spiritualis'. Joachim never advanced his doctrine of the third age to a point of danger to ecclesiastical authority, but his optimistic expectations concerning history had a far-reaching influence in the following centuries among groups who often carried his ideas to revolutionary conclusions, notably the *Spiritual Franciscans and *Fraticelli, who believed themselves to be Joachim's new order of spiritual men. It was his ideas which inspired the attempt by the Spiritual Franciscan, Gerard of Borgo San Donnino, in 1254 to complete Joachim's pattern of threes by proclaiming an Eternal Evangel (excerpts from Joachim's works) which had superseded the OT and NT. Joachim's conceptions continued to captivate the imagination of individuals throughout the later Middle Ages.

There are modern edd. of his *Tractatus super Quatuor Evangelia* by E. Buonaiuti (Fonti per Storia d' Italia, 1930), of his *Liber Contra Lombardum* by C. Ottaviano (Reale Accademia d' Italia. Studi e documenti iii, 1934), of his *Expositio de Articulis Fidei* by E. Buonaiuti (R. Istituto Storico Italiano per il Medio Evo. Fonti per la storia d' Italia, 1936), and of his *Liber Figurarum* by L. Tondelli (2 vols., Turin, 1936; ed. 2, Turin, 1953, vol. i ed. L. Tondelli, vol. ii ed. L. Tondelli, Marjorie E. Reeves, and Beatrice M. Hirsch-Reich). P. Fournier, *Étude sur Joachim de Flora et ses doctrines* (1909). H. Grundmann, *Studien über Joachim von Floris* (Beiträge zur Kulturgeschichte des Mittelalters und der Renaissance, xxxii; 1927); id., *Neue Forschungen über Joachim von Fiore* (Münstersche Forschungen, Hft. 1; 1950). E. Buonaiuti, *Gioacchino da Fiore. I tempi, la vita, il messaggio* (1931). E. Anitchkof, *Joachim de Flore et les milieux courtois* (Collezione di Studi meridionali, 1931). F. Foberti, *Gioacchino da Fiore.* Nuovi studi critici sulla mistica e la religiosità in Calabria (Florence, 1934); id., *Gioacchino da Fiore e il gioacchinismo antico e moderno* (Padua, 1942). J. C. Huck, *Joachim von Floris und die joachitische Literatur* (1938). H. Bett, *Joachim of Flora* ('Great Medieval Churchmen', 1931).

JOAN, Pope. The legend of a female Pope first appears in the (13th cent.) *Dominican chronicler, Jean de Mailly, and was repeated in various versions by historical writers of the following centuries. The gist of the story is that about the year 1100 (later forms say after St. *Leo IV, d. 855) a woman in male disguise, after a distinguished career as a scholar, succeeded to the chair of St. Peter. After reigning more than two years she gave birth to a child during a procession to the *Lateran and died immediately afterwards. There is no evidence whatever in favour of the tale, but it was widely believed in the Middle Ages. To-day it is rejected as an invention by all serious scholars. J. J. I. *Döllinger explained it as an ancient Roman folk-tale.

J. J. I. Döllinger, *Die Papst-Fabeln des Mittelalters* (1863), pp. 1–45 (Eng. tr., 1871, pp. 1–67); E. Vacandard, *Etudes de critique et d'histoire religieuse*, Ser. 4 (1923), pp. 15–39 (La Papesse Jeanne). See also entry *Blondel* (David).

JOAN OF ARC, St. (1412–31), called 'La Pucelle', the 'Maid of Orléans'. The setting of her life was the Hundred Years' War. The daughter of a peasant, she was born and brought up in Domrémy, Champagne. A pious child, she experienced in 1425 the first of her supernatural manifestations, which she described as a voice accompanied by a blaze of light. Gradually her 'voices' increased and she was able to distinguish St. *Michael, St. *Catherine, St. *Margaret and others, who revealed to Joan her mission to save France. She was unsuccessful in an attempt in 1428 to persuade the French commander at Vaucouleurs of the genuiness of her visions; but after her prophecies had been fulfilled in 1429 she was sent to the King (Charles VII), who was convinced when he recognized him in disguise. Joan then gave the King a secret sign, which she never revealed. After close examination of her case by a body of theologians at Poitiers, it was decided to allow her to lead an expedition to Orléans. Clad in a suit of white armour and bearing a banner with a symbol of the Trinity and the words 'Jesus, Maria', she worked wonders by her presence and the city was relieved. After a short campaign in the Loire, she persuaded Charles VII to proceed to *Reims for his coronation, which took place on 17 July 1429, with Joan at his side. The relief of Orléans and the crowning of the Dauphin virtually saved France. After six months of military inactivity fresh campaigns took place in the spring of 1430 in which she was less successful. She was taken prisoner near Compiègne on 24 May 1430, sold to the English by the Duke of Burgundy on 21 Nov. 1430, and appeared before the court of the Bp. of Beauvais (Pierre Cauchon) at Rouen on 21 Feb. 1431 on a charge of

witchcraft and heresy. After further examination in her cell, a summary of her statements was compiled. The judges of the episcopal court declared her visions 'false and diabolical' and the summary was also denounced by the university of *Paris. After some form of recantation on 23 May, she resumed male attire, which she had agreed to abandon, and on 29 May was condemned as a relapsed heretic and on 30 May burnt at Rouen. The determination of her captors to encompass her death is a measure of the influence she exerted on her followers. A revision of her trial by an appellate court appointed by the Pope *Calistus III declared her innocent in 1456. Canonized on 9 May 1920 by *Benedict XV as a holy maiden, she is the second patron of France. Feast day, 30 May.

J. Quicherat (ed.), *Procès de condamnation et de réhabilitation de Jeanne d'Arc* (5 vols., 1841–9); P. Champion (ed.), *Procès de condamnation de Jeanne d'Arc* (2 vols., 1920–1), with introd., Fr. tr., and notes; Eng. tr. of documents of the trial by W. P. Barrett, *The Trial of Joan of Arc* (1931). Studies include those by H. Wallon (2 vols., Paris, 1860), M. Sépet (ib., 1869), J. B. J. Ayrolles (ib., 1890), P. H. Dunaud (ib., 1907), A. France (2 vols., ib., 1907–8), A. Lang (London, 1908), G. Hanotaux (Paris, 1911), A. Fabre (ib., 1912), G. Goyau (ib., 1920), A. B. Paine (2 vols., New York, 1925), J. Calmette (Paris, 1946), and J. Cordier (ib., 1948).

JOASAPH, St. See *Josaphat, St.*

JOB, Book of. The main portion of the book, which is in poetic form, is preceded by a prose Prologue (1 and 2); it is followed by an Epilogue (42. 7–17). Discussions between Job and his three friends appear in three cycles (3–14, 15–21, 22–31), culminating in an appeal to the Almighty. There follow the speeches of Elihu (32–7), which are sometimes regarded as an intrusion since they add nothing to the arguments of the friends and interrupt the connexion of chs. 31 and 38. The Divine reply and Job's acceptance of it is recorded in chs. 38–42. 6.

The main subject of the Book is the perennial problem of innocent suffering. Although no final solution is reached, the Book offers the most thorough treatment of it in the OT. Job rejects the traditional view that suffering is the result of sin, for he has no doubt of his innocence. It is rather in his disinterested piety, which is vindicated in the Epilogue, that the purpose of his suffering is to be sought. Already in the NT (cf. Jas. 5. 11), the patience of Job was proverbial. Owing to the universal nature of the subject matter of the book, considerations of historical background and date are of little importance except for the critical student. Various dates between the 5th and 2nd cents. B.C. have been suggested by modern scholars.

Modern commentaries include those by L. Hirzel (Kurzgefasstes exegetisches Handbuch zum Alten Testament, ii; 1839; ed. 3, by A. *Dillmann, 1869), A. B. *Davidson (Camb. Bib., AV, 1884), K. *Budde (H.K.A.T., Abteilung 2, Bd. i; 1896), B. Duhm (K.H.C., xiv; 1897), E. C. S. Gibson ('Oxford Commentaries' [West. Comm.], 1899), A. S. *Peake (Cent. Bib.; 1905), S. R. *Driver-G. B. *Gray (I.C.C.; 1921), C. J. Ball (Oxford, 1922, including translation into English verse), P. Dhorme, O.P. (Études Bibliques;

1926), N. Peters (E.H., xxi; 1928), G. Hölscher (H.A.T., Reihe 1, Bd. xvii; 1937), and E. J. Kissane (Dublin, 1937). T. K. *Cheyne, *Job and Solomon* (1887), pp. 12–115. G. Richter, *Textstudien zum Buche Hiob* (Beiträge zur Wissenschaft vom Alten und Neuen Testament, Folge 3, vii; 1927). J. Lindblom, *Boken om Job* (Lund, 1940). W. B. Stevenson, *The Poem of Job*. A Literary Study with a New Translation (Schweich Lectures, 1943; 1947). Id., *Critical Notes on the Hebrew Text of the Poem of Job* (1951). E. F. Sutcliffe, S.J., 'Notes on Job, Textual and Exegetical' in *Biblica*, xxx (1949), pp. 66–90. and xxxi (1950), pp. 365–78. A. S. Peake, *The Problem of Suffering in the Old Testament* (Hartley Lectures for 1904; 1904), pp. 83–103. H. W. *Robinson, *The Cross of Job* (1916); J. E. McFadyen, *The Problem of Pain*. A Study in the Book of Job [1917]. M. Jastrow, *The Book of Job*. Its Origin, Growth and Interpretation (Philadelphia, 1920); E. G. Kraeling, *The Book of the Ways of God* (S.P.C.K., 1938).

JOCISTS. The organized association of factory workers in the RC Church known as the **Jeunesse Ouvrière Chrétienne (J.O.C.).** It endeavours to bring Christian moral principles to bear on modern industry and keep the young of the working classes within the life of the Church. As an organization it grew up after the war of 1914–18 in and around Brussels, under the guidance of the Abbé Cardijn and the inspiration of the ideals of *Leo XIII's *Rerum Novarum*. The title was adopted in 1924, and in 1926 the movement spread to France. The unit of organization is the section, usually in the parish, 30–40 sections forming a regional federation. Corresponding associations have also been created for agricultural workers (J.A.C.; *Jeunesse Agricole Chrétienne*) and sailors (J.M.C.; *Jeunesse Maritime Chrétienne*).

JOEL, The Book of. One of the twelve *Minor Prophets of the OT. Apart from the Book nothing is known of 'Joel, the son of Pethuel', though he is generally thought to have been a Judaean by birth. The prophecy, for the most part written in poetic form, has two sections. The first (1. 1–2. 17) tells of a plague of locusts and its results, and draws against this background a picture of the approaching Day of the Lord with its call to repentance. The rest of the Book (2. 18–3. 21) foretells the future outpouring of the Spirit on all flesh, the final salvation of Judah, and the destruction of foreign nations, all subjects of the kind more fully developed in 'the Apocalyptic literature'. The passage predicting the outpouring of the Spirit of God and its effects (2. 28–32) is cited in Acts 2. 17–21 as foreshadowing the gift of the Holy Spirit at Pentecost.

Commentaries by S. R. *Driver (Camb. Bib., AV, on Joel and Amos, 1897, pp. 9–91), J. A. Bewer (I.C.C. on Mic., Zeph., Nah., Hab., Obad., and Joel, 1912; sep. pagination) and G. W. Wade (West. Comm. on Mic., Obad., Joel, and Jon., 1925; sep. pagination). W. Baumgartner, 'Joel 1 und 2' in *Beiträge zur alttestamentlichen Wissenschaft Karl Budde zum siebzigsten Geburtstag überreicht* (Beihefte zur Z.A.T.W., xxxiv, 1920), pp. 10–19. L. Dennefeld, 'Les Problèmes du livre de Joël' in *Rev. S.R.*, iv (1924), pp. 555–575, v (1925), pp. 35–57, 591–608, vi (1926), pp. 26–49. Further Commentaries under *Minor Prophets*.

JOHANNINE COMMA (also known as the 'Three Witnesses'). An interpolation in the text of 1 Jn. 5. 7 f., viz. the words in italics in the following passage from the AV: 'For there are three that bear record *in heaven, the Father, the Word, and the Holy Ghost, and these Three are One. And there are three that bear witness in earth* the Spirit, and the Water and the Blood, and these three agree in one'. They occur only in MSS (almost exclusively Latin) of a late date, are omitted in the RV, and are certainly not part of the original text of the Epistle. The origin of the interpolation is obscure. Traces of a mystical interpretation of the phrase about the Spirit, the Water, and the Blood, applying it to the Trinity, are to be found in *Cyprian and *Augustine; but the earliest evidence for the insertion of a gloss in the text of the Epistle comes from a MS. of *Priscillianist provenance discovered by G. Schepss at Würzburg in 1885. Later the insertion is found in African authors. It would thus seem to have originated in N. Africa or Spain and to have found its way into the Latin Bibles used in those districts (both *Old Latin and *Vulgate), possibly under the stress of *Arian persecution. It is absent from St. Jerome's original text of the Vulgate.

K. Künstle, *Das Comma Ioanneum auf seine Herkunft untersucht* (1905); E. Riggenbach, *Das Comma Johanneum* (Beiträge zur Förderung christlicher Theologie, xxxi, Hft. 4; 1928; posthumous). See also Commentaries on 1 Jn., esp. A. E. Brooke, 'The Johannine Epistles' (I.C.C., 1912), pp. 154–65.

JOHN, St., Apostle. Acc. to tradition, the author of the Fourth Gospel, the Book of Revelation, and three of the Catholic Epistles. He was the son of Zebedee (Mt. 4. 21), and together with St. *Peter and his brother, St. *James, belonged to the inner group of disciples who were present at the raising of Jairus's daughter (Lk. 8. 51), the *Transfiguration (Mt. 17. 1), and the Agony in the Garden (Mt. 26. 37). He and his brother were of impetuous character, hence the Lord designated them Boanerges, i.e. 'sons of thunder' (Mk. 3. 17), but they were also generous, offering to drink with Him the cup of suffering (Mt. 20. 22). In Acts John is frequently mentioned with St. Peter (3. 1 and 11), with whom he is imprisoned and appears before the Sanhedrin (4. 1–21). Later he is sent to Samaria with Peter, to transmit the Holy Ghost to the new converts (8. 14 f.). He was present also at the Apostles' Council at *Jerusalem (Gal. 2. 9). In the Fourth Gospel John is never mentioned by name, but tradition identifies him with the anonymous disciple to whom St. *John the Baptist shows the Lamb of God (1. 35–40) and with the disciple 'whom Jesus loved', who reclined on His bosom at the Last Supper (13. 23), to whom He entrusted His Mother at the foot of the Cross (19. 26), who ran with Peter to the tomb on the morning of the Resurrection (20. 2–8), and who recognized the Risen Lord at the Sea of Tiberias (21. 7). On this last occasion our Lord spoke to him the words which were interpreted as meaning that he would not die. (This traditional identification of the 'beloved disciple' with John, the son of Zebedee, has been contested in modern times;

and the idea has been put forward, notably by H. Delff, W. *Bousset, and H. B. *Swete, that he was not one of the Twelve, but a Jerusalem disciple. Against this view defenders of tradition have argued that the Beloved Disciple, just as the John of the Synoptics and of Acts, is always shown in close association with St. Peter and that the consistent omission of so important a disciple as St. John is inexplicable except on the assumption that for intrinsic reasons he is referred to under some other designation.) Acc. to tradition he later went to Asia Minor and settled at Ephesus, was exiled to *Patmos under *Domitian, where he wrote the Book of Revelation (Rev. 1. 9) and returned to *Ephesus under Nerva, where he wrote the Gospel and the Epistles in his old age. Against this tradition, Mk. 10. 39 has sometimes been urged by critics to be a 'vaticinium ex eventu', implying that St. John suffered martyrdom together with St. James. Support for this theory is also found in an alleged passage from *Papias mentioning the death of one John at the hands of the Jews, and a notice on the death of 'John and James' in several *martyrologies. This evidence for John's early death, however, is very inconclusive. Defenders of the traditional view observe that the terms of the prophecy in Mk. 10. 39 are quite vague, and the Papias passage may embody a tradition relating to St. John the Baptist. As to the martyrologies, that of Carthage mentions explicitly John the Baptist on the same day as St. James, so that it seems probable that the mention in other martyrologies of St. John the brother of James on the same day is due to a confusion between the two Johns. Both the question of the identity of the Beloved Disciple and that of the date of St. John's death have played a considerable part in the controversy on the authorship of the Gospel of St. John (q.v.). Feast day, 27 Dec. Acc. to later legend, St. John was ordered by Domitian to be thrown into a cauldron of boiling oil 'before the Latin Gate', i.e. the gate leading southwards from Rome to Latium, and came out unharmed. This event is commemorated in his feast 'ante portam Latinam' on 6 May.

The main literature is contained in commentaries and studies on the Gospel and Epp. of St. John and the Book of Rev. (qq.v.) and in general works on the NT. Works specifically on the Apostle and his theology as a whole include P. J. Gloag, *Introduction to the Johannine Writings* (1891), G. B. Stevens, *The Johannine Theology* (1894), P. W. *Schmiedel, *The Johannine Writings* (Eng. tr. of various items; 1908), G. G. Findlay, *Fellowship in the Life Eternal* (1909), and J. E. *Carpenter, *The Johannine Writings* (1927). The early martyrdom of the Apostle is defended by E. *Schwartz, *Über den Tod der Söhne Zebedaei* (Abh. (Gött.), N.F., vii, No. 5; 1904). T. B. *Strong in *H.D.B.*, ii (1899), pp. 680–94; P. W. Schmiedel in *E.Bi.*, ii (1901), cols. 2503–62, s.v. 'John, Son of Zebedee'.

JOHN, Acts of. A Greek apocryphal treatise, not later than the early 3rd cent., describing events in the life of the Apostle, St. *John. Large parts of it have come down to us in a number of scattered MSS., all incomplete. A fragment, discovered by M. R. James in 1886, contains an extended account of Christ's passion in highly *Docetic language, and a hymn which at a much later date was used by the *Priscillianists. A long account of the death of St. John has also survived. As the events described are mainly connected with *Ephesus, it is likely that the treatise is of Ephesian provenance. It was known to *Clement of Alexandria, and apparently also to the author of *Monarchian Prologues to the Gospels. It was ascribed, esp. in later times, to a certain *Leucius.

Reff. in *Eusebius, *H.E.*, III., xxv 6, *Epiphanius, *Haer.*, xlvii. 1, and *Philaster, *Haer.*, 88. Text in R. A. *Lipsius–M. Bonnet, *Acta Apostolorum Apocrypha*, II (1; 1898), pp. 151–216. Eng. tr. by M. R. James, *The Apocryphal New Testament* (1924), pp. 228–70; new frag. in B. P. Grenfell and A. S. Hunt, *The Oxyrhynchus Papyri*, vi (1908), pp. 12–18 (No. 850). Analysis of fragg. and later revisions of text in Altaner (ed. 1951), p. 56. The *Acta Ioannis*, attributed to a certain Prochorus and publd. by T. *Zahn (Erlangen, 1880), are a later (5th cent.) orthodox revision of the orig. Gnostic Acts. J. Quasten, *Patrology*, i (Utrecht, 1950), pp. 134–6.

JOHN, Epistles of St. There are three '*Catholic Epistles' which tradition ascribes to St. John, the Apostle and author of the Fourth Gospel. The longest and most important of them is the first. It is reckoned by *Eusebius among the 'homologoumena' and is attested by *Papias, *Polycarp, the *Muratorian Canon, and *Irenaeus. Modern scholars who defend the Apostolic authorship of the Gospel commonly also admit that of this Epistle. Among those who reject it opinion is divided. Some, e.g. A. *Harnack, attribute it to the author of the Gospel; others, e.g. C. H. *Dodd, distinguish their authors. The other two Epistles are intimately connected with each other. They were, however, not generally admitted as authentic in antiquity. Eusebius placed them among the 'antilegomena' and St. *Jerome reports that many attributed them to one 'John the Presbyter' because of their opening words. They are not contained in the Syriac (*Peshitta) Version, and many modern critics do not assign them to the same author as the First Epistle. The Second Epistle is addressed to 'the elect lady and her children', which words are generally believed to refer not to a person but to a church; the Third to a Christian named Gaius.

The First Epistle may be considered as a practical application of the doctrines of the Fourth Gospel. The letter opposes false doctrines on the Person of Christ. Those who do not confess that Jesus is the Christ, or who deny that He came 'in the flesh', but try to substitute some more 'spiritual' religion, are not of God; they are 'antichrists' (4. 1–3). The advocates of such doctrines are 'false brethren', for they sin against the command of neighbourly love (4. 20). The conception of God as Light and Life, prominent in the Gospel, recurs in the First Epistle. Special stress is laid on the Love of God, which manifested itself principally in the Son, who was sent into the world as a propitiation for sin to give eternal life to all believers (4. 9–10). The Divinity of Christ is clearly affirmed (ch. 3). He is the Saviour of the world to which He gives life (5. 12 f.), but the world that does not accept Him lies in the evil one (5. 19), whose marks are the lust of the flesh and of the eyes and the vainglory of life (2. 16). Christ has come by water and blood (5. 6), an allusion to His Death and probably also to the Sacraments. He is our propitiation; His Blood purifies us from all sin (1. 7). In Him we possess Eternal Life (5. 11, 13) so that we become children of God (3. 1) capable of imitating His sanctity, justice, and love (3. 3, 7, 16). The Second Epistle insists esp. on the necessity of professing the right doctrine (2 Jn. 9) and of avoiding communion with the teachers of error (vv. 10, 11), and the Third on hospitality, reprimanding one Diotrephes for lacking the practice of this virtue. The teaching of all three Epistles centres in the love of one's neighbour, for our love of God is best proved by the practice of fraternal charity. On 1 Jn. 5. 7 f. see *Johannine Comma*.

Patristic Commentaries include the 'Adumbrationes' of St. *Clement of Alexandria (i.e. Lat. tr. of part of Clement's 'Hypotyposeis' made by *Cassiodorus c. 540) and the 'Decem Tractatus' of St. *Augustine. The more important modern Commentaries on the Epp. are those of B. F. *Westcott (London, 1883), A. Plummer (Camb. Bib., 1884), A. E. Brooke (I.C.C., 1912), E. C. *Hoskyns in C. *Gore–H. L. Goudge–A. Guillaume (ed.), *A New Commentary on Holy Scripture* (1928), pp. 658–73, and C. H. Dodd (Moff. Comm., 1946); also H. Windisch (Hb. N.T., iv, Hft. 2; 1911, on the Catholic Epistles; ed. 2, xv, 1930, pp. 106–44) and J. Chaine (Études bibliques, 1939, on the Catholic Epistles, pp. 97–260). F. D. *Maurice, *The Epistles of St. John* (1857); C. *Gore, *The Epistles of St. John* (1920). A. *Harnack, *Über den dritten Johannesbrief* (T.U., xv, Hft. 3; 1897). S. D. F. Salmond in *H.D.B.*, ii (1899), pp. 728–42, s.v.; R. Leconte in *Dict. Bibl.*, Suppl., iv (1949), cols. 797–815, s.v. 'Jean (Épitres de saint)'. See also bibl. to *John, St.*

JOHN, Gospel of St. The Fourth Gospel, which both in contents and outlook differs notably from the preceding three 'Synoptics', raises a series of problems generally known as the 'Johannine Question'. Acc. to an unbroken tradition going back to the second half of the 2nd cent. and attested by *Irenaeus, *Clement of Alexandria, and the *Muratorian Canon, it was written by St. John the Apostle. This attribution was contested only by the sect of the *Alogi and their Roman follower, *Gaius. That the Gospel was known already in the first half of the 2nd cent. seems probable from texts of St. *Polycarp and St. *Ignatius of Antioch, reproducing Johannine ideas; while the early acceptance of a Gospel, written probably in the last years of the 1st cent. and so different from the three authoritative Synoptics, has to many appeared a sufficient proof of its Apostolic origin. This, however, is contested by a large body of modern scholars whose positions vary from a complete rejection of both its authenticity and its historicity to the admission of Apostolic inspiration and a certain historical value. The unity of the book has been frequently disputed, esp. by German scholars, e.g. J. *Wellhausen, R. *Bultmann, and others, and also by A. *Loisy. Where its unity is admitted, its attribution to *John the Presbyter [cf. p. 740] is favoured. This theory has been defended, e.g. by A. *Harnack, W. *Sanday, W. *Bousset, and B. H. *Streeter. It rests on a passage from Papias, preserved by *Eusebius (*H.E.*, III, xxxix, 4), where there is

a reference to John in the list of the Apostles and immediately afterwards another mention of a John, called the 'Elder' (πρεσβύτερος). From this passage, from which Eusebius himself concludes that there were two Johns living in *Ephesus at the same time, one the Apostle and the other the 'Elder', modern scholars have suggested that in fact only one John was then living at Ephesus, viz. John the Elder, who was also the author of the Gospel, and that tradition confused him with the Apostle. This hypothesis, however, has been rejected by many conservative scholars, who maintain that the Apostle's authorship is supported not only by tradition but also by internal evidence. In the Prologue of the Gospel the author apparently presents himself as an eye-witness (1. 14), and this testimony is held to be borne out by several details, such as the specified day and hour of certain events (e.g. 1. 29, 35, 39; 4. 6, &c.). On the traditional view that the Beloved Disciple is identical with St. John (see art. *John, St.*) his testimony in 19. 35 and that of his followers in 21. 24 are an additional proof of Apostolic authorship. On this assumption the reason commonly given for the Gospel's omission of the name of St. John is the humility of the Apostle. While he avoided putting himself forward, he left sufficient indications of his identity for those who knew him.

A further objection to Apostolic authorship is seen in the divergence between the Fourth Gospel and the Synoptics, notably the shifting of our Lord's activities from *Galilee to *Jerusalem and the extension of His ministry from the one year of the Synoptics to some three in all. Moreover, while the latter place the expulsion of the moneylenders from the Temple at the close of His ministry, John records it at the beginning. Another striking divergence is the changing of the date of the *Last Supper and the *Crucifixion from the 14th and 15th Nisan to the 13th and 14th. Apart from these details the whole tenor of the Gospel is different from that of the Synoptics. Our Lord's teaching is not given in Parables and pithy sayings, but in long discourses; His Divinity is far more emphasized; very important events such as the institution of the Eucharist at the Last Supper are left out, while others, the omission of which in the Synoptics is difficult to explain, e.g. the Raising of Lazarus (11. 1–44) and the Feetwashing (13. 1–15), are included. These striking differences have been explained by conservative scholars on various lines. It is suggested that St. John presupposed the knowledge of the Synoptics in his readers, and his Gospel, whilst correcting them in some details, is concerned not to reproduce the popular teaching of Christ, which is given by Matthew, Mark, and Luke, but the higher doctrines reserved for His disciples, which were relegated to the background in the catechetical instructions which furnished material of the other three.

The Gospel also raises some textual problems. The so-called '*Pericope adulterae' (7. 53–8. 11; q.v.) cannot have been part of the original text; it is missing from most of the best

Greek codices, though it is found in the *Codex Bezae, and is almost certainly an interpolation. Another difficulty is the present place of chs. 15 and 16, which seem originally to have preceded ch. 14. Ch. 21, too, must be a later addition; but all except the last two verses (21. 24 f.) were probably by the author of the Gospel, and written to combat the belief that the Beloved Disciple would not die.

The purpose of the Gospel as stated in 20. 31 is to strengthen the readers' faith in Jesus as the Christ and the Son of God, so that they may have life in His name. The Prologue (1. 1–18), with which the Gospel begins, has given rise to much speculation. Whereas most commentators believe it to contain the key to the whole, others, e.g. A. Harnack, defend the opinion that it was added afterwards to make the Johannine doctrine acceptable to Hellenistic readers. The general view, however, is that the *Logos (q.v.) doctrine of the Prologue is simply the statement of the theology of the Incarnation in philosophical terms; and that though the word Λόγος does not recur in the Gospel, the idea underlies its whole teaching. The principal theme of the Gospel is the progressive manifestation of the Divine Word, the Light in the darkness. In the first four chapters this Light begins to shine and is received by men with joy. But when, in chs. 5 and 6, our Lord's teaching becomes more definite, men take sides for or against Him. Chs. 7–12 show the formation of the two parties; while opposition increases, the disciples gather more closely round their Master. In chs. 13–17 He is surrounded by a small group of followers to whom He reveals the secret of His Person and of His teaching. In chs. 18–19 the powers of darkness seem to have conquered. But this victory is only apparent, and the concluding chs. 20–21 show the final triumph of the Risen Christ.

The Gospel teaches a high Christological doctrine. Though all the faithful are the children of God, Jesus is His Son in a special sense: He is the Logos, the Only-Begotten of the Father (3. 16–18). Both in the Prologue and in the Gospel His pre-existence is repeatedly affirmed (e.g. 1. 1–5; 8. 58; 17. 5). He Himself clearly states His equality with God, hence He is accused of blasphemy by the Jews (5. 18). He enjoys omniscience (16. 30), He and the Father are one (10. 30), and all that belongs to the Father belongs also to Him (16. 15). At the same time He also teaches His dependence on the Father as Son (5. 19, 26) and His inferiority as man to the Father (14. 28), a statement which provided the *Arians with one of their chief arguments. The Incarnate Word was sent into the world to be its light and its life (1. 4–9), two conceptions which frequently recur in the Gospel; through Him alone can men go to the Father (14. 6), for He is the Good Shepherd who lays down His life for His sheep (10. 11–16). He has brought man salvation by revealing God in His own Person, for to know Christ is to know the Father (14. 7) and in Him man has eternal life. This latter conception largely

replaces, as well as supplements, the Synoptic teaching on the Kingdom. Eternal life, as understood by St. John, begins already here on earth through faith in Christ (5. 24; 6. 47); its principle is the mystic union of the believer with his Lord (14. 20), most clearly expressed in the allegory of the Vine (15. 1–7) and in the so-called High-Priestly Prayer (ch. 17, esp. v. 23). This union is operated by the Holy Ghost, the Paraclete, who dwells in the faithful (14. 17 and 26) and is their guide into the fullness of truth (16. 13). The effects of this union of Christ with the soul are the loving observance of His Commandments (14. 21), perfect peace and interior joy even in the midst of persecution (14. 27; 15. 11 and 20), and union of the faithful among themselves, a union that is modelled on the union of the Father with the Son (esp. 17. 20–24). The eschatological elements which are prominent in the Fourth Gospel as well as in the Synoptics appear here in a variant form. Resurrection and judgement begin already in this life; the future is contained in the present and the terms of the eternal in the temporal.

*Clement of Alexandria called the Fourth Gospel a 'spiritual Gospel'. It is evidently not a simple account of our Lord's miracles and popular teaching, but a deeply meditated representation of His Person and doctrine by a contemplative conscious of inspiration by the Holy Ghost. It may be regarded as the necessary complement of the picture of Christ drawn by the Synoptics, designed to show forth His Divinity and the sublimity of His teaching.

Ancient Gk. commentaries include those of the Gnostic *Heracleon (fragmentary), *Origen (only eight out of thirty-two books survive), *Chrysostom, *Theodore of Mopsuestia (many Gk. fragments and complete in Syr.), *Cyril of Alexandria, *Theophylact and *Euthymius Zigabenus; the most important Lat. work is St. *Augustine's collection of Tractates on the Gospel. Notable pre-19th cent. modern commentaries include those of J. *Calvin and J. *Maldonatus (qq.v.). Much later criticism of the Gospel is foreshadowed in K. G. *Bretschneider, *Probabilia de Evangelii et Epistolarum . . . Joannis Apostoli Indole et Origine* (Leipzig, 1820).

Modern commentaries include those of B. *Weiss (K.E.K., Abt. ii, ed. 6; 1880), B. F. *Westcott (Speaker's Commentary, 1881; Gk. text, 2 vols., London, 1908), A. *Loisy (Paris, 1903), T. *Zahn (in his own *Kommentar zum Neuen Testament*, iv; 1908), J. *Wellhausen (Berlin, 1908), W. Bauer (Hb. N.T., iv; 1912), M. J. *Lagrange, O.P. (Études bibliques, 1924), J. H. *Bernard (2 vols., I.C.C., 1928), G. H. C. Macgregor (Moff. Comm., 1928), the fine, but unfinished, work of E. C. *Hoskyns (ed. F. N. Davey, 2 vols., London, 1940), R. *Bultmann (K.E.K., Abt. ii, ed. 11; 1941, appendix, 1950), C. K. Barrett (1955), R. H. *Lightfoot (1956).

Studies in the 'Johannine Question': W. *Sanday, *The Authorship and Historical Character of the Fourth Gospel* (1872); J. *Drummond, *An Enquiry into the Character and Authorship of the Fourth Gospel* (1903); W. Sanday, *The Criticism of the Fourth Gospel* (1905); E. F. Scott, *The Fourth Gospel. Its Purpose and Theology* (1906); M. Lepin, *L'Origine du quatrième évangile* (1907) and *La Valeur historique du quatrième évangile* (1910); B. W. Bacon, *The Fourth Gospel in Research and Debate* (1910); B. Weiss, *Das Johannesevangelium als einheitliches Werk* (1912); H. L. Jackson, *The Problem of the Fourth Gospel* (1918); C. F. Burney, *The Aramaic Origin of the Fourth Gospel* (1922); W. F. Howard, *The Fourth Gospel in Recent Criticism and Interpretation* (1931); J. Donovan, *The Authorship of St. John's Gospel* (1936); E. Percy, *Untersuchungen über den Ursprung der johanneischen Theologie* (Lund, 1939); W. F. Howard, *Christianity according to St. John* (1943); J. N. Sanders, *The Fourth Gospel in the Early Church* (1943); C. H. *Dodd, *The Interpretation of the Fourth Gospel* (1953).

McNeile, pp. 267-300. F. *von Hügel in *E.B.* (ed. 11), xv (1911), pp. 452-8. E. B. Allo, O.P., in *Dict. Bibl.*, Suppl. iv (1949), cols. 815-43, s.v. 'Jean (Évangile de Saint)'.

JOHN XII, XXII, XXIII, Popes.   See after *John Peckham.*

JOHN, King of England.   See after *John Gualbert.*

JOHN OF ANTIOCH (d. 441), Bp. of *Antioch from 429.   The leader of the moderate Easterns in the *Nestorian controversy, he gave active support to his friend, Nestorius, in his dispute with *Cyril of Alexandria.   In 431 he failed to arrive at the Council of *Ephesus in time for its opening meeting (22 June); and Cyril, suspecting him (probably wrongly) of employing Fabian tactics to aid his friend, refused to wait and proceeded to condemn Nestorius forthwith.   When John eventually reached Ephesus a few days later, he held a counter-council which condemned Cyril and vindicated Nestorius.   In 433 he became reconciled with Cyril on the basis of a theological formula devised as a compromise; but John thereby lost many supporters in his own patriarchate.   A few of his letters are extant.

For his Letters see J. P. Migne, *PG*, lxxvii, 1449-62. See also bibl. to *Cyril of Alexandria* and to *Ephesus* (Council of, 431).

JOHN OF ÁVILA, Blessed (1500-69), Spanish mystic, 'Apostle of Andalusia'.   Born near Toledo, he studied law at Salamanca (1514-15), but, shrinking from a worldly career, he returned home and for three years devoted himself to austerity and prayer; he then studied philosophy and theology under D. *Soto at Alcalá.   Selling all his property on the death of his parents, he was ordained in 1525 and prepared for missionary work in Mexico in 1527.   In 1528, however, he was persuaded by the Abp. of Seville (A. de Manrique) to divert his efforts to reviving the faith in Andalusia, where he began preaching in 1529.   Summoned before the *Inquisition of Seville on a charge of preaching rigorism and exaggerating the dangers of wealth, he was promptly acquitted and widely acclaimed.   After a ministry of nine years in Andalusia, he returned to Seville.   He visited Cordova, Granada and various other Spanish towns.   During the last seventeen years of his life he was in constant physical pain.

John of Avila was one of the most effective preachers of his time, St. *Francis Borgia and St. *John of God being among the many who owed to him their conversion.   He was also the trusted counsellor of St. *Teresa of Ávila and his association with the early *Jesuits did much to foster the spread of the Order in Spain.   Among his works the best known are his *Audi Filia* (c. 1530), a treatise on Christian perfection addressed to a young nun named

Doña Sancha Carillo, and his Spiritual Letters. He was beatified in 1894.   Feast day, 10 May.

His Works were ed. at Madrid, 1588 (repr., 1941). Early Life by his disciple, St. *Luís of Granada (1588).   Modern Life and new ed. of his Works in preparation by Luigi Sala Balust.   Other lives by Martín Ruiz (Madrid, 1618), Longaro degli Oddi, S.J. (Rome, 1754; Eng. tr. by J. G. Macleod, S.J., 1898), and J. M. de Buck (Louvain, 1927). There is a specialist review *Maestro Ávila* (Montilla, 1946 ff.)

JOHN THE BAPTIST, St., The 'Forerunner of Christ'.   He was the son of Zacharias, a priest of the *Temple, and of Elizabeth, a kinswoman of the BVM, from whom he was born in old age.   His birth had been foretold by an angel (Lk. 1. 13-20) who had instructed Zacharias that he should be called John.   On the fulfilment of this injunction his father uttered the *Benedictus (q.v.).   John appeared c. A.D. 27 as a mission preacher on the banks of the *Jordan demanding repentance and baptism from his hearers in view of the approach of the *Kingdom of God.   His dress and diet (locusts and wild honey) were reminiscent of the OT prophets, though some of his preaching foreshadowed that of Christ.   Large crowds were attracted to him and among those who submitted to his baptism was the Lord Himself.   He recognized the Lord as the promised *Messiah and willingly accepted the fact that his own influence must decline as the Lord's increased.   At least three of the Twelve Apostles had been his disciples.   Later his denunciation of *Herod Antipas for his marriage led to his imprisonment and subsequent beheading (Mt. 14. 1-12).   In his life he denied that he was *Elijah, but the Lord was understood to have accepted the identification (Mt. 17. 13).   His influence twenty years later is attested in the Acts (18. 25, 19. 1-7).   He is highly revered by the *Mandaeans (q.v.), who just possibly have some remote connexion with St. John's original disciples.

Outside the NT, John is also mentioned by *Josephus (*Antiq.* XVIII, v, 2) in a passage of which there is no good reason to doubt the authenticity.   Here the place of his imprisonment and death are given as the fortress of Machaerus by the Dead Sea.   He was believed to have been buried at Sebaste, Samaria, where his tomb was honoured in the 4th cent.   On its desecration under *Julian the Apostate (c. 362) his relics appear to have been scattered, numerous churches claiming to possess them.

Acc. to tradition (*Origen, *Ambrose, *Jerome, and *Leo the Great), John the Baptist was endowed with pre-natal grace at the time of the *Visitation of the BVM (Lk. 1. 41).   Consequently the Feast of his Nativity, originally celebrated in connexion with the *Epiphany but from c. the late 4th cent. fixed on June 24 in the West and 25 in the East (six months before *Christmas), was regarded as of greater solemnity than that of his death ('Decollation'), observed 29 Aug. from c. 5th cent. The liturgy for the feast of his Nativity has retained certain affinities with that of Christmas, but because of its date the feast has become linked with certain customs connected with the summer solstice. The early importance of his cult is testified by his place in the *Canon of the Mass and in the *Confiteor.

In art, at first depicted only in connexion with the Baptism of the Lord, he is later represented as an ascetic preacher wearing camel hair and carrying a staff and scroll saying 'Ecce Agnus Dei'; he often bears a book or dish with a lamb on it. In Greek art he usually appears with the wings of a messenger.

M. Goguel, *Au seuil de l'évangile: Jean-Baptiste* (1928; with esp. ref. to his relations to Christ). L. J. M. Bebb in *H.D.B.*, ii (1899), pp. 677–80; J. C. Lambert in *D.C.G.*, i (1906), pp. 861–6; C. L. Souvay in *C.E.*, viii (1910), pp. 486–91; H. *Leclercq, O.S.B., in *D.A.C.L.*, vii (pt. 2, 1927), cols. 2167–84. B. Mariani, E. Josi, P. Toschi, &c., in *E.C.*, vi (1951), cols. 515–27, s.v. 'Giovanni Battista'. Also, on the theological aspects of John's Baptism, H. Houbaut in *D.T.C.*, viii (pt. 1, 1924), cols. 646–56, s.v. 'Jean-Baptiste (Baptême de saint'). [C. H. Kraeling, *John the Baptist* (New York, 1951).]

JOHN BAPTIST DE LA SALLE, St.
(1651–1719), founder of the Institute of the Brothers of Christian Schools. Born at *Reims of noble family, he received the tonsure in 1662 and was installed as Canon of Reims in 1667. After studying at the seminary of *Saint-Sulpice from 1670 to 1672, he was ordained priest in 1678. In 1679 he assisted in the opening of two free schools in Reims where he soon became interested in fostering religious principles in the teachers. The original group, which he had taken into his own house in 1681, having resisted his attempt to enforce a semi-monastic discipline, soon left him; but in 1682 others came forward. Resigning his canonry in 1683, he distributed his fortune to the poor (1684) and devoted himself to the training of his new community. In 1688 he took charge of the free school in the parish of Saint-Sulpice, founded by J. J. *Olier. In 1699 he opened in Paris the first Sunday Schools giving technical and religious instruction to the sons of artisans; and he was also asked by *James II to educate the Irish boys of his court. In subsequent years schools were started in other parts of France and beyond. In 1690 he finally decided to exclude priests from the Order and in 1693 he drew up the first rule. Although officially deposed in 1702, he retained personal control of the Institute until 1717.

Apart from his spiritual importance, de La Salle is significant as a pioneer in educational practice. First in the field for training colleges for teachers, as distinct from ecclesiastical seminaries, he popularized the teaching of the vernacular in French schools and the use of the simultaneous method. His boarding school at Saint-Yon (est. 1705) has been considered the prototype of modern secondary educational institutions. His published works include *Méditations pour tous les dimanches de l'année* (c. 1710) and *Conduite des écoles chrétiennes* (1720; Eng. tr., New York, 1935). He was canonized in 1900. Feast day, 15 May.

Letters and Documents, ed. W. J. Battersby (London, 1952), with introd. Eng. tr. of his two volumes of Meditations by id. (London, 1953); of his *Conduite des écoles chrétiennes* (orig. publd. Avignon, 1720) by F. de La Fontainerie (New York and London, 1935). The principal

authority is the life by his friend, J. B. Blain (2 vols., Rouen, 1733). Other lives include those by J. P. Garreau (Rouen, 1760; abridged Eng. tr., 1843), A. Ravelet (Paris, 1847), 'Un Frère des écoles chrétiennes' [Frère Lucard] (Rouen, 1874), J. Guibert (Paris, 1900), A. Delaire (ed. 4, 'Les Saints', 1902), and F. *Thompson (London, 1911). W. J. Battersby, *De La Salle. A Pioneer of Modern Education* (1949); id., *De La Salle. Saint and Spiritual Writer* (1950). Mrs. R. F. Wilson, *The Christian Brothers. Their Origin and Work* (1883); G. Rigault, *L'Institut des Frères des Écoles Chrétiennes* ('Les Grands Ordres monastiques' [1928]). Heimbucher, ii, pp. 433–44, with bibl.

JOHN BAPTIST MARY VIANNEY, St.
See *Curé d'Ars, The*.

JOHN OF BEVERLEY, St.
(d. 721), Bp. of *York. A monk of St. *Hilda's double-abbey at *Whitby and a diligent scholar and teacher, he was consecrated Bp. of *Hexham c. 687. In 705 he was translated to the see of York, then being claimed by *Wilfred. Before his death he retired to the abbey at Inderawood, afterwards *Beverley, of which he had himself been the founder. The reputation he acquired for sanctity during his lifetime increased after his death, and in the Middle Ages he enjoyed a widespread cultus in England, and many miracles were attributed to his prayers. *Henry V ascribed the victory of Agincourt (1415) to his intercession and in 1416 ordered his feast to be kept throughout England. Feast days, 7 May (death) and 25 Oct. (translation of relics).

The chief authority for his life is *Bede, *H.E.*, iv and v. A Life by Folcard, based on Bede, in J. Raine, *The Historians of the Church of York and its Archbishops*, i (Rolls Series, 1879), pp. 239–91. W. Hunt in *D.N.B.*, xxix (1892), p. 435 f.

JOHN BOSCO, St. See *Bosco, St. John.*

JOHN CAPISTRAN, St. See *Giovanni Capistrano, St.*

JOHN CAPREOLUS. See *Capreolus.*

JOHN CHRYSOSTOM, St. See *Chrysostom, St. John.*

JOHN CLIMACUS, St. (c. 570–649).
Ascetic and writer on the spiritual life. He was also known as σχολαστικός, but is not to be confused with *John Scholasticus, Patr. of Constantinople (q.v.). At first a monk of *Sinai, he became an *anchorite and later Abbot of Sinai. His celebrated 'Ladder of Paradise' (κλῖμαξ τοῦ παραδείσου) treats of the monastic virtues and vices, the anchoritic and coenobitic life, and the nature of complete dispassionateness (ἀπάθεια), which is upheld as the ideal of Christian perfection. There are 30 'steps of the ladder' (i.e. 30 chapters) to correspond with the age of Christ at His Baptism. Feast day, 30 Mar.

There is no critical text. Ed. M. Rader, S.J. (Paris, 1633); repr., with additional material, in J. P. Migne, *PG*, lxxxviii, 585–1248. Medieval Lat. trr. by Ambrogio *Traversari and others; a Spanish tr. of one of these Lat. texts of John Climacus was destined to be the first book to be printed in the New World (Mexico, 1532). Eng. tr. by

Father Robert, Mount St. Bernard's Abbey, Leicester (London, 1858). Bardenhewer, v, pp. 79-82; Altaner (ed. 1950), p. 468. Krumbacher, p. 143 f. L. Petit in *D.T.C.*, viii (pt. 1; 1924), cols. 690-3, s.v. '30. Jean Climaque'; A. Michel in *L.Th.K.*, v (1933), col. 508 f., s.v. 'Johannes Klimakos'.

JOHN OF THE CROSS, St. (1542–91).

Mystical Doctor and joint founder of the Discalced *Carmelites. The son of a poor family of noble origin, he entered the Carmelite monastery at Medina del Campo in 1563, studied theology at Salamanca (1564–7), and was ordained priest in 1567. Dissatisfied with the prevalent laxity of his order, he considered becoming a *Carthusian, but he was dissuaded by St. *Teresa. Then with her aid he introduced her Reform among the friars. He was subsequently Master of the Carmelite College at Alcalá de Henares (1570–2) and Confessor of the Convent of the Incarnation at Avila from 1572 to 1577. A staunch defender of the Teresian Reform, he was imprisoned in the Carmelite monastery at Toledo by order of his general, who was in favour of the Mitigated Observance. After nine months of great hardships he escaped (1578) to the solitary monastery of Calvario. In the meantime the separation between the Calced and the Discalced Carmelites had been effected. In 1579–81 St. John was rector of the college at Baëza; in 1581 he went to Granada, where he became acquainted with the Arabian mystics; from 1588 he was prior at Segovia. When he became again involved in the disputes of the order his superiors, who distrusted him, sent him to one of their poorest monasteries, where he fell dangerously ill. His desire for sufferings being amply granted, he died at Ubeda in 1591. He was beatified in 1675, canonized in 1726, and declared '*Doctor of the Church' in 1926. Feast day, 24 Nov.

His chief works, which form a connected whole of mystic doctrine, are *The Ascent of Mount Carmel*, *The Dark Night of the Soul*, *The Spiritual Canticle*, and *The Living Flame of Love*. The 'Ascent' and the 'Dark Night' deal with the purgation of the soul by the 'night of the senses' when, becoming detached from all sensible devotion, the soul maintains itself in pure faith. This, usually after a period of rest, is followed by a second purification, the 'night of the spirit', when the soul is further spiritualized by the Divine action, normally accompanied by intense sufferings, in order to fit it for the transforming Union described in the glowing language of the Living Flame. St. John of the Cross' mystic doctrine rests on his own personal experience nourished by the study of Scripture and the discipline of the *Thomist philosophy and aided by his keen psychological insight. His austerity was tempered by the gentleness of the poet. His works, lately made accessible in a critical translation, address themselves primarily to contemplatives and particularly to spiritual directors.

The best ed. of his collected works is that of Silverio de Santa Teresa, O.C.D. (Biblioteca Mística Carmelitana, vols. x-xiii, Burgos, 1929-31); Eng. tr. by E. A. Peers (3 vols., London, 1934–5; ed. 2, with additional material, 3 vols., 1953). J. Baruzi, *Saint Jean de la Croix et le problème de l'expérience mystique* (Paris thesis, 1924), with bibl. Bruno [de Jésus Marie], O.D.C., *Saint Jean de la Croix* (1929; Eng. tr., 1932). Crisógono de Jesús Sacramentado, *San Juan de la Cruz: su obra científica y su obra literaria* (2 vols., 1929). B. Frost, *Saint John of the Cross* (1937). E. A. Peers, *Spirit of Flame. A Study of St. John of the Cross* (1943); id., *Handbook of the Life and Times of Saint Teresa and Saint John of the Cross* (1954). Efrén de la Madre de Dios, O.D.C., *San Juan de la Cruz y el misterio de la Santísima Trinidad en la vida espiritual* (1947), with bibl. Other studies include those of David Lewis (London, 1897) and [M.] Deminuid ('Les Saints', ed. 2, 1916). Luís de San José, O.D.C., *Concordancias de las obras y escritos del Doctor de la Iglesia San Juan de la Cruz* (Burgos, 1948). B. Zimmerman, O.D.C., in *C.E.*, viii (1910), p. 480 f., s.v.; Pascal du S. Sacrement, O.D.C., in *D.T.C.*, viii (pt. 1; 1924), cols. 767–87, s.v. 'Jean de la Croix'; A. Mager in *L.Th.K.*, v (1933), cols. 509–12, s.v. 'Johannes v. Kreuz', with further bibl.

JOHN OF DAMASCUS, St. (c. 675–c. 749),

Greek theologian and '*Doctor of the Church'. Little is known of his life, and such sources as exist are in considerable conflict. Born of a rich Christian family of *Damascus, he succeeded his father as the chief representative ('Logothete') of the Christians to the Caliph. c. 716 he was compelled for his faith to abandon this office and withdrew to the monastery of St. *Sabas near *Jerusalem where he became a priest. He was a strong defender of *Images in the *Iconoclastic Controversy, writing three discourses on the subject between 726 and 730. Acc. to his biographer, Stephen Thaumaturgus, he died in 749.

His most important work, the 'Fount of Wisdom' (Πηγὴ γνώσεως), was written at the suggestion of his former fellow-monk, *Cosmas Melodus, Bp. of Maïuma. It is divided into three parts, dealing with philosophy ('Dialectica'), heresies, and the Orthodox faith ('De Fide Orthodoxa'), the most important of the three. For his philosophical doctrines he is indebted to *Aristotle, though he also borrowed from *Plato through *Maximus the Confessor, whereas the book of heresies is for the most part a reproduction of the 'Anakephalaiosis', attributed to St. *Epiphanius. The 'De Fide Orthodoxa' is a comprehensive presentation of the teaching of the Greek Fathers on the main Christian doctrines, esp. the Trinity, Creation, and the Incarnation; the Sacraments, Mariology, Images, and other subjects are also treated, but less systematically. In his demonstration of the existence and unity of God he adduces the metaphysical arguments from the contingency of creatures and the order of the universe. His Trinitarian theology sums up the doctrine esp. of the *Cappadocian Fathers and develops the conception of περιχώρησις ('circumincession') in order to express the Inner-Trinitarian relations. His angelology reproduces that of St. *Gregory of Nazianzus, his favourite Father, and of the Pseudo-*Dionysius. His treatment of the Incarnation is a representative synthesis of Greek theological thought, finding its end in the restoration of fallen man to his former state. He teaches that in the *Hypostatic Union the Word served as 'hypostasis' ('Person') to the humanity which He took; hence he adopted the *Enhypostasia of *Leontius of Byzantium, which he interprets along the lines of the '*Communicatio Idiomatum'. He saw in the interpenetration of the two natures in Christ the formation of '*Theandric Activities', a term he takes over from Pseudo-Dionysius, interpreting it in an orthodox sense. A corollary of his Christological doctrine was his fully developed Mariology. He teaches the Divine maternity of Mary, her exemption from all stain of sin, and her assumption into heaven. In the doctrine of the Eucharist he emphasizes the Real Presence of the Body and Blood of Christ almost to the exclusion of the accidents of bread and wine.

His other great work, the 'Sacra Parallela', preserved only in fragments, is a vast compilation of Scriptural and patristic texts on the Christian moral and ascetical life. It received its name from the parallel treatment of virtues and vices in its third part. He also wrote a comprehensive commentary on the Pauline Epp. and several homilies of a strongly dogmatic bent, e.g. on the Transfiguration, on Holy Saturday, and on the death of the Virgin. Beside his prose works he composed a number of poems which form part of the Greek Liturgy, though not all of those attributed to him are authentic. Some of these have found their way into modern English hymn-books, e.g. 'Come, ye faithful, raise the strain' and 'The Day of Resurrection! Earth tell it out abroad' (both in J. M. *Neale's renderings). The Life of *Barlaam and Joasaph (q.v.) is apparently (so J. M. Hoeck, O.S.B.) also a genuine work of the Damascene, though modern scholars have widely questioned it.

St. John of Damascus exercised a considerable influence on later theology. 'De Fide Orthodoxa', in the inadequate translation of Burgundio of Pisa, was known to *Peter Lombard and St. *Thomas Aquinas, and his authority was invoked in favour of the Latin doctrine of the *Double Procession of the Holy Ghost by the Unionist Greek theologians of the later 13th cent. and by Card. *Bessarion at the Council of *Florence. All through the Middle Ages his works were used by the Greeks and esp. by the Slavs, though they were never commented on nor led to the formation of a school as did those of Peter Lombard and St. Thomas in the West. In modern times they have retained their influence in the formation of E. theologians, though supplemented by later W. writers (RC and Protestant). St. John of Damascus, whose cult developed soon after his death, was declared a doctor of the Church by *Leo XIII in 1890. Feast day, in the Greek Church, 4 Dec.; in the W., 27 Mar.

Earliest collected ed. by M. *Le Quien, O.P. (2 vols. fol., Paris, 1712, with important prolegomena and dissertations); repr. in J. P. Migne, PG, xciv–xcvi, with additions from A. *Gallandi, A. *Mai, and others. Eng. tr. of 'De Fide Orthodoxa' by S. D. F. Salmond (N.P.N.C.F., Ser. 2, ix, 1899). Arabic Life by Michael of Antioch (1085; ed. by C. Bacha, Harisa (Lebanon), 1912; Germ. tr. by G. Graf in Der Katholik, xciii (1913), pp. 164–90, 320–31); this Arabic life was tr. into Gk. by Patr. John VIII of Jerusalem. On the details of St. John's life see M. Jugie, A.A., 'La Vie de saint Jean Damascène' in É.O., xxiii (1924), pp. 137–61] id., 'Une Nouvelle Vie et un nouvel écrit de saint Jean

Damascène', ib., xxviii (1929), pp. 35–41. Modern studies of his life and writings by J. Langen (Gotha, 1879), J. H. Lupton ('The Fathers for English Readers', London, 1883), K. J. Diobuniotes (Athens, 1903), V. Ermoni ('La Pensée chrétienne', Paris, 1904), and J. Nasrallah ('Les Souvenirs chrétiens de Damas', ii, Paris, 1950). On the Sacra Parallela, F. *Loofs, Studien über die dem Johannes von Damaskus zugeschriebenen Parallelen (1892); K. Holl, Die Sacra Parallela des Johannes Damascenus (T.U., xvi, Hft. 1; 1896); id., Fragmenta vornicänischer Kirchenväter aus den Sacra Parallela (ib., xx, Hft. 2; 1899). J. Bilz, Die Trinitätslehre des hl. Johannes von Damaskus (Forschungen zur christlichen Literatur- und Dogmengeschichte, ix, Hft. 3; 1909), J. M. Hoeck, O.S.B., 'Stand und Aufgaben der Damaskenos Forschung' in O.C.P., xvii (1951), pp. 5–60. Bardenhewer, v, 51–65; Altaner (ed. 1950), pp. 474–8; Krumbacher, pp. 68–71, 674–6. F. Kattenbusch in P.R.E. (ed. 3), ix (1901), pp. 286–300; M. Jugie, A.A., in D.T.C., viii (pt. i; 1924), cols. 693–751, s.v. '31. Jean Damascène (Saint)'; id. in L.Th.K., v (1933), cols. 488–91. See also bibl. to Iconoclastic Controversy.

JOHN EUDES, St. See Eudes, St. John.

JOHN THE FASTER (d. 595). John IV, Patriarch of *Constantinople from 582. His renown as an ascetic won him the title of 'Faster' (ὁ νηστευτής, 'jejunator'). Though personally unambitious, he used his great influence at court to gain for his see supremacy over the Churches of the E. and equality with Rome. When in 588 he assumed the challenging title of 'Oecumenical [οἰκουμενικός, "Universal"] Patriarch' (a style which had earlier been applied to his predecessors by *Justinian), Pope Pelagius II, and later St. *Gregory the Great, protested, the latter interpreting the description as a claim to be sole bishop and source of the episcopate. Their objections, however, did not prevent John from bequeathing the description to his successors. Attributed to him is a manual for confessors, commonly known as his 'Penitential' ('Ακολουθία καὶ τάξις ἐπὶ ἐξομολογουμένων), but it is of much later date, probably c. 1100. His only genuine writing which survives appears to be a sermon on 'Repentance, Self-control and Virginity', largely based on St. *Chrysostom.

J. P. Migne, PG, lxxxviii., 1887–1978. Bardenhewer, v, 74 f., with bibl. R. Janin, A.A., in D.T.C., viii (pt. i, 1924), col. 828 f., s.v. 'Jean IV le Jeûneur'.

JOHN OF FIDANZA. See St. Bonaventura.

JOHN FISHER, St. See Fisher, St. John.

JOHN OF GOD, St. (1495–1550). Founder of the 'Order of Charity for the Service of the Sick', or '*Brothers Hospitallers' (q.v.). He was born in *Portugal and, after a pious upbringing, joined a company of foot soldiers and forsook the practice of religion. At the age of about 40 he changed his mode of life in an attempt to atone for his past waywardness. He hoped for martyrdom in Morocco; but, this being denied him, he returned to the south of *Spain and spread the faith by hawking tracts and pictures until in 1538 he was converted to a life of great sanctity by Blessed *John of Ávila. At first his excesses of penitence and devotion caused him to be treated as a lunatic, but a further interview with John of Ávila directed his energies to the care of the sick and poor. After his death his order gradually took shape. He was canonized in 1690 and in 1886 declared by *Leo XIII the heavenly patron of all hospitals and sick folk. He is also often regarded as the patron of printers and booksellers. Feast day, 8 Mar.

Life, written within twenty years of his death, by Francis de Castro, Rector of the Hospital of St. John at Granada, publ. at Granada, 1588; Lat. tr., 1623; excerpts (Lat.) in *AA.SS.*, Mar. I (1668), pp. 814–35, excerpts from early 17th cent. life, ib., pp. 835–58. Modern studies include those of L. Saglier (Paris, 1877), E. Baillon (London, 1884), I. M. Magnin (Lille, 1887; Eng. tr., 1936), and I. Giordani (Florence, 1947). Florence M. Rudge in *C.E.*, viii (1910), p. 472 f.; G. Russotto, F.B.F., in *E.C.*, vi (1951), col. 554 f.

JOHN GUALBERT, St. (*c.* 990–1073).
The founder of the *Vallumbrosan Order (q.v.). After generously pardoning on a *Good Friday the murderer of one of his relatives, he entered the *Benedictine monastery of San Miniato, near Florence. Some four years later he left this house for *Camaldoli; and, at a date which cannot be fixed, he left for the place later known as Vallombrosa, where he collected around him a body of monks who lived under a modified form of the Benedictine Rule, austere in its demands and adapted to the conditions of a semi-hermit existence. In the later part of his life, John Gualbert took a prominent part in assisting the Papacy in its struggles against simony. Feast day, 12 July.

The earliest authority is the life of Andrew of Strumi, who became Abbot of Vallombrosa in 1085 (d. 1097), pr. in *AA.SS.*, Jul. III (1723), pp. 343–65; also ed. F. Baethgen in *M.G.H.*, Scriptores, xxx (pt. 2; 1934), pp. 1080–1104, with introd. pp. 1076–8. Life by St. Atto, later Bp. of Pistoia (d. 22 May 1153), also pr. in *AA.SS.*, loc. cit., pp. 365–82. Third life (12th cent.) first pr. by R. Davidsohn, *Forschungen zur älteren Geschichte von Florenz*, i (Berlin, 1896), pp. 55–60, with introd. pp. 50–4; also ed. F. Baethgen, op. cit., pp. 1104–10, with introd. p. 1078 f. Further sources in *B.H.L.*, p. 651 f. (Nos. 4397–406) and Suppl. (1911), p. 176. D. de Franchi, *Historia del Patriarcha S. Giovan Gualberto* (Florence, 1640). D. F. Tarani, *Della vita di S. Giovanni Gualberto* (Udine, 1903); S. Casini, *Storia di Giovanni Gualberto Fiorentino* (Alba, 1927). Further life by A. Savani (Rome, 1950). H. Kiene, O.S.B., in *L.Th.K.*, v (1933), col. 501 f., s.v.

JOHN, KING OF ENGLAND (1167–1216),
King from 1199. He was the youngest son of Henry II and Eleanor of Aquitaine. He was early nicknamed Lackland because not provided like his brothers with an apanage of land by his father, though he was Henry's favourite and richly endowed with castles and rents. In 1177 he was made 'King of Ireland,' which he was sent to govern in 1185. Alienating the Irish by his insolence and misrule, he was recalled after a few months. In 1189 he took part in the conspiracy of his brother Richard and the King of France against his father, whose death was hastened by this treachery. After his accession (1189) Richard I confirmed him in his possessions, which were increased by his marriage to Isabella of Gloucester. During Richard's absence on the Third *Crusade John expelled his chancellor, William Longchamp, won the support of France, declared that Richard was dead, and demanded the oath

of fealty from his lords. The barons, however, refused him allegiance and, after the archbishops and bishops had excommunicated him, made war on him. After Richard's return (1194) the brothers were reconciled; John assisted the King against Philip of France; and Richard named John as his successor. On his accession (1199) John was recognized by England and Normandy, and in 1202 defeated Anjou and Brittany, who urged the claims of his nephew, Arthur (whom John murdered in 1203). During the following years he lost most of his possessions in France, and with the death of *Hubert of Canterbury in 1205 he was deprived of the only counsellor able to exercise on his acts a measure of restraint. The election of a new archbishop involved him in a quarrel with the chapter of *Canterbury, and when *Innocent III appointed Stephen *Langton (1207) John refused to recognize him. In 1208 England was placed under an *interdict and in 1212 John was excommunicated and declared deposed. The hatred of his barons as well as of the common people, exasperated by his continual misgovernment and heavy taxation, rendered his position desperate. In 1213 he made his submission to the Pope, promised full reconciliation and restitution, and placed England and Ireland under the suzerainty of Innocent and his successors. The last years of his reign were troubled by renewed war with France in which he was defeated in 1214. In 1215 the barons obtained the famous grant of Magna Carta, but soon afterwards John regretted his action and civil war broke out, France intervening on the side of the barons. John died during the struggle, leaving his kingdom in confusion. His character, a mixture of brutality, cowardice, and sloth, caused him to be generally hated and despised. His private life was scandalously immoral, though occasionally he gave way to religious emotion; his constant quarrels with both the Church and his own subjects brought great unhappiness and disaster.

The principal modern studies are Kate Norgate, *John Lackland* (London, 1902), and S. Painter, *The Reign of King John* (Baltimore, 1949). Other studies by J. Lehmann (Historische Studien, xlv; 1904) and E. B. d'Auvergne (London, 1934). C. R. Cheney, 'King John and the Papal Interdict' in *Bulletin of the John Rylands Library*, xxxi (1948), pp. 295–317; id., 'King John's Reaction to the Interdict of England' in *Transactions of the Royal Historical Society*, 4th Ser., xxxi (1949), pp. 129–50. F. M. Powicke in *C. Med. H.*, vi (1929), pp. 204–51, with details of sources and other bibl. pp. 881–7; A. L. Poole, *From Doomsday Book to Magna Carta* (Oxford History of England, iii; 1951), esp. pp. 425–86. W. Hunt in *D.N.B.*, xxix (1892), pp. 402–17, with full reff. to original sources.

JOHN LATERAN, Church of St. See *Lateran Basilica*.

JOHN MALALAS (later 6th cent.), i.e.
'John Rhetor' or 'Scholasticus', Byzantine chronicler. He is prob. to be identified with the *John Scholasticus who became Patr. of *Constantinople (d. 577; q.v.). His 'Chronography' (Χρονογραφία) in 18 Books (Bks. 1–17 from the *Monophysite standpoint; Bk. 18

orthodox), woven round the fortunes of *Antioch, is a primary source of religious and secular history, written in the 'vulgar' Greek of his age. The text originally went down to 574, but now survives only to 563. His work was closely followed by many later chronographers and annalists.

'Chronicle' (Gk. text preserved only in Bod. Barocc. gr. 182), ed. L. Dindorf, in C.S.H. Byz., 1831; repr. J. P. Migne, *PG*, xcvii, 9–790. Crit. text of Bks. IX–XII, ed. A. Schenk Graf von Stauffenberg, *Die römische Kaisergeschichte bei Malalas* (1931), with imp. commentary. W. Weber, 'Studien zur Chronik des Malalas' in *Festgabe für A. Deissmann* (1927), pp. 20–66. Krumbacher, pp. 325–34.

JOHN MARK, St. See *Mark, St.*

JOHN OF MATHA, St. (d. 1213), founder of the *Trinitarian Order. Practically all that is known of him is that he was a native of Provence, founded his Order for the redemption of captives and died at Rome on 17 Dec. 1213. The abundant details in the older biographies are based on spurious records fabricated in the 15th and 16th cents. Feast day, 8 Feb.

Uncritical lives include those of G. Gonzales de Ávila (Madrid, 1630), J. M. Prat, S.J. (Paris, 1846), and le Père Calixte de la Providence, Trinitarian (ib., 1867). Much early material is also pr. in Antoninus ab Assumptione, Trinitarian, *Monumenta Ordinis Excalceatorum SS. Trinitatis Redemptionis Captivorum ad Provinciam S.P.N. Ioannis de Matha Spectantia* (Rome, 1915). N. Schuhmacher, *Der hl. Johannes von Matha* (Klosterneuburg, 1936). See also bibl. to *Trinitarians*.

JOHN MOSCHUS, St. See *Moschus, John.*

JOHN OF NEPOMUK, St. (c. 1340–1393), Bohemian martyr. As vicar-general of the Archdiocese of Prague, John resisted the attempts of Wenceslas IV to suppress an abbey in order to create a see for one of his favourites and to interfere with clerical prerogatives. By the King's orders he was drowned in the Moldau in consequence; but his recovered body became the centre of a widespread cultus and he was canonized in 1729. Tradition credits him with having incensed the monarch by refusing to betray the Queen by breaking the *seal of the confessional. The details of his life are shrouded in obscurity, and some have held that two Johns suffered martyrdom in similar circumstances at the hands of Wenceslas. Feast day, 16 May.

Life by B. Balbino, S.J. (written in 1670), in *AA.SS.*, Mai. III (1680), pp. 668–80. Acts of the Process of his Canonization, publ. Verona, 1725. J. T. A. Berghauer, *Proto-martyr Poenitentiae eiusque Sigilli Custos semper Fidelis Divus Joannes Nepomucenus* (Augsburg, 1736). E. Reimann, 'Johann von Nepomuk nach der Sage und nach der Geschichte' in *Historische Zeitschrift*, xxvii (1872), pp. 225–81. Modern studies by A. H. Wratislaw (London, 1873), A. L. Frind (Prague, 1879; new ed. with crit. notes by W. Frind, ib., 1929), and J. Weisskopf (Vienna, 1931).

JOHN OF PARMA (1209–89), *Franciscan Minister General. He taught logic at Parma for several years, where he took the Franciscan habit, probably in 1233, and was later sent to

*Paris to continue his studies. A popular teacher and preacher, he was elected Minister General of his order in 1247, and as such endeavoured to restore its asceticism and discipline to the original standards of St. *Francis. In pursuit of this aim he carried out visitations throughout Europe, journeying to France, England, Spain, and Greece, and working, but without success, for the reunion of East and West. But his austerity and his leanings towards the teaching of *Joachim of Flora and the attribution to him of the authorship of Gerard of Borgo San Donnino's 'Introductorius Evangelii Aeterni' made him many enemies, and he was accused of heresy in Rome. He resigned his office in 1257, suggesting *St. Bonaventure as his successor. On the examination of his doctrine he narrowly escaped condemnation and retired into the hermitage of Greccio, where for thirty-two years he led a solitary life of penance and contemplation. In 1289 he was sent once more on an embassy to Greece on matters of reunion, but died on his way at Camerino. Many miracles were reported at his tomb, but owing to his Joachimite views his cultus was not confirmed until 1777. Feast day, 20 Mar.

Lives by F. Camerini (Ravenna, 1730) and I. Affo (Parma, 1777). René de Nantes, 'Quelques Pages d'histoire franciscaine' in *Études franciscaines*, xv (1906), VI, 'Le Bienheureux Jean de Parme', pp. 148–67, and VII, 'Le B. Jean de Parme et le joachimisme', pp. 277–300. E. d'Alençon, O.F.M., in *D.T.C.*, viii (pt. 1; 1924), cols. 794–6, s.v. 'Jean de Parme'.

JOHN AND PAUL, Sts. Two Roman martyrs of the 4th cent. of whom virtually nothing further is known. Their 'Acta', whose trustworthiness, however, is doubtful, testify to their having served Constantia, daughter of the Emp. *Constantine, and been instrumental in the conversion to Christianity of one of his generals, and having been finally martyred by the Emp. *Julian for their firm adherence to the Christian faith. A cult of these saints existed from the latter half of the 4th cent. and their names stand in the Roman *Canon of the Mass. A Council at *Oxford in 1222 made the hearing of Mass by all the faithful of England obligatory on their feast day, 26 June.

V. L. Kennedy, C.S.B., *The Saints of the Canon of the Mass* (Rome, 1938), pp. 131–7. P. F. de Cavalieri, 'Note agiografiche' in *S.T.*, ix (1902), pp. 53–65, and xxvii (1915), pp. 41–62. For their reputed house on the Celian Hill, see P. Germano di S. Stanislao, *La casa celimontana dei SS. Martiri Giovanni e Paolo* (1894), and V. E. Gasdia, *La casa pagano-cristiana del Celio* (1937), and bibl. to *Rome* (Churches).

JOHN PECKHAM. See *Peckham, John.*

JOHN XII (d. 964), Pope from 955. Octavian was the son of the Roman patrician, Alberic the younger, who, after the death of his mother, Marozia, had become the absolute ruler of Rome and obliged the noblemen of the city to make his son Pope on the death of Agapetus II. Octavian, who took the name of John XII, thus became Pope at the early age of 18. His

lack of experience and his addiction to pleasure and vice soon gave grave scandal to Christendom. The main cause of the troubles of his pontificate was his decision to call in Otto I from Germany to help him against the rulers of N. Italy, King Berengar II and his son, Adalbert. Otto arrived in Rome in 962 and was crowned emperor by John, who sanctioned the erection of the archbishopric of Magdeburg and of the bishopric of Merseburg. In exchange the Emperor granted the famous 'Privilegium Ottonis', by which the Carolingian donations were considerably enlarged, but which also confirmed the rights of the Emperor in the Papal elections, conceded to Lothar I in 824. As soon as Otto had left Rome, the Pope, regretting his action, began to establish relations with Otto's enemy, Berengar, whose son he received with great honours at Rome. At the news of this treacherous move the Emperor, who returned in 963, received the support of a large section of the Roman population, and John and Adalbert were compelled to flee. In the same year Otto called a synod at Rome and caused the Pope to be deposed for immoral life, and a layman (Leo VIII) to be elected in his place, who received all the orders within two days. When Otto had left Rome, in 964, John returned and revenged himself on the Emperor's partisans. He then called a synod which deprived Leo and cancelled all actions of the previous synod. He died while Otto was on his way back, leaving the Papacy in a much enfeebled position to his successor, Benedict V.

'Epistolae et Privilegia' in J. P. Migne, *PL*, cxxxiii, 1013–41. P. Jaffé, *Regesta Pontificum Romanorum*, i (ed. 2 by W. Wattenbach, Leipzig, 1885), pp. 463–7. *L.P.* (Duchesne), ii, 246–9. T. Sickel, *Das Privilegium Otto I für die römische Kirche vom Jahre 962* (1883). L. *Duchesne, Les Premiers Temps de l'état pontifical* (ed. 2, 1904), pp. 337–51. Mann, iv (1910), pp. 241–72. Fliche–Martin, vii (1940), pp. 44–5, with reff. E. Amann in *D.T.C.*, viii (pt. 1; 1924), cols. 619–26, s.v. 'Jean XII', with further reff. to sources; G. B. Picotti in *E.C.*, vi (1951), col. 587 f., s.v. 'Giovanni XII'.

JOHN XXII (1249–1334), Pope from 1316. Jacques d'Euse, a native of Cahors, after studying law at Paris and other French universities, was appointed Bp. of Fréjus by *Boniface VIII in 1300, Bp. of *Avignon in 1310, and Card. Bp. of Porto in 1312. Elected Pope in 1316 as the candidate of Robert of Anjou, he fixed his residence at Avignon, where he remained for the rest of his life. His reign was filled with theological and political conflicts. Almost at once he became involved in the difficulties threatening to split the *Franciscan Order (q.v.) and in 1317 dissolved the party of the *Spirituals, whose doctrines he denounced as heretical. Soon afterwards he condemned the thesis, held by the bulk of the Franciscans, that the poverty of Christ and His Apostles was absolute. His decision won the assent of the majority of the order, but several of the more fanatical Franciscans fled to the Pope's enemy, Louis of Bavaria, who gave them his support. In 1324 the Pope declared Louis a heretic and the quarrel became the occasion of

a violent literary feud in which *William of Occam and John of Jandun (d. 1328) took part. The literary conflict culminated in *Marsilius of Padua's 'Defensor Pacis' (anathematized by John in 1327), which upheld the absolute supremacy of the Emperor over the Pope, as one who may be elected, censured, and deposed at the Imperial pleasure. Louis then seized Rome, installed himself in the *Vatican, and set up as Antipope (1328) a Spiritual Franciscan under the name of Nicholas V, who, however, was forced to submit to John two years later; and Louis himself had eventually to take steps for reconciliation.

In his last years the Pope was involved in a purely theological dispute on the *Beatific Vision. He opposed the general opinion and denied its enjoyment to the souls of the blessed before the Last Judgement, a doctrine for which he met with strong resistance from the Masters of the University of Paris.

John was a capable administrator, enlarged and reorganized the Curia, put the Papal finances on a sound basis (though the new taxes were generally condemned at the time), and strengthened the hierarchy by founding new, and defining the frontiers of old, dioceses. The authorship of the famous prayer *Anima Christi*, used and popularized by St. *Ignatius of Loyola, has been assigned to him.

S. Riezler (ed.), *Vatikanische Akten zur deutschen Geschichte in der Zeit Kaiser Ludwigs des Bayern* (1891), pp. 1–577. G. Mollat (ed.), *Jean XXII (1316–1334)*. Lettres communes (Bibliothèque des Écoles Françaises d'Athènes et de Rome, Sér. 3, i bis, 16 vols. bound in 13, 1904–47). A. Coulon (ed.), *Lettres secrètes et curiales du Pape Jean XXII . . . relatives à France* (ib., i; 5 fascc. [to 1323]; 1906–13). A. Fayen (ed.), *Lettres de Jean XXII* [concerning the Low Countries] (Analecta Vaticano-Belgica publiés par l'Institut historique Belge de Rome, ii–iii; 1908–12). A. L. Tàutu (ed.), *Acta Ioannis XXII* (Pontificia Commissio ad redigendum Codicem Iuris Canonici Orientalis Fontes, Series III, vol. vi, Tom. 2; Rome, 1952). E. *Baluze, *Vitae Paparum Avenionensium*, ed. G. Mollat, i (1916), pp. 107–94 V. Verlaque, *Jean XXII, sa vie et ses œuvres d'après des documents inédits* (1883). N. Valois, 'Jean Duèse, pape sous le nom de Jean XXII' in *Histoire littéraire de la France*, xxxiv (1914), pp. 391–630. E. Sol, *Un des Plus Grands Papes de l'histoire, Jean XXII* (1948; uncritical). C. Müller, *Der Kampf Ludwigs des Baiern mit der römischen Curie*, i (1879). W. Preger, 'Die Politik des Papstes Johann XXII in Bezug auf Italien und Deutschland' in *Abh.* (Bayr.), xvii (1886), pp. 499–593; H. Otto, 'Zur italienischen Politik Johanns XXII' in *Quellen und Forschungen aus italienischen Archiven und Bibliotheken*, xiv (1911), pp. 140–265, with texts. A. Esch, *Die Ehedispense Johanns XXII und ihre Beziehung zur Politik* (Historische Studien, clxxxiii; 1929). Pastor, i (1891), pp. 58–83. G. Mollat, *Les Papes d'Avignon* (ed. 9 [1949]), pp. 38–67, with detailed bibl. J. P. Kirsch in *C.E.*, viii (1910), pp. 431–4, s.v.; G. Mollat in *D.T.C.*, viii (pt. 1; 1924), cols. 633–41, s.v. 'Jean XXII'; id. in *E.C.*, vi (1951), col. 592 f., s.v. 'Giovanni XXII'; all with bibl.

JOHN XXIII (d. 1419), Antipope to Popes *Benedict XIII and Gregory XII from 1410 to 1415. Baldassare Cossa was the descendant of a noble but impoverished Neapolitan family. After a military career during which he is said to have engaged in piracy, he studied law at *Bologna and entered the service of the *Curia. Boniface IX, who appreciated his administrative and military talents, created him cardinal in 1402, and made him legate of Romandiola in 1403 and of Bologna in 1409. He was crowned Pope in 1410, but the validity of his election has been contested as being simoniacal. Of the three Popes then existing he had the largest number of supporters, esp. after Ladislaus of Naples, defeated at Roccasecca on 19 May 1411, transferred his allegiance from Gregory XII to John. In 1412 he called a synod at Rome which was very poorly attended and soon dissolved. In 1413, at the persuasion of King Sigismund, he convoked a General Council to end the W. Schism, which met at *Constance in 1414. Though he promised to cede his claims to the Papacy if Gregory XII and Benedict XIII would do the same, his sincerity was suspected, and he actually fled soon afterwards, so as to deprive the Council of its authority, under the pretext that he enjoyed no liberty. After being brought back by force he was imprisoned and deposed (1415), accepting his fate with unexpected meekness. He was held a prisoner in Germany for three years, but was set free in 1419, when he recognized *Martin V, who made him Card. Bp. of Tusculum. He died soon afterwards.

J. Schwerdfeger, *Papst Johann XXIII und die Wahl Sigismunds zum römischen König, 1410* (1895). H. Finke, 'Zur Charakteristik des Hauptanklägers Johannes XIII auf dem Konstanzer Konzil' in *Miscellanea Francesco Ehrle*, iii (S.T., xxxix; 1924), pp. 157–63. Pastor, i (1891), pp. 191–9 and 212 f. G. Mollat in *D.T.C.*, viii (pt. 1; 1924), cols. 641–4, s.v. 'Jean XXIII', with reff. to sources. P. Paschini in *E.C.*, iv (1950), col. 708 f., s.v. 'Cossa, Baldassare'. See also bibl. to *Constance, Council of.*

JOHN THE PRESBYTER. The term 'the Presbyter' ('elder', Gr. πρεσβύτερος) is applied to himself by the author of 2 and 3 Jn. while a 'John the Presbyter' is referred to by *Papias (*Eusebius, *HE*, III, xxxix, 4); but the inference to be drawn from these data is disputed. (1) Some think that Papias's evidence points to the existence at *Ephesus of a second John besides the Apostle (the son of Zebedee), and ascribe to him the Canonical Gospel of Jn. and the three Johannine Epistles; this was the view of B. H. *Streeter, for whom 2 and 3 Jn. were 'the author's signature' to the Gospel and First Epistle, and of J. H. *Bernard. Among those who have held this view, some (J. H. Bernard) identify the 'Beloved Disciple' of the Gospel (Jn. 13. 23, 20. 2, 21. 15–23) with the Apostle, others (W. *Sanday, H. B. *Swete) equate him with the Presbyter. (2) Acc. to others, e.g. J. *Moffatt, merely the last two Epistles and possibly the Apocalypse (Rev.) are to be attributed to 'John the Presbyter'; the ascription of 2 and 3 Jn. to him was a view already known to *Jerome (*De vir. illustr.* 9, 18). (3) But the common view of Christian tradition, viz. that 'the Presbyter' was a local designation for the Apostle himself (cf. e.g. 1 Pet. 5. 1 where St. *Peter is apparently termed a presbyter) still has its advocates.

See bibl. to *John, Gospel of St.*

JOHN OF RAGUSA (d. *c.* 1443), *Dominican theologian. John Stoicovic was a native of Ragusa who entered the Dominican Order at an early age, and in 1420 became master of theology at Paris. In 1422 he attended the

Council of Pavia as legate of the university, and in 1431 *Martin V sent him to the Council of *Basle as Papal theologian, where he preached the opening sermon. In 1435 and 1437 he acted as legate to the Council of Constantinople in order to gain the Greeks for union with Rome, and the sending of an embassy by John Palaeologus was largely due to his influence. In 1438 he seems to have been made Bp. of Ardijsek and in 1440 cardinal by Felix V, though some authors assert that he remained faithful to the allegiance of *Eugenius IV, from whom he received the bishopric of Argos. Several of his writings have been printed, among them a treatise 'De Communione sub utraque Specie' against the *Hussites, a history of the Council of Basle and an unfinished history of the negotiations for union with the Greeks.

He is not to be confounded with Cardinal Giovanni Dominici (1356–1420), also known as 'John of Ragusa' who was appointed Abp. of Ragusa in 1407 and took a prominent part at the Council of *Constance (q.v.).

Several of his writings are contained in the Conciliar collections of *Basle. J. Quétif, O.P.–J. Échard, O.P., *Scriptores Ordinis Praedicatorum*, i (1719), 797–9. B. Altaner in *L.Th.K.*, v (1933), col. 527; U. Vincentini in *E.C.*, vi (1951), col. 601, s.v. 'Giovanni di Ragusa'.

JOHN OF RUYSBROECK. See *Ruysbroeck, John of.*

JOHN OF ST. THOMAS (1589–1644). Spanish *Dominican theologian. He was so named from his whole-hearted devotion to the teaching of St. *Thomas Aquinas. A native of Lisbon, he studied at Coimbra and Louvain, and in 1612 entered the *Dominican Order at Madrid. For much of his life he taught at Alcalá. As against the modified Thomism of the *Jesuit theologians, F. de *Suarez and G. *Vazquez, John's system claimed to follow exactly the principles of St. Thomas in that it paid heed not only to Aquinas' conclusions, but also to the concatenation of the arguments by which he reached them. His chief work was his *Cursus theologicus*, a commentary on the 'Summa Theologica' of St. Thomas (1637–1667), of which the first four vols. were published during his lifetime.

The *Cursus Theologicus* (except vol. v) was reissued at Lyons, 1663 (vol. viii, 1667); modern reissue by the *Benedictines of *Solesmes (Paris, 1931–46). John's Spanish works incl. *Explicación de la doctrina cristiana y la obligación de los fieles en creer y obrar* (Madrid, 1640) and *Práctica y consideración para ayudar a bien morir* (Saragossa, 1645). Life by D. Ramirez, O.P., prefixed to vol. 1 of *Cursus Theologicus*; another by Échard to vol. 8 of the same work (1667). T. Trapiello, O.P., *Juan de Santo Tomás y sus obras* (Oviedo, 1889). V. Bertrán de Heredia, 'La enseñanza de S. Tomás en la Universidad de Alcalá' in *La Ciencia tomista*, xiv (1916, ii), pp. 267–97. *La Ciencia tomista*, lxix (1945), is devoted to John of St. Thomas. J. M. Ramírez in *D.T.C.*, viii (1924), cols. 803–8.

JOHN OF SALISBURY (*c.* 1115–80), medieval philosopher. A native of *Salisbury, he studied at *Paris under *Abelard, *William of Conches, and *Gilbert de la Porrée, and perhaps also at *Chartres. After entering the

Papal service, he returned to England (1153–4). Here he became chief minister and secretary successively to *Theobald and Thomas *Becket, Abps. of *Canterbury, supporting Becket in his quarrel with Henry II; he was present at *Canterbury on the fatal 29 Dec. 1170. In 1176 he became Bp. of Chartres, where he remained for the rest of his life. An accomplished Latinist and man of letters, he was one of the leaders of the literary renaissance of the 12th cent. He was the first important medieval writer who was acquainted with the whole of *Aristotle's 'Organon' (i.e. the corpus of his logical writings). His interests, however, were less exclusively logical and metaphysical than those of the rising Scholasticism. His two principal writings are his 'Policraticus, sive de nugis curialium et de vestigiis philosophorum', a treatise on the state, and his 'Metalogicon', a defence of the study of logic and metaphysics against a body of obscurantists whom he named 'Cornificians'. Several of his 'Letters' also survive and are an important historical source for the contest between Henry and Becket.

Works ed. by J. A. Giles (5 vols., Oxford, 1848); repr. in J. P. Migne, *PL*, cxcix, 1–1040. Crit. edd. of his *Policraticus* by C. C. J. *Webb (2 vols., Oxford, 1909), of his *Historia Pontificalis* by R. L. Poole (Oxford, 1927), and of his *Metalogicon* by C. C. J. Webb (Oxford, 1929). Eng. tr. of *Policraticus* IV–VI, with selections from VII and VIII, by J. Dickinson (New York, 1927), of id., I–III, with selections from VII and VIII by J. B. Pike (Minneapolis, 1938). C. C. J. Webb, *John of Salisbury* ('Great Medieval Churchmen', 1932). H. Liebeschütz, *Medieval Humanism in the Life and Writings of John of Salisbury* (Studies of the Warburg Institute, xvii, 1950). R. L. Poole, 'The Early Correspondence of John of Salisbury' in the *Proceedings of the British Academy*, xi (1924–5), pp. 27–53; Helen Waddell, 'John of Salisbury' in *Essays and Studies by Members of the English Association*, xiii, ed. C. F. E. Spurgeon (1928), No. 2, pp. 28–51. Crit. ed. of his Letters, ed. W. J. Millor, S.J., &c., London, 1955 ff. R. L. Poole in *D.N.B.*, xxix (1892), pp. 439–46.

JOHN SCHOLASTICUS (d. 577), John III, Patriarch of *Constantinople from 565. In his early years he was a lawyer (σχολαστικός) at *Antioch, where he made a famous collection ('Synagoge') of Canons. Later, after he had become patriarch, he re-edited and enriched it from the 'Novellae' of *Justinian, and the work became one of the primary sources for subsequent E. canon law. He is also said to have written a 'Catechetical Oration' on the Trinity. He is not to be confounded with *John Climacus, also known as 'John Scholasticus', but is prob. to be identified with *John Malalas (q.v.).

'Synagoge', ed., with Lat. tr., by G. E. Heimbach, Ἀνέκδοτα, ii (Leipzig, 1840), pp. 202–34. Crit. ed. by V. N. Beneševic (*Abh.* (Bayr.), N.F., xiv, 1937). E. *Schwartz, *Die Kanonessammlung von Johannes Scholastikos* (*Sb.* (Bayr.), 1933, Hft. 6). On his identity with John Malalas, cf. J. Haury, 'Johannes Malalas identisch mit dem Patriarchen Johannes Scholastikos' in *B.Z.*, ix (1900), pp. 337–56. Bardenhewer, v, 75 f. L. Petit in *D.T.C.*, viii (pt. 1; 1924), cols. 829–31, s.v. '77. Jean le Scolastique'; F. Dölger in *L.Th.K.*, v (1933), col. 530 f., s.v. (assumes his identity with John Malalas).

JOHN THE SCOT. See *Erigena*.

JOHN OF WESEL (John Rucherat or Ruchrat) (*c*. 1400–81), ecclesiastical reformer.

A native of Oberwesel am Rhein, he was educated at Erfurt university where he was rector in 1456–7. Later he became canon at Worms (1460), professor at Basle (1461), and cathedral-preacher (*Domprediger*) at Worms (1463). Charged with preaching *Hussite doctrines on the Church and Sacraments, he was deposed by Reinhard, Bp. of Worms, from his preaching office in 1477 and in 1479 tried by the *Inquisition. After a public recantation at Worms on 21 Feb. 1479, he was sentenced to lifelong confinement in the *Augustinian monastery at Mainz, where he died some two years later. Several of his writings, many of them still unpublished, survive, among them a 'Commentary on the Sentences' (from his Erfurt period), a treatise against *Indulgences (1475), and a work on the *Immaculate Conception. He rejected *Original Sin, *Transubstantiation, compulsory fasting, *Indulgences, and *Extreme Unction, and held that Scripture alone was the final authority in faith.

C. Ullmann, *Johann Wesel, ein Vorgänger Luthers* (1834). G. Shadé, *Essai sur Jean de Wesel, précurseur de la Réformation* (thesis, Strassburg, 1856). N. Paulus, 'Johann von Wesel über Busssacrament und Ablass' in *Z.K.T.*, xxiv (1900), pp. 644–56; id., 'Die verloren geglaubten philosophischen Schriften des Johann von Wesel', ib., xxvii (1903), p. 601 f. G. Ritter, *Studien zur Spätscholastik*, iii, 'Neue Quellenstücke zur Theologie des Johann von Wesel' (*Sb.* (Heid.), Jahr. 1926/27, Abhandlung 5). O. Clemen in *P.R.E.* (ed. 3), xxi (1908), pp. 127–31, s.v. 'Wesel, Johann von', with bibl.

JOHNSON, JOHN (1662–1725), English theologian. Educated at Magdalene and Corpus Christi colleges, Cambridge, he became Vicar of Boughton-under-the-Blean in 1687, of St. John's, Margate, in 1697, and of Cranbrook, Kent, in 1710. He wrote several works, the theology of which has considerable affinities with that of the *Nonjurors, among whom he had close personal friends. His best known treatise is his *Unbloody Sacrifice and Altar, Unvailed and Supported, in which the Nature of the Eucharist is explained according to the Sentiments of the Christian Church in the Four First Centuries* (1714–18), in which he affirmed that the sacrifice is 'proper', 'expiatory', and 'propitiatory', and described the elements after the Consecration as the 'Sacramental' or 'Eucharistical body and blood' of our Lord. He held, however, that Christ was present in the elements in power and effect rather than in actuality. He also wrote *The Propitiatory Oblation in the Holy Eucharist* (1710).

The Unbloody Sacrifice was repr. in L.A.C.T., 1847. Posthumous Life by T. *Brett prefixed (pp. i–lvi) to three posthumous tracts by Johnson, viz. (1) 'The Primitive Communicant', (2) 'A Sermon . . . on Numb. xi. 29', and (3) 'An Explanation of Daniel's Prophecy of the LXX Weeks' (1748). J. H. Overton in *D.N.B.*, xxx (1892), p. 906.

JOHNSON, SAMUEL (1709–84), author, lexicographer, and conversationalist. His religious beliefs and practice were of a standard rare in the C of E in the 18th cent. He ascribes his conversion as a young man to reading W. *Law's *Serious Call*, and, although unlike

Law he was never a *Nonjuror, he was a strong
*High Churchman, regular and sincere in his
religious duties, and very generous to his
friends and to the poor. He sometimes caused
surprise by his marked tolerance of RC-ism,
while he was at no pains to conceal his dislike
of Presbyterianism and Nonconformity.

Collected Works ed. by his friend and executor, Sir John
Hawkins (11 vols., London, 1787), with life as vol. i; vols.
xii and xiii, 'Debates in Parliament', 1787, and xiv and xv.,
1788–9, by different edd. Not included in this collected ed.
was his *Prayers and Meditations* ed. G. Strahan (London,
1785); modern ed., with introd. by E. Trueblood (New
York, 1945; London, 1947). Critical ed. of his Poems by
D. N. Smith–E. L. McAdam (Oxford, 1941). There is no
modern ed. of his works as a whole. H. L. Piozzi (ed.),
Letters to and from the late Samuel Johnson (1788); id.,
Anecdotes of the late Samuel Johnson (1786). J. Boswell's
Life (2 vols., 1791; ed. 3 by E. Malone, 4 vols., 1799);
id., *The Journal of a Tour to the Hebrides with Samuel
Johnson* (1785); these two last also ed. J. W. Crocker
(5 vols., London, 1831), and G. B. Hill (6 vols., ib., 1887;
revised L. F. Powell, 6 vols., Oxford, 1934–50). Other early
lives by A. Murphy (London, 1792; repr. in his ed. of
Johnson's Works, 12 vols., 1796) and R. Anderson (London,
1795). Modern studies include those of L. Stephen ('English
Men of Letters', 1878), F. Grant (London, 1887), W.
Raleigh (Oxford, 1910), P. H. Houston (Cambridge, Mass.,
1923), O. F. Christie (London, 1924), C. Hollis (ib., 1928),
H. Kingsmill (ib. [1933]), S. C. Roberts (ib., 1935), J. W.
Krutch (New York, 1944; London, 1948), C. E. Vulliamy
(London, 1946), and Jean H. Hagstrum (Minneapolis,
1952). [R. Armitage,] *Doctor Johnson, his religious life and
death* (1850). W. H. *Hutton, *Burford Papers* (1905),
pp. 277–81 ('The Religion of Dr. Johnson'); W. T. Cairns,
The Religion of Dr. Johnson and Other Essays (1946),
pp. 1–23. The classic art. of T. B. Macaulay, written for
E.B. (ed. 7), is repr., with note by T. Seccombe, in *E.B.*
(ed. 11), xi (1911), pp. 463–71. M. C. Struble, *A Johnson
Handbook* (New York, 1933). W. P. Courtney–D. N. Smith,
A Bibliography of Samuel Johnson (1915); suppl. by R. W.
Chapman in *Oxford Bibliographical Society Proceedings and
Papers*, v (1939), pp. 116–66. G. Saintsbury in *E.B.* (ed.
11), xv (1911), p. 492 f. D. N. Smith in *C.B.E.L.*, pp.
613–28 for further bibl.

JOINVILLE, JEAN (c. 1224–1319), French
historian. Seneschal of Champagne from 1233,
Joinville accompanied St. *Louis IX to Egypt
and Palestine on the Sixth *Crusade in 1248.
In this disastrous venture, both he and the King
were taken prisoners. In 1254 they returned to
France, and Joinville spent most of the rest of
his life upon his estates, except when in attendance at court. He declined to accompany the
King on the Crusade of 1270. In 1282 he was
one of the chief witnesses for Louis's canonization and was present at the exhumation of his
body in 1298. During the next ten years he
wrote his famous life of the King, *Le Livre des
saintes paroles et des bonnes actions de St.
Louis*, at the request of Queen Jeanne. It is
the work of an old man, garrulous and discursive, but it gives a charming account of its
hero, contains an illuminating picture of the
Crusade of 1248, and is full of accurate observations. A 'Credo' which he drew up at Acre
in 1252 while on the Crusade epitomizes his
religious faith.

His History of St. Louis was first publ. at Poitiers in 1547;
crit. ed. of his Works by N. de Wailly (Paris, 1867; revised,
1874); best Eng. tr. by Joan Evans (Newtown, 1937;
London, 1938), with good introd. A. Firmin–Didot, *Études
sur la vie et les travaux de Jean Sire de Joinville* (Paris, 2 pts.
1870); H. F. Delaborde, *Jean de Joinville et les seigneurs de
Joinville* (1894). G. P[aris], 'Jean, Sire de Joinville' in
Histoire littéraire de la France, xxxii (1898), pp. 291–459.

JONAH, Book of. This Book, which is
included among the twelve *Minor Prophets,
is unlike the other prophetical books in being
almost entirely in narrative form. It describes
Jehovah's call to Jonah to go to Nineveh, the
Assyrian capital, to preach repentance, his
disobedience, his attempted escape by sea to
Tarshish, his punishment of being thrown
overboard and swallowed by a great fish (a
'whale'), his deliverance after three days and
nights, and the final success of his mission to
the Gentiles (chs. 1, 3, 4). The psalm in ch. 2 is
generally held by modern critics to be a compilation of material from the *Psalter and
without reference to the rest of the Book. The
aim of the Book is primarily didactic, seeking
to stress God's care for Gentiles and Jews alike.
Considerations of language, style, and theology
have led recent scholars to assign the Book to
the post-exilic period, and to hold that it
belongs to a time when *Judaism was in
danger of becoming narrowly exclusive. The
'sign of Jonah' was regarded in NT times as
a prophecy of our Lord's *Resurrection, and
used by Him (Mt. 12. 40, 16. 4, Lk. 11. 30)
to assure the *Scribes and *Pharisees that
through His death Gentiles as well as Jews
would be converted and saved.

Commentaries by T. T. Perowne (Camb. Bib., AV; 1878),
J. A. Bewer (I.C.C. on Hag., Zech., Mal., and Jon., 1912;
sep. pagination), G. W. Wade (West Comm. on Mic., Obad.,
Joel, and Jon., 1925, pp. 120–46). H. Schmidt, *Jona. Eine
Untersuchung zur vergleichenden Religionsgeschichte*
(Forschungen zur Religion und Literatur des Alten und
Neuen Testaments, ix; 1907). A. Feuillet in *Dict. Bibl.*,
Suppl. iv (1949), cols. 1104–31. Further commentaries
under *Minor Prophets*.

JONAS, JUSTUS (1493–1555), orig. 'Jodo-
cus Koch', German reformer. Educated at
the universities of Erfurt and *Wittenberg, in
1518 he was appointed professor of law at
Erfurt and canon of the church of St. Severus.
In 1519 he was elected rector of the university,
where he introduced Greek and Hebrew into
the curriculum. A great admirer of D.
*Erasmus and M. *Luther, he accompanied
the latter to *Worms in 1521. The Elector of
Saxony then appointed him professor of canon
law at Wittenberg, and henceforward Jonas
took a prominent part in the Protestant cause,
notably at the *Marburg Conference (1529),
the Diet of *Augsburg (1530), and in reform
at Halle (1541). His greatest service to the
Reformation Movement was his translation of
the writings of Luther and *Melanchthon. In
1546 he preached Luther's funeral sermon.
After the outbreak of the Schmalkaldic war he
was for a time a fugitive, but in 1553 was appointed superintendent at Eisfeld, where he
remained till his death.

Briefwechsel, ed. G. Kawerau (2 vols., Halle, 1884–5). P.
Kalkoff, *Humanismus und Reformation in Erfurt* (1926).
G. Kawerau in *P.R.E.* (ed. 3), ix (1901), pp. 341–6. Schot-
tenloher, i (1933), p. 391 f. (Nos. 9436–53).

JONES, GRIFFITH (1683–1761), the
founder of the Welsh circulating schools. Of
Nonconformist parentage, he was received
into the C of E, ordained in 1708, and became
rector of Llanddowror in 1716. He set himself

to further social and religious reforms and to this end made successful preaching tours. In 1730 he began to found his 'circulating schools' for adults and children, with travelling teachers who instructed their pupils in reading the Welsh Bible. Largely through help from England, e.g. from the *S.P.C.K., the scheme rapidly developed, so that at his death over 3,000 of these greatly valued institutions were in existence. Jones published annually *Welsh Piety*, an account of the work and progress of his schools. He was also the author of a large number of writings in Welsh.

Lives by David Jones, Vicar of Penmaenmawr (1902), David Ambrose Jones (in Welsh, 1923), R. T. Jenkins (1930), F. A. Cavenagh (Univ. of Wales Press Board, 1930), and Evan John Davies (1930). T. Kelly, *Griffith Jones, Llanddowror*. Pioneer in Adult Education (1950). R. Williams in *D.N.B.*, xxx (1892), p. 102 f., s.v.

JONES, INIGO (1573–1652), English architect. He was the son of a cloth worker. During the last years of the 16th cent. he visited Italy, where he was deeply impressed by A. Palladio. In 1605 he was appointed architect to the Queen (Anne), and in 1612 he went to Italy again, making a long stay at Vicenza. After his return to England in 1614, he was appointed surveyor general of the royal buildings by *James I, and later served on the commission for the restoration of old *St. Paul's. Under *Charles I he was also employed as a designer of masques, and as such had frequent disputes with Ben Jonson. Despite the influence of Palladio, Inigo Jones preserved his originality and his love of simplicity and spaciousness which made him an inspirer of generations of English architects. He was hampered, however, in the full development of his powers by the unsettled political conditions, which hindered the carrying-out of great designs. Among his best-known ecclesiastical works are Lincoln's Inn Chapel (1617–23) and St. Paul's, Covent Garden (1631–8, rebuilt to his design 1795). It is uncertain whether the porch of St. Mary the Virgin, *Oxford, is rightly attributed to him. A fine collection of his drawings is preserved at Worcester College, Oxford.

Inigo Jones. A Life of the Architect by P. Cunningham. . . . Remarks on Some of his Sketches for Masks and Dramas by J. R. Planché . . . (Shakespeare Society; 1848), Life, pp. 1–51. S. C. Ramsey, *Inigo Jones* (1924); J. A. Gotch, *Inigo Jones* (1928); J. Lees-Milne, *The Age of Inigo Jones* (1953). W. J. Loftie, *Inigo Jones and Wren, or the Rise and Decline of Modern Architecture in England* (1893), ch. v, pp. 109–47. *D.N.B.*, xxx (1892), pp. 111–19.

JONES, RUFUS MATTHEW (1863–1948), American *Quaker. Educated at Haverford College and in Europe, he was principal of Oak Grove Seminary from 1889 to 1893 and professor of philosophy at Haverford College from 1904 to 1934. Among his many works are: *A Dynamic Faith* (1901), *Social Law in the Spiritual World* (1904), *Studies in Mystical Religion* (1909), *Spiritual Reformers in the 16th and 17th Centuries* (1914), *The Later Periods of Quakerism* (1921), *The Faith and Practice of the Quakers* (1927), *New Studies in Mystical*

Religion (1927), *George Fox* (1930), *The Testimony of the Soul* (1936).

H. E. *Fosdick (ed.), *Rufus Jones Speaks to Our Times*. An Anthology (New York, 1951; London, 1953). H. H. Brinton (ed.), *Children of Light*. In Honour of Rufus M. Jones (New York, 1938), with introd. by H. H. Brinton, pp. ix–xii, and list of Jones' Works, pp. 407–11.

JONES, WILLIAM, 'of Nayland' (1726–1800), Anglican divine. A native of Lowick in Northants, he was educated at Charterhouse and at University College, Oxford, where with his friend, G. *Horne, he studied the writings of J. *Hutchinson. Having been ordained in 1751 he held several curacies, and became rector of Pluckley, Kent, in 1765. In 1777 he accepted the perpetual curacy of Nayland, Suffolk, whence his traditional epithet. He endeavoured to keep alive the High Church traditions of the *Nonjurors. His best-known work, *The Catholic Doctrine of the Trinity* (1756), sought to prove from Scriptural texts that the Trinitarian dogma is contained in the Bible. In his later work on the same subject, *A Short Way to Truth* (1792), he attempts to find arguments for the doctrine of the Trinity in nature, e.g. in the three primary colours, the three dimensions, and other groups of three. In 1792 he assisted in the formation of a 'Society for the Reformation of Principles', designed to counteract the influence of the French Revolution. His sound and solid piety finds expression in *The Scholar armed against the Errors of the Time* (1792).

The Theological, Philosophical and Miscellaneous Works of the Rev. William Jones [ed. W. Stevens] (12 vols., London, 1801), with short account of his life and writings by the editor, i, pp. l–lv. Further Sermons (*Sermons on Various Subjects and Occasions*), ed. W. H. Walker [grandson] (2 vols., London, 1830). W. H. Teale, *Lives of English Divines* (1866), pp. 345–419. J. H. Overton in *D.N.B.*, xxx (1892), p. 177 f.; S. L. Ollard in *D.E.C.H.*, p. 303.

JORDAN, River. Formed from the waters of four streams which converge in the upper part of the plain of Lake Huleh, the Jordan expands into Lake Huleh (poss. the 'Waters of Merom' of Josh. 11. 5), flows through a narrow gorge and then forms a delta at the head of the Sea of *Galilee (q.v.). Emerging from the south of the lake, it meanders for 200 miles before it eventually enters the *Dead Sea (65 miles distant). The fault which contains it extends from northern Syria to Ezion-geber on the eastern arm of the *Red Sea.

Flowing through a steep unfertile valley in the centre of Palestine, the Jordan was a natural barrier between the settled and the nomadic population. By their passage of the Jordan, when its waters were miraculously divided, the *Hebrews first entered the Promised Land (Josh. 3. 16); it was the scene of Elijah's ascent to Heaven (2 Kgs. 2. 11); in its waters Naaman the Syrian cleansed (2 Kgs. 5. 12) after he had contrasted it unfavourably with the rivers of his own land. In NT times St. *John the Baptist preached on its banks and the Lord Himself was among those baptized in its waters (Mt. 3. 13). From these associations it became an emblem of the achievement of purity (esp. in baptism) and of man's last hindrance to his final blessedness.

W. Libbey–F. E. Hoskins, *The Jordan Valley and Petra* (2 vols., 1905); N. Glueck, *The River Jordan* (1946). G. A. *Smith, *The Historical Geography of the Holy Land* (ed. 25, 1931), pp. 405–96. F. M. Abel, O.P., *Géographie de la Palestine*, i (1933), pp. 161–78.

JOSAPHAT, St., also 'Joasaph'. In medieval legend, the son of an Indian king, Abenner, who was converted to Christianity by the hermit Barlaam. The name 'Josaphat' appears to be a corruption of 'Bodisatva' (Bodhisattva), a title of the Buddha. He is commemorated in the *Roman Martyrology on 27 Nov. See also *Barlaam and Joasaph, Sts*.

JOSEPH, St. The spouse of the BVM. He figures prominently in the two Infancy narratives of the Gospels—in Mt. 1–2 and to a less extent in Lk. 1–2. Both state that Mary was 'betrothed' to him at the time of our Lord's birth, but both emphasize her virginity. He was a pious Jew of Davidic descent (Mt. 1. 19 f., Lk. 2. 4) but of humble situation, and acc. to Mt. 13. 55 a carpenter ($\tau\epsilon\kappa\tau\omega\nu$). Christ grew up in his household at Nazareth for at least 12 years (Lk. 2. 42, 51). Afterwards Joseph is mentioned only once by name in the NT (Lk. 4. 22; cf. Mt. 13. 55, Mk. 6. 3), but he is often referred to in later traditions. In the 'Protevangelium of *James' he is said to have been very old at the time of his marriage to Mary; and as a pattern of holiness he is the subject of various legends. The special veneration of St. Joseph seems to have originated in the E., where the apocryphal 'History of Joseph the Carpenter' (4th–7th cents.) enjoyed considerable popularity. It developed comparatively late in the W. Church, though a commemoration is mentioned in the Irish *Félire* of Oengus, assigned to the 9th cent. Among the earliest promoters of his cult are St. *Bernardino of Siena and John *Gerson in the 15th cent., who laid its theological foundations by drawing out the implications of his office as foster-father of Jesus, and whose teaching found liturgical expression in the introduction of his feast (19 Mar.) into the Roman Calendar in 1479. The devotion was popularized esp. by St. *Teresa and St. *Francis of Sales. In 1714 *Clement XI composed a special office for his feast, and in 1729 *Benedict XIII inserted his name in the Litany of the Saints. He was declared 'Patron of the Universal Church' by *Pius IX in 1870, when his principal feast (apart from 19 Mar.) became his 'Patronage', since 1914 celebrated on the 3rd Wednesday after Easter. His pre-eminent sanctity, which places him next to the BVM among the saints, was confirmed by *Leo XIII in his encyclical 'Quanquam pluries' of 1889. St. Joseph is invoked as the patron of a good death; the month of March and each Wednesday are dedicated to him. He is usually represented with the Child Jesus and lily or staff.

A. H. Lépicier, *Tractatus de S. Joseph* (Paris [1908]). O. Pfülf, 'Die Verehrung des hl. Joseph in der Geschichte' in *Stimmen aus Maria Laach*, xxxviii (1890), pp. 137–61 and

282–302; C. A., 'Le Développement historique du culte de S. Joseph' in *R. Bén.*, xiv (1897), pp. 104–14, 145–55, and 203–9. J. Seitz, *Die Verehrung des hl. Joseph in ihrer geschichtlichen Entwickelung bis zum Konzil von Trient* (1908). A. Michel in *D.T.C.*, viii (1924), cols. 1510–21, s.v. with bibl.

JOSEPH OF ARIMATHAEA, St. The 'councillor' ($\beta o\nu\lambda\epsilon\nu\tau\eta\varsigma$, Lk. 23. 50) who after the Crucifixion requested from Pilate the body of Christ and gave it burial the same day (Mt. 27. 60, Mk. 15. 46, Lk. 23. 53; cf. Jn. 19. 42. &c.). He is described as a 'good and a just man' ($\alpha\nu\eta\rho$ $\alpha\gamma\alpha\theta\delta\varsigma$ $\kappa\alpha\dot{\iota}$ $\delta\dot{\iota}\kappa\alpha\iota o\varsigma$; Lk. 23. 50) and as a disciple, 'but secretly for fear of the Jews' (Jn. 19. 38). Acc. to the apocryphal 'Gospel of *Nicodemus' he played an important part in the foundation of the first Christian community at Lydda. In the 'De Antiquitate Glastoniensis Ecclesiae' (*c.* 1130) of *William of Malmesbury occurs the earliest mention of the story that St. Joseph came to England with the Holy Grail and built the first church in the country at *Glastonbury, but the passage relating this incident is an addition to the book, at least a hundred years later. Feast day, 17 Mar.

E. von Dobschütz, 'Joseph von Arimathia' in *Z.K.G.*, xxiii (1902), pp. 1–17; T. Kluge, 'Die apokryphe Erzählung des Joseph von Aramathäa über den Bau der ersten christlichen Kirche in Lydda' in *Oriens Christianus*, N.S., iv (1914), pp. 24–38.

JOSEPH CALASANCTIUS, St. (1556–1648), in religion 'a Matre Dei', founder of the *Piarists (q.v.). The son of Don Pedro Calasanza and Donna Maria Gastonia, he was born near Petralta de la Sal in Aragon. He studied in several Spanish universities including Valencia and Alcalá and, renouncing marriage, was ordained priest in 1583 by the Bp. of Urgel. After holding administrative appointments in Spain, he went to Rome in 1592, where he was patronized by the *Colonna family. Here he became very active in good works, and after a time interested himself esp. in the education of homeless and neglected children. Under his influence the first free school was established at Rome in Nov. 1597. To give permanence and inspiration to the work, which grew rapidly, he established the Piarist Order in a house at S. Andrea della Valle in 1602. The work was transferred in 1612 to the Torres Palace, adjoining S. Pantaleone, where Joseph spent the rest of his life. He was accused to the Holy Office by rival influences in his institute, being at one stage arrested and saved from imprisonment only by the intervention of Card. Cesarini. It was not until 1645 that his authority in the institute was restored. He was beatified in 1748 and canonized in 1767. Feast day, 27 Aug.

Letters ed. L. Picanyol, Piarist (Rome, 1950 ff.), with introd. in vol. i, pp. ix–xliv. The chief source is the material submitted for his beatification and canonization. Lives by V. Talenti (Rome, 1753; repr. Florence, 1917), U. Tosetti (Rome, 1767; also later edd.), N. Tommaséo (ib., 1847, and later edd.), J. Timon-David (2 vols., Marseilles, 1884), W. E. Hubert (Mainz, 1886), Josef Calasanz Heidenreich (Vienna, 1907), G. Giovannozzi (Florence, 1930), and Calasanz Bau (Madrid, 1949). In English there is a trans. of an Ital. life in the series, 'The Saints and Servants of God', ed. F. W. *Faber, 1850. See also bibl. to *Piarists*.

JOSEPH OF CUPERTINO, St. (1603–1663). Joseph Desa was the son of a poor carpenter at Cupertino, in the kingdom of Naples, and very backward as a youth. After being refused admission by the Conventual *Friars Minor because of his ignorance and being dismissed by the *Capuchins on account of his awkwardness, he at last succeeded in being employed as a stable-boy at the Franciscan convent of La Grotella, nr. Cupertino. He became a choir religious in 1625 and was ordained priest in 1628. His subsequent life is said to have been a series of miracles and ecstasies, remarkable for the supposedly well-authenticated phenomena of levitation accompanying them. Through the disturbance they caused, Joseph was not allowed for 35 years to take part in the community duties such as choir or the common meals in the refectory, and was even denounced to the *Inquisition. From 1653 the ecclesiastical authorities removed him from the curiosity of the people to out-of-the-way convents of the *Capuchins, and in 1657 to the Conventual house at Osimo, where he remained in strict seclusion for the rest of his life. He was also said to have had the gift of reading consciences. It is related that a meeting with him decided the conversion of the Lutheran duke, John Frederick of Brunswick, to the Catholic faith. He was canonized by *Clement XIII in 1767. Feast day, 18 Sept.

D. Bernino, *Vita del Padre Fr. Giuseppe da Copertino* (1722; Fr. tr., 1856); [A. Pastrovicchi, O.M.C.] *Compendio della vita, virtù, e miracoli del B. Giuseppe da Copertino* (1753; Eng. tr., 1918). E. M. Franciosi, *Vita di S. Giuseppe da Copertino* (Recanati, 1925). F. Mershman in *C.E.*, viii (1910), p. 520 f.

JOSEPH THE HYMNOGRAPHER, St. (*c.* 810 – 86), the most voluminous of the Greek hymn-writers. In 830 he left his native Sicily when invaded by the Arabs for the monastic life at Thessalonica. Some time later he went on to *Constantinople, which he left for *Rome during the *Iconoclastic persecution (841). Captured by pirates, he was for several years a slave in Crete, but eventually escaped and *c.* 850 established a monastery at Constantinople. He suffered a further exile in the Chersonese for his defence of the Icons and yet another in the company of *Photius. He is reputed to have composed 1,000 canons, over 200 being contained in the *Menaion under the acrostic of his name. He also gave the final form to the *Parakletike. He has often been confused with Joseph of Thessalonica (also 'Joseph of the Studium'), the brother of *Theodore Studites. Feast day in the E. Church, 3 Apr.

Text of canons in J. P. Migne, *PG*, cv. 983–1426, with introds. and Gk. life by John the Deacon, cols. 925–82; cf. also *Anal. Boll.*, lxv (1947), pp. 134–8. *AA.SS.*, Apr. I (1675), pp. 266–76, and *Bolletino della Badia greca di Grottaferrata*, xi (1948), pp. 87–98, 177–92. C. van de Vorst, 'Note sur St. Joseph l'Hymnographe' in *Anal Boll.*, xxxviii (1920), pp. 148–54.

JOSEPHINISM. The principles which actuated the ecclesiastical reforms of Joseph II, Holy Roman Emperor from 1765 to 1790.

They included religious toleration, the right of the state to regulate ecclesiastical affairs and to reform ecclesiastical abuses, irrespective of Rome, and the restriction of the rights and powers of the Pope within spiritual limits, as laid down by *Febronius. They issued in the Toleration Edict of 1781, which granted all religious bodies the right to practise their beliefs unhindered, the suppression of certain religious orders, the transference of monasteries from the jurisdiction of the Pope to that of the diocesan bishops, and the requirement of civil consent for the publication of any Papal bull, brief or other document. A similar policy was introduced into Tuscany, under the direction of his brother Leopold, the Grand Duke, who was assisted by Scipio de' *Ricci, Bp. of Pistoia. Josephinism completely collapsed with the Emperor's death.

There is an immense lit. Docc. in F. Maass, *Der Josephinismus. Quellen zu seiner Geschichte in Österreich, 1760–1790* Fontes Rerum Austriacarum, Abt. ii, vols. 71, 72; 1951–3. Studies in English include S. K. Padover, *The Revolutionary Emperor Joseph II* (1934), and Sr. Mary C. Goodwin, *The Papal Conflict with Josephinism* (New York, 1938). G. Mollat in *D.T.C.*, viii (pt. 2; 1925), cols. 1543–7; E. Tomek in *L.Th.K.*, v (1933), cols. 572–5, s.v. 'Joseph II', and M. E. Viora in *E.C.*, vi (1951), col. 812 f., all with bibl. See also bibl. to *Febronianism*.

JOSEPHUS, FLAVIUS (*c.* 37–c. 100), Jewish historian. He was a native of Palestine of priestly descent who received a thorough education based on study of the Jewish Law. Having lived for three years in the desert as the disciple of the hermit Bannos, he became a *Pharisee. In 64 he went to Rome to plead for the release of some of his fellow-Jews, and after enlisting the sympathies of the Emp. *Nero's wife, Poppea, returned to Palestine. In 66 he took a leading part in the Jewish war. In 67 he was besieged in Jotopata, but escaped death and was taken prisoner by Vespasian, whose favour he won by prophesying that he would become emperor. On the fulfilment of the prophecy in 69 Josephus was set at liberty and took the name of 'Flavius'. During the siege of *Jerusalem (70) he acted as interpreter to Titus, with whom he returned to Rome, as his surrender had earned him the hostility of the Jews. In Rome he was highly honoured by Vespasian as well as by his successors, Titus and *Domitian, and received the Roman citizenship and a pension which enabled him to devote himself entirely to literary work. In 77–8 he published his 'Jewish War' (Περὶ τοῦ Ἰουδαϊκοῦ πολέμου), probably written originally in Aramaic. It opens with an historical summary of the events from the time of Antiochus Epiphanes to the outbreak of the war. The latter part is largely an eye-witness account, though supplemented by borrowings from other authors. Though the introduction promises an impartial treatment of the subject, the work is written from the standpoint of a Jew trying to gain the sympathy of the Roman public and therefore omits or minimizes all that might offend Roman susceptibilities, such as the activities of the *Zealots and the importance of the Messianic hope. He brought out *c.* 94

his second great work, the 'Antiquities of the Jews' ('Ιουδαϊκὴ 'Αρχαιολογία), the 20 books of which trace the history of the Jews from the creation of the world to the end of the Jewish war. Down to *c.* 400 B.C. Josephus mainly reproduces the Bible narratives; later he uses many other sources, among them Dionysius of Halicarnassus and Nicolaus of Damascus, as well as Apocryphal books. The famous reference to Christ in 18. 3. 3, calling Him 'a wise man, if indeed one should call him a man', is in its present form not authentic. The most generally accepted opinion is that Josephus mentioned our Lord, as he refers to Him later on in a passage on St. James, but that the passage just referred to was interpolated by a Christian writer at an early date, certainly before the time of *Eusebius who already knows it in its present form (*H.E.*, I. xi. 7 f.). There are also two minor works extant, an autobiography and 'Contra Apionem', in the latter of which he tries to prove the unique validity of the Jewish conception of history.

The works of Josephus were highly appreciated by the Fathers, e.g. *Jerome, whom they furnished with a wealth of materials for their apologetics.

Editio princeps of the Gk. text of his works, with Lat. tr. [ed. A. P. Arlenius], Basle, 1544. Best crit. ed. is that of B. Niese (6 vols. and index, Berlin, 1887–95); also ed. S. A. Naber (Teubner, 6 vols., 1888–96). Ed. based on Niese and Naber, with modern Eng. tr., by H. St. J. Thackeray (Loeb, 1926 ff.). Older Eng. tr. by W. *Whiston (2 vols., London, 1737), frequently repr.; revised by A. R. Shilleto, with topographical notes by C. W. Wilson (Bohn's Standard Library, 5 vols., 1889–90). N. Bentwich, *Josephus* (Philadelphia, 1914). R. Laqueur, *Der jüdische Historiker Flavius Josephus* (1920). H. St. J. Thackeray, *Josephus, the Man and the Historian* (Hilda Stich Stoock Lectures; New York, 1929). R. Eisler, 'Ιησοῦς Βασιλεὺς οὐ Βασιλεύσας (2 vols. Lfgng., 1928–30; uncritical and untrustworthy). S. Zeitlin, *Josephus on Jesus* (Philadelphia, 1931). A. *Schlatter, *Die Theologie des Judentums nach dem Bericht des Josephus* (Beiträge zur Förderung christlicher Theologie, 2 Reihe, xxvi; 1932). B. Bienert, *Der älteste nichtchristliche Jesusbericht: Josephus über Jesus* (Theologische Arbeiten zur Bibel-, Kirchen- und Geistesgeschichte, ix; 1936). Eng. tr. of the portion of the Slavonic text on St. *John the Baptist in F. J. Foakes Jackson–K. *Lake (edd.), *The Beginnings of Christianity*, i (1920), pp. 433–5. On the relation of St. *Luke to Josephus see H. J. Cadbury and the editors, ib., ii (1922), pp. 355–8, and works there cited. H. St. J. Thackeray, *A Lexicon to Josephus* (Publications of the Alexander Kohut Memorial Foundation; Paris, 1930 ff.). E. *Schürer, *Geschichte des jüdischen Volkes im Zeitalter Jesu Christi*, i (ed. 4, 1901), pp. 75–106, with bibl. to date. H. St. J. Thackeray in *H.D.B.*, Extra Vol. (1904), pp. 461–73. R. J. H. Shutt, *Studies in Josephus* (S.P.C.K., 1961).

JOSHUA, Book of. The first of the 'historical books' in the OT and, acc. to the Hebrew division, the first of the 'Former Prophets'. It traces the history of the Israelites from the death of *Moses to the death of his successor, Joshua, and gives an account of the entry into and conquest of Palestine, its partition among the twelve tribes, and Joshua's last speeches. Among the better-known incidents in the Book are the hiding of the spies in *Jericho by Rahab the harlot (2), the miraculous crossing of the *Jordan commemorated by the twelve stones representing the twelve tribes of Israel (3 f.), the Fall of Jericho (6), and the standing still of the sun on Gibeon (10). Chs. 12–21 record in detail the division

of Palestine among the twelve tribes. The narrative thus relates to events shortly after the *Exodus (q.v.), which is assigned by Biblical scholars to different dates between *c.* 1500 and 1200 B.C. The composition of the Book, however, is very much later, and though some of its sources may date from the 9th cent. B.C., or even earlier, the Book probably did not reach its present form before the 6th cent. or later. It is generally agreed that the compiler made some use of the recognized sources of the *Pentateuch, and this fact has often led scholars to class Joshua with the five Books of the Law in what is termed the '*Hexateuch'. As in the case of the other historical books of the OT, the history has been interpreted in the light of the author's religious beliefs e.g. its description of the speedy and complete conquest of Canaan in the post-Exodus period is at variance with the account in the Book of *Judges.

Commentaries by H. W. *Robinson (Cent. Bib. on Deut. and Jos., 1907, pp. 271–385), G. A. *Cooke (Camb. Bib., RV, 1918), H. Holzinger (K.H.C., Abt. vi; 1901), C. Steuernagel (H.K.A.T., Abt. i, Bd. iii, on Deut., Jos., 1899, pt. 2, pp. 131–248), and M. Noth (H.A.T., Reihe i, Bd. vii, 1938). J. Garstang, *Joshua–Judges* (1931), pp. 3–260. G. F. Moore in *E.Bi.*, ii (1901), cols. 2600–10; S. Lyonnet, S.J., in *Dict. Bibl.*, Suppl. iv (1949), cols. 1131–43.

JOVIAN (*c.* 332–64), Roman Emperor from June 363 to Feb. 364. He was born at Singidunum in Moesia. On the Emp. *Julian's fatal expedition against the Persians he was captain of his bodyguard; and when, after Julian's death (26 June 363), Sallust, the Prefect of the East, had declined to receive the purple at the hands of the army, Jovian was chosen. He was forced to conclude a humiliating peace with Sapor II, King of the Persians, abandoning Nisibis and the other territories conquered under *Diocletian in 298, and the Christian Kingdom of *Armenia. In the theological disputes he supported orthodoxy and on his way back to the West he received St. *Athanasius, who presented a Confession of Faith at *Edessa and prob. accompanied the Emperor to *Antioch. Before reaching *Constantinople, Jovian died suddenly one night (17 Feb. 364) at Dadastana, apparently through overeating or suffocation. His support of orthodoxy made him for Catholics a welcome successor to Julian; and in *Syriac literature he even became the subject of a Christian romance.

The chief source is Ammianus Marcellinus, xxv, 5–10. Further information will be found in the Church Historians, *Socrates (*H.E.*, iii, 22–6), *Sozomen (*H.E.*, vi, 3–6), and *Theodoret (*H.E.*, iv, 1–4). J. *Wordsworth in *D.C.B.*, iii (1882), pp. 461–5; O. Seeck in *P.W.*, ix (pt. 2; 1916), cols. 2006–11, s.v. 'Jovianus'.

JOVINIAN (d. *c.* 405). An unorthodox monk, condemned by synods at Rome (under *Siricius) and at Milan (under St. *Ambrose in 393). He denied that virginity as such was a higher state than marriage, and that abstinence as such was better than thankful eating. He also attacked the tendency to associate differences of reward in heaven with different earthly states (virgins, widows, wives; monks, priests, laymen), and shared the disbelief of

*Helvidius in the perpetual virginity of *Mary. *Jerome (*Adversus Jovinianum*, i–ii, A.D. 392) and *Augustine (in *De bono conjugali* and *De sancta virginitate*, A.D. 401) both wrote against him.

Jovinian's own writings are lost. W. Haller, *Jovinianus* in *Texte und Untersuchungen*, Bd. xvii, No. 2 (1897; a comprehensive study). J. Forget in *D.T.C.*, viii (pt. 2; 1925), cols. 1577–80; A. Amore in *E.C.*, vi (1951), col. 646 f.

JOWETT, BENJAMIN (1817–93), Master of Balliol College, Oxford. Educated at St. Paul's School under John Sleath, Jowett entered Balliol in 1836 where he was elected a Fellow while still an undergraduate. He held a succession of College offices, finally becoming Master (1870). He was ordained deacon in 1842 and priest in 1845. In 1855 he succeeded T. *Gaisford as Regius professor of Greek.

In strong contrast with his early colleague, W. G. *Ward, Jowett distrusted logic and, under the influence of Greek studies and German philosophy (esp. G. W. F. *Hegel), became a keen theological liberal. His classical learning was almost unrivalled in his day in Oxford. He issued a successful and popular translation of *Plato (4 vols., 1871; ed. 3, 5 vols., 1892), and secured the introduction of Plato into the *Litt. Hum.* course for students. His theological views were first elaborated in his *Commentaries on the Epp. of St. Paul* (Thess., Gal., and Rom.; 2 vols., 1835). His exegesis may have wanted philological exactness, but the treatment was fresh and original. The work contained a personal and subjective exposition of the *Atonement which he redrafted in a 2nd edition (1859) to meet objections, but without modifying it. His essay on 'the Interpretation of Scripture' in *Essays and Reviews* (1860, q.v.) was one of the most debated items in the book; and henceforth Jowett's orthodoxy remained under grave suspicion and he ceased to write on theological subjects. He continued, however, to take an active part in academic affairs, instituting reforms in the interests of poorer students, and he secured for his college a unique place in the University. His other publications include translations of *Thucydides* (2 vols., 1881) and *Aristotle's Politics* (2 vols., 1885).

Evelyn Abbott and L. Campbell, *The Life and Letters of Benjamin Jowett* (2 vols., 1897); L. A. Tollemache, *Benjamin Jowett* (1895); G. Faber, *Jowett* (1957). E. Abbott in *D.N.B.*, Suppl. iii (1901), pp. 49–56.

JOYFUL MYSTERIES, The Five. The first chaplet of the *Rosary (q.v.), consisting of (1) the *Annunciation, (2) the *Visitation, (3) the Nativity of Christ, (4) the *Presentation of Christ in the Temple, and (5) the finding of the Child Jesus in the Temple.

JUBE (pron. as two syllables). The rood loft dividing the nave of a church from the choir. The name is said to derive from the words 'Jube, domne, benedicere' ('Pray, sir, a blessing'), pronounced by the *deacon before the reading of the Gospel, which took place on the rood loft in medieval times.

JUBILATE (Lat., 'O be joyful'). The first word of Ps. 100, to which it thus gives the name. It is provided as an alternative to the *Benedictus at Morning Prayer in the BCP. The rubric requires its use only when the Benedictus occurs elsewhere in the service, though it is apparently permitted on other days. It was first inserted in 1552, probably owing to the dislike of the extreme Reformers for the traditional *canticles (so also Pss. 98 and 67 at Evening Prayer).

JUBILATE SUNDAY. The Third Sunday after *Easter, so called because the first words of the *Introit of the Latin Mass are *Jubilate Deo, omnis terra* (Ps. 66. 1; *Vg.* Ps. 65. 1).

JUBILEE, Year of. (a) Acc. to the Jewish Law (Lev. 25), a year occurring once every fifty years, when Jewish slaves regained their freedom, and land reverted to its former owners. (b) In the RC Church, a 'year of remission' or '*Holy Year' (q.v.) in which a special indulgence is granted to Catholics who visit *Rome and fulfil certain conditions.

JUBILEES, Book of. An apocryphal Jewish work, also called 'The Little Genesis'. It reinterprets the Genesis narrative of the creation and other events under a scheme of dating by years, weeks of years, and 'jubilees' (Lev. 25. 11), in the interests of Jewish priestly law and ceremonial. It is written to show that the *Law, with its prescriptions about feasts, the Sabbath, offerings, abstinence from blood and from fornication (which for the writer includes intermarriage with Gentiles), and such matters, was promulgated in these patriarchal times, and indeed existed eternally with God in heaven. The Book was written between 135 B.C. and *c.* 96 B.C. by a writer of nationalist and rigoristic outlook, who deplored contemporary laxity. Though the original Hebrew (or perhaps Aramaic) text of the Book is lost, it survives in whole or in part in a number of versions, of which the Ethiopic is the most important. Its narrative form is an outstanding early example of *Midrash.

Ethiopic text first publd. by A. *Dillmann (Kiel, 1859); Lat. fragments ed. A. M. Ceriani, *Monumenta Sacra et Profana*, i (Milan, 1861), pp. 15–54; Syriac fragment, ii (ib., 1863), p. ix f. Crit. ed. of Ethiopic text, with other fragments, by R. H. *Charles (Anecdota Oxoniensia, Semitic Series, viii; Oxford, 1895); Eng. tr., with commentary and notes, by id. (London, 1902). Further Syriac fragments ed., with commentary, by E. Tisserant, in *R. Bibl.*, xxx (1921), pp. 55–86 and 206–32. R. H. Charles in id. (ed.), *The Apocrypha and Pseudepigrapha of the Old Testament in English*, ii (1913), pp. 1–82, largely repr. from his vol. cited above. R. H. Pfeiffer, *History of New Testament Times with an Introduction to the Apocrypha* (New York, 1949; London, 1954), pp. 68–70, with bibl. p. 539 f. J. B. Frey in *Dict. Bibl.*, Suppl. i (1928), cols. 371–80, s.v. 'Apocryphes de l'Ancien Testament (2)', with bibl.

JUDAEA. The region reoccupied by the Jews in 537 B.C. after the *Babylonian Captivity, and the most southern of the three districts, Galilee, Samaria, and Judaea, into which Palestine, west of the *Jordan, was divided in Christ's time. The word was sometimes used, e.g. in Lk. 23. 5 (RV; 'Jewry', AV), of the whole of Palestine.

JUDAH, Tribe of. The most powerful of the twelve tribes of Israel. Possibly its earlier tribal history is represented in the story of Judah, the fourth son of Jacob (Israel) (Gen. 29. 35, and ch. 38). Already in the reigns of *David and *Solomon (c. 1000 B.C.) Judah was the predominant tribe. Afterwards, with Benjamin, it formed a separate kingdom which outlasted that of the northern tribes, and in general maintained a purer religious faith.

JUDAISM. The faith and practice of the Jewish people. Judaism shares with Christianity and Islam the belief in one universal God, conceived as personal, Who is the Creator of the universe and the highest Source of values.

I. The words 'Jew' and 'Judaism', in their original Hebrew and Greek forms (Heb. *Yehudi*; Gk. 'Ιουδαῖος), are ultimately derived from the name of Judah, the Southern Kingdom in Palestine, which came to an end with the Babylonian Exile (586 B.C.). The changed circumstances of the Exile were the historical setting of the rise of Judaism. Notably, they led to the redrafting of tradition and the transference of emphasis from cultus to teaching and ethics. These conditions also strongly influenced cosmology, angelology, and eschatology, with the subsequent contrast between the present and future 'ages'. In a wider sense, however, Judaism may be said to go back to the Patriarchs and their election very many centuries earlier. See also *Israel*.

II. The Jewish community in general may be characterized as follows:

(a) GEOGRAPHICALLY, by their centres of concentration which have lain in the Near East, Europe, and, esp. since the 19th cent., in America.

(b) POLITICALLY, by three States, viz., the Hebrew monarchy founded by *Saul (c. 1025 B.C.) with a divided kingdom from *Solomon's death (933 B.C.) until the Exile (586 B.C.), the rise of the *Hasmonean rule (from 165 B.C.), and the State of Israel (from 1948).

(c) ECONOMICALLY, by their distribution along the trading centres and routes of the ancient and modern worlds.

(d) STATISTICALLY, by an expansion into millions at the beginning of the Christian era (7 per cent of the Roman Empire, acc. to A. *Harnack), a reduction to c. 1½ millions by the end of the Middle Ages, and an increasing expansion with the emancipation (c. 11¾ millions at present (c. 1955), of which 29 per cent are in Europe and the U.S.S.R., 51 per cent in America, and over 12 per cent in Israel).

(e) LINGUISTICALLY, by the constantly revived use of the Biblical languages, *Hebrew and *Aramaic; in addition the use of Greek and Arabic in the ancient and medieval, and Yiddish, German, and English in the modern, periods.

(f) JURIDICALLY, by the seven Noachidian laws (against murder, &c.), the division into revealed and rational laws (with emphasis on assistance to the poor, orphan, and stranger), traditional methods of interpretation of law (*Hillel and *Shammai; schools of *Akiba and Ismael; Palestinian, Babylonian, and European academies), the development of large lawcodes, and a rich literature of case *responsa*.

(g) THEOLOGICALLY, by belief in a central revelation on Mt. *Sinai, ethical *Monotheism, God's thirteen qualities (Ex. 34. 6), the Covenant and the election of Israel, resurrection, and future Messianism as represented in written *Torah ('instruction'). Sacred and secular being undivided, there is no word for 'religion' in classical Hebrew (later *dath*, etc.). In character, Torah may be '*Halakhah' (i.e. normative religious statute', e.g. that of R. Samuel, d. 254) or '*Haggadah' (i.e. exposition of non-legal matter).

(h) PHILOSOPHICALLY, by a triple set of influences, viz. in ancient times through Hellenism; in the Middle Ages through the Mu'tazilite Kalām, *Neo-Platonism, *Aristotelianism; and lastly through modern, largely idealistic, philosophy. Outstanding thinkers have been in the first period *Philo of Alexandria; in the second Seadiah ben Joseph (882–942), *Avicebron, Judah Halevi (c. 1085–c. 1140), and M. *Maimonides; in the third B. de *Spinoza, M. Mendelssohn (1729–86), H. Cohen (1842–1918), L. Baeck (1873–1956), M. *Buber, and F. Rosenzweig (1886–1929).

(i) SOCIALLY, by several groups and schisms. Besides the *Samaritan schism, the principal early groupings were the *Sadducees (aristocratic minority, rationalist; acceptance of written Torah only), *Pharisees ('those who separate themselves', extending the revelation to oral Torah; progressive interpretation of tradition), *Essenes (monastic; common property; celibacy), the *Damascus sect of the New Covenant, and the *Karaïtes (since the 8th cent. Mikra only; stringent religious law, e.g. as to incest and the *Sabbath). Modern Rabbinic Judaism is divided into the 'priestly' group (S. R. Hirsch), Talmud- and Torah-centred orthodoxy, and the 19th–20th cent. 'historical', and in ritual 'progressive', Reform.

(j) LITURGICALLY, by the division of their rites into Palestinian (subsequently, e.g., Ashkenazi-Polish and Italian) and Babylonian (subsequently Sephardi), by the emphasis on the Sabbath for rest and joy, and by the close association of religious and national elements in the festivals.

Jewish influences on early Christian worship may include the recital of the *Lord's Prayer three times a day (*Didache*, viii, 3); the *Passover, *Kiddush or *Chaburah rites as influencing the *Eucharist; the 'Qedusha' as the prototype of the *Sanctus; and the use of Scripture-readings in worship. There are also the obvious festival correspondences: Sabbath/Sunday; Passover/Easter; Pentecost/Whitsuntide; three fasts after Nisan-Tishri/Embertide-fasts; etc. Apart from Christianity, the Stoa, Gnosis, Islam, and Socialism have all been influenced by Judaism.

III. The sociological form of Jewish community life, particularly since the age of Roman legislation, has been that of loosely associated congregations (cf. St. *Paul's visits to those of Syria, Cyprus, Asia Minor, etc.). In Palestine these congregations centred round the Second *Temple, later round the patriarchal house. In the *Diaspora strictly organized communities, which were more or less autonomous, existed in Hellenistic Egypt, Mesopotamia, Spain, and Poland. Elsewhere there were individual overseers, e.g. in medieval England (presbyteratus . . . judaeorum totius Angliae, 12th-13th cent.); the inscriptions of the Roman catacombs and Constantine's law for Cologne (321) show the kind of offices held in such congregations. Esp. since the Middle Ages, Jewish congregations have been mainly of an urban character. Apart from Jerusalem, the oldest extant Jewish communities are those of Rome (139 B.C.; Jewish workmen at the Colosseum), Athens (cf. Acts 17. 16 f.), Cologne (321), and Constantinople (under *Theodosius the Great); others include London (under William II, 1087–1100) and Vienna (regulations of Raffelstaetten, 906 A.D.).

IV. The history of the Jews falls into three major periods: (a) Oriental (down to 12th cent. A.D.); (b) European (139 B.C.–A.D. 1492); and (c) Universal (1492–1948).

(a) The first period may be divided (i) from the migrations of the Hebrews and the Patriarchs (2nd millennium B.C.) to the end of Persian rule in Judaea (332 B.C.). Its outstanding features are the Mosaic age with the Exodus from Egypt, the conquest of Canaan, the Solomonic Temple, classical Prophecy, the Assyrian exile (722), the Babylonian Exile (586–538), the Persian support for the restored community in Judah (Cyrus, 538, Artaxerxes I and *Nehemiah c. 444), and the reforms of *Josiah (622) before, and of *Ezra (457 or 397) and the sopherim after, the Babylonian Exile. (ii) From Alexander the Great to the Roman destruction of the Temple and Jerusalem (A.D. 70). It is marked by an autonomous high-priesthood carrying on from the Persians to the Greeks; Jewish Hellenism with the Septuagint, Philo, and *Josephus; the rise of the Hasmonean and Herodian kingdoms; dependence on Rome (province from 63 B.C.); the Pharisaic movement, and a powerful Diaspora. (iii) A third, creative stage of Jewish history extends from the rise of the academy at *Jamnia under Johanan b. Zakkai (after A.D. 70) to the end of the Babylonian academies. Its main factors are the abortive *Bar-Cochba war (A.D. 132–35); the rise of the Palestinian patriarchate sponsoring works like the *Mishnah, Tannaitic Midrashim, the Palestinian *Talmud, and liturgical poetry (Kalir, Yannai, etc.). Within the transition from Parthian to Sassanid rule, and later to Islam, come the growing independence of the Babylonian Diaspora (after 200) with its exilarchs (worldly leaders, 2nd–9th cent.), gaonim (spiritual heads of the academies, c. 590 to the 13th cent., with authority as far as India and Arabia following Benjamin of Tudela, 12th cent.), and the

Babylonian Talmud (fundamental for later Judaism up to the 19th cent.); finally the schism of the Karaïtes (revival in Czarist Russia; c. 12,000 in 1937).

(b) The European period reaches from the first dated testimony (edict of the Praetor Hispalus, 139 B.C.) to the end of Jewish community life in Spain and Portugal (1492 and 1497). Its landmarks are the rise of new centres in Spain, France, and Germany (in the 12th cent. 80–90 per cent still in the Near East); the protective legislation of Pope *Gregory the Great (c. 600; decrees 'sicut Judaeis'); the golden era in Spain; the institution of 'servi camerae imperialis' (since *Louis the Pious); the set-back through the *Crusades, the Black Death (1348–9), and the emigration movement to Eastern Europe. To this period belong the development of medieval philosophy and mysticism, the extensive commentation of the Bible, Talmud, Zohar, and vast legal codifications.

(c) The principal landmarks of the modern period appear at the death of Uriel da Costa (1640), the French revolution (1789, Mirabeau, etc.), and in the age of emancipation extending from Moses Mendelssohn (d. 1786) to the 'minority clauses' of the Versailles Treaty (1919), and in its final outcome to the establishment of the State of Israel (1948). Among the principal features of the period are the Eastern European Kahal ('community-organization' and Wa'ad, c. 1580–1761), the rise of Hasidism, the London Chief Rabbinate (since 1757–8), the French Consistoire (since 1808), and the gradual secularization and participation in European and American life and letters. The last phase shows the Romanoff repression since Czar Alexander III (1881), the rise of political Zionism (Balfour Declaration, 1917), Russian Birobidzhan (1928), a flourishing secular Hebrew literature, and the scientific New Learning (*Wissenschaft des Judentums*, orig. based on classical scholarship).

I. Epstein, *The Jewish Way of Life* (1946). L. Baeck, *Das Wesen des Judentums* (1905; Eng. tr. as *The Essence of Judaism*, 1936). Id., *Wege im Judentum*. Aufsätze und Reden (1933); id., *Aus drei Jahrtausenden*. Wissenschaftliche Untersuchungen und Abhandlungen zur Geschichte des jüdischen Glaubens (1938). H. Graetz, *Geschichte der Juden* (11 vols., 1853–75, often revised by the author; Eng. tr., 5 vols., 1891–5). L. Finkelstein (ed.), *The Jews*. Their History, Culture and Religion (2 vols., New York, 1949). S. W. Baron, *A Social and Religious History of the Jews* (3 vols., New York, 1937; ed. 2, 1952 ff.). C. F. Moore, *Judaism in the First Centuries of the Christian Era*. The Age of the Tannaim (3 vols., Cambridge, Mass., 1927–30). J. Bonsirven, S.J., *Le Judaïsme palestinien au temps de Jésus Christ* (Bibliothèque de Théologie Historique, 2 vols., 1935). S. Singer (ed.), *The Authorized Daily Prayer Book of the United Hebrew Congregations of the British Empire* (1891); I. Abrahams, *Companion* to the preceding item (1922). Periodical Jewish publications include *Monatschrift für Geschichte und Wissenschaft des Judenthums* (Dresden and other places, 1852 ff.), *Jewish Quarterly Review* (Philadelphia, 1888 ff.), *Revue des Études juives* (Paris, 1880 ff.), *Hebrew Union College Annual* (Cincinnati, 1924 ff.) and *Jewish Social Studies* (New York, 1939 ff.); and for bibl., *Kirjath Sepher* (Jerusalem, 1924 ff.) The chief dictionaries are *The Jewish Encyclopedia*, ed. S. Singer (12 vols., New York–London, 1901–6), and the *Encyclopædia Judaica*, ed. J. Klatzin and others (10 vols., Berlin, 1928–34). I. Abrahams in *E.B.* (ed. 11), xv (1911), pp. 371–410, s.v. 'Jews'; H. Loewe in *H.E.R.E.*, vii (1914), pp. 581–609, s.v. 'Judaism'. I. Epstein in *E.B.* (ed. 14; revised 1954), pp. 165–8; J. Bonsirven, S.J., in *Dict. Bibl.*, Suppl. iv (1949), cols. 1143–1285.

JUDAIZERS. In the early Church a section of Jewish Christians who regarded the OT Levitical laws as still binding on all Christians. They tried to enforce on the faithful such practices as circumcision and the distinction between clean and unclean meats. Their initial success brought upon them the strong opposition of St. *Paul, much of whose writing was concerned with refuting their errors.

JUDAS ISCARIOT. The Apostle who betrayed Christ to the Jewish *Sanhedrin (Mk. 14. 10 f. and 43 f., Jn. 13. 2, 18. 3 ff.). The Gospels leave his motive uncertain, as the hint given in Jn. 12. 6 is not supported by the other three. His suicide is recorded in three places—in Mt. 27. 3–5, in Acts. 1. 16–20, and in *Papias—but the accounts differ in their details. He has been regarded with universal abhorrence in the Christian Church, though he was venerated in the *Gnostic sect of the *Cainites. It is noteworthy that whereas nearly all the other Apostles were Galilaeans, the epithet 'Iscariot' (Heb., 'man of Kerioth', a place in S. Palestine) implies that Judas was from *Judaea.

Besides commentaries on the Gospels, C. Daub, *Judas Iscariot, oder Böse in Verhältniss zum Guten* (2 Hft., Heidelberg, 1816–18). D. Haugg, *Judas Iskarioth in den neutestamentlichen Berichten* (1930). A. Spiteri, *Die Frage der Judaskommunion neu untersucht* (Theologische Studien der Oesterr. Leo-Gesellschaft, xxiii; 1918). C. C. Torrey, 'The Name "Iscariot" ' in *H.T.R.*, xxxvi (1943), pp. 51–62. Note on Acts 1. 18 by A. D. Knox, 'The Death of Judas' in *J.T.S.*, xxv (1924), p. 289 f.; J. Herber, 'La Mort de Judas' in *Revue de l'Histoire des Religions*, cxxix (1945), pp. 47–56. P. F. Baum, 'The Mediaeval Legend of Judas Iscariot' in *Publications of the Modern Language Association of America*, N.S., xxiv (1916), pp. 481–632, with reff. to the extensive earlier lit. on this subject. S. P. Carey, *Jesus and Judas* (1931; popular). A. Plummer in *H.D.B.*, ii (1899), pp. 796–799, s.v.; J. G. Tasker in *D.C.G.*, i (1906), pp. 907–13, s.v.; both with reff. F. W. Maier in *L.Th.K.*, v (1933), col. 671 f., s.v., with detailed bibl.

JUDAS MACCABAEUS (d. 161 B.C.), leader of the Jews in the revolt against the Syrians. The third son of the priest, Mattathias (d. 166), who nominated him to succeed him as captain of the hosts, he won a series of spectacular victories against the Syrians in the years 166–164. In 165 he purified the *Temple and restored its worship, and in 163, partly because of dynastic troubles of the Syrians, was able to obtain full religious liberty from *Antiochus IV, Epiphanes (173–162). After defeating the Idumaeans, the Beanites and the Ammonites, he eventually overcame the opposition of the Hellenizing party among the Jews in a battle near Beth-horon in 161. He asserted political independence by entering into negotiations with Rome to aid him against the Syrians. Although his mission was diplomatically successful, before the results were known he was defeated by the Syrian general, Bacchides, and killed in a battle near Eleasa. His career is recounted in the Books of *Maccabees (q.v.).

Monographs by C. R. Conder (London, 1879), H. Weiss (Freiburg i.Br., 1897), and A. M. Hyamson (London, 1935). E. *Schürer, *Geschichte des jüdischen Volkes im Zeitalter Jesu Christi*, i (ed. 4; 1901), pp. 210–22. E. Beurlier in *Dict.*

Bibl., iii (1903), cols. 1790–1802, s.v. 'Judas Machabée'. [O.] Wolff in *P.W.*, ix (pt. 1; 1916), cols. 2461–4, s.v. 'Judas Makkabaios'. See also works cited under *Maccabees* (family) and *Maccabees, Books of.*

JUDE, St., *Apostle. In Lk. 6. 16 he is referred to as 'Judas of James' and in Jn. 14. 22 as 'Judas, not Iscariot'. He is generally taken to be the same person as *Thaddaeus or Lebbaeus, who is mentioned at the corresponding place in Mt. and Mk. The description 'of James' in Lk. 6. 16 is most naturally interpreted 'son of James' (RV), but the Apostle has generally been identified, at least in the W., with Jude the 'brother of *James' (Jude 1), one of the *Brethren of the Lord and the author of the Ep. of *Jude (q.v.). The apocryphal 'Passion of *Simon and Jude' describes the preaching and martyrdom of these two Apostles in Persia, and in the W. Church the two saints are commemorated together. Feast day, with St. Simon, 28 Oct.

Jude's descendants are mentioned by *Eusebius, *H.E.*, iii, 19 f. and 32, citing *Hegesippus. On the Passion of St. Simon and St. Jude see R. A. *Lipsius, *Die apokryphen Apostelgeschichten und Apostellegenden*, ii (pt. 2; 1884), pp. 142–200. J. van Hecke, S.J., in *AA.SS.*, Oct. XII (1867), pp. 437–49. R. Sinker in *D.C.A.*, i (1875), pp. 891–3, s.v. 'Jude the Apostle, St., Legend and Festival of'; A. Plummer in W. Smith–J. M. Fuller (edd.), *A Dictionary of the Bible*, i (pt. 2; 1893), p. 1835, s.v.; G. T. Purves in *H.D.B.*, ii (1899), p. 799, s.v.; J. G. Tasker in *D.C.G.*, i (1906), p. 906 f., s.v., with reff. See also introd. to commentaries on *Jude, Epistle of*, cited s.v., and bibl. to *Brethren of the Lord.*

JUDE, Epistle of St. One of the '*Catholic Epistles' of the NT. It purports to be written by 'Jude . . . brother of James', who is identified by *Origen, St. *Jerome, and others as the *Apostle, 'Judas of James', of Lk. 6. 16 and Acts 1. 13. The aim of the Epistle was to combat the spread of dangerous doctrines through false teachers 'having not the Spirit', whose immoral life it denounces. It was recognized as canonical by the *Muratorian Canon, *Clement of Alexandria, and *Tertullian, though *Eusebius puts it among the 'Antilegomena'. The doubts were due chiefly to vv. 9 and 14 which seem to reproduce passages from the apocryphal 'Assumption of *Moses' and 'Book of *Enoch'. The date is generally assigned to the close of the Apostolic age, perhaps before the destruction of *Jerusalem, which is not mentioned among the calamities enumerated in vv. 5–7. The striking similarities between the Ep. of Jude and 2 Pet. are most probably due to the use made of it by the latter.

Modern commentaries by C. *Bigg (I.C.C., with 1–2 Pet., 1901, pp. 305–44), J. B. Mayor (London, 1907), J. W. C. Wand (West. Comm., with 1–2 Pet., 1934, pp. 187–231), J. *Moffatt (Moffatt Comm., with other General Epistles, 1928, pp. 215–46), and J. Chaîne (Études bibliques, with other Catholic Epistles, 1939, pp. 261–337). McNeile, pp. 239–44. F. H. Chase in *H.D.B.*, ii (1899), pp. 799–806, s.v., with full bibl.; B. W. Bacon in *E.B.* (ed. 11), xv (1911), pp. 536–8, s.v.; A. S. Peake in *D.A.C.*, i (1915), pp. 658–60.

JUDGES, Book of. The Book traces the history of the Israelites from *Joshua's death to the beginning of the monarchy, describing incidents connected with the conquest of Palestine, and woven round the names of several leaders ('judges') who ruled the country before the time of *Saul. It professes at the outset (1. 1) to be a sequel to the Book of Joshua (q.v.), but in fact covers the same period. Its account of the entry of the Israelites into *Canaan, which depicts the settlement as gradual and spread over many years, is prob. more accurate than that in Josh., which claims for Israel the credit of a swift and thorough victory.

After an introductory section describing the attempts of the Israelites to secure a footing at Hebron, Debir, and Bethel (1. 2–2. 5), the exploits of the judges are described in turn. Of these the most notable are Ehud (3. 12–30); Deborah, the prophetess (4, 5); Gideon, also called Jerubbaal (6–8); Abimelech (9); Jephthah (11, 12); and *Samson (13–16). The compiler of the Book has supplied a framework which enabled a continuous historical narrative to be constructed out of what were probably really separate and unrelated histories of the individual judges, and has used it to illustrate his philosophy of history (2. 11–19), which saw a regular sequence of sin, punishment, penitence, and deliverance. The concluding chapters of the Book (17–21) contain incidents relating to the period, but outside this framework.

The Book throws valuable light on the pre-monarchical period, esp. on the beliefs of the early Israelites and the relation of their faith to the already existing religion in Canaan. The Hebrew text, which is often corrupt, may sometimes be restored from the Greek. It is probable that some of the *Pentateuchal sources persist in Judges.

Commentaries by G. F. Moore (I.C.C., 1895), G. A. Cooke (Camb. Bib., RV, 1913), C. F. *Burney (London, 1918), K. *Budde (K.H.C., Abt. vii; 1897), W. Nowack (H.K.A.T., Abt. 1, Bd. iv, on Judges, Ruth, and Sam., 1902, pp. 1–178), M. J. *Lagrange, O.P. (Études bibliques, 1903). J. Garstang, *Joshua–Judges* (1931), pp. 3–115, 263–343. G. F. Moore in *E.Bi.*, iii (1902), cols. 2633–40, s.v.

JUDGEMENT, General (Particular).
See *General (Particular) Judgement*.

JUDICA SUNDAY.
The fifth Sunday in Lent ('*Passion Sunday'), so named from the opening words of the *Introit at the Mass (Ps. 43. 1: 'Give sentence with me, O God').

JUDICIAL COMMITTEE OF THE PRIVY COUNCIL.
A Court of Appeal constituted by an Act of 1833 to regularize the extensive jurisdiction of the King in Council. It took over the ecclesiastical jurisdiction of the High Court of Delegates which arose out of the statute of *Henry VIII abolishing appeals to Rome. Hence it determines appeals from both the Court of *Arches and the provincial Court of *York. It gained much notoriety through a series of ritual and doctrinal cases brought before it in the 19th cent., of which the *Gorham case was the most celebrated. See also *Lincoln Judgement*.

JUDITH, Book of,
OT Apocryphal Book. The Book relates how Nebuchadnezzar, 'who reigned over the Assyrians in Nineveh' (1. 1), failed to gain the support of certain nations, including the Jews, in his conflict with Arphaxad, King of the Medes, and determined to punish them by his general Holofernes (1. 1–2. 13). At first the Jews decided to resist (2. 14–4.-end). But when their city Bethulia (otherwise not identifiable) was besieged and deprived of its water supply, they weaken through the persuasions of Ozias (5–7). Judith, a young and beautiful widow of great piety, upbraids Ozias and promises to deliver her people. She makes her way to the camp of Holofernes, who is captivated by her charms (10–12), and, having enticed him into a state of drunkenness, seizes a sword, cuts off his head and carries it back in a bag to Bethulia (13). The head is publicly displayed (14), the Israelites are encouraged to advance, and the Assyrians flee in panic (15). The narrative concludes with Judith's hymn of thanksgiving (16).

The whole book is wildly unhistorical and was prob. never intended to be read as history. Its orig. language was Heb., but it now exists only in Gk. versions. It prob. dates from the Maccabean period, though some modern scholars have connected it with the time of Artaxerxes Ochus (359–338), chiefly because a Cappadocian named Holofernes fought in his armies. In the Christian Church it was known to *Clement of Rome, *Clement of Alexandria, and *Origen. In the Roman Breviary, the 'Hymn of Judith' (16. 2–17) is recited at *Lauds on Wednesdays.

Commentaries by O. F. Fritzsche (Kurzgefasstes exegetisches Handbuch zu den Apokryphen des Alten Testaments, ii; Leipzig, 1853, pp. 113–211); A. Scholz (Würzburg, 1887; ed. 2, 1896); C. J. Ball in H. Wace (ed.), *Apocrypha*, i (1888), pp. 241–360; M. Lohr in E. Kautzsch (ed.), *Die Apokryphen und Pseudepigraphen des Alten Testaments*, i (1900), pp. 147–64; F. Steinmetzer (Leipzig, 1907); and A. E. Cowley in R. H. *Charles (ed.), *The Apocrypha and Pseudepigrapha of the Old Testament*, i (1913), pp. 242–67. C. Meyer, S.J., 'Zur Entstehungsgeschichte des Buches Judith' in *Biblica*, iii (1922), pp. 193–203. F. Zimmermann, 'Aids for the Recovery of the Hebrew Original of Judith' in *Journal of Biblical Literature*, lvii (1938), pp. 67–74. E. *Schürer, *Geschichte des jüdischen Volkes im Zeitalter Jesu Christi*, iii (ed. 4; 1909), pp. 230–7, with detailed bibl. to date. R. H. Pfeiffer, *History of New Testament Times with an Introduction to the Apocrypha* (New York, 1949; London [1954]), pp. 285–303, with bibl. reff. A. Lefèvre, S.J., in *Dict. Bibl.*, Suppl. iv (1949), cols. 1315–19, s.v. See also bibl. to *Apocrypha*.

JUDSON, ADONIRAM (1788–1850),
American *Baptist missionary to Burma. He was born at Malden, Mass., and educated at Brown university (1804–7). In 1808 he entered the Andover Theological Seminary, and in 1810 went to England to confer with the *L.M.S. and to seek for co-operation with the American Board of Foreign Missions in the East. Having been ordained a *Congregational minister in 1812, he sailed for Calcutta. On reaching Serampore, Judson became a Baptist. After permission to continue in the territories of the East India Company was refused, he went to Mauritius, and in 1813 to Rangoon, where he began to translate the Bible into

Burmese. During the war with England in 1824–5 he was imprisoned. In 1829 he transferred the seat of the mission to Moulmein, but travelled also among the Karens, a tribe living farther north, where he met with great success. In 1842 he began work on a Burmese dictionary which was eventually completed in 1849. He died soon afterwards on a voyage undertaken to recover his broken health. His first wife, Ann Hasseltine (d. 1826), and his second wife, Sarah Boardman, gave him notable assistance in his work and are remembered on their own account.

Lives by F. Wayland (London, 2 vols., 1853), L. Bonar (London, 1871), and Edward Judson (son; London, 1883). W. H. Allison in *Dict. Amer. Biog.*, x (1933), p. 234 f.

JULIAN THE APOSTATE (332–63), 'Flavius Claudius Julianus', Roman Emperor from 361. He was born at *Constantinople, the nephew of *Constantine the Great (Emp. 311–37) and cousin of Constantius II (Emp. 337–61). In 337, after the murder of all his near male relations except his half-brother, Gallus, Julian, a very precocious child, was entrusted to the care of a eunuch, Mardonius, and *Eusebius of Nicomedia. Already possessing strong pagan leanings, he was banished with Gallus in 345 to the remote fortress of Macellum in Cappadocia, where efforts were made to bring him under Christian influences. In 351, when Gallus was made Caesar, Julian became free to leave Cappadocia. He went first to *Constantinople and then to Nicomedia, where before long he was won to *Neoplatonism, mainly through the influence of the Sophist, Maximus of Ephesus. After Gallus's execution (end of 354), Julian was held captive at *Milan; but in 355 he gained permission to visit the schools at Athens, where he was initiated into the Eleusinian mysteries. Among his fellow-students at Athens was St.*Gregory of Nazianzen. On 6 Nov. 355 he was presented to the army as Caesar. He soon justified his nomination by his successes in a difficult military situation, in Aug. 357 inflicting a decisive defeat on the Alamanni at Strassburg. He also carried through some drastic administrative reforms in Gaul. When Constantius, jealous of Julian's popularity, sought to take over the flower of Julian's army for his Persian campaigns, the soldiers resisted and proclaimed Julian Emperor (360). Civil war was only prevented by Constantius's death in Nov. 361.

Now that he was sole Emperor, Julian embarked on an ambitious programme for reform. With regard to the Church, his policy was to degrade Christianity and promote paganism by every means short of open persecution. He sought to re-establish the heathen worship throughout the empire; ordered all instruction in the Imperial schools to be completely paganized; retracted the legal and financial privileges accorded to the Christians by his predecessors; published polemical treatises against Christian doctrine; and even inflicted barbarous sentences on persons guilty only of Christian faith and practice. He also attempted to weaken the Church internally by allowing all exiled Bishops to return to their sees with a view to creating dissensions. At the same time, he attempted to reform the morals and elevate the theology of paganism, himself giving (it must be allowed) a conspicuous example of austerity and purpose.

Having spent the winter of 361–2 at Constantinople, in May 362 he set out for *Antioch in preparation for a campaign against the Persians. In Asia Minor and Syria his strict discipline and strong anti-Christian policy made him very unpopular. In March 363 he set out for Mesopotamia. On 26 June 363 he was struck by an arrow and died the same night. The well-known story that he died with the words 'Vicisti Galilaee' ('Thou hast conquered, Galilean!') is a late embellishment of a passage in Theodoret (*H.E.*, iii, 25).

Julian was an extensive author. His chief writings are (1) a set of eight Orations, including two panegyrics on Constantius, two on true and false cynicism, and theosophical orations on King Helios and on the Mother of the Gods; (2) a set of letters, more than eighty of which have come down under Julian's name (some perh. spurious); (3) 'Symposium' or 'Caesares', a satire on the vices of past Emperors; (4) 'Misopogon' (the 'Beard Hater'), a satire written at Antioch on the licentiousness of the inhabitants; (5) some epigrams. Unique interest attaches to (6) his 'Adversus Christianos', written during the Persian campaign. Though no MS. of this last survives, nearly the whole text can be recovered from *Cyril of Alexandria's refutation of the work.

Collected edd. by E. Spanheim (Leipzig, 1696), F. C. Hertlein (2 vols., Teubn., 1875–6), W. C. Wright (with Eng. tr., 3 vols., Loeb, 1913–23), and crit. ed., incorporating six new letters discovered by A. Papadopoulos-Kerameus at Halki in 1884, by J. Bidez (Collection Guillaume Budé, 1924 ff., with Fr. tr.). Letters also ed. L. H. Heyler (Mainz, 1828). His work against the Christians ed. from Cyr. Alex. by C. J. Neumann (Scriptorum Graecorum qui Christianam impugnaverunt religionem quae supersunt, fasc. iii; Leipzig, 1880).

The chief ancient authority for his life is Ammianus Marcellinus (*Hist.*, xv, 8–xxv). Other pagan sources are Libanius, Eunapius and Claudius Mamertinus. Christian writers (naturally all very hostile) include, besides the Church Historians and Chroniclers, some poems of St. *Ephraem Syrus, two invectives of St. *Gregory of Nazianzus, and St. Cyril of Alexandria's reply already mentioned.

The study of J. Bidez, *La Vie de l'Empereur Julien* (Collection des Études anciennes publiée sous le patronage de l'Association Guillaume Budé, 1930), supersedes all earlier works. Older lives by G. H. Rendall (Cambridge, 1879), Alice Gardner ('Heroes of the Nations', New York and London, 1905), G. Negri (Milan, 1901; Eng. tr., 2 vols., 1905), and P. Allard (3 vols., Paris, 1900–3). There are also full accounts by J. *Wordsworth in *D.C.B.*, iii (1882), pp. 483–525; A. *Harnack in *P.R.E.* (ed. 3), ix (1900), pp. 609–19; and E. von Borries in *P.W.*, x (pt. 1; 1917), cols. 26–91, all s.v.

JULIAN (*c.* 386–454), *Pelagian Bp. of Eclanum, in Apulia, from *c.* 416. On his refusal to subscribe, in 417, the condemnation of *Pelagianism published by *Zosimus, he was deprived of his see and banished. He travelled widely in search of protection or toleration, appealing in turn to *Theodore of Mopsuestia, *Nestorius, *Sixtus III, and others; but was repeatedly condemned in various local councils, and repeatedly exiled by the civil powers. He is believed to have died in Sicily. His writings, which are preserved only fragmentarily in *Augustine's quotations, belong to the period 418–26. He seems to have possessed keen dialectical ability, as well as philosophical insight. His account of the worth and powers of human nature is coherent, and his indictment of Augustine's doctrine of the total depravity of fallen man (which he held to be a consequence of the *Manichaean errors of Augustine's youth), although couched in rather scurrilous terms, is powerful; but his conception of human self-sufficiency is not easily reconciled with the Christian doctrine of man's sinfulness.

Julian's attack on the Augustinian doctrine of grace was developed esp. in his four books 'Ad Turbantium' and his eight 'Ad Florum'; large portions of both survive in Augustine's replies. Recently certain exegetical works have been attributed (somewhat doubtfully) to Julian by G. *Morin, O.S.B., and A. Vaccari, S.J. A. Bruckner, *Julian von Eclanum, sein Leben und seine Lehre* (T.U., xv, 3; 1897); id., *Die vier Bücher Julians von Aeclanum an Turbantius* (1910). G. Morin, 'Un Ouvrage restitué à Julien d'Éclane' in *R. Bén.*, xxx (1913), pp. 1–24; A. Vaccari, S.J., *Un commento a Giobbe di Giuliano di Eclano* (1915). A. d'Alès, 'Julien d'Éclane, exégète' in *Rech. S.R.*, vi (1916), pp. 311–324. J. Forget in *D.T.C.*, viii (1924), cols. 1926–31.

JULIAN (d. after 518), Bp. of Halicarnassus in Caria. He was a *Monophysite who, on being deposed from his see *c.* 518, took refuge at *Alexandria, where he became the leader of the party known to their opponents as '*Aphthartodocetae' (teachers of the incorruptibility of the Body of Christ) or 'Phantasiastae' (teachers of a merely phenomenal Body of Christ). He wrote four works directed against *Severus of Antioch of which a large series of fragments have survived. Some of his letters have also been recovered. The Commentary on Job formerly ascribed to him appears to be the work of an unknown *Arian author of the 4th cent.

The standard work is R. Draguet, *Julien d'Halicarnasse et sa controverse avec Sévère d'Antioche sur l'incorruptibilité du corps du Christ* (Louvain, 1924; with fragments in Syr. and Gk. retransl., also full bibl.). Id., 'Pièces de polémique antijulianiste' in *Muséon*, xliv (1931), pp. 255–317 (text and Lat. tr.). Other texts in *Severi Antijulianistica*, I (ed. A. Sanda, Beyrout, 1931). M. Jugie, A.A., 'Julien d'Halicarnasse et Sévère d'Antioche' in *É.O.*, xxiv (1925), pp. 129–62, 256–85. Bardenhewer, v, 2–6. R. Draguet in *D.T.C.*, viii (pt. 2; 1925), cols. 1931–40, and A. Mayer in *E.C.*, vi (1951), col. 739 f.

JULIAN OF NORWICH (*c.* 1342–after 1413), English mystic. Little is known of her life except that she prob. lived as an *anchoress, outside the walls of St. Julian's church, *Norwich. Acc. to her own account she received on 8 May 1373 a series of 15 revelations in a state of ecstasy, lasting 5 hours. One other vision followed the next day, and her book, *The Sixteen Revelations of Divine Love*, was written twenty years after, as the fruit of her meditations on the original experience which consisted chiefly in visions of the Passion and of the Holy Trinity. The account of these visions is embedded in reflections on the mysteries of the faith, on prayer, and esp. on the love of God. In Divine Love lies the clue to all problems of existence, particularly that

of evil, which, lacking the Divine reality, is but an aberration of the human will that serves to reveal the more clearly the merciful love of God. Julian seems to have written her work under *Neo-Platonist influences, perh. mediated through the writings of Walter *Hilton and the '*Cloud of Unknowing'.

There are three primary MSS. of the Revelations, two in the Brit. Mus. and one in Paris. The last (Bibl. Nat., Fonds Anglais No. 40 (Bibl. Bigotiana 388), 16th cent.) ed. by S. de Cressy (no place, 1670; re-ed. G. H. Parker, London-Leicester, 1843, and G. *Tyrrell, London, 1902). One of the MSS. in the Brit. Mus. (Sloane 2499; 17th cent.) ed. P. H. Collins (London, 1877) and Grace Warrack (ib., 1901) and Dom [G.] R. Hudleston, O.S.B. (Orchard Books, xii, 1927), with notes on MSS. and early edd.; the other (Addit. MS. 37790; early 15th cent.) ed. D. Harford, *The Comfortable Words* (London [1911]). R. H. Thouless, *The Lady Julian. A Psychological Study* (1924); P. F. Chambers, *Julian o Norwich. An Appreciation and an Anthology* (1955).

JULIANA OF LIÉGE, St. (1192–1258), champion of the Feast of *Corpus Christi. Born at Retinnes, near Liége, and bereft of her parents, she was placed in the *Augustinian convent of Mont Cornillon, near Liége, where she made rapid spiritual progress and experienced visions. Once professed (1206), she devoted all her energies to securing the establishment of a Feast of *Corpus Christi. In 1230 she became superior; but meeting with great opposition in the convent, she was forced to leave and took refuge in the city of Liége. Here, through the intervention of a recluse at St. Martin's church, she won to her cause John of Lausanne, one of the canons, who secured in turn the warm interest of James Pantaléon, then Archdeacon of Liége, and later Pope *Urban IV. The Bp. of Liége having obtained her restoration for a brief space, the feast was formally proclaimed in 1246 to be observed in the diocese of Liége for the next year. But the Bishop died (16 Oct. 1246) before the year was up; the feast was not repeated in Juliana's lifetime; and she herself was again exiled and passed the last years of her life first in a monastery near Namur and later as a recluse at Fosses. The real reward of her efforts was the institution of the Feast of Corpus Christi after her death by Urban IV in 1264. Her cultus was confirmed in 1869. Feast day, 5 Apr.

Latin tr. of contemporary Fr. life (1258–62) in *AA.SS.*, Apr. I (1675), pp. 443–75. Later lives by U. Berlière, O.S.B. (anon., Namur, 1884), G. Simenon (Brussels, 1946) and J. Coenen ('Heiligen van onzen Stam', Bruges, 1946). E. Denis, *La Vraie Histoire de sainte Julienne de Liége et l'institution de la Fête-Dieu* (Tournai, 1935). F. Baix-C. Lambot, O.S.B., *La Dévotion à l'eucharistie et VIIe centenaire de la Fête-Dieu* (Namur, 1946), passim. K. Hofmann in *L.Th.K.*, v (1933), col. 712 f. A. Piolanti in *E.C.*, vi (1951), cols. 736–8, with bibl.

JÜLICHER, ADOLF (1857–1938), NT scholar. Born at Falkenberg, he received a pastoral appointment at Rummelsburg near Berlin in 1882. From 1889 to 1923 he was professor of theology at Marburg. His two principal writings were *Die Gleichnisreden Jesu* (2 vols., 1888–9), in which he insisted that the Lord's *Parables must be understood as real similes and not as allegories, and *Die

Einleitung in das Neue Testament (1894; Eng. trans. 1904), a careful critical introduction to the NT writings. He also made extensive studies in the *Old Latin versions of the NT (*Itala*. I: 'Matthäus-Evangelium', 1938). His other writings included *Paulus und Jesus* (1907), *Hat Jesus gelebt?* (1910) and an edition of St. *Vincent of Lérin's *Commonitorium* (1895).

Festgabe für A. Jülicher, hrsg. von R. *Bultmann und H. von Soden (1927).

JULIUS I, St. (d. 352), Pope from 337. In the *Arian struggle he was a strong supporter of orthodoxy and one of the chief influences leading to its ultimate triumph. He gave shelter to *Marcellus of Ancyra at Rome after his condemnation at the Council of *Constantinople (336), and later to *Athanasius after his escape from *Alexandria in 339. In 342–3 he convoked the Council of *Sardica, which consolidated the W. against Arianism and pronounced Athanasius the rightful occupant of his see. Through the appellate jurisdiction allowed by can. 3 (Gk.) of the Council to Julius as Bp. of Rome, his name has secured notoriety in connexion with the rise of the Papal claims. Two of Julius's letters, which survive in Greek, are evidence of his remarkable statesmanship. His pontificate was marked by the building of two new churches in Rome, S. Maria in Trastevere and the Basilica Julia (now the Church of the Twelve Apostles). Feast day, 12 Apr.

The two letters mentioned are preserved in Athanasius, *Apologia c. Arianos*, 21–35 and 52 f. Other (spurious) Epp. attributed to him are by *Apollinarian writers; texts in H. *Lietzmann, *Apollinarius von Laodicea und seine Schule*, i (1904), pp. 185–93, 193–203, 256–62, 283–6, 292 f., 307–10, 310–18, 318. Material on Julius collected in J. P. Migne, *PL*, viii, 857–994. Bardenhewer, iii, pp. 583–5. J. Barmby in *D.C.B.*, iii (1882), pp. 526–32; J. P. Kirsch in *C.E.*, viii (1910), p. 561.

JULIUS II (1443–1513), Pope from 1503. Giuliano della Rovere was the descendant of an impoverished noble family of Albissola, nr. Savona. He lived for some time at a house of Conventual *Franciscans under the supervision of his uncle, Francesco della Rovere. On the latter's accession to the Papacy as *Sixtus IV in 1471 he was created cardinal and loaded with benefices, holding several bishoprics and abbacies in *commendam. He took part in many political missions, and under *Innocent VIII, whose election he had secured by means of bribery, continued to play a leading role in Papal affairs. When in 1492 his personal enemy, Rodrigo Borgia, was elected as *Alexander VI he fled to Charles VIII of France, and even after a formal reconciliation with the Pope in 1498 continued to live in hiding, mostly in N. Italy. After Alexander's death in 1503 he returned to Rome, and after the short reign of Pius III was himself elected Pope in the same year, having promised the cardinals to continue the war against the Turks, to call a General Council within two years, and to follow their advice in all matters of importance. These undertakings, however, which would have seriously limited the Papal power, he did not carry into effect. The

principal achievement of his Pontificate was the restoration and enlargement of the temporal power, which was to safeguard Papal independence in times to come. To assist this end he drove Caesar *Borgia from Italy in 1504. In 1506 he conducted an expedition against Perugia and *Bologna, both of which submitted to his sovereignty, and in 1509 he joined the League of Cambrai against *Venice, which had frequently violated Papal claims. After the city had been defeated with the help of France he turned against the latter and, in 1511, founded the Holy League, including England, Spain, Venice, and Switzerland, for the purpose of defeating it. Louis XII replied by calling a council to depose the Pope at Pisa in 1511. After Julius had deprived the rebellious cardinals who attended the Council of their dignity it retired to *Milan, where Julius was declared suspended in 1512. At the same time the Pope called a Council at the Lateran and won the Emp. Maximilian over to his side. The *Pragmatic Sanction was condemned and France thus remained isolated. The death of Julius on 20–21 Feb. 1513, however, ended the conflict.

Though Julius II was chiefly a statesman and a military leader, he initiated certain important ecclesiastical reforms. His constitution 'De fratrum nostrorum' (1503) declared null and void every pontifical election brought about by simony. He was a patron of Renaissance art and recognized the genius of *Raphael, *Michelangelo, and Bramante. In 1506 he laid the cornerstone of the Basilica of *St. Peter. Among the many immortal works inspired by his generosity are Michelangelo's statue of Moses in San Pietro in Vincoli, the paintings in the *Sistine Chapel, and Raphael's frescoes in the Vatican. His indulgence for the rebuilding of St. Peter's was the occasion later of M. *Luther's 95 Theses. His war-like character was scathingly attacked by D. *Erasmus in his *Moriae Encomium* ('Praise of Folly').

A. J. Dumesnil, *Histoire de Jules II* (1873); M. Brosch, *Papst Julius II* (1878); E. Rodocanachi, *Le Pontificat de Jules II* (1928). Pastor, vi (1923), pp. 185–607. M. Ott in *C.E.*, viii (1910), pp. 262–4, s.v.; G. Mollat in *D.T.C.*, vii (pt. 2, 1925), cols. 1918–20, s.v. 'Jules II'; G. B. Picotti in *E.C.*, vi (1951), cols. 750–58, s.v. 'Giulio II'.

JULIUS III (1487–1555), Pope from 1550. Giammaria Ciocchi del Monte studied jurisprudence at Perugia and Siena, was made Abp. of Siponto in 1511, and under *Clement VII and *Paul III held administrative posts in Rome and the Papal states. He was taken as a hostage by the Imperial forces after the sack of Rome in 1527. In 1545 he opened the Council of *Trent as its first president and Papal legate, and had an important share in its transference to Bologna in 1547. Elected Pope in 1550 after a long and stormy conclave, in 1551 he commanded the Council to resume its sessions, but had to suspend it in the next year owing to political difficulties. During his pontificate he did much for the *Jesuit Order, which he confirmed and endowed with new privileges. On the death of *Edward VI in 1553, he sent Cardinal R. *Pole to England with far-reaching faculties. During the last three years of his life, however, Julius III more and more lost interest in the reform of the Church. His love of the arts — he was a protector of *Michelangelo—and of pomp, as well as his nepotism, range him with the typical Renaissance Popes.

The principal source is A. Massarelli, *Diaria*, v–vii (ed. S. Merkle, *Concilii Tridentini Diariorum*, ii, Freiburg i.Br., 1911, pp. 1–249). V. Schweitzer, *Zur Geschichte der Reform unter Julius III* (Görres-Gesellschaft 3; 1907). G. De Leva, 'La elezione di Papa Giulio III' in *Rivista Storica Italiana*, i (1884), pp. 22–38. Hefele–Leclercq, ix (pt. 1; 1930), pp. 443–527, esp. pp. 46–50. Pastor, xiii (1924). Fliche–Martin, xviii (1948), pp. 105–45, with reff. G. Mollat in *D.T.C.*, viii (pt. 2; 1925), col. 1920 f., s.v.; G. B. Picotti in *E.C.*, vi (1951), cols. 758–605, s.v. 'Giulio III'.

JULIUS AFRICANUS, SEXTUS (*c.* 160–*c.* 240), Christian writer. He was born prob. at *Jerusalem (not, as *Suidas asserts, in Libya) and lived for several years at *Emmaus. From Emmaus he went on a successful embassy to the Emp. Heliogabalus (218–22) for the restoration of the township, which led to its being rebuilt as Nicopolis. He also enjoyed close relations with the royal house of *Edessa. Later, under the Emp. Alexander Severus (222–35), he was instrumental in the erection of the public library in the *Pantheon at *Rome. He also had connexions at *Alexandria with Heraclas and *Origen. Despite a later tradition (Dionysius bar-Salibi) to the contrary, it is unlikely that he was ever ordained.

His chief work was a 'History of the World' (Χρονογραφίαι) to A.D. 217 in five Books, of which fragments are preserved in *Eusebius's 'Chronicle', *George Syncellus, and other writers. He held that the world would last for 6000 years from the Creation and that the Birth of Christ, which he antedated in relation to his own times by three years, took place in the year 5500. His 'Embroidered Girdles' (Κεστοί) is an encyclopaedic work in 24 Books, dedicated to Alexander Severus, on natural history, medicine, military science, magic, and miscellaneous subjects. This, too, survives only in fragments. He was also the author of two letters, one to Origen contesting the genuineness of the story of *Susanna and the other to a certain Aristides on the Genealogies of Christ in Mk. and Lk., both epistles showing good critical powers.

Fragments collected by M. J. *Routh, *Reliquiae Sacrae* (ed. 2, 1844), ii, pp. 238–309; repr. in J. P. Migne, *PG*, x, 63–94. New ed. of *Epp.* by W. Reichardt in T.U., xxxiv, 3 (1909); of frs. of Κεστοί by J. R. Vieillefond (1932). His 'Ep. to Origen' will be found in all editions of Origen. Newly recovered frs. in B. P. Grenfell–A. S. Hunt, *The Oxyrhynchus Papyri*, iii (1903), pp. 36–41; others ed. by J. R. Vieillefond in *Revue des Études grecques*, xlvi (1933), pp. 197–203. H. Gelzer, *Sextus Julius Africanus und die byzantinische Chronographie* (2 vols., 1880–98); F. Granger, 'Julius Africanus and the Library of the Pantheon' in *J.T.S.*, xxxiv (1933), pp. 157–66. See also artt. s.vv. by É. Amann in *D.T.C.*, viii (1924), cols. 1921–5, with bibl., and by W. Kroll–J. Sickenberger in P.W., x (1919), cols. 116–25; also A. *Harnack in *P.R.E.* (ed. 3), ix (1901), p. 627 f. (brief).

JUMIÈGES (Lat., Gemeticum), Benedictine Abbey on the Lower Seine 17 miles W. of Rouen. Founded in 654 by St. *Philibert (q.v.), it rapidly developed in size and influence, sending missionaries to England and Ireland. In 841 it was plundered by the Normans and ten years later almost completely destroyed. After restoration and a second destruction, it rose to become one of the chief cultural centres in N. Europe, and through the patronage of *William the Conqueror, under whom the partly surviving abbey church was built (1040–1067), it became the richest monastery in Normandy, continuing to prosper through most of the Middle Ages. Robbed in 1562 by the *Huguenots, it was restored in 1573, and in the 17th cent. became linked to the *Maurist reform. Benedictine life finally came to an end in 1790, after which the buildings were largely destroyed. Since 1918 its imposing ruins have been under State protection.

J. Loth (ed.), *Histoire de l'abbaye royale de Sainte-Pierre de Jumièges par un religieux bénédictin de la congrégation de Saint-Maur* (3 vols., Rouen, 1882–5). R. Martin du Gard, *L'Abbaye de Jumièges. Étude archéologique des ruines* (Montdidier, 1909). J. J. Vernier (ed.), *Chartes de l'abbaye de Jumièges (v. 825 à 1204), conservées aux archives de la Seine-Inférieure* (2 vols., Rouen, 1916). G. Cyprian Alston, O.S.B., in *C.E.*, viii (1910), p. 566, s.v.; H. *Leclercq, O.S.B., in *D.A.C.L.*, viii (pt. 1; 1928), cols. 412–20, s.v., both with bibl. L. M. Cottineau, O.S.B., *Répertoire topo-bibliographique des abbayes et prieurés* (Mâcon, 1935), cols. 1496–9, s.v., for detailed reff. Also *Jumièges. Congrès Scientifique du XIIe Centenaire* (2 vols., Rouen, 1955).

JUMPERS. A nickname of the Welsh *Calvinistic Methodists, from their former custom of 'leaping for joy' at their meetings.

JUNG CODEX, The. A prob. 4th cent. MS. discovered with twelve others at Nag Hammadi near the Nile, 60 miles below Luxor, and acquired in 1952 by the 'Jung Institute for Analytical Psychology' at Zürich. It consists of four books: an 'Epistle of *James' (not the NT Epistle), the 'Gospel of Truth', an 'Epistle to Rheginos', and a 'Tract on the Three Natures'. All are translations of 2nd cent. Gk. texts and of *Gnostic (prob. *Valentinian) origin. It has been argued that Valentinus himself was the author of the second and third items, and his pupil, *Heracleon, of the fourth; in any case it is a primary source for the history of Egyptian Gnosticism. The author of the Gospel of Truth shows acquaintance with most of the Books of the NT. The recognition of its importance was largely due to G. Quispel of the University of Utrecht.

Coptic text of 'Evangelium Veritatis' (Codex Jung fol. viii–xvi, xix–xxii) ed. M. Malinine, H. C. Puech, and G. Quispel (Zürich, 1956), with facsimiles. F. L. Cross (tr. and ed.), *The Jung Codex*. Three Studies by H. C. Puech, G. Quispel, and W. C. van Unnik (1955), with bibl. of earlier lit., p. 130 f. H. C. Puech–G. Quispel, 'Les Écrits gnostiques du codex Jung' in *Vigiliae Christianae*, viii (1954), pp. 1–51; idd., 'Le Quatrième Écrit gnostique du codex Jung', ib., ix (1955), pp. 65–102. Eng. tr. of The Gospel of Truth, with comm., by K. Grobel (London, 1960).

JURAVIT DOMINUS (Lat., 'The Lord hath sworn'). The votive Mass instituted by *Pius XI to implement the contents of his encyclical 'Ad Catholici Sacerdotii' (1935) on the Christian priesthood. It is so named from the first words of its *introit.

JURIEU, PIERRE (1637–1713), French *Calvinist controversialist. A grandson of the Reformed theologian, P. *du Moulin, he was born at Mer, in the diocese of Blois, where his father was a minister. Having studied Protestant theology at Sedan, he came to England, where he completed his education under the guidance of his uncles, A. Rivet and C. and L. du Moulin, and himself received Anglican orders. On his return to France (1660) he was elected minister of Mer in the place of his father and reordained in the Calvinist form. In 1674 he was appointed professor of Hebrew at the Protestant academy of Sedan, and soon became involved in a number of controversies, notably with J. B. *Bossuet and A. *Arnauld. His *Apologie pour la morale des Réformés* (1675) attempts to prove, against the Catholics, that the Calvinist doctrine of *Predestination is not prejudicial to morality, and in his *Traité de la puissance de l'Église* (1677) he defends the Calvinist belief in the authority of synods against Bossuet as well as against his own uncle, du Moulin, who had become an Independent. In 1680 he published anonymously *La Politique du clergé de France* and consequently was watched by the police. When, in 1681, the academy at Sedan was closed he accepted a professorship at Rotterdam. Here he continued his controversy with Arnauld, against whom he wrote his *Examen de l'eucharistie de l'Église romaine* (1682). It was followed by the important *Histoire du calvinisme et du papisme* (1683), directed against L. Maimbourg. After the revocation of the Edict of *Nantes (1685) he did much for the Calvinist refugees from France. In 1686 he wrote *L'Accomplissement des prophéties, ou la délivrance de l'Église*, predicting the universal triumph of Protestantism for the year 1689. From 1686 to 1689 he published his *Lettres pastorales*, containing recitals of the sufferings of the French Protestants, which were a great success. From 1689 to 1702 he was employed by the Admiralty in London as an agent against France, which he sought to stir up to civil war. In 1704 appeared his last important work, *Histoire critique des dogmes et des cultes* (Eng. trans., 1715). Jurieu defended the claims of strict Calvinism against the RC Church as well as against other forms of Protestantism. He looked on the 'pure preaching of the Word' and the 'right dispensation of the Sacraments' as the signs of the true Church, and wished to confine its membership to narrow limits.

C. E. Mégnin, *Pierre Jurieu* (thesis, Strasbourg, 1854). C. van Oordt, *P. Jurieu, historien, apologiste de la Réformation* (thesis, Geneva, 1879). M. J. Denis, 'Bayle et Jurieu' in *Mémoires de l'Académie Nationale des Sciences, Arts et Belles-Lettres de Caen*, Partie littéraire (1886), pp. 54–132. R. Lureau, *Les Doctrines politiques de Jurieu, 1637–1713* (Bordeaux thesis, 1904). R. Struman, 'La Perpétuité de la foi dans la controverse Bossuet–Jurieu, 1686–1691' in *R.H.E.*, xxxvii (1941), pp. 145–89. G. H. Dodge, *The Political Theory of the Huguenots of the Dispersion, with special Reference to the Thought and Influence of Pierre Jurieu* (New York and London, 1947), with bibl. A. G. C. A. Bonet-Maury in *P.R.E.* (ed. 3), ix (1901), pp. 637–40, s.v.; A. Humbert in *D.T.C.*, viii (pt. 2; 1925), cols. 1996–2001, s.v.

JUS DEVOLUTUM. In the Church of *Scotland, the right devolving on a *presbytery to elect a minister to a vacant charge when the congregation, after nine months, has failed to make an appointment. It is only rarely exercised, as an extension of time, if requested, can be granted to the congregation concerned.

JUSTIFICATION (Lat. *justificatio*; cf. Gk. δικαίωσις). Whereas the Lat. word is unambiguous (*justum facere*, 'to make just'), it has been widely held that in the NT (and esp. in St. *Paul) the Gk. δικαίοω and its cognates are to be understood as a legal metaphor and that they mean not 'to make righteous' but 'to pronounce righteous'. If this is so, it is etymologically inaccurate to render δικαίοω by 'justify' (though in fact this translation is regularly used).

The word is used theologically in several senses. It may mean:

(1) In an active sense, the act whereby God makes a man just. Acc. to St. *Thomas Aquinas, God thereby conveys the gift of sanctifying grace to the man's soul.

(2) In a passive sense, the change in a man's condition whereby he passes from the state of sin to that of righteousness.

(3) Esp. in Protestant theology, the act whereby God, in virtue of the Sacrifice of Christ, acquits a man of the punishment due to his sins and in His mercy treats him as though he were righteous. M. *Luther held that such justification was granted to men in response to the disposition of faith alone (*sola fides*) and that it brought with it the imputation to the sinner of the merits of Christ.

The subject is treated in all works on Christian Dogmatics and in commentaries on the Pauline Epistles. The classical study of the Protestant doctrine is A. *Ritschl, *Die christliche Lehre von der Rechtfertigung und Versöhnung* (3 vols., 1870–74). J. H. *Newman, *Lectures on Justification* (1838). J. Buchanan, *The Doctrine of Justification* (Cunningham Lectures, 1867). E. Böhl, *Von der Rechtfertigung durch den Glauben* (1890). T. Häring, Δικαιοσύνη Θεοῦ *bei Paulus* (1896). J. *Denney, *The Christian Doctrine of Reconciliation* (Cunningham Lectures for 1917; 1917). H. Rückert, *Die Rechtfertigungslehre auf dem Tridentinischen Konzil* (Arbeiten zur Kirchengeschichte, iii; 1925). L. H. Ihmels in *P.R.E.* (ed. 3), xvi (1905), pp. 482–515, s.v. 'Rechtfertigung'. J. G. Simpson in *H.E.R.E.*, vii (1914), pp. 615–19, s.v. J. Rivière in *D.T.C.*, viii (pt. 2; 1925), cols. 2042–2227, s.v. E. Vischer–O. Scheel–P. Kalweit in *R.G.G.* (ed. 2), iv (1930), cols. 1745–65, s.v. 'Rechtfertigung'. G. Schrenk in *T.W.B.*, ii (1935), pp. 176–229, s.v. δίκη δίκαιος, &c.

JUSTIN MARTYR, St. (c. 100–c. 165), early Christian *Apologist. He was born of pagan parents at Flavia Neapolis ('Nablus'), the ancient Shechem in *Samaria. After a long search after the truth in pagan philosophies (*Stoicism, *Aristotelianism, *Pythagoreanism, and finally *Platonism), Justin at last embraced Christianity (c. 130). For a time he taught at *Ephesus, where he engaged in his Disputation with Trypho the Jew (c. 135). Later he moved to *Rome, where he opened a Christian school, having *Tatian (q.v.) as one of his pupils. Here he wrote his 'First Apology' (c. 155), addressed to the Emp. Antoninus Pius and his adopted sons (*Marcus Aurelius and Lucius Verus), and soon afterwards issued his 'Dialogue with Trypho'. His 'Second Apology', addressed to the Roman Senate, was apparently written shortly after the accession of Marcus Aurelius (161). He and some of his disciples were denounced as Christians c. 165 (acc. to Tatian, by the Cynic philosopher Crescens); and on refusing to sacrifice they were scourged and beheaded.

The authentic record of their martyrdom ('Martyrium S. Iustini et Sociorum'), based on an official court report, survives. Feast day in the E. 1 June, in the W. 14 April.

Justin is the most outstanding of the 'Apologists'. Though of no great philosophical or literary skill, he is the first Christian thinker to seek to reconcile the claims of faith and reason. He held that traces of the truth were to be found in the pagan thinkers, since all men shared in the 'generative' or 'germinative' Word (λόγος σπερματικός); but Christianity alone was the truly rational creed. The reason why the Word became incarnate was to teach men the truth and to redeem them from the power of the demons. Justin's stress on the transcendence of God (derived from his Platonism) led him into subordinationism in his doctrine of the Son (or Logos); but in intention his theology was orthodox. He also taught a form of *Millenarianism.

Of his writings his 'First Apology' is concerned to expound the doctrines just outlined. It also replies to the charges of immorality preferred against the early Church. Its later chapters are of great interest through their account of contemporary Christian Baptismal ceremonies and Eucharistic belief and practice. The 'Second Apology' is mainly concerned with rebutting certain specific charges against the Christians. In the 'Dialogue with Trypho', three main ideas are developed: viz. the transitoriness of the Old Covenant and its precepts, the identity of the Logos with the God who appears in the OT, and the vocation of the Gentiles to take the place of Israel.

A large number of other works have circulated from early times under Justin's name, all of them spurious. One group belongs to the late 2nd and 3rd cents. and consists of an 'Address to the Greeks', an 'Exhortation to the Greeks', and a work 'On the Monarchy of God'. Another group are probably all the work of a single author of the Aristotelean school (4th–5th cent.). Yet another pseudo-Justinian work —the 'Expositio Rectae Fidei'—has now been proved by J. Lebon and R. V. Sellers to be a work of *Theodoret.

Of the earlier editions of Justin, the best is that of P. *Maran, O.S.B. (Paris, 1742). The only complete modern critical edition is that of J. C. T. Otto (3 vols., Jena, 1842–1848; ed. 3 in 5 vols., 1876–81). J. P. *Migne, PG, vi (1857). Apologies, ed. with notes by A. W. F. Blunt (1911). Eng. trans. in A.N.C.L. (1867). A. L. Feder, Justins des Märtyrers Lehre von Jesus Christus (1906); J. Rivière, Saint Justin et les apologistes du IIe siècle (1907); M. J. Lagrange, O.P., Saint Justin (1914); E. R. Goodenough, The Theology of Justin Martyr (1923).

B. *Capelle, O.S.B., 'Le Rescrit d'Hadrien et S. Justin' in R. Bén., xxxix (1927), pp. 365–8. J. Lebon, 'Restitutions à Théodoret de Cyr. II: L' Ἔκθεσις τῆς ὀρθῆς πίστεως pseudo-justinienne, œuvre de Théodoret' in R.H.E., xxvi (1930), pp. 536–50; R. V. Sellers, 'Pseudo-Justin's Expositio Rectae Fidei: A Work of Theodoret of Cyrus' in J.T.S., xlvi (1945), pp. 145–60. W. Schmid, 'Die Textüberlieferung der Apologie des Justin' in Z.N T W., xl (1941), pp. 87–138. Bardenhewer, i, 206–62; Altaner (ed. 1951), pp. 90–5. H. S. *Holland in D.C.B., iii (1882), pp. 560–87, s.v. 'Justinus (2) Martyr, St.'; G. Bardy in D.T C., viii (pt. 2; 1925), cols. 2228–77, s.v. 'Justin'; P. Toschi in E.C., vi (1951), cols. 841–5, s.v. 'Giustino'.

JUSTINA, St. See Cyprian, St., of Antioch.

JUSTINIAN I (483–565), Roman Emperor from 527. He was the most energetic of the early Byzantine Emperors, making it his aim to restore the political and religious unity of the empire in E. and W. He reconquered N. Africa from the Vandals and Italy from the Goths. A great builder, he erected many *basilicas at *Constantinople (including *Santa Sophia), *Ravenna, and elsewhere; and a sound juridical basis for the empire was established by his new legal Code (see foll. entry). As the champion of orthodoxy he persecuted the *Montanists, whom he almost exterminated, closed the celebrated ancient philosophical schools at Athens in 529, and forced many pagans to accept baptism. His unsuccessful efforts to bring back the *Monophysites issued not only in his condemnation of the memory, as well as some alleged doctrines, of *Origen (see Origenism), but also in the *Three Chapters controversy (which led to the Second Council of *Constantinople, 553), in the humiliation of Pope *Vigilius, and in a schism in the W.

W. G. Holmes, The Age of Justinian and Theodora (2 vols., 1905–7). P. N. Ure, Justinian and his Age (Pelican Book, A 217; 1951). C. Diehl, Justinien et la civilisation byzantine au VIe siècle (1901); W. Schubart, Justinian und Theodora [1943]. A. Knecht, Die Religionspolitik Kaiser Justinians I (1896). Krumbacher (ed. 2), pp. 57 f., 928–41; Bardenhewer, v, 20–4. J. Bryce in D.C.B., iii (1882), pp. 538–559; M. Jugie, A.A., in D.T.C., viii (pt. 2; 1925), cols. 2277–2290, s.v.; H. *Leclercq, O.S.B., in D.A.C.L., viii (pt. 1; 1928), cols. 507–604, s.v.; F. Dölger in L.Th.K., v (1933), cols. 730–2, s.v., with further bibl. P. de Francisci–A. M. Schneider in E.C., vi (1951), cols. 834–41, s.v. 'Giustiniano'.

JUSTINIAN, The Code of. This revision, enlargement and rearrangement of the *Theodosian Code (q.v.) was published by *Justinian (q.v.) in 529. It survives only in a revised edition embodying later constitutions which dates from 534. It was supplemented by further constitutions known as 'Novellae' and, in the sphere of case law, by (1) the 'Digest' (533), a comprehensive set of passages from juristic text-books and commentaries of the classical period, and (2) the 'Institutes of Justinian' (533), a revised and modified edition of those of Gaius with extracts from similar works. Together the Code, Novellae, Digest and Institutes constituted the Corpus Juris Civilis, which became the authoritative and ordered statement of Roman Law, purged of all that was obsolete or contradictory. The insistence that the monarch's will was supreme (regis voluntas suprema lex) legitimized the control of the State over ecclesiastical affairs which has characterized the subsequent history of the Byzantine Church. The Code much influenced the development of *Canon Law in the West, esp. in the later Middle Ages.

Standard edd. of the Code by P. Krueger (Berlin, 1877); of the Digest by T. *Mommsen (2 vols., ib., 1870); of the Institutes by P. Krueger (ib., 1869); and of the Novellae by R. Schoell–G. Kroll (ib., 1895). The text of the Institutes was repr., with Eng. tr., by J. B. Moyle (2 vols., Oxford, 1883); Eng. tr. of the Digest by C. H. Munro (2 vols., Cambridge, 1904–9). R. Mayr, Vocabularium Codicis Justiniani (2 vols., Prague, 1923–5). P. Collinet, Études historiques sur le droit de Justinien (5 vols., 1912–53); H. S. Alivisatos, Die kirchliche Gesetzgebung des Kaisers

Justinian I (Neue Studien zur Geschichte der Theologie und der Kirche 17, 1913). G. Mollat in *D.D.C.*, iv (1949), cols. 644–81, s.v. 'Corpus Juris Civilis', with bibl.

JUSTUS, St. (d. *c.* 627), Abp. of *Canterbury. He was sent to England in 601 in Pope *Gregory's second band of missionaries. When *Ethelbert created a second Kentish see at *Rochester in 604, St. *Augustine appointed Justus its first bishop. In the pagan reaction under Eadbald, he fled, with *Mellitus, Bp. of London, to Gaul, but came back when the Kentish Church again received royal protection. On the death of Mellitus (624), Justus succeeded him at Canterbury where he consecrated St. *Paulinus for mission work in Northumbria. He was buried at St. Augustine's Abbey, Canterbury. Feast day, 10 Nov.

The main source is *Bede, *H.E.*, i, 29, ii, 3–9 and 18; cf. ed. C. Plummer, ii (Oxford, 1896), pp. 78 f., 81 f., 90, 92 f., 110. There is an 11th cent. life by a monk, *Goscelin, mainly based on Bede, pr. by H. *Delehaye, S.J., in *AA.SS.*, Nov. IV (1925), pp. 535–7, with comm., pp. 532–5.

JUVENAL (d. 458), Bp. of *Jerusalem from *c.* 422. Nothing is known of his early life. His chief ambition seems to have been to make *Jerusalem into a '*Patriarchal see' at the expense of the metropolitical see of *Caesarea and the 'Patriarchal see' of *Antioch. For this purpose he sided with *Cyril, Bp. of Alexandria, against *Nestorius at the Council of *Ephesus in 431, asserting that the Bp. of Antioch (John) 'ought to have obeyed the apostolic see of Jerusalem, by which the throne of Antioch should be corrected and judged'. But Cyril, though glad of his support, refused to further his claims. In the *Eutychian controversy he figured as the chief supporter of *Dioscorus, the successor of Cyril, in his violent proceedings at the *Latrocinium of Ephesus (449). But when two years later Dioscorus was tried at the Council of *Chalcedon, Juvenal went over to the winning side and voted for his condemnation. As a reward, perhaps, he secured the Council's recognition of Jerusalem as a Patriarchal see with jurisdiction over the whole of Palestine. On his return he was faced by a revolt organized by the monks who favoured Dioscorus, and only the action of the Imperial government enabled him to regain his see. In parts of the E. he is revered as a saint; feast day, 2 July.

S. Vaillé, A.A., 'Formation du patriarcat de Jérusalem' in *É.O.* (1910), pp. 325–36. F. M. Abel, O.P., 'St. Cyrille d'Alexandrie dans ses rapports avec la Palestine' in *Kyrilliana, 444–1944* (Cairo, 1947), pp. 214–20. E. Venables in *D.C.B.*, iii (1882), pp. 595–8, s.v. 'Juvenalis (2)'; J. P. Kirsch in *L.Th.K.*, v (1933), col. 734 s.v.

JUVENCUS, CAIUS VETTIUS AQUILINUS (early 4th cent.), Christian Latin poet. He was a Spanish presbyter of noble descent, who wrote *c.* 330 a harmony of the four Gospels in some 3,200 lines of hexameter verse, emphasizing the transitoriness of the created universe and contrasting it with the glory and eternity of the Christian hope. The author's purpose was evidently to provide Christian readers with religious poetry to take the place of the popular pagan works. In its execution his work shows at every turn the influence of the study of *Virgil.

Works in J. P. Migne, *PL*, xix, 9–388; crit. edd. of his *Libri Evangeliorum IIII* by C. Marold (Teubner ed., 1886) and J. Huemer (C.S.E.L., xxiv; 1891) K. Marold, 'Ueber das Evangelienbuch des Juvencus in seinem Verhältniss zum Bibeltext' in *Zeitschrift für wissenschaftliche Theologie*, xxxiii (1890), pp. 329–41. J. T. Hatfield, *A Study of Juvencus* (Johns Hopkins University Diss., Bonn, 1890). N. Hansson, *Textkritisches zu Juvencus* (Lund, 1950). Raby, p. 17 f., with bibl. p. 464.

JUXON, WILLIAM (1582–1663), Abp. of *Canterbury. He was educated at St. John's College, Oxford, where he studied law, and in 1609 became Vicar of St. Giles, Oxford. In 1621 he succeeded his friend, W. *Laud, as president of St. John's College, and actively assisted him in his revision of the university statutes. In 1633 he succeeded him as Bp. of London. Though known to be a High Churchman, he had a reputation for tolerance, and this fact, combined with his integrity and generosity, led him to be trusted by Churchmen of all types. After Laud's imprisonment, he became the regular adviser of *Charles I, whom he attended on his execution (1649). A little later he was deprived of his bishopric; but otherwise he was practically unmolested under the Commonwealth. At the Restoration he was the obvious choice for the see of Canterbury, but survived for only three years.

W. H. Marah, *Memoirs of Archbishop Juxon and his Times* (1869). W. H *Hutton in *D.N.B.*, xxx (1892), pp. 233–7.

K

KABBALA. See *Cabbala*.

KAFTAN, JULIUS WILHELM MARTIN (1848–1926), Protestant theologian. A native of Schleswig, he became professor of systematic theology at *Basle in 1881 and of apologetics and the philosophy of religion at Berlin in 1883. He sought to reinterpret the *Ritschlian Soteriology so as to allow an adequate place for personal experience in religion. Believing that St. Paul's system of theology was the outcome of reflection on his vision of Christ on the Damascus road, he held that the Atonement must be understood by mystical and ethical categories, and that there was no place in the doctrine of Christ's work for any notion of satisfaction or of the reconciliation of God with man (as contrasted with that of man with God). His writings include *Das Wesen der christlichen Religion* (1881), *Die Wahrheit der christlichen Religion* (1888), and a *Dogmatik* (1897 and many later editions). Among his more recent works were *Kant, der Philosoph des Protestantismus* (1905) and *Jesus und Paulus* (1907).

His elder brother, THEODOR KAFTAN (b. 1847), who was General-superintendent for Schleswig from 1886 to 1917, was also a theologian of some influence, who held similar beliefs.

J. W. M. Kaftan, *Neutestamentliche Theologie* (1927; from his remains). Short autobiography in *Die Religionswissenschaft der Gegenwart in Selbstdarstellungen*, iv (1928), pp. 201–310.
On Theodor Kaftan, *Erlebnisse und Beobachtungen . . . von ihm selbst erzählt* (Kiel, 1924; ed. 2, Gütersloh, 1931).

KAGAWA, TOYOHIKO (1888–1960), Japanese Christian social reformer. He came of a wealthy family and received his early education in a Buddhist monastery. After conversion to Christianity and disinheritance by his family, he studied at the *Presbyterian seminary at Kobe from 1905 to 1908. Here he became acutely conscious of Christian responsibility in the face of existing social evils and spent several years among the poor in the bad slums of Shinkawa. In 1914 he went to Princeton, U.S.A., to study modern social techniques, and after returning to Japan in 1917 devoted himself entirely to the improvement of social conditions. In 1921 he founded the first Labour Union and the first Peasant Union in the country; in 1923 he organized relief work after the Yokohama earthquake; in 1928 he founded the National Anti-War League; and in 1930 he established the Kingdom of God Movement to promote conversions to Christianity. In 1940, he was imprisoned for a time as a pacifist. After the War he became a leader in the movement for democracy in Japan.

Kagawa has expounded his ideals in innumerable writings, among them *The Religion of Jesus* (Eng. tr., 1931), *New Life through God* (Eng. tr., 1932), *Christ and Japan* (Eng. tr., 1934), *Songs from the Slums* (Eng. tr., 1935), *Meditations on the Cross* (Eng. tr., 1936), *Brotherhood Economics* (Rauschenbusch Lectures, 1937), and *The Two Kingdoms* (Eng. tr. 1941; another Eng. tr., New York [1941], as *Behold the Man*). They reflect the influence of many spiritual writers and mystics of the West, among them J. *Wesley, G. *Fox, and Mme *Guyon.

There is a biog. introd. by Eleanor M. Hinder–Helen F. Topping in J. F. Gressitt's trans. into English of Kagawa's *Love the Law of Life* (1930), pp. 1–37. W. Axling, *Kagawa* (1932; ed. 8 revised, 1946).

KAISERSWERTH. The band of Protestant *deaconesses in this Rhineland town was begun by T. Fliedner in 1836 to meet the need of the reformed Churches for an organization of women devoted to the care of the sick and the education of neglected children, on the same lines as the corresponding institutes in the RC Church. The house at Kaiserswerth trains three kinds of deaconesses, who devote themselves either to the care of the sick and the poor, or to teaching, or to parish work. Candidates must be unmarried or widows and undertake to remain in the institute for five years, and are governed by a clergyman who is assisted by a woman superior. The Kaiserswerth deaconesses not only supply numerous charitable institutions in Germany with workers, but also have branches in other places, e.g. at *Jerusalem, *Alexandria, and Cairo. See also *Deaconess*.

J. Disselhoff, *Das Diakonissen-Mutterhaus zu Kaiserswerth a. Rhein und seine Töchterhäuser* (rev. ed., 1903; Eng. tr., 1883).

KANT, IMMANUEL (1724–1804), German philosopher. He was born and died at Königsberg in East Prussia and never went beyond the confines of the province. In early life he was attracted to the study of mathematics and physics, and retained interest in the natural sciences throughout his life. After some years as a private tutor, he became a Privatdozent at Königsberg University in 1755, and in 1770 Professor of Logic, holding the post until his death. His dissertation *De Mundi Sensibilis et Intelligibilis Forma et Principiis* (1770) marks an important stage in his development, but it was not until after another eleven years (during which Kant wrote practically nothing) that he expounded his epoch-making 'Critical Philosophy' in *Der Kritik der reinen Vernunft* (1781). Its treatment of the problems of speculative philosophy was carried further in his *Prolegomena zu einer jeden künftigen Metaphysik* (1783), and esp. in the second (and in essentials final) edition of the *Kritik der reinen Vernunft* (1787). The *Kritik der praktischen Vernunft*

(1788) and the *Kritik der Urtheilskraft* (1790) applied the principles of the earlier *Kritiken* to the problems of morals and to those of teleology and aesthetics respectively. In 1792 the divergence of Kant's teaching from orthodox *Lutheranism brought him into difficulties with the Prussian government. He was not prevented, however, from completing the publication of his *Religion innerhalb der Grenzen der blossen Vernunft* in 1793, the last of his large-scale works. His later writings include a monograph, *Zum ewigen Frieden* (1795). In his last years, as shown by his MSS. (publd. in their fullest form by E. Adickes as *Kant's Opus Postumum,* 1920), Kant moved towards a position more akin to that of B. *Spinoza.

It would seem that Kant's main object was to discover a definitive rationale for the admitted validity of mathematics and natural science (esp. the *Newtonian physics). This meant finding a way out of the deadlock arising from the co-existence, on the one hand, of Continental 'rationalism' (R. *Descartes, B. Spinoza, G. W. *Leibniz, and C. *Wolff), and, on the other, of English empiricism (J. *Locke, G. *Berkeley, D. *Hume). He felt that there could be only one solution, namely that it was the understanding (*Verstand*) which prescribed to nature her laws. The validity of the causal law ('every event has a cause') rests not on some constraining principle in the external world of nature, but in the fact that consciousness is so constituted that it cannot but so interpret the empirical *data* which it receives. Knowledge is thus the result of a synthesis between an intellectual act (through the twelve 'categories') and what is presented to the mind from without. The latter is received by the understanding under the two 'forms of perception' (*Anschauungsformen*) of space and time.

In holding that all knowledge required an ingredient derived from nature, Kant cut at the root of traditional metaphysics, with its claim to provide knowledge of subjects which wholly transcended human nature. For being thus constituted the human mind could have no knowledge of the three central 'Ideas' (*Ideen*) of Metaphysics : God, Freedom, and Immortality. The three traditional proofs of God's existence (*Ontological, *Cosmological, and *Teleological) were all invalidated.

But while insisting that Natural Theology was an illusion, Kant believed that the validity of the Ideas could be established in another way. The stern voice of conscience in man assures him of truths which reason is impotent to establish. Kant summarized this belief in his dictum: 'I had to remove knowledge to make room for faith'. The sense of duty assures us of Freedom. And correlative with this belief in Freedom are those in Immortality and in a Divine Being, since the maladjustment of virtue and happiness in the present world requires a righteous God Who will vindicate the claims of justice, and another world for His operation.

In his treatise on *Religion* (1793) Kant elaborated his ethical doctrines in relation to the traditional theology of Lutheranism. Its four sections treat of: (1) the existence of radical evil in human nature; (2) the conflict of the good and evil principles; (3) the victory of the good principle and the foundation of a Kingdom of God on earth; and (4) religion and priestcraft. Despite his constant use of accustomed theological terminology, his presentation of religion did not transcend the limits of morality, and he expressly defined religion as the recognition of all our duties as Divine commands. The moral law had no purpose beyond itself. There was no place for mystical experience, no need for a personal redeemer, and no place (as in traditional Christianity) for the historical as such. Kant once expressed the view that as a man advanced in moral perception he found the practice of prayer increasingly unprofitable. Miracles, if they ever happened, could have no religious significance.

Kant made no attempt to round off his beliefs into a system. This task was soon undertaken by others, who constructed on a Kantian basis a series of grandly conceived systems. J. G. *Fichte, F. W. J. *Schelling, and G. W. F. *Hegel (*Absolute Idealism) were all directly inspired by and looked back to Kant. In the latter part of the 19th cent. there arose in Germany a widespread and diversified philosophical movement seeking inspiration in a more literal interpretation of Kant. In Great Britain a similar, but independent, movement drew its inspiration from Kant and Hegel conjointly, its leading members being T. H. *Green, F. H. *Bradley, and B. *Bosanquet, and this in turn had a marked influence on Anglican Theology (C. C. J. *Webb, W. *Temple, A. E. *Taylor). The moralism of Kant and his critique of metaphysics have made him congenial to some Protestant theologians. RC philosophical theologians tend to see in Kant esp. the critic of the (scholastic) Proofs of God's Existence and hence to be very critical of him.

Collected edition of Kant's *Werke* by G. Hartenstein (1867–9). The best critical edition is that of the Berlin Academy (1900 onwards; still unfinished). Most of the individual writings are obtainable in convenient form, with introductions and notes, in the *Philosophische Bibliothek* (publd. F. Meiner, Leipzig). His more important writings exist in English translations. The best version of the *Critique of Pure Reason* is by N. Kemp Smith (1929). From the vast literature, the following is a small selection: J. Watson, *Kant and his English Critics* (1881); W. Wallace, *Kant* (1882); H. Cohen, *Kants Theorie der Erfahrung* (2nd ed., 1885); E. *Caird, *The Critical Philosophy of Immanuel Kant* (2 vols., 1889); H. A. Prichard, *Kant's Theory of Knowledge* (1909); N. K. Smith, *A Commentary to Kant's 'Critique of Pure Reason'* (1918); A. C. Ewing, *Kant's Treatment of Causality* (1924); C. C. J. Webb, *Kant's Philosophy of Religion* (1926); F. E. England, *Kant's Conception of God, with a translation of the 'Nova Dilucidatio'* (1929); A. D. *Lindsay, *Kant* (1934); H. J. Paton, *Kant's Metaphysic of Experience* (2 vols., 1936); H. J. de Vleeschauer, *La Déduction transcendentale dans l'œuvre de Kant* (3 vols., 1934–1937). A. C. Ewing, *A Short Commentary on Kant's Critique of Pure Reason* (1938); T. D. Weldon, *Introduction to Kant's Critique of Pure Reason* (1945); H. J. Paton, *The Categorical Imperative. A Study in Kant's Moral Philosophy* [1947]; A. H. Smith, *Kantian Studies* (1947). Überweg, iii, 488–620, with bibl. pp. 709–58. R. Adamson in *E.B.* (ed. 11), xv (1911), pp. 662–72; E. *Troeltsch in *H.E.R.E.*, vii (1914), pp. 653–9, s.v.; P. Charles, S.J., in *D.T.C.*, viii (pt. 2; 1925), cols. 2297–331, s.v. 'Kant et le kantisme' (on theological aspects of Kant's writings); W. Bruhn in *R.G.G.* (ed. 2), iii (1929). cols. 607–13, with bibl.

KARAITES (Heb. קָרָא, 'to read'). A Jewish sect, dating from the 8th cent. A.D., which rejects rabbinical tradition and the *Talmud, and bases its teaching solely on the Scriptures. It survives in Egypt, the Crimea, and parts of Turkey, and now numbers some 10,000 members.

The leading authority is S. A. Poznański (1864–1921), whose works are listed in the *Livre d'hommage à la mémoire du Dr Samuel Poznański* (1927), pp. xxix–xxxix. See also I. Markon, J. Heller, and M. Balaban in *Encyclopaedia Judaica*, ix (Berlin, 1923), cols. 923–54, s.v. 'Karäer', with bibl. Z. Ankori, *Karaites in Byzantium* (New York, 1959).

KARLSTADT. See *Carlstadt*.

KATTENBUSCH, FERDINAND (1851–1935), historian of the Creeds and theologian. A pupil of A. *Ritschl, he became professor of systematic theology at Giessen (1878), Göttingen (1904), and Halle (1906). His principal work, *Das apostolische Symbol* (i, 1894; ii, 1900), was an erudite treatise built on the researches of C. P. *Caspari, which brought together a vast body of literary material, ancient and modern, on the history of the *Apostles' Creed. He dated the Old Roman Creed at *c.* A.D. 100. Many of his views, however, lacked clear outlines and changed as he was writing the work. Kattenbusch also contributed to the history of the Reformation Confessions and M. *Luther's personal theology and, in his later years, concerned himself with systematic theology. Among his many other publications were *Luthers Lehre vom unfreien Willen und von der Prädestination* (1875; ed. 2, 1905); 'Der Quellort der Kirchenidee' in the *Harnack Festgabe* (1921; The *Quellort* was Dan. 7); *Die Vorzugsstellung des Petrus und der Charakter der Urgemeinde* (1922); and *Das Unbedingte und der Unbegreifbare* (1927).

H. Mulert in *R.G.G.* (ed. 2), iii (1929), col. 702 f., with list of Kattenbusch's works.

KEBLE, JOHN (1792–1866), *Tractarian leader and author of the *Christian Year* (q.v.). He was the son of John Keble, vicar of Coln St. Aldwyn, a priest of the High Church school. Born at Fairford, after a brilliant career at Corpus Christi College, Oxford, he was elected in 1811 at the age of 19 to one of the much coveted Fellowships of Oriel. In 1815 he was ordained deacon and in 1816 priest. In 1817 he became a tutor at Oriel, but resigned in 1823 to assist his father in his country cure in the Cotswolds. There he composed the poems which, at the insistence of close friends, he published in 1827 in the *Christian Year*. In 1831 he was elected professor of poetry in succession to H. H. *Milman. With many of his friends at Oxford and elsewhere (J. H. *Newman, I. *Williams, R. H. *Froude, E. B. *Pusey, W. *Palmer of Worcester College, J. B. *Mozley, H. J. *Rose), he became increasingly conscious of the dangers threatening the C of E from the reforming and liberal movements, and on 14

July 1833 preached before the University an assize sermon on *National Apostasy* (q.v.), directed esp. against the proposed suppression of ten Irish bishoprics. From now on he took a leading part in the *Oxford Movement. He co-operated with Newman in the issue of the *Tracts for the Times*, to which he himself contributed Nos. 4, 13, 40, 52, 54, 57, 60, 78 and 89. No. 4, which bore the title 'Adherence to the Apostolical Succession the safest Course', was a brief but forceful appeal to the clergy to take a high view of their privileges and duties. In 1836 he issued a learned edition of R. *Hooker's *Works* and in 1838, with Newman and Pusey, he became one of the editors of the *Library of the Fathers* to which he himself contributed the translation of St. *Irenaeus (publd. posthumously, 1872). His publication, with Newman, of the *Remains* (1838–9) of their close friend, R. H. *Froude (q.v.), provoked a storm. His tract No. 89, 'On the Mysticism attributed to the Early Fathers of the Church' (1840–1), a defence of Alexandrian theology and religious 'reserve', also met with a very hostile reception. After the cessation of the *Tracts*, he continued the close friend and adviser of Newman until his secession in 1845.

After 1845 Keble remained the firm associate of Pusey and co-operated with him in keeping the High Church Movement steadily attached to the C of E. In 1857 he published two pamphlets against the *Divorce Act, as well as a treatise *On Eucharistical Adoration*, defending the doctrine of the *Real Presence from its attack in the G. A. *Denison case. In 1863 he issued a *Life* of T. *Wilson, Bp. of *Sodor and Man (d. 1755). His later poetry included contributions to the *Lyra Apostolica* (1836), an English rendering of the *Psalter* (1839) and *Lyra Innocentium* (1846).

Meanwhile, since 1836, Keble had been Vicar of Hursley, near Winchester. He was never offered (and never wished for) preferment, remaining at Hursley, a devoted parish priest, for the rest of his life. He died at Bournemouth on 29 Mar. 1866. His beauty of character impressed all who came into contact with him, and his advice on spiritual matters, always given with great diffidence, was widely sought after. In 1870 Keble College, Oxford, was founded in his memory, with E. S. *Talbot as the first warden.

A set of *Letters of Spiritual Counsel and Guidance* (1870) was ed. by R. J. Wilson. *Memoir*, with many extracts from letters, by Sir J. T. Coleridge (1869). Lives by W. *Lock (1893); E. F. L. Wood, later Lord Halifax (1909); and K. Ingram (1933). H. P. *Liddon, *Clerical Life and Work* (1895), serm. xiii, and R. W. *Church, *The Oxford Movement* (1890), ch. ii. S. L. Ollard in *D.E.C.H.* (ed. 3), pp. 314–16.

KEIM, KARL THEODOR (1825–78), Protestant historian and Biblical scholar. After studying under F. C. *Baur, he became lecturer at *Tübingen in 1851 and pastor at Esslingen in Württemberg in 1856. From 1860 to 1873 he was professor of theology at Zürich, from 1873 till shortly before his death at Giessen. In his earlier years his chief interests were the history of the 4th cent. and of the Reformation. His most important works of this period were 'Die römischen Toleranzedicte für das Christenthum (311–13)', in the *Theologische Jahrbücher*, xi (1852) pp. 207–59, *Schwäbische Reformationsgeschichte bis zum Augsburger Reichstag* (1855), and *Der Uebertritt Konstantins des Grossen* (1862). After his appointment to Zürich, Keim concerned himself esp. with the Apostolic age and the doctrine of the Person of Christ. His principal work, *Die Geschichte Jesu von Nazareth* (3 vols., 1867–72), is a somewhat rationalistic presentation of the life of Christ, but less radical than that of the Tübingen school in which he had been educated. He rejected the supernatural element in the Gospels, including the Resurrection. He denied any historicity to the Fourth Gospel, but asserted the priority of Mt. His view of the Person of Christ exercised considerable influence on the more moderate liberal school of Continental Protestant theology.

J. A. Porret, *Trois Vies de Jésus*. Strauss, Renan, Keim (Geneva, 1893), pp. 33–52. A. *Schweitzer, *Von Reimarus zu Wrede* (1906), pp. 209–12 (Eng. tr., 1910, pp. 210–14). H. Ziegler in *P.R.E.* (ed. 3), x (1901), pp. 198–202, s.v.

KEITH, GEORGE (c. 1639–1716), 'Christian *Quaker'. Born in Aberdeen, he was educated for the *Presbyterian ministry at Marischal College, but in 1662 became a Quaker. After several imprisonments for preaching, he eventually emigrated to America in 1688. There he became suspect among his fellow-Quakers for denying the 'sufficiency of the light within', and was interdicted from preaching. He then proceeded to gather followers around him whom he called the 'Christian Quakers'. In 1694 he returned to England, and for the next six years administered Baptism and the Lord's Supper, though still professing Quaker convictions. In 1700 he conformed to the Anglican Church; and, after ordination, he conducted from 1702 to 1704 a successful mission in America as one of the first missionaries sent out by the *S.P.G. In 1705 he became rector of Edburton in Sussex. His writings include *The Deism of William *Penn and his Brethren* (1699) and *The Standard of the Quakers examined* (1702), the latter directed against R. *Barclay.

E. W. Kirby, *George Keith, 1638–1716* (The American Historical Association, New York and London, 1942), with full bibl. A. Gordon in *D.N.B.*, xxx (1892), pp. 318–21, s.v., with further reff.

KELLS, The Book of. See *Book of Kells, The*.

KEMPE, JOHN (c. 1380–1454), Abp. of *Canterbury. He first became prominent in the ecclesiastical courts and in 1415 was made *Dean of Arches. He filled in turn the sees of *Rochester (1419), *Chichester (1421), London (1421), *York (1425), and Canterbury (1452). He was a prominent member of the Council of Regency for *Henry VI, in which he was a

supporter of H. *Beaufort. During the years following 1430 he was a strong but ineffectual advocate of a policy of peace with France. In 1439 he was made cardinal. In his later years he espoused the Lancastrian cause, and checked the Kentish rebellion of 1450; but he died before the struggle was far advanced. He was far more a politician than a Churchman, and took little interest in the care of his dioceses.

W. F. *Hook, *Lives of the Archbishops of Canterbury*, v (1867), pp. 188–267. T. F. Tout in *D.N.B.*, xxx (1892), pp. 384–8, s.v. 'Kemp, John' [date of death erroneously given as 1447].

KEMPE, MARGERY (c. 1373–after 1433), author of the *Book of Margery Kempe*. Born at Lynn, Norfolk, the daughter of John Burnham (d. 1413), who was five times Mayor of Lynn, c. 1393 she married John Kempe (d. prob. 1431), burgess of Lynn, by whom she had 14 children. After she had received several visions following a period of madness, she and her husband went on a pilgrimage to *Canterbury. Her fervent denunciation of all pleasure aroused stiff opposition and the first taunts of *Lollardy, which later developed into formal accusations. In 1413 Margery and John took vows of chastity before Philip *Repingdon, Bp. of *Lincoln. She publicly rebuked Abp. *Arundel for the behaviour of his followers. In 1413 she went on a pilgrimage to the Holy Land. On her return she was prob. encouraged by *Julian of Norwich. She visited *Compostella in 1417 and *Norway and Danzig in 1433.

The *Book of Margery Kempe*, which is almost the sole source of information about the authoress, describes her travels and mystical experiences. She was endowed with the gift of tears and seems to have been favoured with singular signs of Christ's love, whereby for long periods she enjoyed consciousness of close communion with Him and developed a strong compassion for the sins of the world. Only one MS. of the Book, which was at one time in the possession of the *Carthusian house of Mountgrace and at least since 1754 has been in the Butler-Bowdon family, is now known to exist. Unrepresentative selections, prob. from another MS., were published by W. Worde (prob. 1501).

Worde's extracts reissued by H. Pepwell (London, 1521), repr. in E. G. Gardner (ed.), *The Cell of Self-Knowledge* (1910), pp. 51–9. Crit. ed. of the whole book by S. B. Meech–H. E. Allen (E.E.T.S., Orig. Ser., ccxii ff., 1940 ff.); modern version by W. Butler-Bowdon (London, 1936). K. Cholmeley, *Margery Kempe*. Genius and Mystic (1947).

KEMPIS, THOMAS À. See *Thomas à Kempis*.

KEN, THOMAS (1637–1711), Bp. of *Bath and Wells. He was educated at Winchester and Hart Hall, Oxford, and in 1657 became a Fellow of New College, Oxford. After several pastoral cures he taught at Winchester College from 1672. Here he wrote a manual of devotion for boys and possibly his **two**

famous morning and evening hymns, 'Awake, my soul, and with the sun' and 'Glory to Thee, my God, this night' (*Eng. Hymnal*, 257 and 267). In 1679 *Charles II appointed him chaplain to Princess Mary at the Hague, where he braved the anger of William of Orange in a matrimonial case. In 1683 as chaplain to *Charles II he refused the use of his house to the royal mistress, Nell Gwyn. The King respected his boldness and, in 1684, conferred on him the bishopric of Bath and Wells, and it was Ken who gave the King absolution on his deathbed. Though one of the *Seven Bishops who refused to read the *Declaration of Indulgence at the command of *James II, he declined to take the oath to William. Deposition from his see followed, and Ken then allied himself with the *Non-jurors. For the rest of his life he lived in retirement, refusing the offer of reinstatement on the death of Kidder (1703), who had held the see since his deposition. He opposed, however, the consecration of further nonjuring bishops. He lived an ascetic life as a celibate, and, true to the Laudian tradition, he wrote in his will, 'I die in the Holy Catholic and Apostolic Faith, professed by the whole Church, before the disunion of East and West: more particularly I die in the communion of the Church of England, as it stands distinguished from all Papal and Puritan Innovations'. His *Exposition on the Church Catechism; or, The Practice of Divine Love* (1685) is a classical expression of Laudian doctrine.

[Poetic] Works ed. W. Hawkins (4 vols., London, 1721); Prose Works ed. J. T. Round (ib., 1838), with life by W. Hawkins (orig. publd., London, 1713) repr., pp. 1–23. Other lives by W. L. Bowles (2 vols. bound in 1, London, 1830), J. L. Anderson (anon., London, 1851), E. H. Plumptre (2 vols., ib., 1888; ed. 2, 1890), and F. A. Clarke ('Leaders of Religion', London, 1896). E. Marston, *Thomas Ken and Izaak Walton* (1908), pp. 3–78. Life by H. A. L. Rice (S.P.C.K., 1958). W. Hunt in *D.N.B.*, xxx (1892), pp. 399–404.

KENITES. An obscure Semitic clan which belonged to the south of Palestine. It had several associations with the Hebrews, esp. the tribe of Judah, e.g. *Moses' father-in-law was a Kenite (Ex. 18) and the *Rechabites were apparently of Kenite origin (1 Chron. 2. 55); and it has sometimes been held that they exercised an important influence on the shaping of Hebrew religion. The name is perhaps to be associated with 'Cain' (Gen. 4. 1).

KENNETT, ROBERT HATCH (1864–1932), OT and Semitic scholar. He was educated at Merchant Taylors School and Queens' College, Cambridge, where he was elected a Fellow in 1888. From 1903 until his death he was Regius Professor of Hebrew and Canon of *Ely. He became a well-known figure in OT scholarship by his unconventional theses, e.g. a late dating for *Deuteronomy and the defence of a *Maccabean date for the Pss. and other portions of the OT. His writings include two series of Schweich Lectures (publd. in 1910 and 1933), a collection of *Old Testament Essays* (1928), and many other essays and articles.

Collection of his Essays, under the title *The Church of Israel*, posthumously ed. S. A. *Cook (Cambridge, 1933), with study of Kennett's 'Contribution to Biblical Research', pp. xv–liii, and list of his chief writings, p. lv f. Id. in *D.N.B., 1931–1940* (1949), p. 505 f.

KENNETT, WHITE (1660–1728), Bp. of *Peterborough. Educated at *Westminster and at St. Edmund Hall, Oxford, he was successively vicar of Ambrosden, Oxon (1685), tutor and vice-principal of St. Edmund Hall (c. 1690), Archdeacon of Huntingdon (1701), and Dean (1707) and Bp. (1718) of Peterborough. He was an active supporter of the Revolution of 1689, became a leading Low Churchman, and in the *Bangorian controversy opposed the proceedings against B. *Hoadly. He was, however, a close friend of G. *Hickes the *Nonjuror, whom he encouraged in the preparation of his *Thesaurus*. A keen antiquary, he was the author of a long list of works including sermons. Among them were *Parochial Antiquities* (1695; a history of Ambrosden, &c.), *Ecclesiastical Synods and Parliamentary Convocations* (1701), *Compleat History of England* (1706), and *Register and Chronicle, Ecclesiastical and Civil* (1728). Kennett urged that in every collegiate church a dignity should be reserved for a student of its antiquities, and founded an Antiquarian and Historical Library for the use of his cathedral.

Many of Kennett's valuable unpublished collections are preserved in the British Museum. Anonymous life [by William Newton] (London, 1730). Modern life by G. V. Bennett (Thirlwall Prize Essay for 1955; C. H. S., 1957). T. Cooper in *D.N.B.*, xxxi (1892), pp. 2–6.

KENNICOTT, BENJAMIN (1718–83), Biblical scholar and Hebraist. By the generosity of friends he was enabled to enter Wadham College, Oxford, in 1744, where, while still an undergraduate, he published two dissertations. From 1747 to 1771 he was a Fellow of Exeter College, from 1767 to 1783 Radcliffe Librarian, and from 1770 till his death Canon of Christ Church. His life-work was the critical study of the Hebrew text of the OT, in which he was assisted by collations of MSS. from many parts of Europe. His wife, whom he married in 1771, gave him considerable help in his researches. Their fruits were collected in his *Vetus Testamentum Hebraicum cum variis lectionibus* (2 vols., 1776–1780), a work which established the important negative conclusion that the variants in the Heb. MSS. of the OT are so slight as to be of minimal importance for establishing the correct text.

W. P. Courtney in *D.N.B.*, xxxi (1892), pp. 10–12. W. Michels in *Dict. Bibl.*, iii (1903), cols. 1887–9, s.v.

KENOTIC THEORIES. Certain theories which are concerned to explain the condescension involved in the Incarnation. The title comes from the Greek word (κενόω) in Phil. 2. 7, translated in the RV '*emptied* himself'. A number of 19th cent. *Lutheran theologians held that the Divine Son abandoned His attributes of deity, such as omnipotence, omniscience, and cosmic sovereignty, in order to become man. A more moderate theory, defended by C. *Gore, maintained that, within the sphere of the Incarnation, the deity so restrained its activity as to allow the existence in our Lord of a limited and genuinely human consciousness. Traditional orthodoxy has generally admitted a self-emptying of the Lord's deity only in the sense that, while remaining unimpaired, it accepted union with a physically limited humanity.

The early exponents of the modern theory were G. Thomassius (*Beiträge zur kirchlichen Christologie*, 1845, and *Christi Person und Werke*, 1853) and W. F. Gess (*Die Lehre von der Person Christi*, 1854). Gore's modified form of this appears in his *Bampton Lectures and, more fully, in his essay 'The Consciousness of Our Lord in His Mortal Life' in *Dissertations on Subjects connected with the Incarnation* (1895), pp. 69–226. Imp. artt. by F. *Loofs in *P.R.E.* (ed. 3), x (1901), pp. 246–63, and in *H.E.R.E.*, vii (1914), pp. 680–7; and esp. the valuable study by P. Henry, S.J., in *Dict. Bibl.*, Suppl. x [1950], cols. 1–161, s.v. 'Kenose', with bibl. Cf. also E. H. Gifford, *The Incarnation*. A Study of Phil. ii. 5–11 (1897), and W. *Sanday, *Christologies Ancient and Modern* (1910), esp. pp. 71–8.

KENSIT, JOHN (1853–1902), Protestant propagandist.

An early supporter of the more extreme type of Protestantism, he started the City Protestant bookshop in Paternoster Row in 1885 and later used the *Churchman's Magazine* for the propagation of his opinions. In 1890 he became secretary of the newly founded 'Protestant Truth Society' and from that date took an increasingly violent and individualist stand against what he believed to be romanizing tendencies in the C of E. From 1898 to 1902 he organized resistance to the growth of 'ritualism' in the dioceses of London (e.g. at St. Ethelburga's, Bishopsgate) and Liverpool, causing considerable friction and disturbance wherever he went. At the general election of 1900 he unsuccessfully contested Brighton as an Independent Conservative.

J. C. Wilcox, *John Kensit*, Reformer and Martyr [c. 1903].

KENT, Maid of. See *Barton, Elizabeth*.

KENTIGERN, St. (d. 603), also known as St. Mungo,

missionary in Scotland. Acc. to late but perhaps not untrustworthy sources, Kentigern, the grandson of a British prince in S. Scotland, was brought up by St. Serf in a monastic school at Culross on the Firth of Forth; later became a missionary to the Britons of Strathclyde, and was consecrated their bishop; after being driven out by persecution, preached in Cumberland and in Wales (where he is said to have founded the monastery at *St. Asaph); and eventually returned to Scotland, where he was active in planting or restoring Christianity in the district around Glasgow. His reputed tomb is in Glasgow Cathedral. Feast day, 13 Jan.

Fragment of the Life by an unknown 12th cent. author pr. by C. I[nnes] in the *Registrum Episcopatus Glasguensis*, i (for the Maitland Club, 1843), pp. lxxviii–lxxxvi. The life by Jocelin, monk of Furness (c. 1185), is to be found in J. Pinkerton, *Vitae Antiquae Sanctorum qui habitaverunt in ea parte Britanniae nunc vocata Scotia* (1789), pp. 198–297 (Eng.

tr. by W. M. Metcalfe, 1895, pp. 175–280). Both repr. with trans. in A. P. Forbes, *Lives of S. Ninian and S. Kentigern* (1874; The Historians of Scotland, vol. v). Short modern life by H. L. Simpson, *Saint Mungo* (1918). G. W. Sprott in *D.N.B.*, xxxi (1892), p. 26 f.

KEPLER, JOHN (1571–1630), German astronomer.

He was educated at *Tübingen, where he received instruction in *Copernican principles, and in 1594 was appointed professor of mathematics at Graz. In 1600 he went to Prague to Tycho Brahe, where he became court astronomer in 1601. In 1613 he took part in the Diet of Ratisbon, where he defended the Gregorian reform of the calendar against the many attacks of his fellow-Protestants. He was led to his discovery of the three laws of planetary motion, to which his fame is chiefly due, by *Neo-Platonist mystical doctrines. His understanding of nature was essentially pantheistic, despite his belief in the traditional authority of the Bible, and he held the world to be an order expressing the being of God Himself, particularly in the relations between the sun, the image of God the Father, and the planets. The appearance of a new star in 1604–5 caused him to propose in his *De Jesu Christi Servatoris Nostri Vero Anno Natalitio* (1606) and later writings a new theory concerning the star of the *Magi, which he tried to explain by the unusual conjunction of Mars, Saturn, and Jupiter in the sign of the Taurus, calculated by him for the beginning of the year 6 B.C.

Works ed. C. Frisch (8 vols., Frankfurt a.M., 1858–71), also ed. W. von Dyck–M. Caspar–F. Hammer (Munich, 1937 ff.). Letters ed. M. Caspar–W. von Dyck (2 vols.; Munich and Berlin, 1930). A. Müller, S.J., *Johann Keppler, der Gesetzgeber der neueren Astronomie* (Ergänzungsheft zu den *Stimmen aus Maria Laach*, lxxxiii; 1903); M. Caspar, *Johann Kepler* (Stuttgart, 1948); Carola Baumgardt, *Johannes Kepler*. Life and Letters (1952). L. Schuster, *Johann Kepler und die grossen kirchlichen Streitfragen seiner Zeit* (1888); L. Günther, *Kepler und die Theologie* (1905). *Johann Kepler, 1571–1630*. A Tercentenary Commemoration of his Life and Work. A Series of Papers prepared under the Auspices of the History of Science Society (Baltimore, 1931), with bibl. of his works pp. 86–112 and comm. pp. 113–33. K. Stöckl (ed.), *Kepler-Festschrift. Teil I* (Berichte des Naturwissenschaftlichen Vereins zu Regensburg, xix, 1930; all publd.). M. Caspar (ed.), *Bibliographia Kepleriana* (Munich, 1936).

KERYGMA (Gk. κήρυγμα, 'preaching').

The element of proclamation in Christian apologetic, as contrasted with '*Didache' or its instructional aspects.

KERYGMA PETRI. See *Peter, Preaching of*.

KESWICK CONVENTION.

An annual gathering of Evangelical Christians for prayer, Bible study, and addresses. It began at Keswick in 1875 with the aim of 'the promotion of Practical Holiness'. Its motto is 'All One in Christ Jesus'. The meeting is for a week every year, and it attracts visitors from many countries.

C. F. Harford (ed.), *The Keswick Convention* [1907]; W. B. Sloan, *These Sixty Years*. The Keswick Convention (1935); S. Barabas, *So Great Salvation*. The History and Message of the Keswick Convention (1952). The Convention also publishes an annual report, *Keswick Week*.

KETHUBIM (Heb. כְּתוּבִים, 'writings'). The Jewish name for the third and last division of the OT, more commonly known to Christian scholars as the '*Hagiographa' (q.v.).

KETTELER, WILHELM EMMANUEL (1811–77), Bp. of Mainz from 1850. Ordained priest in 1844, he made it his main life-work to free the RC Church in Germany from state control. His keen interest in social questions is reflected in his *Die Arbeiterfrage und das Christenthum* (1864). He also took a prominent part at the *Vatican Council of 1869–70, opposing the dogma on the ground that its promulgation was 'inopportune' and returning to Germany before the voting took place. After the decrees had been promulgated, however, he accepted them (Aug. 1870). In the *Kulturkampf he warmly and successfully championed the cause of the Church.

Writings ed. J. Mumbauer (3 vols., Kempten, 1911). Sermons ed. I. M. Raich (2 vols., Mainz, 1878); correspondence ed. id. (ib., 1879). Lives by O. Pfülf (3 vols., Mainz, 1899), F. Vigener (Munich, 1924), and W. Geiger (Freiburg, i.Br., 1933). L. Lenhart in *L.Th.K.*, v (1933), cols. 936–9, with bibl.

KETTLEWELL, JOHN (1653–95), devotional writer and *Nonjuror. He was educated at St. Edmund Hall, Oxford, and became Fellow of Lincoln College in 1675, where he was tutor from 1677 to 1684. He was ordained in 1678 and about the same time wrote his first book, *The Measures of Christian Obedience*, which, however, was not published till 1681. It had a great success and led to his appointment as vicar of Coleshill, Warwickshire, in 1682. In 1687 he wrote a popular devotional work, *The Practical Believer*, which was widely read. During the revolution of 1689 he preached against rebellion under any pretext, an attitude which resulted in his being deprived of his living in 1690. He spent his remaining years in retirement in London, writing devotional books and controversial tracts. His *Companion for the Persecuted* (1693) was esteemed as a book of comfort among his Nonjuring fellow-sufferers. His advocacy of a relief fund for the deprived clergy came to nothing owing to the opposition of the government.

Complete Works (2 vols., 1719). [F. Lee] *Memoirs of the Life of Mr. John Kettlewell* (1718; reprinted in K.'s works); T. T. *Carter (ed.), *The Life and Times of John Kettlewell* (1895). W. D. Macray in *D.N.B.*, xxxi (1892), pp. 80–2.

KEVIN, St. (d. 618), also named 'Coemgen', Abbot of Glendalough, Co. Wicklow. The sources for his life are late and untrustworthy. Acc. to these, he was born in Leinster of royal descent, given the name of Kevin (i.e. 'fair-begotten') at his baptism, and educated by St. *Petrock during the latter's stay in Ireland. For a time he settled at Disert-Coemgen, where Refert church now stands, and later established his permanent foundation at Glendalough, the parent of several other monasteries and destined to become, with its seven churches, one of the chief centres of pilgrimage in Ireland. He was on intimate terms with St. Kieran of Clonmacnoise. He is said to have lived to the great age of 120. Feast day, 3 June.

Three Irish lives pr. by C. Plummer in *Bethada Naem nÉrenn* (1922), i, 125–167; Eng. tr., ii, 121–161. One of the Latin lives is contained in C. Plummer, *Vitae Sanctorum Hiberniae*, i (1910), pp. 234–57, the other in C. de Smedt, S.J., and J. de Backer, S.J., *Acta Sanctorum Hiberniae ex Codice Salmanticensi* (1888), pp. 837–44.

KHOMIAKOFF, ALEXIS STEPANOVICH (1804–60), Russian philosophical theologian. He was born at Moscow into a family which fled with him from the city in 1812, when their house was burnt by the French. Later he studied literature and mathematics at the university of Moscow. After two attempts at a military career (1822 and 1828), he abandoned it for the study of art. After marriage in 1836 he found his vocation in the service of 'true Russia' and became with Ivan Kiréevski one of the founders of the Slavophil movement, which he sought to build up on Orthodox Christianity. He attacked the scholastic rationalism ('Aristotelianism') of W. philosophy and was esp. critical of German *Idealism (F. W. J. *Schelling and G. W. F. *Hegel), then influential in Russia. Over against the RC ('unity without freedom') and Protestant ('freedom without unity') conceptions of the Church, Khomiakoff saw in the Orthodox Church an organic society of which Christ was the Head and the Holy Spirit the Soul and whose essence was 'freedom in the spirit at one with itself'. Of this Church the essential quality was inward holiness, and those who partook of it could be saved even though not in external communion with it. Here, as in other dogmatic matters, Khomiakoff's liberal and independent attitude came under ecclesiastical suspicion. His writings were largely occasional. From 1856 until his death he collaborated in the *Rousskaia Beseda*, a review newly founded to further Slavophil ideals. A number of essays and polemical writings which originally appeared in French were re-issued by his son, Dmitri Alexéevitch Khomiakoff, as *L'Église latine et le protestantisme au point de vue de l'Église d'Orient* (Lausanne, 1872).

Khomiakoff also cultivated close relations with some English theologians, notably (from 1844) W. *Palmer ('of Magdalen'), with whom he stayed on a visit to Oxford in 1847, and W. J. Birkbeck. The latter included several of his papers in *Russia and the English Church during the Last Fifty Years* (vol. i, all publd.; 1895).

Collected edition of his works by his son, D. A. Khomiakoff (8 vols., Moscow, 1900). Life by V. Z. Zavitnevitch (2 vols., Kiev, 1902–13); study by N. *Berdyaev (Moscow, 1912). G. Samarine, *Préface aux œuvres théologiques de A. S. Khomiakoff* (Unam Sanctam 7, 1939). A. Gratieux, *A. S. Khomiakoff et le mouvement slavophile* (2 vols., Unam Sanctam 5 and 6, 1939).

KIDDUSH (Heb. קִדּוּשׁ 'sanctification'). The Jewish ceremony of the sanctification of the *Sabbath or other holy day. The rite, full directions for which are given in the *Mishnah (*Pesachim*, 10), is thought to go back to pre-Christian times. On Friday afternoon the household assembled for the evening meal and, at the beginning of the Sabbath, the head filled a cup of wine and water and said over it the Kiddush or 'Blessing' of the day. The same custom was observed on the eves of festivals, when the Kiddush made ref. to the festival as well as to the Sabbath. It has been argued that the custom was observed also by *chaburoth, and that Christ's blessing of the cup at the *Last Supper was the Kiddush of the *Passover. This theory is defended by alleged reminiscences of the idea and phraseology of the Kiddush in Eucharistic prayers, quoted or described in early Christian writings, e.g. the *Didache, *Ignatius, and *Justin. This theory presupposes the *Synoptic synchronism of the Last Supper with the Passover meal. Other scholars, preferring the Johannine dating of the Last Supper twenty-four hours before the Passover, hold that the blessing over the cup was the ordinary Jewish *berakah at the end of a chaburah meal.

J. Elbogen, 'Eingang und Ausgang des Sabbats nach Talmudischen Quellen' in *Festschrift zu Israel Lewy's siebzigstem Geburtstag* (Breslau, 1911), pp. 173–87. The identification of the Last Supper with the Kiddush ceremony, orig. suggested by F. Spitta, was first defended by G. H. Box, 'The Jewish Antecedents of the Eucharist', in *J.T.S.*, iii (1901–2), pp. 357–69. W. O. E. Oesterley, *The Jewish Background of the Christian Liturgy* (1925), esp. pp. 79–81 and 167–77; H. *Lietzmann, *Messe und Herrenmahl* (1926), pp. 202–10; F. Gavin, *The Jewish Antecedents of the Christian Sacraments* (1928), esp. pp. 64–69. L. N. Dembitz in *J.E.*, vii (1904), p. 483, s.v.

KIDRON. See *Cedron*.

KIERKEGAARD, SØREN AABY (1813–1855), Danish philosopher. The son of a wealthy hosier who was a devout *Lutheran, he spent practically his whole life at Copenhagen. After a secluded and unhappy childhood his university years were given over partly to idleness and amusements, partly to an inborn melancholy. He passed his theological examination in 1840, and in the following year became engaged to Regina Olsen; but feeling marriage to be impossible, he broke off the engagement shortly afterwards. In the twelve years from 1843, the year of the publication of his first book, *Enten-Eller* ('Either-Or'), till his death, he produced the series of works which were to place him in the first rank of modern philosophical writers, though his influence was hampered for a long time by the fact of his writing in Danish. In 1846 he was subjected to a long and cruel attack by the comic Copenhagen paper, *Den Corsaren*, and in 1854 he launched his great assault on the Established Church, criticizing it because it had sought to accommodate the Christian revelation to human desires.

He was one of the most personal of thinkers, and his successive publications mark the development of his thought from the aesthetic to the religious and soon to the definitely Christian point of view. He was reared in the atmosphere of *Hegelian dialectics—the only philosophy then taught in Denmark—and attacked this pantheistic falsification of Christianity as 'the system', esp. in the *Philosophiske Smuler* (1844; Eng. trans., 'Philosophical Fragments') and *Afsluttende uvidenskabelig Efterskrift* (1846; 'Concluding Unscientific Postscript'). He opposed to it his own powerful '*existential' dialectics, pointing out with uncompromising vigour, though often in abstruse terminology, the dialectics involved in the position of man 'existing before God'. The whole complex of sin and redemption was described with profound psychological insight in *Begrebet Angest* (1844; Eng. trans., 'The Concept of Dread') and *Sygdommen til Döden* (1849; Eng. trans., 'Sickness unto Death'). His thought, though deeply original and in its ascetic tendencies showing a marked leaning to Catholic ideals, reflects at many points its Lutheran ancestry, e.g. in its opposition of faith to reason and the stress laid on the relation of the individual soul with God almost to the exclusion of the idea of a Christian community. His often-repeated statement, 'truth is subjectivity', though it should not be understood in the sense of a shallow individualism, links up truth with the existing subject instead of with its object, and so, in the last resort, makes its communication to other subjects impossible. Kierkegaard draws the theological consequences from this position by denying the possibility of an objective system of doctrinal truths.

As contrasted with his philosophical writings, his properly religious books, e.g. the *Christelige Taler* (1850; Eng. trans., 'Christian Discourses') and *Indövelse i Christendom* (1850; Eng. trans., 'Training in Christianity'), have aroused less interest, but they are in many respects of great devotional value and show a profound understanding of the redemptive work of Christ and the meaning of the Cross. His total influence on contemporary thought is very considerable. Both the *Dialectical Theology of K. *Barth and his followers, and the *Existential philosophy esp. as expounded by M. Heidegger, owe their inspiration to him.

Collected ed. of *Samlede Vaerker* by A. B. Drachmann–J. L. Heiberg–H. O. Lange (15 vols., Copenhagen, 1901–36); of his 'Papirer' ed. P. A. Heiberg–V. Kuhr–E. Torsting (11 vols. in 19 parts, Copenhagen, 1909–38). Eng. tr. of most of his works, mainly by W. Lowrie, A. Dru, D. F. Swenson, and Lilian Swenson, publd. 1936 ff. (mostly 1938–44), esp. at Princeton, N.J., and London; list of these to 1944 in W. Lowrie's shorter life (v. infra), rev. impr. 1944, pp. 261–3. Selection from his *Journals* tr. and ed. A. Dru (London-Princeton, 1938). Life by W. Lowrie (Princeton-London, 1938); shorter life by id. (Princeton-London, 1942). R. Bretall (ed.), *A. Kierkegaard Anthology* (Princeton, London, 1947). G. Brandes, *Sören Kierkegaard* (Copenhagen, 1877; Germ. tr., Leipzig, 1879). J. Wahl, *Études kierkegaardiennes* (1938; with bibl.); E. Hirsch, *Kierkegaard Studien* (2 vols., 1933); E. L. Allen, *Kierkegaard. His Life and Thought* (1935); R. Thomte, *Kierkegaard's Philosophy of Religion* (Princeton-London, 1948). A. Grieve in *H.E.R.E.*, vii (1914), pp. 696–700, s.v.; E. Geismar in *R.G.G.* (ed. 2), iii (1929), cols. 747–51, s.v.

KIKUYU. The village in British E. Africa where a Missionary Conference of Anglicans, Presbyterians, and other Protestants was held in June 1913, under the leadership of the Bps. of Mombasa (W. G. Peel) and Uganda (J. J. Willis). A federation of the constituent Churches was proposed, on the basis of common acceptance of the *Apostles' and *Nicene Creeds and the recognition of common membership between the Churches in the federation, carrying with it the right of receiving Communion in any of them. Strong opposition was raised by F. *Weston, Bp. of Zanzibar, who appealed to the Abp. of *Canterbury. The latter gave his 'opinion' that Nonconformists in these areas might be admitted to Communion in Anglican churches, but that Anglicans should not seek Communion at the hands of Nonconformist ministers.

J. J. Willis, *The Kikuyu Conference* (1914); [R. T. *Davidson] Abp. of Canterbury, *Kikuyu* (Easter, 1915); H. M. Smith, *Frank* [Weston], *Bp. of Zanzibar* (S.P.C.K., 1926), ch. viii.

KILHAM, ALEXANDER (1762–98). Founder of the '*Methodist New Connexion'. The son of *Methodist parents, he was admitted a preacher in 1785. After J. *Wesley's death in 1791, he became leader of the radical wing of the movement and advocated complete separation from the Established Church. In several pamphlets he expounded his views with vigour, and even violence, and in 1796 was in consequence expelled by the Methodist Conference. In 1798 he founded the New Connexion, but died later in the same year.

Autobiography publd. Nottingham [*c.* 1799]. Anon. life, based on materials supplied by his widow and daughter (London, 1838). Shorter life by W. J. Townsend (ib., [*c.* 1889]). A. Gordon in *D.N.B.*, xxxi (1892), p. 102 f.

KILIAN, St. (d. *c.* 689), 'Apostle of Franconia'. A native of *Ireland, Kilian was probably already a bishop when he went as a missionary to the Franks and established his headquarters at Würzburg. Acc. to the most ancient account, he converted the local ruler, Duke Gozbert, and much of the population of E. Franconia and Thuringia, before he was put to death in the duke's absence through the enmity of his wife. His feast day, 8 July, is that of the solemn translation of his remains in 752 to the cathedral of Würzburg, of which he is the patron saint.

His *Acta* and *Passio*, pr. in *AA.SS.*, Jul. II (1721), pp. 612–18. Modern crit. ed. of *Passio Kiliani Martyris* by W. Levison in *M.G.H.*, Scriptores Rerum Merovingicarum, v (1910), pp. 711–28 (text, pp. 722–8). F. Emmerich, *Der heilige Kilian* (1896).

KILWARDBY, ROBERT (d. 1279), Abp. of *Canterbury. A master in arts of the university of Paris, it was only after some years in this secular career that he entered the *Dominican Order, of which he became provincial prior for England in 1261. He was consecrated Abp. of Canterbury in 1273, on the nomination of Pope *Gregory X, and was assiduous in visitations and in works of charity. In 1278 he was made a cardinal, and translated to the see of Porto in Italy, to which he took some of

the property of the see of Canterbury, including, it is said, the registers and judicial records. In his philosophical doctrines he was strongly opposed to the Aristotelianism of his fellow-Dominican, St. *Thomas Aquinas. His many metaphysical writings include an extensive (unpublished) Commentary on the *Sentences. He died at Viterbo.

The *Injunctions of Archbishop Kilwardby* (on his Visitation of the University of Oxford in 1276), ed. by H. W. G[arrod] and privately pr. (Oxford, 1929). Kilwardby's *Quaestio De Natura Theologiae*, ed. F. Stegmüller (Opuscula et Textus Historiam Ecclesiae Eiusque Vitam atque Doctrinam Illustrantia, Series Scholastica, ed. M. *Grabmann–F. Pelster, S.J., fasc. xvii, 1935). F. *Ehrle, S.J., 'Ein Schreiben des Erzbischofs von Canterbury Robert Kilwardby zur Rechtfertigung seiner Lehrverurtheilung von 18. März 1277' in *Archiv für Literatur- und Kirchengeschichte des Mittelalters*, v (1889), pp. 607–32, with text. L. Baur, *Dominicus Gundissalinus, De Divisione Philosophiae* (Beiträge zur Geschichte der Philosophie des Mittelalters, iv, Hftt. 2–3, 1903), pp. 368–80. M. D. Chenu, O.P., 'Le "De Spiritu Imaginativo" de Robert Kilwardby (d. 1279)' in *Revue des Sciences philosophiques et théologiques*, xv (1926), pp. 507–17; id., 'Le "De Conscientia" de R. Kilwardby, O.P., d. 1279'. ib., xvi (1927), pp. 318–26, with text of questions; F. Stegmüller, 'Les Questiones du commentaire des sentences de Robert Kilwardby' in *R.T.A.M.*, vi (1934), pp. 55–79, with reff. D. A. Callus, O.P., 'The "Tabulae Super Originalia Patrum" of Robert Kilwardby O.P.' in *Studia Mediaevalia in Honorem Admodum Reverendi Patris Raymundi Josephi Martin Ordinis Praedicatorum S. Theologiae Magistri LXXum Natalem Diem Agentis* (Bruges [1949]), pp. 243–70. The principal authority for his life is Nicolaus Trivet, O.P., *Annales Sex Regum Angliae* (ed. T. Hog, London, 1848, p. 278 f.). Ellen M. F. Sommer-Seckendorff, *Studies in the Life of Robert Kilwardby O.P.* (Dissertationes Historicae, fasc. viii; Rome 1937), with bibl. Überweg, ii, 493–7, with bibl. p. 764; Quétif–Échard, i, pp. 374–80. M. D. Chenu, O.P., in *D.T.C.*, viii (pt. 2; 1925), cols. 2354–6, s.v., with bibl.

KINDRED AND AFFINITY, Table of. This table, published by Abp. M. *Parker in 1563 and printed by custom at the end of the BCP, is based on the degrees of intermarriage prohibited in Lev. 18. It follows J. *Calvin's interpretation, namely that marriage is forbidden between any two persons related more nearly than, or as nearly as, any pair mentioned in Lev. 18, in contrast with M. *Luther's view, favoured by *Henry VIII, that only those marriages are forbidden by God's law which are expressly named in Lev. 18. The intention of the table was to set out clearly the marriages forbidden by Divine law and therefore incapable of being allowed by dispensation. Can. 99 of 1603 gave the table canonical authority in the C of E. In 1946 it was subjected to amendment by canon.

Kindred and Affinity as Impediments to Marriage, being the Report of a Commission appointed by his Grace the Abp. of Canterbury (S.P.C.K., 1940).

KING, EDWARD (1829–1910), Bp. of *Lincoln. He was successively assistant curate of Wheatley, Oxon (1855), chaplain of Cuddesdon Theological College (1858), principal of Cuddesdon (1863), Regius professor of pastoral theology at Oxford (1873), and Bp. of Lincoln (1885). A man of great holiness of life, he is most remembered for his teaching on the pastoral duties of the clergy, and for his fatherly care for individuals, both as priest and bishop. He was a Tractarian High Churchman, and a friend of E. B. *Pusey and H. P.

*Liddon. In 1888 a 'ritual prosecution' was brought against him by the *Church Association, and in 1890 decided in the court of the Abp. of *Canterbury (E. W. *Benson) substantially in his favour (see *Lincoln Judgement*).

Spiritual Letters of Edward King, ed. B. W. Randolph (1910). Life by G. W. E. Russell (1912). B. W. Randolph and J. W. Townroe, The Mind and Work of Bishop King (1918). G. W. E. Russell in D.N.B., 1901–1911, pp. 397–400.

KING JAMES VERSION. A title used, esp. in America, for the English translation of the Bible commonly known in England as the *Authorized Version (1611).

KING'S BOOK, The. The name commonly given to the *Necessary Doctrine and Erudition for any Christian Man*, put forth by *Henry VIII in the summer of 1543 after it had been presented to *Convocation earlier in the year. It was based upon the *Bishops' Book of 1537, but except for the fact that the King's supremacy was more strongly asserted, its theology was a reaction in a Catholic direction. *Transubstantiation was more clearly defined, some additional articles on Free Will, Good Works, &c., were added, and fuller treatment was given to such subjects as Justification. It was provided with a preface, apparently written by Henry VIII himself, and a preliminary article on Faith, probably the work of T. *Cranmer. In 1544 a free translation in Latin appeared, entitled *Pia et Catholica Christiani Hominis Institutio*.

The King's Book, ed. by T. A. *Lacey (S.P.C.K., 1932). There is an earlier edition by C. *Lloyd (Oxford, 1825 and 1856).

KING'S BOOKS, The. See *Valor Ecclesiasticus*.

KING'S COLLEGE, LONDON. The College was incorporated in 1829 to provide an education on Anglican principles. It was designed as a counterweight to the undenominational University College, London, established by charter in 1827 (then the only English college of University status for Nonconformists, who were still excluded from Oxford and Cambridge). In 1836, a charter incorporating the university for conferring degrees recognized it as a constituent part of the University of London. The opening of the theological department in 1846 was soon followed by a fierce controversy involving the removal of F. D. *Maurice from his position as lecturer in 1853. A residential hall for those in the department preparing for Holy Orders was established at Mecklenburgh Square in 1902; in 1913 it was transferred to Vincent Square. The 'Associateship of King's College' (A.K.C.) is an academic qualification often taken by nongraduate ordinands of the C of E. On 1 Jan. 1910, King's College was incorporated in the University of London.

F. J. C. Hearnshaw, History of King's College, London, 1828–1928 (1929). Much historical information is to be found in the Calendar of King's College, publd. annually.

KING'S CONFESSION, The. The very Protestant statement of belief drawn up by John Craig (c. 1512–1600) in 1581 when it was feared that Popery might be revived in Scotland through the recent arrival of the Duke of Lennox from France. Its formal title was 'A Short and General Confession of the True Christian Faith and Religion according to God's Word and Acts of our Parliaments', but as it was signed by the King (*James [VI of Scotland]) and his household, it was commonly known as the 'King's Confession'. All parish clergy (and from 1585 also all graduates) were required to sign it. It was reaffirmed in 1590 and 1595, and was the basis of the '*National Covenant' of 1638. See also *Covenanters*.

Text (Eng. and Lat.) in P. *Schaff, A History of the Creeds of Christendom, iii (1877), pp. 480–5. See further bibl. s.v. Covenanters.

KING'S EVIL, Touching for the. The tradition that there existed some virtue in the royal touch for healing the 'King's evil', or scrofula, is said to date from the time of *Edward the Confessor (d. 1066). The practice certainly goes back to the reign of Henry VII, and probably much further. *James I encouraged the custom as a proof of his *Divine Right, and it has been estimated that *Charles II touched in all as many as 100,000 persons. Queen *Anne was the last sovereign to perform it, among those whom she touched being the infant Samuel *Johnson. There was often printed a form of service for the touching in editions of the BCP between the reign of *Charles I and 1719.

M. Bloch, Les Rois thaumaturges (1924).

KINGDOM OF GOD, The. The roots of the conception of the Kingdom of God (Gk. ἡ βασιλεία τοῦ θεοῦ) in Christ's teaching and elsewhere in the NT lie in Hebrew thought, acc. to which the word translated 'Kingdom' (מלכות) means rather the possession or exercise, than the sphere, of kingship. God was eternally king (Pss. 97, 99 etc.) in heaven. But owing to the existence of godless heathen empires His kingship was not visibly and outwardly effective on earth, though it would become so at the 'Day of the Lord' or the Day of Final Judgement. It thus came about that though some of the Rabbis suggest the conception of a spiritual and invisible kingdom of God in this life to which the good man might belong, the phrase 'the Kingdom of God' would normally have been understood in the time of Christ in an eschatological sense. For the righteous, who alone would enter it, it would bring blessings, often conceived in a quite materialistic way (cf. *Enoch 10. 17 ff.). Its establishment would involve the punishment of the wicked, esp. the overthrow of heathen political powers and the transference of power to 'the saints', i.e. Israel, who would henceforth be ruled by God Himself, or by God's Anointed One, the *Messiah (Christ).

In the NT the theme of the Kingdom of God ('Kingdom of Heaven' in Mt.) becomes central. St. *John Baptist proclaimed to his hearers that the Kingdom was at hand (Mt.

3. 2) and Christ began His Ministry with the same message (Mt. 4. 17). Our Lord, however, was to modify profoundly the idea of the Kingdom of God by His further teaching. In contrast to the many who thought mainly of the visible reward to be given to the righteous by an immediate intervention of God (cf. Lk. 19. 11) and even to the apostles who after the Resurrection still looked for a quasi-political kingdom under Jesus as Messiah (Acts 1. 6), Christ stressed the ethical and religious qualities demanded of those who were to enjoy ('enter' or 'receive') the Kingdom: these included the giving-up, if necessary, of home and family, and of every hindrance, even the loss of an eye or a hand (Mk. 9. 47), together with constant watchfulness (Mt. 25. 1–13; cf. Mt. 5. 20, 7. 21). Self-righteous Jews would be excluded from the kingdom (Mt. 8. 11 f.), the rich barely admitted (Mk. 10. 23), and it belonged especially to the humble and childlike (Mt. 5. 3, 10; Mk. 10. 15, cf. John 3. 3–5). In many parables beginning with words such as 'The Kingdom of Heaven is like' the nature of the kingdom is expounded and popular ideas of it corrected. In any attempt to integrate the Lord's teaching into a whole, three diverse aspects of the Kingdom must be considered.

(a) *The Kingdom as future.* To some extent Christ seems to have accepted the current expectation of a future earthly manifestation of the kingdom, i.e. that it would 'come' in a sense in which it was not yet present when He spoke about it. He taught the disciples to pray 'Thy kingdom come' (Mt. 6. 10) and many of the parables speak of a period of growth or waiting, followed by a harvest or a coming (e.g. the Tares, the Ten Virgins), thus suggesting that the full manifestation of the Kingdom is in the future; and the Church has traditionally linked this with the belief in Christ's *Second Coming professed in the Creeds, and with the idea of the Judgement, *Eternal Life, and the *Resurrection of the Body. Christ also promised, acc. to Mk. 9. 1 (cf. Mt. 16. 28, Lk. 9. 27) that some of His hearers would live to 'see the kingdom of God come with power'. Though difficulties were early felt in the Church because the hope of an early return of Christ which such words aroused was not fulfilled (cf. 2 Pet. 3. 4), orthodox thought has steadily continued to believe in a future manifestation of the kingdom of God, however delayed. Theologians of liberal tendencies (the most notable exception is A. *Schweitzer, q.v.) have tended, on the other hand, to replace the expectation of a sudden future revelation of the kingdom by the hope of the progressive realization of better conditions of human life, moral and material, and this ideal state of human affairs has sometimes been loosely identified with the realization of 'the Kingdom of God'.

(b) *The Kingdom as present.* In Christ's teaching, the kingdom of God is also declared to be actually present as He spoke and its coming is represented as a present, but hidden, reality. Such appears to be the sense of the verb 'is at hand' (ἤγγικεν, lit. 'has come near') in Mt. 3. 2; 4. 17. His works of healing, done 'by the finger of God', were evidence that 'the kingdom of God is upon you' (Mt. 12. 28) and, in contrast to the wish for a dramatic manifestation of the kingdom Christ taught that 'the kingdom of God is within you' or 'in the midst of you' (ἐντὸς ὑμῶν, Lk. 17. 21). It is possible that this conception of the Kingdom as a present reality occupied relatively a considerably more prominent place in the Lord's teaching than it fills in the Gospels and elsewhere in the NT where its centrality may have been displaced by the widespread expectation of the early Christians that a visible kingdom was on the point of appearing. That the Kingdom continued to be understood as present is shown by such expressions as 'made us to be a kingdom and priests to God' (Rev. 1. 6, 9; 5. 10), and 'translated us into the kingdom of His son' (Col. 1. 13) where the kingdom is an actual possession of Christians already, 'not eating and drinking, but righteousness and peace and joy in the Holy Ghost' (Rom. 14. 17). This, in the traditional orthodox view, does not exclude a future manifestation of the same kingdom in its power and glory, where all the evil which now opposes it shall be done away. The 'realized eschatology' of C. H. *Dodd, however, holds that Christ taught only one coming of the kingdom, namely that inaugurated by His own ministry, death and resurrection, and that the only fuller realization than this is the life of eternity realized for each Christian after earthly death.

(c) *The Kingdom as the Church.* The conception of the kingdom of God as a present reality, including spiritually all who are God's true subjects, suggests a close relation between the Kingdom and the *Church; but in the NT the two terms are not closely related, unless Christ's promise to St. *Peter to give him 'the keys of the kingdom' (Mt. 16. 19) refers to Peter's position in the Apostolic Church on earth. Before St. *Augustine the identification of the kingdom of God with the Church on earth never seems to have been made, but from then on it became general. St. Augustine, distinguishing between the elect who are predestined to salvation, and the visible Church which contains an admixture of evil men, identified the body of the elect with the *Kingdom of God, or the Kingdom of Christ, as opposed to 'the kingdom of the devil', and also with the 'City of God' (*civitas Dei*) as opposed to the earthly city (*civitas terrena*). Though strictly this identification applied to the invisible body of the elect, Augustine tended to speak as if it applied to the visible hierarchical Church, and in this he was followed, with even less reserve, by medieval thought generally.

KINGS, Books of. These two Books are the principal source for the history of the Jewish monarchy from the accession of *Solomon (c. 970 B.C.) to the Fall of *Jerusalem

(586 B.C.). They carry on the history begun in the Books of *Samuel, of which they are structurally a continuation. The division into two books is not original, but comes from the Greek translators, who also grouped them with the Books of Samuel and designated them as the four 'Books of the Reigns'. Hence I and II Kings of the AV became *III* and *IV Regum* in the *Vulgate and III and IV Kings in the *Douai version.

The First Book opens with an account of the events leading up to the accession of Solomon (1 Kgs. 1–2). The reign of Solomon, esp. the building of the Temple, is described with great fullness (3–11). The history of the two separate kingdoms of Judah and Israel, formed from the partition of Solomon's domains at his death, then follows on a carefully arranged plan, the events of each reign being fitted into a standard framework which allowed the events of the two kingdoms to be treated alternately. Specially detailed accounts are given of the work of the prophets *Elijah and *Elisha. This plan is adopted down to the fall of the kingdom of Israel to Assyria in 721 B.C. (2 Kgs. 17), after which the narrative is concerned solely with Judah (2 Kgs. 18–25). Of the later kings, the writer paid special attention to Josiah, whose reforming work he deservedly commended.

The author's main interest throughout is religious. This is seen from the way in which events and reigns of religious significance are described in great detail whereas those of the highest political importance are often passed over very cursorily. Modern critics have come to see close affinities between the theological outlook of the author and that reflected in the Book of *Deuteronomy, and to find in this a principle governing the sentences passed upon the reigns of the different kings. The author of the Books evidently had access to excellent contemporary sources of history. Some of these are cited in the text, e.g. the 'Acts of Solomon', the 'Chronicles of the Kings of Israel' and 'of Judah', whereas others that are not named, such as official documents and prophetic memoirs, were also clearly used. Comparison with the Books of *Chronicles shows that the chronicler in turn made extensive use of the Books of Samuel and Kings.

Commentaries by J. Skinner (Cent. Bib., 1904), W. E. Barnes (Camb. Bib., RV, 2 vols., 1908), J. A. Montgomery (posthumous, ed. H. S. Gehman, I.C.C., 1951), I. Benzinger (K.H.C., Abt. ix; 1899), R. Kittel (H.K.A.T., Abt. 1, Bd. v; 1900), and A. Sanda (E.H., ix, 2 vols., 1911–12). C. F. *Burney, *Notes on the Hebrew Text of the Books of Kings* (1903). I. Benzinger, *Jahvist und Elohist in den Königsbüchern* (Beiträge zur Wissenschaft vom Alten Testament, N.F., ii; 1921). J. Begrich, *Die Chronologie der Könige von Israel und Juda und die Quellen des Rahmens der Königsbücher* (Beiträge zur historischen Theologie, iii; 1929).

KINGSHIP OF CHRIST, Feast of the. See *Christ the King, Feast of.*

KINGSLEY, CHARLES (1819–75), Anglican divine, social reformer and novelist. Born at Holne in Devonshire, he was educated locally, at *King's College, London (1836–8),

and at Magdalene College, Cambridge (1838–1842). In 1842 he was ordained to the curacy of Eversley, Hants, where he became vicar in 1844 and spent most of the rest of his life. From 1860 to 1869 he was Professor of modern history at Cambridge (a post for which he came to recognize that he was ill-qualified; it required only a short period of residence each year). Later he held canonries at *Chester (1869–73) and *Westminster (1873–5).

Kingsley, who fell under the influence of F. D. Maurice and T. *Carlyle, became keenly interested in the movement for social reform. He was a leading spirit in the *Christian Socialist Movement (q.v.), but he looked to the extension of the co-operative principle and educational and sanitary reform rather than radical political change for the amelioration of the people. He was at first the principal pamphleteer and spokesman of the group and under the pseudonym 'Parson Lot' contributed to *Politics for the People* (1848) and *The Christian Socialist* (1850–1). He was strongly averse to all forms of asceticism (monasticism; clerical celibacy; anti-tobacco) and as such a critic of *Tractarian ideals. He soon came to be regarded as a leading exponent of 'muscular Christianity'.

The Saint's Tragedy (1848; preface by F. D. *Maurice), written in dramatic form, developed out of a life of St. *Elizabeth of Hungary, begun in 1842 as a critique of asceticism. His principal novels were *Yeast* (1850; orig. publd. by 'Parson Lot' in *Fraser's Magazine*, 1848), *Alton Locke* (1850), *Hypatia* (1853; on the factions in the Church of *Alexandria in the early 5th cent.), *Westward Ho!* (1855), *The Heroes* (1856), *Two Years Ago* (1857) and *Hereward the Wake* (1866). An ill-considered jibe at J. H. *Newman in 1863 ('Truth for its own sake has never been a virtue of the Roman clergy. Father Newman informs us that it need not and on the whole ought not to be') led to the publication of the latter's *Apologia* (q.v.) in 1864. To this period his popular children's book, *The Water-Babies* (1863), also belongs.

The novelist Henry Kingsley (1830–76), the author of *Ravenshoe* (1862), was a younger brother.

Collected Works (28 vols., 1880–5; 19 vols., 1901–3). Life by his widow (2 vols., 1877; abridgements, 1879, 1883). C. W. Stubbs, *Charles Kingsley and the Christian Social Movement* (1899); G. Kendall, *Charles Kingsley and his Ideas* (1946). Other studies by M. F. Thorp (Princeton, 1937) and U. C. Pope-Hennessy (London, 1948). L. Stephen in *D.N.B.*, xxxi (1892), pp 175–81.

KIRK. The Scottish equivalent of 'Church'. Although the Church of Scotland has ceased to be officially designated 'The Kirk' since the *Westminster Assembly (1645–8), the term is retained in the name of its lowest court, the *kirk-session, and popularly the old Presbyterian Establishment is still occasionally called 'the Auld Kirk'.

KIRK, KENNETH ESCOTT (1886–1954), Bp. of *Oxford. Educated at St. John's College, Oxford, he was ordained deacon in 1912 and priest in 1913. He was Chaplain to the Forces (1914–19), Fellow and chaplain of Trinity College, Oxford (1922–33), and Regius Prof. of moral and pastoral theology (1932–7). In 1937 he became Bp. of Oxford. He was the most outstanding of modern Anglican writers on moral theology and Christian spirituality. His principal writings include *Some Principles of Moral Theology* (1920), *Ignorance, Faith, and Conformity* (1925), *Conscience and its Problems* (1927), and *The Vision of God* (1931; the *Bampton Lectures for 1928). Kirk also published a commentary on Rom. (Clarendon Bible, 1937) and edited *Personal Ethics* (1934), *The Study of Theology* (1939), and *The Apostolic Ministry* (1946).

Collected addresses and papers, *Beauty and Bands*, ed. E. W. Kemp (1955). E. W. Kemp, *The Life and Letters of Kenneth Escott Kirk* (1959).

KIRK-SESSION, also known simply as the **Session**. The lowest court in the Church of *Scotland and other Presbyterian Churches. It consists of the minister and elders of a local congregation. Its main duties are to supervise and control the congregation and to keep the Communion roll up to date.

KISS OF PEACE, also **PAX**. The mutual greeting of the faithful in the Eucharistic Liturgy, as a sign of their love and union. It is first mentioned by St.* Justin Martyr (2nd cent.) and is probably a usage of the Apostolic period (cf. Rom. 16. 16, 1 Pet. 5. 14, &c.). In the E., *Gallican, and *Mozarabic rites the Peace is given before or after the offering of the Oblations, a position suggested by Mt. 5. 23 f.; in the Roman and *Ambrosian rites it is given later in the service, viz. shortly before Communion. Originally an actual kiss, the form of the Peace has been modified in all rites. In the W. the present practice is for the person giving and the person receiving the Peace to face each other, to put their hands on each other's shoulders, and then bow their heads. The celebrant first 'kisses' the deacon, then the deacon the subdeacon, and then the subdeacon delivers the 'kiss' to the clergy in choir. The Pax is not given on *Maundy Thursday, *Good Friday or *Holy Saturday, or in Masses for the Dead; and its use is confined to High Mass. Among the *Nestorians, a Kiss of Peace is given also at the conclusion of the evening office, and a similar usage once obtained also among the Celtic monks of *Ireland. See also *Pax Brede*.

Jungmann, *M.S.*, ii (ed. 1949), pp. 389–403; Eng. tr., pp. 321–32, with reff. H. Thurston, S.J., in *C.E.*, viii (1910), pp. 663–5, s.v.; F. *Cabrol, O.S.B., in *D.A.C.L.*, ii (1910), cols. 117–30, s.v. 'Baiser'.

KITTO, JOHN (1804–54), writer on Biblical subjects. From his earliest days a delicate child and a great lover of books, he was prevented by health from following his father's trade of stonemasonry and for a time he was apprenticed to a shoemaker. Eventually he was enabled to go to the Islington Missionary College where he was trained to be a printer. After working in Malta (1827–9) and travelling to Persia, he devoted his time to writing. His best-known work was the *Pictorial Bible* (2 vols., 1835–8). Among his other books were *The History of Palestine* (1843) and the *Cyclopaedia of Biblical Literature* (2 vols., 1843–5). In 1848 he founded the *Journal of Sacred Literature* which he edited until 1853. Often in pecuniary difficulties, he was awarded a Civil List pension in 1850.

J. Kitto, *The Lost Senses* (1845; autobiographical). J. E. Ryland, *Memoirs of Kitto* (1856); J. Eadie, *Life of Kitto* (1857).

KLOPSTOCK, FRIEDRICH GOTTLIEB (1724–1803), German poet. The son of a lawyer, he was born at Quedlinburg and studied at Schulpforta (1739–45), Jena (1745–1746) and Leipzig (1746–8). He completed *c.* 1746 the first section of an epic in prose inspired by a translation (1732) by J. Bodmer (1698–1783) of J. *Milton's *Paradise Lost. At Leipzig he began to transpose it into hexameters and in 1748 issued part of it in the *Bremer Beiträge* as the first three cantos of *Der Messias* (completed 1773); though published anonymously, its authorship was soon known. In 1751 he was offered a pension by King Frederick V of Denmark to enable him to complete *Der Messias*. He resided at Copenhagen until 1770, when he retired to Hamburg. In 1789 he was visited by S. T. *Coleridge and W. *Wordsworth.

The publication of the earlier parts of *Der Messias* marked a new epoch in German literature. The poem, consisting of nearly twenty thousand lines distributed in twenty cantos, is concerned with the Passion and forty days after the Resurrection. It not only describes events on earth, but introduces hosts of angels and devils, even the Trinity itself appearing, giving to every event and action its deeper significance. In the opening portions, its bold suggestion of intensity and infinity raised reflective German poetry to a new level; but later the theme became wearisome. Moreover Klopstock's fear of anthropomorphism made his descriptions vague and his characters lifeless. From a literary point of view the work is important as the first modern German epic.

In his lyric poetry Klopstock adapted classical metres. For the most part he rejected rhyme and developed a free rhythmic form. The poems of his earlier years, such as *An des Dichters Freunde* (1747), *An Fanny* (1748) and *An Gott* (1748), are filled with religious fervour. These were followed by his calmer nature poems, such as *Der Zürcher See* (1750) and *Die Frühlingsfeier* (1759). His later poems, largely inspired by the German past, also expressed his disappointment in the French Revolution. In 1758 and 1769 he published two volumes of *Geistliche Lieder* and in 1771 a collection of *Oden*. He also wrote religious and bardic drama, incl. *Der Tod Adams* (1757), *Salomo* (1764), and *David* (1777), the last two in verse. He devoted the last years of his life to philology.

Collected edd. of his Works, 12 vols., Leipzig, 1798–1817. 18 vols., ib. 1823–30 (vols. xiii–xviii ed. A. L. Back–A. R. C. Spindler). K. [E. C.] Schmidt (ed.), *Klopstock und seine Freunde.* Briefwechsel der Familie Klopstock unter sich und zwischen dieser Familie, Gleim, Schmidt, Fanny, Meta und andern Freuden (2 vols., 1810; Eng. tr., with biographical note, 1814). Further correspondence ed. I. M. Lappenberg (Brunswick, 1867). Eng. tr. of *Der Messias* [by J. Collyer], 2 vols., London, 1763. Standard life by F. Muncker (Stuttgart, 1888). E. Bailly, *Étude sur la vie et les œuvres de Frédéric Gottlieb Klopstock* (Lyons thesis; Paris, 1888). There is a very considerable literature, mainly in German, partially listed in *Der Grosse Brockhaus*, vi (ed. vi; 1955), p. 437, s.v.

KLOSTERNEUBURG. A celebrated monastery of *canons regular of St. *Augustine, nr. Vienna. It was founded not later than 1108 by Margrave Leopold III and his consort, Agnes, for secular canons, and was given to the Augustinian Canons in 1133. As it became very rich, it was frequently raided in times of war and civil strife, e.g. during the *Hussite wars, in the Reformation period, and in the wars against the Turks. It possesses great art treasures, e.g. the famous 'Verdun Altar' and precious stained glass dating from the 13th to the 15th cents., as well as a large library with important MSS. and incunabula. Its present buildings date from the finest period of the Austrian Baroque. In recent times Klosterneuburg has become noted for its active support of the *Liturgical Movement, fostered esp. by Pius Parsch, the editor of several liturgical periodicals.

There is a considerable literature, of which the chief items to date are listed by V. O. Ludwig in *L.Th.K.*, vi (1934), col. 54 f., s.v. Catalogue of MSS. ed. H. Pfeiffer–B. Černík (i, Vienna, 1922; ii, Klosterneuburg, 1931): of the 'Kunst-Sammlungen', ed. by the Director of the Kunsthistorisches Museum at Vienna (1937 ff.; pt. 1 at Klosterneuburg; pts. 3 ff. at Vienna). Cf. also S. Schmidt in *E.C.*, vii (1951), cols. 718–20, s.v.

KNEELERS. See *Genuflectentes*.

KNEELING, Declaration on. See *Black Rubric*.

KNIGHTS HOSPITALLER; KNIGHTS OF MALTA; and KNIGHTS OF RHODES. See *Hospitallers*.

KNIGHTS TEMPLAR. See *Templars*.

KNOX, ALEXANDER (1757–1831), pre-*Tractarian Anglican divine. He was a descendant of J. *Knox, the Scottish Reformer. In much of his teaching he anticipated the *Oxford Movement. Thus he affirmed that the C of E was not a 'protestant' Church, but a reformed branch of the Church Catholic, and he stressed the need for adherence to *Apostolic Succession, the BCP, and the *Thirty-Nine Articles. From his intimate friend, J. *Wesley, he learnt the value of frequent communion and for many years worked in harmony with Bp. J. *Jebb, whose *Thirty Years' Correspondence* gives a valuable picture of him.

His writings were collected as *The Remains of Alexander Knox*, by Hornby (4 vols., 1834–7). J. H. Overton in *D.N.B.*, xxxi (1892), p. 304 f., with further reff.

KNOX, EDMUND ARBUTHNOTT (1847–1937), Bp. of Manchester. Educated at Corpus Christi College, Oxford, he held a Fellowship at Merton from 1869 to 1884, and after various parochial charges became (suffragan) Bp. of Coventry in 1894. From 1903 to 1921 he was Bp. of Manchester. He was one of the most prominent *Evangelicals of his generation, a great preacher (esp. famed were his missions on the Blackpool sands), and a strong advocate of Church schools. His writings include *Sacrifice or Sacrament* (1914), a defence of the Protestant Doctrine of the Lord's Supper, and *On What Authority?* (1922), attacking the liberal school of Biblical Critics. After his retirement he continued to take an active part in ecclesiastical affairs and vigorously opposed the Revised Prayer Book (rejected 1927 and 1928). He was also the author of an interesting study, *The Tractarian Movement, 1833–1845* (1933).

His son, RONALD ARBUTHNOTT KNOX (1888–1957), was received into the RC Church in 1917. His writings include *Some Loose Stones* (1913; a reply to *Foundations*), *A Spiritual Aeneid* (1918; autobiographical), and *Essays in Satire* (1928; collected papers). He also published a new translation of the Bible, based on the Vulgate text (NT, 1945; OT, 2 vols., 1949).

E. A. Knox, *Reminiscences of an Octogenarian, 1847–1934* (1935). L. W. Grensted in *D.N.B., 1931–1940*, p. 516 f.

KNOX, JOHN (*c.* 1513–72), Scottish Reformer. He was born at Haddington, educated at Glasgow and possibly St. Andrews, received minor orders, perhaps even the priesthood, and set up as a notary in his native town. Having given up his profession he became a private tutor *c.* 1544, and soon afterwards, under the influence of the reforming G. *Wishart, embraced the principles of the Reformation. In 1547 he became preacher at St. Andrews; at the capture of the castle by the French galleys he was taken prisoner and sent to France, but released in 1549, when he came to England. In 1551 he was made chaplain to *Edward VI and as such assisted in the final stages of the revision of the Second Prayer Book; he appears to have been chiefly responsible for the *Black Rubric. In 1553 he went as a preacher to Bucks, but on *Mary's accession fled to the Continent. He met J. *Calvin at Geneva, and in 1554 was for a short time pastor of the English refugees at Frankfurt, but was expelled after a dispute over matters of Sunday worship. In 1555 he returned to Scotland. Here his preaching and writing met with great success, but the continuing persecution of Protestants led him to accept a call to the English church at Geneva in 1556, where he published several tracts concerning the situation in Scotland, among them *The First Blast of the Trumpet against the Monstrous Regiment of Women* (1558), a violent diatribe against Mary of Guise, asserting that government by a woman is contrary to the law of nature and to Divine ordinance. This pamphlet, which appeared shortly before the accession of *Elizabeth, earned him the hostility of the English Queen, who refused to let him pass through England on his way back to Scotland in 1559.

Becoming leader of the Reforming party, he devoted himself to preaching and to procuring money and troops from England. After the death of Mary of Guise (1560), he drew up the *Scottish Confession (q.v.), and brought into being a commission which abolished the authority of the Pope, 'idolatry', and the Mass, the celebration and attendance of which was forbidden under pain of death. The First Book of *Discipline (q.v.) was largely his work. About the same time his only theological work, the Treatise on Predestination (1560), appeared at Geneva; it is an exposition of rigid *Predestinationism. After *Mary Stuart's return to Scotland (1561), Knox came into repeated conflicts with the Queen over the question of having Mass celebrated for her as well as over the worldliness of her court, on both of which subjects he preached violent sermons. The 'Book of *Common Order' (1556–64), the Scottish service book, was largely his work. In 1567 he preached daily against the Queen, and after her abdication preached the sermon at the coronation of *James and became closely connected with the regent, Lord Murray. After the murder of Murray in 1570, Knox's political power diminished, and it was only after his death that his cause finally triumphed. Narrow, bigoted, and outspoken, Knox easily made enemies; yet fearless and straightforward, he wielded an enormous influence. His principal work is the History of the Reformation of Religion within the Realm of Scotland. An early (unfinished) edition was issued by T. Vautrollier in 1587 and immediately seized and suppressed. The first complete edition appeared in 1644.

His works were edited by D. Laing (6 vols., 1846–64). Lives by T. McCrie (1811) and P. Hume Brown (1895). Modern ed. of his History of the Reformation in Scotland by W. C. Dickinson (London, 2 vols., 1949). A. Loy, John Knox and the Reformation (1905); E. Muir, John Knox (1929); Lord Eustace Percy, John Knox (n.d. [c. 1940]). Æ. Mackay in D.N.B., xxxi (1892), pp. 308–28.

KOCH, JOHANN. See Cocceius, Johannes.

KOHLER, CHRISTIAN and HIERONYMUS. See Brügglers.

KONKORDIENFORMEL. See Concord, Formula of.

KORAN (Arab., Qu'ran, 'recitation'). The sacred Book of Mohammedanism, largely compiled from Jewish and Christian sources, esp. the *Haggadah and the NT apocrypha. It consists of 114 chapters (sūras) supposed to have been communicated to Mohammed through the mediation of an angel and now arranged in order of length, beginning with the longest. The Koran teaches God's oneness, righteousness, and omnipotence, condemns idolatry and gives instruction on Islamic

morality and institutions. The book contains vivid and sensuous descriptions of heaven and hell and warnings of the approach of the last day and judgement of the world. It was probably written in Mohammed's lifetime, but the present text and arrangement date from the recension of the Caliph Uthman (643–56).

The first Eng. tr. direct from the Arabic was that of George Sale (London, 1734). Later trr. by J. M. Rodwell (London, 1861; reissued in Everyman's Library, 1909) and E. H. Palmer (Sacred Books of the East, vi and ix, 2 vols., Oxford, 1880). For scholarly purposes the best is that of Richard Bell (2 vols., Edinburgh, 1937–9). R. Bell, Introduction to the Qur'ân (1953). H. Hirschfeld, Beiträge zur Erklärung des Korân (1886). J. Horovitz, Koranische Untersuchungen (Studien zur Geschichte und Kultur des islamischen Orients, iv; 1926). E. M. Wherry, A Comprehensive Commentary on the Qurán (Trübner's Oriental Series, 4 vols., 1882–6). T. Noeldeke, Geschichte des Quoráns (1860; ed. 2 by F. Schwally, &c., 3 vols., 1909–38).

KORIDETHI CODEX, The. A MS. of the Gospels in rough *uncials (known to textual critics as Θ), and dating probably from the 9th cent. It is now at Tiflis, but it formerly belonged to the monastery of Koridethi, near the Caspian Sea. Its text of Mk., which differs widely from that of this Gospel in the other uncial MSS. and is akin to that of two groups of *minuscules (those designated by the numbers 1–118–131–209 and 13–69–124–346), was named by B. H. *Streeter, in the belief that it represented the text of the Gospel current at *Caesarea in Palestine in the 3rd cent., the '*Caesarean Text' (q.v.).

The MS., found in the church of St. Kerykos and Julitta at Koridethi, was first publd. (in facsimiles) by the Imperial Moscow Archaeological Society at Moscow, 1907; later ed. by G. Beermann–C. R. Gregory, Leipzig, 1913, with a study of the history of the MS. based on its many marginal notes in Gk. and Gruse. K. *Lake–R. P. Blake, 'The Text of the Gospels and the Koridethi Codex' in H.T.R., xvi (1923), pp. 267–86; B. H. Streeter, The Four Gospels (1924), esp. ch. iv. B. Botte, O.S.B., in Dict. Bibl., Suppl. v ('1950'), cols. 192–6.

KORNTHAL, NW of Stuttgart, *Pietist settlement. It was founded in 1819 as a centre of Pietist life in opposition to the increasing rationalism of the contemporary *Lutheran state-Church. Its members accepted the *Augsburg Confession with a few alterations, but their teaching was coloured by belief in the speedy coming of the *Millennium. Inspired by *Moravian influence, their daily life was strictly regulated down to matters of food and clothing, and they were exempted by the civil power from taking the oath and from military service. Their principal achievements were educational institutions for boys, girls, and neglected children, and missionary work on the lines of the '*Innere Mission'. In 1955, the membership of the community was c. 1250.

J. Hesse, Korntal einst und jetzt (Stuttgart, 1910). H. Schmidt–C. Kolb in P.R.E. (ed. 3), xi (1902), pp. 38–47, s.v., with reff. to earlier litt. See also bibl. to Pietism.

KRAUS, FRANZ XAVER (1840–1901), ecclesiastical historian. After studying at several German universities, he was ordained priest in 1864, and in 1872 became professor-extraordinary of the history of Christian art at the university of Strassburg. In 1878 he was appointed professor of Church history at Freiburg, where he filled a number of important civil offices and came into repute as a scholar of great learning. His political theories, which upheld the rights of the state against interference from the Church, led the government to support his candidature for the episcopate, but opposition from the ecclesiastical authorities prevented the appointment being made. Some of his books also gave offence to his religious superiors through their political teaching. He remained in communion with the RC Church, however, till his death. The most considerable of his numerous works was his *Geschichte der christlichen Kunst* (2 vols., 1896–1900; the last section of the work was completed posthumously in 1908 by Joseph Sauer). His other writings include *Roma sotterranea* (1873), *Realencyklopædie der christlichen Altertümer* (2 vols., 1882–6), *Die christlichen Inschriften der Rheinlande* (2 vols., 1890–4), a book on *Dante (1897), of whom Kraus was a deep student, and an essay on Cavour (posthumous, 1902). In 1904 a 'Krausgesellschaft' was formed to further his supposed ecclesiastico-political doctrines.

Two collections of *Essays* were publishe (Berlin, 1896–1901). Lives by K. Braig (Freiburg i.Br., 1902) and E. Hauviller (Colmar, 1904). Artt. by J. Sauer in *Lexikon für Theologie und Kirche*, vi (1934), cols. 233 f. and by H. *Leclercq, O.S.B., in *D.A.C.L.*, viii (pt. 1; 1928), cols. 854–73 (with full bibl. of Kraus's works; but scornful of him as a scholar). Notice by K. Künstle in *R.H.E.*, iii (1902), pp. 431–41.

KRÜDENER, BARBARA JULIANA FREIFRAU VON (1764–1824), *Pietist. After deserting her Russian husband and forming a liaison with a young French officer at Paris—during which period of her life she wrote a novel, *Valérie* (2 vols., 1803)—she was suddenly converted during a sojourn at Riga in the summer of 1804. She became an ardent devotee of the German Pietistic Movement, and in 1815 exercised great influence on the Czar Alexander I, proclaiming that *Napoleon was the Apollyon of Rev. 9. 11 and thus winning the Czar's support for the idea of the *Holy Alliance.

C. Eynard, *Vie de Madame de Krudener* (2 vols., 1849). P. L. Jacob (pseudonym of P. Lacroix), *Madame de Krudener*. Ses lettres et ses ouvrages inédits (1880). C. Ford, *The Life and Letters of Madame de Krudener* (1893). H. von Redern, *Zwei Welten.* Das Leben von Julian von Krüdener (1927); A. Hermant, *Madame de Krüdener, l'amie de Tsar Alexandre* (1934). E. J. Knapton, *The Lady of the Holy Alliance.* The Life of Julie de Krüdener (New York, 1939), with full bibl.

KUENEN, ABRAHAM (1828–91), Dutch OT scholar. Appointed professor at Leyden in 1855, he became one of the most prominent advocates of liberal theological thought in Holland. At first he was a follower of H. G. A. *Ewald, under whose influence he wrote his *Historisch-Kritisch Onderzoek* (3 vols., 1861–5; 2nd edition, 1885–93; trans. in part into English by J. W. *Colenso [1865] by whom Kuenen was much influenced); but he later came to hold the current opinion that the priestly code (P) was the latest element in the Pentateuch.

His later views were embodied in his book *De Godsdienst van Israel* (1869–70; Eng. trans., *The Religion of Israel*, 1874–5) and in the *De profeten en de profetee onder Israel* (1875; Eng. trans., *The Prophets and Prophecy in Israel*, 1877). He delivered the *Hibbert Lectures in 1882 on *National Religion and Universal Religion*.

K. Budde (ed. and tr.), *Gesammelte Abhandlungen zur biblischen Wissenschaft* (1894; with full bibl. of Kuenen's writings, compiled by W. C. van Manen). P. H. Wicksteed in *J.Q.R.*, iv (1892), pp. 571–605. A. Kamphausen in *P.R.E.* (ed. 3), xi (1902), pp. 162–70, s.v., with bibl.

KULTURKAMPF. The repressive political movement in Germany in the 1870s against the RC Church. It was mainly inspired by Bismarck, who feared that the influence of Catholicism would endanger the unity of the German Empire.

In its earlier years the conflict was very bitter, provoked chiefly by the anti-Catholic legislation. In 1871 Bismarck suppressed the Catholic department of the Prussian Ministry of Public Worship, and in 1872 appointed P. L. A. *Falk Minister of Public Worship, under whose aegis the *Jesuits were expelled, education was brought under the control of the state, and the famous '*May laws' (1873) were passed. The opposition to this legislation was very strong, and several Catholic bishops, including Cardinal M. H. von Ledóchowski of Gnesen-Posen and K. Martin of Paderborn, were imprisoned. The German embassy at the Vatican was also recalled, and owing to the condemnatory tenor of the encyclical 'Quod nunquam' (7 Feb. 1875) the RC Church was deprived of all financial assistance from the state. Further, the religious orders were ordered to leave the country.

Bismarck, however, had misunderstood the extent and strength of the opposition, and gradually became convinced that a concordat with the Vatican was the better solution. He also hoped by a change of tactics to gain the aid of the Catholic Church in the fight against Social Democracy. Hence at the end of the '70s the previous policy was reversed and peace was made with the new Pope, *Leo XIII. By 1887 most of the anti-Catholic laws, with the exception of that expelling the Jesuits, had been nullified. The Kulturkampf had the undesigned effect of creating in some measure a religious revival inside Germany. It certainly strengthened the hold of Roman Catholicism on the German people in the latter years of the 19th cent.

The literature, of various categories, is immense. The standard work is J. B. Kissling, *Geschichte des Kulturkampfs im Deutschen Reich* (3 vols., 1911–16). G. Goyau, *Bismarck et l'Eglise.* Le Culturkampf, 1870–1878 (4 vols., 1911–13). From a Protestant standpoint, E. Foerster, *Adalbert Falk* (1927); id., 'Liberalismus und Kulturkampf' in *Z.K.G.*, xlvii (1928), pp. 543–59. E. Foerster in *R.G.G.* (ed. 2), iii (1929), cols. 1352–9, s.v., and A. Schnütgen in *L.Th.K.*, vi (1934), cols. 294–7, s.v.

KUYPER, ABRAHAM (1837–1920), Dutch *Calvinist theologian and politician. Educated at *Leyden, he was pastor of the Dutch

Reformed Church at Beesd from 1863. In 1879 he set out the ideas of the anti-revolutionary party, whose leader he had become, in his book *Ons Program*. He later became a professor of the Calvinistic university which he had founded at Amsterdam, and in 1886 he established the strictly Calvinistic Reformed Church Community. In 1898 he went to America to give the Stone Lectures, published in England in 1932 under the title *Calvinism*. Regarding Calvinism as a way of life satisfying all the needs of modern man, he presented it both as a religious belief opposed to *Liberal Protestantism and in its bearings on contemporary social and political life. He endeavoured to apply these principles in the responsible position he held as Minister of the Interior from 1901 to 1905. In 1903 he was opposed by the Dutch Socialists for using parliamentary legislation to crush a railway strike, and during the South African War he urged Holland to mediate between the Boers and the British. In his later years he led the anti-revolutionary party in the Upper Chamber.

Kuyper was the author of some 150 writings, the more considerable of which are listed by M. C. van M. Broekman in *R.G.G.* (ed. 2), iii (1929), col. 1443, s.v. Lives by P. A. Diepenhorst (Volksuniversiteits Bibliotheek, No. 50; Haarlem, 1931) and P. Kasteel ([Louvain], 1938), with detailed bibl. B. D. Eerdmans, *De Theologie van Dr. Abraham Kuyper* (1909); S. J. Ridderbos, *De Theologische Cultuurbeschouwing van Abraham Kuyper* (1947).

KYRIALE. The Latin liturgical book containing the musical chant for the *Ordinary of the *Mass. It is so named from its opening part, the *Kyrie, which is the first item in the Mass which is sung. As a separate book it seems to owe its existence to printers who sought to satisfy the convenience of choirs wanting the fixed parts of the Mass in a different book from that containing the variable parts such as the *Gradual. *Pius X issued an authoritative revision known as the *Kyriale Vaticanum*, with the music for 18 different plain-chant Masses. The name 'Graduale' is occasionally used to cover the Kyriale as well as the Gradual in its proper sense.

KYRIE ELEISON (Gk. Κύριε ἐλέησον, 'Lord, have mercy'). A brief prayer for Divine mercy which from an early date has been used in the liturgical worship of the Church. The use of the words in non-Christian cultus is also attested (cf. *Epictetus, *Diss.* ii. 7). In Christian usage they appear to have originated in Syria in the 4th cent. and to have reached the S. of France by the 6th. In the E. it is a response made by the deacon to prayers and litanies offered by the celebrant, whereas in the W. it is used as an independent formulary, e.g. in the Roman Mass the celebrant repeats with the server three times the words 'Kyrie eleison', three times 'Christe eleison', and three times again 'Kyrie eleison' (the three groups being conceived as directed to the Father, Son, and Holy Ghost respectively). In the Eucharistic rite of the BCP of 1549, the Kyrie survived in an English translation ('Lord, have mercy upon us'), but in 1552 the Ten Commandments were substituted and have been prescribed here ever since, though reversion to the use of the Kyries has been widely adopted unofficially. Their use in an English form at *Mattins, *Evensong, and the *Litany has been continuous since 1549.

E. *Bishop, *Liturgica Historica* (1918), ch. vi, pp. 116–36. B. *Capelle, 'Le Kyrie de la messe et le pape Gélase' in *R. Bén.*, xlvi (1934), pp. 126–44. C. Callewaert, 'Les Étapes de l'histoire du kyrie' in *R.H.E.*, xxxviii (1942), pp. 20–45. Jungmann, i (ed. 1949), pp. 412–29.

LABADISTS. A Protestant sect named after Jean de Labadie (1610–74), its founder, who had been a *Jesuit from 1625 to 1639, had joined the Reformed Church at Montauban in 1650, and after preaching at various places on the Continent, esp. in Holland, settled temporarily in 1670 at Herford in Westphalia with about 55 followers. On being forced to leave Herford in 1672, he moved first to Bremen and later to Altona, where he died. His followers held extreme *Pietist views. They believed that the Bible could be understood only by the immediate inspiration of the Holy Spirit, rarely celebrated the Eucharist, and held that marriage with an unregenerate person was not binding; and they were organized on a communistic basis. They survived de Labadie's death by some 50 years.

H. van Berkum, *De Labadie en de Labadisten* (2 pts., Sneek, 1851). A. *Ritschl, *Geschichte des Pietismus*, i (1880), pp. 194–268. K. D. Schmidt, 'Labadie und Spener. Literarkritischer Vergleich der "Pia Desideria" Speners mit Labadies Schriften "La Réformation de l'Église par le pastorat" und "L'Exercise prophétique" ' in *Z.K.G.*, xlvi (1927), pp. 566–83. On Labadie, see also L. Marchal in *D.T.C.*, viii (pt. 2; 1925), cols. 2383-5, s.v.

LABARUM. The military standard adopted by the Emp. *Constantine after his vision. In form it seems to have been an adaptation of the Roman cavalry standard, with the pagan emblems replaced by a Christian monogram, viz. the two Greek letters Χ and Ρ (the first two of ΧΡΙΣΤΟΣ, 'Christ') intersecting. It was at first the banner of only the W. Empire, but after Licinius's defeat at the battle of Chrysopolis (324) was adopted by the E. as well. The name is probably an incorrect form of *laureum*, a Latin word used by the Roman soldiery for a standard (*vexillum*).

For the extensive modern literature, with a discussion, see N. H. Baynes, *Constantine the Great and the Christian Church* (1929), pp. 60-5.

LABBE, PHILIPPE (1607–67), Church historian. In 1623 he entered the *Jesuit Order. A prolific writer and compiler, he published over 80 works, of which the most important was his collection of the Church Councils under the title *Sacrosancta Concilia ad Regiam Editionem exacta*. Before his death, vols. 1–8 and 12–15 had been printed, but they were not published until 1671–3. The outstanding volumes were completed by his fellow-Jesuit, G. Cossart. This collection, the most extensive of its age, was later incorporated into the *Concilia* of J. D. *Mansi.

H. *Quentin, O.S.B., *J. D. Mansi et les grandes collections conciliaires* (1900), pp. 29–33 and 182 f. Sommervogel, iv (1893), cols., 1295-1328.

LABERTHONNIÈRE, LUCIEN (1860–1932), RC *Modernist theologian. In 1886 he was ordained priest as an *Oratorian. He taught at the Collège at Juilly (1887) and at the École Massillon at Paris (1896), and in 1900 became rector of the Collège at Juilly. From 1905 to 1913 he edited the *Annales de philosophie chrétienne*. He joined with M. *Blondel in a vigorous attack on C. Maurras and the *Action Française. In theology he upheld against Scholastic dogmatism a pragmatic view of religious truth, which he expounded in *Essais de philosophie religieuse* (1903) and his *Réalisme chrétien et l'idéalisme grec* (1904). Both works were put on the *Index in 1906, and in 1913 he was prohibited from all further publication. His writings exercised considerable influence on G. *Tyrrell.

His posthumous writings incl. *Études sur Descartes* (2 vols., 1935; put on Index, 2 Dec. 1936) and *Études de philosophie cartésienne et premiers écrits philosophiques* (1937; put on Index, 26 Mar. 1941). Study by E. Castelli (Milan, 1927), with bibl. T. Friedel, *Pages choisies de Lucien Laberthonnière* (1931). C. Testore in *E.C.*, vii (1951), cols. 775-7, s.v., with bibl.

LABRE, St. BENEDICT JOSEPH (1748–1783), pilgrim and mendicant saint. Born at Amettes near Boulogne, he showed pious dispositions from childhood and was strongly drawn to one of the religious orders. After vain attempts to be received by the *Trappists, *Carthusians, and *Cistercians, he was rejected by all as unsuitable to community life and found his vocation in a life of solitude and pilgrimage. He visited most of the leading sanctuaries of Europe (some many times) among them *Loreto, *Assisi, Naples, and Bari in Italy, *Einsiedeln in Switzerland, Paray-le-Monial in *France, and *Compostela in *Spain. Every where he begged his food, giving away the alms offered him and spending much of his time in churches. For his last few years he lived at Rome, except for an annual pilgrimage to Loreto. Here he became a familiar figure in the city, known from his devotion to the *Quarant' Ore* as the 'Saint of the *Forty Hours'. Exhausted by his austerities, he died outside his favourite church, Sta. Maria dei Monti, in Holy Week 1783. A local cultus soon developed; and he was pronounced Venerable by *Pius IX in 1859 and canonized by *Leo XIII in 1881. Feast day, 16 Apr.

G. L. Marconi (his confessor), *Ragguaglio della vita del servo di Dio, Benedetto Labre Francese* (1783; abridged Eng. version, 1786). F. Gaguère, *Le Saint Pauvre de Jésus-Christ, Benoît-Joseph Labre* (Avignon, 1936). Other modern lives by A. M. Coltrato (Rome, 1807; Eng. tr., 1850), F. J. M. Desnoyers (2 vols., Lille, 1857), L. Abineau (Paris, 1873), N. Heim (Kempten, 1903), C. L. White (London [1906]), and J. Mantenay ('Les Saints', 1908); also centenary studies by J. Riverain (Paris, 1948) and A. de La Gorce (Paris, 1948).

LACEY, THOMAS ALEXANDER (1853–1931), Anglican divine. Educated at Balliol College, Oxford, he was ordained in 1876 and after holding various scholastic and parochial appointments became Canon of *Worcester in 1918. Brilliant, versatile, and learned, and imbued with a sympathetic understanding of modern problems, he became known as an effective, and at times distinctly original, apologist for the *Anglo-Catholic presentation of the Christian faith. Throughout his life he was devoted to the cause of reunion. He took an active part at Rome in 1894 when a Papal commission was examining the validity of *Anglican ordinations, supplying, in conjunction with his friend Fr. F. W. Puller, S.S.J.E., much of the material from the Anglican side. His most important writings were *De Hierarchia Anglicana Dissertatio Apologetica* (1895; in conjunction with E. Denny); *A Roman Diary and other Documents relating to the Papal Enquiry into English Ordinations, MDCCCXCVI* (1910); *Marriage in Church and State* (1912; revised by R. C. Mortimer, 1947); *Nature, Miracle, and Sin* (on St. *Augustine; 1916); and *Unity and Schism* (1917). He was joint editor of the *English Hymnal* and translated for it many Latin hymns.

Wayfarer's Essays [collection of Lacey's papers ed., with short memoir (pp. v–xi) and list of his books (p. xiii f.), by Arnold Wilson] (1934). C. B. Mortlock in *D.N.B., 1931–1940*, p. 519 f., s.v.

LACHMANN, KARL (1793–1851), philologist and textual critic. From 1825 to 1827 he was extraordinary, and from 1827 till his death ordinary, professor of classical and German philology at Berlin. Lachmann was the first scholar to produce an edition of the Greek NT text in which the *textus receptus was abandoned in favour of that of the oldest Greek MSS. He aimed at presenting the text, not as it was originally composed by the inspired writers of the NT, but as it circulated in E. Christendom at the end of the 4th cent.; and though his *modus operandi*, partly conditioned by this limited aim, suffered from being over-mechanical, he gave the impulse to the later work of C. *Tischendorf and B. F. *Westcott–F. J. A. *Hort. He issued two editions of the Greek text, the smaller in 1831 and a fuller edition in 2 vols. in 1842–50. Lachmann was also the first scholar to put the *Marcan hypothesis on a sound footing, which he did in an article in the *Studien und Kritiken* for 1835. His great services to the study of classical antiquity do not call for consideration here.

K. Lachmann, 'Rechenschaft über seine Ausgabe des Neuen Testaments' in *Theologische Studien und Kritiken*, iii (1830), pp. 817–45; id., 'De Ordine Narrationum in Evangeliis Synopticis', ib., viii (1835), pp. 570–90. Letters to M. Haupt ed. by J. Vahlen (1892); letters to Lachmann (1814–50), ed. A. Leitzmann in *Abh.* (Berl.), 1915, No. 1 ; A. Leitzmann, *Briefe Karl Lachmanns* (ib., 1942, No. 8). Life by M. Hertz (Berlin, 1851). A. Rüegg, *Die neutestamentliche Textkritik seit Lachmann* (Zürich, 1892). E. Michels in *Dict. Bibl.*, iv (1908), cols. 27–9, s.v.

LACORDAIRE, HENRI DOMINIQUE (1802–61), French *Dominican preacher. He was born at Recey-sur-Ource, and, after losing his faith at an early age, became a disciple of J.-J. *Rousseau. He studied law at Dijon and *Paris and speedily made a reputation as an

orator at the Paris bar. In 1824 he was converted, entered the seminary at Issy, and was ordained priest at *St.-Sulpice in 1827. In the next year he was appointed chaplain to the Convent of the *Visitation in Paris. In 1830 he became a contributor to F. de *Lamennais' periodical *L'Avenir*, but severed connexion with it on its condemnation by *Gregory XVI in 1832. He replied to Lamennais's *Paroles d'un croyant* (1834) with *Considérations sur le Système de M. de Lamennais* (1834). In 1835–1836 he gave his first two series of famous Conferences at *Notre-Dame which drew a vast concourse, largely from the *intelligentsia*. His political liberalism and *Ultramontane theology aroused distrust, however, and at the height of his influence he retired to Rome. Here, in 1839, after making a retreat under the direction of Dom P. *Guéranger, then engaged in restoring the *Benedictine Order in France, he entered the Dominican Order with the intention of re-establishing this Order also in France. After his return to Paris in 1841 he resumed his Conferences, and preached also in other cities (Bordeaux, Nancy, etc.). In 1843 he established at Nancy the first Dominican house in France since the suppression of the Order in 1790; and in 1850 he was appointed provincial of the newly founded French Dominican province. In his later years he devoted himself chiefly to organizing the new province and in fostering the liberal movement in politics. In 1860 he was elected a member of the Academy. If hardly a profound theologian or philosopher, he was fully conversant with the religious needs of his time. His most influential work was his *Conférences de Notre-Dame de Paris* (4 vols., 1844–51), directed esp. to unbelievers. His other writings include *Vie de S. Dominique* (1841), and *Vie de Ste Marie Madeleine* (1860), both with many inspired passages but of no value as histories, and *Le Testament* (1863; a posthumous autobiographical work ed. by C. R. F. *Montalembert).

Editions of his works include those in 6 vols., Paris, 1857–61, 9 vols., ib., 1872, and 4 vols., ib., 1912. Among the numerous collections of his correspondence, listed in detail by H. D. Noble, O.P., cited *infra*, that of most general interest is his *Lettres à des jeunes gens* ed. H. Perreyre (Paris, [1862]; Eng. tr., 1902). G. Ledos, *Morceaux choisis et bibliographie de Lacordaire* [1923], for full list of his works. The numerous studies include the primary lives by C. R. F. Montalambert (Paris, 1862; Eng. tr., 1863), B. Chocarne, O.P. (Paris, 1866; Eng. tr., Dublin [1868]), and [J. T.] Foisset (2 vols., Paris, 1870). Further studies by A. Ricard, *L'École menaisienne*, iii (1882); [O.B.P.G. de Cléron], Comte de Haussonville ('Les Grands Écrivains français', 1895; Eng. tr., 1913); G. Ledos ('Les Grands Hommes de l'Église au XIXᵉ siècle', i, Paris, 1902); J. Bézy (Paris, 1910). J. Favre, *Lacordaire orateur. Sa formation et la chronologie de ses œuvres* (1906). [E.] G. Ledos–L. Pauthe, *Lacordaire. Son œuvre, sa survie et son actualité* (1911). In English there are popular lives by Mrs. H. L. S. Lear (London, 1883) and M. V. Woodgate (ib., 1939). P. Spencer, *Politics of Belief in Nineteenth Century France* (1954), pp. 17–115. H. D. Noble in *D.T.C.*, viii (pt. 2; 1925), cols. 2394–424, s.v., with detailed bibl.

LACTANTIUS (*c.*240–*c.* 320), Christian apologist. A pupil of *Arnobius, Lucius Caecilius Firmianus Lactantius was appointed by *Diocletian a teacher of rhetoric at Nicomedia; but on his conversion to Christianity (*c.* 300), he was deprived of his post. Later the Emp. *Constantine made him tutor to his son Crispus. His important surviving works are 'Divinae Institutiones' (304–11), a treatise which sought to commend the truth of Christianity to men of letters and thereby for the first time to set out in Latin a systematic account of the Christian attitude to life; 'De Opificio Dei', an attempt to prove the existence of God from the marvels of the human body; 'De Ira Dei', which deals with God's punishment of human crime; and 'De Mortibus Persecutorum', which describes with a wealth of lurid detail the horrible deaths of the persecutors of the Church. The authenticity of the last-mentioned treatise, formerly widely contested, notably by S. Brandt (1891) and more recently by J. W. P. Borleffs (1930), is now very generally admitted (O. Seeck, 1895; R. Pichon, 1901; A. Maddalena, 1934–5). In his style Lactantius was deliberately Ciceronian, in his theology almost deistic.

*Jerome, *De Viris Illustribus*, 80. Lactantius's writings have been constantly reissued since the 15th cent. *Editio princeps* of 'Divinae Institutiones', 'De Ira Dei' and 'De Opificio Dei' publd. at Subiaco, 1465 (the earliest dated printed book issued in Italy). The text of J. B. le Brun–N. Lenglet du Fresnoy (2 vols., Paris, 1748) is repr. in J. P. Migne, *PL*, vi and vii. Crit. text by S. Brandt and G. Laubmann (C.S.E.L., xix and xxvii; 1890–97). Eng. tr. by W. Fletcher (A.N.C.L., xxi and xxii; 1871). Eng. tr. of Lactantius' own Epitome of the 'Divine Institutes', with text and commentary, by E. H. Blakeney (S.P.C.K., 1950). R. Pichon, *Lactance*: études sur le mouvement philosophique et religieux sous le règne de Constantin (1901); P. Monceaux, *Histoire littéraire de l'Afrique chrétienne*, iii (1905), pp. 287–359. J. W. P. Borleffs, 'An scripsit Lactantius Libellum qui est *De Mortibus Persecutorum*' in *Mnemosune*. Bibliotheca Philogica Batava, lviii (1930), pp. 223–92. A. Maddalena, 'Per la definizione storica del "De Mortibus Persecutorum"' in *Atti del Reale Istituto Veneto di Scienze, Lettere ed Arti*, xciv (1934–5), pp. 557–88. M. Pellegrino, *Studi sull' antica apologetica* (1947), pp. 151–207 (argues Lactantius dependent on *Minucius Felix). On Lactantius's language, see Christine Mohrmann in *Vigiliae Christianae*, ii (1948), pp. 165–76. H. *Lietzmann in *P.W.*, xii (pt. 1; 1924), cols. 351–6, s.v. 'Lactantius (1)'. É. Amann in *D.T.C.*, viii (pt. 2; 1925), cols. 2425–44, s.v. 'Lactance'; H. *Leclercq, O.S.B., in *D.A.C.L.*, viii (pt. 1; 1928), cols. 1018–41, s.v. 'Lactance'; M. Pellegrino in *E.C.*, vii (1951), cols. 951–4, s.v. 'Lattanzio'.

LACTICINIA. Milk and foods such as cheese or butter, made from milk, which (as well as meat and eggs) were often forbidden on fast days in the early Church, and this is still the rule for many fast days in the E. Church.

LADISLAUS, St. (1040–95), King of Hungary. He was elected by the nobles in 1077; but the first years of his reign were troubled by the conspiracies of Solomon, son of a former king and rival claimant to the throne, who was finally defeated in 1089. In the *Investiture struggle between the German Emperor and the Pope he took the side of *Gregory VII and Victor III, and he laboured incessantly to spread the Christian faith among his subjects, esp. in Croatia and Dalmatia which he annexed in 1091. He built many churches, obtained the canonization of *Stephen I and his son, Emeric, and promulgated a series of laws on religious and civil matters at the Synod of Szabolcs (1092).

When *Urban II, however, claimed suzerainty over part of his country, he refused to recognize the Pope as his temporal lord though acknowledging him as his spiritual father. Venerated as a saint by his people, he was canonized in 1192. Feast day, 27 June.

Vita from 15th cent. MS. ed. by L. S. Endlicher, *Rerum Hungaricarum Monumenta Arpadiana* (St. Gall, 1849), pp. 235–44, with his laws, ib., pp. 325–48. R. F. Kaindal, 'Studien zu den ungarischen Geschichtsquellen' in *Archiv für österreichische Geschichte*, xci (1902), Section XV, 'Die Legenden des Heil. Ladislaus', pp. 46–53.

LADY, Our. A common designation in use among Catholics for the BVM. It is derived from the Latin 'Domina nostra'. Since 1559 the feast of the *Annunciation has been described in the Table of Lessons in the BCP as the 'Annunciation of our Lady'. In earlier times, the Annunciation (25 Mar.) was known as 'Our Lady in Lent' or 'in March'; the *Assumption (15 Aug.) as 'Our Lady in Harvest'; and the *Conception (8 Dec.) as 'Our Lady in December'.

LADY CHAPEL. A chapel dedicated to the BVM ('Our Lady') when it forms part of a larger church. From the 13th cent. onwards the practice of constructing such chapels, often as later additions and to the east of the High Altar, became common in England, e.g. Henry VII's Chapel at *Westminster Abbey.

LADY DAY. The feast of the *Annunciation of the BVM, 25 Mar. The name was used in earlier times of any feast of our Lady. In the Middle Ages and later 25 Mar. was reckoned the first day of the civil year. It is still a quarter day and Old Lady Day (6 April) still starts the fiscal year in Great Britain, e.g. for income tax purposes.

LAETARE SUNDAY. The Fourth Sunday in *Lent ('Mid-Lent Sunday', *Mi-carême*), so named from the opening words of the *Introit at the Mass (Is. 66. 10: 'Rejoice ye with Jerusalem'). In W. Christendom certain relaxations of the penitential observances of Lent are allowed, e.g. the wearing of rose-pink instead of purple vestments. The Sunday is also known as *Mothering Sunday and *Refreshment Sunday.

LAETENTUR COELI (Lat., 'Let the heavens rejoice'). Two important theological documents, so named from their opening words. (They are otherwise quite unrelated.) (1) The Greek Formulary of Union, sent on 23 Apr. 433 by *Cyril, Patr. of *Alexandria, to *John, Bp. of Antioch, embodying the terms of reunion agreed upon by both parties, after John had previously given qualified support to the teaching of Cyril's adversary, *Nestorius. Inasmuch as the document was formally approved by the Council of *Chalcedon (451), it possesses *oecumenical authority. It expounds, in Alexandrian terms, the orthodox doctrine of the Person of Christ, insisting on the *theotokos and both the unity of person and the distinction of the natures.

(2) The bull issued by Pope *Eugenius IV on 6 July 1439 decreeing the union settled at the Council of *Florence between the Orthodox E. Church and the W. It laid down that the Orthodox should accept, *inter alia*, the doctrine of the *Double Procession of the Holy Ghost and the primacy of the see of Rome. It had been signed by Latins and Greeks alike on the previous day. See also *Florence, Council of*.

(1) The formulary (Gk. opening, εὐφραινέσθωσαν οἱ οὐρανοί) is *Ep.* xxxix of the correspondence of Cyril of Alexandria (J. P. Migne, *PG*, lxxvii, 173–82). It has often been repr. in collections of 'Oecumenical Documents', e.g. T. H. Bindley, *Oecumenical Documents of the Faith* (ed. 4 by F. W. Green, 1950), pp. 138–48. The only critical text is in E. *Schwartz, *A.C.O.*, I., i. 4, pp. 15–20.
(2) Text in G. Hoffmann, S.J. (ed.), *Concilium Florentinum.* Documenta et Scriptores, Series A. Epistolae Pontificiae ad Conciiium Florentinum Spectantes, pars ii (Rome, 1944), pp. 68–79. Lat. text of the principal clauses repr. in Denz.–Bann. (ed. 1952), p. 252 f. (Nos. 691–4). See also bibl. to *Florence, Council of.*

LAGARDE, PAUL ANTON DE (1827–91), Protestant theologian and critic. In 1854 he exchanged his earlier name of Bötticher for de Lagarde. From 1854 to 1866 he was a schoolmaster at Berlin, and from 1869 till his death Prof. at Göttingen. His strong opposition to all forms of liberalism and economic materialism, his hatred of the Jews, and his intensely national feeling anticipated many subsequent developments in German thought. On the other hand he was a keen upholder of the rights of individual personality and deprecated any attempt to set up the state as an absolute norm. Possessed of untiring industry and an extraordinary range of knowledge, he produced several erudite editions of classical and patristic works. Among those of importance to the ecclesiastical historian are *Didascalia Apostolorum Syriace* (1854), *Onomastica Sacra* (1870), *Psalterium iuxta Hebraeos Hieronymi* (1874), *Aegyptiaca* (1883), *Septuaginta Studien* (1891; 1892), as well as an edition of part of the *Lucianic Recension of the *Septuagint (1883).

Anna de Lagarde (widow), *Paul de Lagarde.* Erinnerungen aus seiner Leben zusammengestellt (Göttingen, 1894). Other studies by L. Schemann (Leipzig, 1919), A. Rahlfs (Mitteilungen des Septuginta-Unternehmens der Wissenschaften zu Göttingen, iv, Hft. 1; 1928), and L. Schmid (Tübinger Studien zur systematischen Theologie, Hft. iv; Stuttgart, 1935). H. H. Schaeder, 'Paul de Lagarde als Orientforscher' in *Orientalistische Literarzeitung*, xlv (1942), cols. 1–13 (hostile). E. Littmann in *R.G.G.* (ed. 2), iii (1929), col. 1452 f.; F. X. Schühlein in *L.Th.K.*, vi (1934), col. 334 f., s.v.

LAGRANGE, MARIE JOSEPH (1855–1938), Biblical scholar. He entered the *Dominican Order in 1879. In 1890 he founded at *Jerusalem the 'École Pratique d'Études Bibliques', and in 1892 the *Revue Biblique [Internationale]. He gave his warm support to *Leo XIII's efforts to encourage the critical study of the Bible in the RC Church, and in 1902 was appointed a member of the *Biblical Commission. In matters of

OT criticism, which was the chief field of his earlier labours, perhaps his position approached as nearly to that of the *Higher Critics as was compatible with Catholic orthodoxy. His sympathies with the critical position became manifest in a memorandum which he presented in 1897 to the International Congress of Catholics at Fribourg (Switzerland) and later published in the *Revue Biblique* (Jan. 1898). His monumental commentaries on the four Gospels (*Marc*, 1911; *Luc*, 1920; *Matthieu*, 1923; *Jean*, 1925) at once established themselves as standard works.

L. H. Vincent, O.P., 'Le Père Lagrange' in *R. Bib.*, xlvii (1938), pp. 321–54. Id. (ed.), *Mémorial Lagrange* (Paris, 1940), with an 'Essai d'une bibliographie sommaire du Père Lagrange' by id., pp. 1–11. *L'Œuvre exégétique et historique du R.P. Lagrange*, with pref. by A. Liénart (Cahiers de la Nouvelle Journée, xxviii [1935]). F. M. Braun, *L'Œuvre du Père Lagrange* (1943).

LAINEZ, JAMES. See *Laynez, James.*

LAITY (from Gk. λαός, people). Members of the Christian Churches who do not belong to the clergy. The distinction between the two is most marked in the RC and the Greek Churches, less so in the C of E, and least in the Free Churches, whilst sects like the *Quakers admit no distinctions at all. The laity owe allegiance to the clergy in spiritual matters and have the right to turn to them for guidance and help. In most Churches they are also bound to contribute to the support of their ministers. In the RC Church laymen have no jurisdiction in ecclesiastical matters, though, in the course of history, secular authorities have from time to time usurped this power.

LAKE, KIRSOPP (1872–1946), Biblical and patristic scholar. Educated at Lincoln College, Oxford, he was ordained in 1895, and after holding two curacies in England, was professor of NT exegesis at *Leyden from 1904 to 1914. Later he held professorships at Harvard university, U.S.A. Esp. in his earlier years he was a provocative NT critic. In his *Historical Evidence for the Resurrection of Jesus Christ* (1907) he challenged the sufficiency of the evidence for the empty tomb, and in his *Earlier Epistles of St. Paul* (1911) maintained that the course of primitive Christianity was profoundly affected by the influence of the mystery religions. These books were followed by *The Beginnings of Christianity: The Acts of the Apostles* (5 vols., 1920–33), a co-operative work in the editing of which he was associated with F. J. Foakes Jackson. Throughout his life he was a devoted student of the palaeography of Greek MSS. *The Early Days of Monasticism on Mount *Athos* (1909) was the fruit of an early visit to Greece for the study of MSS., and from 1934 onwards he edited with his wife *Monumenta Palaeographica Vetera, First Series*, a fine set of facsimiles of 'Dated Greek Minuscule Manuscripts to the Year 1200'. From 1934 until his death he and his wife also edited the series *Studies and Documents*, with contributions by R. P. Blake, C. Bonner, R. P. Casey, C. H. Kraeling and others.

R. P. Casev–S. Lake–A. K. Lake (edd.), *Quantulacumque*. Studies presented to Kirsopp Lake by Pupils, Colleagues and Friends [1937], with biogr. note by Gerard Kirsopp Lake (son), p. vii f.

LAMB. The use of a lamb as a svmbol of Christ is based on such passages as Jn. 1. 29, Rev. 5. 12. Occasionally in early times a lamb with or near a cross was used to represent the sacrifice of Christ, e.g. in a 3rd cent. inscription in the *Catacomb of San Callisto. Common types of symbolism represent the lamb as standing on Mt. *Sion (cf. Rev. 14. 1), from which flow the four rivers of Paradise, or as carrying a crook and milk-pail (cf. Rev. 7. 17). Other passages in the NT (e.g. Jn. 10. 14) suggest the representation of the Christian believers as sheep, and where this symbolism is used the Good Shepherd carries His lambs or, alternatively, stands among them. See also *Paschal Lamb*.

J. A. Martigny, *Étude archéologique sur l'Agneau et le Bon-Pasteur* [1860]. F. Meinecke, *Das Symbol des apokalyptischen Christuslammes als Triumphbekenntnis der Reichskirche* (Diss. Strassburg, Frankturt a.M., 1908). F. Gerke, 'Der Ursprung der Lämmerallegorien in der altchristlichen Plastik' in *Z.N.T.W.*, xxxiii (1934), pp. 160–96. A. de Waal in F. X. Kraus (ed.), *Real-Encyclopädie der christlichen Alterthümer*, ii (1886), cols. 264–7, s.v. 'Lamm'; H. *Leclercq, O.S.B., in *D.A.C.L.*, i (pt. 1, 1907), cols. 877–905, s.v. 'Agneau'; A. Romeo–A. Ferrua, S.J., in *E.C.*, i (1948), cols. 459–64, s.v. 'Agnello', with further bibl.

LAMBERT, St. (*c.* 635–*c.* 700), also 'Landebertus', martyr. He was Bp. of Maestricht from *c.* 670 till his death, though from *c.* 675 to 682 he was, for political causes, exiled from his see at the monastery of Stavelot. In his later life he worked zealously as a missionary in what is now Brabant. It seems indisputable that he suffered a violent death, but the circumstances are differently recorded. Acc. to some authorities it occurred in a blood feud, while there is another story (insufficiently attested) that it was the result of his outspoken reproof of Pepin of Heristal, Mayor of the Palace, for adultery. He was succeeded by St. *Hubert, who transferred the see to Liége. Feast day, 17 Sept.; of the 'Translation' (of Lambert's remains to Liége *c.* 715), 31 May.

Life (*c.* 730 A.D.) by Godescalcus, deacon of Liége, and three other medieval lives, pr. in *AA.SS.*. Sept. V (1755), pp. 574–617; J. Demarteau, *Vie la plus ancienne de S. Lambert* (Liége, 1890), incl. text of first, pp. 39–64; crit. ed. of the four lives by B. Krusch in *M.G.H.*, Scriptores Rerum Merovingicarum, vi (1913), pp. 299–429; H. Moretus in *Anal. Boll.*, xxxiii (1914), pp. 247–9. G. Kurth, *Études franques*, ii (1919), No. xviii, 'Le *Vita Sancti Lamberti* et M. Krusch', pp. 319–47.

LAMBERT OF HERSFELD (*c.* 1024–post 1077), medieval annalist. He entered the *Benedictine Order in 1058. Of his writings, much the most important is his *Annals*, covering the history of the world to 1077. For the period to 1040 he copies earlier writers; from 1040 to 1068 he is fuller, and contributes original matter from his own knowledge; while

from 1068 to 1077 he is very full indeed, and a valuable source, though at times inaccurate and frequently biased.

The best ed. of his *Opera* by O. Holder-Egger in *Scriptores Rerum Germanicarum* (Hanover and Leipzig, 1894). Id. 'Studien zu Lambert von Hersfeld' in *N.A.*, xix (1894), pp. 141–213, 369–430, and 507–74. Full bibl. in W. Wattenbach–R. Holtzmann, *Deutschlands Geschichtsquellen im Mittelalter*. Deutsche Kaiserzeit, Band i, Heft 3 (1948), pp. 456–73.

LAMBERT, FRANCIS (1486–1530), Reformer of Hesse. Of noble birth, he entered the *Franciscan Order at *Avignon in 1501 and soon acquired fame as a powerful preacher. On a journey in 1522 he established relations with H. *Zwingli and the other Swiss Reformers, left his order, and travelled under a false name to *Wittenberg (1523) where M. *Luther obtained a pension for him from the Elector, and where he married. In 1524 he went to Metz, but not being well received he moved to Strassburg, where he lived in poverty, writing several treatises and commentaries on the OT prophets. In 1526 he was called to Hesse by the Landgraf *Philip. Here he took a prominent part in the Homberg Synod, was charged with the preparation of the new Protestant 'Church Order' for Hesse, and in 1527 became professor of exegesis at the newly founded Marburg university. His increasing inclination towards the Zwinglian view of the Eucharist lost him more and more the sympathies of his Lutheran fellow-Reformers. He was the author of commentaries on the Song of Songs (1524) and the Apocalypse (1528), and of several polemical writings including an attack on D. *Erasmus (1525).

Studies by L. Ruffet (Paris, 1873) and R. L. Winters (Philadelphia, 1938). W. Maurer, 'Franz Lambert von Avignon und das Verfassungsideal der *Reformatio Ecclesiarum Hassiae* von 1526' in *Z.K.G.*, xlviii (1929), pp. 208–60. J. A. Wagenmann–C. Mirbt in *P.R.E.* (ed. 3), xi (1902), pp. 220–3: W. Koehler in *R.G.G.* (ed. 2), iii (1929), col. 1462 f. Schottenloher, i (1933), p. 426 (Nos. 10,223–33).

LAMBETH. For over 600 years Lambeth has been the London residence of the Abps. of *Canterbury. Abp. *Baldwin (1185–90) acquired from the possessions of the see of *Rochester the manor of Lambeth and the manor-house, which was called 'Lambeth House' until about 1658, when, owing to the decay of the palace at Canterbury, the title of palace was transferred to Lambeth. The chapel, built in 1245 by Abp. Boniface in the early English style, is the oldest part of the building. The South Gateway with its two towers was erected by Cardinal John Morton (Abp., 1486–1501). The Water Tower, known in recent times as the 'Lollards' Tower' (on the supposition that *Lollards were imprisoned in it), is a massive square keep, erected by Abp. H. *Chichele in 1434. Abp. M. *Parker was consecrated at Lambeth in 1559 and is the only archbishop buried in the palace. The Great Hall, built by Abp. W. *Juxon in 1663, contains part of the Library (founded by Abp. R. *Bancroft in 1610), which has some 2,000 MSS., including the Registers of the archbishops from 1279 to

1744. The part of the palace actually occupied by recent archbishops dates from 1829–34. It was seriously damaged in 1940 in an air raid; restorations were completed c. 1956.

E. W. Brayley–W. Herbert, *Lambeth Palace* (1806); J. C. Browne, *Lambeth Palace and its Associations* (1882). Catalogues of the MSS. in the archiepiscopal library by H. J. Todd (London, 1812) and M. R. James–C. Jenkins (5 parts, Cambridge, 1930–2); of some early pr. books by S. R. *Maitland (London, 1843); index of Eng. pr. books up to 1550 by id. (ib., 1845).

LAMBETH ARTICLES.

Nine theological propositions compiled at Lambeth in 1595 by a committee that met under Abp. J. *Whitgift. Drawn up in the interests of a pronounced *Calvinism, they maintained the *Supralapsarian doctrine that God from all eternity had predestined by an unchangeable decree a definite number of persons to salvation, and that the elect were saved not because God had foreseen their merits but through His good pleasure alone. Although they represented a considerable body of Puritan opinion at the time, they were never formally authorized and strongly disapproved of by *Elizabeth I.

The text is in E. *Cardwell, *Documentary Annals of the C of E* (1839), ii, 30–4.

LAMBETH CONFERENCES.

Assemblies of the bishops of the whole Anglican Communion held about once every ten years at *Lambeth Palace under the presidency of the Abp. of *Canterbury. The demand for these Conferences came from the synod of the Anglican Church in *Canada, held in 1865, with a view to counteracting the unsettling effects of the case of Bp. J. *Colenso and of the publication of *Essays and Reviews. After the original idea of a Council authorized to define doctrine had been abandoned owing to strenuous opposition, the first Conference, with 76 bishops, was held in 1867 by Abp. C. T. *Longley and issued an 'Address to the Faithful'. The following Conferences have been attended by increasing numbers of bishops. That of 1908, with 242 bishops, was preceded by a large Pan-Anglican Congress, composed of some 7,000 clerical and lay delegates. That of 1920, with 252 bishops, was esp. important for its 'Appeal to all Christian People' for Reunion, which was sent to the heads of the Christian communities throughout the world. The resolutions of these Conferences, though not binding, are significant expressions of the opinions of the Anglican episcopate.

The *Reports* are published immediately after each Conference by the S.P.C.K.

LAMBETH DEGREES.

The degrees in Divinity, Arts, Law, Medicine, and Music, which the Abp. of Canterbury confers from time to time in virtue of 25 Hen. VIII, c. 21, which committed to his immediate possession many rights previously enjoyed by the Primate as '*Legatus natus' of the Pope. Their recipients usually wear the academic dress of the university to which the Archbishop belongs.

LAMBETH OPINIONS, The.

The first 'Lambeth Opinion' was delivered on 31 July 1899, by the Abps. of Canterbury (F. *Temple) and York (W. D. Maclagan), at *Lambeth Palace, in response to questions raised by some of the English bishops. It stated that the liturgical use of *incense and the carrying of lights in procession were 'neither enjoined nor permitted' in the C of E. In the matter of incense, however, the archbishops added that there was nothing to prevent its use for sweetening the atmosphere of a church and that it was not in itself an undesirable accompaniment to Divine service. A year later (1 May 1900) the two archbishops issued further opinions (on this occasion that of Canterbury was separate from that of York, though they agreed in substance) denying the legality of *Reservation of the Sacrament. These opinions are sometimes described as the 'Lambeth Judgements', but less correctly as the two archbishops did not sit as an ecclesiastical court.

The official texts were publd. by Macmillan under the titles *The Archbishops on the Lawfulness of the Liturgical Use of Incense and the Carrying of Lights in Procession* (1899); *The Archbishop of Canterbury on Reservation of the Sacrament* (1900, signed F. Cantuar); *Archbishop of York on Reservation of Sacrament* (1900).

LAMBETH QUADRILATERAL (1888).

A slightly revised edition of the four Articles agreed upon at the General Convention of the (Anglican) Protestant Episcopal Church held at Chicago in 1886. In this revised form the Articles were approved by the Lambeth Conference of 1888 as stating from the Anglican standpoint the essentials for a reunited Christian Church. The text of the Articles is as follows:

'A. The Holy Scriptures of the Old and New Testaments, as "containing all things necessary to salvation", and as being the rule and ultimate standard of faith.

'B. The Apostles' Creed, as the Baptismal Symbol; and the Nicene Creed, as the sufficient statement of the Christian Faith.

'C. The two Sacraments ordained by Christ Himself—Baptism and the Supper of the Lord—ministered with unfailing use of Christ's Words of Institution, and of the elements ordained by Him.

'D. The Historic Episcopate, locally adapted in the methods of its administration to the varying needs of the nations and peoples called of God into the Unity of His Church'.

LAMENNAIS, FÉLICITÉ ROBERT DE

(1782–1854), French religious and political author. He was a member of a well-to-do family of St.-Malo. While still a child he read widely, esp. J.-J. *Rousseau, whose influence contributed to his loss of religious faith at an early age. But under the guidance of his brother Jean Marie (c. 1780–1860), who had become a priest, he was converted and made his first communion at the age of 22. He was appointed professor of mathematics at the episcopal college of St.-Malo in 1804; later he retired to the country house of his grandfather, La Chênaie, which became the centre of his circle of like-minded friends. In 1808 he published his *Réflexions sur l'état de l'Église*, written in collaboration with his brother. The book aimed at showing the futility of trust in individual reason, which led to rationalism, atheism, and intellectual anarchy, and called for systematic clerical organization. This demand brought him into conflict with Napoleon's policy and caused him to flee to London during the Hundred Days in 1815. After his return, under the influence of his brother and against his own inclinations, he became a priest in 1816.

In 1818 he published the first volume of his chief work, the *Essai sur l'indifférence en matière de religion*. Lamennais here developed the principle of authority, which he equated with the 'raison générale' or 'sens commun'. He maintained that the individual is dependent on the community for his knowledge of the truth; to isolate oneself is to doubt; and toleration is an evil. His eloquence gained him fervent disciples, esp. among the *Ultramontanists and Royalists, and effected many conversions; but its ideas were suspect esp. to the *Sulpicians and *Jesuits and opposed by the *Gallicans. The later volumes of the work (1820, 1823) were still more opposed to the traditional doctrines. They equated Catholic Christianity with the religion of all mankind, denied the supernatural, and proclaimed subjects freed from loyalty to their temporal sovereigns when rulers refused to conform their conduct to Christian ideals. In order to counteract the evils of the time he desired a theocracy, with the Pope as supreme leader of kings and peoples. The work received the approval of Pope *Leo XII, who possibly intended to make him a cardinal. In *Des progrès de la Révolution* (1829) he prophesied an impending revolution and demanded the separation both of the Church and of the entire educational system from the state, as well as the freedom of the press. In order to carry out these ideas he founded a religious congregation, the short-lived Congrégation de St. Pierre (1828), an Agence Générale pour la Défense de la Liberté Religieuse (1830), and the paper *L'Avenir* (1830-1), and won the co-operation of a number of brilliant younger religious thinkers, among them C. de *Montalembert and H. *Lacordaire. He asserted that the essence of Christianity was freedom, but freedom understood in a political sense and guaranteed by the Papacy. In the last number of *L'Avenir* he launched the 'Acte d'Union', in which he called for the union of all freedom-loving men. Convinced that the Pope would put himself at the head of this crusade for freedom, he went to Rome in 1832 to defend his ideas before *Gregory XVI, which were, however, condemned in the encyclical '*Mirari vos' of 15 Aug. 1832. Lamennais, though submitting externally, retired to La Chênaie where he wrote his reply, the famous *Paroles d'un croyant* (1834). Though admitting the authority of the Church in questions of faith, he denied it in the sphere of politics. In

apocalyptic language he presented a picture of the ideal community in which production and consumption were to be harmoniously balanced. The book caused a tremendous excitement throughout Europe; it was condemned in the encyclical '*Singulari nos' (q.v.) of 25 June 1834. Lamennais's friends submitted, but he himself left the Church.

From this time Lamennais's interests became more and more exclusively political. He gave his views on the social needs of the times in *Le Livre du Peuple* (1837; Eng. tr., 1838) and *L'Esclavage moderne* (1839; Eng. tr., 1840). The *Discussions critiques* (1841) marked the final end of his Christian faith. He denied the whole supernatural order together with the doctrinal beliefs of Catholicism and tended more and more to a vague pantheism, expressed also in *Esquisse d'une philosophie* (4 vols., 1841-6). In 1846 he published a translation of the Gospels with commentary, *Les Évangiles*, which was placed on the Index. In the Revolution of 1848 he became a member of Parliament, but the political reaction of 1852 completely disillusioned him. All efforts, even those of the new Pope *Pius IX, to reconcile him to the Church were in vain. An extraordinarily gifted writer, Lamennais was one of the greatest inspirers of the new social and political ideas of the 19th and 20th cents. as well as a forerunner of *Modernism.

Œuvres complètes (12 vols. bound in 6, Paris, 1836-7); *Œuvres posthumes*, ed. E. D. Forgues (2 vols., ib., 1856-9); *Œuvres inédites*, ed. A. Blaize (2 vols., ib., 1866). Among the various later collections of his letters the most substantial are *Correspondance inédite entre Lamennais et le Baron de Vitrolles . . . 1819-1853*, ed. E. Forgues (Paris, 1886), and *Lettres inédites de Lamennais à Montalembert*, ed. id. (ib., 1898). There is a considerable literature about the various aspects of Lamennais's life, thought, and influence, esp. in French, but no fully documented biography. The two best general studies are C. Boutard, *Lamennais. Sa vie et ses doctrines* (3 vols., 1905-13); F. Duine, *La Mennais. Sa vie, ses idées, ses ouvrages, d'après les sources imprimées et les documents inédits* (1922). Further items listed in F. Duine, *Essai de bibliographie de Félicité Robert de La Mennais* (1923). In English the main items include W. Gibson, *The Abbé de Lamennais and the Liberal Catholic Movement in France* (1896), J. H. Laski, *Authority in the Modern State* (New Haven, 1919), pp. 189-280 (ch. 3); E. L. Woodward, *Three Studies in European Conservatism* (1929), pp. 248-75 ('Gregory XVI and Lamennais'); A. R. Vidler, *Prophecy and Papacy. A Study of Lamennais, the Church, and the Revolution* (Birkbeck Lectures, 1952-1953; 1954), with reff. A. Fonck in *D.T.C.*, viii (pt. 2; 1925), cols. 2473-2526, s.v., with detailed bibl. Ippolito Vittorio in *E.C.*, vi (1951), cols. 849-58, s.v. with more recent items.

LAMENTABILI. The decree of the *Holy Office issued on 3 July 1907 in which 65 propositions believed to be derived from the teaching of the contemporary *Modernists on the subjects of the Church, of Revelation, of Christ, and of the Sacraments, were condemned. It was shortly afterwards followed by the encyclical 'Pascendi' (8 Sept. 1907).

Text in *A.S.S.*, xl (1907), pp. 470-8; operative clauses in Denz.-Bann. (ed. 16-17, 1928), Nos. 2001-65. F. Heiner, *Der Neue Syllabus Pius X* (1907). J. Rivière, *Le Modernisme dans l'Église* (1929), pp. 331-48.

LAMENTATIONS OF JEREMIAH. In the Hebrew Bible, as one of the five *Megilloth, this Book is placed in the third main division of the OT, called the 'Writings' (*Kethubim). In the English Bible, as in the *Septuagint and *Vulgate, it follows Jer. The Book consists of five chapters, all dealing with the desolation of Judah after the destruction of Jerusalem in 586 B.C. They show considerable, if somewhat laboured, literary art, extensive use being made of acrostic arrangement and the greater part of the Book being composed in a peculiar metre used in Hebrew dirges (the 'Qinah' metre). Traditionally the Book has been ascribed to the prophet *Jeremiah, but the tradition may not be more than a misinterpretation of 2 Chr. 35. 25, and the tendency of modern Biblical scholarship is against this attribution and to put it later (e.g. 5th cent. B.C.). In Jewish worship it was appointed to be read at the annual commemoration of the destruction of Jerusalem, and in the Christian Church it has been commonly interpreted in reference to Christ's Passion.

Commentaries by A. W. Streane (Camb. Bib., AV; 1881), A. S. *Peake (Cent. Bib., with pt. 2 of Jer. [c. 1912], pp. 289–350), M. Löhr (H.K.A.T., Abt. 3, Bd. ii, Thiel 2; 1894), K. *Budde (K.A.T., Abt. xvii, on Song of Sol., Ruth, Lam,. Eccles., and Est., 1898, pp. 70–105), W. Rudolph (K.A.T., xvi, 3; 1939), M. Haller (H.A.T., Reihe 1, Bd. xviii, on Ruth, Song of Sol., Eccles., Lam., and Esther, 1940, pp. 91–113). H. Jahnow, Das hebräische Leichenlied im Rahmen der Völkerdichtung (Beihefte zur Z.A.T.W., xxxvi; 1923). H. Wiesmann, S.J., 'Zur Charakteristik der Klagelieder des Jeremias' in Bonner Zeitschrift für Theologie und Seelsorge, v (1928), pp. 97–118; id., 'Die literarische Art der Klagelieder des Jeremias' in T.Q., cx (1929), pp. 381–428; id., 'Der geschichtliche Hintergrund des Büchleins der Klagelieder' in Biblische Zeitschrift, xxiii (1935–6), pp. 20–43; id., 'Der Verfasser des Büchleins der Klagelieder ein Augenzeuge der behandelten Ereignisse' in Biblica, xvii (1936), pp. 71–84. N. K. Gottwald, Studies in the Book of Lamentations (Studies in Biblical Theology, 14, 1954).

LAMMAS DAY. The term 'Lammas', denoting 1 August, is found in the work of King *Alfred and was common throughout the Middle Ages; though now archaic, it occurs in the BCP. Etymologically it derives from 'loaf' and 'mass', and in the early English Church it was customary to consecrate bread made from the first-ripe corn at Mass on this day, prob. in thanksgiving for the harvest. A later explanation (dating from the 15th cent.) suggested that it derived from 'lamb' and 'Mass', denoting the time at which a feudal tribute of lambs was paid (at *York). The day, to which some chronological significance always seems to have attached, is observed as a quarter-day in Scotland. It is also the feast of St. *Peter ad Vincula ('St. Peter's Chains'; cf. Acts 12. 3, 6 f.).

LAMPS. These were probably used in Christian worship from the first, as it usually took place at night, but of ceremonial use there is no early evidence. From the time of *Constantine, however, lamps were burnt in large candelabra during the Liturgy, and for a long time this custom continued in E. worship. In the W. it became customary to burn lights—lamps or candles indifferently—before shrines and relics, at least as early as the 9th cent. The burning of lamps before the altar, and, in particular, of a perpetual white lamp before the reserved Sacrament, came into general use in the W. in the 13th cent., but the latter was not held to be obligatory before the 16th cent. See also Candle.

Rohault, vi (1888), pp. 1–58. C. Babington, 'Lamps' in D.C.A., ii (1880), pp. 919–23; H. *Leclercq, O.S.B., in D.A.C.L., viii (pt. 2; 1928), cols. 1086–221, s.v. 'Lampes', with full reff.

LANCE (liturgical). In the Byzantine rites, a small knife (Gk. λόγχη), shaped like a lance, with a handle ending in a small cross, which is used to cut the Eucharistic bread at the *Proskomide.

LANCE, The Holy. A relic, believed to be the lance mentioned in Jn. 19. 34 as having been used by a Roman soldier for piercing the Lord's dead body. The first record of its existence occurs in the 6th cent., when the pilgrim, St. Antoninus of Piacenza, states that he had seen it at *Jerusalem in the basilica of Mount Sion. Its presence there is also attested by *Cassiodorus and St. *Gregory of Tours. At the capture of Jerusalem by the Persians in 615, it fell into the hands of the pagans, together with the other relics of the Passion; but its point, which had been broken off, was saved and given to Nicetas, who brought it to *Constantinople, where it was kept in *Santa Sophia, set in an icon. In 1241 it was given to St. *Louis and preserved in the *Sainte-Chapelle together with the *Crown of Thorns. It disappeared during the French Revolution. The other part of the Lance was stated to have been seen in Jerusalem by the Frankish pilgrim, Arculf (c. 670), but after that nothing is heard of it until it reappears in Constantinople before the 10th cent. In 1492 it fell into the hands of the Turks, who sent it to the Pope as a present. Since then it has been kept at Rome under the dome of St. Peter, but its authenticity has always been doubted.

There have been several other relics, claimed to be the Holy Lance. One of them was found by the Crusaders at Antioch in 1098 in consequence of a vision. Another was kept among the Imperial insignia of the Holy Roman Empire, having been taken to Prague by Charles IV in 1350, to Nuremberg in 1424, and finally to Vienna in 1800. A special Feast of the Holy Lance was kept in Germany, on the Friday after the Octave of Easter. A Feast of the Holy Lance and Nails is celebrated by the *Passionists on the Friday of the first week in Lent.

F. de Mély, Exuviae Sacrae Constantinopolitanae (Paris, 1904), pp. 22–163. C. Rohault de Fleury, Mémoire sur les instruments de la Passion de N.-S. J.-C. (1870), pp. 272–5. H. Thurston, S.J., in C.E., viii (1910), p. 773 f., s.v.

LANFRANC (c. 1005–89), Abp. of *Canterbury. He was born at Pavia, and after having been a lawyer, left his country c. 1035, probably for political reasons, and went to France. He opened a school at Avranches in Normandy in 1039 and c. 1042 entered the newly founded abbey of *Bec. In 1045 he was made prior and head of the monastery school, which, under him, became one of the most celebrated of the time, numbering among its pupils *Ivo of Chartres, *Anselm of Canterbury, and the future Pope *Alexander II. His theological importance rests chiefly on his participation in the Eucharistic controversy with *Berengar of Tours. In 1049 he met Leo IX at the Council of *Reims, and the Pope took him with him to the Councils of *Rome and of *Vercelli (1050), where Berengar was condemned. In 1053 he was ordered to leave the country by Duke William, because he disapproved of his marriage with Matilda, which was within the forbidden degrees. But before the decree of exile was put into effect he brought about a reconciliation and successfully pleaded William's cause with the Pope. Accordingly c. 1063 the Duke made him Abbot of St. Stephen's, Caen, the erection of which had been imposed as part of the penance for the unlawful marriage. Henceforth he was William's most trusted counsellor, and probably a warm supporter of the Conquest of 1066.

After the deposition of Abp. *Stigand on grounds of simony and uncanonical election (1070), Lanfranc was consecrated Abp. of Canterbury. Soon, however, he had difficulties with the newly appointed Abp. Thomas of York, who refused to recognize the supremacy of Canterbury and claimed the dioceses of *Worcester, *Lichfield, and *Dorchester for his obedience. The disputes were carried before the Pope in 1071, but Alexander II referred them to a council of bishops and abbots which met at *Winchester in 1072 under the presidency of the Papal legate Hubert. It resulted in a decisive victory for Lanfranc. The documents by which he supported his claims have now been proved to be falsifications, though H. Böhmer's assertion that the archbishop himself perpetrated the fraud has been generally rejected as incompatible with all the other evidence concerning Lanfranc's character. Lanfranc's policy, carried out in full harmony with the King and supported by the monastic element, was to replace Saxon bishops and abbots by Normans, a measure which brought the English Church into closer contact with the Continent and with the reform movement of *Gregory VII, but lost it some of its indigenous customs. The reforms, however, which were discussed esp. at the important Council of London in 1075, did not carry out the Gregorian programme in its entirety, but were partly adapted to the special English circumstances. Thus, though celibacy was enforced for canons as well as for deacons to be ordained in the future, married priests were allowed to retain their wives. On the other hand the prohibition of lay investiture remained altogether a dead letter, owing to the Conqueror's system of feudal tenure of landed Church property, for which he exacted homage. On account of these modifications of the Papal policy Lanfranc's relations with Gregory VII were generally cool, and in the schism of the Anti-Pope Clement III (1080) he maintained a strict neutrality. His last years were darkened

by the death of William the Conqueror (1087) and the difficulties caused by his lawless successor, William Rufus. Lanfranc was succeeded at Canterbury by St. Anselm.

Lanfranc's chief theological work is his treatise 'De Sacramento Corporis et Sanguinis Christi', written c. 1070 against Berengar. In it he attacked esp. Berengar's rationalistic tendencies which would see in the Eucharist a mere symbol. He maintained that the Sacred Species contain the invisible Body of Christ, which is identical with the Body born of the BVM, but is hidden under the different signs of Bread and Wine. Among his other writings are the 'Statuta sive Decreta pro Ordine S. Benedicti', an exposition of the Benedictine Rule containing valuable material on the Liturgy and on details of the monastic life, and 'Epistolae Decretales', important esp. for the history of canon law.

First collected ed. of his works by L. *d'Achéry, O.S.B. (fol., Paris, 1648); also ed. J. A. Giles (2 vols., Oxford, 1844; based on ed. d'Achéry), repr. in J. P. Migne, PL, cl. Crit. ed. of the 'Decreta Lanfranci Monachi Cantuariensibus transmissa',with Eng. tr., by [M.] D. Knowles, O.S.B. (Medieval Classics, London, 1951). Early life by Milo Crispin (precentor at Bec; d. 1149; of no great historical value) pr. among his works (ed. 1648, pp. 1–16; also in later edd.); it may be supplemented by the 'Vita Herluini' (first Abbot of Bec) by Gilbert Crispin, also pr. among Lanfranc's works (ed. 1648, appendix, pp. 32–40; also in later edd.). A. J. Macdonald, Lanfranc. A Study of his Life, Work, and Writing (1926). Earlier study by J. de Crozals (Paris, 1877). H. Boehmer, Die Fälschungen Erzbischof Lanfranks von Canterbury (Studien zur Geschichte der Theologie und der Kirche, viii, Hft. i; 1902), with text. J. A. *Robinson, 'Lanfranc's Monastic Constitutions' in J.T.S., x (1909), pp. 375–88. Z. N. Brooke, The English Church and the Papacy from the Conquest to the Reign of John (1931), pp. 57–83 and 117–31. W. Hunt in D.N.B., xxxii (1892), pp. 83–9; H. W. C. Davis in D.E.C.H., p. 310 f.; É. Amann–A. Gaudel in D.T.C., viii (pt. 2; 1925), cols. 2558–70, all s.v. See also bibl. to Berengar and Gregory VII.

LANG, COSMO GORDON (1864–1945), Abp. of *Canterbury. A Scotsman by birth and of *Presbyterian upbringing, he was educated at Glasgow University and at Balliol College, Oxford, and then studied for the Bar. In 1888 he was elected to a fellowship at All Souls College, Oxford. In 1890 he was ordained in the C of E, and after working as a curate of Leeds Parish Church from 1890 to 1893 under E. S. *Talbot, he returned to Oxford to become Dean of Divinity at Magdalen, and from 1894 to 1896 was vicar of St. Mary's, the university church. From 1896 to 1901 he was vicar of Portsea. In 1901 he became (suffragan) Bp. of Stepney and in 1908 Abp. of *York. He was translated to Canterbury in 1928 and resigned in 1942. In Dec. 1936 he played an important part in public affairs in connexion with the abdication of Edward VIII.

J. G. Lockhart, Cosmo Gordon Lang (1949). A. C. Don in D.N.B., 1941–1950 (1959), pp. 474–8.

LANGE, JOHANN PETER (1802–84), German Protestant theologian. After studying at Bonn, he published in 1836 a vigorous attack on D. F. *Strauss's Leben Jesu entitled Über den geschichtlichen Charakter der kanonischen Evangelien and thus became a recognized leader of the *Vermittlungstheologie. In 1841 he was appointed professor at Zürich and in

1854 at Bonn. His many books on Biblical and doctrinal subjects were written under the influence of F. D. E. *Schleiermacher. They included a *Leben Jesu* (3 vols., 1844–7; Eng. trans. 4 vols., 1872), a *Christliche Dogmatik* (3 vols., 1849–52), and several commentaries in a composite work on the Bible.

J. P. *Lange's Gedichte* (Essen, 1843). W. Krafft in *P.R.E.* (ed. 3), xi (1902), pp. 264–8.

LANGTON, STEPHEN (d. 1228), Abp. of *Canterbury. He was of English extraction, but migrated to *Paris as a student and became one of the principal theologians of the university. In 1206 *Innocent III, with whom he had established a close friendship while at *Paris, created him a cardinal, and in 1207 nominated and consecrated him to the see of Canterbury, but owing to *John's opposition, Langton could not land in England until 1213, and he resided in the interval at Pontigny. He showed marked sympathy with the barons, and it was probably he who suggested that they should take their stand on the charter of Henry I which served as the model for Magna Carta. On the Carta itself Langton's name heads the list of the counsellors by whose advice John professed to be acting. In his later life Langton warmly supported the regency in its struggles against baronial insubordination. He upheld the privileges of Canterbury, and established the claim of the Abp. of Canterbury to be the Pope's 'legatus natus'. At a synod at Oseney (1222) he promulgated, besides the decrees of the Fourth *Lateran Council (1215), special constitutions for the English Church. Little of his private life is known but he was 'perhaps the greatest of our medieval Archbishops' (H. W. C. Davis).

Commentary on the Sentences of *Peter Lombard (known also as Langton's 'Summa') ed., with full reff. to previous discussions on attribution to Langton, by A. M. Landgraf (B.G.P.M., xxxvii, Hft. 1; 1952). Episcopal Acta transcribed and ed. Kathleen Major (*Canterbury and York Society, l; 1950). No contemporary biography has survived, but there are many reff. to him in the correspondence of Innocent III. The best modern study is F. M. Powicke, *Stephen Langton* (Ford Lectures for 1927; 1928). Earlier lives by M. *Pattison (J. H. *Newman (ed.), *Lives of the English Saints*, 1845; ed. 2, vol. vi, 1901, pp. 239–380), C. E. Maurice (London, 1872) and J. R. Leeming (ib., 1915). T. F. Tout in *D.N.B.*, xxxii (1892), pp. 122–32; H. W. C. Davis in *D.E.C.H.*, p. 311 f.

LAODICEA. A Hellenistic city of the Roman province of Asia. It was the seat of an early Christian Church to which St. *Paul wrote an epistle (Col. 4. 16), perhaps the same as the extant Eph. The city was reproved at a somewhat later date by the writer of *Rev. (3. 14 ff.) for being 'neither cold nor hot'. It was materially very prosperous in Apostolic times, and a bishopric of some importance for several centuries. It is not to be confounded with the town of Laodicea on the Syrian coast, the home of *Apollinarius.

W. M. *Ramsay, *Cities and Bishoprics of Phrygia*, i (1895), pp. 32–83; id., *Letters to the Seven Churches* (1904), pp. 413–30.

LAODICEA, Canons of. A set of 60 4th-cent. canons which were embodied in the early collections of ecclesiastical law. They fall into two groups, acc. to their opening words (1–19: περὶ τοῦ and 20–59: ὅτι οὐ δεῖ). Among the subjects dealt with are the treatment of heretics (*Quartodecimans, *Novatianists, *Montanists etc.), liturgy, penance, Church order, and the observance of *Lent. Nothing definite is known of the 'Council of Laodicea', though a mention of the *Photinians in can. 7 points to a date not before *c.* 345 and prob. the Council took place at least 20 years later. Acc. to A. Boudinhon, the 'canons' are really subject-headings of canons issued by earlier 4th cent. councils, among them that of *Nicaea (325) and an otherwise unknown Council of Laodicea. The last canon (No. 60) contains a list of the Canonical Scriptural Books closely akin to that of *Apostolic Canons*, can. 85 (84), e.g. it omits the OT Apocrypha and Rev. Acc. to T. *Zahn and others (against C. J. *Hefele), this canon is prob. a later addition.

Hardouin, i (1715), cols. 777–92; Mansi, ii (1759), cols. 563–604. Canons also in Lauchert, pp. 72–9; crit. ed. of Lat. texts in *E.O.M.I.A.*, II, iii (1939), pp. 321–400. Hefele-Leclercq, i (2; 1907), pp. 989–1028. A. Boudinhon, 'Note sur le concile de Laodicée' in *Congrès scientifique international des Catholiques tenu à Paris, 1888* (1889), ii, pp. 420–447 (resumed in Hefele-Leclercq, loc. cit., pp. 992–4, note). On Canon lx, see B. F. *Westcott, *A General Survey of the History of the Canon of the New Testament* (1855), pp. 498–508; T. Zahn, *Geschichte des Neutestamentlichen Kanons*, ii (pt. 1; 1890), pp. 193–202. É. Amann in *D.T.C.*, viii (pt. 2; 1925), cols. 2611–15, s.v.

LAODICEANS, The Epistle to the. A Latin apocryphal Ep. of St. *Paul. The work, which is found in many 6–15th cent. Lat. MSS. of the NT and in early printed editions of the Bible, is an artless collection of St. Paul's own words (esp. from Phil.), which was doubtless produced to meet the demand suggested by Col. 4. 16. It appears to date from the 4th–5th cent. and was prob. originally issued in Greek. A. *Harnack sought to prove, without success, that it was a 2nd-cent. *Marcionite forgery. The first clear mention of it occurs in St. *Augustine, the earlier references to an 'Ep. to the Laodiceans' (*Muratorian Canon; *Jerome, *De vir. ill.* 5) prob. being to MSS. of St. Paul's (canonical) Ep. to the *Ephesians, which read 'Laodicea' for 'Ephesus' at 1. 1.

Crit. ed. of Lat. text, with discussion, in J. B. *Lightfoot, *St. Paul's Epistles to the Colossians and to Philemon* (ed. 1879), pp. 274–300 (actual text, pp. 287–9). Eng. tr. in M. R. James, *The Apocryphal New Testament* (1924), pp. 478–80. B. Carra de Vaux, 'L'Épître aux Laodicéens en arabe' in *R. Bibl.*, v (1896), pp. 221–6, with Arabic text, p. 223 f. A. von Harnack, 'Der Apokryphe Brief des Apostels Paulus an die Laodicener, eine marcionitische Fälschung aus die 2. Hälfte des 2. Jahrhunderts' in *Sb.* (Berl.), 1923, pp. 235–45. K. Pink, 'Die pseudopaulinischen Briefe II. Der Laodizenerbrief' in *Biblica*, vi (1925), pp. 179–92. G. Quispel, 'De Brief aan de Laodicensen een marcionitische Vervalsing' in *Nederlands Theologisch Tijdschrift*, v (1950–1), pp. 43–6. Bardenhewer, i (1913), pp. 598–600, with earlier bibl. É. Amann in *Dict. Bibl.*, Suppl. i (1928), col. 519 f., s.v. 'Apocryphes du Nouveau Testament, IV, 2'.

LAPCLOTH. See *Gremial*.

LAPIDE, CORNELIUS À. See *Cornelius à Lapide*.

LAPSI (Lat. 'the fallen'). Those who in varying degrees denied the Christian faith under persecution. At first apostasy was held to be an unforgivable sin, but, when the problem became serious in the Decian persecution of 250-1, the Church, guided largely by St. *Cyprian, decided to readmit such persons after penance and probation, a decision which led the *Novatianist rigorists to make open schism. The Councils of *Elvira (306), *Arles (314), *Ancyra (314), and *Nicaea (325) also legislated on the subject. See also *Traditors*.

LARDNER, NATHANIEL (1684-1768), Nonconformist apologist. He was a native of Hawkhurst in Kent, studied at Utrecht and *Leyden (1699-1703), and became an Independent minister in 1709. After being private chaplain and tutor from 1713 to 1721, he began to give lectures in 1723. These developed into his famous work on *The Credibility of the Gospel History* (14 vols., 1727-57), in which he set himself the task of reconciling the discrepancies in the Biblical narratives. Its valuable collection of materials on the date and authorship of the NT books, together with a large apparatus of footnotes, made the work a mine of information for scholars, for whom it was of greater service than the ordinary reader, for whom it was originally intended. Lardner's interpretation is based on patristic texts as well as on the commentaries of H. *Grotius. He also published sermons and a *Letter concerning the Logos* (1759), expounding his Christological doctrine.

Works [ed. B. Cole], 11 vols., London, 1788, with life by A. Kippis in vol. i, pp. i-cviii. A more important authority for his life is the anonymous *Memoirs of the Life and Writings of the late Reverend Nathaniel Lardner, . . .* with a Catalogue of his Works [by Joseph Jennings] publd. along with eight of Lardner's Sermons (London, 1769), memoir, pp. 1-134. A. Gordon in *D.N.B.*, xxxii (1892), pp. 147-51.

LA SALETTE. The village in the Alps near Grenoble, where on 19 Sept. 1846 a peasant boy and girl saw a vision of the BVM, who through them gave 'to all her people' a promise of the Divine Mercy after repentance. A special secret, communicated by the Virgin to each child, was afterwards sent to *Pius IX. At first doubts were thrown on the vision; but a commission appointed by the Bp. of Grenoble convinced itself of its reality, and miraculous cures were soon alleged to occur. Pilgrimages quickly followed, and in 1852 the first stone of the present church was laid on the scene of the vision. The church has been served from the first by religious known as the 'Missionaries of La Salette'. Many thousands annually make pilgrimages to the 'Virgin of the Alps'.

There is a vast literature, mostly of little critical value. More substantial works include I. Bertrand, *La Salette* (1888); id., *La Salette. Documents et bibliographie pour servir de pièces justificatives à l'ouvrage portant le même titre* (1889); J. Giray, *Les Miracles de La Salette* (2 vols., Grenoble, 1921). In English there is a popular account by J. S. Kennedy, *Light on the Mountains. The Story of La Salette* (Dublin, 1954). L. Clugnet in *C.E.*, ix (1910), p. 8 f., s.v., and P. Ramers in *L.Th.K.*, ix (1937), col. 118 f., s.v. 'Salette', both with bibl.

LAS CASAS, BARTOLOMÉ DE (1474-1566), Spanish missionary to the New World, sometimes known as 'The Apostle of the Indies'. Originally a lawyer, he accompanied the Spanish governor, Ovanda, to Hispaniola (Cuba) in 1502, and was ordained priest in 1510. From this time he devoted himself to the interests of the Indians by opposing, both in America and at the court of Spain, the cruel methods of exploitation of the Spanish settlers. These activities were strongly resented by his countrymen, and in 1515 he went back to Spain where he successfully presented the cause of the Indians to *Charles V. He returned to America with far-reaching powers; but though supported by his fellow-clergy and many settlers, his projects of colonization miscarried owing to a revolt of the Indians (1521). Two years later Las Casas joined the *Dominicans. He continued to labour for the Indians and put together many lurid reports on the abuses of the settlers, notably his famous *Destrucción des las Indias* (publd. 1552), in which he may sometimes have transgressed the limits of truth in his accusations against the Spanish colonists. In 1543 he became Bp. of Chiapa in Mexico, but he left his diocese in 1551 to retire to Valladolid, where he zealously continued to champion the rights of the Indians in numerous publications. He favoured the importation of negro slaves into America, a practice which had long existed and was not then considered contrary to Christian morals. He died at the age of 92, having pleaded the cause of the natives of Guatemala with *Philip II shortly before his death.

Colección de las obras del obispo de Chiapa, don Bartolomé de las Casas, ed. J. A. Llorente (2 vols., Paris, 1822). There is much biogr. material in A. Dávila Padilla, *Historia de la undación y discurso de la provincia de Santiago de México de la Orden de Predicadores* (Madrid, 1596). Lives by A. Helps (1868), C. Gutiérrez (1878), A. M. Fabie (Colección de documentos inéditos para la historia de España, lxx, 1879 [cf. also lxxi, 1879, pp. 459-64], Madrid, 1879), A. Weijers (Haarlem, 1890), E. Vacas Galindo (Madrid, 1908), F. A. MacNutt (New York, 1909), F. J. de Ortueta (Madrid, 1920), M. Brion (Paris, 1927), L. U. Hanke (The Hague, 1951), and H. Daniel-Rops (pseud., 1951). L. U. Hanke, *Bartolomé de Las Casas. Bookman, Scholar and Propagandist* (Rosenbach Lectures, Univ. of Pennsylvania; 1952). J. Sabin, *A List of the Printed Editions of the Works of Fray Bartolomé de Las Casas* (1870).

LASKI or À LASCO, JOHN (1499-1560), Protestant Reformer. He was a Polish nobleman by birth, who, after studying at *Bologna from 1514 to 1517, visited Basle in 1523, where he met D. *Erasmus and later lived in his house for nearly a year (1524-5). Soon he developed some sympathies with the Reformers, though they were not sufficiently pronounced to prevent his becoming Bp. of Vesprim in 1529 and Archdeacon of Warsaw in 1538. Later (1538), however, he declined the offer of a further bishopric and avowed his belief in the Reformed faith. He made his way to Emden in Holland where he was appointed Pastor in 1542. His sympathies were soon seen to be with the more extreme *Calvinist party among the Reformers. Having made friends with J. *Hooper, he came to England in 1548 at the invitation of T. *Cranmer to advise on the projected reforms and returned in 1550 to become superintendent of the Foreign Protestants in London. He is generally held to have influenced the BCP of 1552. After 1553 he lived for the rest of his life in several places on the Continent.

Works ed. by A. Kuyper (2 vols., Amsterdam, 1866). H. Dalton, *Johannes a Lasco* (Gotha, 1881; earlier part tr. into Eng. by M. J. Evans, 1886); G. Pascal, *Jean de Lasco, baron de Pologne, évêque catholique, réformateur protestant, 1496–1560*. Son temps, sa vie, ses œuvres (1894); *Lasciana* (1898). Further life by P. Bartels (Leben und ausgewählte Schriften der Väter und Begründer der reformirten Kirche, ix, 1860). [K. A. R.] Kruscke, *Johannes a Lasco und der Sacramentsstreit* (Studien zur Geschichte der Theologie und der Kirche, VII, Hft. i; 1901). Further bibl. in K. Schottenloher (ed.), *Bibliographie zur deutschen Geschichte im Zeitalter der Glaubensspaltung*, i (1933), nos. 10324–10364, p. 431 f. H. Dalton in *P.R.E.* (ed. 3), xi (1902), pp. 292–6, also with bibl.

LAST GOSPEL. A second reading from the Gospels which takes place at the very end of Mass in the modern W. rite. In medieval times it was said as a private devotion by the celebrant as he went back to the sacristy, but it is now read by the priest at the altar aloud. The usual Last Gospel is Jn. 1. 1–14; but when the Mass of a Sunday or important *feast or *feria is displaced by a greater festival, the Gospel of the displaced Mass is read here. At the Third Mass of *Christmas, the Gospel for the *Epiphany (Mt. 2. 1–12) is read as the Last Gospel, as Jn. 1. 1–14 has already been read as the proper Gospel of the Mass. The Last Gospel is never sung.

Jungmann (ed. 1949), ii, 542–9.

LAST JUDGEMENT. See *General Judgement*.

LAST SUPPER. The final meal of Christ with His Apostles on the night before the Crucifixion. It was followed by the washing of the Apostles' feet (see *Pedilavium*) and the institution of the *Eucharist. Traditionally it has been held that the meal was the *Passover, in agreement with the *Synoptic Gospels, which appear to put it on the evening when the *Passover celebrations began and the paschal lamb was consumed. The Gospel of St. *John, however, asserts that the Crucifixion itself took place on the 'preparation' (παρασκευή) of the Passover, i.e. a few hours before the Passover meal. If the latter assertion is correct, we may regard the Last Supper as an anticipation of the Passover meal or, perhaps less probably, as either a *Kiddush or some other form of religious meal, such as was celebrated by families or groups of friends. See also *Eucharist, Chaburah, Kiddush*, and *Passover*.

LAST THINGS, The. See *Eschatology*.

LATERAN BASILICA, The (S. Giovanni in Laterano). The present basilica stands on the site of an ancient palace on the Celian Hill at Rome which formerly belonged to the family of the Laterani. This palace, part of the dowry of Fausta, the wife of the Emp. *Constantine, who gave it to the Church, was the official residence (*patriarchium*) of the Popes from the 4th cent. until their departure for *Avignon (1309); it covered a much larger area than the present buildings. In 1308 it was nearly all destroyed by fire; only the 'Sancta Sanctorum' chapel now survives (see *Scala Sancta*). In 1586 *Sixtus V entrusted Domenico Fontana (1543–1607) with the erection of a new palace. This building remained unoccupied until 1693 when it was converted by Innocent XII into an asylum for orphans; in 1843 it was transformed into a museum for antiquities, Christian (*Museo Cristiano*) and classical (*Museo Profano*). For the *Lateran Councils, see foll. entry.

The Lateran Basilica, which remains the cathedral church of Rome ('omnium urbis et orbis ecclesiarum mater et caput'), is one of the four 'Major *Basilicas'. The original dedication was to the Redeemer (S. Salvator); but after destruction by an earthquake in 896 the church was rebuilt by Sergius III (904–11), who dedicated it to St. *John Baptist (with whom has since been associated St. *John the Apostle). After the fire of 1308, it was restored by *Clement V (1305–14); but it was again burnt down in 1360. The present church was built under the direction of a succession of Popes beginning with *Urban V, among the architects being D. Fontana (1543–1604) and F. Borromini (1599–1667). The façade to the E. (*c.* 1734) is by Alessandro Galilei (1691–1737). On the NW. is an octagonal baptistery (S. Giovanni in Fonte), the traditional site of Constantine's baptism by Pope *Sylvester in 324 (in fact Constantine was baptized on his deathbed near Nicomedia in 337); its real founder appears to have been *Sixtus III (432–40).

A. Valentini, *La Patriarcale Basilica Lateranense* (2 vols., fol., 1836). J. Sauer in *L.Th.K.*, vi (1934), cols. 401–4, s.v. 'Lateran, I. Palast'; E. Josi in *E.C.*, x (1953), cols. 1213–20, s.v. 'Roma. V. Topografia, ii. San Giovanni in Laterano e il Patriarchium', with bibl., incl. studies on recent excavations.

LATERAN COUNCILS. A series of councils were held in the Lateran Palace at Rome from the 7th to the 18th cents. Five of these rank as *oecumenical and are thus of special interest, viz.:

(1) First (1123). Convoked by *Callistus II for the solemn confirmation of the Concordat of *Worms which ended the *Investiture contest. Twenty-two disciplinary canons were also promulgated, most of them repeating and emphasizing previous decrees.

(2) Second (1139). Convoked by Innocent II for the reformation of the Church after the schism which had taken place at his election. It issued 30 canons, and condemned the followers of *Arnold of Brescia.

(3) Third (1179). Convoked by *Alexander III to remove the traces of the schism of the antipope Callixtus III. The most important decree of the Council concerned Papal elections. The right to elect the Pope was restricted to the

college of cardinals, and a two-thirds majority was declared necessary. Another important canon (can. 18) provided for the establishment at every cathedral of a school for clerics.

(4) Fourth (1215). Convoked by *Innocent III, it was much the most important of the Lateran Councils. In the course of it an official definition of the doctrine of the *Eucharist (in which the word 'transubstantiate' is used officially for the first time) was given, and annual confession for all Christian people was enacted. Rules were made concerning preaching in cathedral churches; bishops were reminded of their duties as teachers; and steps were taken to withdraw ecclesiastical countenance from judicial *ordeals. The foundation of new religious orders was also forbidden, one consequence of which was that St. *Dominic was compelled to take an already existing rule as the basis of his Friars Preachers.

(5) Fifth (1512–17). Convened by Pope *Julius II, the Council's immediate purpose was to invalidate the decrees of the antipapal Council of Pisa convoked by Louis XII of France. It promulgated a few minor reforms, but left the main causes of the *Reformation untouched.

(1) Hardouin, vi (pt. 2), cols. 1109–18; Mansi, xxi (1776), cols. 277–304. Hefele–Leclercq, v (pt. 1; 1912), pp. 630–44. A. Fliche in Fliche–Martin, viii (1946), pp. 391–5. See also bibl. to Callistus II and below.
(2) Hardouin, vi (pt. 2), cols. 1207–18; Mansi, xxi (1776), cols. 525–46. Hefele–Leclercq, v (pt. 1; 1912), pp. 721–46. See also bibl. to *Innocent II* and *Arnold of Brescia* and below.
(3) Hardouin, vi (pt. 2), cols. 1671–1876; Mansi, xxii (1778), cols. 209–468. Hefele–Leclercq, v (pt. 2; 1913), pp. 1086–112. See also below.
(4) Hardouin, viii, cols. 1–86; Mansi, xxii (1778), cols. 953–1086. Hefele–Leclercq, v (pt. 2; 1913), pp. 1316–98. A. Luchaire, *Innocent III* (6 vols., 1904–8), esp. vol. vi, 'Le Concile de Latran et la réforme de l'Église'. A. Fliche in Fliche–Martin, x (1950), pp. 194–211. See also other works cited under *Innocent III* and below.
V. Tizzani. *I concili lateranesi* (1878). F. Vernet in *D.T.C.*, viii (pt. 2; 1925), cols. 2628–67, s.v. 'Latran (Ier, IIe, IIIe et IVe Concile[s] œcuménique[s] de)'; R. Naz in *D.D.C.*, vi ('1955'), cols. 344–53, s.v. 'Latran (Conciles de)'.

LATERAN TREATY, The.

This treaty, signed on 11 Feb. 1929, 'finally and irrevocably' settled the Roman question, and established the *Vatican City as a sovereign state. The Holy See recognized the Italian state with Rome as capital. The Italian state recognized 'the Catholic, Apostolic and Roman Religion as the sole religion of the State', 'the sovereign independence of the Holy See in the international field', and the Holy See's 'sovereign jurisdiction' in the Vatican City. Attached to the Treaty was a *Concordat which provided for Catholic religious instruction in the schools, the civil recognition of marriage performed in accordance with canon law, the freedom of *Catholic Action on condition of its being non-politically conducted, and the swearing of an oath of allegiance to the King by bishops before taking possession of their dioceses.

Text in *A.A.S.*, xxi (1929), pp. 209–74, followed by text of Concordat, pp. 274–94, with 'Processo–Verbale', p. 295. V. Del Giudice, *La questione romana e i rapporti tra stato e chiesa fino alla conciliazione* (1947), pp. 247–79. D. A. Binchy, *Church and State in Fascist Italy* (1941). R. Danielo in *E.C.*, ix (1953), cols. 990–5, s.v. 'Patti lateranensi'. See further 'lives' of Pope Pius XI cited s.v.

LATIMER, HUGH

LATIMER, HUGH (c. 1485–1555), Bp. of *Worcester and Reformer. He was the son of a yeoman farmer of Thurcaston in Leicestershire, educated at Cambridge, and in 1510 elected Fellow of Clare Hall. In his earlier years he was an ardent opponent of the New Learning. He was ordained priest, and in 1522 his eloquence and zeal in reforming abuses and defending social justice led the University to license him as one of the 12 preachers commissioned to preach anywhere in England. From c. 1523 his opinions began to become suspect to the ecclesiastical authorities, and when in 1525 he declined the request of his bishop, N. West of *Ely, to preach a sermon against M. *Luther, he was forbidden to preach in the diocese. After skilfully defending himself before T. *Wolsey, he was again allowed to preach throughout England. The directness of his method, his understanding of human character, his homely style, and his ready wit won his sermons increasing influence. A sermon before *Henry VIII in Lent 1530, though it attacked the use of temporal weapons for the defence of God's Word, won him the royal favour, and in 1531 he was given the living of West Kington, Wilts. But his preaching, which now openly challenged ecclesiastical authority and spread Protestant doctrines, was censured by Convocation in Mar. 1532. Later in the year he submitted.

After T. *Cranmer's appointment to *Canterbury (1533), Latimer's position improved, and when, in 1534, Henry formally broke with the Pope, Latimer became one of the King's chief advisers. In 1535 he was appointed Bp. of Worcester. In his sermons he continued to denounce social injustices and other contemporary corruptions, attacking also Catholic teaching on purgatory, images, etc. He also supported the King in the *Dissolution of the Monasteries. In 1538 he preached at the execution of John Forest, and in the same year approved the putting to death of the family of R. *Pole. But his career was cut short in 1539 when, in acc. with his Protestant beliefs, he opposed the Act of the *Six Articles, and resigned his see on hearing from T. *Cromwell that this was the King's wish. Taken into custody, he was freed in 1540, but ordered to leave London and forbidden to preach. Very little is known of the next few years of his life. In 1546 he was confined to the Tower, but was released on *Edward VI's accession in the following year. On New Year's Day, 1548, he preached his famous sermon 'Of the Plough' at Paul's Cross, and became very popular as a court preacher, continuing to denounce social and ecclesiastical abuses and supporting the government of Somerset. On the accession of *Mary he was arrested and committed to the Tower (1553). In 1554, together with T. Cranmer and N. *Ridley, he was taken to Oxford to dispute with Catholic theologians of both universities esp. on *Transubstantiation and the Sacrifice of the Mass. Having refused to accept the medieval doctrine, he was excommunicated. He was examined again in 1555 and, after a renewed refusal to recant, was burnt with Ridley at Oxford on 16 Oct. 1555.

Collected ed. of his *Sermons* (2 vols., London, 1758), with life in vol. i, pp. ix–lxxxvii; *Sermons and Remains*, ed. G. E. Corrie (*Parker Society, xvi and xx; 1844–5, with extract from J. *Foxe, *Acts and Monuments* repr. in vol. i, pp. ix-xxxi). Lives by R. Demaus (Religious Tract Society, London, 1869; many subsequent edd.), R. M. Carlyle–A. J. Carlyle (London, 1899), H. S. Darby (ib., 1953), and A. G. Chester (Philadelphia, 1954, with detailed bibl.). J. *Gairdner in *D.N.B.*, xxxii (1892), pp. 171–9.

LATITUDINARIANISM. A term oppro-
briously applied in the 17th cent. to the out-look of a group of Anglican divines who, while continuing to conform with the C of E, at-tached relatively little importance to matters of dogmatic truth, ecclesiastical organization, and liturgical practice. It found characteristic representatives in the '*Cambridge Platonists'. In general the sympathies of Latitudinarian divines lay with the *Arminian theology. Their views did much to prepare the way for the religious temper of England in the 18th cent.

LA TRAPPE, Notre-Dame de. Abbey nr.
Soligny, Normandy, which gives its name to the *Trappist reform, instituted here by A. de *Rancé. It was founded as a *Benedictine monastery in 1122. In 1148 it adopted the *Cistercian reform, but since the early part of the 16th cent. it had fallen on evil days through the custom of appointing *com-mendatory abbots. De Rancé, who had been appointed *in commendam c.* 1636, introduced his celebrated reform in 1664 (see *Trappists*). After a period of great prosperity the com-munity was dispersed under the Revolution in 1790. The abbey was refounded in 1817 and now ranks second after Cîteaux.

H. de Charencey (ed.), *Cartulaire de l'abbaye de Notre-Dame de la Trappe* [Alençon, 1889]. Id., *Histoire de l'abbaye de la Grande-Trappe* (2 vols., Mortagne, 1896–1911). G. Grandpré, *L'Abbaye de la Trappe* (1827); P. P[icquignot], *La Trappe mieux connue, ou Aperçu descriptif et raisonné sur le monastère de la Maison-Dieu, Notre-Dame de la Trappe, près Mortagne, diocèse de Séez* (1834). L. H. Cottineau, O.S.B., *Répertoire topo-bibliographique des abbayes et prieurés* (Mâcon, 1935), col. 3201 f. for further bibl. See also bibl. to *Trappists*.

LATRIA (λατρεία), as contrasted with 'Dulia'
(δουλεία; q.v.), that fullness of Divine worship which may be paid to God alone.

LATROCINIUM (i.e. 'Robber Council').
The Council held at *Ephesus in Aug. 449. Summoned by *Theodosius II, to deal with difficulties arising out of the condemnation of *Eutyches for unorthodoxy at a synod at *Constantinople (the σύνοδος ἐνδημοῦσα) in Nov. 448 (see *Monophysites*), it was under the domination of *Dioscorus, Patr. of Alexandria, a strong upholder of Monophysitism. Eutyches was acquitted of heresy and reinstated in his monastery, Flavian and other bishops were deposed, and the Roman legates, who had brought with them St. Leo's *Tome, were insulted. Its decisions were reversed by the Council of *Chalcedon in 451. The name 'Latrocinium' was derived from Leo's letter (Ep. 95) to the Empress Pulcheria, where he describes the synod as 'non iudicium, sed latrocinium'.

Hefele-Leclercq (pt. i; 1908), pp. 555–621. P. Martin, *Le Pseudo-Synode connu dans l'histoire sous le nom de Brigan-dage d'Éphèse, étudié d'après ses actes retrouvés en syriaque* (Paris, 1875); S. G. F. Perry, *The Second Synod of Ephesus* (Dartford, 1881).

LATTER-DAY SAINTS. See *Mormons.*

LAUD, WILLIAM (1573–1645), Abp. of
*Canterbury. The son of a master tailor, he was born at Reading and educated at St. John's College, *Oxford, of which he became a Fellow in 1593. In 1601 he received holy orders, and in 1611 he was made President of St. John's. From a very early date he opposed the pre-vailing *Calvinist theology, and sought to restore something of the pre-Reformation litur-gical practice to the C of E. In 1616 he was made Dean of *Gloucester, where he moved the communion table to the east end of the choir, an action that brought him into violent conflict with his bishop. On being appointed Bp. of *St. Davids in 1621, he resigned the presidentship of St. John's. In 1622 he con-ducted a controversy with the Jesuit, J. Percy, commonly known as '*Fisher the Jesuit' (q.v.), in which he maintained that the RC Church and the C of E are both parts of the same Church Catholic. Under *Charles I his in-fluence increased. In 1626 he was translated to *Bath and Wells, and in 1628 to London. In 1629 he became chancellor of the university of Oxford, where he carried through many necessary and permanent reforms, codifying the statutes, enforcing discipline, instituting professorships in Hebrew and Arabic, and presenting a large collection of MSS. to the *Bodleian Library, including the so-called 'Codex Laudianus' of Acts. He did much to encourage individual scholars, and among those who enjoyed his patronage were J. *Hales and W. *Chillingworth. In 1633 he was again translated and became Abp. of Canterbury.

For some years past Laud had been taking a leading part in the administration of the country, and now his work on the *High Com-mission and his attempts to impose liturgical uniformity by force increasingly aroused the intense hostility of the *Puritans. Among the chief grievances were that he made the com-munion table rather than the pulpit the centre of the church, that he suppressed the Puritan *lecturers, and that he punished all opposition to his designs with heavy penalties. His at-tempts to enforce his reforms in Scotland (1637) proved the turning point of his career. At the sitting of Convocation in 1640 he introduced new canons, proclaiming the *Divine right of kings, and compelling whole classes of men to swear never to 'consent to alter the government of this Church by archbishops, deans, and arch-deacons, &c'. This formula, known as the 'etcetera oath', exposed him to general ridicule and had to be suspended at the order of the King. Soon afterwards he was impeached by the Long Parliament. In 1641 he was imprisoned in the Tower, but his trial only began in 1644. It is generally held to have been conducted without regard for the demands of justice, the Commons imposing their will on the Lords by force. He was executed on Tower Hill, London, on 10 Jan. 1645, after repudiating the accusation of 'Popery' and declaring his adherence to the Protestant Church of England.

Laud's apparent failure arose from his inability to understand the popular leaning towards Puritanism and the hatred aroused by his violent measures against all who did not share his own views on ritual. In doctrinal matters he showed himself broad-minded and conciliatory. He delighted in the material aggrandizement of the national Church and its prelates, but thereby promoted its identification with a political party. He left a remarkable private diary recording esp. the events of his last years.

Works ed. W. Scott-J. Bliss (L.A.C.T., 7 vols., 1847-60). Apart from the records among the State Papers, the principal authority is the life by his disciple, P. *Heylyn, *Cyprianus Anglicus* (London, 1668). Modern lives by C. W. Le Bas (London, 1836; repr. among his works), A. C. Benson (London, 1887), W. H. *Hutton (ib., 1895), W. L. Mackintosh (ib., 1907), A. S. Duncan-Jones (ib., 1927) and H. R. Trevor-Roper (ib., 1940). E. C. E. Bourne, *The Anglicanism of William Laud* (1947). Catalogue of the MSS. which he presented to the Bodleian Library by H. O. Coxe, *Catalogi Codicum Manuscriptorum Bibliothecae Bodleianae* pars prima (Oxford, 1853), cols. 491-582, and pars secunda (1858-85). S. R. Gardiner in *D.N.B.*, xxxii (1892), pp. 185-94; W. H. Hutton in *D.E.C.H.*, pp. 316-20.

LAUDA SION. The opening words, and hence the name, of the *sequence for the feast of *Corpus Christi, composed for the occasion by St. *Thomas Aquinas (*c.* 1264). Summoning the Church (here addressed as Sion) to the adoration of the Eucharist, it contains a doctrinal exposition of the Presence, closely following that in the *Summa Theologica*. The hymn combines with close philosophical reasoning a severity of form and economy of expression which give it a grandeur and austerity lost in most English translations. These include versions by R. *Crashaw, E. B. *Pusey, F. *Oakeley, and E. *Caswall; the most familiar, 'Laud, O Sion, thy Salvation', is the work of several authors.

Crit. ed. of text in G. M. Dreves (ed.), *Lateinische Hymnendichter des Mittelalters* (A.H.M.A., 1; 1907), p. 584 f. Raby, pp. 405-8, with reff. and bibl., p. 483.

LAUDS. The traditional morning prayer of the W. Church, one of the oldest parts of the Divine Office. Before the reform of the *Breviary (q.v.) by *Pius X, it had six or seven Psalms (as is still the case in the Monastic Office), always including Pss. 148-50 in which the word *laudate* (Lat. 'praise ye . . .') frequently recurs, whence its name. To-day it consists of four Psalms and one OT Canticle with their *antiphons, Little Chapter, hymn and versicle, all of which are variable; these are followed by the '*Benedictus', the *preces* (a series of versicles and responses beginning with *Kyrie and *Pater; these are said only on

the *ferias of *Advent and *Lent and on certain vigils and *Ember Days), the *collect of the day, and *commemorations, if they occur. Nowadays Lauds is normally joined to *Matins and said overnight by anticipation, except in religious orders who rise for the Night Office, when it is sung in the early morning. In the BCP parts of Lauds and Matins were combined to form the service of Morning Prayer.

C. Callewaert, 'De Laudibus Matutinis' in *Collationes Brugenses*, xxvii (1927), pp. 383-9, 448-51, xxviii (1928), pp. 63-72, 152-66, 245-50, and 328-38; repr. in his *Sacris Erudiri* (Steenbrugge, 1940), pp. 53-89. G. *Morin, O.S.B., 'Les Laudes du Dimanche du IVe au VIIe Siècle' in *Le Messager des Fidèles* [later *R. Bén.*], vi (1889), pp. 301-4. I. M. Hanssens, S.J., *Aux origines de la prière liturgique. Nature et genèse de l'office des matines* (Analecta Gregoriana, lvii; 1952), passim. H. *Leclercq, O.S.B., in *D.A.C.L.*, viii (pt. 2; 1929), cols. 1887-98.

LAURA (Gk. λαύρα). In the early Church a colony of *anchorites who, while living in separate huts, were subject to a single abbot. The oldest lauras were founded in Palestine in the early 4th cent., where for some centuries they continued to flourish. Esp. famous were those under the direction of St. Euthymius the Great (d. 473) and his pupil, St. *Sabas (d. 532), the founder of the Laura, Mar Saba (μεγίστη λαύρα), south-east of Jerusalem.

LAURENCE, St. (d. 258), deacon and martyr. He was one of the seven deacons at Rome during the pontificate of Sixtus II (257-8), and suffered martyrdom in the persecution under Valerian. Acc. to a tradition handed down by St. *Ambrose, *Prudentius, and others, on being asked by the prefect of Rome to deliver up the treasure of the Church, he assembled the poor among whom he had distributed the ecclesiastical possessions and presented them to the prefect, saying, 'These are the treasure of the Church', an action for which he was punished by being slowly roasted to death on a gridiron. This story has been widely rejected by modern scholars, who maintain that he was beheaded like Sixtus II and other contemporary martyrs. He was one of the most famous saints of the Roman Church. During the reign of *Constantine a chapel was built over his tomb in a *catacomb (Cyriaca) on the Via Tiburtina, and this was enlarged by Pelagius II (579-90) into a basilica, the present San Lorenzo fuori le Mura. His feast occurs in the Roman 'Depositio Martyrum' of the 4th cent. and his name is also found in the *Canon of the Mass and in the Litanies. Feast day, 10 Aug.

AA.SS., Aug. II (1735), pp. 485-532. *Bibliotheca Hagiographica Latina*, ed. Soc. Boll. (Brussels, 1898-1901), pp. 708-12 (Nos. 4751-89), and suppl. (ib., 1911), p. 187 f. P. F. de' Cavalieri, 'S. Lorenzo e il supplizio della graticola' in *R.Q.*, xiv (1900), pp. 159-76; id., *Note agiografiche*, v (S.T., xxvii, 1915), No. 3, 'Assum est, versa et manduca', pp. 65-82. H. Grisar, S.J., 'Zum ältesten Kultus des Märtyrers Laurentius' in *Z.K.T.*, xxvii (1903), pp. 133-8. V. L. Kennedy, C.S.B., *The Saints of the Canon of the Mass* (Studi di Antichità Cristiana, xiv; 1938), esp. pp. 124-8, with reff. L. *Duchesne, 'Le Sanctuaire de saint Laurent' in *Mélanges d'Archéologie et d'Histoire*, xxxix (1921), pp. 3-24. H. *Leclercq, O.S.B., in *D.A.C.L.*, viii (pt. 2; 1929), cols. 1917-61, s.v. 'Laurent'. See also bibl. to *Sixtus II*.

'LAUSANNE'. The first Conference of the *Oecumenical Movement of '*Faith and Order' held at Lausanne under Bp. C. H. *Brent in 1927. It aimed at promoting doctrinal unity among the diverse branches of Christianity, about 90 different Churches being represented. Among those not represented were the RC Church, the Russian Orthodox, and several *Baptist Churches. The subjects discussed were the call to unity, the message of the Church to the world, the essence of the Church, Episcopacy and Apostolic succession, the Sacraments, and the Unity of Christendom in general. Great differences became apparent esp. as regards the doctrine of the Sacraments, of which the Orthodox recognized seven and the *Quakers none. The difficulties were emphasized by the Greek Abp. Germanos, who declared a union impossible without the acceptance of the Seven Oecumenical Councils. None the less, the Conference did much to stimulate interest in reunion and to encourage theological cooperation.

Faith and Order. Proceedings of the World Conference, Lausanne, August 3–21, 1927. Edited by H. N. Bate (1928). Convictions. A Selection from the Responses of the Churches to the Report of the World Conference on Faith and Order, held at Lausanne in 1927. Edited by L. Hodgson, with the assistance of H. N. Bate and R. W. Brown (1934).

LAVABO (Lat. 'I will wash'). The washing of the celebrant's fingers after the offering of the oblations in the Mass, so called from the initial Latin word of Ps. 26. 6–end (Vulg., Ps. 25. 6–end) with the recitation of which the celebrant accompanies the action.

Jungmann (ed. 1949), ii, 91–8.

LAW, Canon. See Canon Law.

LAW, Natural. See Natural Law.

LAW, WILLIAM (1686–1761), *Nonjuror and spiritual writer. He was born at Kings Cliffe, Northants, and educated at Emmanuel College, Cambridge, of which he became a Fellow in 1711. On the accession of George I Law refused the Oath of Allegiance, was deprived of his fellowship, and became a Nonjuror. From 1727 to 1737 he lived in the household of the *Gibbons at Putney as tutor to the father of the historian. In 1740 he retired to Kings Cliffe, where he was joined later by a Mrs. Hutcheson and Miss Hester Gibbon with whom he organized schools and almshouses, and, until his death, led a life of great simplicity, devotion, and pursuits of charity.

Among his earlier writings are Three Letters to the Bishop of Bangor (1717) which were welcomed as a convincing reply to B. *Hoadly's attack on High Church principles, and in 1726 appeared his Absolute Unlawfulness of the Stage Entertainmeut, a strong but somewhat one-sided attack on the evils of the contemporary theatre. In the same year he published the first of his treatises, On Christian Perfection, which was followed, in 1728, by the most famous of his works, A Serious Call to a Devout and Holy Life. Inspired by the teaching of J. *Tauler, J. *Ruysbroeck, *Thomas à Kempis, and other orthodox spiritual writers, the book is a forceful exhortation to embrace the Christian life in its moral and ascetical fullness. The author recommends the exercise of the moral virtues and meditation and ascetical practices; corporate worship, however, finds little place. He insists esp. on the virtues practised in everyday life, temperance, humility, and self-denial, all animated by the intention to glorify God, to which every human activity should be directed. The simplicity of its teaching and its vigorous style soon established the work as a classic, which has probably had more influence than any other post-Reformation spiritual book except the *Pilgrim's Progress, and was greatly appreciated e.g. by J. *Wesley, G. *Whitefield, and H. *Venn. In 1732 he published his Case of Reason against M. *Tindal and the *Latitudinarian position generally; and his attitude towards Rome is to be found in his Letters to a Lady inclined to enter the Church of Rome (1779). He became acquainted c. 1734 with the writings of the German Protestant mystic, J. *Boehme, whose influence is noticeable in his later works, esp. The Spirit of Prayer (2 parts, 1749–50) and The Spirit of Love (2 parts, 1752 and 1754), which emphasize the indwelling of Christ in the soul. This development of his spirituality estranged many of his former disciples, e.g. Wesley, and led him, though he always remained faithful to the C of E, to a doctrine resembling the *Quaker conception of the *Inner Light'.

Collected ed. of his works, 9 vols., London, each with a general title-page, 1762 (sets being made up from various edd.). Works also ed. 'G. Moreton', 9 vols., privately pr., London, 1892–3. New ed. of the Liberal and Mystical Writings of William Law, with Introd. by W. S. Palmer (London, 1908); Selected Mystical Writings of William Law, ed. with notes and studies by S. [H.] Hobhouse (London, 1938). There has been a steady flow of edd. of A Serious Call to a Devout Life. J. H. Overton, William Law, Nonjuror and Mystic (1881). S. [H.] Hobhouse, William Law and Eighteenth Century Quakerism, with some unpublished Letters and Fragments (1927). A. W. Hopkinson, About William Law. A Running Commentary on his Works (S.P.C.K., 1948). E. W. Baker, A Herald of the Evangelical Revival. A Critical Inquiry into the Relation of William Law to John Wesley and the Beginnings of Methodism (1948). Caroline F. E. Spurgeon, 'William Law and the Mystics' in A. W. Ward–A. R. Waller (edd.), The Cambridge History of English Literature, ix (1912), pp. 305–28, with bibl., pp. 510–12. A. W. Harrison in C.B.E.L., ii, p. 858. L. Stephen in D.N.B., xxxii (1892), pp. 236–40.

LAWRENCE, Brother. See Brother Lawrence.

LAWRENCE, St. See Laurence, St.

LAXISM. A system in *Moral Theology which relaxed the obligations of natural and positive law on grounds deemed by its critics to be insufficient. It developed in the 17th cent., when modern conditions, e.g. the growing practice of taking interest on money loans, hitherto forbidden by the Church as usury, raised several difficult cases of conscience. Its formulation is connected with the appearance of *Probabilism (q.v.), of which it may be considered a perversion. First attacked in France, esp. in B. *Pascal's *Lettres provinciales* (1657), it was rather clumsily defended by the *Jesuit, G. Pirot, in *L'Apologie des casuistes* (1657), which provoked great scandal. In 1658 certain propositions in Pirot's book which asserted that even the slightest degree of probability, derived either from reason or from authority, suffices to excuse from sin were condemned by the *Sorbonne, and in 1659 the *Holy Office censured the book itself. In 1665 and 1666 *Alexander VII condemned Laxism, and in 1679 *Innocent XI condemned 65 propositions drawn from Laxist casuists.

M. Petrocchi, *Il problema del lassismo nel secolo XVII* (1953), with reff. A. Degert, 'Réaction des "Provinciales" sur la théologie morale en France' in *Bulletin de Littérature ecclésiastique publié par l'Institut Catholique de Toulouse*, Sér. 5, v (1913), pp. 400–20 and 442–51. A. Molien–É. Amann in *D.T.C.*, ix (pt. 1; 1926), cols. 37–86, s.v. 'Laxisme'. See also works cited s.v. 'Probabilism'.

LAY BROTHER, LAY SISTER. A member of a religious order who is not bound to the recitation of the Divine Office and is occupied in manual work. The institution, which originated in the 11th cent., arose from the increasingly general custom of admitting monks to the priesthood and freeing them from manual labour. At the same time a similar development took place in the orders of women, where lay sisters were employed to leave the 'choir nuns' free for the Office, mental prayer, and intellectual pursuits. Lay Brothers and Sisters have usually a long novitiate and wear a slightly different habit (Lay Sisters white instead of black veils). They are bound to assist at daily Mass and to recite a short office, which normally consists of a certain number of Paters, Aves, and Glorias, though in some orders the *Little Office of Our Lady is said.

LAY READER. In the C of E, a layman licensed to conduct religious services. The history of the office in its present form dates from 1866, when the Bp. of *Gloucester and Bristol admitted the first Reader in the C of E. The number of Readers gradually increased and in 1905 the Bishops issued rules governing their status, duties, form of admission, etc. (revised in 1921 and 1940). The duties which may be assigned to them include the reading of *Morning and *Evening Prayer (except the Absolution) and of the *Litany, the publication of *Banns of Marriage, the preaching of a sermon except at the Holy Communion, the catechizing of children and the receiving of alms; and generally giving the incumbent such assistance in his pastoral work as he may direct. Exceptionally a Lay Reader may also read the Epistle at the Eucharist and administer the chalice. Readers are formally admitted to their office by a Bishop, from whom they may also receive a licence either for a particular parish or for the diocese generally. In each diocese there is provision for a Readers' Board on which the Readers are represented.

LAY RECTOR. In the C of E, a layman receiving the rectorial tithes of a benefice. By custom he enjoys the right to the chief seat in the chancel of the parish church for himself and his family and the freehold of the whole church, but this gives him no right of possession or of entering it when not open for divine service. He also has the duty of repairing the chancel, for the neglect of which duty he may be sued in the county court. He may compound for this liability, however, with the Board of Finance subject to the approval of the Diocesan Dilapidations Board.

LAYING ON OF HANDS. See *Hands, Laying on of*.

LAYMEN. See *Laity*.

LAYNEZ, JAMES (1512–65), second *General of the *Jesuits. After studying at the university of Alcalá, he joined St. *Ignatius Loyola in Paris and with him helped to found the Jesuit Order. He was appointed professor of scholastic theology at the Sapienza at Rome, and was largely responsible for crushing incipient Protestant opinion at Piacenza and other cities in N. Italy. He took a very prominent part in the Council of *Trent, where he represented the more irreconcilable elements (e.g. on *justification) and was one of the supporters of Papal absolutism. On Ignatius's death (1556) Laynez succeeded him first as 'General-Vicar' and (from 1558) as General. His rule was notable for the continued success and expansion of the order.

Lainii Monumenta. Epistolae et Acta Patris Jacobi Lainii (8 vols., Monumenta Historica Societatis Jesu, Madrid, 1912–17); his *Disputationes Tridentinae*, ed. H. Grisar, S.J. (2 vols., Innsbruck, 1886). Lives by P. de Ribaneira, S.J. (Madrid, 1594), and F. Dilarino (pseudonym of C. M. Rinaldi, S.J., Rome, 1672). Modern studies by G. Boero (Florence, 1880; Fr. tr. 1894), A. Martínez de Azagra y Beladiez (Madrid, 1933), H. Fichter, S.J. (St. Louis, 1944), and F. Cereceda, S.J. (2 vols., Madrid, 1945–6). J. Brodrick, S.J., *The Progress of the Jesuits, 1556–79* (1946), pp. 66–111. P. Dudon, 'Le Projet de Somme théologique du P. Jacques Laynez' in *Recherches de Science religieuse*, xxi (1931), pp. 361–74. A. Martini, S.J., in *E.C.*, vii (1951), cols. 819–21, s.v. 'Lainez, Diego'.

LAZARISTS. The name popularly given to the 'Congregation of the Mission' (C.M.), a congregation of secular priests living under religious vows, founded by St. *Vincent de Paul in 1625. The name comes from the priory of St.-Lazare, which was Vincent's headquarters in Paris. At first they were confined to France and territories under French influence, but have now spread all over the world. The original work of the congregation was the preaching of missions in the various parishes of France, and conducting *retreats. Later they established seminaries. Only with great reluctance, however, did they accept the charge of parishes. Outside France the work of the Lazarists lay for many years chiefly in Tunis and Algiers, where they brought succour to the Christian captives of the Barbary pirates, and in Madagascar.

P. Coste, *La Congrégation de la mission dite de Saint-Lazare* (1927). Heimbucher, ii, pp. 574–86, with bibl., and p. 670.

LAZARUS. (1) The brother of Martha and Mary, and intimate friend of Jesus who raised him from the dead (Jn. 11. 1–44). Of his subsequent life nothing is told in the NT. Acc. to E. tradition he and his sisters and some friends were put into a leaking boat by the Jews and, being miraculously preserved, landed on Cyprus where he was made bishop at Kition. In 890 his supposed relics were translated to *Constantinople, where a church was built in his honour by *Leo VI ('the Philosopher'). In the 11th cent. the legend spread in the W. that he had been Bp. of Marseilles and martyred under *Domitian, a story probably due to the confusion with a 5th cent. Bp. Lazarus of Aix whose epitaph is preserved in the crypt of St. Victor's at Marseilles, or, alternatively, with St. Nazarius, Bp. of Autun. Devotion to Lazarus appears to have been widespread in the early Church. The 'Peregrinatio *Etheriae' describes a procession to *Bethany on the Saturday before *Palm Sunday to the church erected over his tomb. On this day ('Lazarus Saturday') his feast is still observed in the E.; the W. Church keeps it on 17 Dec.

(2) The name of the beggar in Christ's parable of Dives and Lazarus (Lk. 16. 19–31), venerated as the patron of lepers in the Middle Ages.

On (1), M. J. *Lagrange, O.P., *St. Jean* (1925), pp. 295–318. On the legend, see G. *Morin, O.S.B., 'Saint Lazare et saint Maximin' in *Mémoires de la Société des Antiquaires de France*, lvi (1897), pp. 27–51, and L. *Duchesne, *Fastes épiscopaux de l'ancienne Gaule*, i (ed. 2, 1907), pp. 321–59. On the iconography, H. Leclercq, O.S.B., in *D.A.C.L.*, viii (pt. 2; 1929), cols. 2009–86, s.v., and E. Josi in *E.C.*, vii (1951), cols. 996–8. See also bibl. to *Mary Magdalene* and *Martha*.

LEANDER, St. (*c.* 550–600 or 601), Bp. of Seville, probably from 584. He was the brother of St. *Isidore. *c.* 582 he went on an embassy to *Constantinople, where he made the acquaintance of *Gregory the Great, and on his return was appointed to the see of Seville (*c.* 584). He took a prominent part in furthering the cause of Catholic orthodoxy in Spain against the *Arianism of the Visigoths, and in 589 presided over the celebrated Synod of *Toledo. A rule for nuns (*Regula sanctimonialium*) and a Homily delivered at the Synod of Toledo are among his few surviving works. Feast day, 27 Feb.

The Rule for Nuns and Homily repr. in J. P. Migne, *PL*, lxxii, 869–98; modern ed. of the rule, with full introd., by A. C. Vega, O.S.A. (1948). The principal authority is Isidore of Seville, *De Viris Illustribus*, xli. J. Madoz, S.J., study of the 'Libellus de Institutione Virginum' in *Anal. Boll.*, lxvii (1949), pp. 407–24. Mrs. Humphry Ward in *D.C.B.*, iii (1882), pp. 637–40.

LEAVENED BREAD. See *Bread, Leavened and Unleavened*.

LEBBAEUS. An alternative name for *Thaddaeus, found in some (apparently not the best) MSS. of Mt. 10. 3 and also in the *Western text of Mk. 3. 18. In the AV it occurs only at the former place, and in the RV not at all.

LE BRUN, PIERRE (1661–1729), French liturgical scholar. A native of Brignoles he entered the *Oratory *c.* 1682. Having studied theology at Marseilles and Toulouse, he taught philosophy at Toulon and theology at Grenoble. In 1690 he was called to the seminary of Saint-Magloire where he lectured on the Scriptures, the Councils and Church history. His principal liturgical work, *Explication littérale, historique et dogmatique des prières et des cérémonies de la sainte messe* (4 vols., 1716–26), embodied many extended studies. In its important preface he takes up an intermediary position between the excessive symbolism of the Middle Ages and an exaggerated naturalism. In the later volumes, which contain much curious information about usages in the French churches, he gives detailed studies of the various rites, stressing their unanimity in regard to liturgical essentials. In his *Défense de l'ancien sentiment sur la forme de la consécration* (1727) he maintained that the *Epiclesis was an integral element in Eucharistic consecration. He also advocated a more understanding participation in the Liturgy by the laity, for whom he compiled a liturgical prayer book, *Heures ou manuel pour assister à la messe* (1716).

New ed. of *L'Explication de la messe* (Lex Orandi, No. 9, 1949) by E. Bonnardet, Cong. Orat., with biography, full acct. of Lebrun's works, earlier edd., and bibl., pp. xi–xxxiii. A Lat. text of the *Explication littérale*, publd. by J. A. Dalmasius (Venice, 4 vols., 1770). A. Molien in *D.T.C.*, ix (1926), cols. 101–3, s.v., and H. *Leclercq, O.S.B., in *D.A.C.L.*, viii (pt. 2; 1929), cols. 2218–29.

LECLERC, JEAN (1657–1736), 'Clericus', *Arminian theologian and Biblical scholar. He was born at Geneva, studied at Grenoble and Saumur, and later gave up *Calvinism, in which he had been brought up, and became an Arminian. In 1684 he was appointed professor of philosophy, afterwards of church history, at the *Remonstrant College at Amsterdam, where he met J. *Locke. In his first work, *Liberii de Sancto Amore Epistolae Theologicae* (1679) he stated his theological convictions, explaining the mysteries of the *Trinity, the *Incarnation and *Original Sin on rationalistic lines. In *Sentiments de quelques théologiens de Hollande* (1685) he attacked R. *Simon, esp. his plan of a *polyglot Bible, and denied the Mosaic authorship of the *Pentateuch. In 1696 he published an *Ars Critica*, and in 1699 a harmony of the Gospels, *Harmonia Evangelica*, in Greek and Latin. He brought out a Commentary on the Pentateuch in 1699, an annotated translation of the NT in 1703, and Commentaries on the historical books of the OT in 1708 and on the Psalms, the writings of Solomon and the prophets in 1731. He made a new edition of the 'Apostolic Fathers' of J. B. *Cotelier and revised writings of D. *Petavius, H. *Grotius, and others; he also edited three influential periodical works, *Bibliothèque universelle et historique* (26 vols.,

1686–93), *Bibliothèque choisie* (28 vols., 1703–1713), and *Bibliothèque ancienne et moderne* (29 vols., 1714–30). A champion of freedom of thought and an enemy of all dogmatism, he defended the unlimited rights of reason in the domain of faith. He held very advanced critical views on the inspiration of Scripture, which he denied altogether for Job, Proverbs, Ecclesiastes, and the Song of Songs. The historic portions of the Pentateuch he assigned to King Josiah (637–608).

Vita et Opera ad annum 1711, publd. Amsterdam, 1711. Studies by A. des Amorie van der Hoeven (ib., 1843) and J. Collen (thesis, Geneva, 1884). J. Carreyre in *D.T.C.*, ix (pt. 1; 1926), cols. 105–7. Annie Barnes, *Jean Leclerc (1657–1736) et la République des lettres* (Paris, 1938).

LECLERCQ, HENRI (1869–1945), *Benedictine scholar. A native of Tournai (Belgium), he became a naturalized French subject and after profession at *Solesmes was sent to Farnborough Abbey in 1896. He was ordained priest in 1898. From 1914 till his death he lived in London, where he became a very familiar reader at the British Museum. He was a prolific and voluminous editor and writer, esp. concerned with the history of Latin Christianity. His numerous publications include *L'Afrique chrétienne* (2 vols., 1904); *L'Espagne chrétienne* (1906); *Manuel d'archéologie chrétienne depuis les origines jusqu'au VIIIᵉ siècle* (2 vols., 1907); *Monumenta Ecclesiae Liturgica* (4 vols., 1900 ff.), in conjunction with F. *Cabrol, a collection of early liturgical documents; *Histoire des conciles* (10 vols., 1907–38), a completely recast French edition of K. J. *Hefele's *Conciliengeschichte*; and almost innumerable articles in the *Dictionnaire d'archéologie chrétienne et de liturgie* (ed. by F. Cabrol and himself, 1903–53), the later volumes being almost wholly Leclercq's work. He also wrote *Histoire de la régence pendant la minorité de Louis XV* (3 vols., 1921). The range of his writing led it to suffer seriously in accuracy and to compel him to borrow extensively from other writers so that his work can seldom be used without checking. It is, however, always readable, and often clothed in a lively and controversial style.

Brief notice by E. Josi in *E.C.*, vii (1951), cols. 1013 f., s.v.

LECTERN (Lat. *legere*, 'to read'). A bookstand used to support the liturgical books, usually of wood or metal and movable, and often taking the form of an eagle or pelican with outstretched wings. A light folding lectern is sometimes used for supporting the book at the reading of the Gospel at *High Mass.

J. C. Cox, *Pulpits, Lecterns and Organs in English Churches* (1915), pp. 163–203.

LECTIONARY. A book containing the extracts ('pericopes') from Scripture appointed to be read at public worship. The apportionment of particular extracts to particular days begins in the 4th cent. Originally the beginning (*incipit*) and ending (*explicit*) of each pericope was noted in the margin of the church Bible, and a 'capitulary', or table of *incipits*

and *explicits*, was made for reference. Later the pericopes were collected into lectionaries, those for the Mass being further separated into *Epistolaries and *Evangeliaries. The Lessons which are read at *Matins and *Evensong in the C of E are regulated by a lectionary ('Table of Lessons') issued in 1871, or, alternatively, by a revised Table of 1922. In 1944 a further revision of the BCP Lectionary, with new alternative lessons for Sundays and certain Holy Days, was issued (further revised in 1946); and in 1956 a full revision (including week-days) was introduced for experimental use.

LECTOR, also 'Reader'. In the E and RC Churches, one of the *Minor Orders of the ministry. In early times his main function was to read the OT Prophecies, the Epistle, and in some places (e.g. Africa, Spain) the Gospel. The first traces of the order may be seen in Col. 4. 16 and Rev. 1. 3, and express mention of a liturgical reader is found in St. *Justin (*Apol.*, I, lxvii, 3 f.). From the end of the 2nd cent. there is plentiful but widely scattered evidence, e.g. St. *Cyprian (*Epp.* 29; 38. 2; 39. 4). Can. 10 of *Antioch (330 or 341) sanctioned their ordination by *chorepiscopi. In Syria (*Ap. Const.*, viii, 2) and elsewhere they were appointed by the laying on of hands, accompanied in the W. ('Conc. Carth. IV', can. 8) by the delivery of a codex. The Council of *Laodicea (4th cent., can. 23) forbade the wearing of the '*orarion' by a lector. Since the Middle Ages the office has been ranked as the second of the four Minor Orders, though its liturgical functions have been almost lost and it is now only a stepping-stone to the *Major Orders. In the E Church, the normal practice nowadays is for the lector to be ordained also subdeacon and deacon at the same service.

A. *Harnack, *Die Quellen der sogenannten Apostolischen Kirchenordnung* (T.U., ii, Hft. 5, 1886), pp. 57–100, 'Über den Ursprung des Lectorats und den anderen niederen Weihen'. F. Wieland, *Die genetische Entwicklung der sog. Ordines Minores in den drei ersten Jahrhunderten* (R.Q., Supplementheft vii; 1897), pp. 67–114 and 165–72. H. *Leclercq, O.S.B., in *D.A.C.L.*, viii (pt. 2; 1929), cols. 2241–69, s.v. 'Lecteur'; J. Quasten in *L.Th.K.*, vi (1934), col. 479 f., s.v. 'Lektor', with bibl.

LECTURERS. In the 16th and 17th cents., unordained ministers appointed by Parliament to particular parishes and charged with lecturing in church on the Christian faith. The system, which was esp. popular with the *Puritans, was bitterly resisted by most of the clergy. The lecturer was supported voluntarily by the parishioners on whose recommendation he was usually appointed. The *Journals of Parliament* from 1641 to 1643 mention the appointment or confirmation of appointment of some 190 lecturers.

LEDGER, St. See *Leodegar, St.*

LEE, FREDERICK GEORGE (1832–1902), theological writer. From 1867 to 1899 he was vicar of All Saints', Lambeth. He actively promoted reunion between the C of E and the RC Church, and to this end helped to found the *A.P.U.C. in 1857 and started the *Union Review* in 1863. It appears that *c*. 1877 he was secretly consecrated Bp. at or near *Venice by some prelate in communion with the see of Rome and took the title of 'Bp. of *Dorchester (Oxon)' (see *Episcopi Vagantes*). He also took a prominent part in furthering the ceremonial revival in the C of E. His voluminous writings, the historical ones mostly very partisan, include *Historical Sketches of the Reformation* (1879) and a *Glossary of Liturgical and Ecclesiastical Terms* (1877). His widely used *Directorium Anglicanum* (1865; a much revised edition of an earlier book issued by J. *Purchas in 1858) was a manual of directions for clergy at the altar. In 1901 he became a RC.

H. R. T. Brandreth, *Dr. Lee of Lambeth*. A Chapter in Parenthesis in the History of the Oxford Movement (1951). W. G. D. Fletcher in *D.N.B., 1901–1911*, ii, pp. 440–42.

LEEN, EDWARD (1885–1944), Irish spiritual writer. A native of Co. Limerick, he entered the Congregation of the Holy Ghost and studied at Rockwell College and Rome. He was ordained priest in 1914, became dean of studies at Blackrock College in 1922, and its president in 1925. From 1939 he was superior of the house of his congregation at Kimmage. Leen was among the most popular RC spiritual authors. Among his best-known works are *Progress through Mental Prayer* (1935), containing practical instructions on the lower stages of mental prayer up to the Prayer of Quiet; *The Holy Ghost* (1936), considered esp. in His workings in souls; *Why the Cross* (1938), meditations on the problem of pain; and *The Church before Pilate* (1939). He also wrote numerous pamphlets and articles on Catholic education.

His *The Voice of A Priest* was posthumously ed. by B. J. Kelly, C.S.Sp. (1947), with introd., 'Father Leen; the Man and his Teaching. An Appreciation', pp. 3–19; fourteen of his talks on the BVM were also posthumously published, *Our Blessed Mother*. Talks on Our Lady by Edward Leen . . . and John Kearney, ed. id. (Dublin, 1947), pp. 1–106, with introd. pp. vi–ix.

LEFÈVRE D'ÉTAPLES, JACQUES. See *Faber, Jacobus*.

LEGATE, Papal. A personal representative of the *Holy See who has been entrusted with its authority. Papal legates are of three kinds —legates *a latere*, *nuncios, and *legati nati*. Legates *a latere*, to whom the term 'Papal Legate' in common usage is esp. applied, are persons deputed for important missions of a temporary character. This office is now confined to cardinals. Nuncios, also known as *legati missi*, have functions corresponding to those of the ambassadors of secular states. *Legati nati* were the holders of certain offices which conveyed a legatine status *ex officio*, e.g. before the Reformation the Abp. of *Canterbury was such a *legatus natus*, and performed some of the functions which would now be carried out by a nuncio. Though a Papal legate is usually fortified with abundant jurisdiction, the Council of *Trent regulated that his powers should not completely override those of the bishops of the country to which he is sent. See also *Apostolic Delegate; Nuncio*.

LEGER, St. See *Leodegar, St.*

LEIBNIZ, GOTTFRIED WILHELM (1646–1716), philosopher. He was a native of Leipzig, where after a precocious boyhood he entered the university in 1661 as a student of law. Here philosophy and mathematics soon became his chief interests, and in 1663 he wrote a dissertation on the Principle of Individuation, a subject which remained of permanent interest to him. A tract, *De Arte Combinatoria*, which elaborated a new system of symbolic logic, followed in 1666. In 1667 he declined a chair at Altorf, the university town attached to Nuremberg. Shortly afterwards his friendship with J. C. von Boyneburg (1622–72) introduced him to the Elector of Mainz, who employed him on several political projects, including a plan to persuade Louis XIV to divert his attention from Germany to an attack on Egypt. Contacts with French *savants* while in Paris on this mission much widened his outlook; and it was at about this date that he made his celebrated discovery of the infinitesimal calculus. In 1673 he changed to the service of the Duke of Brunswick-Lüneburg, in the employ of whose family he remained for the rest of his life, residing from 1676 at Hanover. Here his main official task was the assembly of a vast body of material relating to the history of the House of Brunswick. But he developed and maintained a great number of other interests. A Protestant by upbringing, he engaged in correspondence with J. B. *Bossuet on Christian reunion, and to this end published his *Systema Theologicum* (1686). The Prussian Academy, founded in 1700, was virtually Leibniz's creation, and he also exerted himself to promote the erection of similar institutions in other European states. Most of his philosophical writings date from the last sixteen years of his life in which he conducted a large correspondence with A. *Arnauld, S. *Clarke and others. He also contributed to learned journals, and wrote an extensive critique of J. *Locke's *Essay*, which owing to Locke's death in 1704, he withheld from publication. (It was first issued by R. E. Raspe in 1765.) In 1710 appeared his *Essais de Théodicée sur la bonté de Dieu, la liberté de l'homme et l'origine de mal*, his one considerable theological work. In 1714 he wrote the *Monadologie* (publd. 1720) and *Principes de la nature et de la grâce* (publd. 1718), which though brief contain the only systematic account of his metaphysical doctrines. Throughout his life Leibniz was ardently devoted to the cause of international peace.

Acc. to the *Monadology*, the universe consisted of an infinite number of 'monads', i.e. simple substances, and nothing else. These monads are indivisible, yet, unlike the atoms of Democritus, ever-active. As every monad contains within itself the whole infinity of substance, each is a living mirror of all existence. Each is, however, limited and different from all the rest, as it mirrors the universe in its own way. All difference is relative and gradual, not absolute, and the universe is governed by a law of continuity. The monads form a continuously ascending series from the lowest, which is next to nothing, to the highest, which is God. Yet though Leibniz sometimes described God as the highest of the monads, he could not avoid the difficulties in the way of reconciling the inclusion of God in the monadic series with the Christian doctrine of the Divine transcendence. In some places he speaks as though God were outside the series and the cause of the monads' existence, or as though they proceeded from Him by 'fulgurations'. A radical optimism pervaded his whole system, expressed in his belief that this world is 'the best of all possible worlds'.

Leibniz defended the validity of the traditional proofs of God's existence, though he thought that they needed modification in detail, notably the *Ontological Proof. In general he was much more favourably disposed towards Scholastic principles than most philosophers who had come under the influence of F. *Bacon and R. *Descartes, and he firmly believed in final causes. He believed that one of the merits of his doctrine of substance was that it was in harmony with *transubstantiation and *consubstantiation alike.

Of the large collection of Leibniz's papers at Hanover, many remain unpublished. The best editions of his philosophical works are those of J. E. Erdmann (Berlin, 1840) and of C. J. Gerhardt (7 vols., 1875–90). A complete edition is in course of publication by the Berlin Academy. R. Latta, The Monadology and other Writings (Eng. transl. with introductions and notes, 1898). L. Couturat, Opuscules et fragments inédits (1903). B. Russell, A Critical Exposition of the Philosophy of Leibniz (1900). Other studies by K. Fischer (1855), J. T. Merz (1884), L. Stein (1890), L. Couturat (1901), E. Cassirer (1902), B. Jansen (1920). A. Görland, Der Gottesbegriff bei Leibniz (1907). G. J. Jordan, The Reunion of the Churches (1927). Good survey of modern literature in D. Mahnke, 'Leibnizens Synthese von Universal-Mathematik und Individual-Metaphysik' in E. *Husserl's Jahrbuch, vii (1925), pp. 305–612. Überweg, iii, 299–340, with bibl., pp. 673–81. W. R. Sorley in E.B. (ed. 11), xvi (1911), pp. 385–90, s.v.; A. Boehm in D.T.C., ix (pt. 1; 1926), cols. 173–95, s.v.; H. Hoffmann in R.G.G. (ed. 2), iii (1929), cols. 1555–8, s.v.; B. Jansen, S.J., in L.Th.K., vi (1934), cols. 460–3, s.v.

LEIDEN. See *Leyden.*

LEIGHTON, ROBERT (1611–84), Abp. of Glasgow. Ordained in 1641, he became principal of Edinburgh University in 1653, Bp. of Dunblane in 1661, and Abp. of Glasgow in 1670. He laboured hard for the restoration of Church unity in Scotland, but being neither a consistent Presbyterian nor a typical Episcopalian, he failed in his hopes of accommodating the two systems. He purposed to retire from his bishopric of Dunblane when the Government continued persecuting the *Covenanters (1665), but on being reassured by *Charles II, relented. He finally resigned his archbishopric

in 1674 after vainly redoubling his efforts towards conciliation.

His writings have never been satisfactorily edited. Early editions by J. Fall (1692–1708) and P. *Doddridge (2 vols., 1748). More recent ed. by W. West (vols. ii–vii), 1869–75; vol. i never publd.). Selections ed. by W. Blair (1883). D. Butler, Life and Letters of Robert Leighton (1903); E. A. *Knox, Robert Leighton, Archbishop of Glasgow [1931]. G. W. Sprott in D.N.B., xxxiii (1893), pp. 4–7.

LEIPZIG, Disputation of. The disputation held at Leipzig from 27 June to 16 July 1519, under the order of George, Duke of Saxony 1500–39), was provoked by J. *Eck's challenge of *Carlstadt. It began with a rather academic discussion between the two opponents on the relations of grace and free will, but the appearance of M. *Luther on 4 July turned the disputation to the question of the doctrinal authority of the Church. Under the pressure of Eck, Luther was led to the decisive statement that Councils not only may err, but actually have erred, holding that among the doctrines of J. *Hus condemned at *Constance some were very Christian and evangelical, and that the same Council had been wrong in affirming the primacy of the Pope. The disputation resulted in the clearing of the issues on both sides and furnished Rome with new material for the process against Luther.

Text in Kidd, pp. 44–51. H. Emser, De Disputatione Lipsicensi, quantum ad Boemos obiter deflexa est, 1519; ed. F. X. Thurnhofer (Corpus Catholicorum, Hft. 4, 1921). J. C. Seidemann, Die Leipziger Disputation im Jahre 1519 (1843). Schottenloher, i (1933), p. 557 (Nos. 13,015–30).

LE NEVE, JOHN (1679–1741), English antiquary. He was educated at Eton and at Trinity College, Cambridge. His *Fasti Ecclesiae Anglicanae, or an Essay towards deducing a regular Succession of all principal Dignitaries in every Cathedral in those parts of Great Britain called England and Wales* (fol., 1716), based on the collections of White *Kennett, was a work of immense industry and has remained a standard treatise on matters of ecclesiastical chronology, &c. His other publications include a Life of R. *Field, Dean of Gloucester (1716; but perhaps only the preface is Le Neve's own work), and *The Lives and Characters . . . of all the Protestant Bishops in the Church of England since the Reformation* (1720). By a curious irony the exact date of his own death is unknown.

His Fasti Ecclesiae Anglicanae was 'corrected and continued from the Year M.DCC.XV. to the present time' by T. D. Hardy (3 vols., Oxford, 1854), with biog. note of Le Neve in vol. i, pp. xiii–xx. W. Rye in D.N.B., xxxiii (1893), p. 35 f.

LE NOURRY, DENIS NICOLAS (1647–1724), *Maurist historian. Educated by the *Oratorians, in 1665 he joined the *Benedictine Order at *Jumièges. From c. 1685 till his death he lived at *Paris. He took part in preparing some of the standard editions of the Fathers, notably of *Cassiodorus (with J. Garet) and St. *Ambrose (with J. du Frische). His own principal work was his *Apparatus ad Bibliothecam Maximam Veterum Patrum et Antiquorum*

Scriptorum (2 vols., 1703 and 1715), a very learned set of dissertations on several of the leading early Fathers and their writings, issued as an Appendix to the Lyons *Bibliotheca*. His *Liber ad Donatum Confessorem de Mortibus Persecutorum* (1710) is notable as the first modern attempt to prove that *Lactantius did not write the treatise 'On the Deaths of Persecutors'.

J. Baudot in *D.T.C.*, ix (pt. 1; 1926), cols. 217 f., s.v., with bibl.

LENT. The fast of forty days before *Easter. In the first three centuries the period of fasting in preparation for Easter did not, as a rule, exceed two or three days, as is evident from a statement of *Irenaeus recorded by *Eusebius (*Hist. Eccl.* 5. 2). The first mention of a period of forty days (τεσσαρακοστή), prob. of Lent, occurs in the Canons of *Nicaea (A.D. 325; can. 5). The custom may have originated in the prescribed fast of candidates for baptism, and the number forty was evidently suggested by the forty days' fasts of *Moses, *Elijah, and esp. our Lord Himself, though till a much later date the period was reckoned differently in the different Churches. In the E. Churches the Lenten Fast was observed during seven weeks, but as Saturdays and Sundays (except *Holy Saturday) were exempt there were only thirty-six actual fast days. The W. Church, on the other hand, fasted during six weeks but also counted thirty-six days, as they normally left out only the Sundays. Only in *Jerusalem were the actual forty days observed as early as the 4th cent. by fasting on five days for eight weeks. Local customs, however, long varied and acc. to *Socrates (*Hist. Eccl.* 5. 22) even a fast of three weeks or a fortnight was called τεσσαρακοστή. The number of forty was not made up in the Latin Church until the 7th cent. when the four days from *Ash Wednesday to the First Sunday in Lent were added, a practice first attested by the *Gelasian Sacramentary and spreading from Rome throughout the W.

During the early centuries the observance of the fast was very strict. Only one meal a day, taken towards evening, was allowed, and flesh-meat and fish, and in most places also eggs and *lacticinia*, were absolutely forbidden. From the 9th cent. onwards the practice began to be considerably relaxed. The hour for breaking the fast was gradually anticipated to three o'clock in the afternoon, and by the 15th cent. it had become the general custom even for religious to eat at noon. These relaxations entailed not only the anticipation of the evening office of *Vespers to before midday (in order to keep the rule of not eating before Vespers), but also the concession of a 'collation' in the evening. This consisted originally only in a drink, but from the 13th cent. included some light food. Fish was allowed throughout the Middle Ages, and from the 15th cent. abstinence from *lacticinia* came to be more and more generally dispensed.

In modern times the Lenten fast has been much alleviated. Apart from the actual fast, Lent is normally observed as a time of penance by abstaining from festivities (including the solemnization of marriage), by almsgiving, and by devoting more than the usual time to religious exercises. See also *Refreshment Sunday*, *Holy Week*.

The observance of Lent continued in the C of E after the Reformation. It was expressly prescribed by the BCP, and sometimes enforced even by secular authorities. Dispensations allowing the use of meat were issued in special cases, e.g. by Abp. W. *Juxon. Falling into comparative disuse in the 18th cent., it was revived by the Tractarians in the 19th and is now widely kept.

H. Thurston, S.J., *Lent and Holy Week* (1904); J. Dowden, *The Church Year and Calendar* (1910), pp. 79–85. F. X. Funk, *Kirchengeschichtliche Abhandlungen und Untersuchungen*, i (1897), 'Die Entwickelung des Osterfastens', No. ix, pp. 241–78. C. Callewaert, *Sacris Erudiri* (Steenbrugge, 1940), pp. 449–671. R. Sinker in *D.C.A.*, ii (1880), pp. 972–7; H. Thurston in *C.E.*, ix (1910), pp. 152–4; E. Vacardard in *D.T.C.*, ii (1905), cols. 1724–50, and in *D.A.C.L.*, ii (pt. 2; 1910), cols. 2139–58, both s.v. 'Carême'; P. Siffrin, O.S.B., in *E.C.*, x (1953), cols. 379 f., s.v. 'Quaresima', all with bibl.

LEO I, St. (d. 461), 'Leo the Great', Pope from 440. Little is known of his early life beyond the fact that as a Roman deacon he opposed *Pelagianism. His Papacy is remarkable chiefly through the enormous extent to which he advanced and consolidated the influence of the Roman see. At a time of general disorder, he sought to strengthen the Church by energetic central government, based on a firm belief that the supremacy of his see was of Divine and Scriptural authority, and he pressed his claims to jurisdiction in Africa, Spain, and Gaul. He also secured from *Valentinian III a rescript which recognized his jurisdiction over all the W. provinces. Though his jurisdiction was not recognized in the E., he was drawn into E. affairs by the *Eutychian controversy, and his support was coveted by all parties. His legates presided over the Council of *Chalcedon (451), where his *Tome (449) was accepted as a standard of Christological orthodoxy. In the political sphere he also much increased Papal prestige by persuading the Huns to withdraw beyond the Danube (452) and securing concessions when the Vandals took Rome (455). Doctrinally Leo was clear and forcible, but not profound. He knew no Greek. His extant works are 96 sermons and 143 letters. He was declared by *Benedict XIV a '*Doctor of the Church'. Feast day, in the E., 18 Feb.; in the W., 11 Apr.

Works ed. by P. *Quesnel (2 vols., Paris, 1675; strongly *Gallicanist) and by P. and H. *Ballerini (3 vols., Venice, 1753–7, with replies to Quesnel's Disquisitions from the *Ultramontane standpoint); both deservedly famous Patristic editions. The latter is repr. in J. P. Migne, *PL*, liv–lvi. Modern crit. ed. of Leo's Epistles in E. *Schwartz, *A.C.O.*, II, 4 (1932). Eng. tr. of Letters by C. L. Feltoe (1896). C. *Gore, *Leo the Great* (n.d.; popular); W. *Bright, *Sermons of S. Leo the Great on the Incarnation* (1862; ed. 2, 1886); T. [G.] Jalland, *The Life and Times of St. Leo the Great* (1941). A. Regnier, *S. Léon le Grand* ('Les Saints'; 1910). Good arts. by P. *Batiffol in *D.T.C.*, s.v., ix, cols. 218–301, and H. *Lietzmann in *P.W.*, xii (2), cols. 1962–73.

LEO III, St. (d. 816), Pope. A Roman priest of humble birth and blameless character, he was unanimously elected Pope in 795. From the beginning of his reign he had to contend with the opposition of the ambitious relatives of his predecessor, *Hadrian I, who, during the procession of St. Mark's Day in 799, set on him and tried to mutilate him. After recovering from his wounds he fled to *Charlemagne, to whom he had sent the keys of the *confessio* of St. Peter in 795, and who now provided him with an escort back to Rome. In 800 Charles having come himself to investigate the charges brought against the Pope, Leo cleared himself by an oath of compurgation. On Christmas Day, two days later, he crowned Charles Roman Emperor, thus inaugurating a new age in Europe. At Charlemagne's instigation the Pope took severe measures against the *Adoptianist heresy, but refused to accede to the Emperor's request to include the *Filioque* in the *Nicene Creed, in order not to alienate the Greeks. Several times he intervened in the differences between the Abps. of *Canterbury and the Anglo-Saxon kings, excommunicating the usurper of the throne of Kent, Eadbert Praen, and withdrawing the *pallium from *Lichfield. In the E. he encouraged the monks in their opposition to the Emp. Constantine VI, who had divorced his wife. After Charlemagne's death in 814, trouble began again for the Pope, who had to crush another conspiracy against himself and, shortly afterwards, revolts of nobles and peasants of the Campagna by the help of the Duke of Spoleto. Assisted by Charlemagne's rich gifts, Leo III did much to adorn the churches in Rome and other cities of Italy and was an efficient and charitable ruler of the *Patrimony. He was canonized in 1673. Feast day, 12 June.

Some of his Correspondence and Privilegia are repr., mainly from J. D. *Mansi, in J. P. Migne, *PL*, cii, 1023–72; ten letters also ed. P. Jaffé, *Bibliotheca Rerum Germanicarum*, iv, Monumenta Carolina (Berlin, 1867), pp. 307–34. Id., *Regesta Pontificum Romanorum*, i (ed. 2 by W. Wattenbach, Leipzig, 1885), pp. 307–16. *L.P.* (Duchesne), ii, pp. 1–48. C. Huelsen, 'Osservazioni sulla biografia di Leone III nel "Liber Pontificalis"' in *Atti della Pontificia Accademia Romana di Archeologia*, Ser. 3, Rendiconti, i (1923), pp. 107–19. L. *Duchesne, *Les Premiers Temps de l'état pontifical* (ed. 2; 1904), pp. 167–88. Mann, ii (1906), pp. 1–110. Fliche–Martin, vi (1937), pp. 148–203. É. Amann in *D.T.C.*, ix (pt. 1; 1926) cols. 304–12, s.v. 'Léon III'; L. Gulli in *E.C.*, vii (1951), cols. 1144–6, s.v. 'Leone III'. See also bibl. to *Charlemagne*.

LEO IV, St. (d. 855), Pope. A native of Rome, he became cardinal-priest of the *titulus* of the *Quattro Coronati and in 847 was elected to succeed Sergius II. He at once set about repairing the damage done by the Saracens (846), putting a wall, 40 ft. high, round the part of Rome on the right of the Tiber (henceforward the 'Leonine City'); he restored many churches (*Vatican, *Lateran, St. Martin's, Quattro Coronati); and he rebuilt and fortified ravaged cities (Porto, Subiaco). In 850 he crowned Louis, the son of Lothaire, as co-Emperor. In 853 he is said to have 'hallowed' the young *Alfred as future King of

England. Among those whom he sought to bring under his authority were *Anastasius Bibliothecarius (later anti-Pope), John, Abp. of Ravenna, *Hincmar of Reims and Nomenoe, Duke of Brittany. He was keenly interested in the liturgical chant and the *Asperges is ascribed to him. A terrible conflagration in the Borgo, said to have been extinguished in answer to Leo's prayers, is the subject of *Raphael's celebrated fresco in the Stanza dell' Incendio in the Vatican. Feast day, 17 July.

Various 'Epistolae et Decreta et Homilia' in J. P. Migne, *PL*, cxv, 629–84; fragg. of his Register ed. P. Ewald in *N.A.*, v (1879), pp. 375–98, and ed. A. de Hirsch-Gereuth in *M.G.H.*, Epistolae, v (1899), pp. 585–612. *L.P.* (Duchesne), ii, 106–39. L. *Duchesne, *Les Premiers Temps de l'état pontifical* (ed. 2, 1904), pp. 217–29. Mann, ii (1906), pp. 258–307. É. Amann in Fliche–Martin, vi (1931), pp. 281–8. Id. in *D.T.C.*, ix (pt. 1; 1926), cols. 312–16, s.v. 'Léon IV', with further bibl.

LEO IX, St. (1002–54), Pope from 1048. His original name was Bruno. A native of Alsace of noble birth, he was educated at Toul, where he was later successively canon and, from 1026, bishop. He became a keen supporter of the *Cluniac monastic reform. Through the influence of Henry III, whose favour he had secured, he was elected Pope in 1048, and at once began to reform the Church from its decadence of a century and a half. In his pastoral zeal and personal humility, he did much to foster a wholly new ideal of the Papacy. At the Easter Synod of 1049 celibacy was enforced on all clergy from the rank of *subdeacon upwards and shortly afterwards Councils were held at Pavia, *Reims, and Mainz, at which decrees were promulgated against *simony and other abuses. In carrying out his programme Leo travelled extensively and was assisted by several able advisers, among them Hildebrand (*Gregory VII), *Humbert, and St. *Peter Damian. At the Easter Synod at Rome in 1050, *Berengar of Tours was condemned for his Eucharistic doctrine. The latter years of his pontificate were marred by defeat at the hands of the Normans at Civitella (18 June 1053) and the break with the E. Church. He has a place in the *Roman Martyrology for 19 Apr.

Contemporary biography ed. A. Poncelet, 'Vie et miracles du Pape S. Léon IX', in *Anal. Boll.*, xxv (1906), pp. 258–97, with further notes ib., xxvi (1907), pp. 302–4. O. Delarc, *Un Pape alsacien. Essai historique sur saint Léon IX et son temps* (1876). E. Martin, *St. Léon IX, 1002–1054* ('Les Saints'; 1904). J. Drehmann, *Leo IX und die Simonie* (Beiträge zur Kulturgeschichte des Mittelalters, Hft. 2; 1908); P. P. Brucker, *L'Alsace et l'Église au temps du Pape St. Léon IX* (2 vols., 1889). A. Fliche, *La Reforme grégorienne*, i (S.S.L.. vi; 1924), pp. 129–59; J. Gay, *Les Papes du XIe siècle et la chrétienté* (1926), pp. 121–67. Mann, iv (1910), pp. 18–182, with reff. to sources. É. Amann in *D.T.C.*, ix (pt. 1; 1926), cols. 320–9, s.v. 'Léon IX', with bibl.

LEO X (1475–1521), Pope from 1513. Giovanni de' Medici was the second son of 'Lorenzo the Magnificent'. He was destined early for an ecclesiastical career and created a cardinal in 1489, but not invested with the insignia of office until he had completed three years' study of theology and canon law at Pisa. After the expulsion of his family from Florence in 1494 he led a wandering and almost Bohemian life in Germany, Holland, and France, returning to Rome in 1500. Towards the end of the pontificate of *Julius II, the affairs of the young cardinal began to improve. In 1511 he became legate in *Bologna and the Romagna, and in 1513, at the age of 38, he was elected Pope.

The high hopes which had been placed upon him were soon disappointed. Leo was, indeed, a person of moral life and sincerely religious, but he was pleasure-loving, easy-going, and far too liberal with money and offices. Within two years he had squandered the fortune left by Julius II and was in serious financial embarrassment. In politics, concern for the independence of the Papal states led him to pursue a shifting course. Eventually he concluded a concordat with Francis I of France (in place of the *Pragmatic Sanction of Bourges) which firmly established royal influence over the French Church (1516). He was completely blind to what was involved in the revolt of M. *Luther, whom he excommunicated in 1520.

Regesta ed. J. *Hergenröther (2 vols. only, to 16 Oct. 1515; Freiburg i.Br., 1884–91). Life by Paolo Giovio, Bp. of Nocera (Florence, 1548). W. Roscoe, *The Life and Pontificate of Leo the Tenth* (4 vols., 1805). E. Rodocanachi, *Le Pontificat de Léon X* (1931). F. S. Nitti, *Leone X e la sua politica* (1892). G. B. Picotti, *La giovinezza di Leone X* [1928]. G. Truc, *Léon X et son siècle* (1941). H. M. Vaughan, *The Medici Popes* (1908), pp. 1–284. Pastor vii and viii (1908), with full bibl. K. Löffler in *C.E.*, ix (1910), pp. 162–166, s.v.; G. Mollat in *D.T.C.*, ix (pt. 1; 1926), cols. 329–32, s.v. 'Léon X', with bibl.; G. B. Picotti in *E.C.*, vii (1951), cols. 1150–55, s.v. 'Leone X', with further bibl. See also bibl. to *Reformation*.

LEO XIII (1810–1903), Pope from 1878. Vincenzo Gioacchino Pecci was a native of Carpineto. He was educated by the *Jesuits of Viterbo and later studied at the 'Academy of Noble Ecclesiastics' in Rome. Ordained priest in 1837, he was sent on a mission to Benevento in the next year. In 1843 he was appointed nuncio to Brussels, where he gained considerable diplomatic experience. On missions to London, *Paris, *Cologne, and many other European cities he became acquainted with modern social questions which were to play an important part in his pontificate. In 1846 *Gregory XVI made him Bp. of Perugia, and in 1853 he was created cardinal by *Pius IX. When, in 1860, Perugia passed under the secular power of Piedmont, the Cardinal opposed the new laws, esp. the suppression of ecclesiastical jurisdiction, the institution of civil marriage, and the spoliation of the religious orders.

After his election to the Papacy in 1878, Leo outlined his programme of reconciling the Church with modern civilization in his first encyclical, 'Inscrutabili Dei Consilio' (21 Apr. 1878). This aim, largely a reversal of the policy of *Pius IX, determined his attitude towards the great powers. He restored good relations with Germany after the *Kulturkampf by procuring the gradual abolition of the *May Laws in 1886 and 1887, and with Belgium after the victory of the Catholic party

in 1884. In 1892 he established an Apostolic Delegation in Washington, and he renewed contacts with Russia and Japan. The improvement of relations with Gt. Britain found expression in King Edward VII's visit to the *Vatican in 1903. His policy failed, however, in the Italian question; the Pope remained the 'Prisoner of the Vatican', and the prohibition of the participation of Catholics in Italian politics was retained. In France, too, relations between Church and state deteriorated, and the Pope's last years were darkened by the increasingly anti-Catholic legislation, esp. the *Associations Laws of 1901.

Leo XIII's pontificate was esp. important for the lead he gave on the burning political and social questions of his time. In some notable encyclicals he developed the Christian doctrine of the state on the basis of St. *Thomas Aquinas. In 'Immortale Dei' (1 Nov. 1885) he defined the respective spheres of spiritual and temporal power; 'Libertas Praestantissimum' (20 June 1888) deals with the freedom of citizens, and 'Graves de Communi' (18 Jan. 1901) with Christian democracy. He upheld the dignity and rights of the state, whether monarchy or republic, and emphasized the compatibility of Catholic teaching with a moderate democracy. His most important pronouncement on social questions was the famous '*Rerum Novarum' (q.v.) of 15 May 1891. Among his activities in the doctrinal sphere his injunction of the study of St. Thomas Aquinas by '*Aeterni Patris' (q.v.) of 4 Aug. 1879 had far-reaching consequences, leading to a great revival of Thomist studies. In 1883 he opened the Vatican archives to historical research; he encouraged the study of the Bible in the encyclical '*Providentissimus Deus' (18 Nov. 1893) and instituted the *Biblical Commission in 1902. He gave a limited measure of encouragement to the new methods of Biblical criticism, which ceased in the pontificate of his successor. His attitude to other Christian Churches is marked by the letter 'Praeclara' of 1894, in which he invited Greeks and Protestants of all shades to unite with Rome; but he rejected the conception of union as a federation of Churches in the encyclical '*Satis Cognitum' of 1896. In his Apostolic Letter 'Ad Anglos' (1895) he encouraged Anglican aspirations to union as promoted by Lord *Halifax and the *English Church Union, and in the same year appointed a commission for the investigation of *Anglican Ordinations. They were rejected as invalid in '*Apostolicae Curae' (1896). Leo XIII promoted the spiritual life of the Church in many encyclicals dealing with the redemptive work of Christ, the Eucharist, and devotion to the BVM and the *Rosary; and he sought to renew the spirit of St. *Francis by modifying the rules of the *Third Order in accordance with the requirements of his times. Following a revelation received by Mary von Droste-Vischering, religious of the Good Shepherd of Angers, he consecrated the whole human race to the Divine *Heart of Jesus in the jubilee year 1900. He also encouraged the work of the missions, esp. the formation of a native clergy. In 1887 he condemned 40 propositions from the works of A. *Rosmini contradicting the doctrine of St. Thomas, and in 1899 he censured in 'Testem Benevolentiae' the teaching known as '*Americanism'.

Acta (22 vols., index and appendix, Rome, 1881–1905); Allocutiones, Epistolae, Constitutiones, aliaque Acta Praecipua (8 vols., Bruges, 1887–1910). Carmina, Inscriptiones, Numismata, ed. J. Bach (Cologne, 1903). The basic life is that of C. de T'Serclaes (3 vols., Bruges, 1894–1906). The many others include those by M. Spahn (Munich, 1905), E. Soderini (3 vols., Milan, 1932–3; Eng. tr. of vols. i and ii, 1934–5), R. Fülöp-Miller (Leipzig, 1935, with bibl., pp. 206–15; Eng. tr., 1937), and F. Hayward (Paris, 1937). E. Lecanuet, La Vie de l'Église sous Léon XIII (1930). U. Benigni in C.E., ix (1910), pp. 167–73, s.v.; G. Goyau in D.T.C., ix (pt. 1; 1926), cols. 334–59, s.v. 'Léon XIII'; E. Martire, S.J., in E.C., viii (1951), cols. 1158–63, s.v. 'Leone XIII', all with bibl. See also bibl. to Anglican Orders.

LEO III (c. 675–740), Byzantine Emperor, usually 'the Isaurian', but more correctly the Syrian. Born at Germanicia in Commagene, he won distinction as a soldier and became commander of the eastern army under Anastasius II. In 717 he was elected Emperor in place of the usurper Theodosius III. In the same year began the siege of *Constantinople by the Saracens, ending with Leo's victory in 718, which saved Europe from Islam. After the Mohammedan danger had been removed he effected many administrative reforms, and in 726 issued a new code of law, the 'Ecloge'. He also introduced reforms in the religious sphere. From 726 to 729 he published a number of edicts against image worship and thus initiated the *Iconoclastic Controversy. In 730 he replaced the Patriarch *Germanus I, an upholder of images, by Anastasius, against popular opinion, which was supported by the monks and the majority of Byzantine theologians. The defence of the veneration of images by the Popes, *Gregory II and Gregory III, in letters and synodal decrees caused the Emperor to annex the Papal Patrimonies in Southern Italy and the province of Illyria; he failed, however, to abolish image worship. In 740 he won another decisive victory over the Arabs, and thus at his death left the Empire well consolidated.

Eng. tr. of the Ecloge by E. H. Freshfield, with full introd. (Cambridge, 1926). K. Schenk, Kaiser Leon III. Ein Beitrag zur Geschichte des Bilderstreits (Inaugural Diss., Halle, 1880); id., 'Kaiser Leons III Walten im Innern' in B.Z., v (1896), pp. 257–310. G. Findlay, A History of Greece (ed. H. F. Tozer) ii (1877), pp. 13–44. A. A. Vasiliev, History of the Byzantine Empire, 324–1453 (Eng. tr. from Russian, ed. 2, Oxford, 1952), pp. 234–59. C. Diehl in C. Med. H., iv (1923), pp. 2–12, with bibl., pp. 795–7. See also bibl. to Iconoclastic Controversy.

LEO VI (866–912), currently known as **Leo the Philosopher** or **Leo Sapiens**, Byzantine Emperor. Succeeding Basil I in 886, he opened his reign by banishing the Patr. of Constantinople, *Photius, to a monastery and installing his brother, Stephen, in his place, thus restoring normal relations with the W. In the disputes that followed his fourth marriage, he appealed from the Patriarch, now Nicolas Mysticus, to the Pope, who recognized

the validity of the marriage against the Patriarch, and Leo then deposed Nicolas in favour of Euthymius I. The extensive writings of the Emperor contain many novellae and other items of ecclesiastical legislation, two homilies attacking the double procession of the Holy Ghost, and hymns and treatises in honour of the BVM.

Collection of his Works in J. P. Migne, PG, cvii; further panegyrics ed. by Akakios, monk of Mt. *Athos (Athens, 1868); funeral oration of his father ed. A. Vogt–I. Hausherr, S.J. (Orientalia Christiana, vol. xxvi, No. 1 (fasc. 77); 1932). Study (in Russian) by N. Popov (Moscow, 1892). M Mitard, 'Études sur le règne de Léon VI' in B.Z., xii (1903), pp. 585–94. C. Diehl, Figures byzantines (1906), ch. 8, 'Les Quatres Mariages de l'Empereur Léon VI', pp. 181–215. L. Petit, 'Notes sur les homélies de Léon le Sage' in É.O., ii (1899–1900), pp. 245–9; D. Serruys, 'Les Homélies de Léon le Sage' in B.Z., xii (1903), pp. 167–70. S. Salaville, A.A., in D.T.C., ix (1926), cols. 365–94, s.v. 'Léon VI le Sage'.

LEODEGAR, St., Ledger, or **Leger** (c. 616–79), Bp. of Autun. He was made archdeacon at an early age by his uncle, Bp. Dido of Poitiers, and became Abbot of St. Maxentius in 653, where he introduced the Rule of St. *Benedict. In 663 he became Bp. of Autun and later imposed the Rule on all the religious houses in his diocese. He prob. also ordered his clergy to adopt the *Athanasian Creed, possibly as a safeguard against the *Monothelete heresy. After the death of Clotaire III in 670 Leodegar became involved in the struggles between the claimants to the throne, in the course of which he was successively banished, blinded (676), and tortured, and finally beheaded by his opponents. Though killed in a political cause he was soon regarded as a saint and martyr, and his cultus became popular throughout France. Feast day, 2 (occasionally 3) Oct.

Two lives, formerly believed to be nearly contemporary, but prob. much later though based on an early life now lost, pr., with full comm., in AA.SS., Oct. I (1765), pp. 355–491. Also ed., with attempted reconstruction of original life, by B. Krusch in M.G.H., Scriptores Rerum Merovingicarum, v (1910), pp. 249–362. Id., 'Die älteste Vita Leudegarii' in N.A., xvi (1891), pp. 565–96. [Fr.] Camerlinck, O.P., Saint Léger, évêque d'Autun ('Les Saints', 1910). A. Lesage, Le Fondateur de Liège. Le martyr saint Léger, évêque d'Autun. Sa première sepulture à Saint-Trond (1919). H. *Leclercq, O.S.B., in D.A.C.L., viii (pt. 2, 1929), cols. 2460–92, s.v. 'Léger'.

LEONARD, St. (6th cent.), hermit. Despite his great popularity in the Middle Ages, nothing was heard of him before the 11th cent. Acc. to the 'Vita' (c. 1050), he was a Frankish nobleman of the court of King *Clovis, whom St. *Remigius converted to Christianity. He lived in a cell at Noblac, nr. Limoges, and later founded a monastery. His cult spread in the 12th cent. to England, France, Italy, and Germany, and many churches were dedicated to him. He is the special patron of prisoners and also of peasants and of the sick. Feast day, 6 Nov.

Excerpts of the Vita ed. B. Krusch in M.G.H., Scriptores Rerum Merovingicarum, iii (1896), pp. 394–9; full text in AA.SS., Nov. III (1910), pp. 149–55, with comm. by A. Poncelet, S.J., pp. 139–49, and other material pp. 155–209. F. Arbellot, Vie de saint Léonard, solitaire de Limousin, ses miracles et son culte (1883). J. A. Aich, Leonard, der grosse Patron des Volkes (Vienna, 1928).

LEONARDO DA VINCI (1452–1519), Italian painter and scholar. The natural son of a Florentine notary and a peasant woman, he became a pupil of A. del Verrocchio at Florence where he stayed till 1482. From 1483 to 1499 he lived at Milan, and during this period executed some of his best-known works, among them the *Virgin of the Rocks* and the *Last Supper* (1495–8), the latter done on the refectory wall of the Dominican convent of Sta Maria delle Grazie. The originality of the *Last Supper* lay in that it depicted not the institution of the Eucharist but the moment of the announcement of the betrayal, the quiet superiority of the sublime figure of Christ dominating a scene filled with human emotions and agitation. When the French invaded Milan (1499), Leonardo left and began to lead a nomadic life mainly devoted to scientific and scholarly work. In this he covered an enormous field of knowledge, and made creative contributions to such different branches as geological research and the construction of guns and even air-machines. To this period belong his *St. Anne, Mona Lisa*, and a weak *St. John the Baptist*. With his complete mastery of technique, Leonardo introduced the style of the High Renaissance.

Reproductions of his pictures (in black and white) ed. H. Bodmer (Klassiker der Kunst in Gesamtausgaben, xxxix [1931]); smaller collection of reproductions (incl. some colour plates) ed. L. Goldscheider (Phaidon Press, London, 1943). Drawings ed., with introd. and notes, by A. E. Popham (London, 1946). K. [M.] Clark, *A Catalogue of the Drawings of Leonardo da Vinci in the Collection of his Majesty the King at Windsor Castle* (2 vols., with reproductions, 1935). Literary Works, with Eng. tr., ed. J. P. Richter (London, 1883; ed. 2 by J. P. Richter–I. A. Richter, 2 vols., 1939). Facsimile reproduction of his MSS., with transcription and Fr. tr., by M. C. Ravaisson–Mollien (6 vols., Paris, 1881–91). The Notebooks of Leonardo da Vinci tr. into English by E. MacCurdy (2 vols., London, 1906; ed. 2, 1938); selections ed. I. A. Richter (World's Classics, dxxx; 1952). General studies include those by W. von Seidlitz (2 vols., Berlin, 1909), E. McCurdy (London, 1928). Studies dealing specifically with his art by E. Müntz (Paris, 1899; Eng. tr., 2 vols., 1898), O. Siren (Stockholm, 1911; Eng. tr., 1916), E. Hildebrandt (Berlin, 1927), E. McCurdy (London, 1933), and K. [M.] Clark (Ryerson Lectures for 1936; Cambridge, 1939). E. Solmi, *Scritti vinciani* (1924). I. B. Hart, *The Mechanical Investigations of Leonardo da Vinci* (1925). J. P. McCurrich, *Leonardo da Vinci, the Anatomist* (Carnegie Institution of Washington Publication, ccccxi; 1930). Lorna Lewis, *Leonardo the Inventor and Pioneer* (1937). E. Verga, *Bibliografia vinciana, 1493–1930* (2 vols., 1931). S. Colvin in *E.B.* (ed. 11), xvi (1911), pp. 444–54, s.v.; G. Castelfranco in *E.C.*, vii (1951), cols. 1120–33, s.v., both with bibl.

LEONINE CITY (Lat. *Civitas Leonina*; Ital. *Città Leonina*). The part of Rome on the right bank of the Tiber, fortified with a wall by Pope Leo IV in 848–52. Besides the *Vatican, it contains the Castello S. Angelo.

LEONINE PRAYERS. In the Roman rite, the prayers recited in the vernacular by priest and people at the end of Mass. Their present form (three *Hail Mary*'s, the *Salve Regina*, a collect *Deus Refugium Nostrum*, an invocation of St. *Michael) goes back to *Leo XIII. In 1859 *Pius IX had introduced for local use similar prayers for the preservation of the Papal States, which continued to be said, even

after the end of the temporal power in 1870; in 1884 Leo XIII extended their use to the whole world, with special reference to the last stages of the *Kulturkampf*; and in 1886 he reissued them in a revised form, adding the invocation of St. *Michael. A final petition ('Most Sacred Heart of Jesus, have mercy on us', three times), apparently still optional, was added by *Pius X in 1904.

Jungmann (ed. 1949), ii, pp. 552–6.

LEONINE SACRAMENTARY. The earliest surviving book of *Mass prayers acc. to the Roman Rite. It exists in a single MS. of the early 7th cent., preserved in the Chapter Library at *Verona (cod. lxxxv), and was first published in 1735 by J. Bianchini. Its attribution to Pope *Leo I (*d.* 461) is quite arbitrary, though certain of its prayers may well be Leo's compositions. The Sacramentary is a fragment, possessing no *Ordinary or *Canon of the Mass, and contains solely the variable parts of the liturgy, and these only for certain months of the year.

J. Bianchini, *Vitae Romanorum Pontificum*, IV (1735,) pp. xii–lvii. Bianchini's text repr. by L. A. *Muratori (Venice, 1748) and J. A. *Assemani (Rome, 1754); rev. text by P. and H. *Ballerini in *S. Leonis Opera*, ii (Venice, 1756), cols. 1–160, repr. J. P. Migne, *PL*, lv. 21–156. Modern ed. by C. L. Feltoe (Cambridge, 1896). P. Bruylants, 'Concordance verbale du sacramentaire léonien' in *Archivum Latinitatis Medii Aevi*, Nos. 18–19 (Brussels, 1945–8). Fundamental is A. Stuiber, *Libelli Sacramentorum Romani* (Theophaneia, 6, Bonn, 1950), who demonstrates that the work is not a Sacramentary in the proper sense, but a private collection of Mass *libelli* which had circulated independently. Other important recent studies include B. *Capelle, O.S.B., 'Messes du pape S. Gélase dans le sacramentaire léonien' in *R. Bén.*, lvi (1945–6), pp. 12–41; id., 'Retouches gélasiennes dans le sacramentaire léonien' in ib., lxi (1951), pp. 3–14; C. Callewaert, 'St. Léon le Grand et les textes du Léonien' in *Sacris Erudiri*, i (1948), pp. 35–132; C. Coebergh, O.S.B., 'St. Gélase I, auteur principal du soi-disant sacramentaire léonien' in *E.L.*, lxiv (1950), pp. 214–37, and lxv (1951), pp. 171–81. F. *Cabrol, O.S.B., in *D.A.C.L.*, viii (pt. 2; 1929), cols. 2549–73; A. Bugnini in *E.C.*, x (1953), cols. 1560–4, s.v. 'Sacramentario, II', both with bibl. Crit. ed. ('Sacramentarium Veronense') by L. C. Mohlberg, O.S.B., and others (Rome, 1956).

LEONTIUS OF BYZANTIUM (6th cent.), anti-*Monophysite theologian. He is prob. to be distinguished from the Scythian monk of the same name who took a prominent part in the *Theopaschite controversy and with whom, until recently, he has been identified; on the other hand, he seems to be the same person as the *Origenist Leontius mentioned in *Cyril of Scythopolis's 'Vita S. Sabae' (so E. *Schwartz). Despite his theological importance, virtually nothing is known of his life. He was a staunch upholder of the *Chalcedonian Christology which he interpreted on Cyrilline principles, introducing the notion of the *Enhypostasia (q.v.). In his polemic he made full use of contemporary philosophy (*Aristotelianism in logic, *Neo-Platonism in psychology). His chief theological work is his 'Libri III contra Nestorianos et Eutychianos' (*c.* 543–4), of which Bk. II took the form of a dialogue between an Orthodox and an *Aphthartodocetist, and Bk. III is directed esp. against *Theodore of Mopsuestia. He also wrote two works against *Severus of Antioch ('Solutio Argumentorum Severi' and 'Triginta Capitula adv. Nestorium'). He is prob. also the author (despite some modern doubts) of *Adversus Fraudes Apollinistarum*, a work of considerable critical acumen on the forgeries of the *Apollinarians (q.v.).

Of other works traditionally ascribed to him, the 'De Sectis' (perh. to be ascribed to *Theodore of Raïthu) is certainly not his, while the 'Adv. Nestorianos' and 'Contra Monophysitas' are to be assigned to a hitherto unrecognized 'Leontius of Jerusalem'.

Works in J. P. Migne, *PG*, lxxxvi, 1185–2016. F. *Loofs, *Das Leben und die polemischen Werke des Leontius von Byzantium* (1887; important, but mostly superseded); J. P. Jungklas, *Leontius von Byzanz* (Paderborn, 1908); V. Grumel, A.A., in *D.T.C.*, ix (pt. 1; 1926), cols. 400–26. All these largely superseded by E. Schwartz, *Kyrillos von Skythopolis* (T.U., xlix, Hft. 2, 1939), p. 388, n. 2; M. Richard, 'Léonce de Jérusalem et Léonce de Byzance' in *Mélanges de Science religieuse*, i (1944), pp. 35–88; and B. Altaner, 'Der griechische Theologe Leontius und Leontius der skythische Mönch' in *T.Q.*, cxxxviii (1947), pp 147–65. Altaner (ed. 1950), p. 460 f.; E. Peterson in *E.C.*, vii (1951), col. 1168 f., s.v. 'Leonzio di Bisanzio'.

LEPANTO, Battle of. The naval battle, fought on 7 Oct. 1571 in which the 'Christian League', created chiefly by the efforts of *Pius V between Venice and Spain, with help from the Papal states and Genoa, decisively beat the Turks, who were threatening W. civilization. Lepanto, on the northern entrance to the Gulf of Corinth, is the ancient Naupactos. In thanksgiving for the victory, the Pope instituted a special feast of Our Lady on 7 Oct., which since 1573 has been kept as the Feast of the *Rosary (q.v.).

LEPORIUS (early 5th cent.), monk. Probably a native of Trier (so G. *Morin), he issued a letter in which he taught the essential similarity between Christ's moral experience and our own, and other doctrines akin to *Pelagianism and early *Nestorianism. Rebuked by several of the bishops of S. Gaul, Leporius and his followers fled to Africa where he was brought into contact with St. *Augustine (*Ep. 219, ad Proculum et Cylinnium*); and he publicly confessed his error at Carthage in a 'Libellus Emendationis', subscribed by *Aurelius, Bp. of Carthage, and Augustine.

'Libellus' first publd. by J. *Sirmond, S.J., *Opuscula Dogmatica Veterum Quinque Scriptorum* (Paris, 1630), pp. 1–34; repr. in J. P. Migne, *PL*, xxxi, 1221–30. G. Morin, O.S.B., 'Notes d'ancienne littérature chrétienne: v, Solution d'un problème d'histoire littéraire: le diocèse d'origine de Leporius, théologien gaulois du Vᵉ siècle' in *R. Bén.*, xiv (1897), p. 102 f. Bardenhewer, iv, 542 f. H. W. Phillott in *D.C.B.*, iii (1882), p. 702 f.; É. Amann in *D.T.C.*, ix (pt. 1; 1926), cols. 434–40.

LE QUIEN, MICHEL (1661–1733), patristic scholar. In 1681 he entered the *Dominican Order at Paris, where he spent most of his life. His two principal works were (1) *Oriens Christianus* (published posthumously [1740] in 3 vols.), in which he collected a vast amount of material on the history of the E. Churches, and (2) his edition of the works of St. *John

of Damascus (1712), still the standard text. His other writings included *La Nullité des ordinations anglicanes* (2 vols., 1725) and *La Nullité des ordinations anglicanes démontrée de nouveau* (2 vols., 1730), both in answer to P. *Courayer's book on the subject.

Quétif-Échard, ii (1721), pp. 808–10. J. Carreyre in *D.T.C.*, ix (pt. i; 1926), cols. 441–3, s.v., with bibl.

LÉRINS. The ancient name of two islands off Cannes in the Mediterranean, on the smaller of which (formerly 'Lerinum', now 'St.-Honorat') a celebrated abbey was founded by St. *Honoratus *c.* 410. It was the nursery of a long line of scholars and bishops, among them St. *Patrick (Apostle of *Ireland), St. *Hilary (Bp. of Arles), St. *Vincent (author of the *Commonitorium*), St. *Lupus (Bp. of Troyes), and St. *Caesarius (Bp. of Arles). Its religious history continued unbroken down to 1788, when it was secularized. Since 1871 a *Cistercian convent has been re-established on the island.

L. Alliez, *Histoire du monastère de Lérins* (2 vols., 1862); H. Moris, *L'Abbaye de Lérins*. Histoire et monuments (1909); A. C. Cooper-Marsdin, *The History of the Islands of the Lerins* (Cambridge, 1913; uncritical). V. Barralis, *Chronologia Sanctorum et aliorum Virorum illustrium ac Abbatum Sacrae Insulae Lerinensis* (Lyons, 1613). 'Cartulary' of Lérins, ed. H. Moris and E. Blanc (2 vols. Paris, 1883–1905); reconstructed 'Bullarium', ed. L. H. Labande in *Annales de la Société des Lettres, Sciences et des Arts des Alpes Maritimes*, xxiv (1922–3), pp. 117–98. H. *Leclercq, O.S.B., in *D.A.C.L.*, viii (pt. 2, 1929), cols. 2596–627; K. Hoffmann in *L.Th.K.*, vi (1934), col. 517 f., both with full bibl.

LESLIE, CHARLES (1650–1722), *Nonjuring divine. After studying law at *Trinity College, Dublin, he was ordained in 1680 and presented in 1686 to the chancellorship of Connor. Refusal to take the oaths at the Revolution of 1688 deprived him of his benefice, and in 1689 he withdrew to London. Here he continued an ardent Jacobite and, after the failure of the 1715 rebellion, he joined the Pretender and accompanied him to Rome. His voluminous writings are learned and ranked highly as controversial productions in his day. The most celebrated was his attack on the *Deist philosophy—*A Short and Easy Method with the Deists, wherein the Certainty of the Christian Religion is demonstrated by Infallible Proof from Four Rules, which are incompatible to any Imposture that ever yet has been, or that can possibly be* (ed. 1, 1698 [with a slightly variant title]; ed. 2, 1699). Leslie's other works included *The Snake in the Grass* (1696), against the *Quakers; *Gallienus Redivivus* (1695), an important historical authority for the facts of the Glencoe massacre; and *The Case Stated between the Church of Rome and the Church of England* (1713), in which the strong anti-Roman sentiments which, despite his political allegiance, he retained till his death found expression.

Collected ed. of his *Theological Works* (2 vols., London, 1721); fuller ed. (7 vols., Oxford, 1832), with life of author from *Biographia Britannica* and list of other works, vol. i, pp. i–xii. R. J. Leslie, *Life and Writings of Charles Leslie* (1885). J. M. Rigg in *D.N.B.*, xxxiii (1893), pp. 77–83.

LESLIE, JOHN (1527-96), Bp. of Ross. Born at Kingussie in Inverness-shire, he was educated at King's College, Aberdeen. In 1549 he studied theology at *Paris, and later canon and civil law at Poitiers. Returning to Scotland in 1554 he was ordained priest in 1558, and in 1559 received the parsonage of Oyne. He strongly opposed the introduction of the Reformation and in 1561 took part in a disputation at Edinburgh with J. *Knox and J. Willocks (d. 1585). Later in the year he went to France where he visited *Mary Queen of Scots at Vitry, being one of her chief supporters. In 1562 he was appointed professor of canon law at Aberdeen, and in 1566 Bp. of Ross. In 1569 he became Mary's ambassador to *Elizabeth, at the same time keeping up communications between her and her adherents in Scotland. In 1571 he was imprisoned at *Ely and then in the Tower for assisting Mary in her pro-jected marriage with the Duke of Norfolk, but was set free in 1573 on condition that he left Great Britain. Proceeding to Paris and Rome he tried to arrange the capture and Catholic education of the young James VI (later *James I of England) and to further other plans in the Catholic interest. In 1578 he published at Rome his *De Origine, Moribus, et Rebus Gestis Scotorum*, which had been partly written origin-ally in Scottish and intended for Queen Mary. The latter part is an important authority for contemporary history. In 1579 he was ap-pointed suffragan bishop and vicar-general of Rouen, and in 1593 Bp. of Coutances; but unable to reach his diocese he spent his last years with the *Augustinian Canons at Guirten-burg, near Brussels. His other writings include *A Defence of the Honour of . . . Mary, Queen of Scotland* (1569) under the pseudonym 'Euse-bius Dicæophile'; *De Illustrium Feminarum in Republica Administranda Authoritate Libellus* (1580); and *De Titulo et Jure Mariae Scot. Reg., quo Regni Angliae Successionem sibi juste Vindi-cat* (1580).

Contemporary Eng. version of the latter part of his *De Origine, Moribus et Gestis Scotorum*, beginning at the reign of James II (1436), ed. for the Bannatyne Club, xxxix (1830); a Scottish version of the history made by Fr. James Dalrymple in 1596, ed. by E. G. Cody, O.S.B., for the Scottish Text Society (2 vols., 1888-95). His 'Narrative of the Progress of Events in Scotland, 1562-1571', is also printed in W. Forbes-Leith, S.J. (ed.), *Narratives of Scottish Catholics under Mary Stuart and James VI* (1885), pp. 85-126; a letter from him to Cardinal de Cosmo (June, 1579), ib., pp. 134-40. His Diary from Apr. 11 to Oct. 16, 1571, in *The Bannatyne Miscellany*, iii (1855), pp. 111-56. Short life printed at Brussels, 1596, repr. in J. Anderson (ed.), *Collections Relating to the History of Mary Queen of Scotland*, i (1727), pp. 1-19; Eng. tr. in vol. iii (1727), pp. vii-xx. T. F. Henderson in *D.N.B.*, xxxiii (1893), pp. 93-9.

LESSER ENTRANCE, The (Gk. ἡ μικρὰ εἴσοδος). In the E. Church, the procession at the *Liturgy with the *Gospel Book. In origin it marks the first intervention in the service of the Bishop, who at this point is fetched from the nave. The procession now takes place whether or not the Bishop is present in person. See also *Greater Entrance*.

LESSING, GOTTHOLD EPHRAIM (1729-81), one of the principal figures of the

*Aufklärung. As the eldest son of a *Lutheran pastor he was intended to study theology, but soon took up a literary career and made him-self a name as a dramatic and art critic and a playwright. In his later years he was chiefly concerned with theological and philosophical problems, his interest receiving a strong stimulus from the fragments of H. S. *Rei-marus which Lessing edited (1774-8). He saw the essence of religion in a purely humanitarian morality independent of all historical revela-tion, and embodied his views in the principal figure of the play *Nathan der Weise* (1779), an ideal Jew of serene tolerance, benevolence, and generosity, conceived on the lines of enlightened rationalism. His chief theoretical writings on the same subject are *Ernst und Falk* (1778-80) and *Die Erziehung des Men-schengeschlechts* (1780), in which he laid the foundations of the Protestant Liberalism that was to hold sway in Germany throughout the 19th cent. He rejected Christianity as an historical religion on the ground that 'the accidental truths of history can never become the proof of necessary truths of reason', and that the disinterested search for truth was in-trinsically preferable to its possession.

Besides publishing the remains of Reimarus, the so-called *Wolfenbüttel Fragments* (7 parts, 1774-8, q.v.), Lessing himself made original studies in Gospel origins. In his *Neue Hypo-these über die Evangelisten als blosse menschliche Geschichtsschreiber betrachtet* (1788) he argued that an Aramaic original underlay St. *Matthew's Gospel, and that this was known to, and supplemented by, Mk. and Lk. He also discovered, in 1770, an incomplete MS. of *Berengar's famous treatise on the *Eucharist (*De Sacra Coena*), the text of which was first publd. by A. F. and F. T. Vischer in 1834.

The collected edd. of Lessing's works include those by J. F. Schinck (32 vols., Berlin, 1825-8), K. *Lachmann (13 vols., Berlin, 1838-40), W. von Maltzahn (12 vols., Leipzig, 1853-7), F. Muncker (23 vols., Stuttgart, 1886-1924), and J. Petersen-W. von Olshausen (25 vols., Berlin, 1925-9, incl., as vols. xx-xxiii, the 2nd ed. of his 'Theo-logical Writings' ed. L. Zscharnack, 4 vols., Berlin 1929). Lives by C. G. Lessing (3 vols., Berlin, 1793-5), T. W. Danzel (2 vols., Leipzig, 1850-4), H. Düntzer (ib., 1882), and E. Schmidt (2 vols., Berlin, 1884-92). Lives in English by J. Sime (2 vols., London, 1877), Helen Zimmern (ib., 1878), and T. W. Rolleston (ib., 1889). W. Oehlke, *Lessing und seine Zeit* (2 vols., 1919). J. G. Robertson, *Lessing's Dramatic Theory* (1939). L. Zscharnack, *Lessing und Semler. Ein Beitrag zur Entstehungsgeschichte des Rationalismus und der kritischen Theologie* (1905). F. *Loofs, *Lessings Stellung zum Christentum* (Lecture before Univ. of Halle, 1910, with bibl.). E. Zeller, 'Lessing als Theolog' in *Historische Zeitschrift*, xxiii (1870), pp. 342-83; repr. in Zeller's *Vorträge und Abhandlungen*, ii (1877), pp. 283-327. Überweg, iii, 470, 476-81, 706-8. J. Sime-J. G. Robertson in *E.B.* (ed. 11), xvi (1911), pp. 496-9, s.v.; Edna Purdie in *Chambers's Encyclopaedia* (ed. 1950), viii, pp. 491-3 s.v. *Selected Theological Writings* with introd. by H. Chadwick (London, 1956).

LESSIUS, LEONHARD (1554 - 1623), *Jesuit theologian. A native of Brecht, near Antwerp, he taught philosophy at *Douai from 1574 to 1581 and at Louvain from 1585 to 1600, and studied for a time under F. *Suarez at Rome. Among his pupils was *Cornelius à Lapide. He took a prominent part in the controversies then raging on the nature of grace (see *De Auxiliis*), defending a position closely akin to that of L. *Molina, with the result that in 1587 M. *Baius secured the censure by the Louvain Theological Faculty of 34 theses taken from his writings. His principal work on the subject of grace was his *De gratia efficaci* (Antwerp, 1610). He also wrote extensively on moral theology, his *De justitia et jure* (1605) being one of the earliest treatises to investigate the ethics of economics.

Opuscula Varia (Paris, 1626). Works listed in Sommervogel, iv (1893), cols. 1726–51, and ix (1900), col. 588 f. L. Scotts, *De Vita et Moribus R.P. Leonardi Lessii Liber* (Paris, 1644). K. van Sull, S.J., *Leonardus Lessius, 1554–1623* (Wetteren, 1923). V. Brants, 'L'Économie politique et sociale dans les écrits de L. Lessius (1554–1623)' in *Revue d'Histoire Ecclésiastique*, xiii (1912), pp. 73–89, 302–18; R. Galdos, S.J., 'De Authenticitate Horologii Passionis Dominicae apud Leonardum Lessium' in *Gregorianum*, xxii (1941), pp. 161–70. J. de Ghellinck, S.J., in *C.E.*, ix (1910), p. 192 f.

LETTERS OF BUSINESS. The document issued by the Crown from time to time since the reign of *Anne to the English *Convocations permitting them to prepare canons on a prescribed subject. Without these Letters any such action is now of doubtful legality. The Letters do not dispense the Convocations from the necessity of obtaining a further licence before any canons so prepared may be enacted.

LETTERS COMMENDATORY. The document issued by an ecclesiastical superior to one of his clerical subjects when travelling, testifying that he is of irreproachable morals and doctrine.

LETTERS DIMISSORY. In the C of E the licence which the Bishop of a diocese where a candidate for Holy Orders has his title issues to the Bishop of another diocese to perform the ministerial act of Ordination when the former Bishop finds it inconvenient or impossible to ordain the candidate. By can. 34 of 1604, the Bishop who ordains must require the production of such letters from the candidate. They are to be distinguished from 'Letters of Request', which ask the ordaining bishop to examine as well as to ordain the candidate. The practice of providing a candidate with such Letters directed to 'any Bishop' (*literae dimissoriae ad omnes*) was formerly a common practice, despite the abuse to which it was open; and, though now obsolete, it still appears to be legal. During the vacancy of a see the issue of such Letters is vested in the guardian of the spiritualities.

LETTERS OF ORDERS. A certificate issued to those who have been ordained, bearing the seal and signature of the officiating bishop. The Anglican can. 39 (of 1604) requires them to be shown to the bishop before *institution to a benefice, except when the presentee was ordained by the instituting bishop. Formerly Letters of Orders were the normal means of proving a claim to *benefit of clergy.

LETTERS TESTIMONIAL. The certificate 'under the seal of some college in Cambridge or Oxford, where before he remained, or of three or four grave ministers together with the subscription and testimony of other credible persons', which a candidate for ordination in the C of E is required to present to the ordaining bishop by can. 34 of 1604.

LEUCIUS. The name of a (real or fictitious) companion of St. *John the Apostle, to whom *inter alia* the apocryphal 'Acts of *John' is attributed. From the time of *Photius (Bibl. cod. 114), he was generally known as Leucius Charinus.

LEUTHOLF, HIOB. See *Ludolf, Hiob*.

LEVELLERS. 17th cent. English political and religious party. They were opposed to kingship and advocated complete freedom in religion and manhood suffrage. The name, to which they themselves objected, first occurs in 1647. Mainly supported by the Army, they found their chief leader in J. Lilburne, who, in *The Case of the Army Truly Stated* (1647), urged the dissolution of Parliament and its re-establishment on democratic lines. In 1648 Lilburne was temporarily imprisoned and his party was treated by O. *Cromwell with marked suspicion. After the execution of *Charles I (1649), they resumed their agitation, demanding the dissolution of the council of state and a reformed Parliament; and Lilburne and other leaders were again arrested. Soon afterwards they lost in importance, though they tried to make contact with *Charles II in exile. By the *Restoration (1660) they had almost completely disappeared.

W. Haller and G. Davies (ed.), *The Leveller Tracts* (New York, 1944); M. D. Wolfe (ed.), *Leveller Manifestoes of the Puritan Revolution* (1944); W. Haller (ed.), *Tracts on Liberty in the Puritan Revolution* (Records of Civilization, Sources and Studies, xviii, 3 vols., New York, 1934–7); A. S. P. Woodhouse (ed.), *Puritanism and Liberty*. Being the Army Debates (1646–9) from the Clarke Manuscripts with Supplementary Documents (1939). T. C. Pease, *The Leveller Movement*. A Study in the historical and political theory of the English Great Civil War (1916); M. James, *Social Problems and Policy during the Puritan Revolution, 1640–1660* (1930), passim; J. Holorenshaw, *The Levellers and the English Revolution* (The New People's Library, xxi, 1939); M. A. Gibb, *John Lilburne the Leveller*. A Christian Democrat (1947), incl. bibl.; W. Schenk, *The Concern for Social Justice in the Puritan Revolution* (1948); D B. Robertson, *The Religious Foundations of Leveller Democracy* (New York, 1951).

LEVI, SON OF ALPHAEUS. The tax-gatherer whom our Lord called to be one of His disciples (Mk. 2. 14). He is apparently to be identified with St. *Matthew (Mt. 9. 9; 10. 3).

LEVIATHAN. The animal referred to by this name in Job 41 and Ps. 74. 14 is probably the crocodile. On the other hand, the leviathan of Ps. 104. 26 is a sea animal, perhaps the whale. The name was transferred mythologically to the devil (cf. Job. 3. 8 [RV], Is.

27. 1). T. *Hobbes gave his famous treatise (1651) on 'the matter, form and power of a Commonwealth, ecclesiastical and civil' this title on the ground that the commonwealth was 'that great Leviathan, or rather, to speak more reverently . . . that mortal god, to which we owe under the immortal God, our peace and defence'.

LEVIRATE MARRIAGE (Lat. *levir*, 'husband's brother'). The marriage of a man with his brother's widow. The Mosaic legislation (Deut. 25. 5–10) required that if a man died, leaving his widow without offspring, his surviving brother should marry the widow so that he might not be without descendants. Reference is made to the practice in the question on the *Resurrection put by the *Sadducees (Mk. 12. 19, &c.); but it seems probable that by NT times the requirement was already a dead letter. In the *Talmud, the subject is dealt with in the tractate 'Jebamoth'. For canonical legislation, see *Affinity*.

LEVITES. The ministers of the sanctuary in ancient *Israel, supposed to be all of one tribe and descended from Levi, the son of *Jacob. *Moses and *Aaron were both of this tribe. Before the fall of Judah in 586 B.C., all the members of the tribe of Levi acted as priests, the terms 'priest' and 'Levite' being then interchangeable. Later, when the priesthood became reserved to the descendants of the family of Aaron alone, the title came to be restricted to the members of the *remaining* (non-Aaronic) families of the tribe, whose duties were the lower ones of acting as the servants of the Temple. In the Middle Ages, the term *levita* was applied to deacons.

The subject is regularly discussed in works on the Pentateuch and in histories of the OT sacrificial system. A. van Hoonacker, *Le Sacerdoce lévitique dans la loi et dans l'histoire des Hébreux* (Louvain–London, 1899). G. B. *Gray, *Sacrifice in the Old Testament* (1925), pp. 241–55. G. A. Cooke in *H.D.B.*, iii (1900), pp. 99–102, s.v. 'Levi'; W. Baudissin, ib., iv (1902), pp. 66–97, s.v. 'Priests and Levites'; W. R. *Smith–A. Bertholet in *E.Bi.*, iii (1902), cols. 2770–6, s.v.; G. Hölscher in *P.W.*, xii (pt. 2; 1925), cols. 2155–208, s.v. 'Levi'; S. Mowinckel in *R.G.G.* (ed. 2), iii (1929), cols. 1601–3, s.v. 'Levi und Leviten'.

LEVITICUS, Book of. The third Book of the *Pentateuch. The Book consists almost wholly of legislation, the general subjects of which are sacrifice (1–10), ritual purification and holiness (11–26), and vows and tithes (27). Acc. to modern critical theories, the bulk of the Book, except chs. 17–26, is derived from the Priestly document ('P') and is thus not earlier than the 6th cent., while 17–26, which form a clearly defined unity and are generally known as 'The Code of *Holiness' (q.v.), seem to be older than the rest. The language and theology of Lev. are reflected in the terminology and conceptions of certain NT writers, notably the author of *Heb., where the priesthood of Christ is contrasted with the Levitical priesthood, and the ritual and aim of the Jewish Day of *Atonement (Lev. 16, 23. 26 ff.) are explained as receiving their full significance and final realization in Christ's atoning death (Heb. 9 and 10).

Commentaries by A. R. S. Kennedy (Cent. Bib. on Lev., Num., c. 1910, pp. 3–182), A. T. Chapman–A. W. Streane (Camb. Bibl., RV, 1914), A. Bertholet (K.H.C., Abt. iii; 1901), B. Baentsch (K.H.A.T., Abt. 1, Bd. ii, on Ex., Lev., Num.; 1903, pp. 306–441), D. Hoffmann (2 vols., Berlin, 1905–6). B. D. Eerdman, *Alttestamentliche Studien*, iv, Das Buch Leviticus (1912). G. F. Moore in *E.Bi.*, iii (1902), cols. 2776–93, s.v.

LEYDEN. To mark its heroic defence against the Spanish (1574), William of Orange, in 1575, gave the city a university with a special college for the study of the Reformed Religion. At first it was a stronghold of *Calvinist orthodoxy and a refuge of the English *Puritans; from 1609 to 1620 it gave hospitality to the *Pilgrim Fathers. About the same time the *Arminians engaged in religious disputes with the *Gomarists; other great 17th cent. controversies connected with the name of the city concerned the theology of J. *Cocceius and the *Cartesian philosophy, which had been defended by A. van der Heyden. The *Elzevir family of printers had their headquarters here; but, despite the imprint 'Lugdunum Batavorum' on books issued from Leyden, the modern city has no connexion with this Roman town. The more famous theologians, historians, and scientists of the university include H. *Saravia, J. Lipsius (1580–1655), C. *Salmasius, G. J. *Voss, H. *Grotius, D. Heinsius (1547–1606), and J. J. *Scaliger. To-day Leyden is a celebrated centre of philological, esp. oriental, studies.

P. J. Blok, *Geschiedenis eener Hollandsche Stad* (4 vols., 1910–18). P. C. Molhuysen (ed.), *Bronnen tot de Geschiedenis der Leidsche Universiteit* (7 vols., 1913–24); id., *Geschiedenis der Universiteits-Bibliothek te Leiden* (1905). A. Eekhof in *R.G.G.* (ed. 2), iii (1929), col. 1559 f., s.v., with bibl.

LIBELLATICI. The name given to those who during the *Decian persecution (249–51) had procured certificates ('libelli pacis') by purchase from the civil authorities stating that they had sacrificed to the pagan idols when, in fact, no such sacrifice had been offered. The practice was condemned by the Church authorities, but those guilty of the circumvention were treated more leniently than those who had actually sacrificed (the 'sacrificati').

The chief authority is the correspondence of St. *Cyprian and the same writer's *De Lapsis*. Several actual *libelli*, from among the Egyptian papyri, have been publd. since 1897 by U. Wilcken, C. Wessely, P. M. Mayer, and others; cf. summary report in J. R. Knipfing, '*Libelli* of the Decian Persecution', in *H.T.R.*, xvi (1923), pp. 345–90. A. Bludau, *Die ägyptischen* Libelli *und die Christenverfolgung des Kaisers Decius* (*R.Q.*, Suppl. xxvii; 1931). J. Bridge in *C.E.*, ix (1910), p. 211 f.

LIBER ANTIPHONARIUS. See *Antiphonary*.

LIBER CENSUUM. The official register of the Roman Church, which recorded the dues (*census*) payable by various institutions, esp. monasteries, churches, cities, dominions, and kingdoms, to the Holy See. It was drawn up by Cencio Savelli, the 'camerarius' of Popes Clement III (Pope, 1187–91) and *Celestine III (Pope, 1191–8). It drew extensively on the *Liber Canonum* of the younger *Anselm of Lucca, the *Collectio Canonum* attributed to Deusdedit (Pope, 616–18), the *Liber Politicus* of Canon Benedict (*fl. c.* 1140), and other sources. The original MS. is preserved in the *Vatican (lat. 8466). Besides the list of *census*, it contains a list of the bishoprics and monasteries directly dependent on the Holy See, a treatise *Mirabilia Urbis Romae*, and other documents.

Crit. ed. by P. Fabre (d. 1899)–L. *Duchesne, completed by G. Mollat (3 vols., Bibliothèque des Écoles Françaises d'Athènes et de Rome, Sér. 2; '1910'–52). P. Fabre, *Étude sur le* Liber Censuum *de l'Église de Rome* (1892). H. *Leclercq, O.S.B., in *D.A.C.L.*, ix (pt. 1; 1929), cols. 180–220, s.v. 'Liber Censuum Romanae Ecclesiae', with further bibl. M. Michaud in *D.D.C.*, iii (1942), cols. 233–55, s.v. 'Censuum (Liber).' L. Spätling, O.F.M., in *E.C.*, vii (1951), cols. 1260–2.

LIBER COMICUS. See *Comes*.

LIBER DE CAUSIS. A treatise, consisting for the most part of extracts from Proclus's 'Elements of Theology', which was put together in Arabic by an unknown Mohammedan philosopher *c.* 850. It exercised an important influence on medieval philosophy through Gerard of Cremona, who translated it into Latin at Toledo between 1167 and 1187. He announced it as a work of *Aristotle, with the result that many *Neo-Platonist doctrines were mistakenly held to be Aristotelean. St. *Albertus Magnus attributed it to one 'David the Jew'. *William of Moerbeke's translation of Proclus's 'Elements of Theology' into Latin (completed on 18 May 1268) revealed to St. *Thomas Aquinas and medieval philosophers generally the true character of the 'Liber de causis'.

The text is in *S. Thomae Aquinatis Opuscula Omnia*, ed. P. Mandonnet, O.P. (Paris, 1927), i, 193–311.

LIBER GRADUALIS. See *Gradual*.

LIBER PONTIFICALIS (Lat., 'the Papal Book'). A collection of early Papal biographies. The account of each Pope is written acc. to a regular plan, with stereotyped *formulae* and exact chronological *data*. The biographies of the earliest Popes are quite short, but from the 4th cent. onwards they tend gradually to increase in size until those of the 8th–9th cents. have the dimensions of a small book. The whole is prefaced by an apocryphal letter of Pope *Damasus to St. *Jerome, begging him to provide a history of the Popes from St. Peter down to his own times. The work is issued in a series of 'editions', which were brought up to date by the addition of later Lives. The earliest form of it, which was dependent on the *Liberian Catalogue (354), appears to have been the work of a Roman presbyter at the time of Boniface II (530–2). Subsequent redactions carry the history down to the death of *Martin V (1431), and even later.

Important crit. edd. by L. *Duchesne (2 vols., Bibliothèque des Écoles Françaises d'Athènes et de Rome, 2e Sér. iii, 1886–92) and T. *Mommsen (*M.G.H.*, Gesta Pontificum Romanorum, i, vol. i, to 715 A.D., all publd., 1898).

L. Duchesne, *Étude sur le* Liber Pontificalis (Bibliothèque des Écoles Francaises d'Athènes et de Rome, 1e Sér. i, 1877; esp. on MSS.); id., 'La Nouvelle Édition du *Liber Pontificalis*' [of Mommsen] in *Mélanges d'Archéologie et d'Histoire* xviii (1898), pp. 381–417. J. B. *Lightfoot, *Apostolic Fathers*, I, i (S. Clement of Rome; ed. 2, 1890), pp. 303–25. E. Caspar, *Geschichte des Papsttums*, ii (1933), pp. 314–20. J. P. Kirsch in *C.E.*, ix (1910), pp. 224–6; H. *Leclercq, O.S.B., in *D.A.C.L.*, ix (pt. 1; 1930), cols. 354–460; E. Josi in *E.C.*, vii (1951), cols. 1278–82; all s.v. and with further bibl.

LIBER PRAEDESTINATUS. See *Praedestinatus*.

LIBER REGALIS. The Book containing the English *Coronation Service introduced for the crowning of Edward II in 1308. The rubrics were extended for Richard II (1377). The Book was translated into English for *James I (1603), and continued in use until discarded by *James II in 1685. Its unknown compiler possessed considerable competence and knowledge. Among its many new features were the introduction of the seven *Penitential Psalms, of the **Veni Creator Spiritus*, and the homage of the peers after the enthronement. Several 14th and 15th cent. MSS. survive.

Liber Regalis, ed. Lord Beauchamp. The Roxburghe Club (1871); E. C. Ratcliff, *The English Coronation Service* (1936); R. H. Murray, *The King's Crowning* (1936).

LIBER SACRAMENTORUM. See *Sacramentary*.

LIBER VITAE (Lat., 'Book of Life'). A name occasionally given in the early Church to the *Diptychs, i.e. the list of those who were recognized members of the Christian community. It was doubtless derived from the references in Scripture to the '*Book of Life' (e.g. Rev. 3. 5).

LIBERAL ARTS, The Seven. See *Seven Liberal Arts, The*.

LIBERAL EVANGELICALISM. The outlook of those within the C of E who, while maintaining their spiritual kinship with the *Evangelical Revival, are concerned to re-state old truths, e.g. concerning the Atonement and the Authority of the Bible, in terms thought to be more consonant with modern thought with its stress on historical method and the philosophy of personality. The *Anglican Evangelical Group Movement (q.v.) exists to further these aims.

T. G. Rogers (ed.), *Liberal Evangelicalism*. By Members of the Church of England (1923).

LIBERALISM. The word, which came into use early in the 19th cent., has been defined as 'the holding of liberal opinions in politics or theology'. In theology it has been used with many different shades of meaning. If taken to mean freedom from bigotry and readiness to welcome new ideas or proposals for reform, it is a characteristic which many people will readily profess, but in itself it gives no indication of their beliefs or aspirations. There have been 'Liberal Catholics', 'Liberal Protestants', and 'Liberal Evangelicals'; but all that they have had in common is a general tendency to favour freedom and progress. Such a tendency may lead to many different results. The 'Liberal Catholics' who formed a distinguished group in the RC Church in the 19th cent. were for the most part theologically orthodox, but they favoured political democracy and ecclesiastical reform. Père D. *Lacordaire (1802–61), the famous French Dominican, said: 'I die a penitent Catholic, but an impenitent Liberal.' 'Liberal Protestantism', on the other hand, developed into an anti-dogmatic and humanitarian reconstruction of the Christian faith, which until recently appeared to be gaining ground in nearly all the Protestant churches.

The word is sometimes also used of the belief in secular or anthropocentric humanism which has its origins in the Renaissance and which is quite inconsistent with Biblical and dogmatic orthodoxy. It was in this sense that the *Tractarians were fiercely opposed to Liberalism. On the other hand, by many orthodox Christians the word 'liberal' is felt to have positive associations of great value. Hence the confusion which surrounds its use.

LIBERIAN CATALOGUE. An early list of the Popes down to *Liberius (352–66). It is one of the items in a collection of documents made by a compiler known (since T. Mommsen's studies) as the '*Chronographer of 354' (q.v.). Its earlier section, which goes down to Pope Pontianus (230–5) and appears to be dependent on a list in the 'Chronicle' of St. *Hippolytus, is less reliable than its latter half. First edited by the Jesuit, A. Bucherius, at Antwerp in 1636, it used sometimes to be called the 'Bucerian Catalogue'.

For editions, see art. *Chronographer of A.D. 354.* Text also pr. in *L.P.* (ed. Duchesne), i (1886), pp. 1–12. Critical discussions in H. *Lietzmann, *Petrus und Paulus in Rom* (ed. 2, 1927), esp. pp. 1–28, and E. Caspar, *Die älteste römische Bischofsliste* (Schriften der Königsberger gelehrten Gesellschaft ii, Geisteswissenschaftliche Klasse, Hft. 4; 1926), pp. [170–8] (pp. 384–92 of vol. ii of the Schriften).

LIBERIUS. Pope from 352 to 366. Ordered by the Arian Emperor, *Constantius, to assent to the condemnation of St. *Athanasius as a rebel, Liberius refused and was banished from Rome in 355. In 357 he submitted to Constantius, and in 358 he was permitted to reoccupy his see, having in the interval signed an Arian formulary. The identification of this formula is uncertain, but that it was heretical seems beyond dispute. Both St. *Jerome and St. Athanasius agree, however, that Liberius's subscription was forced. He built a celebrated church on the Esquiline Hill (the 'Basilica Liberiana') which was the ancestor of the present *Sta Maria Maggiore. Though his name does not appear in modern calendars, his feast occurs on 23 Sept. in the *Hieronymian Martyrology.

Letters and other writings mainly repr. from P. *Coustant in J. P. Migne, *PL*, viii, 1349–1410; crit. text of the nine Epp. found in *Hilary by A. L. Feder (C.S.E.L., lxv, 1916). A Sermon of Liberius survives in a modified form in *Ambrose, *De virginibus*, III, 1–3 (text in *PL*., viii, 1345–50). The four celebrated letters which afford the evidence for his 'Fall' ('Studens paci', 'Pro deifico', 'Quia scio', 'Non doceo') all appear to date, assuming their genuineness, from the spring of 357; against the attacks of K. J. *Hefele, F. Savio, S.J., and J. *Chapman, O.S.B., their genuineness is defended by L. *Duchesne, A. *Wilmart, O.S.B., and A. L. Feder. L. Duchesne, 'Libère et Fortunatien' in *Mélanges d'Archéologie et d'Histoire*, xxviii (1908), pp. 31–78; J. Chapman, 'The Contested Letters of Pope Liberius' in *R. Bén.*, xxvii (1910), pp. 22–40, 172–203, 325–351; A. L. Feder, *Studien zu Hilarius von Poitiers*, I (Vienna, 1910), pp. 153–83; cf. also *L.P.* (Duchesne), i, 207–10. E. Caspar, *Geschichte des Papsttums*, i (1930), pp. 166–95. Bardenhewer, iii, 585–8. J. Chapman in *C.E.*, ix (1910), pp. 217–23; H. *Leclercq, O.S.B., in *D.A.C.L.*, ix (pt. 1; 1930), cols. 497–530; É. Amann in *D.T.C.*, ix (pt. 1; 1926), cols. 631–59; V. Monachino in *E.C.*, vii (1951), cols. 1269–72.

LIBRARY OF THE FATHERS, The. The series of English translations of selected writings of the early Christian Fathers, published under the inspiration of the *Oxford Movement. The first volume to appear was the *Confessions* of St. *Augustine (1838; edited by E. B. *Pusey).

LIBRI CAROLINI. See *Caroline Books.*

LICENCES, Marriage. See *Marriage Licences.*

LICHFIELD. The seat of the Mercian diocese under St. *Chad, it was constituted by King *Offa for a brief period (786–803) an archiepiscopal see. Despite the nominal removal of the see to *Chester in 1075 and to Coventry in 1095, Lichfield remained throughout the Middle Ages the centre of episcopal administration in the diocese. The formation of the Chester diocese in 1541, and various 19th cent. changes, greatly reduced its importance. The present cathedral dates mainly from the 13th cent. There is an Anglican theological college in the city which was founded in 1857.

E. Hobhouse, 'The Register of Roger of Norbury, Bishop of Lichfield and Coventry, from A.D. 1322 to A.D. 1358. An Abstract of Contents and Remarks' in *Collections for a History of Staffordshire edited by the Williams Salt Archaeological Society*, i (1880), pp. 241–88; Registers of Bishop Robert de Stretton, 1358–1385, abstracted into English by R. A. Wilson (ib., N.S., viii and x, pt. 2; 1905–7); H. E. Savage (ed.), *The Great Register of Lichfield Cathedral known as Magnum Registrum Album* (ib. for 1924; 1926). J. C. Cox, *Catalogue of the Muniments and Manuscript Books pertaining to the Dean and Chapter of Lichfield: Analysis of the Magnum Registrum Album; Catalogue of the Muniments of the Lichfield Vicars* (ib., vi, pt. 2; 1886); 'The Muniments of the Dean and Chapter of Lichfield' in the *Fourteenth Report of the Historical Manuscripts Commission*, Appendix viii (1895), pp. 205–36. T. Harwood, *The History and Antiquities of the Church and City of Lichfield* (Gloucester, 1806). A. B. Clifton, *The Cathedral Church of Lichfield* (Bell's Cathedral Series, 1898). R. Willis, 'On the Foundations of Early Buildings recently discovered in Lichfield Cathedral' in *The Archaeological Journal*, xviii (1861), pp. 1–24. T. Barns in *D.E.C.H.* (1912), pp. 322–6, s.v.

LICH-GATE. See *Lych-Gate.*

LIDDELL, HENRY GEORGE (1811–98), Greek lexicographer. He was educated at Charterhouse and *Christ Church, Oxford, where he became tutor (1836) and censor (1845). He was later head master of Westminster (1846–55) and Dean of Christ Church (1855–91). In 1852 he was appointed to sit on the commission for University Reform. Later he was prime negotiator in the radical plan of internal reconstruction embodied in the Christ Church, Oxford, Act of 1867. The famous Greek Lexicon, in which Liddell had the collaboration of R. *Scott (q.v.), appeared in a modest form in 1843, the original edition being based on the Greek-German lexicon of F. Passow, professor at Breslau. It was constantly revised and extended during Liddell's lifetime, the last (8th) edition being issued in 1897. It was later completely recast by H. Stuart Jones (1867–1939) and R. McKenzie (1887–1937), who greatly enlarged it by full attention to recent archaeological and papyrological discoveries, but with the exclusion of *patristic usages (issued in 10 parts, 1925–1940).

Memoir by H. L. Thompson (London, 1899). Id. in *D.N.B.*, Suppl. iii (1901), pp. 94–6.

LIDDON, HENRY PARRY (1829–90), Canon of *St. Paul's. He was a native of North Stoneham, Hants, and educated at Christ Church, *Oxford. He was successively curate of Wantage (1852–54), first vice-principal of Cuddesdon Theological College (1854–1859), and vice-principal of St. Edmund Hall, Oxford (1859–62), where he exercised great influence in face of the post-Tractarian Oxford liberalism. In 1864 he was appointed prebendary of *Salisbury and in 1870 Canon of St. Paul's, where his powerful preaching attracted large audiences. In 1870 he was also appointed Dean Ireland professor of exegesis at Oxford; this combination of offices strengthened his influence in the C of E, which he used chiefly for reviving Catholic principles. He also stood firmly against the attempts made in the 'seventies to lessen or abandon the use of the *Athanasian Creed in the C of E services. After resigning his professorship in 1882 he travelled extensively, esp. in Palestine and Egypt. He was much interested in the *Old Catholics and visited J. J. I. von *Döllinger in Munich. In 1886 he was made chancellor of St. Paul's. In his last years he watched with growing apprehension the spread of critical doctrines of the OT among the younger generation even of his own party, and the publication of *Lux Mundi (1889) was a great grief to him. He was also a considerable, if hardly an original, theologian, whose *Bampton Lectures for 1866, on *The Divinity of Christ* (1867), were deservedly held in high repute. His intense admiration for E. B. *Pusey led him to devote himself assiduously in his later years to writing Pusey's Life (4 vols., posthumous, 1893–7). He also published *University Sermons* (1865; Second Series, 1879), *Some Elements of Religion* (1872;

Lent Lectures, delivered 1870), *Easter in St. Paul's* (1885; sermons), *Advent in St. Paul's* (1888), *Clerical Life and Work* (posthumous, 1895), and other volumes of sermons. Liddon House, in South Audley Street, was founded in his memory as a religious centre in London for educated Anglican Churchmen.

J. O. Johnston, *Life and Letters of Henry Parry Liddon* (London, 1904). Shorter life by G. W. E. Russell (London, 1905). Centenary memoir with contributions by W. M. Whitley, T. B. *Strong, D. *Stone, E. S. *Talbot, and A. B. Emden (London, 1929). H. Scott *Holland in *D.N.B.*, xxxiii (1893), pp. 223–8.

LIEBER, THOMAS. See *Erastianism*.

LIETZMANN, HANS (1875–1942), Church historian. He studied philosophy and theology at Jena and Bonn from 1893 to 1898. After being lecturer at Bonn from 1900 he was appointed professor at Jena in 1905. In 1924 he succeeded A. *Harnack at Berlin. His early studies were largely in the little-worked Greek patristic *catenae, which bore fruit in a Catalogue (1902; in conjunction with G. Karo) and a series of *Catenenstudien* under his editorship. In 1904 there followed *Apollinaris von Laodicea und seine Schule*, which by a fresh attempt to distinguish the genuine and spurious works completely transformed Apollinarian studies. *Petrus und Paulus in Rom* (1915; ed. 2, 1927) was the outcome of long archaeological and chronological researches. In the field of liturgy, he published an edition of the *Gregorian Sacramentary* which derived from the ancient Aachen MS. (1921), and *Messe und Herrenmahl* (1926) in which he sought to trace the Eucharistic Rite back to two distinct primitive types. In his later years he issued a manual of Church history, *Geschichte der alten Kirche* (4 vols., 1932–44; Eng. trans. 1937–1951). From 1902 onwards he edited *Kleine Texte für Vorlesungen und Übungen*, from 1906 the *Handbuch zum Neuen Testament* (to which he himself contributed the commentaries on Rom., Cor., and Gal.), and from 1920 the *Zeitschrift für die neutestamentliche Wissenschaft*.

Gedächtnissrede by H. Bornkamm and bibl. by K. Aland (490 items) in *Z.N.T.W.*, xli (1942), pp. 1–33. Three volumes of Lietzmann's *Kleine Schriften* ed. K. Aland in T.U., lxvii (1958), lxviii (1958), and lxxiv (1962; with reissue of items by H. Bornkamm and K. Aland just mentioned.

'LIFE AND WORK'. The branch of the *Oecumenical Movement concerned with the relation of the Christian faith to society, politics, and economics. It held notable conferences at *Stockholm (1925) and *Oxford (1937). It owed its existence esp. to N. *Söderblom. See also *Faith and Order*, *Reunion*, and *World Council of Churches*.

LIGHT OF THE WORLD, The. (Lat. *Lux Mundi*). A title of Christ, derived from Jn. 8. 12. It is the subject of Holman *Hunt's famous picture (of which the artist painted two copies, the one at Keble College, *Oxford, and the other at *St. Paul's Cathedral).

LIGHTFOOT, JOHN (1602–75), Biblical and *Rabbinic scholar. Educated at Christ's College, Cambridge, he was from 1630 to 1642 rector of Ashley, Staffs. In 1643 he became one of the original and more influential members of the *Westminster Assembly, opposing the extreme *Presbyterians. In 1643 he became master of Catherine Hall, Cambridge, and rector of Much Munden, Herts, and held both offices for the rest of his life. He early developed an interest in Hebrew and Talmudic studies and in 1629 published *Erubhin; or Miscellanies, Christian and Judaical*, followed later by a book on *Genesis* (1642) and many further learned writings. He also materially assisted B. *Walton with the *Polyglott Bible which appeared in 1657. His best-known work, his series of *Horae Hebraicae et Talmudicae* (6 vols.; 1658–78), was designed to show the bearing of Jewish studies on the interpretation of the NT. It is a mine of information and has never been wholly superseded.

Works in Eng. ed. G. Bright (2 vols., London, 1684); in Lat. [ed. J. Texelius] (2 vols., Rotterdam, 1686), also ed. J. Leusden (2 vols., Utrecht, 1699). Complete works ed. J. R. Pitman (13 vols., London, 1822–5), J. Hamilton in *D.N.B.*, xxxiii (1893), pp. 229–31.

LIGHTFOOT, JOSEPH BARBER (1828–1889), Bp. of *Durham. He was educated at King Edward's School, Birmingham, where he came under the strong influence of James Prince Lee (1804–69) and made a lifelong friendship with E. W. *Benson (q.v.). In 1847 he entered Trinity College, Cambridge, where he was a private pupil of B. F. *Westcott (q.v.) and in 1852 was elected Fellow. He was ordained deacon in 1854 and priest in 1858, in both cases by J. P. Lee (Bp. of Manchester since 1847). Becoming a tutor at Trinity College in 1857, he made classical and Biblical subjects his main interest and was one of the founders and editors of the *Journal of Classical and Sacred Philology* (Mar. 1854–Dec. 1859). In 1861 he succeeded C. J. *Ellicott as Hulsean professor of divinity, his lectures on the NT being the basis of his later commentaries. In 1871 he was appointed a Canon of *St. Paul's and in 1875 Lady Margaret professor of divinity at Cambridge. From 1870 to 1880 he was also one of the leading members of the Company of Revisers of the NT. Having accepted the see of Durham with great reluctance (1879), he here proved himself a remarkably successful administrator, did much for the adornment of Auckland Castle and personally trained many promising men for the priesthood.

The excellence of Lightfoot's critical work on the NT and the Fathers, which from the first won the highest recognition in Britain and beyond, has stood the test of time. His first important study, 'Recent Editions of St. Paul's Epistles' in the *Journal of Classical and Sacred Philology* for Mar. 1856, was a critique of the works of A. P. *Stanley and B. *Jowett. His famous commentaries on St. Paul's Epistles—*Galatians* (1865), *Philippians* (1868), and *Colossians with Philemon* (1875)—followed.

All were marked by a wide and original Patristic and classical erudition, lucid presentation, freedom from technicalities, and avoidance of sectional controversies; esp. notable were their long dissertations, e.g. the well-known essay on 'The Christian Ministry' in *Philippians*. The same qualities marked his work on the Apostolic Fathers, which perhaps showed an even greater mastery of learning and technique. His first edition of *Clement of Rome* appeared in 1869 (Appendix, 1877), a second and much extended recasting, revised in the light of the newly recovered full text, in 1890. In 1885 there followed his famous *Ignatius* (2 vols. in 3, 1885; ed. 2, 1889), which finally disposed of W. *Cureton's contention that only the three Epp. in the Syriac recension were genuine. His other writings included *A Fresh Revision of the New Testament* (1871), the valuable art. 'Eusebius of Caesarea' in the *Dictionary of Christian Biography* (vol. ii, 1880), *Leaders of the Northern Church* (1890), and several volumes of Sermons.

Brief account (attributed to H. W. Watkins) in *Quarterly Review*, clxxvi (1893), pp. 73–105, repr. separately, with prefatory note by B. F. *Westcott (London, 1894). G. R. Eden–F. C. Macdonald (edd.), *Lightfoot of Durham. Memoirs and Appreciations* (1932). A. C. Benson, *The Leaves of the Tree* (1911), pp. 187–211. F. J. A. *Hort in *D.N.B.*, xxxiii (1893), pp. 232–40.

LIGHTFOOT, ROBERT HENRY (1883–1953), NT scholar. Educated at Eton and at Worcester College, Oxford, he was ordained priest in 1910. After teaching at Wells Theological College (1912–19), he became Fellow of Lincoln College (1919–21) and of New College (1921–50), Oxford, and Dean Ireland Professor of the Exegesis of Holy Scripture (1934–49). His chief publications were *History and Interpretation in the Gospels* (*Bampton Lectures for 1934; 1935), *Locality and Doctrine in the Gospels* (1938), *The Gospel Message of St. Mark* (1950), and *St. John's Gospel* (1956; ed. C. F. Evans). From 1941 until his death he edited the *Journal of Theological Studies*. His work was marked by accuracy and caution, deference to German *Form-criticism, and, largely through the influence of this last, scepticism with respect to the historicity of the Synoptic narratives. Of deep, if reticent, Christian faith, Lightfoot exercised a considerable influence, esp. on a group of younger Oxford NT students.

D. E. Nineham (ed.), *Studies in the Gospels. Essays in Memory of R. H. Lightfoot* (1955), with memoir by D. E. Nineham, pp. vi–xvi. Obituary notice by R. L. P. Milburn in *Proceedings of the British Academy*, xl (1954), pp. 253–61.

LIGHTS, Feast of. See *Dedication* (*Jewish Feast of the*).

LIGUORI, St. ALPHONSUS. See *Alphonsus Liguori, St.*

LIMBO. In Latin theology the abode of souls excluded from the full blessedness of the beatific vision, but not condemned to any other punishment. There are distinguished (1) the *limbus patrum*, in which the saints of the Old

Covenant remained until Christ's coming and redemption of the world; and (2) the *limbus infantium*, the everlasting state of those who die unregenerate, e.g. unbaptized infants, and hence in *original sin, but innocent of personal guilt. Those in limbo are held to be excluded from supernatural beatitude, but, acc. to St. *Thomas Aquinas, enjoy full natural happiness. St. *Augustine, however, esp. in combating the *Pelagians, taught that all who die unbaptized, being in original sin, suffer some degree of positive punishment.

LIMINA APOSTOLORUM. See *Ad Limina Apostolorum*.

LINACRE, THOMAS (c. 1460–1524), humanist and founder of the Royal College of Physicians. He was among the first to cultivate Greek letters in England. He was educated at *Canterbury Cathedral School and at Oxford and in 1484 became a Fellow of All Souls. Soon afterwards he made his way to Italy, where he became the pupil of Angelo Poliziano, and after ten years, spent mainly in the study of medicine and the classics, he returned to Oxford and was at once recognized as one of the foremost humanist scholars of England. *Henry VIII on his accession made him the King's physician, and many great statesmen (e.g. T. *Wolsey, W. *Warham) were his patients. He was also the intimate friend of J. *Colet, D. *Erasmus, and T. *More. In 1520 he was ordained priest. The College for which he secured the royal charter (23 Sept. 1518) was designed to regulate the practice of medicine and to discourage the quacks who flourished at the time in London. He also founded chairs of medicine at Oxford and Cambridge. Among his writings are a treatise on Latin composition and Latin translations from Galen.

J. N. Johnson, *Life of Thomas Linacre* (1835). Shorter studies are the Linacre Lecture by W. Osler, *Thomas Linacre* (1908), and a sketch in R. T. Williamson's *English Physicians of the Past* (1923), pp. 7–19. J. F. Paine in *D.N.B.*, xxxiii (1893), pp. 266–71 [cf. P. S. Allen in *E.H.R.*, xviii (1903), pp. 514–17].

LINCOLN. A see was established here by Bp. Remigius (d. 1092) who transferred it from *Dorchester, Oxon, and the diocese became the largest in England, extending from the Thames to the Humber, and including the present dioceses of *Oxford, *Peterborough, and Leicester, as well as the present Lincoln. The cathedral, begun in 1086 and largely completed before 1300, contains fine Early English and Decorated architecture. Among celebrated Bps. of Lincoln are St. *Hugh (1186–1200), R. *Grosseteste (1235–53), Richard *Fleming (1420–31), Thomas *Barlow (1675–1691), W. *Wake (1705–16), E. *Gibson (1716–23), and E. *King (1885–1910).

W. P. W. Phillimore (ed.), *Rotuli Hugonis de Welles, Episcopi Lincolniensis A.D. MCCIX–MCCXXXV* (Cant. and York Society, i, iii, and iv; 1907–9, and in The Lincoln Record Society, iii, vi, and ix, 1912–4); F. N. Davis (ed.), *Rotuli Roberti Grosseteste, Episcopi Lincolniensis A.D. MCCXXXV–MCCLIII* (Cant. and York Society, x; 1913, and, with the *Rotulus Henrici de Lixington, Episcopi Lin-*

colniensis MCCLIV–MCCLIX, in The Lincoln Record Society, xi; 1914); id.–C. W. Foster–A. H. Thompson (edd.), *Rotuli Ricardi Gravesend* [Bp., 1258–79] (Cant. and York Society, xxxi; 1925, and Linc. Record Society, xx; 1925); Rosalind M. T. Hill (ed.), *The Rolls and Register of Bishop Oliver Sutton, 1280–1299* (Linc. Record Society, xxxix and xliii; 1948–50). A. H. Thompson, 'Registers of John Gynewell, Bishop of Lincoln, for the Years 1347–1350' in the *Archaeological Journal*, lxviii (1911), pp. 301–60, with extracts. C. W. Foster (ed.), *Lincoln Episcopal Records in the Time of Thomas Cooper . . . Bishop of Lincoln A.D. 1571 to A.D. 1584* (Linc. Record Society, ii; 1912). A. H. Thompson (ed.), *Visitations of Religious Houses in the Diocese of Lincoln* [1420–49] (ib., vii, xiv, and xxi; 1914–29). R. E. G. Cole (ed.), *Chapter Acts of the Cathedral Church of St. Mary of Lincoln A.D. 1520–1559* (ib., xii, xiii, and xv; 1915–20). C. W. Foster–Kathleen Major (edd.), *The Registrum Antiquissimum of the Cathedral Church of Lincoln* (ib., xxvii, xxviii, xxix, xxxii, xxxiv, xli, xlvi to 1950; 1931 ff.). A. H. Thompson (ed.) *Visitations in the Diocese C. W. Foster, The State of the Church in the Reigns of Elizabeth and James I as Illustrated by Documents Relating to the Diocese of Lincoln*, vol. i (ib., xxiii; 1926). H. Bradshaw–of *Lincoln 1517–1531* (ib., xxxiii, xxxv, and xxxvii; 1940–44). C. *Wordsworth (edd.), *Statutes of Lincoln Cathedral* (2 vols., 1892–7). J. A. Bennett, 'The Manuscripts of the Dean and Chapter of Lincoln' in the *Twelfth Report of the Historical Manuscripts Commission*, Appendix, Part IX (1891), pp. 553–72; those in 'The Registry of the Bishop of Lincoln' are described ib., pp. 573–9. G. F. Apthorp, *A Catalogue of the Books and Manuscripts in the Library of Lincoln Cathedral* (Lincoln, 1859). W. *Dugdale, *Monasticon Anglicanum*, vi (pt. 3; 1830), pp. 1266–92. B. Willis, *A Survey of the Cathedrals of Lincoln, Ely, Oxford and Peterborough* (1730), pp. 1–330. A. F. Kendrick, *The Cathedral Church of Lincoln* (Bell's Cathedral Series, 1898). J. H. Srawley, *The Story of Lincoln Minster* (1933). Phyllis Wragge, 'Lincoln Cathedral' in *V.C.H.*, Lincoln, ii (1906), pp. 80–96, with reff. E. Venables, 'Some Account of the Recent Discoveries of the Foundations of the Eastern Termination of Lincoln Minster, as erected by St. Hugh' in *The Archaeological Journal*, xlv (1887), pp. 194–202. J. W. F. Hill, *Medieval Lincoln* (1948). W. Hunt in *D.E.C.H.*, pp. 328–32, s.v.

LINCOLN, Use of. The liturgical usage adopted in the vast pre-Reformation diocese of Lincoln and referred to by T. *Cranmer in the preface to the 1549 BCP (see *Concerning the Service of the Church*). Among the few traces of it which have survived are three leaves of a 15th cent. MS. Missal *secundum usum Lincoln.*, now among the Tanner MSS. in the *Bodleian Library (MS. 9824).

LINCOLN JUDGEMENT, The. The Judgement, given in 1890 by E. W. *Benson, Abp. of Canterbury, upon the complaints made two years before by the *Church Association against Edward *King, Bp. of Lincoln, for consecrating the Eucharist in the eastward position, having lighted candles on the Altar, mixing water and wine in the Chalice, allowing the *Agnus Dei to be sung after the Consecration, absolving and blessing with the *sign of the Cross, and taking the ablutions of the sacred vessels. The Judgement upheld the Bishop in the main, but ordered that the Chalice must be mixed, if at all, before the service, that the *manual acts of consecration must be visible to the people, and that the sign of the Cross may not be used. The Judgement was notable in that it ignored previous decisions of the secular courts and the *Judicial Committee of the Privy Council.

E. S. Roscoe, *The Bishop of Lincoln's Case. A Report of the Proceedings in the Court of the Archbishop of Canterbury . . .* (1889). *Read and Others v. the Lord Bishop of Lincoln*: Judgment, Nov. 21, 1890.

LINDISFARNE. From the 11th cent. it has also been called 'Holy Island'. Its history begins with St. *Aidan's arrival from *Iona in 635 when it became a missionary centre and episcopal see, and a large number of churches were founded by its efforts from Edinburgh to the Humber and beyond. Among those educated in the monastery were St. *Chad, St. *Egbert, St. Oswy, and St. *Wilfred. The church was rebuilt by Aidan's successor, St. *Finan (d. 661). In the latter part of the 7th cent. the Scoto-Irish monks, with some of their English brethren, withdrew to Iona, as they disliked the Roman discipline agreed upon at the Synod of *Whitby (664): and from that time the monastery became 'Italo-Saxon'. St. *Cuthbert's association with it added to its celebrity. In 793 and again in 875 the monastery and church were pillaged by the Danes and the monks fled. Eardulf (d. 900), the last of the 16 bishops, fixed his see in 875 at Chester-le-Street, but it was transferred to *Durham in 995. From 1082 to the Dissolution there was continuous monastic life on the island. The abbey church was a small copy of Durham cathedral, and dedicated to St. Cuthbert.

The MS. known as the 'Lindisfarne Gospels', now in the British Museum (Cotton MSS., Nero D iv), was written by Bishop Eadfrid c. 700 'in honour of St. Cuthbert'. Its *uncial script of an Irish style doubtless indicates the persisting influence of the Irish period of the monastery. An interlinear translation into Anglo-Saxon was added c. 950 by a priest, Aldred.

'Annales Lindisfarnenses et Cantuarienses a. 618–690', ed. G. H. Pertz in *M.G.H.*, Scriptores, iv (1841), p. 1 f.; 'Annales Lindisfarnenses' [A.D. 532–993], ed. id., ib., xix (1866), pp. 502–7. W. *Dugdale *Monasticon Anglicanum*, i (ed. 1846), pp. 220–52. J. Raine, *The History and Antiquities of North Durham* (1852), pp. 73–188.
Lindisfarne Gospels, ed. by J. Stevenson–G. Waring (Surtees Society, xxviii, xxxix, xliii, and xlviii; 1854–65), and by W. K. Skeat, *The Holy Gospels in Anglo-Saxon, Northumbrian, and Old Mercian Versions* (1871–87). Lat. text collated in the ed. of the *Vulgate by J. *Wordsworth–H. J. White (Oxford, 1889). Plates, with introd. by E. G. Millar (British Museum, 1923). Facsimile ed., with introd. by T. J. Brown–R. L. S. Bruce-Mitford–A. S. C. Ross (Olten-Bern, 1956), with Index Verborum of Anglo-Saxon Gloss. The *Liber Vitae Ecclesiae Dunelmensis* (also in the Brit. Mus. Cotton MS., Domitian A., vii) contains the names of the benefactors of the Church of St. Cuthbert, Lindisfarne, and others entitled to commemoration. Begun in the 9th cent. (prob. c. 840) and written in silver and gold, it was later removed to Durham; ed. J. Stevenson (Surtees Society, xiii; 1841); facsimile ed. by A. H. Thompson (ib., cxxxvi; 1923). H. *Leclercq, O.S.B., in *D.A.C.L.*, ix (pt. 1; 1930), cols. 1186–92 s.v.

LINDSAY, THOMAS MARTIN (1843–1914), Church historian. He was educated at Glasgow and Edinburgh, and was for a time assistant at the latter to A. C. *Fraser in philosophy. He decided, however, to become a minister in the Free Church of Scotland, and in 1873 he became professor of church history at the theological college at Glasgow. His main interest was the history of the Protestant Reformation on the Continent, his two principal books being *Luther and the German Reformation* (1900) and *A History of the Reformation in Europe* (2 vols., 1906, 1907). His other writings include *The Church and the Ministry*

in the Early Centuries (Cunningham Lectures, 1903).

His son, Alexander, first LORD LINDSAY OF BIRKER (1879–1952), Master of Balliol College, Oxford (1924–49), took a prominent and effective part in furthering Christian principles in their bearing on social and ethical problems. In addition to philosophical works, notably studies of H. *Bergson (1911) and I. *Kant (1934), he wrote on personal, social, and political ethics.

A Collection of *College Addresses: and Sermons preached on Various Occasions by the late Thomas Martin Lindsay*, ed. by A. D. Lindsay, son (Glasgow, 1915). *Letters of Principal T. M. Lindsay to Janet Ross* (1923), with introd. by Janet [A.] Ross, pp. v–x. R. S. Tait in *D.N.B.*, *1912–1921* (1927), p. 338 f., s.v. On Wallace Martin Lindsay (1858–1937), eminent Latinist, editor of St. *Isidore's *Etymologiae* (2 vols., 1911), and brother of T. M. Lindsay, see H. J. Rose in *Proceedings of the British Academy*, xxiii (1937), pp. 487–512, and C. J. Fordyce in *D.N.B.*, *1931–1940* (1949), p. 537 f.

LINDSEY, THEOPHILUS (1723–1808), English *Unitarian. Educated at Leeds and at St. John's College, Cambridge, of which he was later elected a Fellow (1747), he became rector of Kirkby Wiske, Yorks, in 1753 and of Puddletown, Dorset, in 1756. In 1760 he married the stepdaughter of his friend, Archdeacon Francis Blackburne (1705–87), with whose *Latitudinarian ideas he was much in sympathy. In 1763 he became vicar of Catterick. Having become doubtful about the doctrine of the Trinity, he supported Blackburne in the controversy arising out of the latter's *Confessional* (1766) and, stimulated in his unorthodoxy by friendship with J. *Priestley, he joined in the 'Feathers Tavern' petition to Parliament of several Latitudinarians (J. Jebb, Bp. E. Law, &c.) against subscription to the *Thirty-Nine Articles. The failure of the petition and a change in his own intellectual position led him to adopt Unitarianism. He went to London, where, from 1774, he conducted services in Essex Street. His writings include *Apology on Resigning the Vicarage of Catterick* (1774), *A Sequel to the Apology* (1776), *Historical View of the State of the Unitarian Doctrine and Worship from the Reformation to our own Time* (1783), *Vindiciae Priestleianae* (1788), and *Conversations on the Divine Government* (1802).

Collected ed. of his *Sermons* (2 vols., London, 1810). T. Belsham, *Memoirs of . . . Theophilus Lindsey . . . including a Brief Analysis of his Works* (1812). H. McLachlan, *Letters of Theophilus Lindsey* (Publications of the University of Manchester, cxxxiv; 1920), with introductory 'Sketch of the Life of Theophilus Lindsey', pp. ix–xii. A. Nicholson in *D.N.B.*, xxxiii (1893), p. 317 f.

LINGARD, JOHN (1771–1851), English historian. He came from an old Lincolnshire RC family who had migrated to *Winchester, where he was born. He entered the English College at *Douai in 1782, but had to leave in 1793 on account of the French war. Having finished his theological studies at Crook Hall, nr. *Durham, he was ordained priest in 1795, made prefect of studies, and taught natural and moral philosophy. In 1806 he published his *Antiquities of the Anglo-Saxon Church* (ed. 3, much enlarged, 1845), and in 1808 he went to

Ushaw, where he helped with the foundation of the College and became its vice-president. In 1811 he moved to Hornby, nr. Lancaster, a small country mission, where he spent most of the rest of his life writing. In 1817 he paid a visit to *Rome, where he negotiated the re-opening of the *English College. In 1819 appeared the first three volumes of his *History of England*, the great work on which rests his fame. The eighth and last volume was published in 1830, carrying the history down to 1688. The work had a great success, which it owed esp. to its objectivity, its extensive use of contemporary documents, and the new light in which it viewed esp. such controversial periods as the *Reformation. It was translated into many European languages and earned its author the triple doctorate of theology, canon, and civil law from *Pius VII in 1821. There is some evidence that Leo XII created him cardinal *in petto* in 1826. Among his many other writings are a *New Version of the Four Gospels* (1836) and manuals of prayer and instructions as well as some controversial treatises.

J. Hughes, *John Lingard* (1907); M. Haile and E. Binney, *Life and Letters of John Lingard* (1911). T. Cooper in *D.N.B.*, xxxiii (1893), pp. 320–3.

LINUS, St. Acc. to all the early episcopal lists, Linus was the first Bp. of Rome after the Apostles Peter and Paul, but nothing else is known with certainty about him. A Christian of this name sends greetings, perhaps from Rome, in 2 Tim. 4. 21; and *Irenaeus and *Eusebius of Caesarea identify him with the Bishop. Feast day, 23 Sept.

St. Linus is mentioned by *Irenaeus, *Adv. Haer.*, III, iii, 3, and *Eusebius, *H.E.*, iii, 2, and v, 6. *L.P.* (Duchesne), i. 121. *AA.SS.*, Sept. VI (1757), pp. 539–45. J. B. *Lightfoot, *The Apostolic Fathers*, i (pt. 1; ed. 2, 1890), pp. 76–9. V. L. Kennedy, C.S.B., *The Saints of the Canon of the Mass* (Studi di Antichità Cristiana, xiv; 1938), esp. pp. 111–13. É. Amann in *D.T.C.*, ix (pt. 1; 1926), col. 772, s.v. 'Lin', with further reff.

LION. The lion appears in early Christian art esp. in two connexions. (1) In representations of the story of *Daniel, conceived as a 'type' of God's redemption of His chosen people. This occurs among the earliest *catacomb paintings. (2) As the symbol of St. *Mark. This symbolism, based on Ezek. 1 and Rev. 4, was discussed by St. *Jerome and St. *Augustine. In art its use dates from the 5th cent.

H. *Leclercq, O.S.B., in *D.A.C.L.*, ix (pt. 1; 1930), cols. 1198–207, s.v.

LIPPI, Fra FILIPPO (*c.* 1406–69), Italian painter. Educated at a *Carmelite convent near Florence, he took the habit in 1420. When his artistic talent was discovered he received a great many orders for work, but he began to lead an immoral life and in the event was released from his vows by *Pius II and allowed to marry. Among his principal pictures are the *Coronation of the Blessed Virgin* (1441), the *Vision of St. *Bernard* (1447), and his great fresco works of St. *John the Baptist

and St. *Stephen* (1452–64). Though he belonged to the second generation of the Renaissance and his art did not reach the spiritual heights of a Fra *Angelico, it was far from the pagan style of somewhat later times. He exercised a considerable influence on the subsequent development of devotional art, and his pictures of the Annunciation became the usual models for the theme in the future. He was the father of the painter Filippino Lippi (*c.* 1457–1504).

Studies, with reproductions, by E. C. Strutt (London, 1901) and Henriette Mendelsohn (Berlin, 1909). [G.] Gronau in *Allgemeines Lexikon der bildenden Künstler* begr. von U. Thieme–F. Becker, xxiii (ed. H. Vollmer; 1929), pp. 271–4, s.v., with detailed bibl. Studies on Filippino Lippi by A. Scharf (Vienna, 1935) and Katherine B. Neilson (Harvard-Radcliffe Fine Arts Series, Cambridge, Mass., 1938) and [G.] Gronau, loc. cit., pp. 268–70.

LIPSIUS, RICHARD ADELBERT (1830–1892), German Protestant theologian. He studied at Leipzig, and after holding other academic appointments became professor of systematic theology at Jena in 1871. In his *Pilatusakten* (1871; new ed., 1886) and his *Die Apokryphen, Apostelgeschichten und Apostellegenden* (4 vols., 1883–90) he did much towards unravelling problems connected with early Christian apocryphal literature, and in 1891 he edited, in association with M. Bonnet, the still standard collection of Apocryphal Acts. He also made researches into the early history of the Popes, arguing that St. Peter was never in Rome, and into the literary relationships of the early anti-heretical Christian writings. A pronounced liberal in dogmatic theology, he set out his systematic doctrines in a *Lehrbuch der evangelisch-protestantischen Dogmatik* (1876) and in *Philosophie und Religion* (1885); but he differed from A. *Ritschl and his disciples in a greater readiness to draw on the theoretical aspects of I. *Kant's idealism. He also issued a commentary on Gal., Rom., and Phil. (1891).

His other writings include *Zur Quellenkritik des Epiphanios* (Vienna, 1868), *Chronologie der römischen Bischöfe* (Kiel, 1869), *Die Quellen der römischen Petrussage* (Kiel, 1872), and *Die Quellen der ältesten Ketzergeschichte* (Leipzig, 1875). A. Neumann, *Grundlagen und Grundzüge der Weltanschauung von R. A. Lipsius* (1896). F. R. Lipsius in *P.R.E.* (ed. 3), xi (1902), pp. 520–4, and F. Traub in *R.G.G.* (ed. 2), iii (1929), col. 1667 f., both with bibl.

LISLE, AMBROSE LISLE MARCH PHILLIPPS DE. See *De Lisle, Ambrose Lisle March Phillipps*.

LISMORE, The Book of. A collection of the Lives of the Irish saints, written in medieval Irish, which was found in the castle at Lismore in 1814.

Whitley Stokes, 'Lives of Saints from the Book of Lismore' in *Anecdota Oxoniensia* (1890).

LITANY (Gk. λιτανεία, 'a supplication'). A form of prayer consisting of a series of petitions or biddings which are sung or said by a deacon, a priest, or cantors, and to which the people make fixed responses, e.g. *Kyrie eleison*,

'Grant, Lord', 'We beseech thee, hear us', &c. The Litany apparently originated at *Antioch in the 4th cent., and thence by way of Asia Minor passed to *Constantinople, whence it spread to the rest of the E. Litanies said by the deacon (ἐκτεναί) figure largely in the Greek liturgies, being the principal element of the devotion of the congregation, from whom the main parts of the service which take place in the sanctuary are concealed by the *iconostasis. From Constantinople the Litany spread also to Rome and the W. Pope *Gelasius I (492–6) instituted a litanic intercession into the Mass of which the 'ninefold Kyrie' is the sole surviving relic. The litany became also a favourite form of private prayer. Invocations of saints were a feature in many litanies (see Litany of the Saints). The procession of St. *Mark's Day, instituted at Rome in the 5th cent. or earlier to replace a similar pagan observance, acquired the name of litaniae majores, while the *Rogations were by contrast known as the litaniae minores.

N. Serarius, S.J., Litaneutici seu de Litaniis (Cologne, 1609; repr. in his Opuscula Theologica, iii (Mainz, 1611), pp. 60–94). L. Eisenhofer, Handbuch der katholischen Liturgik, i (1932), pp. 193–202. A. *Baumstark, Liturgie comparée (ed. 3 by B. Botte, O.S.B., 1953), pp. 80–90. H. J. Hotham in D.C.A., ii (1880), pp. 999–1005, s.v.; F. *Cabrol, O.S.B., in D.A.C.L., ix (pt. 2; 1930), cols. 1540–71, s.v. 'Litanies', with bibl.; E. Vykoukal, O.S.B., in L.Th.K., vi (1934), cols. 598–601, s.v. 'Litanei'; E. Cattaneo in E.C., vii (1951), cols. 1417–21, s.v. 'Litanie'. See also bibl. to Kyrie Eleison and Rogation Days.

LITANY, The (BCP). The form of 'general supplication' appointed to be sung or said after *Morning Prayer on *Sundays, *Wednesdays, and *Fridays. It is also included, with the addition of special suffrages, in the rites of *Ordination. It falls into two parts: (1) the invocation of the Persons of the Trinity, the deprecations, the obsecrations, the intercessions, and a final section consisting of invocations, *Kyrie eleison and the Lord's Prayer; and (2) versicles and responses, followed by collects, which are an adaptation of a special intercession in time of war. The Litany was first issued by T. *Cranmer in 1544 for use in the processions ordered by *Henry VIII at a time when England was at war with Scotland and France. Cranmer drew mostly on the Latin litanies then in use in England, esp. the *Sarum *Rogationtide Litany, but also on M. *Luther's 'Latin Litany' of 1529 and the Deacon's Litany in the 'Liturgy of St. John *Chrysostom'. Though he added little or nothing of his own, he made a notable change in the rhythm by grouping several suffrages under one response. In 1544 the invocations of the Trinity were followed by three invocations of saints; these were omitted when the Litany was included in the First BCP (1549). Minor changes were made in later versions of the BCP and the collects at the end have been altered several times. The appointment of Wednesday and Friday as Litany days coincides with Lutheran usage.

Text of the Litanies of 1544, 1552, and 1661, with indication of sources, in F. E. *Brightman, The English Rite, i (1915), pp. 174–91. W. H. Karslake, The Litany of the English Church Considered in its History, its Plan, and the Manner in which it is Intended to be Used (1876). E. G. C. F. Atchley, The People's Prayers. Being some Considerations on the Use of the Litany in Public Worship (*Alcuin Club Tracts, vi; 1906). Cf. also Brightman, op. cit., pp. lviii–lxviii, and see bibl. to Book of Common Prayer.

LITANY DESK. In the C of E, a low movable desk placed in the midst of the church, within or without the chancel, at which the minister kneels to recite the Litany in acc. with *Injunctions 24 of 1547 and 18 of 1559.

LITANY OF LORETO, The. A Litany in honour of the BVM, consisting of a series of invocations of our Lady under various honorific titles, such as 'Mother of Divine grace', 'Virgin most prudent', 'Queen of Angels', &c., each followed by the request: 'Pray for us'. It derives its name from the famous Italian shrine, where its use is attested for the year 1558; but it is doubtful whether it was first sung at *Loreto and did not rather arise under *Dominican influence in the confraternities of the Rosary and thence make its way to the shrine. It is a simplified version of older Litanies of our Lady, which first appeared in the 12th cent. It was approved and indulgenced by *Sixtus V in 1587, and again by *Clement VIII in 1601. In the course of time more titles were added to the original series, e.g. 'Queen of the Most Holy Rosary', 'Queen conceived without Original Sin', and 'Mother of Good Counsel' by *Leo XIII, and 'Queen of Peace' by *Benedict XV in 1917. It is often recited in RC churches at the service of *Benediction, and in many religious orders, e.g. by the *Carmelites, every day after Vespers, and by the Dominicans on Saturdays after *Compline.

A. De Santi, S.J., Le Litanie lauretane (1897; Fr. tr., 1900). J. Sauren, Die lauretanische Litanei nach Ursprung, Geschichte und Inhalt dargestellt (Kempten, 1895). A. De Santi in C.E., ix (1910), pp. 286–90, s.v.

LITANY OF THE SAINTS, The. In the W. Church this litany is in regular use. It consists of invocations for mercy and deliverance addressed to the three Persons of the Trinity and for intercession to the BVM and a list of prophets, patriarchs, angels, apostles, saints, confessors, and virgins individually and in classes. Early forms of such a litany are found in the East from the end of the 3rd cent. and in the West from the late 5th cent. A later stage is represented in the 'Athelstan Psalter' (9th cent.), the *Stowe Missal and the 'Book of *Cerne'. The list of saints invoked varied locally and increased in length through the Middle Ages until in 1570 it became necessary to obtain papal licence to differ from the use of Rome. In the RC Church it is commonly used in three basic forms: (1) the Greater Litany used esp. on the *Rogation days, on the Feast of St. Mark, for special penitential and intercessory processions, and certain other special occasions, such as the conferring of Major Orders and the laying of the foundation stone of a new church; (2) A shortened form used on *Holy Saturday and the vigil of *Pentecost; and (3) An abbreviated form used at the *Commendatio Animae* in which the invocations and supplications are for the benefit of the departing soul. In private devotional usage, litanies with a variant list of saints are also in common use. See also *Deprecatio Gelasii.*

H. Samson, *Die Allerheiligen-Litanei geschichtlich, liturgisch und ascetisch erklärt* (1894). F. Mersham in *C.E.*, ix (1910), p. 291 f., s.v.

LITERATE. In the C of E a cleric who has been admitted to holy orders without a university degree. Canon 58 of 1604 permits such ministers 'to wear upon their surplices, instead of hoods, some decent *tippet of black, so it be not silk'.

LITTLE ENTRANCE. See *Lesser Entrance.*

LITTLE FLOWER OF JESUS, The. A popular designation of St. *Teresa of Lisieux (q.v.) who frequently so describes herself in her autobiography.

LITTLE FLOWERS OF ST. FRANCIS (the 'Fioretti'). A classic collection of legends and traditions about St. *Francis of Assisi (d. 1226) and his companions. It gives an exquisite picture of the religious life and spirit of the early Franciscans. It was written in the Italian of Tuscany *c.* 1322, though it is probably a translation from a Latin original, itself based on the 'Actus Beati Francisci et Sociorum ejus' and other sources. The earliest known MS. (A.D. 1390) is at Berlin, and the first printed edition was issued at Vicenza in 1476.

There is an English version in the Everyman's Library, No. 485, and another in verse by J. Rhoades, in The World's Classics, No. 265.

LITTLE GIDDING. A manor in Huntingdonshire where the Ferrar family lived under a definite religious rule from 1625 to 1646. The household, some forty persons in all, consisted of Nicholas *Ferrar, in deacon's orders, his mother Mary, and the families of his brother and sister. A systematic rule of devotion and work was followed, and there were daily services and employment such as bookbinding, dispensing, and a school for village children. The house was visited by *Charles I and G. *Herbert. After Nicholas Ferrar's death in 1637, the community continued until raided by O. *Cromwell's soldiers in Nov. 1646. Though the house has now disappeared, the church still stands. For further details of the life at Little Gidding, see *Ferrar, Nicholas.*

The Arminian Nunnery; or a Brief Description and Relation of the late erected Monastical Place, called the Arminian Nunnery, at Little Gidding in Huntingdonshire (1641). H. Collett, *Little Gidding and its Founder* (1925). J. E. Acland, *Little Gidding and its Inmates in the Time of Charles I* (1903). Appendix on 'Little Gidding' by W. Page in *The Victoria History of the County of Huntingdon*, i (1926), pp. 399–406. E. C. Sharland (ed.), *The Story Books of Little Gidding* (1899). See also bibl. s.v. *Ferrar*, Nicholas.

LITTLE LABYRINTH, The. A lost 3rd cent. treatise which was directed against the *Adoptionist heretics, *Theodotus and *Artemon. It is referred to under this title (ὁ σμικρὸς λαβύρινθος) by *Theodoret (*Haer. Fab. Comp.* ii, 5), who ascribes it to *Origen, and two passages are quoted by *Eusebius (*HE*, v, 28). Its authorship was assigned with some probability by J. B. *Lightfoot and A. *Harnack, who are followed by O. *Bardenhewer, to St. *Hippolytus, though G. *Salmon wished to attribute it to *Gaius. It is to be distinguished from another writing, the 'Labyrinth', mentioned by *Photius (Cod. 48), which is very probably to be identified with Book X of St. *Hippolytus' *Refutatio.*

J. B. Lightfoot, *St. Clement of Rome*, ii (ed. 1890), pp. 377–80. Bardenhewer, ii, 567 f. G. Salmon in *D.C.B.*, i (1877), pp. 384–6, s.v. 'Caius (2)'.

LITTLE OFFICE OF OUR LADY (Officium Parvum Beatae Mariae Virginis). A brief office in honour of the BVM. It is modelled on the Divine *Office and thus contains the usual seven hours; but Matins has only one *Nocturn with three Psalms and three Lessons, the Psalms of the other hours do not vary acc. to the different days of the week, and much of the additional material such as responsories and versicles is cut out. The Little Office of Our Lady was first known in the 10th cent. It originated in the religious orders, being early adopted by the *Cistercians and *Camaldulensians, and was later taken over by the secular clergy. It was retained at the *Breviary Reform of *Pius V in 1568, though the obligation of its recitation was no longer binding under sin. *Pius X removed the obligation altogether, though recommending it as a private devotion. In modern times it has become the ordinary form of vocal prayer of a great number of the new female congregations, and its recitation is also normally enjoined on *Tertiaries.

Facsimile ed. of two 11th-cent. MSS. ed., with introd., by E. S. Dewick (*Henry Bradshaw Society, xxi; 1902), with reff.; a 15th-cent. MS. ed. H. Littlehales, *The Prymer or Lay Folks' Prayer Book* (E.E.T.S., Orig. Series, cv, cix, 1895–7), with important essay by E. *Bishop, 'The Origin of the Prymer', pp. xi–xxxviii, repr. in Bishop's *Liturgica Historica* (1918), pp. 211–27. E. Taunton, *The Little Office of Our Lady.* A Treatise Theoretical, Practical, and Exegetical (1903). E. Hoskins, *Horae Beatae Mariae Virginis or Sarum and York Primers with Kindred Books and Primers of the Reformed Roman Use* (1901). H. Bohatta, *Bibliographie des Livres d'heures* (Vienna, 1909). L. A. St. L. Toke in *C.E.*, ix (1910), p. 294 f. A. Manser, O.S.B., in *L.Th.K.*, vi (1935), col. 686, s.v. 'Officium' for further reff.

LITTLEDALE, RICHARD FREDERICK (1833–90), liturgical writer and Anglo-Catholic apologist. He came of an Irish family but lived in England from *c.* 1855, holding curacies from 1856 to 1861, when ill-health forced him to abandon parochial work. His *Plain Reasons against joining the Church of Rome* (1880) enjoyed a wide circulation. He also completed J. M. *Neale's *Commentary on the Psalms from Primitive and Medieval Writers* (4 vols., 1860–1874). With J. E. Vaux, he was the first editor of *The Priest's Prayer Book* (1864).

G. C. Boase in *D.N.B.*, xxxiii (1893), p. 364 f., s.v.

LITURGICAL COLOURS. See *Colours, Liturgical.*

LITURGICAL MOVEMENT. A Movement of which the object is the restoration of the active participation by the people in the official worship of the Church. In the RC Church the revival may be traced to P. L. P. *Guéranger (q.v.), but it received its chief impetus from the directions of *Pius X relating to church music (1903) and to the promotion of Eucharistic piety and frequent communion. It has been fostered esp. by the *Benedictines, e.g. the abbey of *Maredsous in Belgium and that of *Maria Laach in Germany. From c. 1910 the movement spread to Holland, Spain, Italy, and England, where Cardinal N. *Wiseman was its forerunner in the 19th and Abbot F. *Cabrol one of its chief exponents in the 20th cent. In recent times it has made much progress in America and even in the Far East, e.g. in the Benedictine Mission of Korea. Among the practical aims of the Movement is the education of the laity to a deeper appreciation of the Liturgy, which is encouraged by communal recitation or chanting of the responses at *Mass, Sunday *Vespers and *Compline, to a better understanding of the Church's Year, and, as a result, to a closer connexion between liturgical worship and private devotion.

The renewed interest in the Liturgy has not been confined to the RC Church. The Ritualist Movement, inaugurated by the *Tractarians to give sacramental worship a central place in the C of E, has steadily grown and, on a far smaller scale, the German 'Hochkirche' of F. *Heiler and other similar Movements on the Continent. The underlying cause of this general trend of return to liturgical worship is the reaction from the subjectivism by which all the Christian Churches have been more or less affected since the 16th cent.

O. Rousseau, O.S.B., *Histoire du mouvement liturgique. Esquisse historique depuis le début du XIXe siècle jusqu'au pontificat de Pie X* (Lex Orandi, iii, 1945), with bibl.; J. H. Srawley, *The Liturgical Movement. Its Origin and Growth* (*Alcuin Club Tracts, xxvii, 1954). E. B. Koenker, *The Liturgical Renaissance in the Roman Catholic Church* (Chicago, 1954). *La Participation active des fidèles au cultes* (Cours et conférences des Semaines Liturgiques, xi; Louvain, 1933). E. Cattaneo in *E.C.*, vii (1951), col. 1439 f., s.v. 'Liturgia, IV: movimento liturgico', with further bibl. col. 1442. For the revival in England see also bibl. to *Oxford Movement*.

LITURGIOLOGY. A cumbersome term for the scientific study of liturgies and related subjects. Its first appearance is in the title of J. M. *Neale's *Essays on Liturgiology and Church History* (1863).

LITURGY (Gk. λειτουργία, from λεώς, 'people' and ἔργον, 'work'). The original Gk. word was used of a public duty of any kind, not only religious, but by the time of the *Septuagint it had come to be applied particularly to the services of the *Temple. The word in English is used in two senses, viz. (1) Of all the prescribed services of the Church, e.g. incl. the

canonical hours, as contrasted with private devotion. And (2), specifically as a title of the *Eucharist (as the chief act of public worship). It is commonly so used among the Eastern Churches. In derived senses the word is further used (1) of the written texts which order such services (e.g. the 'Liturgy of St. John Chrysostom'), and (2) as a general name for the branch of study (more cumbrously 'liturgiology') which concerns itself with these Liturgies.

Among the classical collections of liturgical documents and texts are those of J. *Mabillon, E. *Martène, B. *Gavanti, G. M. *Tommasi, E. *Renaudot (qq.v.). Cf. also F. *Cabrol, O.S.B.-H. *Leclercq, O.S.B., *Monumenta Ecclesiae Liturgica*, I: Relliquiae Liturgicae Vetustissimae (Paris, 1900–2), F. E. *Brightman, *Liturgies Eastern and Western*, i (Eastern Liturgies, 1895; all publd.), and J. Quasten (ed.), *Monumenta Eucharistica et Liturgica Vetustissima* (Florilegium Patristicum, vii, Bonn, 1935) Imp. modern studies include P. *Guéranger, O.S.B., *Institutiones Liturgicae* (4 vols., Paris, 1878–85); L. *Duchesne, *Origines du culte chrétien* (1889); C. Harris–W. K. Lowther Clarke (edd.), *Liturgy and Worship*. A Companion to the Prayer Books of the Anglican Communion (1932); N. Micklem (ed.), *Christian Worship*. Studies in its History and Meaning by Members of Mansfield College (1936); L. Eisenhofer, *Grundriss der Liturgik des römischen Ritus* (1924; ed. 5, J. Lechner, 1950); id., *Handbuch der Katholischen Liturgik* (2 vols., 1932–3); C. Callewaert, *Liturgicae Institutiones*: De Sacra Liturgia universim (Bruges, 1933); A. *Baumstark, *Liturgie comparée* (Chevetogne, 1939); R. Aigrain (ed.), *Liturgia*. Encyclopédie populaire des connaissances liturgiques (1947). Among Periodicals devoted mainly or exclusively to the furtherance of liturgical studies are *Ephemerides Liturgicae* (Rome, 1887 ff.); *Les Questions liturgiques et paroissiales* (Louvain, 1911 ff.); *Jahrbuch für Liturgiewissenschaft* (1921 ff.), contd. since 1951 as *Archiv für Liturgiewissenschaft*; *Ambrosius* (Milan, 1925 ff.), and *Sacris Erudiri* (Bruges, 1948 ff.); also the series *Liturgiegeschichtliche Quellen und Forschungen* and the *D.A.C.L.* (unhappily its interesting and often sparkling artt. suffer from innumerable inaccuracies). On the whole subject, A. Baumstark, *Vom geschichtlichen Werden der Liturgie* (Ecclesia Orans 10; 1923), and K. Mohlberg, O.S.B. *Ziele und Aufgaben der liturgiegeschichtlichen Forschungen* (Münster i.W., 1919). A. G. Martimort and others, *L'Église en prière*. Introduction à la liturgie [1962].

LIUDHARD, St. (d. c. 602), chaplain of Queen Bertha, who brought him from Gaul to England, as was arranged by the terms of her marriage to *Ethelbert, king of Kent (*Bede, *H.E.*, i, 25). He probably ministered in St. Martin's Church at *Canterbury. *William of Malmesbury (untrustworthy) represents him as having been prominent in preparing for the evangelization of Kent by the Roman mission of St. *Augustine. Feast day, 4 Feb.

The principal authority is Bede, *H.E.*, i, 25; notes in ed. by C. Plummer, ii (Oxford, 1896), p. 42. Later lives listed in T. D. Hardy, *Descriptive Catalogue of Materials Relating to the History of Great Britain and Ireland to the End of the Reign of Henry VII*, i (pt. 1; Rolls Series, 1862), p. 175 f. William of Malmesbury, *Gesta Regum*, i, 9 (ed. W. *Stubbs, i, Rolls Series, 1887, p. 13).

LIUTPRAND (c. 922–c. 972), Bp. of Cremona. Of a noble Lombard family, he was ordained deacon at Pavia and later became Chancellor to Berengar of Italy, who sent him in 949 on an embassy to the Byzantine court. On his subsequent disgrace, he attached himself to the Emp. Otto I, who made him Bp. of Cremona in 961. In 963 he was sent as an ambassador to Rome, where he took part in the assembly which deposed *John XII, and later (968) to *Constantinople, where he negotiated the marriage between Otto's son (afterwards Otto II) and Theophano, the daughter of the Byzantine Emperor. Liutprand is the chief authority for the Italian history of his period, but he allowed rhetoric and prejudice to obscure accuracy and objectivity. His principal writings were 'Antapodosis', which relates the events from 888 to 949; 'Historia Ottonis', which covers the years 960–4; and a 'Relatio de Legatione Constantinopolitana' of the years 968–9. The ascription of the *Liber Pontificalis to him is erroneous.

Collected ed. of his Works by H. de la Higuera–L. Ramirez de Prado (Antwerp, 1640); crit. edd. by G. H. Pertz in *M.G.H.*, Scriptores, iii (1839), pp. 264–363, and J. Becker (Scriptores Rerum Germanicarum in Usum Scholarum, Hannover and Leipzig, 1915), with introd. pp. v–xxxvii. Eng. tr. by F. A. Wright (Broadway Medieval Library, 1930), with introd. pp. 1–24. M. Lintzel *Studien über Liutprand von Cremona* (Historische Studien, Hft. 233; 1933), with further reff.

LIVERPOOL CATHEDRALS. (1) *The Anglican Cathedral*. Designed by G. G. *Scott (RC; b. 1880) in the Romantic Gothic style on a vast scale, and built on high ground, it will eventually dominate Merseyside. The foundation stone was laid by Edward VII in 1904, and within 50 years the chancel, central space, Lady Chapel, first transepts, chapter house, Chapel of the Holy Ghost, and the tower, have been finished. It will have the highest interior of all English Cathedrals. (2) *The RC Cathedral*. It has been planned by Sir Edwin Lutyens (C of E; 1869–1944) in a modern free Byzantine style, surmounted by a dome, and, like the Anglican cathedral, is being built on high ground. The foundation stone was laid in 1934.

LIVINGSTONE, DAVID (1813–73), African missionary and explorer. A native of Blantyre in Lanarkshire, he educated himself by omnivorous reading while employed in a cotton factory. The study of Thomas Dick's *Philosophy of a Future State* determined him to devote his life to missionary work and the alleviation of human suffering; and, after attending medical classes in Glasgow he went to London in 1838, where he joined the *London Missionary Society, at first contemplating work in *China. In 1840, inspired by R. *Moffat, he embarked for the Cape of Good Hope and for some years worked as a missionary in the Bechuana country. Here he became possessed of a passionate interest in all aspects of Africa and its peoples, spending several years in labours full of adventures and winning the confidence of the Africans by his medical work and schools. Reports of his explorations and experiences aroused wide interest at home, incl. that of scientific bodies such as the Royal Geographical Society; and on his return to England in 1856 he was received with unbounded enthusiasm. In 1857 he published his *Missionary Travels and Researches in South Africa*. In 1858 he resumed his travels in Africa, no longer under the auspices of the L.M.S. as he had ceased to be a missionary in

the conventional sense, and in 1859 he discovered the lakes of Shirwa and Nyasa. In 1861 he gave pioneer help to the *U.M.C.A. (q.v.). During a second stay in England (1864–5) he published *The Zambesi and its Tributaries* (1865). After his return to Africa he explored the basin of the Upper Nile and discovered Lake Bangweulu in 1868. In his last years he was much hampered in his long journeys of exploration by ill health; and in 1871 he was discovered in a state of exhaustion by H. M. Stanley of the *New York Herald*. He died on 1 May 1873 in the village of Ilala and was buried in *Westminster Abbey.

Livingstone's *Last Journals in Central Africa from 1865 to his Death*, ed. H. Waller (2 vols., London, 1874). D. Chamberlin (ed.), *Some Letters from Livingstone, 1840–1872* (ib., 1940). J. I. Macnair (ed.), *Livingstone's Travels* (ib., 1954). Lives include those of W. G. Blaikie (London, 1880; the official biography), T. Hughes (ib., 1889), H. H. Johnston (ib., 1891), R. J. Campbell (ib., 1929), D. C. Somervell (ib., 1936), J. I. Macnair (ib., 1940) and J. Simmonds (ib., 1955). R. Coupland, *Livingstone's Last Journey* (1945). R. H. Vetch in *D.N.B.*, xxxiii (1893), pp. 384–96.

LLANDAFF. Cathedral city in Wales, two miles NW of Cardiff. The ancient diocese comprised Monmouthshire, Glamorgan, and some parishes in *Hereford and Brecon. In 1921 the dioceses of Monmouth and Swansea-and-Brecon were formed out of it. Its early history, down to 1132, is told in the 'Book of Llandaff', which, however, is not a trustworthy authority. Acc. to this the first church was built in Llandaff by King *Lucius in the 2nd cent. The monastery itself seems not to have been founded by St. *Dubricius or Dyfrig (d. *c.* 546), whose name survives in Llandaff, but by his disciple, St. *Teilo (d. *c.* 560), who became its first abbot and bishop, a combination not unusual in early medieval Britain. The first abbots of Llandaff were styled 'archbishops', but the title probably expressed only the primacy of an episcopal abbot of the principal abbey over those of the subordinate monasteries. With the change from the monastic to the diocesan episcopate the diocesans were styled bishops, and in 1107 became suffragans of *Canterbury. In 1120 Bp. Urban (1107–33) began to build its cathedral. Bp. Anthony Kitchin (d. 1563) was the only English bishop to take the Oath of Supremacy in 1559. In the early years of the Elizabethan Reformation the diocese was a centre of *recusancy, but in the later 17th cent. it became a stronghold of *Puritanism. During the 18th and the first half of the 19th cent. Llandaff was unfortunate in its bishops, who were mostly Englishmen with little interest in their diocese; but from the middle of the 19th cent. Church life revived. Between 1844 and 1869 the medieval cathedral, which since the Reformation had been in ruins, was restored. Many new churches and mission halls were built, and in 1907 St. Michael's Theological College was founded. The cathedral was badly damaged in an air raid in 1941.

The 'Book of Llandaff' was ed., with Eng. tr., by W. J. Rees (Welsh Manuscript Society, i, 1840); suppl. notes by T. Wakeman appended (sep. pagination) to W. J. Rees,

Lives of the Cambro-British Saints (ib., iv, 1853). Text reproduced from the Gwysaney MS., with transcription, by I. G. Evans and J. Rhys (Series of Old Welsh Texts, iv, Oxford, 1894), with full reff. J. A. Bradney (ed.), *Acts of the Bishops of Llandaff* [1660–1724] (4 books in 3 vols., Llandaff Records, ii–iv, 1908–12). W. de G. Birch, *Memorials of the See and Cathedral of Llandaff* (Neath, 1912). B. Willis, *A Survey of the Cathedral Church of Llandaff* (1719). E. J. Newell, *Llandaff* (Diocesan Histories; 1902); E. C. M. Willmott, *The Cathedral Church of Llandaff* (Bell's Cathedral Series; 1907); E. [A.] Foord, *St. David's, Llandaff and Brecon* (Cathedrals, Abbeys, and Famous Churches; 1925), pp. 97–124. G. E. Halliday, *Llandaff Church Plate* [of the Diocese] (1901). J. Fisher in *D.E.C.H.*, pp. 333–5, s.v.

LLOYD, CHARLES (1784–1829), Bp. of Oxford from 1827. After a brilliant career at Christ Church, Oxford, where he was in turn lecturer, tutor, and censor, he was appointed Regius professor of divinity in 1822, an office which he retained until his death. In his theological position he in several ways anticipated the *Oxford Movement and J. H. *Newman, E. B. *Pusey, and R. H. *Froude all came under his influence. He is said to have emphasized, as *Tract 90* did later, the importance of distinguishing between the decrees of the Council of *Trent and many popular aspects of the modern RC system, and insisted in a way then quite unusual upon the primitive and medieval elements in the BCP.

R. Garnett in *D.N.B.*, xxxiii (1893), pp. 411–14.

L.M.S. The 'London Missionary Society' was founded in 1795 by a body of *Congregationalists, *Anglicans, *Presbyterians, and *Wesleyans who combined to promote Christian missions to the heathen. The first 29 missionaries under its auspices sailed to Tahiti in 1796. It was one of its principles that individual missionaries should be left free to choose whatever form of Church government they held right. In recent times the Society, which carries on extensive work in *China, *India, S.E. Asia, S. and E. Africa and the *South Sea Islands, has been maintained almost exclusively by Congregationalists.

R. Lovett, *The History of the London Missionary Society, 1795–1895* (2 vols., 1899); N. Goodall, *A History of the London Missionary Society, 1895–1945* (1954).

LOCK, WALTER (1846–1933), Warden of *Keble College, Oxford. Educated at Marlborough and Corpus Christi College, Oxford, he became a Fellow of Magdalen in 1869 and one of the original tutors of Keble in 1870. In 1873 he was ordained priest. From 1895 to 1919 he held the Dean Ireland chair of Exegesis and from 1919 to 1927 the Lady Margaret chair of Divinity. From 1897 to 1920 he was also Warden of Keble. One of the liberal post-*Tractarian theologians, he contributed the essay on 'The Church' to *Lux Mundi* (1889). His writings, all in a lucid and graceful style, include a biography of John *Keble (1893), a commentary on the *Pastoral Epistles (1924), and an attractive collection of *Oxford Memories* (1932).

D. C. Simpson in *D.N.B., 1931–1940*, p. 240 f.

LOCKE, JOHN (1632–1704), English philosopher. A native of Somerset, he was educated at Westminster School and *Christ Church, Oxford, where he was deeply influenced by the works of R. *Descartes, whose emphasis on reason made a lasting impression on him. In 1666 he became acquainted with Lord Ashley, later first Earl of Shaftesbury, who made him his secretary, and with whom he moved to London. In 1675 he went to France, returning to England in 1679, but after the fall of Shaftesbury escaped to Holland in 1683, where he remained till 1689. After the accession of William and Mary he once more returned to London. From 1691 till his death he lived in the manor house of Otes, in Essex.

Locke was the foremost defender of free inquiry and toleration in the later 17th cent. His system is a combination of Christian rationalism and empiricism. In the *Letters concerning Toleration* (1689, 1690, and 1692) he pleaded for religious liberty for all except atheists and RCs, who were excluded because he held them to be a danger to the state. His ideal was a national Church with an all-embracing creed that made ample allowance for individual opinion, on the ground that human understanding was too limited for one man to impose his beliefs on another. In 1690 he published his *Two Treatises of Government*, expounding the principles of the Whig Revolution of 1688. They were hardly profound, but their historical importance was great through their influence in the following century. The substance of his philosophical thought is contained in the famous *Essay concerning Human Understanding* (1690). In it he attacks the Platonist conception of 'innate ideas'. The human mind is a *tabula rasa* and all our ideas come from experience, i.e. from sensation or reflexion, knowledge through reason being, acc. to him, a 'natural revelation'. Pure reality cannot be grasped by the human mind; consequently there is no sure basis for metaphysics, and substance is 'an uncertain supposition of we know not what'. The spirituality of the soul, though not certain, is at least probable; the existence of God, on the other hand, can be discovered with certainty by reason, and His law gives men their rule of conduct.

Locke's religious ideas were further developed in the *Reasonableness of Christianity as Delivered in the Scriptures* (1695). Here he maintains that the only secure basis of Christianity is its reasonableness, though he accepts the miracles recorded in Scripture as proofs of its Divine origin. Reason, however, has the last word in the acceptance of the supernatural and the interpretation of Scripture. The essence of Christianity is the acknowledgement of Christ as the Messiah, Who was sent into the world chiefly to spread the true knowledge of God and of our duties. All other doctrines are secondary and incapable of conclusive proof. The book roused much controversy, among its critics being John Edwards (1637–1716), J. *Sergeant and Thomas Burnet (1635–1715). In his last years Locke devoted himself to the study of Scripture; the outcome was two posthumous works, *A Paraphrase and Notes on the Epistles of St. Paul* (1705-7) and *A Discourse on Miracles* (1706).

Many collected edd. of his Works. They include 3 vols., fol., London, 1714; and ed. E. Law, Bp. of Carlisle, 4 vols., London, 1777. The best ed. of the *Essay*, with introd. and notes, is that of A. C. *Fraser, 2 vols., Oxford, 1894. *An Early Draft of Locke's Essay* [MS. dating from 1671]. Together with excerpts from his Journal, ed. R. I. Aaron-Jocelyn Gibb (1936). A somewhat later draft, also from 1671, publd. by B. Rand (Cambridge, Mass., 1931). The best life of Locke is that of H. R. Fox Bourne (2 vols., London, 1876). Other lives, with studies of Locke's philosophy, by T. H. Fowler ('English Men of Letters', Oxford, 1880), A. C. Fraser ('Blackwood's Philosophical Classics', 1890), S. Alexander ('Philosophies Ancient and Modern', 1908), and R. I. Aaron ('Leaders of Philosophy', Oxford, 1937). H. MacLachlan, *The Religious Opinions of Milton, Locke and Newton* (Publications of the University of Manchester, cclxxvi, Theological Series, vi; 1941), pp. 67-114. H. Ollion, *La Philosophie générale de John Locke* (1909). J. W. Gough, *John Locke's Political Philosophy* (1950). H. O. Christophersen, *A Bibliographical Introduction to the Study of John Locke* (Skrifter utgitt av det Norske Videnskaps-Akademi. Hist.-filos. Kl. 1930. No. 8). Überweg, iii, pp. 351-69, 685-7. L. Stephen in *D.N.B.*, xxxiv (1893), pp. 27-36; A. C. Fraser in *E.B.* (ed. 11), xvi (1911), pp. 844-52; H. Barker in *H.E.R.E.*, viii (1915), pp. 116-20.

LOCULUS. (1) The commonest type of tomb in the *catacombs, in the form of a horizontal rectangular niche. The *loculi* are cut, one above another, in the sides of the corridors. Each is closed at the front by a tile or marble slab which bears the epitaph. (2) A name sometimes given to the hole ('sepulchre') which contains the relics in a fixed altar.

On (1) H. Leclercq, O.S.B., in *D.A.C.L.*, ix (pt. 2; 1930), cols. 1934-43, s.v., with reff. E. Diehl, *Inscriptiones Latinae Christianae Veteres* (3 vols., Berlin, 1925-31), esp. vol. ii, pp. 222-32 and 279-86.

LOGIA (Gk. λόγια, 'sayings'). A supposed collection of the sayings of Christ which circulated in the early Church. The use of the word in this connexion derives from the statement of *Papias that 'Matthew compiled the logia (τὰ λόγια) in the Hebrew language, and each person interpreted them as he was able'. As many scholars have held that the reference here is to the lost document ' *Q' (q.v.) which was drawn upon by Mt. and Lk., the expression 'the Logia' has been widely used as a synonym for 'Q'. The word is also used of the ' *Sayings of Jesus' (q.v.) discovered at *Oxyrhynchus in 1897 and 1904.

LOGOS (Gk. Λόγος, 'Word' or 'Reason'). The expression is used in (esp. Greek) theology for the 'Word of God', the Second Person of the *Trinity. The term was known both in Jewish and pagan antiquity. Heraclitus (*c.* 500 B.C.) conceived it in a pantheistic way as the universal reason governing and permeating the world, and the *Stoics took it over and popularized it. In the Platonized thought of *Alexandria, its character changed from an immanent power to an intermediary agent between God and the world and as such influenced *Philo. He connected it with the Biblical conception of Gen. 1. 3 and Ps. 33. 9

where it signified the act of creation, and with passages such as Wisd. 9. 15 ff. where it is almost treated as a *hypostasis.

In the NT the term is confined to the Johannine writings (Jn. 1. 1 ff., 1 Jn. 1. 1, Rev. 19. 13 [but cf. Heb. 4. 12]), though the idea occurs also in St. *Paul. In the Prologue of the Fourth Gospel the Logos is described as God from eternity, the Creative Word (cf. Gen. 1. 3), who (and this is entirely new) became incarnate in the man Jesus of Nazareth. In recent times there has been much discussion about the source of the Johannine conception, theories being advanced so far apart as that it was inspired by Palestinian Judaism or by a Mandaean hymn (R. *Bultmann). Its relation to the Gospel has also been disputed since A. *Harnack contended that the Logos was only introduced to interest a philosophic public and was unconnected with the body of the Gospel.

In patristic times the Logos doctrine was taken up by St. *Ignatius and developed by the *Apologists of the 2nd cent. The latter saw in it a welcome means of making the Christian teaching acceptable to Hellenistic philosophy, but did not always escape the danger of falling into unsound *Gnostic speculations. *Justin Martyr, e.g., held that the Logos was generated by an act of will of the Father with a view to creation, and *Theophilus, following the Stoics, distinguished the λόγος ἐνδιάθετος, i.e. the Logos immanent in God before creation, from the λόγος προφορικός, i.e. the Logos externalized as the instrument of creation. *Clement of Alexandria made the Logos doctrine a chief part of his teaching, whilst *Irenaeus pointed out the dangers of going into too detailed speculations. St. *Athanasius is among the first to give a comprehensive and completely satisfactory presentation of the Christian Logos conception by linking it up with the whole doctrine of Redemption. St. *Augustine connected it with the image of the Trinity in the human soul. The whole complex of earlier teaching was eventually systematized in the teaching of the Schoolmen, esp. in the Summa of St. *Thomas Aquinas.

A. Aall, *Der Logos. Geschichte seiner Entwickelung in der griechischen Philosophie und der christlichen Literatur* (2 vols., 1896-9). J. Réville, *La Doctrine du Logos dans le quatrième évangile et dans les œuvres de Philon* (1881). J. Lebreton, *Histoire du dogme de la Trinité des origines au concile de Nicée*, i (1910), pp. 41-73; Eng. tr., i (1939), pp. 40-60. W. R. *Inge in *H.E.R.E.*, viii (1915), pp. 133-8, s.v.; H. Leisegang in *P.W.*, xiii (1926), cols. 1035-81, s.v.; E. Krebs in *L.Th.K.*, vi (1934), cols. 628-31, s.v.; A. Michel in *D.T.C.*, xv (pt. 2; 1950, cols. 2639-72, s.v. 'Verbe'; P. de Ambroggi in *E.C.*, vii (1951), cols. 1481-6, s.v.

LOISY, ALFRED FIRMIN (1857-1940), French *Modernist Biblical scholar. A native of Ambrières in French Lorraine, he entered the seminary at Châlons-sur-Marne in 1874 and was ordained priest in 1879. In 1881 he resumed his studies at the *Institut Catholique in *Paris, where he came under the influence of L. *Duchesne and, in the same year, was charged with teaching Hebrew and OT. From 1882 to 1885 he attended the lectures of

E. *Renan and became attracted to pantheism. Though by 1886 his faith in traditional Catholicism had been completely shaken, he remained in the RC Church with a view to modernizing her teaching. In 1889 he was given the chair of Sacred Scripture at the Institut, but his critical views aroused opposition and in 1892 he was allowed to teach only Assyrian and Hebrew; and after publishing his theories in his periodical *L'Enseignement biblique* (1892–3) he had to leave the Institut. After the appearance of the encyclical '*Providentissimus Deus' (18 Nov. 1893) he gave up his journal and from 1894 to 1899 was chaplain to the *Dominican teaching nuns at Neuilly. From 1900 he taught at the École Pratique des Hautes Études.

In 1902 Loisy published *L'Évangile et l'Église* in reply to A. *Harnack's *Wesen des Christentums* (1900). As against Harnack, who sought to base Christianity on the teaching of the historic Jesus apart from later dogmatic accretions, Loisy maintained that its essence was to be sought in the faith of the developed Church as expanded under the guidance of the Spirit. The fact that Christ did not found a Church nor institute Sacraments did not detract from their central place in the Christian life. The book was at once condemned by the Abp. of Paris. In 1903 Loisy published three further writings, *Le Quatrième Évangile*, *Le Discours sur la Montagne*, and *Autour d'un petit livre*, the last dealing with the controversy aroused by *L'Évangile et l'Église*. All these writings were at once placed on the *Index (1903). In 1904 he resigned his post at the École des Hautes Études and retired to the country. After the decree '*Lamentabili' (2 July 1907) and the encyclical 'Pascendi' (6 Sept. 1907) he published his *Simples Réflexions* (1908) on these documents, as well as his great work *Les Évangiles synoptiques* in which he treated the Gospels in open defiance of the ecclesiastical directions. Two months later he was excommunicated. He had abandoned his priestly functions in 1906.

From 1909 to 1930 Loisy was professor of the history of religions at the Collège de France. Among his many publications during this latter period are *Les Mystères païens et le mystère chrétien* (1914) and *La Religion* (1917), in both of which he asserts the strong influence of the pagan mystery religions on Christianity. *Les Livres du Nouveau Testament* (1922) develops this idea and reflects the influence of recent *Form-critical methods. In 1930–1 he published his voluminous *Mémoires pour servir à l'histoire religieuse de notre temps*, which embody extensive information on his own life and on the history of *Modernism. His final views on the NT are summed up in the *Naissance du christianisme* (1933) in which he treated the Gospels not as historical documents but as catechetical and cultural literature with but very slight historical basis.

Loisy was a brilliant but undisciplined critic. He had a wide knowledge of German Biblical criticism from which he borrowed ideas which he often illuminated with flashes of insight. Much of his Biblical work does not seem, however, to have convinced even himself, and he readily abandoned his theories without misgivings. He regarded himself as, and is generally held to be, the true founder of Modernism in France.

His *Mémoires*, already referred to, can be supplemented by M. D. Petre, *Alfred Loisy: His Religious Significance* (1944). See also F. *von Hügel, *Select Letters, 1896–1924*, ed. by B. Holland (1927); M. J. Lagrange, O.P., *M. Loisy et le modernisme* (1932); A. R. Vidler, *The Modernist Movement in the Roman Catholic Church* (1934), pp. 67–139.

LOLLARDY. A 'Lollard' was originally a follower of J. *Wycliffe; later, the name was applied somewhat vaguely to anyone seriously critical of the Church—knights who hankered after Church property, dissatisfied tenants of an oppressive abbey, parishioners who refused to pay tithes, and apocalyptic visionaries. The original meaning of the term would appear to be a 'chanter' and so a 'mumbler of prayers' (cf. Old Dutch, *lollen* or *lullen*, 'to sing'); but possibly it comes from the Latin *lollium* ('tares'). Its first official use occurs in 1382 when Abp. W. *Courtenay condemned the teachings of Wycliffe.

The Lollards, following Wycliffe, based their teaching on personal faith, Divine election, and, above all, the Bible. The Scriptures were the sole authority in religion and every man had the right to read and interpret them for himself. The Lollards commonly attacked clerical *celibacy, *transubstantiation, *indulgences, and *pilgrimages; and they held that the validity of priestly acts was determined by the priest's moral character and that endowments, the Pope, and the hierarchy were all unscriptural. They propagated their teaching by men known as 'Poor Preachers'.

The movement may be divided into two phases. In the first, which extended till the end of the 14th cent., it was mainly academic. Rigorous persecution, esp. the passing of *De Haeretico Comburendo* (1401), and the burning of Sawtre, caused most of the early leaders to recant. After 1400 the movement became more popular; its social teaching became more pronounced, and its adherents, drawn increasingly from the poorer classes, sought to achieve their ends by active revolt.

The Lollards, despite persistent persecution, remained fairly active until the middle of the 15th cent. and then gradually dwindled. The movement was also powerful in Scotland and exercised an important influence on the development of the *Hussite rising in Bohemia.

J. *Gairdner, *Lollardy and the Reformation in England* (4 vols., 1908–13); R. L. Poole, *Wycliffe and Movements for Reform* (1889); H. B. Workman, *John Wyclif: A Study of the English Medieval Church* (2 vols., 1926); B. L. Manning, *The People's Faith in the Time of Wyclif* (1918); K. B. McFarlane, *John Wycliffe and the Beginnings of English Nonconformity* (1952).

LOMBARD, PETER. See *Peter Lombard*.

LONDON. See *Bow Church, Brompton Oratory, St. Paul's Cathedral, Westminster Abbey* and *Westminster Cathedral*.

LONDON MISSIONARY SOCIETY. See *L.M.S.*

LONGINUS, St. (prob. from Gk. λόγχη, 'lance'). The name traditionally given to the soldier who pierced the side of Christ with his spear. It can be traced back to the apocryphal 'Acts of *Pilate', one version of which also gives it to the centurion who, standing by the Cross, confessed Christ as the Son of God. In the later forms of the legend the two persons are often confused. *Bede, who is followed by many medieval authors, among them the author of the *Golden Legend, reports that he was martyred for his faith at Caesarea in Cappadocia in A.D. 58 and gives as his feast, which occurs in several old martyrologies, 15 Mar.

'Acta' of Longinus the soldier and of Longinus the centurion pr., with discussion as to whether both were the same person, in *AA.SS.*, Mar. II (1668), pp. 376–90. 'Martyrium Sancti Longini Centurionis' of *Hesychius of Jerusalem pr. in J. P. Migne, *PG*, xciii, 1546–60; Gk. text of 'Martyrium . . . Sancti Longini Centurionis' in *Simeon Metaphrastes, ib., cxv, 32–41. The cultus of the centurion (unnamed) in Cappadocia is attested by *Gregory of Nyssa, *Ep.*, xvii (*PG*, xlvi, 1061). K. Burdach, 'Der Longinus-Speer in eschatologischen Lichte' in *Sb.* (Berl.), 1920, pp. 294–321. F. J. Dölger, *Antike und Christentum*, iv (1934), pp. 81–94 ('Die Blutsalbung des Soldaten mit der Lanze im Passionsspiel *Christus Patiens*'). Rose J. Peebles, *The Legend of Longinus in Ecclesiastical Tradition and in English Literature and its Connection with the Grail* (Diss., Bryn Mawr College Monographs, Monograph Series, ix; Baltimore, 1911).

LONGLAND, JOHN (1473–1547), Bp. of *Lincoln. After a long period of study at Oxford, where he became Fellow of Magdalen, Longland was made Dean of *Salisbury in 1514, and Bp. of Lincoln in 1521. He was a staunch upholder of the royal supremacy, and as *Henry VIII's confessor took a prominent part in furthering the divorce proceedings with Catherine of Aragon. A preacher and a humanist of considerable repute, he enjoyed the warm friendship of D. *Erasmus.

'Injunctions of John Longland, Bishop of Lincoln, to certain Monasteries in his Diocese', from his Register, ed. E. Peacock in *Archaeologia*, xlvii (pt. i; 1882), pp. 49–64; further extracts in A. Clark (ed.), *Lincoln Diocese Documents, 1450–1544* (E.E.T.S., Original Series, cxliv; 1914), pp. 133–244 and 245–54, incl. text of Longland's directions for publication in his diocese of Henry VIII's repudiation of the Pope's Supremacy, pp. 188–91. H. Maynard Smith, *Henry VIII and the Reformation* (1948), passim, and other works cited s.v. *Henry VIII*. J. H. Lupton in *D.N.B.*, xxxiv (1893), p. 120 f.

LONGLEY, CHARLES THOMAS (1794–1868), Abp. of *Canterbury. He was educated at Christ Church, Oxford, where he taught for several years. In 1829 he was appointed head master of Harrow. Later he became Bp. of *Ripon (1836) and of *Durham (1856), and Abp. of *York (1860) and of Canterbury (1862). At Ripon he aroused much feeling through his suppression of the 'Romanizing' at E. B. *Pusey's newly built church of St. Saviour's, Leeds. At Canterbury he proceeded as far as he could against J. W. *Colenso without provoking a conflict with the law. The most memorable event of his rather undistinguished

archiepiscopate was the first *Lambeth Conference.

G. C. Boase in *D.N.B.*, xxxiv (1893), p. 121 f.

LOOFS, FRIEDRICH (1858–1928), historian of doctrine. He studied at Leipzig, where under A.*Harnack he became a keen student of the history of dogma, and at Göttingen, where A. *Ritschl stimulated his more systematic interests. From 1882 to 1887 he taught at Leipzig. In 1887 he became extraordinary, and 1888 full, professor at Halle, where he remained till his death. He took a prominent part in Lutheran ecclesiastical affairs, becoming a member of the Saxon Consistory in 1910. Among many important essays in patristic subjects are a monograph on *Leontius of Byzantium (1887), his significant *Leitfaden zur Dogmengeschichte* (1890), works on the 'Sacra Parallela' of St. *John of Damascus (1892) and *Eustathius of Sebaste (1898), a collection of the then known *Nestoriana* (1905), and a comprehensive study of *Paul of Samosata (1924). He also took an active part in opposing E. *Haeckel's materialism in his *Anti-Haeckel* (1900; Eng. trans., 1903). An original interpretation of *Nestorian teaching was presented in *Nestorius and his Place in the History of Christian Doctrine* (1914), the substance of four lectures delivered at London in 1913.

Autobiographical notice in *Die Religionswissenschaft der Gegenwart in Selbstdarstellungen* (ed. E. Stange), ii (1926), pp. 119–60, with bibl.

LOPEZ, GREGORY (1611–91), first native Chinese bishop. His native name was A-lu. Born of pagan parents in the city of Fogan in N.E. Fukien, he embraced Christianity when he grew up and was baptized by the *Franciscans. He studied for a time at Manila, where in 1651 he joined the *Dominican Order. In 1656 he was ordained the first Chinese priest. His success and zeal led the French bishops in Tonkin and Siam to induce Clement X to offer him the titular bishopric of Basilea in N. Africa and the office of vicar-apostolic of Nanking. Lopez, however, modestly declined the promotion. In 1679 *Innocent XI repeated the offer of a bishopric; but now the Dominicans at Manila demanded a European associate to advise Lopez, who again declined, this time on the ground that such an associate would limit his freedom. He was eventually consecrated in 1685 at Canton at the hands of Italian Franciscans. Later he was promoted to the new see of Nanking, but did not live to employ the title. There was no further native RC bishop in China until 1918.

Quétif-Échard, ii, 708 f.; Eng. tr. by A. C. Moule in *The New China Review*, i (Hongkong, 1919), pp. 480–7; suppl. note by id., ib., iii (1921), p. 138 f. J. de Moidrey, S.J., *La Hiérarchie catholique en Chine, en Corée, et au Japon, 1307–1914* (Variétés sinologiques, No. 38; 1914), pp 22–4. B. M. Biermann, O.P., *Die Anfänge der neueren Dominikanermission in China*, pt. 1 (1927), esp. pp. 90–2 and 129–33. See also works cited s.v. *China*.

LORD OF HOSTS. This Divine title occurs in the OT no less than 282 times, all except 36 of them in the Prophetical writings. In its earliest usage among the Hebrews, it was probably based on the belief that it was their God *Jehovah who led and defended their armies against their enemies (cf., e.g., Ex. 7. 4, where the forces of Israel are described as 'the hosts of the Lord'), but in later times its reference was to God's dominion in majesty and power over the angels and other celestial beings and, a fortiori, His supremacy over the destinies of men. In the NT, apart from a quotation from Is. 1. 9 in Rom. 9. 29, the expression occurs only in Jas. 5. 4, and is rendered in both places 'Lord of *Sabaoth'.

S. R. *Driver in *H.D.B.*, iii (1900), p. 137 f.; E. Kautzsch in *P.R.E.* (ed. 3), xxi (1908), pp. 620–27, s.v. 'Zebaoth', with full bibl.; H. *Gunkel in *R.G.G.* (ed. 2), v (1931), col. 2085 f.

LORD OF MISRULE. See *Misrule, Lord of.*

LORD'S DAY, The. A Christian appellation of *Sunday, based on Rev. 1. 10 (ἡ κυριακὴ ἡμέρα). In recent times it has been used (esp. by Protestants) when special stress is laid on the sacred character of the day. In the 17th–18th cents., however, the title 'Lord's Day' (without the article) was fairly widely used as an ordinary name for the day, and not only among *Puritans. The Lord's Day Observance Society, founded in 1831 by Daniel Wilson, Bp. of Calcutta, has as its two principal objects the diffusion of information about the blessings of Sunday and the promotion of its observance as a weekly day of rest and worship.

LORD'S PRAYER, The (Lat. *Oratio Dominica* or *Pater Noster*). The prayer, 'Our Father', taught by our Lord to the Apostles. In the NT it is given in two slightly different forms, viz. in Mt. 6. 9–13, in the teaching on prayer in the *Sermon on the Mount, and in Lk. 11. 2–4, where Christ gives it to His disciples in answer to their request 'Lord, teach us to pray'. The form in Mt. is that universally used by Christians; that in Lk. is shorter. A concluding doxology was probably added in early times, for it occurs in the *Didache, and, in a longer form, corresponding to that in the BCP, in the Liturgy of St. *Chrysostom; it was taken over into some Gospel MSS.

The Lord's Prayer is usually divided into the address and seven petitions, the first three asking for the glorification of God, the latter four being requests for the chief physical and spiritual needs of man. As a prayer given to the Church by our Lord Himself, it has always been regarded by Christians as uniquely sacred.

From early times the Lord's Prayer was taught to the *catechumens at *Baptism and used in the Liturgy. St. *Cyprian already calls it 'the public and common prayer'. It has also regularly found a place in the celebration of the Eucharist. The first witness to it in this connexion is St. *Cyril of Jerusalem (c. 350). Acc. to St. *Augustine and to the *Ambrosian and *Mozarabic Liturgies, it was said after the Breaking of the Bread,

immediately before the *Kiss of Peace and the Communion. St. *Gregory the Great (d. 604), however, following the Greek Liturgies, placed it at the end of the Canon, before the Breaking of the Bread. He also appears to have held the opinion that the Apostles used the Lord's Prayer to consecrate the Eucharist. In the BCP, since 1552, it has followed the Communion. In the Divine *Office the Prayer has also occupied a prominent place. It is mentioned as part of *Lauds and *Vespers by the Synod of Gerona of 517, and St. *Benedict prescribed it in his rule for all the Canonical Hours. St. *Pius V, in 1568, regulated its present use in the *Breviary.

The Lord's Prayer has played a prominent part in Christian devotion. *Tertullian called it the 'epitome of the whole Gospel' (*breviarium totius evangelii*) and St. Augustine the source of all other prayers. It has been frequently expounded, either in commentaries on the Gospels or in separate treatises, notably by St. *Thomas Aquinas and St. *Teresa of Avila.

The version of the Lord's Prayer in common use in England among Catholics and Protestants alike owes its general acceptance to an ordinance of *Henry VIII in 1541. It follows closely the form of the Prayer in W. *Tyndale's version of the NT. The concluding Doxology, however, which was not traditional in the liturgical tradition of Western Christendom, is first found in the Scottish BCP of 1637, whence it was taken over in many places in the revision of 1662.

Patristic commentaries include *Tertullian, *De Oratione*, i–x, *Origen, *De Oratione*, esp. xxii–xxx, Cyprian, *De Dominica Oratione*, and Augustine, *De Sermone Domini in Monte*, ii, 15–39. F. H. Chase, *The Lord's Prayer in the Early Church* (Texts and Studies, I, 3, Cambridge, 1891). G. Walter, *Untersuchungen zur Geschichte der griechischen Vaterunser-Exegese* (1914). G. Friedlander, *The Jewish Sources of the Sermon on the Mount* (1911), pp. 152–65. P. Fiebig, *Das Vaterunser*. Ursprung, Sinn, und Bedeutung des christlichen Hauptgebetes (Gütersloh, 1927). A. Harnack, 'Über einige Worte Jesu, die nicht in den kanonischen Evangelien stehen. Anhang: Die ursprüngliche Gestalt der Vaterunsers' in *Sb.* (Berl.), 1904, pp. 195–208. J. Haussleiter in *P.R.E.* (ed. 3), xx (1908), pp. 43f–45, s.v. 'Vaterunser'; E. *Nestle–J. C. Lambert in *D.C.G.*, ii (1908), pp. 57–63, s.v., with full bibl. p. 60; H. Thurston, S.J., in *C.E.*, ix (1910), p. 356 f., s.v.; H. *Leclercq, O.S.B., in *D.A.C.L.*, xii (pt. 2; 1936), cols. 2244–55, s.v. 'Oraison dominicale'; G. Stano in *E.C.*, ix (1952), cols. 943–6, s.v. 'Pater Noster'.

LORD'S SUPPER, The. A title for the Holy Communion, in use esp. among Protestants. It is taken from 1 Cor. 11. 20 (τὸ κυριακὸν δεῖπνον), where the rendering 'Lord's Supper' is found in the English version of J. *Wycliffe (1382). Its occurrence in the title of N. *Ridley's *Brief Declaration of the Lord's Supper*, written in 1554 while its author was in prison, helped to popularize the name. See also *Eucharist*.

LORETO, near Ancona in Italy, is the site of the Holy House, alleged to have been inhabited by the BVM at the time of the *Annunciation and to have been miraculously transported by angels from *Nazareth to Tersatz in Dalmatia in 1291 and thence by the same agency to

Loreto in 1295. The earliest attestation of the legend is an account of the sanctuary written c. 1470. The whole story is now commonly regarded as unhistorical, not least by RC writers of unquestioned orthodoxy. See also *Litany of Loreto*.

The traditional account in H. Tursellinus, *Lauretanae Historiae Libri V* (1597), and P. V. Martorelli, *Teatro istorico della S. Casa Nazarena* (3 vols., fol., 1732–5). Somewhat more critical, J. A. Vogel, *De Ecclesiis Recanatensi et Lauretana* (1859; but written in 1806), and Mgr Leopardi, *La santa casa di Loreto* (Lugano, 1841). The attack on the tradition, led by H. Grisar, S.J., at the Munich Congress in 1900, was brought to a conclusion by C. U. J. Chevalier, *Notre-Dame de Lorette*. Étude historique sur l'authenticité de la santa casa (1906). See also A. Boudinhon, *La Question de Loretto* (1910).

LORIC OF ST. PATRICK. See *Breastplate of St. Patrick*.

LOS VON ROM (Germ., free from Rome'). A vigorous anti-Roman Movement begun in Austria in 1897 and fostered by the Pan-German party, who aimed at the incorporation of an Austria, freed from the Pope, into Germany under the protection of the Protestant Hohenzollern Emperors. The Movement, which owed its name to the shout of a student at the Deutscher Volkstag at Vienna (1897), came to have its centre at Innsbruck. Its chief organization was the 'Ulrich-Hutten-Bund', and among its principal leaders were G. von Schönerer, V. Eisenkolb, and Superintendent F. Meyer. Its influence was increased by the unsatisfactory situation of the Church in Austria, e.g. the unwieldy size of the dioceses, the lack of German priests, and esp. the anti-clerical spirit of the secondary schools. Though most of those who left the RC Church (up to 1914 c. 75,000) became nominal Protestants, the Movement was essentially anti-Christian, as the Pan-Germans favoured a neo-pagan 'German' religion, an aim later realized on a much greater scale by the National Socialists. From Austria parallel Los von Rom movements spread to other countries, e.g. *Poland (see Mariaviten), *France, *Belgium, *Ceylon, and *Mexico, but with comparatively little success.

P. Bräunlich, *Berichte über den Fortgang der 'Los von Rom-Bewegung'* (I. Reihe, Htt. 1–10, II Reihe, Hftt. 1–10; 1899–1910). H. Mulert in *R.G.G.* (ed. 2), iii (1929), cols. 1726–8 s.v.; K. Algermissen in *L.Th.K.*, vi (1934), cols. 652–4, s.v.

LOTZE, HERMANN (1817–81), logician and metaphysician. A native of Bautzen, he studied medicine and philosophy at Leipzig. After teaching for a short time at Leipzig (1839–42), he became Prof. of Philosophy at Göttingen (1842; full Prof. 1844), where he remained until called to Berlin (1881) shortly before his death. He combined a firm belief in the reign of scientific law with conviction of the need for metaphysics, and opposed alike the theory of a specific *Lebenskraft* in nature ('vitalism') and the *a priori* constructions of the German *Idealists (F. W. J. von *Schelling, G. W. F. *Hegel). He was insistent that philosophy must be rooted in the natural sciences, in which

he retained his interest until his death. He had a firm faith in *theism; and, believing in the validity of moral judgements, he became an early exponent of 'value philosophy'. His doctrines, first formulated in his *Metaphysik* (1841) and *Logik* (1843), were elaborated in a semi-popular form in his *Microcosmus* (3 vols., 1856–64; Eng. tr., 2 vols., 1885). He devoted his later years to the elaboration of a *System der Philosophie*, of which only two volumes were publd., the *Logik* (1874; Eng. tr. by B. *Bosanquet, 1884) and *Metaphysik* (1879; Eng. tr. by id., 1884). His other writings include *Über den Begriff der Schönheit* (1845), *Über Bedingungen der Kunstschönheit* (1847), *Allgemeine Physiologie des körperlichen Lebens* (1851), *Medicinische Psychologie* (1852), and *Geschichte der Aesthetik in Deutschland* (1868).

Lotze's main Works have been reissued, with introds., in the *Philosophische Bibliothek*. *Kleine Schriften*, ed. by D. Peipers, 3 vols., 1885–91. T. M. *Lindsay, 'Hermann Lotze' in *Mind*, i (1876), pp. 363–82. E. Pfleiderer, *Lotze's philosophische Weltanschauung nach ihren Grundzügen* (1882); E. von *Hartmann, *Lotzes Philosophie* (1888); H. Jones, *A Critical Account of the Philosophy of Lotze* (1895); R. Falckenberg, *Hermann Lotze* (1901); M. Wentscher, *Hermann Lotze* (vol. i, 1913), and other works; P. Gese, *Lotze's Religionsphilosophie* (1916); E. E. Thomas, *Lotze's Theory of Reality* (1921). Überweg, iv, pp. 299–308 and 703–5, with full bibl.

LOU, TSENG-TSIANG (1871–1949), Chinese statesman and Benedictine monk and abbot. His baptismal name was Jean-Jacques and at confirmation he took the further name of René. The son of a Protestant catechist, he was born at Shanghai and educated at Shanghai and Peking. He was successively secretary to the Chinese Legation at St. Petersburg (1893–1906), Minister at the Hague (1907–11) and at St. Petersburg (1911–12), and Foreign Minister (1912–20; with brief interruptions). In 1912 and 1915 he was also Prime Minister and from 1922 to 1927 Chinese Minister at Berne. In Oct. 1911 he was received into the RC Church. After the death of his wife (a Belgian whom he had married in 1899) in 1926, he entered the *Benedictine Abbey of St.-André, near Bruges (1927), where he was later professed as Dom Pierre Célestin Lou. In 1946 he was appointed Titular Abbot of St.-Pierre-de-Gand by *Pius XII. His intention of returning to the East to establish a Benedictine Congregation in China was prevented by ill-health. As a Christian statesman, he had been a reformer not a revolutionary. In the sphere of religion he saw in Christianity the fulfilment of Confucianism, finding St. *John's doctrine of the *Logos paralleled by Lao-Tse's teaching of the Tao. He believed Classical Chinese to be the appropriate liturgical language for the worship of his countrymen. His writings include *Souvenirs et pensées* (1945), and *La Rencontre des humanités* (1949; posthumous).

Wu Ching-Hioung, *Dom Lou. Sa vie spirituelle* [1949].

LOUIS OF GRANADA. See *Luis of Granada*.

LOUIS I (778–840) (**the Pious** or **le Dé-bonnaire**). The third son of *Charlemagne (d. 814), by whom he was appointed king of Aquitaine in 781 and joint emperor in 813. His reign was marked by growing political disturbance, caused chiefly by his struggles with his sons. In 817 he associated Lothair with him in the Empire and gave subordinate kingships to his younger sons, Pepin and Louis. This arrangement was upset by the King's second marriage to Judith and the subsequent birth of another son, Charles, upon whom Louis showered all his favour. He was deposed by the assembly of Compiègne in 833 and compelled by the bishops to appear in a penitent's garb. He was restored, however, at Metz in 835 and survived till 840. In spite of his weak and indecisive character, Louis had undoubted religious interests and was a patron of learning, and in his reign much of the real work of the Carolingian scholars came to fruition. He furthered ecclesiastical reorganization in many parts of Germany and the monastic reforms of *Benedict of Aniane, as well as St. *Anskar's missionary work in Scandinavia.

J. F. Böhmer, *Die Regesten des Kaiserreichs unter den Karolingern* (ed. 2 by E. Mühlbacher, 1908), pp. 234–412. Life by Theganus, written n 835, ed. G. H. Pertz in *M.G.H.*, Scriptores, ii (1829), pp. 589–603; further early life by an anonymous writer known as the 'Astronomer', ib., pp. 604–48. B. Simson, *Jahrbücher des fränkischen Reiches unter Ludwig dem Frommen* (Jahrbücher der deutschen Geschichte, 2 vols. in one, 1874–6). R. Poupardin in *C. Med. H.*, iii (1922), pp. 1–22, with bibl. pp. 583–6; F. Lot–C. Pfister–F. L. Ganshof, *Les Destinées de l'empire en occident de 395 à 888* (1928), pp. 473–97. Fliche–Martin, vi (1937), pp. 201–28 and 247–66, with further bibl.

LOUIS IX, St. (1214–70), King of France. Born at Poissy, he was the son of Louis VIII (d. 1226) and Blanche of Castile (d. 1252), who acted as regent during his minority. In 1226 he was crowned at *Reims, in 1234 he married Margaret of Provence, and in 1236 he began his personal rule. In 1242 he secured the submission of Raymond of Toulouse and defeated Henry III of England at Taillebourg thus securing acknowledged suzerainty over Guienne. Having resolved during an illness in 1244 to take the cross, he sailed to Egypt in 1248 and captured Damietta in 1249; but owing to floods and lack of co-operation the crusaders were routed in 1250 and Louis IX taken prisoner. Securing his own release by the surrender of Damietta and that of his men by the payment of their ransoms, he proceeded to Syria in 1250 to fortify the strongholds still in Christian hands. He returned to France in 1254, imposed peace on Flanders in 1256 and signed the Treaties of Corbeil with Aragon in 1258 and of Paris with Henry III in 1259, the terms of both illustrating his desire for equity and a lasting settlement. In 1263 he arbitrated between Henry III and his barons. Having planned a further crusade to the Holy Land in 1267, he embarked on 1 July 1270 and landed at Tunis where he died of dysentery on 25 Aug.

In his austere and prayerful private life, his energy, his determination that every man

should have his due, and the paramount consideration which he gave to the defence of the Holy Land, Louis embodied the highest ideals of medieval kingship. He reformed the administration of France, frequently meting out justice himself. He built the *Sainte-Chapelle in Paris (1245–8) for the *Crown of Thorns which he had acquired from the Emp. Baldwin II in 1239, endowed various religious houses and supported the theological college founded by Robert de *Sorbonne in 1257. He was canonized by *Boniface VIII in 1297. Feast day, 25 Aug.

The instructions which St. Louis compiled for his son, known as *Les Établissements de saint Louis*, were ed. P. Viollet (Société de l'Histoire de France, 4 vols., 1881–6). The principal authority is the life by J. *Joinville (q.v. for edd. and translations). Life by William of Saint-Pathus, written some time between 1302 and 1307, ed. H. F. Delaborde (Collection de textes pour servir à l'étude et à l'enseignement de l'histoire; 1899); also publd. in Les Classiques français du moyen-âge, lxx; 1931. Lives by Geoffrey of Beaulieu, O.P., and William of Chartres, O.P., his confessors and chaplains, pr., with other material, in *AA.SS.*, Aug. V (1741), pp. 275–672. *B.H.L.*, pp. 747–50 (Nos. 5034–52), and Suppl., p. 201 f. L. S. le N. *Tillemont, *Vie de saint Louis*, first ed. in full, J. de Gaulle (6 vols.), Société de l'Histoire de France; 1847–51). Modern lives by H. Wallon (2 vols., Paris, 1875), M. Sepet ('Les Saints', 1898; Eng. tr., 1899), F. Perry ('Heroes of the Nations', 1902), G. Goyau (Paris, 1928), J. Boulenger (ib., 1929), and 'Franc-Nohain' (pseudonym, Paris, 1932). C. Petit-Dutaillis in *C. Med. H.*, vi (1929), pp. 331–61 (ch. 10, 'Saint Louis'), with bibl. pp. 904–8.

LOURDES. Famous French place of pilgrimage in the Department of Hautes-Pyrénées. In 1858 the 14-year-old peasant girl, *Bernadette Soubirous, had visions of the BVM in the grotto of a rock at Lourdes in which the Virgin told her that she was the Immaculate Conception. At the same time a spring appeared; miraculous healings were soon reported to have taken place; and the faithful began to flock to Lourdes. In 1862 the pilgrimage received official ecclesiastical recognition, a church was built above the grotto, and beside it from 1883 to 1901 the magnificent church of the Rosary. Since then millions of pilgrims have visited the shrine, a medical bureau has been established to investigate the character of the cures, and an enormous literature, much of it controversial, has sprung up around it. In 1891 a local feast of the apparition of Our Lady of Lourdes (11 Feb.) was sanctioned, and extended to the universal Church by *Pius X in 1907.

L. Cros, *Histoire de Notre-Dame de Lourdes d'après les documents et les témoins* (3 vols., 1925–6); further collection of testimonies in 'Hommage à la bienheureuse Bernadette Soubirous' in *Revue d'Ascétique et de Mystique*, xii (1929), pp. 6–174. There is also a very large number of popular studies such as J. Jørgensen, *Lourdes* (Copenhagen, 1910; Eng. tr., 1914). G. Bertrin in *C.E.*, ix (1910), pp. 389–91, s.v.; M. Gaspari in *E.C.*, vii (1951), cols. 1580–3, s.v., with further bibl. See also bibl. to *Bernadette, St.*

LOVE. In the NT the principle of God's action and of man's response. Of the words in Greek for 'love', neither φιλία ('dutiful' or 'filial affection') nor ἔρως ('passionate emotion') is adequate to the Christian conception, which the NT expresses by ἀγάπη, a word hardly used before, except occasionally in the LXX.

As a supernatural Christian virtue, ἀγάπη is often (esp. in the AV) translated as "*charity', for which the RV substitutes 'love'. But the Christian use of the word 'love' is more general, and it is misleading to confine it to denote a single human virtue, even though supernatural. In its wider sense, it is not only the motive principle of the perfect relation between God and man, but also constitutes the essential nature of God Himself (see e.g. 1 Jn. passim).

W. Lütgert, *Die Liebe im Neuen Testament* (1905). M. Scheler, *Zur Phänomenologie und Theorie der Sympathiegefühle und von Liebe und Hass* (1913; ed. 2 as *Wesen und Formen der Sympathie*, 1923). B. B. Warfield, 'The Terminology of Love in the New Testament' in *Princeton Theological Review*, xvi (1918), pp. 1–45 and 153–203. J. *Moffatt, Love in the New Testament* (1929). H. Scholz, *Eros und Caritas*. Die platonische Liebe und die Liebe im Sinne des Christentums (1929). J. Ziegler, *Die Liebe Gottes bei den Propheten* (Würzburg thesis; Alttestament-Abhandlungen, xi, Hft. 3; 1930). H. Preisker, *Die urchristliche Botschaft von der Liebe Gottes im Licht der vergleichenden Religionsgeschichte* (1930). A. Nygren, *Den Kristna Kärlekstanken genom tiderna*. Eros och Agape (2 vols., 1930–6; Eng. tr. (*Agape and Eros*), in 3 vols., 1932–9, pt. i by A. G. Hebert, S.S.M., and pt. ii, 2 vols., by P. S. Watson; new tr. by P. S. Watson, 1953). C. E. Raven, *Jesus and the Gospel of Love* (Albert Robertson Lectures for 1931; 1931). H. Riesenfeld, 'Étude bibliographique sur la notion biblique d''ΑΓΑΠΗ' in *Coniectanea Neotestamentica*, v (Uppsala, 1941), pp. 1–32. M. C. *D'Arcy, S.J., *The Mind and Heart of Love* (1945). V. Warnack, *Agape*. Die Liebe als Grundmotiv der neutestamentlichen Theologie (1951). G. Quell–E. Stauffer in *T.W.B.*, i (1933), cols. 20–55, s.v. 'ἀγαπάω'; Eng. tr. of this art., with bibl., by J. R. Coates (London, 1949).

LOVE, CHRISTOPHER (1618–51) *Puritan minister. A native of Cardiff, he was converted at the age of 14 by W. Erbury (1604-54), who enabled him to study at New Inn Hall, Oxford (1635–9). In 1639 he went to London, where he refused to be ordained by a bishop. After an unsuccessful attempt to secure *Presbyterian ordination in Scotland, he returned to England (c. 1641) and was imprisoned at Newcastle for his outspoken criticisms of the BCP. Soon after the outbreak of the Civil War he became chaplain to Colonel J. Venn's regiment and was ordained. Through his zeal for Presbyterianism he incurred the hostility of the *Independents, and in 1651 was accused of conspiracy with *Charles Stuart (II) and *Henrietta Maria for the overthrow of the Commonwealth. He was executed on Tower Hill after having disclosed the plot. Among his writings are *The Debauched Cavalier* (1642), *England's Distemper* (1645), and several posthumous collections of Sermons.

Sixteen of his Sermons on 2 Pet. 1. 10 were publd. under the title *A Treatise of Effectual Calling and Election* (London, 1653), and another twenty-seven sermons preached shortly before his death as *The Combat between the Flesh and Spirit* (ib., 1654). *Select Works* (2 vols., Glasgow, 1805–6); *Remains of Christopher Love*, ed. W. Ward–E. Davies (London, 1807), with sketch of his life, pp. iii–xii. His *Several Petitions to Parliament and his last Speech and Prayer*, with other material, publd. as *Mr. Love's Case* (London, 1651). *The Life, Trial and Martyrdom of the Rev. Christopher Love* (The Gospel Atlas, No. 1 [1855]), with various of his letters. B. Brook, *The Lives of the Puritans*, iii (1813), pp. 115–38. W. A. Shaw in *D.N.B.*, xxxiv (1893), p. 155 f.

LOW CHURCHMEN. The group in the C of E which gives a relatively unimportant or 'low' place to the claims of the episcopate, priesthood, and sacraments, and generally approximates in its beliefs to those of Protestant Nonconformists. The term 'Low Churchman', which dates from the early 18th cent., was coined in contrast to "*High Churchman', but orig. used of the *Latitudinarian (liberal) group. It went out of use again; and when revived in the mid-19th cent. it was applied to the *Evangelicals, whereas the liberal group then came to be dubbed "*Broad Churchmen'. See also *Evangelicalism.*

LOW MASS. In the W. Church, the simplified form of Mass in most frequent use. It grew up in the Middle Ages, when the practice of each priest saying a Mass daily became common and the elaborate ceremonial and considerable number of assistants traditionally required for the Liturgy were no longer practicable. In a Low Mass there are no ministers to assist the priest except a single server; there is no choir; and no part of the service is sung by the celebrant. The celebrating priest, therefore, in the absence of both *subdeacon and *deacon, reads the Epistle and Gospel himself. Except in cathedral and capitular churches, Low Mass is the usual form of Mass celebrated except on Sundays and the greater feast days; and even on these all except one of the Masses in a given church will usually be Low Masses. Low Mass is unknown in the E., though some *Uniat bodies have adopted a somewhat similar form of celebration. See also *High Mass.*

Jungmann (1949), i, 269–94; Eng. tr. (1951), pp. 212–233.

LOW SUNDAY. The first Sunday after *Easter, probably so called in contrast to the 'high' feast of Easter Sunday itself. In Latin it is termed *Dominica in albis.*

LOWDER, CHARLES FUGE (1820–80), vicar of St. Peter's, London Docks. Educated at Exeter College, Oxford, he was ordained priest in 1844, and in 1851 became curate at the *Anglo-Catholic parish of St. Barnabas, Pimlico. In 1856 he joined the staff of St. George's in the East, where he took a leading part in the first regular mission work in East London, with A. H. *Mackonochie as his colleague from 1858. The advanced ceremonial led to fierce riots. His mission work expanded, however, and he built the church of St. Peter's, London Docks (1860–6). Known always as 'Father Lowder', he was the means of bringing many thousands of East Londoners to the Christian faith.

Anonymous life by Maria Trench (London, 1881). W. A. J. Archbold in *D.N.B.*, xxxiv (1893), p. 187; S. L. Ollard in *D.E.C.H.*, p. 342 f.

LOWTH, ROBERT (1710–87), Bp. of London. He was educated at Winchester and at New College, Oxford. From 1741 to 1750 he was professor of poetry at Oxford, and later Bp. successively of *St. David's (1766), of

Oxford (also 1766), and of London (1777). His chief contributions to Biblical learning arose from his study of the forms of Hebrew poetry. In his *De sacra poesi Hebraeorum Praelectiones Academicae* (1753; J. D. *Michaelis added notes in 1775 ; Eng. trans. of this expanded revision, 1793) he recognized the existence of 'parallelism' as a regular device of the Hebrew poet. In a controversy with W. *Warburton, Lowth defended the extreme antiquity of the Book of *Job. His commentary on *Isaiah (1778) pointed the way to later criticism of that Book.

Sermons and Other Remains of Robert Lowth, ed. P. Hall (London, 1834), with introductory Memoir, pp. 1-42. Short *Memoirs of the Life and Writings of . . . Robert Lowth* (London, 1787). W. Hunt in *D.N.B.*, xxxiv (1893), pp. 214-16.

LOYOLA, St. IGNATIUS. See *Ignatius Loyola, St.*

LUBBERTUS, SIBRANDUS (1556/7–1625), Dutch *Calvinist theologian. Educated at *Wittenberg, *Marburg, Geneva (where he sat under T. *Beza), and Basle, in 1585 he became professor of dogmatics at Franeker university, combining his duties in the faculty with pastoral work. Before long he was one of the foremost upholders of orthodox Calvinism in Holland against the rising *Arminianism. In 1607 he took a prominent part in the Hague Conference which was planning the suppression of Arminian doctrines, and also corresponded extensively with theologians (among them A. *Melville and G. *Abbot) to warn them against Arminius' teaching. His works were for the most part controversial. He attacked the Arminianism of P. Bertius in his *Epistolica Disceptatio de Fide Justificante, nostraque coram Deo Justificatione* (1612), C. *Vorstius in two writings (1611, 1613), and the *Pietas Ordinum Hollandiae et Westfrisiae* of H. *Grotius (1613) in his *Responsio ad Pietatem Grotii* (1614). He also wrote several treatises against the RC Church and *Socinianism.

His other writings include *De Principiis Christianorum Dogmatum* (1591; ed. 2, 1595), *De Papa Romano* (1594), *De Ecclesia* (1609), and *De Jesu Christo Servatore contra Faustum Socinum* (1611). At the Synod of *Dort (1618), at which he was a prominent defender of the Calvinist position, he was appointed to the Commission preparing the new version of the OT. S. D. van Veen in *P.R.E.* (ed. 3), xi (1902), p. 653 f, s.v. with bibl.

LÜBER, THOMAS. See *Erastianism.*

LUCAR, CYRIL (1572–1638), Greek theologian. He was a Cretan by birth. After studying at *Venice and Padua, where he came into contact with Latin thought, he became *syncellus to Meletios Pegas, Patr. of *Alexandria, whom he succeeded in 1602. Hitherto he had viewed the Roman Catholic Church with respect and warmth, but he now became more and more friendly disposed towards the Reformed Churches. His sympathies towards

the C of E were expressed in his despatch of *Metrophanes Critopoulos to study at Oxford in 1616. In 1620 he was appointed Patr. of *Constantinople, an appointment as welcome to the Protestants, esp. the Dutch, as disagreeable to the *Jesuits. Henceforth his Protestant views became more and more pronounced and in 1623 he underwent a sentence of banishment, though later he was given permission to return. *c.* 1625 he sent to G. *Abbot, Abp. of Canterbury, the famous '*Codex Alexandrinus'. With the support and encouragement of the *Calvinist theologian, Antoine Léger, a translation of the Bible into the vernacular for the use of his flock was begun, schools were re-established, and possibly—though this is disputed—a catechism was prepared. In 1629 Cyril published his *Confessio*, a thoroughly Calvinistic interpretation of the faith of the Greek Orthodox Church, Eight years later he was accused of inciting the Cossacks against the Turkish Government and strangled by the Janissaries at the command of the Sultan Murad. He was the first important theologian of the E. Church since the fall of Constantinople in 1453, and his name dominated the theology of the Greek Church in the 17th cent. His characteristic doctrines were repudiated at the Synod of *Jerusalem (q.v.; 1672).

For his 'Confession', see E. Kimmel, *Libri Symbolici Ecclesiae Orientalis* (1843), pp. 24–44. P. *Schaff, *The Creeds of Christendom,* i (1881), pp. 54–7. Studies by P. Trivier (Paris, 1877) and S. Germanos (London, S.P.C.K., 1951; brief). V. Semnoz, 'Les Dernières Années du patriarche Cyrille Lucar' in *É.O.,* vi (1903), pp. 97–107. P. Meyer in *P.R.E.* (ed. 3), xi (1902), pp. 682–90, with full bibl., and C. Emereau in *D.T.C.,* ix (pt. 1; 1926), cols. 1003–19, s.v., with bibl.

LUCIAN OF ANTIOCH, St. (d. 312), theologian and martyr. A presbyter of *Antioch, he founded an influential theological school of which both *Arius and *Eusebius of Nicomedia were members; indeed his *subordinationist teaching seems to have been the immediate source of the Arian heresy. Only a few fragments of his writings have survived; but the second of the four Creeds put forward by the Council of *Antioch in 341 was perhaps his composition. He was a keen Biblical student, who revised the text of *Septuagint, as well as that of the four Gospels (see *Lucianic Text*). His reputation for sanctity was not less than his fame as a scholar; and after enduring many tortures he was martyred at Nicomedia in 312. The long-prevalent view that he was a pupil of *Paul of Samosata has recently been disputed by F. *Loofs and G. *Bardy. Feast day, 7 Jan.

Fgmts. collected in M. J. *Routh, *Reliquiae Sacrae* (ed. 2, iv, 1846), pp. 3–10 (texts), 11–17 (notes). Eusebius, *H.E.*, VIII, xiii, 2, and IX, vi, 3; Jerome, *De Vir. Illustr.,* 77. 'Vita' in *Philostorgius, *H.E.* (ed. J. Bidez in G.C.S., pp. 184–201). G. Bardy, *Recherches sur Lucien d'Antioche et son école* (1936). H. B. *Swete, *An Introduction to the Old Testament in Greek* (1900), pp. 80–5. G. Mercati, 'Di alcune testimonianze antiche sulle cure bibliche di S. Luciano', in *Biblica,* xxiv (1943), pp. 1–17. Bardenhewer, ii, 279–85; Altaner (ed. 1950), p. 178 f. G. Bardy in *D.T.C.,* ix (pt. 1; 1926), 1024–31; A. Vaccari, S.J., in *E.C.,* vii (1951), col. 1625 f.

LUCIAN OF SAMOSATA (*c.* 115–*c.* 200), pagan satirist. His interest to the student of early Christianity lies chiefly in some references in his 'Alexander of Abonuteichos' and esp. in 'De Morte Peregrini'. The latter treats of the philosopher Peregrinus, a historical person who exchanged paganism for Christianity and was even imprisoned for his faith; but later he apostatized and became a cynic. Being expelled from Rome he made his way to Athens, where he burned himself at a stake during the Olympic Games, in order, as he said, to crown an exemplary life by an exemplary death. In his account of Peregrinus's life, Lucian depicts the Christians as kindly but credulous. He describes the generosity with which they looked after their fellow-believer, Peregrinus, when imprisoned; but believing that the philosopher was an impostor, he scoffs at their simplicity.

The '*Philopatris*' (q.v.), which purports to be a work of Lucian and directly attacks Christianity, is of much later date, prob. 10th cent.

Editio princeps of his collected works, Florence, 1496; modern edd. by C. Jacobitz (4 vols., Leipzig, 1836–41; 3 vols., Teub., 1852–3, and subsequent edd.), J. Sommerbrodt (3 vols. in 5 parts, Berlin, 1886–99; incomplete, but good critical apparatus), and N. Nilén (Teub., 1906 ff.). Modern Eng. tr. (repr. text from Teub. edd. of C. Jacobitz and N. Nilén), by A. M. Harmon (8 vols., Loeb, 1913 ff.). M. Croiset, *Essai sur la vie et les œuvres de Lucien* (1882). M. Caster, *Lucien et la pensée religieuse de son temps* (1937; with bibl.). C. R. Thompson, *The Translations of Lucian by Erasmus and St. Thomas More* (Ithaca, New York, 1940). A. *Harnack in P.R.E.* (ed. 3), xi (1902), pp. 659–66, s.v.; [R. W. O.] Helm in *P.W.*, xiii (pt. 2; 1927), cols. 1725–77, s.v.; H. *Leclercq, O.S.B., in *D.A.C.L.*, ix (pt. 2; 1930), cols. 2619–35, s.v.; W. M. Edwards in *O.C.D.*, p. 515, s.v.; N. Turchi in *E.C.*, vii (1951), col. 1626 f., s.v.

LUCIANIC TEXT. The text of the Gk. Bible, as revised by *Lucian of Antioch (q.v.). As regards the OT, Lucian's revision of the *Septuagint almost at once became the accepted standard in Syria, Asia Minor, and *Constantinople. Acc. to P. de *Lagarde, it is closely followed in the MS. which underlies the *Complutensian Polyglott. In the case of the NT, the researches of F. J. A. *Hort and H. von *Soden indicate that Lucian's text is that now represented by the great body of the surviving Gk. MSS. and is thus embodied in the 'Textus Receptus' (q.v.) and the AV. Its marks are the elimination of barbarisms and obscurities, the conflation of variant readings, intelligibility and smoothness. It is also known to modern scholars as the 'Byzantine' (or, as proposed by B. F. *Westcott–F. J. A. Hort, but their nomenclature has not been generally followed, as the 'Syrian') text.

LUCIFER (Lat., 'light-bearer'), in Is. 14. 12 (Vulgate, followed by AV), an epithet of the King of Babylon. Taken in conjunction with Lk. 10. 18 it was used as a synonym for the devil by St. *Jerome and other Fathers. With the use of the word in classical mythology for the planet Venus may be compared the RV rendering 'daystar' in Is. 14. 12. The imagery is applied to Christ in 2 Pet. 1. 19 (φωσφόρος,

'daystar'), Rev. 22. 16 (ὁ ἀστὴρ ὁ πρωϊνός, 'the morning star') and in the *Exultet.

LUCIFER (d. 370 or 371), Bp. of Cagliari. A fiercely anti-Arian theologian, at the first session of the Council of Milan (354) he resisted the proposal to condemn *Athanasius with such vehemence that the Arians prevailed on *Constantius to confine him for three days in the Imperial Palace. His personal altercations with the Emperor which followed led to his banishment first to Palestine and later to the Thebaid (Egypt). During his exile he addressed several violent writings to Constantius with the evident, but unsuccessful, intent of courting martyrdom. They include 'De non conveniendo cum haereticis', 'De regibus apostaticis', and 'De S. Athanasio'. Soon after the accession of *Julian, in common with the exiled bishops generally, he was released (362). He then made his way to Antioch, where he vigorously resisted all conciliatory action towards repentant Arians, and by consecrating Paulinus, an Antiochene presbyter, bishop, created an unfortunate schism. A little later, it appears, he went back to his see. Whether or not he was ever formally excommunicated is uncertain, though this is suggested by passages in St. *Ambrose and St. *Augustine, and St. *Jerome refers to his followers as 'Luciferians'.

His writings survive in the single MS. Cod. Vat. 133 (s. ix/x). J. P. Migne, *PL*, xiii. 767–1038. Best ed. by W. Hartel in *C.S.E.L.*, xiv (1886). G. Krüger, *Lucifer Bischof von Cagliari und das Schisma der Luciferianer* (1886); F. Piva, *Lucifero di Cagliari contro l' imperatore Costanzo* (Trent, 1928); G. Thörnell, *Studia Luciferiana* (Uppsala, 1934). A. M. Coleman, *The Biblical Text of Lucifer of Cagliari* (Welwyn, 1927; 8 pp.). Bardenhewer, iii, pp. 469–77. É. Amann in *D.T.C.*, ix (pt. 1; 1926), cols. 1032–44.

LUCINA. Several pious women of this name figure in the early traditions and legends of the Roman Church. Acc. to the *Liber Pontificalis (s.v. *Cornelius, A.D. 251–3), a certain Lucina removed the bodies of Sts. *Peter and *Paul from their resting place at the *catacombs ('ad Catacumbas'), and laid that of St. Paul in her own property on the *Ostian Way. It appears that she or another Lucina was buried in another property, the 'Crypt of Lucina', on the *Appian Way. G. B. *de Rossi sought to identify the Lucina who gives her name to the crypt with *Pomponia Graecina (1st cent.; q.v.).

J. P. Kirsch, *Die römischen Titelkirchen im Altertum* (1918), pp. 80–4; H. *Lietzmann, *Petrus und Paulus in Rom* (ed. 2, 1927), pp. 179–89. G. Belvederi, 'Le cripte di Lucina' in *Rivista di Archeologia cristiana*, xxi (1945), pp. 121–64. H. *Leclercq, O.S.B., in *D.A.C.L.*, ix (pt. 2; 1930), cols. 2636–61, s.v. 'Lucine (Crypte de)'; J. P. Kirsch in *L.Th.K.*, vi (1934), col. 679, s.v.; E. Josi in *E.C.*, vii (1951), col. 1631 f., s.v. See also bibl. to *Pomponia Graecina.

LUCIUS. In legend, the first Christian king of Britain. Acc. to an early form of the story (based apparently on a statement in the *'Liber Pontificalis' that a British king, Lucius, sent a request to the Pope that he might become a Christian), Lucius successfully appealed to Pope Eleutherus (174–89) for Christian teachers to be sent to England, and together with large numbers of his subjects received baptism at their hands; the heathen temples were converted into Christian churches; the heathen priesthood abandoned their pagan functions for the Christian ministry; and Lucius finally died at *Gloucester in 156. In later times (9th to 16th cents.) the legend was considerably embellished. King Lucius becomes the son of *Simon of Cyrene, is converted by St. *Timothy, and goes as a missionary to Rhaetia, where he establishes himself as the first Bp. of Chur and is martyred by stoning. The details of the later story are apparently due to the conflation of legends about the King of Britain with independent traditions about a Lucius of Chur, who was possibly a historical person. A. *Harnack suggested that the statement in the 'Liber Pontificalis' is due to a confusion between 'Britain' and 'Britis', a name for *Edessa, and that the king mentioned was really *Abgar IX of that city.

The story is related by *Bede, H.E., i, 4, and v, 24 (cf. notes to ed. C. Plummer, ii, Oxford, 1896, p. 14, with useful reff.); *William of Malmesbury, De Antiquitate Glastoniensis Ecclesiae, ii, and *Geoffrey of Monmouth, Historia Regum Britanniae, iv, 19, and v, 1. A. Harnack, 'Der Brief des britischen Königs Lucius an den Papst Eleutherus' in Sb. (Berl.), 1904, I, pp. 909–16. A. W. Haddan–W. *Stubbs, Councils and Ecclesiastical Documents Relating to Great Britain and Ireland, i (1869), p. 25 f. J. Gammack in D.C.B., iii (1882), pp. 754–6, s.v. 'Lucius (16)'.

LUCY, St. Acc. to tradition, she was a native of Syracuse who openly proclaimed her Christian faith by distributing her goods to the poor at the height of the *Diocletianic persecution. For this act she was denounced to the authorities by the young man to whom she had been betrothed by her parents, and suffered martyrdom in 303. She was much venerated in the early Church, as is shown by her inclusion in the *Canon of the Roman and *Ambrosian Mass. Feast day 13 Dec.

The details of the acta (prob. 5th–6th cent., surviving in various Gk. and Lat. recensions) from which the story derives are untrustworthy. The Gk. passio was ed. by G. di Giovanni (Palermo, 1758) and C. Barreca (Rome, 1902), the Lat. passio frequently, e.g. in A. Beaugrand, Sainte Lucie (1882). The acta were utilized by St. *Aldhelm in Tractatus de Laudibus Virginitalis, 42 (PL, lxxxix, 142) and in his poem De Laudibus Virginum (PL, lxxxix, 269 f.). There is also a long poem by *Sigebert of Gembloux in her honour. The most reliable authority for her early cult appears to be an inscription described by P. Orsi, 'Insigne epigrafe del cimitero di S. Giovanni in Siracusa' in Römische Quartalschrift, ix (1895), pp. 299–308. G. Goyau, Sainte Lucie (1921). Collection of pictures ed. M. Capdevila, Iconografía de Santa Lucía (Barcelona, 1949). H. *Leclercq, O.S.B., in D.A.C.L., ix (pt. 2; 1930), cols. 2616–18, s.v. 'Lucie (Sainte)'; A. Bigelmair in L.Th.K., vi (1934), cols. 674–6, s.v. 'Lucia', with further bibl.

LUDLOW, JOHN MALCOLM FORBES (1821–1911). The founder of *Christian Socialism. Educated in France, where he got to know F. C. M. Fourier and other Socialist pioneers, he came to London in 1838, and in 1843 he was called to the bar at Lincoln's Inn. In a letter to F. D. *Maurice from *Paris after the Revolution of 1848, he insisted that 'the

new Socialism must be Christianized'. He soon became active in literary propaganda, helped to form some co-operative associations for production, which, however, were short-lived, and was largely responsible for promoting the Industrial and Provident Societies Act of 1852. Later he co-operated with Maurice in the founding of the Working Men's College, where he taught for many years. Although overshadowed in public estimation by Maurice and C. *Kingsley, Ludlow was the real founder of the movement and remained its organizer and co-ordinator. A member of the C of E, he believed in Socialism as the truest expression of democracy, but was also convinced that Christian Socialism was possible only if political and industrial emancipation were accompanied by an education spiritual and moral as well as intellectual. Ludlow was well versed in law, politics, and economics, and an accomplished linguist. His influence did much to prevent in England the antagonism between the Church and Socialism that exists in most other countries.

C. E. Raven, Christian Socialism, 1848–1854 (1920), pp. 54–75, 106–12, 137–49, 154–67, 185–94, 245–9, 290–301, 317–25, 369 f., 372–4, 376, and passim. Sir Norman Moore in D.N.B., 1901–1911 (1912), p. 487 f., s.v. Life by N. C. Masterman (Cambridge, 1963).

LUDOLF, HIOB (1624–1704), also spelled 'Leutholf', German orientalist. A native of Erfurt, after studying there and at *Leyden, he travelled extensively to increase his linguistic knowledge. Having met with an Abyssinian scholar in Italy, he induced him to teach him *Ethiopic. His record of what he learnt of the pronunciation of the language is valuable, since at that date Ethiopic was still spoken in places in Abyssinia. From 1652 to 1678 he was in the employment of the Duke of Saxe-Gotha. In 1683 he visited England to try to establish trade with Abyssinia, but, owing to obstacles raised by the Abyssinian Church, met with no success. For the rest of his life he devoted himself to study. His many publications did much to introduce to the W. a knowledge of Ethiopic sources and history, which did not advance appreciably till the work of A. *Dillmann. They include a Grammatica Aethiopica (1661; ed. 2, much enlarged and improved, 1702), a Historia Aethiopica (1681), and a Commentarius ad suam Historiam Aethopicam (1691). In the last-named, the '*Apostolic Tradition' of St. *Hippolytus was first made accessible to W. scholars.

His correspondence with Leibniz (mainly on linguistic subjects) was ed. by A. B. Michaelis (Göttingen, 1755). Eng. tr. of his 'New History of Ethiopia' by 'J. P., Gent.' (London, 1682). J. Fleming, 'Hiob Ludolf. Ein Beitrag zur Geschichte der orientalischen Philologie' in Beiträge für Assyriologie, i (1890), pp. 537–58, ii (1894), pp. 63–110, incl. extracts of docc. in Ethiopic, with Germ. tr. C. F. Bauer, Hiob Ludolf. Der Begründer der äthiopischen Sprachwissenschaft und des äthiopischen Buchdrucks (1937; brief, with specimens of his Ethiopic type and bibl.). F. Schühlein in L.Th.K., vi (1934), col. 684.

LUDOLF OF SAXONY (c. 1300–78), also 'Ludolf the *Carthusian', spiritual writer. Little is known of his life. After some 30 years as a *Dominican, he joined the Carthusians at Strassburg in 1340 and became Prior of the Charterhouse at Coblence in 1343, but in 1348 resumed his status as an ordinary monk and spent the rest of his life at Mainz and Strassburg, mainly in prayer. His two principal works are a 'Commentary on the Psalms' and his celebrated 'Vita Christi'. The latter, much more than a biography, with doctrinal, spiritual, and moral instructions as well as prayers and extensive Patristic citations, became very popular. It was first printed in 1474 at Strassburg and Cologne, and has been very frequently reissued in a great many languages. Parallels make it probable that Ludolf influenced the '*Imitation of Christ', but the attempt to ascribe the Imitation itself to Ludolf seems to have failed.

His Comm. on the Psalms was first printed by J. Wimpfeling at Speyer c. 1491. Best modern ed. of his *Vita Christi* by L. M. Rigollot (Paris, 1870). P. Pourrat, S.J., *La Spiritualité chrétienne*, ii (1923), pp. 484–8. Full bibl. list in U. Chevalier, *Répertoire des sources historiques du moyen-âge*. Biogr. II, (1907), col. 2923. A. Mougel, O. Cart., in *C.E.*, ix (1910), p. 416.

LUGO, JOHN DE (1583–1660), Spanish *Jesuit. After studying law at Salamanca till 1603, he entered the Society in that year. From 1611 he taught philosophy at several Spanish colleges, and from 1616 theology at Valladolid. Called to Rome in 1621, he soon achieved international fame as a theologian, and was made cardinal by *Urban VIII in 1643. During these years were published his chief works, *De Incarnatione* (1633), *De Sacramentis in Genere* (1636), *De Virtute Fidei Divinae* (1646), *Responsa Moralia* (1651). An independent thinker, Lugo is chiefly important for his teaching on faith and on the sacrifice of the Mass. He held that God gives light sufficient for salvation to every soul, so that all men of good will can find among the errors of their human religious or philosophical systems the elements of Divine truth which will enable them to be saved. In his Eucharistic teaching he emphasized the element of destruction as the distinctive characteristic of sacrificial worship. He held that in the act of Consecration, Christ's human nature is in some manner 'destroyed' by being changed into a lower state from which the normal human activities are excluded and the primary object of its existence is henceforward to be consumed as food. His contributions to dogmatic theology, combined with his luminous exposition of many problems of moral theology, caused St. *Alphonsus Liguori to regard Lugo as 'the most important theologian after St. *Thomas Aquinas'.

Works listed in Sommervogel, v (1894), cols. 176–80, and ix (1900), col. 619 f. D. *Stone, *A History of the Doctrine of the Holy Eucharist*, ii (1909), pp. 373–7. P. Bernard in *D.T.C.*, ix (pt. i, 1926), col. 1071 f.

LUIS OF GRANADA (1505–88), Spanish spiritual author. Born of poor parents, in 1524 he entered the *Dominican convent of the Holy Cross at Granada. As a student at Valladolid, he came under the influence of the Humanist Movement. In 1544 he was sent to Cordova to reform the convent Scala Coeli, where he spent the next ten years, restoring discipline and evangelizing the neighbouring peasants. In 1554 he founded a convent at Badajoz, and in 1557 was elected provincial of his order for Portugal. His devotion and learning attracted the attention of the Queen Regent, who made him her confessor, but he refused her offer of the archiepiscopal see of Braga, for which he recommended his fellow-Dominican, *Bartholomew of the Martyrs.

Luis's most considerable works, are his ascetical treatises, written in the vernacular. In the *Libro de la oración* (1553) he urged the practice of meditation and gave a detailed method, suitable for beginners and simpler than that of St. *Ignatius of Loyola, which laid esp. stress on the preparation of the heart. The book also contained 14 meditations on the Passion and on the Last Things, two for each day of the week. The popular *Guía de pecadores* (1555; 'Guide of Sinners') was a treatise on the Christian virtues and the principal vices, based on the relevant articles of the 'Summa Theologica' of St. *Thomas Aquinas. Though both books were placed on the *Index in 1559, owing to the Spanish *Inquisition's fears of false mysticism, they were republished in 1567 after the Pope and the Council of *Trent had fully approved them. Luis also wrote *Memorial de la vida cristiana* (1566), followed by a sequel, *Adiciones al Memorial* (1574), which aimed at giving a complete summary of the ascetical life, as well as biographies of Bartholomew of the Martyrs and *John of Ávila. He exercised a profound influence on generations of subsequent spiritual writers, esp. through St. *Francis of Sales, who in his *Introduction to the Devout Life* drew largely on Luis's *Libro de la oración*. His published Sermons were also widely read.

Collected edd. of his works by D. Sánchez (Madrid, 1679); also in 9 vols., ib., 1730, with life by L. Múñoz forming vol. ix; in 'Biblioteca des autores españoles' (3 vols., 1848–9); crit. ed. by J. Cuervo [Arango y Rodrigeuz Trelles], O.P. (Madrid, 1906 ff.). Id. *Biografia de Fr. Luis de Granada* (ib., 1895), and other works by the same author. M. Llaneza, *Bibliografia del V.P.M. Fr. Luis de Granada, O.P.* (4 vols., Salamanca, 1926–8). M. Baumgarten, 'Zu den geistlichen Schriften des Dominikaners Fray Luis de Granada' in *T.Q.*, cvii (1926), pp. 267–83. E. A. Peers, *Studies in the Spanish Mystics*, i (1927), pp. 33–76. Quétif-Échard, ii, 285–91. Pourrat, iii (1925), pp. 143–53; Eng. tr., iii (1927), pp. 95–101. M. H. Lavocat in *D.T.C.*, ix (pt. i; 1926) cols. 953–9, s.v. 'Louis de Grenade', with further bibl.

LUITPRAND. See *Liutprand*.

LUKE, St. Evangelist; acc. to tradition the author of the Third Gospel and of *Acts. Several facts of his life can be gathered from the Pauline Epp. and from Acts, if the 'we-sections' (Acts 16. 10–17; 20. 5–21. 18; 27. 1–28. 16) are parts of his travel journal. Acc. to Col. 4. 11, 14 he was a gentile, an inference corroborated by his idiomatic Greek, and a physician. He accompanied St. Paul on his Second Missionary Journey from Troas to Philippi (Acts 16. 10–17) and on the Third from Philippi to *Jerusalem (Acts 20. 5–21. 18), and he went with him to Rome, where he stayed during his captivity (Col. 4. 14, 2 Tim. 4. 11). If a variant in *Codex Bezae (D, 11. 28) be correct, he would have been one of the first members of the Christian community at *Antioch, a hypothesis made plausible by his interest in and detailed information about the early Antiochene Christians and supported by statements in *Eusebius, St. *Jerome, and others. Acc. to a tradition recorded in the *Anti-Marcionite Prologues, St. Luke was unmarried, wrote his Gospel in Greece, and died at the age of 84. *Origen is the first to identify him with 'the brother' of 2 Cor. 8. 18, a view followed by the Anglican collect for his feast. In 356–7 *Constantius II had his relics translated from Thebes in Boeotia to *Constantinople, where they were preserved at the Church of the Apostles, built soon afterwards. The *Acta* of his alleged martyrdom are legendary.

St. Luke is the patron of doctors. Acc. to later legends he was one of the Seventy of Lk. 10. 1, the unnamed disciple of *Emmaus (Lk. 24. 13–35), and a painter, and in the Middle Ages a picture of our Lady in *Santa Maria Maggiore, Rome, was ascribed to him. He is therefore also the patron of artists. Feast day, 18 Oct.

For bibl., see works cited under foll. entry. On the cult of St. Luke, cf. K. Hofmann in *L.Th.K.*, vi (1934), cols. 709 f., s.v. 'Lukas'.

LUKE, Gospel of St. The third of the Synoptic Gospels. Its authorship has been attributed from the end of the 2nd cent. to *Luke (q.v.), the companion of St. *Paul, on the authority of St. *Irenaeus and *Tertullian. This statement has been generally accepted on the grounds that there is no reason why a Gospel should have been falsely assigned to a comparatively unimportant personage. The date is doubtful. Some scholars, among them A. *Harnack, put it before the death of St. Paul (64), because Acts, which it precedes, contains indications of a date prior to the martyrdom of the Apostle. A serious objection to this view is the prediction, in 19. 43 f. and 21. 20, 24, of the fall of *Jerusalem (70) in much more precise terms than in any of the other Gospels, which has determined many scholars to assign to the Gospel a date between A.D. 70 and 100. If the supposed dependence of passages in it on *Josephus could be established, this would seem to require a date at the end of the 1st cent.

The author sets out his purpose in a brief Prologue (1. 1–4). Acc. to most modern critics the Gospel is composed of two main sources, *Mark and the so-called *'Q'; the material proper to Lk. is assigned to a special source called L, and the Birth stories (chs. 1, 2) are believed to be derived from a Jewish Christian source. Some critics (B. H. *Streeter, V. Taylor) have argued that the present Gospel is made up of an original first draft, which they call 'Proto-Luke', consisting of Q and L, to which a later editor added

sections of Mk. The Passion Narrative also seems to be derived from an independent source. Acc. to the author's own testimony in the Prologue, he collected his materials from eye - witnesses, among whom conservative scholars commonly see in the Virgin herself the principal authority for the Birth stories.

The special characteristic of the Gospel, which is written in idiomatic Greek, is its insistence on the Life, Death and Teaching of Christ as a message of universal salvation addressed to all men. The author carefully translates all Hebrew terms, lays comparatively little stress on the fulfilment of OT prophecies, and omits whatever might offend pagan readers, e.g. the prohibition to the Disciples to preach to the Gentiles and the reproach addressed to the Canaanitish woman. On the other hand, he emphasizes our Lord's loving-kindness and human understanding, e.g. in the Parable of the Prodigal (15. 11–32), His words to the women of Jerusalem (23. 27–31), and the promise to the good thief (23. 43), all peculiar to Lk. The Lord Himself is pre-eminently the Saviour of all men (the terms σωτήρ and σωτηρία do not occur in the other Synoptics). He has a special care for the outcasts, and side by side with its gentleness, the Gospel preaches an austere love of poverty in its absolute version of the first *Beatitude (6. 20) and in the Parable of Dives and Lazarus (16. 19–31), which is not recorded in the other Synoptics. St. Luke is, moreover, the evangelist of the Holy Ghost, whose action he constantly affirms in the work of the Incarnation (1. 35) as well as on our Lord Himself (4. 1), on His disciples (12. 12), and, indeed, on all Christians (11. 13). He is the evangelist of prayer, to which he gives a greater part in his picture of Christ than the others, and his Gospel is also the Gospel of women. It is Mary, not, as in Mt., *Joseph, who plays the principal part in the Lucan Birth stories, and there are many figures of women about whom nothing is said in the other Gospels, e.g. the Virgin's cousin Elizabeth (1. 5–66), the woman who was a sinner (7. 37–50), the widow of Nain (7. 11–17), and the woman in the crowd who blessed Christ's Mother (11. 27). This gracious humanity, accompanied by a strong sense of the supernatural, which is shown in the working of the Spirit and the ministry of the angels, make the peculiar charm of the Gospel, from which, at all times, saints as well as artists have drawn inspiration.

Commentaries: A. *Plummer (1896, Int. Crit. Comm.); J. *Wellhausen (1904); T. *Zahn (1913); M. J. *Lagrange (1921); L. Ragg (1922, West. Comm.); B. S. Easton (1926); H. Balmforth (1930, Clar. Bible); W. Manson (1930, Moff. Comm.); J. M. Creed (1930); A. Schlatter (1931); H. K. Luce (1933, Camb. Gk. Test.). Special studies: W. K. Hobart, *The Medical Language of St. Luke* (1882); A. Harnack, *Lukas der Arzt* (1906; Eng. trans., *Luke the Physician*, 1907); B. Weiss, *Die Quellen des Lukas Evangeliums* (1907); E. W. Lummis, *How Luke was Written* (1915); H. J. Cadbury, *The Style and Literary Method of Luke* (1920); H. McLachlan, *St. Luke, the Man and his Work* (1920); A. T. Robertson, *Luke the Historian in the Light of Research* (1920); B. H. Streeter, *The Four Gospels* (1924), pp. 199–270; H. J. Cadbury, *The Making of Luke-Acts* (1927); V. Taylor, *Behind the Third Gospel*. A Study of the Proto-Luke Hypothesis (1926). Comm. by A. R. C. Leaney (London, 1958).

LULL, RAYMOND (*c.* 1235-*c.* 1315), the 'Enlightened Doctor' ('doctor illuminatus'). At an early age he entered the service of King James I of Aragon and, both before and after his marriage, led a worldly life until his conversion at the age of 30. He then became a *Franciscan tertiary, and gave himself up to an attempt to convert the Mohammedans. He traversed Europe in an effort to enlist support for his plans, but with little practical result beyond the foundation of the college of Miramar (1276) for the study of Arabic. His own missionary activities led him through Africa and Asia as far as the Indian frontiers. In the intervals between his journeys he taught at Montpellier and Paris, where he refuted Latin *Averroism. He died a martyr's death at Bougie in N. Africa, stoned by the Moslems. Lull's literary activity (in Latin, Catalan, and Arabic) was prodigious. His theology is deeply influenced by medieval *Augustinianism, esp. the doctrines of St. *Bonaventure. In his opposition to Averroism, which completely severed theological from philosophical truth, he was led into the opposite extreme of identifying them and maintaining that even the deepest mysteries of the Christian faith can be proved by logical argument. In his ambitious work entitled 'Ars Magna' he attempted to work out a method by which all possible knowledge could be reduced to, or derived from, certain first principles. The supposed dangers in this confusion of faith and reason led to the condemnation of his teaching by *Gregory XI in 1376. His poetical writings give him an important place in the history of Catalan literature.

As a mystic Lull has been considered the forerunner of St. *Teresa and St. *John of the Cross. His conception of the mystic life centres in the contemplation of the Divine perfections, which is achieved by the purification of memory, understanding, and will, and results in action for the greater glory of God. He was one of the most ardent defenders of the *Immaculate Conception in the Middle Ages. His cult, which developed soon after his death, was hindered by the ecclesiastical authorities owing to the difficulties in his teaching, but it was approved by *Pius IX in 1847. Interest in him has been steadily growing in recent times.

First crit. ed. of his *Opera* by I. Salzinger (8 vols., 'i-vi' and 'ix-x', Mainz, 1721-48). There are Eng. trr. from the Catalan by E. A. Peers of his *Blanquerna*. A Thirteenth-Century Romance (London [1926]), *The Book of the Lover and the Beloved* (ib., 1923), *The Art of Contemplation* (ib., 1925), *The Tree of Life* (ib., 1926), and *The Book of the Beasts* (ib., 1927). The principal authority for his life is a contemporary Life surviving in Lat. and Catalan. Lat. text in *A.A.SS.*, Jun. V (1709), pp. 661-8, with other material, pp. 633-61 and 668-70; crit. ed. by B. de Gaiffier, S.J., in *Anal. Boll.*, xlviii (1930), pp. 130-78, with reff. *Histoire littéraire de la France*, xxix (1885), pp. 1-386, with detailed list of works and edd. E. A. Peers, *Ramón Lull.* A Biography (1929) with full bibl. reff. O. Keicher, O.F.M., *Raymundus Lullus und seine Stellung zur arabischen Philosophie.* Mit einem Anhang, enthaltend die zum ersten Male veröffentlichte 'Declaratio Raymundi per Modum Dialogi Edita' (Beiträge zur Geschichte der Philosophie des Mittelalters, vii, Hftt. 4-5; 1909). E. Longpré, O.F.M., in *D.T.C.*, ix (pt. I; 1926), cols. 1072-1141, s.v., with full bibl.

LULLUS, St. (d. 786), Bp. of Mainz. Like St. *Boniface an Anglo-Saxon, he was educated and ordained deacon at *Malmesbury. Proceeding to Rome and then to Germany, he became closely associated with Boniface, on whose behalf he went on a mission to Pope *Zacharias in 751. Having been promised by *Pepin the Younger succession to Boniface in the see of Mainz, he was consecrated a *chorepiscopus *c.* 752. After Boniface's death (754), however, a long dispute ensued between Lullus and Sturmius, the Abbot of *Fulda, when Lullus attempted to end the exemption of Fulda from the jurisdiction of Mainz and its direct dependence on Rome, which his predecessor had secured; and Lullus did not receive the *pallium* till *c.* 781. After his failure over Fulda, Lullus founded a separate monastery at Hersfeld, where he was afterwards buried. His influence and reputation for learning are reflected in his large correspondence with many of the leading figures of his time. Feast day, 16 Oct.

Letters of St. Boniface and St. Lullus ed. E. Dümmler in *M.G.H.*, Epistolae, iii (1892), pp. 215-433; also ed. M. Tangl (*M.G.H.*, Epistolae Selectae, i; 1916). J. F. Böhmer-C. Will (edd.), *Regesten zur Geschichte der Mainzer Erzbischöfe,* i (Innsbruck, 1887), pp. 34-45. Life by *Lambert of Hersfeld pr. among the latter's works (ed. O. Holder-Egger, Hanover, &c., 1894), pp. 305-40. O. Holder-Egger, 'Ueber die *Vita Lulli* und ihren Verfasser' in *N.A.*, ix (1884), pp. 285-320; id., 'Studien zu Lambert von Hersfeld', III, v, 'Ueber die letzten Capitel der *Vita Lulli* und die Verwendung dieser *Vita* für die Kritik der Annalen, ib., xix (1894), pp. 509-37. E. Schröder, 'Urkundenstudien eines Germanisten', v, 'Zur Ueberlieferung und Kritik des Breviarium S. Lulli' in *Mitteilungen des Instituts für Oesterreichische Geschichtsforschung,* xx (1899), pp. 361-76. T. Schieffer, 'Angelsachsen und Franken' in *Akademie der Wissenschaften und der Literatur* [in Mainz]. Abhandlungen der Geistes- und Sozialwissenschaftlichen Klasse, Jahr. 1950, No. 20, pt. 2, II, 'Erzbischof Lul und die Anfänge des Mainzer Sprengels', pp. 1471-1529. For Lullus's Profession of Faith see W. Levison, *England and the Continent in the Eighth Century* (Ford Lectures for 1943; 1946) Appendix II, pp. 233-40; text repr. in T. Schieffer, op. cit., pp. 1535-9. W. *Stubbs in *D.C.B.*, iii (1882), pp. 757-61.

LUNA, PEDRO DE. See *Benedict XIII.*

LUND. Constituted a bishopric suffragan to Hamburg-Bremen in the middle of the 10th cent., it was established as an independent archbishopric in 1104. Apart from a brief period from 1133 onwards, it continued to possess its archiepiscopal status till the see was suppressed in 1536. The university dates from 1668. In the 19th cent. its theological faculty stood for a conservative and 'High Church' tradition in contrast to the liberalizing theology of *Upsala. From 15 to 28 Aug. 1952, it was the scene of a Conference of the Faith and Order Commission of the *World Council of Churches on 'The Church, Ways of Worship and Intercommunion'.

L. Weibull (ed.), *Diplomatarium Diocesis Lundensis.* Lunds Arkestifts Urkundsbok (Lund, 1900 ff.). Studies on the Cathedral by O. Rydbeck (Lund, 1915), E. H. G. Wrangel (ib., 1923), and E. Newman (2 vols., Stockholm, 1946). M. J. J. Weibull, *Lunds Universitets Historia* (ed. L. Weibull-C. G. Weibull; Lund, 1918). The Transactions of the Third World Conference on Faith and Order held at Lund, Aug. 1952, ed. O. S. Tomkins (London, 1953).

LUPERCALIA. A pagan fertility festival which continued to be observed on 15 Feb. in Christian Rome until *Gelasius I superseded it in 494 with the Feast of the *Purification (2 Feb.).

LUPUS, St. (*c.* 383–479), Bp. of Troyes. After seven years in wedlock with Pimeniola, the sister of St. *Hilary of Arles, he and his wife agreed to separate and devote themselves more strictly to religion. Having made his way to *Lérins, Lupus there embraced the monastic life in 426. Shortly afterwards (427), however, he accepted the bishopric of Troyes, and held the see for some fifty years. The supposition that he was associated with St. *Germanus of Auxerre in his mission to Britain against the *Pelagians in 429 rests on insufficient evidence, and the story that by his entreaties he preserved his country from the ravages of *Attila and his Huns is almost certainly fictitious. Feast day, 29 July.

Two of his letters, pr. in J. P. Migne, *PL*, lxviii, 63–8, survive. His Life (prob. 8th cent. and of little value) has been ed. by B. Krusch in *M.G.H.*, Scriptores Rerum Merovingicarum, vii (1920), pp. 284–302.

LUPUS, SERVATUS (*c.* 805–62), Abbot of Ferrières. Born in the diocese of Sens he entered the abbey of Ferrières at an early age. *C.* 829 he went to *Fulda where he studied under *Rabanus Maurus and met *Gottschalk (q.v.) with whom he remained in contact throughout his life. In 836 he returned to Ferrières, was presented at the court of Louis the Pious, and gained the favour of the Empress Judith. In 840 he became Abbot of Ferrières. A humanist rather than a theologian, he became one of the chief figures of the *Carolingian Renaissance, and made his abbey an important centre of learning. He also took part in many synods, among them Germigny (843), and even in some military enterprises. His comparatively few writings include a 'Life of St. Wigbert' (836) and a disputed 'Life of St. Maximin of Trier' (839). His collection of 132 letters, addressed to famous correspondents such as Benedict III, Charles the Bald, *Hincmar of Reims, and Rabanus Maurus are a primary source for the history of his era. His principal theological work, the 'Liber de Tribus Questionibus' (*c.* 850), which arose out of the controversy provoked by Gottschalk, defended an integral *Augustinianism, though in a less rigid sense than Gottschalk. He affirmed that in fallen man freewill left to its own powers was capable only of evil, that there was a predestination to hell as well as to eternal life, and that the text of 1 Tim. 2. 4, acc. to which it is God's will that all men should be saved, is to be interpreted in a restricted sense as applying only to the elect. The work is supplemented by the 'Collectaneum de Tribus Questionibus', a body of materials of interest for its wide acquaintance with the Fathers.

Collected ed. of his works by É. *Baluze (Paris, 1664; ed. 2, Antwerp, 1710, repr. in J. P. Migne, *PL*, cxix,

427–700). Crit. edd. of his Vita Wigberti by O. Holder-Egger in *M.G.H.*, Scriptores, xv, (pt. 1; 1887), pp. 36–43, and of his letters by G. Desdevises du Dezert (Bibliothèque de l'École des Hautes Études. Sciences philologiques et historiques, lxxvii; 1888; author's chronology generally rejected), by E. Dümmler in *M.G.H.*, Epistolae, vi (1925), pp. 1–126, and by L. Levillian (Les Classiques de l'histoire de France publiés sous la direction de Louis Halphen et sous les auspices de l'Association Guillaume Budé, x and xvi; 1927–35). F. Sprotte, *Biographie des Abtes Servatus Lupus von Ferrières* (1880). E. von Severus, O.S.B., *Lupus von Ferrières. Gestalt und Wert eines Vermittlers antiken Geistesgutes an das Mittelalter in IX. Jahrhundert* (Beiträge zur Geschichte des alten Mönchtums und des Benediktinerordens, xxi; 1940). W. Levison, 'Eine Predigt des Lupus von Ferrières' in *Kultur- und Universalgeschichte Walter Goetz zu seinem 60. Geburtstage dargebracht* (1927), pp. 3–14. C. H. Beeson, *Lupus of Ferrières as a Scribe and Text Critic.* A Study of his Autograph Copy of Cicero's *De Oratione* . . . with a Facsimile of the Manuscript (The Mediaeval Academy of America Publication, No. 4; Cambridge, Mass., 1930). Z. C. Snijders, *Het Latijn der Brieven van Lupus van Ferrières* (Amsterdam, 1943). Manitius, i (1911), pp. 483–90. É. Amann in *D.T.C.*, ix (pt. 1; 1926), cols. 963–7, s.v. 'Loup, Servat', with notes of early edd. of individual works and other bibl.

LUTHER, MARTIN (1483–1546), founder of the German Reformation. The son of a miner at Mansfeld in Saxony, he was educated at the Cathedral School at Magdeburg, at Eisenach, and at Erfurt university (1501–5), where he studied esp. philosophy. In 1505 he entered the monastery of the *Augustinian Hermits at Erfurt, in fulfilment of a vow made during a thunderstorm. He was ordained priest in 1507, and in the following year was sent as lecturer to the recently founded university of *Wittenberg, continuing his studies and lecturing on moral philosophy. In 1510 he was sent to Rome on affairs of his order. Soon after his return to Wittenberg in 1511 he became doctor of theology and professor of Scripture, holding this post till his death. In 1515 he was made vicar of his order, an office entailing the charge of 11 Augustinian monasteries.

From now onwards his teaching diverged increasingly from the traditional Catholic beliefs and began to assume a characteristic shape. He was influenced by the *Nominalism taught at the contemporary universities and the exaggerated pessimism prevalent in the Augustinian Order; but the chief factor in its development seems to have been in his own passionate and melancholy nature. Anxiety about his own salvation caused him many scruples; and the fact that the routine of the religious life failed to bring him confidence and relief led him at last to give up such of his regular religious duties as the daily celebration of Mass and the recital of the Divine Office. About this time took place also the so-called 'Turmerlebnis' ('Tower experience', usually dated between 1512 and 1515). This took the form of a sudden revelation which convinced him of the essence of the Gospel, namely that faith alone justifies without works, and gave him a belief destined to become the cornerstone of his creed. He found support for this doctrine in certain passages in St. *Augustine's anti-*Pelagian writings as well as in the mystics, esp. J. *Tauler and the *Theologia Germanica, with their emphasis on the nothingness of man before God. From 1516 he gradually came to deny, as a consequence of his belief that faith entails the certitude of salvation for every Christian, the necessity for the mediatorial function of the Church and the priesthood. When in 1517 J. *Tetzel preached on the *Indulgences granted by *Leo X for contributions to the renovation of St. Peter's in Rome, the crisis came. Against the Indulgences Luther drew up his famous 95 theses, which he affixed to the door of the Schlosskirche at Wittenberg. Within a fortnight they had spread throughout Germany, where they were welcomed esp. by the Humanists and other circles desiring the reform of the Church.

In the fierce conflict which soon arose, the attack on Luther was conducted at first esp. by J. *Eck. The ecclesiastical authorities hoped to settle the affair by means of monastic discipline; but at the chapter of the order, held at Heidelberg in 1518, Luther conducted a disputation in the course of which he won over several of his brethren, among them M. *Bucer, and the rift only grew greater. In the same year Luther was tried in Rome for spreading heretical doctrines. He was also summoned before Card. *Cajetan at Augsburg but, refusing to recant, he fled to Wittenberg under the protection of his prince, the Elector *Frederick III of Saxony. Negotiations with the Papal camerarius, C. von *Miltitz, achieved nothing more than a promise from Luther that he would keep silence if his opponents did the same. At a disputation held with Eck at Leipzig in 1519 he denied both the primacy of the Pope and the infallibility of the General Councils.

In 1520 the break with the Medieval Church was completed by his three celebrated reforming writings of that year. The first, *An den christlichen Adel deutscher Nation*, was addressed to the German princes, whom he invited to take the reform of the Church into their own hands, and to abolish tributes to Rome, the celibacy of the clergy, Masses for the dead, pilgrimages, religious orders, and other Catholic practices and institutions. The tremendous success which greeted this pamphlet led him to issue his *De Captivitate Babylonica Ecclesiae* (publd. in Latin and German, *Von der babylonischen Gefangenschaft der Kirche*). He considered that the Babylonian captivity of the Church consisted in the denial to the laity of Communion under both kinds, and in the doctrines of *Transubstantiation and the sacrifice of the Mass. Only Baptism and the Eucharist were held to be Sacraments. In the last of the trilogy, *Von der Freiheit eines Christenmenschen*, he proclaimed the liberation of the Christian by faith, which frees him from the obligation of performing good works. By the bull '*Exsurge Domine' of 15 June 1520, 41 of Luther's theses were censured as heretical; his writings were ordered to be destroyed; and he himself was threatened with the ban if he did not retract within 60 days. Luther replied by burning the bull together with a number of Catholic books, and was duly excommunicated by the

bull 'Decet Romanum Pontificem' of 3 Jan. 1521.

Summoned before the Diet of *Worms in 1521, where he again refused to recant, Luther was put under the ban of the Empire. The Elector of Saxony, however, fearing for his safety, arranged a simulated attack on him and had him brought to the *Wartburg, nr. Eisenach, where he spent the next eight months fighting his doubts as to the rightfulness of his action as temptations of the devil, and regarding his condemnation by Church and State as trials sent to confirm his mission. He also wrote many pamphlets, e.g. against monastic vows and the Sacrifice of the Mass. Much the most enduring of his literary productions begun in this period was his fine translation of the Bible. The first version in German from the original text, it is remarkable for its power and warmth. In its successful use of popular speech, it brought the Bible to life in the German language, and made it henceforward a dominant influence in German religion. It also contributed largely to the formation of the modern German tongue.

While Luther was living in seclusion at the Wartburg his ideas spread rapidly throughout the country. Hand in hand with the revival of popular religious enthusiasm went the abandonment of many traditional practices. Priests married, monks and nuns left their monasteries. *Carlstadt, however, joined the *Anabaptists and, seeking to destroy all altars, images, and crucifixes, proceeded to such lengths that, in 1522, Luther found it necessary to leave the Wartburg and return to Wittenberg to restore order with the help of the secular authorities. He resumed his lectures and abolished many Catholic practices, including private Mass, Confession, and fasts. In 1524 he finally discarded his religious habit, and in the next year, shortly after the death of the Elector, who had discountenanced marriages between priests and religious, married the former *Cistercian nun, Catherine von Bora. In the same year he advised the German princes to wage war against the peasants who had risen in arms, an attitude which cost him the sympathies of a large section of the population. (See *Peasants' Revolt, The*).

The religious and political situation, however, continued to favour the spread of his teaching. His noble German hymns, which gave the congregation a larger part in the service, won many for his innovations; and his work was facilitated esp. by the decision of the Diet of *Speyer in 1529, which established the right of the princes to organize national Churches. Already the movement had spread to other countries. But now differences among the Reformers began to be serious. At the Colloquy of *Marburg (1529), a deep cleavage between Luther and H. *Zwingli on the nature of the Eucharistic Presence revealed itself. In 1530, though prevented from appearing at the Diet of *Augsburg on account of the ban of the Empire, he approved of the comparatively conciliatory '*Augsburg Confession' (Confessio Augustana), drawn up by P. *Melanchthon, but discountenanced all further attempts at restoring union with the Catholic Church. In the *Schmalkalden Articles (1537) the doctrinal differences between Luther and Rome were further emphasized. In 1539 he sanctioned the bigamous marriage of *Philip of Hesse, in a written document, though he later endeavoured to minimize his responsibility for this action. His last years were darkened by the increasing dissensions among his adherents, which could only be subdued by placing the cause of doctrinal unity in the hands of the secular authorities.

Apart from his three writings of 1520, Luther published a great number of works, mostly small occasional pamphlets, with no attempt at a systematic elaboration of his doctrine. Among them is the treatise *De Votis Monasticis* (1521), in which he presented the religious life as it appeared to him after he had broken away from it. His passionate reply to *Henry VIII's *Defence of the Seven Sacraments*, entitled *Contra Henricum Regem Anglicum* (1522), lost him the sympathies of England. His views on the incapability of the human will to follow the good are laid down in *De Servo Arbitrio* (1525), a reply to *Erasmus's *De Libero Arbitrio*. His *Kleiner Katechismus* and *Grosser Katechismus* (both 1529) were designed to propagate his teaching among the people. From 1529 to his death his disciples wrote down the *Tischreden*, conversations at table with his family and friends, in which he developed all his favourite ideas. His writings contain many passages of deep religious feeling, but he also gives free play to his love of abuse and obscenities and his hatred of the Papacy, the bitterest attack on which was his last work, *Wider das Papsttum zu Rom, vom Teufel gestiftet* (1545).

Luther's character, very complex in itself, has attracted both fervent admiration and violent enmity. His deep emotions completely controlled his powers of judgement. His great command of language and his successful oratory won him a wide popular hearing, but in controversy he had few scruples as to the character of his arguments, and to attempt to assess conflicting evidence dispassionately was quite foreign to his nature. His central doctrines were a mirror of his temperament and of his own experiences. His deep pessimism led him to affirm the total depravity of mankind and the uselessness of human reason, whereas his personal need for a 'gracious God' created the doctrine of the imputation of Christ's merits by faith alone, without any human co-operation. Even Baptism could not restore man's freedom for the good. The movements of concupiscence which remain after Baptism he held to be mortal sins. Man is, in fact, wholly under the power of evil and can do nothing but sin. Justification is something which is accomplished in man by a kind of legal fiction, acc. to which God regards sinful man as righteous, owing to the merits of Christ, though in reality he remains as sinful as before. In the famous hymn, 'Ein' feste Burg ist unser Gott', Luther expressed his thought: 'Es ist

O.D.C.C.—2 E

doch unser Tun umsonst, auch in dem besten Leben' ('All we do is in vain, even in the best life'). But the complete uselessness and even sinfulness of all human activity which would logically follow from such teaching were never admitted either by Luther himself or by his followers. The negative attitude to religious human effort, however, showed itself in the growing dichotomy of interior religious and exterior behaviour, with the consequence that Luther left the latter, including all outward manifestations of religion, to be entirely regulated by the secular powers. See *Lutheranism*.

The standard critical ed. of Luther's works is the 'Weimarer Ausgabe' ed. J. C. F. Knaake and others (Weimar, 1883 ff.). It contains his writings, lectures, table talk, correspondence, and material on his tr. of the Bible. Of older edd. the chief is the 'Erlangen Ausgabe', ed. J. G. Plochmann–J. K. Irmischer (67 vols., Erlangen, 1826–57). Luther's Correspondence was also ed. by E. L. Enders–G. Kawerau (19 vols., Frankfurt a.M., 1884–1932). Selected docc. on Luther's mental development to 1519, ed. O. Scheel (Sammlung ausgewählter kirchen- und dogmengeschichtlicher Quellenschriften, Reihe ii, Hft. 9; 1911). Few of his works have been tr. into English. Selection by B. L. Woolf (London, 1952 ff.). Older Eng. tr. of his 'Primary Works', ed. H. Wace–C. A. Buchheim (London, 1896); of Comm. on Gal., ed. P. S. Watson (London, 1953); of Selected Letters by Margaret A. Currie (ib., 1908). Eng. tr. of complete works ed. J. Pelikan and H. T. Lehmann (St. Louis, Mo., and Philadelphia, 1958 ff.).

The chief modern biographies are those of J. Köstlin (2 vols., Elberfeld, 1875; revised ed. by G. Kawerau, 1903; Eng. tr., 1883), H. S. *Denifle, O.P. (2 vols., Mainz, 1904–7, vol. 2 with co-operation of A. M. Weiss, O.P.); H. Grisar, S.J. (3 vols., Freiburg i.Br., 1912; Eng. tr., 6 vols., 1913–17). O. Scheel (2 vols., Tübingen, 1916–17), and R. Thiel (2 vols., Berlin, 1933–5); also R. H. Bainton, *Here I Stand. A Life of Martin Luther* (1951). C. Beard, *Martin Luther and the Reformation in Germany until the Close of the Diet of Worms*, (ed. J. F. Smith, 1889); J. Mackinnon, *Luther and the Reformation* (4 vols., 1925–30).

On his theology, T. Harnack, *Luther's Theologie mit besonderer Beziehung auf seine Versöhnungs- und Erlösungslehre* (2 vols., 1862–86); J. Köstlin, *Luthers Theologie* (2 vols., 1863; Eng. tr., 2 vols., Philadelphia, Pa., 1897); R. Seeberg, *Dogmengeschichte*, Bd. iv, i; Die Lehre Luthers (1917); K. Holl, *Gesammelte Aufsätze*, Bd. 1, Luther (1921); E. Seeberg, *Luther's Theologie* (2 vols., 1929–37); H. H. Kramm, *The Theology of Martin Luther* (1947); P. S. Watson, *Let God be God!* An Interpretation of the Theology of Martin Luther (1947); E. G. Rupp, *The Righteousness of God*. Luther Studies (1953). E. Hirsch, *Lutherstudien* (2 vols., 1954). K. Aland, *Hilfsbuch zum Lutherstudien* (1956).

On special points, H. Boehmer, *Luther im Lichte der neueren Forschung* (1904; ed. 5, 1918; Eng. tr., 1930); K. Müller, *Luther und Karlstadt* (1907); H. Boehmer, *Luthers Romfahrt* (1914); H. Bornkamm, *Luther und Böhme* (1925). H. Preuss, *Martin Luther. Der Künstler* (1931). W. Link, *Das Ringen Luthers um die Freiheit der Theologie von der Philosophie* (1940).

Index of *Luthers Schriften*, ed. G. Kawerau (Halle, 1917; ed. 2, Leipzig, 1929). Recent publications listed in the *Jahrbuch der Luthergesellschaft* (Wittenberg, 1920 ff.).

J. Köstlin in *P.R.E.* (ed. 3), xi (1902), pp. 720–56, s.v.; T. M. Lindsay in *E.B.* (ed. 11), xvii (1911), pp. 133–40; J. Paquier in *D.T.C.*, ix (pt. 1; 1926), cols. 1146–335, s.v.; F. Blanke in *R.G.G.* (ed. 2), iii (1929), cols. 1755–74, s.v., with extensive bibl.; J. Mackinnon in *E.B.* (ed. 14), xiv (1929), pp. 491–8; A. Bigelmair in *L'Th.K.*, vi (1934), cols. 721–32. See also bibl. to *Reformation*.

LUTHERANISM.

The teaching of M. *Luther found early systematic expression in several formularies of which the chief were his own *Catechisms* (1529), the *Augsberg Confession* (1530), the *Articles of* *Schmalkalden* (1537), and the *Formula of* *Concord* (1577), all of which were combined in the *Book of Concord* of 1580 (qq.v.). In these the Scriptures are affirmed to be the sole rule of faith, to which the Creeds and other traditional statements of belief are all subordinated. The principal Lutheran tenet is *justification by faith alone (*sola fide*). As *Original Righteousness, which at the creation was an integral part of human nature, was irretrievably lost by the Fall, man was henceforward no longer free to do the good but now lives in bondage to the rule of sin. Redemption consists in his justification by faith in Christ, by reason of which, though in fact as great a sinner as before, he is accounted righteous in the sight of God without co-operation on his part. The strongest emphasis was laid on the all-pervading action of God, and hence the soteriological aspects of Christianity became central. The danger of a thoroughgoing *quietism which might have been expected from the denial of human freedom was averted by the practical sense of the Reformer and by subsequent developments which interpreted Luther's own doctrines with greater latitude than their supporters usually readily admitted.

In the later 16th and early 17th cents. these doctrines were elaborated in a scholastic mould which give it a severely intellectual cast. Against this scholastic 'Orthodoxy' the *Pietism of the later 17th cent. strongly reacted. Even the *sola fide* teaching was abandoned and the necessity of personal sanctification emphasized. In the 18th cent. Rationalism made great inroads into Lutheranism and led to an increasing depreciation of all supernatural elements in Christianity, though here again the movement of N. L. von *Zinzendorf and of the *Herrnhuters was a reaction on Pietist lines. In the 19th cent. German Lutheranism underwent a crisis when Frederick William III of Prussia decreed (1817) the union between Lutherans and Reformed in his kingdom. The formation of the 'Altlutheraner' in 1830 and an increasing doctrinal imprecision on the part of the State Church were the results. This development was fostered by a growing interest in Biblical criticism, which threatened to remove the Lutheran foundations. In recent times, however, several factors have combined to bring about a revival of Lutheran orthodoxy, notably the teaching of K. *Barth who, though a *Calvinist, has exercised a powerful influence on all Continental Protestant bodies, and the persecution of Christianity by the Third Reich, which produced a great renewal of the religious spirit among both pastors and congregations. See also *Confessing Church*.

After the end of the war (1945) attempts were made to unite all the Lutheran Churches in Germany in a 'United Evangelical Lutheran Church of Germany' (VELKD, *Vereinigte Evangelisch-Lutherische Kirche Deutschlands*) inside the looser framework of the new federal 'Evangelical Church in Germany' (EKD, *Evangelische Kirche in Deutschland*); the latter, which was formally constituted in July 1948 at Eisenach under the presidency of Theophil Wurm, Bp. of Württemberg, embraces Lutherans, Calvinists, and 'United'. By the end of 1949 all the Lutheran Churches in Germany except those of Oldenburg and Württemberg (but not of course the Lutheran majorities in

the 'United Churches', e.g. of Prussia) had joined the former. Its original Chairman was Hans Meiser, Bp. of Bavaria, its Vice-Chairman, Hans Lilje, Bp. of Hanover. In 1949 Bp. Lilje was also elected Vice-Chairman of the Council of the 'Evangelical Church in Germany'.

Apart from Germany, its country of origin, where it is the faith of about two-thirds of the population, Lutheranism is the official religion in the Scandinavian countries including Finland, and counts a large body of adherents in the U.S.A. It is usually organized in state Churches, the head of the state being at the same time the chief authority of the Church, and it has thus contributed to the modern growth of state absolutism and nationalism. Religious questions are settled either by secular legislation or by a consistorium appointed by the government. There is only one order of clergy, normally examined and provided for by the government. The superior officials in the German Lutheran Churches, who are appointed by the state, are the '*General Superintendents', though under the Third Reich the title of 'Bishop' was revived, which had been kept in *Denmark and *Sweden. Both clergy and laity are organized in synods. The worship varies in the different countries; but its principal feature is always the sermon, set in the framework of a vernacular Liturgy. Holy Communion is received rarely, preferably on Good Friday. Lutheranism has always favoured a sound elementary and secondary education as well as theological and Biblical studies, and such modern branches of Biblical knowledge as *Textual Criticism, *Higher Criticism, and *Form Criticism have been to a very great extent the creation of Lutheran scholars.

Die Bekenntnisschriften der evangelisch-lutherischen Kirche, ed. by the Deutscher Evangelischer Kirchenausschuss (Göttingen, 1930). There is a collection of early Lutheran confessions pr., with Eng. tr., in P. *Schaff, *A History of the Creeds of Christendom*, iii (1877), pp. 1–189, with comment in vol. i (1877), pp. 211–353. 16th cent. 'Kirchenordnung', ed. E. Sehling (Leipzig, 1902 ff.). W. Elert, *Morphologie des Luthertums* (2 vols., 1931–2); id., *Der christliche Glaube*. Grundlinien der lutherischen Dogmatik (1940); id., *Das christliche Ethos*. Grundlinien der lutherischen Ethik (1949). E. Schlink, *Theologie der lutherischen Bekenntnisschriften* (1940; with bibl.); P. Althaus, *Die christliche Wahrheit*. Lehrbuch der Dogmatik (2 vols., 1947–8). I. A. *Dorner, *Geschichte der Protestantischen Theologie* (1867; Eng. tr., 2 vols., 1871); P. Tschackert, *Die Entstehung der lutherischen und der reformierten Kirchenlehre samt ihren innerprotestantischen Gegensätzen* [to 1580] (1910); H. Leube, *Kalvinismus und Luthertum im Zeitalter der Orthodoxie* (vol. i only publd., 1928); H. E. Weber, *Reformation, Orthodoxie und Rationalismus* (Beiträge zur Förderung christlicher Theologie, Reihe 2, Bde. xxxv, li, etc., 1937 ff.); H. Stephan, *Geschichte der evangelischen Theologie seit dem Idealismus* (Sammlung Töpelmann, Reihe 1, ix; 1938); id., *Luther in den Wandlungen seiner Kirche* (ed. 2, 1951). E. Fischer, *Zur Geschichte der evangelischen Beichte* (Studien zur Geschichte der Theologie und der Kirche, viii, Hft. 2, and ix, Hft. 4; 1902–3); E. *Troeltsch, *Die Soziallehren der christlichen Kirchen und Gruppen* (1912), pp. 427–605 (Eng. tr., 1931, ii, 461–576). R. Rocholl, *Geschichte der Evangelischen Kirche in Deutschland* (1897). A. L. Drummond, *German Protestantism since Luther* (1951). A. Jundt, *Histoire résumée de l'Église luthérienne en France* (1935). A. R. Wentz, *The Lutheran Church in American History* (Philadelphia, [1923]). V. Firm, *The Crisis in American Lutheran Theology*. A Study of the Issue between American Lutheranism and Old Lutheranism (New York, 1927). J. A. McHugh, O.P., in *C.E.*, ix (1910), pp. 458–63, s.v.; H. E. Jacobs in *H.E.R.E.*, viii (1915), pp. 202–4, s.v.; W. Elert in *R.G.G.* (ed. 2), iii (1929), cols. 1779–87, s.v. 'Luthertum'; K. Algermissen in *L.Th.K.*, vi (1934), cols. 732–9, s.v. 'Luthertum'. See also bibl. to preceding entry and to individual countries where Lutherans are the main religious body.

LUX MUNDI. A 'Series of Studies in the Religion of the Incarnation' published in 1889 by a group of Oxford Anglican teachers under the editorship of C. *Gore, then Principal of Pusey House. The other contributors included H. S. *Holland, E. S. *Talbot, R. C. *Moberly and F. *Paget. Its purpose was 'to put the Catholic faith into its right relation to modern intellectual and moral problems'. At the time interest in the book was directed esp. to a few pages in Gore's own essay on 'The Holy Spirit and Inspiration', in which by accepting in principle the new critical views of the OT, he definitely broke with the conservative position of E. B. *Pusey and the *Tractarians. For this reason the book caused grave distress to many of the older school of High Churchmen, e.g. H. P. *Liddon.

LUXEUIL. The abbey, established *c.* 590 by St. *Columbanus on the site of the Roman Luxovium (about 20 miles north-east of Vesoul), soon became the most important in France. The abbey of *Corbie was founded *c.* 660 by some of its monks. Destroyed in 732 by the *Saracens, under *Charlemagne it was re-established, henceforward under the *Benedictine Rule. The abbey ceased to exist in 1790, though the abbey church is still in use as a parish church.

'Chronicon Luxoviense Breve' (from origins to 1039), ed. G. H. Pertz in *M.G.H.*, Scriptores, iii (1839), pp. 219–21; H. Baumont, *Étude historique sur l'abbaye de Luxeuil, 590–1790* (Luxeuil, 1895); E. de Beauséjour, *L'Église abbatiale de Luxeuil* (Besançon, 1891). H. *Leclercq, O.S.B., in *D.A.C.L.*, ix (pt. 2; 1930), cols. 2722–87, s.v., with full bibl. Lectionary of Luxeuil [Par. Lat. 9427], ed. P. Salmon, O.S.B., 1944. *Mélanges colombaniens.* Congrès International d'Études Colombaniennes. Luxeuil, 20–23 juil. 1950 (Paris, 1951).

LXX. An abbreviation in common use for the *Septuagint (q.v.).

LYCH-GATE (Old Eng. *lic* [cf. Ger. *Leiche*], 'corpse'). The roofed gateway to a churchyard beneath which the coffin is set down to await the arrival of the officiating minister.

LYING. A lie is a statement not in accordance with the mind of the speaker, made with the intention of deceiving. In the OT the practice of lying is denounced as an attribute of sinners (Lev. 19. 11, Ps. 5. 6, Prov. 6. 17), though it is sometimes recorded of otherwise righteous people, e.g. of *Abraham (Gen. 20. 2), *Jacob (Gen. 27. 32), and *David (1 Sam. 21. 2). These lies, however, are usually regarded as excusable because they were told in cases of necessity without the intention to hurt. In the NT the standard is higher, and lying is so abhorrent that for the disciple a simple affirmation of the truth is to take the place of an oath (Mt. 5. 37). St. Paul, too, exhorts Christians to put away falsehood (Eph. 4. 25, Col. 3. 9), and in the Bk. of Rev. the virgins who follow the Lamb are praised because 'in their mouth was found no lie' (14. 5). The NT teaching is followed by the Fathers, though with slight divergences. Some of them, e.g. *Origen, St. *Hilary, St. *Jerome and St. *Chrysostom, held that a lie may be lawful, e.g. in order to save an innocent man from death. St. *Augustine, however, and following him, St. *Thomas Aquinas, hold that lying is always sinful, because it perverts the nature of human speech, which is meant to express man's thought, not to disguise it. Acc. to St. Thomas lies are never lawful, and even 'officious' lies, i.e. those told for the benefit of someone without the intention of deceiving, and 'jocose' lies, told for amusement, are reprehensible. St. Thomas admits, however, that in certain cases it may be prudent to hide the truth under some 'dissimulation'. In modern times the problem of the lawfulness of lying in these cases, when, e.g., human life would be endangered or a secret violated not only by speaking the truth but also by preserving silence, has given rise to several theories attempting a solution. They either permit *mental reservation (q.v.) or assert that not everyone has the right to the truth (so, e.g., H. *Grotius and S. *Pufendorf), or, what seems most in agreement with common sense, that there may arise conflicts of duty in which the choice of a lie is a lesser evil. These, however, are exceptional cases which do not prejudice the general obligation of speaking the truth, without which an ordered human society which is built on mutual trust would become impossible.

LYNDHURST, Act of Lord. The Act (5 & 6 Will. IV, c. 54) passed in 1835 making all future marriages within the *prohibited degrees (e.g. marriage with a deceased wife's sister) *ipso facto* null and void, and not voidable (as had been the previous rule) only by an explicit pronouncement of the ecclesiastical courts.

LYNDWOOD, WILLIAM (1375 – 1446), English canonist and Bp. of *St. David's. Educated at Gonville and Caius College, Cambridge, he became Fellow of Pembroke Hall and later migrated to Oxford. In 1414 he was appointed by Abp. H. *Chichele his *Official Principal; in 1426 he became Dean of the *Arches; in 1433 Keeper of the Privy Seal; in 1434 Archdeacon of Stow; and in 1442 Bp. of St. David's. He was closely associated with Chichele in his proceedings against the *Lollards. His celebrated *Provinciale* (completed 1433) is a digest in five books of the synodical constitutions of the province of Canterbury from Abp. S. *Langton (1222) down to Abp. H. Chichele (1416), with glosses, and remains a standard authority on English ecclesiastical law and his text of the constitutions is that generally used for official purposes. As F. W. *Maitland pointed out, Lyndwood regarded the law of the C of E as dependent on the Papal codes and held that local constitutions must be interpreted in accordance with Papal law. Similarly the Archbishop's legislative and jurisdictional authority is superior to that of the provincial councils, but the Archbishop himself is bound by the legatine constitutions.

The latest and best ed. of Lyndwood's *Provinciale* is that publd. at Oxford, 1679. Text of Canons (only) repr. by J. V. Bullard–H. Chalmer Bell, London, 1929. J. M. Rigg in *D.N.B.*, xxxiv (1893), pp. 340–42.

LYNE, JOSEPH LEYCESTER. See *Ignatius, Father.*

LYONS, Council of (1245). Acc. to RC numbering the 13th *Oecumenial Council. The Council was convoked by *Innocent IV to deal with what, in his opening sermon, he called the five wounds of the Church, viz. the bad lives of the clergy and faithful, the danger of the Saracens, the Greek Schism, the invasion of Hungary by the Tatars, and the rupture between the Church and the Emp. *Frederick II. The bishops present, who did not greatly exceed 150, came chiefly from France, Italy, and Spain. The principal achievement of the Council was the formal deposition of the Emperor, who had been repeatedly excommunicated for having imprisoned cardinals and bishops on their way to a Council convoked by *Gregory IX, for being suspect of heresy through his association with the Saracens, and for pursuing a violently anti-ecclesiastical policy in Sicily. The objections of Thaddaeus of Suessa, Frederick's ambassador, that the accused had not been cited to the Council, that it was wholly irregular for the Pope to be plaintiff and judge at once, and that the Council was not truly oecumenical, were overruled. At the last session the *Dominicans and *Franciscans were charged with the publication of the decree throughout Christendom. The Council also enjoined the preaching of a Crusade for the liberation of the Holy Land from the Saracens, which, however, came to nothing.

Hardouin, vii, cols. 375–406; Mansi, xxiii (1779), cols. 605–86. Hefele–Leclercq, v (pt. 2; 1913), pp. 1633–79. J. B. Martin, *Conciles et bullaires du diocèse de Lyon* (Lyons thesis; 1905), pp. 252–83 and 624–9. Contemporary accounts of the Council in the 'Brevis nota eorum quae in primo Concilio Lugdunensi Generali gesta sunt' (repr. in Mansi, loc. cit., cols. 610–13), and by *Matthew Paris, *Chronica Majora*, under the year 1245 (ed. H. R. Luard, iv, R.S. 1877, pp. 430–79). M. Tangl, 'Die sogennante *Brevis Nota* über das Lyoner Concil von 1245' in *Mittheilungen des Instituts für Oesterreichische Geschichtsforschung*, xii (1891), pp. 246–53. T. G. von Karajan, 'Zur Geschichte des Concils von Lyon 1245' in *Denkschriften der kaiserlichen Akademie der Wissenschaften*. Phil. hist., Kl., ii (Vienna, 1851), pp. 67–100, with texts, pp. 103–17. S. Kuttner, 'Die Konstitutionen der ersten allgemeinen Konzils von Lyon' in *Studia et Documenta Historiae et Iuris*, vi (Rome, 1940), pp. 70–131. F. Vernet in *D.T.C.*, ix (pt. 1; 1926), cols. 1361–74, s.v. 'Lyon (Ier Concile œcuménique de)', with detailed bibl. See further bibl. to *Gregory IX* and *Innocent IV*.

LYONS, Council of (1274). Acc. to RC numbering the 14th *Oecumenical Council. It was convoked by *Gregory X to bring about the union with the Greek Church, the liberation

of the Holy Land, and the reform of morals. It was attended by about 500 bishops, 60 abbots, and 1000 other prelates. Among its better-known members were St. *Albert the Great, St. *Bonaventure, St. Philip Benizi, General of the *Servites, and the *Dominicans, Humbert de Romanis and Peter of Tarentaise, the future Innocent V. St. *Thomas Aquinas died on the way to the Council. The desire of the Greeks for reunion with Rome arose chiefly from their fear of Charles of Anjou, who sought to become Latin Emp. of Constantinople. The legates of the Greek Emperor, Michael VIII Paleologus, presented letters declaring their adherence to the obedience of the RC Church and to the articles of faith which the Apostolic nuncios had asked them to subscribe, and at the High Mass, at which St. Bonaventure preached the sermon, they repeated three times the *Filioque of the Creed. Besides defining in detail the *Double Procession of the Holy Ghost, the Council gave rulings about the election of the Pope in *conclave, suppressed some of the newly founded mendicant orders while approving esp. the Dominicans and *Franciscans, and deposed several prelates. Its principal achievement, the union of the Churches, proved ephemeral; it came to an end in 1289.

Hardouin, vii, cols. 669–722; Mansi, xxiv (1780), cols. 38–136. Hefele–Leclercq, vi (pt. 1; 1914), pp. 153–209. J. B. Martin, *Conciles et bullaires du diocèse de Lyon* (Lyons thesis; 1905), pp. 403–61 and 651–6. H. Finke, *Konzilienstudien zur Geschichte des 13. Jahrhunderts* (Ergänzungen und Berichtigungen zu Hefele–Knöpfler 'Conciliengeschichte', Band v und vi; 1891), pp. 1–18. W. Norden, *Das Papsttum und Byzanz*. Die Trennung der beiden Mächte und das Problem ihrer Wiedervereinigung bis zum Untergange des byzantinischen Reiches, 1453 (1903), esp. pp. 520–36. E. Göller, 'Zur Geschichte des zweiten Lyoner Konzils und des *Liber Sextus*' in *R.Q.*, xx (1906), pp. 81–7. M. Villain, 'La Question de l'union des Églises entre Grecs et Latins depuis le concile de Lyon jusqu'à celui de Florence' in *R.H.E.*, xvii (1921), pp. 260–305, 515–32, xviii (1922), pp. 20–60. A. Fliche, 'Le Problème oriental au second concile œcuménique de Lyon (1274)' in *O.C.P.*, xiii (1947), pp. 475–85. S. Kuttner, 'Conciliar Law in the Making. The Lyonese Constitutions (1274) of Gregory X in a MS. at Washington' in *Miscellanea Pio Paschini*, ii (Lateranum, N.S., xv; 1949), pp. 39–81, with useful reff. A. Fliche in Fliche–Martin, x (1950), pp. 487–503, with bibl. F. Vernet–V. Grumel, A.A., in *D.T.C.*, ix (pt. 1; 1926), cols. 1374–1410, s.v. 'Lyon (IIe Concile œcuménique de)', with detailed bibl.; M. Jugie, A.A., in *E.C.*, vii (1951), cols. 1398–1401, s.v. 'Lione, Secundo Concilio'.

LYONS, Rite of, the ancient modification of the Roman Rite which survives at Lyons. Acc. to Dom D. Bruenner, its characteristic ceremonies were the ancient Papal usages as adapted by *Charlemagne for his palace chapel at Aachen and introduced thence to Lyons by Bp. Leidrad *c.* 810. The Pontifical High Mass is celebrated with great splendour, the bishop being assisted by six priests (in *chasubles), seven deacons (in *dalmatics), seven subdeacons (in *tunics), seven acolytes (in *albs), and seven clerics (in capes).

D. Bruenner, O.S.B., *L'Ancienne Liturgie romaine*. Le rite lyonnais (1935).

LYRA. See *Nicolaus of Lyra.*

M

MAASSEN, FRIEDRICH (1823–1900), historian of early canon law. He began life as an advocate in N. Germany; but, finding himself debarred from public office through his conversion to the RC faith in 1851, he decided to devote himself to academic teaching, and later held professorships at Innsbruck (1857), Gratz (1860), and Vienna (1871). He was at first a strong opponent of the decrees of the *Vatican Council on Papal Infallibility, but in the *Kulturkampf he strenuously defended the claims of the RC Church. Of the first importance were his studies in the history of the ecclesiastical canons, embodied in his *Geschichte der Quellen und der Literatur des canonischen Rechts im Abendlande bis zum Ausgange des Mittelalters* (Bd. I, 1870 [all published]), which were the basis of the later researches of E. *Schwartz, C. H. *Turner and others. Among his other writings were his *Pseudoisidorstudien* (1885).

Obituary notice by R. von Scherer in *Historisches Jahrbuch*, xxi (1900), pp. 640–2. R. Naz in *D.D.C.*, vi ('1956'), cols. 687–9, s.v.

MABILLON, JEAN (1632–1707), *Maurist scholar. He entered the *Benedictine Order at St.-Remy in 1653 and spent most of his life (from 1664) at *St.-Germain-des-Prés. Prob. the most erudite and discerning of all the Maurists, he rendered immense services to historical research. In his *De Re Diplomatica* (1681), conceived as a reply to attacks on his order by the *Bollandist, D. *Papebroch, he put the study of palaeography for the first time on a scientific footing. In all, he produced some twenty folio works, including an edition of St. *Bernard (1667); the *Acta* of the Benedictine saints (with J. L. *D'Achéry; 9 vols., 1668–1701); the first four volumes of the Benedictine *Annales* (to A.D. 1066; 1703–7); and several collections of documents including a set of the *Ordines Romani. The attacks made by the *Trappist, J. A. le B. de *Rancé, on the engagement of religious in scholarly pursuits provoked his *Traité des études monastiques* (1691).

T. *Ruinart, O.S.B., *Abrégé de la vie de Dom Jean Mabillon* (1709; mod. ed. in 'Collection Pax', xxxv, 1933). [R. P. Tassin, O.S.B.], *Histoire littéraire de la congrégation de St.-Maur* (1770), pp. 205–69. Later Lives by M. Jadart (Reims, 1876), E. de Broglie (2 vols., Paris, 1888), and S. Bäumer (Augsburg, 1892). A. M. P. Ingold, *Mabillon en Alsace* (1902); J. Koesters, *Studien zu Mabillons römischen Ordines* (1905); F. *Cabrol, O.S.B., *Mabillon et les études liturgiques* (1908); J. B. Monnoyeur, O.S.B., *Un Grand Moine; Dom Jean Mabillon* (1933); E. Heer, O.S.B., *Johannes Mabillon und die Schweizer Benediktiner*. Ein Beitrag zur Geschichte der historischen Quellenforschung in 17. und 18. Jahrhundert [1938]. H. *Leclercq, O.S.B., in *D.A.C.L.*, x (pt. i; 1931), cols. 427–724, s.v.

MACARIUS, St., of Alexandria (4th cent.), Egyptian hermit. (He is often confused with *Macarius the Egyptian, q.v.). He retired into the desert at the age of 40 and seems to have lived near St. *Antony. He was persecuted by the Arian Patr. of Alexandria and, like Macarius the Egyptian, was a miracle-worker of repute. A monastic rule has been ascribed to him, probably erroneously. Feast day, 2 (or 19) Jan.

On the various Macarii see C. *Butler, *The Lausiac History of Palladius*, ii (1904), p. 193 f. The early authorities for Macarius the Alexandrian are *Palladius, *Hist. Laus.* 18, and *Rufinus, *Hist. Mon.*, 29, and *H.E.*, 2. 4. Coptic Life, ed. by E. Amélineau in *Annales du Musée Guimet*, xxv (1894), pp. 235–61. Writings ascribed to him in J. P. Migne, *PG*, xxxiv ('Rule', cols. 967–70 [Lat.], 'Sermo de Exitu Statuque Animarum post hanc Vitam', 385–92). See also É. Amann in *D.T.C.*, ix (1926), col. 1440 f., s.v.

MACARIUS, St., of Egypt (*c.* 300–*c.* 390), also known as **Macarius the Elder** or **Macarius the Citizen** (πολιτικός). Our knowledge of him derives from *Palladius's 'Lausiac History' and *Rufinus' 'History of the Monks' (apparently independent). He was a native of Upper Egypt who, at the age of about 30, joined a colony of monks in the desert of Scete, then a centre of Egyptian monasticism. He soon became renowned for his sanctity and miracles, and was ordained priest *c.* 340. Neither the 'Lausiac History' nor Rufinus mention any works of Macarius of Egypt, though the writings ascribed to him fill the greater part of a volume of J. P. *Migne's *Patrologia Graeca*. Feast day, 15 (or 19) Jan.

The fifty Homilies (ὁμιλίαι πνευματικαί) traditionally attributed to him are of uncertain authorship. They seem to have been largely influenced by non-Christian forms of mysticism, and it has been argued (e.g. by Dom L. Villecourt and G. L. Marriott) that their teaching betrays heretical elements of a *Messalian (Euchite) kind. They were probably produced not in Egypt but in *Constantinople or farther east. A set of seven further homilies was discovered by G. L. Marriott in a *Bodleian MS. (cod. Barocc. 213) and published in the *Harvard Theological Studies*, v (1918).

Palladius, *Hist. Laus.*, xvii; Rufinus, *Hist. Mon.*, xxviii. The Fifty Homilies were first pr. by J. Picus (Paris, 1559; repr. in J. P. Migne, *PG*, xxxiv, 449–822). Other writings also in J. P. Migne, *PG*, xxxiv. Crit. Lat. text of the (spurious) *ep. ad filios Dei* [*PG*, xxxiv, 406–10] ed. A. *Wilmart, O.S.B., in *Revue d'Ascétique et de Mystique*, i (1920), pp. 58–83; Syr. text ed. G. L. Marriott in *J.T.S.*, xx (1918–19), pp. 42–4. Eng. tr. of Fifty Homilies by A. J. Mason, S.P.C.K., 1921. L. Villecourt, O.S.B., 'La Date et l'origine des "Homélies spirituelles" attribuées à Macaire' in *Comptes-Rendus des séances de l'Académie des Inscriptions et des Belles-Lettres* (Paris, 1920), pp. 250–8. J. Stoffels, *Die mystische Theologie Makarius des Agypters* (1908). J. Stiglmayr, S.J., *Sachliches und Sprachliches bei Makarius* (Innsbruck, 1912). H. Dörries, *Symeon von Mesopotamien. Die Überlieferung der messalianischen 'Makarius'-Schriften* (T.U., lv, Hft. 1; 1941; claims to isolate the Messalian Catechism); E. Klostermann, *Symeon und Makarius* (*Abh.* (Berl.), 1943, Hft. 11). Bardenhewer, iii, 87–93 and 668 f.; Altaner (ed. 1950), pp. 224–6. É. Amann in *D.T.C.*, xi (pt. 1; 1926), cols. 1452–5, s.v.; E. Peterson in *E.C.*, vii (1951), col. 1740 f., s.v. 'Macario il Grande'.

MACARIUS, St. (d. *c.* 334), Bp. of *Jerusalem from *c.* 313. A strong upholder of orthodoxy against *Arianism, he was present at the Council of *Nicaea (325) where it has been suggested (F. J. A. *Hort) that he took a prominent part in drafting the Creed and also (with less probability) that he had a 'passage of arms' on the privileges of his see with his metropolitan, *Eusebius of Caesarea (A. P. *Stanley, followed by J. B. *Lightfoot). Soon after the Council he was commissioned by *Constantine to build the Church of the *Holy Sepulchre at Jerusalem after St. *Helena's invention of the Cross (326). Later he and his fellow-bishops of Palestine received a further letter from Constantine providing for the erection of a church at Mamre. Feast day, 10 Mar.

.Constantine's letter to Macarius are preserved in *Eusebius, *Vita Constantini*, iii, 30–2 and 52 f. F. J. A. Hort, *Two Dissertations* (1876), p. 59. A. P. Stanley, *Lectures on the History of the Eastern Church* (1861), p. 193 f.

MACARIUS MAGNES (4th–5th cent.), Christian apologist. Nothing is known of his life, unless he is to be identified with the Bp. of Magnesia who was the accuser of Heraclides of Ephesus at the Synod of the *Oak (403). He was the author of an apology in five books known as the 'Apocriticus', Μονογενὴς ἤ Ἀποκριτικὸς πρὸς Ἕλληνας περὶ τῶν ἀπορουμένων ἐν τῇ Καινῇ Διαθήκῃ ζητημάτων καὶ λύσεων, in which the objections which a learned and clever Neo-Platonist (perhaps *Porphyry) had raised against the Christian faith were (not altogether effectively) attacked. In the 9th cent. the treatise was used by the *Iconoclasts in defence of their doctrines, and in the 16th cent. it was quoted by F. *Torres from a copy in the *Marciana. Later the MS. was lost and the text not recovered till 1867, when a defective MS. was found at Athens; but this appears now to have also been lost. There also survive fragments of a (spurious) series of 'Homilies on Genesis' ascribed to the same writer.

Text of 'Apocriticus' ed. C. Blondel [–P. Foucart] (Paris, 1876). L. *Duchesne, *De Macario Magnete et Scriptis ejus* (Paris, 1877, with text of the spurious Gen. fragments, pp. 39–43). Eng. tr. of 'Apocriticus' by T. W. Crafer (S.P.C.K., 1919). On the MS. tradition, G. Schalkhausser, *Zu den Schriften des Makarios von Magnesia* (T.U., xxxi, Hft. 4; 1907). T. W. Crafer, 'Macarius Magnesius. A Neglected Apologist' in *J.T.S.*, viii (1906–7), pp. 401–23, 546–71. Bardenhewer, iv (1924), pp. 189–95; Altaner (ed. 1951), p. 290. G. *Salmon in *D.C.B.*, iii (1882), pp. 766–771; G. Bardy in *D.T.C.*, ix (pt. 2; 1927), cols. 1456–9.

MACARIUS OF MOSCOW (1816–82), Metropolitan of Moscow. Michael Bulgakov, son of a country priest, was educated at the seminary of Kursk and at the ecclesiastical academy of Kiev. After finishing his studies he became a monk, taking the name of Macarius, and later was appointed assistant lecturer in ecclesiastical and civil history at Kiev. From 1842 to 1857 he was professor of dogmatic theology at the academy of St. Petersburg. In 1857 he was appointed Bp. of Tambov, in 1859 transferred to Charkov, and in 1868 to Vilna. He became Metrop. of Moscow

in 1879. He is the best representative of 19th cent. Russian theologians. His two most important works, which were translated into several languages, were the *Introduction à la théologie dogmatique orthodoxe* (1847) and *Théologie dogmatique orthodoxe* (5 vols., 1845–1853). They reflect the official orthodoxy which was imposed on the Russian Church by Protasov to counteract Protestant influences, and are based on the Scriptures, the tradition as recognized by the Orthodox Church, and on arguments from reason. He also wrote a comprehensive *History of the Russian Church* (12 vols., 1857–82), which he traces from its beginnings to the Council of Moscow of 1667.

Life by T. Titov (2 vols., Kiev, 1895–8, in Russian). M. Jugie in *D.T.C.*, ix (1926), col. 1443 f., s.v. 'Macaire Bulgakov'; A. M. Ammann in *É.C.*, vii (1951), col. 1743 f.

MACAULAY, ZACHARY (1768–1838), Anglican Evangelical and philanthropist and father of Thomas Babington Macaulay (1800–1859), the historian. At the age of sixteen he went to Jamaica where he became manager of an estate which used slave labour. Disgust at the conditions under which the slaves worked determined him to wage war on the practice of slavery, and on returning to England in 1792 he made the cause of abolition his main concern. In 1793 he became governor of the colony of Sierra Leone, where he remained intermittently until 1799. A member of the '*Clapham Sect', he became deeply interested in the work of the *B.F.B.S. and of the *C.M.S. From 1802 to 1816 he edited the *Christian Observer*, the organ of the Clapham Sect. He was also one of the founders of London University.

Viscountess Knutsford [M. J. Holland, granddaughter], *Life and Letters of Zachary Macaulay* (1900). C. Z. Booth, *Zachary Macaulay. His Part in the Movement for the Abolition of the Slave Trade and of Slavery* (1934). L. Stephen in *D.N.B.*, xxxiv (1893), pp. 418–20. See also bibl. to *Clapham Sect*.

MACCABEES. The celebrated Jewish family, which was mainly instrumental in freeing Judaea from the Syrian yoke, and thus at a very critical period of its history stemming the threatened destruction of Judaism by the advance of Hellenism. The revolt was begun in 168 BC.. when Mattathias, then an aged priest, killed an apostate Jew who was about to offer sacrifice to Zeus on the abomination of desolation set up by *Antiochus Epiphanes in the Temple precincts at *Jerusalem. The struggle was carried on by his five sons, three of whom in turn, *Judas (who in the *Apocrypha is alone given the epithet 'Maccabaeus', Gk. Μακκαβαῖος meaning perhaps 'hammerer' or 'extinguisher'), Jonathan, and Simon, led the Jews in their struggle. Acc. to *Josephus (*Antiq.* 12. 6. 1), Mattathias was the great-great-grandson of Hasmon, and they are thus often known as the 'Hasmonaeans'.

The principal authority for the history of the family, besides Josephus, is I and II Macc. (see following entry). E. *Schürer, *Geschichte des jüdischen Volkes im Zeitalter*

Jesu Christi, i (ed. 4; 1901), pp. 200–301, with genealogical table, p. 779. A. W. Streane, *The Age of the Maccabees* (1898). A. Momigliano, *Prime linee di storia della tradizione maccabaica* (1930). E. Bickermann, *Die Makkabäer* (1935; Eng. tr., New York, 1947). F. M. Abel, O.P., 'Topographie des campagnes machabéennes' in *R. Bibl.*, xxxii (1923), pp. 495–521; xxxiii (1924), pp. 201–17, 371–87; xxxiv (1925), pp. 194–216; xxxv (1926), pp. 206–22 and 510–33. W. Fairweather in *H.D.B.*, iii (1900), pp. 181–7, s.v.; C. C. Torrey in *E.Bi.*, iii (1902), cols. 2850–8, s.v.; E. Beurlier in *Dict. Bibl.*, iv (1908), cols. 479–88, s.v. 'Machabées'.

MACCABEES, Books of.

Four Books, so called after the hero of the first two, *Judas Maccabaeus, are found in certain MSS. of the *Septuagint, of which the first two are included in the *Canon of the Greek and Latin Churches and the *Apocrypha of the English Bible. A fifth Book, contained in the Ambrosian *Peshitta (B.21 Inf.) and thus designated by Henry Cotton (1789–1879), appears to be merely a Syriac version of *Josephus, *The Wars of the Jews*, book vi.

The First Book consists of a history of the Jews from the accession of *Antiochus Epiphanes (175 B.C.) to the death of Simon Maccabaeus in 135 B.C. After a brief note on the reign of Alexander, it describes the desecration of the *Temple and the resistance of Mattathias the priest, continued by his sons, Judas, Jonathan and Simon Maccabaeus. It closes with the escape of Simon's son, John Hyrcanus, on a note of reassurance for the future. Extant only in Greek, though written in Hebrew (known to St. *Jerome, *Prol. Gal. ad Lib. Reg.*) it appears to have been the work of a Palestinian Jew of nationalist sympathies, prob. *c.* 100 B.C. It is the primary historical source for the period.

The Second Book describes the history of the Maccabean wars from the close of the reign of the Syrian king Seleucus IV (176 B.C.) to the victory of Judas Maccabaeus over Nicanor and the death of the latter (161 B.C.). It appears to have been written in Greek by a Jew of *Pharisaic sympathies some time after the composition of Book I and before 70 A.D. An epitome of a larger work by Jason of Cyrene (otherwise unknown; 2. 23) and of little historical value, it has a marked devotional note, emphasizing the care of God for His people in all things.

The Third Book describes the attempt of Ptolemy IV to enter the Sanctuary of the Temple (217 B.C.), his frustration, and his unsuccessful attempt to take vengeance on the Jews of Egypt. It appears to have been written in Greek, prob. by an Alexandrian Jew between 100 B.C. and 70 A.D., and is prob. thus named on the analogy of the events described with those of the Maccabaean period. Listed in the Biblical catalogue in the *Apostolic Canons (can. 85), the Book appears to have been held in high esteem in the early Church, but its canonicity is now admitted only by the Syriac Church.

The Fourth Book is a Greek philosophical treatise addressed to Jews on the supremacy of devout reason over the passions, illustrated by examples from the history of the Maccabees. The work was erroneously attributed to

*Josephus by *Eusebius, '*Suidas' and others. It was prob. written by a Hellenistic Jew of Alexandria at some time later than Book II and before 70 A.D.

The Books of the Maccabees contain important doctrinal teaching on immortality (2 Macc. 7. 9, 23, 37 and 4 Macc.), the value of suffering as a means of expiation (2 Macc. 7, 39 f.) and prayers for the dead (2 Macc. 12. 43–5). This last passage has played an important part in the defence of the doctrine of *Purgatory.

The Gk. text of I–IV Macc. is pr. in H. B. *Swete, *The Old Testament in Greek*, iii (1894), pp. 586–762; crit. ed. of Syriac text of IV Macc. by R. L. Bensley (Cambridge, 1895). H. Cotton, *The Five Books of Maccabees in English*, with notes (Oxford, 1832). Modern commentaries on I and II Macc. by C. G. Keil (Biblischer Commentar über das Alte Testament. Suppl. Band, Leipzig, 1875), J. Knabenbauer, S.J. (Cursus Scripturae Sacrae; Paris, 1907), W. O. E. Oesterley in R. H. *Charles (ed.), *The Apocrypha and Pseudepigrapha of the Old Testament*, i (1913), pp. 59–124 (on I Macc.), and J. Moffatt, ib., pp. 125–54 (on II Macc.), C. Gutberlet, (Alttestamentliche Abhandlungen, viii, Hftt. iii–iv; 1920. on I Macc.; ib., x, Hftt. iii–iv; 1927, on II Macc.), H. Bévenot, O.S.B. (Das Heilige Schrift des Alten Testaments, 1931), and F. M. Abel, O.P. (Études bibliques, 1949), with bibl.; also on I Macc. by W. Fairweather–J. S. Black (Cambridge Bible, 1897), S. Zeitlin (Jewish Apocryphal Literature, New York, 1950), and J. C. Dancy (Oxford, 1954); on III Macc. by C. Emmet in R. H. Charles (ed.), op. cit., pp. 155–73, and on IV Macc. by R. B. Townshend, ib., ii, 653–85, and A. Dupont-Sommer (Bibliothèque de l'École des Hautes Études, cclxxiv; 1939), and on III and IV Macc. by M. Hadas (Jewish Apocryphal Literature, New York, 1953). D. de Bruyne, O.S.B.–B. Sodar, O.S.B. (edd.), *Les Anciennes Traductions latines des* [I and II] *Machabées* (Anecdota Maredsolana, iv; 1932). J. *Wellhausen, 'Ueber den geschichtlichen Wert des Zweiten Makkabäerbuchs im Verhältnis zum Ersten' in *Nach.* (Gött.), 1905, pp. 117–63. B. Niese, *Kritik der beiden Makkabäerbücher* (1900). H. W. Ettelson, 'The Integrity of I Maccabees' in *Transactions of the Connecticut Academy of Arts and Sciences*, xxvii (1925), pp. 249–384. R. H. Pfeiffer, *History of New Testament Times with an Introduction to the Apocrypha* (New York [1949], London [1954]), pp. 461–522 [on I and II Macc.], with bibl. on I–III Macc., p. 537 f., and on IV Macc., p. 540. W. Fairweather in *H.D.B.*, iii (1900), pp. 187–96, s.v.; C. C. Torrey in *E.Bi.*, iii (1902), cols. 2857–86, s.v.; A. Lefèvre in *Dict. Bibl.*, Suppl. iv ('1953'), cols. 597–612, s.v. 'Maccabées (Livres I et II de'); J. B. Frey, ib., i (1928), cols. 428–30, s.v. 'Apocryphes de l'Ancien Testament', 12. Le IIIe Livre des Machabées', with bibl., and cols. 445–7, s.v. 'Apocryphes de l'Ancien Testament, 14. Le IVe Livre des Machabées', also with bibl. See also bibl. to *Apocrypha*.

MACCABEES, Feast of the Holy.

The feast kept in the W. Church on 1 Aug. to commemorate the seven Jewish brethren whose sufferings and deaths are described in 2 Macc. 7. The incident, which is doubtless referred to in Heb. 11. 35, struck the imagination of the early Christians and was celebrated by many of the Church fathers, notably St. *Gregory of Nazianzum (*Serm.* 15) and St. *Augustine (*Serm.* 300–2). The reputed relics of the martyrs were honoured at Antioch, the scene of their deaths, and later at S. Pietro in Vincoli in Rome (see *Lammas Day*, also observed on 1 Aug.). In the W. Church this is the only feast of any OT saint which has more than local observance.

M. Maas, 'Die Maccabäer als christliche Heilige' in *Monatschrift für Geschichte und Wissenschaft des Judenthums*, xliv (1900), pp. 145–56; H. Bévenot, O.S.B., 'The Holy Machabees' in *The Month*, cl (1927), pp. 107–14. On the early veneration of the Maccabees at Antioch, where the cultus prob. originated, see also H. *Leclercq, O.S.B., in

D.A.C.L., i (pt. 2; 1907), cols. 2375-9, s.v. 'Antioche (archéologie), IV: La Basilique et le culte des Macchabées'; cf. ib., x (pt. 1; 1931), cols. 724-7. H. Bévenot, O.S.B., in *L.Th.K.*, vi (1934), col. 818, s.v. 'Makkabäische Brüder'.

MACDONALD, GEORGE (1824–1905), Scottish novelist and poet. Educated at the university of Aberdeen and at Highbury College, London, he became a *Congregational minister, but in 1853 left the ministry to devote himself to literature. His writings, largely based on the life and customs of N.E. Scotland, include the novels *David Elginbrod* (1863), *Alec Forbes of Howglen* (1865), *Malcolm* (1875), and *Donal Grant* (3 vols., 1883). In his books MacDonald reveals firm religious faith, moral enthusiasm, and Christian optimism. He was also the author of several religious books, including *Unspoken Sermons* (1867, 1885, 1889) and the *Miracles of our Lord* (1886).

The Poetical Works of George MacDonald (2 vols., 1893). His Romance, *Lilith* (1895), was ed. by Greville MacDonald (son) (1924), with introd., pp. ix–xx. C. S. Lewis (ed.), *George MacDonald. An Anthology* (1946), with introd. preface, pp. 10–22. J. M. Bulloch, 'A Bibliography of George MacDonald' in the *Aberdeen University Library Bulletin*, v (1925), pp. 679–747, also issued separately (1925). J. Johnson, *George MacDonald*. A Biographical and Critical Appreciation (1906). Greville MacDonald (son), *George MacDonald and his Wife* (1924). Ronald MacDonald (son), 'George MacDonald: A Personal Note' in F. Watson (ed.), *From a Northern Window*. Papers, Critical, Historical and Imaginative (1911), pp. 55–113. A. Matheson in *D.N.B.*, *1901-1911*, pp. 513–15. S. J. Looker in *C.B.E.L.*, iii, p. 494 f.

MACE, DANIEL (d. *c.* 1753), NT textual critic. Little is known of his life beyond the fact that he was a *Presbyterian clergyman who ministered at Newbury from 1727 till his death. He anticipated conclusions which only met with general acceptance among textual critics over a century later, e.g. he disproved the authenticity of the text relating to the *Three Witnesses (1 Jn. 5. 7). His results were incorporated in *The New Testament in Greek and English* (2 vols., 1729), to which a reply in defence of the *textus receptus* was issued shortly afterwards by L. Twells (d. 1742).

H. McLachlan, 'An Almost Forgotten Pioneer in New Testament Criticism', *Hibbert Journal*, xxxvii (1939), pp. 617–25. A. Gordon in *D.N.B.*, xxxv (1893), p. 68 f.

MACEDONIUS (d. *c.* 362), Bp. of *Constantinople. In the divisions which followed the death of *Eusebius of Nicomedia (*c.* 341) he was one of the rival claimants to the see, and seems to have gained possession of it *c.* 342. He strongly supported the *Semi-Arian cause and defended his position at the Council of *Seleucia in 359. In 360 he was deposed by the Arian Council of Constantinople. From the end of the 4th cent. onwards he has been regarded as the founder of the '*Pneumatomachi' (q.v.) and thus caused the sect to be known as the 'Macedonians'; but it is doubtful how far this association is correct, as it seems clear that disputes about the Divinity of the Holy Spirit did not arise until after Macedonius' deposition. It is not known whether he left any writings.

F. *Loofs in *P.R.E.* (ed. 3), xii (1903), pp. 41–8, s.v.; G. Bardy in *D.T.C.*, ix (1926), cols. 1464–78, s.v., both with bibl. See also bibl. to *Pneumatomachi*.

MACHUTUS [otherwise **Malo, Maclovius, Maclou**], **St.** (d. *c.* 640), early Breton saint. Acc. to tradition, he was of either Welsh or Breton descent, and trained in the monastic life by St. *Brendan. He settled at Aleth, opposite the present town of St.-Malo, and is said to have lived an ascetic life, preached with great success, and founded several monasteries in the surrounding districts. One tradition asserts that he accompanied St. Brendan on his journey to *Iona. Feast day, 15 Nov.

Two Lives (both *c.* A.D. 850–900) exist, the one by the deacon Bili of Aleth, ed. by F. Plaine, O.S.B., in *Bulletins et Mémoires de la Société archéologique du département d'Ille-et-Vilaine*, xvi (1883), pp. 167–256; the other by an Anon. of Saintes, ed. by A. de La Borderie, ib., pp. 267–93. For texts, cf. also F. Lot, *Mélanges d'histoire bretonne* (1907), pp. 294–329, and 331–430; and id., 'Les Diverses Rédactions de la vie de saint Malo', ib., pp. 97–206. L. *Duchesne, 'La Vie de saint Malo. Étude critique' in *Revue celtique*, xi (1890), pp. 1–22 A. Poncelet, 'Une Source de la vie de S. Malo par Bili' in *Anal. Boll.*, xxiv (1905), pp. 483–6.

MACKAY, ALEXANDER MURDOCH (1849–90), *C.M.S. Missionary in Uganda. The son of a Free Church minister, he was educated at Edinburgh, where he studied classics, mathematics, and esp. engineering. In 1873 he went to Germany, where he obtained a position as a draftsman in Berlin. His thoughts had long turned to missionary work, and in 1876, despite the offer of a lucrative post, he was accepted by the C.M.S. for work in Africa. Having embarked for Victoria Nyanza, he finally reached Uganda in 1878 after constructing 230 miles of road. His printing of part of the Scriptures in Swahili interested King Mtesa, and he was granted permission to carry on missionary work. Soon, however, he met with opposition both from RCs and from Moslems. In 1884, when King Mtesa was succeeded on the throne of Uganda by Mwanga, Mackay was threatened with expulsion, but allowed to remain by reason of his engineering skill. The Christians meanwhile had to face fierce persecution, and many were slain. In 1887 Mackay was expelled, and settled at Usambiro on the southern end of Lake Victoria, where he reduced the vernacular of Uganda to writing, and then translated the Scriptures into it. His life was cut short by an attack of malaria in 1890.

A. M. Mackay, *Pioneer Missionary of the C.M.S. Uganda*, by his sister [Mrs. J. W. Harrison], (1890). A. H. Millar in *D.N.B.*, xxxv (1893), p. 118.

MACKINTOSH, HUGH ROSS (1870–1936), Scottish theologian. After a distinguished university career at Edinburgh, he studied at Marburg, specializing in philosophy. He was ordained in 1897, and after some years of effective and diligent pastoral work at Tayport and at Beechgrove Church, Aberdeen, he was appointed professor of systematic theology at New College, Edinburgh, in 1904. Here he exercised great influence as a teacher. He showed marked sympathy with the Liberal Movement in German Protestant theology and made it one of his chief objects to make German doctrines better known in Britain. In 1932 he was elected Moderator of the

General Assembly of the Church of Scotland. Among his written works the more important are *The Doctrine of the Person of Christ* (1912), in which he showed himself critical of the *Chalcedonian Christology and defended a modified *Kenotic doctrine, *The Christian Experience of Forgiveness* (1927), and *Types of Modern Theology* (1937, posthumous).

Sermons (1938), with Memoir by A. B. Macaulay, pp. 1–33, and list of his chief publications, p. ix. D. M. Baillie in *D.N.B., 1931–1940*, p. 581 f.

MACKONOCHIE, ALEXANDER HERIOT (1825–87), *Anglo-Catholic leader.

Educated at Wadham College, Oxford, he was ordained in 1849, and served in turn under W. J. *Butler at Wantage (1852–8) and C. F. *Lowder at St. George's in the East (1858–62). By 1862, when he was put in charge of the newly built church of St. Alban's, Holborn, he was recognized as an advanced 'ritualist', and from 1867 onwards was constantly prosecuted by the *Church Association for his ceremonial practices (e.g. the *mixed chalice and *altar lights). He eventually resigned in 1882, though he worked unofficially in the parish from 1883 until his sudden death in the Highlands in Dec. 1887.

E. A. Towle, *A. H. Mackonochie* (1890). W. A. J. Archbold in *D.N.B.*, xxxv (1893), p. 185 f.

MACLAREN, ALEXANDER (1826–1910), *Baptist preacher and expositor. Trained at Glasgow university and Stepney College, after twelve years as minister in Southampton (1846–58) he moved to Manchester and from the pulpit of Union Chapel (1858–1903) achieved a world-wide reputation by his sermons and writings. Twice President of the Baptist Union (1875; 1901), he also presided at the first Congress of the Baptist World Alliance in 1905.

G. G. Atkins (ed.), *The Best of Alexander Maclaren* (New York, 1949), with introd. pp. vii–xix (London, 1950, with introd. pp. 7–22). G. Eayrs, *An Index to Expositions of Holy Scripture by Alexander Maclaren* (1912), with an Appreciation of Dr. Maclaren by W. R. *Nicoll (repr. from the *British Weekly*), pp. v–xviii. D. Williamson–J. H. Shakespeare, *The Life of Alexander Maclaren* (1910); E. T. McLaren (cousin and sister-in-law), *Dr. McLaren of Manchester*. A Sketch (1911). A. Gordon in *D.N.B., 1901–1911*, p. 534, with list of publications.

MACLEOD, NORMAN (1812–72), Scottish divine. Educated at Glasgow and Edinburgh (under T. *Chalmers), he travelled on the Continent before his ordination in 1838. After holding appointments at Loudoun, Ayrshire, and Dalkeith, he became minister of the Barony Church, Glasgow, in 1851, and chaplain to Queen Victoria in 1857, with whom he was a great favourite. In 1869 he was elected Moderator of the General Assembly of the Church of Scotland. He was one of the most prominent and respected parochial ministers in Scotland in the 19th cent. Besides being the editor of the successful periodical *Good Words* (from 1860), he was the author of several books, among the best-known being his *Reminiscences of a Highland Parish* (1867).

O.D.C.C.–2 E 2

Memoir by his brother, Donald Macleod (2 vols., London, 1876). Shorter study by J. Wellwood ('Famous Scots Series', Edinburgh and London [1897]). T. Hamilton in *D.N.B.*, xxxv (1893), p. 217 f.

MACRINA, St. (c. 327–379), the elder sister of St. *Basil the Great and St. *Gregory of Nyssa. She is sometimes known as 'Macrina the Younger' to distinguish her from 'Macrina the Elder', her paternal grandmother. By her strength of character, she exercised a deep influence upon her brothers, esp. in winning Basil from a promising secular career for the Christian priesthood. She also established a flourishing community on the family estate in Pontus. The chief source for knowledge of her life is Gregory of Nyssa's *Vita Macrinae Junioris*, which also preserves a vivid account of their meeting on her deathbed. Her competence as a theologian is attested by the same writer's *De Anima ac Resurrectione*. Feast day, 19 July [of Macrina the Elder, 14 Jan.].

For the *Vita* see J. P. Migne, *PG*, xlvi, 959–1000. There is an Eng. trans., with Introduction, by W. K. L. Clarke (S.P.C.K., 1916).

MADAURAN MARTYRS, The (2nd cent.), first reputed Christian martyrs in Africa. The four martyrs, all of whom had Punic names (Namphamo, Miggin, Lucitas, Samae), supposedly suffered at Madura in 180. Our knowledge of them comes from Maximus of Madaura, a pagan grammarian of the late 4th cent., who inveighs against the populace for deserting the pagan cults and visiting the tombs of such uncultured barbarians. But J. H. Baxter has argued that the evidence is very insecure.

Maximus' letters and St. *Augustine's reply are contained in *S. Augustini Opera* (ed. Ben.), Epp. xvi, xvii. See also J. B. *Lightfoot, *Ignatius*, vol. i, pp. 506–8 (Note ζ). J. H. Baxter, 'The Martyrs of Madaura, A.D. 180', in *J.T.S.*, xxvi (1924–5), pp. 21–37.

MADEBA MAP. A map of Palestine and the Near East in coloured mosaics, uncovered in 1896 at Madeba to the east of the Dead Sea. It dates from the 5th–6th cents. and throws important light on the history of Palestinian topography.

M. J. *Lagrange, 'La Mosaïque géographique de Mâdaba' in *R. Bibl.*, vi (1897), pp. 165–84; C. Clermont-Ganneau *Receuil d'Archéologie orientale*, ii (1898), pp. 161–75 [Eng tr. in *Quarterly Statement of the Palestine Exploration Fund* (1897), pp. 213–25]; J. Germer-Durand, *La Carte de Madaba* (1897); A. Schulten, 'Die Mosaikkarte von Madaba und ihr Verhältnis zu den ältesten Karten und Beschreibungen des heiligen Landes' in *Abh.* (Gött.), N.F., iv, Hft. 2 (1900). H. *Leclercq, O.S.B., in *D.A.C.L.*, x (1931), cols. 806–85, s.v. 'Madaba' (with reproductions).

MADONNA, Ital. for 'My Lady'. A designation of the BVM, used esp. with reference to statues and pictures of her, e.g. 'The *Sistine Madonna'. The Madonna lily is the White Lily (*Lilium candidum*), which on account of its pure whiteness is a frequent emblem of Mary in art.

MADRAS CONFERENCE (1938). See *Tambaram Conference*.

MADRIGAL (apparently from early Ital. *mandriale*, 'pastoral'). The word denotes originally a type of poetry, and then, from its musical setting, a polyphonic song without instrumental accompaniment. In the 16th cent. the madrigals were adapted to devotional purposes, esp. in Italy, where G. P. da *Palestrina wrote his *Madrigali Spirituali*, much used by St. *Philip Neri in his popular services at the Oratory. In England the madrigals are usually entirely secular.

A. Einstein, *The Italian Madrigal* (3 vols., Princeton, 1949). E. H. Fellowes, *The English Madrigal Composers* (1921). E. J. Dent in *Grove's Dictionary of Music and Musicians*, ed. 5, by E. Blom, v (1954), pp. 488–98, with bibl.

MAFFEI, FRANCESCO SCIPIO (1675–1755), polyhistorian. A native of *Verona, he studied under the *Jesuits at Parma, fought in the Spanish Succession War, and became the friend of *Benedict XIV. He took a lively and practical interest in a variety of problems, attacking duelling (1710) and magic (1754) and defending the theatre (1713), which he actively fostered. In 1710 he founded the *Giornale de' letterati d' Italia* (ed. successively by A. and P. C. Zeno, 40 vols., Venice, 1710–40), with the *Osservazioni letterarie* (Verona, 6 vols., 1737–40), as a supplement. After extensive travels he published *Verona illustrata* (4 vols., Verona, 1731–2). In the contemporary controversies on grace, he attacked the *Jansenists in *De Haeresi Semipelagiana* (Rovereto, 1743) and other writings. His defence of usury in *Dell' impiego del danaro* (Verona, 1744) provoked Benedict XIV's encyclical of 1 Nov. 1745; but Maffei's work was not actually condemned and a 2nd edition appeared in 1746. His historical studies bore fruit in an edition of *Hilary of Poitiers (2 vols., Verona, 1730, a revision of the text of P. *Coustant) and other treatises. He also edited for the first time the 'Historia Acephala', a primary source for the Life of St. *Athanasius, from Cod. Ver. LX (58) (*Osservazioni letterarie*, iii (1738), pp. 60–83).

Opere (ed. A. Rubbi), 21 vols., Venice, 1790. *Opuscoli letterarii di Scipione Maffei con alcune sue lettere edite e inedite* (Venice, 1829). Modern ed. of *Opere drammatiche e poesie* by A. Avena (Bari, 1928). On his important contributions to palaeography, see L. Traube, *Vorlesungen und Abhandlungen* (ed. F. Boll), i (1909), pp. 43–8 (in 'Geschichte der Paläographie', pp. 1–80); cf. also W. Telfer, 'The Codex Verona LX (58)' in *H.T.R.*, xxxvi (1943), pp. 169–246, esp. pp. 228–31. Modern study by G. Silvestri (Treviso, 1954). C. Carletti in *E.C.*, vii (1951), col. 1812 f., s v.

MAGDALENE, ST. MARY. See *Mary Magdalene, St.*

MAGDALENES. In reference to St. *Mary Magdalene, the word has often been applied to reformed prostitutes. As a title it was widely adopted in the Middle Ages by religious communities consisting of penitent women ('*White Ladies'), to whom others of blameless lives often joined themselves. These communities, widely established in the 13th cent. in Germany, France, Belgium, Italy, Spain, and Portugal, often followed the Rule of St. *Augustine, though many German houses were affiliated to *Dominicans and *Franciscans. They are now almost extinct. The 'Magdalonettes', an order of Magdalens founded for the reformation of women in 1618 by Père Athanase Molé, a *Capuchin, is also extinct.

MAGDEBURG, Centuriators of. See *Centuriators of Magdeburg*.

MAGI, The. The first Gentiles to believe in Christ (Mt. 2. 1–12). Guided by a mysterious star, they came from the East to *Bethlehem with gifts of gold, frankincense, and myrrh for the Christ Child. They are called in the NT μάγοι (sages). The idea that they were kings first appears in Christian tradition in *Tertullian, who calls them *fere reges* ('almost kings'; *Adv. Jud.* 9 and *Adv. Marc.* 3. 13), and it became general from the 6th cent., on the basis of the implied reference in Ps. 72 (71), 10. The NT account says nothing on their number. *Origen is the first to give it as three, probably on account of their three gifts, and this has become the general tradition. Their names, Gaspar, Melchior, and Balthasar, are first mentioned in the 6th cent. *Excerpta Latina Barbari* and later in a quotation of St. *Bede from the *Collectanea et Flores*. In the Middle Ages they were venerated as saints, and the Milanese claimed to possess their relics, brought from *Constantinople in the 5th cent. These were taken to Germany by *Frederick Barbarossa in 1162, and are now enshrined in *Cologne Cathedral. The Adoration of the Magi early became one of the most popular subjects of representation in art, the first extant painting being in the 'Cappella greca' of the Priscilla Catacomb dating from the 2nd cent.

H. Kehrer, *Die hl. drei Könige in Literatur und Kunst* (2 vols., 1908–9). P. V. M. Benecke in *H.D.B.*, iii (1900), pp. 203–6, s.v.; F. Homes Dudden in *D.C.G.*, ii (1908), pp. 97–101, s.v., with bibl. R. Hindrenger in *L.Th.K.*, ii (1931), cols. 451–4, s.v. 'Drei Könige', with bibl. For iconography, H. *Leclercq, O.S.B., in *D.A.C.L.*, x (1931), cols. 980–1067, s.v. 'Mages'.

MAGNIFICAT. The Song of Praise (Lk. 1. 46–55) sung by the BVM when her cousin *Elizabeth had greeted her as the mother of the Lord. It is so named from the opening word of the Latin text, 'Magnificat anima mea Dominum' ('My soul doth magnify the Lord'). From a very early date, probably since St. *Benedict, it has been the canticle of *Vespers of the W. Church, and its importance is emphasized by its special antiphons and the incensing of the altar at solemn Vespers. It has been adopted at Evensong in the BCP. In the Greek Church it is used on certain days in the morning office (the *Orthros), sometimes in conjunction with the '*Benedictus'. Its language, which is steeped in the poetic tradition of the OT, shows notable resemblances to that of the 'Song of Hannah' (1 Sam. 2. 1 ff.), a fact which, in conjunction with some weak textual evidence (Lk. 1. 46 in a few MSS.: *et ait Elisabeth*), led A. *Loisy (1897) and A. *Harnack (1900) to argue not very convincingly that Luke attributed it originally to Elizabeth and not to Mary.

H. P. *Liddon, *The Magnificat*. Sermons in St. Paul's (1889). A. *Harnack, 'Das Magnificat der Elisabet (Luc. 1, 46–55) nebst einigen Bemerkungen zu Luc. 1 and 2' in *Sb.* (Berl.), 1900, pp. 538–56. L. Pirot in *Dict. Bibl.*, Suppl. ii (1934), cols. 1269–72, s.v. 'Évangile et commission biblique' with bibl. A. E. Burn in *D.C.G.*, ii (1917), pp. 101–3, s.v.; H. T. Henry in *C.E.*, ix (1910), pp. 534–6.

MAGNUS, St. (1), martyr. The supposed existence of the saint of this name occurring in the Roman martyrology for 19 Aug., where he is asserted to have suffered in the Decian persecution, seems to have arisen from a blunder. In Latin lists 'St. Andrew the Tribune', who in Greek calendars is described as the 'Megalomartyr' (μεγαλομάρτυς, i.e. the Great Martyr), became *Andreas Tribunus Magnus Martyr*; and this description was later erroneously understood to refer to two saints, Andrew the Tribune and Magnus the Martyr.

(2), (d. *c.* 750), Apostle of the Allgäu, Bavaria. Very little is known about him, as the one surviving Life, in which his relations with St. *Gall and St. *Columbanus are described, is obviously so full of anachronisms and errors as to make it of little value for historical purposes. Feast day, 6 Sept.

(3), (d. 1116), son of Earl Erlin, ruler of the Orkneys. Having been captured by the Norwegian king, Magnus Barefoot, he escaped to Malcolm III of Scotland (d. 1093), and later lived in the house of a British bishop. During the latter part of his life he devoted himself to prayer and penance. After Magnus Barefoot's death he returned to the Orkneys, where he shared the government with his cousin, Hakon, who treacherously killed him. Because of his saintly life he was soon venerated as a martyr though he did not die for the faith. He is supposed to have appeared to Robert Bruce before the battle of Bannockburn (1314) and promised him victory. Feast day, 16 Apr.

MAHOMETANISM. See *Islam*.

MAI, ANGELO (1782–1854), Italian philologist and palaeographer. Born of poor parents, he was educated at the Collegium Romanum and for a time belonged to the *Jesuit Order. In 1813 he was appointed custodian of the *Ambrosiana at Milan, and in 1819 prefect of the *Vatican library. In 1838 he became cardinal. He was renowned esp. as a reader of *palimpsests. He published four large collections of classical and theological texts, chiefly based on unpublished MSS. in the Vatican and Ambrosian libraries, viz. *Classicorum Auctorum* (10 vols., 1828–38), *Scriptorum Veterum Nova Collectio* (10 vols., 1830–8), *Spicilegium Romanum* (10 vols., 1839–44), and *Nova Patrum Bibliotheca* (8 vols., 1844–71; vols. 9 (1888) and 10 (1905) added later by J. Cozza-Luzi).

Lives by B. Prina (Bergamo, 1882) and G. Poletto (Bergamo, 1882; ed. 2, Siena, 1886). A. Bonnetty, *Table alphabétique analytique et raisonnée de tous les auteurs sacrés et profanes qui ont été découverts et édités récemment dans les 43 vol. publiés par le cardinal Mai* (1850). J. Cozza-Luzi, *Epistolario del cardinale Angelo Mai* (Bergamo, 1883); id., 'I grandi lavori del cardinale Mai' in *Bessarione*, vii (1904), pp. 103–33; viii (1905), pp. 59–74; ix (1905), pp. 308–17; x (1906), pp. 169–82. G. Gervasoni, *L' ambiente letterario milanese nel secondo decennio dell' ottocento*. Angelo Mai alla Bibliotheca Ambrosiana (Fontes ambrosiani xi, Florence, 1936), with full bibl. S. Timpanaro, 'Angelo Mai' in *Atene e Roma*, N.S., i (1956), pp. 3–34. H. *Leclercq, O.S.B., in *D.A.C.L.*, x (i; 1931), cols. 1196–202, s.v.

MAID OF KENT. See *Barton, Elizabeth*.

MAID OF ORLEANS. See *Joan of Arc, St.*

MAIER, JOHANNES. See *Eck, Johann*.

MAIMONIDES, MOSES (1135–1204), Jewish philosopher. He is known to Jewish writers as 'Rambam' (the consonants being the initial letters of 'Rabbi Moses ben Maimon'). Born at Cordova, he received a comprehensive education from his father, a learned *Talmudist. During an anti-Jewish persecution (1149) he fled and settled in Fez, where he wrote his 'Epistle on Apostasy' to strengthen his co-religionists against Mohammedanism. In 1165 he had to leave Morocco and, after a brief stay in Palestine, finally settled at Fostat (Cairo) where he became head of the Jewish community. In 1168 he completed his commentary on the *Mishnah, known as the *Siraj* or 'Luminary'; it was a notable contribution to exegesis and scholarship. He brought out *c.* 1180 his 'Mishneh Torah' in Hebrew, a Talmudic code in fourteen parts arranged by subject matter, which was often commented on; it consists of a classification of Jewish religious doctrines, their interpretation by the masters, and their moral and philosophical implications. All his other works were written in Arabic. In 1190 appeared his principal treatise, the 'Guide for the Perplexed' (*Dux Neutrorum sive Dubiorum*). Its purpose was to achieve a working harmony between reason and faith. Its three parts treat of (1) the idea of God; (2) the arguments for the existence of God, His manifestations, the world of spirits, the creation of the world in time, and prophecy; and (3) the interpretation of *Ezekiel's vision, the problem of evil, the end of creation, Divine Providence and Divine knowledge. Maimonides' aim was to achieve a synthesis of the data of the Jewish revelation and the findings of human reason proposed by *Aristotle. His work had a profound influence on the Christian thought of the Middle Ages, esp. on St. *Albert the Great and St. *Thomas Aquinas.

Maimonides' works have been repeatedly repr. from the 15th cent. onwards, but there is no collected ed. The principal ed. of his 'Guide' (Arab. text) is that of S. Munk, with Fr. tr. (3 vols., Paris, 1856–66); Eng. tr. by M. Friedländer (3 vols., London, 1881–5). Eng. tr. (in progress) of the *Mishneh Torah* by J. J. Rabinowitz, H. Danby, H. Klein, and others (Yale Judaica Series, ed. J. Obermann, New Haven, Conn., 1949 ff.). Eng. tr. from various works by A. Cohen as *The Teachings of Maimonides* (1927).

Studies by A. Geiger (Breslau, 1850), D. Yellin–I. Abrahams (London, 1903), J. Müntz (Frankfurt am Main, 1912), A. Heschel (Berlin, 1935), and S. Zeitlin (New York, 1935). W. Bacher–M. Brann–D. Simsonsen–J. Guttmann, *Moses ben Maimon. Sein Leben, seine Werke und sein Einfluss.* *Zur Erinnerung an den siebenhundertsten Todestag des Maimonides* (2 vols., 1908–14). I. Epstein (ed.), *Moses Maimonides, 1135–1204.* Anglo-Jewish Papers in connexion with the eighth centenary of his birth (1935), with bibl. of Eng. works, pp. 231–48. S. W. Baron (ed.), *Essays on Maimonides.* An Octocentennial Volume (New York, 1941). A. Rohner, O.P., *Das Schöpfungsproblem bei Moses Maimonides, Albertus Magnus und Thomas von Aquin* (B.G.P.M., xi, Hft. 5; 1913), pp. 1–44. L. Roth, *The Guide* for the Perplexed. *Moses Maimonides* (1948). B. Z. Bokser, *The Legacy of Maimonides* (New York, 1950). Überweg, ii, 339–41, with bibl. p. 727. I. Broydé–J. Z. Lauterbach in *J.E.* (1905), pp. 73–86, s.v. 'Moses ben Maimon'.

MAISTRE, J. M. COMTE DE. See *De Maistre, J. M. Comte*.

MAITLAND, FREDERIC WILLIAM (1850–1906), historian. The grandson of S. R. *Maitland, he was educated at Eton and at Trinity College, Cambridge, and called to the bar at Lincoln's Inn in 1876. In 1884 he was appointed reader in, and in 1888 Downing professor of, English law at Cambridge. In his *Roman Canon Law in the C of E* (1898) he maintained against nearly all previous writers, including W. *Stubbs (who was convinced by Maitland's arguments), that in the Middle Ages the English secular courts recognized the Roman canon law as binding on the English clergy apart from its re-enactment in the English synods. His crucial instance was the legitimation of natural-born children by subsequent matrimony. He also contributed the essay on 'The Anglican Settlement and the Scottish Reformation' to the *Cambridge Modern History* (vol. ii, ch. 16) and was the author of a large number of other historical writings.

Collected Papers, ed. H. A. L. Fisher (3 vols., Cambridge, 1911); some of these, with additions, ed. H. D. Hazeltine–G. Lapsley–P. H. Winfield, as *Selected Essays* (ib., 1936). A. L. Smith, *Frederick William Maitland.* Two Lectures and a Bibliography (Oxford, 1908). Fuller list by H. A. L. Fisher (Cambridge, 1910). B. F. Lock in *D.N.B., 1901–1911,* pp. 552–5.

MAITLAND, SAMUEL ROFFEY (1792–1866), ecclesiastical historian. He was educated at St. John's and Trinity Colleges, Cambridge, and called to the bar, but soon abandoned the idea of a legal profession. In 1821 he was ordained deacon in the C of E (previously he had been a Nonconformist), and from 1823 to 1827 was Perpetual Curate of Christ Church, *Gloucester. He then travelled abroad for some years, taking a keen interest in missionary work among the Jews. In 1838 he was appointed *Lambeth librarian. Maitland was a student of immense industry with a great variety of interests. Among his many writings were: *Facts and Documents illustrative of the History, Doctrine, and Rites of the Ancient Albigenses and Waldenses* (1832), a work which was occasioned by a controversy with the *Irvingites; *The Dark Ages* (1844); and *Essays on Subjects connected with the Reformation in England* (1849). The two works last named had first appeared in the *British Magazine*, of which Maitland took over the editorship from H. J. *Rose in 1839.

A. Jessopp in *D.N.B.*, xxxv (1893), pp. 371–4, s.v., with notes on MS sources.

MAJOR ORDERS. The higher grades of the Christian ministry in contradistinction from the *Minor Orders (q.v.). Since the time of *Innocent III, the *subdiaconate has been accounted a major order and the diaconate and the priesthood reckoned as the other two to preserve the original number of three in all. In earlier times the episcopate was more commonly reckoned as an order distinct from the priesthood. This distinctness of the episcopal order was denied by St. *Thomas Aquinas and again by the Council of *Trent (sess. xxiii, cap. 2). Acc. to modern RC practice no one can receive major orders who has not previously received the minor orders; and those on whom they are conferred are bound to celibacy and the recitation of the Divine Office.

MAJORISTIC CONTROVERSY. The controversy aroused among the German Protestants in 1551 through the teaching of Georg Major (or Maier; 1502–74) to the effect that the performance of good works was necessary to a Christian man's salvation. This teaching was promptly attacked by M. *Flacius, N. Amsdorf (1483–1565), and others as opposed to the *Lutheran doctrine of *justification by faith only. Though Major elaborated further, and perhaps modified, his teachings, he continued to hold that good works were necessary, though he allowed they were only a *token* of man's justification (which was by faith alone). He received very little support from his contemporaries.

G. Major's *Werke* were ed. in 3 vols., Wittenberg (1569–70; many works omitted). O. Ritschl, *Dogmengeschichte des Protestantismus,* ii (1912), esp. pp. 371–98. G. Kawerau in *P.R.E.* (ed. 3), xii (1903), pp. 85–91, s.v. 'Major, Georg'.

MAJUSCULE SCRIPT. See *Uncial Script*.

MALABAR CHRISTIANS. A group of Christians of S.W. *India, living on the coast in the district of Travancore and Cochin, also known as 'Thomas Christians'. They follow the 'Acts of *Thomas' (q.v.) in tracing their origin to St. *Thomas the Apostle, who acc. to their tradition landed in these parts and crossed to Madras, near which city his shrine is marked by a cross bearing a 7th cent. Pahlavi inscription. More reliance is to be put on the assertion of *Cosmas Indicopleustes that there were Christians in India before 550. These early Christians were probably of E. Syrian origin, and for many centuries maintained a connexion with the *Nestorian Patriarch of Bagdad, from whom they obtained new bishops in 1490. Their Nestorianism was not marked, however, and in the 16th cent. the Portuguese recognized them as orthodox. At the Synod of *Diamper (1599) they formally abjured Nestorius and allied themselves with Rome. Interference with their customs caused a break with the W. in 1653; but in 1662 many returned to communion with Rome while the rest joined themselves to the *Jacobites, and these two groups have existed alongside each other ever since. The latter group has been disturbed by constant internal dissensions and been frequently in conflict with its Jacobite Patriarch, and in 1925 it opened negotiations for reunion with Rome. The result was the creation of the Malankarese *Uniat Church (q.v.) in 1930. There has also been some *rapprochement* between the Jacobites and the C of E.

Each of these three groups has its special liturgy. The Catholics of 1662 use the Nestorian Liturgy of *Addai and Mari, very slightly Romanized. The Jacobites adopted the W. Syrian Antiochene Liturgy and those who joined the Malankarese Church were allowed to retain this liturgy. All use Syriac and the vernacular in their liturgies.

M. Geddes, *The History of the Church of Malabar from the Time of its first being discovered by the Portuguese in the Year 1501* (tr. from the Portuguese into English, London, 1694). J. F. Raulin, *Historia Ecclesiae Malabaricae cum Diamperitana Synodo* (Rome, 1745). W. Germann, *Die Kirche der Thomaschristen* (Gütersloh, 1877). G. M. Rae, *The Syrian Church in India* (1892). J. C. Panjikaran, *The Syrian Church in Malabar* (Trichinopoly, 1914); id., *Christianity in Malabar*, with special reference to the St. Thomas Christians of the Syro-Malabar Rite (Orientalia Christiana, fasc. xxiii; 1926). T. K. Joseph, *Malabar Christians and their Ancient Documents* (Trivandrum, 1929). F. E. Keay, *A History of the Syrian Church of India* (S.P.C.K. [1938]). L. W. Brown, *The Indian Christians of St. Thomas* (1956). R. H. *Connolly, 'The Work of Menezes on the Malabar Liturgy' in *J.T.S.*, xv (1914), pp. 396–425, 569–89, with addition by E. *Bishop, pp. 589–93. L. K. Ananthakrishna Ayyar, *Anthropology of the Syrian Christians* (Ernakulam, 1926). G. B. Howard, *The Christians of St. Thomas and their Liturgies* (1864; with trr. of several liturgies). W. Logan, *Malabar*, i (Madras, 1887), pp. 199–213. A. *Fortescue *The Lesser Eastern Churches* (1913), pp. 353–79; D. Attwater, *The Catholic Eastern Churches* (revised ed. Milwaukee, Wisc., 1937) pp. 243–55. A. J. Maclean in *H.E.R.E.*, xii (1921), pp. 178–80, s.v. 'Syrian Christians, 9'. É. Amann in *D.T.C.*, ix (pt. 2; 1927), cols. 1704–45, s.v. 'Malabres (Rites)'. E. Tisserant, ib., xiv. (pt. 2; 1941), cols. 3080–162, s.v. 'Syro-Malabare (Église)'. See also bibl. to *India, Christianity in*, and *Thomas, St.*

MALACHI, Book of. The last of the 12 *Minor Prophets and the last Book of the OT, acc. to the English order. The Heb. 'Malachi' (מַלְאָכִי) means 'my messenger', and the word is probably not to be considered the actual name of the prophet, although a few scholars hold that one of *Ezra's assistants was so called. The writer, whoever he was, begins by emphasizing the love of God for His people (1. 2–5), which is only reciprocated by insincere worship and empty, corrupt, and unworthy priestcraft (1. 6–2. 9); he then condemns the practice of mixed marriages and divorce (2. 10–16); he announces that a day of judgement will surely come (2. 17–3. 6), and that happiness and prosperity can be restored only by the regular payment of tithes and other dues (3. 7–12); he touches on the age-long problem of innocent suffering and the ultimate reward of the righteous (3. 13–4. 3); and in

conclusion he exhorts his readers to keep the law of *Moses (4. 4–6).

The attitude (typified by Ezra) of superiority over all non-Jews is replaced in this Book by a lofty universalism. The language and thought of the Book are those of the age following the Exile (i.e. after 538), and the Jewish *Temple has evidently been rebuilt. Contemporary Jewish expectations for the future may be seen in the role given to *Elijah (4. 5; cf. Lk. 1. 17). The passage about the 'pure offering' in 1. 11 is often quoted in Christian tradition from St. *Justin Martyr onwards as a prophecy of the *Eucharist.

Commentaries by W. E. Barnes (Cam. Bib., RV, 1917), J. M. P. Smith (I.C.C. on Hag., Zech., Mal., Jon., 1912; separate pagination). A. von Bulmerincq, *Einleitung in das Buch des Propheten Maleachi* (Acta et Commentationes Universitatis Dorpatensis B. Humaniora, i, pt. 2; iii, pt. 1; vii, pt. 1; 1921–6); id., *Kommentar* (ib., xv, pt. 1; xix, pt. 1; xxiii, pt. 2; xxvi, pt. 1; xxvii, pt. 2; 1929–32). O. Holtzmann, 'Der Prophet Maleachi und der Ursprung des Pharisäerbundes' in *Archiv für Religionswissenschaft*, xxix (1931), pp. 1–21. Further commentaries under *Minor Prophets*.

MALACHY, St. (1094–1148), Abp. of *Armagh. He was one of the foremost figures in *Ireland in the Middle Ages. A strong supporter of Roman practices and customs, he became involved in a long struggle between the pro- and anti-Roman parties, and was for several years unable to secure possession of the see of Armagh to which he had been nominated in 1129. In 1139 he set out for Rome to seek the *pallium from Innocent II, and on the way met St. *Bernard at *Clairvaux, who became his close friend and biographer. Though the Pope received him favourably, he refused to grant the pallium until assured of the real situation in Ireland. On the return journey St. Malachy again visited Clairvaux, and taking thence four of its monks, introduced the *Cistercian Order into Ireland. In 1148 he was dispatched on a second visit to Rome to obtain the pallium, but died at Clairvaux on the way in the arms of St. Bernard. Feast day, 3 Nov.

The so-called 'Prophecies of Malachy', contained in a document composed apparently in 1590, are erroneously ascribed to him. They purport to give a concise motto for every Pope from Celestine II (1143-4) to 'Peter II' at the end of the world (*In persecutione extrema S.R. Ecclesiae sedebit Petrus II Romanus*). *Pius IX, e.g., corresponded with *crux de cruce*; *Pius X with *ignis ardens*; and *Pius XII is *papa angelicus*. But singularly inappropriate was the description of *Benedict XIV as a 'rustic animal' (*animal rurale*).

Life and two metrical sermons by St. Bernard of Clairvaux ed. J. *Mabillon, O.S.B., in his ed. of St. Bernard's Works, repr. in J. P. Migne, *PL*, clxxxii, 1073–118, and clxxxiii, 481–90. Eng. tr., with good introd., by H. J. Lawlor (S.P.C.K., texts, 1920). E. Vacandard, 'Un Évêque d'Irlande, au XIIᵉ siècle. Saint Malachie O'Margair' in *R.Q.H.*, lii (1892), pp. 5–72. Popular modern life by A. J. Luddy (Dublin, 1930).

The Prophecies were first pr. by A. Wion, O.S.B., *Lignum Vitae, Ornamentum et Decus Ecclesiae*, i (Venice, 1595), pp. 307–11. A. *Harnack, 'Über den Verfasser und den Zweck der Prophetia Malachie de Summis Pontificibus (1590)' in *Z.K.G.*, iii (1879), pp. 315–24. H. Thurston, S.J.,

The War and the Prophets (1915), pp. 120–61 ('The So Called Prophecy and St. Malachy'). J. F. Kenney, *Sources of the Early History of Ireland*, i (New York, 1929), pp. 764–7, with further bibl. Further bibl. also by A. Bigelmair, S.J., in *L.Th.K.*, vi (1934), col. 822, s.v.; A. Ghinato, O.F.M., in *E.C.*, vii (1951), col. 1884 f.

MALALAS, JOHN. See *John Malalas.*

MALANKARESE CHURCH. The group of *Malabar Christians (q.v.) who entered into communion with Rome in 1930. An unsuccessful attempt of a section of the Jacobite Malabarese at reunion with the W. was made *c.* 1870 by their Bishop, Mar Dionysius IV. The group, which eventually became *Uniat in 1930, consisted of Mar Ivanios (who had shortly before been raised to the rank of metropolitan) and his suffragan, Mar Theophilus, with some 10,000 followers. By the papal constitution *Christo pastorum principi* of 11 June 1932, Trivandrum was made the metropolitan see. They retain their ancient Antiochene rite.

D. Attwater, *The Catholic Eastern Churches* (Milwaukee, Wisc. [1935], pp. 196–99. M. Ivanios, 'The Malabar Reunion' in *Pax*, xxi (1931), pp. 1–4. See also bibl., s.v. 'Malabar Christians'.

MALCHION (3rd cent.), *Antiochene presbyter. He was head of the Hellenic rhetorical school at Antioch and chosen for his orthodoxy and great learning to interrogate *Paul of Samosata at the Council of Antioch (*c.* 270). He successfully forced Paul to reveal his heretical doctrines and, acc. to St. *Jerome, himself composed the synodical letter which condemned them.

The chief early authorities are *Eusebius, *H.E.*, VII, 29 f., and *Jerome, *De vir. ill.*, 71. The (scattered) fragments of Malchion's Dialogue with Paul, taken down in shorthand, have been collected by F. *Loofs, *Paulus von Samosata* (T.U., xliv, No. 5, 1924), pp. 334–7. Cf. also G. Bardy, *Paul de Samosate* (1923), and H. de Riedmatten, O.P., *Les Actes du procès de Paul de Samosate* (Paradosis, vi, Fribourg, 1952). Brief art. by G. Bardy in *D.T.C.*, ix (pt. 2; 1927), cols. 1765 f., s.v.

MALDONADO, JUAN (1533–83), 'Maldonatus', Spanish theologian and exegete. After being educated at the university of Salamanca, he entered the *Jesuit Order in 1562. In 1564 he became professor at the Jesuit Collège de Clermont at Paris, where his theological lectures attracted enormous audiences. In 1574 the *Sorbonne attacked his teaching as heretical; but, though vindicated by the Bp. of Paris in 1576, he withdrew from Paris. His work went far towards rescuing Catholic theology from the barbarous language and barrenness of ideas then prevalent, and his commentaries on the Gospels (2 vols., 1596–7) are held in deservedly high repute. All his writings are posthumous, and some of those attributed to him are to be treated with caution, as they appear to be inaccurate reproductions of notes taken down at his lectures.

Opera Varia Theologica, publ. in 3 vols. (Paris, 1677), with short life in vol. iii. R. Galdos, S.J. (ed.), *Miscellanea de Maldonato anno ab eius nativitate quater centenario, 1534²–1934* (Madrid, 1947), with life, pp. 11–6, and bibl.,

pp. 17–21, and certain of his Orations. J. M. Prat, S.J., *Maldonat et l'université de Paris au XVIᵉ siècle* (Paris, 1856). A. Astrain, S.J., *Historia de la Compañia de Jesús en la asistencia de España*, ii (1905), pp. 357–65. J. Iturrioz, 'Maldonado en Salamanca' in *Estudios eclesiásticos*, xvi (1942), pp. 221–34. Sommervogel, v (1894), cols. 403–14, and ix (1900), col. 631. É. Amann in *D.T.C.*, ix (pt. 2; 1927), cols. 1772–6, s.v. 'Maldonat'; A. Carrozzini, S.J., in *E.C.*, vii (1951), col. 1902, s.v.

MALEBRANCHE, NICOLAS (1638–1715), French philosopher. He became an *Oratorian in 1660. His most important works are *Recherche de la vérité* (1674) and *Traité de la nature et de la grâce* (1680). Some of his positions derive from *Augustine and *Descartes, but his system is profoundly original. He denied that any action of matter upon mind was possible, and explained sensation as the effect of a new creative act in the mental order to correspond with things in the physical creation ('*Occasionalism'). His principle of *simplicité des moyens* (that God exhibits His omnipotence by acting always in the simplest possible way) led him into a form of *Ontologism, in which God was the immediate cause of all human knowledge, and the 'place of our ideas'; consequently, he taught that our first and simplest idea is that of the infinite. Again, the complexity of the natural creation as a whole was justified in his system solely by the fact of its being eternally ordained (as the simplest possible means) towards the Incarnation of the Word and the reign of grace. A. *Arnauld, J. B. *Bossuet, and F. *Fénelon wrote against various aspects of his doctrine during his lifetime.

Crit. ed. of Malebranche's works by D. Roustan (Paris, 1938 ff.). Older edd. by E. de Genoude–H. de Lourdoueix (2 vols., Paris, 1837) and (less complete) by J. Simon (2 vols., Paris, 1842). Besides various older trr. of Malebranche's writings, there is a good Eng. tr. of the *Dialogues on Metaphysics and on Religion* by M. Ginsberg ('Library of Philosophy', 1923.) E. A. Blampignon, *Étude sur Malebranche d'après des documents manuscrits, suivie d'une correspondance inédite* (1862). Studies by L. Ollé-Laprune (2 vols., Paris, 1870–2), H. Joly ('Les Grands Philosophes', 1901), and R. W. Church (London, 1931). J. Vidgrain, *Le Christianisme dans la philosophie de Malebranche* (1923); H. Gouhier, *La Philosophie de Malebranche et son expérience religieuse* (1926). Überweg, iii, 265–8, with bibl., p. 663 f. J. Bridge, S.J., in *C.E.*, ix (1910), p. 568 f, s.v.; J. Wehrlé in *D.T.C.*, ix (pt. 2; 1927), cols. 1776–1804, s.v.

MALINES CONVERSATIONS. The meetings of a group of Anglican and RC theologians held at Malines between 1921 and 1925 under the presidency of Cardinal D. J. *Mercier. The initiative came from Lord *Halifax. The others who took part were, on the Anglican side, J. A. *Robinson, W. H. *Frere, C. *Gore, and Dr. B. J. Kidd (the Warden of Keble), and on the Roman side Mgr J. E. van Roey, the Abbé F. Portal, P. *Batiffol, and the Abbé H. Hemmer; and all the meetings except the first took place with the cognizance of the Holy See and the Abp. of *Canterbury. It was agreed that the Pope should be given primacy of honour; that the Body and Blood of Christ are indeed taken in the Eucharist; that the Sacrifice of the Eucharist is a true sacrifice, but after a mystical manner; that Episcopacy is by Divine law; and that

Communion in both kinds is a matter of discipline not of dogma. The more Protestant sections of the C of E viewed the Conversations with great suspicion, and the publication of the Report was long delayed for fear that it might fan the opposition to the Revised Prayer Book. Lord Halifax, however, published it early in 1928. Though the Conversations issued in no tangible result and further progress was hindered by *Pius XI's encyclical '*Mortalium Animos' (1928), they indirectly stimulated the movement for co-operation between the C of E and the RC Church.

Halifax, *The Conversations at Malines, 1921–5* (1930); W. H. *Frere, *Recollections of Malines* (1935); G. K. A. Bell, *Randall Davidson* (1935), ch. lxxix; J. G. Lockhart, *Viscount Halifax*, vol. ii (1936), chs. xviii–xxii. J. de Bivort de la Saudée, *Anglicains et Catholiques* (2 vols., Brussels, 1949), with docc. in vol. ii.

MALLEOLUS (or MALLEUS) HAERETICORUM (Lat., 'Hammer of the Heretics'). A title applied to various persons who contended vigorously with heretics, among them St. *Antony of Padua, St. Peter *Canisius, and Johann *Faber (1478–1541).

MALMESBURY. The town, formerly the seat of a *Benedictine abbey, traces its origin to the Scottish or Irish monk Maildulf, who founded a school there *c.* 635. It developed into a monastery under his pupil, St. *Aldhelm, who became its first abbot and later Bp. of *Sherborne. The house flourished under him and his successors, and enjoyed the favour of many English kings, Athelstan, William the Conqueror, and later Richard II and *Henry V, among them. Throughout the Middle Ages it remained one of the principal English monasteries and sent its mitred abbots to Parliament; its most famous member was the historian, *William of Malmesbury. The monastery was dissolved in 1539. The principal portions of the abbey that remain now form the parish church of St. Mary and St. Aldhelm.

J. S. Brewer and C. T. Martin (edd.), *Registrum Malmesburiense* (R.S., 2 vols., 1879–80). T. Perkins, *The Abbey Churches of Bath and Malmesbury and the Church of Saint Laurence, Bradford-on-Avon* (Bell's Cathedral Series, 1901), pp. 33–101; R. H. Luce, *Pages from the History of the Benedictine Monastery of Malmesbury* (Devizes, 1929). H. Breakspear, 'Malmesbury Abbey' in *Archaeologia*, lxiv (1913), pp. 399–436. W. *Dugdale, *Monasticon Anglicanum*, i (ed. 1817), pp. 253–64.

MALO, St. See *Machutus, St.*

MALTA, KNIGHTS OF. See *Hospitallers.*

MALTESE CROSS. A black cross of eight points on a white ground, so named because it was adopted by the Knights of Malta, i.e. the *Hospitallers of St. John of Jerusalem.

MALVERN CONFERENCE. The Anglican Conference which met at Malvern, 7–10 Jan. 1941, under the presidency of Abp. W.

*Temple, to consider in the light of the Christian faith the crisis confronting civilization. The speakers included Sir R. Acland, V. A. Demant, T. S. *Eliot, H. A. Hodges, D. M. Mackinnon, J. M. Murry, and Miss D. L. Sayers. In its 'findings', which were esp. concerned with the relation of the Church to economic life, the Conference asserted its belief that the continued private ownership of the industrial resources of the country imperilled the Christian doctrine of man, and it urged that the C of E should radically reform its own economic and administrative system.

The Resolutions were issued as a leaflet entitled *The Life of the Church and the Order of Society* by the *Industrial Christian Fellowship. Most of the papers read were printed in *Malvern 1941* (1941).

MAMERTINE PRISON. A building in the centre of Rome consisting of two cells, one above the other, in which, acc. to tradition, St. Peter was imprisoned and converted his two gaolers, Processus and Martinianus. It was certainly in use as a prison from Republican times. The small church of San Giuseppe dei Falegnami now stands above the site.

H. Grisar, S.J., 'Der mamertinische Kerker und die römischen Traditionen vom Gefängnisse und den Ketten Petri' in *Z.K.T.*, xx (1896), pp. 102–20. L. *Duchesne, 'Le Forum Chrétien' in *Mélanges de littérature et d'histoire religieuses publiés à l'occasion du jubilé épiscopal de Mgr de Cabrières*, i (1899), II, 'La Prison mamertine', pp. 128–31. H. *Leclercq, O.S.B., in *D.A.C.L.*, x (pt. 1; 1931), cols. 1356–60, s.v.

MAMERTUS, St. (d. *c.* 475), Abp. of Vienne in Gaul from *c.* 461. He was the brother of *Claudianus Mamertus (q.v.). For consecrating a Bishop of Die and overriding the attempted settlement of the conflicting claims of the sees of Arles and Vienne (450), he received a rebuke from Pope Hilary (464). He is esp. remembered for having introduced (*c.* 470) the 'litanies' on the days immediately preceding *Ascension Day as an act of intercession against earthquakes and other perils, a practice which led later to the institution of the *Rogation Days. Feast day, 11 May.

*Avitus, *Homilia de Rogationibus* (*PL*, lix, 289–94). *AA.SS.*, Mai. II (1680), pp. 629–31. J. P. Kirsch in *C.E.*, ix (1910), p. 580. See also bibl. to *Rogation Days.*

MAN, Isle of. See *Sodor and Man.*

MANASSES, Prayer of. This short book in the OT *Apocrypha consists of a penitential prayer put into the mouth of Manasseh, King of Judah (2 Kgs. 21. 1–18). Though the prayer contains no reference to Manasseh by name (apart from the heading) and in content resembles some of the *Penitential Psalms, there are some indications that it was composed with Manasseh's situation in view. In some early Greek Bibles it was appended to the Psalter, and its use in the early Christian Church is attested by its embodiment in the

*Didascalia and the *Apostolic Constitutions. All that can be said with certainty about its date is that it must be earlier than that of the Didascalia (early 3rd cent.). It was never included in the *Vulgate.

The numerous edd. of the *LXX* text include that of H. B. *Swete, *The Old Testament in Greek*, iii (1894), pp. 802–4. The Syriac text from the Didascalia ed., with Fr. tr. and introd., by F. Nau in *Revue de l'Orient chrétien*, xiii (1908), pp. 134–41. H. E. *Ryle in R. H. *Charles (ed.), *The Apocrypha and Pseudepigrapha of the Old Testament*, i (1913), pp. 612–19. R. H. Pfeiffer, *New Testament Times, with an Introduction to the Apocrypha* (New York [1949], London [1954]), pp. 457–60. F. C. Porter in *H.D.B.*, iii (1900), p. 232 f., s.v.; F. Prat, S.J., in *Dict. Bibl.*, iv (1908), cols. 654–83, s.v. 'Manassé (Prière de)'; J. B. Frey, *ibid.*, Suppl. i (1928), cols. 442–5, s.v., 'Apocryphes de l'Ancien Testament 13'. See also bibl. to *Apocrypha*.

MANDAEANS (also known as the Naso-reans and Christians of St. John). A *Gnostic sect which originated as a small community to the east of the *Jordan in the 1st or 2nd cent. A.D., and still survives south of Bagdad. Their extant writings, the chief of which is the *Ginza* or 'Treasure', date from the 7th or 8th cent. and are a farrago of inconsistent teachings, mostly akin to *Manichaean dualism. They taught that man's soul, unwillingly imprisoned in the body and persecuted by demons, will finally be freed by the redeemer, *Manda da Hayyê*, the personified 'Knowledge of Life' (sometimes also called *Hibel*, or *Enos Uthra*), who was himself once on earth and defeated the powers of darkness, and hence can guide souls through the heavenly spheres. These notions may be of Christian origin and really refer to Jesus Christ, though the sect has been very hostile to Christianity since Byzantine times. To assist man to prepare for his ascension after death, frequent baptism is enjoined. As St. *John the Baptist plays a large part in Mandaean writings (esp. in those dating from the Islamic period), some scholars have held that the sect must trace its ancestry to the Baptist himself (cf., e.g., Acts 19. 2 f.). But the dating is very uncertain, and the Mandaeans are more probably a late offshoot of Christianity than pre-Christian.

Modern crit. edd. of several Mandaean texts by M. Lidzbarski, incl. *Das Johannesbuch der Mandäer* (2 parts, Giessen, 1905–15), *Mandäische Liturgien* (*Abh.* (Gött.), xvii, Hft. 1; 1920), and *Ginza, der Schatz oder das grosse Buch der Mandäer* (Quellen der Religionsgeschichte, xiii; 1925 [Germ. tr.]). W. Brandt, *Die mandäische Religion. Ihre Entwicklung und ihre geschichtliche Bedeutung* (1889); id., *Mandäische Schriften* (1893). S. A. Pallis, *Mandaeische Studier*, i (all publd., Copenhagen, 1919; Eng. tr., London–Copenhagen, 1926). H. Odeberg, *Die mandäische Religions-anschauung* (Upsala, 1930). Ethel S. Drower, *The Mandaeans of Iraq and Iran. Their Cults, Customs, Magic, Legends, and Folklore* (1937). R. *Bultmann, 'Die Bedeutung der neuerschlossene mandäischen und manichäischen Quellen für das Verständnis des Johannesevangeliums' in *Z.N.T.W.*, xxiv (1925), pp. 100–46; id., *Das Evangelium des Johannes* (K.E.K., ed. 10, 1941; Ergänzungsheft, 1953). H. *Lietzmann, 'Ein Beitrag zur Mandaërfrage' in *Sb.* (Berl.), 1930, pp. 596–608. C. H. Dodd, *The Interpretation of the Fourth Gospel* (1953), pp. 115–30. On the language, T. Nöldeke, *Mandäische Grammatik* (1875). S. A. Pallis, *Essay on Mandaean Bibliography, 1560–1930* (London–Copenhagen, 1933). K. Kessler, 'Mandäer' in *P.R.E.* (ed. 3), xii (1903), pp. 155–83; K. Kessler–G. W. Thatcher in *E.B.* (ed. 11), xvii (1911), pp. 554–7; G. Bardy in *D.T.C.*, ix (pt. 2; 1927), cols. 1812–24; J. Schmitt in *Dict. Bibl.*, Suppl. v ('1954'), cols. 758–88, s.v. 'Mandéisme', with recent bibl.

MANDE, HENDRIK (*c.* 1360–1431), one of the *Brethren of the Common Life. He came under the influence of G. *Groote and *Florentius Radewyns and, at some date after 1390, entered the monastery at *Windesheim, where he was subject to visionary experiences. Here he wrote in Flemish twelve mystical tracts which embodied and developed many of J. Ruysbroek's ideas.

The chief source is Ian *Busch, *Chronicon Windeshemense* (ed. K. Grube, Halle, 1886), pp. 122–35. G. Visser, *Hendrik Mande. Bijdrage tot de Kennis der Noord-Nederlandsche Mystiek* (The Hague, 1899; with reprint of five of Mande's writings). Anthology in B. Spaapen, *Hendrik Mande* (Tielt, 1951). L. Schulze in *P.R.E.* (ed. 3), xii (1903), pp. 183–8.

MANES AND MANICHAEISM. It is impossible to state in brief compass the facts relating to the life of Manes (or, acc. to the usual W. form of his name, 'Manichaeus'), the founder of Manichaeism, as the relatively late sources of his life are mutually contradictory in their details. The chief sources are: (1) The writings of certain of the Church Fathers, notably St. *Ephraim Syrus, *Titus of Bostra, *Serapion of Thmuis, and esp. St. *Augustine of Hippo (who was himself a Manichee for nine years before his conversion); (2) a report of a reputed dialogue between Manes and a bishop, Archelaus, the so-called 'Acta Archelai', which was issued by one Hegemonius; (3) references in various mediaeval Mohammedan historians who came across Manichaeism in Babylonia, notably Al-Biruni; (4) a collection of Manichaean documents, discovered in 1904–5 at Turfan and elsewhere in Chinese Turkestan, and published by F. W. K. Müller and others; (5) another collection of Manichaean documents of the 3rd and 4th cents. found in 1933 in Egypt and published by C. Schmidt, H. J. Polotsky, and others, which, if not from Manes himself, embody the teaching of his earliest disciples.

From our extant sources it would seem that Manes (*c.* 215–275) was born at Seleucia-Ctesiphon, the capital of the Persian Empire, that he began his own special teaching *c.* 240, that opposition from the *Zoroastrians forced him into exile in India, and that he propagated his teaching rapidly by preaching far and wide in the E., that he returned to the capital after the coronation of Sapor I in 242, who first gave him active support and then attacked him, and that under his second successor, Bahram I, he was put to death by being flayed alive, and his disciples banished.

His system was apparently a hotch-potch of many long-dead heresies. It was based on a supposed primeval conflict between light and darkness, combined with ascetic beliefs which may have been of *Mandaean origin. It taught that the object of the practice of religion was to release the particles of light which Satan had stolen from the world of Light and imprisoned in man's brain, and that Jesus, Buddha, the Prophets, and Manes had been sent to help in this task. This dualism is explained in poetic fashion, the whole forming a system of religious knowledge rather than a code of ethics.

To achieve this end, severe asceticism, including vegetarianism, was practised. There existed in the sect a hierarchy of grades professing different standards of austerity. Their enemies attributed to them many abominable practices, but St. *Augustine, with his exceptional opportunities for being well informed, nowhere criticized their morals.

The sect spread rapidly. It appears to have been established in Egypt before the end of the 3rd cent., and at Rome early in the 4th. In the later 4th cent. Manichaeans were numerous in Africa. How far the sect directly influenced such heretics as the *Albigensians, *Bogomiles, and the *Paulicians is disputed; for some similarities of practice would account for the charges of 'Manichaeism' laid against them. On the other hand, the Turfan fragments attest its survival in Chinese Turkestan down to the 13th cent.

The first critical study of the subject was Isaac de Beausobre, *Histoire critique de Manichée et du manichéisme* (2 vols., Amsterdam, 1734–9). Important later works include F. C. *Baur, *Das manichäische Religionssystem* (1831); G. Flügel, *Mani, seine Lehre, seine Schriften* (1862). E. Rochat, *Essai sur Mani et sa doctrine* (Geneva, 1897). F. Cumont–M. A. Kugener, *Recherches sur le manichéisme* (2 vols., 1908–12). P. Alfaric, *Les Écritures manichéennes* (2 vols., 1918–19). F. C. *Burkitt, *The Religion of the Manichees* (Donnellan Lectures for 1924; 1925). A. V. W. Jackson, *Researches in Manichaeism* (Columbia University Indo-Iranian Series, xiii; 1932). H. C. Puech, *Le Manichéisme* (1949). K. Kessler in *P.R.E.* (ed. 3), xii (1903), pp. 193–228, s.v. 'Mani, Manichäer'; A. *Harnack–F. C. *Conybeare in *E.B.* (ed. 11), xvii (1911), pp. 572–8, s.v. 'Manichaeism'; H. J. Polotsky in *P.W.*, Suppl. Band vi (1935), cols. 240–71, s.v. 'Manichäismus'; D. Obolensky in *Chambers's Encyclopaedia* (ed. 1950), ix, p. 61, s.v. 'Manichaeism'.

MANIPLE. A strip of silk, two to four inches wide and a little over a yard in length, worn over the left arm by the ministers at Mass. In origin it was a handkerchief carried, as pagan and Christian monuments attest, on the left hand. It was first used liturgically in Rome, but in the 6th cent. is found in *Ravenna, and by the 9th cent. was in use all over Europe. In the Middle Ages it was sometimes worn by all clerks, and not as now confined to those who have at least the rank of *subdeacon. Its colour now accords with that of the liturgical season and it usually carries three crosses.

Braun, *L.G.*, pp. 515–61. J. Braun, S.J., in *C.E.*, ix (1910), p. 601 f.

MANNA. The food miraculously provided for the *Israelites on their pilgrimage through the wilderness from Egypt to the *Holy Land (Exod. 16). It was a white substance which fell along with the dew, and was collected every morning except on the *Sabbath, for which an additional portion was gathered on the previous day. Christ speaks of Himself as the True Bread from Heaven (Jn. 6); and by a natural symbolism it has been widely regarded as a type of the Christian Eucharist, e.g. in 1 Cor. 10. 3 and in the hymn 'O esca viatorum' (Eng. tr. in *Eng. Hymnal*, No. 321).

MANNERS-SUTTON, CHARLES (1755–1828), Abp. of *Canterbury. A grandson of the Duke of Rutland, he was educated at Emmanuel College, Cambridge. In 1791 he became Dean of *Peterborough and in 1792 Bp. of *Norwich. In 1794 he was appointed Dean of Windsor *in commendam* and lived on intimate terms with the family of George III. In 1805 he became Abp. of Canterbury. A High Churchman of the old school, he was dignified, gracious, and highly respected. He was opposed to RC emancipation, but favoured concessions to dissenters. He gave his active support in the foundation of the *National Society (for the education of the poor) in 1811, and guided and helped the *S.P.C.K. He also used his influence on behalf of the foundation of the Anglican episcopate in *India.

A. W. Rowden, *The Primates of the First Four Georges* (1916), pp. 380–426. J. H. Overton in *D.N.B.*, xxxvi (1893), p. 57 f.

MANNING, HENRY EDWARD (1808–92), Abp. of *Westminster. The youngest son of William Manning, M.P., he was educated at Harrow and Balliol College, Oxford. His early ambition was for a parliamentary career, but his father's bankruptcy compelled him to accept a clerkship in the Colonial Office. In 1832 he was elected to a fellowship at Merton College, and in the same year he returned to Oxford and was ordained deacon. In Jan. 1833 he went as curate to John Sargent, rector of Lavington, whom he succeeded in May, and whose daughter, Caroline (d. 1837), he married in Nov. In 1841 he became Archdeacon of *Chichester. Manning, who had begun life as an Evangelical, now gradually swung round to the *Tractarian side. He contributed No. 78 to the *Tracts for the Times*, and after J. H. *Newman's secession (1845) he was looked on as one of the leaders of the *Oxford Movement. He had disapproved, however, of the contents of *Tract Ninety, and on 5 Nov. 1843 preached a strongly anti-Papal sermon before the University. The *Gorham Judgement destroyed his faith in Anglicanism, and in 1851 he was received into the RC Church. Two months later he was ordained priest by N. *Wiseman, and after studying for two years at *Rome, was made provost of the Westminster Metropolitan Chapter in 1857. In 1865 he succeeded Wiseman as Abp. of Westminster. At the *Vatican Council (1869–70) he was a staunch supporter of Papal *Infallibility, taking a vow to do his utmost to secure its promulgation. His bitter hostility to the admission of RCs to the Universities and other differences completely alienated him from Newman after 1866. After 1875, when he was made a cardinal, he was prominent in social work of all kinds, and in 1889 mediated successfully in the London Dock Strike. His body was buried in Kensal Green Cemetery, but was later brought back to Westminster Cathedral, which he had founded.

Official life by E. S. Purcell (2 vols., London, 1896; cynical, also inaccurate). In a similar vein L. Strachey, *Eminent Victorians* (1918), pp. 3–115 ('Cardinal Manning'). Other lives by A. W. Hutton (London, 1892, with list of

Manning's works; rev. ed., 'English Leaders of Religion', 1894), S. Leslie (ib. 1921) and V. A. McClelland (ib., 1962). J. E. C. Bodley, *Cardinal Manning* [and other Essays] (1912), pp. 1–65. J. M. Rigg in *D.N.B.*, xxxvi (1893), pp. 62–8; A. W. Hutton in *E.B.* (ed. 11), xvii (1911), pp. 589–591.

MANSE. The dwelling-house, esp. in *Scotland, of a minister. When his residence in it is obligatory and it is used for the purposes of his ministry, the rates and taxes are payable by the Church as occupier as well as owner. In the old Church of Scotland, if the manse was not in a state of tenantable repair, an allowance in lieu of rent called 'manse maill' was paid to the incumbent by the *heritors, but by Act of Parliament, 1925, the rights of property have been transferred to the General Trustees of the Church.

MANSEL, HENRY LONGUEVILLE, (1820–71), Anglican divine. He was successively scholar (1839) and tutor (1844) of St. John's College, Oxford. In 1859 he became the first Waynflete professor of moral and metaphysical philosophy at Oxford, in 1866 (somewhat incongruously) Regius professor of ecclesiastical history, and in 1868 Dean of St. Paul's. He delivered a course of *Bampton Lectures in 1858 on *The Limits of Religious Thought*, in which he argued that the human intellect acquired its knowledge of the nature of God from supernatural revelation alone. His contentions, which had been reached esp. from study of the doctrines of Sir William Hamilton, provoked much hostile criticism, notably from F. D. *Maurice and J. S. *Mill. Mansel's other writings include *Artis Logicae Rudimenta* (1849), a widely used compendium of logic based on H. *Aldrich's manual; the *Limits of Demonstrative Science* (1853); the article 'Metaphysics' in the 8th edition of the *Encyclopaedia Britannica* (1857); and a set of lectures on the *Gnostic Heresies* (1875; issued by J. B. *Lightfoot). His witty pen was often employed in matters of domestic controversy in the university, e.g. *Phrontisterion, or, Oxford in the 19th Century* (1852), a satire on the University Commission of 1850.

A collection of Mansel's *Letters, Lectures and Reviews*, including the *Phrontisterion*, ed. H. W. Chandler (London, 1873); sixteen lectures delivered at Oxford in 1868; *Gnostic Heresies in the First and Second Centuries* (London, 1875), ed. J. B. *Lightfoot, with sketch of Mansel's Work, Life, and Character by the Earl of Carnarvon, pp. v–xxii. The *Phrontisterion* was repr. in *Three Oxford Ironies*, ed. G. Gordon (London, 1927), pp. 77–102, with introd., pp. 17–23. J W. *Burgon, *The Lives of Twelve Good Men*, ii (1888), pp. 149–237. L. Stephen in *D.N.B.*, xxxvi (1893), pp. 81–3.

MANSI, GIOVANNI DOMENICO (1692–1769), canonist and Abp. of Lucca. A native of Lucca, where he spent most of his life, he was professed a Clerk Regular of the Mother of God in 1710 and in 1765 was elected Abp. of Lucca. In 1724 he published *Tractatus de Casibus et Censuris Reservatis*, his only considerable original work. But he issued a vast series of publications in which his own part usually did not go beyond annotations (some 90 folio vols. have Mansi's name on their

titles). The most celebrated was his edition of the Councils. In its original shape it was designed as a supplement to N. Coleti's collection (1728–33) and issued in 6 vols. (1748–52). Its success encouraged Mansi to produce his well-known 'Amplissima', the *Sacrorum Conciliorum Nova et Amplissima Collectio* (31 vols., 1758–98). It goes down to the Council of *Florence, but Mansi himself supervised only the first 14 vols. Its only real merit is its completeness. The editing is poor and uncritical and the older editions are often to be preferred. Among earlier scholars whose writings (in whole or part) Mansi re-edited were C. *Baronius (1738–56). J. A. *Fabricius (1754), *Pius II (Aeneas Silvius Piccolomini, 1755), and E. *Baluze (1761).

H. *Quentin, O.S.B., *J. D. Mansi et les grandes collections conciliaires* (1900). Hefele–Leclercq, I, i (1907), pp. 111–14. A. Boudinhon in *C.E.*, ix (1910), p. 609 f.

MANT, RICHARD (1776–1848), Bp. of Down, Connor, and Dromore. Educated at Winchester and Trinity College, Oxford, he was elected a Fellow of Oriel College in 1798 and ordained deacon in 1802. After holding several livings, he was appointed Bp. of Killaloe and Kilfenoragh in 1820, and of Down and Connor in 1823 (with Dromore from 1842). His best known work, which he prepared with G. D'Oyly (d. 1846), was an edition of the Bible with notes selected from Anglican divines (1814). His other writings include an annotated *Book of Common Prayer* (1820) and, the fruit of wide research, a *History of the Church of Ireland* (1840). He was also the author of 'Bright the vision that delighted' and other well-known hymns, as well as of much indifferent poetry.

Memoirs by [E.] Berens (London, 1849) and Walter-Bishop Mant (Dublin, 1857). Detailed list of his publd. works in H. Cotton (ed.), *Fasti Ecclesiae Hibernicae*, iii (Dublin, 1849), pp. 213–17. A. Gordon in *D.N.B.*, xxxvi (1893), pp. 96–8.

MANTEGNA, ANDREA (1431–1506), Italian painter. Adopted as a child by the painter, Francesco Squarcione, he received an artistic education from early youth. His series of fresco paintings representing the *Martyrdom of St. James and St. Christopher* (1448–57), in the Church of the Eremitani at Padua, established his reputation as the first painter of the city. A second sequence, finished in 1474, treats of scenes from the *Life of Marquess Lodovico Gonzaga*, and the third, now at Hampton Court, the *Triumph of Caesar* (1484–92). A distinct line of development is noticeable in his altar pictures. His earliest works follow the traditional side-by-side grouping of single saints' figures, e.g. *St. Luke's Altar* (1453–4) of St. Giustina's at Padua, now in the Brera at Milan; but his later altar-pieces, e.g. that of San Zeno at Venice (1455–9), which exhibit Venetian influence in their closely knit composition, the triptych of the *Adoration of the Magi* (c. 1464), the *Madonna della Vittoria* (1495–6, Louvre), and the

Madonna and Saints, 1497), show considerable freedom of composition. One of his last works, the famous *Dead Christ* in the Brera of Milan, is remarkable for its virtuosity in foreshortening the body. Mantegna's copper engravings, which are among the earliest Italian specimens of this technique, are remarkable for the austerity of their style.

Paintings and engravings (in black and white) ed., with introd., by G. Knapp (Klassiker der Kunst in Gesamtausgaben, xvi; 1910); smaller collection of plates in colour ed., with introd., by R. H. Wilenski, *Mantegna and the Paduan School* ('The Faber Gallery', 1947). P. Kristeller, *Andrea Mantegna* (Berlin–Leipzig, 1902; Eng. tr., 1901), with plates and original docc. C. Yriarte, *Mantegna*. Sa vie, sa maison, son tombeau, son œuvre dans les musées et les collections (1910). G. Fiocco, *L' arte di Andrea Mantegna* (Bologna, 1927); id., *Mantegna* (Milan [1937]), with plates and bibl. Other studies by H. Thode (Künstler-Monographien ed. H. Knackfuss, xii; 1897), Maud Cruttwell (London, 1901), A. Blum ('Les Grands Artistes', 1911), Mrs. Arthur Bell (London [1911]), and W. Boeck (Heimbücher der Kunst ed. F. Winkler, Burg b.M. [1942]), with plates. G. Fiocco in U. Thieme–F. Becker (founders), *Allgemeines Lexikon der bildenden Künstler von der Antike bis zur Gegenwart*, xxiv (ed. H. Vollmer; 1930), pp. 37–43, s.v., with detailed bibl.

MANTELLETA. In the W. Church a short mantle open in front and reaching to the knees which is reserved for the use of cardinals, bishops, and other prelates of rank. The material and colour depend not only on the rank of the wearer, but also on the particular occasion on which it is used.

The principal legislation governing the behaviour and dress of the senior members of the RC hierarchy is in the Motu Proprio of *Pius X, pr. in *Decreta Authentica Congregationis Sacrorum Rituum*, vi (Appendix i; 1912), No. 4154, pp. 55–64. J. Braun, S.J., in *C.E.*, ix (1910), p. 611, s.v.; P. Siffrin, O.S.B., in *E.C.*, vii (1951), col. 1985 f., s.v.

MANTELLONE. A purple-coloured mantle of silk or wool, worn by certain lesser prelates of the Papal court. It is fastened at the neck, and reaches to the ground and has slits through which the arms are placed.

G. Felici in *E.C.*, vii (1951), col. 1986 f., s.v. T. Ortolan in *D.T.C.*, iii (1908), col. 1972, s.v. 'Cour romaine'. See also bibl. to previous entry.

MANTUM. A red mantle of the Pope which from the 11th to the 14th cents. played an important part in the Papal elections, since the investiture with it (the so-called *immantatio*) expressed the transference to the Pope of his rights to govern the Church.

MANUAL ACTS, The. The rubrics in the 1662 BCP require the celebrant of Holy Communion at the consecration to take the paten into his hands, to break the bread, lay his hand upon it, and to perform corresponding acts at the consecration of the wine. In 1549 the rubrics were less detailed, while from 1552 to 1662 they were omitted altogether, though some of the traditional ceremonies at the consecration no doubt continued. In the *Ridsdale case (1875–7) the Privy Council held that the rubric at the head of the Prayer of Consecration requiring the priest to break the bread

'before the people' meant that he must not intentionally stand at the consecration so as to prevent the congregation from seeing the manual acts. This decision was reaffirmed in substance in the *Lincoln Judgement (q.v.). It is now rarely observed except among Evangelicals. See also '*North End*', The.

V. Staley, *The Manual Acts* (*Alcuin Club Prayer Book Revision Pamphlets, iv, 1913).

MANUALE (Lat., 'a book of handy size'). In the Middle Ages the usual name for the book containing the forms prescribed to the parish priest for the administration of the sacraments. It now commonly goes by the name of the *Rituale (q.v.).

MANUSCRIPTS OF THE BIBLE. Hebrew MSS. of the OT are mostly of no great age, by reason of the rule, laid down in the *Talmud, that worn or defective copies of the Holy Scriptures must be buried. The earliest extant complete MSS. of the OT belong to the 10th cent. A.D. All contain the text as fixed by Jewish scholars some centuries earlier; and owing to the extreme care prescribed for their copying, the variations in them are of small importance. This text, known as the '*Massoretic Text', is therefore securely established. For the earlier history of the OT text the evidence is mainly that of the *Samaritan and Greek versions (see *Septuagint), which were made before the Massoretic text was fixed. See also *Dead Sea Scrolls*.

The Greek MSS. of the Bible, both OT and NT, fall into three groups: (1) *Papyri*, covering the period from the 3rd cent. B.C. to the 4th cent. A.D. (see *Papyrology*). The earliest now extant are some small fragments of Deut., 2nd cent. B.C.; a tiny scrap of St. Jn., early 2nd cent. A.D.; much of Num. and Deut., early 2nd cent. A.D.; most of the Pauline Epistles, and substantial portions of the Gospels and Acts, Is., Ezek., Dan., and Est., early 3rd cent. A.D. (see *Chester Beatty Papyri*); (2) *Vellum *uncials* of various dates, from the 4th to the 9th cents., beginning with the *Codex Vaticanus, and the *Codex Sinaiticus of the early 4th cent.; (3) *Vellum minuscules*, from the 9th cent. to the invention of printing, of which there are over 4,000, including service books. The earliest printed texts of the Greek NT were taken from a few late minuscule MSS., and the AV was translated from these. The RV represents a revision of this text by the help of the earliest MSS.

For determining the text, esp. of the NT, the MSS. of certain of the versions from the Greek are of very great value. The *Syriac versions, which circulated in the Syriac-speaking lands to the east of Antioch, include the *Old Syriac, the *Peshitta (early 5th cent.), and the *Harklean versions. Of the Latin versions, the most celebrated is the *Vulgate of St. *Jerome, though the '*Old Latin' versions are often of even greater value to the textual critic. Among the other translations of greater or less use for determining the correct text are the *Coptic,

*Armenian, *Georgian, *Gothic, and *Ethiopic versions.

Textually, the MSS. and versions of the NT fall into the following main groups: (1) *Byzantine*, traceable probably to a revision made at Antioch late in the 4th cent., and producing eventually the standard text used in the Greek Church. This is found in the great mass of later Greek MSS.; (2) *Alexandrian*, or '*Neutral', of the Codices Vaticanus and Sinaiticus and other early MSS., now widely considered the best; (3) *Caesarean*, used by *Origen in his later works, found partially in the *Chester Beatty papyri of the Gospels and in a few other MSS; (4) *Western*, found in the Greco-Latin MSS. (Bezae, Claromontanus, &c.), the Old Latin version, *Cyprian, &c.; (5) *Syriac*, in the *Old Syriac version, and partially in other Syriac and Armenian versions.

The standard ed. of the Massoretic text is that of C. D. Ginsburg (4 vols., London, 1880–1905). F. G. Kenyon, *Our Bible and the Ancient Manuscripts* (1895; ed. 4, 1939). Id., *The Text of the Greek Bible* (1937), esp. pp. 66–110; B. J. Roberts, *The Old Testament Text and Versions* (Cardiff, 1951), pp. 1–100 passim. C. Van Puyvelde, O.S.B.–B. Botte, O.S.B., in *Dict. Bibl.*, Suppl. v ('1954'), cols. 793–835, s.v. 'Manuscrits bibliques'. See also bibl. to *Massoretes* and individual MSS. and subjects referred to above.

MAPHRIAN (Syriac *mafriano*, 'one who bears fruit', i.e. 'a consecrator'). The title of the bishop of the *Jacobite Syrians who holds rank immediately after the Patriarch.

MARAN , PRUDENTIUS (1683 - 1762), *Maurist scholar. Born at Sézanne, he entered the Benedictine Order at St.-Faron, near Meaux, in 1703. Later he moved to *St.-Germain-des-Prés where he co-operated with A. A. Touttée (1677–1718) in his edition of St. *Cyril of Jerusalem (publd. 1720). In 1734 he was driven from St.-Germain-des-Prés for supposed leanings to *Jansenism. From 1737 until his death he was at the abbey of Blancs-Manteaux. Of his patristic editions his masterpiece was his edition of St. *Justin Martyr and the other *Apologists (1742) with learned prolegomena. He also completed the editions of St. *Cyprian, begun by E. *Baluze (1726), and of St. *Basil, begun by Julien Garnier (1730). His other writings (anon.) include a *Dissertation sur les Sémiariens* (1722; in defence of Touttée's edition of St. Cyril), and *La Divinité de Jésus Christ prouvée contre les Hérétiques et les Déistes* (3 vols., 1751).

[R. P. Tassin, O.S.B.], *Histoire littéraire de la congrégation de Saint-Maur* (Brussels, 1770), pp. 741–9. J. Baudot, O.S.B., in *D.T.C.*, ix (pt. 2; 1937), cols. 1933–6, s.v. See also bibl. to *Maurists*.

MARANATHA. This Aramaic word, which occurs at 1 Cor. 16. 22, was understood by the Christian Fathers as 'Our Lord has come', but it is probably more correctly rendered by the imperative 'O Lord, come' (cf. Rev. 22. 20). Its use by St. *Paul reflects the strong eschatological hopes of the early Church.

See Commentaries to 1 Cor. 16. 22 and *Didache*, x, 6 (the only other literary occurrence of the word). J. H. Thayer in *H.D.B.*, iii (1900), pp. 241–3; H. *Leclercq, O.S.B., in *D.A.C.L.*, x (pt. 2; 1932), col. 1729 f.; and esp. K. G. Kuhn in *T.W.B.*, iv (1942), pp. 470–5.

MARBECKE, JOHN. See *Merbecke, John*.

MARBURG, Colloquy of (1529). The meeting convoked by *Philip of Hesse with a view to achieving unity between the Saxon and the Swiss Reformers. It met in the castle at Marburg-on-the-Lahn on 1–3 Oct. 1529, with M. *Luther and P. *Melanchthon representing the Saxons, and H. *Zwingli, J. *Oecolampadius, and M. *Bucer the Swiss. In 14 of the 15 'Marburg Articles' which Luther, commissioned by Philip of Hesse, had drawn up, agreement between the two parties was reached; but the conference failed through Zwingli's refusal to accept the Lutheran doctrine of the Eucharist ('*Consubstantiation') contained in the remaining article. Shortly after the conference had dispersed, Luther revised these articles. In this form, as the 'Articles of *Schwabach', they became the first of the Lutheran Symbolical Books and thus led on to the *Augsburg Confession (q.v.) of 1530.

Text in H. Heppe (ed.), *Die fünfzehn Marburger Artikel vom 3. Oktober 1529 nach dem wieder aufgefundenen Autographen der Reformatoren als Facsimile veröffentlicht* (Cassel, 1847; ed. 2, 1854). 'Relatio Rodolphi Collini de Colloquio Marburgensi' in *Zuinglii Opera*, ed. M. Schuler–J. Schulthess, IV (Zürich, 1841), pp. 173–82, mostly repr. in B. J. Kidd, *Documents Illustrative of the Continental Reformation* (1911), No. 109, pp. 247–54. A. Erichson, *Das Marburger Religionsgespräch . . . nach ungedruckten Strassburger Urkunden* (Strassburg, 1880); W. Köhler, *Das Marburger Religions-Gespräch.* Versuch einer Rekonstruktion (Schriften des Vereins für Reformationsgeschichte, No. 148, 1929). Schottenloher, iv (1938), p. 533 f. (Nos. 41337a–62). T Kolde in *P.R.E.* (ed. 3), xii (1903), pp. 248–55, s.v.

MARBURG, University of. Founded by *Philip, Landgraf of Hesse, in 1527, it was the first Protestant university established in Europe. Its theological faculty, esp. since the middle of the 19th cent., has been famous through its long line of distinguished professors (including W. *Herrmann, K. *Budde, A. *Harnack, C. Mirbt, R. *Otto, H. Hermelink, F. *Heiler, R. *Bultmann). The university was also the centre of an influential philosophical school (the 'Marburg School'), which on Neo-Kantian principles conceived of religion as purely immanental. The chief representatives of this school were H. Cohen, P. Natorp, E. Cassirer, and (in his first phase) N. Hartmann.

Die Philipps-Universität zu Marburg, 1527–1927. Fünf Kapitel aus der Geschichte der Universität Marburg, 1527–1866, von H. Hermelink und S. A. Kaehler; Die Universität Marburg seit 1866—in Einzeldarstellungen (Marburg, 1927). F. Gundlach (ed.), *Die akademischen Lehrer der Philipps-Universität in Marburg von 1527 bis 1910* (Veröffentlichungen der Historischen Kommission für Hessen und Waldeck, No. 15, Marburg, 1927). K. Hofmann in *L.Th.K.*, vi (1934), col. 865 f., s.v., with further bibl.

MARCA, PIERRE DE (1594–1662), French canonist. After filling several important civil offices, he was commissioned by the King to publish his *Dissertationes de Concordia Sacer-dotii et Imperii* (1641). A defence of *Galli-canist doctrines, it was put on the *Index in the following year. In 1642 he was ordained priest (having been widowed in 1631); but though nominated by the King in 1643 to the Bpric. of Conserans, he did not obtain Papal confirmation until 1647. In 1652 he became Abp. of Toulouse and in 1662, shortly before his death, Abp. of Paris. A much enlarged edition of the *Dissertationes* was issued in 1663 by É. *Baluze, but this too was put on the Index in 1664.

Early lives by É. *Baluze, in the form of 'Epistola ad Clarissimum et Eruditissimum Virum Samuelem Sorbe-rium', prefixed to his ed. of Marca's *Dissertationes de Concordia Sacerdotii et Imperii* (Paris, 1663), pp. 1–32; and P. de Forget, prefixed to his collection of Marca's *Dissertationes Posthumae* (Paris, 1669). F. Gaquère, *Pierre de Marca, 1594–1662*. Sa vie, ses œuvres, son gallicanisme (1932). J. Carreyre in *D.T.C.*, ix (pt. 2; 1927), cols. 1087–91, s.v.

MARCAN HYPOTHESIS, The.

The theory that St. Mark's is the earliest of the four Gospels and that in its presentation of the life of Christ the facts of history are set down with a minimum of disarrangement, interpretation, and embellishment. The Hypothesis was first put on a seemingly secure footing in 1835 by K. *Lachmann, who based his case on an analysis of the literary relationship between the three *Synoptic Gospels. It was adopted almost at once by C. H. Weisse (1801–66) and C. G. Wilke (1788–1854), and in the latter part of the 19th cent. became very generally accepted. Later study, though leaving the literary priority of Mark generally unchal-lenged, has tended to discover a much greater element of theological interpretation in the Gospel.

MARCELLA, St.

(325–410), Christian ascetic. Of a noble Roman family, she determined to devote herself, after the early death of her husband, to a life of charitable works, study, and asceticism. Her palace on the Aventine Hill became a centre of Christian influence and St. *Jerome once referred to her as 'the glory of the ladies of Rome'. She suffered bodily ill-treatment at the hands of the Goths when they captured Rome in 410 and died from its effects. Feast day, 31 Jan.

Practically all our information is derived from the Epp. of St. Jerome, esp. Ep. 127 (J. P. Migne, *PL*, xxii, 1087–95). F. Cavallera, *St. Jérôme*. Sa vie et son œuvre, l, i (Spici-legium Sacrum Lovaniense. Études et documents, i; 1922), pp. 85–9 and 114–19.

MARCELLINA, St.

(c. 330–c. 398), the sister of St. *Ambrose. After the death of her father, she assisted her mother in the education of her brother, and was consecrated a virgin by Pope *Liberius in 353. Later she lived at Milan with her brother, who tried to dissuade her from her excessive austerities. St. Am-brose dedicated to her his three sermons 'De Virginibus'. Feast day, 17 July.

For Ambrose's three sermons, *De Virginibus*, see J. P. Migne, *PL*, xvi, 187–232. Marcellina was also the recipient

---

of Ambrose's three *Epp.*, 20, 22, and 41 (ib., 994–1002, 1019–26, and 1115–21), and she is mentioned in his *De Excessu Satyri*, 33 and 76. A Lat. panegyric, pr. by B. Mombritius, is repr. in the *A A.SS.*, Jul. IV (1725), pp. 234–8.

MARCELLUS

(d. *c.* 374), Bp. of *Ancyra and a strong supporter of the *Homoousion at the Council of *Nicaea. In 336 he was deposed from his see on the ground of certain statements in his work against the Arian *Asterius. He was restored on the death of *Constantine (337), but *c.* 339 again expelled. The W. accepted his orthodoxy at Councils held at Rome *c.* 340 and at *Sardica in 343, on the ground that the offending passages were merely conjectures. The E. was more critical of his orthodoxy and here the Nicene party found his support embarrassing. Marcellus taught that in the Unity of the Godhead the Son and the Spirit only emerged as independent entities for the purposes of Creation and Redemption. After the redemptive work is achieved they will be resumed again into the Divine Unity and 'God will be all in all'. The clause in the *Nicene Creed, 'whose Kingdom shall have no end', was inserted to combat his teaching. The Creed which Marcellus embodied in his Ep. to Pope *Julius (in *Epiphanius, *Haer*, lxxii) is generally considered a primary witness for the history of the *Old Roman Creed.

Fragments coll. by C. H. G. Rettberg (Göttingen, 1794)' crit. ed. by E. Klostermann in *Eusebius' Werke*, vol. 4 (*G.C.S.*, 1906), pp. 183–215 (129 items). T. *Zahn, *Marcellus von Ancyra* (1867); F. *Loofs, 'Die Trinitätslehre von Marcellus von Ancyra' in *Sb.* (Berl.), 1902, pp. 764–81; W. Gericke, *Marcell von Ancyra* (1940). M. Richard, 'Un Opuscule méconnu de Marcel évêque d'Ancyre' in *Mélanges de Science religieuse*, vi (1949), pp. 5–28 (attributes to Marcellus the 'De S. Ecclesia' ascribed to Anthimus of Nicomedia). Bardenhewer, iii, pp. 117–22; Altaner (ed. 1950), p. 248. M. D. Chenu, O.P., in *D.T.C.*, ix (pt. 2, 1927), cols. 1993–8, s.v. 'Marcel d'Ancyre'.

MARCIAN

(396–457), the soldier who by his marriage with *Pulcheria, the sister of the Emp. *Theodosius II, became the E. Emperor in 450. His financial reforms made his reign one of considerable prosperity. Theologically his rule was marked by his successful repression of *Monophysitism, Marcian himself attending personally at the sixth session of the Council of *Chalcedon (451) and even resorting to arms to enforce its theological decrees. He stood in good relations with Pope *Leo I (440–61), his correspondence with whom has survived.

MARCIANA.

The famous library at Venice, named after St. *Mark, the patron saint of the city. The real nucleus of the library was the valuable collection of (largely Greek) MSS. made in the 15th cent. by Cardinal *Bessarione, though tradition attributes its beginnings to *Petrarch (1362). Besides a large number of important classical, Biblical, and patristic MSS., the library contains the autographs of Bessarion's 'Encomium on Trebizond' and of P. *Sarpi's *History of the Council of Trent* as well as many early printed works. Since 1904, the library has been housed in the Palazzo della Zecca (the Mint).

J. Valentinelli (ed.), *Bibliotheca Manuscripta ad S. Marci Venetiarum*. Codices Latini (6 vols., 1868–73); A. M. Zanetti–A. Bongiovanni, *Graeca D. Marci Bibliotheca Codicum Manu Scriptorum per Titulos Digesta* (1740); C. Castellani (ed.), *Catalogus Codicum Graecorum qui in Bibliothecam D. Marci Venetiarum inde ad ann. MDCCXL. ad haec usque tempora inlati sunt* (1895). H. Omont, *Inventaire des manuscrits grecs et latins donnés à Saint-Marc de Venice par le cardinal Bessarion en 1468* (1894). H. *Delehaye, S.J., 'Catalogus Codicum Hagiographicorum Graecorum Bibliothecae D. Marci Venetiarum' in *Anal. Boll.*, xxiv (1905), pp. 169–256.

MARCION (d. *c.* 160), heretic. He was a native of Sinope in Pontus and a wealthy shipowner. Acc. to *Hippolytus (*Syntagma* ap. *Epiphanius, *Haer.* 42) he was the son of a Bishop who excommunicated him on grounds of immorality. Making his way to Rome *c.* 140, he attached himself to the local orthodox Church. In the next few years he worked out his system and began to organize his followers as a separate community; and in 144 he was formally excommunicated. From now on, apparently from Rome as a centre, he devoted his gifts as an organizer to the propagation of his views and established compact communities over a large part of the Empire which admitted converts of every age, rank, and background. His many and widely scattered orthodox opponents (among them *Dionysius of *Corinth, *Irenaeus of Lyons, *Theophilus of *Antioch, Philip of Gortyna, *Tertullian at Carthage, Hippolytus and *Rhodo at Rome, *Bardesanes at *Edessa) sufficiently attest Marcion's success. His followers were certainly the chief danger to the Church from dogmatic unorthodoxy in the latter half of the 2nd cent. By the end of the 3rd cent., most of the Marcionite communities had been absorbed in *Manichaeism, but they continued to exist in small numbers down to a much later date.

Marcion's central thesis was that the Christian Gospel was wholly a Gospel of Love to the absolute exclusion of Law. This doctrine, which he expounded esp. in his 'Antitheses', led him to reject completely the OT. The Creator God or *Demiurge, revealed in the OT from Gen. 1 onwards as wholly a God of Law, had nothing in common with the God of Jesus Christ. Study of the OT indicated that this Jewish God constantly involved himself in contradictory courses of action, that he was fickle, capricious, ignorant, despotic, cruel. Utterly different was the Supreme God of Love Whom Jesus came to reveal. It was His purpose to overthrow the Demiurge.

Acc. to Marcion, this contrast of law and spirit was fully understood by St. *Paul alone, the Twelve Apostles and Evangelists being largely blinded to the truth by the remnants of Jewish influence. Hence for Marcion the only Canonical Scriptures were ten of the Epp. of St. Paul (he rejected the *Pastorals) and an edited recension of the Gospel of St. *Luke. He seems to have encouraged in his disciples a close study of the Bible and to have rejected all *allegorical methods of exegesis. He even exercised a certain influence on the history of the Catholic Bible. His brief introductions

('Prologues') to the Pauline Epp. found their way into Latin Biblical MSS. of orthodox *provenance*, while his rejection of three of the Gospels compelled the Church to differentiate between true and spurious works and construct its own *Canon. His Christology was *Docetic. Christ, Who was an embodiment of the Father, suddenly appeared preaching and teaching in the Synagogue at *Capernaum. His Passion and Death were the work of the Creator God.

Marcion's writings have all been lost; but it is possible to deduce a good deal about them and to reconstruct much of his Biblical text, esp. from the invective of Tertullian. He has often been reckoned among the *Gnostics, but it is clear that he would have had little sympathy with their mythological speculations. He inculcated a severe morality and some of his followers suffered in the persecutions.

Marcion is discussed in all histories of early Christian doctrine. The chief ancient sources are *Irenaeus, *Tertullian (esp. 'Adv. Marcionem' and 'De Praescriptione Haereticorum'), *Clement of Alexandria, *Origen, *Adamantius, and the anti-heretical writers generally. The standard modern work, with full analysis of sources and attempted reconstruction of Marcion's Biblical text, is A. *Harnack, *Marcion. Das Evangelium vom fremden Gott* (T.U., xlv; 1921); its value as a history is not seriously affected by its attempt to see in Marcion a precursor of classical Protestantism. Id., *Neue Studien zu Marcion* (ib., xliv, Hft. 4; 1923). E. C. Blackman, *Marcion and his Influence* (1948). J. Knox, *Marcion and the New Testament*. An Essay in the Early History of the Canon (Chicago, 1942). M. J. Lagrange, 'Les Prologues prétendus marcionites' in *R. Bibl.*, xxxv (1926), pp. 161–73; id., 'Saint Paul ou Marcion', ib., xli (1932), pp. 5–30. Bardenhewer, i, 371–6; Altaner (ed. 1950), p. 106 f. G. *Salmon in *D.C.B.*, iii (1882), pp. 816–824; G. Krüger in *P.R.E.* (ed. 3), xii (1903), pp. 266–77; É. Amann in *D.T.C.*, ix (pt. 2; 1927), cols. 2009–32. See also bibl. to *Gnosticism*.

MARCIONITE PROLOGUES, The. A set of short introductory prologues to each of the Pauline Epistles which are to be found in a majority of the best MSS. of the *Vulgate. That they originated in *Marcionite circles is now generally admitted. H. *Lietzmann explains the unexpected introduction of heretical prologues into the Vulgate on the supposition that it was Marcionite teachers at *Rome who first translated the Pauline Epistles from Greek into Latin in the latter part of the 2nd cent.

Text pr. in J. *Wordsworth–H. J. White, *Novum Testamentum Latine*, II, i (1913), p. 41 f., and in A. *Harnack, *Marcion* (T.U., xlv, 1921), pp. 136*–8*. D. de Bruyne, O.S.B., 'Prologues bibliques d'origine marcionite' in *R. Bén.*, xiv (1907), pp. 1–16; A. Harnack, 'Der marcionitische Ursprung der ältesten Vulgata-Prologe zu den Paulusbriefen' in *Z.N.T.W.*, xxiv (1925), pp. 204–18. The Marcionite *provenance* of the Prologues, which is accepted also by P. Corssen, J. R. *Harris, T. *Zahn, J. A. *Robinson, H. *Lietzmann, A. *Souter, is contested by W. Mundle, ib., xxiv (1925), pp. 56–77, and M. J. *Lagrange in *R. Bibl.*, xxxv (1926), pp. 161–73.

MARCOSIANS, the followers of the *Gnostic Marcus, a disciple of *Valentinus. Acc. to *Irenaeus, from whom our knowledge of the sect is derived, they flourished in the Rhône valley in the middle of the 2nd cent. Irenaeus represents Marcus as a charlatan, who made use of magical devices esp. to deceive women to be his prophetesses, and his followers as indulging in elaborate sacramental rites and fantastic speculations about numbers. As Scriptures they used the 'Acts of *Thomas' and other apocryphal books. They represent Gnosticism in its later and most decadent phase.

Irenaeus, *Adv. Haer.*, I, 7–14 (ed. W. W. Harvey), is the sole source; both *Hippolytus, *Ref.* vi, 39–55, and *Epiphanius, *Haer.*, xxxiv, refer explicitly to Irenaeus. F. M. M. Sagnard, O.P., *La Gnose valentinienne et le témoignage de St. Irénée* (1947), pp. 358–86. G. *Salmon in *D.C.B.*, iii (1882), pp. 827–9, s.v., and É. Amann in *D.T.C.*, ix (1926), cols. 1960–2, s.v.

MARCUS, *Gnostic heretic. See preceding entry.

MARCUS AURELIUS (121–80), Roman Emperor from 161. The adopted son of his predecessor, Antoninus Pius (138–61), whose daughter, Faustina (d. 175), he had married, he cherished a noble ideal of life, in essentials a tempered form of *Stoicism. He was deeply concerned for the moral strength and material prosperity of the Empire, and devoted his whole energies to its interests. This firmness of purpose brought him into conflict with the Christian Church, which not only proclaimed an ethic irreconcilable with that of Stoicism, but, in its uncompromising resistance to the official state religion and its inculcation of principles recognizing the equality of Roman and barbarian alike, was radically opposed to Marcus' political ideals. A number of Christian writers addressed 'Apologies' to him, including *Athenagoras and (probably) *Theophilus of Antioch, whose works survive, and *Miltiades, Claudius *Apollinaris and *Melito, Bp. of Sardis, whose apologies are lost. Marcus Aurelius set down his ideals of conduct in Greek in his twelve books of 'Thoughts' or 'Meditations', a work of sincerity and deep feeling but without philosophical originality. In form they are essentially occasional utterances, composed at intervals in the course of his official duties and campaigns.

Editio princeps of his 'Thoughts' by G. Xylandrus (Zürich, 1558). Crit. ed., with English tr. and commentary, by A. S. L. Farquharson (posthumously publd. by J. Sparrow; 2 vols., Oxford, 1944). Other convenient edd. by J. Stich (Teubn., 1882) and, with Fr. tr., by A. I. Trannoy (Collection des Universités de France publiée sous le patronage de l'Association Guillaume Budé; 1939). Convenient Eng. tr. by J. Jackson (World's Classics [1906]). Critical studies of his life by H. D. Sedgwick (New Haven–London, 1921) and G. Loisel (Paris, 1929); studies also by E. *Renan (vol. vii of his *Histoire des origines du christianisme*, 1882; Eng. tr. [1904]), C. C. Dove (London, 1930), F. H. Hayward (ib., 1935), and J. Lindsay (ib., 1936). A. v. Premerstein, 'Untersuchungen zur Geschichte des Kaisers Marcus' in *Klio*. Beiträge zur alten Geschichte, xi (1911), pp. 355–66, xii (1912), pp. 139–78, and xiii (1913), pp. 70–104. M. J. Lagrange, O.P., 'Marc-Aurèle' in *R. Bibl.*, N.S., x [xxij] (1913), pp. 243–59, 394–420, and 568–87. W. Weber in *C.A.H.*, xi (1936), pp. 340–76, with bibl., p. 895. J. Dartigue-Peyrou, *Marc-Aurèle dans les rapports avec le christianisme* (Paris thesis, 1897). P. von Rohden–H. von Arnim in *P.W.*, i (1894), cols. 2279–309, s.v. 'Annius (93)'.

MARCUS DIADOCHUS. The reputed author of a 4th cent. sermon against the *Arians. It has been suggested that the name 'Marcus' arose out of a MS. confusion for

'Blessed Diadochus' (μακάριος Διάδοχος). He is not to be identified, however, with *Diadochus of Photice.

The sermon is printed in J. P. Migne, *PG*, lxv, 1149–66. Bardenhewer, iv, p. 186.

MARCUS EREMITA. See *Mark the Hermit*.

MAREDSOUS. The seat of a Belgian *Benedictine abbey, founded in 1872 as a daughter house of *Beuron in Germany. It is a noted centre of scholarship and publishes the *Revue Bénédictine* (from 1890; originally, from 1884, the *Messager des fidèles*) and the collection *Anecdota Maredsolana* (from 1893). Dom Columba *Marmion was Abbot from 1909 to 1923. After the war of 1914–18, Maredsous separated from Beuron, and became one of the constituent abbeys in the newly constituted 'Belgian Congregation' of the order.

L. H. Cottineau, O.S.B., *Répertoire topo-bibliographique des abbayes et prieurés* (Mâcon, 1939), col. 1744, with good bibl. A. Pratesi in *E.C.*, viii (1952), col. 61 f., s.v.

MARGARET, St., of Antioch (in Pisidia). She is also known as St. Marina. A reputed martyr of the *Diocletianic persecution, of whom, however, nothing certain is known. From an early date she was honoured in the E. Church, and from the 7th cent. also in the W., though devotion to her did not become popular in the W. till the 12th. In more recent times she has been included among the fourteen *Auxiliary saints, and is invoked esp. by women in travail. In art she is often represented with a dragon (representing the devil). Many of the numerous legends which have gathered round her have also attached themselves to St. *Pelagia (q.v.). Feast day in the W., 20 July; in the E., 13 July.

AA.SS., Jul. V (1727), pp. 22–44. *B.H.L.*, p. 787 f. (Nos. 5303–13). H. *Delehaye, S.J., *Les Légendes hagiographiques* (1905), pp. 222–34. A. Zimmermann in *L.Th.K.*, vi (1934), col. 888. See also bibl. to *Pelagia*, St.

MARGARET, 'Lady' (c. 1441–1509). Margaret Beaufort, Countess of Richmond and Derby. She was the daughter of the 1st Duke of Somerset and was married to *Henry VI's half-brother, Edmund Tudor, the Earl of Richmond, c. 1454. He died in 1456, before the birth of his son, the later Henry VII. In 1459 she married a distant cousin, Lord Henry Stafford. During the misfortunes of the house of Lancaster she lived in retirement, in fear for the life of her son who, after the death of Henry VI (1471), lived in exile in Brittany. The later years of her second marriage she spent chiefly at Woking. After Stafford's death (1482) she married Lord Stanley, afterwards Earl of Derby. She had a considerable part in the insurrection which ended in the decisive victory of Bosworth (1485) and in the accession of her son as Henry VII, for whom she had arranged a marriage with Elizabeth of York to reconcile the rival houses. She used her important position as the King's mother mostly for religious and educational interests. In 1495 she became acquainted with J. *Fisher, whom she later chose as her spiritual director. Under his guidance she took religious vows and gave herself up to a life of prayer and good works, reciting the Divine Office as well as the Office of Our Lady and hearing several Masses every day. She also was a 'Sister' of many religious houses, among them *Charterhouse, *Durham, and *Westminster. Fisher also encouraged the foundations by which her name still survives in the older universities. She established the Lady Margaret professorships (originally readerships) at Oxford (1502) and Cambridge (1503) as well as a preachership at Cambridge (1504), and founded Christ's College, Cambridge, in 1505. Her other foundation, St. John's College, Cambridge, was completed only after her death.

Her translation from the Fr. of the *Imitation of Christ, Book iv, was orig. publd. by Richard Pynson at London, 1503; reissued by Wynkyn de Worde, ib., c. 1504. There is a very fine repr. of the latter pr. at Campden, Glos., and publd. at London, 1904. C. H. Cooper, Memoir of Margaret Countess of Richmond and Derby (posthumously publd. by J. E. B. Mayor, Cambridge, 1874), with orig. docc. Other lives by Caroline A. Halstead (London, 1836), Margaret Domville (ib., 1899), and Enid M. G. Routh (ib., 1924). H. A. Tipping in D.N.B., iv (1885), p. 48 f., s.v. 'Beaufort, Margaret'.

MARGARET CLITHEROW, Bl. See Clitherow, Margaret.

MARGARET MARY ALACOQUE, St.
(1647–90), *Visitandine, chief founder of devotion to the *Sacred Heart (q.v.). After an unhappy childhood—she was for years unable to leave her bed, and later had to suffer much from unsympathetic relatives — she entered the Convent of the Visitation at Paray-le-Monial in central France in 1671, where she subsequently became Novice Mistress and Assistant Superior. Here she received several revelations of the Sacred Heart, the first in Dec. 1673, and the final one 18 months later. The visions revealed to her the form of the devotion, the chief features being Holy Communion on the *First Friday of each month, the Holy Hour on Thursdays, and the Feast of the Sacred Heart. Her visions were at first treated with contempt by her superiors, who regarded them as delusions, but under the influence of her temporary confessor, Bl. Claude de la Colombière, S.J. (d. 1682), the opposition softened and eventually ceased. The devotion, however, was not officially recognized till 75 years after her death. She was beatified in 1864 and canonized in 1920. Feast day, 17 Oct.

Crit. ed. of Vie et œuvres de la bienheureuse Margarite-Marie Alacoque by L. Gauthey (ed. 3 [definitive ed.], 3 vols., Paris, 1915; including the best text of her autobiography, also publd. separately, 1920). The standard lives are those by J. J. Languet (Paris, 1729; ed. L. Gauthey, 1890; Eng. tr. in the series 'The Saints and Servants of God', ed. F. W. *Faber, 1850), E. Bougaud (Paris, 1874; Eng. tr., New York, 1920), and A. Hamon, S.J. (Paris, 1907; vol. i of his Histoire de la dévotion au sacré-cœur; frequently publd. separately). Among the better-known popular lives is that of Mgr M. Deminuid ('Les Saints', 1912); in English there

are lives by G. Tickell, S.J. (London, 1869), and A. Barry, C.SS.R. (London [1890]). Pourrat, iv, 402–19. See also bibl. to Sacred Heart.

MARGARET OF SCOTLAND, St. (c.
1045–93), wife of Malcolm III of Scotland, and granddaughter of the English king, Edmund Ironside. She was probably born in Hungary. In 1067, after the battle of Hastings, she left England with her mother and sister and found refuge at the court of Malcolm, to whom she was married in 1070, despite a leaning to the religious life. At her instigation many abuses were reformed, and synods held to regulate the Lenten Fast and Easter Communion and the observance of the prohibited degrees in marriage. Her great personal piety found expression in her practice of prayer and fasting, in her charity to the poor, and in the royal benefactions to religion in her lifetime, which included the foundation of the Church of the Holy Trinity at Dunfermline. She was canonized by *Innocent IV in 1250. She died on 16 Nov., in some places observed as her feast day. There seems no satisfactory explanation of the date of her feast day in the *Roman Martyrology of 1584, namely 10 June, to which, after being transferred to 8 July, it was restored by *Innocent XII in 1693 (at the request of the deposed *James II to mark the birthday of his son).

Life by Turgot, her confessor and later Bp. of St. Andrews, pr. in AA.SS., Jun. II (1698), pp. 328–35. Eng. tr. by W. Forbes-Leith, S.J. (ed. 2, Edinburgh, 1884). Modern ed. of the life in [J.] Pinkerton's Lives of the Scottish Saints revised and enlarged by W. M. Metcalfe, ii (Paisley, 1889), pp. 159–82; Eng. tr. by W. M. Metcalfe, Ancient Lives of Scottish Saints (ib., 1895), pp. 298–321. Modern lives and studies by S. Cowan (Newcastle-on-Tyne, 1911), Lucy Menzies (London, 1925), T. R. Barnett (Edinburgh and London, 1926), and an anonymous life (London and Edinburgh, 1911). W. M. Bryce, 'Saint Margaret of Scotland and her Chapel in the Castle of Edinburgh' in The Book of the Old Edinburgh Club, v (Edinburgh, 1912), pp. 1–66.

MARHEINEKE, PHILIPP KONRAD
(1780–1846), Protestant theologian. From 1811 till his death he was professor at Berlin, and from 1820 in charge also of the important Dreifaltigkeitskirche. A warm admirer of the philosophy of G. W. F. *Hegel, then exercising a dominating influence on all aspects of German culture, Marheineke sought to invoke its support for the Christian faith, though not without radically transforming it. He professed to be, in Hegelian language, a 'theologian of the concept' (Begriffstheologe), as opposed to a 'theologian of faith' (the standpoint of traditional historic Christianity) or 'of feeling' (F. D. E. *Schleiermacher). Characteristic of his theological method and attitude was his thesis that 'the Church is the truth (Wahrheit) of the State, the State the reality (Wirklichkeit) of the Church'. The Protestant and Catholic Confessions were to be united in a higher Hegelian synthesis. His writings include a Symbolik (3 vols., 1810–14), which brought him into conflict with J. A. *Möhler), a history of the German Reformation (2 vols., 1816), and Die Bedeutung der Hegelschen Philosophie in der christlichen Theologie (1842). Much of his most characteristic teaching was formulated in his

lectures, many of which were published by his pupils soon after his death.

His theological lectures were ed. by S. Matthies–W. Vatke (4 vols., Berlin, 1847–9). A. Weber, *Le Système dogmatique de P. C. Marheineke* (Strassburg, 1857). Margaret E. Ihle, *P. K. Marheineke*. Der Einfluss der Philosophie auf sein theologisches System (Diss., Leipzig, 1938). G. Frank in *P.R.E.* (ed. 3), xii (1903), pp. 304–9, s.v.

MARIA LAACH ('Maria ad lacum'), *Benedictine abbey some 15 miles north-west of Coblence, founded in 1093. The fine Romanesque church, with five towers and a dome, was completed in 1156. In 1802, the troubles of the French Revolution brought the life of the monastery to an end; in 1815 the buildings passed into the possession of the Prussian state; and in 1820 they became private property. In 1863 they were recovered for ecclesiastical purposes by the *Jesuits, who used them as a centre of studies until 1872. They finally reverted to the Benedictines of the *Beuron Congregation in 1892. The monks have actively prosecuted liturgical studies, edited the *Jahrbuch für Liturgiewissenschaft* (1921 onwards), and taken an active part in fostering the *Liturgical Movement.

A. Schippers, O.S.B., *Das Laacher Münster* (1927), and other works by this author. L. H. Cottineau, O.S.B., *Répertoire topo-bibliographique des abbayes et prieurés* (Mâcon, 1939), col. 1533 f., with good bibl. I. Herwegen, O.S.B., in *C.E.*, ix (1910), p. 658, also with bibl.

MARIANA, JUAN (1536–1623 [? 1624]), Spanish *Jesuit. He joined the order in 1554, and held teaching appointments at Rome (1561–4), Sicily (1564–9), Paris (1569–74), and Toledo (from 1574). He became famous by his book *De Rege et Regis Institutione* (1559), justifying tyrannicide. The book encouraged the belief that the Jesuits were responsible for the assassination of *Henry IV of France and the *Gunpowder Plot in England, and in 1610 the Jesuit General C. *Aquaviva expressly forbade members of the order to teach this doctrine. Mariana is also one of the foremost historians of Spain (the 'Spanish Livy'). In 1592 he issued his *Historia de rebus Hispaniae* and in 1601 *Historia general de España* (2 vols.).

An Eng. tr. of his *History of Spain* was publd. at London, 1699. G. Cirot, *Études sur l'historiographie espagnole.* viii (1905). M. Ballesteros-Gaibrois, *Juan de Mariana* (2 vols., Santander, 1938–9). J. Laures, S.J., *The Political Economy of Juan de Mariana* (New York, 1928); M. B. Amzalak, *As teorias monetárias do Padre João de Mariana* (1944). B. Antoniades, 'Die Staatslehre des Mariana' in *Archiv für Geschichte der Philosophie*, xxi (1908), pp. 166–95. F. Asensio, 'El profesorado de Juan de Mariana y su influjo en la vida del escritor' in *Hispana*, liii (1953), pp. 581–639. Sommervogel, v (1894), cols. 547–67. A. Lehmkuhl in *C.E.*, ix (1910), p. 659 f., s.v.; E. Amann in *D.T.C.*, ix (pt. 2; 1927), cols. 2336–8, s.v.; C. Testore, S.J., in *E.C.*, viii (1952), col. 146 f., s.v., with bibl.

MARIANISTS. The 'Society of Mary', of Bordeaux (to be distinguished from the *Marists, q.v.). The congregation, which was founded at Bordeaux in 1817 by the theologian William Joseph Chaminade (1761–1850), and recognized by the Pope in 1865 and again in 1891, consists of priests and laymen. It was instituted to fight religious indifference, and

its members, who devote themselves esp. to educational work, add to the three vows of poverty, chastity, and obedience a fourth, promising stability in the service of the BVM, which is expressed in the daily recitation of the *Rosary and of the Little Office of Our Lady. The congregation, which is governed by a Superior General with his seat at Nivelles (Belgium), spread rapidly in many European countries as well as in America and Asia. The members of the female Institute, the 'Daughters of Mary', founded in 1816, also devote themselves to education; their constitutions were finally confirmed in 1888.

Lives of the founder by J. Simler (Paris, 1901), H. Rousseau, S.M. (ib., 1913), and G. Goyau (ib., 1914). M. Heimbucher, *Die Orden und Kongregationen der katholischen Kirche*, ii (ed. 3; 1934), pp. 445–7. E. Scherer, S.M., in *E.C.*, xi (1953), col. 864 f., s.v. 'Società di Maria', with bibl.

MARIAVITES. A Polish sect, founded in 1906 by J. Kowalski, a priest of Warsaw, and Felicia Kozlowska, a *Tertiary sister (d. 1922), on their excommunication from the RC Church. Many years earlier the latter had laid claim to private revelations and these formed the doctrinal basis of the new communities. Their name is derived from their profession of great devotion to the BVM ('qui Mariae vitam imitantur'). They acknowledged the first seven *Oecumenical Councils, accepted the '*Filioque' as a 'theological opinion', and incorporated into their practice many ascetic elements, combined with some unconventional arrangements about the marriage of the clergy. Relations having been established with the *Old Catholics, in 1909 Kowalski was consecrated a bishop by the Abp. of Utrecht; and in 1911 they were officially recognized by the Duma. But after a few brief years of prosperity their numbers and influence declined, their discipline deteriorated, and in 1924 the Old Catholics severed communion with them.

K. Gajowski, *Mariavitensekte. Einige Blätter aus der neuesten Kirchengeschichte* Russisch-Polens (Cracow, 1911); A. Rhode, *Bei den Mariaviten.* Eindrücke von einer neuen romfreien katholischen Kirche (1911). R. Janin, 'Les Mariavites et l'orthodoxie' in *É.O.*, xxx (1927), pp. 216–20; M. Niwinski, 'Les Mariavites de Pologne' in *Revue apologétique*, liv (1932), pp. 570–80. C. Neuhaus in *R.G.G.* (ed. 2), iii (1929), cols. 2000–4, s.v. 'Mariaviten'.

MARIOLATRY. A term derived from 'Maria' and '*latria*' (Gk. λατρεία, worship), denoting erroneous attribution of Divine honours to the BVM. An early instance of it is found in the 4th cent. when the sect of the *Collyridians was condemned by St. *Epiphanius for offering sacrificial worship to Mary. A more recent example is the cult of the BVM in the Eucharist, advocated by the Franciscan *Recollect, Z. de Someire, and condemned by *Benedict XIV. By Protestants the word is often employed in an abusive sense of what they consider the excessive devotion to the BVM in the RC Church.

MARIOLOGY. The systematic study of the person of the Blessed Virgin *Mary and of her place in the economy of the *Incarnation.

MARISCO, ADAM DE. See *Adam Marsh*.

MARISTS. The 'Society of Mary' was founded at Lyons in 1824 by the Ven. Jean Claude Marie Colin (1790–1875). It was approved by *Gregory XVI in 1836, when the first 20 Marists took simple perpetual vows and the W. Pacific was allotted to them as their special mission field, and finally sanctioned in 1873. It spread rapidly in many European countries, in N. America, and esp. in Australia and New Zealand, and was introduced in England by N. *Wiseman in 1850. The congregation comprises priests and lay brothers whose main activities are educational and missionary work. Their rule, which is based on that of the *Jesuits, aims esp. at fostering devotion to our Lady. Several other institutes are connected with the Marists, among them the Marist Schoolbrothers founded in 1817 by the Ven. Marcellin Joseph Benedict Champagnat and approved by the Holy See in 1863 and 1903, the Marist Sisters (Sisters of the Holy Name of Mary), founded by Colin in 1816 for the education of young girls, and the Third Order of the Society of Mary, founded in 1850 for persons living in the world, with its seat in Rome.

There is a brief life of Colin by G. Goyau (Paris, 1910). Heimbucher, ii, 374–7, with bibl. J. F. Sollier, S.M., in *C.E.*, ix (1910), p. 751 f., s.v. 'Mary, Society of'.

MARITAIN, JACQUES (b. 1882), French *Thomist philosopher. He was born in *Paris and studied at the *Sorbonne, where he came under the influence of H. *Bergson. His friendship with L. Bloy contributed decisively to his conversion to the Catholic Church in 1906. In 1907 and 1908 he studied biology at Heidelberg under H. Driesch, and in the following years devoted himself to the study of St. *Thomas Aquinas. This interest became the inspiration of his life-work, which may be summarized as the application of Thomist philosophy to the issues of modern culture. In 1914 he became professor at the *Institut Catholique de Paris, and from 1933 he taught at the Institute of Mediaeval Studies at Toronto. In the divisions in French politics before 1939, Maritain associated himself closely with the more democratic Catholic wing. From 1945 to 1948 he was French Ambassador to the Holy See. In 1948 he was appointed Prof. of Philosophy at Princeton University.

His first considerable work, *La Philosophie bergsonienne* (1914), is a vigorous criticism of the thought of his former master. In *Art et scolastique* (1920; Eng. trans., 1930), which made a deep impression on artists as well as theorists of art, he applied Thomist principles to aesthetics. In 1925 there followed *Trois Réformateurs* (Eng. trans., 1928), which contains short but penetrating studies of M. *Luther, R. *Descartes, and J.-J. *Rousseau. Acc. to Maritain their work was marked respectively by the placing of self in the centre of the religious life and the transformation of objective faith into subjective confidence

(Luther), by the 'sin of angelism', which refuses to recognize the dependence of human knowledge on sense experience (Descartes), and by the identification of sanctity with 'pure nature', aiming at a religious conception of life without the aid of either reason or grace (Rousseau). In his *Primauté du spirituel* (1927; Eng. trans., *The Things that are not Caesar's*, 1930), inspired by the Papal condemnation of the '*Action française', he studied the relations between Catholic doctrine and politics, esp. the exercise of the indirect power of the Church in the temporal sphere and the consequences of the primacy of the spiritual for the modern world. In *Les Degrés du savoir* (1932; Eng. trans., 1937), he traverses the whole field of knowledge from science and metaphysics to the supra-rational knowledge of the mystics, exemplified esp. by St. *Augustine and St. *John of the Cross. In *Humanisme intégral* (1936; Eng. trans., 1938), he dealt with the tragedy of secular humanism and the ideal and possibility of a new Christian order. His more recent writings include *Les Droits de l'homme et la loi naturelle* (1942; Eng. tr., 1944) and *Redeeming the Time* (1943).

The Maritain Volume of the Thomist (publ. as vol. v of the Thomist), Dedicated to Jacques Maritain on the Occasion of his Sixtieth Birthday (New York, 1943), incl. bibl. of his works 1910–42, and of writings about him, by R. Byrns, pp. 345–71; *Jacques Maritain*. Son œuvre philosophique (Bibliothèque de la Revue Thomiste [1949]), incl. 'Bibliographie résumée des écrits de Jacques Maritain', pp. 24–32. G. B. Phelan, *Jacques Maritain* (1937).

MARIUS MERCATOR (early 5th cent.). A Latin Christian writer, probably of African birth. A friend and disciple of St. *Augustine, he wrote *c.* 418 at Rome against *Pelagius. Some ten years later, when in Constantinople, perhaps as the agent of Pope *Celestine (422–432), he again wrote in defence of orthodoxy, this time attacking both *Nestorians and Pelagians. A collection of his writings, compiled about 100 years after his time, has survived in a Vatican MS. (Cod. Vat. Pal. 234). It consists largely of Mercator's translations of and replies to Nestorius's writings, made (acc. to E. *Schwartz) for the Latin-speaking monks of Thrace, and is one of the more important sources for our knowledge of Nestorius's doctrines.

Writings ed. J. *Garnier, S.J. (Paris, 1673; repr. in J. P. Migne, *PL*, xlviii), on the basis of a Beauvais MS., since lost. Another ed. by É. *Baluze (Paris, 1684) from Vat. Pal. 234. Crit. text, with discussion, by E. Schwartz in *A.C.O.*, I, v, (1), pp. 5–70 (only the texts on pp. 3–36 belong to Marius Mercator; the remainder, incl. the Counter-Anathematisms of Nestorius, commonly ascribed to him, appear to be of much later date). Bardenhewer, iv, 525–9. W. Eltester in *P.W.*, xiv (1930), cols. 1831–5; C. Vogel in *E.C.*, viii (1952), col. 166.

MARK, St., Evangelist. John Mark, the cousin of St. *Barnabas (Col. 4. 10), a Jew, and perhaps a minor minister of the synagogue (Acts 13. 5, Gk. ὑπηρέτης), set out with St. Barnabas and St. *Paul on their first missionary journey, but for reasons which failed to satisfy St. Paul turned back (Acts 12. 25, 13. 13, 15. 37 ff.). Afterwards he was in Rome with

St. Paul (Col. 4. 10, Philem. 24, 2 Tim. 4. 11), and St. *Peter (1 Pet. 5. 13), whose 'interpreter' (ἑρμηνευτής), acc. to *Papias, he was; and it was no doubt in Italy, if not at *Rome itself, that he wrote his Gospel. Acc. to *Eusebius, he afterwards went to *Alexandria and was its first bishop, while in later tradition he is also associated with *Venice. Feast day, 25 Apr.

The processional Major Litanies (*Litaniae Majores*) traditionally observed at Rome on 25 Apr. appear to have arisen quite independently of the feast. They go back to the time of St. *Gregory the Great (d. 604) when they were introduced as a Christian substitute for the pagan *robigalia* on that day.

AA.SS., Apr. III (1675), pp. 344–58, and Sept. VII (1760), pp. 379–90. The tradition that Mark was κολοβοδάκτυλος (prob. 'stump-fingered', i.e. of Mk. himself, and not an allusion to the brevity of his Gospel) is found in the *Anti-Marcionite Prologue and in St. *Hippolytus, *Haer.*, vii, 30. On his founding of the Church of Alexandria, cf. *Eusebius, *H.E.*, II, xvi, 1, and xxiv, 1. H. B. *Swete, *The Gospel according to St. Mark* (1898), pp. ix–xxiii. F. H. Chase in *H.D.B.*, iii (1900), pp. 245–8, s.v. 'Mark (John)'; A. *Jülicher in *P.R.E.* (ed. 3), xii (1903), pp. 288–97, s.v., 'Marcus im NT'; U. Holzmeister, S.J., in *L.Th.K.*, vi (1934), col. 955 f.; P. de Ambroggi–W. Wehr–P. Toschi in *E.C.*, viii (1952), cols. 41–9. On the Major Litanies, see L. *Duchesne, *Christian Worship* (Eng. trans., ed. 1919), p. 288.

MARK, Gospel of St. (1) *Authorship, Date and Place of Origin.* The Gospel was known in the 1st cent. and, acc. to the view at present most widely held, was used by both Matthew and Luke (see *Marcan Hypothesis*). The earliest definite tradition about it is due to *Papias. He states that the Gospel was written by St. *Mark, who drew his information from the teaching of St. *Peter. The connexion of Mark with Peter has earlier testimony in 1 Pet. 5. 13. Later tradition follows the statements of Papias.

The external tradition about the Gospel must be controlled by the internal evidence of the Book itself. It seems that the author had considerable knowledge of Palestine and yet was not bound by narrow Jewish sympathies. The same double background is reflected in the traces of both Aramaic and Latin which the Greek of the Gospel betrays. The Latinisms support the presumption, based on the traditional connexion with Peter, that the Gospel was written in Rome, as also does Mark's dating of the Crucifixion on the 15th *Nisan, in agreement with the Roman view in subsequent controversy. Whether or not there is to be found in the Gospel such a particular interest in Peter as might have been expected if the Petrine origin described by Papias is to be maintained is a matter of dispute among critics. The date suggested by the Gospel itself is early. Not all those who had known our Lord personally were dead (cf. 9. 1).

There seems to be no good reason why the Gospel should not have been written by John *Mark, esp. as it is unlikely that tradition would wrongly have assigned a Gospel to so unimportant a character. It has been suggested that the account of the young man in *Gethsemane (14. 51 f.) is the 'artist's signature', and that Mark himself is intended.

(2) *Sources and Composition.* It is likely that St. Mark had to collect for himself the material of which his Gospel is composed. Even if Papias was wrong in ascribing the Marcan material to Peter, he was no doubt correct in describing it as having first existed in the form of oral teaching (see *Form Criticism*). There are, however, traces of written sources in Mk. At some points there is contact between Mk. and *'Q' (see *Synoptic Problem*), and it is possible that 'Q' was known to Mark. The detection of other sources can only be conjectural; but, e.g., it may be that the parallel narratives of 6. 32–7. 37, and 8. 1–26 come from written sources, while in ch. 13 there are traces of earlier (and perhaps Jewish) material. It is also possible that Mark derived his self-contained 'Passion narrative' from a previously written document.

(3) *Character and Purpose.* Mk. is written in 'Koine *Greek', i.e. in the popular language that was the *lingua franca* of the E. Mediterranean. It is the least cultured and the least grammatical of the Gospels, though the author shows considerable talent and power in writing narrative. His style is Semitic in colouring, and it may be that in places Mark was translating an Aramaic document; in any case much of the material of the Gospel seems to bear a Palestinian stamp.

The Gospel is arranged as a continuous narrative. The simple outline of events to which the sources are subordinated corresponds with that implied in the speeches attributed to Peter and Paul in Acts. The story opens with the preaching of *John the Baptist, represented as the fulfilment of prophecy. After the Baptism and Temptation of our Lord, the Messianic ministry at once begins. Disciples are called, miracles are performed, teaching, chiefly in the form of parables, is given. The whole emphasizes the idea of fulfilment; the Kingdom of God, though still the object of hope, is also present in the person of the Messiah (who chooses rather the title '*Son of Man') and among those who follow Him. The narrative is sharply broken at 8. 27 ff. by the confession of Peter that Jesus is the Messiah. Immediately, and from that point continuously, the burden of our Lord's teaching is that as Messiah He must suffer, die, and rise from the dead. The story of the Passion includes the account of the Last Supper and describes the death of Christ as the fulfilment of OT prophecy. The Crucifixion is followed by the Resurrection; but Mark's Gospel concludes abruptly at 16. 8 perhaps because Mark intended it to end there, perhaps because its end has been lost. 16. 9–20 is one of two early supplements added to the Gospel. They do not appear in the oldest MSS., but are of very early date. See also *Aristion*.

The purpose of the Gospel is shown both in the sources and in the evangelist's arrangement of them. He wishes to witness to Jesus as the Messiah. His Messiahship was attested at His baptism. As such He is recognized by demons and finally by men, though He claims the title for Himself only before the High Priest. As Messiah He died. Mark's own definition of his work and its subject is given in 1. 1, echoed in 15. 39. His Gospel was written around the themes of the Church's preaching—the Kingdom of God, the Messiah, and the suffering Son of Man.

(4) *Conclusion.* It is clear that Mark's purpose is 'evangelistic' and thus by no means corresponds with that of the modern historian. Does this mean that he tells us nothing on which we may rely as historical truth? Admittedly Mk. is in the first place evidence for the tradition of its own time. But though in that tradition history and its interpretation were already mingled, the history did not cease to be history because it was interpreted. Mk. gives us a patchwork of tradition; but on analysis every part of it bears witness, in its own way, to a 'Jesus of History' behind it.

The Patristic and Medieval Commentators paid scant attention to St. Mark's Gospel, probably because of its brevity and the inclusion of nearly all its matter in the other Synoptics. Those who commented on it include *Victor of Antioch, *Theophylact, and *Euthymius Zigabenus among the Greeks and *Bede among the Latins. In modern times, on the other hand, it has attracted close attention from all students of the Gospels. Commentaries include those of E. P. Gould (I.C.C., 1896), H. B. *Swete (London, 1898), J.*Wellhausen, (Berlin, 1903), E. Klostermann (H.N.T., 1907), M. J. *Lagrange (Études bibliques, 1911), A. *Loisy (Paris, 1912), A. E. J. Rawlinson (West. Comm., 1925), A. W. F. Blunt (Clar. Bib., 1929), E. Lohmeyer (K.E.K., ed. 10; 1937), B. H. Branscomb (Moff. Comm., 1937), J. [D.] Schniewind (Neue Testament Deutsch 1; Göttingen, 1937), V. Taylor (London, 1952) and S. E. Johnson (London, 1960).
Other studies include E. Wendling, *Die Entstehung des Marcus-Evangeliums.* Philologische Untersuchungen (1908). B. W. Bacon, *Is Mark a Roman Gospel?* (Harvard Theological Studies, vii; 1919). M. Werner, *Der Einfluss paulinischer Theologie im Markusevangelium* (Beiheft i, zur *Z.N.T.W.*; 1923). B. W. Bacon, *The Gospel of Mark.* Its Composition and Date (New Haven, Conn., 1925). R. H. Lightfoot, *The Gospel Message of St. Mark* (1950). A. M. Farrer, *A Study in St. Mark* (1951). See also bibl. to *Synoptic Problem.*

MARK, Liturgy of St. The traditional Greek Eucharistic Liturgy of the Church of *Alexandria, formerly used by the Egyptian *Melchites. It survives in three late MSS., the Cod. Rossanensis (Vat. gr. 1970; saec. xiii), the Rotulus Vaticanus (Vat. gr. 2281; saec. xiii), and the Rotulus Messanensis (Cod. Messin. gr. 177; saec. xii). Behind these texts, all much altered by foreign influences (*Constantinople and/or *Jerusalem), lies a primitive local Egyptian text, in which the great intercessory prayer stood before the *Preface and there was no *Benedictus at the end of the *Sanctus. Recently (1928) a fragment of the authentic text of the Liturgy has been recovered on a Strassburg Papyrus (4th–5th cent.). A modified form of the rite in Coptic (known alternatively as 'The Coptic Liturgy of St. Mark' or 'of St. Cyril') is still in use among the Coptic *Monophysites, another form of it, in Ethiopic, among the Abyssinians.

Text in E. *Renaudot, *Liturgiarum Orientalium Collectio,* i (Paris, 1716), pp. 131–65; in C. A. Swainson, *The Greek Liturgies* (1884), pp. 2–73; and in Brightman, *L.E.W.*, pp. 115–88. Papyrus fragment of authentic text ed. M. Andrieu-P. Collomp, 'Fragments sur papyrus de l'anaphore

de saint Marc' in *Rev. S.R.*, viii (1928), pp. 480–515; text repr. in *Florilegium Patristicum*, fasc. vii., 1 (ed. 2 by J. Quasten, 1935), pp. 44–8; shorter fragment ed. C. H. Roberts, *Catalogue of the Greek and Latin Papyri in the John Rylands Library, Manchester*, iii (Manchester, 1938), pp. 25–8 (Papyrus No. 465). A. Gastoué-H. *Leclercq, O.S.B., in *D.A.C.L.*, i (pt. 1; 1907), cols. 1182–204, s.v. 'Alexandrie (liturgie)', with full bibl.; A. *Fortescue in *C.E.*, i (1907), pp. 303–6, s.v. 'Alexandrine Liturgy'; A. Raes, S.J., in *E.C.*, i (1949), cols. 769–73, s.v. 'Alessandria d' Egitto. 5, Il rito alessandrino'.

MARK THE HERMIT (*fl. c.* 400), ascetical writer. Like his contemporary, *Nilus the Ascetic, he was a pupil of St. *Chrysostom. Most of the details of his life are obscure, though it is likely that at one time he was an abbot at *Ancyra and later a hermit, perhaps in the desert of Judaea. His writings, for the most part of a practical character, include treatises 'On Fasting', 'On Repentance', 'On the Spiritual Law', and 'On Those who suppose Justification is from Works'. His vigorous attack on human merit in the last-named writing commended him to older Protestant theologians. A work 'On Temperance' (κεφάλαια νηπτικά), which is ascribed to him, certainly belongs to a later writer.

Works in J. P. Migne, *PL*, lxv, 893–1140. Partial ed. by F. *Ducaeus, S.J., in his *Bibliotheca Veterum Patrum*, i (Paris, 1624), pp. 869–984 (repr. from the ed. of G. Morel, Paris, 1563). The Gk. text of Mark's 'De Jejunio' and 'De Melchisedek' were first publd. by B. M. Remondini (Rome, 1748). His 'Adversus Nestorianos', first publd. from a 13th cent. Jerusalem MS. by A. Papadopoulos-Kerameus at St. Petersburg in 1891, was issued in an improved text by J. Kunze, *Markus Eremita* (1895; important study, esp. on Mark's Baptismal Creed), pp. 6–30. Bardenhewer, iv (1924), pp. 178–86; Altaner (ed. 1951), p. 291 f. É. Amann in *D.T.C.*, ix (pt. 2; 1927), cols. 1964–8, s.v. 'Marc l'Ermite'; H. Dörries in *P.W.*, xiv (1930), cols. 1867–9, s.v. 'Markus (6)'.

MARKS OF THE CHURCH. See *Notes of the Church.*

MARMION, COLUMBA (1858–1923), Abbot of *Maredsous. He was an Irishman by birth, who, though he lived mainly surrounded by French culture, retained his Irish characteristics and sympathies till his death. In 1886 he entered the Benedictine house at Maredsous; in 1899 he became prior of the Abbey of Mont-César at Louvain; and from 1909 till his death was Abbot of Maredsous. Basing his teaching on the Christocentric teaching of St. *Paul, he drew largely on the patristic and liturgical traditions of *Benedictine monasticism, without at the same time failing to appreciate *Thomist theology. He was an unusually gifted spiritual writer and director, whose main works, the fruit of series of spiritual addresses, are *Le Christ, vie de l'âme* (1918, over 100,000 copies issued), *Le Christ dans ses mystères* (1919), and *Le Christ, idéal du moine* (1922).

Life by R. Thibaut (Maredsous, 1929; Eng. tr., 1932).

MARNIX, PHILIPP VAN (1538–98), Baron de Sainte-Aldegonde, Dutch Protestant theologian and statesmen. Between 1562 and 1569 he won fame by his Protestant and nationalist writings, of which the most celebrated was the bitterly satirical *De biënkorf der heilige roomsche kerche* (1569; Eng. trans. by G. Gilpin, 1579). *c.* 1566–7 he took up arms as an anti-Spanish leader, and formed a close friendship with William the Silent, whose constant adviser he became. He was made the first burgomaster of Antwerp in 1584, but lost his political influence in the next year by his surrender of the town to Alexander of Parma. A personal disciple of J. *Calvin and T. *Beza, his theology was rigidly Calvinist. Down to his death he was engaged on a Dutch version of the Bible.

Œuvres de P. de Marnix de Sainte-Aldegonde, with introd. by E. Quinet (9 vols., Brussels, 1857–60); *Godsdienstige en Kerkelijke Geschriften*, ed. J. J. van Toorenenbergen (3 vols., The Hague, 1871–91). W. A. Nolet, *Marnix als Theoloog*. Historische Inleiding (1948), with bibl. T. Schott–S. D. van Veen in *P.R.E.* (ed. 3), xii (1903), pp. 347–55, s.v., and A. Eekhof in *R.G.G.* (ed. 2), iii (1929), col. 2022, s.v., both with bibl.

MARONITES. A Christian community of Syrian origin, the greater part of whom still live in their native land of Lebanon, though some are to be found elsewhere in Syria and Palestine, and there are colonies also in Cyprus, Alexandria, and the U.S.A. Since 1181, when they were brought into relation with the Crusaders, they have been in formal communion with the RC Church.

By their own theologians it is claimed that their existence can be traced back to St. Maro, a friend of St. *Chrysostom (d. 407), whose disciples shortly after his death founded the monastery on the Orontes that now goes by his name and that the modern Maronites derive directly from this foundation. It seems certain, however, that their origin does not go back beyond the 7th cent., and that their existence as a separate body arose out of their adoption of *Monothelite doctrines and their consequent excommunication at the Council of *Constantinople in 680. Their monastery on Mt. Lebanon was destroyed by the Arab invasion at the beginning of the 10th cent. Since their union with Rome in the 12th cent., relations with the W. have been continuously maintained. In 1584 *Gregory XIII founded a Maronite college in Rome, which was later the home of the *Assemani and several other notable scholars. In recent times they have suffered severe treatment at the hands of the Turks and the Druses.

As a *Uniat body they possess their own liturgy, which is in essence an Antiochene rite in the Syriac language, much modified by Latin influences. Their hierarchy consists of a *patriarch (whose see town is Jebeil [? Gebal]), 8 bishops (Aleppo, Baalbek, Beirut, Cyprus, Damascus, Sidon, Tyre, Tripoli), besides a patriarchal vicar in Egypt and 7 titular bishops.

T. Anaissi (ed.), *Bullarium Maronitarum* (Rome, 1911). P.Dib (ed.), *Quelques Documents pour servir à l'histoire des Maronites* (1945). M. *Lequien, O.P., *Oriens Christianus*, iii (Rome, 1740), cols. 1–100. P.Dib, *L'Église maronite*, vol. i, 'L'Église maronite jusqu'à la fin du moyen-âge' (1930). Id., *Étude sur la liturgie maronite* [*c.* 1920]. Id. in *Codificazione Canonica Orientale*, Fonti, fasc., viii (Rome, 1932), pp. 90–116; P. Sfair, ib., fasc. xii, *Ius Particulare Maroniti-*

arum (ib., 1933). D. Attwater, *The Catholic Eastern Churches* (Milwaukee, 1935), pp. 180–95. D. G. Hogarth in *E.B.* (ed. 11), xvii (1911), p. 747 f.; P. Dib. in *D.T.C.*, x (pt. 1; 1928), cols. 1–142, s.v., with full bibl.; P. Sfair–A. Raes, S.J., in *E.C.*, viii (1952), cols. 177–84, s.v. 'Maroniti', with bibl.

MAROT, CLÉMENT (*c.* 1497–1544), French hymn-writer. Having entered the service of Marguerite d'Angoulême ('Margaret of Navarre'), he was brought into contact with an early form of *Huguenot teaching, and in 1527 openly avowed his adhesion to Protestantism. In 1535 he was compelled to flee to Ferrara, but became reconciled to Catholicism in the next year. His French version of some selected Psalms (1538) was warmly welcomed (despite the religious vacillations of its composer) by the French Protestants, who were in great need of a hymn-book. He soon became suspect once more of Protestant sympathies, and this time took refuge at Geneva. When, in 1562, T. *Beza added to a collection of 49 of Marot's Psalms the remaining 101, the first complete Protestant Psalter in verse was brought into being.

Œuvres de Clément Marot, ed. G. Guiffrey (5 vols., Paris, 1875–1931; vol. i, life of Marot, ed. by R. Yve-Plessis, vols. iv and v ed. by J. Plattard). O. Douen, *Clément Marot et le psautier huguenot* (2 vols., 1878–9). P. A. Becker, *Clement Marot. Sein Leben und seine Dichtung* (1926). J. Plattard, 'Marot. Sa carrière poétique. Son œuvre' in *Revue des Cours et Conférences*, xxxix (1938), part. i, pp. 27–41, 129–41, 235–49, 345–59, 463–76, 632–43, 723–36, and pt. ii, pp. 68–83, 177–91, 271–9, 372–84, 441–53, 553–61, 640–51, and 728–34; also separately as vol. xlvi of the Bibliothèque de la Revue des Cours et Conférences, 1939.

MARPRELATE TRACTS, The. A series of violent and frequently scurrilous *Puritan tracts attacking *Episcopacy, issued under the pseudonym of Martin Marprelate in 1588 and 1589. They were prob. occasioned by the decree of Abp. J. *Whitgift in 1586 requiring ecclesiastical approval for all publications. The titles (abbreviated) of the seven which survive are *The Epistle*, *The Epitome*, *Hay any Work for Cooper*, *Minerall and Metaphysical School-points*, *Theses Martinianae*, *The Just Censure and Reproof* and *The Protestation*. They appear to have been published successively at Molesey (nr. Kingston-on-Thames), Fawsley House (nr. Daventry, Northants), Norton, Wolston (both Worcs.), Coventry and in or near Manchester. Among those accused of writing them were Job Throckmorton (1545–1601; prob. one of the authors) and J. *Udall, who both denied the charges, and J. *Penry, who was executed. Replies were published by T. Cooper, Bp. of Winchester, R. *Bancroft, J. Lyly, and T. Nash. The tracts themselves, though prob. the most brilliant prose satire of the period, by their violence aroused hostility rather than sympathy for the Puritan party.

Modern ed. of Tracts with hist. notes by W. Pierce (London, 1911). See also W. Pierce, *An Historical Introduction to the Marprelate Tracts* (1908). J. D. Wilson–A. F. S. Pearson in *C.B.E.L.*, i, pp. 688–94.

MARRIAGE. See *Matrimony*.

MARRIAGE LICENCES. Licences to dispense with the necessity of *banns have been granted by bishops since the early 14th cent. The power to issue such licences was confirmed to them in 1534 by the Peter's Pence Act (25 Hen. VIII, c. 21). In 1753 Lord *Hardwicke's Marriage Act (26 Geo II, c. 23) enacted that marriages solemnized without banns or licence should be void according to the secular law although acc. to Anglican Church law they were irregular but valid. It was repealed in 1823 when the Marriage Act of that year (4 Geo IV, c. 76) declared clandestine marriages valid, but the officiating minister a felon.

Acc. to canon 101 of 1604, marriage licences may be issued by those having episcopal authority or the commissary for faculties, vicars-general of the Archbishops and Bishops *sede plena* or *sede vacante*, the guardian of the spiritualities, or ordinaries exercising the right of episcopal jurisdiction in the several jurisdictions respectively, but in practice they are generally granted by *surrogates appointed by the chancellor. They are entirely a matter of grace. The 1823 Marriage Act requires that before a licence is granted one of the parties shall swear before the surrogate that he knows of no impediment or suit pending in any court to bar the marriage and that one of the parties has for the past fifteen days had his abode in the parish or chapelry in which the marriage is to be solemnized.

The power to grant special licences to marry at any time and in any church, chapel or other suitable or convenient place was exercised in both provinces by the Abps. of *Canterbury as *legati nati*. It was confirmed to them by the Peter's Pence Act, and specifically reserved in the Marriage Act of 1823. The fee is now £25.

Acc. to the Marriage Act of 1836 (6 and 7 Will. IV, c. 85) superintendent registrars may issue licences for marriages in the office of a registrar or a nonconformist place of worship but not acc. to the rite of the C of E or in any church or chapel belonging to it or licensed for the celebration of divine worship acc. to its rites.

R. Phillimore, *The Ecclesiastical Law of the Church of England* (ed. 2, 1895), pp. 607-17; H. W. Cripps, *A Practical Treatise on the Law Relating to the Church and Clergy* (ed. 8, 1937), pp. 547-51.

MARRIOTT, CHARLES (1811–58), English divine. He was educated at Exeter and Balliol Colleges, Oxford, and in 1833 was elected a Fellow of Oriel, where he became closely associated with several of the *Tractarian leaders and a devoted disciple of J. H. *Newman. After Newman seceded to the RC Church Marriott remained with E. B. *Pusey a leader in Oxford of the High Church Movement. As a religious counsellor, he exercised a wide influence, esp. on young men. From 1839 to 1841 he was the first principal of Chichester Theological College, and from 1850 to 1855 vicar of the University Church at Oxford. From 1841 onwards he collaborated with Pusey and J. *Keble in producing the *Library of the

Fathers, and bore the chief burden of the work of direction.

J. W. *Burgon, *Lives of Twelve Good Men* (1888), i, 296–373 (No. 3: 'The Man of Saintly Life'); R. W. *Church, *The Oxford Movement* (1891), ch. 5. J. H. Overton in *D.N.B.*, xxxvi (1893), pp. 196-8.

MARROW CONTROVERSY, The. A protracted controversy in the Church of *Scotland arising out of the condemnation by the *General Assembly in 1720 of *The Marrow of Modern Divinity*, a book written in 1645 by 'E. F.', a 'poor inhabitant' of London (apparently *not* Edward Fisher, *fl.* 1627–55), and republished in 1719. The book which advocated strongly *Calvinist doctrines, was held to favour *Antinomianism.

MARSH, HERBERT (1757–1839), Bp. of *Peterborough. Educated at King's School, *Canterbury, and St. John's College, Cambridge, of which he was elected a Fellow in 1779, he studied in Germany under J. D. *Michaelis. Here he became conversant with the prevalent critical methods, esp. as applied to the Gospels, and after his return translated into English Michaelis's *Introduction to the New Testament* (4 vols., 1793–1801), adding a 'hypothesis' of his own on the mutual relations of the Gospels for which he was much attacked by the more conservative English theologians. His *History of the Politics of Great Britain and France* (2 vols., 1799), a work in defence of recent British foreign policy, attracted the attention of W. Pitt, who granted Marsh a pension. In 1805 he preached a series of sermons against the *Calvinist doctrines of *justification and the inamissibility of grace which provoked a violent controversy with the *Evangelicals. In 1807 he was elected Lady Margaret professor of divinity at Cambridge, holding the post until his death. His lectures on Biblical criticism (1809–16), among the first to popularize German critical methods in England, were enthusiastically listened to by the University and *The History of Sacred Criticism* (1809) was based on the first of his courses. In 1814 he issued a *Comparative View of the Churches of England and Rome*, and in 1815 *Horae Pelasgicae* (Part I, all publd.), a learned study of the origin and language of the Pelasgi. In 1816 he was appointed Bp. of *Llandaff and three years later translated to Peterborough. The early years of his episcopate were marked by controversy arising from his anti-Evangelical measures and his refusal to license clergy of Calvinist beliefs. His profound and extensive erudition, his clear and active mind, his belief in the Establishment, his ideal of rigid uniformity in matters of doctrine and liturgical practice, and his capacity for business, made him the foremost English bishop of his age.

E. Venables in *D.N.B.*, xxxvi (1893), pp. 211-15.

MARSIGLIO OF PADUA (c. 1275–1342). Italian scholar and author of the 'Defensor Pacis'. After studying at Padua, he went to

Paris *c.* 1311 to devote himself to medicine, was made rector of the university in 1313, and, after a period in N. Italy and Avignon, practised medicine and possibly studied theology in Paris from 1320. In 1324 he completed the 'Defensor Pacis', his principal work, written probably in collaboration with John of Jandun. When, in 1326, his authorship became known he fled to the Emperor, Louis of Bavaria, who had just been excommunicated. In 1327 *John XXII condemned five propositions of the 'Defensor' and excommunicated its author. From 1327 to 1329 Marsilius accompanied the Emperor to Rome, where he was made Imperial Vicar. After the failure of Louis's policy he spent the remainder of his life at the court of Munich.

The 'Defensor Pacis' is one of the most challenging works produced in the Middle Ages. Acc. to Marsilius, the state is the great unifying power of society to which the Church must be completely subordinated. It derives its authority from the people, who retain the right to censure and depose the Emperor. The Church, on the other hand, has no inherent jurisdiction whether spiritual or temporal. All her rights in this regard are given her by the state, which may withdraw them at will. She may own no property, but only use what the state lends her; her hierarchy is not of Divine but of purely human institution; St. Peter was never given the primacy, and the Papacy owes its prerogatives chiefly to the *Donation of the Emp. *Constantine (a document the authenticity of which Marsilius did not doubt). The principal authority in all ecclesiastical matters is the *General Council, which should be composed of priests and laymen. These ideas, which ran counter to the whole medieval conception of society, made Marsilius of Padua a forerunner of the Reformers, modern democracy, and even totalitarianism.

The 'Defensor Pacis' was first printed in 1522 and put on the *Index in 1559.

Crit. edd. of the *Defensor Pacis* by C. W. Previté-Orton (Cambridge, 1928), with introd. and notes, and by R. Scholz (Fontes Iuris Germanici Antiqui in Usum Scholarum; Hanover, 1933). The *Defensor Minor* was ed. by C. K. Brampton (Birmingham, 1922). A. Gewirth, *Marsilius of Padua, the Defender of Peace* (2 vols., Records of Civilization. Sources and Studies, New York, 1951 ff., vol. 2 to include Eng. tr. of the *Defensor Pacis*). E. Emerton, *The Defensor Pacis of Marsiglio of Padua. A Critical Study* (Harvard Theological Studies, viii; 1920). F. Battaglia, *Marsilio da Padova e la filosofia politica del medio evo* (Studi filosofici, secondo serie, iv; Florence, 1928); G. de Lagarde, *La Naissance de l'esprit laïque au déclin du moyen-âge*, ii, 'Marsile de Padoue ou le premier théoricien de l'état laïque' (Saint-Paul-Trois-Châteaux (Drôme), 1934). A. Checchini–N. Bobbio (edd.), *Marsilio da Padova. Studi raccolti nel VI centenario della morte* (Pubblicazione della Facoltà di Giurisprudenza della R. Università di Padova, iii; 1942). J. Haller, 'Zur Lebensgeschichte des Marsilius von Padua' in *Z.K.G.*, xlviii (1929), pp. 166–97. J. Sullivan, 'Marsiglio of Padua and William of Ockham' in *The American Historical Review*, ii (1897), pp. 409–26 and 539–610; N. Valois, 'Jean de Jandun et Marsile de Padoue, auteurs du *Defensor Pacis*' in *Histoire littéraire de la France*, xxxiii (1906), pp. 528–623; E. R. Avondo, 'Il *Defensor Pacis* di Marsilio da Padova' in *Rivista storica italiana*, xli (1924), pp. 113–66; G. de Lagarde, 'Marsile de Padoue et Guillaume de Nogaret' in *Revue historique de Droit français et étranger*, sér. 4, xi (1932), pp. 463–90; C. W. Previté-Orton, 'Marsilius of Padua' in *Proceedings of the British Academy*, xxi (1935), pp. 137–83, with bibl. notes; R. Scholz, 'Marsilius von Padua und die Genesis des modernen Staatsbewusstseins' in *H.Z.*, clvi (1937), pp. 88–103. A. P. d'Entrèves, *The Medieval Contribution to Political Thought* (1939), chs. 3 and 4, pp. 44–87. J. Rivière in *D.T.C.*, xii (pt. 1; 1928), cols. 153–77, s.v. 'Marsile de Padoue', with bibl.

MARTÈNE, EDMOND (1654–1739), liturgist. In 1672 Martène made his profession as a *Benedictine at the *Maurist house at *Reims and was later sent to *St.-Germain-des-Prés to be trained under J. L. *D'Achéry and J. *Mabillon. Of his many writings the chief is his *De antiquis ecclesiae ritibus* (3 vols., Rouen, 1700–2), a large collection of liturgical texts, with disquisitions on their historical significance. This he supplemented in 1706 by a *Tractatus de antiqua ecclesiae disciplina*. From 1708 till 1715 he worked on the *Gallia Christiana*, travelling extensively with Ursin Durand (d. 1773) through France and Belgium in search of MSS. and other materials. Later the two scholars visited many religious houses of the Netherlands and Germany for documents, which were embodied in their *Veterum scriptorum et monumentorum ecclesiasticorum et dogmaticorum amplissima collectio* (9 vols. fol., 1724–33). He was also sole compiler of the *Annales Ordinis S. Benedicti*, vol. vi (1739), begun by Mabillon.

[R. P. Tassin] *Histoire littéraire de la congrégation de Saint-Maur* (1770), pp. 542–63. H. Bremond, *Histoire littéraire du sentiment religieux en France*, vi (1922), ch. 6: 'Dom Martin et Dom Martène', pp. 177–226. H. Wilhelm-U. Berlière, *Nouveau Supplément à l'histoire littéraire de la congrégation de St.-Maur*, ii (Maredsous, 1931), pp. 48–57. H. *Leclercq, O.S.B., in *D.A.C.L.*, x (pt. 2; 1932), cols. 2297–322.

MARTENSEN, HANS LASSEN (1808–84), Danish Protestant theologian. He was a native of Flensburg, studied theology at Copenhagen university (1827–32), and after further studies in Germany and at Paris he became lecturer at Copenhagen in 1838 and professor of systematic theology in 1840. From 1854 till his death he was Bp. of Seeland as successor of J. P. Mynster. His chief purpose was to set forth a harmonious view of all the departments of human life with Christ at its centre. He was greatly influenced by F. E. D. *Schleiermacher, G. W. F. *Hegel, and esp. F. X. von Baader (1765–1841). In 1840 he published a study of Master *Eckhart, and in 1841 *Grundrids til Moralphilosophiens System*, an introduction to the study of moral philosophy. In 1849 appeared Martensen's principal work *Den Christelige Dogmatik* (Eng. trans., 1866), which rests on the principle of the harmony between faith and knowledge, in the light of which he interpreted the *Lutheran system of doctrine. His interest in theosophical speculation is noticeable in *Den Christelige Ethik* (3 vols., 1871–8, Eng. trans., 1873–81). In the course of this work he treated of the existence of corporality in the Godhead, which he conceived as the principle of order in nature and a plenitude of forces and potencies. This notion found full expression in a work on *Jacob *Boehme* (1881; Eng. trans., 1885), in which he placed beside the Trinity a fourth elemental principle, the Uncreated Light.

Martensen also took part in many controversies. In 1843 he attacked the *Baptists in a treatise on Baptism. After the publication of his work on Christian Doctrine he became involved in a lengthy controversy with S. *Kierkegaard and his disciples, who, as defenders of the irreconcilable antagonism between faith and reason, attacked Martensen's harmonizing theology. He also wrote against Catholicism, *Katholizismus und Protestantismus* (1874), and published many volumes of sermons.

Coll. of his lesser works ed. Julius Martensen, Copenhagen, 1885, with detailed bibl. Eng. tr. of his *Jacob Boehme* (London, 1885); new ed., with notes by S. Hobhouse (ib., 1949). Correspondence with J. A. *Dorner, ed. posthumously, 2 vols., Berlin, 1888. Martensen wrote some autobiographical reflections, publd., Copenhagen, 1882–3 (German tr., 3 vols., 1883–4). Lives by V. Nannestad (Copenhagen, 1897), and S. Arildsen (vol. i, all publd., Copenhagen, 1932). P. Madsen in *P.R.E.* (ed. 3), xii (1903), pp. 373–9.

MAR THOMA CHURCH. See *Malabar Christians*.

MARTHA, St.

The sister of *Mary and *Lazarus, who received Christ in her house during His ministry. From the incident related in Lk. 10. 38–42, she is commonly regarded as typifying the 'active' Christian life as contrasted with Mary, who typifies the 'contemplative'. Acc. to a medieval legend, Martha, Mary, and Lazarus came to the south of France and founded churches at Marseilles, Aix, *Avignon, and other places. Feast day, 29 July.

On the legend, besides the collections of docc. listed under *Mary Magdalene*, q.v., L. *Duchesne, *Fastes épiscopaux de l'ancien Gaule*, i (1894), pp. 310–44 ('La Légende de sainte Marie-Madeleine', esp. sect. 3, pp. 325–9), 'La Légende de sainte Marthe'; G. de Manteyer, 'Les Légendes saintes de Provence et le Martyrologe d'Arles–Toulon' in *Mélanges d'Archéologie et d'Histoire*, xvii (1897), pp. 467–89; G. *Morin, O.S.B., 'La Formation des légendes provençales. Faits et aperçus nouveaux' in *R. Bén.*, xxvi (1909), pp. 24–33, with reff. to earlier lit.; E. Vacandard, 'La Venue de Lazare et Marie-Madeleine en Provence' in *R.Q.H.*, c (1924), pp. 257–305; H. *Leclercq, O.S.B., in *D.A.C.L.*, viii (pt. 1; 1929), cols. 2044–86, s.v. 'Lazare', with detailed bibl. H. Lesêtre in *Dict. Bibl.*, iv (1908), col. 825 f., s.v. 'Marthe'; D. Smith in *D.C.G.*, ii (1908), p. 138 f., s.v. See also bibl. to *Lazarus*.

MARTIN, St. (d. 397), Bp. of Tours and a patron saint of France.

He was probably born in 335, though 316 is given in some sources. The son of a pagan, Martin early became a *catechumen. He served in the Roman army until, after he had given half his cloak to a beggar at Amiens, a vision of Christ impelled him to baptism and the religious life. Obtaining his discharge, he visited Pannonia, Milan (from which he was driven by its Arian bishop, *Auxentius), and Illyricum. In 360 he joined *Hilary at Poitiers and founded the monastery of Ligugé, the first in Gaul. Becoming Bp. of Tours in 372, he encouraged the spread of monasticism in Gaul, his own foundation outside Tours being particularly influential, and set himself to evangelize the hitherto neglected countryside, into which he introduced a rudimentary parochial system. His protest against the execution of *Priscillian by Maximus in 386 raised important issues in the relations between Church and state. He wrote nothing, but his life was recorded by his friend *Sulpicius Severus. The uncritical collection of his miracles by *Gregory of Tours added to his fame, but obscured his real importance. Feast day, 11 Nov.

The *Vita* by Sulpicius, to which are appended three *Epistulae* and two *Libri Dialogorum*, pr. in J. P. Migne, *PL*, xx, 159–222. Cf. also Gregory of Tours, *Hist. Franc.* (i, 36–8, 43). The most complete collection of material is A. Lecoy de la Marche, *St. Martin* (Tours, 1881). The thesis of É. C. Babut, in his *St. Martin de Tours* (1912), denying all historical value to the Life by Sulpicius, is severely criticized by H. *Delehaye, S.J., 'St. Martin et Sulpice Sévère', in *Anal. Boll.*, xxxviii (1920), pp. 1–136; cf. also C. Jullian, 'Remarques critiques sur les sources de la vie de S. Martin' in *Revue des Études anciennes*, xxiv (1922), pp. 37–47, 123–8, 229–35, and 306–12, and xxv (1923), pp. 49–55, 139–43, and 234–49. Other lives by P. Monceaux (Paris, 1926, with tr. of Sulpicius's Life; Eng. tr., 1928) and A. Regnier ('Les Saints', 1907). J. Costanza, *La leggenda di S. Martino nel medio evo* (Palermo, 1921). L. Clugnet in *C.E.*, ix (1910), p. 732 f., s.v.; É. Amann in *D.T.C.*, x (pt. 1; 1928), cols. 211–14, s.v.; P. Toschi in *E.C.*, viii (1952), cols. 228–32, s.v. 'Martino di Tours'.

MARTIN, St. (c. 520–80), Abp. of Braga.

He was a Pannonian by birth. After becoming a monk in Palestine, he travelled to Spain, where he became successively Abbot and Bp. of Dumio and later Abp. of Braga. He was active in furthering the conversion of the remaining *Arians in Portugal to Catholicism. He wrote a letter to a bishop, Boniface, 'De Trina Mersione', opposing the Spanish practice of using one immersion only at baptism, which, adopted probably through fear of Arianism, he considered to smack of *Sabellianism. He also wrote several moral treatises, among them the 'Formula Vitae Honestae' and the 'De Ira' (both based on *Seneca), and also compiled an important collection of canons, the so-called 'Capitula Martini', relating to the duties and status of clergy and laity. A sermon 'De correctione rusticorum' has considerable interest for the light it throws on the older pagan beliefs of the country population of Portugal. Feast day, 20 Mar.

J. P. Migne, *PL*, lxxii, 17–52 (from A. *Gallandi), and lxxxiv, 574–86 ('Capitula Martini'). Mod. crit. ed. of Works by C. W. Barlow (New Haven, Conn., 1950). C. P. *Caspari, *Martin von Braccaras Schrift De Correctione Rusticorum* (Christiania, 1883), with imp. introd. The chief authorities for his life are St. *Gregory of Tours and *Venantius Fortunatus; also St. *Isidore of Seville, *De Vir. Ill.*, 35. E. Bickel, 'Die Schrift des Martin von Bracara *Formula Vitae Honestae*' in *Rheinisches Museum*, NF, lx (1905), pp. 505–51. J. Madoz, S.J., 'Una nueva recensión del *De Correctione Rusticorum* de Martino de Braga' in *Estudios eclesiásticos*, xix (1945), pp. 335–53. Bardenhewer, v, 379–88; Altaner, p. 445. É. Amann in *D.T.C.*, x (pt. 1; 1928), cols. 203–7.

MARTIN I, St. (d. 655), Pope from 649.

He was a vigorous opponent of the *Monothelites. Before his election as Pope had been confirmed from Constantinople by the Emp. Constans II, Martin had condemned *Monothelitism at a Synod at the *Lateran in 649. When Constans found Martin unwilling to sign the *Typos, he tried to induce his exarch, Olympius, to seize the Pope's person, but in vain. Olympius's successor, Theodore Calliopas, did so, however, and after a year in captivity at Naxos on the way, Martin arrived at Constantinople in Dec. 654. Here he was condemned to exile, though the sentence was commuted to banishment to the Chersonesus (Crimea), where he died soon afterwards. He is the last of the Popes who is venerated as a martyr, and is actually mentioned by name in the *Canon of the Mass in the *Bobbio Missal. Feast day in the W., 12 Nov.; in the E., 13 Apr.

A few of his letters and privilegia repr. from G. D. *Mansi in J. P. Migne, PL, lxxxvii, 119–211; others calendared in P. Jaffé (ed.), Regesta Pontificum Romanorum, i (ed. G. Wattenbach, Leipzig, 1885), pp. 230–4. L.P. (Duchesne), i, pp. 336–40. *Anastasius Bibliothecarius in J. P. Migne, PL, cxxix, 586–604. P. Peeters, S.J., 'Une Vie grecque du pape S. Martin I' in Anal. Boll., li (1933), pp. 225–62, with text. W. M. Peitz, S.J., 'Martin I und Maximus Confessor. Beiträge zur Geschichte des Monotheletenstreites in den Jahren 645–68' in Hist. J., xxxviii (1917), pp. 213–36 and 429–58. E. Caspar, 'Die Lateransynode von 649' in Z.K.G., li (1932), pp. 75–137. Hefele–Leclercq, iii (pt. 1; 1909), pp. 435–61. E. Michael, S.J., 'Wann ist Papst Martin I bei seiner Exilierung nach Constantinopel gekommen?' in Z.K.T., xvi (1892), pp. 375–80. L. *Duchesne, L'Église au VIe siècle (1925), pp. 441–53. L. Bréhier in Fliche–Martin, v (1938), pp. 166–72. Mann, i (pt. i; 1902), pp. 385–405. É. Amann in D.T.C., x (pt. 1; 1928), cols. 182–94, s.v.; S. Majarelli, O.F.M., in E.C., viii (1952), col. 224, s.v. 'Martino I', with bibl.

MARTIN IV (c. 1210–85), Pope from 1281. Simon de Brie (or Brion) was a native of Touraine. After being canon and treasurer at St. Martin's at Tours, he was appointed Chancellor of France by *Louis IX in 1260. In 1261 Urban VI created him Cardinal-priest of St. Cecilia. As Papal legate he conducted the negotiations for the crown of Sicily with Charles of Anjou and presided over several French synods, including that held at Bourges in 1276. In 1281 he was elected Pope at Viterbo against his will through the influence of Charles of Anjou, on whom he remained dependent throughout his pontificate. He restored Charles to the influential position of Roman Senator of which Nicholas III had deprived him, and with a view to assisting the planned attack on the Greek Empire he excommunicated in 1281 its Emperor, Michael Palaeologus, thus destroying the union between the Latin and Greek Churches achieved at the Council of *Lyons in 1274. His unpopularity with the Roman people led to his expulsion from the city, and he died at Perugia. He was a supporter of the *Franciscan Order, whose privileges he extended by the bull 'Ad fructus uberes' in 1281.

Les Registres de Martin IV, 1281–1285 (Bibliothèque des Écoles Françaises d'Athènes et de Rome, Ser. 2, xvi; 1935). Two contemporary biographies repr. in L.P. (Duchesne), ii, 459–65. N. Backes, Kardinal Simon de Brion (Papst Martin IV) (Breslau Diss., Berlin, 1910), with bibl. p. 10 f. Mann, xvi (1932), pp. 171–356. É. Amann in D.T.C., x (pt. i; 1928), cols. 194–7, s.v.

MARTIN V (1368–1431), Pope. Oddo (Otto) Colonna, a man of simple tastes and free from intrigue, was unanimously elected Pope at the Council of *Constance in 1417. His reign marked the end of the Great Schism, the Antipope Clement VIII submitting to him in 1429. Three years after his election, Martin entered Rome, then in a ruinous condition,

and restored its churches and other public buildings. In the Papal States he also re-established order with the help of his relatives, among whom he distributed honours and offices. He greatly strengthened the Papal power by dissolving the Council of Constance in 1418, and that of Pavia and Siena in 1424. In the following years he curtailed the liberties of the Church of France and increased the influence of the Papacy in England, though he failed to secure the repeal of the Statutes of *Provisors and *Praemunire. His attempts at suppressing the *Hussites and at restoring union with the Greek Church were also unsuccessful.

E. v. Ottenthal, 'Die Bullenregister Martin V und Eugen IV' in Mittheilungen des Instituts für Oesterreichische Geschichtsforschung, Ergänzungsband, i (1885), pp. 401–589, esp. pp. 401–568. F. Baix, La Chambre apostolique et les 'Libri Annatarum' de Martin V, 1417–1431 (pt. 1, Introduction et Textes; Analecta Vaticano-Belgica, xiv; 1942). K. A. Finke, Martin V und Aragon (Historische Studien, cccxl; 1938). Id., 'Martin V und Bologna (1428–1429)' in Quellen und Forschungen aus italienischen Archiven und Bibliotheken herausgegeben vom preussischen historischen Institut in Rom, xxiii (1931–2), pp. 182–217. Pastor, i, 208–82. G. Mollat in D.T.C., x (pt. 1; 1928), cols. 197–202, s.v.; G. B. Picotti in E.C., viii (1952), cols. 225–8, s.v. 'Martino V'.

MARTIN, GREGORY (d. 1582), Biblical translator. One of the original scholars of St. John's College, Oxford, he became a tutor in the household of Thomas Howard, Duke of Norfolk. On the Duke's imprisonment for Catholicism, Martin escaped to *Douai, where he joined W. *Allen. In 1573 he was ordained priest. After some time in *Rome he returned to Douai in 1578, where he spent most of the rest of his life translating the *Vulgate into English. He died on 28 Oct. 1582, the year in which the NT appeared at Reims. See also Douai-Reims Bible.

T. Cooper in D.N.B., xxxvi (1893), pp. 277–9; B. Ward in C.E., ix (1910), p. 727 f., s.v., both with further bibl. reff.

MARTINEAU, JAMES (1805–1900), *Unitarian divine. He was the brother of Harriet Martineau (1802–76). Educated at Norwich Grammar School, he was converted in 1822 and in the same year entered Manchester College at York. After work as a Unitarian minister at Dublin and Liverpool, during which he became increasingly interested in problems of philosophy, he became professor of philosophy (1840) at, and afterwards principal of, Manchester New College (1869), but continued his pastoral activities. He was a strong and ardent upholder of the theist position against the negations of physical science and elaborated the 'Design argument' with the modifications made necessary by the Darwinian theory of evolution; and did much to convince many of his contemporaries of all shades of theological belief that the Monism of H. *Spencer and the Materialism of John Tyndall (1820–93) did not cover all the facts. In Types of Ethical Theory (2 vols., 1885) and in A Study of Religion (2 vols., 1888) he found powerful arguments for theism in the facts of the moral consciousness and the existence of the laws of nature. He inspired great confidence through his intense moral earnestness, his passionate faith in God, and his massive power of reasoning. He also did much for the organization of the Unitarian body in England and Ireland.

Martineau's other writings include *A Study of Spinoza* (1882), *The Seat of Authority in Religion* (1890), and some collections of Hymns and 'Home Prayers'.

Essays, Reviews and Addresses. Selected and revised by the Author (4 vols., 1890–1). *Life and Letters*, ed. J. *Drummond–C. B. Upton (London, 1902). A. H. G. Craufurd, *Recollections of James Martineau* (1903). Other lives by A. W. Jackson (London, 1900) and J. E. *Carpenter (ib., 1905). H. *Sidgwick, *Lectures on the Ethics of T. H. Green, Mr. Herbert Spencer and J. Martineau* (1902; posthumous), pp. 313–74. A. Gordon in *D.N.B.*, Suppl. iii (1901), pp. 146–51. A. M. *Fairbairn in *E.B.* (ed. 11), xvii (1911), pp. 797–800 s.v.

MARTYN, HENRY (1781–1812), Anglican missionary. He was born at *Truro and studied at St. John's College, Cambridge (1797–1801), of which he became a Fellow in 1802. His acquaintance with C. *Simeon awakened his interest in missionary work, and having been ordained deacon in 1803, he became a chaplain of the East India Company at Calcutta in 1805. Besides doing missionary work among the natives he translated the NT into Hindustani and Persian, the Psalms into Persian, and the BCP into Hindustani. He also prepared a translation of the NT into Arabic. On his way back from Persia he died at Tokat, where he was given Christian burial by the *Armenian clergy. His life of devotion to the cause of the missions made a great impression in Gt. Britain and he became the hero of several literary publications.

Journals and Letters of the Rev. Henry Martyn, ed. S. *Wilberforce (2 vols., London, 1837). Lives by J. Sargent (London, 1819) and G. Smith (ib., 1892); more popular accounts by Jessie Page (ib., [1891]) and C. E. Padwick (London, 1922). Unsigned article in *D.N.B.*, xxxvi (1893), pp. 315–17.

MARTYR (Gk. μάρτυς, 'witness'). The term was originally used of the Apostles as witnesses of Christ's life and resurrection (e.g. Acts 1. 8, 1. 22), but with the spread of persecution it was reserved to those who had undergone hardships for the faith, and finally it was restricted to those who had suffered death. The age before *Constantine was the classic period of martyrs, esp. the era of *Diocletian. As martyrdom usually involved severe physical and moral sufferings before the execution, those who had remained steadfast were soon accorded particular honours by the Church. From the earliest time martyrdom, the 'baptism of blood', was considered an equivalent of normal baptism where this had not been received. Since the end of the 2nd cent. the anniversary of the martyr's death (*natalis*, i.e. his [heavenly] birthday) was kept as a feast with a liturgical celebration at his tomb; and later churches were frequently built on the site. The fame of the martyrs often spread beyond their city and

country. They were venerated as powerful intercessors, their relics were sought after, and their lives widely read and often embellished by numerous legends.

In the Roman liturgy Martyrs rank before all other saints. The liturgical colour is red, to signify that they shed their blood for the faith, and acc. to current RC practice relics of martyrs must be contained in every consecrated altar.

The large periodical literature on the concept of martyrdom in the early Church, beginning with F. *Kattenbusch, 'Die Märtyrertitel' in *Z.N.T.W.*, iv (1903), pp. 111–27, is listed in the dictt. mentioned below. H. *Delehaye, S.J., *Les Origines du culte des martyrs* (Subsidia Hagiographica, xx; 1912); id., *Les Passions des martyrs et les genres littéraires* (1921). O. Michel, *Prophet und Märtyrer* (Beiträge zur Förderung christlicher Theologie, xxxvii, Hft. 2; 1932); H. von Campenhausen, *Die Idee des Martyriums in der alten Kirche* (1935); E. Günther, Μάρτυς. Die Geschichte eines Wortes (1941). M. M. Hassett in *C.E.*, ix (1910), pp. 736–40, s.v.; H. *Leclercq, O.S.B., in *D.A.C.L.*, x (pt. 2; 1932), cols. 2359–512, s.v.; J. P. Kirsch in *L.Th.K.*, vi (1934), cols. 995–8, s.v.; E. Peterson–A. P. Frutaz–S. Indelicato in *E.C.*, viii (1952), cols. 233–44, s.v. 'Martirio e martire'. H. Strathmann in *T.W.B.*, iv [1939], pp. 477–520, s.v. 'μάρτυς', &c.

MARTYR, PETER. See *Peter Martyr*.

MARTYRIUM (Gk. μαρτύριον). A church built over the tomb or relics of a *martyr or occasionally a church built just in honour of a martyr. The cleric in charge of such a church was sometimes known as the 'martyrarius'.

A. Grabar, *Martyrium*. Recherches sur le culte des reliques et l'art chrétien antique (Collège de France. Fondation Schlumberger pour les Études byzantines, 2 vols., 1946; Album, 1943). H. *Leclercq, O.S.B., in *D.A.C.L.*, x (pt. 2; 1932), cols. 2512–23, s.v.

MARTYROLOGY. An official register of Christian martyrs. As distinct from individual 'Passions' describing the martyrdoms of those who have suffered for the Christian faith, martyrologies are collective in structure. The earliest are calendars, merely naming the martyr and the place of martyrdom under the day of the festival. They may be local, like the calendars of Rome (354) and Carthage (c. 505), or general, like the '*Hieronymian Martyrology' (q.v.) and the 'Breviarium Syriacum' (411). The later 'historical' martyrologies, notably those of *Bede (c. 730), *Florus of Lyons, *Rabanus, *Ado, and *Usuard (all 9th cent.), add stories of martyrs from sources of varying value. The '*Roman Martyrology' (q.v.; 1584) is a revision of Usuard's. The practice of reading in choir at *Prime the martyrology for the day is already laid down by *Chrodegang of Metz and in the Aachen Capitula of 817, and is still preceptive in religious houses.

The standard source is the magisterial ed. and discussion of the 'Hieronymian Martyrology' in *AA.SS.*, Nov. II, i (1894); new ed. by H. *Quentin, O.S.B., with important notes by H. *Delehaye, S.J., in *AA.SS.*, Nov. II, ii (1931). H. Achelis, *Die Martyrologien. Ihre Geschichte und ihr Wert* (*Abh.* (Gött.), N.F., iii, Hft. 3; 1900). H. Quentin, O.S.B., *Les Martyrologes historiques du moyen-âge* (1908). J. Baudot, *Le Martyrologe* (1911). H. Delehaye, S.J., in *C.E.*, ix (1910), p. 741 f., s.v.; H. Leclercq, O.S.B., in *D.A.C.L.*, x (pt. 2; 1932), cols. 2523–619, s.v.; J. P. Kirsch in *L.Th.K.*, vi (1934), cols. 1000–2, s.v.; A. Bugnini, C.M., in *E.C.*, viii (1952), cols. 244–58, s.v. 'Martirologio'. See also bibl. to separate Martyrologies and authors mentioned above.

MARTYRS, Acts of the. See *Acts of the Martyrs.*

MARTYRS, Era of the. See *Diocletianic Era.*

MARTYRS, Four Crowned. See *Quattro Coronati.*

MARUCCHI, ORAZIO (1852–1931), Italian archaeologist. Under the influence of G. B. *De Rossi, the *catacombs of Rome became the chief object of his research. In 1879 he founded the 'Collegium Cultorum Martyrum' and in quick succession became Scriptor of the *Vatican Library, director of the *Lateran Museum, lecturer on Christian archaeology at several institutes, and, after De Rossi's death (1894), editor of the *Nuovo Bullettino di Archeologia Cristiana*. As secretary of the pontifical 'Commissione di Archeologia Sacra', he conducted the excavations of many famous tombs, such as the 'Coemeterium Valentini' (1876 ff.) and parts of the Catacomb of *Priscilla. Owing to the considerable diversity of his interests, his work was sometimes wanting in precision in its details. Among his principal writings are *Éléments d'archéologie chrétienne* (1900–3) and *Le Catacombe romane* (1903; ed. 2, 1933), besides a great number of contributions to learned periodicals.

Marucchi's *Le catacombe romane* was publ. posthumously by E. Josi [1933], with biogr. introd., pp. xix–xxxi. C. Cecchelli, 'Scrittori contemporanei di cose romane. Orazio Marucchi' in *Archivio della R. Società Romano di Storia Patria*, lii (1929; stampato nel 1931), pp. 381–406, with list of his works, pp. 407–52. H. *Leclercq, O.S.B., in *D.A.C.L.*, x (pt. 2; 1932), cols. 2619–38, s.v.

MARY, The Blessed Virgin, the Mother of Christ. The place accorded to her in Catholic theology and devotion issues from the position which she fills in the economy of revelation as the Mother of the Redeemer. She is accounted pre-eminent among the *Saints (q.v.).

In the NT accounts the Blessed Virgin naturally figures very prominently in the birth stories of Mt. (1; 2) and esp. Lk. (1; 2). Though mentioned several times during the years of our Lord's public ministry, she is mostly in the background; but she reappears at the foot of the Cross (Jn. 19. 25) to take her part in the Passion. In the Upper Room at Jerusalem she witnessed the growth of the infant Church under the action of the Holy Spirit (Acts 1. 14). Both her Divine maternity and her virginity are clearly stated in the Gospels: Mary has really conceived and given birth to Jesus, the Son of God (Lk. 1. 31–33) without losing her virginity (Mt. 1. 20 and 23; Lk. 1. 34 f.). See also *Virgin Birth.*

From these few, but significant, Biblical data have issued a series of theological statements on the one hand and the development of devotion to Mary on the other. The famous title *Theotokos (θεοτόκος), in use among theologians at least since the 4th cent., became the touchstone of orthodoxy in the *Nestorian controversy. Her perpetual virginity, asserted by *Hilary of Poitiers and *Didymus, the latter of whom gave her the title 'ever virgin' (ἀειπάρθενος), was defended by St. *Ambrose (c. 390) against *Jovinian and explicitly taught by the orthodox Fathers from the 5th cent. onwards. Her supreme dignity as the Mother of God was praised in exalted terms by such Eastern Fathers as St. *Ephrem, St. *Germanus of Constantinople, and St. *John of Damascus. In the W. St. *Anselm and others formulated their belief in the dignity of Our Lady on the principle that Mary must possess all privileges possible to a creature which are in harmony with her office as Mother of God. This, in its turn, led to the doctrine of the *Immaculate Conception as formulated by *Duns Scotus and ultimately defined for RCs by *Pius IX in 1854. Acc. to RC teaching a further consequence of her Divine maternity is her secondary mediatorship. Hence the antithesis between Eve, cause of our death (Gen. 3), and Mary, cause of our salvation, which was drawn out, e.g., by St. *Justin, St. *Irenaeus, *Tertullian, and reproduced by St. *Cyril of Jerusalem, St. *Epiphanius, and others. In the 8th cent. St. John of Damascus calls her mediatrix (μεσῖτις), and St. *Andrew of Crete mediatrix of grace, whereas a few centuries later in the W. St. *Bernard formally teaches a certain subordinate co-operation of Mary in our redemption. This last consideration was developed and clarified by modern RC theologians such as F. *Suarez, S.J. It is also maintained that the BVM, being the mother of the Author of all grace, obtains all graces for us by her maternal intercession, an office indicated by the title 'Mediatrix of All Graces'. This doctrine was defended by St. *Alphonsus of Liguori, the great panegyrist of the *Glories of Mary*, and sanctioned by *Benedict XV, who approved a Mass and Office of Our Lady under this title. In 1950, the doctrine of her Corporal *Assumption into heaven, long held as a pious tradition, was formally defined as a doctrine of faith by *Pius XII.

Devotion to Mary and belief in the efficacy of her intercession is probably very old. St. *Gregory of Nazianzus mentions recourse to her protection as of common usage, and her pictures in the catacombs may indicate an even earlier cult. This cult received considerable impetus from the definition of the Council of *Ephesus (431), esp. in the E. There devotion to the Theotokos became so strong that her name was even substituted in the official Service Books in the place of that of our Lord at the end of many liturgical prayers. In the Latin Church St. *Thomas Aquinas formulated the doctrine of the ''hyperdulia' proper to her, which, though infinitely inferior to the 'latria' (worship of adoration) due to her

Divine Son, yet far surpasses that befitting angels and saints.

Since the Reformation, when the excessive devotion to Our Lady provoked a strong reaction among Protestants, the defence of its legitimacy has been a recurrent task for RC theologians. Some cultus of the BVM is held to be a necessary element in the spiritual life of the Catholic and this devotion must not be confined to purely exterior practices. Among the liturgical Marian devotions are the '*Little Office of Our Lady', which originated in the medieval monasteries, the Marian antiphons, and the Saturday Office and Mass of Our Lady; whereas popular piety finds expression in the *Rosary, the *Angelus, May devotions, pilgrimages (esp. to *Lourdes), and other devotional exercises. Under the influence of the *Oxford Movement, there has been an important revival of devotion to Our Lady in the C of E since the middle of the 19th cent. The way was prepared by such language as J. *Keble's 'Ave Maria! Thou whose name All but adoring love may claim', and contemporary sentiment is reflected in the re-establishment of the shrine at *Walsingham.

The six principal feasts observed in the W. Church are those of the (Immaculate) Conception (8 Dec.), the *Nativity (8 Sept.), the *Annunciation (25 Mar.), the *Purification (2 Feb.), the *Visitation (2 July), and the Assumption (15 Aug.). In addition to these there are a large number of lesser feasts, many of them of local commemoration. Among those of universal observance in the Latin Church are the two feasts of the Seven Sorrows (the Friday after *Passion Sunday and 15 Sept.), the Name of Mary (12 Sept.), the Presentation of Mary in the Temple (21 Nov.), Our Lady of Mt. *Carmel (16 July), and Our Lady of the Snows (5 Aug.). Of the first six feasts, the calendar in the BCP contains all except the Assumption (this last retained in the Oxford University Calendar); but only the Annunciation and the Purification have a proper Collect, Epistle and Gospel.

Classical discussions include St. *Thomas Aquinas, *S.T.*, iii, qq. 27–30, and P. *Canisius, *De Beata Maria Virgine* (Ingoldstadt, 1577). A. T. Wirgman, *The Blessed Virgin and all the Company of Heaven* (1905), pp. 1–214; T. E. Bridgett, C.SS.R., *Our Lady's Dowry; Or, How England gained and lost that Title* (1875); J. Guitton, *La Vierge Marie* (1949; Eng. tr., 1952). I. Marracci, *Biblioteca Mariana* (2 vols., Rome, 1648); J. J. Bourassé, *Summa Aurea de Laudibus Beatissimae Virginis Mariae* (13 vols., Paris, 1862–6). J. H. Schütz, *Summa Mariana*. Allgemeines Handbuch der Marienverehrung für Priester, Theologiestudierende und gebildete Laien (5 vols., 1903–21). H. du Manoir de Juaye, S.J. (ed.), *Maria*. Études sur la Sainte Vierge (3 vols., 1949–54). F. A. Lehner, *Die Marienverehrung in den ersten Jahrhunderten* (1886). S. Beissel, S.J., *Geschichte der Verehrung Marias in Deutschland während des Mittelalters* (1909); id., *Geschichte der Verehrung Marias im 16. und 17. Jahrundert* (1910). J. H. *Newman, *Letter to the Rev. E. B. Pusey, D.D., on his recent Eirenicon* (1866). [Anna B.] Jameson, *Legends of the Madonna, as represented in the Fine Arts* (1852). A. J. Maas, S.J., in *C.E.*, xv (1912), pp. 464–72 [c. 16 pages], s.v. 'Virgin Mary, The Blessed'; H. Thurston, S.J., ib., pp. 459–64, s.v. 'Virgin Mary, Devotion to the'; J. Cooper in *H.E.R.E.*, viii (1915), pp. 474–80, s.v. 'Mary'; H. *Leclercq, O.S.B., in *D.A.C.L.*, x (pt. 2; 1932), cols. 1982–2043, s.v. 'Marie, Mère de Dieu'; P. de Ambroggi and others in *E.C.*, viii (1952), cols. 76–118, s.v. 'Maria'. See also bibls. to *Annunciation*, *Assumption*, and other Feasts of the B.V.M.

MARY, Gospel of. An apocryphal *Gnostic Gospel which exists in an unpublished 5th cent. *Coptic papyrus MS. at Berlin. In it the Virgin describes a vision in which the progress of the Gnostic through the seven planetary spheres is explained.

The earliest ref. to the Gospel in print is by C. Schmidt, 'Ein vorirenaeisches gnostisches Originalwerk in koptischer Sprache' in *Sb.* (Berl.), 1896 (pt. 2), pp. 839–46. A fragment of a Gk. text (Pap. Ryl., III, 463) was publd., with introd. and notes, by C. H. Roberts in his *Catalogue of the Greek and Latin Papyri in the John Rylands Library, Manchester*, iii (Manchester, 1938), pp. 18–23. S. G. Kapsomenos, 'Τὸ κατὰ Μαριὰμ Ἀπόκρυφον Εὐαγγέλιον' in 'Ἀθηνᾶ, xlix (1939), pp. 177–86.

MARY, Gospel of the Birth of. An apocryphal book containing a narrative of the birth of the BVM to St. *Joachim and St. *Anne, her life in the Temple from the age of 3 to 12 years, her betrothal to St. *Joseph, the *Annunciation, and the *Virgin Birth of Christ. It is a Latin work of the Middle Ages, though in a preface sometimes attached to it it is attributed to St. *Jerome, who is stated to have composed it after a Hebrew original. Its compiler drew largely on the canonical Gospels and other sources, esp. the Book of *James (the 'Protevangelium').

The text is taken over almost bodily in the '*Golden Legend' (q.v.). Crit. ed. by C. *Tischendorf (ed.), *Evangelia Apocrypha* (ed. 2, Leipzig, 1876), pp. 113–21. Brief summary of contents in M. R. James, *The Apocryphal New Testament* (1924), p. 79 f. Bardenhewer, i, p. 536 f.

MARY OF EGYPT, St. (5th cent.), penitent. She was the subject of many elaborate and widely popular legends. After a career of infamy at Alexandria as an actress and courtesan, she is said to have been converted on the threshold of the Holy Sepulchre at *Jerusalem and fled to the desert east of Palestine to expiate her sins. Here she is recorded to have lived a life of complete isolation for forty-seven years, and then made the acquaintance of a priest, Zosimus, who gave her communion and prepared her for death. Feast day in the E., 1 Apr.; in the W., 2 (also 3 and 9) Apr.

The earliest account of St. Mary of Egypt is in *Cyril of Scythopolis' 'Life of St. Cyriacus'. This material was developed in legendary fashion by *Sophronius of Jerusalem (7th cent.). *A.A.SS.*, Apr. I (1675), pp. 67–90, with Gk. text, pp. xiii–xxi (of which Lat. tr., pp. 76–82). F. Delmas, 'Remarques sur la vie de Ste Marie l'Égyptienne' in *É.O.*, iv (1900–1), pp. 35–42; id., 'Encore Ste Marie l'Égyptienne', ib., v (1901–2), pp. 15–17. H. *Leclercq, O.S.B., in *D.A.C.L.*, x (pt. 2; 1932), cols. 2128–36, s.v. 'Marie l'Égyptienne', with bibl.; A. Amore, O.F.M., in *E.C.*, viii (1952), col. 120 f., s.v. 'Maria Egiziaca'.

MARY OF THE INCARNATION, Blessed (1566–1618). See *Acarie, Madame*.

MARY OF THE INCARNATION, Ven. (1599–1672). See *Guyard, Marie*.

MARY MAGDALENE, St. A follower of Christ out of whom He is said to have cast 'seven devils' and who ministered to Him in Galilee (Lk. 8. 2). Later she stood by His cross at the Crucifixion (Mk. 15. 40), with

two other women discovered the empty tomb
and heard the angelic announcement of His
*Resurrection (Mk. 16. 1 ff., &c.), and was
granted an appearance of the Risen Christ
early on the same day (Mt. 28. 9, Jn. 20. 11 ff.).
From early times she has been identified with
the 'woman which was a sinner' who anointed
Christ's feet in Simon's house (Lk. 7. 37),
and with Mary the sister of *Martha, who also
anointed Him (Jn. 12. 3); but the Gospels give
no real support to either identification. Acc.
to early legend in the E. Church, St. Mary
Magdalen went to *Ephesus with St. *John and
died there, whence her body was later taken to
*Constantinople. In the W. a very popular but
late and quite unfounded legend had arisen by
the 9th cent. that she, with Martha and
*Lazarus, came to the south of France by sea,
and in the Middle Ages her supposed tomb
was venerated at Aix-en-Provence. Feast day,
22 July.

Popular modern lives include those of H. D. *Lacordaire
(Paris, 1860; Eng. tr. 1880), E. Prats-de-Mollo (3 vols.,
Tournai, 1882), M. M. Sicard, O.P. (3 vols., Paris, 1910),
J. Brierre (Liége, 1933), Edith Olivier (London, 1934),
V. McNabb, O.P. (ib., 1940), and R. Buckberger, O.P. (Paris
[1952]; Eng. tr., 1954). Eng. tr. of 14th cent. Italian life by
Valentina Hawtrey (London, 1904) [E. M. Faillon (ed.)],
*Monuments inédits sur l'apostolat de sainte Marie-Madeleine
en Provence et les autres apostles de cette contrée* (publd. by
J. P. *Migne, 2 vols., 1848); C. Chabaneau (ed.), *Sainte
Marie-Madeleine dans la littérature provençale*. Receuil des
textes provençaux en prose et en vers relatifs à cette sainte
(1887). Classical studies by J. *Faber Stapulensis (Paris,
1517 and 1519). *AA.SS.*, Jul. V (1727), pp. 187–225.
M. J. *Lagrange, O.P., 'Jésus a-t-il été oint plusieurs fois
et par plusieurs femmes?' in *R. Bibl.*, ix (1912), pp. 504–32.
U. Holzmeister, S.J., 'Die Magdalenfrage in der kirchlichen
Überlieferung' in *Z.K.T.*, xlvi (1922), pp. 402–22 and
556–84. J. Sickenberger, 'Ist die Magdalen-Frage wirklich
unlösbar?' in *Biblische Zeitschrift*, xvii (1926), pp. 63–74.
Helen M. Garth, *Saint Mary Magdalen in Mediaeval
Literature* (Johns Hopkins University Studies in Histori-
cal and Political Science. Series xlvii, No. 3; 1950).
N. Hansel, *Die Maria-Magdalena-Legende* (Greifswalder
Beiträge zur Literatur- und Stilforschung, xvi, IIft. 1;
1937). A. Pissier, *Le Culte de sainte Marie-Madeleine à
Vézelay* (1923). For other works on the legend of her
connexion with S. France, see bibl. to *Martha*, St. J. B.
Mayor in *H.D.B.*, iii (1900), pp. 284–6, s.v. 'Mary V'; H.
Lesêtre in *Dict. Bibl.*, iv (1908), cols. 809–18, s.v. 'Marie-
Madeleine'; H. Pope, O.P., in *C.E.*, ix (1910), p. 761 f., s.v.;
A. Schwessinger–J. Sauer in *L.Th.K.*, vi (1934), cols. 902–4,
s.v. 'Maria Magdalena'; P. de Ambroggi–E. Battisti in
E.C., vii (1952), cols. 138–43, s.v. 'Maria Maddalena'. See
also commentaries to Gospels.

MARY MAGDALENE OF PAZZI, St.
(1566–1607), *Carmelite mystic. Born of a
noble family of Florence, she entered the
Carmelite convent in her native town in 1582
and was professed during a grave illness two
years later. In 1598 she was made novice-
mistress and later subprioress. During the
first years after her profession she was severely
tried by spiritual desolation, temptations, and
physical sufferings, but from 1590 her life
became a series of ecstasies during which she
often gave spiritual counsels which were taken
down by her fellow-nuns and published after
her death. She was an ardent believer in the
value of suffering for the spiritual life and the
salvation of souls, and the last three years of
her life were spent bedridden in constant pain
and often in great spiritual aridity. She was
canonized in 1669. Feast day, 29 May.

Works ed. L. M. Brancaccius, Florence, 1609; selections
tr. into Fr. from the ed. of Naples, 1750, by A. Bruniaux,
O.S.B., 2 vols., Paris, 1873. The best ed., including letters
previously unpubld., is that issued under the patronage
of Card. A. Bausa, Florence, 1893. Modern selection of her
ecstasies and letters by M. Vaussard (Florence, 1924). Early
lives in Italian by V. Puccini, Carmelite, her last confessor
(first draft written in 1609; final version publd. Florence,
1621), and V. Cepari, S.J., also her confessor (written *c.*
1626; first publd., Rome, 1669); both translated into Lat.
and pr., with introd. and other material, in *AA.SS.*, Mai. VI
(1688), pp. 177–351; Eng. tr. of life by V. Cepari in the
series 'The Saints and Servants of God' (ed. F. W. *Faber,
1849). Modern lives by la Vicomtesse de Beausire-Seysell
(Paris, 1913) and M. Vaussard ('Les Saints', 1925). Pourrat,
iii, 349–51 and 369–73.

MARY MAJOR, Church of St. See *Santa
Maria Maggiore, Rome.*

MARY, Queen of Scots (1542–87). She was
the only daughter of James V who died when
she was a few days old, leaving her heiress to
the throne of Scotland, of which she was
crowned Queen in 1543. Her mother was
Mary of Lorraine (or 'Mary of Guise', 1515–
1560). In 1548 she was sent to France for her
education, and in 1558 married to the Dauphin
Francis, becoming Queen Consort in 1559.
After the early death of Francis (1560) she
returned to Scotland (1561) where J. *Knox
and his followers introduced the Reformation
and thus stirred up bitter hatred against the RC
Church. Mary had a series of stormy interviews with Knox, but she remained impervious
to her arguments as well as her charm. In
other quarters her policy of moderation won
her many adherents, though it disappointed her
Catholic subjects as well as the Pope. In 1565
she married her cousin Henry Stuart, Lord
Darnley. The match was approved both by
the Pope and *Philip of Spain, and by Darnley
she became the mother of the future James VI
of Scotland (*James I of England) in 1566.
In 1566 Darnley instigated the murder of
Mary's secretary, David Rizzio, of whom he
had become jealous. This murder caused her
complete estrangement from Darnley, who, in
1567, was assassinated by James Hepburn,
Earl of Bothwell, who had become her
favourite. In the same year Bothwell obtained
a divorce from his wife and married Mary,
after he had been tried for the murder of
Darnley but found not guilty by judges who are
generally held not to have been impartial. This
marriage, which was concluded acc. to the
Protestant rite, was denounced by the Pope
and opposed by most European courts. How
far she was implicated in the murder of Darnley is still disputed; the verdict depends chiefly
on the contested authenticity of the so-called
Casket Letters, purporting to have been written
by Mary to Bothwell. Soon after this third
marriage the Protestant lords rose against her,
defeated her army at Carberry Hill, and imprisoned her in Lochleven Castle. Bothwell,
whom she refused to give up, fled to Denmark;
the rebellious lords established Protestantism
as the religion of the country and suppressed
Catholicism. In 1567 Mary signed her abdication and James VI was crowned king. In 1568

she escaped from Lochleven and raised an army, but was once more defeated at Langside. She fled to England, where she was imprisoned and tried by a commission, which produced the *Casket Letters* against her with a series of the most humiliating accusations against which she refused to defend herself. The commission of peers gave an open verdict, stating that nothing derogatory to her had been proved. This verdict restored her reputation, which had been gravely injured by the Bothwell marriage, and *Pius V wrote her a conciliatory letter. *Elizabeth I, however, who, on account of the illegitimacy of her birth, feared for the security of her throne as long as Mary was at liberty, continued to hold her in close captivity. There was a proposal, supported by the Catholic powers, to have her marriage with Bothwell annulled, to enable her to marry the Duke of Norfolk; but when a Catholic uprising in the north failed, the scheme came to nothing and Norfolk was executed (1572). For the next 14 years Mary was held a prisoner, guarded first by the Earl of Shrewsbury and later by Sir Amias Paulet. Her secret correspondence was watched by spies, and an unguarded letter, written in 1586, brought about her condemnation. She met her death at Fotheringay on 8 Feb. 1587 with great courage.

A. Labanoff, *Lettres, instructions, et mémoires de Marie Stuart* (7 vols., 1844); A. Teulet, *Lettres de Marie Stuart* (1859); *Calendar of State Papers, Scotland.* J. H. Pollen, S.J., *Papal Negotiations with Mary, Queen of Scots, etc.* (Scot. Hist. Soc., xxxvii, 1901); id., *A Letter from Mary, Queen of Scots, to the Duke of Guise* (ib., xliii, 1904); id., *Mary, Queen of Scots, and the Babington Plot* (ib., 3rd Ser., iii, 1922). Modern Biographies by F. A. M. Mignet (1851), D. Hay Fleming (1898), T. F. Henderson (1905), S. Zweig (1935). See also J. D. Leader, *Mary, Queen of Scots, in Captivity* (1880). On the Casket Letter controversy, W. Goodall, *Examination of the Letters said to be written by Mary, Queen of Scots, to Bothwell* (2 vols., 1754); T. F. Henderson, *The Casket Letters* (1890); A. Lang, *The Mystery of Mary Stuart* (1904). T. F. Henderson in *D.N.B.*, xxxvi (1893), pp. 373–90.

MARY TUDOR (1516–58), Queen of England from 1553. The daughter of *Henry VIII and Catharine of Aragon, she was betrothed to the Dauphin of France in 1518, and in 1522 by the Treaty of Windsor to the Emp. *Charles V, who, however, married a Portuguese princess in 1526. The disgrace and unhappiness of her mother and the subsequent separation made a deep impression on her. In 1532 she was sent to Richmond, and, during Anne Boleyn's life and some time afterwards, she was in disfavour. She was excluded from the succession at the birth of *Elizabeth (1533), regarded as the King's bastard, and placed in the humiliating position of lady-in-waiting to Anne Boleyn's daughter. In 1536 she signed a document acknowledging Henry's religious supremacy and the illegitimacy of her mother's marriage, and so was received back to favour, under the influence of Jane Seymour. In 1537 she was godmother to the future *Edward VI, and during the next years lived quietly in retirement. After Henry's last marriage she was on affectionate terms with Catharine Parr, and in 1544 was given the second place in the succession, after Edward, during whose reign she

continued to live in obscurity. She made a courageous stand against the demand of the Protector *Somerset that she should give up her chaplain and conform to the Established Church.

On Edward's death (1553) Mary became Queen, despite an effort of a small Protestant group to put Lady Jane Grey in her place. Her accession was welcomed with enthusiasm by the supporters of the old religion, and, acting on the advice of the Emperor, she showed at first leniency to her Protestant opponents though proscribing their religion. She was crowned by Stephen *Gardiner, Bp. of *Winchester, and soon afterwards betrothed to *Philip II of Spain despite the opposition of Parliament. In 1554 she displayed great courage in quelling Thomas Wyatt's plot, and resolved to rule henceforth with greater sternness. Among the many victims of the persecution following the plot were Jane Grey and her husband; and Elizabeth, who had possibly been implicated, was committed to the Tower. In July 1554 Philip landed in England, but the marriage proved a failure and was disliked by the people. Early in 1555 R. *Pole, who had arrived in England at the end of 1554, reconciled the country to the Papacy. In the same year Gardiner had the Heresy Bill and the Bishops' Courts restored, and the trials for heresy began, the steadfastness of the condemned greatly serving the cause of Protestantism. This persecution and her inability to have children lost her the affection of her people; Philip returned to the Continent; and in 1555 Mary also lost Gardiner, her trusted Chancellor. In 1555–6 T. *Cranmer, H. *Latimer, N. *Ridley, J. *Hooper, and others were burned as heretics; and new conspiracies, with Elizabeth at their centre, were discovered and severely quelled. In 1557 further measures were adopted against heretics; Philip, needing English aid against France, temporarily returned to the Queen; and war was declared on France in June, the French being defeated at St.-Quentin. But in 1558 Calais fell, a blow which severely damaged Mary's remaining prestige. From this time her health began to fail, and she died at St. James's Palace on 17 Nov. 1558.

P. F. Tytler, *England under the Reigns of Edward VI and Mary*, ii (1839), pp. 186–500. Modern lives by J. M. Stone (London, 1901), B. White (ib., 1935), and H. F. M. Prescott (ib., 1940), with bibl. J. D. Mackie, *The Early Tudors, 1485–1558* (The Oxford History of England, vii; 1952), pp. 526–61. S. Lee in *D.N.B.*, xxxvi (1893), pp. 333–54.

MARYS IN THE NT. Besides (1) the Virgin *Mary and (2) St. *Mary Magdalene, there are four (or perhaps three) others. These are (3) 'The wife of Clopas' (Jn. 19. 25), who stood by the Cross. Some have identified her with '[Christ's] mother's sister' (ib.), but it is possible that different women are meant. (4) 'The mother of James and Joses' (Mk. 15. 40), who stood by the Cross and was a witness of the Empty Tomb (Mk. 16. 1). She may well be the same as (3); on this assumption her sons *James and Joses have been identified with the

*Brethren of the Lord of those names. (5) Mary of Bethany, the sister of *Martha and *Lazarus (Jn. 11. 1 ff.), who sat at Christ's feet (Lk. 10. 38 ff.). Acc. to Jn. 11. 2, she 'anointed the Lord with ointment and wiped his feet with her hair', as is also related of an unnamed woman in Lk. 7. 37; cf. Mk. 14. 3. She is perh. to be identified with St. Mary Magdalene (q.v.). (6) 'The mother of John *Mark' (Acts 12. 12).

MASKELL, WILLIAM (c. 1814–90), ecclesiastical antiquary. Educated at University College, Oxford, he became an extreme High Churchman and took holy orders in 1837. His two books, *The Ancient Liturgy of the Church of England* (1844) and *Monumenta Ritualia Ecclesiae Anglicanae* (1846), were important contributions to the revival of liturgical studies in the C of E. As chaplain to H. *Phillpotts, Bp. of Exeter, Maskell conducted the examination of G. C. *Gorham when presented to the vicarage of Brampford Speke; and the issue of the case led Maskell to secede to the Church of Rome in 1850. He never received Roman ordination, but devoted himself to antiquarian studies and public service in the county of Cornwall.

J. M. Rigg in *D.N.B.*, xxxvi (1893), p. 413 f., s.v.

MASON, FRANCIS (1566–1621), Archdeacon of Norfolk. He was educated at Oriel College, Oxford, and later had connexions with Merton and Brasenose Colleges. His best-known writing was his *Of the Consecration of the Bishops in the C of E* (1613), written with the encouragement of Abp. G. *Abbot in refutation of the recently fabricated *Nag's Head Fable. Composed in dialogue form and in an entertaining style and drawing on the records of *Lambeth Palace, it sought to establish the validity of the consecration esp. of M. *Parker. In reply to several attacks by RC writers, Mason revised and enlarged the work, and in this form it was reissued posthumously in a Latin translation by N. Brent in 1625. Its spirited defence of the C of E against Rome procured for him the title 'Vindex Ecclesiae Anglicanae'.

A. Wood, *Athenae Oxonienses* (ed. P. Bliss), ii (1815), cols. 305–8. B. Porter in *D.N.B.*, xxxvi (1893), pp. 417–19.

MASS (Lat. *missa*). A title of the *Eucharist (q.v.). The word is a late form of *missio* (cf. late Lat. *ascensa* for *ascensio*, *collecta* for *collectio*), itself derived from *mittere*, 'to send'. (The older attempts to trace it back to a Heb. root may safely be dismissed). St. *Avitus of Vienne (c. 500) refers to its use, in churches and in the law courts, for the dismissal of the people (*ep. 1 ad Gundobald*; *PL*, lix. 186). The same use is attested by St. *Isidore of Seville (*Etymol. 6. 19. 4*). But the word had long been current also for the service from which the people were dismissed. St. *Ambrose (*ep. 20*; *PL*, xvi, 995) already applies to the Eucharist the expression 'missam facere' ('to perform the Mass'). The term was also used

(less commonly) of other services, e.g., in the Rule of St. *Benedict, of the Divine Office. In the present Roman Rite '*Ite, missa est' remains a regular form of dismissal at the end of Mass. The word was retained by T. *Cranmer in the 1549 BCP ('The Supper of the Lord and the Holy Communion, commonly called the Mass'), but disappeared from later editions. In modern times it has come to be associated with the doctrine of the Eucharistic Sacrifice and in the C of E its use as a title of the Eucharist has been revived by High Churchmen.

J. A. Jungmann, S.J., 'Zur Bedeutungsgeschichte des Wortes *Missa*' in Z.K.T., lxiv (1940), pp. 26–37. Jungmann, i (ed. 1949), pp. 222–4 (Eng. tr., i, 1951, pp. 173–5). L. Eisenhofer, *Grundriss der Liturgik des römischen Ritus* (ed. 1950), p. 161 f., with further bibl. A. *Fortescue in C.E., ix (1910), pp. 790–92, s.v. 'Mass, Liturgy of the. A. Name and Definition'.

MASS OF THE CATECHUMENS. See *Catechumens, Mass of the.*

MASS OF THE FAITHFUL. See *Faithful, Mass of the.*

'MASSA CANDIDA' ('White Lump'). See *Utica, The Martyrs of.*

MASSILLON, JEAN-BAPTISTE (1663–1742), French *Oratorian preacher. A native of Hyères in Provence, he joined the Oratory in 1681, was ordained priest in 1691, and in 1696 was appointed by L. A. *de Noailles, Abp. of *Paris, Director of the Seminary of St.-Magloire at Paris. From 1699 he often preached before Louis XIV (who voiced the *mot* that whereas hitherto he had been very satisfied with his preachers, after hearing Massillon he was very ill-satisfied with himself). In 1717 he was nominated Bp. of Clermont (consecrated 1718) and in 1719 became a Member of the Academy. He was one of the foremost preachers of a great generation, much respected even by leaders of the *Aufklärung (Voltaire, J. le R. *d'Alembert). If his classical style fell short of the sublimity of J.-B. *Bossuet, his sermons were marked by unsurpassed brilliance, colour, and vehemence and he was unrivalled as a preacher of moral seriousness. Among his most celebrated sermons were the discourse 'On the Fewness of the Elect' (1704) and his series of *Lent sermons ('Le Petit Carême') delivered before Louis XV in 1718. He preached the funeral orations of C. de N. de Villeroy, Abp. of Lyons (1693), of Louis XIV 'le Grand' (1715; which began *Dieu seul est grand*) and of Liselotte of the Palatinate, Duchess of Orleans (1723). He spent his last twenty years in the devoted service of his diocese.

Sermons ed. by Joseph Massillon, Cong. Orat. (nephew), in 15 vols. (Paris, 1745–9); later ed. of his *Œuvres complètes* by E. A. Blampignon (Bar-le-Duc, 3 vols., 1865–7). M. A. Bayle, *Massillon, étude historique et littéraire* (1867)· E. A. Blampignon, *Vie de Massillon d'après des documents inédits* (1879); id., *L'Épiscopat de Massillon* (1884); J. Janin, *Massillon et l'éloquence de la chaire* (1882); A. A. L. Pauthe, *Massillon* (1908). Other studies by J. de la Porte (Paris,

1820), A. Laurent (Tours, 1870) and F. Brunetière (Paris, 1882). Shorter works by E. Chazel (Paris, 1874), B. Attaix (Toulouse, 1882), and G. Chabert (Montauban, 1890). A. M. P. Ingold, *L'Oratoire et le jansénisme au temps de Massillon* (1880). A. Dégert in *C.É.*, x (1911), p. 34 f.

MASSORETES. The Jewish grammarians who between the 6th and 10th cents. A.D. introduced into the Hebrew text of the OT, hitherto unpointed, a system of *vowel points and accents. They based their work on the traditional pronunciation of the *Synagogues and Schools, which they aimed at preserving free from corruption at a time when Hebrew was becoming less and less a spoken language. So called from the Hebrew word 'Mas(s)oreth' (מסרה), which means, probably, 'tradition', the text produced by their labours is known as the 'Massoretic Text'.

Ed. of Massorah from MSS. by C. D. Ginsburg (4 vols., fol., London, 1880–1905). Classical study is J. Buxtorf (the elder), *Tiberias sive Commentarius Masorethicus Triplex* (Basle, 1620). C. D. Ginsburg, *Introduction to the Massoretico-Critical Edition of the Hebrew Bible* (1897). P. Kahle, *Der masoretische Text des Alten Testaments nach der Überlieferung der babylonischen Juden* (1902); id., *Masoreten des Ostens* (1913); id., *Masoreten des Westens* (2 vols., 1927–30). H. Hyvernat, 'Petit Introduction à l'étude de la Massore' in *R. Bibl.*, xi (1902), pp. 551–63, and xii (1903), pp. 529–49; continued as 'La Langue de la Massore', ib., N.S., i [xiii] (1904), pp. 521–46, and N.S., ii [xiv] (1904), pp. 203–34 and 515–42. B. J. Roberts, 'The Emergence of the Tiberian Massoretic Text' in *J.T.S.*, xlix (1948), pp. 8–16. H. L. Strack in *P.R.E.* (ed. 3), xii (1903), pp. 393–9, s.v. 'Masora'; L. Bigot in *D.T.C.*, x (pt. 1; 1928), cols. 265–78, s.v. 'Massore (texte hébreu de la)'; F. Spadafora in *E.C.*, viii (1952), cols. 280–2, s.v. 'Masora'.

MASTER OF MISRULE. See *Misrule, Lord of.*

MASTER OF THE SENTENCES, The (Lat. *Magister Sententiarum*). A title in use from the 12th cent. onwards for *Peter Lombard (d. *c.* 1160) on account of the central place which his 'Libri Sententiarum' occupied as a textbook in the medieval schools.

MATERIAL SIN. An action which though in itself ('materially') contrary to the Divine law is not culpable, because the agent acted either in ignorance (e.g. when someone takes another's property, believing it to be his own) or under external constraint. It is contrasted with '*Formal Sin' (q.v.).

MATHEW, ARNOLD HARRIS (1853–1919), *Old Catholic bishop. Educated for the Anglican ministry, he was ordained priest in the RC Church in 1878; but in 1892 he lost his status by a marriage and later was allowed to officiate in the C of E with the sanction of Abp. F. *Temple. On 28 Apr. 1908 he received episcopal consecration at Utrecht from the Dutch Old Catholic Church as their Archbishop in Great Britain. In 1910, however, he was repudiated by the Dutch Old Catholics on the ground that his consecration had been obtained under a misconception of the extent of his following in England (which appears to have been virtually non-existent). He continued to describe himself as 'Archbishop of the London Area' and (later) as 'Archbishop and Metropolitan of the English Catholic Church', and left irregular episcopal successions (see *Episcopi Vagantes*) which were repudiated by the *Lambeth Conference of 1920. See also *Old Catholics.*

A. H. Mathew, *An Episcopal Odyssey. An Open Letter to His Grace the Right Hon. and Most Rev. Randall Thomas Davidson, D.D. . . .* (privately printed, Kingsdown, Kent, 1915), with documents. H. R. T. Brandreth, O.G.S., *Episcopi Vagantes and the Anglican Church* (1947), pp. 12–30, with bibl. p. 71 f.

MATHURINS. Another name for members of the *Trinitarian Order (q.v.), founded for the redemption of Christian captives in 1198 by *St. John of Matha.

MATILDA OF MAGDEBURG, St. See *Mechtilde of Magdeburg, St.*

MATINS. See *Mattins.*

MATRIMONY. The Christian conception of marriage, though it claims to be based on the natural law, differs sharply from earlier practice, whether Jewish or pagan, and also from modern secular usage, notably in the equality it gives to the woman and the indissolubility it ascribes to the marriage bond.

Early Hebrew law, which was founded on marriage by purchase, assigned a low status to the woman, who became in effect the property of her husband, though he could not sell her (Ex. 21. 7). The woman could neither own nor inherit property and had no rights of divorce, while the man might divorce her for some 'uncleanness' (Deut. 24. 1). Polygamy was practised, sometimes with the consent of the wife, as in the case of Sarah (Gen. 16. 2) that the bond might be preserved, but in later Judaism there was a growing realization that monogamy represented the ideal.

Roman matrimonial practice was in many ways more influential in the formation of Christian doctrine. Though under the Empire divorce was readily available to both parties, the jurist Modestinus could define marriage as 'a life-long partnership, and a sharing of civil and religious rights' (*consortium omnis vitae, divini et humani iuris communicatio,* L. 1, Dig. xxiii, 2), while the legal commonplace that it was not consummation but consent that made a marriage was equally agreeable to Christian belief. One part of Roman law, however, that there could be no marriage between bond and free, was repugnant to Christian sentiment and set aside in the 3rd cent.

In His teaching about matrimony Our Lord was concerned to restore it to its original place in God's plan, and therefore abrogated the Mosaic toleration of divorce (Mt. 5. 31 f., 19. 3–9; Mk. 10. 2–12; Lk. 16. 18) and condemned remarriage. The 'Matthean exception' permitting remarriage (19. 9), which conflicts with the other Gospels, the rest of the NT and the general tradition of the Church, is perhaps to be understood as an early gloss to render the Christian law easier. In Rom. 7. 2 f. and 1 Cor. 7. 10–14 St. *Paul reasserts the Lord's teaching, while in Eph. 5. 22–33 he brings in a new aspect, comparing the union with the relation between Christ and His Church. Like St. *Peter (1 Pet. 3. 1–7) he assigns the governance of the household to the husband, but emphasizes the duty of love towards the wife, who is an equal partner (1 Cor. 7. 3 f.). In 1 Cor. 7. 15 he states the '*Pauline Privilege', i.e. that where there had been a marriage between unbaptized, a partner who has been converted is not bound by the marriage bond if the unbelieving partner deserts by reason of the conversion. This principle has been developed in RC moral theology (*CIC*, 1120–7) and has on occasion been greatly widened.

While matrimony is exhibited in the NT as a wholly honourable estate, virginity is more highly commended (Mt. 19. 10–12, 1 Cor. 7, passim). A passage in the Apocalypse ('these are they which were not defiled with women; for they are virgins', Rev. 14. 4) is out of harmony with the rest of the NT and has not influenced the main stream of Christian belief; it bears signs of *Encratite influence.

The preface to the Marriage Service in the BCP aptly sums up the ends of marriage. It defines its purposes as the procreation of children, the avoidance of sin, and mutual society. The first of these, universally understood as the prime end, demands that the good of the children (*bonum prolis*) be put before all other considerations. This has led many Christian moralists to repudiate all methods of family limitation. The 'avoidance of sin', though founded on Scripture (1 Cor. 7. 2, 9), derives chiefly from the teaching of St. *Augustine, who concentrated on the negative aspects of the union and did not see in matrimony a means of grace. The reluctance of the BCP to entitle it a Sacrament (though it is so called in the *Homilies; '*Hom. against Swearing and Perjury*, Part i') arises from the same hesitation of theologians to recognize as such a rite which did not appear to be manifestly productive of grace. But it was already reckoned a Sacrament by *Hincmar of Reims (d. 882), and from St. *Thomas Aquinas onwards the Schoolmen taught that it conferred grace. Its sacramental status is usually deduced from Eph. 5. 22–33, esp. 5. 32. Matrimony is accounted peculiar among the sacraments in that the parties themselves are ministers, the priest being only the appointed witness.

It was only in the 11th cent. that the claim of the Church to exclusive jurisdiction over matrimonial cases was conceded. The Reformation in England did not affect this, and the first breach with Canon Law was effected by Lord *Hardwicke's Marriage Act of 1753 (26 Geo. II, cap. 35), concerning clandestine marriages, and more notably by the Marriage Act of 1836 (6 & 7 Will. IV, cap. 85) establishing civil marriage. In 1857 the Divorce and Matrimonial Causes Act (20 & 21 Vict. cap.

85) abolished the jurisdiction of the ecclesiastical courts, and also allowed divorce *a vinculo* for adultery when allied to cruelty or desertion (hitherto it had only been available by Act of Parliament). This has been modified by the Matrimonial Causes Act of 1923 (13 & 14 Geo. V, cap. 19), granting divorce for adultery only, and that of 1937 (1 Edw. VIII & 1 Geo. VI, cap. 57), which widened the grounds of divorce to include desertion, cruelty and insanity. Agitation continues in favour of making divorce still easier.

Civil legislation has not affected the belief of the Church, both Roman Catholics and Anglicans maintaining that indissolubility is of divine institution. Suits of nullity (i.e. to obtain a declaration that there has been no true marriage) are allowed on various grounds by RC courts. In the Orthodox Church divorce was already formally tolerated in Byzantine times and it is still recognized.

The principle that any Christian man or woman may marry has naturally been subjected to limitation (see *Affinity*). The lifelong character of Christian marriage prohibits bigamy, which has been felony in England since 1604. The minimum age for marriage, which has varied, was fixed by the Age of Marriage Act of 1929 (19 & 20 Geo. V, cap. 36) at 16 for both parties, marriage below this age being void. The various restrictions are divided by Canon Law into impedient and diriment *impediments, of which the former admit of dispensation and the latter not.

As the Church took over the Roman view of marriage as the consent of the parties, a certain publicity has always been required. Apart from the period 1753–1823 English civil law has accepted the teaching of the canonists that clandestine marriages are valid but irregular. The necessary publicity is secured by the publishing of banns on three consecutive Sundays or holy-days in the parishes of residence of both parties, and the celebration of marriage in one or the other (since the Marriage Measure of 1930 alternatively banns may be published and marriage celebrated in the usual place of worship of one party). Marriages may also be celebrated by licence, obtainable from *surrogates, or by special licence (normally only for weddings in nonparochial churches), obtainable from the Abp. of Canterbury, in virtue of his original legatine authority. Similar publicity is required for a civil marriage. Canon 62 of 1604 fixed the hours when marriages might be solemnized as between 8 a.m. and noon, but the latter was extended in 1886 to 3 p.m., and in 1934 to 6 p.m., and Convocation amended the Canon accordingly. See also *Marriage Licences*.

Practice varies among the Christian bodies concerning clerical marriage. While the Orthodox Church preserves the primitive practice, that ordinands must either be already married or elect to remain celibate, the Roman Church (at least for all who follow the Lat. rite) has enforced celibacy, while the Anglican Church (Art. xxxii) and Nonconformist bodies allow a free choice.

Studies free from technicalities by Anglican writers include O. D. Watkins, *Holy Matrimony* (1895); T. A. *Lacey, *Marriage in Church and State* (1912; rev. ed. by R. C. Mortimer, 1947); K. E. *Kirk, *Marriage and Divorce* (1933; rev. ed., 1948); by a RC writer, G. H. Joyce, S.J., *Christian Marriage* (1933). Official RC teaching in the encyclicals of *Leo XIII, 'Arcanum Divinae Sapientiae' (10 Feb., 1880), and *Pius XI, 'Casti Connubii' (31 Dec. 1930), and *C.I.C.*, Cans. 1012–143. G. *Perrone, *De Matrimonio Christiano* (3 vols., Rome, 1858). D. Palmieri, *De Matrimonio Christiano* (Paris, 1880). A. Esmein, *Le Mariage en droit canonique* (Paris, 1891). P. Gasparri, *Tractatus Canonicus de Matrimonia* (2 vols., 1891). E. Friedberg, *Das Recht der Eheschliessung in seiner geschichtlichen Entwicklung* (Leipzig, 1865). J. Freisen, *Geschichte des canonischen Eherechts bis zum Verfall der Glossenlitteratur* (Tübingen, 1888). J. Zhishman, *Das Eherecht der orientalischen Kirche* (1863–5). On the comparative study of the institution, E. Westermarck, *The History of Human Marriage* (1891 [partly issued, Helsingsfors, 1889]; ed. 5, rewritten, 3 vols., 1921). F. Meyrick in *D.C.A.*, ii (1880), pp. 1092–114, s.v. 'Marriage'; various authors in *C.E.*, ix (1910), pp. 691–715, s.v. 'Marriage'; W. M. Foley in *H.E.R.E.*, viii (1915), pp. 433–43, s.v. 'Marriage (Christian)'; L. Godefroy–G. Le Bras–M. Jugie, A.A., in *D.T.C.*, ix (pt. 2, 1927) cols. 2044–335, s.v. 'Mariage'; various authors in *E.C.*, viii (1952), cols. 407–75, s.v. 'Matrimonio', all with bibl.

MATTER. In medieval philosophy, the stuff underlying all material existence before it is determined and actualized by *form (q.v.). The conception is derived from *Aristotle, where it is used to explain the fact of change in the physical world. Since one substance passes into another, originates and decays, but never springs from nothing nor turns into nothing, Aristotle postulated 'matter' (ὕλη) as a common substratum. It is the mere potentiality of physical being and becoming, and hence no immediate object for the intellect, but something that can be known only through the body in which it is actualized by the form.

The conception was developed and applied by the Schoolmen of the 13th cent. to the Sacraments. They substituted the terms 'matter' and 'form' for the older expressions 'things' and 'words'. The matter was the sensible element in the Sacraments, e.g. the water of *Baptism and the bread and wine of the *Eucharist. Though possessing a certain significance (cleansing and nourishing) in itself, the Sacramental matter or action needed for its perfection a more decisive determination, which it receives through the form, i.e. the accompanying words. The Scholastic terminology was accepted by Pope *Eugenius IV in his instruction to the Armenians and by the Council of *Trent; but it is not easily adapted to certain Sacraments, e.g. matrimony.

MATTHEW, St., Apostle and Evangelist. Acc. to Mt. (9. 9), he was the tax-gatherer called by Christ from the receipt of custom, whom Mk. (2. 14) and Lk. (5. 27) call 'Levi'. He may well have borne both names. He was evidently a Jew, and acc. to *Papias made a collection of Christ's sayings in Hebrew. He is traditionally the author of the First Gospel (see foll. entry).

Acc. to *Eusebius (*HE*, III, xxiv) St. Matthew preached to the Hebrews. Other traditions about his later life conflict and merit little credence. The *Roman Martyrology states that he was martyred 'in Ethiopia', the *Hieronymianum puts his death 'in Persia in the town of 'Tarrium' (perhaps Tarsuana east of the Persian Gulf, so A. von Gutschmid), while some apocryphal Greek Acts (prob. *Gnostic) state that he suffered in Pontus. In later times, Salerno and other places laid claim to his relics. He is credited with a 6th-cent. apocryphal Lat. work on the Lord's Infancy (*De Ortu Beatae Mariae et Infantia Salvatoris*), an adaptation of the *Protevangelium of St. James. In Christian symbolism he has commonly (*Irenaeus, *Jerome, *Augustine) been allotted the figure of a man (cf. Rev. 4. 7) on the ground that his Genealogy (1. 1–17) emphasizes the Lord's human origin. In art he is depicted with a sword, a money-bag, or a carpenter's square. Feast day in the E. 16 Nov., in the W. 21 Sept. *Bede has a sermon for the feast.

'Passio' in R. A. *Lipsius–M. Bonnet (edd.), *Acta Apostolorum Apocrypha*, ii (pt. 1; Leipzig, 1898), pp. 217–62. *AA.SS.*, Sept. VI (1757), pp. 194–227. E. Mangenot in *Dict. Bibl.*, iv (1908), cols. 872–6, s.v. 'Matthieu (Saint)'.

MATTHEW, Gospel acc. to St. Traditionally held to be the oldest of the four, the Gospel acc. to St. *Matthew (q.v.) stands first in the *Canon. It was prob. known to the author of the *Didache (perh. *c*. 100 A.D.) and St. *Ignatius of Antioch (*c*. 110 A.D.); and from the time of St. *Irenaeus onwards was regularly ascribed to the Apostle Matthew by name. *Papias (*c*. 130 A.D.) records that Matthew wrote the 'Logia' (τὰ λογία) 'in the Hebrew tongue'; and if the reference be to our Gospel, this is still earlier evidence for its ascription to him. It is perhaps to be dated *c*. 80 A.D.; but all the evidence is so indirect that it is consistent with any date between *c*. 65 A.D. and *c*. 100 A.D.

Modern scholars commonly hold that Mt. drew extensively on Mk., which he expanded with the aid of *'Q' (though this dependence is generally denied by Eng. RC scholars, e.g. J. *Chapman and B. C. Butler; also by A. M. Farrer). If so, the early tradition that the Gospel was written in 'Hebrew' (by which Aramaic was prob. meant) is untenable. The chief objection to its ascription to St Matthew is that to supposing an Apostle would have had such extensive recourse to a work of St. Mark.

The subject-matter of the Gospel is: A *Genealogy of Christ (1. 1–17), an 'Infancy Narrative' (1. 18–2 end; quite independent of that of Lk.), the mission of St. *John Baptist (3. 1–12), the Baptism and Temptation of Christ (3. 13–4. 17), His Mission in Galilee (4. 18–15. 20), His work further afield including His revelation of His Messiahship to St. *Peter at *Caesarea Philippi (15. 21–18 end), His Last Journey to Jerusalem (19 f.), concluding with the account of His last week, Passion and Resurrection (21–28). From 3. 1 onwards, Mt. appears to derive the bulk of his narrative material from Mk. (almost all of which Gospel is incorporated); but whereas in 3–13, he interpolates long sections of 'discourse' into the Marcan framework, in the rest of his Gospel he follows Mk. much more closely. In addition to the (mainly discourse) material which is paralleled in Lk. (i.e. the 'Q' material), there are considerable sections peculiar to Mt. These last are often described as 'M'. In general, Mt. shows a tendency to group together similar material which is scattered in Lk., e.g. the contents of 'The *Sermon on the Mount' (Mt. 5–7).

Among the characteristics of the Gospel are the fullness with which it records Our Lord's teaching; its special interest in the relation of the Gospel to Jewish Law, with its stress on Christianity as the 'New Law'; the special commission given to St. Peter (16. 17–20), and the record of the post-Resurrection appearances in Galilee (28). Its author is sometimes regarded as the most 'ecclesiastical' of the Evangelists (the only two occurrences of ἐκκλησία in the Gospels being at 16. 18 and 18. 17). The Gk. of the Gospel is 'correct, if rather colourless' (J. H. Moulton). Mt. avoids some of Mk.'s undignified words and is more concise, but much of Mk.'s unconscious and naïve artistry is lost. Of the three Synoptic Gospels it is that best adapted to public reading; and it has probably always been the best-known of them.

Patristic commentaries in Gk. include those of *Origen, St. John *Chrysostom, and *Peter of Laodicea; in Lat., those of *Hilary of Poitiers, St. *Jerome, St. *Augustine, and *Bede. Modern commentaries include those by T. *Zahn (Kommentar zum Neuen Testament ed., id., i; 1903), J. *Wellhausen (Berlin, 1904), W. C. Allen (I.C.C., 1907), A. Plummer (London, 1909), E. Klostermann (Hb.N.T., v, 1909, pp. 121–52; ed. 2, iii, 1927), A. H. McNeile (London, 1915), P. A. Micklem (West. Comm., 1917), G. H. Box (Cent. Bibl., 1922), M. J. *Lagrange, O.P. (Études Bibliques, 1923), T. H. Robinson (Moff. Comm., 1928), and F. W. Green (Clar. Bib., 1936). B. W. Bacon, Studies in Matthew (1930); G. D. Kilpatrick, The Origins of the Gospel according to St. Matthew (1946). E. Massaux, Influence de l'évangile de saint Matthieu sur la littérature chrétienne avant saint Irénée (Louvain, 1950). J. Chapman, O.S.B., Matthew, Mark and Luke (posthumous, 1937); B. C. Butler, O.S.B., The Originality of St. Matthew (1951); A. M. Farrer, St. Matthew and St. Mark (The Edward Cadbury Lectures, 1953–4; 1954). More recent Comm. by E. Lohmeyer–W. Schmauch (K.E.K., 1956). J. V. Bartlet in H.D.B., iii (1900), pp. 296–305, s.v.; L. Vaganay in Dict. Bibl., Suppl. v ('1954'), cols. 940–56. Recent Comm. by F. V. Filson (London, 1960). See also Synoptic Problem.

MATTHEW OF AQUASPARTA (c. 1240–1302), *Franciscan philosopher. A native of Aquasparta in Umbria, he became a Franciscan and studied at Todi and, under St. *Bonaventure, at Paris. In 1281 he succeeded John *Peckham as lector sacri palatii at Rome. In 1287 he became General of his Order, in 1288 Cardinal, and in 1291 Cardinal Bp. of Porto and Rufina. He stood high in the confidence of *Boniface VIII, who entrusted him with political missions. His writings (mostly unprinted) include sermons and Biblical commentaries (Job, Pss., Dan., Mt., Rom., etc.) and a commentary on the *Sentences, as well as 'Quaestiones Disputatae'. Against the rising *Aristotelianism (St. *Thomas Aquinas) he defended the *Augustinian theory of cognition, which he elaborated in great detail, holding that whatever is certainly known is known by means of rationes aeternae. Yet, like Bonaventure, he allowed that an empiri-

cal element entered into our knowledge. He also followed the Franciscan tradition in defending the *Ontological argument for the Being of God.

His Quaestiones Disputatae de Fide et de Cognitione publd. in the Bibliotheca Franciscana Scholastica Medii Aevi, i, Quaracchi, 1903; Quaestiones Disputatae de Christo (ib., ii, 1914); Quaestiones Disputatae de Gratia, ed. V. Doucet, O.F.M. (ib., xi; 1935). M. *Grabmann, Die philosophische und theologische Erkenntnislehre des Kardinals Matthaeus ab Aquasparta (Theologische Studien der Leo-Gesellschaft, xiv; 1906). E. Longpré, O.F.M., 'Thomas d'York et Matthieu d'Aquasparta. Textes inédites sur le problème de la création' in Archives d'Histoire doctrinale et littéraire, i (1926–7), pp. 267–308, notably pp. 272 and 293–308. Überweg, ii, 478–84, with bibl. p. 761 f. E. Longpré, O.F.M., in D.T.C., x (pt. 1; 1928), cols. 375–89, s.v.

MATTHEW PARIS (c. 1199–1259), medieval chronicler. He became a member of the Benedictine monastery of *St. Albans in 1217 and, as an expert scribe and illuminator, annalist of the monastery in 1236. His chief claim to fame lies in his Chronica Majora, a history of the world from the Creation to 1259. Its earlier sections are almost entirely a transcription of Roger of Wendover's Flores Historiarum, but its later pages are his own careful narration of contemporary events. The work is characterized by trenchant criticism of ecclesiastical abuses (in particular, Papal venality) and of Henry III's employment of foreigners in England, and was the fruit of his own experiences at St. Albans and his wide travels, both at home and abroad. Matthew was also the author of a Historia Anglorum sive Historia Minor, an abridgment of his longer history.

Extracts from his Works ed. F. Liebermann in M.G.H., Scriptores, xxviii (1888), pp. 74–455. His Chronica Majora, ed. H. R. Luard (7 vols., R.S., 1872–83); his Historia Anglorum, ed. F. Madden (3 vols., ib., 1866–9), with biogr. preface in vol. iii, pp. vii–liv; the part of the Gesta Monasterii Sancti Albani which is prob. mainly his work, ed. H. T. Riley in Gesta Abbatum Monasterii Sancti Albani a Thoma Walsingham, i (ib., 1867), pp. 3–324. The section of his Historia Anglorum dealing with the period 1235–73 is tr. into Eng. by J. A. Giles (Bohn's Antiquarian Library, 3 vols., 1852–4). A. Jessopp, Studies by a Recluse (1893), pp. 14–20 and 45–60. V. H. Galbraith, Roger Wendover and Matthew Paris (lecture; 1944). W. Hunt in D.N.B., xliii (1895), pp. 207–13, s.v. 'Paris, Matthew'.

MATTHEW'S BIBLE. This edition of the English Bible was issued in 1537. It was a revision of the work of W. *Tyndale, pieced out with Tyndale's unpublished MSS. and portions of M. *Coverdale's OT, with expository notes drawn from Conrad Pellican (1478–1556). Printed at Antwerp in 1537, it was dedicated to *Henry VIII, who licensed it for general reading. 'Thomas Matthew', the name of the supposed editor, was a mere alias for John *Rogers (q.v.).

J. Isaacs in The Bible in its Ancient and English Versions (ed. H. W. Robinson, 1940), pp. 172–175. W. T. Whitley, 'Thomas Matthew's Bible' in the C.Q.R. vol. cxxv (Oct. 1937), pp. 48–69. Whitley's attempt to defend the existence of Thomas Matthew as a real person has been disposed of by J. F. Mozley, William Tyndale (1937), Appendix E.

MATTHIAS, St., Apostle. He was chosen after the Ascension by lot to fill the vacancy in the Twelve left by the treachery of *Judas Iscariot (Acts 1. 15–26). It is implied that he

had been a follower of Christ from the beginning of His ministry, but he is not mentioned elsewhere in the NT. Acc. to apocryphal traditions, he (or, acc. to some versions, *Matthew) preached the Gospel in Ethiopia, or among the 'Anthropophagi', while the *Gnostic *Basilides claimed that he had derived his doctrines from a private tradition going back to St. Matthias. *Eusebius (H.E., I. xii. 3, II. i. 1) and St. *Epiphanius (Pan. i. 22) believed that he was one of our Lord's 'Seventy Disciples' (Lk. 10. 1). Feast day in the W., 24 (or, in leap year, 25) Feb.; in the Greek Church, 9 Aug.

AA.SS., Feb. III (1658), pp. 431-54. H. Cowan in H.D.B., iii (1900), p. 305 f., s.v. with bibl.; E. Jacquier in C.E., x (1911), p. 66, s.v. On his election see also comm. on Acts (s.v.), esp. that of E. Jacquier (ed. 2, Paris, 1926), pp. 30-41.

MATTHIAS, Gospel of St. A lost apocryphal Gospel, mentioned by *Origen, Hom. I in Lc. and other early Christian writers. Perhaps it is to be identified with the treatise referred to by *Clement of Alexandria as 'the Traditions of Matthias' (Strom. II. ix. 45, &c.).

Bardenhewer, i (1913), pp. 529 f. and 532, with further bibl. É. Amann in Dict. Bibl., Suppl. i (1928), col. 478 f., s.v. 'Apocryphes du Nouveau Testament. II. 2. Évangile de Matthias', also with bibl. reff.

MATTINS (1). In the W. the Breviary Office for the night, derived from the *Vigils of the primitive Church and so called ('vigiliae') until the 11th cent. It was originally performed at midnight, but in the Rule of St. *Benedict it was prescribed for the eighth hour of the night, i.e. 2 a.m. In some religious orders one or other practice is still the custom, but since the Middle Ages the tendency to 'anticipate', i.e. to say Mattins on the night before, has steadily increased and is now the rule for the secular clergy as well as for many regulars. After the silent recitation of *Paternoster, *Ave Maria, and *Credo, the night office is introduced by the versicles 'Domine, labia mea aperies' and 'Deus, in adiutorium meum intende', followed by the *Invitatory (q.v.) and a hymn which varies acc. to feast and season. On Sundays and feasts of *double and *semi-double rank there follow three *Nocturns, each consisting of three Psalms with their antiphons, versicle, Paternoster, and a short prayer called Absolutio, to which are joined three Lessons, each of which is preceded by a benediction. The Lessons of the First Nocturn are always taken from Scripture, those of the second are usually historical, and those of the third from a homily on the Gospel of the day. *Simple feasts and ferias have only one Nocturn, consisting of nine Psalms and three Lessons, and Easter and Pentecost with their Octaves only three Psalms and three Lessons. The Office concludes with the *Te Deum, which is said on all Sundays except those of *Advent and from *Septuagesima to *Palm Sunday, on all feasts, and on the ferias of Paschal time. In choir it is immediately followed by *Lauds, but in private recitation the latter may be said separately, in which case Mattins is terminated by a prayer with Paternoster.

(2) The designation, retained in the 1549 Book, but dropped in 1552, is also in current use for the service of 'Morning Prayer' in the Anglican BCP. The office was based on the Medieval Mattins with supplements from *Prime. Its structure is in essence identical with that of *Evensong (q.v.) except that Ps. 95 is sung as an *Invitatory before the Psalms for the day (except on the 19th day of the month, when it is in the ordinary course of the Pss., and on *Easter Day when a special anthem is ordered). Also on thirteen feast days in the year the *Athanasian Creed is ordered to be said in substitution of the *Apostles' Creed, but in modern times this rubric has been widely disregarded. Between the First (OT) and Second (NT) Lessons, the Canticle '*Te Deum' or as an alternative, mainly in penitential seasons, 'Benedicite' is said or sung and after the Second Lesson the *Benedictus (or Ps. 100, Jubilate Deo).

(1) P. *Batiffol, Histoire du bréviaire romain (1895), pp. 90-9 (ed. 3, 1911, pp. 117-28; Eng. tr., 1912, pp. 75-83) and passim. J. A. Jungmann, S.J., 'Beiträge zur Geschichte der Gebetsliturgie I. Die Entstehung der Matutin' in Z.K.T., lxxii (1950), pp. 66-79. J. M. Hanssens, S.J., Aux origines de la prière liturgique. Nature et genèse de l'office des matines (Analecta Gregoriana, lvii; 1952).

(2) F. Procter-W. H. *Frere, A New History of the Book of Common Prayer (1901), esp. pp. 368-401. F. E. *Brightman, The English Rite, i (1915), esp. pp. lxxxv-xcii.

MATTINS OF BRUGES. The massacre of the French lodged in Bruges by the Flemish inhabitants at daybreak on 18 May 1302. Those who fell had been marked out by their inability to pronounce a prearranged Flemish shibboleth.

The principal authority is the contemporary author of the Annales Gandenses (ed. F. Funck-Bretano, Collection de textes pour servir à l'étude et à l'enseignement de l'histoire, xviii; 1896, pp. 24-6, with notes). E. Vanden-Bussche, 'Les Matines de Bruges. Note pour l'histoire de Jean Breidel et Pierre de Coninc' in La Flandre. Revue des Monuments d'Histoire et d'Antiquités, xii (1881), pp. 319-28. J. Frederichs, 'Note sur le cri de guerre des matines brugeoises' in Compte-Rendu des séances de la Commission royale d'Histoire, Ser. 5, iii (1893), pp. 263-74. F. Funck-Brentano, Philippe le Bel en Flandre (1896), pp. 388-94. H. Pirenne, Histoire de Belgique, i (1900), p. 382, with note on sources; id. in C. Med. H., viii (1936), p. 339 f.

MAUNDY THURSDAY. The traditional English name for the Thursday preceding *Easter, derived from the first antiphon of the ceremony of the washing of the feet, 'mandatum novum' (Jn. 13. 34). Its special celebration in commemoration of our Lord's Institution of the Eucharist on that day is attested already for the 4th cent. by the Council of *Hippo (393). Two other traditional liturgical features are the Blessing of the Holy Oils and the Reconciliation of Penitents, though the latter has long been obsolete. Two or even three Masses were celebrated on the day in the early centuries, but the *Gregorian Sacramentary and the oldest *Ordines Romani allow only one. In the W. Church peculiarities of the Maundy

Thursday Mass are the solemn ringing, at the '*Gloria in excelsis', of all the bells, henceforward silent till the Easter Vigil; the consecration of a second Host for the Mass of the *Presanctified on Good Friday, which is carried in procession to the Altar of *Repose after the Mass; the omission of the *Kiss of Peace in commemoration of the kiss of *Judas; and the general communion of the clergy. In cathedral churches the Holy *Oils are blessed during the Mass. After *Vespers the altars are stripped and the holy water stoups emptied. In some churches the altars are then ceremonially washed. The Maundy Thursday ceremonies conclude with the *Pedilavium (washing of the feet), which is performed by bishops in their cathedrals, by abbots in their monastery churches, and formerly also by certain sovereigns, of which the 'Maundy Ceremony' at *Westminster Abbey is an abbreviated survival. See also Green Thursday and Sheer Thursday.

J. W. Tyrer, Historical survey of Holy Week, its Services and Ceremonial (*Alcuin Club Collections, xxix; 1932), pp. 79–115. H. Thurston, S.J., Lent and Holy Week (1904), pp. 274–325. L. Eisenhofer, Handbuch der katholischen Liturgik, i (1932), pp. 511–23. A. *Wilmart, O.S.B., Auteurs spirituels et textes dévots du moyen-âge latin (1932), No. 2, 'L'Hymne de la charité pour le Jeudi-Saint', pp. 26–36.

MAURICE, St., Primicerius ('leader') of the *Theban Legion. Acc. to the 5th cent. 'Passio Agaunensium Martyrum', a composition of *Eucherius of Lyons, the Emp. Maximian (Caesar from 286 to 305) took an army to Gaul during *Diocletian's persecution, which included a wholly Christian 'Theban legion' (from the Thebaïd, Egypt) commanded by Mauricius. As it refused to sacrifice, it was massacred by Maximian at Agaunum (now St. Maurice-en-Valais; not to be confounded with other places of the same name, e.g. St. Moritz in the Engadine). The story, though unhistorical in this form, may spring from some action of Christian soldiers during Maximian's campaign against the Bagaudae (286). Feast day, 22 Sept.

The best text of the 'Passio Acaunensium Martyrum' is that ed. B. Krusch in M.G.H., Scriptores Rerum Merovingicarum, iii (1896), pp. 20–41. Further details of edd. and other sources in B.H.L., pp. 841–4 (Nos. 5737–64), and suppl., p. 224 f. AA.SS., Sept. VI (1757), pp. 308–403 and 895–926. Of the considerable literature the fullest account is that of J. Bernard de Montmélian, Saint Maurice et la légion thébéenne (2 vols., 1888; detailed but not entirely accurate); among the more reliable discussions is that of M. Besson, Monasticon Acaunense (Fribourg, 1913). H. *Leclercq, O.S.B., in D.A.C.L., x (pt. 2; 1932), cols. 2699–2729, s.v., with detailed bibl.

MAURICE, FREDERICK DENISON (1805–72), Anglican divine. He was born at Normanstone, near Lowestoft, the son of a *Unitarian minister. After a boyhood spent among long and painful religious disputes in his family he entered Trinity College, Cambridge, in 1823, where F. *Field was his tutor, with a view to becoming a barrister. In 1825 he migrated with his close friend, John Sterling, to Trinity Hall. Refusal to subscribe the *Thirty-Nine *Articles excluded him from a degree and fellowship and he moved to London, where he wrote in defence of social reforms, criticizing the Benthamite materialism.

Having gradually accepted the Anglican faith, in 1830 Maurice went up to Exeter College, Oxford, and in 1834 was ordained to the curacy of Bubbenhall, Warwickshire. Here he wrote Eustace Conway (1834), an autobiographical novel, and Subscription No Bondage (1835), a pamphlet defending the imposition of religious tests at the universities. In 1836 he became chaplain of Guy's Hospital, where he lectured regularly on moral philosophy and wrote his most enduring book, The Kingdom of Christ; or Hints to a Quaker concerning the Principle, Constitution and Ordinances of the Catholic Church (1838). Its philosophical, yet fundamentally orthodox, presentation of theology was misunderstood and subjected to attacks from all ecclesiastical angles. In 1840 he was elected Professor of English Literature and History at *King's College, London; in 1845 Warburtonian Lecturer (his lectures, The Epistle to the Hebrews, 1846, contained a reply to J. H. *Newman's Theory of Development); in 1846 Chaplain at Lincoln's Inn; and in 1846 Professor of Theology in the newly created Theological School at King's College.

Maurice, who had been deeply moved by the political events of 1848, now became actively interested again in the application of Christian principles to social reform. Acquaintance with J. M. F. *Ludlow led to the formation of the *Christian Socialists (q.v.), which brought him into close contact with C. *Kingsley and others. But his orthodoxy was constantly under suspicion and in 1853 his Theological Essays, in which he attacked the popular view of the endlessness of future punishment and maintained that in the NT '*Eternity' had nothing to do with time, provoked a crisis which resulted in his resignation from King's College. In 1854 he started a 'Working Men's College' in London to promote his socialistic ideals. In What is Revelation? (1859) he made a fierce attack on the *Bampton Lectures of H. L. *Mansel (1858) who had defended Theism on the basis of the limitations of human reason and by implication repudiated philosophical theology. In 1860 he was appointed to the chapel of St. Peter's, Vere Street, and in 1866 Knightbridge Professor of Moral Philosophy at Cambridge. In 1870 he became incumbent of St. Edward's, Cambridge. Among his other writings were Three Letters to the Rev. W. *Palmer (1842; defending the *Jerusalem Bishopric), The Lord's Prayer (1848), The Old Testament (1851), The Unity of the New Testament (1854), The Epistles of St. John (1857), The Gospel of St. John (1857), The Gospel of the Kingdom of Heaven (1864) and The Conscience, Lectures on Casuistry, (1868). He also wrote a long article 'Moral and Metaphysical Philosophy', originally published in the Encyclopaedia Metropolitana and later expanded and reissued in various forms. Many of his other writings were subjected to considerable revision in their later editions.

Life and Letters, ed. by his son, Frederick Maurice (2 vols.; 1884); C. F. G. Masterman, *F. D. Maurice* (1907); C. Jenkins, *F. D. Maurice and the New Reformation* (1938), M. B. Reckitt, *Maurice to Temple*. Scott Holland Memorial Lectures, 1946 (1947); F. Higham, *F. D. Maurice* (1947); A. R. Vidler, *The Theology of F. D. Maurice* (1948; publd. U.S.A., 1947, as *Witness to the Light*); A. M. Ramsey, *F. D. Maurice and the Conflict of Modern Theology* (1951). L. Stephen in *D.N.B.*, xxxvii (1894), pp. 77–104.

MAURISTS, The. The *Benedictine monks of the Congregation of St.-Maur. The Congregation, which takes its name from St. *Maurus (6th cent., q.v.), was founded in 1621, to represent in France the reform initiated in the Abbey of Saint-Vanne (Lorraine) in 1600. From 1672 onwards, the Maurists devoted themselves largely to historical and literary works, and many of their productions in this field are monuments of scholarship, which constitute the chief glory of the Congregation. Among their members were J. *Mabillon, B. de *Montfaucon, R. Massuet, C. de la Rue, L. *D'Achéry, F. Aubert, and many others whose names are familiar to patristic students. Some of the monks became supporters of *Jansenism, and towards the end of the 18th cent. the Congregation suffered a tendency towards abusive relaxation of discipline. Suppressed in 1790 by the Revolutionary government, it was finally dissolved by *Pius VII in 1818.

E. *Martène, O.S.B., contd. by J. Fortet, O.S.B., *Histoire de la congrégation de Saint-Maur*, ed. G. Charvin, O.S.B. (Annales de la France Monastique, xxxi, xxxii, xxxiii, xxxiv, xxxv, xlii, xliii, xlvi, xlvii; 1928–43). B. Pez, O.S.B., *Bibliotheca Benedictino-Mauriana seu de Ortu, Vitis et Scriptis Patrum Benedictinorum a Celeberrima Congregatione S. Mauri in Francia* (Augsburg, 1716). P. Le Cerf, O.S.B., *Bibliothèque historique et critique des auteurs de la congrégation de St.-Maur* (The Hague, 1726). [R. P. Tassin] *Histoire littéraire de la congrégation de Saint-Maur, ordre de S.-Benoît* (Brussels, 1770); suppl. by U. Robert (Paris, 1881); further suppl. by H. Wilhelm-U. Berlière, O.S.B. (ib., 1908). C. De Lama, *Bibliothèque des écrivains de la congrégation de Saint-Maur, ordre de Saint-Benoît en France* (1882). C. McCarthy, *The Lives of the Principal Benedictine Writers of the Congregation of St. Maur* (1868). E. Chavin de Malan, *Histoire de D. Mabillon et de la congrégation de Saint-Maur* (1843). E. de Broglie, *Mabillon et la société de l'abbaye de Saint-Germain-des-Prés à la fin du XVIᵉ siècle, 1664–1707* (2 vols., 1888); id., *La Société de l'abbaye de S.-Germain-des-Prés au XVIIIᵉ siècle*. Bernard de Montfaucon et les Bernardins 1715–1750 (2 vols., 1891). M. Heimbucher, *Die Orden und Kongregationen der katholischen Kirche*, i (ed. 3, 1933), pp. 235–41, with further bibl. J. Baudot in *D.T.C.*, x (1928), cols. 405–43, s.v.

MAURUS, St. (6th cent.), disciple of St. *Benedict of Nursia. Nothing certain is known of him. Acc. to a biography ascribed to his companion, Faustus of *Monte Cassino (acc. to H. *Delehaye and others a 9th cent. forgery by Abbot Odo of Glanfeuil), he made his way to France in 543, where he founded the abbey of Glanfeuil, afterwards St.-Maur-sur-Loire; and, after resigning the abbacy to Bertulf in 581, spent the rest of his life in solitude and contemplation. He is the patron of charcoal-burners, and is invoked against gout and other diseases. Feast day, 15 Jan.

Life ascribed to Faustus of Monte Cassino pr. in *Acta Sanctorum Ordinis S. Benedicti*, i (Paris, 1668), pp. 275–98;

also, with other material, in *AA.SS.*, Jun. I (1643), pp. 1038–62. A. Giry, 'La Vie de saint Maur du Pseudo-Faustus' in *Bibliothèque de l'École des Chartes*, lvii (1898), pp. 149–52. B. F. Adloch, O.S.B., 'Die Benedictiner-Tradition über den hl. Maurus und Abt Odo von Glanfeuil' in *Studien und Mitteilungen aus dem Benedictiner- und dem Cistercienser-Orden*, xix (1898), pp. 310–26; id., 'Zur Vita S. Mauri', ib., xxvi (1905), pp. 3–22 and 202–26; id., ''Les Légendes hagiographiques'', und die ''Vita Sancti Mauri'' per Faustum', ib., xxviii (1907), p. 101, all with reff. to other litt. H. *Leclercq, O.S.B., in *D.A.C.L.*, vi (pt. 1; 1924), cols. 1285–319, s.v. 'Glanfeuil', with full discussion of authenticity of life, and bibl.

MAXIMILIAN, St. (d. 295), also Marmilian, martyr. He is recorded to have been executed at Theveste in Numidia, his native town, because he refused to serve in the Roman army. Feast day, 12 Mar.

'Acta' pr. in T. *Ruinart (ed.), *Acta Primorum Martyrum Sincera et Selecta* (Paris, 1689), pp. 309–11; A. *Harnack, *Militia Christi*. Die christliche Religion und der Soldatenstand in den ersten Jahrhunderten (1905), pp. 114–17; and in R. Knopf (ed.), *Ausgewählte Märtyrerakten* (ed. 3 by G. Krüger; 1929), p. 86 f.; for earlier edd. see *B.H.L.*, p. 850 (No. 5813). H. *Delehaye, S.J., *Les Passions des martyrs et les genres littéraires* (1921), pp. 104–10. C. J. Cadoux, *The Early Christian Attitude to War* (1919), pp. 149–51. H *Leclercq, O.S.B., in *D.A.C.L.*, xi (pt. 1; 1933), cols. 1133–7, s.v. 'Militarisme XIII, le martyre du conscrit Maximilien', with bibl.

MAXIMUS, St. (*c.* 380–*c.* 470), Bp. of Turin. Little is known of his life beyond the facts that he witnessed the martyrdom of three missionary bishops in 397 at 'Anaunia' in the Rhaetian Alps and attended synods at Milan in 451 and Rome in 465. Many of his discourses survive, which, since first edited by B. Bruni in 1784, are commonly divided into 'Homilies' (118), 'Sermons' (116), and 'Tractates' (6); but several of those ascribed to him are spurious, some 40 belonging to Maximinus, Bp. of the Goths. They are for the most part short, pithily expressed, sometimes over rhetorical, and marked by a strong popular appeal. They throw much light on the history of the liturgy and the survival of paganism in N. Italy. Some newly discovered homilies were published by U. Moricca in 1929. Feast day, 25 June.

Editio princeps (only 74 sermons), by J. Gymnicus (Cologne, 1535). The ed. of B. Bruni (Rome, 1784) is repr. in J. P. Migne, *PL*, lvii. Crit. edd. of selected sermons (including some previously unknown) by A. Spagnolo–C. H. *Turner in *J.T.S.*, xvi (1914–15), pp. 161–76, 314–22; xvii (1915–16), pp. 225–35, 321–37; xx (1918–19), pp. 289–310; acc. to B. *Capelle, O.S.B. *R. Bén.*, xxxiv (1922), pp. 81–108, all these sermons really belong to Maximinus the Arian. U. Moricca, 'Il Codice Casanatense, 1338, II. Ventiquattro omilie inedite di Massimo di Torino' in *Bilychnis*, xxxiii (1929), pp. 1–22, 81–93. Bardenhewer, iv, 610–13; Altaner (ed. 1951), p. 407. G. M. Rolando in *E.C.*, viii (1952), cols. 311 f., s.v. 'Massimo di Torino'.

MAXIMUS, St., 'Confessor' (*c.* 580–662), Greek theologian and ascetic writer. A member of the old Byzantine aristocracy, after holding the post of Imperial Secretary under the Emp. *Heraclius, *c.* 614, he became a monk (later abbot) of the monastery of Chrysopolis. During the Persian invasion (626) he fled to Africa. From *c.* 640 onwards he was a determined opponent of *Monothelitism. After Pyrrhus, the temporarily deposed Monothelite

Patriarch of *Constantinople, had declared his defeat in a dispute at Carthage (645), Maximus procured the condemnation of the heresy by several African Synods, and also had a share in its condemnation by the *Lateran Council of 649. In 653 he was brought to Constantinople, where pressure was put upon him to obtain his adherence to the 'Typus' of Constantius II. On his refusal he was exiled to Thrace. In 661 he was again brought to the capital and severely questioned; a probably true tradition says that on this occasion his tongue and his right hand were cut off. He was then exiled to the Caucasus, but died soon afterwards.

Maximus Confessor was a prolific writer on doctrinal, ascetical, exegetical, and liturgical subjects. His works include the 'Quaestiones ad Thalassium', 65 questions and answers on difficult passages of Scripture, the 'Ambigua', an exegetical work on *Gregory of Nazianzus, Paraphrases on the works of Pseudo-*Dionysius, several dogmatic treatises against the *Monophysites and Monothelites, the 'Liber Asceticus' and 'Capita de Caritate', and the 'Mystagogia', a mystical interpretation of the Liturgy. He maintained that the purpose of history was the Incarnation of the Son of God and the divinization ($\theta\acute{\epsilon}\omega\sigma\iota s$) of man, which consisted in the restoration of the Image impaired by Original Sin. Man, created in an incorruptible nature devoid of passion, caused evil to come into the world by his desire for pleasure, which destroyed the dominion of reason over the senses; hence Christ had to redeem the race by pain to restore the equilibrium. It was through the Incarnate Word, the centre of Maximus's speculative as of his mystical doctrine, that man is not only freed from ignorance but given the power to practise virtue. The goal of the human life, attained through abnegation, is union with God by charity. Feast day in the W., 13 Aug.

Works ed. F. *Combefis, 2 vols., Paris, 1675 (the projected third vol. never appeared). The Scholia to St. *Gregory Nazianzen and the Ps.-*Dionysius were first pr. in F. Oehler, Anecdota Graeca, i (Halle, 1857). All these repr. in J. P. Migne, PG, xc and xci, and (scholia to Ps.-Dionysius), ib., iv, 15–432 and 527–76. His 'Computus Ecclesiasticus' is in J. P. Migne, PG, xix, 1217–80 (among the works of *Eusebius of Caesarea). Fr. tr. of 'Capita de Caritate' ed. J. Pegon, S.J., in S.C., ix (1943). On the life of Maximus, repr. from Combefis in PG, xv, 68–109, cf. R. Devreesse, 'La Vie de saint Maxime le Confesseur et ses Recensions' in Anal. Boll., xlvi (1928), pp. 5–49. H. U. von Balthasar, Kosmische Liturgie: Maximus Bekenner. Höhe und Krise des griechischen Weltbildes (1941; ed. 2, 1961; Fr. tr., 1947); I. Hausherr, S.J., Philautie. De la tendresse pour soi à la charité selon Saint Maxime le Confesseur (Orientalia Christiana Analecta, cxxxvii; 1952). P. Sherwood, O.S.B., An Annotated Date-List of the Works of Maximus the Confessor (Studia Anselmiana, xxx; 1952); id., The Earlier Ambigua of Saint Maximus the Confessor and his Refutation of Origenism (ib., xxxvi; 1955). Krumbacher, pp. 61–4; Bardenhewer, v. 28–35; Altaner (ed. 1951), pp. 470–3. J. A. Wagenmann–R. Seeberg in P.R.E. (ed. 3), xii (1903), pp. 457–70; V. Grumel, A.A., in D.T.C., x (pt. 1; 1928), cols. 448–9; I. Hausherr, S.J., in E.C., viii (1952), col. 307 f., with further bibl.

MAXIMUS THE CYNIC (4th cent.), intruded Bp. of *Constantinople. After a disreputable early life at *Alexandria, he conceived the idea of supplanting St. *Gregory Nazianzen, and with the support of Peter II,

Bp. of Alexandria, went to Constantinople (379), where he ingratiated himself with Gregory, who even pronounced a panegyric on him in his presence. One night in 380, when Gregory was ill, he was consecrated to the see. He then set out immediately for Thessalonica to secure the recognition of the Emp. *Theodosius, but in this he was unsuccessful. The Council of *Constantinople of 381 (can. 4) declared that Maximus 'neither is nor was a bishop'. Meanwhile, Peter recognized what Maximus was worth and withdrew his support. However, Maximus convinced St. *Ambrose and others in the W., where only his version of events was known and believed, of his claims, and some W. synods threatened to break off all relations with the E. Church if Maximus were not restored to his see; but at the Council of Rome in 382 they were undeceived and abandoned him. He professed to combine belief in the Cynic philosophy with profession of the Nicene faith.

The chief sources are Gregory Naz. Orat., xxv; id., De Vita Sua (Poema de Seipso), ll. 745–1029; Ambrose, Ep. 13; *Sozomen, H.E., VII, ix; *Theodoret, H.E., V, viii. E. Venables in D.C.B., iii (1882), pp. 878–80.

MAX MÜLLER, FRIEDRICH (1823–1900), comparative philologist and religious writer. A native of Dessau in Germany, he was educated at the universities of Leipzig (1841–3) and Berlin (1844–5), and in 1845 went to Paris, where he began to work on an editio princeps of the Rig-Veda. In 1846 he came to England, and in 1848 went to Oxford to supervise its printing (6 vols., 1849–75). In 1850 he was appointed deputy, and in 1854 full, Taylorian professor of modern European languages. He was elected a Fellow of All Souls in 1858. In 1859 he published his History of Ancient Sanskrit Literature, important esp. for its studies in chronology. Having failed to secure the Sanskrit professorship at Oxford in 1860, he devoted himself largely to other studies, esp. to comparative philology, on which he lectured at the Royal Institution in 1861 and 1863. In 1868 he was appointed to the chair of comparative philology at Oxford, founded esp. for him. In 1875 he undertook the edition of The Sacred Books of the East, a series of translations of E. religious classics in 51 vols., over thirty of which are devoted to the religions of India. Much of his work on the comparative study of religions is embodied in The Origin and Growth of Religion (*Hibbert Lectures (1878) and the *Gifford Lectures from 1888 to 1892, on Natural Religion (1889), Physical Religion (1891), Anthropological Religion (1892), and Theosophy, or Psychological Religion (1893)). He also interested himself in comparative mythology, on which he wrote a large work, Contributions to the Science of Mythology (1897).

Max Müller was among the most learned and popular figures in post-*Tractarian Oxford. Through the influence of C. C. J. *Bunsen, his work also attracted the attention of the Queen and the Prince Consort. His wide range of interests, his facility of expression, and his readiness to put forward highly speculative (and often inadequately tested) theories made his writings congenial to the religious liberals of his age. Though mostly without permanent theological importance, they exercised a great influence on the ideas of the later 19th cent.

A collected edition of his works appeared in 1898–1903. His *Life and Letters* (2 vols., London, 1902) were edited by his widow. A. A. Macdonell in *D.N.B.*, Suppl. iii (1901), pp. 151–7.

MAY LAWS. The legislation associated with Bismarck's *Kulturkampf* and directed against the RC Church in Germany. These laws, passed in May 1873 under the direction of P. L. A. *Falk, were based on the theory of the absolute supremacy of the state. They limited the extent of the disciplinary powers of the Church, instituted a Supreme Ecclesiastical Court whose members were appointed by the Emperor and directly under state control, ordered all ordinands to pass through a state Gymnasium and to take a state examination (the '*Kultur-Examen*'), and brought all ecclesiastical seminaries under state control. The laws, with others of a similar nature, were condemned by *Pius IX in the encyclical 'Quod nunquam' (1875) as subversive of the constitution and rights of the Church, and also strongly opposed by many German Protestants.

P. Hinschius, *Die preussischen Kirchengesetze des Jahres 1873* (1873), with full text. Eng. tr. of the most important clauses in R. G. D. Laffan (ed.), *Select Documents of European History*, iii, ed. H. Butterfield (1931), p. 167 f. The encyclical 'Quod Nunquam' is pr. in Mirbt, No. 613, pp. 471–3, with further reff. See also bibl. to *Kulturkampf*.

MAYNE, CUTHBERT (1543–77), the first RC seminary priest executed in England. Born in Devon, he was ordained at the age of 18. At St. John's College, Oxford, he came under the influence of E. *Campion, and secretly became a RC. He then entered the English College at *Douai, where he was ordained to the RC priesthood. In 1576 he was sent on the English Mission and became chaplain to a landowner in Cornwall, passing as his steward. In 1577, however, a search was made, and Mayne was found concealed. On being tried at Launceston, he was sentenced to death. As it was difficult to find grounds for a capital charge, as the Act of Parliament making it high treason to receive orders abroad had not yet been passed, he was condemned on the alleged grounds of denying the Queen's spiritual supremacy, saying Mass, possessing a printed copy of a bull for a jubilee, and wearing an *Agnus Dei. He was executed at Launceston on 29 Nov. 1577. He was beatified in 1888. Feast day, 29 Nov.

W. *Allen, *A Brief History of the Glorious Martyrdom of Twelve Reverend Priests, Father Edmund Campion and his Companions* ([1582]; ed. J. H. Pollen, S.J., 1908, pp. 104–10). R. A. McElroy, C.R.L., *Blessed Cuthbert Mayne*. Protomartyr of the English Seminaries (1929). E. S. Knox, Cong. Orat., in B. Camm, O.S.B. (ed.), *Lives of the English Martyrs Declared Blessed by Pope Leo XIII in 1886 and 1895*, ii (1905), pp. 204–22 and 656. T. Cooper in *D.N.B.*, xxxviii (1894), p. 161 f., s.v. for further reff.

MAYNOOTH COLLEGE. The 'Royal Catholic College' at Maynooth, Co. Kildare, 15 miles north-west of Dublin, established in 1795 by the Irish Parliament for the education of RC clergy for Ireland. The present building was erected by A. W. *Pugin from funds supplied by Parliament in 1846. Until the disestablishment of the (Anglican) Church of Ireland in 1869, when the payment was commuted, the College was supported by an annual grant, originally of £8,000, but in 1845 raised by Sir Robert Peel from £9,500 to £26,000.

J. Healy, *Maynooth College*. Its Centenary History (1895).

MAZARIN, JULES (1602–61), French statesman and cardinal. A native of Piscina in the Abruzzi, he was educated by the *Jesuits and accompanied Jerome *Colonna to the university of Alcalá. On his return to Rome *c.* 1622, he graduated as a doctor of laws and became a captain in the army of the Colonna. His diplomatic skill soon attracted the attention of *Urban VIII, who in 1629 gave him the difficult task of ending the war of the Mantuan succession. From 1632 to 1634, and again from 1636 to 1640, he was vice-legate at *Avignon, where he warmly promoted French interests. In 1639 he became a naturalized Frenchman and in 1640 formally entered the service of Louis XIV. At the King's instigation he was created cardinal in 1641, and in 1642 he succeeded A. J. *Richelieu as prime minister. He continued Richelieu's policy and from now on practically ruled France till his death. At the Peace of *Westphalia (1648) he was successful in enlarging French territory, but could not prevent the economic disintegration of his country nor the civil wars of the Fronde (1648–53). He himself encountered violent attacks by venomous pasquinades, which led to his temporary banishment (1651–2). Towards the *Huguenots he pursued a policy of reconciliation, maintaining the edicts in their favour and employing their brilliant men in the service of France. In the *Jansenist controversy he furthered the acceptance of *Innocent X's constitution '*Cum Occasione' (1653). He maintained French influence in the Baltic, concluded a trade treaty with Oliver *Cromwell, carried on a successful war with Spain, and eventually secured the marriage of Louis XIV to the Infanta, Maria Theresa, and the victorious Treaty of the Pyrenees (1659). Though he never received Major Orders, he held the see of Metz and a great number of abbeys, using their incomes to amass a large fortune. With part of this last he founded the Collège Mazarin for students from the four provinces which were added to France under his government, and bequeathed to it his valuable library. See also foll. entry.

Lettres du cardinal Mazarin pendant son ministère, ed. [P.] A. Chéruel–G. d'Avenel (9 vols., Collection de documents inédits sur l'histoire de France publiés par les soins du Ministère de l'Instruction Publique, 1e sér., Histoire politique; 1872–1906). C. Moreau (ed.), *Choix de Mazarinades* (2 vols., Societé de l'Histoire de France, 1853); id., *Bibliographie des Mazarinades* (2 vols., ib., 1850–51). Modern studies of Mazarin by A. Hassall ('Foreign Statesmen', 1903); K. Federn (Munich, 1922), with bibl.; and

U. Silvagni (Turin, 1928); also by M. Boulenger ('Les Leçons du passé', 1929) and A. Bailly (Paris, 1935). H. Coville, *Étude sur Mazarin et ses démêlés avec le pape Innocent X, 1644-1648* (Bibliothèque de l'École des Hautes Études. Science historique et philologique, ccx; 1914). V. Tornetta, 'La politica del Mazzarino verso il Papato (1644-1646)' in *Archivio storico italiano*, xcix, Disp. iii-iv for 1941 (1942), pp. 86-116, and c, Disp. i-ii for 1942 (1943), pp. 95-134. [P.] A. Chéruel, *Histoire de France pendant la minorité de Louis XIV* (3 vols., 1879); id., *Histoire de France sous le ministère de Mazarin* (3 vols., 1882), with reff. to earlier works. E. Lavisse, *Histoire de France depuis les origines jusqu'à la révolution*, vii (pt. 1; 1905), pp. 1-117, 'Le Période mazarine'. H. M. Stephens in *E.B.* (ed. 11), xvii (1911), p. 940 f., s.v.; G. Goyau in *C.E.*, x (1911), p. 92 f., s.v.

MAZARIN BIBLE. The name commonly given to the rare and beautiful Bible printed by J. *Gutenberg at Mainz *c.* 1455. It is so called because the copy which first attracted the attention of bibliographers was discovered in the library of Card. J.*Mazarin. Prob. the first book to be printed in Europe, it was issued in two volumes, in double columns, with 42 lines to the column. Some forty copies are said to survive, but only two of these (at Munich and at Vienna) are known to be absolutely complete. See also *Constance Missal.*

Readings cited in the *Biblia Sacra iuxta Latinam Vulgatam Versionem ad Codicum Fidem iussu Pii PP. XI* (Romae Typis Polyglottis Vaticanis, 1926 ff.). H. *Quentin, O.S.B., *Mémoire sur l'établissement du texte de la Vulgate*, part i (Collectanea Biblica Latina, vi; 1922), pp. 75-7. Darlow-Moule, ii (1911), p. 905 f.

MAZZOLINI, SYLVESTER. See *Prierias, Sylvester.*

MECHITARISTS. A community of *Uniat *Armenian monks, founded at *Constantinople in 1701. They live under a modified form of the *Benedictine Rule. Founded by Mechitar of Sebaste (1676-1749), an Armenian priest who had submitted to Rome and been ordained in the RC Church in 1696, the community was driven from Constantinople in 1703 and took refuge in Modon in the Morea, then Venetian territory. Upon the conquest of the Morea by the Turks, the Venetian senate gave the community the island of San Lazzaro, *Venice, where it settled in 1717. Another section of the community later established itself at Vienna. The Mechitarists devote themselves to study, education, and missionary work, and have issued many important Armenian publications from their printing-houses in Venice and Vienna. They use the Armenian liturgy.

V. Langlois, *Notice sur le couvent arménien de l'île de St.-Lazare* (Venice, 1869; Eng. tr., Venice, 1874). V. Inglisian in *L.Th.K.*, vii (1935), cols. 34 f.

MECHLIN, Conversations of. See *Malines Conversations.*

MECHTHILD, St. (*c.* 1210-*c.* 1280), of Magdeburg, medieval German mystic and spiritual writer. Descended from a noble family in Saxony, in a desire for humiliations she left her home (*c.* 1230) and became a *Béguine at Magdeburg, where she led a life of prayer and

penance. At the order of her *Dominican confessor she wrote down her visions (1250-69) under the title 'Das fliessende Licht der Gottheit'. Later she found refuge in the *Cistercian convent at Helfta (1270), where she added a further volume to her book. Her work, written in a forceful and poetic style, deeply influenced German medieval mysticism. Among her visions was a revelation of the *Sacred Heart. Her work, no longer extant in the original Low German, has survived in Middle High German and Latin translations.

She has often been confounded with St. MECHTILD OF HELFTA, or HACKEBORN, her contemporary. Feast day, 19 Nov.

The best text of her revelations is the Middle High German tr. of Henry of Nördlingen and the *Friends of God at Basle in 1344-5; the MS., discovered in 1860, was ed. by G. Morel (Ratisbon, 1869); Eng. tr. by Lucy Menzies (London, 1953), with introd. and bibl. H. Stierling, *Studien zu Mechthild von Magdeburg* (Göttingen Diss., 1907). J. Ancelot-Hustache, *Mechtilde de Magdebourg, 1207-1282. Étude de psychologie religieuse* (thesis, Paris, 1926). H. Neumann, 'Problemata Mechtildiana' in *Zeitschrift für deutsches Altertum und deutsche Litteratur*, lxxxii (1948-50), pp. 143-72. W. Preger, *Geschichte der deutschen Mystik im Mittelalter*, i (1874), pp. 91-112; E. Michael, S.J., 'Die Angaben über die Chronologie zur Geschichte der Mystikerin Mechthild von Magdeburg sind vielfach sehr verworren' in *Z.K.T.*, xxv (1901), pp. 177-80. Alice Kemp-Welch, *Of Six Mediaeval Women* (1913), pp. 57-82.

MEDE, JOSEPH (1586-1638), also 'Mead'. Biblical scholar. He was a native of Berden in Essex and educated at Christ's College, Cambridge, of which he was elected a Fellow in 1613, and where he remained for the rest of his life. He was a scholar of encyclopaedic knowledge. Though regarding the Pope as the antichrist, he admitted that the RC Church taught the principal doctrines of Christianity, and defended the sacrificial aspect of the Eucharist. Mede's best-known work, *Clavis Apocalyptica* (1627), is an interpretation of the Book of Rev. on the principle that its visions form an organic and related whole in chronological order; the Day of Judgement is a period of a thousand years of peace for the Church on earth. His millenarian doctrines were partly influenced by the astrological studies of his youth. Among his other writings are treatises *Of the Name Altar* (1637) and on *The Apostasy of the Latter Times* (1641).

Collected Works, 2 vols., London, 1648; enlarged ed. [by J. Worthington], 2 vols., ib., 1663-4; further extension, 2 vols., ib., 1672. Brief Life appended to his posthumously publd. *Diatribae*. Discourses on Divers Texts of Scripture (4 parts, 1643-52); Life, pt. iv. pp. 675 ff. [no pagination]. A. Gordon in *D.N.B.*, xxxvii (1894), pp. 178-80, s.v. 'Mead'.

MEDINA, BARTOLOMEO (1527-80), Spanish *Dominican theologian. He taught theology first at the college of Alcalá, and from 1576 to his death as principal professor at the university of Salamanca, his main interest being the commentation of St. *Thomas Aquinas. He has been given the title of 'Father of *Probabilism', though whether he was the real author of this doctrine is still a matter of controversy. His opinions on the subject are laid down in an essay inserted in his Commentary on the 'Prima Secundae' of St.

Thomas, where he defends the view that of two opinions both of which are probable, though in an unequal degree, the less probable may be followed. This thesis was immediately taken up and defended by other Dominicans, esp. D. *Bañez, though in the subsequent development of the doctrine, in which the notion of the 'probable' was more and more enlarged, the *Jesuits had the main share in upholding it, whilst Dominican moralists came to reject it. See also *Salmanticenses*.

His Comm. on *Summa Theol.* II (2) was issued at Salamanca, 1577; on III, qq. 1–9, ib., 1578; and *Breve Instruction de comme se ha de administrar el sacramento de la penitencia* (ib., 1580). I. G. Menéndez Reigada, 'El pseudo-probabilismo de Fray Bartolomé de Medina' in *La Ciencia Tomista*, xx (1928), pp. 35–57; M. M. Gorce, 'Le Sens du mot "Probable" et les origines du probabilisme' in *Rev. S.R.*, x (1930), pp. 460–4. M. M. Gorce in *D.T.C.*, x (pt. i; 1928), cols. 481–5, s.v., with bibl.

MEDITATION. As the term is used by exponents of Christian spirituality, mental prayer in its discursive form. It is the type of mental prayer appropriate to beginners and as such accounted its lowest stage; and it is commonly contrasted with *Contemplation (q.v.). Its method is the devout reflection on a chosen (often Biblical) theme, with a view to deepening spiritual insight and stimulating the will and affections. Among the many methods of meditation advocated by modern schools of spirituality, that expounded by St. *Ignatius Loyola in the *Spiritual Exercises* (originally intended for use by the novices of his Society) is prob. that most widely used.

MEGILLOTH (Heb. מְגִלּוֹת, 'rolls'). The name given to five Books in the OT, all of them in the third and latest section of the OT *canon known as the '*Hagiographa', which were read by the Jews on certain feast days. They were the Song of *Solomon (read at the *Passover), *Ruth (at the Feast of *Weeks), the *Lamentations of Jeremiah (at the anniversary of the Chaldean destruction of *Jerusalem), *Ecclesiastes (at the Feast of *Tabernacles), and *Esther (at the Feast of *Purim).

MEINRAD, St. (d. 861), Patron of *Einsiedeln (q.v.). Born in the E. of *France, he became a monk at *Reichenau and for several years was active in teaching and pastoral work. In middle life he felt called to greater austerity, left his monastery and eventually settled at the spot in the Swiss forests where Einsiedeln ('hermitage') now stands, and here lived the life of a hermit for 25 years. A statue of the Virgin, given to him by a Benedictine abbess and placed in his chapel, is still venerated at Einsiedeln. He was put to death by two ruffians to whom he had given hospitality. His body was taken back to Reichenau and he became venerated as a martyr. Feast day, 21 Jan. His symbol is two ravens.

The earliest life was orig. ed. by S. Brandt (Basle, 1496); this was also repr. from ed. of C. Hartmann (1612), with introd., in *AA.SS.*, Jan. II (1643), pp. 381–5; also ed., O. Holder-Egger, in *M.G.H.*, Scriptores, xv (pt. 1; 1887),

pp. 444–8, and in O. Ringholz, O.S.B., *Geschichte des fürstlichen Benediktinerstiftes U.L.F. Einsiedeln*, i (Einsiedeln, etc., 1904), pp. 648–51; life written in 1378 by Gergius de Gengenbach, pr. ib., pp. 654–7. The Einsiedeln 'Blockbuch' of 1450, with legends of St. Meinrad, ed. G. Morell (ib., 1861). K. Brandes, *Der heilige Meinrad und Wallfahrt von Einsiedeln* (ib., 1861; Fr. tr., 1861). O. Ringholz, O.S.B., *Meinrads-Büchlein*. Das Leben und Verehrung des Märtyrs von Einsiedeln (Einsiedeln, &c., 1905), pp. 1–80. See also works cited under *Einsiedeln*.

MEKITARISTS. See *Mechitarists*.

MELANCHTHON, PHILIPP (1497–1560), Protestant Reformer. His real name was 'Schwarzerd' and his mother was a niece of J. *Reuchlin. He studied at Heidelberg (from 1509) and *Tübingen (from 1512), and in 1518 became professor of Greek at *Wittenberg. Here he exercised a great influence, lecturing in the spirit of the Renaissance. He soon fell under the spell of M. *Luther, whose teachings he helped to cast into a more rational and systematic form. In 1519 he took part in the *Leipzig Disputation and a controversy with *Carlstadt followed. In 1521 he found himself the leader of the Reformation Movement during Luther's confinement in the Wartburg. The original edition of his *Loci Communes* (1521) was the first ordered presentation of Reformation doctrine. In the following years his energies were largely taken up with translating and commenting on the Bible. He took part in the Diet of *Speyer (1529) and the Colloquy of *Marburg (1529), at the latter strongly opposing the Eucharistic doctrine of H. *Zwingli. The leading figure at the Diet of *Augsburg (1530), he was mainly responsible for the Augsburg Confession, and great hopes were placed on his conciliatory spirit as a basis of restoring peace and unity. In 1537 he signed the *Schmalkaldic Articles with the reservation that he would accept the Papacy in a modified form. In his later years he was largely concerned in the organization of the Church of Saxony on a semi-episcopal basis and in the *Adiaphoristic, the *Cryptocalvinistic, and other controversies.

Melanchthon's attitude to Christianity was far more humanistic than that of most of the Reformers. He cared for learning as such, and left a deep mark on upper schools and universities, for which he wrote textbooks that lasted for several generations. His own doctrines went through many stages, which are reflected in the successive editions of his *Loci Communes*. His commentaries on Scripture broke new ground. They discarded the medieval 'four senses', treated the NT like the classics, and emphasized the need of history and archaeology for their understanding. He was always conciliatory, and at times even weak, for he advised both *Henry VIII and *Philip of Hesse to take two wives.

Collected Works and Letters ed. K. G. Bretschneider–E. Bindseil (Corpus Reformatorum, i–xxviii; Brunswick, 1834–60), works omitted from this collection publd. as *Supplementa Melanchthonia* (Leipzig, 1910 ff.). Separate modern edd. of *Loci Communes* by G. L. Plitt (Erlangen, 1864; rev. T. Kolder, ib., 1890; ed. 4, ib., 1925; Eng. tr. by C. L. Hill (Boston, Mass., 1944); of *Der Unterricht der Visitatoren* by

H. *Lietzmann (1912); ot Correspondence by O. Clemen (vol. i, all publd. 1926). Lives by R. Schaefer (Gütersloh, 1894) and G. Ellinger (Berlin, 1902). E. *Troeltsch, *Vernunft und Offenbarung bei Johann Gerhard und Melanchthon* (Göttingen Diss., 1891). H. Maier, *An der Grenze der Philosophie* (1909), pp. 1–139, 'Melanchthon als Philosoph'. O. Clemen, *Studien zu Melanchthons Reden und Gedichten* (1913). C. Hartfelder, *Melanchthon als praeceptor Germaniae* (1889). F. Hildebrandt, *Melanchthon, Alien or Ally?* (1946). O. Kirn in *P.R.E.* (ed. 3), xii (1903), pp. 513–48; J. Paquier in *D.T.C.*, x (pt. 1; 1928), cols. 502–13; G. Ellinger in *R.G.G.* (ed. 2), iii (1929), cols. 2074–82.

MELANIA, St. (*c.* 345–410), 'the Elder'. A Roman lady of aristocratic descent, she adopted the ascetic life under St. *Jerome's influence, left Rome in 372 for Egypt and Palestine, and founded a monastery on the Mount of *Olives. In 397 she returned to Italy with *Rufinus of Aquileia. In 408 she fled before the Goths by way of Sicily and Africa to *Jerusalem, where she died.

The chief sources are the 'Life' of St. Melania the Younger (see below), and scattered reff. in *Palladius's *Lausiac History* and in the *Epp.* of *Jerome and *Paulinus of Nola. W. H. Fremantle in *D.C.B.*, iii (1882), p. 888 f. See also bibl. to foll. entry.

MELANIA, St. (*c.* 383–438), 'the Younger', granddaughter of preceding. She fled with her husband Pinian to Africa, where they founded two monasteries at Tagaste. Later they joined St. *Jerome and entered monasteries at *Bethlehem. After Pinian's death (431), Melania founded another monastery on the Mount of *Olives. She also visited *Constantinople, but returned to *Jerusalem to die. Feast day, 31 Dec.

Lat. life ed. [prob. H. *Delehaye, S.J.] in *Anal. Boll.*, viii (1889), pp. 16–63 (incomplete); Gk. life ed. H. D[elehaye, S.J.], ib., xxii (1903), pp. 5–50. Complete Lat. text, with Gk. text, ed. Card. M. Rampolla del Tindaro (Rome, fol., 1905). It is disputed whether the Gk. or Lat. text is the original; cf. A. d'Alès, 'Les Deux Vies de sainte Mélanie la Jeune' in *Anal. Boll.*, xxv (1906), pp. 401–50. Life by G. Goyau ('Les Saints', 1908). W. H. Fremantle in *D.C.B.*, iii (1882), p. 889, s.v.; H. *Leclercq, O.S.B., in *D.A.C.L.*, xi (pt. 1; 1933), cols. 209–30, s.v. 'Mélanie la Jeune (Sainte)'; J. P. Kirsch in *L.Th.K.*, vii (1935), col. 60, s.v.

MELCHIADES, St. See *Miltiades, St.*

MELCHIORITES. See *Hoffmann, Melchior.*

MELCHISEDECH. An alternative spelling of *Melchizedek (q.v.).

MELCHITES. This term, derived from the Gk. form of the Syriac adjective *mălkāyā*, 'imperial', is used of those Christians of Syria and Egypt who, refusing *Monophysitism and accepting the Definition of Faith of the Council of *Chalcedon (451), remained in communion with the Imperial see of Constantinople as 'Emperor's men'. The Greek *Uniats of Syria and Egypt are also commonly termed Melchites.

MELCHIZEDEK. Acc. to Gen. 14. 18, the 'King of Salem' and 'Priest of the Most High God' who offered *Abraham bread and wine

as he was returning from his defeat of the four kings. The only other mention of him in the OT occurs in Ps. 110. 4, where the Messiah is styled 'a priest for ever after the order of Melchizedek'. Both these passages were used by the author of the Ep. to the Hebrews (6. 20; 7. 1 ff.) to prove the superiority of the priesthood of Christ, prefigured by Melchizedek, over that of Aaron and the Levites. From the time of *Clement of Alexandria (*c.* 200) onwards his offering of bread and wine has been regarded as a type of the Eucharist, esp. in the W., and *Cyprian argued from it the necessity of using wine, and not merely water, for the celebration of the Christian sacrifice. In the same connexion the name of Melchizedek has been introduced into the Roman *Canon of the Mass, where his offering is mentioned together with those of Abel and Abraham as an acceptable sacrifice typifying that of Christ on the Cross. Another liturgical mention occurs in the first antiphon of the *Vespers of *Corpus Christi, where Christ is called in the words of Ps. 110 'Sacerdos in aeternum ... secundum ordinem Melchisedech'. In the first Christian centuries several heretical interpretations of his person were condemned by the Fathers, e.g. the belief that he was a power of God superior to Christ (by St. *Epiphanius), that he was the Holy Ghost (by St. *Ambrose), and that he was an incarnation of the Logos (by *Marcus Eremita).

See Commentaries *ad loca.* G. Bardy, 'Melchisédech dans la tradition patristique' in *R. Bibl.*, xxxv (1926), pp. 496–509, and xxxvi (1927), pp. 25–45; G. Wuttke, *Melchisedek der Priesterkönig von Salem.* Eine Studie zur Geschichte der Exegese (Beihefte zum Z.N.T.W., No. 5, 1927); A. Vaccari, S.J., 'Melchisedek, Rex Salem, proferens panem et vinum' in *Verbum Domini*, xviii (1938), pp. 208–14, 235–43. On the 'Melchisedekians', described by *Epiphanius (*Haer.*, lv), see also G. Bardy in *D.T.C.*, x (pt. 1; 1928), cols. 513–16, s.v. 'Melchisédéciens'.

MELITIAN SCHISMS. Two 4th cent. schisms go under this name:

(1) That due to Melitius (often, but wrongly, spelled 'Meletius'), Bp. of Lycopolis in Egypt. It arose out of Melitius's objections to the terms laid down by *Peter, Bp. of Alexandria, during a lull in the Diocletian persecution *c.* 306, for the return of the lapsed to the Church. Thinking the conditions too lax, Melitius created disturbances, and ordained some of his supporters, whereupon he was excommunicated by Peter. After a further period of persecution, during which Peter was martyred and he himself banished to the mines, he returned to Egypt and founded a schismatic church with clergy of his own ordination.

The schism continued to flourish for several decades. At the *Council of Nicaea (325), where the matter was raised, it was determined that Melitian clergy should be allowed to continue their functions, but to be subordinate to *Alexander (who had meanwhile succeeded Peter). Their bishops, if legally elected, might take the places of the Catholic bishops when the latter died. Melitius himself was to retain the title of bishop, but to have no see. On the accession of St. *Athanasius (328), however, this arrangement broke down, as the Melitians, encouraged by *Eusebius of Nicomedia, again went into schism. Melitius was succeeded by John Arkaph of Memphis. The sect continued, and evidence for the life of Melitian monastic communities has recently come to light in a number of British Museum papyri. It seems to have survived as a small body down to the 8th cent.

(2) The 4th cent. schism at Antioch which followed the leadership of Melitius. See the next entry.

The chief authorities for the Egyptian Schism are the Melitian documents in the *Theodosian Codex (Ver., lx [58]); the recently recovered papyri, ed., with introd., in H. I. Bell, *Jews and Christians in Egypt* (1924), pp. 38–99; scattered reff. in *Athanasius; and *Epiphanius, *Haer.*, lxviii. E. *Schwartz, 'Zur Geschichte des Athanasius' in *Nach.* (Gött.), 1905, pp. 164–87; F. H. Kettler, 'Der meletanische Streit in Agypten' in *Z.N.T.W.*, xxxv (1936), pp. 155–93. F. J. Foakes–Jackson in *H.E.R.E.*, viii (1915), p. 538, s.v. 'Meletianism'; É. Amann in *D.T.C.*, x (pt. 1; 1928), cols. 531–6; C. Vagaggini, O.S.B., in *E.C.*, viii (1952), col. 640 f., s.v. 'Melezio (Melizio) di Licipoli'.

MELITIUS, St. (d. 381), Bp. of *Antioch from 360. He was translated from the see of Sebaste to Antioch in 360, and both *Arians and *Nicenes looked for his support. An orthodox inaugural sermon on Prov. 8. 22 led to his immediate exile by the Emp. Constantius; but when he returned in 362 under *Julian, he failed to secure the support of *Athanasius for his claim to the see. He was twice banished under Valens, from 365 to 366 and from 371 to 378, St. *Basil being unswerving in support for his claims, but Alexandria wavering and Rome hostile. He was finally restored in 378 and presided at the Council of *Constantinople of 381, during which he died. The schism at Antioch called by his name (not to be confused with the *Melitian Schism in Egypt half a century earlier) arose from the presence of two rival orthodox parties at Antioch which failed to co-operate. The supporters of *Eustathius (Bp. of Antioch *c.* 324–30) suspected the theology of Melitius and created the schism by securing the consecration of one Paulinus in 362. Though it lasted until after the death of Melitius, canonical right was on the side of Melitius. Feast day, 12 Feb.

F. Cavallera, *Le Schisme d'Antioche* (1905), passim. F. *Loofs in *P.R.E.* (ed. 3), xii (1903), pp. 552–8, s.v., and É. Amann in *D.T.C.*, x (1930), cols. 520–31, s.v., both with bibls. G. Bardy, 'Le Concile d'Antioche (379)' in *R. Bén.*, xlv (1933), pp. 196–213.

MELITO, St. (d. *c.* 190), Bp. of Sardis. He was a prolific writer greatly respected by his contemporaries, but very little of his work has survived. Recently, however, a treatise on 'The Lord's Passion' has been recovered in a *Chester Beatty–Michigan papyrus. In a highly rhetorical style full of hymnodic passages, it is an early example of devotional Christian literature in a time chiefly known by its apologetics. Melito, whom the author of the '*Little Labyrinth' praised as a representative of orthodox Christology, here shows himself deeply imbued with the sense of the Divinity of Christ, whom he calls 'by nature both God

and man' (φύσει θεὸς ὢν καὶ ἄνθρωπος), and freely uses the theological principle of the *communicatio idiomatum* as a means to heighten the effect, as when he exclaims, 'He who hung the earth is hanged, he who fixed the heavens is fixed'. Melito's lost writings include an 'apology' addressed to *Marcus Aurelius, and treatises on a large variety of subjects, e.g. on the *Quartodeciman practice (which he defended), the Incarnation, Baptism, and Sunday. Feast day, 1 Apr.

The papyrus containing the 'Homily on the Passion' (which is shared between Mr. A. Chester Beatty and the University of Michigan) was ed. by C. Bonner (*Studies and Documents*, ed. K. *Lake and Silva Lake, xii, 1940). Coll. of fragments in J. C. T. Otto (ed.), *Corpus Apologetarum*, ix (Jena 1872), pp. 374–478, 497–512; also in M. J. *Routh, *Reliquiae Sacrae*, i (ed. 2, 1846), pp. 113–53. E. J. Wellesz, 'Melito's Homily on the Passion. An Investigation into the Sources of Byzantine Hymnography' in *J.T.S.*, xliv (1943), pp. 41–52. A. Wifstrand, 'The Homily of Melito on the Passion' in *Vigiliae Christianae*, ii (1948), pp. 201–23. Older lit. in Bardenhewer, i, 455–65. J. Quasten, *Patrology*, i (1950), pp. 242–8, with further bibl. É. Amann in *D.T.C.*, x (pt. 1; 1928), cols. 540–7. E. Peterson in *E.C.*, viii (1952), col. 645 f. See also F. L. Cross, *The Early Christian Fathers* (1960), pp. 103–9.

MELLITUS, St. (d. 624), Abp. of *Canterbury. Sent to England by St. *Gregory I in 601, he was consecrated by St. *Augustine missionary bishop for the East Saxons in 604, with London (where *Ethelbert built the church of St. Paul for him) as his headquarters. After some years, evangelization was arrested by the accessions of two kings of the East Saxons and of Kent who were hostile to Christianity, and Mellitus was forced to take refuge for a time in Gaul. In 619, soon after his return to England, he succeeded Laurentius as the third Abp. of Canterbury (619). Feast day, 24 Apr.

The main source is *Bede, *H.E.*, i, 29 f., and ii, 3–7; cf. ed. C. Plummer, ii (Oxford, 1896), pp. 78–90 passim. W. *Stubbs in *D.C.B.*, iii (1882), p. 90 f.

MELVILLE, ANDREW (1545–1622), Scottish *Presbyterian Reformer and theologian. He was born at Baldovie, nr. Montrose, and educated at St. Andrews, where he was the only member of the university who knew Greek. In 1564 he went to Paris to study oriental languages, and thence to Poitiers (1566) where he read civil law. The political troubles in France led him to retire to Geneva in 1569, where T. *Beza procured him the professorship of humanity at the Academy. On his return to Scotland in 1574 he became principal of Glasgow university. His educational reforms, which included a new plan of studies and the establishment of chairs in languages, science, philosophy, and theology, met with great success. He also took an active part in abolishing what was left of Episcopalianism. In 1575 he was entrusted with the drawing-up of the 'Second Book of *Discipline' (q.v.), which discarded the last traces of prelacy and was largely inspired by the Genevan model. In 1578 he was appointed commissioner for the visitation of St. Andrews, and in 1580 he became principal of St. Mary's College, St. Andrews. When Moderator of the General Assembly of 1582, he prosecuted R. Montgomery, one of the '*tulchan' bishops, who had accepted the see of

Glasgow from the Duke of Lennox on condition that the bulk of the revenues reverted to the Duke. Thereby brought into opposition to *James VI [I], he was charged at Edinburgh in 1584 with treason, and fled to England to escape imprisonment and possible death. In 1585 he returned to Scotland, was again Moderator of the General Assembly in 1587, and became rector of St. Andrews in 1590. His attacks on the King's interference in religious matters led to the loss of his rectorship in 1597, but he was made Dean of the Theological Faculty at St. Andrews in 1599. After the accession of James to the English throne he again incurred the royal displeasure by insisting on the right of a free Assembly and was summoned to London in 1606. A sarcastic Latin poem on Anglican worship caused him to be charged before the Privy Council and confined to the Tower in 1607, whence he was released in 1611 on being offered the chair of Biblical theology at Sedan university. Here he spent the remaining years of his life. Though his bitter invective frequently marred the success of his work, his reform of the Scottish universities and of Scottish Presbyterianism are lasting achievements. Among his writings are Latin poems on Biblical subjects, the finest of which is the *Carmen Mosis* (1573); a treatise on Free-Will (1597); and a commentary on Romans (publd. 1850).

The standard modern work is the life by T. McCrie (2 vols. bound in 1; Edinburgh, 1819; ed. 2, 1823). Popular life by W. Morrison ('Famous Scots Series' [1899]). Study by S. Mechie in R. S. Wright (ed.), *Fathers of the Kirk* (1960), pp. 37–48. A. Gordon in *D.N.B.*, xxxvii (1894), pp. 230–7, with further reff.

MEMLING or MEMLINC, HANS (*c.* 1430–1494), Flemish painter. A Fleming by birth, he is said to have been a pupil of Roger van der Weyden, but little that is definite is known of his life. He apparently settled in Bruges, and became an inmate of St. John's Hospital, where much of his work may be seen. His paintings, notable for their colour and harmony, include the Shrine of St. *Ursula and several Madonnas and altar-pieces.

Reproductions of his pictures, with introd. by K. Voll (Klassiker der Kunst in Gesamtausgaben, xiv; 1909). Details of his 'Passionsaltar' at Lübeck ed. C. G. Heise (Hamburg, 1950). J. Du Jardin, *Hans Memling*. Son temps, sa vie et sa culture (Antwerp, 1897); F. Bock, *Memling-Studien* (Düsseldorf, 1900); L. von Baldass, *Hans Memling* (Vienna [1942]). M. J. Friedländer, *Die altniederländische Malerei*, vi (1928), pp. 9–70, with plates i–lxvi; id., 'Noch etwas über das Verhältnis Roger van der Weydens zu Memling' in *Oud-Holland*, lxi (1946), pp. 11–19. Id., *Memling* (Palet Series, xliv; Amsterdam [1949]). Other studies include works by W. H. J. Weale (printed for the Arundel Society, 1865; also in the series 'The Great Masters in Painting and Sculpture', 1901, and, with H. C. Weale, in the series 'Masterpieces in Colour' [1909]), [J.] A. [X.] Michiels (Verviers [1883]), M. Vioux (Paris [1924]), A. Goffin (in Fr., Brussels, 1925; in Dutch, ib., 1926), and G. Huisman (Paris, 1934). H. Vollmer in U. Thieme–F. Becker (founders), *Allgemeines Lexikon der bildenden Künstler von der Antike bis zur Gegenwart*, xxiv (ed. H. Vollmer; 1930), pp. 374–7, s.v., with detailed bibl.

MEMORARE (Lat., 'Remember'). A widely used intercessory prayer addressed to the BVM. It is commonly ascribed to St. *Bernard of Clairvaux, prob. owing to a confusion with Claude Bernard ('The Poor Priest'; 1588–

1641), who popularized the prayer; but its real author is unknown. The earliest known texts date from the late 15th cent. where they are embodied in a much longer prayer to the BVM. In 1846 Pope *Pius IX attached considerable indulgences to its recitation, and it is included in the 1849 ed. of the *Raccolta. The most popular Eng. version begins, 'Remember, O most loving Virgin Mary'.

N. Paulus, 'Das Alter des Gebetes *Memorare*' in *Z.K.T.*, xxvi (1902), pp. 604–6. H. Thurston, S.J., 'The *Memorare*' in *The Month*, cxxxii (1918), pp. 269–78, repr. in his *Familiar Prayers*, ed. P. Grosjean, S.J. (1953), No. ix, pp. 152–63, with reff.

MEMORIALE RITUUM. A Latin liturgical book, also known as the **Rituale parvum**, containing the forms used in the blessing of candles (for *Candlemas), ashes (for *Ash Wednesday), and palms (for *Palm Sunday), as well as the service for the last three days in *Holy Week in the shortened form usual in smaller RC parish churches. The book was first issued in 1725 for use at Rome by *Benedict XIII, and nearly a hundred years later (1821) approved by *Pius VII for the whole Church of the Roman rite.

P. Siffrin in *E.C.*, viii (1952), cols. 666 f., s.v.

MEMPHITIC. See *Bohairic*.

MEMRA (Aram. מֵימְרָא, 'word'). The word was used in a specifically theological sense in Jewish literature esp. for the Divine creative Word (see *Logos*), manifesting God's power in the material world and in the human mind, and acting as His agent and as the mediator between God and men. In the *Targums 'Memra' is sometimes used where the OT has '*Jehovah', to avoid anthropomorphism. The Memra concept possibly underlies the 'Logos' or 'Word' of Jn. 1. 1–14.

MENAION Gk. μηναῖον, from μήν, 'month'). In the E. Church, the name given to each of the twelve liturgical books (one for each month) which contain the variable parts of the Divine *Office for the immovable feasts. They correspond with the 'proprium sanctorum' in the W. The series begins with the Greek ecclesiastical year, in September. An appendix contains the rite for the saints which have no *proper office, corresponding to the 'commune sanctorum' of the Latin *Breviary. See also *Menologion*.

MENAS, St. (*c.* 3rd–4th cent.), Egyptian martyr. He was probably born and martyred in Egypt, but his story was apparently fused with that of a soldier executed in Phrygia under the Emp. *Diocletian, possibly another Menas, possibly St. Gordian. His reputed birthplace, to the south-west of Lake Mareotis, became an important pilgrimage centre, associated with miraculous cures by water. The church and town were excavated in 1905–8, and *ampullae bearing a figure of Menas between camels are common. He was held to be esp. the patron of merchants, and his cult spread to Constantinople, Rome, Gaul, and Germany. Feast day, 11 Nov.

'Acta S. Menae' (Gk. text; with Lat. tr.) in *Anal. Boll.*, iii (1884), pp. 258–70. The primary sources are the Reports of C. M. Kaufmann (3 vols., Cairo, 1906–8), who directed the Frankfurt expedition to the site. C. M. Kaufmann, *Die Menasstadt und das Nationalheiligtum der altchristlichen Ägypter in der westalexandrinischen Wüste* (1910); R. Miedema, *De heilige Menas* (Rotterdam, 1913). Margaret A. Murray, 'St. Menas of Alexandria' in *Proceedings of the Society of Biblical Archaeology*, xxix (1907), pp. 25–30, 51–60, and 112–22 (with plates). H. *Delehaye, S.J., 'L'Invention des reliques de St. Ménas à Constantinople' in *Anal. Boll.*, xxix (1910), pp. 117–50. H. *Leclercq, O.S.B., in *D.A.C.L.*, xi (pt. 1; 1933), cols. 324–97, s.v., with bibl.

MENAS, St. (d. 552), also Mennas, Patr. of Constantinople from 536. He was consecrated by the Pope Agapetus (535–6) to succeed the *Monophysite, Anthimus. In 543 he presided over an anti-Origenist Council. At the beginning of the *Three Chapters' controversy (543) he subscribed with some hesitation to the Imperial Edict and forced his suffragans to do the same. But on their complaining to the vacillating Pope, *Vigilius (537–55), Menas was excommunicated, first in 547, and again in 551. In neither instance did the sentence last for long and he died in full communion with the Papacy. His patriarchate marks a high-water mark of Papal influence at Constantinople. Feast day, 25 Aug.

AA.SS., Aug. V (1741), p. 164 f. The chief documents of Menas' patriarchate are calendared in V. Grumel, A.A., *Régestes des actes du patriarcat de Constantinople*, I (i) (Socii Assumptionistae Chalcedonenses, 1932), pp. 94–8. W. M. Sinclair in *D.C.B.*, iii (1882), pp. 902 f.

MENDICANT FRIARS. Members of those orders which were forbidden to own property in common. Unlike the monks, they work or beg for their living and are not bound to one convent by a vow of 'stability'. In the Middle Ages their activities were carried on chiefly in towns, and their privileges, esp. exemption from episcopal jurisdiction and extensive faculties for preaching and hearing confessions, roused much hostility among the bishops and the secular clergy as well as in the universities. Opposition was particularly strong at *Paris, where it was led by William of St. Amour and where St. *Thomas Aquinas and St. *Bonaventure wrote in their defence. In 1256, the dispute was settled in their favour by Alexander IV.

Originally restricted to the *Franciscans and *Dominicans, the name and privileges of Mendicant Friars were given to the *Carmelites by *Innocent IV in 1245, to the Hermits of St. *Augustine by Alexander IV in 1256, and to the *Servites by *Martin V in 1424, several other orders following later. Acc. to the *Codex (can. 621), the friars are allowed, with the permission of their superiors, to beg for alms in the dioceses where their houses are situated; in other dioceses they have to ask the permission of the bishop.

F. Vernet, *Les Ordres mendiants* (Bibliothèque Catholique des Sciences Religieuses, 1933). L. Gillet, *Histoire artistique des ordres mendiants*. Étude sur l'art religieux en Europe du XIII⁰ au XVI⁰ siècle (1912). See further bibl. under separate Mendicant Orders.

MENNONITES, the followers of Menno Simons (1496–1561), from whom they take their name. At one time parish priest in Dutch Friesland, he renounced his connexions with the RC Church in 1536 and joined the *Anabaptists, then suffering severe persecution and obloquy after the attempted Kingdom of the Saints at Münster. For twenty-five years he shepherded and reorganized the stricken companies in Holland and the neighbouring territories. His views, which were similar to those of the Swiss Brethren, included stress on believers' baptism, a connexional type of Church organization with an emphasis on the responsibilities and rights of the local congregation, a rejection of Christian participation in the magistracy, and non-resistance. John *Smyth and other English Separatist exiles in Holland were in friendly touch with Mennonites. In the 17th and 18th cents. the Mennonites became a numerous and influential community in Holland; certain branches adopted *Socinian views. The number of Mennonites to-day is said to be over 500,000. Of these there are about 70,000 in Holland, 12,500 in Germany, and uncertain numbers in European and Asiatic Russia. There are 50,000 in Canada and 250,000 in the United States (where there has been much internal division).

Common ground of the different Mennonite communities is the rejection of Church organization, *Infant Baptism, and the *Real Presence in the Eucharist. Every congregation is independent and the Lord's Supper is administered by elders chosen by the community; and both men and women may preach. Most of them refuse military service and the taking of the oath and any public office. On the other hand, they recognize no common doctrine, so that some of them are practically Unitarians in their views while others hold the doctrine of the Trinity.

Anna Brons, *Ursprung, Entwicklung und Schicksale der Altevangelischen Taufgesinnten oder Mennoniten in kurzen Zügen übersichtlich dargestellt* (Norden, 1884). C. H. A. van der Smissen (ed.), *Kurzgefasste Geschichte und Glaubenslehre der Altevangelischen Taufgesinnten oder Mennoniten* (Summerfield, Ill., 1895). C. H. Wedel, *Abriss der Geschichte der Mennoniten* (4 vols., Newton, Kansas, 1900–4). J. C. Wenger, *Glimpses of Mennonite History* (Scottdale, Pa., 1940). R. Friedmann, *Mennonite Piety through the Centuries*. Its Genius and its Literature (Studies in Anabaptist and Mennonite History, vii; Goshen, Indiana, 1949). Life of Menno Simons in English by J. Horsch (Scottdale, Pa., 1916). S. Cramer in *P.R.E.*, xii (1903), pp. 594–616, s.v. 'Mennoniten'; cf. id., ib., pp. 586–94, s.v. 'Menno Simons'. W. J. Kühler in *H.E.R.E.*, viii (1915), pp. 551–4, s.v., with bibl.

MENOLOGION (Gk. μηνολόγιον, from μήν, 'month'). In the E. Church a liturgical book containing the lives of the saints, arranged by months throughout the ecclesiastical year (which begins with September). The word is used in a variety of senses, being applied to several distinct books current in the E. Church corresponding to the description just given, e.g. counterparts of the W. '*Proper of the Saints' (the 'Menaion', q.v.), '*Martyrology, and '*Acta Sanctorum'. One of the most celebrated menologia is that compiled by *Simeon Metaphrastes. The term has also been applied (in the W.) to private non-liturgical collections of the lives of saintly persons.

[H.*Delehaye, S.J.,] 'Le Synaxaire de Sirmond' in *Anal. Boll.*, xiv (1895), pp. 149–434; [id.] 'Les Ménologes grecs', ib., xvi (1897), pp. 311–29; [id.] 'Le Ménologe de Métaphraste', ib., xvii (1898), pp. 448–52. Id., *AA.SS.*, Propylaeum ad Nov. (1902), pp. iv–lxxvi. H. Thurston, S.J., in *C.E.*, x (1911), p. 191 f., s.v. 'Menologium'; H. *Leclercq, O.S.B., in *D.A.C.L.*, xi (pt. 1; 1933), cols. 419–30, s.v.; H. Engberding, O.S.B., in *L.Th.K.*, vii (1935), col. 87 f., s.v. See also bibl. to *Simeon Metaphrastes*.

MENSA (Lat., 'table'). In early Christian times the word was applied esp. to the large tablets of stone set over or near a grave, and used apparently for receiving food for meals in memory of the deceased. A large number of such *mensae* have been recovered from N. Africa, and in recent times also from N. Germany (Bonn, Xanten). In Africa their use was widespread among the pagans, and the superstitious and unbecoming nature of the associated rites led St. *Augustine and other Christian theologians to denounce them.

The word is also in common use among liturgists for the flat stone which forms the top of an altar. Acc. to modern Roman requirements, it must consist of a single, unbroken piece of non-crumbling stone (*CIC*, 1198, 1).

H. *Leclercq, O.S.B., in *D.A.C.L.*, xi (pt. 1; 1933), cols. 440–53, s.v. On the use of the word in the second sense, see Braun, *C.A.*, i (1924), pp. 245–316, with pll. 41–5.

MENTAL PRAYER. See *Meditation*.

MENTAL RESERVATION. The conflict which may arise between the duty of telling the truth and that of keeping a secret has caused the development of the doctrine of mental reservation. RC moral theology distinguishes between *restrictio pure mentalis*, ('strict mental reservation') and *restrictio late mentalis* ('wide mental reservation'). In the former a qualification is added mentally which completely alters the statement pronounced, so that the hearer is necessarily deceived; and in this form it was condemned by *Innocent XI in 1679. In the 'wide mental reservation', on the other hand, words are used which, acc. to the circumstances, are susceptible of more than one interpretation, without the speaker giving an indication as to the sense in which he uses them. The wide mental reservation may be used when the person who puts a question has no right to the truth, or else only where a professional secret is involved, as, e.g., in the case of a priest denying knowledge of a fact with the mental reservation 'apart from confession'. In instances such as these the deception of the hearer is allowable for a good reason and involves no sin on the part

of the speaker. In an extreme form, it was developed by the *Jesuit theologian J. Caramuel, in his *Haplotes de restrictionibus mentalibus* (Leyden, 1672).

MERBECKE or MARBECK, JOHN (d. *c.* 1585), English divine and musician. Appointed organist at St. George's Chapel, *Windsor, in 1541, he was condemned to the stake for heresy in 1544 because he had written the first *concordance in English of the Bible. He was pardoned, however, through the influence of Bp. Stephen *Gardiner, and the concordance was published in 1550 with a dedication to *Edward VI. In 1550 he produced his *Book of Common Prayer Noted*, in which the plainchant is adapted to Edward VI's first (1549) liturgy. He continued his musical and theological studies for some years and apparently died about 1585. His son, Roger Merbecke (1536–1605), provost of Oriel College, Oxford, was chief physician to Queen *Elizabeth I.

E. H. Fellowes, *The Office of the Holy Communion as set by John Merbecke* (1949). Id. in *Grove's Dictionary of Music and Musicians* (ed. 5 by E. Blom), v (1954), pp. 561–3, s.v. 'Marbeck'.

MERCATI, GIOVANNI (1866–1957), Prefect of the *Vatican Library. Born in 1866 at Villa Gàida in the province of Reggio Emilia, he was ordained priest in 1889, and from 1893 until 1919 was on the staff of the 'Bibliotheca *Ambrosiana' at *Milan. In 1898 he was nominated Scriptor of the Greek Language at the Vatican Library, pro-Prefect in 1918, and Prefect in 1919. In 1936 he was created cardinal. Mercati wrote innumerable studies, esp. on matters of Patristic and palaeographical interest; and he was one of the editors of the Catalogue of the Vatican Gk. MSS. (1923 ff.).

His brothers, ANGELO MERCATI (1870–1955) and SILVIO GIUSEPPE MERCATI (b. 1877) were also distinguished scholars.

Mercati's chief papers to date assembled in *Opere minori raccolte in occasione del settantesimo natalizio sotto gli auspicii di S.S. Pio XI.*, ed. A. M. Albareda, O.S.B. (S.T., lxxvi–lxxx; 5 vols., 1937–41), with biog. notice and bibliography [for years 1890–1941] in vol. lxxx. *Miscellanea Giovanni Mercati* (S.T., cxxi–cxxvi; 6 vols., 1946), to commemorate Mercati's 80th birthday.

MERCATOR, MARIUS. See *Marius Mercator*.

MERCEDARIANS. A religious order of men founded *c.* 1220 by St. *Peter Nolasco (hence also known as 'Nolascans') with the twofold object of tending the sick and rescuing Christians who had been taken prisoner by the Moors. They owed their rule to St. *Raymond of Pennafort. In addition to the usual three vows, a fourth was added pledging them to offer their own persons as hostages if needed for the redemption of Christian captives. They rapidly spread through W. Europe, and as some of their members accompanied Columbus to the New World, many of their houses became established in Latin

America. A corresponding order of nuns was founded at Seville in 1568. In modern times the two orders have declined in numbers and influence. They took their name from their dedication to Our Lady of Mercy (Orden de Nuestra Señora de la Merced).

A. Remon, Mercedarian, *Historia general de la orden de Nuestra Señora de la Merced Redención de Cautivos* (2 vols., Madrid, 1618); M. Salmeron, Mercedarian, *Recuerdos históricos y políticos de los servicios que los generales y varones ilustres de la religión de Nuestra Señora de la Merced, Redención de Cautivos* (Valencia, 1646). M. Even, *Une Page de l'histoire de la charité dans l'Église catholique*. L'Ordre de la Merci pour la Rédemption des Captifs (ed. 2, revised and enlarged for the 7th centenary of the foundation of the Order; Rome, 1918). F. D. Gazulla, Mercedarian, *La orden de Nuestra Señora de la Merced*. Estudios historicocríticos, 1218-1317 (1934). P. N. Pérez, Mercedarian, *Religiosos de la Merced que pasaron a la América Española, 1514-1777* (Seville, 1924). Heimbucher, i, 571-6, with detailed bibl. J. M. Besse, O.S.B., in *C.E.*, x (1911), p. 197 f., s.v. See also bibl. to *Raymond of Penafort*.

MERCIER, DÉSIRÉ JOSEPH (1851-1926), Belgian philosopher and prelate. Educated at Malines and Louvain and ordained to the priesthood in 1874, in 1877 he became Prof. of Philosophy at the Petit Séminaire at Malines and in 1882 first Prof. of Thomist Philosophy at Louvain. From the first he was an ardent promoter of the Thomist revival heralded by *Aeterni Patris* (1879), esp. interesting himself in the application of Thomist principles to modern science. The new school ('Neo-Scholasticism') developed in conscious opposition both to the Scientific *Positivism of J. S. Mill and H. *Spencer and to the Neo-Kantian Idealism. Under Mercier's inspiration an Institute of Philosophy was founded at Louvain which gave a prominent place to experimental methods. Mercier expounded his own philosophical position in a tetralogy—*Psychologie* (1892), *Logique* (1894), *Métaphysique* (1894), and *Critériologie* (1899). He was also mainly responsible for the *Revue Néoscolastique de Philosophie* (1894 ff.).

In 1906 Mercier was made Abp. of Malines and in 1907 created a cardinal. He was in many ways a model prelate, ever concerned for the spiritual life of his clergy and people. He naturally had little interest in the activist philosophy of the *Modernist school; and in his Lenten Pastoral for 1908 he denounced G. *Tyrrell, who replied in his *Medievalism* (1908). During the World War of 1914-18 he strenuously upheld Belgian interests against the German invaders, and encouraged resistance by his own example. Prompted by his desire for the promotion of Christian unity, he was the leading spirit on the RC side in the Conversations at *Malines (1921, 1923, 1925, q.v.), which were cut short by his death.

Mercier's correspondence with the German Government during the occupation, 1914-18, ed. F. Mayence (Brussels, 1919; Eng. tr. as *Cardinal Mercier's Own Story*, 1920). His *Œuvres pastorales* were publd. in 7 vols., Brussels-Louvain, 1911-29. Commemorative vol. under the title *Le Cardinal Mercier (1851-1926)*, publd. Brussels, 1927, with list of his works, pp. 341-72. Other lives include those by G. Ramaekers (Brussels, 1926), G. Goyau (London, 1926; popular), H. L. Dubly (Paris, 1927; Eng. tr., 1928), A. P. Laveille (Paris, 1927; Eng. tr., New York, 1928), and J. A. Gade (New York, 1934). A. Bolton, *A Catholic Memorial of Lord Halifax and Cardinal Mercier* (1935), esp. pp. 109-37.

J. J. Harnett, 'Désiré Mercier and the Neo-Scholastic Revival' in *The New Scholasticism*, xviii (1944), pp. 303-33. The centenary of his birth was marked by celebrations at Louvain; a commemorative vol. was prepared by L. de Raeymaeker and others, *Le Cardinal Mercier. Fondateur de l'Institut Supérieur de Philosophie à l'Université de Louvain* [1952].

MERCY, Corporal Works of. See *Corporal Works of Mercy*.

MERCY, Sisters of. See *Sisters of Mercy*.

MERCY, Spiritual Works of. See *Spiritual Works of Mercy*.

MERCY-SEAT. In the Jewish Temple, the covering of solid gold laid on the '*Ark of the Covenant' which was conceived to be God's resting-place. The Hebrew (כַּפֹּרֶת), Greek (LXX, ἱλαστήριον), and Latin (*Vulgate, *propitiatorium*) words are all connected with the idea of 'propitiation'. The AV rendering 'Mercy Seat' goes back to W. *Tyndale's version, following M. *Luther's *Gnadenstuhl*.

G. A. *Deissmann in *E Bi.*, iii (1902), cols. 3027-35, s.v.; J. Herrmann-F. Büchsel in *T.W.B.*, iii (1938), pp. 319-24, s.v. 'ἱλαστήριον'. See also bibl. to *Ark* (2).

MERIT. In the theological sense of the term, 'merit' designates man's right to be rewarded for a work done for God. The conception has its foundation in the Bible, where both in the OT and the NT rewards are promised to the just for their good works (e.g. Exod. 23. 20-22, Deut. 5. 28-33 and passim, Mt. 5. 3-12, 6. 4, 6. 19 f., 7. 21). The term appears to have been first employed by *Tertullian, who already recognizes diversity of merit followed by diversity of reward, 'Quomodo multae mansiones apud Patrem si non pro varietate meritorum?' (*Scorp.* 6). This doctrine was endorsed by *Cyprian, *Augustine (partly), and the later Fathers, until the theology of merit was fully developed by the Schoolmen. These last distinguish two kinds of merit, *meritum de condigno* and *meritum de congruo*. *Condign merit confers a claim to reward due in justice to services rendered, whilst *congruous merit may only claim the reward on grounds of fitness. In the relation between God and man, condignity of merit in the strict sense is impossible owing to the creature's absolute dependence on the Creator. It is, however, admitted in the sense that God, by His free promise, has bound Himself to confer rewards on certain works. The following are the conditions to be fulfilled in order to obtain merit *de condigno*. The work must be morally good, be done freely, be assisted by actual grace, performed with a supernatural motive (whether with charity or whether faith alone is sufficient is contested by theologians) in the sphere of this life (*in statu viae*), be done in the state of grace, and, lastly, God must have promised to reward it. Merit *de congruo* is held to be conferred on similar conditions except for the state of grace, which is not considered always necessary.

The traditional doctrine of merit was repudiated by the Reformers, esp. by M. *Luther, who taught the sinfulness of all human works whether done before or after justification. Most subsequent Protestant theology has denied that merit is a valid Christian category. The medieval doctrine was reformulated by the Council of *Trent, which, while maintaining the impossibility of meriting the initial grace of justification, emphasized the reality of human merit, based on the supernatural life communicated by Christ as the head to the members of His Mystical Body.

H. Schultz, 'Der sittliche Begriff des Verdienstes und seine Anwendung auf das Verständnis des Werkes Christi' in *Theologische Studien und Kritiken*, lxvii (1894), pp. 7–50, 245–314, 553–614. K. H. Wirth, *Der 'Verdienst'-Begriff in der christlichen Kirche* (2 vols., 1892–1901; on Tertullian and Cyprian). J. Kunze in *P.R.E.* (ed. 3), xx (1908), pp. 500–8, s.v. 'Verdienst'; J. Pohle in *C.E.*, x (1911), pp. 202–8, s.v.; R. S. Franks in *H.E.R.E.*, viii (1915), pp. 561–5, s.v. 'Merit (Christian)'; J. Rivière in *D.T.C.*, x (pt. 1; 1928), cols. 574–85, s.v. 'Mérite', with extensive bibl.

MERLE D'AUBIGNÉ, JEAN HENRI
(1794–1872), Swiss historian of the *Reformation. The son of French Protestant refugee parents, he studied at Berlin under J. A. W. *Neander and W. M. L. *de Wette. After taking charge of the French Protestant church in Hamburg from 1819 to 1823, he became pastor to a congregation and court preacher at Brussels. In 1831 he returned to Geneva as professor of Church history in the new theological faculty. Here he wrote his *Histoire de la Réformation du XVIe siècle* (5 vols., 1835–53). Written in an easy and graphic style, the book won great popularity; but its author's enthusiasm sometimes overrode the demands of historical accuracy. His *Histoire de la Réformation en Europe au temps de Calvin* (8 vols., 1863–78) was a more finished, if less popular, work.

J. Bonnet, *Notice sur la vie et les écrits de M. Merle d'Aubigné* (1874; 32 pp.). R. Kayser, 'Henri Merle d'Aubigné und die Anfänge der Erweckung in Hamburg' in *Zeitschrift des Vereins für Hamburgische Geschichte*, xxx (1920), pp. 106–35. Duchemin in *P.R.E.* (ed. 3), xii (1903), pp. 637–43.

MERRY DEL VAL, RAFAEL (1865–1930),
Cardinal. The son of Don Rafael Merry del Val, secretary to the Spanish Legation in London, he was educated by the *Jesuits at Namur and Brussels, at Ushaw College, *Durham (1883–5), and at the Roman Accademia dei Nobili (1885–91). He was ordained priest in 1888. Singled out by *Leo XIII for the Papal service, he became secretary to the commission which pronounced against *Anglican Ordinations (1896). In 1897 he was entrusted with important negotiations in *Canada on the schools question which arose out of the Manitoba Laws of 1890. In 1900 he became titular Abp. of *Nicaea. In 1903, he was created Cardinal and also Secretary of State by *Pius X, with whose intransigent policy (*Loi de Séparation* in France, anti-*Modernism) he became closely identified. After he had ceased to be Secretary of State, in acc. with custom, on the

Pope's death, he became Secretary of the *Holy Office, where he unobtrusively exercised great influence. He had a strong pastoral sense; and he often regretted that his career gave him only limited scope (e.g. through spiritual correspondence) for its exercise. His tomb in the crypt of St. Peter's Rome, near that of Pius X, is inscribed 'Da mihi animas. Caetera tolle.'

Lives by F. A. Forbes (London, 1932) and P. Cenci (Rome' 1933; with pref. by E. Pacelli, afterwards *Pius XII).

MERSCH, EMIL (1890–1940), *Jesuit theologian. He was ordained priest at Louvain in 1917 and taught philosophy at Namur from 1920 to 1935. Throughout his life his aim was to construct a theological synthesis in terms of the 'Mystical Body of Christ'. In *Le Corps mystique de Christ*. Études de théologie historique (2 vols., Louvain, 1933; Eng. tr., *The Whole Christ*, Milwaukee, 1938), he traced the development of the doctrine of the Church, so understood, through history; in *La Théologie du corps mystique* (ed. J. Levie, S.J.; 2 vols., Louvain, 1946; posthumous) he expounded the doctrine from a more systematic standpoint. He was killed at Lens in an air attack on 23 May 1940.

Memoir by J. Levie, S.J., prefixed to Mersch's *La Théologie du corps mystique*, I, pp. vii–xxxiii, with full list of Mersch's writings, pp. xxxi–xxxiii. G. Dejaifve, S.J., 'La Théologie du corps mystique du P. Em. Mersch' in *Nouvelle Revue Théologique*, lxxvii (1945), pp. 408–16.

MERSENNE, MARIN (1588–1648), French philosopher, scientist, and theologian. He was educated at the *Jesuit College at La Flèche, where he formed a lifelong friendship with his younger fellow-pupil, R. *Descartes. In 1611 he joined the *Minims and finally settled in 1620 at the convent of L'Annonciade at Paris. Though himself the author of several works, among them *Quaestiones celeberrimae in Genesim* (1623), *L'Impiété des déistes* (1624), and *La Vérité des sciences* (1624), 'Père Mersenne' (as he was universally known) fills a place in the history of modern philosophy which rests on the links that he forged by his friendship and correspondence between many of the leading French philosophers and scientists of his day. In this way he did much to foster the new scientific movement and also to prevent it from developing in an anti-religious direction.

Correspondance de Mersenne, crit. ed. by Mme P. Tannery and C. de Waard (3 vols., Paris, 1932, 1936, 1949). Contemporary Life by Hilarion de Coste (Paris, 1649; new ed. by B. T. de Sarrogue, with unpubld. letters, Paris, 1932). R. Lenoble, *Mersenne ou la naissance du mécanisme* (1943). H. Ludwig, *Marin Mersenne und seine Musiklehre* (1935). Überweg, iii, pp. 172, 180–2, 649. E. Dumoutet in *D.T.C.*, x (pt. i; 1928), col. 788 f.

MESHA, Inscription of. See *Moabite Stone*.

MESROB, St. (c. 345–440), historian and Patr. of *Armenia. Over a long period he was coadjutor-bishop to the patriarch Sahak, and on Sahak's death in 440 succeeded to the office, but died himself within less than six months. Zealous for a Christian national culture in

Armenia, he made it one of his main objects to eliminate from Armenian life all traces of Syriac institutions. His ardent love of learning induced him to compose for the Armenians an alphabet which was adopted in 406; and, gathering round him a band of keen scholars (among them, acc. to a doubtful tradition, *Moses of Chorene), he sent some of his disciples as far as Rome in search of MSS. of the Scriptures and of ecclesiastical and profane writers. In the Armenian Bible, based on the Syriac and issued c. 410, Mesrob was himself the translator of the NT and Prov.; and later (c. 433) he assisted in its revision with the use of Gk. MSS. He also did much to encourage the development of monastic institutions. Feast days in the Armenian *menology, 19 Feb. and 25 Nov. (the latter also in W. calendars).

Armenian Lives, of uncertain trustworthiness, by Koriun, his pupil (ed. Venice, 1833), and by Lazarus Pharbetzi. Many sermons, theological discourses, hymns, and other writings which pass under the name of *Gregory the Illuminator are prob. the work of St. Mesrob. Bardenhewer, v, 197–201. J. Marquart, *Über den Ursprung des armenischen Alphabets in Verbindung mit den Biographie des heiligen Mast'oc* (Vienna, 1917). J. Karst in *D.T.C.*, x (pt. i; 1928), cols. 789–92, and A. Merk, S.J., in *L.Th.K.*, vii (1935), cols. 113 f.

MESSALIANS, also known as the **Euchites** (Εὐχῖται), a pietistic mendicant sect. Their name is derived from a Syriac word which, like the corresponding Greek, means 'praying people'. They appear to have originated in Mesopotamia soon after the middle of the 4th cent. and to have spread to Syria, Asia Minor, Thrace, &c., and later to Egypt. They were attacked by *Amphilochius of Iconium, Flavian of Antioch, and St. *Epiphanius, and condemned at the Council of *Ephesus of 431. They survived, however, down to the 7th cent. They held that in consequence of Adam's sin everyone had a demon substantially united with his soul, and that this demon, which was not expelled by baptism, was completely liberated only by concentrated and ceaseless prayer, the aim of which was to eliminate all passion and desire. Those who had in this way become spiritual and perfect received an immediate vision of the Holy Trinity. The Messalians also laid great stress on the efficacy of ascetic practice.

The earliest mention of the sect is in *Ephraim Syrus, *Hom.*, xxii, against heresy; fuller details (but unreliable) in Epiphanius, *Haer.*, lxxx ('Contra Messalianos'). The main sources are conveniently collected by M. Kmosko in the preface to his ed. of the 'Liber Graduum' in *Patrologia Syriaca* (ed. R. Graffin), iii (Paris, 1926), cols. clxxi–ccxciii. The Homilies of (Ps.) *Macarius of Egypt appear to be of Messalian origin. I. Hausherr, S.J., 'L'Erreur fondamentale et la logique du messalianisme' in *O.C.P.*, i (1935), pp. 328–60. H. Dörries, *Symeon von Mesopotamien. Die Überlieferung der messalianischen 'Makarios' Schriften* (T.U., lv, Hft. 1; 1941). G. Bonwetsch in *P.R.E.* (ed. 3), xii (1903), pp. 661–4, s.v.; É. Amann in *D.T.C.*, x (pt. 1; 1928), cols. 792–5, s.v.; E. Peterson in *E.C.*, viii (1952), cols. 841 f., s.v.

MESSIAH. In Jewish theology, the person, whether earthly or supernatural, invested by God with special powers and functions, who is destined to appear as the divinely appointed deliverer and ruler of Israel. The Hebrew word 'Messiah' (lit. 'anointed') was used, among others, to designate this expected Deliverer. In the *Septuagint it is translated χριστός, *christos* (from χρίω, 'anoint'), whence the title *Christ (q.v.) given to Jesus of Nazareth, who, acc. to the most fundamental Christian belief, is the Messiah foretold in the OT. In Christian usage, as in Jn. 1. 41, 4. 25, the term 'Messiah' is generally used to denote the future Deliverer of Jewish expectation without reference to the fulfilment of that expectation in Our Lord.

Under the Hebrew monarchy, anointing was the sacrament of accession to the kingship, denoting particularly the king's divine appointment (1 Sam. 10. 1, 16. 1–13); the king, as 'the Lord's anointed', was held to be sacrosanct (1 Sam. 24. 4–6). Acc. to 2 Sam. 7. 12–13 the promise was made to *David through Nathan the prophet that the throne of his 'seed' would be established 'for ever'. Under the later monarchy, when the kingdom of Judah was threatened by Assyria and then by Babylon, the appearance of a future king of the house of David whose rule would be glorious, wise, and secure, in contrast to Judah's present weakness and danger, was foretold by *Isaiah and *Jeremiah. Although apparently a human monarch, sitting on the throne of David, he is called by unique titles (Is. 9. 6–7) and to be endowed with special spiritual gifts (11. 1–2). He will be a righteous judge, vindicating the poor and meek (9. 7, 11. 3–4) and destroying the wicked 'with the breath of his lips' (11. 4), and his reign will be a time of supernatural harmony and peace (11. 6–8) and of spiritual blessing for mankind (11. 9–10). Such a Davidic king is foretold also in Jer. 23. 5–6 (cf. 33. 15–17) and the advent of a great ruler from *Bethlehem, the city of David, is prophesied in Mic. 5. 2. In Jer. 23. 7–8 the prophecy of the Davidic ruler is followed by another predicting the return of all Israelite exiles, which will inaugurate a new age, as did the *Exodus from Egypt (cf. the prophecy of a New Covenant, replacing that of Sinai, in Jer. 31. 31 ff.). Further mention of a new age is found in Is. 2. 4 ff. (Mic. 4. 1 ff.) and elsewhere, though generally without mention of any ruler over Israel other than God Himself (cf. Is. 24. 23). The description in Ps. 2 of the unshakable dominion of the Lord's anointed, against whom the nations rage, even if it referred originally to a king of Israel contemporary with the Psalmist or to the dynasty of David personified (cf. Jer. 30. 8–9), was later understood by the Jews of the Messiah. The references in Ps. 110, of uncertain date, to a ruler in *Jerusalem who is also a priest 'after the order of *Melchizedek' and to the destruction of kings in the day when God 'shall judge among the nations', were understood in the same way (cf. Mt. 22. 42).

The hope of a restoration of the Davidic monarchy was not quenched by the Exile (Ezek. 34. 23–4). Indeed, shortly after the return it seemed possible that the kingship might be immediately restored in the person of the Davidic prince Zerubbabel (cf. Zech. 3.8, 4.6–10), in association with Joshua the *High Priest. But in fact it was the High Priests alone who became the secular rulers of Israel down to the time of the *Maccabees, from whom (and not from the Davidic line) the Hasmonaean rulers sprang. The growth of *Apocalyptic literature reflects that in the last two cents. B.C. the expectation of a New Age became more vivid and detailed, but also that it did not always include the idea of a personal Messiah. In Dan. 7. 1–14 (c. 165 B.C.) the ultimate destruction of the heathen kingdoms (represented by beasts) at God's judgement on the world is foretold. Their dominion will be handed over to 'one like unto a *son of man', who is shown (Dan. 7. 17 ff.) to represent 'the people of the saints of the Most High'. In the Similitudes of *Enoch, however, the term 'Son of Man' (1 Enoch 46. 2, etc.) is used of the Messiah ('the Anointed', 52. 4, also called 'the Elect One, and 'the Righteous One'), a supernatural being in human form existing in heaven and associated with God in His divine kingship, who will be revealed at the Last Judgement, destroy the wicked, and rule over a purified and blessed Israel. In the Pss. of *Solomon (17. 23 ff.), which portray the condition of Israel in the glorious future age, their king is described as 'the Lord's Anointed' (i.e. Messiah or Christ, cf. Lk. 2. 26).

From passages such as these it is evident that among the Jews, particularly in Palestine, in the time of Christ expectation of the advent of a Deliverer and Ruler, generally known as the Messiah (Christ), was widespread. His character and function might be variously conceived. As in the earlier prophets, he was usually (but not in Enoch) expected to be (unlike the reigning Herodian family) of the legitimate line of David (Mt. 2. 4–5, 22. 42), and to restore the independence and empire enjoyed under David and Solomon (Acts 1. 6). Such a kingdom might be conceived politically (cf. Jn. 6. 15) as armed revolt against Rome or, more spiritually, as securing the blessings of religious freedom for Israel (Lk. 1. 74–80) and the enlightenment of the Gentiles (Lk. 2. 32).

Acc. to the *Synoptic Gospels, the Messiahship of Jesus was expressly proclaimed by angels at His birth (Lk. 2. 11). It was also divinely attested before His birth, and at His Baptism, in other, but no less definite, terms (Mt. 1. 21–3, Lk. 1. 32–3, Mk. 1. 11). In His public ministry His Messiahship was acclaimed at first only by demoniacs (Mk. 3. 11, 5. 7; Lk. 4. 41), and suspected by John the Baptist (Mt. 11. 3), while the disciples wondered at the mystery of His Person (Mk. 4. 41). He Himself in this period did not openly acknowledge His Messiahship. Acc. to W. *Wrede, Jesus did not in fact claim to be the Messiah; but it is fundamental to the narrative of the Synoptic Gospels that St. *Peter's explicit confession of Him at Caesarea Philippi as the Christ (Mk. 8. 29; Mt. 16. 16 ff.), was a turning point in His ministry, and this He did not disclaim but, acc. to Mt. 16. 17, acknowledged

fully. But He still enjoined secrecy on His disciples regarding the Messiahship, doubtless because of its current political implications and of the need to bring about a profound transformation, in the minds of His followers, of even the traditional religious idea of Messiahship, preparing them for its fulfilment through His Passion and Resurrection (Mk. 8. 31; 9. 31; 10. 33) rather than by the immediate establishment of a visible *Kingdom of God. In this transformed sense in which, e.g., the prophecies of the Suffering Servant of the Lord in Is. (42. 1–9; 49. 2–6; 50. 4–11; 52.13 –53.12) and of the king 'meek and lowly, riding upon an ass' (Zech. 9. 9), were revealed as Messianic, Jesus undoubtedly acknowledged Himself to be the Messiah, and when asked a direct question on the point by the High Priest at His trial, He replied in the affirmative (Mk. 14. 62). Acc. to St. *John's Gospel, Jesus spoke of Himself on various occasions throughout his ministry as the Messiah (4. 26), or in terms that implied His unique divine Sonship (5. 18, 8. 42–58, etc.) and to some extent the latter language is paralleled in the Synoptics (Mt. 11. 25–7, Lk. 10. 21–2). In all four Gospels He is reported as speaking of Himself as Son of Man (q.v.); and after the Resurrection He further taught His own identity with the Messiah of OT expectation (Lk. 24. 26–7).
See also *Christology*.

Among modern works: J. *Drummond, *The Jewish Messiah* (1877); V. H. Stanton, *The Jewish and Christian Messiah* (1886); W. *Wrede, *Das Messiasgeheimnis in den Evangelien* (1901; ed. 2, 1913); A. *Schweitzer, *The Quest of the Historical Jesus* (Eng. trans., 1910); E. F. Scott, *The Kingdom and the Messiah* (1911); W. *Bousset, *Kyrios Christos* (1913; ed. 2, 1921); A. Lukyn Williams, *The Hebrew-Christian Messiah* (1916); A. E. J. Rawlinson, *The New Testament Doctrine of the Christ* (1926); M. J. *Lagrange, O.P., *Le Judaïsme avant Jésus-Christ* (1931); A. G. Hebert, S.S.M., *The Throne of David*. A Study of the Fulfilment of the Old Testament in Jesus Christ and His Church (1941); W. Manson, *Jesus the Messiah* (1943). V. H. Stanton in *H.D.B.*, iii (1900), pp. 352–7, s.v.; W. Fairweather, ib., Extra Vol. (1904), pp. 295–302 s.v. 'Development of Doctrine in the Apocryphal Period. V: The Messianic Hope'; W. R. *Smith–O. C. Whitehouse in *E.B.* (ed. 11), xviii (1911), pp. 191–4, s.v.; C. W. Emmet in *H.E.R.E.*, viii (1915), pp. 570–81, s.v.; L. Dennefeld in *D.T.C.*, x (pt. 2; 1929), cols. 1404–1568, s.v. 'Messianisme'; F. Spadafora in *E.C.*, viii (1952), cols. 843–9, s.v. 'Messia e messianismo'.

METAPHRAST, The. A traditional name for the Byzantine hagiographer, *Simeon (q.v.; *fl. c.* 960), also called **Logothetes,** derived from his 'metaphrase' of older versions of the saints' lives.

METAPHYSICAL POETS. The term was first applied by Dr. S. *Johnson to a group of 17th cent. poets (J. *Donne, G. *Herbert, T. *Traherne, and H. *Vaughan, etc.) in a derogatory sense, implying boastful exhibition of wit and learning in fanciful 'conceits' and extravagant metaphors. During the 19th cent., and esp. in recent times, the Metaphysical Poets have come to be more favourably judged. Apart from their exaggerations of style, their works are of high poetical quality and considerable religious feeling, with a strong appreciation of Christian dogma and worship.

Metaphysical Lyrics and Poems of the Seventeenth Century. Donne to Butler. Selected and Edited by H. J. C. Grierson (1921), with introd. pp. xiii-lviii. J. B. Leishman, *The Metaphysical Poets.* Donne, Herbert, Vaughan, Traherne (1934); Joan Bennett, *Four Metaphysical Poets.* Donne, Herbert, Vaughan, Crashaw (1934; ed. 2, 1953). H. C. White, *The Metaphysical Poets.* A Study in Religious Experience (1936). Molly M. Mahood, *Poetry and Humanism* (1950).

METAPHYSICAL SOCIETY, The. A society founded in 1869 by Sir James Knowles (1831–1908; editor successively of the *Contemporary Review* and, from 1877, of the *Nineteenth Century*), with the encouragement of Tennyson to foster constructive debate between the leading exponents of science and religion. Among its members were H. Acland, H. *Alford, A. J. *Balfour, W. B. Carpenter, R. W. *Church, J. B. *Dalgairns, A. C. *Fraser, J. A. Froude, F. A. *Gasquet, W. E. *Gladstone, T. H. *Huxley, W. C. Magee, H. E. *Manning, J. *Martineau, F. D. *Maurice, J. Morley, J. B. *Mozley, M. *Pattison, G. Croom Robertson, J. R. *Seeley, H. *Sidgwick, A. P. *Stanley, Leslie Stephen, James Sully, and C. *Thirlwall. The last meeting of the society was held on 16 May 1880. Many of its members, however, were later prominent in the 'Synthetic Society' (1869–1908), founded with similar but rather more definitely religious interests.

A. W. Brown, *The Metaphysical Society* (New York, 1947).

METAPHYSICS. The name given by the Greek editors of *Aristotle to his 'First Philosophy', and by analogy to all philosophical treatises concerning cognate topics. The title was merely intended to indicate the position of the books on this subject in the Aristotelian *corpus*—τὰ μετὰ τὰ φυσικά, 'the [books] that succeed the *Physics*'. The precise scope of metaphysical inquiry is very hard to define. To Aristotelians, it is the study of being *qua* being; to idealists, that of the ultimate implication of experience, cognitional, volitional, and aesthetic; to modern realists that of the most pervasive features of reality (self-consistency, spatial and temporal relatedness, causality, substantiality, &c.). Contemporary philosophy tends to be radically empiricist, and criticizes the notion of metaphysical inquiry on the ground that it involves the constant assertion of statements unverifiable in principle. Thus it dismisses G. W. *Leibniz' metaphysics as a philosophical romance, and has suggested that most philosophers should publish their writings in periodicals devoted to literary matters. Christian theology has historically tended to take a realist metaphysics more or less for granted (see *Analogy*; *Thomas Aquinas, St.*), but in Protestantism, both liberal (e.g. A. *Ritschl) and neo-orthodox (e.g. K. *Barth, E. *Brunner), the influence of I. *Kant's substitution of ethics for metaphysics has been considerable.

Since nearly the whole range of philosophical speculation has at different times been comprised under the term 'Metaphysics', the literature is virtually limitless. Good

general orientations in A. E. *Taylor, *Elements of Metaphysics* (1903), and J. S. Mackenzie, *Elements of Constructive Philosophy* (1917). See also bibls. to such entries as *Plato*; *Aristotle*; *Neoplatonism*; *Scholasticism*; *Descartes, R.*; *Spinoza, B.*; *Leibniz, G. W.*; *Wolf, C.*; *Kant, I.*; *Fichte, J. G.*; *Schelling, F. W. J. von*; *Hegel, G. W. F.*; *Lotze, H.*; *Dilthey, W.*; *Bradley, F. H.*; *Bosanquet, B.*; *Croce, B.*; *Pattison, A. S. Pringle*; *Phenomenology*; *Existentialism.* Further, M. Heidegger, *Sein und Zeit* (1927); id., *Kant und das Problem der Metaphysik* (1929); N. Hartmann, *Das Problem des geistigen Seins* (1933); id., *Zur Grundlegung der Ontologie* (1935); R. G. Collingwood, *Philosophical Essays* (2 vols., 1933–40).

METEMPSYCHOSIS. The doctrine that souls migrate from one body into another until complete purification has been achieved. The belief is widespread, esp. in India, where it forms an integral part of Brahmanism and Buddhism; but it is also found in the later Jewish teaching of the *Cabbala and among many savage races. In pre-Christian Europe its most outstanding advocates were *Plato and Pythagoras, both of whom were probably influenced by Orphism, and the doctrine was generally accepted among the later Platonists, by whom the word μετεμψύχωσις was in current use. In the Christian era *Origen's doctrine of the pre-existence of souls often approached actual metempsychosis. It was frequently attacked, e.g. by St. *Augustine and by *Aeneas of Gaza, and it was implicitly condemned by the Councils of *Lyons (1274) and *Florence (1439) which affirmed that the souls go immediately to heaven, purgatory, or hell. In modern times belief in metempsychosis was revived by Giordano *Bruno, G. E. *Lessing, Charles Fourier, and others, and recently it has come to the fore through the spread of *Spiritualism and *Theosophy. Its attraction lies partly in its claim to provide a morally satisfying explanation of the inequalities of fortune and character among mankind, which it ascribes to deeds done in former lives. Belief in metempsychosis is fundamentally at variance with the Christian doctrine of the resurrection of the body.

METHODISM. The system of religious faith and practice promoted, orig. at Oxford in 1729, by John and Charles *Wesley and their followers. Since the organization of the movement as a separate denomination, the designation has been confined to members of this Church and the other Churches derived from it. The circumstances of the original application of the word 'Methodist' to the followers of the Wesleys (first recorded instance, 1733) have never been satisfactorily explained. The word is occasionally met with in a not dissimilar sense in the 17th cent.

Most of the Methodist Churches, including the influential Methodist Episcopal Church of the U.S.A., are *Arminian in their theological sympathies. The '*Calvinistic Methodists' (q.v.) of Wales, however, are *predestinarian and federated with the Presbyterian Churches. See also *Wesley, John* and *Charles*; *Whitefield, George*; *Bible Christians*; *Methodist Churches*; *Methodist New Connexion*; *United Methodist Church*; and *United Methodist Free Churches.*

METHODIST CHURCHES. In 1784 J. Wesley (q.v.) made provision for the continuance as a corporate body of the 'Yearly Conference of the People called Methodists' by nominating under a deed poll 100 persons whom he declared to be its members and laying down the method by which their successors were to be appointed. The Conference had power to appoint preachers to the various 'Preaching Houses' (later 'chapels') the ownership of which was vested in boards of trustees acc. to a model trust deed, which since 1763 had already specified Wesley's *Notes on the New Testament* (1754) and his four volumes of sermons as a doctrinal standard. Provision was made for the case of preachers who should be, like J. and C. *Wesley, clergy of the C of E, but in fact there were few such. On Wesley's death in 1791 the future relations of Methodism with the C of E were a matter of dispute, but the 'Plan of Pacification' adopted by the Conference of 1795 led to the administration of the sacraments (i.e. Baptism and esp. Holy Communion) in all Methodist chapels and the declaration that the admission of a preacher to 'full connexion with the Conference' conferred ministerial rights without any form of ordination. Ordination by the imposition of the hands of ministers was again adopted by the Conference in 1836.

The secession of the *Methodist New Connexion (q.v.) in 1797 was relatively small, the great majority of Methodists remaining in connexion with the Conference thus constituted by Wesley, and organized acc. to his principles in local societies and circuits. There were further small secessions in 1805, of a body mainly in the N. of England who later became the 'Independent Methodists', in 1810 of the followers of H. Bourne who became the *Primitive Methodist Church (q.v.), and in 1815 of those of W. Bryan, known as the *Bible Christians (q.v.). The causes were in both cases matters of discipline and polity, not of doctrine. Similar disagreements with the official policy arising out of such matters as the installation of an organ in a chapel at Leeds (1827) and the foundation of a theological college for the training of ministers (1835) led to the formation of the Wesleyan Methodist Association. A more serious controversy over the expulsion of three ministers in 1849 led to the formation of the Wesleyan Reformers. These two bodies united in 1857 as the *United Methodist Free Churches (q.v.). The original body of Methodists continued, considerably weakened by these latter secessions. In course of time more friendly relations between all branches of Methodism were re-established and all took part, with Methodist Churches abroad, in a decennial Ecumenical Conference (first held 1881). In 1907 the Methodist New Connexion, the Bible Christians, and the United Methodist Free Churches came together in a union as the *United Methodist Church (q.v.), and this itself reunited in 1932 with the original or 'Wesleyan' Methodist Church and the Primi-

tive Methodist Church to form the Methodist Church in Great Britain as it now exists. The Calvinistic Methodists in Wales, followers of G. *Whitefield rather than of Wesley, are the only other substantial body bearing the Methodist name to remain separate.

The Methodist Church considers itself part of the Church Universal but claims no rights for its particular form of Church order *iure divino*, believing in the priesthood of all believers and following in organization the principles laid down by Wesley for the pastoral oversight of the societies of Methodists which had grown up as a result of his preaching. Though not usually so called, the resulting organization is in principle, in the judgement of at least one Methodist scholar (H. B. Workman), presbyterian. The supreme authority is the Conference, the legal successor of that originally constituted by Wesley, and now regulated in Statute law by the Methodist Church Union Act, 1929, which took effect in 1932. It consists of 325 ministers and 325 laymen elected by and representing the local synods; the ministers sit separately in 'Ministerial Session' to decide affairs concerning ministers, but decisions affecting the whole Church are taken by the full conference ('Representative Session'). A minister as Chairman and, for the Representative Session, a layman as Vice-Chairman are elected annually by the Conference. The Conference delegates certain duties to the Synods, held twice yearly in each district, of which there are 46 in Great Britain, containing mostly about 20 or 30 Circuits in each; it also appoints ministers as Chairmen of each District and Superintendents of each circuit, the latter consisting normally of a number of local 'societies' (Wesley's term for the local bodies of Methodists), which form the several churches or chapels of the denomination. A distinction is made between adherents who may be in fact regular members of a congregation, and 'members' who have been formally admitted to the Church. 'All persons are welcomed into membership of the Methodist Church who sincerely desire to be saved from their sins through faith in the Lord Jesus Christ and evidence the same in life and conduct. . . .' Those who apply on this basis are admitted first for a probationary period and then (after baptism, if previously unbaptized), by a public service of reception into membership at which the Holy Communion is celebrated. Acc. to Wesley's system, which is peculiar to Methodism, 'All members shall have their names entered on a Class Book, shall be placed under the pastoral care of a Class Leader, and shall receive a Quarterly Ticket of Membership'. The weekly class-meeting for 'fellowship in Christian experience' has from the beginning been a valuable institution. On removing to another place a member receives a recommendation which entitles him to membership in another local society.

In each circuit there is a Quarterly Meeting consisting of ministers and lay office-holders, including Class Leaders, and in each Society there is a Leaders' Meeting on the same basis. A meeting of all Church members is held annually in each Society to appoint representatives to the Leaders' Meeting and for fellowship and consultation, but it has none of the powers of a Church Meeting in the Congregational or Independent Churches. Ministers are not 'called' to particular churches, but may be invited, the appointment being made by authority of the Conference, which also regulates the whole organization of Districts and Circuits, sets up special missions (e.g. to Seamen, Miners, etc.) and controls other central organizations and committees, which are responsible to it. It governs the training and ordination of ministers and the reception into communion of any who wish to join the Methodist Ministry from other bodies.

By tradition Methodism has an active concern with both evangelism and social welfare and by means of its centralized organization it is able to make co-ordinated efforts in these directions. Under the leadership of Hugh Price *Hughes (q.v.) the Methodist Forward Movement was active from 1885 in founding Missions in various parts of London, beginning with the East London Mission in Stepney, and in Manchester. Hughes's preaching at the West London Mission (from 1887) was a notable force in presenting Christianity as intimately concerned with social betterment and public morals: it was through his influence that the phrase 'the Nonconformist conscience' gained currency in connexion with the divorce suit involving C. S. Parnell (1846–91), and Hughes willingly accepted the phrase as a description of his standpoint. J. Scott Lidgett (1854–1953), founder in 1891 of the Bermondsey Mission and its Warden till 1949, was another outstanding figure.

Methodism outside Great Britain dates from the lifetime of Wesley, who in 1784 'set apart' T. Coke (1747–1814) and others for N. America, where by 1791 there were already 42,265 members of Methodist Societies, compared with 71,688 in Great Britain. With the growth of the U.S.A. (see *U.S.A., Christianity in*) Methodist numbers increased and now greatly exceed those in Britain. From the Civil War until 1939 there were two main Churches, in North and South respectively, which are now reunited, but there are also many smaller Methodist bodies. Wesley had 'set apart' Coke as 'Superintendent'; Coke, with others, ordained F. *Asbury (1745–1816) to the same office, and himself, against Wesley's opinion, took the title of 'bishop'; and American Methodism is largely 'episcopal' in possessing superintendents who are called bishops, though claiming no Episcopal Orders in the Catholic sense. There are also Methodist Churches under separate Conferences in *Ireland, Australasia (so-called, but mainly in *Australia) *New Zealand, and *South Africa; in *Canada Methodists have entered the United Church of Canada, and in S. India the Church of *South India. In N. India, *China, *Burma, and East, Central, and *West Africa there are Methodist Districts and Mission Stations in connexion with the vigorous work of the (British) Methodist Missionary Society (founded 1813), and in other parts of the world are missions resulting from the work of American Methodists. The world total of Methodist members c. 1950 was approaching 12 million, of whom over 10 million were in the U.S.A. and about 750,000 in Great Britain.

W. J. Townsend–H. B. Workman–G. Eayrs (edd.), *A New History of Methodism* (2 vols., 1909). J. R. Gregory, *A History of Methodism chiefly for the Use of Students* (2 vols., 1911). J. Scott Lidgett–B. H. Reed (edd.), *Methodism in the Modern World* (1926). A. W. Harrison and others, *The Methodist Church. Its Origin, Divisions and Reunion* (1932). F. Baker, *A Charge to Keep*. An Introduction to the People Called Methodists (1947). H. Bett, *The Spirit of Methodism* (1937). R. F. Wearmouth, *Methodism and the Common People of the Eighteenth Century* (1945); id., *Methodism and the Working Class Movements in England, 1800–1850* (1937); W. J. Warner, *The Wesleyan Movement in the Industrial Revolution* (1930). M. Edwards, *Methodism and England*. A Study of Methodism in its Social and Political Aspects during the Period 1850–1932 (1943); also other works by this author. T. B. Shepherd, *Methodism and the Literature of the Eighteenth Century* (1940). J. M. Buckley, *A History of Methodists in the United States* (American Church History, v; 1896); G. Alexander, *History of the Methodist Episcopal Church South* (ib., xi; 1894, pp. 1–142). W. W. Sweet, *Methodism in American History* (New York, 1933). I. F. MacLeister, *History of the Wesleyan Methodist Church of America* (Syracuse, N.Y., 1934). G. G. Findlay–W. W. Holdsworth, *The History of the Wesleyan Methodist Missionary Society* (5 vols., 1921–4). M. H. Harper, *Ecclesiastical Organization and Administration in the Methodist Episcopal Church in India* (Chicago Diss., Lucknow, 1936). H. Spencer–E. Finch, *The Constitutional Practice and Discipline of the Methodist Church* (1951), with text of historical docc. pp. 229–317. G. G. Findlay in *H.E.R.E.*, viii (1915), pp. 603–12, s.v. 'Methodism'. See also bibl. to *Primitive Methodist Church*; *Wesley, J*.

METHODIST NEW CONNEXION. The group of Methodists which in 1797 seceded from the *Wesleyan Methodist Church and in the union of 1907 was incorporated in the United Methodist Church.

This, the first of the Methodist secessions, originated six years after the death of *J. Wesley (1791). The leader of the 'reforming' movement which led to the disruption, Alexander *Kilham (q.v.), was ordained a minister in the Methodist Church in 1792. In the controversy on the relationship of Methodism to the C of E, he strongly supported complete separation, contending that Methodists should have the right to receive Communion from their own preachers. He also desired the lay members of the Church to take a much greater part in its administration than government through Wesley's Conference of preachers allowed. Kilham embodied his proposals for reform in a booklet in which he also exposed what seemed to him abuses of the existing system. His writings and agitation led to his trial by the Wesleyan Conference of 1796 and expulsion.

In 1797 Kilham and his supporters summoned a Convention to negotiate with the Conference; but as the Conference's concessions did not affect the central issue, viz., the representation of the laity in the ruling courts of the Church, Kilham at once founded the 'New Itinerancy' or 'Methodist New Connexion'. When its second Conference was held, a year later, the denomination had 15 ministers. On Kilham's death in 1798 he was succeeded by William Thom; and, despite the early loss of its first leader and great poverty, the New Connexion rapidly grew. The New Connexion differed from Wesleyan Methodism solely in the matter of Church government, and made neither doctrinal nor liturgical changes.

In 1907 the Methodist New Connexion united with the *Bible Christians and the *United Methodist Free Churches to form the *United Methodist Church.

For bibl. see previous entry.

METHODIUS and CYRIL, Sts. See Cyril and Methodius, Sts.

METHODIUS OF OLYMPUS, St. (d. c. 311), bishop in Lycia. Very few biographical details are known. St. *Jerome's assertion (De Vir. Illus., lxxxiii) that he was also Bp. of Tyre, and probably, too, that of ''*Leontius of Byzantium' (De Sectis, III, i) that he was Bp. of Patara, seem mistaken. He was apparently put to death in the concluding years of the *Diocletianic Persecution. Feast day, 18 Sept.

One of the first assailants of *Origen—perhaps the reason for the absence of mention of him by *Eusebius—Methodius wrote extensively, though only a small portion of his works has been preserved. The 'Symposium, or Banquet of the Ten Virgins' (Συμπόσιον, ἢ περὶ ἀγνείας) alone remains entire. Written in dialogue form after the manner of *Plato, it extols the excellence of virginity. At the end is a hymn to Christ as the Bridegroom of the Church. In a treatise on the Resurrection ('Ἀγλαοφῶν, ἢ περὶ τῆς ἀναστάσεως) he upheld against Origen the identity of the resurrection body with that worn in this life. His work on Free-Will (Περὶ τοῦ Αὐτεξουσίου) is a defence of human liberty against the fatalism of the *Gnostics. Considerable portions of the Greek text of these two writings has come down. His other works, surviving only in Slavonic, include writings on the food laws of the OT, on the mystical interpretation of the references to leprosy in Lev. 13, and on the leech in Prov. 30. 15. His lost writings include an extensive work against *Porphyry, commentaries on Genesis and the Song of Songs, and a treatise on the Pythonissa directed against Origen.

Earliest collection of Methodius's writings ed. (with those of other Fathers) by F. *Combefis, Paris, 1644; the 'Symposium', however, was first publd. by L. *Allatius, Rome, 1656. Crit. ed. by G. N. Bonwetsch (G.C.S., xxvii; 1917). Slavonic version of 'De Autexousio' with Gk. texts, ed. A. Vaillant in P.O., xxii. 5 (1930). Collected works also in J. P. Migne, PG, xviii, 9–408. Eng. tr. by W. R. Clark in A.N.C.L., xiv (1869), pp. 1–230. G. N. Bonwetsch, Die Theologie des Methodius von Olympus (1903); J. Farges, Les Idées morales et religieuses de Méthode d'Olympe (1929). Bardenhewer, ii, 334–51; Altaner (ed. 1951), p. 179 f. G. *Salmon in D.C.B., iii (1882), pp. 909–11; É. Amann in D.T.C., x (pt. 2; 1929), cols. 1606–14; E. Beck in E.C., viii (1952), cols. 888–90, s.v. 'Metodio di Olimpo'. Eng. ed. of his 'Symposium' by H. Musurillo, S.J. (A.C.W., 1958).

METHUSELAH. The eighth in the list of antediluvian patriarchs in Gen. 5 and the longest lived (969 years; Gen. 5. 27). He appears in the parallel list in Gen. 4 as 'Methusael' (RV 'Methushael') (v. 18).

METRICAL PSALTERS. At the Reformation metrical psalmody was introduced in the French and Swiss Reformed Churches as a more Biblical form of musical worship than the German *Lutheran hymns. In England metrical versions of the Psalms first appeared under *Edward VI. They were issued by T. *Sternhold (d. 1549) and others. In 1556 the Marian exiles in Geneva, doubtless inspired by the work of C. *Marot (q.v.) and L. Bourgeois (c. 1510–?), published along with their Book of Common Order fifty-one metrical psalms composed by Sternhold, J. Hopkins (d. c. 1570), and W. *Whittingham (d. 1579). In 1562 the first complete Anglo-Genevan edition was printed in England. Until the middle of the 19th cent., when the use of metrical psalmody waned, many English versions were produced. The most widely used of these was the New Version of the Psalms (1696) of N. *Tate and N. Brady.

In Scotland the use of a metrical psalter, fostered by 'Sang Schules', became a permanent and characteristic feature of national worship. The Anglo-Genevan version was printed with additions in 1564 (with 105 tunes). An important harmonized edition followed in 1635. In 1650 in place of this Old Version the Scottish General Assembly adopted, in a much revised form, the simple, rugged and dignified version of Francis Rouse, which had earlier been commended by the *Westminster Assembly and approved by the English House of Commons. The Assembly made no provision, however, for music for the new book and gradually many of the old tunes were forgotten. A new edition, The Scottish Psalter (1929), with tunes true to the old tradition, is now in use in Scottish and other Presbyterian churches.

N. Livingston (ed.), The Scottish Metrical Psalter of A.D. 1635 reprinted in full from the original work . . . and . . . illustrated by Dissertations, Notes, and Facsimiles (Glasgow, 1864). F. Bovet, Histoire du psautier des Églises réformées (1872). O. Douen, Clément Marot et le psautier huguenot. Étude historique, littéraire, musicale et bibliographique (2 vols., 1878–9), with specimens of early melodies by various authors. H. Kling, 'Les Compositeurs de la musique du psautier huguenot genevois' in Rivista musicale italiana, vi (1899), pp. 496–530. M. Patrick, Four Centuries of Scottish Psalmody (1949).

METROPHANES CRITOPOULOS (1589–1639). A Greek monk of Mt. *Athos who was sent by Cyril *Lucar to study theology in England under the direction of G. *Abbot. From 1617 to 1622 he was at Balliol College, *Oxford, and then in London, partly with Abbot, until 1624. After visiting Universities and Protestant Churches in Germany (1624–7) and Switzerland (1627), he returned via *Venice (1627–30) to Egypt in 1631. In 1633 he became Metropolitan of Memphis in Egypt, and in 1636 Patriarch of Alexandria. In 1638 he signed the anathemas pronounced against Cyril Lucar for Calvinism. His works include a 'Ὁμολογία τῆς ἀνατολικῆς ἐκκλησίας (ed. J. Horne, Helmstädt, 1661).

His 'Ὁμολογία τῆς ἀνατολικῆς ἐκκλησίας (Wolfenbüttel MS. 1048) has also been ed. by H. Weissenborn in E. J. Kimmel, Monumenta Fidei Ecclesiae Orientalis, ii (1850), pp. 1–213. Studies by J. A. Dietelmair (Altdorf, 1769), A. K. Demetracopoulos (Leipzig, 1870; Gk.), G. Mazarakē (Cairo, 1884; Gk.), M. Renierē (Athens, 1893), K. J. Dyobuniotes (ib., 1915), and I. N. Karmirē (ib., 1937 and 1948). J. Kemke, *Patricius Junius* (Leipzig, 1898), pp. 124–30. E. Legrand, *Bibliographie hellénistique . . . du XVIIᵉ Siècle*, v (1903), pp. 192–218. V. Grumel, A.A., in *D.T.C.*, x (pt. 2; 1929), cols. 1622–7, s.v.

METROPOLITAN. The title of a bishop exercising provincial, and not merely diocesan, powers. The organization of the early Church broadly followed that of the Roman Empire. Each city, with its territory, was governed by a bishop, and in each province the bishop of the civil metropolis (normally) came to possess rights over his comprovincial bishops, later called suffragans. These rights were determined by local custom before the Council of *Nicaea (325), whose 4th canon, in which the title metropolitan first appears, began the gradual process of legal definition. The duties and rights of a metropolitan have varied in time and place. Chief among them are the summoning and presidency of provincial synods, the visitation of dioceses, the care of vacant sees, some share in the appointment and consecration of suffragans and some disciplinary powers over them. Owing to *Diocletian's grouping of civil provinces into civil dioceses, metropolitans were in time subordinated to synods of the civil diocese or to a superior bishop (*exarch, *patriarch). The W. Church saw many conflicts between metropolitans and Popes, the latter being generally victorious (see *Pallium*). Provincial organization continues in episcopal Churches (*Canterbury, *York), though the metropolitical see is not always the civil capital. In the early Church, the metropolitan of some African provinces was the bishop senior by consecration. Metropolitans have commonly the titles of *archbishop and *primate.

MEXICO, Christianity in. The pre-Spanish Aztec empire of Mexico appears to have had vague traditions of Biblical and Christian ideas, but their source cannot be traced. But within five years of the first Spanish invasion (1519) *Franciscan and other missionaries arrived. Conversions were numerous, though not always entirely voluntary, and Mexican Christians have, from the first, kept much of the old paganism under an outward profession of Christianity. Throughout Mexican history from the 16th cent. onwards, hardly any Christians of other denominations have entered the country to challenge the prevailing RC-ism.

Mexican independence was won in 1821, after many revolts, but the influence of the Church remained very powerful in the political and financial fields, until the measures of President Juárez, which separated Church and state, nationalized Church property, and forbade the participation of the Church in state affairs, were embodied in the constitution after his death in 1872. The constitution of 1917 further provided that the Church is incapable of owning property, that churches must be under state supervision, and that all priests must be Mexican-born and excluded from politics. These enactments were not put into force until 1926, when, after a stand against them by the clergy, action was taken which resulted in the closing of the churches, the deportation of the episcopate, and the execution of many priests and lay persons, upon suspicion of political activity directed against the government. In later years the ban against foreign ecclesiastics has been extended to non-RCs.

M. Cuevas, *Historia de la Iglesia en México* (5 vols., Tlalpam, 1921–8). C. S. Braden, *Religious Aspects of the Conquest of Mexico* (Durham, N.C., 1930). J. Ramirez Canañas, *La relaciones entre México y el Vatican* (Archivo histórico diplomático mexicano, xxvii, Mexico, 1928: docc. with notes). G. Decorme, *La obra de los Jesuitas mexicanos durante la época colonial, 1572–1767* (Mexico, 1941). P. Ricard, *La 'Conquête spirituelle' du Mexique. Essai sur l'apostolat et les méthodes missionnaires des ordres mendiants en Nouvelle-Espagne de 1523 à 1572* (thesis, Paris, 1933). W. H. Callcott, *Church and State in Mexico, 1822–1857* (Durham, N.C. [c. 1926]). On the post-1917 crisis, L. C. Balderrama, *El clero y el gobierno de México* (2 vols., Mexico, 1927), with docc.; C. S. Macfarland, *Chaos in Mexico. The Conflict of Church and State* (London and New York, 1935); W. Parson, S.J., *Mexican Martyrdom* (New York, 1936). G. Baez Camargo-K. G. Grubb, *Religion in the Republic of Mexico* (Evangelical survey, London, 1935). J. M. Davis, *The Economic Basis of the Evangelical Church in Mexico* (ib. and New York, 1940). Latourette, iii, 108–23, and vi, 72–7 passim and 113–15, and vii, 176–81, with further reff.

MEYER, HEINRICH AUGUST WILHELM (1800–73), German NT scholar. Born at Gotha, he studied theology at the university of Jena and held various ecclesiastical offices at Hanover. The chief work of his life was his editorship of the well-known *Kritischexegetischer Kommentar zum Neuen Testament* (16 vols., 1832–52; Eng. trans., 20 vols., 1873–95) to which he himself contributed the Gospels, the Acts, and most of the Pauline epistles. It was highly praised for its completeness and philological exactness, and has been constantly revised and rewritten by a long series of distinguished scholars down to the present time. Meyer also published an edition of the text of the NT, with a trans. (2 vols., Göttingen, 1829), and a Latin version of the Symbolical Books of the *Lutheran Church (1830).

F. Düsterdieck in *P.R.E.* (ed. 3), xiii (1903), pp. 39–42.

MEYNELL, ALICE CHRISTIANA GERTRUDE (1847–1922), *née* Thompson, poet and essayist. Having become a RC *c.* 1872, she married Wilfrid Meynell in 1877, to whom she gave much help in his literary work. Throughout her life she contributed to several magazines a large number of essays, e.g. on contemporary authors such as Tennyson, Swinburne, and the Pre-Raphaelites. A great part of her work both in prose and verse has religion as its subject or background. Her verse, collections of which appeared at intervals from *Preludes* (1875) to the posthumously edited *Last Poems* in 1923, developed from the more emotional poetry of her earlier period to the subtle thought and restrained language of her riper years. In 1912 she published *Mary, the Mother of Jesus*, a collection of essays. Her writing was much appreciated by the most exacting critics of her time, among them men of such different views and temperament as G. Meredith and Coventry *Patmore.

The Poems of Alice Meynell. Complete Edition (1923); *Selected Poems of Alice Meynell* (1930), with introd. note by W.[ilfred] M.[eynell], pp. vii–xi; selection of her *Prose and Poetry.* Centenary volume ed. by F. P., V. M., O. S., and F. M. (1947), with biog. and crit. introd. by V. Sackville-West, pp. 7–26. Viola Meynell (daughter), *Alice Meynell. A Memoir* (1929). A. K. Tuell, *Mrs. Meynell and her Literary Generation* (New York, 1925). F. Page in *D.N.B.*, *1922–1930*, pp. 584–6. R. D. Coole–H. B. Grimsditch in *C.B.E.L.*, iii, p. 348 f.

MICAH, Book of. The sixth of the *Minor Prophets. From Mic. 1. 1 it appears that the author after whom the book is named lived in the 8th cent. B.C. and began to prophesy (Mic. 1. 5–7) before the fall of *Samaria (721). The first three chapters are generally accepted as the genuine work of this author, who is mentioned by *Jeremiah (Jer. 26. 17–19) as preaching with some success. They foretell the destruction of Samaria and of *Jerusalem. The rest of the book is prob. of much later date. Chs. 4–5, which predict the regeneration of the people and the advent of a *Messiah, prob. date from the period of the *Deutero-Isaiah, or poss. even from the 2nd cent. B.C. The last two chs., which are occupied with a dispute between Jehovah and his people, are prob. a collection of sayings of different periods, in some cases (e.g. 7. 7–20) even from that of the *Maccabees. Conservative exegetes uphold the unity of the book on stylistic grounds.

The component parts of the Book of Micah contain the fundamental ideas of *Amos, *Hosea and *Isaiah respectively. The Book contains the first prophecy of the destruction of the *Temple (Mic. 3. 11) as a punishment for presumption on the trust in divine protection. In Mic. 6. 8 it reaches one of the highest levels of the OT when it sums up true religion as justice, mercy and humble communion with God. The complaints of Jehovah in Mic. 6. 1–8 are the model on which have been formed the *Reproaches of the Mass of the *Presanctified on *Good Friday.

Commentaries by T. K. *Cheyne (Camb. Bib., AV, 1882), J. M. P. Smith (I.C.C. on Mic., Zeph., Nah., Hab., Obad., Joel, 1912, pp. 5–156), and G. W. Wade (West. Comm. on Mic., Obad., Joel, Jon., 1925, pp. 1–66). H. Gunkel, 'Der Micha-Schluss. Zur Einführung in die literaturgeschichtliche Arbeit am Alten Testament' in *Zeitschrift für Semitistik und verwandte Gebiete*, ii (1923), pp. 145–78. J. Lindblom, *Micha literarisch untersucht* (Acta Academiae Aboensis Humaniora, vi, 2; 1929). W. Nowack in *H.D.B.*, iii (1900), pp. 358–60, s.v.; W. R. *Smith–T. K. *Cheyne in *E.Bi.*, iii (1902), cols. 3068–74, s.v.; W. R. Smith–H. W. *Robinson in *E.B.* (ed. 11), xviii (1911), pp. 356–8, s.v. Further commentaries under *Minor Prophets*.

MI-CARÊME. See *Laetare Sunday*.

MICHAEL THE ARCHANGEL, St. He is mentioned four times in Scripture, twice in Dan. (10. 13 ff. and 12. 1), where he is represented as the helper of the Chosen People, once in Jude (v. 9), disputing with the devil over the body of *Moses, and once in Rev. (12. 7–9), fighting the dragon. He also plays an important part in the apocryphal literature, e.g. in

the 'Assumption of *Moses', in '*Enoch', and in the 'Ascension of *Isaiah' (qq.v.), where he appears as 'the great captain' 'who is set over the best part of mankind'. In connexion with the Scriptural and apocryphal passages he was early regarded in the Church as the helper of Christian armies against the heathen, and as a protector of individual Christians against the devil, esp. at the hour of death, when he conducts the souls to God, a belief still found in the Offertory of the Roman Mass for the Dead: 'Signifer S. Michael repraesentet eas in lucem sanctam'.

His cult originated in Phrygia where he was chiefly venerated as a healer, and many hot springs were dedicated to him both in Greece and Asia. The cult soon spread to the W., and in the *Leonine Sacramentary St. Michael is named in four of the five Masses for 30 Sept. of a dedication festival of a basilica erected in his honour on the Via Salaria. This feast, which is kept throughout the Church on 29 Sept., is identical with that of the BCP of St. Michael and All Angels. The cult of St. Michael in the W. Church received a strong impetus by the famous apparition on Mt. Garganus in the time of Pope *Gelasius, (492–6), in commemoration of which a feast is still kept in the RC Church on 8 May. Throughout the Middle Ages St. Michael enjoyed general veneration. His feast, 'Michaelmas Day', is connected with many popular usages and numerous churches are dedicated to him. He is usually represented with a sword, standing over, or fighting with, a dragon.

AA.SS., Sept. VIII (1762), pp. 4–123. W. Lueken, *Michael. Eine Darstellung und Vergleichung der jüdischen und der morgenländisch-christlichen Tradition vom Erzengel Michael* (1898). O. Rojdestvensky, *Le Culte de St. Michel et le moyen-âge latin* (1922); A. M. Renner, *Der Erzengel Michael in der Geistes- und Kunstgeschichte* (Saarbrücken, 1927). R. H. *Charles in *H.D.B.*, iii (1900), p. 362 f.; G. Löw, C.SS.R.–E. Josi, &c., in *E.C.*, viii (1952), cols. 948–54.

MICHAEL CERULARIUS (d. 1058), Patr. of *Constantinople from 1043, under whom the breach between the Eastern and Western Churches was finally consummated. Destined for a political career, he was deeply moved by the suicide of his brother in 1040 and suddenly became a monk. In outlook he was violently anti-Latin, fiercely attacking the *filioque and unleavened *bread in the Eucharist. The attempted mediation at Constantinople between a Roman legation, led by Cardinal *Humbert of Silva Candida, and the E. Emp., Constantine IX (Monomachus), failed; the Latins laid a bull of excommunication against the Easterns on the altar of *Santa Sophia; and Cerularius replied by anathemas (21 and 24 June 1054) and an encyclical embodying the Byzantine case. In his last years he probably took part in the political plot to put Isaac Comnenus on the throne in place of Michael VI (Stratiotikos).

Collection of his works in J. P. Migne, *PG*, cxx, 719–820, with reff., but incl. also material of an anterior date. Some of his correspondence also pr. in C. Will (ed.), *Acta et Scripta quae de Controversiis Ecclesiae Graecae et Latinae Saeculo*

Undecimo Composita Exstant (Leipzig–Marburg, 1861), pp. 65–85, 89–92, 153 f., and 172–204. V. Grumel, A.A. (ed.), *Les Régestes des actes du patriarcat de Constantinople*, I, iii (1947), pp. 1–16 (Nos. 856–86). A. Michel, *Humbert und Kerullarios* (Quellen und Forschungen aus dem Gebiete der Geschichte herausg. von der Görres-Gesellschaft, xxi and xxiii, 1925–30). Id., 'Verstreute Kerullarios- und Humbert-Texte' in *R.Q.*, xxxix (1931), pp. 355–76. M. Jugie, A.A., *Le Schisme byzantin* (1941), pp. 187–246. A. Laurent, A.A., 'Le Titre de patriarche œcuménique et Michel Cérulaire à propos de deux de ses sceaux inédits' in *Miscellanea Giovanni Mercati*, iii (S.T., cxxiii; 1946), pp. 373–86. A. *Fortescue in C.E.*, x (1911), p. 273 f., s.v.; É. Amann in *D.T.C.*, x (pt. 2; 1929), cols. 1677–1703, s.v. 'Michel (4) Cérulaire', with detailed reff.; A. Michel in *L.Th.K.*, vii (1935), col. 165 f., s.v. 'Michael Cärularius', for further bibl.

MICHAEL PSELLOS, See *Psellos, Michael*.

MICHAELIS, JOHANN DAVID (1717–1791), German Protestant theologian. He was professor of oriental languages and theology at Göttingen from 1746 to his death, and is important chiefly for his studies in Hebrew and Arabic and his research work on the early versions of the Bible, esp. the *Peshitto. In 1750 he published his critical *Einleitung in das NT*, and from 1769 to 1791 his influential annotated translation of the OT in 13 volumes. In his famous *Mosäisches Recht* (6 vols., 1770–1775; Eng. tr., 4 vols., 1840) he treated the legislation of the Pentateuch as a human achievement, and thus appeared to deny its character as Divine Revelation. His rationalist methods as well as his comprehensive linguistic studies had a far-reaching influence on the development of German Biblical criticism.

Michaelis's correspondence was ed. by J. G. Buhle, 3 vols., Leipzig, 1794–6. J. M. Hassencamp, *Leben des Herrn Johann David Michaelis, von ihm selbst beschrieben* (Rinteln, 1793). Oration ('Festrede') by R. Smend (Göttingen, 1898). R. Kittel in *P.R.E.* (ed. 3), xiii (1903), pp. 54–6.

MICHELANGELO (1475–1564), Italian Renaissance artist. Michelangiolo Buonarroti was the son of the Podestà of the village of Caprese. In 1488 he became the pupil of the Florentine painters Domenico and Davide Ghirlandaio, but, following his attraction for sculpture, went the next year to Bertoldo, a disciple of Donatello, who introduced him into the circle of Lorenzo the Magnificent (de' Medici). Here he learnt to appreciate the classic ideal of sensuous beauty, which was for a long time to struggle in him with the ideal of religious asceticism represented by his older contemporary *Savonarola. In 1496 he went to Rome, where he did a *Pietà* (finished in 1501) in which Christian austerity and classic beauty are admirably harmonized. During a temporary stay at Florence he carved his famous *David* (1502–4) as a symbol of the deliverance of the city from Cesare Borgia. In 1505 *Julius II called him back to Rome to execute the Papal tomb. His design, which was on so grand a scale that it would have been almost impossible to carry it through in a lifetime, seems to have been meant to represent the three orders of Nature, Law, and Grace in their relation to the Papacy. Its most important finished work is the great figure of *Moses* representing to perfection the majestic wrath of the Law-Giver of the Old Dispensation.

Between 1508 and 1512, under pressure from Julius II, Michelangelo painted the celebrated frescoes on the ceiling of the *Sistine Chapel. Their subject is the *praeparatio evangelica*, leading from the Creation of the world through temptation and sin to the Prophets of the OT and the Sybils of the Gentiles. The two frescoes representing the 'Creation of Light' and the 'Creation of Man' are among the most grandiose paintings of all time, combining in the Creator human tenderness with stupendous force. The artist continued in Papal employment under *Leo X and his successors, executing for them parts of his plan for a mortuary chapel of the Medici in San Lorenzo with its famous figures of Night and Day, Morning and Evening, representing the frailty of human greatness. From 1534 to 1541 he was engaged on the *Last Judgement* in the Sistine Chapel. After the death of his friend, Vittoria Colonna (1547), to whom he addressed many sonnets full of devotion and religious feeling, he was entrusted with the direction of the building of *St. Peter's, and he was engaged on this work till his death.

Editions of his letters by G. Milanesi (Florence, 1875); of his poems by C. Frey (Berlin, 1897). His sonnets were repr., with Eng. tr. and introd. by J. A. Symonds (London, 1950). Collection of reproductions (in black and white), ed. F. Knapp (Klassiker der Kunst in Gesamtausgaben, vii; 1906); of his painting, ed. L. Goldscheider (Phaidon Press, London [1939]); of his sculpture, by id. (ib. [1940]); of his drawings, by K. Frey (3 vols., Berlin, 1909–11), and selections by L. Goldscheider (Phaidon Press, 1951); selection of his paintings. sculpture, and architecture (some in colour), ed. id. (ib., 1953). Lives by C. Vasari (Florence, 1550), ed. K. Frey (Munich, 1911); by A. Condivi (Rome, 1553), ed. A. Maraini (Florence, 1927); an Eng. tr. of the latter was publd. at London, 1903. Modern studies by J. [A.] Symonds (2 vols., London, 1892), C. Justi (Leipzig, 1900), H. Thode (6 vols. bound in 7, Berlin, 1902–13), K. Frey (vol. i only publd., Berlin, 1907), G. Brandes (2 vols., Copenhagen, London, etc., 1921–31), A. Venturi (Rome, 1926; Eng. tr. 1928), J. H. Whitehouse–C. Rocke (London, 1934), David Lord Finlayson (New York–London, 1935), a series of studies by C. de Tolnay (Princeton, 1943 ff.), and studies by G. *Papini (Milan, 1949) and Agnes Allen (London, 1953). S. Colvin in *E.B.* (ed. 1), xviii (1911), pp. 362–9, sv. K. Tolnai in *Allgemeines Lexikon der bildenden Künstler* begründet von U. Thieme–F. Becker, xxiv, ed. H. Vollmer (1930), pp. 515–525, s.v., with detailed bibl.

MICHIGAN PAPYRUS OF ACTS. A 3rd–4th cent. fragment discovered in Egypt and now at Ann Arbor, Michigan (No. 1571), containing, in a very mutilated condition, the text of Acts 18. 27–19. 6 on the recto and 19. 12–16 on the verso. Apart from its early date, it is of great interest for its close affinities with the *Western text of the NT, which thus provide new evidence for the currency of that text in Egypt.

H. A. Sanders, 'A Papyrus Fragment of Acts in the Michigan Collection' in *H.T.R.*, xx (1927), pp. 1–19, with text p. 4 f. and facsimile reprod. between pp. 8 and 9. Text and facsimile reproduced, with discussion, in F. J. Foakes Jackson–K. *Lake, *The Beginnings of Christianity*, v (1933), pp. 262–8. A. C. Clark, 'The Michigan Fragment of the Acts' in *J.T.S.*, xxix (1928), pp. 18–28.

MICROLOGUS. An 11th cent. Roman *Mass book, attesting several practices, e.g. the omission of *Gloria in Excelsis* in *Advent and *Septuagesima and the use of *Placeat tibi after the dismissal, which later became universal in the Latin West. There is still never more than one *collect, the *Creed has not yet been introduced, *incense at the *Offertory is discouraged, and there is no Offertory prayer. The work was prob. composed by Bernold (*c.* 1054–1100), monk of Schaffhausen and strong defender of *Gregory VII (not, as was formerly held, by St. *Ivo of Chartres).

Editio princeps (incomplete), Paris, 1510. First complete ed. by J. Pamelius, Antwerp, 1560 (repr. in J. P. Migne, *PL*, cli, 973–1022). S. B[aeumer], O.S.B., 'L'Auteur du Micrologue' in *R. Bén.*, viii (1891), pp. 193–201, incl. text of two additional chapters, p. 200 f. G. *M[orin], O.S.B., 'Que "L'Auteur du Micrologue" est Bernold de Constance', ib., pp. 385–95; S. Bäumer, O.S.B., 'Der Micrologus ein Werk Bernold's von Konstanz' in *N.A.*, xviii (1892–3), pp. 429–46. F. *Cabrol, O.S.B., in *D.A.C.L.*, ii (pt. 1; 1910), cols. 817–20, s.v. 'Bernold (de Constance) et le Micrologue' and H. *Leclercq, O.S.B., ib., xi (pt. 1; 1933), cols. 908–12, s.v. 'Micrologue'; S. Mattei in *E.C.*, viii (1952), col. 979 f., s.v. 'Micrologus de Ecclesiasticis Observationibus'.

MIDDLE AGES, The. The era preceding the Renaissance, formerly taken to date from the fall of the W. Roman Empire in 476, but in more recent writers from *c.* 1100, and extending down to the end of the 15th cent. The conception of the 'medium aevum' is to be found in the writings of Flavio Biondo (1388–1463), and was in established use by 1467. Once viewed as a sterile period, it has come to be regarded as one of the most creative and fruitful periods in the world's history. For the historian of Christianity it has special interest as the age which approached most nearly the realization of Christendom as a cultural unity.

G. Gordon, *Medium Aevum and the Middle Age* (Society for Pure English. Tract xix; 1925).

MIDDLETON, THOMAS FANSHAWE (1769–1822), Bp. of Calcutta. After graduating at Pembroke College, Cambridge, he was ordained in 1792 and held a number of livings before being appointed vicar of St. Pancras in 1811. Three years later he was consecrated first Bishop of Calcutta, constituted as a vast diocese covering all the territories of the East India Company. His episcopate witnessed a great advance in Church life, including the foundation of the Bishop's College at Calcutta, a training college for missionaries in Asia, in 1820. Despite a somewhat chill exterior, Middleton was a man of great ability as well as a scholar of note, his chief work being *The Doctrine of the Greek Article applied to the Criticism and Illustration of the New Testament* (1808; revised ed. by H. J. *Rose, 1833).

C. W. Le Bas, *Life of T. F. Middleton* (2 vols., 1831). W. Wroth in *D.N.B.*, xxxvii (1894), pp. 363–5.

MID-LENT. See *Laetare Sunday*.

MIDRASH (Heb., 'investigation'). A Jewish method of Scriptural exegesis directed to the discovery in the sacred text of a meaning deeper than the literal one. The word appears in 2 Chr. 13. 22 and 24. 27 (E.V., 'commentary'), but has here scarcely acquired its technical meaning. Its basis was the belief that every detail of the text was significant, since it was all of Divine origin. It was of two kinds.

'Midrash Halacha' was concerned with the derivation of the '*Halacha' (Oral Law) from the Bible, while 'Midrash Haggadah' was the exposition of the non-legal parts of Scripture for purposes of edification. It originated in the period of the Soferim ('scribes'), of whom, acc. to Jewish tradition, *Ezra was the first. The earliest collections of Midrashim come, however, from the 2nd cent. A.D., although, since the scribes sought to preserve traditional material, much of their content is considerably older. Their study has illuminated many references in the Gospels to Jewish beliefs and practices and tended to confirm the general accuracy of the Gospel picture of contemporary Judaism.

Among the more important edd. are those of GEN. RABBAH by J. Theodor–C. Albeck (Berlin, 1912–29) and smaller Midrashim, ed. J. D. Eisenstein (New York, 1915) and S. A. Wertheimer (ed. 2, Jerusalem, 1950–3). The principal translations include: of the Tannaitic Midrashim, EXOD. tr. into Lat. by B. Ugolini, *Thesaurus Antiquitatum Sacrarum*, xiv (Venice, 1752), cols. i–dlxxxvi; tr. into Eng. by J. Lauterbach (Philadelphia, Pa., 1933) and into German by J. Winter–A. Wünsche (Leipzig, 1909); LEV. tr. into Lat. by B. Ugolini, op. cit., cols. dlxxxvii–mdcxxx; of NUM. and DEUT. also into Lat. by id., op. cit., xv (ib., 1753), cols. i–dccccxvi; of the earliest exegetical Midrashim, GEN. RABBAH, etc., into Eng. by H. Freedman–M. Simon and others (10 vols., London, 1939); Pentateuch-Scrolls tr. into Germ. by A. Wünsche (8 vols., Leipzig, 1880–3); of the Homiletic Midrashim, Pesikhta tr. into Germ. by A. Wünsche (Leipzig, 1885) and smaller collections tr. into Germ. by id., 5 vols. (ib., 1907–10); other exegetical Midrashim, Lekah tobh (wrongly called Pesikhta) on LEV.–DEUT. tr. into Lat. by B. Ugolini, op. cit., xv, cols. dccccxvi–mccxxvi, and xvi (ib., 1754); Midrash on Pss. into Germ. by A. Wünsche (2 vols., Trier, 1891–3); on PROV. into Germ. by id. (Leipzig, 1885). Index to Midrashic interpretations on the whole OT by A. Hyman, *Torah ha-Kethubhah we-ha-mesurah* (3 vols., Tel Aviv, 1937–40). L. Zunz, *Die gottesdienstlichen Vorträge der Juden* (1832; ed. 3, in Hebrew, Jerusalem, 1947). D. Hoffmann, *Zur Einleitung in die halachischen Midraschim* (Beilage zum Jahresbericht des Rabbiner-Seminars zu Berlin pro 1886–7 [1887]). W. Bacher, *Die exegetische Terminologie der jüdischen Traditionsliteratur* (2 parts [1899–]1905). H. Strack, *Einleitung in Talmud und Midraš* (ed. 5, 1930), pp. 195–226 (Eng. tr., Philadelphia, Pa., 1945), pp. 201–34 and 331–49. M. Waxman, *A History of Jewish Literature from the Close of the Bible to our own Days*, i (New York, 1930), pp. 138–52.

MIGETIUS (8th cent.), Spanish heretic. The little that is known of him comes from the letters of his opponents, esp. *Elipandus. He seems, perhaps under *Priscillianist influences, to have taught the curious doctrine that God was revealed successively in David (as Father), in Jesus (as Son), and in St. Paul (as Holy Ghost). He was condemned at synods held at Seville in 782 and 785.

É. Amann in *D.T.C.*, x (pt. 2; 1929), cols. 1720–2, s.v. See also bibls. to *Adoptianism* and *Elipandus*.

MIGNE, JACQUES PAUL (1800–75), editor and publisher of theological literature. A parish priest near Orléans from 1824 to 1833, he then went to Paris, where he founded a printing-house and published an immense collection of religious texts and dictionaries, notably the *Patrologia Latina*, a corpus of Latin ecclesiastical writers up to *Innocent III (217 vols., 1844–55), and the *Patrologia Graeca*, of Greek writers to 1439 (162 vols., Greek text with Latin trans., 1857–66). He used many editions since superseded and printers' errors abound, but for most of the authors the collections remain the standard means of reference and citation. Migne's commercial activities were disliked by H. L. Quelen, Abp. of Paris (1817–39); but subsequent archbishops were more favourable. In 1868 his workshops and stereotype moulds were destroyed by fire.

Useful index to *PG* by F. Cavallera (Paris, 1912); to the same series there is also a more elaborate *Index Locupletissimus* by T. Hopfner (2 vols., ib., 1928–45). P. Glorieux, *Pour revaloriser Migne. Tables rectificatives* (Mélanges de Science religieuse, IXᵉ Année, 1952. Cahier Supplémentaire). P. de Labriolle, 'Quelques Documents sur J. P. Migne, l'éditeur des deux Patrologies' in *Bulletin d'ancienne Littérature et d'Archéologie chrétiennes*, iii (1913), pp. 203–9. F. de Mely, 'L'Abbé Migne, l'homme et l'œuvre' in *Revue archéologique*, Sér. 5, i for Jan.–Jun. 1915 (1914), pp. 203–58. J. de Ghellinck, S.J., *Patristique et Moyen-Age*, ii (1947), pp. 23 f. L. Marchal in *D.T.C.*, x (pt. 2; 1929), cols. 1722–40, s.v.; H. *Leclercq, O.S.B., in *D.A.C.L.*, xi (pt. 1; 1933), cols. 941–57, s.v.

MILAN, Edict of. Early in 313, the Emps. *Constantine and Licinius met at Milan and agreed to recognize the legal personality of the Christian Churches and to tolerate all religions equally. Their policy marked the triumph of Christianity over *persecution, but did not 'establish' the Church. The document commonly known as the 'Edict of Milan' (it is not an edict and was not issued at Milan) is to be found in divergent forms, in *Lactantius (*De Mortibus Persecutorum*, xlviii) and *Eusebius (*Hist. Eccl.*, x. v).

O. Seeck, 'Das sogenannte Edikt von Mailand' in *Z.K.T.*, xii (1891), pp. 381–6. N. H. Baynes, *Constantine the Great and the Christian Church* (Raleigh Lecture for 1929; 1930), pp. 69–74 (full and valuable bibl.).

MILANESE RITE. See *Ambrosian Rite*.

MILDRED, St. (c. 700), Abbess of Minster-in-Thanet. Acc. to late and not wholly reliable sources (among them, *Goscelin, Thorn, *William of Malmesbury), she was the granddaughter of Penda, King of Mercia, and daughter of St. Ermenburga, the foundress and abbess of the nunnery at Minster. She was sent for education to the convent of Chelles near Paris, whence, after resisting strong inducements to marriage, she returned to Minster, and became a nun at her mother's house, later succeeding her as abbess. After the destruction of Minster by the Danes in 1011, two of the monasteries at *Canterbury (St. Augustine's and St. Gregory's) laid claim to the possession of her relics; the resulting dispute provoked Goscelin's 'Libellus contra usurpatores S. Mildrithae'. Later her remains found their way to Deventer in Holland. Feast day, 13 July (more recently, 20 Feb.).

Life repr. from J. Capgrave, with introd. and other late material, in *AA.SS.*, Jul. III (1723), pp. 512–23. Earlier material described in Hardy, i (pt. 1; 1862), pp. 376–84. *B.H.L.*, ii, 820 (Nos. 5960–94). W. *Stubbs in *D.C.B.*, iii (1882), p. 914 f., s.v.

MILIC, JOHN (d. 1374), pre-*Hussite reformer. After holding offices in the Imperial chancery of Charles IV, he abandoned (before the end of 1363) all his temporal interests and at Prague and elsewhere vigorously preached against the vices of the clergy. In 1367 he was imprisoned by the *Inquisition at Rome. His writings include a *Libellus de Antichristo* and many Latin sermons.

J. Loserth in *P.R.E.* (ed. 3), xiii (1903), pp. 68–72, s.v. 'Militsch von Kremsier'.

MILITANT, The Church. The body of Christians still on earth, as distinct from those in *Purgatory (*expectant), and those in *heaven (*triumphant) (see *Communion of Saints*). Cf. the 'Prayer for the Church Militant' in the BCP.

MILL, JOHN. See *Mills, John*.

MILL, WILLIAM HODGE (1792–1853), English orientalist and High Church divine. Educated at Trinity College, Cambridge, where he was elected Fellow in 1814, he was from 1820 to 1838 the first principal of Bishop's College, Calcutta. Here he became keenly interested in Arabic and Sanscrit studies and assisted with the publication of works in the Indian vernaculars for spreading the Christian faith. Forced through ill-health to return to England in 1838, he became chaplain to Abp. W. *Howley and *Hulsean advocate (1839) and later Regius professor of Hebrew at Cambridge (1848). His support of the 'Cambridge *Camden Society' did much to further the interests of Tractarian principles at the university.

His *Lectures on the Catechism*, delivered in the Parish Church of Brasted, Kent, were posthumously ed. by B. *Webb, his son-in-law (1856), who also ed., with notes, a second ed. of his *Five Sermons on the Temptation of Christ Our Lord in the Wilderness* preached before the University of Cambridge in Lent 1844 (1873). C. Bendall in *D.N.B.*, xxxvii (1894), p. 400, s.v.

MILLENARIANISM. The belief in a future 'millennium', i.e. in a thousand years preceding the Second Coming of Christ, during which He will reign upon earth in a kingdom of His saints and at its conclusion take them with Him into heaven. It is a Christian adaptation of conceptions of the Messianic kingdom on earth, such as were popular in late pre-Christian Jewish apocalyptic speculation, esp. in Dan., 2 Esdr., and the non-canonical Book of *Enoch.

Christian advocates of this teaching base their case mainly on the Book of Rev., by interpreting, e.g., ch. 20 in a strictly literal sense. In the early Church, Millenarianism was upheld principally among the *Gnostics and *Montanists, but also accepted by more orthodox writers, such as St. *Justin Martyr, St. *Irenaeus, and St. *Hippolytus of Rome. But though primitive Millenarianism lingered on in some places down to the end of the 4th cent., it received its death-blow from *Origen. In medieval times, though various apocalyptic opinions became current, e.g. among certain 13th cent. sectarians, Millenarianism properly so called was but rarely met with. At the *Reformation the *Anabaptists, as well as the *Bohemian and *Moravian Brethren, were Millenarians in the strictest sense, while the 17th cent. *Independents in England appear to have held similar views. In Germany the Millenarian view gained its widest currency in the *Pietist Movement of the 17th and 18th cents., while in the 19th cent. new advocates of apocalyptic and Millenarian views arose in the U.S.A. and in Great Britain, among them the *Irvingites, *Mormons, and *Adventists. Though Millenarianism has never been formally rejected by orthodox Christianity, it may be doubted whether there is adequate justification for it either in Scripture or in Christian tradition.

L. Atzberger, *Geschichte der christlichen Eschatologie innerhalb der vornicänischen Zeit* (1896), passim. V. Ermoni, 'Les Phases successives de l'erreur millénariste' in *R.H.Q.*, lxx (1901), pp. 353–88. L. Gry, *Le Millénarisme dans ses origines et son développement* [1904]. R. Janin, A.A., 'Le Millénarisme et l'Église grecque' in *É.O.*, xxvii (1928), pp. 201–210. J. Daniélou, S.J., 'La Typologie millénariste de la semaine dans le christianisme primitif' in *Vigiliae Christianae*, ii (1948), pp. 1–16. G. Bardy in *D.T.C.*, x (pt. 2; 1929), cols. 1760–3, s.v.; K. Algermissen in *L.Th.K.*, ii (1931), cols. 864–7, s.v. 'Chiliasmus'; H. *Leclercq, O.S.B. in *D.A.C.L.*, xi (pt. 1; 1933), cols. 1181–95, s.v.; A. Piolanti in *E.C.*, viii (1952), cols. 1008–11, s.v.; W. Bauer in *R.A.C.*, ii (1954), cols. 1073–8, s.v. 'Chiliasmus'; all with bibl. See also bibl. to *Eschatology, Adventists, Jehovah's Witnesses, Plymouth Brethren, Seventh Day Adventists*, etc.

MILLENARY PETITION. The petition presented in Apr. 1603 by the Puritans to *James I on his way from Scotland to London, in which they prayed to be relieved from their 'common burden of human rites and ceremonies'. It was so called from the thousand ministers whose wishes it professed to embody. The practices objected to included the cross in Baptism, *Confirmation, the surplice, the ring in marriage, the length of the service, the profanation of the Lord's Day, bowing at the name of Jesus, and the reading of the *Apocrypha in the lessons; but to avoid giving offence nothing was said against episcopacy as such. It was the immediate occasion of the *Hampton Court Conference (q.v.).

Text in T. *Fuller, *The Church History of Britain from the Birth of Jesus Christ to the Year M.DC.XLVIII* (1655), Book x, pp. 21–3 [Fuller's comments (p. 7; cf. also p. 23 f.) have very frequently been repeated]. Text also in Gee-Hardy, pp. 508–11 (No. 88). Useful note in S. R. Gardiner, *History of England from the Accession of James I to the Disgrace of Chief Justice Coke*, i (1863), p. 163 (note 1). See also bibl. to *Hampton Court Conference, James I*, and *Puritans*.

MILLS, JOHN (1645–1707), NT textual critic. From 1670 to 1682 he was a fellow of Queen's College, Oxford, and from 1685 till his death principal of St. Edmund Hall. His edition of the Greek text of the NT, published in 1707, was a great advance on any of its predecessors, as Mills added to it a critical apparatus containing the readings of nearly 100 MSS. He was also the first to lay down the principles of sound NT textual criticism. His correct name appears to have been 'Mills', not (as commonly given) 'Mill'.

D. *Whitby, *Examen Variantium Lectionum J. Milii . . . in Novum Testamentum* (Leyden, 1724; hostile). A. Fox, *John Mill and Richard Bentley. A Study of the Textual Criticism of the New Testament 1675–1729* (1954), pp. 3–102. B. Porter in *D.N.B.*, xxxvii (1894), pp. 388–90.

MILMAN, HENRY HART (1791–1868), Dean of St. Paul's. After a brilliant career at Oxford, Milman was ordained in 1816 and in 1818 appointed rector of St. Mary's, Reading. In early life he was known esp. as a poet and writer of plays, and held from 1821 to 1831 the professorship of poetry at Oxford, where he was the immediate predecessor of J. *Keble. In 1827 he delivered some undistinguished *Bampton Lectures on *The Character and Conduct of the Apostles considered as an Evidence of Christianity*. His *History of the Jews* (1829; anon.) first brought his name prominently before the theological world. The freedom and freshness with which it handled the OT narratives, treating the Jews as an oriental tribe and attaching relatively little weight to the influence of the miraculous, met with much criticism. In 1835 Peel made him rector of St. Margaret's, Westminster, and in 1849 he became Dean of St. Paul's. While in the latter office he published his well-known treatise on the *History of Latin Christianity* (1855), a work which, despite many blemishes in matters of detail, treated a vast subject with balance, candour, and sympathy, and did much to foster the intelligent study of medieval life and institutions. Among his other writings were editions of E. *Gibbon's *Decline and Fall* (1838) and of his Life and Correspondence (1839), a *History of Christianity to the Abolition of Paganism in The Roman Empire* (1840) and *Annals of St. Paul's Cathedral* (1868; posthumous).

The standard life is by his son, Arthur Milman (London, 1900; not entirely satisfactory). Shorter, but good, accounts which supplement the life, by A. P. *Stanley in *Macmillan's Magazine*, xix (1869), pp. 177–87; repr. in Stanley's *Essays chiefly on Questions of Church and State* (1870), pp. 572–91; [J. S. *Howson] in *The Quarterly Review*, cxxvi (1869), pp. 218–47; W. E. H. Lecky in *The Edinburgh Review*, cxci (1900), pp. 510–27; repr. in Lecky's *Historical and Political Essays* (1908), pp. 249–74; C. [H. E.] Smyth, *Dean Milman* (S.P.C.K., 1949). R. Garnett in *D.N.B.*, xxxvi (1894), pp. 1–4.

MILNER, ISAAC. See *Milner, Joseph*.

MILNER, JOHN (1752–1826), RC apologist. Educated at the English College at *Douai, he was ordained priest in 1777. He soon returned to England as a zealous propagandist for his creed, where, however, his extreme claims in the matter of Catholic Emancipation alienated many of his co-religionists. In 1803 he was appointed titular Bp. of Castabala and *Vicar-Apostolic of the Midland District. As an enthusiastic *Ultramontane, he eagerly pressed the case for Papal Infallibility. His chief work, *The End of Religious Controversy* (written 1801–2; published 1818; new edition by L. Rivington, 1896), forcefully presented the RC case in a series of letters, and has gone through many editions.

F. C. Husenbeth, *Life of John Milner* (1862). T. Cooper in *D.N.B.*, xxxviii (1894), pp. 14–16.

MILNER, JOSEPH (1744–97), *Evangelical divine. He was educated at Leeds grammar school and Catharine Hall, Cambridge. After ordination he was curate at Thorp Arch near Tadcaster, Yorks, until 1768 when he moved to Hull. In 1770 he became an ardent Evangelical, and for the rest of his life was successively curate and vicar of North Ferriby on the Humber. Shortly before his death, mainly through the efforts of W. *Wilberforce, he was presented to the living of Holy Trinity, Hull. His *History of the Church of Christ*, largely put into shape and extended by his brother, Isaac Milner (1750–1820, from 1791 Dean of *Carlisle) was brought out in stages between 1794 and 1809. Though inaccurate and uncritical, it won great popularity. Among Joseph Milner's other writings were *Gibbon's Account of Christianity Considered* (1781) and *Essays on Several Religious Subjects* (1789). After his death many of his sermons (*Practical Sermons*, 4 vols., 1800–30) were published.

Life by Isaac Milner, prefixed to Joseph Milner's *Practical Sermons* (London, 1800). J. H. Overton in *D.N.B.*, xxxviii (1894), p. 17 f.

MILTIADES (2nd cent.), early Christian *Apologist. *Tertullian (*Adv. Valent.* v) and *Eusebius (*H.E.*, V, xvii, 1 and 5) mention him as having written against the pagans and the Jews, as well as against the *Montanists and *Valentinians; but all his works are lost. He wrote in Asia Minor.

Testimonia on Miltiades assembled in J. C. T. Otto (ed.), *Corpus Apologetarum Christianorum Saeculi Secundi*, ix (Jena, 1872), pp. 364–73. Bardenhewer, i (1913), pp. 284–6. G. *Salmon in *D.C.B.*, iii (1882), p. 916 f., s.v.; E. Amann in *D.T.C.*, x (pt. 2; 1929), col. 1765, s.v.

MILTIADES, St. (d. 314), less correctly, Melchiades, Pope from 310 (or perhaps 311). Acc. to the *Liber Pontificalis*, he was an African by birth. His pontificate was remarkable for *Constantine's victory over Maxentius and the issue of the Edict of *Milan. In Oct. 313 he held a Council at the *Lateran at which *Donatism was condemned. J. B. *De Rossi believed, but on evidence now generally thought insufficient, that he had discovered his tomb in the Catacomb of St. Callistus. Feast day, 10 Dec.

L.P. (Duchesne), i, 8 f., 74 f., 168 f. E. Caspar, *Geschichte des Papsttums*, i (1930), pp. 103–15. J. B. de Rossi, *Roma sotterranea cristiana*, ii (1867), pp. 188–90 and pl. xxiii. H. *Leclercq, O.S.B., in *D.A.C.L.*, xi (pt. i; 1933), cols 1199–203, s.v.

MILTITZ, CARL VON (*c*. 1480–1529), Papal nuncio. Born near Meissen of a noble Saxon family, after studying at Mainz, Trier, and *Cologne, he made his way to *Rome where he was appointed Papal chamberlain (*c*. 1514) and acted as agent of *Frederick the Wise (III), Elector of Saxony. After Card. T. de V. *Cajetan's attempts to silence M. *Luther had failed, Miltitz, as a German who knew the Germans, was deputed, on pretence of taking the coveted *Golden Rose to Frederick, to negotiate with the Reformer. At a first meeting, held at Altenburg (4–6 Jan.

1519), Luther agreed to cease from further action pending reference of the matter to a German bishop, but made no offer of recantation. Miltitz then proceeded to Leipzig, where, in the hope of restraining the movement, he disavowed and attacked J. *Tetzel. He soon discovered that nothing could be achieved by conciliation and two further meetings with Luther, at Liebenwerda (5 Oct. 1519) and Lichtenberg, near *Wittenberg (12 Oct. 1520), were fruitless. After a further visit to Rome, he returned to Germany, where he spent his last years at Mainz and Meissen. He was accidentally drowned in the Main on 20 Nov. 1529 and was buried in Mainz Cathedral.

H. A. Creutzberg, *Karl von Miltitz, 1490–1529*. Sein Leben und seine geschichtliche Bedeutung (Studien und Darstellungen aus dem Gebiet der Geschichte, vi, Hft. 1; 1907). P. Kalkoff, *Die Miltitziade*. Eine kritische Nachlese zur Geschichte des Ablassstreites (1911).

MILTON, JOHN (1608–74), poet and controversialist. The son of a scrivener, he was educated at St. Paul's School, London, and at Christ's College, Cambridge (1625–32), where he won a high reputation for his scholarship and literary gifts; his famous *Ode on the Morning of Christ's Nativity* (1629) belongs to this period. From 1632 to 1638 he lived on his father's estate at Horton in Buckinghamshire. Having abandoned his original intention of taking orders because of the 'tyranny' that had invaded the Church under Abp. W. *Laud, he devoted himself entirely to scholarship and literature. Among his finest poems of this period are *L'Allegro* and *Il Penseroso*, expressing the two sides of his nature, torn between the desire for pleasure and the love of meditation and silence. In his *Comus, a Mask presented at Ludlow Castle*, 1634, he sings the praises of chastity in a dramatic poem. In 1637 he wrote the monody *Lycidas* on the death of a friend, containing a bitter satire on the clergy, one of his main themes in later years. Next year he travelled in Italy, and after his return moved to London, where he spent many years in political and religious controversy. In 1641 he joined the *Presbyterians and took part in the famous '*Smectymnuus' affair, and about the same time wrote *The Reason of Church Government Urged against Prelacy*, a bitter attack on the priesthood in which he saw only an instrument of tyranny. In 1643 he married Mary Powell, a member of a strongly Royalist family. She left him shortly afterwards, and as a result of his matrimonial misfortune he wrote *The Doctrine and Discipline of Divorce* (1643), in which he made a passionate appeal for the solubility of marriage on the grounds of incompatibility of character and declared the sanctity and sacramental character of marriage to be a clerical invention. The treatise, which roused a heated discussion, caused his break with the Presbyterians. Its publication without a licence from the censor led the case to be submitted to Parliament and drew from Milton the celebrated *Areopagitica* (1644) in defence of the freedom of the press. The book had a great success, and Parliament dropped the case. From this time his religious views tended more and more towards the *Independents, and he came to regard sects and schisms as a sign of health in the body politic. In 1645 he was reconciled to his wife, and in the same year published the first collection of his *Poems*. From 1649 Milton supported the new government. He defended the execution of the King in his *Tenure of Kings and Magistrates* (1649) and accepted a government post as secretary for foreign tongues, which involved chiefly the drafting of letters in Latin to foreign governments. In the same year he published *Eikonoklastes*, his reply to the royalist pamphlet *Eikon Basilike*. In 1651 he wrote his *Pro Populo Anglicano Defensio*, an answer to the accusations of regicide levelled (esp. by *Salmasius) against the English people. It was followed by the *Defensio Secunda* (1654). In 1651 he became totally blind, and in 1652 he lost his wife. Despite his admiration for O. *Cromwell he disagreed with the ecclesiastical policy of his later years, which ran counter to Milton's main idea of a complete disestablishment of Churches everywhere. After Cromwell's death his chief preoccupation was to prevent the re-establishment of the monarchy, and after the Restoration he was for a short time imprisoned. With the fall of his religious and political hopes he turned once more to poetry, and from 1658 to 1665 wrote his greatest work *Paradise Lost* (q.v., publd. 1667), in which he undertook to 'justify the ways of God to man' and to show the cause of evil and injustice in the world. In 1671 appeared its sequel *Paradise Regained*, which dealt with the temptation of Christ in the wilderness, and *Samson Agonistes*. In the latter, which described in dramatic form the last hours of Samson 'before the prison in Gaza', the blind hero partly represented Milton himself, a trait that added poignancy to the masterly representation of the tragic death of the OT hero. Milton's theological testament is contained in the treatise *De Doctrina Christiana*, which was published posthumously. It teaches much unorthodox doctrine, denying the coeternity and coequality of the Divine Persons as well as the dogma of creation *ex nihilo*, and asserting that matter is inherent in God. Despite his attachment to the Puritan party, his independent outlook can hardly be forced under a party label. His theological as well as his political opinions were highly individualistic and a strange blend of love of order and hierarchical values with the revolutionary ideas of a mind wishing to be a law to itself.

Collected ed. of his works in prose and verse by J. Milford (8 vols., London, 1851); fuller ed. by F. A. Patterson and others (18 vols. in 21 parts, New York, 1931–8, with index, 2 vols., ib., 1940). First ed. of his collected verse, 5 parts, fol., London, 1695; modern edd. include those by J. Bradshaw (Aldine ed. of British Poets, 2 vols., London, 1892), H. C. Beeching (Oxford, 1900), W. A. Wright (Cambridge, 1903), H. J. C. Grierson (London, 1925 ff.), H. F. Fletcher (Boston, Mass., 1941), and Helen Darbishire (Oxford, 1952 ff.); prose writings ed. J. *Toland (3 vols., fol., 'Amsterdam' [London], 1698); also ed. C. Symmons (7 vols., London, 1806) and J. A. St. John (5 vols., London, 1848–53). *Private Corre-spondence and Academic Exercises* tr. into Eng. by P. B. Tillyard, ed., with introd., by E. M. W. Tillyard (Cambridge, 1932), S. *Johnson, *The Lives of the English Poets*, i (Dublin, 1779), pp. 137–230 (often reprinted). Helen Darbishire (ed.), *The Early Lives of Milton* (1932), with useful introd. J. M. French (ed.), *The Life Records of John Milton* (New Brunswick, N.J., 1949 ff.). Standard life by D. Masson (6 vols., London, 1859–80, index, 1894). Other general studies include those by M. *Pattison ('English Men of Letters', 1879), R. Garnett (London, 1890), W. Raleigh (ib., 1900), E. M. W. Tillyard (ib., 1930), H. *Belloc (ib., 1935), F. E. Hutchinson (ib., 1946), and J. H. Hanford (ib., 1950). J. H. Hanford, *A Milton Handbook* (1926); E. M. W. Tillyard, *The Miltonic Setting, Past and Present* (1938); id., *Studies in Milton* (1951). D. Saurat, *La Pensée de Milton* (Paris thesis, 1920), expanded and tr. as *Milton, Man and Thinker* (1925). Dora N. Raymond, *Oliver's Secretary*. John Milton in an Era of Revolt (New York, 1932); D. M Wolfe, *Milton in the Puritan Revolution* (1931); A. Barker, *Milton and the Puritan Dilemma, 1641–1660* (University of Toronto, Department of English, Studies and Texts, i; 1942). A. Sewell, *A Study in Milton's Religious Doctrine* (1939). H. F. Fletcher, *The Use of the Bible in Milton's Prose* (University of Illinois Studies in Language and Literature, xiv, No. 3, 1929). R. D. Havens, *The Influence of Milton on English Poetry* (Cambridge, Mass., 1922). J. Bradshaw, *A Concordance to the Poetical Works of John Milton* (1894). D. H. Stevens, *Reference Guide to Milton from 1800 to the Present Day* (Chicago, 1930); addenda by H. F. Fletcher (University of Illinois Studies in Language and Literature, xvi, No. 1; 1931). G. Saintsbury in A. W. Ward–A. R. Waller (edd.), *The Cambridge History of English Literature*, vii (1911), pp. 95–141, with bibl. by G. A. Brown, pp. 413–23; further bibl. by D. H. Stevens in *C.B.E.L.*, i, 463–73. L. Stephen in *D.N.B.*, xxxviii (1894), pp. 24–41.

MILVIAN BRIDGE, Battle of the.

The battle on 28 Oct. 312 between the Emps. *Constantine and Maxentius (Emperor in Italy and Africa). Maxentius, who had made a sortie from Rome, met his rival advancing from the north, and after being outmanoeuvred was defeated at the 'Saxa Rubra' on the Flaminian Way. On taking flight he was drowned in the Tiber some five miles nearer Rome at the Ponte Milvio (whence the battle is somewhat inaccurately named). The battle was decisive for the history of Christianity, for it enabled Constantine to establish himself with Licinius as joint Emperor and thus prepared the way for the 'Edict of *Milan'.

N. H. Baynes, *Constantine the Great and the Christian Church* (Raleigh Lecture for 1929; 1930), p. 65 f. (full and valuable bibl.).

MINIMS (Ordo Fratrum Minimorum).

The order of friars founded in 1435 by St. *Francis of Paola. As their name indicates, they meant to practise humility as their chief virtue, regarding themselves as the least (*minimi*) of all religious. Their first rule, confirmed by *Alexander VI in 1493, was based on that of St. *Francis of Assisi, whereas the second one, sanctioned by the same Pope in 1501, was more or less independent. Its special characteristic is the fourth vow of perpetual abstinence not only from flesh meat, and fish, but also from eggs, cheese, butter, and milk. The superiors of the Minims are called 'correctors', the 'corrector-general' being elected for 6 years, the 'corrector-provincial' for 3. The members of the order wear a black habit. The order spread quickly and had already 5 provinces in Italy, France, Spain, and Germany at the death of its founder. It reached its greatest expansion in the first half of the 16th cent. with about 450 convents, but suffered severely in the times of revolution and secularization from 1791 to 1870. To-day it leads a very precarious existence in Italy and Spain. Its Second Order of enclosed nuns became extinct in 1903, but the *Third Order for people living in the world still exists.

G. Moretti, *Acta Capitulorum Generalium Ordinis Minimorum* (2 vols., Rome, 1916). G. M. Roberti, *Disegno storico dell' ordine dei Minimi* (3 vols., 1902–22), S. Mortola, *Martiri Minimi* (Genoa, 1926). Heimbucher, ii, 48–52, with bibl. L. Oliger, O.F.M., in *C.E.*, x (1911), p. 325 f., s.v.; G. Moretti in *E.C.*, viii (1952), cols. 1036–40, s.v. 'Minimi', with bibl.

MINISTER (Lat. 'servant'). A person officially charged to perform spiritual functions in the Christian Church. As a general designation for any clergyman, it is used esp. in nonepiscopal bodies. In the BCP it usually means the conductor of a service who may or may not be a priest. A Minister is also one who assists the higher orders in discharging their functions, and in this sense the *Deacon and *Subdeacon at *High Mass are known as the 'Sacred Ministers'. In yet another sense, the word is used semi-technically of one who 'administers' the outward and visible signs of a Sacrament. Thus should a layman baptize in a case of necessity, he would in that case be the 'minister' of the Sacrament.

MINOR CANON. A cleric attached to a cathedral or collegiate church to assist in the rendering of the daily service. He holds a position analogous to that of a *canon, but is not a member of the *chapter. In cathedrals of the 'Old Foundation' the Minor Canons are often known as 'Vicars Choral'. Originally the corporation of Minor Canons at *St. Paul's Cathedral consisted of 12 members, but by the 'St. Paul's Minor Canonries Act' (1840; 3 & 4 Vict. c. 113) the number was reduced to six (two retaining the title of 'cardinal').

MINOR ORDERS. The inferior degrees of the ministry, below the three *Major Orders of *bishops, *priests, and *deacons, to which, in the W., have been added *subdeacons. The latter were formally placed among the major orders by *Innocent III in 1207; until then they were commonly reckoned as minor orders, as they still are in the E. In the W. Church there are four minor orders, viz. porters, *lectors, *exorcists, and *acolytes, which are first mentioned in a letter of Pope *Cornelius to Fabius of Antioch in 252. In the E., since the *Trullan Council of 692, lectors and cantors have survived, whereas the other three, porters, exorcists, and acolytes, have been merged in the subdiaconate.

The rite by which minor orders are conferred differs essentially from ordination to holy orders. In the W. it has remained in essentials as laid down in the '*Statuta Ecclesiae Antiqua' (*c.* 500). It consists chiefly in a benediction and the handing-over of the instruments required by the different offices. Acc. to present RC usage the four minor orders are normally conferred on the same day. They are conferred by a bishop, but an abbot who has received the episcopal benediction may confer them on his own subjects. As the liturgical functions of the minor orders have been taken over either by the priesthood, as in the case of exorcism, or by the laity, as in the case of serving Mass, they are now no more than transitory stages to the priesthood and are usually conferred on students during their time at the seminary. Clerks in minor orders enjoy ecclesiastical privileges, but are not bound to celibacy.

MINOR PROPHETS, The. In the OT the authors of the twelve shorter Prophetic Books, as contrasted with the three Major Prophets—*Isaiah, *Jeremiah, and *Ezekiel. They are *Hosea, *Joel, *Amos, *Obadiah, *Jonah, *Micah, *Nahum, *Habakkuk, *Zephaniah, *Haggai, *Zechariah, and *Malachi. This, the usual order, is apparently based on chronological considerations, the place of Jonah doubtless being determined by his identification with the prophet of the same name in 2 Kgs. 14. 25. In the Greek Bible they were termed collectively the 'Twelve' (δωδεκαπρόφητον). *Daniel (acc. to modern critics on account of its late date) was assigned by the Jews to the *Hagiographa, and thus not included in the Hebrew Bibles in either Prophetic group, though in the Greek Bible he was grouped with Isaiah, Jeremiah, and Ezekiel to form the 'Four' (οἱ τέσσαρες).

Modern commentaries on the Minor Prophets include those by E. B. *Pusey (London, 1860, with index vol. 1891), J. Knabenbauer, S.J. (Cursus Scripturae Sacrae, 2 vols., Paris, 1886), J. *Wellhausen (Skizzen und Vorarbeiten by id., v; Berlin, 1892), G. A. *Smith (Expositor's Bible, 2 vols., 1896–8), W. Nowack (H.K.A.T., Abt. 3, Bd. iv; 1897), R. F. Horton–S. R. Driver (Cent. Bib., 2 vols. [1904–6]), K. Marti (K.H.A.T., Abt., xiii; 1904), A. van Hoonacker (Études Bibliques, 1908), E. Sellin (K.A.T., xii; 1922), T. H. Robinson–F. Horst (H.A.T., Reihe 1, Bd. xiv; 1936 ff.), and A. Weiser (Das Alte Testament Deutsch, xxiv–xxv; 1949). See also bibl. to individual Books.

MINORITES. An older name for the *Franciscan 'Friars Minor'. The street in London called the 'Minories' (E.C.3) takes its name from a convent of the 'Minoresses' (Minorite nuns).

MINSTER (Lat. *monasterium*, 'monastery'; cf. Ger. *Münster*). A name applied to certain cathedrals and other large churches in England, esp. the cathedrals of *York, *Lincoln, *Ripon, *Southwell, and *Lichfield, and the churches at *Beverley, Wimborne, &c. As a common noun it originally meant any monastic establishment or its church, whether strictly a monastery (e.g. the abbey at *Westminster), or a house or college of secular canons (which was also often called 'monasterium' in the Middle Ages), such as were all those mentioned above. The word 'minster' also occurs in place-names (e.g. Minster Lovell), usually implying the site of a house of secular canons.

MINUCIUS FELIX (2nd or 3rd cent.), author of the 'Octavius'. Apparently an African, he wrote in Latin an elegant defence of Christianity in the form of a conversation between Octavius, a Christian, and Caecilius, a pagan, who was converted by the argument. The book refutes the common charges against Christians (see *Persecutions*), argues the case for monotheism and providence, and attacks pagan mythology, but says little of specifically Christian doctrines. It is probably a 3rd cent. work, dependent on *Tertullian's 'Apology' (197), though some scholars believe it to be Tertullian's source.

The 'Octavius' survives in a poor text in Cod. Par. 1661 (saec. ix), where it appears as Bk. VIII of *Arnobius *Adversus Nationes*. *Editio princeps* in Works of Arnobius, ed. Rome. 1543. Crit. edd. by C. Halm (C.S.E.L., 1867), J. P. Waltzing (Louvain, 1903; ed. Teub., Leipzig, 1926), G. Rauschen (Bonn, 1913), J. Martin (Bonn, 1930), G. H. Rendall (Loeb, 1931), and M. Pellegrino (Turin, 1950; with Introd. and Comm.). J. P. Migne, *PL*, iii. 193–652. Further Eng. trr. by R. E. Wallis in A.N.C.L., xiii (1869), pp. 451–517, and by J. H. Freese (Early Church Classics, 1918). P. Monceaux, *Histoire littéraire de l'Afrique chrétienne*, i (1901), pp. 463–508. H. J. Baylis, *Minucius Felix and his Place among the Early Fathers of the Latin Church* (S.P.C.K., 1928). Bardenhewer, i, 329–43; Altaner (ed. 1950), pp. 120–2, with bibl.

MINUSCULE SCRIPT. See *Cursive Script*.

MIRACLE. Acc. to the traditional view, a miracle is a sensible fact (*opus sensibile*) produced by the special intervention of God for a religious end, transcending the normal order of things usually termed the Law of Nature. The possibility of miracles began to be questioned with the rise of modern science in the 17th and 18th cents., with its ever growing tendency to regard the world in which we live as a closed system, subject to the laws of nature, and to exclude all interference from a higher power. Neither *pantheism (B. *Spinoza, G. W. F. *Hegel), which identifies God with the Law of Nature, nor *Deism (J. *Toland, M. *Tindal), which separates God from the world, nor 18th cent. thought as represented by the scepticism of D. *Hume, accorded a place to supernatural intervention. Thus the miracles of Scripture and Church history were normally regarded as facts within the sphere of natural explanation, misrepresented by credulous contemporaries, and the term 'miracle' came to be treated as a cover for human ignorance. Such views were widely held by rationalistic exponents of Christianity in the 19th cent., e.g. E. *Renan, D. F. *Strauss, T. H. *Huxley, and M. *Arnold.

In support of the traditional belief it is argued that on a genuinely theistic view miracles are not only possible but even probable, for if God be held to be the supreme First Cause responsible for, but not subject to, the Laws of Nature, it would be likely that He should, from time to time, act directly without the intervention of secondary causes. The latest developments in the field of science, which move further and further away from a hard-and-fast determinism, may indicate an

approaching reconciliation between the Christian tradition and modern scientific research.

Whereas Protestant orthodoxy normally confines itself to belief in the miracles recorded in Scripture, Catholic orthodoxy claims that miracles have at all times occurred within the pale of the Church. The reputed cures at *Lourdes are among the best known, and acc. to RC *canon law (*CIC*, can. 2117), two to four well-authenticated miracles after death are required for the beatification of a saint, though belief in any of these miracles is not demanded of the faithful as *de fide*.

J. B. *Mozley, *Eight Lectures on Miracles* [*Bampton Lectures] (1865); F. R. Tennant, *Miracle and its Philosophical Presuppositions*, Three Lectures (1925). On the NT miracles, R. C. *Trench, *Notes on the Miracles of our Lord* (1846); A. C. Headlam, *The Miracles of the New Testament* (1914); A. Richardson, *The Miracle-Stories of the Gospels* (1941); C. S. Lewis, *Miracles*. A Preliminary Study (1947). A. Fridrichsen, *Le Problème du miracle dans le christianisme primitif* (Études d'histoire et de philosophie religieuses 12, Strassburg, 1925).

MIRACLE PLAY. See *Mystery Play*.

MIRARI VOS. *Gregory XVI's encyclical (15 Aug. 1832) condemning the social and political doctrines of F. R. de *Lamennais and his circle. Without naming Lamennais it censured his writings in defence of social liberty as inciting to sedition and as contrary to the spirit of obedience inculcated by the Gospel, as well as his teaching on the liberty of worship and of the press as opposed to the maxims of the Church. Its reactionary standpoint foreshadowed the *Syllabus Errorum* of 1864. After Lamennais's reply in *Paroles d'un croyant* the Pope reiterated the condemnations in the encyclical 'Singulari Nos' of 25 June 1834.

Text of 'Mirari Vos' is pr. among the *Acta Gregorii Papae XVI*, ed. A. M. Bernasconius, i (Rome, 1901), pp. 169–74; text of 'Singulari Nos', ib., iii (Rome, 1902), pp. 356–8; the principal clauses are repr. in Denz.–Bann. (ed. 1952), p. 447 f. (Nos. 1613–16) and p. 448 f. (No. 1617) respectively, with reff. to other edd. of texts. See also bibl. to *Lamennais*.

MIRFIELD. See *Community of the Resurrection*.

MIRK, JOHN. See *Myrc, John*.

MISERERE. A common designation of Ps. 51 (Vulg. 50) derived from the initial word of the Latin version, 'Miserere mei, Deus'. The term is sometimes inaccurately applied to the '*misericord'.

MISERICORD (Lat. *misericordia*, 'mercy'). The projection on the underside of a hinged seat of a choir-stall, commonly said to have been designed to provide support to those incapable of standing for long periods during Divine worship. The term is also sometimes used of a room set apart in a monastery for the use of those monks whose health or age requires some relaxation of the observance of the rule.

F. Bond, *Wood Carvings in English Churches*, i, 'Misericords' (1910), with bibl. M. D. Anderson, *Misericords* (King Penguin Books, lxxii; 1954).

MISHNAH (Heb., מִשְׁנָה, 'instruction'). The authoritative collection of the Jewish Oral Law which, in different recensions, forms the basis of both the Palestinian and Babylonian versions of the *Talmud. Acc. to a prob. correct tradition, the Mishnah itself was compiled by R. Judah ha-Nasi (135–c. 220). From the early 3rd cent. A.D. it supplanted the numerous earlier collections and so put an end to much confusion. It is not an original work but a redaction of earlier material, and it is written in the Hebrew characteristic of Jewish scholars of the time. Each of the six divisions—Seeds (laws on agriculture), Festivals, Women (marriage laws), Injuries (civil and criminal law), Holy Things (ritual law), Purifications—is divided into parts ('Tractates'), the parts urther subdivided into chapters, and the chapters into paragraphs. Among the Tractates are the well-known 'Yoma' (on the Day of *Atonement) and the '*Pirqe Aboth' (q.v.).

The Mishnah and Talmud have had an influence on the life of Judaism second only to that of the Scriptures, and its study is an essential part of Jewish education. Its authority rests on the view that the Oral Law was given to Moses on *Sinai at the same time as the Written Law and so is of Divine origin, a view originally peculiar to the *Pharisees, but which, through the leading part they took in the reorganization of Jewish life after the fall of Jerusalem in A.D. 70, became that generally accepted by Judaism. In a wider sense the word 'Mishnah' was used of the teaching and learning of the tradition and then of the tradition itself, the study of which goes back at least to the 2nd cent. B.C. See also *Tosefta*.

Editio princeps publd. at Naples, 1492. There is no crit. ed. of the Heb. text; the ed. with most comprehensive comm. is that publd. by Widow Romm and Brothers, Vilna, ed. 50, 6 vols., 1922. There are many translations of the Mishnah into Western languages; good Eng. version by H. Danby, Oxford, 1933, with introd. and notes. Concordance to Heb. text by H. J. Kassowski (2 vols., Frankfurt a.M., 1927). C. Albeck, *Untersuchungen über die Redaktion der Mischna* (Veröffentlichungen der Akademie für die Wissenschaft des Judentums, Talmudische Sektion, ii; 1923). S. Rosenblatt, *The Interpretation of the Bible in the Mishnah* (Baltimore, 1935). H. Strack, *Einleitung in Talmud und Midras* (ed. 5, 1930), pp. 23–64; Eng. tr. (Philadelphia, 1945), pp. 26–64. The best general study is that by J. N. Epstein (in Hebrew; 2 vols., Jerusalem, 1948). Mod. ed., with Eng. tr., by P. Blackman, 7 vols., London, 1951–6. J. Z. Lauterbach in *J.E.*, viii (1904), pp. 609–19, s.v.

MISRULE, Lord of, also known as the **Abbot (or Master) of Misrule.** In medieval times, a person selected to preside over the Christmas revels and games. The custom was closely connected with the 'Feast of *Fools' kept at this season, it being the practice to nominate at the celebration a 'precentor of the fools' (*praecentor stultorum*). In a secularized form the institution survived till the 17th cent. See also *Boy Bishop*; *Asses, Feast of.*

E. K. Chambers, *The Medieval Stage* (1903), i, 390–419 ('Masks and Misrule').

MISSA CANTATA (Lat. 'Sung Mass'). In the W. Church the form of celebrating Mass in which the celebrant and congregation sing the liturgical parts of the rite set to music for High Mass, but without *deacon and *subdeacon. It is in essence a simplification of High Mass, esp. used in places where there are insufficient ministers for the full ceremonial.

Jungmann (ed. 1949), pp. 263–9; Eng. tr. (1951), pp. 207–12.

MISSA CATECHUMENORUM. See *Catechumens, Mass of the.*

MISSA FIDELIUM. See *Faithful, Mass of the.*

MISSA ILLYRICA. A mass *ordo* published by M. *Flacius 'Illyricus' at Strassburg in 1557. Acc. to J. Braun, it was composed at Minden for the use of Bp. Sigebert (c. 1030). (F. *Cabrol's contention that it came from the Court of Charlemagne rests on a confusion between *Alcuin and the Ps.-Alcuin of the 10th cent.) It is characterized by the unusually large number of 'apologiae' (i.e. avowals of personal unworthiness interpolated into the Liturgy by the Celebrant) at various points of the rite. Flacius, who argued that the rite was free from the corruptions of Medieval Eucharistic doctrine, wrongly dated the Mass at c. 700. The stir which its publication created among 16th cent. theologians and liturgists was in no way justified by its contents.

The text is repr. in E. *Martène, *De antiquis Ecclesiae Ritibus* (Rouen, 1700), Lib. I, cap. 4, Ordo 4 (vol. i, pp. 481–513); also in J. P. Migne, *PL*, cxxxviii, 1305–36. J. Braun, 'Alter und Herkunft der sog. *Missa Illyrica*' in *Stimmen aus Maria Laach*, lxix (1905, ii), pp. 143–55. F. Cabrol, O.S.B., in *D.A.C.L.*, v (pt. 2; 1923), cols. 1625–35, s.v. 'Flacius Illyricus (La Messe latine de)'.

MISSAL (Lat. *Liber missalis*, also *Missale*). The book containing all that is necessary to be sung or said at, with ceremonial directions for, the celebration of the *Mass throughout the year. As a liturgical book, the Missal began to make its appearance with the 10th cent. as a combination of the *Antiphonary, the *Gradual, the *Epistolary and *Evangeliary, and the *Ordo with the *Sacramentary.

Selection of early Missals pr. in the publications of the Surtees Society and of the *Henry Bradshaw Society and in the *Beuron *Texte und Arbeiten.* The growth of the Missal is discussed in all histories of the Roman Mass; brief account in P. *Batiffol, *Leçons sur la messe* (ed. 2, 1919), pp. 1–10. A. Ebner, *Quellen und Forschungen zur Geschichte und Kunstgeschichte des Missale Romanum im Mittelalater.* Iter Italicum (1896). J. Baudot, O.S.B., *Le Missel romain. Ses origines, son histoire* (2 vols., 1912). A. *Baumstark, *Missale Romanum* (Eindhoven, 1930). H. Grisar, S.J., *Das Missale im Lichte der römischen Stadtgeschichte* (1925). J. B. Ferreres, *Historia del misal romano* (Barcelona, 1929). W. H. I. Weale, *Bibliographia Liturgica.* Catalogus Missalium Ritus Latini . . . Impressorum (London, 1886; ed. H. Bohatta, 1948). F. *Cabrol, O.S.B., in *D.A.C.L.*, xi (pt. 2; 1934), cols. 1431–68 and 1468–94, s.v. 'Missel' and 'Missel romain'; A. P. Frutaz-G. Ronci in *E.C.*, viii (1952), cols. 831–41, s.v. 'Messale'.

MISSALE FRANCORUM. An incomplete Sacramentary, formerly thought to be of Gallican *provenance*, but now generally recognized to be closely related to the (Roman) *Gelasian Sacramentary. It contains rites of Ordination, of the blessing of virgins and widows, and of the consecration of altars, and eleven Masses, concluding with the *Canon of the *Roman Mass as far as *Nobis quoque peccatoribus*. The MS., which is in *uncials, was written in France *c.* 700. In the 13th cent. it was in the possession of the abbey of *St.-Denis and is now in the *Vatican Library (Lat. Reg. 257).

The text has been edited by G. M.*Tommasi (Rome, 1680), J. *Mabillon (Paris, 1685; reprinted in J. P. *Migne, *PL*, lxxii, 317-40), and by L. A. *Muratori (Venice, 1748).

MISSALE GOTHICUM. A *Gallican *Sacramentary, now in the *Vatican (Reg. 317). It contains Masses of the season from Christmas Eve to Whitsunday interspersed with some for saints' days, and followed by Masses for the *Common of Saints, six Sunday Masses, and a fragment of a Mass for use on ferias described as 'romensis'. Some of its formularies are Roman, but the arrangement throughout is acc. to the order of the Gallican Mass. It was written for use in a French church *c.* 700. The misleading title, 'Missale Gothicum', which was added to the MS. in the 15th cent., wrongly suggested to G. M. *Tommasi, its first editor, that it was from the province of Narbonne when under Visigothic rule. It was prob. drawn up for the Church of Autun.

Earlier editions by G. M. Tomasi (Rome, 1680), J. *Mabillon (Paris, 1685; reprinted in J. P. Migne, *PL*, lxxii, 225-318), L. A. *Muratori (Venice, 1748), A. F. Vezzozi (Rome, 1747), and J. M. *Neale (Burntisland, 1855). Critical edition, with introduction and notes, by H. M. Bannister in the *Henry Bradshaw Society's texts, vols. lii (1917 for 1916) and liv (1919 for 1917). Facsimile edition by C. Mohlberg, O.S.B., 2 vols. (Tafelband and Textband), Augsburg, 1929.

MISSALE SPECIALE CONSTANTI-ENSE. See *Constance Missal*.

MISSIONS. Missionary enterprise, i.e. the propagation of the Christian faith among non-Christian people, was one of the main tasks of the Christian Church from its beginning. It was, indeed, implicit in the Lord's teaching (e.g. Mt. 28. 19; Lk. 24. 47). Apart from the labours of St. *Paul and the legendary missionary journeys attributed to the Apostles, unknown missionaries soon carried the Christian Gospel to the far corners of the Roman world (including Britain). In the early period one should notice *Pantaenus in 'India' (*c.* 190), St. *Gregory the Illuminator in Armenia (*c.* 312), the Arian *Ulfilas among the Goths (*c.* 325), *Frumentius in Abyssinia (*c.* 330) and the remarkable developments in the *Nestorian Church of the East, whose missionaries penetrated as far as *Ceylon, *Malabar and *China (where the Church was esp. active during the 7th and 8th cents.). In the West, St. *Patrick's work in *Ireland (early 5th cent.) was followed by intensive *Celtic missionary enterprise embracing *Scotland (where St. *Columba established the monastery of *Iona, and further advance was made during the 5th to 7th cents. by St. *Ninian, St. *Kentigern, and St. Maol Rubh', Gaul (where St. *Columbanus worked), and England, where St. *Aidan's work in the North was supplemented in the South by the Roman missions of St. *Augustine

and St. *Birinus (7th cent.). So successful was the evangelization of Great Britain, that in the 8th cent. English missionaries took a prominent part in evangelizing the more pagan parts of Europe. Most notable was the work of St. *Willibrord (in Frisia) and St. *Boniface (in Thuringia and Hesse). The conversion of Scandinavia (where the task was long and difficult) also owed much to English missionary enterprise. Of the missionaries to *Sweden in the 9th cent. St. *Anskar is the most notable. The conquests of *Charlemagne (d. 814) were accompanied by the forcible baptism of the vanquished to the Christian faith. In Slavonic lands the chief missionaries were St. *Cyril and St. Methodius (9th cent.), Bulgaria witnessing a struggle between the rival 'missionary' interests of Rome and Constantinople. This early stage of missionary enterprise culminated in the conversion of the *Poles, the Magyars (esp. through St. *Stephen in the 10th cent.), and the *Russians (esp. through St. *Vladimir, 986-1015).

The medieval period proper witnessed three aspects of missionary work:

(1) Efforts were made to convert the remaining heathen tribes in Europe. The task was gradually completed through the labours of St. *Adalbert (the martyr-apostle of Prussia), Vicelin (among the Wends), Meinhard and Albert of Apeldern (in Livonia), the Teutonic Knights and others.

(2) Missions among the Moslems were initiated. Though St. *Francis of Assisi may well claim to have begun this branch of missionary activity, the missions were overshadowed by the Crusades until the end of the medieval period. The need for more specific missionary work was urged, however, by the Spanish mystic, Raymond *Lull, who died a martyr at Bougie, North Africa, in 1315.

(3) Work was carried on further afield among Tartars, Chinese, and, to a lesser extent, Indians (e.g. Bishop Jordanus in the 14th cent.). In 1245 *Innocent IV sent two embassies, whilst a few years later St. *Louis IX sent a Franciscan, William of Rubruck, to the Mongols. The Emperor Kublai, whose court the Polo brothers visited at the end of the 13th cent., apparently asked for more information about Christianity, and, although his request went for the moment unanswered, missionaries very soon penetrated his dominions. The Franciscan, John de Monte Corvino, who worked for over thirty years in China until his death in 1328, made many converts, and even hoped to convert the Emperor himself. His work included a translation of the NT and Pss. The success of such missionary enterprise was impeded by the nationalist and isolationist policy pursued by the Ming dynasty, whilst in the Nearer East, for which *John XXII had appointed an archbishop with his seat at the Ilkhan's capital, Sultaniyah, in 1318, further advance was stayed by the invasions of Timur (1380-1405).

With the Reformation missionary enterprise slackened, particularly in the Reformed

Churches which were busily engaged in establishing themselves against the attacks of the *Counter-Reformation, whilst the seas were chiefly the preserve of Roman *Spain and *Portugal. In addition, the ultra-Calvinist *predestinarianism held by some of the Churches was not conducive to further evangelism, while the rise of individualism, sponsored by the Reformation, was more likely to encourage civil strife between the denominations that had sprung up than to call forth a concerted effort to evangelize the non-Christian world. In the Roman Church, however, the Counter-Reformation brought with it a rebirth of missionary work. New gains were sought to counteract the losses in north-western Europe, and the *Dominicans, *Franciscans, *Augustinians and newly formed *Jesuits did heroic work in the Americas, in India, *Japan, and China (where the RC Church flourished in the 17th cent.), whilst work was later begun in Africa. In 1622 Gregory XV formed the *Congregatio de propaganda fide* (popularly, the *Propaganda), which subsequently had the general supervision of all missionary work. In the 18th cent. the religious climate and political conditions in Europe brought missionary expansion temporarily to a standstill. But early in the 19th cent. the RC foreign missions, supported by such societies as the 'Association for the Propagation of the Faith' (founded 1822), experienced a powerful revival. Notable in this last period has been the prominence given to charitable and educational works and also the important part taken by women religious, who had hitherto been practically excluded from the apostolate abroad. It has been estimated that the number of converts to Catholicism from paganism in mission areas in the 19th cent. was over 8,000,000.

In the Reformed Churches there was, at first, little activity, but gradually Societies sprang up. In England a Corporation for the Propagation of the Gospel in New England was founded in 1649, but more important were the establishment of the *S.P.C.K. (1698) and the *S.P.G. (1701), both largely inspired by Dr. Thomas *Bray. None the less, the main success and burden of missionary work rested with the *Moravians, who under the inspiration of Count N. L. *Zinzendorf regarded themselves as a Missionary community, and the Danish-Halle missions in India. Through the influence of the *Evangelical Revival, fostered in England by the work of the *Wesleys and G. *Whitefield, a new impetus was given to evangelization on a world-wide scale, which has caused Prof. K. Latourette to speak of the 19th cent. as the 'Great Century' in this respect. The *Methodist Missionary Society dates its origin from 1786 and the Baptist Missionary Society from 1792, the Baptist, W. *Carey, sailing for India in 1793. They were followed by the founding of the London Missionary Society (*L.M.S., 1795), the Church Missionary Society (*C.M.S., 1799), the *British and Foreign Bible Society (1804), and the London Society for Promoting Christianity amongst the Jews (1809). In the meantime,

similar organizations were springing up in America, Germany, France, Scandinavia, and Holland. The phenomenal expansion of the work saw the rise of innumerable Societies, most being specialized in their sphere of activity. Among the larger of these in England were the South American Missionary Society (1844), the Melanesian Mission (1846), and the *Universities' Mission to Central Africa (1859), the last-named being the outcome of the challenge sent out by D. *Livingstone.

The evangelistic missions held by D. L. *Moody in America and England were largely responsible for the rise of a distinctive feature in more modern missionary effort—the interdenominational Missionary Society. Of such Societies the largest is the *China Inland Mission (1865), founded by J. Hudson *Taylor, but many have in the 20th cent. reached large proportions, with work in most parts of the world.

In addition, there has been a vast advance in the scope and method of evangelistic work, esp. in connexion with native literature, education, and medical service, whilst the rise of an indigenous Church has been sponsored in many lands (e.g. Nippon Sei Ko Kwei and the *South India Church). The development of the last century was witnessed at the *Tambaram Conference (1938), when there were present representatives from lands that had not been evangelized 100 years before.

Missionary enthusiasm has continued unabated in the 20th cent. despite the obstacles presented by two major wars, although the new commitments of the missionary societies have not always been accompanied by an adequate intake of recruits. Such movements as the Student Volunteer Movement and the Inter-Varsity Missionary Fellowship have, however, been instrumental in keeping alive the challenge. It is generally recognized that a new stage in missionary work has been reached, where direct evangelism becomes subordinate to the establishing and strengthening of the native Churches, although fields for pioneering still remain in South America, Central Asia and parts of Africa and Europe.

K. S. Latourette, *History of the Expansion of Christianity* (7 vols., 1939–45). Also A. Grant, *The Past and Prospective Extension of the Gospel* (*Bampton Lectures for 1843; repr. 1910); G. Warneck, *Geschichte der protestantischen Missionen* (ed. 10, 1913; Eng. trans., ed. 7, 1901); Louise Creighton, *Missions* (H.U.L., 1912); C. H. Robinson, *History of Christian Missions* (1915); B. Arens, S.J., *Handbuch der katholischen Missionen* (1925); J. T. Addison, *The Medieval Missionary* (1936); H. Kraemer, *The Christian Message in a Non-Christian World* (1938); J. I. Parker, *Interpretative Statistical Survey of the World Mission of the Christian Church* (1938); G. Phillips, *The Gospel in the World* (1939); J. J. Considine, *Across a World* (1942); E. A. Payne, *The Church Awakes* (1942); M. S. Bates, *Data on the Distribution of the Missionary Enterprise* (1943); S. Bolshakoff, *The Foreign Missions of the Russian Orthodox Church* (1943); G. Phillips, *The Transmission of the Faith* (1946). Also Reports of the International Missionary Conferences at *Edinburgh (1910), Jerusalem (1928), and Tambaram (1938), and histories of individual missionary societies, missionary orders, and countries.

MIT BRENNENDER SORGE (Ger., 'with burning anxiety'). The German encyclical of *Pius XI read from all Roman Catholic pulpits in Germany on *Palm Sunday, 21 Mar. 1937. In it the Pope, whose fear of Communism had induced him to make a Concordat with A. Hitler in 1933, gave unequivocal expression to his belief that Nazism is fundamentally unchristian. It denounced Nazi breaches of the Concordat, and attacked the idea of a German National Church, the abolition of the OT from the schools, and other views typical of the '*German-Christians' which the Nazis were imposing on the Church.

Text in *A.A.S.*, xxix (1937), ling. Ger., pp. 145–67; ling. Ital., pp. 168–88.

MITHRAISM. The cult of Mithras, an old Persian and Indian sun-god, which spread over the empire of Alexander the Great, is said to have reached Rome in 67 B.C. Commodus (180–92) made it an Imperial cult. Its monuments are very common in the frontier districts of the Roman Empire, for Mithras had a great appeal to soldiers. All creatures were supposed to be sprung from the bull which he had overcome and sacrificed before he ascended into heaven, where he guaranteed a blessed immortality to those who had been initiated into his mysteries—by baptism, purification by honey, and the use of bread, water, and wine consecrated by priests, called 'fathers', who enjoined a high moral code. The similarities with Christianity were so striking to *Tertullian that he tried to explain them by supposing that the devil had inspired a deliberate parody of the Christian sacraments. Possibly the resemblances are due partly to mutual influence, and also to common affinities with primitive religion and the meeting of a common need. Mithraism was almost completely superseded by Christianity in the 4th cent.

The primary collection of sources is F. Cumont, *Textes et monuments figurés relatifs aux mystères de Mithra* (2 vols., Brussels, 1896–9). Id., *Les Mystères de Mithra* (ib., 1900; ed. 3, 1913; Eng. tr., Chicago, 1903); an abridgment of Cumont's earlier work with addit. bibl. A. Dieterich; *Eine Mithrasliturgie* (1903; ed. 2, 1910). F. Saxl, *Mithras. Typengeschichtliche Untersuchungen* (1931). M. J. Vermaseren, *De Mithrasdienst in Rome* (Nijmegen, 1951). W. J. Phythian Adams, *Mithraism* (Religions Ancient and Modern, 1915). L. Patterson, *Mithraism and Christianity* (1921). H. S. Jones in *H.E.R.E.*, viii (1915), pp. 752–9. J. Lippl in *L.Th.K.*, vii (1935), cols. 239–42. E. Wüst in *P.W.*, xv (pt. 2; 1932), cols. 2131–55.

MITRE (Gk. μίτρα, 'turban'). The liturgical head-dress and part of the insignia of a bishop in the W. Church. It is shield-shaped and was originally always of white linen, but now the common material is embroidered satin, which is often jewelled. Two fringed lappets (*infulae* or *fanones*) hang down at the back. The mitre is not found before the 11th cent. and apparently took its origin in the '*camelaucum' of the Pope, an unofficial hat worn chiefly in procession. In certain cases permission to wear it has been granted to prelates other than bishops, notably to many *abbots and the members of certain cathedral chapters, e.g. Lucca, *Ravenna. It is worn in the W. Church at all solemn functions, but is removed

during the prayers (cf. 1 Cor. 11. 4) and the *canon of the Mass. In modern practice, three types of mitre are distinguished, viz. (1) the Precious Mitre, adorned with gold and precious stones, worn on Feasts and ordinary Sundays; (2) the Golden Mitre, of cloth-of-gold, worn in penitential seasons and when the Bishop has to remain seated during a sacred function; and (3) the Simple Mitre, of plain white silk or linen, worn at funerals, on Good Friday, at the blessing of the candles at *Candlemas, and on certain other occasions.

Though the frontispiece of T. *Cranmer's 'Catechism' depicts bishops wearing mitres, this attire was rarely, if ever, used in the C of E from the Reformation to the 19th cent., except at *coronations (down to that of George III). In the E. Church mitres are not worn, the corresponding head-dress being a metal crown.

J. Braun, *L.G.* (1907), pp. 424–98; P. Hofmeister, O.S.B., *Mitra und Stab der wirklichen Prälaten ohne bischöflichen Charakter* (Kirchenrechtliche Abhandlungen, Hft. 104; 1928), passim; T. Klauser, *Der Ursprung der bischöflichen Insignien und Ehrenrechte* (Bonner Akademische Reden, No. 1 [1949]), pp. 17–22. J. Braun, S.J., in *C.E.*, x (1911), pp. 404–6, with illustrations.

MIXED CHALICE. The practice of mixing water with wine for drinking was general in the ancient world. From allusions in the writings of *Justin Martyr, *Irenaeus, *Clement of Alexandria, and *Cyprian, it would appear that the ancient Church continued at the *Eucharist what had probably been the practice of the Lord at the *Last Supper; and, with the exception of the *Armenian, the historic Liturgies all enjoin or presuppose the mixture of water with the wine in the Eucharistic chalice. The First BCP of 1549 directed the continuance of this traditional usage; but the direction disappeared in the Book of 1552 and was not restored in 1662. The usage was not wholly abandoned however, and its widespread revival during last century was the subject of controversy between the adherents of the *Anglo-Catholic Revival and their opponents. The usage was declared to be not contrary to the law of the C of E by Abp. E. W. *Benson's *Lincoln Judgement (1890). See also *Six Points*.

MIXED MARRIAGE. A marriage between Christians of different religious allegiances. A marriage is so described esp. when one of the parties is a RC. The main body of modern RC legislation on such marriages, which are tolerated only in exceptional cases, is to be found in the *Codex (CIC, cans. 1060–4).

MOABITE STONE (c. 850 B.C.). An inscription in Moabite (virtually a Hebrew dialect) discovered by F. Klein at Dîbân E. of the Dead Sea (the Biblical Dibon, Num. 21. 30, etc.) in 1868, and commemorating the successes gained by Mesha, King of Moab, against Israel. The text, which has several points of contact with the Biblical Book of Kings, points to a close kinship between the

Moabite religion of Chemosh and the contemporary conception of *Yahweh in Israel. The stone was broken up by the local Bedouin during its removal; but a squeeze had already been taken and this, together with many fragments of the stone, are preserved in the Louvre at *Paris.

Crit. edd. of the text by G. A. Cooke, *A Text-Book of North Semitic Inscriptions* (1903), with Eng. tr. and comm., pp. 1–14; M. Lidzbarski, *Altsemitische Texte*, i (1907), pp. 5–9. W. H. Bennett in *H.D.B.*, iii (1900), pp. 406–8, with text, p. 404, and illustration of stone, p. 405, s.v. 'Moab, Moabites, iii, B'; S. R. *Driver in *E.Bi.*, iii (1902), cols. 3039–48, s.v. 'Mesha'.

MOBERLY, ROBERT CAMPBELL (1845–1903), *Anglican theologian. He was the son of George Moberly, Bp. of *Salisbury, 1869–1885. Educated at New College, Oxford, he became Regius Prof. of Pastoral Theology and Canon of Christ Church, Oxford (1892–1903). He belonged to the school of High Churchmen which produced *Lux Mundi* (1889), to which he contributed 'The Incarnation as the Basis of Dogma'. His two principal works were *Ministerial Priesthood* (1897), a theological study of the Christian ministry, with a notable appendix on the validity of *Anglican Ordinations, and *Atonement and Personality* (1901), perhaps the most original and profound study of the *Atonement in modern Anglican theology. His other writings include *Sorrow, Sin and Beauty* (1889), *Christ our Life* (sermons; 1902), *Undenominationalism as a Principle of Primary Education* (1902), and *Problems and Principles* (collected papers, 1904; posthumous).

His son, Sir WALTER HAMILTON MOBERLY (b. 1881), who has held several distinguished academic and civil appointments, contributed the essays on 'The Atonement' and 'God and the Absolute' to *Foundations* (1912).

Appreciations of R. C. Moberly by W. *Sanday in *J.T.S.*, v (1903), pp. 481–99, and by W. H. Moberly [son], ib., vi (1905), pp. 1–19. H. S. *Holland, *Personal Studies* (1905), pp. 272–9. A. Clark in *D.N.B.*, *1901–1911*, pp. 624–6.

MODALISM. In the early Church a form of unorthodox teaching on the Trinity which denied the permanence of the three Persons and maintained that the distinctions in the Godhead were only transitory. Among its leading exponents were *Praxeas, *Noetus, and Sabellius (see *Sabellianism*). It was a form of *Monarchianism (q.v.) and also known as *Patripassianism.

For Bibl. see s.v. *Monarchianism*.

MODERATES. In the Church of *Scotland, the party in the ascendant in the second half of the 18th cent. which held a more moderate conception of doctrine and discipline than their opponents (the 'Evangelicals'). They sought to be friends of learning, culture, and order and emphasized morality rather than dogma. They were opposed to the abolition of lay patronage, insisting that presbyteries should induct patrons' presentees acc. to the law of the land, whether the people called them or not. The

*Disruption of 1843 (q.v.) under T. *Chalmers was largely inspired by hostility to the principles of the Moderates.

MODERATOR. In *Presbyterian church courts the Moderator is the presbyter appointed *primus inter pares* to constitute the court and to preside over its proceedings. He has only a casting vote. In the lowest court, the *Kirk-session, the minister is Moderator *ex officio*. In *presbyteries and synods, one of the members, as a rule a minister, is appointed Moderator for a term, generally six months. The Moderator of the *General Assembly is elected for a year. In the Church of Scotland, the Moderator of the General Assembly is given the courtesy title 'Right Reverend' during his period of office and afterwards is styled 'Very Reverend'. Although it is inaccurate to speak of him as the Moderator of the Church, he serves as its representative, wears distinctive dress, and in court precedence in Scotland he comes before the peers.

MODERN CHURCHMEN'S UNION. An Anglican society, founded in 1898 as the 'Churchmen's Union' (till 1928), for the advancement of liberal religious thought, esp. in the C of E. Among its aims are to uphold the comprehensiveness of the C of E and to maintain the legitimacy of doctrinal re-statement and the adjustment of the forms of worship in acc. with the believed requirements of modern discovery. Its policy has been marked by hostility to *Anglo-Catholic and RC ideals and (esp. latterly) to socialistic programmes of reform in Church or state. Among those who have taken a prominent part in the movement are H. *Rashdall, W. R. *Inge, E. W. Barnes (Bp. of Birmingham 1924), and K. *Lake. *The Modern Churchman* (1911 ff.), founded by H. D. A. Major (b. 1871; principal of Ripon Hall, Oxford, 1919–48), serves as an organ of the Union.

MODERN DEVOTION. See *Devotio Moderna*.

MODERNISM. A movement within the RC Church which aimed at bringing the tradition of Catholic belief into closer relation with the modern outlook in philosophy, the historical and other sciences and social ideas. It arose spontaneously and independently in several different countries in the later years of the 19th cent. In France, where it was most vigorous, it was fostered in its earlier years esp. by a number of professors at the *Institut Catholique at Paris, notably L. *Duchesne (who himself, however, stood apart from the Movement when it had developed) and his pupils. It reached the height of its influence in the first years of the present century. It was formally condemned by St. *Pius X in 1907.

The Modernists, having no common programme, differed widely among themselves.

The leading ideas and tendencies to be found in the Movement were:

(1) The whole-hearted adoption of the critical view of the Bible, by this date generally accepted outside the RC Church. The Bible was to be understood as the record of a real unfolding of Divine truth in history. Abandoning artificial attempts at harmonizing inconsistencies, the Modernists recognized that the Biblical writers were subject to many of the limitations of other historians. They approached the Scriptural record with considerable independence, indeed often with much greater scepticism than the Protestant scholars. In the nineties they found encouragement in *Leo XIII's two-edged *Providentissimus Deus (1893).

(2) A strong inclination to reject the 'intellectualism' of the Scholastic theology and correspondingly to subordinate doctrine to practice. Many of the Modernists accepted a philosophy of 'action' (M. *Blondel) and welcomed the *Pragmatism of W. *James and the Intuitionism of H. *Bergson. They sought the essence of Christianity in life rather than in an intellectual system or creed.

(3) A teleological attitude to history, finding the meaning of the historic process in its issue rather than in its origins. Since the Church's growth took place under the guidance of the Spirit, the essence of the Gospel will lie in its full expansion rather than in its primitive historic kernel. This belief was sometimes reflected in an extreme historical scepticism about Christian origins. Thus, whether or not the historic Jesus founded a Church was a question of small importance and one to which we should never know the answer: the significant fact was that the seed then sown had developed into the world-wide institution for bringing men into touch with supernatural reality and saving their souls; the Mass was to be understood in its developed glory, and this would remain whether or not the historic Christ instituted it.

Among the leaders in the Modernist Movement were, in France, A. *Loisy, M. Blondel, E. I. Mignot (1842–1918; Abp. of Albi from 1899), L. *Laberthonnière, and Édouard Le Roy (1870–1954); in Italy, Romolo Murri (1870–1944) and A. *Fogazzaro; and in the British Isles, F. *von Hügel and G. *Tyrrell. In some ways von Hügel filled a special position in the Movement as the chief link between the Modernists in the different countries.

The accession of Leo XIII (Pope, 1878–1903) gave those who held liberal views considerable encouragement, for Leo had a real respect for learning and sought to abandon the isolationism of his predecessor. But his tolerance of Modernism prob. rested rather on grounds of expediency than on any personal sympathy with its ideals; and in his later years he became increasingly critical of the Movement. His successor, St. Pius X (Pope, 1903–1914), wholly distrusted the Movement from the first. Officially described as the 'synthesis of all the heresies', Modernism was finally condemned in 1907 by the decree '*Lamentabili'

and the encyclical 'Pascendi'. These decrees were carried into effect by the *motu proprio* 'Sacrorum Antistitum' (1910), imposing on all suspect clerics an Anti-Modernist oath. While the clergy who had been identified with the Movement were for the most part excommunicated, the laymen, such as von Hügel and Blondel, were generally left untouched.

With regard to the word 'Modernism', it should be noted that it was apparently not applied to the Movement until after the turn of the present century. In a wider sense the term Modernist has been used more recently of radical critics of traditional theology in the non-RC Churches, esp. of the thought of those associated with the *Modern Churchman's Union' (q.v.).

For the official condemnation of Modernism, see bibl. to the encyclical, *Lamentabili*. Other primary sources for the history of the Movement are the works of A. Loisy (esp. *Mémoires*, 3 vols., 1930–1), G. Tyrrell and F. von Hügel (esp. *Selected Letters*, 1927). The most comprehensive single study is J. Rivière, *Le Modernisme dans l'Église. Étude d'histoire religieuse contemporaine* (1929). Good summary also in A. R. Vidler, *The Modernist Movement in the Roman Church* (1934). A. L. Lilley, *Modernism. A Record and a Review* (1908); P. *Sabatier, *Les Modernistes* (1909); J. Kübel, *Geschichte des katholischen Modernismus* (1909); J. Schnitzer, 'Der katholische Modernismus' in *Zeitschrift für Politik*, v (1912), pp. 1–218 (later issued separately with modifications, Berlin, 1912); A. Houtin, *Histoire du modernisme catholique* ('1913' [publd. 1912]); Maude D. Petre, *Modernism. Its Failure and its Fruits* (1918). A. L. Lilley in *H.E.R.E.*, viii (1915), pp. 763–8, s.v.; J. Rivière in *D.T.C.*, x (pt. 2; 1935), cols. 2009–47, s.v. 'Modernisme'; W. Reinhard in *L.Th.K.*, vii (1935), cols. 249–54, s.v. 'Modernismus'; C. Fabro in *E.C.*, viii (1952), cols. 1188–96, s.v. 'Modernismo'.

MOFFAT, ROBERT (1795–1883), pioneer missionary in *South Africa. Born at Ormiston, East Lothian, he was apprenticed as a gardener, and having come to Cheshire in 1813, he was drawn under *Wesleyan influence to missionary work. In 1815 he became engaged to Mary Smith (1795–1870), his employer's daughter, who was to be a constant assistant in his work and whom he married at Cape Town in 1819. Becoming a *Congregationalist he was accepted in 1816 as a candidate by the *London Missionary Society and sent to South Africa. He arrived at Cape Town on 13 Jan. 1817 and proceeded north east to Namaqualand where he stayed over a year. Here he succeeded in converting the Hottentot chief known as Africaner, and by reconciling him to the British Government gained official support. From 1821 to 1830 he worked among the Bechuanas, where the inter-tribal warfare brought him many adventures. In 1825 the Bechuanas began to lay out for him a new station at Kuruman, where a native convert organized the erection of a school-house. Moffat then began a translation of the Gospel of Lk. into Sechwana and in 1830 the printing started at Cape Town. This was the first of a series of translations which extended to hymns and other literature and which laid the foundations for subsequent missionary enterprise. Meanwhile he had established his first contact with the Matabele tribe (1829–30), to which other visits followed in 1835, 1854, 1857, and 1859–60. In 1839 he returned to England and in 1840 persuaded D. *Livingstone, his future son-in-law, to go out to Africa. In 1843 he returned to S. Africa, where he remained until 1870. In 1857 he completed his translation of the Bible. His publications include *Missionary Labours and Scenes in Southern Africa* (1842), *Rivers of Water in a Dry Place* (1863), and *The Bible translated into Sechwana* (1872).

J. P. R. Wallis (ed.), *The Matabele Journals of Robert Moffat, 1829–60* (Government Archives of Southern Rhodesia, Oppenheimer Series, i, 2 vols., 1945); L. Schapera (ed.), *Apprenticeship at Kuruman, being the Journals and Letters of Robert and Mary Moffat, 1820–28* (Central African Archives, Oppenheimer Series, v, 1951). J. S. Moffat (son), *The Lives of Robert and Mary Moffat* (1885). E. W. Smith, *Robert Moffat*, One of God's Gardeners (1925). Other Lives by A. Manning (London, 1875), W. Walters (ib., 1881), D. J. Deane (ib., 1887), and J. J. Ellis (ib., 1929). R. H. Vetch in *D.N.B.*, xxxviii (1894), pp. 97–101.

MOFFATT, JAMES (1870–1944), NT scholar. A native of Glasgow, where he was educated at the University and the Free Church College, he was ordained in 1896, and after some years in the ministry of the Free Church of Scotland taught at Mansfield College, Oxford, from 1911 to 1915 and at Glasgow from 1915 to 1927. From 1927 to 1939 he was professor of Church history in the *Union Theological Seminary, New York. Encyclopaedic and versatile, he became well known as a writer in many fields. His *Introduction to the Literature of the NT* (1911) is a comprehensive survey of modern NT scholarship, written from the standpoint of a somewhat advanced criticism. His translation of the Bible, written in a colloquial style which in the NT makes full use of modern studies in Hellenistic Greek and often brings out the connexion of ideas in a way that the older versions fail to achieve, has been widely read. The NT appeared in 1913, the OT (generally regarded as less satisfactory critically) in 1924, and the whole was revised in 1935. Moffatt also edited a complete commentary on the NT (17 vols., 1928–49) for which his version is taken as the textual basis, and to which he has himself contributed the volumes on 1 Cor. and the General Epp. Besides many other writings on Biblical matters and Church history, he has also produced works on general English literature, among them a primer to the novels of G. Meredith.

E. F. Scott in *D.N.B., 1941–1950*, p. 602 f., s.v.

MOGILA, PETER (1597–1646), Orthodox theologian. A Wallachian of noble birth, he studied at the university of Paris, and became abbot of a monastery at Kiev in 1627 and Metropolitan of Kiev in 1632. The most important of his writings was the 'Confession', the first draft of which he prepared at the behest of Abbot Kosslowski of Kiev with the aid of three bishops in 1638. A comprehensive survey of the faith of the Greek Orthodox Church, it was formally approved by the foremost Orthodox patriarchs in 1642–3, was first published in 1645 as Ὀρθόδοξος ὁμολογία τῆς πίστεως τῆς καθολικῆς καὶ ἀποστολικῆς ἐκκλησίας τῆς ἀνατολικῆς, and again approved by the Synod of *Jerusalem in 1672. It remains one of the primary witnesses to Orthodox doctrine. Mogila also issued in 1645 his very widely circulated 'Catechism'.

The Gk. text of his Confession is pr., with modern Lat. tr., in E. J. Kimmel, *Monumenta Fidei Ecclesiae Orientalis*, i (Jena, 1850), pp. 55–324; also, with introd., in J. Michalcescu, Θησαυρὸς τῆς Ὀρθοδοξίας Die Bekenntnisse und die wichtigsten Glaubenszeugnisse der griechisch-orientalischen Kirche (Leipzig, 1904), pp. 22–122. Early Lat. tr. in Par. gr. 1265, ed., with notes and imp. introd., by A. Malvy–M. Viller (Orientalia Christiana, x, fasc. 39, 1927). Eng. tr. of Gk. text by Philip Lodvel (orig. publd. 1772), ed. J. J. Overbeck (London, 1898). The classical study on Mogila is the work (in Russian) of S. Golubev (2 vols., Kiev, 1883–98). M. Jugie, A.A., in *D.T.C.*, x (pt. 2; 1929), cols. 2063–81, s.v. 'Moghila', with full bibl.

MOHAMMEDANISM. See *Islam*.

MÖHLER, JOHANN ADAM (1796–1838), RC historian and theologian. He was educated at Ellwangen and the University of *Tübingen, and in 1819 ordained priest. In 1828 he became professor of Church history at Tübingen, later (1835) moving to Munich. Shortly before his death he was appointed Dean of Würzburg Cathedral. His work did much towards the needed theological revival within the Church, though his *Symbolik, oder Darstellung der dogmatischen Gegensätze der Katholiken und Protestanten nach ihren öffentlichen Bekenntnisschriften* (1832; Eng. trans., 1843), a treatise which sought to reckon with the situation created by F. D. E. *Schleiermacher in theology and G. W. F. *Hegel in philosophy, caused offence to many of his more conservative fellow-Catholics. He is perhaps the most considerable RC apologist since J. B. *Bossuet. His other works include *Die Einheit der Kirche oder das Princip des Katholizismus* (1825; Fr. trans. in 'Unam Sanctam', ii, 1939) and a Life of *Athanasius (2 vols., 1827), and, among posthumous writings, a commentary on Romans (1845) and a Church History (3 vols., ed. by P. B. *Gams, 1867–70).

Works ed. S. Lösch, Munich, 1928 ff. Collected essays ed. J. J. I. *Döllinger, 2 vols., Ratisbon, 1839–40. Studies by J. *Friedrich (Munich, 1894; with unpublished docc.) and A. Knöpfler (ib., 1896). P. Chaillet, S.J. (ed.), *L'Église est une.* Hommage à Möhler (1939). Y. M. J. Congar, O.P., *Esquisse du mystère de l'Église* (Unam Sanctam, viii; 1941), pp. 129–65. S. Bolshakoff, *The Doctrine of the Unity of the Church in the Works of Khomyakov and Moehler* (1946), pp. 217–62. A. Schmid, 'Der geistige Entwicklungsgang Johann Adam Möhlers' in *Hist. J.*, xviii (1897), pp. 322–56 and 572–99. J. A. Wagenmann in *P.R.E.* (ed. 3), xiii (1903), pp. 203–8; S. Lösch in *L.Th.K.*, vii (1935), col. 256 f.; A. Piolanti in *E.C.*, viii (1952), cols. 1208–11, s.v.

MOLINA, LUIS DE (1535–1600), Spanish theologian. In 1553 he entered the *Jesuit Order, and later taught at Coimbra (1563–7), and Evora (1568–83). He then spent several years at Lisbon writing, and in 1588 published, his *Concordia liberi arbitrii cum gratiae donis*. In 1590 he retired to Cuenca, where he remained until, in the year of his death, he was appointed professor of moral theology at Madrid.

The term 'Molinism' is used loosely by theologians to describe doctrines of grace of the kind elaborated in de Molina's *Concordia*

(1588) and unified (in spite of divergences of detail) by the central tenet that the efficacy of grace has its ultimate foundation, not within the substance of the Divine gift of grace itself (*ab intrinseco*), but in the Divinely foreknown fact of free human co-operation with this gift. It is claimed that human free-will is not adequately safeguarded by any other system. The Divine foreknowledge of free human actions is held to imply a knowledge, peculiar to God Himself, of hypothetical future contingents; and it is maintained that this *scientia conditionata* or *media* is therefore fundamental.

The system, which was widely adopted by the *Jesuits, was soon attacked by conservative theologians, esp. the *Dominicans, and the ensuing controversies '*De Auxiliis' were the subject of a special Congregation in Rome (1598–1607). The points at issue, however, were left undecided and Molinism is still taught side by side with *Thomism and other established systems in the Catholic schools.

F. Stegmüller (ed.), *Geschichte des Molinismus*, i, Neue Molinaschriften [all publd.] (B.G.P.M., xxxii; 1935). E. Vansteenberghe in *D.T.C.*, x (pt. 2; 1929), cols. 2094–187, s.v. 'Molinisme', with detailed bibl. On Molina, Sommervogel, v (1894), cols. 1167–79; E. Vansteenberghe in *D.T.C.*, x (pt. 2; 1929), cols. 2184–7. J. Pohle in *C.E.*, x (1911), pp. 437–41, s.v., with bibl.; F. Stegmüller in *L.Th.K.*, vii (1935), col. 262 f., s.v. 'Molinismus', and col. 261, s.v. 'Molina', the latter with list of specialized artt.; C. Baisi in *E.C.*, viii (1952), col. 1223 f., s.v. 'Molinismo', with further bibl.

MOLINAEUS, PETRUS. See *Du Moulin, Pierre.*

MOLINOS, MIGUEL DE (*c.* 1640–97), Spanish *Quietist. Born at Muniesa near Saragossa in Spain, he studied theology, obtained his doctor's degree, and was sent to Rome in 1663. Here he soon became one of the most celebrated confessors and spiritual directors, and the friend of many prelates, among them the future Pope *Innocent XI. His fame grew after the publication of his *Spiritual Guide* (*Guida spirituale, che disinvolge l' anima e la conduce per l' interior camino all' acquisito della perfetta contemplazione e del ricco tesoro della pace interiore*; 1675), in which he recommended the prayer of acquired contemplation and an excessive indifference to the soul. He was accused of error by the *Jesuits and the *Dominicans, with the result that his accusers were censured. In his account of the spiritual life, as expounded in his letters of direction rather than in the *Guide*, he found the state of perfection in perpetual union with and complete transformation into God, to which all external observances, mortifications, and even the resisting of temptation, were a hindrance. The soul, beginning with devotion to the Church and progressing to devotion to Jesus (Who was *deiformis non deus*), finally rose superior to both in devotion to God alone. Hence the state of perfection was to be attained by the total annihilation of the will. In consequence of this doctrine the nuns whom he directed began to refuse to recite their office

and to go to confession, discarded their rosaries and holy pictures, and generally disturbed discipline in their houses. In 1685 the storm broke and Molinos was imprisoned. Two years later his teaching was condemned and, though he recanted, he was sentenced to life-long imprisonment on charges of immorality. Throughout his process and imprisonment he showed the imperturbable serenity of soul described in the *Guide*, and as the letters on which the charges against him were based have never been published, his life and character remain something of an enigma. His teaching had a great influence in *Pietist circles and was defended by A. H. *Francke and G. *Arnold.

His Letters are kept under seal in the archives of the *Holy Office. The basis of the charges were a set of 263 'Theses Damnandae', printed in *Analecta Juris Pontificii*, x (1869), cols. 574–94; the 68 errors condemned on 28 Aug. 1687 and inserted by Innocent XI on 19 Nov. 1687 in the bull *Coelestis Pastor* are pr. in Denz.–Bann. (ed. 12, 1913), Nos. 1221–88. Life by P. Dudon (very hostile; Paris, 1921), with bibl. M. Petrocchi, *Il quietismo italiano del seicento* (Storia e Letteratura, 20, 1948), passim; R. A. Knox, *Enthusiasm* (1951), pp. 295–318. J. Paquier in *D.T.C.*, x (pt. 2; 1929), cols. 2187–92, s.v.

MOMMSEN, THEODOR (1817–1903), historian of Rome and jurist. He was a native of Schleswig. After studying law at Kiel and taking part in the political agitation which led later (1864) to the separation of Schleswig-Holstein from Denmark, he was professor in turn at Leipzig (1848), Breslau (1854), and Berlin (1858). He had also travelled widely in Italy collecting inscriptions. Between 1854 and 1856 he wrote his *History of Rome* (Eng. trans., 1862–6), and for twenty-five years edited the *Corpus Inscriptionum Latinarum* (vol. i, 1861). In 1884 appeared his *Provinces of the Roman Empire* (Eng. trans., 1886). He also wrote fundamental treatises on Roman Public Law, Roman Coinage, and Roman Criminal Law. He touched the field of NT studies in his treatment of Roman Law, and of Church History in his study of the relations between Church and state in the Persecutions; and he produced fine editions of the *Liber Pontificalis* (1898) and of some of the works of *Cassiodorus.

Gesammelte Schriften (8 vols. only publ., Berlin, 1905–13). E. *Schwartz (ed.), *Mommsen und Wilamowitz. Briefwechsel, 1872–1903* (1935), with introd. pp. v–xviii. L. M. Hartmann, *Theodor Mommsen. Eine biographische Skizze* (1908). *Theodor Mommsen als Schriftsteller. Ein Verzeichnis seiner Schriften von Karl Zangemeister, ed. E. Jacobs (1905). K. Rossmann, *Wissenschaft, Ethik und Politik. Erörterung des Grundsatzes der Voraussetzunglosigkeit in der Forschung* (1949) [on T. Mommsen, esp. pp. 20–52]. Adelheid Mommsen (daughter), *Theodor Mommsen im Kreise der Seinen* (1936). G. P. Gooch, *History and Historians in the Nineteenth Century* (1913), pp. 454–65.

MOMMSEN CATALOGUE, The. Also known as the **Cheltenham List**. The early list of Biblical Books discovered in 1885 by T. *Mommsen in the *Phillipps MS. 12266 at Cheltenham (10th cent.) and first published in *Hermes*, xxi (1886), pp. 142–56. The list dates from the year 359. Notable points about it are the number of the Psalms (151, not 150), the order of the Gospels (Mt., Mk., Jn., Lk.), the omission of Heb., the inclusion of Rev., and an abridged list of the *Catholic Epp. (Jas. and Jude wanting). It is generally agreed that the list is of Western origin.

W. *Sanday, 'The Cheltenham List of the Canonical Books of the OT and NT and of the Writings of Cyprian' in *Studia Biblica et Ecclesiastica*, iii, § vi (1891), pp. 217-325.

MONACHISM. See *Monasticism*.

MONARCHIANISM. A theological movement in the 2nd and 3rd cents. In its attempt to safeguard *Monotheism and the Unity ('Monarchy') of the Godhead, the movement became heretical, as it failed to do justice to the independent subsistence of the Son. There were two distinct groups of Monarchian theologians. (1) The '*Adoptionist' or 'Dynamic' Monarchians, which included two persons named *Theodotus, *Artemon, and perhaps also *Paul of Samosata. They maintained that Jesus was God only in the sense that a power or influence from the Father rested upon His human person. (2) The 'Modalist' Monarchians or *Sabellians, of whom the most notable were *Noetus, *Praxeas, and Sabellius. They held that in the Godhead the only differentiation was a mere succession of modes or operations. They were also called '*Patripassians', as it was a corollary of their doctrine that the Father suffered as the Son. The term 'Monarchian', in itself susceptible of a perfectly orthodox meaning, was brought into general use for such heretical teaching by *Tertullian (*Adv. Praxean*, iii and ix).

A. *Harnack, *History of Dogma* (Eng. tr.), iii (1897), ch. i, pp. 1-118. A. Harnack in *P.R.E.* (ed. 3), xiii (1903), pp. 303-36, s.v.; J. *Chapman, O.S.B., in *C.E.*, x (1911), pp. 448-51, s.v.; G. Bardy in *D.T.C.*, x (pt. 2; 1929), cols. 2193-209.

MONARCHIAN PROLOGUES, The. The short introductory narrative passages, also known as the **Arguments**, prefixed in many MSS. of the *Vulgate to each of the four Gospels. They contain brief accounts of the respective evangelists and of their supposed objects in writing the Gospels. Their Latin is very involved and their meaning uncommonly obscure; but it was obviously one of their purposes to inculcate a particular dogmatic position. Until the present century it was widely held that they were of 2nd-3rd cent. date and came from *Monarchian sources; hence their name. Most recent critics, however (e.g. J. *Chapman [who held that they were *Priscillianist and drawn up at *Lérins], D. de Bruyne, A. *Harnack), have put them in the 4th cent. Recent study has also made it probable that they are dependent on the *Anti-Marcionite Prologues (q.v.).

Text ed. by H. *Lietzmann in Kleine Texte, No. 1 (1908; ed. 4, 1933). P. Corssen, *Monarchianische Prologe zu den vier Evangelien* (*Texte und Untersuchungen*, Bd., xv, Hft. 1, 1896); J. Chapman, O.S.B., *Notes on the Early History of the Vulgate Gospels* (1908), pp. 217-88: A. *Baumstark, Note on 'Liturgischer Nachhall der "monarchianischen" Evangelienprologe' in *J.L.W.*, xii (1932), pp. 194-7 (argues prologues of Roman origin, 3rd cent.).

MONASTERY. The house of a religious community. The Lat. *monasterium*, with its English form '*minster', was formerly vaguely applied to large churches whether served by religious or by secular priests. The modern usage of confining the word to describe male religious establishments and calling those of the other sex 'convents' has no authority behind it.

MONASTIC BREVIARY. The *Breviary used by all monks and nuns following the Rule of St. *Benedict. It developed out of the directions given by St. Benedict in chs. 8-19 of his rule, and was revised by *Paul V (1608-1611) on the lines of the Roman Breviary, but unlike the latter has not been subsequently reformed. Among its distinctive features are a different distribution of the Psalms, the omission of the *Nunc Dimittis at *Compline, and alterations in the text of some of the hymns. It is noteworthy that the Benedictines have no Missal of their own, but use the *Missale Romanum*.

MONASTICISM. Christian Monasticism owes its origin to the desire of leading a life of perfection in greater security than is normally possible in the world. The chief aim of the monk, therefore, is personal sanctification by fulfilling the *Counsels of Perfection in the three vows of poverty, chastity, and obedience. Of these the last is the most characteristic of the *coenobitic life, as the other two may also be practised in the world. The day of the monk is spent in the two activities of prayer and work (*ora et labora*), the 'Opus Dei', or Divine Office, being the centre and source from which both his private prayer and his work draw their inspiration. The scope of his work, originally restricted to manual labour, grew apace with the development of the monasteries, extending to copying MSS., teaching, art, and all kinds of scholarly research, so that in the Middle Ages the monks were among the chief teachers of Europe and an influential civilizing power.

Christian Monasticism originated in Egypt, where St. *Antony is usually regarded as its founder It was introduced in the W. in the 4th cent. The first monks in Gaul, Italy, and elsewhere followed E. models, esp. the rules of *Pachomius and of *Basil, and neither *Martin of Tours nor John *Cassian made any substantial contribution to the old ideals, which were often marked by extreme austerity. A new departure was made by St. *Benedict (480-543) who produced his famous rule, the first detailed piece of monastic legislation adapted to European needs. It soon superseded all other rules, and from the 8th to the 12th cent. Benedictine Monasticism was the only form of the religious life known to the W. With the rise of the *Mendicant orders Monasticism properly so called declined, but benefited from the great spiritual revival at the time of the Counter-Reformation. As the chief exponent of the liturgical tradition it plays an important part in modern Roman Catholicism.

See also under the various religious orders.

There is an immense literature; many of the principal items are listed under the separate Orders. Useful survey of existing Orders and Congregations in M. Heimbucher, *Die Orden und Kongregationen der katholischen Kirche* (ed. 3, 2 vols., 1933–4); older survey in [P. Helyot (–M. Bullot)], *Histoire des ordres monastiques, religieux et militaires, et des congrégations séculières de l'un et l'autre sexe* (8 vols., 1714–19). J. O. Hannay, *The Spirit and Origin of Christian Monasticism* (1903); H. B. Workman, *The Evolution of the Monastic Ideal from the Earliest Times to the Coming of the Friars* (1913). On the early history of E. Monasticism, the chief works are O. Zöckler, *Kritische Geschichte der Askese* (1863; ed. 2 as *Askese und Mönchtum*, 2 vols., 1897); P. Ladeuze, *Étude sur le cénobitisme pakhomien pendant le IVe siécle et la première moitié du Ve* (Louvain diss., Paris, 1898); J. M. Besse, O.S.B., *Les Moines d'orient antérieurs au concile de Chalcédoine, 451* (1900); S. Schiwietz, *Das morgen-ländische Mönchtum* (3 vols., 1904–38); K. Heussi, *Der Ursprung des Mönchtums* (1936). Cf. also E. Herman, S.J., 'Ricerche sulle istituzioni monastiche bizantine. Typika ktetorika, caristicari e monasteri "liberi" ' in *O.C.P.*, vi (1940), pp. 293–375. For its early history in the West, besides the books of J. O. Hannay and H. B. Workman already cited, L. Gougaud, O.S.B., *Les Chrétientés celtiques* (1911; Eng. tr., 1932); J. Ryan, S.J., *Irish Monasticism. Origins and Early Development* (1931). On the monastic ideal, G. *Morin, O.S.B., *L'Idéal monastique et la vie chrétienne des premiers jours* (1912; 1914). G. R. Huddleston, O.S.B.–F. J. Bacchus–A. *Fortescue in *C.E.*, x (1911), pp. 459–76, s.v., with bibl.; E. C. *Butler, O.S.B., in *E.B.* (ed. 11), xviii (1911), pp. 687–91, s.v.; F. *Cabrol, O.S.B., in *H.E.R.E.*, viii (1915), pp. 781–97, s.v.; A. Wuyts, S.J.–F. Antonelli, O.F.M.–A. Pazzini in *E.C.*, viii (1952), cols. 1236–57, s.v. 'Monachismo'.

On monasticism in medieval England, D. Knowles, O.S.B., *The Religious Orders in England* (3 vols. in 4, 1940–59). Id. and R. N. Hadcock, *Medieval Religious Houses in England and Wales* (1953).

MONASTICON ANGLICANUM. The title under which Sir William *Dugdale published a vast collection of monastic charters and other sources relating to the history of English monasteries and collegiate churches in the Middle Ages. It was a cooperative work based in the main on the collections of Roger Dodsworth, and issued in three vols. in 1655, 1661, and 1673 respectively.

The best ed. is that of J. Caley, H. Ellis, and B. Blandinel (6 vols., London, 1817–30; new ed., 8 vols., 1846).

M O N E, FRANZ JOSEPH (1796–1871), German historian and liturgical scholar. He was a native of Baden and studied at Heidelberg university, where he was professor from 1819 to 1827. From 1827 to 1831 he taught at Louvain, returned to Heidelberg in 1831, and in 1835 was appointed director of the Baden Archives, a post he held till 1868. He did important research work on Latin medieval literature and early German history. His chief liturgical publication was his *Lateinische und griechische Messen aus dem zweiten bis sechsten Jahrhundert* (1850), which contains the text of eleven Masses of the pure Gallican type, notable for the absence of all reference to the cycle of liturgical feasts. He also published a collection of medieval hymns, *Lateinische Hymnen des Mittelalters* (1853–5).

The 'Masses of Mone' are repr. in J. P. Migne, *P.L.*, cxxxviii, 863–82. A. *Wilmart, O.S.B., 'L'Âge et l'ordre des messes de Mone' in *R. Bén.*, xxviii (1911), pp. 377–90.

MONICA, St. (c. 331–87), mother of St. *Augustine of Hippo (q.v.). (In the oldest MSS. the spelling is 'Monnica'.) Presumably a native of Tagaste, she was of Christian upbringing. Her husband, Patricius, a *vir curialis*, though a formal member of the Christian community, seems to have been of dissolute habits and a violent temper. At the age of forty Monica was left a widow. Of her three children (Augustine, Navigius, Perpetua), Augustine was the eldest; and, in acc. with a common custom of the time, Monica had him enrolled as a catechumen without having him baptized. Apprehensive at her son's waywardness she earnestly prayed for his conversion, and after Augustine had set out for Italy (383) she resolved to follow him. From *Rome she pursued him to Milan where she came under the influence of St. *Ambrose, took a devout part in public worship and witnessed her son's conversion. She and Augustine then retired to Cassiciacum where she appears as an interlocutor in the dialogues 'De Ordine' and 'De Beata Vita'. Having set out with Augustine on his return to Africa, she died at *Ostia on the way.

A cult of St. Monica began to develop in the later Middle Ages and in 1430 *Martin V transferred her supposed relics from Ostia to Rome where they rest in the church of S. Agostino. She has often been chosen as the patron of associations of Christian mothers. Feast day, 4 May.

The main source is St. Augustine, *Confessions*, Bk. IX. *AA.SS.*, Mai. I (1680), pp. 473–92. Modern Lives by É. H. Bougaud (Paris, 1865; Eng. tr. by Lady Herbert of Lea, 1894) and F. A. Forbes ('Standard-bearers of the Faith', 1915; slight). P. Henry, S.J., *La Vision d'Ostie. Sa place dans la vie et l'œuvre de St. Augustin* (1938). H. C. G. *Moule in *D.C.B.*, iii (1882), pp. 932–4, s.v.; H. *Leclercq, O.S.B., in *D.A.C.L.*, xi (pt. 2; 1934), cols. 2232–56, s.v.; and E. Romanelli in *E.C.*, viii (1952), cols. 1290 f., s.v., with bibl.

MONISM. The philosophy which seeks to explain all that is in terms of a single reality. The term was first used by C. *Wolff. Typical exponents of different varieties of Monism are the earliest Greek philosophers, e.g. Thales of Miletus (who held that everything was a form of water), *Plotinus, B. *Spinoza, and G. W. F. *Hegel. Modern forms of Monism (E. *Haeckel) are often esp. concerned to eliminate the dualism of the physical and the psychical by postulating a reality transcending these, of which both are modes. Materialism is another form of Monism. All forms of Monism are in conflict with the Christian belief in a radical distinction between the various grades of being.

MONK. A word of uncertain origin popularly used of any member of a religious community for men, living under the vows of poverty, chastity, and obedience. Though it has never acquired a clear-cut technical sense, its use is properly confined to those bodies in which community life is an integral element, and not extended to religious of such later developments of the monastic ideal as *canons regular, *mendicants, and *clerks regular. See also *Monastery*, *Monasticism*.

MONNICA, St. See *Monica, St.*

MONOGENES, The (Gk. μονογενής, 'only-begotten'). The hymn beginning 'Ο Μονογενής Υἱὸς καὶ Λόγος τοῦ Θεοῦ, addressed to the Triumphant Redeemer, which forms the conclusion of the second *antiphon in the *Enarxis of the Byzantine Liturgies. It also occurs in the Liturgies of St. *James and St. *Mark, where it is found at the *Little Entrance, probably its original position. It is traditionally ascribed to the Emp. *Justinian (527–65).

Gk. text in Brightman, *L.E.W.*, p. 365 f. J. Puyade, O.S.B., 'Le Tropaire 'Ο Μονογενής' in *Revue de l'Orient chrétien*, xvii (1912), pp. 253–67, with Syriac and Gk. text; V. Grumel, A.A., 'L'Auteur et la date de composition du tropaire 'Ο Μονογενής' in *E.O.*, xxii (1923), pp. 398–418.

MONOLATRY (Gr. μονός 'single', +λατρεία, 'worship'). Restriction of worship to one god, when other gods may be held to exist. The term was introduced *c.* 1880 by J. *Wellhausen and taken up by W. R. *Smith. It has been held by some OT historians to be a necessary stage in the transition from polytheism to monotheism, and to have marked Israel's religious condition from the time of the *Sinai Covenant (Exod. 24) to that of the prophets.

MONOPHYSITISM (from Gk. μόνος, 'one', and φύσις, 'nature'). The doctrine that in the Person of the Incarnate Christ there was but a single, and that a Divine, Nature, as against the Orthodox teaching of a double Nature, Divine and Human, after the Incarnation. Its adherents came into being as a distinct body immediately after the Council of *Chalcedon (451), which formally defined the Dyophysite doctrine. In essentials Monophysite teaching was already taught by *Apollinarius of Laodicea (d. *c.* 390), but its real formulation was the work of *Eutyches (d. 454), whose teaching was attacked in the *Tome of St. *Leo I (449) and expressly condemned at Chalcedon. Eutyches claimed (with what justice was, and is, disputed) to be only reasserting the teaching of St. *Cyril of Alexandria (d. 444). From the first, Eutychian doctrines found a ready welcome in Alexandria. Among Eutyches's early followers were *Timothy Aelurus and *Peter the Fuller (qq.v.).

Many variant forms of Monophysitism soon developed. An extreme type was that held by the followers of *Julian, Bp. of Halicarnassus ('Julianists'), who taught the incorruptibility and immortality of the Body of the Human Christ from the first moment of the Incarnation; this group was dubbed by their opponents '*Aphthartodocetae', or 'Phantasiastae'. Opposed to them were the followers of *Severus, Patr. of Antioch, who held a doctrine much closer to Catholic teaching and whose only divergence from orthodoxy may have been terminological; they in turn were termed by the Julianists 'Corrupticolae'. What was really another form of Monophysite doctrine was the *Theopaschitism (q.v.) of the 6th cent.

During the later 5th and the 6th cents. many attempts were made at reconciling the Monophysites to the Catholics. The Emp. *Zeno (474–91) drew up the *Henotikon (q.v.) to replace the Chalcedonian definition; but his formula was rejected by the Pope as well as by the extremist Egyptian Monophysites and resulted in the *Acacian schism. *Justinian I (527–65) also earnestly sought to win them over, even attempting to make the Monophysite Anthimus Patr. of *Constantinople. But despite all these efforts the break became final when, in the 6th cent., Monophysitism consolidated itself in three great Churches, (1) the *Copts and *Abyssinians, (2) the Syrian *Jacobites, so called after their leader *Jacob Baradaeus, and (3) the *Armenians. All these bodies accept the fathers of the Church prior to Chalcedon, and in their official professions of faith and their liturgical documents even appear to confess the orthodox Christology but in Monophysite terms, though individual members have sometimes followed the heterodox teaching of Eutyches and his disciples.

Recently the subject has attracted much attention. Important new work in A. Grillmeier, S.J.–H. Bacht, S.J. (edd.), *Das Konzil von Chalcedon. Geschichte und Gegenwart* (3 vols., 1951–4), notably the essays in Bd. i by J. Lebon, C. Moeller, and M. Richard; this treatise has full bibl. reff. The radical differences between the Eutychian and Severian doctrines were first emphasized in J. Lebon, *Le Monophysisme sévérien* (Louvain, 1909). Cf. also R. Draguet, *Julien d'Halicarnasse et sa controverse avec Sévère d'Antioche sur l'incorruptibilité du corps du Christ* (ib., 1924). A. A. Luce, *Monophysitism Past and Present. A Study in Christology* (1920). W. A. Wigram, *The Separation of the Monophysites* (1923). G. Krüger in *H.E.R.E.*, viii (1915), pp. 811–17, s.v.; M. Jugie, A.A., in *D.T.C.*, x (pt. 2; 1929), cols. 2216–51, s.v. 'Monophysisme', with bibl.; id., ib., cols. 2251–306, s.v. 'Monophysite (Église copte)'; id. in *E.C.*, viii (1952), cols. 1299–1302, s.v. 'Monofisiti'. See also bibl. to *Eutyches* and other Monophysite leaders cited in entry.

MONOTHEISM. Belief in one personal and transcendent God, as opposed to polytheism on the one hand and *pantheism on the other. Acc. to traditional Christian teaching it was the original religion of man revealed to our first parents, but subsequently lost by most men as a consequence of the Fall. In the 19th cent., under the influence of the newly aroused interest in comparative religion and natural science, this account of the beginnings of Monotheism was largely abandoned in favour of the evolutionary theory. Acc. to this view, defended by E. B. Tylor and many others, the religious beliefs of mankind have progressed from *animism by way of polytheism to Monotheism as the last link in a long chain of development. To-day this theory is less widely held. It is pointed out that on the one hand neither *Judaism nor Christianity nor *Mohammedanism, the three great monotheistic religions properly so called, have grown up as developments of polytheism but rather in opposition to it, and the same may be said of the Monotheism of Greek philosophy. On the other hand, known polytheistic religions do not show signs of issuing in Monotheism, whereas, acc. to some scholars, there is evidence among primitive peoples for a residue of Monotheism, belief in the 'High God', inherited from a forgotten past. See also *Henotheism*.

It is sometimes alleged against Christianity that it does not profess pure Monotheism because of its dogma of the Holy *Trinity (q.v.). Christian orthodoxy, however, has consistently denied this charge, maintaining that though there are Three Persons in the One Godhead, yet, as the *Athanasian Creed affirms, there are 'not three Gods, but One God'.

The subject is regularly discussed in works on the Philosophy of Religion and Christian Doctrine. W. Schmidt, *Der Ursprung der Gottesidee* (1912 ff. [9 vols. to 1949]). E. Peterson, *Der Monotheismus als politisches Problem*. Ein Beitrag zur Geschichte der politischen Theologie im Imperium Romanum (1935). J. Royce in *H.E.R.E.*, viii (1915), pp. 817-21, s.v. [philosophical]; R. Pettazzoni in *R.G.G.* (ed. 2), iv (1930), cols. 185-91, s.v. 'Monotheismus und Polytheismus. I: Religionsgeschichtlich'; P. Palazzini-L. Vannicelli in *E.C.*, viii (1952), cols. 1311-19, s.v. 'Monoteismo'. See also bibl. to art. *God*.

MONOTHELITISM (Gk. μονοθελῆται, from μόνος, 'one', and θέλειν, 'to will'; the more correct, but less usual, spelling of the word is 'Monotheletism'). A 7th cent. heresy confessing only one will in the God-man. The heresy was of political rather than of religious origin, being designed to rally the *Monophysites to their orthodox (*Chalcedonian) fellow-Christians when division endangered the Empire, faced with Persian and later with Mohammedan invasions. In 624 conferences of the Monophysite leaders with the Emp. *Heraclius resulted in producing a formula seemingly acceptable to both, which asserted two natures in Christ but only one mode of activity (μία ἐνέργεια). The solution was referred to *Sergius, the Patr. of *Constantinople, who, having found a similar formula in the writings of St. *Cyril of *Alexandria, approved the Imperial expedient. When, by this means, Cyrus of Alexandria had reconciled a large number of Monophysites to the Church, its success seemed to prove its truth. It was vigorously rejected, however, by *Sophronius of *Jerusalem, whose opposition caused Sergius *c.* 634 to write to Pope *Honorius (q.v.). In two unguarded letters the Pope approved the patriarch's conduct and himself used the unfortunate expression of 'one will' in Christ, which henceforth replaced the 'one energy'. Honorius's term was taken up in the '*Ecthesis' (Ἔκθεσις), probably drawn up by Sergius and issued by Heraclius in 638. This Ecthesis, the chief document of the Monothelites properly so called, forbids the mention of one or two energies and admits only one will (ἓν θέλημα) in Christ. In two Councils held at Constantinople in 638 and 639 the E. Church accepted the Ecthesis. But the successors of Honorius, Severinus, John IV, and Theodore I, all condemned Monothelitism, so that the Emp. Constans II, in order to obtain religious peace, withdrew the Ecthesis in 648, replacing it by another document, the so-called *Typos. In it he rejected both the monothelitic and the dyothelitic formulas and forbade their use. This, however, did not solve the question, and the Typos was condemned at

the *Lateran Council of 649. The controversy was finally settled by the Council of Constantinople in 680, which confirmed the decisions of a synod held at *Rome in 679. The Council condemned the Monothelitic formulas and their adherents, and proclaimed the existence of two wills in Christ, Divine and human, to be the orthodox faith.

Theologically, the issues at stake in the controversy were closely similar to those raised by Monophysitism (q.v.).

The main sources are preserved in the Acta of the 7th cent. Councils, pr. in the standard collections of J. *Hardouin and J. D. *Mansi; much material also in the writings of St. *Maximus Confessor and St. *Anastasius of Sinai (qq.v.). L. J. Tixeront, *Histoire des dogmes*, iii (1912), pp. 160-92. V. Grumel, A.A., 'Recherches sur l'histoire du monothélisme' in *É.O.*, xxvii (1928), pp. 6-16, 257-77, xxviii (1929), pp. 19-34, 272-82, and xxix (1930), pp. 16-28. G. Krüger in *P.R.E.* (ed. 3), xiii (1903), pp. 401-13, s.v. 'Monotheleten', with full bibl.; id. in *H.E.R.E.*, viii (1915). pp. 821-5, s.vv.; M. Jugie, A.A., in *D.T.C.*, x (pt. 2; 1929). cols. 2307-23, s.v. 'Monothélisme'; A. Mayer, O.S.B., in *E.C.*, viii (1952), cols. 1319-24, s.v. 'Monotelismo', with bibl.

MONSIGNOR, usually abbreviated Mgr. In the RC Church, an ecclesiastical title attached to an office or distinction ordinarily bestowed by the Pope. It is also used in some countries, e.g. France (in the form Monseigneur), as a regular style for archbishops and bishops.

MONSTRANCE. The vessel, also known as an 'ostensorium', used for exposing the Eucharistic Host for veneration. In its modern form it consists of a frame of golden or silver rays in the centre of which is a receptacle with a glass window through which the Host may be seen by the people. When the cultus of the Blessed Sacrament began to spread in the later Middle Ages, the Host was at first venerated in the closed *ciborium, but later the bowl was elongated and made transparent, and by the 16th cent. the monstrance had assumed its present shape.

Braun, *A.G.* (1932), pp. 348-411, with plates 62-78.

MONTAGU, or MONTAGUE, RICHARD (1577-1641), successively Bp. of *Chichester and *Norwich. Educated at Eton and King's College, Cambridge, he held two country benefices before he was appointed Dean of *Hereford in 1616, and in the following year Canon of *Windsor. An eloquent but somewhat violent champion of the C of E, he claimed 'to stand in the gap against puritanism and popery, the Scylla and Charybdis of Ancient Piety'. His *Appello Caesarem*, a defence against charges of Popery and *Arminianism, was condemned by Parliament (1626), but this did not prevent its bringing Montagu into favour with *Charles I, who appointed him to the see of Chichester in 1628. At both Chichester and Norwich, whither he was translated in 1638, he showed himself a stern opponent of Puritanism, a faithful shepherd of his dioceses, and a follower of Abp. W. *Laud. An erudite if somewhat cumbrous scholar, his best known books, apart from his controversial writings, are *Eusebii De Demonstratione Evangelica* (1628) and *De Originibus Ecclesiasticis* (1636).

Extracts in P. E. More–F. L. Cross, *Anglicanism* (1935), Nos. 3, 137, 160, 237. W. H. *Hutton in *D.N.B.*, xxxviii (1894), pp. 266–70.

MONTAIGNE, MICHEL DE (1533–92). French essayist. Of noble family, he was born at the Château de Montaigne in Périgord, and received his earliest training from a German tutor with no knowledge of French, so that he might learn Latin as his mother-tongue. At the age of six he was sent to school at the Collège de Guienne, Bordeaux. Later he studied law, prob. at Toulouse. In his youth he came much under the influence of *Raymond of Sebonde's *Theologia Naturalis* which his father had invited him to translate (publd. 1569). *C.* 1556 he became a counsellor in the *Cour des Aides* at Périgueux which was incorporated soon afterwards in the Parlement of Bordeaux. In 1565 he married Françoise de la Chassaigne who brought him a large dowry. In 1570 he sold his post as counsellor; in 1571 he retired to the Château de Montaigne which he had inherited on his father's death (1568); and in the next nine years he wrote most of the *Essais* for the first two Books (publd. 1580). In 1580 he set out on the extensive travels in Switzerland, Bavaria, the Tyrol, and Italy (where he spent much time at *Rome and Lucca), described in his *Journal de voyage* (first publd. 1774; new ed. by A. d' Ancona, 1895; Eng. trans., W. G. Waters, 1903). From 1581 until 1585 he held the mayoralty of Bordeaux. In 1588 he published a new edition of the *Essais*, adding as a Third Book those written after his resumption of leisure in 1585.

In his first group of *Essais* Montaigne propounded a scarcely christianized form of Neo-Stoic moral theory; but after undergoing a crisis of scepticism *c.* 1576, he inclined towards an Epicurean, or even a Cyrenaic, attitude to life, distinguished by certain reservations. The good life, he held, consisted in a due development of the whole of human nature, including its nobler aspects. In speculative matters he was an acute critic, but hardly a creative thinker; and his sceptical motto '*Que sais-je?*' indicates his reluctance to accept any fixed position. Though his religious opinions were expressed with prudent reserve, he was always a professing Catholic; but he made no attempt to justify his faith otherwise than by a pragmatic appeal to tradition and to the power of Divine grace, which he does not at all relate to the workings and exigencies of human nature. His influence upon French and English thought was considerable (F. *Bacon, B. *Pascal). What especially impressed his more immediate posterity was his presentation of ancient philosophy as a self-sufficient ethical system, independently of religious principles and sanctions.

The best ed. of his complete works is that of A. Armaingaud (12 vols., Paris, 1924–41). Among the many modern edd. of his *Essais*, the standard text is that of F. Strowski and others (5 vols., Bordeaux, 1906–33). An Eng. tr. of his *Essais* by J. Florio was publd. London, 1603; many subsequent edd., incl. that of J. I. M. Stewart (2 vols., London,

1931); further early Eng. tr. by C. Cotton (London, 1685; also frequently edited). Modern Eng. tr. by E. J. Trechmann (2 vols., London, 1927), with introd. by J. M. Robertson in vol. i, pp. xix–l. The considerable modern literature includes studies by P. Stapfer ('Les Grands Écrivains français', 1895), M. E. Lowndes (Cambridge, 1898), Grace Norton (New York–London, 1904), E. Dowden ('French Men of Letters', 1905), F. Strowski ('Les Grands Philosophes', 1906), R. W. Bond (London, 1906), Edith Sichel (ib., 1911), Irene C. Willis (ib., 1927), J. Plattard (Paris, 1933), P. Villey ('Maîtres des littératures', 1933; and other works by this author), A. M. Boase (London, 1935), and H. Friedrich (Bern, 1949). M. Dréano, *La Pensée religieuse de Montaigne* (Paris thesis, 1936). C. Dédéyan, *Montaigne chez ses amis anglo-saxons* (Études de littérature étrangère et comparée, 2 vols. [*c.* 1946]). S. A. Tannenbaum, *Michel Eyquem de Montaigne.* A Concise Bibliography (New York, 1942). Überweg, iii, 162–5, with bibl. p. 648. G. Saintsbury in *E.B.* (ed. 11), xvii (1911), pp. 748–50, s.v.; C. Constantin in *D.T.C.*, x (pt. 2; 1929), cols. 2338–44, s.v., with bibl.

MONTALEMBERT, CHARLES RENÉ FORBES (1810–70), French RC historian. He was the son of a French *émigré* and born in London. An ardent religious *liberal who desired to see the Church freed of state control, he soon associated himself with the movement sponsored by F. R. de *Lamennais and H. *Lacordaire, and enthusiastically supported Lamennais's newspaper, *L'Avenir*. A journey to Rome to win Papal support, however, proved fruitless, and when in 1832 *Gregory XVI condemned liberalism in his '*Mirari Vos', Montalembert submitted and ceased to propagate his views, though he did not altogether abandon them. From 1848 to 1857 he sat in the French Chamber of Deputies, where he became a vehement champion of Catholic principles. His revived advocacy of liberal views, notably in *Des intérêts catholiques au XIXe siècle* (1852), in *Le Correspondant*, and at the Congress of Malines in 1863, made him an object of dislike to more reactionary Catholics. His historical writings were composed under the influence of the *Romantic Movement. Their style was polished and eloquent, and their purpose edifying, but as works of history they were uncritical. The best known is his *Moines d'occident* (5 vols., 1860–7; Eng. trans., 1896), which developed out of a study of the life of St. *Bernard of Clairvaux. A successful earlier work was his *Vie de Ste Élisabeth de Hongrie* (1836, Eng. : rans., 1904).

Collected Works in 9 vols. (Paris, 1860–8). His addresses ed. by C. de Meaux (Montalembert's son-in-law; Paris, 3 vols., ed. 2, 1892). *Lettres à un ami de collège* [L. Cornudet] (Paris, 1873); much enlarged ed., Paris, 1905. Letters to F. R. de Lamennais, ed. by G. Goyau and P. de Lallemand (Paris [1932]). E. Lecanuet, *Montalembert d'après son journal et sa correspondance* (3 vols., 1895–1902). Shorter lives by Mrs. M. O. Oliphant (2 vols., London, 1873), L. Bouthors (Abbeville, 1896), V. Bucaille (Paris, 1927), and A. Trannoy (Paris, 1947). P. de Lallemand, *Montalembert et ses amis dans le romantisme (1830–40)* (1927); id., *Montalembert et ses relations littéraires avec l'étranger jusqu'en 1840* (1927); A. Trannoy, *Le Romantisme politique de Montalembert avant 1843* (1942). G. Goyau in *C.E.*, x (1911), pp. 513–16.

MONTANISM. An apocalyptic movement in the latter half of the 2nd cent. which is to be traced back to one Montanus in Phrygia. It lived in expectation of the speedy outpouring of the Holy Spirit on the Church, of which it saw the first manifestation in its own prophets and prophetesses. Montanus himself, who began to prophesy either in 172 (*Eusebius' *Chronicle*) or 156–7 (*Epiphanius, *Haer.*, xlviii. 1), proclaimed that the Heavenly Jerusalem would soon descend near Pepuza in Phrygia. Closely associated with him were two women, Prisca and Maximilla.

The movement soon developed ascetic traits which became esp. prominent in an offshoot of Montanism in Roman Africa. Here, where *c.* 206 it won the allegiance of *Tertullian (q.v.), it disallowed second marriages, condemned the existing regulations on fasting as too lax, imposing a discipline of its own, and forbade flight in persecution. Tertullian also condemned the penitential discipline current at Rome for its leniency and termed the Catholics 'Psychics' (*psychici*), or 'animal men', as opposed to their own members who were the 'Pneumatics' (*pneumatici*) or 'Spirit-filled'.

Certain elements in the movement (enthusiasm, prophecy) had their parallels in primitive Christianity, and in modern times it has sometimes been regarded (e.g. by A. *Harnack) as an attempt to revert to primitive fervour in the face of a growing institutionalism and secularization of the Church. More probably the movement is to be understood as an early instance of the apocalyptic groups which have constantly sprung up in Christian history. It was attacked by a large number of orthodox writings most of which have unhappily been lost, among them those of Claudius *Apollinarius, *Miltiades, and *Rhodo. It was formally condemned by Asiatic Synods before A.D. 200 and also, after some hesitation, by Pope *Zephyrinus.

The chief sources are to be found in P. de Labriolle, *Les Sources de l'histoire du montanisme* (1913). Among Patristic writers they include Hippolytus's *Syntagma* (lost in its orig. form; but in substance in later writers), Eusebius, *H.E.*, V, xvi f., and Epiphanius, *Haer.*, xlviii; and the later writings of Tertullian. G. N. Bonwetsch, *Die Geschichte des Montanismus* (1881); P. de Labriolle, *La Crise montaniste* (1913), with full bibl.; B. Poschmann, *Paenitentia Secunda*. Die kirchliche Busse im ältesten Christentum bis Cyprian und Origenes (1940), pp. 261–348 G. *Salmon in *D.C.B.*, iii (1882), pp. 935–45, s.v. 'Montanus'; G. Bardy in *D.T.C.*, x (pt. ii; 1929), cols. 2355–70, s.v.

MONTBOISSIER, Peter of. See *Peter the Venerable*.

MONTE CASSINO. The principal monastery of the *Benedictine Order, founded by St. *Benedict *c.* 529 when he migrated from *Subiaco; it lies midway between Rome and Naples. He and his sister St. *Scholastica were buried there. The buildings were destroyed by the Lombards *c.* 585, and the monks fled to the *Lateran basilica. The monastery was rebuilt by Abbot Petronax in 720, but was destroyed yet again by the Saracens in 884 and by the Normans in 1046. The house reached the peak of its prosperity under Desiderius (Abbot, 1058–87, later Pope Victor III) and Oderisius (1095–1105), when the church was consecrated (1071) and the fame of the scriptorium established. With varying prosperity it has remained the chief house of

the order. In 1866 it was declared a national monument by the Italian government, with the monks as guardians. The buildings were almost totally destroyed in 1944, but have been restored. See also *Cassinese Congregation*.

There is a Chronicle of the Abbey (A.D. 529–1075) by Leo of Ostia, contd. by Peter the Deacon (A.D. 1075–1139), ed. W. Wattenbach in *M.G.H.*, Scriptores vii (1846), pp. 551–844; also the 'Annales Casinenses' (1000–1212) ed. G. H. Pertz, ib., xix (1866), pp. 303–20; further 'Annales Casinenses ex Annalibus Montis Casini Antiquis et Continuatis Excerpti' (1000–98) ed. G. Smidt, ib., xxx (pt. 2; 1934), pp. 1385–1429. E. Gattula, O.S.B., *Historia Abbatiae Cassinensis* (2 pts., Venice, 1733); id., *Ad Historiam Abbatiae Cassinensis Accessiones* (2 pts., ib., 1734), with original sources. L. Tosti, O.S.B., *Storia della badia di Monte-Cassino* (3 vols., Naples, 1842–3). On the Cassinese Manuscripts, *Bibliotheca Casinensis seu Codicum MSS. . . . Series* (5 vols., Monte Cassino, 1873–94); *Codicum Casinensium Manuscriptorum Catalogus* (3 vols., 1915–41). *Spicilegium Casinense*, complectens Analecta Sacra et Profana e Codd. Casinensibus Aliarumque Bibliothecarum Collecta atque Edita Cura et Studio Monachorum S. Benedicti Archicoenobii Montis Casini (Monte Casino, 1893 ff.). Series of specialized studies in *Miscellanea Cassinense*, ossia Nuovi contributi alla storia, alle scienze e arti religiose (Monte Cassino, 1897 ff.). *Casinensia*. Miscellanea di studi cassinesi pubblicati in occasione del XIV centenario della fondazione della badia di Monte-Cassino (Monte Cassino, 1929). Further bibl. in L. H. Cottineau, O.S.B., *Répertoire topo-bibliographique des abbayes et prieurés* (Mâcon, 1935), cols. 1913–16. G. R. Huddleston, O.S.B., in *C.E.*, x (1911), pp. 526–8, s.v.; H. *Leclercq, O.S.B., in *D.A.C.L.*, xi (pt. 2; 1934), cols. 2451–84, s.v. 'Mont-Cassin'; V. Redlich, O.S.B., in *L.Th.K.*, vii (1935), cols. 298–301, s.v., with bibl. A. Mancone, O.S.B., in *E.C.*, viii (1952), cols. 1350–6, s.v.

MONTEFIORE, CLAUDE JOSEPH GOLDSMID (1858–1938), Biblical student and prominent advocate of 'Liberal Judaism'. A Jew by religion, he was educated at Balliol College, Oxford, under B. *Jowett, with T. H. *Green as his tutor, who imbued him with an idealist outlook on life. His writings, based on a wide, rather than deep, learning, include a set of *Hibbert Lectures on *The Origin and Development of the Religion of the Ancient Hebrews* (1892); *The Synoptic Gospels* (2 vols., 1909; ed. 2, much revised, 1927); *Liberal Judaism and Hellenism* (1918); and *Rabbinic Literature and Gospel Teachings* (1930). In his insistence on the importance of the Rabbinic writings for the understanding of the NT, he was at one with his friend, Israel *Abrahams (1858–1925), with whom he worked in close conjunction.

Speculum Religionis. Being Essays and Studies in Religion and Literature from Plato to von Hügel, with an introduction by F. C. Burkitt . . . presented . . . to . . . C. G. Montefiore (1929). Lucy Cohen, *Some Recollections of Claude Goldsmid Montefiore* (1940), with bibl. H. Danby in *D.N.B., 1931–1940*, p. 624 f.

MONTES PIETATIS. In the later Middle Ages, charitable institutions for lending money in cases of necessity. The first was started by Michael Northburgh (d. 1361), Bp. of London, but failed because it charged no interest. From the middle of the 15th cent., Italian *Franciscans established many successful *montes* which charged a low contribution towards expenses. They were opposed esp. by the *Dominicans on the ground that they offended against the canonical prohibition of *usury, but were

approved by *Leo X at the Fifth *Lateran Council in 1515. They then spread to the Low Countries, France, Spain, and Germany, but failed in England. In modern times they have been superseded in some countries by secular institutions with similar objects.

U. Benigni in *C.E.*, x (1911), pp. 534–6, s.v., and G. Coniglio in *E.C.*, viii (1952), cols. 1378–80, s.v. 'Monti di pietà', both with extensive bibl.

MONTESQUIEU, CHARLES LOUIS JOSEPH DE SECONDAT, Baron de la Brède et de (1689–1755), French historian and philosopher. He was educated by the *Oratorians at Juilly and studied law at Bordeaux, where he became counsellor of the Parliament of the town in 1714, but soon embraced a literary career. In 1721 he published anonymously his *Lettres persanes*, a witty satire on European society which had a resounding success. The *Lettres* criticized Louis XIV's government and the Catholic Church, ridiculing esp. the dogmas of the *Trinity and of *Transubstantiation, and accusing Christianity of the worst crimes. In 1728 he was elected a member of the French Academy, and after travelling several years in Europe and England, he wrote his *Considérations sur les causes de la grandeur et de la décadence des Romains* (also anonymous; 1734). Its thesis was that the history of empires was governed by moral and physical causes, and, apart from the writings of G. *Vico, it may be considered the first important work on the philosophy of history. In 1748 Montesquieu published at Geneva his most important work, the *Esprit des lois* (2 vols.), strongly influenced by J. *Locke and Viscount Bolingbroke, and defending the English principle of the division of powers as the safeguard of liberty and the way to an ideal form of government. In *L'Esprit des lois* he takes a more positive view of religion than in *Lettres persanes*, regarding Christianity as a powerful moral force in society which, though directly occupied only with the next life, makes for order and happiness in this; but he strongly attacked clerical celibacy and doctrinal intolerance, and the book was placed on the *Index in 1752. Montesquieu's ideas were later taken up and developed by A. de Tocqueville (1805–1859).

The standard ed. of his works is that by E. Laboulaye (7 vols., Paris, 1875–9); more recent ed. by A. Masson and others (3 vols., Paris, 1950–5). Eng. tr. of works so far publd., 4 vols., London, 1777. The extensive literature on Montesquieu includes studies by L. Vian (Paris, 1878), A. Sorel ('Les Grands Écrivains français', 1887; Eng. tr., 1887), J. Dedieu ('Les Grands Philosophes', 1913; also shorter study, 'Le Livre de l'étudiant', xii; [1941]), and G. Lanson ('Réformateurs sociaux', 1932). H. Barckhausen, *Montesquieu, ses idées et ses œuvres d'après les papiers de La Brède* (1907). J. Dedieu, *Montesquieu et la tradition politique anglaise en France* (Bordeaux thesis; Paris, 1909). F. T. H. Fletcher, *Montesquieu and English Politics, 1750–1800* (1939), W. Struck, *Montesquieu als Politiker* (Historische Studien, ccxxviii; 1933). E. Vidal, *Saggio sul Montesquieu* (Pubblicazioni dell' Istituto di Filosofia del Diretto dell Università di Roma, xvii; 1950); with bibl. G. Saintsbury in *E.B.* (ed. 11), xvii (1911), pp. 775–8, s.v.; A. Degert in *C.E.*, x (1911), pp. 536–8, s.v.; C. Constantin in *D.T.C.*, x (pt. 2; 1929), cols. 2377–88, s.v.; S. Cotta–C. Testore, S.J., in *E.C.*, viii (1952), col. 1369 f., s.v., for further bibl.

MONTFAUCON, BERNARD DE (1655–1741), one of the foremost *Maurist patristic scholars. After embarking on a military career he joined the Maurist Benedictine congregation in 1676. He produced splendid editions of St. *Athanasius (3 vols., 1698), of the '*Hexapla' of *Origen (2 vols., 1713), and of St. *Chrysostom (13 vols., 1718–38). In his *Collectio nova patrum et scriptorum graecorum* (2 vols., 1706), he printed for the first time many previously unedited texts. His *Palaeographia graeca* (1708) virtually created the science of Greek palaeography. His other writings include his survey of MSS in his *Bibliotheca Bibliothecarum* (2 vols., 1739), the work by which he is prob. best known, treatises incorporating masses of material on French historical antiquities and a defence (1699) of the Benedictine ed. of St. *Augustine against *Jesuit attacks.

E. de Broglie, *La Société de l'abbaye de Saint-Germain-des-Prés au XVIIIe siècle*: Bernard de Montfaucon et les Bernardins (2 vols., 1891). M. Valéry, *Correspondence inédite de Mabillon et de Montfaucon avec l'Italie* (3 vols., 1846). List of Montfaucon's works with short Life in [R. P. Tassin], *Histoire littéraire de la congrégation de Saint-Maur*, ii (Brussels, 1770), pp. 585–616. The W. *Leclercq, O.S.B., in *D.A.C.L.*, xi (pt. 2; 1934), cols. 2608–72; E. Peterson in *E.C.*, viii (1952), cols. 1374–6, for further bibl.

MONTH'S MIND. The *Requiem Mass celebrated on the 30th day after death or burial. The custom of observing this day as the conclusion of a thirty-days mourning was known already to the Jews (cf. Num. 20. 29; Deut. 34. 8) and the Greeks. For the W. Church it is attested in the 'Dialogues' of St. *Gregory the Great (iv. 55) and the *Gelasian Sacramentary, which has a special Mass for it.

MONT-ST.-MICHEL. The abbey and fortress of this name lies on a rocky island a mile or so off the north coast of France, near St.-Malo. An oratory is said to have been established there by St. Aubert, Bp. of Avranches (early 8th cent.), in obedience to the commands of an apparition of St. *Michael. In 966 a *Benedictine monastery was founded on the mount, to which a fortress was added later; and the sanctuary gradually became the most famous of all shrines dedicated to St. Michael. The monastery is now secularized, but the buildings remain, surmounted by a Gothic spire on which is a statue of St. Michael. St. Michael's Mount, Cornwall, is an English counterpart on a smaller scale and of less fame.

S. Luce (ed.), *Chronique du Mont-Saint-Michel, 1343–1468* (Société des Anciens Textes, 2 vols., 1879–83). E. Corroyer, *Description de l'abbaye du Mont-Saint-Michel et de ses abords, précédée d'une notice historique* (1877); P. M. Brin-E. Corroyer, *Saint Michel et le Mont-Saint-Michel* (1880); G. Dubouchet, *L'Abbaye du Mont-St-Michel* (1895). P. Gout, *Le Mont-Saint-Michel*. Histoire de l'abbaye et de la ville. Étude archéologique et architecturale des monuments (2 vols., 1910). H. J. L. J. Massé, *A Short History and Description of the Church and Abbey of Mont S. Michel* (Bell's Handbooks to Continental Churches, 1902). L. H. Cottineau, O.S.B., *Répertoire topo-bibliographique des abbayes et prieurés* (1935), cols. 1897–1908, s.v., with full bibl.

MONTSERRAT (Lat. *Mons Serratus*). This celebrated mountain near Barcelona is surrounded by legends which locate there the

Castle of the Holy Grail. The *Benedictine monastery, whose church enshrines the famous image of 'Our Lady of Montserrat' (traditionally held to be the work of St. *Luke), and which is known to have existed before the 10th cent., was raised to the rank of an abbey in 1410. After a short period of decline it was reformed at the end of the 15th cent. and became a popular place of pilgrimage. One of its most distinguished visitors was St. *Ignatius Loyola who hung up his sword there after his conversion. Partly destroyed in the Napoleonic wars of 1811–12, and sacked by Spanish militia in 1820 and 1834, the abbey was abolished in 1835. It was restored, however, in 1844 and in 1862 affiliated to the congregation of *Subiaco, of which it is now the principal monastery in the Spanish province. Its monks are famous for their researches into Catalonian culture and folklore and their interest in sacred music. They also care for the numerous pilgrims who visit the shrine.

G. de Argais, *La perla de Cataluña. Historia de Nuestra Señora de Montserrate* (Madrid, 1677). M. Muntados, O.S.B., *Montserrat*. Su pasado, sa presente y su porver ó lo que fué hasta su destrucción en 1811 y lo que será en adelante (Manresa, 1867). *Analecta Montserratensia* (Montserrat, 1918 ff.). A. Mundó, O.S.B., in *E.C.*, viii (1954), cols. 1327–30, s.v. 'Monserrato', with bibl. Further bibl. in L. H. Cottineau, O.S.B., *Répertoire topo-bibliographique des abbayes et prieurés* (1935), col. 1977 f., s.v.

MOODY, DWIGHT LYMAN (1837–99), evangelist. The son of a bricklayer, he left his home at Northfield, Mass., in 1854 for work in Boston. After reception into the *Congregational Church in 1856, he moved to Chicago where he prospered in business (which he abandoned in 1860) and entered on successful evangelical work in connexion with his Sunday School. During the Civil and Spanish wars (1861–65) he worked under the *Y.M.C.A., labouring particularly to evangelize the wounded. Returning to Chicago in 1865, he organized several state and international Sunday School teachers' Conventions, during which he met Ira David Sankey (1840–1908) who joined him in 1870 and regularly accompanied his preaching with singing and organ-playing. After a first visit to England in 1867, he returned with Sankey on a preaching tour from 1872 to 1875, in the course of which the 'Sankey and Moody Hymn Book' was published (1873) with many of the songs used by Sankey and other revivalists who found the hymns in use in England unsuited to their type of appeal. The tour through England, Scotland, and Ireland, which was supported by clergy of all denominations, met a wide and enthusiastic response. After conducting a similar mission to Brooklyn, Philadelphia, and New York during the winter of 1875–6 and to Boston in 1877, Moody founded the Northfield Seminary for Young Women in 1879 and the Mount Hermon School for Young Men in 1881. After a second tour in Great Britain from 1881 to 1884, during which he made his first appeal to the academic world, he began organizing

annual student conferences for Bible Study. In 1891–2 he paid a further visit to England. In 1893 he organized a mission in connexion with the World Fair at Chicago, out of which grew the Bible Institute Colportage Association, for the production of cheap religious literature (founded 1895).

Moody's success as an evangelistic preacher was the fruit of his undaunted courage in pursuing converts in spite of all opposition, the frankness, vigour, and urgency of his appeal, and the use of the inquiry-room and other revivalist methods.

W. R. Moody (son), *The Life of Dwight L. Moody* [1900]. L. A. Weigle in *Dict. Amer. Biog.*, xiii (1934), pp. 103–6.

MOORE, AUBREY LACKINGTON (1848–1890), Anglican theologian. Educated at St. Paul's School and Exeter College, Oxford, he was successively Fellow of St. John's College, Oxford (1872–6), rector of Frenchay, Glos. (1876–81), and tutor of Keble College (1881–1890). His keen intellect, equally at home in philosophy and the natural sciences, and a rare depth of spiritual power made him one of the chief religious influences in Oxford. His publications included the essay on 'The Christian Doctrine of God' in *Lux Mundi* (1889), a collection of papers on *Science and the Faith* (1889), and *Lectures on the History of the Reformation* (1890; posthumous); but these books in no sense reflect his real abilities.

R. D. Middleton, 'Aubrey Moore' in *Theology*, li (1948), pp. 85–9. H. E. D. Blakiston in *D.N.B.*, xxxviii (1894), p. 342.

MORAL PHILOSOPHY. In current usage, the branch of philosophy which examines the goodness and rightness of human actions apart from any considerations derived from a supernatural revelation. The word is thus merely another name for what philosophers also term 'ethics'.

MORAL REARMAMENT (M.R.A.). The watchword of the campaign for moral and spiritual regeneration on the principle of the *Oxford Group, launched by F. N. D. *Buchman in June 1938. It won considerable public support and held its first Assembly at Interlaken, Switzerland, in Sept. 1938. Since 1946 further Assemblies have been held at Caux-sur-Montreux, Switzerland.

MORAL THEOLOGY. The science of Christian conduct, treating of God as man's last end, and of the means by which He may be attained. Its sources are the precepts of Revelation, as contained in the OT and NT, esp. in the *Decalogue and the *Sermon on the Mount, reason enlightened by faith, and the tradition of the Church, including the lives and teachings of the saints. There are three principal methods followed in Moral Theology, the application of which largely coincides with the three periods of Church history. They are:

the Positive method, simply stating moral principles and doctrines without entering deeply into discussions (*patristic); the *Scholastic method, aiming at a scientific statement and systematic arrangement of moral teaching (medieval); and the *Casuistic method, which applies moral principles to individual cases (modern). Of these the first is esp. suited for preaching, the second for study and apologetics, and the third for the practice of the confessional.

The '*Didache' perhaps contains what can be called the earliest treatise of Moral Theology in its teaching of the Two Ways, and the 'Shepherd' of *Hermas gives an actual compendium of Christian moral teaching in the twelve 'Mandates'. *Clement of Alexandria produced guides to the Christian life in the 'Protrepticus' and 'Paedagogus', which give a detailed description of the morality of the true Christian. *Tertullian taught that the Will of God was the first principle of the moral life, and he and St. *Cyprian wrote several practical treatises on such subjects of Christian morality as Patience, Almsgiving, and Virginity. With the wholesale conversion of pagans in the 4th cent. strict moral teaching became particularly urgent. It was given in the E., among others, by the *Cappadocian Fathers, St. *Basil and the two *Gregories, and by St. *Cyril of Jerusalem, esp. in his 'Catecheses'. In the W. St. *Ambrose produced a Christian counterpart to Cicero's 'De Officiis' in his 'De Officiis Ministrorum'. St. *Augustine established charity as the fundamental principle of Christian morality, from which flow all other virtues, esp. in his 'Enchiridion' and 'De Moribus'; he also wrote smaller treatises on Marriage, Continence, and similar subjects. The moral teaching of antiquity was summed up by St. *Gregory I in his 'Moralium Libri XXV' and 'Liber Regulae Pastoralis', in which, at the same time, were laid the foundations of medieval developments.

The first indication of new needs was the appearance of the '*Penitential Books', dating from the 5th–7th cents. They deal in a practical way with the requirements of the newly converted barbarians and reflect the ensuing gradual attenuation of the penitential practice of the Church. The true founder of Moral Theology in the modern sense, however, is St. *Thomas Aquinas. Building on St. Augustine and *Aristotle, he devoted the whole of the second part of his 'Summa Theologica' to the subject of Moral Theology, treating it from the point of view of the speculative theologian, and linking it closely to the whole organism of natural and supernatural virtues and to the gifts of the Holy Ghost. At the same time precursors of modern casuistry made their appearance with *Raymond de Peñafort's famous 'Summa de Poenitentia' (c. 1235), a compilation of relevant passages from the Fathers, Councils, and Papal decisions, and a century later, with the even more practical so-called 'Summa Astensis' of an unknown Franciscan of Asti, in Italy (c. 1317). In the 14th and 15th cents. a large number of similar Summae were produced, usually arranged in alphabetical order, one of the most celebrated being the 'Summa Theologica Moralis' of St. *Antoninus of Florence, which proved a mine of information for all subsequent manuals of casuistry.

The modern period, which may be dated from the Council of *Trent, is marked in the RC church esp. by the many commentaries on the 'Summa Theologica', by the controversies over different systems of morality, esp. *Probabilism (q.v.), and by the numerous special manuals and treatises on Moral Theology, produced largely by members of the *Dominican and *Jesuit Orders. This development was greatly fostered by the increased frequency of sacramental confession. Among the commentaries on the second part of the 'Summa' those by B. de Medina (1527–31), G. *Vasquez, F. *Suarez, and D. *Bañez are held in great esteem by RC moralists, as is also the comprehensive work of the *Salmanticenses Cursus Theologiae Moralis (1665 ff.) Of the casuists M. de *Sa's Aphorismi Confessariorum (1595) was widely used, and J. de *Lugo's Disputationes scholasticae et morales (1644) is still frequently regarded as the classical textbook of casuistry. The most famous moral theologian of modern times, whose work received the special approval of the RC Church, is St. *Alphonsus Liguori, whose Theologia Moralis (1753–5) finally established the milder Probabilist and *Equiprobabilist method for resolving doubtful cases against the harsher *Probabiliorism, at that time largely followed in France and Italy. Most modern RC handbooks on Moral Theology are strongly influenced by the Liguorian teaching. It should, however, be remembered that the various modern systems only apply to the comparatively unimportant sphere of uncertain cases, and that the great principles of Catholic Moral Theology are the same whatever the particular casuistic doctrines an author may follow.

In the C of E the problems of Moral Theology received the attention of many writers in the 17th and early 18th cents., notably Jeremy *Taylor and R. *Sanderson. The Catholic revival of the 19th cent. produced little more than adaptations of current RC handbooks, but more recently some serious efforts have been made to lay the foundations of a body of Moral Theology adapted to the needs of the Anglican Church.

The active cultivation of the subject in modern times, esp. in the RC Church, has issued in innumerable handbooks, mainly in Latin. Recent treatises include those of A. Lehmkuhl, S.J. (2 vols., Freiburg i.Br., 1883), A. Ballerini–D. Palmieri (7 vols., Prato, 1889–93), A. *Tanquerey (3 vols., Paris-Rome, 1902), A. Koch (Freiburg i.Br., 1905 [in German]; Eng. tr. by A. Preuss, 5 vols., St. Louis, Mo., 1921–8), T. Slater (2 vols., New York, 1908), D. M. Prümmer, O.P. (3 vols., Freiburg i.Br., 1915). J. Mausbach, Die katholische Moral, ihre Methoden, Grundsätze und Aufgaben (1901; ed. 5, with title, Die katholische Moral und ihre Gegner, 1921). Anglican books on the subject include several writings of K. E. *Kirk (q.v.); also R. C. Mortimer, The Elements of Moral Theology (1947). An adapted version of J. J. Gaume's treatise, ed. E. B. *Pusey (1877), was much used by English confessors in the later 19th cent. J. J. I. von *Döllinger–F. H. Reusch, Geschichte der Moralstreitigkeiten in der römisch-katholischen Kirche seit dem sechzehnten Jahrhundert (2 vols., 1889). K. Hilgenreiner in L.Th.K., vii (1935), cols. 319–22, s.v.

MORALITY PLAY, or MORALITY. A form of drama, popular in the 15th and 16th cents., in which a moral truth or lesson was inculcated by the chief characters personifying various abstract qualities. It was a development from the earlier *Mystery Plays. Originally the interest of these plays was mainly religious, but from the end of the 15th cent. onwards they became more secular in character, though in their later form they were sometimes used, e.g., for defending Protestantism against Catholicism. 'Everyman', the best known of them, is a translation from a Dutch original. The name 'Morality', which is derived from the French, was not applied to them till the late 18th cent.

A collection of *English Miracle Plays, Moralities and Interludes* [extracts] was ed., with useful introd., by A. W. Pollard (1890; ed. 8, 1927). S. W. Clarke, *The Miracle Play in England* [1897]; E. H. Moore, *English Miracle Plays and Moralities* (1907), with bibl. H. Craig, *English Religious Drama of the Middle Ages* (1955), esp. pp. 321–53, with reff. W. W. Greg, 'Bibliographical and Textual Problems of the English Miracle Cycles' in *The Library*, 3rd Series, v (1914), pp. 1–30, 168–205, 280–319, and 365–99. G. R. Coffman, 'The Miracle Play in England. Nomenclature' in *Publications of the Modern Language Association of America*, xxxi (1916), pp. 448–65; id., 'The Miracle Play in England. Some Records of Presentation, and Notes on Preserved Plays' in *Studies in Philology*, xvi (1919), pp. 56–66. K. Young, 'Concerning the Origin of the Miracle Play' in *The Manly Anniversary Studies in Language and Literature* (1923), pp. 254–68; J. M. Manly, 'The Miracle Play in Mediaeval England' in *Transactions of the Royal Society of Literature of the United Kingdom*, New Series, vii (1927), pp. 133–53. See also bibl. to *Mystery Plays*; also to *Drama*.

MORAVIAN BRETHREN. The name in common use for the Protestant Church which is the direct continuation of the *Bohemian Brethren (q.v.) after their 'renewal' at *Herrnhut under Count N. L. von *Zinzendorf in 1722. From now on there was a strong *Pietist element in the community, a consequence of Zinzendorf's influence; and they also became closely linked to the *Lutheran Church, in which they considered themselves a group (*ecclesiola*).

From an early date they were active missionaries. In 1732 two brethren went out to the negroes of St. Thomas (West Indies) and in 1733 a mission was begun in Greenland. In 1738 Peter Bohler, one of their number, established a 'religious society' at Fetter Lane, London, where he exercised a deep influence on J. *Wesley (q.v.).

In theology the Moravians have always distrusted doctrinal formulae, the *Easter Litany (q.v.) tending to take the place of a dogmatic creed; but they give a limited recognition to the *Augsburg Confession. They have retained the offices of *Bishop, *Presbyter, and *Deacon; but these offices do not wholly correspond with their Catholic counterparts. In general they have stood for a simple and unworldly form of Christianity. They publish annually a 'Text Book', with appointed OT and NT texts for daily use, to foster fellowship among their groups. In their services the use of hymns, mainly of German origin, plays an important part. Their prayers for public use are prefixed to modern editions of *The Moravian Hymn Book*.

The Moravian Church now has four provinces, viz. Europe (Germany, Holland, Switzerland, Denmark), Britain, N. America, and S. America; more than half of their number are now in N. America. For the most part they live in settlements in rural areas.

D. Cranz, *Alte und neue Brüder-Historie oder Kurzgefasste Geschichte der Evangelischen Brüder-Unität in den altern zeiten und insonderheit in dem gegenwärtigen Jahrhundert* (Barby, 1771; Eng. tr., 1780). E. A. Schweinitz, *History of the Moravian Church known as Unitas Fratrum* (Bethlehem, Pa., 1885); E. A. Senft, *L'Église de l'Unité des Frères* (Neuchâtel, 1888); J. E. Hutton, *Short History of the Moravian Church* (London, 1895; enlarged ed., 1900); E. R. Hassé, *The Moravians* ('Leaders of Revivals' [1911]); E. Langton, *History of the Moravian Church* (1956). J. T. Hamilton, *History of the Moravian Church during the Eighteenth and Nineteenth Centuries* (Bethlehem, Pa., 1900). W. G. Addison, *The Renewed Church of the United Brethren, 1722–1930* (1930). W. Marx, *Die Saalkirche der deutschen Brüdergemeine im 18. Jahrhundert* (Studien über christliche Denkmäler, xxii, 1931). H. Pleijel, *Das Kirchenproblem der Brüdergemeine in Schweden.* Eine kirchliche Studie (Lunds Universitets Årsskrift, N.F., Avd. 1, Bd. xxxiii, Nr. 6; 1938). J. T. Hamilton, 'A History of the *Unitas Fratrum* or Moravian Church in the United States of America' in *American Church History Series*, viii (New York, 1895), pp. 425–508. J. J. Sessler, *Communal Pietism among Early American Moravians* (New York, 1933). E. A. Senft, *Les Missions moraves chez les peuples païens* (Neuchâtel, 1890); J. E. Hutton, *A History of Moravian Missions* [1922]. D. Cranz, *Historie von Grönland enthaltend die Beschreibung des Landes und der Einwohner u. insbesondere die Geschichte der dortigen Mission der evangelischen Brüder zu Neu-Herrnhut und Lichtenfels* (Barby, 1765; Eng. tr., 2 vols., 1767; abridged ed. with continuation, 2 vols., 1820). J. H. Clewell, *History of Wachovia, The Moravian Church in North Carolina, 1752–1902* (New York, 1902). R. T. Jenkins, *The Moravian Brethren in North Wales* (Y Cymmrodor, xlv; 1938). J. E. Hutton, 'The Moravian Contribution to the Evangelical Revival in England, 1742–1755' in T. F. Tout–J. Tait (edd.), *Historical Essays by Members of the Owens College, Manchester.* Published in Commemoration of its Jubilee, 1851–1901 (1902), pp. 423–52, with reff. J. E. Hutton in *E.B.* (ed. 11), xviii (1911), p. 818 f., s.v.; E. R. Hassé in *H.E.R.E.*, viii (1915), pp. 837–41, s.v. On the early history see also bibl. to *Bohemian Brethren*.

MORE, DAME GERTRUDE (1606–33), *Benedictine nun and spiritual writer. A direct descendant of St. Thomas *More, she entered the house of the English Benedictine congregation at Cambrai in 1623 as one of its first postulants. During her novitiate she was much troubled by scruples and temptations, which continued after she had made her vows, until she came under the direction of Dom Augustine *Baker. On account of her repute for sanctity she was nearly made abbess at the age of 23. She died four years later of smallpox. Her writings, which were published after her death as *The Holy Practices of a Divine Lover* (Paris, 1657) and *Confessiones Amantis* (Paris, 1658), contain affective meditations of considerable beauty and an apology for her way of prayer.

Her Life, written by her director, Augustine Baker, was lost to sight until comparatively recent times. The first half of Baker's MS., recovered in Germany *c.* 1850, is in the possession of Stanbrook Abbey, Worcs.; the whole Life, somewhat abbreviated by a copyist, has since been identified in another MS. now at Ampleforth Abbey. The Life was first pr. by Dom Benedict Weld-Blundell in a volume entitled *The Inner Life of Dame Gertrude More* (London, 1911; the editor appears to have dealt rather freely with the text and, somewhat misleadingly, omitted to print Baker's name on the title-page). Modern edd. of her 'Devotions' by H. Collins (London, 1873), of the *Holy Practices* by H. Lane Fox, O.S.B. (London, 1909), and of her 'Writings' by B. Weld-Blundell, O.S.B. (1911). Life by H. Collins (London, 1875).

MORE, HANNAH (1745–1833), religious writer and philanthropist. Born at Stapleton, Glos, she was educated by her father and from *c.* 1757 at the school established by her sisters in Bristol. Visiting London *c.* 1773, she became acquainted with the literary circle of Edmund Burke (1729–97), Joshua Reynolds (1723–92), David Garrick (1717–79) and S. *Johnson, who encouraged her to publish plays and poems. After Garrick's death she devoted herself more to religious activities. She published a series of *Sacred Dramas* for the instruction of young persons in 1782 and *Thoughts on the Importance of the Manners of the Great to General Society* (anon.) in 1788; this last had a very wide circulation. In 1787 she became closely acquainted with W. *Wilberforce and also with J. *Newton who became her spiritual adviser. While visiting the Mendips with W. Wilberforce in 1789, they were both struck by the ignorance of the country and the appalling lack of religious provision. Under his influence she established schools at Cheddar and in the neighbouring villages at a time when schemes of popular education were almost unprecedented; religious education was combined with a training in spinning, which was also designed to relieve poverty. She also established friendly societies and other philanthropic organizations for the relief and education of adults. In spite of initial opposition from the landowners, and later from some of the clergy who accused her of *Methodist leanings, her system of schools was finally commended by R. Beadon, Bp. of Bath and Wells from 1802 to 1824. Four of the schools which she founded survived. Between 1793 and 1799 she wrote a large number of Tracts designed to counteract the influence of the French Revolution (collected under the title *Cheap Repository Tracts*). Moving to Barley Wood in 1802, she came into closer contact with the *Clapham Sect and in 1809 anonymously published *Coelebs in Search of a Wife* (2 vols.), the most popular of her books. On the abolition of slavery in *Ceylon she wrote a poetical dialogue which was set to music by C. *Wesley. Although suffering from ill-health during the last years of her life, she continued to write religious and moral treatises. Her later published works include *Practical Piety* (2 vols., 1811), *Christian Morals* (2 vols., 1813) and *Moral Sketches of Prevailing Opinions and Manners, Foreign and Domestic* (1819).

Collected ed. of her Works in 8 vols., London, 1801; revised ed., 11 vols., ib., 1830. William Roberts, *Memoirs of the Life and Correspondence of Mrs. Hannah More* (4 vols., 1834); Arthur Roberts (ed.), *Letters of Hannah More to Zachary Macaulay* (1860); selected letters ed. R. Brimley Johnson (London, 1925). Further contemporary life by H. Thompson (London, 1838); modern lives by C. M. *Yonge ('Eminent Women Series', 1888), and M. G. Jones (Cambridge, 1952, with list of 'Cheap Repository Tracts' ascribed to Mrs. More, p. 272 f.). L. Stephen in *D.N.B.*, xxxviii (1894), pp. 414–20.

MORE, HENRY (1614–87), '*Cambridge Platonist'. Educated at Christ's College, of which he became a Fellow in 1639, he remained in Cambridge all his life, despite the fact that he was offered several rich preferments. His chief interests were theological, philosophical, and ethical. Among his principal works were *Antidote against Atheism* (1653), *Manual of Ethics* (1666), *Divine Dialogues* (1668), and *Manual of Metaphysics* (1671). In these discursive writings he sought to vindicate theism and immortality against the materialism represented by T. *Hobbes. He emphasized in particular the instinctive reasonableness of Divine truth and affirmed the existence of a higher principle, 'more noble and inward than reason itself', which he termed the 'Divine Sagacity'. He held that it was possible to apprehend this higher truth only through the cultivation of a righteous disposition and a free intellect, though afterwards this intuitive instinct might be confirmed by the methods of reason. He also defended innate ideas and notions, and postulated the existence of a Spirit of Nature or 'anima mundi'. Despite his curiously superstitious leanings, he had a high reputation for learning and saintliness.

Works collected in 3 vols., fol., London, 1675–9. Philosophical works previously issued, London, 1662; ed. 4, 1712. Modern ed. of selection of his philosophical works, with introd. and notes, by Flora I. Mackinnon (New York, 1925); philosophical poems ed. G. Bulloch (Publications of the University of Manchester, ccix; English Series, No. xx; 1931). Life by Richard Ward, rector of Belton (London, 1710; ed. M. F. Howard, ib., 1911). J. Tulloch, *Rational Theology in England in the Seventeenth Century*, ii (1872), pp. 303–409; F. J. Powicke, *The Cambridge Platonists* (1926), pp. 150–73. J. H. Overton in *D.N.B.*, xxxviii (1894), pp. 421–3.

MORE, St. THOMAS (1478–1535), Lord Chancellor of England. The son of Sir John More, he became a member of the household of Abp. J. Morton at the age of 13. His early study of the classics won his lifelong interest. At the desire of his father he began to study law in 1494 and was called to the bar in 1501. For three successive years he was lecturer at Furnival's Inn and in 1504 entered Parliament. About this time he felt drawn to the religious life, but finally decided that he was not called to celibacy; and he married in 1505, but without abandoning his strict manner of life and his religious practices. His house in Chelsea became a centre of intellectual life, being frequented by men like D. *Erasmus, J. *Colet, and W. *Grocyn. With the accession of *Henry VIII in 1509, his brilliant public career began. Made Under-Sheriff of London in 1510, he was sent as an envoy to Flanders in 1515 and there wrote his most famous work, the *Utopia* (publd. 1516). In it he described an ideal community living acc. to the natural law and practising a natural religion, with many satiric side-thrusts at contemporary abuses. In 1518 he was made Master of Requests and Privy Councillor, was knighted three years later, elected Speaker of the House of Commons in 1523, high steward of Cambridge university and chancellor of the Duchy of Lancaster in 1525, and finally, in 1529, appointed Lord Chancellor to succeed T. *Wolsey.

During these years, when the *Lutheran controversy had roused all Europe, More became involved through the need for an answer to M. *Luther's attack on Henry VIII's *Assertio Septem Sacramentorum*. Under the pseudonym of Gulielmus Rosseus More replied in his *Responsio ad convitia Martini Lutheri* (1523). Among his other controversial writings are treatises on the veneration of saints and images and on the punishment of heretics. The turning point in his fortunes came when he opposed the King in the matter of his divorce. Having tendered his resignation in 1532, an action that lost him almost his entire income, he lived in retirement for 18 months until, in 1534, he refused to take the oath on the Act of Succession and was confined in the Tower. Here he remained for 15 months, making his imprisonment an occasion of prayer and penance, and writing devotional books, the finest of which is the *Dialogue of Comfort against Tribulation*. On 1 July 1535 he was accused of high treason on the ground of having opposed the Act of Supremacy, and was beheaded on Tower Hill five days later (6 July). He was beatified by *Leo XIII in 1886 and canonized by *Pius XI in 1935. Feast day, 9 July.

Eng. works ed. by his nephew William Rastell (London, 1557); Lat. works publd. at Louvain, 1565, and at Frankfurt a.M., 1689. Modern ed. by W. E. Campbell (1931 ff.). Crit. ed. of *Utopia* by A. W. Reed (London, 1929). The earliest Life, based on orig. documents, is that of William Roper, More's son-in-law (first pr., Paris, 1626; new edd., London, 1925 and 1935); other early Lives by Thomas Stapleton (*Tres Thomae*, Douai, 1588; Eng. tr., P. E. Hallett, 1928), Nicholas Harpsfield (d. 1575; Harleian MS. 6253; ed. E. V. Hitchcock, London, 1932), and Cresacre More, his great-grandson (London, 1626). Modern Lives by T. E. Bridgett (London, 1891), W. H. *Hutton (London, 1895), H. *Bremond ('Les Saints', Paris, 1904), G. R. Potter (London, 1925), C. Hollis (ib., 1934), R. W. Chambers (ib., 1935). E. E. Reynolds (ib., 1953), and L. Paul (ib., 1953). E. M. G. Routh, *Sir Thomas More and his Friends, 1477-1535* (1934). S. Lee in *D.N.B.*, xxxviii (1894), pp. 429-49.

MORIN, GERMAIN (1861-1946), *patristic scholar. A native of Caen, in 1881 he became a Benedictine monk at *Maredsous in Belgium. From 1907 to 1916, and again in his later years, he resided chiefly at Munich. He made many important original contributions to Latin patristics and liturgy, mostly in the *Revue Bénédictine*, and published an outstanding edition of the works of St. *Caesarius of Arles (1937-42). He also issued collections of previously unpublished sermons of St. *Jerome (1897, 1903) and of St. *Augustine (1917, 1930).

J. Madoz, S.J., 'La carrera científica de Dom G. Morin, O.S.B.' in *Estudios eclesiásticos*, xx (1946), pp. 487-507; P. Borella, 'Dom Germain Morin, O.S.B. (1861-1946)', in *E.L.*, lxi (1947), pp. 55-76, with notes on Morin's writings.

MORIN, JEAN (1591-1659), *Oratorian theologian. The son of *Calvinist parents, he was converted to Catholicism in 1617 under the influence of P. de *Berulle, became an Oratorian in the following year, and devoted his life almost wholly to studies in patristics and the text of the Bible. At the invitation of Pope *Urban VIII he spent nine months in Rome in 1639-40 as theological adviser in the matter of *orders during the attempts to reunite the E. and W. Churches. His works included *De patriarcharum et primatum origine . . . atque antiqua et primigenia censurarum in clericos praxi* (1626), *Biblia LXX interpretum Graeco-Latina* (3 vols., 1628), *Exercitationes ecclesiasticae in utrumque Samaritanorum Pentateuchum* (1631) and *De Sacris Ecclesiae Ordinationibus* (1655). A notable item in the last-named work was its rejection of the view formerly widely held among Latin theologians that the Tradition of the *Instruments constituted the *matter of the Sacrament of Orders.

R. *Simon in *Antiquitates Ecclesiae Orientalis cum Notis et Vita I. Morini* (London, 1682), pp. 1-117 (hostile, Simon having then left the *Oratory). A. Molien in *D.T.C.*, x (pt. 2; 1929), cols. 2486-9.

MORISON, JAMES (1816-93), founder of the '*Evangelical Union'. Educated at Edinburgh university, he was trained for the ministry of the *United Secession Church. In 1839 he was appointed to the charge of Cabrach and in 1840 to a church at Kilmarnock. His preaching of the universal atonement of Christ and the publication of his beliefs in a short tract, *The Question 'What must I do to be saved?' Answered* (1840), led his teachings to be challenged as incompatible with the *Westminster Confession, and in 1841 he was expelled from the United Secession Church. In 1843, with three other ministers and nine laymen, he founded at Kilmarnock the '*Evangelical Union', and later was joined by others. In 1851 he left for Glasgow. He retired from active work in 1884.

Memorial Volume ed. G. G[ladstone] (on occasion of Morison's ministerial jubilee; 1889). Lives by W. Adamson (London, 1898) and [W. H.] O. Smeaton (Edinburgh, 1901). A. C. Rutherford, *Morisonianism examined and set aside* (ed. 3, 1850), and J. B. Johnstone, *Who are the Limitarians? or, Gospel-Grace versus Morisonian Exclusiveness* (ed. 2, 1852). A. Gordon in *D.N.B.*, xxxix (1894), p. 57 f.

MORITZ, St. See *Maurice, St.*

MORLEY, GEORGE (1597-1684), Bp. of *Winchester. Educated at Westminster and at Christ Church, Oxford, he became rector of Mildenhall, Wilts, in 1641. He was ejected as a royalist in 1648 and was abroad until the Restoration, conducting services in many places for the Anglican exiles. Soon after his return (1660) he became Dean of Christ Church and later in the year Bp. of *Worcester. On 23 Apr. 1661 he preached the Coronation Sermon and in May took a prominent part at the *Savoy Conference. He was translated to Winchester in 1662. Despite his close associations with the High Church party, his theology was *Calvinistic. His writings, however, were short and mostly occasional. He was a great benefactor notably to the diocese of Winchester, and rebuilt Wolvesey Palace. He was also the patron of T. *Ken, whom he made his chaplain in 1665.

A. Wood, *Athenae Oxonienses* (ed. P. Bliss), iv (1820), cols. 149-58. W. Hunt in *D.N.B.*, xxxix (1894), pp. 74-8.

MORMONS. The popular name for the 'Church of Jesus Christ of Latter-Day Saints'. They were founded at Manchester, New York, in 1830, by one, Joseph Smith (1805–44), who claimed to have discovered through a revelation the 'Book of Mormon', which became the Bible of the Latter-Day Saints. In 1843 Smith had another revelation sanctioning polygamy, and the lawfulness or otherwise of this practice is still a disputed point among Mormons. In 1844 Smith was killed by a mob. Brigham Young (1801–77) succeeded him and removed the headquarters of the sect to Salt Lake City, Utah, in 1847. The practice of polygamy brought them into conflict with the Federal Government until 1890 when the President of the Mormons advised his followers to conform to the law. Utah was admitted to the Union in 1896. In the U.S. census of 1936 they numbered just under 775,000, but by 1958 their numbers appear to have increased to over a million.

The Book of Mormon, orig. publ. New York, 1830, ed. O. Pratt (Salt Lake City, 1903; Liverpool, 1909). The Pearl of Great Price. Being a Choice Selection from the Revelations, Translations, and Narrations of Joseph Smith (Liverpool, 1882; ed. J. E. Talmage, Salt Lake City, 1902). W. A. Linn, The Story of the Mormons from the Date of their Origin to the Year 1901 (1902), with reff. R. C. Webb, The Real Mormonism (New York, 1916). On Joseph Smith, see Lucy Smith (mother), Biographical Sketches of Joseph Smith the Prophet and his Progenitors for many Generations (Liverpool, 1853). I. W. Riley, The Founder of Mormonism. A Psychological Study of Joseph Smith, Jr. (1903). Id. in H.E.R.E., xi (1920), pp. 82–90, s.v. 'Saints, Latter Day', with analytical bibl.

MORNING PRAYER. See Mattins.

MORONE, GIOVANNI (1509–80), Bp. of Modena. He came of an old and distinguished family of Milan, where his father, Ieronimo Morone (d. 1529), was chancellor. In 1529 he was nominated Bp. of Modena by *Clement VII, but was prevented by the opposition of Cardinal Ippolito d' Este from taking possession of his see. After various diplomatic missions on behalf of the Pope, he became nuncio to Germany in 1536 and was present at the Diets of *Hagenau (1540), *Ratisbon (1541), and *Speyer (1542). Like J. *Sadoleto, he showed considerable sympathy with the Reformers' grievances and tried to establish less embittered relations. In 1542 he was created cardinal and nominated with Paul Parisio and R. *Pole to preside over the forthcoming Council at *Trent, but though his reforming zeal did much to keep the prospect of the Council alive he did not eventually take part at the opening group of sessions. In 1557 he was incarcerated by *Paul IV in the Castel Sant' Angelo for supposed heresy on justification, the invocation of saints, and the veneration of relics. He was completely cleared of these charges under the more liberal *Pius IV, who employed him during the concluding sessions of the Council of Trent to win the goodwill of the secular powers needed to ensure the Council's success. In his later years he was employed on diplomatic missions to Genoa (1575) and Augsburg (1576), and 1578–9, as Cardinal Protector of England, he took an active part in administering the *English College at Rome.

F. Dittrich (ed.), Nuntiaturberichte Giovanni Morones vom deutschen Königshofe, 1539, 1540 (Quellen und Forschungen aus dem Gebiete der Geschichte. In Verbindung mit ihrem historischen Institut in Rom herausgegeben von der Görres-Gesellschaft, i, Teil 1; 1892); W. Friedensburg (ed.), Nuntiatur des Morone, 1536–1538 (Nuntiaturberichte aus Deutschland, Abt. 1, Bd. ii; 1892); id. (ed.), Nuntiaturen Fabio Mignanelli's 1538–1539 und Giovanni Morone's Bischofs von Modena 1539 (ib., iii; 1893); id. (ed.), Nuntiaturen Giovanni Morone's Bischofs von Modena, 1539 Juli–Oktober (ib., iv; 1893); L. Cardauns (ed.), Nuntiaturen Morones und Poggios Legationen Farneses und Cervinis, 1539–1540 (ib., v; 1909); id. (ed.), Gesandtschaft Campegios, Nuntiaturen Morones und Poggios, 1540–1541 (ib., vi; 1910). The evidence of Alfonso Salmerone, S.J., given before the *Inquisition in Morone's trial (1555) is pr. in P. Tacchi Venturi, S.J., Storia della Compagnia di Gesù in Italia, i (1910), pp. 533–49. Modern life by N. Bernabei (Modena, 1885). There is also a shorter study by C. Cantù (Memorie del Reale Istituto Lombardo di Scienze e Lettere. Classe di Lettere e Scienze Morali e Politiche, x (Ser. 3, i; 1867). G. Constant, La Légation du Cardinal Morone près l'empereur et le concile de Trent, avril–décembre, 1563 (Bibliothèque de l'École des Hautes Études, ccxxxiii; 1922). H. Thurston, S.J., in C.E., x (1911), p. 575 f., s.v.; F. Lauchert in L.Th.K., vii (1935), col. 332, s.v., with bibl.; P. Paschini in E.C., viii (1952), cols. 1420–4, s.v. See also bibl. to Trent, Council of.

MORRIS, WILLIAM (1834–96), English artist and author. He was educated at Marlborough and Exeter College, Oxford, where contact with the *Oxford Movement stimulated his interest in the Middle Ages. In 1854 he almost became an RC. He then studied Anglican theology, but abandoning his plan of taking Orders, warmly embraced the intellectual and social movement associated with the names of T. *Carlyle, J. *Ruskin, and C. *Kingsley. Visits to N. France in 1854 and 1855 aroused his enthusiasm for French Gothic, and in 1856 he began to study under G. E. *Street. D. G. *Rossetti, however, persuaded him to give up architecture and, like his life-long friend, E. Burne-Jones, to devote his energies to painting. Meanwhile he had launched the Oxford and Cambridge Magazine (Jan. 1856), and in 1858 published a volume of poetry, The Defence of Guenevere, which was appreciated by a discriminating public. In 1861 he founded a firm to realize his ideal of giving artistic form to the objects of everyday life. In 1866 he began a series of romances, modelled on G. *Chaucer. The first, The Life and Death of Jason, was published in 1867; but it was the others, with the single title The Earthly Paradise (3 vols., 1868–70), that established his literary fame. In 1872 he published Love is Enough, a poem in medieval alliterative verse, in 1875 a very free translation of the Aeneid, and in 1876 the epic poem Sigurd the Volsung. In the following years he became increasingly convinced that the prerequisite of healthy art was a sound social life, and that this could be achieved only by the regeneration of society. In 1883 he became a member of the Democratic Federation and in 1884 the leader of the Socialist League, which sought to promote a social revolution and issued the periodical Commonweal. His Dream of John *Ball (1888) gives a philosophy of history. When his socialist ideas seemed destined to remain unfulfilled, he again turned to romances, dealing either with the remote past, as in *The House of the Wolfings* (1889), or with the distant future, as the Utopian *News from Nowhere* (1891). In 1890 he founded the famous Kelmscott Press, of which the finest production, the Kelmscott Chaucer, was completed in the year of his death. Morris's main ideal, to which all his various activities were devoted, was the re-integration of life and art, the unity of which he held had been broken up by the specialization and mechanization which had begun at the end of the Middle Ages.

Collected ed. of his works, 24 vols., London, 1910-15, with introd. by his daughter, May Morris, in vol. i, pp. ix-xxxi. Extracts from his writings also ed., with introd., by May Morris (2 vols., Oxford, 1936). The primary authority is the life by J. W. Mackail (2 vols., London, 1899). Other studies include those by A. Vallance (London, 1897), A. Noyes ('English Men of Letters', 1908), H. Jackson (London, 1908; revised ed., 1926), J. Drinkwater (London, 1912), A. Compton-Rickett (ib., 1913), A. Clutton-Brock (ib. [1914]), J. B. Glasier (ib., 1921), P. Bloomfield (ib., 1934), L. E. Grey (Princeton, N.J., 1937; London, 1949), Margaret R. Grennan (Morningside Heights, N.Y., 1945), E. and S. Godwin, *The Warrior Band* (London, 1947), and Esther Meynell (London, 1947). H. B. Forman, *The Books of William Morris Described with some Account of his Doings in Literature and in the allied Crafts* (1897). T. Scott, *A Bibliography of the Works of William Morris* (1897). A. Vallance, *The Art of William Morris* (1897, with reproductions); G. H. Crow, *William Morris, Designer* (The Studio special number, 1934). H. H. Sparling, *The Kelmscott Press and William Morris* (1924). Anna A. von Helmholtz-Phelan, *The Social Philosophy of William Morris* (Durham, N.C., 1927). J. W. Mackail in *D.N.B.*, Suppl. iii (1901), pp. 197-203.

MORRISON, ROBERT (1782-1834), first Protestant Missionary in *China. He was a native of Morpeth in Northumberland, received an elementary education at Newcastle, and was apprenticed to a last-maker. In his spare time he studied theology. In 1798 he joined the *Presbyterian Church, and in 1803 went to London where he entered the Hoxton Academy. In 1804 he became a member of the *L.M.S., went to the Missionary Academy at Gosport, and after studying medicine and astronomy as well as some Chinese, was ordained and sent to Canton in 1807. Here with great difficulty he secured lessons in Chinese, which could not then be taught to foreigners. In 1809 he became translator to the East India Company. In 1814 he published a Chinese grammar and a translation of the NT, based partly on an old *Jesuit version. In 1818 he finished a translation of the OT, and in 1818 he founded the Anglo-Chinese College at Malacca (charter, 1820). His chief work, the Chinese Dictionary, appeared in 6 vols. in 1821 and remained a standard work for a long time. It was followed, in 1823, by the publication of the whole Chinese Bible in 21 vols. In 1824 he went to England, but returned to Canton in 1826, where he spent the remaining years of his life. He also translated the BCP and a large number of hymns and tracts.

Memoires of the Life and Labours of Robert Morrison, compiled by his widow, with critical notes of his Chinese works by S. Kidd (2 vols., 1839). M. Broomhall, *Robert Morrison* (1925). R. K. Douglas in *D.N.B.*, xxxix (1894), p. 111 f.

MORTAL SIN. Acc. to Catholic teaching, mortal sin (cf. 1 Jn. 5. 16) consists in a deliber-

ate act of turning away from God as man's last end by seeking his satisfaction in a creature. This frustration of God's purpose is held to involve the loss of sanctifying grace and eternal damnation. A sin in order to be mortal must be committed with a clear knowledge of its guilt and with full consent of the will, and must concern a 'grave matter'. It is required that where circumstances allow every mortal sin be confessed to a priest; but if such confession is impossible, the desire to do so and an act of contrition are sufficient for obtaining God's pardon. See also *Venial Sin*.

MORTALIUM ANIMOS. The Papal encyclical, issued on 6 Jan. 1928, 'On Fostering True Religious Unity', which forbade RC's to take part in such reunion movements as *Faith and Order.

Text in *A.A.S.*, xx (1928), pp. 5-16.

MORTIFICATION. An ecclesiastical term used to describe the action of the 'killing' or 'deadening' of the flesh and its lusts (cf. Rom. 8. 13; also Col. 3. 5, Gal. 5. 24) through ascetic practices, and more particularly through the infliction of bodily discomfort and even bodily hurt. Fasting and abstention from pleasure are among the many means of mortification. Its chief aim is by breaking bad habits to lead men into better and holier ways.

MORTMAIN. A term used for land held by an ecclesiastical or other corporation that cannot be alienated. Statutes of Mortmain with the purpose of setting limitations on the Church's power of acquiring property date from an early period. In England, the Magna Carta as revised by Henry III in the autumn of 1217 prohibited the transfer of land to an ecclesiastical corporation without the lord's permission. A further law—*Statutum de viris religiosis* (7 Edw. I, st. 2; 1279)—forbade anyone under pain of forfeiture to buy, sell, or receive lands or tenements and thereby cause them to come into Mortmain (*per quod ad manum mortuam terrae et tenementa hujusmodi deveniant quoquo modo*). The laws, which met with indifferent success and were constantly evaded, were often re-enacted and altered. Of more recent statutes, that of 1736 imposing restrictions on the devising of property to ecclesiastical uses is commonly known as the Mortmain Act (9 Geo. II, c. 36). The present law in England is regulated by the Mortmain and Charitable Uses Act of 1888 (51 & 52 Vict. c. 42) and its subsequent amendments.

Text of the third issue of Magna Carta (1217), ch. 43, is repr. in W. *Stubbs (ed.), *Select Charters and other Illustrations of English Constitutional History* (ed. 9, by H. W. C. Davis, 1913), p. 343; that of the Mortmain Act of 1279, with introd., ib., pp. 450-2; Eng. tr. of the latter in Gee-Hardy, p. 81 f. (No. xxviii). L. Shelford, *A Practical Treatise on the Law of Mortmain and Charitable Uses and Trusts* (1826), esp. pp. 1-266, with Eng. tr. of the relevant statutes in appendix. T. F. T. Plucknett, *Legislation of Edward I* (Ford Lectures, 1947; 1949), pp. 94-102. K. L. Wood-Legh, *Studies in Church Life under Edward III* (1934), esp. pp. 60-88 ('Alienations in Mortmain'). G. Gross,

'Mortmain in Medieval Boroughs' in *American Historical Review*, xii (1907), pp. 733–42; Helena M. Chew, 'Mortmain in Medieval London' in *E.H.R.*, lx (1945), pp. 1–15. On more recent legislation, O. D. Tudor, *On Charities* (ed. 5, by H. G. Carter–F. M. Crashaw, 1929), pp. 413–72, with texts of the 1888, 1891, and 1892 Acts. W. Kahl, *Die deutschen Amortisationsgesetze* (1879). C. W. Sloane in *C.E.*, x (1911), pp. 579–82, s.v.; G. Crosse in *D.E.C.H.*, p. 377, s.v. On mortmain in France, E. Magnin in *D.D.C.*, i (1935), cols. 468–71, s.v. 'Amortissement', with bibl.

MORTON, THOMAS (1564–1659), Bp. of *Durham. He was educated at *York and Halifax and at St. John's College, Cambridge, where he was elected Fellow in 1586 and taught logic for several years. In 1598 he became rector of Long Marston, near York, and later Dean of *Gloucester (1606), Dean of *Winchester (1609), Canon of York (1610), Bp. of *Chester (1616), of *Lichfield and Coventry (1618), and of Durham (1632). On the abolition of episcopacy in 1646 he was deprived and lived for the rest of his life in retirement. He was a well-known anti-Roman controversialist, among his numerous writings being *Apologia Catholica* (1605), prob. written with the assistance of J. *Donne; *A Catholic Appeal* (1609); *Of the Institution of the Sacrament of the Blessed Body and Blood of Christ* (1631); and *De Eucharistia Controversiae Decisio* (1640).

Funeral Sermon by J. Barwick, Dean of St. Paul's, with Life of Morton appended (London, 1660). Another Life 'begun by R. B., Secretary to his Lordship [i.e. Richard Baddeley] . . . and finished by J. N., D.D., his Lordship's Chaplain [Joseph Naylor]' (York, 1669). P. E. More and F. L. Cross, *Anglicanism* (1935), No. 206. R. B. Prosser in *D.N.B.*, xxxix (1894), pp. 160–6.

MOSCHUS, JOHN (*c.* 550–619), 'Eukratas', spiritual writer. In *c.* 575 he retired from the world to the monastery of St. Theodosius, near *Jerusalem. Later he journeyed widely, visiting or settling at many notable centres of monasticism, among them Egypt, Mt. *Sinai, *Antioch, *Cyprus, and Rome. His 'Pratum Spirituale' (Λειμών, i.e. 'The Meadow') contains a large collection of anecdotes on the monastic life, derived from his personal experience and from communications of others. The book became extremely popular as a devotional manual and its text was continually added to and revised.

Gk. text, ed. by F. *Ducaeus in *Bibliotheca Veterum Patrum*, ii (1624), pp. 1057–1169, and J. B. *Cotelerius, *Ecclesiae Graecae Monumenta*, ii (Paris, 1681, pp. 341–456), supplemental chapters from MS. Par. Reg. 2464, pr. in J. P. Migne, *PG*, lxxxvii. 2851–3112; Lat. tr. by St. Ambrose *Traversari, orig. publd. Venice, 1475, repr. in *PL*, lxxiv. 119–240. Fr. tr., by M. J. Rouët de Journel, S.J., with introd. and notes, in S.C. No. 12 (Paris, 1946). N. H. Baynes, 'The *Pratum Spirituale*' in *O.C.P.*, xiii (1937), pp. 404–14; E. Mioni, 'Il *Pratum Spirituale* di Giovanni Mosco', ib., xvii (1951), pp. 61–4. Bardenhewer, v, pp. 131–5.

MOSES, the Founder and Lawgiver of Israel, who, acting on a Divine commission, led the Hebrew people out of their Egyptian bondage and brought them, after forty years' wandering in the deserts, to the *Jordan, preparatory to their entry into the Promised Land.

Acc. to the Pentateuchal narratives, where Moses is the central figure in all five Books except Gen., his birth took place at a time when all Hebrew male children were under sentence of drowning by a decree of Pharaoh (Ex. 1. 22). The infant Moses owed his escape to being hidden in a basket by the Nile and rescued by Pharaoh's daughter (2. 1–10). When he had grown to full estate, having killed an Egyptian overseer who had struck one of the Israelites, he took refuge in the deserts with Jethro (Reuel), the 'priest of Midian' (Ex. 2. 11–22). Here he married Jethro's daughter, Zipporah, and after leading a shepherd's life for forty years received the revelation of Jehovah and his call in the Burning Bush on Mt. *Sinai (Ex. 3–6). On his return to Egypt he met with the strongest opposition from Pharaoh, but with Jehovah's help, mediated esp. through the ten plagues, and the assistance of his elder brother, *Aaron, he gradually broke down the king's vacillation; and on the night of the *Passover (Ex. 12) when all the firstborn of the Egyptians, both men and cattle, were killed, the king finally yielded and Moses and his people went forth (Ex. 7–12). The pursuing Pharaoh and his forces were drowned in the Red Sea (Ex. 14 f.).

Moses now had to lead the Israelites through the desert. The people, ever ready to rebel by reason of the trials of the long journey, were several times pacified by miracles, among them the gift of '*manna' from Heaven (Ex. 16) and water from a rock at Massah and Meribah (Ex. 17. 1–8). Three months after the Exodus, Mt. Sinai was reached, where Moses received the Ten *Commandments (q.v.) and the 'Book of the Covenant'. After the Book had been read to the people and the covenant ratified, Moses returned to the Mount, where he remained for forty days and forty nights and received from Jehovah two Tables on which were engraven the Law (Ex. 24). Meanwhile the people, impatient at the delay, had caused Aaron to make an idol in the form of the Golden Calf (Ex. 32). Seized with wrath at this apostasy, Moses broke the Tables and entrusted the tribe of *Levi, which had remained faithful, with the execution of justice. Afterwards he interceded with Jehovah and obtained forgiveness for the people and freshly inscribed Tables of stone were given him.

On reaching the Desert of Paran, Moses despatched spies to the Promised Land. All except Joshua and Caleb brought back exaggerated accounts of the strength of the inhabitants (Num. 13); and the Israelites again turned against Moses. The Divine sentence was that they were to wander in the desert for forty years, and that none save Joshua and Caleb would enter Palestine (Num. 14). Later the same punishment was meted out to Moses and Aaron (Num. 20). Little is recorded of the remaining thirty-eight years in the desert. Shortly before his death Moses led the Israelites to the land E. of Jordan and was himself granted a sight of the Promised Land from Mt. *Pisgah. He then blessed the tribes of Israel (Deut. 33) and died on Mt. Nebo in Moab.

Such, in bare outline, is the Pentateuchal narrative. Acc. to the traditional view (nowhere, however, implied in the Pentateuch itself and not easily compatible with its record of Moses' own death), the whole narrative was the work of Moses and therefore self-authenticating. Modern scholars are almost unanimous in finding interwoven in these Books a number of independent documents of widely differing dates and of varying degrees of historicity. The extent to which the Biblical account is capable of being controlled by other historical evidence or archaeological *data* being small, the historicity of the narrative has to be estimated mainly on grounds of general probability esp. in relation to what is known of the relative antiquity of the sources. Opinions range from those which would regard the narratives as substantially true to those which deny the historical existence of Moses altogether (G. Hölscher, E. Meyer). The great majority of Biblical scholars would at least agree that some such commanding figure as Moses is presupposed by the unity of the Israelite tribes and that it is highly unlikely that the Hebrew People would have sought their beginnings in bondage unless such had been the fact. The dates assigned to Moses vary widely (see art. *Exodus*).

In Christian tradition Moses takes a prominent place. In the Gospels he appears at the Transfiguration Scene as the Representative of the Law (Matt. 17. 3 and parallels). In Heb. 3. 1–6 his mission is compared with that of Christ on a lower plane. A Jewish tradition preserved in the 'Assumption of *Moses', acc. to which St. *Michael and the Devil contested for the body of Moses, is alluded to in Ep. of Jude (ver. 9). In later tradition he became the subject of many, often extravagant, legends.

Besides commentaries on the Pentateuch and histories of Israel, P. Volz, *Mose* (Tübingen, 1907; ed. 2, 1932); H. Gressmann, *Moses und seine Zeit* (1913); E. Sellin, *Moses und seine Bedeutung für die israelitisch-jüdische Religionsgeschichte* (1922). M. Buber, *Moses* (Oxford, 1946); E. Auerbach, *Moses* (Amsterdam, 1953 [in German]). H. Cazelles and others, *Moses, l'homme de l'alliance* (special issue of Cahiers Sioniens, 1955). W. H. Bennett in *H.D.B.*, iii (1900), pp. 438–48; E. Mangenot in *Dict. Bibl.*, iv (1908), cols. 1189–1215; H. *Gunkel in *R.G.G.* (ed. 2), iv (1930), cols. 230–7.

MOSES, The Assumption of ('Ἀνάλημψις or Διαθήκη Μωυσέως). A composite Jewish work, written in Hebrew or Aramaic during the first half of the 1st cent. A.D. It contained a speech of *Moses to *Joshua, prophesying the history of the Israelite nation, and probably also an account of Moses' death and taking up into heaven. It appears to have been the work of a *Pharisee who wished to protest against the rapid secularization of his party and recall it to the Law and the old ideals. It was soon translated into Greek, and a few phrases of this edition are probably preserved in Acts 7. 36 and Jude 9, 16, 18. Part of a Latin version, made from the Greek, survives; but for the rest, apart from one or two brief fragments, the work has been lost.

Lat. text, discovered and publd. by A. M. Ceriani (ed.), *Monumenta Sacra et Profana*, i (Milan, 1861), pp. 55–64. Crit. ed. by R. H. *Charles, *The Assumption of Moses translated from the Latin Sixth Century MS.* (1897). Id. in

R. H. Charles (ed.), *The Apocrypha and Pseudepigrapha of the Old Testament*, ii (1913), pp. 407–24. G. Hölscher, 'Über die Entstehung der "Himmelfahrt Moses" ' in *Z.N.T.W.*, xvii (1916), pp. 108–27 and 149–58. G. Kuhn, 'Zur Assumptio Mosis' in *Z.A.T.W.*, xliii (1925), pp. 124–9. E. *Schürer, *Geschichte des jüdischen Volkes im Zeitalter Jesu Christi*, iii (ed. 4; 1909), pp. 294–305, with bibl. F. C. *Burkitt in *H.D.B.*, iii (1900), pp. 448–50, s.v.; J. B. Frey in *Dict. Bibl.*, Suppl. i (1928), cols. 403–9, s.v. 'Apocryphes de l'Ancien Testament, 6', with bibl.

MOSES BEN MAIMON. See *Maimonides*.

MOSES OF CHORENE, *Armenian Christian scholar. Acc. to Armenian tradition, he was a disciple, and perhaps also a nephew, of St. *Mesrob, and thus belonged to the latter part of the 5th cent. But the 'History of Armenia', with which his name is esp. associated, is in parts at least a much later work, and the balance of more recent critical opinion puts Moses in the 8th cent. The 'History' was written with an avowedly patriotic purpose; and though its contents seem much less reliable than older scholars used to suppose, it remains a work of the first importance for the primitive history of Armenia, not least through its incorporation of many literary remains of the pre-Christian period. Moses was also the author of a 'Geography' which, however, is little more than a revision of that of Pappus. Other writings attributed to him include a treatise on rhetoric, a 'Letter on the Assumption of the BVM', a homily on Christ's Transfiguration, and a collection of hymns used in Armenian Church worship.

Moses' collected works (Arm. text) publd. by the *Mechitarists of Venice in 1843 and 1865; the 'History' at Amsterdam, 1695, and again at Venice, 1881. Lat. tr. of History by W. and G. *Whiston (London, 1736). A. Carrière, *Moïse de Khoren et les généalogies patriarcales* (1891); id., *Nouvelles Sources de Moïse de Khoren* (1893–4) and other works all defending Moses not before 7th-8th cents. F. C. *Conybeare, 'The Date of Moses of Khoren' in *B.Z.*, x (1901), pp. 489–504 (defends authenticity of History). Bardenhewer, v, pp. 189–95. P. N. Akinian in *P.W.*, Suppl. 6 (1935), cols. 534–41.

MOSES MAIMONIDES. See *Maimonides*.

MOSHEIM, JOHANN LORENZ VON (1694–1755), ecclesiastical historian and divine. Educated at the university of Kiel, in 1723 he became professor of theology at Helmstedt and in 1747 at Göttingen, in the founding of which university he himself had taken an important part. His historical work was marked by a hitherto unprecedented objectivity and penetration and he may be considered the first of modern ecclesiastical historians. His *Institutiones historiae ecclesiasticae* (1726; Eng. trans. by J. Murdock, 1841) went through many editions and revisions. He was also an excellent preacher. His numerous writings include *Sittenlehre der heiligen Schrift* (5 vols., 1735–1753), a *Ketzer-Geschichte* (2 vols., 1746–48), and *De rebus Christianorum ante Constantinum Magnum Commentarii* (1753).

K. Heussi, *Die Kirchengeschichtsschreibung J. L. von Mosheims* (1904); id., *J. L. Mosheim* (1906). N. Bonwetsch in *P.R.E.* (ed. 3), xiii (1903), pp. 502–6, with bibl.

MOSLEMS. See *Islam*.

MOSQUE OF OMAR. See *Dome of the Rock*.

MOTET. Term of uncertain origin (perhaps from the French *mot*, 'word', or Lat. *motus*, 'movement'). One of the most important forms of polyphonal chant. Probably of secular origin, it came into liturgical worship from the beginning of the 13th cent., either following or replacing the *Offertory at Mass. In its classical form it is founded on the Gregorian tones of the Mass to which it belongs. At first it was almost entirely restricted to France, the first known examples being in Philip de Vitry's 'Ars Compositionis de Motetis' (*c.* 1320). From *c.* 1400 it became popular also in other European countries, esp. Italy and Germany, and in England. From the end of the 15th cent. onwards the composition of motets made much progress and the development reached its height at the end of the 16th cent. with Orlando di Lasso, G. P. *Palestrina, and others. In the later 17th cent. instrumental accompaniment was introduced, a practice which continued till the 20th cent., when a return to the older traditions was encouraged by a *Motu Proprio* of St. *Pius X. Many of the great Continental composers such as G. Allegri, J. S. *Bach, G. F. *Handel, and W. A. Mozart have written some of the finest specimens of this form of music. Among well-known English composers of motets are J. Taverner, T. *Tallis, W. *Byrd, and H. *Purcell.

H. Leichtentritt, *Geschichte der Motette* (1908). H. C. Colles in *Grove's Dictionary of Music and Musicians* (ed. 5 by E. Blom), v (1954), pp. 912–15, with bibl.

MOTHER OF GOD. See *Theotokos*.

MOTHERING SUNDAY. The Fourth Sunday in Lent, also known as *Laetare Sunday. The name has been referred (1) to the custom in some parts of England of paying a visit to one's mother on this day; or (2) to the practice of visiting the cathedral or mother church on this day; or (3) to the words occurring in the *epistle for the day, 'Jerusalem . . . which is the mother of us all' (Gal. 4. 26).

MOTT, JOHN RALEIGH (1865–19   ), American *Methodist. After studying at Upper Iowa and Cornell universities, he became student secretary of the International Committee of the *Y.M.C.A. (1888), chairman of the executive committee of the Student Volunteer Movement, and then in 1895 general secretary of the World Student Christian Federation, for whose formation he was largely responsible. In 1901 he was appointed assistant general secretary of the Y.M.C.A. He is chiefly known for his zealous propaganda on behalf of missions, based upon the watchword 'The Evangelization of the World in our Generation', and he acted as chairman of the committee which called the first International Missionary Conference at

*Edinburgh (1910). His numerous books, relating to missionary work, include *The Evangelization of the World in this Generation* (1900) *The Present-Day Summons to the World Mission of Christianity* (1932) and his collected *Addresses and Papers* (6 vols., New York, 1946–7).

Addresses and Papers (6 vols., New York, 1946–7). B. Mathews, *John R. Mott*. World Citizen (1934).

MOTU PROPRIO (Lat., 'on his own impulse'). A letter, addressed by the Pope either to the Church at large or to some part of it or to some particular persons, which has been written on his personal initiative and bears his personal signature.

MOULE, HANDLEY CARR GLYN (1841–1920), Bp. of *Durham. He had a brilliant career at Trinity College, Cambridge, where he was elected a Fellow in 1865. After a period as a master at Marlborough College (1865–7) he was ordained at *Ely and acted for some years as his father's curate at Fordington, Dorset, returning temporarily to Cambridge from 1873 to 1877. On the establishment of Ridley Hall, Cambridge, in 1881 as a theological college on *Evangelical principles, Moule became its first Principal and became a leading influence for Evangelicalism at Cambridge. In 1899 he was elected Norris Professor of Divinity and in 1901 he succeeded B. F. *Westcott as Bp. of Durham, where he continued to promote Evangelical ideals. His writings include *Outlines of Christian Doctrine* (1889), *Veni Creator* (1890), *Charles Simeon* (1892), *Philippian Studies* (1897), *Colossian Studies* (1898), *Ephesian Studies* (1900), and *Christus Consolator* (1915).

J. B. Harford (ed.), *Letters and Poems of Bishop Moule* [1922]. Life by J. B. Harford–F. C. Macdonald (London [1922]). J. Baird, *The Spiritual Unfolding of Bishop H. C. G. Moule* [1926]. W. *Lock in *D.N.B.*, *1912–1921*, p. 390 f.

MOULTON, WILLIAM FIDDIAN (1835–1898), Biblical student. Having entered the *Wesleyan ministry in 1858, he was at once appointed to a teaching post at Richmond College, which he held till 1874. In the latter year he became the first head master of the Leys School, Cambridge. He was one of the foremost authorities on NT Greek in his day. In 1870 he became secretary of one of the NT committees occupied on the *RV, and work in connexion with the RV filled a great part of his life. His published writings include a fresh Eng. trans. of J. G. B. *Winer's *Grammar of NT Greek* (1870) and, in conjunction with A. S. Geden, a *Concordance* (1897) to the Greek NT.

His elder son, JAMES HOPE MOULTON (1863–1917), also did important work in the same field, esp. in bringing to bear on NT Greek the new evidence from non-literary papyri (the significance of which he had come to understand through the writings of A. *Deissmann). His brilliant 'Prolegomena' (vol. i, 1906) to his *Grammar of the New Testament Greek* embodied many of his conclusions. In conjunction with G. Milligan he began in 1914 the issue of his important *Vocabulary of the Greek Testament, illustrated from the Papyri and other non-literary Sources* (completed in 1930). He was also the author of *Early Zoroastrianism* (*Hibbert Lectures for 1912; 1913). He lost his life through submarine action in the Mediterranean in 1917.

Memoir ot W. F. Moulton by W. Fiddian Moulton (son), with chapter on his biblical work and opinions by J. H. Moulton (London, 1899). Shorter sketch by G. G. Findlay (ib., 1910). G. Le G. Norgate in *D.N.B.*, Suppl. iii (1901), p. 204 f.
Life of J. H. Moulton by his brother [W. Fiddian Moulton] (London, 1919). A. S. *Peake in *D.N.B., 1912-1921*, p. 391 f.

MOUNT OF OLIVES, The. See *Olives, The Mount of.*

MOVABLE FEASTS. Annual ecclesiastical feasts which do not fall on a fixed date in the secular calendar, but vary acc. to certain determined rules. Thus *Easter Day is the first Sunday after the ('ecclesiastical') full moon between 21 Mar. and 18 Apr., and a number of other feasts fall at a fixed number of days or weeks from Easter. *Advent Sunday is the Sunday falling on or nearest to 30 Nov.

MOZARABIC RITE. The name given to the ancient liturgical forms which were in use in the Iberian Peninsula from the earliest times until the 11th cent. It is, however, a misnomer, for the term Mozarabic is correctly applied only to the part of Spain which fell under Moorish rule after 711.

The earliest reference to liturgy in Spain occurs in the letter (A.D. 538) of Pope *Vigilius to Profuturus, Bp. of Braga, in reply to a request for liturgical information. For the following three cents. we are dependent for material on the Spanish Councils and Fathers, esp. St. *Isidore's *De Ecclesiasticis Officiis.* The earliest extant MS. service book is of the 9th cent. The Rite contained in these sources remained in general use (in spite of efforts to get rid of it on the charge of *adoptianism in the 9th cent.) until the 11th cent.; and even its 'abolition' by Popes *Alexander II and *Gregory VII did not prevent its survival in some Moorish provinces until they were taken from the Moors in the 14th–15th cents. After the final conquest of the Moors, Cardinal *Ximenes, Abp. of Toledo from 1495 to 1517, secured the preservation of the Rite by setting apart a chapel in *Toledo Cathedral and six parish churches in the city for its celebration, and by causing a *Missal and *Breviary to be printed. The Mozarabic Rite has thus survived to the present day, though it now seems to be little regarded, even by its appointed custodians. With the jealously preserved *Ambrosian Rite at Milan, it is the only extant Latin non-Roman rite in the RC Church.

The Mozarabic Mass is of a '*Gallican' type. Each Mass in the *Sacramentary consists of nine prayers, varying in text, which form the framework of the liturgy. After the three lections (the first generally from the OT) have

been read and the appropriate chant sung, there follow the first two prayers and the *Diptychs. After the fourth prayer there occurs the *Kiss of Peace. The fifth is the 'illatio' or *Preface, leading to '*Sanctus' and '*Benedictus'. The Words of *Institution ('missa secreta') constitute the only part of the Mass said silently. Until 924 their text began *Dominus noster Jesus Christus, in qua nocte tradebatur*, and they are found in this form in the only extant Sacramentary (9th cent.); but since 924 the Roman text, *Qui pridie*, &c., has taken its place. The prayer 'post Pridie' is sometimes a form of *epiclesis. The *fraction of the *Host into nine pieces, of which seven are arranged in the form of a cross, representing the mysteries of our Lord's life, is similar to *Gallican and *Celtic practice. After the *Creed, the '*Paternoster' and *Embolism lead up to the 'commixtio' and the recitation of the 'Sancta Sanctis'. The last of the nine prayers is the 'benedictio', and this is followed by the *Communion and *Dismissal ('absolutio').

The Occasional Offices in Spain have long been entirely Roman, for the 'Liber Ordinum', in which the Mozarabic forms were contained, was lost for centuries and never printed. Baptism seems to have been administered with either one or three 'mersiones' (*Conc. Toled.*, 633, can. 6) and, until the Council of Braga of 563, with a form slightly varying from the Roman; it also (as at one time in Milan and Gaul) included the '*pedilavium'.

The extant MS. service-books are the 'Liber Ordinum' (Ritual and Pontifical), the 'Liber Sacramentorum' (Missal), the 'Comes' (Masslectionary), and the 'Psalterium'. The Mozarabic Rite is sometimes held to have influenced English liturgical books by way of Ireland, and the Roman books also include Mozarabic material in the prayers of the *Rituale for the dying and the dead. At a later date its 'benedictio fontis' was used in compiling the *Baptismal Office of the 1549 *BCP.

The *editio princeps* of the Missal was the *Missale Mixtum secundum Regulam Beati Isidori, dictum Mozarabes* (Toledo, 1500). Later ed. by A. Lesley, S.J., Rome, 1755; repr. in J. P. Migne, *PL*, lxxxv. *Editio princeps* of the Breviary was the *Breviarium secundum Regulam Beati Isidori* (Toledo, 1502); also ed. F. A. Lorenzana, Madrid, 1775; repr., Rome, 1804; also in J. P. Migne, *PL*, lxxxvi. M. Férotin, O.S.B. (ed.), *Le Liber Ordinum en usage dans l'Église wisigothique et mozarabe de l'Espagne du cinquième au onzième siècle* (Monumenta Ecclesiae Liturgica, v; Paris, 1904); id. (ed.), *Le Liber Mozarabicus Sacramentorum et les manuscrits mozarabes* (ib., vi; 1912). J. P. Gilson (ed.), *The Mozarabic Psalter MS.*, British Museum, Add. 30851 (*Henry Bradshaw Society, xxx for 1905; 1905). W. C. Bishop, *The Mozarabic and Ambrosian Rites* (*Alcuin Club Tracts, xv; 1924), pp. 1–97. H. Jenner in *C.E.*, x (1911), pp. 611–23, s.v.; F. *Cabrol, O.S.B., in *D.A.C.L.*, xii (pt. 1; 1935), cols. 390–491, s.v. 'Mozarabe Liturgie'; L. Casanas Guasch in *E.C.*, viii (1952), cols. 1496–1503 (with illustrations), s.v. 'Mozarabica Liturgia'.

MOZLEY, JAMES BOWLING (1813–78), post-*Tractarian theologian. Educated at Oriel College, Oxford, where his brother, Thomas (q.v.), became a Fellow, he was himself elected to a fellowship at Magdalen in 1840. From the first he had taken a keen interest in the *Oxford Movement, and after the secession of J. H. *Newman in 1845 was for a time one of its foremost representatives in Oxford. Largely under the influence of the *Gorham case, he was led to modify his Tractarian beliefs in a more moderate direction, though he continued a strong Churchman. His books include *On the Augustinian Doctrine of Predestination* (1855) and *On the Primitive Doctrine of Baptismal Regeneration* (1856); but much of his most brilliant writing is to be found in his essays and articles, collected as *Essays Historical and Theological* (2 vols., 1878). His *Bampton Lectures on 'Miracles' (1865) were acclaimed a masterly contribution to a then very pressing issue. From 1871 till his death he was Regius professor of divinity at Oxford. From 1856 he also held the living of Old Shoreham in Sussex, where he died on 4 Jan. 1878.

Collected ed. of *University and other Sermons* (1876). Mozley's *Essays, Historical and Theological* (2 vols., 1878; with biogr. introd., i, pp. xi–xlviii), and *Letters* (1885; also with biogr. introd. pp. 1–30), both ed. by his sister, Anne Mosley (1809–91). His fine sermon on 'The Reversal of Human Judgment', repr. in H. H. *Henson (ed.), *Selected English Sermons* ('The World's Classics', 1939), pp. 279–304. W. A. Greenhill in *D.N.B.*, xxxix (1894), pp. 249–51.

MOZLEY, THOMAS (1806–93), divine and journalist. The brother of J. B. *Mozley, he was educated at Oriel College, Oxford (where J. H. *Newman was his tutor), and elected a Fellow of the College in 1829. He was ordained in 1831, and held a succession of parochial appointments. At the outset of the *Tractarian Movement he was a keen supporter and wrote extensively for its organ, the *British Critic*, himself assuming the editorship from 1841 till its cessation in 1843. From 1844 onwards he was a constant contributor to *The Times* newspaper. His writings include *Reminiscences, chiefly of Oriel College and the Oxford Movement* (2 vols., 1882), valuable for the light it throws on many aspects of the *Oxford Movement, and *Letters from Rome on the Occasion of the* [*Vatican] *Council, 1869–1870* (2 vols., 1891). Though a gifted writer, Mozley was apt to be inaccurate in his record of facts.

There is no Life, but much is to be gleaned from scattered reff. to him in the literature of the Oxford Movement. A. F. Pollard in *D.N.B.*, xxxix (1894), p. 251 f., s.v.

MOZZETTA. A short cape-like garment to which a small hood is attached, worn by the Pope, cardinals, exempt abbots, abbots-general, and other privileged dignitaries. It came into use in the later Middle Ages. Its colour depends on the office of the wearer and the occasion on which it is worn.

MUGGLETONIANS. A sect founded *c.* 1651 by Ludowicke Muggleton (1609–98) and his cousin, John Reeve (1608–58), who claimed to be the 'two witnesses' of Rev. 11. 3–6. They denied the doctrine of the Holy Trinity, and held that during the period of the Incarnation the government of heaven was left to *Elijah.

Believing that God would never again interfere with the world after His revelation to Muggleton and Reeve, they condemned prayer and preaching. They also taught that matter was eternal and reason the creation of the devil. As a very small sect, the Muggletonians continued at least until 1868.

A. Jessopp, *The Coming of the Friars and Other Historical Essays* (1889), ch. vii, 'The Prophet of Walnut Tree Yard', pp. 302–43. W. T. Whitley in *H.E.R.E.*, viii (1915), p. 871, s.v., with bibl.

MÜLLER, F. MAX. See *Max Müller, Friedrich*.

MÜLLER, GEORGE (1805–98), philanthropist and preacher. He was born near Halberstadt in Germany, but later became a British subject. Though intended for the ministry Müller was profligate as a youth until in 1825, while a student at Halle, he came into contact with a group of earnest Christians. Under their influence he experienced a sudden change and became a man of self-abnegation, devoting himself exclusively to religious work. In 1829 he came to London to take up an appointment for the Society for Promoting Christianity among the Jews. Forced by ill-health to leave London in 1830 he moved to Teignmouth, where he associated himself with the *Plymouth Brethren, resigned from his previous appointment, and became a preacher to the local community. Believing that temporal as well as spiritual needs could be supplied through faith and prayer, he abolished pew rents and refused a salary, supporting himself and his charitable work with offerings from his followers. Two years later he moved to Bristol, where he devoted his life to the care of orphan children, relying on voluntary contributions which flowed in through the deep impression made by his *Narrative of the Lord's Dealings with George Müller* (Part i, 1837; ii, 1841). Starting with only a few children, he eventually had 2,000 under his care, accommodated in large houses at Ashley Down, near Bristol. At the age of 70, leaving this work in the hands of his daughter and her husband, James Wright, Müller set out with his second wife on a preaching mission to Europe, America, India, Australia, and China extending over 17 years. He died at Bristol.

Autobiography of George Müller compiled by G. F. Bergin, with preface and concluding chapter by A. T. Pierson (London, 1905). Mrs. [S. G.] Müller, *Preaching Tours and Missionary Labours of George Müller* (1883), with introd. by George Müller, pp. iii–xiv. E. K. Groves (nephew), *George Müller and his Successors* (1906). Lives by F. G. Warne (London [1898]; enlarged [1935]); A. T. Pierson (ib., 1899; with additions [1949]) and W. H. Harding (ib., 1914). T. B. Johnstone in *D.N.B.*, Suppl. iii (1901), p. 208 f.

MÜLLER, JULIUS (1801–78), German Protestant theologian. He studied law at Breslau and Göttingen universities, but finding his spiritual aspirations unsatisfied, under the influence of F. A. G. *Tholuck, who urged him to come to Berlin (1823), he studied theology. In 1825 he was ordained pastor at Breslau. In

1831 he was appointed university preacher at Göttingen, and in 1835 professor of dogmatics at *Marburg. Here he upheld a conservative Protestant theology against the *Hegelianism of the *Tübingen School, esp. F. C. *Baur, and the *Leben Jesu* of D. F. *Strauss. In 1839 he was appointed to the chair of theology at Halle. In his principal work, *Die christliche Lehre von der Sünde* (vol i. 1839; ii, 1844), he sought to interpret the fact of sin on the assumption of an extra-temporal fall occasioned by a free and intelligible act of decision on the part of each individual. As one of the most prominent theologians of his time he took a leading part in the negotiations for the Prussian Evangelical Union. In 1850 he founded, with A. *Neander and K. I. *Nitzsch, the *Deutsche Zeitschrift für christliche Wissenschaft und christliches Leben*; most of his contributions to it were collected in the *Dogmatische Abhandlungen* (1870).

Life by his son-in-law, L. Schultze (Bremen, 1879); also L. Schultze, *D. Julius Müller als Ethiker und die Glaubensfrage mit Bezug auf das Apostolicum* (1895). D. Hupfeld in *P.R.E.* (ed. 3), xiii (1903), pp. 529–34.

MÜLLER, LUDWIG (1883–1946), German *Reichsbischof. He was born at Gütersloh and educated at Münster i.W. When an army chaplain at Königsberg, he met Hitler (1926) who in 1933 made him his confidential adviser in Church matters; and, under strong Nazi pressure, he was elected Bp. of Prussia and also Reichsbischof. Resistance from the embryonic Confessing Church to his Aryanizing policy led to his virtual supersession in 1935 by the appointment of H. Kerrl as Minister for Church Affairs, though Müller nominally remained in office. In 1936 he published a Germanized Version of the Sermon on the Mount.

MUNGO, St. See *Kentigern, St.*

MUNIFICENTISSIMUS DEUS. The opening words and hence the name of the Apostolic Constitution issued by *Pius XII on 1 Nov. 1950 defining the doctrine of the *Assumption of the BVM (q.v.). The Pope acknowledged the petitions of the faithful and, recalling the action of *Pius IX in defining the doctrine of the *Immaculate Conception, from which the doctrine of the Assumption seemed to follow, briefly traced the history of the doctrine through the earliest sources and the works of later theologians and in the Liturgy. He concluded by declaring and defining it as a matter of divinely revealed dogma that the BVM 'having completed her earthly course was in body and soul assumed into heavenly glory', to deny which would incur the wrath of Almighty God and the Holy Apostles.

The constitution was issued in answer to repeated demands, esp. from 1870 onwards, which had grown much stronger and more highly organized in the period immediately preceding its publication. The definition of the dogma aroused considerable opposition among members of the Eastern Churches and among some Anglicans who feared that it would impede any plans for union, though the statement of the doctrine was very moderate.

Text in *A.A.S.*, xlii (1950), pp. 253–73. B. *Capelle, O.S.B., 'Théologie de l'Assomption d'après la bulle "Munificentissimus Deus" ' in *Nouvelle Revue théologique*, lxxii (1950), pp. 1009–27.

MÜNSTER, SEBASTIAN (1489–1552), Hebrew scholar. He studied at Heidelberg, *Tübingen, and Vienna and later entered the *Franciscan Order, which he abandoned for Protestantism. From 1529 until his death he taught at Basel. He produced the first German edition of the Hebrew Bible (2 vols., Basel, 1534–5; with a literal Latin version and notes), extensive use of which was made by M. *Coverdale for the OT of the *Great Bible (1539). His most widely read work, his *Cosmographia Universalis* (Basel, 1544), was a geographical description of the world after the manner of Strabo, written in German. He also issued Hebrew (1525) and Chaldee (1527) grammars.

V. Hantzsch, *Sebastian Münster. Leben, Werke, wissenschaftliche Bedeutung* (*Abh.* (Sächs.), xxiii, Hft. 3; 1898). A. Wolkenhauer, *Sebastian Münsters handschriftliches Kollegienbuch aus den Jahren 1515–1518 und seine Kartin* (*Abh.* (Gött.), N.F., xi, Hft. 3; 1909).

MÜNZER, THOMAS (c. 1490–1525), German *Anabaptist. A native of Stolberg in the Harz mountains, he studied at Leipzig and Frankfurt. In 1519 after an unsettled life he became confessor at a convent of nuns in Thuringia, and in the same year probably met M. *Luther at Leipzig. Under the influence of *Joachim of Fiore, J. *Hus, and others, he became a Protestant preacher at *Zwickau in 1520, demanding radical religious and social reform. He laid claim to immediate inspiration by the Holy Ghost and sought to establish a community of similarly inspired followers. After expulsion on account of the subversive tendencies of his preaching, he sought to establish in Bohemia a spiritual 'Church' among the Hussites, but was soon driven out again. In 1522 he seems to have had disputes with Luther at *Wittenberg, and in 1523 he went to Alstedt. Here he organized the first services in German, which reflect his learning and abilities as a translator. He proceeded to attack Luther, the Scriptural principle, and Infant Baptism, and preached revolt and wild threats against all his opponents. Driven from Alstedt at Luther's instigation (1524), he went to Mühlhausen in Thuringia, where he again preached open revolt. Once more expelled he went to S. Germany, but returned to Mühlhausen after a few months and tried to link up his movement with the *Peasants' Revolt, placing himself at the head of the rebels. After the defeat at the battle of Frankenhausen (1525) he was captured and executed.

Briefwechsel, ed. H. Böhmer-P. Kirn (Leipzig-Berlin, 1931); *Politische Schriften*, ed. C. Hinrichs (Hallische Monographien ed. O. Eissfeldt, 17; 1950); [Selected] *Schriften*, ed.

O. H. Brandt (Jena, 1933), with full introd. Modern ed. of his *Deutsche Messen und Kirchenämter* by O. J. Mehl (Grimmen, 1937). General studies by E. Bloch (Munich, 1922), with bibl.; J. Zimmermann (Berlin, 1925). L. G. Walter, *Thomas Münzer . . . et les luttes sociales à l'époque de la Réforme* (1927). A. Lohmann, *Zur geistigen Entwicklung Thomas Müntzers* (Beiträge zur Kulturgeschichte des Mittelalters und der Renaissance, xlvii; 1931). E. Sommer, *Die Sendung Thomas Münsers.* Taboritentum und Bauernkrieg in Deutschland (1948). T. Kolde in *P.R.E.* (ed. 3), xiii (1903), pp. 556–66, s.v.; W. Koehler in *R.G.G.* (ed. 2), iv (1930), cols. 279–81, s.v.

MURATORI, LUDOVICO ANTONIO

(1672–1750), librarian and archivist to the Duke of Modena. He published many collections of theological and historical sources, notably the corpus of medieval (500–1500) writers on Italian history (*Rerum Italicarum Scriptores*, 25 vols., 1723–51). His theological writings, often pseudonymous, provoked attacks on his orthodoxy, but he was protected by *Benedict XIV. See also foll. entry.

Collected Works ed. at Arezzo (13 vols., 1767–73) and at Venice (48 vols., 1790–1800). *Epistolario*, ed. M. Campori (14 vols., Modena, 1901–22). Life by his nephew, Gian Francesco Soli Muratori (Modena, 1756). A. C. Jemolo, 'Il pensiero religioso di Ludovico Antonio Muratori' in *Rivista trimestrale di Studi filosofici e religiosi*, iv (1923), pp. 23–78. E. Raimondi, 'I padri maurini e l' opera del Muratori' in *Giornale storico della Letteratura italiana*, vol. cxxviii (1951), p. 429–71, and cxxix (1952), pp. 145–78. G. Cavazzuti, *Lodovico Antonio Muratori, 1672–1750* (1950). H. *Leclercq, O.S.B., in *D.A.C.L.*, xii (pt. 1; 1935), cols. 536–43, and F. Cognasso in *E.C.*, viii (1952), cols. 1523–7, with bibl.

MURATORIAN CANON.

The oldest extant list of NT writings, discovered by L. A. *Muratori in an 8th-cent. *Ambrosiana MS. (J. 101 up.). It is generally held to date from the (later) 2nd cent., because *Pius I, *Hermas, *Marcion, *Basilides and *Montanus are mentioned as contemporaries of the author. The list comprises 85 lines; the beginning and probably also the end are missing; for it starts with what must be the conclusion of a notice on St. Mark and continues with accounts of Luke and John, enumerated as the third and fourth Gospels respectively. It mentions all the NT books except Heb., Jas., and 1 and 2 Pet., and also the *Apocalypse of Peter and the Wisdom of *Solomon, though with a *caveat*. It rejects the 'Pastor' of Hermas, the Marcionite Epistles of St. *Paul to *Laodicea and *Alexandria, and a series of other *Gnostic and Montanist writings. The Canon is written in very bad Latin, full of orthographical and grammatical errors. Some scholars believe it to be a translation from the Greek; J. B. *Lightfoot and others have attributed it to St. *Hippolytus.

The Muratorian Canon was first published by Muratori in *Antiquitates Italicae Medii Aevi*, III (Milan, 1740), pp. 851–854. Facsimile ed. by S. P. *Tregelles, *Canon Muratorianus* (1867). Revised text by E. S. Buchanan in *Journal of Theological Studies*, viii (1906–7), pp. 537–45. Commentaries, with text, in NT Handbooks, e.g. T. *Zahn in *Geschichte des Neutestamentlichen Kanons*, II, 1 (1890), pp. 1–143; B. F. *Westcott, *A General Survey of the Canon of the New Testament* (ed. 1, 1855), Appendix C. S. Ritter, 'Il Frammento muratoriano' in *Rivista di Archeologia cristiana*, iii (1926), pp. 213–63, with text, pp. 245–54, and bibl., pp. 226–32. Bardenhewer, ii, 610–12; Altaner (ed. 1951), p. 117. H. *Leclercq, O.S.B., in *D.A.C.L.*, xii (pt. 1; 1935), cols. 543–60, s.v. 'Muratorianum', with good photographic reproductions and full bibl. J. Schmid in *L.Th.K.*, vii (1935), col. 382 f., s.v.

MURILLO, BARTHOLOMÉ ESTEBÁN

(1617–82), Spanish painter. Except for a period of study under D. R. Velazquez in Madrid, Murillo spent all his life in Seville. He is esp. known as the painter of the 'Immaculate Conception', which he executed more than twenty times. His other paintings include the 'Angels' Kitchen' (1646), the 'Birth of the Virgin' (1655), and the 'Holy Family' (1670), all in the Louvre, and two of the 'Madonna and Child', the one at Florence and the other at Rome.

Reproductions of his paintings (in black and white), ed. A. L. Mayer (Klassiker der Kunst in Gesamtausgaben, xxii; 1913); small collection of plates in colour publd. by the Medici Society (London, 1954). C. Justi, *Murillo* (Leipzig, 1892; ed. 2, 1904). Other studies by A. F. Calvert (London, 1907), P. Lafond ('Les Grands Artistes' [1907]), and S. Montoto (Seville, 1923). C. B. Curtis, *Velázquez and Murillo.* A Descriptive and Historical Catalogue of the Works of . . . Velázquez and Bartolomé Esteban Murillo (1888), pp. 109–352, A. L. Mayer in *Allgemeines Lexikon der bildenden Künstler* begründet von U. Thieme–F. Becker, xxv, ed. H. Vollmer (1931), pp. 285–7, s.v., with detailed bibl.

MYCONIUS, FRIEDRICH (c. 1491–1546),

*Lutheran Reformer of Thuringia. Born at Lichtenfels on the Main, he studied at Annaberg, where in 1510 he encountered J. *Tetzel on the subject of indulgences. After entering the *Franciscan Order (14 July 1510) he was transferred to Leipzig, and in 1512 to Weimar. In his studies he found no satisfaction in the Scholastic theology, but was deeply impressed by the teaching of St. *Augustine. In 1516 he was ordained priest and soon became known in Weimar as a persuasive preacher. Growing sympathy with M. *Luther's attack on *Indulgences (1517) made his position difficult. In 1524 he left the Franciscan Order and in the same year was appointed by Duke Johann preacher at Gotha where he married, reformed the schools, and exercised a powerful moral influence. In correspondence with Luther from 1525 and with P. *Melanchthon from 1527, he played a leading part in the Reform Movement. He was present at the Conferences at *Marburg (1529), *Wittenberg (1536), *Schmalkalden (1537), Frankfurt and Nuremberg (1539) and *Hagenau (1540). In 1538 he visited England on the embassy which hoped to win *Henry VIII for the *Augsburg Confession. He returned to Gotha in 1540.

Although known in his lifetime mainly as a preacher, Myconius also wrote extensively. His main work, *Historia Reformationis*, written in conjunction with J. Heller (ed. by E. S. Cyprian, 1715; modern ed. by O. Clemen, 1914), is a valuable contemporary source esp. for the movement in Thuringia. He also wrote tracts in the vernacular, among them *Wie man die Einfältigen, und sonderlich die Kranken, im Christenthum unterrichten soll* (1539).

P. Scherffig, *Friedrich Mekum von Lichtenfels* (Quellen und Darstellungen aus der Geschichte des Reformationsjahrhunderts, xii; 1909). O. Schmidt–G. Kawerau in *P.R.E.* (ed. 3), xiii (1903), pp. 603–7, and xxiv (1913), p. 191. Schottenloher, ii (1935), p. 83 f. (Nos. 16188–211).

MYCONIUS, OSWALD (1488–1552), originally Geisshäusler, Swiss Reformer and humanist. It appears that the name 'Myconius' was given him by D. *Erasmus. A native of Lucerne, he studied at Basle from 1510 to 1514. In 1516 he went to Zürich, where he became the cathedral schoolmaster and induced the chapter to elect his friend, H. *Zwingli, as people's priest. From 1520 to 1522 he taught at Lucerne; but soon becoming an upholder of the Reformed cause, he was compelled, on account of his Protestant sympathies, to leave the city. In 1523 he was back in Zürich, where he collaborated closely with Zwingli in the propagation of the Reformation. In 1532 he became the successor of J. *Oecolampadius at Basle, remaining here for the rest of his life. His undogmatic temper, which found expression in a desire to reach a compromise with the Lutheran theologians on the matter of *Consubstantiation, aroused distrust among the stricter Zwinglians. Among his works are a Life of Zwingli (1536), the Basle Confession of 1534, and commentaries on several Biblical books.

K. R. Hagenbach, *Johann Oekolampad und Oswald Myconius* (Leben und ausgewählte Schriften der Väter und Begründer der reformierten Kirche, ii; 1859), pp. 309–462; P. Wernle, *Calvin und Basel bis zum Tode des Myconius, 1535–52* (Programm zur Rektoratsfeier der Universität Basel, 1910). B. Riggenbach–E. Egli in *P.R.E.* (ed. 3), xiii (1903), p. 607 f.

MYRC, JOHN, also spelled 'Mirc' (*fl. c.* 1400), religious writer. Beyond the fact that he was the prior of the *canons regular of Lilleshall in Shropshire, nothing is known of his life. His surviving writings are his *Liber Festialis*, a collection of sermons for the higher festivals of the Christian year, beginning with the first Sunday in *Advent; a *Manuale Sacerdotum*; and *Instructions for Parish Priests*, an English poem written in rhyming couplets for the instruction of the clergy in their various duties. His works are important sources for the Church life of his age.

The works mentioned survive in several MSS. (Brit. Mus., Bod., Camb. Univ. Lib.). Early printed edd. of the 'Liber Festialis' by W. *Caxton (1483) and Wynkyn de Worde (1493). His 'Instructions for Parish Priests' were ed. by E. Peacock, with Introd. Note by H. Bradshaw, by the E.E.T.S. (Orig. ser., xxxi, 1868; rev. ed., F. J. Furnivall, 1902). M. Bateson in *D.N.B.*, xxxviii (1893), p. 50 f., s.v. 'Mirk'.

MYSTERIES OF THE ROSARY. The fifteen subjects of meditation connected with the fifteen *decades of the *Rosary. They are divided into three groups of five, corresponding to the three *chaplets of which the devotion is composed, and known as the *Joyful, *Sorrowful, and *Glorious Mysteries (qq.v.). The whole in order forms an epitome of the lives of Christ and His Mother.

MYSTERY PLAYS. The religious dramas ('mysteries') of the Middle Ages are commonly held to have developed from the dramatic parts of the Liturgy, esp. in the offices of *Holy Week and *Easter, though it has also been argued (O. Cargill) that they were composed by individual authors from Biblical and other sources. The most important and impressive were the Passion Plays, but the *Corpus Christi processions offered an occasion for an elaborate representation of Gospel stories, while Antichrist, the Parable of the Wise and Foolish Virgins, and the Last Judgement were other popular themes. Among the non-Biblical subjects adopted later were the legends of St. *Catherine, St. *Dorothy, St. *George, and the *Invention of the Cross. The plays were commonly performed out of doors, on temporary or fixed stages. From the 16th cent., there was a general decay; but since the 19th cent., largely through the success of the *Oberammergau Passion Play, there has been a widespread revival, esp. on the Continent, to which the plays of P. *Claudel in France and of H. von Hofmannsthal in Germany and Austria have contributed. See also *Drama, Christian*.

E. K. Chambers, *The Medieval Stage*, ii (1903), pp. 1–176; K. Young, *The Drama of the Medieval Church* (2 vols., 1933). H. Craig, *English Religious Drama in the Middle Ages* (1955). Grace Frank, *The Medieval French Drama* (1954), pp. 1–202. L. Petit de Julleville, *Les Mystères* (2 vols., 1880). C. Davidson, *Studies in the English Mystery Plays* (Yale Diss., New Haven, 1892). P. E. Kretzmann, *The Liturgical Element in the Earliest Forms of the Medieval Drama, with special Reference to the English and German Plays* (University of Minnesota Studies in Language and Literature, iv; 1916). O. Cargill, *Drama and Liturgy* (Columbia University Studies in English and Comparative Literature, New York, 1930). W. Creizenach in *Cambridge History of English Literature*, ed. A. W. Ward–A. R. Waller, v (1910), pp. 36–60 ('Early Religious Drama'), with bibl. pp. 387–94; further bibl. in *C.B.E.L.*, i, 275–9 and 513–17. See also bibl. to *Morality Play*; also to *Drama*.

MYSTICAL THEOLOGY. In Catholic theology, the science of the spiritual life, in so far as this is dependent on the operation of Divine grace. It is commonly contrasted with *Ascetical Theology (q.v.), which treats of the spiritual life, so far as it can be pursued without supernatural assistance.

MYSTICISM. In general, an immediate knowledge of God attained in this present life through personal religious experience. It is primarily a state of prayer and as such admits of various degrees from short and rare Divine 'touches' to the practically permanent union with God in the so-called 'mystic marriage'. The surest proof adduced by the mystics themselves for the genuineness of their experience is its effect, viz. its fruit in such things as an increase of humility, charity, and love of suffering. Mysticism is a widespread experience not only in Christianity but also in many non-Christian religions, e.g. Buddhism, Taoism, Hinduism, and Islam.

Distinctive of the Christian form of mysticism is its emphasis on two elements often absent elsewhere. In contrast to all pancosmic conceptions of the underlying Reality as an impersonal Unity, it recognizes that the Reality to which it penetrates transcends the soul and the cosmos. And in place of all notions of absorption of the soul into the divine ('Thou art in me and I am in Thee:

and Thy attributes are my attributes' in the Egyptian *Book of the Dead*; much Oriental and *Neo-Platonic religion), it posits that the union is one of love and will in which the distinction between Creator and creature is permanently retained.

Psycho-physical phenomena such as dreams, locutions, trances, visions, and ecstasies, have been frequent concomitants of mystical experience. But while these are recognized by Christian spiritual writers as possible accessories of true mystical insight, they are not held to be essential to it, and indeed are considered to be sometimes hindrances to its proper realization. In the highest state of spiritual marriage they normally cease.

Christian thinkers have differed in their attitudes to mysticism. Some (esp. Protestant) theologians (E. *Brunner; R. *Niebuhr) hold it to be essentially anti-Christian on the ground that its close link with the Neo-Platonic outlook seems nearer to pagan gnosis than to the Gospel's offer of salvation. It has also been suspected on account of its supposed pantheistic dangers (J. W. *Oman; P. E. More). But even if spiritual writers who uphold mysticism sometimes appear too ready to cut through the concrete historical and particular problems to which the Christian Gospel ministers, it would seem difficult to reject all that the Christian mystics have contributed to a deepened understanding of Christian Truth or to disregard the large extent to which their findings have influenced theology. On the other hand, to look upon mystical union as the very essence of Christianity (W. R. *Inge; N. *Berdyaev) must certainly be accounted an exaggeration.

A measure of mysticism is met with so widely in Christian life at its more serious levels that it is impossible to put the Christian mystics into a separate class. There are passages in St. *John's Gospel, St. *Paul's Epistles, and the Bk. of *Revelation which mark their authors as having personally enjoyed mystical experience. In any attempted list of Christian mystics the following would certainly have to be included: St. *Clement of Alexandria, St. *Gregory of Nyssa, St. *Augustine, St. *Dionysius the Areopagite, *Hugh of St.-Victor, St. *Bernard, St. *Mechthild, *Richard of St.-Victor, St. *Hildegard, St. *Francis of Assisi, St. *Bonaventure, St. *Gertrude 'the Great', *Eckhart, R. *Rolle,

J. *Tauler, *Henry Suso, St. *Catherine of Siena, J. *Ruysbroeck, W. *Hilton, the author of the *Theologia Germanica, *Julian of Norwich, St. *Catherine of Genoa, S. *Franck, St. *Teresa of Ávila, St. *Luis of Granada, St. *John of the Cross, J. *Boehme, R. *Crashaw, G. *Foxe, H. *Vaughan, M. de *Molinos, F. *Fénelon, Mme *Guyon, W. *Law, St. Gemma *Galgani, St. *Grignion of Montfort, and Charles *de Foucauld.

All works on Christian spirituality are necessarily largely concerned with Mysticism. Books treating the subject historically include P. Pourrat, P.S.S., *La Spiritualité chrétienne* (4 vols., 1918-28); K. E. *Kirk, *The Vision of God* (Bampton Lectures for 1928; 1931); W. R. *Inge, *Christian Mysticism* (Bampton Lectures for 1899; 1899); id., *Studies of English Mystics* (St. Margaret's Lectures for 1905; 1906), H. *Bremond, *Histoire littéraire du sentiment religieux en France depuis la fin des guerres de religion jusqu'à nos jours* (11 vols., index, 1916-36; Eng. tr., 1928 ff.). [E.] C. Butler, O.S.B., *Western Mysticism. The Teaching of SS. Augustine, Gregory and Bernard on Contemplation and the Contemplative Life* (1922). E. *Underhill, *Mysticism* (1911); id., *Practical Mysticism* (1914); id., *The Mystics of the Church* (1925) and other works. On some less well-known mystics, H. Thurston, S.J., *Surprising Mystics* (ed. J. H. Crehan, S.J., 1955). Among philosophical discussions of the subject (from varying standpoints) may be mentioned J. [J.] *Görres, *Die christliche Mystik* (4 vols. in 5 parts, 1836-42); W. *James, *The Varieties of Religious Experience* (Gifford Lectures for 1901-2; 1902), pp. 379-429; E. Lehmann, *Mystik i Hedenskab og Kristendom* (Copenhagen, 1904; Eng. tr., 1910); F. *von Hügel, *The Mystical Element of Religion, as studied in St. Catherine of Genoa and her Friends* (2 vols., 1908); E. I. Watkin, *The Philosophy of Mysticism* (1920); M. *Grabmann, *Wesen und Grundlagen der katholischen Mystik* (Der katholische Gedanke, ii, 1922); J. Maréchal, S.J., *Études sur la psychologie des mystiques* (Museum Lessianum, Section philosophique, ii and xix, 1924-37; Eng. tr. of vol. i, 1924); E. *Brunner, *Die Mystik und das Wort. Der Gegensatz zwischen moderner Religionsauffassung und christlichen Glauben dargestellt an der Theologie Schleiermachers* (1924); H. Thurston, S.J., *The Physical Phenomena of Mysticism* (ed. J. H. Crehan, 1952). Works of a more avowedly practical character include A. Saudreau, O.P., *Les Degrés de la vie spirituelle* (2 vols., 1896); id., *La Vie d'union à Dieu et les moyens d'y arriver d'après les grands maîtres de la spiritualité* (1900 ; Eng. tr. of ed. 3, 1927); id., *L'État mystique, sa nature, ses phases* (1903; Eng. tr., 1924); id., *Les Faits extraordinaires de la vie spirituelle* (1908). A. Poulain, S.J., *Des grâces d'oraison* (1901; Eng. tr., 1910). There are several periodicals devoted to the subject, including *La Vie spirituelle* (Paris, 1919 ff.; Dominican), *Revue d'Ascétique et de Mystique* (Toulouse, 1920 ff.; Jesuit), *Zeitschrift für Aszese und Mystik* (Innsbruck-Würzburg, 1926 ff.; since 1947, *Geist und Leben*), *Études carmélitaines* (Paris, 1911 ff.); also *Dictionnaire de spiritualité*, ed. M. Viller, S.J., and others (1937 ff.). R. M. *Jones and other writers in *H.E.R.E.*, ix (1917), pp. 83-177, s.v. 'Mysticism' [in Christian and non-Christian religions]; A. Fonck in *D.T.C.*, x (pt. 2; 1929), cols. 2599-2674, s.v. 'Mystique (Théologie)'; E. Mura in *E.C.*, viii (1952), cols. 1135-43, s.v. 'Mistica'.

NAASSENES

NAASSENES (Heb. *שׁחָנ*, 'serpent'). A *Gnostic sect whose members, in pretended hostility to the God of the Jews who had trampled down the serpent's wisdom (Gen. 3. 14 f.), worshipped the serpent. They appear to have been a branch of the *Ophites. An account of them is given by *Hippolytus (*Haer.* 5. 6–17).

Texts from Hippolytus repr., with notes, in W. Völker, *Quellen zur Geschichte der christlichen Gnosis* (Sammlung ausgewählter kirchen- und dogmengeschichtliche Quellenschriften, N.F., v; 1932), pp. 11–27. R. *Reitzenstein, *Poimandres* (1904), pp. 81–101. See also bibl. to *Ophites.*

NAG'S HEAD STORY, The

NAG'S HEAD STORY, The. This tale was apparently fabricated early in the 17th cent. to discredit the validity of M. *Parker's episcopal consecration. It alleged that when Parker found himself unable to obtain regular consecration, some clerics met at the Nag's Head tavern in Cheapside, and that there J. *Scory, the deprived Bp. of *Chichester, and himself affirmed not to have been properly consecrated, constituted Parker and the others bishops by placing a Bible on the neck of each in turn with the words 'Take thou authority to preach the Word of God sincerely'. The story was first put into circulation by C. Holywood, S.J., in 1604; and though soon discredited, it continued to reappear in the controversial literature on the validity of *Anglican Ordinations till beyond the middle of the 19th cent.

Christopher [Holywood], S.J., *De Investiganda Vera ac Visibili Christi Ecclesia Libellus* (Antwerp, 1604), p. 17 f. The earliest attempt to discredit the story is that in F. *Mason, *The Consecration of the Bishops of the Church of England* (1613), p. 123 f. See also bibl. to *Anglican Ordinations* and *Parker, M.*

NAHUM, Book of

NAHUM, Book of. One of the twelve '*Minor Prophets'. It mainly relates to the fall of Nineveh (612 B.C.), here depicted as so certain and imminent that it is generally supposed that the oracle may be dated about 613 B.C. The opening verses (1. 2–2. 2) contain a psalm which, although it forms a fitting introduction to what follows, has no reference to Nineveh, the main subject of the Book; and on this ground, combined with its (imperfectly preserved) acrostic form, some attribute the psalm to an independent source. Various theories have been advanced to explain the one fact stated in connexion with the person of Nahum, that he was 'an Elkoshite' (1. 1). Some fix the site of Elkosh near Nineveh; others follow St. *Jerome and place it in *Galilee (cf. the derivation of *Capernaum as 'village of Nahum'); others again prefer a site in Judah. The prophecy, being confined to the subject of Nineveh and its destruction, makes no specific allusions to any future hope and destiny connected with the *Messiah.

Commentaries by A. B. *Davidson (Camb. Bib., AV, on Nah., Hab., and Zeph., 1896, pp. 9–44) and J. M. P. Smith (I.C.C. on Mic., Zeph., Nah., Hab., Obad., and Joel, 1912, pp. 267–363) and G. G. V. Stonehouse (West. Comm. on Zeph., Nah., and Hab., 1929, pp. 73–140). W. R. Arnold, 'The Composition of Nahum 1–2:3' in *Z.A.T.W.*, xxi (1901), pp. 225–65. A. Haldar, *Studies in the Book of Nahum* (Uppsala Universitets Årsskrift, 1946, Pt. 7; 1947), with bibl. A. R. S. Kennedy in *H.D.B.*, iii (1900), pp. 473–7. See also bibl. to *Minor Prophets.*

NAME OF JESUS

NAME OF JESUS. In consequence of the close relation between name and person, the Name of Jesus is used in the NT as a synonym for Jesus Himself, denoting His character and authority. The disciples perform miracles and exorcisms 'in the name of Jesus', i.e. by His power (Mk. 9. 37 ff., Acts 4. 30), and regularly baptize in it (Acts 2. 38, 8. 16, &c.), and St. Paul esp. insists on its efficacy for our justification (1 Cor. 6. 11) and the obligation of Christians to venerate it above all other names (Phil. 2, 9 f.). This reverence for, and confidence in, the Name of Jesus has found expression in the Church from early times, e.g. in its use in exorcisms and the medieval custom of giving medals with the monogram 'IHS' (q.v.) to newly baptized infants. In the 15th cent. devotion to the Holy Name was popularized by the *Franciscans, St. *Bernardino of Siena and St. *Giovanni Capistrano, to whom also the Litany of the Holy Name, used since the 15th cent. and approved for the universal RC Church by *Leo XIII in 1886, possibly owes its origin. See also foll. entry.

A. Cabassut, O.S.B., 'La Dévotion au nom de Jésus dans l'Église d'occident' in *La Vie spirituelle*, lxxxvi (1952), pp. 46–69.

NAME OF JESUS, Feast of the

NAME OF JESUS, Feast of the. This feast, which had been celebrated locally at the end of the Middle Ages, was officially granted to the *Franciscans in 1530 for commemoration on 14 Jan. The observance gradually spread until it was finally prescribed in 1721 by Innocent XIII for the whole RC Church on the Second Sunday after *Epiphany. The Office and Mass were composed by Bernardino dei Busti (d. 1500), while the celebrated office hymns, '*Jesu dulcis memoria', 'Jesu Rex admirabilis', and 'Jesu decus angelicum', were the work of an uncertain 13th cent. author. The date of the feast was again modified in the Latin Church by *Pius X, who fixed it for the Sunday between the *Circumcision (1 Jan.) and the *Epiphany (6 Jan.) or, if in any year there is no such Sunday, on 2 Jan. Acc. to late medieval practice in England, as embodied in the later forms of the *Sarum Rite, the feast was observed on 7 Aug., and on this date, assigned to it in the calendar of the BCP, it is commonly observed in the Anglican Communion.

For relevant clauses of Pius X's *motu proprio* 'Abhinc duos annos' of 23 Oct. 1913 fixing the new date of the Feast, see *A.A.S.*, v (1913), pp. 458–60. G. Löw, C.SS.R., in *E.C.*, viii (1952), col. 1919 f., s.v. 'Nome di Gesù, Festa del'.

NANTES, Edict of. The edict which ended the French wars of religion, signed by *Henry IV at Nantes on 13 Apr. 1598. The *Huguenots were allowed free exercise of their religion except in certain towns, civil equality, and fair administration of justice, and were provided with a state subsidy for the support of their troops and pastors. Its terms were sometimes much infringed in the 17th cent., notably by A. *Richelieu. It was finally revoked on 18 Oct. 1685 by Louis XIV, under pressure from Mme de Maintenon and Père La Chaise.

[E. Benoist], *Histoire de l'édit de Nantes* (24 books in 5 vols., Delft, 1693-5), with text of Edict in vol. i, pp. (62-94), and of Revocation in vol. v, pp. (184-6); Eng. tr. of Books 1-11 (2 vols., 1694), with Eng. tr. of text of Edict, i, 526-62. Text of Edict repr. in J. Dumont (ed.), *Corps universel diplomatique de droit des gens*, v (Amsterdam, 1728), No. CCLII, pp. 545-57; extracts in Eng. tr. in H. Bettenson (ed.), *Documents of the Christian Church* (1943), p. 302 f. Operative clauses of Revocation repr. in [J. A. L.] Jourdan-... Decrusy-[F. A.] Isambert[-A. H. Taillandier], *Recueil général des anciennes lois françaises*, xix [c. 1830], pp. 530-4, and in Mirbt, No. 536, p. 390 f.

NARSAI (d. c. 503), also Narses, *Nestorian theologian. In early life he was a professor at the School of *Edessa under the presidency of the Nestorian *Barsumas, from c. 437. Upon the expulsion of Barsumas from Edessa in 457, Narsai accompanied him to Nisibis, assisted him to found the Nestorian School there, and presided over it until his death. Narsai was one of the formative theologians of the Nestorian Church. He wrote an extensive set of commentaries on the OT, but these appear to have been completely lost. Of his many hymns, however—the fame of which gained for him the description 'Harp of the Spirit'— several have survived. Certain of these (the 'Liturgical Homilies') afford important evidence for the early history of the E. Syrian rites of *Baptism and the *Eucharist.

Syriac text of Works ed. A. Mingana (2 vols., Mosul, 1905; editing partly in Syriac). Eng. tr. of four of the 'Liturgical Homilies', with critical discussions, by R. H. *Connolly (Texts and Studies, viii, 1, Cambridge, 1909). A. *Baumstark, *Geschichte der syrischen Literatur* (1922), pp. 109-13. Bardenhewer, iv, 407-10. E. Tisserant in *D.T.C.*, xi (pt. 1; 1931), cols. 26-30; H. *Leclercq, O.S.B., in *D.A.C.L.*, xii (pt. 1; 1935), cols. 884-8.

NARTHEX (Gk. νάρθηξ, lit. 'a small case'). In a Byzantine church, the antechamber to the nave, from which it is separated by columns, rails, or a wall. *Catechumens, candidates for baptism, and penitents occupied the narthex. It is to be distinguished from the 'exonarthex', or porch, opening on to the street.

H. *Leclercq, O.S.B., in *D.A.C.L.*, xii (1935), col. 888 f., s.v.; M. Zocca in *E.C.*, viii (1952), cols. 1659-61, s.v. 'Nartece'.

NASH PAPYRUS, The. The oldest surviving MS. of any portion of the Hebrew OT. It is a small fragment of papyrus, acquired by W. L. Nash in 1902, and perhaps to be dated (so W. F. Albright) as early as the 2nd cent. B.C. (and not 2nd cent. A.D., as was at first thought). It contains the Ten *Commandments in substantially the Deuteronomic text (Deut. 5.

6-21), with the 6th and 7th Commandments transposed (cf. Lk. 18. 20), followed by a brief introductory passage and then the *Shema. Points of contact with the *Septuagint indicate that it may have transmitted a text of the OT nearer to that of the original Hebrew than that in any of the standard Hebrew MSS. The fragment is in the Cambridge University Library (Or. 233).

S. A. *Cook, 'A Pre-Massoretic Biblical Papyrus' in the *Proc. of the Soc. of Biblical Archaeology*, xxv (1903), pp. 34-56 (with facsimile).

NASOREAN. See *Nazarene*.

NATALIS, ALEXANDER (1639-1724), Church historian. In 1655 he entered the *Dominican Order at Paris, where he spent nearly all his life. Possessed of strong sympathies with *Jansenism, he became one of the *Appellants who in 1714 opposed the '*Unigenitus'. The most important of his writings is his *Selecta Historiae Ecclesiasticae Capita* (24 vols., 1676-86), a treatise of great erudition; but though the earlier volumes had been praised by *Innocent XI in 1682, Natalis's treatment of the conflict between the Empire and the Papacy caused the whole work to be put on the *Index two years later. Natalis himself tried in vain to make the work unobjectionable by a revision in 1699, but it was only after this had been followed by two further banned editions that the work was finally removed from the Index in 1734. Among Natalis's other writings was a *Theologia dogmatica et moralis* (10 vols., 1694).

P. Mandonnet in *D.T.C.*, i (1903), cols. 769-72, s.v. 'Alexandre (Noël)', with bibl.

NATALITIA (Lat., 'birthday'). In the early cents. this word was used of the death-days of Christians, and esp. of martyrs, in the sense of their birthday into eternal life. In later Christian usage, the word sometimes meant no more than 'anniversary', the *Gelasian Sacramentary, e.g., employing it of the anniversary of a bishop's consecration.

NATHANAEL. One of the first disciples of Jesus, Who recommended him for his sincerity (Jn. 1. 47). He was a native of Cana (Jn. 21. 2) and his call is related in Jn. 1. 43-51. In spite of this his name is not included among those of the Twelve Apostles. From the 9th cent. he was identified with St. *Bartholomew by Elias of Damascus, *Ebedjesus, and other *Nestorians. In the W. this conjecture is first mentioned by *Rupert of Deutz in the 12th cent., and was adopted later by Cornelius Jansenius the Elder (1510-76). The identification is now widely accepted by Biblical scholars.

The identity of Nathanael and Bartholomew has been accepted by J. H. *Newman, H. G. A. *Ewald, H. *Alford, G. Milligan, E. *Renan, F. W. *Farrar, B. F. *Westcott, T. *Zahn, and others. H. Cowan in *H.D.B.*, iii (1900), p. 488 f., s.v.

NATIONAL ANTHEM, The. See *God save the King*.

NATIONAL APOSTASY, Sermon on. The sermon with this title preached by J. *Keble on 14 July 1833 in the church of St. Mary the Virgin, Oxford, before the Judges of Assize and commonly regarded as the beginning of the *Oxford Movement (q.v.). Its aim was to promote action in defence of the Church, esp. in view of the proposed suppression of ten Irish bishoprics. The text was 1 Sam. 12. 23.

The Sermon was publd. at Oxford in 1833 immediately after delivery; repr., ed. R. J. E. Boggis, Torquay, 1931; also London [publd. A. R. Mowbray], 1931. Its traditional place as inaugurating the Oxford Movement appears to derive from a passage in J. H. *Newman's *Apologia*; cf. F. L. Cross, *John Henry Newman* (1933), Appendix IV, 'The Myth of July 14, 1833' (p. 162 f.).

NATIONAL ASSEMBLY OF THE CHURCH OF ENGLAND. See *Church Assembly*.

NATIONAL COUNCIL OF THE EVANGELICAL FREE CHURCHES. An association of the Free Churches, formed in 1896 for mutual consultation, co-operation, and witness. It succeeded in uniting these Churches in action, as, e.g., against the Education Bill of 1902, and in the holding of joint missions in different parts of the country. It was merged in 1939 in the *Free Church Federal Council.

NATIONAL COVENANT, The (1638). The Covenant of the Scottish *Presbyterians inaugurated in the Greyfriars churchyard at Edinburgh on 28 Feb. 1638, as an answer to the attempt to impose on the Scottish Church the 1637 BCP. It consisted of the *King's Confession of 1581, with many additions by A. *Henderson and others and concluded with an oath. See also *Covenanters*.

Text pr. in S. R. Gardiner (ed.), *The Constitutional Documents of the Puritan Revolution* (1889), pp. 54–64.

NATIONAL SOCIETY, The. The popular name of the Society formed in 1811 (incorporated 1817) as 'The National Society for the Education of the Poor in the Principles of the Established Church'. With the British and Foreign Schools Society (founded 1807), a mainly Nonconformist body, it was a principal agent in promoting popular education in England and Wales before the setting up by the State of School Boards in 1870. It sponsored A. Bell's system of teaching through monitors or pupil-teachers under a master, and worked by means of a model school (established in Baldwin's Gardens, London, in 1812) and by advice and grants-in-aid to diocesan and other local societies and to individual Church schools. A government grant was first received in 1833. It also undertook the training of teachers, St. Mark's College, Chelsea (now amalgamated with St.

John's College, Battersea, as the College of St. Mark and St. John), being opened in 1841. After 1870 its schools (the 'National' Schools) remained in existence as 'non-provided' schools independent of the system of education under the School Boards; in 1902 these schools began to receive financial aid from the Local Authorities but remained distinct from the State Schools under the 'Dual System'. Under the Act of 1944 such schools became either 'Aided' or 'Controlled' by the Local Authority, with greater or less scope for distinctive Church teaching, respectively. In 1934 the Society received a Supplemental Charter and changed its full name to 'The National Society for the Promotion of Religious Education in accordance with the principles of the Church of England'. Its main activities up to 1948 included (1) the provision to diocesan and parochial authorities of expert advice, and of facilities for exchange of information and co-ordination of action, in all matters concerning religious education, esp. the legal position and efficient conduct of Church schools, and (2) the representation of Church opinion in educational matters to the government; it is also (3) trustee for St. Mark and St. John's and three other C of E training colleges for teachers, and for two C of E boarding schools and some other institutions, and (4) it assists the work of all C of E teachers' training colleges, and the training of ordinands in matters connected with the teaching work of the clergy, arranges courses for Sunday School teachers, and conducts other miscellaneous activities.

In 1948 the C of E Council for Education was set up by the *Church Assembly. Under this Council are five Departmental Councils, including two (the Schools' Council and the Children's Council) which are affiliated to the National Society. Some of the previous activities of the National Society then began to be taken over by the Departmental Councils, but the National Society still retains its independent status.

Much information in annual reports of the National Society (1811 ff.). C. K. F. Brown, *The Church's Part in Education, 1833–1941, with Special Reference to the Work of the National Society* (1942), with bibl.

NATIVITY OF OUR LORD, Feast of the. See *Christmas*.

NATIVITY OF ST. JOHN THE BAPTIST. A feast observed on 24 June, at any rate since the 4th cent., to commemorate the miraculous birth of the Baptist, recorded in Lk. 1. It was one of the earliest feasts to find a place in the Christian calendar. St. *Augustine (*Serm.* 287, 4) explained the special appropriateness of the date selected, as after this Feast the days begin to get shorter, whereas after the Feast of Christ's Nativity they begin to grow longer (cf. Jn. 3. 30).

G. *Morin, 'La Date de la Saint-Jean. Solution d'un problème liturgique au IVe siècle' in *Le Messager des Fidèles* [later *R. Bén.*], v (1888), pp. 257–64. H. *Leclercq, O.S.B., in *D.A.C.L.*, vii (pt. 2; 1927), cols. 2171–4.

NATIVITY OF THE BLESSED VIRGIN.
This feast, which is celebrated in the W. Church and by the Greeks on 8 Sept., is attested for the 8th cent. in the E. by two sermons of St. *Andrew of Crete. Though referred to in Rome by Pope *Sergius (687–701) and in some MSS. of the *Gelasian and *Gregorian Sacramentaries, it was not generally observed in the W. until the 11th cent. It has survived in the calendar of the BCP. The choice of 8 Sept. for the feast is unexplained.

F. G. Holweck in *C.E.* x (1911), p. 712 f.; G. Löw, C.SS.R., in *E.C.*, viii (1952), cols. 1678–80.

NATURAL LAW.
In a theological context, the law inherent in the nature of rational creatures whereby they duly order their conduct with respect to God, their neighbour, and themselves. The chief NT text on which the Christian teaching on the subject rests is Rom. 2. 14 f., where St. *Paul affirms that 'when Gentiles, which have no law, do by nature the things of the law, these, having no law, are a law to themselves; in that they shew the work of the law written in their hearts, their conscience bearing witness therewith'. This law, being perceived by the light of reason, is a matter of obligation for every human being who enjoys the use of his rational faculties. The universal claim of the Natural Law has been defended philosophically on the ground that men everywhere and at all times have acknowledged some moral code, however imperfect, resting on the fundamental principle that good is to be done and evil avoided. The *Commandments of the Decalogue, except that of the sanctification of the Sabbath, all belong to the Natural Law. The fact that the Natural Law can be known by unaided human reason was denied, e.g., by *Traditionalism; its dependence on God as the author of nature is denied by Rationalism; and its very existence by many modern philosophers.

N. Micklem, *The Theology of Law* (1943); J. Dalby, *The Catholic Conception of the Law of Nature* (1943); A. R. Vidler–W. A. Whitehouse (edd.), *Natural Law. A Christian Reconsideration* (1946). O. Gierke, *Das deutsche Genossenschaftsrecht*, iv (1913; Eng. tr., *Natural Law and the Theory of Society, 1500–1800*, 2 vols., 1934); E. *Brunner, *Gerechtigkeit. Eine Lehre von den Grundgesetzen der Gesellschaftsordnung* (1943; Eng. tr. as *Justice and the Social Order*, 1945). C. G. Haines, *The Revival of Natural Law Concepts* (Harvard Studies in Jurisprudence, iv; 1930). C. H. *Dodd, 'Natural Law in the New Testament' in *Theology*, xlix (1946), pp. 128–33 and 161–7; repr. in C. H. Dodd, *New Testament Studies* (1953), pp. 129–142.

NATURAL THEOLOGY.
The body of knowledge about God which may be obtained by human reason alone without the aid of Revelation and hence to be contrasted with 'Revealed Theology'. The distinction was worked out in the Middle Ages at great length, and is based on such passages as Rom. 1. 18 ff., acc. to which man is capable of arriving at certain religious truths by applying his natural powers of discursive thought. In a definition of the *Vatican Council (*De fid. cath.* cap. 2, can. 2) the possibility of this knowledge is explained by the dependence of the creature upon God. The chief objects of Natural Theology

are God in so far as He is known through His works, the human soul, its freedom and immortality, and *Natural Law. Hence, strictly speaking, Natural Theology is part of philosophy and treated as such in the systems of Scholasticism. Reformation theology generally rejected the competence of fallen human reason to engage in Natural Theology; and in recent times this incompetence has been reasserted with emphasis by K. *Barth and the *Dialectical School.

NAUMBURG CONVENTION.
A meeting of princes and representatives of the German Protestant leaders, held at Naumburg from 20 Jan. to 8 Feb. 1561, with a view to securing doctrinal unity, esp. in the matter of the *Eucharist. The proposed agreement on the basis of the *Augsburg Confession failed, as the *Calvinists stood by the 'variata' edition of 1540 and the *Lutherans by the 'invariata' of 1531. An invitation from the Pope to send legates to the Council of *Trent was rejected, nominally through objection to the form of address ('Dilecto filio') in the Papal letter, which was returned unopened.

J. H. Gelbke, *Der Naumburgische Fürstentag, oder wichtige Urkunden und Acten den, wegen erneuerter Unterschrift der Augspurgischen Confession und Beschickung des Concilii zu Trident, von den protestantischen Fürsten und Ständen in Deutschland 1561 zu Naumburg an der Saale gehaltenen Convent betreffend* (1793). R. Calinich, *Der Naumburgische Fürstentag, 1561* (1870). G. Kawerau in *P.R.E.* (ed. 3), xiii (1903), pp. 661–9. Schottenloher, iv (1938), p. 462 (Nos. 40411—25).

NAVE.
That part of a church, between the main front and the chancel and choir, which is assigned to the laity. It is often separated from the sanctuary by a screen, and from the side aisles by columns or pillars. The term is generally thought to be derived from the Lat. *navis*, 'ship', this being a symbol of the Church, but it may be a corrupt form of the Gk. *vaós*, 'temple'.

NAYLER, JAMES
(*c.* 1618–1660), *Quaker. Born near Wakefield, Yorks, from 1643 to 1651 he served with some distinction in the Parliamentary army, in which he was noted as an Independent preacher. He retired, perhaps with consumption, to a farm near his former home, where, shortly after joining the C of E, he was convinced by G. *Fox at the end of 1651 of the Quaker doctrine of the Inner Light. At the outset he was second only to Fox in the leadership of the movement. He was partially responsible for the conversion of the family of Judge Fell of Swarthmoor Hall, Lancs, which soon became a noted centre of Quakerism. In 1652 he preached widely in the N. of England and was imprisoned at Appleby. From the summer of 1655 he was in sole charge of the flourishing London Society until June of the following year. About that time he came under the influence of a group of *Ranters, led by one Martha Simmonds (d. 1665), who, confusing the doctrine of the Inner Light with a belief in absolute unity with God, tried to worship him

as Christ. At first Nayler resisted his devotees and set out to visit Fox who was imprisoned in Launceston castle. Apprehended on the way as a Quaker he was confined in the late summer of 1656 in *Exeter gaol. Here he was accredited with having raised a woman from the dead and in September, under the influence of Martha Simmonds, quarrelled with Fox. As soon as he was released (Oct. 1656) he proceeded to Bristol which he entered with his followers in the manner that the Lord entered Jerusalem. After examination by a Committee of the second Protectorate Parliament, he was very severely punished for blasphemy. He appears to have repented by c. 1657, was released from prison by the Long Parliament in 1659, reconciled with Fox in 1660 and eventually restored to much of his former popularity. He wrote many tracts, among them *How Sin is Strengthened and How it is Overcome* (1657).

A Collection of Sundry Books, Epistles and Papers written by James Nayler (1716). M. R. Brailsford, *A Quaker from Cromwell's Army* (1927); E. Fogelklou, *Koåkaren James Nayler. Ein Sällsam Gestalt i Religionens Historia* (1929; Eng. tr., 1931). A. Gordon in *D.N.B.*, xl (1894), pp. 130–3.

NAZARENE. The term has been applied in a Christian context in several senses. In several of these the form 'Nasorean' is also found.

(1) In the NT Christ is called 'Jesus the Nazarene', *i.e.* 'of *Nazareth', from the place of His residence. In Mt. 2. 23 it is said to have been prophesied that the Christ should 'be called a Nazarene', but the original ref. and meaning of this prophecy, which is not found in the OT, is doubtful. Perhaps the original ref. here was not to Nazareth (so M. Lidzbarski, R. *Reitzenstein), though it is so understood by the Evangelist. In Mt., Jn. and Acts the form is Ναζωραῖος, in Mk. Ναζαρηνός, while in Lk. both forms occur.

(2) The 'Nazarenes' appears as a Jewish term for the early Christians in Acts 24. 5, and continued to be so used for some centuries. It is sometimes met with in Jewish literature in the form 'Nozri'.

(3) 'Nazarenes' occurs also as a name given by 4th-cent. writers to groups of Christians of Jewish race in Syria, who continued to obey much of the Jewish Law though they were otherwise orthodox Christians. They used a version of the Gospel in Aramaic, known as the 'Gospel acc. to the *Hebrews' (which has hence sometimes been termed the 'Gospel of the Nazarenes'). The sect had no doubt existed from the earliest times of Christianity.

(4) The *Mandaeans (q.v.) are described as Nasoreans in some of their earliest literature.

NAZARETH. The village in Galilee which was the home of the BVM and St. *Joseph, and where Christ was brought up and lived till the beginning of His ministry. It lies on a hill verlooking the valley of Esdraelon. Today the town is a popular place of pilgrimage, many of its shrines having been rebuilt after their destruction by the Mohammedans in the Middle Ages. Among its more important sanctuaries are the 'Church of the Annunciation', believed to be erected over the house of Mary, the 'Church of the Nutrition' (now the Church of St. Joseph), on the traditional site of that of St. Joseph, and the beautiful 'St. Mary's Well'. See also *Nazarene*.

T. Tobler, *Nazareth* (Berlin, 1868); G. le Hardy, *Histoire de Nazareth et de ses sanctuaires. Étude chronologique des documents* (1905). P. P. Viaud, *Nazareth et ses deux églises de l'Annonciation et de St.-Joseph d'après les fouilles récentes* (1910); C. Kopp, 'Beiträge zur Geschichte Nazareths' in *Journal of the Palestine Oriental Society*, xviii (1938), pp. 187–228 (useful bibl., pp. 224–8), xix ('1939–40'), pp. 82–119, 253–85, xx (1940), pp. 29–42, and xxi (1948), pp. 148–64.

NAZARITES (so AV; in RV, more correctly, 'Nazirites'). A body of Israelites specially consecrated to the service of God who were under vows to abstain from eating or drinking the produce of the vine, to let their hair grow, and to avoid defilement by contact with a dead body (Num. 6). Originally the vow seems to have been for life (e.g. that of *Samson), but later it was limited to a definite period. If the Nazirite suffered defilement by the sudden death of someone beside him, he must undergo purification by shaving and burning his hair and renewing his vow. St. *Paul demonstrated his loyalty to Judaism by joining with certain Jewish Christians who were completing such vows at Jerusalem (Acts 21, 23–6).

See commentaries on Num. 6. G. B. *Gray, 'The Nazarite' in *J.T.S.*, i (1899–1900), pp. 201–11. K. v. Orelli in *P.R.E.* (ed. 3), xiii (1903), pp. 653–5; D. Eaton in *H.D.B.*, iii (1900), pp. 497–501, s.v.; W. R. *Smith–T. K. *Cheyne in *E.Bi.*, iii (1902), cols. 3362–4, s.v.

NAZARIUS, St. A martyr whose body St. *Ambrose discovered in a garden outside Milan c. 395 and translated to the Church of the Apostles in the city, which was afterwards re-dedicated to St. Nazarius. In the same garden, St. Ambrose later discovered the body of another martyr, St. Celsus. Nothing else is known of the saints, the later '*Passions' being purely fictitious. The two saints appear together in the Ambrosian calendar on 28 July, and on 10 May there is also a feast of the 'Translation of St. Nazarius'.

The primary source is *Paulinus of Nola, *Vita S. Ambrosii*, xxxii f. (*PL.* xiv, 38 f.). Text of 'Passions' in *AA.SS.*, Jul. VI (1729), pp. 503–34. H. *Leclercq, O.S.B., in *D.A.C.L.*, xi (pt. 1; 1933), cols. 1057–60, s.v. 'Milan: xxvii, Saint-Nazaire'.

NEAL, DANIEL (1678–1743), historian of the *Puritans. After being educated at Merchant Taylors' School, he trained for the dissenting ministry, studying at Utrecht and *Leyden. He returned to London in 1703 to be assistant (1704), and two years later (1706) full, pastor of the Independent congregation in Aldersgate Street, a position he retained until his death. Here he was recognized as one of the best Puritan preachers of his day. Of great historical interest are his *History of New England, containing an Impartial Account of the Civil and Ecclesiastical Affairs of the Country* to the Year of Our Lord 1700 (2 vols., 1720), and esp. his History of the Puritans, 1517–1688 (1732–8), both valuable compilations, though the latter suffers from a strong Puritan bias. Neal also wrote a book defending inoculation against smallpox (1722).

Neal's History of the Puritans was ed. J. Toulmin (5 vols., Bath, 1793–7; repr. London, 1822), with life in vol. i, pp. xvi–xxxiii. J. B. Mullinger in D.N.B., xl (1894), pp. 134–6.

NEALE, JOHN MASON (1818–66), Anglican author and hymn-writer. He was educated at Sherborne and Trinity College, Cambridge, where he became imbued with High Church ideals, and in 1839, with his lifelong friend, B. *Webb, was one of the founders of the *Cambridge Camden Society (q.v.). Ordained in 1842, he was presented to the living of Crawley, Sussex, but ill-health prevented his being instituted, and he spent the next three winters in Madeira. From 1846 till his death he held the wardenship of Sackville College, E. Grinstead, at a salary of £28 a year, dividing his activities between his manifold literary work and the Sisterhood of St. Margaret which he founded in 1854. This community, whose rules were framed on those of St. *Francis of Sales' Visitation and St. *Vincent de Paul's Sisters of Charity, was founded esp. for the education of girls and the care of the sick, and though at first it met with violent opposition, and even rioting, from Protestant quarters, it developed into one of the leading religious communities in the C of E. Neale's ritualistic practices led to his inhibition by the Bp. of *Chichester (A. T. Gilbert) from 1847 to 1863.

Neale, who was a man of remarkably versatile gifts, excelled as a hymn writer. Among the favourites of his own compositions are 'O happy band of pilgrims' and 'Art thou weary' and of his translations from Lat. and Gk. hymns, 'Jerusalem the Golden' and 'Christian, dost thou see them?' His collections have also played a decisive part in modern Anglican worship. In the Hymnal Noted (two parts, 1852 and 1854), 94 out of 105 hymns are from his pen, and the *Hymns Ancient and Modern owes very much to his inspiration. His Commentary on the Psalms, begun in Madeira and completed by R. F. Littledale (4 vols., publd. 1860–74), is in essence a compilation from patristic and medieval authors. The History of the Holy Eastern Church (publd. in 5 vols., 1847–73) is a useful collection of material, his linguistic gifts — he knew about twenty languages—enabling him to make use of many original documents. Neale was also the author of numerous children's books, e.g. the popular Duchenier, or The Revolt of La Vendée (1847) and The Farm of Aptonga (1856), stories written to present Christian teaching in a simple and attractive form. The warmth of his devotional nature comes out clearly in his sermons, largely inspired by medieval models. Characteristic are his Sermons on the Song of Songs (c.1858), Sermons on the Black-Letter Days, or Minor Festivals of the Church of England (1868), and Sermons preached in Sackville College Chapel (2 vols.,

1871–2). Worn out by his immense labours, he died when not yet 50 years of age.

Selections from the Writings of John Mason Neale was publd., London, 1884. Letters selected and ed. Mary S. Lawson (daughter), London, 1910; Collected Hymns, Sequences, and Carols also ed. Mary S. Lawson, ib., 1914. Memoir by Eleanor A. Towle, ib., 1906. J. H. Overton in D.N.B., xl (1894), pp. 143–6, with further reff.

NEANDER, JOACHIM (1650–80), German hymn-writer. After a somewhat riotous student life, he was converted in 1670 by hearing T. Under-Eyck, the pastor of St. Martin's church at Bremen. In 1673–4, during a winter at Frankfurt, where he made the acquaintance of P. J. *Spener, he became an ardent adherent of the *Pietist Movement. Most of his hymns date from the years 1674 to 1679, when he was rector of the Latin School of Düsseldorf. They reflect not only his deep Pietist faith but also his intense love of the beauties of nature. Many of them have been translated into English, perhaps the best known being 'Praise to the Lord, the Almighty'.

His 'Hymns' were first ed. at Bremen, 1680; later edd., with additional hymns, include those of Berlin, 1707, and Amsterdam, 1725. J. F. Iken, Joachim Neander, sein Leben und seine Lieder (1880). J. Mearns in J. Julian (ed.), A Dictionary of Hymnology (ed. 2, 1907), pp. 790–2. E. Simons in P.R.E. (ed. 3), xiii (1903), pp. 687–90, s.v.; P. Glaue in R.G.G. (ed. 2), iv (1930), col. 476 f., s.v.

NEANDER, JOHANN AUGUST WILHELM (1789–1850), ecclesiastical historian. David Mendel was a Jew by birth. After coming under the influence of F. D. E. *Schleiermacher, he was baptized in 1806 and took the name of Neander. At first interested in speculative theology, he soon turned to Church history and taught this subject at Berlin from 1813 till his death. His early works were monographs on *Julian the Apostate (1812), St. *Bernard (1813), *Gnosticism (1818), St. *Chrysostom (1822), and *Tertullian (1824); also Denkwürdigkeiten (1823–4). His General Church History (6 vols., 1826–52), which went down to c. 1450, followed. It was based on a wide study of original sources, somewhat uncritically treated, however, and exercised great influence. Unlike J. L. *Mosheim, whose interest was in institutions, Neander paid most attention to persons, and made it his aim to discover in Church history the interpenetration of human life by the Divine. A convinced Protestant, though eirenic in temper, he regarded outward ordinances, esp. the priesthood, as dangerous to Christian simplicity. Neander also wrote on the Life of Christ (1837; in reply to D. *Strauss).

Collected ed. of Neander's works, 14 vols., Gotha, 1862–7 P. *Schaff, Erinnerungen an Neander (Gotha, 1886); A. F. J. Wiegand, Neanders Leben (Erfurt, 1889). Commemorative discourse by A. *Harnack (Berlin, 1889). K. R. Hagenbach, 'Neander's Verdienste um die Kirchengeschichte' in Theologische Studien und Kritiken, xxiv (1851), pp. 543–94. G. Uhlhorn in P.R.E. (ed. 3), xiii (1903), pp. 679–87; K. Bauer in R.G.G. (ed. 2), iv (1930), col. 475 f., both s.v., with bibl.

NECTARIUS, St. (d. 397), Bp. of *Constantinople. He was born at Tarsus in Cilicia and rose to the office of praetor at Constantinople.

Though unbaptized he was selected by *Theodosius I in 381 to succeed St. *Gregory Nazianzen in the imperial see. After baptism he was consecrated Bp. and presided over the final stages of the (2nd) *Oecumenical Council, then in session. J. Kunze suggested that Nectarius's formal profession of his faith at the Council in the words of the *Niceno-Constantinopolitan Creed accounts for the association of this Creed with the Council. Despite his long episcopate, little is recorded of him. He died on 27 Sept. 397 and he was succeeded by St. John *Chrysostom. A sermon by him on a certain St. Theodore, perhaps a martyr under *Julian (d. 363), survives. Feast day, 11 Oct.

*Socrates, H.E., V, viii, and *Sozomen, H.E., VII, xvi. His Sermon on St. Theodore will be found in J. P. Migne, PG, xxxix, 1821–40 (from Cod. Nann. 134, saec. xiii; repr. from A. *Gallandi). J. Kunze, Das Nicänisch-Konstantinopolitanische Symbol (1898). W. M. Sinclair in D.C.B., iv (1887), pp. 11–14.

NECTARIUS (1605–c. 1680), Patr. of *Jerusalem from 1661 to 1669. Educated by the monks of *Sinai, he became a monk and later studied under the Neo-Aristotelian Theophilus Corydalleus at *Athens. He was a vigorous opponent of all W. theology, attacking at once the Roman claims and the Calvinist doctrines of Cyril *Lucar. In 1662 he expressed his warm approval of the 'Confession' of Peter *Mogila, and in 1672 he took a prominent part in the Synod of *Jerusalem. His treatise against the Papacy (περὶ τῆς ἀρχῆς τοῦ πάπα ἀντιρρήσεις) was published by his successor, *Dositheus, in 1682.

V. Grumel, A.A., in D.T.C., xi (pt. 1; 1931), cols. 56–8, with full bibl.

NEHEMIAH, Jewish leader of the post-exilic period. His activities are recorded in the Books of *Ezra and Nehemiah. The cupbearer to the Persian king, Artaxerxes (probably the first of that name, 'Longimanus'), he obtained leave to visit Palestine on a mission of help, and, accompanied by an escort provided by the king, arrived in *Jerusalem in 444 B.C. (Neh. 1 f.). Here, despite much hostility from the local officials and reports of a threatened attack from Samaria, he supervised the speedy completion of the rebuilding of the city walls (Neh. 2–6). Nehemiah's period of leave soon ended and he had to return to the Persian court. In 432 B.C., however, he made a second journey to Jerusalem, and now introduced some important moral and religious reforms, insisting, e.g., on *Sabbath observance and denouncing inter-marriage between Jews and non-Jews (Neh. 13). His work was carried further by *Ezra (q.v.), who probably lived some fifty years later.

For bibl. see Comm. to Books of *Ezra and Nehemiah and other works cited s.v. L. W. Batten in H.D.B., iii (1900), pp. 507–10. Further studies listed in articles by H. Kaupel in L.Th.K., vii (1935), cols. 478–81, s.v. 'Nehemias' and G. Rinaldi, C.R.S., in E.C., viii (1952), col. 1727 f., s.v. 'Neemia'.

NEHEMIAH, Book of. See Ezra and Nehemiah, Books of.

NELSON, ROBERT (1656–1715), *Nonjuring layman. Convinced of pronounced Church principles by G. *Bull, who was his private tutor, he strongly disapproved of the Revolution of 1688 and went abroad to avoid it. When he returned in 1691, he made friends with many of the leading Nonjurors, and became one himself. He did not, however, altogether sever his connexions with the 'Conformists', and eventually returned to the Established Church in 1710, though remaining a Jacobite in his political sympathies. Throughout his life he generously supported many philanthropic objects, notably the *S.P.C.K. and the *S.P.G. His publications include a Companion for the Festivals and Fasts of the C of E (1704), a book which long continued very popular, and a Life of Bishop Bull (1713).

C. F. Secretan, Memoirs of the Life and Times of the pious Robert Nelson (1860). L. Stephen in D.N.B., xl (1894), pp. 210–12.

NEMESIUS OF EMESA (fl. c. 390), Christian philosopher. Beyond the fact that he was Bp. of Emesa in Syria, nothing is known of his life. His treatise Περὶ Φύσεως Ἀνθρώπου ('On Human Nature') is an attempt to construct on a mainly *Platonic basis a doctrine of the soul agreeable with the Christian revelation. Probably through confusion with the similar title of St. *Gregory of Nyssa's anthropological treatise Περὶ Κατασκευῆς Ἀνθρώπου, Nemesius's book was often cited as Gregory's in the Middle Ages. It was much used by St. *John of Damascus and, in Latin revisions, by several of the Schoolmen, notably Sts. *Albertus Magnus and *Thomas Aquinas.

Gk. text first publd. by N. Ellebod (Antwerp, 1565; based on two inferior MSS.). Later edd. by J. *Fell (Oxford, 1671; mainly reprod. of Ellebod) and C. F. Matthaei (Halle, 1802); this last repr. in J. P. Migne, PG, xl, 504–817. Eng. tr., with introd. and notes, by W. Telfer in Library of Christian Classics, iv (1955), pp. 201–466. Lat. tr. by N. Alfanus, Abp. of Salerno, ed. C. Burkhard (Teub., 1917). W. Jaeger, Nemesios von Emesa. Quellenforschungen zum Neuplatonismus und seinen Anfängen bei Poseidonios (1914). E. Skard, 'Nemesiosstudien' in Symbolae Osloenses, xv–xvi (1936), pp. 23–43; xvii (1937), pp. 9–25; xviii (1938), pp. 31–41; xix (1939), pp. 46–56; xxii (1942), pp. 40–8. Überweg, ii, 118, 120 f., with bibl. in i, 198*; Bardenhewer, iv, 275–80; Altaner (ed. 1950), p. 201. E. Venables in D.C.B., iv (1887), p. 16, s.v.; E. Amann in D.T.C., xi (pt. 1; 1931), cols. 62–7, s.v. 'Némésius d'Émèse'.

NEOCAESAREA, Council of. A Cappadocian Council of uncertain date (probably early 4th cent., before 325). It passed 15 canons concerned chiefly with disciplinary and marriage questions. Along with those of *Ancyra and *Gangra, the canons of this Council formed the earliest Greek corpus canonum (with the canons of *Nicaea prefixed). They were translated into Latin before A.D. 451, and thus became a constituent part of the canon law of both E. and W.

Hardouin, i, cols. 281–6; Mansi, ii (1759), cols. 539–52. Canons also in Lauchert, p. 35 f.; crit. ed. of Lat. texts in E.O.M.I.A., II (pt. 1; 1907). Hefele–Leclercq, i (pt. 1; 1907), pp. 326–34.

NEOPHYTE (Gk. νεόφυτος, lit. 'newly planted'). The word occurs in 1 Tim. 3. 6 in the sense of 'newly converted' and was generally used in the early Church of the recently baptized. In acc. with St. Paul's admonition not to make a neophyte a bishop, the First Council of Nicaea (A.D. 325, can. 2) postponed the admission of neophytes to holy orders until the bishop deemed them sufficiently strong in the faith.

NEO-PLATONISM. The philosophical system of *Plotinus (c. 205–269) and his successors. It drew its inspiration and ideas from *Plato, but its beliefs were more closely knit and its purposes more directly religious. In its earlier phases, it was esp. centred at *Alexandria, which had long since displaced *Athens as the intellectual centre of the Roman world. The system soon spread to *Rome (where Plotinus himself taught from 244 onwards) and the rest of the Empire; and by the early 5th cent. it had gained a firm footing at Athens. Its most outstanding representatives after Plotinus were *Porphyry (c. 232–303; q.v.), *Iamblichus (c. 250–c. 330; q.v.), Eunapius of Sardis (b. 346), Proclus (410–85, an encyclopaedic thinker, 'the Aristotle of Neo-Platonism' [E. R. Dodds]), and the Latin Neo-platonist, Chalcidius.

The main formative influences on Neo-Platonism are somewhat obscure. Plotinus expresses his special indebtedness to *Ammonius Saccas, of whom, however, very little is known. While a sympathetic interest in Platonic doctrines had long existed among religious philosophers, both Jewish (*Philo) and Christian (*Pantaenus, *Clement of Alexandria, *Origen), at Alexandria, it is not clear that Plotinus himself drew directly on any of these thinkers. He has closer affinities with some of the later pagan philosophers notably Maximus of Tyre (c. 125–85), an itinerant sophist, and esp. Numenius of Apamea (c. 150–200), a Neo-Pythagorean, for whom Plato was 'Atticizing Moses' (Μωυσῆς Ἀττικίζων). The contacts of Alexandria with the East lend some colour to the view that some of the more theosophic elements in Neo-Platonism were derived from Persia (which Plotinus had visited in the Emp. Gordian's military expedition) or India.

The main purpose of the Neo-Platonists was to provide a sound and satisfying intellectual basis for a rational life. In the ultimate One which lies behind all experience, the dualism between Thought and Reality was to be overcome. This One can be known by man only by the method of abstraction. He must gradually divest his experience of all that is specifically human, so that in the end, when all attributes have been removed, only God is left. Yet the Neo-Platonists were too serious to rest in a merely negative agnosticism, and maintained that the Absolute which, as Plotinus said, 'has its centre everywhere but its circumference nowhere', could be reached by mystical experience.

The more ardent and thorough-going Neo-Platonists were necessarily hostile to Christianity, esp. its doctrine of an Incarnation in history and its rejection of the ancient philosophies. On the other hand, Neo-Platonist influences gradually made themselves felt on Christian theology. They came in partly from their diffusive impact on the whole of the later Roman world; for outside the circle of its professed adherents, it was scarcely possible to distinguish the Neo-Platonist elements from those which were Platonist and idealistic in a broader sense. For the influence of the latter see the entry *Platonism*. Instances of more specifically Neo-Platonist influences in Christianity may be seen in the writings of *Synesius, Bp. of Ptolemais, in those of the Pseudo-*Dionysius (who was esp. dependent on Proclus) and in the Medieval thinkers who drew on the '*Liber de Causis' (q.v.).

E. R. Dodds, *Select Passages Illustrating Neo-Platonism* (text, 1924; Eng. tr., 1923). C. *Bigg, *Neo-Platonism* (1895); T. Whittaker, *The Neo-Platonists* (1901). J. Simon, *Histoire de l'école d'Alexandrie* (1845); A. Richter, *Neo-Platonische Studien* (5 vols., 1864–7); A. E. Chaignet, *Histoire de la psychologie des Grecs*, vols. iv and v (1893). E. R. Dodds, *Proclus' 'Elements of Theology'* (1933). Überweg, i, 590–655, with bibl. pp. 186*–200*. W. R. *Inge in *H.E.R.E.*, ix (1917), pp. 307–19. See also bibliographies to *Plotinus*, *Porphyry*, and *Iamblichus*.

NEOSTADIENSIUM ADMONITIO. The reply made by the members of the 'Reformed' (*Calvinist) church at Heidelberg to the Lutheran 'Formula of *Concord' (1580). It was issued in 1581 by Z. Ursinus (1534–83) at Neustadt a.d. Haardt, whither the Heidelberg Calvinists had been forced to flee. It sets out in 12 chapters the more distinctive tenets of Calvinism.

Text pr. in Z. Ursini's *Opera Theologica* (ed. 2 by Q. Reuter), ii (Heidelberg, 1612), cols. 893–1138. E. F. K. Müller in *P.R.E.* (ed. 3), xiii (1903), p. 709 f., s.v., with bibl.

NEOT, St. (c. 9th cent.), Saxon saint. He is known only from late and untrustworthy medieval legends, acc. to which he was a monk of *Glastonbury who in search of solitude retired to the place now known as St. Neot in Cornwall. He is said to have been visited and held in much honour by King *Alfred. After his death his relics are reputed to have found their way to St. Neots, Huntingdonshire. Feast day, 31 July.

A contemporary biography appears to have been lost. Four medieval lives survive: an Anglo-Saxon life (MS. Cotton Vespasian D., xiv), pr. by G. C. Gorham, *The History and Antiquities of Eynesbury and St. Neot's in Huntingdonshire; and of St. Neot's in the County of Cornwall* (1820), pp. 256–61; a 12th cent. Lat. life pr. by J. Whitaker, *The Life of Saint Neot* (1809), pp. 339–65, with extracts in G. C. Gorham, op. cit., pp. 261–3; a 13th-14th cent. anonymous Lat. life, from which the legends regarding his residence in Cornwall are derived, pr. in *AA.SS.*, Jul. VII (1731, pp 319–29; a 14th cent. metrical life, depending upon the last, pr. in J. Whitaker, op. cit., pp. 317–38. S. Baring-Gould-J. Fisher, *The Lives of the British Saints*, iv (1913), pp. 4–10. Study by G. H. Doble in 'Cornish Saints' Series, No. 21 (Exeter, 1929). Hardy, i (pt. 2), pp. 538–49. M. Bateson in *D.N.B.*, xl (1894), p. 221 f.

NEPOMUK, JOHN OF. See *John of Nepomuk*.

NEPOTISM. The bestowal of office or patronage on one's relations. The term is used esp. of the widespread abuse of the practice by certain 16th cent. Popes, e.g. *Clement VII and the Medici, *Paul III and the Farnese. The practice was condemned by St. *Pius V in the bull 'Admonet Nos' (1567).

NEREUS AND ACHILLEUS, Sts. (perhaps 1st cent.), Roman martyrs. Their remains are in the Cemetery of St. *Domitilla on the Via Ardeatina. Acc. to the inscription by Pope *Damasus on their tomb they were soldiers, acc. to their legendary 'Acta', eunuchs in Domitilla's household. These 'Acta' assert that all three were transported to the island of Terracina, where Nereus and Achilleus were beheaded and Domitilla burnt. The church built over their tomb dates from the later 4th cent. Feast day, in conjunction with St. Domitilla and St. *Pancras, 12 May.

Early Lat. tr. of Acta in *AA.SS.*, Mai. III (1680), pp. 6–13, with introd., pp. 4–6, and other material, pp. 13–16. Gk. text first ed. A. Wirth (Leipzig, 1890); also ed., with Germ. tr., by H. Achelis (T.U., xi, Hft. 2; 1893). F. Schaefer, 'Die Acten der heiligen Nereus und Achilleus' in *R.Q.*, viii (1894), pp. 89–119. G. B. *de Rossi, 'Scoperta della basilica di S. Petronilla. Col sepolcro dei martiri Nereo ed Achilleo nel cimitero di Domitilla' in *Bullettino di Archeologia cristiana*, Ser. 2, v (1874), pp. 5–35; id., 'Insigni scoperte nel cimitero di Domitilla: I, notizie preliminari sul sepolcro di S. Petronilla: scoperta d' un singolare monumento del sepolcro-altare dei martiri Nereo ed Achilleo', ib., vi (1875), pp. 5–11. J. P. Kirsch, *Die römischen Titelkirchen* (Studien zur Geschichte und Kultur des Altertums, ix, Hftt. 1–2; 1918), pp. 90–4 ('Titulus de Fasciola oder SS. Nerei et Achillei'). P. F. de' Cavalieri, *Note agiografiche*, ii (S.T., xxii; 1909), pp. 43–55 ('I SS. Nereo ed Achilleo nell' epigramma damasiano'). H. *Leclercq, O.S.B., in *D.A.C.L.*, xii (pt. 1; 1935), cols. 1111–23, s.v. 'Nérée et Achillée'.

NERI, St. PHILIP. See *Philip Neri, St.*

NERO, CLAUDIUS (37–68 A.D.), Roman Emperor from 54. The last Emperor of the Julian-Claudian line, Nero was born at Antium (Anzio), the son of Domitius and Agrippina, who was the sister of the Emp. Caligula. On his mother's second marriage to the Emp. Claudius in 49, Nero was adopted by his stepfather and, after Claudius's murder, proclaimed his successor by the Praetorians. The first five years of his reign were a time of great prosperity, acc. to Trajan far superior to any other period of imperial rule. Claudius's schemes for the water and corn supplies were completed and the frontiers of the Empire strengthened. But before long Nero fell under the influence of Poppaea, the wife of his friend Salvius Otho, and increasingly abandoned himself to his whims. He was ruthless in resisting all opposition. In 59 he planned the murder of Agrippina, and in 62 he divorced his wife, Octavia (the daughter of Claudius), and married Poppaea, who now assumed the title of Augusta. His unrelieved extravagance led to grave financial difficulties and the debasement of the coinage. Even his supporters were greatly scandalized at his unbecoming public appearances in plays and other performances. In 62, after reviving the law of *maiestas*, he caused a number of wealthy nobles to be executed on suspicion. In 64 he was suspected of causing the fire which destroyed a large part of Rome (18–24 July) and thereby aroused still further discontent. Increasing unpopularity provoked revolts in Spain and Africa, and Nero, finding himself deserted by the Praetorians, committed suicide on 9 June 68.

Nero was the Caesar to whom St. *Paul appealed when accused by the Jews at *Caesarea before Festus (Acts 25. 10); but it is unknown whether Nero took any personal part in the Apostle's trial. Acc. to *Tacitus (*Annales*, XV, xliv, 3), Nero sought to fix on the Christians at Rome the responsibility for the fire of 64 and severely punished them not only as incendiaries but also for their 'hatred of the human race' (*odium humani generis*). Acc. to a well-founded tradition, both St. *Peter and St. *Paul suffered martyrdom at Rome later in his reign. After Nero's death there was a widespread popular belief that the tyrant would return ('Nero redivivus') and this myth is perhaps in view in the references to the Beast in Rev. 13. 11–18, esp. as the 'Number of the Beast', viz. 666, corresponds to 'Neron Caesar' in Gk. notation. See also *Tacitus, Number of the Beast*.

The principal sources are Tacitus, *Annales*, xiii–xvi; *Suetonius, 'Nero'; and Dio Cassius, *Hist.*, lxi–lxiii. M. P. Charlesworth (ed.), *Documents illustrating the Reigns of Claudius and Nero* (1939), pp. 31–42. B. W. Henderson, *The Life and Principate of the Emperor Nero* (1903). On Nero's persecution of the Christians see also, in addition to the items cited s.v. Persecutions, C. F. Arnold, *Die neronische Christenverfolgung* (1888); E. Zeller, 'Das *odium generis humani* der Christen' in *Zeitschrift für wissenschaftliche Theologie*, xxxiv (1891), pp. 356–67. On the responsibility for the fire of Rome, see esp. C. Pascal, *L' incendio di Roma e i primi cristiani* (1900; fire kindled by the Christians), and A. Profumo, *Le fonti ed i tempi della incendia neroniano* (1905; Nero's sole responsibility); cf. also C. Hülsen, 'The Burning of Rome under Nero' in *American Journal of Archaeology*, xiii (1909), pp. 45–8. A. Momigliano in *C.A.H.*, x (1934), pp. 702–42, with bibl. pp. 978–84. H. Cowan in *H.D.B.*, iii (1900), pp. 514–18, s.v.; H. *Leclercq, O.S.B., in *D.A.C.L.*, xii (pt. 1; 1935), cols. 1124–50, s.v. 'Néron', with bibl.

NERSES, St. (d. c. 373), sixth *Catholicos of the *Armenian Church. A direct descendant of *Gregory the Illuminator, he was educated at Caesarea in Cappadocia and held office at the royal court. After the death of his wife he became an ecclesiastic, and, having been elected Catholicos (perh. c. 363), undertoook the reform of the Armenian Church. At the Council of Ashtishat (c. 365) he promulgated a number of decrees, e.g. against marriages between relations and on fasting. He also founded many hospitals and orphanages. He was deposed and exiled for criticizing the dissolute life of King Arshak III. Though restored under Arshak's successor Pap (369), he also incurred the new King's hostility whom he censured for his immorality and was poisoned by him during a meal. His son, St. *Isaac the Great (q.v.), became one of his successors. Feast day, 19 Nov.

J. Markwart, *Die Entstehung der armenischen Bistümer*. Kritische Untersuchung der armenischen Überlieferung (Orientalia Christiana, xxvii, 2 [No. 80]; 1932, pp. 139–236), esp. pp. 223–33. Fr. Tournebize in *D.H.G.E.*, iv (1930), col. 297 f., s.v. 'Arménie'.

NESTLE, EBERHARD (1851–1913), Biblical scholar. From 1883 to 1898 he held professorships at Ulm and *Tübingen, and from 1898 appointments at the Evangelical Theological Seminary at Maulbronn. His early work was done on the text of the *Septuagint. He increasingly interested himself, however, in the NT, and in 1898 published the first edition of his Greek NT text, which, though somewhat mechanically constructed from the existing editions of C. *Tischendorf, B. F. *Westcott–F. J. A. *Hort, and B. *Weiss, came to be very widely used. In 1904 this text was adopted by the *British and Foreign Bible Society in place of the *Textus receptus. Nestle also wrote many grammars and other aids to Biblical study.

Nestle's Gk. text of the NT in its successive German edd. has been constantly revised (ed. from the 10th ed., 1914, onwards, by his son, Erwin Nestle). The apparatus was radically altered in the 13th ed. (1927) and notable improvements were also made in the text in the 17th ed. (1941). J. Schmid in *L.Th.K.*, vii (1935), col. 492, s.v., with further reff.

NESTORIANISM. The doctrine that there were two separate Persons in the Incarnate Christ, the one Divine and the other Human, as opposed to the orthodox doctrine that the Incarnate Christ was a single Person, at once God and man. It was characterized by the rejection of the term *Theotokos (q.v.).

Nestorius (d. *c.* 451), from whom the heresy takes its name, was a native of Germanicia in Syria Euphratensis. He entered a monastery at *Antioch, where he became imbued with the principles of the Antiochene theological School, and prob. studied under *Theodore of Mopsuestia. Soon he acquired a great reputation as a preacher; and in 428, when the see of *Constantinople became vacant, *Theodosius II, overriding the claims of the local candidates, invited Nestorius to fill the see. Nestorius at once proclaimed himself a zealous upholder of orthodoxy, eager to rid the city of heretics and schismatics. When his chaplain Anastasius preached against the use of the Theotokos as savouring of heresy (*Apollinarianism), Nestorius gave him full support. A violent controversy developed round the propriety of a term which had long been used by theologians of the highest orthodoxy and was now gaining in popularity since it gave theological expression to the growing devotion to the Virgin as the Mother of God. Nestorius's opponents succeeded in winning the support of St. *Cyril of Alexandria and the Egyptian monks to their cause. Both sides having appealed to Rome, at a Council held there in August 430, Nestorius's teaching was condemned by Pope *Celestine and Cyril was commissioned to pronounce sentence of deposition on Nestorius, if he would not submit. In Nov. 430 Cyril took action and on 7 Dec. 430 delivered his sentence into Nestorius's hands by legates sent to Constantinople, condemning Nestorius in a set of twelve anathemas and requiring him to retract within ten days. Meanwhile the Emp. had arranged a General

Council to meet at *Ephesus in the following summer. It assembled on 22 June 431 and pronounced sentence of deposition on Nestorius (see *Ephesus*, Council of). Theodosius eventually acquiesced in its decision and Nestorius was sent back to his monastery at Antioch. In 435 Theodosius had his books condemned, and in 436 Nestorius was banished to Upper Egypt where he died several years later (date unknown).

Nestorius's principal writings were his letters and sermons, which, however, for the most part, survive only in fragments. He was also the author of an extensive treatise, publd. in his last years and known as the 'Bazaar of Heracleides'. This was discovered *c.* 1895 and first publd. in 1910. Written when the theological climate had completely changed, Nestorius is here claiming that his own beliefs were identical with those then being sustained (against the *Eutychians) by the orthodox. The twelve 'Counter Anathemas' long ascribed to Nestorius have been shown by E. *Schwartz to be of much later date.

Opinion is widely divided as to what the doctrine of Nestorius really was and in how far it was heretical. His sustained objection to the term 'Theotokos' has traditionally been held to imply that he asserted not only two different natures, but also two different persons in Christ, the one the man, born of Mary. But we must not overlook that he repeatedly affirmed the oneness of Christ, though he preferred to speak of conjunction (συνάφεια) rather than of union (ἔνωσις). His fear of the Monophysite tendencies, which were actually to come into the open a few years later, led him to reject Cyril's conception of a hypostatic union (ἔνωσις καθ' ὑπόστασιν), substituting for it a union of the will (κατ' εὐδοκίαν). The latter term certainly savoured of *Adoptianism, of which he was actually, though unjustly, accused. Certainly his zeal for upholding the integrity of the two natures, which he believed to be both self-subsisting and therefore incapable of being physically united in the Person of the God-man, caused him to fall into unguarded language, and the fact that his own friends finally abandoned him supports the view that, by trying to defend, he actually compromised the Antiochene Christology.

After the Council of Ephesus the E. Bishops who refused to accept the Formula of 433 gradually constituted themselves a separate Nestorian Church. It had its centre in Persia where the Christian community ('East Syrians'), whose independence of Antioch had been recognized since the Synod of Markabta (424), claimed to go back to Apostolic times. Within the Empire at *Edessa (Ur-hai, the 'Athens of Syria') a strong school of Nestorian theology developed under *Ibas, who had supported Nestorius at Ephesus (Bp. of Edessa from 435). After *Chalcedon (451) the hostility of the Monophysites to the Edessene school led many Nestorianizers to migrate to Persian territory. From the later 5th cent. several of the Persian kings, notably Peroz (457–84), actively supported them and under *Zeno they were finally expelled from Edessa in 489. The Nestorian school at Nisibis, which had been founded by *Barsumas (a pupil of Ibas and Bp. of Nisibis from 457), thus gradually supplanted Edessa as the main seat of Nestorian culture. At one time it had as many as 800 students and it is said to have inspired *Cassiodorus's school at Vivarium.

The ecclesiastical centre and see of the Patriarch (the 'Catholicos'; from 498 he took the title of 'Patriarch of the East') was fixed at Seleucia-Ctesiphon on the Tigris. In 484 Babaeus or Babowai, Patr. from 457, was put to death on the ground of conspiring with *Constantinople. From the early 6th cent. the Nestorian Church was active in missionary work and established Christian settlements in Arabia (see Cosmas Indicopleustes), *India (see Malabar Christians), and Turkestan (see Sigan-fu Stone). Despite occasional persecution from the ruling power the Church continued over several centuries in a relatively flourishing condition. In the 6th cent. it owed much to the successful administration of Mar Aba I (540–52), a convert from *Zoroastrianism, while monasticism was put on a sound footing by Abraham of Kaskar (491–586), the founder of the monastery on Mt. Izala, near Nisibis, and Mar Babai the Great (569–628). The latter, a considerable theologian, also defined Nestorian principles in his Book of the Union (sc. of the Godhead and manhood in Christ).

Within twenty years of Mohammed's death (632) the Arab conquest of Persia was complete (651). The Christians met with moderately good treatment under the Caliphate which constituted them (like the Jews and Zoroastrians) a separate melet. Nisibis, with Jundishapur and Merv, flourished as centres of Nestorian culture. In the short reign of Omar II, a zealous Mohammedan (717–20), the Nestorians were faced with a temporary persecution, owing to the rigid enforcement of Islamic laws. C. 775 the Patriarchal see was moved from Seleucia-Ctesiphon to Baghdad, and the Patriarch was for some centuries a considerable political figure. *Thomas of Marga's Book of Governors (c. 840) bears testimony to the ascetic and historical interests of the 9th cent. Another period of repression occurred under Mutawakkil (847–861). They suffered severely from the Mongol and other invasions of the 13th and 14th cents. A remnant who escaped capture by Timur (Tamerlane) fled to the mountains of Kurdistan where their descendants have survived until modern times under the name of *Assyrian Christians (q.v.).

The chief documents bearing on the original Nestorian controversy, incl. most of the surviving fragments and letters of Nestorius himself, will be found in the printed edd. (J. *Hardouin, J. D. *Mansi, and others) of the acta of the Council of Ephesus (q.v.); crit. text now publd. by E. Schwartz in A.C.O. The 'Bazaar of Heracleides' was first brought to the general notice of scholars by J. F. Bethune Baker, Nestorius and his Teaching (1908; with extracts from the 'Bazaar' tr. [by R. H. *Connolly]). Syr. text of 'Bazaar' ed. for the first time by P. Bedjan (Paris, 1910); Fr. tr. by F. Nau (Paris, 1910); Eng. tr., with introd. and studies, by G. R. *Driver–L. Hodgson (Oxford, 1925). Nestorius's fragments are collected in F. *Loofs, Nestoriana

(Halle, 1905). On the true authorship of the Counter-anathemas, commonly ascribed to Nestorius, cf. E. Schwartz, Die Gegenanathematismen des Nestorius (Sb. (Bayr), 1922, Hft. 1). On the historical course of the conflict, L. *Duchesne, Histoire ancienne de l'Église, iii (1910), pp. 313–88 (very critical of Cyril's handling of Nestorius); M. Jugie, A.A., Nestorius et la controverse nestorienne (1912; more sympathetic to Cyril). J. P. Junglas, Die Irrlehre des Nestorius (Trier, 1912); F. Loofs, Nestorius and his Place in the History of Christian Doctrine (1914). R. V. Sellers, Two Ancient Christologies (C.H.S., 1940), esp. pp. 107–201. Bardenhewer, iv, 2–5, 74–8; Altaner (ed. 1951), p. 293 f. F. Loofs in P.R.E. (ed. 3), xiii (1903), pp. 736–49, and xxiv (1913), pp. 239–44, both s.v. 'Nestorius'; A. J. Maclean in H.E.R.E., ix (1917), pp. 323–32, s.v.; É. Amann in D.T.C., xi (pt. 1; 1931), cols. 76–157, s.v. 'Nestorius'. See also bibl. to Ephesus, Council of.

The chief literature on the Nestorians from the next generation onwards is surveyed and annotated in J. S. *Assemani, Bibliotheca Orientalis, iii (1; Rome, 1725; 'De Scriptoribus Syris Nestorianis'. The series opens with the Catalogue of *Ebed-jesu, with extensive annotation) and iii (2; Rome, 1728; 'Dissertatio de Syris Nestorianis'). J. Labourt, Le Christianisme dans l'empire perse sous la dynastie sassanide, 224–632 (1904). W. A. Wigram, An Introduction to the History of the Assyrian Church, 100–640 A.D. (1910). B. J. Kidd, The Churches of Eastern Christendom from A.D. 451 to the Present Time (1927), pp. 91–5, 415–24, with bibl. reff. pp. 515–17. G. P. Badger, The Nestorians and their Rituals (2 vols., 1852; descriptive account of contemporary practice as seen by a missionary, with Eng. tr. of Nestorian liturgical texts). A. J. Maclean–W. H. Browne, The Catholicos of the East and his People. Being the Impressions of Five Years' Work in the 'Archbishop of Canterbury's Assyrian Mission' (1892). A. R. Vine, The Nestorian Churches (1937; popular). A. J. Grieve–J. A. L. Riley in E.B. (ed. 11), xix (1911), pp. 407–9, s.v. 'Nestorians'; E. Tisserant–É. Amann in D.T.C., xi (pt. 1; 1931), cols. 157–32, s.v. 'Nestorius. 2. L'Église nestorienne'; M. Jugie, A.A.–G. de Vries, S.J., in E.C., viii (1952), cols. 1780–7, s.v. 'Nestorio e nestorianesmo'. See also bibl. to Assyrian Church.

NESTORIAN STONE, The. See Sigan Fu Stone, The.

NE TEMERE.

The decree (2 Aug. 1907) of the Sacred *Congregation of the Council, promulgated by *Pius X to come into force on 19 Apr. 1908, putting the matrimonial legislation of the RC Church on a new basis. It was designed to remedy the confusions created by the Tridentine Tametsi decree (q.v.) (1563). Earlier attempts at revision were *Benedict XIV's Matrimonia quae in locis (4 Nov. 1741) exempting Belgium and Holland from the operation of Tametsi and Pius X's constitution Provida sapientiaque (18 Jan. 1906) suspending its application in Germany for mixed marriages and the marriages of non-Catholics. The new regulations of Ne Temere were to be of universal application. No marriage between persons baptized as Catholics or who have been received into Catholic communion is valid unless celebrated before the parish priest or the Ordinary or a priest delegated by one or other of these. The same ruling holds if only one of the contracting parties is a Catholic. Hence while the RC Church now declines to recognize marriages in which a RC is involved, if solemnized before a Protestant minister or merely by a civil contract, it allows the marriage of two non-Catholics. To make 'surprise marriages' (mariages à la gaulmine) impossible, the decree also laid down that the parish priest must formally ask and receive the consent of the parties. The rulings of Ne Temere, with minor modifications, were taken over into the new *Codex (can. 1094-1103).

Text in *A.S.S.*, xl (1907), pp. 527-30. See also bibl. to *Matrimony*.

NETHERLANDS, Christianity in the.
See *Holland, Christianity in.*

NETTER, THOMAS (*c.* 1377-1430), *Carmelite theologian. Born at Saffron Walden in Essex, he was sent by his superiors to study in Oxford, where he gained a reputation for sound scholarship ('Doctor praestantissimus'). In 1409 he was sent to the Council of *Pisa as the representative of King Henry IV, whose adviser he had become, and on his return to England took an active part in the struggle against the followers of J. *Wycliffe. Henry V chose him for his confessor and, after Netter had been elected Provincial of the English Carmelites in 1414, appointed him one of his mandatories to the Council of *Constance. In 1419 he was sent on a political mission to Poland. Later he became spiritual adviser to *Henry VI, his former pupil. The latter part of his life appears to have been chiefly taken up with the composition of his main work 'Doctrinale antiquitatum fidei ecclesiae catholicae', in which he sought to refute the doctrines of Wycliffe and the *Hussites from the teaching of the Bible and the Fathers.

The best ed. of his 'Doctrinale' is that of B. Blanciotti, Ord. Carm. (3 vols., Venice, 1757-9), with introd., vol. i, pp. ix-xviii. Life herein contained repr. in *Analecta Ordinis Carmelitarum*, i (1909), pp. 298-303, 329-35, and 361-5. Earlier edd. of the 'Doctrinale', 3 vols., Paris, *c.* 1520-32, and 3 vols., Venice, 1571. Various letters, with brief introd., in B. Zimmerman, O.C.D. (ed.), *Monumenta Historica Carmelitana*, i (Lérins, 1907), pp. 442-82. The 'Fasciculi Zizaniorum' (a collection of anti-Wycliffite docc.), traditionally, but erroneously, attributed to Netter, ed. in part by W. W. Shirley (R.S., 1858). P. R. McCaffrey, Ord. Carm., *The White Friars*. An Outline Carmelite History with Special Reference to the English-Speaking Provinces (Dublin, 1936), pp. 143-51. C. L. Kingsford in *D.N.B.*, xl (1894), pp. 231-4; Nilo di San Brocardo, O.C.D., in *E.C.*, viii (1952), col. 1787 f., s.v., with more recent bibl.

NEUMANN, THERESE (1898-1962), of Konnersreuth in Bavaria, stigmatized visionary. After a normal childhood and youth, Therese Neumann lost her health in 1918 through overstrain in helping to put out a fire. Having become bedridden in the same year and blind in 1919, she regained her sight in 1923 on the day of the beatification of *Teresa of Lisieux. Two years later, on the day of the canonization of the same saint, she became able to walk again. During Lent 1926 she began to have visions of the Passion and received the *stigmata, which remained visible and bled on Fridays. She was reputed to have taken no solid food after 1922, and after 1927 no nourishment whatever except daily Holy Communion. After her visions she was usually in an abnormal state of absorption during which she was credited with supernatural faculties such as ability to read consciences and to discern the authenticity of relics. The events of Konnersreuth, which soon became a place of pilgrimage for the curious as well as the devout, were for

years a topic of lively discussion; but the RC ecclesiastical authorities have abstained from any pronouncement on the case.

L. Witt, *Das kleine Leben der stigmatisierten Jungfrau Therese von Konnersreuth* (1927); F. Gerlich, *Die stigmatisierte Therese Neumann* (2 vols., 1927); F. X. Huber, *Das Mysterium von Konnersreuth* (1950). Among the many other sympathetic works those available in English include studies by R. W. Hynek (ed. 3, Prague, 1932; Eng. tr., 1932, with bibl.), C. E. Roy–W. A. Joyce (London, 1936), and J. Teodorowicz (Salzburg, 1936; Eng. tr., St. Louis, Mo., 1940). More critical studies by J. Deutsch, *Aerztliche Kritik an Konnersreuth* (1938); B. Poray Madeyski, *Le Cas de la visionnaire stigmatisée*. Thérèse Neumann de Konnersreuth (1940); other studies by Hilda C. Graef (Cork, 1950) and P. Siwek, S.J. (Paris, 1950; Eng. tr., Dublin, 1954). 'M.S.' in *L.Th.K.*, vi (1935), cols. 512-15, s.v.

NEUME (1) From Gk. πνεῦμα, 'breath'. In plainsong, a prolonged group of notes, sung to a single syllable, esp. at the end of the '*Alleluia' and in the *responsories of the Mass. (2) From Gk. νεῦμα, 'sign'. The sign employed in the earliest plainsong to indicate the melody. These signs are probably derived from the accent-marks of the grammarians. They are thought to date from the 8th cent.

NEUTRAL TEXT, The. The type of text of the Greek NT represented by the two MSS., *Codex Vaticanus and *Codex Sinaiticus, and so designated by F. J. A. *Hort because it was supposed to be less subject to corrupting influences of editorial revision than any other. There seems little doubt that the origin of the text is to be connected with Egypt (though either or both MSS. may have been actually written elsewhere); and some scholars have believed it to be the work of *Hesychius, an Alexandrian who is known to have revised the *Septuagint.

B. F. Westcott and F. J. A. Hort, *The New Testament in the original Greek*, i (1881), esp. pp. 126-30 ('The Neutral Text and its Preservation').

NEVIN, JOHN WILLIAMSON (1803-86), American Protestant theologian. He was a native of Pennsylvania, of *Presbyterian upbringing and Scottish descent. From 1823 to 1828 he studied at Princeton Theological Seminary, being for part of the time in charge of the classes of Charles *Hodge. In 1828 he published his widely used *Summary of Biblical Antiquities* (2 vols.). From 1830 to 1840 he was professor of Biblical literature at the Western Theological Seminary at Allegheny, Pa. Here, under the influence of the writings of J. A. W. *Neander, he gradually abandoned the dogmas of Presbyterianism for a more liberal theology, and became closely associated with P. *Schaff. In 1840 he became professor of theology in the Mercersburg (Pa.) Theological Seminary, a 'German Reformed' institution, where, having transferred his allegiance from the Presbyterian to this Reformed Church, he gained an increasing influence. In 1843 he attacked the then prevailing methods of revivalist preaching in *The Anxious Bench: A Tract for the Times*. In 1844 Schaff joined him from Germany, and the theological doctrines for which both stood became known as the 'Mercersburg Theology'. In 1846 he published *The Mystical Presence*, a defence of a doctrine of the Eucharist which conceded a 'Real Presence' and advocated a more sacramental conception of Christianity than is ordinarily held among Protestants. In 1853 he retired into private life on account of weak health, but from 1861 to 1866 he again lectured at Mercersburg, and from 1866 to 1876 was president of the reorganized Franklin and Marshall College in that city.

T. Appel, *The Life and Work of John Williamson Nevin* (1889). W. W. Sweet in *Dict. Amer. Biog.*, xiii (1934), p. 442 f.

NEW CHURCH. See *Swedenborg, Emmanuel.*

NEW JERUSALEM CHURCH. See *Swedenborg, Emmanuel.*

NEW ROME. A name for *Constantinople, which, acc. to *Sozomen (*Hist. Eccl.*, ii, 3), was given to the city by the Emp. *Constantine himself. The Council of Constantinople of 381 laid down (can. 3) that 'the Bp. of Constantinople was to have honorary pre-eminence (ἔχειν τὰ πρεσβεῖα τῆς τιμῆς) after the Bp. of Rome, because Constantinople is New Rome (διὰ τὸ εἶναι αὐτὴν νέαν 'Ρώμην)'.

NEW TESTAMENT (Gk. Καινὴ Διαθήκη; Lat. *Novum Testamentum*). In the sense of 'new dispensation', a term denoting the Canonical Books belonging exclusively to the Church, in contradistinction to those styled *Old Testament (q.v.) which the Church shares with the Synagogue. The use of the word διαθήκη for the records of the OT dispensation has its roots in St. *Paul (2 Cor. 3. 14) and from *Tertullian onwards 'Novum Testamentum' came to be accepted as a technical term. The NT contains the four Gospels, Acts, the Pauline and the 'Catholic' Epistles, and the Book of Revelation. See also *Canon of Scripture.*

NEW YEAR'S DAY. In the pre-Christian era it was celebrated with great solemnity both by the Jews, who reckoned the year from the Feast of the New Moon at the end of Sept., and in the pagan empire. Acc. to the Julian Calendar, the Roman year began on 1 Jan., and the day was marked by the 'Saturnalia'. Christians were not only forbidden to participate in these festivities, but even had special fasts and Masses of expiation on the day, facts attested by the Second Council of Tours (567) and several Sacramentaries containing Masses and Offices 'ad prohibendum ab idolis'. The later Christian practice of reckoning the beginning of the year varied acc. to the different countries. In England from early times the year began with the Feast of the *Annunciation (25 Mar.), in Germany with *Christmas, and in France and the Low Countries with *Easter. Since *Gregory XIII's reform of the calendar in 1582, 1 Jan. came to be generally adopted as the first day of the year on the Continent, though this date was not accepted

in England until 1752. In the Orthodox E. Church, New Year's Day (here, 1 Sept.) is solemnized in many hymns, but in the W. the day has no liturgical significance, except for the fact of its coinciding with the Feast of the *Circumcision (q.v.). In England the custom of an informal 'watch-night' service, however, on the night of 31 Dec.–1 Jan. is often met with, esp. in the *Methodist Church.

F. Bünger, *Geschichte der Neujahrsfeier in der Kirche* (1911).

NEW ZEALAND, Christianity in. Europeans first made permanent settlements in New Zealand in 1805, and the first missionaries arrived in 1814. Missionary work, in the usual sense, has long ceased, as all the Maoris (now some 4 per cent of the population) profess Christianity, and the Church is self-supporting. The majority of the inhabitants are Anglicans; but there are also a large number of Scottish Presbyterians, while the RC Church, which established its first bishopric in 1848, and the *Methodists, form large minorities. The Anglican see of New Zealand (later called Auckland) was set up in 1841, with G. A. *Selwyn (q.v.) as the first bishop. In his diocese the first Anglican ecclesiastical synod since the suppression of *Convocation in 1717 met in 1844. The diocese was soon divided, and within a hundred years from its foundation comprised nine sees. In 1928 a Maori (F. A. Bennett) was consecrated Assistant Bishop of Waiapu, to supervise the work of the Church among the Maoris.

W. Williams, *Christianity among the New Zealanders* (London, 1867); H. Jacobs, *New Zealand* ('Colonial Church Histories'; S.P.C.K. [c. 1889]); H. T. Purchas, *A History of the English Church in New Zealand* (Christchurch and London, 1914). W. Yate, *An Account of New Zealand: and of the Formation and Progress of the Church Missionary Society's Mission in the North Island* (London, 1835). H. L. Clarke, *Constitutional Church Government* (1924), pp. 168–95. R. Dickson, *History of the Presbyterian Church of New Zealand* (Dunedin, 1899); J. R. Elder, *The History of the Presbyterian Church of New Zealand* (Christchurch, 1940). J. A. Scott in *C.E.*, xi (1911), pp. 41–3, s.v. Latourette, v, 177–97, and vii, 190–2, with further bibl. reff.

NEWMAN, JOHN HENRY (1801–90), *Tractarian leader and later Cardinal. He was brought up in the C of E under Evangelical influence. He entered Trinity College, Oxford, in June 1817, became Fellow of Oriel in 1822, and was ordained deacon in 1824. In 1825 he was appointed vice-principal of Alban Hall by R. *Whately, and in 1828 vicar of St. Mary's, Oxford. In 1832–3 he toured S. Europe and on returning became intimately associated with the *Oxford Movement, in which he was the leading spirit. His sermons in St. Mary's, published as *Parochial and Plain Sermons* (1834–42), had a profound influence on the religious life not only of Oxford but of the whole country. Their spirituality was based on a systematic study of the Fathers which bore fruit in the *Arians of the Fourth Century* (1833), whereas the *Tracts for the Times* (1833–41), 24 of which came from his pen, were popular statements of his religious position. Directed 'against Popery and Dissent', they defended his thesis of the 'Via media', i.e. the belief that the C of E held an intermediate position, represented by the patristic tradition, as against modern Romanism on the one hand and modern Protestantism on the other. This belief received developed expression in his *Lectures on the Prophetical Office of the Church* (1837) and in his *Lectures on Justification* (1838). In the famous *Tract No. 90* (1841) he advocated the interpretation of the *Thirty-Nine Articles in a sense generally congruous with the decrees of *Trent. The Tract, which caused a violent controversy, was condemned by the Hebdomadal Board, and R. *Bagot, Bp. of Oxford, imposed silence on its author. Meanwhile, from 1839 onwards, Newman began to have doubts about the claims of the Anglican Church, and from 1841 onwards he gradually gave up his position in Oxford, living from 1842 at the neighbouring village of Little-more, which was at that date part of the ecclesiastical parish of St. Mary's. Here he set up a semi-monastic establishment and, during the next years, lived in retirement with a few friends. He resigned the incumbency of St. Mary's on 18 Sept. 1843, preaching a few days later a celebrated sermon in Littlemore church on 'The Parting of Friends'. On 9 Oct. 1845 he was received into the RC Church. Almost immediately afterwards he issued his *Essay on the Development of Christian Doctrine* in defence of his change of allegiance.

Having been ordained in Rome, he established the *Oratorians at Birmingham in 1849, was in Ireland as rector of Dublin University from 1854 to 1858, and, on his return to England, became involved in the affair of the *Rambler*, a periodical which published a disparaging review of a book by H. E. *Manning for which Newman was held responsible. This incident was the immediate cause of rupture between the two men and of Newman's strained relations with Rome during the following years. In 1864 a controversy with C. *Kingsley resulted in his *Apologia pro vita sua*, which, by its combination of frankness and delicacy, won him the sympathies of RCs and others alike. In the next year he wrote the *Dream of *Gerontius* depicting the journey of the soul to God at the hour of death, an almost Dantesque poem inspired by the Requiem Offices. In 1870 he published the *Grammar of Assent*, the work which contains much of his ripest thought. It is esp. remarkable for its differentiation between real and notional assent, its analysis of the function of the conscience in our knowledge of God and of the role of the 'illative sense', i.e. the faculty of judging from given facts by processes outside the limits of strict logic, in reaching religious certitude. In 1877 he was elected an Honorary Fellow of Trinity College, and two years later *Leo XIII made him Cardinal-Deacon of St. George in Velabro.

Newman's thought was nourished by the Fathers rather than by the Schoolmen, and his main contribution to the thought of his age lay much more in the fields of psychological analysis and acute moral perception than in matters strictly theological. His fruitful use of the idea of development, in its application to the growth of Christian doctrine, and his profound insight into the nature and motives of religious faith, place him in the first rank of modern Christian thinkers. His ideals for Christian religious education were set forth in his *Idea of a University* (1852). Though unsuccessful in most of his undertakings in the RC Church during his lifetime, his genius has come to be more and more recognized after his death, and his influence both on the restoration of RC-ism in England and the advance of Catholic ideas in the C of E can hardly be exaggerated.

His more important writings have often been reissued, notably *Parochial and Plain Sermons, The Idea of a University*, the *Apologia*, and *The Dream of Gerontius*. For his earlier life, his autobiographical *Apologia pro vita sua* (q.v., 1864) is the fundamental source, though its scope is limited by its purpose of self-defence. Further primary material, for his Anglican period, in Anne Mozley, *Letters and Correspondence of J. H. Newman during his Life in the English Church* (2 vols., 1891); for his RC period (esp.), in W. Ward, *The Life of John Henry Newman* (2 vols., 1912). Correspondence with J. Keble and others, ed. at the Birmingham Oratory (London, 1917). There is also abundant material in the biographies of his associates in the Oxford Movement. Other lives by R. H. *Hutton ('English Leaders of Religion', London, 1891), W. Barry (London, 1904), H. *Bremond (Paris, 1906; Eng. tr., 1907), J. Lewis May (London, 1929), F. L. Cross (London, 1933), R. Sencourt (pseud., London, 1948), and L. Bouyer, Cong. Orat. (Paris, 1952). E. A. *Abbott, *The Anglican Career of Cardinal Newman* (2 vols., 1892; hostile); J. Guitton, *La Philosophie de Newman* (1933), with bibl.; G. C. Faber, *Oxford Apostles* (1933); D. Gorce, *Newman et les pères* [1934]; Maisie Ward, *Young Mr. Newman* (1948); R. D. Middleton, *Newman and Bloxam* (1947); id., *Newman at Oxford* (1950); J. Rickaby, S.J., *Index to the Works of John Henry Newman* (1914). W. S. Lilly in *D.N.B.*, xl (1894), pp. 340–51. Letters and Diaries, ed. C. S. Dessain, Cong. Or. (London, 1961 ff.). Life by [L.] Meriol Trevor (2 vols., London, 1962).

NEWTON, ISAAC (1642–1727), mathematician and natural philosopher. He was educated at Grantham School and Trinity College, Cambridge, of which he was elected Fellow in 1667. In 1669 he succeeded I. *Barrow as Lucasian Prof. of mathematics. In 1688–1689 and 1703–5 he represented the university in the House of Commons, but he never took much interest in politics. After 1694 he moved to London, being appointed Master of the Mint in 1699 and knighted by Queen *Anne in 1705. He had been a member of the Royal Society since 1672 and was its president from 1703 until his death.

Newton was the most eminent physicist of his day, and his work is a landmark in the study of mathematics. Among his principal achievements are the formulation of the law of gravitation, the discovery of the differential calculus, and the first correct analysis of white light. In his celebrated *Philosophiae Naturalis Principia Mathematica* (1687) he gives expression also to his religious convictions. Belief in God rests for him chiefly on the admirable order of the universe. He acknowledges the Divine transcendence, omnipotence, and perfection, and combats the pantheistic idea of a world soul. God is the Supreme Being with complete authority over the material universe as well as over human souls, which owe Him absolute submission.

Though a conforming Churchman, Newton was not orthodox. He denied the doctrine of the Trinity on the ground that such a belief was inaccessible to reason. He was a friend of the *Cambridge Platonist, H. *More, whose millenarian interests he shared; some of his speculations in this field were embodied in his *Observations on the Prophecies of Daniel and the Apocalypse of St. John* (posthumous, 1733). His more exclusively scientific works include *Optics* (1704) and *Arithmetica Universalis* (1707).

Collected works ed. S. *Horsley (5 vols., London, 1779–1785). The standard life is that of D. Brewster (2 vols., London, 1855). More modern account by L. T. More (New York–London, 1934). Other lives by R. de Villamil (London [1931]), J. W. N. Sullivan (ib., 1938), E. N. da C. Andrade (ib., 1950), and S. I. Wawilow (Berlin, 1951), with bibl. L. Bloch, *La Philosophie de Newton* (Paris thesis, 1908). Hélène Metzger, *Attraction universelle et religion naturelle chez quelques commentateurs anglais de Newton* (1938). Überweg, iii, 371–3, with bibl. p. 687 f. R. T. Glazebrook in *D.N.B.*, xl (1894), pp. 371–93.

NEWTON, JOHN (1725–1807), Evangelical divine. The son of a shipmaster, he was impressed into naval service, where he had an adventurous career, and was converted on 10 Mar. (*N.S.*, 21), 1748. From 1755 to 1760 he was the surveyor of the tides at Liverpool. At this time he came under the influence of G. *Whitefield, and also began studying Latin, Hebrew, Greek, and Syriac. On being offered the curacy of Olney, he was ordained by the Bp. of *Lincoln in 1764. Here he became a close friend of W. *Cowper and collaborated with him in the production of the *Olney Hymns* (1779). In 1780 he was appointed rector of St. Mary Woolnoth, London, and held this post until his death. Among the better known of his hymns, which are remarkable for their directness and simplicity, are 'Glorious things of Thee are spoken' and 'How sweet the Name of Jesus sounds'. He was also the author of several prose writings; among them are *Authentic Narrative of some . . . Particulars in the Life of John Newton* (1764), *A Review of Ecclesiastical History* (1769), several collections of moving letters, and some sermons. In theology he was a pronounced *Calvinist and much influenced many leaders in the *Evangelical Revival, among them T. *Scott, W. *Wilberforce (whom he also aided in his campaign against slavery), C. *Simeon and Hannah *More.

Coll. ed. of his Works by R. Cecil (6 vols., London, 1808). Newton published much of his religious correspondence anonymously in *Omicron* (1774), *Cardiphonia* (2 vols., 1781), *Letters to a Wife* (2 vols., 1793), and *Letters to Rev. W. Bull* (posthumous, 1847). F. J. Hamilton (ed.), '*Out of the Depths*', *being the Autobiography of the Rev. John Newton* (1916). Memoir by R. Cecil (London, 1808). Other Lives by R. Bickersteth (London, 1865), J. Bull (ib., c. 1868), and B. Martin (ib., 1950). H. L. Bennett in *D.N.B.*, xl (1894), pp. 235–8.

NICAEA, First Council of (325). The first *Oecumenical Council, summoned by the Emp. *Constantine within a few months of his conquest of the Eastern provinces, primarily to deal with the *Arian Controversy. The *acta* of the synod (if such ever existed) have been lost, the only authentic documents surviving

from the Council being the Creed, the Synodal Letter, and the collection of twenty Canons.

The Council, which had been orig. convened to Ancyra, assembled at Nicaea (now Isnik) in Bithynia in the early summer of 325 (traditionally 20 May). It appears to have begun with informal discussion between the Arians and Orthodox, which was followed by a solemn opening by Constantine himself. Constantine's main interest was to secure unity rather than any predetermined theological verdict. After the Emperor's opening speech, the presidency prob. passed to *Hosius of Cordova, who had accompanied Constantine from the W., though there is also some authority for the view that *Eustathius, Bp. of Antioch, presided. An Arian creed submitted by *Eusebius of Nicomedia was at once rejected. *Eusebius of Caesarea then laid before the Council the Baptismal Creed of his own Palestinian community, and this, supplemented by the word '*Homoousios', was received by the Council as orthodox. But the Creed formally promulgated by the Council was not this Creed but another, prob. a revision of the Baptismal Creed of *Jerusalem (see *Nicene Creed*). This Creed, with four Anti-Arian anathemas attached, was subscribed by all the Bishops present except two (Theonas of Marmarica and Secundus of Ptolemais); and these last were deposed and banished. In the Arian struggle at the Council it would seem that *Athanasius, who was present as the deacon of his Bishop, *Alexander of *Alexandria, was the leading champion of orthodoxy. The Council also reached decisions on the *Melitian Schism in Egypt and the *Paschal Controversy (qq.v.). It closed on 25 July. Some modern scholars (E. *Schwartz and others) have argued that this closure was only an adjournment, and that a second and concluding session of the Council met in 327.

The number of bishops who attended the Council is not known, since the signature lists are defective. The traditional number, which goes back to a late writing of Athanasius (*Ep. ad Afros*, 2), is 318, probably a symbolical figure, based on the number of *Abraham's servants (Gen. 14. 14). The Council, however, became generally known as 'the synod of the 318 Fathers'. Apparently the only representatives from the W. apart from Hosius were two priests representing the Pope of Rome, and the Bps. of Carthage, Milan, Dijon, and two others.

It is difficult to integrate what we learn from the twenty genuine surviving Canons with our other information about the Council. Can. 6 laid down the precedence due to metropolitan sees, and was later constantly invoked in support of the claims of Rome; cans. 10–14 are a short penitential code, dealing with the treatment of the lapsed in the recent persecutions; can. 13 ordered that no one who sought it was to be refused the *viaticum; can. 19 dealt with the followers of *Paul of Samosata; can. 20 laid down that prayer should be said standing during the Paschal Season. Before long these canons were universally accepted both in E.

and W.; and several independent versions survive from the 4th and 5th cents. They were normally given pride of place in the canonical collections and, prob. through this cause, the canons of other Councils (notably *Sardica, q.v.) were apt to be cited as Nicene because they followed on without a break.

The genuine documents, together with a large collection of *spuria*, are pr. in all the principal Conciliar Collections. Hardouin, i, cols. 309–528; Mansi, ii (1759), cols. 635–1082; Hefele–Leclercq, i (pt. 1; 1907), pp. 335–632. Text of Canons also in Lauchert, pp. 37–43; crit. text of Lat. versions in *E.O.M.I.A.*, esp. I, ii (1904). W.*Bright, *Notes on the Canons of the First Four General Councils* (ed. 2, 1892), pp. 1–89. G. Bardy in Fliche–Martin, iii (1936), pp. 69–95, with good bibl. A. E. Burn, *The Council of Nicaea* (1925). P. Batiffol, 'Les Sources de l'histoire du concile de Nicée' in *É.O.*, xxiv (1925), pp. 385–402, xxvi (1927), pp. 5–17. On the lists of Bishops present, see paper by E. Honigmann, 'Recherches sur les listes des pères de Nicée et de Constantinople' in *Byzantion*, xi (1936), pp. 429–49, esp. pp. 429–39. G. Bardy, 'Sur la réitération du concile de Nicée (327)' in *Rech. S.R.*, xxiii (1933), pp. 430–50. F. Haase, *Die koptischen Quellen zum Konzil von Nicäa.* Übersetzt und untersucht (Studien zur Geschichte und Kultur des Altertums, x, Hft. 4; 1920). C. A. Bernoulli in *P.R.E.* (ed. 3), xiv (1904), pp. 9–18; G. Fritz in *D.T.C.*, xi (pt. 1; 1931), cols. 399–417, s.v. 'Nicée (1er Concile de)'; I. O. de Urbina, S.J., in *E.C.*, viii (1952), cols. 1828–32.

NICAEA, Second Council of (787).
The Seventh General Council was convoked by the Empress Irene at the instigation of the Patr. *Tarasius of Constantinople in order to end the *Iconoclastic Controversy. Pope *Hadrian I accepted the invitation of the Empress and sent two legates on condition that the Iconoclastic Synod of Hieria (753) was condemned. The patriarchs of *Alexandria, *Antioch, and *Jerusalem, then subject to the Khalifs, were unable to come and were each represented by two monks. The Council met on 17 Aug. 786 in the church of the Holy Apostles at *Constantinople, but was immediately broken up by iconoclastic soldiers and did not reassemble till 24 Sept. 787, this time in the church of St. Sophia at Nicaea, where Tarasius presided. The Council declared its adherence to the doctrine on the veneration (προσκύνησις) of images expounded by the Pope in his letter to the Empress, adding that they are honoured with a relative cult (σχετικῷ ποθῷ), whereas absolute adoration (λατρεία) is reserved to God alone, the honour given to the image passing on to its prototype. The decree promulgating the doctrine was signed by all present and by the Empress and her son Constantine, and the iconoclasts were anathematized.

The 22 canons drawn up by the Council deal with disciplinary matters; they declare null the election by a secular authority of bishops, priests, and deacons, condemn simony, forbid priests to leave their diocese without permission of the bishop, enjoin simplicity of life on all clerics, and forbid the stay of women in bishops' houses and monasteries of men as well as the erection of double monasteries.

Hardouin, iv, cols. 3–820; Mansi, xii (1766), cols. 951–1154, and xiii (1767), cols. 1–820. Canons also in Lauchert, pp. 139–51. Hefele–Leclercq, iii (pt. 2; 1910), pp. 741–98. E. Amann in Fliche–Martin, vi (1937), pp. 114–20. G. Fritz in *D.T.C.*, xi (pt. 1; 1932), cols. 417–41, s.v. 'Nicée (IIe Concile de)', with text of canons and Fr. tr. See also bibl. to *Iconoclastic Controversy*; also *Caroline Books*.

NICENE CREED, The.
Two Creeds currently so named must be distinguished:

(1) The Nicene Creed properly so called, issued in 325 by the Council of *Nicaea (q.v.) and known to scholars as N. This Creed was drawn up at the Council to defend the Orthodox Faith against the *Arians and includes the word '*Homoousios'. Compared with later conciliar Creeds it is relatively short, concluding with the words 'And in the Holy Spirit'. Appended to it were four anathemas against Arianism, which came to be regarded as an integral part of the text. It was probably based on the Baptismal Creed of *Jerusalem (H. *Lietzmann), not, as older scholars held, through a misunderstanding of a statement of *Eusebius of Caesarea, on that of Caesarea in Palestine (F. J. A. *Hort, A. E. Burn, E. C. S. Gibson).

(2) In common parlance, the 'Nicene Creed' more often means the considerably longer formula which bears this title in the *Thirty-Nine Articles and is in regular use in the *Eucharistic worship of the Church, both in East and West. It is also known as the 'Niceno-Constantinopolitan Creed', and is referred to as C. It differs from N. in that, *inter alia*, (1) the second section on the Person of Christ is longer; (2) the phrase in N. 'from the substance of the Father' (ἐκ τῆς οὐσίας τοῦ πατρός), as an explanation of 'Homoousios' is wanting; (3) the third section contains an extended statement on the status and work of the Holy Ghost; and (4) after this follow assertions of belief in the Church, Baptism, the Resurrection of the Dead, and Eternal Life. Also it has no anathemas. Since the time of that of *Chalcedon of 451 it has been regarded as the Creed of the Council of *Constantinople of 381; but the earliest authorities connecting it with Constantinople date from *c.* 449–50. If this tradition is to be accepted, it may have been put forward at the Council as a profession of faith by *Cyril of Jerusalem, or alternatively by *Nectarius (both of whom figured prominently there). But, apart from the want of any contemporary evidence, there are other grounds for dissociating the Creed from Constantinople. Its occurrence in St.*Epiphanius's *Ancoratus* (374) would be decisive if its position in this treatise were established; but there are grounds for believing that N., not C., originally stood in the text here. Whatever its origin, it is probable that, like N., it ultimately derives from the Baptismal Creed of Jerusalem.

Its use in Eucharistic Worship after the Gospel apparently began at Antioch under *Peter the Fuller (476–88) and gradually spread through E. and W. In the early Middle Ages, the *Filioque (q.v.) was added to it in the W. In the Roman Rite its use at Mass is confined to Sundays, the greater Feasts, and the Feasts of *Doctors. In the E. it is regularly used as a Baptismal Creed. It has been widely accepted in modern times as a proposed basis of Christian unity, e.g. in the *Lambeth Quadrilateral (1888).

Both Creeds, N. and C., are discussed in A. E. Burn, *An Introduction to the Creeds and to the Te Deum* (1899), pp. 72–

123; id., *The Nicene Creed* (Oxford Church Text Books, 1909). I. Ortiz de Urbina, S.J., *Il simbolo niceno* (Consejo Superior de Investigaciones Científicas, 1947). J. N. D. Kelly, *Early Christian Creeds* (1950), pp. 205–62.

On (1), see also F. *Loofs, 'Das Nicänum' in *Festgabe von Fachgenossen und Freunden Karl Müller zum siebzigsten Geburtstag dargebracht* (1922), pp. 68–82; H. Lietzmann, 'Symbolstudien XIII' in *Z.N.T.W.*, xxiv (1925), pp. 193–202, with 'Kritischer Epilog' by A. *Harnack, p. 203. Hefele–Leclercq, i (pt. 1; 1907), pp. 442–8.

On (2), F. J. A. *Hort, *Two Dissertations* (1876), pp. 73–150 ('On the Constantinopolitan Creed and other Eastern Creeds of the Fourth Century'); J. Kunze, *Das nicänisch-konstantinopolitanische Symbol* (1898); E. C. S. Gibson, *The Three Creeds* (Oxford Library of Practical Theology, 1908), pp. 115–77.

On the use of the Nicene Creed [C] at the Eucharist, cf. B. *Capelle, O.S.B., 'L'Introduction du symbole à la messe' in *Mélanges Joseph de Ghellinck*, ii (Museum Lessianum. Sect. hist., xiv, 1951), pp. 1003–27, and Jungmann, *S.M.*, i (ed. 1949), pp. 569–84; Eng. tr., i, (pt. 1), pp. 461–74.

NICEPHORUS, St. (*c.* 758–829), Patr. of *Constantinople. His father had occupied high office under the Emp. Constantine Copronymus and suffered in the *Iconoclastic Controversy for his defence of images. Nicephorus inherited his father's beliefs and represented the Emperor at the Second Council of *Nicaea (787). Later he withdrew from court life and founded a monastery on the Propontis whither he retired, but without himself becoming a monk. The Emp. Constantine VI and his mother, Irene, recalled him to Constantinople, where the Emp. Nicephorus made him patriarch on the death of *Tarasius (806) though he was not yet in holy orders. In recompense for the Imperial favour the Emperor demanded his reinstatement of the priest Joseph, who had been deposed in 797 for blessing the adulterous marriage of Constantine VI. After some hesitation Nicephorus gave way, and at a synod held in 806 or 807 rehabilitated Joseph. After the death of the Emperor and of his son Stauracius (811), he renewed the original sentence against Joseph. In 813 he crowned the Emp. Leo V ('the Armenian'), who resumed the Iconoclastic policy of his predecessors in the 8th cent. Nicephorus resisted, but was abandoned by the majority of his bishops, who supported the Emperor. In 815 he was exiled and retired to his former monastery again, where he spent the remainder of his life, devoting himself to the cause of the Images and to study. Despite the opposition of the *Studites, who could not forgive his weakness in the Adulterine Controversy, his relics were translated to Constantinople in 847, and he received the title of a confessor of the faith. Feast day in the Greek Church, 2 June; in the Latin Church, 13 Mar.

Among his writings on the Image controversy are 'Apologeticus Minor' and 'Apologeticus Major' (both 817) and 'Libri Tres Antirrhetici'. Of particular value is his 'Ιστορία σύντομος or 'Breviarium Nicephori', a Byzantine history from 602 to 770, highly praised by *Photius for its accuracy and literary excellence. He also compiled a Chronicle, Χρονογραφία σύντομος, reaching from Adam to the year of his own death.

V. Grumel, A.A. (ed.), *Les Régestes des actes du patriarcat de Constantinople*, i (fasc. 2; 1936), pp. 23–40 (Nos. 374–407).

Collection of his works in J. P. Migne, *PG*, c, 169–1068; further 'Antirrhetici' in J. B. *Pitra (ed.), *Spicilegium Solesmense*, i (1852), pp. 302–504, and iv (1858), pp. 233–380; *Opuscula Historica* [i.e. his 'Ιστορία σύντομος and Χρονογραφία σύντομος], ed. C. de Boor (Teub., 1880). Life by his pupil, the Deacon Ignatius, pr. in *AA.SS.*, Mar. II (1648), pp. 704–27, Gk. text, with Lat. tr., pp. 294–321, and introd., p. 293; repr. in J. P. Migne, op. cit., cols. 41–160; also in C. de Boor, op. cit., pp. 139–217. Krumbacher, pp. 71–3. R. Janin, A.A., in *D.T.C.*, xi (pt. 1; 1931), cols. 452–5, s.v. 'Nicéphore de Constantinople'. P. J. Alexander, *The Patriarch Nicephorus of Constantinople* (1958).

NICEPHORUS CALLISTUS (*c.* 1256–*c.* 1335), 'Xanthopoulos', Byzantine historian. Little is known of his life. Apparently a native of *Constantinople and a priest of *Santa Sophia, whose library he utilized for his works, at the end of his life he seems to have become a monk. He belonged to the party of the Emp. Andronicus II (reigned 1282–1328), whose ecclesiastical policy, in contrast to that of his father Michael Palaeologus, supported Greek orthodoxy against the Latinizers. His principal work, a 'Church History', narrates in 18 books the events from the birth of Christ to the death of the Phocas (610). At the end of the introduction there is a summary of five more books, probably never executed, which were to continue the narrative to the death of *Leo the Philosopher (912). The History has been held to rest on an anonymous 10th cent. work; it certainly draws extensively, either directly or through an unknown intermediary, on the Ecclesiastical Histories of *Eusebius, *Socrates, *Sozomen, *Theodoret, and *Evagrius. It is none the less an important source for certain of the early controversies and heresies as well as for the history of Byzantine legends, but its value throughout depends on that of the earlier material used. In 1555 it was translated into Latin and played an important part in the controversial literature of the time, furnishing material for the defence of images and relics. Among his other writings, several of them in iambics, are liturgical, exegetical, and hagiographical works.

His Church History was publd. in Lat. tr. by J. Lange, Basle, 1555; Gk. text with Lat. tr. by J. Lange, ed. F. *Ducaeus, 2 vols., Paris, 1630, repr. J. P. Migne, *PG*, cxlv, 559–1332, cxlvi, and cxlvii, 9–448; other works repr. ib., cxlvii, 449–634, with note from J. A. *Fabricius, ib., cxlv, 549–58. A. Papadopoulos–Kerameus, 'Νικηφόρος Κάλλιστος Ξανθόπουλος' in *B.Z.*, xi (1902), pp. 38–49, incl. a few texts. *Progymnasmata*, ed. J. Gettner, ib., xxxiii (1933), pp. 1–12 and 255–70 (text, pp. 7–12), with useful introd. Krumbacher, pp. 291–3. M. Jugie, A.A., in *D.T.C.*, xi (pt. 1; 1931), cols. 446–52, s.v.

NICETA, St. (d. *c.* 414), ecclesiastical writer. He was Bp. of Remesiana (Bela Palanka in Yugoslavia) from *c.* 370 onwards. His literary importance arises esp. from his contacts through his geographical situation with both E. and W. His writings, mainly ascribed to other authors in later times, have been largely restored to him by A. E. Burn (d. 1927). His *Explanatio Symboli* is a primary witness for the history of the *Apostles' Creed, containing, e.g., the oldest attestation for the words 'communio sanctorum'; *De Diversis Appellationibus* is a tract on the titles of Christ; *De Ratione Fidei* and *De Spiritu Sancto* are respectively directed against *Arianism and the *Pneumatomachoi; *De Vigiliis* and *De Psalmodiae Bono* are of liturgical interest. Both G. *Morin and A. E. Burn also ascribe to Niceta the authorship of the celebrated hymn '*Te Deum Laudamus'. Feast day, 22 June.

Crit. ed. of principal texts in A. E. Burn, *Niceta of Remesiana*. His Life and Works (1905); of 'De Vigiliis' and 'De Psalmodiae Bono' by C. H. *Turner in *J.T.S.*, xxii (1920-1), pp. 305-20, and xxiv (1922-3), pp. 225-50. W. A. Patin, *Niceta, Bischof von Remesiana, als Schriftsteller und Theologe* (1909). J. Zeiller, *Les Origines chrétiennes dans les provinces danubiennes de l'empire romain* (Bibliothèque des Écoles françaises d'Athènes et de Rome, cxii, 1918), pp. 549-58. G. Morin, O.S.B., 'Nouvelles Recherches sur l'auteur du *Te Deum*' in *R. Bén*, xi (1894), pp. 49-77; id., 'Notes additionnelles à l'étude sur l'auteur du *Te Deum*', ib., 337-45; id., 'Le *Te Deum*, type anonyme d'anaphore latine préhistorique?', ib., xxiv (1907), pp. 180-223. C. H. Turner, 'Niceta and Ambrosiaster, I' in *J.T.S.*, vii (1905-6), pp. 203-19. Bardenhewer, iii, 598-605; Altaner (ed. 1951), p. 342. E. Amann in *D.T.C.*, xi (pt. 1; 1931), cols. 477-9; E. Peterson in *E.C.*, viii (1952), col. 1838 f. See also bibl. to *Te Deum*.

NICETAS ACOMINATOS (d. after 1210), Byzantine scholar. A native of Chonia (i.e. Colossae; hence also 'Nicetas Choniates') and the son of a wealthy family, he studied at *Constantinople where he rose rapidly in the Imperial service. He was governor of the province of Philippopolis when the Emp. *Frederick Barbarossa passed through on the Third *Crusade (1189). His dealings with the Crusaders at this time led him to become closely connected with the Eastern Court in the next years. On the Fall of Constantinople (1204) he fled to *Nicaea, where he passed the rest of his life. His writings include a 'Treasury of Orthodoxy' (Θησαυρὸς 'Ορθοδοξίας), a comprehensive work in 27 books (written between 1204 and 1210) against contemporary heresies, intended to supplement *Euthymius Zigabenus's 'Panoplia Dogmatike'; and a History (Χρονικὴ Διήγησις) of the period 1180–1206 in 21 books covering the reigns of the last Comneni. The former is the main source for the Councils held between 1156 and 1166; the latter is esp. valuable for its account of the capture of Constantinople by the Latins in 1204. His elder brother, MICHAEL ACOMINATOS (c. 1140–c. 1215), who became Abp. of *Athens in 1175, was also a famous scholar, his writings including numerous sermons, verses and a collection of letters.

Collection of Nicetas's writings in J. P. Migne, *PG*, cxxxix, 287-1444, and cxl, 9-284; and of those of Michael, ib., 299-382. Krumbacher, pp. 281-6 and 92 f. (on Nicetas); pp. 468-470 (on Michael). L. Petit, A.A., in *D.T.C.*, i (1903), cols. 189 f., s.v. 'Acominatos, Nicétas'; T. J. Shahan in *C.E.*, i (1907), p. 239 f., s.v. 'Akominatos'; V. Laurent, A.A., in *L.Th.K.*, i (1930), col. 189 f., s.v. 'Akominatos', with reff.

NICHOLAS, St., Bp. of Myra in Lycia. Though one of the most popular saints in both the Greek and Latin Churches, scarcely anything is historically certain about him. Acc. to tradition, he was imprisoned during the *Diocletianic persecution and afterwards released, and was present at the Council of *Nicaea. The latter supposition is most improbable as he is not in any of the early lists of

bishops present at the Council, nor referred to in the writings of *Athanasius. He is first definitely met with in the Church of 'St. Priscus and St. Nicholas', built by the Emp. *Justinian (d. 565) at *Constantinople. His cult became popular in the W. after the inhabitants of Bari claimed to have got possession of his remains on 9 May 1087.

St. Nicholas is regarded as the patron saint of sailors, and churches under his dedication are often built so that they could be seen off the coast as landmarks. He is also the patron saint of children, bringing them gifts on 6 Dec. (whence 'Santa Claus', an American corruption of 'Saint Nicholas'). And he is also the patron saint of Russia. His symbol is sometimes three bags of gold, the dowry he is supposed to have given to three girls to save them from degradation, sometimes three children standing in a tub at his side, a representation which has been variously explained. Feast day, 6 Dec.

N. C. Falconius (ed.), *Sancti . . . Nicolae Acta Primigenia* (Naples, 1751; Gk. text with Lat. tr.); more crit. ed. by G. Anrich, *Hagios Nikolaos. Der heilige Nikolaos in der griechischen Kirche. Texte und Untersuchungen* (2 vols., 1913-17). 12th cent. life by Norman poet Wace, ed. Mary S. Crawford (thesis, Philadelphia, 1923). K. Meisen, *Nikolauskult und Nikolausbrauch in Abendlande* (1931). J. Laroche, *Vie de S. Nicolas, évêque de Myre* [c. 1892]. E. Crozier, *The Life and Legends of Saint Nicholas, Patron Saint of Children* (1949). K. Künstle, *Ikonographie der christlichen Kunst*, ii (1926), pp. 459-64. M. Ott in *C.E.*, xi (1911), p. 63 f., s.v., with bibl.; N. Meisen in *L.Th.K.*, vii (1935), col. 582 f., s.v. 'Nikolaus'; E. Battisti in *E.C.*, viii (1952), cols. 1848-51, s.v. 'Nicola di Mira'.

NICHOLAS I, St. (d. 867), Pope from 858. He was one of the most forceful of the early medieval Popes. Of a noble Roman family, he entered the service of the Curia under Pope Sergius II (844-7) and was made subdeacon; having become deacon under *Leo IV (847-55), he gained a decisive influence in the affairs of the Holy See under Benedict III (855-8), and on his death he was elected to succeed him (858). One of the chief events of his rule was the long-drawn-out struggle with the E. Church over the deposition of Ignatius by the Emp. Michael III and the appointment of *Photius to the see of Constantinople. The latter, though at first seeking Rome's approval of his accession, became more and more embittered when Nicholas, refusing to sanction the illegality of the proceedings, anathematized him and restored Ignatius at the Synod at Rome in 863. The situation was further aggravated by the readiness of the Pope to respond, in 866, to the advances of the newly converted Bulgars, whom he tried to win over to the see of Rome and for whom he wrote his famous 'Responsa Nicolai ad consulta Bulgarorum', a kind of summary on Christian faith and discipline. To this supposed encroachment on his rights, Photius replied in 867 by declaring the Pope deposed, but was himself deprived of his office in the same year. In the W. Nicholas had to contend with similar difficulties in upholding the Papal authority. He vigorously defended the sanctity of marriage in the divorce case of Lothair II of Lorraine, deposing the two Abps. of *Cologne and Trier who had connived at his bigamous marriage, and effecting a temporary reconciliation between the king and his consort. He successfully asserted the supremacy of the see of Rome against Abp. John of *Ravenna, who, counting on Imperial support, had violated the rights of property of the Holy See and tyrannized over his subjects. Similarly *Hincmar of Reims was obliged to acknowledge the right of the Papacy to intervene in disputes. There are grounds for believing that the '*False Decretals' were already received in Rome during his pontificate, though probably not before 864, and that Nicholas himself was influenced by them in his attitude to Hincmar. Apart from his decisive effect on the prestige of the Papacy in political matters, Nicholas was a man of high personal integrity, fully conscious of the responsibilities which he owed to his position. Feast day, 13 Nov.

Letters pr. in J. P. Migne, *PL*, cxix, 753–1212. Crit. ed. by E. Perels in *M.G.H.*, Epistolae, vi (1925), pp. 257–690. *L.P.* (Duchesne), ii, 151–72. Lives by J. Roy ('Les Saints', 1899) and J. Richterich (Berne, 1903; by an *Old Catholic). F. Dvornik, *The Photian Schism* (1948), passim. A. Greinacher, *Die Anschauungen des Papstes Nikolaus I über das Verhältnis von Staat und Kirche* (Abhandlungen zur mittleren und neueren Geschichte, x; 1909); E. Perels, *Papst Nikolaus I und Anastasius Bibliothecarius* (1920); J. Haller, *Nikolaus I und Pseudo-Isidor* (1936). L. *Duchesne, *Les Premiers Temps de l'état pontifical* (ed. 2, 1904), pp. 235–45 (Eng. tr., 1908, pp. 155–62). J. P. Kirsch in *C.E.*, xi (1911), p. 54 f.; É. Amann in *D.T.C.*, xi (pt. 1; 1931), cols. 506–26.

NICHOLAS V (1397–1455), Pope from 1447. Thomas Parentucelli, the son of a doctor of Sarzana, studied theology at *Bologna where Bp., later Cardinal, Nicholas Albergati became his protector. Appointed Bp. of Bologna after Albergati's death (1444), he was Papal Legate at the Diet of Frankfurt, where he worked so successfully for the recognition of *Eugenius IV by the German princes that he was created Cardinal in 1446. In 1447 he was elected Pope. By his conciliatory spirit and great diplomatic skill he obtained the recognition of the Papal rights in the matter of benefices and bishoprics by the Concordat of Vienna in 1448 and, in the following year, put an end to the schism by receiving the submission of the antipope, Felix V, and that of the Council of *Basle before its dissolution. In thanksgiving for the restoration of unity he decreed a *Jubilee in 1450, and immediately after sent out his legates to reform abuses—Cardinal *Nicholas of Cusa and St. *Giovanni Capistrano to N. and S. Germany respectively, and Cardinal D'Estouteville to France. In 1452 he crowned Frederick III of Habsburg German Emperor (the last Imperial Coronation in Rome). At the same time he restored order in the States of the Church and suppressed the revolt of Stefano Porcaro (1453) who attempted to overthrow the papal régime and declare Rome a republic. After the fall of *Constantinople (1453) he tried in vain to incite the European princes to a crusade against the Turks, and anxiety for the state of Christendom probably hastened his death. An enthusiastic lover of arts and science, Nicholas restored many ruined churches, planned to rebuild the *Vatican and St. Peter's, and founded the Vatican Library. He was the first, and probably the best, of the Renaissance Popes, of blameless personal life, free from nepotism and anxious to reconcile religion with the new learning.

The principal authorities are the lives by Vespasiano da Bisticci (d. 1498) in *Vite di uomini illustri del secolo XV* (ed. Ludovico Frati, Bologna, 1892, pp. 26–65) and B. *Platina, *Vitae Pontificum* (Venice, 1479; no pagination). J. Manetti (d. 1459), 'Vita Nicolai V' in L. A. *Muratori (ed.), *Rerum Italicarum Scriptores*, iii (pt. 2; Milan, 1734), cols. 907–60. Modern life by G. Sforza (Lucca, 1884; Germ. tr., 1887). K. Pleyer, *Die Politik Nikolaus V* (1927). Pastor, ii (1891), pp. 3–314, with bibl. Fliche–Martin, xv (1951), pp. 15–38. G. Mollat in *D.T.C.*, xi (pt. 1; 1931), cols. 541–8, s.v. 'Nicolas V'; F. X. Seppelt in *L.Th.K.*, vii (1935), col. 587, s.v. 'Nikolaus V', for further bibl.; L. Simeoni, O.F.M., in *E.C.*, viii (1952), col. 1826, s.v. 'Niccolò V'.

NICHOLAS OF BASLE (d. c. 1395), medieval heretic. He was a *Beghard who preached and propagated his opinions esp. in the district round Basle. Claiming to be inspired, he taught that all those submitting to his direction were sinless and need not obey any authority. For many years he evaded the *Inquisition but was eventually seized and burned at the stake in Vienna. At one time he was identified (esp. by K. Schmidt) with the mysterious 'Friend of God from the Oberland' who plays an important part in the writings of the Strassburg ascetic, Rulman Merswin, but H. S. *Denifle has convincingly argued that this figure is a literary creation of Merswin himself.

K. Schmidt (ed.), *Nicolaus von Basel. Leben und ausgewählte Schriften* (1866); id. *Nicolaus von Basel: Bericht von der Bekehrung Taulers* (1875). H. S. Denifle, O.P., 'Der Gottesfreund im Oberland und Nikolaus von Basel. Eine kritische Studie' in *Historisch-politische Blätter für das katholische Deutschland*, lxxv (1875), pp. 17–34, 93–122, 245–66, and 340–54.

NICHOLAS BREAKSPEAR. See *Hadrian IV*.

NICHOLAS CABASILAS. See *Cabasilas, Nicholas*.

NICHOLAS OF CUSA (c. 1400–64), German cardinal and philosopher. He was a native of the village of Cues, on the Moselle. After studying at Heidelberg (1416) and Padua (1417), he entered Cologne university in 1425, where he became doctor of canon law. Having been ordained priest in 1430, he was made Dean of St. Florin's at Coblence in 1431. In 1433 he took part in the Council of *Basle as an advocate in a dispute concerning the possession of the archiepiscopal see of Trier. He also worked for the reconciliation of the *Hussites to the Church and in 1433 procured the acceptance of the *Calixtines by the Council. In the same year he wrote his famous work, *De Concordantia Catholica*, in which he outlined a comprehensive programme for the reform of Church and Empire. Though he originally favoured the Conciliar Movement, the revolutionary proceedings of the Council and its failure to bring about a union with the Greeks estranged him from the majority of its supporters. From 1437 he devoted himself entirely to the cause of the Pope, being sent in that year by *Eugenius IV to *Constantinople in the interests of reunion. In the following years he worked for the Papal cause at the Diets of Mainz (1441), Frankfurt (1442), and Nuremberg (1444). When in 1448 a reconciliation was effected between the Pope and the Empire which culminated in the Concordat of Vienna, *Nicholas V rewarded him by creating him cardinal. In 1450 he was appointed Bp. of Brixen (in the Tyrol) and Papal legate for the German-speaking countries. As such, besides publishing the Jubilee Indulgences, he was authorized to hold provincial synods and to visit monasteries and remove abuses. In 1452 he took possession of his diocese, where he worked with great zeal for the reform of the morals of clergy and people. When a conflict with Duke Sigismund forced him to leave his diocese, he went to Rome, where *Pius II appointed him in 1459 his vicar-general with the task of reforming and governing Rome and the patrimony of St. Peter. After an apparent reconciliation he returned to Brixen, but Sigismund soon declared war on him and besieged him in the fortress of Bruneck, which he was forced to surrender. He once more went to Rome, where he spent the rest of his life as Camerarius of the Sacred College.

In intellectual outlook Nicholas was a forerunner of the Renaissance. His principal work, De Docta Ignorantia (completed, 1440), was a defence of his two celebrated principles, 'docta ignorantia' and 'coincidentia oppositorum'. 'Docta ignorantia' was the highest stage of intellectual apprehension accessible to the human intellect, since Truth, which is absolute, one, and infinitely simple, is unknowable to man. Knowledge by contrast is relative, multiple, complex, and at best only approximate. The road to Truth therefore leads beyond reason and the principle of contradiction; it is only by intuition that we can discover God, the 'coincidentia oppositorum', wherein all contradictions meet. This description is meant to indicate that God is at once infinitely great and infinitely small, the maximum and the minimum, the centre and the circumference of the world, everywhere and nowhere, neither One nor Three, but Triune.

Nicholas's general cast of thought has many affinities with *Neo-Platonism; and among those who esp. influenced him were St. *Augustine, Proclus (410–85) and *Dionysius the Areopagite, and of medieval thinkers, esp. St. *Bonaventure and Master *Eckhart. He held the common Platonist view that mathematics is the supreme science. He also had considerable critical gifts as a historian, rejecting e.g. the authenticity of the *False Decretals and of the *Donation of Constantine.

His other writings include an Apologia Doctae Ignorantiae, a reply to a charge of pantheism by John Wenck, professor of theology at Heidelberg; De Quaerendo Deum (1445);

Idiotae Libri (1450), four dialogues on the ways that lead to wisdom and on the human soul; De Non Aliud (1462), an attempted synthesis of the *Aristotelian and *Platonist conceptions of God; and De Apice Theoriae (1463–4), a final summary.

Editio princeps of his collected works, 2 vols., Strassburg, c. 1490; until the present century the standard ed. was that issued in 3 vols., Basle, 1565. Crit. ed. under the auspices of the Heidelberg Academy, by E. Hoffmann, R. Klibansky, and others (14 vols., 1932 ff.). Further collection of 'Cusanus-Texte' in the Sb. (Heid.), ed. E. Hoffmann–R. Klibansky (1928–9, Hft. 3), G. Kallen (1935–6, Hft. 3), J. Koch (1935–6, Hft. 2), L. Bauer (1940–1, Hft. 4), J. Koch (1941–2, Hft. 1), id. (1942–3, Hft. 2), id. (1944–8, Hft. 3), G. von Bredow (1955, Hft. 2), etc. Philosophische Schriften, ed., with important introd., by A. Petzelt (Stuttgart, 1949 ff.), Eng. tr. of 'De Visione Dei' by E. G. Salter (London, 1928) and of 'De Docta Ignorantia' by G. Heron, O.F.M. (ib., 1954). Substantial general studies by F. A. Scharpff (Tübingen, 1871), E. Vansteenberghe (Paris thesis, Lille, 1920, with detailed bibl.), P. Rotta (Pubblicazioni della Università Cattolica del Sacro Cuore, Ser. 1, xii [1928], also with bibl.), and M. Patronnier de Gandillac, La Philosophie de Nicolas de Cues (Paris thesis [1941], with further bibl.). More popular introductions by H. Bett ('Great Medieval Churchmen', London, 1932), P. Mennicken (Leipzig, 1932; ed. 2, Trier, 1950), and R. Gradi, Il pensiero del Cusano (Problemi d' oggi. Collana di Filosofia e Storia della Filosofia, Ser. 2, vii, Padua, 1941). J. Uebinger, Die Gotteslehre des Nikolaus Cusanus (1888). E. Vansteenberghe, Autour de la docte ignorance (Paris thesis, Münster i.W. [c. 1921]). J. Lenz, Die Docta Ignorantia oder die mystische Gotteserkenntnis des Nikolaus Cusanus in ihren philosophischen Grundlagen (Abhandlungen zur Philosophie und Psychologie der Religion, iii; 1923); 'Cusanus-Studien' in Sb. (Heidelberg), by R. Klibansky (1929–30, Hft. 3), M. Honecker (1937–8, Hft. 2), Elisabeth Bohnenstädt (1938–9, Hft. 1), R. Cruetz (1938–9, Hft. 3), M. Honecker (1939–40, Hft. 2), O. Menzel (1940–1, Hft. 6), E. Hoffmann (1941–2, Hft. 4), etc.; R. Haubst, Studien zu Nikolaus von Kues und Johannes Wenk aus Handschriften der Vatikanischen Bibliothek (B.G.P.M., xxxviii, Hft. 1; [1955]), esp. pp. 1–32; E. F. Jacob, 'Nicolas of Cusa' in F. J. C. Hearnshaw (ed.), The Social and Political Ideas of Some Great Thinkers of the Renaissance and Reformation (1925), pp. 32–59; id., 'Cusanus the Theologian' in Bulletin of the John Rylands Library, xxi (1937), pp. 406–24. Überweg, iii, 72–89, with bibl. p. 636 f. E. Vansteenberghe in D.T.C., xi (pt. 1; 1931), cols. 601–12, s.v. 'Nicolas (24) de Cusa'; R. Klibansky in Enciclopedia italiana, xxiv (1934), pp. 761–3, s.v. 'Niccolà da Cusa'; P. Rotta in E.C., viii (1952), cols. 1819–22, s.v. 'Niccolà Cusano'.

NICHOLAS OF FLÜE, St. (1417–87),

'Brother Klaus', Swiss ascetic. The son of wealthy peasants, he distinguished himself as a soldier and later as a cantonal councillor and judge (1459). In 1467 he obtained the consent of his wife to leave her and their ten children, to lead the life of a hermit in the Ranft valley, near Sachseln, in Switzerland. Here, where he is said to have lived for 19 years with no food save the Eucharist, his reputation for sanctity attracted many visitors from all parts of Europe seeking his advice. His great influence showed itself in 1481 when a dispute between the delegates of the Swiss confederates at Stans that threatened to result in civil war was settled by his counsel. He was beatified in 1669 and canonized in 1947. Feast day, 21 Mar.; in Switzerland (of which he is the Patron Saint), 25 Sept.

Fundamental study by R. Durrer, Bruder Klaus. Die ältesten Quellen über den seligen Nikolaus von Flüe, sein Leben und seinen Einfluss (2 vols., Sarnen, 1917–21), orig. planned to mark the fifth centenary of his birth, with text of life by Henry of Gundelfingen (d. 1490) and other primary material. Other studies include those of J. Ming (4 vols., Luzern, 1861–78), H. Federer ('Die Schweiz im deutschen

Geistesleben', xiv; 1928), Agnes von Segesser (Fribourg, Switzerland, 1936), A. Andrey (Geneva, 1939), G. Méautis (Neuchâtel, 1940), C. Journet (ed. 2, Collection des Cahiers du Rhône, v; 1947) with texts, and R. Centlivres (Geneva, 1947). *Letterae Decretales* in *A.A.S.*, xl (1948), pp. 49–63. C. Trezzini in *E.C.*, viii (1952), cols. 1846 f., s.v. 'Nicola della Flue', with useful reff.

NICHOLAS OF HEREFORD (d. *c.* 1420), *Lollard writer. While a Fellow of Queen's College, Oxford, he became an ardent supporter of J. *Wycliffe, and in 1382 began to preach Wycliffite doctrines. For this he was condemned and excommunicated. An expedition to Rome to appeal against the sentence was unsuccessful, and imprisonment followed. Escaping, he returned to England and resumed his Lollard activities, esp. in the West Country. He seems to have recanted about 1391. Later he became chancellor and treasurer of *Hereford Cathedral. In 1417 he resigned the latter post, was professed in a *Carthusian monk, and died a few years later. Nicholas of Hereford probably took a prominent part with J. *Purvey in the translation of the Bible into English.

The principal chronicle sources include the *Fasciculi Zizaniorum* (ed. W. W. Shirley, R.S., 1858, pp. 289–329) and Henry Knighton, *Chronicon* (ed. J. R. Lumby, ii, Rolls Series, 1895, pp. 170–4). M. Deanesly, *The Lollard Bible and Other Medieval Biblical Versions* (1920), esp. pp. 232–6, 253–67, and 286–8; K. B. McFarlane, *John Wycliffe and the Beginnings of English Nonconformity* (1952), pp. 107–12 and 126–9. C. L. Kingsford in *D.N.B.*, xl (1894), pp. 418–20.

NICHOLAS OF LYRA (*c.* 1270–1340), *Franciscan scholar. A student of theology and later (after 1308) a regent master in the university of *Paris, Nicholas was the best-equipped Biblical scholar of the Middle Ages. In addition to a wide knowledge of the history of Christian exegesis, he knew Hebrew (but not Greek), and was familiar with the commentaries of many of the Jewish expositors, notably *Rashi. As against the current allegoristic interpretations of the Bible, he set himself to arrive at the exact and literal sense, and R. *Simon once stated that no one down to his day since the time of St. *Jerome had contributed as much to the understanding of the OT. Nicholas's principal work was his 'Postillae perpetuae in universam S. Scripturam'. It was the first Biblical commentary printed and became very popular. His commentaries have commonly been supposed, perhaps wrongly, to have greatly influenced M. *Luther ('Si Lyra non lyrasset, Lutherus non saltasset'). Nicholas also wrote on the *Eucharist, the *Beatific Vision, and other subjects.

Postilla Litteralis, first publ. Rome, 5 vols., 1471–2. P. Glorieux, *Répertoire des maîtres en théologie de Paris au XIII*e *siècle*, ii (1934), pp. 215–31, with details of MSS. and edd. H. Labrosse, 'Sources de la biographie de Nicolas de Lyra' in *Études Franciscaines*, xvi (1906), pp. 383–404; id., 'Biographie de Nicolas de Lyre', ib., xvii (1907), pp. 489–505 and 593–608; id., 'Œuvres de Nicolas de Lyre. Sources bibliographiques', ib., xix (1908), pp. 41–52; id., 'Œuvres de Nicolas de Lyre. Catalogue des œuvres', ib., pp. 153–75 and 368–79, and xxxv (1923), pp. 171–87 and 400–32. C. V. Langlois, 'Nicolas de Lyre, frère mineur' in *Histoire littéraire de la France*, xxxvi (1927), pp. 355–400, with reff. P. Vernet in *D.T.C.*, ix (pt. 1; 1926), cols. 1410–22, s.v. 'Lyre, Nicole de', with bibl.

NICHOLAS OF ORESME. See *Oresme, Nicolas.*

NICHOLAS OF TOLENTINO, St. (*c.* 1245–1306), *Augustinian friar. Born at Sant' Angelo in the March of Ancona, he made his profession as an Augustinian hermit *c.* 1253. His life was pious but uneventful, devoted to preaching and pastoral work among the poor and destitute and, it is recorded, graced by frequent miracles. His last thirty years were spent at Tolentino, where fragments of his body, which are reputed to bleed shortly before great calamities (e.g. in 1452 before the Fall of *Constantinople, in 1510 before the Reformation), are interred. He was canonized by *Eugenius IV in 1446. Feast day, 10 Sept.

The principal authority is the contemporary life by Pietro di Monte Rubiano, his fellow Augustinian hermit, written in 1326; repr. in *AA.SS.*, Sept. III (1750), pp. 644–64, with other material, pp. 664–743, and introd., pp. 636–44. Popular modern lives by A. Tonna-Barthet (Paris, 1896), 'l'Abbé H.P.' (ib., 1899), and E. A. Foran, O.S.A. (London, 1920). W. Hümpfner, O.E.S.A., in *L.Th.K.*, vii (1935), col. 589 f.

NICHOLAS, HENRY (*c.* 1502–*c.* 1580), or Hendrik Niclaes, founder of the *Anabaptist sect of '*Familists' (q.v.). He was probably a native of Münster in Westphalia, of a devout RC family, and at an early age began to have visions. Later he became a mercer. After being imprisoned for heresy he went to Amsterdam *c.* 1531. Here in 1539 or 1540 he believed he had Divine communications commanding him to found a new sect, the 'Family of Love' or 'Familia Caritatis'. In 1540 he went to Emden, where he spent the next twenty years of his life and wrote a large number of books, the best known being the *Mirror of Justice*, which was published anonymously. In 1560 the authorities at Emden took steps against his sectarian activities, and he spent the last years of his life as a fugitive in several towns of Holland and Germany. His teaching, which was a kind of mystic pantheism with antinomian features, and was apparently much influenced by the Dutch Anabaptist, David Joris (d. 1556), found many adherents esp. in Holland and England, where he had travelled probably in 1552 or 1553. His books were all placed on the *Index.

F. Nippold, 'Heinrich Niclaes und das Haus der Liebe. Ein monographischer Versuch aus der Secten-Geschichte der Reformationszeit' in *Zeitschrift für die historische Theologie*, xxxii (1862), pp. 323–402 and 473–563. Charlotte Fell-Smith in *D.N.B.*, xl (1894), pp. 427–31, with reff. to sources. See also bibl. to *Familists.*

NICLAES, HENDRIK. See *Nicholas, Henry.*

NICODEMUS. The Jew learned in the Law and a member of the council of the *Sanhedrin, who came to Jesus by night and evoked the discourse narrated in Jn. 3. 1–15 on Christian rebirth. He is afterwards shown as a partial sympathizer with Christ (Jn. 7. 50), and as helping *Joseph of Arimathaea to give Him burial (Jn. 19. 39).

NICODEMUS, Gospel of. See *Pilate, Acts of.*

NICOLAITANS. Sectaries mentioned in the NT only at Rev. 2. 6 and 2. 14 f., where they appear as the advocates of a return to pagan morals, esp. in the matters of sexual practices and idolatrous worship. It is possible that the word 'Nicolaitans' is allegorical, being a Grecized form of the Hebrew 'Balaam' (cf. Rev. 2. 14), and that the persons referred to in Rev. had no real existence as a sect. A *Gnostic sect of this name, however, is alluded to by *Irenaeus, *Clement of Alexandria, and *Tertullian; and Irenaeus affirms that they were founded by the Nicolas of Antioch mentioned in Acts 6. 5, though this is perhaps no more than a conjecture. Indeed, it is not impossible that all references to them in Christian tradition are merely deductions from Rev. At any rate, the sect seems to have come to an end by *c.* A.D. 200. In the Middle Ages the term was sometimes applied to married priests by the upholders of clerical celibacy.

See Commentaries on Rev. 2. H. Cowan in *H.D.B.*, iii (1900), p. 547 f.; F. Sieffert in *P.R.E.* (ed. 3), xiv (1904), pp. 63–8; R. W. Moss in *H.E.R.E.*, ix (1917), pp. 363–6; E. Amann in *D.T.C.*, xi (pt. 1; 1931), cols. 499–506.

NICOLE, PIERRE (1625–95), French theologian and controversialist. A native of *Chartres, he studied philosophy and theology at *Paris, taking his theological degree (baccalaureus) in 1649. Subsequently he went to teach at *Port-Royal, where he formed a close friendship with A. *Arnauld, in collaboration with whom many of his works were written. He accompanied him to Paris in 1655, and later shared his exile in the Netherlands (1679), but returned to France in 1683, after submitting to the Abp. of Paris. A great number of his writings deal with the *Jansenist controversy and are directed against *Jesuit authors, but in general they were more moderate in tone than most Jansenist works. In 1658 he published a Latin version of B. *Pascal's *Lettres provinciales* with additional articles on *Probabilism and on the Love of God, and later opposed the signature of the formularies (see *Jansenism*) in his *Dix Lettres sur l'hérésie imaginaire* (1664–5). At the same time he defended the doctrines of the *Real Presence and of *Transubstantiation in *La Perpétuité de la foi de l'Église catholique touchant l'eucharistie* (1664), directed against *Calvinism, and in 1665 published *Apologie pour les religieuses de Port-Royal*. The controversy with the Protestants was continued in *Préjugés légitimes contre les calvinistes* (1671), and the first version of his principal work, the *Essais de morale*, appeared from 1671 to 1678 (4 vols.). In these essays he showed great originality of outlook in his application of Christian teaching to the detail of everyday life. They are also penetrated by the pessimism which characterized Jansenist writers in their emphasis on the frailty of human nature and its incapacity for the good. His spiritual teaching, given in the

Traité de l'oraison (1679), is strongly biased against mysticism. His last work was a refutation of *Quietism, *Réfutation des principales erreurs des quiétistes* (1695). Written at the instigation of J. B. *Bossuet, it was directed esp. against M. de *Molinos and Mme *Guyon. In the posthumous *Traité de la grâce générale* (2 vols., 1715) the Jansenist position is definitely abandoned, and he defends the universal saving will of God and the sufficiency of grace for all men.

Life by C. P. Goujet in the *Continuation des essais de morale* [de P. Nicole], xiv (2 pts., 'Luxembourg', 1732). Modern study by E. Thouverez ('Les Moralistes chrétiens', Paris, 1926). Bremond, iv (1920), pp. 418–588. J. Carreyre in *D.T.C.*, xi (1931), cols. 634–46, s.v. See also bibl. to *Jansenism* and *Port-Royal*.

NICOLL, WILLIAM ROBERTSON (1851–1923), editor. Ordained in 1874 to the Free Church of Scotland, he became minister at Kelso in 1877. In 1885, however, he was compelled through ill-health to resign his charge and go south, and for the rest of his life devoted his energies to successful editorial work, mainly with the assistance of the publishing house of Hodder & Stoughton. From 1885 till his death he edited the *Expositor*, a semi-popular monthly journal in which he enlisted the help of many leading scholars. From 1886 Nicoll also issued the *British Weekly*, a penny weekly in which current policy and affairs were discussed from a Christian (mainly Nonconformist) standpoint, Nicoll himself regularly contributing to its columns under the pseudonym of 'Claudius Clear'.

Life and Letters ed. by T. H. Darlow (1925), with bibl. J. *Denney, *Letters . . . to W. Robertson Nicoll, 1893–1917* [1920]. J. T. Stoddart in *D.N.B., 1922–1930*, p. 636 f.

NICOLO DE' TUDESCHI. See *Panormitanus*.

NICOMEDES, St., early Christian martyr. His name occurs in both the *Gelasian Sacramentary and the Roman *Martyrology under the date 15 Sept., but it is wanting from the oldest MSS. of the *Hieronymian Martyrology. From refs. in three 7th-cent. itineraries, it would appear that he was buried in a catacomb on the Via Nomentana near the wall of *Rome. There is mention in the 5th cent. of a titular church at Rome dedicated to him. Nothing certain, however, is known of his date or the circumstances of his death. In the BCP calendar (here 'Nicomede') his feast is observed on 1 June, the date of the dedication of a church at Rome rebuilt in the 7th cent.

A.A.SS., Sept. V (1755), pp. 5–12. J. P. Kirsch in *L.Th.K.*, vii (1935), col. 591. E. Josi in *E.C.*, viii (1952), col. 1863 f., s.v. 'Nicomede, Cimitero di', with bibl. reff. to archaeological papers by G. B. *de Rossi, O. *Marucchi, and others.

NIEBUHR, REINHOLD (b. 1892), American theologian. A native of Wright City, Mo., he was educated at Elmhurst College (1910) and Yale University (1914), and ordained in 1915. He was pastor at the Bethel Evangelical church of Detroit from 1915 to 1928, when he was appointed professor of Applied Christianity at the *Union Theological Seminary in New York City.

Niebuhr's aim is to expound a 'vital prophetic Christianity' which shall preserve the integrity of the Christian Revelation and at the same time relate it to social and international ethics. He has been much influenced by the *Dialectical Theology of K. *Barth, and finds a central place for myth and paradox in theology. But he insists against Barth that Christianity has a direct prophetical vocation in relation to culture. The theology of the Creeds in its traditional form he rejects as a spurious metaphysics which reduces true Christian faith to logical nonsense: it also gives insufficient place to original sin.

Niebuhr's principal work is The Nature and Destiny of Man (*Gifford Lectures for 1939; 2 vols., 1941-3). He has also expounded his views in innumerable addresses and essays. His other writings (often collections of papers) include Does Civilization need Religion? (1928), Moral Man and Immoral Society (1932), An Interpretation of Christian Ethics (1936), Beyond Tragedy (1938), and Christian Realism and Political Problems (1954).

His younger brother, HELMUT RICHARD NIEBUHR (b. 1894), prof. of Christian Ethics at the Yale Divinity School from 1938, is also an influential theologian. He is the author of The Social Sources of Denominationalism (New York, [1929]), The Kingdom of God in America (ib., 1937) and Christ and Culture (ib., 1951; London, 1952), and other works.

G. H. C. Macgregor, The Relevance of the Impossible. A Reply to Reinhold Niebuhr (1941). D. R. Davies, Reinhold Niebuhr. Prophet from America (Modern Christian Revolutionaries; [1946]). G. Hammar, Christian Realism in Contemporary American Theology. A Study of Reinhold Niebuhr, W. M. Horton, and H. P. Van Dusen (Uppsala, 1940), pp. 167–253. See also Reinhold Niebuhr (ed. C. W. Kegley–R. W. Bretall; New York, 1956). G. Harland, The Thought of Reinhold Niebuhr (New York, 1960).

NIEHEIM, Dietrich of. See Dietrich of Nieheim.

NIEMÖLLER, MARTIN (b. 1892), German *Lutheran pastor. The son of a Westphalian pastor, he served as a submarine commander during the war of 1914–18. In 1924 he was ordained minister of the Protestant church in Westphalia and in 1931 appointed pastor at Berlin-Dahlem. He at first welcomed National Socialism, but later opposed it on account of its pagan tendencies and supported the '*Confessing Church'. His anti-Nazi religious activities led to his arrest in 1937 and confinement in a concentration camp. Several offers of release were made to him on certain conditions, but he preferred imprisonment to giving up his convictions. A strong character as well as a picturesque personality, he became the symbolical figure of the Protestant opposition to National Socialism. After the Second World War, Niemöller became head of the Foreign Relations department of the Evangelical Church in Germany and Vice-Chairman

of its Council until 1949. In 1947 he was elected Kirchenpräsident of the Territorial Church of Hesse.

Pastor Niemöller and his Creed (Eng. trans., with a foreword by the Bp. of Chichester [G. K. A. Bell], 1939).

NIETZSCHE, FRIEDRICH WILHELM (1844–1900), German philosopher. The son of a Lutheran pastor in the Prussian province of Saxony, he was educated at the public school of Schulpforta, near Naumburg. In 1864 he went to Bonn university and in the following year to Leipzig, where he studied philology. In 1869 he accepted a professorship at Basle which he resigned in 1879, owing to ill-health. He had already published several books, among them Menschliches, Allzumenschliches (1878; Eng. trans. Human, All too Human, 1911), and now devoted himself entirely to literary activities, writing in quick succession Die fröhliche Wissenschaft (1882); Also sprach Zarathustra (1883–91; Engl. trans. Thus Spake Zarathustra, 1896); Jenseits von Gut und Böse (1886; Engl. trans. Beyond Good and Evil, 1907); Die Genealogie der Moral (1887); Der Antichrist (1888); and Der Wille zur Macht (posthumous, 1901). In the beginning of 1889 Nietzsche lost his reason, and, nursed first by his mother, then by his widowed sister, he died on 25 Aug. 1900 after being an invalid for nearly twelve years.

Nietzsche was a prophet rather than a systematic thinker. His chief work, Zarathustra, written in fine poetic language, consists entirely of aphorisms. In his years at Leipzig he came under the influence of the works of A. *Schopenhauer whose atheism and deprecation of reason in favour of the will attracted him. On this atheistic and irrational foundation he constructed a philosophy of life by which he claimed to inaugurate a 'transvaluation of all values'. Acc. to this doctrine life is the will to power; but power, not as exercised collectively by the masses, but the power of the great individual which he calls Übermensch ('superman'). The superman, though an ideal to be realized only in the future, has been adumbrated by personalities like Cesare Borgia and Napoleon; he may be described as a magnified man, disciplined and perfected in both mental and physical strength, serene and pitiless, ruthlessly pursuing his path of success and victory and without moral scruples. In order to make the superman possible the present values which are derived from Christianity must be abolished, since they are the portion of the weak and disinherited 'herd' who, by proclaiming humility, kindness, pity, and the like as virtues, have succeeded in putting themselves into power to the detriment of the strong.

There are several German edd. of Nietzsche's works, of which the best is the large octavo ed. of Leipzig, 1901–13, in 19 vols. (vols. i–viii, Werke, 1905–10; vols. ix–xvi, Nachlass, 1901–11; vols. xvii–xix, Philologica, 1910–13). Eng. tr. of 'Complete Works' ed. O. Levy in 18 vols., 1909–13. There are several collections of his Letters, from which a selection was publd. in Eng. tr. by O. Levy (New York, etc., 1921). Official life by Elisabeth Förster-Nietzsche, his sister (2 vols. bound in 3, Leipzig, 1895–1904; shorter version as Der junge Nietzsche (1912; Eng. tr., 1912) and *Der einsame Nietzsche* (1914; Eng. tr. [1915])). Fullest life and account in English by M. A. Mügge (London, 1908, with bibl.). There are innumerable studies of his philosophy; they include those by H. Lichtenberger (Paris, 1898; Eng. tr. 1910), G. Brandes (various artt., collected in Eng. tr., London, 1914), F. Copleston, S.J. (Bellarmine Series, vii, London, 1942), W. A. Kaufmann (Princeton, N.J., 1950). Überweg, iv, 543–51, with bibl. pp. 716–20. H. Ellis in *H.E.R.E.*, ix (1917), pp. 366–70; T. Odenwald in *R.G.G.* (ed. 2), iv (1930), cols. 552–6; T. Steinbuchel in *L.Th.K.*, vii (1935), cols. 561–4, with bibl.

NIGHT OFFICE. Another name for *Mattins, the liturgical *office prescribed for the night.

NIGHTINGALE, FLORENCE (1820–1910), reformer of hospital nursing. She was born at Florence, whence her Christian name. At an early age she began to interest herself in nursing, and from *c.* 1844 undertook regular hospital visiting. On a journey to Egypt in 1849–50 she studied the nursing system of the Sisters of Charity of St. *Vincent de Paul at *Alexandria, and soon afterwards visited T. Fliedner's deaconesses at *Kaiserswerth, where she was trained for several months in 1851. In 1853 she was made head of a hospital for invalid gentlewomen in Harley Street. In 1854 she offered to go to the Crimea to organize the nursing of the sick and wounded English soldiers. She established her headquarters at Scutari, where the barrack hospital was in a state of indescribable neglect; but her indefatigable devotion soon improved conditions and considerably reduced the death-rate. She returned to England in 1856. In recognition of her services the Nightingale School and Home for Nurses was founded at St. Thomas's Hospital in 1860, though owing to her weakened health she could take no more than an advisory part in its work. Her experience was also placed at the disposal of the governments concerned in the American Civil War of 1861–4 and the Franco–German War of 1870–1. She took an active interest in the establishment of several nursing societies and in the sanitary reforms carried out in the Indian army as well as among Indians. Her chief work, *Notes on Nursing* (1859), went through many editions.

Lives by Sarah A. Tooley (London, 1904), E. T. Cook (2 vols., ib., 1913), I. Cooper Willis (ib., 1931) and [Mrs.] Cecil Woodham-Smith (ib., 1950). S. Paget in *D.N.B.*, *1901-1911*, iii, pp. 15–19.

NIHILIANISM. The Christological doctrine that Christ, in His human nature, was 'nothing', His essential Being being contained in His Godhead alone. It was defended by a number of 12th cent. theologians (among them Peter of Poitiers, d. 1205) who claimed to deduce it from the teaching of *Peter Lombard. It was condemned by Pope *Alexander III in 1170 and 1177.

E. Portalié in *D.T.C.*, i (1903), cols. 413–18, s.v. 'Adoptianisme [au XIIᵉ siècle]'; G. H. Joyce, S.J., in *H.E.R.E.*, ix (1917), pp. 370–2, s.v.

NIKON (1605–81), Patr. of Moscow. After a monastic education he married and became a secular priest, but separated from his wife, who entered a convent, and himself became a monk of the Solovietski monastery on the White Sea. A quarrel with the monks led him to transfer his membership to the Kojeozerski community, of which he became *hegumen (abbot) in 1642. On a journey to Moscow in 1646 the Tsar Alexis appointed him archimandrite of the Novospaski monastery at Moscow, and, three years later, Metropolitan of Novgorod; and when, in 1652, the Patr. of Moscow died, he was elected in his place by order of the Tsar. As Patriarch, Nikon at once began important reforms. One of his principal concerns was to carry through a much-needed revision of the Russian liturgy. He sought to bring the prescriptions of the service books into conformity with Greek usages and, taking expert advice, to eradicate many of their long-standing corruptions. He had such details settled as the making of the sign of the cross with three fingers instead of with two and the use of the threefold Alleluia. These reforms, which were carried out with the aid of the civil power with great rigour, gained the Patriarch many enemies.

From 1652 to 1658 his influence with the Tsar was immense, but in the latter year, probably owing to his claims of complete independence in ecclesiastical matters, he fell from Imperial favour. After his resignation had been accepted by the Tsar, he retired to the monastery of the 'New Jerusalem' which he had founded. In the following years he tried to regain his position, but in 1667, at the Council of Moscow, he was finally deposed and sentenced to banishment. His liturgical reforms were sanctioned, however, and the formation of the schismatical sect of the *Old Believers followed. After 14 years of severe imprisonment Alexis' successor, Feodor II, recalled Nikon to Moscow, but he died on the way and was buried with patriarchal honours. Subsequently all decrees against him were revoked at the bidding of the Tsar, and he is now recognized as perhaps the greatest bishop of the Russian Church.

W. Palmer, *The Patriarch and the Tsar* (6 vols., 1871–6), with Eng. tr. of numerous primary documents. The main literature, which is extensive, is in Russian. In Eng. there is a brief life [by R. Thornton] in *Lives of Eminent Russian Prelates* (1854), pp. 1–38. A. *Fortescue in *C.E.*, xi (1911), p. 77 f., s.v.; J. Ledit, S.J., in *D.T.C.*, xi (pt. 1; 1931), cols. 646–55, s.v. 'Nicon (1)'. See also works cited under *Russia, Christianity in*, and *Old Believers*.

NILUS THE ASCETIC, St. (d. *c.* 430), Bp. of Ancyra, also (erroneously) known as 'Nilus of Sinai'. Acc. to the traditional account (*Nicephorus Callistus; a set of 'Narrationes'; Byzantine *Synaxaria), Nilus was a high officer at the *Constantinopolitan court who with his son, Theodulus, became a hermit on Mt. *Sinai. In 410, when the monks were attacked by hordes of robbers, Nilus escaped, but Theodulus was captured and sold into slavery. After many adventures both were ordained by the Bp. of Eleusa in Palestine who sent them back to Sinai.

In recent times this account has been

generally rejected (K. Heussi and others). It appears that Nilus was in fact a native of Ancyra who studied at Constantinople where he became the disciple of St. John *Chrysostom. He then became the founder and superior of a monastery near Ancyra, whence he conducted a large correspondence and exerted a wide influence on his contemporaries.

His writings deal mainly with ascetic and moral subjects. They include 'De Monachorum Praestantia', 'De Monastica Exercitatione', 'De Voluntaria Paupertate', and also a collection of 1061 letters (mainly genuine, but some of them only epistolary in form and in fact excerpts from other Patristic writers). The 'Tractatus ad Eulogium' and the 'De Oratione' attributed to him appear to belong to *Evagrius Ponticus, while the 'De Octo Vitiosis Cogitationibus' is a compilation from *Cassian. Nilus's ideal of the spiritual life is a 'Christian philosophy' ($\phi\iota\lambda o\sigma o\phi\epsilon\hat{\iota}\nu$ $\kappa\alpha\tau\grave{\alpha}$ $X\rho\iota\sigma\tau\acute{o}\nu$) based on a 'moderated poverty' ($\mu\acute{\epsilon}\sigma\eta$ $\grave{\alpha}\kappa\tau\eta\mu o\sigma\acute{\upsilon}\nu\eta$). Feast day, 12 Nov.

Works in J. P. Migne, *PG*, lxxix (unsatisfactory). The traditional account of Nilus is based on seven 'Narrationes de Caede Monachorum et de Theodulo Filio' (ib., cols. 589–694). Modern studies include F. Degenhart, *Der hl. Nilus Sinaita*. Sein Leben und seine Lehre vom Mönchtum (Beiträge zur Geschichte des alten Mönchtums und des Benediktinerordens, vi; 1915); K. Heussi, *Untersuchungen zu Nilus dem Asketen* (T.U., xlii, Hft. 2; 1917); F. Degenhart, *Neue Beiträge zur Nilus-Forschung* (1918; reply to preceding work); K. Heussi, *Das Nilus Problem* (1921; a further reply). I. Hausherr, S.J., 'Le Traité de l'oraison d'Évagre le Pontique (pseudo-Nil)' in *Revue d'Ascétique et de Mystique*, xv (1934), pp. 34–93 and 113–70. Bardenhewer, iv, 161–178; Altaner (ed. 1951), p. 291. M. T. Disdier in *D.T.C.*, xi (pt. 1; 1931), cols. 661–74; I. Hausherr, S.J., in *E.C.*, viii (1952), col. 1882 f.

NIMBUS. See *Halo*.

NIMROD. Acc. to Gen. 10. 8–10, Nimrod was the first of the 'heroes' and a 'mighty hunter before the Lord', and founded the Assyrian Empire. In Babylonian mythology he is paralleled by the figure of *Gilgamesh, the tyrant of Erech. The only other references to him in the Bible are at 1 Chr. 1. 10 and Mic. 5. 6.

NINE FRIDAYS. See *First Fridays*.

NINEVEH, Fast of. A two-weeks' pre-*Lenten fast kept esp. in the dissident Eastern Churches (*Nestorians, *Jacobites, *Copts, and *Armenians). It is usually observed about a month before Lent begins, except in the Armenian Church where it immediately precedes the Lenten fast.

NINIAN, St. (c. 360–c. 432), Scottish missionary. There are two accounts of his life, viz. a summary notice in *Bede's 'Ecclesiastical History' and a more elaborate but less trustworthy 12th cent. 'Vita' by St. *Ailred. The son of a converted chieftain of the Cumbrian Britons, he went to Rome as a youth where he was instructed in the faith. After being consecrated bishop in 394, probably by Pope *Siricius, he set out to convert Scotland. Making the acquaintance of St. *Martin as he travelled through Tours on the way, he later dedicated to him the church which he founded at Whithorn in Wigtownshire. This church, called 'Candida Casa' (White House), probably on account of the colour of its stones, became a centre whence Ninian and his monks went out to convert the neighbouring Britons and also the Picts of the former Roman province of Valentia; and it long continued a seat of learning for the Welsh and Irish missionaries. In the Middle Ages Ninian's tomb in the church was a favourite shrine of pilgrimage. Feast day, 16 Sept.

Bede, *H.E.* III. iv. 1; cf. notes in ed. C. Plummer, ii (Oxford, 1896), pp. 128–30. Life by Ailred ed. J. Pinkerton, *Vitae Antiquae Sanctorum qui habitaverunt in . . . Scotia* (London, 1789), pp. 1–23. Life (14th cent.) in Old English in W. M. Metcalfe (ed.), *The Legends of SS. Ninian and Machor* (1904), pp. 40–83, with notes pp. 138–63, and Eng. tr. of life by Aelred, pp. 187–209. Modern study by A. B. Scott (London, 1916). W. D. Simpson, *Saint Ninian and the Origins of the Christian Church in Scotland* (1940). See also A. O. Anderson, 'Ninian and the Southern Picts' in *Scottish Historical Review*, xxvii (1948), pp. 25–47.

NISAN. The opening month in the Jewish year, roughly corresponding to April. It was the month in which the *Passover was held, the Passover Lamb being slain in the afternoon of the 14th day of Nisan. The name appears to be Babylonian and to have been substituted by the Jews from the time of the Exile (6th cent. B.C.) for its older Hebrew name of 'Abib'.

NITRIAN DESERT. The region in Libya lying to the west of the mouths of the Nile, and celebrated as a centre of early Christian monasticism. In the latter part of the 4th cent. an enormous colony of hermits was founded here, chiefly under the influence of Ammon, one of the *Tall Brothers. Of the still extant Coptic monasteries, one, the 'Dēr as-Surjān', i.e. the 'Monastery of the Syrians', formerly possessed a valuable collection of *Syriac MSS. which were acquired partly by the *Assemani for the *Vatican Library (in 1707 and 1745), partly by H. *Tattam (1841 and 1843) and W. *Cureton (1847) for the British Museum.

NITZSCH, KARL IMMANUEL (1787–1868), German *Lutheran theologian. Educated at Schulpforta and *Wittenberg, he became Privatdozent of theology in 1810 and assistant preacher at the Schlosskirche at Wittenberg in 1811. In 1822 he accepted a professorship at Bonn university, and in 1847 was called to Berlin to succeed P. K. *Marheineke, where he was made provost of the Nicolaikirche in 1854. His principal works are the *System der christlichen Lehre* (1829; Eng. trans. by R. Montgomery and J. Hennen, 1849) and *Praktische Theologie* (1847–67). Nitzsch is one of the chief representatives of the German '*Vermittlungstheologie'. As an opponent of contemporary unbelieving rationalism he rejected a purely speculative interpretation of Christianity and emphasized esp. the immediacy of religious feeling, which, acc. to him, produces the foundations of religious knowledge. As a member of the Supreme Church Council he was an active promoter of the Evangelical Union of the Prussian Churches (1817).

Life by W. Beyschlag (Berlin, 1872). Friedrich Nitzsch in *P.R.E.* (ed. 3), xiv (1904), pp. 128–36, s.v.

NOAH (otherwise 'Noe'). A son of Lamech, and tenth in descent from *Adam. Acc. to the story in *Genesis (6–9), Noah and his family alone were saved in an ark of gopher-wood, when the rest of mankind were destroyed in the *Flood. He took with him into the ark specimens of all kinds of living creatures whereby the species were providentially preserved. From Noah, therefore, the entire surviving human race descended, through his three sons, Shem, Ham, and Japheth. To Noah is also attributed the discovery of viticulture (Gen. 9. 20).

Other races have traditions of a great flood in very early times. In classical literature the story of Noah is closely paralleled by the legend of Deucalion. See also *Gilgamesh, The Epic of.*

P. Lundberg, *La Typologie baptismale dans l'ancienne Église* (Acta Seminarii Neotestamenticii Upsaliensis, x; Leipzig and Uppsala, 1942), pp. 73–116. See also comm. to Genesis cited s.v., and bibl. to *Ark* and *Flood.*

NOAILLES, L. A. DE. See *De Noailles, L. A.*

NOBILI, ROBERT DE. See *De Nobili, Robert.*

NOBIS QUOQUE PECCATORIBUS (Lat. 'To us sinners, also'). The opening words of the section of the Roman *Canon of the Mass in which the celebrant prays for admission into the company of the saints, several of whom he mentions by name. At these words he strikes his breast and raises his voice slightly. In the *Ambrosian Rite the words are in the variant form '*Nobis quoque minimis et peccatoribus*'.

V. L. Kennedy, C.S.B., *The Saints of the Canon of the Mass* (Studi di Antichità Cristiana, xiv, 1938), pp. 34–8 and 189–199, who defends the improbable thesis that the *Nobis quoque peccatoribus*, like *Communicantes*, was first introduced into the Roman Canon by Pope *Gelasius I (492–6). Jungmann (ed. 1952), ii, 309–22.

NOBLE GUARD. The bodyguard, consisting in all of 77 men of noble rank, which attends on the Pope at public functions. They were instituted with their present title by *Pius VII in 1801, but owing to political difficulties they did not come into effective being till later. They received the basis of their present constitution in 1815. They wear an impressive military uniform, and their commander is always a Roman prince. See also *Palatine Guard, Swiss Guard.*

G. Felice in *E.C.*, vi (1951), col. 1203 f., s.v. 'Guardia nobile pontificia', with bibl. and illustr.

NOCTURN. A division of the 'night office' (*Mattins, q.v.) of the *Breviary. In the Roman Breviary, on Sundays, on all feasts above the rank of a *Simple, and in the Office of the Dead, there are three Nocturns, consisting of three Psalms and three Lessons each. On simple feasts and ferias there is only one Nocturn comprising nine Psalms and three Lessons. Before the Breviary Reform of *Pius X the single Nocturn of the ferias contained twelve Psalms. In the *Monastic Breviary, however, there are two Nocturns with six Psalms each on ferias, and three Nocturns with twelve Psalms in all, three Canticles and twelve Lessons on Sundays and feasts. In earlier usage, the term Nocturn was applied to the whole of the night office, including *Lauds, and not limited to its constituent parts.

NOETICS (from Gk. νοητικός, 'pertaining to the mind or intellect'). Term applied to an early 19th cent. group of thinkers, Whigs in politics, who were members of the Senior Common Room of Oriel College, Oxford. The chief were E. *Copleston and E. *Hawkins (successively Provosts of Oriel College), R. *Whately and R. D. *Hampden. They freely criticized traditional religious orthodoxy, and sought to increase the comprehensiveness of the C of E. The later Noetics came into sharp conflict with the *Tractarians.

W. Tuckwell, *Pre-Tractarian Oxford. A Reminiscence of the Oriel 'Noetics'* (1909).

NOETUS (*c.* 200), heretic. Our knowledge of him comes chiefly from *Hippolytus (*Haer.*, ix. 7–10; *Cont. Noetum*), acc. to whom he was a native of Smyrna. He was probably the first to teach *Patripassian doctrines, viz. that it was God the Father who in the Incarnation was born, suffered, and died. He also rejected the Logos doctrine, admitted only a purely allegorical interpretation of the Prologue of St. John's Gospel, and accused his opponents of ditheism. He was condemned by an assembly of presbyters at Smyrna *c.* 200. Hippolytus asserts also that through his disciple, Epigonus, Patripassian teaching made its way from Asia Minor to Rome.

Further reff. in Hippolytus, *Haer.*, ix, 2, and x, 27; *Epiphanius, *Haer.*, lvii; and *Theodoret, *Haer. Fab.*, iii, 3. Crit. text of Hippolytus *Contra Noetum*, with discussion (much challenged), by P. Nautin, Paris, 1949. For further bibl. see under *Monarchianism.*

NOLASCANS. See *Mercedarians.*

NOMINALISM. The theory of knowledge which denies reality to universal concepts. In the controversy on *Universals, partly occasioned by the famous text in *Porphyry's 'Isagoge', which occupied medieval philosophers esp. in the 11th and 12th cents., a form of Nominalism was first evolved by *Roscellinus and later by *Abelard. It was directed against the Platonist *Realists who held that universals, such as genus and species, had a separate existence apart from the individuals which are tributary to them. In opposition to this teaching, Roscellinus carried the denial of the unity of species to a point which led him into *Tritheism. Abelard, on the other hand, though severely criticizing the doctrine of the separate existence of the universals, which he calls 'names' ('voces', 'nomina'), as opposed to 'things' ('res'), does not seem to have denied that the resemblances among individual things justify the use of universals for establishing knowledge, so that he has often been represented as a forerunner of Moderate Realism rather than as a Nominalist properly so called.

A far more pronounced form of Nominalism made its appearance in the 14th cent. with *William of Occam. He asserted that the universal is not found at all in reality, but only in the human mind ('in anima'), for every substance is radically individual. Acc. to him the resemblance between two men does not lead to the conclusion that they share a common nature; universals, therefore, are no more than vocal sounds ('flatus vocis'). Thus our first knowledge is an intuition of the individual, accompanying sensation. In its application to theology, which was made by Occam himself, but more esp. by Gabriel *Biel, Nominalism, which conceives God exclusively as omnipotence and mercy, denies the plurality of His attributes and the distinction between His Intellect and His Will. It simplifies His Being to such a degree that the reality of the Three Persons which depends on formal distinctions and real relations can be accepted only on the authority of faith. Nor can reason demonstrate that the First Cause of the existing universe is the One God. Thus Nominalism in its theological consequences withdrew almost all the data of faith from the realm of reason and paved the way for the disintegration of Scholasticism.

C. S. Barach, *Zur Geschichte des Nominalismus vor Roscellin* (1866). J. Reiners, *Der Nominalismus in der Frühscholastik* (B.G.P.M., VIII, 5, 1910). A. Vigneaux in *D.T.C.*, xi (pt. 1; 1931), cols. 717–84. See also bibl. to *William of Occam*.

NOMOCANON (Gk. νόμος, 'a law', and κανών, 'canon'). In the E. Church, a collection of ecclesiastical canons and Imperial laws, arranged acc. to subject-matter. The earliest (c. 600) derives from *John Scholasticus (q.v.). This is a later conflation of two legal collections, themselves compiled by John, viz. (1) a collection of canons arranged in 50 tituli, the outline of which is preserved in all subsequent editions of the Nomocanon, and (2) a collection of Imperial laws arranged in 87 capitula which are re-sorted acc. to the 50 headings of the Nomocanon.

NONCONFORMIST CHAPELS ACT, 1844. Introduced by Lord Lyndhurst, it laid down that where no particular religious doctrine or mode of worship is prescribed by the Trust Deeds, the usage of the congregation for the past twenty-five years is to be taken as conclusive evidence of what may properly be done in such meeting-houses.

The Act, which is entitled in 'An Act for the Regulation of Suits Relating to Meeting Houses and other Property held for Religious Purposes by Persons Dissenting from the United Churches of England and Ireland' (7 and 8 Vict. cap. 45), is pr. in *The Statutes of the United Kingdom of Great Britain and Ireland*, xvii, ed. N. Simons (1845), p. 125 f.

NONCONFORMITY. Refusal to conform to the doctrines, polity or discipline of any Established Church. Originally in the 17th cent. used of those who agreed with the doctrines of the C of E but refused to conform to its discipline and practice, particularly in matters of ceremony, the term has come to be applied to all dissenters, esp. those of Protestant sympathies. Among the groups to whom the term is commonly applied are the *Presbyterians (in England), the *Congregationalists, *Methodists, *Quakers, and *Baptists (qq.v.).

C. S. Horne, *A Popular History of the Free Churches* (1903). W. B. Selbie, *Nonconformity. Its Origin and Progress* (H.U.L. [1912]); H. Davies, *The English Free Churches* (ib., 1952). G. L. Turner (ed.), *Original Records of Early Nonconformity under Persecution and Indulgence* (3 vols., 1911–14). H. W. Clark, *History of English Nonconformity from Wiclif to the Close of the Nineteenth Century* (2 vols., 1911). C. Burrage, *The Early English Dissenters in the Light of Modern Research, 1550–1641* (2 vols., 1912). A. [H.] Lincoln, *Some Political and Social Ideas of English Dissent, 1763–1800* (Prince Consort Prize for 1934; 1938). E. A. Payne, *The Free Church Tradition in the Life of England* (1944); J. W. Grant, *Free Churchmanship in England, 1870–1940, with special Reference to Congregationalism* (1955). H. McLachlan, *English Education under the Test Acts being the History of the Nonconformist Academies, 1662–1820* (Publications of the University of Manchester No. ccxiii; Historical Series No. lix; 1931). C. Ord in *D.E.C.H.*, pp. 391–410, s.v.; W. F. Adeney in *H.E.R.E.*, ix (1917), pp. 381–93, s.v.; T. F. Glasson in *D.E.C.H.* (ed. 3, 1948), pp. 403–22, s.v. See also bibl. to separate nonconforming bodies.

NON EXPEDIT (Lat., 'It is not expedient'). The name given, from its opening words, to an official RC decree, issued on 29 Feb. 1868, forbidding Catholics in Italy to take part in the polling at civil elections. Its object was to counter the threat to the territorial possessions of the Papacy from the movement for a united Italy.

U. Benigni in *C.E.*, xi (1911), p. 98 f., s.v.; A. Vian in *E.C.*, viii (1952), cols. 1930–2, s.v.; both with bibl., but neither gives ref. to text.

NONE. The last of the Little Hours. It is appointed to be recited at the ninth hour, i.e. 3 P.M. It is now said in many orders either immediately after the principal Mass (hence 'noon') or together with the other Little Hours. For the structure of the service, see *Terce*.

NONJURORS, The (English). The title is used of members of the C of E who after 1688 scrupled to take the Oath of Allegiance to William and Mary on the grounds that by so doing they would break their previous oath to *James II and his successors. They numbered eight bishops, some 400 priests, and a few laymen. The deprived bishops were Abp. W. *Sancroft of *Canterbury and Bps. T. *Ken of *Bath and Wells, F. Turner of *Ely, T. White of *Peterborough, W. Lloyd of *Norwich, R. Frampton of *Gloucester, J. Lake of *Chichester, and W. Thomas of *Worcester, the last two of whom died before sentence against them could be carried out (1689). T. Cartwright (d. 1689), Bp. of *Chester, who had followed *James II to France, should perhaps also be added. All were deprived by Act of Parliament and their successors appointed in the same way; hence the Nonjuring clergy still regarded them as their lawful bishops. To ensure the episcopal succession they soon began to consecrate successors in secret, G. *Hickes and T. Wagstaffe (with the respective titles of Thetford and Ipswich) being the first thus consecrated (1694) after the *congé d'élire had been received from the exiled *James II. The Nonjurors were divided on the question of the lawfulness of worshipping in the parish church; the majority preferred their own services, which, of course, were illegal. In 1716, after the death of Hickes, the controversy between *Usagers (q.v.) and Non-Usagers over questions of ritual produced a serious division which was not healed till 1732. From 1716 to 1725 they carried on abortive negotiations for union with the E. Churches. In addition to internal dissensions, the fear of a restoration of the Stuarts, esp. in the early Hanoverian period, considerably weakened their position. In the latter part of the 18th cent. they gradually disappeared through absorption into the Established Church. Their guiding principles had been the sanctity of the Oath and the distinctive Anglican doctrine of the *Divine Right of Kings and the duty of passive obedience. They held a high conception of the Church as a spiritual society with its own laws, and laid particular emphasis on the external forms of worship, which tendencies link them with the *Caroline divines of the 17th and the *Tractarians of the 19th cents. They produced a number of good devotional writers. Among their more distinguished clergy were J. *Kettlewell, C. *Leslie, and W. *Law, well-known laymen being H. *Dodwell and T. *Hearne.

T. Lathbury, *A History of the Nonjurors* (1845); J. H. Overton, *The Nonjurors* (1902); H. Broxap, *The Later Nonjurors* (1924). S. L. Ollard in *D.E.C.H.* (1912), pp. 410–14, s.v. The Nonjurors' liturgies of 1718 and 1734 are printed by W. J. Grisbrooke, *Anglican Liturgies of the Seventeenth and Eighteenth Centuries* (Alcuin Club Collections xl, 1958), pp. 273–316, with comm., pp. 71–135.

NONNUS OF PANOPOLIS (c. 400). The

probable author of two Greek poems in hexameters, the one Διονυσιακά, a descriptive account of the journey of the god Dionysus to India, and the other a 'Paraphrase (μεταβολή) of the Fourth Gospel'. The latter, of which only part (3750 lines) has survived, has a certain value for the light it throws on the text of the Bible, but is otherwise of scant interest. Nothing further is known of their author, and some unsuccessful attempts have been made to assign the 'Paraphrase' to otherwise known writers, e.g. to *Apollinarius of Laodicea.

Best crit. text of 'Paraphrase' ed. A. Scheindler (Teub., 1881) and of 'Dionysiaca' ed. A. Ludwich (ib., 1909); the 'Paraphrase', repr. from ed. D. Heinsius (Leyden, 1627), also in J. P. Migne, *PG*, xliii, 749–920. R. Janssen, *Das Johannes-Evangelium nach der Paraphrase des Nonnus Panopolitanus* (T.U., xxiii, Hft. 4; 1903). J. Golega, *Studien über die Evangelien-Dichtung des Nonnus von Panopolis* (1930). R. Keydell, 'Über die Echtheit der Bibeldichtungen des Apollinaris und des Nonnos' in *B.Z.*, xxxiii (1933), pp. 243–54. Bardenhewer, iv, 122–4; Altaner (ed. 1951), p. 242. É. Amann in *D.T.C.*, xi (pt. 1; 1931), cols. 793–5; R. Keydell in *P.W.*, xvii (pt. 1; 1936), cols. 904–20.

NORBERT, St. (c. 1080–1134), founder of

the *Premonstratensians and Abp. of Magdeburg. The younger son of a noble family of Xanten, Norbert early became subdeacon and canon of St. Victor's in his native town, but led a worldly life at the courts of Abp. Frederick I of Cologne and the Emp. Henry V. Having avoided the priesthood and declined the Bpric. of Cambrai in 1113, he was converted in 1115 when in danger of death during a thunderstorm. After some time in retirement at the abbey of Siegburg near Cologne, whose Abbot Cuno became his spiritual director, he was ordained priest in the same year, and, having taken the monastic habit, endeavoured to reform his brother canons at Xanten. These, who resented his zeal, accused him at the Synod of Fritzlar in 1118 of making innovations and of preaching without authorization; and in reply he resigned his canonry, sold his property, and went to Pope Gelasius II at St.-Gilles in Languedoc. After the Pope had given him permission to preach wherever he wished, he travelled as an itinerant preacher through N. France and soon became renowned for his eloquence and his miracles. In 1120, supported by Bartholomew, Bp. of Laon, he founded the Order of the Premonstratensians in the valley of Prémontré. He travelled in France, Belgium, and Germany, preaching everywhere, and successfully fighting the heresy of Tanchelm at Antwerp (1124). Early in 1126 he obtained at Rome the recognition of his order from Pope Honorius II, and in the same year was appointed Abp. of Magdeburg. His zeal for the reformation of his clergy and the recovery of alienated Church property made him many enemies and led to attempts against his life; but he won the confidence and favour of the Emp. Lothair II, and accompanied him in 1132–3 to Rome where he supported Innocent II against the antipope, Anacletus. He also prevented the outbreak of fresh quarrels about the *Investiture, in recognition of which service the Pope extended his metropolitan jurisdiction to the whole of Poland. In 1133 Lothair made him Chancellor for Italy, but his activities were cut short by his early death. In 1582 he was canonized by *Gregory XIII. Feast day, 6 June.

The principal authority is a life written between 1157 and 1161, falsely attributed to Hugh of Prémonstré, ed R. Wilmans in *M.G.H.*, Scriptores, xii (1856), pp. 663–706; excerpts, from a later redaction, in *AA.SS.*, Jun. I (1695), pp. 819–58. R. Rosenmund, *Die ältesten Biographieen des heiligen Norbert* (1874). Modern lives by G. Madelaine, O.Praem. (Lille, 1886), and F. A. Žák, O.Praem. (Vienna, 1900). Also by É. Maire ('Les Saints', 1922). Short study by M. Geudens, O.Praem. (London, 1886).

NORIS, HENRI (1631–1704), cardinal and theologian. The descendant of an English family, he studied with the *Jesuits at Rimini, where he entered the Order of *Augustinian Hermits out of devotion to St. *Augustine. From the age of 27 he taught theology and Church history at Pesaro and Perugia, and from 1674 to 1692 at Padua. In 1692 Innocent XII called him to Rome, making him First Custodian of the *Vatican Library and, in 1695, creating him cardinal. His most important work is the *Historia Pelagiana et Dissertatio de Synodo V Oecumenica* (1673), a history of the *Pelagian Controversy, followed by a defence of the Augustinian doctrine of grace (against that held by L. de *Molina). The book, though approved by the Holy See, raised a great deal of controversy, and, in 1676, was denounced to the Holy Office for renewing the errors of M. *Baius and C. *Jansenius. Noris was acquitted of heresy, but forty years after his death the Spanish *Inquisition renewed the accusation, placing the book on the *Index. His teaching was finally rehabilitated in 1748 by *Benedict XIV who ordered Noris' books to be removed from the Index.

Collected works ed. P. and G. *Ballerini (4 vols., Verona, 1729–32), with life in vol. iv, pp. xiii–xlii; suppl. of letters in Ital. (Padua, 1741). F. Bonnard in *D.T.C.*, xi (pt. i; 1931), cols. 796–802.

NORRIS, JOHN (1657–1711), English divine. He is generally reckoned the last of the *Cambridge Platonists. Educated at Winchester and Exeter College, Oxford, and later elected to a Fellowship at All Souls, he became rector of Newton St. Loe, Somerset, in 1689. From 1691 until his death he was rector of Bemerton. His philosophy was mainly derived from the writings of N. *Malebranche, whose *Recherche de la vérité* (1674) made a great impression on him. Like Malebranche, he combined Cartesianism with a Platonic mysticism. His most elaborate work, his *Essay towards the Theory of the Ideal or Intelligible World* (2 vols., 1701, 1704), though tedious in its style, contained some penetrating criticisms of J. *Locke's *Essay* (1690). His other writings include an *Account of Reason and Faith* (1697), a reply to the *Deistic doctrines of J. *Toland's *Christianity not Mysterious* (1690).

In 1687, Norris issued *A Collection of Miscellanies*. A. *Wood, *Athenae Oxonienses* (ed. P. Bliss), iv (1820), cols. 584–6. F. I. MacKinnon, *The Philosophy of John Norris of Bemerton* (Philosophical Monographs, I, No. 2, New York, 1910). L. Stephen in *D.N.B.*, xli (1895), pp. 132–4.

'NORTH END', The. The position sometimes adopted at the Communion table by the celebrant of the *Eucharist in the C of E. It has been held to be required by certain rubrics in the BCP (see *Eastward Position*). It is now confined to pronounced Evangelicals; but where adopted, its use is generally defended with vigour on the ground that it rules out any ascription of a priestly or mediatorial function to the celebrant. Until comparatively recently, however, it was not a mark of doctrinal belief, such High Churchmen as C. *Wheatley and E. B. *Pusey having celebrated at the North End.

NORWAY, Christianity in. Attempts were made by enlightened kings to introduce Christianity to Norway in the 9th and 10th cents., but without permanent success. Under St. *Olave (d. 1030) the country was finally converted, though largely at the point of the sword. In 1152 jurisdiction over the Norwegian Church, which had previously rested in the see of *Lund, in *Sweden, was transferred to the Bp. of Trondhjem (Nidaros). Little is known of the subsequent history of the Norwegian Church down to the Reformation.

Although suppression of the monasteries began under Christian II (1513–23), the Reformation in Norway was largely imposed by the Danish conquerors, when her independent existence ceased in 1537. Lutheranism became the state religion, in the radical form favoured by *Denmark rather than the more moderate form adopted by Sweden, and no other form of religion was recognized or tolerated until 1845. Since that date both RC-ism and Protestant dissent have to some degree spread their influence. In 1814 the Danish power was shaken off, and the country united to Sweden; and in 1905 Norway became once more an independent state. During the German occupation of 1940–5, the Church was a focus of resistance under the leadership of Eivind *Berggrav, Bp. of Oslo.

J. R. Keyser, *Den Norske Kirkes Historie under Katholicismen* (2 vols., Kristiania, 1856–8). A. C. Bang, *Den Norske Kirkes Historie* (ib., 1912). F. Siegmund–Schultze (ed.), *Ekklesia. Eine Sammlung von Selbstdarstellungen der christlichen Kirchen*, Bd. ii, fasc. 6 (1936), with bibl. I. Welle, *Norges Kirkehistorie* (Oslo, 1948). J. B. Metzler, *Die apostolischen Vikariate des Nordens, ihre Entstehung, ihre Entwicklung und ihre Verwalter* (Paderborn, 1919). K. Gjerset, *History of the Norwegian People* (New York, 1932), esp. pts. i, pp. 174–97, 345–55, 427–34, ii, 134–42, 294–300, with reff.

NORWICH. Although Eorpwald, King of East Anglia (d. 628), embraced the Christian faith, the real conversion of the country dates from the reign of his brother Sigeberht (d. 637), when Honorius, Abp. of *Canterbury (627–53), sent St. *Felix to be Bp. of Dunwich. About the same time St. Fursey (d. 650) founded a monastery, prob. at Burghcastle, on land provided by the King. In 673 St. *Theodore, Abp. of Canterbury, divided the diocese between the North Folk and the South Folk, Dunwich remaining the see of the latter, while Elmham became a new see for Norfolk. There is a gap in the recorded succession of East Anglian bishops between 870 and 956, when the area was perhaps under the episcopal jurisdiction of London. Shortly before 1075, Herfast (Bp. 1070–85) moved his see from Elmham to Thetford, whence in 1094 Herbert of Losinga (c. 1054–1119) transferred it to Norwich. Here in 1096 he founded the Cathedral of the Holy and Undivided Trinity, poss. as a penance for simony, and constituted it a monastic church under the *Benedictine Rule. The limits of the diocese remained practically unchanged until 1837 when the archdeaconry of Sudbury was transferred to *Ely. In 1914 the archdeaconry of Suffolk was incorporated in the new diocese of St. Edmundsbury and Ipswich. The diocese of Norwich now corresponds roughly with the county of Norfolk.

The Cathedral is mainly a Norman building with a 15th cent. spire and fine 15th and 16th cent. vaulted roofs. The nave has an altar at the East end, behind which is the stone pulpitum, supporting the organ. The choir has an ambulatory with radiating chapels, and a semicircular apse. Here are the Jesus Chapel, St. Luke's Chapel, used as the parish church, and the Bauchun chapel, used as the Consistory Court. A bridge on the N. side is believed to have led to a chapel for relics. The Lady Chapel, at the extreme East, built by Walter de Suffield (Bp. 1245–57), was later ruined, but rebuilt in 1930–2. The two-storied cloisters are 14th cent. and contain a remarkable series of roof-bosses. The late Norman Bishop's throne in the Byzantine position behind the altar is unique in England. In the Cathedral Library is an exceptionally complete set of Obedientiary Rolls.

The Bp. of Norwich owes his unique position as a mitred Abbot to the fact that when *Henry VIII confiscated the episcopal revenues he substituted those of the Abbey of St. Benet, together with those of Hickling. Notable Bishops include, besides Herbert of Losinga (1091–1119) and Henry Despenser, the 'fighting bishop' (1370–1406), J. *Overall (1618–19), F. *White (1629–31), M. Wren (1635–8; uncle of Christopher *Wren), R. *Montague (1638–1641), J. *Hall (1641–56), E. *Reynolds (1661–1676), and A. *Sparrow (1676–85).

H. T. Riley, 'Norwich: The Bishop's Registry' in the *First Report of the Royal Commission on Historical Manuscripts* (1874), Appendix, p. 86 f.; id., 'Norwich; The Dean and Chapter', ib., pp. 87–9. A. Jessopp (ed.), *Visitations of the Diocese of Norwich A.D. 1492–1532* (Camden Society, Second Series, xliii; 1888). J. F. Williams (ed.), *Diocese of Norwich. Bishop Redman's Visitation, 1597.* Presentments in the Archdeaconries of Norwich, Norfolk and Suffolk (Norfolk Record Society, xviii; 1946). H. W. Saunders (ed.), *The First Register of Norwich Cathedral Priory* (ib., xi; 1939). Id., *An Introduction to the Obedientiary and Manor Rolls of Norwich Cathedral Priory* (1930). Bartholomew de Cotton, 'Annales Ecclesiae Norwicensis' and continuation in H. *Wharton, *Anglia Sacra*, i (1691), pp. 397–417. W. *Dugdale, *Monasticon Anglicanum*, iv (ed. 1823), pp. 1–24. F. Blomefield, *An Essay towards the Topographical History of the County of Norfolk*, iii (1806), pp. 445–671, and iv (1806), pp. 1–64. J. Britton, *The History and Antiquities of the See and Cathedral Church of Norwich* (1816). A. Jessopp, *Norwich* (Diocesan Histories; 1884); C. H. B. Quennell, *The Cathedral Church of Norwich* (Bell's Cathedral Series, 1898). H. Leeds, *Norwich Cathedral Past and Present* (1910). D. H. S. Cranage (ed.), *Thirteen-Hundredth Anniversary of the Diocese of East Anglia* (Norwich, 1930). D. J. Stewart (from Memoranda of R. Willis), 'Notes on Norwich Cathedral' in *The Archaeological Journal*, xxxii (1875), pp. 16–47 and 155–87. J. C. Cox on 'The Cathedral Priory of the Holy Trinity, Norwich', in *The Victoria History of the County of Norfolk*, ii, ed. W. Page (1906), pp. 317–28; also id. on the ecclesiastical history of the county, ib., pp. 213–317. Indices to wills in the consistory courts and other similar material also published by the Norfolk Record Society and the Norfolk and Norwich Archaeological Society.

NOTARIES. Specially appointed persons who confirm and attest the truth of any deeds or writings in order to render them authentic. It is a rule of *canon law that the evidence of one notary is equivalent to that of two witnesses; hence the signed statement of a notary is unchallengeable evidence in a court of law. In the Middle Ages their appointment lay with the Pope or his delegates, and their work was and remains international. By 25 Hen. VIII, c. 21, sect. 3, the right of appointing notaries was transferred to the Abp. of *Canterbury who acted through his Master of Faculties. Nowadays the English notary, who is an ecclesiastical officer, is nominated by the judge of the provincial courts of Canterbury and *York.

NOTES OF THE CHURCH, The. The four characteristic marks of the Church first enumerated in the so-called *Nicene Creed, i.e. one, holy, catholic, and apostolic. Though forming the opening words of *Boniface VIII's bull '*Unam Sanctam', they were not generally discussed until the Reformation, when RC theologians utilized them to discern the true Church among the rival claims of the different Christian Communions. Since then, they have been employed as a particular mode of apologetics ('via notarum'). From about the middle of the 16th cent., treatises 'De notis Ecclesiae' became very numerous, though the notes were not at first confined to the four of the Creed. Thus St. Robert *Bellarmine enumerated as many as fifteen notes, though he held that these fifteen were ultimately reducible to four. Under the stress of controversy the positions were clarified and the exact meaning of the word defined. The term was taken over by the *Tractarians in order to demonstrate the Catholicity of the C of E, and a doctrine of the Church, based on its four notes, was elaborated with some fullness by W. *Palmer in his *Treatise on the Church of Christ* (2 vols., 1833). For a much earlier dispute about the notes of holiness and catholicity, see *Optatus*.

D. *Stone, *The Notes of the Church* (1910). G. Thils, *Les Notes de l'Église dans l'apologétique catholique depuis la Réforme* (Gembloux, 1937).

NOTKER. Among several monks of the *Benedictine monastery of St. *Gall of this name the two best known are:

(1) **Notker Balbulus** (*c.* 840–912), 'the Stammerer'. He entered the monastery of St. Gall in his youth, was made librarian in 890, then guest-master, and finally master of the monastic school, where Solomon III, later Bp. of Constance, was among his pupils. He is famous for his literary work, esp. his compilation of *sequences and his introduction of them into the Liturgy. He also continued the 'Breviarium Regum Francorum' attributed to Erchanbert, wrote a metrical 'Vita' of St. Gall, and is the probable author of the 'Gesta Caroli Magni', a collection of stories about *Charlemagne circulated under the designation of 'a monk of St. Gall'. His biographer,

Ekkehart IV, praises him as a vessel of the Holy Ghost, stammering of tongue but not of spirit. Soon venerated as a saint, his cult was approved by *Leo X for St. Gall in 1512 and for the diocese of Constance a year later. Commemoration, 6 Apr.

(2) **Notker Labeo** (c. 950–1022), called also 'Notker the German'. He entered the monastery of St. Gall as a boy and later became master of the monastic school, which office he retained till his death. To make Latin literature more accessible to his pupils, he took the unprecedented step of translating many classical and other writings into German, among them works by Cato, Vergil, Terence, as well as the 'Job' and the 'Moralia' of St. *Gregory. All, however, are now lost except *Boethius's 'De consolatione philosophiae', Martianus Capella's 'De nuptiis Philologiae et Mercurii', *Aristotle's 'De categoriis' and 'De interpretatione', and the Psalter. He also wrote several works in Latin and a treatise on choral music in German. His vigorous style and his ability to translate philosophical terms into the as yet undeveloped Old High German have been deservedly admired.

(1) Collection of his works in J. P. Migne, *PL*, cxxxi, 993–1178; Sequences also ed. C. Blume, S.J.–H. M. Bannister (A.H.M.A., liii; 1911); modern ed. of his poetical works, with full introd., by W. von den Steinen, *Notker der Dichter und seine geistige Welt* (Bern, 2 vols., 1948); 'Vita S. Galli' also ed. K. Strecker in *N.A.*, xxxviii (1913), pp. 59–93 (with introd. in German), and in *M.G.H.*, Poetae, iv (pt. 2; 1923), pp. 1093–108 (with introd. in Lat.). The 'Gesta Caroli Magni' have frequently been edited; classical ed. by P. Jaffé, *Monumenta Carolina* (Bibliotheca Rerum Germanicarum, iv; Berlin, 1867), pp. 628–700. Life of Notker by Ekkehart IV is pr. in *AA.SS.*, Apr. I (1675), pp. 579–96, with process of canonization, pp. 596–604. Useful biographical note in L. *d'Achery, O.S.B.–J. *Mabillon, O.S.B. *Acta Sanctorum Ordinis Sancti Benedicti*, v (Paris, 1635), pp. 11–22; repr. in J. P. Migne, op. cit., cols. 983–94. J. Schwalm–P. von Winterfield, 'Zu Notker dem Stammler' in *N.A.*, xxvii (1902), pp. 740–51. P. von Winterfield, 'Rhythmen- und Sequenzenstudien, vii, Welche Sequenzen hat Notker verfasst?' in *Zeitschrift für deutsches Altertum und deutsche Litteratur*, xlvii (1904), pp. 321–99. Raby, pp. 210–14, with bibl. p. 476. G. Meyer von Knonau in *P.R.E.*, xiv (ed. 3), (1904), pp. 218–20, s.v. 'Notker, Mönche vom Kloster St. Gallen'; É. Amann in *D.T.C.*, xi (pt. 1; 1931), col. 805 f., s.v. 'Notker le Bègue'; J. Beckmann in *L.Th.K.*, vii (1935), col. 633 f., s.v. 'Notker der Stammler'; K. Langosch in Stammler, v (1955), cols. 735–75.
(2) Editions of his works by P. Piper (Germanischer Bücherschatz herausgegeben A. Holder, viii–x; Freiburg i.Br., 1882–3) and E. H. Sehrt–T. Starck (Altdeutsche Textbibliothek begründet von H. Paul, xxxii–xxxiv, xxxvii, xl; 1933 ff.). P. [T.] Hoffmann, *Die Mischprosa Notkers des Deutschen* (Palaestra, lviii; 1910); id., *Der mittelalterliche Mensch gesehen aus Welt und Umwelt Notkers des Deutschen* (1922). H. Naumann, *Notkers Boethius. Untersuchungen über Quellen und Stil* (Quellen und Forschungen zur Sprach- und Culturgeschichte der Germanischen Völker, cxxi; 1913). Manitius, ii (1923), pp. 694–99; K. Löffler in *C.E.*, xi (1911), p. 125 f.; É. Amman in *D.T.C.*, xi (pt. 1; 1931), col. 806 f.; E. Karg-Gasterstädt in Stammler, v (1955), cols. 775–90.

NOTKER (c. 940–1008) Bp. of Liége. Of a noble Swabian family he was perhaps educated at St. *Gall, but he was not provost there as stated by the 'Hildesheim Chronicle'. Nominated Imperial chaplain in Italy in 969, he was made Bp. of Liége by the Emp. Otto I in 972 and throughout his life defended German interests both in Italy and Lorraine. He established the temporal sovereignty of the bishops of his diocese, which he embellished with many fine buildings. At the same time he improved the moral and intellectual standard of his clergy and reformed the abbey of Lobbes. He was a great benefactor of the Liége schools, to which he attracted celebrated scholars. The many Lives of saints attributed to him are the works of his friend, Abbot Heriger of Lobbes, to which he lent his name.

Works attributed to him in J. P. Migne, *PL*, cxxxix, 1135–68. Anonymous Life, written in the late 12th cent. and incorporated in the 13th cent. 'Gesta Episcoporum Leodiensium' of Giles of Orval, ed. J. Heller in *M.G.H.*, Scriptores, xxv (1880), pp. 57–63; also ed., with detailed introd., by G. Kurth in *Compte-Rendu des séances de la commission royale d'histoire, ou Receuil de ses bulletins*, Sér. 4, xvii (Brussels, 1890), pp. 365–422. G. Kurth, *Notger de Liége et la civilisation au Xᵉ siècle* (2 vols., 1905), with repr. of the Life in vol. ii, pp. 10–15. Manitius ii (1923), pp. 219–22. É. Amann in *D.T.C.*, xi (pt. 1; 1931), cols. 807–9, s.v.

NOTRE-DAME, PARIS. The cathedral church of Paris. Built in the early French Gothic style on the Ile de la Cité, it was begun in 1163 and consecrated in 1182; and became an accepted model for several other French cathedrals. The western front was added in 1200–20. The church was desecrated in the French Revolution, when the 'Feast of Reason' was celebrated in it in 1793, but it was reopened for Christian worship in 1795, at first for the '*Constitutional Church'. Victor Hugo's *Notre-Dame de Paris* (1831) awakened a fresh interest in its glories and from 1845 onwards its fabric was restored.

B. Guérard (ed.), *Cartulaire de l'église Notre-Dame de Paris* (Collection de Documents Inédits sur l'Histoire de France, Sér. I, Collection des Cartulaires de France, iv–vii; 1850). F. de Guilhermy–E. Viollet-le-Duc, *Description de Notre-Dame, cathédrale de Paris* (1856). M. Aubert, *Notre-Dame de Paris. Sa place dans l'histoire de l'architecture du XIIᵉ au XIVᵉ siècle* (1920). P. *Batiffol, *Notre-Dame de Paris dans l'histoire et dans la dévotion de la France* (1917). A. Temko, *Notre-Dame of Paris. The Biography of a Cathedral* (1956). See also bibl. to *Paris*.

NOVALIS. The pseudonym of **Friedrich Leopold Freiherr von Hardenberg** (1772–1801), the German Romantic poet. To his parents, who belonged to the *Moravian sect, he owed the deep religious strain in his character which he never lost. He was educated at the universities of Jena, Leipzig (where he made friends with F. *Schlegel), and *Wittenberg. His poetic genius, inspired by passion for the girl Sophie von Kühn, found its best expression in the beautiful *Hymnen an die Nacht* (1800) evoked by grief at her early death (1797). His marked leanings towards Catholicism became apparent in this, as also in his essay *Die Christenheit oder Europa* (1799; publd. 1826), Later he studied geology under Prof. A. G. Werner (1750–1817), whom he immortalized as the 'Meister' in one of his two great unfinished prose romances, *Die Lehrlinge zu Sais*. His other chief work, *Heinrich von Ofterdingen*, records much of his spiritual history under the allegory of a search for a mysterious 'blue flower'. He died of phthisis on 25 Mar. 1801.

His works, mostly fragments, were ed. by his two associates, Ludwig Tieck and Friedrich Schlegel (2 vols., Berlin, 1802), often repr. Modern edd. by E. Heilborn

(2 vols., Berlin, 1901), J. Minor (4 vols., Jena, 1907), P. Kluckhohn (4 vols., Leipzig [1929]); and E. Wasmuth (3 vols., Berlin, 1943). Correspondence with Friedrich and August Wilhelm, Charlotte and Caroline Schlegel ed. J. M. Raich (Mainz, 1880). Novalis has been the subject of innumerable studies in Germany, esp. from the literary standpoint. T. *Carlyle discusses him in a review of his collected works in *The Foreign Review*, iii (1829), pp. 97–141. A. Schubart, *Novalis' Leben, Dichten und Denken* (1887); E. Heilborn, *Novalis der Romantiker* (1901); E. Hederer, *Novalis* (Vienna, 1949). W. *Dilthey, *Das Erlebnis und die Dichtung* (1906), pp. 201–82. In Eng. there is a popular introd. by P. Spring, *Novalis, Pioneer of the Spirit* (Winter Park, Florida, 1946). K. J. Obenauer in *R.G.G.* (ed. 2), iv (1930), cols. 599–602.

NOVATIANISM. A rigorist schism in the W. Church which arose out of the *Decian persecution (A.D. 249–50). Its leader, Novatian, was a Roman presbyter and the author of an important (and completely orthodox) work on the doctrine of the Trinity. Details about the life of Novatian are limited and not entirely consistent. Apparently because disappointed by the election of *Cornelius as Pope (251), he joined the rigorist party, which deprecated concessions to those who had compromised with paganism, and was consecrated rival Bp. of Rome. Novatianist views were approved by *Antioch, but rejected by *Dionysius at Alexandria. Novatian himself suffered martyrdom under Valerian in 257–8.

Though doctrinally orthodox, the Novatianists were excommunicated. One of their bishops, Acesius, after accepting the *Nicene decisions on *Arianism and the *Paschal Controversy, was rebuked by *Constantine himself at the Council for persisting in schism. Can. 8 of Nicaea also elaborated the terms on which Novatianists could be received back into Catholic communion. A Novatianist Church persisted into the 5th cent. and, in isolated communities, even later.

The chief authority on Novatian is Cyprian's 'Epistles'. Of the earlier edd. of the 'De Trinitate', the best is that of J. Jackson in his ed. of Novatian's works (London, 1728), pp. 1–250; this ed., repr. from A. *Gallandi, in J. P. Migne, *PL*, iii, 911–82. Crit. ed. by W. Yorke Fausset (Cambridge Patristic Texts, 1909). Eng. tr. by H. Moore (Translations of Christian Literature, Series 2; S.P.C.K., 1919). A. d'Alès, S.J., *Novatien. Étude sur la théologie romaine au milieu du troisième siècle* (1924). Bardenhewer, ii, 624–35; Altaner (ed. 1951), pp. 140–2. A. *Harnack in *P.R.E.* (ed. 3), xiv (1904), pp. 223–42; H. Koch in *P.W.*, xxxiii (1936), cols. 1138–56; É. Amann in *D.T.C.*, xi (pt. 1; 1931), cols. 816–49; A. Mayer, O.S.B., in *E.C.*, viii (1952), cols. 1976–80, s.v. 'Novaziano e novazianismo'.

NOVELLO, VINCENT (1781–1861), Church musician. Born of mixed Italian and English parents, he was appointed organist of the Portuguese Embassy chapel as early as 1797, and from 1840 to 1843 was organist of the RC church in Moorfields. From 1849 till his death he lived at Nice. He was one of the founders of the London Philharmonic Society and of the Choral Harmonists' Society. He is esp. remembered for his editions of sacred music and for his rehabilitation of such great works as the Masses of J. Haydn and W. A. Mozart and the music of G. P. da *Palestrina in England. Among his chief publications were: *A Selection of Sacred Music* (2 vols., 1811), *Twelve Easy Masses* (3 vols., 1816), *The*

Fitzwilliam Music (i.e. the Musical MSS. in the Fitzwilliam Museum, Cambridge; 5 vols., 1825), **Purcell's Sacred Music* (5 vols., 1829).

M. Cowden Clarke (daughter), *The Life and Labours of Vincent Novello* [1864]. P. M. Young in *Grove's Dictionary of Music and Musicians* (ed. 5 by E. Blom), vi (1954), pp. 113–15.

NOVENA. In the W. Church, a term applied to a period of nine-days' private or public devotion, by which it is hoped to obtain some special grace. The general observance of Novenas is quite modern, dating only from the 17th cent., though it is modelled on the nine-days' preparation of the Apostles and the BVM for the descent of the Spirit at *Pentecost (Acts 1. 13 f.) and there are other instances of a nine-days' preparation earlier. Novenas may be arranged either in circumstances of special peril or need, or as a recurrent devotion, and, in the RC Church, *indulgences have sometimes been attached to their observance.

J. Hilgers, S.J., in *C.E.*, xi (1911), pp. 141–4, s.v.; G. Löw, C.SS.R., in *E.C.*, xii (1954), col. 518, s.v. 'Triduo, ottavario, novena'.

NOVICE. A probationary member of a monastic community. The period of probation generally lasts at least a year. During this time the Novice is under the authority of the superior, and wears the dress and follows the rule of the community. A Novice may be dismissed from the community at any stage of his or her novitiate, and may also leave at any time without incurring ecclesiastical penalties. Admission to the novitiate, marked by the wearing of the habit of the community for the first time, is known as the 'clothing'. Usually admission to the novitiate takes place only after a period already spent as a '*postulant' (q.v.).

NOWELL, ALEXANDER (c. 1507–1602), Dean of *St. Paul's. He was educated at Brasenose College, Oxford, where in 1526 he became a Fellow. In *Mary's first Parliament he was returned as the member for Looe, but was not allowed to take his seat on the ground that he was already a member of *Convocation. After some years in exile during Mary's reign he returned on *Elizabeth's accession and in 1560 was appointed Dean of St. Paul's. He wrote three 'Catechisms'—the 'Large', the 'Middle', and the 'Small'. The last-named, published in 1572, so closely resembles that of the 1549 BCP that it has been argued that Nowell wrote this as well. The additions of 1604 to the BCP Catechism were certainly taken (by J. *Overall) in substance from Nowell's 'Small Catechism'. The 'Large Catechism' was probably approved by Convocation in 1563, though it was not printed till 1570.

Life by R. Churton (Oxford, 1809). W. Hunt in *D.N.B.*, xli (1895), pp. 243–50.

NULLITY. In canon law the absence of legal validity from an act or contract, owing to the omission of an integral requirement. Thus a pretended marriage is invalidated from the outset through the existence of one or more impediments, e.g. the relation of the parties to one another within the *prohibited degrees, the intention of one or both of the parties to form a union which was not indissoluble, *clandestinity (acc. to the Tridentine legislation), restraint on the free consent of one or both of the parties.

By the Matrimonial Causes Act of 1937, four specific grounds for a civil decree of nullity were recognized: (1) non-consummation of the marriage through the wilful refusal of the respondent; (2) insanity or epilepsy; (3) venereal disease in a communicable form in the respondent; and (4) pregnancy of the respondent by some other person than the petitioner. In (2), (3), and (4), the petitioner has to establish his ignorance of the facts at the time of marriage. A difficult ecclesiastical problem is raised by (1), since it professes to establish the 'nullity' of a marriage on the ground of facts which have happened *since* the marriage. Provided that at least one of the parties has acted in good faith, the union remains, even after a sentence of nullity, a 'putative marriage' and the children are considered 'legitimate'. See also *Matrimony* and *Divorce*.

The Report of a Commission on the subject appointed by the Abpp. of *Canterbury and *York in 1949 at the request of the *Convocations was publd. under the title *The Church and the Law of Nullity of Marriage* (S.P.C.K., 1955).

NUMBER OF THE BEAST, The.

The number 666 (or acc. to some MSS., 616) in Rev. 13. 18. As in both Gk. and Heb. each letter of the alphabet represented a figure as well as a sound, every name could be represented by a number corresponding to the sum of its letters. Innumerable explanations have been given of the cryptogram. The most prob. is that '*Nero Caesar' is intended. In Heb. letters it adds up to 666 (with the form 'Neron') or to 616 (with 'Nero'). This is esp. appropriate for the 'man of sin' if 666 is read, since here each digit is one less than seven, the perfect number. St. *Irenaeus proposed 'Euanthas', 'Lateinos' or 'Teitan' (*Adv. Haer.* V, xxx, 3). The many ingenious attempts to refer it to such persons as Mohammed, the Pope, Napoleon or M. *Luther may be safely dismissed.

NUMBERS, Book of.

The fourth Book of the *Pentateuch. Its English title, which follows that of the Greek and Latin versions, is explained by its two records of a census (1–4 and 26). The Hebrew title, 'Bemidhbar' (Heb. בְּמִדְבַּר. the fourth word, meaning 'in the wilderness'), is more appropriate, however, as the bulk of the Book narrates the experiences of the Israelites during their wilderness wanderings down to the time of *Joshua's appointment as *Moses' successor. The Book centres in the person of Moses and, besides its main narrative, contains large sections of miscellaneous laws and ceremonial

directions. It includes the well-known episodes of the twelve spies (13), of the revolt of Korah, Dathan, and Abiram (16), and of Balaam's mission to Balak (22 f.). To the last of these there are references in the NT (2 Pet. 2. 15, Jude 11, Rev. 2. 14). The form of priestly blessing in 6. 24–6 is frequently used in the Christian Church.

Commentaries by G. B. *Gray (I.C.C., 1903), A. H. McNeile (Camb. Bib., RV, 1911), L. Elliott Binns (West. Comm., 1927), H. Holzinger (K.H.C., Abt. iv; 1903), B. Baentsch (K.H.A.T., Abt. i, Bd. ii, on Ex., Lev., and Num.; 1903, pp. 443–699). G. F. Moore in *E.Bi.*, iii (1902), cols. 3439–49, s.v.

NUMINOUS.

A word coined by R. *Otto to denote the elements of a non-rational and amoral kind in what is experienced in religion as the 'holy'. The Numinous is thus held to include feelings of awe and self-abasement (at the *Mysterium Tremendum*) as well as an element of religious fascination (the *fascinans*). Otto developed his psychological analyses for the first time in *Das Heilige* (1917; Eng. trans. by J. W. Harvey, 1923).

NUN.

A member of a religious order or congregation of women living under the vows of poverty, chastity, and obedience. In RC *Canon Law (*CIC*, 488, § 7) only those living under 'solemn vows' are accounted Nuns (*moniales*) in the technical sense, those under 'simple vows' being properly called 'sisters' (*sorores*). The *Carthusians require complete bodily integrity, but other orders receive widows and penitents by dispensation.

NUN OF KENT, The.

See *Barton, Elizabeth*.

NUN'S RULE, The.

See *Ancren Riwle, The*.

NUNC DIMITTIS.

The Song of *Simeon (Lk. 2. 29–32), so named from its initial words in the *Vulgate version. It has formed part of daily prayers since the 4th cent., its use being already prescribed in the '*Apostolic Constitutions' (vii, 48). In the E. Rite it is said at *Vespers. In the Roman and many other W. breviaries its use is ordered at *Compline, whence it passed to the *Evensong of the BCP. In the *Monastic Breviary, however, it finds no regular place. It is also part of the celebrant's final devotions in the Liturgy of St. *Chrysostom, and in the Roman Rite it is sung at the *Candlemas Procession.

NUNCIO.

A permanent diplomatic representative of the *Holy See accredited to a civil government and often of ambassadorial status. He acts also as a link between Rome and the Church of the state to which he is accredited. The Nuncio was originally a fiscal officer, charged with the collection of Papal tithe and other money contributions, and only from the time of the *Counter-Reformation have his functions been diplomatic. See also *Apostolic Delegate*; *Papal Legate*.

NUPTIAL MASS. The wedding Mass which follows on the celebration of the marriage and contains the nuptial blessing. It is a votive Mass consisting of suitable lessons, chants, and prayers and is to be found in a form similar to its present one already in the *Leonine, *Gelasian, and *Gregorian Sacramentaries. Acc. to the law of the RC Church, it may be celebrated except in the 'closed times' (from the first Sunday of *Advent to the Octave of the *Epiphany and from *Ash Wednesday to *Low Sunday) on any day except Sundays, Holidays of *Obligation, *doubles of the first and second class, and certain privileged ferias and Octaves. On these latter days the Mass of the day is said instead and the prayers of the nuptial blessing are inserted and a commemoration of the Nuptial Mass is made. *Mixed marriages may not be accompanied by the Nuptial Mass (*CIC*, can. 1102, § 2).

NUREMBERG DECLARATION, The. The statement of belief issued by a group of 14 German Catholic professors and teachers which met at Nuremberg on 25–6 Aug. 1870 in protest against the decrees of the *Vatican Council on the Papal claims (promulgated 18 July 1870). Those present included J. J. I. von *Döllinger (Munich), J. *Friedrich (Munich), W. C. Reischl (Munich), F. H. *Reusch (Bonn), J. F. von Schulte (Prague). The manifesto denied that the recent Vatican Council was a true *Oecumenical Council, repudiated the relevant chapters of *Pastor Aeternus*, maintained that Papal infallibility would destroy civil liberties, and demanded an unfettered General Council which should meet north of the Alps. The declaration was later signed by 33 professors and teachers, priests and laymen. Its signatories formed the nucleus of the *Old Catholic Movement (q.v.).

The text is in J. F. von Schulte, *Der Altkatholizismus* (1887), pp. 14–16. C. B. Moss, *The Old Catholic Movement* (1948), p. 227 f.

O

OAK, Synod of the. The synod held under an Imperial order in July 403, at a suburb of *Chalcedon called 'The Oak'. Its object was to remove St. *Chrysostom from his see of *Constantinople. Held under the presidency of Paul, the Exarch of Heraclea (390–403), it was attended by 36 (or possibly 45) bishops, of whom all but 7 were from Egypt and all were Chrysostom's enemies. After Chrysostom had been condemned on several fabricated counts, ranging from favouring *Origenism to eating lozenges in church, the Emp. Arcadius (395–408) accepted the synod's decision and exiled Chrysostom to Bithynia. The riotous indignation of the people of Constantinople, together with the occurrence of an earthquake, frightened the Empress and he was recalled a few days later.

'Acta' (prob. genuine) survive in *Photius, Cod. lix (*PG*, ciii, 105–13). Hardouin, i, cols. 1037–42; Mansi, iii (1759), cols. 1141–54; Hefele–Leclercq, ii (pt. 1; 1908), pp. 137–54. P. Ubaldi, 'La sinodo "ad Quercum" dell' anno 403' in *Memorie della Reale Accademia delle Scienze di Torino.* Serie secunda, lii (1903), Scienze morali, storiche e filologiche, pp. 33–97. See also bibl. to Origenism.

OAKELEY, FREDERICK (1802–80), *Tractarian divine. Educated at Christ Church, Oxford, he was elected to a chaplain-fellowship at Balliol in 1827, where the influence of W. G. *Ward, then also a Fellow of Balliol, led to his accepting Tractarian teaching. From 1839 to 1845 Oakeley was in charge of the Margaret Chapel, London, on the site of the present church of All Saints, Margaret Street, and under his ministry the chapel became a centre of Tractarian worship in London. When the rift began to appear in the Oxford Movement, Oakeley was on the pro-Roman side; and on 29 Oct. 1845, three weeks after J. H. *Newman, he was received into the RC Church. Ordained priest in that Church in 1847, he was a canon of the diocese of Westminster from 1852 until his death. His writings include *Whitehall Chapel Sermons* (1837), *The Church of the Bible* (1857), *Historical Notes on the Tractarian Movement* (1865) and *The Priest to the Mission* (1871). He also wrote frequently for the *British Critic* and the *Dublin Review*.

In March 1880 Oakeley contributed 'Personal Recollections of Oxford from 1820 to 1845' to *The Month*, repr. in Miss L. M. Q. Couch (ed.), *Reminiscences of Oxford* (Oxf. Hist. Soc., xxii, 1892), pp. 301–45. There is no Life, but he figures extensively in the lit. of the Oxford Movement, e.g. in Wilfred Ward, *W. G. Ward and the Oxford Movement* (1889), passim. C. R. Beazley in *D.N.B.*, xli (1895), p. 286 f.

O-ANTIPHONS (also known as the **Greater Antiphons**). The *Antiphons sung before and after *Magnificat at *Vespers, acc. to Roman use, on the seven days preceding Christmas Eve, i.e. from 17 to 23 Dec. The name is derived from their initial 'O', viz. 'O Sapientia', 'O Adonai', 'O Radix Jesse', 'O Clavis David', 'O Oriens', 'O Rex gentium',

and 'O Emmanuel'. The *Sarum Use began the Antiphons on 16 Dec., and provided an additional 'O' for 23 Dec., viz. 'O Virgo virginum', and this arrangement is reflected by the insertion of 'O Sapientia' for 16 Dec. in the calendar of the BCP. The authorship and date of composition of the Antiphons are alike unknown; but they were already in use by the 8th cent.

H. Thurston, S.J., 'The Great Antiphons. Heralds of Christmas' in *The Month*, cvi (1905), pp. 616–31; A. Weber, 'Die sieben O-Antiphonen der Adventsliturgie' in *Pastor Bonus*, xix (1906–7), pp. 109–19; C. Callewaert, 'De groote Adventsantifonen O' in *Liturgisch Tijdschrift*, ii (1911–12), pp. 1–13, repr. in id., *Sacris Erudiri* (1940), pp. 405–18, with further bibl.

OATES, TITUS (1649–1705), conspirator. The son of an *Anabaptist preacher, Oates owes his notoriety to the part he played in the '*Popish Plot'. In the unsettled state of the times he managed to inflame public opinion by spreading stories of alleged RC intrigues to assassinate *Charles II and place his brother, *James, on the throne. The public panic lasted from 1678 to 1681, and many innocent persons were condemned and executed on his false testimony.

T. Seccombe (ed.), *Lives of Twelve Bad Men* (1894), No. v, 'Titus Oates', by id., pp. 95–154. Jane Lane, *Titus Oates* (1949), with reff. and bibl. T. Seccombe in *D.N.B.*, xli (1895), pp. 296–303.

OATH. Several Christian bodies, e.g. the *Waldensians, *Baptists, *Mennonites, and *Quakers, have interpreted Mt. 5. 33–7 as forbidding every oath; but the prohibition is more generally understood as primarily directed against the habit of promiscuous and unnecessary swearing such as prevailed among the Jews in the time of Christ.

Acc. to general Christian teaching, an oath, though not desirable, may be required by human weakness and is admissible for reasons of serious necessity. It must be concerned only with what one knows to be true, its object must be morally good, and in order to be valid it must be taken with the intention to swear. The taking of an oath is often surrounded with solemnity, ecclesiastical oaths, e.g., being sworn before the Crucifix and accompanied by the touching of the Gospel Book. An oath may be either assertory, i.e. referring to a fact past or present, or promissory, relating to the future; and in important matters it is held by moral theologians to be binding under grave sin.

J. E. Tyler, *Oaths. Their Origin, Nature and History* (1834). E. B. Tylor in *Encyclopaedia Britannica* (ed. 11), xix (1911), pp. 939–43, s.v.; N. Iung in *D.T.C.*, xiv (pt. 2; 1941), cols. 1940–56, s.v. 'Serment'.

OATH OF ALLEGIANCE. See *Allegiance, Oath of.*

OBADIAH, Book of. One of the *Minor Prophets and the shortest Book of the OT. It foretells the punishment of the Edomites, the traditional foes of the Jews, in the coming Day of the Lord. The close relation of the opening verses to Jer. 49. 14–16 has been variously interpreted, some claiming priority for the Obadiah version, others postulating an independent earlier prophecy as the source of both later documents. Reference to the destruction of *Jerusalem (ver. 11) seems to require a date later than 586 B.C. for the final compilation of the Book.

Commentaries by T. T. Perowne (Camb. Bibl., AV, Obad. and Jonah, 1883, pp. 8–42), J. A. Bewer (I.C.C. on Micah, Zeph., Nah., Hab., Obad., and Joel, 1912; sep. pagination), and G. W. Wade (West Comm. on Micah, Obad., Joel, and Jonah, 1925; sep. pagination). W. Rudolph, 'Obadja' in *Z.A.T.W.*, xlix (1931), pp. 222–31, with bibl. W. R. *Smith–T. K. *Cheyne in *E.Bi.*, iii (1902), cols. 3454–62; W. R. Smith–H. W. *Robinson in *E.B.* (ed. 11), xix (1911), p. 944 f. See also bibl. to *Minor Prophets*.

OBEDIENCE. The moral virtue which inclines a man to carry out the will of his lawful superior. Its exercise is necessary for the upholding of the order established in the world by both natural and positive law. Absolute obedience is due only to God, whereas obedience to men is limited by the bounds of authority and by the claims of conscience. Spiritual writers distinguish three degrees of lawful obedience, viz. mere external obedience, willing submission to an order though its wisdom may be doubted, and blind obedience, i.e. submission of the personal judgement to that of the superior, except, of course, in cases of obviously sinful commands. Obedience is enjoined by Christ (Jn. 15. 10), who by His perfect obedience unto death (Phil. 2. 8, Heb. 5. 8) is its supreme example. It came to be one of the three *vows by which a religious binds himself to obey his superiors acc. to the rule and constitutions of his order or congregation. Acc. to RC canon law, canonical obedience is due from all cardinals, metropolitans, bishops, and exempt abbots to the Pope, and from all priests to their bishops. It is promised by oath (*juramentum obedientiae*) and may be enforced by punishment. In the C of E every cleric before *institution to a benefice is required to take an oath of obedience to the Bishop of the Diocese in all things lawful and honest.

OBEDIENTIARY. A now almost obsolete name of the permanent officials in a monastery, appointed by a superior. It was used, e.g., of the sacristan, the cantor, the cellarer, &c., but generally not of the prior and sub-prior.

OBERAMMERGAU, in Upper Bavaria. To express gratitude for the cessation of a plague in 1633, the villagers vowed to enact the Passion and Death of our Lord at intervals of ten years. Performances took place every tenth year from 1634 to 1674, and in the decimal years from 1680 onwards, the only exceptions being 1870, when it was omitted on account of the Franco-

Prussian War; 1920, when world conditions led it to be postponed to 1922; and 1940. An extra performance took place in 1934 to commemorate the 300th anniversary of the first performance. The play, which takes some eight hours, is produced and acted by some 700 natives of the village, and is repeated many times through the summer.

There are Eng. trr. of the Passion Play by Mary F. Drew (London, 1881; ed. 2, ib., 1910) and Maria Trench (anon., ib., 1890; ed. 2 with name of translator, ib., 1910). O. Günzler–A. Zwink, *Oberammergau. Berühmtes Dorf—berühmte Gäste. 3 Jahrhunderte Passionsspiel im Spiegel seiner Besucher* (1950).

OBLATE (Lat. *oblatus*, 'offerred'). The word has several eccl. senses. (1) In the early Middle Ages, it was esp. applied to children dedicated to a monastery by their parents and placed there to be brought up. (2) Later, after this practice had been abandoned, it became widely used of laity who lived at a monastery or in close connexion with it, but who did not take full religious vows. (3) In modern times it has been adopted in the title of certain communities of the RC Church, e.g. the 'Oblates Regular of St. Benedict' (see foll. entry), the 'Oblates of Mary Immaculate' (founded 1816) and the 'Oblates of St. *Charles Borromeo' (founded by H. E. *Manning, 1857).

OBLATES REGULAR OF ST. BENEDICT. The 'Oblates of Mary' were founded by St. *Frances of Rome (q.v.) in 1425 as an association of noble Roman ladies, affiliated to the White *Benedictines ('Olivetans') of Sta Maria Nuova (afterwards Sta Francesca Romana). In 1433, with the approval of *Eugenius IV, St. Frances formed them into the Oblate Congregation of Tor de' Specchi, at the foot of the Capitol, Rome, where they still reside. Following her adaptation of the Benedictine Rule, they give themselves to prayer and good works, but without vows, strict enclosure, or giving up their property, and they make revocable promises of obedience to the Mother President. They wear black dresses with white gauze veils. Besides the original house in Rome, there are others in Switzerland and in the *United States.

Heimbucher, i, 310 f.

OBLATIONS (Lat. *oblationes, oblata*; Gk. προσφορά). In Christian usage, the term is applied both to the bread and wine offered for consecration in the Eucharist, and also to any other kind of gift (e.g. grapes, oil, cheese, altar cloths, &c.) presented by the faithful at Mass for the use of the clergy, the sick, the poor, the church, &c. In the Prayer for the Church Militant in the BCP, oblations, as distinguished from 'alms', originally meant money to be devoted to other purposes than the relief of the poor, but the authority of Bp. Simon *Patrick (1626–1707) can be invoked for interpreting oblations here as meaning bread and wine. See also *Offertory*.

J. Dowden, ' "Our Alms and Oblations": An Historical Study' in *J.T.S.*, i (1899-1900), pp. 321-46; repr., with additions, in id., *Further Studies in the Prayer-Book* (1908), pp. 176-222.

OBLIGATION, Feasts of. See *Feasts of Obligation*.

O'BRYAN, WILLIAM. See *Bible Christians*.

OBSCURANTISM. Active opposition, esp. from supposedly religious motives, to intellectual enlightenment. Christians have sometimes been charged with it by secular critics, and professing Christians have also sometimes made the charge against one another, but it has rarely, if ever, been admitted. The word probably derives ultimately from the famous *Epistolae Obscurorum Virorum* (1515-17).

OBSERVANTINES (Fratres de Observantia), also 'Observants'. Those members of the *Franciscan Order who claimed to 'observe' exactly the primitive Rule of St. *Francis, as confirmed by Pope *Honorius III on 29 Nov. 1223. The movement, which started in Italy in 1368 as a protest against the lax and secularizing elements which had been present in the order almost from the first, drew its inspiration largely from the *Spiritual Franciscans. In the 16th cent. the Observantines became divided into several branches, among them the *Capuchins, the Reformed, and the *Recollects, but these were all incorporated in 1897 into the single Order of *Friars Minor by *Leo XIII's bull 'Felicitate quadam'. See also *Conventuals*.

Bernardin of Aquila, O.F.M., *Chronica Fratrum Minorum Observantiae*, ed. L. Lemmens, O.F.M. (Rome, 1902). Heimbucher, i, 709-24. See also works cited under *Franciscan Order*; also bibl. to *Capuchins* and *Recollects*.

OCCAM, WILLIAM OF. See *William of Occam*.

OCCASIONAL CONFORMITY ACT, The. The Act, finally passed in 1711 (10 Anne, c. 2), to restrain Dissenters from receiving the Sacrament in the C of E to qualify for Government posts. It laid down that if after 25 March 1712 any civil or military officer in receipt of a salary, who had been obliged to receive the Sacrament, should after admission to office be discovered at a conventicle, he should forfeit £40, cease to hold office, and no longer be eligible for any employment in England. If, however, the convicted person conformed to the C of E for one year after his conviction, then his eligibility for office was restored. An earlier bill against occasional conformity (imposing still larger penalties) had been introduced into the Commons in 1702 and succeeding years, but always rejected by the Whig Lords. The Act of 1711 proved a failure in operation; and in 1719, to conciliate the Nonconformists, it was repealed by 5 Geo. I, c. 4.

OCCASIONAL OFFICES. In the BCP, the services which, in distinction from the constant offices of the Church (viz. *Mattins and *Evensong and the *Holy Communion), are used only as occasion may demand. They include *Baptism, *Confirmation, *Matrimony, *Visitation of the Sick, Communion of the Sick, Burial of the Dead, and the *Commination.

OCCASIONAL PRAYERS. In the BCP, the collection of eleven prayers prescribed for use 'upon several [i.e. appropriate] occasions' 'before the two final prayers of the Litany, or of Morning and Evening Prayer'. They include prayers for use in various times of adversity, two for the *Ember Weeks, and the 'Collect and Prayer for all Conditions of Men' (prob. by P. *Gunning, d. 1684). They first appeared in their present position at the 1661 revision of the BCP. In the proposed revision of 1928, many occasional prayers were added.

OCCASIONALISM (Lat. *occasio*, 'event'). The philosophical theory of the relation of mind to matter which denies that finite things have efficient causality and postulates that God always intervenes to bring about a change in matter when a change occurs in mind and vice versa. It was formulated to avoid the difficulties confronting the dualism of R. *Descartes. Among its principal exponents were A. *Geulincx (d. 1669) and N. *Malebranche (d. 1715); in the latter it assumed a form very near to *Pantheism. It never had any considerable following and soon suffered eclipse by G. W. *Leibniz's doctrine of 'Pre-established Harmony'. In the 19th cent. a form of occasionalism was revived by Hermann Lotze (1817-81).

Überweg, iii, 261-9, with bibl. p. 663 f. F. R. Tennant in *H.E.R.E.*, ix (1917), p. 443 f, s.v. See also bibl. to *Geulincx, A.*, and *Malebranche, N.*

OCCURRENCE. The falling of two feasts (or other commemorations) on the same day in the ecclesiastical calendar, e.g. the coincidence of *Christmas Day with a Sunday. In the W. Church the feast of higher rank is kept in such cases, the inferior one ordinarily being 'commemorated' by the recitation of its proper *collect after that of the greater feast. In some cases, however, where the one feast is of very high rank, the lesser is entirely unnoticed. When the feast displaced is a Sunday or other great holy day, its service is read on the first free day following.

OCHINO, BERNARDINO (1487-1564) Protestant Reformer. A native of Siena, he joined the *Observantine Franciscans and rose to be their general. In 1534 he transferred to the still more austere *Capuchins, of whom he was twice (in 1538 and 1541) the vicar-general. His preaching was so eloquent and moving that *Charles V said of him, 'That man is enough to make the stones weep'. Contact with *Peter Martyr (Vermigli) led him to accept Protestant doctrines, and in 1541 he became a Lutheran. He was cited before the Inquisition, but escaped to Geneva. From 1545 to 1547 he was minister to the Italian Protestants at Augsburg. In the latter year T. *Cranmer invited him to England and secured for him a Prebend of *Canterbury and a royal pension, and Ochino gave himself up to writing *The Usurped Primacy of the Bishop of Rome* and the *Labyrinth*, the latter attacking the *Calvinistic doctrine of *Predestination. On *Mary's accession he returned to Switzerland and in 1555 was appointed a pastor at Zürich, but on account of his *Thirty Dialogues* (1563), which proved him unsound on the doctrine of the *Trinity and on monogamy, he was expelled from his office. He then went to Poland, but was not allowed to remain there, and died at Slavkow (Austerlitz) in Moravia.

Life by C. Benrath (Leipzig, 1875; ed. 2, 1892; Eng. tr. by H. Zimmern, 1876); this work contains a full analysis and list of Ochino's writings. R. H. Bainton, *Bernardino Ochino* (Florence, 1940). J. M. Rigg in *D.N.B.*, xli (1895), pp. 350–3.

OCKHAM. See *William of Occam.*

'O COME, ALL YE FAITHFUL'. See *Adeste Fideles.*

O COME, O COME, EMMANUEL. See *Veni, Veni, Emmanuel.*

O'CONNELL, DANIEL (1775–1847), Irish politician. Educated at the colleges of St.-Omer and *Douai (1792), he returned to England in 1793, entered Lincoln's Inn in the following year, and was called to the Irish bar in 1798. In 1800 he made his first appearance on a public platform, on behalf of the Irish Catholics, denouncing the Union. He soon became a successful lawyer, married in 1802, and from 1805 began to gain more and more influence as a Catholic leader. In 1813 he opposed the Bill of Emancipation introduced by H. Grattan which contained the royal veto for the elections of bishops, a condition unacceptable to both Irish clergy and people though favoured by RCs in England. The next years were a long-drawn-out struggle between O'Connell and Sir R. Peel, who suppressed all Catholic organizations started by the former. In 1823, however, O'Connell formed the *Catholic Association with the object of securing Catholic emancipation by legal means. It quickly spread throughout the country and became so powerful an instrument that it was proscribed by Act of Parliament in 1825. But it continued its work under another name and under the leadership of O'Connell, who, in 1828, was returned as M.P. for Clare by the small freeholders of the county. The Roman Catholic Emancipation Act followed in the next year. From now onwards O'Connell began to work for the Repeal of the Union. He fought against Lord Grey's Coercion Bill of 1833 and, in 1840, founded his Repeal Association. From 1841 to 1843 he was Lord Mayor of Dublin, an office which he endeavoured to fill with complete impartiality. In 1843 he resumed his agitation for Repeal, holding a number of 'monster meetings' of which the most famous was that on the hill of Tara. In the same year he was arrested on a charge of creating disaffection and stirring up the people, and in 1844, after trial, condemned to a year's imprisonment. Though freed on appealing to the House of Lords, his health had suffered, and henceforward his policy, which wavered between Repeal and Federalism, lacked firmness. He also quarrelled with the Young Ireland Party. Acclaimed as the 'Liberator' by his countrymen, O'Connell's influence on Irish history was profound. He was a stirring orator who could sway the masses, but his agitation always stopped short of violence and was untarnished by selfish motives.

Life and Speeches of Daniel O'Connell ed. by his son, John O'Connell (2 vols., Dublin, 1846); *Select Speeches* also ed. by his son, John O'Connell (2 vols., ib., 1854–5); *Correspondence* ed. W. J. Fitzpatrick (2 vols., London, 1888). A. Houston, *Daniel O'Connell. His Early Life and Journal, 1795–1802* (London, 1906). Other studies by W. Fagan (2 vols., Cork, 1847–8; ends 1837), W. J. O'N. Daunt (2 vols. London, 1848), M. F. Cusack (London, 1872), J. A. Hamilton (ib., 1888), R. Dunlop ('Heroes of the Nations', New York and London, 1900), M. Macdonagh (London [1903]), and D. Gwynn (ib. [c. 1930]). S. O'Faoláin, *King of the Beggars.* A Life of Daniel O'Connell, the Irish Liberator, in a study of the Rise of Modern Irish Democracy, 1775–1847 (London, 1938). M. Tierney (ed.), *Daniel O'Connell.* Nine Centenary Essays (Dublin, 1949). R. Dunlop in *D.N.B.*, xli (1895), pp. 371–389.

OCTATEUCH. The first eight Books of the OT, i.e. the *Pentateuch with the three additional Books of *Joshua, *Judges, and *Ruth.

OCTAVARIUM. A collection of lessons, supplementary to those of the *Breviary, for use in the 2nd and 3rd *nocturns of the *Mattins of *Octaves which are of only local observance.

OCTAVE (Lat. *octava*, sc. *dies*, 'eighth day'; formerly used only in the plural). In Christian liturgical usage, the eighth day after a feast, reckoning inclusively, and so always falling on the same day of the week as the feast itself; some commemoration of the more important feasts is usually made on this day. Later the term was applied to the whole period of these eight days, during which the observance of certain major feasts came to be continued. The practice was prob. suggested by the OT usage of an eighth-day celebration of the 'Feast of Tabernacles' (Lev. 23. 36) and the 'Dedication of the Temple' (2 Chr. 7. 9), and first introduced under *Constantine (d. 337) when the dedication festivities of the basilicas at *Jerusalem and Tyre were extended over the same period. The liturgical feasts to be first dignified with an Octave were *Easter, *Pentecost, and, in the E., *Epiphany, the reason being possibly to provide a time of recollection for the newly baptized. From the 7th cent. saints' feasts also began to have Octaves, among the oldest being those of Sts. *Peter and Paul, St. *Lawrence, and St. *Agnes, which were long observed in the Roman Rite. From the 12th cent., however, the custom was introduced of observing also the days between the first and the eighth day as well as the eighth day itself. The number of feasts with Octaves was also greatly increased during the Middle Ages; they were reduced, however, by the Breviary reforms of St. *Pius V and St. *Pius X. By a decree of the Congregation of *Rites dated 23 Mar. 1955, all octaves were suppressed in the Latin rite except those of *Christmas, *Easter, and *Pentecost.

G. Löw, C.SS.R., in *E.C.*, ix (1952), cols. 451–3, s.v. 'Ottava'.

OCTOECHOS (Gk. ὀκτώηχος [βίβλος], 'the book of eight tones'). A liturgical book in the E. Church which contains the variable parts of the services from the first Sunday after Whitsun till the tenth Sunday before Easter. Since these variable parts recur every eight weeks in the same order, only eight sets of tones (ὀκτὼ ἦχοι), one for each week, are provided; hence the name.

ODA, St. See *Odo, St.*

ODES OF SOLOMON. See *Solomon, Odes of.*

ODILIA, St. (d. *c.* 720), also Othilia, the patroness of Alsace. She is said to have been the daughter of Adalricus, a Frankish lord, and been born blind but later miraculously recovered her sight. Having been granted by Adalricus his castle at Hohenburg (now the Odilienberg) above Obernai in the Vosges Mountains, she founded a large nunnery which she ruled as Abbess. In the Middle Ages the abbey was granted exceptional privileges and became a famous centre of pilgrimage (visited by *Charlemagne, St. *Leo IX and perhaps Richard I of England). In the last hundred years it has again been much visited. The water of the well is said to cure diseased eyes. Feast day, 13 Dec.

Crit. edd. of 10th cent. Life (of little historical value) by C. Pfister in *Anal. Boll.*, xiii (1894), pp. 5–32, and W. Levison in *M.G.H.*, Scriptores Rerum Merovingicarum, vi (1913), pp. 24–50, with useful introd. Modern lives by H. Welschinger ('Les Saints', 1901; quite uncritical), C. Wehrmeister, O.S.B. (St. Ottilien, Oberbayern, 1902; also uncritical), and C. Champion ('L'Art et les saints', 1930). M. Sapet, 'Observations sur la légende de sainte Odile' in *Bibliothèque de l'École des Chartes*, lxiii (1902), pp. 517–36; C. Pfister, *Pages alsaciennes* (Publications de la Faculté des Lettres de l'Université de Strasbourg, xl; 1927), pp. 87–119 ('La Légende de sainte Odile'), with reff. to the earlier works of the author. H. *Leclercq, O.S.B., in *D.A.C.L.*, xii (pt. 2; 1936), cols. 1921–34, s.v. 'Odile', with full bibl.

ODILO, St. (*c.* 962–1048), fifth Abbot of *Cluny. He entered the monastery in 991 and became abbot three years later. He was a man of high virtue as well as of great administrative abilities, under whose government the number of Cluniac houses rose from 37 to 65 and their influence spread throughout Christendom. The order was further strengthened by his plan of centralization, whereby most of the reformed monasteries were made directly dependent on Cluny. Odilo spent much of his time travelling in the interests of the Church and of his order, being highly esteemed by both Popes and Emperors; and the establishment of the '*Truce of God' for the South of France and Italy was largely his work. He has left a permanent mark on the Liturgy by introducing the commemoration of *All Souls' Day (2 Nov.), which, at first a local observance at Cluny, was soon extended to the whole W. Church. Though severe with himself he was gentle with others, and the great famines of the time, esp. between 1028 and 1033, gave scope to his charity which saved many from death. He was canonized in 1063. Feast days, 1 or 2 Jan.; in the order, 29 Apr.

Collection of St. Odilo's works in M. Marrier, O.S.B. (ed.); *Bibliotheca Cluniacensis* (Paris, 1614; repr., 1915), cols. 338–408, with extracts of the life by his disciple Iotsaldus, monk of Cluny, cols. 1813–24, and life by *Peter Damian, cols. 315–32; works, with life by Iotsaldus and other biographical material repr. from L. *d'Achery, O.S.B.–J. *Mabillon, O.S.B.–T. *Ruinart, O.S.B. (edd.), *Acta Sanctorum Ordinis Sancti Benedicti*, vi (pt. 1; Paris, 1701), pp. 631–710 (text of life by Iotsaldus, pp. 679–710), in J. P. Migne, *PL*, cxlii, 831–1038. E. Sackur, 'Handschriftliches aus Frankreich, II, Zu Iotsaldi *Vita Odilonis* und Verse auf Odilo' in *N.A.*, xv (1889), pp. 117–26, with texts. Id., 'Ein Schreiben Odilo's von Cluni an Heinrich III vom Oktober 1046', ib., xxiv (1899), pp. 728–35, also with text. Crit. ed. of excerpts of life by Iotsaldus by G. Waitz in *M.G.H.*, Scriptores, xv (pt. 2; 1888), pp. 813–20. O. Ringholz, O.S.B., *Der heilige Abt Odilo von Cluny in seinem Leben und Wirken* (1885). Popular lives by P. Jardet (Lyons, 1898) and L. Coté, *Un Moine de l'an mille* (Moulins, 1949). C. Schmitt, O.F.M., in *E.C.*, ix (1952), col. 71 f., s.v. 'Odilone', with further bibl. See also bibl. to *Cluny, Order of*.

ODIUM THEOLOGICUM (Lat., 'theological hatred'). A proverbial expression for the ill-feeling to which theological controversy frequently gives rise.

ODO, St. (879–942), Abbot of *Cluny. The son of Abbo, a Frankish knight of Maine, he was born at Tours and brought up in the family of William, Duke of Aquitaine, who later (910) founded the abbey of Cluny. At the age of 19 he was instituted to a canonry at St.-Martin's, Tours, and then made his way to Paris, where he studied under *Remigius of Auxerre. After returning to Tours he was deeply affected by reading the Rule of St. *Benedict and three years later gave up his canonry and was admitted by St. Berno to the monastery of Baume (909). On the foundation of Cluny in the next year, Berno put Odo in charge of the monastery school at Baume. In 927 he succeeded Berno as Abbot of Cluny, where he was mainly instrumental in raising the monastery to the high position it held in the next centuries. During his abbacy the monastic church of SS. Peter and Paul was completed and the influence of Cluny over other monasteries was greatly extended, largely through a privilege of John XI (931). On his first visit to Rome (936) he took an important part in the conflict between Hugh, 'King of Italy', and the Patrician Alberic, and also won over several Italian monasteries (S. Maria on the Aventine, *St. Paul's Outside the Walls, *Monte Cassino, *Subiaco) to Cluniac principles. His writings include a Life of Gerald of Aurillac, three books of moral essays, ('Collationes'), some sermons, an epic ('Occupatio') on the Redemption and twelve choral antiphons in honour of St. *Martin. Feast day, 18 Nov. (by the Benedictines, 29 April).

Collection of his works pr. in M. Marrier, O.S.B. (ed.), *Bibliotheca Cluniacensis* (Paris, 1614; repr. 1915), cols. 65–264, with life of St. Odo by his disciple, John, monk of Cluny, ib., cols. 13–56; further collection of his works, from various sources, repr. in J. P. Migne, *PL*, cxxxiii, 105–845, with life by John, cols. 43–86, and 12th cent. life by Nalgodus, monk of Cluny, cols. 85–104 (both repr. from L. *d'Achery, O.S.B.–J. *Mabillon, O.S.B. (edd.), *Acta Sanctorum Ordinis Sancti Benedicti*, v (1685), pp. 150–99). Odo's 'Occupatio' was first ed. A. Swoboda (Teubn., 1900). E. Sackur, 'Handschriftliches aus Frankreich, I. Zur Vita Odilo Abbatis Cluniacensis auctore Iohanne' in *N.A.*, xv (1889), pp. 105–16. Modern life by [A.] du Bourg, O.S.B. ('Les Saints', 1905). A. Hessel, 'Odo von Cluni und das französische Kulturproblem im früheren Mittelalter' in *H.Z.*, cxxviii (1923), pp. 1–25. É. Amman in *D.T.C.*, xi (pt. 1; 1931), cols. 937–9, s.v. 'Odon de Cluny'; C. Schmitt, O.F.M., in *E.C.*, ix (1952), cols. 65–7, s.v. 'Oddone', with bibl. See also bibl. to *Cluny, Order of*.

ODO, St. (d. 959), or 'Odo the Good', also 'Oda', Abp. of *Canterbury. He is said to have been the son of a Dane and originally a pagan. In 927 he became Bp. of Ramsbury. On Abp. Wulfhelm's death in 942, Odo at first declined the see of Canterbury offered him by King Edmund, on the ground of not being a monk; but on the king's persistence he received the *Benedictine habit from *Fleury and accepted the office. He was very active in restoring the cathedral buildings and in raising the morals and discipline of the clergy. He was also a staunch defender of the privileges of the Church. Feast day, 4 July

Life by *Eadmer pr. in *AA.SS.*, Jul. II (1721), pp. 67–73, where, however, it is wrongly ascribed to Osbern. More reliable information is to be found scattered in the contemporary life of his nephew, St. *Oswald, Abp. of York (q.v.). W. F. *Hook, *Lives of the Archbishops of Canterbury*, i (1860), pp. 360–81. W. Hunt in *D.N.B.*, xli (1895), pp. 421–3.

ODO (c. 1036–97), Bp. of Bayeux. He was a uterine half-brother of William the Conqueror who gave him the see of Bayeux while still a youth (c. 1050). His career was mainly that of a soldier and a statesman. In 1066 he founded the priory of St.-Vigor at Bayeux, colonizing it from the abbey of Mont-St.-Michel. He fought in person at the Battle of Hastings (14 Oct. 1066), armed with a mace so that as a cleric he might not shed blood. In 1067 he became Earl of Kent and for several years a trusted minister of William I. He appropriated many ecclesiastical lands which he distributed among his supporters until *Lanfranc secured their restoration. In 1080 he was sent North to punish the Northumbrians for the murder of Walcher, Bp. of *Durham. In 1082 he fell into disgrace, ap-

parently for having planned a military expedition to Italy, and was kept in prison until William was on his death-bed (1087). After his release he returned to Kent and under Rufus organized a rebellion designed to put his nephew, Duke Robert, on the throne. When it failed he returned to Normandy. He actively supported the First *Crusade and himself set out with Robert for Palestine in Sept. 1096, but died on the way at Palermo. He rebuilt Bayeux cathedral (completed c. 1076) and perhaps commissioned the celebrated *Bayeux tapestry (q.v.).

E. A. Freeman, *The History of the Norman Conquest of England* (6 vols., 1867–79), esp. vol. ii, pp. 210–12, iii, pp. 379 f., 451, 463 f., iv, passim, and v, pp. 76 and 79; F. M. Stenton, *Anglo-Saxon England* (1943), pp. 591–643 passim. On the question of his connexion with the Bayeux Tapestry, E. A. Freeman, op. cit., vol. iii, pp. 570–5; see also bibl. s.v. 'Bayeux Tapestry'. C. L. Kingsford in *D.N.B.*, xli (1895), pp. 424–6.

OECOLAMPADIUS, JOHN (1482–1531), German Reformer. His real name was 'Hussgen'. A native of Weinsberg (Palatinate), he was appointed cathedral preacher at Basle in 1515, where he soon showed strong reforming proclivities, but after championing M. *Luther's position for a time, he abandoned it, and in 1520 entered a monastery. He soon changed again, and in 1522 definitely threw in his lot with the Reformers. On his return to Basle in the same year, his influence led to the adoption of the Reformation principles in the city, and in 1528 he secured their acceptance in the canton of Berne. In the latter year he also married. At the Colloquy of *Marburg (1529) he defended the Eucharistic doctrine of H. *Zwingli. He was not, however, a great theologian, and he owed his influence rather to the trust put in his leadership than to any theological gifts. The *Anabaptists for a time claimed that he shared their views, but in a disputation he disavowed their doctrines. His successor at Basle was O. *Myconius.

E. Staehelin (ed.), *Briefe und Akten zum Leben Oekolampads* (vol. i, 1499–1526, Quellen und Forschungen zur Reformationsgeschichte, x, vol. ii, 1527–93, ib., xix; 1927–34). Life by W. F. *Capito prefixed to his ed. of Oecolampadius' Comm. on Ezek. (Strassburg, 1534 [no pagination]); also to the ed. of *Ioannis Oecolampadii et Huldrichi Zwingli Epistolae* (Basle, 1536 [no pagination]; Eng. tr. in [H. Bennet], *A Famous and Godly History* (1561 [no pagination]). Modern lives by J. J. *Herzog (2 vols., Basle, 1843) and K. R. Hagenbach (Leben und ausgewählte Schriften der Väter und Begründer der reformirten Kirche, ii, 1859, pp. 3–306). E. Staehelin, *Das theologische Lebenswerk Johannes Oekolampads* (Quellen und Forschungen zur Reformationsgeschichte, xxi; 1939). W. Hadorn in *P.R.E.* (ed. 3), xiv (1904), pp. 286–99, s.v.; L. Cristiani in *D.T.C.*, xi (pt. 1; cols. 947–51, s.v. 'Oecolampades'; E. F. J. Müller in *L.Th.K.*, vii (1935), cols. 691–3, s.v. 'Ökolampadius', with further bibl.

OECUMENICAL COUNCILS (Gk. οἰκουμένη, 'the whole inhabited world'). Assemblies of bishops and other ecclesiastical representatives of the whole world whose decisions on doctrine, cultus, discipline, &c., are considered binding on all Christians. Acc. to the teaching of most Christian communions outside the RC Church there have been no Oecumenical Councils since the schism between E. and W., the last being the Second of *Nicaea in 787. Acc. to present RC *canon law (*CIC*, cans. 222–9), an Oecumenical Council must be convened by the Pope, and its decrees have binding force only if sanctioned and promulgated by the Holy See; they are then infallible. As the oecumenicity of a Council is now held to depend on the co-operation of the Pope, the *Gallican doctrine that there can be an appeal from the Pope to a Council is inadmissible. The death of the Pope suspends the Council until it be reopened by his successor. As well as cardinals, archbishops and bishops, abbots and prelates nullius, and most generals of orders with solemn vows have the right to vote, and eminent theologians are usually invited in an advisory capacity.

Seven councils are commonly held both in E. and W. to be oecumenical. These are, with their dates and the chief subjects dealt with: (1) *Nicaea (325, *Arianism); (2) Constantinople I (381, *Apollinarianism); (3) *Ephesus (431, *Nestorianism); (4) *Chalcedon (451, *Eutychianism); (5) Constantinople II (553, *Three Chapters Controversy); (6) Constantinople III (680–1, *Monothelitism); (7) Nicaea II (787, *Iconoclasm).

The RC Church reckons the following 13 further Councils as possessing oecumenical authority: (8) Constantinople IV (869–70, *Photian Schism); (9) *Lateran I (1123, *Investiture Controversy); (10) Lateran II (1139, *Arnold of Brescia, &c.); (11) Lateran III (1179, Papal elections, &c.); (12) Lateran IV (1215, *Waldenses, &c.); (13) *Lyons I (1245, *Frederick II); (14) Lyons II (1274, Reunion, &c.); (15) *Vienne (1311–12, *Templars); (16) Constance (1414–18, *Schism— the oecumenicity of the Council before the election of *Martin V is disputed); (17) Ferrara-*Florence (1438–9, Union with the Greeks); (18) Lateran V (1512–17, Reform); (19) *Trent (1545–63, *Protestantism and Reform); (20) *Vatican (1869–70, Papal Infallibility, &c.).

In the C of E the *Thirty-Nine Articles assert that General Councils 'may err, and sometimes have erred, even in things pertaining unto God', and that what they ordain is to be tested by reference to Scripture (Art. 21). The *Reformatio Legum Ecclesiasticarum (1553) states that General Councils are regarded with honour and that the decisions of the first Four in particular are 'accepted and received with great reverence' (*De Summa Trinitate et Fide Catholica*, ch. 14). By 1 Eliz. cap. 1 (sect. xxxvi) the powers of those assigned to correct ecclesiastical abuses were limited in matters of heresy by the decisions of the first Four Councils and the authority of the Canonical Scriptures. R. *Hooker and L. *Andrewes uphold the authority of the first Four, while the Book of Homilies ('against Peril of Idolatry', pt. ii), R. *Field and H. *Hammond accept the first Six. It appears, however, that such Councils are ultimately revered in the C of E on the ground that their decisions are acceptable rather than vice versa.

OECUMENICAL MOVEMENT. The movement in the Church towards the recovery of the unity of all believers in Christ, transcending differences of creed, ritual, and polity. It endeavours to give expression to that unity by closer relations in conference, both for co-operation in common Christian tasks and with a view to the ultimate reunion of the Churches. This aspiration has never been alive to the same extent as in the present century. The present movement dates from the *Edinburgh Missionary Conference of 1910, and in the next three decades flowed in the two main channels, '*Life and Work' concerned with the application of Christianity to social, economic and political life, and '*Faith and Order' concerned with more specifically theological and ecclesiastical questions (qq.v.). In 1937, at conferences at *Oxford and *Edinburgh, it was resolved to unite the two movements and the *World Council of Churches (q.v.) came into being. For fuller details, see art. *Reunion*.

G. K. A. Bell (ed.), *Documents on Christian Unity 1920–4* (1924); id., Second Series (1930); id., Third Series 1930–48 (1948); Fourth Series 1948–57 (1958). Studies include G. J. Slosser *Christian Unity. Its History and Challenge in all Communions, in all Lands* (1929). K. [D.] Mackenzie (ed.), *Union of Christendom* (2 vols., 1938), Ruth Rouse–S. C. Neill (edd.), *A History of the Ecumenical Movement, 1517–1948* (1954). G. K. A. Bell, *Christian Unity. The Anglican Position* (Olaus Petri Lectures at Upsala University, October, 1946; 1948). *Irénikon*. Bulletin mensuel des moines de l'union des Églises, Prieuré d'Amay s. Meuse, also Collections (1926–8; the two series were amalgamated and six numbers a year issued 1929–39; four numbers a year 1940–52; three numbers a year 1953 ff.); *The Ecumenical Review* (4 numbers a year, Geneva, 1948 ff.). *Oecumenica*. Revue de l'Anglicanisme et des Questions œcuméniques (7 vols., each in 3 parts, 1934–9). N. Goodall, *The Ecumenical Movement. What it is and what it does* (1961).

OECUMENICAL PATRIARCH, The. (Gk. οἰκουμενικὸς πατριάρχης). The style borne by the Abps. or Patrs. of *Constantinople since the 6th cent. It was occasionally used also of other prelates from the middle of the 5th cent. Its exact significance is nowhere officially defined, but the title has been attacked in the W. as incompatible with the claims of the see of Rome.

OECUMENIUS (6th cent.), author of the oldest extant Greek Comm. on Rev., to whom tradition has assigned the designations 'Rhetor' and 'Philosopher'. Little is known of his life, but he appears to have been a contemporary and supporter of *Severus of Antioch. His Comm., one of but three on the Apocalypse in Greek from the first millennium, was rediscovered by F. Diekamp and published by H. C. Hoskier in 1928. The exposition, vigorous, modest, but uneven, accepts the Apocalypse as a divinely inspired canonical Book, relevant not only for its immediate situation but for the understanding of the past and the future. It cites no earlier comm., but its authorities include St. *Athanasius, St. *Basil, St. *Gregory Nazianzen, and *Evagrius. This 6th-cent. expositor is not to be confused with Oecumenius, Bp. of Tricca in Thessaly (10th cent.), to whom commentaries on Acts, the Pauline and Catholic Epistles have been ascribed.

H. C. Hoskier (ed.), *The Complete Commentary of Oecumenius on the Apocalypse* (University of Michigan Studies. Humanistic Series, xxiii, 1928). F. Diekamp, 'Mittheilungen über den neuaufgefundenen Commentar des Oekumenius zur Apokalypse' in *Sb.* (Berl.) (1901) (2), pp. 1046–56; id., 'Neues über die Handschriften des Oekumenius-Kommentares zur Apokalypse' in *Biblica*, x (1929), pp. 81–4. A. Spitaler, 'Zur Klärung des Ökumeniusproblems' in *Oriens Christianus*, Ser. 3, ix (1934), pp. 208–15; additional notes by J. Schmid, ib., pp. 216–18. J. Schmid, 'Ökumenios der Apokalypsen-Ausleger und Ökumenios der Bischof von Trikka' in *Byzantinisch-neugriechische Jahrbücher*, xiv (1938), pp. 322–30.

OEKONOMOS, CONSTANTINOS. See *Oikonomos, Constantine.*

OENGUS, St.

(8th–9th cent.), Irish saint, commonly, though perhaps erroneously, called the *Culdee, author of the Félire, or Festology of Saints known by his name. Of royal birth, he was educated at the monastic school at Clonenagh, Ireland, and lived as a hermit first at Disertbeagh, on the banks of the R. Nore, and later in a more solitary district, now known as Dysert Enos, nr. Maryborough. He is recorded to have communed with angels and attracted a crowd of disciples. He subsequently joined the fraternity of Tallaght, nr. Dublin, where, at first concealing his identity, he was employed on various menial duties. He collaborated with S. Maelruain (d. 787) on the compilation of the Martyrology of Tallaght, a prose catalogue of Irish saints, which is prob. the oldest of the Irish martyrologies. He began his own Festology at Clonenagh and finished it at Tallaght early in the 9th cent. Before his death in either 819, 824, or 839, he became both abbot and bishop. Feast day, 11 March.

W. Stokes (ed.), *Félire Oengusso Céli Dé.* The Martyrology of Oengus the Culdee (*Henry Bradshaw Society, xxix, 1905 with tr. and notes). Life from Colgan pr. in *AA.SS.*, Mar. II (1668), pp. 85–8. 'The Life and Works of St. Aengusius Hagiographus, or St. Aengus the Culdee' in *The Irish Ecclesiastical Record*, v (1869), pp. 1–29, 73–81, and 97–108.

OFFA

(d. 796), King of the Mercians from 757. He gained the throne after the short civil war which followed the death of Ethelbald and he gradually secured dominion, either directly or as overlord, over the whole of England south of the Humber. The result of the Battle of Otford with the Kentishmen in 776 is disputed, but at any rate by 785 his authority over Kent was established. In 779 he subjected the West Saxons near Bensington (Benson) in Oxfordshire. These conquests made him the most powerful English sovereign before the 10th cent. and in his charters he styled himself *rex Anglorum* or *rex totius Anglorum patriae.* The surviving portions of Offa's Dyke, constructed as a bulwark against the Welsh, are an index of his military strength. He governed well, was respected by *Charlemagne and gave his support to the Church. His influence with the Pope permitted the creation of the new archbishopric at *Lichfield (787–8, suppressed 803). He appears to have been a generous benefactor of the

monasteries, even though some of the charters displaying his grants must be discounted as forgeries. He is the reputed founder of the abbeys of *St. Albans and *Bath.

Charters printed in J. M. Kemble (ed.), *Codex Diplomaticus Aevi Saxonici*, i (1839), pp. 146–205, and in W. de Gray Birch (ed.), *Cartularium Saxonicum.* A Collection of Charters Relating to Anglo-Saxon History, i (1885), pp. 316–82; one, granting some land in Worcs to the Bishop, pr., with Eng. tr., in A. J. Robertson (ed.), *Anglo-Saxon Charters* (1939), pp. 3–5. F. M. Stenton, *Anglo-Saxon England* (1943), pp. 204–23. W. *Stubbs in *D.C.B.*, iv (1887), pp. 68–71; W. Hunt in *D.N.B.*, xlii (1895), pp. 2–5.

OFFERTORY.

In the Eucharistic liturgy: (1) The worshippers' offering of the bread and wine (and water) to be consecrated. In the Roman and derived rites, including the Anglican liturgy, it takes place at a relatively late point in the service (after the lections and the Creed), viz. at what was originally the beginning of the 'Mass of the Faithful'. It is now performed by the celebrant on behalf of the people, though at Milan representatives of the people ('*vecchioni') still offer the gifts. The prayers in the Roman rite which accompany the offering of the bread ('Suscipe, sancte Pater') and wine ('Offerimus tibi, Domine, calicem salutaris') are of late date and did not establish themselves until the later Middle Ages. In the Eastern rites, the offertory, with its elaborate cutting up and arranging of the bread, takes place at the *Prothesis at the outset of the whole service (see *Proskomide), the elements being solemnly brought to the altar at the '*Great Entrance' (ἡ μεγάλη εἴσοδος).

(2) The word is also used for the short anthem, first mentioned in St. *Augustine (*Retract.*, II, xi), sung in the Roman rite at the time of the act of offering. Originally a whole psalm, by the 8th cent. it had been reduced to one or two verses and it now consists (except at *Requiem Masses) of only an antiphon, proper to each Mass.

Full discussion, with bibl. reff., in Jungmann, *M.S.*, ii (ed. 1952), pp. 3–125; Eng. tr., ii, pp. 1–100. Further discussion, with additional reff., in L. Eisenhofer–J. Lechner, *Grundriss der Liturgik des römischen Ritus* (ed. 1950), pp. 201–8. G. P. Wetter, *Altchristliche Liturgien* (2 vols., 1921–2), passim. L. Beauduin, O.S.B., 'L'Offertoire, jadis et aujourd'hui' in *Questions liturgiques et paroissiales*, vi (1921), pp. 30–45; B. *Capelle, O.S.B., 'L'Offertoire', ib., xvii (1932), pp. 57–67; id., 'Quête et offertoire' in *La Maison Dieu*, vi (1950), pp. 121–40. A. Clark, 'The Function of the Offertory Rite in the Mass' in *E.L.*, lxiv (1950), pp. 309–44. A. *Fortescue in *C.E.*, xi (1911), pp. 217–19, s.v.; F. *Cabrol, O.S.B., in *D.A.C.L.*, xii (pt. 2; 1936), cols. 1946–62, s.v. 'Offertoire'.

OFFICE, Divine (*Officium Divinum*).

In the W. Church, the obligatory vocal prayer of the Church, recited by priests, religious, and clerics upon whom this duty is imposed. The practice of saying prayers at fixed hours of day or night was general among the Jews, from whom the primitive Christians took it over (cf. Acts 10. 6, 9; 16. 25). It probably developed as a preparation for the Eucharist from the Vigils kept before the great feasts, and by the end of the 5th cent. consisted, in monastic usage, of the 'Night Office' (*Mattins), and the seven 'Day Hours', viz. *Lauds, *Prime, *Terce, *Sext, *None, *Vespers, and *Compline (q.v.). The arrangement of the offices was fixed in detail by St. *Benedict, who named it the 'work of God' (*opus Dei*), taking as his basis the Roman use. This same use was later introduced in England (7th cent.), the Frankish kingdom (8th cent.), and Spain (11th cent.). In its essential elements the 6th cent. office is identical with the present one in the RC Church, all eight hours comprising psalms, hymns, lessons, antiphons, responses and versicles, and prayers. At the Reformation, their place was taken in the C of E by the two offices of Morning and Evening Prayer ('Mattins' and 'Evensong'). See also *Breviary*.

OFFICE, Holy. See *Holy Office*.

OFFICE HYMNS. *Hymns appear as a fixed part of the Monastic Office already in the Rule of St. *Benedict, though they were not generally used in the Roman Liturgy till the 13th cent. A trace of their absence from the rite is still discernible in the fact that in the Roman Breviary *Mattins of the *Epiphany, the *Triduum of *Holy Week, *Easter and its Octave, and the Office of the *Dead have no hymns. At all other times a hymn is sung at Mattins and the Little Hours before, and at *Lauds, *Vespers, and *Compline after, the Psalms. The hymns of the Little Hours and Compline are the same throughout the year; those of the other hours vary acc. to feasts and seasons. The hymns of the former, as well as others in the same rhythm (iambic dimeters), vary their concluding verse, normally a doxology to the Bl. Trinity, on some feasts and octaves. Many ancient Office Hymns are contained (in English versions) in modern hymnals, e.g. 'Lucis Creator Optime' ('O Blest Creator of the Light'; from Sunday Vespers), 'Te lucis ante terminum' ('Before the Ending of the Day'; from Compline), '*Pange, lingua, gloriosi Corporis mysterium' ('Of the glorious Body telling'; from the Vespers of *Corpus Christi).

OFFICIAL PRINCIPAL, also 'Official'. In ecclesiastical law, the person to whom a bishop formerly entrusted the exercise of his coercive jurisdiction, and hence nowadays the judge in an ecclesiastical court. Against his sentence there is no appeal to the bishop. Since the bishop also has the right of sitting with the Official Principal in the court (a practice in fact seldom adopted), the court is known as the '*Consistory Court' (the two together forming *unum consistorium*).

OIKONOMOS, CONSTANTINE (1780–1857), *Greek scholar and theologian. A keen Greek patriot, his ecclesiastical career was more than once interrupted by political activities. He was the author of a very long and elaborate work on the *Septuagint entitled Περὶ τῶν ο´ Ἑρμηνευτῶν (i.e. *On the Seventy Interpreters*, Athens, 4 vols., 1844–9) which, though setting out from wrong premisses (e.g. belief in the inspired character of the Septuagintal text as against the Hebrew), contains many valuable investigations. Oikonomos also wrote several works on philology and the history of literature. He made it one of his chief aims to oppose W. influences in Greek religious life, which had assumed increasing prominence since the middle of the 18th cent.

Works partly repr. by his son, Sophocles Oikonomos (3 vols., Athens, 1862–6). P. Meyer in *P.R.E.* (ed. 3), xiv (1904), pp. 299–304, s.v. 'Oekonomos'; A. Bigelmair in *L.Th.K.*, vi (1935), col. 688 f., s.v., with bibl.

OILS, Holy. See *Chrism*.

OLAVE, St. (995–1030), OLAF HARALDS-SÖN, Patron Saint of *Norway and King of Norway from 1016 to 1029. During his lifetime he was known as 'the Fat'. After some years spent fighting the Danes in England, where he was converted to the Christian faith, he returned to Norway in 1015, and by defeating Earl Sweyn at the battle of Nesje in 1016, became king of the country. The harshness of his methods provoked fierce resistance from his subjects and in 1029 the nobles, who had rallied round Canute the Great, forced him to flee to Russia; and when in the following year he tried to regain his kingdom he was killed at the battle of Stiklestad. His shrine at Nidaros (Trondhjem) was a famous place of pilgrimage in the Middle Ages. Feast day, 29 July.

He is not to be confused with OLAF TRYGGVESSÖN (969–1000), King of Norway from 995.

Life by Augustine, Bp. of Trondheim (1161–88), pr. in *AA.SS.*, Jul. IV (1731), pp. 113–15; also ed., with useful introd., by F. Metcalfe, *Passio et Miracula Beati Olaui* (Oxford, 1881). The Saga of St. Olave written by Snorre Sturlason (1175–1241) was ed. P. A. Munch–C. R. Unger (Christiania, 1853); also ed. O. A. Johnsen–J. Helgason (Norsk Historisk Kjeldeskrift-Institut, 2 vols., Oslo, 1941). Eng. tr. of Snorre Sturlason's *Heimskringla* or the Lives of the Norse Kings by E. Monsen–A. H. Smith (Cambridge, 1932), pp. 218–474. Modern lives by J. F. Vicary (London, 1886), C. Riesteren (Avignon, 1930), and O. Moberg (Lund, 1941). B. Dickins, 'The Cult of S. Olave in the British Isles' in *Saga-Book of the Viking Society*, xii (1945), pp. 53–80, with reff.

OLD BELIEVERS. The section of the Russian Orthodox Church which refused to accept the liturgical reforms of the patriarch, *Nikon (d. 1681). They were excommunicated in 1667, called 'Raskolniki', i.e. schismatics, and violently persecuted, esp. during the first 80 years of the schism and again under Nicholas I (1825–55). They included a great body of peasants and many of the more devout priests, and received large reinforcements when Peter the Great (1682–1725), whom they believed to be the Antichrist, tried to Europeanize Russia. Since, however, no bishops seceded from the Established Church, they were left without a hierarchy and split up into two sections: the one, called 'Popovtsy', who sought for means of establishing their own priesthood, the other, 'Bezpopovtsy', who denied its necessity. The former had to be content with the ministrations of discontented priests coming to them from the Orthodox Church until, in 1846, a deposed bishop, Ambrose of Bosnia, joined them and established a hierarchy. From that time the Popovtsy steadily increased in number and importance (though part of them were reconciled to the Church) and they were officially recognized by the state in 1881. The Bezpopovtsys, on the other hand, split up into a great number of sects, many of them adopting the most extravagant doctrines and practices, but they remained a comparatively small minority.

The main literature is in Russian. Other works include F. C. *Conybeare, *Russian Dissenters* (Harvard Theological Studies, x; 1921), pp. 13–258, with reff.; F. Knie, *Die russisch-schismatische Kirche* (Graz, 1894); P. Pascal, *Avvakum et les débuts du Raskol. La crise religieuse au XVII siècle en Russie* (Paris thesis; Ligugé, 1938), with bibl. Baron A. von Stromberg in *H.E.R.E.*, xi (1920), pp. 332–9, s.v. 'Sects (Russian)'. See further, bibl. to *Russia, Christianity in*; also to *Nikon*.

OLD CATHOLICS. A group of small national Churches, consisting of Christians who have at various times separated from Rome. Since 1932 they have been in full Communion with the C of E. They are composed of three sections:

(1) The Church of Utrecht, with three bishops, which separated from Rome in 1724 (see *Holland, Christianity in*).

(2) The German, Austrian, and Swiss Old Catholic Churches. This group of Churches was created from those Christians who refused to accept the dogmas of the Infallibility and universal ordinary jurisdiction of the Pope, as defined by the *Vatican Council of 1870, and seceded from the RC Church shortly afterwards. The movement was temporarily strengthened by those who joined them for political reasons, owing to the strained relations between the Prussian Government and the Roman Curia (see *Kulturkampf*). Their organization was partly the work of Conferences, presided over by von *Döllinger at *Bonn in 1874 and 1875, and attended by members of the Old Catholic, Anglican, Orthodox, Lutheran, and other Churches, among the Anglican representatives being the Bps. of *Winchester (E. H. *Browne) and Gibraltar (C. W. Sandford), and H. P. *Liddon. The Old Catholics received their episcopal succession from the Church of Utrecht; the first German bishop, J. H. Reinkens (with see at Bonn), was consecrated in 1874, and the first Swiss bishop, E. Herzog (with see at Berne), in 1876. Owing to the opposition of the government, bishops were not consecrated for the Austrian communities till much later. A bishop of Warnsdorf (Bohemia) was consecrated in 1924 and of Vienna in 1925. In 1939 the three bishoprics of Bonn, Warnsdorf, and Vienna were united into one Church. They have since been separated.

(3) Some small groups of Slav origin. National Church movements among the Poles in U.S.A. (1897) and the Croats (1924) have resulted in the establishment of the 'National Polish Church', with four bishoprics in America

and one in Poland, and of the 'Yugoslav Old Catholic Church' (see also *Mariavites*).

The doctrinal basis of the Old Catholic Churches is the 'Declaration of *Utrecht' (q.v.), agreed upon by the five Old Catholic bishops in 1889. The Old Catholics recognize the same seven *Oecumenical Councils as the E. Orthodox Church, and those doctrines accepted by the Church before the Great Schism of 1054. The bishops, as well as the rest of the clergy, are permitted to marry. All services are in the vernacular. In some countries communion is given in both kinds. Auricular confession is not compulsory.

The Old Catholic communion formally recognized *Anglican ordinations in 1925, and entered into full communion with the C of E in 1932, on the basis of an agreement reached at Bonn on 2 July 1931. The American Episcopal Church, and most other Anglican Churches, have since also established intercommunion. Old Catholic bishops have twice taken part in the consecration of Anglican bishops in London, using their own formula (*Accipe Spiritum Sanctum*, &c.), and in 1937 Anglican bishops took part in the consecration of Andreas Rinkel as Abp. of Utrecht. There are no Old Catholic communities in any English-speaking country except U.S.A. where their work is entirely among Poles and other foreigners. Various small sects which sometimes call themselves 'Old Catholic' are not recognized by the Old Catholic Churches referred to above.

F. Siegmund-Schultze (ed.), *Ekklesia. Eine Sammlung von Selbstdarstellungen der christlichen Kirchen* III, ii (1935), 'Die altkatholische Kirche'; C. B. Moss, *The Old Catholic Movement. Its Origins and History* (1948), J. M. *Neale, *History of the So-called Jansenist Church of Holland* (1853); J. F. von Schulte, *Der Altkatholizimus. Geschichte seiner Entwicklung, inneren Gestaltung und rechtlichen Stellung in Deutschland* (1887), with docc. and bibl.; Paulin Gschwind, *Geschichte der Entstehung der christkatholischen Kirche der Schweiz* (2 vols., Berne, 1904–1910). Quarterly periodical *Revue internationale de Théologie* (Berne, 1893–1910), with changed title *Internationale kirchliche Zeitschrift* (ib., 1911 ff.). See also the Reports of Old Catholic International Conferences. J. F. von Schulte in *P.R.E.* (ed. 3), i (1896), pp. 415–25, s.v. 'Altkatholizismus'; E. Moog in *R.G.G.* (ed. 2), i (1927), cols. 276–80, s.v. 'Altkatholiken'; J. Troxler in *L.Th.K.*, i (1930), cols. 318–22, s.v. 'Altkatholiken'.

OLD LATIN VERSIONS, The. The Latin versions of the Scriptures in use in the Church before the issue of the 'authorized' (*Vulgate) version of St. *Jerome at the bidding of Pope *Damasus. In S. Gaul and N. Africa a vernacular translation was needed sooner than in Rome (where the use of Greek continued until well into the 3rd cent. and all the earliest bishops bore Greek names), and the existence of the Scriptures in Latin in those two provinces is attested before the end of the 2nd cent. Several independent versions came into currency. One form, known as the 'African Old Latin', is very clearly defined. Its African *provenance* is proved by its use in the Biblical quotations in St. *Cyprian, and it is represented by the fragmentary 'Codex Bobiensis' ('k', 4th–5th cent., now at Turin; see *Bobbio*), less exactly by the 'Palatinus ('e', 5th cent., at Vienna), and to a great extent in the Greco-Latin *Codex Bezae (q.v., for the Gospels and Acts) and Codex Claromontanus ('d', now at Paris; for the Pauline Epistles). The 'African Old Latin has many contacts with the so-called *Western text. The form in which the Old Latin circulated in Europe is less defined. It has been generally supposed that there are two main types—the 'Italic' (represented by the MSS. *f* [at Brescia] and *q* [at Munich]) and the 'European' (represented by the MSS. *b* [at Verona] and *a* [at Vercelli]). The MSS. of the Old Latin text differ greatly among themselves, and it was largely the desire to remedy the inconveniences arising out of such differences that led Jerome (who asserted that there were almost as many different texts as MSS.) to undertake his Vulgate. See also *Itala*.

The fullest presentation of the evidence for the whole Bible is still Pierre *Sabatier, O.S.B., *Bibliorum Sacrorum Latinae Versiones Antiquae, seu Vetus Italica* (3 vols., fol. Reims, 1743[-9]; repr. Paris, 1751). This is being superseded for the OT by B. Fischer, O.S.B. (ed.), *Vetus Latina* (Freiburg i.Br., 1949 ff.); for the NT by A. *Jülicher (ed.), *Itala. Das Neue Testament in altlateinischer Überlieferung* (Berlin, 1938 ff.). Several of the chief MSS. were printed separately by the Clarendon Press in the series of *Old Latin Biblical Texts*, 1883 ff. T. A. Marazuela, *La Vetus Latina Hispana* (Madrid, 1953 ff.). F. Stummer, *Einführung in die lateinische Bibel* (1928), pp. 4–76 ('Die lateinische Bibel vor Hieronymus'). H. Rönsch, *Itala und Vulgata* (1869; ed. 2, 1875; mainly philological); F. C. *Burkitt, *The Old Latin and the Itala* (Texts and Studies, iv, No. 3; Cambridge, 1896). H. von Soden, *Das lateinische Neue Testament in Afrika zur Zeit Cyprians nach Bibelhandschriften und Väterzeugnissen* (T.U., xxxiii; 1909). A. V. Billen, *The Old Latin Texts of the Heptateuch* (1925). M. J. Lagrange, O.P., *Introduction à l'étude du Nouveau Testament*, II (ii), (1935), pp. 240–81, 421–36, 488–500, 539–51, 598–612. H. F. D. Sparks in H. W. *Robinson (ed.), *The Bible in its Ancient and English Versions* (1940), pp. 100–10. H. A. A. Kennedy in *H.D.B.*, iii (1900), pp. 47–62, s.v. 'Latin Versions, The Old'. See also bibl. to *Vulgate*.

OLD ROMAN CREED, The.

An earlier and shorter form of the Apostles' Creed (q.v.), which at least from the end of the 2nd cent. was the official creed of the Church of *Rome. It is first found in the *Apostolic Tradition* of St. *Hippolytus (d. 235) and is attested in an almost identical form in the 4th cent. by *Marcellus of Ancyra (ap. *Epiphanius, *Haer.* 72, 3) and *Rufinus of Aquileia (*Comm. in Symbol.*). It is also found in Codex E of Acts in the *Bodleian (Laud. gr. 35) and in an 8th cent. MS. in the British Museum (Cotton. 2 A XX). In 1919 it was the subject of three brilliant papers by K. Holl, A. *Harnack, and H. *Lietzmann in the *Sitzungsberichte* of the Prussian Academy.

The subject is necessarily discussed in all books dealing with the history of the *Apostles' Creed (see bibl.). J. *Ussher, *De Romanae Ecclesiae Symbolo Apostolico Veteri, aliisque Fidei Formulis* (London, 1647). Modern studies dealing specifically with the Old Roman Creed include the brilliant essays by K. Holl, 'Zur Auslegung des 2. Artikels des sog. apostolischen Glaubensbekenntnisses' in *Sb.* (Berl.), 1919, pp. 2–11; A. *Harnack, 'Zur Abhandlung des Hrn. Holl: Zur Auslegung des 2. Artikels des sog. apostolischen Glaubensbekenntnisses', ib., pp. 112–16; H. *Lietzmann, 'Die Urform des apostolischen Glaubensbekenntnisses', ib., pp. 269–74. B. *Capelle, O.S.B., 'Le Symbole romain au second siècle' in *R. Bén.*, xxxix (1927), pp. 33–45; id., 'Les Origines du symbole romain' in *R.T.A.M.*, ii (1930), pp. 5–20. J. N. D. Kelly, *Early Christian Creeds* (1950), esp. pp. 100–66. Bardenhewer, i, 82–90; Altaner (ed. 1951), pp. 35–7.

OLD SYRIAC VERSIONS, The.

The Syriac translations of the NT which circulated in the Syriac-speaking Church before the construction of the *Peshitta ('Vulgate') version early in the 5th cent. Only two MSS. of these versions are known, both of the Gospels. The 'Curetonian' recovered by H. *Tattam from Egypt in 1842 was printed privately by W. *Cureton in 1848 and published in 1858. The 'Sinaitic' was found and photographed towards the end of the 19th cent. in the monastery of St. Catherine on Mt. *Sinai by Mrs. Lewis and Mrs. Gibson of Cambridge. (The latter is not to be confounded with the Greek *Codex Sinaiticus discovered by C. *Tischendorf). The existence of an Old Syriac text of Acts is attested by St.*Ephraim Syrus's Commentary (which has survived, however, only in *Armenian). The readings of the Old Syriac NT are closely allied to those of the so-called *Western text.

The best ed. of the Curetonian text (Sinaitic as *apparatus*) is in F. C. *Burkitt, *Evangelion Da-Mepharreshe* (2 vols., Cambridge, 1904), of the Sinaitic text (Curetonian as *apparatus*) is that of Mrs. A. S. Lewis (London, 1910). Facsimile ed. of the Sinaitic text by A. Hjelt (Helsingfors, 1930). W. Cureton, *Remains of a very antient Recension of the Four Gospels in Syriac* (1858), and R. L. Bensly-J. R. *Harris-F. C. Burkitt, *The Four Gospels in Syriac transcribed from the Sinaitic Palimpsest* (with introd. by A. S. Lewis, 1894). A. Hjelt, 'Die altsyrische Evangelienübersetzung und Tatians Diatessaron besonders in ihrem gegenseitigen Verhältnis', in T. *Zahn, *Forschungen zur Geschichte des neutestamentlichen Kanons*, vii (pt. 1; 1903); Hjelt defends priority of Old Syriac over the Diatessaron.

OLD TESTAMENT (Gk. Παλαιὰ Διαθήκη, Lat. Vetus Testamentum).

Term denoting the collection of Canonical Books which the Christian Church shares with the Synagogue. Traditionally it is divided into three parts, viz., the Law, the Prophets, and the Writings. The 'Law' (*Torah) is coincident with the *Pentateuch; the 'Prophets' include most of the historical Books and the Major and *Minor Prophets (but not *Daniel); the *Writings are the Books of latest date. Like the NT, the OT Books are regarded as inspired in the Church, which from the time of *Marcion has consistently defended them against attacks.

OLDCASTLE, Sir JOHN (c. 1378?–1417),

*Lollard leader and rebel. He was a knight of Herefordshire who became, by his marriage in 1408, Lord Cobham. In 1413 he was accused of heresy before Convocation, and upheld Lollard opinions. He was given forty days to recant, but escaped from the Tower of London before their expiration. He then put himself at the head of a conspiracy for a Lollard rebellion, which, however, collapsed. He remained in hiding till 1417, when he was captured and executed. He was reputed to have been the boon companion of the young Henry V, and this traditional figure of Sir John Oldcastle was the basis of Shakespeare's Falstaff.

W. T. Waugh, 'Sir John Oldcastle' in *E.H.R.*, xx (1905), pp. 434–56 and 637–58; H. G. Richardson, 'John Oldcastle in hiding, Aug.-Oct. 1417', ib., lv (1940), pp. 432–8. K. B. McFarlane, *John Wycliffe and the Beginnings of English Nonconformity* (1953), pp. 160–83. J. Tait in *D.N.B.*, xlii (1895), pp. 68–93.

OLIER, JEAN-JACQUES (1608–57), founder of the Society and seminary of *Saint-Sulpice (q.v.). A native of *Paris, he studied classics at the *Jesuit Collège de la Trinité at Lyons from 1617 to 1624, philosophy at the Collège de Harcourt in Paris from 1624 to 1627 and theology at the *Sorbonne from 1627 to 1630. At an early age he was provided with ecclesiastical benefices and rose to become a popular preacher. Having made his way to Rome in 1630 to study Hebrew, he lost his sight. He was cured and converted to a life of godliness during a pilgrimage to *Loreto. He returned to Paris in 1631. Ordained priest in 1633, under the influence first of St. *Vincent de Paul and then of Père C. de *Condren, he conducted missions to Auvergne in 1634 and 1636–37 and to Brittany in 1638 and 1639. After an unsuccessful attempt at *Chartres, in 1641 he established a seminary at Vaugirard. In 1642 he took charge of the parish of Saint-Sulpice in Paris, which was in a degraded condition, hoping with the assistance of the seminary which he transferred there, to Christianize the Sorbonne and reform the neighbourhood. Dividing the parish into eight districts, each under a priest, he established catechetical centres to educate the ignorant and combat *Calvinism and *Jansenism, founded homes for women, and did much to relieve distress. Among the rich he led the movement against duelling.

The seminary at Saint-Sulpice, which was marked by the close association of masters and students, became a model for other dioceses, to some of whom Olier lent priests to found similar seminaries. The society was not so much a religious congregation as a community of secular priests following a common life. In 1657 he sent priests from Saint-Sulpice to the colony in Montreal, which he had conceived as a community dedicated to the honour of the Blessed Virgin.

His mysticism is in the tradition of St. Vincent de Paul and St. John *Eudes. His published writings include *La Journée chrétienne* (1655); *Catéchisme chrétien pour la vie intérieure* (1656); *Explication des cérémonies de la grand' messe de paroisse selon l'usage romain* ('1657'; really 1656); *Introduction à la vie et aux vertus chrétiennes* (1657); *Traité des saints ordres* (1675); *Lettres spirituelles* (1672); and *Pietas Seminarii Sancti Sulpitii* (1815).

Œuvres ed. J. P. *Migne (Paris, 1856). Modern lives by E. M. Faillon (2 vols., Paris, 1841; Eng. life by E. H. Thompson based entirely on that of Faillon, London, 1861), G. M. de Fruges (Paris [1904]), L. A. F. Monieur, P.S.S. (vol. i only; posthumously publd. by E. L[évesque], Paris, 1914), P. Pourrat, P.S.S. (Paris, 1932), and A. Portaluppi (Milan, 1947). H. I. Ichard, P.S.S., *Doctrine de M. Olier expliquée par sa vie et ses écrits* (1889; ed. 2, 1891). C. Letourneau, *La Mission de Jean-Jacques Olier et la fondation des grands séminaires en France* (1906). Bremond, iii (1921), pp. 419–507. E. Lévesque in *D.T.C.*, xi (pt. 1; 1931), cols. 963–82, s.v., with detailed bibl.

OLIVES, Mount of. The highest point in the range of hills to the E. of *Jerusalem, rising to 2600 ft. above sea-level, and separated from the city by the Valley of Jehoshaphat through which flows the brook *Cedron. Near its foot is the Garden of *Gethsemane (q.v.). It was aptly described by A. P. *Stanley as in NT times 'The Park' of Jerusalem. From the frequent reff. in the Gospels it would appear that Christ often resorted to the Mt. of Olives. He was met here by the crowd on *Palm Sunday (Mk. 11. 1 and 11. 7), and from its summit He ascended to Heaven (Acts 1. 2–12). The traditional site of the Ascension was marked by a Church known as the 'Imbomon' (ἐν βωμῷ; prob. 'at the summit'), built by a matron Poemenia before 378. Another church on the slopes, the 'Eleona' (ὁ Ἐλαίων; 'the olive yard'), also dating from the 4th cent., was built over a grotto where Christ was believed to have discoursed to the disciples on the Last Things (Mk. 13).

The most comprehensive study is H. Vincent, O.P.–F. M. Abel, O.P., *Jérusalem*: II, Jérusalem nouvelle (1914), pp. 328–419 (iii, 'Les Sanctuaires du mont des Oliviers').

OLIVETAN (c. 1506–38), Protestant Reformer. His real name was Pierre Robert; he is supposed to have been dubbed 'Olivetanus' from burning the midnight oil. A native of Noyon in Picardy and a cousin of J. *Calvin, he began his studies at Orléans in 1528. Here his adoption of *Lutheran doctrines forced him to flee to Strassburg, where he became a competent Hebrew and Greek scholar. From 1532 to 1535 he preached Reformation doctrines to the *Waldenses in Piedmont and for the purposes of his mission work translated the Bible into French. The OT was done direct from the Hebrew, but the *Apocrypha and NT were only a revision of the version of *Faber Stapulensis. He was materially assisted in this work by Calvin, who also contributed the prefaces. The version was published at Neufchâtel in June 1535. In his last years he helped Calvin in organizing the Reformation at Geneva.

Short study by C. A. Négrier (Montauban Diss., 1891). G. Bonet-Maury in *P.R.E.* (ed. 3), xiv (1904), p. 363 f, s.v.

OLIVETANS ('The Order of Our Lady of Mount Olivet'). An independent branch of the *Benedictine Order founded in 1319 by Giovanni Tolomei (St. Bernard Ptolomei, d. 1348) at Monte Oliveto, near Siena. They follow a strict interpretation of the rule, for a period in their history were total abstainers from wine, and wear a white habit. They have now only a few houses, among them the former Abbey of *Bec.

S. Lancellotti, *Historiae Olivetae* (Venice, 1623). Anthony of Braga's *Chronicon Montis Oliveti* (1313–1450) ed. P. Lugano, O.S.B. (Spicilegium Montolivetense i; Florence, 1901). P. Lugano, O.S.B., *Origine e primordi dell'ordine di Montoliveto, 1313-1450* (ib., ii; 1903). J. I. Cummins, O.S.B., 'The Olivetan Constitutions' in *Ampleforth Journal*, ii (1897), pp. 149–64. Life of Giovanni Tolomei by B. M. Maréchaux, O.S.B. (Paris, 1888). Heimbucher, i, 214–17, with bibl. J. C. Almond, O.S.B., in *C.E.*, xi (1911), p. 244, s.v.

OLIVI, PETRUS JOANNIS (c. 1248–98), *Spiritual Franciscan. Born at Sérignan in Hérault, Languedoc, at the age of 12 he entered the *Franciscan Order and studied at *Paris and possibly at *Oxford. His zeal for the strict observance of the rule led him to be consulted by Nicholas III in 1279 about Franciscan poverty. As leader of the rigorists in the Order, he was accused of heresy in the General Chapter of Strassburg in 1282; and after examination by seven masters his works were censured in thirty-four propositions (1283). At the General Chapter of Montpellier (1287), however, he established his orthodoxy, which was confirmed at Paris in 1292. He became lector in various convents (Nîmes, Florence, Montpellier). After his death the Spiritual Franciscans accorded him exaggerated veneration and though in the decretal 'Fidei Catholicae Fundamento' at the Council of *Vienne in 1311 certain propositions believed to be his (on the moment at which the Lord's body was transfixed by the lance; on the manner of the soul's union with the body; on the baptism of infants) were repudiated, his name was not mentioned. In 1326 *John XXII condemned his *Postilla super Apocalypsim* (publ. 1700). His other works include the *Quaestiones*, a commentary on the *Sentences, Tractatus de Sacramentis, Tractatus de Virtutibus, Tractatus de Quantitate*, Commentaries on Genesis, Job, the Psalms, the Proverbs, Ecclesiastes, the Song of Solomon, Lamentations, Ezekiel, the Lesser Prophets, the Four Gospels, and the Epp. to the Romans and Corinthians, *Expositio Dionysii de Angelica Hierarchia* and various works on the Franciscan Order.

'Quaestiones in Secundum Librum Sententiarum', ed. B. Jansen (Bibliotheca Franciscana Scholastica Medii Aevi, iv–vi; 1922–6); 'Quaestio de Angelicis Influentiis', ed. F. Delorme, O.F.M., in his ed. of St. *Bonaventure's 'Collationes in Hexaëmeron' (ib., viii; 1934), pp. 363–417; extracts from further works ed. id., 'Textes franciscaines, I. L'Explication littérale du *Pater* selon Pierre-Jean Olivi' in *Archivio italiano per la Storia della Pietà*, i (1951), pp. 181–203. F. *Ehrle, 'Petrus Johannis Olivi, sein Leben und seine Schriften' in *Archiv für Litteratur- und Kirchengeschichte*, iii (1887), pp. 409–552. B. Jansen, *Die Erkenntnislehre Olivis* (1921). Überweg, ii, 490–2, with bibl. p. 763. B. Jansen in *L.Th.K.*, vii (1935), cols. 709–11, s.v., with bibl. F. Callaey in *D.T.C.*, xi (pt. 1; 1931), cols. 982–991, s.v. 'Olieu', with bibl.; id. in *E.C.*, ix (1952), cols. 103–5, s.v., with bibl.

OLLÉ-LAPRUNE, LÉON (1839–98), French philosopher. From 1875 he was professor of philosophy at the École Normale Supérieure at Paris, where he became the leading lay exponent in France of a Catholic system of philosophy. He stressed the limits of a purely intellectual approach to the issues of philosophy along lines which had affinities with the teaching of J. H. *Newman in England, and in his emphasis on the part played by the will and the heart in cognition prepared the ground for such later influences in French culture as H. *Bergson, M. *Blondel, and the *Modernist Movement. His writings include *La Philosophie de Malebranche* (1870), *De la certitude morale* (1880), and *La Philosophie et le temps présent* (1890).

M. Blondel, *Léon Ollé-Laprune. L'achèvement et l'avenir de son œuvre* (Paris, 1923). Brief sketches by G. L.

Fonsegrive (Paris, 1898; also in the series 'Science et Religion', No. 628; 1912), M. Blondel (Paris, 1899) and L. Crippa (Brescia, 1947, with bibl.). E. Boutroux, 'Notice sur la vie et les œuvres de M. Léon Ollé-Laprune' in *Mémoires de l'Académie des Sciences Morales et Politiques de l'Institut de France*, xxv (1907), pp. 207–42. G. Goyau in *C.E.*, xi (1911), p. 246 f., s.v.; L. Crippa in *E.C.*, ix (1952), col. 107 f., s.v. See also bibl. to *Modernism*.

OLSHAUSEN, HERMANN (1796–1839), Protestant theologian. He studied at Berlin where he was greatly influenced by F. D. E. *Schleiermacher and J. A. W. *Neander. In 1821 he became professor at Königsberg and in 1834 at Erlangen. His main interest was in NT exegesis, his chief work being a large-scale commentary on the NT (1830 ff.; Eng. trans. 4 vols. 1847–49). His brother, Justus Olshausen (1800–82), was an orientalist of some repute.

L. Pelt in *P.R.E.* (ed. 3), xiv (1904), pp. 366–8, s.v.

OMAN, JOHN WOOD (1860–1939), *Presbyterian theologian. From 1889 to 1907 he was minister at Alnwick, Northumberland. From 1907 to 1935 he was professor at, and from 1925 to 1935 principal of, Westminster College, Cambridge. His early interest in F. D. E. *Schleiermacher, of whose *Speeches on Religion* he published a translation in 1893, indicates the direction of his thought. Holding the uniqueness and independence of the religious consciousness as an immediate, self-authenticating awareness of the Supernatural, he nevertheless insisted that it should not be isolated from other spheres of experience. In *The Natural and the Supernatural* (1931) he set forth a powerful philosophic justification of his position. Esp. important in this work is his treatment of the idea of the sacred, which differed notably from, as it had in fact antedated in his class-room teaching, R. *Otto's treatment of the 'Holy'. On the side of doctrine, Oman's theology might be said to be the theology of 'sincerity'. The inner authority of truth determined his understanding of personality, of sin and grace, of the Church, sacraments, and ministry. His other writings include his *Vision and Authority* (1902), *The Church and the Divine Order* (1911), *Grace and Personality* (1917).

Memoirs of the author by G. Alexander and H. H. Farmer prefixed to Oman's posthumously publd. *Honest Religion* (1941), pp. xv–xxv and xxvi–xxxii respectively. *A Dialogue with God and Other Sermons and Addresses* was also posthumously publd. by F. H. Ballard [son-in-law] (London [1952]). Obituary note by F. R. Tennant in *Proceedings of the British Academy*, xxv (1939), pp. 333–8, with portrait. H. H. Farmer in *D.N.B.*, *1931–1940* (1949), p. 657 f.

OMAR, Mosque of. See *Dome of the Rock*.

OMBRELLINO. In the W. Church the small umbrella-like canopy of white silk carried over the Blessed Sacrament when it is moved informally from one place to another.

OMOPHORION.

OMOPHORION. The long scarf, originally of wool and now a piece of embroidered white silk or velvet, about 10 inches wide, worn in the E. Church by Bishops round the shoulder and falling loose towards the ground. It corresponds to the *pallium in the Latin Church. It is worn at the Liturgy. There are two forms, a larger one worn until the end of the Epistle (when it is laid aside as a sign of self-effacement for the reading of the Gospel) and a shorter one from the *Cherubicon until the end of the service.

Braun, L.G., pp. 664–74.

ONEIDA COMMUNITY, The.

ONEIDA COMMUNITY, The. A Christian communist society established in 1848 at Oneida, Madison County, N.Y., by John Noyes (1811–86). The body were also known as the **Perfectionists**, from their insistence that true sinlessness could be realized though communion with Christ. They also maintained that marriage was not a binding contract between husband and wife, but an arrangement under the control of the community. At first their activities were mainly agricultural, but later they included industry and the Community became a very prosperous body. In 1881 it was formed into a joint-stock company.

J. H. Noyes, *History of American Socialisms* (1870), pp. 614–45; C. Nordhoff, *The Communistic Societies of the United States* (1875), pp. 257–301; A. Estlake, *The Oneida Community* (1900); W. A. Hinds, *American Communities* (Oneida, N.Y., 1878), pp. 117–41 and 170 f.; R. A. Parker, *Yankee Saint. John Humphrey Noyes and the Oneida Community* (1935).

ONESIMUS, St.

ONESIMUS, St. The Phrygian slave on whose behalf St. *Paul wrote his Ep. to *Philemon. St. Paul perhaps plays on his name, which means 'profitable', in Philem. ver. 11 ('which in time past was to thee unprofitable, ἄχρηστον, but now profitable, εὔχρηστον, to thee and to me'). Acc. to tradition, he suffered martyrdom. Feast day, 16 Feb.

W. *Lock in *H.D.B.*, iii (1900), p. 622. The NT Onesimus has often been identified with the Onesimus, Bp. of Ephesus, mentioned in *Ignatius, *Ad. Eph.*, i, 3; but the name is too common to make this more than a conjecture.

ONTOLOGICAL ARGUMENT, The.

ONTOLOGICAL ARGUMENT, The. The *a priori* argument for the Being of God on the ground that the existence of the idea of God necessarily involves the objective existence of God. It was first elaborated by St. *Anselm, who urged that since by the very notion of God we mean 'that than which nothing greater can be conceived' (*id quo nihil majus cogitari possit*), if we were to suppose that God did not exist we should be involved in contradiction, since we could at once conceive of an entity greater than a non-existing God, namely a God who existed. The argument was criticized by St. *Thomas Aquinas, and also by I. *Kant, on the ground that existence is not a predicate. It has found modern defenders in R. *Descartes, G. W. F. *Hegel and C. C. J. *Webb.

The subject regularly finds a place in philosophical discussions of Christian apologetics, as well as in works on the philosophers mentioned above. Anselm's classical formulation of the argument is to be found in his *Proslogion* (PL,

clviii, 223–42); Eng. tr. in *The Devotions of Saint Anselm* ed. C. C. J. Webb (London, 1903), pp. 3–46, with note on the argument, pp. 46–53. Good discussion also in C. C. J. Webb, *Problems in the Relations of God and Man* (1911), pp. 173–88. A. Koyré, *L'Idée de Dieu dans la philosophie de St. Anselme* (1923), passim. E. *Caird, 'Anselm's Argument for the Being of God' in *J.T.S.*, i (1899–1900), pp. 23–39. L. Pelloux in *E.C.*, ix (1952), col. 145 f., s.v. 'Ontologico, Argomento'.

ONTOLOGISM.

ONTOLOGISM. A philosophical system favoured by certain Catholic philosophers, chiefly in Italy and France, during the 19th cent. The name first appears in the *Introduzione allo studio della filosofia* (1840) of the Italian statesman V. *Gioberti, who, with A. *Rosmini, may be regarded as the principal exponent of the system. Ontologism claims descent from *Plato and *Augustine, and positions akin to those of the ontologists are common to the whole Augustinian tradition of philosophers (e.g. St. *Anselm, R. *Descartes N. *Malebranche). In reaction from the sceptical trend of post-Kantian speculation, the ontologists asserted that God Himself is the guarantee of the validity of human ideas; that all human knowledge, itself a mode of truth, implies an immediate intuition of uncreated Truth; and that the idea of being, which is the first and simplest idea of all, is an immediate perception of absolute Being. A set of seven 'Errores Ontologistarum' was condemned by the *Inquisition on 18 Sept. 1861.

The condemned propositions are repr. in Denz.–Bann. (ed. 17, Freiburg i.Br., 1928), p. 447 (Nos. 1659–65). G. M. Sauvage in *C.E.*, xi (1911), p. 259 f., s.v.; A. Fonck in *D.T.C.*, xi (pt. 1; 1931), cols. 1000–61, s.v. 'Ontologisme', with full bibl.; L. Pelloux in *E.C.*, ix (1952), cols. 146–50, s.v. 'Ontologismo'. See also bibl. to *Gioberti, V.*, and *Rosmini-Serbati, A.*

ONTOLOGY

ONTOLOGY (from Gk. τὸ ὄν, stem ὀντ-, 'that which is'; λόγος, 'discourse'). The branch of metaphysics which deals with being in general as distinct from being-such-and-such. It is closely connected with the theory of knowledge (epistemology), and also, if we may assume real things exist independently of the mind which knows them, contrasted with it. The relation of sensation to the object perceived, and the forms of unity of being, are the object of ontological studies. The repudiation of 'ontological thinking' (as illustrated by the famous *Ontological Argument) is general among most modern philosophers, notably among the disciples of I. *Kant and recent empiricists.

OPHITES.

OPHITES. An early sect of *Gnostics whose opposition to the God of the OT led them to glorify his opponent, the serpent (Gk. ὄφις) as the Liberator and Illuminator of mankind. They held the Fall to be a progress from ignorance to knowledge and a positive advantage to mankind. The *Naassenes were a branch of the Ophites, and similar doctrines were taught by the 'Cainites' and 'Sethites'.

R. A. *Lipsius, 'Ueber die ophitischen Systeme' in *Zeitschrift für wissenschaftliche Theologie*, vi (1863), pp. 410–457. A. Hönig, *Die Ophiten* (1889). G. *Salmon in *D.C.B.*, iv (1887), pp. 80–8, s.v. É. Amann in *D.T.C.*, xi (pt. 1; 1931), cols. 1063–75, s.v. See also bibl. to *Gnosticism.

OPTATUS, St. (*fl.* 370), Bp. of Milevis in N. Africa. Nothing is known of him save his treatise 'Against Parmenian the Donatist' (Bp. of Carthage), of which Books I–VI appeared about 367, and a revision, with Book VII, about 385. Book I relates the origins of *Donatism and II–VI argue that the Donatist sect cannot be the One, Holy Catholic Church. The argument turns mainly on the lack of 'catholicity' among the Donatists, but Optatus also attacks their claim to 'holiness'. Book III has some treatment of the problem of Church and state; V discusses baptism; and VII offers repentant Donatists readmission to the Church. An appendix ('dossier') of important historical documents has deservedly received much attention from modern scholars. Optatus's telling arguments formed the starting-point for St. *Augustine's developed refutation of Donatism. Feast day, 4 June.

Editio princeps by J. *Cochlaeus (Mainz, 1549; based on a single indifferent MS.). Best of earlier edd. by L. E. P. *Dupin (Paris, 1700); repr. in J. P. Migne, *PL*, xi, 759–1556. Crit. ed. by C. Ziwsa (C.S.E.L., lvi; 1893). Eng. tr. with introd. and notes by O. R. Vassall-Phillips, C.SS.R. (London, 1917). Bardenhewer, iii, 491–4; Altaner (ed. 1951), p. 324 f. H. W. Phillott in *D.C.B.*, iv (1887), pp. 90–3, s.v.; E. Amann in *D.T.C.*, xi (pt. i; 1931), cols. 1077–84, s.v. 'Optat de Milève'; A. Pincherle in *E.C.*, ix (1952), cols. 449–51, s.v. 'Ottato di Milevi'.
On the 'dossier', see also D. Völter, *Der Ursprung des Donatismus* (1883); O. Seeck, 'Urkundenfälschungen des 4. Jahrhunderts. I. Das Urkundenbuch des Optatus' in *Z.K.G.*, xxx (1909), pp. 181–227; L. *Duchesne, 'Le Dossier du donatisme' in *Mélanges d'Archéologie et d'Histoire publiés par l'École française de Rome*, x (1890), pp. 589–650; N. H. Baynes, 'Optatus' in *J.T.S.*, xxvi (1925), pp. 37–44 and 404–6. C. H. *Turner, 'Adversaria Critica: Notes on the Anti-Donatist Dossier and on Optatus, Books I, II', ib., xxvii (1926), pp. 283–96.
See also bibl. to *Donatism*.

OPTION. The right formerly possessed by an archbishop when about to consecrate a bishop of choosing within the latter's see some benefice to which he could act as patron at the next vacancy. The word is also used of the right of members of certain monastic chapters to secure at choice a particular benefice or title. *Cardinals have such an option on the *title they assume.

OPUS DEI (Lat., 'the work of God'). An old *Benedictine designation of the Divine *Office, to express the belief that this, the monk's special duty of prayer, is his first responsibility to God.

OPUS OPERATUM. See *Ex opere operato*.

ORACLES, Sibylline. See *Sibylline Oracles*.

ORANGE, Councils of. Two synods held at Orange ('Arausio') in the south of France in 441 and 529 respectively. The former, which took place under the presidency of St. *Hilary of Arles, issued 30 canons, which deal mainly with disciplinary matters. The latter is of great importance for its 25 dogmatic

capitula. These *capitula* upheld many of St. Augustine's doctrines on the nature of grace as against the *Semi-Pelagianism then being advocated by *Faustus of Riez, though it repudiated any predestination of man to evil. Later these decrees were confirmed by Pope Boniface II (531).

On the Council of 441, Hardouin, i, cols. 1783–8; Mansi, vi (1761), cols. 433–52. Hefele–Leclercq, ii (pt. i; 1908), pp. 430–54, with bibl. reff. See also bibl. to *Hilary of Arles*.
On the Council of 529, Hardouin, ii, cols. 1097–104; Mansi, viii (1762), cols. 711–24; 'capitula' also ed. A. *Hahn, *Bibliothek der Symbole und Glaubensregeln der alten Kirche* (ed. 3 by G. L. Hahn; 1897), pp. 220–7 (par. 174), and ed. F. *Maassen in *M.G.H.*, Legum Sectio III, Concilia, i (1893), pp. 44–54. J. Ernst, 'Zur Erklärung des 22. Kanons von Orange' in *Z.K.T.*, xix (1895), pp. 177–85. M. Cappuyns, O.S.B., 'L'Origine des "Capitula" d'Orange 529' in *R.T.A.M.*, vi (1939), pp. 121–42. G. Fritz in *D.T.C.*, xi (pt. i; 1931), cols. 1087–103, s.v. 'Orange (Deuxième Concile de)'.

ORANGISM. The movement defending the cause of Protestantism in Ireland, maintained by the Orange Association (founded, 1795). The word Orange in this connexion probably derives directly or mediately from King William 'of Orange' (i.e. William III), and thus ultimately from the town of Orange in the South of France (cf. previous entry). Members of the Orange Association are known as Orangemen.

ORARION (Gk. ὡράριον). In the E. Church, the deacon's stole. It is a narrow band of silk, worn over the left shoulder, and hangs straight down back and front. While reciting prayers, the deacon holds it in his hand. At the time of Communion, it is crossed round the body.

ORATE, FRATRES (Lat. 'pray, brethren'). The opening words and hence the name of the sentence addressed by the celebrant to the people at *Mass, after the *Offertory and before the *Secret. It asks the prayers of the people before the *Canon, and with the response emphasises the unity of the congregation with the priest in the offering of the Sacrifice. The formula seems to have originated in Italy in the 11th cent.

Jungmann, *M.S.* (1949), ii, 99–108; Eng. tr., ii, 82–90.

ORATORIANS. (1) THE ORATORY OF ST. PHILIP NERI. This, the original 'Oratory', grew out of the community of priests that had gathered round the saint (1564), the name being prob. derived from the oratory at S. Girolamo, Rome, where they held their 'Exercises'. In 1575 they were erected into a congregation, and in 1612 their constitutions were sanctioned by *Paul V. The congregation spread quickly through Italy, France, and Spain. Though almost destroyed by the revolutions of the 18th and early 19th cents., they have revived in many countries. J. H. *Newman introduced them into England, founding the Oratory at Old Oscott in 1847 and that in London two years later, which moved to its present site in Kensington in 1854.

St. Philip's Oratory is a congregation of secular priests living in community without vows, and supporting themselves by their private means. Each house is independent and elects its superior for three years. There is no central organization. The chief task of the Oratorians is to lead men to God by prayer, popular preaching—they have a daily evening service with sermon in all their churches—and the Sacraments; and there is always a priest in the confessional. In conformity with the intentions of their founder, they lay great stress on attractive services and esp. on good music; the modern 'oratorio' grew out of the *laudi spirituali* sung in their devotional exercises, of which many were composed by *Palestrina, one of the saint's penitents. The congregation has produced a number of scholars, among whom C. *Baronius and J. D. *Mansi are the best known.

(2) THE FRENCH ORATORY was founded in 1611 by P. de *Bérulle at Paris, and approved by Papal bull under the name of the 'Oratoire de Jésus-Christ' in 1613. It spread quickly through France and other European countries, esp. the Netherlands. Like the institute of St. Philip, it was intended for the sanctification of secular priests and for the rehabilitation of the priestly office among the laity. Though formed on the Italian model, the French Oratory differs mainly in that it is a centralized organization governed by a Superior-General. One of its chief activities was the training of priests in *seminaries, run on the lines laid down by the Council of *Trent. The popularity of the French Oratory was temporarily eclipsed by the *Jansenist propensities of some of its members, esp. the two Superior-Generals, Père A. L. de Sainte-Marthe (1672–96) and Père de La Tour (1696–1733). The Oratory was dissolved in the French Revolution, but re-established in 1852 by L. P. Pététot and A. J. A. *Gratry as 'Oratoire de Jésus-Christ et de Marie Immaculée'.

The Oratorians, who have been excellent educationists and directors, have contributed much to the furtherance of popular devotion in France. Despite the Jansenist troubles, the Christ-centred spirituality of their founder, Bérulle, has been one of the chief characteristics of the congregation. Many of its members have been distinguished for their holiness and scholarship, e.g. C. de *Condren, N. *Malebranche, J. B. *Massillon, and J. *Morinus. St. John *Eudes, though he later left the Oratory to found his own congregations, was deeply imbued with the Oratorian spirit.

(1) The principal material for the early history of the order is contained in the lives of St. Philip Neri, cited s.v. C. A. Kneller, 'Das Oratorium des hl. Philipp Neri und das musikalische Oratorium' in *Z.K.T.*, xli (1917), pp. 246–82, with reff. A. George, *L'Oratoire* ('Les Grandes Ordres monastiques', 1928), pp. 1–33, with bibl. p. 231 f. Heimbucher, ii, 562–6. H. Bowden in *C.E.*, xi (1911), pp. 272–4, s.v. 'Oratory of Saint Philip Neri'. See also bibl. to foll. entry.

(2) L. Batterel (d. 1749), *Mémoires domestiques pour servir à l'histoire de l'Oratoire* (ed. A. M. P. Ingold–E. Bonnardet, 'Documents pour servir à l'histoire religieuse des XVIIᵉ et XVIIIᵉ siècles', 5 vols., 1902–11). M. Leherpeur, *L'Oratoire de France* (1926); A. George, *op. cit.*, pp. 34–230, with bibl. pp. 232–7. A. [L. A.] Perraud, *L'Oratoire de France au XVIIᵉ et au XIXᵉ siècle* (1865). A. M. P. Ingold, *L'Oratoire et la Révolution* (1883), and other works of this author. Id., *Essai de bibliographie oratorienne* (2 vols., 1880–2). *Bibliothèque oratorienne* (13 vols., Paris, 1880–92). Bremond, iii (1921), esp. ch. 3, 'L'Oratoire', pp. 155–221. Heimbucher, ii, 566–71. A. M. P. Ingold in *C.E.*, xi (1911), p. 274 f., s.v.; A. Molien in *D.T.C.*, xi (pt. 1; 1931), cols. 1104–38, s.v. 'Oratoire des Jésus (Congrégation de l'). See also bibl. to *Bérulle, P. de*, and *Gratry, A. J. A.*

ORATORIO. The musical setting of a religious libretto for chorus, orchestra (or other accompaniment), and soloists, without (in modern practice) the use of dramatic action, scenery, or dresses, though these adjuncts were sometimes employed until *c.* 1730. Oratorio apparently derives from the dramatic services of St. *Philip Neri (d. 1595) at the *Oratory in Rome. The first known oratorio in the present sense was performed at Santa Maria in Vallicella in Rome in 1600. The most celebrated oratorios of the 18th cent. are those of G. F. *Handel, esp. his *Saul* (1738), *Israel in Egypt* (1739), *Samson* (1741), and *Messiah* (1742). In the 19th cent. the oratorio reached its greatest popularity, notably in England, but with few exceptions, such as F. Mendelssohn's *St. Paul* (1836) and *Elijah* (1846), the compositions of the period were of little value. In more recent times England alone has maintained a considerable interest in oratorio, largely through the influence of annual musical festivals and local amateur choral societies. Among the more significant modern works are Sir E. *Elgar's *Dream of *Gerontius* (1900) and *Apostles* (1903) and A. Honegger's *King David* (1921).

The standard general work is A. Schering, *Geschichte des Oratoriums* (Kleine Handbücher der Musikgeschichte nach Gattungen, iii; 1911). Shorter study by F. Raugel, *L'Oratorio* (Paris, 1948). W. S. Rockstro–E. Walker in *Grove's Dictionary of Music and Musicians* (ed. 5 by E. Blom), vi (1954), pp. 247–62, s.v., with bibl. D. F. Tovey in *E.B.* (ed. 11), xx (1911), pp. 161–4, s.v.

ORATORY (Lat. *oratorium*, 'place of prayer'). The term, used in antiquity for both churches and private chapels, has come to be restricted since the Middle Ages to places of worship other than the parish church. Their origin probably goes back to the chapels built over the tombs of the martyrs in early times. Their use became more frequent in the early Middle Ages, when churches tended to be restricted to cities, and places of worship were needed for the country districts.

For the legal position of oratories in the C of E see *Private Chapels Act* (1871). In the RC Church their status has been regulated by Canon Law (*CIC*, 1188–96). This distinguishes three kinds of oratories, public, semi-public, and private. Public oratories, which may be erected for communities as well as for private individuals, are distinguished from the other two by the fact that all the faithful have right of access at least during the times of Divine Service. Like churches, they are canonically erected by the bishop and consecrated or blessed; all sacred functions, such as *High and *Low Masses, *Benediction services, etc., may be performed in them. Semi-public oratories, on the other hand, which may be erected for religious communities or groups of lay people, are not freely accessible; such are, e.g., many convent chapels. The permission of the Ordinary is required for their erection, and for the most part all religious functions may be performed in them as in public oratories, but they are without certain privileges such as the right to a title, bells, burials, etc. Private oratories are rooms set apart for devotional purposes in private houses; no permission is required for their erection, but Mass may not be celebrated in them except on particular occasions with the permission of the Ordinary. For habitual celebration a Papal Indult is required, but it usually covers only one Low Mass a day except for the great feasts. The Blessed Sacrament may be reserved only if an Apostolic Indult has been granted.

ORATORY, The. The name is used absolutely of the *Oratorians (q.v.) or 'Congregation of the Oratory'. It is also often applied to churches belonging to the Congregation, e.g. the Brompton Oratory, London.

ORDEALS (Lat. *judicium Dei*). A method of judicial trial among Teutonic peoples in which the innocence of the accused person was determined by the results of some physical test to which he was submitted. The result was regarded as the immediate judgement of God. Such ordeals were pre-Christian in origin; but in Christian times they were sanctioned by the Church and conducted under the direction of the clergy. There were four kinds of Ordeal in Anglo-Saxon law. (1) That of hot iron, in which the accused carried a ball of hot iron in his hand for nine steps. (2) That of hot water, in which he plunged his arm into a cauldron either to the wrist or to the elbow, according to the gravity of the charge. After both of these the member was bound up and examined at the end of three days by the priest; and if the wound was festering, the man was held guilty. (3) That of cold water into which the man was thrown, his innocence being revealed by his sinking. And (4) that of the morsel, in which the accused was given a piece of bread or cheese an ounce in weight to swallow. If it stuck in his throat, he was found guilty. There was also the Ordeal by battle, though this was not used by the Anglo-Saxons, and that of walking blindfold between red-hot ploughshares. The Ordeal always took place after Mass, at which the accused had communicated. In England, the Ordeal began to be disused after the Norman Conquest, and eventually disappeared after the Fourth *Lateran Council (1215) had forbidden clergy to take part in the practice.

Collection of primary material ed. P. Browe, S.J., *De Ordaliis* (Pontificia Universitas Gregoriana. Textus et Documenta in Usum Exercitationum et Praelectionum Academicarum, Series Theologica, ii and iv; 1932–3). H. C. Lea, *Superstition and Force* (Philadelphia, 1866; ed. 3, 1876), pp. 217–370 of ed. 3. F. Paletta, *Le ordalie.* Studio di storia del diritto e scienze del diritto comparato (R. Università di Torino. Istituto di Esercitazioni nelle Scienze Giuridico-Politiche, Memoria, vii; 1890). E. Vacandard, 'L'Église et les ordalies au XIIᵉ siècle' in *R.Q.H.*, liii (1893), pp. 185–200; id., *Études de critique et d'histoire religieuse*, Sér. i (1905), pp. 191–215 ('L'Église et les ordalies'). A. Esmein, *Les Ordalies dans l'Église gallicane au IXᵉ siècle* (1898). R. Köstler, 'Der Anteil des Christentums an den Ordalien' in *Zeitschrift der Savigny-Stiftung für Rechtsgeschichte*, xlvi (Kan. Abt., ii; 1912), pp. 208–48; G. Schreiber, 'Kirchliches Abgabenwesen an französischen Eigenkirchen aus Anlass von Ordalien (Oblationes Campionum, Oblationes Pugilum, Oblationes Bellorum, Oblationes Iudiciorum). Zugleich ein Beitrag zur gregorianisch-kluniazensischen Reform und zur Geschichte und Liturgik der Traditionsnotizen', ib., xlix (Kan. Abt., v; 1915), pp. 414–83. S. Grelewski, *La Réaction contre les ordalies en France depuis le IXᵉ siècle jusqu'au décret de Gratien* (Strassburg thesis, 1924). P. Fournier, 'Quelques Observations sur l'histoire des ordalies au moyen-âge' in *Mélanges Gustave Glotz*, ii (1932), pp. 367–76. J. P. Kirsch in *C.E.*, xi (1911), pp. 276–8, s.v.; A. E. Crawley and others in *H.E.R.E.*, ix (1917), pp. 507–33, s.v., esp. P. Vinogradoff, pp. 519–21, s.v. 'Ordeal (Christian)'. A. Michel in *D.T.C.*, xi (pt. 1; 1932), cols. 1139–52, s.v. 'Ordalies'; R. Hindringer in *L.Th.K.*, iv (1932), cols. 614–16, s.v. 'Gottesurteile', with bibl.; H. *Leclercq, O.S.B., in *D.A.C.L.*, xii (pt. 2; 1936), cols. 2377–90, s.v. 'Ordalie', also with bibl.

ORDER OF THE COMMUNION, The. See *Communion, The Order of the.*

ORDER OF PREACHERS. See *Dominican Order.*

ORDERS, Anglican. See *Anglican Ordinations.*

ORDERS, Holy. See *Holy Orders.*

ORDERS, Minor. See *Minor Orders.*

ORDERS, Religious. See *Religious Orders.*

ORDERS AND ORDINATION.
1. *Origins.* The Ministry of the Christian Church traces its beginnings to the Lord's commissioning of the Twelve (Mt. 10. 1–5, Mk. 3. 13–19, Lk. 6. 12–18) and the Seventy (Lk. 10. 1) to the work of the kingdom. This Ministry, so far from coming to an end at His death, received a new power and wider responsibilities after Pentecost (Acts 2. 1–13) when the Twelve assumed direction of the primitive community (Acts 2. 14, 3. 1–10, 4. 23–31, etc.). From the first its external form was largely influenced by Jewish synagogual practice, which had itself been moulded by the OT, but its development was necessarily conditioned also by the practical needs of the nascent Church. The view that its structure followed secular and pagan models in the contemporary Hellenistic world (E. *Hatch) no longer finds much favour. In the Apostolic band the place of leadership was assumed by St. *Peter (Acts 1. 15, 2. 37, 4. 8, 5. 8, 10. 1–11, 18, 15. 7; cf. Mt. 16. 16–18), and at the outset

an attempt was made to preserve the original number by the election of *Matthias to remedy the defection of *Judas (Acts 1. 15–26).

II. *Appointment of Ministers in the NT.* The chief NT passages in which a reference to Ordination may be discovered are: (1) The appointment of the Seven by the laying on of hands (Acts 6). (2) The commissioning of Barnabas and Saul with laying on of hands and prayer by the prophets and teachers at Antioch (Acts 13. 1–3). (3) The mention of 'bishops' (ἐπίσκοποι) by St. Paul in his speech at Miletus as men whom 'the Holy Ghost had appointed to tend the Church of God' (Acts 20. 28). (4) St. Paul's admonition to *Timothy not to neglect the gift (χάρισμα) bestowed on him by prophecy with the laying on of the hands of the presbytery (1 Tim. 4. 14) and 'to stir up the gift which was in him through the laying on of his [St. Paul's] hands' (2 Tim. 1. 6). (5) St. Paul's warning to Timothy not to lay hands hastily on anyone (1 Tim. 5. 22). In such passages the act of Ordination would seem to be conceived as a function of the whole Church, acting through its existing Ministers; the rite is considered to convey to the candidate the gifts of the Spirit in such measure as he needs them for his new office and work.

III. *Gradation in the Ministry.* In the NT we discover several grades of ministry co-existing (1 Cor. 12. 28, Eph. 4. 11). A broad distinction seems to lie between a 'missionary, (also termed by modern scholars 'itinerant' 'apostolic', and 'charismatic', but the last term may be misleading) and a 'local' or 'settled' ministry. The former is represented by the 'Apostles' (a term used to cover more than the Twelve, Acts 14. 14, Rom. 6. 7, Gal. 1. 19) and also the '*Prophets' (q.v.; cf. *Didache 10. 7 and 13. 1–7), the latter by Bishops (1 Tim. 3. 2, Tit. 1. 7), 'Presbyters' (Acts 11. 30, 14. 23, 1 Tim. 5. 17, Jas. 5. 14), and 'Deacons' (Phil. 1. 1, 1 Tim. 3. 8). This second group in the NT is the nucleus of the traditional threefold ministry, though it should be observed that in the NT the terms 'Bishop' and 'Presbyter' seem often interchangeable (contested, however, by A. M. Farrer and others). Other titles of ministers found in the NT are 'pastors', 'teachers', 'evangelists'.

By the middle of the 3rd cent. considerably more differentiation had come about. At Rome under Pope *Cornelius (251–3) there were, besides the Bishop, forty-six Presbyters, seven Deacons, seven Sub-deacons, forty-two Acolytes and fifty-two Exorcists, Readers and Door-keepers (*Eusebius, *HE*, VI, xliii, 11). But it was long before uniformity was reached. The *Statuta Ecclesiae Antiqua (prob. Gallic, 5th cent.) has nine distinct orders; St. *John of Damascus has five; *Innocent III has six. By the later Middle Ages it was the prevalent view that there were seven orders, but there were different methods of reckoning, largely through contending theories on the relation of the priesthood and the episcopate. For St. *Thomas, who held that the ultimate purpose of Holy Order lay in its relation to the Eucharist, the priesthood was the highest grade, since

the priest possessed the power of consecrating the Sacrament; and this appears to be the view officially countenanced by the Council of *Trent. A distinction had come to be drawn, esp. in the W. between the '*Major Orders' (Bishop, Priest, Deacon, Sub-deacon) and the *Minor Orders (Acolytes, Exorcists, Readers, Door-keepers). The distinction in current speech between 'consecration' to the episcopate and 'ordination' to the other Orders was unknown in early times.

IV. *Order as a Sacrament.* Acc. to traditional Catholic theology the gift of Order is a Sacrament. The Council of Trent (Sess. xxii) defines it as a Sacrament instituted by Christ (can. 3) and as conveying the Holy Ghost (can. 4). Like Baptism Order is held to impart an indelible *character. Hence a cleric if degraded does not lose the gift of Orders and on restoration is not 're-ordained'; and though the civil law may treat a cleric who has executed a deed of relinquishment under the Clerical Disabilities Act of 1870 as a layman, from the standpoint of the Church he remains a priest or deacon. But where there is grave doubt (e.g. through loss of records) whether ordination has been validly administered, it may be, and sometimes is, repeated 'conditionally'.

Despite the various grades in the ministry it is agreed that there is but a single Sacrament of Orders. It is widely denied, however, that the orders lower than the diaconate can be reckoned a Sacrament. In the Middle Ages they were commonly so regarded (St. Thomas, *S.T.*, Suppl. 94. qu. 7, art. 3); but RC theologians now reject this view on the ground that they are of ecclesiastical (and not Divine) institution.

In the *Thirty-Nine Articles (art. 25) Orders is included among 'the five commonly called Sacraments' which 'are not to be counted for Sacraments of the Gospel'. In the Protestant Churches the Sacramental nature of Orders is commonly denied.

V. *The Recipient of Orders.* The traditional view is that only a baptized and confirmed male person can be validly ordained. The candidate must be of good moral character and convinced that he has a Divine call ('vocation') to the office. For the Ordination to be regular the candidate must also be of due age (in the C of E 24 years for the priesthood, 30 years for the episcopate; see *Age, Canonical*) and not be excommunicate; and (a matter esp. stressed by RC theologians) the *interstices must have been duly observed. The candidate also generally needs a '*title' to the cure of souls; in the C of E the principal exception is the tenure of Fellowships at Colleges at Oxford and Cambridge. By 28 & 29 Vict., cap. 122, an ordinand in the C of E is further required to make and subscribe a 'Declaration of Assent' to the Thirty-Nine Articles, to the BCP and to the Ordination Service, and to make Oaths of Allegiance to the Sovereign and of canonical obedience to the Bishop. The duties of the respective offices in the Anglican ministry are well set out in the

*Ordinal. In the RC Church, the specific obligations incurred by the reception of Major Orders include, acc. to W. discipline, celibacy (q.v.) and the recitation of the Divine Office (q.v.).

VI. *The Minister of Orders.* Traditional theology also holds that the Sacrament of Orders can be validly conferred only by a duly consecrated Bishop, acting as the minister of Christ and the successor of the Apostles. The episcopate is thus held to create a historical link between the Church of Apostolic times and that of to-day and is both the means and assurance of the continuity of office and of the transmission of grace (see *Apostolic Succession*); and on these grounds the episcopate is held to be of the *esse* of the Church. The privilege of conferring minor orders, which has occasionally been conceded to Abbots and other Priests, is justified on the ground that these Orders are not Sacraments (cf. § IV above).

There is, however, a small body of evidence that in the early Church ordination was occasionally conferred by clerics other than Bishops. St. *Jerome asserts that down to the middle of the 3rd cent. the Bp. of Alexandria was elected and consecrated by the presbyters of the city (*Ep.* 146); the 13th can. of *Ancyra may provide for ordination by presbyters (but the text is disputed); and it was sometimes allowed that suffering for the faith in time of persecution was the equivalent of ordination (e.g. St. *Hippolytus, *Ap. Trad.* x. 1).

Since the purpose of Ordination is to qualify a man for office in the Church, it might seem that outside the Church Orders could not be given. Such was the usual view of the early Church, and it is still that held in the East. But since the time of St. *Augustine, whose influence here was paramount, it has been generally maintained in the W. that, even when in heresy or schism, a Bishop can validly ordain (as he can validly baptize and validly celebrate the Eucharist). Hence the RC Church does not 're-ordain' Bishops and Priests from the Orthodox Church should they be received into communion with the Pope, but accepts their previous Ordination as valid. Similarly Priests of the RC Church who join the C of E are not re-ordained, though for certain technical reasons (see *Anglican Ordinations*) the RC Church does not recognize Ordinations conferred in the C of E.

VII. *Rites of Ordination.* The earliest known rite of Ordination is that in the *Apostolic Tradition* of Hippolytus (*c.* 215); and from the 4th cent. several survive, e.g. the Liturgy of St. *Serapion, and those in the *Apostolic Constitutions* and the *Statuta Ecclesiae Antiqua* (see *Church Orders*). Traditionally Ordination has always taken place in the context of the Eucharist, but for long, esp. in the E., the rite continued very simple. In the W. it became the custom for the newly ordained presbyters to *concelebrate with the ordaining Bishop. Gradually elaborations were introduced esp. to signify the ordinand's new office. The Gospels were delivered to the Deacon (in earlier times to the Reader), while by the later Middle Ages the delivery of the Paten and Chalice with the elements prepared for the Mass to candidates for the priesthood had become sufficiently established for it to be regarded as the essence ('matter') of the rite (see *Instruments, Tradition of the*).

It became usual both in E. and W. for Bishops to be consecrated on a Sunday, e.g. the BCP orders that the rite is 'always to be performed upon some Sunday or Holy-day'. In the W. the ordination of Priests and Deacons became customary at the *Ember (esp. December) seasons; and this has remained the practice of the C of E though the rule of can. 31 (confining all Ordinations to the Sunday following the Ember Weeks) is no longer rigidly observed. The BCP provides special prayers for daily use in the Ember Weeks on behalf of those to be admitted to Orders.

J. *Morin, Cong. Orat., *De Sacris Ecclesiae Ordinationibus* (Paris, 1655); J. B. *Lightfoot, *St. Paul's Epistle to the Philippians* (1868), pp. 179–267 ('The Christian Ministry'); E. *Hatch, *The Organization of the Early Christian Churches* (*Bampton Lectures for 1880; 1880); C. *Gore, *The Church and the Ministry* (1888; new ed. by C. H. *Turner, 1919); F. J. A. *Hort, *The Christian Ecclesia* (1897); R. C. *Moberly, *Ministerial Priesthood* (1897); W. *Sanday, *The Conception of Priesthood in the Early Church and in the Church of England* (1898); J. *Wordsworth, *The Ministry of Grace* (1900); T. M. *Lindsay, *The Church and the Ministry in the Early Centuries* (1903); A. R. Whitham, *Holy Orders* (1910); D. *Stone, *Episcopacy and Valid Orders in the Primitive Church* (1910); H. B. *Swete, *Essays on the Early History of the Church and the Ministry* (1918; esp. essay on 'Apostolic Succession' by C. H. Turner). J. Tixeront, *L'Ordre et les ordinations* (1924); B. H. *Streeter, *The Primitive Church studied with special reference to the Origins of the Christian Ministry* (1939). J. P. Whitney, *The Episcopate and the Reformation* (1917). J. N. Ainslie, *The Doctrines of Ministerial Order in the Reformed Churches of the 16th and 17th Centuries* (1940). A. C. *Headlam, *The Doctrine of the Church and Christian Reunion* (Bampton Lectures for 1920; 1920). J. W. Hunkin, *Episcopal Ordination and Confirmation in Relation to Inter-Communion and Reunion* (1929); K. D. Mackenzie, *The Case for Episcopacy* (1929); C. Jenkins–K. D. Mackenzie (edd.), *Episcopacy, Ancient and Modern* (1930); R. Dunkerley (ed.), *The Ministry and the Sacraments* (1946); S. Neill, *The Ministry of the Church* (1947); T. W. Manson, *The Church's Ministry* (1948); K. E. *Kirk (ed.), *The Apostolic Ministry* (1946); E. R. Fairweather, *Episcopacy and Reunion* (Toronto, 1952; London, 1953); K. M. Carey (ed.), *The Historic Episcopacy in the Fullness of the Church* (1954). N. Sykes, *Old Priest and New Presbyter.* The Anglican Attitude to Episcopacy, Presbyterianism and Papacy since the Reformation (1956). See also bibl. to art. *Bishop.*

ORDINAL (Lat. *ordinale*). (1) In the Middle Ages, a manual to acquaint the priest with the Office to be recited in acc. with variations in the ecclesiastical year.

(2) In the C of E, the 'Form and Manner of Making, Ordaining and Consecrating of Bishops, Priests and Deacons according to the Order of the Church of England'. This use of the word dates only from *c.* 1600. There have been four English Ordinals. (i) The first was published in March 1550 ('1549'). It was the work of six Bishops and six other scholars, appointed by an Order in Council of 31 Jan. 1550, as decreed by Act of Parliament (3 & 4 Edw. VI, c. 12). Though bound up with copies of the BCP, neither this nor the later Ordinals is properly a part of the Book. It

was modelled on the rite in the medieval *Sarum *Pontifical. Ordination was to take place on a Sunday or Holy Day. The Exhortation and Examination in the Ordering of Priests were mainly based on a draft by M. *Bucer. At the imposition of hands the formula was 'Receive the Holy Ghost. Whose sins thou dost forgive they are forgiven; whose sins thou dost retain they are retained. And be thou a faithful dispenser of the Word of God and of His Holy Sacraments. In the Name of the Father and of the Son and of the Holy Ghost. Amen'; and at the delivery of the Bible and the chalice with the bread, 'Take thou authority to preach the Word of God and to minister the Holy Sacraments in this congregation'. In the Consecration of Bishops, the medieval ceremonies of anointing, putting on of gloves, and delivery of the ring and mitre were omitted. No provision was made for the minor orders. (ii) In 1552, the chief alterations were the omission of certain ceremonies, e.g. in the Ordering of Priests, the correction of the *Instruments. (iii) In 1559 the changes were negligible except in the wording of the Oath (now of 'the Queen's Sovereignty' instead of 'the King's Supremacy'). (iv) In 1662 some important modifications were made, notably in the Ordering of Priests, the change of the formula accompanying the imposition of hands to 'Receive the Holy Ghost *for the office and work of a priest in the Church of God, now committed unto thee by imposition of our hands*. Whose sins, etc.'

The 1550 Ordinal is printed in *The Liturgies . . . of King Edward VI* (ed. *Parker Society by J. Ketley, 1844), pp. 159–86, and in the Everyman's Library edition of the *First and Second Prayer Books of King Edward VI* (1910), pp. 291–317. F. Procter–W. H. *Frere, *A New History of the Book of Common Prayer* (1901), pp. 648–73.

ORDINARY. In canon law, an ecclesiastic in the exercise of the jurisdiction permanently and irremovably annexed to his office. Such jurisdiction extends over his rights of teaching, governing, adjudicating, and administering the Sacraments. In the RC Church the term is defined as including, besides the Pope who possesses a plenitude of immediate ordinary jurisdiction, all diocesan bishops, abbots, apostolic administrators or vicars, prelates or prefects with some territorial jurisdiction, their officials and vicars-general, and in the vacancy of a see, the vicar capitular or lawful administrator (*CIC*, 198, §§ 1–2). The meaning of the term in the BCP is not precisely determined; it may refer either to the Bishop or the Archdeacon. The parish priest may be regarded as possessing ordinary jurisdiction of an inferior kind, but he may not delegate it against the will of his superior ordinary.

ORDINARY OF THE MASS, The (Lat. *Ordo Missae*). The invariable or almost invariable part of the *Mass, as distinguished from the parts which vary with the ecclesiastical calendar, called the *Proper. It comprises the preparatory prayers, the *Kyrie, *Gloria and

*Creed, the *Preface and *Sanctus, the *Canon, *Paternoster, *Fraction and *Agnus Dei, part of the Communion and post - Communion devotions, and the *Last Gospel. The Canon, however, is sometimes distinguished from the Ordinary, the two together being termed the 'Ordinary and Canon of the Mass'.

ORDINATION. See *Orders and Ordination*.

ORDINATIONS, Anglican. See *Anglican Orders*.

ORDINES ROMANI. The ancient collections of ceremonial directions for the performance of the Roman rite and thus the ancestors of the *Caeremoniale Romanum, the *Caeremoniale Episcoporum, and the *Pontificale. The name apparently does not go back behind the 8th cent., but the earliest surviving Ordines received substantially their present form in the 6th cent. The first to be printed in modern times, the so-called 'Ordo romanus vulgatus', was edited by G. *Cassander in 1561 (Cologne) and more adequately by Melchior Hittorp in 1568 (also Cologne). This Ordo (Mabillon's Ordo II) appears to have been compiled in Gaul in the 10th cent. Far more important was the collection of fifteen Ordines published by J. *Mabillon in his *Musaeum Italicum*, vol. ii (1689). These Ordines (still distinguished by Mabillon's enumeration) are of varying dates from the 9th to the 15th cent. and of unique interest for the history of the ceremonial development of the Roman rite. Ordo I, one of the earliest and the ancestor of several others in the collection, describes the Pope's stational Mass at Rome, probably in the time of St. *Gregory (d. 604). Probably the earliest of all is Ordo VII, almost all of which is found in the *Gelasian Sacramentary.

Text of J. Mabillon repr. in J. P. Migne, *PL*, lxxxviii 851–1408. Crit. ed. by M. Andrieu, *Les Ordines Romani du haut moyen-âge* (S.S.L., xi, xxiii, xxiv, and xxviii; 1931–56), with valuable investigation of sources and interrelations, superseding all earlier work on the *Ordines*. *Ordo Romanus Primus* also ed. by E. G. C. F. Atchley, with introd., Eng. tr., and notes (L.L.F., vi; 1905). H. Thurston, S.J., in *C.E.*, xi (1911), pp. 284–8; A. Bugnini in *E.C.*, ix (1952), cols. 243–8.

ORESME, NICOLAS (*c.* 1320–82), French medieval philosopher. He studied at Paris (from 1348), and after filling several ecclesiastical offices was appointed Bp. of Lisieux in 1377. His writings, which are partly in Latin, partly in French, treat of two separate branches of knowledge, viz. economics and politics, and natural science. In the former field his book *De l'origine, nature et mutation des monnaies* exercised great influence on the development of medieval economic ideas; in the latter, in *De coelo et mundo*, he carried further *Buridan's theory of the earth's motion and met objections with arguments which partly anticipated N. *Copernicus. In other respects he was a forerunner of R. *Descartes (by laying the foundations of analytical geometry) and of G. *Galileo (in formulating the law of motion for falling bodies).

Modern edd. of his *Tractatus de Origine, Natura, Jure et Mutationibus Monetarum*, by M. L. Wolowski (Paris, 1864; Lat. and Fr. texts, together with biogr. introd.); Lat. text, with Germ. tr. by E. Schorer (Jena, 1937); of his *Livre de Éthiques d'Aristote* (a Fr. tr. made at the request of King Charles V in 1370), by A. D. Menut (New York, 1940). His Fr. tr. and comm. on Aristotle's *De Caelo et Mundo*, first publ. by A. D. Menut–A. J. Demony, C.S.B., in *Mediaeval Studies*, iii (Toronto, 1941), pp. 185–280, iv (1942), pp. 159–297, and v (1943), pp. 167–333. [L.] F. Meunier, *Essai sur la vie et les ouvrages de Nicole Oresme* (Paris thesis, 1857). E. Bridley, *La Théorie de la monnaie au XIVᵉ siècle*. Nicole Oresme (1906). E. Borchert, *Die Lehre von der Bewegung bei Nicolaus Oresme* (B.G.P.M., xxxi, Hft. 3; 1934); id., *Der Einfluss des Nominalismus auf die Christologie der Spätscholastik nach dem Traktat* De Communicatione Idiomatum *des Nicolaus Oresme* (ib., xxxv; Hftt. 4–5; 1940). G. W. Coopland, *Nicole Oresme and the Astrologers*. A Study of his *Livre de divinations* (Liverpool, 1952). Überweg, ii, 595 f. and 599 f., with bibl. p. 784. É. Amann in *D.T.C.*, xi (pt. 2; 1932), cols. 1405–10, s.v. Crit ed. of *De Moneta* by C. Johnson (Medieval Texts, 1956).

ORGANIC ARTICLES, The. The provisions of Napoleon (1802) to regulate public worship and the relations of Church and state in France. They included (1) governmental control over Papal documents entering France, and over the powers of ecclesiastical councils and synods; (2) a limited state control of seminaries and clergy, requiring *inter alia* the teaching of the *Gallican Articles; (3) state regulation of processions and clerical dress; and (4) state regulation of stipends and parish boundaries. Napoleon sought to defend this radical and sudden modification of the *Concordat (1801) on the ground that the Articles were supplementary and explanatory. The Pope objected to them from the first, and in fact the Articles were less and less enforced, though they were not finally repealed till the separation of Church and state in 1905.

The text is in C. Mirbt, *Quellen zur Geschichte des Papsttums und des römischen Katholizismus*, No. 559 (ed. 4, 1924), and J. E. C. Bodley, *The Church in France* (1906), pp. 121–34.

ORGANS. The use of an organ is recorded at *Malmesbury in the early 8th cent., and in the 10th cent. instances at *Glastonbury, *Winchester, and elsewhere are known. By the 13th cent. they were common in the larger parish churches and by the end of the Middle Ages almost universal. Their use was objected to by the more puritanically minded of the Reformers, notably E. *Grindal, and a motion in the Lower House of Canterbury Convocation on 13 Feb. 1562 for the removal of all organs from churches was defeated by a single vote. A petition of the Puritans in 1586 for the removal of cathedral organs was also unsuccessful, and organs thus survived till the middle of the 17th cent. In 1644, however, legislation for the destruction of organs and their cases was carried through, and in consequence very few pre-Commonwealth organs now exist. They were reintroduced after the Restoration (1660), among the most famous organ-builders being 'Father *Smith' and René (Renatus) Harris (?1640–?1715). In the 18th cent., barrel organs, with a limited selection of tunes, were widely used.

E. J. Hopkins–E. F. Rimbault, *The Organ, its History and Construction* (1855); W. L. Sumner, *The Organ*. Its Evolution, Principles of Construction and Use (1952). J. *Stainer,

The Organ [c. 1878]. A. M. Richardson, *Modern Organ Accompaniment* (1907). N. A. Bonavia-Hunt, *The Church Organ* (Church Music Monographs, No. 2; 1920). M. P. Conway, *Playing a Church Organ* (1949). E. Freeman, *English Organ-Cases* (1921). F. W. Thornsby, *Dictionary of Organs and Organists* (Bournemouth, 1912). *Grove's Dictionary of Music and Musicians* (ed. 5 by E. Blom), vi (1954), pp. 282–337.

ORIENS CHRISTIANUS. The title of two quite distinct publications.

(1) M. *Le Quien's work on the Eastern Church. It contains an enormous collection of geographical and historical material, arranged acc. to the four E. Patriarchates and, despite the inaccuracies incidental to a pioneer work of vast dimensions, has not been superseded. Le Quien worked on it from 1718 till his death in 1733, issuing a prospectus of the work in 1722; but it was not published till 1740, when it appeared in three folio volumes.

(2) A German periodical devoted to Oriental studies publd. at Leipzig under the direction of A. *Baumstark. It appeared in three series, viz. the Original Series, 8 vols., 1901–10; a 'Neue Serie', 14 vols., 1911–25; and the Third Series, 14 vols., 1927 ['1926']–1941. The periodical was revived on new lines, under the auspices of the Görres-Gesellschaft, and a Fourth Series publd. at Wiesbaden, 1953 ff.

On (1), H. *Leclercq, O.S.B., in *D.A.C.L.*, viii (pt. 2; 1929), cols. 2593–6, s.v. 'Le Quien'; S. Vailhé, A.A., in *C.E.*, ix (1910), p. 188, s.v. 'Le Quien'.

ORIENTATION. The construction of a church so that its longer axis runs east and west. The earliest (4th cent.) basilicas in Rome had a façade to the east and an *apse for the altar at the west, so that the celebrant at the Eucharist, standing behind the altar, faced east. The high altar of Byzantine churches, on the other hand, was placed in an eastern apse, a practice followed later esp. in England, Germany, and Spain. Elsewhere custom has been more variable. Though orientation is derived historically from a pagan habit of praying towards the sunrise, Christians have seen in its adoption symbolic reference to Christ as the Rising Sun.

H. Nissen, *Orientation*. Studien zur Geschichte der Religion (3 Hftt., 1906–10), esp. pp. 391–459 ('Das Christentum'). F. J. Doelger, *Sol Salutis*. Gebet und Gesang im christlichen Altertum mit besonderer Rücksicht auf die Ostung in Gebet und Liturgie (Liturgische Forschungen, iv–v, 1920). F. v. Duhn, 'Bemerkungen zur Orientierung von Kirchen und Gräbern' in *Archiv für Religionswissenschaft*, xix (1916–19), pp. 441–51. E. Weigand, 'Die Ostung in der frühchristlichen Architektur' in *Festschrift für Sebastian Merkle zu seinem 60. Geburtstage* (1922), pp. 370–85. T. D. Atkinson in *H.E.R.E.*, x (1918), pp. 73–88, s.v. 'Points of the Compass'. O. Rühle in *R.G.G.* (ed. 2), iv (1930), cols. 778–80, s.v.; J. Sauer in *L.Th.K.*, vii (1935), cols. 826–8, s.v. 'Ostung', with bibl.; H. *Leclercq, O.S.B., in *D.A.C.L.*, xii (pt. 2; 1936), cols. 2665–9, s.v.

ORIGEN (c. 185–c. 254), Alexandrian Biblical critic, exegete, theologian and spiritual writer. The facts of his life are recorded by *Eusebius. He was born in Egypt, probably at *Alexandria, where he received a thoroughly Christian education in the house of his parents. He studied in the *Catechetical School under *Clement. During the persecution in Alexandria in 202 when his father, Leonidas, was killed, he was prevented from seeking martyrdom only by a ruse of his mother, who hid his clothes. When peace was restored Origen took the place of his master, Clement, who had fled, as head of the school. He now began to lead a strictly ascetical life of fastings, vigils, and voluntary poverty, and, in an excess of zeal, mutilated himself, misinterpreting Mt. 19. 12 in a literal sense. In order to gain a deeper influence on his pupils he studied pagan philosophy and literature under *Ammonius Saccas. He undertook several journeys, one to Rome, where he heard a sermon of St. *Hippolytus, and one to Arabia. When, in 215, troubles broke out in Alexandria in connexion with a visit of the Emp. Caracalla, he went to Palestine, where he was asked to preach by the Bps. of *Caesarea and *Aelia. As he was only a layman, this was regarded as a breach of the Alexandrian ecclesiastical discipline, in consequence of which he was recalled by his bishop, *Demetrius. From c. 218 to 230 he devoted himself almost without interruption to literary activities. In 230 he went again to Palestine, where he was ordained priest by the same bishops who had invited him to preach on his previous visit. As a consequence Bp. Demetrius deprived him of his chair, deposed him from the priesthood, and sent him into exile, not, as later opponents asserted, because of doctrinal offences, but for the irregularity of his ordination. He found a refuge at Caesarea (231), where he established a school which soon became famous, and where he continued his literary work and devoted himself to preaching. In 250, in the persecution of *Decius, he was imprisoned and subjected to prolonged torture, which he survived only a few years.

Origen was a very fertile author. Many of his writings have perished and most of the others survive only in fragments or in Latin translations. The main reasons for this almost complete loss of the originals are the later condemnations of his teaching and the exorbitant length and diffusiveness of his works. His chief work on Biblical criticism is his famous '*Hexapla' (q.v.). Among his many exegetical works are *scholia* on Exod., Lev., and Num., commentaries on almost all the books of the Bible, most of which survive only in small fragments, and many homilies, which are among the oldest examples of Christian preaching. Large portions of the Commentaries on Mt. and Jn., however, have been preserved, as well as considerable sections (in *Rufinus's Lat. trans.) of those on the Song of Solomon and Rom.

The most important of Origen's theological works is the 'De Principiis' (Περὶ Ἀρχῶν), conceived as a systematic exposition of Christian doctrine in four books treating of God and the heavenly beings, of man and the material world, of free-will and its consequences, and of Holy Scripture. The original text has almost completely disappeared, and the work is extant only in the not very reliable Latin translation of *Rufinus and the more faithful, but fragmentary, rendering of St. *Jerome. Of his other theological works nearly all are lost. His two ascetical works, 'Exhortation to Martyrdom', written during the persecution of Maximin in 235, and 'On Prayer', were much read in antiquity. He also wrote an important apologetic work against *Celsus (q.v.).

Origen was essentially a Biblical scholar whose thought was nourished on Scripture, the inspiration and integrity of which he affirmed esp. against the *Marcionites. He recognized a triple sense, literal, moral, and allegorical, of which he preferred the last. He justified this choice on many grounds, esp. the contention that the whole universe is pervaded with symbols and types of the invisible world. All things had a double aspect, one corporeal and sensible, which is accessible to all, the other spiritual and mystical, known only to the perfect. This led him to distinguish between two classes of Christians, the simple, who have to be satisfied with faith in Christ crucified, and the perfect, who ascend beyond this to the contemplation of the Word dwelling with the Father.

The point of departure of Origen's doctrinal teaching was faith in the unity of God, who is altogether transcendent. This unity did not exclude the Trinity of the Persons. He taught the eternal generation of the Son and the eternity of the Holy Ghost, though he was uncertain as to His nature and as to His relation to the Father and to the Son. He has often been accused of teaching *Subordinationism, notably by *Epiphanius and Jerome. It seems that his thought on this subject was still in flux; for though in his 'Treatise on Prayer' he taught that prayer ought to be addressed only to the Father, in his homilies he prayed also directly to Christ. Moreover, there are passages in which he holds the Father to be the absolute, and the Son only relative Truth, whereas in others he declares them both to be perfect Truth. These contradictions are partly explicable by the opposition within himself between the thinker concerned to defend his system and the Christian praying and meditating in harmony with the Church.

His philosophical speculations often issued in audacious theories, though, in the absence of the original texts, it is not always easy to say whether he held them as certain or merely stated them as hypotheses, or even simply repeated the ideas of other thinkers. He affirmed that creation was eternal in the belief that without an existing world God would have been inactive and not omnipotent. He held Him to be finite, because if He were infinite He could not think Himself. Among his most controverted theories was his teaching on souls and their destiny. All spirits were created equal, but through the exercise of their free-will they developed in hierarchical order and some fell into sin and so became either demons or souls, imprisoned in bodies. Death does not finally decide the fate of the soul, which may turn into a demon or an angel. This ascent and descent goes on uninterruptedly until the final '*Apocatastasis' (q.v.) when all creatures, even the devil, will be saved. There is also a strong current of mysticism in Origen.

He held that true knowledge was the participation of the purified soul in the Wisdom of the Word and a way towards Deification and union with Christ. In the course of the disputes on *Origenism (q.v.) his teaching has often been misrepresented, and owing to the loss of the originals of most of his works, a satisfactory reconstruction of his authentic thought is not always possible.

The earliest printed editions were confined to Origen's Lat. works. Greek works ed. P. D. *Huet, Bp. of Avranches (2 vols., fol., Rouen, 1668; with important introd., still valuable, repr. in J. P. Migne, *PG*, xvii, 633–1284). The best complete ed. (without, however, the *Hexapla fragments) is still that of the *Maurist, C. de La Rue, O.S.B., 4 vols., fol., Paris, 1733–59 (vol. iv completed by his nephew, C. Vincent de La Rue, O.S.B.); repr. in J. P. Migne, *PG*, xi–xvii. Another ed. by C. H. E. Lommatzsch, 25 vols., Berlin, 1831–48. Modern crit. ed. of separate texts in G.C.S., incl. *Cont. Celsum* (ed. P. Koetschau, 1899), *Comm. in Jn.* (ed. E. Preuschen, 1903), *De Principiis* (ed. P. Koetschau, 1913), *Comm. in Matt.* (ed. E. Klostermann–E. Benz–L. Früchtel, 1933–55), *Hom. in Luc.* (ed. M. Rauer, 1930). R. Cadiou, *Commentaires inédits des psaumes* (1935). Text of Origen's 'Discourse with Heracleides', discovered in 1941 on Toura papyrus, ed. J. Scherer (Publications de la Société Fouad I de Papyrologie. Textes et Documents, ix, Cairo, 1949). The 'Philocalia' (excerpts from Origen, collected by St. Gregory Nazianzen and St. Basil), ed. J. A. *Robinson, Cambridge, 1893. For the *Tractatus Origenis, see s.v. Eng. tr. (incomplete) of his collected works in A.N.C.L. Modern translations of *Contra Celsum* by H. Chadwick (Cambridge, 1953), of *De Principiis* by G. W. Butterworth (S.P.C.K., London, 1936), of *De Oratione* by E. G. Jay (S.P.C.K., London, 1954), of *De Oratione* and *Exhortatio ad Martyrium* by J. J. O'Meara, (A.C.W. 19, 1954), of *Philocalia* by G. Lewis (Edinburgh, 1911). Fr. tr. of Homm. on Ex. (S.C., xvi; 1947), Homm. on Numbers (ib., xxix; 1951), of Homm. on Cant. (ib., xxxvii; 1954). Studies on Origen's life and work as a whole by E. R. Redepenning (2 vols., Bonn, 1841–6), E. de Faye (3 vols., Paris, 1923–8), J. Daniélou, S.J. (Paris, 1948; Eng. tr., 1955). R. Cadiou, *Introduction au système d'Origène* (1932); id., *La Jeunesse d'Origène* (1935). W. Völker, *Das Vollkommenheitsideal des Origenes* (1931); Hal Koch, *Pronoia und Paideusis*. Studien über Origenes und sein Verhältniss zum Platonismus (Arbeiten zur Kirchengeschichte 22, 1934;) A. Lieske, *Die Theologie der Logosmystik bei Origenes* (1938). H. de Lubac, S.J., *Histoire et esprit*. L'Intelligence des Écritures d'après Origène (1950). A. *Harnack, *Der kirchengeschichtliche Ertrag der exegetischen Arbeiten des Origenes* (T.U., xlii, Hft. 3; 1918). R. P. C. Hanson, *Origen's Doctrine of Tradition* (1954). Bardenhewer, ii, 96–194; Altaner (ed. 1951), pp. 165–74. Important art. by B. F. *Westcott in *D.C.B.*, iv (1887; but art. dated 1882), 96–142. E. Preuschen in *P.R.E.* (ed. 3), xiv (1904), pp. 467–88; G. Bardy in *D.T.C.*, xi (pt. 2; 1932), cols. 1489–1565. B. Drewery, *Origen and the Doctrine of Grace* (1960). See also bibl. to *Alexandrine Theology, Celsus, Hexapla.

ORIGENISM.

The group of theories enunciated by, or attributed to, *Origen (q.v.). Among Origen's earliest opponents was *Methodius of Olympus, who rejected esp. his teaching on the pre-existence of souls and his denial of the identity between the mortal and the resurrection bodies. In the 4th cent. the attacks of the Anti-Origenists were directed mainly against the Trinitarian doctrine of the 'De Principiis'. He was further accused of teaching *metempsychosis and of interpreting the Scriptures only allegorically. But his supporters were also numerous. The martyr St. *Pamphilus wrote in his defence, and later, Sts. *Athanasius, *Basil, and *Gregory of Nazianzus esteemed him highly, and St. *Didymus endeavoured to prove his Trinitarian orthodoxy. The first great controversy was inaugurated by St. *Epiphanius (between c. 375 and

377), who, in his 64th heresy, gives a very one-sided account of his doctrines. Epiphanius's attack was taken up by St. *Jerome. Having first been an ardent defender of Origen, Jerome changed his views in 395, on the occasion of a visit of Epiphanius to *Jerusalem, and attempted to obtain a condemnation of Origen from its bishop, John. In this he failed, and John even obtained a sentence of exile against Jerome from the secular authorities, which, however, was not carried out. For a time John and Jerome were reconciled through the good offices of *Theophilus of Alexandria, at that time an adherent of Origen. The peace was interrupted when, in 398, *Rufinus returned from *Rome with his Latin translation of the 'De Principiis', in the preface of which he referred to Jerome's former Origenistic leanings. The controversy reached its climax when, in 400, a Council at Alexandria convoked by Theophilus, who had become an opponent, condemned Origenism. Pope Anastasius I and the Bps. of Palestine and Syria adhered to the condemnation, and Theophilus continued his campaign. In his Festal Letter of 402 he called Origen the 'hydra of heresies' and he expelled from their monasteries the famous '*Tall Brothers' (q.v.) and other supporters of Origenism, who found refuge with St. *Chrysostom at *Constantinople.

The controversy flared up again in the 6th cent., being described in detail in the 'Life of St. Sabas' by *Cyril of Scythopolis. Origenism had been propagated esp. in the New Laura, nr. Jerusalem, whose monks had separated from the Great Laura, but it found adherents also in the latter, and c. 542 it had strong partisans throughout Palestine. Its Palestinian opponents, however, obtained from the Emp. *Justinian the famous letter to Mennas, Patr. of Constantinople, in which Origen is numbered among the most pernicious heretics. At the Emperor's command a Council was convoked at Constantinople in 543, and an edict drawn up in accordance with Justinian's views giving a long list of Origenistic errors and their refutation, which was signed by Pope *Vigilius and the E. patriarchs. The Origenist monks at Jerusalem split into two parties: the Isochrists, who held that at the Apocatastasis all men would become equal to Christ, and the Protoctists, who seem to have regarded the soul of Christ not as equal to the other souls but as the most excellent of creatures. These latter, after renouncing the doctrine of the pre-existence of souls, made common cause with the orthodox against the Isochrists. The Origenistic controversy was ended by the Second Council of *Constantinople (553), when Origen's teaching was condemned, though it is uncertain whether the Council examined his case afresh or simply adhered to the decision of the synod of 543. All the bishops submitted except Alexander of Abila, who was deposed.

L. B. Radford, *Three Teachers of Alexandria, Theognostus, Pierius and Peter*. A Study in the Early History of Origenism and Anti-Origenism (1908); K. Holl, 'Die Zeitfolge des ersten origenistischen Streits' in *Sb.* (Berl.), 1916, pp. 226–55, repr. in *Gesammelte Aufsätze*, ii (1928), pp. 310–35. F. Diekamp, *Die origenistischen Streitigkeiten im sechsten*

Jahrhundert und das fünfte allgemeine Konzil (1899). A. W. W. D. [prob. A. W. W. Dale] in *D.C.B.*, iv (1887), pp. 142–56; N. Bonwetsch in *P.R.E.* (ed. 3), xiv (1904), pp. 489–93; A. d'Alès in *Dictionnaire apologétique de la foi catholique* (ed. 4 by A. d'Alès) iii (1926), cols. 1228–58, s.v. 'Origénisme', with bibl.; G. Fritz in *D.T.C.*, xi (pt. 2; 1932), cols. 1565–88, s.v. 'Origénisme'.

ORIGINAL RIGHTEOUSNESS (*Justitia Originalis*).

Acc. to Catholic theology, God's gratuitous impartation to man of perfect rectitude in his original condition before the *Fall. The state of Original Righteousness in which man was first created is held to have included freedom from concupiscence, bodily immortality and impassibility, and happiness.

ORIGINAL SIN.

In Christian theology, the state of sin in which humankind has been held captive since the *Fall (q.v.). Catholic theologians hold that its essential element is the loss of sanctifying grace. (It is also held by RCs that the BVM was by a special dispensation preserved from the stain of original sin: see *Immaculate Conception.*)

The Scriptural foundation of the doctrine is the Pauline teaching that 'through one man (i.e. Adam) sin entered into the world' so that, 'by the trespass of the one the many died' (cf. Rom. 5. 12–21). The doctrine, the significance of which was obscured by other preoccupations in the age of the *Apostolic Fathers and the *Apologists, began to be developed in the struggle against the *Gnostic errors by St. *Irenaeus. As against the dualist systems of the heretics, he defended the teaching that evil came into the world through the sin of Adam. *Origen has the conception of man's fallen state, but in him it is bound up with speculations on the prenatal sins of souls. *Methodius, while attacking Origen's more speculative theses, argued that the full effects of the Fall could be seen in man's inherent corruptibility (φθορά). St. *Athanasius in his treatise 'De Incarnatione' anticipated later developments by teaching that the chief result of the sin of Adam, which consisted in the abuse of his liberty, was the loss of the grace of conformity to the image of God, by which he and his descendants were reduced to their natural condition (εἰς τὸ κατὰ φύσιν). *Didymus of Alexandria taught clearly the transmission of the stain of Original Sin by natural propagation, and St. *Chrysostom is explicit on the consequences of concupiscence. *Theodore of Mopsuestia seems to have been the only Greek Father of the first four cents. who explicitly denied it, placing sin entirely in the will without allowing for the possibility of a moral stain on human nature.

To try to answer whether the Greek Fathers taught the transmission of the guilt itself or only of its consequences is fruitless. At most their language is vague, and the precise formulation of the doctrine was reserved to the West. Here *Tertullian, St.*Cyprian, and St. *Ambrose taught the solidarity of the whole human race with Adam not only in the consequences of his sin but in the sin itself, which

is transmitted through natural generation, and the so-called '*Ambrosiaster' found its Scriptural proof in Rom. 5. 12, translating ἐφ' ᾧ by *in quo* and referring it to Adam, 'in whom all have sinned'. In this he was followed by St. *Augustine, who in his 'Quaestiones ad Simplicianum' (396–7) and other pre-Pelagian writings, taught that Adam's guilt is transmitted to his descendants by concupiscence, thus making of humanity a *massa damnata* and much enfeebling, though not destroying, the freedom of the will. In the struggle against Pelagianism the principles of the Augustinian doctrine were confirmed by many Councils, esp. the Second of *Orange (529).

With the existence of Original Sin firmly established, the medieval theologians were particularly occupied with its nature and transmission. St. *Anselm of Canterbury was the first to open up new ways of thought in which he was followed by the great 13th cent. Schoolmen. He defines Original Sin as the 'privation of the righteousness which every man ought to possess', thus separating it from concupiscence with which the disciples of St. Augustine had often identified it. It is transmitted by generation, because the whole human race was present in Adam *seminaliter*. His ideas were not immediately taken up. Whilst *Abelard was condemned by the Council of Sens (1140) for refusing to recognize Original Sin as guilt, other 12th cent. theologians, e.g. *Peter Lombard, identified it with concupiscence. This latter conception was rejected in the next century by *Alexander of Hales and *Albert the Great, who distinguish a formal element, viz. privation of original righteousness, from the material element of concupiscence. All of them hold that it is transmitted by the concupiscence accompanying the conjugal act. St. *Thomas, who treated the subject five times (esp. in 'De Malo' and in 'Summa Theol.' II (1) qq. lxxxi–lxxxiv), brought in a new element by distinguishing, in the state of Adam before the Fall, 'pure nature' (*pura naturalia*) from the supernatural gifts which perfected it. Hence Original Sin consists in the loss of these supernatural privileges which had directed man to his supernatural end and enabled him to keep his inferior powers in submission to reason, a rectitude not natural to a being compounded of soul and body such as man. This conception entails a more optimistic view of man than that of St. Augustine and his successors in that it leaves to the reason, will, and passions of fallen man their natural powers. Acc. to St. Thomas, Original Sin is transmitted not as the personal fault of Adam but as a state of human nature, yet constituting a fault inasmuch as all men are regarded as members of one great organism of which Adam was the first mover. Thus through his sin his descendants incur a culpability similar to that of the hand which executes a murder, moved by the human will. The instrument of transmission is generation, regardless of the accompanying concupiscence.

The Thomist synthesis was not at once

accepted everywhere. The old rigorous Augustinianism persisted among the *Franciscans, and esp. in the religious family of St. Augustine, whereas, on the other hand, the rationalist tendencies of Abelard were voiced by others who denied the guilt (*reatus culpae*), recognizing only its punitive consequences (*reatus poenae*). The more prominent Scholastics, however, such as *Duns Scotus, *William of Ockham, and their disciples, accepted the Thomist principles, but while defining Original Sin exclusively as lack of original righteousness (*carentia justitiae originalis debitae*), tended to eliminate the element of concupiscence.

In the subsequent controversy with the Reformers the teaching was made increasingly precise; to the exaggerated pessimism of M. *Luther and J. *Calvin who equated Original Sin with concupiscence and affirmed that it completely destroyed liberty and persisted even after baptism, the Council of *Trent opposed the teaching of the Schoolmen, without, however, pronouncing on points still disputed by Catholic theologians. In re-stating the doctrine of St. Thomas, Dominic *Soto eliminated the element of concupiscence altogether from the definition and identified Original Sin with the loss of sanctifying grace. His views had a far-reaching influence, being accepted by authorities like F. *Suarez, R. *Bellarmine, and the *Salmanticenses, and are again widely discussed to-day. But the official decisions of the RC Church followed the teaching of the older theologians. In his condemnation of M. *Baius (1567), St. *Pius V, going beyond Trent, sanctioned the Thomist distinction between nature and supernature in the state of Paradise, condemned the identification of Original Sin with concupiscence, and admitted the possibility of the right use of the freedom of the will in the unbaptized. In the 17th and 18th cents. the *Jesuits developed the doctrine along the lines of moderated optimism traced by the Schoolmen, whereas the French theologians of *Jansenist leanings, such as the circle of *Port Royal and J. B. *Bossuet, inclined towards the old Augustinian pessimism. From the 18th cent. onwards the influence of rationalism and natural science has tended to attenuate the dogma of Original Sin, which has been given up almost completely by Liberal Protestantism and Modernism, but is strongly reaffirmed by modern RC orthodox theologians and, in its Protestant version, esp. by K. *Barth and his school.

F. R. Tennant, *The Origin and Propagation of Sin* (Hulsean Lectures for 1901–2; 1902); id., *The Sources of the Doctrines of the Fall and Original Sin* (1903); id., *The Concept of Sin* (1912), passim; C. W. Formby, *The Unveiling of the Fall* (1923); N. P. *Williams, *The Ideas of the Fall and of Original Sin* (Bampton Lectures for 1924; 1927), with formularies repr., pp. 537–50. R. M. Martin (ed.), *La Controverse sur le péché originel au début du XIVe siècle. Textes inédits* (S.S.L., x; 1930). A. Gaudel–M. Jugie, A.A., in *D.T.C.*, xii (pt. 1; 1933), cols. 275–623, s.v. 'Péché originel', with bibl. cols. 605 f. and 623. H. Lange in *L.Th.K.*, iii (1931), cols. 740–6, s.v. 'Erbsünde'; F. Spadafora–P. Parente in *E.C.*, ix (1952), cols. 1027–39, s.v. 'Peccato originale', with bibl. See also bibl. to *Augustine*, *St.*, and commentaries to *Romans, Epistle to the*.

ORNAMENTS RUBRIC, The. The common name for the ruling, inserted in the 1559 BCP at the beginning of the order for Morning and Evening Prayer, that the ornaments of the Church and the ministers should be those in use 'by the authority of Parliament in the second year of the reign of King *Edward VI.' The Act of *Uniformity of 1559, to which this Book was attached, added the qualification that such use should continue 'until other order shall be therein taken by the authority of the Queen's Majesty, with the advice of her commissioners appointed and authorized under the great seal of England for causes ecclesiastical, or of the Metropolitan of this realm'. The interpretation of this rubric has been a vexed question since the 16th cent. The only explicit statement about the ornaments is contained in the Prayer Book of 1549, but that Book was authorized by Parliament in the third (not the second) year of Edward VI. The *Judicial Committee of the Privy Council have twice ruled that Abp. M. *Parker's '*Advertisements' (1566) were the 'other order' foreshadowed in the Act; but their ruling has been widely disputed, esp. since the Advertisements had no statutory authority, nor can they be regarded as overriding the later re-enactment of the rubric by Parliament in 1604 and 1662. The whole question seems too complex to permit of any certain solution.

The Ornaments of the Church and its Ministers. Convocation of Canterbury. Upper House Report No. 416. Report of the sub-committee appointed February 1907 to draw up a Historical Memorandum on the Ornaments of the Church and its Ministers (1908). J. T. Micklethwaite, *The Ornaments of the Rubric* (*Alcuin Club Tracts, i; 1897). W. H. *Frere in *D.E.C.H.*, pp. 425–7.

OROSIUS (early 5th cent.), Paulus Orosius, historian. A native of Braga, who as a young presbyter had written a 'Commonitorium' against *Priscillianism, he migrated to Africa in 414 where he was befriended by St. *Augustine. Shortly afterwards Augustine sent him to Palestine to enlist St. *Jerome in the fight against *Pelagianism. When, however, the Council of Diospolis (in Palestine) of 415 upheld Pelagius, Orosius composed a 'Liber Apologeticus', defending himself against the charge of heresy. In 416 he returned to the W. and in 417 undertook, at Augustine's request and in the spirit of his 'City of God', a 'Historia adversus Paganos' which, by insisting both on the providential control of history and the calamities of the past, attacked the pagan complaint that Rome's troubles were due to her abandonment of the gods. Books I–II reach to the foundation of Rome, III–VI to the birth of Christ, and VII to A.D. 417. Only after A.D. 378 is it of any real historical value.

Ed. by S. Haverkamp (Leyden, 1738), repr. with additions in J. P. Migne, *PL*, xxxi. Modern ed. of 'Historia' and 'Liber Apologeticus' by C. Zangemeister (*C.S.E.L.*, vol. v, 1882); also by I. W. Raymond (with Eng. tr., New York, 1936); of 'Commonitorium' by G. Schepss (*C.S.E.L.*, vol. xvii, 1889, pp. 149–57). J. Svennung, *Orosiana* (Upsala, 1922); H. Hagendahl, *Orosius und Justinus* (Göteborg, 1941). Bardenhewer, iv, 529–33; Altaner (ed. 1950), p. 207 f.

ORSISIUS, St. (d. *c.* 380), also 'Orsiesius' and 'Horsi-isi', ascetic and Abbot of Tabenne (an island in the Nile). He was a disciple and close friend of St. *Pachomius who set him over the monastery of Chenobosci. On Pachomius's death (348) he succeeded him (after a few days'interval under Petronius) as *hegumen of Tabenne. The opposition to his strict rule led him to resign in favour of St. Theodore (d. 368), but he resumed the oversight of the monastery on the latter's death. He wrote a 'Doctrina de Institutione Monachorum' (probably in Coptic), which was commended by *Gennadius; it survives in a Latin version, probably the work of St. *Jerome. He was warmly supported by St. *Athanasius, from whom two letters to Orsisius survive. Feast day, 15 June.

Jerome's text of 'Doctrina de Institutione Monachorum' repr. in J. P. Migne, *PG*, xl, 869–94; also in *PL*, ciii, 453–76. Text of Athanasius's two Epp. to Orsisius in id., *PG*, xxvi, 977–80. P. Ladeuze, *Étude sur le cénobitisme pakhômien* (Diss., Louvain, 1898), esp. pp. 155–255. Bardenhewer, iii, 85–7.

ORTHODOXY. Right belief, as contrasted with heresy. The word is used esp. of those Churches in E. Christendom which are in communion with *Constantinople, collectively described in ancient times as the 'holy, orthodox, catholic, apostolic Eastern Church' (ἡ ἁγία ὀρθόδοξος καθολικὴ ἀποστολικὴ ἀνατολικὴ ἐκκλησία) to distinguish it from such separated bodies as the *Nestorians and *Jacobites. See also following entry.

ORTHODOXY, Feast of. The feast established in 842 to celebrate the final downfall of the *Iconoclastic party and the restoration of the icons. Since then it has been solemnly kept in the E. Church both by Orthodox and *Uniats on the First Sunday of *Lent, and has come to commemorate the triumph of the right faith not only over Iconoclasm but over all heresies. A list of heretics, and another of several saints and pious emperors, is read out in the *Synodicon, and old triumphal hymns, composed by martyrs of the Iconoclast persecution, are chanted during the procession of crosses and icons.

ORTHROS (Gk. ὄρθρος, 'dawn'). The name in the E. Church for the morning *office which corresponds to *Lauds in the W.

ORTLIEB OF STRASSBURG (*c.* A.D. 1200), founder of an ascetic sect ('Ortlibarii'). Very little is known of him beyond the fact that his teaching was condemned by *Innocent III. His followers, who appealed against the tenets of the external Church to the inner authority of the Spirit, maintained the eternity of the world and unorthodox doctrines of the Trinity and the Incarnation. Their teaching had affinities with that of the *Waldenses and *Cathari; but in neither case has historic contact been established.

The principal source for the doctrines ascribed to the sect is the 'Anonymus of Passau contra Waldenses', pr. in the *Bibliotheca Maxima Veterum Patrum*, xxv (Lyons, 1677), pp. 262–77. W. Preger, *Geschichte der deutschen Mystik im Mittelalter*, i (1874), pp. 191–6; H. Reuter, *Geschichte der religiösen Aufklärung im Mittelalter*, ii (1877), pp. 237–40, with notes, p. 375 f. S. M. Deutsch in *P.R.E.* (ed. 3), xiv (1904), pp. 498–501, with bibl.; F. Rabenek in *L.Th.K.*, vii (1935), col. 791 f., s.v. 'Ortlieber'. See also works cited under *Joachim of Fiore* and *Waldenses*.

O SALUTARIS HOSTIA (Lat., 'O Saving Victim'). The last two verses of St. *Thomas Aquinas's hymn 'Verbum Supernum Prodiens', written *c.* 1263 for use on the Feast of *Corpus Christi. In the RC Church it is sung at the opening of the tabernacle at the service of *Benediction. There are many English translations of the complete hymn, and still more of its two concluding verses, the most familiar being E. *Caswall's 'O Saving Victim! Opening wide The Gate of Heaven to man below, &c.' (1849).

Crit. ed. of text by C. M. Drewes (ed.), *Lateinische Hymnendichter des Mittelalters*, ii (A.H.M.A.; 1; 1907), p. 588 f. Raby, p. 409 f., with bibl. p. 483.

O SAPIENTIA (Lat., 'O Wisdom'). The initial apostrophe of the first of the *O Antiphons. The words appeared in the *Sarum calendar as an entry against 16 Dec. Omitted from the calendar of the BCP of 1549, owing to the discontinuance of the Antiphons, they were restored in 1661. In non-English calendars the date is 17 Dec.

OSCULATORIUM. See *Pax Brede.*

OSIANDER, ANDREAS (1498–1552), Reformation theologian. Ordained priest at Eichstätt in 1520, he joined the *Lutherans in 1522 and took part in the *Marburg Colloquy of 1529 and the *Augsburg Diet of 1530. He was also one of the signatories of the *Schmalkalden Articles (1537). In 1549 he became professor at Königsberg, where he published his *De Justificatione* (1550). A violent and bitter controversialist, he opposed Luther's doctrine of *justification by faith, maintaining that justification was not a mere imputation of Christ's merits, but a substantial transference of His righteousness to the believer. His other writings include a revised edition of the *Vulgate and a 'Harmony' of the Gospels, the first of its kind. His niece, Margaret Osiander, became the wife of T. *Cranmer (1532).

Study by W. Möller (Leben und ausgewählte Schriften der Väter und Begründer der lutherischen Kirche, ed. I. Hartmann and others, v; Elberfeld, 1870). E. Hirsch, *Die Theologie des Andreas Osiander und ihre geschichtlichen Voraussetzungen* (1919); id., 'Osianders Schirmschrift zum Nürnberger Reichstage' in *Z.K.G.*, xliii (1924), pp. 417–22. Further bibl. in Schottenloher, ii (1935), pp. 107–9 (Nos. 16668–16712a). W. Müller–P. Tschackert in *P.R.E.* (ed. 3), xiv (1904), pp. 501–9, s.v.; Prof. Blanke in *R.G.G.* (ed. 2), iv (1930), col. 817 f., s.v.; L. Cristiani in *D.T.C.*, ix (pt. 2; 1932), cols. 1652–5, s.v.; J. B. Götz in *L.Th.K.*, vii (1935), col. 797 f., s.v., all with bibl.

OSMUND, St. (d. 1099), Bp. of *Salisbury. A Norman by race, being the son of the Count of Séez, Osmund followed William I to England. Later he became his chancellor and assisted with the compilation of Domesday Book. As a reward for his services he was created Bp. of Salisbury in 1078. An energetic and practical organizer, he gave the new see its cathedral (at *Sarum; not the present one at Salisbury which dates from 1225) and the constitution of its cathedral chapter, which became the model of many other foundations. Acc. to some authorities he also instituted the Sarum liturgical use: but the definitive formation of this is probably not older than Richard *Poore (dean and bishop, 1198 – 1228). He was canonized on 1 Jan. 1457. Feast day, 4 Dec.; in the Anglican S. African calendar, 16 July.

Vetus Registrum Sarisberiense alias dictum S. Osmundi Episcopi, ed. W. H. Rich Jones (2 vols., Rolls Series, 1883–1884). A. R. Malden (ed.), *The Canonization of Saint Osmund from the Manuscript Records in the Muniment Room of Salisbury Cathedral . . .* with introduction and notes (Wilts Record Society, 1901). The main chronicle sources include *William of Malmesbury, *Gesta Pontificum Anglorum*, esp. ii, 83, and v, 267 and 269 (ed. N. E. S. A. Hamilton, Rolls Series, 1870, pp. 183 f., 424 f., and 428 f.), and *Simeon of Durham, *Auctarium de Injusta Vexatione Willelmi I*, xix, and id., *Historia Regum*, clxxiii and clxxxi (*Opera*, ed. T. Arnold, 2 vols., Rolls Series, 1882–5, vol. i, p. 193, and vol. ii, pp. 219 and 230). Modern Life by W. J. Torrance (London [*c*. 1919]). See also bibl. s.v. 'Salisbury, Use of'.

OSSERVATORE ROMANO (Ital., 'The Roman Observer'). The official newspaper of the *Vatican, founded in 1861 and published daily except on Sundays. In addition to news of religious interest, it publishes reports and comments on political and social events.

OSSIUS. Probably the correct spelling of the name of the celebrated 4th cent. Bp. of Cordova commonly known as *Hosius (q.v.).

C. H. *Turner, 'Ossius (Hosius) of Cordova', in *J.T.S.*, xii (1910–11), pp. 275–7.

OSTENSORY (Lat. *ostensorium*). A receptacle for showing objects of religious devotion to the people. The word is now commonly restricted to the *monstrance (q.v.), used for the exposition of the Blessed Sacrament; but in earlier times it was applied to other vessels with a transparent casing, e.g. those for the exposition of relics.

OSTIAN WAY, The (Lat. *Via Ostiensis*). The ancient road which led from Rome to the seaport of Ostia, 14 miles distant at the mouth of the Tiber on its left bank. On its west side, about two miles from the centre of Rome, lies the church of San Paolo fuori le Mura. This site has been held to be the resting-place of the remains of St. *Paul at least from the end of the 2nd cent., for the presbyter *Gaius (*c*. A.D. 200) recorded that the tombs (τρόπαια) of Sts. Peter and Paul were located (respectively) in his day at the *Vatican and on the Ostian Way. The Bp. of Ostia is the senior cardinal-bishop and 'Dean of the Sacred College'. He has the privilege of consecrating a new Pope if the candidate is not already in episcopal orders.

*Eusebius, *Hist. Eccl.* ii, 25. 6–7.

OSTIARIUS. See *Doorkeeper*.

OSWALD, St. (*c*. 605–42), King of Northumbria, and martyr. The son of Ethelfrith, King of Northumbria, Oswald was forced to flee to Scotland when Edwin seized the kingdom after his father's death in 616. He was converted later to the Christian faith by the monks of St. *Columba at *Iona. After Edwin's death (633), he returned and, after erecting a wooden cross on the battlefield and commanding his soldiers to pray, defeated the British king, Caedwalla, at Hevenfelt. Encouraged by his victory, he began to establish Christianity in his kingdom and appealed to Iona for missionaries. St. *Aidan was sent for the work, and having been given the isle of *Lindisfarne as his see, by his gentleness and with the co-operation of the king, who often acted as his interpreter, achieved the conversion of a large part of the country. In the seventh year of his reign Oswald was killed in battle by the pagan Penda of Mercia, who mutilated his body. His head, which was deposited in St. *Cuthbert's coffin in 875, was found at *Durham in 1827. He was honoured as a martyr not only by the English but also on the Continent throughout the Middle Ages. Feast day, 5 Aug.; in some places, 8 or 9 Aug.

The principal authority is *Bede, *H.E.*, ii, 5, 14, 20, iii, 1–3, 6 f., 9–14, 23 f., and iv, 14; notes to ed. C. Plummer, ii (Oxford, 1896), esp. pp. 86, 116, 119–24, 138, 140 f., 152–65. 11th cent. life by Drogo pr. in *AA.SS.*, Aug. II (1735), pp. 94–103; life by Reginald of Durham (1162), most of which is pr. among the works of *Simeon of Durham ed. T. Arnold, i (R.S.), 1882), pp. 326–85, with introd., p. xli. Life [by F. W. *Faber] in *The Lives of the English Saints* [written at the suggestion of J. H. *Newman], 1844; ed. A. W. Hutton, iv (1901), pp. 209–39. Elizabeth W. Grierson, *The Story of the Northumbrian Saints* (1913), pp. 3–41. B. Colgrave in C. F. Battiscombe (ed.), *The Relics of Saint Cuthbert* (1956), pp. 116–8, with further reff. J. Raine in *D.C.B.*, iv (1887), p. 163 f., s.v. 'Oswald (1)', W. Hunt in *D.N.B.*, xlii (1895), pp. 321–3, with further reff. On the late medieval widely circulating legend about St. Oswald, see M. Förster in *L.Th.K.*, vii (1935), col. 829 f., s.v., with bibl. reff.

OSWALD, St. (d. 992), Abp. of *York. A Dane by birth, Oswald studied in the household of his uncle, Abp. *Odo of Canterbury, and later at the Benedictine monastery of *Fleury where he was ordained. He returned to England in 959 and in 962 was consecrated Bp. of *Worcester by St. *Dunstan. He took an active part in the reform of abuses and established many monasteries, the most famous of which was the abbey of Ramsey in Huntingdonshire. In 972 he was made Abp. of York, though he retained the see of Worcester in order to promote his monastic reforms. The latter were seriously endangered by Elfhere, King of Mercia, who broke up many of Oswald's communities, though he spared Ramsey. Besides reforming the morals of his clergy he took pains to improve their theological knowledge and himself wrote two treatises and several synodal decrees. Feast day, 28 Feb.

The principal authority is an anonymous life, written within ten years of St. Oswald's death, prob. by a monk of Ramsey; it survives in only one MS. (Brit. Mus. Cotton MS., Nero E 1); ed. J. Raine, *The Historians of the Church of York and its Archbishops*, i (R.S., 1879), pp. 399-475, with introd., pp. lxv-lxvii. The life by *Eadmer, pr. ib., ii (R.S., 1886), pp. 1-59, adds a certain amount of information. Other lives, of little historical value, ib., pp. 60-97 and 489-512, with introd., pp. ix-xi. J. Armitage *Robinson, *St. Oswald and the Church of Worcester* (British Academy Supplementary Papers, v; 1919); E. H. Pearce, *St. Oswald of Worcester and the Church of York* (York Minster Historical Tracts, iv [1928]). [M.] D. Knowles, O.S.B., *The Monastic Order in England* (1949), pp. 40-56. W. Hunt in *D.N.B.*, xliii (1895), pp. 323-5, with further reff.

OSWIN, St. (d. 651), Anglo-Saxon King. After the murder of his father, Osric, King of Deira, by Caedwalla (634), Oswin was taken to Wessex for safety. Returning on the death of his cousin, St. *Oswald, King of Northumbria (642), he became (the last) King of Deira, while Bernicia, the other part of Northumbria, passed under the rule of another cousin, Oswy. When open conflict broke out with Oswy, Oswin took refuge at Gilling, near Richmond, Yorks, where he was murdered. He was a devout Christian and a close friend of St. *Aidan. His tomb at Gilling became a place of pilgrimage until, in the Danish invasions, it was removed to Tynemouth. Feast day, 20 Aug.

The principal authority is *Bede, *H.E.*, iii, 14; notes to ed. C. Plummer, ii (Oxford, 1896), p. 163 f. There is a 12th cent. life by a monk of *St. Albans resident at Tynemouth, based on the account of Bede, but with additional material on St. Oswin's translation and the miracles connected with him; it is mostly pr. in J. Raine (ed.), *Miscellanea Biographica* (Surtees Society, viii; 1838), pp. 1-59. Life [by F. W. *Faber] in *The Lives of the English Saints* [written at the suggestion of J. H. *Newman], 1844; ed. A. W. Hutton, iv (1901), pp. 240-70. J. Raine in *D.C.B.*, iv (1887), p. 165, s.v. 'Oswin (1)'; C. L. Kingsford in *D.N.B.*, xliii (1895), p. 332 f.; W. Hunt in *D.E.C.H.*, p. 428 f., s.v.

OTHILIA, St. See *Odilia, St.*

OTTLEY, ROBERT LAWRENCE (1856-1933), Anglican theologian. A native of Richmond in Yorkshire, he was educated at King's School, *Canterbury, and Pembroke College, *Oxford. After being vice-principal of Cuddesdon College from 1886 to 1890 he became Dean of Divinity at Magdalen College, Oxford, in 1890, and principal of Pusey House in 1893. From 1903 till his death he was Canon of Christ Church and Regius professor of pastoral theology at Oxford. His writings cover a wide range of theological subjects. In 1893 he issued a study of *Lancelot *Andrewes* and in 1896 *The Doctrine of the Incarnation*, a student's manual outlining the history of the doctrine from NT times to M. *Luther and R. *Hooker, with particular emphasis on the patristic period. In 1897 he published his *Bampton Lectures on *Aspects of the Old Testament*, in 1898 *The Hebrew Prophets*, and in 1905 *The Religion of Israel. Christian Ideas and Ideals* (1909), designed esp. for candidates for holy orders, contains much practical advice

on the formation of the Christian character; and this theme was also taken up in *The Rule of Life and Love* (1913) and *Christian Morals* (1915). In *Studies in the Confessions of St. *Augustine* (1919) he examined esp. the influences exercised on the saint by *Manichaeism, *Neo-Platonism, and the personal friendship of St. *Ambrose.

OTTO, St. (1062/3-1139), Bp. of Bamberg, the **Apostle of Pomerania**. Born of a noble family of Swabia, he entered the service of the Emp. *Henry IV before 1090, and was made chancellor in 1101. In 1102 Henry named him Bp. of Bamberg, but in 1105 he joined the party of Henry V and was consecrated in Rome in the following year. Though in the *Investiture controversy his sympathies were with the Pope, he tried to maintain a neutral attitude which led to his temporary suspension by Adalbert of Mainz at the Synod of Fritzlar in 1118. At the Congress of Würzburg (1121) he endeavoured to restore peace, which was finally obtained by the Concordat of *Worms in 1122. Throughout these years Otto devoted himself to the reform of his diocese, taking part in the foundation of over 20 monasteries and completing the cathedral. In 1124 he went on a missionary journey to Pomerania at the instigation of Duke Boleslas III of Poland who had obtained the Pomeranians' promise to accept the Christian faith as a condition of the peace made between the two peoples in 1120. Having gained the confidence of the Pomeranians by his liberality, he converted many of the most important towns and, on a second journey four years later, also the greater part of the nobles, though a bishopric was not established till after his death. He was canonized in 1189. Feast day, 30 Sept.; in the Roman Martyrology, 2 July.

A. Ussermann, *Episcopatus Bambergensis* (Germania Sacra [iv], St. Blasien, 1802), pp. 50-95; repr. in J. P. Migne, *PL*, clxxiii, 1267-1314, with correspondence and other material, cols. 1313-80. Lives by Ebo, monk of St. Michael's, Bamberg (d. 1163), and Herbord, also monk of St. Michael's, Bamberg (d. 1168; 'Dialogus de Vita Ottonis'), ed. R. Knöpke in *M.G.H.*, Scriptores, xii (1856), pp. 774-83 [the latter, however, not complete text]; life by a monk of Prüfening (prob. slightly later than the other two), also ed. id., ib., pp. 883-903; other material, pp. 903-19, and introd., pp. 721-46. Full text of life by Herbord ed. O. Holder-Egger, ib., xv (pt. 2; 1888), pp. 1151-69. The Prüfening *Vita* also ed. A. Hofmeister (Denkmäler der Pommerschen Geschichte, i; 1924). *B.H.L.*, ii, 923-6 (Nos. 6392-47). Eng. tr. of Books II and III of life by Ebo, with additional matter from life by Herbord, by C. H. Robinson (S.P.C.K. Translations of Christian Literature, Series 2, Latin Texts; 1920, not wholly satisfactory). Modern life by G. Juritsch (Gotha, 1889). K. Löffler in *C.E.*, xi (1911), p. 353 f., s.v.; A. Zimmermann, O.S.B., in *L.Th.K.*, vii (1935), cols. 836-8, s.v., with bibl.

OTTO OF FREISING (c. 1110/15-58), Bp. of Freising. He was the son of Leopold III, Margrave of Austria, and uncle of *Frederick Barbarossa. He studied at Paris under *Abelard and *Hugh of St.-Victor, and entered the *Cistercian abbey of Morimond in Champagne in 1132, where he became abbot c. 1136. Appointed Bp. of Freising in 1138, he reformed his diocese, took part in the

Second *Crusade (1147–8), and was one of the first theologians to introduce the study of *Aristotle into Germany. He is chiefly important as a historian, his principal works being 'Chronicon seu historia de duabus civitatibus' (1143–6) and 'Gesta Friderici' (1156–8). In the former he modified St. *Augustine's conception of the 'two cities', seeing their union in the Catholic Church as the continuation of the Roman Empire. In the latter he described the history of the first part of Barbarossa's reign, largely on the basis of original documents.

The best ed. of his *Chronicon* is that of A. Hofmeister (Scriptores Rerum Germanicarum in Usum Scholarum, Hanover–Berlin, 1912); of his *Gesta Friderici* that of G. Waitz–B. de Simson (ib., 1912). Eng. tr. of the former by C. C. Mierow (Records of Civilization. Sources and Studies, New York, 1928) and of the latter by id. (ib., 1953), both with introd. J. Hashagen, *Otto von Freising als Geschichtsphilosoph und Kirchenpolitiker* (Leipziger Studien aus dem Gebiet der Geschichte, vii, Hft. 2; 1900). J. Schmidlin, *Die Geschichtsphilosophie und kirchenpolitische Weltanschauung Ottos von Freising* (Studien und Darstellungen aus der Geschichte. Im Auftrage der Görres-Gesellschaft und in Verbindung mit der Redaktion des *Historischen Jahrbuches*, iv, Hftt. 2–3; 1906). P. Brezzi, 'Ottone di Frisinga' in *Bulletino dell' Istituto Storico Italiano per il Medio Evo e Archivio Muratoriano*, liv (1939), pp. 130–328. Manitius, iii (1931), 376–88. J. Spörl in *L.Th.K.*, vii (1935), col. 842 f.

OTTO, RUDOLF (1869–1937), Protestant theologian. From 1904 to 1917 he was professor of systematic theology at Breslau, and from 1917 to 1929 at Marburg. His analysis of religion in *Das Heilige* (1917; Eng. trans., by J. W. Harvey, *The Idea of the Holy*, 1923) rested on a wide knowledge of *comparative religion, contemporary oriental thought, and the natural sciences. Its central theme was insistence on the part played by the *numinous in the religious consciousness. Despite its professed emphasis on the 'irrational' moments in religion, Otto's understanding of religion had close affinities with that of F. D. E. *Schleiermacher (whose *Reden über die Religion* he edited, 1899). His other writings include *Naturalistische und religiöse Weltansicht* (1904; Eng. tr. 1907), *Kantisch-Fries'sche Religionsphilosophie* (1909), *Goethe und Darwin* (1909), *West-östliche Mystik* (1926), *Die Gnadenreligion Indiens und das Christentum* (1930) and *Reich Gottes und Menschensohn* (1934; Eng. trans., *The Kingdom of God and the Son of Man*, 1938).

H. Frick (ed.), *Rudolf Otto Festgruss* (1931); *Rudolf Otto Gedächtnisfeier* (1938).

OUEN, St. (c. 610–84) (also **Audoin** or **Owen**), Abp. of Rouen. He was a native of Sancy, nr. Soissons, and spent part of his youth at the court of King Clothaire II. There he became the friend of St. *Eligius, whose Life (no longer extant in its orig. form) may be his work. Under Dagobert I he became referendary or chancellor. In 634 he founded a monastery called Resbac, the present Rebais, but was prevented from becoming a monk there by King Dagobert. After being ordained priest he was consecrated Bp. of Rouen in 641. He encouraged scholarship, founded

many monasteries, and fought simony and other serious abuses. He was employed on several political missions by the Merovingian kings, among them the arrangement of a peace between the Franks of Austrasia and Neustria. He is remembered esp. by the famous church dedicated to him at Rouen, where his body was interred. Feast day, 24 Aug.

Crit. ed. of the life of St. Eligius ascribed to St. Ouen, ed. B. Krusch in *M.G.H.*, Scriptores Rerum Merovingicarum, iv (1902), pp. 634–741. The earliest life of St. Ouen, dating from the 8th cent., ed. W. Levison, ib., v (1910), pp. 536–67; earlier ed. in *AA.SS.*, Aug. IV (1739), pp. 805–9; one 9th cent. life is also pr. ib., pp. 810–19; a second was first ed. E. P. Savage in *Anal. Boll.*, v (1886), pp. 67–146. Good modern study by E. Vacandard (Paris, 1902).

OUR FATHER. See *Lord's Prayer.*

OVERALL, JOHN (1560–1619), Bp. of *Norwich. He was educated at Cambridge, where in 1581 he became a Fellow of Trinity College and from 1595 to 1607 was the Regius professor of theology. In 1602 he succeeded A. *Nowell as Dean of St. Paul's, and in 1605 became *prolocutor of the Lower House of *Convocation. He was consecrated Bp. of Coventry and Lichfield in 1614 and translated to Norwich in 1618. The section on the Sacraments in the BCP Catechism was drawn up by Overall on the basis of that in Nowell's 'Small Catechism' of 1572. He was also responsible for a set of canons on the relations of Church and state, compiled in 1606 with the *Gunpowder Plot in view and known as his 'Convocation Book'. *James I, however, prohibited its acceptance by Convocation, as Overall defended teaching on the *Divine right of kings which appeared to justify a successful rebellion and permit the institution of 'new forms of government' (can. 28); and the publication of the Book was delayed till 1690. Overall also assisted in the translation of the AV Bible.

His 'Convocation Book', orig. ed. W. *Sancroft, London, 1690, was repr. in the L.A.C.T., 1844. A. Gordon in *D.N.B.*, xlii (1895), pp. 375–7; B. Blaxland in *D.E.C.H.*, p. 429, s.v.

OVERBECK, FRANZ (1837–1905), Protestant theologian. He was born in St. Petersburg and taught Church History at Jena (1864–1870) and 'critical theology' at Basle (1870–97). Holding that the Christian Gospel was wholly eschatological and world-negating, he came to reject completely historic Christianity and expounded in his lectures a 'secular Church history' (*profane Kirchengeschichte*) in which the course of ecclesiastical history was understood as a radical departure from the original revelation in Scripture. Liberal and apologetic theology were also alike essentially un-Christian. In his critique of immanental religious notions Overbeck has exercised considerable influence on the modern *Dialectical Theology. His writings include *Über die Christlichkeit unserer heutigen Theologie* (1873; ed. 2, 1903), *Studien zur Geschichte der alten Kirche* (1875), and

Christentum und Kultur (posthumous, 1919). He was for many years a close friend of F. *Nietzsche.

Correspondence with F. Nietzsche ed. R. Oehler–C. A. Bernoulli (Leipzig, 1916). C. A. Bernoulli, *Franz Overbeck und Friedrich Nietzsche*. Eine Freundschaft (2 vols., Jena, 1908; with list of writings, i, 439–44). K. *Barth, *Die Theologie und die Kirche*. Gesammelte Vorträge, ii (1928), pp. 1–25. E. Vischer in *P.R.E.* (ed. 3), xxiv (1913), pp. 295–302; L. Zscharnack in *R.G.G.* (ed. 2), iv (1930), col. 843 f., s.v.

OWEN, JOHN (1616–83), *Puritan divine and statesman. He was educated at Queen's College, Oxford, but ejected in 1637 under W. *Laud's Statutes. In 1642 he obtained the living of Fordham in Essex, and in 1647 became pastor of Coggeshall. Originally a strong *Calvinist, he had come to believe with J. *Milton that 'new presbyter was but old priest writ large', and took up the more tolerant Independent position. His preaching won the ear of O. *Cromwell who in 1651 made him dean of Christ Church and in the following year vice-chancellor of the university. In 1654 he sat for a short time in Parliament, was one of Cromwell's *Triers, and a member of the *Savoy Conference. The Restoration drove him to London, where he continued to preach and write until his death. He was a voluminous author, often in controversy with R. *Baxter, *Arminians, and *Anglicans, but always tolerant and fair. Many of his writings show deep spiritual insight and a firm grasp of NT Christianity.

Works ed. by T. Russell with memoir by W. Orme (21 vols., 1826) and by W. H. Goold with Life by A. Thomson (24 vols., 1850–55). J. *Moffatt, *The Golden Book of John Owen* (1904). Brief modern Life by J. Moffatt [1911]. J. M. Rigg in *D.N.B.*, xlii (1895), pp. 424–8.

OXFORD. The ecclesiastical history of Oxford appears to begin with St. *Frideswide (d. 735), around whose shrine the town grew up. By the end of the 11th cent. there were secular canons at the Priory of St. Frideswide, who were replaced in the 12th cent. by *Augustinian canons. In 1129, Oseney Priory was founded outside the town, also for Augustinian canons, and in the latter half of the 13th cent. Rewley Abbey ('de regali loco') for *Cistercians. Throughout the Middle Ages Oxford was in the diocese of *Lincoln, but in 1542 *Henry VIII created the See of Oxford, selecting the suppressed Oseney Abbey as the cathedral church and appointing Robert King, the last abbot, as the (first) bishop. In 1546 the seat of the bishopric was transferred to King's (previously 'Cardinal') College, founded by T. *Wolsey around the St. Frideswide's Priory, which had been suppressed in 1524. The priory church then became the cathedral and the college was renamed '*Christ Church'. Since 1635, the bishop's official residence has been at the village of Cuddesdon, some six miles to the east of the city. Among notable recent bishops of Oxford are S. *Wilberforce (1846–69), W. *Stubbs (1889–1901), F. *Paget (1901–11), C. *Gore (1911–19), T. B. *Strong (1925–37), and K. E. *Kirk (1937–54).

The origins of the university are also obscure. The traditional view that it was founded by *Alfred the Great rests on a manifestly forged passage, wrongly attributed to Asser's 'Life of Alfred'. The supposition, formerly popular, that it developed out of the monastic schools is also very unlikely. The university was probably in origin a secular foundation, whose beginnings go back to the latter half of the 12th cent. H. *Rashdall maintained that the creation of a *Studium Generale* at Oxford is to be ascribed to an edict of 1167, which forbade students to go abroad, and that it was modelled on the *Studium* at Paris. In 1214 the first reference to a chancellor is found; he derived his authority from the Bp. of *Lincoln (in whose diocese Oxford then was). By c. 1230 Oxford was already a famous university. Between 1220 and 1270 came the Friars,— *Black, *Grey, *White, and *Austin. Out of the boarding-houses under religious and secular control emerged the colleges, the first of which were Merton (founded outside Oxford, and removed to its present site, 1264) and Balliol (founded in 1263). In 1571 the university was incorporated by Act of Parliament, and henceforward subscription to the *Thirty-nine Articles was required from all its members. In the 17th cent. its statutes were radically remodelled by W. *Laud, who gave them the form which they still possess to-day. Except at certain Halls, religious tests no longer exist. The close and continuous connexion of the university with the life of the Church is shewn by the trials of T. *Cranmer, N. *Ridley, and H. *Latimer in the University Church of St. Mary (1555), the early history of the *Wesleys, and the '*Oxford Movement' in the 19th cent.

For works on Oxford Cathedral see bibl. to *Christ Church*. On the University, H. C. Maxwell Lyte, *A History of the University of Oxford from the Earliest Times to the Year 1530* (1886); C. E. Mallet, *A History of the University of Oxford* (3 vols., 1924–7); H. *Rashdall, *The Universities of Europe in the Middle Ages*, iii (ed. F. M. Powicke–A. B. Emden, 1936), pp. 1–273; *V.C.H.*, Oxford iii, ed. H. E. Salter–Mary Lobel (1954). *City of Oxford* (The Royal Commission on Historical Monuments, 1939). [R. W. Chapman], *Some Account of the Oxford University Press, 1468–1926*) (1926). The 'Oxford Historical Society', founded 1884 for the publication of material on the history of the University and City and neighbourhood, has issued over 100 vols. A. B. Emden, *A Biographical Register of the University of Oxford* (1957 ff.). See also bibl. to *Bodleian Library*.

OXFORD CONFERENCE (1937). The second Conference of the '*Life and Work' branch of the *Oecumenical Movement held at Oxford 12–26 July, 1937, under the general title of 'Church, Community, and State'. There were 425 delegates representing all the more important religious bodies except the RC Church and the German Evangelical Church (then under Nazi control). The report is in eight volumes ('The Church Community and State Series'), including a preliminary volume (vol. i) on the Church, by W. A. Visser't Hooft and J. H. Oldham and a collected summary, *The Churches Survey their Task* (vol. viii). The remaining six volumes, which embody papers, are entitled respectively *The Christian Understanding of Man* (T. E.

Jessop, E. *Brunner, A. M. Farrer, etc.), *The Kingdom of God and History* (C. H. *Dodd, E. Bevan, C. Dawson, H. Wendland, H. G. Wood, etc.), *The Christian Faith and the Common Life* (M. *Dibelius, W. *Temple, R. *Niebuhr, H. H. Farmer, etc.), *Church and Community* (E. Barker, H. Lilje, S. Zankov, K. S. Latourette, M. Boegner, etc.), *Church Community and State in Relation to Education* (F. Clarke, C. R. Morris, P. H. Kohnstamm, etc.) and *The Universal Church and the World of Nations* (A. Zimmern, J. F. Dulles, V. A. Demant, O. Piper, C. E. Raven, etc.). It was agreed to take steps for the fusion of the 'Life and Work' Movement with that of '*Faith and Order', which held a Conference at *Edinburgh (q.v.) a week or two later. The first oecumenical council of the united bodies was held in 1948 at *Amsterdam (q.v.). See also *World Council of Churches*.

'OXFORD GROUP'. The religious movement founded and directed by F. N. D. *Buchman (q.v.). After an experience of conversion at the *Keswick Convention of 1908, Buchman returned to America and did not again visit England until 1920. At Cambridge, and a little later at Oxford, his evangelism made a profound impression on several undergraduates and in the next years, but esp. in and after 1926, his following increased in both Universities, and esp. in Oxford, where he received the active support of certain senior members of the University. In 1929 Buchman, with a group of followers, some of them Oxford men, visited South Africa where the movement became locally known as 'the Oxford Group', a name which it adopted for general use; despite opposition, esp. from members of Oxford University, in Parliament and in the press, it obtained legal incorporation under this name in 1939, but was still often referred to by outsiders as 'Buchmanism', or, more non-committally, as 'the Group Movement'. The most rapid spread of the movement in England was probably in the early thirties and its appeal in the first instance was to the professional and upper classes rather than the less well-to-do. In 1938 the '*Moral Rearmament' movement was launched under Buchman's leadership, and more attention was thenceforward paid to national and international questions, and the support of trade unionists and industrial workers sought. International assemblies were held, in 1946, and following years, at Caux, Switzerland. The movement has permanent secretarial and administrative headquarters in Los Angeles, U.S.A., London, and Caux, and is active in western democratic (but esp. English-speaking) countries generally. It has experienced both Fascist and Communist opposition.

Buchman, referred to inside the movement as 'Frank', is looked up to as the leader and pioneer of this new and more authentic form of the Christian life, and his influence and that of his immediate associates is very great. The movement supports some whole-time workers,

either permanently or for limited periods, but otherwise it has no regular ministry nor meeting-places of a denominational type. It works through personal contact, through the writings of Buchman and others (e.g. A. J. Russell's *For Sinners Only*, many times reprinted, and more recently the books of Peter Howard) and its own publications in pamphlet or magazine form. It holds meetings and conferences (or 'house-parties') in premises hired or temporarily owned *ad hoc*.

The movement met with considerable opposition from the more cultured English circles, religious and secular, on its first appearance, both for its allegedly disingenuous use of the name 'Oxford', and on religious grounds, e.g. that the conversions it secured were spiritually unsound and often only temporary, that its 'sharing' and 'guidance' were ill-advised and were pressed on converts indiscriminately without any true attempt at the cure of souls, and generally that its leaders and enthusiastic adherents were unqualified for the task they assumed and tended to an arrogant disregard of all older Christian bodies. On behalf of the movement it was urged that such charges were no more justified than similar accusations made by cultured contemporaries against the *Methodists, some of the Reformers, or even the early Church itself; that the Groups presented Christianity in a language and manner which enabled it to reach many whom the Church had failed to reach; and that it was the mission of the Groups to shake the older Christian bodies out of their complacency. On some of these grounds it was given more or less qualified approval by some Anglican bishops and other clergymen and ministers.

Of Buchman's own writings (1937 and after, mostly of little documentary importance), *Remaking the World* (1947), a collection of speeches on Moral Rearmament, may be considered typical. Popular expositions of Group principles (omitting many ephemeral tracts) include A. J. Russell, *For Sinners Only* (1932, see text of entry); J. C. Winslow, *Why I believe in the Oxford Group*, with foreword by F. Westcott, Metropolitan of India (1934); Peter Howard, *Ideas have Legs* (1945); id., *That Man Frank Buchman* (1946); G. A. West (Bp. of Rangoon), *The World that Works* (1945). A good short statement is J. P. Thornton-Duesbery, *The Oxford Group. A Brief Account of its Principles and Growth* (1947). Views by outsiders, necessarily critical, are H. H. *Henson, *The Group Movement* (1933; ed. 2., 1934); R. H. S. Crossman (ed.) *Oxford and the Groups* (1934). Also G. Williamson, *Inside Buchmanism* (1950).

OXFORD MOVEMENT, The. The movement (1833–45) within the C of E, centred at Oxford, which aimed at restoring the High Church ideals of the 17th cent. Several causes contributed to its growth. The progressive decline of Church life and the spread of 'Liberalism' in theology were causing grave misgivings among Churchmen; on the other hand, the works of C. *Lloyd and others, coupled with the Romantic Movement, had led to a new interest in many elements in primitive and medieval Christianity. Among the more immediate causes were the fear that the *Catholic Emancipation Act (1829) would lead many Anglicans into the RC Church, the anxiety occasioned by the passing of the

Reform Bill (1832) and the plan to suppress ten Irish bishoprics. The latter proposal evoked from J. *Keble on 14 July 1833 a sermon delivered in the university pulpit at Oxford on '*National Apostasy', which, after J. H. *Newman, is usually regarded as the beginning of the Movement.

Its chief object was the defence of the C of E as a Divine institution, of the doctrine of the Apostolic Succession, and of the BCP as a rule of faith. These aims were realized esp. through the famous *Tracts for the Times, begun by Newman in 1833. The Movement, whose acknowledged leaders were Keble, Newman, and E. B. *Pusey, soon gained many influential supporters, among them R. H. *Froude, R. W. *Church, R. I. *Wilberforce, C. *Marriott, and I. *Williams. The liberal party in the University and the bishops, however, soon began to attack it; among its early opponents were T. *Arnold, R. *Whately, and R. D. *Hampden. Within the Movement itself there gradually arose a party which tended more and more towards submission to Rome. In 1841 Newman published his famous Tract 90, which was condemned by many bishops, and in 1842 he retired to Littlemore.

After W. G. *Ward's book, The Ideal of a Christian Church (1844), had been censured by the Convocation of Oxford on 13 Feb. 1845, Ward, F. W. *Faber, and several of their circle were received into the Church of Rome, and Newman followed later in the same year. But the majority remained in the C of E, and their views began to gain ground. In 1850 the *Gorham Case (q.v.) again brought about a number of conversions to Roman Catholicism, among them being H. E. *Manning and R. I. Wilberforce. The Movement, however, continued to spread despite the hostility of the press and of the government, which chose the majority of bishops from the ranks of its opponents. Its influence was exercised esp. in the sphere of worship and ceremonial, which came to play a much larger part in the life of the C of E than in the 18th and early 19th cents. At the same time the dignity and responsibility of the ministry was emphasized, not only in the directly religious but also in the social sphere, the slum settlements being among its most notable achievements. The institution of religious community life, too, is due to the Oxford Movement, being a natural result of the ideals it propagated. As a movement with close associations with a university it made considerable contributions to scholarship. In 1836 Keble, Newman, and Pusey began to edit the *Library of the Fathers, and a few years later the Library of Anglo-Catholic Theology was begun as a corpus of *Caroline theology. The principles of the Movement, esp. its concern for a higher standard of worship, gradually influenced not only all groups within the C of E, but even many Nonconformists, and have decisively affected the pattern of contemporary Church life in Great Britain and beyond.

There is an immense literature. Besides the writings, tracts, and innumerable controversial pamphlets of the

leaders and their opponents, the biographies supply much primary material. The three fundamental historical sources are J. H. Newman, Apologia pro Vita Sua (1864); H. P. *Liddon, Life of E. B. Pusey (4 vols., 1893–7), and R. W. *Church, The Oxford Movement. Twelve Years, 1833–45 (1891). A contemporary account (partly written in self-defence) is W. *Palmer, A Narrative of Events connected with the Publication of Tracts for the Times (1843). Modern studies include S. Baring Gould, The Church Revival (1914); S. L. Ollard, A Short History of the Oxford Movement (1915); E. A. *Knox, The Tractarian Movement (1933). P. Thureau-Dangin, La Renaissance catholique en Angleterre au XIXᵉ siècle (3 vols., 1899–1906; Eng. tr., 2 vols., 1914); C. P. S. Clarke, The Oxford Movement and After (1932); C. Dawson, The Spirit of the Oxford Movement (1933). W. H. Hutton in A. W. Ward–A. R. Waller (edd.), The Cambridge History of English Literature, xii (1915), pp. 253–78, with bibl., pp. 453–63; further bibl. by S. L. Ollard in C.B.E.L., iii, 853–60. Id. in D.E.C.H., pp. 429–32; id. in H.E.R.E., ix (1917), pp. 585–9. [W.] O. Chadwick (ed.), The Mind of the Oxford Movement (1960).

OXYRHYNCHUS PAPYRI.
The collection of many thousand fragments of papyri, found from 1897 onwards at Oxyrhynchus, a centre of Christian culture in the 4th cent., some 10 miles west of the Nile, near the modern Behnesa. The most celebrated are two series of '*Sayings of Jesus' (Nos. 1 and 654; q.v.). Among others of Christian interest are a letter of *Peter, the martyred Bp. of Alexandria (d. 311), found together with an ecclesiastical calendar of A.D. 535–6 (No. 1357), and a Christian hymn with musical notation which is the oldest known piece of ecclesiastical music (No. 1786; late 3rd cent.).

The papyri are being ed., with Eng. tr., by B. P. Grenfell, A. S. Hunt, H. I. Bell, C. H. Roberts, E. P. Wegener, and E. Lobel for the Egypt Exploration Fund, Graeco-Roman Branch (London, 1898 ff.). B. P. Grenfell–A. S. Hunt (edd.), Hellenica Oxyrhynchia (O.C.T., 1909).

OZANAM, ANTOINE FRÉDÉRIC (1813–1853),
French scholar and founder of the 'Society of St. *Vincent de Paul'. At the age of 18 he wrote a pamphlet against C. H. *Saint-Simon, and two years later, while studying law and literature at Paris, founded the Society of St. Vincent de Paul, an association of laymen for personal service among the poor. During his early years in Paris Ozanam made the acquaintance of R. *Chateaubriand, C. F. R. *Montalembert, H. D. *Lacordaire, and other progressive thinkers who became closely associated with the revival of Catholicism in France. In 1839 he published a brilliant thesis on the philosophy of *Dante; in 1841 he became assistant professor of foreign literature at the Sorbonne, and simultaneously professor of rhetoric at the Collège Stanislas, then under the direction of A. J. A. *Gratry; and in 1844 full professor at the Sorbonne. On the bases of researches in Italian libraries (1846) he edited some early *Franciscan poetry (Poètes franciscains en Italie au XIIIᵉ siècle, 1852), of much importance for the history of medieval spirituality. Together with Lacordaire he founded the Ère nouvelle in 1848 as a mouthpiece of their ideas on Catholic socialism. In the next year he published his influential work La Civilisation chrétienne chez les Francs, in which he described the influence of the Church on the education of the Teutonic tribes. A keen advocate of political liberalism, he became the

subject of many sharp attacks, and spent his last years away from public life in work for his Society and in travelling.

Collected ed. of his works, with preface signed J. J. Ampère, 8 vols., Paris, '1855', with life by H. D. Lacordaire (dated '1856') appended to vol. i [separate pagination]. Life by his brother, Charles Alphonse Ozanam (Paris, 1879). The numerous other studies include those of Kathleen O'Meara (Edinburgh, 1876), C. Huit (Lyons, 1888), L. Baunard (Paris, 1913; Eng. tr., Dublin [1925]), G. Goyau and others (Paris, 1913; to mark the centenary of his birth), J. C. Crighton (Port-Louis, 1933), H. L. Hughes (London, 1933) and the vol. issued by the Society of St. Paul to mark the centenary of its foundation, *L'Œuvre d'Ozanam à travers le monde, 1833–1933* (1933). L. Curnier, *La Jeunesse de Frédéric Ozanam* (1888). J. Méjecaze, *Fr. Ozanam et l'Église catholique* (Toulouse thesis; Lyons-Paris, 1932); id., *Fr. Ozanam et les lettres* (ib., 1932). A. Foucault, *La Société de Saint Vincent de Paul. Histoire de cent ans* (1933). E. Galopin, *Essai de bibliographie chronologique sur Antoine Frédéric Ozanam* (1933). C. Constantin in *D.T.C.*, xi (pt. 2; 1936), cols. 1706–10, s.v.; P. Paschini in *E.C.*, ix (1952), cols. 487–9, s.v., both with bibl.

P

'P'. The name usually given since J. *Wellhausen to the 'Priestly source' held to be embodied in the *Pentateuch. It is marked by a preponderance in general of ritual and ceremonial enactments over narrative (e.g. Exod. 25–40, Lev. (all), and much of Num.), a formal style sometimes rising to great dignity (e.g. the first account of Creation, Gen. 1. 1–2. 3), the avoidance of anthropomorphic or primitive ideas of God (contrast, e.g., Gen. 3. 8, J), the use of a historical framework linking events by means of genealogies, and the inclusion of numerical information (sometimes historically improbable, e.g. Exod. 12. 37). The priesthood is conceived as limited to the sons of *Aaron (not merely to the tribe of Levi as in '*D'), and the divine Name 'Jehovah' (Yahweh; AV and RV 'the LORD') is used only after its revelation to Moses, related in Exod. 3 (not from the first as in '*J'). Although it is increasingly agreed that 'P' embodies earlier matter, in its final edaction it is the latest element in the Pentateuch, dating from the Exile (586–38 B.C.) or after, though not later than c. 400 B.C. See also *Holiness, Code of*.

PACELLI, Cardinal. See *Pius XII, Pope*.

PACHOMIUS, St. (c. 290–346), the founder of *coenobitic Christian monasticism. It is difficult to disentangle fact and legend from the many late Lives. He appears to have been born in Upper Egypt, to have served against his will in the army, and after his release to have been converted and baptized. After some three years' discipleship to the hermit Palaemon, he built a monastery at Tabennisi on the right bank of the Nile (c. 320), to which large numbers of monks were soon attracted by the repute of his sanctity. Other monasteries soon followed, so that by the time of his death there were nine monasteries for men and two for women under his rule. They served as a model for the monastic foundations of St. *Basil later in the century. The 'Rule of Pachomius' in its original form no longer survives. Feast day, 14 May; in the Coptic Church, 9 May.

Brief notices in *Palladius, *Historia Lausiaca*, 32 (ed. C. Butler, O.S.B., pp. 87–97), and in Sozomen, *H.E.*, III, xiv. His *Rule* and eleven of his *Epp.* survive in a Lat. tr. by St. *Jerome (*PL*, xxiii, 61–99), with fragments of the Rule also in Gk. and Copt. Several Copt., Gk., Syr., and Arab. Lives of Pachomius also exist; Gk. Lives ed. by F. Halkin, S.J., *S. Pachomii Vitae Graecae* (Brussels, 1932); Coptic Lives (Bohairic and Sahidic) ed. L. T. Lefort (C.S.C.O., 1925–34). E. Amélineau, *Histoire de St. Pakhôme et de ses communautés*. Documents coptes et arabes inédits (Annales du Musée Guimet, No. 17, 1889), with text of an Arab. Life. Syr. Life ed. P. Bedjan in *Acta Martyrum et Sanctorum*, v (Paris, 1895), pp. 122–76. P. Ledeuze, *Étude sur le cénobitisme pakhômien pendant le quatrième siècle et la première moitié du cinquième* (1888); G. Grützmacher, *Pachomius und das älteste Klosterleben* (1896). A. Boon, *Pachomiana Latina. Règle et épîtres de St. Pachôme, épître de St. Théodore* et *Liber* de St. Orsiesius (Louvain, 1932). V. Monachino in *E.C.*, ix (1952), cols. 511–14, s.v., with bibl.

PACIAN, St. (4th cent.), Bp. of Barcelona. A Spaniard by birth, he warmly defended the Catholic doctrine of the forgiveness of sins against the *Novatianists, then a flourishing body in Spain. Besides three letters, a short treatise, *Paraenesis ad Poenitentiam*, survives. Pacian is esp. remembered for the epigrammatic passage which occurs in one of his letters (*Ep.* i, 4), 'My name is Christian; my surname is Catholic' (*Christianus mihi nomen est, catholicus vero cognomen*). To his son, Flavius Dexter, who became pretorian prefect under Honorius, St. *Jerome dedicated his *De Viris Illustribus*. Feast day, 9 Mar.

Works first ed. by F. du Tillet (Paris, 1538), repr. in J. P. Migne, *PL*, xiii, 1051–94. Modern ed. by P. H. Peyrot (Zwolle, 1896). A. Grube⁻, *Studien zu Pacianus von Barcelona* (1901; philological); R. Kauer, *Studien zu Pacianus* (1902). Bardenhewer, iii, 401–3; Altaner (ed. 1950), p. 322 f. É. Amann in *D.T.C.*, xi (pt. 2; 1932), cols. 1718–21, s.v. 'Pacien'; J. Zellinger in *L.Th.K.*, vii (1935), col. 862 f., s.v., with bibl.; G. Madoz, S.J., in *E.C.*, ix (1952), col. 504 f., with further bibl.

PACIFISM. See *War, Christian Attitude to*.

PADRE. Popular designation of a chaplain in the Army, Navy, and Air Force and frequently used of all clergymen. *Padre* is the Italian, Spanish, and Portuguese for 'Father', and hence became a common title for a priest. The term is supposed to have been picked up by the British army in India.

PAEDOBAPTISM. See *Infant Baptism*.

PAGET, FRANCIS (1851–1911), Bp. of *Oxford. Educated at Shrewsbury and *Christ Church, Oxford, he became a senior student of Christ Church in 1873, Regius professor of pastoral theology in 1885, Dean of Christ Church in 1892, and Bp. of Oxford in 1901. Except from 1882 to 1885, when he held the vicarage of Bromsgrove, his work lay in Oxford throughout his life. He warmly supported the reinterpretation of *Tractarian principles by the *Lux Mundi group and himself contributed the essay on 'Sacraments' to the volume (1889). He also completed R. W. *Church's revision of J. *Keble's edition of R. *Hooker's *Ecclesiastical Polity* (1883–8) and wrote *An Introduction to the Fifth Book* of Hooker's treatise (1899). His fine spirituality is reflected in his *Spirit of Discipline* (1891), which contains a notable essay on '*Accidie'. He also took an important part in ecclesiastical politics, and was one of the most influential members of the Royal Commission on Ecclesiastical Discipline (1904–6).

Stephen Paget and J. M. C. Crum, *Francis Paget* (1913). E. H. Pearce in *D.N.B.*, 1901–11, iii (1912), p. 62 f.

PAGET, HENRY LUKE (1852–1932), Bp. of *Chester. Brother of the preceding, he was educated at Shrewsbury and *Christ Church, Oxford, ordained in 1877, and worked extensively in the East End of London, founding the Christ Church Mission at Poplar in 1879. Later he became Bp. of Ipswich (1906–9), of Stepney (1909–19), and of Chester (1919–32). Personal contact as a young man with E. B. *Pusey, J. H. *Newman, E. *King, and H. P. *Liddon had imbued him with the *Tractarian ideals; and he was a typical representative of the best Anglican pastors of his generation.

Elma K. Paget (widow), *Henry Luke Paget.* Portrait and Frame (1939).

PAGI, ANTOINE (1624–99), French Church historian. A native of Rognes in Provence, he studied with the *Jesuits at Aix and entered the Order of Conventual *Franciscans at an early age. He frequently filled the office of *Provincial. His principal work is the *Critica historico-chronologica*, a learned attempt to correct the errors contained in the *Annals* of C. *Baronius. The first volume of it appeared in 1689; the complete work, in 4 vols., was edited posthumously by his nephew, François Pagi, in 1705. Among his other writings are the *Dissertatio hypatica* (1682) on the Roman consuls, and a Latin edition of the sermons of St. *Anthony of Padua (1685).

A. Teetaert, O.F.M.Cap., in *D.T.C.*, xi (pt. 2; 1932), col. 1728 f., s.v.

PAGNINUS, SANTES (d. 1541), *Dominican scholar. A native of Lucca, he was the first modern scholar to render the whole Bible from the original languages. His Latin version, which he completed c. 1518, was remarkably literal. It was published at Lyons in 1528 (ed. 2, Cologne, 1541) and was extensively drawn on by M. *Coverdale in preparing the *Great Bible (1539). He was also the compiler of a Hebrew Lexicon.

G. Pagnino, *Vita di S. Pagnino Lucchese, dell' ordine de' predicatori* (Rome, 1653). T. M. Centi, 'L' attività letteraria di Santi Pagnini nel campo della scienze bibliche' in *Archivum Fratrum Praedicatorum*, xv (1945, pp. 5–51. (Quétif–Échard, ii, pp. 114–18.

PAIN BÉNIT. The blessed bread which in French and Canadian churches is often distributed to the people after High Mass. It has its counterpart among the E. Orthodox, where the so-called 'antidoron' (ἀντίδωρον), i.e. what remains of the loaves from which the Eucharistic Bread is cut, is held to share in the liturgical offering, and is distributed as a consolation to those unable to receive Holy Communion. The modern French custom distinguishes carefully between the Eucharistic Bread and the *pain bénit* by assigning to the latter a special blessing and regarding it as at most a symbol of charity and spiritual unity.

PAINE, THOMAS (1737–1809), political reformer and author of the *Rights of Man*. He was a native of Thetford in Norfolk and,

though confirmed in the C of E, was greatly influenced by the principles of the *Quakers, of which his father was a member. He was of an adventurous spirit, and after a chequered career as a sailor, staymaker, excise officer, and usher went to America in 1774 at the suggestion of Benjamin Franklin. There he became an editor, attacked slavery, and agitated for the emancipation of women. In 1776 he issued his pamphlet *Common Sense* in favour of American independence, which soon made him famous. During the American War he wrote a series of pamphlets entitled *The Crisis.* He also devoted himself to the invention of an iron bridge which he exhibited in England after his return in 1787. In 1791 he published the first part of his famous *Rights of Man* in reply to E. Burke's *Reflections on the Revolution in France*. After the publication of the second part (1792) he fled to Paris to escape arrest. Here he was received with enthusiasm, but he lost his influence after the fall of the Girondists in 1793 and was arrested in the same year, after completing the first part of his *Age of Reason* (1794). He was released in 1794, having written the second part of his work in prison (publd. 1795). The *Age of Reason*, which aroused fierce opposition both in Britain and America, reflected the Quaker influence of his youth as well as that of contemporary *Deism in its negative estimate of revealed religion, whose beliefs and institutions are ridiculed as full of superstition and bad faith. In 1802 he returned to America, where he spent his last years in disappointment, having lost most of his former friends through his political opinions and his hostility to Christianity.

Collected Works ed. M. D. Conway (4 vols., New York–London, 1894–6) and P. S. Foner (2 vols., New York, 1945), with biographical introd. in i, pp. ix–xlvi. Modern edd. of *The Rights of Man* (1937) and *The Age of Reason* (1938) in the 'Thinkers' Library'. The standard life is that of M. D. Conway (2 vols., New York–London, 1892). Modern studies by F. J. Gould (London, 1925), Mary A. Best (ib., 1927), H. Pearson (ib., 1937), H. [M.] Fast (ib., 1945), and W. E. Woodward (ib., 1946). L. Stephen in *D.N.B.*, xliii (1895), pp. 69–79, with refl. to earlier works.

PALAMAS. See *Gregory Polamas*.

PALATINE GUARD. A corps of militia in the Papal service. It was created in 1850 by *Pius IX as the 'Guardia Palatina d' Onore' out of two existing bodies, the *civici scelti* and the *capotori*; but since 1870 their numbers have been greatly reduced. A company is always stationed in the Cortile del Maresciallo during a Papal *conclave. Their dress is a uniform of dark blue and a peaked cap with a plume of feathers. See also *Noble Guard, Swiss Guard*.

G. Felici in *E.C.*, vi (1951), cols. 1204–6, s.v. 'Guardia palatina d' onore', with bibl. and illustr.

PALESTINE EXPLORATION FUND. A fund and society founded in London in 1865 for the purpose of surveying and mapping W. Palestine and excavating important sites. A similar fund, organized in Germany in 1887, surveyed Palestine east of Jordan. The most valuable work of the English society has been done at Lachish and Gezer. From 1865 to 1936 the society published a *Quarterly Statement* devoted to Biblical archaeology, which since 1937 has been continued as the *Palestine Exploration Quarterly*.

PALESTINIAN SYRIAC TEXT OF THE NT.

A version of the NT in the Palestinian dialect of Syriac which, acc. to F. C. *Burkitt, originated at *Antioch in the 6th cent. Its text is attested mainly in *lectionaries. The relatively primitive character of its readings is shown by the fact that they often agree with those of the *Codex Vaticanus (B) against the great majority of later MSS.

The principal texts are contained in P. de *Lagarde, *Bibliotheca Syriaca* (Göttingen, 1892), Agnes S. Lewis and Margaret D. Gibson, *The Palestinian Syriac Lectionary of the Gospels* (1899) and *Studia Sinaitica*, No. vi (1897). F. C. Burkitt, 'Christian Palestinian Literature' in *J.T.S.*, ii (1900–1), pp. 174–185.

PALESTRINA, GIOVANNI PIERLUIGI DA

(*c.* 1525–94), Italian composer. He received his musical education at Rome and, in 1544, became organist of the cathedral of his native town Palestrina. In 1551 Pope *Julius III appointed him musical instructor at the Capella Giulia of St. Peter's with the title of 'Magister Capellae'. About this time St. *Philip Neri became his friend and confessor, and under his influence Palestrina devoted himself increasingly to the interests of the Church. In 1555 the Pope made him a member of the Papal choir despite his being married, but this office he had to resign a few months later under *Paul IV. In the same year he was appointed 'Maestro della Capella' of St. John *Lateran, where he composed among other things the famous *Improperia*, first performed in 1561. From 1561 to 1571 he held a similar post at *Santa Maria Maggiore and here probably composed his celebrated *Missa Papae Marcelli*, which met the requirements of the decree on church music of the 22nd session of the Council of *Trent. In 1565 Palestrina was nominated Composer of the Papal Chapel, a post specially created for him and which he justified by producing an enormous number of Masses and motets. In 1570 he was charged with the music of St. Philip Neri's *Oratory. For this purpose he wrote many of his spiritual *madrigals. In the following year he was appointed choirmaster of St. Peter's, a post he filled till his death. Among the best-known works of this last period of his life are the *Motets* to words taken from the Song of Songs, dedicated to *Gregory XIII, and the Mass *Assumpta est Maria*, first performed in 1585.

Palestrina's music, coinciding with a time of vigorous ecclesiastical reforms, is deeply religious. In an age when ecclesiastical music had suffered greatly from secular influences, the austere polyphony of Palestrina's work won the approval of the Church authorities and became one of the most important factors in the subsequent development of sacred music.

Complete Works ed. T. de Witt–F. Epagne–F. Commer–F. X. Haberl (33 vols., Breitkopf–Härtel, Leipzig [1862–1907]); also ed. R. Casimiri–L. Virgili, etc. (Rome, 1939 ff.). G. Baini, *Memorie storico-critiche della vita e delle opere di Giovanni Pierluigi Palestrina* (2 vols., 1828). R. Casimiri, *Nuovi documenti biografici* (2 fascc., 1918–22). Other studies include those of M. Brenet (Paris, 1906), Z. K. Pyne (London, 1922), A. Cametti (Milan [1925]), F. Raugel (Paris, 1930), and H. Coates (London, 1938). K. G. Fellerer, *Der Palestrinastil und seine Bedeutung in der vokalen Kirchenmusik des achtzehnten Jahrhunderts* (1929). K. Jeppesen, *Palestrinastil met scerligt henblik paa dissonansbehandlingen* (1923; Eng. tr., 1927, revised ed., 1946). H. Coates in *Grove's Dictionary of Music and Musicians* (ed. 5 by E. Blom), vi (1954), pp. 506–25, s.v.

PALEY, WILLIAM

(1743–1805), author of the *Evidences of Christianity*. Educated at Christ's College, Cambridge, where his unusual abilities, esp. in mathematics, attracted much attention, he was elected Fellow in 1766 and soon became a much-sought-after lecturer. His first book, *The Principles of Moral and Political Philosophy* (1785), an expansion of his lectures on ethics, was at once adopted at Cambridge as a standard textbook. This was followed in 1790 by his *Horae Paulinae*, written to prove the historicity of the NT by a comparison of the accounts of St. *Paul in the Epistles and Acts; it was the only really original work which Paley wrote. In 1794 appeared the first edition of the famous *View of the Evidences of Christianity*. Though its arguments added little that was new, the work became extremely popular from its effective presentation of the facts and its pellucid style. In estimating its external and somewhat mechanical view of revelation, it must be remembered that Paley shared this with his age. His last book, *Natural Theology* (1802), covers in more thorough fashion parts of the same groundwork as the *Evidences*. In 1776 Paley became Rector of Musgrave, Westmorland, and in 1782 Archdeacon of *Carlisle; but the *latitudinarianism of his younger days is said to have debarred him from the ecclesiastical preferment which usually fell to men of his abilities.

Editions of his Works with Life by A. Chalmers (5 vols., 1819), by Edmund Paley (son, 7 vols., 1825), by R. Lyman with memoir (4 vols., 1825), and in one vol. (1831). G. W. Meadley, *Memoirs of William Paley* (1809). L. Stephen in *D.N.B.*, xliii (1895), pp. 101–7.

PALIMPSEST

(Gk. πάλιν, 'again', ψάω, 'I rub'). A vellum or papyrus MS. from which the original writing has been erased or obliterated and the surface then used for some (usually quite different) writing. Of Biblical MSS., the best-known instance is the so-called *Codex Ephraemi ('C') of the Gk. NT. Many of the sheets of the original 5th cent. MS. (which appears to have contained a complete OT and NT) have been lost or thrown away, and the remainder cleaned and written over in the 12th cent. with some writings of St. *Ephraem Syrus. Formerly chemical reagents were much used to reveal the underlying writings, but it is now possible to secure in many cases at least equally successful results by photography, which has the great advantage that there is no risk of damage to the MS. Instances are known of 'double palimpsests', where the MS. has received three texts.

F. Mone, *De Libris Palimpsestis tam Latinis quam Graecis* (Carlsruhe, 1855). E. Chatelain, *Les Palimpsestes latins* (École Pratique des Hautes Études. Section des Sciences Historiques et Philologiques, 1904). A. Dold [O.S.B.], 'Palimpsest-Handschriften. Ihre Erschliessung einst und jetzt; ihre Bedeutung' in *Gutenberg-Jahrbuch* [xxv] (1950), pp. 16–24; also a number of other articles by this author (list of his works in *Colligere Fragmenta*. Festschrift Alban Dold zum 70. Geburtstag ed. B. Fischer, O.S.B.–V. Fiala [Texte und Arbeiten [the organ of the Palimpsest Institute founded by Dold at Beuron], i, Hft. 2; 1952], pp. ix–xx). E. M. Thompson, *An Introduction to Greek and Latin Palaeography* (1912), pp. 64–6. A. Dold, O.S.B., in *E.C.*, ix (1951), cols. 632–5, s.v. 'Palinsesto', with bibl.

PALL. Originally the same word as *pallium, it has been applied to several kinds of cloth covering. In ecclesiastical usage it denotes esp. (1) the small linen cloth with which the chalice is covered at the Eucharist, stiffened in its modern form by a piece of cardboard; and (2) a cloth, commonly of black, purple, or white velvet, which is spread over the coffin at funerals.

PALLADIUS (*c.* 365–425), historian of early monasticism. Probably a native of Galatia, he spent several years with the monks of Egypt and Palestine, returning in 400 to Asia Minor, where he became Bp. of Helenopolis in Bithynia. As a friend of St. *Chrysostom he was forced into exile in 406, though he returned to Asia Minor later (*c.* 412). Both St. *Jerome and St. *Epiphanius accused him of *Origenism, but it is not clear that the charge was well founded. His famous 'Lausiac History' (so named from its dedication to Lausus, the chamberlain of *Theodosius II) of the 'Friends of God' (φιλόθεοι, i.e. the monks), composed *c.* 419, is the most valuable single writing that survives for the history of early monasticism. If somewhat credulous about stories relating to the Egyptian monks, it is the work of a writer indubitably sincere and unquestionably religious. Palladius is probably also the author of a 'Dialogue' on the life of St. Chrysostom.

Gk. text of 'Lausiac History' first ed. J. Meursius, Leyden, 1616. New ed. by F. *Ducaeus in his *Bibliotheca Veterum Patrum*, ii (Paris, 1624), pp. 893–1053; repr. in J. P. Migne, *PG*, xxxiv, 991–1262. Crit. text, with introd. and discussion in [E.] C. Butler (Texts and Studies, vi, Nos. 1 and 2; Cambridge, 1898–1904). Eng. tr. by W. K. L. Clarke (Translations of Christian Literature, Series 1, Greek Texts; S.P.C.K., 1918). The 'Dialogus' was first pr. by E. Bigot, Paris, 1680; repr. by B. de *Montfaucon in his ed. of Chrysostom, xiii (Paris, 1738), pp. 1–89, and in J. P. Migne, *PG*, xlvii, 5–82. Crit. ed. by P. R. Coleman-Norton (Cambridge, 1928). Eng. tr. by H. Moore (Translations of Christian Literature, Series 1, Greek Texts; S.P.C.K., 1921). E. Preuschen, *Palladius und Rufinus*. Ein Beitrag zur Quellenkunde des ältesten Mönchtums (1897); R. *Reitzenstein, *Historia Monachorum und Historia Lausiaca* (1916); W. *Bousset, 'Komposition und Charakter der Historia Lausiaca' in *Nach.* (Gött.), 1917, pp. 173–217. E. *Schwartz, 'Palladiana' in *Z.N.T.W.*, xxxvi (1937), pp. 161–204. Bardenhewer, iv, 148–57; Altaner (ed. 1951), p. 188 f. (with bibl. of important artt. by R. Draguet and others). O. Zöckler in *P.R.E.* (ed. 3), xiv (1904), pp. 609–12; A. *Fortescue in *C.E.*, xi (1911), p 425 f.; É. Amann in *D.T.C.*, xi (pt. 2; 1932), cols. 1823–30.

PALLADIUS, St. (5th cent.), early Irish missionary. Acc. to *Prosper of Aquitaine, he persuaded Pope *Celestine I to send St. *Germanus, Bp. of Auxerre, to stamp out the *Pelagian heresy in Britain and was later himself consecrated by the same Pope, who sent him to the Irish as their first bishop. He worked in Wicklow, where the sites of three of his churches have been identified. His mission seems, however, to have met with little success and he eventually left for Scotland where he probably died shortly afterwards. It is uncertain whether he was of British or Roman origin. Neither the medieval Scottish tradition that he did mission preaching in Scotland for twenty-three years nor the attempt (elaborated esp. by H. Zimmer) to identify him with St. *Patrick seems defensible. Feast day, 7 July.

The principal sources are the Chronicle of Prosper of Aquitaine (for edd. of which see art. *Prosper*) and material incorporated into the lives of St. Patrick. H. Zimmer in *P.R.E.* (ed. 3), x (1901), pp. 214–18, s.v. 'Keltische Kirche' (Eng. tr. of art. by A. Meyer as *The Celtic Church in Britain and Ireland* (1902), pp. 32–9). J. B. Bury, *St. Patrick and his Place in History* (1905), esp. pp. 54–8, with note on Palladius, pp. 342–4, and full reff. L. Gougaud, O.S.B., *Les Chrétientés celtiques* (Bibliothèque de l'Enseignement de l'Histoire Ecclésiastique, 1911), pp. 38–41 (Eng. tr., 1932, pp. 29–31). J. L. G. Meissner, 'The British Tradition of St. Patrick's Life' in *Proceedings of the Royal Irish Academy*, xl (1932), pp. 356–84, esp. pp. 369–77; id. in W. A. Phillips (ed.), *History of the Church of Ireland*, i (1933), pp. 376–8 (Appendix E, 'The Mission of Palladius'). G. T. Stokes in *D.C.B.*, iv (1887), p. 176 f., s.v.; C. R. Beazley in *D.N.B.*, xliii (1895), p. 112 f. See also bibl. to *Ireland, Christianity in*, and *Patrick, St.*

PALLIUM. In ecclesiastical usage, the circular band of white woollen material with two hanging strips and marked with six dark purple crosses which is worn on the shoulders by the Pope and granted by him to archbishops (and occasionally also to other bishops) of the RC Church. It is held to symbolize the 'plenitude of the pontifical office' and participation in the authority of the Pope. No archbishop may exercise jurisdiction till it has been petitioned for and granted. It is made from the wool of lambs blessed on St. *Agnes' Day in the Church of St. Agnese fuori le mura while the *Agnus Dei is being sung, and, before dispatch, rests for a night on the tomb of St. *Peter in the Vatican basilica. The early history of the Pallium is very obscure. It seems to have been worn at first by archbishops and to have had no connexion with Rome, still less with the investment of Papal authority. At a later stage, after the Pope had himself assumed it, he seems occasionally to have sent it to individual prelates as a mark of special honour, and in this way its reception became much coveted. Not until the 9th cent. were all metropolitans required to petition for it. Its E. counterpart is the '*omophorion' (ὠμοφόριον), which the E. patriarchs transmit to their metropolitans. The Pallium naturally went out of use in the C of E at the *Reformation, though it still appears in some armorial bearings where it appears (as in a front or back view of the wearer) in the shape of the letter Y.

N. de Bralion, Cong. Orat., *Pallium Archiepiscopale* (Paris, 1648). P. de *Marca, De Concordia Sacerdotii et Imperii* (ib., 1663), pp. 79–88. H. Thurston, S.J., *The Pallium* (Historical Papers ed. J. Morris, S.J., iv [c. 1893]). H. Grisar, S.J., 'Das römische Pallium und die ältesten liturgischen Schärpen' in S. Ehses (ed.), *Festschrift zum elfhundertjährigen Jubiläum des Deutschen Campo Santo in Rom* (1897), pp. 83–114. J. W. Legg, 'The Blessing of the Episcopal Ornament called the Pall' in *Yorkshire Archaeological Journal*, xv (1898), pp. 121–41. J. Wilpert, 'Der Parallelismus in der Entwicklung der *toga* und des *pallium*' in *B.Z.*, viii (1899), pp. 490–2. Braun, *L.G.*, pp. 620–76; Braun, *L.P.*, pp. 143–51. J. Braun, S.J., in *C.E.*, xi (1911), pp. 427–9; s.v.; H. *Leclercq, O.S.B., in *D.A.C.L.*, xiii (pt. 1; 1937), pp. 931–40, s.v., with detailed bibl.; P. Siffrin in *E.C.*, ix (1952), col. 644 f., s.v. 'Pallio', with more recent bibl.

PALLOTTINI FATHERS, The. A society of RC priests, lay brothers, sisters and associates, founded in 1835 by Bl. Vincent Pallotti (1795–1850), an Italian of noble descent, who after ordination as priest (1818) devoted his life to apostolic work in Rome. Since 1854 the Fathers have been known as the 'Pious Society of Missions' (P.S.M.; *Pia Societas Missionum*). Their original aims closely resembled those of *Catholic Action of which *Pius XI saw in Pallotti a forerunner. They work in Italy and many distant lands (*Brazil, N. America, *Australia) as well as in *Poland and Germany. The sisters (*Congregatio Missionum Pallotinarum*) were founded by Pallotti in 1843 as a separate Congregation. One of their chief interests is the return of the Oriental Christians to the RC Church. To this end they have fostered since 1836 the observance of the Octave of the Epiphany as a special time of prayer.

[J. Hettenkofer], *Historia Piae Societatis Missionum* (Rome, 1935); id., *Historia Societatis Apostolatus Catholici, 1935–1950* (ib., 1950). M. Heimbucher, *Die Orden und Kongregationen der katholischen Kirche*, ii (ed. 3, 1934), pp. 614–19, with detailed bibl.

PALM SUNDAY (*Dominica in Palmis*). The Sunday before *Easter which introduces *Holy Week. The distinctive ceremonies of the day are the blessing of the palms and the procession, representing our Lord's triumphal entry into *Jerusalem a week before the Resurrection. The Palm Sunday procession is attested for Jerusalem as early as the 4th cent. by the 'Peregrinatio Etheriae' (see *Etheria*). In the W. it is first met with in the *Gallican 'Sacramentary of *Bobbio' (7th/8th cent.) which also contains a blessing of the palms, to be carried as symbols of the victory of Christ and protection against the devil. In the Middle Ages the procession usually set out from one church and made its way to another, where the palms were blessed and distributed, and then returned to the church from which it had started. Frequently a representation of Christ, e.g. the Gospel book or a crucifix or a carved figure seated on a wooden ass, was carried in the procession. The use of the Blessed Sacrament for the purpose was ordered by Abp. *Lanfranc for the cathedral at *Canterbury c. 1078, and thence spread to Rouen and several places in England.

A very elaborate rite for the blessing of the palms developed during the early Middle Ages, similar in structure to the Mass. In the C of E the ceremony was abolished by an Order in Council in Jan. 1549 and has never been included in the BCP. In the RC Church it was radically simplified by the decree 'Maxima Redemptionis Nostrae Mysteria' of 16 Nov. 1955 which revised the whole Liturgy for Holy Week. According to this rite, after the palms have been blessed and distributed to the clergy and also to the people (except in places where the people bring their own and hold them during a general blessing), the Gospel (Matt. 21. 1–9) is read by the deacon, and the clergy and people process behind an unveiled Cross for some distance, if possible outside the church, singing a hymn (traditionally the 'Gloria, Laus' 'All Glory, Laud and Honour' by *Theodulph of Orléans). After returning to the church, or in another church, a solemn Mass follows, which includes the chanting of the Passion acc. to St. Matthew. The proper colour for the procession is red, for the Mass purple; and the day is now no longer known as 'Palm Sunday,' but as the 'Second *Passion Sunday'. In the Byzantine Rite the Liturgy is followed by a procession in which the celebrant carries the *icon of the day.

The texts for the Latin Rite are pr. in the Roman Missal with the rest of the Palm Sunday proper. H. Thurston, S.J., *Lent and Holy Week* (1904), pp. 191–237. A. Franz, *Die kirchlichen Benediktionen im Mittelalter*, i (1909), pp. 470–505. L. Eisenhofer, *Handbuch der katholischen Liturgik*, i (1932), pp. 504–11. A. *Baumstark, 'Orientalisches in den Texten der abendländischen Palmfeier' in *J.L.W.*, vii (1927), pp. 148–53; id., 'La Solennité des Palmes dans l'ancienne et la nouvelle Rome' in *Irénikon*, xiii (1936), pp. 3–24. C. Callewaert, 'De Palmwijding en de Palmprocessie' in *Tijdschrift voor Liturgie*, x (1929), pp. 66–70, repr. in Callewaert's *Sacris Erudiri*. Fragmenta Liturgica collecta a Monachis Sancti Petri de Aldenburgo in Steenbrugge (Steenbrugge, 1940), pp. 701–11. O. Casel, O.S.B., 'Die Präfation der Palmenweihe' in *J.L.W.*, ii (1922), pp. 107–9; id., 'Zur Präfation der Palmenweihe', ib., iii (1923), p. 120; id., 'Neue Beiträge zur Geschichte der Palmweihepräfation', ib., iv (1929), pp. 183–5. F. Mersham, O.S.B., in *C.E.*, xi (1911), p. 432 f., s.v.; H. *Leclercq, O.S.B., in *D.A.C.L.*, xiv (pt. 1; 1948), cols. 2060–4, s.v. 'Rameaux (Dimanche de)'; P. Siffrin, O.S.B., in *E.C.*. ix (1952), cols. 654–6, s.v. 'Palme, Domenica delle'.

PALMER, ROUNDELL (1812–95). First Earl of Selborne, Lord Chancellor, and High Churchman. Educated at Rugby, Winchester, and Trinity College, Oxford, he was elected a Fellow of Magdalen in 1835. His brilliant abilities led him to rise rapidly in his profession; he was Lord Chancellor in 1872–4 and again in 1880–5. A devoted member of the C of E, he admired the leaders of the *Oxford Movement, actively supported I. *Williams's candidature for the Poetry Professorship, and expressed his belief that the condemnation of E. B. *Pusey's 1843 Sermon was illegal. Until 1869 he was opposed to the entrance of Dissenters to Oxford university. His writings include *The Book of Praise* (1863), a hymnal on historical principles, *Notes on Some Passages in the Liturgical History of the English Church* (1878), *A Defence of the Church of England against Disestablishment* (1886), and *Ancient Facts and Fictions concerning Churches and Tithes* (1888). He also contributed the art.

'Hymns' to the 9th ed. of the *Encyclopaedia Britannica*.

Palmer's *Letters to his Son on Religion* were posthumously publd. London, 1898; also *The Catholic and Apostolic Church*. Letters to his Son, ib., 1899. Autobiographical *Memorials*, ed. by his daughter, Sophia M. Palmer (Part I, Family and Personal, 2 vols., London, 1896; Part II, Personal and Political, 2 vols., ib., 1898). J. M. Rigg in *D.N.B.*, xliii (1895), pp. 150-4.

PALMER, WILLIAM (1803-85), Fellow of Worcester College, Oxford (from 1831), and *Tractarian theologian. His *Origines Liturgicae* (1832), a learned treatise on the history of the English liturgy, brought him into relations with J. *Keble, H. J. *Rose, and others who led the *Oxford Movement in the next years. A rigid High Churchman who was strongly opposed both to Popery and Dissent, he expounded what he conceived to be the Anglican doctrine of the Church (roughly the so-called *Branch Theory) in his *Treatise on the Church of Christ* (2 vols., 1838) with learning and lucidity. When under the influence of such men as J. H. *Newman and esp. W. G. *Ward the Oxford Movement became less anti-Roman in its ideals, W. Palmer gave public expression to his misgivings in his *Narrative of Events connected with the Publication of Tracts for the Times* (1843). In 1846 he issued a reply to J. H. Newman's *Doctrine of Development*. The Roman Jesuit theologian, G. *Perrone, described him as 'theologorum Oxoniensium facile princeps'.

G. Goodwin in *D.N.B.*, xliii (1895), pp. 168-70, with reff.

PALMER, WILLIAM (1811-79), Fellow of Magdalen College, Oxford (from 1832), and divine. Though for his day an extreme High Churchman, he took little direct part in the *Oxford Movement. In 1840 and 1842 he paid visits to Russia, provided with letters of commendation from the revered president of his college (M. J. *Routh), to explore the possibilities of intercommunion between the Anglican and Orthodox Churches, and did much to foster interest in the E. Church in Great Britain. Between these two visits he made strong protests against the proposed Anglo-Lutheran *Jerusalem Bishopric plan. Distressed by the *Gorham case, he tentatively considered seceding to the Orthodox Church; but deciding against this step because the Easterns insisted on his 'rebaptism', he eventually joined the RC Church in 1855. His writings include *Dissertations on Subjects relating to the Orthodox or Eastern-Catholic Communion* (1853), *Notes of a Visit to the Russian Church in the Years 1840, 1841* (ed. J. H. *Newman; 1882), and works on archaeology.

J. M. Rigg in *D.N.B.*, xliii (1895), p. 167 f.

PAMMACHIUS, St. (c. 340-410), Roman Christian. A senator of the Furian family, he was a friend of St. *Jerome who dedicated to him several works, among them the Commentaries on the Minor Prophets (406) and on

Daniel (407). After the death of his wife, the daughter of St. *Paula, he took the monastic habit and spent his possessions on works of piety, among them the famous hospital for pilgrims at Portus and the church of SS. Giovanni e Paolo (excavated in 1887) in Rome. Of a peace-loving character, he disapproved of the lack of moderation in Jerome's attack on *Jovinian and of the violent controversy between Jerome and *Rufinus on the subject of *Origen. His intervention in the *Donatist schism in Numidia, where he owned estates, earned him a laudatory letter from St. *Augustine (401). He died in the invasion of the Goths in 410. Feast day, 30 Aug.

The chief sources are St. Jerome, *Epp.*, xlviii f., lvii, lxvi, lxxxiii f., and xcviii; St. Augustine, Ep. lviii, and *Palladius, *Historica Lausiaca*, cxxii. J. Pinius, S.J., in *AA.SS.*, Aug. VI (1743), pp. 555-63, incl. relevant texts of works cited above. On the *tituli S. Pammachii*, later SS. *Johanni et Pauli*, cf. J. P. Kirsch, *Die römischen Titelkirchen im Altertum* (Studien zur Geschichte und Kultur des Altertums, ix; 1918), pp. 26-33. W. H. Fremantle in *D.C.B.*, iv (1887), p. 178.

PAMPHILUS, St. (c. 240-309), disciple of *Origen. A native of Berytus, he received his education at *Alexandria, and later directed a theological school at *Caesarea in Palestine, where he was martyred. Having conceived a very high regard for the teachings of *Origen, he prepared during imprisonment in the persecution of Maximinus Daza an 'Apology' on his behalf. In this work he was much assisted by *Eusebius of Caesarea, who in turn held Pamphilus in immense veneration. Of the five books of the 'Apology' which are Pamphilus's own, only the first survives, and this in a Latin version of doubtful accuracy made by *Rufinus of Aquileia. After Pamphilus's martyrdom, Eusebius added a sixth book to the 'Apology', wrote Pamphilus's Life (now lost, except for a few fragments), and took for himself the name of 'Eusebius of Pamphilus' (ὁ τοῦ Παμφίλου). His large library survived at Caesarea until destroyed by the Arabs in the 7th cent. Feast day in the E., 16 Feb. (the day of his martyrdom); in the W., 1 June.

Rufinus' version of Bk. I of Pamphilus's *Apology*, with 'Admonitio' of C. de La Rue, in J. P. Migne, *PG*, xvii, 521-616. Fgmt. of Eusebius's *Life* in *Jerome, Adv. Rufin.*, i, 9. Eusebius, *H.E.*, VII, xxxii, 25, and *De Mart. Pal.*, xi, 3; Jerome, *De Vir. Illustr.*, 75; *Photius, Cod.* 118. Bardenhewer, ii, 287-92; Altaner (ed. 1950), p. 178. G. Bardy in *D.T.C.*, xi (pt. 2; 1932), cols. 1839-41.

PANAGIA (Gk. παναγία, 'all holy'). A favourite title of the BVM in the E. Church. The word is also used (1) of a small folding case containing an image of the BVM which Greek bishops wear on the breast suspended on a chain; and (2) of bread (ἄρτος τῆς παναγίας) which is solemnly blessed in honour of the BVM.

PANCRAS, St. (d. 304), martyr. There are no reliable historical data about him. Acc. to an early tradition he was a Phrygian by race and a member of the Roman Church, who at the age of 14 was martyred on the Via Aurelia during the *Diocletianic persecution. Devotion to him became very popular, esp. in Rome where his church gave one of the cardinals his title. Feast day, 12 May.

St. Pancras railway station in London is named after the dedication of the church of the parish in which it is situate.

His 'Acta' survive in several recensions both in Lat. and Gk. A Lat. text from several MSS. is pr., with discussion, in *AA.SS.*, Mai. III (1680), pp. 17–22; other Lat. MSS. in *Anal. Boll.*, ii (1883), pp. 289–91, and x (1891), pp. 53–6. P. Franchi de' Cavalieri, *Hagiographica* (S.T., xix; 1908), pp. 77–105 ('Della leggenda di S. Pancrazio Romano'), with Gk. text of 'Acta', pp. 109–12. *B.H.L.*, p. 928 f. (Nos. 6420–28), and supplement, p. 242. S. Pesarini, 'Studi sopra alcune basiliche cristiane di Roma, I, La cripta di S. Pancrazio e la sua basilica sulla Via Aurelia' in *Nuovo Bulletino di Archeologia cristiana*, xxviii (1922), pp. 71–81; J. P. Kirsch, 'Le memorie dei martiri sulle Vie Aurelia e Cornelia I, Gruppo del cimitero di S. Pancrazio, S. Pancratius' in *Miscellanea Francesco Ehrle*, ii (S.T., xxxviii; 1924), pp. 65–8. H. *Leclercq, O.S.B., in *D.A.C.L.*, xiii (pt. 1; 1937), cols. 1001–14, with reff.; E. Josi in *E.C.*, ix (1952), col. 674 f., s.v. 'Pancrazio'.

PANENTHEISM (Gk. πᾶν, 'everything'; ἐν, 'in'; θεός, 'God'). The belief that the Being of God includes and penetrates the whole universe, so that every part of it exists in Him, but (as against *Pantheism, q.v.) that His Being is more than, and is not exhausted by, the universe. The word was coined by K. C. F. Krause (1781–1832) for his own system. N. *Malebranche's doctrines approximated to Panentheism.

PANGE LINGUA. The title of two famous Latin hymns, viz. the Passiontide hymn by *Venantius Fortunatus (d. 610) (*Pange lingua gloriosi proelium certaminis*), and the *Corpus Christi hymn by St. *Thomas Aquinas (d. 1274) (*Pange lingua gloriosi corporis mysterium*). On the latter see also *Tantum Ergo*.

PANNYCHIS (Gk. παννυχίς). In the E. Church the liturgical preparation for a feast, and thus the counterpart of the *vigil in the W. It lasts through the whole night, in contrast with the ἀγρυπνία, a rite which occupies only part of the night. The word occurs already in St. *Athanasius (*Apol. ad Const.* 25).

PANORMITANUS (1386–1445), also known as **Abbas Modernus** and **Siculus**, canonist. A Sicilian by birth, Nicolò de' Tudeschi entered the *Benedictine Order *c.* 1400, and after studying under F. *Zabarella (1405–6), taught at Parma, Siena, and *Bologna. In 1425 he became abbot of Maniacio, near Messina, and in 1435 Abp. of Palermo (hence Panormitanus). At first he supported *Eugenius IV but later sided with the antipope, Felix V (by whom he was made a cardinal), defending in his *Tractatus de Concilio Basiliensi* the Pope's inferiority to a *General Council. His principal writings were his works on canon law, which included commentaries on the *Decretals of Gregory IX, on the *Sext, and on the *Clementines.

Many of his works were pr. in the 15th cent. Collected edd. 8 vols., Venice, 1592, and 9 vols., ib., 1617. J. Schweizer, *Nicolaus de' Tudeschi, Archiepiscopus Panormitanus et S.R.E. Cardinalis. Seine Tätigkeit am Basler Konzil* (Strassburg, 1924).

PANPSYCHISM. The doctrine advocated by G. T. *Fechner (1801–87) and other 19th cent. philosophers that everything in the universe is endowed with a measure of consciousness. It has found little favour with Christian theologians. A similar doctrine was expressly repudiated by St. *Thomas Aquinas (*Sum. Theol.* I, q. 18, a. 1).

PANTAENUS, St. (d. *c.* A.D. 190). The first known head of the *Catechetical School at Alexandria. Probably a native of Sicily, he was converted from paganism to the Christian faith and taught at Alexandria (where he greatly influenced his more celebrated disciple, *Clement) from *c.* 180 till his death. It appears that he never composed any treatises. Acc. to *Eusebius (*H.E.*, V. x. 2), he preached the Gospel in 'India'. Feast day, 7 July; in the Coptic Church, 22 June.

J. Munck, *Untersuchungen über Klemens von Alexandria* (Forschungen zur Kirchen- und Geistesgeschichte, ii; 1933), pp. 151–204 [critique of W. *Bousset's theory of a 'Pantaenus Source' in Clement]. Bardenhewer, ii, 37–40. E. Peterson in *E.C.*, ix (1952), col. 693 f.

PANTALEON, St. (d. *c.* 305), martyr. His name means 'the All-merciful' (παντελεήμων). Nothing is known with certainty about him. Acc. to one form of the legends, he was a physician to the Emp. Galerius at Nicomedia who, after having been converted to Christianity in his early years by his mother, was led into apostasy by the worldly attractions of court life. Reconverted by a Christian called Hermolaus, he suffered martyrdom when *Diocletian gave orders to purge the court of Christians. His cult has been very popular, esp. in the E.; and in the Middle Ages he was honoured as one of the patron saints of physicians, second only to St. *Luke. He is accounted one of the fourteen *Auxiliary Saints. Feast day, 27 July; also other dates.

Gk. text of 'Passio' in the works of *Simeon Metaphrastes pr. in J. P. Migne, *PG*, cxv, 448–77; Lat. tr. of this, and other material, with commentary, in *AA.SS.*, Jul. VI (1729), pp. 397–427. Further reff. in *B.H.L.*, pp. 929–32 (Nos. 6429–48), and suppl., p. 243; *B.H.G.*, p. 196 f. (Nos. 1413–18); *B.H.O.*, p. 183 (Nos. 835–7). H. *Delehaye, S.J., *Les Origines du culte des martyrs* (Subsidia Hagiographica, xx; 1912), p. 181 f. For popular account of the liquefaction of the relic of his blood, very similar to that recorded of St. Januarius (q.v.), I. R. Grant, *The Testimony of Blood* (1929), pp. 17–44. A Bigelmair in *L.Th.K.*, vii (1935), col. 918, s.v.

PANTHEISM. (Gk. πᾶν, 'all', and θεός, 'God'). The belief or theory that God and the universe are identical. The word appears to be coinage of J. *Toland, the *Deist, in 1705 and to have been employed shortly afterwards by his opponents. Pantheistic systems, however, go back to very early times. It is a type of thought esp. found in Hinduism. Acc. as it interprets the universe in terms of God or God in terms of the universe, its attitude is religious or materialistic. Of the former type the most extreme representative in modern times was B. *Spinoza (1632–77) with his immanental formula, 'God or Nature' (*Deus* *sive Natura*). In the 19th cent. the German Idealists (F. W. J. von *Schelling, G. W. F. *Hegel) and the British *Absolute Idealists (F. H. *Bradley, B. *Bosanquet) taught philosophical doctrines akin to pantheism. Mysticism, with its passionate search for God in nature and desire for union with the Divine, has often verged on pantheism. Among Christian thinkers of pantheistic tendencies may be named St. *Dionysius the Areopagite, *Erigena and *Nicholas of Cusa; and such mystics as *Eckhart and Jacob *Boehme.

C. E. Plumptre, *History of Pantheism* (2 vols., 1881); W. S. Urquhart, *Pantheism and the Value of Life* (1919). A. E. Garvie–F. Thilly–A. S. Geden in *H.E.R.E.*, ix (1917), pp. 609–20, s.v.; F. A. Schalck in *D.T.C.*, xi (pt. 2; 1932), cols. 1855–74, s.v. 'Panthéisme'; K. Algermissen in *L.Th.K.*, vii (1935), cols. 918–22, s.v. 'Pantheismus'; M. F. Sciacca in *E.C.*, ix (1952), cols. 686–93, s.v. 'Panteismo'.

PAPA ANGELICUS (also **Pastor Angelicus**). A belief which arose in Italy in the earlier half of the 13th cent. and recorded by Roger *Bacon (*Opus Tertium*, xxiv), to the effect that a Pope would arise who would revive Apostolic simplicity and zeal in the Church and inaugurate a new age. It was developed in apocryphal writings and prophecies of the 14th cent., e.g. those of Telesphorus of Cosenza (1386). In St. *Malachy's prophecy the 106th Pope, i.e. *Pius XII (1940–   ), is so designated.

'PAPAL AGGRESSION'. The name popularly given to the action of Pope *Pius IX making England and Wales, by Letters Apostolic, *Universalis Ecclesiae* (29 Sept. 1850), an ecclesiastical province of the RC Church, with a hierarchy consisting of an archbishop and twelve *suffragans all with territorial titles. The wording of the brief was provocative, e.g. by its reference to the C of E as 'the Anglican Schism'. An unexpected and almost fanatical storm of indignation spread through Great Britain under the leadership of Lord John Russell (1792–1878), culminating in the passing of the *Ecclesiastical Titles Act of 1851 (q.v.).

PAPAL LEGATE. See *Legate, Papal.*

PAPAL STATES. See *States of the Church.*

PAPEBROCH, DANIEL (1628–1714), (or van Papenbroeck), *Bollandist hagiographer. In 1659 he became J. Bollandus's assistant and continued till his death to take an active part in the compilation of the '*Acta Sanctorum', though he was forced to interrupt his work for a time by blindness. His name appears for the first time in 'Martius I' (1668), and for the last in 'Junius V' (1709), i.e. on 18 volumes in all. Bitter criticism from the *Carmelites, the foundation of whose order by *Elijah he denied, led to his denunciation at Rome and in Spain for heresy, and in 1695 14 volumes of

the 'Acta' were put on the *Index. Papenbroeck also drew up a set of rules of a drastically critical kind for the science of diplomatic.

J. Pien, S.J., in *AA.SS.*, Jun. VI (1715), pp. 3–21. H. *Delehaye, S.J., *L'Œuvre des Bollandistes* (1920), pp. 31–40. Sommervogel, vi (1895), cols. 178–85. H. *Leclercq, O.S.B., in *D.A.C.L.*, xiii (pt. 1; 1937), cols. 1345–58, s.v.; C. Testore, S.J., in *E.C.*, ix (1952), col. 780 f., s.v., with bibl.

PAPHNUTIUS, St. (d. *c.* 360), Bp. of the Upper Thebaid. He was an Egyptian monk, who had been a disciple of St. *Antony. He suffered such hardship and cruelty during the persecution of Maximin Daza (305–313) that at the Council of *Nicaea his mutilated body was an object of wonder and veneration to the assembled bishops. Acc. to *Socrates (*H.E.*, i, 11) and *Sozomen (*H.E.*, i, 23), he dissuaded the Council from ordering all clergy to put away their wives. Feast day, 11 Sept.

Gk. text of 'Passio' ed. H. *Delehaye, S.J., in *Anal. Boll.*, xl (1922), pp. 328–43. Lat. tr. in *AA.SS.*, Sept. VI (1757), pp. 681–8. For his views on celibacy, G. *Bickell, 'Der Cölibat eine apostolische Anordnung' in *Z.K.T.*, ii (1878), pp. 26–64, 57–62. H. *Leclercq, O.S.B., in *D.A.C.L.*, xiii (pt. 1; 1937), cols. 1358–61, s.v. 'Paphnuce'.

PAPIAS (*c.* 60–130), Bp. of Hierapolis in Asia Minor. Nothing is known of his life, apart from the statement of St. *Irenaeus that he was a 'man of long ago' (ἀρχαῖος ἀνήρ) and the disciple of one 'John' and a companion of St. *Polycarp. His work, Λογίων Κυριακῶν Ἐξηγήσεις ('Expositions of the Oracles of the Lord'), in five books survives only in quotations in Irenaeus and *Eusebius. Apparently his work contained many oral traditions and legendary accounts as well as Gospel material. In the famous fragments on the origin of the Gospels of St. *Matthew and St. *Mark he states, on the authority of 'the Elder', that Mark, having become the interpreter of St. Peter, set down accurately (ἀκριβῶς), though not in order (οὐ μέντοι τάξει), everything that he remembered of the words and actions of the Lord, and that St. Matthew composed 'the oracles' (τὰ λόγια) in Hebrew, and that everyone translated them as best he could. Of his theology we only know that he held *Millenarian views, believing that there would be a period of a thousand years after the Resurrection during which the Kingdom of Christ would be set up on earth in a material form.

The fragments have often been repr., conveniently, with Eng. tr., in J. B. *Lightfoot, *Apostolic Fathers* (ed. J. R. Harmer, 1891), pp. 514–35. T. *Zahn, 'Apostel und Apostelschüler in der Provinz Asiens' in id., *Forschungen zur Geschichte des neutestamentlichen Kanons*, vi (1900), pp. 109–57. J. *Chapman, O.S.B., *John the Presbyter and the Fourth Gospel* (1911). H. J. Lawlor, 'Eusebius on Papias' in *Hermathena*, xix [No. 43] (1922), pp. 167–222. Bardenhewer, i, 445–54; Altaner (ed. 1951), p. 83 f. G. Bardy in *D.T.C.*, xi (pt. 2; 1932), cols. 1944–7, s.v.; E. Peterson in *E.C.*, ix (1952), col. 781 f., s.v. 'Papia di Gerapoli'.

PAPINI, GIOVANNI (1881–1956), Italian author. In his early years he followed various trends of modern philosophy, esp. the *pragmatism of W. *James, and in his own periodicals, *Leonardo* (1902) and *Lacerba*

(1913), as well as in several volumes of essays, treated metaphysical and moral questions with originality and often with violence. In 1912 he published *Un uomo finito*, a novel reflecting his interior struggle between his philosophical speculations and the desire for faith, which he at last resolved by acceptance of the Catholic creed. The outcome of his conversion was the *Storia di Cristo* (1921; Eng. trans. *The Story of Christ*, 1923), his most successful book, in which he traces the earthly life of Christ, His effect on His contemporaries and the uniqueness of His Person and message in the world of antiquity, with great poetical insight. It was followed in 1929 by a Life of St. *Augustine (Eng. trans., 1930), a psychological study, but less successful than the earlier work.

A. Viviani, *Gianfalco*. Storia e vita (1934); M. Apollonio, *Papini* ('Guide di cultura contemporanea', 1944).

PAPYROLOGY. The science of dealing with MSS. on papyrus. Papyrus is a writing material made out of the fibres of the stem of a water plant which formerly grew plentifully in the Nile. It was used in ancient Egypt and became the chief material for books in the Greco-Roman world from the 5th cent. B.C. (and probably earlier) to the 4th cent. A.D., when it gradually gave way to vellum. It was manufactured in sheets, which were fastened together to form rolls of any desired length up to about 35 feet. This was the form in which most books of the NT were written, and for pagan literature the roll predominates until the 4th cent. A.D. Such a roll would not contain more than a single Gospel. But from the latter part of the first cent. an alternative form, that of the 'codex', which could contain much more matter, came into use, and this was predominantly used for Christian books. In the codex, sheets of papyrus were folded in two and formed into quires, as in a modern printed book. At first codices were composed of single quires, consisting of any number of folded sheets, from one to fifty or more; eventually it was found more convenient to form quires of not more than 8 sheets, making 16 leaves or 32 pages, and (as in modern books) to make up the codex from several such quires. The writing on a roll was in columns of about $2\frac{1}{2}$ to $3\frac{1}{2}$ inches wide, and was normally on one side of the roll only; but in case of an excess of matter, it might be written 'within and without' (Ezek. 2. 10, Rev. 5. 1).

Papyrus manuscripts have survived hardly anywhere but in the dry soil of Egypt, where they were first found in 1778; but it is only since 1877 that they have been discovered in any large numbers, and still more recently that they have become important for the Bible text.

Useful directory to the many series of published papyri in H. G. *Liddell–R. *Scott, *A Greek-English Lexicon* (rev. ed., 1940), pp. xliii–xlv. Large collection of historical and legal texts assembled in L. Mitteis–U. Wilcken, *Grundzüge und Chrestomathie der Papyruskunde* (4 vols., 1912). A. S. Hunt–C. C. Edgar (ed.), *Select Papyri* (2 vols., Loeb, 1932ff.).–G. Milligan, *Selections from the Greek Papyri* (1910). General introd. to subject by W. Schubart, *Einführung in die Papyruskunde* (1917). Lexicon by F. Preisigke, *Wörterbuch der griechischen Papyruskunden* (2 vols., 1925–7; suppl. 1931). Grammar by E. Mayser (2 vols.; Bd. ii in 3 parts; Berlin, 1906–34). *Archiv für Papyrusforschung und verwandte Gebiete* (begun by U. Wilcken, 1900 ff.). J. G. Winter, *Life and Letters in the Papyri* (University of Michigan Press, 1933). Vocabulary of NT Gk. usage by J. H. *Moulton–G. Milligan, *The Vocabulary of the Greek Testament Illustrated from the Papyri and other non-literary Sources* (1914–30). On the bearing of the papyri on NT studies, G. Milligan, *Here and There among the Papyri* (1922). A. S. Hunt in *E.B.* (ed. 14), xvii (1929), pp. 243–6, s.v., with bibl. C. H. Roberts in *O.C.D.*, p. 645 f., s.v. See also bibl. to *Chester Beatty Papyri* and *Oxyrhynchus Papyri*.

PARABLES (Gk. παραβολή). The name given to similitudes drawn from nature or from human affairs, esp. those suggesting or containing a short narrative, which our Lord used to convey a spiritual meaning. No sharp line distinguishes the Parables from the minor metaphors and similes which are a feature of Christ's teaching, but between 30 and 40 distinct Parables can be recognized in the *Synoptic Gospels. In St. John's Gospel there are no Parables, though there are sayings of Christ, e.g. about Himself as the *Good Shepherd, of a similar character. A few of the Parables (e.g. that of The Sower) are found in all three Synoptists but most of them are contained in Mt. and Lk. only, a great number, including several of the best known, being in Lk. alone (e.g. The *Good Samaritan, The Prodigal Son, *Dives and Lazarus).

The Parables are one of the most distinctive features of Christ's teaching. They are not to be conceived as allegories, in which every detail has a meaning, nor yet simply as anecdotes of which the purpose is to convey a purely moral lesson. They vary greatly in the closeness or otherwise of the story to the reality it is desired to illustrate. But there is one main point of comparison in each Parable, and apart from this the details may, or may not, have a particular meaning.

The most widely read of the older works was R. C. *Trench, *Notes on the Parables of Our Lord* (1841). Recent studies include A. T. Cadoux, *The Parables of Jesus*. Their Art and Use (1931); C. H. *Dodd, *The Parables of the Kingdom* (1935); W. O. E. Oesterley, *The Gospel Parables in the Light of their Jewish Background* (1936); B. T. D. Smith, *The Parables of the Synoptic Gospels* (1937). A. B. *Bruce, *The Parabolic Teaching of Christ* (1882). T. W. Manson, *The Teaching of Jesus* (1931), pp. 57–81. A. *Jülicher, *Die Gleichnisreden Jesu* (2 vols., 1888–99). C. A. Bugge, *Die Haupt-Parabeln Jesu* (1903); P. Fiebig, *Die Gleichnisreden Jesu im Lichte der rabbinischen Gleichnisse des neutestamentlichen Zeitalters* (1912). J. Jeremias, *Die Gleichnisse Jesu* (Zürich, 1947; Eng. tr., 1954). G. Heinrici in *P.R.E.* (ed., 3), vi (1899), pp. 688–703, s.v. 'Gleichnisse Jesu'; E. König–A. Plummer in *H.D.B.*, iii (1900), pp. 660–5, s.v.; W. J. Moulton in *D.C.G.*, ii (1908), pp. 312–17, s.v.; F. Hauck in *T.W.B.*, v [1955], pp. 741–59, s.v. 'παραβολή'.

PARABOLANI (Gk. παραβολᾶνοι, 'those who disregard', sc. their lives; cf. Phil. 2. 30). They were an association of men, orig. at Alexandria but later also at *Constantinople, devoted to nursing the sick, who probably originated in a period of epidemics. They are mentioned in two laws of the 'Codex Theodosianus', XVI, 2 (de episcopis 42 and 43 of A.D. 416 and 418), reproduced in the 'Codex Justinianus' I, 3 (de episcopis 18). Acc. to these laws, which fixed their number at 500, later at 600, we learn that the Parabolani were clerics under episcopal supervision and exempt from public duties. They were forbidden to visit theatres and law courts. They seem to have played a considerable part in the public life of Alexandria and are believed to have had a share in the murder of the philosopher *Hypatia (415). They also took part in the *Latrocinium of *Ephesus (449).

J. *Bingham, *Origines sive Antiquitates Ecclesiasticae*, liber 1, cap. ii, para. 9, and liber 3, cap. ix (vol. i, ed. 1708, p. 20 f, and ii, 1709, pp. 45–50). E. Venables in *D.C.A.*, ii (1880), p. 1551 f., s.v.

PARACELSUS. The name coined for himself by Theophrastus Bombastus von Hohenheim (1493–1541), Swiss physician. Educated at the university of Basle, he studied alchemy and chemistry under Abbot J. *Trithemius of Sponheim. He was appointed city physician at Basle, but his open opposition to the prevailing system of medicine, based on Galen and *Avicenna, forced him to leave in 1528. For the rest of his life he was moving from place to place. His great advances in therapeutics rested on his belief that its principles were to be derived from the study of nature and not from scholastic disputations. Yet his empiricism did not prevent his elaborating a mystical theosophy on a *Neo-Platonic basis, in which he held that just as we know nature only to the extent that we are ourselves nature, so we know God only in so far as we are God. Paracelsus also made important contributions to the study of chemistry.

Works ed. J. Huserum (4 parts, Basle, 1589–99). Crit. ed. by K. Sudhoff–W. Matthiessen, etc. (Munich–Berlin, 1922 ff.). Eng. tr. of his *Hermetic and Alchemical Writings* by A. E. Waite (2 vols., London, 1894) and of his *Select Works* by N. Guterman (ib., 1951). The very considerable literature on Paracelsus includes studies in English by F. Hartmann (London, 1877), Anna M. Stobbart (ib., 1911), J. M. Stillman (Chicago–London, 1920, with useful bibl.), and J. Hargrave (London, 1951; more popular). F. Mook, *Theophrastus Paracelsus. Eine kritische Studie* (1876); J Ferguson, *Bibliographica Paracelsica* (5 parts, privately printed, Glasgow, 1877–93). K. Sudhoff, *Versuch einer Kritik der Echtheit der paracelsischen Schriften* (i, Bibliographia Paracelsica; ii, Paracelsus-Handschriften, 1894–9). F. Strunz, *Theophrastus Paracelsus, sein Leben und seine Persönlichkeit* (1903), and other writings by same author. C. G. Jung, *Paracelsica*. Zwei Vorlesungen über den Arzt und Philosophen Theophrastus (Zürich–Leipzig, 1942). Unsigned art. in *E.B.* (ed. 11), xx (1911), p. 749 f., s.v.; L. Sendfelder in *C.E.*, xi (1911), p. 468 f., s.v., with reff.; L. Baur in *L.Th.K.*, vii (1935), cols. 946–8, s.v., with bibl.; N. Turchi in *E.C.*, ix (1952), col. 791 f., s.v., for further bibl.

PARACLETE (Gk. παράκλητος, 'advocate'). Johannine epithet of the Holy Ghost. It is traditionally translated 'Comforter'. Though used of Christ in 1 Jn. 2. 1 and, by implication, in Jn. 14. 16, it is ordinarily applied to the Holy Spirit (Jn. 14. 16; 16. 7, &c.). *Origen interpreted the word as meaning 'Intercessor' where the reference is to our Lord, as 'Consoler' (for the loss of Christ) where it is to the Holy Ghost. This latter meaning, though not found outside the NT, may be defended by the context, and was indeed that generally accepted by the Fathers. But it describes the mission of the Holy Ghost, which is to

strengthen and guide the Church into all truth' less fully than the renderings 'Helper'' 'Counsellor', or the *Vulgate translation 'Advocate', preferred by many modern commentators. Several scholars are in favour of simply transcribing the Greek word as was done in several ancient versions of the NT.

Many important discussions will be found in Commentaries, ad locc.; cf., e.g., those of B. F. *Westcott and J. H. *Bernard on Jn., and of A. E. Brooke on 1 Jn. H. Saase, 'Der Paraklet im Johannesevangelium' in *Z.N.T.W.*, xxiv (1925), pp. 260–77; H. Windisch, 'Die fünf Johanneischen Parakletsprüche' in *Festgabe Adolf Jülicher zum 70. Geburtstag* (1927), pp. 110–37; G. Bornkamm, 'Der Paraklet im Johannesevangelium' in *Festschrift R. Bultmann zum 65. Geburtstag überreicht* (1949), pp. 12–35. J. *Hastings in *H.D.B.*, iii (1900), pp. 665–8, s.v. J. Behm in *T.W.B.*, v (1954), pp. 798–812, with bibl.

PARACLETICE. See *Parakletike*.

PARADIGM. The title given by M. *Dibelius and other *Form-critics to passages in the Gospels which contain narratives woven round a particular saying of Christ in order to drive its teaching home. They are held to have received their present literary form from their use as illustrations in preaching. Dibelius enumerates eight cases in St. *Mark's Gospel where the type is perfect, viz. the Sick of the Palsy (2. 1–12), the Question of Fasting (2. 18 f.), the Plucking of the Ears of Corn (2. 23–8), the Man with the Withered Hand (3. 1–5), the Relatives of Christ (3. 31–5), Christ's Blessing of the Children (10. 13–16), the Tribute Money (12. 13–17), and the Anointing in Bethany (14. 3–9).

M. *Dibelius, *From Tradition to Gospel* (Eng. trans., 1934), ch. iii.

PARADISE. The word is probably of Persian origin (Zend, *pairidaêza*; Gk. παράδεισος), denoting an enclosed park or pleasure-ground. In Gen. 2 and 3 it occurs only in the *Septuagint text, not in the Hebrew, and is applied to the garden planted by God in Eden, the ideal abode of Adam and Eve which soon became the scene of man's temptation and fall. In later Jewish literature it came more and more to signify a state of blessedness whether material (much of the *Rabbinic literature) or spiritual (so Ecclus. 24. 25–30 and Pss. Sol. 14. 2), and with this latter meaning the word is used in the NT, where it occurs three times. In Lk. 23. 43 it has been variously interpreted as referring either to the intermediate state of the just before the Resurrection (*Limbo) or as a synonym of the heaven of the blessed. In this second sense it is used in the two other NT passages, 2 Cor. 12. 4 and Rev. 2. 7. In patristic and medieval literature there was much speculation both as to the conditions of the primeval paradise and, esp. in later times, on the Intermediate State and the distinction between a terrestrial and a heavenly paradise. In modern popular usage paradise usually denotes the state of future bliss. See also *Beatific Vision*.

For 'paradise' as an architectural term see *Parvis*.

'PARADISE LOST'. The magnificent epic of J. *Milton (q.v.), describing the *Fall of Man, and its consequences. It was the first original non-dramatic work to be written in English in blank verse. For vastness in conception and grandeur in treatment it is surpassed in modern literature only by *Dante's *Divina commedia. Its theology shows traces of Milton's *Arianism and his lack of sympathy with organized religion; but its main themes are those common to the main stream of Christian doctrine. Milton prob. did not complete it until 1667, and on 27 Apr. 1667 he disposed of the copyright for the sum of £5, with the contingency of three further instalments of the same sum if additional editions were needed.

Facsimile of first ed. prepared by J. Isaacs, pr. at the Golden Cockerel Press [Waltham S. Lawrence], 1937. Modern ed., with full notes, by A. W. Verity (Cambridge, 1910); cf. also edd. of Milton's Poetical Works, cited s.v. Milton, esp. that of Helen Darbishire, vol. i (Oxford, 1952). N. Bøgholm, Milton and Paradise Lost (Copenhagen-London, 1932). G. McColley, Paradise Lost. An Account of its Growth and Major Origins, with a Discussion of Milton's Use of Sources and Literary Patterns (Chicago, 1940). C. S. Lewis, A Preface to Paradise Lost (Ballard Matthews Lectures for 1941; 1942). [J. N.] D. Bush, Paradise Lost in Our Time (Ithaca, N.Y., 1945); J. S. Diekhoff, Milton's Paradise Lost. A Commentary on the Argument (New York, 1946). B. Ragan, Paradise Lost and the Seventeenth Century Reader (1947); A. J. A. Waldock, Paradise Lost and its Critics (1947); A. H. Gilbert, On the Composition of Paradise Lost (Chapel Hill, N.C., 1947). See also works cited s.v. Milton, John.

PARAGRAPH BIBLES. In 1755 a NT arranged in paragraphs (as opposed to the usual AV practice of arrangement in verses), with a revised text, was issued by J. *Wesley. In 1838 the *Religious Tract Society published an edition with the AV text in paragraphs; and other similar editions followed. It is the arrangement adopted in the *Revised Version and most other modern translations.

PARAKLETIKE. (Gk. παρακλητική, 'supplicatory [prayer]'), the service book of the E. Church with the ferial offices. They are arranged on a recurring system of eight weeks.

PARALIPOMENON, Books of. The title in the *Vulgate for the two Books of *Chronicles (q.v.). It was taken over by St. *Jerome from the *Septuagint, where the title of 1 (2) Chron. is 'the first (second) book of the things omitted concerning the Kings of Judah' (παραλειπομένων βασιλέων 'Ιούδα α' [β']), a description which implies that the Books are supplementary to 1 and 2 Kings.

PARALLELISM, Poetic. This characteristic of Hebrew poetry was first analysed by R. *Lowth in his De sacra poesi Hebraeorum (Oxford, 1753). Such parallelism is not confined to the poetical books of the Bible but it is also an essential element in Assyrian and Babylonian hymns. Parallelism is ordinarily of three kinds:

(1) Synonymous Parallelism, which is the most usual form, consisting in the simple repetition of the same thought in slightly different words, e.g. 'Hear my crying, O God: Give ear unto my prayer' (Ps. 61. 1).

(2) Antithetical Parallelism, produced by contrasting the first member with the second. This form is very frequent in the Bk. of Prov., e.g. 'A merry heart doeth good like a medicine: But a broken spirit drieth the bones' (Prov. 17. 22).

(3) Synthetic Parallelism, in which the first member is developed or completed by a similar thought in the second (or third, in the case of triplets), e.g. 'The kings of the earth stand up: And the rulers take counsel together: Against the Lord and against His Anointed' (Ps. 2. 2).

Apart from these chief forms some commentators have claimed to find others, such as 'climactic', 'introverted', 'stairlike', and 'emblematic' Parallelism, but they are in general less easily discernible.

PARAPHRASES OF ERASMUS, The. The Commentary on the Gospels written by D. *Erasmus which *Edward VI in his *Injunctions of 1547 ordered to be set up in all parish churches 'in some convenient place' where the 'parishioners may most commodiously resort unto the same and read the same'. The section on St. John's Gospel was translated into English by the Princess *Mary.

PARASCEVE. See Preparation, Day of.

PARCLOSE. In ecclesiastical architecture, a screen or set of railings, usually standing at the east end of the *aisle of a church, for enclosing a *chantry altar for *requiems and one or more seats for members of the family of the deceased. After the Reformation, these enclosures developed into the 'family pew'.

PARDON. (1) Another name for an '*Indulgence', found, e.g., in Art. 22 of the *Thirty-Nine Articles. In the later Middle Ages, the right to share in an indulgence was hawked around Europe by the 'Pardoners', denounced by G.*Chaucer, W. Langland, and J.*Wycliffe. Such Pardons were a source of great profit to the ecclesiastical authorities and were frequently used to obtain money for building purposes, as for *St. Peter's, Rome, and the completion of *York Minster.

(2) In Brittany, the feast of the patron saint of a church at which an indulgence may be gained. These Pardons are held in many places between *Easter and *Michaelmas. The celebrations are preceded by Confession on the night before and start early in the morning with Mass, and much of the day is given to prayer. The most dramatic element in the proceedings is the procession round the church or village

in which relics or other votive objects are carried and the pilgrims assist in their best national costumes. They are commonly accompanied by a village fair. Among the more famous Breton Pardons are those of St. Jean-du-Doigt near Morlaix (24 June), and St. Anne d'Auray in Morbihan (24 July).

PARIS. The city, which is first mentioned by Caesar as 'Lutetia Parisiorum', was a centre of Christianity at a very early date. Acc. to St. *Gregory of Tours, St. *Denis, its first bishop, was one of the seven bishops sent out by Pope *Fabian *c.* 250. During the invasion of the Huns it was protected by St. *Geneviève, who is still venerated as its patroness. From the end of the 5th cent. it increased considerably in political and religious importance. Many churches were built, and during the frequent absence of the Merovingian kings the episcopal power developed. In the 9th cent. *Notre-Dame and the abbey of *St.-Germain-des-Prés became the most powerful factors in its life. Under Hugh Capet (987–96) it became the official capital of France. The beginnings of its famous University date from the 12th cent., when *Peter Lombard taught at the Cathedral School of Notre-Dame, *Hugh and *Richard at St.-Victor, and *Abelard at Ste-Geneviève. The University as an established community of masters and pupils appears at the end of the 12th cent. It was styled 'Universitas magistrorum' in 1207 and received its statutes from *Innocent III in 1215. Many privileges were bestowed on it, making it a body independent of bishops, king, and Parliament. Between 1215 and 1225 developed the so-called 'nations', Gallicani, Normanni, Picardi, and Angli (the last being replaced by the Alemanni after the Hundred Years War), and soon afterwards the four faculties of theology, law, medicine, and arts. Masters and pupils lived in colleges, the most famous of which was the *Sorbonne; religious in the houses of their orders ('studia generalia'), the *Dominicans, e.g., at St.-Jacques. In the 13th cent. Paris was the centre of Scholasticism, counting among its teachers the *Franciscans *Alexander of Hales and St. *Bonaventure, the Dominicans St. *Albert the Great and St. *Thomas Aquinas, and the seculars *William of Auxerre, *Henry of Ghent, and the *Averroist *Siger of Brabant. St. Albert, St. Bonaventure, and St. Thomas took part in the great controversy between the *Mendicant orders and the seculars, who, represented esp. by William of St.-Amour (d. *c.* 1273), were jealous of the growing influence of the religious, in whose favour the quarrel was decided by Alexander IV in 1256. The University continued to play an important part in the time of the W. Schism and of the Reform Councils, when some of its most learned men, such as J. *Gerson and Peter *d'Ailly, favoured the Conciliar party. At the end of the 14th cent. its decadence set in, caused by the general decline of Scholasticism as well as by the Schism and the war with England, in the course of

which Paris was under English occupation from 1420 to 1436. Under Francis I and Catherine of Medici the city became the centre of the French Renaissance, supported by its bishop, the poet Jean du Bellay (1532–51). From 1568 to 1662 the see was occupied by the Gondi family, under whom occurred the massacres of St. *Bartholomew's Night (1572). It became an archdiocese in 1622. During the 17th cent. the city witnessed a religious regeneration brought about by the activities of St. *Francis de Sales, St. *Vincent de Paul, P. de *Bérulle, and P. *Olier, who counteracted *Jansenism and *Gallicanism which numbered many adherents in the capital, esp. at the University. In the 18th cent. Paris became a centre of Rationalism and 'Enlightenment'; religion suffered its most serious eclipse during the Revolutions of 1789, 1830, and 1848. In the first of these the old University was abolished; a new one was established in 1806 by the combination of the three faculties of arts, medicine, and law, but without theology, which, since 1875, had been represented by the *Institut Catholique.

Paris has always been famous for its churches and monasteries, among the chief of which are Notre-Dame (q.v.) and the former Benedictine abbey St.-Germain-des-Prés. Other famous religious houses were the Benedictine abbeys of *St.-Denis and St.-Maur-des-Fossés, the Augustinian monasteries of St.-Geneviève and St.-Victor, and the houses of *Benedictine nuns, Montmartre and *Port-Royal, all of which perished in the Revolution of 1789. Foremost among modern churches are *St.-Sulpice with its 18 chapels, Notre-Dame-des-Victoires, a popular place of pilgrimage, La Madeleine, built in the form of a Greek Temple, and the Sacré-Cœur on Montmartre, built in Byzantine-Romanesque style from 1875 to 1919.

See also *Sorbonne, Sainte-Chapelle.*

T. Okey, *Paris and its Story* (1904; enlarged ed., 1906). L. Dubech-P. d'Espezel, *Histoire de Paris* (1926; ed. with illustrations, 2 vols., 1931). B. Maurel, *Paris. Ses origines, ses croissance, son histoire* (1932). L. Brossolette, *Paris et sa région à travers l'histoire* (1933). On the University, H. *Denifle, O.P.–A. Chatelain edd.), *Chartularium Universitatis Parisiensis* (4 vols., Paris, 1889–97); idd. and others (edd.), *Auctarium Chartularii Universitatis Parisiensis* (ib., 1894 ff.). C. E. Du Boulay, *Historia Universitatis Parisiensis* (6 vols., ib., 1665–73). J. B. L. Crevier, *Histoire de l'université de Paris, depuis son origine jusqu'à l'année 1600* (7 vols., 1761); E. Dubarle, *Histoire de l'université, depuis son origine jusqu'à nos jours* (2 vols., 1829). L. Liard, *L'Université de Paris* (Les Grandes Institutions de France, 1909). The best account of the medieval university, with bibl., is that in H. *Rashdall, *The Universities of Europe in the Middle Ages*, i (ed. F. M. Powicke–A. B. Emden, 1936), pp. 268–584. C. Jourdain, *Histoire de l'université de Paris au XVIIe et XVIIIe siècle* (2 pts., 1862–6). P. Glorieux, *Répertoire des maîtres en théologie de Paris au XIIIe siècle* (Études de Philosophie médiévale, xvi–xviii; 1932–4). On the ecclesiastical history, J. Lebeuf, *Histoire de la ville et de tout le diocès de Paris* (15 vols., 1754–8). J. Rupp, *Histoire de l'église de Paris* (Bibliothèque Chrétienne d'Histoire, 1948). P. Pisani, *L'Église de Paris et la Révolution* (4 vols., Bibliothèque d'Histoire religieuse, 1908–11). G. d'Avenel, *Les Évêques et archevêques de Paris depuis saint Denys jusqu'à nos jours* (2 vols., Tournai, 1878). See also works cited under *France, Christianity in.* G. Goyau in *C.E.*, xi (1911), pp. 480–95, s.v. 'Paris, Archdiocese of'; P. Ferret, ib., pp. 495–8, s.v. 'Paris, University of'; A. P. Frutaz–G. Rupp–M. Briek–I. Cecchetti–E. Josi in *E.C.*, ix (1952), cols. 825–37, s.v. 'Parigi', with detailed bibl. H. *Leclercq, O.S.B., in

D.A.C.L., xiii (pt. 1; 1938), cols. 1696–1959, s.v. 'Paris [Histoire]', with full bibl.; cols. 1959–2074, s.v. 'Paris (La Bibliothèque Nationale); cols. 2074–160, s.v. 'Paris (Manuscrits liturgiques de)'.

PARIS, MATTHEW. See *Matthew Paris*.

PARISH.

In England, an area under the spiritual care of a C of E clergyman (the '*incumbent' or, in the correct meaning of the word, the 'curate'), to whose religious ministrations all its inhabitants are entitled. The incumbent, who receives his income wholly or in part from funds specially allocated to the parish, is nominated by the *patron of the benefice, and can only be removed from his cure in very exceptional cases ('freehold of the clergy'). The word comes from the Gk. παροικία, 'district', via the late Lat. *parochia*. Originally the παροικία was the ecclesiastical area under the bishop (the modern 'diocese'), but from the later 4th cent. it came to be applied to the subdivisions of the diocese, which the bishop put in charge of resident presbyters. In England the establishment of the parochial system has been traditionally attributed to Abp. *Theodore (7th cent.); but it is now commonly held (after Ulrich Stutz) that its roots, including its form of patronage, must be sought in the relations (of Teutonic ancestry) of landlord and pagan priest in pre-Christian times when the owner of land was bound to provide facilities for worship for his dependants, appointing a priest as his agent for the purpose. The compromise reached at the Third *Lateran Council of 1179, which gave the Bishop the right of *institution, strengthened the incumbent against his patron, though once instituted he still preserved his freehold against his bishop.

From a very early date the English parish has also been an important unit of civil administration. Except in the N. of England, where a parish might contain more than one town, the parish and the township were normally conterminous. To meet the growth and changing distribution of population, esp. since the Industrial Revolution, many new parishes have been formed. An Act of 1710 (9 Anne cap. 22) provided for 50 additional parishes in London; and the Church Building Acts of 1818 and 1824 set up many more new parishes. But as each case required a separate Act of Parliament, until recent times action was slow and costly. The present practice is much simpler. Schemes are drawn up by the *Church Commission (until 1948 the *Ecclesiastical Commission) and confirmed by Order in Council. Since the abolition of Church Rates in 1868 the civil importance of the parish has much declined.

The custom of marking the boundaries by '*beating the bounds' on the *Rogation Days is still observed in some parishes.

P. D. Thomson, *Parish and Parish Church*. Their Place and Influence in History (Baird Lecture for 1935; 1948). A. *Gasquet, *Parish Life in Medieval England* (The Antiquary's Books, 1906); E. L. Cutts, *Parish Priests and their People in the Middle Ages in England* (1914). J. C. Cox,

The English Parish Church. An Account of the Chief Building Types and of their Material during Nine Centuries (1914; with additional chapters by C. B. Ford, 1935). Id., *The Parish Registers of England* (The Antiquary's Books, 1910). E. Tyrrell-Green, *Parish Church Architecture* (1924). U. Stutz, *Die Eigenkirche als Element des mittelalterlich-germanischen Kirchenrechtes* (Basel Inaugural Lecture; Berlin, 1895; Eng. tr. by G. Barraclough, *Mediaeval Germany*, ii, 1938, pp. 35–70). E. Stolz, 'Παροικία, parochia und parochus', in *T.Q.*, lxxxix (1907), pp. 424–48; id., 'Zur Geschichte des Terminus *Parochus*', ib., xcv (1913), pp. 193–203; id., 'Parochus', ib., pp. 1–8. P. de Labriolle, 'Paroecia' in *Rech. S.R.*, xviii (1928), pp. 60–72. H. Boehmer, 'Das Eigenkirche in England' in *Texte und Forschungen zur englischen Kulturgeschichte*. Festgabe für Felix Liebermann (1921), pp. 301–53. H. W. Cripps, *A Practical Treatise on the Law Relating to the Church and Clergy* (ed. 8 by K. M. Macmorran, 1937), esp. pp. 178–98. E. W. Watson in *D.E.C.H.*, pp. 441–5, s.v. U. Stutz in *P.R.E.* (ed. 3), xxiii (1913), pp. 364–77, s.v. 'Eigenkirche', with bibl. A. M. Koeniger–K. Algermissen in *L.Th.K.*, viii (1936), cols. 188–194, s.v. 'Pfarrei', with detailed bibl. incl. useful reff. to further specialized artt. by U. Stutz.

PARISH CLERK.

The church official, either a layman or in orders, but usually the former, who in England assists the priest, chiefly by making the responses of the congregation in the services, and sometimes in reading the epistle. He also helps in the general care of the church. The office, which is known from the time of St. *Augustine of Canterbury, could be held only by men of some education. Until 1921 the office was freehold, but since then the parish clerk is appointed and dismissed by the incumbent and the *Parochial Church Council acting jointly. In the old 'three-decker' pulpits, the lowest stage was assigned to the clerk.

The conditions of the appointment of (lay) Parish Clerks are laid down in the Book of *Canons of 1604, can. 91; of persons in Holy Orders in 7 & 8 Vict. c. 59. J. Christie, *Some Account of Parish Clerks, more especially of the Ancient Fraternity (Bretherne and Sisterne) of S. Nicholas, now known as the Worshipful Company of Parish Clerks* (privately printed for the Company, 1893). J. Wickham Legg (ed.), *The Clerk's Book of 1549* (*Henry Bradshaw Society, xxv; 1903), with good general introd., pp. xvii–lxii. P. H. Ditchfield, *The Parish Clerk* (1907). [E. G.] C. [F.] Atchley, *The Parish Clerk, and his Right to Read the Liturgical Epistle* (*Alcuin Club Tracts, iv; 1903).

PARKER, JOSEPH (1830–1902), *Congregationalist divine.

A native of Hexham, he was for a time a *Wesleyan local preacher, but in 1852 returned to Congregationalism and became an assistant to John Campbell at the Moorfields Tabernacle in London. After ministering at Banbury (1853–8) and Manchester (1858–69), he accepted in 1869 a call to the Poultry Street Chapel, where his power and dramatic oratory in the pulpit attracted a large congregation. By 1874 he had completed the City Temple on Holborn Viaduct, and here ministered with great influence until his death. His publications include *The People's Bible* (25 vols., 1883–95); *Ecce Deus* (1867), a reply to J. R. *Seeley's *Ecce Homo*; *A Preacher's Life* (1899), autobiographical; and many volumes of sermons. Throughout his life he was a strong advocate of temperance.

Lives by A. Dawson (London, 1901), W. Adamson (Glasgow–London, 1902), and G. H. Pike (London, 1904). A. Gordon in *D.N.B.*, *1901–1911*, pp. 71–3, with further reff.

PARKER, MATTHEW (1504–75), Abp. of *Canterbury. Educated at Corpus Christi College, Cambridge, where he was elected a Fellow in 1527, Parker soon identified himself with the groups of moderate reformers. Under *Henry VIII and *Edward VI he received several preferments, and in the latter reign took advantage of the permission to the clergy to marry. Under *Mary he was deprived, and lived in obscurity till 1559, when *Elizabeth I chose him for the vacant Abpric. of Canterbury. After accepting it with much reluctance, he was consecrated at *Lambeth Palace on 17 Dec. 1559 by four bishops who had held sees in Edward VI's reign. His main objects as primate were to preserve the settlement of 1559 from further change and to rejoin as far as possible the links with the past. To this end he took part in the issue of the *Thirty-Nine Articles and of the ['*Bishops' Bible', and published in 1566 his ['*Advertisements' on ritual matters, which commanded, *inter alia*, the use of the surplice. Henceforward he had to face considerable opposition from the *Puritan party which embodied its aims in the *Admonition to Parliament* (1572). Parker was a wise and tolerant, though hardly a forceful, archbishop, preferring scholarship to controversy. He issued editions of the works of many medieval chroniclers, among them Matthew of Westminster (1567–70), *Matthew Paris (1571) and Thomas of Walsingham (1574). The most considerable of his own writings was his *De Antiquitate Ecclesiae et Privilegiis Ecclesiae Cantuariensis cum Archiepiscopis eius lxx* (1572). A large collection of the MSS. collected by or for him survives in the library of his college at Cambridge.

Correspondence from 1535 to 1575 ed. J. Bruce–T. T. Perowne (*Parker Society, 1853). Episcopal Register, Book I (1559–71) transcribed by E. Margaret Thompson and ed., with introd., by W. H. *Frere (*Canterbury and York Society, xxxv–xxxvi; 1928). The primary authority is the life by J. *Strype (London, 1711). Modern lives by W. M. Kennedy ('Makers of National History', 1908) and Edith W. Perry, *Under Four Tudors* (1940). J. B. Mullinger in *D.N.B.*, xliii (1895), pp. 254–64; W. H. Frere in *D.E.C.H.*, p. 445 f. Modern life by V. J. K. Brook (Oxford, 1962). See also bibl. to *Anglican Ordinations*.

PARKER, THEODORE (1810–60), American *Unitarian preacher and reformer. The son of a New England yeoman farmer, he graduated at Harvard in 1836. Here he taught himself many oriental languages and began a translation of M. L. *de Wette's *Einleitung in das Alte Testament* (publd. 1843). In 1837 he was ordained first pastor of the parish (Unitarian) church in W. Roxbury, Mass. By 1841 he had come to hold, through the influence of R. W. *Emerson and D. *Strauss, much more liberal views than those of Unitarian orthodoxy and his associates consequently denounced him. In his *Discourse of Matters Pertaining to Religion* (1842) he expounded his radical views, maintaining that the permanent essence of Christianity was the influence of Jesus and that belief in miracles was unnecessary. The work, which was widely read, won him some new followers esp. in Europe (among them J. *Martineau), but confirmed the orthodox

Unitarians in their distrust of him. From 1845 till his death he ministered to a congregation at Boston, U.S.A., taking an increasingly active part in social reform movements. He became a fervent advocate of temperance, prison reform, and of education for women, and the leader in Boston of the Anti-Slavery Crusade.

J. Weiss. *Life and Correspondence of Theodore Parker* (New York, 1864); J. W. Chadwick, *T. Parker* (Boston, 1900). F. R. Christie in *Dict. Amer. Biog.*, xiv (1934), pp. 238–40.

PARKER SOCIETY, The. A society established in 1840 under the leadership of the Earl of *Shaftesbury and some other prominent *Evangelicals, including Edward Bickersteth of the *C.M.S., to issue 'the works of the Fathers and early writers of the Reformed Church'. Its publications include editions of the works and letters of M. *Parker (from whom it took its name), T. *Cranmer, J. *Jewel, and others. Like the contemporary 'Library of the Fathers' (q.v.) and 'Library of Anglo-Catholic Theology' (1841 ff.), of which it was a kind of Protestant counterpart, these publications were of great service to historical and theological learning.

PAROCHIAL CHURCH COUNCIL. A council set up in every parish in the C of E by the Parochial Church Councils (Powers) Measure, 1921 (subsequently amended, 1929), to give the laity a share in parochial administration. At an annual meeting the qualified electors in every parish elect lay representatives to the Council, which also includes the incumbent, the churchwardens, and any lay representatives on the Diocesan or Ruridecanal Conference. It must meet at least four times a year. Its primary duty is 'to co-operate with the incumbent in the initiation, conduct, and development of Church work both within the parish and outside'. Most of the powers formerly possessed by the vestry and the churchwardens which relate to the financial affairs of the church, as well as the maintenance of its fabric and ornaments, have been transferred to the Parochial Church Council.

PAROISSIEN. The name for various prayer-books in the vernacular designed for the use of the laity which have been published in France since the 17th cent. They usually contain, besides private devotional exercises, a considerable amount of liturgical matter, such as translations of the *Masses and *Vespers for Sundays and feasts, as well as the Holy Week services, often together with the proper musical notation. Though lineally descended from the Medieval *Primers, the popularity of the Paroissien in the 17th cent. was chiefly inspired by the desire for vernacular forms of worship.

PAROUSIA (Gk. παρουσία, 'presence' or 'arrival'). In its English form, the word is employed (following NT usage) to denote particularly the future return of Christ in glory (the 'Second Coming') to judge the living and the dead, and to terminate the present world order. Primitive Christianity believed the event to be imminent and this belief has been revived from time to time in the history of the Church. The prevailing Christian tradition, while maintaining that our Lord's words attest the certainty of a final *General Judgement which will mark the end of the present order and the entry of redeemed humanity into the resurrection-life in heaven, has been opposed to speculation as to the exact time and manner of the Coming. It is believed that in the Judgement humanity will be confronted by the risen and glorified Christ. The supposition that Christ, when He returned, would first reign for a long period on earth (the *Millennium, q.v.) was held in some early Christian circles, but it has not been generally followed.

Besides the discussions of the NT evidence in the writings of J. *Weiss and A. *Schweitzer, cited in the entries s.vv., F. Tillmann, *Die Wiederkunft Christi nach den paulinischen Briefen* (Biblische Studien, xiv, Hftt. 1–2; 1909); H. D. Wendland, *Die Eschatologie des Reiches Gottes bei Jesus* (1931); F. Guntermann, *Die Eschatologie des heiligen Paulus* (1932); R. *Otto, *Reich Gottes und Menschensohn* (1934; Eng. tr., 1938); J. Héring, *Le Royaume de Dieu et sa venue. Étude sur l'espérance de Jésus de l'apôtre Paul* (Études d'Histoire et de Philosophie religieuses, xxxv; 1937); E. Walter, *Das Kommen des Herrn* (Leben aus dem Wort, iv, 2 vols., 1941–7). T. F. Glasson, *The Second Advent. The Origin of the New Testament Doctrine* (1945); id., *His Appearing and His Kingdom.* The Christian Hope in the Light of History (1953). W. A. *Brown in *H.D.B.*, iii (1900), pp. 674–80, s.v.; S. H. Hooke in *D.A.C.*, ii (1918), pp. 123–31, s.v.; J. Chaine in *D.T.C.*, xi (pt. 2; 1932), cols. 2043–54, s.v. 'Parousie'; A. Romeo in *E.C.*, ix (1952), cols. 875–82, s.v. 'Parusia'; A. Oepke in *T.W.B.*, v (1954), pp. 856–69, s.v. 'παρουσία, πάρειμι'.

PARSON. Properly, the holder of an ecclesiastical benefice who has full possession of its rights, i.e. a *rector. This use was general until the 17th cent., e.g. E. *Stillingfleet wrote in a charge of 1691: 'A vicar cannot appoint a vicar, but a parson may'. Its current use for any (esp. C of E) clergyman has now completely superseded its orig. sense.

The ecclesiastical use of the Lat. *persona* appears to date from the 11th cent., e.g. Council of *Clermont (1095), can. 3. Acc. to English legal writers (E. Coke, W. Blackstone) it derives from the view of the Parson as the legal 'person' by whom the property of God (or of the Patron Saint or of the church) in the parish was actually held; he was the person to sue or to be sued. C. D. *Du Cange, however, derives the usage from *persona* as equivalent to *dignitas*, meaning a 'personage' or 'dignitary', while H. Schaefer (*Pfarrkirche und Stift im deutschen Mittelalter*, 1903, para. 19), pointing out that *persona* was most frequently used of an absentee rector, often a layman, has suggested that the word is to be deduced from the use of *persona* as a role. The civil law sense seems the most likely origin of the English usage.

PARSONS, ROBERT (1546–1610), also 'Persons', *Jesuit missionary. After holding a Fellowship at Balliol College, Oxford (1568–74), Parsons left England and was received into the RC Church at Louvain; and in 1575 became a Jesuit at Rome. Chosen with E. *Campion to lead the Jesuit Mission, he was sent to England in 1580, but soon afterwards was forced to flee to the Continent, whilst Campion was arrested and executed (1581). Parsons subsequently engaged in plotting with the more extreme RCs against *Elizabeth I, and was thus among those responsible for causing the Government to take severer measures against the whole body of *Recusants. He vigorously supported the Jesuits in their struggle with the secular clergy, and also succeeded in retaining for his order control over RC policy in England. In *The Conference about the Next Succession to the Crown of England* (1594), published under the name of Doleman, he insisted on the right of subjects to set aside, on religious grounds, the heir to the throne, and in the course of the work set forth the claims of the Infanta.

'Memoirs', ed. by J. H. Pollen, S.J., in *Catholic Record Society Publications*, ii (1906), pp. 1–161 and iv (1907), pp. 1–161. T. G. Law in *D.N.B.*, xliii (1895), pp. 411–18.

PARTICULAR BAPTISTS. The group of Baptists whose theology was essentially *Calvinistic as contrasted with the *Arminianism of the *General Baptists. Their polity was similar to that of the *Independents, but a considerable place was given to 'associations' of local Churches. The first Particular Baptist community in England was established at Southwark from 1633 onwards. In 1891 the General Baptists of the New Connexion joined the Baptist Union which had been formed among the Particular Baptists.

PARTICULAR JUDGEMENT. In Catholic theology, the judgement on each individual soul immediately on its separation from the body. It is thus prior to and quite distinct from the *General Judgement (q.v.) on the Last Day. In the bull 'Benedictus Deus' (1336) Benedict XII upheld the teaching that the Particular Judgement admits the souls at once either to the *Beatific Vision, to *purgatory, or to *hell, thus excluding an intermediate state of sleep or partial happiness or suffering between the day of death and the final resurrection of the body, such as had been envisaged by certain older theologians, e.g. St. *Justin, *Tertullian, and St. *Ambrose. The chief Scriptural evidence for the doctrine is found in the Parable of Dives and Lazarus (Lk. 16. 19) and in Christ's words to the penitent thief (Lk. 23. 43). There is no universally accepted teaching as regards the circumstances of the Particular Judgement, but acc. to the common opinion of Catholic theologians, it occurs at the time of death and consists in an interior illumination which makes known to the separated soul its state in relation to God.

PARVIS (Fr., from Lat. *paradisus*). Originally the court in front of a cathedral or other large church, esp. when, as at *St. Peter's, Rome, surrounded by a colonnade. The word came to be also used of the portico of a church porch. In modern times it is often erroneously applied to the room over such a porch, apparently through a misunderstood reference in F. Blomefield's *Norfolk* (ii, p. 748; *c*. 1744), which mentions a school kept in the parvis of St. Martin's Church, Norwich, in 1300.

O.E.D., vii (1909), p. 517, s.v.

PASCAL, BLAISE (1623–62), French theologian, mathematician, and savant. The son of Étienne Pascal, President of the local court of exchequer and a man of culture, he was born at Clermont-Ferrand; his mother died when he was four and in 1631 his father transferred the family to Paris, until his appointment as Intendant of Normandy in 1639. Pascal was educated privately by his father together with his two sisters, Gilberte (b. 1620; in 1641 she married her cousin, Florin Périer) and Jacqueline (b. 1625). He showed great precocity, and in Rouen engaged in various mathematical experiments, incl. those which led to the invention of the barometer. Having been brought up to regard matters of faith as beyond reason, he came into contact with the *Jansenists in 1646 (his 'first conversion'), and in the next year secured the condemnation of an ex-*Capuchin monk who maintained that reason could comprehend the mysteries of faith. A few months later he entered into direct communication with *Port-Royal, but was not yet prepared to accept all its demands. Leaving Rouen in 1648, the family returned to Paris in 1650. In 1651 his father died, and shortly afterwards Jacqueline, despite the opposition of her brother, entered the convent of Port-Royal. Pascal continued his scientific pursuits and enjoyed the society of Paris. On 23 Nov. 1654 his 'definitive conversion' took place, when he discovered the 'God of Abraham, the God of Isaac, the God of Jacob, and not of philosophers and men of science'; at the time he made a record of the experience which he carried on his person for the rest of his life. In 1655 he retired to a strict retreat near Port-Royal-des-Champs, where he spent most of his remaining eight years, though he never became one of the Solitaires. He was in bad health from 1658 until his death.

The condemnation of A. *Arnauld by the Sorbonne in 1655 prompted his famous attack on the *Jesuits in his *Lettres écrites à un provincial*, commonly known as his 'Lettres provinciales' (18 in all). The first was printed on 23 Jan. 1656, the rest followed shortly afterwards (1656–7). The first four and the last two were directly concerned with the immediate issue as a personal quarrel. The remaining twelve, attacking the Jesuit theories of grace (*Molinism) and moral theology (*Probabilism), were intended to expose the immoral character of their casuistry and to oppose to it the rigorist morality of the Jansenists, with its aim of restoring the disciplinary practices and austerity of the primitive Church. The work was condemned by the Congregation of the *Index in 1657 but continued to provoke violent controversy. The literary history of the *Pensées* begins with the publication of selections from his notes in 1670, eight years after his death; the remaining fragments were stuck into an album regardless of sequence; the whole has subsequently been frequently re-edited. The work was designed as a vindication of the truth of Christianity against the indifference of the *libertins* whom, though inaccessible to philosophical reasoning, Pascal hoped to convince by the presentation of facts and fulfilment of prophecy and by an appeal to the heart. Apart from its brilliant style, it owes its force to the wealth of personal experience and psychological perception which it embodies. The intention of writing such a book may have dated from his second conversion (1654), or more prob. from the time of the miraculous cure of his niece by the Holy Thorn (1656). At the time of his death only bundles of material had been collected.

Pascal's religion was centred on the Person of Christ as Saviour and based on his personal experience. Here, as in his scientific investigations, his thought was deeply influenced by his interest in experimental knowledge. Nourished on the *Augustinianism of Port-Royal, his deepest experience was that of man's tragic situation between greatness and misery, to escape from which he plunges into distractions. From this state only faith can free him, since human existence is confronted with the necessity of making a decision for or against God. The element of risk in the life of faith and emphasis on the will are characteristic of Pascal, who confesses that the 'heart has its reasons of which reason knows not'. He does not, however, thereby exclude the use of reason from demonstrating the truth of faith. His scientific works include *Expériences nouvelles touchant le vuide* (1647); *Récit de la grande expérience de l'équilibre des liqueurs* (by B. P., 1648), and *Traités de l'équilibre des liqueurs et de la pesanteur de la masse de l'air* (1647). Pascal was ridiculed by *Voltaire and the *Encyclopedists of the 18th cent., but in the 19th cent. there came a revival of interest, which continues.

The best ed. of Pascal's *Œuvres complètes* is that of L. C. Brunschvicg–F. Boutroux–F. Gazier (14 vols., Grands Écrivains de la France, Paris, 1904–14). Among the more important edd. of the *Lettres provinciales* are those of E. Havet (2 vols., Paris, 1885) and H. F. Stewart (Manchester University Press, 1920); of the *Pensées* those of E. Havet (Paris, 1852), G. Michaut (Collectanea Friburgensia, vi; Fribourg, Switzerland, 1896), L. Brunschvicg (facsimile of Bibl. Nat. MS. Fonds français 9209; Paris, 1905), and H. F. Stewart (London, 1950; with Eng. tr.). Of the large literature on Pascal, the following studies are among the most important: E. Boutroux, *Pascal* (Les Grands Écrivains français, 1900; Eng. tr., 1902); F. Strowski, *Pascal et son temps* (3 vols., 1907); H. F. Stewart, *The Holiness of Pascal* (Hulsean Lectures, 1914–15; 1915), J. Chevalier, *Pascal* ([1922]; Eng. tr., 1930); L. C. Brunschvicg, *Le Génie de Pascal* (1924); H. F. Stewart, *The Secret of Pascal* (1941); E. Cailliet, *The Clue to Pascal* (1944). E. Jovy, *Études pascaliennes* (8 vols., 1927–32). On Pascal's relation to Fr. thought in the present century, Dorothy M. Eastwood, *The Revival of Pascal* (1936). C. C. J. *Webb, *Pascal's Philosophy of Religion* (1929); H. F. Stewart, *Pascal's Apology for Religion* (1942). G. Saintsbury–G. Chrystal in *E.B.* (ed. 11), xx (1911), pp. 878–81; C. Constantin in *D.T.C.*, xi (pt. 2; 1932), cols. 2074–203; W. F. Cobb in *H.E.R.E.*, ix (1917), pp. 652–8, s.v. See also bibl. to *Port-Royal*.

PASCH (Aram. אֲסְפָא, Gk. πάσχα, 'passover'). A name formerly in fairly wide currency in England both for the Jewish *Passover and the Christian festival of *Easter (qq.v.). See also *Passion*.

PASCHAL II (d. 1118), Pope from 1099. Ranierus, a native of Galeata near *Ravenna, entered a *Cluniac monastery as a boy. Sent to Rome on some business of his convent, he attracted the notice of *Gregory VII, who made him cardinal-priest of San Clemente in c. 1080. In 1099 he was elected Pope. His pontificate is marked by a renewal of the *Investiture struggle with the Emp. *Henry IV. In England the difficulties, which had culminated in 1105 in the excommunication of several of Henry I's advisers, were solved in 1106 when investiture by ring and staff was abandoned by the king and replaced by the feudal oath to be taken by all bishops before their consecration. In Germany things proved much more difficult. Paschal disregarded all advances of the Emp. Henry IV, whose excommunication he confirmed at the Council of Rome in 1102, and gave his support to the revolt of his son, later Henry V. When the new Emperor followed the practice of lay investiture, Paschal opposed him at the synods of Guastalla (1106) and Troyes (1107), where he declared deposed all bishops who had received it, and secured the re-enforcement of these decisions at Benevento in 1108 and at a Council held in Rome in 1110. When Henry V came to Rome in the ensuing year to be crowned, the Pope, after further negotiations and conflict, refused the Emperor lay investiture as well as coronation. Henry replied by taking the Pope prisoner and extorting from him the Treaty of Ponte Mammolo, in which Paschal promised the Emperor on oath to grant lay investiture, never to anathematize him, and to crown him. This treaty roused the indignation esp. of the Gregorian party and was declared null and void by the Lateran Council of 1112. After several synods both in France and Germany had excommunicated Henry, the Pope in 1116, at another Lateran Council, formally condemned the treaty that had been wrested from him. When the Emperor marched on Rome again in the following year, Paschal II fled to Benevento and died on his return in 1118, leaving the question of investiture unsolved.

His Register has not survived; collection of letters in J. P. Migne, *PL*, clxiii, 31–448. Jaffé, i, 702–72. *L.P.* (Duchesne), ii, 296–310. B. Monod, *Essai sur les rapports de Pascal II avec Philippe Iᵉʳ* (Bibliothèque de l'École des Hautes Études, clxiv; 1907). Mann, viii (1910), pp. 1–119. A. Fliche in Fliche-Martin, viii (1944), pp. 338–75, with bibl. C. Mirbt in *P.R.E.* (ed. 3), xiv (1904), pp. 717–24, s.v. 'Paschalis II'; É. Amann in *D.T.C.*, xi (pt. 2; 1932), cols. 2057–74; s.v. 'Pascal II'; G. Mollat in *E.C.*, ix (1952), cols. 902–4, s.v. 'Pasquale II'. See also bibl. *Investiture Controversy*, and *Henry IV*.

PASCHAL BAYLON, St. (1540–92) *Franciscan lay brother. The son of peasant parents, he was born at Torre Hermosa, on the borders of Castile and Aragon, on Whitsunday, 1540, and christened 'Pascua' after the feast. From his seventh to his twenty-fourth year he minded his father's sheep, leading a life of austerity and prayerfulness which was graced (it is recorded) by various miracles. In obedience to a vision he entered the neighbouring convent of the Franciscans of the Alcantarine reform where he practised extreme mortification. Throughout his life he was particularly devoted to the cult of the Blessed Sacrament. During a mission to *France he defended the doctrine of the *Real Presence at the risk of his life, and was roughly handled by the *Calvinists. He was canonized in 1690 and on 28 Nov. 1897 he was declared by *Leo XIII in the encyclical 'Providentissimus Deus' (not to be confused with that of 1893 on the Study of Scripture with the same title) patron of *Eucharistic Congresses and Associations. He is usually depicted in the act of adoration before the Host. Feast day 17 May.

J. Sala, O.F.M. (ed.), *Opúsculos de S. Pascual Bailón* (Toledo, 1911), with useful introd. The primary authorities are the Spanish *Chronicon del B. Fray P. Baylon de la Orden del P. S. Francisco* by his friend, J. Ximénez, Valencia, 1601, and the account written in connection with h's canonization by C. de Arta (It. tr., Venice, 1673). Lat. tr. of abstracts of these pr. in *AA.SS.*, Mai IV (1685), pp. 49–132. Modern studies by L. A. de Porrentruy, O.M.C. (Paris, 1899), and A. Groeteken, O.F.M. (Einsiedeln, 1909). P. M. Mansuy, O.F.M., *Le Patron des congrès et des œuvres eucharistiques, saint Pascal Baylon* (ed. 2, 1910).

PASCHAL CANDLE. In the W. Church, the candle placed on a large separate candlestick in the north side of the *sanctuary which is lighted esp. at liturgical functions throughout Eastertide. It is solemnly lit by the *deacon from the new fire during the singing of the *Exultet on *Holy Saturday, five grains of incense being then inserted into its stem. It is extinguished after the Gospel on *Ascension Day.

U. Berlière, O.S.B., 'Le Cierge pascal' in *Le Messager des Fidèles* (later *Rev. Bén.*), v (1888), pp. 106–16; H. P. Feasey, O.S.B., 'The Paschal Candle' in *The Ecclesiastical Review*, xxxiv (1906), pp. 353–71; id., 'The Paschal Preconium', ib., xxxvi (1907), pp. 248–61; H. J. Heuser, 'The Tenebrae and the New Light of the Holy Fire', ib., pp. 225–31. C. E. Hammond in *D.C.A.*, ii (1880), p. 1564, s.v. 'Paschal Taper'; H. *Leclercq, O.S.B., in *D.A.C.L.*, xiii (pt. 2; 1938), cols. 1559–71, s.v. 'Pâques'. See also bibl. to *Exultet*.

PASCHAL CHRONICLE. See *Chronicon Paschale*.

PASCHAL CONTROVERSIES. Among the many controversies in the early Church over the complex question as to how to settle the date of *Easter (the Christian 'Passover' or 'Pasch') were:

(1) Whether Easter should be observed, after the Jewish manner, on a fixed day of the lunar month (14 Nisan) or always on (the following) Sunday. The former practice was the ancient tradition in Asia Minor. On this dispute, see *Quartodecimanism*.

(2) The divergences arising from the *Antiochene and *Alexandrian methods of determining the 'Paschal Moon', the Antiochenes being content to accept the Jewish reckoning whereas at Alexandria an independent

calculation was made. Acc. to Alexandrian practice, Easter was always put after the vernal equinox. The decision at *Nicaea (325) in favour of Alexandrian practice was generally accepted, except by a small group of schismatics (Audiani, Protopaschites).

(3) Differences in the 4th and 5th cents. between the Roman and Alexandrine methods of computation, through the use of divergent 'paschal cycles', Alexandria having long accepted the *Anatolian 19-years cycle whereas Rome used an older 84-year cycle. Further, while the Alexandrians allowed Easter to be kept on the 15th of the month if a Sunday, it was never observed at Rome before the 16th; also the latest date for keeping Easter at Alexandria was 25 Apr., but at Rome 21 Apr. Thus we learn from St. *Augustine (*Ep.* 23) that in 387 Easter was observed in Gaul on 21 Mar., in Italy on 18 Apr., and at Alexandria on 25 Apr. From the 5th cent., Rome increasingly followed the Alexandrian computation, which was formally adopted in the W. by *Dionysius Exiguus (525); but as late as 455 there had been seven days' difference between the Alexandrian and the Roman Easter.

(4) Until the time of *Charlemagne (*c.* 742–814), considerable uncertainty existed in Gaul, owing to the adoption of Victorius of Aquitaine's Paschal Tables (drawn up in Rome in 457, but never much used in the City) with their cycle of 532 years.

(5) The possession by the Celtic Churches of their own method of computation led to a long quarrel in the British Isles after the arrival of the Roman missionaries. As late as 651 Queen Eanfleda, who followed the Roman rule, was keeping *Palm Sunday and fasting on the same day that her husband, Oswy, King of Northumbria, was celebrating Easter (*Bede, *H.E.*,III,xxv). The Roman custom was accepted for Northumbria by the Synod of *Whitby (664), and imposed on the whole of England by Abp. *Theodore in 669.

A large number of the older works on the subject are listed by H. *Leclercq, O.S.B., in *D.A.C.L.*, xiii (pt. 2; 1938), cols. 1571–4, s.v. 'Pâques'. Since the researches of L. *Duchesne and B. Krusch, earlier works are only of historical interest. L. Duchesne, 'La Question de la Pâque au concile de Nicée' in *R.Q.H.*, xxviii (1880), pp. 1–42. B. Krusch, *Studien zur christlich-mittelalterlichen Chronologie. Der 84-jährige Ostercyclus und seine Quellen* (1880). Id., 'Die Einführung des griechischen Paschalritus im Abendlande' in *N.A.*, ix (1883), pp. 99–169. J. Schmid, *Die Osterfrage auf dem ersten allgemeinen Konzil von Nicäa* (Vienna, 1905). E. *Schwartz, *Christliche und jüdische Ostertafeln* (*Abh.* (Gött.), N.F., viii, Hft. 6; 1905); id., 'Osterbetrachtungen' in *Z.N.T.W.*, vii (1906), pp. 1–33. F. E. *Brightman, 'The Quartodeciman Question' in *J.T.S.*, xxv (1924), pp. 254–70. G. Fritz in *D.T.C.*, xi (pt. 2; 1932), cols. 1948–70, s.v. 'Pâques, Les Controverses pascales'.

PASCHAL LAMB. Originally, the lamb eaten at the Jewish *Passover. The lambs were sacrificed in the *Temple on the afternoon of 14 *Nisan, then taken by the people to their homes and eaten during the night (cf. Exod. 12). The fulfilment of the Jewish Passover in Christ (cf. 1 Cor. 5. 7, 'Christ our Passover is sacrificed for us'; Jn. 1. 29, 'Behold the Lamb of God') has made Him for Christians the 'Paschal Lamb'. See also *Lamb*.

PASCHASINUS (*c.* 440), Bp. of Lilybaeum (now Marsala) in Sicily. Pope *Leo the Great assisted him when his diocese was devastated by the Vandals. When asked by Leo his opinion in the *Paschal Controversy, he replied in favour of the Alexandrian as against the Roman usage. In 451 he was one of the Papal legates at the Council of *Chalcedon, where he vigorously objected to the presence of *Dioscorus. There is nothing known about him after the Council.

The chief source is his correspondence with Leo ('Leo', *Ep.* 3, 'De Paschate anni 444' and Leo, *Ep.* 88) and scattered references in the *Acta* of Chalcedon (q.v.).

PASCHASIUS RADBERTUS, St. (*c.* 785–*c.* 860), *Benedictine theologian. He entered the monastery at *Corbie under its abbot, Adalhard, whom he accompanied into Saxony in 822. Elected abbot *c.* 844, he attended the Council of Paris in 847, but resigned *c.* 853 and henceforth devoted himself entirely to study. The most important of his works, which comprise also a Life of abbot Adalhard and a very learned commentary on St. Matthew, is his treatise 'De Corpore et Sanguine Domini' (831, revised 844) which was composed for the instruction of the Saxon monks. The work is the first doctrinal monograph on the Eucharist. In maintaining the real Presence of Christ in the Eucharist, Radbertus specified it further as the flesh born of Mary, which had suffered on the Cross and risen again, and which is miraculously multiplied by the omnipotence of God at each consecration. At the same time he insisted on the spiritual mode of this Presence, but without defining it, though there seem to be indications of his implicit acceptance of the later doctrine of *transubstantiation. By eating this flesh men are incorporated into the mystical Body of Christ which is the Church. Radbertus's doctrine was sharply attacked by *Ratramnus and *Rabanus Maurus, who opposed to his emphatic realism, which was sometimes marred by unfortunate comparisons and illustrations, their more spiritual conceptions of the Divine presence. Feast day, 26 Apr.

Collection of his works ed. J. *Sirmond, S.J. (Paris, 1618); repr. with additional works from other sources in J. P. Migne, *PL*, cxx. Crit. edd. of his Poems by L. Traube in *M.G.H.*, Poetae, iii (1896), pp. 38–53, with further notes, p. 746 f.; of various 'Epistolae' (incl. extracts of his works) by E. Duemmler, ib., Epistolae, vi (1925), pp. 133–49; and of his 'Epitaphium Arsenii' by id. (*Abh.* (Berl.), aus den Jahren 1899 und 1900 (1900), Hft. 2); also of 12th–13th cent. life of Paschasius, ed. O. Holder-Egger, *M.G.H.*, Scriptores, xv (pt. 1; 1887), pp. 452–4. Studies, mainly of his Eucharistic doctrine, by E. Choisy (Geneva, 1888), J. Ernst (Freiburg i.Br., 1896), H. Peltier (Strassburg thesis; Amiens, 1938), W. Kahles (Emsdetten, 1938), and C. Gliozzo (Palermo, 1945). D. *Stone, *A History of the Doctrine of the Holy Eucharist*, i (1909), pp. 216–22. J. Pohle in *C.E.*, xi (1911), p. 518, s.v.; H. Peltier in *D.T.C.*, xiii (pt. 2; 1937), cols. 1628–39, s.v. 'Radbert, Paschase'.

PASSION, The (Lat. '*passio*', lit. 'suffering'). The term is used absolutely of the Lord's Redemptive Suffering during the last days of His earthly life, and esp. of His Crucifixion. The word 'Pasch' or 'Passover' (Gk. Πάσχα), commonly applied in the early Church to the joint annual commemoration of the Redemptive Death and Resurrection of Christ (i.e. to 'Good Friday' and 'Easter' together), was often held by a false etymology to be derived from the Greek πάσχω ('to suffer'). See also *Passion Sunday, Passiontide.*

PASSION, Musical Settings of the. From at least the 4th cent. the Gospel narratives of the Passion were recited in church during *Holy Week with musical settings, St. *Gregory Nazianzen, e.g., recording such a recitation with choruses interspersed. During the Middle Ages all or part of the narrative was chanted to plainsong, and in the 15th cent. motet choruses were added. *C.* 1525, Johann Walther (1496–1570), M. *Luther's musical adviser, produced a Passion in German, the first to be written in a vernacular language, while in the next cent. Heinrich Schütz (1585–1672) developed the practice of assigning the characters to different vocal soloists. From the end of the 17th cent. lyric poems were sung in comment and chorales were added to be sung by the congregation; and an orchestra was also introduced. The greatest Passions of this type were the 'St. John Passion' (1723) and esp. the 'St. Matthew Passion' (1729) of J. S. *Bach.

[L.] O. Kade, *Die ältere Passionskomposition bis zum Jahre 1631* (Gütersloh, 1893). W. Lott, 'Zur Geschichte der Passionskomposition von 1650–1800' in *Archiv für Musikwissenschaft*, iii (1921), pp. 285–320. C. S. Terry–W. L. Smoldon in *Grove's Dictionary of Music and Musicians* (ed. 5 by E. Blom), vi (1954), pp. 577–87, s.v. 'Passion Music', with bibl. See also bibl. to *Oratorio, Bach* and other individual composers.

PASSION PLAYS. See *Drama;* also *Oberammergau.*

PASSION SUNDAY. The fifth Sunday in Lent, sometimes called *Judica Sunday from the *Introit for the day. In the RC Church since 1956 it has been officially named the 'First Passion Sunday', while *Palm Sunday has now become the 'Second Passion Sunday'. For the liturgical usages which begin on this day, see *Passiontide.*

PASSIONAL (Lat. *Liber Passionarius*). The word is used for various Latin liturgical books:
(1) The series of lections from the Lives or Acts of the Saints read at *Mattins on their feast days.
(2) A book containing the narratives of our Lord's Passion from the four Gospels.
(3) The particular *Evangeliarium, also known as 'King Aethelstan's Book', on which the English kings from Henry I to Edward III took the Coronation Oath. It contained the Gospel of St. John complete, followed by the Passions of Matthew, Mark, and Luke.

PASSIONISTS. The popular name for the members of the 'Congregation of Discalced Clerks of the Most Holy Cross and Passion of our Lord Jesus Christ'. The congregation was founded by St. *Paul of the Cross, who drew up its rule in 1720 and erected the first house, the 'Retreat' on Monte Argentaro, in 1737.

After some mitigations the rule was approved by *Benedict XIV in 1741 and 1746, and in 1769 confirmed by *Clement XIV, who at the same time conferred the privileges of the old orders on the new congregation. It soon spread throughout Europe and beyond. In 1841 the Passionists came to England, where they were the first religious after the Reformation to lead a strict community life and wear their habit in public. Among them was Fr. Dominic Barberi who received J. H. *Newman into the RC Church. The Passionists stress the contemplative life as the foundation of their apostolic work; and they take a further fourth vow promising to further the memory of Christ's Passion in the souls of the faithful. Their chief activities are the giving of missions and retreats. Their habit is black with the badge of the Passion, a white heart with the inscription 'Jesu XPI Passio', surmounted by a cross. The Passionist nuns, founded by St. Paul of the Cross together with Mother Mary Crucifixa in 1771, are strictly enclosed and contemplative; they, too, take a vow to practise devotion to the Passion.

F. Ward, C.P., *The Passionists* (New York, 1923). Gaétan du Saint Nom de Marie, C.P., *S. Paul de la Croix et l'Institut des Passionnistes* (Tirlemont, 1934). Heimbucher, ii, 341–5. A. Devine, C.P., in *C.E.*, xi (1911), pp. 521–5, s.v.; E. Krempel, C.P., in *L.Th.K.*, vii (1935), cols. 1015–17, s.v. 'Passionisten', with bibl.; Mauro dell' Immacolata, C.P., in *E.C.*, iii (1950), cols. 1441–3, s.v. 'Chierici Scalzi della SS.ma Croce e Passione di N.S. Gesu Cristo', also with bibl.

PASSIONS. The detailed and professedly contemporary accounts of the early Christian martyrdoms. They are commonly distinguished from the '*Acts' (q.v.), in which the narrative follows (or, at least, is intended to give the impression of following) the shorthand report taken down for official purposes.

PASSIONTIDE. The last two weeks of *Lent, extending from *Passion Sunday till *Holy Saturday (the *vigil of Easter). Acc. to W. practice, all crucifixes, pictures, and images in church are veiled in purple during this period, the crucifixes being unveiled again on Good Friday and other objects during the Easter Eve ceremonies. 'Gloria Patri' is omitted from the Pss., from the *Introit at Mass, and at '*Venite' at Matins. In English pre-Reformation practice the Lenten array of unbleached linen gave place in Passiontide to a deep red, as the liturgical colour, but in modern usage Lenten purple continues throughout, except for the Mass of *Maundy Thursday, which is in white, and on *Good Friday, when black is used.

PASSOVER. The Jewish festival celebrated every spring in commemoration of the *Exodus. Its chief feature was the sacrificial meal, culminating in the eating of the *paschal lamb, which was followed by the Feast of Unleavened Bread, lasting seven days. In NT times, the Passover meal united the members of all Jewish families or groups from sunset till midnight on 15 Nisan. Its last celebration by our Lord was, if the chronology of the

*Synoptic Gospels be followed, the occasion of the institution of the Eucharist of which the Jewish feast was the adumbration. See also *Eucharist, Paschal Lamb.*

The early history is discussed in all commentaries on Exodus and Leviticus. Good summary in G. B. *Gray, *Sacrifice in the Old Testament* (1925), esp. pp. 337–97. The first English scholar to defend the view that the orig. setting of the Passover was the sacrifice of firstlings and that it was unrelated to the Exodus was W. R. *Smith, *Lectures on the Religion of the Semites* (Burnett Lectures, 1888–9; 1889), p. 445 f. (following J. *Wellhausen). For post-OT period, W. O. E. Oesterley–G. H. Box, *The Religion and Worship of the Synagogue* (1907), pp. 355–66. The later method of observance was laid down in the *Mishnah, esp. in the tractate *Pesahim*; on this cf. H. L. Strack, *Pesahim. Der Misnatraktat Passafest, mit Berücksichtigung des Neuen Testaments und der jetzigen Passafeier der Juden* (Schriften des Institutum Judaicum in Berlin, xl; 1911). On its relation to Eucharist, G. *Bickell, *Messe und Pascha* (1872; Eng. tr., 1891); J. Jeremias, *Die Abendmahlsworte Jesu* (1935; ed. 3, 1956; Eng. tr., 1955), with full bibl. Christine Mohrmann, 'Pascha, Passio, Transitus' in *E.L.*, lxvi (1952), pp. 37–52. W. J. Moulton in *H.D.B.*, iii (1900), pp. 684–92, s.v.; I. Benziger in *E.Bi.*, iii (1902), cols. 3589–601, s.v.; J. Jacobs in *E.B.* (ed. 11), xx (1911), pp. 888–90, s.v.; J. Jeremias in *T.W.B.*, v (1954), pp. 895–903, sv. πάσχα; S. Zedda–P. Siffrin, O.S.B., in *E.C.*, ix (1952), cols. 894–901, s.v. 'Pasqua'.

PASTOPHORION. (Gk. παστοφόριον). In the E. Church, the sacristy adjacent to the *apse, used at least from the end of the 4th cent. (*Apostolic Constitutions*, VIII, xiii) for the reservation of the Sacrament.

PASTOR AETERNUS. The title (from its opening words) of the 'First Dogmatic Constitution on the Church of Christ', issued at the concluding session of the *Vatican Council on 18 July 1870. It defined the primacy and infallibility of the Pope.

Text in *A.S.S.*, vi (1870), pp. 40–7, and in *Acta et Decreta Sacrorum Conciliorum Recentiorum*. Collectio Lacensis, vii (Freiburg i.Br., 1890), cols. 426–32; also pr. Denz.-Bann. (ed. 1952), Nos. 1821–40, pp. 501–8, and, with Eng. tr., in [E.] Cuthbert Butler, O.S.B., *The Vatican Council*, ii (1930), pp. 276–95.

PASTOR OF HERMAS. See *Shepherd of Hermas.*

PASTOR, LUDWIG (1854–1928), historian of the Popes. He was a native of Aachen and, though his father had been a Protestant, was brought up a Catholic after his mother had become a widow. At the age of 19 he conceived the plan of writing a history of the Popes. After studying at Louvain, Vienna, and other universities he continued his researches at Rome. In 1880 he became lecturer at Innsbruck university, where he was appointed professor in 1887. In 1901 he became director of the Austrian Historical Institute in Rome, and in 1921 Austrian ambassador to the Holy See. His principal work is the *Geschichte der Päpste seit dem Ausgang des Mittelalters* (16 vols., 1886–1933), which has been translated into several languages. Based on extensive research in the archives of over 200 European cities, it aims at giving in vivid language a balanced representation of the history of Catholicism in modern times.

Diaries, Letters, and Memoirs ed. W. Wühr (Heidelberg, 1950), with bibl. pp. 918–20. Eng. tr. of his *Geschichte der Päpste* by F. I. Antrobus, Cong. Orat., R. F. Kerr, Cong. Orat., E. Graf, O.S.B., and E. F. Peeler (40 vols., 1891–1953). Appreciations by J. P. Dengel in *Hist. J.*, xlix (1929), pp. 1–32; W. Goetz in *Historische Zeitschrift*, cxlv (1932), pp. 550–63 (cf. ib., cxlvi, 1932, pp. 510–15); and A. Pelzer in *R.H.E.*, xlvi (1951), pp. 192–201, with reff. F. Cognassi in *E.C.*, ix (1952), cols. 925–8, s.v.

PASTORAL EPISTLES, The. The three latest Pauline Epp. (1, 2 Tim., Tit.), apparently first so described by P. Anton (1726). They were written to inculcate the characteristic Christian virtues, esp. as required in those holding pastoral office in the Church, and to encourage steadfastness in belief. Differences in language, style, and theological standpoint from the other Epp. in the Pauline *corpus* make their ascription to St. Paul doubtful. Many modern scholars, however, hold that they embody fragments of St. Paul's writing, worked up by a later hand. If genuine they certainly date from the end of St. Paul's life. For details see entries on the separate Epp.

Pauli Antonii . . . Exegetische Abhandlung der Pastoral-Briefe Pauli an Timotheum und Titum, im Jahr 1726 und 1727 öffentlich vorgetragen, nunmehr aber nach bisheriger Methode treulich mitgetheilet von J. A. Meyer (2 parts, Halle, 1753–5). P. N. Harrison, *The Problem of the Pastoral Epistles* (1921), pp. 13–16.

PASTORAL LETTERS (Lat. *litterae pastorales*). Official Letters addressed by a bishop to all members of his diocese. Many RC bishops make a practice of publishing such letters to be read from the pulpit, e.g. at the beginning of *Lent. They are commonly distinguished from 'encyclical letters' (*litterae encyclicae*) from a bishop, addressed only to his clergy.

PASTORAL STAFF. Another name for the *Crosier (q.v.). The distinction drawn by many 19th cent. antiquarians between the staff and the crosier was without authority. See *Crosier.*

PASTORALIA. The branch of theology concerned with the principles regulating the life and conduct of the parish priest. Among the subjects which it normally includes are : (1) the methods of public worship and administration of the Sacraments; (2) preaching and sermon construction; (3) the care of the sick and dying; (4) the study of moral theology. All exponents of the subject are agreed that the personal training of the pastor himself in prayer and devotion to his calling are the precondition of all success.

PATARINES also 'Patarelli'. The term first appears in the 11th cent. at Milan as the designation of a Catholic party favoured by Popes Stephen IX and *Alexander II, which contended for the *celibacy of the clergy and against *simony. The word is generally believed to be derived from 'pataria', a low quarter of Milan, where they held their assemblies. Under the leadership of the Milanese deacon, Arialdus, the Patarines played an important part in the politics of the city, whose archbishop, Guy, they forced to abdicate in 1066. When, in 1071, *Henry IV invested his successor, they began to oppose lay *investiture. After the death, in 1075, of their leader, Erlembald, who had succeeded Arialdus, they ceased to exist.

In the 12th cent. the name was used as a synonym for *Cathari, e.g. in can. 27 of the Third *Lateran Council (1179), and in the 13th and 14th cents. for heretics in general, though how the word came to have this wider connotation is uncertain.

J. Goetz, 'Kritische Beiträge zur Geschichte der Pataria' in *Archiv für Kulturgeschichte*, xii (1914), pp. 17–55 and 164–94; S. M. Brown, 'Movimenti politico-religiosi a Milano ai tempi della pataria' in *Archivio storico lombardo*, lviii (1931), pp. 227–78, with reff. G. Schwartz, 'Die Herkunft des Namens Pataria' in *Archiv für Kulturgeschichte*, xii (1914), pp. 402–10. C. Mirbt in *P.R.E.* (ed. 3), xiv (1904), pp. 761–4, s.v. 'Pataria'; É. Amann in *D.T.C.*, xi (pt. 2; 1932), cols. 224–6, s.v. 'Patarins', with details on sources; F. Cognasso in *E.C.*, ix (1952), cols. 936–9, s.v. 'Pataria'.

PATEN. The dish, now usually of silver or gold, on which the species of bread is placed at the celebration of the Eucharist. In the early cents., patens were of sufficient size to take the large loaves offered by the people and distributed at the Communion, but their modern counterparts in the W. are usually quite small, esp. where, as is always the case in the RC Church, wafer bread is used. The corresponding vessel in the E., the *discos (δίσκος), is larger and often possesses a foot.

Rohault, iv [1887], pp. 154–67, with plates cccxv–cccxvii. Braun, *C.A.*, pp. 197–246, with plates 41–7. W. W. Watts, *Catalogue of Chalices and other Communion Vessels* (Victoria and Albert Museum, 1922), pp. 39–46. H. *Leclercq, O.S.B., in *D.A.C.L.*, xiii (pt. 2; 1938), cols. 2392–414, s.v. 'Patène'.

PATER NOSTER. See *Lord's Prayer, The.*

PATMORE, COVENTRY KERSEY DIGHTON (1823–96), poet. He was educated privately and began to write poetry at an early age, publishing his first verse (*Poems*) in 1844. Compelled, owing to his father's unfortunate financial speculations, to earn his living, he was appointed supernumerary assistant in the printed book department of the British Museum and filled this post for nearly 20 years. In 1847 he married the daughter of a *Congregationalist minister; she contributed inspiration as well as valuable criticism to his poetry. In 1854 and the following years there appeared the various parts of *The Angel in the House*, a set of poems forming a panegyric on married love and endowing seemingly trivial incidents with both charm and depth. After the death of his wife in 1862, he went to Rome, where in 1864 he was received into the RC Church and in the same year married a second time. In 1877 he published *The Unknown Eros*, a collection of odes, some of them of great musical beauty and almost mystical depth. In 1880 he lost his second wife and in the following year married for the third time. In 1895 he published his last work. This book, a prose volume *Rod, Root, and Flower*, consists chiefly of meditations on the same lines as the mystical poems in *The Unknown Eros*. It probably contains much of the substance of a work he had destroyed, called *Sponsa Dei*, in which he had embodied his religious ideas. As a religious poet Patmore is often of impressive beauty, though his conception of 'the relation of the soul to Christ as his betrothed wife' is sometimes unduly laboured.

Collected edd. of his Poems, 4 vols., London, 1879; repr., 2 vols., ib., 1886; London, 1906, with introd. by B. Champneys, pp. xvii–xlvii, and ed. F. Page (Oxford Edition of Standard Authors, London, 1949). B. Champneys, *Memoirs and Correspondence of Coventry Patmore* (2 vols., 1900). Other studies by E. Gosse (London, 1905), O. [H.] Burdett (ib., 1921), F. Page (ib., 1933), and Derek [C.] Patmore (ib., 1949). R. Garnett in *D.N.B.*, Suppl. iii (1901), pp. 249–52. B. I. Evans in *C.B.E.L.*, iii, p. 270 f.

PATMOS. The small island in the Aegean off the coast of Asia Minor on which St. *John the Divine saw the *Apocalypse (Rev. 1. 9; the sole NT ref.). Acc. to a tradition found in St. *Irenaeus (*Adv. Haer.* V, xxx), *Eusebius (*H.E.* III, xviii) and St. *Jerome (*De Vir. Ill.* 9), John was exiled to Patmos under *Domitian (A.D. 81–96) and returned to *Ephesus under Nerva (A.D. 96–8). The apocryphal 'Acts of *John' (q.v.) narrate several miracles which the Apostle performed here. In 1088, St. Christodulus, who had been granted a bull by the Emp. Alexis Comnenus (1081–1118), founded a monastery on a peak in the middle of the island, which rapidly grew in importance. The monastery amassed a valuable collection of MSS. (of which a 13th cent. list survives in the *Vatican, publd. by A. *Mai, Cod. gr. 1205), but many have since been dispersed (the famous 9th cent. codex of *Plato is in the *Bodleian). The Abbot is directly subject to the Patr. of *Constantinople. A grotto in the hill-side (τὸ σπήλαιον τῆς Ἀποκαλύψεως) is pointed out as the place where the Apostle received his vision.

V. Guérin, *Description de l'île de Patmos et de l'île de Samos* (1856), pp. 1–120; W. E. Geil, *The Isle called Patmos* (1897). H. F. Tozer, *The Islands of the Aegean* (1890), pp. 178–98. G. Hofmann, S.J., *Patmos und Rom*. Darstellung der Beziehungen zwischen dem griechischen Johanneskloster und der römischen Kirche (Orientalia Christiana, fasc. 41; 1928). Catalogue of the MSS. of the monastery by J. Sakkelion (Athens, 1890). J. Frings, 'Das Patmosexil des Apostels Johannes nach Apc. 1, 9' in *T.Q.*, civ (1923), pp. 20–31. F. C. *Conybeare in *H.D.B.*, iii (1900), p. 693 f., s.v.; H. *Leclercq, O.S.B., in *D.A.C.L.*, xiii (pt. 1; 1938), cols. 2424–40, s.v. See also Comm. to *Revelation*, Book of.

PATON, JOHN GIBSON (1824 - 1907), missionary to the New Hebrides. Born at Kirkmahoe, Dumfriesshire, of parents who belonged to the rigid '*Reformed Presbyterian Church of Scotland', he gained his education under great difficulties. After ten years as a missionary in a poor part of Glasgow, he offered himself in 1857 as an assistant to John Inglis, the sole missionary of the Reformed Presbyterian Church in foreign work, for service in the New Hebrides. He arrived with his wife at Aneityum on 30 Aug. 1858 and shortly afterwards moved to the island of Tanna, where he and his wife were the only white people in a land of very primitive savages. In the next year his wife gave birth to a child and both died. In 1861, after many trials, he just escaped from Tanna with his life and made his way to New South Wales. Here he successfully aroused interest in missionary work in the New Hebrides; and after a visit to Scotland, where he married again, he returned to the Pacific on mission service in 1865. From 1866 to 1881 he had his headquarters on the island of Aniwa, subsequently at Melbourne. His autobiography, written in the form of notes, was put into shape by his brother, Rev. James Paton (1843–1906), and from its publication in 1889 did much to stimulate support for his cause.

The principal material is to be found in his own works. Popular life by C. D. Michael (London [1912]). Sir Everard im Thurn in *D.N.B.*, *1901–1911*, iii (1912), p. 77 f.

PATON, WILLIAM (1886–1943), *Presbyterian minister and writer on missionary subjects. Born in London, he received his education at Pembroke College, Oxford, and Westminster College, Cambridge. In 1911 he became Missionary Secretary to the Student Christian Movement in England and maintained his keen interest in missionary and ecumenical activities throughout his life. His earliest books on this subject are *Jesus Christ and the World's Religions* (1916) and *Social Ideas in India* (1919). From 1922 to 1927 he was General Secretary of the National Christian Council of India, Burma, and Ceylon, and subsequently held the position of Secretary to the International Missionary Council and Editor of the *International Review of Missions*. Among his later publications are *Alexander Duff* (1922), *The Faiths of Mankind* (1932), *World Community* (1938), *The Message of the World-wide Church* (1940), and *The Church and the New Order* (1941).

Life by Margaret Sinclair (London, 1949).

PATRIARCH (Biblical). Lit. the father or ruler of a family or tribe. In the Scriptures the term is applied to the antediluvian fathers of the human race, and, more frequently, to *Abraham, *Isaac, *Jacob, and the twelve sons of Jacob (Gen. 12–50; cf. Acts 7. 8 f., Heb. 7. 4). In Acts 2. 29 the word is applied to *David.

PATRIARCH (Ecclesiastical). A title, dating from the 6th cent., for the bishops of the five chief sees of Christendom, *Rome, *Alexandria, *Antioch, *Constantinople, and *Jerusalem. Their jurisdiction extended over the adjoining territories, and included the right of ordaining '*metropolitans', i.e. bishops of the principal sees under them, of trying the same when accused, and of hearing appeals from their judgements. The earliest bishops exercising such powers, though not so named, were those of Rome (over the whole or part of Italy), Alexandria (over Egypt and Libya), and Antioch (over large parts of Asia Minor). These three were recognized by the Council of *Nicaea (325). But at *Chalcedon (451)

O.D.C.C.—2 L

Jerusalem secured recognition as well as Constantinople, whose jurisdiction over Thrace, Asia, and Pontus was exercised henceforward in spite of protests from Rome. See also *Oecumenical Patriarch*.

PATRIARCHS, The Testaments of the. See *Testaments of the XII Patriarchs, The*.

PATRICK, St. (*c.* 389–*c.* 461), 'Apostle of the Irish'. The son of a Romano-British deacon, Calpurnius, he was born in a village called Bannavem, prob. in Britain or Gaul, and at the age of 16 captured by raiders and taken as a slave to *Ireland. After minding herds for six years, prob. in Antrim or Mayo, in obedience to a vision he escaped and travelled two hundred miles to a ship whose crew reluctantly took him on board. After they had landed, prob. in Gaul, their provisions ran out and, at the prayers of St. Patrick, they found a herd of swine. Soon after his return to his family, he received a vision bidding him evangelize Ireland. He appears to have studied in the monastery of *Lérins (perhaps from 412 to 415), and to have proceeded to Auxerre, where he was prob. ordained deacon by St. Amator *c.* 417. In 431 he was sent to assist *Palladius in Ireland and on the latter's death consecrated Bishop by St. *Germanus (432). Working at first prob. in Leinster or Ulster, he is supposed to have tried to convert his former master, who committed suicide at his approach. After founding a church in Sabal Patraic (later called Saul), he proceeded to the court of the High King Laoghaire (d. 458) at Tara, Meath. In spite of determined opposition from the Druids, whom he is supposed to have defeated by miraculous means, he gained toleration for Christianity and converted several members of the royal family. He preached extensively in Connaught, Leinster, and Meath, establishing numerous churches and some religious communities. After visiting Rome *c.* 442, in 444 he founded the Cathedral Church of *Armagh, which soon became the educational and administrative centre of the Irish Church. The 'Collectio Canonum Hiberniae', if genuinely of his period, was prob. issued by a synod held towards the end of his life. The story of his forty days fast on Croagh Patrick is usually assigned to the same period.

In Ireland St. Patrick organized the scattered Christian communities which he found in the north, did much to convert the pagan west and brought the country into much closer relations with the rest of the Western Church. He encouraged the study of Latin and tried to raise the general standards of scholarship. His 'Confessions', written *c.* 450 as an apology against his detractors, and his letter to Coroticus, are the chief sources for his life. The earliest accounts by others are full of the miraculous; and the chronology of his life remains obscure. The '*Breastplate' (q.v.) attributed to him is supposed to have been used against the spells of the Druids. His cult, which grew very shortly after his death, has flourished continuously. Feast day, 17 March. See also *St. Patrick's Purgatory*.

Lat. Writings ed. N. J. D. White in *Proceedings of the Royal Irish Academy*, xxv (1905), pp. 201–326; popular ed. by id., 'Texts for Students', iv, 1918; Eng. tr. by id., ib., v, 1918, and, with Life by Muirchu (7th cent.), and full notes. Id., *St. Patrick*. His Writings and Life (Translations of Christian Literature, Series v, 1920); with fuller *apparatus criticus* by L. Bieler (ed.), '*Libri Epistolarum Sancti Patricii Episcopi*. Introduction, Text and Commentary' (linguistic), in *Classica et Mediaevalia*, xi (1950), pp. 1–150, and xii (1951), pp. 79–214. W. Stokes, *The Tripartite Life of Patrick with other Documents relating to that Saint* (R.S., 1887). Ludwig Bieler, *Codices Patriciani Latini*. A Descriptive Catalogue of Latin Manuscripts Relating to St. Patrick (Dublin, 1942); J. F. Kenney, *The Sources for the Early History of Ireland*, i (New York, 1929), pp. 331–56 and passim (see index). J. H. Todd, *St. Patrick, Apostle of Ireland* (1864); J. B. Bury, *The Life of St. Patrick and his Place in History* (1905); L. Bieler in A.C.W. 17 (Eng. tr. of writings of St. Patrick and St. Secundinus with useful notes; 1953). E. MacNeill, *St. Patrick, Apostle of Ireland* (1934). On the identification of St. Patrick with Palladius, H. Zimmer, *The Celtic Church in Britain and Ireland* (1902), pp. 7–39; T. F. O'Rahilly, *The Two Patricks*. A Lecture on the History of Christianity in Fifth Century Ireland (Dublin, 1942). T. Olden in *D.N.B.*, xliv (1895), pp. 38–42.

PATRICK, SIMON (1625–1707), Bp. of *Ely. A native of Gainsborough, Lincs., he was educated at Queens' College, Cambridge, where he came under the influence of the '*Cambridge Platonist', John *Smith. In 1648 he was ordained a Presbyterian minister; but the study of H. *Hammond and H. *Thorndike determined him to seek episcopal ordination. In 1654 he received holy orders from J. *Hall, Bp. of *Norwich, and became successively vicar of Battersea (1658), rector of St. Paul's, Covent Garden (1662), and Dean of *Peterborough (1679), which he held together with his previous living. He was a prominent and sincere *Latitudinarian. In 1687 he resisted the reading of the Declaration of Indulgence, and in 1688 took the Oath of Allegiance to William and Mary. In the same year he was appointed Bp. of *Chichester. He was translated to Ely in 1691. As bishop he was a warm supporter of the *S.P.C.K., which he helped to found, and of the *S.P.G. He wrote extensively. In 1664 he published *The Parable of the Pilgrim*, an allegory similar to, but not influenced by, J. *Bunyan's *Pilgrim's Progress*. He commented on and paraphrased all the books of the OT from Genesis to the Song of Solomon (10 vols., 1695–1710), and wrote many controversial treatises against both *Nonconformists and RCs, among them *A Friendly Debate between a Conformist and a Nonconformist* (1669), *A Full View of the Doctrines and Practices of the Ancient Church* (1688), and *Texts Examined which Papists cite out of the Bible* (also 1688). He also published devotional books, e.g. *The Devout Christian Instructed how to Pray* (1672), *The Glorious Epiphany* (1675), and *A Treatise of Repentance and Fasting* (1686).

Works, incl. his autobiography, which was first publd. Oxford, 1839, but excluding his commentaries, ed. A. Taylor, 9 vols., Oxford, 1858. J. H. Overton in *D.N.B.*, xliv (1895), pp. 45–7.

PATRIMONY OF ST. PETER, The. The estates belonging to the Church of Rome.

Although the Church of Rome had long been wealthy, persecutions had prevented the acquisition of permanent property until an edict of *Constantine (*Cod. Theod.* XVI, 2, 4) made it legal to leave property to the Church. In the following period, up to 600, economic conditions encouraged large donations of land and commendations. Parallels between the *patrimonium ecclesiae* and the *patrimonium principis* suggest that the *Donation of Constantine, though forged, represented the truth in substance and that much Imperial property was given to the Church. By gifts and inheritance the patrimony came to include lands in Sicily (confiscated by Emp. *Leo II in 730), Illyria, Gaul, Corsica, Sardinia, around Hippo in Africa, as well as vast estates in Italy. They were governed by a centralized administration which facilitated the extension of Papal influence. The revenues were employed not only for administrative purposes, but widely for the relief of the poor, redemption of captives and later for defence. As the further patrimonies were conquered, Popes concentrated on the defence of the regions round Rome, esp. the exarchate of *Ravenna and the Duchy of Rome. When the castle of Sutri was captured in 727, the Lombard king Luitprand 'restored' it 'as a gift to the Blessed Apostles Peter and Paul'. In 753 *Stephen II appealed for protection to *Pepin, King of the Franks, who agreed to give the Pope certain lands to be conquered from the Lombards. By the Donations of 754 and 756 Pepin gave to St. Peter territory in the exarchate of Ravenna, the Duchy of Rome and the districts of Venetia and Istria, and renouncing the Byzantine authority, founded the papal states independent of any temporal power.

The term was applied in medieval usage to the environs of Rome. It is used loosely for the *States of the Church (q.v.) as a whole.

The primary sources include the *Liber Censuum and the *Liber Pontificalis (qq.v.). P. Fabre, *De Patrimoniis Romanae Ecclesiae usque ad Aetatem Carolinorum* (Paris thesis; Lille, 1892). G. Schnürer, *Die Entstehung des Kirchenstaates* (1894). L. *Duchesne, *Les Premiers Temps de l'état pontifical* (1898; ed. 2, 1904; Eng. tr., 1908). A. Crivellucci, 'Delle origini dello stato pontificio' in *Studi storici*, x (1901), pp. 3–39, 289–329, xi (1902), pp. 37–86, 409–39, xii (1903), pp. 113–40, 413–52, xiv (1905), pp. 3–27. E. Spearing, *The Patrimony of the Roman Church in the Time of Gregory the Great* (posthumously ed. Evelyn M. Spearing, 1918). H. Grisar, S.J., 'Ein Rundgang durch die Patrimonien des heiligen Stuhles um das Jahr 600' in *Z.K.T.*, i (1877), pp. 321–60; id., 'Verwaltung und Haushalt der päpstlichen Patrimonien um das Jahr 600', ib., pp. 526–563. R. Macaigne, *L'Église mérovingienne et l'état pontifical* (1929). R. Aigrain in Fliche–Martin, v (1938), pp. 543–53, with bibl. G. Schnürer in *C.E.*, xiv (1912), pp. 257–61, s.v. 'States of the Church, I', with bibl. O. Bertolini in *E.C.*, ix (1952), cols. 957–60, s.v. 'Patrimonio di S. Pietro'.

PATRIPASSIANISM. A form of *Monarchianism (q.v.) which arose in the early 3rd cent. and held that God the Father suffered as the Son. It is also known as '*Sabellianism'.

PATRISTICS. The branch of theological study which deals with the writings of the Fathers (*patres*). Sometimes the title 'Fathers' is given to important Christian writers of all ages down to the 13th cent., when the 'Schoolmen' took their place. In stricter usage it belongs to those teachers who wrote between the end of the 1st cent. (when the NT had been almost, if not quite, completed) and the close of the 8th cent.; and this is the period commonly termed the 'Patristic Age'. The study of Patristic literature is closely allied both with Church history and with the history of early doctrine, since this literature is the chief evidence both for the events and for the ideas of these times. The leading Fathers were the authors of much work vital to Christianity. They defended the Gospel against heresies and misunderstandings; they composed extensive commentaries on the Bible, explanatory, doctrinal, and practical, and published innumerable sermons, largely on the same subject; they exhibited the meaning and implications of the *Creeds; they recorded past and current events in Church history; and they related the Christian faith to the best thought of their own age. See also foll. entry.

The earliest essays in Patristic study were the catalogues of Christian writers compiled by St. *Jerome, *Gennadius of Marseilles, St. *Isidore of Seville, St. *Ildefonsus of Toledo, and *Photius. Later similar catalogues are due to *Sigebert of Gembloux, *Honorius of Autun, and the *Anonymus Mellicensis* (of Melk in Lower Austria, c. 1135), and to (pseudo-) *Henry of Ghent. The more imp. early printed collections include the *Bibliotheca SS. Patrum* (ed. M. de La Bigne, 8 vols., Paris, 1575, with later suppl.; more comprehensive new ed., 14 vols., Cologne, 1618, suppl. 1622; further extended as *Maxima Bibliotheca Veterum Patrum*, 27 vols., Lyons, 1677) and those of F. *Ducaeus, L. *D'Achéry, J. *Sirmond, J. B. *Cotelier, and F. *Combefis. A new era in the editing of Patristic texts was inaugurated by the *Maurists (q.v.). Later collections are due to J. E. *Grabe, B. de *Montfaucon, and A. *Gallandi, and, in the 19th cent., to M. J. *Routh, A. *Mai (contd. by J. Cozza-Luzi) and J. B. *Pitra. J. P. *Migne's vast *Patrologiae* ('Latina' and 'Graeca') incorporated nearly all the Gk. and Lat. texts hitherto in print. The chief recent collections, edited on modern critical methods, are the *Corpus Scriptorum Ecclesiasticorum Latinorum* ('C.S.E.L.', Vienna, 1866 ff.), *Die griechischen christlichen Schriftsteller der ersten drei Jahrhunderte* (Leipzig, 1897 ff.), the *Patrologia Orientalis* (ed. R. Graffin and F. Nau, Paris, 1907 ff.), and the *Corpus Scriptorum Christianorum Orientalium* (C.S.C.O., Paris, 1903 ff.). Of Eng. trr. of the Fathers, the principal series are The *Library of the Fathers* (1838 ff.), *The Ante-Nicene Christian Library* (28 vols., 1886–1900), and a large collection of separate texts publd. by the *S.P.C.K. Good Fr. edd. of many Patristic texts in *Sources chrétiennes* (Paris, 1941 ff.). For modern Patrologies, see foll. entry. J. de Ghellinck, *Patristique et moyen-âge* (3 vols., 1946–8); B. Altaner, 'Der Stand der patrologischen Wissenschaft und das Problem einer neuen altchristlichen Literaturgeschichte' in *Miscellanea Giovanni Mercati*, i (S.T., cxxi, 1946), pp. 483–520. On the knowledge of Gk. Patristic literature in the West, see P. Courcelle, *Les Lettres grecques en occident* (1943), and A. Siegmund, *Die Überlieferung der griechischen Literatur in der lateinischen Kirche bis zum 12. Jahrhundert* (1949). New series of Lat. texts entitled *Corpus Christianorum*, ed. by the Monks of Steenbrugge, Belgium (Turnhout, 1953 ff.). Reports of the Second and Third International Conferences on Patristic Studies held in Oxford have been published under the title *Studia Patristica* (T.U. lxiii and lxiv, 1957; lxxviii–lxxxi, 1961–2). F. L. Cross, *The Early Christian Fathers* (1960). *Bibliographia Patristica* I ff., ed. W. Schneemelcher (Berlin, annually, for 1956 ff.).

PATROLOGY. In older English writers, the term Patrology was synonymous with *Patristics (q.v.), esp. in its doctrinal aspects, but it is now in current use for a systematically arranged manual on the patristic literature. Among the more important of recent Patrologies are A. *Harnack's *Geschichte der altchristlichen Literatur bis Eusebius* (3 vols., 1893–1904) and O. *Bardenhewer's *Patrologie*

(1894; Eng. trans., 1908) and *Geschichte der altkirchlichen Literatur* (5 vols., 1902–31).

Among older works of similar scope, the most ambitious are the *compendia* of J. A. *Fabricius (q.v.). More recent works include J. A. *Möhler, *Patrologie* (i [all publd.], 1840); I. Fessler, *Institutiones Patrologiae* (2 vols., Innsbruck, 1850–1; ed. 2 by B. Jungmann, 1890–6); F. Cayré, A.A., *Précis de patrologie* (2 vols., 1927–30; ed. 3, 3 vols., 1945); B. Steidle, O.S.B., *Patrologia* (Freiburg i.Br., 1937); B. Altaner, *Patrologie* (1938; ed. 6, 1960; Eng. tr., 1960); J. Quasten, *Patrology*. I: The Beginnings of Patristic Literature (Utrecht, 1950); II: The Ante-Nicene Literature after Irenaeus (ib., 1953); III: The Golden Age of Greek Patristic Literature (ib., 1960). For the Lat. Fathers, cf. also P. de Labriolle, *Histoire de la littérature latine chrétienne* (1920; new ed. by G. Bardy, 1947; Eng. tr., 1924) and the invaluable *Clavis Patrum Latinorum* (ed. E. Dekkers, O.S.B., in *Sacris Erudiri*, iii, Steenbrugge, 1951; ed. 2, 1961).

PATRON SAINT. A saint who, by tradition or otherwise, has been chosen as the special intercessor and advocate in heaven of a particular place, person, or organization. The custom of having patron saints for churches arose from the practice of building churches over the tombs of martyrs. The expression 'titular' is also used in the same sense. Since the middle of the 19th cent. the traditional celebration of the patronal feasts of churches has been widely revived in the C of E. See also *Dedication of Churches*.

PATTESON, JOHN COLERIDGE (1827–1871), Bp. of Melanesia. Educated at Eton (where he came under the influence of G. A. *Selwyn) and Balliol College, Oxford, he was ordained in 1853. In 1855 at Selwyn's persuasion he set out for the South Seas, to found the Melanesian Mission. He toured the islands in the *Southern Cross*, learnt many of the languages, founded a college on Norfolk Island for the training of native boys, and was remarkably successful in his pastoral and educational work. In 1861 he was consecrated the first Bp. of Melanesia. On 20 Sept. 1871 he was murdered on the island of Nukapu, where he had landed alone, in revenge for the kidnapping of some of the inhabitants by white men a few months earlier. His fate made a deep impression in England and aroused much interest in missionary work and in the labour conditions of Polynesia.

The standard life is that of Charlotte M. *Yonge (2 vols., London, 1874 [1873]); shorter life by F. H. L. Paton (London [c. 1930]). W. H. Fremantle in *D.N.B.*, xlvii (1895), pp. 53–6; R. W. Codrington in *D.E.C.H.*, p. 450 f., s.v.

PATTISON, ANDREW SETH PRINGLE- (1856–1931), until 1898 Andrew SETH, Scottish philosopher. He was educated at the Royal High School, Edinburgh, at Edinburgh University, and at Berlin, Jena, and Göttingen, where he studied under H. Lotze. After holding chairs at Cardiff (1883–7) and St. Andrews (1887–91), he became Prof. of Logic and Metaphysics at Edinburgh (1891–1919). He showed marked sympathy with German Idealism (I. *Kant, and esp. G. W. F. *Hegel) but he sought to free it from *pantheism and to safeguard the claims of the human person. He held that 'God or the Absolute', although not Himself an individual among others, was the source of individuation. His chief writings were *Scottish Philosophy* (1885), *Hegelianism and Personality* (1887), *Man's Place in the Cosmos* (1897), *The Idea of God in the Light of Recent Philosophy* (Gifford Lectures for 1912–1913; 1917), *The Idea of Immortality* (1922), and *Studies in the Philosophy of Religion* (1930).

Pattison's *The Balfour Lectures on Realism* was posthumously ed. by G. F. Barbour (1933), with memoir, pp. 3–46. Memoir by J. B. Cooper in *Proceedings of the British Academy*, xxii (1931), pp. 447–61; J. B. Baillie, 'Pringle Pattison as Philosopher', ib., pp. 461–89. J. Laird in *D.N.B., 1931–1940*, p. 678 f.

PATTISON, MARK (1813–84), Rector of Lincoln College, Oxford. In 1832 he entered Oriel College, then suffering from E. *Hawkins's removal of J. H. *Newman, R. H. *Froude, and R. I. *Wilberforce from their tutorships, and, being mainly dependent on his own resources, came to assimilate a wide range of largely out-of-the-way knowledge. Before long he came under the religious influence of Newman, contributed to some of his translations for the *Library of the Fathers*, and from about 1838 to 1848 was a keen *Tractarian. Later his enthusiasm for the Oxford Movement declined and with it his faith in institutional Christianity. He became keenly interested, however, in educational and university reform, and did good work among his pupils and as a university examiner. His very extensive writing largely took the form of essays and articles on literary subjects, but his *Isaac *Casaubon* (1875) was an enduring contribution to the history of modern scholarship. His posthumous *Memoirs* (1885) reflect the fierce anti-Tractarianism of his last years.

A selection of his Essays was publd. by his friend, Henry Nettleship (2 vols., 1889). L. A. Tollemache, *Recollections of Pattison* (1885). V. H. H. Green, *Oxford Common Room. A Study of Lincoln College and Mark Pattison* (1957). R. C. Christie in *D.N.B.*, xliv (1895), pp. 58–63.

PAUL, St. (d. *c.* A.D. 65), the 'Apostle of the Gentiles'. Born during the first years of the Christian era, the future St. Paul, originally 'Saul', was the son of a Jew of the tribe of Benjamin, possessed of Roman citizenship and a native of Tarsus in Cilicia. He was brought up a *Pharisee (Acts 26. 5) and had his education, in part at least, at *Jerusalem, where he studied under the famous Rabbi *Gamaliel (Acts 22. 3). This, and his life 'in the Jews' religion' (Gal. 1. 14), brought him his experience of the Law and a thorough knowledge of the Scriptures, as well as his well-known habit of arguing from isolated texts. As a Jew of the Dispersion he spoke and wrote Greek. He had probably received a better formal education than any other NT writer or Apostle.

Within a few years of the Crucifixion, St. Paul came in contact with the new 'Way' of the followers of Jesus, almost certainly in Palestine, and, meeting it with intense opposition, assisted at the martyrdom of St. *Stephen, when he guarded the clothes of those who stoned him (Acts 7. 58). On a mission to Damascus to arrest some Christians and bring them to Jerusalem for trial occurred the decisive event. His conversion is told three times in Acts, viz. at 9. 1–19, 22. 5–16, and 26. 12–18. Acc. to these accounts, which vary only in details, St. Paul saw a great light and heard the words: 'Saul, Saul, why persecutest thou Me?', and, in reply to his question, 'Who art thou, Lord?', received the answer 'I am Jesus, Whom thou persecutest', words which, through their identification of Christ with His followers, contain in germ the future characteristic Pauline doctrine of the Church.

The call to the Christian life and apostolate was at once accepted. Soon afterwards he received Baptism and the imposition of hands from Ananias (Acts 9. 17 f.) and then departed to Arabia (Gal. 1. 17; not mentioned in Acts), perhaps to prepare himself by solitude and prayer for his future ministry. Three years later he returned to Damascus, whence he was compelled to make a secret escape from the hostility of Aretas, the Nabataean King, by being let down the city wall in a basket (Acts 9. 23–25; 2 Cor. 11. 32 f.). After a visit to Jerusalem, where he was received, but not unnaturally, with suspicion until *Barnabas allayed doubts, he went to Caesarea, Syria, and Cilicia (Acts 9. 30; Gal. 1. 21–24). Nothing is known of his activities until Barnabas a few years later fetched him from Tarsus to enlist his help in the conversion of *Antioch (Acts 11. 25 f.). *C.* A.D. 44 the two Apostles went to Jerusalem during a famine to take food to the Christian community. (For the question whether this visit is to be identified with that recorded in Gal. 2. 1–10, see *Galatians*; in the traditional view the visit of Gal. 2 is to be identified with that of Acts 15.) It has been suggested that the ecstasy mentioned in 2 Cor. 12. 2–4 took place during this period, perhaps as the immediate preparation for St. Paul's apostolate in the pagan world.

After his return (Acts 12. 25) the 'prophets and teachers' of the Church at Antioch, following an inspiration of the Holy Ghost, sent him and Barnabas out on the so-called First Missionary Journey. They set sail for Cyprus, accompanied by John *Mark. During this journey Barnabas, hitherto the leader, ceded his place to Paul (the change in name from Saul at this point, Acts 13. 9, may indicate this reversal of roles). After leaving *Cyprus the Apostles went to Asia Minor where, to Paul's great disappointment, Mark left them. At Antioch of Pisidia Paul preached after his custom in the synagogue, and was opposed by the Jews. Openly proclaiming his intention of turning to the Gentiles, he won many converts (Acts 13. 48), and at Lystra, where he healed a cripple, the pagans even mistook him and Barnabas for gods (14. 11 f.). Here as elsewhere the Jews stirred up trouble, but their opposition only served to confirm Paul in his mission and convince him that 'through many tribulations we must enter into the kingdom of God' (14. 22). The Apostles returned overland to Antioch (*c.* 49) where they described to the Christian community the success of their work among the Gentiles (14. 27).

This rapid growth of Gentile Christianity raised serious issues for the nascent Church. With its relations with Judaism as yet undefined, St. Paul found himself faced with opposition from Jewish Christians who came to Antioch asserting that without circumcision Gentiles could not be saved. Accordingly he and Barnabas went up to Jerusalem to discuss the question with Peter, James, and the other Apostles (Acts 15). The decrees of this first Council of the Church (the exact import of which is much debated) were at any rate in principle a victory for Paul. The Law was not to be imposed on Gentile Christians and his Mission to the Gentiles was recognized by the Jerusalem Church (Gal. 2. 6–9; Acts 15). After the Council ended he returned to Antioch.

Having separated from Barnabas, St. Paul now set out on his Second Missionary Journey, accompanied by Silas. He revisited the Churches in the interior of Asia Minor, founded on his first journey, and from Lystra he took *Timothy with him (Acts 16. 1–3). He then evangelized the Galatians. Frustrated by Divine intervention, as he believed, from going on to Bithynia, he responded to a dream vision bidding him cross over to Macedonia and thus extend the sphere of his ministry to Europe (Acts 16. 9 f.). Having reached Philippi he and his companions stayed in the house of Lydia, his first Macedonian convert (Acts 16. 15). The exorcism of a maid possessed with a 'spirit of divination' led to his imprisonment, but having converted his jailer and family he was publicly freed by the magistrates when they learned he was a Roman citizen (16. 38 f.). From Philippi he went to Thessalonica and Beroea, where he converted many Gentiles; but in both places troubles were stirred up by the Jews and he was forced to leave. At *Athens, where he was confronted on Mars' Hill with a philosophically interested audience, he changed his method of preaching, but with ill success (Acts 17. 16–34). His teaching was met with unwonted indifference and he went to *Corinth, where he stayed for a long time. The fact that this stay was during *Gallio's proconsulship (Acts 18.12) enables us to establish the chronology of St. Paul's travels with tolerable accuracy, since an inscription determines this date as 51 or 52. At Corinth he wrote his two Epp. to the Thessalonians, founded a flourishing Church, and after 18 months of strenuous work returned to Antioch.

Soon afterwards he set out on his Third Missionary Journey. First he went to *Ephesus (Acts 19. 1), where he completed the conversion of catechumens who had received only the 'Baptism of John (Baptist)'. Here he stayed for two years, teaching in the 'School of Tyrannus' (Acts 19. 10), working many miracles and, despite strenuous opposition, gaining a large number of converts. The communities in the hinterland (Colossae, *Philadelphia, Hierapolis, *Laodicea) which were later to be such prominent centres of Christian life probably owe their beginnings to St. Paul's long stay at Ephesus. Here he also wrote 1 *Corinthians. Eventually driven from the city by riots of the silversmiths, whose trade in shrines of the goddess Diana was seriously

threatened by the spread of Christianity, he went to Macedonia, where *Titus brought him consoling news from Corinth (2 Cor. 7. 6 f.) and where he wrote 2 Corinthians. He then spent three months in Achaia (Acts 20. 1–3), probably at Corinth (A.D. 57), where he wrote *Romans to prepare the way for the visit he was already planning to the capital (Rom. 15. 22–24). He then set out for Jerusalem with the delegates of the Churches of Asia and Greece with contributions collected to relieve the poverty of the mother Church (1 Cor. 16. 3 f.; Rom. 15. 25–26). On the way he bade farewell at Miletus to the Elders of the Church of Ephesus who had come to meet him, and predicted his imprisonment (Acts 20. 22 f.).

At Jerusalem he was met by the anticipated hostile reception. Accused of teaching transgression of the Law, he was beaten by the mob and only rescued by Roman soldiers who put him under protective arrest in the castle (Acts 21. 27–36) whence, addressing the crowd, he recounted his conversion. His mention of his mission to the Gentiles again provoked a tumult and the chief captain only desisted of his decision to examine his prisoner by scourging on learning that he was a Roman citizen. Brought before the *Sanhedrin (Acts 22. 30), St. Paul skilfully divided Pharisees and Sadducees by referring to the doctrine of the resurrection (Acts 23. 1–10). Information of a plot against Paul's life led the chief captain to send him under strong escort to the governor Felix at Caesarea (23. 23 f.), where he was treated leniently. His trial, however, was deferred for two years, and not resumed until Felix was succeeded by Festus (A.D. 59). St. Paul now appealed to Caesar, i.e. for a trial at Rome. Before embarking he was brought before the Jewish King Agrippa whom he deeply impressed (Acts 25. 13–27). On the voyage to Rome he suffered shipwreck before Malta, the details of which are described at length in Acts 27. After wintering in Malta, where he is said to have cured many sick people, he reached Rome where he was kept in mitigated custody in a house of his own. It is the common opinion that he wrote the '*Captivity Epistles' (Phil., Col., Philem., and Eph.) while awaiting his trial, though it has also been argued that some or all of them were written during an earlier imprisonment at Ephesus or from Caesarea.

Acts ends with the statement that St. Paul remained in captivity in Rome for two years. For the remainder of his life we depend on material to be gleaned from the *Pastoral Epp. and tradition. Acc. to St. *Clement of Rome, writing about 30 years after his death (Ep. i. 5), he went to the 'limits of the Occident' (τὸ τέρμα τῆς δύσεως), a statement which (unless τῆς δύσεως is to be taken as a defining genitive) would give point to his own assertion (Rom. 15. 24 and 28) that after visiting Rome he proposed to go on to Spain; and several of the Fathers (e.g. *Cyril of Jerusalem, *Epiphanius, *Chrysostom, and *Jerome) accept the tradition of this visit to Spain. If the Pastoral Epp. are genuine, they are presumably to be placed after his return from Spain. Acc. to their evidence he would have revisited Ephesus, Macedonia, and Greece. It would seem that he was finally once more arrested, perhaps at Troas (cf. 2 Tim. 4. 13), taken to Rome and slain in the Neronian persecution (acc. to *Eusebius, in A.D. 67). *Tertullian (*De Praescr.*, xxxvi) adds that he was beheaded.

Acc. to a tradition, first found in the apocryphal Acts of St. Paul (see next entry) and repeated by St. *Gregory the Great and the itineraries of the 7th and following cents., the scene of St. Paul's martyrdom was on the left bank of the Tiber, about three miles from Rome; this place, known as Ad Aquas Salvias, was renamed *Tre Fontane from the legend that when St. Paul's head bounced three times three fountains sprang forth. His body was then taken to a cemetery on the *Ostian Way nearer Rome, belonging to a Christian matron Lucina, and buried on the site of the present basilica of S. Paolo fuori le Mura. On 29 June 258, when the Christian tombs were threatened with desecration in the Valerianic persecution, it was apparently transferred for a time, along with that of St. Peter, to a locality described as 'Ad Catacumbas' on the *Appian Way. After its return to its former resting place, the Emp. *Constantine erected the famous basilica on the site (see *St. Paul's outside the Walls*). A joint feast for the two Apostles on 29 June was instituted in the West. By the 7th cent. it was customary, in addition to the Mass at the Vatican for the two Apostles on 29 June, to observe a special commemoration for St. Paul on the following day.

St. Paul is the most powerful human personality in the history of the Church. From the decisive revelation on the way to Damascus his life was dominated by an ardent devotion to Christ, who was henceforward the centre both of his preaching and teaching and of his personal faith and life. For the sake of Christ he strove to make himself 'all things to all men' (1 Cor. 9. 22), exposed himself to all kinds of dangers, and took upon himself the care of his many Churches. In the celebrated hymn to 'charity' in 1 Cor. 13 he unconsciously drew his own portrait, as it had developed in a life of constant self-denial and communion with his Lord.

In his Epistles, nearly all written to meet the needs of the moment, St. Paul laid the foundations (for the most part unbeknown to himself) on which subsequent Christian theology has built. His doctrine was first worked out in the struggle against the Judaizers, to whose rigid conception of the *Mosaic Law he opposed the freedom of the Gospel as the only efficacious means of salvation. Sinful humanity is redeemed and justified by Divine grace through faith in Jesus Christ, who by His Life, Death, and Resurrection abrogated the old Law and ushered in the new era of the Spirit (esp. Gal. and Rom.). Christ is not only the Messiah in whom the OT promises are fulfilled, but the eternal, pre-existent Son of God through whom all things were created (Phil. 2. 6; Col. 1. 15–17) and who, after the humiliations of His earthly life and His sacrificial Death on the Cross, was exalted to the right hand of God and receives the homage of all creation (Phil. 2. 9–11). As such He is the Head of a new and redeemed humanity, the New 'Israel of God', in which Jew and Gentile are made one (Eph. 2. 14–19), the Church; and at the same time He is identified with the Church as His Mystical Body so that St. Paul can claim to fill up in his flesh what is lacking in the afflictions of Christ 'for his body's sake, which is the Church' (Col. 1. 24). Thus the sufferings of the members of the Church become the sufferings of Christ and contribute to the perfection of the Body; and the true Christian lives no longer his own life, but Christ lives in him (Gal. 2. 20), transforming him into the likeness of his Saviour already in this life, and fully in the resurrection.

This new life, which is no longer 'according to the flesh' (κατὰ σάρκα), by which St. Paul ordinarily means man in his fallen state, but 'according to the Spirit' (κατὰ πνεῦμα), begins in Baptism. Through Baptism the believer shares in Christ's death and resurrection (Rom. 6. 3–6) and is enabled to meet the moral and spiritual demands of this new life through the power of the Holy Spirit (Gal. 5. 16), sent by God into his heart (Gal. 4. 6) as a personal guide and friend. It is the fellowship or communion of the Holy Spirit (Phil. 2. 1), bound together by the bond of charity (Col. 3. 14). This fellowship is both maintained and expressed in the Eucharist, the Christian sacrifice, the 'communion in the body of Christ' (1 Cor. 10. 16, κοινωνία τοῦ σώματος τοῦ Χριστοῦ), and the memorial of His death (1 Cor. 11. 20–34, 10. 16–21), and it will be fully realized at the end of the ages when the Lord shall return in glory, a glory in which the faithful both living and dead will share (1 Thess. 4. 13–17). Its essential mark is love, which will continue in the life of glory, when prophecies shall be done away and tongues shall cease, and we shall no longer see in a mirror darkly, but face to face (1 Cor. 13). The urgency of its proclamation is the greater for St. Paul in view of his expectation (esp. stressed in his earlier Epp.) of the speedy return of Christ to judge the world.

The influence of Pauline thought has permeated all subsequent theology. His doctrine of grace, predestination and free-will, less emphasized in the Greek Church, was developed and expanded by St. *Augustine in his struggle with *Pelagius and came again to the fore in the controversy between *Gottschalk and *Hincmar of Reims. The Augustinian interpretation of St. Paul's teaching on grace has furnished the principal points in the controversies between *Thomism and *Molinism, *Jansenism and the *Jesuit theologians, *Calvinism and *Arminianism. St. Paul's doctrine of *justification by faith also provided the foundation of *Lutheranism, and his predestinationism gave Calvinism its central dogma. In the 17th cent. H. *Grotius and others made a new approach to St. Paul by an exegesis which sought to exclude doctrinal considerations, and this ideal was increasingly upheld during the 18th and 19th cents. The brilliant reconstruction of the beginnings of Christianity by the *Tübingen School also created a lively interest in St. Paul, the effects of which are still felt. Paul came to be widely regarded as the creator of the whole doctrinal and ecclesiastical system presupposed in his Epp. More recently, R. *Reitzenstein and A. *Deissmann have endeavoured to explain Paulinism in terms of the Hellenistic mystery religions and Hellenistic Judaism respectively. A reaction from the Liberal Protestant separation between Jesus and Paul is to be seen in A. *Schweitzer, who finds the key to the understanding of both Jesus and Paul in Jewish eschatology, while the work of J. *Weiss and the *Form-critics has led to a fuller recognition of the inheritance received by St. Paul from the primitive Church as well as of the Hebraic character of his thought.

From the vast literature only a few works can be mentioned. Among the principal are W. J. *Conybeare and J. S. *Howson, *The Life and Epistles of St. Paul* (2 vols., 1851); A. *Sabatier, *L'Apôtre Paul* (1871; Eng. trans. 1891); W. M. *Ramsay, *St. Paul the Traveller and the Roman Citizen* (1895) and other works; W. *Wrede, *Paulus* (1905); A. Deissmann, *Paulus* (1911; ed. 2, 1925; Eng. trans. 1926); K. *Lake, *The Earlier Epistles of St. Paul. Their Motive and Origin* (1911); P. Gardner, *The Religious Experience of St. Paul* (1911); A. H. McNeile, *St. Paul. His Life, Letters, and Christian Doctrine* (1920); T. R. Glover, *Paul of Tarsus* (1925); W. L. Knox, *St. Paul and the Church of Jerusalem* (1925); id., *St. Paul* (1932); A. D. Nock, *St. Paul* (1938) H.U.L.; W. L. Knox, *St. Paul and the Church of the Gentiles* (1939).
Among studies in his theology: O. Pfleiderer, *Der Paulinismus* (1873; Eng. tr., 2 vols., 1877); A. B. *Bruce, *St. Paul's Conception of Christianity* (1894); F. Prat, S.J., *La Théologie de saint Paul* (2 vols., 1908; Eng. trans. 1926–7); C. H. *Dodd, *The Meaning of Paul for To-day* (1920); C. A. A. Scott, *Christianity according to St. Paul* (1927); A. M. Hunter, *Paul and his Predecessors* (1940). Studies on special subjects: O. Pfleiderer, *The Influence of the Apostle Paul* (1885, *Hibbert Lectures); A. Schweitzer, *Geschichte der paulinischen Forschung von der Reformation bis auf die Gegenwart* (1911; Eng. trans., *Paul and his Interpreters*, 1912). H. A. A. Kennedy, *St. Paul and the Mystery-Religions* (1913); W. H. P. Hatch, *The Pauline Idea of Faith in its Relation to Jewish and Hellenistic Religion* (Cambridge, Mass., 1917); A. Deissmann, *The Religion of Jesus and the Faith of Paul* (1923); A. Schweitzer, *Die Mystik des Apostels Paulus* (1930; Eng. trans., *The Mysticism of Paul the Apostle*, 1931); L. Cerfaux, *La Théologie de l'Église suivant saint Paul* (Unam Sanctam, x; 1942); W. D. Davies, *Paul and Rabbinic Judaism* (1948); *Studia Paulina. In Honorem J. de Zwaan* (Haarlem, 1953); L. Cerfaux, *Le Christ dans la théologie de saint Paul* (1951).
G. G. Findlay in *H.D.B.*, iii (1900), pp. 696–731; E. *Hatch–W. C. *van Manen in *E.Bi.*, iii (1902), cols. 3603–3638; J. Stalker in *D.A.C.*, ii (1918), pp. 138–59; J. B. Colon in *D.T.C.*, xi (pt. 2; 1932), cols. 2330–2490; F. W. Maier in *L.Th.K.*, viii (1936), cols. 27–43, all s.v.

PAUL, Acts of St. An apocryphal Book, written in Greek and put into circulation in the latter half of the 2nd cent. Unlike most apocryphal 'Acts', it appears to have been the work of an orthodox Christian. It was compiled in Asia Minor, and is contained in its completest form in Coptic in a Heidelberg papyrus which C. Schmidt pieced together in 1904 from some 2000 fragments. Its reconstruction proved that a number of short treatises which had circulated independently and had been known to earlier scholars were all parts of this single work, among them the 'Martyrdom of St. Paul', the 'Acts of *Paul

and Thecla', and the 'Third Ep. of St. Paul to the *Corinthians' (qq.v.). Several passages of the Gk. text have long been known, the most important of them one publd. by C. Schmidt in 1936 from the Hamburg Public Library. It is now established that the work made use of the 'Acts of *Peter'.
The Acts, which were designed to glorify St. Paul's achievements, were based on the canonical Acts of the Apostles and Pauline Epistles. The author, however, had little regard for historical truth, and it was doubtless the romancing character of the Acts rather than any heretical bias in their teaching that caused him, as *Tertullian relates in his 'De Baptismo' (17), to be deprived of his office of presbyter. The Acts were used by *Origen, *Hippolytus, and *Cyprian.

Older ed. of texts in R. A. *Lipsius–M. Bonnet (edd.), *Acta Apostolorum Apocrypha*, i (Leipzig, 1891), pp. 23–44, 104–17, and 235–72. Heidelberg text in *Acta Pauli aus der Heidelberger koptischen Papyrushandschrift Nr. 1* (1904; with facsimile in separate Tafelband, 1904, and Zusätze, 1905); id., 'Ein neues Fragment der Heidelberger Acta Pauli' in *Sb.* (Berl.), 1909, pp. 216–20; id., ΠΡΑΞΕΙΣ ΠΑΥΛΟΥ. Acta Pauli nach dem Papyrus der Hamburger Staats- und Universitäts-Bibliothek (Veröffentlichungen aus der Hamburger Staats- und Universitäts-Bibliothek, N.F., ii; 1936). Further fragment ed. G. D. Kilpatrick–C. H. Roberts in *J.T.S.*, xlvii (1946), pp. 196–9. Eng. tr. in M. R. James (ed.), *The Apocryphal New Testament* (1924), pp. 270–99, with important Appendix [by J. W. B. Barns] in id., '1953 reprint (corrected)', pp. 570–8. L. Vouaux, *Les Actes de Paul et ses lettres apocryphes*. Introduction, textes, traduction et commentaire (1913). E. Peterson, 'Einige Bemerkungen zum Hamburger Papyrusfragment der Acta Pauli' in *Vigiliae Christianae*, iii (1949), pp. 142–62. J. Quasten, *Patrology*, i (Utrecht, 1950), pp. 130–2. Bardenhewer, i, 554–64; Altaner (ed. 1951), pp. 53–5.

PAUL, Apocalypse of St. An apocryphal apocalypse, written in Greek and dating from the latter half of the 4th cent., which describes in detail what St. Paul saw when he was taken up into the 'third heaven' (2 Cor. 12. 2). It narrates that St. Paul was led into paradise, where in the city of God he met all the blessed, —in one quarter the *Prophets, in another the *Holy Innocents, in another *Abraham, *Isaac, and *Jacob, and in the fourth those who had wholeheartedly devoted themselves to God. The treatise, which was known to St. *Augustine (c. 416), became very popular, and was translated into Latin, Syriac, Coptic, and Ethiopic. It also enjoyed a great vogue in the Middle Ages, being quoted by *Dante (*Inferno*, 2. 28). The 'Apocalypse of St. Paul' of *Gnostic origin, mentioned by St. *Epiphanius (*Haer.*, 38. 2), appears to have been an independent work of which nothing has survived.

Gk. text in C. *Tischendorf, *Apocalypses Apocryphae* (Leipzig, 1866), pp. 34–69. Crit. ed. by M. R. James (ed.), *Apocrypha Anecdota* (Texts and Studies, ii, No. 3; Cambridge, 1893), pp. 11–42. Syr. text ed. G. Riciotti in *Orientalia*, ii (Rome, 1933), pp. 1–25, 120–49. Lat. text ed. in several recensions, with full discussion, by T. Silverstein (Studies and Documents ed. K. *Lake–S. Lake, iv, 1935). Eng. tr. in M. R. James (ed.), *The Apocryphal New Testament* (1924), pp. 525–55. C. H. Kraeling, 'The Apocalypse of Paul and the *Iranische Erlösungsmysterium*' in *H.T.R.*, xxiv (1931), pp. 209–44; R. P. Casey, 'The Apocalypse of Paul' in *J.T.S.*, xxiv (1933), pp. 1–32. J. Quasten, *Patrology*, i (Utrecht, 1950), pp. 146–9. Bardenhewer, i, 615–20; Altaner (ed. 1951), p. 65 f.

PAUL, Clerks Regular of St. See *Barnabites.*

PAUL, Martyrdom of St. An apocryphal account of the death of St. *Paul dating from the latter part of the 2nd cent. It forms the concluding section of the 'Acts of *Paul' (q.v.). It describes how St. Paul was brought to the presence of *Nero at Rome, sentenced to death, and led to execution by the prefect, Longus, and the centurion, Cestus (who were converted). The 'Martyrdom' survives in the two Greek MSS. which also contain the 'Acts of *Peter'.

Two Gk. texts with a Lat. tr. in R. A. *Lipsius–M. Bonnet (edd.), *Acta Apostolorum Apocrypha*, i (Leipzig, 1891), pp. 104–17. Eng. tr. in M. R. James (ed.), *The Apocryphal New Testament* (1924), pp. 293–6. For further items see bibl. to *Paul, Acts of.*

PAUL AND THECLA, Acts of Sts. An apocryphal work describing the adventures of Sts. *Paul and *Thecla, which was part of the 'Acts of *Paul' (q.v.). Its great popularity in the early Church is shown by its existence not only in the original Greek, but also in five separate Latin translations, as well as in Syriac, Armenian, Slavonic, and Arabic. The 'Acts' describe how St. Paul, after his flight from Antioch in Pisidia (Acts 13. 51), arrived at Iconium, where in the house of Onesiphorus he preached the benefits of chastity and thereby won St. Thecla away from Thamyris to whom she was betrothed. In consequence, Paul was charged before the civil authorities and beaten, while Thecla was condemned to death by burning, but miraculously saved. Other incidents in various parts of Asia Minor are described in the lives of both Paul and Thecla, and the 'Acts' conclude with the record of Thecla's death at Seleucia. It is not impossible that the 'Acts' contain a kernel of historical truth.

Gk. text pr. in R. A. *Lipsius–M. Bonnet (edd.), *Acta Apocrypha Apostolorum*, i (Leipzig, 1891), pp. 235–72. Syr. text ed. W. Wright, *Apocryphal Acts of the Apostles* (1871), i, 128–69; Eng. tr., ii, 116–45. Ethiopic text ed., with Eng. tr. and introd., by E. J. Goodspeed in *American Journal of Semitic Languages and Literatures*, xvii (1900–1), pp. 65–95. Armenian text publd. at Venice, 1874; Eng. tr. of this text by F. C. *Conybeare, *The Apology and Acts of Apollonius and other Monuments of Early Christianity* (1894), pp. 61–88, with introd., pp. 49–60. For important Coptic text, see *Paul, Acts of.* Eng. tr. in M. R. James (ed.), *The Apocryphal New Testament* (1924), pp. 272–81. W. M. *Ramsay, *The Church in the Roman Empire before A.D. 170* (1893), pp. 375–428. C. Holzhey, *Die Thekla-Akten. Ihre Verbreitung und Beurtheilung in der Kirche* (Veröffentlichungen aus dem kirchen-historischen Seminar München, Reihe II, vii; 1905). Bardenhewer, i, 561–4. C. Holzhey in *L.Th.K.*, x (1938), cols. 28–30.

PAUL III (1468–1549), Pope from 1534. Alessandro Farnese was educated at Rome and Florence at the court of Lorenzo the Magnificent, and created cardinal-deacon by *Alexander VI in 1493. He held numerous benefices, among them the Bprics. of Parma and Ostia, became Dean of the Sacred College under *Leo X, and was unanimously elected to the Papacy on 13 Oct. 1534. Though in his personal life a typical Renaissance Pope—he

had three sons and a daughter, was much given to worldly pleasures, and indulged in unlimited nepotism—he was an efficient promoter of the inner reform of the Church. He created as cardinals men of virtue and scholarship like R. *Pole, G. P. Caraffa (*Paul IV), and G. *Morone (1509–80), established ecclesiastical commissions to draw up plans for the reform of the Church, and favoured the new orders, e.g. the *Ursulines, the *Barnabites, and esp. the *Jesuits which he approved in 1540 by the bull '*Regimini militantis Ecclesiae'. In 1542 he restored the *Inquisition, and above all fought hard against the opposition to a General Council which finally opened at *Trent in 1545. He was, however, less successful in his political efforts to check the spread of Protestantism. The religious colloquies in Germany and the wars of the Emperor whom he supported could not restore unity, and the bull which he published against *Henry VIII in 1538 alienated England still further from Rome. His last years were darkened by the death of his son and the revolt of his grandson, Ottavio, who took the part of the Emperor against him. Like his immediate predecessors, Paul III was a friend of art and scholarship. He appointed prominent theologians to the chairs of the Roman university, enriched the *Vatican Library with valuable MSS., and made *Michelangelo architect-in-chief of *St. Peter's.

The best collection of his bulls is that in the *Bullarum Diplomatum et Privilegiorum Sanctorum Romanorum Pontificum Taurinensis Editio*, vi (Turin, 1860), pp. 173–401. There is a good modern study by C. Capasso (2 vols., Messina, 1923–4 [on wrappers '1925']). L. Cardauns, 'Paul III, Karl V und Franz I in den Jahren 1535 und 1536' in *Quellen und Forschungen aus italienischen Archiven und Bibliotheken* herausgegeben vom koenigl. Preussischen Historischen Institut in Rom, xi (1908), pp. 147–244. L. Dorez, *La Cour du Pape Paul III d'après les registres de la Trésorerie Secrète (Collection F. de Navenne)* (2 vols., 1932). W. Friedensburg, *Kaiser Karl V und Papst Paul III.* (Schriften des Vereins für Reformationsgeschichte No. 153; 1932). W. H. Edwards, *Paulus III oder die geistliche Gegenreformation* (1933). Pastor, xi and xii (1912), with full bibl. R. O. Zöpffel–K. Benrath in *P.R.E.* (ed. 3), xv (1904), pp. 31–9, s.v., with bibl.; J. F. Loughlin in *C.E.*, xi (1911), pp. 579–81, s.v.; L. Marchal in *D.T.C.*, xii (pt. 1; 1933), cols. 9–20, s.v., with detailed bibl.; H. Jedin in *E.C.*, ix (1952), cols. 734–6, s.v. 'Paolo III'. See also bibl. to *Trent, Council of.*

PAUL IV (1476–1559), the first of the *Counter-Reformation Popes (from 1555). Giovanni Pietro (Giampietro) Caraffa came of a distinguished Neapolitan family. Having been brought up by his uncle, Oliviero Caraffa (1430–1511), into close relations with the *curia, he became possessed from early life with a keen enthusiasm for the reform of abuses. From 1504 to 1524 he was Bp. of Chieti (Theate), sitting in 1520 on the commission at Rome appointed to deal with the affair of M. *Luther. In 1524 he resigned his bishopric in order to found, in conjunction with St. *Cajetan, the *Theatine Order, which was named after him and in which he continued to be one of the chief movers. In 1536 he became Abp. of Naples and was created cardinal, and in 1542 he reorganized the *Inquisition. Finally in 1555 he was elected Pope. Despite his age he acted with great determination, though his actions in his later years seem to have been motivated more by a lust for power and the advancement of his relatives than by devotion to the highest needs of the Church. His unpopularity was increased by his political sympathies, hatred of Spain making him quarrel with *Mary Tudor; and his opposition to anything savouring of *Protestantism was so violent that its effect was only to consolidate the Protestant forces.

The best collection of his bulls is that in the *Bullarum Diplomatum et Privilegiorum Sanctorum Romanorum Pontificum Taurinensis Editio*, vi (Turin, 1860), pp. 489–566. R. Ancel, O.S.B. (ed.), *Nonciatures de France*. Nonciatures de Paul IV [to 4 July 1557] (Archives de l'Histoire Religieuse de la France, 2 vols., 1909–11). A. Caraccioli, *Collectanea Historica de Vita Pauli Quarti* (Cologne, 1612). C. Bromato, Theatine, *Storia di Paolo IV* (2 vols., Ravenna, 1748–53). G. M. Monti, *Ricerche su Paolo IV Carafa* (Benevento, 1925). G. Duruy, *Le Cardinal Carlo Carafa (1519–1561)*. Étude sur le pontificat de Paul IV (1882). L. Riess, *Die Politik Pauls IV und seiner Nepoten* (Historische Studien, lxvii; 1909). There is also a series of important articles by R. Ancel, listed in *D.T.C.* (vide infra). Pastor, xiv (1924), pp. 56–426, with full bibl. to date of German ed. G. Mollat in *D.T.C.*, xii (pt. 1; 1933), cols. 20–3, s.v., with detailed bibl.; F. X. Seppelt in *L.Th.K.*, viii (1936), col. 14 f., s.v., with bibl.; H. Jedin in *E.C.*, ix (1952), cols. 736–8, s.v. 'Paolo IV'.

PAUL V (1552–1621), Pope from 1605. Camillo Borghese was a descendant of a noble Sienese family. He studied law at Perugia and Padua, was created Cardinal in 1596, Papal Vicar in 1603, and elected and crowned Pope in May 1605. The first years of his reign were troubled by the conflict with *Venice, whose government had attacked ecclesiastical immunities and liberties by promulgating two laws (1604 and 1605) which forbade the erection of religious buildings without the consent of the Senate and the donation or sale of secular property to the Church. After a refusal to repeal these laws, the Pope excommunicated the Senate and put the city under the *interdict. In the theological controversy which ensued, he was defended by R. *Bellarmine and C. *Baronius against the *Servite, P. *Sarpi, who in the interests of Venice denied all temporal power and privileges to the Church. About the same time the English question became once more acute in consequence of the Oath of Allegiance required by *James I, which the Pope condemned in two Briefs in 1606 and 1607. This step gave rise to a dispute between the archpriest, G. *Blackwell, who defended the Oath, and the *Jesuits, who insisted on the right of the Pope to depose kings, and later between James I himself and Bellarmine. In his Continental policy Paul V preserved a neutral attitude between the two rival powers France and Spain, whom he tried to reconcile in order to present a united Christian front to the Turks. After futile efforts at re-establishing the Roman Church in Russia, he lived to see the beginnings of the *Thirty Years War in Germany. He died of a stroke soon after the celebrations of the Catholic victory in the Battle of the White Mountain. A man of blameless life (except for his nepotism) and a skilful canonist, he endeavoured from the beginning of his reign

to enforce the decrees of the Council of *Trent. He fostered the work of the Congregations devoted to education and care of the sick as well as the missions, notably those in Africa and *Canada; and many popular saints were canonized or beatified by him, among them *Charles Borromeo and *Frances of Rome. He was also greatly devoted to the city of Rome, among the works which he carried through being the completion of St. Peter's and the extension of the *Vatican Library.

Life by A. Bzovius, O.P. (Rome, 1626). [C. P. Goujet]. *Histoire du pontificat de Paul V* (2 vols., Amsterdam, 1765). E. Cornet, *Paolo e la Repubblica Veneto*. Giornale dal 22 ottobre 1605–9 giugno 1607. Corredato di note e documenti (Vienna, 1859). A. Nürnberger, 'Papst Paul V und das venezianische Interdict' in *Hist.J.*, iv (1883), pp. 189–209 and 473–515; id., 'Documente zum Ausgleich zwischen Paul V und der Republik Venedig' in *R.Q.*, ii (1888), pp. 64–80, 248–76, and 354–67. C. P. de Magistris, *Per la storia del componimento della contesta tra la Repubblica Veneto e Paulo V, 1605–1607*. Documenti (posthumously publd., Turin, 1941). J. M. Pou y Marti, O.F.M., 'La intervención española en el conflicto entre Paulo V y Venecia (1605–1607)' in *Miscellanea Pio Paschini*, ii (Lateranum, N.S., xv; 1949), pp. 359–81. Pastor, xxv and xxvi (1937), with full bibl. to date of German ed. R. O. Zöpffel–K. Benrath in *P.R.E.* (ed. 3), xv (1904), pp. 44–9, s.v.; J. F. Loughlin in *C.E.*, xi (1911), p. 581 f., s.v.; L. Marchal in *D.T.C.*, xii (pt. 1; 1933), cols. 23–37, s.v., with detailed bibl. G. B. Picotti in *E.C.*, ix (1952), cols. 738–41, s.v. 'Paolo V'. See also bibl. to *Sarpi, P.

PAUL OF CONSTANTINOPLE, St. (d. 350). A native of *Thessalonica, he succeeded Alexander in the see of *Constantinople in 336. He was soon displaced by the Arian *Macedonius, who had the support of the Emp. Constantius; and though he regained his see he was soon after removed again and went into exile in the W. Under pressure from Constans, the Emp. of the W., he again recovered his see, but after the death of Constans (350) he was once again exiled, first to Singara in Mesopotamia, then to Emesa, and finally to Cucusus in Armenia where he was strangled. He was a zealous upholder of orthodoxy and a close associate of St. *Athanasius and Pope *Julius. Feast day, 7 June.

The literary reff. to Paul are scattered. W. Telfer, 'Paul of Constantinople' in *H.T.R.*, xliii (1950), pp. 31–92, with reff.

PAUL OF THE CROSS, St. (1694–1775), founder of the *Passionists. Paul Francis Danei was the eldest son of an impoverished noble family, who led a life of prayer and great austerity in the world until, in 1720, a vision inspired him to found a religious order in honour of the Passion of our Lord. In a 40-days' retreat he drew up its rule, which is in substance that still followed by his congregation. In 1725 he obtained permission to receive novices from *Benedict XIII, who ordained him and his brother priests in 1727. He then retired to Monte Argentaro where, faced with great difficulties (desertion of novices, threat of war), he laboured as a missionary among the people. In 1737 the first Passionist 'Retreat' was opened. In 1744 St. Paul moved to the second house near Vetralla, was elected Superior-General three years later, and from 1769 till his death lived in Rome. He was one of the most celebrated preachers of his age, esp. on account of his stirring meditations on the Passion, and famous as a miracle worker and spiritual director. He was canonized in 1867. Feast day, 28 Apr.

Lettere di S. Paolo della Croce, ed. Amadeo della Madre del Buon Pastore, C.P. (4 vols., Rome, 1924). The primary life is that by the Bl. Vincenzo Maria Strambi, C.P. (Rome, 1786; Eng. tr., 'Saints and Servants of God', 2 vols., 1853). Modern studies include those by Pius a Spiritu Sancto [A. Devine], C.P. (Dublin–London, 1867; revised ed., London, 1924), F. Liphold (Dülmen, 1930), Gaïtan du S. Nom de Marie [J. Cajetan], C.P. (Tirlemont, 1934), and Father Edmund [J. E. Burke], C.P. (Dublin, 1946), with bibl. Gaëtan du S. Nom de Marie, Oraison et ascension mystique de S. Paul de la Croix (Museum Lessianum, 1930); id., Doctrine de S. Paul de la Croix sur l'oraison et la mystique (ib., 1932). A. Devine, C.P., in C.E., xi (1911), p. 590, s.v.; Giacinto del S. Crocifisso, C.P., in E.C., ix (1952), cols. 727–30, s.v. 'Paolo della Croce', with bibl. See also bibl. to Passionists.

PAUL THE DEACON (c. 720–c. 800), also 'Paulus Levita' or 'Warnefridi', 'Father of Italian History', chronicler. Of noble Lombard descent, he received an exceptionally good education, prob. at the court of Pavia, where he later taught Adelperga, the daughter of King Desiderius (756–74). He entered the *Benedictine monastery of St. Peter at Civate c. 774, leaving shortly afterwards for *Monte Cassino. In 782 he visited *Charlemagne on behalf of a brother implicated in a revolt at Friuli in 776. Received with honour on account of his learning and culture, he remained in Francia until c. 786 composing a history of the diocese of Metz ('Gesta Episcoporum Mettensium') and various didactic works. After his return to Monte Cassino he undertook his most important work, the 'Historia Gentis Langobardorum', an incomplete history in five books from 568 to the death of Luitprand (744). Based largely on documents no longer extant, it is the principal source for the Lombard history of the period, being esp. valuable for Franco-Lombard relations and its vivid picture of the life of the time. His 'Historia Romana', supplementing and continuing the 'Breviarium' of Eutropius to 553, which was undertaken at the request of Adelperga, is of much less historical value. In his later years he composed some important liturgical works, including a compilation of lessons for the Night Office and, at the request of Charlemagne, a collection of Homilies (*'Homiliarium') which were ordered to be used throughout the Empire. He also wrote an Expositio super Regulam S. Benedicti, a life of St. *Gregory and various epitaphs and poems, including 'Ut queant laxis'.

Collection of his works in J. P. Migne, PL, xcv, 433–1710. His Comm. on the Rule of St. Benedict was first publd. by the monks of *Monte Cassino (Monte Cassino, 1880). Crit. ed. of Books xi–xvi of his 'Historia Romana' by H. Droysen in M.G.H., Auctores Antiquissimi, ii (1879), pp. 185–224; of his 'Historiae Langobardorum' by L. Bethmann–G. Waitz, ib., Scriptores Rerum Langobardicarum et Italicarum Saec. vi–ix. (1879), pp. 12–187; of his poetry by E. Duemmler, ib., Poetae, i (1880), pp. 35–50, also ed. K. Neff (Quellen und Untersuchungen zur lateinischen Philologie des Mittelalters, iii, Hft. 4; 1908); and of his Life of Gregory I by H. Grisar, S.J., in Z.K.T., xi (1887), pp. 158–73. There is an Eng. tr. of his 'Historia Langobardorum' by W. D. Foulke (Philadelphia and New York, 1907). T. *Mommsen, 'Die Quellen der Langobardengeschichte des Paulus Diaconus' in N.A., v

(1879), pp. 51–103; G. Waitz, 'Zur Frage nach den Quellen der Historia Langobardorum', ib., pp. 415–24. A. Crivelluci, 'Per l' edizione della Historia Romana di Paolo Diacono' in Bullettino dell' Istituto Storico Italiano, No. 40 (1921), pp. 7–103. P. Paschini in E.C., ix (1952), cols. 730–2, s.v. 'Paolo Diacono'.

PAUL THE HERMIT, St. See Paul of Thebes, St.

PAUL OF SAMOSATA (3rd cent.), heretical Bp. of *Antioch. A native of Samosata who became a man of considerable wealth, he was Procurator Ducenarius to Zenobia, Queen of Palmyra (overthrown, 272) and c. 260 became Bp. of Antioch. His teaching on the Person of Christ was condemned at two, or poss. three, Synods at Antioch and in 268 he was deposed from his see. He taught a form of Dynamic *Monarchianism, in which the Godhead was a closely knit Trinity of Father, Wisdom and Word and until creation formed a single *hypostasis. In Christology he was a precursor of *Nestorius, holding that from the Incarnation the Word rested upon the human Jesus as one person upon another, and that the Incarnate Christ differed only in degree from the Prophets. In the course of the controversy the famous '*Homousios' first came into dispute. The chief sources for the conflict are (1) a synodal letter of the Antiochene Synod of 268, partly preserved by *Eusebius (H.E., VII, xxx); (2) a stenographic report of a disputation at this Synod between Paul and an *Origenist presbyter of Antioch named Malchion; and (3) the so-called 'Hymenaeus Epistle', a letter addressed to Paul by Hymenaeus and five other Bishops. The extant fragments of Paul's 'Addresses to Sabinus' are probably fabrications. Paul's followers ('*Paulianists'; q.v.) long survived his death.

G. Bardy, Paul de Samosate. Étude historique (S.S.L., iv; 1923; new ed. 1929); F. *Loofs, Paulus von Samosata (T.U., xl, Hft. 5; 1924); H. de Riedmatten, O.P., Les Actes du procès de Paul de Samosate. Etude sur la christologie du III au IVe siècle (Paradosis vi; 1952). Collection of fragments in H. de Riedmatten, op. cit., pp. 135–58 (superseding that of H. J. Lawlor in J.T.S., xix (1917–18), pp. 20–45 and 115–21). A. v. *Harnack, 'Die Reden Pauls von Samosata an Sabinus (Zenobia?) und seine Christologie' in Sb. (Berl.), 1924, pp. 130–51. E. *Schwartz, Eine fingierte Korrespondenz mit Paulus dem Samosatener (Sb. (Bayr.), 1927, Hft. 3). P. Galtier, [S.J.,] ὁμοούσιος de Paul de Samosate' in Rech.S.R., xii (1922), pp. 30–45. Bardenhewer, ii, pp. 275–9; Altaner (ed. 1951), p. 178. G. Bardy in D.T.C., xii (pt. 1; 1933), cols. 46–51.

PAUL THE SILENTIARY. See Paulus Silentiarius.

PAUL OF THEBES, St. (d. c. 340), traditionally the first Christian hermit. Acc. to St. *Jerome's Vita Pauli, the sole authority, Paul was a native of the Thebaid. During the *Decian Persecution (249–51) he fled to the desert where he lived for some hundred years a life of prayer and penitence in a cave. St. *Antony is said to have visited him when 113 years old and later to have buried him, wrapping him in the mantle which he had himself received from St. *Athanasius.

The details of this narrative, which find no

corroboration from other sources, are open to considerable suspicion. In later art, Paul is commonly represented with a palm tree or two lions. Feast Day, 15 Jan.

Jerome's *Vita Pauli* (J. P. Migne, *PL*, xxiii, 17–28) is prob. the source of the various Gk. and Oriental Lives; cf. J. Bidez, *Deux Versions grecques inédites de la vie de Paul de Thèbes, publiées avec une introduction* (Ghent, 1900). On his possible identification with a 'Paul of Oxyrhynchus' cf. H. *Delehaye, S.J., 'La Personnalité historique de S. Paul de Thèbes', in *Anal. Boll.*, xliv (1926), pp. 64–9.

PAULA, St. (347–404), Roman matron. At the age of 33, then a mother of five children (among them St. *Eustochium), this Roman lady of noble birth dedicated herself to a life of devotion. In 385 she and Eustochium both followed St. *Jerome to Palestine; and after visiting the Holy places and the hermits in the Egyptian deserts, she settled permanently in *Bethlehem from 386 where she founded a convent of monks and another of nuns. Feast day, 26 Jan.

Her character is vividly described by Jerome in *Ep.* 108, written shortly after her death (J. P. Migne, *PL*, xxii, 878 ff.).

PAULIANISTS. The followers of *Paul of Samosata. Presumably because they repudiated the *Trinity, the 19th canon of the Council of *Nicaea (325) required that they should be *rebaptized on being received back into Catholic communion.

PAULICIANS. The members of a sect of the Byzantine Empire. Their name may be derived from St. *Paul, whom they held in special veneration, or, more probably, from *Paul of Samosata, with whom they had affinities. The origins of the sect are obscure; their true founder seems to have been Constantine of Mananali, a *Manichaean village near Samosata, who established a community at Kibossa in Armenia under Constantius II (641–68). Under Constantine Pogonatus they were persecuted and their founder was stoned (*c.* 684). In the 9th cent. they suffered again under Emp. Leo the Armenian, and the Empress Theodora tried to exterminate them. In consequence many of them assisted the Saracens in their raids on the Empire and adopted Mohammedanism. Those who sought refuge in Bulgaria seem to have amalgamated with the *Bogomiles in the 10th cent. It seems that they ceased to exist as an independent sect in the 12th cent.

The Paulicians professed a Dualistic doctrine, distinguishing between the good God, the Lord of Heaven and creator of souls, and the evil God, the Demiurge and ruler of the material universe. Holding all matter to be evil they denied the reality of Christ's Body and of the Redemption and considered Christ's most important work His teaching. From this contempt of His Body they were led to reject the Cross and all images. Instead they honoured the Book of the Gospels. Like *Marcion, they repudiated the OT and held St. *Luke and the Pauline Epp. in particular

esteem. Originally they were organized in four grades of apostles, prophets, itinerants, and copyists, but later only the latter two remained, the itinerants being the superiors and the copyists being entrusted with transcribing the Sacred Books and keeping order in church. Their dualistic doctrines seem frequently to have led to grave moral disorders.

The primary sources include Petrus Siculus, 'Historia Haereseos Manichaeorum qui et Pauliciani' in J. P. Migne, *PG*, civ, 1239–1304; id., 'Sermones contra Paulicianos', ib., 1305–50. *Euthymius Zigabenus, 'Panoplia Dogmatica, tit.', xxiv', ib., cxxx, 1189–244. K. Ter-Mkrttschian, *Die Paulikianer im byzantinischen Kaiserreich und verwandte ketzerische Erscheinungen in Armenien* (1893; with Armenian sources). F. C. *Conybeare, *The Key of Truth.* Manual of the Paulician Church of Armenia (1898). Id. in *E.B.* (ed. 11), xx (1911), pp. 959–62, s.v.; R. Janin, A.A., in *D.T.C.*, xii (pt. 1; 1933), cols. 56–62, s.v. 'Pauliciens'.

PAULINE PRIVILEGE. The privilege conceded by St. *Paul (1 Cor. 7. 15) to the partner of a heathen marriage to contract a new marriage on becoming a Christian, if the other (non-Christian) partner wished to separate or put serious obstacles in the way of the convert's faith and practice. There is little evidence of its exercise in the earliest times, but its use is attested by *Chrysostom and *Ambrosiaster. The right gradually became established in *canon law and is now provided for in the *Codex Iuris Canonici (cans. 1120–7). See also *Divorce*.

G. H. Joyce, S.J., *Christian Marriage* (1933), ch. xi.

PAULINUS, St. (*c.* 726–802), Bp. of Aquileia. Born not far from Friuli, he became an assiduous and learned scholar. In 776 *Charlemagne summoned him to the Frankish court, where he made the close acquaintance of *Alcuin and other leading men of learning, and in 787 appointed him Patr. of Aquileia. Here he took a leading part in ecclesiastical affairs, notably in the relations between the Byzantine Church and the W. He also took a prominent share in the suppression of *Adoptianism, notably at the Councils of Regensburg (792), Frankfurt (794), and Friuli (796), and in the conversion of the pagans in the Tyrol and adjacent provinces. His writings include two anti-Adoptianist works—'Libellus Sacrosyllabus contra Elipandum' and 'Libri iii contra Felicem'; several poems ('rhythms'), e.g., on the death of his friend, Heric, and on the destruction of Aquileia; and hymns for ecclesiastical feasts in his own church. Feast day, 28 Jan. (otherwise, 11 Jan. and 2 Mar.).

Works ed. J. F. Madrisius, Cong. Orat. (Venice, 1737), repr. in J. P. Migne, *PL*, xcix, 9–683. Modern ed. of his Epp. by E. Dümmler in *M.G.H.*, Epistolae, iv (1895), pp. 516–27; of his Poems by id., ib., Poetae, i (1881), pp. 123–48. Manitius, i (1911), pp. 368–70. J. Reviron in *D.T.C.*, xii (pt. 1; 1933), cols. 62–7, with bibl.

PAULINUS, St. (353/4–431), Bp. of Nola. The son of a noble and wealthy family at Bordeaux, Paulinus seems to have received a good education, counting among his teachers the famous *Ausonius. After a short public career and a few years of cultured leisure, he was baptized by St. Delphinus, Bp. of Bordeaux, in 390, and, in agreement with his Spanish wife, Therasia, retired from the world and began to distribute his enormous fortune to the Church and the poor. On a journey to Spain he was ordained priest at Barcelona in 394 on the insistence of the people. Shortly afterwards he settled at Nola, near the tomb of St. Felix, where he and his wife founded a home for monks and poor and themselves led a life of great austerity. Here, in 409, Paulinus was made bishop. His widespread corre-pondence kept him in touch with several famous Christians of his time, many of whom were his intimate friends, such as St. *Martin of Tours, St. *Ambrose, St. *Augustine, and Pope Anastasius I. Apart from his letters, many of which survive, his poetic works have attracted special attention and place him beside *Prudentius as the foremost Christian Latin poet of the patristic period. Most of his poems were written for the annual celebrations in honour of St. Felix and are of great interest as throwing light on the cult of saints and popular customs of that time. Paulinus still uses the old classical forms with great skill, but fills them with the new Christian spirit of hope and charity, the combination of old and new being one of the greatest charms of his poetry. Feast day, 22 June. See also *Bells*.

Early edd. of his works by F. *Ducaeus, S.J.-H. Rosweyde, S.J. (Antwerp, 1622), J. B. Le Brun (2 vols., Paris, 1685), and L. A. *Muratori (Verona, 1736). Muratori's text is repr. in J. P. Migne, *PL*, lxi. Crit. ed. by W. Hartel (C.S.E.L., xxix and xxx; 1894). Life by A. Baudrillart ('Les Saints', 1905). Other studies by A. Buse (Ratisbon, 1856), F. Lagrange (Paris, 1877), P. Fabre (Strassburg, 1948), and id. (Paris, 1949). P. Courcelle, 'Paulin de Nole et saint Jérôme' in *Revue des Études latines*, xxv (1947), pp. 250–80. Raby, pp. 168–71, with bibl. p. 473. Bardenhewer, iii, 569–82. K. Löffler in *C.E.*, xi (1911), p. 585 f. É. Amann in *D.T.C.*, xii (pt. 1; 1933), cols. 68–71, s.v., with bibl. E. Rapisarda in *E.C.*, ix (1952), cols. 701–3, s.v. 'Paolino, vescovo di Nola', also with bibl.

PAULINUS, St. (d. 358), Bp. of Trier. He was a disciple of St. Maximin, whom he succeeded in the see of Trier. A strong opponent of Arianism, he was banished after the Synod of *Arles of 353 to Phrygia where he died in exile. His relics were brought back to Trier in 396, where they have since remained. Feast day, 31 Aug.

A.A.SS., Aug. VI (1743), pp. 668–79, with 8th–9th cent. life, pp. 676–9. S. A. Bennett in *D.C.B.*, iv (1887), p. 232, s.v. 'Paulinus (4).'.

PAULINUS, St. (d. 644) Bp. of *York. In 601 he was sent to England by Pope *Gregory to reinforce the mission of St. *Augustine; and when in 625 Edwin, King of Northumbria, married Ethelburga of Kent, Paulinus was consecrated bishop and went with her to York. As a result of his preaching, Edwin and his chiefs accepted Christianity at the assembly of Goodmanham (627). A cathedral was begun at York, and, assisted by James the Deacon, Paulinus taught the faith there until 633 when, upon Edwin's defeat by the heathen Cadwallon, he returned with Ethelburga to Kent and became Bp. of *Rochester. Feast day, 10 Oct.

The principal authority is *Bede, *H.E.*, i, 29; ii, 9, 12–14, 16–18, 20; iii, 1; iv, 23; v, 24; notes to ed. by C. Plummer, ii (Oxford, 1896), esp. pp. 93 f., 100 f., 117 f., 161 f. Hardy, i, pt. 1 (1862), p. 229 f. R. H. Hodgkin, *A History of the Anglo-Saxons*, i (1935), pp. 273–80. J. Raine in *D.C.B.*, iv (1887), p. 248 f., s.v., with reff.; W. H. *Hutton in *D.E.C.H.* (1912), p. 451, s.v.

PAULISTS. The popular name for members of 'The Missionary Society of St. Paul the Apostle in the State of New York', founded by I. T. *Hecker in 1858 to further the work and interests of the RC Church in the U.S.A. Its members live under a rule based on that of the *Redemptorists, of which order Hecker had previously been a member. Through the supposed connexion of Hecker with *Americanism, the Society was under suspicion for a time.

Heimbucher, ii, 619–21. See also bibl. to *Americanism* and *Hecker, I. T.*

PAULUS OROSIUS. See *Orosius*.

PAULUS SILENTIARIUS (6th cent.; a *silentiarius* was an usher who maintained silence in the Imperial Palace), Christian poet. He wrote during the reign of *Justinian (Emp. 527–65). His principal work, a hymn to mark the consecration on 24 Dec. 562, gives a full description (ἔκφρασις) of the church and pulpit (ἄμβων) in fluent hexameters, and is of great interest for the history of Byzantine art. Paulus also wrote some 80 epigrams, preserved in the Greek anthology. A poem on the Baths of Pythia in Bithynia has also, but wrongly, been ascribed to him.

Paulus's *Ecphrasis* and *Ambo*, ed. I. Bekker (C.S.H. Byz., 1837); repr. in J. P. Migne, PG, lxxxvi, 2119–58 and 2251–64, with C. D. *du Cange's commentary on the former, also repr. from Bekker, cols. 2159–252. Crit. ed. in P. Friedländer, *Johannes von Gaza und Paulus Silentiarius* (1912), pp. 225–65, with notes pp. 266–305. K. Praechter, 'Zum Bädergedichte des Paulos Silentiarios' in *B.Z.*, xiii (1904), pp. 1–12. S. G. *Mercati, 'Intorno all' autore del carme εἰς τὰ Πυθίοις Θερμά (Leone Magistro Choirosphaktes)' in *Rivista degli Studi orientali*, x (1923–5), pp. 212–48. W. von Christ, *Geschichte der griechischen Literatur*, ii (ed. 6 by W. Schmid–O. Stählin, 1924), pp. 977 f. and 980. Bardenhewer, v, 24 f. W. Peck in *P.W.*, xviii (pt. 4; 1949), cols. 2363–72, s.v. 'Paulus 10'.

PAULUS, HEINRICH EBERHARD GOTTLOB (1761–1851), German orientalist and theologian. He was professor of oriental languages at Jena from 1789 to 1793, and of exegetical theology from 1793 to 1803. After other appointments, he held the chair of exegesis and ecclesiastical history at Heidelberg from 1811 to 1844. His most important works were *Leben Jesu als Grundlage einer reinen Geschichte des Urchristenthums* (2 vols., 1828) and an *Exegetisches Handbuch über die drei ersten Evangelien* (3 vols., 1830–3) in which he made a fruitless attempt to reconcile belief in the substantial accuracy of the Gospel narrative with disbelief in the miracles and the supernatural. His influence gradually waned before the more radical scepticism of D. F. *Strauss.

He publd. his autobiographical *Skizzen aus meiner Bildungs- und Lebens-Geschichte* (Heidelberg, 1839). Frh. C. A. von Reichlin-Meldegg (Paulus' son-in-law), *H. E. G. Paulus und seine Zeit* (2 vols., 1853). A. *Schweitzer, *Geschichte der Leben-Jesu-Forschung* (ed. 2, 1913), pp. 49–58. K. F. A. Kahnis–P. Tschackert in *P.R.E.* (ed. 3), xv (1904), pp. 88–92.

PAX. See *Kiss of Peace* and foll. entry.

PAX BREDE (also Pax or Osculatorium). A small plate of ivory, metal, or wood, with a representation of the Crucifixion or other religious subject on the face and a projecting handle on the back, used at Mass for conveying the *Kiss of Peace (q.v.) esp. to those in choir and to the laity. It is kissed first by the cele-brant and then by the others who receive it in turn. Pax bredes came into general use in the later Middle Ages prob. under *Franciscan influence. They have been widely retained by the *Dominicans and *Carthusians and recently there has been a tendency to reintro-duce them elsewhere.

Jungmann, ii (ed. 1949), p. 398 f. (Eng. tr., ii, 328 f.). F. *Cabrol, O.S.B., in *D.A.C.L.*, ii (1910), cols. 128 f., s.v. 'Baiser. vi: *Osculatorium.*'

PEACE OF THE CHURCH, The. The term is applied:
(1) To the new situation in the Church when persecution ceased with the 'Edict of *Milan' in 313; also, in a more specialized sense,
(2) To the temporary cessation of the *Jan-senist conflict in 1668, brought about when Pope Clement IX accepted the submission of the four French bishops (28 Sept.) and Louis XIV ordered all parties to the dispute to refrain from further conflict. The settlement, also known as the 'Clementine Peace' ('Pax Clementina'), was formally ratified by Clement IX in four briefs dated 19 Jan. 1669.

PEACOCK, REGINALD. See *Pecock, Reginald.*

PEAKE, ARTHUR SAMUEL (1865–1929), Biblical scholar. The son of a *Primitive Methodist minister, he was educated at St. John's College, Oxford, and in 1890 elected a Fellow of Merton. In 1892 he was appointed tutor in charge of the curriculum at the newly-founded Hartley Primitive Methodist College, Manchester, where his influence was such that he raised the whole standard of the ministry of the Methodist Church. In 1904 he also became the first occupant of the Rylands Chair of Biblical Criticism and Exegesis at Manchester university. An accurate, balanced, and cautious scholar, he possessed a vast knowledge of current Biblical literature. The works by which he is best remembered are *The Bible, its Origin, its Significance, and its Abiding Worth* (1913), *The Problem of Suffering in the Old Testament* (1904), and esp. his editorship of a *Commentary on the Bible* in one volume

(1919). He also took an active part in the ecclesiastical affairs of the Free Churches and the reunion movement among Methodist bodies and beyond. He was never ordained.

Supplement to Peake's Commentary, ed. A. J. Grieve (London, 1936). A Collection of his minor works, mainly obituary notices of other scholars, ed. W. F. Howard, under the title *Recollections and Appreciations* (ib., 1938). Memoir of Peake by his eldest son, Leslie S. Peake (ib., 1930). C. H. *Dodd in *D.N.B.*, *1922–1930* p. 657 f. New ed. of *Peake's Commentary* ed. M. Black and H. H. Rowley (London, 1962).

PEARSON, JOHN (1613–86), Bp. of *Chester. He was educated at Eton and Queens' College, Cambridge, and ordained in 1639. During the Civil War he supported the Royalist cause, under the Commonwealth lived in semi-retirement in London, and after the Restoration became Master successively of Jesus College (1660) and of Trinity College (1662), Cambridge, and also (from 1661) Lady Margaret professor of divinity. At the *Savoy Conference in 1661 he championed the cause of episcopacy. In 1673 he became Bp. of Chester. He was perhaps the most erudite and profound divine of a learned and theo-logical age. His classical *Exposition of the Creed* (1659), in origin a series of lectures extending over several years at St. Clement's, Eastcheap, reveals his firm grasp of funda-mental principles, his delight in clear and accurate statement, and his judicious and sober temper, while the notes which illustrate the text reflect his remarkable knowledge, esp. of the Christian Fathers. Addressed to a more scholarly public is his *Vindiciae Epistolarum S. Ignatii* (1672), an elaborate defence of the authenticity of the Epp. of St. *Ignatius against the attacks of J. *Daillé, of which the con-clusions have only been strengthened by the intensive work of such later scholars as W. *Cureton, J. B. *Lightfoot, and T. *Zahn. Pearson also wrote a great number of minor works, largely concerned to uphold the position of the C of E against Rome and Nonconformity.

Life by E. Churton, prefixed to Pearson's *Minor Theo-logical Works* (2 vols., Oxford, 1844), i, pp. xiii–cxxxvi. S. Cheetham, 'John Pearson' in A. Barry (ed.), *Masters in English Theology* (1877), pp. 213–40. F. Sanders in *D.N.B.*, xliv (1895), pp. 168–73.

PEARSON, JOHN LOUGHBOROUGH (1817–97), architect. His work, which was mainly geometrical-gothic and ecclesiastical, was characterized by accurate scholarship, refined detail, elegant proportion, and noble vaulting. The best known example is *Truro Cathedral (1880). Among his other notable churches are St. Peter's, Vauxhall (1864), St. Augustine's, Kilburn (1870), St. John's, Red Lion Square (1874), and St. Stephen's, Bournemouth (1889). He was also a careful and conservative restorer of many ancient churches, and practically rebuilt the front of the north transept of *Westminster Abbey.

J. E. Newberry, 'The Work of John L. Pearson, R.A.', in *The Architectural Review*, i (1897), pp. 1–11, 69–82. Memoir of 'The Late John Loughborough Pearson, R.A.', in *Journal of the Royal Institute of British Architects*, Ser. 3, v (1898), pp. 113–21. P. Waterhouse in *D.N.B.*, Suppl. iii (1901), pp. 255–8.

PEASANTS' REVOLT, The. The insurrection of the German peasants in 1524–6. It arose from the economic distress of a large part of the German peasantry which had produced such movements as the *Bundschuh* (from 1493) on the Upper Rhine and the *Armer Konrad* in Württemberg. They were stimulated by the doctrines of certain of the Reformers, esp. T. *Münzer, which incited the peasants to seek greater freedom by violent means, and supported also by townspeople and a number of knights and apostate priests dissatisfied with the existing order of things. They set out their grievances in the *Twelve Articles drawn up at Memmingen (Mar. 1525), demanding *inter alia* the abolition of certain taxes and of serfdom, and the freedom of election of their pastors. To these religious privileges were soon added, and before long mob violence began to rage. Devoid of proper leadership, the peasants burned down castles and monasteries and proposed to destroy all authority. M. *Luther, who at first had attempted to mediate between landlords and peasants, was soon disgusted with the brutality of the rebels, and in 1525 issued his famous pamphlet *Wider die mördischen und räubischen Rotten der Bauern*. His advocacy of their merciless extermination cost him much of his popularity. The movement was ruthlessly stamped out by the armies of the *Schwäbischer Bund*, the union of Protestant princes, in the same year. The last remnants fled into the mountains of Salzburg and the Tyrol, where they survived for another year. The war resulted in a further deterioration of the lot of the peasants and in a consolidation of the power of the Lutheran princes.

O. H. Brandt (ed.), *Der grosse Bauernkrieg*. Zeitgenössische Berichte, Aussagen und Aktenstücke (1925). A. F. Pollard in *C.M.H.*, ii (1903), ch. vi: 'Social Revolution and Catholic Reaction in Germany', esp. pp. 174–97; bibl. pp. 752–4. Further bibl. in Schottenloher, iv (1938), pp. 52–80 (Nos. 34765–35241). Brief art., with bibl., by F. Zoepfl in *L.Th.K.*, ii (1931), col. 41 f. Cf. also W. Stolze in *R.G.G.* (ed. 2), i (1927), cols. 805–10, s.v. 'Bauernkrieg'.

PECKHAM, JOHN (c. 1225–92), also Pecham, Abp. of *Canterbury. He was born at Patcham (formerly Pecham), Sussex, and probably educated by the monks of Lewes. After joining the *Franciscans c. 1250 he studied at Oxford and Paris, where he was a pupil of St. *Bonaventure. He returned to Oxford c. 1272 where he was the first to dispute 'de Quodlibetis'. He proceeded to Rome in 1276 and became *lector sacri palatii*. In 1279 he succeeded Robert *Kilwardby (O.P.) as Abp. of Canterbury, being the Papal candidate in opposition to Robert Burnell, Bp. of Bath and Wells, who was the nominee of Edward I. He was henceforward a strenuous defender of the Papal claims and promptly inaugurated a vigorous policy of ecclesiastical reform. At a provincial Council at Reading on 31 July 1279, he legislated against pluralities and other abuses. At another Council at Lambeth (1281) he sought to suppress abuses concerning the Eucharist. He also concerned himself with raising the standard of the clergy; took active steps to encourage preaching; and reformed

the financial administration of many religious houses. His reforms brought him into conflict both with the King and many of the clergy, e.g. St. *Thomas of Hereford.

In theology Peckham was a strong upholder of the Franciscan tradition. He wrote several works on scientific subjects, among them 'Perspectiva Communis', 'De Sphaera', and 'Theorica Planetarum'; also 'Questiones Disputatae et Quodlibeta' and a commentary on Bk. I of the Sentences. He was opposed to the Thomistic doctrine of the soul. In his theory of knowledge he followed *Matthew of Aquasparta and Bonaventure in teaching that certainty was attainable through direct contact with the Divine uncreated Light. He also wrote some hymns and an Office for Trinity Sunday.

Registrum Epistolarum Fratris Johannis Peckham, ed. C. T. Martin (3 vols., R.S., 1882–5); a more complete ed. of his Register in The *Canterbury and York Society*, parts xiv and xvii (to 1287; 1908, 1910 ff.) For edd. of Works see A. Teetaert, Ord. Cap., in *D.T.C.*, xii (pt. 1; 1933), cols. 100–140, s.v. 'Pecham', with bibl., esp. cols. 107–25, and D. L. Douie, *Archbishop Pecham* (1952), with full reff. P. Glorieux, *Répertoire des maîtres en théologie de Paris au XIIIᵉ siècle*, ii (Études de Philosophie médiévale, xviii; 1934), pp. 87–98; V. Doucet, O.F.M., 'Supplément au "Répertoire des maîtres en théologie de Paris au XIII siècle"' in *A.F.H.*, xxvii (1934), No. 316, p. 548 f. H. Spettmann, O.F.M., 'Quellenkritisches zur Biographie des Johannes Pecham O.F.M. (†1292)' in *Franziskanische Studien*, ii (1915), pp. 170–207; 266–85; M. D. Knowles, O.S.B., 'Some Aspects of the Career of Archbishop Pecham' in *E.H.R.*, lvii (1942), pp. 1–18; 178–201. D. L. Douie, 'Archbishop Pecham's Sermons and Collations' in R. W. Hunt-W. A. Pantin-R. W. Southern (edd.), *Studies in Medieval History Presented to Frederick Maurice Powicke* (1948), pp. 269–82. C. L. Kingsford in *D.N.B.*, xliv (1895), pp. 190–7.

PECOCK, REGINALD (c. 1393–1461), Bp. of *Chichester. A Welshman by birth, he was educated at Oriel College, Oxford, of which he became a Fellow. In 1431 he was appointed master of Whittington College, London, and subsequently, through court influence, Bp. of *St. Asaph in 1444 and of Chichester in 1450. His antagonism to the Yorkist party and his theological writings having made him unpopular, he was accused of heresy in 1457, and although he recanted, he was deprived of his bishopric and confined in Thorney Abbey where he died probably in 1461.

Pecock's thought, which is embodied in his best-known work *The Repressor of Overmuch Wijting* [i.e. *Blaming*] *of the Clergy*, written to controvert the *Lollards, is notable for its very marked emphasis on the 'law of kind', 'written in mennis soulis with the finger of God', to which the Scriptures are merely subordinate and supplementary. Much of his work is an apologia for the Church against the Lollards, of whose doctrines he gives a penetrating analysis. Although his writings were medieval in form, Pecock's critical faculty and his use of the English language make him one of the most significant figures of the 15th cent.

There are modern edd. of 'The Repressor' by C. Babington (2 vols., R.S., 1860), his 'Book of Faith' by J. L. Morison (Glasgow, 1909), 'The Donet' by E. V. Hitchcock (E.E.T.S., clvi, 1921), 'The Follower to the Donet' by id. (ib., clxiv, 1924), and of 'The Rule of Christian Religion' by W. C.

Greet (ib., clxxi, 1927). Life by J. Lewis (London, 1744). V. H. H. Green, *Bishop Reginald Pecock*. A Study in Ecclesiastical History and Thought (Thirlwall Prize, 1941; 1945), incl. bibl. A. M. Cooke in *D.N.B.*, xliv (1895), pp. 198–202.

PECTORAL CROSS. A cross of precious metal worn on the breast and suspended by a chain which goes round the neck. In the C of E its use is almost exclusively confined to bishops; but in the RC Church cardinals and abbots as well as certain other privileged persons also wear it, the last-named only during public worship.

PECULIAR PEOPLE, The, also 'Plumstead Peculiars'. A small sect of faith-healers, founded in London in 1838. On the basis of Jas. 5. 14 they reject medical aid, and in cases of illness rely on anointing with oil and prayer. They are mostly humble folk, held in high respect by their neighbours.

PEDILAVIUM (Lat., 'washing of the feet'). The ceremony of the washing of the feet traditionally performed on *Maundy Thursday (q.v.) in cathedral and abbey churches. It is attested by the 17th Synod of Toledo in 694 and, for Rome, in the 10th of the '*Ordines Romani'. The ceremony begins with the recital of the Gospel narrative (Jn. 13) by the deacon, after which the superior washes, dries, and kisses the right foot of the persons chosen for the Pedilavium, while several antiphons are chanted. The rite concludes with the recital of a number of versicles and a prayer.

D. Stiefenhofer, 'Die liturgische Fusswaschung am Gründonnerstag' in *Festgabe Alois Knöpfler* (1917), pp. 325–339. A. Malvy, S.J., in *D.T.C.*, ix (pt. 1; 1926), cols. 16–36, s.v. 'Lavement des pieds'; H. *Leclercq, O.S.B., in *D.A.C.L.*, viii (pt. 2; 1929), cols. 2002–9, s.v. 'Lavement (Lavage liturgique de la tête, des mains, des pieds)'.

PEDROG, St. See *Petrock, St.*

PEEL PARISH. In the C of E, a district taken out of another parish and not containing any existing church. If needful it may be constituted a separate parish with the consent of the Bishop by a scheme drawn up by the *Ecclesiastical (now *Church) Commissioners. The patronage is in the Crown and the Bishop alternately. Such parishes were first set up by Act of Parliament (6 & 7 Vict., cap. 37) in 1843, when Sir Robert Peel was Prime Minister.

PÉGUY, CHARLES PIERRE (1873–1914), French writer. He came of a peasant and artisan family of Orléans, and was educated at Paris at the École Normale Supérieure and the *Sorbonne; but he gave up his studies to manage a bookshop in the rue de la Sorbonne, which became a centre of intellectual activity. At first an ardent socialist and Dreyfusard, he later became a mystical nationalist with a strong sympathy for medieval Catholicism. His philosophy was much influenced by H. *Bergson. His attachment to France found early expression in the drama, *Jeanne d'Arc* (1897), publd. in collaboration with Marcel Baudouin under the pseudonym 'Pierre Baudouin'. As an anti-clerical he remained estranged from his Catholic contemporaries and, though his Medievalism and Incarnationalism led him to uphold the alliance of Christianity with socialism, he was distrusted by republicans and socialists alike because of his pessimism on the future of the secular order. In the *Cahiers de la Quinzaine* (founded by Péguy, 1900) he endeavoured to vindicate his position as an ardent Catholic and a socialist, himself contributing to it *Notre Patrie* (1905), *De la situation faite au parti intellectuel dans le monde moderne* (1906), *Le Mystère de la charité de Jeanne d'Arc* (1910), *Victor-Marie, Comte Hugo* (1911), *Le Mystère des Saints Innocents* (1912), *L'Argent* (1913), and other items. He had a strong faith in the Eucharist which domestic circumstances made it impossible for him to receive. Despite his strange style, in which logic and syntax are alike wanting, and the remoteness of some of his preoccupations, he exercised a deep influence on later French Catholic writers, esp. in regard to politics. He lost his life in the Battle of the Marne on 5 Sept. 1914.

Eng. tr. of selections from Péguy's works by A. and J. Green, *Charles Péguy*: Basic Verities (1943), and *Charles Péguy*: Men and Saints (1947). J. and J. Tharaud, *Notre Cher Péguy* (2 vols., 1926); D. Halévy, *Péguy et les Cahiers de la Quinzaine* (1941; Eng. tr., 1946); R. Rolland, *Péguy* (2 vols., 1944); J. Delaporte, *Connaissance de Péguy* (2 vols., c. 1944). Yvonne Servais, *Charles Péguy*. The Pursuit of Salvation (1953); A. Dru, *Péguy* (London, 1956).

PELAGIA, St. (d. *c.* 311), virgin and martyr. Her name occurs in the canon of the *Ambrosian Mass of Milan, and her fate is known from mentions of her in St. *Ambrose (*PL*, xvi, 229–32 and 1093) and in St. *Chrysostom (*PG*, l, 579–85). She was a 15-year-old girl of *Antioch who, when during one of the persecutions (probably that under *Diocletian) her house was surrounded by soldiers, threw herself out of a window into the sea to preserve her chastity. Feast day, 9 June.

To the name of this historical person a legend became attached of a 4th cent. actress of Antioch who was suddenly converted by St. Nonnus, Bp. of *Edessa, and went to *Jerusalem in men's clothes, where she lived as a recluse in a grotto of the Mt. of *Olives practising severe penances. Feast day, 8 Oct.

The story of a third Pelagia, a virgin martyr of *Tarsus, seems to be a combination of the former two. This Pelagia is supposed to have been burned to death for refusing to become the mistress of the Emperor. Her feast is also on 8 Oct. in E. calendars, in the Roman martyrology on 4 May. H. Usener's attempt to explain the cultus of Pelagia as a Christian adaptation of the myth of Astarte has been severely handled by H. *Delehaye.

The legend of St. Pelagia appears to have close connexions with that of St. *Margaret (q.v.).

For the legends, besides the items cited in the text, see *B.H.G.* (ed. 2, 1909), Nos. 1478–80, and *B.H.L*, Nos. 6605–

6611. H. Usener, *Legenden der hl. Pelagia* (1879); H. *Delehaye, S.J., *Les Légendes hagiographiques* (1905), pp. 222–34. J. P. Kirsch in *C.E.*, xi (1911), p. 601 f.; A. Zimmermann, O.S.B., in *L.Th.K.*, viii (1936), col. 62 f.

PELAGIANISM. The theological system which held that a man took the initial and fundamental steps towards salvation by his own efforts apart from the assistance of Divine *Grace.

The teaching owes its formulation to Pelagius, a British (or, acc. to some writers, Irish) lay monk who came to *Rome in the time of Pope Anastasius (399–401), where he acquired a reputation for learning and devotion and engaged in various literary works, incl. a Commentary on St. *Paul's Epp. Having heard a bishop cite the words in St. *Augustine's *Confessions* (x, 40) in relation to the gift of continence: 'Grant what Thou commandest and command what Thou wilt' (*Da quod iubes et iube quod vis*), Pelagius attacked them on the ground that they imperilled the whole moral law. If a man were not himself responsible for his good and evil deeds, there was nothing to restrain him from indulgence in sin. Pelagius soon gained a considerable following at Rome, among his warm supporters being *Celestius (q.v.).

After the fall of Rome to Alaric (410) both Pelagius and Celestius made their way to Africa. Here St. Augustine, after some preliminary hesitation, soon became one of Pelagius's strongest critics, and vigorously attacked Pelagian doctrines in 'De Peccatorum Meritis' and 'De Spiritu et Littera' (both 412). Meanwhile Pelagius made his way to Palestine, where, though accused of heresy at the Synods of *Jerusalem and Diospolis (Lydda), both held in 415, he succeeded in clearing himself and avoiding censure. In the same year St. Augustine directed a further work against Pelagius's doctrines, viz. his 'De Natura et Gratia', while St. *Jerome published his three 'Dialogi adversus Pelagianos'. Pelagius's issue of his treatise 'De Libero Arbitrio' led to a condemnation of his teaching by two African Councils at Carthage and Mileve in 416. In 417 Pope *Innocent I (401–17) endorsed the condemnations and declared Pelagius and Celestius excommunicated; and in the same year St. Augustine wrote an account of the heresy and of the Synod of Diospolis in his 'De Gestis Pelagii'. Under Innocent's successor, *Zosimus (417–19), Pelagius's case was taken up again at Rome. At first Zosimus, on the basis of a 'Libellus Fidei' in which Pelagius epitomized his creed, pronounced him innocent, but, after a renewed investigation and another Council at Carthage (418), which issued a set of nine canons on the subject which later became famous, the Pope retracted his earlier decision and confirmed the verdict of his predecessor in his 'Epistola Tractoria' (418). After this date there is no more direct information about Pelagius, but he is believed to have died in Palestine.

The rejection of Pelagianism was accepted by the whole Church, excepting a small circle that gathered round *Julian of Eclanum, who conducted a violent polemic against St. Augustine, accusing him of *Manichaeism. St. Augustine's 'Contra Duas Epistolas Pelagianorum' (420) and 'Contra Julianum' (421) are replies to these accusations. In 429 *Nestorius intervened with the Pope in favour of Julian and his friends; but *Marius Mercator wrote against them his 'Commonitorium super Nomine Caelestii' (429), which led to their banishment, in 430, by Emp. *Theodosius II. The heresy was again condemned at the Council of *Ephesus (431). It continued in the W., esp. in Gaul and Britain, where its chief representatives were Agricola and *Fastidius, and among its principal opponents St. *Germanus of Auxerre and St. *Lupus of Troyes. It was once more condemned by the Second Council of *Orange (529), and finally disappeared in the second half of the 6th cent.

The chief heresies with which the Pelagians were charged were (acc. to a list of theses against Celestius drawn up by Paulinus of Milan in 411–12): (1) that Adam would have died, even if he had not sinned; (2) that the sin of Adam injured himself alone and not the whole human race; (3) that new-born children are in the same condition as Adam was before he fell; (4) that the whole human race does not die because of Adam's death or sin, nor will it rise again because of Christ's resurrection; (5) that the law as well as the Gospel offers entrance to heaven; (6) that even before the Coming of Christ there were men wholly without sin.

See also *Semi-Pelagianism.*

Owing to Pelagius's condemnation his extensive writings have been largely lost or transmitted under other names. The most considerable surviving work is his 'Commentary on St. Paul's Epp.' (on all thirteen, but not Heb.; written in Rome before 410), which has come down in a worked-over form ascribed to Jerome (*PL*, xxx, 645–902) and to *Primasius of Hadrumetum (ib., lxviii, 413–686). The orig. text, which survives in a 9th cent. *Reichenau MS. (now at Karlsruhe), and two other MSS (Coll. Boll. Ox. 157 and Coll. Mert. Ox. 26), was discovered by A. *Souter; and ed. by him with introd. (Texts and Studies, ix, 1–3; Cambridge, 1922–1931). Other works which are certainly the work of Pelagius are his 'Ep. ad Demetriadem', addressed to a Roman lady of high standing who became a nun (wrongly incl. among the works of Augustine and Jerome, *PL*, xxx, 15–45, and xxxiii, 1099–1120), and the short 'Libellus Fidei ad Innocentium Papam' (ib., xlviii, 488–91). G. de Plinval has defended as indisputably the work of Pelagius a small collection of Epp. and other writings brought together in C. P. *Caspari, *Briefe, Abhandlungen und Predigten* (Christiania, 1890), pp. 3–167 (with comm. pp. 223–389 and hence known as the 'Corpus Casparianum'), as well as a number of other lesser writings. For further details see Altaner, cited below.

The classical account of the subject is H. *Noris, *Historia Pelagiana* (Padua, 1673; with strong *Jansenist leanings). Modern studies include A. Souter, *The Earliest Latin Commentaries on the Epistles of St. Paul* (1927), pp. 205–30; G. de Plinval, 'Recherches sur l'œuvre littéraire de Pélage, in *Revue de Philologie, de Littérature et d'Histoire anciennes*-Sér. 3, viii (1934), pp. 9–42; id., *Pélage*. Ses écrits, sa vie et sa réforme (Lausanne, 1943); id., *Essai sur le style et la langue de Pélage, suivi du traité inédit* De Induratione Cordis Pharaonis (Collectanea Friburgensia, Nouvelle Série, xxxi; 1947). H. Zimmer, *Pelagius in Irland*. Texte und Untersuchungen zur patristischen Litteratur (1901). Useful collection of texts in A. Bruckner, *Quellen zur Geschichte des pelagianischen Streites* (Sammlung ausgewählter kirchen-und dogmengeschichtlicher Quellenschriften, Reihe 2, vii; 1906). Bardenhewer, iv, 513–15; Altaner (ed. 1951), pp. 327–9. F. *Loofs in *P.R.E.* (ed. 3), xv (1904), pp. 747–74, s.v. 'Pelagius und der pelagianische Streit' [at end of the volume]; R. Hedde, O.P.–E. Amann in *D.T.C.*, xii (pt. 1; 1933), cols. 675–715. J. Ferguson, *Pelagius* (Cambridge, 1956).

PELICAN. The image of the Pelican, 'vulning herself' with her beak to feed her young with her blood, has been widely used in Christian symbolism to typify the Lord's redeeming work, esp. as mediated through the Blessed Sacrament. Well-known instances are the first line of the 6th stanza of '*Adoro te devote', and the figure of the Pelican on the column in the quadrangle of Corpus Christi College, Oxford. At *Durham the Blessed Sacrament used to be reserved in a silver Pelican suspended over the high altar.

W. Lampen, O.F.M., ' "Pie Pelicane, Jesu Domine" ' in *Antonianum*, xxi (1946), pp. 68–92. A. P. Frutaz in *E.C.*, ix (1952), col. 1088 f., s.v. 'Pellicano'. See also works cited under *Iconography*.

PENANCE. Of the earliest history of the Sacrament of Penance very little is known. By the 3rd cent. there had emerged a developed system of public Penance which was regarded as a 'second Baptism'. After the sinner, voluntarily or under threat of excommunication, had asked the Bishop for Penance, he was enrolled in the order of *penitents, excluded from Communion, and committed to a severe course of prayer, fasting, and almsgiving. At the end of a period whose length was determined by the gravity of the sin, the sinner was reconciled and rejoined the congregation of the faithful. Certain inhibitions, however, attached to him for life, e.g. he must not be a soldier and he might not marry. The outstanding characteristics of this system were (1) the enrolment into the distinct order of penitents, (2) it could be undergone only once in a lifetime, and (3) the enforcement of lifelong continence. Because of these characteristics the system broke down. Except for persons of great devotion and almost monastic vocation, Penance was nearly always postponed to the eve of death.

In consequence, a new system was developed through the influence of *Celtic or *Anglo-Saxon monk-missionaries, which was administered by means of the *Penitential Books (q.v.). This differed from the earlier system in the absence of the three features mentioned above; but the Penance remained public, long, and arduous, even in the new. Confession of the details of sin, which had probably never been public in the old system, was secret. Absolution, at any rate at the start of the new system, was withheld until completion of the Penance. Gradually it was pushed back until it was granted on confession and before the Penance was begun. From this developed the 'private Penance' of to-day, with its confession, absolution, and light formal penance. The private Penance received its charter at the Fourth *Lateran Council (1215), which required every Christian to confess his sins in Penance at least once a year.

Penance means 'poena', i.e. punishment. It was apparently the doctrine of the early Church that sins must be atoned for in part by the punishment of the sinner, on the ground that it was better to endure the punishment in this world than in the next. Though the essential part played in the redemption of sin by Christ's *Atonement on the Cross was never overlooked, yet great weight was always attached to the amends offered by the penitent and the use of the word '*satisfaction' for the Penance as well as its relative severity reflected this belief. But from the first another idea was also present, viz. that the practice of asceticism controlled and eradicated the passions which led to the sin, and by enforcing a semi-retirement from the world shielded the sinner from further temptations. Hence the Penance is often called a 'heavenly medicine', which heals the wounds inflicted by sin. These ideas are carried over into the Celtic system, together with the more secular purpose of enforcing obedience to the law and exercising over barbarians a moderating and civilizing influence. The Penance consisted generally of fasts (of greater or less severity), continence, pilgrimages, floggings, and imprisonment. Owing to the grave inconvenience and interruption to ordinary life occasioned by long and arduous Penances, the system of commutation grew up. A Penance of years or a lengthy pilgrimage could be compressed into a single day by the payment of money or its place taken by the repeated repetition of the Psalter in a position of physical discomfort. From this idea of commutation probably developed the later practice of *indulgences. This practice also owes much to the greater doctrinal precision of the *Schoolmen, who distinguished between 'culpa' and 'poena', and between 'poena damnationis' and 'poena temporalis', the last alone being the object of Penance. 'Culpa' and 'poena damnationis' were held to be removed by contrition and absolution, whereas 'poena temporalis' required the Penance of the sinner or its equivalent drawn from the treasury of *Merit.

Useful historical account in O. D. Watkins, *A History of Penance* (2 vols., 1920). The many RC dogmatic treatises include D. Palmieri, S.J., *Tractatus de Poenitentia* (Rome, 1879), and P. Galtier, S.J., *De Poenitentia* (Paris, 1923; ed. 2, Rome, 1950). J. Morinus [*Morin], *Commentarius Historicus de Disciplina in Administratione Sacramenti Poenitentiae* (Paris, fol. 1651). Modern studies on the early history of penance include P. *Batiffol, 'Les Origines de la pénitence' in *Études d'Histoire et de Théologie positive*, i (1902), pp. 43–222. G. Rauschen, *Eucharistie und Bussakrament in den ersten sechs Jahrhunderten der Kirche* (1908), pp. 105–200. B. Poschmann, *Die abendländische Kirchenbusse im Ausgang des christlichen Altertums* (Münchener Studien zur historischen Theologie, vii; 1928); id., *Die abendländische Kirchenbusse im frühen Mittelalter* (Breslauer Studien zur historischen Theologie, xvi; 1930); id., *Paenitentia Secunda*. Die kirchliche Busse im ältesten Christentum bis Cyprian und Origenes (Theophaneia, i; 1940). P. Galtier, S.J., *L'Église et la rémission des péchés aux premiers siècles* (1932); id., *Aux origines du sacrament de pénitence* (Analecta Gregoriana, liv; 1951), and other works by this author; R. C. Mortimer, *The Origins of Private Penance in the Western Church* (1939). E. J. Hanna in *C.E.*, xi (1911), pp. 618–35; E. L. van Becelaere–O. D. Watkins in *H.E.R.E.*, ix (1917), pp. 711–720, s.v.; É. Amann–A. Michel–M. Jugie, A.A., in *D.T.C.*, xii (pt. 1; 1933), cols. 722–1138, s.v. 'Pénitence'; A. Landgraf in *L.Th.K.*, ii (1931), cols. 661–4, s.v. 'Busse I–IV'; A. Mayer, O.S.B.–A. Gennaro, O.S.B.–A. Raes, S.J.–M. Federici in *E.C.*, ix (1952), cols. 1104–33, s.v. 'Penitenza'.

PENINGTON, ISAAC, the 'Younger' (1616–79), also spelled Pennington, *Puritan and *Quaker. He was the eldest son of Sir Isaac Penington (c. 1590–1661), Lord Mayor of London (1642–4), and educated at Catharine Hall, Cambridge. After years of religious perplexity, during which he attached himself for a time to the *Independents, he heard George *Fox speak near Luton in 1657 and, together with his wife, joined the Quaker body. His conversion was an important accession of strength to the Quakers, who hitherto had had no one of his station in their ranks. From 1658 Quaker worship took place at 'The Grange', his house at Chalfont St. Peter. After 1660 he was imprisoned several times; his house and other property confiscated; and his health progressively undermined by the severity of prison life. At Jordans, Chalfont St. Giles, where he was buried, a meeting house that still survives was built on his property. He wrote many books and pamphlets, all of them in a spirit quite free from controversial bitterness, which were of great assistance in the building up of the new Quaker Society.

Works (2 parts, London, 1681, 1680). J. G. Bevan, *Memoirs of the Life of Isaac Pennington*; to which is added a review of his writings (1807). M. Webb, *The Penns and Peningtons of the 17th Century* (1867). C. F. Smith in *D.N.B.*, xliv (1895), pp. 297–300.

PENITENTIAL BOOKS.

A set of books containing directions to confessors in the form of prayers, questions to be asked, and exhaustive lists of sins with the appropriate penance prescribed. Of *Celtic origin (the earliest are the two series of canons ascribed to St. *Patrick and dating from the 5th cent.), they spread with the Celtic and Anglo-Saxon missions all over Europe, the best known being that ascribed to Abp. *Theodore (668–90). They were far more flexible than the ancient penitential system which they practically superseded, and their wide use and popularity effected a degree of uniformity in discipline.

Selection of texts, with discussion, pr. by F. W. H. Wasserschleben (Halle, 1851(and H. J. Schmitz (vol. i, Mainz, 1883; vol. ii, Düsseldorf, 1898). Eng. trr. (various items) by J. T. McNeill–Helena M. Gamer (Records of Civilization, xxix; New York, 1938). F. W. H. Wasserschleben, *Beiträge zur Geschichte der vorgratianischen Kirchenrechtsquellen* (1839); E. Friedberg, *Aus deutschen Bussbüchern*. (1868). T. P. Oakley, *English Penitential Discipline and Anglo-Saxon Law in their Joint Influence* (Studies in History, Economics, and Public Law ed. by the Faculty of Political Science of Columbia University, cvii, fasc. 2; New York, 1923). E. Stolz in *L.Th.K.*, ii (1931), cols. 655–7, s.v. 'Bussbücher; G. Le Bras in *D.T.C.*, xii (pt. i; 1933), cols. 1160–79, s.v. 'Pénitentiels'; C. Vogel in *E.C.*, ix (1952), cols. 1131–3, s.v. 'Penitenziali, Libri'.

PENITENTIAL PSALMS.
See *Seven Penitential Psalms.*

PENITENTIARY.
In the RC Church a Penitentiary in general is a cleric charged with oversight of the administration of the Sacrament of *Penance in a particular area. A Canon Penitentiary is a member of a cathedral chapter specially empowered to hear confessions through the whole diocese. The 'Grand Penitentiary' is the *Cardinal who presides over a tribunal which deals with all important matters affecting the Sacrament.

PENITENTS.
In the ancient system of public *penance (q.v.), Penitents were segregated from the rest of the congregation by wearing a special robe, having close-cropped hair and worshipping apart in the Church. Here, towards the west end of the nave, placed between the *catechumens and the faithful, they received from the bishop special laying-on of hands each Sunday. In the E. Church, though not in the W., the order of Penitents may have been divided into four stages though the prevalence of this procedure has been contested by F. X. Funk and E. *Schwartz. The Penitent remained in the order till he was readmitted to Communion. Certain disabilities attached to him for life.

The disciplinary regulations controlling the exercise of Penance in the early Church will be found in the primitive collections of canons (for bibl. see *Canon Law*). E. Vacandard, *La Pénitence publique dans l'Église primitive* (2 vols., 1903). F. X. Funk, *Kirchengeschichtliche Abhandlungen und Untersuchungen*, i (1897), pp. 151–209; E. Schwartz, *Busstufen und Katechumenatsklassen* (Schriften der wissenschaftlichen Gesellschaft in Strassburg, vii; 1911). G. Mead in *D.C.A.*, ii (1880), pp. 1591–6, s.v. 'Penitence, iii: The Penitential Stations' (useful collection of material, but assumes older view).

PENN, WILLIAM (1644–1718),
*Quaker and founder of Pennsylvania. The eldest son of Admiral Sir William Penn (1621–70), who captured Jamaica from the Dutch (May 1655), he was for a time an undergraduate at Christ Church, Oxford, whence he was sent down in 1661 for refusal to conform with the restored Anglicanism. After some years of travel abroad he was admitted in 1665 a student at Lincoln's Inn. A sermon of Thomas Loe, an Oxford tradesman with whom he had been acquainted since boyhood, which he heard at Cork in 1665, had a decisive influence and henceforward he attached himself to the Quakers. He soon began writing in defence of his newly won faith and in 1668 his *The Sandy Foundation Shaken*, an attack on the orthodox doctrines of the *Trinity and *Atonement and the *Calvinistic account of *Justification, led to his imprisonment in the Tower. During his confinement he wrote *No Cross, No Crown* (1669), a recognized classic of Quaker practice. In 1670 his acquittal at the Old Bailey by the jury, who gave a verdict against the ruling of the Court and were forthwith imprisoned, led to the famous 'Bushell's Case' in which twelve judges unanimously upheld the jury's rights and declared their imprisonment illegal. During the 'seventies Penn became increasingly interested in the foundation of a colony in America which would assure liberty of conscience for Quakers and others, and eventually in 1682 he obtained by letters patent grants of East New Jersey and Pennsylvania. In the same year he founded the 'Free Society of Traders of Pennsylvania', drew up a constitution for the colony which permitted all forms of worship compatible with monotheism and religious liberty, and himself sailed for America. After establishing the colony he returned to England in 1684. Believing that *James II, with whom he had had relations from the days of his father's admiral-

ship, was a true advocate of toleration, he expressed the Quakers' thanks for the *Declaration of Indulgence (1687) in a loyal address and followed it with a pamphlet, *Good Advice to the Church of England, Roman Catholics and Protestant Dissenters*. For a short time after the Revolution he was held to bail as one of James's adherents. In 1692 he was deprived by an order in council of the Governorship of Pennsylvania and in his enforced leisure wrote *The Fruits of Solitude*. In 1693 he resumed his practice of itinerant preaching and in 1696 wrote his *Primitive Christianity*, upholding the identity of Quaker principles with those of the early Church. In 1699 he paid a second visit to Pennsylvania, intending to settle there for good, but in 1701 the proposal to introduce legislation changing the status of the province into a Crown Colony brought him back to England, where he lived successively at Kensington, Knightsbridge, Brentford, and Field Ruscombe (near Twyford). He is buried at Jordans, near Chalfont St. Giles. His prolific writings were almost all occasional.

Collected ed. of his works (2 vols., fol., London, 1726), with life, written by Joseph Besse eight years after Penn's death, pr. anon. in vol. i, pp. 1–150. Other lives by T. Clarkson (2 vols., London, 1813), S. M. Janney (Philadelphia, 1851; ed. 2, 1856; with many useful original docc.); W. Hepworth Dixon (London, 1851; popular and inaccurate in detail); J. Stoughton (ib., 1882); A. G. Buell (New York, 1904); Mrs. Coloquhoun Grant (London, c. 1907); Mabel R. Brailsford (ib., 1930); B. Dobrée (ib., 1932); C. E. Vulliamy (ib., 1933); and W. I. Hull (ib., 1937). J. M. Rigg in *D.N.B.*, xliv (1895), pp. 311–20; R. W. Kelsey in *Dict. Amer. Biog.*, xiv (1934), pp. 433–7. See also bibl. to *Friends, Society of.*

PENRY, JOHN (1559–93), *Brownist. Of Welsh descent, he was educated at Peterhouse, Cambridge, and St. Alban's Hall, Oxford. After leaving Oxford, he quickly came into conflict with the bishops on account of his *Puritan ideas. His *Equity of an Humble Supplication in the behalf of the Country of Wales, that some Order may be taken for the Preaching of the Gospel among those People* (1587), an attack on the C of E, angered Abp. J. *Whitgift, who brought him before the Court of High Commission. In 1588, when the scurrilous *Marprelate tracts appeared, Penry was suspected of being their author, and in consequence of these suspicions fled to Scotland early in 1590, where he remained for nearly three years. On his return to England in the autumn of 1592 he became an adherent of the Separatist Church of R. *Browne. Now considered a danger to the Church, he was hanged on 29 May 1593, on an ill-grounded charge of treason.

An Account of Penry's Trial, in Lat. (but with extracts from his works in English), together with a collection of citations apparently collected for his trial and which Penry intended to present to Queen *Elizabeth I, the original MS. of his defence against his first indictment and some of his final remarks to Lord Burghley on the day of his execution, were ed., with introd., by C. Burrage (Oxford, 1913). The Note-Book containing the passages mainly responsible for his condemnation, ed. A. Peel (Camden Society, 3rd Series, lxvii; 1944). Lives by J. Waddington (London, 1854), H. M. White (ib. [1899]; popular), and W. Pierce (ib., 1923, with good bibl.). S. Lee in *D.N.B.*, xliv (1895), pp. 346–50. See also bibl. to *Marprelate Tracts.*

PENTATEUCH. A title in general use among Biblical scholars for the five 'Books of *Moses', *Genesis, *Exodus, *Leviticus, *Numbers, and *Deuteronomy. Most Biblical critics hold that these books are made up of various written documents dating from the 9th to the 4th cent. B.C. See also entries '*J', '*E', '*P', and '*D', and *Holiness, Code of.*

PENTECOST (Gk. πεντηκοστή, the 'fiftieth day'). The name was first given to the Jewish Feast of Weeks, which fell on the 50th day after the *Passover, when the first-fruits of the corn harvest were presented (Deut. 16. 9) and, in most later times, the giving of the Law of Moses was commemorated. As the Holy Ghost descended on the Apostles on this, the 50th day after the Resurrection (Acts 2. 1), the name was applied by the Church to the feast celebrating this event, popularly called *Whitsunday (q.v.). In early times, e.g. in the *Nicene canons (can. 20), the word 'Pentecost' was also used for the whole period between Easter and Whitsunday, i.e. the Paschal time, during which no fast was allowed, prayer was only made standing, and the *Alleluia was sung more frequently. For further liturgical details see *Whitsunday*.

On the Hebrew feast, see e.g. G. T. Purves in *H.D.B.*, iii (1900), pp. 739–42, s.v. For the Christian feast see bibl. to *Whitsunday.*

PENTECOSTAL CHURCHES. The Pentecostal Movement began in the first years of the 20th cent. among believers who sought a baptism in the Holy Spirit accompanied by speaking with tongues similar to instances recorded in Acts. Manifestations of this nature, occurring in some special meetings in Los Angeles in Apr. 1906, were the first to attract world-wide attention. The Movement spread rapidly.

In Britain it can be dated from Sept. 1907, when T. B. Barratt, a Methodist minister in Oslo, who had made contact with the Pentecostal Movement in New York, was invited by A. A. Boddy of All Saints' Parish Church, Sunderland, to conduct some special revival meetings. As a result, small Pentecostal Meetings sprang up all over the British Isles emphasizing charismatic Christianity, and mostly led by laymen.

The Pentecostal Movement received its greatest impetus in the British Isles between 1925 and 1935 under the fervent preaching of the Welsh evangelists, Stephen and George Jeffreys, and Edward Jeffreys, a nephew. Divine Healing had always played a part in the little Pentecostal Assemblies, but great 'Evangelistic and Divine Healing' campaigns caught the public imagination and filled on occasion the largest halls in the land.

At first the groups of Pentecostal believers were reluctant to organize; but in 1915 the 'Elim Foursquare Gospel Alliance' came into being under George Jeffreys in Monaghan, Ireland. In 1924 the 'Assemblies of God in Great Britain and Ireland' was constituted by about 70 independent assemblies agreeing to form a recognized Fellowship. This is the largest Pentecostal denomination in Britain. The chief difference between these two main streams of the British Movement is that while 'Assemblies of God' maintain congregational government, 'Elim' is more centralized. There are also some other smaller Groups. Altogether there were in 1955 about 1000 Pentecostal churches in the British Isles with a probable membership of something over 50,000.

The Movement has attained its greatest dimensions in North America, Scandinavia, and Brazil, where there are some local churches with up to 6000 members, and an aggregate membership totalling around 2 millions. The largest Group is known as 'Assemblies of God, U.S.A.'

D. Gee, *The Pentecostal Movement. A Short History and an Interpretation for British Readers* (1941; enlarged ed., 1949).

PENTECOSTARION (Gk. πεντηκοστάριον). In the E. Church, the liturgical book which contains the variable prayers and lections for the season between *Easter and the Sunday after *Pentecost inclusive.

PEPIN III (714–68), 'Pepin the Short', Frankish king. The son of *Charles Martel, he was educated by the monks of *St.-Denis, near *Paris, and with his brother, Carloman, succeeded to his father's office of Mayor of the Palace of the Frankish Kingdom in 741. In 747 Carloman retired into a monastery, leaving Pepin sole ruler. With the assent of Pope *Zacharias he was elected king by the nobles in 751 in place of the purely nominal Merovingian, Childeric III, and anointed by St. *Boniface. In 754 the ceremony was repeated by the Pope himself, *Stephen (II) III, from whom he received the title 'patricius' in exchange for his promise to win back for him the exarchate of *Ravenna and the rights and territories of the Roman republic. Having defeated the Lombards under Aistulf in the same year and again in 756, Pepin fulfilled his promise by giving to the Pope the territories drawn up in the no-longer-extant document called the 'Donation of Pepin'. He thus laid the foundation of the States of the Church and constituted himself and his successors protectors of the Holy See. Throughout his reign he took an active part in the ecclesiastical reforms inaugurated by St. Boniface and thereby considerably increased the prestige of the Church among his people. He died at St. Denis on 24 Sept. 768 and was succeeded by his son *Charlemagne.

A. Dopsch–J. Lechner–M. Tang–E. Mühlbacher (edd.), *Die Urkunden Pippins, Karlmanns und Karls des Grossen* (M.G.H. Diplomata Karolinorum, i; 1906), pp. 1–60. G. Paris, 'La Légende de Pépin "le Bref" ' in *Mélanges Julien Havet* (1895), pp. 603–32. M. Tang, 'Die Epoche Pippins' in *N.A.*, xxxix (1914), pp. 259–77, with reff. to earlier works. E. Caspar, *Pippin und die römische Kirche* (1914); C. Rodenburg, *Pippin, Karlmann und Papst Stephan II* (Historische Studien, clii; 1923). L. Levillain, 'L'Avènement de la dynastie carolingienne et les origines de l'État pontifical (749–757)' in *Bibliothèque de l'École des Chartes*, xciv (1933),

pp. 225–95. E. Perels, 'Pippins Erhebung zum König' in *Z.K.G.*, liii (1934), pp. 400–11. O. Bertolini, 'Il problema delle origini del potere temporale dei papi nei suoi presupposti teoreti ciniziali: il concetto di "Restitutio" nelle prime cessioni territoriali (756–757) alla chiesa di Roma' in *Miscellanea Pio Paschini*, i (Lateranum, N.S., xiv; 1948), pp. 103–71.

PERCEVAL, ARTHUR PHILIP (1799–1853), *Tractarian theologian. He was educated at Oriel College, and from 1821 to 1825 held a fellowship at All Souls, Oxford. In 1824 he became rector of East Horsley in Surrey; from 1826 until deprived in 1850 he was a royal chaplain. In the early stages of the *Oxford Movement he was one of its chief supporters, being present at the celebrated conference at Hadleigh in July 1833. In his *Churchman's Manual*, a set of questions and answers conceived as a supplement to the *Catechism in the BCP and issued shortly after the Conference, he stressed the *Apostolic Succession and thus produced a useful complement to No. 1 of the *Tracts for the Times*. In 1842 he published *A Collection of Papers Connected with the Theological Movement of 1833*, largely in defence of J. H. *Newman's 'Tract No. 90'. He had himself been the author of Tracts Nos. 23, 35, and 36. Queen Victoria deprived him of his chaplaincy because of his opposition to the *Gorham Judgement (1850).

A. F. Pollard in *D.N.B.*, xliv (1895), p. 368.

PERCIVAL, JOHN (1834–1918), Bp. of *Hereford. Elected Fellow of Queen's College, Oxford, in 1858, he became successively first head master of Clifton College (1862), president of Trinity College, Oxford (1878), head master of Rugby (1887), and Bp. of Hereford (1895). He was keenly interested in religious and secular education, and did much to promote the university extension movement and the higher education of women; and as head master of Clifton exercised a great spiritual influence on his school. During his latter years, he sought to further the cause of reunion between the C of E and the Nonconformist Churches, and met with the opposition both of *Convocation and of his own clergy when he invited Nonconformists to receive Communion in Hereford Cathedral.

W. *Temple, *Life of Bishop Percival* (1921). G. F. Bradby in *D.N.B., 1912–1921*, p. 432 f.

PERCY, JOHN. See *Fisher the Jesuit*.

PEREGRINATIO ETHERIAE (or Silviae). See *Etheria, Pilgrimage of*.

PERFECTION, Christian. Acc. to the classical teaching on the spiritual life, Christian perfection consists in charity, which St. Paul calls 'the bond of perfection' (Col. 3. 14). It is enjoined by our Lord on all men in the double commandment to love God and our neighbour (Mt. 22. 37–9) and in the *Sermon on the Mount ('Be ye therefore perfect as your heavenly Father is perfect'; Mt. 5. 48). Certain passages, however, seem to indicate the impossibility of perfection in this life. Thus in 1 Jn. 1. 8 the assertion that we have no sin is said to spring from self-deception, and the Ep. of St. *James (3. 2) teaches that 'in many things we all stumble'. The same apparent contradiction occurs in Phil., where St. *Paul admits on the one hand that he is not yet perfect (3. 12), and on the other numbers himself among such 'as be perfect' (3. 15). A solution of the difficulty is given by the conception of different degrees of perfection, the supreme degree, i.e. absolute perfection, belonging to God alone.

The conception of Perfection has played a prominent part in *Methodism. In his earlier years J. *Wesley assigned it an important place in his system. Acc. to Methodist spiritual writers the entrance on the way of perfection takes place some time after conversion; it is instantaneous, and those who receive the experience, known as the 'Great Salvation', are thereby convinced that all sin has been completely and permanently rooted out in them. Those that are made perfect in this way pray constantly without interruption, they feel nothing but love, and are restored to the original image of God.

St. *Thomas Aquinas, *De Perfectione Vitae Spiritualis*; F. *Suarez, *De Statu Perfectionis*; J. Wesley, *Plain Account of Christian Perfection* (1765); R. Garrigou-Lagrange, *Perfection chrétienne et contemplation* (1923); R. N. Flew, *The Idea of Perfection in Christian Theology* (1934).

PERFECTION, Counsels of. See *Counsels of Perfection*.

PERFECTIONISTS. See *Oneida Community*.

PERGAMUM. The town was situated *c.* 50 miles north of Smyrna and *c.* 15 miles from the sea, on a hill 1000 feet above the surrounding plain. In the 2nd cent. B.C. it became one of the greatest centres of art and culture in the ancient world, reaching the height of its glory in the reign of Eumenes II (197–159). This Eumenes erected the great altar of Zeus the Saviour (now in the Pergamon Museum, Berlin) with the frieze depicting the gods and goddesses of Hellas hurling back the earthborn giants, typifying the triumph of civilization over barbarism. To the same period belongs the invention of parchment ('pergamena carta') as a substitute for papyrus.

To the NT student the chief interest of Pergamum lies in its being one of the 'Seven Churches' in Rev. (2. 12–17). Here it is referred to as the place 'where Satan's throne is' and 'where Satan dwelleth' (2. 13). As Pergamum was the first city in Asia to receive permission to worship the living ruler, the allusion here is presumably to Emperorworship. This permission had been granted by Octavian (Augustus) in 29 B.C. although the temple was not erected until 19 B.C. Pergamum was also one of the chief centres of the worship of the healing god Aesculapius, and a large 'Aesculapium' was uncovered by German excavators in 1928. The modern town is known as Bergama.

Inscriptions and other antiquities in *Altertümer von Pergamon*, publd. by the Königliches Museum at Berlin (10 vols. + plates, var. dates, 1885–1937). T. Wiegand, *Bericht über die Ausgrabungen in Pergamon in 1927* (*Abh.* (Berl.), 1928, Hft. 3); id., *Zweiter Bericht über die Ausgrabungen in Pergamon, 1928–32: Das Asklepieion* (ib., 1932, Hft. 5). G. Cardinali, *Il regno di Pergamo* (Studi di Storia Antica Pubblicati da Giulio Beloch, v; 1906). E. V. Hansen, *The Attalids of Pergamon* (Cornell Studies in Classical Philology, New York, 1947), with bibl. pp. xix–xxii. W. M. *Ramsay, *Letters to the Seven Churches of Asia and their Place in the Plan of the Apocalypse* (1904), pp. 281–315. Id. in *H.D.B.*, iii (1900), pp. 749–52, s.v.; W. Zschietzschmann in *P.W.*, xix (pt. 1; 1937), cols. 1235–63 (Nachträge, s.v. 'Pergamon').

PERICOPE (Gk. περικοπή, 'section'). A passage from the Scriptures, esp. one appointed to be read in the Church services. The use of such prescribed portions of Scripture in the Eucharist appears to date from the 4th–5th cents. In earlier times, both in E. and W., the passages were selected at choice by the officiating clergy.

Περικοπή for a section of the Bible occurs as early as St. *Justin, *Dial. c. Tryph.*, lxv. 3. W. Caspari in *P.R.E.* (ed. 3), xv (1904), pp. 131–59, s.v. 'Perikopen', where the writer shows that the word was first used as a liturgical term by Protestant writers of the 16th cent.

PERICOPE ADULTERAE, i.e. Jn. 7. 53–8. 11. These verses, which narrate our Lord's compassionate dealing with the woman taken in the act of adultery, are certainly not part of the original text of St. John's Gospel. They are not found in any of the early Greek MSS., with the one exception of *Codex Bezae, and they are also wanting in many of the more important MSS. of the Syriac, Latin, and Coptic versions. Nor does any Greek commentator before *Euthymius Zigabenus (*c.* A.D. 1118) discuss the passage. On the other hand, there are no sufficient reasons for doubting the historicity of the incident the passage records. Our Lord's dealings with the woman and her accusers are wholly of a piece with other incidents in the Gospels; and the facts that it is definitely referred to in a passage in the 3rd cent. *Didascalia Apostolorum* (ii. 24; ed. R. H. *Connolly, p. 76), and was perhaps known to *Papias, point to its primitiveness. In the *Ferrar group of MSS., the passage is placed after Lk. 21. 38.

Commentary, with discussion of textual problem, in J. H. *Bernard, '*St. John*' (I.C.C., 1928), pp. 715–21.

PERIPATETIC (Gk. περιπατητής, 'one who walks about'). A philosopher of the school of *Aristotle. The name was adopted in reference to Aristotle's practice of teaching while moving about in a covered walk (περίπατος) in the Lyceum at Athens.

PERKINS, WILLIAM (1558–1602), *Puritan theologian. Educated at Christ's College, Cambridge, where he was a Fellow from 1584 to 1594, he soon became prominent in the university by his preaching, lectures, and writings as a vigorous anti-Romanist theologian and a supporter of Puritan principles. His writings, mainly occasional, were marked by candour, an honest desire to understand his opponents, and, despite his use of the traditional scholastic methods which still survived at Cambridge, an evident concern for history. They include his *Reformed Catholike* (1597) on the Roman controversy, which W. Bishop, titular Bp. of *Chalcedon (d. 1624), answered in his *Reformation of a Catholic Deformed by W. Perkins* (2 pts., 1604, 1607), and *De Praedestinationis Modo et Ordine* (1598), which evoked a reply from J. *Arminius in the same year. His works were held in high repute throughout the 17th cent. by theologians with Calvinist sympathies. They also include *An Exposition of the Lord's Prayer* (1582) and *An Exposition of the Symbol or Creed of the Apostles* (1595).

The numerous collected edd. of his works (all very incomplete) include those publd. at Cambridge, 1603; ib., 1605; 3 vols., fol., ib., 1608–9, and 3 vols. fol., London-Cambridge, 1612–13. J. B. Mullinger in *D.N.B.*, xlv (1896), pp. 6–9, with list of his works.

PERPETUA, St. (d. 7 Mar. 203), African martyr. When in 202 Septimius Severus forbade conversions to Christianity, Perpetua and other African catechumens were imprisoned and, after their baptism, condemned to execution in the arena at Carthage. The *Passion* of St. Perpetua is a contemporary account, possibly edited by *Tertullian, which records, besides the story of her martyrdom, the interesting visions of Perpetua and the priest, Saturus. The basilica of Sts. Perpetua and Felicitas was among the most important in Carthage. Feast day, now 6 Mar. (transferred to make 7 Mar. free for St. Thomas *Aquinas).

Crit. ed. of Lat. text of *Passio* by J. A. *Robinson (Texts and Studies, i, No. 2, Cambridge, 1891). Text also ed., with Eng. tr., by W. H. Shewring (London, 1931). Gk. text first ed. from a Jerusalem MS. by J. R. *Harris–S. K. Gifford, London, 1890 (Harris' defence of the priority of the Gk. text has been generally rejected by later scholars; cf. J. A. Robinson, loc. cit., pp. 2–15). Another ed. of Lat. and Gk. texts by C. I. M. I. van Beek (Florilegium Patristicum, xliii; Bonn, 1938). Eng. tr. in E. C. E. Owen, *Some Authentic Acts of the Early Martyrs* (1927), pp. 74–92, with notes, pp. 148–58. P. Franchi de Cavalieri, *La Passio SS. Perpetuae et Felicitatis* (R.Q. Supplementheft v; 1896). Further advocacy of Tertullian's editorship, besides that of J. A. Robinson, loc. cit., pp. 47–58, in A. d'Alès, S.J., 'L'Auteur de la *Passio Perpetuae*' in *R.H.E.*, viii (1907), pp. 5–18, and P. de Labriolle, 'Tertullien, auteur du prologue et de la continuation de la Passion de Perpétue et Félicité' in *Bulletin d'ancienne Littérature et d'Archéologie chrétiennes*, iii (1913), pp. 126–32; Tertullian's editorship has been challenged, however, by E. Rupprecht, 'Bemerkungen zur Passio SS. Perpetuae et Felicitatis' in *Rheinisches Museum für Philologie*, xc (1941), pp. 177–92. V. L. Kennedy, C.S.B., *The Saints of the Canon of the Mass* (Studi di Antichità cristiana, xiv; 1938), pp. 161–8. Bardenhewer, ii, 682–6; Altaner (ed. 1951), p. 185 f. J. P. Kirsch in *C.E.*, vi (1909), p. 29, s.v. 'Felicitas and Perpetua'; H. *Leclercq, O.S.B., in *D.A.C.L.*, xiv (pt. 1; 1939), cols. 393–444, s.v. 'Perpétue et Félicité (Saintes), with bibl. E. Peterson–A. Amore–E. Josi in *E.C.*, ix (1952), cols. 1191–3.

PERPETUAL CURATE. A clerk who officiates in a parish or district to which he is nominated by the *Impropriator and licensed by the Bishop. Exemption from the Appropriation of Benefices Act, 1404 (4 Hen. IV, c. 12) was allowed to benefices granted *ad mensam monachorum* and in certain other cases. When, after the dissolution of the monasteries, these exempt parishes passed to *lay rectors, these rectors were obliged to nominate some particular person to the *Ordinary for his licence to serve the cure. Curates thus licensed became perpetual, removable only by revocation of the licence of the Ordinary. Perpetual curacies were not formerly adjudged ecclesiastical *benefices, but were declared to be so by the *Pluralities Act, 1838 (1 & 2 Vict. c. 106, s. 124). Those augmented from *Queen Anne's Bounty were declared (1 Geo. I, Stat. 2, c. 10, s. 4) perpetual cures and the incumbents bodies politic. Under the Church Building Act, 1845 (8 & 9 Vict. c. 70, s. 9 and 17), the ministers of new churches of separate parishes, ecclesiastical districts, consolidated chapelries and district chapelries are also perpetual curates, as are the ministers appointed to new districts or parishes under the Church Building and New Building Acts (1 & 2 Will. IV c. 38, s. 12; 2 & 3 Vict. c. 49, s. 2; and 6 & 7 Vict. c. 37, s. 12). Perpetual curates obtain possession of their benefices by licence from the Bishop without Institution or Induction. They are commonly styled '*vicars.'

PERRONE, GIOVANNI (1794–1876), Italian theologian. He joined the *Jesuit Order in 1815 and in 1824 was made professor of dogmatic theology in the Roman College, a post which he held (not quite continuously) till his death. His *Praelectiones Theologicae* (9 vols., 1835–42) were one of the most widely used books on Catholic dogmatics in the 19th cent.

His other writings include *De Immaculato B.V. Mariae Virginis Conceptu* (Rome, 1847), *Il protestantesimo e la regola di fede* (3 vols., Rome, 1853), *De Matrimonio Christiano* (3 vols., Rome, 1858) and *De Romani Pontificis Infallibilitate* (Turin, 1874). C. Sommervogel, S.J., *Bibliothèque de la Compagnie de Jésus*, vi (1895), cols. 558–71. T. Lynch (ed.), 'The Newman–Perrone paper on Development' in *Gregorianum*, xvi (1935), pp. 402–47; F. Cavallera, S.J., 'Le Document Newman–Perrone et le développement du dogme' in *Bulletin de Littérature ecclésiastique*, xlvii (1946), pp. 132–42.

PER SALTUM (Lat., 'by a leap'). A term used of the conferring of a particular rank of orders when the candidate has not previously received the lower grades, e.g. of the ordination of a man to the priesthood who is not already a deacon. In canon law it is held that such ordinations are valid, except possibly to the episcopate (owing to the dispute as to whether or not the episcopate is a distinct order), but they are held to be gravely irregular and to preclude the person so ordained from proceeding further. They are prohibited in the C.I.C., can. 977. In early times, however, ordinations *per saltum* were of common occurrence. See also *Interstices*.

PERSECUTION. See *Toleration*.

PERSECUTIONS, Early Christian. The Roman government commonly tolerated such foreign religions as were no danger to morality and discipline; and though it did not recognize all religious bodies as legal corporations, it did not always suppress unrecognized religions. Since national religions were respected, Christianity at first sheltered under Jewish privileges, but as the distinction became clear and Gentile Christians refused Emperor-worship, their loyalty might be suspected; and before they were sufficiently numerous to appear politically dangerous, they earned dislike by aloofness from society, while mis-understandings among non-Christians about the *Agape and the *Eucharist aroused scandal. Persecution by the state began almost accidentally and remained intermittent. Until 250 its extent was determined more by local feeling than Imperial policy. Its legal basis remains obscure, since Ulpian's collection of anti-Christian measures has perished. Although *Orosius popularized the notion of ten persecutors (numbered below), the truth is less simple.

(1) *Nero, says *Tacitus, used Christians as scapegoats for the fire of Rome (A.D. 64; see artt. *Peter, *Paul). There is no evidence of persecution outside Rome (anticipated by 1 *Pet.), unless *Rev. is of this date. But, though Nero's victims were condemned for arson and not for holding a particular creed, a precedent was set for treating Christians generally as criminals, and condemning them 'for the Name' [i.e. of Christ] by summary magisterial jurisdiction (coercitio). Some hold that Nero explicitly forbade Christianity.

(2) *Domitian (95) executed Flavius Cle-mens and *Glabrio and banished *Domitilla for 'atheism'. They were perhaps Christians, but his motives were political and personal. Rev. refers to wider persecution, probably in this reign, for refusal to worship the Emperor.

(3) Trajan's correspondence with *Pliny (112) reveals Christian trials in Bithynia. Trajan would not tolerate Christianity alto-gether (*Ignatius), but ordered Pliny not to search for the Christians. This restriction was binding on all magistrates.

Under Hadrian and Antoninus Pius (117–161) toleration tended to outweigh repression. Churches held property, but by grace, not law. It is possible, but improbable, that they were regarded as burial clubs (see Catacombs). The authenticity of Hadrian's rescript forbidding the execution of Christians unless guilty of a specific crime is doubtful, since contemporary acts of *martyrs suggest that persistent profession of Christianity was sufficient ground for condemnation.

(4) *Marcus Aurelius disliked Christians and sanctioned severe persecution at Lyons (177). Another martyr was the Apologist, *Justin. *Celsus and Fronto give explanations of the current anti-Christian feeling. Chris-tians wished to whitewash this 'good' Emperor (*Thundering Legion), but it was the bad Commodus who gave them rest (180–92).

(5) Under Septimius Severus, *Tertullian appealed for toleration. Severus forbade fresh conversions (*Perpetua), but was not an active persecutor. A long period of peace followed his death in 211, broken only momentarily by

(6) Maximinus Thrax (235). Perhaps his motive was to reverse the policy of his hated predecessor, Alexander Severus, who was ap-parently well disposed towards the Christians.

(7) *Decius changed the situation. His order (250) that all his subjects should sacrifice to the state gods under pain of death, though partly inspired by the desire for a mass demonstration of religious loyalty, was a systematic attack on Christianity, which might by now be considered a serious threat to the state. Many were punished and many apostatized; but the Church recovered under such leaders as *Cyprian.

(8) Valerian's method was less wholesale. In 257 Christians were forbidden to assemble and many bishops were arrested. Next year, Valerian ordered the execution of all clergy and laymen of high rank who would not abjure. But Gallienus (260) cancelled these measures, restored Church property, and ushered in a long peace. For, despite Orosius,

(9) Aurelian did not seriously trouble the Church.

(10) *Diocletian (284–305) continued the policy of toleration until 303 when, influenced probably by Galerius, he ordered that all churches should be destroyed and the Scrip-tures burnt. A stronger edict in 304 sanctioned the bloodshed from which he at first shrank. This persecution, described by *Lactantius and *Eusebius, continued after Diocletian's abdication, its intensity varying according to the policy of the rulers who shared the Empire. In the W. Constantius did little; in Syria Maximin proved ferocious. Bloodshed, how-ever, failed to achieve its purpose and sickened the people. In 311 the dying Galerius issued an edict of toleration, Maximin was eventually forced to follow his example (312), and *Con-stantine and Licinius proclaimed complete religious liberty (see Milan, Edict of). Though Licinius (321) and *Julian (361–3) launched new attacks, substantial toleration had been assured. Before long toleration turned to privilege and the Church committed itself to the coercion of belief (*Theodosius I).

The question of the extent of the persecutions, the civil status of the Church in pre-Nicene times, and the legal enactments under which persecution was carried out, have been the subject of much discussion; and the matter is dealt with in all histories of the Early Church.

Introductory account in H. B. Workman, Persecution in the Early Church (36th Fernley Lecture, 1906). P. Allard, Histoire des persécutions pendant les deux premiers siècles (1885), followed by four further vols. with similar titles (5 vols. in all, 1885–90); T. *Mommsen, 'Der Religionsfrevel nach römischem Recht' in Historische Zeitschrift, lxiv (1890), pp. 389–429; W. M. *Ramsay, The Church in the Roman Empire before A.D. 170 (1893); E. G. Hardy, Christianity and the Roman Government (1894); M. Conrat, Die Christenver-folgungen im römischen Reiche vom Standpunkt des Juristen (1897); C. Callewaert, 'Les Premiers Chrétiens furent-ils persécutés par édits généraux ou par mesure de police?' in R.H.E., ii (1901), pp. 771–97; iii (1902), pp. 5–15, 324–48, 601–14; A. Linsenmayer, Die Bekämpfung des Christentums durch den römischen Staat bis zum Tode des Kaisers Julian (1905); L. H. Canfield, The Early Persecutions of the Chris-tians (Studies in History, Economics and Public Law, ed. by the Faculty of Political Science of Columbia University, lv. 2; New York, 1913). H. M. Last, 'The Study of the

"Persecutions"' in *Journal of Roman Studies*, xxvii(1937), pp. 80–92. H. Grégoire, with the collaboration of P. Orgels, J. Moreau, and A. Maricq, *Les Persécutions dans l'empire romain* (Académie Royale de Belgique. Classe de Lettres, et des Sciences Morales et Politiques. Mémoires. Collection in 8o, xlvi, Brussels, 1950).

Studies on particular persecutions include C. F. Arnold, *Die neronische Christenverfolgung* (1888); R. L. P. Milburn, 'The Persecution of Domitian' in *C.Q.R.*, cxxxix (1945), pp. 154–64; J. A. F. Gregg, *The Decian Persecution* (1897); A. J. Mason, *The Persecution of Diocletian* (1876). See also bibls. to individual emperors.

A. *Harnack in *P.R.E.* (ed. 3), iii (1897), pp. 823–8, s.v. 'Christenverfolgungen'; H. M. Gwatkin in *H.E.R.E.*, ix (1917), pp. 742–9, s.v. 'Persecution (Early Church)'; H. *Leclercq, O.S.B., in *D.A.C.L.*, iv (1921), cols. 1565–1648, s.v. 'Droit persécuteur'; A. Bigelmair in *L.Th.K.*, ii (1931), cols. 912–17, s.v. 'Christenvenfolgungen'.

PERSEVERANCE.

In addition to its general meaning, the word is used technically in connexion with the doctrine of *predestination to mean steady continuance, after conversion, in the faith and life proper to the attainment of eternal life. St. *Augustine held that God bestowed on those elected to salvation, not only the initial call to be baptized and accept the Christian faith, but also the gift of such final perseverance. *Calvinism maintained that the elect could be certain that God would never allow them to fall away from Him. Outside Calvinism it would generally be held that none can be personally certain of persevering to the end and that the gift must be sought by prayer and effort.

PERSIA, Christianity in.

See *Nestorianism*.

PERSON OF CHRIST.

See *Christology*, also *Incarnation*.

PERSONS, ROBERT.

See *Parsons, Robert*.

PERTH, Articles of

(1618). Five articles forced on the Church in *Scotland at Perth in 1618 by *James I. They required (1) kneeling at Communion; (2) the observance of Easter and Christmas; (3) Confirmation; (4) provision for administering Communion to the dying in their houses; and (5) Baptism on the Sunday following the child's birth. In 1621, much to the horror of older Scottish Churchmen, the articles were carried with a majority through the Scottish parliament.

The text will be found in J. *Spotswood, *The History of the Church of Scotland* (1655), p. 538 f.

PERUGINO, PIETRO VANNUCCI

(1446–1524), Italian painter of the Umbrian school. He studied first at Perugia and afterwards at Florence under Verrocchio, where he learned the art of composition and perspective in which he became a master. In 1482 he painted the *Delivery of the Keys to St. Peter* in the *Sistine Chapel. (His other frescoes in the Chapel gave way to *Michelangelo's *Last Judgement*). The devotional warmth of his style soon caused a great demand for his religious pictures, and among his masterpieces were the *Adoration of the Holy Child* (1491),

the *Vision of St. Bernard* (c. 1494), and the *Preparation for the Tomb* (1495). In 1496 he completed his greatest work, the well-known fresco of the *Crucifixion* in St. Maria Maddalena dei Pazzi at Florence. After that his art showed a marked decline.

Reproductions of his paintings (in black and white) ed. W. Bombe (Klassiker der Kunst in Gesamtausgaben, v; 1914), with introd. pp. ix–xxxiii. F. Canuti, *Il Perugino* (2 vols., Siena [1931]), also with reproductions, and bibl. i, pp. 395–407. Other studies include those by G. C. Williamson (London, 1900), E. Hutton (London [1906]), F. Knapp (Bielefeld–Leipzig, 1907), U. Gnoli (Spoleto [1923]), and J. Alazard ('Les Grands Artistes', Paris, 1927). W. Bombe in *Allgemeines Lexikon der bildenden Künstler von der Antike bis zur Gegenwart* begründet von U. Thieme–F. Becker, xxvi (ed. H. Vollmer; 1932), pp. 450–2, s.v., with bibl. W. M. Rossetti in *E.B.* (ed. 11), xxi (1911), p. 279 f.

PESHITTA, The.

From the early 5th cent., the official text of the Bible in Syriac-speaking Christian lands. (The word 'Peshitta' means literally 'simple', or, as applied to a text, 'current'.) The NT portion has been very generally held to have been the work of *Rabbula, Bp. of Edessa from 411 to 435. If so, it was probably produced partly to provide a version of the Gospels to supplant the '*Diatessaron', then in common use, which was objected to both for its artificial form and as the work of a heretic (*Tatian). The NT did not include the Book of Rev., nor the four lesser *Catholic Epistles (2 Pet., 2 and 3 Jn., and Jude). Some 250 MSS. have survived, the oldest dating from the 5th cent.

Older edd. of NT by E. Widmanstadt (Vienna, 1555) and J. Leusden–C. Schaaf (Leiden, 1709). Best ed. of Peshitta Gospels by P. E. *Pusey–G. H. Williams (Oxford, 1901); complete ed. of NT ed. *British and Foreign Bible Society, London, 1905–20. Editions of the OT include the London *Polyglott (1657) and that of S. Lee (London, 1823). L. Haefeli, *Die Peschitta des Alten Testaments* (Alttestamentliche Abhandlungen, xi, Hft. 1; 1927), with full bibl. F. C. *Burkitt, *S. Ephraim's Quotations from the Gospel* (Texts and Studies, vii, No. 2; Cambridge, 1901); A. Vööbus, *Investigations into the Text of the New Testament used by Rabbula of Edessa* (Contributions of Baltic University, lix; Pinneberg, 1947); id., *Researches on the Circulation of the Peshitta in the Middle of the Fifth Century* (ib., lxiv; 1948). M. Black, 'Rabbula of Edessa and the Peshitta' in *Bulletin of the John Rylands Library*, xxxiii (1951), pp. 203–10; id., 'The New Testament Peshitta and its Predecessors' in *Studiorum Novi Testamenti Societas*, Bulletin i (1950), pp. 51–62.

PETAVIUS, DIONYSIUS

(1583–1652), Denis Pétau, *Jesuit historian and theologian. A native of Orléans, he studied at Paris where I. *Casaubon aroused his interest in the Fathers. In 1603 he was appointed a lecturer at Bourges, resigning in 1605 to become a Jesuit. He became professor of rhetoric at Reims (1609), La Flèche (1612), and finally at the College de *Clermont at Paris (1618), wher in 1621 he was given the chair of Dogmatic Theology. He lived at Paris for the rest of his life, one of the most brilliant and learned scholars of his age. His *Opus de Doctrina Temporum* (2 vols., 1627), in substance a thorough revision and expansion of J. J. *Scaliger's *De Emendatione Temporum* (1583), was a fundamental contribution to the study of ancient chronology; in 1633 he issued an abridged edition with the title *Rationarium Temporum*. He also published notable editions of the writings of *Synesius (1612; new ed. 1633) and St. *Epiphanius (1622; not superseded until K. Holl's edition of 1915–33).

Petavius was also an outstanding dogmatic theologian, strictly orthodox in doctrine but one of the first to accept the idea of doctrinal development (here he influenced J. H. *Newman) and to concede the imperfections of much Patristic teaching judged by later standards. His vast and still valuable *De Theologicis Dogmatibus* (vols. i–iii, 1644; vol. iv, 1650) was unfinished at the time of his death. G. *Bull's famous *Defensio Fidei Nicaenae* (1685) was written primarily to defend the orthodoxy of pre-Nicene teaching on the Trinity against Petavius's criticisms. His *De la pénitence publique et de la préparation à la communion* (1644) was an attack on A. *Arnauld's *Fréquente Communion* (1643).

The primary source is the life [by F. Oudin, S.J.] in [J. P.] Nicéron, *Barnabite, *Mémoires pour servir à l'histoire des hommes illustres dans la république des lettres*, xxxvii (1737), pp. 81–234. Full life by J. C. Vital Châtellain (Paris, 1884). Shorter study by J. Martin ('Science et religion. Les Grands Théologiens', fasc. 545; 1910). Dr. Kuhn, 'Ehrenrettung des Dionysius Petavius und der katholischen Auffassung der Dogmengeschichte' in *T.Q.*, xix (1850), pp. 249–93. P. Galtier, S.J., 'Petau et la préface de son "De Trinitate"' in *Rech. S.R.*, xxi (1931), pp. 462–76. Sommervogel, vi (1895), cols. 588–616. J. de Ghellinck, S.J., in *C.E.*, xi (1911), p. 743 f., s.v. 'Pétau'; P. Galtier, S.J., in *D.T.C.*, xii (pt. 1; 1933), cols. 1313–37, s.v. 'Pétau'.

PETER, St., Prince of the *Apostles. Our knowledge of his life and personality is derived chiefly from the Gospels, Acts, St. Paul's Ep. to the Galatians, and tradition. Acc. to the Gospel of St. John he was a native of Bethsaida, a village near the lake Tiberias (Jn. 1. 44); but when our Lord began His public ministry he is found at Capernaum (Mt. 8. 5, 14). In the Johannine account (1. 35–42) he was introduced to our Lord by his brother Andrew and given the name 'Cephas', probably the Aramaic equivalent of the Greek 'Peter' ($\pi\acute{\epsilon}\tau\rho\alpha$, 'rock'). Shortly afterwards he was present at the miracle of Cana (Jn. 2. 2 and 11). Another meeting is recorded by the Synoptists (Mt. 4. 18–22; cf. Lk. 5. 1–11) at which, at our Lord's command, he catches a large draught of fishes. Christ then cures Peter's mother-in-law of a fever, and from this time Peter's house and his boat are always at His disposal when He is in Capernaum. Some time later he is formally called to become an Apostle. In all the lists of the Twelve he is named first; he is present on all those occasions when only a small 'inner group' is admitted, viz. at the raising of Jairus's daughter (Mt. 9. 18–26), at the Transfiguration (Mt. 17. 1–8), and at the Agony in the Garden (Mt. 26. 37). He usually takes the lead and is the mouthpiece of the Apostles; he walks on the water (Mt. 14. 22–33) and speaks for the others when they declare their readiness to continue following Christ (Jn. 6. 66–9). After his confession of faith at *Caesarea Philippi (Mt. 16. 13–20), when he professes his belief that Jesus is the Christ, the Son of the living God, our Lord tells him that this truth has not been revealed to him by flesh and blood, but by the Father in Heaven. The

Apostle then receives the promise 'Thou art Peter, and on this rock will I build my Church' together with the keys of heaven and the power of binding and loosing (ver. 18 f.). This passage, on which the claims of the Popes are esp. based, has raised much controversy. Its authenticity is now very widely acknowledged by NT critics, though it is much disputed whether the 'rock' refers to Peter himself or to his faith. The main argument against its Papal interpretation, however, is that Christ's words envisage only Peter, not his successors. Peter's confession of faith is soon followed by a sharp rebuke, when, animated by his natural love for his Master, the Apostle objects to His prediction of the Passion (16. 22 f.). Together with John he is entrusted with the preparations for the *Last Supper, during which the Lord reaffirms his pre-eminence (Lk. 22. 31 f.). His impulsive love leads him to protest at the foot-washing (Jn. 13. 6–10), and, on the way to the Mount of Olives, to his boast that he will never leave his Lord, answered by the prediction of his triple denial (Mt. 26. 31–35). At the arrest of Jesus he strikes off the ear of a servant of the high priest (Jn. 18. 10), but then, like the other disciples, leaves Him (Mt. 26. 56). He follows, however, from afar (Mt. 26. 58) to the court of the high priest. There he is accused of being one of our Lord's followers, but denies three times that he knows Him, then remembers His prediction and bitterly repents (Mt. 26. 69–75). After the Resurrection he is favoured with a special appearance of the risen Christ (Lk. 24. 34). Acc. to the Johannine account our Lord appears to him and several other disciples at the Sea of Tiberias, where he makes reparation for his triple denial by a triple protestation of love and receives the charge to feed His sheep and the prediction of his martyrdom (Jn. 21).

After the Ascension Peter immediately takes the lead of the Apostles in designating the successor of Judas (Acts 1. 15–22) and throughout the first half of Acts he appears as their head. He speaks on the day of *Pentecost (Acts 2. 14–41); he is the first of the Apostles to perform a miracle in the name of Jesus (3. 1–10); he is the speaker when brought before the *Sanhedrin with John (4. 1–21); and he pronounces the condemnation of Ananias and Sapphira (5. 1–11). He also is the greatest miracle-worker among the Apostles, whose shadow even heals the sick (5. 15); he opens the Church to the Gentiles by admitting Cornelius (10. 1–11, 18), and his authority is again evident at the Apostles' Council at Jerusalem (15. 7–11). Of the later years of his Apostolate outside Palestine very little is known. His visit to *Antioch is mentioned by St. Paul in Gal. 2. 11–21, who sharply rebukes him for giving way to the demands of the Jewish Christians to dissociate himself from the Gentiles. Possibly he visited Corinth, as a party of 'Cephas' existed in that city (1 Cor. 1. 12).

The tradition connecting St. Peter with *Rome (q.v.) is early and unrivalled by any competing indication of his later life. Against it can be placed only the silence of the NT on the subject; but even here Rom. 15. 20–22 may point to the presence of another Apostle in Rome before St. Paul wrote, while the identification of 'Babylon' in 1 Pet. 5. 13 (see *Peter, Epp. of*) with Rome seems highly probable. St. *Clement of Rome (*I Clem.* 5) conjoins Peter and Paul as the outstanding heroes of the Faith and prob. implies (μαρτυ-ρήσας) that Peter suffered martyrdom. St. *Ignatius uses words (*Rom.* 4. 2) which suggest that Peter and Paul were the Apostles of special authority for the Roman Church, and St. *Irenaeus (*Adv. Haer.*, III, i, 2; III, iii, 1) states definitely that they founded that Church and instituted its episcopal succession. Other early witnesses to the tradition are *Gaius of Rome and *Dionysius of Corinth, both cited by *Eusebius (*H.E.*, II, xxv, 5–8), who also (*H.E.*, III, i, 2 f.) quotes a statement of *Origen that Peter was crucified head downwards, having requested this form of death. That Peter, when 'old', was crucified is also borne out by Jn. 21. 18 f. The later tradition (first found in St. *Jerome) which attributes to him an episcopate (or apostolate) in Rome of twenty-five years preceding his martyrdom is less well supported. His death is placed by Eusebius in the reign of *Nero (54–68) and was prob. in the *persecution of 64, not, as Eusebius himself asserts (*Chron.*), in 68. That he and St. Paul suffered on the same day is perhaps a mistaken deduction from their common feast (prob. date of translation of their relics, not of martyrdom) on 29 June. See also entry *Quo Vadis*.

St. Peter was above all a man of action, ardent and impetuous. His passionate love of Christ, though at first mixed with self-esteem and unable to stand up to severe trials, was purified by failure and suffering. After Pentecost he was the true leader of the Church, who fearlessly faced persecution, and whose humility is strikingly shown in the Gospel of St. *Mark, which, as is widely acknowledged, reproduces the Petrine teaching, and where his person appears in a far less favourable light than in any of the others. For the Epistles of St. Peter, see the following entries. There are considerable historical reasons for believing that his tomb in St. Peter's in Rome is authentic. Feast day, together with St. Paul, 29 June. For the Feast of St. Peter's Chains (1 Aug.), see *Lammas Day*.

Modern study with good discussion of the main historical questions in O. Cullmann, *Petrus*. Jünger, Apostel, Märtyrer (Zürich, 1952; Eng. tr., 1953). The best comprehensive discussions tend to be in dictionaries. F. J. Foakes Jackson, *Peter, Prince of Apostles* (1927). C. H. *Turner, 'St. Peter in the New Testament' in *Theology*, xiii (1926), pp. 66–78; repr. in id., *Catholic and Apostolic* (1931), pp. 181–205. Popular studies by A. T. Robertson (New York, 1933, with bibl.) and J. A. Findlay (London, 1935). H. *Lietzmann, *Petrus und Paulus in Rom* (1915; ed. 2, Arbeiten zur Kirchengeschichte, i; 1927). A. Schlatter, *Petrus und Paulus nach dem ersten Petrusbrief* (1937). Recent work on the question of Peter's connexion with Rome includes C. Heussi, *War Petrus in Rom?* (1936); id., *War Petrus wirklich römischer Märtyrer?* (1937; reply to critique by H. Lietzmann). F. H. Chase in *H.D.B.*, iii (1900), pp. 756–79, s.v. 'Peter (Simon)'; P. W. *Schmiedel in *E.Bi.*, iv (1903), cols. 4559–627, s.v. 'Simon Peter'; F. Sieffert in *P.R.E.* (ed. 3), xv (1904), pp. 186–212, s.v. 'Petrus, der Apostel'; K. *Lake in *E.B.* (ed. 11), xxi (1911),

pp. 285–8, s.v.; S. J. Case in *D.A.C.*, ii (1918), pp. 191–201, s.v.; E. Fascher in *P.W.*, xix (pt. 2; 1938), cols. 1335–61, s.v. 'Petrus (121)'; P. de Ambroggi, E. Josi, and others in *E.C.*, ix (1952), cols. 1400–27, s.v. 'Pietro apostolo'. J. Lowe, *St. Peter* (three lectures, 1956).

PETER, Acts of St. An apocryphal Book composed in Greek *c.* 150–200, perhaps in Asia Minor, which internal evidence shows to have been dependent on the 'Acts of *John'. Apart from the 'Martyrdom of St. *Peter' which forms part of it and survives in Greek as well as in several versions, it is preserved *in toto* in Latin in a Vercelli MS. A Coptic fragment also survives which describes St. Peter's miraculous treatment of his paralytic daughter. In the Martyrdom are recorded both the '*Quo Vadis' incident and the crucifixion of St. Peter head downwards. In places its teaching has a *Docetic ring, perhaps occasioned by the writer's limited theological capacities rather than by any connexion with unorthodox circles.

Lat. text of 'Martyrdom' in R. A. *Lipsius–M. Bonnet (edd.), *Acta Apostolorum Apocrypha*, i (Leipzig, 1891), pp. 1–22; Eng. tr. in M. R. James (ed.), *The Apocryphal New Testament* (1924), pp. 330–6. Lat. text ('Actus Vercellenses'; a variant form describing Peter's victory over Simon Magus in the Roman forum), together with the Gk. text on opposite pages where it corresponds, in R. A. Lipsius–M. Bonnet, op. cit., pp. 45–103; Eng. tr. in M. R. James, op. cit., pp. 304–30. Coptic fragment ed. C. Schmidt, *Die alten Petrusakten im Zusammenhang der Apokryphen Apostelliteratur nebst einem neuentdeckten Fragment* (T.U., xxiv, Hft. 1; 1903), pp. 3–7, with Germ. tr., pp. 7–10; Eng. tr. from the Germ. in M. R. James, op. cit., pp. 300–2. Further Gk. fragment in B. P. Grenfell–A. S. Hunt, *The Oxyrhynchus Papyri*, vi (1908), pp. 6–12. L. Vouaux, *Les Actes de Pierre* (1922; text, Fr. tr. and comm., with good bibl.). J. Quasten, *Patrology*, i (Utrecht, 1950), pp. 133–5. Bardenhewer, i, 550–4; Altaner (ed. 1950), p. 55. E. Amann in *Dibt. Bibl.* Suppl. i (1928), cols. 496–501.

PETER, Apocalypse of St. This, the most important of the apocryphal apocalypses, dates from the early 2nd cent. Small portions of it have survived in quotations in *Clement of Alexandria and others, and in some scattered fragments (see *Akhmîm Fragment*); and an Ethiopic version, in a modified form, was discovered by S. Grébaut in 1910. The Apocalypse describes how our Lord granted to the Apostles a vision of their brethren in the next world and of their rewards. Both Clement and the *Muratorian Fragment held it to be Scripture; and acc. to *Sozomen (5th cent.) it was still read in his day on *Good Friday in some Palestinian churches.

Akhmîm fragment of Gk. text ed. A. Lods in *Mémoires publiés par les membres de la Mission Archéologique Française du Caire*, ix (1892), pp. 224–8; repr. by E. Klostermann, *Apocrypha*, i (Kleine Texte, ed. H. *Lietzmann, iii, 1921), pp. 8–12; Eng. tr. in M. R. James (ed.), *The Apocryphal New Testament* (1924), pp. 507–10; there is a small Gk. papyrus fragment in the *Bodleian Library (MS. Gr. th. f. 4 (P)); Eng. tr. in M. R. James, op. cit., p. 510; cf. M. R. James, 'The Rainer Fragment of the Apocalypse of Peter' in *J.T.S.*, xxxii (1931–2), pp. 270–9, with text. Ethiopic text ed. S. Grébaut in *Revue de l'Orient chrétien*, xv (1910), pp. 199–208, 307–16, 425–33, with Fr. tr., pp. 208–14, 316–323, 433–9; mainly tr. into Eng. in M. R. James (ed.), *The Apocryphal New Testament* (1924), pp. 510–20; cf. M. R. James, 'A New Text of the Apocalypse of Peter' in *J.T.S.*, xii (1910–11), pp. 36–54. Eng. tr. of the extracts from Clement of Alexandria, *Methodius of Olympus, *Macarius Magnes, etc., in M. R. James, *The Apocryphal New Testament* (1924), p. 505 f. Sozomen, *H.E.*, vii, 19. M. R. James,

'The Recovery of the Apocalypse of Peter' in *C.Q.R.*, lxxx (1915), pp. 1–36. Bardenhewer, i, 610–15; Altaner (ed. 1951), p. 62. É. Amann in *Dict. Bibl.*, Suppl. i (1928), cols. 525–7, with bibl.

PETER, Epistles of St. There are two Epistles ascribed to St. *Peter in the NT.

(1) The First Epistle of Peter was written from *Rome (if this is the city referred to in 5. 13 as 'Babylon') to Christian communities in 'Pontus, Galatia, Cappadocia, Asia, and Bithynia' (1. 1), i.e. all lands in what is now Asia Minor, to encourage them under persecution. The author reminds his readers that, as the chosen people of God, they are heirs to the glorious promises made to Israel of old and insists on the central place in the Christian plan of salvation of Christ's redeeming death and resurrection, at once the basis of the Christian life and the great example to those in suffering (1. 2–25). As believers, they are called to love one another, to advance in grace, to live soberly and humbly, to look for the coming of Christ, and esp. to witness by their good lives in their heathen surroundings, whence trials are constantly awaited (2–5).

The Epistle was sent to Asia Minor by the hands of Silvanus (5. 12). If tradition is correct in attributing it to St. Peter, its *terminus ad quem* is the date of his death, i.e. probably *c.* 65. Its Petrine authorship, however, has been often questioned. It is urged that its literary style is not that of a Galilean fisherman; that passages in the Epistle reflect Pauline teaching; and that persecution of the Church in Asia Minor at so early a date is otherwise unattested. These objections, however, are far from conclusive and critical opinion is still in the balance. External evidence for ascribing it to St. Peter goes back to St. *Irenaeus (*adv. Haer.* IV, xix, 1) and *Clement of Alexandria (*Strom.* III, 18 [110]).

(2) The Second Epistle, though it is written as if by St. Peter, with a ref. to his presence at the *Transfiguration (1. 18; cf. Mk. 9. 2), is markedly different from the First in contents and manner, e.g. in the treatment of redemption with which it opens. Its main message is a warning against false and ungodly teachers, upon whom the future judgements of God are prophesied from the OT and Jewish writings. The chief passage in which this warning is given (2. 1–3. 3) is parallel to Jude 4–18, from which it is almost certainly borrowed.

There are several indications that the Epistle is of a late date. Thus the passage (3. 3 ff.) dealing with the delay of the Coming of the Lord presupposes that the first generation of Christians had passed away. The author classes the Epp. of St. Paul as 'scripture' (3. 16), a position which they apparently did not attain until some considerable time after the Apostle's death. It is first definitely referred to by *Origen (in *Eusebius, *Hist. Eccl.* VI, xxv, 8) in the 3rd cent., and he writes of it as of disputed authenticity. It also has some close points of literary contact with the 'Apocalypse of *Peter' (q.v.). These indications of date, and the difference in style and interest from 1 Peter, make it virtually impossible to hold that St. Peter was the author. The Epistle was received into the *Canon with considerable hesitation. Its date is probably the second or third Christian generation, perhaps *c.* A.D. 150.

Modern commentaries on BOTH EPP. include those of C. F. Keil (Leipzig, 1883, with Jud., pp. 1–297), R. Knopf (K.E.K., xii, ed. 5, 1887, with Jud.; ed. 7, 1912, pp. 1–201 and 246–328), C. Bigg (I.C.C., 1901, with Jud., pp. 1–304), H. Windisch (Hb. N.T., iv, Th. 2, 1911, on the Catholic Epp.; ed. 2, xv, 1930, pp. 50–105; ed. 3, by H. Preisker, 1951, with addenda, pp. 152–63), J. *Moffatt (Moffatt Comm., 1928, on General Epp., pp. 85–213), and J. W. C. Wand (West. Comm., 1934, with Jud., pp. 1–186); on 1 PET. only, by F. J. A. *Hort (London, 1896; on 1 Pet. 1.1–2.17 only), J. H. B. Masterman (ib., 1900), E. G. Selwyn (ib., 1946), and F. W. Beare (Oxford, 1947); on 2 PET. only, by J. Chaine (Études Bibliques, ed. 2, 1939, on Catholic Epp., pp. 1–96). J. M. Usteri, *Wissenschaftlicher und praktischer Commentar über den ersten Petrusbrief* (2 Thll., Zürich, 1887). D. E. J. Voelker, *Der erste Petrusbrief*. Seine Entstehung und Stellung in der Geschichte des Urchristentums (1906). R. Perdelwitz, *Die Mysterienreligion und das Problem des I. Petrusbriefes* (1911). B. H. *Streeter, *The Primitive Church* (1929), pp. 115–30. F. L. Cross, *1 Peter. A Paschal Liturgy* (1954). F. *Spitta, *Der zweite Brief des Petrus und der Brief des Judas* (1885); J. B. Mayor, *The Epistle of St. Jude and the Second Epistle of St. Peter* (1915). F. H. Chase in *H.D.B.*, iii (1900), pp. 779–96 (on 1 Pet.) and 796–818 (on 2 Pet.); O. Cone in *E.Bi.*, iii (1902), cols. 3677–84; S. J. Case in *D.A.C.*, ii (1918), pp. 201–9.

PETER, Gospel of St. An early apocryphal Gospel of which the only surviving section is contained in the *Akhmîm Fragment, discovered in 1886–7. Acc. to *Serapion, Bp. of Antioch (*c.* 190), it was in use at Rhossus in his time, and in the next cent. *Origen knew of its existence. It seems to have been a largely legendary work, the author of which had strong antipathies to the Jews and was *Docetic in his theological standpoint. It was probably written in Syria about the middle of the 2nd cent.

Editio princeps of the Akhmîm fragment ed. A. Lods in *Mémoires publiés par les membres de la Mission Archéologique Française du Caire*, ix (1893, pp. 218–24, with facsimiles in plates II–VI. Text also ed., with introd., notes, and Eng. tr., by H. B. *Swete (London, 1893); among many other edd., convenient reprint in E. Klostermann, *Apocrypha*, i (Kleine Texte ed. H. *Lietzmann, iii; 1908), pp. 4–8. Eng. tr. of extracts (Origen, *In Matt.*, x, 17; Serapion ap. *Eusebius, *H.E.*, VI, xii, 2–6; Eusebius, *H.E.*, III, iii, 2; *Theodoret, *Haer. Fab.*, ii, 2] in M. R. James, *The Apocryphal New Testament* (1924), p. 13 f. Fr. tr. of complete text, with full commentary and bibl., by L. Vaganay (Études Bibliques, 1930). J. A. *Robinson in id.–M. R. James, *The Gospel according to Peter and the Revelation of Peter* (1892), pp. 13–36. Bardenhewer, i, 524–9. J. Quasten, *Patrology*, i (Utrecht, 1950), p. 114 f.

PETER, Liturgy of St. A Mass combining elements from the Byzantine and Roman rites which was probably drawn up for the use of Greek communities in Italy, but may have been put together only as a literary experiment. The canon is that of the Roman Mass. It was first published, apparently from Vat. graec. 1970 (saec. xii), by G. Linden in *Apologia pro Liturgia Petri Apostoli et Commentarius in eandem cum Missa Apostolica Petri Apostoli* (Antwerp, 1589, and Paris, 1595).

Text in C. A. Swainson, *The Greek Liturgies* (1884), pp. 191–203. Brightman, *L.E.W.*, i, p. xci, with reff. to other editions. H. W. Codrington, *The Liturgy of St. Peter*. With

Preface and Introduction by P. de Meester, O.S.B. (Liturgie-geschichtliche Quellen und Forschungen, Hft. 30, 1936). J. M. Hanssens, S.J., 'La Liturgie romano-byzantine de saint Pierre' in *O.C.P.*, iv (1938), pp. 235–58; v (1939), pp. 103–50.

PETER, Martyrdom of St. See *Peter, Acts of St.*

PETER, Patrimony of St. See *Patrimony of St. Peter.*

PETER, Preaching of St. (Gk. Κήρυγμα Πέτρου). A treatise, of which but few fragments survive, purporting to be the work of the Apostle St. *Peter, but probably dating from the earlier half of the 2nd cent. It was very popular in the early Church and known in its entirety to *Clement of Alexandria. Apparently intended for missionary propaganda, it emphasized the superiority of Christian monotheism to the current beliefs of Greeks and Jews. *Origen thought that it was possibly genuine in whole or in part.

Fragments collected by A. *Hilgenfeld, *Novum Testamentum extra Canonem Receptum*, iv (Leipzig, 1866), pp. 52–67, incl. introd. and notes. Fragments from Clement of Alexandria pr. in E. Klostermann, *Apocrypha*, i (Kleine Texte ed. H. *Lietzmann, iii, 1908), pp. 13–16; Eng. tr. of these latter in M. R. James, *The Apocryphal New Testament* (1924), pp. 16–19. E. von Dobschütz, *Das Kerygma Petri kritisch untersucht* (T.U., xi, Hft. 1; 1893). A. Hilgenfeld, 'Das Κήρυγμα Πέτρου (καὶ Παύλου)' in *Zeitschrift für wissenschaftliche Theologie*, xxxvi (1893), pp. 518–41. Bardenhewer, i, 547–50.

PETER OF ALCÁNTARA, St. (1499–1562), founder of the Spanish *Discalced Franciscans. A native of Alcántara, he studied at Salamanca (1513–14), but having early been attracted to the practice of asceticism, took the habit of the *Observantist Franciscans in 1515. Ordained priest in 1524, he became superior of different houses and, from 1538 to 1541, provincial of the province of St. Gabriel, whose strictness he increased by the addition of several constitutions. On the expiration of his office he retired to a hermitage near Lisbon where he was soon joined by other like-minded friars, so that he could establish several communities, which were later (1560) erected into a province. Having returned to Spain c. 1553, he realized his exalted ideals of austerity in the little convent at Pedroso, founded c. 1556, on which his congregation, the 'Alcantarines', was subsequently modelled. Soon he became much sought after as a spiritual director; and he was for a time the confessor of St. *Teresa, whose way of prayer he defended against her opponents and whom he guided in her reform of the *Carmelite Order. His *Tratado de la oración y meditación* (1556; Eng. trans., 1926) has been very popular and was translated into many languages. Lately his authorship has been contested, owing to its striking similarity to a book by St. Luís de Granada on the same subject, but the question of mutual dependence has so far not been decided. He was canonized in 1669. Feast day, 19 Oct.

Lives by F. Marchese (Rome, 1667) and Alonso de S. Bernardo (Naples, 1710). Cf. also *AA.SS.*, Oct. VIII (1866), pp. 623–809. The first to ascribe the substance of the *Tratado* to Luís of Granada was J. Cuervo, O.P., in his Biogr. of Luís (Madrid, 1896); here and in later writings Cuervo argued that it was dependent on Luís's *Libro de la oración* and on the second part of his *Guía de pecadores*. On the other hand the priority of Peter's *Tratado* has been defended by Michael Ange, O.Cap., in *Études franciscaines*, xxxvi (1924), pp. 63–83 and 141–66, and ib., xlix (1937), pp. 92–105 and 189–212, and elsewhere; for Ange, Luís's *Libro* is an expanded revision of the *Tratado* (MS. not later than 1535) with the design of making it more scholarly. A. Teetaert, O.Cap., in *D.T.C.*, xii (pt. 2; 1935), cols. 1793–1800, with bibl.

PETER OF ALEXANDRIA, St. (d. prob. 311), Bp. of Alexandria from 300. Peter is described by *Eusebius as 'a model bishop, remarkable alike for his virtuous life and for his keen study of the Scriptures'. He survived the persecution of *Diocletian, and drew up rules governing the readmission to the Church of those who had lapsed from Christianity under the influence of fear or torture. When, in 306, persecution began again, Peter went into hiding, and another bishop, *Melitius, subsequently claimed authority over Alexandria. It seems that Peter came back to his see when peace was restored in 311, but was beheaded in the persecution of Maximin shortly afterwards. Feast day, 26 Nov.

Fragments in M. J. *Routh (ed.), *Reliquiae Sacrae* (ed. 2 Oxford, 1846), iv, 19–82. J. P. Migne, *PG*, xviii, 449–522. Eng. tr. by J. B. H. Hawkins in A.N.C.L., xiv (1869), pp. 269–332, incl. introd. For more recently discovered fragments, cf. Altaner (ed. 1950), p. 177. Eusebius, *H.E.*, VII, xxxii, 31; VIII, xiii, 7; and IX, xiv, 2. L. B. Radford, *Three Teachers of Alexandria*. Theognostus, Pierius and Peter (1908), pp. 58–86. W. Telfer, 'St. Peter of Alexandria and Arius' in *Anal. Boll.*, lxvii (1949), pp. 117–30. Bardenhewer, ii, 239–47; J. Quasten, *Patrology*, ii (Utrecht, 1953), pp. 113–18. G. Fritz in *D.T.C.*, xii (pt. 2; 1935), cols. 1802–4; F. H. Kettler in *P.W.*, xix (pt. 2; 1938), cols. 1281–8, s.v. 'Petros I'.

PETER DE BRUYS (d. c. 1140), medieval heretic. He is known through the writings of *Peter the Venerable and *Abelard. It would appear that he was a priest who was deprived of his office and then began to preach in Dauphiné and Provence. He rejected infant baptism, the Mass, church buildings (because every place is equally suitable for prayer), prayers for the dead, the veneration of the Cross (as being the instrument of crucifying Christ afresh) as well as large parts of the Scriptures and the authority of the Church. He gained a considerable number of followers, called 'Petrobrusians', who ill-treated priests and incited monks to marry. His teaching was frequently condemned, e.g. by the second *Lateran Council in 1139. He himself was thrown into the flames at St.-Gilles, near Nîmes, by the people infuriated at his burning the crosses.

The principal sources are Peter the Venerable, 'Tractatus adversos Petrobrusianos Haereticos' (J. P. Migne, *PL*, clxxxix, 719–850), and Peter Abelard, 'Introductio ad Theologiam', ii, 4 (ib., clxxviii, 1056). [J. J.] I. von *Döllinger, *Beiträge zur Sektengeschichte des Mittelalters*, i (1890), pp. 75–97 ('Petrus von Bruys und Heinrich von Toulouse'); E. Vacandard, 'Les Origines de l'hérésie albigeoise' in *R.Q.H.*, lv (1894), pp. 50–83, esp. pp. 67–72. J. Kramp, S.J., 'Chronologisches zu Peters des Ehrwürdigen *Epistola adversus Petrobrusianos*' in *Miscellanea Francesco*

Ehrle, i (S.T., xxxvii; 1923), pp. 71–9. J. C. Reagan, 'Did the Petrobrusians Teach Salvation by Faith Alone?' in *The Journal of Religion*, vii (1927), pp. 81–91, with reff. F. Vernet in *D.T.C.*, ii (1905), cols. 1151–6, s.v. 'Bruys, Pierre de'.

PETER OF CANDIA. See *Alexander V.*

PETER CANISIUS, St. See *Canisius, St. Peter.*

PETER CELESTINE, St. See *Celestine V.*

PETER CHRYSOLOGUS, St. See *Chrysologus, St. Peter.*

PETER CLAVER, St. (1581–1654), 'Apostle of the Negroes'. A native of Verdu in Catalonia, he entered the *Jesuit novitiate at Tarragona in 1601. While studying at Palma, Majorca, he was inspired by St. Alphonsus Rodríguez with a longing to convert the heathen in the New World. In 1610 he landed at Cartagena in what is now Colombia and at once began ministering to the slaves who were brought over in terrible conditions from W. Africa. In 1615 he was ordained priest. He declared himself 'the slave of the negroes for ever' and despite much opposition from slave owners and people of fashion, he championed their cause and devoted himself for long years to their temporal and spiritual welfare. He is said to have instructed and baptized over 300,000 negroes. He was canonized by *Leo XIII in 1888. Feast day, 9 Sept.

J. Fernández, S.J., *Apostólica y penitente vida de el V.P. Pedro Claver* (Saragossa, 1666). Other Lives by B. G. Fleuriau (Paris, 1751; Eng. tr., 1849), J. Charruau (Paris, 1914), and G. Ledos (Paris, 1923). A. Lunn, *A Saint in the Slave Trade*. Peter Claver (1935).

PETER COMESTOR (d. *c.* 1179), Biblical scholar. Acc. to *Henry of Ghent he was a native of Troyes, where he was Dean of the cathedral from 1147 to 1164. In 1164 he became Chancellor of the University of *Paris. Towards the end of his life he retired to the monastery of St.-*Victor. His chief works are his 'Historia Scholastica' and his Sermons. The 'Historia' is a continuous history from the Creation to the end of the period covered by Acts, based on the text of the OT, the Gospels, and Acts, with many Scriptural quotations and literal and allegorical explanations frequently reflecting the tenets of contemporary science. The works of the Fathers and of pagan authors are used to fill up the gaps of the Biblical narrative. The 'Historia' became the standard work on Biblical history for the Middle Ages, was translated into several languages, and frequently annotated and commented on, e.g. by Stephen *Langton. In matters of theology he belonged to the school which adopted a more critical attitude to the Sentences of *Peter Lombard.

The 'Historia Scholastica', first pr. at Strassburg *c.* 1470, is repr. from the ed. of E. Navarro, O.S.B. (Madrid, 1699), in J. P. Migne, *PL*, cxcviii, 1049 (text 1053)–1722; the

'Sermons', erroneously attributed to Peter of Blois in *Maxima Bibliotheca Veterum Patrum*, xxiv (1677), pp. 1386–1463, are reprinted with correct ascription in J. P. Migne, ib., 1721–1844. Crit. text of the 'Tractatus De Sacramentis' with full bibl. by R. M. Martin, O.P., as appendix (S.S.L., xvii; 1937). R. M. Martin, O.P., 'Notes sur l'œuvre littéraire de Pierre le Mangeur' in *R.T.A.M.*, iii (1931), pp. 54–66; A. Landgraf, 'Recherches sur les écrits de Pierre le Mangeur', ib., pp. 292–306, 341–72. See also B. Smalley, *The Study of the Bible in the Middle Ages* (1941; rev. ed., 1951), ch. v. and passim. J. de Ghellinck, S.J., in *C.E.*, xi (1911), p. 763 f., s.v.; N. Iung in *D.T.C.*, xii (pt. 2; 1935), cols. 1918–22, s.v. 'Pierre Comestor'.

PETER'S CHAINS, Feast of St. See *Lammas Day.*

PETER DAMIAN, St. (1007–72), reformer and Doctor of the Church. Born at *Ravenna of poor parents, he had to tend the swine in his youth; but when his intelligence was recognized, he was sent to study at Faenza and Parma. In 1035 he entered the *Benedictine hermitage at Fonte Avella where he began to lead a life of extreme austerity. *C.* 1043 he was chosen prior and spent the next years founding new monasteries and reforming old ones; and before long he became famous as an uncompromising preacher against the worldliness and simoniacal practices of the clergy. In 1057 he was made Cardinal Bishop of *Ostia much against his will, and as such took a prominent part in the work of ecclesiastical reform and the struggle against the various antipopes, esp. Honorius II. Though he seems to have been relieved of his cardinalate by *Alexander II, he was sent several times on diplomatic missions to France and Germany. He died on a journey back from his native town, Ravenna, which he had reconciled to the Pope.

During his life Peter enjoyed great authority in the Church, owing to his learning, zeal, and integrity. In his numerous writings he enjoined strict monastic discipline and severe mortification, and denounced immorality and simony. He also treated of doctrinal matters, esp. *purgatory, the *Eucharist, and the validity of the Sacraments administered by simoniacal priests. The last of these he defended at a time when the teaching of the Church on this point was still in flux. He was never formally canonized, but since his death a local cult has existed in several places, and in 1828 Leo XII extended his feast to the universal Church, at the same time pronouncing him a 'Doctor of the Church'. He is said to have adopted the title Damian in gratitude to his brother of that name who had arranged for his education. His writings include 'Liber Gomorrhianus' (against clerical marriage), 'Liber Gratissimus' (in defence of the validity of simoniacal ordinations) and 'Disceptatio Synodalis'. Feast day, 23 Feb.

Works ed. C. Cajetan (4 vols., Rome, 1606–40), repr. in J. P. Migne, *PL.*, cxliv and cxlv. Better ed., 4 vols., Venice [–Bassano], 1783. Crit. ed. of his 'Liber Gratissimus' by L. de Heinemann in *M.G.H.*, Libelli de Lite Imperatorum et Pontificum in Saeculis XI et XII, i (1891), pp. 15–75; of his 'De Divina Omnipotentia' and other opuscula by P. Brezzi–B. Nardi (Florence, 1943); and of his hymns by G. M. Dreves, S.J., *Lateinische Hymnendichter des Mittelalters*, i (A.H.M.A., xlviii; 1905), pp. 29–78. Life by his disciple, John of Lodi, O.S.B., pr. in the ed. of his works by

C. Cajetan, i, pp. v–xviii; repr. in *AA.SS.*, Feb. III (1658), pp. 416–27, and in J. P. Migne, *PL*, cxliv, 113–46. A. Capecelatro, *Storia di S. Pier Damiano e del suo tempo* (1862). Other modern studies by F. Neukirch (vol. i only [to 1059], Leipzig, 1875), J. Kleinermanns (Steyl, 1882), and R. Biron, O.S.B. ('Les Saints', 1908). J. A. Enders, *Petrus Damianus und die weltliche Wissenschaft* (B.G.P.M., viii, Hft. 3; 1910). H. von Schubert, 'Petrus Damiani als Kirchen-politiker' in *Festgabe von Fachgenossen und Freunden Karl Müller zum siebzigsten Geburtstag dargebracht* (1922), pp. 83–102. J. P. Whitney, *Hildebrandine Essays* (1932), pp. 95–120. Raby, pp. 250–6. Überweg, ii, 187–9; Manitius, iii, 68–75. L. A. St. L. Toke in *C.E.*, xi (1911), p. 764 f., s.v.; G. Bareille in *D.T.C.*, iv (1911), cols. 40–54, s.v. 'Damien (2), Saint Pierre'; P. Palazzini in *E.C.*, ix (1952), cols. 1377–1380, s.v. 'Pier Damian', all with bibl. See also bibl. to *Gregory VII*.

PETER THE FULLER (d. 488), *Monophysite Patr. of *Antioch. Acc. to an uncertain tradition, recorded by a 6th cent. monk, Alexander of Cyprus, Peter had been a monk of the convent of the *Acoemetae at *Constantinople, where he practised the trade of a fuller. Expelled for his Monophysite leanings, he went to *Chalcedon, but after a brief stay returned and became known to the Emp.*Zeno the Isaurian, whom he accompanied to Antioch *c.* 470. Here he joined the *Apollinarians and violently opposed Martyrius, Bp. of Antioch, a supporter of the Chalcedonian Definition. During an absence of Martyrius, in search of assistance against the Apollinarians in Constantinople, Peter, backed by Zeno, had himself made bishop in his place (470). *Gennadius of Constantinople, however, obtained a decree of exile against him which was commuted to imprisonment in the convent of the Acoemetae. In 475 he succeeded in regaining his see, but in 477 he was once more deposed and interned, this time with the *Messalians. In 482 he gave his assent to Zeno's '*Henoticon' and again became Patr. of Antioch, where he remained till his death. At a Council he succeeded in inducing his bishops to assent to the Emperor's formula. He is chiefly remembered for his addition to the *Trisagion of the Monophysite clause ὁ σταυρωθεὶς δι' ἡμᾶς ('who was crucified for us'). Acc. to *Theodore Lector he also introduced the recitation of the *Nicene Creed at the *Eucharist, the solemn blessing of the *chrism, and the commemoration of the *Theotokos at every service.

Theodore Lector, *H.E.*, i, 20–2 (repr. in J. P. Migne, *PG*, lxxxvi (1), 175–8). E. Venables in *D.C.B.*, iv (1887), pp. 338–40, s.v. 'Petrus (10)'; G. Fritz in *D.T.C.*, xii (pt. 2; 1935), cols. 1933–5, s.v. 'Pierre le Foulon'.

PETER GONZALES, St. See *Elmo, St.*

PETER THE HERMIT (1050?–1115). He was one of the most eloquent preachers of the First *Crusade, inaugurated by *Urban II in 1095 at the Council of *Clermont. In 1096 he led a band of enthusiastic country folk as far as Civitot where most of them were killed by the Turks while he had gone back to *Constantinople to ask for help from the Emp. Alexius. On his return he collected the survivors with whom he joined the main army under *Godfrey of Bouillon. During the siege of Antioch (1098) he made an unsuccessful attempt to escape but later apparently regained

his reputation and entered Jerusalem with the victorious army. On his return to Europe he became prior of the *Augustinian monastery of Neufmoutier (Huy) which he had helped to found. After his death he became the hero of many legends. The story, repeated by *Anna Comnena, that it was he who conceived the idea of the Crusades on a pilgrimage to Jerusalem is an invention. Commemoration on 8 July.

P. d'Outreman, S.J., *La Vie du vénérable Pierre l'Hermite* (Mons, 1632; mod. ed., Clermont, 1895). H. Hagenmeyer, *Peter der Eremite* (1879; Fr. tr., 1883). Y. Le Febvre, *Pierre l'Ermite et la croisade* (Amiens, 1946). See also works cited under *Crusades*.

PETER OF LAODICEA (*c.* 7th–8th cent.), Gk. Patristic writer and reputed Commentator on the Gospels. His name is attached to extracts from Gospel commentaries in two late MSS., though in others the passages are anonymous. In 1908 C. F. G. Heinrici argued that they were actually the work of this author; but further investigation has made this improbable. The only undoubted work of Peter's to survive is a short 'Exposition of the Lord's Prayer'.

The 'Expositio in Orationem Domini' and other fragments in J. P. Migne, *PG*, lxxxvi (2), 3321–36. The surviving portions of his supposed Comm. on Mt., ed. C. F. G. Heinrici (Beiträge zur Geschichte und Erklärung des Neuen Testamentes, v; 1908). M. Rauer, *Der dem Petrus von Laodicea zugeschriebene Lukaskommentar* (Neutestamentliche Abhandlungen, viii, Hft. 2; 1920). Krumbacher, p. 136 f. R. Devreesse in *Dict. Bibl.*, Suppl. i (1928), cols. 1165–7, s.v. 'Chaînes exégétiques grecques'.

PETER LOMBARD (*c.* 1100–60), the 'Master of the Sentences'. He was born near Novara in Lombardy, and after studying at *Bologna and *Reims, came to Paris *c.* 1139, where he taught at the Cathedral School. In 1148 he opposed *Gilbert de La Porrée at the Council of Reims, and in 1159, shortly before his death, was appointed Bp. of Paris. His Commentaries on the Pauline Epistles and on the Psalms were probably written before 1143, and his chief work, the 'Sententiarum libri quatuor', between 1148 and 1150. This last work, to which he owes his fame, is arranged in four books, on (1) the Trinity, (2) the Creation and Sin, (3) the Incarnation and the Virtues, and (4) the Sacraments and the Four Last Things. It contains a wealth of quotations from the Latin Fathers, esp. Sts. *Augustine and *Hilary, as well as (of the Greeks) from St. *John of Damascus, hitherto almost unknown in the W. After Peter Lombard's death the book was violently attacked by *Walter of St.-Victor on the ground of its *Abelardian Christological '*Nihilianism', i.e. the doctrine that Christ acc. to His humanity is nothing (*quod Christus secundum quod est homo non est aliquid*), which, however, was apparently given only as an opinion. Later, under the influence of *Joachim of Fiore's 'Liber de vera et falsa philosophia', which attacked Peter Lombard's Trinitarian teaching, efforts were made to have the work censured at the Fourth *Lateran Council in 1215, with the result that Joachim's doctrine was rejected and the 'Sentences' pronounced orthodox. After this rehabilitation it became the standard textbook of Catholic theology during the Middle Ages, despite the early rejection of several opinions advanced in it, e.g. the identification of the Holy Spirit with the virtue of charity. Its teaching on the Sacraments marked an important development; Peter Lombard is one of the first to insist on the number seven, to distinguish them (like *Alexander of Hales later) from the *sacramentals, and to clarify the conception by asserting the efficacity and causality of the sign. The book, which owed its success chiefly to its lucid arrangement, its comprehensiveness, and its absence of individuality, was commented on by nearly all theologians of repute and even versified. It was finally superseded as a textbook by the 'Summa' of St. *Thomas Aquinas, but in the 17th cent. commentaries were still produced, among the last being that of the *Jesuit, J. M. de Ripalda (1635).

Works collected in J. P. Migne, PL, cxci and cxcii. Crit. ed. of the text of the Sentences in the ed. of the Commentary on them by St. *Bonaventura, Opera, ed. by the Franciscans at Quaracchi, i–iv (Quaracchi, 1882–9); text of the Sentences also ed. separately, 2 vols., ib., 1916. F. Protois, Pierre Lombard, évêque de Paris. . . . Son époque, sa vie, ses écrits, son influence (thesis, Paris, 1880). J. N. Espenberger, Die Philosophie des Petrus Lombardus und ihre Stellung im zwölften Jahrhundert (B.G.P.M., iii, Hft. 5; 1901). O. Baltzer, Die Sentenzen des Petrus Lombardus (Studien zur Geschichte der Theologie und der Kirche, viii, Hft. 3; 1902). J. Schupp, Die Gnadenlehre des Petrus Lombardus (1932). F. Stegmüller (ed.), Repertorium Commentariorum in Sententias Petri Lombardi (2 vols., Würzburg, 1947). There is an important series of artt., mainly by J. de Ghellinck, S.J., listed by id. in D.T.C., vide infra. J. de Ghellinck, S.J., Le Mouvement théologique du XIIe siècle (1914), pp. 73–244 (ed. 2, Museum Lessianum, Section Historique, x; 1948, pp. 113–373). Überweg, ii, 274–6, with bibl. p. 710 f. J. de Ghellinck, S.J., in D.T.C., xii (pt. 2; 1935), cols. 1941–2019, s.v. 'Pierre Lombard', with good bibl. R. Seeberg in P.R.E. (ed. 3), xi (1902), pp. 630–42, s.v. 'Lombardus, Petrus'; J. de Ghellinck, S.J., in C.E., xi (1911), p. 768 f., s.v.

PETER MARTYR, St. (1205–52), Inquisitor. Born at *Verona (hence known also as **Veronensis**) of parents of the *Cathari sect, received into the *Dominican Order in 1221 at *Bologna by St. *Dominic himself, and eventually elected prior of several houses, he was appointed *Inquisitor for N. Italy by Pope *Gregory IX in 1251. He gained a great reputation as a preacher and wonder-worker, and successfully reconciled large numbers of Cathari, at the same time forcing others into exile. While journeying from Como to Milan he was attacked by two assassins, one of whom clove his head with an axe and stabbed his companion. After commending himself and his murderer to God, he wrote on the ground in his own blood (so tradition affirms) the words 'Credo in Deum', received another blow, and died. Fra *Angelico has depicted him in a famous painting in the convent of S. Marco, Florence, with wounded head, his finger to his lips. Feast day, 29 Apr. He was the patron of Inquisitors.

Life by Thomas Agni de Lentino, O.P., written before 1257, pr. from a redaction made c. 1517 in AA.SS., Apr. III (1675), pp. 686–719; other material, pp. 678–86; Gerard de Fracheto, O.P. (d. 1271), Vitae Fratrum Ordinis Praedi-

catorum, ed. B. M. de Reichert, O.P. (Monumenta Ordinis Praedicatorum, i, Rome, 1897), pp. 236–48. Life by P. T. Campana (Milan, 1741). F. T. Perrens, 'Saint Pierre Martyr et l'hérésie des Patarins à Florence' in Revue historique, ii (1876), pp. 337–66. G. Meersseman, O.P., 'Études sur les anciennes confréries dominicaines, II. Les confréries de saint Pierre Martyr' in Archivum Fratrum Praedicatorum, xxi (1951), pp. 51–196, with docc. A. Redigouda in E.C., x (1952), col. 1450, s.v. 'Pietro de Verona' for further bibl.

PETER MARTYR (1500–62), an Anglicized form of 'Pietro Martire Vermigli', Reformer. He was born at Florence, the son of Stefano Vermigli (a follower of *Savonarola), who, having lost several children, vowed to dedicate any that lived to St. Peter Martyr (see previous entry). After education at Fiesole by the *Augustinians and joining that order, he became in 1530 abbot of the Augustinians at Spoleto, and in 1533 prior of St. Petrus-ad-aram at Naples. He was now a serious student of the Bible, and was much impressed by a reading of M. *Bucer's Commentaries on the Gospels and Psalms, and H. *Zwingli's De vera et falsa religione. The sympathy with the Reformers which he displayed in his lectures led him to be accused of error and prohibited from preaching, though the prohibition was removed, on appeal to Rome, through the help of R. *Pole and other friends. In 1542, however, he was forced to flee from Italy and take refuge at Zürich and Basel, and lastly at Strassburg, where, with Bucer's help, he was appointed professor of theology (1542). Here he married Catherine Dammartin, a nun. At T. *Cranmer's invitation he came to England with B. *Ochino in 1547, was given a government pension of 40 marks, made Regius professor of divinity at Oxford (1548), and took part in a great disputation (1549) on the Eucharist. He was consulted on the BCP of 1552, and was one of the commissioners for the reform of canon law. In 1553 his wife died, and was buried in *Christ Church Cathedral, Oxford, near the tomb of St. *Frideswide, but, at the order of Cardinal Pole, the body was subsequently disinterred. (In 1558 her remains were mingled with the supposed relics of St. Frideswide and buried at the north-east end of the cathedral; hence N. *Sanders' epigram 'hic requiescit religio cum superstitione'). At *Mary's accession, Martyr was imprisoned, but after six months was allowed, through S. *Gardiner's influence, to go to Strassburg, where he was reappointed professor of theology (1554). In 1556, owing to opposition to his Eucharistic views, he removed to Zürich, where he became professor of Hebrew, maintaining a long correspondence on English affairs with J. *Jewel, R. *Cox, John Parkhurst, and Edwin *Sandys.

Some of his correspondence is included in the Zürich Letters ed. H. Robinson (*Parker Society, 4 vols., 1842–5). The primary source is J. Simler, Oratio de Vita et Obitu (Zürich, 1563; it was also appended to the collection of Martyr's miscellaneous works publd. under the title Loci Communes Sacrarum Literarum, Zürich, 1563; Eng. tr. of the latter, with the Oratio appended, by A. Marten, London, 1583). F. C. Schlosser, Leben des Theodor de Beza und des Peter Martyr Vermilli (Heidelberg, 1809), pp. 363–514. Further life by C. Schmidt (Leben und ausgewählte Schriften der Väter und Begründer der Reformirten Kirche, vii; Elberfeld, 1858). M. Young, *The Life and Times of Aonio Paleario*, i (1860), pp. 397–493. A. Gordon in *D.N.B.*, lviii (1899), pp. 253–6, s.v. 'Vermigli'.

PETER MOGILA. See *Mogila, Peter*.

PETER MONGO (d. 490) (Gk. Μογγός, 'stammerer'), *Monophysite Patr. of *Alexandria. In 477 he was elected the successor of the Monophysite, *Timothy Aelurus. The Emp. *Zeno forced him to abandon his see temporarily, but he was restored on accepting the *Henoticon. Rejecting the decisions of *Chalcedon, he remained a staunch supporter of *Acacius, the schismatic Patr. of *Constantinople. While his acceptance of the Henoticon annoyed the extreme Monophysites in Alexandria, his endeavours to placate them by a Monophysite interpretation of it also offended the orthodox. The compromise served, however, to maintain peaceful relations with Constantinople during the patriarchate of Acacius. Euphemius, who became Patr. of Constantinople in 490, had his name erased from the *diptychs and intended to depose him, an action prevented by Mongo's death.

The sources include *Evagrius, *H.E.*, iii, *Zacharias Scholasticus, *H.E.*, v, and Theophanes, *Chronogr.*, 194. I. Rucker in *L.Th.K.*, viii (1936), col. 170 f.

PETER NOLASCO, St. (*c.* 1189–*c.* 1256), *Mercedarian. The facts of his life are much contested. Acc. to a late tradition he took part in the *Crusade against the *Albigensians and became the tutor of James I of Aragon. He is usually regarded as the joint-founder, with St. *Raymond of Penafort (from whom they received the rule), of the order of Mercedarians for the ransom of Christian prisoners from the Saracens. He redeemed 400 captives on a journey to Valencia and Granada, and went himself twice to Africa as ransomer. He ceased to rule the order after 1249, giving place to William of Bas. In 1628 he was canonized by *Urban VIII. Feast day, 28 (formerly 31) Jan.

Lives by F. Zumel, Mercedarian, pr. in *AA.SS.*, Jan. II (1643), pp. 981–8, F. Olignano, Mercedarian (Naples, 1668), F. Colombo (Madrid, 1674) and P. N. Pérez, Mercedarian (Barcelona, 1915; It. tr., 1921). See also bibl. to *Mercedarians* and *Raymond of Penafort*.

PETER'S PENCE (Lat. *denarii S. Petri*), also 'Rome-Scot', an ecclesiastical tax formerly paid in England to the Pope. It was first paid by King *Offa after the visit of the two Papal legates concerned in the erection of the Archbishopric of *Lichfield in 787, and appears to have been continued by Offa's successors. *William of Malmesbury records that it was paid by King Aethelwulf (d. 858), the father of *Alfred the Great. After a lapse it was renewed by *William I. At one time a levy, collected at midsummer on all but the poorest houses, in the 12th cent. it was commuted by the Bishops to an annual sum of £199 : 6 : 8. It was finally abolished by *Henry VIII in 1534.

Act forbidding the payment (25 Hen. VIII, c. 21) repr. in Gee-Hardy, pp. 209–32 (No. 53). P. Fabre, 'Recherches

sur le denier de saint Pierre en Angleterre au moyen-âge' in *Mélanges G. B. de Rossi* (Supplément aux Mélanges d'Archéologie et d'Histoire publiés par l'École française de Rome, xii; 1892), pp. 159–82; O. Jensen, 'The "Denarius Sancti Petri" in England' in *Transactions of the Royal Historical Society*, New Series, xv (1901), pp. 171–247. W. E. Lunt, *Papal Revenues in the Middle Ages* (Records of Civilization, xix; New York, 1934), i, 65–71, with documents, ii, 55–81; id., *Financial Relations of the Papacy with England to 1327* (Studies in Anglo-Papal Relations during the Middle Ages, i; The Mediaeval Academy of America Publication No. 22; 1939), pp. 3–84, both with reff. E. W. Watson in *D.E.C.H.*, p. 457 f.

PETER OF TARANTAISE, St. (d. 1175). (Not to be confounded with Pope Innocent V (1276), also 'Peter of Tarantaise'.) A native of the Dauphiné, at the age of 20 he became a *Cistercian monk at the Abbey of Bonnevaux, founded by St. *Bernard, where he lived a life of great piety. In 1142 he was appointed Abp. of Tarantaise (Moutiers, in Savoy), and with great difficulty thoroughly reformed his diocese, founding many hospitals. His practice of distributing free bread and soup ('May Bread') in the weeks before harvest is said to have survived until the Revolution. In 1155 he sought release in flight, but being discovered as a lay brother in a Swiss monastery he was compelled to return to his see. He stood high in the confidence of the Popes and was commissioned to try to reconcile Prince Henry (later Henry II) of England and Louis VII of France. Feast day, 8 May.

AA.SS., Mai II. (1680), pp. 320–45, incl. life by Godfrey, Abbot of Hauteville, written at the request of Pope Lucius III and completed before 1185. J. M. Chevray, *La Vie de saint Pierre II, archevêque de Tarentaise* (1841). H. Brultey, *Saint Pierre de Tarentaise*. Ses miracles, ses reliques, son culte (Besançon, 1874). Un Moine de Tamié [i.e. A. Dimier], *saint Pierre de Tarentaise*. Essai historique (Ligugé, 1935).

PETER THE VENERABLE (*c.* 1092–1156), eighth Abbot of *Cluny. A descendant of the noble family of Montboissier, he was educated at the monastery of Sauxillanges of the congregation of Cluny, under whose abbot St. *Hugh he made his profession at the age of 17. After being prior at Vézelay and Domène (1120), he was elected abbot of Cluny in 1122. Against much opposition he carried through important reforms, esp. in the financial and educational spheres, in the two general chapters of 1132 and 1146 by enforcing the detailed constitutions which he had drawn up for the congregation. His interest in the pursuit of studies at Cluny brought about a controversy with his intimate friend, St. *Bernard, who wished to see the monastic life confined to prayer and manual work. In 1130 Peter supported Innocent II against the antipope Anacletus II, himself a Cluniac monk, and in 1140 he gave shelter to *Abelard first at Cluny and later at the priory of St.-Marcel-de-Chalon. Between his numerous journeys, which took him twice to Spain (1126 and 1141), twice to England, and six times to Rome, he frequently retired to a hermitage to devote himself to study and meditation. He was the first to have the *Koran translated into Latin (completed 1143) and himself wrote against the Saracens. His works, among which are treatises against *Peter de Bruys and against the Jews (c. 1140), a number of sermons, and some poems, show comparatively little acquaintance with the Fathers but profound knowledge of the Scriptures, and a preference for the literal sense which causes him to avoid allegorical speculations. His moderation and gentleness earned him the veneration of his contemporaries, though in the eyes of posterity he was eclipsed by the great figure of his friend, St. Bernard. Though honoured as a saint, he was never canonized. Commemoration in several martyrologies is on 29 Dec.

Collected ed. of his works, Paris, 1522 (very incomplete); further collection, incl. text of statutes of Cluny during his time, in M. Marrier, O.S.B. (ed.), *Bibliotheca Cluniacensis* (Paris, 1614), cols. 621–1420; works repr., with additions from E. *Martène and elsewhere (details in *D.T.C.*, vide infra), in J. P. Migne, *PL*, clxxxix, 61–1054. Life by his friend, Rudolphus, pr. from a MS. no longer known in E. Martène, O.S.B.–U. Durand, O.S.B. (edd.), *Veterum Scriptorum et Monumentorum Amplissima Collectio*, vi (Paris, 1729), cols. 1187–202; repr. in J. P. Migne, op. cit., cols. 15–28. Further life in M. Marrier, op. cit., cols. 589–602, repr. with other biogr. material in J. P. Migne, op. cit., cols. 27–62. J. H. Pignot, *Histoire de l'ordre de Cluny depuis la fondation de l'abbaye jusqu'à la mort de Pierre-le-Vénérable*, iii (1868), pp. 47–609. Other modern studies by J. d'Avenel (Paris, 1874), M. Demimuid (ib., 1876), and J. Leclercq, O.S.B. ('Figures monastiques'; Abbaye S. Wandrille, 1946), with bibl. Festschrift commemorating the 8th centenary of his death ed. G. Constance–J. Kritzeck (Studia Anselmiana, xl; 1957). W. Watkins, 'Peter the Venerable' in *The Downside Review*, liv (1936), pp. 1–17. M. Manitius, 'Zu Petrus' von Cluny patristischen Kenntnissen' in *Speculum*, iii (1928), pp. 582–7. A. *Wilmart, O.S.B., 'Le Poème apologétique de Pierre le Vénérable et les poèmes connexes' in *R.Bén.*, li (1939), pp. 53–69. Manitius, iii, 136–44. G. Grützmacher in *P.R.E.* (ed. 3), xv (1904), pp. 222–6, s.v. 'Petrus der Ehrwürdige'; P. Séjourné, O.S.B., in *D.T.C.*, xii (pt. 2; 1935), cols. 2065–81, s.v. 'Pierre le Vénérable'. See also bibl. to *Peter de Bruys*.

PETER OF VERONA, St. See *Peter Martyr, St.*

PETERBOROUGH.

At the Saxon village of Medehamstede, which had existed on the site, a monastery was established c. 655, Peada, son of Penda, King of the Mercians, being one of its founders. After the monastery church had been destroyed by the Danes in 870, it was rebuilt c. 970 by *Ethelwold, Bp. of *Winchester, who dedicated it to St. Peter, and hence the village came to be called 'Peterborough'. This church being accidentally burnt in 1116, the foundations of a new church were laid in the following year. It was completed in 1237 and consecrated by R. *Grosseteste, Bp. of *Lincoln, and in 1541 became the cathedral of the newly constituted diocese. It embraces eight periods of construction from Norman to Perpendicular. Catherine of Aragon was buried here in 1536 and *Mary Queen of Scots in 1587, Mary's body being removed to *Westminster Abbey in 1612. In 1895 the site of a cruciform Saxon church was discovered under the south transept.

Chronicon Petroburgense, ed. T. Stapleton (Camden Society, xlvii; 1849). G. Butler, *Statutes of Peterborough Cathedral* (1853; Eng. tr.). W. T. Mellows (ed.), *Peterborough Local Administration. Parochial Government before the Reformation. Churchwardens' Accounts 1467–1573 with supplementary documents 1107–1488* (Northampton Record Society, ix; Kettering, 1939); id., *Peterborough Local Administration. The Last Days of Peterborough. Being Part I of Tudor Documents, a Series relating chiefly to the Surrender of the Monastery, the Administration of its*

Temporalities during the Interregnum before the Establishment of the Cathedral, the Early Government of the Cathedral by the Dean and Chapter, and the Tudor Bishops of the Diocese of Peterborough (ib., xiii; 1947); id., *Peterborough Local Administration. The Foundation of Peterborough Cathedral A.D. 1541. Being Part II of Tudor Documents* (ib., xii; 1941). 'The Manuscripts of the Dean and Chapter of Peterborough' are described by J. A. Bennett in the *Twelfth Report of the Historical Manuscripts Commission*, Appendix, Part ix (1891), pp. 580–5. M. R. James, *Lists of Manuscripts Formerly in Peterborough Abbey Library* (Suppl. to the Bibliographical Society's Transactions, No. v; 1926). S. Gunton, *The History of the Church of Peterborough* (1686). W. *Dugdale, *Monasticon Anglicanum*, i (ed. 1817), pp. 344–404. B. Willis, *A Survey of the Cathedrals of Lincoln, Ely, Oxford and Peterborough* (1730), pp. 475–540. W. D. Sweeting, *The Cathedral Church of Peterborough* (Bell's Cathedral Series, 1898). J. C. Cox in *The Victoria History of the County of Northampton*, ii, ed. R. M. Serjeantson–W. R. D. Adkins (1906), pp. 83–95, with reff. G. F. Assinder in *D.E.C.H.* (1912), pp. 455–7, s.v.

PETITE ÉGLISE.

The body of French Catholics who refused to recognize the *Concordat of 1801 (q.v.) and separated themselves from the communion of the Pope. Its members, who were known by various names, such as 'Illuminés' and 'Fidèles', remained faithful to a number of exiled bishops who had resisted the Pope's order to resign their old dioceses, and met in private houses for worship. When at the restoration, between 1817 and 1818, all schismatic bishops were reconciled to the Holy See except the Bp. of Blois, he came to be regarded as the head of the Petite Église till his death in 1829, which left them without a bishop. From that date their number rapidly decreased, esp. after their last priest died in 1847. By 1900 the schism had practically ceased to exist.

PETRARCH, FRANCESCO (1304–74),

Italian poet and humanist. He spent part of his youth at Carpentras, near *Avignon, where his father had settled after being exiled from Florence for embracing, like *Dante, the cause of the White Guelphs. After studying law at Montpellier from 1319 to 1323 and at *Bologna from 1323 to 1325, he received minor orders at Avignon in 1326 which enabled him to hold several benefices. In 1327 he first saw Laura, who was to inspire his most famous poems collected in the 'Canzoniere'. From 1330 to 1337 he journeyed through N. France, Germany, and Italy, visiting many scholars and copying classical MSS. until, in 1337, he settled down to a life of solitude at Vaucluse where most of his important works were written. His poems on Laura and his epic 'Africa' (begun in 1338) on Scipio Africanus won him the poet's crown in 1341. In the following year he wrote the treatise 'De Contemptu Mundi', consisting of three dialogues between himself and St. *Augustine, who seeks to turn the poet's mind from the transitory things of this world to thoughts of eternal life. In 1347 Petrarch joined the short lived republican movement of Cola di *Rienzi and in 1350 began his famous friendship with Boccaccio. In the following years he was employed on several political embassies, e.g. to the Emp. Charles IV at Prague (1356). The last years of his life were spent again in retirement at Padua and the neighbouring village of

Arquà. His religious nature, which was often in conflict with the sensuousness of the fame-loving poet and the passion of the scholar for pagan culture, found expression in several Latin treatises. 'De Otio Religiosorum' (begun in 1347), dedicated to the *Carthusians of Montrieu, is a panegyric on the contemplative life; 'De Vita Solitaria' (1356) is a praise of solitude; and in the 'De Remediis Utriusque Fortunae' (1358–66) the ageing poet meditates on the transitoriness of human life. His last great poetical work, the 'Trionfi', strongly influenced by Dante's *Divina commedia, cele-brates in allegorical form the triumph of the Divine over all things and the ultimate redemp-tion of man from the dominion of the senses.

Editio princeps of his collected works, Basel, 1496 (Lat. works only); fuller ed. [by J. Herold] (4 vols. bound in 1, ib., 1554). A. Hortis (ed.), Scritti inediti di Francesco Petrarca (Trieste, 1874). Crit. text in the Edizione nazionale delle opere di Francesco Petrarca by various edd. (Florence, 1926 ff.). Eng. tr. of his sonnets by W. D. Foulke (London, 1915) and J. Auslander (ib., 1931), and of his 'De Vita Solitaria' by J. Zeitlin (Urbana, Ill., 1924). The fullest account in Eng. is E. H. R. Tatham, Francesco Petrarca . . . His Life and Correspondence (2 vols., 1925–6). The very extensive literature includes general studies by F. di Sanctis (Naples, 1869; ed. B. *Croce, 1907), L. Geiger (Leipzig, 1874), G. Koerting (ib., 1878), J. H. Robinson (New York–London, 1898; with Eng. tr. of extracts of his letters), G. Finza (Florence, 1900), H. C. Hollway-Calthorp (London, 1907), Maud F. Jerrold (ib., 1909), E. Wolf (Beiträge zur Kulturgeschichte des Mittelalters und der Renaissance, xxviii; 1926), L. Tonelli (Milan, 1930), and H. W. Eppelsheimer (Frankfurt a.Main, 1934). P. de Nolhac, Pétrarque et l'humanisme (Bibliothèque de l'École des Hautes-Études. Sciences Philologiques et Historiques, xci; 1892; revised ed., Bibliothèque Littéraire de la Renais-sance, Nouvelle Série, i and ii; 1907). J. H. Whitfield, Petrarch and the Renaissance (1943). Collection of essays by M. A. Potter (posthumous, Harvard Studies in Romance Languages, iii; 1917) and E. H. Wilkins (in English, Rome, 1951), as well as a large number of commemorative vol-umes. The Catalogue of the Petrarch Collection Bequeathed by W. Fiske [to the Cornell University Library], compiled by Mary Fowler (1916), contains extensive bibl. to date. J. A. Symonds in E.B. (ed. 11), xxi (1911), pp. 310–15, s.v.; E. Carrara in Enciclopedia italiana, xxvii (1935), pp. 8–23, s.v. 'Petrarca', with full bibl.; P. G. Ricci in E.C., ix (1952), cols. 1288–99, s.v. 'Petrarca', with more recent bibl.

PETRI, OLAUS (1493–1552), Swedish Re-former. The son of a blacksmith of Örebro, he was educated at *Wittenberg and, returning home imbued with strict *Lutheran views, was made master of the chapter school at Strengnäs, and later appointed city clerk at Stockholm (1524). Gaining the favour of Gustavus Vasa, by whom he was later made chancellor (1531), he became the leading ex-ponent of doctrinal change in Sweden. After his marriage in 1525 he produced a continuous stream of tracts, pamphlets, and a book of homilies, which were widely read. In 1529 he published the first Swedish service book, Een Handbock pää Swensko. The latter years of his life (after 1539) were spent in retirement.

His brother, LAURENTIUS PETRI (1499–1573), was also a leading Reformer. He took a prominent part in the translation of the NT into Swedish (1526) and was appointed the first Protestant Abp. of *Upsala (1531).

Collected Works (4 vols., Upsala, 1914–17). The Manual of Olavus Petri (ed. E. E. Yelverton, Church Historical Society, 1953). Lives by R. Holm (Upsala, 1917) and H. Schück (Stockholm, 1893). J. E. Berggren, 'Olaus Petris

reformatoriska grundtankar' in Upsala Universitets Årsskrift (1899), pp. 1–17. C. J. I. Bergendoff, Olaus Petri and the Ecclesiastical Transformation in Sweden (New York, 1928). E. Newman in R.G.G. (ed. 2), iv (1930), col. 1103.

PETROBRUSIANS. See Peter de Bruys.

PETROCK, St. (6th cent.) also 'Pedrog', 'the captain of Cornish saints' (T. *Fuller). He is said to have been the son of a Welsh chieftain who after studying in Ireland (where he is said to have instructed St. *Kevin) made his way to Cornwall and founded monasteries at Padstow (i.e. 'Petrockstowe') and Bodmin. It is almost impossible to disentangle the facts of his life from the extravagant embellishments of later times. In 1177 his relics were stolen from Bodmin by a Breton canon and given to the abbey of St.-Méen, but Henry II secured their restoration. Many churches in Cornwall and Devon bear his dedication; and he is also venerated in Brittany as St. Perreux. He is commonly represented with a stag. Feast day, 4 June.

14th cent. life by John of Tynemouth repr. in AA.SS., Jun. I (1695), pp. 400–2. G. H. Doble, Saint Petrock, Abbot and Confessor ('Cornish Saints' Series, No. 11 [c. 1929]), with Eng. tr. of Life in MS. Bibl. Nat. Lat. 9889. C. W. Boase in D.C.B., iv (1887), p. 326 f.

PETRONIUS, St. (early 5th cent.), Bp. of *Bologna. He was perhaps the son of Pe-tronius, a praefectus praetorio in Gaul (402–8). He appears to have made a pilgrimage to Palestine in early life, visiting the monks and holy places, and after becoming Bp. of Bologna (c. 432) to have erected a church, dedicated to St. Stephen, modelled on the *Constantinian buildings in *Jerusalem. Various extant writings have been assigned to him, mostly in-correctly. His cultus at Bologna rapidly de-veloped after the appearance of a historically worthless 'Life' in the 12th cent., and in 1141 his relics were discovered. The present church of St. Petronius, a fine Gothic structure, was begun in 1390 and completed in the 17th cent. Feast day, 4 Oct.

*Gennadius, De Viris Illustribus, xli. The 12th-cent. life (of little historical value) and other later material is pr., with good introductory discussion, in AA.SS., Oct. II (1768), pp. 422–70. Full study by F. Lanzoni (Rome, 1907). Id., 'Le fonti della Vita S. Petronii' in Romagna, vii (1910), pp. 269–77. F. H. B. Daniell in D.C.B., iv (1887), p. 328 f.

PEW. At first the customary postures of the worshippers in the W., as to this day in E. churches, were standing and kneeling, and no seats were provided for the congregation. Later on, as a concession to the infirm, stone seats were attached to the walls, or, more rarely, to the piers of the nave; and by the end of the 13th cent. many English churches appear to have been equipped also with a number of fixed wooden benches. These were often known as 'Pews' (probably derived from the Latin 'podium') and meaning a seat raised up above floor-level. Such Pews, even in village churches, were sometimes elaborately carved, at the ends and on the back, with figures of saints, symbols of the Passion of Christ, or grotesque animals. As fine a set as any in England is to be seen at Fressingfield, in Suffolk.

A. Heales, *The History and Law of Church Seats or Pews* (2 vols., 1872). J. C. Cox, *Bench Ends in English Churches* (1916). G. W. O. Addleshaw–F. Etchells, *The Architectural Setting of Anglican Worship* (1948), pp. 86–98. See also J. M. *Neale, *The History of Pews* (Paper read before the *Cambridge Camden Society, 22 Nov. 1841; 1841; Suppl., 1842; ed. 3, incl. suppl. and additions, 1843).

PFAFF FRAGMENTS OF IRENAEUS.
Four fragments first publd. in S. *Maffei's *Giornale de' letterati d' Italia* in 1713 by C. M. Pfaff (d. 1760), who alleged that he had found them in the Turin library and believed them to be written by St. *Irenaeus. Among other subjects they dealt with 'true Gnosis' and the 'new oblation' (i.e. the Eucharist). Though their Irenaean authorship was constantly challenged from the outset, they were regularly quoted and discussed down to the end of the 19th cent., when A. *Harnack showed convincingly that they were a fabrication of Pfaff himself. He proved that they made use of the (late) *Textus Receptus of the NT and of the defective printed editions of the Greek text of Irenaeus current in the early 18th cent., as well as reflected Pfaff's own theological tenets, e.g. the *Lutheran doctrine of the Eucharist.

A. Harnack, *Die Pfaff'schen Irenäus-Fragmente als Fälschungen Pfaffs nachgewiesen* (T.U., xx, Hft. 3; 1900), a magisterial monograph. On Pfaff himself, cf. E. Preuschen in *P.R.E.* (ed. 3), xv (1904), pp. 233–7, with useful bibl.

PFLUG, JULIUS VON (1499–1564), Bp. of
Naumburg. Of Saxon descent, he was educated at Leipzig, *Bologna, and Padua, and appointed Provost of Zeitz in 1522 and Dean of Meissen in 1537. His humanistic sympathies made him eager for peace with the Protestants and to that end he took part in several conferences, e.g. at Leipzig in 1534 and at *Ratisbon in 1541. He indicated his willingness even to tolerate a married clergy and communion in two kinds. In 1541 he was elected Bp. of Naumburg-Zeitz, but as the Elector Johann Friedrich of Saxony refused to acknowledge him, he was unable to take possession of his see till after the Elector's defeat at Mühlberg in 1547. The 'Interim of *Augsburg' (1648; q.v.) was largely Pflug's work. His rule was much disturbed by the Protestantism in his diocese. In his theology, he was much influenced by G. *Contarini.

The sources are scattered. Schottenloher, ii (1935), p. 138 (Nos. 17222–17232b). G. Kawerau in *P.R.E.* (ed. 3), xv (1904), pp. 260–3; L. Cristiani in *D.T.C.*, xii (pt. 1; 1933), cols. 1366–9; A. Herte in *L.Th.K.*, viii (1936), col. 208, all sv., and with bibl. See also bibl. to *Augsburg* (Interim of).

PHANAR, The. The official residence and
court of the *Oecumenical Patriarch at *Constantinople. It is in the Greek quarter of the city, on the Golden Horn.

PHARISEES (Aram. פְּרִישִׁין, 'separated ones';
Gk. Φαρισαῖοι). Jewish religious party, known chiefly through *Josephus, the *Talmud, and the NT. They accepted the name already applied to them by their opponents in the time of John Hyrcanus I (135–104 B.C.), when they first appeared as a distinct party, in the belief that their 'separation' was pleasing to God. They upheld the strict legalistic Judaism of the *Chasidim (q.v.), whose successors they were; but unlike the *Sadducees they put the oral additions which had become attached to Mosaic Law on the same level of importance as the Law itself. They also fostered synagogue worship. They opposed John Hyrcanus for religious reasons and instigated a revolt against Alexander Jannaeus (103–76 B.C.), but were favoured by Alexander's widow, Alexandra (76–67 B.C.). They gradually secured a large following among the common people, who admired their austerity and shared their hatred of the pagan rulers and the sacerdotal caste. In the Gospels they appear as the chief opponents of the Lord, whom they attacked, e.g., for forgiving sins, breaking the Sabbath, and consorting with sinners. Christ repeatedly denounced their purely external observance of the Law, their multitude of formalistic precepts which even they themselves could not keep (e.g., Mt. 23. 13–36), and their self-righteousness (Lk. 18. 9–14). During the Passion they remained in the background, when their place was taken by the Sadducees. After the Resurrection they appear less hostile to the nascent Church than the Sadducees; they share its belief in the resurrection and a retribution in the next world, in angels, in human freedom and Divine Providence; and it was a Pharisee, Gamaliel, who publicly defended the Apostles before the Sanhedrin (Acts 5. 34–40). After the fall of *Jerusalem (A.D. 70) they disappear from history; but their influence survived in the teaching of the Rabbis and the *Mishnah. Several modern scholars have questioned whether the Pharisees depicted in the Gospels are representative of the party as a whole.

The primary authority, apart from the NT, is *Josephus. J. *Wellhausen, *Die Pharisäer und die Sadducäer* (1874). A. T. Robinson, *The Pharisees and Jesus* (The Stone Lectures for 1915–16, Studies in Theology, 1920). L. Finkelstein, *The Pharisees. The Sociological Background of their Faith* (2 vols., Philadelphia, Pa., 1940). W. Foerster, 'Der Ursprung des Pharisäismus' in *Z.N.T.W.*, xxxiv (1935), pp. 35–51. E. *Schürer, *Geschichte des jüdischen Volkes im Zeitalter Jesu Christi*, ii (ed. 4, 1907), pp. 449–75, with bibl. pp. 447–9. T. W. Manson, 'Sadduccee and Pharisee—The Origin and Significance of the Names', in *Bulletin of the John Rylands Library*, xxii (1938), pp. 144–59, esp. pp. 153–9. A. E. F. Sieffert in *P.R.E.* (ed. 3), xv (1904), pp. 264–92, s.v. 'Pharisäer und Sadducäer'; D. Eaton in *H.D.B.*, iii (1900), pp. 821–9, s.v.; H. M. Scott in *D.C.G.*, ii (1908), pp. 351–6, s.v.

PHELONION (Gk. φελόνιον). The E.
form of the *chasuble. In shape it is somewhat like the W. Gothic vestment, but is gathered up in front instead of at the sides, so that when in use it looks more like a *cope.

Braun, *L.G.*, pp. 234–9.

PHENOMENALISM. (1) The belief that
what we term physical objects have no existence except as experienced as 'sense data' in men (or animals) who perceive them.

(2) The theory that such objects, though they may in reality exist, can be known only as the experiences ('sense data') which they occasion in us.

(3) As used by E. *Caird and N. Kemp Smith, the theory of knowledge expounded in, or implied by, *The Critique of Pure Reason* of I. *Kant, on the basis of his fundamental distinction between appearance and reality.

PHENOMENOLOGY (Gk., τὰ φαινόμενα, 'appearance', and λογία, 'discourse'), lit. 'the science of *phenomena*'. The term was occasionally employed by I. *Kant in its literal sense. By G. W. F. *Hegel, whose first large philosophical treatise bore the title *Phänomenologie des Geistes* (1807), it was applied to the description of the stages whereby the mind (*Geist*) develops from naïve consciousness (for Hegel, sense perception) to absolute knowledge. In recent times, however, it has been used esp. of the philosophical doctrines of Edmund Husserl (1859–1938) and his school. Acc. to Husserl phenomenology is a descriptive science concerned with the discovery and analysis of essences and essential meanings. It professes to exclude all metaphysical questions; but much in Husserl's first elaboration of the science tended towards a *Platonic realism. These Platonist elements were developed by his disciples and used e.g. by Max Scheler and Johannes Hessen for the defence of a Christian metaphysic of an *Augustinian (non-Thomistic) type. Husserl himself in his later writings embraced a form of Subjective Idealism.

Husserl, who already employed the phenomenological method in parts of the *Logische Untersuchungen* (2 vols. in 3, 1900), developed it in academic lectures in the years 1900–13 and systematically elaborated it in the programmatic *Ideen zu einer reinen Phänomenologie und phänomenologischen Philosophie* (1913; Eng. trans. by W. R. Boyce Gibson, *Ideas*, 1931). The chief organ of the Phenomenological Movement was the *Jahrbuch für Philosophie und phanomenologische Forschung* (11 vols., 1913–30). Phenomenology was the most influential movement in German Philosophy in the period 1910–33; but Husserl's Jewish ancestry brought it to an end with the arrival of the Nazis.

Until his last years, Husserl showed reluctance to publish. His later writings include *Vorlesungen zur Phänomenologie des inneren Zeitbewusstseins* (ed. M. Heidegger, 1928), *Formale und transzendentale Logik* (1929), *Méditations cartésiennes* (1931) and *Erfahrung und Urteil* (1939). Among Scheler's chief works were *Der Formalismus in der Ethik und die materiale Wertethik* (2 pts., 1913–16), *Vom Ewigen im Menschen* (collected essays, 1921), *Die Wissensformen und die Gesellschaft* (1926) and *Die Stellung des Menschen im Kosmos* (1928). J. Hessen, *Augustins Metaphysik der Erkenntnis* (1931). A. Metzger, *Phänomenologie und Metaphysik* (1933). The drastic redirection of Phenomenology in M. Heidegger makes it difficult to regard him and his followers as Phenomenologists (see also on Heidegger art. *Existentialism*).

PHILADELPHIA. A city of the Roman province of Asia. It was the seat of one of the '*Seven Churches of Asia', addressed in Rev. 2–3, and was there commended for its faithfulness and given promises for the future (3. 7–13). The circumstances in which this Church was founded are unknown. In the 14th cent. the city was a Christian stronghold and withstood several sieges by the Turks.

W. M. *Ramsay, *The Letters to the Seven Churches of Asia* (1904), pp. 391–412, with notes, p. 446. Id. in *H.D.B.*, iii (1900), pp. 830–2, s.v.

PHILADELPHIANS. A religious sect which flourished at the end of the 17th cent. Their doctrines derived ultimately from J. *Boehme, whose notions were eagerly adopted by John Pordage (1607–81), rector of Bradfield, Berks. There gathered round Pordage, who was ejected from his living by the *Triers in 1655, but reinstated in 1660, a group of followers who shared his enthusiasm for Boehme, the chief of them being a Mrs. Jane Leade (1623–1704), who from her childhood had experienced visions which from 1670 she recorded in a diary entitled *A Fountain of Gardens*. In 1670 the group was organized as the Philadelphian Society for the Advancement of Piety and Divine Philosophy, the term 'Society' being preferred to 'Church' as its members were to retain their respective ecclesiastical allegiances. They professed a kind of nature pantheism, imbued with esoteric and pseudo-mystical teachings, and held that their souls were immediately illuminated by the Holy Spirit. Its headquarters later removed from Bradfield to London. A certain Francis Lee (1661–1719), who had been a Fellow of St. John's College, Oxford, but refused the oaths on William III's accession, was much impressed by Mrs. Leade's writings, which he had come across in Holland and, becoming an ardent disciple, was instrumental in spreading Philadelphian doctrines on the Continent. A formal confession of belief was drawn up in 1703; but the Society rapidly declined after Mrs. Leade's death in 1704.

A number of Mrs Jane Leade's works were reissued in the 19th cent., incl. *The Wars of David* and other works, repr. 1816 and 1886; *The Revelation of Revelations*, repr. 1884, and *The Wonders of God's Creation*, repr. 1887. W. T. Whitley in *H.E.R.E.*, ix (1917), p. 836 f., s.v., with bibl.

PHILARET, THEODORE NIKITICH ROMANOV (c. 1553–1633), Patr. of Moscow and founder of the Romanov dynasty. Under his cousin, Theodore I (d. 1598), the last Tsar of the House of Rurik, he fought against the Swedes in 1590, and in 1593–4 conducted negotiations with the Emp. Rudolph II. Banished into a monastery by Boris Godunov (1598–1605), Theodore's successor, he was released by Pseudo-Dimitri I, who made him Metropolitan of Rostov. In 1610 he was imprisoned by the Poles. On their expulsion his son Michael was elected Tsar (1613), but Philaret was not freed until the truce of Deulino in 1619. In the same year he was made patriarch and until his death remained the virtual ruler of Russia, introducing measures to stop the migration of the serfs from the land into the steppes and reorganizing the army. A zealous reformer, he made it his aim to establish a seminary in each diocese and to encourage the study of theology. He also founded the Patriarchal Library.

R. N. Bain, *The First Romanovs* (1905), pp. 47–61. P. Pascal, *Avvakum et les débuts du Raskol. La crise religieuse au XVIIe siècle en Russie* (Paris thesis, Ligugé, 1938), esp. pp. 25–30. R. N. Bain in *E.B.* (ed. 11), xxi (1911), p. 373 f., s.v. See also bibl. to *Russia, Christianity in.*

PHILARET DROZDOV (1782–1867), Russian theologian and Metropolitan of Moscow. Educated at the Troitskii laura, near Moscow, he became lecturer at its seminary in 1803, and in 1808 took the monastic habit. In the same year he was called to the seminary at St. Petersburg as professor of philosophy, and subsequently taught most branches of theology at the Ecclesiastical Academy. His rise to high office took place very rapidly. In 1818 he became a member of the Holy Synod, in 1820 Bp. of Jaroslav, and in 1821 he was transferred to Moscow with the title of Archbishop, which was changed into that of Metropolitan in 1826. He was an exemplary bishop, famous for his sermons and the wise administration of his diocese as well as for his profound influence in Church and state. He was the author of many theological works, but his best-known writing is his *Christian Catechism of the Orthodox Catholic Eastern Greco-Russian Church* (1823). It is composed of three parts, dealing with (1) the Nicene Creed, (2) the Lord's Prayer and the Beatitudes, and (3) the Decalogue. It underwent several redactions through the attempt of the procurator, Protasov, an opponent of the infiltration of *Lutheran teaching into the Russian Church, to eliminate its supposedly Protestant elements which Philaret had imbibed in his youth esp. through the works of T. Prokopovitch (1681–1736). Though its doctrinal authority has been contested by other sections of the E. Church, it had a great influence on 19th cent. Russian theology and has frequently been commented on.

Eng. tr. of his *Christian Catechism* conveniently repr. from the trans. of R. W. Blackmore in P. *Schaff, *The Creeds of Christendom*, ii (1877), pp. 445–542. Fr. tr. of *Selected Sermons* by A. Serpinet (3 vols., Paris, 1866); Germ. tr. of his Christian Catechism by Dr. Blumenthal (Frankfurt a.M., 1872). M. Jugie, A.A., in *D.T.C.*, xiii (pt. 1; 1933), cols. 1376–95, with bibl. (mainly Russian). See also bibl. to *Russia, Christianity in.*

PHILASTER, St. (d. *c.* 397), more correctly 'Filaster', Bp. of Brescia and anti-heretical writer. After travel undertaken for the purpose of preaching the Gospel and of confounding the *Arians and other heretics, he became Bp. of Brescia towards the end of the 4th cent. *c.* 385 he wrote a treatise designed to refute 28 Jewish and 128 Christian heresies. This work, which may have been partly based on the 'Syntagma' of *Hippolytus, suffers from clumsy arrangement and a certain lack of proportion. Thus, the number of those stigmatized includes not only such notable heretics as *Simon Magus but also persons whose sole aberration was to believe that the stars occupied a fixed place in the sky instead of being set in position every evening by God. Despite its limitations, how-

ever, the book seems to have filled a real need in the W., and was freely used by St. *Augustine. He was succeeded in his see by St. *Gaudentius. Feast day, 18 July.

Liber de Haeresibus first ed. by J. Sichard (Basle, 1528); later edd. by J. A. *Fabricius (Hamburg, 1721), P. Galeardi (Brescia, 1738; repr. in J. P. Migne, *PL*, xii, 1111–302), and F. Marx (C.S.E.L., 1898). R. A. *Lipsius, *Zur Quellenkritik des Epiphanios* (1865); id., *Die Quellen der ältesten Ketzergeschichte neu untersucht* (1875), pp. 91–137. P. C. Juret, 'Étude grammaticale sur le latin de S. Filastrius' in *Romanische Forschungen*, xix (1906), pp. 130–320. Bardenhewer, iii, pp. 481–5.

PHILEAS, St. (d. *c.* 307), Bp. of Thmuis in Lower Egypt. Of noble birth and great wealth, he was imprisoned, tried before the prefect, Culcianus, and executed at *Alexandria. A Roman official, Philoromus, suffered at the same time. A letter to his flock from his dungeon (in *Eusebius, *H.E.*, VIII, x) and the *acta* of his trial (acc. to *Tillemont, T. *Ruinart, P. Allard, L. *Duchesne, and A. *Harnack, authentic; but challenged by C. Schmidt and E. *Schwartz) survive. Feast day, 4 Feb.

The chief authority is Eusebius, *H.E.*, VIII, ix, 7 f., and x (with additions in *Rufinus's Lat. version). Epistle (from Eusebius, l.c.) and Acts pr. in R. Knopf–G. Krüger (edd.), *Ausgewählte Märtyrerakten* (Sammlung ausgewählter kirchen- und dogmengeschichtliche Quellenschriften, N.F., iii; 1929), pp. 111–16. Lat. version pr. in T. Ruinart, O.S.B. (ed.), *Acta Primorum Martyrum Sincera* (Paris, 1689), pp. 323–5. Bardenhewer, ii, 247–9. H. *Leclercq, O.S.B., in *D.A.C.L.*, xiv (pt. 1; 1939), cols. 703–9, s.v. 'Philéas et Philorome', with bibl.

PHILEMON. The recipient of St. *Paul's brief epistle of that name. He was a Christian of Colossae or the neighbourhood, whose slave, *Onesimus, had run away, and somehow came to meet St. Paul, either in *Rome or, if G. S. Duncan is right, in *Ephesus. St. Paul sent Onesimus, now a Christian and therefore a 'beloved brother', back to his master with this epistle, which was a tactful plea for his forgiveness. The letter was undoubtedly written and sent with the Ep. to the *Colossians. Acc. to tradition, Philemon and his wife, Appia, were martyred at Colossæ. Feast day, 22 Nov.

Modern commentaries on the Ep. include those of J. B. *Lightfoot (London, 1875, with Col., pp. 369–412), M. R. Vincent (I.C.C., 1897, with Phil., pp. 171–94), E. L. Williams (Camb. Bib., Gk. text, 1907, with Col., pp. lxvi–lxxiii and 172–207), M. *Dibelius (Hb.N.T. Lfg. 21, 1911; ed. 2, xii, 1927; ed. 3 by H. Greeven, 1953, with Col. and Eph., pp. 101–8), E. Lohmeyer (K.E.K., ix, Hft. 2, ed. 8, 1930, with Phil. and Col., pp. 171–92, with bibl. p. 194), E. F. Scott (Moffatt Comm., 1930, with Col. and Eph., pp. 95–115), and L. B. Radford (West. Comm., 1931, with Col., pp. 323–367). J. Knox, *Philemon among the Letters of Paul. A New View of its Place and Importance* (Chicago, 1935). E. R. Goodenough, 'Paul and Onesimus' in *H.T.R.*, xxii (1929), pp. 181–3. G. S. Duncan, *St. Paul's Ephesian Ministry* (1929), pp. 72–5. J. H. *Bernard in *H.D.B.*, iii (1900), pp. 832–4, s.v.; W. C. *van Manen in *E.Bi.*, iii (1902), cols. 3693–7, s.v.; Teodorico da Castel San Pietro, O.F.M., in *E.C.*, v (1950), col. 1294 f., s.v. 'Filemone, Epistola a', with further bibl. C. F. D. Moule, *The Epistles of Paul the Apostle to the Colossians and Philemon* (Cambridge, 1957), pp. 1–42 and 140–9.

PHILIBERT, St. (d. 684), founder and first abbot of *Jumièges. Under the influence of St. *Ouen he took the monastic habit at Rebais, of which he became abbot. Led by the refractory character of his monks to retire to Neustria, he here founded the monastery of Jumièges on some land given him by Clovis II.

In 674 his reproval of Ebroin, the mayor of the palace, for gross injustice was followed by his expulsion, and he retired first to Poitiers and later to the island of Her (now Noirmoutier, orig. 'Hermonasterium') where he established another monastery. Feast day, 20 August.

The principal source is the 9th-cent. life by the monk Ermentarius, pr. in *AA.SS.*, Aug. IV (1739), pp. 75–80; also ed. R. Poupardin, *Monuments de l'histoire des abbayes de Saint-Philibert* (Collection de textes pour servir à l'étude et à l'enseignement de l'histoire, xxxviii; 1905), pp. 3–18, with full discussion; also ed. W. Levison in *M.G.H.*, Scriptores Rerum Merovingicarum, v (1910), pp. 583–604, with discussion, pp. 568–83. 'Vita et Miracula in Translationibus' also by Ermentarius in *AA.SS.*, loc. cit., p. 68, in R. Poupardin, op. cit., p. 1 f., and ed. Levison, op. cit., pp. 604–6. The much later 'Liber Miraculorum' also in *AA.SS.*, loc. cit., pp. 81–95, and in R. Poupardin, op. cit., pp. 19–70. Modern life by L. Jaud (Paris, 1910). See also bibl. to *Jumièges*.

PHILIPS IN THE NEW TESTAMENT.

(1) PHILIP THE APOSTLE is mentioned in the Synoptic Gospels and in Acts 1. 13 as one of the Twelve, but Jn. alone supplies any details. Jn. 1. 43–51, where he is described as 'from Bethsaida', describes how he obeyed the call of Jesus and then persuaded *Nathanael to appear before Jesus. In Jn. 6. 5–7 Philip, present at the feeding of the 5,000, observes that two hundred pennyworth of bread would not provide even a scanty meal for those assembled. Philip is again referred to in Jn. 12. 21 f., and Jn. 14. 8 f. records his request to Jesus, 'Shew us the Father', and its answer. The Apostle's subsequent career is obscure, and in legend is confused with that of Philip the Evangelist. *Polycrates of Ephesus connects him with Asia and declares that he died, apparently from natural causes, at Hierapolis; but other traditions describe him as having suffered crucifixion so that, in medieval art, his symbol—when not loaves, as suggested by Jn. 6.—is a tall cross. Feast day in the E, 14 Nov.; in the W (jointly with St. *James the Less), 1 May.

(2) PHILIP THE EVANGELIST was one of the Seven ('*Deacons' whose appointment is recorded in Acts 6. Concerned to proclaim the Gospel to the Gentiles, he was successful in winning over the Samaritans from belief in the sorceries of *Simon Magus to Christianity (Acts 8. 9–13). After the conversion and baptism of the Ethiopian eunuch (Acts 8. 26–39) Philip went on a missionary tour from Ashdod northwards. He settled at Caesarea, with his four daughters who were noted for their prophetic powers, and here he gave hospitality to St. *Paul (Acts 21. 8). Uncertainty shrouds the latter years of Philip. One tradition makes him Bp. of Tralles, in Lydia. Feast day, 6 June.

(3) PHILIP THE TETRARCH. One of the sons of *Herod the Great, he was ruler from 4 B.C. to A.D. 34 of 'the region of Ituraea and Trachonitis' (Lk. 3. 1). Acc. to *Josephus (*Antiq.* XVIII, iv, 6), he ruled with moderation, simplicity and good sense.

PHILIP THE ARABIAN, Roman Emperor from 244 to 249. He celebrated in 248 with the utmost magnificence the thousandth anniversary of Rome's foundation, but was harassed by invasions and revolutions, and met his death when fighting against *Decius in 249. *Eusebius records that Philip was a Christian and gives an edifying story of his submission to a bishop (later identified with *Babylas of Antioch) who debarred him from church until he had made confession of his sins. But Philip was probably commended by Christian writers simply because they detested his rival Decius, though a tradition that *Origen addressed a letter to him and another to his wife may testify to Philip's sympathetic interest in Christianity.

The ancient authorities include *Eusebius, *H.E.*, vi, 34, and *Zosimus, *H.E.*, i, 19–22. H. M. D. Parker, *A History of the Roman World from A.D. 138 to 337* (1935), pp. 150–7. E. Stein in *P.W.*, x (pt. 1; 1917), cols. 755–70, s.v. 'Julius (Phillipus) 386'.

PHILIP II (1527–98), King of Spain and Naples (1556), and of Portugal (1580). His marriage in 1554 to *Mary Tudor (d. 1558) gave him a short-lived influence in English affairs. The main object of his reign was the defence of the Catholic faith against Protestantism, a task he undertook in the interests of religion as well as of royal absolutism. This double motive sometimes brought him into conflict with the Papacy and the Reformers alike. In the beginning of his reign he had a quarrel with Pope *Paul IV who was forced to give in, and a war with the French who were defeated. In Spain he suppressed *Lutheranism, mainly through the instrument of the *Inquisition, and subdued the Moriscoes. The Turks were defeated in the battle of *Lepanto (1571) and Portugal conquered in 1580. In the Low Countries he was less successful and, chiefly through the reckless cruelty of Alva, lost the northern provinces in his attempt to uproot Calvinism. Still less successful were his efforts in *Elizabeth I's reign to regain England for Catholicism, which culminated in the destruction of the Armada (1588) and the loss of Spanish sea power. His ambitions in France, which he hoped to save from Protestantism by putting his daughter Isabella on the throne, were frustrated by the conversion of *Henry IV. He was undoubtedly a man of great industry and of real devotion to duty, his religion, his country, and his family, but also cold and suspicious, and lacking in the gentler qualities of mercy and forgiveness. His character has in turns been blackened and whitewashed by historians and poets (Schiller, 'Don Carlos') according to their prejudices. The Escurial is a fitting expression of his personality.

Much of his correspondence has been publd. in the *Colección de documentos inéditos para la historia de España*, esp. vols. ii–vi, xxvii–xliii, 1 f., lxviii, and lxxxvii–cii (Madrid, 1843–92) passim; incl. the *Correspondencia de Felipe II con sus embajadores en la corte de Inglaterra 1558 á 1584* as vols. lxxxvii and lxxxix–xcii, 1886–8; detailed list in L. Pfandl, see below, pp. 558–60. W. H. Prescott, *History of the Reign of Philip II, King of Spain* (2 vols., 1855, vol. 3, 1858). H. Forneron, *Histoire de Philippe II* (4 vols., 1880–2). M. A. S. Hume, *Philip II of Spain* ('Foreign Statesmen', 1897). L. Pfandl, *Philipp II*. Gemälde eines Lebens und einer Zeit (1938), with full bibl. M. Tomás, *Felipe II, rey de España y monarca del universo* (Saragossa, 1939). R. Altamira y Crevea, *Ensayo sombre Felipe II hombre de estado: su sicología general y su individualidad humana* (Publicaciones del Instituto de Historia, Ser. 1; num. xvi; Mexico, 1950). J. Casson, *La Vie de Philippe II* (Vies des hommes illustres, No. xxix; 1927). D. Loth, *Philip II of Spain* (London, 1932); W. T. Walsh, *Philip II* (New York and London, 1938). J. H. Mariéjol, *Master of the Armada*: the Life and Reign of Philip II of Spain (Eng. tr. from Fr.; 1933). R. B. Merriman, *The Rise of the Spanish Empire in the Old World and the New*, iv (1934).

PHILIP (1504–67), Landgraf of Hesse. He was the ablest of the German princes who supported M. *Luther. Declared of age in 1518, he led the suppression of the *Peasants' Revolt (1525) and, though there seems to have been no popular sympathy for it, determined to introduce the Reformation into Hesse. In 1527 he founded the university of *Marburg as a school for Protestant theologians. Two years later he signed the Protest of *Speyer and summoned the Conference of Marburg, which failed, however, to bring about an understanding between M. Luther and H. *Zwingli on the subject of the Real Presence in the Eucharist. Philip's policy of uniting the Protestant princes was more successful. In 1530 the *Schmalkaldic League was founded with himself and the Elector of Saxony as leaders, but the dissension between the two Protestant parties largely hampered its striking power. This, as well as the whole cause of Protestantism, was further impaired by Philip's bigamous marriage (1540) which had been approved by Luther. Seriously compromised among his own followers, Philip now made peace with the Emperor and thereby lost his leadership of the Protestant party. His policy during the next years was wavering, resulting in the Schmalkalden War (1546–7) at the end of which he was imprisoned. Set free in 1552, he devoted his remaining years to the work of reunion between Catholics and Protestants.

Philip of Hesse figures prominently in all works on the *Lutheran Reformation. *Festschrift zum Gedächtnis Philipps des Grossmütigen* ed. Verein für hessische Geschichte und Landeskunde (Cassel, 1904). W. W. Rockwell, *Die Doppelehe des Landgrafen Philipp von Hessen* (1904). Further bibl. in Schottenloher, iii (1936), pp. 190–8 (Nos. 30326–30483). T. Kolde in *P.R.E.* (ed. 3), xv (1904), pp. 296–316; W. Koehler in *R.G.G.* (ed. 2), iv (1930), col. 1182 f., both with bibl.

PHILIP NERI, St. (1515–95), the 'Apostle of Rome'. Son of a Florentine notary, he was educated by the *Dominicans of San Marco and later became a business apprentice. Resolving to give himself entirely to God, he went to Rome in 1533. Here he undertook the education of the two sons of a Florentine countryman, leading at the same time a very austere life. In 1535 he began to study philosophy and theology, but after three years sold his books and gave himself up to works of charity and instruction, spending the nights in prayer, mostly in the *catacomb of St. Sebastiano on the *Appian Way. Here he experienced in 1544 the ecstasy which is believed to have miraculously enlarged his heart. In 1548 he became the co-founder of the Confraternity of the Most Holy Trinity for the care of pilgrims

and convalescents which, in the year of the *Jubilee, 1575, assisted 145,000 pilgrims. In 1551, after being ordained, he went to live in a community of priests at San Girolamo, where his confessional soon became the centre of his apostolate and where he held spiritual conferences for men and boys often combined with visits to the Seven Churches. From these activities, which attracted more and more priests to the community, sprang the Congregation of the Oratory (see *Oratorians*), probably so called from the room at San Girolamo where the meetings were held. By 1575, when the Oratory was finally approved by *Gregory XIII, Philip Neri had become the most popular figure in Rome. His advice and direction were sought by Popes and cardinals no less than by the common people, and in 1593 he prevented a serious conflict between France and the Holy See by insisting on the absolution of *Henry IV. His chief characteristics were his gentleness and gaiety. Venerated as a saint during his lifetime, he was canonized by Gregory XV in 1622. Feast day, 26 May.

The primary source is the Process of Canonization. It supplied the main material for the first and fundamental life, written in Lat., by A. Gallonio, Cong. Orat. (Rome, 1600; repr. in *AA.SS.*, Mai. vi (1688), pp. 463–524). An Ital. tr., said to be clearer and more complete, was publd. at Rome, 1601. Other early lives by P. J. Bacci, Cong. Orat. (Rome, 1622; ed. G. F. Ricci, 1678; Eng. tr., Paris, 1659; Eng. tr. of ed. of 1837 by F. W. *Faber (Saints and Servants of God, 2 vols., 1847); new ed. of Eng. tr. by F. I. Antrobus, Cong. Orat. (2 vols., 1902)), G. Crispino (Naples, 1675; Eng. tr. of last part by F. W. Faber, 1850) and J. Bernabei, Cong. Orat., pr in *AA.SS.*, loc. cit., pp. 524–649. The standard modern work is that of L. Poncelle–L. Bordet (Paris, 1929; Eng. tr., 1932), with full discussion of sources. Other modern lives include those of M. A. Bayle (Paris, 1859), A. Capecelatro (2 vols., Naples, 1879; Eng. tr., 2 vols., 1882; abridged ed. of Eng. tr., 1926), R. F. Kerr, Cong. Orat. (London, c. 1903; new ed., 1927), V. J. Matthews, Cong. Orat. (London, 1934), M. V. Magni (Florence, 1937) and A. Baudrillart ('Les Saints', 1939). C. Gasbarri, Cong. Orat., in *E.C.*, v (1951), cols. 1327–31, s.v. 'Filippo Neri'. See also bibl. to *Oratorians* (1).

PHILIP SIDETES (early 5th cent.), historian. A native of Side, in Pamphylia, he removed to *Constantinople early in the 5th cent. where he became the friend of St. *Chrysostom, who ordained him deacon. After having become a priest he was three times an unsuccessful candidate for the patriarchate. He wrote a voluminous historical work, Χριστιανικὴ Ἱστορία, in 36 books which, to judge by *Socrates, appears to have been a hotch-potch of miscellaneous learning and to have dealt with the whole period from the creation of the world until A.D. 430. Only small fragments of this work remain, including the much-discussed assertion that *Papias had stated that *John the Divine and his brother, *James, were martyred by the Jews. A defence of Christianity against *Julian the Apostate, mentioned by Socrates, seems to be wholly lost.

The fragment on the Alexandrian *Catechetical School was publd. by H. *Dodwell in his *Dissertationes in Irenaeum* (Oxford, 1689), p. 488; on this cf. C. de Boor, 'Zur Kenntnis der Handschriften der griechischen Kirchenhistoriker. Codex Baroccianus 142' in *Z.K.T.*, vi (1884), pp. 478–94, esp. p. 487 (variant readings). Id., *Neue Fragmente des Papias, Hegesippus und Pierius . . . aus der Kirchengeschichte des Philippus Sidetes* (T.U., v, Hft. 2; 1885), pp. 165–84. E. Bratke, *Das sogenannte Religionsgespräch* am Hof der Sasaniden (ib., xix, Hft. 3; 1899), esp. pp. 157–64. Bardenhewer, iv, 135–7. [H.G.] Opitz in P.W., xix (pt. 2; 1938), col. 2350 f., s.v. 'Philippos 41'.

PHILIPPIANS, Epistle to the. One of the so-called '*Captivity Epistles' of St. *Paul, the authenticity of which is solidly attested by antiquity and almost unanimously accepted by modern scholars. It is addressed to the Christian community at Philippi in Macedonia, the first of the Churches founded by St. Paul in Europe, to which he was united by ties of particular affection and tenderness. Acc. to the Apostle's own account, the Philippian Epaphroditus had come with presents from the community to relieve his needs during his imprisonment. This is generally held to refer to his captivity in *Rome; and, though some scholars, e.g. G. S. Duncan, A. *Deissmann, and K. *Lake, believe it to have been at *Ephesus, and E. Lohmeyer at the Palestinian *Caesarea, the reff. to the Praetorian guard and to the members of 'Caesar's household' would seem to favour the traditional opinion. Its date has also been a matter of discussion. Some, e.g. J. B. *Lightfoot and F. W. *Farrar, assign it to the beginning of his captivity, whereas most critics, among them T. *Zahn, W. M. *Ramsay, and M. R. Vincent, place it at the end of his process of appeal, mainly on the grounds that internal evidence suggests a considerable missionary activity of the Apostle in Rome and a long drawn-out trial, soon to be brought to a happy conclusion. The unity of the Epistle has been contested, e.g. by A. *Loisy, because of the sudden attack on the Judaizers in 3. 1b ff., but the apparent break has been explained by others as due to the informal character of the letter which follows the successive emotions of the writer or on other grounds (T. *Zahn, M. *Dibelius, M. Jones).

After thanking the Philippians for their assistance (1. 1–11), St. Paul tells them of the success of his preaching in his captivity (1. 12–18) and asks them to make his joy perfect by charity, self-denial, and humility, of which Christ is the sublime example (1. 19 – 2. 11). He, too, wishes to give them joy and therefore promises to send them *Timothy and Epaphroditus (2. 12–30). After warning them against Judaizers he again exhorts them to lead a blameless life of peace and concord (3. 1 – 4. 7) and ends with a doxology and salutations (4. 8–23). The whole letter breathes spiritual joy and peace.

Despite its personal character the Epistle contains in 2. 5–11 a Christological passage of great doctrinal importance. These verses present Christ who, pre-existing 'in the form of God', was 'found in fashion as a man' and 'humbled Himself', and was consequently 'highly exalted' by God, as the sublime example of humility. There have been different interpretations of the passage, bearing esp. on the sense of ἁρπαγμός (AV, 'robbery'; RV, 'prize') in v. 6 and of ἑαυτὸν ἐκένωσε (AV, 'made Himself of no reputation'; RV, 'emptied Himself') in v. 7. Acc. to the Greek Fathers

of the first five cents., ἁρπαγμός is to be taken in its passive sense, as 'prey', and the meaning of the passage is that Christ did not cling to His Divine equality as to a prey which he might lose, but voluntarily renounced it when taking the form of a man. The Latin Fathers, on the other hand, taking the term in its active sense as 'robbery', interpret it as to mean that though Christ, being God, could not consider His Divine prerogatives a robbery, He yet voluntarily renounced them. Either interpretation is doctrinally correct, though the former is generally held to be the better exegesis. As regards the other difficulty, the Fathers of the first five cents. are almost unanimous in referring the ἐκένωσε of v. 7 to the Divine Will of the Word, understanding the Incarnation as an act of humility and self-abnegation on the part of the Divine Son. Some modern exegetes, on the other hand, following *Pelagius and *Ambrosiaster, understand it of the human will, because, acc. to them, the virtues of humility and self-abnegation are incompatible with the Divine perfections. For modern Protestant interpretations, see *Kenotic Theory*. The whole passage is one of the finest examples of NT Christology and has often been used, e.g. in the *Arian controversy, as a Scriptural proof of the orthodox doctrine.

Modern commentaries include those of C. J. *Ellicott (London, 1857, with Col. and Philem., pp. 1–105), B. *Weiss (Berlin, 1859), J. B. *Lightfoot (London, 1868), C. J. *Vaughan (ib., 1885), H. C. G. Moule (Camb. Bib., Greek Text, 1897), M. R. Vincent (I.C.C., with Philem., 1897, pp. 1–54), E. Haupt (K.E.K., viii and ix on the Gefangenschaftsbriefe, ed. 6, 1897), M. *Dibelius (Hb.N.T., 1911, with Thess.; ed. 3, xi, 1937, pp. 59–98), M. Jones (West. Comm., 1918), A. Plummer (London, 1919), J. H. Michael (Moffatt Comm., 1928), E. Lohmeyer (K.E.K., ix, Hft. 1, ed. 8; 1928), K. *Barth (Munich, 1928), W. Michaelis (Theologischer Handkommentar zum Neuen Testament bearbeitet von P. Althaus, etc., xi; Leipzig, 1935), P. Bonnard (Commentaire au Nouveau Testament, x; Neuchâtel–Paris, 1950, pp. 7–87). W. Lütgert, Die Vollkommenen im Philipperbrief und die Enthusiasten in Thessalonich (1909). P. Feine, Die Abfassung des Philipperbriefes in Ephesus (1916). J. Gibb in H.D.B., iii (1900), pp. 840–4; D. Mackenzie in D.A.C., ii (1918), pp. 216–27; P. Feine in R.G.G. (ed. 2), iv (1930), cols. 1184–8. Recent Comm. by F. W. Beare (London, 1959).

PHILIPPISTS. The followers of the *Lutheran theologian, Philip *Melanchthon ('Dr. Philippus'), also known as '*Crypto-Calvinists', and '*Synergists' (qq.v.).

PHILIP'S LENT, St. A name in use in the E. Church for the period from 15 Nov. to 24 Dec., i.e. the counterpart of *Advent in the W. Church. It is so named because it begins on the day following the Feast of St. Philip (14 Nov. in the E.).

PHILLIMORE, ROBERT JOSEPH (1810–1885), English judge. Educated at Westminster and at Christ Church, Oxford, he became a prominent Anglican High Churchman, numbering among his friends W. E. *Gladstone, G. A. *Denison, and H. P. *Liddon. In 1841 he was called to the bar at the Middle Temple. He held a succession of ecclesiastical appointments and in 1867 became *Dean of Arches.

In 1868 in the case against A. H. *Mackonochie, in which he had first appeared as defending counsel, he delivered judgement declaring the legality of altar lights and of kneeling during the prayer of consecration. The Judicature Act of 1875 caused him to resign his ecclesiastical judgeship. Deeply learned, he was the author of several legal writings, and his *Ecclesiastical Law of the Church of England* (2 vols., 1873; ed. 2, 1895) remains a standard treatise. His other writings include *Thoughts on the Law of Divorce in England* (1844) and *Commentaries upon International Law* (4 vols., 1854–61).

His son, W. G. F. PHILLIMORE (High Court Judge, 1897–1913, and Lord Justice of Appeal, 1913–16), also appeared as counsel in many ritual cases.

R. J. Phillimore himself published a collection of *The Principal Ecclesiastical Judgements delivered in the Court of Arches, 1867 to 1875* [by himself] (1876). W. P. W. Phillimore–W. G. F. Phillimore, *Genealogy of the Family of Phillimore* (Devizes, 1922), pp. 240–52. J. A. Hamilton in *D.N.B.*, xlv (1896), pp. 186–8; G. Crosse in *D.E.C.H.*, p. 458. On W. G. F. Phillimore, John, Baron Sankey, in *D.N.B.*, 1922–1930, p. 677 f.

PHILLIPPS, AMBROSE LISLE. See *De Lisle, Ambrose Lisle March Phillipps.*

PHILLIPPS MANUSCRIPTS, The. The famous collection of MSS. assembled at Cheltenham in the 19th cent. by the antiquary, Sir Thomas Phillipps (1792–1872). Phillipps, who had been educated at Rugby and University College, Oxford, began his collection by purchasing the bulk of the Meerman Collection at the Hague in 1824. Later acquisitions included the 9th cent. MSS. of Professor van Ess of Darmstadt, the Muschenbroek Collection of Chronicles and other documents on Dutch history, the Williams Collection (incl. Bp. Gundulf's Bible), the Knaresborough MSS. on Mexico, many MSS. on the history of Wales and of Ireland, as well as some Gk. MSS (incl. an illuminated 10th–11th cent. Dioscorides). His library was orig. located at Middle Hill, near Broadway, Worcs, whence Phillipps transferred it to Thirlestane House, Cheltenham, in 1862. The collection passed at his death into the hands of his younger daughter, Mrs. Fenwick. The MSS. have since been gradually sold, the greater part of the Meerman Collection being now in the Staatsbibliothek at Berlin. See also *Mommsen Catalogue.*

Phillipps, who had installed a printing press at Middle Hill, printed his own catalogue in fol., successive sections appearing as the collection grew: *Catalogus Librorum Manuscriptorum in Bibliotheca D. Thomae Phillipps* (1824–[1867]). A. N. L. Munby, *Phillipps Studies* (1951 ff.; orig. designed to extend to 12 vols.).

PHILLPOTTS, HENRY (1778–1869), Bp. of *Exeter. He was educated at Corpus Christi College, Oxford, and in 1795 elected a Fellow of Magdalen. From 1805 to 1826 he held a number of benefices in the diocese of *Durham. In 1828 he was appointed Dean of *Chester, and in 1830 Bp. of Exeter. An old-fashioned High Churchman, he was throughout his episcopate in sympathy with the *Oxford Movement (q.v.). He greatly desired to raise the standard of public worship and in 1844 ordered the surplice to be worn at all ministrations in his diocese, though the order raised so fierce a storm that it had to be withdrawn. His refusal to institute G. C. *Gorham (q.v.), who had been presented to the living of Brampford Speke, on the grounds of his denial of baptismal regeneration, gave rise to one of the most famous ecclesiastical law-suits in the 19th cent. He was also a champion of the revival of religious orders in the Anglican Church and aided the efforts of E. B. *Pusey for the sisterhood at Devonport founded by Miss P. L. *Sellon.

A Life was begun by R. N. Shutte (vol. i only, London, 1863 [to 1832]; publication was suspended on an injunction granted to Phillpotts). Brief sketch by E. C. S. Gibson in W. E. Collins (ed.), *Typical English Churchmen* (1902), pp. 299–323. Full life by G. C. B. Davies (C.H.S., 1954), with bibl. J. C. S. Nias, O.G.S., *Gorham and the Bishop of Exeter* (ib., 1951). J. A. Hamilton in *D.N.B.*, xlv (1896), pp. 222–5.

PHILO (*c.* 20 B.C.–*c.* A.D. 50), Jewish thinker and exegete. He belonged to a prosperous priestly family of Alexandria; but nothing is known of his life except that in 39 he took part in an embassy to *Rome, described in his *Legatio ad Caium*, to plead the religious rights of the Jews with Emp. Caligula. He was the most important figure among the Hellenistic Jews of his age and a fertile author. His numerous writings include: (1) Philosophical works, written in his youth, among them *De Aeternitate Mundi*, *Quod omnis probus liber sit*, and *De Providentia*; (2) Exegetical writings on the *Pentateuch; incl. *Quaestiones et Solutiones in Genesim et Exodum* and *Legum Allegoriae*; and (3) Historical and apologetic writings, incl. *De Vita Mosis*, *De Vita Contemplativa* (on the *Therapeutae, q.v.), and *Contra Flaccum* (against Flaccus, Procurator of Egypt, A.D. 32–8).

In his religious outlook, Philo was essentially an eclectic. He reproduced a variety of doctrines, gathered from contemporary philosophical systems as well as from Jewish sources, without welding them into an harmonious whole. His most influential achievement was his development of the allegorical interpretation of Scripture which enabled him to discover much of Greek philosophy in the OT, and to combine the respect of his religion for the Pentateuchal law with his personal aspirations towards a more spiritual interpretation of it. In his theological ideas also, Greek and Jewish elements were interwoven. On the one hand he emphasized the complete transcendence of God, whom he asserted to be above virtue, above knowledge, and even above the Good, while on the other he maintained that God was the Father who governed the world as well as each individual soul by His Providence. He accorded a central place in his system to the *Logos who was at once the creative power which orders the world and the intermediary through whom men know God. It was the Logos who spoke to *Moses in the burning bush, and who is represented in the OT under the figure of the *high priest. As a spiritual leader, Philo stands in the tradition of the philosophical mystics. The highest grade of the inner life is ecstasy, which conveys the felt Presence of God to the soul.

Philo's influence was esp. strong in the Alexandrine school of theology. *Clement and *Origen used him freely, and through them and later through St. *Ambrose and other Latin Fathers his allegorical interpretation of Scripture became an accepted form of Biblical exegesis in the Christian Church. His influence on the Logos doctrine of the Fourth Gospel and of the Apologists, notably St. *Justin, has often been alleged, but in recent times the differences between the Christian and the Philonic conceptions have been very widely admitted.

Editio princeps of his collected works, Paris, 1522; much improved ed., with Lat. tr., by T. Mangey (2 vols., London, 1742); crit. ed. by L. Cohn–P. Wendland–S. Reiter (6 vols., Berlin, 1896–1915; index by I. Leisegang, 2 pts., 1926–30). Eng. tr. by H. Colson–G. H. Whitaker–R. Marcus (Loeb, 1929 ff.). 'De Vita Contemplativa' also ed., with full notes, by F. C. *Conybeare (Oxford, 1895); 'In Flaccum' ed., with Eng. tr., by H. Box (London, 1939). H. E. *Ryle, *Philo and Holy Scripture* (1895); P. Katz, *Philo's Bible*. The Aberrant Text of Bible Quotations in some Philonic Writings and its Place in the Textual History of the Greek Bible (1950). J. *Drummond, *Philo Judaeus* (2 vols., London, 1888); H. A. A. Kennedy, *Philo's Contribution to Religion* (1919); E. R. Goodenough, *An Introduction to Philo Judaeus* (New Haven, Conn., 1940); H. A. Wolfson, *Philo*. Foundations of Religious Philosophy in Judaism, Christianity and Islam (2 vols., Cambridge, Mass., 1947). E. Bréhier, *Les Idées philosophiques et religieuses de Philon d'Alexandrie* (Paris thesis, 1907; ed. 2, Études de Philosophie médiévale, viii; 1925). J. Pascher, Ἡ Βασιλικὴ Ὁδός. Der Königsweg zu Wiedergeburt und Vergottung bei Philo von Alexandreia (Studien zur Geschichte und Kultur des Altertums, xvii, Hftt. 3–4; 1931). I. Heinemann, *Philos griechische und jüdische Bildung* (1932). F. Geiger, *Philon von Alexandreia als sozialer Denker* (Tübinger Beiträge zur Altertumswissenschaft, xiv; 1932). E. R. Goodenough, *The Politics of Philo Judaeus* (New Haven, Conn., 1938), with General Bibliography of Philo by H. L. Goodhart–E. R. Goodenough, pp. 127–321. W. Völker, *Fortschritt und Vollendung bei Philo von Alexandrien* (T.U., xlix; 1938). E. Stein, *Die allegorische Exegese des Philo aus Alexandreia* (Beiheft zur Z.A.T.W., li; 1929); id., *Philo und der Midrasch* (ib., lvii; 1931). E. *Schürer, *Geschichte des jüdischen Volkes im Zeitalter Jesu Christi*, iii (ed. 4; 1909), pp. 633–716. Überweg, i, 567–9, 572–8, with bibl. pp. 181*–3*. A. Edersheim in *D.C.B.*, iv (1887), pp. 357–89, s.v.; C. Siegfried–J. Z. Lauterbach in *J.E.*, x (1905), pp. 6–19, s.v.; E. Schürer–C. Bigg in *E.B.* (ed. 11), xxi (1911), pp. 409–13, s.v.; H. Leisegang in *P.W.*, xx (pt. 1; 1941), cols. 1–50, s.v. 'Philon (41)'; F. Spadafora in *E.C.*, v (1951), cols. 1345–8, s.v. 'Filone', with further bibl.

PHILOCALIAN CALENDAR, The.

A name sometimes given to the list of Roman bishops (also known as the '*Liberian Catalogue') compiled by the '*Chronographer of 354' (q.v.). It takes this name from the fact that part of the document in which it occurs was illuminated by the artist, Furius Dionysius Philocalus (prob. better Filocalus).

On Filocalus, also known for his skilful incision of *Damasus' metrical inscriptions, see H. *Leclercq, O.S.B., in *D.A.C.L.*, v (pt. 2; 1923), cols. 1594–600, s.v. For further bibl. see s.v. *Chronographer of 354*.

PHILOMENA, St.

She was formerly held to be a virgin martyr of the early Church. Her cultus dates from 1802 when a *loculus was

found in the Catacomb of St. Priscilla, near Rome, closed with three tiles on which were painted the letters LUMENA / PAX TE/ CUM FI, which, arranged in the right order, read 'Pax tecum Filumena'. Taken in conjunction with an *ampulla supposed to have contained blood, the bones found in the tomb were held to be those of a martyred Christian virgin. She came to be venerated as a saint when many miracles took place at the translation of her relics to Mugnano in 1805. A proper Office and Mass were granted to her by *Pius IX in 1855, and she temporarily became one of the most popular saints on account of the devotion to her of the *Curé d'Ars. Subsequent research, however, has cast grave doubt on the connexion between the relics and the tiles, which seem to have belonged to another grave, so that nothing seems known about the saint venerated under this name. Feast day, 11 Aug.

The identification was first made by F. di Lucia, *Relazione istorica della traslazione del sacro corpo di Santa Filomena* (ed. 4, 1833). It was refuted by A. de Waal, 'Die Grabschrift der Philumena aus dem Coemeterium der Priscilla' in *R.Q.*, xii (1898), pp. 43–54; O. *Marucchi, 'Osservazioni archeologiche sulla iscrizione di S. Filomena' in *Miscellanea di Storia ecclesiastica e di Studi ausiliari*, ii (1904), pp. 365–86; id., 'Studio archeologico sulla celebre iscrizione di Filumena scoperta nel cimitero di Priscilla' in *Nuovo Bullettino di Archeologia cristiana*, xii (1906), pp. 253–300. F. Tronchu, *La 'Petite Sainte' du curé d'Ars*. Sainte Philomène (Lyons, 1924). In Eng. there is a popular, mainly devotional, account by Cecily Hallack (Dublin [1936]). H. *Leclercq, O.S.B., in *D.A.C.L.*, v (pt. 2; 1923), cols. 1600–2, s.v. 'Filumena', with detailed bibl.

PHILOPATRIS.

A Greek dialogue, formerly thought to be a veiled attack on Christianity by *Lucian of Samosata. The scene is laid at *Constantinople where one Triephon, converted to the Christian faith, is transported into the third heaven and engages in a discussion on paganism, which concludes with reflections on the political situation of the time. The work, long assigned to the reign of *Julian (361–3), has been commonly put since B. G. Niebuhr in the time of Nicephorus Phocas (963–9).

The text is pr. in many edd. of the works of Lucian of Samosata (q.v.), e.g. that of C. Jacobitz, iii (Teub. ed. of 1886, pp. 411–25); also ed. C. B. Hase appended to his ed. of the History of Leo the Deacon (C.S.H. Byz., xxv; 1828), pp. 324–42. B. G. Niebuhr, *Kleine historische und philologische Schriften*, ii (1843), pp. 73–8 ('Ueber das Alter des Dialogus Philopatris'). E. von Dobschütz in *P.R.E.* (ed. 3), xv (1904), pp. 363–5, s.v.; there is a summary of this art. in English in *E.B.* (ed. 11), xxi (1911), p. 439, s.v.

PHILOSOPHIC SIN.

Acts of sin held to violate the natural order of reason without consciously transgressing the Divine law, and hence not to merit the punishments meted out to offences against the latter. The theory that sin under such conditions is possible presupposes the existence of a distinction between the Divine and natural moral law of contestable validity and was censured by Pope *Alexander VIII on 24 Aug. 1690.

Pope Alexander VIII's condemnation of 24 Aug. 1690 is pr. in C. Duplessis d'Argentré (ed.), *Collectio Judiciorum de Novis Erroribus*, iii (Paris, etc., 1736), p. 365; main clauses repr. in Denz.–Bann. (ed. 1952), p. 382 f. (No. 1289 f.). H.

Beylard, 'Le Péché philosophique. Quelques précisions historiques et doctrinales' in *Nouvelle Revue théologique*, lxii (1935), pp. 591–616 and 673–98. T. Deman, O.P., in *D.T.C.*, xii (pt. 1; 1933), cols. 255–72, s.v. 'Péché. IX', with bibl. col. 275.

PHILOSOPHY OF RELIGION.

The notion of the philosophy of religion as a distinct discipline was the creation of the *Aufklärung*. The term is first met with in Germany in the last years of the 18th cent. Early occurrences in titles are J. C. G. Schaumann, *Philosophie der Religion* (1793) and J. Berger, *Geschichte der Religionsphilosophie* (1800). Properly its aim, as the expression implies, is the philosophical investigation of the particular group of phenomena covered by the terms 'religion' and 'religious experience'. It studies the essence, content, origin, and, to some extent, value of religion as a factor in human life. In general it does not profess to take cognizance of the traditional distinction between natural and revealed religion. Indeed, the latter only comes within its province at all in so far as it is held to be a factor in human experience. On the other hand, the philosophy of religion is concerned, at least indirectly, with the traditional themes of natural theology, e.g. I. *Kant's three 'Ideas' (God, freedom, and immortality), since consideration of these subjects naturally arises out of the study of religious experience. In recent times, the place to be assigned to history in a philosophical account of religion has attracted a great deal of attention among religious philosophers.

As a separate discipline, the philosophy of religion has been cultivated mainly by Christians with liberal leanings. Catholic theologians have more commonly envisaged the matters at issue from the standpoint of natural theology and formulated their philosophical beliefs in terms of objective metaphysics. Orthodox Protestantism has also tended to regard the subject as irrelevant to the real issues of faith, and in recent times the very notion of a philosophy of religion has been criticized by several theologians of the *Barthian School.

J. Baillie, *Our Knowledge of God* (1939); E. Bevan, *Symbolism and Belief* (Gifford Lectures [='G.L.'], 1938); W. G. de Burgh, *Morality and Religion* (G.L., 1938); E. *Brunner, *Religionsphilosophie evangelischer Theologie* (1926; Eng. trans., 1937); J. *Caird, *Introduction to the Philosophy of Religion* (1880); A. Caldecott–H. R. Mackintosh, *Selections from the Literature of Theism* (1904); V. A. Demant, *The Religious Prospect* (1939); D. M. Emmet, *The Nature of Metaphysical Thinking* (1945); R. Flint, *Theism* (1877); F. *von Hügel, *Essays and Addresses on the Philosophy of Religion* (1921); id., Second Series (1926); G. H. Joyce, S.J., *Principles of Natural Theology* (1923); J. *Martineau, *A Study of Religion* (2 vols., 1888); id., *The Seat of Authority in Religion* (1890); E. L. Mascall, *He Who Is*. A Study in Traditional Theism (1943); id., *Existence and Analogy*. A Sequel to *He Who Is* (1949); W. R. Matthews, *God in Christian Thought and Experience* (1930); J. W. *Oman, *The Natural and the Supernatural* (1931); A. S. Pringle-*Pattison, *The Idea of God in the Light of Recent Philosophy* (G.L., 1917); A. E. *Taylor, art. 'Theism' in J. Hastings' *E.R.E.*, xii (1921), pp. 261–87; id., *The Faith of a Moralist* (G.L., 2 vols., 1930); id., *Philosophical Studies* (1934); W. *Temple, *Nature, Man and God* (G.L., 1934); F. R. Tennant, *Philosophical Theology*, vol. i: The Soul and its Faculties (1935), vol. ii: The Word, the Soul and God (1937); E. *Troeltsch, *Gesammelte Schriften* (4 vols., 1912–25).

W. Wallace, *Lectures and Essays on Natural Theology and Ethics* (ed. E. Caird, 1898); C. C. J. *Webb, *Problems in the Relations of God and Man* (1911); id., *Studies in the History of Natural Theology* (1915); id., *God and Personality* (G.L. i, 1918); id., *Divine Personality and Human Life* (G.L., ii, 1920).

PHILOSTORGIUS (c. 368–c. 439), *Arian ecclesiastical historian. A native of Borissus in Cappadocia Secunda, Philostorgius became a follower and warm admirer of *Eunomius (q.v.) and spent most of his active life in *Constantinople. His principal work, a 'History of the Church' from the Arian standpoint for the period c. 300–430, survives only in fragments, esp. in the 'Passion of Artemius' (Artemius was an Arian martyr, c. 362), and in an epitome by *Photius who writes very disparagingly of its author. His work was inaccurate and biased, but what survives is of value through its use of excellent sources as well as on account of Philostorgius's descriptions of several of the chief Arian personalities.

Editio princeps of fragments by J. Gothofredus (Geneva, 1643); they are also pr. in J. P. Migne, *PG*, lxv, 459–624; crit. ed., with important introd., by J. Bidez (G.C.S., xxi; 1913). Text of 'Vita Constantini', incorporating further passages from Philostorgius, in H. G. Opitz, 'Die *Vita Constantini* des Codex Angelicus 22' in *Byzantion*, ix (1934), pp. 535–93. P. *Batiffol, *Quaestiones Philostorgianae* (thesis, Paris, 1891). Bardenhewer, iv, 132–5; Altaner (ed. 1951), p. 203. G. Fritz in *D.T.C.*, xiv (pt. 2; 1935), cols. 1495–1498, s.v.

PHILOXENIAN VERSION OF THE NT.

The Syriac version of the NT made from the Greek in 508 for *Philoxenus (q.v.) by Polycarp, a *chorepiscopus. Unlike the *Peshitta, it contained the four lesser Catholic Epistles (2 Pet., 2 & 3 Jn., Jude) and the Book of Rev. In 616 it was drastically revised throughout (except for its non-Peshitta Books just named) by Thomas of Harkel, and its original text has thus been almost completely lost. In the lesser Catholic Epp. and Rev., where the original readings survive, the text is of the common *Lucianic type. See also *Harclean Version*.

Editio princeps of the four Philomenian Epps. by E. *Pococke, Leyden, 1630; modern ed. by J. Gwynn, Text and Translation Society, London–Oxford, 1909. Philoxenian text of Rev. first discovered and publd. by J. Gwynn, *The Apocalypse of St. John in a Syriac Version hitherto Unknown* (Dublin–London, 1897). J. Lebon, 'La Version philoxénienne de la Bible' in *R.H.E.*, xii (1911), pp. 414–436. A. *Baumstark, *Geschichte der syrischen Literatur* (1922), p. 144 f.

PHILOXENUS (c. 440–523), Bp. of Mabbug (Hierapolis), to which office he was appointed in 485 by *Peter the Fuller. He was a leading *Monophysite, with views approximating to those of *Julian of Halicarnassus, and one of the most learned Syrian theologians. His extensive writings include a set of thirteen 'Discourses on the Christian Life' and some works on the Incarnation. He also conducted a large correspondence which has partly survived. See also preceding entry.

Philoxenus's remains have been publd. in a variety of places. The more important collections include an edition of his Discourses, with Eng. tr., by E. A. W. Budge (2 vols., London [1893]–1894; from Brit. Mus. MSS.); his 'Tractatus de Trinitate et Incarnatione' ed., with Lat. tr., by A. Vaschalde (C.S.C.O., Scriptores Syri, Ser. 2, xxvii; 1907), and 'Dissertationes Decem de Uno e Sancta Trinitate Incorporato et Passo', also with Lat. tr., by M. Brière in *P.O.*, xv (1927), pp. 441–542 [2 Diss. only so far publd.]. Edd. of further works listed in Bardenhewer and dictt. cited below. More recently a Letter sent to a friend has been ed. by E. Olinder (Göteborgs Högskolas Årsskrift, lvi, 1950, No. 1). W. Wright, *A Short History of Syriac Literature* (1894), pp. 72–6; A. *Baumstark, *Geschichte der syrischen Literatur* (1922), pp. 141–4. Bardenhewer, iv, pp. 417–21; Altaner (ed. 1951), p. 303 f. G. Krüger in *P.R.E.* (ed. 3), xv (1894), pp. 367–70; E. Tisserant in *D.T.C.*, xii (pt. 2; 1935), cols. 1509–32; A. Rücker in *L.Th.K.*, viii (1936), col. 248 f.

PHILPOT, JOHN (1516–55), Reformation divine. The facts known with certainty about his life are few. After being educated at *Winchester and New College, *Oxford, where he held a Fellowship from 1534 to 1539, he went abroad and developed doubts of the traditional Catholic doctrines. A controversial discussion with a *Franciscan friar near Padua almost led to his seizure by the *Inquisition. At an unknown date under *Edward VI (1547–1553) he became Archdeacon of Winchester. An attack on *Transubstantiation in the first Convocation of Mary's reign (1553) was followed by imprisonment. In Oct. 1555, despite E. *Bonner's defence, he was convicted, and on 18 Dec. burnt at *Smithfield. Besides many occasional writings dealing with current controversies he translated some of J. *Calvin's Homilies and *Chrysostom 'Against Heresies'.

Extant works, with account of his 'Examination' taken mainly from J. *Foxe, *Acts and Monuments*, ed. R. Eden (*Parker Society, 1842), with biogr. introd., pp. i–xxii. W. A. J. Archbold in *D.N.B.*, xlv (1896), p. 226 f.; C. P. S. Clarke in *D.E.C.H.*, p. 459.

PHOCAS, St. (d. 117), Bp. of Sinope in Pontus. A martyr of this name who suffered under Trajan by suffocation in a bath is commemorated in the *Roman Martyrology on 14 July. He has constantly been confused with 'St. Phocas the Gardener', commemorated in the W. Church on 23 July and in the E. on 22 Sept., who is stated to have been martyred in the *Diocletianic Persecution, as well as with St. Phocas of Antioch, named in the Roman Martyrology on 5 Mar. St. Phocas the Gardener was the subject of a panegyric pronounced in 400 by Asterius, Bp. of Amasea. When the various traditions had become fused, the cult of St. Phocas became very popular, esp. among seafaring people, perhaps through a superficial resemblance of his name to φώκη, 'seal'. Several attempts (for the most part unconvincing) have been made in recent times by students of folk-lore to connect the cultus of St. Phocas with pagan myths.

Gk. text of Asterius's panegyric on Phocas the Gardener in *AA.SS.*, Sept. VI (1757), pp. 294–9. K. Lübeck, 'Der hl. Phocas von Sinope' in *Hist. Jahr.*, xxx (1909), pp. 743–61. C. Van de Vorst, 'Saint Phocas' in *Anal. Boll.*, xxx (1911), pp. 252–72, with discussion of the relation of the various saints of this name and full reff. to earlier lit.; various primary texts, ib., pp. 272–95.

PHOCYLIDES, Pseudo-. The name given to the author of 230 hexameters inserted into the work of Phocylides of Miletus (6th cent.

B.C.). The strictly ethical character of the poem, combined with the absence of specifically Jewish allusions, and esp. of all ref. to Jewish ceremonial law, has suggested that the author was a Christian (A. *Harnack); on the other hand, there is no mention of Christ or of anything definitely Christian, while the moral teaching seems closely to follow that of the OT. The poem may have been written at any time within the period of the Judaeo-Hellenistic civilization up to *c.* A.D. 150. It was widely used as a school-book in the Byzantine period and has survived in many MSS.

Crit. ed. by T. Bergk, *Poetae Lyrici Graeci* (Leipzig, 1843), pp. 342–55. Eng. tr. by W. Hewett (Watford, 1840). J. Bernays, *Ueber das phokylideische Gedicht*. Ein Beitrag zur hellenistischen Litteratur (1856); cf. review by A. Harnack in *T.L.Z.*, x (1885), col. 160. E. *Schürer, *Geschichte des üdischen Volkes*, iii (ed. 4, 1909), pp. 617–22, with bibl.

PHOEBADIUS, St. (d. *c.* 395), also 'Fiari', Bp. of Agen (Agennum) in Guyenne. A friend of St. *Hilary of Poitiers, he was a strong opponent of *Arianism and attacked the *Sirmian formula of 357 in his 'Liber contra Arianos' (partly based on *Tertullian). In 359 he signed the formula of *Ariminum, but vigorously denounced the Council when he realized its import. A work, 'De Fide Orthodoxa contra Arianos', also passes under his name, but this probably belongs to *Gregory of Elvira. Feast day, 26 April.

J. P. Migne, *PL*, xx, 13–30. *Jerome, *De Viris Illustribus*, cviii.

PHOENIX (Gk. φοῖνιξ), a gorgeously arrayed mythical bird which was the subject of several legends in antiquity, notably one to the effect that after living five or six hundred years it burnt itself to ashes and then came back to life again with renewed youth. From St. *Clement of Rome (*Ep. ad Cor.*, xxv) and *Tertullian (*De Res. Carnis*, xiii) onwards, Christian writers frequently regarded it as an image of the Resurrection. *Lactantius wrote a special hymn on the religious significance of the phoenix (*De Ave Phoenice*). From *Constantinian times the phoenix was occasionally (but somewhat rarely) used in Christian art, representations of it being found, e.g., in the Roman Churches of Sts. *Cosmas and Damian, St. Praxedes and St. Cecilia.

F. Schöll, *Vom Vogel Phönix* (Akademische Rede; Heidelberg, 1890). R. St. J. Thackeray in *D.C.A.*, ii (1880), p. 1633, s.v.; J. Sauer in *L.Th.K.*, viii (1936), col. 251 f., s.v. 'Phönix'; H. *Leclercq, O.S.B., in *D.A.C.L.*, xiv (pt. 1; 1939), cols. 682–91, s.v. 'Phénix'; E. Josi in *E.C.*, v (1950), col. 1151 f., s.v. 'Fenice'.

PHOS HILARON (Gk. φῶς ἱλαρόν). In the E. Church, the hymn sung at 'Hesperinos' (the counterpart of the W. *Vespers) during 'the lighting of the lamps' and the central item in the office. It is found already in St. *Basil (*De Spir. Sanct.* 73). Translations by J. *Keble ('Hail Gladdening Light') and by R. S. *Bridges ('O Gladsome Light, O Grace') have found their way into English hymnals.

Text pr., with Lat. tr., in M. J. *Routh, *Reliquiae Sacrae*, iii (Oxford, 1815), p. 299, with notes, pp. 300–4; and in H. A. Daniel, *Thesaurus Hymnologicus*, iii (Leipzig, 1846), p. 5, repr. by J. Julian in id. (ed.), *A Dictionary of Hymnology* (1892), p. 894, s.v., with list of Eng. trr.

PHOTINUS (4th cent.), heretic. A pupil of *Marcellus of Ancyra, he became Bp. of Sirmium *c.* 344. He was recognized as a man of learning and eloquence. Though involved in the condemnation of Marcellus by a Council of Antioch *c.* 345, he retained his see until 351, when he was deposed and exiled after his errors had been exposed at a Council called by the Emp. Constantius at Sirmium. None of his writings have survived and his doctrine is variously described by his detractors. It was clearly a form of *Sabellianism. Acc. to St. *Augustine, he denied the pre-existence of Christ, though he allowed that He was born of the Virgin and was endowed with superhuman excellences. His followers, the 'Photinians', were formally condemned at the Council of *Constantinople in 381.

The primary sources are scattered. D. *Petavius, *De Photino Haeretico eiusque Damnatione* (Paris, 1636). Bardenhewer, iii, 123 f. F. *Loofs in *P.R.E.* (ed. 3), xv (1904), pp. 372–4, and G. Bardy in *D.T.C.*, xii (pt. 2; 1935), cols. 1532–6, both s.v.

PHOTIUS (*c.* 810–95), Patriarch of *Constantinople. Of a noble Constantinopolitan family, he received a good education and gave up his original plan of entering a monastery for the career of a scholar and statesman. Close relations with the court made him the first Imperial Secretary and, in 838, Imperial Ambassador to Assyria. When the Emp. Michael III deposed Ignatius, Patr. of Constantinople, in 858, Photius, still a layman, was appointed his successor. He was consecrated by his friend, Gregory Asbestas, Abp. of Syracuse, whom Ignatius had himself deposed. On Ignatius' refusal to abdicate, Michael and Photius sent an embassy to Pope *Nicholas I, asking for legates to a synod at Constantinople which, besides regulating the *Iconoclastic Controversy, should also settle the dispute of the two Patriarchs. Nicholas's legates exceeded their powers, probably under pressure from the Eastern court, and took part in the Synod of 861 which deposed Ignatius. In 862 the Pope, in letters to Photius and to Michael III, blamed his legates' conduct and complained that his former letter had been tampered with at Constantinople; and, at a synod at Rome (863), annulled the proceedings at Constantinople. He maintained that Ignatius was still Patriarch; and after the arrival of an embassy from Ignatius declared Photius deposed and his friend, Gregory Asbestas, deprived of the priesthood and of all ecclesiastical offices. All clerics promoted by Photius were also deposed, and the deposition of Ignatius declared null and void. This assertion of Papal authority naturally gave great offence at Constantinople. Photius himself kept silence, but the Emperor wrote a strongly worded letter to the Pope who, in 865, declared himself ready to reopen the case. A reconciliation was prevented by the dispute whether Christianity in Bulgaria, then being converted, was to depend on Rome or on Constantinople. In 867 Photius, in an encyclical, denounced the presence of Latin missionaries in Bulgaria as an intrusion, and also gave an exposition of his objections to the *Filioque clause in the creed. In the same year, at a Council at Constantinople, sentence of deposition was pronounced against the Pope, who was declared anathema and excommunicated.

With the accession of Basil (867), the murderer and successor of the Emp. Michael, the situation changed. Ignatius was reinstated, and a sentence of a Council at Rome in 869, anathematizing Photius, was confirmed by the Council of Constantinople of 869–70, later counted as the 8th General Council by the Latins. The restored harmony between E. and W. was of short duration. When Ignatius consecrated an archbishop and bishops for the Bulgarians (870) he was threatened by the Pope with excommunication. This action at Rome assured him continuance in his see, and it was only after Ignatius's death (877) that Photius, by order of the Emperor, once more became Patriarch. At a council held at Constantinople in 879–80 the Papal legates seem to have approved Photius and annulled the decision of the Council of 869–70. (That the Papal legates acted thus in 879–80 is maintained by most modern scholars following F. Dvornik, against the earlier view of e.g. J. *Hergenröther and K. J. *Hefele.)

The causes of the renewed outbreak of the controversy are obscure. When Leo VI became Emperor (886) he at once deposed Photius, who was perhaps excommunicated by Pope *Formosus in 892, though Dvornik holds that the relevant Papal letter had been falsified at Constantinople by the anti-Photian party. After his deposition Photius disappears from history; he died at the Convent of Armeniaki towards the end of the 9th cent. Though his schism is only one among many similar episodes in the history of the relations between the Greek and Latin Churches, it had grave consequences for the future. It accentuated the conflict between the Roman claim to be the centre of unity for Christendom and the Greek conception of the five patriarchates of almost equal status. Moreover, Photius was the first theologian to accuse Rome of innovating in the matter of the Filioque. Hence in the 13th and 14th cents. the name of Photius became the watchword of those who opposed the union of the two Churches.

Photius was a scholar of wide interests and encyclopaedic knowledge. His most important work, his 'Bibliotheca' or 'Myriobiblion', is a description of several hundred books, often with exhaustive analyses and copious extracts. It is an invaluable mine of information, as a great number of the works mentioned in it are now lost. The 'Amphilochia', written during his first exile, deals mainly with exegetical and doctrinal problems; his treatises against the *Manicheans are chiefly concerned with the *Paulicians. The 'Treatise on the Holy Ghost', written after his second deposition, has furnished all subsequent Greek theologians with their objections to the W. dogma. The 'Nomocanon', which is sometimes attributed to him, is not really his, though he may have re-edited it. A number of his homilies and letters have also been preserved. In the Greek Church Photius is venerated as a Saint; he is also the patron of a guild for English members of the Orthodox Church. Feast day, 6 Feb.

The only collected ed. of Photius's writings is that of J. P. Migne, *PG*, ci–civ, which Migne prepared with the help of J. B. Malou, Bp. of Bruges, and J. *Hergenröther. Other sources include J. Hergenröther, *Monumenta Graeca ad Photium eiusque Historiam Pertinentia* (Ratisbon, 1869), and A. Papadopoulos-Kerameus, Φωτιακά (St. Petersburg, 1897). Earlier works are now superseded by F. Dvornik, *The Photian Schism*. History and Legend (1948), with full bibl., incorporating the results of Dvornik's earlier papers on the subject. Of the older works, J. Hergenröther, *Photius, Patriarch von Konstantinopel* (3 vols., 1867–9), is still valuable. V. Grumel, A.A., 'La Liquidation de la querelle photienne' in *É.O.*, xxxiii (1934), pp. 257–88. Krumbacher, pp. 73–9 and 515–24. É. Amann in *D.T.C.*, xii (pt. 2; 1935), cols. 1536–1604, with bibl. G. Hofmann in *L.Th.K.*, viii (1936), cols. 254–8.

PHYLACTERY (Gk. φυλακτήριον ; Heb. *Tephillin*). A small leather case containing vellum strips inscribed with four passages from the OT, viz. Ex. 13. 1–10, Ex. 13. 11–16, Deut. 6. 4–9, Deut. 11. 13–21. They have been worn by orthodox Jews from pre-Christian times on the forehead and arm during morning prayer on all days except the Sabbath and certain festivals, to remind them of their obligation to keep the law. The *Pharisees and scribes were condemned by Christ for their ostentatious broadening of their phylacteries (Mt. 23. 5).

There is a brief monograph by G. Langer, *Die jüdischen Gebetsriemen* (1931). H. L. Strack–P. Billerbeck, *Kommentar zum Neuen Testament aus Talmud und Midrasch*, iv (1928), pp. 250–76 (Elfter Exkurs, 'Die Tephillin oder Gebetsriemen'). A. R. S. Kennedy in *H.D.B.*, iii (1900), pp. 869–74; s.v.; H. Lesêtre in *Dict. Bibl.*, v (1912), cols. 349–53, s.v. 'Phylactères', with illustrations. See also commentaries to Ex., Deut., and Mt.

PHYSICO-THEOLOGICAL ARGU-MENT. The name commonly applied in the 18th cent., e.g. by I. *Kant, to the *Teleological Argument for the existence of God. In 1713 William Derham (Canon of Windsor from 1716; d. 1735) published two series of *Boyle Lectures under the title *Physico-Theology; or, a Demonstration of the Being and Attributes of God from His Works of Creation*, which won great popularity and, through translations issued a few years later in Italian, French, and Dutch, probably did much towards bringing the expression into general currency.

'PIA DESIDERIA.' P. J. *Spener's book which aimed at fostering a religious revival in German Protestantism and thus created the *Pietist Movement. Written in German, it was published in 1675 at Frankfurt, where Spener was then pastor. He stated his main immediate objectives under the head of six 'simple proposals' (*einfältige Vorschläge*), viz. (1) an intensified study of the Bible, aiming at enhanced personal devotion as the chief end;

(2) a fuller exercise by the laity of their spiritual priesthood; (3) emphasis on the practical, as opposed to the merely intellectual, side of Christianity, culminating in the spirit of love; (4) the manifestation of charity in religious controversy, which by the sympathetic presentation of truth should seek to win the heart rather than to gain controversial victory; (5) the reorganization of theological studies at the universities and the establishment of higher standards of religious life among both professors and students; (6) the reform and revival of preaching with a view to edification. The book also looked forward to an age of prosperity for the Church when these ideals would be largely realized, after the conversion of the Jews and the fall of Papal Rome. Spener further developed his programme in *Das geistliche Priesterthum* (1677) and *Allgemeine Gottesgelehrtheit* (1680).

For bibl. see *Spener, P. J.*

PIARISTS. An order of Clerics Regular for the education of the young. Their name derives from the last word of their Latin designation, 'Regulares pauperes Matris Dei scholarum piarum'. They were founded in 1597 by St. *Joseph Calasanctius, who in that year opened the first free elementary boys' school in Europe, to educate the children at large in the streets of Rome. The school, which in 1612 counted 1,200 children, was a great success, and its teachers were recognized as a congregation by *Paul V in 1617. In 1621 Gregory XV made it an order, whose members added to the three vows of religion a fourth to devote themselves to the education of the young. In 1622 it received all the privileges of the *Mendicant orders. In 1645, owing to the intrigues of one of its members, the order was degraded into an association. In 1656, however, it was once more set up as a congregation, and in 1669 Clement IX restored it as an order with all its former privileges. From that time it flourished in many parts of Central, E. and S. Europe, esp. in Spain, as well as in Latin America. After the dissolution of the *Jesuit Order the Piarists rendered esp. valuable services to the Church in carrying on Catholic education. They are governed by a Praepositus Generalis, helped by four Assistants General, who all reside in Rome. In their teaching they pay particular attention to mathematical studies.

L. Picanyol (Piarist), *Brevis Conspectus Historico-Statisticus Ordinis Scholarum Piarum* (Rome, 1932). Letters of St. Joseph Calasanctius ed. by id. (Rome, 1950 ff.); principal lives by V. Talenti (Rome, 1753; modern ed., Florence, 1917) and U. Tosetti (Rome, 1767). Heimbucher, ii, 121–30, with further bibl. L. Picanyol in *E.C.*, iii (1950), cols. 1438–41, s.v. 'Chierici Regolari, iii, Chierici Regolari Poveri della Madre di Dio delle Scuole Pie', also with bibl.

PICA. See *Pie*.

PICO DELLA MIRANDOLA, GIO-VANNI (1463–94), Italian nobleman, scholar, and mystical writer. After studying at

*Bologna he spent many years wandering among schools of learning in Italy and France and collecting a library. Besides being a good classic, he knew also Hebrew, Aramaic, and Arabic; and he was the first to seek in the *Cabbala a clue to the Christian mysteries. His vivid imagination led him to many unorthodox views, several of which found expression in a set of 900 theses on a great diversity of topics which he proposed to defend in 1486. As, however, some of them appeared to Innocent VIII definitely heretical, Pico abandoned the enterprise, and for the rest of his life lived in great simplicity. On his deathbed he was clothed in the *Dominican habit by G. *Savonarola.

Collections of his works (2 parts, Bologna, 1495–6), with life by his nephew, Giovanni Francesco Pico prefixed [no pagination]; also Venice, 1498; much improved ed., Paris, 1601 (repr. life [no pagination]). Crit. ed. of his 'De Hominis Dignitate', 'Heptaplus', and 'De Ente et Uno' by E. Garin (Edizione Nazionale dei Classici del Pensiero Italiano, i, Florence, 1942), and of his 'Disquisitiones Adversus Astrologiam Divinatricem' by id. (ib., ii and iii; 1946–52). His 'Liber de Imaginatione' ed., with Eng. tr., by H. Caplan (Cornell Studies in English, ix; 1930). The life by his nephew, three of his letters and certain other works were tr. into Eng. by Sir Thomas *More (London, [c. 1510]; modern ed. with introd. by J. M. Rigg, London, 1890; also among the works of Sir Thomas More). Modern studies by G. Semprini (Todi, 1921), E. Anagnine (Bari, 1937), L. Gautier Vignal (Paris [1937]), and E. Garin (Pubblicazioni della R. Università degli Studi di Firenze, Facoltà di Lettere e Filosofia, serie 3, v; 1937), and A. Dulles, *Princeps Concordiae*. Pico della Mirandola and the Scholastic Tradition (Harvard Phi Beta Prize Essay for 1940; Cambridge, Mass., 1941). A. J. Festugière, O.P., 'Studia Mirandulana' in *Archives d'Histoire doctrinale et littéraire du Moyen-Âge*, vii (vol. for 1932; 1933), pp. 143–50, with text of 'De Ente et Uno', pp. 208–24, and Fr. tr., pp. 225–50. P. Kibre, *The Library of Pico della Mirandola* (New York, 1936). Überweg, iii, 20 f., with bibl. p. 629*. F. Bonnard in *D.T.C.*, xii (pt. 2; 1935), cols. 1605–7, s.v. 'Pic de la Mirandole'; B. Nardi in *E.C.*, ix (1952), cols. 1351–5, s.v.

PIE, or PICA. The name given in England in the 15th cent. to the *Ordinale* or *Directorium*, the book of directions for saying the service, and relating its various parts, esp. the *occurrence and *concurrence of *movable and immovable feasts. This work, which took the place of the modern *Ordo recitandi divini officii* or Kalendar, is censured in the Preface to the 1549 BCP (since 1662 headed 'Concerning the Service of the Church') for 'the number and hardness of its rules'.

PIERRE D'AILLY. See *D'Ailly, Pierre*.

PIETÀ. A representation, often in sculpture, of the BVM lamenting over the dead body of Christ, which she holds on her knees. Of 13th cent. German origin, it reached its perfection in Renaissance Italy, as may be seen from the famous work by *Michelangelo in St. Peter's, Rome.

J. Sauer in *L.Th.K.*, viii (1936), cols. 268–70, with bibl.

PIETISM. A 17th cent. movement in the German *Lutheran Church, started by P. J. *Spener (q.v.) with the purpose of infusing

new life into the lifeless official Protestantism of its time. Spener was convinced that by its exclusive stress on dogmatic orthodoxy, Lutheranism had ceased to be a living faith, and with a view to reform put forth a set of six proposals for restoring true religion in his *Pia Desideria* (1675). The movement began with religious meetings in his house. He instituted devotional circles for prayer, Bible reading, &c., and proclaimed the universal priesthood of all the faithful, without, however, intending to separate from the Church. The movement quickly won support from a large body of pastors and in P. *Gerhardt it found a hymn-writer whose compositions did much to spread its ideals. But a clash with the orthodox became inevitable when his friend and disciple, A. H. *Francke (d. 1727), attacked the Leipzig theologians, demanding the conversion of lectures into devotional meetings and condemning wholesale philosophy, doctrine, and homiletics. Francke had to leave Leipzig, but before long a new university was founded by Frederick III at Halle (1694) which for several years was the centre of the movement. A body, chiefly of younger theologians, helped to carry the movement throughout Protestant Germany. Through want of consistent leadership, however, the movement took on different aspects in the different districts. In Halle it developed into a hard-and-fast system of penance, grace, and rebirth, while at *Herrnhut, in the settlement of Spener's godson, Count von *Zinzendorf, it consisted chiefly in personal devotion to the Redeemer. In its various forms Pietism has lasted into the present century, and has affected many similar movements in other countries, J. *Wesley's *Methodism among them. In modern times German theologians have differed widely in their assessments of Pietism. It was vigorously attacked, in common with other forms of mysticism, by A. *Ritschl and his school.

The literature is nearly all in German, the standard work being A. Ritschl, *Geschichte des Pietismus* (3 vols., 1880–6). H. Schmid, *Die Geschichte des Pietismus* (1863); [F.] A. [G.] *Tholuck, *Geschichte des Rationalismus*, i, Geschichte des Pietismus und des ersten Stadiums der Aufklärung (1865), pp. 9–91; H. Heppe, *Geschichte des Pietismus und der Mystik in der reformierten Kirche, namentlich der Niederlande* (1879). E. Sachsse, *Ursprung und Wesen des Pietismus* (1884). C. Mirbt in *P.R.E.* (ed. 3), xv (1904), pp. 774–815, s.v. 'Pietismus' [at end of the vol.]; E. S. Waterhouse in *H.E.R.E.*, x (1918), pp. 6–9, s.v.; H. Leube in *R.G.G.* (ed. 2), iv (1930), cols. 1250–61, s.v. 'Pietismus', with full bibl.; K. Algermissen in *L.Th.K.*, viii (1936), cols. 270–2, s.v. 'Pietismus'. See also bibl. to *Spener, P. J.*, and *Francke, A. H.*

PIGHI, ALBERT (c. 1490–1542), theologian. A native of Kampen in Holland, he studied at Louvain and *Cologne and in 1523 was called to Rome by *Hadrian VI. Here he took a prominent part in writing on the main issues of his time. In 1525 he wrote a treatise *Adversus Graecorum Errores* (preserved in MS. in the *Vatican Library) to pave the way for reunion with the Orthodox Church. He also prepared a memorandum, since lost, on *Henry VIII's divorce project. His principal work, *Hierarchiae Ecclesiasticae Assertio* (Cologne, 1538), was an elaborate defence of *tradition as a source of Christian truth co-ordinate with Scripture. In his opposition to M. *Luther and J. *Calvin he emphasized human free-will to such an extent as to imperil belief in *Original Sin. On the other hand he formulated a doctrine of justification which had affinities with Luther's teaching and was repudiated at the Council of *Trent. At the Colloquy of *Ratisbon (1541), he took part on the Catholic side.

Correspondence ed. W. Friedensburg in *Z.K.G.*, xxiii (1902), pp. 110–55. [A.] Linsenmann, 'Albertus Pighius und sein theologischer Standpunkt' in *T.Q.*, xlviii (1866), pp. 571–644. H. Jedin, *Studien über die Schriftstellertätigkeit Albert Pigges* (Reformationsgeschichtliche Studien und Texte, lv; 1931). É. Amann in *D.T.C.*, xii (pt. 2; 1935), cols. 2094–2104, s.v., with useful bibl.

PILATE, PONTIUS. The governor ('procurator') of Judaea from A.D. 26 to 36 under whom Christ was crucified. The Gospels represent him as at first well disposed towards Jesus, but as having finally yielded to the populace through fear of the consequences of an acquittal. The data as to his character contained in *Josephus and *Philo are in full accord with the NT narratives, their additional evidence showing him in anything but a favourable light. The tradition in *Eusebius (*Hist. Eccl.* ii, 7) that he committed suicide may well be correct. Late legends embroidered this theme in the interest of Christianity, and also gave the name of his wife (Mt. 27. 19) as 'Claudia Procula'. In the *Coptic Church he is revered as a martyr (feast day, 25 June). See also foll. entry.

The principal authorities, apart from the NT, include *Philo, *Leg. ad Gaium*, xxxviii; *Josephus, *Antiquitates*, xviii, 3, and *Bell. Jud.*, ii, 8 f. E. *Schürer, *Geschichte des jüdischen Volkes im Zeitalter Jesu Christi*, i (ed. 3, 1901), pp. 488–93, with reff. to earlier lit. M. J. Ollivier, O.P., 'Ponce Pilate et les Pontii' in *R. Bibl.*, v (1896), pp. 247–54 and 549–60. M *Dibelius, ' "Herodes und Pilatus" ' in *Z.N.T.W.*, xvi (1915), pp. 113–26. U. Holzmeister, S.J., 'Wann war Pilatus Prokurator von Judaea?' in *Biblica*, xiii (1932), pp. 228–32. E. von Dobschütz in *P.R.E.* (ed. 3), xv (1904), pp. 397–401, s.v. 'Pilatus'. G. T. Purves in *H.D.B.*, iii (1900), pp. 875–9; A. *Souter in *D.C.G.*, ii (1908), pp. 363–6.

PILATE, Acts of. An apocryphal work giving an account of the trial, death, and resurrection of Christ. In some MSS. an independent treatise on the *Descent of Christ into *Hades is attached to it. From the 13th cent. onwards, the two together have been sometimes known as the 'Gospel of *Nicodemus'.

The first part, the 'Acts' proper, is generally held to be not earlier than the 4th cent., though references to the existence of Acts of Pilate in earlier writers, notably in *Justin Martyr (*Apol.* i, 35; 48) have led some scholars to contend that the book is based on a 2nd cent. original, and that this work may even have been founded on authentic records of Christ's trial. It seems more probable, however, that Justin was referring to an independent treatise. As it is known that fictitious accounts of the trial were put into circulation under the Emp. Maximin (early 4th cent.) in the interests of paganism, it is not impossible

that the Acts of Pilate were compiled as a reply. The book draws extensively on the four canonical Gospels, to which it is evidently seeking to provide supplementary material, including fresh grounds for belief in Christ's *Resurrection.

The second part purports to have been written by the two sons of the aged *Simeon, Carinus and Leucius. It describes with much detail the effect of Christ's presence among the imprisoned souls in Hades (cf. 1 Pet. 3. 19, on which it is based).

The two documents were probably not united before the 5th cent.

Lat. and Gk. recensions ed. C. *Tischendorf, *Evangelia Apocrypha* (Leipzig, 1853), pp. 203–412 (ed. 2, 1876, pp. 210–434); Eng. tr. in M. R. James, *The Apocryphal New Testament* (1924), pp. 94–146. Further ed. of Lat. and Gk. in parallel cols. by P. Vannutelli (Rome, 1938). Coptic text ed. E. Revillout in *P.O.*, ix (1913), pp. 57–132. Syriac text ed., with Lat. tr., by I. E. Rahmani, *Studia Syriaca*, ii (Charfat, 1908). Armenian text, retranslated into Lat. and Gk., by F. C. *Conybeare in *Studia Biblica et Ecclesiastica*, iv (Oxford, 1896), pp. 59–132. R. A. *Lipsius, *Die Pilatus-Akten kritisch untersucht* (1871). J. Quasten, *Patrology*, i (Utrecht, 1950), pp. 115–18. Bardenhewer, i, 543–7; Altaner (ed. 1950), p. 51 f. E. von Dobschütz in *H.D.B.*, iii (1900), pp. 544–7, with bibl.

PILGRIM FATHERS, The. The founders of the colony of Plymouth, Massachusetts, who set sail from Holland and England in the *Mayflower* in Sept. 1620. The title 'Pilgrim Fathers' is comparatively modern. In 1630 William Bradford, the Governor, wrote of his company as 'pilgrims' (with a ref. to Heb. 11. 13), and such language was gradually adopted in New England, e.g. on 22 Dec. 1798 a feast of the 'Sons' or 'Heirs of the Pilgrims' was held at Boston, at which the memory of 'the Fathers' was celebrated. In this way the phrase 'Pilgrim Fathers' eventually came into common use.

C. M. Andrews, *The Colonial Period of American History* (4 vols., 1934–8), esp. i, 249–78, with full bibl. notes on primary sources.

PILGRIMAGES. Journeys to holy places undertaken from motives of devotion in order to obtain supernatural help or as acts of penance or thanksgiving. The practice of pilgrimages is common to most higher religions, e.g. Hinduism (Benares) and Islam (Mecca), and is due to the natural desire of men to visit the places where their great heroes have lived and died and to the deep-seated conviction that certain localities are particularly favoured by the Godhead. In Christianity the fact of the Incarnation is the sufficient explanation of the early custom of visiting the places consecrated by the presence of Christ. The practice received a strong impulse from the conversion of *Constantine, followed by the visit of the Empress *Helena to *Jerusalem (326), and later in the 4th cent. from the example of St. *Jerome. The 'Peregrinatio *Etheriae' (q.v.) is an illuminating account of one of these pilgrimages in the early Church. Almost on an equal footing with those to Palestine were pilgrimages to Rome, to the tomb of the Apostles, Peter and Paul ('ad limina Apostolorum'), which came to be much frequented by Anglo-Saxon princes and nobles. To these the growing veneration of saints and images soon added many others, the most famous being Santiago de *Compostela. From the 8th cent. the practice of imposing a pilgrimage in the place of a public penance added to the number of pilgrims, so that throughout the Middle Ages they were organized on a grand scale and provided for by special ecclesiastical and civil legislation. Abuses which had already called forth the censure of St. *Chrysostom and St. Jerome increased with the popularity of the devotion and were satirized by *Erasmus in his 'Religious Pilgrimage'. The Reformation marked a notable setback, but the growth of popular piety in the period of the *Counter-Reformation led to a revival of the practice. In modern times, *Lourdes has acquired an unrivalled fame as a place of pilgrimage, and in England the restoration of the shrines of Our Lady of *Walsingham has once more attracted Anglican and RC worshippers.

P. Geyer (ed.), *Itinera Hierosolymitana Saeculi iiii–viii* (C.S.E.L., xxxix; 1898). Further primary texts publd. in The Library of the Palestine Pilgrims' Text Society, vols. i–xii (London, 1888–97). B. Kötting, *Peregrinatio Religiosa. Wallfahrten in der Antike und das Pilgerwesen in der alten Kirche* (1950). L. Lalanne, 'Les Pèlerinages en Terre Sainte avant les Croisades' in *Bibliothèque de l'École des Chartes*, vii (1845–6), pp. 1–32; L. Le Grand, 'Les Pèlerinages en Terre Sainte au moyen-âge' in *R.Q.H.*, lxxv (1904), pp. 382–402. G. Bardy, 'Pèlerinages à Rome vers la fin du IVe siècle' in *Anal. Boll.*, lxvii (1949), pp. 224–35. S. Heath, *Pilgrim Life in the Middle Ages* (1911). G. H. Jones, *Celtic Britain and the Pilgrim Movement* (Y Cymmrodor. The Magazine of the Society of Cymmrodorion, xxiii; 1912). Bede Camm, O.S.B., *Forgotten Shrines* (1910); id., *Pilgrim Paths in Latin Lands* (1923). Bede Jarrett, O.P., in *C.E.*, xii (1911), pp. 85–99, s.v.; K. Hofmann in *L.Th.K.*, xii (1938), cols. 735–40, s.v. 'Wallfahrt'; H. *Leclercq, O.S.B., in *D.A.C.L.*, xiv (pt. 1; 1939), cols. 65–176, s.v. 'Pèlerinages aux lieux saints', with bibl.; id., ib., cols. 40–65, s.v. 'Pèlerinage à Rome'; G. Mollat-G. Anichini in *E.C.*, ix (1952), cols. 1080–6, s.v. 'Pellegrinaggio'.

PILGRIMAGE OF GRACE, The. A popular religious rising in the N. of England in defence of the suppressed religious houses and against the autocratic religious policy of T. *Cromwell. By the end of 1536 R. *Aske, who led the rebellion, had assembled between 30,000 and 40,000 men and the Abp. of *York (E. Lee) and the chief of the gentry took refuge in Pontefract Castle. Aske's success was such that he was soon able to open negotiations at Doncaster on equal terms with the Duke of Norfolk and the Earl of Shrewsbury, who had been sent to suppress the Pilgrimage. Provided with a safe-conduct, he was favourably received in London by *Henry VIII, and having obtained an assurance that the grievances would be redressed and the promise of a Parliament at York, he returned home early in 1537. It seems doubtful, however, whether the Government's intentions were honourable at any stage. At any rate, a fresh outbreak of rebellion gave them the excuse for breaking off negotiations and renewing the attack, and, on the ground of his having had communications with the Imperial ambassador, Aske was sentenced to death for high treason, paraded and despatched to the north on 28 June 1537 and executed at York in the following month.

M. H. Dodds–R. Dodds, *The Pilgrimage of Grace, 1536–37, and the Exeter Conspiracy, 1538* (2 vols., 1915). M. Bateson, 'The Pilgrimage of Grace' in *E.H.R.*, v (1890), pp. 330–45; id., 'Aske's Examination', ib., pp. 750–3; A. G. Dickens, 'The Yorkshire Submission to Henry VIII, 1541', ib., liii (1938), pp. 267–75.

PILGRIM'S PROGRESS, The. The First Part of the masterpiece of J. *Bunyan (q.v.), prob. written not (as traditionally held) during his long imprisonment in Bedford gaol (1660–1672), but during a second six months' confinement in 1676, was published in February 1678 (N.S.); a fresh edition, with many additions, appeared later in the same year; while the Second Part, depicting 'the manner of setting out of Christian's wife and children', did not appear until 1684. Attempts to identify an underlying medieval or Renaissance model have failed. Bunyan had but the most meagre historical knowledge and interests; and it is far more probable that the work owes everything to his own originality.

Its unrivalled place in the world's religious literature rests on its artless directness, its imaginative power, the homeliness and rusticity of its method and its plainness of style, which give it its universal appeal, even to the most simple-minded. The persons and incidents encountered by Christian on his journey from the 'City of Destruction' to the 'Heavenly City'—'Evangelist', 'Mr. Worldly-Wiseman', 'Mr. Legality' and his son 'Civility', 'Mr. Talkative, the son of Mr. Saywell, who dwelt in Prating Row', 'Mr. Facing-both-ways', and 'Greatheart', and, of places, the 'Slough of Despond', the 'Hill of Difficulty' the 'House Beautiful' (supposed to have been modelled on an actual house in Houghton Park), the 'Valley of the Shadow of the Death', and 'Vanity Fair'—have become part and parcel of the language of religion in England.

The book, which circulated at first mainly in uneducated circles and whose supreme qualities were only gradually recognized, has appeared in a vast number of editions, and been translated into well over 100 languages. It has also been the subject of many adaptations (issued under similar titles), for the most part wholly without independent merit. The well-known hymn, 'He who would valiant be', is a modification of some lines sung by the pilgrims on the way to the 'Enchanted Ground'.

Good modern ed. by J. B. Wharey (Oxford, 1928), with full discussion of earlier edd. and bibl. See also bibl. to *Bunyan*.

PILKINGTON, JAMES (c. 1520–76), Bp. of *Durham. A native of Lancs, he was educated at Pembroke Hall and St. John's College, Cambridge. In 1539 he was elected a Fellow, and in 1550 President, of St. John's College. In warm sympathy with the Reformation, he disputed at Cambridge, on 24 June 1549, against *Transubstantiation. During the Marian Persecution he lived principally at Protestant centres on the Continent. Returning to England from Frankfurt after Mary's death in 1558, he now became a prominent member of the Protestant party in the C of E. He took an active part in the revision of the BCP and, as Master of St. John's and Regius professor of divinity at Cambridge, upheld the tenets of Reformation theology in the university. Towards the end of 1560 he was appointed Bp. of Durham, thus becoming the first Protestant occupant of the see. His strong support of the Protestant cause in his diocese provoked much hostility and he and his family fled when the insurgents broke into Durham Cathedral during the Northern Rebellion of 1569. He upheld the temporal rights of his see with vigour, but failed as an administrator, allowing many of the buildings in his diocese to fall into neglect and decay. His writings include commentaries on *Haggai (*Aggeus*, 1560), *Obadiah (*Abdias*, publd. with a new edition of *Aggeus*, 1562), and *Nehemiah (1585, ed. posthumously by John Fox), as well as a treatise on 'The Burning of Paul's Church in London [4 June 1561] by Lightning'.

Works ed. J. Scholefield (*Parker Society, 1842), with biographical introd., pp. i–xvi. Episcopal Register ed. and calendared by Gladys Hinde (Surtees Society, clxi, 1952, pp. 140–82). J. Pilkington, *The History of the Lancashire Family of Pilkington and its Branches from 1066 to 1600* (ed. 2, Liverpool, 1894), pp. 43–9, with portrait, and text of his will, pp. 94–7. C. W. Sutton in *D.N.B.*, xlv (1896), pp. 293–5.

PILLAR SAINTS. See *Stylites*.

PIN, L. E. DU. See *Dupin, L. E.*

PIONIUS, St. (d. 250), martyr. He was executed at Smyrna during the *Decian persecution, having been arrested while celebrating the anniversary of the martyrdom of St. *Polycarp. The 'Acta Pionii', which describe his death, were known to *Eusebius, and are reliable documents. It was he who was responsible for the preservation of the 'Martyrium Polycarpi', but the attribution to him of the extant Life of St. Polycarp is probably incorrect, though its authenticity has been recently defended (e.g. by C. J. Cadoux). Feast day in the E., 11 Mar.; in Latin martyrologies, 1 Feb.

Eusebius, *H.E.* IV. xv. 46 f. The Greek 'Acta' (contemporary, but with slight 4th cent. revision) discovered by O. von Gebhardt in 1896 in the Cod. Ven. Marc. 359. Text in id., *Acta Martyrum Selecta* (1902), pp. 96–114; Lat. text in *AA.SS.*, Feb. I (1735), pp. 40–6. E. *Schwartz, *De Pionio et Polycarpo* (Göttingen, 1905); H. *Delehaye, S.J., *Les Passions des martyrs et les genres littéraires* (1921), pp. 28–59. L. Wohleb, 'Die Überlieferung des Pionios-Martyriums' in *R.Q.*, xxxvii (1929), pp. 173–7. C. J. Cadoux, *Ancient Smyrna* (1938), pp. 306–10 note.

PIPPIN III. See *Pepin III.*

PIRCKHEIMER, WILLIBALD (1470–1530), German humanist. Born at Eichstätt, he studied Greek at Padua (1489) and Law at Pavia (1492). In 1497 he became a town councillor at Nuremberg, where his house soon became a centre of learning. In 1499 he led the Nuremberg contingent in the Swiss War, of which he wrote a famous history, *Bellum Helveticum* (first publd. 1610). After his return he devoted himself to the translation of the Greek classics and Fathers into Latin, as well as to historical, astronomical, and artistic studies. He became a friend of A. *Dürer and a defender of J. *Reuchlin. At the beginning of the Reformation he favoured M. *Luther, whose chief opponent, J. *Eck, he attacked in the virulent pamphlet *Eccius Dedolatus*, now generally acknowledged to be his work. He regretted, however, Luther's break with the Church. In 1521, under the influence of his brilliant and devout sister, Charitas, abbess of the convent of *Poor Clares at Nuremberg, he asked to be absolved from the ban of excommunication which he had incurred as a follower of the Reformer. In his later years he completely abandoned Luther. His last work is an apology for the persecuted convent of his sister, entitled *Oratio Apologetica* (1529).

Collected ed. of Pirckheimer's works ed. M. Goldas (Frankfurt a.M., 1610). Modern ed. of *Eccius Dedolatus* by S. Szamatólski (Berlin, 1891); of his writings on the Swiss War (from the autograph in the Brit. Mus.) and his Autobiography by K. Rück (Munich, 1895). Correspondence ed. E. Reicke (vol. i, Munich, 1940). Lives by F. Roth (Halle, 1887) and E. Reicke ('Deutsche Volkheit', Jena, 1930). P. Drews, *Willibald Pirckheimers Stellung zur Reformation* (1887). F. List in *P.R.E.* (ed. 3), xv (1904), pp. 405–9, with bibl.; K. Löffler in *C.E.*, xii (1911), p. 109.

PIRMINIUS, St. (d. 753), perhaps 'Priminius', first Abbot of *Reichenau. He was probably of Visigothic nationality (not Frankish, Irish, or Anglo-Saxon). With the protection of *Charles Martel he founded Reichenau (724) and other monasteries among the Alamanni in Baden and in Alsace, which became important centres of religious and cultural development. His *Scarapsus* (also *Dicta Pirmini*), which circulated widely in Carolingian times, is of interest as the earliest document containing the *Apostles' Creed in its present form. Feast day, 3 Nov.

Life (9th cent.) and other material in *AA.SS.*, Nov. II (pt. 1; 1894), pp. 2–56. 'Dicta Abbatis Pirminii, de Singulis Libris Canonicis Scarapsus', ed. C. P. *Caspari in his *Kirchenhistorische Anecdota*, i (1883), pp. 149–93. G. Jecker, *Die Heimat des hl. Pirmin des Apostels der Alamannen* (Beiträge zur Geschichte des alten Mönchtums und des Benediktinerordens, xiii; 1927), with text of 'Dicta', pp. 34–73. F. Flaskamp, 'Zur Pirminforschung' in *Z.K.G.*, xliv (1925), pp. 199–202. On his connexions with the Apostles' Creed, see J. N. D. Kelly, *Early Christian Creeds* (1950), esp. pp. 407–9. A. Köhler–A. *Hauck in *P.R.E.* (ed. 3), xv (1904), pp. 409–12.

PIRQE ABOTH (Heb. אֲבוֹת פִּרְקֵי, 'Sayings [lit. 'Sections'] of the Fathers'). A set of Jewish aphorisms on Wisdom, similar to those in Ecclus. They are assigned to some sixty different doctors and preserved in the *Mishnah as a separate tractate. Many are purely utilitarian, others are on a high moral level and constant stress is laid on the study of the Law. The collection appears to date from the period A.D. 70–170. There are several points of contact with the sayings in the Gospels.

Modern edition by C. Taylor (1877; ed. 2, 1900). Translations in R. H. *Charles, *Apocrypha and Pseudepigrapha of the *Old Testament* (1913), pp. 686–714; W. O. E. Oesterley–G. H. Box (S.P.C.K., 1919). Also in H. Danby, *The Mishnah* (1933), pp. 446–61.

PISA, Council of. It was convoked by the cardinals in 1409 in order to end the Great Schism which had divided W. Christendom since 1378. Though both Popes held rival councils, *Benedict XIII at Perpignan and Gregory XII at Cividale near Aquileia, the assembly at Pisa was fairly representative, comprising besides a number of prelates the ambassadors of most European princes. After declaring itself canonically convoked and *oecumenical, the Council deposed both Popes as schismatics and heretics and elected Cardinal Peter Philargi, who took the name of *Alexander V, promised to work for the reform of the Church, and dissolved the Council.

The authority of the Council of Pisa has been much discussed. It is not recognized by the RC Church as oecumenical, e.g. on the ground of its not having been convoked by the Pope, but it was defended by J. *Gerson and P. *D'Ailly and later by the *Gallicans. Though it did not end the Schism, which, on the contrary, became worse than before by the existence of three Popes, it is generally admitted that it paved the way for the final solution found at the Council of *Constance (1415).

Hardouin, viii, cols. 1–204; Mansi, xxvi (1784), cols. 1131–256, xxvii (1784), cols. 1–502. Crit. ed. of the Acta by J. Vincke, in *R.Q.*, xlvi (1941), pp. 81–331. Id., *Briefe zum Pisaner Konzil* (Beiträge zur Kirchen- und Rechtsgeschichte, i; 1940); id., *Schriftstücke zum Pisaner Konzil. Ein Kampf um die öffentliche Meinung* (ib., iii; 1942). Hefele–Leclercq, vii (pt. 1; 1914), pp. 1–69. J. Lenfant, *Histoire du concile de Pise, et de ce qui s'est passé de mémorable depuis ce concile jusqu'au concile de Constance* (2 vols., Amsterdam, 1724). F. Bliemetzrieder, *Das Generalkonzil im grossen abendländischen Schisma* (1904), esp. pp. 221–329. L. Schmitz, 'Zur Geschichte des Konzils von Pisa 1409' in *R.Q.*, ix (1895), pp. 351–75. O. Günther, 'Zur Vorgeschichte des Konzils von Pisa' in *N.A.*, xli (1919), pp. 632–76. G. Mollat in *D.T.C.*, xii (pt. 2; 1935), cols. 2128–30, s.v. J. Beckmann in *L.Th.K.*, viii (1936), col. 291 f., s.v.

PISCINA (Lat., 'basin'). A niche in the wall on the Epistle side of the altar for the ablutions of the priest's hands and of the chalice and paten at Mass. It is usually furnished with a shelf to hold the cruets and has a drain (*sacrarium*) connected with the earth, to receive the water used for the ceremonies. The piscina is of medieval origin; in a few English parish churches and in the crypt of *Gloucester Cathedral, piscinas date back to the Norman period. Sometimes two piscinas were set side by side, the one perhaps being reserved for the washing of the priest's hands, the other for the cleansing of the sacred vessels. They are often richly decorated.

Rohault, iii (1883), pp. 140–4. F. Bond, *The Chancel of English Churches* (1916), pp. 143–63.

PISGAH (Vulg. 'Phasga'). The mountain to the east of the river *Jordan where *Moses was granted a sight of the Holy Land at the end of his life and the promise made that his descendants would possess it (Dt. 34. 1–4).

Biblical students are not agreed whether the Hebrew word (הַפִּסְגָּה) is a proper or a common noun. This revelation to Moses is the source of such phrases as a 'Pisgah view', a 'Pisgah prospect', for any vision or hope of which a man will not himself see the realization.

PISTIS SOPHIA. This curious work, a product of 3rd cent. Egyptian Christianity, is contained in a solitary *Coptic MS. in the British Museum (Add. 5114), formerly the property of Dr. Anthony Askew (d. 1774). It purports to record instructions given by Jesus to certain disciples at the end of a twelve-year sojourn upon earth after the Resurrection. With fantastic imagery, based largely upon that of the *Gnostic thinker, *Valentinus, and interspersed with jejune canticles, it relates the salvation of the personified 'Pistis Sophia' (i.e. Philosophy) from a demon named 'Self-Will'. Ascetic rules are appended which a man must follow if he is to escape the menace of evil powers and win through to the Kingdom of Light. In his own strange fashion the author emphasizes above all things the condescending Incarnation of Jesus, who is the greatest yet simplest of all Mysteries and in whom the contradictions of the universe are explained. The work appears to be a translation from the Greek. Acc. to C. Schmidt, the MS. dates from the later 4th cent.

Text ed., with Lat. tr., by M. G. Schwartze–J. H. Petermann (Berlin, 1851); Fr. tr. by E. Amélineau (Paris, 1895); Eng. tr. by G. Horner, with introd. by F. Legge (London, 1924). Modern ed. of Coptic text by C. Schmidt (Copenhagen, 1925) and Germ. tr. by id. (Leipzig, 1925). A. *Harnack, *Über das gnostische Buch* Pistis Sophia (T.U., vii, Hft. 2, 1891, pp. 1–114). F. C. *Burkitt, 'Pistis Sophia' in *J.T.S.*, xxiii (1921–2), pp. 271–80; id., 'Pistis Sophia' and the Coptic Language', ib., xxvii (1925–6), pp. 148–57. Bardenhewer, i, 354–6, 357 f.; Altaner (ed. 1951), p. 107 f. J. *Moffatt in *H.E.R.E.*, x (1918), pp. 45–8, with full bibl. to date; E. Peterson in *E.C.*, ix (1952), col. 1574, with further bibl.

PISTOIA, Synod of (1786). The Synod met under the presidency of Scipio de' *Ricci, Bp. of Pistoia-Prato, to give support to the policy of Leopold II, Grand Duke of Tuscany (1765–1790), who was strongly in favour of a reform of the Church along the lines pursued by *Gallicanism in France and *Josephinism in Austria-Hungary. The Synod adopted the Four *Gallican Articles of 1682, based the authority of the Church upon the consent of the body as a whole, and that of bishops upon the assent of their clergy in synod, and held that the jurisdiction of a diocesan bishop is independent of the Pope. It exalted the civil power, and also decreed alterations in religious practice, requiring that there should be one altar only in each church, and one Mass only each Sunday; it also condemned the use of Latin in service, and the cult of the *Sacred Heart. Not unnaturally the proposals aroused popular opposition as well as official displeasure. In 1790 Ricci resigned his see; but on the issue of the bull '*Auctorem Fidei', condemning 85 of the Pistoian articles, Ricci recanted.

The acts of the synod were publd. in 1786 in Lat. and Ital. at Florence, and in Fr. at Pistoia; ed. 2 of the Lat. and Ital., Florence, 1788, and of the Fr., Pistoia-Paris, 1789. Mansi (cont. by J. B. Martin–L. Petit, A.A.), xxxviii (Paris, 1907), cols. 989–1282. Much primary information in de' Ricci's *Memorie* and in his letters. J. Carreyre in *D.T.C.*, xii (pt. 2; 1935), cols. 2134–230, s.v. 'Pistoie (Synode de)', with bibl. J. B. Peterson in *C.É.*, xii (1911), p. 116 f., s.v. See also bibl. to *Ricci, S. de'* and *Auctorem Fidei*; also lives of *Pius VI*.

PITHOU, PIERRE (1539–96), *Gallican theologian. He came of a family of distinguished jurists. Brought up a Calvinist and called to the bar at Paris in 1560, he was converted to Catholicism in 1573. Later he received legal appointments from *Henry IV, whom he supported in his struggles with the League. Besides important political writings, which include his *Satire ménippée* (1593) and editions of several texts of the classics, he prepared for publication (in conjunction with his brother, François) a text of the *Corpus Iuris Canonici* (issued in 1687). In his treatise, *Les Libertés de l'Église gallicane* (1594), the leading principles of Gallicanism were formulated for the first time. His extensive collection of MSS., some of them of great value for the text of the early conciliar canons, is now in the Bibliothèque Nationale at Paris.

Collected ed. of Pithou's *Opera Sacra, Iuridica, Historica, Miscellanea*, Paris, 1609, with life by I. Mercerus, dated 1597, pp. 819–27. [P. J.] Grosley, *Vie de Pierre Pithou; avec quelques mémoires sur son père, et sur ses frères* (2 vols., 1756), vol. i, and vol. ii, pp. 1–105. G. Goyau in *C.É.*, xii (1911), p. 118 f., s.v.; J. Carreyre in *D.T.C.*, xii (pt. 2; 1935), cols. 2235–8, s.v.

PITRA, JEAN BAPTISTE FRANÇOIS (1812–89), *patristic scholar. He was ordained priest in 1836, and his reputation as an archaeologist was soon established by his decipherment (1839) of the 'Inscription of Autun', a (probably 3rd cent.) grave inscription. In 1843 he was professed as a Benedictine at *Solesmes, and for a short time he gave valuable co-operation to J. P. *Migne in the editing of his *Patrologiae*. He then travelled widely in search of MSS., in 1858 at the behest of *Pius IX visiting several Russian libraries. His knowledge of many branches of patristic and Byzantine literature was unrivalled. Having been created cardinal in 1863, in 1869 he was appointed Librarian of the *Vatican, in which capacity *Leo XIII employed him to catalogue the Palatine Greek codices in the library. His publications include *Spicilegium Solesmense* (4 vols., 1852–8) and *Analecta Sacra* (8 vols., 1876–91), both containing many previously unpublished patristic texts, and an important collection of canonical material, *Iuris Ecclesiastici Graecorum Historia et Monumenta* (2 vols., 1864–8).

Lives by F. *Cabrol, O.S.B. (Paris, 1893), and A. Battandier (ib., 1896). There is also a short biographical introd. by A. Battandier prefixed to the posthumously publd. vol. vi of the *Analecta Sacra* (Paris-Rome, 1891), pp. viii–xix. List of his works in F. Cabrol, O.S.B. (ed.), *Bibliographie des Bénédictines de la Congrégation de France* (Solesmes, 1889), pp. 37–52 and 197. M. Ott in *C.É.*, xii (1911), p. 119 f.; P. Séjourné, O.S.B., in *D.T.C.*, xii (pt. 2; 1935), cols. 2238–45, s.v.

PIUS I, St. (d. *c.* 154), Bp. of *Rome from *c.* 140. Acc. to the *Liber Pontificalis* he was a native of Aquileia and acc. to the *Muratorian Fragment he was the brother of *Hermas, the author of the 'Shepherd', but nothing certain is known of his pontificate. The tradition that he was a martyr has no early authority. Feast day, 11 July.

L.P. (Duchesne), i, 132 f. J. Barmby in *D.C.B.*, iv (1887), p. 416 f., s.v.; É. Amann in *D.T.C.*, xii (pt. 2; 1935), col. 1612 f., s.v. 'Pie Iᵉʳ'.

PIUS II (1405–64), (Aeneas Sylvius), Pope from 1458. Enea Silvio de' Piccolomini, born of a poor noble family at Corsignano (near Siena), studied at Siena and Florence, where he became one of the greatest representatives of the humanism of his age. In 1432 he went to the Council of *Basle as secretary of Cardinal D. Capranica, and later served several other prelates in the same capacity; and in 1435 he was sent on a secret mission to *Scotland by Cardinal N. Albergati. On his return to Basle in the following year his personal influence on the Council began to increase; he supported the adversaries of Pope *Eugenius IV and worked for the antipope, Felix V, who made him his secretary in 1439 after Enea had refused to take orders on account of his dissolute life. In the service of Felix he became an eloquent advocate of the Conciliar Theory set forth in his *Libellus Dialogorum de Concilii Auctoritate* (1440). Crowned Imperial poet by the Emp. Frederick III in 1442, he became his secretary in the same year. In 1444 he wrote his much-admired love story, *Euryalus and Lucretia*. In 1445 he left the party of the antipope, was absolved of excommunication, and reconciled to Eugenius IV, to whom he now rendered valuable services by winning over the Emperor to his side and breaking up the Electors' League. At the same time he reformed his moral life and, in 1446, received holy orders. Appointed Bp. of Trieste by *Nicolas V in 1447, he was transferred to Siena in 1450. From the fall of *Constantinople in 1453 he began to work enthusiastically for a *Crusade. In 1456 he was created cardinal by *Calixtus III, whom, after a fierce conflict in the *conclave, he succeeded in 1458.

Pius II now subordinated all other interests to the war against the Turks who became a daily increasing menace to Europe. When the Congress of Mantua (1459–60) had revealed the selfishness and lack of solidarity of the European princes, the Pope took the initiative in proclaiming a three-years Crusade. At the end of the Congress he promulgated the bull 'Execrabilis' (18 Jan. 1460), in which he condemned the practice of appealing to a General Council. He won a victory for these doctrines in Louis XI's repeal of the *Pragmatic Sanction of Bourges in 1461, but Bohemia under Podiebrad and a great number of German princes were in more or less open revolt against Pius, invoking his own former views in their support. This led him to publish his bull, 'In minoribus agentes' (26 Apr. 1463), in which occur the famous words 'Aeneam rejicite,

Pium suscipe', retracting his earlier political doctrines. As he could not expect more than a strictly limited support from the European powers, Pius resolved, in 1463, to put himself at the head of the Crusaders, but he died at Ancona, soon afterwards. His character and motives have been variously judged; but he was at least one of the best Popes of his age.

Opera, publ. Basle, 1551; *Orationes Politicae et Ecclesiasticae*, ed. G. D. *Mansi (3 pts. in 2 vols., Lucca, 1755–9); *Epistolae*, ed. R. Wolkan (Fontes Rerum Austriacarum, lxi, lxii, lxvii, and lxviii; 1909–18). 'Aeneae Silvii Piccolomini Senensis qui postea fuit Pius II P.M. Opera Inedita descripsit ex codicibus Chisianis vulgavit notisque illustravit J. Cugnoni' in *Atti della R. Accademia dei Lincei*, ser. 3, Memorie della Classe di Scienze morali, storiche e filologiche, viii (1883), pp. 319–686. Eng. tr. of his Commentaries on the memorable events of his times by F. A. Gragg, with introd. and notes by L. C. Gabel (Smith College Studies in History, xxii, Nos. 1–2, xxv, Nos. 1–4, xxx, xxxv; Northampton, Mass., 1937 ff.). G. Voigt, *Enea Silvio de' Piccolomini, als Papst Pius der Zweite und sein Zeitalter* (3 vols., 1856–63). A. Weiss, *Aeneas Sylvius Piccolomini als Papst Pius II*. Sein Leben und Einfluss auf die literarische Cultur Deutschlands (1897). W. Boulting, *Aeneas Silvius . . . Orator, Man of Letters, Statesman and Pope* (1908); Cecilia M. Ady, *Pius II. . . . The Humanist Pope* (1913). T. Buyken, *Enea Silvio Piccolomini. Sein Leben und Wirken bis zum Episkopat* (1931). G. Paparelli, *Enea Silvio Piccolomini: Pio II* (1950). Pastor, iii (1894), with full bibl. to date. Fliche–Martin, xv (1951), esp. pp. 46–65, with bibl. E. Vansteenberghe in *D.T.C.*, xii (pt. 2, 1935), cols. 1613–32, s.v. 'Pie II', with bibl.; G. B. Picotti in *E.C.*, ix (1952), cols. 1492–6, s.v. 'Pio II', with bibl.

PIUS IV (1499–1565), Pope from 1559. Gian Angelo Medici, son of a Milanese family, after studying medicine and law at Pavia, came to Rome in 1527 where he held several offices at the Curia. Having been made Abp. of Ragusa in 1545, he was created cardinal by *Paul III in 1549, and under Julius III (1550–1555) was Papal legate in Romagna. Elected Pope in 1559, he reversed the anti-Imperial policy of his predecessor, *Paul IV, whose relatives he brought to trial. If he could be charged with nepotism this at least had beneficial results for the Church in the cardinalate of his nephew, St. *Charles Borromeo. Probably his greatest achievement was the reassembling and successful conclusion of the Council of *Trent (1562–3), whose decrees he began to put into execution during the last two years of his reign. He published a new *Index in 1564, prepared the edition of the 'Roman *Catechism', imposed the 'Professio fidei Tridentina' on all holders of an ecclesiastical office, and reformed the *Sacred College. At the instance of the Emperor he conceded the chalice to the laity of Germany, Austria, Hungary, and several other countries (1564), to check the spread of Protestantism, a measure abolished by his successors. An unsuccessful attempt on his life was made in the last year of his pontificate, owing to the dissatisfaction of the heavily taxed subjects of the states of the Church.

Bullarum, Diplomatum et Privilegiorum S.R. Pontificum Taurinensis editio, vi (Naples, 1860), pp. 489–566, and vii (ib., 1882), pp. 1–422. Docc. also in J. Susta (ed.), *Die römische Kurie und das Conzil von Trient unter Pius IV* (4 vols., 1904–14). G. Constant, *Concession à l'Allemagne de la communion sous les deux espèces. Étude sur les débuts de la réforme catholique en Allemagne, 1548–1621* (Bibliothèque des Écoles Françaises d'Athènes et de Rome, cxxviii, 2 vols., 1923). J. Birkner, 'Das Konzil von Trient und die Reform des Kardinalkollegiums unter Pius IV' in

Hist. J., lii (1932), pp. 340–55. Pastor, xv and xvi (1928), with bibl.; Fliche–Martin, xvii (1948), pp. 148–222. G. Constant in *D.T.C.*, xii (pt. 2; 1935), cols. 1633–47, s.v. 'Pie IV', with bibl.; H. Jedin in *E.C.*, ix (1952), cols. 1496–8, s.v. 'Pio IV', with bibl. See also bibl. to *Trent, Council of*.

PIUS V, St. (1504–72), Pope from 1566. Michele Ghislieri entered the *Dominican Order at the age of 14, was ordained priest in 1528, and subsequently lectured in philosophy and theology and held the offices of novice master and prior in his order. Conspicuous for his zeal and austerity of life, he was made Commissary General of the *Inquisition in 1551 by Cardinal G. P. Caraffa, who, having become Pope under the name of *Paul IV, appointed him Bp. of Nepi and Sutri in 1556 and created him cardinal in the following year, at the same time making him 'Inquisitor General of Christendom'. He opposed vigorously the nepotism of Paul's successor, *Pius IV (1559–65), on whose death he was unanimously elected Pope (1566). Throughout his short but important pontificate he worked zealously for the reform of the Church. Continuing to observe the ascetical practices of the religious life, he transformed his household into a model of regularity, a task in which he was generously assisted by St. *Charles Borromeo. He compelled bishops and clergy to accept the recommendations of the Council of *Trent, had the Roman *Catechism completed (1566) and translated into several languages, reformed the *Breviary (1568) and the *Missal (1570), and ordered a new complete edition of the works of St. *Thomas Aquinas (1570), whom he had declared '*Doctor of the Church' in 1567. In his struggle against the spread of the Reformation he made successful use of the Inquisition in Spain and Italy, but his excommunication of Queen *Elizabeth I in 1570 is generally considered a mistake as it seriously aggravated the position of RCs in England. Politically his reign was marked by the decisive victory over the Turks of the combined Papal, Spanish, and Venetian fleets at *Lepanto in 1571. He was canonized in 1712. Feast day, 5 May.

Bullarum, Diplomatum et Privilegiorum S.R. Pontificum Taurinensis Editio, vii (Naples, 1882), pp. 422–973. Epp. ed. F. Goubau (Antwerp, 1640); later collections of his Epp. ed. de Potter (Brussels, 1827), W. E. Schwartz (Paderborn, 1889), and L. Serrano, O.S.B. (4 vols., Madrid, 1914). The oldest life, anon. but almost certainly by Tommaso Porcacchi (d. 1585), ed., with other docc., by F. Van Ortroy in *Anal. Boll.*, xxxiii (1914), pp. 187–215. Other early lives by G. Catena (Rome, 1586) and J. A. Gabutius (Rome, 1605; repr. in *AA.SS.*, Mai. I (1680), pp. 617–714). Modern lives by J. Mendham (London, 1832), [A. F. P.] de Fallow (2 vols., Paris, 1844), C. M. Antony (London, 1911), and G. Grente ('Les Saints', 1914). O. Braunsberger, S.J., *Pius V und die deutschen Katholiken* (Stimmen aus Maria-Laach, Ergänzungshft., cviii; 1912); C. Hirschauer, *La Politique de St Pie V en France, 1566–1572* (Bibliothèque des Écoles Françaises d'Athènes et de Rome, cxx; 1922). Pastor, xvii and xviii (1929), with full bibl. and notes on sources. R. Hedde, O.P.–E. Amann in *D.T.C.*, xii (pt. 2; 1935), cols. 1647–53, s.v. 'Pie V', with bibl.; H. Jedin in *E.C.*, ix (1952), cols. 1498–500, s.v. 'Pio V', with bibl.

PIUS VI (1717–99), Pope from 1775. Giovanni Angelico Braschi, of a noble family of Cesena, was educated by the *Jesuits and, after having studied law, became secretary to Cardinal Raffo in 1740. Appointed Papal secretary and Canon of St. Peter's in 1755, he was ordained priest three years later. In 1766 *Clement XIII made him treasurer of the Roman Church, and his successor, *Clement XIV, created him cardinal in 1773. Elected Pope in 1775, his rule was marked by the struggle against the rising tide of atheism and secularism. Local Roman affairs, such as the draining of the Pontine marshes, the reorganization of the finances of the states of the Church, and the embellishment of the Vatican Museum and St. Peter's, at first claimed his attention. Before long he became involved in a struggle against '*Febronianism' (q.v.); and though Hontheim made his submission in 1778, his ideas led to practical results in the ecclesiastical reforms of Joseph II (see *Josephinism), who forbade the Austrian bishops to apply for dispensations to Rome and secularized a great number of monasteries. A visit of Pius to Vienna, in 1782, remained without result; Joseph's example was followed by his brother, Leopold, Grand Duke of Tuscany; and Febronianist doctrines were adopted in 1786 at the Synod of *Pistoia under the leadership of Bp. Scipio de' *Ricci. In 1794 Pius formally condemned Febronian teaching in the bull '*Auctorem fidei' (q.v.). Meanwhile, under pressure from Catharine II, Pius, who had already granted Frederick II an exemption from the decree of suppression for individual Jesuits in Silesia, permitted the continuation of the *Jesuits in Russia (1783–4). In 1791, after Louis XVI had sanctioned the *Civil Constitution of the Clergy, a decree subjecting the French clergy to the secular authorities (1790), Pius condemned it as schismatical and heretical and suspended all priests and prelates who had taken the civil oath. In the same year France annexed the Papal territories of *Avignon and Venaissin. The strained relations between the two powers led to the occupation of the States of the Church by Napoleon, and the occupation was only terminated by the Peace of Tolentino (1797), which required the surrender of Ferrara, Bologna, and the Romagna, and, in addition, many valuable MSS. and works of art. In the same year the French general, Duphot, was killed in an attempt to stir up revolution in Rome, whereupon Berthier occupied the city in the following year and declared it a republic. Pius VI was taken prisoner and, in spite of his age and infirmity, removed first to Siena and Florence, then (1799) to Bologna, and thence through several other places across the Alps to Briançon, Grenoble, and Valence, where he died. In his troubled reign Papal prestige was at its lowest before its regeneration in the 19th cent.

Bullarii Romani Continuatio coll. A. A. Barbèri, v–x (Rome, 1842–5). *Collectio Brevium atque Instructionum SS. D. N. Pii Papae VI quae ad Praesentes Gallicanarum Ecclesiarum Calamitates pertinent* (2 pts., Augsburg, 1796). [J. F. de Bourgoing], *Mémoires historiques et philosophiques sur Pie VI et son pontificat* (2 vols., [1798–1800]). P. P. Wolf, *Geschichte der römischkatholischen Kirche unter der Regierung Pius des Sechsten* (7 vols., 1793–1802). G. B. Tavanti, *Fasti del S.P. Pio VI* (3 vols., 1804). I. Bertrand, *Le Pontificat de Pie VI et l'athéisme révolutionnaire* (2 vols., 1879). J. M. Gendry, *Pius VI* (2 vols., [1906]). A. Latreille, *L'Église catholique et la Révolution française*, i, Le pontificat de Pie VI et la crise française, 1775–1799 (1946). Pastor, xxxix–xl (1952–3), with full reff. Fliche–Martin, xx (1949), pp. 17–158. G. Bourgin in *D.T.C.*, xii (pt. 2; 1935), cols. 1653–69, s.v. 'Pie VI', with bibl.; V. E. Giuntella in *E.C.*, ix (1952), cols. 1500–4, s.v. 'Pio VI'.

PIUS VII (1740–1823), Pope from 1800. Gregorio Barnaba Chiaramonti took the *Benedictine habit at the age of 16. In 1775 *Pius VI appointed him abbot of San Callisto at Rome and, in 1782, Bp. of Tivoli. Three years later he was translated to Imola and created cardinal, and in 1800 elected Pope at Venice. The main problem confronting him concerned the relations between Church and state in France. By the *Concordat of 1801 (q.v.), negotiated between Napoleon and Cardinal *Consalvi, religion had been restored in France; but the success of the plan was vitiated by the secretly drawn-up *Organic Articles (q.v.), published simultaneously, against the Gallican tendencies of which the Pope protested in vain. A concordat with the Italian republic followed in 1803; and at the same time the Church in Germany was seriously threatened by extensive secularizations. In 1804 Napoleon was proclaimed Emperor and the Pope accepted his invitation to consecrate him in Paris, but did not obtain the hoped-for concessions. In 1805 Napoleon occupied Ancona, despite the protests of the Pope who had to dismiss Consalvi in the following year. When, in 1808, a French army entered Rome, Pius VII considered himself a prisoner and refused negotiations, and in 1809 the States of the Church were incorporated into the French Empire. When Pius in protest excommunicated the responsible parties by the bull 'Quum memoranda', he was arrested and deported to Grenoble and thence to Savona. In 1811, separated from all his advisers, he assented to a new mode of the institution of bishops by the metropolitans without cognizance of the Pope, which had been propounded by the Council of Paris convoked by Napoleon in the same year. In 1812 he was brought to Fontainebleau where, after a long illness and under pressure, he made far-reaching concessions to the Emperor, published by the latter in 1813 as the 'Concordat of Fontainebleau' and revoked by the Pope two months later. After the fall of Napoleon, Pius VII returned to Rome in 1814 and, in the same year, re-established the *Jesuit Order. The Congress of Vienna (1815) restored the states of the Church, which were reorganized by Consalvi. New concordats were concluded with Bavaria and Sardinia in 1817, with Naples and Russia in 1818, and with Prussia in 1821. In 1821 the Pope also published a bull against the *Carbonari, who were responsible for the revolution in Naples. Despite his political preoccupations, Pius VII favoured art and science; he made valuable additions to the *Vatican Library and established new chairs in the Roman College. His reign marks a transition between the troubles of the French

Revolution and the quiet pontificates that were to follow.

Bullarii Romani Continuatio, coll. A. A. Barbèri, xi–xv (Rome, 1846–53). [A. F.] Artaud [de Montor], *Histoire du Pape Pie VII* (2 vols., 1836). Mary H. Allies, *The Life of Pope Pius VII* ('Quarterly Series', xvii; 1875). H. Chotard, *Le Pape Pie VII à Savone* (1887). [J. O. B. de C.] d'Haussonville, *L'Église romaine et le premier empire, 1800–1814* (5 vols., 1868–9). I. Rinieri, *La diplomazia pontificia nel secolo XIX*, i, 'Il concordato tra Pio VII e il Primo Console anno 1800–1802' (1902); id., *Napoleone e Pio VII (1804–1813)*, vol. i, 1804–8, only publ. (1906). A. Latreille, *L'Église catholique et la Révolution française*, ii, L'Ère napoléonienne et la crise européenne, 1800–1815 (1950). Fliche–Martin, xx (1949), pp. 161–376, with bibl. p. 9 f. G. Bourgin in *D.T.C.*, xii (pt. 2; 1935), cols. 1670–83, s.v. 'Pie VII', with bibl.; F. Cognasso in *E.C.*, ix (1952), cols. 1504–8, cols. 1504–8, s.v. 'Pio VII', with bibl.

PIUS IX (1792–1878), Pope from 1846. Giovanni Maria Mastai-Ferretti was ordained priest in 1819, took part in a Papal mission to Chile in 1823–5, was appointed Abp. of Spoleto in 1827, Bp. of Imola in 1832, and created cardinal in 1840. On the death of *Gregory XVI (1846), who had estranged the Italian people by his oppressive measures, he was elected Pope owing to his reputation as a partisan of liberal ideas. He inaugurated his reign with a general amnesty of political prisoners and exiles and showed himself favourable to the movement of national unity; but his concessions came too late, and when, in 1848, he refused to make war on Austria, he lost popular favour and, in November of the same year, was besieged by the revolutionaries in the Quirinal. He succeeded in escaping to Gaeta, whence he addressed an appeal to the Catholic European powers for the restoration of the Papal state, which was effected after the occupation of Rome by the French army in 1849. From his return to Rome, in 1850, Pius abandoned his liberal attitude in politics. He saw his temporal power gradually decrease, as the Romagna was lost in 1859 and Umbria and the Marches in 1860, until, after the seizure of Rome by Victor Emmanuel on 20 Sept. 1870, he was virtually deprived of all temporal sovereignty by the Law of *Guarantees of 13 May 1871, against which the Pope solemnly protested.

Though an apparent failure from a political point of view, the pontificate of Pius IX was one of striking success in its spiritual and ecclesiastical achievements. The erection of many new dioceses and missionary centres, as well as the restoration of the hierarchy in England (1850) and Holland (1853) and the conclusion of *concordats with many European and American governments, testified to a vigorous life within the Church. His definition of the *Immaculate Conception of the BVM in 1854 gave an enormous stimulus to Catholic devotion, while the issue of the '*Syllabus errorum' and the encyclical '*Quanta cura' in 1864 conserved the traditional beliefs of Catholicism by their condemnation of contemporary rationalism, pantheism, religious liberalism, and other forms of modern philosophy. The most important event of all in his reign was the definition of Papal Infallibility by the *Vatican Council of 1869–70 which, though it gave rise

to the *Old Catholic schism and the *Kulturkampf in Germany, by the increased authority it added to the Papacy on the spiritual plane, in the end more than compensated for the loss in temporal dominion that marked his pontificate. He was the first Pope whose reign extended over the 25 years traditionally ascribed to the rule of St. Peter.

His Acta were publd., 7 vols., Rome [c. 1854–78]; the official docc. for the latter part of his pontificate are also in *A.S.S.* G. Maioli (ed.), *Pio IX. Da vescovo a pontifice. Lettere al* Card. Luigi Amat, agosto 1839–luglio 1848 (Collezione storica del Risorgimento, Ser. 2, xxxviii; 1949). The numerous lives include those by A. de Saint-Albin (Paris, 1860; ed. 2, 1870; new ed., with continuation, 3 vols., 1878), J. M. Stepischnegg (2 vols., Vienna, 1879), B. Castaldi (Rome, 1882), E. Clerici (Milan, 1928), F. Hayward (Paris, 1948), and E. E. Y. Hales (London, 1954). R. Aubert, *Le Pontificat de Pie IX, 1846–1878* (Fliche–Martin, xxi; 1952), with good bibl. R. Ballerini, S.J., *Les Premières Pages du pontificat du Pape Pie IX* (posthumously publd., 1909). A. M. Ghisalberti, *Nuove ricerche sugli inizi del pontificato di Pio IX e sulla consulta di stato* (Regio Istituto per la Storia del Risorgimento italiano, Biblioteca Scientifica, Ser. 2, xxx; 1939). P. Pirri, S.J., *Pio IX e Vittorio Emanuele II dal loro carteggio privato* (Miscellanea Historiae Pontificiae, viii, etc., 1944 ff.). D. Demarco, *Pio IX e la rivoluzione romana del 1848* (Collezione storica del Risorgimento italiano, Ser. 2, xxxvi; 1947). In Eng. there is a brief sketch by J. H. Williams (London, [c. 1920]). M. Ott in *C.E.*, xii (1911), pp. 134–7, s.v.; G. Mollat in *D.T.C.*, xii (pt. 2; 1935), cols. 1868–1716, s.v. 'Pie IX'; P. Pirri, S.J., in *E.C.*, ix (1952), cols. 1510–23, s.v. 'Pio IX', with bibl.

PIUS X, St. (1835–1914), Pope from 1903. Giuseppe Melchior Sarto, born of a poor family at Riese in Upper Venetia, entered the seminary at Padua in 1850, was ordained priest in 1858, became chaplain at Tombolo in the same year, and, in 1867, archpriest of Salzano. In 1875 he was made canon of Treviso, where he was also chancellor to the bishop and spiritual director of the episcopal seminary, and, in 1884, he was appointed Bp. of Mantua. In 1893 *Leo XIII created him cardinal and Patr. of *Venice. Elected Pope in 1903, he chose as his guiding principle 'instaurare omnia in Christo' (Eph. 1. 10, quoted in his encyclical of 4 Oct. 1903), with the implication that, in contrast to his predecessor Leo XIII, he intended to be a religious rather than a political Pope. Events, however, frequently forced him into political action. When, in 1905, the French government effected the separation of Church and state and proposed the formation of the '*associations cultuelles', which were to take possession of the remaining Church property and to be responsible to the civil authorities, Pius X condemned them in two encyclicals (1906), a brave step which, at the price of material ruin, secured the independence of the Church in France from state interference. In 1911 *Portugal followed the example of the French government.

Like his predecessor, Pius took a leading part in the social questions of the time. In the encyclical 'Il fermo proposito' (1905) he laid down the principles of '*Catholic Action', which had assumed rather disquieting features in Italy. Social action and the solution of the labour problem were only parts, though important parts, of the whole of Catholic Action, while its chief aim was to restore Christ to His rightful place within the home, the schools, and society in general. In 1910 he condemned the 'Sillon', a French social movement attempting to spread and adapt the ideas of the French Revolution, and in 1914 the '*Action Française', founded by C. Maurras, which worked on opposite, but equally dangerous lines, advocating an intransigent nationalism based on a union between the positivism of A. *Comte and the organization of the RC Church. He saw another grave danger, threatening the purity of Catholic doctrine itself, in the spread of *Modernism, which he condemned in the decree '*Lamentabili' and the encyclical 'Pascendi' of 1907, and again by a 'motu proprio' ('Sacrorum antistitum') three years later which introduced the anti-Modernist oath, and as an antidote to the new errors particularly recommended the study of *Thomism.

In addition to these protective measures, Pius X undertook a series of difficult reforms. Among them were the codification of the new *canon law (promulgated under *Benedict XV in 1917), which occupied almost the whole of his reign, and administrative changes which involved esp. the *Roman Congregations. His interest in liturgical matters showed itself in the Breviary Reform and in his decrees on sacred music, notably the 'motu proprio' of 1903 restoring the Gregorian chant to its traditional place in the Liturgy. Pius X has become particularly popular as the 'Pope of frequent Communion', and by recommending daily Communion in the decree of 1905 and children's Communion a year later, has given a lasting stimulus to the spiritual life of the faithful. He was venerated as a saint even during his lifetime, and many miracles have been attributed to his intercession. He was beatified in 1951 and canonized in 1954.

Acta publ. Rome, 5 vols., 1905–14. F. A. Forbes, Life of Pius X ('Heroes of the Church'; 1918); R. Bazin, Pie X (Paris, [1928]; Eng. tr., 1928); B. Pierami, Vita del servo di Dio, Pio X (1925; Eng. tr., 1928); Katherine Burton, The Great Mantle. The Life of Giuseppe Melchiore Sarto, Pope Pius X (Dublin, 1951). An Eng. tr. of Card. R. *Merry del Val's Memories of Pope Pius X was publ. London, 1939. É. Amann in D.T.C., xii (pt. 2; 1935), cols. 1716–40, s.v. 'Pie X', with reff.; G. Urbani in E.C., ix (1952), cols. 1523–30, s.v. 'Pio X', with bibl.

PIUS XI (1857–1939), Pope from 1922. Achille Ambrogio Damiano Ratti was ordained priest in 1879, taught dogmatics at the Grand Seminary at Milan from 1883 to 1888, and in 1888 was elected to the College of Doctors at the *Ambrosian Library, of which he became prefect in 1907. In 1912 he was made vice-prefect of the *Vatican Library. At the end of the war of 1914–18 he became Apostolic Visitor to Poland, in 1919 Nuncio and Titular Abp. of Lepanto, in 1921 Cardinal and Abp. of Milan, and in 1922 he was elected Pope. He made 'the restoration of all things in Christ,' symbolized in the institution of the Feast of *Christ the King (1925), the chief object of his pontificate. His great encyclicals, of which '*Quadragesimo Anno' (1931) is the best known, deal with the same problem under its educational and social aspects. The most

important political event of his reign was the *Lateran Treaty (1929; q.v.). The spiritual life of the Church was fostered by the celebration of the Jubilee in 1925 which became the occasion of many canonizations (that of St. *Teresa of the Child Jesus among them), by his support of the apostolate of the laity in the Catholic Action Movement, and by several encyclicals recommending increased religious devotion. The last years of the Pope were overshadowed by the development of events in Europe, esp. the persecution of the Church in Germany (encyclical: '*Mit brennender Sorge') and the spread of atheism and neo-paganism.

His official acts are pr. in the A.A.S., xiv (1922), p. 158–xxxi (1939), p. 83. Eng. tr. of selected encyclicals to date, with introd., by J. H. Ryan (St. Louis, Mo.–London, 1927). A collection of his Scritti storici was publd., Florence, [c. 1932], with introd. by P. Bellezza, 'L' opera scientifica e letteraria di Achille Ratti', pp. vii–xlii; six of these essays were tr. into Eng. by E. Bulloch as Essays in History written between the Years 1896–1912 (London, [1934]). A. P. Frutaz in E.C., ix (1952), cols. 1531–43, s.v. 'Pio XI', with list of some of the many lives of this Pope.

PIUS XII (1876–1958), Pope from 1939. Educated at the *Gregorian University and the Roman Seminary, Eugenio Pacelli was ordained priest in 1899 and entered the Papal Secretariat of State under *Leo XIII in 1901. In 1914 he was appointed Secretary of Extraordinary Ecclesiastical Affairs and, three years later, titular Abp. of Sardes and Apostolic *Nuncio to Bavaria. In this last capacity he took an active part in the peace efforts of *Benedict XV. In 1920 he became Nuncio to the German Republic at Berlin, where, as dean of the Diplomatic Corps, he exercised considerable influence. In 1924 he concluded a favourable concordat with Bavaria, in 1929 a less satisfactory one with Prussia. In 1930 *Pius XI created him cardinal and appointed him Papal Secretary of State. In 1933 he promoted a concordat with the National Socialist German government, though its constant violations by Hitler and the deteriorating position of the Church in Germany soon created grave difficulties. Between 1934 and 1938 he undertook many journeys as Cardinal Legate to *Eucharistic Congresses in Europe and America, and on other missions.

On 2 Mar. 1939, Pacelli was elected Pope and took the name of Pius XII. His elevation, contrary to the tradition against electing the Papal Secretary of State, reflected the need for an experienced politician and diplomat to guide the Church through the grave dangers that threatened. His first encyclical, '*Summi Pontificatus' (20 Oct. 1939; q.v.) published in the first weeks of the War (1939–45), was an appeal to mankind to restore to God His due place in the life of the world and unite in defence of natural law. There soon followed his 'Christmas Allocution' (1939) which laid down the basic principles of a lasting peace in 'Five Peace Points', viz. (1) recognition of the right of every nation to life and independence, (2) true disarmament both material and spiritual, (3) institution of an international court to guarantee the peace, (4) the recognition of the rights of minorities, and (5) the acquisition of a true Christian spirit among the nations. Throughout the War, and afterwards, he laboured to relieve distress, esp. among prisoners. In 1943 he issued the encyclical 'Mystici Corporis Christi' (29 June) emphasizing the unity of the Church in the Mystical Body of Christ, at the same time condemning the errors of *Quietism. It was supplemented by 'Mediator Dei' (20 Nov. 1947) on the Liturgy, which, while expressing sympathy with movements for *Liturgical Reform, incl. the desire for the vernacular, reaffirmed the duty to conform to the rite prescribed by the Holy See. In the encyclical 'Divino Afflante Spiritu' (30 Sept. 1943), he stressed the need for Catholic exegetes to follow the literal meaning of Scripture whenever possible. The encyclical '*Humani Generis' (12 Aug. 1950; q.v.) was directed against certain modern tendencies in (esp. RC) theology. 'Orientalis Ecclesiae Decus' (9 Apr. 1944) and 'Orientalis Omnes Ecclesiae' (23 Dec. 1945; directed esp. to the *Ruthenians) were both designed to foster closer relations with the *Uniat Churches. Among his other important acts were the declaration of the year 1950 as a *Holy Year, the creation of thirty-two cardinals in 1946 and twenty-four in 1953, in each case drawn from a wide variety of countries, thirteen canonizations and esp. the definition in the encyclical '*Munificentissimus Deus' (1 Nov. 1950) of the doctrine of the *Assumption of the BVM (q.v.).

Official docc. are to be found in the *A.A.S.* for the years of his pontificate. The best work so far publd. in English is the study by O. Halecki (London, 1954).

PLACEBO (Lat., 'I will please'). A traditional title for the *Vespers of the Dead, derived from the *antiphon (Ps. 116 [114]. 9; Vulg. *Placebo Domino in regione vivorum*) with which the office opens. See also *Dirge*.

PLACET. See *Exequatur*.

PLACIDIA, GALLA. See *Galla Placidia*.

PLANETA. An alternative name, found already in the Fourth Council of *Toledo (633; can. 28), for the *chasuble. The Lat. word is perh. from the Gk. πλανήτης, 'wanderer', as a garment orig. worn when travelling.

PLANTIN BIBLES. The Bibles issued by the Antwerp printer, Christophe Plantin (1514–1589), celebrated for the beauty and accuracy of their execution. Besides separate editions of the Hebrew, Latin, and Dutch text, Plantin published an elaborate *Polyglott Bible in 8 folio volumes (1569–73), known as the *Biblia Regia*. He was also extensively employed for printing service-books.

PLATINA, BARTOLOMEO (1421–81), Italian humanist. Born at Piadena (hence

'Platina', his family name was Sacchi), near Mantua, he went to Florence in 1457 to study Greek under Argyropolis. Proceeding to Rome in 1462, he was patronized by *Pius II, but when Paul II succeeded in 1464, he lost favour and was imprisoned. He again came into favour under *Sixtus IV, who made him librarian of the *Vatican (1475), and it was while holding this office that he compiled his *Lives of the Popes* (*Liber de vita Christi ac de vitis summorum pontificum omnium*, Venice, 1479). The work is written in a flowing, readable style, but is uncritical. A mention in its pages of the prayers and curses of *Callistus III in 1456 against the Turks, followed by a reference in the same context to the appearance of Halley's comet, gave rise to the fable, frequently repeated in the 19th cent., that the Pope had excommunicated the comet.

The original MS. of his lives of the Popes, which has often been edited, is preserved in the Vatican (Cod. 2044). Eng. tr. with continuation to date by P. *Rycaut (London, fol., 1685); more modern tr. by W. Benham (ib., 2 vols. [1888]). G. J. Schorn, 'Die Quellen zu den *Vitae Pontificum Romanorum* des Bartolomeo Platina' in *R.Q.*, xxvii (1913) pp. 3*–19* and 57*–84*.

PLATO (427–347 B.C.), Greek philosopher. He was a native of Athens, of a noble family, and destined for a political career. In his early years he was introduced to the doctrines of Heraclitus and in 407 (if not earlier) became a pupil of Socrates. Affection for his master and the love for philosophy turned him away from public life after Socrates's execution (399). He withdrew from Athens, taking refuge for a time with Eucleides at Megara. In the next two years he travelled widely (Egypt, Cyrene, Magna Graecia, Sicily, &c.). Returning to Athens *c.* 387, he established a school on the outskirts of the city near the grove sacred to Academus (hence the 'Academy', which had a continuous life until its dissolution by *Justinian in A.D. 529). At the age of sixty (367) he was unexpectedly invited to take a part in politics. Dion, a leader at the court of the youthful Dionysius II (367–45), tyrant of Syracuse, was anxious to set up a liberal state on the model of the *Republic* and invited Plato to instruct Dionysius about the 'philosopher-king'. The enterprise met with small success and in 366 both Dion and Plato were forced to leave Syracuse. In 361 he paid a fruitless visit to Sicily to try to reconcile Dionysius with Dion. Apart from this Sicilian venture Plato seems to have spent the last forty years of his life at the Academy.

With the exception of a small collection of *Epistles*, Plato's writings are in the form of Dialogues, often with Socrates as the principal speaker and various critics or pupils, after whom the Dialogues are usually named, taking part in the discussion. It is often uncertain how far the speeches represent the real or supposed teaching of the interlocutors, and how far they voice Plato's own beliefs. Their literary artistry (directness, dramatic tensions, irony), intellectual breadth, and moral seriousness are supreme. There is no contemporary record of their chronological arrangement, which must be determined mainly by internal criteria. Evidence is sometimes afforded by the historic setting of the Dialogues, though here again it is apt to be doubtful how far Plato meant the history to be taken literally. More reliable criteria are the intrinsic probabilities of Plato's philosophic development, general considerations of subject-matter (e.g. the Dialogues in which Socrates is central are presumably to be put first), Plato's references back to earlier Dialogues (e.g. of the *Timaeus* to the *Republic*), and the growth of Plato's dramatic power. These evidences converge on conclusions about which there is a fair measure of agreement among scholars. The correctness of these conclusions is confirmed by philological ('stylometric') considerations (W. Lutoslawski) and, under the influence of Isocrates, the absence of stylistic hiatus in the later Dialogues.

The principal Dialogues, in their approximate order of composition, are:

(1) The *Socratic Dialogues*, a large group, including the *Gorgias, Meno, Euthyphro, Apology*, and *Crito*. Their common subject is the nature of virtue and whether or not it can be taught. The three last-mentioned are linked with the trial and death of Socrates. The *Euthyphro* deals with correct behaviour towards the gods (ὁσιότης), the *Apology* ('the Hellenic counterpart of Book II of the **Imitation*', A. E. *Taylor) with the fear of doing wrong, and the *Crito* with the duty of loyalty to the state.

In the next four dialogues (2–5), Plato's philosophical and dramatic power is at its highest:

(2) *Phaedo*, on immortality. The divine and enduring soul which shares in the eternal Forms is here contrasted with the mutable human body.

(3) *Symposium*, on the nature of eros, true beauty, and the life of contemplation. The love of earthly beauty can lead the soul onwards to the love of wisdom and of the Form of beauty itself.

(4) *Protagoras*, on the nature of the good, whether virtue is one or many, and on the identity of knowledge and goodness.

(5) *Republic*, generally considered the supreme creation of Plato. Its twofold theme is the nature of right conduct and the ideal political state. Consideration of man's threefold psychological constitution leads to the famous description of the ideal city-state (the philosopher-king, the guardians, community of goods, etc.). The object of the moral quest is no longer a particular ethical Form but the Form of the Good (ἰδέα τἀγαθοῦ) as such, held to underlie all the changing and particular facts in the world. Book VII contains the well-known analogy of human life in which men who live in a cavern see only the shadows of real objects (i.e. the Forms) reflected on the opposite wall.

(6) *Phaedrus*, on persuasion and eros and their part in our perception of the Forms.

(7) *Theaetetus*, on the nature of knowledge (ἐπιστήμη), which is held to be judgement, i.e. the union of true opinion (δόξα) with reason (λόγος).

(8) *Parmenides*, on the relation of likeness and unlikeness, of the one and the many, expounded by the Eleatic philosophers. The Dialogue seems to be a direct attack on the theory of Forms; J. Burnet and A. E. Taylor, however, hold that it is really directed against the existence of sensibles. Perhaps its chief purpose is to parody some false method of argument.

(9) The pair *Sophistes* and *Politicus* (or *Statesman*). Their respective subjects (metaphysics; politics) differ widely, but the two Dialogues are closely connected and of the same date. The *Sophistes* examines the relation of being and becoming, posed by difficulties in the Eleatic teaching. It is argued that 'not being', no less than 'being', exists. The *Politicus* reiterates and develops the teaching of the *Republic* that good government should be left to experts.

(10) *Philebus*, on the nature of pleasure in its relation to the good life. The goodness of a thing lies in the unity of beauty, symmetry, and truth.

(11) *Timaeus*, on cosmology and natural science. Here, as in the *Laws*, the dialogue form has virtually been abandoned in favour of didactic exposition. The universe is described as a single living sphere, composed of soul and body. Besides the world and the model after which it was built there is a third entity, the receptacle (χώρα), in which the world becomes. The world itself is composed of the traditional four elements. Plato also gives an elaborate account of man and his various affections. Through a Latin translation by Chalcidius, known to the earlier Middle Ages, the *Timaeus* was for several centuries the best known of Plato's writings.

(12) *Laws*, on politics. This, the longest of the Dialogues, is in the form of a speech put into the mouth of an Athenian Stranger. The treatise, which was apparently left unfinished, reasserts the communistic teaching of the *Republic*, but with differences of detail. The constitution of the state must avoid the extremes of despotism and freedom. 'Examiners' and a 'Nocturnal Council' are to be in charge of the laws, which here occupy a more prominent place in the constitution than in the *Republic* and the *Politicus*. Great stress is laid on the importance of religious belief. Everyone is to be taught astronomy since God's existence can be deduced from the study of the stars, while atheists who persist in their heresy are to be put to death.

In the earlier Dialogues the main emphasis is ethical. They insist *inter alia* that the cultivation of mind and will, 'goodness of soul', is the chief business of life; that this is attained by a rational insight into the nature of goodness, truth, and beauty; that morality and the claims of the enlightened conscience are to be respected in political life; and that the rational moral personality is created by the 'recollection' (ἀνάμνησις) of what the soul knows of these values. Since the soul naturally aims at what it believes to be good, wrongdoing is the pursuit of a falsely conceived good.

These doctrines are all based on a metaphysic, developed esp. in the later Dialogues, which contrasts the world of sense and everyday experience with a true and higher world of 'Ideas' (or better 'Forms'). These 'Forms' are 'present to' individual entities, and by grasping the eternal Forms and participating in them the soul attains its true well-being and is lifted above the flux of 'becoming'. The secret of human destiny is to be found in the soul's search for the good which it sees but does not possess.

Plato's two principal discussions of theology in the narrower sense are in the *Timaeus* and Book X of the *Laws*. The *Timaeus* describes how the Demiurge (δημιουργός, 'artisan' or 'craftsman'), who is assumed to be identical with God, brings the world into being, how He makes it as an image (εἰκών) of an eternal archetype, and how He enables it to share in His perfection by putting into it mind (νοῦς) or soul (ψυχή). Later critics disagreed as to whether (as *Aristotle held) the *Timaeus* taught that the world had a beginning (was γεννητός) or (as the Neo-Platonists maintained) was eternal. The *Timaeus* also contains Plato's exposition of time as a 'moving image of eternity'.

The *Laws* X embodies the earliest known exposition of natural theology, viz. a form of the *cosmological argument based on the belief that all motions ultimately require at their head a 'perfectly good soul' (ἀρίστη ψυχή). The existence of a second maleficent world-soul, identified with necessity (ἀνάγκη), is also defended. (1) Atheism, (2) the view that the gods are indifferent to human conduct, and (3) the notion that the gods can be deterred from the execution of justice by human offerings, are all rejected as morally pernicious. The evil consequences of wrong belief make it the duty of the state to impose orthodoxy, where necessary by force.

It remains obscure how Plato related the highest of the Forms (the 'Form of the Good') to God as the Supreme Soul. In the *Timaeus* the Forms are the thoughts of God (νοήματα Θεοῦ). But on the other hand, since God also created the universe after the pattern of the Forms, He would seem to be in some sense subordinate to them. On this matter Plato betrays no great concern for consistency. It was only among the more theologically interested Platonists of later times that the problem became a matter of debate.

TEXT. Editio princeps: Aldine, Venice, 1513. H. *Stephanus (3 vols., 1578; still used for refs. to Plato); the effective editor was Serranus, who also made the Lat. version. G. Stallbaum (12 vols., 1821–5); id., ed. in one vol., 1850. J. Burnet in *Oxford Classical Texts* (5 vols., 1899–1907). Separate editions (usually with texts, introductions and notes) of *Phaedo* by J. Burnet (1913); of *Republic* by J. Adam (1902); of *Euthyphro, Apology, and Crito* by J. Burnet (1924); of *Theaetetus* by L. Campbell (1861); of *Sophistes* and *Politicus* by L. Campbell (1867); and many others. TRANSLATIONS. Complete Eng. version by B. *Jowett (4 vols., 1871; ed. 2, 5 vols., 1875; ed. 4, revised, 4 vols., 1953). Versions of *Republic* by A. D. Lindsay (Everyman's Library, 1908) and F. M. Cornford (1941), *Parmenides* (1934), *Timaeus and Critias* (1929) and *Laws* (1934) by A. E. Taylor; and others.

COMMENTARIES. On the *Gorgias* by W. H. Thompson (1871); on the *Phaedo* by J. Burnet (1911); on the *Republic*, lectures by R. L. *Nettleship (publd. 1897) and B. *Bosanquet (1895); on the *Phaedrus* by W. H. Thompson (1868); on the *Parmenides* by W. Waddell (1894), J. Wahl (1926) and F. M. Cornford (1939); on the *Philebus* by E. Poste (1860) and R. G. Bury (1897); on the *Timaeus* by T. H. Martin (1841), R. D. Archer-Hind (1888), J. Cook Wilson (1899), A. E. Taylor (1928), and F. M. Cornford (1937); on the *Laws* by C. Ritter (1896); and many others.
WORKS. G. Grote, *Plato and the other Companions of Socrates* (1865); H. Bonitz, *Platonische Studien* (1886); C. Ritter, *Untersuchungen über Platon* (1888); W. Pater, *Plato and Platonism* (1893); W. Lutoslawski, *The Origin and Growth of Plato's Logic* (1897); P. Shorey, *The Unity of Plato's Thought* (Chicago, 1903); P. Natorp, *Platos Ideenlehre* (1903; ed. 2., 1921); H. Raeder, *Platons philosophische Entwickelung* (Leipzig, 1905); J. A. Stewart, *The Myths of Plato* (1905); J. A. Stewart, *Plato's Doctrine of Ideas* (1909); N. Hartmann, *Platos Logik des Seins* (1909); C. Ritter, *Platon. Sein Leben, seine Schriften, seine Lehre* (2 vols., Munich, 1910, 1923); id., *Neue Untersuchungen über Platon* (Munich, 1910); A. E. Taylor, *Varia Socratica* (1911); L. Parmentier, *La Chronologie des dialogues de Platon* (Brussels, 1913); J. Burnet, *Greek Philosophy*. Part I: Thales to Plato (1914); U. von Wilamowitz-Moellendorff, *Platon* (2 vols., 1917–18); E. Barker, *Greek Political Theory*. Plato and his Predecessors (1918); J. Stenzel, *Zahl und Gestalt bei Platon und Aristoteles* (1924); A. E. Taylor, *Plato*. The Man and his Work (1926); J. Stenzel, *Plato der Erzieher* (1928); G. C. Field, *Plato and his Contemporaries* (1930); C. Ritter *The Essence of Plato's Philosophy* (Eng. trans., 1933; orig. German, 1931); L. Robin, *Platon* (1935); A. J. Festugière, *Contemplation et vie selon Platon* (1936); W. F. R. Hardie, *A Study in Plato* (1936); H. Gauss, *Plato's Conception of Philosophy* (1937); J. Stenzel, *Plato's Method of Dialectic* (Eng. trans., 1940); G. C. Field, *The Philosophy of Plato* (H.U.L., 1949). DICTIONARIES. L. Campbell in *E.B.* (ed. 11, xxi (1911), pp. 808–25; H. Jackson in *H.E.R.E.*, x (1918), pp. 54–61, s.v. 'Plato and Platonism'; H. Leisegang in *P.W.*, xl (1950), cols. 2342–2537.

PLATONISM.

After the death of *Plato (q.v.), his nephew, Speusippus, succeeded him as head of the Academy at Athens (347–339) which with varying fortunes persisted until its closure by *Justinian in A.D. 529. But in the Hellenistic Age Plato's doctrines had a wide following which extended far beyond the direct influence of any institution. Their impact on later Judaism is to be seen in the Book of *Wisdom and the system of *Philo. In the 3rd cent. A.D. a thorough recasting of Plato's system ('*Neo-Platonism') was elaborated by *Plotinus (205–270) whose disciple, *Porphyry (232–c. 305), developed it in conscious opposition to Christianity. Proclus, the last considerable head of the Academy and a celebrated commentator on Plato's writings, died in 485.

The beginnings of an interweaving of Platonism with Christian thought go back to *Clement of Alexandria and *Origen. Of perhaps even greater moment for the history of Christian theology was the fact that the thought of St. *Augustine was radically influenced, largely through *Victorinus Afer, by Platonic doctrines. The authority accorded to his teaching throughout the Middle Ages did much to secure for many Platonic notions a permanent place in Latin Christianity. Henceforward the Platonic Forms were regularly reinterpreted as the creative thoughts of God. The relevance of Platonism for Christian mysticism was appreciated by *Dionysius the Areopagite and other spiritual writers, Eastern (St. *John Climacus) and Western (St. *Bernard of Clairvaux, the *Victorines). Other *media* through which Platonic doctrines reached the Medieval Church were *Boethius, who translated Porphyry into Latin, John Scotus *Erigena (q.v.), and a Latin version by Chalcidius of Plato's *Timaeus*. Even the supposed eclipse of Plato by *Aristotle as 'the Philosopher' *par excellence* in the 13th cent. was only apparent, for, as A. E. *Taylor and others have pointed out, St. Thomas's teaching remained fundamentally Platonist.

The Renaissance led to a revival of interest in Plato himself in such scholars as Marsilio *Ficino. In the 16th cent. there was a steady stream of Platonist influence on religion in England (J. *Colet, St. J. *Fisher, St. T. *More, R. *Hooker). In the 17th cent. the *Cambridge Platonists urged the return of Christian theology to 'its old loving nurse, the Platonic philosophy' and found in its doctrine of the inwardness of morality and religion the best antidote to the controversial aridities of contemporary *Calvinism and the secularism of T. *Hobbes. Strong Platonist influences were also present in many English theologians of the 19th cent. (B. *Jowett, F. D. *Maurice, C. *Kingsley, the *Lux Mundi* School). Among recent philosophers A. N. Whitehead has defended a Platonist cosmology. On the other hand, Protestant orthodoxy on the Continent, with its distrust of natural reason, has commonly been hostile to Platonism and in the present century there has been much theological criticism of Greek metaphysics.

A. E. Taylor, *Platonism and its Influence* (1925); C. Bigg, *The Christian Platonists of Alexandria* (1886); R. Klibansky, *The Platonic Tradition during the Middle Ages* (1939); W. R. *Inge, *The Platonic Tradition in English Religious Thought* (1926); A. Fox, *Plato and the Christians* (1957; selected passages). R. Arnou in *D.T.C.*, xii (pt. 2; 1935), cols. 2258–392, s.v. 'Platonisme des Pères'.

PLAYS, Passion. See *Mystery Plays*; also *Oberammergau*.

PLENARY INDULGENCE. In modern RC theology an *Indulgence (q.v.) which is held to remit the whole of the temporal punishment due to an individual's sins. The petitioner may apply it either to himself or to the profit of a soul, or souls, in purgatory. As it is held that its efficacy depends on the perfection of the soul's disposition (of which no one can ever be certain), there is always an element of doubt as to whether a soul has profited to the full by a particular plenary indulgence. Acc. to current teaching a plenary indulgence cannot normally be gained more than once on the same day (*CIC*, can. 928). The earliest known example of the issue of a plenary indulgence was the promise of *Urban II at the Council of *Clermont (1095) that all penance incurred by Crusaders who confessed their sins should be remitted. As the issue of plenary indulgences became more common in the 12th and 13th cents. it was much debated (St. *Albert the Great, St. *Thomas Aquinas, Pope *Hadrian VI) whether plenary indulgences covered penances which ought to have been enjoined as well as those that had actually been imposed. It was the former

view which gradually became generally accepted. Nowadays plenary indulgences are normally granted for the recitation under prescribed conditions of certain prayers or for other devotional exercises.

PLETHON, GEORGIUS GEMISTUS. See *Gemistus Plethon, Georgius*.

PLINY'S LETTER TO TRAJAN. The famous letter (*c.* 112) in which the younger Pliny, as governor of Bithynia, asked the Emp. Trajan whether Christians should be punished 'for the name' or only for specific crimes. He had already, he stated, executed some Christians, but since further investigation of their customs (on which Pliny's description throws valuable light) had revealed their good character, he now hints at toleration (see *Persecutions*). This, as a principle, the Emp. Trajan would not allow, but he forbade the governor to initiate prosecutions or to act on anonymous accusations, and agreed that apostates might be pardoned.

Pliny, *Letters*, x, 96–7. There is a translation in B. J. Kidd, *Documents illustrative of the History of the Church*, vol. i (1920), No. 14.

PLOTINUS (*c.* 205–270), *Neo-Platonist philosopher and mystic. He was a native of Lycopolis, and acc. to his friend and pupil, *Porphyry, became interested in philosophy at the age of 28 and was for eleven years a disciple of *Ammonius Saccas. He later accompanied Emp. Gordian (d. 243) on an expedition to Persia to make himself acquainted with E. thought. After his return he established his own school in Rome in 244. At the age of 51 he began to write, and after his death Porphyry published his 54 treatises, arranging them in six 'Enneads' (Gk. ἐννεάδες, 'groups of nine').

Owing to the difficulty of his style and subject-matter Plotinus has been variously interpreted, and it is disputed whether his thought is fundamentally pantheistic or tending towards Theism. He rejects the *Gnostic dualism as vigorously as the Christian conception of a historic Redemption, opposing to either his system of an intellectualist mysticism. Its main concern on the speculative side is with the relations between unity and multiplicity. At the summit of the hierarchy of beings there is the One (τὸ ̔Έν) or the Good, the first principle, absolutely simple and self-sufficient, whose intimate life is incomprehensible. Beneath it is the intelligible world of ideas (Νοῦς), and on a still lower plane there is the World Soul (Ψυχή), the third member of the Plotinian Triad. This last is the intermediary between the intelligible and the material world, which, since matter holds the lowest place in the Plotinian system, is the furthest removed from the One. The World Soul has created all material things and orders the universe. Individual souls separate from this World Soul by a mysterious process. They are all homogeneous and have a capacity for the spiritual life, for, in their highest point, they are capable of contemplation.

Contemplation, which occupies a central position in Plotinus's system, is the most perfect activity, for by it souls can attain union with God. In order to reach this its last end the soul has to prepare itself by purity of heart and ascetical practices, turning away from all sensible things. It must devote itself to re-collection, in which memory, sensibility, and discursive reasoning progressively disappear, until it reaches a state in which it 'feels' an ineffable Presence in an ecstasy of 'joyous stupor' and blissful plenitude. The chief difference between this so-called 'natural mysticism' and that of the orthodox Christian mystics is that, in Plotinus's system, union is reached by the unaided effort of the soul, whereas in Catholic teaching it is the work of Divine grace. Despite this fundamental difference Plotinus seems to have exercised indirectly much influence on Christian thought, esp. on St. *Augustine and *Dionysius the Pseudo-Areopagite, and, through them, on the theologians and mystics of the Middle Ages.

Editio princeps of Gk. text of Enneads, Basle, 1580, with M. *Ficino's Lat. tr. Later edd. by F. Creuzer, 3 vols., Oxford, 1835; A. Kirchhoff, Teub., 2 vols., 1856; R. Volkmann, ib., 2 vols., 1883–4; E. Bréhier, Collection des Universités de France, 7 vols., 1924–38, with Fr. tr. Crit. text edd., P. Henry, S.J.–H. R. Schwyzer (Museum Lessianum, Series Philosophica, Paris, etc., 1951 ff.). Eng. tr. of Enneads, with Porphyry's *Life*, by S. Mackenna (5 vols., London, 1917–30). W. R. *Inge, *The Philosophy of Plotinus* (Gifford Lectures, 1918; subjective); F. Heinemann, *Plotin* (1921); R. Arnou, *Le Désir de Dieu dans la philosophie de Plotin* (1921); E. Bréhier, *La Philosophie de Plotin* (1928); J. Guitton, *Le Temps et l'éternité chez Plotin et saint Augustin* (1933); P. Henry, S.J., *Plotin et l'Occident* (S.S.L., xv; 1934); G. Barion, *Plotin und Augustinus.* Untersuchungen zum Gottesproblem (1935); P. Henry, S.J., *Études plotiniennes* (2 vols., Museum Lessianum. Section philosophique, xx and xxi; 1938–41); A. Dahl, *Augustin und Plotin.* Philosophische Untersuchungen zum Trinitätsproblem und zur Nuslehre (Lund, 1945); P. E. More, *Hellenistic Philosophies* (The Greek Tradition, ii, Princeton, N.J., 1923), pp. 172–259. H. R. Schwyzer in *P.W.*, xli (1951), cols. 471–591, with bibl. See also bibl. to *Neo-Platonism*.

PLUMSTEAD PECULIARS. See *Peculiar People*.

PLUNKET, Bl. OLIVER (1629–81), RC Abp. of *Armagh. Of noble family, he was born at Loughcrew, nr. Oldcastle, Co. Meath, and studied and later taught at Rome. In 1654 he was ordained priest, for some years acted as the representative of the Irish Bishops at Rome, and in 1669 was appointed Abp. of Armagh. Consecrated at Ghent, he returned to Ireland where he administered his diocese energetically, raising the standards of education and morality in the face of constant hardship. During the persecutions which began in 1673 he remained in Ireland and in the fury engendered by the *Titus Oates Plot, he was arrested (1679), tried in London, and executed for treason at Tyburn on 1 July (O.S.), 1681. His head, taken to Rome in 1684, has been at Drogheda since 1722, where it is now venerated in the Blessed Oliver Plunket

Memorial Church. He was beatified in 1920. Feast day, 11 July.

Report of his last speech and confession publd. at London, 1681; repr. with other papers, by E. Horne, O.S.B., in *Downside Review*, xxxix (1921), pp. 99–105. *The Trial and Condemnation of Edw. Fitz-Harris . . . as also . . . of Dr. Oliver Plunket . . .* (London, 1681), pp. 61–103. Another contemporary account of his martyrdom ('Vita et Mors Gloriosa Illustrissimi D. Oliverii Plunketti'), ed. by P. F. Moran in his *Spicilegium Ossoriense*, iii (Dublin, 1884), pp. 102–8. Memoirs compiled from orig. sources, also by P. F. Moran (Dublin, 1861). Other modern lives by 'A Sister of Notre-Dame' (London, 1920) and H. [Mrs. T.] Concannon (London, 1935). A. Curtayne, *The Trial of Oliver Plunkett* (1953). R. Bagwell in *D.N.B.*, xlv (1896), pp. 442–5.

PLURALISM. The view that the world contains or consists of a plurality of things or states ultimately distinct, and hence the contradiction of '*Monism' (q.v.).

W. James, *A Pluralistic Universe* (1909); J. Ward, *The Realm of Ends, or Pluralism and Theism* (1911).

PLURALITIES ACT, 1838 (1 and 2 Vict. cap. 106). An Act forbidding any clergyman simultaneously to hold more than one ecclesiastical benefice with cure of souls except, by dispensation of the Abp. of *Canterbury, in the case of two livings with a population of under 3,000 where the travelling distance between the churches was less than ten miles and the joint annual income under £1,000. Cathedral preferments were included within the terms of the Act, though an Archdeacon was in certain cases permitted to hold two benefices or one benefice and one cathedral preferment in addition to his archdeaconry. Acceptance of a second benefice contrary to the terms of the Act rendered the former preferment void. The Act, which also provided more stringent regulations for residence, supplemented the *Canons of 1603 (can. 41) which prohibited the issue of licences to hold two or more benefices over 30 miles apart. The Act was modified by the Pluralities Act, 1850, acc. to which the churches of benefices held in conjunction were to be under three miles apart and the annual value of one under £100, the Pluralities Acts Amendment Act, 1885, which allowed the distance between the churches to be four miles and provided that the annual income of one should not exceed £200, and the Pluralities Measure, 1930, which raised the annual income permissible in cases of plurality to £400. The Benefices Act, 1898, and the Union of Benefices Measure, 1923, were concerned with the administration of the Act. The terms of the Act are virtually abrogated by the Pastoral Reorganization Measure, 1949.

R. *Phillimore, *The Ecclesiastical Law of the Church of England*, ii (ed. 2, 1895), pp. 898–906; H. W. Cripps, *A Practical Treatise on the Law relating to the Church and Clergy* (ed. 8 by K. M. Macmorran, 1937), pp. 299–302.

PLUVIAL (Lat. *Pluviale*). An alternative name for the *cope, probably from its having been originally a rain-cloak. In its English form the word is now almost obsolete.

PLYMOUTH BRETHREN. A Christian religious body, so named because its first centre in England was established by J. N. Darby (1800–82), a former Anglican priest, at Plymouth in 1830. They had been founded in *Ireland by Darby two or three years earlier. Among their early converts was S. P.*Tregelles, the Biblical scholar. Their teaching combines elements from *Calvinism and *Pietism and emphasis has often been laid on an expected *Millennium. Their moral outlook is *Puritanical and they renounce many secular occupations, allowing only those compatible with NT standards (e.g. medicine, handicrafts). They have no organized ministry, though great stress is laid on the Breaking of the Bread each Sunday, partly as a symbol of Christian union and partly as the appointed means of showing forth Christ's death. Their outlook on the Bible is conservative. They also stress the complete autonomy of the local church.

In spite of their emphasis on Christian unity as a principle, the Plymouth Brethren tended from the first to split into separate groups. Controversies on the human nature of Christ and subsequently on Church government led to the fundamental division in 1849 between the 'Open Brethren' and the 'Exclusive Brethren'; and within these groups there are several sub-divisions. Though numerically few, the Plymouth Brethren are widely distributed, esp. in Great Britain and Ireland, on the Continent of Europe (esp. Switzerland, France, and Italy), and in the U.S.A., and are very active in missionary work esp. in India, E. Asia, Central Africa, and S. America.

Collected Writings of J. N. Darby ed. W. Kelly (34 vols., London, [1867–c. 1900], with index [1902]); short modern life by W. G. Turner (London, 1926). A. Miller, "The Brethren" (commonly so-called). A Brief Sketch of their Origin, Progress and Testimony [1880]. J. S. Teulon, The History and Teaching of the Plymouth Brethren (S.P.C.K., [1883]). W. B. Neatby, A History of the Plymouth Brethren (1901). T. S. Veitch, The Story of the Brethren Movement. A Simple and Straightforward Account of the Features and Failures to Carry out the Principles of Scripture during the last hundred years [1933]; D. J. Beattie, Brethren. The Story of a Great Recovery (Kilmarnock, [1940]). J. McCulloch in H.E.R.E., ii (1909), pp. 843–8, s.v. 'Brethren (Plymouth)'.

PNEUMATOMACHI (Gk. πνευματομάχοι). 4th cent. heretics who denied the full Godhead of the Holy Ghost. They are perhaps the 'Tropici' of St. *Athanasius in his Epp. to *Serapion of Thmuis (between 355 and 361), but came to the fore only in 373, when *Eustathius of Sebaste became their head after breaking with his former friend St. *Basil the Great. They were condemned by Pope *Damasus in 374, and their teaching was repeatedly attacked by the three great *Cappadocian Fathers and St. *Didymus. The sect had reached its full development c. 380, containing a more conservative section which, while rejecting the Divinity of the Holy Ghost, accepted the consubstantiality of the Son, and a radical party, which denied also the latter. At the Council of *Constantinople (381; can. 1) they were anathematized. The historians *Socrates and *Sozo-

men as well as the Latin Fathers, St. *Jerome, *Rufinus, and others, regard *Macedonius (q.v.) as their founder, but as he disappeared from the forefront of theological controversy after his deposition in 360 and as his name does not occur in contemporary anti-Pneumatomachian writings, this statement seems to be unfounded. It is possible that after Macedonius's death his followers amalgamated with the Pneumatomachi, and that the identification is to be so explained. The sect disappeared after 383, when they became victims of the Theodosian anti-heretical laws.

T. Schermann, Die Gottheit des heiligen Geistes nach den griechischen Vätern des vierten Jahrhunderts (1901). J. P. Arendzen in C.E., xii (1911), p. 174; A. Stohr in L.Th.K., viii (1936), cols. 334–6; and C. Vagaggini in E.C., ix (1952), cols. 1641–3, all s.v. See also bibl. to Macedonius.

POCOCKE, EDWARD (1604–91), orientalist. Educated at Magdalen Hall and Corpus Christi College, Oxford, he became a Fellow of the latter society in 1628 and was English chaplain at Aleppo from 1630 to 1635. Here he perfected his knowledge of Arabic, collected a large number of valuable MSS., and on his return was appointed by W. *Laud first professor of Arabic at Oxford. In 1648 he succeeded to the chair of Hebrew but his royalist views led to his temporary suspension. His erudition was immense. He took an active part in the preparation of B. *Walton's '*Polyglott Bible' (1657), and in 1660, at the expense of R. *Boyle, published an Arabic edition of H. *Grotius's De veritate christianae religionis for the furtherance of Christianity among Moslems. In 1663 he issued the Arabic text (with a Latin translation) of the Historia Compendiosa Dynastiarum of *Bar Hebraeus (Abu-l-Faraj). He also published large parts of the BCP in Arabic.

L. Twells (ed.), The Theological Works of the Learned Dr. Pocock (2 vols., 1740), with full biography and correspondence. S. Lane-Poole in D.N.B., xlvi (1896), pp. 7–12.

POIMANDRES (Gk. ποιμάνδρης, apptly. 'the Shepherd of Men'). The first treatise in the corpus of *Hermetic writings (q.v.), though in its text the name of Hermes does not occur. It describes a vision seen under the guidance of Poimandres, a semi-divine being who is termed 'the Mind of the Sovereignty' (ὁ τῆς αὐθεντίας νοῦς) and treats of the creation of the universe and man, the union of spirit with matter following the Fall, and the method of redemption by knowledge (γνῶσις). The writer's nearest associations are with *Gnosticism; but there are parallels with the NT, e.g. the description of the Divine as 'light' and 'life' and the doctrine that the Divine *Logos was active in creation (cf. Jn. 1. 2–4). At times, the language closely approximates to that of the *Septuagint, which was certainly known to the author. The work was written in Egypt early in the Christian era, perhaps (C. H. *Dodd) not long after A.D. 100. It was first published in a Lat. rendering by Marsilius *Ficinus (*Venice, date uncertain; acc. to R. *Reitzenstein, 1463).

Text in *Hermetis Trismegisti Poemander*, ed. G. Parthey, Berlin, 1854; and (with much highly conjectural emendation) in W. Scott, *Hermetica*, i (1924). C. H. Dodd, *The Bible and the Greeks* (1935), pp. 99-248. R. Reitzenstein, *Poimandres*. Studien zur griechisch-ägyptischen und frühchristlichen Literatur (1904).

POINTS, Hebrew. See *Vowel Points*.

POIRET, PIERRE (1646–1719), French Protestant mystic.

After being preacher at Heidelberg (1668) and Anweiler (1672), he resigned his office in 1676 and became the companion of the visionary, Antoinette *Bourignon, whose ideas he subsequently interpreted in *L'Économie divine* (7 vols., 1687). After her death in 1680, he lived at Amsterdam and from 1688 at Rijnsburg. He was a keen student of mysticism, esp. as found in his contemporaries, J. *Boehme and Mme *Guyon (whose works he edited in 1704), and, of earlier writers, of *Thomas à Kempis and J. *Tauler. He laid stress on the relevance of the Cartesian philosophy to the study of mysticism. His most important work, *Bibliotheca mysticorum* (1708), contains much valuable out-of-the-way information on minor writers on mystic subjects. After his death Poiret's influence was chiefly exercised through his disciple, G. *Tersteegen, and, less directly, on the whole *Pietistic Movement.

M. Wieser, *Peter Poiret. Der Vater der romanischen Mystik in Deutschland* (1932). S. Cramer in *P.R.E.* (ed. 3), xv (1904), pp. 491-7, with discussion of sources and bibl.

POISSY, Colloquy of (Disputatio Pussicena).

A Conference held in 1561 at Poissy (on the Seine, not far from Paris) between the French bishops under Cardinal F. de Tournon and the Protestant ministers led by T. *Beza, to consider the religious situation created by the progress of the Reformed doctrines. It had been summoned by *Catherine de' Medici. Among the Catholic spokesmen was J. *Laynez, the General of the *Jesuits, and among the Protestants *Peter Martyr. Though it failed to secure dogmatic agreement between the two parties on the Eucharist, it prepared the way for the edict of Jan. 1562, which gave official recognition and a measure of freedom to French Protestants.

H. Klipffel, *Le Colloque de Poissy*. Étude sur la crise religieuse et politique de 1561 (1867). J. Roserot de Melin, 'Rome et Poissy (1560–1561)' in *Mélanges d'Archéologie et d'Histoire*, xxxix (1921-2), pp. 47-151. E. Lachenmann in *P.R.E.* (ed. 3), xv (1904), pp. 497-504.

POLAND, Christianity in.

Poland received Christianity in the latter half of the 10th cent., probably from Moravia. In 966 the Prince Mieczyslaw I was baptized, and in 1000 Gnesen became a metropolitical see. (The alleged earlier dependence of the Church on the see of Magdeburg seems to have been disproved by modern research.) There were strong anti-Christian outbreaks between 1034 and 1040 and many martyrdoms. Throughout the 11th and 12th cents. the country was devastated by civil wars and disorders, and the Synod of Leczyca (1180) had to take special measures against robbers of churches. The fact that the *Hildebrandine reforms (11th cent.) had been carried out by royal power in the teeth of the opposition of bishops and clergy had brought the Church strongly under state control, but early in the 13th cent. this control was shaken off and the Church was reorganized in conformity with current canon law. In the same century the Tartar invasions stirred up a revival of Christianity, which later (c. 1400) manifested itself in missions to Lithuania.

In the early 15th cent. some of the nobility supported the *Hussites and the *Inquisition was introduced. In the 16th cent. the *Reformation also made headway esp. among the nobility, who had long chafed at the dual control of King and Church. A religious war followed, while internal reform of the Church was effectively prevented by the papal legate, J. F. Commendone; but by the Conference of Warsaw in 1573 mutual toleration was secured. After the Conference the RCs increased their influence by judicious reforms, while dissensions diminished the strength of their opponents. In 1595 the *Ruthenian Church renounced communion with *Constantinople and submitted to Rome, and shortly after the *Armenians in Poland accepted *Uniat status.

In the 17th cent. the RC majority succeeded in making toleration a dead letter. In the 18th the Protestants, though not formally persecuted, were still under restrictions, until the Confederation of Radom (1767) provided for complete religious freedom. The continual wars acted to the detriment of religion and opened the way for the growth of *Freemasonry, which fomented anti-Church feeling. The partition of Poland in 1772–3 between Russia, Austria, and Prussia was a disaster for the RC Church. The Russians put endless restrictions upon RCs and in 1831 compelled the Uniat Easterns to give up their communion with Rome; Prussia also interfered with the freedom of its RC subjects; and Austria placed the RCs under strict State supervision, and prevented control from Rome. With the independence of Poland in 1919 the influence of the RC Church revived, though the Orthodox retained their hold on many of the eastern parts.

Both Orthodox and RC Churches suffered severely under German and Russian occupation in 1939–45, and the setting up of a Communist-controlled government in 1945 led to the continuance of severe difficulties, esp. for the RCs.

See also *Old Catholics* and *Mariavites*.

K. Völker, *Kirchengeschichte Polens* (1930), with detailed bibl. F. Siegmund-Schultze (ed.), *Ekklesia*, v, 2 (Lfg. 21, Die evangelischen Kirchen in Polen; 1938), also with detailed bibl. V. Krasinski, *Historical Sketch of the Rise, Progress and Decline of the Reformation in Poland* (2 vols., 1838-40). K. Völker, *Der Protestantismus in Poland auf Grund der einheimischen Geschichtschreibung dargestellt* (1910); T. Wotschke, *Geschichte der Reformation in Polen* (Studien zur Kultur und Geschichte der Reformation herausgegeben vom Verein für Reformationsgeschichte, fasc. i; 1911). P. Fox, *The Reformation in Poland. Some Social and Economic Aspects* (Baltimore, 1924). J. Bois, 'L'Église orthodoxe en

Pologne avant le partage de 1772' in *Échos d'Orient*, xii (1909), pp. 227–33, 292–7; id., 'Lutte de l'orthodoxie contre l'union en Pologne avant 1772', ib., pp. 349–54. and xiii (1910), pp. 25–34 and 87–94. L. Lescœur, *L'Église catholique en Pologne sous le gouvernement russe, depuis le premier partage jusqu'à nos jours* (1860; ed. 2, revised, 2 vols., 1876); E. Likowski, *Geschichte des allmaeligen Verfalls der Unirten Ruthenischen Kirche im XVIII. und XIX. Jahrhundert unter polnischem und russischem Scepter* (Germ. tr., 2 vols., 1885–7); id., *Die ruthenisch-römische Kirchenvereinigung, genannt Union zu Brest* (1904). T. Andrews, *The Polish National Church in America and Poland* (1953), passim. See also bibl. to *Ruthenian Churches*.

POLE, REGINALD (1500–58), Abp. of *Canterbury. Of the blood royal by his mother, Margaret, Countess of Salisbury and niece of Edward IV, he was educated at the Sheen Charterhouse, and Magdalen College, Oxford, and given ecclesiastical preferment by *Henry VIII while still in his teens and a layman. In 1521 he went to Padua, and for several years was in close contact with the later Italian Renaissance, corresponding with T. *More and D. *Erasmus, and visiting Rome and Paris. In 1530 Henry, anxious for help over his divorce, offered him the sees of *York or *Winchester, but Pole declined both, and, in 1534–6, wrote *Pro Ecclesiasticae Unitatis Defensione*, censuring the King's conduct. *Paul III summoned him in 1536 to confer about a general council, put him on a committee for the reform of discipline, and (after his ordination as deacon) created him a cardinal. In 1538, indignation at *Rome over the destruction of *Becket's shrine caused Pole to be sent as legate on a fruitless mission to persuade Spain and France to break with England, and in 1539 an Act of Attainder was passed against him and his family. On hearing of his mother's execution (1541) he exclaimed, 'I am the son of a martyr.' That year G. *Contarini took counsel with Pole, before the Diet of *Ratisbon, with a view to conciliating the Protestants, whose views on justification were not unlike Pole's own; and in 1542 he was one of the three legates appointed to preside at the Council of *Trent, which did not meet, however, until 1545. In 1547 he urged *Somerset to treat with the Holy See, and on Paul III's death (1549) was nearly elected Pope. On *Edward VI's death in 1553 *Julius III appointed him legate in England, and, after the removal of his attainder he reached Dover in Nov. 1554, formally absolved Parliament from schism, and presided over a synod of both *convocations. On 20 Mar. 1557 he was ordained priest at the Greyfriars, Greenwich, and consecrated Abp. of Canterbury two days later. By the outbreak of war between *Paul IV (Caraffa) and *Philip of Spain, the Queen became the Pope's enemy, and the Pope cancelled Pole's legation, accusing him also of doctrinal unsoundness. He died only twelve hours after the Queen. Pole was a man of pure morals, sincere piety, and ascetical habits, and animated by a remarkable singleness of purpose.

Standard ed. of his *Epistolae*, incl. some other writings, ed. Card. A. M. Quirini (Brescia, 5 vols., 1744–57). J. *Gairdner, *Letters and Papers of Henry VIII*; Rawdon Brown, *Calendar of State Papers*. Venetian, vols. v and vi

(both passim). Lives by L. Beccadelli (Lat., Venice, 1563; Eng tr., 1766), T. Phillips (Oxford, 1764), Athanasius Zimmermann (Ratisbon, 1893), M. Haile (London, 1910), R. Biron and J. Barennes (Paris, 1922), and W. Schenk (London, 1950; imp., with useful note on sources, p. 170 f.). J. Gairdner in *D.N.B.*, xlvi (1896), pp. 35–46.

POLITARCHS (Gk. πολιτάρχης). A comparatively rare title for magistrates in the Greco-Roman world, used in the NT only of the city magistrates of Thessalonica (Acts 17. 6, 8; AV, 'the rulers of the city'). The accuracy of St. *Luke's usage is proved by the occurrence of the word on several inscriptions which come from Thessalonica.

E. de W. Burton, 'The Politarchs' in *The American Journal of Theology*, ii (1898), pp. 598–632.

POLITIQUES. French political party which advocated religious toleration esp. after the Massacre of St. *Bartholomew's night (q.v.). They made an alliance with the *Huguenots and subsequently many of them supported *Henry IV.

POLYCARP, St. (*c.* 69–*c.* 155), Bp. of Smyrna. He seems to have been the leading Christian figure in Roman Asia in the middle of the 2nd cent., and his long life (about which unfortunately little is known) is thus an important link between the *Apostolic Age and the great Christian writers (e.g. St. *Irenaeus) who flourished at the end of the 2nd cent. A staunch defender of orthodoxy, he devoted much of his energy to combating such heretics as the *Marcionites and *Valentinians. A letter addressed to him by St. *Ignatius has survived, as well as his own 'Ep. to Philippians' (perhaps a combination of two epistles of different dates; so P. N. Harrison). The latter is important for its testimony to the NT, e.g. it quotes 1 Jn. 4. 3. At the end of his life, when Polycarp paid a visit to Rome to visit the bishop, Anicetus, and to discuss, among other things, the date of keeping the Easter festival, it was agreed that each Church should maintain its own custom and that Asia should continue the *Quartodeciman practice. Soon after his return to Smyrna, Polycarp was arrested during a public (pagan) festival and, proclaiming that he had served Christ for 86 years, he refused to recant his faith and was burnt to death (A.D. 155 or 156). The 'Martyrium Polycarpi', written from Smyrna by request of the Church at Philomelium, gives an account of his trial and martyrdom. St. Irenaeus says that Polycarp 'had intercourse with John [the Apostle or Elder?] and with the rest of those who had seen the Lord'. Feast day, 26 Jan.

Texts, incl. 'Martyrium Polycarpi', will be found in edd. of the Apostolic Fathers; with esp. valuable comm. and notes in ed. J. B. *Lightfoot (Part II, 3 vols., 1885). P. N. Harrison, *Polycarp's Two Epistles to the Philippians* (1936). On the date of the martyrdom, see C. H. *Turner in *Studia Biblica et Ecclesiastica*, ii (1890), pp. 105–55 [defends 23 Feb. 155]; also H. Grégoire–P. Orgels, 'La Véritable Date du martyre de Polycarpe (23 Fevr. 177) et le *Corpus Polycarpianum*' in *Anal. Boll.*, lxix (1951), pp. 1–38 [much contested]. Bardenhewer, i, 160–70; Altaner (ed. 1951), pp. 81–3. G. *Salmon in *D.C.B.*, iv (1887), pp. 423–31, s.v.; G. N. Bonwetsch in *P.R.E.* (ed. 3), xv (1904), pp. 535–7, s.v. 'Polykarp'; G. Fritz in *D.T.C.*, xii (pt. 2; 1935), cols. 2515–20, s.v. 'Polycarpe'; J. Quasten in *L.Th.K.*, viii (1936), col. 360 f., s.v. 'Polykarp'; E. Peterson in *E.C.*, ix (1952), col. 1670 f., s.v. 'Policarpo'. See also entry *Pionius* and bibl. there cited.

POLYCHRONIUS (d. *c.* 430), Bp. of Apamaea in Syria. He was the brother of *Theodore, Bp. of Mopsuestia. A Biblical exegete of the *Antiochene school, he wrote commentaries on Job, Daniel, and Ezekiel, of which considerable fragments survive, chiefly in *catenae*. It is probable that the fragments on other Books. (Prov., Eccles., Song of Songs, &c.), come from another writer of the same name. He expressly condemned the *Alexandrine method of allegorical exegesis.

Fgmts. on Job ed. P. *Young in *Catena Graecorum Patrum in Jobum* (London, 1637); repr. in J. P. Migne, *PG*, xciii, cols. 13–468. Other fgmts. ed. A. *Mai whence repr. in J. P. Migne, *PG*, clxii (very rare). O. *Bardenhewer, *Polychronius von Apamea* (1879). Bardenhewer, iii, 322–4.

POLYCRATES (2nd cent.), Bp. of *Ephesus. He was the leading *Quartodeciman of Asia who, after assembling in synod about 190, sturdily opposed Pope *Victor in his attempts to secure that the feast of *Easter should be uniformly celebrated on a Sunday. In consequence, Victor withdrew from communion with Polycrates. The incident, which is all that is known of Polycrates, is an important illustration of the early claims of the Roman see.

Extracts from Polycrates' letter are preserved in *Eusebius, *H.E.*, V, xxiv, 2–8, and III, xxxi, 3. E. Peterson in *E.C.*, ix (1952), col. 1672 f.

POLYGLOT BIBLES. A 'Polyglot Bible' is a single Bible containing the text in a number of languages. Such Bibles were issued esp. in the 16th and 17th cents. The most celebrated is the '*Complutensian Polyglot', in 6 vols. (1522), produced under the patronage of Cardinal *Ximenes, containing the OT in Hebrew, Latin, and Greek, and the NT in Greek and Latin. Other Polyglot Bibles are those of Antwerp (1569–72) in 8 vols., adding the Syriac NT, with a Latin trans.; of Paris (1629–45) in 10 vols., adding the Arabic, with a Latin translation, and the *Samaritan Pentateuch; and of London (1657), by B. *Walton in six vols., containing the Hebrew, Greek, Latin, Syriac, Ethiopic, Arabic, and Persian, all with Latin translations, as well as the Samaritan Pentateuch, various *Targums, and selected readings of the *Codex Alexandrinus. 'Diglot Bibles' (Greco-Latin, Greco-Coptic, and later Coptic-Arabic) are known from the 5th cent. onwards, but there is no proof of early polyglots.

POMPONAZZI, PIETRO (1464–1525). The most outstanding philosopher of the Italian Renaissance. He taught successively at Padua, Ferrara, and *Bologna. Under the influence esp. of the Aristotelian commentator, Alex-

O.D.C.C.–2 N

ander of Aphrodisias (*c.* A.D. 200; whence Pomponazzi's disciples were termed 'Alexandrists'), he expounded *Aristotle in a way at variance with that of the regnant Scholasticism, maintaining, e.g., in his *De immortalitate animae* (1516) that it was possible to demonstrate by the natural reason the mortality of the human soul. He argued that the only sense in which one could speak legitimately of the immateriality and immortality of the soul was in reference to its capacity for reflective knowledge and conceiving universal concepts, a capacity which accorded it a status between the brutes on the one hand and the angelic beings on the other. Pomponazzi maintained, however, that these doctrines need cause no offence to the Christian, since they were merely the deductions of human reason and were transcended by the supernatural revelation made to the Church. Two later treatises *De Incantationibus* and *De Fato*, were published posthumously at Basle.

F. Fiorentino, *Pietro Pomponazzi. Studi storici sulla scuola bolognese-padovana del sec. XVI* (Florence, 1868; still important); id., *Studi e ritratti della rinascenza* (Bari, 1911), pp. 1–79. A. H. Douglas, *The Philosophy and Psychology of P. Pomponazzi* (ed. C. Douglas and R. P. Hardie, 1910); C. C. J. *Webb, *Studies in the History of Natural Theology* (1915), pp. 313–43. L. Ferri, *La psicologia di P. Pomponazzi, secondo un MS. della Bibl. Angelica di Roma* (1877). B. Nardi in *E.C.*, ix (1952), cols. 1731–4, s.v.

POMPONIA GRAECINA (1st cent.). Wife of Aulus Plautius, the conqueror of Britain, and prob. an early convert to Christianity. Acc. to *Tacitus (*Annales*, xiii, 32), she was accused by her husband of foreign superstition (*superstitio externa*), but acquitted. A Gk. inscription to 'Pomponios Grecinos', perhaps a descendant, has been found in the catacomb of St. *Callistus. She has been identified (not very convincingly) by G. B. *de Rossi and others with the Roman matron *Lucina (q.v.) of the 'Crypt of Lucina'.

G. B. de Rossi, *La Roma sotterranea cristiana*, i (1864), p. 319 f., and ii (1867), pp. 362–5. H. *Leclercq, O.S.B., in *D.A.C.L.*, i (pt. 2; 1907), col. 2847 f., s.v. 'Aristocratiques (Classes), II', with bibl.

PONTIFEX MAXIMUS (Lat., 'Supreme Pontiff'). Originally a pagan title of the chief priest at Rome, *Tertullian used it satirically in one of his *Montanist writings (*De pudicitia*, 1) of the Pope, and from the 5th cent. onwards it was a regular title of honour for the Popes, and occasionally used also of other bishops. In later times the title has been confined to the Roman Pontiff. Cf. the Italian 'Sommo Pontefice' and the French 'Souverain Pontife'.

PONTIFICAL, the liturgical book of the W. Church containing the prayers and ceremonies for rites restricted to the bishop, e.g. *Confirmation and Holy *Orders, the *consecration of churches, etc. It does not contain, however, the Pontifical Mass. Pontificals developed from the older *Sacramentaries and can be traced back to the 8th cent. A famous early example is that ascribed to *Egbert, Abp. of

York (732–6). At first they contained much that had no exclusively episcopal reference, but in course of time these non-episcopal elements were gradually eliminated. In their contents and form they differed widely throughout the Middle Ages; and though a pontifical was printed at Rome as early as 1485, uniformity was not achieved till *Clement VIII issued an authoritative edition in 1596. This was followed by later revisions of much less importance in 1644, 1752, and 1888.

The substance of the Roman Pontificals is largely taken from the '*Ordines Romani' (q.v., incl. bibl.). P. de Puniet, O.S.B., *Le Pontificale romain* (2 vols., 1930–1; Eng. tr., 1932); V. Leroquais, *Les Pontificaux Manuscrits des bibliothèques publiques de France* (4 vols., 1937). H. Leclercq, O.S.B., in *D.A.C.L.*, xiv (pt. 1; 1939), cols. 1428–45.

PONTIFICALS (Lat. *Pontificalia*). The insignia of the episcopal order worn by a prelate when celebrating Pontifical Mass. Those common to all prelates, as enumerated by *Pius VII in *Decet Romanos* (1823), are the buskins (silk leg-coverings), *sandals, *gloves, *dalmatic, *tunicle, *ring, *pectoral cross, and *mitre. The *Codex (*CIC*, §337, 2), however, refers to the *pastoral staff and the mitre as the characteristic 'insignia pontificalia'. The word is also applied to episcopal functions at which these insignia are worn.

T. Klauser, *Der Ursprung der bischöflichen Insignien und Ehrenrechte* (Lecture; 1948).

PONTIUS, St. (d. *c.* 260), biographer of St. *Cyprian. He was Cyprian's deacon at Carthage and followed him into exile at Curubis. His *Vita et Passio Cypriani*, more an edifying panegyric than a work of history, is the earliest Christian biography. Feast day, 8 Mar. (He is to be distinguished from the Roman martyr St. Pontius [3rd cent.]; feast day, 14 May.)

Crit. text of *Vita Cypriani* ed. W. Hartel in C.S.E.L., iii (1) (1868), pp. xc–cx. Eng. tr. in A.N.C.L., viii (Writings of Cyprian, vol. i), pp. xiii–xxxi. A. *Harnack, *Das Leben Cyprians von Pontius* (T.U., xxxix, Hft. 3; 1913; perhaps overestimates the historical value of the *Vita*). P. Corssen, 'Das Martyrium des Bischofs Cyprian. II. Das Verhältnis des sog. *Vita Cypriani* zu den Cypriansakten' in *Z.N.T.W.*, xv (1914), pp. 285–316, xvi (1915), pp. 54–92, 198–230; 'IV. Pontius' Verhältnis zu Cyprian als Mensch und Schriftsteller', xviii (1917–18), pp. 118–39, and 'V. Die literarische Charakter und die Tendenz der Schrift des Pontius', ib., pp. 203–233 (defends authenticity of *Vita* against R. *Reitzenstein). M. Pellegrino in *E.C.*, ix (1952), col. 175 f., s.v. 'Ponzio'.

PONTIUS PILATE. See *Pilate, Pontius*.

POOR CLARES, Fr., Clarisses. The 'Second Order' of St. *Francis, founded by him and St. *Clare between 1212 and 1214. It received its first rule in 1219 from Cardinal Ugolino (later *Gregory IX), and spread rapidly through Italy, and later all over Europe. In 1247 *Innocent IV sanctioned a second rule containing several moderations, esp. regarding poverty, and six years later a third and much stricter one, based on that of St. Francis and enjoining complete poverty both individual and corporate. This rule was not accepted by all convents, and in 1263 Urban IV sanctioned a milder one which was observed by the majority, those nuns who follow it being hence called 'Urbanists'. The order was thoroughly reformed in the 15th cent. by St. *Colette, who restored the principle of strict poverty in her houses; and since then the Urbanists and the Colettines have remained the two chief branches of the order. The majority of Poor Clare convents are strictly contemplative, devoted to prayer, penance, and manual work. They have the strictest enclosure, practise severe fasts and other austerities, rise for the Night Office, and are regarded as the most austere women's order of the RC Church. Their habit, which, like that of the Franciscans, has no *scapular, is of dark frieze with a cord girdle, and they wear a black veil and cloth sandals on bare feet.

Histoire abrégée de l'ordre de Sainte Claire d'Assise. Édition des Monastères des Clarisses Colettines à Lyon et à Tournai (1906). G. Daval, O.F.M., *Les Clarisses* (Les Grands Ordres religieux, 1924); J. Ancelot-Hustache, *Les Clarisses* (Les Grands Ordres monastiques, 1929). *Saint Clare and her Order.* A Story of Seven Centuries by the author of 'The Enclosed Nun' (1912). E. Lempp, 'Die Anfänge des Clarissenordens' in *Z.K.G.*, xiii (1892), pp. 181–245; L. Lemmens, O.F.M., 'Die Anfänge des Clarissenordens' in *R.Q.*, xvi (1902), pp. 93–124. L. Oliger, O.F.M., 'De Origine Regularum Ordinis S. Clarae' in *A.F.H.*, v (1912), pp. 181–209 and 413–47. E. Wauer, *Entstehung und Ausbreitung des Klarissenordens besonders in den deutschen Minoritenprovinzen* (1906); A. F. C. Bourdillon, *The Order of Minoresses in England* (Manchester University thesis; British Society of Franciscan Studies, xii; 1926); H. Concannon, *The Poor Clares in Ireland, A.D. 1629–A.D. 1929* (Dublin, 1929). Heimbucher, i, 815–28, with bibl. See also bibl. to *Clare, St.*

POOR MEN OF LYONS. The name under which Pope Lucius III condemned the *Waldensians (q.v.) in 1184.

POORE, RICHARD (d. 1237), Bp. of *Salisbury. His name also occurs in the forms **Poor, Poure**, and **Le Poor**. Elected Dean of *Sarum *c.* 1197, he was twice unsuccessful as a candidate for the sees of *Winchester (1204) and *Durham (1213), but was elected Bp. of *Chichester in 1214 and translated to Salisbury three years later. In 1219 he removed his see from Old Sarum to its present site, and in the next year began the erection of the present cathedral where he consecrated a temporary high altar in the Lady Chapel in 1225. About the same time he drew up the Salisbury Constitutions and probably gave the 'Use of Sarum' (q.v.) its final form. In 1228 he was translated to the see of Durham. In 1230 he refounded a convent of nuns at Tarrant (who later embraced the *Cistercian rule), a fact which has suggested that he is the author of the '*Ancren Riwle', addressed to anchoresses at Tarrant.

The 'Constitutiones Ricardi [Poore], Episcopi Sarum', pr. in W. [H.] Rich Jones–W. Dunn Macray (edd.), *Charters and Documents illustrating the History of the Cathedral, City, and Diocese of Salisbury, in the Twelfth and Thirteenth Centuries* (R.S., 1891), No. cxli, pp. 128–63, with other information, passim. See also W. H. Rich Jones (ed.), *The Register of S. Osmund* (2 vols., R.S., 1883–4), i, 284–379, and ii, 4–100 passim, and introd., ii, pp. xcviii–cxxxi passim. C. R. Cheney, *English Synodalia of the Thirteenth Century* (1941), pp. 51–89. On his conjectured authorship of the *Ancren Riwle* see bibl. s.v. H. E. D. Blakiston in *D.N.B.*, xlvi (1896), pp. 106–9.

POPE, The (Gk. πάπας, Lat. *papa*, 'father'). The title, though now restricted to the Bp. of Rome, was in early times used in the W. of any Bishop. In the E. it was apparently confined to the Bp. of Alexandria who was regularly styled πάπας; but in modern popular usage the word is applied in the Orthodox Churches to all priests (cf. the use of 'father', q.v., in the W.). At the Synod of Pavia on 20 Sept. 998, the Abp. of Milan was rebuked for calling himself 'Pope', and in 1073 *Gregory VII, in a Council at Rome, formally prohibited its use by any other Bishop than the Bp. of Rome.

B. Labanca, 'Del nome Papa nelle chiese cristiane di Oriente ed Occidente' in *Actes du Douzième Congrès International des Orientalistes, Rome, 1899*, III, ii (Florence, 1902), pp. 47–101, with bibl.

POPE JOAN. See *Joan, Pope*.

POPE, WILLIAM BURT (1822–1903), *Wesleyan theologian. He was born at Horton in Nova Scotia, and after studying privately entered the Methodist Theological Institution at Hoxton in 1840. From 1842 he was a minister in several cities, including Dover, London, Manchester, and Leeds. In 1860 he became editor of the *London Quarterly Review* and in 1867 was appointed tutor of systematic theology at Didsbury. In 1876 he went to America as delegate to the General Conference of the Methodist Episcopal Church at Baltimore, and in 1877 he presided over the Wesleyan Conference at Bristol. He resigned his tutorship at Didsbury College in 1886. He enjoyed a high reputation as a theologian in the Methodist Church. His principal work, the *Compendium of Christian Theology* (3 vols., 1875), contains an elaborate and sympathetic defence of the Methodist doctrine of Christian perfection. He also published several volumes of sermons and translations from the German.

Life by R. W. Moss (London, c. 1909). C. H. Irwin in *D.N.B.*, *1901–1911*, iii, 127.

POPERY. This hostile designation for the specific doctrines and practices of the RC Church is already found in 1534 in W. *Tyndale and has been in common use since.

POPERY, The Declaration Against. The declaration imposed by 30 Car. II, Cap. I, St. II (3), 1677, requiring all Members of Parliament to denounce transubstantiation, the Mass, and the Invocation of Saints as idolatrous. It was abolished in 1778 when another and less exacting Oath was substituted for it.

POPISH PLOT, The. The supposed plot to murder *Charles II which T. *Oates (q.v.) claimed that he had discovered in 1678. Despite the great sensation it created, it seems to have been a pure invention of Oates.

[F.] J. Pollock, *The Popish Plot* (1903; ed. 2, 1944). See also bibl. to *Oates, Titus*.

POPPY HEADS. In ecclesiology, the ornamented finials at the tops of bench-ends, in form somewhat resembling a fleur de lys. They became common in the 15th cent., esp. in E. Anglia, where many fine examples can still be seen, and were widely copied. It is uncertain whether the name has any connexion with the poppy flower. Possibly it derives from the Fr. *poupée*, a 'figurehead' or 'puppet'.

J. C. Cox, *Bench Ends in English Churches* (1916), esp. pp. 12–16. F. Bond, *Wood Carvings in English Churches*, ii (1910), esp. p. 6 f.

PORPHYRY (c. 232–303), *Neoplatonist philosopher. Of pagan family, possibly orig. called 'Malchus', he was brought up at Tyre, and in his youth visited Syria, Palestine and Alexandria. It is possible that he was at one time a Christian (so *Socrates and Aristocritus [5th cent.], followed by A. *Harnack; denied by J. Bidez), but he clearly did not hold the faith by the time of the persecution of the Emp. *Decius in 250. He studied philosophy at *Athens and was finally convinced of Neoplatonist principles by *Plotinus, whom he met at *Rome in 262. Just before the death of the latter (270) he went to Sicily, where he published many of his philosophical works, but towards the end of his life he returned to Rome and taught with considerable success, numbering *Iamblichus among his pupils.

After investigating with sympathetic interest the religious systems current in Asia, Porphyry adopted an attitude of scepticism towards all popular religion, enforced by esp. bitterness against the Christians. In his Πρὸς Ἀνεβώ he pointed out the contradictions in popular superstition. Of more lasting significance was his treatise in fifteen books against the Christians (Κατὰ Χριστιανῶν); it was condemned to be burnt in 448 and survives only in fragments in works written mainly to refute it. Porphyry seems to have observed a certain restraint in his remarks about Christ Himself, whom he admired as a teacher; but he considered the apparent failure of His life proof that He was not divine, and he launched his most bitter invective against the Apostles and leaders of the Church, which he finally condemned for the lack of patriotism in resisting the religious revival fostered by the Emps. Decius and Aurelian. His exposure of the alleged inconsistencies of the Gospels and his attack on the OT (e.g. the date of the Book of *Daniel) was sufficiently forceful to draw detailed refutations from St. *Methodius of Olympus, *Eusebius of Caesarea, *Apollinarius of Laodicea and others.

His numerous philosophical works, primarily intended to draw the soul from contact with the sensible world and turn it to the contemplation of intelligible reality, are important not so much for their originality as for their clear exposition, development and preservation of much that was obscurely put in Plotinus and others. They include, besides various commentaries on the Categories of *Aristotle, Περὶ τῆς ἐκ λογιῶν φιλοσοφίας, Περὶ ἀγαλμάτων, Φιλόσοφος ἱστορία and Ἀφορμαὶ πρὸς τὰ νοητά.

He also wrote a life of Plotinus and edited his works (after 300), and composed various treatises on astronomy, mathematics, grammar and rhetoric, a philological dissertation on Homer, a commentary on Ptolemy's *Harmonica* and on various other technical subjects. His 'Introduction to the *Categories* of Aristotle' (Εἰσαγωγή) became a standard work in the medieval schools.

No collected edition of Porphyry's works exists, the different items being printed in a variety of places; careful list in J. Bidez, op. cit. infra, pp. 63*–73*. *Opuscula Selecta* ed. A. Nauck (Teubn., 1886). For Porphyry's life the chief sources are his own 'Life of Plotinus' (crit. ed. in *Plotini Opera*, ed. P. Henry, S.J.–H. R. Schwyzer, Paris, i (1951), pp. 1–41) and the entry in *Suidas' Lexicon, s.v. The material is fully surveyed in J. Bidez, *Vie de Porphyre avec les fragments des traités* Περὶ Ἀγαλμάτων *et* De Regressu Animae (Université de Gand. Recueil de Travaux publiés par la Faculté de Philosophie et Lettres, xliii; 1913). A. *Harnack, *Kritik des Neuen Testaments von einem Philosophen des 3. Jahrhunderts* (T.U., xxxvii, Hft. 4; 1911); id., *Porphyrius 'Gegen die Christen', 15 Bücher. Zeugnisse, Fragmente und Referate* (*Abh.* (Berl.), 1916, Hft. 1; acc. to Harnack and others, Porphyry was the pagan philosopher extensively cited in *Macarius Magnes' *Apocriticus*). H. Raeder, *Porphyrios fra Tyros, Videnskabmand og Mystiker* (Studier fra Sprog- og Oldtidsforskning, No. 188, Copenhagen, 1942). P. de Labriolle, *La Réaction païenne* (1934), pp. 223–96. W. Theiler, *Porphyrius und Augustinus* (Halle, 1933). Überweg, i, 597–9, 609–12, with bibl. p. 190* f. L. Vaganay in *D.T.C.*, xii (pt. 2; 1935), cols. 2555–90, s.v. 'Porphyre', with bibl.; R. Beutler in *P.W.*, xxii (pt. 1; 1953), cols. 275–313, s.v. 'Porphyrios'.

PORRECTIO INSTRUMENTORUM. See *Instruments, Tradition of the.*

PORTA SANTA. See *Holy Door.*

PORTAS. See *Portiforium.*

PORTER. See *Doorkeeper.*

PORTEUS, BEILBY (1731–1808), Bp. of London. Of American descent, he was educated at Christ's College, Cambridge, and after holding various parochial appointments became Bp. of *Chester in 1776 and of London in 1787. He identified himself with the practical ideals of the rising *Evangelical school, energetically furthering many of their reforms, e.g. promoting mission work among negro slaves in America and securing the due observance of the Christian Holy Days. He was also an eager supporter of the *C.M.S. and of the *British and Foreign Bible Society. A keen *Sabbatarian, he actively opposed the practice of Sunday concerts by professional performers in private houses, as well as Sunday debating societies. In 1767 he preached a sermon at Cambridge, some extracts from which, falling into the hands of John Norris (1734–77), moved him to found the Norrisian chair in divinity. Theologically, he was out of sympathy with the *Calvinism currently upheld by the Evangelicals and to this extent did not fully accept all their teaching.

Collected ed. of his Works (35 Sermons, 24 Lectures and various Tracts) in 6 vols., London, 1811, with life by R. Hodgson as vol. i. J. H. Overton in *D.N.B.*, xlv (1896), pp. 195–7, with further reff.

PORTIFORIUM. A name used in England in the Middle Ages for the *Breviary. Other forms of the word are 'Portas', 'Portuary', and 'Portuis'.

PORTIUNCULA. The Umbrian village, also known as Santa Maria degli Angeli, about 2 miles from *Asissi, where St. *Francis received his vocation on 24 Feb. 1208. He made it his headquarters for the rest of his life, and clothed St. *Clare here in 1212. The cell in which he died (3 Oct. 1226) is surrounded by an imposing church, largely rebuilt after an earthquake in 1832. The town gives its name to the 'Portiuncula *Indulgence' which is now to be obtained by visiting certain churches (esp. those immediately connected with the Franciscan Order) on 2 Aug. or the Sunday following. The evidence for connecting the Indulgence with St. Francis himself is unconvincing, though the practice of seeking the indulgence at the Portiuncula chapel (to which it was originally confined) is well attested before the end of the 13th cent.

A. Teetaert, O.S.F.C., in *D.T.C.*, xii (pt. 2; 1935), cols 2602–11, s.v. 'Portioncule', with selection from the immense literature.

PORT-ROYAL, Convent of, *Jansenist centre. A convent of *Cistercian nuns was originally founded at Port-Royal, a marshy site some 18 miles SW. of *Paris (hence 'Port-Royal-des-Champs'), in 1204. After an uneventful history it suddenly came into prominence in the early 17th cent. under the direction of the Abbess, Angélique *Arnauld (q.v.). After an experience of conversion in 1608, she introduced radical reforms into the discipline of the Convent, and from 1622 Port-Royal began to attract large numbers of novices. By 1625 the Convent had become so overcrowded that a new house was established in Paris in the Faubourg St.-Jacques ('Port-Royal-de-Paris'); and hither all the nuns were transferred shortly afterwards.

From 1633 onwards the influence of *Saint-Cyran upon the convent became paramount; and after 1637 a number of his converts lived as *Solitaires* in the neighbourhood of the convent (at first in Paris, later at the older house of Port-Royal-des-Champs), devoting themselves to the interests of the nuns, to the education of a few boys, and to literary pursuits. By 1648, through the labours of these men, Port-Royal-des-Champs had become habitable enough to receive some of the nuns; and henceforward the two houses existed with a single conventual organization. Meanwhile under Saint-Cyran's direction Port-Royal had become the leading centre of *Jansenist influence in France. Blaise *Pascal was closely linked with it, esp. in his later years, and his sister, Jacqueline, was professed here as a nun.

When in 1661 the nuns of Port-Royal refused to subscribe the condemnation of *Jansenism, certain measures affecting the prosperity of the convent were taken by the civil power, and in

1664 a real persecution began; but very few of the nuns were persuaded to sign the 'formulary' until after the *Peace of the Church (1668). In 1669 the two houses were legally separated, Port-Royal-de-Paris being given over to the nuns who had submitted before 1668, while the Jansenist majority were established in Port-Royal-des-Champs. A period of prosperity followed, cut short in 1679, after the recrudescence of the Jansenist controversy, when the convent was forbidden to take boarders or receive any more novices. Subsequently further measures were taken to the prejudice of its temporalities. In 1705 *Clement XI published a bull condemning those who, in signing the anti-Jansenist formulary of *Alexander VII, used mental reservations: the nuns of Port-Royal refused to accept this new definition, and, after a short persecution, were finally dispersed in 1709. The buildings were subsequently destroyed, and the site desecrated (1710–13).

A. de Dion (ed.), *Cartulaire de l'abbaye de Porrois au diocèse de Paris plus connue sous son nom mystique Port-Royal*, i, 1204–80 [all publd.] (1903). The fundamental modern critical work is that of C. A. Sainte-Beuve, *Port-Royal* (5 vols., 1840–59, and index, 1861; modern ed. by J. Pommier, 1937). The more important earlier works include [C. Clémencet, O.S.B.] *Histoire générale de Port-Roïal* (10 vols., Amsterdam, 1755–7); id., *Histoire littéraire de Port-Royal*, ed. [R. F. W.] Guettée (Paris, 1868); J. Racine (the poet), *Abrégé de l'histoire de Port-Royal* (1742–54; ed. A. Gazier, 1908); and H. Reuchlin, *Geschichte von Port-Royal. Der Kampf des reformirten und des jesuitischen Katholicismus und Louis XIII und XIV* (2 vols. 1839–44). C. *Beard, *Port-Royal* (2 vols., 1861). C. Gazier, *Histoire du monastère de Port-Royal* (1929); id., *Les Belles Amies de Port-Royal* (1930); id., *Ces Messieurs de Port-Royal. Documents inédits* (1932), and other works of this author. G. Denis, *Port-Royal. Conférences données à la Salle du Chapeau Rouge de Nantes en 1924* [1931]. J. Laporte, *La Doctrine de Port-Royal* (1923; ed. 2, enlarged, 2 vols., Bibliothèque d'Histoire de la Philosophie, 1951–2). A. Maulvault, *Répertoire alphabétique des personnes et des choses de Port-Royal* (1902). Popular sketches by Ethel Romanes, *The Story of Port-Royal* (1907); Lilian Rea, *The Enthusiasts of Port-Royal* (1912). Bremond, esp. vol. iv. See also bibl. to *Jansenism*.

PORTUARY. See *Portiforium*.

PORTUGAL, Christianity in. The independent history of Portugal begins in the 12th cent., when she became free from Spain and a self-governing vassal of the Papacy. At this time the country was much influenced in religious matters by the new *Cistercian Order, and in particular had the closest relations with the house at *Clairvaux. Under Sancho I (reigned 1185–1211) a strong nationalist and anti-Papal movement began which even *Innocent III could not finally crush. The submission of Sancho in 1210 produced only a temporary settlement and the disputes arising from the movement lasted through much of the 13th cent. The *Mendicant Orders which entered the country at that period proved valuable allies to the Popes in the quarrel. In the Great Schism, anti-Spanish feeling kept the Portuguese bishops on the Papal side.

Early in the 15th cent. began the Portuguese conquests abroad, which by the middle of the next cent. had built up a great empire in Africa, *India, and America. Missionaries went with empire-builders throughout the new dominions, and partly by their preaching, and partly by the assistance of the secular power, secured mass conversions. But the immoral and tyrannous conduct of the civil governors and traders and the readiness of the Church to accept nominal conversion at its face value made much of this activity of little worth.

In Portugal itself reform of the bishops and clergy at the end of the 15th cent. had anticipated the *Reformation, which had no influence in the country. The Jewish problem arose at a later date than in Spain, and it was not until 1536 that, under the influence of the civil power, the *Inquisition was set up. Many of the Jews were forced to mass conversions, but for several generations these 'New Christians', as they were called, were placed on an inferior footing to the old.

From 1580 to 1640 the crown of Portugal was worn by the kings of Spain. From 1640 to 1668 a war of independence was waged in which the Papacy was in open military alliance with Spain, but eventually Portugal secured her freedom.

The 19th cent. saw the conflict of the Church with organized political and religious liberalism. In Portugal Catholicism triumphed in the Concordat of 1886, and even since the Radical revolution of 1910 the country has been predominantly RC. In 1910 the teaching of religion in primary schools was forbidden, the religious orders were expelled, and their property was confiscated. The RC Church was disestablished in 1911 in Portugal, and in 1913 in the Portuguese colonies. After the revolution of 1917 certain of the exiles were recalled, and in 1918 relations with the *Vatican were officially resumed. Except the toleration of the religious orders (which in practice is allowed), the existing relations between Church and state were formally regularized in 1933. In recent times there is said to have been a considerable religious revival in Portugal in consequence of the occurrences at *Fatima (q.v.) in 1917.

F. de Almeida, *História da igreja em Portugal* (4 vols., 1910–22). C. Erdmann, *Papsturkunden in Portugal* (*Abh.* (Gött.), N.F. xx, Hft. 3; 1927); id., *Das Papsttum und Portugal im ersten Jahrhundert der portugiesischen Geschichte* (*Abh.* (Berl.) 1928, Hft. 5). D. A. Reuter, *Königtum und Episkopat in Portugal im 13. Jahrhundert* (Abhandlungen zur mittleren und neueren Geschichte, lxix; 1928). A. Herculano, *História da origem e estabelecimento da Inquisacão em Portugal* (3 vols., 1852; Eng. tr. by J. C. Branner, Stanford University Publications, History, Economics and Political Science, vol. i, No. 2; Stanford, Cal., 1926). F. Rodrigues, S.J., *História da Companhia de Jesus en assistência de Portugal* (1931 ff.). E. Moreira, *The Significance of Portugal. A Study of Evangelical Progress* (1933). G. V. de Pinas Martins and R. Danieli in *E.C.*, x (1952), col. 1796 f., s.v. 'Portogallo'.

PORTUIS. See *Portiforium*.

POSITIVE THEOLOGY. The branch of theology which treats of matters of historic and particular fact, custom, or enactment, as opposed to '*natural theology' (or 'natural religion'), which deals with religious principles and laws of universal validity.

POSITIVISM. In its orig. and narrower sense, the system of the French thinker Auguste *Comte (q.v.), which confined intellectual inquiry to observable ('positive') facts and their relations, and eschewed all consideration of ultimate issues, incl. those of philosophy and theology. Its most prominent English exponent was Frederic Harrison (1831–1923); but similar doctrines were taught by H. *Spencer and other defenders of *Agnosticism. The term has now come to be used in a wider sense for any form of philosophical outlook which rejects metaphysics, esp. when the physical sciences are regarded as offering the norm of knowledge. One school which flourished in Great Britain, esp. in the late 'thirties, came to be known as 'Logical Positivism'. Its leading advocate was A. J. Ayer.

POSSIDIUS, St. (c. 370–c. 440), biographer of St. *Augustine. A converted pagan, he lived in the monastery at Hippo until he became Bp. of Calama in Numidia in 397. He helped Augustine in his struggle against *Donatism and *Pelagianism, was with him when he died, and left, besides a list of his works, a short but valuable sketch of his life.

His 'Vita Augustini', commonly pr. in the earlier edd. of St. Augustine, is repr. in J. P. Migne, *PL*, xxxii, 31–66. Crit. edd. by H. T. Weiskotten, Princeton, N.J., 1919, with Eng. tr.; A. Vega, Escurial, 1943; and M. Pellegrino, 'Verba Seniorum', Turin, [c. 1954]. Another Eng. tr. in E. A. Foran, O.S.A., *The Augustinians, from St. Augustine to the Union*, 1256 (1938), pp. ix–xii and 1–36. Study and Germ. tr. by A. *Harnack in *Abh.* (Berl.), 1930, Hft. 1. Possidius's 'Operum S. Augustini Elenchus', ed. A.*Wilmart, O.S.B., in *Miscellanea Agostiniana*, ii (1931), pp. 149–233. Bardenhewer, iv, 428, 441, 443, 445; Altaner (ed. 1951), 364. M. Pellegrino in *E.C.*, ix (1952), col. 1838, s.v. 'Possidio'.

POSTCOMMUNION. In the Roman *Mass the prayer, similar in structure to the *Collect, which follows the priest's communion. In early times it was the last item in the Mass. When more than one Collect has been recited, there is a corresponding increase in the number of the Postcommunions. The counterpart in the Anglican BCP is the pair of alternative prayers beginning 'O Lord and Heavenly Father' and 'Almighty and Everliving God' (since 1552 separated from the Blessing by the transposition of the '*Gloria in excelsis' from the early part of the rite). The name Postcommunion is first found in the *Gelasian Sacramentary.

Jungmann (ed. 1952), ii, 520–7.

POSTIL, also 'Apostil'. This word (Lat. *postilla*) which in the Middle Ages was used of a gloss on a scriptural text, came to be applied esp. to a homily on the Gospel or Epistle for the day or to a book of homilies. It is perhaps derived from *post illa*, meaning 'After those [words of scripture]'.

POSTLAPSARIANISM. See *Sublapsarianism*.

POST-SANCTUS. The prayer in the Eucharistic Liturgy which in the *Gallican Rite followed the *Sanctus and varied according to the feast commemorated. It survives in the *Mozarabic Rite.

POSTULANT. One who is undergoing a preliminary stage of testing as a candidate for a religious order before admission to the *novitiate. The period of postulancy varies in length acc. to the religious order and the circumstances of the candidate, but it commonly extends over several months, which are spent at the religious house where the candidate expects later to be professed.

POTENTIANA, St. See *Pudentiana, St.*

POTHINUS, St. (c. 87–177), first Bp. of Lyons. He was probably a native of Asia Minor and a disciple of St. *Polycarp, and if so would have brought Asian influences to early Christianity in the south of Gaul. The circumstances of his death are described in the 'Ep. of the Churches of Vienne and Lyons' (ap. *Eusebius, *Hist. Eccl.*, v. i). Feast day (with his companions in martyrdom), 2 June.

Eusebius, *H.E.*, V, 1 f. T. Richoud, *Le Premier Évêque de Lugdunum* (Lyons, 1900). On the persecution of 177, J. B. *Lightfoot, *The Apostolic Fathers*, i (pt. 2; ed. 2, 1889), p. 515 f.; a number of reff. to recent discussions by A. *Harnack and P. Allard can be found in J. W. Thompson, 'The Alleged Persecution of the Christians at Lyons in 177' in *The American Journal of Theology*, xvii (1913), pp. 249–258; U. Kahrstedt, 'Die Märtyrerakten von Lugdunum 177' in *Rheinisches Museum für Philologie*, N.F., lxviii (1913), pp. 395–412. H. Quentin, O.S.B., 'La Liste des martyrs de Lyon de l'an 177' in *Anal. Boll.*, xix (1921), pp. 113–38.

POTTER, JOHN (c. 1674–1747), Abp. of *Canterbury. Educated at Wakefield and University College, Oxford, Potter became successively Fellow of Lincoln (1694), Regius professor of divinity at Oxford (1707), and Bp. of Oxford (1715). He ordained J. *Wesley, with whom he remained on good terms. In 1737 he unexpectedly succeeded W. *Wake as Abp. of Canterbury (E. *Gibson's appointment being thought probable). A Whig, Potter was nevertheless a High Churchman, as his *Discourse of Church Government* (1707) shows. His works include a long-used *Archaeologia Graeca* (2 vols., 1697–9), a fine edition of St. *Clement of Alexandria (1715), and attacks upon B. *Hoadly.

Collected ed. of his *Theological Works* publd. in 3 vols., Oxford, 1753. Life by Robert Anderson, M.D. (1750–1830), prefixed to the ed. of Potter's *Archaeologia Graeca* publd. London, 1818 (vol. i, pp. i–xi), and subsequent edd. A. W. Rowden, *The Primates of the Four Georges* (1916), pp. 115–166. J. H. Lupton in *D.N.B.*, xlvi (1896), p. 216 f.

POWERS. Acc. to medieval angelology, the sixth order of angels in the celestial hierarchy. The word is also used more generally of any celestial being who exercises control or influence over other parts of creation (cf. the English version of the *Te Deum, 'To Thee all angels cry aloud: the heavens and all the powers therein').

PRAEDESTINATUS. A treatise, composed probably at Rome during the Papacy of Sixtus III (432-40), and directed against the extremer forms of the doctrine of *Predestination then being taught under the influence of certain passages in the writings of St. *Augustine. Its standpoint, if not actually *Pelagian, is at least *Semi-Pelagian. Of its three books, the first is mainly a plagiarized reproduction of St. Augustine's 'De haeresibus'; the second purports to be the work of an upholder of St. Augustine's predestination doctrines, though it is almost certainly a composition of the writer of the whole treatise; and the third is a refutation of the second book. It was first edited in 1643 by J. *Sirmond, S.J.

J. Sirmond based his ed. on the MS Reims 40, once in the possession of *Hincmar. Revised text by J. de La Baune, S.J., in his ed. of Sirmond's works (1696); repr. (via A. *Gallandi) in J. P. Migne, PL, liii, 579-692. The work was much discussed in the *Jansenist controversies. H. von Schubert, Der sogenannte Praedestinatus. Ein Beitrag zur Geschichte des Pelagianismus (T.U., xxiv, 4, 1903); G. Bardy, 'Le Souvenir d'Arius dans le Praedestinatus' in R. Bén., xl (1928), pp. 256-61. Bardenhewer, iv, p. 521. É. Amann in D.T.C., xii (pt. 2; 1935), cols. 2775-80, s.v.

PRAEMUNIRE. The title of statutes (first passed in 1353, 1365, and 1393) which were designed to protect rights claimed by the English crown against encroachment by the Papacy. The name can denote the statutes, the offence, the writ, and the punishment. The statute of 1353 forbade the withdrawal from England of cases which should be decided in the king's courts, and the penalties prescribed were in 1393 stiffened and extended to any who should promote any Papal bull or excommunication. In consequence appeals to Rome dwindled. In 1529 *Henry VIII claimed that T. *Wolsey's activities as Papal legate infringed this statute, and, alleging that the acquiescent clergy were no less guilty, in 1531 blackmailed them into submitting to the Royal Supremacy. *Elizabeth used Praemunire to deal with purely civil offences and with RC recusants; and *James I's judges used it to assist the encroachments of temporal upon ecclesiastical courts. A peer charged with Praemunire cannot claim to be tried by his peers, but must submit to trial by jury.

Eng. tr. of First Statute of Praemunire (1353) pr. Gee-Hardy, p. 103 f. (No. xxxv); that of 1393, ib., pp. 122-5 (No. xl). The latter is repr. in H. Bettenson (ed.), Documents of the Christian Church (World's Classics, 1943), pp. 239-42. W. T. Waugh, 'The Great Statute of Praemunire' in E.H.R., xxxvii (1922), pp. 173-205. G. Crosse in D.E.C.H. (1948), p. 487 f., s.v.

PRAEPOSITINUS OF CREMONA (c. 1140-c. 1210), theologian and liturgist. He studied dogmatic theology and canon law at Paris, where he afterwards taught. C. 1194 he became prebendary at Mainz Cathedral, and probably about this time was engaged in missionary

work among the *Cathari. He seems to have resigned his office in 1203, owing to a conflict with *Innocent III over the succession to the see of Mainz, but he must have soon submitted to the Pope, since in 1206 he is known to have been chancellor of *Paris university. He wrote the 'Summa de Officiis', a work in four parts, an explanation of the symbolism of the offices and a principal source of William *Durandus of Mende. The 'Summa contra Haereticos' contains valuable information of the otherwise unknown sect of the Passagians, but its authorship has been contested. He also wrote a 'Summa super Psalterium' and a 'Summa Theologica', which represents the theological teaching of his last period in Paris. Even his latest work is untouched by the new problems raised by the introduction of *Aristotle into the W. It had a considerable influence in his time, esp. on the *Franciscan school (*Alexander of Hales, St. *Bonaventure).

G. Lacombe, Prepositini Cancellarii Parisiensis (1206-1210) Opera Omnia, I (all publd. to 1953): la vie et les œuvres de Prévostin (Bibliothèque thomiste, No. 11, Kain, 1927). Id. in D.T.C., xiii (pt. 1, 1933), cols. 162-9, s.v.; A. Piolanti in E.C., ix (1952), col. 1953.

PRAGMATIC SANCTION (Lat. *Pragmatica Sanctio*). A term orig. employed in later Roman law for an arrangement defining the limits of the sovereign power of a prince, esp. in the matter of royal succession. A pragmatic sanction, published by Philip V, introduced Salic Law into Spain, and another, issued later by Ferdinand VII, revoked it.

The Pragmatic Sanction of Bourges, issued by the French clergy on 7 July 1438 while the Council of *Basle (q.v.) was still in session, was a statement of *Gallicanist principles. It upheld the right of the French Church to administer its temporal property independently of the Papacy and disallowed Papal nominations to vacant benefices. In 1516 it was superseded by the Concordat of *Bologna (q.v.).

Text of the Pragmatic Sanction of Bourges in Ordonnances des rois de France de la troisième race, xiii (ed. M. de Vilevault, 1782), pp. 267-91; summary in Mirbt, No. 398, pp. 232 f.; Eng. tr. in S. Z. Ehler-J. B. Morrall (edd.), Church and State Through the Centuries (1954), pp. 112-21. N. Valois, Histoire de la pragmatique sanction de Bourges sous Charles VII (Archives de l'Histoire de la France; 1906). Hefele-Leclercq, vii (pt. 2; 1916), pp. 1053-61. V. Martin, Les Origines du gallicanisme, ii (1939), pp. 293-324. R. Hedde in D.T.C., xii (pt. 2; 1935), cols. 2781-6, s.v. 'Pragmatique Sanction, II'.

PRAGMATISM (Gr. πράγματα, 'ordinary things', 'affairs'). A system of belief devised by C. S. Peirce, H. *Bergson, F. C. S. Schiller, W. *James, J. Dewey, and others, on the principle that every truth has practical consequences, and that these are a test of its truthfulness. Truth is therefore relative, and the proof of a fact is not an act of the pure reason, but rather an account of how the fact has come to be accepted as justifying itself by practical results. The real is not to be investigated by metaphysical speculation, but rather acc. to the values developed through its being known.

Pragmatism justifies and explains religions acc. as they satisfy psychological criteria, and generate suitable values. In the RC Church the *Modernist Movement was much influenced by Pragmatist ideals, notably in the persons of L. *Laberthonnière and G. *Tyrrell, as well as F. *von Hügel in his earlier life. Pragmatist ideas also exercised a widely diffused influence on religious thought generally, esp. in the period 1901–30.

Personal Idealism (ed. H. Sturt, 1902); J. Dewey, *Studies in Logical Theory* (1903); F. C. S. Schiller, *Humanism* (1903); id., *Studies in Humanism* (1907); W. James, *Pragmatism* (1907); id., *The Meaning of Truth* (1909); H. Vaihinger, *Die Philosophie des Als Ob* (1911). F. C. S. Schiller in *H.E.R.E.*, x (1918), pp. 147–50, s.v., with bibl.

PRASSEDE, St. See *Praxedes, St.*

PRAXEAS (*fl. c.* 200), heretic. The substance of his history and teaching is known only from the treatise 'Adversus Praxean' (*c.* 217) of his vigorous opponent *Tertullian and may thus be somewhat misrepresented. He is said to have arrived in Rome towards the end of the 2nd cent. from Asia, where he had suffered imprisonment for his faith, and to have succeeded in turning the Pope (*Victor or *Zephyrinus) against the *Montanists. He proclaimed himself a leader of the '*Patripassian Monarchians', i.e. of those who were concerned to maintain the unity of the Godhead even at the cost of declaring that God suffered. As Tertullian put it, he 'crucified the Father' (*Patrem crucifixit*) since he conceived of the Godhead as emptied into the person of Christ in order to assume the temporary role of Redeemer. Before the end of his life he recanted his heretical doctrines.

'Praxeas' is prob. a real name and not, as G. B. *de Rossi suggested, a pseudonym ('busybody') for *Noetus or Epigonus. For bibl. see *Monarchianism.*

PRAXEDES, St. (1st–2nd cent.), also Prassede, early martyr at Rome. Acc. to her (spurious) *acta*, she was a Roman virgin who sheltered Christians during the persecution under *Marcus Aurelius. She was buried in the Catacomb of *Priscilla next the grave of St. *Pudentiana and hence (on wholly insufficient grounds) was supposed to have been her sister. The well-known church of Santa Prassede on the Esquiline at Rome (which inspired R. Browning's 'Tomb at St. Praxed's') was built by Paschal I (817–24) on the site of an earlier structure supposed to have stood on the site of her house. Feast day, 21 July.

St. Praxedes and St. Pudentiana are first mentioned in 7th-cent. Roman Itineraries to the Catacombs; they occur only in interpolated texts of the *Hieronymian Martyrology. Later legends make them both daughters of St. *Pudens (q.v.). *A.A.SS.*, Mai. IV (1685), pp. 296–301. A. de Waal, 'Der Titulus Praxedis' in *R.Q.*, xix (1905), pp. 169–80. J. P. Kirsch, *Die römischen Titelkirchen im Altertum* (1918), pp. 149–51. M. Armellini, *Le chiese di Roma dal secolo IV al XIX* (ed. C. Cecchelli, 1942), pp. 296–303 and 1418–20.

PRAYER. Christian prayer rests on two foundations which give it its specific character, belief in the transcendent and personal nature of the God who is revealed in the Bible as Lord of History and Creator of the World, and the acceptance of the intimate relation of God and man disclosed by the atoning work of the Incarnate Christ.

From these truths it follows that petition, invocation and adoration, which also belong to other world-religions, are practised in Christian spirituality under the dominant ideas of (a) submission to the Divine will and (b) recognition of the direct relationship of every creature to God who at once transcends the created order and is immanent in it. Adoration, thanksgiving, penitence and petition are therefore acts directed to God 'through Jesus Christ our Lord' or made 'in the Spirit' (Jude 20). Moreover, the note of the Christian's approach to God is the fruit of '*justification' by Christ.

A further consequence for Christian prayer follows from the theology of the Incarnation. By disclosing a congruity of humanity to deity, though not a unity of essence, this belief supplies a new basis for man's search for God in prayer which leads to the vision of God and union with and likeness to Him. It points to a way of prayer which, though a part of natural religion, occupies besides a large place in the devotional tradition of Christendom, where it is transformed by the Christian belief in God's grace. This type of prayer is the fruit of 'sanctification'.

These two kinds of prayer have been distinguished as vocal prayer and mental prayer. An early statement of such a distinction is in St. *John of Damascus: 'Prayer is either the ascent of the mind to God or the decently beseeching of Him' (*De Fide Orthodoxa*, iii, 24), though it should be noted that vocal prayer includes praise, thanksgiving and penitence, as well as 'beseeching'. St. *Thomas Aquinas, who also clearly distinguishes vocal and mental prayer, divides the former into common and individual prayer (*Summa Theol.*, II (2), q. 83, art. 13). F. *Heiler has differentiated them as the 'prophetic' and the 'mystical' types of prayer, contending that the first only is Biblical and Christian while the second is of *Neo-Platonic affiliation. But this last contention is misleading, and for two reasons. There are elements of 'mysticism' in the Bible and there are ways of contemplation and union with God in the Christian tradition which are not strictly mystical. But the distinction in itself is valid. While, as Heiler points out, Protestant piety confines itself almost entirely to the prophetic type, Catholic and Eastern Orthodox devotion give a prominent place to the mystical as well.

As to vocal prayer, while the *Stoics recognized praise and the summoning of the soul to acquiescence in God's will, but not petition, Christianity allows petitions for benefits and virtues. Though Cicero had recommended prayer to Jupiter for the gifts of fortune, he declared that 'no one has ever referred to God the acquisition of virtue' (*De Natura Deorum*, III, 36), since virtue is a human achievement. By contrast Hebrew and Christian prayer, while asking God for both, regard esp. the practice of virtue as the reward of prayer. *Solomon besought the Lord for virtue (1 Kgs. 3. 9) and for benefits (8. 22–53). To the Hebrew requirement of holiness as a precondition of true prayer, Christianity adds the converse that true holiness only comes of prayer.

As regards Christ's own authority, it must be observed that He participated in the public worship of the synagogue (Mk. 1. 21). When He expressly mentions prayer, however, it is always of a private kind: 'Enter into thy closet' (Mt. 6. 6); and on occasion He Himself went into the desert (Mk. 6. 31, 32; Lk. 5. 16), to a solitary place (Mk. 1. 35), to a mountain (Lk. 9. 28, Mk. 6. 46), and to Gethsemane (Lk. 22. 39–41, Mk. 14. 32) to pray. This double prayer life adumbrates the distinction between common and private prayer in the life of the Church. Common prayer may be further divided into liturgical (*Eucharist, Hours of Prayer) and informal gatherings for prayer and praise. Liturgical prayer is normally a regular cycle of worshipful action, with variations only according to festival or fast and to the turn of the year, month, week or day. Informal common worship expresses aspirations and needs of the moment, as does also extempore individual prayer.

In the NT prayer is an art to be learnt; hence the pattern given in the *Lord's Prayer. Prayer is also a weapon in the cosmic spiritual battle of good and evil (Mt. 17. 21); Jesus prays for power to raise *Lazarus (Jn. 11. 41 f.) and to endure the Passion (Mt. 26. 39, Mk. 14. 35 f., Lk. 22. 42).

As to Mental Prayer, the name is unsatisfactory for it includes the direction of the affections as well as of thought and also contemplation which is a kind of spiritual looking or gaze. On the other hand, 'contemplative prayer' is not wide enough to include meditation and acts of the affections. The medieval rendering of the description of John of Damascus, quoted above, as 'the ascent of the mind to God' ('Ascensus Intellectus in Deum') has given a too intellectual appearance to mental prayer, at least for those who do not understand 'intellectus' as the faculty of spiritual vision, in distinction from 'ratio' which is the discursive reason. The main schools of mental prayer recognize that its 'ordinary ways' include discursive meditation, affective prayer and contemplation (with the prayer of loving regard and prayer of simplicity), while its 'extra-ordinary ways' comprise mystical and supernatural experiences. (See Mysticism). The *Cloud of Unknowing is commonly regarded as a reliable guide to contemplative prayer for those without mystical gifts.

Many methods of meditation and of contemplative prayer have been advocated by Christian spiritual writers; and a stream of teachers of prayer such as *Clement of Alexandria, *Origen, *Cassian, St. *Bernard, St. *Thomas Aquinas, *Thomas à Kempis, St. *Peter of Alcantara, St. *Ignatius Loyola, St. *Teresa of Ávila, St.

*John of the Cross, *Fénelon, J. B. *Bossuet, and W. *Law, not to mention more recent guides, have expounded their principles.

There has been a continuous stream of literature on the practice and philosophy of Christian prayer from *Tertullian and *Origen onwards. Many of these studies are cited under their authors, notably the various exponents of Mysticism. Useful guides to the subject generally include P. Pourrat, P.S.S., La Spiritualité chrétienne (4 vols., 1918–1928; Eng. tr. of vols. 1–3, 1922–7); F. *Heiler, Das Gebet. Eine religionsgeschichtliche und religionspsychologische Untersuchung (1918; abbreviated Eng. tr. by S. McComb-J. E. Park, New York, 1932); and the writings of Evelyn *Underhill (q v.). Modern studies on the nature and philosophy of prayer include H. P. *Liddon, Some Elements of Religion (1872), Lect. v ('Prayer, the Characteristic Action of Religion'), pp. 165–203; A. Poulain, S.J., Des Grâces d'oraison (1901; Eng. tr., 1910); A. J. Worlledge, Prayer (Oxford Library of Practical Theology, 1902); J. *Hastings, The Christian Doctrine of Prayer (1915); B. H. *Streeter (ed.), Concerning Prayer. Its Nature, its Difficulties and its Value (1916); F. Ménégoz, Le Problème de la prière (Études d'Histoire et de Philosophie religieuse, xiii; 1925); E. J. Bicknell, In Defence of Christian Prayer (1925); B. Frost, The Art of Mental Prayer (1931); F. P. Harton, The Elements of the Spiritual Life (1932); D. Jenkins, Prayer and the Service of God (1944); H. Northcott, C.R., The Venture of Prayer (1950). 'Prayer' in various religions in H.E.R.E., x (1918), pp. 154–205, by various writers, incl. F. Perles on 'Prayer (Jewish)', pp. 191–6, C. F. D'Arcy on 'Prayer (Christian, Theological)', pp. 171–7, and R. M. Woolley on 'Prayer (Christian, Liturgical), pp. 177–80; A. Fonck in D.T.C., xiii (pt. 1; 1936), cols. 169–244. See also bibl. to Liturgy, Mysticism.

PRAYER OF MANASSES. See Manasses, Prayer of.

PRAYERS FOR THE DEAD. See Dead, Prayers for the.

PREACHERS, Order of. See Dominican Order.

PREACHING OF PETER. See Peter, Preaching of St.

PREBEND and PREBENDARY. A cathedral benefice and its holder. Though in the early Middle Ages reformers constantly aimed at maintaining the common life under rule for the *canons of cathedral and collegiate foundations, in the majority of such foundations this ideal was frankly abandoned and the endowment divided up into separate portions, each designed for the support of one member of the chapter. These acquired the name of 'prebends' from the fact that they supplied or furnished (praebere) a living to their holders, who in turn came to be known as 'prebendaries'. The prebend normally consisted of the revenue from one manor of the cathedral estates, a fact which accounts for the territorial names still attached to the prebendal stalls in many English cathedrals. In English cathedrals of the 'Old Foundation' the ancient prebends have been kept in name, though the transference of their attached incomes to the *Ecclesiastical Commission by the 19th cent. legislation has made them in nearly all cases honorary offices only. In the former monastic cathedrals, reorganized by *Henry VIII at the *Dissolution and known as cathedrals of the

'New Foundation', prebends in the proper sense do not exist, though 'prebendary' became the normal appellation of the members of the chapters of these churches until the 19th cent. when the title of 'canon' replaced it in general usage.

PRECENTOR. In *Cathedrals, the cleric responsible for the direction of the choral services. In those of the 'Old Foundation' he is a member of the chapter who ranks next to the Dean, and commonly delegates his duties to a deputy known as the *succentor. In cathedrals of the 'New Foundation', however, his status is the lower one of *minor canon or chaplain.

PRECEPT (Lat. *praeceptum*). In moral theology, a matter of obligation, as contrasted with a '*counsel' (q.v.), which is only a matter of persuasion. For Precepts of the Church, see *Commandments of the Church*.

PRECEPTORY. Among the *Templars a community established on one of their provincial estates. The corresponding institution among the *Hospitallers was a '*Commandery'.

PRECES FERIALES (Lat. 'ferial prayers'). In W. service-books, a short series of prayers said esp. on ferial (non-festal) days consisting of *Kyrie Eleison*, *Paternoster and versicles and responses. In the present Roman Breviary they stand immediately before the collect and are recited in the ferial office in penitential seasons. In the BCP they are represented by the prayers at *Mattins and *Evensong between the Creed and the Collects, and are said or sung throughout the year.

PRECES PRIVATAE. The Latin book of devotion issued by *Elizabeth I in 1564 with the title *Preces Privatae in Studiosorum Gratiam Collectae et Regia Autoritate Approbatae*. It was a manual of prayers largely based on the BCP, and thus carried on the tradition of the medieval English *Primers which were compilations for private use based on the liturgical services. A later edition of 1573 contained additional devotions compiled by St. John *Fisher. Apart from its title it has no connexion with the celebrated 'Preces Privatae' of L. *Andrewes (q.v.).

It is printed in *Private Prayers of the Reign of Queen Elizabeth* (Parker Society, 1851), pp. 209-428.

PRECIOUS BLOOD, Devotion to the. The Blood of Christ, shed during the Passion, has been honoured and regarded as of redeeming virtue since the Apostolic Age, esp. in connexion with the Eucharist. Beyrout, Bruges, Saintes, the English monasteries of Ashridge and Hailes, and various other churches have claimed to possess particles of it. Such relics have been greatly venerated, although St. *Thomas Aquinas (S.T. 3a., q.

54, a. 3) maintained that all the particles of the Blood of Christ shed during the Passion were reassumed by Him at His Resurrection, and that such relics must have flowed from an image of Christ. *Benedict XIV, admitting that some particles might not have been assumed, maintained that not being united to the Godhead, they were to be venerated rather than adored. The *Dominicans held that the Precious Blood was an essential part of the Sacred Humanity; the *Franciscans that it was concomitant only. Since the Council of *Trent the former view has tended to prevail among RC theologians. Feasts in honour of the Precious Blood were celebrated by various orders in the 19th cent. In 1849 *Pius IX, while at Gaeta, extended the Feast to the whole Church, assigning to it the first Sunday in July, altered by *Pius X in 1914 to 1 July. The whole month of July is unofficially connected with the devotion. The Friday after the fourth Sunday in Lent is also celebrated by the *Passionists and various other orders, of whom several are dedicated to the Precious Blood. The (RC) Cathedral Church of the Archdiocese of *Westminster is dedicated to the Most Precious Blood.

The decree of *Pius XI raising the Feast to a Double of the First Class is pr. in *A.A.S.*, xxvi (1934), p. 559 f. F. W. *Faber, *The Precious Blood, or the Price of our Salvation* (1860; devotional). M. D. Chenu, O.P., in *D.T.C.*, xiv (pt. 1; 1939), cols. 1094-7, s.v. 'Sang du Christ'; A. P. Frutaz in *E.C.*, x (1953), cols., 1778-80, s.v. 'Sangue preziosissimo di N.S. Gesù Cristo'.

PRECISIAN. A name widely used of the *Puritans in the 16th and 17th cents. on account of their punctiliousness in observing external religious rules and forms.

PREDELLA. (1) The platform (foot-pace) on the uppermost of the steps to an altar, on which the priest stands when celebrating Mass. (2) The lowest piece of a *reredos, immediately above the altar. The word is the Ital. *predella*, 'foot-stool', 'kneeling-stool'.

PREDESTINATION (from Lat. 'praedestinare', Vulg. trans. of Gk. προορίζειν, 'foreordain'). The Divine decree acc. to which certain persons are infallibly guided to eternal salvation. The doctrine is not explicitly taught in the OT, but adumbrations of it may be found in the conception of the 'Book of Life' (Ps. 69. 29, Exod. 32. 32, Dan. 12. 1). Predestination is presupposed in the Gospels, e.g. Mt. 20. 23, where our Lord tells the Apostles that the sitting on His right or left is reserved 'for them for whom it hath been prepared of my Father', and in Jn. 10. 29 where He tells the Jews that no one can snatch from Him the sheep given Him by the Father. The most explicit teaching in the NT is in St. *Paul, esp. in the crucial text Rom. 8. 28-30, where the Apostle traces the process of the salvation of those 'that are called according to His purpose' from foreknowledge and predestination to vocation, justification, and glorification. The theme is resumed in Eph. 1. 3–14, where is added the factor of *election (q.v.), inserted between foreknowledge and predestination. In the same text great stress is laid on the gratuity of it 'according to the good pleasure of His will'. This is still more emphasized in 2 Tim. 1. 9, where it is affirmed that God has called us 'not according to our works, but according to His own purpose and grace', and in 1 Cor. 4. 7, where the Apostle asks 'What hast thou that thou didst not receive?'

In the W. the *Pelagian controversy caused a thorough investigation of the doctrine, which St. *Augustine developed on the basis of St. Paul's teaching. For him the mystery of Predestination consists in the inaccessibility to the human mind of the reasons for the Divine choice, which, nevertheless, is made in perfect justice. In his view it is the vocation not only to grace but also to glory. It contains the gift of final perseverance (donum perseverantiae) and depends not on human acceptance but on the eternal decree of God and is therefore infallible, without, however, acc. to Augustine, violating free-will. Evil enters into the plan of Predestination in so far as it is permitted by God in view of a greater good.

St. Augustine's doctrine was defended by St. *Prosper of Aquitaine. The 6th cent. Semi-Pelagian *Faustus of Riez attacked it, but he was opposed by St. *Fulgentius and St. *Caesarius of Arles. The latter's influence led to the acceptance of the Augustinian teaching by the Council of *Orange (529), which ended the quarrel between Augustinians and Anti-Augustinians. In the 9th cent. the discussions were revived by the monk *Gottschalk (q.v.), who seems to have propagated an exaggerated Augustinianism, teaching a double predestination to eternal life and eternal death. This doctrine was condemned by the Synod of *Quiercy in 849.

The medieval teaching was based on St. Augustine, but took into account also the Greek doctrine, esp. as represented by St. *John of Damascus, who followed *Origen and stressed the universal saving will of God. Acc. to him God 'antecedently' wills the universal salvation of all men, but, in consequence of their sins, He wills eternal punishment for some. The reconciliation of this view with the Divine omnipotence and the efficacy of grace, stressed by St. Augustine, was undertaken by the Schoolmen. *Peter Lombard emphasized the absence, in God, of all passivity or dependence on the decisions of creatures, and St. *Bonaventure asserted the principle of the Divine predilection, which is the cause, not the effect, of the greater or lesser goodness of creatures. St. *Thomas Aquinas based the reconciliation of the universal saving will of God with the mystery of Predestination on the same principle, viz. that the love of God is the cause of the goodness of things (Amor Dei est causa bonitatis rerum).

The problem was again a matter of fundamental concern to the Reformers. J. *Calvin made the doctrine of Predestination one of the corner-stones of his system. Rejecting the universal saving will of God, he maintained that Christ's atoning death was offered for the elect alone. He added to the gratuitous predestination of the elect the equally gratuitous and positive reprobation of the damned, to whom salvation is denied from all eternity without any fault on their part. Calvin's disciples, however, were divided into Ante- or *Supralapsarians and *Sublapsarians (qq.v.). The Calvinist doctrine of Predestination, which was not accepted by the *Arminians (q.v.), was imposed by the Synod of *Dort (1618–19) and by the *Westminster Assembly (1647), which declared that at least after Adam's Fall God does not will the salvation of all men and that Christ died only for the elect.

The post-Tridentine RC theologians formulated their doctrine of Predestination with particular emphasis on the freedom of the human will. Among the systems devised to reconcile the latter with the dogma of Predestination was that of L. de *Molina (see Molinism), who abandoned the principle of Divine predilection and taught predestination post praevisa merita. F. *Suarez, *Bellarmine, and most other Jesuit theologians except the strict Molinists recognize the gratuity of Predestination and its priority to the prevision of merits, though denying the intrinsic efficacy of the Divine decree independently of human consent. The controversy between Thomist and Jesuit theologians on these points still continues.

The number of the predestined has been a matter for speculation from early times. Acc. to the teaching of the majority of the Fathers and theologians, who based their belief on passages such as Mt. 22. 14, it was smaller than that of the reprobate. The tendency of most modern theologians who have been bold enough to seek an answer to this and other such questions has been towards a more optimistic view.

On the Biblical teaching on Predestination, see esp. commentaries on the OT Prophets and Rom. and works on the theology of St. Paul. The more important post-Biblical discussions include Origen, De Principiis, ii and iii; St. Augustine, De Praedestinatione Sanctorum; and Calvin, Institutes, iii. Modern discussions will be found in treatises on dogmatic theology. J. B. *Mozley, A Treatise on the Augustinian Doctrine of Predestination (1855); W. A. Copinger, A Treatise on Predestination, Election and Grace (1889), with bibl. R. Garrigou-Lagrange, O.P., La Prédestination des saints et la grâce (1936). G. Hoennicke in P.R.E. (ed. 3), xv (1904), pp. 581–6, s.v. 'Prädestination I. Schriftlehre'; E. F. K. Müller, ib., pp. 586–602, s.v. 'Prädestination II. Kirchenlehre'; J. Pohle in C.E., xii (1911), pp. 376–84, s.vv. 'Predestinarianism' and 'Predestination'; A. S. Martin in H.E.R.E., x (1918), pp. 225–35, s.v.; A. Lemonnyer, O.P.–H. D. Simonin, O.P.–R. Garrigou-Lagrange, O.P.–B. Lavaud, O.P., in D.T.C., xii (pt. 2; 1935), cols. 2809–3022, s.v. 'Prédestination'; R. Garrigou-Lagrange, O.P., in E.C., ix (1952), cols. 1907–12, s.v. 'Predestinazione'.

PREDESTINATUS. See Praedestinatus.

PRE-ESTABLISHED HARMONY. In the system of G. W. *Leibniz, the predetermined harmony between all the 'simple substances' (monads) in the universe. Leibniz believed that God had established such a harmony before creation, which explained the apparent interaction between mind and body in the world of experience. See also *Occasionalism*.

PREFACE. In the Eucharist, the words which introduce the central part of the service. It begins with the '*Sursum Corda' and ends with the '*Sanctus'. The main part of it is an ascription of praise to the Creator in union with the worship of the whole angelic company. It varies acc. to the feast observed. In W. liturgies there is a common form into which a 'proper' is interpolated on the greater feast days. The BCP provides 'proper prefaces' for *Christmas, *Easter, *Ascensiontide, and *Whitsuntide, and on *Trinity Sunday, while in the Roman Rite still more propers are in use, though their present number is small compared with that of earlier times. The oldest surviving Roman *Sacramentary, the *Leonine, had a separate Preface for every Mass, the *Gelasian had 54, but in the *Gregorian Sacramentary their number had fallen to ten. In the E. Church the Preface does not change with the season. Historically the Preface is the first part of the prayer of *consecration or *canon; but in the Roman Mass it is now a separate entity from the canon, and in the BCP it is divided from the consecratory prayer by the 'Prayer of *Humble Access'.

Jungmann, ii (ed. 1949), esp. pp. 140–56 (Eng. tr., pp. 115–28). H. *Leclercq, O.S.B., in *D.A.C.L.*, xiv (pt. 1; 1948), cols. 1704–16, s.v., with reff.

PRELATE. A term originally of wide connotation, it gradually acquired a purely ecclesiastical reference and still later came to be restricted to Church officials of high rank. In the C of E the title is restricted nowadays to bishops. In the Roman Church it was long used of important ecclesiastics having an independent jurisdiction, but it is now also applied to a variety of officers attached to the Roman court who may have only an honorary dignity. The term 'prelacy', which denotes the system of ecclesiastical government by bishops, is commonly used only in a hostile sense.

PREMONSTRATENSIAN CANONS, also 'Norbertines' and, in England, 'White Canons' from the colour of their habit, an order founded by St. *Norbert (q.v.) at Prémontré, near Laon, in 1120. The basis of the rule was the so-called rule of St. *Augustine, with additional austerities, e.g. entire abstinence from meat. In its details, the Premonstratensian life also came under *Cistercian influences through Norbert's friendship with St. *Bernard of Clairvaux. In 1126 the order received papal approbation and quickly spread over W. Europe, their earliest English house being at Newhouse in Lincoln (c. 1143). They became powerful in Hungary and also took an active part in evangelizing the lands between the Elbe and the Oder. Relaxation in the severity of the original rule led to several

reforms and the creation of more or less independent congregations, notably in Spain where a virtually self-contained body was established *c.* 1573. The order suffered severely from the French Revolution and had become nearly extinct in the early 19th cent. More recently it has re-established its influence and is esp. strong in Belgium, with its headquarters at Tongerloo.

Numerous studies of primary importance in *Analectes de l'ordre de Prémontré*, ed. M. van Waefelghem (12 vols., Brussels, 1905–14); contd. as *Analecta Praemonstratensia* (Tongerloo, 1925 ff.). C. L. Hugo, *Sacri et Canonici Ordinis Praemonstratensis Annales* (2 vols., Nancy, 1734–5). F. Petit, Ord. Praem., *L'Ordre de Prémontré* ('Les Ordres religieux'; 1927). F. Petit, O. Praem., *La Spiritualité des Prémontrés aux XIIe et XIIIe siècles* (Études de Théologie et d'Histoire de Spiritualité, x; 1947). J. Le Paige, *Bibliotheca Praemonstratensis Ordinis* (Paris, 1633). L. Goovaerts, *Écrivains, artistes et savants de l'ordre de Prémontré*. Dictionnaire bio-bibliographique (4 vols., bound in 3, 1899–1917). F. Winter, *Die Prämonstratenser des zwölften Jahrhunderts und ihre Bedeutung für das nordöstliche Deutschland* (1865). F. A. *Gasquet (ed.), *Collectanea Anglo-Premonstratensia*. Documents drawn from the Original Register of the Order, now in the Bodleian Library, Oxford, and the Transcript of another Register in the British Museum (Camden Society Third Series, xii; 1906). H. M. Colvin, *The White Canons in England* (1951), with bibl. R. van Waefelghem, *Répertoire des sources imprimées et manuscrites relatives à l'histoire et à la liturgie des monastères de l'ordre de Prémontré* (1930). M. Heimbucher, *Die Orden und Kongregationen der katholischen Kirche*, i (ed. 3; 1933), pp. 432–48, and ii (1934), p. 657 f.

PREPARATION, The. In the W. Church the opening prayers at *Mass, recited alternately by the priest and ministers (or *server) at the foot of the *altar. It consists usually of Ps. 43 (Vulg. 42), a confession of sin, and two prayers preceded by four *versicles and responses. In the Roman Rite it dates in a shorter form from the 11th cent., and in substantially its present form from *c.* 1300.

Jungmann (ed. 1952), i, 377–409.

PREPARATION, Day of (Gk. παρασκευή). A name given by the Jews to Fridays, i.e. the day preceding, and thus employed in 'preparation' for, the *Sabbath (hence also προσάββατον). The title was perhaps used occasionally also of the day before certain other of the greater feasts, e.g. the *Passover. In all four Gospels, the Crucifixion is recorded to have taken place on the Preparation (Mt. 27. 62, Mk. 15. 42, Lk. 23. 54, Jn. 19. 14, 31, 42).

PRESANCTIFIED, Mass of the (Gk. λειτουργία τῶν προηγιασμένων). A shortened form of the Eucharistic Liturgy without consecration, a *Host consecrated at a previous Mass being used for Communion. It is attested as an approved custom for the E. by can. 52 of the *Quinisextum (692), and in the Byzantine Rite it was formerly celebrated on most week-days in *Lent, though now it takes place ordinarily only on the *Wednesdays and *Fridays. In the Latin Church it is restricted to *Good Friday. It first appears in Gaul. It is described in the *Gelasian Sacramentary and was in general use in Rome by the 9th cent. In its present form it is preceded by the

*Adoration of the Cross and the procession of the Blessed Sacrament back from the Altar of *Repose. After the Host has been incensed and elevated, the priest says the pre-Communion prayers, communicates, and performs the usual ablutions. In the Middle Ages all present at the Mass of the Presanctified received Holy Communion. In modern times this has been restricted by RC discipline until recently to the celebrant; but General Communion has now been restored.

The text of the various rites will be found in the standard edd. of the Liturgies. Earlier expositions incl. St. *Theodore Studites, *Explicatio Divinae Liturgiae Praesanctificatorum* (PG, xcix, 1687 f.), and L. *Allatius, *De Missa Praesanctificatorum* (1648). I. Ziadé in *D.T.C.*, xiii (pt. 1; 1936), cols. 77–111. G. *Dix, O.S.B., 'The Christian Passover' in *Laudate*, xiii (1935), pp. 2–18; repr. sep. as *The Mass of the Presanctified*.

PRESBYTER.
The earliest organization of the Christian Churches in Palestine resembled that of the Jewish synagogues, each of which was administered by a board of 'elders' (πρεσβύτεροι, i.e. 'presbyters'). Acts 11. 30 and 15. 22 witness to this collegiate system of Church government at *Jerusalem, and Acts 14. 23 mentions the appointment of Presbyters in the various Churches founded by St. *Paul. At first the Presbyters seem to have been identical with the 'overseers' (ἐπίσκοποι, i.e. 'bishops'), and such passages as Acts 20. 17 f., Phil. 1. 1, and Tit. 1. 5, 7 reveal the terms as interchangeable. But from the 2nd cent. the title of bishop is normally confined to the presidents of these councils of Presbyters, and such 'bishops' came to be distinguished, both in honour and prerogative, from the Presbyters, who were held to derive their authority by delegation from the bishops. The presbyterate, in its developed form, possesses both authority in administration and teaching and the sacerdotal functions foreshadowed by the Jewish priesthood. The English word 'priest' derives ultimately from this root. See also *Bishop*.

For discussion of the office of Presbyter and its relation to that of the Bishop in NT times see works on the early history of the Ministry; some listed above, p. 175, s.v. 'Bishop'. Many theologians now defend the original identity of the two offices. Cf. also J. A. *Robinson in *E.Bi.* iii (1902), cols. 3833–7, s.v.; W. Bauer, *Griechisch-deutsches Wörterbuch zu den Schriften des Neuen Testaments* (ed. 4), col. 1274 f., s.v. 'πρεσβύτερος'.

PRESBYTERIANISM.
Presbyterianism as a form of ecclesiastical polity is essentially government of the Church by presbyters. Its protagonists in the 16th cent. did not regard it as an innovation but as a re-formation after the apostolic model. To-day, however, there are Presbyterians who hold that the NT Church contained episcopal and congregational as well as presbyterian elements, and that Presbyterianism is not *jure divino* the only permissible or valid church polity.

A Presbyterian church is governed by a pyramidal hierarchy of courts,—the *Kirk-session* (consistory) of the particular congregation consisting of the minister and *elders; the *presbytery* (colloquy, *classis*) consisting of

ministers and representative elders of the churches within a prescribed area; *synods* consisting of members of several presbyteries within a larger area; and the final court of appeal, the *General Assembly* consisting of ministers and elders, usually in equal numbers, commissioned by the presbyteries. These courts are representative bodies based ultimately upon popular election.

Divergent views exist as to the relation between the presbyters of the NT and modern elders, some considering the two offices to be identical and others holding that ministers alone are presbyters, the ruling elders being laymen. Some regard *Apostolic Succession through presbyters as an important historical fact, others view it with indifference. Ministers are elected *ad vitam aut culpam* by the people, but their ordination is an act of the presbytery. The standard of education required for the Presbyterian ministry is traditionally high, the minimum curriculum usually including three years in Arts at a university and three years in Theology.

The only Presbyterian State-church is the Church of *Scotland, but it claims and exercises the spiritual independence which is a fundamental principle of all Presbyterians. For most Presbyterians the subordinate standards are those of the Westminster Assembly liberally interpreted, but their supreme rule of faith and life is the Word of God. Their doctrine is traditionally *Calvinistic. Worship is simple, orderly and dignified, but there are High and Low Presbyterian Churchmen, some using a liturgy and others avoiding this set form; all, however, when faithful to the principles and practices of J. *Calvin and J. *Knox, lay emphasis upon the importance of preaching and seek to be true to Apostolic and Catholic usage. The usual Sunday morning canonical service is a truncated Communion service. Holy Communion itself is comparatively infrequently celebrated. Although elders generally assist the minister in the distribution of the elements at the solemn and impressive Communion service it is not, strictly speaking, a sessional act. Discipline is not now exercised so publicly, harshly, and often as formerly; it is largely left in the hands of the minister.

The Alliance of Reformed Churches holding the Presbyterian system, founded in 1875, holds a Council—a Pan-Presbyterian oecumenical assembly without legislative authority—at regular intervals. The membership of the churches here represented now numbers about eleven millions.

See also *Scotland, Christianity in;* and, for the Presbyterian Church of *Wales, *Calvinistic Methodism*.

Useful introd. by J. *Moffatt, *The Presbyterian Church* (1928). J. N. Ogilvie, *The Presbyterian Churches*. Their Place and Power in Modern Christendom (1896; enlarged ed., 1925); G. B. Howard, *The Rise and Progress of Presbyterianism* (1898). J. Macpherson, *Presbyterianism* [1883]. A. Wright, *The Presbyterian Church*. Its Worship, Functions, and Ministerial Orders (1895); W. M. Macphail, *The Presbyterian Church*. A Brief Account of its Doctrine, Worship, and Polity (1908). E. W. Smith, *The Creed of the Presbyterians* (Toronto, 1901). A. H. Drysdale, *History of the Presbyterians in England*. Their Rise, Decline and

Revival (1889). Olive M. Griffiths, *Religion and Learning. A Study in English Presbyterian Thought from the Bartholomew Ejections* [1662] *to the Foundation of the Unitarian Movement* (1935). W. T. Latimer, *A History of the Irish Presbyterians* (Belfast–Edinburgh, [1893]; ed. 2, 1902). C. A. *Briggs, *American Presbyterianism. Its Growth and Early History* (New York, 1885); R. E. Thompson, *A History of the Presbyterian Church in the United States* (American Church History Series, vi, New York, 1895; further information in other vols. in this series, see bibl. to *United States of America*). A. C. Zenos, *Presbyterianism in America. Past, Present and Prospective* (New York, 1937). J. Dall in *H.E.R.E.*, x (1918), pp. 244–70, s.v., with bibl. by J. Herkless, p. 270 f.

PRESBYTERY. (1) The sanctuary or eastern part of the chancel of a church beyond the choir. (2) The residence of (esp.) RC priests. (3) Acc. to current Presbyterian usage, the Church court having oversight and jurisdiction over a certain area, the extent of which is decided by the *General Assembly, and consisting of the ministers and representative elders of the congregations within the bounds. A Presbyterian minister is ordained by it (the ministerial members only joining in the imposition of hands) and is subject to it, and not to his session. It belongs to the Presbytery, not to the court of a particular congregation (*Kirk-session), to see that public worship is in accordance with the law and usage of the Church.

PRESENTATION OF CHRIST IN THE TEMPLE, The. In the BCP an alternative name for the feast of the *Purification of the BVM or *Candlemas (q.v.), kept on 2 Feb.

PRESENTATION OF THE BVM, The (not to be confused with the preceding). In the W. Church, a feast kept on 21 Nov. to commemorate the presentation of the Virgin in the Temple when three years old, as related in the apocryphal 'Book of *James'. The feast was first observed in the E. *c.* the 8th cent., and in the W. gradually established itself in the later Middle Ages. *Sixtus IV received it into the Roman *Breviary, St. *Pius V removed it again, and *Sixtus V made its observance universal in the RC Church in 1585.

M. Zalan, O.S.B., 'Das früheste Vorkommen des Festes Praesentatio B.M.V. im Abendland' in *E.L.*, xli (1927), p. 188 f. Sr. Mary Jerome Kishpaugh, O.P., *The Feast of the Presentation of the Virgin Mary in the Temple* (Catholic University of America, Diss., Washington, D.C., 1941). G. Löw, C.SS.R., in *E.C.*, ix (1952), cols. 1966–8.

PRESTER JOHN (i.e. 'Presbyter' John), legendary medieval Christian king of Asia. The story of an E. *Nestorian priest-king who had defeated the Moslems and would bring help to the Holy Land spread through Europe from the middle of the 12th cent. He is first mentioned in *Otto of Freising's Chronicle and soon afterwards in a letter full of fables, addressed by 'Prester John' to the German Emp. *Frederick I and to the E. Emp. Manual and several other princes. In 1177 Pope *Alexander III wrote a letter, headed 'Indorum Regi, Sacerdotum Sanctissimo' (to the King of the Indies, the most holy priest), which was supposed to be addressed to Prester John. It has been argued, however, that it was meant for

a real historical personage, viz. the King of *Abyssinia, which country was commonly confused with India during the Middle Ages; and this contention gains weight from the fact that in the later Middle Ages Prester John was actually located in Abyssinia. Another theory, based on an account of the 13th cent. *Franciscan missionary, William of Rubruck, identifies him with a Chinese prince, Gor Khan, who defeated the Sultan of Persia in 1141 and founded an empire in which lived a number of Nestorian Christians. The designation 'priest' is held to be due to a confusion of *khan*, 'king', with *kam*, 'priest'. The whole story seems to be a legend of Nestorian origin, but it probably contains a nucleus of historical fact.

Otto of Freising, *Chronicon*, vii, 33. F. Zarnacke, 'Der Priester Johannes' in *Abh.* (Säch.), vii (1879), pp. 827–1030 (with Lat. text of the letter sent to the Emp., pp. 909–24), viii (1883), pp. 1–186. F. Fleuret, 'La Lettre de Prêtre Jean, pseudo-roi d'Abyssinie' in *Mercure de France*, cclxviii (1936), pp. 294–318, with Fr. tr. of the letter, pp. 298–309. E. D. Ross, 'Prester John and the Empire of Ethiopia' in A. P. Newton (ed.), *Travel and Travellers in the Middle Ages* (1926), pp. 174–94, with Eng. tr. of extract of the letter, pp. 174–8. G. Oppert, *Der Presbyter Johann in Sage und Geschichte* (1864). Dr. Bruum, 'Die Verwandlungen des Presbyters Johannes' in *Zeitschrift der Gesellschaft für Erdkunde zu Berlin*, xi (1876), pp. 279–314. C. Marinescu, 'Le Prêtre Jean. Son pays, explication de son nom' in *Académie roumaine.* Bulletin de la Section historique, x (1923), pp. 73–112; id., 'Encore une fois le problème du Prêtre Jean', ib., xxvi (1945), pp. 202–22. L. Olschki, 'Der Brief des Presbyters Johannes' in *Historische Zeitschrift*, cxliv (1931), pp. 1–14. R. Hennig, 'Das Christentum im mittelalterlichen Asien und sein Einfluss auf die Sage vom "Priester Johannes"' in *Historische Vierteljahrschrift*, xxix (1935), pp. 234–52. C. E. Nowell, 'The Historical Prester John' in *Speculum*, xxviii (1953), pp. 435–55.

PREVENIENT GRACE. The species of Actual *Grace which, as an illumination or inspiration of the Holy Spirit, precedes the free determination of the will. It is held to mark the beginning of all activity leading to *justification, which cannot be achieved without it, but its acceptance or rejection depends on man's free choice. Belief in the existence of Prevenient Grace claims Scriptural support in such texts as Ps. 59. 10 (Vulg.), Rom. 8. 30, and 2 Tim. 1. 9. It was defended by St. *Augustine (who often uses the technical term, 'gratia praeveniens') against the *Pelagians, taught by St. *Thomas Aquinas, formally defined by the Council of *Trent, and asserted in the Anglican Article X.

PRICE, RICHARD (1723–91), Nonconformist minister, moral and political philosopher. In 1758 he published *A Review of the Principal Questions in Morals* (ed. 3, 1787), in which he defended a view of ethical action which had many affinities with the teaching later expounded by I. *Kant. He held that the rightness and wrongness of an action belonged to it intrinsically and criticized the 'moral sense' view of ethics which had secured popularity through such writers as Lord *Shaftesbury (d. 1713) and F. Hutcheson (d. 1746). In the fields of politics and economics he advocated the reduction of the National Debt, and strongly supported the cause of American Independence. Though holding opposite views on morals and meta-physics, he became an intimate friend of J. *Priestley. By 1778 both were '*Unitarians', and in 1791 Price became an original member of the Unitarian Society.

Modern ed. of Price's *Review of the Principal Questions in Morals* by D. D. Raphael (Oxford, 1948 [based on ed. 3 of 1787, but repr. preface from ed. 1.]) A list of his works is appended to the sermon preached by J. Priestley on the occasion of his death (London, 1791), pp. 41–5. The principal authority is the Memoir by his nephew, William Morgan (London, 1815). Modern life by R. Thomas (ib., 1924), with detailed list of his works, pp. 173–7, and other bibl. C. B. Cone, *The Torchbearer of Freedom.* The Influence of Richard Price on Eighteenth Century Thought (Kentucky University Press, Lexington, 1952). T. Fowler in *D.N.B.*, xlvi (1896), pp. 334–7. See also bibl. to *Unitarians.*

PRICKET. A stand containing one or more upright spikes on which to fix votive candles.

PRIDE. The first of the seven capital sins, being the inordinate love of one's own excel-lence. It is traditionally believed to have been the sin of the angels and the first man, and is denounced as a vice particularly repugnant to God throughout the OT and NT (e.g. Prov. 16. 18; 1 Pet. 5. 5).

PRIDEAUX, HUMPHREY (1648–1724), Dean of *Norwich from 1702. He was educated at Westminster and at Christ Church, Oxford, where he came under the influence of J. *Fell, and from 1677 onwards held a succession of benefices. As a Low Churchman he welcomed the Revolution of 1688, and supported the pro-posed changes in the BCP with a view to the inclusion of dissenters. His fame rested on two treatises, his *Life of Mahomet* (1697), really a polemical tract against the *Deists, and *The Old and New Testaments connected in the History of the Jews* (2 vols., 1716–18), an ac-count of the history of the Jewish people in the last centuries before the Christian era. He also issued *The Validity of the Orders of the C of E* (1688) and several other pamphlets.

Anon. Life (London, 1748, prob. by T. Birch), from in-formation supplied by his son. *Bibliotheca Cornubiensis*, ii (1878), pp. 527–33. His letters to John Ellis, Under-Secretary of State, 1674–1722, ed. by E. M. Thompson, (Camden Society, N.S., xv, 1875). A. Gordon in *D.N.B.*, xlvi (1896), pp. 354–6.

PRIE-DIEU (Fr., 'pray God'). A small prayer-desk for private use, usually constructed with a sloping ledge and sometimes also a shelf for books. The name appears to date from the early 17th cent.

PRIERIAS, SYLVESTER (1456–1523), Sylvester Mazzolini, opponent of M. *Luther. A native of Priero in Piedmont, he entered the *Dominican Order, taught at *Bologna and *Venice, and from 1508 to 1510 was Vicar General of the province of Lombardy. After being Prior of Cremona, *Leo X appointed him in 1514 to the Dominican chair of theology at the Gymnasium Romanum. His *Summa Summarum quae Silvestrina dicitur* (1515), an alphabetically arranged compendium of moral

theology which won great popularity through its convenience despite its slight intrinsic theo-logical merit, brought his name into promin-ence and in 1515 Leo made him 'Sacri Palatii Magister'. Here he acted as *Inquisitor. He took an active part in condemning J. *Reuchlin and in 1517 entered the lists against M. Luther with his *Dialogus de Potestate Papae.* Some brief and hastily compiled writings against the Reformer were followed in 1519 by a more elaborate *Errata et Argumenta M. Luteris* [sic] *recitata, detecta, repulsa, et copiossime trita* (1520). It is generally agreed that the Papal case suffered in its early stages through not being in more competent hands. He also wrote a commentary on the 'Summa', *Con-flatum ex S. Thoma,* of which that on Part I only was printed (1519).

There is a brief Lat. diss. devoted to his life and works by F. Michalski (Münster i.W., 1892), with detailed list of his Lat. writings, pp. 21–34. F. Lauchert, *Die italienischen literarischen Gegner Luthers* (Erläuterungen und Ergän-zungen zu Janssens Geschichte des deutschen Volkes ed. L. von *Pastor, viii; 1912), pp. 7–30. Quétif–Échard, ii, 55–8. M. M. Gorce, O.P., in *D.T.C.*, x (pt. 1; 1928), cols. 474–7, s.v. 'Mazolini'.

PRIEST. The term 'priest' is etymologically a contraction of '*presbyter' (Gk. πρεσβύτερος 'elder'), but while the AV and RV of the NT regularly render 'πρεσβύτερος' by 'elder', they keep 'priest' and 'priesthood' for the purely sacerdotal terms ἱερεύς and ἱεράτευμα (Lat. *sacerdos* and *sacerdotium*). The latter words are never used in the NT specifically of Christian ministers, though they are applied to the Christian body as a whole (1 Pet. 2. 5 and 9; Rev. 5. 10). By the close of the Old English period the English term priest had become the current word alike for 'presbyter' and 'sacerdos' and so an ambiguous term. The idea and institution of priesthood is found in almost all the great religions, usually connected with the conception of *sacrifice. In some cases the duties attach to the father of the family or the ruler of the tribe or nation, but in most religions a separate order developed.

In the OT it appears that before the age of *Moses the priesthood was patriarchal. The father sacrificed for the family (*Noah, Gen. 8. 20; *Abraham, Gen. 22. 13), the sheik for his tribe (Jethro; Ex. 2. 16) and the prince for his people (*Melchizedek, Gen. 14. 18). Acc. to an early tradition, Moses himself was a priest. At the same time it appears that there was a separate class of priests (Ex. 19. 22), but it was not they whom Moses employed to offer sacrifice, but 'young men' and himself (cf. Ex. 24. 4–8). Later a more formal priesthood seems to have been established. On Mt. Sinai Moses was ordered to consecrate *Aaron and his three sons 'to minister in the priest's office' (Ex. 28. 1). In Ex. 32. 26–9 the tribe of Levi was chosen to be consecrated to the Lord; eventu-ally the *Levites were given charge of the services of the Tabernacle, and only the sons of Aaron were to exercise the functions of the priesthood (Num. *passim*). All subsequent priests were believed to be descendants of Aaron, though various legal fictions mitigated this rule. As the holiness of Israel centred on the Sanctuary, the importance of the priesthood, and esp. of the *High Priest (q.v.), increased with the enhanced place of the Temple in later Judaism. His position, exemplified in the Priestly Code of the Pentateuch, as mediator between God and man, came to be the predominant idea in the Jewish priesthood in the time of Christ.

In the NT all the pre-Christian ideas of priesthood were raised to a new level in the Christian revelation. The idea of Christ as the culmination of the High Priesthood finds clear expression in Heb. 5, where He is described as 'called of God an high priest after the order of Melchisedek' (Heb. 5. 10). The Jewish priesthood is seen as the type of His priesthood, as the Jewish sacrifice was of His Sacrifice. By His Sacrifice as Priest He reconciles God to men, fulfilling what had been foreshadowed by the Jewish sacrifices of the blood of sheep and goats. His own realization of His priesthood is summed up in the 'High Priestly Prayer' in Jn. 17. But though he was in the Sacrifice the Priest, he was also the Victim, the 'Lamb slain from the foundation of the World' (Rev. 13. 8); consequently, while He remains 'our Great High Priest', yet for the continuation of the offering of the Sacrifice, a Christian priesthood was established in the Church. For although in one sense His priesthood is all-sufficient and through Him we have 'access by the one Spirit to the Father' (Eph. 2. 18), and the whole Church is through baptism conceived as sharing in the priesthood, a Christian priesthood was held to be implied in His teaching and, esp. in relation to the Eucharist, came to be regarded as an integral element in the Church.

The idea of priesthood as belonging to the Christian ministry was, however, a gradual development. Apart from a doubtful reference in St. *Ignatius (Phil., 9), the term 'priest' does not appear to have been applied to Christian ministers until the end of the 2nd cent. The 'presbyters' of the NT were not commonly called 'sacerdotes' until the time of St. *Cyprian (Ep. 61). At first the use of the term was commonly confined to Bishops. It appears in St. Cyprian that, while priests shared in the episcopal *sacerdotium*, could offer the Sacrifice of the Eucharist, and by the imposition of hands receive a penitent *lapsus*, these functions were to be exercised only in the absence of the Bishop and seem to have been regarded as delegated by him. With the spread of Christianity in the country and the establishment of parish churches, the presbyters adopted more fully the priestly functions of the Bishop. A letter of *Innocent I to Decentius (A.D. 416) explains that in towns the Eucharist is to be consecrated by the Bishop only and sent to parish priests, but in the outlying churches the priests are to consecrate themselves. When the priest thus independently obtained power to consecrate in the Eucharist and administer most other Sacraments, the way was opened for the fullest

medieval doctrine of the priesthood. This was most fully developed in connexion with the power conferred in *Ordination, esp. when, in the 11th cent., the custom spread of ordaining priests who had no benefice. As the parish priest came to be the normal Celebrant of the Eucharist and customarily to exercise the power of absolution, esp. with the development of eucharistic theology and the obligation of confession (1215), increasingly he came to be regarded as the representative of God to the people rather than the converse. His supernatural powers and functions were emphasized, so that during the Middle Ages, vis-à-vis the laity, a priest acquired a position outside that of the feudal hierarchy. He remained, however, entirely subordinate to his bishop, who retained his superiority in such matters as Ordination and *Confirmation and his canonical jurisdiction, though there remained some doubt as to whether his office was of a different order from that of the priesthood. The validity of the position of a priest always depended upon his ordination.

The tendency of medieval theology to see the priesthood of the clergy almost exclusively in relation to the Mass led to its rejection by the Reformers. The term priest was retained in the BCP apparently in order to make it clear that deacons were not to celebrate the Holy Communion. In general parlance, except in the N. of England, the term 'clergyman' was more frequently used in the C of E to avoid the implications of that of priest. With the revival of Catholic views, however, the term priest has again come into common use. This revival of the term outside the RC Church prob. also reflects a more comprehensive view of the priesthood, which is seen in relation to the whole Church and in so far ministerial rather than dominating, and a fresh recognition of its relation to the priesthood of Christ.

E. O. James, The Nature and Function of Priesthood. A Comparative and Anthropological Study (1955). E. Landtman, The Origin of Priesthood (University of Finland thesis; Ekenaes, 1905).
On priesthood in the OT, W. W. G. Baudissin, Die Geschichte des alttestamentlichen Priesterthums untersucht (1889). E. *Schürer, Geschichte des jüdischen Volkes im Zeitalter Jesu Christi, ii (ed. 4, 1907), pp. 267–363. R. H. *Kennett, Old Testament Essays (1928), pp. 59–90 ('The Jewish Priesthood'). A. C. Welch, Prophet and Priest in Old Israel (1936); J. Hoschander, The Priests and Prophets (posthumously publd., New York, 1938). W. Baudissin in H.D.B., iv (1902), pp. 67–97, s.v. 'Priests and Levites'; J. Köberle in P.R.E. (ed. 3), xvi (1906), pp. 32–47, s.v. 'Priestertum im AT'.
For the origins of the Christian Priesthood, see bibl. to artt. Orders and Ordination and to Bishop, par. 2. Cf. also H. S. Box (ed.), Priesthood (1937). E. *Hatch in D.C.A., ii (1880), pp. 1698–1708, s.v. 'Priest or Presbyter'; L. Kösters, S.J., in L.Th.K., viii (1936), cols. 462–71, s.v. 'Priester'; A. Michel in D.T.C., xiii (pt. 1; 1936), cols. 138–61, s.v. 'Prêtre'; G. Schrenk in T.W.B., iii (1938), cols. 257–84, s.v. 'ἱερεύς'; N. Turchi–A. Romeo in E.C., x (1953), cols. 1532–40, s.v. 'Sacerdozio'. On the conception of priesthood in non-Christian religions, E. Landtman–T. G. Pinches–A. S. Geden–H. J. T. Johnson–A. M. Blackman–W. J. Woodhouse–H. P. Smith–A. B. Keith–E. Edwards–H. Hirschfeld–L. Spence–D. S. Margoliouth–G. J. Laing–U. Holmberg in H.E.R.E., x (1918), pp. 278–336, s.v.

PRIEST, High. See High Priest.

'PRIEST IN ABSOLUTION', The (1866; 1870). A privately printed manual for the use of Anglican confessors, compiled by Rev. J. C. *Chambers (q.v.). The second part, dealing with certain sins which necessarily called for treatment in a technical manual, was sold only to *bona fide* confessors. On Chambers' death (1874), to prevent misuse of the work, the remaining stock and copyright were bought by the Society of the Holy Cross. The work created a storm of protest against the *High Church Movement when, on 14 June 1877, Lord Redesdale, into whose possession by some inadvertence a copy had come, drew attention to its contents in the House of Lords. The attack, in which A. C. *Tait, Abp. of Canterbury, took part, caused for a short time much annoyance to High Churchmen, but it passed without leaving any permanent mark and with Chambers' high character unstained.

R. T. *Davidson–W. Benham, *Life of Archibald Campbell Tait* (1891), ii, 171–84. W. Walsh, *The Secret History of the Oxford Movement* (1897), pp. 93–146 (hostile); J. Embry, *The Catholic Movement and the S.S.C.* (1931), pp. 97–127.

PRIESTLEY, JOSEPH (1733–1804), *Presbyterian minister and scientist. A native of Fieldhead, Yorks, he entered Daventry Academy to train for the *Presbyterian ministry in 1751. In 1755 he became minister at Needham Market, Suffolk, and in 1758 at Nantwich, where he opened a school. His religious beliefs became increasingly unorthodox. He came to hold *Arian views on the Person of Christ, and rejected the doctrine of the *Atonement and the Inspiration of the Bible. In 1761 he became tutor of languages at the newly founded Academy at Warrington, and in 1767 was appointed minister of Mill Hill Chapel, Leeds, where he embraced *Socinianism. Here he brought out the *Theological Repository*, a critical periodical that appeared irregularly and aroused much hostility, favoured the autonomy of the individual congregation and an increase in the number of sects, and complete toleration for RCs; and he attacked the idea of a national Church. In 1772 a librarianship to Lord Shelburne gave him sufficient leisure to pursue his scientific studies which had already gained him a reputation. During this period he published his *Institutes of Natural and Revealed Religion* (3 vols., 1772–4), *Disquisitions relating to Matter and Spirit* (1777), and *A Harmony of the Evangelists* (also 1777). In 1780 he gave up his post with Lord Shelburne and settled at Birmingham, where he became junior minister of the New Meeting Society. In 1782 he published his widely read *History of the Corruptions of Christianity*. He denied the impeccability and infallibility of our Lord, views which he finally elaborated in his *History of Early Opinions concerning Jesus Christ* (1786). The book provoked a violent controversy, his chief orthodox critic being S. *Horsley. In 1791 he became one of the founders of the *Unitarian Society, and in the same year defended the French Revolution in his *Letters to Burke*. The hostility aroused

was such that he had to escape to London, where he became morning preacher at Gravel Pit Chapel, Hackney. In 1794 he went to America, spending the remaining years of his life at Northumberland, Pennsylvania. During this period he adopted the doctrine of universal restitution and of moral progress in life after death. Despite his unorthodoxy on other points he was a firm believer in the mission of Moses and the Messiahship of our Lord. In the realm of science he is known chiefly for his 'discovery' of oxygen in 1774 and for his great work on *Experiments and Observations on Different Kinds of Air* (1774–86).

Theological and Miscellaneous Works, ed. J. T. Rutt (25 vols., London [1817–31]). *Memoirs of Dr. Joseph Priestley, to the Year 1795, written by himself, with a Continuation . . . by his son, J. Priestley* (London, 1806). Modern lives by T. E. Thorpe ('English Men of Science', 1906) and Anne Holt (London, 1931). A. Gordon–P. J. Hartog in *D.N.B.*, xlvi (1896), pp. 357–76.

PRIMASIUS (6th cent.), Bp. of Hadrumetum in N. Africa. His commentary on Rev., which drew extensively on *Tyconius and *Augustine, is of great value for the light it throws on the history of the *Old Latin Version of the NT. A commentary on St. *Paul's Epp. is also attributed to him; but this really belongs to the school of *Cassiodorus. In the *Three Chapters Controversy he was a strong supporter of Pope *Vigilius.

Comm. on Rev. ed. Cologne, 1535; Paris, 1544; Basle, 1544 (all purporting to be *editiones principes*). Works in J. P. Migne, *PL*, lxviii, 407–936. J. Haussleiter, *Leben und Werke des Bischofs Primasius von Hadrumetum* (1887); id., *Die lateinische Apokalypse der alten afrikanischen Kirche* (in T. *Zahn, *Forschungen zur Gesch. des NT Kanons*, iv, 1891, pp. 1–224); id. in *P.R.E.* (ed. 3), xvi (1905), pp. 55–7. H. J. Vogels, *Untersuchungen zur Geschichte der lateinischen Apokalypse-Übersetzung* (1920), pp. 19–36 and 153–64. É. Amann in *D.T.C.*, xiii (pt. 1; 1936), cols. 245–7.

PRIMATE. The title of the bishop of the 'first see' (*prima sedes*), used originally of the *metropolitan of a province, then for a time equated with the *patriarch, and later applied to the chief bishop of a single state or people. The Abp. of *Canterbury is 'Primate of All England', the Abp. of *York 'Primate of England'.

PRIME. The *Office appointed for the first hour, i.e. 6 a.m. Acc. to *Cassian, it was introduced as 'altera matutina' ('Second Mattins') in his monastery at *Bethlehem *c.* 395, and under its name of 'Prima' appears as the first of the Little Hours (see *Terce*) in the Rule of St. *Benedict. At first recited in the dormitory, it was later transferred to the choir and thence passed into the Office of the secular clergy. In its present form it consists of two parts. The first, after the usual opening and the hymn 'Iam lucis orto sidere', contains three Psalms with antiphon to which is added a fourth on certain stated days; and on *Trinity and some other Sundays the 'Quicunque Vult' (see *Athanasian Creed*) is recited as well. The Psalms are followed by a (little) *chapter with 'responsorium breve', the Sunday or ferial prayers, and a concluding prayer. The second part is the originally independent Chapter Office. It begins with the reading of the *Martyrology (if recited in choir) and is followed by several prayers, versicles, and the variable 'lectio brevis', and ends with a benediction.

J. Pargoire, 'Prime et complies' in *Revue d'Histoire et de Littérature religieuses*, iii (1898), pp. 281–8 and 456–67. N. Gihr, *Prim und Komplet des römischen Breviers, liturgisch und aszetisch erklärt* (Theologische Bibliothek, 1907). J. Froger, O.S.B., *Les Origines de prime* (Bibliotheca 'Ephemerides Liturgicae', xix, 1946); crit. reviews by L. Brou in *J.T.S.*, xlviii (1947), p. 240 f., and by E. Cattaneo in *E.L.*, lxi (1947), pp. 366–9. J. M. Hanssens, S.J., *Nature et genèse de l'office des matines* (Analecta Gregoriana, lvii; 1952), passim.

PRIMER, The. See *Prymer, The.*

PRIMICERIUS. The word, derived from 'primus in cera', i.e. 'the first on the waxed table' of names, was applied to the senior in rank of several classes of officials, both ecclesiastical and secular. In the Rule of St. *Chrodegang he was the cleric next below the archdeacon and archpresbyter and charged with the liturgical functions and music of the monastery.

PRIMITIVE METHODIST CHURCH. One of the three *Methodist Churches which united in 1932. It came into being in 1811 in connexion with, but for the most part outside, the *Wesleyan Methodist Church.

The new community developed out of some earlier unofficial Methodist movements. Hugh Bourne, a Methodist, had begun *c.* 1800 an important evangelistic movement near Mow Cop, Staffs, but outside the official structure of Methodism. Another contributory element was the work of Lorenzo Dow, an American Methodist, who in 1807 introduced the Camp Meeting into English Methodism at Mow Cop. This form of meeting, held for a whole day in the open and designed for those not attracted by the ordinary work of the Church, was pronounced by the Wesleyan Conference to be 'highly improper and likely to be of considerable mischief'. When these Camp Meetings were continued, Hugh Bourne, who was now mainly responsible for them, was expelled and in 1810 there came into being as a distinct community the 'Camp Meeting Methodists'. In the same year William Clowes, who had carried Bourne's earlier evangelistic work to Tunstall, was also expelled from the Methodist Church. In 1811 the two bodies united under the name of the Primitive Methodists.

At first the policy of the new society was to cease mission work and consolidate itself; but soon they gave themselves to systematic and widespread evangelism. For several years they met with great success, in spite of persecution, but rapid growth and lack of discipline brought a serious decline in 1825–8. Bourne was able, however, to replace the original organization, whereby administration was carried out chiefly by District Meetings and each district was to a great extent autonomous, by a centralization of authority. In 1843 the Primitive Methodists founded missions in *Australia and *New Zealand; and in 1889 work was begun in Africa also.

Notable features of the Church were its connexion with the Society of *Friends and its use of women as preachers, esp. in its earlier years. In 1932 the Primitive Methodist Church united with the *Wesleyan and *United Methodists to form the present *Methodist Church.

H. B. Kendall, *The Origin and History of the Primitive Methodist Church* (2 vols., [1905]). J. Petty, *The History of the Primitive Methodist Connexion from its Origin to the Conference of 1859* (1860). J. Ritson, *The Romance of Primitive Methodism* (1910). H. Bourne, *History of the Primitive Methodists, Giving an Account of their Rise and Progress to the Year 1823* (1823); J. Watford, ed. W. Antliff, *Memoirs of the Life and Labours of the late Venerable Hugh Bourne* (2 vols., 1855–6). H. B. Kendall, 'The Primitive Methodist Church and the Independent Methodist Churches, 1796–1908' in W. J. Townsend–H. B. Workman–G. Eayrs (edd.), *A New History of Methodism*, i (1919), pp. 555–98. *The Christian Endeavour* (20 vols., 1858–78); cont. as *The Primitive Methodist Quarterly Review* (31 vols., 1879–1909); cont. as *The Holborn Review* (23 vols., 1910–32); in 1932, *The Holborn Review* was amalgamated with *The London Quarterly* to form *The London Quarterly and Holborn Review* (1932 ff.). *Primitive Methodist Year Book* (ceased 1932).

PRIMUS. In the Scottish Episcopal Church, the title of the presiding bishop. The first mention of the office is in 1731 in the 'Articles of Agreement amongst the Bishops of the Church of Scotland'. The principal function of the Primus, who has no metropolitical power, is to convene and preside at meetings of the Episcopal Synod. He is elected by the College of Bishops and the office is attached to no fixed see and not necessarily given by seniority. His title is 'The Most Revd. the Lord Bishop of X, Primus of the Scottish Church'.

PRIOR. The head or deputy head of a monastery. During the early Middle Ages the word was used in a very vague sense and might be applied to various secular officials. Under *Benedictine influence it came to denote the monk who ranked next to the abbot and deputized for him, a post which was sometimes multiplied. Later it was also applied to the heads of houses in the mendicant orders and of the small houses dependent on an abbey. See also *Priory.*

PRIORESS. The head or deputy head of certain houses of nuns. In general the Prioress fulfils the same functions for her house as a *Prior in the corresponding male order. In the case of an abbey she is subject to the *Abbess and the second in command. In the Roman Church the title is confined, strictly speaking, to convents which have Papal approbation and whose members take solemn vows, but it is sometimes used more generally. See also *Priory.*

PRIORY. A religious house presided over by a *prior or *prioress. In certain orders of the Roman Church, esp. those following the Rule of St. *Augustine, the Priory is the normal unit. The Benedictine and allied orders distinguish between 'conventual priories' (self-governing houses) and 'obedientary priories', which are dependencies of abbeys.

PRISCA. The name given to an early Latin version of the canons of certain Greek Councils, viz. those of *Nicaea, *Ancyra, *Neocaesarea, *Gangra, *Antioch, *Chalcedon, and *Constantinople. The translation was made in Italy in the late 5th cent. The two chief MSS. are the 'Chieti MS.' (Vat. Reg. 1997; 9th cent.) and the 'Justel MS.' (Bod. e Mus. 100–2; 6th–7th cents.). The |title 'Prisca', found in the *Ballerini, is taken from a (perhaps misunderstood) reference in *Dionysius Exiguus (*confusione priscae translationis offensus*).

F. *Maassen, *Geschichte der Quellen und der Literatur des canonischen Rechts im Abendlande*, i (1870), pp. 87–100. C. H. *Turner, 'Chapters in the History of Latin MSS. of Canons, 5 and 6' in *J.T.S.*, xxx (1928–9), pp. 337–46, and xxxi (1929–30), pp. 9–20.

PRISCA, St. See *Priscilla, St.*

PRISCILLA, St., also 'Prisca' (1st cent.), an early Christian convert, the wife of Aquila, a Jew of Pontus and (like St. *Paul) a tentmaker. She is mentioned six times in the NT (Acts 18. 2, 18. 18, and 18. 26; Rom. 16. 3; 1 Cor. 16. 19; 2 Tim. 4. 19); in the Pauline Epp., the better attested form in all cases is 'Prisca'. Both she and Aquila, who are found in the NT at *Rome, *Ephesus, and *Corinth, were clearly prominent members in the primitive Church. They were both compelled to leave Rome by the Emp. Claudius's decree (Acts 18. 2), but, unless Rom. 16 is a fragment of an epistle sent by St. Paul to Ephesus, returned later (Rom. 16. 3). The suggestion of A. *Harnack that she and her husband were the authors of the Ep. to the Hebrews has met with little favour. Feast day, 8 July.

In later Roman tradition, a saint with one or other of her names is prominent in two connexions:

(1) Since the 4th cent. a church has existed on the Aventine Hill known as the *titulus S. Priscae*. Acc. to the (late) *Acta S. Priscae*, this church enshrined the remains of the martyr St. Prisca, whose relics had been translated hither from the *Ostian Way. This St. Prisca, who was well known to the medieval hagiographers, is sometimes represented in art between two lions, who are reputed to have refused to attack her. Feast day, 18 Jan.

(2) The 'Coemeterium Priscillae' on the *Via Salaria* was one of the oldest of the *catacombs. It prob. takes its name from a Priscilla quite unconnected with the saint of the *titulus S. Priscae* and perh. a member of the senatorial family of the 'Acilii Glabrones'. It was in this catacomb that J. Wilpert discovered the well-known painting, 'Fractio Panis'. On the site Pope *Silvester built a basilica in which he was himself buried.

There are no sufficient reasons for identifying either of these with the Priscilla of the NT.

A. *Harnack, 'Ueber die beiden Recenzionen der Geschichte der Prisca und des Aquila in Act. Apost; 18. 1–27' in *Sb.* (Berl.), 1900, pp. 2–13. A. C. *Headlam in *H.D.B.*, iv (1902), p. 102 f.; J. E. Roberts in *D.A.C.*, i (1915), p. 87 f. On (1), J. P. Kirsch, *Die römischen Titelkirchen im Altertum* (Studien zur Geschichte und Kultur des Altertums, ix, 1–2; 1918), pp. 101–4, 162 f. H. *Leclercq, O.S.B., in *D.A.C.L.*, xiv (pt. 2; 1948), cols. 1876–87, s.v. 'Prisque (Sainte)'. On (2), see works cited s.v. *Catacombs*. J. Wilpert, *Fractio Panis*. La plus ancienne représentation du sacrifice eucharistique à la Capella Greca découverte et expliquée (1896). H. Leclercq, O.S.B., loc. cit., cols. 1799–1874, s.v. 'Priscille (Cimetière de)', with bibl. E. Josi in *E.C.*, x (1953), cols. 36–40, s.v. 'Priscilla, Cimitero di', with full bibl.

PRISCILLIANISM. The origins of this 4th-5th cent. heresy are obscure. Acc. to the historian *Sulpicius Severus, Priscillian (*c.* 370) was a layman who took up a kind of *Gnosticism introduced into Spain by an Egyptian named Marcus. As a person of education famous for his austerity, he soon found adherents, among them two bishops, Instantius and Salvianus, and a large number of women. In 380 the doctrines attributed to him (though Priscillian was not mentioned by name) were condemned at Saragossa. The canons of this synod forbade mixed gatherings for the reading and interpretation of Scriptures, fasting on Sundays, absence from church during *Lent, and similar unusual practices. Despite this condemnation Priscillian became Bp. of Ávila soon afterwards. In 381 his opponents obtained a decree of exile against him and his followers, who were now described as '*Manicheans'. The exiles went to the S. of France and thence to Rome, where they sought Pope *Damasus' support but failed to obtain a hearing. At Milan they met with a similar rebuff from St. *Ambrose. They succeeded, however, in getting the decree of exile annulled by the secular authorities and returned to Spain, where they won a large following.

Not long after this, Emp. Maximus, seeking the support of the Catholic bishops, had Priscillian tried by a synod at Bordeaux. Priscillian, however, refused to recognize its authority and made his way to Trier to appeal to the Emperor himself (385). Despite the pleadings of St. *Martin of Tours, he and several of his followers were condemned to death on the charge of magic. It was the first instance of capital punishment for heresy in the history of the Church and they were at once venerated as martyrs. The sect flourished esp. after the fall of Maximus in 388, when the province of Galicia became almost entirely Priscillianist. In 400 a Council at *Toledo decreed the deposition of those Priscillianist bishops who would not abandon the heresy and the confirmation in office of those who submitted. The heresy, however, continued throughout the 5th and the first half of the 6th cents. and did not disappear until after its condemnation by the Council of Braga in 563.

Priscillianism, in its fully developed form, seems to have been a kind of Manichean

Dualism with strong *Docetic and *Sabellian elements. It taught a *Modalist doctrine of the Trinity and denied the pre-existence of Christ before His birth from the BVM as well as His real Humanity; hence their fasting on *Christmas Day and on Sunday. Angels and human souls were emanations of the Godhead and souls were united to bodies in punishment of their sins. The devil was not a fallen angel, but the principle of evil, and the body was his creation. Hence marriage, the procreation of children, and the use of flesh-meat were condemned, while, on the other hand, free love was permitted. Though the Priscillianists tried to prove their doctrines from the Bible, they, like their founder, had a marked preference for the apocryphal books.

Eleven treatises found in a MS. at Würzburg under the name of Priscillian ed. G. Schepps, *Priscilliani Quae Supersunt* (C.S.E.L., xviii; 1889). Their authenticity has been challenged by A. *Hilgenfeld, 'Priscillianus und seine neuentdeckten Schriften' in *Zeitschrift für wissenschaftliche Theologie*, xxxv (1892), pp. 1–85; G. *Morin, O.S.B., 'Pro Instantio, contre l'attribution à Priscillien des opuscules du manuscrit de Würzburg' in *R. Bén.*, xxx (1913), pp. 153–73; and M. Hartberger, 'Instantius oder Priscillian' in *T.Q.*, xcv (1913), pp. 401–40; it has been defended by J. Martin, 'Priscillianus oder Instantius' in *Hist. J.*, xlvii (1927), pp. 237–51. D. de Bruyne, O.S.B., 'Fragments retrouvés d'apocryphes priscillianistes' in *R. Bén.*, xxiv (1907), pp. 318–35, with text; G. Morin, O.S.B., 'Un Traité priscillianiste inédit sur la Trinité', ib., xxvi (1909), pp. 255–80, repr., with text, in his *Études, Textes, Découvertes*, i (Anecdota Maredsolana, Ser. Sec., 1913), pp. 151–205. D. de Bruyne, O.S.B., La *Regula Consensoria*, une règle des moines priscillianistes' in *R. Bén.*, xxv (1908), pp. 83–8. F. Paret, *Priscillianus*. Ein Reformator des vierten Jahrhunderts (1891). J. Dierich, *Die Quellen zur Geschichte Priscillians* (Inaugural diss., Breslau, 1897). K. Künstle, *Antipriscilliana*. Dogmengeschichtliche Untersuchungen und Texte aus dem Streite gegen Priscillians Irrlehre (1905). E. C. Babut, *Priscillien et le priscillianisme* (Bibliothèque de l'École des Hautes Études. Sciences Historiques et Philologiques, clxix; 1909). A. Puech, 'Les Origines du priscillianisme et l'orthodoxie de Priscillien' in *Bulletin d'ancienne Littérature et d'Archéologie chrétiennes*, ii (1912), pp. 81–95 and 161–213. J. A. Davids, *De Orosio et Sancto Augustino Priscillianistarum Adversariis*. Commentatio Historica et Philologica (Diss., The Hague, 1930). A. d'Alès, S.J., 'Priscillien' in *Rech. S.R.*, xxiii (1933), pp. 5–44 and 129–75. Id., *Priscillien et l'Espagne chrétienne à la fin du IVe siècle* (1936). J.*Chapman, O.S.B., *Notes on the Early History of the Vulgate Gospels* (1908), pp. 238–70, ch. 13, 'Priscillian the Author of the Prologues'. Bardenhewer, iii, 403–13; Altaner (ed. 1950), p. 326. G. Bardy in *D.T.C.*, xii (pt. 1; 1936), cols. 391–400, s.v. 'Priscillien'.

PRIVATE CHAPELS ACT.

This Act of 1871 (34 & 35 Vict., c. 66), which regulates the status of C of E chapels in schools, hospitals and similar institutions, permits the Bishop of the diocese in which the chapel is situate to license a cleric to serve such chapels, with the right of administering the Lord's Supper. Such a cleric is not subject to interference from the incumbent of the parish, provided that the entire cure of souls, except of those within the institution, is safeguarded to the incumbent. All alms collected in such a chapel can be disposed of as the minister shall determine, subject to the *ordinary's direction.

PRIVILEGED ALTAR.

Acc. to RC canon law (*CIC*, cans. 916–18) an altar at which a *plenary indulgence may be secured for a soul in purgatory by the celebration and application

of a Mass. Ordinaries may appoint one such altar (to be indicated by the legend *altare privilegiatum*) in cathedral, conventual and parish churches. During the *Forty Hours' Devotion and on *All Souls' Day all the altars in a church are accounted privileged.

PRIVILEGED PRESSES, The.

The Oxford and Cambridge University Presses, so called in respect of their right, shared only with the King's (Queen's) Printer, of printing the Book of Common Prayer and, in England, the Authorized Version of the Bible, which are perpetual Crown copyright. The King's Printer holds this right by his Letters Patent of appointment, while the University Presses derive it from their respective Charters. That granted to Cambridge in 1534 conferred the right to print 'all manner of books' (*omnimodos libros*), and this was held to be unimpaired by the monopoly otherwise granted to the Stationers' Company in 1587, and was confirmed in 1628. A similar Charter was granted to Oxford in 1634. As a result, the Authorized Version, printed at first only by the then King's Printer, Robert Barker, was printed, with considerably improved accuracy, at Cambridge in 1629; at Oxford the same rights of printing Bibles and certain other books were claimed, but, by a 'covenant of forbearance' made with the members of the Stationers' Company (including the King's Printer), remained unexercised until 1675. Before 1839 the King's Printer for Scotland held similar exclusive rights in his territory; but an Order in Council of that year empowered the Lord Advocate to license any printer to produce an edition of the AV upon certain conditions.

PRIVY COUNCIL, Judicial Committee of the.

See *Judicial Committee of the Privy Council*.

PROBABILIORISM.

The system of moral theology based on the principle that, if the licitness or illicitness of an action is in doubt, it is lawful to follow the opinion favouring liberty only when it is more probable than the opinion favouring the law. The system was developed by opponents of *Probabilism (q.v.), adopted by the *Dominican Order in 1656, and favoured by several Popes, esp. *Innocent XI. Though paramount in the first half of the 18th cent., it is to-day abandoned by most moral theologians. Chief among the objections to it is its impracticability, as the decision on the relative degrees of probability demanded by it requires more time and skill than is normally at the command of the confessor and his penitent.

PROBABILISM.

The system of *moral theology based on the principle that, if the licitness or illicitness of an action is in doubt, it is lawful to follow a solidly probable opinion favouring liberty, even though the opposing opinion, favouring the law, be more probable.

From the beginning of the 14th cent. the rights of the probable opinion began to be discussed, but Probabilist principles were first fostered esp. in the school of *Salamanca in the 16th cent., where the *Dominican, B. *Medina, in his 'Commentary on the Summa of St. *Thomas Aquinas' (1577), gave this teaching its classical form: 'Si est opinio probabilis, licitum est eam sequi, licet opposita probabilior sit'. From Medina down to 1656 the doctrine reigned almost without opposition, being accepted by both Dominicans (*John of St. Thomas) and *Jesuits (G. *Vazquez, F. *Suarez) alike. The latter developed the 'principle of possession', acc. to which in case of doubt one is not obliged to change the present state of things, i.e. if a law is doubtful, human freedom remains 'in possession'. The system, however, was recognized to be open to the charge of *Laxism, since, under the pretext of making salvation easy it would seem to allow men to act acc. to freedom even on a very slight chance of probability; and already in 1604 abuse of the principle was deplored by the Jesuit General, C. *Aquaviva.

It was not, however, till 1656 that a sharp conflict among moralists broke out. The Dominican general chapter in Rome required members of the order to follow more closely St. Thomas and to adopt a system that came to be known as *Probabiliorism (q.v.). In the same year B. *Pascal began to publish his Lettres provinciales with their violent denunciations, inspired by *Jansenism, of the morality of the Jesuits with whom, since then, Probabilism has increasingly been identified. Several Probabilist propositions savouring of Laxism were condemned by *Alexander VII in 1665 and 1666, and Laxism as a whole by *Innocent XI in 1679. In the following year the Pope ordered the Jesuit General, G. P. Oliva, to permit the teaching of Probabiliorism and to allow criticism of Probabilism in the Society, and in 1687 T. González (1624–1705), who favoured Probabiliorism, was elected General. His Fundamentum Theologiae Moralis (publd. 1694) further impaired the position of Probabilism in the order. On the other hand, '*Tutiorism', a more rigorist system, which had been taught by the Jansenists and J. Sinnich (1603–68) at Louvain, was condemned by *Alexander VIII in 1690. In 1700 the French clergy, under the leadership of J. B. *Bossuet, censured Probabilism and adopted Probabiliorism, which, under Jansenist influence, held sway during the first part of the 18th cent. The vigorous advocacy of Probabiliorism by the Dominican, D. Concina (1687–1756), who attacked the rival teaching in his Storia del probabilismo (1743), provoked a long-drawn-out controversy between Dominicans and Jesuits.

The subsequent rehabilitation of Probabilism is due esp. to the authority of St. *Alphonsus Liguori. After a short period of Probabiliorism, which he abandoned as too rigid, he became a Probabilist; and, though in 1762 he again modified his position and expounded his own theory of '*Equiprobabilism' (q.v.), this

system rests at bottom on a Probabilist foundation. His great prestige as a moralist, esp. after he was canonized (1839) and declared a Doctor of the Church (1871), reflected on the whole Probabilist position, which was further strengthened by the restoration of the Society of Jesus in 1814. Surrounded with safeguards to prevent it from generating into Laxism, Probabilism has since become the official teaching of the Society, and together with Equiprobabilism is the most generally accepted moral system of the RC Church.

M. A. Potton, O.P., De Theoria Probabilitatis (Paris, 1874); F. ter Haar, C.SS.R., De Systemate Morali Antiquorum Probabilistarum (Paderborn, 1894). Id., Das Decret des Papstes Innocenz' XI über den Probabilismus (1904). A. Schmitt, S.J., Zur Geschichte des Probabilismus. Historisch-kritische Untersuchung über die ersten 50 Jahre desselben (1904). T. Richard, O.P., Le Probabilisme moral et philosophique (1922). T. Deman, O.P., in D.T.C., xiii (pt. 1; 1936), cols. 417–619, s.v.; Sisinio da Romallo, O.F.M., in E.C., x (1953), cols. 57–61, s.v. for further bibl. See also bibl. to Moral Theology.

PROBATIONER. In the Presbyterian Churches, the status of one who, after examination and approval by his presbytery, receives a licence to preach. He is also known as a licentiate. The licence empowers him to act as an assistant to a minister, but he may not administer the Sacraments until he is ordained to a charge of his own. In Scotland a probationer who failed to be elected to a church used commonly to be called a 'stickit minister'. The title is also used in a similar sense in the Methodist Churches.

PROBST, FERDINAND (1816–99), liturgical scholar. A pupil of K. J. *Hefele at Tübingen, he was ordained priest in 1840 and became Pastor at Pfärrich near Wangen in 1843, Prof. of Pastoral Theology at Breslau in 1864 and Dean of Breslau Cathedral in 1896. Among Probst's long series of writings were Katholische Moraltheologie (2 vols., 1848–50), Die Liturgie der drei ersten christlichen Jahrhunderte (1870), Sakramente und Sakramentalien (1872), Die ältesten römischen Sakramentarien und Ordines (1892), Die Liturgie des vierten Jahrhunderts (1893) and Die abendländische Messe vom 5. bis 8. Jahrhundert (1896). He was a scholar of great erudition and industry. But his conclusions were marked by an excessive conservatism, and his methods of argumentation were apt to be over-speculative. He held that the Liturgy in *Apostolic Constitutions, Bk. VIII (late 4th cent.), was in almost universal use throughout the Church from the earliest times.

H. *Leclercq, O.S.B., in D.A.C.L., ix (pt. 2; 1930), cols. 1731 f., s.v. 'Liturgistes, iv'.

PROCESS OF CANONIZATION. See Beatification and Canonization.

PROCESSION (Liturgical). Processions are of two different kinds, festival and penitential. Acc. to strict W. use, there is a procession on all Sundays and principal festivals before the High Celebration of the *Eucharist, but in practice this takes place generally only on festivals. The ancient English use was for processions to be held after *Evensong on feasts and on all Saturdays from *Easter to *Advent. The order of procession, acc. to *Sarum Use, is thurifer, cross-bearer, candle-bearers, subdeacon, deacon, celebrant, choir, clergy, bishop (if present); but acc. to modern Roman use the choir walk before the celebrant. Processions are frequently held in the open air as acts of witness, e.g. on *Good Friday or before a parochial mission. *Rogationtide processions are often through the fields to pray for God's blessing on the fruits of the earth. Banners are often carried in procession both to excite devotion and to typify the Church's vocation to conquer like an army the powers of evil. See also *Processional*.

N. Serrarius, *Sacri Peripatetici, sive de Sacris Ecclesiae Catholicae Processionibus libri duo* (Cologne, 1607). C. Dunlop, *Processions*. A Dissertation together with Practical Suggestions (*Alcuin Club Tracts, xx; 1932). H. Thurston, S.J., in *C.E.*, xii (1911), pp. 446–8.

PROCESSION (Theological) (Gk. ἐκπόρευσις, Lat. *processio*). In Trinitarian doctrine, the attribute which distinguishes the Holy Ghost from the two Persons of the Father and the Son. This attibute of the Holy Ghost implied in the NT (cf. e.g. Jn. 15. 26) is asserted in the *Niceno-Constantinopolitan Creed, and is first developed at length by the *Cappadocian Fathers. See also *Double Procession, Filioque*.

PROCESSIONAL. The book containing the text of the litanies, hymns, and prayers formally prescribed for use in processions. In the W. Church, the bulk of it is merely an extract from the "*Ritual", with some supplementary matter derived from the *Missal and the *Pontifical. In the later Middle Ages, 'Processionals' were often adapted to the requirements of local churches and uses, e.g. the widely used 'Sarum Processional'.

PROCLUS, St. (d. 446 or 447), Patr. of *Constantinople. On the death of the Patr. Atticus (425), whose secretary he had been, he was an unsuccessful candidate for the patriarchate, but in 426 he was consecrated Abp. of Cyzicus. Unable to take possession of his see through ecclesiastical differences, he remained in Constantinople as a much-applauded preacher, and here delivered in 428 or 429 a famous sermon on the *Theotokos in the presence of *Nestorius, though Proclus did not take an active part in the subsequent controversy. When he became patriarch in 434, his moderation in the cause of orthodoxy gained him many sympathies and his popularity was enhanced by the solemn translation of the body of St. *Chrysostom which he effected in 438. Among his writings, which consist for the most part of homilies and epistles, is the so-called 'Tome of St. Proclus' (Ep. 2), an exposition of the doctrine of the

one Christ in two natures, addressed to the *Armenians, and directed against *Theodore of Mopsuestia (but without naming him). Traditionally the formula 'One of the Trinity was crucified acc. to the flesh', destined to play an important part in the *Theopaschite Controversy (6th cent.), has been ascribed to him (but mistakenly). The introduction of the *Trisagion into the Liturgy has also been attributed to him. Feast day, 24 Oct.

His writings, first ed. by V. Riccardus (1630), are repr. in J. P. Migne, *PG*, lxv, 651–88. Crit. text of his Sermon on the Theotokos in *A.C.O.*, I, i, 1 (1927), pp. 103–7; of his *Tomus ad Armenios*, ib., IV, ii (1914), pp. 65–8, 187–205. E. *Schwartz, *Konzilstudien* (Schriften der wissenschaftlichen Gesellschaft in Strassburg, Hft. 20, 1914), II. Über echte und unechte Schriften des Bischofs Proklos von Konstantinopel, pp. 18–53. B. Marx, *Procliana*. Untersuchungen über den homiletischen Nachlass des Patriarchen Proklos von Konstantinopel (1940) (Marx ascribes, often on precarious grounds, more than 80 of the sermons preserved in the *spuria* of Chrysostom to Proclus). M. Richard, 'Proclus de Constantinople et le théopaschisme' in *R.H.E.*, xxxviii (1942), pp. 303–31. Bardenhewer, iv, 202–8; Altaner (ed. 1950), p. 294 f.

PROCOPIUS OF CAESAREA (early 6th cent.), Byzantine historian. A native of *Caesarea in Palestine, in 527 he was appointed secretary to Belisarius, whom he accompanied in his campaigns against the Persians, the Vandals, and the Ostrogoths. From 542 he lived in *Constantinople. His writings consist of his 'Histories' (which describe the wars he had himself witnessed), his 'De aedificiis' (an account of the buildings of the Emp. *Justinian), and the so-called 'Anecdota', issued, as the name implies, only after his death. The work of a careful and on the whole impartial author, they are of great historical value and stand in marked contrast to most of the poor compositions of his age. The 'De aedificiis', however, suffers from its excessive flattery of Justinian. The 'Anecdota', not intended for publication, are a bitter invective against the civil and ecclesiastical powers.

Works ed. W. Dindorf in C.S.H. Byz. (3 vols., Bonn, 1833–8). Crit. ed. J. Haury (Teubn., 3 vols., 1905–13); also ed., with Eng. tr., by H. B. Dewing (Loeb, 7 vols., 1914–40). F. Dahn, *Prokopius von Cäsarea* (1865). Krumbacher, pp. 230–6.

PROCOPIUS OF GAZA (c. 475–c. 538), rhetorician and Biblical exegete. He was perh. the foremost figure of the 'School of Gaza', a group of Christian rhetoricians of the 5th–6th cent. His Biblical works consist mainly of extensive extracts from older exegetes (*Philo, *Origen, *Basil, *Theodoret, *Cyril of Alexandria). Of his two Commentaries on the Octateuch the shorter, which is preserved in Cod. Monac. gr. 358, has been published *in toto* in a Lat. transl. and, in fragments, also in the Gk. He also commented on 1 and 2 Sam., 1 and 2 Kgs., and 1 and 2 Chron.; on Is.; and on Cant. His Epp., of which 163 survive, are in an affected and precious style (which, however, made them popular) and without theological interest, but remain, with the funeral oration of his pupil Choricius, the chief source for his life. Acc. to D. Russos and J. Dräseke, some fragments of a work against the *Neo-platonist Proclus (410–85) are to be assigned to Procopius of Gaza; but more recent opinion is against this ascription.

Works first collected in J. P. Migne, *PG*, lxxxvii, 1–2838 (ptt, 1–3); new ed. of 163 of Procopius's Epp. in R. Hercher, *Epistolographi Graeci* (Paris, 1873), pp. 533–98. The chief source for his Life, apart from his Epp., is a Funeral Oration of Choricius of Gaza (Opera, ed. R. Foerster–E. Richtsteig, Teubner ed., 1929, pp. 109–28). L. Eisenhofer, *Procopius von Gaza*. Eine literarhistorische Studie (1897). Barden-hewer, v, 86–91, with bibl.; Altaner (ed. 2, 1950), p. 465 f., with bibl. J. van den Gheyn, S.J., in *Dict. Bibl.*, v (1912), cols. 686–9, s.v. See also bibl. to *Catenae*.

PROCTORS FOR THE CLERGY. The elected representatives of the Anglican clergy who, together with the *ex-officio* members, constitute the Lower Houses of *Convocation of *Canterbury and *York. The canons regulating the existing conditions of election date from 1921 (with an amendment in 1936 to provide for University representation). The proctors are elected on a diocesan basis by all clergy beneficed in the diocese or licensed under seal. See further *Convocations of Canterbury and York*.

PROFESSION, Religious. The taking of the vows of poverty, chastity, and obedience, necessary to the embracing of the 'religious life'. The profession follows upon the novitiate or training period. By can. 574 of the 1918 Roman *Codex Iuris Canonici there must in every case be first a temporary profession of at least three years. At the end of this period the 'professed' may either withdraw again into the world or make a perpetual profession, i.e. take lifelong vows.

PROHIBITED DEGREES. The relationships by blood or marriage which render it unlawful for two persons to marry. Certain relationships, e.g. mother and son, and a man and his wife's mother, prevent marriage in almost every state of society, however primitive. The reasons which underlie these prohibitions are partly biological, but mainly social, e.g. the maintenance of peace and purity in the home. Blood relationships are called 'consanguinity': relationships by marriage, 'affinity'. Such relationships are called in canon law 'degrees' (cf. Lat. *gradus*, 'step').

It is the general practice to compute the nearness of the relationship by the number of persons or steps between the people related and their common ancestors. Thus son to father is one step or the 'first degree', son to grandfather the second, and so on, and such relationship is called *linea recta* or 'direct line'. Brother to sister is one step via the common parent, and so the 'first degree'. First cousin to first cousin is two steps either way to the common ancestor, the grandfather, and so the 'second degree'; this is the 'collateral line'. In the E. Church there is another system of calculation for the collateral line, namely to add the steps between each of the pair related and the common ancestor, e.g. first cousins are

related in the 'fourth degree', there being two steps on either side to the common grandparent.

Ecclesiastical legislation forbidding marriage between persons related within certain degrees is based on the prohibitions in Lev. 18. At one time the W. Church extended the prohibition to the seventh degree. This was reduced to the fourth at the *Lateran Council of 1215, and by the new Roman *Codex Iuris Canonici of 1918 to the third in consanguinity and the second in affinity. The degrees of affinity are calculated in the same way as those of consanguinity, the husband and wife being regarded as identical for this purpose, i.e. a man's wife's first cousin is counted as his own first cousin, to whom he is accordingly related in the second degree of affinity. In the C of E the prohibited degrees are those listed in M. *Parker's Table of *Kindred and Affinity (q.v.) as amended in 1946.

See also *Affinity*.

The principal canons on the subject in the Codex are C.I.C. 96 f., 1042, and 1076. F. X. Wahl, *The Matrimonial Impediments of Consanguinity and Affinity* (Washington, D.C., 1934), with bibl. On the position in C of E, H. W. Cripps, *A Practical Treatise on the Law Relating to the Church and Clergy* (ed. 8 by K. M. Macmorran, 1937), p. 538 f. F. Cimetier in *D.T.C.*, xi (pt. 2; 1932), s.v. 'Parenté (Empêchements de)'. See also bibl. to *Affinity*, *Consanguinity*, and *Matrimony*.

PROLOCUTOR. The title of the president and chairman of each of the Lower Houses of the *Convocations of *Canterbury and *York. He also acts as the representative of his House to the corresponding Upper Houses (of bishops). He is elected to his office by the House to which he belongs.

PROMISED LAND, The. The land of *Canaan, promised to *Abraham and his descendants. Cf. Gen. 12. 7, 13. 15, &c.; and J. *Milton, *Paradise Lost*: 'Over the Promis'd Land to God so dear' (iii. 531).

PROMOTOR FIDEI (Lat., 'promoter of the faith'). The member of the *Congregation of Rites whose duty it is to examine critically the alleged virtues and miracles of a candidate for *beatification or *canonization, and so to prevent any rash decision. The first formal mention of the office seems to be in connexion with the canonization of St. Lawrence Justinian (d. 1456) by *Leo X. In the *Codex Iuris Canonici, his function is described as 'ad ius tuendum' (can. 2010). He is popularly known as 'the *Devil's Advocate' (*advocatus diaboli*).

PRONE. The name was given in medieval N. Europe, including Britain, to the vernacular office attached to the sermon at High Mass on Sundays and other feast days. Its form was at the discretion of the preacher, but it ordinarily consisted of such items as the '*bidding of the bedes' (q.v.) and expositions of the Lord's Prayer and the Creed, as well as notifications of ensuing feasts and fasts and of banns of

marriage and ordination. The name has also been used for sermons, esp. of an expository kind. The word is derived from the Fr. *prône*, orig. a grille which separated the chancel or place where notices were given out from the rest of the church.

PRONOUNCEMENT STORIES. The name proposed by V. Taylor for those passages in the Gospels which M. *Dibelius terms *Paradigms (q.v.) and R. *Bultmann *Apophthegms.

PROPAGANDA, Sacred Congregation of. The *Roman Congregation which is concerned with missions to heathen countries and the administration of territories where there is no properly established hierarchy. It originated in the latter half of the 16th cent. to meet the spiritual needs of the newly discovered heathen populations, as one of the fruits of the general stimulus given to Church organization by the *Counter-Reformation. At first it took the form of a cardinalitial commission 'De propaganda fide', and it was not until 6 June 1622 that Gregory XV created the Congregation of Propaganda by the bull 'Inscrutabili Divinae'. The Congregation was originally composed of 13 cardinals, 2 prelates, a secretary, and a consultor. *Urban VIII further gave the Congregation a prefect-general and a central missionary training seminary, the 'Collegium Urbanum', founded in 1627. Owing to the extensive range of its work the Congregation is now divided into numerous secretariats and commissions; the scope of its jurisdiction is regulated by canon law (*CIC*, can. 252).

Bullarium Pontificium Sacrae Congregationis de Propaganda Fide (5 vols. bound in 3, Rome, 1839–41; appendix, 2 vols., ib., no date); *Collectanea S. Congregationis de Propaganda Fide, seu Decreta, Instructiones, Rescripta pro Apostolicis Missionibus, Ann. 1622–1906* (2 vols., ib., 1907). The present competence of the Congregation is defined in *Pius XI's *motu proprio* 'Sancto Dei Ecclesia' of 25 Mar. 1938, pr. *A.A.S.*, xxx (1938), pp. 154–9. *Catalogus Editionum quae prodierunt ex Typographia Polyglotta Sacrae Congregationis de Propaganda Fide* (ib., 1890). U. Bertini in *E.C.*, iv (1950), cols. 328–30, s.v. 'Congregazioni Romani, vii, S.C. di Propaganda Fide', with bibl. See also works cited under *Roman Congregations*.

PROPER. The part of the *Eucharist and *Offices which changes acc. to the festival or ecclesiastical season. It is thus contrasted with the rest of the service, the invariable '*Ordinary of the Mass'. The 'Proper of Saints' ('Proprium Sanctorum') is the Proper for festivals of fixed date, except those falling between 24 Dec. and 13 Jan.; the 'Proper of Time' ('Proprium Temporum') that for *Sundays, *ferias, and festivals which have no fixed date, and also for all days between 24 Dec. and 13 Jan. Many saints' days share the same Proper with others, and where this is so their Proper is printed once for all in a separate part of the *Missal and *Breviary, under the title '*Common of Saints' ('Commune Sanctorum'). In the BCP, the Proper consists of (1) the *Collect, *Epistle, and *Gospel (with the *Easter Anthems for use at *Matins on *Easter

Day), which are arranged together in the order of the ecclesiastical year, the Proper of Time coming first, and then that of Saints (there being no Common), and (2) the *Prefaces, which are set out in the body of the Communion Service, as in the Roman Missal.

PROPHECY. From the earliest times Christians have believed that already before the Incarnation God the Holy Ghost, as affirmed in the *Nicene Creed, 'spake by the prophets'. Such prophetic inspiration was found esp. in the supernatural knowledge by which holy men were enabled to foresee and foretell, in part, the revelation which was to be given in Christ. It was extended to *Abraham (Jn. 8. 56) and *David (Mk. 12. 35 ff.), but it was pre-eminently the privilege of the Prophets. At the same time it has been generally recognized that the Prophets were the inspired deliverers of God's message not only about the future, but to their own contemporaries, to whom they declared His will, and whom they recalled to His righteousness.

1. *The Name 'Prophet'*. In NT times the Jews applied the term 'the Prophets' to the large section of the OT *Canon intermediate in authority between the ancient 'Law' and the more recent 'Writings'. In this connexion it was customary to distinguish (1) the 'Former Prophets', viz. Jos., Jgs., 1 and 2 Sam., 1 and 2 Kgs., and (2) the 'Latter Prophets', viz. Is., Jer., Ezek. (these, the three Major Prophets) and the twelve *Minor Prophets. But the name of prophet could be applied personally in a wider sense, e.g. to *Moses and the future 'prophet like Moses' who was expected to appear (Deut. 18. 15 ff.), and to David (Acts 2. 29 f.). Christ Himself was considered by some as a prophet (Jn. 4. 19, Mt. 8. 28).

2. *Origins and Characteristics of Prophecy.* The beginnings of Hebrew prophecy can be traced to the early days of the monarchy. 1 Sam. 9 f. already attests the existence of two types of prophets, the Seer (Heb. *ro'eh*), possessed of clairvoyance, like Samuel who was able to show Saul the whereabouts of his lost asses, and the corybantic ecstatic (Heb. *nabi'*), associated with the local shrine, who under the stimulus of music and dancing fell into a frenzy and uttered words not his own, held to be Jehovah's (1 Sam. 10. 10 f., 19. 23 f.). In this ecstatic condition, the prophet gave the impression of madness (cf. 2 Kgs. 9. 11, Jer. 29. 26); and, like *Elijah who ran before Ahab's chariot to Jezreel (1 Kgs. 18. 46), he might be possessed of superhuman strength.

Gradually, however, the ecstatic features became of less importance and the conscious delivery of a Divine message or 'word' became the dominating feature of prophecy. Thus 'the word of the Lord' 'came' to prophets already in the age of Elijah. Side by side with this was the use of symbolic action. Thus Zedekiah foretold the overthrow of the Syrians by equipping himself with horns of iron (1 Kgs. 22. 11): and, in the early period at least, such action was believed not merely to foretell but to influence the future (cf. 2 Kgs. 13. 14–19), being in its beginnings not far from sympathetic magic. Moreover, even among the later prophets words were reinforced by actions. *Isaiah went about naked 'for a sign' (Is. 20), *Jeremiah wore a 'yoke' (or fetters) on his shoulders (Jer. 27), and *Ezekiel performed various symbolic actions (e.g. Ezek. 12). It was, however, essentially the 'word' of Jehovah which controlled the prophet, and his words passed on the Word of God to His people.

3. *The Canonical Prophets.* These prophets fall into four groups: (1) the 8th-century prophets, *Amos, *Hosea, *Micah, and Isaiah; (2) the immediately Pre-exilic prophets (late 7th–early 6th cent.), *Nahum, *Zephaniah, *Habakkuk and Jeremiah; (3) the Exilic prophets, Ezekiel and *Deutero-Isaiah; (4) the Post-exilic prophets, *Haggai, *Zechariah and *Malachi, together with (prob.) *Obadiah, *Joel, and *Jonah, which are less easy to date precisely. The Books in the Bible which bear the names of these Prophets contain mainly or wholly the work of the prophet in question, and are usually the only source of information about the writer, though Isaiah and Jeremiah figure also in the known history of Israel and some other prophets are briefly referred to (Jer. 26. 18, Ez. 5. 1). One book (Malachi) is virtually anonymous, and Is. 40–66 is the work of one or two great unknown prophets of the Exilic and post-exilic period (see *Isaiah, Book of*). In other cases the undisputed work of the prophet has been subjected to some revision and addition, though all the prophetic books show clearly the individualities of their respective original authors.

4. *The Christian Appeal to Prophecy.* Since it is in the Prophets of the OT that most (though not all) of the passages concerning the *Messiah appear, Jews who looked for His coming had an especial interest in the prophets, who, with other inspired writers, had looked for the Messiah 'since the world began' (Lk. 1. 70; cf. Lk. 1. 55, 2 Pet. 1. 21). As we learn from all four Gospels, Christ saw the fulfilment of OT prophecy in His own Ministry and Passion, saying e.g. that 'many prophets and kings' had desired to see what the Disciples were then seeing (Lk. 10. 24) and declaring the fulfilment of Is. 61. 1 in his own Ministry (Lk. 4. 21), and of other prophecies in His Passion and Resurrection (Lk. 18. 31–34, 24. 25–27). He taught the Disciples, however, to see in Himself the fulfilment not only of the writings of the prophets but of 'all the scriptures' (Lk. 24. 27), including the Pss. (Lk. 24. 44; cf. Mk. 12. 10 [Ps. 118. 22], Mk. 12. 36 [Ps. 110. 1]). The Evangelists in their own persons, esp. the author of Mt., point out the fulfilment of OT passages by the events they describe, e.g. Christ's birth from a Virgin was foretold by Is. 7. 14 (Mt. 1. 22) and its occurrence at *Bethlehem by Mic. 5. 2 (Mt. 2. 6), the ministry of St. *John the Baptist by Mal. 3. 1 and Is. 40. 3 (Mk. 1. 2–3, cf. Mt. 3. 3, Lk. 3. 4, Jn. 1. 23), His Passion by Is. 53 (Jn. 12. 38) and particular incidents

of it by Ps. 22. 18, Ex. 12. 46, and Zech. 12. 10 (Jn. 19. 24, 36 f.). In one case, it appears, Christ by His action claimed to be the Person foretold in an OT prophecy, viz. when he entered Jerusalem before His Passion riding upon an ass, in accordance with the words of Zech. 9. 9.

Acc. to Acts, the Apostles began, immediately after *Pentecost, to see the fulfilment of OT passages in Christ's Resurrection and Ascension and the Coming of the Holy Spirit (Acts 2. 14–36, quoting Joel 2. 28–30, Ps. 16. 8–11 and Ps. 110. 1). The appeal to OT prophecy was a constant feature of early Christian preaching (Acts 8. 26–35). St. *Paul in writing to his converts not only reminds them of the universal Christian belief that 'Christ died for our sins acc. to the Scriptures' (1 Cor. 15. 3), but also uses many OT texts in a more individual manner, here doubtless influenced by his rabbinic training as well as by his Christian faith. Thus he interprets the Rock which supplied the Israelites with water in the wilderness (Ex. 17. 6) as a type of Christ (1 Cor. 10. 4). The Ep. to the Hebrews is almost a continuous appeal to OT texts (predominantly in the Law and the Pss. rather than the Prophets) in support of teaching about Christ.

In Christian writers from the *Apostolic Fathers onwards the appeal to the OT Scriptures is continued on the same general lines as in the NT. It is elaborated esp. in the Ep. of *Barnabas, for the author of which all the ceremonial enactments of the OT referred in a hidden manner to the Christian revelation and had been misinterpreted by the Jews. Among the *Apologists it is found esp. in *Justin Martyr whose 'Dialogue with Trypho, the Jew' is naturally much concerned with rival interpretations of the OT. Throughout the Patristic and Medieval periods all who sought to expound Christian doctrine, whether heretical or orthodox, assumed that the inspiration of Scripture guaranteed the prophetic foreknowledge of the Christian revelation, even in its details, so that OT texts might validly be used as arguments, e.g., for specific Christological teaching.

Wide application was given to the allegorical interpretation of OT texts, esp. by the *Alexandrian theologians. By the mystical interpretation of Scripture some Latin and Medieval writers were able to find an appropriate relevance in one OT text or another to almost any conceivable subject. At the Reformation reliance on far-fetched interpretations of the OT tended to be curbed by its controversial weakness, but the principle was not doubted in any quarter and the traditionally accepted uses of OT texts in a Christian sense appear, e.g., in the original chapter-summaries and page-headings of the *Authorized Version for such passages as Is. 49–63 and Ps. 110. It was only with the *Aufklärung* and the rise of a critical approach to history that doubt was cast on the existence of any real anticipation of NT events in such texts as Is. 7. 14. Hence modern expositors of the OT tend to stress that the prophets were originally and primarily 'forth-tellers' of God's will to their contemporaries rather than 'foretellers' of the future; nevertheless their words concerning the glory and dignity of the Messiah, and also His suffering (Is. 53), are real, though not precise, glimpses of an eternal truth about God's nature and purpose which are fully manifested in Christ.

Among the more important of the older discussions are J. Davison, *Discourses on Prophecy* (1824); A. Knobel, *Der Prophetismus der Hebräer* (1837); G. H. A. *Ewald, *Die Propheten des Alten Bundes* (2 vols., 1840–1; Eng. tr. of ed. 2, 5 vols., 1875–81); F. A. G. *Tholuck, *Die Propheten und ihre Weissagungen* (1860); B. Duhm, *Die Theologie der Propheten* (1875); A. Kuenen, *De Profeten en de Profetie onder Israël* (2 vols., 1875; Eng. tr., 1877). In British theology, the modern critical view of the development of Hebrew Prophecy was popularized by W. R. *Smith, *The Prophets of Israel and their Place in History to the Close of the Eighth Century B.C.* (1882; ed. 2, with notes by T. K. *Cheyne, 1895). A. F. Kirkpatrick, *The Doctrine of the Prophets* (Warburtonian Lectures for 1886–1890, 1892); G. Hölscher, *Die Propheten* (1914); M. Buttenwieser, *The Prophets of Israel from the Eighth to the Fifth Century* (New York, 1914); B. Duhm, *Israels Propheten* (1916); T. H. Robinson, *Prophecy and the Prophets in Ancient Israel* (Duckworth's Theology Series, 1923); J. M. P. Smith, *The Prophets and their Times* (Chicago, 1925); A. Lods, *Les Prophètes d'Israel et les débuts du judaïsme* (1935; Eng. tr. in series 'History of Civilization', 1937). A. B. *Davidson in *H.D.B.*, iii (1900), pp. 106–27, s.v. 'Prophecy and Prophets'; T. K. *Cheyne and others in *E.Bi.*, iii (1902), cols. 3853–901, s.v. 'Prophetic Literature'; E. König in *H.E.R.E.*, x (1918), pp. 384–93, s.v. 'Prophecy (Hebrew)'.

PROPHETS (Early Christian). There are several indications, notably the lists in 1 Cor. 12. 28 and Eph. 4. 11, that there existed in the primitive Church a separate group of ministers known as 'prophets'. On the other hand, it would appear that the term 'prophet' might be applied to an elder, a deacon, and even a lay member of the Church, male or female (Acts 15. 32, 21. 9, 21. 10). If the *Didache* could be accepted as an authentic historical document of *c.* 100–20, we should have here clear evidence of the prophets as a group in a primitive itinerant ministry, whose authority, indeed, had already fallen into disrepute; but as many recent writers (J. A. *Robinson, R. H. *Connolly, &c.) hold that the *Didache* is an imaginative reconstruction of primitive Church life from NT tags, the possible invalidation of its witness throws serious doubt on the view of A. *Harnack, A. C. *Headlam and others, which saw in the prophets a well-established order in the sub-Apostolic age. A prominent place was accorded to 'prophets' by the *Montanists, but it is most improbable that these were in any sense successors of the prophets mentioned in the NT.

A. Harnack, *Die Lehre der zwölf Apostel* (T.U., ii, Hftt. 1–2; 1884), pp. 119–31. R. M. Pope in *D.A.C.*, ii (1918), pp. 279–81, s.v. 'Prophecy, Prophet, Prophetess'; E. K. Mitchell in *H.E.R.E.*, x (1918), pp. 382–4, s.v. 'Prophecy (Christian)'.

PROPITIATION. The general meaning of the word is the appeasing of the wrath of the Deity by prayer or sacrifice when a sin or offence has been committed against Him. The word occurs three times in the AV, in connexion with the death of Christ (Rom. 3. 25, 1 Jn. 2. 2, 4. 10; to which RV adds Heb. 2. 17), but it is disputed whether it accurately represents the Greek of these passages (ἱλαστήριον, ἱλασμός). In Christian thought the death of Christ has usually been regarded as a propitiatory sacrifice to the Father for the sins of the world. The conception of the Divine wrath involved is to be understood, however, in harmony with the fact that the sacrifice which appeases it proceeds from the Divine love. Acc. to the Council of *Trent (Sess. xxii, can. 3), the Sacrifice offered in the Eucharist is propitiatory (*propitiatorium*). See also *Atonement, Mercy Seat.*

PROPRIETARY CHAPEL. In the C of E a chapel built by subscription and maintained by private individuals, without constitutional existence or parochial rights. Such chapels were seldom episcopally consecrated though their ministers were normally granted episcopal licences (revocable absolutely at the bishop's will) which could only be issued with the consent of the incumbent of the parish. They were established esp. in fashionable areas (London, watering places); were commonly supported by pew rents, which were often high; and were sometimes centres of extreme Evangelicalism or (less frequently) High Church doctrine. Many such chapels existed in the 18th and early 19th cents; but they are now almost, if not quite, extinct.

R. J. *Phillimore, *The Ecclesiastical Law of the Church of England* (ed. 2 by W. G. F. Phillimore, son; 1895), i, 250–2, 436, and ii, 1459 and 1759; H. W. Cripps, *A Practical Treatise on the Law relating to the Church and Clergy* (ed. 8, by K. M. Macmorran, 1937), pp. 104 f. esp. note m, 209, and 533.

PROSE (Lat. *prosa*). An alternative name, once common in England, for the *Sequence (q.v.). The word has occasionally been applied to other anthems of similar form which have no place in the Liturgy.

PROSELYTE (Gk. προσήλυτος). The word means literally 'stranger' or 'foreign sojourner', and, by an extension, a convert to Judaism. The NT mentions both 'proselytes' and 'God-fearers' (cf., e.g., Acts 2. 10, 13. 43; 10. 2), the distinction being probably that the former underwent circumcision and were therefore reckoned full members of the Jewish Church, whereas the 'God-fearers' were more loosely attached to the Jewish communities. In a wider sense the word has come to be used of a convert to any faith or sect.

PROSKOMIDE (Gk. προσκομιδή). In the E. Church, the preparation of the bread and wine for the Eucharist which takes place before the beginning of the service at the table known as the *prothesis. The priest cuts the bread into pieces with the *lance, and then arranges it on the *discus in a fashion prescribed by the rubrics; then the deacon pours wine and water into the chalice; and the whole is afterwards veiled. At the end of the ceremony the bread and wine are censed and a prayer is said over

them. In origin the Proskomide is the second
part of the *offertory, moved back to the beginning of the service. There are considerable
variations in terminology among liturgical
writers, the Proskomide being sometimes
known as the Prothesis.

PROSPER OF AQUITAINE, St. (c. 390–
c. 463), theologian. Prosper Tiro of Aquitania
was living at Marseilles at the outbreak of
the *Semi-Pelagian controversy (426), probably as a lay monk. In 428 he wrote to
St. *Augustine, whose theology of grace and
predestination he warmly accepted, informing
him of the opposition which his teaching was
encountering among the disciples of *Cassian.
About the same time he wrote a letter to a
certain Rufinus and the 'Carmen de ingratis',
a poem of over a thousand hexameters, both
on the subject of grace. In 431, after St.
Augustine's death, he went to Rome to secure
Pope *Celestine I's support for Augustinian
doctrines and between 431 and 434 published a
number of works in their defence, one of them
directed against St. *Vincent of Lerins, and
another against Cassian. After the latter's
death (c. 435), he became more conciliatory, as
is borne out by his 'Expositio super Psalmos',
and (if, as is now widely held, it be Prosper's)
the 'Capitula Coelestini', written as an appendix to the Pope's letter to the bishops of Gaul,
probably between 435 and 442 from Rome.
In his last period, when he held the office of
secretary to *Leo I, he devoted himself chiefly
to compilations, among them the 'Epigrammata ex sententiis sancti Augustini', versified
excerpts from the works of St. Augustine, and a
'Chronicle' which until 378 follows *Eusebius
and St. *Jerome, but is of value for his
own time (425–455), esp. for the history of
dogma. It would seem that Prosper's theological
opinions developed from the rigid Augustinianism of his earlier controversial writings
to a milder view which rejected predestination
to damnation and affirmed the will of God to
save all men, though believing in fact in the
reprobation of a great number. The canons of
the Council of *Orange of 529 are partly based
on his extracts from St. Augustine, and later
he exercised a considerable influence on the
Carolingian theologians. Feast day, 7 July.

Works ed. J. B. Le Brun des Marettes, O.S.B.–P.
Mangeant, O.S.B., Paris, 1711; repr. with addendum in
J. P. Migne, *PL*, li, 1–868. Crit. text of 'Chronicle' ed. T.
*Mommsen in *M.G.H.*, Auctores Antiquissimi, ix (1892),
pp. 341–499. E. M. Pickman, *The Mind of Latin Christendom* (1937), pp. 418–36. Bardenhewer, iv, 533–41;
Altaner (ed. 1951), pp. 399–401. H. W. Phillott in *D.C.B.*,
iv (1887), pp. 492–7; A. Hauck in *P.R.E.* (ed. 3), xvi (1905),
pp. 123–7; G. Bardy in *D.T.C.*, xiii (pt. 1; 1936), cols.
846–50; J. Martin in *L.Th.K.*, viii (1936), cols. 504–6, with
bibl.

PROSPHORA (Gk. προσφορά). In the E.
Church, the altar bread. It takes the form of
round leavened cakes about 5 inches in dia-
meter and 2 inches thick, of which five are
required for the service. They are solemnly
cut up at the *Proskomide. From the first,

which is divided by a cross into four quarters
containing respectively the Greek letters IC
('Jesus'), XC ('Christ'), NI, KA (νικᾷ,
'conquers'), the principal particle (the 'seal')
is cut out. From the second a particle is
removed in honour of the BVM, and from the
other three, nine further particles in honour of
St. John the Baptist, the Prophets, the Apostles,
&c. The remaining portions, the 'Antidoron',
are not consecrated but distributed later among
the congregation.

PROTASIUS, St. See *Gervasius and
Protasius, Sts.*

PROTESTANT EPISCOPAL CHURCH.
The Church in the *United States of America
in communion with the See of *Canterbury.

The first Anglican church in America was
built at Jamestown, Virginia, in 1607; many
other congregations were established in
different parts of the Continent, all under the
jurisdiction of the Bp. of London; and from
1701 onwards the spread of the Anglican
Church was vigorously furthered by *S.P.G.,
founded in that year. But it was only after
the War of Independence that the Protestant
Episcopal Church was established as an autonomous organization. S. *Seabury (q.v.) was
elected by the clergy of Connecticut as their
bishop, and, after legal difficulties had prevented his consecration in England, he received the episcopal succession in 1784 at the
hands of the Bishops of the (Episcopal)
Church of *Scotland. Further Bishops were
consecrated in England, however, in 1787 and
1790. At a General Convention in 1789 a
constitution and canons were drawn up and
the Prayer Book revised. The Church for a
long time had to meet with considerable prejudice, through its British connexions, but
gradually this feeling lessened, though in
point of numbers it has never quite recovered
from this initial handicap.

The Church was a pioneer in the foundation
of theological seminaries and established the
*General Theological Seminary in New York
as early as 1817. During the Civil War of
1861–5 the Church in the southern states
formed itself into a separate body, but reconciliation followed the peace of 1865. Since
that date the Church has expanded both at
home and abroad, and missionary dioceses
were set up in Alaska, Hawaii, the Philippines,
Porto Rico, Cuba, China, Japan, Hayti,
Liberia, and Brazil. Since 1867 the American
Church has taken a prominent part in all the
*Lambeth Conferences. Further revisions of
the Prayer Book were made in 1892 and in
1928–29.

The constitution of the Church provides
for the laity a greater share in administration
than in England, both in all legislative bodies
and in the vestries of individual churches.
The supreme court in the Church is the
General Convention, which meets every three
years. There are no archbishops, but there is
a Presiding Bishop. Until 1910 he was the

senior bishop by consecration, but is now elected by the General Convention.

Theological and ecclesiastical parties run in some measure upon similar lines to those in the C of E, though the absence of state control encourages freer development. There are numerous Church organizations; and religious communities, both for men and women, made their appearance soon after the middle of the 19th cent.

See also *United States of America, Christianity in.*

W. S. Perry [Bp. of Iowa] (ed.), *Historical Collections relating to the American Colonial Church* (5 vols. in 4, relating to Virginia, Pennsylvania, Massachusetts, Maryland, and Delaware; privately pr. at Hartford, Conn., 1870–78). W. White, Bp. of Pennsylvania, *Memoirs of the Protestant Episcopal Church in the United States of America* (Philadelphia, Pa., 1820), with orig. docc. W. S. Perry, *The History of the American Episcopal Church, 1587–1883* (2 vols., Boston, Mass., 1885). S. M. McConnell, *History of the American Episcopal Church from the Planting of the Colonies to the End of the Civil War* (New York, 1890). C. C. Tiffany, *A History of the Protestant Episcopal Church in the United States of America* (American Church History Series, vii; New York, 1895); L. Coleman, Bp. of Delaware, *The Church in America* (The National Churches, 1895); G. Hodges, *Three Hundred Years of the Episcopal Church in America* (Philadelphia, Pa., 1908). W. W. Manross, *A History of the American Episcopal Church* (New York, 1935). P. M. Dawley, *The Episcopal Church and its Work* (Greenwich, Conn., 1955). C. O. Loveland, *The Critical Years. The Reconstruction of the Anglican Church in the United States of America, 1780–1789* (Greenwich, Conn., 1956). J. T. Addison, *The Episcopal Church in the United States, 1789–1931* (New York, 1951). W. W. Manross, *The Episcopal Church in the United States, 1800–1840* (Columbia University thesis; New York, 1938). G. E. DeMille, *The Catholic Movement in the American Episcopal Church* (Philadelphia, Pa., 1941; ed. 2, enlarged, 1950). W. S. Perry, *The Episcopate in America.* Sketches, Biographical and Bibliographical, of the Bishops of the American Church, with a Preliminary Essay on the Historic Episcopate and Documentary Annals of the Introduction of the Anglican Line of Succession into America (New York, 1895). A. L. Cross, *The Anglican Episcopate and the American Colonies* (Harvard Historical Studies, ix; 1902). E. C. Chorley, *Men and Movements in the American Episcopal Church* (Hale Lectures for 1943; New York, 1946). E. L. Parsons–B. H. Jones, *The American Prayer Book.* Its Origins and Principles (New York, 1937). C. R. Barnes, *The General Convention.* Offices and Officers, 1785–1950 (Philadelphia, Pa., 1951). E. A. White, *Annotated Constitution and Canons for the Government of the Protestant Episcopal Church in the United States of America, adopted in General Convention 1789–1922* (New York, 1924; revised and continued to 1952 by J. A. Dykman, 2 vols., Greenwich, Conn., 1954). H. Lowther Clarke, *Constitutional Church Government in the Dominions Beyond the Seas and in Other Parts of the Anglican Communion* (1924), pp. 196–205. See also bibl. to *United States of America, Christianity in.*

PROTESTANTISM. The system of Christian faith and practice based on acceptance of the principles of the Reformation. The term is derived from the 'Protestatio' of the reforming members of the Diet of *Speyer (1529) against the decisions of the Catholic majority. The word has retained a strongly anti-Roman flavour and is commonly repudiated by those who minimize their difference from Rome.

The chief branches of original Protestantism were *Lutheranism, *Calvinism, and *Zwinglianism (qq.v.). The position of the C of E is disputed. Here strong Calvinist influences have intermingled with older traditions, but it is widely contended that these have not effected any intrinsic modification of the pre-Reformation faith. The term is not used in any edition of the BCP, but from the beginning of the 17th cent. it was adopted as opposed to both Roman Catholicism and Puritanism, e.g. by *Charles I when he affirmed his allegiance to the Protestant religion. After the Restoration, however, it was generally extended to include also the Nonconformists. In this enlarged sense it is now widely used in popular parlance, though a large body of Anglicans deny the Protestant character of the C of E.

The chief characteristics of original Protestantism, common to all its denominations, are the acceptance of the Bible as the only source of revealed truth, the doctrine of justification by faith only, and the universal priesthood of all believers. Protestantism has tended to stress the transcendence of God, laying corresponding emphasis on the effects of the Fall and Original Sin, and the impotence of the unaided human intellect to obtain any knowledge of God, to minimize the liturgical aspects of Christianity, to put preaching and hearing of the Word before Sacramental faith and practice, and, while rejecting asceticism, to uphold for the individual a high, if at times austere, standard of personal morality. The principle of 'private judgement' in the interpretation of Scripture accounts for the great variety of sects and Churches typical of Protestantism, in which many shades of doctrine and practice are found.

The rigid systems of doctrinal orthodoxy elaborated by the earlier Protestant theologians began to suffer dissolution in the 18th cent., esp. under the growth of the new sense of history. G. E. *Lessing and the *Aufklärung distinguished Bible and religion, letter and spirit, theology and religious sentiment, and put all the emphasis on the latter members of these pairs. This one-sided stress on the subjective element in Christianity was further developed by F. D. E. *Schleiermacher, who placed religious experience in the centre of the Christian life. He had a profound influence, esp. on Continental Protestantism, which was later enhanced, and largely superseded, by that of A. *Ritschl (q.v.). Ritschl, though giving the first place not to feelings but to the facts of Scripture, brought back the principle of subjectivism by his theory of 'value judgements'. His contentions about Scripture, notably his assumptions that the fundamental idea of original Christianity was the Kingdom of God and that the Christianity of Jesus differed radically from that of St. *Paul, also won a wide following. Another strong influence on the formation of modern Protestantism was that of A. *Harnack (q.v.), whose *Wesen des Christentums* presented our Lord as the prophet of a religion without priests and dogma, but with the Fatherhood of God and the Brotherhood of men as its central theme. In Calvinism also there has been a tendency to abandon old positions such as the rigid doctrine of Predestination.

These liberal currents, however, have been variously counteracted. From the time of the *Oxford Movement there has been a strong group in the C of E concerned with the defence of traditional doctrine and practice. Recently there has been a similar movement in Germany. S. *Kierkegaard had also endeavoured to infuse a new objectivism into the Protestant Church in *Denmark. And in 18th- and 19th-cent. Protestantism generally, there continued a large body of conservative belief, the strength of which, because it was less vociferous than many of the more academic theologians, has often been much under-estimated. In the present cent. the most influential protagonist of the objective realities of Christianity has been K. *Barth. His *Römerbrief* (1919) marked a decisive break in the universities with the earlier psychological systems and a return to a Theology of Revelation. His influence has been very deep on the Continent as well as in Great Britain and America, where it has done much to break the reign of the more negative elements of German criticism. This return to the foundations coincides with an increasing desire to overcome the old divisions. Union is sought not only among the various Protestant Churches and sects, but also with the Orthodox E. Churches, and the *Oecumenical Movement is a living expression of this desire for unity.

The writings of many of the early leaders are pr. in the *Corpus Reformatorum*, ed. C. G. Bretschneider–H. E. Bindseil and others (Halle, &c., 1834 ff.). Collection of the Protestant confessions tr. into English in P. *Schaff, *The History of the Creeds*, iii (1878), with discussion in vol. i (1878), pp. 203–930. R. W. *Dale, *Protestantism*. Its Ultimate Principle (1874). O. Ritschl, *Dogmengeschichte des Protestantismus*. Grundlagen und Grundzüge der theologischen Gedanken- und Lehrbildung in den protestantischen Kirchen (4 vols., 1908–27). E. *Troeltsch, *Die Bedeutung des Protestantismus für die Entstehung der modernen Welt* (1911; ed. 2, Beiheft ii der *Historische Zeitschrift*, 1924; Eng. tr., 1912). K. *Heim, *Das Wesen des evangelischen Christentums* (1925; Eng. tr. 1935). R. H. Tawney, *Religion and the Rise of Capitalism*. A Historical Study (Holland Memorial Lectures for 1922; 1926). C. J. Cadoux, *Catholicism and Christianity*. A Vindication of Progressive Protestantism (1928). K. Leese, *Die Religion des protestantischen Menschen* (1938). T. Siegfried, *Das protestantische Prinzip in Kirche und Welt* (1939). P. *Tillich, *The Protestant Era* (Chicago, Ill., 1948; London, 1951). J. Dillenberger–C. Welch, *Protestant Christianity interpreted through its Development* (New York, 1954). C. H. H. Wright–C. Neil (edd.), *A Protestant Dictionary* (1904). F. *Kattenbusch in *P.R.E.* (ed. 3), xvi (1905), pp. 135–82; H. Hermelinck in *R.G.G.* (ed. 2), iv (1930), cols. 1582–1600, both s.v. 'Protestantismus'.

PROTEVANGELIUM, The. A modern title of the apocryphal Infancy Narrative, also known as the Book of *James (q.v.). It was so described by G. Postel (d. 1581) whose Lat. transl. of it was published by T. *Bibliander as *Protoevangelion Jacobi, fratris Domini, de natalibus Jesu Christi, et Virginis Mariae; cum Evangelio vitaque S. Marci Evangelistae* (Basle, 1552).

PROTHESIS (Gk. πρόθεσις). In the E. Church, the word is used (1) for the table on which the solemn preparation (*Proskomide) of the Eucharistic gifts takes place; (2) for the chamber to the left of the apse of the church, on the opposite side to the *diaconicon, in which the table just mentioned stands; and (3) for the Proskomide (q.v.) itself.

PROTO-LUKE. A first draft which St.*Luke is supposed to have made of his Gospel. The theory was first developed by B. H. *Streeter in an article in the *Hibbert Journal*, Oct. 1921, and in a fuller form in his *Four Gospels* (1924), ch. viii. It is suggested that Proto-Luke consisted mainly of those sections of the existing Gospel which were peculiar to Luke, together with material derived from '*Q', and that only at a later stage did the Gospel reach its present form by the addition of the Infancy Narratives (ch. 1 and 2) and the matter provided by the Gospel of St. *Mark.

PROTOMARTYR (i.e. First Martyr). A title commonly given to St. *Stephen (Acts 7. 60), and also occasionally to the first martyrs of different countries, e.g. to St. *Alban, the 'Protomartyr of England'.

PROTONOTARY APOSTOLIC. A member of the chief college of prelates in the Roman *Curia. The office, which dates back to very early times, has undergone frequent transformations. At present there are four classes of Protonotaries, the highest group (membership of which is limited to seven holders at any one time) being termed 'protonotarii de numero participantium'.

PROVERBS, Book of. A poetical Book of the OT, part of the '*Hagiographa', and usually placed after the *Psalms. The Book is divided into eight clearly marked sections: (1) chs. 1–9 is a series of counsels given by Divine Wisdom, which '*Solomon' identifies with the 'fear of the Lord'. It ends in the description of the two feasts, of wisdom which leads to understanding (9. 1–6), and of folly which leads to '*Sheol' (9. 13–16). It is followed by (2) chs. 10. 1–22. 16, a second collection also headed 'The Proverbs of Solomon'. These are all simple and unconnected distichs enouncing particular rules of conduct. Section (3), chs. 22.17 – 24.22, entitled 'The Words of the Wise', consists of small groups of practical counsels, more developed than the preceding ones. They are followed by another small collection, (4) 24. 23–34, the 'Sayings of the Wise', containing maxims of behaviour to one's neighbour. (5) Chs. 25–29 purport to be a further collection of 'Proverbs of Solomon, which the men of Hezekiah king of Judah copied out'; they are also chiefly distichs, but in more popular style than the former Solomonic collection. This is followed by section (6), ch. 30, 'The Words of Agar', and (7), 31. 1–9, 'The Words of King Lemuel'. The Book ends with (8), 31. 10–31, an acrostic poem in praise of the virtuous woman. After much hesitation the Jews recognized the Book as Scriptural, but prob. not before the 1st cent. A.D. The Christian Church took the Book over from the Jews in the Greek Bible. It is quoted as Scripture in Rom. 3. 15 and Jas. 4. 6.

Traditionally associated with Solomon, Prov. is most probably a compilation of several collections of proverbs, the compiler being perhaps also the author of the first section, for he distinguishes between the 'Proverbs' of other authors and his own. The ascription of certain sections to Solomon, vigorously contested by most critics, who would refer the whole of the Book to the Hellenistic period, has recently found defenders; for the influence on it of early Egyptian proverb literature (2000–1000 B.C.) is being more and more recognized and would support an earlier date. A satisfactory answer to the questions of times and authors of the other collections is almost impossible. The redaction of the whole may have been made c. 350 or, if the passages on the 'strange woman' be regarded as symbolizing Hellenistic culture, about 300 B.C. The book as a whole was very little commented on in antiquity and the Middle Ages, but frequently in modern times, e.g. by P. *Melanchthon (1525), Card. T. *Cajetan (1542), and J. B. *Bossuet (1693). In the Christian Liturgy it is frequently used, e.g. in the Roman Missal the Praise of Wisdom in 8. 22-35 forms the Epistle for the Feast of the *Immaculate Conception, while the Poem of the Virtuous Woman (31. 10-31) is that for the Common of a Matron (*Missa pro nec Virgine nec Martyre*).

Commentaries by C. H. Toy (I.C.C., 1899), T. T. Perowne (Camb. Bib., AV, 1899), G. C. Martin (Cent. Bib., on Prov., Eccles., and Song of Sol., 1908, pp. 9–207), W. O. E. Oesterley (West. Comm., 1929), K. Marti (K.H.C., xv, 1897), W. Frankenberg (H.K.A.T., Abt. 2, Bd. iii, Theil 1; 1898) and B. Gemser (H.A.T., Reihe 1, Abt., xvi; 1937). S. C. Malan, *Original Notes on the Book of Proverbs* (3 vols., 1889–93). T. K. *Cheyne, *Job and Solomon, or The Wisdom of the Old Testament* (1887), pp. 117–78. A. Hudal, *Die religiösen und sittlichen Ideen des Spruchbuches* (Scripta Pontificii Instituti Biblici, Rome, 1914). G. Boström, *Proverbiastudien. Die Weisheit und das Fremde Weib in Spr. 1–9* (Lunds Universitets Årsskrift N.F. Avd. 1, Bd. xxx, Nr. 3; 1935).

PROVIDENTISSIMUS DEUS (1893). The encyclical on the study of the Holy Scriptures issued by Pope *Leo XIII on 18 Nov. 1893. Its purpose was to give official guidance, esp. to the clergy, in the new situation in Biblical studies brought about by recent discoveries in archaeology and literary criticism. While stressing the importance of the study of the new evidence, it condemned the use made of it in some quarters (with a clear ref. to such scholars as A. F. *Loisy and M. *D'Hulst though they were not mentioned by name). It expressly reaffirmed the pronouncements of the *Tridentine and *Vatican Councils on Biblical Inspiration and on the Scriptural text and asserted that the whole of Scripture was written 'at the dictation of the Holy Ghost' (*Spiritu Sancto dictante*). Both conservatives and liberals appealed to the document; but, in the next decade, owing to the spread of *Modernism (q.v.), the Encyclical was increasingly interpreted in official quarters in a conservative sense. See also *Biblical Commission*.

Two later encyclicals, Pope *Benedict XV's 'Spiritus Paraclitus' (15 Sept. 1920) and Pope *Pius XII's 'Divino Afflante Spiritu' (30 Sept. 1943), both dealt with the same issues as 'Providentissimus Deus' in the light of the further development of Biblical studies. All three reflect the ever-growing interest in the study of the Bible along modern lines in the RC Church.

Text pr. in *A.S.S.*, xxvi (1893–4), pp. 269–92. Extracts in Denz.–Bann. (ed. 1952), pp. 542–8 (Nos. 1941–53). Teodorico da Castel San Pietro in *E.C.*, x (1953), cols. 217–19, s.v.; P. Nober, ib., xi (1953), col. 1162 f., s.v. 'Spiritus Paraclitus'; C. Testore, S.J., ib., iv (1950), col. 1772 f., s.v. 'Divino Afflante Spiritu'.

PROVINCE. A group of *dioceses, territorially contiguous, forming an ecclesiastical unit, so-called because such groups were originally coincident with the Provinces of the Roman Empire. See also *Archbishop*; *Metropolitan*; *Primate*.

PROVINCIAL. An official of a religious order subject to the superior-general. He exercises authority over all houses of the order within a given area, though a house may sometimes be geographically in one province, but subject to the Provincial of another. The office of Provincial, unknown to the old monastic orders, came into being with the more centralized *Mendicant orders, and from them was taken over by the majority of modern orders and congregations. The Provincial is normally elected by the provincial chapter, subject to the approval of the *general chapter; in the *Jesuit Order he is appointed by the *General. The Provincial holds office for a term of years, usually three or six, never for life. His chief duty is to make regular visitations of the houses of his jurisdiction and to supervise the life of the religious and the administration of their property.

PROVISORS, Statutes of. Four laws passed in England in the 14th cent. to check the practice of Papal 'provision', or nomination to vacant benefices over the head of the ordinary patron.

The First, passed in 1351, provided that 'the King and other lords shall present unto Benefices of their own, and not the Bishop of Rome'.

The Second, passed in 1353, imposed the penalties of '*Praemunire for suing in a foreign realm, or impeaching of Judgement given [*sc.* in the English courts]'.

The Third, passed in 1365, confirmed the law of 1351.

The Fourth, passed in 1389, enacted that benefices accepted contrary to the earlier laws of Provisors should be forfeited, and that proceedings should be taken against anyone attempting to enforce a provision by summons or excommunication, and against any prelate enforcing such a provision.

Despite these Statutes, the practice of provision continued down to the *Reformation, and was revived during the reign of *Mary. See also *Praemunire*.

Text, with Eng. tr., in A. J. Stephens, *The Statutes Relating to the Ecclesiastical and Eleemosynary Institutions of England, Wales, Ireland, India, and the Colonies* (1845), pp. 58–66, 67–70, and 84–7. Eng. tr. of the last, reciting in full the Statute of 1351, also in Gee-Hardy, pp. 112-21 (No. xxxix), mainly repr. in H. Bettenson (ed.), *Documents of the Christian Church* ('World's Classics', 1943), pp. 233-9. For general background see G. Barraclough, *Papal Provisions* (1935). G. Crosse in *D.E.C.H.*, p. 476 f.

PROVOST (Lat. *praepositus*, Germ. *Probst*). In early Christian usage the official next in dignity to the abbot of a monastery, but now esp. the head of an ecclesiastical chapter. In England the title is used in the newer dioceses (e.g. Bradford, Derby, Portsmouth) of the head of the cathedral chapter where the cathedral is also a parish church and the Provost is thus also an incumbent with cure of souls. The title is used in a non-ecclesiastical sense for the heads of certain colleges, e.g. of Oriel, Queen's, and Worcester Colleges at Oxford, King's College at Cambridge, and Eton College.

PRUDENTIUS AURELIUS CLEMENS (348–c. 410), Latin poet and hymn-writer. A Spaniard by birth, he practised at the bar and made a successful career in civil administration. The retirement of his later life was occupied in devout exercises and Christian writings. His apologetic poems, 'Apotheosis' (on the theology of the Incarnation), 'Hamartigenia' (against *Marcion), and 'Contra *Symmachum' (on the occasion of a temporary recrudescence of paganism), exhibit his distinction in abstract thought as well as in the imitation of classical models. His hymns are reflective and didactic, rarely less than 100 lines long, and composed in classical metres; extracts from them are found in most W. breviaries. One collection, the *Cathemerinon* (καθημερινῶν), consists of hymns designed for daily use; another, the *Peristephanon* (περὶ στεφάνων) sings the praises of a number of Spanish and Italian martyrs. The 'Psychomachia', a description of Christian asceticism under the allegory of a spiritual warfare, exercised a profound influence upon medieval poetry.

Of the older edd., the best is that of F. Arévalo (2 vols., Rome, 1788-9) with extended comm.; repr. in J. P. Migne, *PL.*, lix and lx. Crit. text by J. Bergman (C.S.E.L., lxi; 1926). Text with Fr. transl., also ed. M. Lavarenne in 'Collection des Universités de France' (1943 ff.); text with Eng. tr. by H. J. Thomson (Loeb, 1949 ff.). R. J. Deferrari-J. Marshall Campbell, *A Concordance of Prudentius* (Cambridge, Mass., 1932). A. S. Walpole, *Early Latin Hymns* (1922), pp. 115-48. A. Puech, *Prudence* (1888); J. Bergman, *A. Prudentius Clemens, der grösste christliche Denker des Altertums* (Dorpat, 1922). M. Lavarenne, *Étude sur la langue du poète Prudence* (1933), with bibl. Bardenhewer, iii, 440-3; Altaner (ed. 1950), pp. 358-61. G. Bardy in *D.T.C.*, xiii (pt. 1, 1936), cols. 1076-9.

PRUDENTIUS, GALINDO (d. 861), Bp. of Troyes. He was a native of Spain, became a chaplain at the court of *Louis the Pious, and, c. 843, Bp. of Troyes. He played an important part in the controversy on *Predestination between *Hincmar of Reims and the monk, *Gottschalk, defending the *Augustinianism of the latter, and denying the general saving will of God. In his 'Epistola ad Hincmarum', he taught the Augustinian doctrine of the double predestination and, in 852, wrote a treatise 'De

Praedestinatione contra Joannem Scotum', i.e. against John Scotus *Erigena, whom Hincmar had called to his aid. Acc. to Hincmar, he signed the four anti-Augustinian propositions of the Synod of *Quiercy (853). In 856, however, he wrote his 'Epistola Tractoria', addressed to Abp. Venilo of Sens, in which he opposed to the decisions of Quiercy four counter-propositions, teaching Augustinian doctrine of the strictest type. Prudentius also wrote a continuation of the 'Annales Bertiniani' for the years 835-861, valuable for the history of the Frankish Empire.

His writings on the predestination controversy were first publd. by G. Mauguin at Paris in 1650. Crit. ed. of his continuation of the 'Annales Bertiniani' by G. H. Pertz in *M.G.H.*, Scriptores, i (1826), pp. 429-54. Collected ed. in J. P. Migne, *PL*, cxv, 965-1458. J. Girgensohn, *Prudentius und die bertinianischen Annalen* (Riga, 1875). Manitius, i, esp. pp. 344-8. H. Peltier in *D.T.C.*, xiii (pt. 1; 1936), cols. 1079-84, s.v. 'Prudence de Troyes'.

PRYMER (Lat. *Primarium*). A devotional book current among the educated laity in the later Middle Ages. Its nucleus was ordinarily the *office of the BVM, compiled for use after the canonical offices, and supplemented by the *Seven Penitential and fifteen *Gradual Psalms, a *litany, and offices for the dead. A considerable part of the 'Prymer' was often in the vernacular, and in this way the laity in England were to some extent prepared for the 'Order of the *Communion' and the BCP. The first complete primer to be printed in England was issued by W. de Worde c. 1494.

A specimen dating from c. 1400 is printed in H. Littlehales, *The Prymer or Prayer Book of the Lay People in the Middle Ages*. Edited . . . from the MS. (G 24) in St. John's College, Cambridge (2 vols., 1891-2).

PRYNNE, WILLIAM (1600–69), *Puritan controversialist. Educated at Bath Grammar School and Oriel College, Oxford, he was admitted at Lincoln's Inn in 1621 and later became a barrister. As a strong and unbending Puritan, he was soon in conflict with the High Church party. In 1627 he published his first book, *The Perpetuity of a Regenerate Man's Estate*. A violent attack on the stage in *Histriomastix* (1632), thought to contain veiled attacks on both *Charles I and *Henrietta Maria, led to his sentence by the Star Chamber on 17 February 1634 to imprisonment for life, a fine of £5,000, expulsion from Lincoln's Inn, the loss of his university degree, and the pillory, where he was to lose both his ears. The whole sentence, except the permanence of the imprisonment and the fine, was carried out. In 1637 an attack on the 'Declaration of *Sports' led to a fresh sentence by the Star Chamber and he was imprisoned first at Caernarvon and then in Mont Orgueil Castle in Jersey; but the unpopularity of ship-money and the metropolitical visitation had changed public opinion and Prynne now met with wide sympathy. When the Long Parliament met in 1640 he was liberated and defended the right of taking up arms against the King, notably in his *The Sovereign Power of Parliaments and Kingdoms* (1643). He also carried on a literary warfare with W. *Laud. On the other hand, his ideal of the supremacy of State over Church put him out of sympathy with the *Independents, whom he attacked in *Twelve Considerable Serious Questions touching Church Government* (1644); and he hated the notion of toleration. In 1648 he issued *The Levellers Levelled*, a defence of the House of Lords. Eventually on 7 Nov. 1648 he obtained a seat (Newport, Cornwall) in the Commons and unexpectedly argued for conciliation with the King and opposed his execution. In consequence he was included in 'Pride's Purge' (6 Dec.) and imprisoned. On 1 Jan. 1649 he published *A Brief Memento to the Present Unparliamentary Junto*. Later in the year he attacked the new tax imposed by the Commonwealth in *A Legal Vindication of the Liberties of England* and embarked on a large-scale work against the new Parliament; and in 1650 he was again imprisoned, without a trial. After his release (1653) he ceased from further attacks on O. *Cromwell's régime and wrote against the Papists and *Quakers. To his annoyance he was excluded from the Rump Parliament (1659) and fearlessly criticized it in a long series of controversial writings. He eventually resumed his seat in Parliament on 21 February 1660 and three days later brought in the bill for the dissolution preparatory to *Charles II's restoration. Shortly after his return, Charles appointed him Keeper of the Tower Records. His strong *Presbyterianism, however, soon brought him into conflict with the reviving *Anglicanism, which he attacked in a long series of publications, among them *A Short, Sober, Pacific Examination of Exuberances in the Common Prayer* (1661) and *Apology for Tender Consciences touching Not Bowing at the Name of Jesus* (1661). But he continued to take a prominent part in Parliamentary affairs until his death. He also wrote extensively in his last years, defending on historical grounds the subjection of the clergy to the Crown.

S. R. Gardiner (ed.), *Documents Relating to the Proceedings against William Prynne in 1634 and 1637* (Camden Society, New Series, xiii; 1877), with the beginning of a life by J. Bruce (d. 1869) [up to 1624], pp. i–xxxv, and list of Prynne's works by Bruce, pp. 101–18. Modern study by E. W. Kirby (Cambridge, Mass., 1931), with list of Prynne's works, pp. 194–207, and other bibl., pp. 207–19. C. H. Firth in *D.N.B.*, xlvi (1896), pp. 432–7; S. R. Gardiner–P. C. Yorke in *E.B.* (ed. 11), xxii (1911), pp. 531–3, s.v.

PSALMS, Book of (Gk. ψαλμοί, 'songs, accompanied by string music'), in the *Septuagint the first of the *Hagiographa, but in the *Vulgate, the AV and RV, preceded by Job. The Book contains 150 Psalms, variously enumerated. By combining Pss. 9 and 10 of the Hebrew *Massoretic text (followed by the BCP version, AV and RV), the Gk. and Lat. (Vulg.) versions, up to Psalm 114, remain one number behind the Hebrew counting (e.g. Ps. 90 AV is Ps. 89 Vulg.); Pss. 114 and 115 (Heb.) are again conflated in Gk. and Lat., but as the following Ps. 116 is divided in two, the Gk. and Lat. numeration is again one behind that of the Heb. up to Ps. 147 which is divided in two in Gk. and Lat. Hence only the first eight and the last three Psalms agree in both enumerations.

The Psalms are now divided into five Books, probably after the model of the Books of the *Pentateuch, viz. 1–41, 42–72, 73–89, 90–106, 107–50, each except the last ending with a doxology. But this division is relatively late. There are clear indications of earlier groupings which point back to independently existing collections, e.g. the concluding notice after 72 ('The prayers of David the son of Jesse are ended'). Thus Pss. 3–41 are all (except 10, a continuation of 9, and 33) headed 'Of David'; 42–49 (except 43, a continuation of 42) 'Of the Sons of Korah'; and 73–83 (also 50) 'Of Asaph'. Other groupings, e.g. the *Gradual Psalms (Pss. 120–34, q.v.) are later. Of 'Alphabetic Psalms', Ps. 119 is the most elaborate, each section of eight verses beginning with a separate letter of the alphabet.

The rubrics in the *Massoretic text and in the Septuagint make it clear that in its present form the Psalter is essentially a liturgical book; it has often been described as 'the hymnal of the Second *Temple'. The whole book is marked by the characteristic poetic form of *Parallelism. From early times attempts have been made to discover a definite metre, but the most that can be said with certainty is that the Pss. have a rhythm of their own and that poetical devices such as refrains and acrostics are frequent.

The popular belief that David was the author of the whole Psalter can no longer be sustained. It was held by many of the Latin Fathers, e.g. St. *Ambrose and St. *Augustine, and not seriously questioned during the Middle Ages nor by the Reformers, except J. *Calvin; but it had been strongly opposed by St. *Jerome. Most modern scholars believe that the Pss. come from a variety of authors and are of widely differing date; but against the view, prevalent in the later 19th cent., that few if any Pss. are pre-exilic, a more moderate opinion has recently been gaining ground. Very few scholars to-day would accept the view maintained by B. Duhm that the bulk of the Psalter belongs to the *Maccabean period. Though we may prefer to assign few, if any, of the Pss. to David, there is no reason to doubt that many of them come from the early days of the Monarchy (so H. Gressmann). Uncertainty also prevails as to the date at which the various collections were made; but these are almost certainly post-exilic.

The subject-matter of the Psalms covers the whole range of the relations between God and man. Jehovah, the eternal, immutable, and omnipotent, is the Creator of the universe which He upholds and governs by His Divine Providence. Himself all-holy, He demands holiness and penitence (see *Penitential Psalms*) from His creatures, but His supreme justice is tempered by His mercy which the Psalmists praise and implore in the language of childlike trust. Friendship and communion with God and the beauty of His Law and His Temple are constant objects of prayer and gratitude. The Psalmists' zeal for the right does not prevent them from giving passionate expression to their desire to see God's vengeance on the wicked (see *Imprecatory Psalms*). The conception of life after death is still mostly confined to the shadowy realm of *Sheol, though a brighter hope is already sometimes envisaged (Pss. 16. 10–12, 49. 15, 73. 23 f.). The aspirations of the Psalmists culminate in the expectation of the *Messiah, the Son of God (Ps. 2) and the great Priest-King (Ps. 110), who will cast down his enemies (Ps. 89) and, having himself suffered, will unite the whole world in his worship (Ps. 22).

Recently the traditional exegesis has been challenged at several points. R. Smend and others have maintained that the 'I' of the Psalms commonly refers not to an individual but to Israel as a nation. Even more radical are the theories of S. Mowinckel (*Psalmenstudien*, 1921), for whom the evil men about whom the Psalmists complain are frequently sorcerers and the Psalms themselves a kind of countercharm. He also held that the so-called 'Accession Psalms' in which Jehovah is described as a king find their origin in an otherwise unknown feast of the Inthronization of Jehovah. It must be admitted that, despite the considerable attention which Mowinckel's theories, which are based on supposed parallels in the Babylonian literature, have received, they have won little acceptance.

In the Christian Church the Psalter has from the first been used for the same purposes as by the Jews. Its intrinsic spiritual depth and beauty made it from the earliest times a regular source of public and private prayer. Instances of its use by the Lord Himself are His self-application of the metaphor of the 'stone which the builders rejected' (118. 22) and His self-defence against the Jews with Ps. 82. 6 'I said, Ye are gods'. On the Cross He voiced both His desolation and His supreme act of surrender in the words of the Psalms (22. 1, 31. 6). Both St. *Paul and the author of Heb. constantly see the Psalmists' teaching fulfilled in Christ. The Patristic tradition follows the same lines.

The Psalter continued to be held in the highest regard in the next generations. Jerome, Ambrose, and many others recommend its regular use. St. Augustine, in his long commentary, finds Christ or His Church prefigured in almost every Psalm. As a book of private and public devotion it has retained its importance throughout the centuries. In the Divine Office of the RC Church it is recited once every week, in the C of E once every month, and both Continental Protestant and English Nonconformist piety have been nourished on it. The Psalms were an integral part of the spiritual life of men as widely apart as *Benedictines and *Puritans, M. *Luther and St. *Francis Xavier, Charles *Wesley and J. H. *Newman.

Commentaries by J. M. *Neale and R. F. *Littledale (mystical interpretation; 4 vols., 1860–74); J. J. S. Perowne (1864); T. K. *Cheyne (1888); F. Baethgen (German, 1892); B. Duhm (German, 1899); A. F. Kirkpatrick (Camb. Bible, 1902); C. A. *Briggs (I.C.C., 2 vols., 1906); P. Boylan (RC, 2 vols., 1920–4); T. E. Bird (RC, 2 vols., 1927); W. E. Barnes (West. Comm., 2 vols., 1931); W. O. E. Oesterley (2 vols., 1939).

W. T. Davison, *The Praises of Israel* (1893); C. L. Marson, *The Psalms at Work* (1894); R. E. *Prothero, *The Psalms in Human Life* (1904); S. R. Driver, *The Parallel Psalter* (1904); S. Mowinkel, *Psalmenstudien* (6 parts, Kristiania, 1921–4); J. P. Peters, *The Psalms as Liturgies* (1922); D. C. Simpson (ed.), *The Psalmists* (1926); A. C. Welch, *The Psalter* (1926); P. S. Waddy, *Homes of the Psalms* (1928); H. N. Snaith, *Studies in the Psalter* (1934); L. James, *Songs of Zion* (1936); W. O. E. Oesterley, *A Fresh Approach to the Psalms* (1937).

PSALMS, Imprecatory. See *Imprecatory Psalms*.

PSALMS, Metrical. See *Metrical Psalms*.

PSALMS OF SOLOMON. See *Solomon, Psalms of*.

PSALTERS, Hieronymian. St. *Jerome issued three separate translations of the Psalms into Latin. (1) A version of the Psalter based wholly on the *Septuagint and issued *c*. 384. Jerome admitted that he produced it hastily (*cursim*). This has commonly been identified with the '*Roman Psalter' (q.v.). (2) The '*Gallican Psalter' (q.v.), based on *Origen's *Hexaplaric text of the Septuagint (in Jerome's time still preserved at *Caesarea). This translation, which was made at *Bethlehem *c*. 392, is the version printed in the editions of the *Vulgate. (3) The 'Hebrew Psalter' ('Psalterium iuxta Hebraeos'), translated *c*. 400 from the Hebrew text. Conservatism in the practice of worship prevented this Psalter from ever replacing the older versions in public use.

The version of the Psalms in the BCP, which is almost that of the '*Great Bible' (1539), was based on M. *Coverdale's translation from the Vulgate, i.e. from the 'Gallican Psalter', and thus embodies many Septuagintal readings not found in the Hebrew.

PSALTERY (Lat. *Psalterium*). In the medieval W. rite, the book which contained the Psalms for recitation at the Divine Office. The arrangement was commonly acc. to the requirements of the Office. Psalteries often contained also the corresponding *antiphons, the *canticles recited in the Office, and other matter such as hymns, litanies, and prayers. When their contents were later incorporated in the *Breviary they fell into disuse.

PSELLUS, MICHAEL (*c*. 1019–*c*. 1078), Byzantine philosopher, historian, theologian, and statesman. He was Imperial secretary to Michael V (1041–2), and secretary of state to his successor, Constantine IX (1042–54). A keen enthusiast for the revival of classical learning and esp. *Platonic philosophy, in 1045 he was appointed the first professor of philosophy at the newly founded university of *Constantinople. Having incurred the disgrace of the Emperor, he entered a monastery in 1054, but soon returned to the court on Constantine's death, where he took part in many intrigues until, in 1072, he fell from favour once more and spent the rest of his life in obscurity.

Psellus wrote a large number of treatises on a wide range of subjects as well as many speeches, letters, and poems. His Χρονογραφία remains an important source for the history of the years 976–1077 and was utilized by later historians such as *Anna Comnena and *Zonaras. His chief theological writings are expositions of various Biblical books including an exegesis of seventy-two psalms in verse, a short treatise against the Latin theologians, and a dialogue Περὶ ἐνεργείας δαιμόνων against the *Messalians. His philosophical works include commentaries on the 'Timaeus' of *Plato and on the Περὶ ἑρμηνείας and other writings of *Aristotle.

Works repr. from various sources in J. P. Migne, *PG*, cxxii, 477–1358. Ed. of his unpubld. *Scripta Minora* begun by E. Kurtz–F. Drexl (Munich, 1936; only one part issued). His Χρονογραφία ('History') ed. C. Sathas, from the only surviving and poor MS., Bibl. Nat. 1712 ('Byzantine Texts' ed. J. B. Bury, London, 1899); Eng. tr. of 'Chronographia' by E. R. A. Sewter (London, 1953). The most important of the older discussions on Psellus is the account in L. *Allatius, *De Psellis et eorum Scriptis* (Rome, 1634); repr. with corrections and additions in J. P. Migne, loc. cit., cols. 477–536. Modern studies include C. Zervos, *Un Philosophe néo-platonicien du XIe siècle* (1920), and E. Renauld, *Étude de la langue et du style de Michel Psellos* (1920). Joan M. Hussey, *Church and Learning in the Byzantine Empire, 867–1185* (1937), incl. bibl. to Psellus, pp. 236–8. Krumbacher, pp. 433–44. M. Jugie, A.A., in *D.T.C.*, xiii (pt. 1; 1936), cols. 1149–58, s.v. 'Psellos (Michel)'; J. Lippl in *L.Th.K.*, viii (1936), col. 547 f.

PSEUDEPIGRAPHA. Writings ascribed to some other than their real author, generally with a view to giving them an enhanced authority. The term is used esp. of the pseudonymous Jewish works, dating from the centuries immediately before and after the beginning of the Christian era, which were excluded from the Greek *Canon of the OT. Among these writings are the 'Book of *Enoch', the 'Assumption of *Moses', the later 'Books of *Baruch', the 'Psalms of *Solomon', and the 'Fourth Book of *Maccabees'. On the other hand, pseudonymous books which occur in the OT or *Apocrypha, e.g. 'the Rest of the Book of *Esther' and the '*Wisdom of Solomon', are by convention not ordinarily reckoned among the Pseudepigrapha.

The most convenient collection of these writings, with full discussion of authorship, dates, &c., is *The Apocrypha and Pseudepigrapha of the Old Testament*, ed. by R. H. *Charles, vol. ii: Pseudepigrapha (1913). For further bibl. see under separate treatises.

PSEUDO-CLEMENTINES. See *Clementine Literature*.

PSEUDO-ISIDORIAN DECRETALS. See *False Decretals*.

PSILANTHROPISM (Gk. ψιλὸς ἄνθρωπος, 'a mere man'). The heretical doctrine that Christ was just a man and not God and man in one Person. In the '*Little Labyrinth', quoted by *Eusebius (*HE*, v, xxviii, 6), *Theo-

dotus the Cobbler is said to have taught that He was a 'mere man' (ψιλὸς ἄνθρωπος). The single word, ψιλάνθρωπος, seems to occur for the first time in *Anastasius of Sinai (Hodegos, xiii; J. P. Migne, *PL*, lxxxiii, 216 C), while the noun 'Psilanthropism' is apparently a 19th cent. coinage.

PSYCHOLOGY OF RELIGION. As a scientific discipline this study dates from the last decades of the 19th cent. when the methods of general psychology were first applied to religious data. It began first in America, whence interest in the science spread to Germany and later to other European countries and to Britain. Its scope is limited by its object, viz. to collect, arrange, and classify the facts of religious experience. The problems of the interpretation and validity of these experiences remain in the end outside its competence and belong to the province of theology. Nevertheless the psychologist's interpretation of religious phenomena will be affected by his individual beliefs. What the student who acknowledges a personal God and a supernatural order regards as providential aids, Divine touches, visions, and revelations, the rationalist will see only as sensations, emotions, and illusions. And in fact some religious understanding is almost essential for an intelligent interpretation of religious phenomena, which, in turn, can prove very valuable in the field of personal ethics and moral theology.

The main sources to which the religious psychologist turns for his material are religious autobiographies, e.g. of St. *Augustine, St. *Teresa, or John *Wesley, *questionnaires*, and personal introspection. Of these the most valuable is the first. *Questionnaires* are apt to be misleading, since they are not normally answered by those most qualified to speak, and personal experience is necessarily strictly limited. Among the chief facts investigated are the feeling of dependence on a Divine Being, conversion experiences, the subjective effects of prayer and worship and the manifold phenomena of mysticism. Modern psychologists assign an important role to the subconscious also in religious manifestations, esp. in the conversion experiences looked for in many Protestant groups.

New lines of research have been opened up by the so-called 'New Psychology' of the Psycho-analytical school. S. Freud's doctrines were developed, and extensively applied therapeutically, on the Continent in the early years of this century, and since the World War of 1914–18 have penetrated widely in Britain. Preoccupation with the sex-instinct led Freud to the view that all religion is but its 'sublimation'. His disciple, C. G. Jung, considers religion the principal factor of integration in human life, the loss of which often means neurosis. He emphasizes the psychological safeguards of dogma and ritual and insists on the importance of symbolism ('archetypes') in psychological life. Jung's ideas have found much approval also among students of religion and led to some fruitful developments, esp.

when taken out of their medical context and applied to normal religious experience.

E. D. Starbuck, *The Psychology of Religion* (1889); W. *James, *The Varieties of Religious Experience* (Gifford Lectures for 1901–2, 1902), W. McDougall, *An Introduction to Social Psychology* (1908); E. S. Ames, *The Psychology of Religious Experience* (1910); J. H. Leuba, *A Psychological Study of Religion* (1912); J. B. Pratt, *The Religious Consciousness*. A Psychological Study (1920); R. H. Thouless, *Introduction to the Psychology of Religion* (1923); J. A. Hadfield, *Psychology and Morals* (1923); W. B. Selbie, *Psychology of Religion* (1924); L. W. Grensted, *Psychology and God* (1930); C. G. Jung, *Psychology and Religion* (1938); V. White, O.P., *God and the Unconscious* (1952).

PTOLEMAIC SYSTEM. The body of astronomical doctrines elaborated by Ptolemy (2nd cent. A.D.) in his Μαθηματικὴ σύνταξις, which explained the apparent motions of the sun, moon and planets on the assumption that the earth was stationary. It was commonly accepted throughout the Middle Ages and later until it was replaced by the *Copernican theory.

PUBLIC WORSHIP REGULATION ACT. The Act (37 & 38 Vict., c. 35) passed in 1874 to suppress the growth of ritualism in the C of E. The Bill, drafted by Abp. A. C. *Tait, was drastically amended in Parliament in a more Protestant and *Erastian direction by Lord *Shaftesbury. It provided for the appointment, by the two Archbishops conjointly, of a barrister or ex-judge as Judge of the provincial courts of *Canterbury and *York to try ritual cases, with an appeal to the Privy Council. Tait secured (against Shaftesbury's wishes) provision for the bishop's veto of proceedings under the Act. The first judge was James Plaisted Baron Penzance, ex-judge of divorce. The imprisonment of four priests (Arthur Tooth, 1877; Thomas Pelham Dale, 1880; Richard William Erraght, 1880; Sidney Faithorn Green, 1881–2) for contumacy between 1877 and 1882 greatly discredited the Act and henceforward it has been virtually obsolete. Lord Penzance retired in 1899 to be succeeded by properly qualified ecclesiastical judges.

PUBLICAN (Gk. τελώνης ; Lat. *publicanus*). In the NT, a member of one of the financial organizations which farmed the taxes in the service of the Roman government. In view of the abuses and corruptions to which the system led, the publicans were the objects of widespread hatred. In the Gospels they are commonly coupled with the 'sinners'. St. *Matthew ('Levi'), one of their number, received the call to be an Apostle from his place of toll (τελώνιον) at *Capernaum (Mt. 9. 9, &c.). *Zacchæus is described as the 'chief publican' (ἀρχιτελώνης) of *Jericho (Lk. 19. 2).

E. *Schürer, *Geschichte des jüdischen Volkes im Zeitalter Jesu Christi*, i (ed. 3, 1901), esp. pp. 477–9, with reff. W. F. Adeney in *H.D.B.*, iv (1902), p. 172 f., s.v.; L. Fillion in *Dict. Bibl.*, v (1912), cols. 858–61, s.v. 'Publicains'; W. Schwahn in *P.W.*, Zweite Reihe, v (pt. 1: 1934), cols. 418–25, s.v. τελῶναι [mainly on 'publicans' in Republican, i.e. pre-N.T., times] ; W. Bauer, *Griechisch-deutsches Wörterbuch zu den Schriften des Neuen Testaments* (ed. 4, 1952), col. 1476, s.v. τελώνης.

PUDENS, St. (Gk. Πούδης). A Christian of *Rome who is mentioned in 2 Tim. 4. 21 as sending greetings along with Eubulus, *Linus, and Claudia to *Timothy. Tradition makes him St. *Peter's host at Rome. He is possibly the Pudens mentioned with Claudia in Martial's 'Epigrams' (4. 13; cf. 11. 53). There are no sufficient grounds for identifying the Pudens of the NT with the Pudens (prob. 3rd cent.) who gave his house on the Vicus Patricius (*titulus Pudentis* or *ecclesia Pudentiana*) to the Roman Church. See also foll. entry. Feast day, 19 May.

On the proposed identifications of the NT Pudens, see W. *Lock in *H.D.B.*, iv (1902), p. 173. J. P. Kirsch, *Die römischen Titelkirchen im Altertum* (Studien zur Geschichte und Kultur des Altertums, ix, Hftt. 1 and 2; 1918), pp. 61–7; A. Petrignani, *La basilica di S. Pudenziana in Roma* (Monumenti di antichità cristiana pubblicati dal Pontificio Istituto di Archeologia Cristiana, Ser. 2, i; 1934). H. *Marucchi in *Dict. Bibl.*, v (1912), cols. 862–8, s.v.; J. P. Kirsch in *L.Th.K.*, viii (1936), col. 560 f., s.v.

PUDENTIANA, St., also 'Potentiana'. Acc. to the Roman *Martyrology, she was a Roman virgin of the early Church, the daughter of St. *Pudens and the sister of St. *Praxedes. Probably the cultus rests on a mistaken popular notion which supposed that the '*ecclesia Pudentiana*' in Rome, really the church of St. Pudens, presupposed a 'St. Pudentiana'. The 'Acta' of Sts. Pudentiana and Praxedes, printed by the *Bollandists, are not earlier than the 8th cent. Feast day, also 19 May.

AA.SS., Mai. IV (1685), pp. 296–301. See also bibl. to preceding entry.

PUFENDORF, SAMUEL (1632–94). The first German professor of natural and international law. The son of a *Lutheran pastor, he became professor successively at Heidelberg (1661) and Lund (1670), historiographer to the court of Sweden (1677), and privy councillor to the Elector of Brandenburg (1688). Developing the system of H. *Grotius, he divided law into natural, civil, and moral, and maintained that while moral law was based on revelation and civil law on the positive enactments of the state, natural law had its basis in the instinct of society, and therefore ultimately in human reason. His chief book is *De Iure Naturae et Gentium* (1672), of which an Eng. trans. was published in 1710 (under the title, *Of the Law of Nature and Nations*). In his *De Habitu Religionis Christianae ad Vitam Civilem* (1687), he expounded the theory of Church government known as ' *Collegialism'. Pufendorf was also the author of many historical writings, among them *Einleitung zu der Historie der vornehmsten Reiche und Staaten . . . in Europa* (Frankfurt a.M., 1682), *Commentariorum de Rebus Suecicis Libri XXVI* (Utrecht, 1686; Eng. tr., with continuation, London, 1702), *De Rebus Gestis Friderici Wilhelmi Magni, Electoris Brandenburgici* (Berlin, 1695), and *De Rebus Gestis Friderici III Electoris Brandenburgici* (ib., 1784).

Photographic reproductions of Pufendorf's *De Officio Hominis et Civis juxta Legem Naturalem* [ed. 1682] with introd. by W. Schücking and Eng. tr. of text by F. G. Moore

(The Classics of International Law, x; 2 vols., New York, London, &c., 1927); of his *Elementorum Jurisprudentiae Universalis Libri Duo* [ed. 1672] with introd. by H. Wehberg and Eng. tr. of text by W. A. Oldfather (The Classics of International Law, xv; 2 vols., Oxford–London, 1931); and of his *De Jure Naturae et Gentium* [ed. 1688] with introd. by W. Simons and Eng. tr. of text by C. H. and W. A. Oldfather (ib., xvii; ib., 1934). Correspondence with Christian Thomasius, 1687–93, ed. E. Gigas (Munich–Leipzig, 1897). F. Lezius, *Der Toleransbegriff Lockes und Pufendorfs* (1900), pp. 58–115. F. Schenke, 'Pufendorfs Kirchenbegriff' in *Zeitschrift der Savigny-Stiftung für Rechtsgeschichte*, Kan. Abt., xiv (1925), pp. 39–61. G. Frank in *P.R.E.* (ed. 3), xvi (1905), pp. 315–18, s.v., with bibl.; G. Fasso in *E.C.*, x (1953), col. 304 f., s.v. for further bibl.

PUGIN, AUGUSTUS WELBY NORTH-MORE (1812–52), architect and *ecclesiologist. He was the chief initiator and inspirer of the 'Gothic Revival'. The son of Auguste-Charles, Comte de Pugin, a French refugee, *c.* 1835 he joined the RC Church, to which his attention had been directed through his admiration of Gothic architecture. Among his very many works were St. George's (RC) Cathedral, Southwark, and the chapel of St. Edmund's College, Ware. He also collaborated with C. Barry in his designs for the Houses of Parliament. His plans often suffered in execution as the money to carry them through was constantly lacking, esp. as the RCs by whom he was chiefly employed were a relatively poor body. Hence his designs often give a more adequate idea of Pugin's ideals than the buildings themselves. He also met with many difficulties from RCs who wanted to model their architecture on Italian prototypes. His most important writings were *The True Principles of Pointed or Christian Architecture* (1841), *An Apology for the Revival of Christian Architecture in England* (1843), and *The Present State of Ecclesiastical Architecture in England* (1843).

B. Ferrey, *Recollections of A. N. Welby Pugin, and his Father, Augustus Pugin* (1861). Modern life by M. Trappes-Lomax (London, 1932), with bibl. D. Gwynn, *Lord Shrewsbury, Pugin and the Catholic Revival* (1946). H. R. Hitchcock, *Early Victorian Architecture in Britain* (2 vols., 1954), esp. i, pp. 56–98, with illustrations in vol. ii, section III. P. Waterhouse in *D.N.B.*, xlvii (1896), pp. 6–10.

PULCHERIA, St. (399–453), E. Empress from 450. She was the daughter of the Emp. Arcadius (395–408), and elder sister of *Theodosius II (408–50); and a woman of uncommon ability and deep piety. From 414 to 416 she was entrusted by the Senate, despite her youth, with the guardianship of her weak-minded brother, Theodosius; and for several years she ran the Imperial palace at *Constantinople on strict and ascetic Christian principles. After Theodosius's marriage (421), she found life at court increasingly difficult, partly because of theological intrigues. A stalwart supporter of orthodoxy, she induced Theodosius to condemn *Nestorius. In 438 she put an end to the schism at Constantinople by bringing thither the bones of St. *Chrysostom. In the *Monophysite controversy she was again on the Orthodox side, and after the momentary triumph of Monophysitism at the *Latrocinium (449), she sought the support of

Pope *Leo I. After the sudden death of Theodosius in 450 she became Empress, taking the aged general and senator, Marcian, as her consort. In the interests of orthodoxy, she forthwith arranged for a General Council to meet at *Chalcedon in 451, and herself attended the sixth session in person. Since the Middle Ages she has been commemorated as a saint. Feast day, 10 Sept.

AA.SS., III (1750), pp. 503–40. Ada B. Teetgen, *Life and Times of the Empress Pulcheria* (popular; 1907). A. Bigelmair in *L.Th.K.*, viii (1936), cols. 563 f.

PULLEN, ROBERT (d. *c.* 1146), theologian. He is one of the earliest known masters in the schools of Oxford, where he began to teach the Scriptures in 1133, being at the same time archdeacon of *Rochester. After the death of Henry I (1135), he went to *Paris where he taught logic and theology, counted *John of Salisbury among his pupils, and was highly esteemed by St. *Bernard on account of his sound doctrine. Called to Rome by Innocent II, he was created cardinal in 1144 by Lucius II, and in the following year made chancellor of the Holy Roman Church, an office he held also under St. Bernard's disciple, *Eugenius III, who became Pope shortly afterwards. He used his influence in Rome against *Abelard and laid down his own doctrine in his 'Sentences', a compilation treating a wide range of theological subjects, but soon to be superseded by the 'Sentences' of *Peter Lombard.

His *Sententiae* are repr. from the ed. of H. Mathoud, O.S.B. (Paris, 1655), in J. P. Migne, *PL*, clxxxvi, 625–1152. F. Courtney, S.J., *Cardinal Robert Pullen.* (Analecta Gregoriana, lxiv, Ser. Theol., Sect. A (No. 10); 1954). F. Pelster, S.J., 'Einige Angaben über Leben und Schriften des Robertus Pullus, Kardinals und Kanzlers der römischen Kirche (d. 1146)' in *Scholastik*, xii (1937), pp. 239–47; A. Landgraf, 'Studien zur Theologie des zwölften Jahrhunderts. II. Literarhistorische Bemerkungen zu den Sentenzen des Robertus Pullus' in *Traditio*, i (1943), pp. 210–22. R. L. Poole, 'The Early Lives of Robert Pullen and Nicholas Breakspear' in A. G. Little–F. M. Powicke (edd.), *Essays in Medieval History Presented to T. F. Tout* (1925), esp. pp. 61–4 (maintains Pullen taught at *Exeter, not at Oxford). H. *Rashdall, *The Universities of Europe in the Middle Ages*, iii (ed. F. M. Powicke–A. B. Emden, 1936), p. 18 f.; id. in *D.N.B.*, xlvii (1896), p. 19 f., s.v.

PULPIT (Lat., *pulpitum*, 'platform'). An elevated stand of stone or wood for the preacher or reader. They first became general in the later Middle Ages. In early Christian times, the bishop preached from his *cathedra. Later the *ambo was used for the sermon and in still later times the rood-loft. Except in cathedrals the north side of the *nave is considered the proper place for the pulpit. Sometimes the workmanship of the pulpit is very elaborate, famous examples being the marble structures at Pisa and Siena and the wooden *baroque pulpits of the Netherlands. Pulpits are also generally found in monastic refectories, and sometimes against the outside wall of a church, e.g. at Magdalen College, Oxford. It is now customary to use the Latin word 'Pulpitum', not for the preaching-stand, but for the stone choir-screen which sometimes separates the choir from the nave in cathedral and monastic churches.

F. T. Dollman, *Examples of Ancient Pulpits Existing in England* (1849); J. C. Cox, *Pulpits, Lecterns and Organs in English Churches* (1915), pp. 1–147.

PURCELL, HENRY (1659–95), English composer. He was born in London and, becoming a choirboy at the *Chapel Royal, began to study music at an early age. From 1675 he tuned the organ, and in 1680 was made organist at *Westminster Abbey, to which in 1682 the office of organist at the Chapel Royal was added. During the next years he devoted himself chiefly to sacred music, among his compositions being a series of *Odes for St. Cecilia's Day*. His most famous ecclesiastical work is the *Te Deum* and *Jubilate* in D (1694), also written for St. Cecilia's Day, which was regularly performed at *St. Paul's Cathedral for half a century. He also composed settings for the *Benedicite* and *Jubilate* in B flat (known as his 'Second Morning Service') and for the *Magnificat* and *Nunc Dimittis* in G minor. His burial service for Queen Mary (d. 1694) contained the well-known anthem 'Thou knowest, Lord'. Many of his anthems are still regularly performed. With the exception of a few early examples of polyphonic composition, their most outstanding feature is Purcell's development of the verse anthem, dimly foreshadowed by W. *Byrd; in the spirit of the Restoration much of the music is elaborate and highly dramatic; the words are nearly always from the OT. They include 'In Thee, O Lord, do I put my trust', 'Thou art He that took me from my mother's womb', 'Save me, O God', 'My beloved spake', 'O Praise God in His Holiness' and the Coronation anthem, 'My heart is inditing of a good matter'. Even apart from his more extensive work in the sphere of secular composition, the technical skill, powers of expression and the beauty of the melodies of his sacred music have deservedly maintained Purcell's reputation among the first rank of English composers.

The best ed. of his works is that publd. by the Purcell Society (London, 1878 ff. [26 vols. to 1928]). Modern lives by W. H. Cummings ('The Great Musicians'; London, 1881); D. [D.] Arundel (London, 1927), H. Dupré (Paris, 1927; Eng. tr., New York, 1928), A. K. Holland (London, 1932; Penguin Books, 1948), and J. A. Westrup ('The Master Musicians'; London, 1937). J. A. F. Maitland in *D.N.B.*, xlvii (1896), pp. 39–44; id., revised by W. B. Squire–H. C. Colles, in *Grove's Dictionary of Music and Musicians*, vi (ed. 5 by E. Blom; 1954), pp. 997–1019, s.v., with detailed bibl.

PURCHAS JUDGEMENT, The. The judgement by the *Judicial Committee of the Privy Council in 1871 that Eucharistic *Vestments, the *Eastward Position, the *Mixed Chalice, and Wafer *Bread were illegal. This decision, which was given when the Rev. John Purchas (1823–72), vicar of St. James', Brighton, had been charged with these and other ritualistic practices, reversed the previous judgement in Purchas's favour by the *Dean of the Arches. The verdict marks a turning point in the ceremonial revival in the C of E in the 19th cent.,

because hitherto such practices had been regarded on nearly all sides as conforming with the letter of the law, whereas from now onwards ritualists were held to be lawbreakers. The judgement was widely disobeyed, however, as without spiritual authority and the Eastward Position was continued, e.g., in *St. Paul's Cathedral.

PURGATIVE WAY, The (*Via Purgativa*). The first stage of mental prayer, acc. to the scheme commonly adopted by *ascetical theologians, and most fully set forth by St. *Teresa and St. *John of the Cross. The chief activity of the soul at this stage is the eradication of bad habits, with repentance for past sins; and to this end the imagination and intellect are called into play. When meditation gives place to increased activity of the affections and will, the soul begins to enter gradually upon the next stage, the '*Illuminative Way'.

PURGATORY. Acc. to RC teaching the place or state of temporal punishment, where those who have died in the grace of God are expiating their *venial faults and such pains as are still due to forgiven *mortal sins, before being admitted to the Beatific Vision. The OT passage most frequently adduced in proof of the doctrine is 2 Macc. 12. 39–45, acc. to which *Judas Maccabaeus 'made the propitiation for them that had died, that they might be released from their sin'. In the NT the words of the Lord on the sin against the Holy Ghost which will be forgiven 'neither in this world nor in that which is to come' (Mt. 12. 31 f.) seem to imply a state beyond the grave in which expiation is still possible. The much-quoted 1 Cor. 3. 11–15 is difficult; but, given the doctrine of Purgatory, the conception of salvation 'yet so as through fire' seems easily applicable to it. As regards the Fathers St. *Clement of Alexandria already asserts that those who, having repented on their deathbed, had no time to perform works of penance in this life, will be sanctified in the next by purifying fire (*Stromateis*, 7. 6), a conception developed by *Origen (*Numbers*, *Hom.* 15; J. P. *Migne, *PG*, xii, 169 f.). Without the conception of Purgatory the general practice of offering prayers and the Holy Sacrifice for the dead, attested by numerous inscriptions and E. Fathers such as St. *Cyril of Jerusalem (*Catech. myst.* 5. 9) and St. *Chrysostom, are held to be unintelligible. St. *Epiphanius even reckons the denial of the utility of prayers for the dead a heresy (*Panarion*, 75. 8), and in the E. liturgies these prayers are a constant feature.

The Latin tradition follows that of the E., but, in accordance with its particular genius, in a more systematic manner. Fairly clear traces of a belief in Purgatory are found already in the visions of Dinocrates, related in the 'Passion of Sts. *Perpetua and Felicitas'. A more developed doctrine is taught by St. *Ambrose, who asserts that the souls of the departed await the end of time in different habitations, their fate varying acc. to their works, though some are already with Christ. The foundation of the medieval doctrine is found in St. *Augustine, who holds that the fate of the individual soul is decided immediately after death, and teaches the absolute certainty of purifying pains in the next life (*De Civ. Dei*, xxi, 13, and ib. 24), whereas St. *Caesarius of Arles already distinguishes between capital sins, which lead to hell, and minor ones, which may be expurgated either by good works on earth or in Purgatory. This doctrine was sanctioned also by St. *Gregory the Great, who taught that the privation of the vision of God was one of the purgatorial pains, and Gregory's position was accepted by many Latin theologians, e.g. the Venerable *Bede. This more explicit teaching on Purgatory was evolved in order to avoid a confusion of thought as to the state of the souls between death and the *General Judgement; its main points were constantly embodied in the practice of the Church esp. in her offering of the Eucharist for the departed and in the Memento of the dead in the Mass, as found e.g. in the Missals of *Bobbio and *Stowe. It was amplified in the Middle Ages esp. by St. *Thomas Aquinas. He taught that the guilt (*culpa*) of venial sin is expiated immediately after death by an act of perfect charity and that only the pain remained to be borne. Acc. to St. Thomas and other Scholastic theologians, the smallest pain in Purgatory is greater than the greatest on earth, it being relieved, however, by the certitude of salvation which establishes the Holy Souls, despite their sufferings, in deep peace. Moreover, they may be helped by the suffrages of the faithful, and esp. by the offering of Mass on their behalf, a belief which St. Thomas bases on the doctrine of the Communion of Saints, from which only the inhabitants of hell and of Limbo are excluded. The official teaching of the RC Church on Purgatory was defined at the Councils of *Lyons (1274) and *Florence (1439) with a view to reconciling the Greeks, who objected esp. to the conception of material fire and to the distinction between guilt and pain. The Latins confined themselves to the two points of the existence of Purgatory and of the usefulness of prayer and pious works offered for the departed; at Florence, agreement was reached on both these questions.

In the W. the existence of Purgatory had been denied in the Middle Ages by some heretical sects such as the *Waldenses and *Albigensians. It was openly rejected by the Reformers, who taught that souls are freed from sin by faith in Christ alone without any works, and therefore, if saved, go straight to heaven. One of the earliest and most explicit attacks on the Reformation teaching was that by St. John *Fisher, *Assertionis Lutheranae Confutatio* (1523), who based himself esp. on the Fathers and on the practice of prayer for the dead from the earliest times. The Council of *Trent reaffirmed the teaching propounded at Lyons and Florence, forbidding all fanciful elaborations, esp. in public sermons. Modern RC divines, besides insisting on the fact that, from her beginnings, the Church has prayed for the dead,

adduce the theological argument of the need for personal expiation within the economy of the Redemption. The RC Church officially encourages the offering of Masses, *indulgences, and public as well as private prayers and works of devotion on behalf of the souls in Purgatory. It is, however, extremely careful in the matter of private revelations on the subject, the most credited being those described in St. *Catherine of Genoa's 'Treatise on Purgatory'. The custom of addressing prayers to the Holy Souls to ask for their intercession is a fairly recent development, advocated, among others, by St. Robert *Bellarmine and St. *Alphonsus Liguori, and accepted by nearly all modern RC theologians.

In the E. Churches belief in Purgatory has been fairly constant. It was reaffirmed by the Synod of *Jerusalem (1672), which taught that, beside the saints and the damned, there is a category of souls sustaining in 'Hades' the punishment of their sins, which, however, might be lightened by the prayers of the Church and of individuals, and esp. by the offering of the Holy Sacrifice. The teaching of the synod was the expression of the faith of most Orthodox Churches, and, with some unessential alterations, was accepted by the Russian Church in 1838.

The conception of Purgatory found its way into the C of E in the form of the 'Intermediate State' as defended by the *Tractarians. There is, however, no generally accepted teaching on the subject. The most widely received opinion would seem to be that this state is not so much a process of purification from sin, as in RC theology, as one of growth and development. Moreover, it is believed to end only with the Last Judgement, the soul being only then admitted to the Beatific Vision.

Besides the immortal description by *Dante in his *Divina commedia*, Book ii, and the account in Aquinas (*Comm. in Lib. IV. Sent.*, dist. xxi, qu. 1) there are classical treatises by R. *Bellarmine, S.J., *Disputationes de Controversiis Fidei*, iii (Ingoldstadt, [1588]), part 2 (Primi Tomi Sexta Controversia: 'De Ecclesia, quae est in Purgatorio'), and F. *Suarez, S.J., *Commentarii ac Disputationes in Tertium Partem Divi Thomae*, iv (Lyons, 1603), pp. 618–55 ('De Purgatorio'). The Tridentine 'Decretum De Purgatorio' is repr. in Denz.–Bann. (ed. 28, 1952), p. 342 (No. 983). The subject is necessarily treated in all books on eschatology, q.v. Modern Catholic works include J. Bautz, *Das Fegfeuer. Im Anschluss an die Scholastik, mit Bezugnahme auf Mystik und Ascetik dargestellt* (1883); J. P. Kirsch, *Die Lehre von der Gemeinschaft der Heiligen im christlichen Alterthum* (Forschungen zur christlichen Litteratur- und Dogmengeschichte, i; 1900; Eng. tr., 1911), passim. F. Schmid, *Das Fegfeuer nach katholischer Lehre* (1904). B. Bartmann, *Das Fegfeuer* (1928; Eng. tr., 1936). Mary of St. Austin, *The Divine Crucible of Purgatory* (posthumously ed. N. Ryan, S.J., 1940). Works by Anglicans include H. W. Luckock, *After Death* (1879); id., *The Intermediate State between Death and Judgement* (1890); E. H. Plumptre, *The Spirits in Prison and Other Studies on the Life after Death* (1884), esp. ch. x, 'The Doctrine of Purgatory', pp. 287–311; A. J. Mason, *Purgatory* [and other Lectures] (1901), esp. pp. 1–57, R. E. Hutton, *The Soul in the Unseen World* (1901). A. d'Alès, S.J., 'La Question du purgatoire au concile de Florence en 1438' in *Gregorianum*, iii (1922), pp. 9–50, with reff. A. Michel–M. Jugie, A.A., in *D.T.C.*, xiii (Pt. 1; 1936), cols. 1163–1357, s.v. 'Purgatoire'. A. Piolanti–W. Wehr in *E.C.*, x (1953), cols. 330–9, s.v. 'Purgatorio', with further bibl.

PURGATORY, St. Patrick's. See *St. Patrick's Purgatory.*

PURIFICATION OF THE BVM. The feast kept on 2 Feb. in commemoration of the BVM's purification in the Temple, recorded in Lk. 2. 21–39. The feast is also known as *Candlemas (q.v.).

PURIFICATOR. A small piece of white linen used at celebrations of the Eucharist to cleanse the chalice after communion. It is folded in three layers and before the service begins is placed on the *chalice beneath the *paten. It is sometimes marked with an embroidered cross to distinguish it from the finger towels used at the *Lavabo.

PURIM. A Jewish festival, celebrated in the spring (14 and 15 Adar), which commemorates the deliverance of the Jews from massacre under the Persian Empire (473 B.C.), as related in the Book of Esther (9. 26 ff.). It is observed primarily as a national and secular, rather than as a religious, festival. There are some grounds for believing that the 'feast of the Jews' of Jn. 5. 1 is the Feast of Purim. 'Purim' has been proved by the texts from Kultepe to be a loan-word of Babylonian origin.

The Heb. name is prob. connected with the Bab. root *pûru*, 'lot' (cf. Est. 3. 7). For the method of observance see the tractate 'Megilla' of the *Talmud. On the many modern theories on the origin of the feast, see J. A. McClymont in *H.D.B.*, iv (1902), p. 174 f. P. Haupt, *Purim* (Beiträge zur Assyriologie und semitischen Sprachwissenschaft, vi, Hft. 2; 1906). See also Commentaries on Esther and H. Lesêtre in *Dict. Bibl.*, v (1912), cols. 338–41, s.v. 'Phurim (Fête des)'. J. Jacobs in *E.B.* (ed. 11), xxii (1911), p. 661 f.

PURITANS, the more extreme English Protestants who, dissatisfied with the Elizabethan Settlement, sought a further purification of the Church from supposedly unscriptural and corrupt forms along the Genevan model. Although never in the majority, they were powerful and influential, esp. among the mercantile classes of the first decades of the 17th cent. They demanded express Scriptural warrant for all the details of public worship, believing that all other forms were popish, superstitious, idolatrous, and anti-Christian. They attacked church ornaments, vestments, surplices, rochets, organs, the sign of the cross, prelacy (notably in the *Marprelate Tracts, q.v.), and ecclesiastical courts, and put corresponding emphasis on preaching, Sunday observance, Church government by presbyters, and the 'tablewise' position of the altar. J. *Whitgift's Articles of 1583 and the Act of 1593 against 'seditious sectaries' were aimed at them. The *Hampton Court Conference (1604), a result of the Puritan *Millenary Petition, only led to increased hostility and they were among the chief enemies of W. *Laud's ecclesiastical and political policy. Their theology was *Calvinist, many of the more extreme Puritans having studied in Holland and at Geneva. Among well-known representatives of the Puritan movement were T. *Cartwright, W. *Travers, R. *Browne, H. *Barrow, W. *Prynne, R. *Leighton, and J. *Milton. The term 'Puritan', which never

had a precise use, ceased to be applicable after 1660.

D. *Neal, *History of the Puritans from 1517 to 1688* (new ed. by J. Toulmin, 5 vols., 1793–7); H. O. Wakeman, *The Church and the Puritans* (1887); W. A. Shaw, *A History of the English Church during the Civil Wars and under the Commonwealth 1640–60* (2 vols., 1900); G. B. Tatham, *The Puritans in Power* (1913); A. F. Scott-Pearson, *Church and State: Political Aspects of Sixteenth-Century Puritanism* (1928); C. E. Whiting, *Studies in English Puritanism, 1660–1688* (1931); W. Haller, *The Rise of Puritanism* (New York, 1938); M. M. Knappen, *Tudor Puritanism* (Chicago, 1939); Horton Davies, *The Worship of the English Puritans* (1948). A. Simpson, *Puritanism in Old and New England* (Charles R. Walgreen Foundation Lectures, Chicago, 1955). J. N. *Figgis in *D.E.C.H.*, pp. 479–82, s.v. 'Puritanism'; H. G. Wood in *H.E.R.E.*, x (1918), pp. 507–15, s.v. 'Puritanism'.

PURVEY, JOHN (*c.* 1353 – *c.* 1428), *Wycliffite preacher. Educated probably at Oxford, he became closely associated with J. Wycliffe (d. 1384) at Lutterworth. His most important achievement was a revision, probably with Wycliffe's full agreement, of the extremely literal and almost unreadable English version of the Bible made by Wycliffe and *Nicholas of Hereford. Begun in Wycliffe's lifetime, it was probably completed at Bristol in 1388. On account of his continued *Lollard activities, Purvey was forbidden to preach and in 1390 was imprisoned. After recanting under pressure (*c.* 1401), he was inducted to the vicarage of West Hythe, Kent; but, finding that he could not conscientiously abandon his former position, he resigned in 1403 and, as far as circumstances allowed, continued to disseminate Lollard doctrine. See also *Bible* (*English Versions*), p. 168.

H. Hargreaves, 'The Latin Text of Purvey's Psalter' in *Medium Aevum*, xxiv (1955), pp. 73–90. M. Deanesly, *The Lollard Bible and Other Medieval Biblical Versions* (1920), esp. pp. 266–85, 334–47, 437–67; id., *The Significance of the Lollard Bible* (Ethel M. Wood Lecture, 1951.) A. Gordon in *D.N.B.*, xlvii (1896), p. 51 f.

PUSEY, EDWARD BOUVERIE (1800–82), *Tractarian leader. He was educated at Eton and at *Christ Church, Oxford, and elected a Fellow of Oriel College in 1823. Not long afterwards he went to Göttingen and Berlin (1825), where he got to know many leading German Biblical critics. During the next years he devoted himself to the study of Hebrew, Arabic, and other Semitic languages both at Oxford and in Germany. In 1828 he published *An Historical Enquiry into the Probable Causes of the Rationalist Character lately predominant in the Theology of Germany* (followed by Part II in 1830), in which he traced German rationalism to the dead orthodoxy of a Protestantism lacking in spiritual vitality; but the book was misunderstood to be a defence of his German masters and later he withdrew it. In 1828 he was ordained deacon and priest and also appointed Regius professor of Hebrew and Canon of Christ Church. He held this office for the rest of his life. At the end of 1833 he became formally attached to the *Oxford Movement by contributing a Tract (No. 18) on *Thoughts on the Benefits of the System of Fasting, Enjoined by our Church* (publd. in 1834), his prestige and erudition proving of great benefit to the cause. In 1836 he published three further Tracts on *Scriptural Views of Holy Baptism* (Nos. 67–9), which taught a very rigorous doctrine on the forgiveness of post-baptismal sin, and which, in their form, were significant as altering the scope of the Tracts from pamphlets to learned treatises. He also gave wholehearted support to the *Library of the Fathers* supplying its first volume (St. *Augustine's *Confessions*, 1838) with a notable preface on the significance of *patristic study. His most influential activity, however, was his preaching. This was eminently practical and was devoted chiefly to inculcating the heinous-ness of sin, the nothingness of the world, and the blessedness of heaven. The death of his wife, in 1839, left an indelible mark on his life; from that time he practised many austerities and took an active interest in the establishment of the religious life in the C of E. When, in 1841, J. H. *Newman, whom he had vigor-ously defended, withdrew from the movement, the leadership devolved on Pusey alone. His sermon on *The Holy Eucharist, a Comfort to the Penitent*, preached before the university in 1843, was condemned by the vice-chancellor and six doctors of Divinity as teaching error, and Pusey was suspended from the university pulpit for two years. The condemnation, however, secured for it wide publicity in its printed form and drew attention to the doctrine of the *Real Presence, of which Pusey remained a devoted defender. In 1845 he assisted in the establishment of the first Anglican sisterhood, and throughout his life he continued to en-courage efforts in this direction. In 1846 he preached another sermon before the university on *The Entire Absolution of the Penitent*, in which he claimed for the C of E the power of the keys and the reality of priestly absolution. The practice of private confession in the modern Anglican Church dates from this work. As the principal champion of the High Church Movement he had frequently to defend its doctrines, e.g. in the *Gorham Case (q.v.), which issued in many conversions to the RC Church, though Pusey then and later spared no effort to dissuade his followers from joining it. He took a leading part in the controversy on the reform of the university, defending the old tutorial system. In 1862 he accused B. *Jowett of teaching unsound doctrine, but the court of the chancellor of the university declined to hear the case. After the judgement of the Privy Council in favour of the authors of *Essays and Reviews* (1860), he wrote his famous letter to J. *Keble on *The Church of England a Portion of Christ's One Holy Catholic Church, and a Means of Restoring Visible Unity. An Eirenicon* (1865). In it he expressed his belief that union with Rome was prevented not so much by the official teaching of the RC Church as by unofficial devotions, e.g. to the BVM, and by the popular conceptions of purgatory and Indulgences. This letter was answered by Newman in 1866. From 1867 he took an active part in the Ritualist controversy. In his sermon *Will Ye also Go Away?* (1867) he again defended the doctrine of the Real

Presence and the corresponding ceremonial. In 1869 he published his second *Eirenicon* in answer to Newman, which dealt chiefly with the *Immaculate Conception, and in 1870 he issued the third, entitled *Is Healthful Reunion Impossible?* principally on the doctrine of purga-tory, the deutero-canonical books, and the Roman supremacy. This he sent to many RC bishops who attended the *Vatican Council, but his hopes were disappointed by the defini-tion of Papal Infallibility. From 1870 to 1873 he fought vigorously for the retention of the *Athanasian Creed, threatened by the Fourth report of the Ritual Commission, which advo-cated its abandonment. In 1880 in *What is of Faith as to Everlasting Punishment?* he de-fended against F. W. *Farrar the eternity of hell, basing himself on Scriptural and patristic teaching. He died at Ascot Priory, Berks, on 16 Sept. 1882 and is buried in the nave of Christ Church cathedral Oxford. After his death his library was bought by his friends, who endowed for it the institution in Oxford known as Pusey House.

Spiritual Letters, ed. J. O. Johnston and W. C. E. Newbolt (1898). Monumental *Life* by H. P. *Liddon (4 vols., 1893–7), with list of Pusey's writings, compiled by Falconer Madan, iv, pp. 395–446. Shorter Lives by Maria Trench (anon.; 1900), G. W. E. Russell (1907), and G. L. Prestige (1933). J. O. Johnston in *D.N.B.*, xlvii (1896), pp. 53–61. G. W. E. Russell in *D.E.C.H.*, pp. 482–6. See also bibl. to *Oxford Movement*.

PUSEY, PHILIP EDWARD (1830–80), *patristic scholar. The only son of E. B. *Pusey, whom he assiduously assisted in his patristic and Semitic studies, he was an inde-fatigable student who, though deaf and a cripple, travelled all over Europe, working at MSS. He edited many of the writings of St. *Cyril of Alexandria, and laid the foundations for a critical edition of the *Peshitta (publd., after further editing, by G. H. Gwilliam, 1901).

H. P. *Liddon, *Life of Edward Bouverie Pusey*, iv (1897), pp. 346–9.

PUSEYISM. A contemporary title for the *Tractarian Movement, generally used in an opprobrious sense, from its leader, E. B. *Pusey. Pusey was prob. singled out as he was the first contributor to the *Tracts for the Times* to append his initials (to No. 18, 21 Dec. 1833), the earlier *Tracts* being anonymous. The term spread rapidly, being met with even in a Greek newspaper as πουζεισμός.

O.E.D., vii (1909), p. 1639, s.v.

PYE. See *Pie*.

PYRRHONISM. Properly, the system of sceptical philosophy expounded *c.* 300 B.C. by the Greek thinker, Pyrrho of Elis. Its charac-teristic doctrine was the denial of all possibility of attaining of certain knowledge. Conceived in an ethical interest, it maintained that when a man had understood the futility of intellectual inquiry, he would not be perturbed nor lose his happiness by disquietude at his inability to arrive at any certain truth. In a wider sense, the term has come to be applied to any sceptical system of thought.

Pyrrho himself left no writings; the propagation of his doctrines was due to his disciple, Timon of Phlius (c. 320–330 B.C.), of whose satirical poems (Σίλλοι) a few fragments survive.

PYX (Gk. πυξίς, 'box-wood vessel'). The word denoted formerly any receptacle destined to contain the reserved *Host, and is still so used officially in the C.I.C. (can. 1270). Acc. to ordinary present terminology it is used esp. of a small, mostly flat, gold or silver-gilt box which is used for carrying the Blessed Sacrament to the sick. For this purpose it is wrapped in a small corporal and placed in a pyx bag hung round the priest's neck. The term is also used for the vessel in which the large Host for exposition is kept in the *Tabernacle.

Q

'Q'. The symbol (usually, perh. wrongly, held to come from Germ. *Quelle*, 'source') for the hypothetical source of those passages in the *Synoptic Gospels where Mt. and Lk. show a close similarity to each other but not to anything in Mk. (See *Synoptic Problem*.) These passages consist largely of sayings of Jesus, but include also some other material, e.g. on St. *John the Baptist (Lk. 3. 17 f., cf. Mt. 3. 12; Lk. 7. 18–23, cf. Mt. 11. 2–6) and the account of the Temptation (Lk. 4. 2–13, cf. Mt. 4. 2–11). The theory, elaborated on the basis of the critical studies of Sir John Hawkins and A. *Harnack, was put into a widely accepted form by B. H. *Streeter, who held: (i) Q was a document (not merely a group of oral traditions) written in Greek; (ii) almost its whole content was used by either Matthew or Luke or both; and (iii) the order of the contents in Lk. is nearer to the original than that in Mt. Acc. to Streeter the existence of Q 'though highly probable, falls just short of certainty'. The existence of such a document is still challenged (J. *Chapman, A. M. Farrer, B. C. Butler, O.S.B.), but the hypothesis continues to enjoy very wide acceptance among scholars.

J. C. Hawkins, *Horae Synopticae* (Oxford, 1899); A Harnack, *Sprüche und Reden Jesu* (1907; Eng. tr., 1908); W. *Sanday (ed.), *Oxford Studies in the Synoptic Problem* (1911); B. H. Streeter, *The Four Gospels* (1924), chs. vii–xi. R. H. *Lightfoot, *History and Interpretation in the Gospels* (1935), p. 27, note 1. J. Chapman, O.S.B., *Matthew, Mark, and Luke* (1937); B. C. Butler, *The Originality of St. Matthew* (1951). A. M. Farrer, 'On Dispensing with Q' in D. E. Nineham (ed.), *Studies in the Gospels*. Essays in Memory of R. H. Lightfoot (1955), pp. 55–86.

Q.A.B. See *Queen Anne's Bounty*.

QARAITES. See *Karaites*.

QORBAN. See *Corban*.

QUADRAGESIMA. Another name for the forty days of *Lent, and, occasionally, for the First Sunday in Lent. The word 'Quadragesimale' has been sometimes used of a set of sermons delivered in Lent.

QUADRAGESIMO ANNO. The encyclical letter of *Pius XI, dated 15 May 1931, confirming and elaborating the theses of *Rerum Novarum* (q.v.). Points esp. stressed are: the evil results of free competition and administrative centralization; the incompatibility of strict Socialism with Catholicism; and the need for a reorganization of society on the model of the 'guild' system.

Text in *A.A.S.*, xxiii (1931), pp. 177–228. An Eng. tr. was publd. by the *Catholic Truth Society under the title *The Social Order* [1931].

QUADRATUS, St. (2nd cent.), the earliest Christian '*Apologist'. *C.* 124 he wrote in Asia Minor an apology for the Christian faith addressed to the Emp. Hadrian, of which a single fragment survives in *Eusebius (*Hist. Eccl.*, IV. iii. 2). Since *Jerome (*de vir. illust.* 19; *ep.* 70) he has been erroneously identified with an early Bp. of Athens of the same name. Feast day, 26 May.

Fragments in M. J. *Routh (ed.), *Reliquiae Sacrae*, i (ed. 2, Oxford, 1846), pp. 69–79, repr. in J. P. Migne, *PG*, v, 1261–6. Bardenhewer, i, 183–7; Altaner (ed. 1950), p. 88. É. Amann in *D.T.C.*, xiii (pt. 2; 1937), cols. 1429–31; E. Peterson in *E.C.*, x (1953), col. 362 f., s.v. 'Quadrato'.

QUADRILATERAL, Lambeth. See *Lambeth Quadrilateral*.

QUADRIVIUM. The medieval name for the group of four sciences consisting of music, arithmetic, geometry, and astronomy, which together with the *trivium (q.v.) of the inferior sciences constituted the *Seven Liberal Arts.

QUAKER. A nickname first given by Justice Bennet in 1650 to George *Fox because he bade the Justice tremble at the Word of the Lord. The word had been used, however, at least as early as 1647 of a foreign religious sect. Early Quakers also explained it by the spiritual trembling sometimes experienced at their religious meetings. See *Friends, Society of*.

See *O.E.D.*, s.v.

QUAM SINGULARI. The decree issued, on 8 Aug. 1910, by the Sacred Congregation of the Sacraments, recommending that children be admitted to receive Holy Communion as soon as they have reached the 'age of discretion' (*aetas discretionis*), i.e. by the tests there given, at the age of about 7 years.

Text in *A.A.S.*, ii (1910), 577-83.

QUANTA CURA. The encyclical, issued by Pope *Pius IX on 8 Dec. 1864, to which the famous *Syllabus (q.v.) condemning the doctrines of *liberalism was attached.

Text in the *A.S.S.*, iii (1867), pp. 160–7; excerpts repr. in Denz.–Bann., Nos. 1688–99.

QUARANT' ORE. See *Forty Hours' Devotion*.

QUARE IMPEDIT. In the C of E a form of legal action by which the right of presentation to an ecclesiastical benefice is tried. It may be brought by a patron against the bishop on his refusal to institute his presentee to a living. Since the passing of the Benefices Act (1898), its use is restricted to cases where the objection to presentation is on the grounds of doctrine or ritual. The name is from the opening words of the writ issued. See also *Duplex Querela*.

QUARLES, FRANCIS (1592–1644), religious poet. He was born at Romford in Essex and educated at Christ's College, Cambridge (1606–9). In 1613 he went to Heidelberg in the retinue of the Princess Palatine, returning to England by 1615. He now began to publish many Biblical paraphrases, among them *Job Militant* (1624) and *Sions Elegies wept by Jeremy* (1624). About 1626 he went to *Dublin, where he became private secretary to J. *Ussher, Abp. of Armagh. In 1630 a collection of his Biblical paraphrases was published with the title *Divine Poems*, and in 1632 there appeared his *Divine Fancies*, a small volume of epigrams and meditations in verse. They were followed by his popular *Emblems* (1635), perhaps the most original of emblem-books, though it was partly derived from two Jesuit manuals, *Pia Desideria* (1624) and *Typus Mundi* (1627). In 1638 Quarles published another emblem-book, *Hieroglyphikes of the Life of Man*. In 1640 he was made chronologer to the city of London. In his later years he wrote chiefly devotional prose. His *Enchiridion* (1640), a collection of thoughts on religion and morals, achieved great popularity, and he also wrote *The Loyall Convert* (1644), a pamphlet defending the Royalist cause, of which he was an ardent partisan. His reputation increased after his death through the publication of his posthumous works, among them *The Shepherd's Oracles* (1646), a satire in verse on the contemporary religious disputes. Though often overlaid with conceits and epithets in the style of his time, Quarles's poetry betrays deep religious feeling, coloured by a keen sense of sin and of the transitoriness of life.

Complete Works ed. A. B. Grosart (Chertsey Worthies' Library, 3 vols., privately pr., 1880–1), with biographical introd., i, pp. ix–lxvi. The primary authority is the brief life by Ursula Quarles, widow, prefixed to Quarles's posthumously publd. *Solomon's Recantation, entitled Ecclesiastes Paraphrased* (1645) [no pagination]. J. Horden, *Francis Quarles (1592–1644)*. A Bibliography of his Works to the Year 1800 (Oxford Bibliographical Society Publications, New Series, ii; 1953), with introd., pp. 1–16. Further bibl. by F. E. Hutchinson in *C.B.E.L.*, i, p. 450 f. S. Lee in *D.N.B.*, xlvii (1896), pp. 92–6.

QUARR ABBEY, near Ryde, Isle of Wight. In 1131 Baldwin de Redvers founded a *Cistercian house on the site, which became the most considerable religious foundation on the island. It survived until the Dissolution in 1537. Soon afterwards the buildings were destroyed, and only a small part of the medieval structure remains. In 1908 the site was acquired by the *Benedictine monks exiled from *Solesmes (q.v.), who had previously (1901) settled at Appledurcombe House, near Wroxall, in the centre of the island. A fine abbey in red brick in a Flemish style was erected (consecrated 1912). After the First World War many of the monks returned to Solesmes. The Abbey is now an independent house of the Solesmes Congregation, and an important centre of liturgical and historical studies.

QUARTODECIMANISM. The early custom in some places of following Jewish practice in always observing *Easter, i.e. the Christian *Passover, on Nisan 14, whatever the day of the week, and not (as elsewhere) on the following Sunday. The tradition was esp. rooted in Asia Minor, where it was believed to derive from St. *John the Apostle, and upheld by *Melito of Sardis and *Apollinarius of Hierapolis. On a visit to Rome *c.* 155 St. *Polycarp, Bp. of Smyrna, sought to persuade Anicetus to conform to Quartodeciman usage. Though the Pope refused, he had no scruples about Polycarp continuing his own custom. Thirty or forty years later a more rigid line was taken up by Pope *Victor, who tried to suppress Quartodecimanism; and when *Polycrates, Bp. of Ephesus, refused to comply, Victor forthwith excommunicated him. Despite this stern measure, which met with a sharp rebuke from St. *Irenaeus (*ap.* Eusebius, *HE*, V, xxiii–xxv), the Asiatic Churches retained their practice for the time being. At a later date the Quartodecimans organized themselves as a separate Church. They survived as a sect down to the 5th cent. See also *Paschal Controversies*.

F. E. *Brightman, 'The Quartodeciman Question' in *J.T.S.*, xxv (1923–4), pp. 254–70. É. Amann in *D.T.C.*, xiii (pt. 2; 1937), cols. 1445–7.

QUASIMODO SUNDAY. A title in the W. Church for *Low Sunday, derived from the opening words of the *Introit at Mass on that day (*Quasi modo geniti*, 'As new-born babes', 1 Pet. 2. 2).

QUATTRO CORONATI (i.e. 'the Four Crowned Ones'). A group of four saints, commemorated in the W. Church on 8 Nov., to whom a famous ancient basilica on the Celian Hill at *Rome is dedicated. Considerable doubt reigns as to which particular saints are intended. The Roman *Martyrology for 8 Nov. supposes the conflation of two groups of five and four martyrs respectively whose names it gives. It appears from other sources that the one group were five sculptors of Pannonia who were martyred for refusing to make a statue of Aesculapius for a heathen temple, and the other group four martyrs who were buried not at Rome but at Albano in the Alban Hills. They are the patrons of stone-masons.

AA.SS., Nov. II (2) (1931), pp. 590 f., and III (1910), pp. 748–84. A. Muñoz, *Il restauro della chiesa e del chiostro dei SS. Quattro Coronati* (1914). J. P. Kirsch in *L.Th.K.*, x (1938), cols., 602 f.; H. Leclercq, O.S.B., in *D.A.C.L.*, xiv (pt. 2; 1948), cols. 2009–14 with bibl.

QUEEN ANNE'S BOUNTY ('Q.A.B.'). A fund formed by Queen *Anne in 1704 to receive the first fruits (*annates) and tenths which had been confiscated by *Henry VIII. On surrendering them for the benefit of the Church, she directed their use for the augmentation of the livings of the poorer Anglican clergy. Grants of capital (not income) were made to poorly endowed benefices; and later the fund was empowered to make loans (from

1777) and disbursements (from 1803) for the building and repair of parsonage houses, etc. Between 1809 and 1820 it received grants of over £1,000,000 from Parliament and at various times large private benefactions. By the Tithe Act of 1925, Q.A.B. was charged with the collection of ecclesiastical tithe rentcharge and its distribution to benefices and ecclesiastical corporations. When the Tithe Act of 1936 extinguished tithe rentcharge, Q.A.B. received Government Stock as compensation. In 1948 Q.A.B. and the *Ecclesiastical Commissioners were united in a new body, the *Church Commissioners for England (q.v.).

A. Savidge, *The Foundation and Early Years of Queen Anne's Bounty* (C.H.S., 1955). G. Crosse in *D.E.C.H.*, p. 486 f., s.v.

QUENTIN, HENRI (1872–1935), *Benedictine scholar. Professed at *Maredsous in 1895, he was transferred to *Solesmes in 1897 and ordained priest in 1902. Five years later *Pius X called him to Rome as a member of the commission on the revision of the *Vulgate, in which capacity he superintended the photographing of most of the important Vulgate MSS. at Paris, Rome, London, and elsewhere, including the entire *Codex Amiatinus at Florence; and he was the principal editor of the text of the *Pentateuch (1926–36). His own writings include *J. D. Mansi et les grandes collections conciliaires* (1900) and *Les Martyrologes historiques du moyen-âge* (1908), the latter containing discussions of the text of the *martyrologies of *Bede and other early medieval compilers. He also issued several writings in defence of his much-contested principles for establishing the Vulgate text. The new Office of the Feast of the *Sacred Heart (1928) was, for the most part, his work.

C. Mohlberg, O.S.B., 'Commemorazione dell' abbate Dom Enrico Quentin' in *Atti della Pontificia Accademia Romana di Archeologia*, Serie III, Rendiconti, xi (for 1935; 1936), pp. 13–39, with list of his works, pp. 34–9.

QUESNEL, PASQUIER (1634 – 1719), French *Jansenist. Educated by the *Jesuits, he studied philosophy and theology at the *Sorbonne and entered the Congregation of the *Oratory in 1657, where he soon was entrusted with the direction of students and became the author of a number of spiritual books. In 1672 he published *Abrégé de la morale de l'Évangile*, with a commendatory preface by the Bp. of Châlons-sur-Marne; its subsequent editions, expanded and revised, became famous under the title of *Le Nouveau Testament en français, avec des réflexions morales sur chaque verset*, usually called *Réflexions morales*. As against the formalized methods of spirituality in the manuals, the work emphasized the value of the close study of the Scriptures in increasing true devotion. In 1675 he published a scholarly edition of the works of St. *Leo which, however, was placed on the Index owing to the *Gallican theories developed in the notes. In 1681 he was removed to Orléans on the charge of upholding Jansenist views. Three years later he refused to subscribe to an anti-Jansenist

formula imposed by his superiors and went to Brussels, where he lived together with A. *Arnauld. In 1703 he was imprisoned by the Abp. of Malines at the instigation of Philip V, but escaped and fled to Holland in the following year. His subsequent life was filled with defences of himself and his *Réflexions* which, commended by the Abp. of *Paris, Cardinal L. A. *de Noailles, went through many editions, but was condemned by a brief of *Clement XI in 1708 and, five years later, by the bull '*Unigenitus'. Among his doctrines condemned by the bull are the theses that no grace is given outside the Church, that grace is irresistible, that without grace man is incapable of any good and that all acts of a sinner, even prayer and attendance at Mass, are sins. Quesnel never accepted the condemnation, and though he asked for and received the Last Sacraments, he appealed to a future General Council for his vindication.

L. Batterel, *Mémoires domestiques pour servir à l'histoire de l'Oratoire* (ed. A. M. P. Ingold, 5 vols., 1902–11), with list of Quesnel's writings, iv, 424–93. *Correspondance de Pasquier Quesnel*, ed. A. Le Roy (2 vols., 1900). *Causa Quesnelliana* (Brussels, 1704; documents ed. by order of the Abp. of Malines). A. Le Roy, *Un Janséniste en exil* (1900; with selection of Quesnel's Letters). L. Ceyssens, 'Les Papiers de Quesnel saisis à Bruxelles et transportés à Paris en 1703 et 1704' in *R.H.E.*, xliv (1949), pp. 508–51. J. Carreyre in *D.T.C.*, xiii (pt. 2; 1937), cols. 1460–1535, s.v. 'Quesnel et le quesnellisme'.

QUICK, OLIVER CHASE (1885 – 1944), Anglican theologian. Educated at Harrow and at Corpus Christi College, Oxford, he was ordained priest in 1912. He was canon-residentiary successively at Newcastle (1920–3), *Carlisle (1923–30), *St. Paul's (1930–4), *Durham (1934–9), and *Christ Church (1939–44; also Regius Professor of Divinity). One of the leading exponents of orthodox Anglicanism, he upheld a position akin to that of *Essays Catholic and Critical* (1926). His approach to doctrinal issues was systematic and synthetic rather than historical, and essentially modern in expression. Among his many writings, all widely read, were *Essays in Orthodoxy* (1916), *Catholic and Protestant Elements in Christianity* (1924), *The Christian Sacraments* (1927), *The Gospel of Divine Action* (1933), *Doctrines of the Creed* (1938), and *The Gospel of the New World* (posthumous, 1944, with a Memoir by W. *Temple).

QUICUNQUE VULT (Lat., 'Whosoever wishes' [*salvus esse*, 'to be saved']). An alternative name for the '*Athanasian Creed' (q.v.) from its opening words.

QUIEN, MICHAEL LE. See *Le Quien, Michael*.

QUIERCY, Synods of. Of the several synods held in the 9th cent. at Quiercy (*palatium Carisiacum*), near Laon, the two most notable are:

(1) Synod of 849, under *Hincmar of Reims. It condemned the strict Augustinianism of *Gottschalk, who was sentenced to degradation and imprisonment at Hautvillers.

(11) Synod of 853, also under Hincmar. It repeated its condemnation of Gottschalk's doctrines, publishing four chapters ('capitula') viz. (1) that God has predestined to *life* only; (2) that human free-will, lost by Adam, was restored to us by Christ; (3) that God would have all men to be saved; and (4) that Jesus Christ suffered for all. These articles were rejected by the Church of Lyons and formally repudiated in 855 by the Council of *Valence (q.v.).

(1) Hardouin, v, cols. 17–20; Mansi, xiv (1769), cols. 919–922. Hefele–Leclercq, iv (pt. 1; 1911), pp. 150–6, and iv (pt. 2; 1911), pp. 1308–10. A. Werminghoff, 'Verzeichnis der Akten fränkischer Synoden von 834–918' in *N.A.*, xxv (1901), pp. 607–78, esp. p. 615.
(11) Hardouin, v, cols. 57 f.; Mansi, xiv (1769), cols. 995–8. Hefele–Leclercq, iv (pt. 1; 1911), pp. 197–9, and iv (pt. 2; 1911), pp. 1324, 1390–98. A. Werminghoff, op. cit., esp. p. 619. B. Lauvaud, O.P., in *D.T.C.*, xii (pt. 2; 1935), cols. 2920–2, s.v. 'Prédestination', with Lat. text and Fr. tr. of the *capitula*.

QUIETISM. The term 'Quietism' which is often used loosely of any system of spirituality minimizing human activity and responsibility, is usually restricted to the teaching of certain 17th cent. writers, esp. that of M. de *Molinos, and, to a lesser degree, Mme *Guyon and Abp. *Fénelon.
The fundamental principle of Quietism is its condemnation of all human effort. Acc. to the Quietists, man, in order to be perfect, must attain complete passivity and annihilation of will, abandoning himself to God to such an extent that he cares neither for heaven nor hell, nor for his own salvation. This state is reached by a certain form of mental prayer in which the soul consciously refuses not only all discursive meditation but any distinct act such as desire for virtue, love of Christ, or adoration of the Divine Persons, but simply rests in the presence of God in pure faith. As this passive prayer expresses the height of perfection, it makes any outward acts of mortification, almsgiving, going to confession, &c., superfluous. Once a man has attained to it, sin is impossible, for then all he does or thinks is the work of God. The devil may, indeed, tempt him and even compel him to commit actions that would be sinful in others, but when his will has become completely annihilated they cease to be sins in him; on the contrary, the man who has reached this state must carefully guard against being disquieted by such distractions, lest he should be disturbed in his state of mystic death. The moral consequences of such teaching are almost indistinguishable from those of pantheism.
Quietism was condemned in the person of M. de Molinos by *Innocent XI in his bull 'Coelestis Pastor' of 19 Nov. 1687. Sixty-eight propositions from Molinos' writings were condemned. Other notable exponents of Quietist teaching were P. M. Petrucci (1636–1701) and the *Barnabite, F. Lacombe, the director of Mme *Guyon.

H. Heppe, *Geschichte der quietistischen Mystik in der katholischen Kirche* (1875). J. Paquier, *Qu'est-ce que le quiétisme?* (1910). M. Petrocchi, *Il quietismo italiano del seicento* (Storia e Letteratura, xx; 1948). R. A. Knox,

Enthusiasm (1950), esp. pp. 231–87. P. Pourrat, P.S.S., *La Spiritualité chrétienne*, iv (ed. 2, 1928), pp. 128–295. Id. in *D.T.C.*, xiii (pt. 2; 1937), cols. 1537–81, s.v. 'Quiétisme'; id. in *Dictionnaire de spiritualité*, i (1937), cols. 25–49, s.v. 'Abandon'; P. Sannazzaro in *E.C.*, x (1953), cols. 412–16, s.v. 'Quietismo', with further bibl. See also works cited under *Fénelon, Molinos*, and *Guyon*.

QUINISEXT SYNOD. See *Trullan Synod*.

QUIÑONES, FRANCISCO DE (d. 1540), reforming cardinal. Born at León of a noble Spanish family, he entered the *Franciscan Order in 1498. In 1517 he became Definitor General and in 1523 and 1526 he was elected Minister *General of the *Observants, in which office he worked for a strengthening of discipline, promoted missions and studies, and induced many Conventuals to join the Observants. In 1526, and esp. in 1527 after the Sack of Rome and the imprisonment of *Clement VII, he mediated successfully between *Charles V and the Pope, who made him cardinal in the same year or early in 1528. From 1529 he took an active part in the question of the divorce of *Henry VIII, defending the interests of Queen Catherine.
It was then that Quiñones, by order of the Pope, devoted himself to the compilation of a new *Breviary, which *Paul III published in 1535, often called the 'Breviary of the Holy Cross' after the cardinal's titular church. It abolished almost entirely the difference of rank in the Feasts as well as *Antiphons, *versicles, the *Little Office of our Lady, and reduced to a minimum the readings from the Lives of the Saints. On the other hand, the whole *Psalter was recited during the week and nearly the whole of the Bible read during the year. The several Hours were almost equal in length, each containing only three Psalms, and Matins on all days only three lessons. A second recension of it appeared in 1536. Although special permission was necessary for the recitation of Quiñones' Breviary, which was originally intended only for private use, it soon began to penetrate even into the public offices of the religious orders and more than a hundred editions appeared between 1536 and 1566. In other quarters it was attacked for its disregard of tradition and it was eventually proscribed by *Paul IV in 1558.
Quiñones' Breviary considerably influenced T. *Cranmer, whose early drafts of a reformed Service Book and Calendar follow it closely; and with its uniformity, its continuous reading of Scripture, the recitation of the whole Psalter during a given period, and the general simplification by cutting out antiphons, responses, and the like, the BCP of 1549 and, through it, the final shape of the BCP, owe a good deal to the 'Breviary of the Holy Cross'.

Quiñones' Breviary of 1535 was repr. by J. Wickham Legg (Cambridge, 1888); the second recension, of 1536, ed. id. (*H.B.S.*, xxxv (text) and xlii (liturgical introd., life of Quiñones, notes and indices), 1908–12). [Fernando] Marquis d'Alcedo, *Le Cardinal Quiñones et la Sainte Ligue* (Bayonne, 1910). J. A. Jungmann, S.J., 'Warum ist das Reformbrevier des Kardinals Quiñones gescheitert?' in *Z.K.T.*, lxxviii (1956), pp. 98–107. See also works cited under *Breviary* and *Common Prayer, Book of*.

QUINQUAGESIMA. Properly the period of fifty days preceding *Easter which begins on the Sunday before *Ash Wednesday; but the word is in general use only for the Sunday mentioned. In earlier times, a new stage in the pre-Lenten discipline, e.g. abstinence from flesh-meat, began on this day. The word is occasionally used also of the fifty days which extend from Easter to *Pentecost.

A. Chavasse, 'Temps de préparation à la Pâques d'après quelques livres liturgiques romains' in *Rech. S.R.*, xxxvii (1950), pp. 125–45, esp. III, 'La "Cinquantaine" préparatoire au jour de Pâques ou Quinquagésime', p. 130. P. Siffrin, O.S.B., in *E.C.*, x (1953), col. 421, s.v. See also bibl. to *Septuagesima* and *Sexagesima*.

QUINQUE VIAE. The five 'ways' or arguments by which St. *Thomas Aquinas (*Summa Theol.* I, q. 2, art. 3) sought to prove the existence of God *a posteriori*, i.e. from those effects of His being which are known to us, viz. (1) that motion implies a first mover; (2) that a sequence of efficient causes and their effects, such as we find in the world, implies an uncaused first cause; (3) that the existence of things which are not self-explanatory, and therefore might logically not exist, implies some necessary being (see *Cosmological Argument*); (4) that the comparisons we make (more or less 'true', 'good', 'noble', &c.) imply a standard of comparison which is itself perfect in all these qualities; (5) that the fulfilment by inanimate or unintelligent objects of an end to which they are evidently designed to work implies a purposive intelligence in their creation and direction (see *Physico-Theological Argument*).

QUIRE. The older spelling, still retained in the BCP, of the word now usually spelt **choir.**

QUIRINUS. The signature over which the series of 69 brilliantly written letters on the *Vatican Council was published in the *Augsburger Allgemeine Zeitung* in 1869–70. The writer is now known to have been J. J. I. von *Döllinger, who relied on material supplied by informants residing in Rome, among them Lord *Acton and J. *Friedrich. The letters, which were directed against the dominant party at the Council which was pressing for the definition of the Pope's Infallibility, maintained that the anti-infallibilist cause suffered from the many non-theological factors working in favour of an early definition, e.g. the Pope's

personal influence and the disproportionate representation of Italians at the Council. Admittedly the work of a strong partisan, they remain one of the primary sources for the history of the Council. See also *Janus.*

An Eng. trans. was published in 1870. See also C. Butler, *The Vatican Council* (1930), vol. i, ch. xiv.

QUMRAN SCROLLS. See *Dead Sea Scrolls.*

QUO VADIS? Acc. to a legend, first found in the 'Acts of St. *Peter' and transmitted by St. *Ambrose, the words 'Domine quo vadis'? (Lat., 'Lord, whither goest Thou?') were spoken by St. *Peter when, fleeing from Rome, he met Christ on the *Appian Way. Our Lord answered: 'I am coming to be crucified again,' words which St. Peter took to mean that He was to suffer again in His disciple; so he turned back to Rome where he was martyred. The small church of S. Maria delle Piante on the Appian Way, commonly called *Domine Quo Vadis*, which was rebuilt early in the 17th cent., commemorates the incident.

The development of the legend can be studied in 'Acts of *Peter', xxxv; *Origen, *Comm. in Joan.*, xx, 12 (*PG*, xiv, 600 B); Ambrose, *Sermo Contra Auxentium* (inter epp. 21 and 22), xiii (*PL*, xvi, 1011).

QUOAD OMNIA. The name given to Scottish parishes to which the ancient *teinds or tithes belonged. They were so called because they were provided *quoad omnia*, i.e. in respect of all things civil and ecclesiastical. If, however, through changed circumstances, e.g. owing to the growth of population, the one parochial church was found insufficient and a portion of the original parish was erected into a parish with a church of its own, the new parish was designated *quoad sacra*, i.e. as provided in respect of ecclesiastical affairs alone. In the pre-union Church of Scotland most of the churches in the cities were in *quoad sacra* parishes, and hence supported not by the teinds but by modern endowments and the liberality of their members. Since the union of 1929 ex-United Free churches have been allotted parishes and in many cases have received a portion of the teind-endowment of the old parish within whose area they stand.

QUOAD SACRA. See *Quoad Omnia.*

R

RABANUS MAURUS (776 or 784–856). Abbot of *Fulda and Abp. of Mainz, one of the greatest theologians of his age. Educated at Fulda and later at Tours under the direction of *Alcuin, he was made master of the monastery school at Fulda on his return, which under him became one of the most influential schools in Europe, counting *Walafrid Strabo and Otfrid of Weissenburg among its pupils. He was ordained priest in 814 and elected abbot in 822, and during the twenty years of his government the abbey of Fulda rapidly developed spiritually and intellectually as well as materially. He resigned his charge in 842, probably owing to difficulties with King Louis the German, and retired to Petersberg near Fulda. There he led a life of prayer and study until, in 847, he was made Abp. of Mainz, where, during his episcopate, three important synods were held in the years 847, 848, and 852. As abbot and archbishop Rabanus Maurus carried forward the evangelization of Germany and with this end in view furthered the learning of monks and clerics for whom he wrote 'De clericorum institutione', a kind of manual, dealing with the Sacraments, public prayer, fasts, and other subjects necessary for their work. He wrote a number of commentaries on the Scriptures, e.g. on the Pentateuch, the Wisdom Books, St. Matthew, and the Pauline Epistles. Of his other writings 'De universo', an encyclopaedic work based on St. *Isidore of Seville's 'Etymologiae' which upheld a mystical interpretation of the world, had considerable success. Rabanus was also a prolific poet, the '*Veni Creator Spiritus' being often attributed to him. He took part in the controversy which centred in the monk *Gottschalk who advocated the doctrine of predestination to damnation, and wrote against the pronounced realism of the sacramental teaching of *Paschasius Radbertus. Though he was not an original thinker and theologian, his sound knowledge, esp. of the Scriptures, the Latin Fathers and the Liturgy, and his zeal for the promotion of learning won him the title of *praeceptor Germaniae*. He was early venerated as a Saint but was not formally canonized. Feast day, 4 Feb.

Works ed. J. Pamelius–G. Colvenerius (6 vols., bound in 3, Cologne, 1626–7); repr. in J. P. Migne, *PL*, cvii–cxii. Modern edd. by E. Dümmler of his letters in *M.G.H.*, Epistolae, v (1898), pp. 379–516, with appendix of fragments pp. 517–33, and of his poems, ib., Poetae, ii (1884), pp. 154–244, with 'Appendix Hymnorum Incertae Originis', pp. 244–258, and by A. Koepler of his *De Institutione Clericorum* (Veröffentlichungen aus dem kirchenhistorischen Seminar München, No. 5; 1901). The primary source for his life is the biography by his disciple Rudolph, monk of Fulda, printed in *AA.SS.*, Feb. I (1658), pp. 512–22. F. Kunstmann, *Hrabanus Magnentius Maurus. Eine historische Monographie* (1841). E. Dümmler, 'Hrabanstudien' in *Sb.* (Berl.), 1898, I, pp. 24–42. J. Hablitzel, *Hrabanus Maurus. Ein Beitrag zur mittelalterlichen Exegese* (Biblische Studien, xi, Hft. 3; 1906). G. M. Dreves, *Hymnologische Studien zu Venantius Fortunatus und Rabanus Maurus* (Veröffentlichungen aus dem kirchenhistorischen Seminar München, III. Reihe No. 3; 1908), pp. 55–136. Raby, pp. 179–81, with bibl. p. 474. A. Manser, O.S.B., in *L.Th.K.*, v (1933), col. 160 f., s.v. 'Hrabanus' for further bibl. H. Petlier in *D.T.C.*, xiii (pt. 2; 1937), cols. 1601–20, s.v.

RABBI (Heb., 'my master'). A Jewish title of respect given to honoured teachers by disciples and others (Mt. 23. 7). Christ is so addressed in the Gospels (Jn. 1. 38, &c.). Shortly after NT times, it became added as a recognized title to the name of Jewish religious teachers, e.g. 'Rabbi Johanan'. Rabbi Judah (A.D. 135–217) was regarded as 'the Rabbi' *par excellence*.

RABBULA (d. 435), Bp. of *Edessa from 412. The leading figure in the Syrian Church in his day, he strongly opposed *Nestorianism, and attacked in particular the writings of *Theodore of Mopsuestia (d. 428). Acc. to F. C. *Burkitt, he compiled the *Peshitta text of the NT in the interests of orthodoxy and issued it to supersede the *Diatessaron of the heretic, *Tatian. He translated into Syriac St. *Cyril of Alexandria's 'De Recta Fide'; and was also the author of many letters and hymns and of a sermon against Nestorius. His successor in the see was the unorthodox *Ibas.

J. J. Overbeck (ed.), *S. Ephraemi Syri, Rabulae Episcopi Edesseni, Balaei aliorumque Opera Selecta* (Oxford, 1865), containing text of *Vita* (pp. 159–209), prose works (pp. 210–44), and some poetical and other texts (pp. 245–48, 362–78). Fr. tr. of Rabbula's Canons by F. Nau, *Ancienne Littérature canonique syriaque*, ii (1906), pp. 83–91, with introd. p. 79 f. M. J. *Lagrange, O.P., *Mélanges d'histoire religieuse* (1915), pp. 185–226 ('Un Évêque syrien du Ve siècle'; repr. from *La Science catholique*, 15 Sept. 1888). P. Peeters, S.J., 'La Vie de Rabboula, évêque de Édesse' in *Rech. S.R.*, xviii (1928), pp. 170–204 [shows unreliability of *Vita*]. W. Wright, *A Short History of Syriac Literature* (1894), pp. 47–9; A. *Baumstark, *Geschichte der syrischen Literatur* (1922), pp. 71–3. Bardenhewer, iv, 388–92. I. Ziadé in *D.T.C.*, xiii (pt. 2; 1937), cols. 1620–6, s.v. 'Rabboula'. See also bibl. to *Peshitta*.

RACCOLTA (Ital., 'collection'). An officially approved RC prayer book containing all the devotions to which Papal *indulgences are attached. The first Raccolta was published in 1807 at Rome by Telesforo Galli.

RACOVIAN CATECHISM, The. The first statement of Socinian principles. Drawn up by Valentin Schmalz and Johannes Völkel on the basis of drafts by F. P. *Socinus, it was published in Polish in 1605 at Racow, an early stronghold of Socinianism in S. Poland. Versions in German (1608) and Latin (1609) followed. It was professedly not a formal confessional creed, designed to be dogmatically imposed on the Socinians, but a body of opinions which would point believers towards eternal life. In eight sections it dealt with (1) the Scriptures (the only source of truth), (2) the way of salvation (knowledge and a holy life), (3) the knowledge of God ('the Supreme

Lord of all things', with rejection of the Trinity), (4) the Person of Christ (a man by his marvellous life and resurrection raised to divine power), (5) the Prophetic Office of Christ, (6) the Kingship of Christ, (7) the Priesthood of Christ, and (8) the Church (the body of Christians who uphold and profess the saving doctrines). A copy of the Latin version, sent to England with a dedication to *James I, was publicly burnt in 1614.

An English version by J.*Biddle was publd. at Amsterdam in 1652; it was formally burnt in 1654 by order of O. *Cromwell. New Eng. ed. by Thomas Rees with Historical Introduction, London, 1818.

RADBERTUS, PASCHASIUS. See *Paschasius Radbertus*.

RADEGUNDE, St. (518–87), the Queen of Clothaire I. The daughter of a prince of Thuringen, she fell into the hands of the Franks after a successful invasion of her country. She was a woman of great piety who did not wish to marry, but as an act of charity consented to become the wife of Clothaire, a man of debased tastes and evil character (c. 540). His murder of her brother gave her an excuse to flee from court (c. 550) and to persuade Médard, Bp. of Noyon, to ordain her a deaconess. Not long afterwards she founded a monastery of nuns outside Poitiers, where the rule of *Caesarius of Arles was adopted. Here she spent the remaining thirty years of her life in prayer, study, and good works. In 569 she obtained for her convent, from the Emp. Justin II, a large fragment of the true cross, which inspired *Venantius Fortunatus to write his famous '*Vexilla regis'. Feast day, 13 Aug.

Contemporary Lives by *Venantius Fortunatus and the nun, Baudonivia, printed in *Acta Sanctorum*, Aug. III (1737), pp. 67–83; crit. ed. by B. Krusch in *M.G.H.*, Scriptores Rerum Merovingicarum, ii (1888), pp. 358–95; the former Life also ed., with Fr. tr., by R. Aigrain (Paris, 1910). Life by *Hildebert of Lavardin in *Acta Sanctorum*, loc. cit., pp. 83–92, repr. in J. P. Migne, *PL*, clxxi, 967–88. Anon. Life attributed to Henry Bradshaw, O.S.B., (d. 1513), printed c. 1508–27, ed. by F. Brittain (Cambridge, 1926). Modern lives by E. de Fleury (Paris, 1843), E. Briand (Poitiers, 1898), and R. Aigrain ('Les Saints', 1918). F. Brittain, *St. Radegund*. Patroness of Jesus College, Cambridge (1925).

RADEWYNS, FLORENTIUS. See *Florentius Radewyns*.

RAIKES, ROBERT (1735–1811), the founder of *Sunday Schools. A native of *Gloucester, he was educated at the College (i.e. Cathedral) School. He became an advocate of many philanthropic causes which he supported in the *Gloucester Journal* (est. 1732), which he inherited from his father in 1757. Stimulated by the neglected condition of the local children and their behaviour on Sundays, he was led to assist in the establishment of a Sunday School in a neighbouring parish; and in 1780 he started a school in his own parish, open on week-days and Sundays, for the teaching of Scripture, reading, and other elementary subjects. Although he had to face opposition

at first from conservatives who felt that popular education spelled revolution, as well as from strict *Sabbatarians, his enthusiasm and use of new methods (phonetics, employment of monitors, &c.) triumphed. In 1783 he felt his school sufficiently established to draw attention to his achievement in his paper. His methods were soon followed by Hannah *More (q.v.) and others, and before his death Sunday Schools had come into being in many places throughout the country.

The basic lives are those by A. Gregory (London, 1877) and that ed. J. H. Harris, with introd. by F. W. *Farrar (Bristol–London, 1899). Other lives by J. H. Harris ('Splendid Lives Series', London [1900]; revised ed. [1928]), T. B. Walters (London, 1930) and G. Kendall (ib., 1939). L. Stephen in *D.N.B.*, xlvii (1896), pp. 168–70.

RAINOLDS, JOHN (1549–1607), also Reynolds, Anglican divine. A native of Pinhoe, Devon, he was educated at Corpus Christi College, Oxford, where he was elected a Fellow in 1568. As reader in Greek in his college (1573–8), he became well known through his successful lectures on *Aristotle's *Rhetoric*. Resigning his Fellowship in 1586, probably through difficulties with William Coke, the president, he taught for a time at Queen's College. In 1593 he became Dean of *Lincoln and in 1598, by an arrangement welcome to Corpus where Coke's rule was much disliked, exchanged this office with the president. By this time Rainolds had won a reputation as a skilled champion of *Calvinism, and at the *Hampton Court Conference (1604) he was the chief representative of the Puritan cause. Among the things in the BCP to which he objected were the *Sign of the Cross in baptism, the ring in marriage, the use of the *Apocrypha, and the *churching of Women. Though the Puritan objections were overruled at the Conference, Rainolds did not fall into favour. He was given a prominent part in preparing the *Authorized Version of the Bible, sitting in the company which translated the Prophets. His high character and wide learning won him respect even from his theological adversaries.

Rainolds's *Orationes Duodecim* were posthumously ed. by his friend and pupil, Henry Jackson (London, 1614). The fifth of them, *Oratio in Laudem Artis Poeticae*, was repr. from a later ed., with introd. (pp. 1–23) and commentary by W. Ringler and Eng. tr. by W. Allen (Princeton Studies in English, xx; Princeton, N.J., 1940). T. Fowler in *D.N.B.*, xlvii (1896), pp. 180–2.

RAMBAM. See *Maimonides*.

RAMBLER, The. A monthly RC periodical, founded by J. M. Capes in 1848, which became an organ of liberal English Catholicism. In 1859 (Lord) *Acton, then one of its proprietors, secured J. H. *Newman as editor. After four months, however, an article by Newman on the place of the laity in the Church was condemned at Rome and he was compelled to retire. Acton himself nominally succeeded to the editorship, though in fact Richard Simpson, an earlier editor, did most of the work. The

Rambler attacked the *Ultramontanism of W. G. *Ward and H. E. *Manning, and in 1862 the latter suppressed it. It was nominally merged in a quarterly, the *Home and Foreign Review* (itself suppressed for similar reasons in 1864).

RAMÓN LULL. See *Lull, Raymond.*

RAMSAY, WILLIAM MITCHELL (1851–1939), NT Scholar. Educated at Aberdeen, Oxford, and Göttingen, he became Fellow successively of Exeter (1882) and Lincoln (1885) Colleges, Oxford. From 1886 to 1911 he was professor of humanity at Aberdeen. He travelled extensively in Asia Minor, and became an eminent authority on its geography and history. He was also a keen student of the NT, making extensive use of his archaeological and other learning in defence of a moderate conservatism. His books include *The Historical Geography of Asia Minor* (1890), *The Church in the Roman Empire* (1893), *The Cities and Bishoprics of Phrygia* (2 vols., 1895, 1897), *St. Paul, the Traveller and Roman Citizen* (1895) and *Was Christ born at Bethlehem?* (1898).

Anatolian Studies presented to Sir William Mitchell Ramsay, ed. W. H. Buckler and W. M. Calder (Manchester, 1923). J. G. C. Anderson in *D.N.B., 1931–1940*, p. 727 f.

RAMUS, PETRUS (Pierre de la Ramée) (1515–72), French humanist. Educated at the College of Navarre, he began publicly to attack *Aristotelianism at Paris university in 1536 when, in his exercise for his Master of Arts, he defended the thesis that all Aristotle's doctrines were false. In 1543 he published his *Aristotelicae Animadversiones* and *Dialecticae Institutiones* which were condemned by the university of Paris. In 1544 Francis I forbade him to teach, but through the influence of his patrons, the Cardinals de Bourbon and de Lorraine, he was appointed president of the College of Presles in 1545 and professor of rhetoric and philosophy at the Collège Royal in 1551. After becoming a *Calvinist in 1562 he went to Germany. He returned to Paris in 1571 and was killed by his enemies in the Massacre of St. *Bartholomew in 1572. To Aristotle's system, which he accused of falsifying the innate logic of the human mind, he opposed his own, a mixture of logic and rhetoric which declared deduction to be the final scientific method. His distinction between *inventio* (idea and definition) and *iudicium* (judgement, conclusion and method) was much discussed, and the quarrel between 'Ramists' and 'Anti-Ramists' agitated the European universities for several years.

Studies by C. Waddington-Kastus (Paris, 1848, in Lat.; ib., 1855, in Fr.), C. Desmaze (ib.; 1867) and F. P. Graves, *Peter Ramus and the Educational Reformation of the Sixteenth Century* (New York, 1912), with bibl. P. Lobstein, *Petrus Ramus als Theologe* (Strassburg, 1878). Überweg, iii, 156–8, with bibl. p. 647.

RANCÉ, ARMAND JEAN LE BOUTHILLIER DE (1626–1700), founder of the *Trappists. Son of the secretary of Maria

de' Medici, he was destined to an ecclesiastical career in order to keep the numerous benefices in the family. He became Canon of Notre-Dame-de-Paris and commendatory Abbot of *La Trappe and several other monasteries *c.* 1636. At the age of twelve he published an edition of Anacreon with a Greek commentary. He soon entered on a worldly and dissipated life in which his ordination to the priesthood in 1651 made no change. The process of his conversion began with the death of the Duchess of Montbazon in 1657 and was completed by that of the Duke Gaston d'Orléans in 1660. He resigned his benefices and gave away his property, took the *Cistercian habit at the novitiate at Perseigne in 1663, and was consecrated abbot of La Trappe in the following year. His next years were spent in bringing back his monastery to the original strictness of the rule to which he added many other austerities. He encountered strong opposition, but nevertheless La Trappe soon became a centre of the spiritual life of France and was frequented by men like J. B. *Bossuet. The publication of Rancé's *Traité de la sainteté et des devoirs de la vie monastique* in 1683 was the occasion of a long-drawn-out controversy with J. *Mabillon on the place of studies in the monastic life, Rancé being unwilling to admit anything but prayer and manual work. He was violently opposed to the semi-*Quietism of F. *Fénelon whom he attacked in two letters to Bossuet (1697); and on account of his excessive austerity he was himself suspected of *Jansenist leanings but, as his letters show, without reason. At La Trappe Rancé was much sought after as a spiritual director, and among those who placed themselves under his guidance was *James II.

Collection of his letters, 2 vols., Paris, 1701–2; modern ed. by B. Gonod (ib., 1846). Primary lives by P. de Maupeou (2 vols., Paris, '1602' [1702]) and J. Marsollier (ib., 1703). Other lives include those of P. Le Nain, O.S.B. (Prior of the Abbey, 2 vols., no place, 1715; ed. 2, Paris, 1719), F. R. de *Chateaubriand (ib., 1844; undertaken in fulfilment of a penance), L. Dubois (2 vols., ib., 1866), B. Schmid, O.S.B. (Regensburg, 1897), H. *Bremond, *L'Abbé Tempête* (Paris, 1929; Eng. tr., 1930; unsympathetic), and A. J. Luddy, O.Cist. (London, 1931; reply to Bremond). J. Carreyre in *D.T.C.*, xiii (pt. 2; 1937), cols. 1652–6, s.v., with bibl. See also bibl. to *Trappists.*

RANKE, LEOPOLD VON (1795–1886), German historian. From 1825 till his death he was professor of history at Berlin. Ranke's work is characterized by emphasis on the primary importance of the study of original sources, by psychological penetration and by a fundamentally objective attitude to history, as well as by understanding of national tendencies in their relation to the history of their age. The most famous of his works was his History of the Popes in the 16th and 17th cents., *Die römischen Päpste, ihre Kirche und ihr Staat* (3 vols., 1834–6), which from the 6th edition (1874) was carried down to 1870. It was based on extensive researches in the libraries of Italy where he collected material for three years (1828–31). In this work he removed the history of the Papacy from denominational polemics and showed the development of the Papal power and its effects on the history of Europe, stressing, however, its political rather than its religious significance. This work was followed by a large-scale history of the Reformation, *Deutsche Geschichte im Zeitalter der Reformation* (6 vols., 1839–47), which it studied in the setting of contemporary European history and with full appreciation of its religious values from the Lutheran point of view.

Sämmtliche Werke (54 vols., Leipzig, 1867–90); also ed. P. Joachimsen, with the co-operation of E. Marcks, F. Meinecke, and H. Oncken (Münich, 1952 ff.) *Das Briefwerk*, ed. W. P. Fuchs (Hamburg, 1949); B. Hoeft–H. Herzfeld (edd.), *Neue Briefe* (1949). His principal works have also been tr. into Eng. E. Guglia, *Leopold von Rankes Leben und Wirken* (1893); H. F. Helmolt, *Leopold von Rankes Leben und Wirken* (1921). T. H. Von Laue, *Leopold Ranke. The Formative Years* (Princeton, 1950), with bibl. G. P. Gooch, *History and Historians in the Nineteenth Century* (1913), pp. 76–102.

RANTERS

A fanatical *antinomian and *pantheistic sect of the mid-17th cent. They appealed to their inward experience of Christ and denied the authority of Scripture, Creeds, and the Ministry. Their revolutionary and immoral doctrines made them the object of deep suspicion. They were at first popularly associated with the *Quakers, who suffered misrepresentation from the confusion. They were fiercely attacked by R. *Baxter. In the 19th cent. the word was applied colloquially to nonconformist (esp. *Primitive Methodist) preachers.

R. Barclay, *The Inner Life of the Religious Societies of the Commonwealth* (1876), pp. 409–74, with repr. of extracts from two Ranter Tracts as appendix to Ch. xvii (sep. pagination). R. M. Jones, *Studies in Mystical Religion* (1909), pp. 467–81. Id. in *H.E.R.E.*, x (1918), pp. 578–80, with reff.

RAPHAEL, St., *Archangel

In the Books of *Tobit and *Enoch, Raphael figures as one of the seven archangels who stand in the presence of God. In Tobit (12. 12, 15) he hears the prayers of holy men and brings them before God. The name in Heb. (רפאל) means 'God heals', and in Enoch (10. 7) he is said to have 'healed' the earth when it was defiled by the sins of the fallen angels. From these Jewish speculations the figure of Raphael passed into Christian tradition. Feast day, 24 Oct.

The principal literature is to be found in commentaries on Enoch and Tobit, cited s.vv. On the Christian feast, L. Eisenhofer, *Handbuch der katholischen Liturgik*, i (1932), p. 602. J. T. Marshall in *H.D.B.*, iv (1902), p. 201, s.v.; A. Penna, C.R.L.-G. Löw, C.SS.R.-M. Donati in *E.C.*, x (1952), cols. 469–73, s.v. 'Raffaele'. See also works cited under *Angels*.

RAPHAEL (1483–1520) (Raffaele Sanzio)

the most famous of the Renaissance painters. From 1499 to 1504 he worked under *Perugino at Perugia, and painted the *Crucifixion* (1502; lately in the Mond Collection, now in the National Gallery) and the *Espousals of the Virgin* (1504; Brera, Milan). In 1504 he migrated to Florence, where he was brought into contact with the greatest artists of the time, among them *Michelangelo, *Leonardo da Vinci, and the Dominican Fra *Bartolommeo. Here he painted the *Madonna del Granduca* (Pitti, Florence) and the *Ansidei Madonna* (London National Gallery). In 1508 he was summoned to Rome by *Julius II to decorate the Vatican 'Stanze'. The series of famous paintings for their walls included the *Disputa* and *St. Peter released from Prison*. He also executed at Rome the *Madonna della Sedia* (1516; Pitti, Florence) and the celebrated *Sistine Madonna* (1516; Dresden). In 1514 *Leo X appointed him chief architect of St. Peter's in succession to Bramante. His last work, *The Transfiguration* (Vatican), was left unfinished and completed by his pupils.

Reproductions of his pictures, in black and white, ed. G. Gronau (Klassiker der Kunst, i; ed. 2, 1905); also by G. Nicodemi (Milan, 1929); collection of colour plates with introd. by W. E. Suida (Phaidon Press, London, 1941). The 'Stanze' are being reprod. in the series Monumenti vaticani di archeologia e d' arte pubblicati per munificenza di Sua Santità Benedetto XV a cura della Pontificia Accademia Romana d' Archeologia, vol. i, &c., 1922 ff. V. Golzio, *Raffaello nei documenti nelle testimonianze dei contemporanei e nella letteratura del suo secolo* (Pontificia Insigne Accademia Artistica dei Virtuosi al Pantheon; Rome, 1936). Modern studies include those of J. D. Passavant (2 parts, Leipzig, 1839; Eng. tr., 1872), E. Muntz (Paris, 1881; Eng. tr. 1882), J. A. Crowe–G. B. Cavalcaselle (2 vols., London, 1882–5), A. P. Oppé (London, 1909), V. Wanscher (Copenhagen, 1919; Eng. tr., 1926), A. Venturi (Rome, 1920), W. Stein (Berlin, 1923), G. Lattanzi (Milan, 1929), and O. Fischel (translated into Eng. and posthumously publd., 2 vols., London, 1948, incl. one vol. of plates). C. [J.] Holmes, *Raphael and the Modern Use of the Classical Tradition* (1933). O. Fischel in *Allgemeines Lexikon der bildenden Künstler von der Antike bis zur Gegenwart* begründet U. Thieme–F. Becker, xxix (ed. H. Vollmer; 1935), cols. 433–46, s.v. 'Santi (Sanzio)', with bibl.

RAPP, JOHANN GEORG (1757–1847)

founder of the *Harmony Society (q. v.).

RAS SHAMRA TABLETS

A collection of cuneiform tablets with mythological poems and ritual prescriptions excavated by C. F. A. Schaeffer at Ras Shamra (anciently Ugarit) in N. Syria from 1929 onwards. The tablets, prob. dating from the 14th cent. B.C. or earlier, are in a hitherto unknown alphabetical script and in a Semitic dialect closely akin to Hebrew. They bear on the development of the alphabet and the language, literature, and religion of Canaan before the Israelite settlement. Their contents show some remarkable correspondences with the OT literature, throwing light on obscure Hebrew words and phrases, on OT religious practices and beliefs, and on the forms of Hebrew poems and their liturgical use. The key to the decipherment of the texts was discovered almost simultaneously by three scholars, H. Bauer, E. Dhorme, O.P., and C. Virolleaud.

Reports of the finds at Minet-el-Beida and Ras Shamra are given by C. F. A. Schaeffer in *Syria*. Revue d'Art et d'Archéologie publiée par l'Institut Français d'Archéologie de Beyrout, x (1929), pp. 285–97; xii (1931), pp. 1–14; xiii (1932), pp. 1–27; xiv (1933), pp. 94–127; xv (1934), pp. 105–131; xvi (1935), pp. 141–76; xvii (1936), pp. 105–49; xviii (1937), pp. 125–54; xix (1938), pp. 193–255, and 312–34; xx (1939), pp. 277–92; xxviii (1951), pp. 1–21. *Mission de Ras-Shamra* dirigée par C. F. A. Schaeffer: i, C. Virolleaud.

La *Légende phénicienne de Daniel* (Haute Commission de la République Française en Syrie et au Liban. Service des Antiquités. Bibliothèque archéologique et historique, xxi; Paris, 1936); ii, id., *La Légende de Kéret, roi des Sidoniens* (ib., xxii; 1936); iii, C. F. A. Schaeffer, *Ugaritica*. Études relatives aux découvertes de Ras Samra (ib., xxxi; 1939); iv, C. Virolleaud, *La Déesse 'Anat*. Poème de Ras-Shamra (ib., xxviii; 1938); v, C. F. A. Schaeffer, *Ugaritica*, ii (ib., xlvii; 1949). Id., *The Cuneiform Texts of Ras Shamra-Ugarit* (Schweich Lectures for 1936; 1939). C. H. Gordon, *Ugaritic Handbook*. Revised Grammar, Paradigms, Texts in transliteration, Comprehensive Glossary (Analecta Orientalia, xxv; 1947); id., *Ugaritic Literature*. A Comprehensive Translation of the Poetic and Prose Texts (Scripta Pontificii Instituti Biblici, xcviii; 1949). G. R. Driver, *Canaanite Myths and Legends* (1956). There are also a number of other important specialized artt. by C. Virolleaud and others in *Syria*, x (1929) and following volumes.

RASHDALL, HASTINGS (1858–1924), moral philosopher and theologian. Educated at Harrow and New College, Oxford, Rashdall taught philosophy at Oxford from 1888 to 1917, first at Hertford College and later (after 1895) at New College. From 1909 to 1917 he also held a canonry at *Hereford. From 1917 till his death he was Dean of *Carlisle. He won fame first as a historian by his *Universities of Europe in the Middle Ages* (3 vols., 1895; new ed. by F. M. Powicke and A. B. Emden, 1936). In 1907 he published an important treatise on moral philosophy, *The Theory of Good and Evil* (2 vols.), in which he expounded an ethical doctrine which he described as 'Ideal *Utilitarianism'. In his *Bampton Lectures for 1915, *The Idea of Atonement in Christian Theology* (1919), he upheld with much vigour the *Abelardian or '*Exemplarist' theory of the Atonement. Rashdall possessed supreme confidence in the capacity of human reason, rightly employed, to arrive at the final truths of religion. He was in consequence an untiring controversialist, and a strong critic of all forms of *pragmatism, *modernism, sentimentalism, and *mysticism.

Three volumes of (largely unpubld.) papers and sermons by Rashdall, ed. H. D. A. Major–F. L. Cross under the titles *Principles and Precepts* (Oxford, 1927), *Ideas and Ideals* (ib., 1928), and *God and Man* (ib., 1930). Life by P. E. Matheson (London, 1928). C. C. J. *Webb in *D.N.B.*, *1922–1930*, pp. 706–9.

RASHI (1040–1105), Jewish Biblical scholar, so called from the initials of his name Rabbi Solomon ben Isaac. After studying at Mainz and Worms he was appointed rabbi in his native city of Troyes. Among the Jews he is still one of the most highly reputed exegetes of the Hebrew Scriptures and the *Talmud. His aim, in opposition to the current exegesis of his time, was to interpret the OT acc. to its literal sense. His commentaries, esp. on Genesis, were used by *Nicholas of Lyra and, through him, are commonly supposed to have influenced M. *Luther. His works were translated into Latin in the 17th and 18th cents., the most complete edition being that of F. Breithaupt (1710, 1713, 1714).

His Comm. on the Pentateuch is ed. with Eng. tr. and notes by M. Rosenbaum–A. M. Silbermann (5 vols., London, 1929–34). L. Zunz, 'Solomon ben Isaac gennant Raschi' in *Zeitschrift für die Wissenschaft des Judentums*, i (1822), pp. 277–384. M. Liber, *Rashi* (Paris, 1906; Eng.

tr., 1906). E. I. J. Rosenthal, 'Rashi and the English Bible' in *Bulletin of the John Rylands Library*, xxiv (1940), pp. 138–67. M. Liber–M. Seligsohn in *J.E.*, x (1905), pp. 324–8.

RASKOLNIKI (Russ., 'schismatics'). A comprehensive name for the section of the Russian Church that refused to accept the reforms of the patriarch *Nikon (d. 1681). They are also known as the '*Old Believers' (q.v.).

RATHERIUS (*c.* 887–974), Bp. of *Verona. A man of a very refractory and ambitious character, he took a prominent part in the ecclesiastical life of the 10th cent. Born in the neighbourhood of Liége, he at first became monk at the abbey of Lobbes in the Hennegau. In 926 he accompanied his abbot, Hilduin, to Italy where he received the see of Verona from Hugo, the King, Hilduin's cousin, in 931. Soon, however, he fell out with the King and was removed from his see. After many changes of fortune, he was made Bp. of Liége in 953, but forced to resign in 955. From 962 to 968 he was again in possession of the Bpric. of Verona. His many writings, mostly of an occasional kind and often full of invective, throw important light on his age.

Works ed. J. and P. *Ballerini (Verona, 1765), with life pp. xxvi–clxxiv; repr. in J. P. Migne, *PL*, cxxxvi, 9–768. Critical ed. of his letters by F. Weigle in *M.G.H.*, Briefe der deutschen Kaiserzeit, i (1949), with bibl. reff. A. Vogel, *Ratherius von Verona und das zehnte Jahrhundert* (2 vols., 1854). G. Pavani, *Un vescovo belga in Italia nel secolo decimo*. Studio storico-critico su Raterio di Verona (1920). G. Monticelli, *Raterio, vescovo di Verona, 890–974* (1938), with bibl. É. Amann in *D.T.C.*, xiii (pt. 2; 1937), cols. 1679–87, s.v. 'Rathier de Vérone'.

RATIO STUDIORUM (Lat., 'the method of the studies'). The abbreviated name for the 'Ratio atque Institutio Studiorum Societatis Jesu', the elaborate code of rules which since the end of the 16th cent. has governed the *Jesuit system of education. After some 15 years of testing and discussion it was finally issued in 1599. In its original form it provided for an education based almost exclusively on the classics and a somewhat rigidly prescribed method of instruction ('praelectiones') which the teacher was required to follow. In recent times the curriculum has been enlarged. While the system undoubtedly fosters thoroughness and great technical perfection, it is sometimes criticized as failing to develop originality.

RATIONALE. The word has several ecclesiastical senses:

(1) Formerly, the breastplate worn by the Jewish high priest.

(2) A liturgical vestment of stuff which was sometimes worn by bishops over the shoulders. It seems to have been looked upon as a kind of substitute for the archiepiscopal *pallium, and to have been in use esp. in Germany. Its use is now confined to the Bps. of Eichstätt, Paderborn, Toul, and Cracow.

(3) An ornament worked in gold sometimes worn by bps. on the breast over the *chasuble when celebrating Mass. Its adoption was never

widespread, though its use survived at *Reims till the beginning of the 16th cent.

(4) A set of liturgical rules, e.g. those of W. *Durandus ('Rationale Divinorum Officiorum', 1286–91). Cf. also the *Rationale upon the Book of Common Prayer* (1657), by A. *Sparrow.

RATISBON, The Conference of (1541).

A reunion conference of three Catholic and three Protestant theologians convened at Ratisbon (Regensburg) from 27 Apr. to 22 May by the Emp. *Charles V. The three Catholics were J. *Eck, Julius Pflug (1449–1564), and John Gropper (1503–59): the three Protestants P. *Melanchthon, M. *Bucer, and Pistorius (1503–83). Though doctrinal agreement was reached on most of the controverted subjects, including the crucial question of *justification, the subsequent hostility of M. *Luther, as well as political rivalries, prevented any reunion being effected.

The *Acta* were publd. by M. Bucer at Strassburg in 1541 (Eng. tr. by M. *Coverdale [Geneva?], 1542). Kidd, pp. 340–346 [incl. Docc. Nos. 136–40]. L. *Pastor, *Die Reunionsbestrebungen während der Regierung Karls V* (1879), pp. 218–278. K. T. Hergang, *Das Religions-Gespräch zu Regensburg i.J. 1541 und das Regensburger Buch nebst andren darauf bezüglichen Schriften jener Zeit* (1858). H. Eells, 'The Origin of the Regensburg Book' in *The Princeton Theological Review*, xxvi (1928), pp. 353–72. Further bibl. in Schottenloher, iv (1938), p. 536 f. (Nos. 41376–89). T. Kolde in *P.R.E.* (ed. 3), xvi (1905), pp. 542–52, s.v. 'Regensburger Religionsgespräch und Regensburger Buch, 1541'.

RATRAMNUS (d. 868).

A monk of *Corbie, who took a prominent part in the theological controversies of his age. In his 'De Praedestinatione', written at the bidding of Charles the Bald, he defended the doctrine of 'double predestination', i.e. to good and evil. His most celebrated writing was his treatise on the *Eucharist, 'De Corpore et Sanguine Domini', in which he attacked the carnal view of the Sacrament defended by *Paschasius Radbertus. Ratramnus's highly individual approach to the doctrine makes it difficult to relate his position to that of later orthodoxy. His book was condemned at the Synod of Vercelli held on 1 Sept. 1050 (where it was wrongly attributed to *Erigena). In the 16th cent. he was claimed (whether justly or not is much disputed) by several of the Reformers, notably N. *Ridley, as supporting their own doctrines. John *Fisher, on the other hand, appealed to his teaching against that of J. *Oecolampadius. In 1559 the treatise was put on the *Index, but removed again in 1900. Ratramnus also wrote a book, 'Contra Graecorum Opposita', against the theology of the E. Church.

Editiones principes of his 'De Corpore et Sanguine Domini', Cologne, 1531; of his 'De Praedestinatione' in G. Mauguin (ed.), *Veterum Auctorum qui IX. saeculo de Praedestinatione et Gratia scripserunt Opera et Fragmenta* (Paris, 1650), pp. 29–102. Collected ed. of his works repr. from various sources in J. P. Migne, *PL*, cxxi, 11–346 and 1153–6. Crit. ed. of six letters by E. Dümmler in *M.G.H.*, Epistolae vi (1925), pp. 149–58. A. *Wilmart, O.S.B., 'L'Opuscule inédit de Ratramne sur la nature de l'âme' in *R. Bén.*, xliii (1931), pp. 207–23, incl. text (abbreviated) from one MS.; full ed. by C. Lambot, O.S.B. (Analecta Mediaevalia Namurcensia, ii; Namur-Paris, [c. 1952]).

Modern Eng. trr. of his 'De Corpore et Sanguine Domini' by 'H. W.'-'W. C. C.' (London, 1838) and W. F. Taylor (ib., 1880). A. Naegle, *Ratramnus und die hl. Eucharistie* (Theologische Studien der Leo-Gesellschaft, v; 1903). D. *Stone, *A History of the Doctrine of the Holy Eucharist*, i (1909), pp. 226–33. J. Dräseke, 'Ratramnus und Photius' in *B.Z.*, xviii (1909), pp. 396–421. Manitius, i, 412–17. G. E. Steitz-A. Hauck in *P.R.E.*, xvi (1905), pp. 463–70; s.v.; H. Peltier in *D.T.C.*, xiii (pt. 2; 1937), cols. 1780–7, s.v. 'Ratramne'. Crit. ed. of 'De Corpore et Sanguine Domini' by J. N. Bakhuizen van den Brink (Amsterdam, 1954). See also works cited under *Paschasius Radbertus*.

RAVENNA.

Acc. to tradition the first Bp. of Ravenna was St. *Apollinaris (q.v.). After the choice of the city in 404 as the Imperial residence by Honorius (395–423), it rapidly grew in importance and wealth. In 493 it fell to *Theodoric the Goth (d. 526), who introduced *Arianism. After the capture of the city for the Byzantine Empire by Belisarius (540) it became the capital of the Exarchate until it fell to the Lombards in 751. It is unrivalled in its mosaics and other remains of early Christian art. The oldest monument is the mausoleum of *Galla Placidia (d. 450), with magnificent mosaics, the most famous that of Christ as the Good Shepherd. Other noted early mosaics are in the Baptistery, a converted Roman bath (449–52), and the chapel of the archiepiscopal palace. Of the churches, the most famous are S. Apollinare Nuovo, originally the Arian cathedral (c. 500), S. Vitale (547), and S. Apollinare in Classe (549; at Classe, some three miles distant). *Dante, who spent the last four years of his life at Ravenna, was buried in the church of S. Francesco (1321). It was a key-point in the German defence in the Second World War, but the only building seriously damaged was S. Giovanni Evangelista. The patron of the city is St. *Vitalis (q.v.). Perhaps its most celebrated Bishop (apart from St. Apollinaris) was St. Peter *Chrysologus (d. 450).

*Agnellus (9th cent.), *Liber Pontificalis Ecclesiae Ravennatis* (crit. ed. by O. Holder-Egger in *M.G.H.*, Scriptores Rerum Langobardicarum et Italicarum Saec. VI–IX (1878), pp. 265–391; also ed. A. Testi Rasponi in L. A. *Muratori, *Rerum Italicarum Scriptores*, new ed. G. Carducci-V. Fiorini, ii, Parte III, 1924 ff.). E. Hutton, *Ravenna* (1913); rev. ed. for the 'The Mediaeval Towns Series', 1926). W. Götz, *Ravenna* (Leipzig, 1901); T. Nediani, *Ravenna* (Florence, 1921); C. O. Nordström, *Ravennastudien* (Stockholm, 1953). S. Muratori, *Ricordi di Ravenna medioevale, nel VI centenario della morte di Dante* (1921). E. Uehli, *Die Mosaiken von Ravenna* (1935). Marion Lawrence, *The Sarcophagi of Ravenna* (Monographs on Archaeology and Fine Arts sponsored by the Archaeological Institute of America and the College Art Association, ii, New York, 1945). O. G. von Simson, *Sacred Fortress. Byzantine Art and Statecraft in Ravenna* (Chicago, 1948). F. *Cabrol, O.S.B., 'Autour de la liturgie de Ravenne. Saint Pierre Chrysologue et le *Rotulus* in *R.Bén.*, xxiii (1906), pp. 489–500. M. Mazzotti in *E.C.*, x (1953), cols. 558–73, s.v., with bibl.

RAYMOND LULL.

See *Lull, Raymond*.

RAYMOND NONNATUS, St. (c. 1204–40),

*Mercedarian missioner. The accounts of his life rest on wholly unreliable sources written in the Mercedarian interest centuries later. Acc. to these he came into the world after his mother had died in labour (hence 'non natus', not born) at Portello in Catalonia. After a most pious childhood, he was given leave by his father to join the Mercedarians, to whom he was admitted at Barcelona by St. *Peter Nolasco. Sent to N. Africa, he redeemed many slaves at Algiers and, when his funds were exhausted, gave himself up in ransom and for some years lived among the Moslems, converting many to the Christian faith. His trials are said to have culminated in an eight months' imprisonment, from which he was ransomed by members of his order. On his return to Spain in 1239, *Gregory IX nominated him cardinal, but in the next year on his way to Rome he died at Cardona, near Barcelona. Feast day, 31 Aug. He is the patron saint of midwives.

There is very little trustworthy information about the Saint. A 16th cent. life is pr. in *A.A.SS.*, Aug. VI (1743), pp. 737–41, with introd., pp. 729–37, and account of the miracles attributed to him, pp. 74–6. See also histories of the *Mercedarians*, cited s.v.

RAYMOND OF PENAFORT, St. (*c.* 1175–1275), Spanish canonist. He studied, and later taught, rhetoric and logic at Barcelona, but resigned his chair in 1210 in order to study law at *Bologna. Here he was made doctor in 1216 and lectured until 1222 when he entered the *Dominican Order. About this time he assisted St. *Peter Nolasco in his foundation of the *Mercedarians (for the redemption of Christian captives), for which he drew up the constitutions and obtained Papal approval in 1235. In 1230, *Gregory IX appointed him his confessor, and later his chaplain and Grand Penitentiary, and charged him with the collection of the pontifical decretals. Completed in 1234, this collection became a standard work which was accepted by the canonists. Between 1223 and 1238 Raymond compiled his *Summa de poenitentia* (also called *Summa casuum*) which exercised a profound influence on the development of the penitential system in the later Middle Ages. In 1236 he went back to Spain for reasons of health, and two years later, much against his will, was elected General of his order. In this last capacity he drew up a revision of the Dominican constitutions which remained in force until 1924. After having resigned his generalship in 1240 he devoted himself esp. to the conversion of Jews and Saracens, and for this purpose founded schools of Hebrew and Arabic. He was held in high esteem by his contemporaries. James I of Aragon was among his penitents, and St. *Thomas Aquinas wrote his *Summa contra Gentiles* at his suggestion. He was canonized by *Clement VIII in 1601. Feast day, 23 Jan.

Collected ed. of his works under the auspices of the Facultad de Derecho, Universidad de Barcelona, by J. R. Serra (Barcelona, 1945 ff. [*Summa Iuris* only item publd. to date (1957)]). Raymond's revision of the Dominican Constitutions ed. H. Denifle, O.P., in id.–F. Ehrle, S.J. (edd.), *Archiv für Literatur und Kirchengeschichte des Mittelalters*, v (1889), pp. 530–64; also ed. R. Creytens, O.P., in *Archivum Fratrum Praedicatorum*, xviii (1948), pp. 5–68, both edd. with introd. Life and canonization from the Bull of Clement VIII, pr. in *A.A.SS.*, Jan. I (1643), pp. 407–19, with account of his miracles by Michael Llot, also taken from the process of canonization, ib., pp. 419–27, with other material, pp. 404–7 and 427–9. F. Balme, O.P.– C. Paban, O.P.–J. Collomb, O.P. (edd.), *Raymundiana; seu Documenta quae pertinent ad S. Raymundi de Penna-*

forti Vitam et Scripta (Monumenta Ordinis Fratrum Praedicatorum Historica 'iv' [vi], fascc. 1 and 2; 1898–1901); further docc. ed. F. Vallis Taberner, 'El diplomatari de Sant Ramón de Penyfort' in *Analecta Sacra Tarraconensia*, v (1929), pp. 249–304. Modern life by id. (Collección pro Ecclesia et Patria, Barcelona, 1936); brief sketch in English by T. M. Schwertner (Milwaukee [1935]). A. Danzas, *Études sur les temps primitifs de l'ordre de St. Dominique*, Ser. 2, i, Saint Raymond de Pennafort et son époque (1885). [D. A.] Mortier, O.P., *Histoire des maîtres généraux de l'ordre des Frères Prêcheurs*, i (1903), pp. 255–85. The numerous controversial works on his relations with the Mercedarians include E. V. Galindo, O.P., *San Raimundo de Peñafort, fundador de la orden de la Merced* (Rome, 1919; maintaining that Mercedarians were founded in 1222 by Raymond, then a Dominican) and the reply by F. Gazulla, Mercedarian (Barcelona, 1920; maintaining that the Order was founded in 1218, before he became a Dominican). Quétif–Échard, i, 106–10. A. Teetaert, O.F.M.Cap., in *D.T.C.*, xiii (pt. 2; 1937), cols. 1806–23, s.v. 'Raymond de Penyafort', with bibl., incl. list of important artt. by the same author.

RAYMOND OF SEBONDE (d. 1432–6), Spanish philosopher. A native of Barcelona, he became professor at the university of Toulouse where he taught theology, philosophy, and medicine. His book, 'Liber Naturae sive Creaturarum', in later printed editions *Theologia Naturalis*, written originally in Spanish, was first published in 1484, and achieved great fame in the 16th cent. through M. de *Montaigne who translated and defended it (1569). Its Prologue gave offence because it over-emphasized the authority of the 'Book or Law of Nature' at the expense of Scripture and tradition, maintaining that it is possible for human reason to discover the contents of the Christian Revelation in nature alone; and it was put on the *Index in 1595. The book itself, however, was highly esteemed, not only by his contemporaries but also by later authorities such as Cardinal Bona and St. Peter *Canisius, for its able defence of the truth and reasonableness of Catholic doctrine on grounds appealing to those who do not accept revelation.

Raymond's *Theologia Naturalis* was often repr. in the 15th–17th cents. Best ed. (but without the preface) by J. Sighart, Sulzbach, 1852. J. H. Probst, *Le Lullisme de Raymond de Sebonde (Ramon de Sibiude)* (Toulouse, 1912); C. de Boer, *Montaigne als 'Apologeet' van Raymond Sebond* (Mededeelingen der Nederlandsche Akademie van Wetenschappen. Afd. Letterkunde, N.R. dl., iii, No. 12, Amsterdam, 1940). C. C. J. *Webb, *Studies in the History of Natural Theology* (1915), pp. 292–312. K. Schaarschmidt in *P.R.E.* (ed. 3), xvi (1905), pp. 415–21, s.v. 'Raimundus Sabieude'.

READER, Lay. See *Lay Reader*.

READERS. See *Lectors*.

REAL PRESENCE, The. In (esp. *Anglican) Eucharistic theology an expression used to cover several doctrines emphasizing the actual Presence of the Body and Blood of Christ in the Sacrament, as contrasted with others that maintain that the Body and Blood are present only figuratively or symbolically. An early instance of its use is in H. *Latimer, who, as reported in J. *Foxe's 'Book of Martyrs' (1563), held that 'this same presence may be called most fitly a real presence, that is, a presence not feigned, but a true and faithful presence'.

REALISM. (1) Any form of belief which is chary of speculation and rooted in sober fact. In this sense, Christianity claims to be realistic as based not on abstract theorizing or symbolic myths, but on historical events known to have happened at a certain time and concerned with the concrete facts of human experience. Thus L. *Laberthonnière contrasted 'Christian Realism' with 'Greek Idealism'.

(2) The philosophical doctrine of the reality of the external world as against the idealistic view that it is constituted by consciousness. In reaction from the classical formulation of Idealism by I. *Kant and his successors (J. G. *Fichte, F. W. J. *Schelling, G. W. F. *Hegel), which exercised such a deep influence on speculative theology throughout the 19th cent., in the present cent. there has set in a strong reaction towards Realism. In philosophy the turning-point was G. E. Moore's 'Refutation of Idealism' in Mind, new ser. xii (1903), pp. 433–53.

(3) In a more technical sense the doctrine that abstract concepts ('universals') have a real existence apart from the individuals ('particulars') in which they are embodied. The doctrine was developed in the Middle Ages on the basis of *Plato's metaphysic, largely out of a constantly discussed passage in *Porphyry's 'Isagoge' on the existence of genera and species. It was professed by *Erigena and *Remigius of Auxerre and, in a modified form, by St. *Anselm in opposition to the *Nominalism (q.v.) of *Roscellinus. It was carried further by *William of Champeaux in the 12th cent., who recognized in the several individuals of the same species an identical reality (eandem rem), modified by *Abelard and, under the influence of *Aristotle, reconstructed by St. *Thomas Aquinas who, rejecting the view that universals exist apart from the individuals (universalia ante res), upheld a 'moderate realism' (universalia in rebus).

RECAPITULATION (Lat. recapitulatio; Gk. ἀνακεφαλαίωσις, a 'summing up', 'summary'). The term is used in its verbal form in Eph. i. 10, where God is said to sum up all things in Christ, and from this passage was taken over by the Fathers. The conception of recapitulation was elaborated esp. by St. *Irenaeus, who interpreted it as both the restoration of fallen humanity to communion with God through the obedience of Christ and as the summing-up of the previous revelations of God in past ages in the Incarnation. Besides these two meanings, which are common in patristic literature, there is a third found in St. *Chrysostom, who applies the word to the reunion of both angels and men under Christ as their common head.

RECARED (d. 601), King of the Visigoths. Having been associated with his father, the *Arian Leovigild, in the government of the country (mainly Spain) from 573, he succeeded him on the throne in 586. In the next year, probably owing to the influence of St. *Leander,

Bp. of Seville, he and his family became Catholics. The step, though followed by several quickly suppressed insurrections on the part of the Arian bishops, helped considerably to pacify the country, in which the Catholic clergy and nobles were more powerful than the Arian Visigoths. The king's action was ratified by the Third Council of Toledo in 589 which regulated the religious situation in a number of canons. The remaining years of the king seem to have been peaceful; he is praised by St. *Isidore of Seville for founding many churches and monasteries.

The main sources for his life are St. Isidore's Historia Gothorum and the Chronicle of John of Biclara, both ed. T. *Mommsen in M.G.H., Chronica Minora, ii (1894), pp. 217–20 and 288–90. Life by M. Hernández Villaescusa (Barcelona, 1890). F. Görres, 'Rekared der Katholiker' in Zeitschrift für wissenschaftliche Theologie, xlii (1899), pp. 270–322. See also Historia de España, iii, 'España visigoda', ed. R. Menéndez Pidal, 1935.

RECEPTIONISM. A form of Eucharistic teaching acc. to which, while the bread and wine continue to exist unchanged after consecration, the faithful communicant receives together with them the true Body and Blood of Christ. Such a doctrine was common among Anglican divines in the 17th cent. Those who lean to such teaching have generally shrunk from giving it precise definition. The word itself is apparently not found before 1867.

RECHABITES. A religious order or clan in Israel, founded by Jehonadab, the son of Rechab, who persuaded Jehu to abolish Tyrian Baal worship (2 Kings 10). The order represented a protest against Canaanite luxury and ways of living and a return to the simplicity and even asceticism of the more nomad life. Like the *Nazarites, they made it a rule to abstain from wine, and they were also opposed to agriculture and the cultivation of vineyards. The title has been adopted in modern times by a society of total abstainers.

RECLUSE. A person who lives apart from the world, esp. for the purpose of religious meditation. In a stricter use, the word is applied to those who have made definite vows to live in this way.

RECOGNITIONS, Clementine. See Clementine Literature.

RECOLLECTION. A term used by spiritual writers to denote the concentration of the soul on the presence of God. It involves the renunciation of all avoidable dissipations and its use is habitually recommended to those who wish to lead an interior life. In a more restricted sense the word is applied to a certain stage of prayer, in which the memory, understanding, and will are held to be stilled by Divine action and the soul left in a state of peace in which grace can work without hindrance.

RECOLLECTS. The title of two separate religious orders:

(1) *The Franciscan Recollects.* A reformed branch of the *Franciscan Observants, started in France at the end of the 16th cent., which spread to Belgium, Germany, Ireland, and the exiled English Friars on the Continent in the course of the 17th cent. In 1897 they were incorporated with the other Observants by *Leo XIII.

(2) *The Augustinian Recollects.* A reformed branch of the *Augustinian Hermits, started in Spain. Their first house was founded at Talavera in 1589, and other monasteries were soon established in many parts of the country. They were erected into a separate province by brief of *Clement VIII in 1602, and in 1621 formed a separate congregation. The congregation became successful as missionaries, esp. in Peru and the Philippines. In 1912 they were constituted into an independent order ('Ordo Eremitarum Recollectorum S. Augustini') with a prior-general at its head.

(1) M. Bihl, O.F.M., in *L.Th.K.*, viii (1936), col. 754, s.v. 'Rekollecten'. See also works cited under *Franciscan Order*.
(2) Andrés de San-Nicolas, *Historia general de los religios descalzos del orden de los Hermitanos del . . . Padre . . . San Agustin* (Madrid, 1644; continued by other members of the Order, making 7 vols. to 1927, publd. Madrid–Barcelona). M. T. Disdier, A.A., in *D.H.G.E.*, v (1931), cols. 851–95, s.v.'Augustin (Ier Ordre de) (Ermites récollets)', with detailed bibl.; G. Fernández, O.R.S.A., in *E.C.*, x (1953), col. 610 f., s.v. 'Recolletti di S. Agostino'. See also works cited under *Augustinian Hermits*.

RECORD, The. The first Anglican weekly newspaper, begun on 1 Jan. 1828. It was from the first strongly *Evangelical, among those concerned in its foundation being J. H. *Newman (then an Evangelical). On 1 Jan. 1949 it was amalgamated with the *Church of England Newspaper* (founded as the *Church Family Newspaper*, 1894).

RECTOR. In the C of E a rector, as distinguished from a *vicar, is a parish incumbent whose *tithes are not impropriate. A '*lay rector' is a layman receiving rectorial tithes or in whom the rectory is vested. In the Scottish universities the 'Rectors' or 'Lord Rectors' are elected officers; in English universities the title is used of the heads of Exeter and Lincoln Colleges, Oxford. On the Continent the title is customary for the heads of universities or for the presidents of their administrative bodies. The heads of *Jesuit houses are also commonly styled rectors.

RECUSANCY. The term, which was earlier employed in a wider sense, came to be used about 1570 of those Romanists who refused to attend the services of the established Church in England. Until the Pope expressly anathematized *Elizabeth I in the bull '*Regnans in excelsis' (1570), recusancy had been rare, since conservative and reactionary elements in the nation had received no clear guidance regarding their attitude towards the Establishment. Recusancy received a powerful impetus from the *Seminarist and *Jesuit invasions, esp. during the years around 1580. By Elizabethan and Jacobean statesmen it was considered a dangerous problem, since, unlike *Puritanism, it had tenacious roots throughout the social structure of certain regions of England, notably in the N. where it was for long thought likely to express itself in the form of armed rebellion. Lancashire and Durham, followed by certain regions of Yorkshire and Wales, took the lead in recusancy during the 16th and 17th cents. Derbyshire, Warwickshire, Staffordshire, Monmouthshire, Herefordshire, and even Hampshire also showed strong recusant parties. That everywhere, except in Lancashire, actual recusants remained a small percentage of the total population, was partly due to a succession of harsh, though irregularly enforced, penal laws. Of these latter, that of 1581, imposing a fine of £20 per month for recusancy, was the most important. Such an enormous exaction was, of course, mainly intended *in terrorem*, since it could only apply to the richest recusants. The number of persons practising recusancy did not increase with the relaxation of the penal laws in the late 17th cent., and registrations of 1715–20 show a proportion of about 5 per cent.

RED HAT. The flat-crowned broad-brimmed hat, with two clusters of 15 tassels, distinctive of a *cardinal. The Pope invests the cardinal with it at the first public *consistory after his appointment, and it is not worn again. After the cardinal's death, it is suspended over his tomb. The expression 'red hat' is often used for the cardinal's office.

RED LETTER DAY. An important feast or saint's day, printed in ecclesiastical calendars in red ink. In the C of E the term is applied to those feasts for which the BCP provides a proper Collect, Epistle, and Gospel, as formerly these feasts were distinguished in the calendar in this way.

RED MASS. Acc. to W. usage, a *votive Mass of the Holy Ghost, so named from the red vestments in which it is celebrated. Such Masses are customarily celebrated with some solemnity at the opening of councils, synods, &c., to invoke the aid and illumination of the Holy Ghost in the deliberations to follow. In England a Red Mass is celebrated at *Westminster Cathedral at the opening of the law term and attended by RC judges.

RED SEA, The. In the Bible, refs. to the 'Red Sea' are exclusively to the part now known as the 'Gulf of Suez'. The crossing of the Red Sea, described with its attendant miracles in Ex. 14 and 15, marked the end of the bondage of the Israelites in Egypt and has ever since been regarded by the Jews as a turning point in their destinies (e.g. Pss. 66. 6; 78. 53; 114. 3). In the NT (1 Cor. 10. 2) it is regarded as a type of Christian Baptism. See also *Exodus*.

On the site of the Crossing (whether at Suez, as traditionally held, or to the N. of the Bitter Lakes, whither the Red Sea perh. extended in earlier times), cf. C. Bourdon, 'La Route de l'Exode, de la Terre de Gessé à Mara' in *R. Bibl.*, xli (1932), pp. 370–92 and 538–49. T. H. Robinson, 'Der Durchzug durch das Rote Meer' in *Z.A.T.W.*, li (1933), pp. 170–3. D. Baldi, O.F.M., in *E.C.*, x (1953), cols. 1389–91, s.v. 'Rosso, Mare'.

REDEMPTION. The idea of redemption is common to many religions, being based on the desire of man to be delivered from sin, suffering, and death. Christianity claims that in it alone has it become a fact through the Incarnation and the Death of Christ. It is viewed by theologians under the double aspect of deliverance from sin and restoration of man and the world to communion with God. Both these aspects are developed in the NT, esp. in the Pauline Epistles, where the 'redemption (ἀπολύτρωσις) through His blood, the forgiveness of our trespasses' (Eph. 1. 7), and 'the dispensation of the fullness of the times, to sum up (ἀνακεφαλαιώσασθαι) all things in Christ' (Eph. 1. 10) are set forth as the interrelated effects of the work of the Redeemer. In patristic thought both sides were somewhat differently emphasized, the Greeks stressing more the restoration of man to the Divine life, whereas the Latin Fathers gave primary importance to the expiation of our sins through the sacrificial death of Christ. In St. *Augustine, and later in *Scholastic theology, Redemption was brought into more direct connexion with *Original Sin which it was held to remove by restoring man to his state of *Original Righteousness, lost by the *Fall of *Adam. From St. *Anselm's *Cur Deus Homo* onwards, the question of the necessity of the Redemption was widely discussed. Anselm held that, given the Divine plan and its violation by the infinite malice of sin, the justice of God which required adequate satisfaction made redemption by the death of the God-man a necessity. This view was abandoned by the Schoolmen, notably St. *Thomas Aquinas, who taught that, though God might have redeemed the world in many other ways, the manner in which He did so was highly 'congruous', because it showed forth His omnipotence, goodness, and wisdom, and the admirable harmony in His Being between Justice and Mercy. Consequently Redemption is the free gift of God to man who could not have redeemed himself, because of the supernatural character of the gifts lost by Original Sin. He maintained that, though it was impossible that sin should be abolished as a physical reality, it could be repaired morally by the objective merits of the Redeemer which, applied to the repentant sinner, enabled him to co-operate with grace towards justification and sanctification.

The theologians of the Reformation claimed to return to the teaching of St. Paul. They denied the idea of Redemption as a restoration to Original Righteousness and, consequently, the possibility of human co-operation with grace other than by faith alone, and placed the exclusive emphasis in the forgiveness of sin and justification by imputation of the righteousness of Christ. Through the teaching of J. *Calvin and later, of C. *Jansenius, the view that Redemption extends only to the predestined was advocated by a number of Protestant and Catholic theologians in the 16th and 17th cents. It was pronounced heretical by *Innocent X in the constitution '*Cum Occasione' (1653). Later, the proposition that Christ died for all the faithful, but for the faithful alone (*pro omnibus et solis fidelibus*), was also condemned by *Alexander VIII (1690). The universality of Redemption, taught already in the NT (e.g. 1 Jn. 2. 2), was thus safeguarded, without, on the other hand, prejudicing the fact that its actual application does not extend to the damned nor, as *Origen believed, to the fallen angels. See also *Atonement*.

REDEMPTORISTS. The common name for the members of the 'Congregation of the Most Holy Redeemer', founded by St. *Alphonsus Maria di Liguori at Scala, Italy, in 1732. The Congregation was instituted for mission work among the poor both in Europe and among the heathen, and it has steadily refused to engage in purely educational activities. The order received the sanction of *Benedict XIV in 1749, and a community of Redemptorist nuns received similar approval in 1750. Despite frequent persecution at the hands of secular governments, it has continued to flourish to the present time. It was introduced into England in 1843. The Congregation is governed by a 'Rector Major', who holds office for life and resides in Rome.

G. Stebbing, C.SS.R., *The Redemptorists* (1924); E. Hosp, C.SS.R., *Die Kongregation des allerheiligsten Erlösers*. Ihr Werden und Wollen (1924); G. Brandhuber, C.SS.R., *Die Redemptoristen, 1732–1932* (1932). M. de Meulemeester, C.SS.R., *Histoire sommaire de la congrégation du T.S. Redempteur* (1950; Eng. tr., Louvain, 1956). J. B. Byrne, C.SS.R., *The Redemptorist Centenaries.* 1732, Founding of the Congregation of the Most Holy Redeemer—1832, Establishment in United States (1932). M. de Meulemeester, C.SS.R.–E. Colet, C.SS.R.–C. Henze, C.SS.R., *Bibliographie générale des écrivains rédemptoristes* (3 vols., 1933–9). Heimbucher, ii (ed. 3; 1934), pp. 345–64 and 667, with bibl. M. de Meulemeester, in *E.C.*, iv (1950), cols. 294–6, s.v. 'Congregazione del S.mo Redemptore', with bibl.

REFORMATIO LEGUM ECCLESIASTICARUM (Lat., 'the Reform of the Ecclesiastical Laws'). The book which was designed to provide a system of order and discipline for the C of E in place of the medieval *canon law. By an Act of 1549 (3 & 4 Edw. VI, c. 11) the King had been empowered to appoint 32 persons to compile a *corpus* of ecclesiastical laws for use in the English spiritual courts. The work was actually taken in hand in 1551 by a body of eight persons, and the Book produced was presented to Parliament in Mar. 1553. Through the King's death in the summer, however, it ceased to be possible to proceed with it, and the Book was first printed by J. *Foxe in 1571. In his preface Foxe confidently affirmed that it would have been sanctioned but for Edward VI's death; but this is highly contestable. Its standpoint was virtually *Calvinist. The Book is of importance for its connexions both in content and language with the *Thirty-Nine Articles.

Modern edition by E. *Cardwell (Oxford, 1850).

REFORMATION, The. This somewhat loose term covers an involved series of changes in W. Christendom between the 14th and 17th cents. They may be said to have begun with the attacks of the *Lollards and their Czech associates, the *Hussites, upon the hierarchical and legalist structure of the Church as a whole. From first to last, however, the Papacy, as most clearly responsible for that structure, attracted strongest criticism. The English statutes of *Provisors and *Praemunire, like the French *Pragmatic Sanction of Bourges (1438), represent the effort of the rising monarchies to curtail Papal influence over their national Churches. Though after the dark periods of the 'Babylonish Captivity' at *Avignon and the Great Schism the Popes had recovered sufficient authority to ride out the storms of the Conciliar Movement, the final collapse of the Council of *Basle in 1449 left European opinion still dissatisfied with many aspects of the Papal monarchy of the Church. If down to the late 15th and early 16th cents. anti-clericalism and divergence from Catholic doctrine remained rare and spasmodic phenomena, discontent continued to simmer against the worldliness and increasing financial exactions that characterized the Papacy as an Italian power.

Consequently, when M. *Luther protested against the corruption of Rome and the great abuses attending the sale of *indulgences, he was breaking no new controversial ground. Most, indeed, of the Reformation movements, like those of the Renaissance, laid stress, not upon innovation, but upon return to a primitive excellence. In due course Luther's study of St. *Augustine led him to question the emphasis of late medieval theology upon 'good works', while his historical studies, based on those of L. *Valla, had raised doubts regarding the validity of Papal claims to supremacy. From these traditionalist origins were derived his attacks upon *Transubstantiation and clerical celibacy as well as his demands for the abolition of Papal power in Germany and for the radical reform of the religious orders. They found pregnant expression in Luther's celebrated treatises of 1520. Four years later, his advocacy of princely authoritarianism during the *Peasants' Revolt helped to ensure the support of his cause by the German princes. The rulers of Saxony, Hesse, Brandenburg, and Brunswick, besides the kings of *Denmark and *Sweden, were won to the reformed beliefs before or shortly after their classical enunciation in the 'Confession of *Augsburg' (1530). These rulers proceeded to regulate the Churches within their territories acc. to Lutheran precept, and henceforth the progress of the Lutheran Reformation lay in the hands of the 'godly prince' to whom the plenitude of power was explicitly confided.

Meanwhile in 1523-4 the Swiss divine H. *Zwingli, motivated at first by studies and beliefs analogous to those of Luther, had captured the support of the civic authorities of Zürich and carried through anti-papal, anti-hierarchic, and anti-monastic reforms in that city. The Zwinglian Movement, far more radical and less scholastic than Lutheranism in its eucharistic and social doctrines, rapidly overran many of the Swiss cantons and most of SW. Germany. It was only the death of Zwingli in warfare against the Catholic cantons in 1531 that ultimately transferred the leadership of the Swiss Reformation from Zürich to Geneva.

Here, in 1539, J. *Calvin finally established an elaborately organized theocracy. In his hands, reforming opinion assumed a more explicitly doctrinal and revolutionary tone. Emphasis upon predestination, it is true, may be traced in the thought of J. *Wycliffe, while Luther himself denied to man freedom or responsibility, as traditionally understood. Yet a massive, coherent, theological system based upon the doctrines of particular election and redemption first appeared in Calvin's *Institutio Christianae Religionis* (1536). This system, with its peculiar appeal to many rising elements in European society, henceforth proved for several generations the driving force of the Reformation, esp. in W. Germany, France, the Netherlands, and Scotland. Like that of Lutheranism, but upon a wider stage, the progress of the Calvinist Reformation became inextricably involved with a series of political struggles, notably the Wars of Religion in France, which ultimately adjusted the position of the *Huguenots, the national revolt which freed the northern Netherlands from Spain, and the *Thirty Years War, which ensured the apotheosis of princely control and incidentally the preservation of N. German Lutheranism under the aegis of Sweden. In Scotland, too, the Calvinist cause, led by J. *Knox and the Lords of the Congregation, triumphed upon a wave of nationalist reaction against French control, parallel to that contemporary English reaction against Spain which contributed so powerfully to the success of the Elizabethan settlement.

Meanwhile, however, the English Reformation had remained an insular process responsive to peculiar political and social forces. *Henry VIII, a convinced traditionalist in both doctrine and Church government, accomplished the overthrow of Papal Supremacy and the *Dissolution of the Monasteries largely in pursuance of a long-standing monarchical policy of extending the sovereignty of the central government into all spheres of the national society. Despite, however, his repression of reforming Continental doctrines, he found himself unable to check the undermining of scholastic theology by humanist Biblical studies. Under *Somerset and T. *Cranmer, the first English Prayer Book of 1549 sketched out that *via media* in religion which was recaptured in 1558-9 by the Elizabethan government after a period of antithetical extremes under Northumberland and *Mary.

Upon this *Erastian basis, which from the first stood firm against the impact of extremist Calvinism upon English religious life, the national Church developed in course of time spiritual and cultural traditions more brilliant than those of the analogous Erastian Churches of Germany. The Calvinist Reformation in England, as a movement extraneous to the national Church, finally allied itself with political forces to form the Puritan Revolution (1640–60). Its force, diminished by sectarian subdivision and by political reaction, proved in the long run insufficient to sweep away the established Church, which enjoyed the support of the monarchy and was now grounded in public opinion. In England, as on the Continent, where the reforming movements were increasingly checked and balanced by the *Counter-Reformation, a considerable degree of stabilization had been attained by the last years of the 17th cent.

Useful primary material collected and translated into English in B. J. *Kidd (ed.), *Documents Illustrative of the Continental Reformation* (1911). For the history of the Reformation in England much basic material is preserved in the works of J. *Foxe and J. *Strype (qq.v.). J. H. *Merle d'Aubigné, *Histoire de la réforme du seizième siècle* (5 vols., 1835–53; complete Eng. tr., 5 vols., 1846–53; popular). L. von *Ranke, *Deutsche Geschichte im Zeitalter der Reformation* (6 vols., 1839–47; Eng. tr. of vols. i–iii, 1845–7). C. Ullmann, *Reformatoren vor der Reformation vornehmlich in Deutschland und den Niederlanden* (2 vols., 1841–2; Eng. tr., 2 vols., 1855). C. Hardwick, *A History of the Christian Church during the Reformation* (1856; ed. 3 by W. *Stubbs, 1872). L. Häusser, *Geschichte des Zeitalters der Reformation, 1517–1648* (ed. W. Oncken, 1868; Eng. tr., 2 vols., 1873). C. *Beard, *The Reformation of the Sixteenth Century in Relation to Modern Thought and Knowledge* (Hibbert Lectures, 1883; 1883). J. Janssen, *Geschichte des deutschen Volkes seit dem Ausgang des Mittelalters* (8 vols., 1878–94; Eng. tr., 16 vols., 1896–1910, + index, 1925). H. B. Workman, *The Dawn of the Reformation* (2 vols., 1901–2). P. Imbart de La Tour, *Les Origines de la réforme* (4 vols., 1905–35; new ed. of vol. ii, with revised bibl., by Yvonne Lanhers, 1946). T. M. *Lindsay, *A History of the Reformation* (2 vols., 1906–7). J. P. Whitney, *The Reformation*. Being an Outline of the History of the Church from A.D. 1503 to A.D. 1648 (1907; new ed. entitled 'The History of the Reformation', C.H.S., 1940). H. *Wace, *Principles of the Reformation, Practical and Historical* (1910). H. Hermelinck, *Reformation und Gegenreformation* (Handbuch der Kirchengeschichte für Studierende, iii; 1911). A. Plummer, *The Continental Reformation in Germany, France and Switzerland, from the Birth of Luther to the Death of Calvin* (1912). Preserved Smith, *The Age of the Reformation* [1921]. E. Eyre (ed.), *European Civilization*. Its Origin and Development, iv. The Reformation (1936). N. Sykes, *The Crisis of the Reformation* (1938). J. Mackinnon, *The Origins of the Reformation* (1939). Also extensive bibl. to date in *C.M.H.*, ii, 'The Reformation' (1903). H. M. Gwatkin in *H.E.R.E.*, x (1918), pp. 609–22, s.v. R. H. Bainton, *The Reformation of the Sixteenth Century* (Kansas, 1952; London, 1953). For further bibl. on the Continental Reformation see works cited in Schottenloher. See also bibl. to *Calvinism* and *Lutheranism*.

REFORMED CHURCHES. The term is sometimes taken to include all the Protestant Churches which have accepted the principles of the *Reformation, but in a narrower and more accurate sense it is used specifically of the *Calvinist bodies, as contrasted esp. with the *Lutherans. This restriction is almost universal with the corresponding French (*Églises réformées*) and the German (*reformierte Kirchen*) expressions. The designation of the Calvinistic Churches as 'ecclesiae reformatae' was already general before the end of the 16th cent.

REFORMED PRESBYTERIAN CHURCH, The. The small body of Scottish Presbyterians, popularly known as *Cameronians, who declined to accept the settlement of 1690 which established the Church of Scotland. They have continued to exist as a separate body until the present day. J. G. *Paton, the missionary to the New Hebrides, was a member of this Church.

REFRESHMENT SUNDAY. A name for the Fourth Sunday in Lent, also known as *Laetare Sunday. The epithet has been explained as referring either to the miracle of the feeding of the five thousand which is the Gospel for the Day (Jn. 6. 1–14) or to the relaxation of Lenten discipline allowed on this day (e.g. the consumption of simnel-cakes).

REFUGE, Cities of. See *Cities of Refuge.*

REGALE (Lat. *regale*, neut. of *regalis*, 'pertaining to the king'). In legal language esp., the right to the revenues of vacant bishoprics and abbeys and to presentation to their dependent benefices claimed by the kings of Europe during the Middle Ages. It was usually held to derive from their position as feudal lords, and taken as analogous to that enjoyed during the minority of a lay-tenant. The claim, consistently denied by the Popes, became closely connected with the *Investiture Controversy. The earliest known trace of it is met with in *France towards the end of the Carolingian period (10th cent.). In England it was successfully asserted by King William II (1087–1100) on the death of *Lanfranc (1089), and later became one of the causes of rejection of the Constitutions of *Clarendon by *Alexander III. In 1176 King Henry II (1154–89) promised to limit the exercise of the right to one year, but it continued, with few exemptions, until the *Reformation. It is still enjoyed by the Crown over the *temporalities of vacant sees (though the revenues are now restored untouched when the newly elected Bishop does homage). In Germany the right was claimed and exercised by Henry V (1106–1125) and his immediate successors, but practically ceased after the death of *Frederick II (1250). In France, where it was claimed not only by the king but also by certain of the more important territorial lords, it was a continual source of friction between the Papacy and the temporal power from the time of St. *Bernard to the end 19th cent.

The term Regale has also, since the 18th cent., been more properly used of the privileges and prerogatives of the Sovereign in general.

REGENERATION. The spiritual rebirth (Gk. παλιγγενεσία), which, acc. to traditional theology, is effected in the soul by Christian Baptism (cf. Tit. 3. 5). See *Baptism.*

REGENSBURG, Conference of. See *Ratisbon, Conference of.*

REGIMINI MILITANTIS ECCLESIAE.
The bull issued by *Paul III on 27 September 1540, instituting the *Jesuit Order. After listing the members of the proposed Society and acknowledging their work at Rome, at their request it established their organization and rule, under the name of the Society of Jesus, for the care of souls in life and doctrine, for the preaching of the faith and for ministry of the word, esp. through education and the confessional. They were to have one Superior, who would consult the whole Society on matters of importance, were to obey the Pope implicitly wherever he might send them, swear obedience to the rule and the Superior, and have no permanent property, except colleges, schools and other things necessary for education. Their numbers were limited to sixty. The Society was permitted to draw up constitutions conformable to the purpose of the Society, and was taken under special papal protection. The terms of the bull implied that much of the work of the Society would be directed towards the conversion of pagans and heretics.

The full text is pr. in Mirbt, pp. 272–6 (No. 430), with reff. See also works cited under *Jesuits.*

REGINA COELI (Lat., 'Queen of Heaven'). The Eastertide anthem to the Blessed Virgin, so named from its opening words. In the Roman Breviary, its recitation after the daily *offices is prescribed from *Compline of *Holy Saturday until the Saturday after *Whitsunday. It also takes the place of the *Angelus in Eastertide. Its authorship is unknown, but it probably dates from the 12th cent.

H. Thurston, S.J., 'The *Regina Caeli*' in *The Month*, cxxi (1913), pp. 384–8, repr. in his *Familiar Prayers*, ed. P. Grosjean, S.J. (1953), pp. 146–51, with reff.

REGINALD OF PIPERNO (*c.* 1230–*c.* 1290), *Dominican friar. Having been chosen by St. *Thomas Aquinas as his confessor at Rome in 1259, he became his inseparable companion. He collected all the saint's writings and took down several of his lectures, among them the Commentary on St. John and part of that on the Pauline Epistles. He also compiled the Supplement to the Third Part of the 'Summa' after St. Thomas's death.

Quétif–Échard, i, 382. M. *Grabmann, *Die Werke des hl. Thomas von Aquin* (ed. 3, B.G.P.M., xxii, Hftt. 1/2; 1949), esp. pp. 298–301. Id. in *L.Th.K.*, viii (1936), col. 722 f.

REGIONARIUS. A name in use at Rome in the earlier Middle Ages for members of the clergy who filled offices dependent on the arrangement of the city into seven ecclesiastical 'regions' (*regiones*), and who were thus distinguished both from the 'Papal' and the 'titular' clergy. See *Title.*

REGISTERS, Episcopal. Many English Episcopal Registers have been printed in the publications of the *Canterbury and York Society (q.v.) and elsewhere. See the bibliographies to the separate dioceses and to individual bishops.

REGIUM DONUM (Lat., 'Royal Gift'). The grant from public funds formerly made to the ministers of certain English *Nonconforming bodies. It originated out of sums which *Charles II ordered to be paid to *Presbyterian ministers after the *Declaration of Indulgence of 1672; but the practice did not become established in England till 1723, in which year a fresh precedent was created by a sum of £500 granted to E. *Calamy by George I. By 1727 all the '*Three Denominations' (*Presbyterians, *Baptists, *Congregationalists) were enjoying it, and it continued until 1851. In *Ireland a *regium donum* to Presbyterian ministers was paid almost continuously from 1690 until the disestablishment of the Irish Church in 1869.

R. W. *Dale, *History of English Congregationalism* (ed. by A. W. W. Dale, 1907), pp. 524–7.

REGIUM PLACET. See *Exequatur.*

REGNANS IN EXCELSIS. The *bull of excommunication published by *Pius V on 25 Feb. 1570, against Queen *Elizabeth I. It was issued after a formal trial of the Queen at Rome, whither a number of English exiles had been summoned to testify to her heretical proceedings. The bull declares Elizabeth a usurper as well as a heretic, absolves her subjects of their allegiance, and orders them to disobey her laws. It thus placed the unfortunate English RCs between conflicting loyalties and evoked as a counterblast the Elizabethan penal laws.

Text in *Bullarum, Diplomatum et Privilegiorum Sanctorum Romanorum Pontificum Taurinensis Editio*, vii (Naples, 1882), p. 810 f.; operative clauses repr. in C. Mirbt, *Quellen zur Geschichte des Papsttums und des römischen Katholizismus* (ed. 4, 1924), No. 491, p. 348 f., with reff. See also bibl. s.v. *Elizabeth I.*

REGULAR (from Lat. *regula*, 'rule'). General term for those members of the clergy who are bound by the vows of religion and live in community, following a rule. They are to be distinguished from the seculars, i.e. priests living in the world. In a narrower sense the expression is restricted to religious who have taken solemn *vows.

REGULAR CANONS. See *Canons Regular.*

REGULAR CLERKS. See *Clerks Regular.*

REGULARIS CONCORDIA. The code of monastic observance in England, drawn up and approved by the Synod of *Winchester (*c.* 970) under the direction of St. *Dunstan, Abp. of *Canterbury and St. *Ethelwold, Bp. of Winchester. Its provisions follow the *Benedictine tradition of *Benedict of Aniane, modified by the *Cluniac reforms and greatly influenced by the customaries of *Fleury, Ghent, and elsewhere. Details are given of the liturgical functions of the day and year and the duties attached to various monastic offices. The important position accorded to the sovereigns as patrons of the monastic life, e.g. the intercession for the King and Queen after all parts of the Office, except *Prime, is peculiar to England. Other English traditions were the allowance of a fire in winter and processions through the streets; notable also is the encouragement given to daily Communion.

Text repr. in J. P. Migne, *PL*, cxxxvii, 475–502. Crit. edd. by W. S. Logeman 'De Consuetudine Monachorum', in *Anglia*, Neue Folge I (1891), pp. 365–448 (glossary, pp. 448–54), and by T. Symons, O.S.B. ('Medieval Classics', 1953).

REICHENAU (Lat. *Augia dives*). A small island in the western arm of Lake Constance famous in the earlier Middle Ages for its Benedictine monastery, founded by St. *Pirminius in 724. It was an important centre of culture when the neighbouring *St. Gall was still insignificant; and in the 9th cent. numbered among its members *Walafrid Strabo and Hatto, Abp. of Mainz. Its collection of MSS. (many of which have been at Karlsruhe since 1805) was already well established by the early part of the 9th cent. The churches still survive and contain interesting remains.

Quellen und Forschungen zur Geschichte der Abtei Reichenau herausg. von der Badischen historischen Kommission (2 vols., Heidelberg, 1890–3). J. Dieterich, *Die Geschichtsquellen des Klosters Reichenau bis zur Mitte des elften Jahrhunderts* (1897). K. Beyerle (ed.), *Die Kultur der Abtei Reichenau. Erinnerungsschrift zur zwölfhundertsten Wiederkehr des Gründungsjahres des Inselklosters, 724–1924* (2 vols., 1925). A. Holder, *Die Reichenauer Handschriften* beschrieben und erlaeutert (Die Handschriften der Grossherzoglich Badischen Hof- und Landesbibliothek in Karlsruhe, v–vii; 1906–18). L. H. Cottineau, O.S.B., *Répertoire topo-bibliographique des abbayes et prieurés* (Mâcon, 1935), cols. 2427–30, s.v., with detailed bibl. H. *Leclercq, O.S.B., in *D.A.C.L.*, xiv (pt. 2; 1948), cols. 2197–2213, s.v., with reff.; E. Josi in *E.C.*, x (1953), cols. 665–8, s.v.

REICHSBISCHOF. The title adopted in May 1933 at the suggestion of a Committee of the German Evangelical Church Federation for the office of head of a united German Evangelical Church, incorporating all the provincial Churches. Its first holder was Friedrich von Bodelschwingh. When the state appointed a Commissar for Prussia, who dismissed many pastors, Bodelschwingh resigned and was succeeded by the *German Christian, Ludwig *Müller.

REIMARUS, HERMANN SAMUEL (1694–1768), *Deist and Biblical critic. A native of Hamburg, he joined the class of J. A. *Fabricius, whose son-in-law he was to become, and later studied theology, classical philology and philosophy at Jena. For a time he was Privatdozent at *Wittenberg and rector of the Hochschule at Wismar; and from 1727 until his death Prof. of Hebrew and Oriental languages at Hamburg. His light duties enabled him to pursue independent studies in

many fields, and between 1744 and 1767 he composed the treatise from which G. E. *Lessing published the notorious *Wolfenbüttel Fragments* (q.v.) in 1774–8. The complete work (which Reimarus kept back from publication during his lifetime) bore in the MS. the title *Apologie oder Schutzschrift für die vernünftigen Verehrer Gottes*. It unreservedly rejected miracles and revelation and sought to convict the Biblical writers of conscious fraud, innumerable contradictions, and fanaticism. The appearance of the fragments produced a sensation in Germany. Further portions were issued by C. A. E. Schmidt (a pseudonym) in 1787 and W. Klose in 1850–2, while D. F. *Strauss in his book on Reimarus (see Bibl.) gave an analysis of the complete work. Reimarus published himself two writings in defence of *Natural Religion on the principles of C. *Wolff, which became very popular, viz. *Abhandlungen von den vornehmsten Wahrheiten der natürlichen Religion* (1754) and *Betrachtungen über die Kunsttriebe der Thiere* (1762), as well as a good edition of Dio Cassius (2 vols., 1750–2).

D. F. Strauss, *Hermann Samuel Reimarus und seine Schutzschrift für die vernünftigen Verehrer Gottes* (1862). A. C. Lundsteen, *Hermann Samuel Reimarus und die Anfänge der Leben-Jesu-Forschung* (Copenhagen, 1939), with bibl. A. *Schweitzer, *Geschichte der Leben-Jesu-Forschung* (ed. 2, 1913), pp. 13–26. L. Zscharnack in *R.G.G.* (ed. 2), iv (1930), col. 1836 f., s.v.; J. Engert in *L.Th.K.*, viii (1936), col. 738 f., s.v.; both with bibl.

REIMS. Acc. to tradition, the episcopal see in the old capital of the *Remi* in Gaul was founded in the second half of the 3rd cent. by St. Sixtus, who was succeeded by St. Sinicius. The first bishop for whom there is historical evidence was Imbetausius (or Bethausius), who took part in the Council of *Arles in 314. The power of the see increased greatly under St. *Remigius (d. 535; q.v.) who baptized *Clovis in 496 and evangelized the surrounding districts, and under the famous *Hincmar (d. 882). From the middle of the 10th cent. the Archbishops were also counts of Reims whose right to crown the French kings was recognized by Pope *Sylvester II in 999 and confirmed as their exclusive privilege by *Alexander III in 1179. One of the most famous consecrations was that of Charles VII in the presence of St. *Joan of Arc in 1429. By the *Concordat of 1801 the Abpric. of Reims was abolished and its territories divided between the dioceses of Meaux and of Metz, but it was restored in 1821.

The cathedral, one of the finest examples of French Gothic, was begun in 1211 and completed in the 14th cent. In 1481 a fire destroyed the roof and spires, and during the First World War (1914–18) the famous western façade with its three portals richly decorated with statues suffered severely. Among the badly damaged parts are the beautiful rose window above the central portal, the statue of Christ (the 'beau Dieu'), and that of the smiling angel. The cathedral was restored after the war and reopened in 1927. It suffered further damage in the Second World

War. Its rich treasury contains many famous relics, e.g. the chalice of St. Remigius and the remains of the Sainte Ampoule (see *Ampulla*). The tomb of St. Remigius in the former Benedictine abbey of St. Remi is a popular place of pilgrimage.

Flodoard (canon of Reims; d. 966), *Historia Remensis Ecclesiae* (ed. G. Colvener, Douai, 1617; ed. and cont. by G. Marlot, O.S.B., 2 vols., Lille–Reims, 1666–79). G. Marlot, O.S.B. (d. 1667), *Histoire de la ville, cité et université de Reims* (ed. J. Lacourt, 4 vols., Reims, 1843–6). G. Boussinesq–G. Laurent, *Histoire de Reims depuis les origines jusqu'à nos jours* (2 vols. in 3 parts, 1933). *Gallia Christiana*, ix (Paris, ed. 1751), pp. 1–322. L. *Duchesne, Fastes épiscopaux de l'ancienne Gaule*, iii (1915), pp. 76–88. The many architectural studies of the Cathedral include those of C. Cerf (2 vols., Reims, 1861), A. Gosset (Paris, 1894), L. Demaison (Petites Monographies des grands Édifices, [1910]), P. Vitry (9 fasc., Paris, 1915–20; mainly plates) and L. Bréhier (Paris, 1916). G. Goyau in *C.E.*, xii (1911), pp. 725–30, s.v.

REIMS NEW TESTAMENT. See *Douai–Reims Bible*.

REINCARNATION. See *Metempsychosis*.

REINKENS, JOSEPH HUBERT (1821–1896), *Old Catholic bishop. In 1850 he became professor of Church history at Breslau, where he published some monographs on *patristics. At the *Vatican Council he was opposed to the definition of Papal Infallibility, and in 1871 joined J. J. I. von *Döllinger in the *Nuremberg Declaration. After excommunication from the RC Church, Reinkens was elected the first bishop of the German Old Catholics at Cologne in 1873, and consecrated by Bp. Hermann Heykamp of Deventer. For the rest of his life he devoted himself to the Old Catholic cause by learned writing and in other ways. In 1874 and 1875 he took a prominent part in the *Bonn Reunion Conferences and in 1876 consecrated Edward Herzog the first Swiss Old Catholic bishop.

His Life was written by his nephew, J. M. Reinkens (Gotha, 1906).

REITZENSTEIN, RICHARD (1861–1931), classical philologist and historian of religions. From 1889 onward he held professorships at several German universities, his final appointment being to Göttingen in 1914. His earlier work was chiefly philological, but later he applied the results of his philological studies to the religious and philosophical movements of the early cents. A.D. and their influence on the development of Christianity. In *Poimandres* (1904) he tried to prove that NT phraseology and ideas are largely derived from *Hermetic sources and that the Christian Churches were modelled on Hermetic communities, while in *Die hellenistischen Mysterienreligionen* (1910; ed. 3, 1927) and other later writings he sought to establish the direct dependence of early Christianity on Hellenistic, *Mandaean, and Iranian ideas. Similar methods were applied to the study of Christian monasticism in *Historia Monachorum und Historia Lausiaca* (1916). Though his brilliant and ingenious theories did not win much acceptance, they brought together much new material for the study of Christianity in relation to its primitive environment.

E. Fraenkel, H. Fränkel, M. Pohlenz, E. Reitzenstein, R. Reitzenstein, E. *Schwartz and J. Stroux, *Festschrift Richard Reitzenstein zum 2. April 1931 dargebracht* (1931), with list of his works by R. Reitzenstein, pp. 160–8.

RELICS. In Christian usage the word is applied to the material remains of a saint after his death, as well as to sacred objects which have been in contact with his body. The veneration of relics is found in many religions, e.g. popular Buddhism, and is based on the natural instinct of men to treat with reverence what is left of the dead they loved. Traces of it may be found in the OT miracles worked through the mantle of *Elijah (2 Kgs. 2. 14) and the bones of *Elisha (2 Kgs. 13. 21), and, in the NT, in the healing power of handkerchiefs that had been in touch with St. *Paul's body (Acts 19. 12). In post-NT times the martyrs' bodies were venerated from an early date, the first certain evidence occurring in the 'Martyrium Polycarpi' (*c.* 156–7) where the relics of St. *Polycarp are described as 'more valuable than precious stones and finer than refined gold' (τιμιώτερα λίθων πολυτελῶν καὶ δοκιμώτερα ὑπὲρ χρυσίον; ch. 18), to be carefully collected and honoured by a memorial service for the saint at the place where they were laid.

The cult of relics spread quickly both in the E. and the W. In Rome it was bound up with the *catacombs where prayer services were held and, from the 4th cent., the Eucharist celebrated over the tombs of the martyrs. The danger of exaggerated worship, caused by the great influx of pagans into the Church after the age of persecution, led *Vigilantius to oppose the cult. Against him St. *Jerome enunciated the principle, already foreshadowed in the 'Martyrium Polycarpi', that the relics of the martyrs are honoured for the sake of Him whose martyrs they are. St. *Augustine added the reason that the bodies served the saints while they lived as organs of the Holy Spirit, and that also the objects they used should be dear to Christians from motives of filial piety. *Gennadius held that they should be honoured as the members of Christ. At the same time the increasing demand for relics led, in the E., to the translating and even dismembering of the bodies, a practice strictly forbidden by the Roman civil law and not introduced into the W. till the 7th and 8th cents. Under the influence of the *Iconoclastic Controversy, the Second Council of *Nicaea (787) anathematized those who despised holy relics and laid down that no church should be consecrated without them. The veneration of relics was approved for the E. Church by the Council of *Constantinople in 1084, though owing to the scarcity of canonizations and the great role played by the *icons it has never held the same place there as in the W. In the W., on the other hand, the cult increased enormously, esp. during the *Crusades, when quantities of relics, often spurious, were brought to Europe from the Holy Land. They were kept in magnificent *reliquaries, carried in procession, and often gave rise to superstitious practices. They were assigned an important place in the Liturgy, the priest saluting the relics which had been enclosed in the altar stone at its consecration by kissing the *mensa* at the beginning of Mass.

The theological foundation of the cult of relics was worked out by the Schoolmen, esp. St. *Thomas, on the principles laid down by St. Jerome and St. Augustine. Stress was laid on the special dignity of the bodies of the saints as temples of the Holy Ghost destined to a glorious resurrection, and the sanction given by the Godhead in making them the occasion of many miracles. In the 16th cent. the doctrine was confirmed by the Council of *Trent against the Reformers. Post-Tridentine theologians have differed as to whether they are to be honoured with the same cult of '*dulia' as the saints or with an inferior one. Acc. to canon law (*CIC*, 1281-9) no relics may be venerated without a written authentication by a cardinal or the local ordinary; and the sale of genuine relics as well as the fabrication or distribution of false ones is punished by excommunication. Among the most famous relics are those of Santiago de *Compostela, the Holy House of *Loreto, and the *Holy Coat of Trier. A feast of Holy Relics is observed in many English RC dioceses on 5 Nov.

S. Beissel, S.J., *Die Verehrung der Heiligen und ihre Reliquien in Deutschland* (Stimmen aus Maria-Laach, Ergänzungshefte, xlvii and liv; 1890-2). H. Siebert, *Beiträge zur vorreformatorischen Heiligen- und Reliquienverehrung* (1907). U. Mioni, *Il culto delle reliquie nella chiesa cattolica* (1908). F. Pfister, *Der Reliquienkult im Altertum* (Versuche und Vorarbeiten, ed. R. Wünsch–L. Deubner, v; 1909). B. Lefeuvre, *Courte Histoire des reliques* (1932). H. Fichtenau, 'Zum Reliquienwesen im früheren Mittelalter' in *Mitteilungen des Instituts für österreichische Geschichtsforschung*, lx (1952), pp. 60-89. H. Thurston, S.J., in *C.E.*, xii (1911), pp. 734-8, s.v.; H. *Leclercq, O.S.B., in *D.A.C.L.*, xiv (pt. 2; 1948), cols. 2294-359, s.v. 'Reliques et reliquiares'; E. Josi–F. Antonelli, O.F.M.– P. Palazzini in *E.C.*, x (1953), cols. 749-60, s.v. 'Reliquie'.

RELIEF ACTS. See *Catholic Relief Acts.*

RELIGIONSGESCHICHTLICHE SCHULE. The 'History of Religion School', an influential group of German Biblical scholars between 1880 and 1920, who advocated extensive use of *data* from the comparative study of religions in the interpretation of Christianity. In contrast to A. *Ritschl, who interpreted the NT in the light of modern doctrinal convictions and largely ignored its historical antecedents, this School reduced dogmatic considerations to a minimum. Further, religious documents must be understood not as isolated expressions of their authors' thoughts and inspirations, but as products of a long and often complex development of the tribe or community. In its philosophy the School was influenced by G. W. F. *Hegel and the concept of evolution, in its historical methods also by L. von *Ranke and T. *Mommsen.

At first the School confined itself to tracing historical developments inside Judaism and Christianity, but it soon came to search for parallels in Egyptian, Babylonian, and various Hellenistic religious systems. Thus H. *Gunkel, H. Gressmann (1877-1927), and W. *Bousset claimed that many Biblical passages were based on the ancient myths not only of the Hebrews but also of e.g. Babylon and Egypt. Bousset and J. *Weiss maintained that the eschatological ideas underlying the terms '*Messiah' and '*Kingdom of God' were largely of non-Jewish origin, while Bousset also claimed to have found extrabiblical antecedents for the term 'Lord'. R. *Reitzenstein, whose imagination admittedly far outran his critical sense, advanced similar claims for such terms as 'Man from Heaven', 'Holy Spirit', and 'Saviour', and he, A. Eichhorn (1856-1926), and W. Heitmüller (1869-1925) upheld the relevance of Gentile 'parallels' for the *Eucharist and *Baptism. Another prominent member of the school was H. *Windisch.

O. Eissfeldt in *R.G.G.* (ed. 2), iv (1930), cols. 1898-1905, s.v., with useful bibl.

RELIGIOUS (Lat. *religiosus*). Technical term for a member of a religious order or congregation. In canon law (*CIC*, can. 487) the religious status is defined as a stable mode of living in community in which the faithful bind themselves by vow to observe, in addition to the precepts, the evangelical *counsels of obedience, chastity, and poverty.

RELIGIOUS DRAMA. See *Drama.*

RELIGIOUS ORDERS IN ANGLICANISM. The revival of religious orders in the Anglican Communion was one of the results of the *Oxford Movement. In 1839 E. B. *Pusey wrote to J. *Keble that he and J. H. *Newman had independently been led to recognize the desirability of some 'Sœurs de Charité' in the Anglican Church and on Trinity Sunday 1841 he received the vows of Marian Rebecca Hughes who in 1849 became the first Superior of the Convent of the Holy Trinity at Oxford. In 1845 he founded the first community at Park Village, Regent's Park, which was later merged in the Society of the Holy Trinity, founded at Devonport by Priscilla Lydia *Sellon in 1848 and now at Ascot. After this, communities followed in rapid succession. Among the most famous are the Community of St. Mary the Virgin, founded in 1848 with the help of W. J. *Butler, vicar of Wantage; the Community of St. John the Baptist, founded in 1852 at Clewer by T. T. *Carter with Harriet Monsell as first superior; the Community of All Saints, founded in 1851 by W. Upton Richards, vicar of All Saints, Margaret Street, London; and the Community of St. Margaret, founded in 1855 at East Grinstead by J. M. *Neale. All these were 'active' or 'mixed' communities, combining the monastic life (with its centre in the daily recitation of the Breviary Offices) with a life of service, and they were among the pioneers in the care for the poor in the slums of great cities which was one of the fruits of the Oxford Movement. It was not until 1907 that, with the foundation of the first enclosed community, the 'Order of the Love of God', at Fairacres, Oxford, the 'contemplative' life was revived.

Communities for men have developed more slowly. J. H. Newman, after he had moved to Littlemore in 1842, lived a community life with some companions and on occasion referred to his establishment as a μονή, but there were no vows. The first religious order of men was the *Society of St. John the Evangelist founded in 1866 at Cowley by R. M. *Benson. The *Community of the Resurrection, founded in 1892 by C. *Gore, while principal of Pusey House, Oxford, has been, since 1898, established at Mirfield, and the Society of the Sacred Mission, founded by H. H. Kelly, in 1891, is now at Kelham; one of the chief works of both of these is the training of ordinands. The English Order of St. Benedict at Nashdom Abbey sprang from the Benedictine community at *Caldey, founded by Aelred Carlyle who later seceded to Rome with most of his monks. More recently an English *Franciscan order has been formed.

From England, this revived religious life has spread throughout the Anglican Communion. Many of the English orders have branch houses in other countries and new communities have grown up in America, Africa, India, and Australasia.

The early communities, though for the most part established in dioceses where the bishop was sympathetic, had no recognized place in the life of the Church and had to face much suspicion and at times active hostility. Since 1861, when the movement was first discussed in *Canterbury Convocation, their contribution to the life of the Church has been increasingly recognized. Following the recommendation made in a report to the *Lambeth Conference of 1930, an 'Advisory Council on the Relation of the Bishops and Religious Communities' was established for Canterbury and York, and it is now possible for communities to receive formal recognition.

A Directory of the Religious Life (1943) and Guide to the Religious Communities of the Anglican Communion (1951) [both] issued by the Advisory Council on Religious Communities under the Chairmanship of the Bishop of Oxford [K. E. *Kirk]. A. T. Cameron (ed.), Directory of Religious Communities of Men and Women and of Deaconess Communities and Institutions in the Anglican Communion (1920; ed. 2, enlarged 1922). P. F. Anson, The Call of the Cloister (1955). S. L. Ollard in D.E.C.H. (ed. 3, 1948), s.v., 'Religious Orders. II: Modern'.

RELIGIOUS TRACT SOCIETY (R.T.S.). The Society was founded in 1799 (incorporated, 1899), with a committee of an equal number of Anglicans and Nonconformists for the publication and dissemination of tracts and other Christian evangelical literature. It published in two hundred languages for missionary purposes and established daughter societies in

*India and *China. During the war of 1914–18 it gratuitously distributed many millions of books and magazines among soldiers, sailors, and prisoners of war. On 14 May 1935 it was absorbed in the *United Society for Christian Literature (q.v.).

W. Jones, The Jubilee Volume of the Religious Tract Society: containing a Record of its Origin, Proceedings, and Results. A.D. 1799–1849 (1850); S. G. Green, The Story of the Religious Tract Society for One Hundred Years (1899); G. Hewitt, Let the People Read. A Short History of the United Society for Christian Literature, 1799; Christian Literature Society for India and Africa, 1858; Christian Literature Society for China (British Support), 1887 (1949). Annual Reports of the Religious Tract Society (London, 1799 ff.).

RELIQUARY. A receptacle for *relics. The oldest reliquaries took the form of caskets, capsules, *ampullas, also of crosses, esp. for relics of the True Cross, of rings and of purses, and from early times they have frequently been of precious material and richly decorated. For the reception of the whole remains of a saint the gabled shrine was a favourite form in the Middle Ages, among famous examples being the silver shrine of the Three Kings at *Cologne (c. 1190–1225) and H. *Memling's reliquary of St. *Ursula at Bruges. At the same period smaller relics were kept in reliquaries of the shape of arms, legs, and esp. heads and busts, while in the later Middle Ages the *monstrance form, which facilitated exposition, became frequent. Besides the varied formalized shapes, caskets and boxes of all sizes and materials have always served as receptacles for relics.

J. Braun, S.J., Die Reliquiare des christlichen Kultes und ihre Entwicklung (1940). H. Thurston, S.J., in C.E., xii (1911), p. 762 f., s.v.

REMBRANDT (1606–69) **(Rembrandt Harmens van Rijn),** Dutch painter. The son of a wealthy miller of *Leyden, he showed an early inclination for his art and, at the age of 25, was one of the most famous portrait painters of his country. In 1631 he moved to Amsterdam, where he lived till his death. In 1634 he married the beautiful Saskia who during the rest of her life was the inspiration of his art. His pictures on Scriptural subjects in these years, which treat mostly of vivid scenes such as the story of Samson, are full of vigour and imagination though they have not reached the spirituality of his later period. With the death of Saskia, in 1642, sorrow entered his life, and his troubles were increased by financial difficulties ending in bankruptcy and, in 1654, the scandal of having a child by his servant, Hendrikje, which brought him into conflict with the Reformed Church at Amsterdam. These sufferings, which threw him more and more into solitude, helped further to deepen and spiritualize his art and to give him an understanding of the Passion—a theme treated in about 90 paintings and etchings—such as few artists have possessed. Characteristic was his treatment of light and shade out of which his human figures appear to grow, thereby producing the impression of a happening beyond space and time. The supernatural atmosphere of the *Last Supper* and the *Disciples at Emmaus*, and the union of Divine majesty and redeeming love in the face of his Christ blessing the children or healing the sick, are unsurpassed in Christian art. Among his last great works is his famous *Return of the Prodigal Son* (Leningrad, c. 1668), a painted confession of faith in the goodness of God expressed in the face and hands of the father who receives the kneeling beggar with infinite love. Rembrandt has rightly been termed the painter of the soul.

Reproductions of his Paintings include that ed. W. R. Valentiner (Klassiker der Kunst in Gesamtausgaben, ii; 1904; further paintings by same editor, ib., xxvii; 1921); also by A. Bredius (Utrecht, 1935; Eng. ed., 1937); of his Drawings, ed. W. R. Valentiner (Klassiker der Kunst in Gesamtausgaben, xxxi, xxxii, &c. [1925] ff.); also ed. O. Benesch (Phaidon Press, London, 6 vols., 1954 ff.; of his Etchings, ed. H. W. Singer (Klassiker der Kunst in Gesamtausgaben, viii; 1906); also ed. Constance Schild (New York, 1937) and L. Münz (Phaidon Press, London, 2 vols., 1952). The very extensive literature includes studies by E. Michel (Paris, 1893; Eng. tr., 2 vols., 1894), C. Neumann (Berlin-Stuttgart, 1902), W. Weisbach (Berlin-Leipzig, 1926) and A. M. Hind (Charles Eliot Norton Lectures, 1930–1; London, 1932). O. Benesch in *Allgemeines Lexikon der bildenden Künstler von der Antike bis zur Gegenwart* begr. U. Thieme–F. Becker, xxix (1935), pp. 259–71. J. F. White–P. G. Konody in *E.B.* (ed. 11), xxiii (1911), pp. 77–81, s.v.

REMIGIUS, St. (*c.* 438–*c.* 533), also 'Remi', 'Apostle of the Franks'. The son of Aemilius, Count of Laon, he studied at *Reims and was acclaimed Abp. of Reims at the age of 22. In 496 he baptized *Clovis I, King of the Salic Franks (481–511), with three thousand of his subjects. He founded Bishoprics at Laon, Tournai, Cambrai, Arras and Térouanne and directed missions to the Morini and the *Arians of Burgundy. Acc. to a legend, first mentioned by *Hincmar of Reims, the *ampulla of chrism traditionally used in the coronation of French kings was brought by a dove in answer to the prayers of St. Remigius at the baptism of Clovis. He is said to have conferred upon Clovis the power of touching for the *king's evil. Feast day 1 Oct., the anniversary of the translation of his relics to the abbey of St. Remi by Pope *Leo IX in 1049, except at Reims (13 Jan.), where his death is commemorated.

Letters, together with the Testament (prob. wrongly) attributed to him, in J. P. Migne, *PL*, lxv, 963–76; crit. ed. of the letters by W. Gundlach in *M.G.H.*, Epistolae, iii (1892), pp. 112–16. *A.A.SS.*, Oct. I (1765), pp. 59–187, incl. text of life traditionally ascribed to *Venantius Fortunatus, pp. 128–30; full text of the life by *Hincmar of Reims ed. B. Krusch in *M.G.H.*, Scriptores Rerum Merovingicarum, iii (1896), pp. 239–349. The traditional account of the baptism of Clovis is also found in *Gregory of Tours, *Historia Francorum*, ii, 23. B. Krusch, 'Reimser Remigius-Fälschungen' in *N.A.*, xx (1895), pp. 511–68. H. Jadart, 'Bibliographie des ouvrages concernant la vie et le culte de saint Remi, évêque de Reims' in *Travaux de l'Académie Nationale de Reims*, lxxxvii (1891), pp. 225–75. More recent study by R. Barroux ('Grandeurs et gloires de l'ancienne France', 1947). A. Manser, O.S.B., in *L.Th.K.*, viii (1936), col. 817 f., s.v., with further reff.; G. Bardy in *D.T.C.*, xiii (pt. 2; 1937), cols. 2379–81, s.v. 'Remi de Reims (Saint)'. See also bibl. to *Reims.

REMIGIUS OF AUXERRE (*c.* 841–*c.* 908), medieval philosopher. Educated at the monastic school of St.-Germain at Auxerre, where he was a pupil of *Heiric and Dunchad, on Heiric's death he succeeded as master of the school. Later he taught at *Reims and *Paris. He became widely known as the author of many philosophical and theological works and commentaries on Gen. and the Pss., though the extent to which he composed these writings himself or merely copied them from other writers of his school is disputed. His commentary on Martianus Capella, derived very largely from *Erigena and Dunchad, had a wide circulation in the Middle Ages. His general philosophical position closely reflects the *Realism of Erigena. He was also the author of a liturgical tractate, 'De Celebratione Missae', which was incorporated into Pseudo-*Alcuin's 'De Divinis Officiis' (ch. 40).

Collection of his works, with notices of his life, in J. P. Migne, *PL*, cxxxi, 47–970. E. K. Rand, *Johannes Scottus* (Quellen und Untersuchungen zur lateinischen Philologie des Mittelalters ed. L. Traube, i, Hft. 2; 1906), pp. 85–106 (Zweiter Teil: Remigius von Auxerre), with the part of the text of the gloss on *Boethius's 'Opuscula Sacra' which Rand ascribes to John Scotus *Erigena, pp. 30–80, and the rest, pp. 99–106; on the authorship of the whole, cf. M. Cappuyns, O.S.B., 'Le Plus Ancienne Commentaire des *Opuscula Sacra* et son origine' in *R.T.A.M.*, iii (1931), pp. 237–72 (ascribes the whole to Remigius). H. F. Stewart, 'A Commentary by Remigius Autissiodorensis on the *De Consolatione Philosophiae* of Boethius' in *J.T.S.*, xvii (1915–16), pp. 22–44, incl. text from a MS. in the Öttingen-Wallerstein collection at Maihingen, collated with the relevant parts of the Trèves MS. used by Rand, and introd. on Remigius. M. Manitius, 'Zwei Remigiuskommentare' in *N.A.*, xlix (1932), pp. 173–83. J. R. Geiselmann, 'Der Einfluss des Remigius von Auxerre auf die Eucharistielehre des Heriger von Lobbes' in *T.Q.*, cxiv (1933), pp. 222–44. *Histoire littéraire de la France*, vi (1742), pp. 99–122. Manitius, i, 504–19, with addenda, ii, 808, and iii, 1063; Überweg, ii, 178–80, with bibl. p. 695. W. Neuss in *L.Th.K.*, viii (1936), col. 815 f.

REMONSTRANCE, The. The statement of Arminian teaching drawn up at Gouda in 1610, after the death of J. *Arminius, in the presence of 46 ministers. It appears to have been compiled by J. Uitenbogaert, though it was often attributed by earlier writers to H. *Grotius and S. *Episcopius. Under five headings it sets out in positive form the leading Arminian doctrines on salvation. Among the Calvinistic doctrines repudiated were both the *Supralapsarian and *Sublapsarian forms of predestination, the doctrine that Christ died only for the elect, and the belief that the saints could not fall from grace. The ensuing conflict was very bitter, for the Remonstrants were suspected of favouring the pro-Spanish party in politics, and the *Contra-Remonstrants, led by F. *Gomar, were aided by Prince Maurice of Orange. As a result the Remonstrants were condemned at the Synod of *Dort (1618–19). See also *Arminianism*.

The text is in P. *Schaff, *The Creeds of Christendom*, iii (1877), pp. 545–9. Cf. also i, pp. 508–19.

RENAN, JOSEPH ERNEST (1823–92), French philosopher, theologian, and orientalist. A native of Tréguier in Brittany, he was invited in 1838 by F.A.P. *Dupanloup (whose attention had been drawn to Renan's brilliance through his sister, Henriette) to join his celebrated seminary of St.-Nicholas-du-Chardonnet at Paris. His study of German theology and Semitic languages led him to have doubts of the truth of Christianity, and in Oct. 1845 he left the seminary of *St.-Sulpice, where he then was. After a somewhat precarious and varied life for several years, he published in 1852 his *Averroès et l'averroïsme*, which at once established his reputation as a scholar. In 1860 he was sent by the Emperor on an archaeological mission to Phoenicia and Syria, and it was while in Palestine that he wrote his celebrated *La Vie de Jésus*. In this book, written in an attractive and vivid style, but in a tone that hardly rang sincere, he repudiated the supernatural element in Christ's life, ignored its moral aspect, and portrayed Him as a charming and amiable Galilean preacher. Its publication in 1863 created an immediate sensation throughout Europe. In Jan. 1862 he had been appointed professor of Hebrew at the Collège de France, but the storm created by his *Vie de Jésus* led to his removal in 1864. For the rest of his life he held no further appointment. His other writings include *Les Apôtres* (1866), *St. Paul* (1869), *Les Évangiles* (1877), *Histoire du peuple d'Israel* (5 vols., 1887–93), and his widely popular *Souvenirs d'enfance et de jeunesse* (1883).

Collected ed. of his works by H. Psichari (Paris, 1947 ff.). Many of his works were translated into English, incl. his *Life of Jesus* (London, 1864, and many later edd.), *Recollections of my Youth* (ib., 1883) and *History of the People of Israel* (3 vols., ib., 1889–91). The many studies in French include J. Pommier, *Ernest Renan d'après des documents inédits* (1923); id., *La Pensée religieuse de Renan* (1925), and id., *La Jeunesse cléricale d'Ernest Renan*. Saint-Sulpice (Strassburg thesis, Strassburg, 1933), with bibl.; M. Weiler, *La Pensée de Renan* (1945); L. Vié, *Renan*. La Guerre de 70 et la "Réforme de la France" (1949), and other works of this author. G. Sorel, *Le Système historique de Renan* (4 vols. bound in 1 [1905–6]). M. J. *Lagrange, O.P., *La Vie de Jésus d'après Renan* (1921; Eng. tr., 1928). P. Alfaric, *Les Manuscrits de la 'Vie de Jésus' d'Ernest Renan* (Publications de la Faculté des Lettres de l'Université de Strasbourg, xc; 1939), with introd., notes, and concordance. H. Girard–H. Moncel, *Bibliographie des œuvres d'Ernest Renan* (Publication de la Société Ernest Renan. Histoire religieuse, i; 1923). Studies in English by Mrs. James Darmester [A. May F. Robinson] (London, 1897), W. Barry (ib., 1905), L. F. Mott (New York–London, 1921), and J. M. Robertson (London, 1924). Agnes M. F. Duclaux (revised) in *E.B.* (ed. 11), xxiii (1911), pp. 93–5, s.v.; J. Schmid in *L.Th.K.*, viii (1936), cols. 823–5, s.v., with bibl.

RENAUDOT, EUSÈBE (1646–1720), orientalist and liturgist. He was a native of *Paris. After a short stay with the *Oratorians he devoted himself entirely to oriental studies and became a member of the Académie Française in 1689. A valued friend and adviser of the leading men of his time, among them J. B. *Bossuet, he accompanied the Cardinal *de Noailles to the conclave of 1700. He never received more than minor orders.

Renaudot's two chief theological writings are his erudite *Historia Jacobitarum Patriarcharum Alexandrinorum* (1713) and his *Liturgiarum Orientalium Collectio* (2 vols., 1716). The latter contains the texts of a great number of E. liturgies with copious notes and commentaries, and is still indispensable for liturgical studies. Renaudot, who was a friend of several *Jansenists, was also the author of the fourth and fifth volumes of the famous *Perpétuité de la foi*, published under the direction of P. *Nicole and A. *Arnauld, in which,

by rich documentation, he upheld the antiquity of the Eucharistic faith of the E. Churches against the *Calvinistic doctrine.

A corrected ed. of Renaudot's *Liturgiarum Orientalium Collectio* was publd., 2 vols., Frankfurt a.M., 1847. Selections from his correspondence ed. F. Duffo (Paris, 1927 and 1931). H. Omont, 'Inventaire sommaire des manuscrits de la collection Renaudot, conservée à la Bibliothèque Nationale' in *Bibliothèque de l'École des Chartes*, li (1890), pp. 270–97. A. Villien, *L'Abbé Eusèbe Renaudot*. Essai sur sa vie et sur son œuvre liturgique (1904). J. Carreyre in *D.T.C.*, xiii (pt. 2; 1937), cols. 2381–3, s.v.; H. *Leclercq, O.S.B., in *D.A.C.L.*, xiv (pt. 2; 1948), cols. 2369–72, s.v.

RENEGADE. One who forsakes his religion for another faith. The term was formerly in current use esp. of Christians who apostatized to *Islam.

RENUNCIATION OF THE DEVIL. The renunciation of Satan at *Baptism is attested in St. *Hippolytus' *Apostolic Tradition*, St. *Cyril of Jerusalem, and St. *Ambrose's *De Mysteriis*, and has been a regular part of almost all Baptismal rites, E. and W. It was presumably designed originally to confirm the candidate in his intention to forsake all heathen worship and ways of life.

REORDINATION. The repetition of an ordination to the priesthood which had been conferred either *extra ecclesiam*, i.e. by an heretical or schismatic bishop, or *intra ecclesiam* but not canonically, e.g. by a deposed or simoniacal bishop. Reordination was frequently practised in the Church down to the 12th cent., when the doctrine of the Sacraments began to receive more precise formulation. The question of reordination first became a practical issue through the rise of schisms and heresies. Implicitly different answers were already given in the 3rd cent. by St. *Cyprian of Carthage and St. *Stephen of Rome, in that the one rejected and the other accepted the validity of heretical Baptism.

In the following cents. the practice of the Church varied. Acc. to the Council of *Nicaea (325, can. 19) ordinations in the different sects were treated differently, whereas the *Apostolic Constitutions and the *Apostolic Canons are hostile to the sacraments of all non-Catholic bodies. In view of the new schisms of the 4th and 5th cents. the practice of reordination was attenuated and often replaced by a ceremony called χειροθεσία which was mentioned in the Canons of Nicaea, and is apparently a supplementary rite distinct from ordination (χειροτονία). The Greek Church, though she repudiated reordination at the *Trullan Council (692; can. 95), has continued to waver in its practice. In the W. St. *Augustine's doctrine of the validity of the sacraments administered by sinful, excommunicated, schismatic, or heretical priests, formed in the course of the *Donatist controversy, slowly gained ground against opposition. Though St. *Gregory the Great expressed himself clearly against reordination, heretical sacraments were viewed with hostility by many subsequent theologians, and reordination was practised, e.g., by the Greek Abp. *Theodore of Canterbury, who, in 669, reordained Ceadda who had been ordained by supposed *Quartodecimans. It was also practised in the case of priests ordained by the irregularly elected Pope Constantine II (767–9), by Pope *Formosus (891–6), and by the 9th-cent. *chorepiscopi, as well as on the simoniacal clergy of the 11th cent. many of whom were reordained by the Pope himself, St. *Leo IX. From the period of *Gregory VII, however, when *Anselm of Lucca defended the validity of heretical sacraments, the Augustinian view became more and more general and was finally formulated by St. *Thomas Aquinas, who rejected the practice of reordination because of the indelible *character bestowed by the Sacrament of Holy Orders on its recipient. This doctrine was formally sanctioned by the Council of *Trent, provided that the sacrament was conferred in the prescribed form and with the right intention.

L. Saltet, Les Réordinations (1907); C. H. *Turner, art. 'Apostolic Succession' in Essays on the Early History of the Church and the Ministry (ed. H. B. *Swete, 1918), esp. pp. 161–79.

REPARATION. The making amends for damage done to another. In moral theology it is generally used in a sense similar to *restitution (q.v.) in cases of personal injury such as homicide, detraction, adultery, &c. For wrongs of this kind reparation cannot be made exactly corresponding to the loss, but takes the form of compensation, already prescribed in the Mosaic Law (Ex. 21. 22 ff.).

In modern devotional language the term is frequently used for the amends made to God for offences against Him by means of prayer and penance. Reparation plays a central part in the *Sacred Heart devotion, esp. with ref. to outrages committed against the Blessed Sacrament, and confraternities and congregations have been established with this and similar ends in view.

REPENTANCE. The condemnation and abhorrence of one's own sins. True repentance or *contrition (as contrasted with mere *attrition) springs from a sense of the outrage which sin commits against the love of God. It includes sorrow for sin committed, confession of guilt, and the purpose of amendment. The Greek word μετάνοια, translated 'repentance' in the English NT, emphasizes the last aspect, while the Latin word penitentia (whence 'penance' and 'penitence') refers in origin to the first two aspects, esp. as expressed in the payment of a penalty. In accord with this distinction in language, Latin teaching has laid special emphasis in *penance on acts of *reparation and *satisfaction for sin.

REPINGTON, PHILIP (d. 1424), Bp. of *Lincoln. He was educated at *Oxford and became an *Augustinian canon of St. Mary-de-Pré, Leicester. In early life he was a supporter of the doctrines of J. *Wycliffe whose sacramental teaching he defended in several sermons. At the Council of Blackfriars (1382) he was suspended and a few weeks later excommunicated at *Canterbury, but he recanted his heresies and was restored to communion in the same year. In 1394 he became Abbot of St. Mary-de-Pré and three years later chancellor of the university of Oxford, an office he held again in 1400 and the two following years. Shortly after his accession in 1399 Henry IV made him his chaplain and confessor, and in 1404 he was appointed Bp. of Lincoln. Four years later Gregory XII created him Cardinal, a dignity rendered doubtful by the deposition of Gregory by the Council of *Pisa in 1409 until it was revalidated in 1415 by the Council of *Constance. He resigned his bishopric in 1419, probably because Henry V had opposed the raising of Henry *Beaufort to the cardinalate.

The primary source for his life is the Fasciculi Zizaniorum ed. W. W. Shirley (Rolls Series, 1858), pp. 289 f., 296–329 passim. 'Cardinal Repyngdon and the Followers of Wycliffe' in The Church Quarterly Review, xix (1884), pp. 59–82. K. B. McFarlane, John Wycliffe and the Beginnings of English Non-conformity (1953), pp. 102 f., 108–15, and 120. C. L. Kingsford in D.N.B., xlviii (1896), pp. 26–8.

REPOSE, Altar of. An altar to which (acc to W. use) the Blessed Sacrament is taken in procession after the Mass of *Maundy Thursday and reserved for communion at the 'Mass of the *Presanctified' on *Good Friday. It is customary to make the Altar of Repose as splendid as possible with lights and flowers, and in many places the faithful watch before it by turns through the entire day and night. It is first mentioned in the 15th cent.

REPROACHES, The (Lat. Improperia). The set of reproofs addressed by the Crucified Saviour to His ungrateful people, which form part of the *Good Friday Liturgy of the Latin Church. They are chanted by two choirs during the *Veneration of the Cross and consist of twelve verses, which set in parallel the Divine compassion for Israel and the outrages inflicted on Christ in His Passion. Each of the first three verses is followed by the *Trisagion sung alternately in Latin and Greek, and each of the other nine by the refrain 'Popule meus, quid feci tibi', &c. The Improperia, which are built up on OT passages, are probably of French origin, dating from the 10th cent. By the 12th cent. they were a fixed part of the Roman Liturgy.

REPROBATION. The act by which God condemns sinners to eternal punishment, and the state of this punishment. In his struggle against *Pelagianism and *Semi-Pelagianism, St. *Augustine sometimes used expressions which might be understood as teaching that there is predestination, on the part of God, to everlasting death, as there is to eternal life. In the 9th cent. the question was agitated in the Frankish Church on account of the bold teaching of the monk, *Gottschalk, who was accused of maintaining that God positively and irresistibly predestined certain men to sin and damnation. His doctrine, vigorously opposed by *Hincmar of Reims, was condemned by the Council of Mainz in 848 and by the first (849) and second (853) Councils of *Quiercy, which rejected all predestination to perdition. The Council of *Valence (855), though using the expression 'predestination to death', was none the less careful to point out that 'the evil deserts precede the just judgement of God'. The doctrine of predestination to eternal punishment was revived by many of the 16th cent. Reformers, esp. J. *Calvin, who taught positive and gratuitous reprobation. Acc. to Calvin God, by an inscrutable decree, Himself incites to sin those whom He has predestined to hell. This teaching was condemned by the Council of *Trent (Sess. VI, can. 6). Somewhat similar doctrines were taught later by M. *Baius and the *Jansenists.

REQUIEM. A Mass offered for the dead, so named from the first word of the opening *antiphon in the Roman rite ('*Requiem* aeternam dona eis Domine'). The Missal contains four classes of Requiems—for *All Souls' Day (2 Nov.); for the day of death or burial (with modifications for the 3rd, 7th, and 30th day after burial); for the anniversary of death; and for 'Daily, i.e. unspecified, Masses for the Dead'. By a concession formerly limited to *Spain, but extended by *Benedict XV to the whole RC Church, every priest is permitted to celebrate three Masses on All Souls' Day, a privilege shared only with *Christmas Day. In general, except on the greater feast days, requiems are offered throughout the year as occasion arises, e.g. on the day of burial of a member of the congregation (often *praesente cadavere*) or of a public figure or by special request. In November, regarded acc. to modern RC custom as the month of the Holy Souls, Masses for the dead are said with particular frequency.

In Requiem Masses black vestments are worn, the candles are of unbleached wax, the Psalm 'Judica Me' is omitted in the *Preparation, the *Sequence (if said) is the *Dies Irae (q.v.), the water is not blessed at the *Offertory, there is a proper *Preface, there is a variant form of the *Agnus Dei, and there is no blessing. On the occasion of a burial the Mass is at once followed by the '*Absolutions of the Dead'.

J. Merk, *Die messliturgische Totenehrung in der römischen Kirche* (1926); E. Freistedt, *Altchristliche Totengedächtnistage und ihre Beziehung zum Jenseitsglauben und Totenkultus der Antike* (Liturgiegeschichtliche Quellen und Forschungen, xxiv; 1928). L. Eisenhofer, *Handbuch der katholischen Liturgik*, ii (1933), pp. 17–19; Jungmann, i, 275–7; Eng. tr., pp. 217–19.

REREDOS. Properly any decoration put up above and behind an altar. The earliest type of such decoration was the painting of scenes or symbols on the walls against which altars backed; but during the Middle Ages a reredos might consist in a rich silken hanging or a piece of jewelled metalwork, as, e.g., at St. Mark's, *Venice. More commonly, painted wooden panels, either fixed or in the form of a triptych, made up the reredos, while another way of providing a reredos that represented Biblical incidents or figures of the saints was to have it carved in stone or alabaster. Where there happened to be no east window behind the altar, a reredos might cover the whole wall, as at New College, Oxford, or—a most elaborate example—at Burgos in Spain.

Braun, *C.A.*, ii (1924), pp. 277–544, with plates 192–336. F. Bond, *The Chancel of English Churches* (1916), pp. 51–100.

RERUM NOVARUM. The encyclical issued by *Leo XIII on 15 May 1891 *De Conditione Opificum*. Its purpose was to apply to the new conditions created by the Industrial Revolution the traditional Catholic teaching on the relationship of a man to his work, profit, masters, and servants. On the ground that society originated in the family, it proclaimed private property a natural right and condemned 'socialism' as infringing it. It upheld wage-settlements by free agreement, the rightfulness of combinations of workers or employers, and above all the ideal of a just wage, defined as 'enough to support the wage-earner in reasonable and frugal comfort' with a family. It maintained that the natural place of women was in the home. It also emphasized the duty of the state to preserve justice and the responsibility of the Church in the moral aspects of employment.

This new concern of the Church for the condition of the workers was heralded as revolutionary and subversive of the established order; but the encyclical has since been widely acclaimed as among the most important modern pronouncements on social justice and has exercised wide influence. On 15 May 1931 *Quadragesimo Anno* (q.v.) was issued by *Pius XI to mark its fortieth anniversary.

Text in *Acta Leonis XIII*, iv (1894), pp. 177–209. H. E. *Manning, *Leo XIII on the Condition of Labour* (1891); H. George, *The Condition of Labour* (1891; rev. ed., 1947, incl. Eng. tr. of text, pp. 99–127).

RESCISSORY ACT. The Act passed by the Scottish Parliament on 28 Mar. 1661 repealing the whole of the legislation enacted since 1633. Its effect was to overthrow *Presbyterianism and restore episcopacy. Its principal author was Sir Archibald Primrose (1616–79).

Text of Act pr. in *The Acts of the Parliaments of Scotland* [1124–1707], ed. T. Thomson–C. Innes for the Record Commission, vii (1820), p. 86 f.

RESERVATION. The practice of keeping the Bread (and occasionally also the Wine) consecrated at the Eucharist, primarily for the purpose of Holy Communion. The earliest mention of Reservation occurs in the First Apology of St. *Justin Martyr (cap. 65). It is frequently referred to in the 2nd–4th cents., e.g. in *Tertullian, St. *Cyprian and St. *Basil. When Communion was frequent but Masses comparatively rare, the faithful kept the Bl. Sacrament in their homes or carried It on their persons, as being the safest places, and this practice long survived; and among the hermits, who often lived at a great distance from a church, the custom survived until the 13th and 14th cents. But from the Constantinian era (4th cent.) the churches were increasingly the ordinary places for reservation. Here the Sacrament was kept either in the sacristy, as is attested for the 6th cent. in Gaul, and still in the 16th cent. for parts of N. Italy, or in the church itself, either in an *aumbry (q.v.) in the wall, or in a *pyx (q.v.) hanging over the altar, or in a *tabernacle (q.v.) on the altar, the last being the normal modern RC practice. From the beginning reservation under the Species of Bread only seems to have been the most common practice both in E. and W. But from the 11th cent. developed the modern E. custom, acc. to which the Host is dipped into the consecrated Wine and then artificially dried. The Sacrament, thus prepared, is used in the E. for the Communion of the sick as well as for the Liturgies of the *Presanctified in the season of *Lent.

In the 16th cent. the First BCP of 1549 provided for the Communion of the sick by reservation of the Sacrament at the open Communion and the carrying of It to the sick man as soon as convenient, though it also allowed the priest to celebrate in the sick person's house. In the Second BCP of 1552, the provision for reservation ceased and it was not replaced in Elizabeth's English Book of 1559. In the Latin Prayer Book of Elizabeth (1560), however, the two provisions for sick Communions in the 1549 BCP came back. The (present) BCP of 1661 retained the regulations of 1559; but, apparently to prevent the use for profane purposes of any of the consecrated Sacrament left over, it ordered that the priest and such other of the communicants as he summoned should reverently consume what remained immediately after the blessing. Anglican divines opposed to the practice have argued that this rubric, in conjunction with the statement in the *Thirty-Nine Articles that the Sacrament of the Lord's Supper was not commanded by Christ's ordinance to be kept, is prohibitive of reservation in the C of E. Those who defend it commonly maintain that in view of the circumstances mentioned the rubric is irrelevant to the issue. As a matter of history, the practice had died out in the C of E, except in very rare instances, before the beginning of the 19th cent., but it has now been widely restored. In the Scottish Episcopal Church it has remained customary and a note in the Scottish Liturgy declares it to be lawful. The rubrics which would have permitted the practice in the proposed English Prayer Books of 1927 and 1928 largely contributed to the defeat of the Prayer Book Measure in Parliament.

D. *Stone, *The Reserved Sacrament* (1917); W. H. Freestone, *The Sacrament Reserved* (Alcuin Club Collections, No. XXI, 1917); *Reservation*. Report of a Conference held at Farnham Castle on 24–27 Oct. 1925 (S.P.C.K., 1926); G. Dix, *A Detection of Aumbries* (1942).

RESERVATION, Mental. See *Mental Reservation.*

RESERVED SINS. In conformity with the early practice, which restricted the administration of penance to a bishop, bishops in the RC Church have retained the right to 'reserve' certain sins to their own jurisdiction. The reservation may be either as to the sin or as to the censure—excommunication, &c.—imposed on the sin, a distinction corresponding to that between the internal and external *forum. Some sins are reserved by a general law, others by a particular enactment. In normal cases absolution for reserved sins may be granted only by the authority making the reservation, his successor, superior, or delegate. But on death-beds, and in cases of great urgency, any priest may absolve, though if a censure is involved subsequent ratification by the proper authority is normally required. A few very grave matters are reserved to the Pope. The system is not so irksome as it sounds on account both of the number of delegates who may absolve and the excepting clause of urgency. In the C of E the practice of such reservation of sins does not obtain.

See *Codex Iuris Canonici*, Nos. 893–900, 2245–54.

RESIDENCE. All clergy are under a grave obligation to reside personally in the place in which they are authorized to minister. From very early times, owing to the frequent abuse of non-residence, this injunction figures in the canons. Combined with the holding of livings in plurality, which non-residence makes possible, the abuse was at its worst during the Middle Ages. The Council of *Trent took reforming action (Sessions IV and XXIII). In RC *canon law, the place and time of residence for all grades of clergy are precisely laid down (*CIC*, cans. 143, 238, 338, and 465). In the C of E residence is required by the English *Canons of 1604, Nos. 41–7.

RESPONSES. See *Versicles.*

RESPONSORY (Lat. *Responsorium*). Liturgical chant consisting of a series of *versicles and responses, the text of which is usually taken from Scripture. The arrangement was designed for the alternate singing of its sentences or lines by the celebrant and choir. The 'cantus responsorius', which is mentioned already by *Tertullian, goes back to the worship of the synagogue. The responsories of the Mass are the *Gradual, the *Alleluia, and formerly also the *Offertory. In the Latin Divine Office the responsories, which generally include the first part of the *'Gloria Patri' and vary acc. to the office, follow the Lessons at Matins. They were prescribed already by the Rule of St. *Benedict (*c.* 530). In the Roman *Breviary a shorter form, called 'responsorium breve', follows the *Little Chapter at the Little Hours and *Compline, in the Monastic Office at *Lauds and *Vespers; they vary only slightly, esp. in Passion- and Paschal-tide.

RESTITUTION. In W. moral theology, the act of 'commutative justice' by which an injury done to the goods or person of another is repaired. The duty of restitution arises from the unjust detention or damage to another's property. If the possessor of another's property has been in good faith, he is bound to make restitution if the goods are still extant, together with the fruits derived from them, unless they have been gained by his own industry. If, however, the property has perished, there is no such obligation. On the other hand, in the case of a possessor in bad faith, he must restore the goods together with a compensation if they have suffered deterioration, and if they have perished he must make restitution acc. to the value they had at the time they were stolen. In the case of possession of property in doubtful faith, the possessor is bound to investigate; but, if the question of ownership cannot be cleared up, he may keep the property. In the case of wilful damage done to another's property restitution must be made as far as possible for the damage done as well as for consequent losses which were to be foreseen. The same principles hold good for the damage to another's reputation, health, life, or chastity.

RESTORATION, The. Among English historians, a title for the re-establishment of the Monarchy under *Charles II in 1660, and by extension the period immediately subsequent to this event. Its use dates from the 18th cent.

RESURRECTION, Community of the. See *Community of the Resurrection.*

RESURRECTION OF CHRIST, The. That the Lord Jesus, after His death and burial, rose again on the third day is a fundamental tenet of Christian belief, asserted in the NT and the Creeds. It was the Resurrection which gave the Apostles, who on Christ's arrest 'all forsook him and fled' (Mk. 14. 50), the renewal of faith and enabled and inspired them to preach the Gospel; and in that preaching the fact of the Resurrection was itself basic (cf. Acts 2. 22–36, 1 Pet. 1. 3). At a date before most of the NT Books were written, St. *Paul testifies to this fact as part of the Gospel which he had 'received' (1 Cor. 15. 1–7), stating that Christ both 'was raised' from the dead and 'was seen' (ὤφθη) by, or 'appeared to', Cephas (*Peter; cf. Lk. 24. 34), to 'the twelve' (Lk. 20. 36 ff.; Jn. 20. 19 ff.), to more than five hundred brethren at once, to *James, and to all the Apostles (cf. perhaps Mt. 28. 16 ff.). It should be noted that the tradition received by St. Paul does not merely say that after His crucifixion Christ 'appeared' to these persons, but, by stating, before mentioning the appearances, that Christ 'was buried' and then 'was raised' (1 Cor. 15. 3 f.), points to an objective Resurrection in which Christ's human body no longer remained in the tomb.

The Gospels amplify this belief of St. Paul by stating that the disciples received their earliest intimation of the Resurrection through the discovery by St. *Mary Magdalene and other women that the body of Christ was missing from the tomb and the words of a 'young man' (or angel) to them that He was risen from the dead (Mk. 16. 1–8, Mt. 28. 1–10, Lk. 24. 1–12, Jn. 20. 1–9). Acc. to Mk. and Mt. the disciples were bidden to go to *Galilee, acc. to Lk. and Jn. Christ showed Himself first in and near *Jerusalem to Mary Magdalene (Jn. 20. 11–18), to Peter (Lk. 24. 34; cf. 1 Cor. 15. 5), to two disciples who were walking to *Emmaus (Lk. 24. 13–35), and to the Apostles who were gathered together in the city (Lk. 24. 36 ff., Jn. 20. 19–23). Jn. records appearances to the Apostles again in Jerusalem a week later (Jn. 20. 24–29), and, later, in Galilee (Jn. 21. 1–23, cf. Mt. 28. 16–20).

It is clear from the NT that the Resurrection was in no sense a restoration of Jesus to an earthly life as He had previously lived it; but neither was it merely a series of visions which assured the disciples that Jesus was still alive and present with them in spiritual power. The event is rather a mighty act of God, by which Jesus 'was raised up' (ἠγέρθη, passive) and exalted by the Father to His rightful position of glory at the Father's right hand (Acts 2. 22–36, etc.). It was the victory of Christ over death, with results not only for Himself but for all Christians (1 Pet. 1. 3 f., cf. 1 Cor. 15. 14), and hence the beginning of a new era (Jn. 20. 17, Mt. 28. 16). It is true that the details of the time and place of the appearances by which the disciples were convinced of this fact and commissioned to proclaim it appear somewhat confusedly in the Gospels. In the genuine text of Mk. the accounts of the Resurrection-appearances are lost, or were perhaps deliberately omitted, though the fear of the women (16. 8) marks the sense of a great supernatural event. While the accounts in Mt. and Lk. might be read as each referring to a single day only, Jn. shows that the events extended over somewhat more than eight days, and Acts (correcting or amplifying Lk. 24) fixes the period at forty days closing with the *Ascension near Jerusalem. To this St. Paul adds the appearance to himself on the Damascus road. But on the significance of the Resurrection as Christ's conquest of death and entrance into His Glory with its far-reaching consequences, all the NT writers are agreed. This is shown by the way in which it is inseparably connected in thought with the Passion (Lk. 24. 26, etc), with the Christian life (Col. 3. 1–11), and even with belief in God (Rom. 4. 24, 1 Pet. 1. 21).

In modern times NT critics have drawn attention to the difficulties in the Gospel accounts of the Resurrection, particularly the discrepancy between the 'Galilee' tradition of Mk. and Mt. and the 'Jerusalem' tradition known to Lk. It has been held by liberal critics (D. *Strauss, E. *Renan) that the whole story sprang from subjective visions first of the women at the tomb and then of other disciples, influenced by their intense love for Christ and their excited mental state. The chief objection to this view is that the disciples clearly had no expectation that Jesus would survive death such as would predispose them to such experiences, but on the contrary were amazed and at first sceptical. Indeed they are expressly said to have distinguished between seeing the spirit of one dead and the experience which they had of Christ's bodily presence (Lk. 24. 37 ff.). Another view (T. *Keim, B. H. *Streeter) is that while the visions which the disciples saw were indeed Divinely authenticated and sufficient evidence that Christ had overcome death and thenceforth reigned in glory, His material body was not actually raised from the tomb. Either the wrong tomb was visited by the women and Peter and John or the body of Jesus had been removed, unknown to them, by some other persons. This conflicts with the evidence of the grave clothes (Jn. 20. 5), to say nothing of the improbability of such an elementary mistake not being discovered within a short time. Advocates of this view often allege on *a priori* grounds that the resuscitation of a material body is irrelevant to the reality of Christ's conquest of death, and its appearance in the Gospel narratives arises from ideas which must be discarded in the light of modern knowledge. But this contention ignores the difference between ideas of the immortality of the soul, which were well known in the contemporary world, and the quite distinct Christian doctrine of the *resurrection of the dead (see foll. ent.), acc. to which not a disembodied spirit, but the complete personality consisting of body and soul, ultimately possesses eternal life.

The subject is treated by St. *Thomas Aquinas, *Summa Theologica*, iii, qq. 54 ('De Qualitate Christi Resurgentis'), 55 ('De Manifestatione Resurrectionis'), and 56 ('De Resurrectionis Christi Causalitate'); also by the commentators on these questions, notably F. *Suarez, S.J. Modern works include B. F. *Westcott, *The Gospel of the Resurrection* (1866); W. Milligan, *The Resurrection of Our Lord* (1881); W. J. Sparrow Simpson, *Our Lord's Resurrection* (1905); id., *The Resurrection and Modern Theology* (1911); B. H. *Streeter in *Foundations* (1912), esp. pp. 127-45; E. G. Selwyn in *Essays, Catholic and Critical* (1926), pp. 279-319; A. M. Ramsey, *The Resurrection of Christ* (1945).

RESURRECTION OF THE DEAD. The

belief that at the *Parousia or 'Second Coming' of Christ departed souls will be restored to a bodily life and the saved will enter in this renewed form upon the life of heaven is a fundamental element in the Christian doctrine of man's final destiny. The doctrine of resurrection appears in a few late passages in the OT; it was held by many Jews at the time of Christ's ministry; and it was clinched for Christian believers by the *Resurrection of Christ Himself. It can be combined with the Greek doctrine of the natural immortality of the soul, but the two doctrines are independent and different, since resurrection implies (1) that the full redeemed life of heaven must include a restoration of the whole psychophysical organism, because man was created by God to be and to remain an embodied spirit;

and (2) that the life after death is wholly the gift of God, and not due to the inherently immortal nature of man's soul. It has at times been the prevailing view that the resurrection will involve a collection and revivifying of the material particles of the dead body. Many theologians, however, following the principles of St. Paul, hold that the resurrection body will be new and 'spiritual' (1 Cor. 15. 35-54), i.e. a body of a new order, the perfect instrument of the spirit, raised above the limitations of the earthly body, with which it will be identical only in the sense that it will be the recognizable organism of the same personality. Commonly it is held that all the dead, whether saved or not, will rise to pass under judgement; but with some support in the NT it may be held that resurrection in any full sense will be confined to those destined to eternal life.

R. H. *Charles, *A Critical History of the Doctrine of a Future Life in Israel, in Judaism and in Christianity* (Jowett Lectures for 1898-9; 1899). J. T. Darragh, *The Resurrection of the Flesh* (S.P.C.K., 1921). W. Milligan, *The Resurrection of the Dead*. An Exposition of 1 Corinthians xv (1894). A. Michel in *D.T.C.*, xiii (pt. 2; 1937), cols. 2502-71, s.v. 'Résurrection des morts'. See also items cited under previous entry.

RETABLE. A structure placed at the back

of an altar in the form either of a ledge on which ornaments may be set or of a frame for decorated panels. The ledge form is also known as a *gradine, the form for panels also as a *reredos.

RETREAT. A period of days spent in silence,

and occupied with meditation and other religious exercises. In essence the practice is older than Christianity, but the forty days Christ spent in the wilderness have been considered to give the ultimate authority for its Christian use. As a formal devotion, retreats were introduced in the *Counter-Reformation period. The *Jesuits, who were the first religious order to include them in their rule, also counselled them to those outside their body. A little later St. *Francis de Sales and St. *Vincent de Paul became strong advocates of the practice. In the 17th cent. retreat houses were instituted, where those who wished to make a retreat might stay for short periods under the guidance of 'conductors'. In the RC Church, the practice of annual retreat became widespread early in the 19th cent., at first for the clergy, both *regular and *secular, but soon also for many of the laity. In the C of E the practice of retreat was adopted under the influence of the *Oxford Movement, the first formal retreat being held in 1856 in Christ Church, Oxford.

R. Schofield (ed.), *Retreats*. Their Value, Organisation and Growth (1915); id., new work with same title but different contributors (1927). A. T. Cameron, *Directory of Retreat Houses and other Places of Retreat* [C of E] (1925). P. Debuchy in *C.E.*, xii (1911), pp. 795-7, s.v. D. *Stone in *H.E.R.E.*, x (1918), p. 743 f., s.v., with bibl.

RETZ, CARDINAL DE (Jean François

Paul de Gondi) (1614-79), Abp. of Paris. Destined to an ecclesiastical career by his family, in whose hands the archiepiscopal see of Paris had been since 1569, he was a member of St. *Vincent de Paul's Tuesday Conferences and was appointed Coadjutor-Archbishop to his uncle, Jean François, in 1643. His inclination towards a secular life and political intrigues led him to take a prominent part in the activities of the Fronde (1648–9) against J. *Mazarin. After being temporarily reconciled to Louis XIV, at whose suggestion he was created Cardinal by *Innocent X in 1652, he soon lost favour and was imprisoned at Mazarin's instigation. On the death of his uncle in 1654, his plenipotentiaries took possession of the see of Paris and, a few months after, he escaped from prison. He went to Spain and from there to Rome, where he took part in the election of *Alexander VII in 1655. After a series of adventures and intrigues in Italy, Germany, and other countries, he returned to Paris in 1661, was finally reconciled to the king, and resigned his see in the following year in exchange for the rich abbey of St. Denis. He took an active part in the subsequent conflicts between Louis XIV and the Popes and in the conclaves which elected Clement IX, Clement X, and *Innocent XI. His *Memoirs*, begun in 1671, are famous for their literary charm and for their political judgements.

Works ed. J. Gourdault–R. Chantelauze, with notes by M. A. Feillet and appendix to his correspondence by C. Cochin (11 vols., Paris, 1870–1920). Memoirs, first publ. 3 vols., Nancy, 1717, first ed. from autograph MSS., Paris, 1837; modern ed. by G. Mongrédien (4 vols., Paris, 1935), with biogr. preface, vol. i, pp. vi–xxxviii and bibl. pp. xli–xliii; Eng. trr. of his Memoirs, London, 1723, 1774, and 1904. M. Topin, *Le Cardinal de Retz* (1863); A. Gazier, *Les Dernières Années du Cardinal de Retz, 1655–1679* (1875); R. Chantelauze, *Le Cardinal de Retz et l'affaire du chapeau* (2 vols., 1878); id., *Le Cardinal de Retz et ses missions diplomatiques à Rome, d'après les documents inédits des archives du Ministère des Affaires Étrangères* (1879). D. Ogg, *Cardinal de Retz, 1613–1679* (1912); L. Batiffol, *Le Cardinal de Retz* (1927); id., *Biographie du Cardinal de Retz* (1929); J. Dyssord (pseudonym of J. M. de Bellaing), *Le Cardinal de Retz: conspirateur né* (1938).

REUCHLIN, JOHANNES (1455–1522), German humanist. He studied Latin and Greek at Freiburg i.Br., *Paris, and Basle, where he compiled a Latin lexicon, *Vocabularius Breviloquus* (1475), which became very popular. Having become a Master of Arts in 1477, he studied law at Orléans and Poitiers and took his degree as licentiate in 1481. In 1482 he accompanied Count Eberhard of Württemberg to Rome as his interpreter and later became his adviser and ambassador. C. 1485 he began to study Hebrew with the help of learned Jews and became interested in *Cabbalistic doctrines, expounding the latter in *De Verbo Mirifico* (1494) and later in *De Arte Cabbalistica* (1517), both full of abstruse speculations on sacred letters. Owing to the hostility of Eberhard's successor he fled to Heidelberg in 1496, where he wrote his spirited Latin comedies *Sergius* and *Henno* in imitation of Terence, and perfected his Hebrew knowledge. After the deposition of Eberhard's son in 1498, he returned to Württemberg, where he became one of the three justices in the

Swabian League in 1502. In 1506 he published his most important work, *De Rudimentis Hebraicis*. Consisting of a Hebrew grammar and lexicon, it placed the hitherto almost neglected scientific study of the Hebrew language on an entirely new basis and became a powerful incentive to the study of the OT in the original. It was supplemented by an edition of the *Seven Penitential Psalms in Hebrew with a Latin translation (1512), and a treatise on Hebrew accents, *De Accentibus et Orthographia Linguae Hebraicae* (1518). The latter years of his life were troubled by his controversy with the Jewish convert, Johann Pfefferkorn, and the *Dominican friars of Cologne on the destruction of the Jewish books, which Reuchlin opposed in the interests of scholarship. Bitter pamphlets were produced on both sides, the most celebrated being the *Epistolae Obscurorum Virorum* (1515–17, q.v., in which Reuchlin and his friends stood for the modern learning against the Dominicans, esp. Jakob von Hochstraten (d. 1527), who represented the old Scholastic tradition. In the course of the controversy Reuchlin became involved in a trial for heresy in which both parties appealed repeatedly to Rome and which was finally decided against him by *Leo X in 1520. As a result his satirical pamphlet, *Augenspiegel* (1511), was forbidden and he was condemned to defray the costs of the trial. Though many of the Reformers took part in the controversy on the side of Reuchlin, he himself remained a loyal Catholic and endeavoured hard to detach his grandnephew, P. *Melanchthon, from his friendship with M. *Luther.

The standard life is that of L. Geiger (Leipzig, 1871). Correspondence ed. id. (Bibliothek des litterarischen Vereins in Stuttgart, cxxvi; 1875). A. Horawitz, 'Zur Biographie und Correspondenz Johannes Reuchlins' in *Sb.* (Wien), lxxxv (1877), pp. 117–90. K. Christ, *Die Bibliothek Reuchlins in Pforzheim* (Beiheft zum Zentralblatt für Bibliothekswesen, lii; 1924). *Festschrift der Stadt Pforzheim zur Erinnerung an dem 400. Todestag Reuchlins* (Pforzheim [1922]). F. Barham, *The Life and Times of John Reuchlin* (1843). S. A. Hirsch, *A Book of Essays* (1905), pp. 116–50 ('Johann Reuchlin, The Father of the Study of Hebrew among Christians'). G. Kawerau in *P.R.E.* (ed. 3), xvi (1905), pp. 680–8, s.v.; W. R. *Smith in *E.B.* (ed. 11), xxiii (1911), pp. 204–6, s.v. K. Bihlmeyer in *L.Th.K.*, viii (1936), col. 847 f., s.v., for further bibl.

REUNION. Desire for the restoration of intercommunion between the Christian Churches has greatly increased since the end of the 19th cent., largely through the common struggle against paganism. The problems vary acc. to the different bodies of Christians between which it is envisaged.

Reunion between the C of E and the RC Church has been often considered since the 17th cent., notably in the time of the *Oxford and post-*Tractarian Movements, and again at the *Malines Conferences (1921–5). Its main conditions on the part of Rome are submission in all matters of doctrine and recognition of Papal supremacy. (See also *Wake, W.*, and *Anglican Ordinations*.)

Reunion with the Orthodox Church has also been frequently attempted by both the Roman and non-Roman Churches. After the

short - lived union between E. and W. at
*Florence (1439) there were other less import-
ant *rapprochements*. Those of the *Non-jurors
(1716–25) came to nothing, as did several
attempts in the 19th cent., including the
Conferences at *Bonn in 1874 and 1875. In
1906 the '*Anglican and Eastern Orthodox
Churches Union' was founded, and the *Lambeth Conference of 1908 appointed a Committee to confer with the E. Patriarchs. In
recent years progress has been made on the
question of the validity of *Anglican Ordinations.

Schemes for reunion between the C of E
and foreign Protestant bodies have often been
under discussion. In 1841 a scheme was set
on foot for a joint Anglican and *Lutheran
Bishop in *Jerusalem, by which the Prussian
King, Frederick William IV, intended to
introduce episcopacy into his Church. The
scheme, which was strenuously opposed by
the High Church party, proved a failure. One
of the few successful attempts at reunion with
foreign religious bodies was that between the
C of E and the *Old Catholics (1932).

There have been several efforts at uniting
English dissenting bodies with the Established
Church. At the Restoration an attempt was
made to 'comprehend' *Presbyterians and
*Independents, but the *Savoy Conference
(1661) failed, and similar suggestions made in
1688 were without success. In the middle of
the 18th cent. there were rather half-hearted
attempts at conversations. In the 19th cent.
reunion between the C of E and the Free
Churches was advocated by T. *Arnold in his
Principles of Church Reform (1832), A. P.
*Stanley (1834), Thomas *Chalmers (1843),
and by W. T. Mowbray, the founder of the
Home Reunion Society (1873). The *Lambeth
Conference of 1888 laid down four conditions
for such reunion known as the '*Lambeth
Quadrilateral' (q.v.). The *Kikuyu Conference (1913, q.v.) showed a widespread desire
among missionaries for federation and intercommunion without waiting for dogmatic
agreements or uniformity in Church order.
As a result of the 'Appeal to all Christian
People', issued by the Lambeth Conference
of 1920, exploratory conversations took place
between representatives of the C of E and the
Federal Council of Evangelical Free Churches
(1920–5), and further conversations followed
the Lambeth Conference of 1930. The main
difficulties have turned on the question of the
ministry and on varied interpretations of what
is meant by the 'historic episcopate'. A third
series of conversations followed a suggestion of
the Abp. of *Canterbury (G. F. Fisher) in 1946,
in a Cambridge University Sermon, that without
surrendering their identity the Free Churches
might 'take episcopacy into their system' and
thus prepare the way for intercommunion in
England.

In other parts of the world a number of
unions have taken place. The Church of
*South India, established in 1947, consists
of those formerly members of the Church
of India, Burma, and Ceylon, and a Church

already uniting former Presbyterians, *Methodists, and *Congregationalists. A scheme for
a united Church of *Ceylon, embracing Anglicans, Methodists, Presbyterians and *Baptists
is under consideration. The United Church
of *Canada was established in 1925 and includes former Presbyterians, Methodists and
Congregationalists. Various Christian bodies
in *Japan have united. The Evangelical and
Reformed Church of the *United States is seeking to unite with the Congregational Christian
Church, and closer relationships which may
lead to union are being fostered between the
Northern Convention Baptists and the *Disciples of Christ.

In 1929 various Presbyterian Churches reunited with the Established Church of *Scotland; and in 1939 Reformed and Free Churches
in *France came together. In 1932 the
Methodist Church of Great Britain was formed
by the union of several Methodist bodies and
in 1939 three Methodist communions in the
United States united.

Almost all interconfessional discussions are
now influenced by the steady growth of world
confessional organizations and by the *Faith
and Order movement which has become a part
of the *World Council of Churches.

See also *Oecumenical Movement.*

G. K. A. Bell (ed.), *Documents on Christian Unity, 1920–
1924* (1924); ib., Second Series, *1924–30* (1930); ib., Third
Series, *1930–48* (1948). J. H. *Shakespeare, *The Churches at
the Cross Roads* (1918); S. L. Ollard, *Reunion* (1919); A. C.
*Headlam, *The Doctrine of the Church and Christian Reunion*
(1920); G. J. Slosser, *Christian Unity. Its History and
Challenge* (1929); H. L. Goudge, *The Church of England and
Reunion* (1938); K. D. Mackenzie (ed.), *Union of Christendom*
(1938); G. K. A. Bell, *Christian Unity.* The Anglican Position
(1948). For the theology of reunion, cf. M. J. Congar,
O. P., *Chrétiens désunis* (1937; Eng. trans., *Divided Christendom*, 1939). H. R. T. Brandreth, *Unity and Reunion.* A
Bibliography (1945; ed. 2 1948).

**REUSCH, FRANZ HEINRICH (1825–
1900),** *Old Catholic theologian. He taught at
Bonn from 1854, holding a full professorship
in OT exegesis from 1861 onwards. Throughout his life he was closely associated with
his former teacher J. J. I. von *Döllinger, and
shared his intellectual ideals as well as his liberal
views of Church history. In 1870 he strongly
opposed the infallibility decrees of the *Vatican
Council and in 1872 was excommunicated on
his refusal to subscribe. Thereafter he took a
leading part in organizing in its earlier years
the *Old Catholic Church and in arranging
the Reunion Conferences which were held at
*Bonn in 1874 and 1875. When, however, the
Old Catholics abolished clerical celibacy in
1878, Reusch objected and retired into lay
communion. An untiring student, Reusch
wrote many books, his earlier ones dealing
with OT subjects and his later ones mainly
with modern ecclesiastical history. Much of
his best work was done in conjunction with
Döllinger, notably a history of post-Tridentine
moral theology (*Geschichte der Moralstreitigkeiten in der römisch-katholischen Kirche seit dem
XVI. Jahrhundert*, 2 vols., 1889). His other
writings include *Luis de Leon und die spanische
Inquisition* (1873); *Der Prozess Galileis und die*

Jesuiten (1879); and *Index der verbotenen Bücher* (2 vols., 1883–5).

Life by L. K. Götz, incl. list of Reusch's works (Gotha, 1901). [Dr.] Menn, 'Fritz Heinrich Reusch als Schriftsteller' in *Revue internationale de Théologie*, xiv (1906), pp. 38–72, 462–8, 729–44; xv (1907), pp. 75–93, 462–80. L. K. Goetz in *P.R.E.* (ed. 3), xvi (1905), pp. 689–91.

REVELATION. In Christian theology the word is used both of the *corpus* of truth about Himself which God discloses to us and of the process by which His communication of it takes place. Traditional theology has tended to conceive of revelation in the latter sense as taking place through propositions; but there has been an increasing tendency among many recent theologians to insist that Divine revelation reaches us largely, and even primarily, through God's activity (His 'mighty acts', *magnalia Dei*; cf. Acts 2. 11), rather than in propositional statements. Since it is commonly held that there are certain truths about God which can be learnt through man's natural endowments (e.g. His existence, which such philosophers as *Aristotle who were outside the Christian covenant believed that they could establish), while others, e.g. the Doctrine of the Holy *Trinity, are not knowable except by faith, Christian philosophers have often held that a sharp distinction must be drawn between 'truths of reason' and 'truths of revelation'. This distinction received its classical elaboration by St. *Thomas Aquinas. It has its counterpart in the antithesis between 'natural theology' and 'revealed theology'. Over against this, there has been another school of theologians who have held that truths of revelation and truths of reason differ only in degree. When revelation has once been formulated, it is known as '*dogma' (q.v.). While Christians of the Protestant tradition hold that all revelation is sufficiently contained in Holy Scripture, Catholics commonly maintain that part of it is also to be found in the unwritten traditions of the Church.

Modern discussions include A. B. *Bruce, *The Chief End of Revelation* (1881); J. R. *Illingworth, *Reason and Revelation. An Essay in Christian Apology* (1902); E. *Brunner, *Philosophie und Offenbarung* (1925); id., *Offenbarung und Vernunft. Die Lehre von der christlichen Glaubenserkenntnis* (Zürich, 1941; Eng. tr. as *Revelation and Reason*, 1947); P. *Tillich, 'Die Idee der Offenbarung' in *Zeitschrift für Theologie und Kirche*, N.F., viii (1927), pp. 403–12; J. Baillie–H. Martin (edd.), *Revelation* (1927); R. *Bultmann, *Der Begriff der Offenbarung im Neuen Testament* (Sammlung gemeinverständischer Vorträge und Schriften aus dem Gebiet der Theologie und Religionsgeschichte, cxxxv; 1929); H. Dieckmann, *De Revelatione Christiana*. Tractatus Philosophico-Historicus (Freiburg i.Br., 1930); J. Baillie, *The Idea of Revelation in the Light of Recent Discussion* (1956). N. Iung in *D.T.C.*, xiii (pt. 2; 1937), cols. 2580–2618, s.v. 'Révélation', with bibl.

REVELATION, Book of. The last Book of the NT and the only one of its Books which is an *Apocalypse. Its author, described in the title as 'John the Divine', has traditionally been identified with St. *John the Apostle.

At the time of writing, the author was in the island of *Patmos 'for the Word of God and the testimony of Jesus' (1. 9). He prefaces his Book with letters to the 'Seven Churches of Asia' (*Ephesus, Smyrna, *Pergamum, *Thyatira, Sardis, *Philadelphia, and *Laodicea). The remainder of the Book consists of a series of visions. In the first the author sees the glory of God and the worship of twenty-four 'elders' and four 'living creatures' (4). A book is seen, sealed with seven seals which Christ alone has power to open (5). As the first six seals are opened, four horsemen appear, the approach of the end is revealed (6), the 144,000 faithful of the twelve tribes of Israel are sealed on the forehead and an innumerable multitude of the redeemed is seen in Heaven (7). The opening of the seventh seal begins a series of seven trumpet-calls, sounded by seven angels and heralding various disasters (8 f.). The voice of 'the seven thunders' is heard; but the seer is bidden not to record it and the angel's book is given him to eat (10. 1–11. 14). The seventh trumpet-call is followed by the proclamation of the Kingdom of God and of Christ (11. 15–19). Then follow two general eschatological visions: a woman who is persecuted by a dragon, and war in heaven between the angelic hosts led by *Michael and *Satan (12); and then a further pair of visions of a beast from the sea which blasphemes against God and a beast from the earth which compels all men to worship the first beast under threat of death (13; see *Number of the Beast*). Next comes the execution of judgement on 'Babylon the Great', followed by world-judgement described under images of the harvest, the vintage, and the 'pouring-out' from seven vials of the wrath of God (14–16). The destruction of Babylon, now described as a harlot 'arrayed in purple and scarlet', is vividly portrayed (17 f.). There follows the 'marriage-supper of Christ' ('the Lamb', also 'the Word of God') who is represented as a warrior riding in triumph. The beast and the 'false prophet' are destroyed in a great battle and Satan is 'bound' for a thousand years (the *Millennium) and finally cast into the lake of brimstone for ever (19 f.). The Book concludes with the general resurrection and judgement of souls, the 'New Heaven and New Earth' and the 'New Jerusalem' (21. 1–22. 5), and an epilogue (22. 6–22. 21).

The Book, which was prob. known to *Papias, is already ascribed by St. *Justin to the Apostle John. This attribution was accepted in the *Muratorian Canon, and by *Tertullian and St. *Hippolytus and (except by *Gaius, who assigned it to *Cerinthus) generally followed in the West. In the East, however, it was widely rejected, notably by *Marcion, the so-called *Alogi, St. *Dionysius of Alexandria (who argued against its Apostolic authorship on the ground of differences in style and content from the Fourth Gospel and believed it to be the work of some other John) and *Eusebius. Some subsequent E. writers and Councils (St. *Cyril of Jerusalem, Council of *Laodicea, St. John *Chrysostom, *Theodore of Mopsuestia, *Theodoret) did not include it in the Canon, and it was omitted originally from the *Peshitta (Syriac) and *Armenian versions.

Its bitterly hostile attitude to Rome indicates that the Book cannot be earlier than the persecution under *Nero in 64. But as it is unlikely that this persecution affected Asia Minor the Book prob. dates from some later persecution, perhaps that of the Emp. *Domitian (81–96). If the 'Number of the Beast' is correctly interpreted as referring to the name of Nero, this would then imply that Domitian was a second Nero, reflecting the current superstition that Nero was not really dead, but would return (*Nero redivivus*) as the leader of barbaric hordes.

The Greek of the Book, both in grammar and vocabulary, is often barbarous. Although there are points of contact with the Fourth Gospel, notably the use of the titles 'Lamb (of God)' and 'Word of God' applied to Christ, not found elsewhere in the NT, there are also wide differences of outlook which seem to many scholars conclusive against a common authorship. Also the fact that the author of Rev. nowhere claims to be an eye-witness of the Incarnate Christ and refers to the twelve Apostles in a reverential and detached manner (21. 14) makes it improbable that he was John the son of Zebedee. It seems reasonable to suppose that the author's real name was indeed John, and that he was an otherwise unknown Christian of Jewish descent living in Asia Minor.

Patristic commentaries include those by *Victorinus of Pettau, *Oecumenius of Tricca, and Andrew of Caesarea (J. P. Migne, *PG*, cvi, 215–486); important medieval commentaries by *Bede, *Richard of St.-Victor, St. *Albert the Great, and *Joachim of Fiore. More modern commentaries include those of T. Brightman (Frankfurt a.M., 1609 [in Lat.]; Eng. tr., 1615), *Cornelius a Lapide (Antwerp, 1627), C. *Vitringa (Franeker, 1705), C. J. *Vaughan (2 vols. London, 1863), W. Milligan (Expositor's Bible, 1889), [H. J.] Holtzmann (H.K.N.T., iv, 1891, on Jn., 1–3 Jn., and Rev., pp. 249–323), W. *Bousset (K.E.K., vi, ed. 5; 1896), J. *Weiss (Forschungen zur Religion und Literatur des Alten und Neuen Testaments, iii; 1904), F. J. A. *Hort (on Rev. 1–3; posthumous, London, 1908), H. B. *Swete (London, 1906), R. H. *Charles (2 vols., I.C.C., 1920), E. B. Allo, O.P. (Études bibliques, 1921), A. *Loisy (Paris, 1923), T. *Zahn (Kommentar zum Neuen Testament, xviii; 2 vols., 1924), E. Lohmeyer (Hb. N.T., xvi; 1926; ed. 2, 1953, with detailed bibl.), W. Hadorn (Theologischer Handkommentar zum Neuen Testament, xviii; 1928), M. Kiddle (Moff. Comm., 1940) and J. Bonsirven, S.J. (Verbum Salutis, xvi; Paris, 1952). Collations of Gk. MSS. by H. C. Hoskier (2 vols., London, 1929). Christopher *Wordsworth, *Lectures on the Apocalypse* (Hulsean Lectures for 1848; 1849); F. D. *Maurice, *Lectures on the Apocalypse* (1861); W. Milligan, *The Revelation of St. John* (1886; enlarged as *Lectures on the Apocalypse*, 1892, and *Discussions on the Apocalypse*, 1893). B. *Weiss, *Die Johannes-Apokalypse.* Textkritische Untersuchungen und Textherstellung (T.U., vii, Hft. 1; 1891). F. Boll, *Aus der Offenbarung Johannis.* Hellenistische Studien zum Weltbild der Apokalypse (Στοιχεῖα, i; 1914). A. S. *Peake, *The Revelation of John* (1919). J. E. Carpenter, *The Johannine Writings.* A Study of the Apocalypse and the Fourth Gospel (1927), pp. 3–188. J. *Oman, *The Text of Revelation* (1928). P. Carrington, *The Meaning of Revelation* (S.P.C.K., 1931). E. F. Scott, *The Book of Revelation* (1939). A. M. Farrer, *The Rebirth of Images.* The Making of St. John's Apocalypse (1949). M. E. Boismard, O.P., ' "L'Apocalypse" ou "Les Apoca.ypses" ' de S. Jean' in *R. Bibl.*, lvi (1949), pp. 507–41; id., 'Notes sur l'Apocalypse', ib., lix (1952), pp. 161–81. W. M. *Ramsay, *The Letters to the Seven Churches of Asia and their Place in the Plan of the Apocalypse* (1904).

REVEREND (Lat. *reverendus*, 'worthy of being revered'). An epithet of respect applied to the clergy since the 15th cent. Since the 17th cent. it has been used as a title prefixed to their names in correspondence. Archbishops and the Bp. of Meath (as the 'Premier Bp. of Ireland') are styled 'Most Reverend', other bishops 'Right Reverend', and deans 'Very Reverend'. Abbesses, prioresses, and other nuns who have the title of 'Mother', are also styled 'Reverend'. The Moderator of the Church of Scotland is 'Right Reverend'. *Carthusian priests are an exception, all except the prior-general being styled not 'Reverend' but 'Venerable'. The legal right of Nonconformists to the title was established by the 'Keat Case' in 1876, when a faculty was ordered for the erection of a tombstone on which a *Wesleyan minister was styled 'Reverend', the incumbent having previously refused to allow it to be set up.

REVISED VERSION OF THE BIBLE, The. See *Bible* (*English Versions*), No. 4.

REVIVALISM. A type of religious worship and practice centring in evangelical revivals, or outbursts of mass religious fervour, and stimulated by intensive preaching and prayer meetings. It has been a common feature of the work of many religious bodies since the *Methodist Movement of the 18th cent., where, under the *Wesleys, G. *Whitefield, and others, it was regularly encouraged. Some bodies, e.g. the *Salvation Army, make revivalism the principal element of all their worship.

REVUE BÉNÉDICTINE. A Belgian periodical devoted esp. to the study of Christian Latin literature, issued quarterly from the abbey of *Maredsous. The first 6 vols., under the direction of Dom G. van Caloen, were issued as *Le Messager des fidèles* (1884–9).

REVUE BIBLIQUE. The quarterly periodical on Biblical studies which is published (at Paris) by the *Dominicans established at the convent of St.-Étienne at *Jerusalem. It was founded by M. J. *Lagrange and its first issue appeared in Jan. 1892. Its contributions on matters of Biblical archaeology tend to be of marked distinction.

REYNOLDS, EDWARD (1599–1676), Bp. of *Norwich. He was educated at Merton College, Oxford, and in 1622 appointed preacher at Lincoln's Inn. He had considerable sympathies with the *Puritan Movement, but, though a member of the *Westminster Assembly, did not take the Covenant until 1644. In 1647 he was one of the parliamentary visitors at Oxford, and in 1648–50 was Dean of *Christ Church, and again in 1659, when he was ejected for refusing to subscribe the Engagement. At the Restoration he conformed and took a prominent part in the efforts then made to effect a reconciliation between Episcopalians and Presbyterians. In

1661 he was made Bp. of Norwich. He published many sermons and short devotional works which maintained a wide popularity down to the early 19th cent.

Collected edd. of his works, London, 1658 and 1679; full ed. by A. Chalmers, 6 vols., ib., 1826, with memoir in vol. i, pp. xvii–lxxiv. W. A. J. Archbold in *D.N.B.*, xlviii (1896), p. 40 f.

REYNOLDS, JOHN. See *Rainolds, John.*

RHABANUS MAURUS. See *Rabanus Maurus.*

RHADAGUNDE, St. See *Radegunde, St.*

RHEIMS. See *Reims.*

RHENANUS, BEATUS (1485–1547), German humanist. A native of Schlettstadt, he studied at *Paris from 1503 to 1507, where Jacob *Faber Stapulensis taught *Aristotelian philosophy. From 1511 to 1526 he lived at Basle, where he became interested in the publishing activities of J. *Froben, and from 1526 onwards at Schlettstadt, here pursuing his philosophical and historical studies. His earliest work was a biography of *Geiler of Kaisersberg (1510). Later he produced many editions of the classics and of the Fathers, e.g. of Velleius Paterculus, from a MS. found by him at Murbach (1520), and of *Tertullian (1521). His studies of German antiquities resulted in the *Rerum Germanicarum Libri Tres* (1531), the best German work in critical historical research of the period. In 1540–1 he published the works of his friend, D. *Erasmus, with a Life, in 9 vols. Like him, Rhenanus at first favoured the Reformers, esp. their rejection of *indulgences and *auricular confession, but he changed his attitude when the revolutionary character of Protestantism became more apparent.

Correspondence ed. A. Horawitz–K. Hartfelder (Leipzig, 1886). The primary authority is the life by J. *Sturm (Basle, 1551). A. Horawitz, 'Beatus Rhenanus. Ein biographischer Versuch' in *Sb.* (Wien), lxx (1872), pp. 189–244; id., 'Des Beatus Rhenanus literarische Thätigkeit in den Jahren 1508–1531', ib., lxxi (1872), pp. 643–90; id., 'Des Beatus Rhenanus literarische Thätigkeit in den Jahren 1530–1547', ib., lxxii (1872), pp. 323–76. G. Knod, *Aus der Bibliothek des Beatus Rhenanus.* Ein Beitrag zur Geschichte des Humanismus (Strassburg, 1889). W. Teichmann, 'Die kirchliche Haltung des Beatus Rhenanus' in *Z.K.G.*, xxvi (1905), pp. 363–81. H. Kaiser, 'Aus den letzten Jahren des Beatus Rhenanus' in *Zeitschrift für die Geschichte des Oberrheins*, lxx (1916), pp. 30–52.

RHODES, KNIGHTS OF. See *Hospitallers.*

RHODO (2nd cent.), anti-*Gnostic apologist. A native of Asia Minor who became, for a time, a disciple of *Tatian at Rome, he wrote under the Emp. Commodus (180–192). His works included a treatise against the *Marcionites and a commentary on the *Hexaemeron (Εἰς τὴν Ἐξαήμερον Ὑπόμνημα).

The few surviving fragments, nearly all from *Eusebius, *H.E.*, v, 13, are pr. in M. J. *Routh (ed.), *Reliquiae Sacrae*, i (ed. 2, Oxford, 1846), pp. 435–46; repr. in J. P. Migne, *PG*, v, 1331–8. Bardenhewer, i, 392–4. J. Zellinger in *L.Th.K.*, viii (1936), col. 865.

RHYTHMICAL OFFICE. A form of the *Breviary office, popular in the Middle Ages, in which besides the hymns almost all the other parts except the psalms and lessons were put into metre or rhyme. It developed from the practice of enlarging on the lives of the saints in the *nocturns by additions in rhythm, and was thus also known as a 'Historia'. The construction of such rhythmical offices was a popular diversion for monks possessed of poetic gifts. Among the better-known writers of these offices are St. *Odo (d. 942) and St. *Odilo (d. 1048), abbots of *Cluny, and *Fulbert, Bp. of Chartres (d. 1028).

RICAUT, PAUL. See *Rycaut, Paul.*

RICCI, MATTEO (1552–1610), *Jesuit missionary in China. He entered the Roman College in 1571, where he was specially trained in mathematics, astronomy, and other branches of natural science. In 1578 he was sent to Goa, and in 1582 to Macao, where he studied the Chinese language and civilization. In 1583 he settled at Chao-K'ing, whence he was expelled in 1589, but went to Shao-chow in the same year, to Nanking in 1599, and finally, in 1601, to Peking, where he stayed till his death. Gaining the esteem of the Chinese by displaying and explaining to them European scientific instruments, esp. clocks and a map of the world, he made many converts by skilfully adapting Christianity to Chinese notions. One of the fruits of his missionary experience was his work *The True Doctrine of God* (1595), written in Chinese, as well as a Chinese translation of the Ten Commandments and a Chinese Catechism, which have become standard manuals for many generations of missionaries. His methods, however, which attempted to recommend Christianity to the Chinese by a far-reaching adaptation to their semi-religious ceremonies, gave rise to a protracted controversy after his death which was finally decided against him by *Clement XI in 1704 and 1715.

Opere storiche, ed. P. Tacchi Venturi, S.J. (2 vols., Macerata, 1911–13). Eng. tr. of his Journals of 1583–1610 by L. J. Gallaher, S.J. (New York, 1953). P. M. D' Elia, S.J. (ed.), *Fonti ricciane*. (Reale Accademia d' Italia, 3 vols., 1942–9). H. Bernard, S.J., *Le Père Matthieu Ricci et la société chinoise de son temps, 1552–1610* (2 vols., Tientsin, 1937). D. Jenks, S.S.M., *Six Great Missionaries of the Sixteenth and Seventeenth Centuries* (1930), pp. 80–110. V. Cronin, *The Wise Man from the West* (popular biography; 1955). Sommervogel, vi (1895), cols. 1792–5.

RICCI, SCIPIONE DE' (1741–1810), ecclesiastical reformer. In 1780 he was created Bp. of Pistoia-Prato in Tuscany at the instance of Leopold I. He took the initiative among the Tuscan prelates in introducing into N. Italy *Josephinist doctrines and a higher standard of morals. To this end he founded in 1783 a theological academy at Prato to which he appointed professors in sympathy with his views and carried through a plan of reform at the Synod of *Pistoia in 1786. He was esp. opposed to the excesses (as he held them) of the current devotions to the *Sacred Heart. His proposals, however, met with much opposition and in 1790 he was deposed from his see and retired into private life. Later he became reconciled to the RC Church.

His *Memorie* (ed. by A. Galli, 2 vols., Florence, 1865) is the chief authority. There is also a full Life by L. J. A. de Potter (3 vols., Brussels, 1825).

RICHARD OF CHICHESTER, St. (1197–1253),

Bp. of *Chichester. He was born at 'Wych' (i.e. Droitwich), and is hence sometimes known as 'Richard of Wych'. After studying at Oxford and Paris, he became chancellor of the university of Oxford in 1235 and a little later, under Abp. St. *Edmund Rich, chancellor of *Canterbury. He accompanied St. Edmund in his exile and was with him on his death-bed (1242). In 1244 he was elected Bp. of Chichester but, on the refusal of Henry III, who favoured Richard Passelew, a rival candidate, to surrender the temporalities of the see, he obtained consecration from *Innocent IV at Lyons in 1245. Only under the threat of excommunication did Henry give way. He was a man of deep spirituality and an excellent administrator of his diocese, where he did much to raise the standard of clerical life. He was canonized by Urban IV in 1262. His shrine in Chichester Cathedral, where many cures are said to have been wrought, was destroyed by order of *Henry VIII in 1538. Feast day, 3 Apr.

His Statutes are printed in D. *Wilkins (ed.), *Concilia Magnae Britanniae et Hiberniae*, i (1737), pp. 688–93; his will, with notes by W. H. Blaauw, in *Sussex Archaeological Collections*, i (1848), pp. 164–92. An almost contemporary life by Ralf Bocking, with account of miracles and the bull of canonization, in *AA.SS.*, April I (1675), pp. 282–318. Further life by J. Capgrave, ib., pp. 278–82. Modern life, based on these two, in J. H. *Newman (anon. ed.), *Lives of the English Saints* (1845). J. H. Cooper, 'Some Notes on the Life of Richard of Chichester' in *Sussex Archaeological Collections*, xliv (1901), pp. 184–203. M. R. Capes, O.S.D., *Richard of Wyche, Labourer, Scholar, Bishop and Saint, 1197–1253* [c. 1913]. There is a further 17th cent. MS. life in the British Museum (Lansdowne, 340). Mrs. Tout in *D.N.B.*, xlviii (1896), pp. 202–4. S. L. Ollard in *D.E.C.H.*, p. 514 f., s.v. 'Richard of Wych'.

RICHARD OF MIDDLETON (d. *c.* 1305),

'Ricardus de Mediavilla', Scholastic philosopher. The site of Middleton, his birthplace, is uncertain. After becoming a *Franciscan, he taught philosophy at *Oxford and *Paris Between 1281 and 1285 he wrote a Commentary on the 'Sentences' of *Peter Lombard, notable for its clarity and precision, in which he abandoned at a number of points the *Augustinian doctrines, traditionally defended in his order, in favour of the teaching of St. *Thomas Aquinas. He rejected the thesis that there was an immediate bond of union between the human intellect and God, the uncreated Light, and also denied the validity of St. *Anselm's *Ontological Argument for the being of God. In his 'Quodlibeta' he showed a keen interest in the phenomena of hypnotism.

His commentary on the Sentences was pr. at Venice, c. 1475, 1489, and 1499; also, with the Quodlibeta, at Brescia, 1591. *Quaestio Disputata de Privilegio Martini Papae IV*, first ed. F. M. Delorme, O.F.M. (Quaracchi, 1925). R. Zavalloni, O.F.M., *Richard de Mediavilla et la controverse sur la pluralité des formes. Textes inédits et étude critique* (Philosophes médiévaux, ii; 1951). E. Hocedez, S.J.,

Richard de Middleton. Sa vie, ses œuvres, sa doctrine (S.S.L., vi; 1925). J. Lechner, *Die Sakramentenlehre des Richard von Mediavilla* (Münchener Studien zur Historischen Theologie, v; 1925). P. Rucker, O.F.M., *Der Ursprung unserer Begriffe nach Richard von Mediavilla* (B.G.P.M., xxxi, Hft. 1; 1934). J. Reuss, 'Die theologische Tugend der Liebe nach der Lehre des Richard von Mediavilla' in *Franziskanische Studien*, xxii (1935), pp. 11–43; V. Heynck, O.F.M., 'Die aktuelle Gnade bei Richard von Mediavilla', ib., pp. 297–325. F. Ott, O.F.M. 'Der Kirchenbegriff bei den Scholastikern, besonders bei Richard von Mediavilla', ib., xxv (1938), pp. 331–53; id., 'Die Lehre von der Kirche oder vom mystichen Leib Christi bei Richard von Mediavilla', ib., xxvi (1939), pp. 38–64, 142–66, and 297–312. W. Lampen, O.F.M., 'De Manuscriptis Richardi de Mediavilla, O.F.M.', in *Antonianum*, xvi (1941), pp. 45–52. P. Glorieux, *La Littérature quodlibétique de 1260–1320*, i (Bibliothèque thomiste, v; 1925), pp. 267–73, ii (ib., xxi; 1935), p. 257. Überweg, ii, 480, 489, and bibl. p. 762. C. L. Kingsford in *D.N.B.*, xxvii (1894), p. 356 f., s.v. 'Middleton'. É. Amann in *D.T.C.*, xiii (pt. 2; 1937), cols. 2669–75, s.v. 'Richard de Mediavilla', with detailed bibl. reff. to date.

RICHARD OF ST.-VICTOR (d. 1173),

*Victorine mystic and theologian. Very little is known of his life, beyond the fact that he was a native of Britain who entered the abbey of St.-Victor, where he became a pupil of *Hugh of St.-Victor. His most important treatise was his 'De Trinitate' in six books, in which his main philosophical doctrines are contained; but he also wrote many other works, largely devoted to Scriptural exegesis, e.g., his 'De praeparatione animi ad contemplationem, seu Liber dictus Benjamin minor' and his 'De gratia contemplationis, seu Benjamin maior'. Despite his mystical temperament, Richard insisted on the importance of demonstration and argument in matters of theology, and he emphasized the folly of contentment with an array of mere authorities. In his stress on the need of an empirical basis for the proof of God's existence, he pointed forward to the position of St. *Thomas Aquinas. But unlike St. Thomas he held that it was possible to arrive at the essentials of the Christian doctrine of the Trinity by the processes of speculative reasoning.

Collected ed. of his *Opera*, Venice, 1506; also ed., with brief life by John of Toulouse, a Victorine (Rotterdam, 1650; repr. in J. P. Migne, *PL*, cxcvi, 1–1378). *Sermones et opuscules spirituels inédits*, ed. J. Châtillon–W. J. Tulloch, with Fr. tr. by J. Barthélemy (Bibliothèque de Spiritualité [Bruges], 1951 ff.). Eng. tr. of Selections from his Spiritual Writings, with introd. by Claire Kirchberger (London, 1957). G. *Morin, O.S.B., 'Le Commentaire sur Nahum du pseudo-Julien, une œuvre de Richard de Saint-Victor?' in *R. Bén.*, xxxvi (1925), p. 404 f. J. Chatillon, 'Le Contenu, l'authenticité et la date du *Liber exceptionum* et des *Sermones Centum* de Richard de Saint-Victor' in *Revue du Moyen-Âge latin*, iv (1948), pp. 23–51 and 343–66; id., '*Misit Herodes Rex Manus*. Un opuscule de Richard de Saint-Victor égaré parmi les œuvres de Fulbert de Chartres', ib., vi (1950), pp. 287–98. G. Buonamici, *Riccardo da S. Vittore* (1898). J. Ebner, *Die Erkenntnisse Richards von St. Viktor* (B.G.P.M., xix, Hft. 4; 1917). C. Ottaviano, 'Riccardo di S. Vittore. La vita, le opere, il pensiero' in *Memorie della R. Accademia Nazionale dei Lincei*. Classe di scienze morali, storiche et filologiche, Ser. 6, iv (1933), pp. 411–541. A. M. Éthier, O.P., *Le 'De Trinitate' de Richard de Saint-Victor* (Publications de l'Institut d'Études Médiévales d'Ottawa, ix; Paris–Ottawa, 1939). L. Otto, *Untersuchungen zur theologischen Briefliteratur der Frühscholastik* (B.G.P.M., xxxiv; 1937), pp. 549–657 ('Die theologischen Briefe Richards von St. Viktor'). E. Kulesza, *La Doctrine mystique de Richard de Saint-Victor* (thesis; Éditions de la *Vie spirituelle*; [1925]); J. Chatillon, 'Les Quatre Degrés de la charité d'après Richard de Saint-Victor' in *Revue d'Ascétique et de Mystique*, xx (1939), pp. 236–48; id., 'Les

Trois Modes de la contemplation selon Richard de Saint-Victor' in *Bulletin de Littérature ecclésiastique*, xli (1940), pp. 2–26. G. Dumeige, *Richard de Saint-Victor et l'idée chrétienne de l'amour* (Paris thesis, 1952), with bibl. pp. 171–185. Survey of recent literature on Richard of St. Victor by J. Châtillon in *Revue du Moyen-Âge latin*, viii (1952), pp. 254–64. Überweg, ii, 267–71, with bibl. p. 710. G. Fritz in *D.T.C.*, xiii (pt. 2; 1937), cols. 2676–95, s.v., with bibl.

RICHELIEU, ARMAND JEAN DU PLESSIS (1585–1642), French cardinal and politician. Destined at first for a military career, he became an ecclesiastic in order to secure the bishopric of Luçon which had originally been intended for his elder brother who entered the *Grande Chartreuse in 1602. Having been nominated bishop by *Henry IV in 1606, he was consecrated at Rome in 1607. He administered his diocese wisely, entrusted the *Capuchins and *Oratorians with missions in all the parishes, and encouraged the conversion of Protestants. Chosen to represent the clergy of Poitou in the States General in 1614, he soon gained influence with the queen mother, Maria de Medici, and the young king, Louis XIII, who appointed him Secretary of State in 1616. Dismissed after the assassination of his protector, C. Concini, he retired to Blois and, in 1618, was exiled to *Avignon. During his enforced leisure he wrote his *Défense des principaux points de la foi catholique* (1617) against the *Huguenots, and his famous catechism, *Instruction du chrétien* (1619), which was translated into many languages. He was recalled to Paris in 1619 owing to the influence of the Capuchin Father Joseph, who became his intimate friend and adviser. In 1620 Richelieu effected the reconciliation between the King and his mother and two years later was created cardinal by Gregory XV. He became president of the Council of Ministers in 1624, and from 1629 was chief minister and actual ruler of France. His policy aimed at the establishment of absolutism in France and at the destruction of the Hapsburg-Spanish power in Europe. For the achievement of the former end he fought the Huguenots, who were allied with the feudal aristocracy. They were defeated at La Rochelle in 1628 and their political privileges were abolished. In his foreign policy, on the other hand, he supported the Protestant German princes and *Gustavus Adolphus of Sweden against the Emperor, thus seriously impeding the work of Catholic restoration in Germany. Though an enemy of the *Jesuits, many of whom denounced his policy, he opposed *Jansenism and dispersed the solitaries of *Port-Royal in 1638. He favoured the independence of the French Church from Rome and was even suspected of aiming at being made 'patriarch' and thus concentrating the supreme spiritual power of France in his hands. Abbot General of *Cluny from 1629, he undertook the reform of the *Benedictine Order. He was a patron of art and literature and, in 1635, founded the French Academy. His *Traité de la perfection du chrétien* was published posthumously (1646); it is a brief exposition of the threefold

way of purgation, illumination, and union, prob. largely influenced by the mystic teaching of Father Joseph. See also *Thirty Years War*.

Lettres, instructions diplomatiques et papiers d'état du Cardinal de Richelieu, ed. M. Avenal (Collection des Documents inédits sur l'Histoire de France, 8 vols., 1853–77); crit. ed. of Richelieu's *Testament politique* by L. André (Paris, 1947); facsimile repr. of the 1642 ed. of Richelieu's *Instruction du chrétien*, publd. at Paris, 1944, to commemorate the third centenary of the foundation of the Imprimerie Nationale de France, founded by Louis XIII on Richelieu's advice in 1640. The best ed. of the *Mémoires du Cardinal de Richelieu* (written after his death) is that publd. by the Société de l'Histoire de France, 1907 ff.; see also the *Rapports et notes sur l'édition* publd. by the same Society, 1905 ff. G. Hanotaux–le Duc de la Force, *Histoire du Cardinal de Richelieu* (1893 ff. [vol. vii, 1947]). Other studies include those of R. Lodge ('Foreign Statesmen', London, 1896), J. B. Perkins ('Heroes of the Nations', New York, &c., 1900), H. *Belloc (London, 1930), A. Bailly (Paris, 1934; Eng. tr., 1936), C. J. Burckhardt (Munich, 1935; abridged Eng. tr., 1940), and L. Batiffol (Paris, 1937). G. Fagniez, *Le Père Joseph et Richelieu, 1577–1638* (2 vols., 1894). S. Leathers in *C.M.H.*, iv (1906), ch. 4, pp. 118–57, with full bibl. to date, pp. 873–83. There is an attractive character study by Aldous Huxley, *Grey Eminence* (1941).

RIDLEY, NICHOLAS (c. 1500–55), Bp. of London. After studying at Cambridge, the *Sorbonne, and Louvain, he became Fellow of Pembroke Hall, Cambridge (c. 1530), chaplain to T. *Cranmer (1537), vicar of Herne in Kent (1538), and master (1540) of Pembroke Hall. In 1547 he became Bp. of *Rochester and in 1550, upon E. *Bonner's deprivation, of London. From c. 1535 he had had definite leanings towards the teachings of the Reformers, partly through the study of *Ratramnus's book on the Eucharist, and from the accession of *Edward VI his Protestantism became pronounced. He assisted in the compilation of the BCP of 1549 and in the establishment of Protestantism at Cambridge University. In 1553 he supported the claims of Lady Jane Grey to the Crown, and on Mary's accession was deprived of his see. After the Oxford disputations (1554) he was excommunicated, and, when heresy was made a capital offence, was burned with H. *Latimer at Oxford, 16 Oct. 1555. Like Latimer, he preached on the social injustices of his age, and a sermon he preached before the King was partly the occasion of the foundation of Christ's Hospital, St. Thomas's Hospital, and Bridewell.

Surviving works ed. H. Christmas (Parker Society, i; 1841), with biographical notice, pp. i–xvi; selections also in *The Fathers of the English Church*, iv (1809), pp. 31–267, with account of his life and martyrdom based on J. *Foxe, pp. 3–25; his *A Brief Declaration of the Lord's Supper*, ed. H. C. G. *Moule (1895), with biographical sketch, pp. 1–68. Gloucester Ridley, *The Life of Nicholas Ridley* (1763). Modern life by J. G. Ridley (London, 1957). W. A. J. Archbold in *D.N.B.*, xlviii (1896), pp. 286–90.

RIDSDALE JUDGEMENT. The judgement of the *Judicial Committee of the Privy Council, pronounced on 12 May 1877, acc. to which Eucharistic vestments were declared illegal in the C of E, but the *Eastward Position permitted, provided it did not conceal from the congregation the *manual acts. The defendant in the case was the Rev. C. J. Ridsdale, vicar of St. Peter's, Folkestone.

The Judgement was fully reported as 'The Folkstone Ritual Case' in *The Times* Monday, 14 May, 1877, pp. 11–13.

RIEMENSCHNEIDER, TILMAN (*c.* 1460–1531), German wood carver and sculptor. He was a native of Osterode (Harz) and lived from 1483 until his death at Würzburg, where he became Bürgermeister in 1520. He took a prominent part on the side of the insurgents in the *Peasants' Revolt of 1525. His work, which was in both wood and stone, was marked by deep religious feeling; and now, after three centuries of neglect, it is considered among the most remarkable of the late Gothic style. In his altar pieces he secured unity by focusing the design on a central point. In place of colour, he achieved his effects by the play of light, the texture of his material and the highly expressive faces of his figures. Among his most notable works are the Altar of the Blessed Sacrament in S. Jakobus, Rothenburg ob der Tauber (1499–1504); the tomb of Rudolf von Scherenberg (1496–9) and carvings in the Lady Chapel (1500–5) and on the High Altar (1508–10) in Würzburg Cathedral; and the tomb of the Emp. Henry II and his wife, Cunigunde, in Bamberg Cathedral (1499–1513).

J. Bier, *Die Jugendwerke Tilman Riemenschneiders* (1925); K. Gerstenberg, *Tilman Riemenschneider* (Vienna, 1943). R. Hoffmann in *L.Th.K.*, viii (1936), col. 890 f.

RIENZO, COLA DI (*c.* 1313–54), i.e. Nicolas [the son] of Lorenzo, Tribune of the Roman people. The son of a Roman inn-keeper, he passed his early years at Anagni, where intensive study of the Latin classical authors inspired him with the idea of restoring Rome to its past greatness. Later he became a notary. In 1343 he was sent on a public mission to Clement VI at *Avignon in a vain attempt to secure the Pope's return to Rome. By describing eloquently the bad rule of the nobles in the city, he gained, however, Clement's confidence and in 1344 he was nominated secretary to the Camera Capitolina.

On his return to Rome Rienzo agitated for the restoration of order and freedom and prepared for revolution. In May 1347 he called the people to the Capitol, gave them a new constitution, and was invested by them with almost dictatorial powers. The Pope sanctioned his action, but his luxurious life and his attempts at uniting all Italy under his leadership soon provoked opposition, and at the instigation of the Papal legate for Italy the Roman barons whom he had expelled rose against him. In Dec. 1347 he fled from Rome and lived for two years with the *Spiritual Franciscans at Monte Maiella. In 1350 he went to Prague to deliver a prophetic message to Charles IV, who arrested him and sent him to Clement VI, who kept him a prisoner. But when, in 1353, Cardinal Albornoz went to Rome to restore order, Innocent VI sent Rienzo with him. He was appointed senator, and triumphantly entered the city in 1354. His cruelty and luxurious life, however, again estranged the people, who soon revolted and killed him while he was trying to escape. Rienzo's career is intelligible only within the setting of his age, in which the religious and supra-national inheritance of the Middle Ages began to give way to the love of antiquity and the beginnings of nationalism characteristic of the Renaissance. He is the hero of one of *Petrarch's odes, of a novel by Baron Lytton (1835) and of the well-known opera by R. Wagner (1842).

Epistolario di Cola di Rienzo, ed. A. Gabrielli (Rome, 1890); ed. with full introd., crit. apparatus, and bibl. by K. Burdach–P. Piur, *Briefwechsel des Cola di Rienzo* (5 vols., Vom Mittelalter zur Reformation. Forschungen zur Geschichte der deutschen Bildung, ii; 1912–29). Anon. contemporary life, once attributed to T. Fortifiocca, publ. by A. Fei, Bracciano, 1624; modern ed. by A. M. Ghisalberti (Florence, 1928). Studies by F. Papencordt (Hamburg and Gotha, 1841), H. J. Schmitz (Sammlung historischer Bildnisse 4, ser. v; 1879), E. Rodocanachi (Paris, 1888), and P. Piur (Vienna, 1931), with bibl. M. E. Cosenza, *Francesco Petrarca and the Revolution of Cola di Rienzo* (Chicago, 1913). Popular studies by Iris Origo (*Tribune of Rome*, 1938) and V. Fleischer (London, 1938); anonymous novel, with much historical material, by Sir Edward Bulwer-Lytton, *Rienzi, the Last of the Tribunes* (3 vols., 1835).

RIEVAULX (i.e., Rye Vale), Yorks. One of the earliest *Cistercian foundations in England. At the invitation of Thurstan (d. 1140), Abp. of *York, a colony of Cistercians, under Abbot William, was sent by St. *Bernard of Clairvaux to England to start a monastery, and in 1131 Walter Espec, who himself joined the community later, provided them with a site about 20 miles north of York. The abbey was dedicated to the BVM. It soon gained repute as a centre of devotion, learning, and agriculture, and several other foundations such as Melrose sprang from it. By the time of St. *Aelred (the 'Bernard of the North'), its third abbot (1147–67), the community numbered 600. Later its importance declined and at the *Dissolution there were only 23 religious beside the abbot. To-day the abbey lies in ruins, but the greater part of the exquisite Early English cruciform church remains, with many of the altars *in situ*.

J. C. Atkinson (ed.), *Cartularium Abbatiae de Rievalle* (Surtees Society, lxxxiii; 1889). W. *Dugdale, *Monasticon Anglicanum*, v (ed. 1825), pp. 274–86. H. A. Rye, 'Rievaulx Abbey, its Canals and Building Stones' in *The Archaeological Journal*, lvii (1900), pp. 69–77. T. M. Fallow in *V.C.H.*, York, iii, ed. W. Page (1913), pp. 149–53; W. H. St. J. Hope in *V.C.H.*, North Riding, i, ed. W. Page (1914), pp. 494–502.

RIGHTEOUSNESS, Original. See *Original Righteousness*.

RIGORISM. In a technical sense the word is used as another name for the system of moral philosophy known as *Tutiorism. Non-technically, it is employed to denote the cult of extreme asceticism and self-denial and rigid keeping of the letter of the law, and thus approximates in meaning to *Puritanism and *formalism.

RIMINI, Synod of. See *Ariminum and Seleucia, Synods of*.

RINGS. Of the ring, which is commonly considered an emblem of fidelity, there have been, and still are, several kinds in Christian use:

(1) Early Christian rings. In the 3rd–4th cents., rings with Christian emblems seem to have been often worn in ordinary life.

(2) Episcopal rings. Rings are first mentioned as an official part of a bishop's insignia of office in the early 7th cent., and became general in the 9th–10th cents. They were emblematic of the bishop's betrothal to his church. Worn on the third finger of the right hand, they were engraved with a signet and sometimes enclosed relics (e.g. the ring of St. *Hugh of Lincoln). To-day the bishop's ring is of gold and usually contains an amethyst. Cardinals, abbots, and some abbesses also wear similar rings.

(3) Nuns' rings. In many female orders, e.g. the *Benedictine and *Cistercian, a ring is conferred at solemn profession.

(4) Wedding rings. Originating in the betrothal rings used by the Romans, they were adopted by Christians at an early date, but customs regarding their use have differed widely. In England down to the end of the 16th cent., the bride wore the ring on her right hand. The present custom of wearing it on the third finger of the left hand is explained by the practice of pronouncing the Trinitarian formula over the thumb and first two fingers, so that the third was reached at the 'Amen' which sealed the marriage rite.

(5) The 'Fisherman's Ring' (*anulus piscatoris*). A gold seal-ring which the cardinal camerlengo places on the finger of a new Pope. Engraved on it is St. *Peter in a boat fishing (cf. Lk. 5. 10), with the Pope's name round it. The earliest mention of it is in a letter of Clement IV (1265). Since the 15th cent. it has been used for sealing Papal briefs. At the death of a Pope it is ceremonially broken up by the camerlengo.

(6) The 'Coronation Ring', in England placed by the Abp. of *Canterbury on the fourth finger of the King's right hand as 'the ensign of Kingly Dignity and of Defence of the Catholic Faith'.

(7) *Rosary rings. These have ten small knobs and are used for saying the rosary. They were in use in the 15th cent. and have been revived in modern times.

RIPALDA, JUAN MARTÍNEZ DE (1594–1648), *Jesuit theologian. One of the most famous theologians of his time, he taught philosophy at Monforte, theology at Salamanca, and, in the last years of his life, moral theology at the Imperial College at Madrid. His chief work is his treatise on the supernatural, *De Ente Supernaturali* (3 vols., 1634, 1645, and 1648, vol. iii being mainly an attack on M. *Baius). Among his other published works are an exposition of the *Master of the Sentences, *Brevis Expositio Magistri Sententiarum* (1635), and the posthumous *De Virtutibus Theologicis* (1652). Several other treatises, among them 'De Visione Dei', 'De Voluntate Dei', and 'De Praedestinatione', are preserved in MS. in the National Library at Salamanca.

A. Astrain, S.J., *Historia de la Compañía de Jesús en la asistencia de España*, v (1916), p. 81. A. Arbeloa Egüas, *La doctrina de la predestinación y de la gracia eficaz en Juan Martínez de Ripalda* (Pamplona, 1950). Sommervogel, v (1894), cols. 640–3. P. Dumont, S.J., in *D.T.C.*, xiii (pt. 2; 1937), cols. 2712–37, s.v.

RIPON (Lat. *Ad Ripam*). *C.* 650 Aldfrid (d. 705), King of Northumbria, founded a monastery at Ripon which he peopled with monks from Melrose, but when shortly afterwards he required them to abandon their *Celtic customs and adopt Roman discipline, Eata, the abbot, St. *Cuthbert, the guestmaster, and others, returned to Melrose, and St. *Wilfrid was elected abbot (661). In 950 the abbey was destroyed by King Edred (d. 955) in his war with the Danes. It was rebuilt later by Abps. of *York. In the 11th cent. *Augustinian canons raised a new church, dedicated to Sts. Peter and Paul, upon the ruins of that of St. Wilfrid. This foundation was dissolved by *Henry VIII, but re-founded in 1604 as a collegiate church. In 1836 the church became the cathedral of the new diocese of Ripon. Beneath it is the 7th cent. crypt known as 'St. Wilfrid's Needle'.

The primary material is ed. by J. T. Fowler, *Memorials of the Church of SS. Peter and Wilfrid, Ripon* (Surtees Society, lxxiv, lxxviii, lxxxi, and cxv; 1881–1908). Id., *Acts of Chapter of the Collegiate Church of SS. Peter and Wilfrid, Ripon, A.D. 1452 to A.D. 1506* (ib., lxiv; 1875). W. *Dugdale, *Monasticon Anglicanum*, ii (ed. 1819), pp. 131–3. C. Hallett, *The Cathedral Church of Ripon* (Bell's Cathedral Series, 1901). A. H. Thompson in *V.C.H.*, York, iii, ed. W. Page (1913), pp. 367–72. G. G. *Scott, 'Ripon Minster' in *The Archaeological Journal*, xxxi (1874), pp. 309–18. R. L. Poole, 'St. Wilfred and the See of Ripon' in *E.H.R.*, xxxiv (1919), pp. 1–24. G. Crosse in *D.E.C.H.* (ed. 3, 1948), p. 536, s.v.

RITA OF CASCIA, St. (1381–1457), *Augustinian nun. Acc. to her biographers, she was a native of Roccaporena in the Apennines who wished from early childhood to become a nun, but was forced by her parents into marriage. For the next 18 years, despite tyrannical treatment from her husband, she behaved as an exemplary wife and mother. When after his death she sought admission to the Augustinian convent at Cascia, she was at first refused, as a widow, but later, owing (it is related) to supernatural intervention, was received and professed, and lived her last years with great austerity. Her symbol is roses, which are blessed in Augustinian churches on her feast day, 22 May.

There is very little early or reliable information. An Italian life by A. Cevallucci is tr. into Lat. in *AA.SS.*, Mai. V (1694), pp. 224–9, with introduction, p. 223 f., and other material pp. 230–2. The many popular lives include those by J. Sicardo, A.A. (Madrid, 1701; modern ed., Naples, 1924), L. Tardi, A.A. (Foligno, 1805; modern ed., 1925; Eng. tr. by R. Connolly, O.S.B., 1903), M. J. Corcoran (New York, 1919), A. C. De Romanis, A.A. (Rome, 1923), and L. Vannutelli, O.E.S.A. (Perugia, 1925). D. Falcioni in *E.C.*, x (1953), col. 994 f., s.v., with further bibl.

RITES, The Congregation of Sacred. This Congregation was established by *Sixtus V in 1588 for the purpose of carrying out the decrees of the Council of *Trent with regard to the uniformity of public worship. It is responsible for the direction of the Liturgy of the Latin Church and everything relating to *canonization, *beatification, and the veneration of *relics, as well as for all *faculties, *indulgences, and *dispensations in liturgical matters. One of its most recent duties, imposed by *Pius XI in 1930, is the correction and improvement of liturgical books. Its decrees are binding on the whole RC Church in the W. Its existence is provided for in the *Codex Iuris Canonici, can. 253.

The Decisions of the Congregation of Sacred Rites prior to 1926 are collected in *Decreta Authentica Congregationis Sacrorum Rituum sub Auspiciis S.D.N. Leonis Papae XIII* (5 vols., Rome, 1898–1901; vols. i–iii, decisions issued from May 1588 to 15 Dec. 1899, Nos. 1–4051, with enumeration of older collections in brackets; vol. iv. the 'Instructio Clementina' with comm. of A. Gardellini and further Suffragia and Adnotationes to decrees; vol. v, index; vol. vi, Appendix I (1912), continuing the decrees to 1911 (Nos. 4052–284) with index; and Appendix II (1927), containing the decrees (4285–404), issued 1912–26; later decrees are published in the *Acta Apostolicae Sedis*. An index of the archives placed in the Bibliothèque Nationale by order of Napoleon I was made by Amedeus Comes de Bourmont and printed in *Anal. Boll.*, v (1886), pp. 147–61. B. Ojetti, S.J., in *C.E.*, xiii (1912), p. 144 f., s.v. 'Roman Congregations', with bibl.; F. Antonelli, O.F.M., in *E.C.*, iv (1950), cols. 330–3, s.v. 'Congregazione romane' with bibl. See also works cited under *Roman Congregations* and *Canonization*.

RITSCHL, ALBRECHT (1822–89), German Protestant theologian. He was the son of Georg Karl Benjamin Ritschl (1783–1858), a pastor at Berlin. After studying at Bonn, Halle, Heidelberg, and *Tübingen, he was successively extraordinary (1851–9) and full (1859–64) Prof. of Theology at Bonn; and then, from 1864 until his death, Prof. of Theology at Göttingen.

Ritschl began his career as a disciple of F. C. *Baur and the *Tübingen School (qq.v.), defending in *Das Evangelium Marcions und das kanonische Evangelium des Lukas* (1846) and *Die Entstehung der altkatholischen Kirche* (ed. 1, 1850) Baur's thesis of the radical conflict in the primitive Church between Petrinism and Paulinism. But his partial independence of Baur was already clear in his *Entstehung* and when in 1857 he issued a second edition of this work, he had completely abandoned the Tübingen doctrines.

From 1852 onwards Ritschl lectured regularly on 'Systematic Theology'. He insisted on the irreducibility of religion to other forms of experience. We apprehend by faith, not by reason, and this faith rests not on the intellectual apprehension of a series of facts but on the making of value-judgements (*Werturtheile*). To take a concrete instance, Our Lord's Divinity is to be understood not as an historical statement of fact but as an expression of the 'Revelational-value' (*Offenbarungswert*) of Christ for the community which trusts in Him as God. The theologian will reject all forms of philosophical Idealism as irrelevant to the Christian faith. Ritschl believed that his doctrines were in essence a reaffirmation of the NT message which, despite their serious endeavours, even the 16th cent. Reformers did not wholly understand.

Ritschl insisted further that it was to a Community, not to individuals, that the Gospel was, and still is, committed. The Church was the immediate subject of Divine revelation and of God's Redemptive work. The forgiveness of sins ('justification') is primarily achieved in and through the Community for which, in His priestly office and in loyalty to His vocation, Christ died; and the final purpose of God for redeemed man is the moral integration of humanity in the Kingdom of God. The 'faith' by which man receives this gift is totally different from every form of mystical experience, of which Ritschl and his followers showed a deep distrust.

Ritschl elaborated his main conceptions in *Die christliche Lehre von der Rechtfertigung und Versöhnung* (3 vols., 1870–4; Eng. tr. of vol. i by J. S. Black, 1872, of vol. iii ed. by H. R. Mackintosh and A. B. Macaulay, 1900). The work exercised an immense influence on the theology of Germany in the latter half of the 19th cent. Of his later writings the two most considerable were *Theologie und Metaphysik* (1881; ed. 2, 1887) and *Geschichte des Pietismus* (3 vols., 1880–6).

The so-called 'Ritschlian School' was characterized by its stress on ethics and on the 'community', and by its repudiation of metaphysics and religious experience. Its principal organs were the *Theologische Literaturzeitung*, founded by E. *Schürer in 1876, *Die christliche Welt* (1887 ff.), and the *Zeitschrift für Theologie und Kirche* (1891 ff.). Apart from a more rigidly 'Ritschlian' inner circle, the school counted a great number of important Protestant theologians among its members, among them J. *Kaftan, W. *Herrmann, F. *Kattenbusch, F. *Loofs, A. *Harnack, and E. *Troeltsch.

There is no collected ed. of Ritschl's works. Life by Otto Ritschl (son), 2 vols., Freiburg i.Br.–Leipzig, 1892–6. The extensive literature in German includes W. Herrmann, *Die evangelische Glaube und die Theologie Albrecht Ritschls* (1890); F. Kattenbusch, *Von Schleiermacher zu Ritschl* (1892); C. von Kügelgen, *Die Dogmatik Albrechts Ritschls* (1898; ed. 2, much altered, 1903); J. Wendland, *Albrecht Ritschl und seine Schüler* (1899); C. Fabricius, *Die Entwicklung in Albrecht Ritschls Theologie von 1874 bis 1889* (1909). A hostile study is O. Pfleiderer, *Die ritschlische Theologie* (1891). Works in English include J. Orr, *The Ritschlian Theology and the Evangelical Faith* (1897); A. E. Garvie, *The Ritschlian Theology* (1899); J. Orr, *Ritschlianism. Expository and Critical Essays* (1903); J. K. Mozley, *Ritschlianism* (1909); R. Mackintosh, *Albrecht Ritschl and his School* (1915). O. Ritschl in *P.R.E.* (ed. 3), xvii (1906), pp. 22–34; H. Stephen in *R.G.G.* (ed. 2), iv (1930), cols. 2043–6, s.v.

RITUAL. Strictly, the prescribed form of words of a liturgical function. By common usage the word is also employed, often in a derogatory sense, of the accompanying ceremonial. In the 19th cent the term 'Ritualist' was commonly used of those who introduced or reintroduced Medieval or modern RC ceremonial practices into the C of E.

RITUAL COMMISSION, The. The Royal Commission created in 1867 to inquire into the differences of ceremonial practice in the C of E. Its appointment followed the creation of a Committee of the *Canterbury Convocation on the subject, set up on the motion of Harvey Goodwin, afterwards Bp. of *Carlisle, early in 1866. Among the Commissioners were Abp. C. T. *Longley, Bp. A. C. *Tait, Bp. S. *Wilberforce, Bp. C. *Thirlwall, Dean R. *Gregory, Dean A. P. *Stanley, and Sir Robert *Phillimore. The Commission published its evidence in four reports issued between 1867 and 1870. The first (1867) confined itself to the question of Eucharistic *vestments; the second (1868) dealt with *incense and *lights; the third (1869) was concerned with the *lectionary; and the fourth (1870) dealt with Prayer Book revision and other subjects. The Commissioners were almost unanimous in their wish to forbid the use of vestments, but in the second and fourth reports there were great divergences of opinion. As a general rule, practices which had prevailed in the C of E for the last 300 years were to be the standard of Anglican usage, and the Bishop, on receiving complaints relating to any variation from such established use from churchwardens or from five resident parishioners, was to enforce obedience. The proposals met with much criticism, esp. from High Churchmen, and failure to bring them into effect led ultimately to the *Public Worship Regulation Act (q.v.).

The reports, with appendices, are to be found respectively among the Parliamentary Papers, 1867, xx, 719–896 (of the MS. pagination of the volumes arranged for the House of Commons) (Cd. 3951); 1868, xxxviii (whole volume; Cd. 4016); 1870, xix, 437–69 (Cd. 17); and 1870, xix, 461–742 (Cd. 218).

RITUALE ROMANUM. The official service-book of the Roman Rite which contains the prayers and formulas for the administration of the Sacraments and other liturgical actions of a priest, apart from the Mass and the Divine Office. It thus includes such rites as *Baptism and *Unction, as well as various blessings. The first edition appeared under *Paul V in 1614 and it was enlarged by *Benedict XIV in 1752. The book was revised in accordance with the new canon law in 1925.

Before the pontificate of Paul V, various dioceses had issued their own *Rituale*. An *editio typica* of the *Rituale Romanum* was issued by Pope *Leo XIII (Ratisbon, 1884). For the decree authorizing the present ed., see *Acta Apostolicae Sedis*, xvii (1925), p. 326. F. A. Zaccaria, *Bibliotheca Ritualis*, i (Rome, 1776), pp. 137–60. L. Eisenhofer, *Handbuch der katholischen Liturgik*, i (1932), pp. 100–13, and, on the Rituale of the Eastern Churches, pp. 111–18. A. *Fortescue in *C.E.*, xiii (1912), pp. 88–90, s.v. 'Ritual'; E. Vykoukal in *L.Th.K.*, viii (1936), cols. 911–13, s.v. 'Rituale'; G. Löw, C.SS.R., in *E.C.*, x (1953), cols. 1010–17, s.v. 'Rituale Romanum', all with further bibl. On the Rituale of the Eastern Churches see also J. *Goar, Εὐχολόγιον sive Rituale Graecorum (Paris, 1647).

RITUS SERVANDUS. Two liturgical items relating to the modern RC Latin rite have this title.

(1) The rules about the customs and ceremonial of the Mass printed (since *Pius V) at the beginning of the *Missal ('Ritus Servandus in Celebratione Missae').

(2) The book, officially approved by the RC hierarchy, containing the directions and prayers for *Benediction of the Blessed Sacrament and certain other non-liturgical services (*Ritus Servandus in Solemni Expositione et Benedictione SS. Sacramenti*). The corresponding book in Ireland is also known as a *Benedictionale*.

ROBBER COUNCIL OF EPHESUS. See *Latrocinium*.

ROBBIA, DELLA. See *Della Robbia*.

ROBERT, St. (c. 1027–1111), Abbot of Molesme. The member of a noble family of Champagne, he entered the abbey of Moutier-la-Celle at the age of 15 and later became prior. After 1060 he was appointed abbot of St.-Michel-de-Tonnerre, but failed to reform its greatly relaxed discipline and returned to Moutier-la-Celle. After a brief period as prior of St.-Aiyoul, some hermits living in the forest of Colan asked to be placed under Robert's direction, and with the approval of the Pope he founded a monastery for them at Molesme (Burgundy) in 1075. The saintly life of its abbot and the original monks caused the house to flourish. But increasing wealth and the influx of unsuitable new members gradually brought about divisions in the community, and in 1098, Robert and several of his monks left Molesme and founded the monastery of *Cîteaux, to be made famous in the following century by St. *Bernard of Clairvaux. When eighteen months later the monks of Molesme asked to have their abbot back, Robert returned and under his government Molesme became a famous Benedictine centre. Permission for his cultus was granted by *Honorius III in 1222. Feast day, 29 Apr.

The principal authority is a 12th cent. life by a monk of Molesme, printed in *AA.SS.*, Apr. III (1675), pp. 668–76; Process of canonization, ib., pp. 676–8. Life repr. in J. P. Migne, *PL*, clvii, 1269–94, with three letters, col. 1293 f. Modern ed. of Life by K. Spahr, S.O.Cist. (Freiburg i.Br., 1944), with bibl. A. Zimmermann in *L.Th.K.*, viii (1936), col. 921 f., s.v.

ROBERT BELLARMINE, St. See *Bellarmine, St.*

ROBERT OF HOLCOT. See *Holcot, Robert.*

ROBERT OF MELUN (d. 1167), Scholastic theologian. An Englishman by birth, he studied at *Paris, where he became the successor of *Abelard at the school on Mount Ste-Geneviève and *John of Salisbury was among his pupils. In 1142 he went to Melun where he directed a school, and in 1148 took part in the condemnation of *Gilbert de La Porrée at the Synod of *Reims. Recalled to England by Henry II c. 1160, he was made Bp. of *Hereford in 1163. Three of his writings are still extant, the most important of them the unfinished theological 'Summa Sententiarum', which also exists in a completed but abridged version. His Trinitarian doctrine, which contradicted that of St. *Bernard, came nearer to Abelard and was generally accepted by the 13th cent. Schoolmen. Acc. to Robert, power is to be esp. attributed to the Father, wisdom to the Son, and goodness to the Holy Ghost, without, however, robbing the other two Persons of the quality predicated in a particular way of the one. The *Victorines, with whom Robert's teaching had many other affinities, accepted his Trinitarian speculations.

Works ed. R. M. Martin, O.P.–R. M. Gallet, O.P. (S.S.L., xiii, xviii, xxi, xxv ff.; 1932 ff.). R. M. Martin, 'L'Œuvre théologique de Robert de Melun' in *R.H.E.*, xv (1920), pp. 456–89, with reff. and biographical introd.; id., 'Les Idées de Robert de Melun sur le péché originel' in *Revue des Sciences philosophiques et théologiques*, vii (1913), pp. 700–725; viii (1914), pp. 439–66; ix (1920), pp. 103–20; xi (1922), pp. 390–415; id., 'Pro Petro Abaelardo. Un Plaidoyer de Robert de Melun contre S. Bernard', ib., xii (1923), pp. 308–33; id., 'L'Immortalité de l'âme d'après Robert de Melun (†1167)' in *Revue néoscolastique de Philosophie*, xxxvi (1934), pp. 128–45. F. Anders, *Die Christologie des Robert von Melun* (Forschungen zur christlichen Literatur- und Dogmengeschichte, xv, Hft. v, 1927); F. Pelster, S.J., 'Literargeschichtliche Beiträge zu Robert von Melun, Bischof von Hereford (†1167)' in *Z.K.T.*, liii (1929), pp. 564–79. A. Landgraf, 'Familienbildung bei Paulinenkommentaren des 12. Jahrhunderts: 2. Robert von Melun und seine Schule' in *Biblica*, xiii (1932), pp. 169–93. F. Bliemetzrieder, 'Robert von Melun und die Schule Anselms von Laon' in *Z.K.G.*, liii (1934), pp. 117–70. Überweg, ii, 276–8, with bibl. p. 711.

ROBERT OF WINCHELSEA. See *Winchelsea, Robert.*

ROBERT, PIERRE. See *Olivetan.*

ROBERTSON, ARCHIBALD (1853–1931), Bp. of *Exeter. Educated at Trinity College, Oxford, of which he was elected a Fellow in 1876, he became Principal of Hatfield Hall, *Durham (1883–97), and later of *King's College, London (1897–1903). From 1903 to 1916 he was Bp. of Exeter. He was the principal Athanasian scholar of his generation. In 1882 and 1893 he issued editions of the text of the *De Incarnatione*, and in 1892 published the *Select Writings of Athanasius*, based on J. H. *Newman's translations, but with the addition of important prolegomena and notes. His other writings include *Regnum Dei* (1901; *Bampton Lectures).

C. Jenkins in *D.N.B., 1931–1940* (1949), p. 734 f., s.v.

ROBERTSON, FREDERICK WILLIAM (1816–53), 'Robertson of Brighton', Anglican preacher. After abandoning an earlier intention of entering the army, he matriculated in 1837 at Brasenose College, Oxford, to prepare for the ministry. In 1840 he was ordained to a title at *Winchester and in 1842 became curate of Christ Church, Cheltenham. Here he gradually abandoned his earlier *Evangelicalism in favour of a *Broad Church type of theology. In 1846 he was for a short time minister of the English Church at Heidel-

berg. After returning to England and working for a brief space as rector of St. Ebbe's, Oxford, he was appointed in 1847 minister of Trinity Chapel, Brighton, a small proprietary chapel. Here his influence as a preacher extended far and wide. Though in no sense a scientific theologian, he appealed through his manifest sincerity, his great spiritual insight, and his remarkable capacity for analysing motive and character. He had a powerful influence with the working classes, at that time largely untouched by the C of E, and some of his best lectures were delivered to working men. The opposition he had to face throughout his time at Brighton, largely through his support of the revolutionary ideas of 1848, hastened his early death.

His sermons and lectures were publd. posthumously from shorthand notes: *Sermons Preached at Brighton* (Series i and ii, 1855; Series iii, 1857; Series iv, 1863); *Lectures and Addresses on Literary and Social Topics* (1858); *Expository Lectures on St. Paul's Epistles to the Corinthians* (1859). Selection of Sermons in *Everyman's Library*, Nos. 37–9 (1906). *Life and Letters*, ed. Stopford A. Brooke (2 vols., London, 1865). Other lives by Frederick Arnold (London, 1886) and H. H. *Henson (London, 1916). R. Garnett in *D.N.B.*, xlviii (1896), pp. 404–7.

ROBINSON, HENRY WHEELER (1872–1945), theologian and OT scholar. Born in Northampton of humble parentage, he was educated for the *Baptist ministry in the universities of Edinburgh and Oxford. After short pastorates at Pitlochry and Coventry, he was appointed in 1906 to the staff of Rawdon Baptist College and quickly made his mark as teacher and writer. From 1920 to 1942 he was Principal of Regent's Park College and was chiefly responsible for its transference from London to Oxford. He was Speaker's Lecturer in the university of Oxford, one of the editors of 'The Library of Constructive Theology', and president of the Baptist Historical Society. His main interests were in the fields of OT theology and the doctrines of the Holy Spirit and redemption. Among his principal writings were *Deuteronomy and Joshua* (Century Bible, 1907), *The Christian Doctrine of Man* (1911), *The Religious Ideas of the Old Testament* (1913), *The Christian Experience of the Holy Spirit* (1928), and *Redemption and Revelation* (1938). A man of wide intellectual interests and deep piety, his influence extended far beyond his own communion.

E. A. Payne, *Henry Wheeler Robinson*. A Memoir (1946).

ROBINSON, JOHN (c. 1575–1625), pastor to the *Pilgrim Fathers. Very little is known about his early life. He was a native of Lincs or Notts, probably studied at Cambridge, was ordained in the C of E, and seems to have held a curacy at *Norwich. He later became a *Puritan, joining the 'gathered Church' at Scrooby Manor, Notts. In 1608, owing to severe measures against Nonconformity, Robinson and his congregation were forced to flee to *Holland. In 1609 he settled at *Leyden, of which university he became a member in 1615. From 1617 he interested himself in the project of his Leyden community to emigrate to America, as their strict *Calvinism had brought them into conflict with the *Arminianism of which Leyden was a centre. Though he was prevented from joining the Pilgrim Fathers in the *Mayflower*, he assisted them in their preparations and encouraged them by his letters. He was an able controversialist; in 1610 he published *Justification of Separation from the Church*, and in his *Apologia* (1619) he defended the principles of Congregationalism. He also wrote *A Defence of the Doctrine Propounded by the Synod of Dort* (1624). His *Observations Divine and Moral*, a collection of 62 essays on spiritual and moral subjects, was published posthumously (1625).

Collected ed. of his works, 3 vols., London, 1851, with memoir by R. Ashton in vol. i, pp. xiii–lxxiv. Modern studies by F. J. Powicke (London, [1920]) and W. H. Burgess (ib., 1920). A. Gordon in *D.N.B.*, xlix (1897), pp. 18–22, with reff. to primary sources.

ROBINSON, JOSEPH ARMITAGE (1858–1933), NT and patristic scholar. Educated at Christ's College, Cambridge, of which he was a Fellow from 1881 to 1899, he was ordained priest in 1882 and devoted himself to patristic studies. In 1891 he founded the series of monographs *Texts and Studies* in which he edited the *Passion of Perpetua* in the same year. In 1893 he published an edition of *Origen's* 'Philocalia'. In 1899 he became a canon, and in 1902 Dean, of *Westminster. In 1903 he published his commentary on *St. Paul's Epistle to the Ephesians* in which he defended the authenticity of the letter on the view that it was an encyclical, combining minute exegesis with a clear exposition of its theology. In 1911 he resigned the Deanery of Westminster to become Dean of *Wells. Here he took a lively interest in the cathedral and the early history of the see and wrote *The Saxon Bishops of Wells* (1919) and *St. Oswald at Worcester* (1919). In 1920 Robinson published an English translation of the recently recovered 'Apostolic Preaching' of St. *Irenaeus and his Donnellan Lectures on *Barnabas, Hermas, and the Didache* in which he attempted to prove a late date for the *Didache. Among his later publications are *The Times of St. Dunstan* (1923) and an enlarged edition of an earlier work on *The Historical Character of the Fourth Gospel* (1929). He was one of the Anglican participants in the *Malines Conversations.

J. M. Creed, 'Joseph Armitage Robinson, 1858–1933' in *Proceedings of the British Academy*, xx (1934), pp. 297–308. C. Jenkins in *D.N.B., 1931–1940* (1949), pp. 743–5, s.v.

ROCH, St. (*c*. 1295–1327), also **ROCCO** (Ital.), healer of the plague-stricken. Very little is known of his life. Acc. to Francis Diedo, his Venetian biographer (1478), he was a native of Montpellier, who on a journey to Italy stopped at the plague-ridden town of Aquapendente, where he cured many by the sign of the cross. He afterwards performed similar miracles at Cesena, Mantua, Modena, Parma, and elsewhere, himself fell a victim at Piacenza, but recovered and returned to his native city. A miraculous cross is said to have been discovered on his body after his death. He was regularly invoked against the plague, notably in an outbreak in 1414 during the Council of *Constance. In 1485 his relics were moved to Venice, where they are still venerated. There is no sufficient evidence for the *Franciscan tradition that he was a *tertiary of the Order. Feast day, 16 Aug.

AA.SS., Aug. III (1727), pp. 380–415. Life by Jehan Phelipot, orig. publ. Brescia, 1494, re-edited by M. Luthard (Paris, &c., 1917), with introd. and notes. Abbé Recluz, *Histoire de saint Roch et de son culte* (Avignon, 1858); J. C. F. Chavanne, *Saint Roch. Histoire complète* (ed. 2, Paris, 1875). G. Ceroni, *San Rocco nella vita, nel culto, nell' arte* (1927); M. Bessodes, *Saint Roch. Histoire et légendes* (Turin and Rome, 1931). A. Fliche, 'Le Problème de saint Roch' in *Anal. Boll.*, lxviii (1950), pp. 343–61, with bibl. A. P. Frutaz in *E.C.*, x (1953), cols. 1054–9, s.v. 'Rocco'.

ROCHESTER (Lat. *Durobrivae* or *Roffa*). This, the oldest and smallest of the suffragan sees of *Canterbury, was founded by St. *Augustine, who consecrated St. *Justus its first bishop in 604. The cathedral, which was dedicated to St. *Andrew and served in early times by a college of secular canons, was damaged in 676 by the Mercians and Danes. Bp. Gundulf (bp., 1077–1108) began a new cathedral, probably at the request of *Lanfranc, and in 1082 replaced the secular canons by Benedictines. His nave is the oldest in England, and a fine example of rich and varied Norman work. The cathedral was consecrated in 1130 by the Abp. of Canterbury in the presence of Henry I, but a fire which occurred at the time damaged much of the cathedral and city. In 1343 the choir was rebuilt and a central tower added (replaced 1825–7) out of the offerings at the shrine of 'St. William of Rochester' (a baker from Perth who was murdered here *c*. 1201, while on pilgrimage; feast day, 23 May). At the *Dissolution, *c*. 1541, the monks were replaced by a dean and six canons (now reduced to four).

C. Johnson (ed.), *Registrum Hamonis Hethe, Diocesis Roffensis A.D. 1319–1352* (*Canterbury and York Society, xlviii and xlix; 1948). 'Ernulfi Episcopi Roffensis Collectanea' in H. *Wharton, *Anglia Sacra*, i (1691), pp. 329–40; 'Annales Ecclesiae Roffensis, ex Historia Ecclesiastica Edmundi de Hadenham', ib., pp. 341–55; William de Dene, 'Historia Roffensis ab anno MCCCXIV. ad MCCCL.', ib., pp. 356–83. T. *Hearne, *Textus Roffensis* (Oxford, 1720; a collection of documents by Ernulf, many of them relating to the see of Rochester). J. Thorpe–J. Thorpe (son) (edd.), *Registrum Roffense: or a Collection of Antient Records, Charters, and Instruments of Divers Kinds, necessary for illustrating the Ecclesiastical History and Antiquities of the Diocese and Cathedral Church of Rochester* (1769); J. Thorpe (ed.), *Custumale Roffense* (London, 1788). W. *Dugdale, *Monasticon Anglicanum*, i (ed. 1817), pp. 153–88. *The History and Antiquities of the Cathedral Church of Rochester* (anon., ascribed to J. Lewis, but generally supposed to have been written by Dr. Rawlinson; 1717). A. I. Pearman, *Rochester* (Diocesan Histories; 1897); G. H. Palmer, *The Cathedral Church of Rochester* (Bell's Cathedral Series, 1897). W. H. St. J. Hope, *The Architectural History of the Cathedral and Monastery of St. Andrew at Rochester* (1900). R. C. Fowler in *V.C.H.*, Kent, ii, ed. W. Page (1926), pp. 121–6. E. M. Blackie in *D.E.C.H.* (1912), pp. 520–3, s.v.

ROCHET. A white linen vestment, resembling the *surplice but with tight sleeves, which is worn by bishops and occasionally by other ecclesiastical dignitaries. It is derived from the *alb, and until the 14th cent. was in use outside Rome by all clerics (and even sacristans). The rochet worn by Anglican bishops under the *chimere has wide lawn sleeves. In the 18th cent. these sleeves developed to such balloon-like dimensions that they were commonly detached from the rest of the garment and sewn on to the chimere separately.

Braun, *L.G.*, pp. 125–35. W. B. Marriott, *Vestiarium Christianum*. The Origin and Gradual Development of the Dress of Holy Ministry in the Church (1868), p. 226.

ROCK, DANIEL (1799–1871), ecclesiologist and antiquary. He was ordained to the RC priesthood in 1824. He took a keen interest in the English medieval religious ceremonial customs, and his chief work, *The Church of our Fathers* (3 vols. in 4, 1849–53), did much to spread knowledge of them, esp. of the *Sarum Rite. His other best-known work is his *Hierurgia, or the Holy Sacrifice of the Mass* (2 vols., 1833). He took an active part in furthering the restoration of the RC hierarchy in England, and in 1852 he was appointed one of the first canons of Southwark RC Cathedral.

His *Church of Our Fathers* was ed. by G. W. Hart–W. H. *Frere, C.R. (4 vols., London, 1903–4), with life by B. W. Kelly, vol. i, pp. xvii–xxvi; his *Hierurgia* was also ed. and rev. by W. H. J. Weale ('Catholic Standard Library', 2 vols., 1892).

ROCOCO. A development of *baroque architecture and decoration, which originated in France and lasted from *c.* 1715 to 1750. It endeavoured to substitute gracefulness for the dignity of the Louis XIV period, but was often over-ornate. The name is derived from the French *rocaille* ('shell-work'), the twisted curves of a shell typifying freedom and irregularity.

ROGATION DAYS (Lat. *rogare*, 'ask'). In W. Christendom certain prescribed days of prayer and fasting in the early summer, on which intercession is made esp. for the harvest. The 'Major Rogation', which is on 25 April, is a Christianized version of the pagan observance of the 'Robiglia', which took the form of processions through the cornfields to pray for the preservation of the crops from mildew. Historically it has no connexion with the Feast of St. *Mark, of later institution, also kept on 25 Apr. The 'Minor Rogations' are kept on the Monday, Tuesday, and Wednesday before *Ascension Day. These rogations, which derive from the processional litanies ordered by St. *Mamertus of Vienne (*c.* 470), when his diocese was troubled by volcanic eruptions, spread through Gaul and later to other places. They are first found at Rome in the *Gregorian Sacramentary. In England they were adopted by the Council of *Clovesho (can. 16).

The outdoor Rogation processions were suppressed in England in 1547, but under Elizabeth I the Royal *Injunctions of 1559 (No. 19) ordered the perambulation of the

parish at Rogationtide and the Second 'Book of *Homilies' contained two homilies for the Rogation Days. The observance is not mentioned in the earlier issues of the BCP. In that of 1662, the three (minor) Rogations (only) were ordered to be observed as 'Days of Fasting and Abstinence'.

D. de Bruyne, O.S.B., 'L'Origine des processions de la chandeleur et des rogations à propos d'un sermon inédit' in *R. Bén.*, xxxiv (1922), pp. 14–26, esp. pp. 14–18. W. E. Scudamore in *D.C.A.*, ii (1880), p. 1809 f., s.v. H. *Leclercq, O.S.B., in *D.A.C.L.*, x (pt. 2; 1932), col. 1740 f., s.v. 'Marc (Procession de saint)'; id., ib., xiv (pt. 2; 1948), cols. 2459–61, s.v. 'Rogations'; P. Siffrin, O.S.B., in *E.C.*, x (1953), cols. 1084–6, s.v. 'Rogazioni'.

ROGER BACON. See *Bacon, Roger*.

ROGERS, JOHN (*c.* 1500–55), editor of '*Matthew's Bible' and first British Protestant Martyr under *Mary. Educated at Pembroke Hall, Cambridge, in 1534 he became chaplain to the English merchants in Antwerp. Soon after meeting W. *Tyndale (d. 1536), then engaged in his translation of the Scriptures, he accepted the Protestant faith. In 1537 under the name of 'Thomas Matthew' he published the first complete version of the Bible in English, which was hence known as 'Matthew's Bible' (q.v.). Rogers's own share in it was confined to contributing some valuable prefaces and marginal notes. At about this time he gave evidence of his Protestantism by marriage. His wife was an Antwerp lady, Adriana de Weyden (later Anglicized as 'Pratt'). Having returned to London in 1548, he was presented in 1550 with the crown livings of St. Margaret Moyses and St. Sepulchre, both in London, and shortly afterwards became prebendary, and then divinity lecturer, at St. Paul's Cathedral. For preaching Protestant doctrine at Paul's Cross at the beginning of Mary's reign, he was first confined to his house, and then taken to Newgate prison, where he was kept for a year with J. *Hooper and others. In Jan. 1555 sentence of death was pronounced for denial of the Papal claims and of the real presence in the *Eucharist, and he was burnt at Smithfield on Feb. 4.

J. L. Chester, *John Rogers*. The Compiler of the First Authorised English Bible; the Pioneer of the English Reformation; and its first Martyr (1861). The attempt of W. T. Whitley, 'Thomas Matthew's Bible' in *The Church Quarterly Review*, cxxv (Oct. 1937), pp. 48–69, to deny that Matthew was an *alias* for John Rogers seems to have failed. Cf. J. F. Mozley, *William Tyndale* (1937), Appendix E, 'Thomas Matthew', p. 354 f.; H. H. Hutson–H. R. Willoughby, *Decisive Data on Thomas Matthew Problems* [Chicago, 1938], with reff. S. Lee in *D.N.B.*, xlix (1897), pp. 126–9.

ROGERS, WILLIAM (1819–96), Anglican educational reformer. Educated at Eton, Balliol College, Oxford, and Durham university, he was ordained deacon in 1843. From 1845 to 1863, while perpetual curate of St. Thomas's, Charterhouse, he devoted himself to the cause of primary education and, winning influential support, erected a large network of very successful schools in his slum parish. When in 1863 he became rector of St Botolph's,

Bishopsgate, he worked on similar lines on behalf of middle-class schools, among them Alleyn's College, Dulwich, of which he was a governor. His attempt to exclude from his schools religious teaching on the ground that the responsibility for this lay with the parents and the clergy, won him the sobriquet of 'Hang Theology Rogers'. He also took a very active part in several local philanthropic works, including the founding of the Bishopsgate Institute (1894).

R. H. Hadden (formerly curate at St. Botolph's; ed.), *Reminiscences of William Rogers* (1888), with foreword by Rogers. T. Seccombe in *D.N.B.*, xlix (1897), p. 145 f.

ROLLE OF HAMPOLE, RICHARD
(c. 1295–1349), English hermit and mystic. The facts of his life have recently been much discussed. A native of Yorkshire, he studied at Oxford. Acc. to the traditional account taken from the office drawn up in view of his (never realized) canonization, he broke off his studies at the age of 19 to become a hermit. The investigations of Dom M. Noetinger, however, based on copies of records of the *Sorbonne and on internal evidence, would suggest that from Oxford he went to Paris, where he finished his theological studies as a master and priest. From c. 1326 onwards he lived as a hermit, first on the estate of his friend John Dalton, later in various other places, frequently preaching and denouncing the vices of the times. His last years were spent at Hampole, not far from Doncaster, near a convent of *Cistercian nuns who were under his spiritual guidance. For a time he was the subject of a considerable cultus (never formally confirmed); feast day, 29 Sept.

Rolle is one of the first religious authors to write in the vernacular as well as in Latin. His Latin works include his 'Incendium Amoris' and his 'Emendatio Vitae'. His devotion to the Lord's sufferings finds expression in the 'Meditation of the Passion', one of the finest and most moving treatises on the subject in English. His authorship of the popular didactic poem 'The Pricke of Conscience' has lately been contested. Of his translations of Biblical books only the Psalms have been printed. His Commentary on the Psalter shows acquaintance with *Peter Lombard and St. *Augustine; among other influences noticeable in his works are *Richard of St. Victor, St. *Bernard, and St. *Gregory. He was also the author of much devotional poetry. Rolle's writings, which were highly esteemed by his contemporaries, were used by the *Lollards with interpolations in the interests of their doctrines.

Many of his works have frequently been edited and translated. C. Horstman (ed.), *Yorkshire Writers*. Richard Rolle of Hampole . . . and his followers (2 vols., 1895–6); *Selected Works of Richard Rolle Hermit*, ed. with introd. by E. C. Heseltine (1930); Hope Emily Allen (ed.), *English Writings of Richard Rolle Hermit of Hampole* (1931). Id., *Writings Ascribed to Richard Rolle Hermit of Hampole and Materials for his Biography* (Modern Language Association of America Monograph Series, iii; 1927), with reff.; Geraldine [E.] Hodgson, *Rolle and 'Our Daily Work'* (1929). Modern ed. of 'Incendium Amoris' by Margaret Deanesly (Manchester, 1915). The principal authority for his life is the

office prepared for his canonization ed. F. Procter, *Brevarium ad Usum Insignis Ecclesie Eboracensis*, ii (Surtees Society, lxxv; 1883), Appendix V, cols. 785–820; crit. ed. by R. M. Woolley (1919). Frances M. M. Comper, *The Life of Richard Rolle*, together with an Edition of his English Lyrics, now for the first time published (1928). Geraldine E. Hodgson, *The Sanity of Mysticism*. A Study of Richard Rolle (1926); M. Noetinger, O.S.B., 'The Biography of Richard Rolle' in *The Month*, cxlvii (1926), pp. 22–33; id. (ed.), *Le Feu de l'amour* (Tours, 1929), introd., pp. i–cx. P. Renaudin, *Quatre Mystiques anglais* (1945), pp. 13–50. More detailed bibl. in F. W. Bateson (ed.), *The Cambridge Bibliography of English Literature*, i (1940), pp. 191–4 and 307 f.

ROLLS CHAPEL, The.
A chapel which once stood on the site of the Public Record Office, London, and from the time of Edward III was annexed to the Keeper of the Rolls ('Custos Rotulorum'). The first chapel was erected in the time of Henry III as part of a foundation for converted Jews, but it was almost entirely rebuilt by Inigo *Jones in 1617. From 1718 to 1726, J. *Butler held the office of Preacher at the Rolls Chapel and delivered his famous sermons here. It was pulled down in the last years of the 19th cent. The Rolls of the Court of Chancery were formerly kept in the chapel.

ROMAINE, WILLIAM (1714–95), *Calvinist preacher.
He was educated at Hertford College, Hart Hall, and *Christ Church, Oxford, and was ordained in 1736. In his early years he followed the scholarly traditions of the C of E, to which he made an important contribution with his edition of the Hebrew Concordance of Marius de Calasio (1748). In 1749 he was appointed lecturer at St. Dunstan's-in-the-West and in 1750 at St. George's, Hanover Square. In 1755 he came under the influence of G. *Whitefield and became one of the principal representatives of rigid Calvinism. His preaching attracted vast crowds of the poor and uneducated, whose presence in church was resented by his fashionable parishioners, so that he had to give up his lectureships. After holding brief appointments at some other London churches he became incumbent of St. Anne's, Blackfriars, in 1766, where his revivalist preaching continued to draw large congregations till his death. He was a powerful preacher; he held an extreme form of predestinationism which he expounded in several writings, e.g. *The Life of Faith* (1763), *The Walk of Faith* (1771), and *The Triumph of Faith* (1795).

Works ed. by his son (8 vols., bound in 4, London, 1796), with life by W. B. Cadogan in vol. vii, pp. 9–111, and list of Romaine's works, ib., pp. 112–16. J. C. *Ryle, *The Christian Leaders of the Last Century* (1869), pp. 149–79. H. L. Bennett in *D.N.B.*, xlix (1897), pp. 175–7.

ROMAN CATHOLICISM.
The term, which denotes the faith and practice of all Christians who are in communion with the Pope, is used in particular of Catholicism as it has developed since the Reformation. On its doctrinal side it is characterized by strict adherence to tradition combined with acceptance of the living voice of the Church, which is held to expound infallibly the revealed truths contained in the deposit of faith. Whereas in the early centuries the Church

had to clarify esp. the great mysteries of the Trinity and the Incarnation, and in the Middle Ages the doctrines concerning the relation of God and man through grace and the sacraments, post-Tridentine theologians have been esp. concerned with the structure and prerogatives of the Church, the position of the BVM in the economy of salvation, leading to the definitions of the dogma of the *Immaculate Conception by *Pius IX in 1854, and of the Corporal *Assumption by *Pius XII in 1950, and the function of the Pope as the Vicar of Christ on earth, culminating in the dogma of Infallibility enunciated at the *Vatican Council of 1870. Another characteristic post-medieval development is the establishment of dogmatic, moral, and ascetical or mystical theology as separate disciplines; but the revival of *Thomism, the theological and philosophical foundation of RC-ism, tends to be a safeguard against overspecialization and to unite the several components of its teaching in one coherent system.

From an external point of view RC-ism presents itself as an elaborately organized hierarchy of bishops and priests with the Pope at its head, built up during a long history and basing its claims on the power entrusted by Christ to His Apostles in general (Jn. 20. 23) and to St. Peter in particular (Mt. 16. 18 f.; Lk. 22. 32; Jn. 21. 15-17), as whose successors the Popes are traditionally regarded. Their supremacy over the Church, though sometimes contested by representatives of the Conciliar Theory and of *Gallicanism, was widely accepted in the W. from early times, as is shown by the appeals to Rome in the *Donatist and *Pelagian controversies of the 4th and 5th cents., and was reaffirmed at *Trent. Acc. to RC teaching this hierarchy represents the Divine authority to which obedience is due, and protects the supernatural life of the Church which flows from Christ, her head, down to her members. This life is mediated esp. by the *Seven Sacraments, which convey sanctifying grace, a conception familiar to the Schoolmen and worked out in detail by the Tridentine and post-Tridentine theologians. If lost by mortal sin, grace can be restored by the Sacrament of *Penance. It is conveyed particularly by Holy Communion, the frequency of which has been encouraged by recent Popes, esp. *Pius X. The centre of the liturgical life of RC-ism is the Mass, which is regarded as an extension of the Incarnation and a bloodless renewal of the sacrifice on Calvary. It is the chief of RC devotions, having its origin in the institution of the Eucharist in the upper room, and assistance at it is compulsory on all Sundays and *Feasts of Obligation. All other devotions are left to the free choice of the individual; among those of post-Reformation times are *Benediction of the Blessed Sacrament, and devotion to the *Sacred Heart and to St. *Joseph, whereas the *Stations of the Cross and the *Rosary are of medieval origin. To these RC-ism adds devotion to particular saints, which dates from the age of the martyrs and has been encouraged by a great number of canonizations in recent times, among the most popular being that to St. *Teresa of Lisieux.

The religious life, confined in the Middle Ages to the comparatively few old orders of monks, friars, canons regular and enclosed nuns, has in post-Reformation Catholicism developed in various ways. The most influential of the modern orders is the Society of Jesus (see *Jesuits*), beside which grew up a multitude of congregations and other associations of both men and women, often pursuing particular aims such as teaching, nursing, and social work. The Jesuits popularized the institution of *retreats, through which the spiritual life of the individual received more attention than in medieval times. On the other hand the *Liturgical Movement, which seeks to increase the dignity and understanding of corporate worship, and the very active interest taken by the Popes in recent times in social problems, tend to establish a balance between the needs of the individual and those of the community which has always been the ideal of Christianity.

Introductions by RCs include K. Adam, *Das Wesen des Katholizismus* (1924; Eng. tr., 1929); C. C. Martindale, S.J., *The Faith of the Roman Church* ('The Faiths'; 1927); R. A. Knox, *The Belief of Catholics* (1927); P. L. T. G. Goyau, *Le Catholicisme* ('Les Religions'; 1931); P. Hughes, *The Faith in Practice*. Catholic Doctrine and Life (1938); T. Corbishley, S.J., *Roman Catholicism* (Hutchinson's University Library, li; 1950).
D. Mathew, *Catholicism in England, 1535-1935*. Portrait of a Minority, its Culture and Tradition (1936). E. I. Watkin, *Roman Catholicism in England* [post-Reformation] (H.U.L., 1957). Works on the earlier period include A. O. Meyer, *England und die katholische Kirche unter Elisabeth* (Bibliothek des kgl. Preussischen Historischen Instituts in Rom, vi, Pt. 1, 1911; Eng. tr., 1916); J. H. Pollen, S.J., *The English Catholics in the Reign of Queen Elizabeth*. A Study of their Politics, Civil Life and Government (1920). B. Magee, *The English Recusants*. A Study of the Post Reformation Catholic Survival and the Operation of the Rucusancy Laws (1938). P. Hughes, *Rome and the Counter-Reformation in England* (1942). W. M. Brady, *Annals of the Catholic Hierarchy in England and Scotland, A.D. 1585-1876* (Rome, 1877; London, 1883). D. [R.] Gwynn, *The Struggle for Catholic Emancipation, 1750-1829* (1928); id., *A Hundred Years of Catholic Emancipation, 1829-1929* (1929). G. A. Beck (ed.), *The English Catholics, 1850-1950*. Essays to Commemorate the Centenary of the Restoration of the Hierarchy of England and Wales (1950). For the 18th and 19th cent. there is much information in the works of Bernard Ward, and the lives of R. *Challoner, J. H. *Newman, W. G. *Ward, H. E. *Manning, W. B. *Ullathorne, and H. *Vaughan (qq.v.). See also the publications of the *Catholic Record Society.
P. F. Anson, *The Catholic Church in Modern Scotland, 1560-1937* (1937), with reff. to earlier works. D. Attwater, *The Catholic Church in Modern Wales*. A Record of the Past Century (1935). For the history of the RC Church in other parts of the world, see bibl. to the various countries. For works on RC theology, see bibl. to *Moral Theology*; *Trent, Council of*; *Vatican Council*, &c. There is also abundant information in *C.E.*, *D.T.C.*, *L.Th.K.*, and *E.C.*; also in W. E. Addis-T. Arnold, *A Catholic Dictionary* (1884; ed. 15 by P. E. Hallett, 1951); and D. Attwater (ed.), *The Catholic Encyclopaedic Dictionary* (1931; revised ed., 1949).

ROMAN CATHOLIC RELIEF ACTS.
See *Catholic Relief*.

ROMAN CONGREGATIONS.
The departments of the *curia for dealing with ecclesiastical affairs, esp. legal and administrative matters. They were established by *Sixtus V in 1588 and reorganized by *Pius X in 1908.

The original number was fourteen, but in the new *Codex Iuris Canonici* (1917; cans. 242–57) the number was fixed at eleven. Each congregation consists of the cardinal prefect and a number of major and minor officers, largely cardinals. The most important is the *Holy Office, which handles questions of faith and morals and, since 1917 when the Congregation of the *Index was abolished, also the censorship of literature. Other influential Congregations are the *Propaganda, which regulates the affairs of the missionary countries, and the Congregation of *Rites, which deals with canonizations, ceremonies of the Church, &c. The publishing organ of the Roman Congregations is the *Acta Apostolicae Sedis.

V. Martin, *Les Congrégations romaines* (1930). V. Bartocetti, V. Santoro, A. Coussa, F. M. Cappello, S.J., G. Mandelli, I.M.C., U. Bertini, F. Antonelli, O.F.M., G. Felici, A. Mauro, I. Cecchetti, N. Del Re, and L. Sandri in *E.C.*, iv (1950), cols. 308–50, s.v. 'Congregazioni romane', with bibl.

ROMAN MARTYROLOGY (*Martyrologium Romanum*). The official *Martyrology of the RC Church. It was compiled by a commission of ten scholars, among them C. *Baronius and A. Agellius (d. 1608), and issued by *Gregory XIII in 1584 to replace the various local adaptations of *Usuard's text current since the later Middle Ages. Several later Popes have subjected it to revisions demanded by the progress in historical knowledge and fresh canonizations. Of these the most radical was that of *Benedict XIV (1748), the principles of which are contained in a prefatory letter to John V, King of Portugal. More recent revisions are due to *Pius IX (1870), *Pius X (1913), and *Benedict XV (1922).

ROMAN PSALTER, The. The text of the Biblical Psalter which was used in all churches in Rome, as well as elsewhere in Italy, down to the time of Pope *Pius V (1566–72), when it was virtually replaced, except at *St. Peter's, Rome, by the '*Gallican Psalter' (q.v.). It has commonly been equated with the revision of the Latin Psalter which St. *Jerome says he compiled hastily ('cursim') on the basis of the *Septuagint, though this identification has recently been challenged. The Roman *Breviary still retains certain passages (outside the continuous text of the Pss.) from this version. See also *Psalters, Hieronymian*.

ROMANOS, St. (d. 556), 'Melodus' (ὁ μελ-ῳδός), Greek hymn-writer. A Syrian by birth, after a short time as deacon at the Church of the Resurrection at Berytus, he made his way to *Constantinople under Patr. Anastasius I (d. 518; not Anastasius II, d. 716, as W. Christ and other scholars), where he wrote some 1,000 hymns. Only about 80 survive, each consisting of 24 or more strophes. They are unsurpassed in early hymnody for inspiration, diction, and poetic quality; and are based on accent and not on the ancient metre (i.e. the quantities of the syllables). In the liturgical books their place has been taken by much inferior compositions; but his celebrated Christmas Day Hymn ('Η παρθένος σήμερον) continued in use at the Christmas Eve banquet in the Imperial Palace down to the 12th cent. Feast day, 1 Oct.

Many of Romanos's hymns are still unpubld.; but a crit. text of Romanos, prepared by P. Maas, is expected [1957]. Individual hymns will be found in W. Christ-M. Paranikas, *Anthologia Graeca Carminum Christianorum* (Leipzig, 1871), pp. 131–40 (2 hymns); J. B. *Pitra, *Analecta Sacra*, i (Paris, 1876), pp. 1–241 (29 items); G. Cammelli, *Romano il Melode*. Inni (1930; 8 hymns with Ital. tr.; the greater part of the book being repr. of earlier edd.), E. Mioni, *Romano il Melode* (1937; 10 further hymns). There is also a very faulty ed. by N. B. Tomadakes (Athens, 1952 ff.); cf. review of part by P. Joannou in *B.Z.*, xlviii (1955), pp. 142–54 with reff. to recent literature on Romanos. K. Krumbacher, 'Studien zu Romanos' in *Sb.* (Bayr.), 1898 (part 2), pp. 69–268; id., 'Umarbeitungen bei Romanos. Mit einem Anhang über das Zeitalter des Romanos', ib., 1899 (pt. 2), pp. 3–155; id., 'Romanos und Kyriakos', ib., 1901, pp. 693–764; id., 'Die Akrostichnis in der griechischen Kirchenpoesie', ib., 1903, pp. 551–690, esp. 'Die Akrostichnis bei Romanos', pp. 559–587; id., 'Miscellen zu Romanos' in *Abh.* (Bayr.), xxiv, Hft. 3 (1909), pp. 1–138. P. Maas, 'Die Chronologie der Hymnen des Romanos' in *B.Z.*, xv (1906), pp. 1–44; 'Romanos auf Papyrus' in *Byzantion*, xiv (1939), p. 381; and numerous other artt. by this author. Krumbacher, pp. 663–71; Bardenhewer, v, 159–65; Altaner (ed. 1951), p. 479. E. Amann in *D.T.C.*, xiii (pt. 2; 1937), cols. 2895–8.

ROMANS, Epistle to the. The longest of St. *Paul's Epistles and the most systematic theologically. The letter was dispatched from *Corinth, prob. *c.* A.D. 58, when St. Paul was about to leave for *Jerusalem at the close of his 'Third Missionary Journey' and was proposing to travel thence to *Rome, which he had not previously visited. It is the only Epistle which St. Paul addressed to a Church not of his own foundation. He writes as one conscious of his Apostolic commission from Christ, yet deferentially, as 'not wishing to build on another man's foundation' (cf. 15. 20).

After a formal opening, St. Paul gives an epitome of the Gospel which he preaches (1. 16 f.) which he makes the burden of his message. The universality of sin, both in the Gentile world with its idolatry and vice, and among the Jews, who have failed to keep the Mosaic law, is shown to be a fact (1. 18–2. 29), and leads to the conclusion that 'by the works of the law'—i.e. by all human efforts at obedience—'no flesh is justified before God' (3. 20). On the contrary, *Justification is given 'apart from law' (3. 21) by the righteousness (or 'righteous act') of God which is revealed in Christ, whom God 'set forth to be a propitiation' to reconcile sinful man to God (3. 25). The method of appropriating this free gift of God is by faith, acc. to the example of *Abraham (4), whose trust in God, rather than any legal observance, was 'counted to him for righteousness' (Gen. 15. 6). By such faith Christians obtain not only peace with God but also the hope of glory and the love of God, imparted through the gift of the Holy Spirit, all of which are mediated by the atoning death of Christ, the Second *Adam (5).

St. Paul next rebuts the objection that in such a situation we might as well continue in sin so that grace might abound. In reply he points to the fact that *Baptism effects a change in character which is (i) a death to sin and a sharing in Christ's death and resurrection, (ii) a transfer, as of a slave, to a new ownership, viz. from sin to righteousness, or (iii) like the death of a spouse, the end of one marriage-bond and the beginning of another (6. 1–7. 4). Lest these analogies might seem to make the 'law' equivalent to 'sin', he elaborates the true purpose of the law in God's design (7. 5–25). It is by the Spirit through Christ that we are freed from sin and the resulting condemnation and that we walk not by the flesh but by the Spirit. The life acc. to the Spirit, in which as 'joint heirs with Christ' we are led to eternal life, is celebrated in a hymn of confidence in the glory of our redemption (8).

The next section deals with the problem of the destiny of Israel. There is a new situation in which, while salvation is now offered freely also to Gentiles, most Jews have rejected it. But, as in His dealings with the patriarchs and Pharaoh, God is sovereign in His choice or rejection of whom He will, even though only a remnant of Israel be saved. St. Paul also recognizes that the falling-away of Israel may be only temporary, to provide an occasion for the bringing in of the Gentiles, and that we can trustfully await the eventual restoration of the unconverted Israelites in God's providence (9–11).

St. Paul now turns to the practical obligations of the Christian life. We are to live not acc. to the fashion of this present world but acc. to the will of God in the unity of the Body of Christ, 'overcoming evil with good' (12). Due obedience must be given to the civil government, for the ruler is a 'minister of God' (13. 1–7). The whole law is summed up in the command to love one's neighbour. All this is the more urgent, as the *Parousia is at hand (13. 8–14). There must be mutual tolerance. Those who do not share the sensitiveness of others about foods and days must respect the consciences of the scrupulous, who in turn must not judge their brethren (14. 1–15. 13).

In the final section St. Paul treats of his personal plans, conveys his greetings to some twenty-five named persons, adds yet a word more on unity, and concludes with further greetings, the 'grace', and a doxology (16. 25–7).

The integrity of the text of Rom. has been much discussed. There is evidence of an ancient recension which ended with ch. 14, followed immediately by 16. 25–27. There are also texts which omit the name 'Rome' in 1. 7 and 1. 15. There is no altogether satisfactory solution of these facts; but it seems more likely that the 'Short Recension' was abbreviated from the full text than that it preceded it. Many modern scholars have also contended (though here without textual evidence) that the long list of personal greetings in ch. 16 mark it as sent orig. to some community other than Rome, most prob. *Ephesus, in which Paul was personally known; but the evidence is not conclusive. The doxology (16. 25–27) appears in varying places in different MS. traditions, and in some is lacking altogether. This indeed may well be by a later hand.

Rom. has always been recognized as a primary contribution to Christian theology. Its influence is perhaps already to be traced in other Books of the NT (e.g. 1 Pet., Heb., Jas.) and it is quoted or alluded to by the Fathers from St. *Clement of Rome onwards. From the 4th cent. it stood first in the traditional *Canon of the Pauline Epp. From *Origen onwards it has been the subject of many commentaries, and its teaching was esp. influential in St. *Augustine's anti-*Pelagian works and has profoundly affected the Christian outlook on such questions as original sin, merit, and justification generally. In a different way, the reading of Rom. 13. 13 f. played a decisive part in St. Augustine's conversion (cf. *Confessions*, viii, 29). Meditation on Rom. 1. 16 f. strongly influenced M. *Luther's conviction of the truth of Justification by faith, and J. *Calvin wrote an important commentary on the Epistle. J. *Wesley's conversion was also connected with his study of it.

The unique theological significance of the Epistle to the Romans, together with its subtle argumentation at some of the crucial points, have attracted most of the greatest exegetes from the 3rd cent. onwards. The principal Gk. commentators are *Origen (whose Comm., written at *Caesarea in his later life, survives, apart from a few fragments, only in *Rufinus's paraphrase) and *Chrysostom (from his Antiochene years). Lat. commentators include *Ambrosiaster, *Pelagius, P. *Abelard, and St. *Thomas Aquinas (a study of exceptional penetration, due, however, more to the theological equipment which Aquinas brought to the Epistle than the close study of the text itself). Luther, despite the place which the teaching of Romans occupies in his theology, wrote no Comm. on Rom. to match his great work on Gal.; but important Commentaries come from P. *Melanchthon (Nuremberg, 1522 on Rom. and Cor.; more fully on Rom. only, Wittenberg, 1532; enlarged ed. Strassburg, 1540) and J. *Calvin (Strassburg, 1540). Among Commentaries publd. in the 19th cent. may be mentioned those of [F.] A. [G.] Tholuck (Halle, 1842; Eng. tr., 2 vols., 1833–6), C. F. A. Fritzsche (3 vols., Halle, 1836–1843), H. A. W. Meyer (K.E.K., Teil 2, iv; 1836; Eng. tr., 2 vols., 1873–4), B. *Jowett (2 vols. with Thess. and Gal., London, 1855, vol. ii), C. J. *Vaughan (Cambridge, 1859), F. *Godet (2 vols., Paris, 1879–80; Eng. tr., 2 vols., 1881), H. C. G. *Moule (Camb. Bib., 1879), B. *Weiss (K.E.K., Abt. iv, ed. 6, 1881), and H. P. *Liddon (posthumous, London, 1893).

For English-speaking students, a new era in the study of Rom. was opened by the Comm. of W. *Sanday–A. C. *Headlam, I.C.C., 1895). Since then there have appeared those of H. *Lietzmann (Hb. N.T. iii, pt. 1; 1906); T. *Zahn (Kommentar zum Neuen Testament, vi; Leipzig, 1910); E. Kühl (Leipzig, 1913); M. J. *Lagrange, O.P. (Études bibliques, 1916); N. P. *Williams in C. *Gore–H. L. Goudge–A. Guillaume (edd.), *A New Commentary on Holy Scripture* (1928), pp. 442–84; C. H. *Dodd (Moff. Comm., 1932); P. Boylan (Dublin, 1934); K. E. *Kirk (Clar. Bib., 1937); A. Nygren (Stockholm, 1944; Eng. tr., 1952); C. K. Barrett (Black's New Testament Commentaries, 1957). Though K. Barth's commentary, *Der Römerbrief* (1918; ed. 6, 1921; Eng. tr., 1933), often throws flashes of illumination on the Epistle, its main significance is as an exposition of the author's theological viewpoint. Other works on Rom. include K. *Lake, *The Earlier Epistles of St. Paul* (1911), pp. 324–420; P. Feine, *Der Römerbrief.* Eine exegetische Studie (1903). W. Luetgert, *Der Römerbrief als historisches Problem* (Beiträge zur Förderung christlicher Theologie, Jahrg. xvii, Hft. 2; 1913); A. *Schlatter, *Gottes Gerechtigkeit. Ein Kommentar zum Römerbrief* (1935). E. Evans, *To the Romans.* An Exposition of the Epistle (1948).

ROMANTICISM. The word is used esp. for the movement in literature and art reasserting passion and imagination in reaction from the classicism and rationalism which marked the 18th cent. As so used, it is a vague term, and describes a mood or tendency rather than a system. It has been applied, however, in a more exact sense to the school which flourished in Germany at the end of the 18th and the beginning of the 19th cent. of which Goethe has been termed the divinity, F. *Schlegel the high priest, and F. D. E. *Schleiermacher, with his definition of religion as 'feeling of dependence,' the prophet. Among its more vigorous Catholic lay exponents was *Chateaubriand; and *Novalis was also a prominent member of the group.

ROMANUS, St. A deacon and exorcist of a church of *Caesarea in Palestine, who was martyred at *Antioch (c. 304) in the *Diocletianic Persecution. The contemporary account of *Eusebius (De mart. Pal., 2) was embellished by later writers. *Prudentius mentions a boy associated with him in martyrdom, whom later tradition, perhaps through some confusion with an authentic Syriac martyr Barlaba or Balaam, names Barulas. The two saints are mentioned together in the Roman Martyrology. Feast day, 18 Nov.

H. *Delehaye, S.J., 'S. Romain martyr d'Antioche' in Anal. Boll. l (1932), pp. 241–83, with text of sources. On the entry in Roman Martyrology, id. in AA.SS., Nov. II (1931), p. 650 f. Id., 'S. Barlaam, martyr à Antioche' in Anal. Boll., xxii (1903), pp. 129–45, with text of 'Passio'.

ROMANUS, St. 'Melodus'. See *Romanos, St.

ROME (Early Christian). An early but not well grounded tradition asserts that St. *Peter reached Rome in A.D. 42. When the Ep. to the *Romans was written (c. A.D. 58), a large Christian community already existed at Rome, and *Suetonius almost certainly refers to Christians in Claud., xxv, 4 (Judaeos impulsore Chresto tumultuantes Roma expulsit). St. Paul arrived between A.D. 59 and 61 (Acts 28. 16) and it is probable that his '*Captivity Epistles', as well as Mk., Lk., Acts, and 1 Pet., were written in Rome. The burning of the City under *Nero (A.D. 64) was a pretext for a general persecution of the Christians (Tacitus, Ann., xv, 44; I Clem. 6) in which it appears that both St. Peter and St. Paul were martyred. Under Vespasian (69–79) and Titus (79–81) the Church grew and attracted persons of every social class, incl. members of the patrician families. *Domitian (81–96) had his cousin, the consul Flavius Clemens, and his cousin's wife, Flavia Domitilla, banished, prob. because they were Christians.

The early Roman Bishops, of whom we have exceptionally reliable lists, were all Greek-speaking before *Victor I (c. 189) and mostly administrators rather than theologians. In the first two cents. the most notable Bishops were St. *Clement I (c. 88–97), author of an Ep. to the Church in Corinth; St. *Telesphorus (c. 126–36), prob. the only martyr among them; St. *Pius I (c. 141–55), brother of the *Hermas who was author of 'The Shep-

herd'; Anicetus (c. 155–66), who received St. *Polycarp of Smyrna and discussed with him the dating of *Easter; and St. Victor I, the first Latin-speaking Bishop, whose action in the *Quartodeciman Controversy reflects the growing importance of the see. St. *Ignatius of Antioch was martyred at Rome (c. 110–17), and under *Marcus Aurelius (A.D. 161–80) the Church was severely persecuted, St. *Justin Martyr and (prob.) St. *Cecilia being among the victims. During the 2nd cent. Christians and semi-Christians of the most diverse views (*Tatian, *Hegesippus, *Valentinus and *Marcion) congregated in Rome.

During the early 3rd cent., a number of *Monarchians of varying schools taught in the capital and were opposed by the rigorist theologian, St. *Hippolytus. Hippolytus's disputes with St. *Callistus (Bp. 217–22) on disciplinary and dogmatic matters led to a serious schism, which continued until the episcopate of Pontian (230–5) when the persecution of Maximin (Emp., 235–8) issued in the exile of the leaders of both parties and their consequent reconciliation. During the persecution of *Decius (249–51) St. *Fabian (Bp. 236–50) was martyred and the see kept vacant for thirteen months. Another rigorist schism, led by the presbyter *Novatian, took place under Fabian's successor, *Cornelius (251–3), who died in exile during the persecution of Gallus. *Stephen I, the next Pope (253–7), is known for his controversy with St. *Cyprian of Carthage about re-baptism. Persecution began once more under Valerian (253–60) who struck both at the clergy and the property of the Church, and in 258 the Bishop, *Sixtus (Xystus) II, and all his deacons, incl. St. *Laurence (q.v.), were martyred. Bishop *Dionysius of Rome (259–68) is best remembered for his intervention in a doctrinal dispute in the Church of Alexandria.

By this date the Roman Church was already highly organized. Under Cornelius there were forty-six presbyters, seven deacons, and a large number of lesser ministers (*Eusebius, H.E., VI, xliii, 11). The considerable property of the Church included private houses (tituli) in the City for worship and burial-places (*catacombs, q.v.) outside the walls. Both these would be made over to the Church by wealthy Christians who would hold them in custody for the community. The administration of this property, together with the relief of a large number of poor, fell to the deacons, each of whom had a district and a staff under him.

Little is recorded of the course of the *Diocletianic persecution at Rome. The accounts both of the lapse and martyrdom of Bp. Marcellinus (296–304) seem equally unreliable. But it is known that the Church's property was confiscated, and that a number of Christians fell away; and it is possible that among the victims was St. *Agnes. With the coup d'état of Maxentius (306), persecution ceased, but the see remained vacant until 308. Bps. Marcellus (308–9) and Eusebius (310) had to face opposition from the lapsed who wished to be readmitted to communion with little or no penance. The disorders which arose led to the exile of both Bishops and their chief opponent, Heraclius. The re-establishment of the *tituli* by Marcellus and the return of the Church's property in 311 under Bp. *Miltiades (311–4) were the prelude to the grant of full toleration. This was achieved by Constantine's victory at the Milvian Bridge (28 Oct. 312) and the so-called Edict of *Milan (313).

The period from 313 to the fall of the Western Empire in 476 saw the steady growth of the authority of the Bishops, or Popes, of Rome. They consistently intervened on the orthodox side in the theological disputes of the time. Their characteristics were common sense, firm adherence to traditional belief, distrust of theological niceties, and support of orthodox leaders in adversity, qualities which made appeal to their authority increasingly general. *Julius I (337–52) and *Liberius (352–66) upheld the Nicene faith against the *Arians, *Damasus I (366–84) condemned *Apollinarianism, *Innocent I (402–17) *Pelagianism, and *Celestine I (422–32) *Nestorianism, while the '*Tome' of St. *Leo I (the Great) (440–61), a masterly statement of the orthodox doctrine of the Incarnation, greatly assisted the defeat of *Eutychianism at the Council of *Chalcedon (451). St. *Athanasius was welcomed in Rome while in exile from 339 to 342, and St. *Cyril of Jerusalem, Flavian of Antioch and St. *Augustine were all supported by the increasingly respected authority of the Roman see in their struggles against heresy.

During this period the disciplinary authority of the Papacy increased steadily despite the exile of Liberius, the intrusion of the anti-pope Felix, and the tumults which accompanied the elections of Damasus and *Boniface (418–22). The Canons of *Sardica (343) and the legislation of Gratian (Emp., 375–83) and *Theodosius (d. 395) firmly established the Roman see as a court of appeal. The earliest genuine decretal dates from the reign of *Siricius (384–99), and Innocent I and Leo I frequently intervened in the affairs of other Churches.

Meanwhile paganism lingered on among the aristocracy much longer in Rome than elsewhere. Not before 382 was Christian influence sufficiently strong to cause the removal, by Gratian, of the Altar of Victory from the Senate-house; but there soon followed the anti-pagan legislation of Theodosius and the decree of Honorius (408) denying the right of property to the pagan religions. The growth of Christianity in Rome in the period is reflected in the building of churches under Pope *Sylvester (314–35) and his successors (see *Rome, Churches of*), the restoration by Pope Damasus of the tombs of the martyrs, the introduction of monastic life by St. Athanasius and St. *Jerome, and the new ('Vulgate') Latin version of the Bible by Jerome at the instance of Damasus.

In political significance Rome suffered greatly after the removal of the capital of the

Empire to *Constantinople (330). Even in the West Milan and later *Ravenna became the effective capitals rather than Rome. In the 5th cent. Italy was invaded thrice, by *Alaric the Goth, Attila the Hun, and Gaiseric the Vandal, and Rome was sacked twice before the final fall of the Western Empire in 476. The rule of Italy passed into the hands first of Odoacer, and then of Theodoric the Ostrogoth, both of whom, as Arians, were not well disposed to the Roman see. Their policy, however, was one of tolerance, and a far greater disaster was the long Gothic War (537–553) during which Rome changed hands several times between Goths and Byzantines, and, at one point, was almost completely abandoned by its inhabitants. The partial conquest of Italy by the Arian Lombards and the decline of the Byzantine power made it necessary for the Popes to assume political authority in Rome. Fortunately for the Papacy, this coincided with the pontificates of the able Pelagius II (579–90), and his greater successor St. *Gregory I ('the Great') (590–604). The defence of the 'Roman Duchy' was assured by the papal policy of holding the balance of power between Byzantines, Lombards, and (later) Franks. Gregory's missionary and pastoral zeal, united with his remarkable statesmanship, make his pontificate one of the outstanding eras in the history of the Papacy. Especially notable was his genius in turning Benedictine monasticism into an instrument for missionary activity. After the Lombards had destroyed practically all monastic life in Italy except in Rome itself, Gregory founded his own monastery on the Celian Hill which gave refuge to Benedict's own community of *Monte Cassino and sent St. Augustine to Britain. By his thought-out revision of the Roman liturgy and chant (see *Schola Cantorum) he gave both the form which became the basis of the worship of the Western Church in the Middle Ages.

Relations between the Papacy and the Byzantine Emperors, the nominal overlords of Rome, deteriorated during the 7th cent. Pope Martin I (649–55) died a prisoner in exile and *Gregory II (715–31) was the chief opponent of the *Iconoclast Emperor, *Leo III (the Isaurian). We have the beginnings of the Temporal Power of the Papacy in the Donation of Sutri to 'St. Peter' (729) by the Lombard King, Luitprand. The growth of the Lombard power led Pope Stephen III (752–7) to appeal in 753 to the Frankish King *Pepin for support and in 773 *Hadrian I (772–95) followed his example with Pepin's son, *Charlemagne. The Frankish intervention led to the destruction of the Lombard kingdom, to the restoration of the Roman Duchy and the Exarchate of Ravenna not to the Byzantine Empire but to the Papacy, and, in 800, to the coronation by St. *Leo III (795–816) in Rome of Charlemagne as Roman Emperor.

See also foll. entry, and under individual Popes.

The most important single early source is the *Liber Pontificalis (q.v.). Much primary material is also to be found in the extant Papal Letters (conveniently catalogued in Jaffé, i). The subject naturally occupies a place in all histories of the early Church, notably those of L. *Duchesne, P. *Batiffol, and H. *Lietzmann, and in C. *Baronius's *Annales*. Much information also in the earlier volumes of F. *Gregorovius, *Geschichte der Stadt Rom im Mittelalter* (8 vols., 1859–72; Eng. tr., 8 vols., 1894–1902). H. Grisar, S.J., *Geschichte Roms und der Päpste im Mittelalter*, i: Rom beim Ausgang der antiken Welt (14 Lieferungen, [1898–] 1901). H. Lietzmann, *Petrus und Paulus in Rom*. Liturgische und archäologische Studien (1915; ed. 2, 1927). E. Caspar, *Geschichte des Papsttums* (2 vols., 1930–3). On the transition to Medieval Rome, cf. also L. Duchesne, *Les Premiers Temps de l'état pontifical, 754–1073* (1898).

ROME, Churches of. From the innumerable Roman churches of historic and ecclesiastical interest, only a selection, necessarily somewhat arbitrary, can be listed in this art. For the four 'Major *Basilicas', (1) *St. Peter's, (2) St. John *Lateran, (3) *Santa Maria Maggiore, and (4) *St. Paul's outside the Walls, see sep. entries.

In addition to these Major Basilicas three further churches (here listed first, Nos. 5, 6, and 7) also take rank as 'Patriarchal Basilicas'.

(5) *S. Croce in Gerusalemme* (Basilica Sessoriana). Founded by St. *Helena *c.* 325 on the site of the Sessorian Palace to enshrine the newly recovered relics of the Passion. Very little of the 4th cent. building remains except a subterranean chapel and the pillars of the nave. A Council met here as early as 433, and at a later date the Pope went barefoot on Good Friday from the Lateran to S. Croce, carrying a relic of the Cross. The church was rebuilt by Lucius II (1144), much restored by *Urban V (1370), and modernized under *Benedict XIV (1744).

(6) *S. Lorenzo fuori le Mura* (4th cent.). In the Cemetery of S. Ciriaco where St. *Laurence was buried. The basilica, already described by *Prudentius (d. *c.* 410), was rebuilt by Pelagius II (578–90) and entirely reconstructed by *Honorius III (d. 1227), who transferred the façade and porch to the W. end. *Pius IX (d. 7 Feb. 1878) is buried in the crypt. The church was damaged by a bomb on 19 July 1943.

(7) *S. Sebastiano fuori le Mura* (4th–5th cent.). On the *Appian Way over the catacombs. The relics of St. *Peter and St. *Paul were prob. removed here during the Valerianic Persecution (258). The church is first mentioned by St. *Gregory the Great (d. 604). It contains the body of St. *Sebastian and a statue of the saint designed by G. L. Bernini (1589–1680); the present church is mainly the work of Card. Scipio Borghese (1612).

(8) *S. Agnese*. On the Via Nomentana, adjoining the catacombs where St. *Agnes was buried. Built under *Constantine (d. 337) or slightly later, the church (now subterranean) has a fine mosaic in the apse depicting St. Agnes with Popes *Symmachus (498–514) and *Honorius I (625–38) on either side. In a chapel is the shrine of St. Emerentiana (feast day, 23 Jan.), her foster sister. Annually on 21 Jan. the lambs to provide wool for the archiepiscopal *pallia are blessed here. The church is served by *Canons Regular of the Lateran.

(9) *S. Clemente*. Near the *Colosseum. The present church dates from the 12th cent. *Paschal II, d. 1118); but excavations begun in 1858 revealed the existence of a much larger church (mentioned by St. *Jerome in 392; the scene of a Council in 417) at a lower level, which was severely damaged at the sack of Rome under Robert Guiscard (1084). The latter has some highly interesting 9th–11th cent. mural paintings depicting the legends of Sts. *Cyril and Methodius and of St. *Clement. The white marble altar canopy, choir screen, and ambones of the present church no doubt belonged to this earlier structure. At a still lower level is a chapel of *Mithras dating from the Imperial Age. The church, with the adjacent priory, is now in the hands of Irish *Dominicans.

(10) *SS. Cosmas & Damiano*. On the edge of the Forum. The first of the Roman churches to be constructed from pagan temples, it consists of the union of two buildings, a round Temple of Romulus (built by the Emp. Maxentius, son of Maximian; d. 312), and a rectangular Temple of the Sacra Urbs (built by Vespasian, d. A.D. 79). They were adapted to Christian worship by Felix IV (528), who inserted the notable mosaics (subjects from the Apocalypse, &c.) and dedicated the church to Sts. *Cosmas and Damian, the two 'anarguroi' who enjoyed great popularity at Rome in the 6th cent.

(11) *S. Francesca Romana* (S. Maria Nuova). In the Forum. *Leo IV (d. 855) erected the church, formerly known as S. Maria Nuova, on a site partly occupied by a ruined Temple of Venus and Rome, to replace the ruined S. Maria Antiqua. The mosaics in the apse date from 1161; the beautiful campanile from the 12th–13th cent. St. *Frances of Rome (q.v.), whose labours were centred here, was buried in the church (1440), which was restored by Carlo Maderna (1556–1629) after her canonization (1608). It is served by *Oblates of the Order of St. Benedict.

(12) The *Gesù*. The principal church of the *Jesuits and one of the most ornate in Rome, enshrining the body of St. *Ignatius Loyola, their founder. It was built (1568–75) in the *Baroque style by Card. Alessandro Farnese (1520–89), nephew of *Paul III after designs by Vignola and Giacomo della Porta.

(13) *SS. Giovanni & Paolo*. On the Celian Hill. Built by Pammachius over the supposed house of the two Roman saints, *John and Paul (4th cent.). Interesting remains of an ancient dwelling (discovered 1887) contain some famous frescoes (Christ between Sts. Michael and Gabriel, Sts. John and Paul). The church, which with other buildings on the Celian Hill was severely damaged by the Normans in the sack of Rome, was enlarged in the 1154, and extensively restored in the late 19th cent. In a chapel lies the body of St. *Paul of the Cross, founder of the *Passionists, who now serve the church.

(14) *S. Gregorio Magno*. Also on the Celian Hill. A monastery was established here in 575 by St. *Gregory the Great (Pope, 590–604) in

his paternal house (*gens Anicii*) and dedicated to St. *Andrew the Apostle. Later *Gregory II (715–31) dedicated it to his earlier namesake. The church, which claims to possess the stone bed and marble chair of the saint (himself buried in St. Peter's), was extensively restored by G. B. Soria in 1633 under Card. Borghese and the interior modernized in 1725–34. It has close connexions with England as the orig. home of St. *Augustine of Canterbury and the titular church of Cards. H. E. *Manning and H. *Vaughan, successive Abps. of *Westminster. There are some modern frescoes by Guido Reni (1574–1642). Since 1573 the church has been served by *Camaldolese.

(15) *S. Maria in Ara Coeli* (so named since 14th cent.). On the site of the ancient Roman citadel and the Temple of Juno Moneta and already mentioned as 'S. Maria de Capitolio' in the 9th cent. It was in this church that E. *Gibbon conceived the plan of his *Decline and Fall*. A chapel in the transept ('Capella Santa di Sant' Elena) marks the spot where, acc. to an early legend, a vision of the Blessed Virgin on an altar in heaven (*ara coeli*) was granted the Emp. Augustus (d. A.D. 14) when sacrificing. Beneath this altar in a porphyry sarcophagus are the reputed remains of St. *Helena. The church was the scene of Marcantonio Colonna's solemn thanksgiving for the victory of *Lepanto (5 Oct. 1571). Since 1280 it has been served by *Franciscans.

(16) *S. Maria in Cosmedin* (also 'Bocca della Verità'). On the site of an ancient temple, perh. the 'Temple of Fortune', and in a region formerly inhabited by Greek refugee Christians, it was prob. so named from its beauty (Gk. κοσμέω, 'adorn'; or perh. from a square named 'Cosmedin' in *Constantinople). The church, which has recently been restored to its austere simplicity, is one of the best examples of an early basilica in Rome (inlaid marble canopy over high altar, ambones, Cosmati pavement); the fine campanile was erected by *Hadrian I (d. 795). Acc. to a late tradition, St. *Augustine of Hippo taught at a neighbouring house.

(17) *S. Maria ad Martyres* (the 'Pantheon'). The foundations go back to a building erected by Marcus Agrippa, son-in-law of the Emp. Augustus, in 27 B.C.; the present round structure and vaulting are due to Hadrian (d. 138) who rebuilt it after it had been struck by lightning. On 13 May 609 it was dedicated as a Christian church by Boniface IV (608–15) under the name of 'S. Maria ad Martyres', large quantities of relics being brought from the catacombs to mark the event and the Feast of *All Saints (orig. 13 May) instituted. *Urban VIII (Maffeo Barberini) removed the bronze panels from the ceiling of the portico to provide metal for the spiral columns for the baldacchino of St. Peter's (hence 'Quod non fecerunt barbari, fecerunt Barberini'). The church contains the tomb of *Raphael.

(18) *S. Maria sopra Minerva*. On the ruins of an ancient temple of Minerva which later became the site of a Greek monastery. The present church (completed 1453), the only Gothic Church in Rome, was begun *c.* 1280 by Fra Sisto and Fra Ristoro, two *Dominicans, and has been continuously served by members of the Order. It contains statues, frescoes, and paintings by *Michelangelo, Filippino Lippi, Giacomo della Porta, and other famous artists.

(19) *S. Pietro in Vincoli* (also 'Basilica Eudoxiana'). The church, which goes back at least to 431, being at first known as *titulus Apostolorum*, was reconstructed by Sixtus III (432–40), to whom the Empress Eudoxia, wife of Valentinian II, presented the reputed chains of St. Peter. Among its monuments are the celebrated *Moses of Michelangelo, a relief of *Nicholas of Cusa, and the tomb of *Julius II (1503–13). It is served by Canons Regular of St. John Lateran.

(20) *S. Prassede*. On the Esquiline. The present church, which contains the reputed remains of St. *Praxedes and St. *Pudentiana, was built by Paschal I (817–24) near an earlier church of the same dedication. A chapel near the W. end contains some furniture which belonged to St. *Charles Borromeo, titular Card. of this church. The 9th cent. mosaics, among the best in Rome, depict subjects from the Apocalypse. A column in the chapel of St. *Zeno is traditionally reckoned that to which Christ was bound. The church, which is served by *Vallumbrosans, inspired R. Browning's 'Tomb at St. Praxed's'.

(21) *S. Pudenziana*. Near the foot of the Esquiline. Its nucleus was the mansion of the senator, Pudens, whose daughters, Praxedes and Pudentiana, are said to have given it to *Pius I (d. 154?). The church was restored as early as the time of *Siricius (d. 395). The apse has some fine early mosaics (4th cent. but much restored; incl. Christ with the Apostles, St. Praxedes, St. Pudentiana). A table in the church is venerated as that on which St. Peter celebrated Mass.

(22) *SS. Quatro Coronati*. On the Celian Hill. As early as the 4th cent. a church (*titulus Aemilianae*) existed on the site; it was later dedicated to the *Quattro Coronati whose bodies it enshrines. After its destruction by Robert Guiscard (1084), it was rebuilt in 1111 by Paschal II, who reduced its size. It is served by *Capuchins.

(23) *S. Sabina*. On the Aventine. Built by an Illyrian priest, Petrus, and consecrated, acc. to tradition, in 432, it is one of the most impressive Roman basilicas (recently admirably restored). It contains a fine series of columns of Parian marble which came from a Temple of Diana and between the vestibule and nave a large wooden door (5th–6th cent.) with a series of remarkable wood-carvings (incl. very early Crucifixion). The church has been served by Dominicans since the time of *Honorius III (d. 1227).

(24) *S. Stefano Rotondo*. On the Celian Hill not far from the Lateran. Prob. orig. a secular building, it was consecrated by Pope *Simplicius (468–83), decorated with marbles in the 6th cent., and adorned with mosaics (Christ above a jewelled cross; Sts. Primus and Felicianus, martyrs from the age of the Persecution of Diocletian) in the 7th cent.

The transverse wall prob. belongs to the time of *Hadrian I (d. 795). Under *Nicholas V (1447–55) a third outside circle of pillars was destroyed and the church correspondingly reduced in size; but it is said to be still the largest circular church in existence. It contains an ancient episcopal throne from which St. Gregory I (d. 604) delivered one of his homilies.

M. Armellini, *Le chiese di Roma dalle loro origini fino al secolo xvi* (1887; new ed., continuing history to 19th cent. ed. C. Cecchelli, 2 vols., 1942). O. *Marucchi, *Basiliques et églises de Rome* (1902). J. P. Kirsch, *Die römischen Titelkirchen im Altertum* (Studien zur Geschichte und Kultur des Altertums, ix, Hftt. 1–2; 1918). Id., *Die Stationskirchen des Missale Romanum* (Ecclesia Orans, xix; 1926). C. Hülsen, *Le chiese di Roma nel medio evo*. Cataloghi ed appunti (1927). F. X. Zimmermann, *Die Kirchen Roms* (1935). R. Krautheimer, *Corpus Basilicarum Christianarum Romae* (Monumenti d' Antichità cristiana pubblicati dal Pontificio Istituto di Archeologia Cristiana, Ser. 2, ii; 1937 ff.). J. Wilpert, *Die römische Mosaiken und Malereien kirchlicher Bauten vom IV. bis XIII. Jahrhundert* (4 vols., 1916). Popular survey in English by R. Thynne, *The Churches of Rome* (1924). U. Benigni in *C.E.*, xiii (1912), pp. 164–79, s.v. 'Rome', esp. pp. 169–75; E. Josi in *E.C.*, x (1953), cols. 1208–45, s.v. 'Roma V: topografia'.

ROMUALD, St. (*c.* 950–1027), founder of the *Camaldolese Order. A nobleman of *Ravenna, he entered the abbey of Sant' Apollinare in Classe through horror at his father having killed a man in a duel. In 998 he was appointed abbot, but the life not proving sufficiently severe, he resigned in the next year and retired to the neighbouring marshes to practise rigid asceticism. In his later years he wandered round Italy, founding hermitages and monasteries, that at Campus Maldoli becoming the centre of the Camaldolese Order. Feast day, 7 Feb.

Fragm. of exposition on Ps. lxviii attrib. to Romuald in J. P. Migne, *PL*, cxl, 1125–8. Life by St. *Peter Damian (*c.* 1040) in *AA.SS.*, Feb. II (1658), pp. 104–24; also repr. from A. *Mai's ed. of Damian's works in J. P. Migne, op. cit., cxliv, 953–1008. Filippo Maria da Napoli, O. Camald., *Delle notizie storiche della vita di San Romoaldo* (Naples, 1716). B. Collina, *Vita di San Romualdo, fondatore della religione camaldolese* (2 pts., Bologne, 1752). W. Franke, *Quellen und Chronologie zur Geschichte Romualdo von Camaldoli und seiner Einsiedlergenossenschaften im Zeitalter Ottos III* (Diss., Halle, 1910); id., *Romuald von Camaldoli und seine Reformtätigkeit zur Zeit Ottos III* (Historische Studien, cvii; 1913). Modern lives by A. Pagnani (Sassoferrato; 1927) and T. Ciampelli (Ravenna, 1927). L. A. St. L. Toke in *C.E.*, xiii (1912), p. 179.

'ROOT AND BRANCH'. An expression originally taken from the wording of the London Petition of 11 Dec. 1640 (itself modelled on Mal. 4. 1) in which it was demanded 'that the said government [i.e. the episcopal system] with all its dependencies, roots, and branches, be abolished'. The petition thus became known as the Root and Branch Petition, and the bill of 1641 embodying its demands the Root and Branch Bill; and the expression hence came to be applied to any thoroughgoing policy.

ROPES, JAMES HARDY (1866–1933), NT scholar. Born at Salem, Massachusetts, he was educated at Harvard and Andover and in Germany. From 1903 until his death he was professor at Harvard university. His principal writings were *Die Sprüche Jesu* (Texte und Untersuchungen, xiv. 2; 1896), an edition of the uncanonical sayings of Christ; a Commentary on the Ep. of St. James (*I.C.C.*, 1916); and an edition of the texts (based on *Codex Vaticanus and *Codex Bezae) of the Acts of the Apostles (*Beginnings of Christianity*, ed. F. J. Foakes-Jackson and K. *Lake, vol. iii, 1926).

E. C. Moore in *Dict. Amer. Biog.*, xvi (1935), p. 151 f.

ROSARY. The devotion to the Fifteen *Mysteries (q.v.) in which fifteen '*decades' of ' *Ave Marias', are recited, each decade being preceded by the *Paternoster and followed by the *Gloria Patri. Ordinarily only a third part of the Rosary, a so-called *chaplet, is said on one occasion. To assist the memory, the prayers are commonly counted on a string of beads. Acc. to a tradition current since the 15th cent., the devotion of the Rosary was founded by St. *Dominic in the course of his missionary work against the *Albigensians; but in fact it seems to have developed gradually, esp. under *Cistercian and Dominican influence. The name of an earlier form of instrument for reciting the rosary (a 'paternoster') survives in 'Paternoster Row' in London, once the residence of craftsmen who made them. In the RC Church the Feast of the Rosary is kept on 7 Oct., the anniversary of the victory of the Christian naval forces over the Turks at *Lepanto (1571), and throughout the month of October special prominence is given to the devotion. See also *Chaplet* and *Rings* (7).

H. Thurston, S.J., 'The Rosary' in *The Month*, xcvi (1900), pp. 403–18, 513–27, 620–37, xcvii (1901), pp. 67–79, 172–88, 286–304, and 384–404. M. Chéry, O.P., *La Théologie du rosaire* (2 vols., 1869); id., *Histoire générale du rosaire et de sa confrérie* (1869); T. Esser, O.P., *Unserer Lieben Frauen Rosenkranz erklärt* (1889); M. D. Chapotin, O.P., *Les Quinze Mystères du saint-rosaire* (1900). H. Holzapfel, O.F.M., *St. Dominicus und der Rosenkranz* (Veröffentlichungen aus dem kirchenhistorischen Seminar München, Nr. 12; 1903). M. M. Gorce, O.P., *Le Rosaire et ses antécédents historiques* (1932). H. Thurston, S.J., in *C.E.*, xiii (1912), pp. 184–7, s.v.; M. M. Gorce, O.P., in *D.T.C.*, xiii (pt. 2; 1937), cols. 2902–11, s.v. 'Rosaire'; P. Paschini-G. Löw, C.SS.R.–W. Wehr in *E.C.*, ix (1953), cols. 1349–54, s.v. 'Rosario', with further bibl.

ROSCELLINUS (d. *c.* 1125), Scholastic philosopher and theologian. The facts of his life are very imperfectly known. Probably a native of Compiègne, he studied at Soissons and *Reims, and later taught as a canon either at Compiègne or at Besançon. He was accused of *Tritheism at a Council at Soissons in 1092, but denied having taught it and went to England, where his doctrines were opposed by St. *Anselm. After his return to France he taught at Loches, Besançon, and Tours, his most famous pupil being P. *Abelard, who attacked his teaching *c.* 1120.

Roscellinus's theories are known principally through the works of his opponents Anselm, Abelard, and *John of Salisbury. He was one of the first and most outstanding defenders of

*Nominalism, and possibly even its founder. He stressed the universal *in voce* to the detriment of the universal *in re*, claiming to establish that a being can have no parts. These philosophical tenets led him to adopt a Tritheist position, on the consideration that if the three Persons of the Trinity were identical in substance as orthodoxy affirms, the Father, in generating the Son, would generate Himself and, on the other hand, the Father and the Holy Spirit would have become incarnate together with the Son.

His sole surviving work, a letter to P. Abelard, is ed. J. A. Schmeller in *Abh.* (Bayr.), v (Hft. 3; 1849), pp. 189–210; repr. in J. P. Migne, *PL*, clxxviii, 357–72; crit. ed. by J. Reiners, *Der Nominalismus in der Frühscholastik* (B.G.P.M., viii, Hft. 5; 1910), pp. 62–80, with discussion of his position, pp. 25–41. Recently discovered letter from Walter of Honnecourt to Roscellinus ed. by G. *Morin, O.S.B., in *Rev. Bén.*, xxii (1905), pp. 172–5. F. Picavet, *Roscelin, philosophe et théologien, d'après la légende et d'après l'histoire* (École pratique des Hautes Études. Section des sciences religieuses. Rapports annuels, 1896; greatly enlarged ed., 1911). Überweg, ii, 206–9, with bibl. p. 701; M. M. Gorce, O.P., in *D.T.C.*, xiii (pt. 2; 1937), cols. 2911–15, s.v., with bibl.

ROSE OF LIMA, St. (1586–1617), the first canonized saint of America. She lived all her life in Lima, Peru, and from childhood practised the severest austerities. In her 20th year she joined the *Third Order of St. *Dominic. A vow of virginity and her strictness of life incurred persecution from her family and friends, and she also suffered intensely from interior desolation. Long sickness and early death crowned her self-sought mortifications. She was canonized by Clement X in 1671 and is the Patroness of S. America and the Philippines. Feast day, 30 Aug.

A.A.SS., Aug. V (1741), pp. 892–1029, incl. text of life by Leonard Hansen, O.P., pr. at Louvain, 1668, pp. 902–84, and bull of canonization, pp. 1027–9. Short life by J. B. Feuillet (Paris, 1671; Eng. tr. in *The Lives of St. Rose of Lima, the Blessed Columba*, &c., ed. by F. W. *Faber, London, 1847, pp. 3–195). M. T. de Bussierre, *Le Pérou et sainte Rose de Lima* (1863); F. M. Capes, *The Flower of the New World*. Being a Short History of St. Rose of Lima (1899). Further bibl. in *E.C.*, x (1953), col. 1338 f., s.v. [unsigned].

ROSE, Golden. See *Golden Rose*.

ROSE, HUGH JAMES (1795–1838), pre-*Tractarian Anglican High Churchman. He was educated at Trinity College, Cambridge, and after ordination as priest in 1819 held the vicarage of Horsham, Sussex, from 1821 to 1830, and of Hadleigh, Suffolk, from 1830 to 1833. A year's absence in Germany from May 1824 bore fruit in *The State of the Protestant Religion in Germany* (1825), designed to counteract the dangers of contemporary rationalism on the Continent. Its hostile tone provoked a reply from E. B. *Pusey, who in his early years was more sympathetically disposed than later towards German theology. In 1832 he founded the *British Magazine* to further High Church doctrines. A meeting in July 1833 in his rectory at Hadleigh, attended by W. *Palmer (of Worcester College), A. P. *Perceval, and R. H. *Froude,

was an important landmark in the beginnings of the Tractarian Movement and indirectly led to the 'Association of Friends of the Church'. Later Rose became somewhat more critical of the Tractarian ideals. In 1833–4 he held the chair of divinity at *Durham University and in 1836 he was appointed Principal of *King's College, London. Rose's other writings include *The Commission and Consequent Duties of the Clergy* (1826), *A Letter to the Lord Bishop of London in Reply to Mr. Pusey's Work on the Causes of Rationalism in Germany* (1829), *Notices of the Mosaic Law* (1831), and *The Gospel an Abiding System* (1832).

J. W. *Burgon, *The Lives of Twelve Good Men*, i (1888), pp. 116–283 (No. 2; 'The Restorer of the Old Paths'). J. M. Rigg in *D.N.B.*, xlix (1897), pp. 240–2. See also bibl. to *Oxford Movement*.

ROSENMÜLLER, ERNST FRIEDRICH KARL (1768–1835), Biblical scholar. From 1792 till his death he taught at Leipzig. He issued a long series of commentaries and other works bearing on Scriptural (esp. OT) exegesis, which drew extensively on rabbinic and patristic sources. They included *Scholia in Vetus Testamentum* (16 parts, 1788–1817), *Handbuch der biblischen Altertumskunde* (4 vols., 1823–31), and a new edition of S. *Bochart's *Hierozoicon* (1793–96).

A. Vogel–G. Frank in *P.R.E.* (ed. 3), xvii (1906), p. 156 f.

ROSETTA STONE, the celebrated basalt stele which provided J. F. Champollion (1790–1832) and others with the key to the Egyptian hieroglyphics. Discovered in 1799 by a French officer in the neighbourhood of Rosetta on the W. bank of the western mouth of the Nile, it records in Egyptian (both hieroglyphics and demotic) and in Greek a decree of the priests assembled at Memphis in favour of Ptolemy V Epiphanes (reigned 204–181 B.C.). At the fall of *Alexandria in 1801 it passed into the hands of the British Government. The interpretation of the demotic text was mainly the work of Thomas Young (1773–1829) who published his conclusions in 1815. The stone is now in the British Museum.

E. A. W. Budge, *The Rosetta Stone and the Decipherment of Egyptian Hieroglyphs* (1929), with Gk., Demotic, and Egyptian texts, Eng. trr., and full bibl.

ROSICRUCIANS. The name assumed by the members of certain secret societies akin to the freemasons, who venerated the emblems of the Rose and the Cross as twin symbols of the Lord's Resurrection and Redemption. Early in the 17th cent. (1604 or 1614) two anonymous writings were published in Germany, the *Chymische Hochzeit Christiani Rosenkreutz* and the *Confessio Fraternitatis*, which are now unanimously assigned to the *Lutheran pastor, J. V. Andreae (1586–1654). They narrate the fabulous story of a certain Christian Rosenkreutz who, having learned the wisdom of the Arabs in the E. became the founder of a secret society devoted to the study of the hidden things of nature and an esoteric and anticatholic kind of Christianity, which acc. to the author was still in existence. The books, meant to be satirical, were taken seriously and aroused a very wide interest. A flood of literature about the mysterious society followed, and the curiosity kindled was so great that even men like R. *Descartes and G. W. *Leibniz tried in vain to get into touch with its genuine members, while a number of new societies with alchemistic tendencies actually came into being under this title. The best-known English representative of these tendencies was Robert Fludd (1574–1637), a London physician who spread Rosicrucian ideas in a number of medico-theosophical books. In the 18th cent. the name 'Gold-und Rosen-kreuzer' ('Gold- and Rosi-crucians') was adopted by a society started at Vienna which, spreading rapidly through Germany, Russia, and Poland, received only freemasons of the master grade and generally followed masonic ideas. One of its most famous members was the Prussian minister, J. C. von Wöllner (1732–1800), through whom Rosicrucian ideas exercised a strong influence on Friedrich Wilhelm II of Prussia; but the society became extinct before the end of the 18th cent.

The considerable literature is mainly the work of authors of Rosicrucian leanings or profession. It includes: A. E. Waite, *The Real History of the Rosicrucians* (1887), with reff. to earlier Eng. litt.; id., *The Brotherhood of the Rosy Cross* (1924); F. Wittemans, *Histoire des Rose-Croix* (ed. 3, 1925; Eng. tr., 1939). R. S. Clymer, *The Rosicrucians. Their Teaching* (Quakertown, Pa., 1923). F. de P. Castells, *Our Ancient Brethren, the Originators of Freemasonry. An Introduction to the History of Rosicrucianism*, dealing with the period A.D. 1300–1600 (1932). W. E. Peuckert, *Die Rosenkreutzer. Zur Geschichte einer Reformation* (1928). R. Kienast, *Johann Valentin Andreae und die vier echten Rosenkreutzer-Schriften* (Palaestra, clii; 1926). J. Twine, *De Geheimen der Rozekruisers Broederschap. Esoteriese Analyse der Fama Fraternitatis, A.D. 1614* (Haarlem, 1939). A. C. Jones in *H.E.R.E.*, x (1918), pp. 856–8, s.v., with bibl.; H. Hermelink in *P.R.E.* (ed. 3), xvii (1906), pp. 150–6, s.v. 'Rosenkreuzer'.

ROSMINI-SERBATI, ANTONIO (1797–1855), Italian philosopher and founder of the 'Institute of Charity'. Born at Rovereto of a noble family, he studied at Padua and was ordained priest in 1821. With the aid of Pius VIII, *Gregory XVI, and *Pius IX, he undertook the renewal of Italian philosophy, beginning with the systematic study of St. *Thomas, a translation of whose *Summa* he had attempted in 1819. Following a suggestion of the Ven. Maddalena di Canossa, the foundress of a society of Daughters of Charity, he established, in 1828, his congregation of the 'Fathers of Charity' (see *Rosminians*), without, however, relaxing his efforts to construct a satifying philosophical synthesis. His first and most important work, *Nuovo saggio sull' origine delle idee*, appeared in 1830 and was supplemented by *Il rinnovamento della filosofia in Italia* in 1836. Through his attack on *Probabilism in his *Trattato della coscienza Morale* (1839) he incurred the hostility of the *Jesuits, and in the following years was

repeatedly accused of *Jansenist and *pantheistic teaching. In 1848 he proposed ecclesiastical reforms in the *Costituzione secondo la giusticia sociale*, which, along with his *Cinque piaghe della chiesa*, was condemned by the Congregation of the *Index in 1849. Rosmini submitted at once and retired to Stresa, where, a year before his death, he had the satisfaction of seeing his works, which had been denounced to the Index in their entirety, returned with a *dimittantur*, i.e. without censure. After his death, however, and esp. after the posthumous publication of his voluminous synthesis *La teosofia* (5 vols., 1859–74), the accusations against his teaching continued and a second examination of his works resulted in a condemnation of 40 propositions by *Leo XIII in 1887–8.

Rosmini's system which shows the influence, besides that of *Plato, St. *Augustine, and St. *Thomas, of R. *Descartes, I. *Kant, G. W. F. *Hegel, and other modern philosophers, is founded on the leading idea of indeterminate being, innate in the human soul. If analysed this idea divides itself into a plurality of other ideas which are identical with those that are in the mind of God. Rosmini distinguished between degrees of being acc. to their completeness, God alone being absolutely complete. The being, however, which actualizes finite nature and which is the object of human intuition, is 'something of God', though not God Himself. Among the 40 condemned propositions were several on this metaphysical doctrine of the idea. Others related to the mystery of the *Trinity, which Rosmini thought capable of rational explanation, to *Transubstantiation, and to *Original Sin which he seems to have believed to be only a physical infection of the human flesh.

His influence, though negligible outside Italy, was considerable in his own country. A number of periodicals were founded after his death with the object of defending his teaching, and A. Manzoni, M. Minghetti, and G. Cavour were among those who came under his influence.

Collected ed. of Rosmini's works, 14 vols., Naples, 1842–5; this is to be supplemented by many posthumous items issued separately, Turin, 1857–74. Those translated into Eng. include *A Catholic Catechism* by W. S. Agar (1849); *The Five Wounds of the Holy Church* (abridged tr.) with introd. by H. P. *Liddon (1883), *Maxims of Christian Perfection* by W. A. Johnson (1889), and *Short Sketch of Modern Philosophies* by W. Lockhart (1882). For his correspondence, *Epistolario completo* (13 vols., Cassale Monferrato, 1887–94); Eng. tr. of 'Selected Letters' by [D. Gazzola] (London, 1901). Lives include those by F. Paoli (2 vols., Turin, 1880), G. B. Pagnani (2 vols., ib., 1880–4; Eng. tr., 1907), G. S. Macwalter (vol. i only, London, 1883) and W. Lockhart (2 vols. [vol. i being a reissue of the previous item without the author's name], London, 1886). Bibliography by C. Caviglione (Turin, 1925). D. Hickey, I.C., in *C.E.*, xiii (1912), pp. 194–8, s.v. 'Rosmini and Rosminianism'; C. Caviglione in *Enciclopedia italiana*, xxx (1936), pp. 123–6, s.v.; G. Bozzetti in *E.C.*, x (1953), cols. 1359–71, s.v.

ROSMINIANS. The 'Fathers of Charity'. The congregation was founded by A. *Rosmini in 1828 and formally approved by *Gregory XVI in 1838. Its chief aim is the sanctification of its members, combined with such works of charity as they may be called upon to perform, e.g. teaching, preaching, popular missions, and literary activities. There are the two grades of presbyters and coadjutors, the presbyters taking a special fourth vow of obedience to the Pope; and persons living in the world may be affiliated to the Institute. The congregation, which was introduced into England by A. Gentili in 1835, now has houses in Italy, England, Eire, and America. The women's branch of the congregation, the 'Sisters of Providence', was founded in 1831–2 and has houses in Italy and England, where they devote themselves esp. to the instruction of converts.

Heimbucher, ii, 634 f. W. H. Pollard in *C.E.*, xiii (1912), pp. 198–201, s.v. See also lives of *Rosmini*, cited s.v.

ROSSETTI, CHRISTINA GEORGINA
(1830–94), poetess. She was a younger sister of M. F. *Rossetti and D. G. *Rossetti, and closely associated with the Pre-Raphaelite Brotherhood. The first of her poems to be published (some had been privately printed earlier) appeared in the *Germ* (1850), the organ of the Brotherhood, under the pseudonym of 'Ellen Alleyne'. Marked by great beauty and care in the selection of words and pervaded by a deep melancholy (not, as is sometimes asserted, morbidity), they are the expression of a strong Christian faith. Besides those dealing with definitely religious subjects, many give expression to the agonies that come from disappointed love. She also wrote a number of religious books, among them *Seek and Find* (1879) and *Time Flies, a Reading Diary* (1885). Her hymns include 'What are these that glow from afar?' and the well-known carol 'In the bleak mid-winter'.

Poetical Works ed. with memoir and notes by William Michael Rossetti, brother (London, 1904; memoir, pp. xlv–lxxi); *Family Letters*, ed. id. (ib., 1908). Further letters in J. C. Troxell (ed.), *Three Rossettis*. Unpublished Letters to and from Dante Gabriel, Christina, William (Cambridge, Mass., 1937), esp. pp. 138–80. Brief memoir by Ellen A. Proctor (S.P.C.K., London, 1895); much fuller life by M. Bell (London, 1898). Modern studies by Mary F. Sandars (London, [1930]), Dorothy M. Stuart ('English Men of Letters', 1930), F. Shove (Cambridge, 1931), Eleanor W. Thomas (Columbia University Studies in English and Comparative Literature, New York, 1931), and Margaret Sawtell (London, 1955). Dorothy M. Stuart, *Christina Rossetti* (English Association Pamphlet No. lxxviii; 1931). R. Garnett in *D.N.B.*, xlix (1897), pp. 282–4. Further bibl. by R. Gathorne-Hardy in *C.B.E.L.*, iii, 273–5. See also bibl. to following entry.

ROSSETTI, DANTE GABRIEL (1828–82),
English Pre-Raphaelite poet and painter. He was for a short time a pupil of Ford Madox Brown, and with J. E. Millais, Holman *Hunt, and T. Woolner, founded the Pre-Raphaelite Brotherhood in 1848. In 1860 he married Elizabeth Siddal, whose death in 1862 marked a turning point in his life. The principal influence of Rossetti's early years was *Dante whom he began to translate in 1845. In his own poetry of this period Christian themes abound, and his ideal of womanhood is expressed by the BVM and Beatrix. Among his poems of this period are 'Ave', a beautiful

prayer to the Blessed Virgin, the well-known 'The Blessed Damozel' (1847) with its Dantesque conception of heaven, and the weird 'Sister Helen' (1850–1), characteristic of his love for mystery and magic. Of his paintings the *Girlhood of Mary Virgin* (1849), *Ecce Ancilla Domini*, the triptych *The Seed of David* in *Llandaff Cathedral, *Beata Beatrix* (1863), and many others, try to recall the spiritual beauty of medieval pictures, an aim which they hardly achieve, however, for lack of simplicity. In the second period, from *c.* 1863 to his death, religious motives disappear, and the inherent sensuality of his poetry and art, which now came more and more to the fore, brought upon him the charge of being a 'fleshly poet'. The eroticism of these years was coupled with a pessimistic outlook on life and an intensified interest in its morbid aspects which comes out, e.g., in his poem 'Rose Mary'.

Collected Works [prose and poetry] ed. William Michael Rossetti [brother] (2 vols., London, 1886; enlarged ed., with dates of composition and first publication of each item, 1911); *Family Letters*, ed. id. (2 vols., ib., 1895), with memoir as vol. i. Further material in id. (ed.), *Praeraphaelite Diaries and Letters* (1900), esp. pp. 3–47 ('Some Early Correspondence of Dante Gabriel Rossetti'); and id., *Rossetti Family Papers, 1862 to 1870* (1903). O. Doughty (ed.), *The Letters of Dante Gabriel Rossetti to his Publisher, F. S. Ellis* (1928); Janet C. Troxell (ed.), *Three Rossettis*. Unpublished Letters To and From Dante Gabriel, Christina, William (Cambridge, Mass., 1937), esp. pp. 3–137. P. F. Baum (ed.), *Dante Gabriel Rossetti's Letters to Fanny Cornforth* (Baltimore, 1940). W. M. Rossetti, *Dante Gabriel Rossetti as Designer and Painter* (1889). W. Sharp, *Dante Gabriel Rossetti*. A Record and a Study (1882); T. H. Caine, *Recollections of Dante Gabriel Rossetti* (1882; fuller ed., 1928). Later general studies include those of A. C. Benson ('English Men of Letters', 1904), H. Dupré (Paris, 1921), E. Waugh (London, 1928), R. L. Mégroz (ib., 1928), D. Larg, *Trial by Virgins* (London, 1933), L. Wolff ('Les Écrivains étrangers', [1934]), O. Doughty, *A Victorian Romantic* (London, 1949), and Helen Rossetti (ib., 1949). Works dealing more specifically with his art, incl. reproductions, by H. C. Marillier (London, 1899); also by F. G. Stephens (London, 1894), F. M. Hueffer (ib., 1902), Esther Wood, *Dante Rossetti and the Pre-Raphaelite Movement* (London, 1904), and E. Radford (London, [1908]. F. Winnar, *The Rossettis and their Circle* (1934; popular). R. Garnett in *D.N.B.*, xlix (1897), pp. 284–9. Further bibl. by J. B. Gregory in *C.B.E.L.*, i, 271–3.

ROSSETTI, MARIA FRANCESCA (1827–
1876), Anglican religious. The eldest of the Rossetti family, she was, in the opinion of her agnostic brother, William (W. M.), 'more warmly and spontaneously devotional than any person I have ever known'. Feeling herself free from domestic responsibilities on his marriage in 1874, she joined the sisterhood of All Saints', Margaret Street, London, but died shortly afterwards. In 1871 she published *A Shadow of Dante*.

The principal sources are W. M. Rossetti's lives of Christina Georgina and Dante Gabriel Rossetti, cited s.vv. R. D. Waller, *The Rossetti Family, 1824–1854* (Manchester, 1932), pp. 171–80. See also other works cited in the two previous entries.

ROSVITHA. See *Hrosvitha*.

ROSY SEQUENCE. A part of the hymn '*Jesu dulcis memoria' (q.v.), used as a sequence for the Feast of the *Holy Name in the *Sarum Gradual. A form of the hymn in 50 stanzas was formerly used as a kind of rosary in five decades.

ROTA SACRA ROMANA. The principal RC tribunal for judging cases brought before the Holy See. It dates from the middle of the 13th cent., and its name appears to derive from the circular table used by the judges at *Avignon. Its power was at a maximum in the 15th and 16th cents., but by the 18th its duties had come to be limited to civil cases, and hence with the cessation of the temporal power in 1870 they ended altogether. In its present form it was created by *Pius X in 1908 by the bull 'Sapienti Consilio'. It now tries all cases except the so-called 'major' cases (*causae maiores*), i.e. grave matters which by their nature or by law are reserved to the Pope himself. It is also a court of appeal for cases tried in episcopal tribunals. The judges, who are known as auditors (*uditori*) and form a college, must be priests who are at least doctors in civil and canon law. The president is called the 'Dean' and is *primus inter pares*. It is prob. best known as the court to which appeals in nullity and other matrimonial cases are referred. In its present form it is governed by cans. 1598–1601 of the *Codex Juris Canonici.

Several collections of the decisions of the Rota in various periods have been publd.; some of the more important are listed in *L.Th.K.*, cit. infra. D. Bernini, *Il tribunale della S. Rota Romana* (fol., 1717). E. Schneider, *Die römische Rota nach geltendem Recht auf geschichtlicher Grundlage*, i. Die Verfassung der Rota (all publd. Görres-Gesellschaft. Veröffentlichungen der Sektion für Rechts- und Sozialwissenschaft, xxii; 1914), with bibl. to date. E. Cerchiari, *Capellani Papae et Apostolicae Sedis Auditores Causarum Sacri Palatii Apostolici seu Sacra Romana Rota ab Origine ad diem usque 20 Septembris 1870*. Relatio historicajuridica (4 vols., Rome, 1919–21). A. Trilhe, 'Les Chapelains du pape, auditeurs des causes du Palais Apostolique ou la Rote Romaine' in *Bulletin de Littérature ecclésiastique*, xxiv (Toulouse, 1923), pp. 348–59. E. Schneider, 'Über den Ursprung und die Bedeutung des Namens *Rota* als Bezeichnung für den obersten päpstlichen Gerichtshof' in *R.Q.*, xli (1933), pp. 29–43, with further reff. U. Benigni in *C.E.*, xiii (1912), p. 205 f., s.v.; E. Schneider in *L.Th.K.*, viii (1936), cols. 1007–9, s.v.; P. Santini in *E.C.*, x (1953), cols. 1393–6, s.v.; id., ib., xii (1954), cols. 502–6, s.v. 'Tribunali ecclesiastici I. iii'. See also works cited s.v. *Curia*.

ROTHE, RICHARD (1799 – 1867), *Lutheran theologian. He taught successively at *Wittenberg (from 1828), Bonn (from 1849), and Heidelberg (from 1854). A disciple of F. D. E. *Schleiermacher and J. A. W. *Neander, he combined an unusually devout and even pietistic spirit with a keenly critical and historical sense. He emphasized the inseparable relation between religion and morals in his great work *Theologische Ethik* (3 vols., 1845–8; 2nd ed., 5 vols., 1867–71). He also wrote a book on the beginnings of the Christian Church (1837). He is best known in Britain by his *Stille Stunden* (1872), a collection of devotional essays and reflections translated under the title *Still Hours* (1886).

Several treatises, based on Rothe's unpublished papers, were issued posthumously. There is a brief sketch by J. Macpherson prefixed to Rothe's *Still Hours* (Eng. tr. by Jane T. Stoddart, 1886), pp. 9–41. Studies on Rothe

include W. Hoenig, *Richard Rothe* (Berlin, 1898), and A. Hausrath, *Richard Rothe und seine Freunde* (2 vols., 1902–6). A. E. F. Sieffert in *P.R.E.* (ed. 3), xvii (1906), pp. 169–78; H. Stephan in *R.G.G.* (ed. 2), iv (1930), cols. 2117–20.

ROTHMANN, BERNT (*c.* 1495–1535), German *Anabaptist leader. In 1529 he was appointed a chaplain of St. Maurice's church outside Münster, but soon joined the Protestant Movement. From 1531 he openly preached *Lutheran doctrines and in 1532 secured by force the possession of the large church of St. Lambert in the city. From 1533 onwards he came to incline increasingly to Anabaptist views, propagated by the adherents of Melchior *Hoffmann, and in 1534 became a member of their sect. He now took part in organizing communism and the burning of books in his 'New Jerusalem' (of which the Bible was to be the only law book), as well as in the introduction of polygamy; he himself had nine wives. When John of Leyden (d. 1535) had been elected 'king' of Münster, Rothmann became his 'court preacher' and published an exposition of Anabaptist teaching in his *Restitution rechter und gesunder christlicher Lehre* and a pamphlet *Von der Rache* (both 1534), in which he incited the people to kill the 'godless'. He died in the occupation of Münster by the troops of the bishop and his allies in 1535.

There is no collected ed. of Rothmann's writings. H. Delmer–R. Krumbholtz (edd.), *Zwei Schriften des Münsterschen Widertäufers Bernhard Rothmann*. Mit einer Einleitung über die zeitgeschichtlichen Verhältnisse (Dortmund, 1904). C. Sepp, *Geschiedkundige Nasporingen*, i (Leyden, 1872), pp. 55–157 ('De veel genoemde en weinig bekende Geschriften van den Wederdooper Bernt Rothmann'). W. Koehler in *R.G.G.* (ed. 2), iv (1930), col. 2121 f., with list of editions of Rothmann's writings and bibl. See also bibl. to *Anabaptists*.

ROUSSEAU, JEAN-JACQUES (1712–78), French author. He was the son of a French refugee family at Geneva, and, though brought up a Calvinist, became a Catholic in 1728 through the influence of Mme de Warens, his benefactress and later his mistress, herself a convert from Protestant Pietism. She had a large share in his religious formation, combining *Deistic beliefs, which excluded doctrines such as Hell and Original Sin, with a kind of *Quietist sentimentalism. During the years spent with her (1731–40), Rousseau completed his sketchy education by omnivorous reading, including the works of R. *Descartes, G. W. *Leibniz, J. *Locke, B. *Pascal, and others. In 1741 he went to Paris, where he met Thérèse Levasseur, a servant girl, by whom he had five children which he placed in a foundlings' hospital. Through D. *Diderot he was introduced to the circle of the *Encyclopaedists, for whom he wrote several contributions. In 1750 he published his *Discours sur les sciences et les arts*, a prize essay for the university of Dijon, in which he defended the thesis that progress in art and science corrupts human morals. In 1754 he returned to Geneva and once more became a Calvinist, and in the same year wrote his *Discours sur l'origine et les fondements de l'inégalité parmi les hommes*. Inspired by

H. *Grotius, S. *Pufendorf, and others, he treated the subject regardless of historical reality, and, on the gratuitous assumption that the primitive man was a free and happy being living in acc. with his instincts, without virtue or vice, alleged that human inequalities arose from the undue development of his social and proprietary instincts. In 1756 Rousseau settled near Montmorency, where he wrote the works which made him world-famous. In *Julie, ou La Nouvelle Héloïse* (1760), a passionate love story, he condemned a society which for the sake of convention divorced love from marriage, and put forward a defence of a natural religion based on an undogmatic personal interpretation of the Gospels which, he maintained, is necessary for morality. In *Émile, ou de l'Éducation* (1762) he developed a Utopian programme of an education far from the corrupting influence of society and in acc. with nature. In the famous chapter entitled 'La Profession de foi du vicaire savoyard' he summed up his religious ideas. He advocated a kind of sentimental Deism, consisting in belief in the existence of God, the soul, a future life, and the necessity of following one's conscience. *Du contrat social* (1762) set out his theory of the just state, resting on the general will of the people, the expression of which are the laws. This, too, contained a chapter on religion, 'De la religion civile', in which 'civic religion' was distinguished from natural religion. The articles of this civic religion, which are fixed and enforced by the state, bear on the same subjects as natural religion, forbid all dogmatic intolerance, and admit only those religions which do not claim to possess the absolute truth. *Émile*, put on the *Index in 1762, and *Du contrat social* were condemned in France and at Geneva, and Rousseau fled first to Neuchâtel, then to Strassburg, and, in 1766-7, he was the guest of D. *Hume. But, suffering from persecution mania, he went back to France, where he married Thérèse Levasseur 'before nature' in 1768, and in 1772 completed his *Confessions*, with their curious mixture of vanity and self-accusation.

After his death Rousseau became one of the most powerful influences in Europe. In France his ideas were taken up by the Revolution, in Germany by the 'Storm and Stress'. His religious impact was the deeper as, unlike *Voltaire, he offered man a sentimental substitute for revealed religion which made few claims on faith or morals but satisfied his emotional needs. It has sometimes been asserted that he served Christianity by propagating its fundamental truths among his unbelieving contemporaries. A juster estimate might point out that, by taking its doctrines out of their supernatural context and by supplanting faith and reason by sentiment, he removed the foundations of sound religion and became a forerunner of humanistic liberalism.

Many edd. of his collected works, incl. that of V. D. Musset-Pathay (24 vols., Paris, 1823-6). M. G. Streckeisen-Moultou (edd.), *Œuvres et correspondance inédites de J.-J. Rousseau* (1861). The fullest ed. of his correspondence is that of T. Dufour (20 vols., Paris, 1924-34). P. P. Plan, *Table de la correspondance générale de J.-J. Rousseau* avec . . . lettres inédites (Société de Publications Romaines et Françaises, xxxix; 1953). There have been innumerable edd. of individual works; useful ed. of his Political Writings, with full introd. and notes in Eng., by C. E. Vaughan (2 vols., Cambridge, 1915). His more important works were translated into English soon after publication; there have been many reprr. and new trr., incl. that of *The Social Contract* by H. J. Tozer (London, 1895) and, with *The Discourses*, by G. D. H. Cole (Everyman's Library, dclx; [1913]); of *Émile* by Barbara Foxley (ib. [1911]); of his *Confessions* (ib., 2 vols., 1931), and by J. M. Cohen (Penguin Classics, 1953). The numerous studies include those of J. Morley (2 vols., London, 1873), M. Giradin (2 vols., Paris, 1875), A. Chuquet ('Les Grands Écrivains français', 1893), Frederika Macdonald (2 vols., London, 1906), J. Lemaître (Paris, [c. 1907]; Eng. tr., 1908), L. Ducros (3 vols., Paris, 1908-20), A. Dide (ib. [1910]), E. Seillière (ib., 1921), C. E. Vulliamy (London, 1931), and R. B. Mowat (ib., 1938). P. M. Masson, *La Religion de J.-J. Rousseau* (3 vols., 1916). A. Schinx, *La Pensée de Jean-Jacques Rousseau* (2 vols., Northampton, Mass., 1929); E. H. Wright, *The Meaning of Rousseau* (1929). C. W. Hendel, *Jean-Jacques Rousseau, Moralist* (2 vols., 1934). H. Roddier, *J.-J. Rousseau en Angleterre au XVIIIᵉ siècle* (Études de Littérature étrangère et comparée [1950]). P. Burgelin, *La Philosophie de l'existence de J.-J. Rousseau* (Bibliothèque de Philosophie contemporaine. Histoire de la Philosophie et Philosophie générale; 1952). J. *Maritain, *Trois Réformateurs*. Luther, Descartes, Rousseau (1925), pp. 131-237, with notes, pp. 267-284; Eng. tr. [1928], pp. 93-164, with notes, pp. 219-341. J. Sénelier, *Bibliographie générale des œuvres de Jean-Jacques Rousseau* [1949]. *Annales de la Société Jean-Jacques Rousseau* (Geneva, 1905 ff.). Überweg, iii, 440-8, with bibl. pp. 700-3. G. Saintsbury in *E.B.* (ed. 11), xxiii (1911), pp. 775-8, s.v.; G. Constantin in *D.T.C.*, xiv (pt. 1; 1939), cols. 102-33, s.v., with bibl.

ROUTH, MARTIN JOSEPH (1755-1854), patristic scholar and president of Magdalen College, Oxford. A strong supporter of the traditional High Church position in Anglican theology, he was much respected and revered by the *Tractarians, J. H. *Newman in dedicating to him his *Lectures on the Prophetical Office of the Church* (1837) declaring that he had 'been reserved to report to a forgetful generation the theology of their fathers'. It was he who advised S. *Seabury, when sent to Europe to inaugurate an episcopal succession in the American (Anglican) Church, to seek it from the Scottish Episcopal Church.

Elected a demy at Magdalen College in 1771, he was ordained deacon in 1777, and, after holding College appointments, was elected president in 1791 (in succession to G. *Horne), to hold the office for sixty-three years. In 1788 he issued a prospectus of his projected *Reliquiae Sacrae*, an edition of scattered pre-Nicene Patristic texts. The work first appeared in 4 vols., Oxford, 1814-18; a complete revision ('ed. altera'), with an additional volume, was issued in 5 vols., 1846-8. Routh also published *Scriptorum Ecclesiasticorum Opuscula Praecipua Quaedam* (2 vols., 1832).

Life by R. D. Middleton (London, 1938). J. W. *Burgon, *Lives of Twelve Good Men*, i (1888), pp. 1-115. G. C. Boase in *D.N.B.*, xlix (1897), pp. 324-7.

ROWITES. The disciples of J. McLeod *Campbell, who was in charge of the parish of Row, near Cardross, Dumbarton, from 1825 to 1830. They are also known as 'Campbellites'.

ROWNTREE, JOSEPH (1836–1925), *Quaker philanthropist and social reformer. Educated at Bootham School, *York, he entered the grocery business established by his father in the city in 1822, and eventually, on the death of his elder brother, Henry Isaac Rowntree, in 1883, became head of the great cocoa business of Rowntree & Co. He was a pioneer in the movement for securing for workpeople reasonable hours and conditions of labour, higher wages, and provision against old age and unemployment. He established three trusts to carry some of his ideals into effect and in 1904 founded the model village of New Earswick. He was an ardent temperance reformer, did much to promote adult education, esp. in the Society of Friends, and took a prominent part in the civic life of York.

A. E. Watkin in *D.N.B., 1922–1930* (1937), p. 731 f., s.v.

ROYAL CHAPELS. See *Chapel Royal.*

ROYAL DECLARATION. See *Declaration of the Sovereign.*

ROYAL SCHOOL OF CHURCH MUSIC (R.S.C.M.). An organization founded in 1927 as the School of English Church Music, and granted its present title in 1945. Till his death in 1947 its Director was Sydney H. Nicholson (b. 1875; organist of *Westminster Abbey, 1918–27). Its work has consisted in advice to choirs affiliated to the School, provision of suitable music, and the organization of choral festivals. In 1929 the College of St. Nicholas was founded at Chislehurst, Kent, to provide courses for organists, choristers, clergy, and ordinands, with both resident and non-resident students. In 1945 the work, interrupted by the War since 1939, was resumed at *Canterbury, and in 1954 was removed to Addington Palace (an archiepiscopal residence 1807–96) near Croydon, Surrey.

RUBRIC, Black. See *Black Rubric.*

RUBRIC, Ornaments. See *Ornaments Rubric.*

RUBRICS. Ritual or ceremonial directions, printed at the beginning of service-books, or in the course of the text. The word originated from the fact that in medieval books they were written in red (Lat. *ruber*), to distinguish them from the text of the services.

RUCHERAT (or **RUCHRAT**), **JOHN.** See *John of Wesel.*

RUFINUS, TYRANNIUS (*c.* 345–410), presbyter of Aquileia. Born near Aquileia in N. Italy, he travelled to the E. about 371 where, after visiting the monks of Egypt, he stayed in Alexandria and *Jerusalem. He returned to Italy in 397. He is mainly important as a translator of Greek theological works into Latin at a time when knowledge of Greek was declining in the W. His free translation of *Origen's 'De Principiis', the only complete text now surviving, was intended to vindicate Origen's orthodoxy, and involved Rufinus in bitter controversy with St. *Jerome, who pointed out the tendentious character of his rendering. He translated also some of Origen's scriptural commentaries, the '*Clementine Recognitions', works of St. *Basil and St. *Gregory of Nazianzus, and, in a free rendering with additions, the 'Ecclesiastical History' of *Eusebius. His commentary on the *Apostles' Creed, perhaps based on the 'Catechetical Discourses' of St. *Cyril of Jerusalem, gives the earliest continuous Latin text of the 4th cent. form of the creed, as used at Aquileia and at Rome. See also *Gelasius of Caesarea.*

D. *Vallarsi projected a collected ed. in 2 vols., fol., but only vol. i, containing Rufinus's independent works, appeared (Verona, 1745); this is repr. in J. P. Migne, *PL*, xxi. Rufinus's translations are generally to be sought in the edd. of their corresponding Gk. authors. His 'Commentary on the Apostles' Creed' has often been printed; convenient ed. by C. A. Heurtley, *De Fide et Symbolo* (Oxford, 1864); Eng. tr., with crit. introd., by J. N. D. Kelly (Ancient Christian Writers, 20, 1955). The most comprehensive study is F. X. Murphy, C.SS.R., *Rufinus of Aquileia, 345–411* (Catholic University of America. Studies in Mediaeval History, N.S., vi; 1945). R. *Reitzenstein, *Historia Monachorum* [by Rufinus] *und Historia Lausiaca* [by *Palladius] (Forschungen zur Religion und Literatur des Alten und Neuen Testaments, N.F., vii; 1916). J. E. L. Oulton, 'Rufinus's Translation of the Church History of Eusebius' in *J.T.S.*, xxx (1928–9), pp. 150–74. Bardenhewer, iii, 549–58; Altaner (ed. 1951), p. 343 f. A. Anwander in *L.Th.K.*, ix (1937), cols. 1–3; G. Bardy in *D.T.C.*, xiv (pt. 1; 1939), cols. 153–60, s.v. 'Rufin'; P. Paschini in *E.C.*, x (1953), cols. 1436–8, s.v. 'Rufino Turannio'.

RUINART, THIERRY (1657–1709), *Maurist patristic scholar. From 1674 he was a monk of St.-Remy at *Reims and from 1682 an assistant to J. *Mabillon at *St.-Germain-des-Prés. The most celebrated of his writings is his *Acta Primorum Martyrum Sincera et Selecta* (1689), a collection to which he admitted only those *acta* of the martyrs which seemed to him authentic, though some of its contents are no longer regarded as genuine to-day. Among his other works was an edition of St. *Gregory of Tours (1699).

V. Thuiller, O.S.B. (ed.), *Ouvrages posthumes de D. Jean Mabillon et de D. Thierri Ruinart* (3 vols., Paris, 1724), vol. ii, pp. 399–544, and vol. iii. Modern ed. of his *Acta Martyrum* (Ratisbon, 1859). H. Jadart, *Dom Thierry Ruinart (1657–1709)*. Notice suivie de documents inédits sur sa famille, sa vie, ses œuvres, ses relations avec D. Mabillon (1886). H. *Leclercq, O.S.B., in *D.A.C.L.*, xv (pt. 1; 1950), cols. 163–82, s.v., with bibl.

RULE, Golden. See *Golden Rule.*

RULE OF ST. BENEDICT. See *Benedict, Rule of.*

RULER. A name formerly applied to those who presided in cathedrals over the singing in the choir, esp. over the psalms. The office, which goes back to medieval times, when the rulers frequently wore copes, was revived in a few places in the C of E in the 19th cent.

RUMANIA, Christianity in. Roman Dacia, which roughly covered the present Rumania, received Christianity through Roman soldiers and colonists by the 4th cent. or earlier. Its earliest liturgy was Latin, and a see was in existence at Tomi (Constanza) in the 4th cent. Under Bulgarian rule its ecclesiastical affairs were placed under *Constantinople, and its worship gradually took on an E. character. In the 14th and 15th cents., when it stood in the outer line of defence of Europe against the Turks, it retained its national religion and culture. Under Turkish rule Christianity was not proscribed, but under the Phanariot hospodars (1721–1812), the episcopate was generally filled by Greeks who upheld Greek customs in ecclesiastical matters. In the 19th cent. Rumania suffered as a victim of the power-politics of Russia, Turkey, and Austria; but after having been ruled by all, collectively or in turn, she began her existence as a virtually self-governing power in 1862. In 1859 she claimed the independence of her national Church from the metropolitan jurisdiction of Constantinople, and in 1885 this claim was allowed by the *Oecumenical Patriarch and a Holy Synod constituted. In 1935, after conversations between Rumanian and Anglican divines, the National Synod recognized the Anglican Communion as part of the Catholic Church, and its orders as valid, equally with those of the RC Church. There are very small RC and Protestant minorities, consisting of immigrants from abroad.

The main literature is in Rumanian. In Eng. there is a brief sketch by M. Beza, *The Rumanian Church* (S.P.C.K., 1943). A. *Fortescue, *The Orthodox Eastern Church* (1907), pp. 328–34; D. Attwater, *The Catholic Eastern Churches* (Milwaukee, Wisc., [1935]; ed. 2 [1946]), pp. 98–103; id., *The Dissident Eastern Churches* (ib., [1937]) pp. 110–18. G. K. A. Bell (ed.), *Documents on Christian Unity*, Third Series, 1930–48, (1948), pp. 43–50 (No. 158 f.). On the general history of the country, N. Iorga, *Histoire des Roumaines et de leur civilisation* (Paris, 1920; ed. 2, Bucarest, 1922; Eng. tr., 1925); R. W. Seton-Watson, *A History of the Roumanians from Roman Times to the Completion of Unity* (1934). J. Lins in *C.E.*, xiii (1912), pp. 224–8, s.v.; E. Herman, S.J., in *L.Th.K.*, ix (1937), cols. 6–11, s.v. 'Rumänien'; G. Caraci, A. Raes, S.J., and others in *E.C.*, x (1953), cols. 1282–1301, s.v. 'Romania'.

RUPERT OF DEUTZ (*c.* 1070–1129 [?1135]), scholastic theologian. After teaching at Liége and Siegburg, he became abbot of Deutz, near Cologne, *c.* 1120. His writings include a treatise 'De Divinis Officiis', largely concerned to expound the ecclesiastical year, and several commentaries, notably one on the Twelve Prophets. Against the dialectic methods introduced into theology under the influence of *Anselm of Laon and *William of Champeaux, Rupert defended the more mystical theology traditional in the *Benedictine Order, with its allegorical interpretation of Scripture. In his teaching on the Eucharist he held a doctrine which had affinities with that of *Impanation, though it won little acceptance, even among his contemporaries.

Early collections of Rupert's works publd. Cologne, 1526; later ed., Cologne, 1540; *Opera Omnia*, ed. M. Pleunich (4 vols. bound in 2, Venice, 1748–51), repr. in J. P. Migne, *PL*, clxvii–clxx. Crit. edd. of his *Chronicon Sancti Laurentii*

Leodiensis by W. Wattenbach in *M.G.H.*, Scriptores, viii (1848), pp. 261–79, of his *De Incendio Tiutiensi* and *de Cunone Episcopo Ratisponensi* by P. Jaffé, ib., xii (1856), pp. 624–39. *Histoire littéraire de la France*, xi (1759), pp. 422–587, with list of edd. of his works. R. Rocholl, *Rupert von Deutz*. Beitrag zur Geschichte der Kirche im XII. Jahrhundert (Gütersloh, 1886). F. Doyen, *Die Eucharistielehre Ruperts von Deutz* (Diss. Metz, 1889). D. *Stone, *A History of the Doctrine of the Holy Eucharist*, i (1909), pp. 291–5. P. Séjourné, O.S.B., in *D.T.C.*, xiv (pt. 1; 1939), cols. 169–205, s.v.

RURAL DEAN. In the C of E, the head of a group of parishes in a given area ('Rural Deanery'). He is appointed by the Bishop of the diocese, usually, but not necessarily, from among the beneficed clergy of the Deanery, and may be removed by the Bishop at any time. The boundaries of a Rural Deanery can, if necessary, be modified under the Archdeaconries and Rural Deaneries Act of 1874 (37 & 38 Vict., cap. 63).

The office is ancient and formerly the duties were important; but they were gradually absorbed by the *Archdeacons. The office was revived in 1836; and since the later 19th cent., Rural Deans have again come to play a considerable part in the life of the diocese, e.g. as a channel of communication between the smaller parishes and the Bishop. The Rural Dean is president of the Ruridecanal Chapter, i.e. the incumbents and clergy licensed under seal in the Deanery.

W. Dansey, *Horae Decanicae Rurales* (2 vols., London, 1835). J. B. Hughes, *Deans Rural*. The History of their Office and Duties (revised ed., 1889). E. W. Watson in *D.E.C.H.*, pp. 527–9, s.v.

RUSKIN, JOHN (1819–1900), art critic and social reformer. The son of a *Puritan mother and an art-loving father, Ruskin was brought up at home. From 1836 to 1840 he studied at *Christ Church, Oxford, where he retained a simple *Evangelical piety and was completely untouched by the *Tractarian Movement. The first book that established his fame was *Modern Painters* (1843, followed till 1860 by 4 more vols.). In this and in later writings (which treat not only of such modern painters as J. M. W. Turner, whose prophet he became, but also of the old Italian masters, esp. Fra *Angelico and Tintoretto), he expounded his spiritual interpretation of art. His main principles are summed up in *The Seven Lamps of Architecture* (1849) as sacrifice, truth, power, beauty, life, memory, and obedience. Closely connected with his moral ideals were his aesthetic views, truth and sincerity being the indispensable foundations of both; for he held that the art and architecture of a people are the expression of its religion and morality. From 1851 to 1853 appeared his *Stones of Venice* with the famous chapter 'On the Nature of Gothic Architecture' which became an important influence in the growth of the Gothic Revival. About the same time he became connected with the Pre-Raphaelites whom he defended in his book on *Preraphaelitism* (1851). His interest in Protestant reunion resulted in his pamphlet *Notes on the Construction of Sheepfolds* (1851), in which he proposed as a basis a simple NT Christianity, rejecting the High Church claims to the priesthood but retaining the episcopate. After the completion of the series *Modern Painters* in 1860, he devoted himself almost entirely to social and economic problems. In *Unto This Last* (1862) he defended the dignity and moral destiny of man. Against J. S. Mill and other contemporary thinkers he stressed nobility of character and aesthetic development as the only true wealth of humanity and upheld national education, organization of labour, old-age pensions, and other social institutions as against the *laissez-faire* principles of the age. In *Time and Tide* (1867), *Munera Pulveris* (1872), and other works, he further elaborated his views. By this date his early Evangelicalism had given place to a vague Theism, and among his ideas for social reforms was the plan of a completely dependent State Church with state-salaried officials and with a minimum of dogma. From 1871 onwards he attempted to put his principles into practice, and he established the 'Guild of St. George', comprising agricultural and also industrial settlements; but they did not succeed. From Brantwood on Coniston Lake he wrote monthly letters 'to the workmen and labourers of Great Britain' which are collected in the volumes of *Fors Clavigera* as a means of propaganda for his ideas. In 1870 he was elected the first professor of fine arts in Oxford. Here he also worked out his social programme, which was among the main influences leading to the establishment of university settlements. From *c.* 1875 he returned to a more Christian standpoint, his partiality for the Middle Ages and his friendship with H. E. *Manning at one time giving rise to the rumour that he was about to become a RC. But the religion of his last period seems to have been rather an undogmatic kind of Bible Christianity without attachment to any Church. From 1884 he lived in retirement.

Best ed. of his Works by E. T. Cook–A. Wedderburn (39 vols., 1903–12). J. H. Whitehouse (ed.), *The Solitary Warrior.* New Letters by Ruskin (1929); Charlotte Quaritch Wrentmore (ed.), *Letters of John Ruskin to Bernard Quaritch, 1867–1880* (1938). W. G. Collingwood, *The Life and Work of John Ruskin* (2 vols., 1893); id., *The Life of John Ruskin* (1900); E. T. Cook, *The Life of John Ruskin* (2 vols., 1911). Other studies by M. Mather (London, 1883), C. Waldstein (ib., 1894), M. H. Spielmann (ib., 1900), Mrs. Meynell (ib., 1900), F. Harrison ('English Men of Letters'; 1902), J. W. Graham (London, 1920), A. Williams-Ellis (ib., 1928), J. Bardoux (ed. 4, Paris, 1931), D. Larg (London, 1932), R. H. Wilenski (ib., 1933), D. Leon (ib., 1949), P. Quennell (ib., 1949) and Joan Evans (ib., 1954). J. A. Hobson, *John Ruskin Social Reformer* (1898). H. G. Pollard in *C.B.E.L.*, iii (1940), pp. 691–707.

RUSSELL, CHARLES TAZE (1852–1916), 'Pastor Russell', founder of the International Bible Students Association, now generally called '*Jehovah's Witnesses' (q.v.). He was a draper of Pittsburg, U.S.A., of Congregational upbringing. His refusal to accept the doctrine of eternal punishment led him to an independent study of the Bible, with the result that, in 1872, he came to believe that the Second, though secret, *Advent of Christ would take place in 1874 and the end of the world in 1914. He set down his convictions in a small book, *The Object and Manner of Our Lord's Return* (no date), which had a large circulation and made him known to a wide public of credulous and uncritical readers. In 1878, when he took the name of 'Pastor' without having received any kind of ordination, he became pastor at an independent church at Pittsburg, and from 1879 he published *The Watchtower*, the magazine of his movement, which found a large public and was translated into several European languages. In 1881 he wrote his principal book, *Food for Thinking Christians*, reissued in 1886 under the title *Millennial Dawn*, and later incorporated in his series of so-called 'Scripture Studies'. In 1884 he founded the Watch Tower Bible and Tract Society, which soon became a flourishing business, bringing out innumerable pamphlets and books. He also engaged in various other commercial ventures (bricks, coal, turpentine). In 1909 his wife obtained a divorce on the grounds of his immoral conduct with members of his 'Church' and he went abroad for a time. In 1911 another scandal followed, brought about by the fraudulent sale of 'miracle wheat' alleged to have marvellous agricultural properties. Despite these scandals the sect continued to flourish, and the outbreak of war in 1914, though very different from the beginning of the millennium which he had prophesied for that year, brought him an increase of popularity. His teaching, which resembles that of other *Adventists in its fanciful interpretations of the Books of Daniel and Revelation, lends itself to political propaganda of a subversive type. It proclaims the approach of a general revolution of the workers which is to be followed by the resurrection of the dead, the Last Judgement, and the Messianic Kingdom on earth. Despite the great parade of learning in his books he was unable to name in the courts the letters of the Greek alphabet. His ideas were developed in a still more anarchist direction by J. F. *Rutherford (q.v.).

E. S. Bates in *Dict. Amer. Biog.*, xvi (1935), p. 240, s.v. See also bibl. to *Jehovah's Witnesses*.

RUSSIA, Christianity in. Christian missionaries first preached extensively in Russia in the 9th and 10th cents. In 988 the Emp. *Vladimir (canonized, 12th cent.) was baptized and established Christianity as the official religion in his dominions. Anxious to bring Russia into closer relationship with Europe, he brought priests from the Byzantine Empire and established a Greek hierarchy under a metropolitan. From the first the Slav tongue was used in worship and gradually a Russian clergy replaced the Greeks. At the Great Schism of 1054 the Russian Church took the E. side. Monastic life began with the coming of the monk Antonius from Mount *Athos in 1051, who established himself in a grotto near Kieff and laid the foundations of the great monastery of Kievo-Petcherskaja. Monasticism spread rapidly, so that by the

12th cent. in Kieff alone there were 17 monasteries.

During the invasions of the Tartars from Mongolia, which began in 1237, several Russian princes suffered martyrdom for their faith. The monastic movement continued to grow, and in 1329 two Russian monks, Sergius and Germanus, founded the famous monastery of Valamo on an islet in Lake Ladoga. Later St. *Sergius Radonejski (1314–92), one of the most honoured saints in Russia, began a reform of monastic life. He founded the monastery of the Most Holy Trinity at Sergievo, and gave the impulse to the wave of monasticism which in the following cent. resulted in the building of monasteries all over Russia. Monasteries supplied bishops, while the secular clergy were commonly married and unlettered. When the Church eventually emerged from the ruins left by the invasions she had become the embodiment of the Russian soul.

In 1328 the metropolitical see had been transferred from Kieff to Moscow. From 1461 to 1589 the Russian Church was divided between two metropolitans, centred at Moscow and Kieff, the former Russian and Orthodox and the latter attempting to assimilate the culture of the W. During the 15th and 16th cents. the missionary activity of the Russians continued to the south and east of their borders.

Russia wholly refused the findings of the Council of *Florence (1439). The advances of Constantinople to the W. Church were used as an argument against the orthodoxy of the Greeks, and towards the end of the 15th cent. the Russian Church refused to receive Greek Metropolitans and Bishops. Two outstanding theologians in the see of Moscow during this period were Macarius (1542–63) and Philip II, the latter slain by the order of Ivan the Terrible (1533–84) in 1573.

In 1551 the famous Council of the Hundred Chapters was called to reform the clergy. It was the climax of a movement for the revival of true monastic poverty, begun by Sergius and continued by Nil Sorski (1433–1508). In the same century there were outbreaks of rationalism and Protestantism, but both were firmly repressed by the civil power. In the reign of Theodore (1584–98), the second son of Ivan the Terrible, the Russian Church realized her greatest ambition in the creation of the Patriarchate of Moscow by Jeremias II, Patriarch of Constantinople (1589). The first Patriarch was Job (1589–1605).

Since the Council of Florence RCs had been severely repressed in the Russian Empire, but their influence had grown, largely from centres of propaganda in *Poland and Lithuania which both acknowledged the Papacy. A *Uniat Church had also come into being in Russia itself at an uncertain date. In 1606 a determined effort was made to set up a RC Czar in the person of Demetrius, but it was checked by his assassination. In the controversies against Rome and the Uniats in the 17th cent. the most outstanding figure was Peter

*Moghila, Metropolitan of Kieff (d. 1646). Chief among the ecclesiastics of this period was *Nikon, Patriarch of Moscow (q.v.; d. 1681), a man of great learning, austere life, and devoted to his Church. His attempted revision of the liturgical books in 1654 produced a storm of protests; and the horror which greeted the order in his first Pastoral letter (Lent 1653) that the sign of the cross be made with three fingers instead of the traditional two, led to the schism of the '*Old Believers' (q.v.), who were henceforward a leading influence in Russian ecclesiastical life. In 1658 Nikon found himself surrounded with hate and retired to one of his monasteries. His expectations of being recalled were not fulfilled, and in 1667 he was solemnly degraded. The 'Old Believers' were excommunicated by the Council of 1667 and expelled from the Church; and Nikon was exiled.

The reign of Peter the Great (1676–1725) saw the final and complete subjugation of the Russian Church to the imperial power. In the Ecclesiastical Regulations of 1720 it was put under the control of a lay synod, whose members did not even need to be Christians. One president at least was a professed rationalist.

From the inclusion of part of Poland in the Russian Empire, which took place by stages at the end of the 18th cent., RC activity was intensified and sternly repressed by imperial ukases. In the reign of Catherine the Great (d. 1796) the *Jesuits, after their suppression by *Benedict XIV in 1773, found a home in Russia, but, proving unwelcome guests, they were shortly afterwards expelled. The RC cause was bound up with Polish and Lithuanian nationalism while these countries were under Russian rule, and even the edict of toleration to all faiths, issued by Nicholas II in 1905, had almost at once to be modified and limited in respect of the RCs.

The Communist Revolution of 1917 brought into power a government which was both committed to the materialist and anti-religious doctrines of Marxism, and also hated the Church as the instrument and associate of Czarism. Public worship was at no time legally forbidden, but very many church buildings were confiscated and secularized, clergy were esp. suspect, and liable to death or banishment to prison camps, churches were forbidden to possess funds or engage in any public activity, and the teaching of religion to any person under 18 was a criminal offence. As between different religions (including Mohammedanism and Judaism, both represented in the country as well as Christianity) and different sects, the state proclaimed official neutrality, but RCism was accorded probably even less freedom than under the Czars. Certain sects, however, such as *Baptists, benefited, relatively to their former state, though they never attracted more than a small fraction of the population. There was also a 'Reform' movement in the Orthodox Church, whose supporters formed a schismatic body, but afterwards returned to the Church.

Organized government 'anti-God' propaganda began in 1929. The Constitution of 1936 enacted 'freedom of religious worship and of anti-religious propaganda'. In 1938 it was reported that anti-religious propaganda was being intensified, but that churches still open were full. At the outbreak of war with Germany in 1941 prayers were said by the Church for the success of Russian arms in defence of the country, and the attitude of the Government was rapidly modified, anti-religious propaganda ceasing almost at once. In 1943 the Holy Synod was allowed to meet and the Metropolitan Sergei elected to the Patriarchate, vacant since the death of the Patriarch *Tikhon in 1924, and two state councils, one for Orthodox and one for all other religious affairs, were set up. Under this régime the Church enjoyed a certain limited freedom, being legally able, e.g., to possess corporate funds, and to set up academies for the training of clergy and for theological study. The number of churches open for worship greatly increased, and at a Synod in 1945, at which 44 dioceses were represented, a successor to the Patriarch Sergei (d. 1944) was elected, and publicly enthroned. Messages of friendship with the C of E were exchanged, and C. F. Garbett, Abp. of York, visited Moscow.

With the defeat of Germany and increasing tension between the U.S.S.R. and the W., government policy was modified. Anti-religious propaganda was restarted, but the Orthodox Church in Russia (as in Russian-dominated Slav lands) retained a certain amount of freedom as long as all contacts with the W. were repudiated. In 1948 the Russian Church publicly celebrated the 500th anniversary of its 'autocephaly' in the presence of representatives of other Orthodox (but no W.) Churches and of the *Oecumenical Patriarch; afterwards a meeting of representatives of Slav Churches passed resolutions hostile to the Vatican and the *World Council of Churches (then meeting at *Amsterdam), and favourable to the Russian government's foreign policy.

The principal material is in Russian and has largely remained untranslated into any W. European language; standard works available in tr. are the histories of the Russian Church by A. N. Murav'ew (orig. publd. in Russian in 1840), translated into Eng. by R. W. Blackmore as *A History of the Church of Russia* (1842), and D. *Philaret, translated into German by Dr. Blumenthal as *Geschichte der Kirche Russlands* (2 vols., 1872). W. H. *Frere, C.R., *Some Links in the Chain of Russian Church History* (1918). Slighter introductory studies include R. F. Bigg-Wither, *A Short History of the Church of Russia* (S.P.C.K., 1920); H. Y. Reyburn, *The Story of the Russian Church* (1924); D. A. Lowrie, *The Light of Russia*. An Introduction to the Russian Church (1924); N. [V.] Brian-Chaninov, *L'Eglise russe* (1927; Eng. tr., 1931); J. N. Danzas [pseudonym for Y. Nikolaev], *L'Itinéraire religieux de la conscience russe* (Collection Istina, ii; 1935; Eng. tr., 1936); N. Zernov, *Moscow the Third Rome* (1937); id., *The Russians and their Church* (S.P.C.K., 1945); E. L. Mascall (ed.), *The Church of God*. An Anglo-Russian Symposium by Members of the Fellowship of St. Alban and St. Sergius (S.P.C.K., 1934). M. Jugie, A.A., *Theologia Dogmatica Christianorum ab Ecclesia Catholica Dissentium*, i–iv (Paris, 1926–31). G. P. Fedotov, *The Russian Religious Mind* (Harvard, Mass.-London, 1946). Id. (ed.), *A Treasury of Russian Spirituality* (1950). See also entry *Macarius of Moscow*. L. K. Goetz, *Staat und Kirche in Altrussland* . . . 988–

1240 (1908). N. de Baumgarten, *Chronologie ecclésiastique de terres russes du Xe au XIIIe siècle* (Orientalia Christiana, xvii, Pt. 1 (No. 58); 1930); id., *Saint Vladimir et la conversion de la Russie* (ib., xxvii, Pt. 1 (No. 79); 1932). J. B. Koncevicius, *Russia's Attitude towards Union with Rome, 9th–16th Centuries* (Catholic University of America thesis; Washington, D.C., 1927), with bibl. P. Pierling, S.J., *La Russie et le saint-siège*. Études diplomatiques (5 vols., 1896–1912). R. S. Latimer, *Under Three Tsars*. Liberty of Conscience in Russia, 1859–1909 (1909), and other works by this author. J. S. Curtiss, *Church and State in Russia*. The Last Years of the Empire, 1900–1917 (New York, 1940); id., *The Russian Church and the Soviet State, 1917–1950* (ib., 1954). F. McCullagh, *The Bolshevik Persecution of Christianity* (1924); M. Spinka, *The Church and the Russian Revolution* (New York, 1927). G. P. Fedotoff, *The Russian Church since the Revolution* (S.P.C.K., 1928). J. F. Hecker, *Religion and Communism*. A Study of Religion and Atheism in Soviet Russia (1933). N. S. Timasheff, *Religion in Soviet Russia, 1917–1942* (1943). J. S. Curtiss, *The Russian Church and the Soviet State, 1917–1950* (Boston, Mass. [1953]).

W. J. Birkbeck (ed.), *Russia and the English Church during the Last Fifty Years*, containing a Correspondence between Mr. William Palmer, Fellow of Magdalen College, Oxford, and M. Khomiakoff, in the Years 1844–1854 (1895); A. Riley (ed.), *Birkbeck and the Russian Church*. Containing Essays and Articles by the late W. J. Birkbeck . . . written in the Years 1888–1915 (1917).

K. K. Grass, *Die russischen Sekten* (2 vols., 1907–9); F. C. Conybeare, *Russian Dissenters* (Harvard Theological Studies, x; 1921). H. Dalton, *Beiträge zur Geschichte der evangelischen Kirche in Russland* (4 vols., 1887–1905). A. W. Fechner, *Chronik der evangelischen Gemeinden in Moskau* (2 vols., Moscow, 1876).

E. Herman, S.J., in *L.Th.K.*, ix (1937), cols. 24–33, s.v. 'Russland', with further bibl.

RUTH, Book of. The Book tells the story of Ruth, a Moabitess, who had married a Jew when he was compelled during a famine in the land of Judah to take refuge in Moab. It is narrated how, after the death of her husband, Ruth determined to return to Judaea with her Hebrew mother-in-law, and how Boaz, a kinsman of her former husband, took her under his protection and married her. The incident is set in the days of the Judges (*c.* 1000 B.C.), and this explains the position of the Book in the English Bible (as in the Greek and Latin Versions) after *Judges. The Book itself, however, is evidently of a relatively late date, certainly not earlier than the Exile (6th cent. B.C.); and in the Hebrew Bible it appears as one of the 'Five *Megilloth', i.e. in the third and latest division of the Hebrew OT. The genealogy at the end (4. 18–22), which may or may not be an addition to the work in its original form, indicates one of the apparent aims of the book, viz. to record the ancestry of *David. The disclosure of the Moabite strain in David's lineage shows that the writer had a broader view on the legitimacy of the marriage of Jews with foreigners than was inculcated by *Nehemiah and *Ezra, and the story may point to his disapproval of the exclusive attitude of the Jews of his time. He probably also wished to insist on the duty of marriage on the part of the next-of-kin with a widow left without male offspring. The genealogy of David is cited by St. *Matthew in his genealogy of Christ (1. 2–6).

Commentaries by G. A. *Cooke (Camb. Bib., RV, 1913), A. Bertholet (K.H.C., xvii, on Song. of Sol., Ruth, Lam., Eccles., and Est., 1898, pp. 49–69), W. Nowack (H.K.A.T., Abt. 1, Bd. iv, on Jgs., Ruth, and Sam., 1902, pp. 179–201), W. Rudolph (K.A.T., xvi, Theil 2, 1939), and M. Haller (H.A.T., Reihe 1, Bd. xviii, on Ruth, Song of Sol., Eccles., Lam., and Est., 1940, pp. 1–20).

RUTHENIAN CHURCHES. This title comprises certain *Uniat Churches mostly found in Polish Galicia, Czechoslovakia, Hungary, and Bohemia, with colonies in N. America and elsewhere. Their ancestors, who were Slavonic converts of St. *Vladimir, formed part of the *Russian Church under the jurisdiction of the Metropolitan of Kiev until his expulsion on the promulgation of the Union of *Florence (1443). In 1485 *Pius III appointed a Catholic metropolitan of Kiev, who, by agreement with Casimir IV of *Poland (1447–92), was permitted to exercise jurisdiction over the eight *eparchies of the province under the control of Poland and Lithuania. Although these Churches reverted to Orthodoxy at the beginning of the 16th cent., in 1595 the Metropolitan of Kiev, and the Bps. of Vladimir, Lutsk, Pololsk, Pinsk and Kholn petitioned for communion with Rome, which was achieved on 23 Dec. 1595 by the Union of *Brest-Litovsk (q.v.). They were joined in 1694 by the Bp. of Przemysl and in 1700 by the Bp. of Lwów. Despite a decree of *Urban VIII (1624), during the 17th cent. the majority of the nobility and landowners in Poland adopted the Latin rite. After the Partition of Poland (1795) most of the Ruthenians, except those of Galicia, passed under the sovereignty of Russia and were gradually suppressed in the early 19th cent. in favour of the Orthodox Church; in the Kholn district (ceded by Austria in 1815) they survived until c. 1875. When toleration was granted to RCs in Russia in 1905, Catholic Byzantines still being illegal, the survivors passed to the Latin rite.

After the Ruthenians of Galicia had come under the sovereignty of Austria, to solve the problems arising from the sees of Lwów and Przemysl being under a different political authority from their metropolitan, Lwów was constituted an Archbishopric in 1807. During the 19th cent. the Galician Ruthenians enjoyed religious toleration, but more recently they have suffered greatly from the political troubles in Eastern Europe, during which considerable ill-feeling between the Latin Poles and Byzantine Ruthenians has been engendered. A Ruthenian College was founded in Rome by *Leo XIII in 1897 (since 1904 in charge of the Ruthenian Basilian monks). The monastic element in the Ruthenian Church appears to be strong, and is esp. fostered by the more austere Studites (founded c. 1900). The Ruthenian liturgy is based on the Byzantine rite with certain modifications adopted from Rome.

There is a further Ruthenian community (the Podcaparthian Ruthenians) granted a separate jurisdiction by the erection of the eparchy of Mukachevo, subject to the primacy of Hungary, by Pope *Clement XIV in 1771. It was created to settle the disputes between the Ruthenian metropolitan north of the Carpathians and the settlement (dating from the 14th cent.) of Little and White Russians south of the Carpathians, brought into communion with Rome in 1625 by the Union of Ungvar.

There are also considerable Ruthenian communities of both jurisdictions in U.S.A. (since c. 1876), *Canada (from the 1890's), *Brazil and the *Argentine.

A. Theiner, *Die neuesten Zustände der katholischen Kirche beider Ritus in Polen und Russland seit Katherina II bis auf unsere Tage* (Augsburg, 1841). J. Pelesz, *Geschichte der Union der ruthenischen Kirche mit Rom* (2 vols., Würzburg, 1878–81). D. Attwater, *The Catholic Eastern Churches* (Milwaukee, Wisc., [1935]), pp. 76–95. A. J. Shipman in *C.E.*, xiii (1912), pp. 277–80, s.vv. 'Ruthenian Rite' and 'Ruthenians'; N. Andrusiak in *D.T.C.*, xiv (pt. 1; 1939), cols. 382–407, s.v. 'Ruthène (Église)'; G. Olšr, S.J.–A. Raes, S.J., in *E.C.*, x (1953), cols. 1482–92, s.v. 'Ruteni'.

RUTHERFORD, JOSEPH FRANKLIN (1869–1941), popularly called 'Judge Rutherford', second head of the American sect of '*Jehovah's Witnesses' (q.v.). He was the descendant of a Baptist family of Morgan County (Mo.). Though he had never studied, he was given an attorney's licence c. 1892. He frequently defended C. T. *Russell (q.v.) in the courts and became a resourceful supporter of his sect and, in 1917, after Russell's death, its head. Under his leadership the organization took on an increasingly revolutionary aspect. In 1918–19 he served a term of imprisonment at Atlanta (Georgia) for insubordination and disloyalty, and he was frequently accused of fraudulent practices, even by his own followers. He originally assigned the Second Coming to 1914. Later he held that Christ had returned invisibly in that year, and that the final Armageddon between Jehovah and Satan was imminent, though no precise date was fixed. He wrote several books including *The Harp of God*, *Deliverance*, and *Creation* (all undated), and innumerable pamphlets propagating his subversive views.

H. Thurston, S.J., '*Judge' Rutherford* (C.T.S. pamphlet, 1940).

RUTHERFORD, MARK, pseudonym of WILLIAM HALE WHITE (1831–1913), author of religious works. The son of William White, a Nonconformist bookseller who was later a doorkeeper of the House of Commons and author of *The Inner Life of the House of Commons* (1897), Hale White had orig. intended to enter the *Congregational ministry. He spent most of his life as a civil servant. He won recognition as a religious author by *The Autobiography of Mark Rutherford* (1881), marked by its unusual combination of spiritual depth, irony, and humour. It was followed by *Mark Rutherford's Deliverance* (1885) and other works, incl. *Catharine Furze* (1893), *Pages from a Journal* (1900), *More Pages from a Journal* (1910), and *Last Pages from a Journal* (posthumous, 1915). He also issued under his real name an Eng. tr. of B. de *Spinoza's writings. Though he has never made more than a limited appeal, the freshness and penetration of his books have won him an assured place among English religious writers.

W. R. *Nicoll, *A Bookman's Letters* (1913), pp. 364–412; repr. separately as *Memories of Mark Rutherford* (1924). A. E. *Taylor, 'The Novels of Mark Rutherford' [a lecture] in *Essays and Studies by Members of the English Association*, v (1914), pp. 51–74. W. Stone, *Religion and Art of William Hale White* ('*Mark Rutherford*') (Stanford University Publications, University Series. Language and Literature, xii; Stanford, California, 1954), with bibl. Studies by Catherine M. Maclean (London, 1955) and I. Stock (ib., 1956). H. W. Massingham in *D.N.B., 1912–1921*, p. 573 f.

RUTHERFORD, SAMUEL (*c.* 1600–61), also 'Rutherfurd', Scottish *Presbyterian divine. After studying at Edinburgh University, he was elected professor of humanity in 1623, but deprived in 1626 for a pre-nuptial scandal. Soon afterwards he became fervently religious. In 1627 he was appointed minister at Anwoth, Kirkcudbrightshire. His *Exercitationes Apologeticae pro Divina Gratia* (Amsterdam, 1636), written from a rigidly *Calvinist standpoint, led to his prosecution before the High Commission, and in 1636 he was deposed and exiled at Aberdeen till 1638. In 1639 he became professor of divinity at, and in 1647 principal of, St. Mary's College, St. Andrews. His *Plea for Presbytery* appeared in 1642. In 1643 he was one of the eight Scottish Commissioners at the *Westminster Assembly and for four years he defended the Presbyterian cause at London. His *Lex Rex, a Dispute for the Just Prerogative of King and People* (1644), which was an attack on monarchical absolutism, brought him considerable repute as a constitutional theorist. There followed *The Divine Right of Church Government and Excommunication* (1646), on behalf of Presbyterian Church polity, and *A Free Disputation against Pretended Liberty of Conscience* (1648), a vigorous defence of religious persecution in reply to J. *Taylor, on the ground that the advocacy of toleration put conscience in the place of God and the Bible. Several devotional writings also belong to these years. At the Restoration (1660) his *Lex Rex* was publicly burnt and a charge of high treason was preferred against him, but he died shortly afterwards.

Collection of his letters publd. under the title *Joshua Redivivus or Mr. Rutherford's Letters* [ed. by R. McWard], no place, 1664; the best ed. is that of A. A. Bonar (London, 1848), with sketch of Rutherford's life, pp. v–xxxiii, frequently republd.; in ed. 1891, there is also a list of Rutherford's works, p. 31 f. A collection of his Sermons also ed. A. A. Bonar (London, 1885). Lives by T. Murray (Edinburgh, 1828), A. Thomson ('Men Worth Remembering', London, 1884), and R. Gilmour (Edinburgh–London, 1904). A. Whyte, *Samuel Rutherford and some of his Correspondents* (Lectures delivered in St. George's Free Church, Edinburgh; 1894). G. W. Sprott in *D.N.B.*, l (1897), pp. 7–9.

RUTILIUS CLAUDIUS NAMATIANUS (5th cent.), Latin poet. In 416 he returned to his native Gaul after some time spent in Rome; in his 'De Reditu Suo' he described the journey homewards. By religion he was almost certainly a pagan, despite C. Schenkl's attempt (1911) to prove him a Christian. He was conservative in his outlook, despised all religious innovations and was esp. critical of the monastic movement which, under St. *Jerome's influence, had then become very popular at Rome. Stilicho he regards not as a restorer of traditional pagan practices (the usual Christian conception of him), but as their uncompromising enemy. His poem

O.D.C.C.–2 Q 2

throws important light on the background of the Church in the period.

Editio princeps by J. B. Pius, Bologna, 1520. Crit. texts by J. Vessereau–F. Préchat (Collection des Universités de France, Paris, 1933; with Fr. tr.) and P. van de Woestijne (Rijksuniversiteit te Gent. Werken uitgegeven door de Faculteit van de Wijsbegeerte en Letteren, Afl. lxxvi; Antwerp, 1936). H. Schenkl, 'Ein spätrömischer Dichter und sein Glaubensbekenntnis' in *Rheinisches Museum für Philologie*, N.F., lxvi (1911), pp. 393–416. F. Vollmer in *P.W.*, 2. Reihe, ii (pt. 1; 1914), cols. 1249–54, s.v. (dismisses view that Rutilius was a Christian).

RUYSBROECK, JAN VAN (1293–1381), Flemish mystic. A native of Ruysbroeck, *c.* 1304 he went to Brussels to his relative J. Hinckaert, canon of St.-Gudule, who educated him. Ordained priest *c.* 1318, he began to lead a life of contemplation, at the same time opposing the mystics known as '*Brethren of the Free Spirit'. In 1343 he retired with Hinckaert and another priest into a hermitage at Groenendael, near Brussels, where, in 1350, he took the habit of *Canons Regular of St. Augustine and was made prior. Here many of his works were written, and Groenendael itself became a school of sanctity which attracted many disciples. Among his writings were *The Adornment of the Spiritual Marriage, The Seven Steps of the Ladder of Spiritual Love, The Book of the Highest Truth*, and *The Mirror of Eternal Salvation*.

Ruysbroeck's treatises, all written in Flemish, made a profound impression on his time. Himself influenced by *Dionysius the Areopagite and possibly also by Master *Eckhart, he became the head of the school called *Devotio Moderna* from which sprang the '*Brethren of the Common Life' and the Canons Regular of *Windesheim, to which belonged such eminent spiritual writers as *Thomas à Kempis and *Dionysius the Carthusian. His cultus was approved by *Pius X in 1908. Feast day, 2 Dec.

Works ed. J. David (6 vols., Ghent, 1856–68) and J. van Mierlo, S.J.–J. B. Poukens, S.J.–L. Reypens, S.J.– D. A. Stracke, S.J.–M. Schurmans, S.J. (4 vols., Amsterdam, 1932–4). Lat. tr. by L. Surius (Cologne, 1552). Fr. tr. by the Benedictines of S. Paul de Wisques (3 vols., Brussels, 1912–30). Eng. trr. from the Flemish of *The Twelve Béguines* by J. Francis (London, 1913), of *The Adornment of the Spiritual Marriage, The Sparkling Stone*, and *The Book of Supreme Truth* by C. A. W. Dom (ib., 1916), and of *The Seven Steps of the Ladder of Spiritual Love* by P. S. Taylor (ib., 1944), and (from Surius's Lat.) of *The Kingdom of the Lovers of God* by T. A. Hyde (ib., 1919). The principal authority for his life is H. Pomerius, *De Origine Monasterii Viridisvallis una cum Vita Joannis Rusbrochii* (first half of the 15th cent.) pr. in *Anal. Boll.*, iv (1885), pp. 257–308. P. O'Sheridan, 'Ce que reste de la plus ancienne vie de Ruysbroeck' in *R.H.E.*, xxi (1925), pp. 51–78 and 215–48, with reff. M. d'Asbeck, *Documents relatifs à Ruysbroeck* [1926], with bibl. Modern lives by W. L. de Vreese (Ghent, 1896), V. Scully, C.R.L., (London, 1910), E. *Underhill (ib., 1915), A. Wautier d'Aygalliers (Paris, 1924; Eng. tr., omitting bibl., 1925). A. Auger, *De Doctrina et Meritis Johannis Ruysbroeck* (Louvain, 1892). G. J. Waffelaert, *L'Union de l'âme aimante avec Dieu . . . d'après la doctrine de Jean Ruysbroeck* (1916); G. Dolezich, *Die Mystik Jan van Ruysbroecks des Wunderbaren* (Breslauer Studien zur historischen Theologie, iv; 1926]; M. d'Asbeck, *La Mystique de Ruysbroeck l'Admirable* (1928). A. Combes, *Essai sur la critique de Ruysbroeck par Gerson* (Études de Théologie et de l'Histoire de la Spiritualité, iv, v, . . . 1945 ff.). A series of important studies on Ruysbroeck's mystical doctrines by A. Ampe (Tielt, 1950 ff.). L. Reypens, S.J., in *E.C.*, x (1953), cols. 1495–7, s.v. 'Ruusbroec, Jan di'.

RYCAUT, PAUL (1628–1700), also 'Ricaut', traveller and author. Born at Aylesford, Kent, after studying at Trinity College, Cambridge, he spent most of his life abroad. In 1661 he was appointed secretary to the British Embassy at *Constantinople, where he collected extensive materials on the life and customs of Turkey and the Moslem religion, which were published later as *The Present State of the Ottoman Empire* (1668; acc. to S. Pepys, an original edition was almost completely destroyed in the Great Fire). From 1667 to 1679 he was consul to the Levant Company at Smyrna. On his return to England, he issued an essay on *The Present State of the Greek and Armenian Churches* (1679), which remains an important contemporary source of information on the Eastern Churches. He was also the author of *The History of the Turkish Empire from the Year 1623 to the Year 1677* (2 parts, 1679–80), and translated a large number of Latin and Greek treatises into English, incl. B. *Platina's *Lives of the Popes* (1685).

T. Seccombe in *D.N.B.*, l (1897), pp. 38–40.

RYLE, HERBERT EDWARD (1856–1925), Dean of *Westminster. The son of J. C. *Ryle, he was educated at Eton and King's College, Cambridge, where in 1881 he was elected a Fellow. Apart from a short period as principal of St. David's College, Lampeter (1886–8), he remained at Cambridge until his appointment to the see of *Exeter in 1900. Translated in 1903 to the see of *Winchester, he resigned this office in 1910 to become Dean of Westminster. From 1919 to 1925 he was *Prolocutor of the Lower House of Convocation of Canterbury. His writings include *The Early Narratives of Genesis* (1892), *The Canon of the OT* (1892), and *Genesis* (Camb. Bible, 1914).

Memoir by M. H. FitzGerald (London, 1928). Id. in *D.N.B., 1922–1930*, pp. 733–5.

RYLE, JOHN CHARLES (1816–1900), Bp. of Liverpool. He was born at Macclesfield and educated at Eton and Christ Church, Oxford. When his wish to become a member of Parliament had been frustrated by lack of financial means, he decided to take orders. He was ordained priest in 1842, and after holding several parochial cures, was consecrated bishop of the newly created Anglican see of Liverpool in 1880, which he held till shortly before his death. A strong Evangelical in his beliefs, he defended his convictions in forceful and simple language in a number of tracts which had a wide circulation. Among his publications are *The Bishop, the Pastor, and the Preacher* (1854; studies on H. *Latimer, R. *Baxter, and G. *Whitefield), *The Christian Leaders of the Last Century* (1869), *What do we owe to the Reformation?* (1877), and *Principles for Churchmen* (1884).

J. M. Rigg in *D.N.B.*, Suppl. iii (1901), p. 334 f., s.v.

RYSWICK CLAUSE, The. The clause 'Religione tamen Catholica Romana in locis sic restitutis, in statu quo nunc est, remanente', inserted into Article IV of the Treaty of Ryswick (30 Oct. 1697). It modifies the general rule that the religious frontiers should revert to their position at the time of the Treaty of Nymegen (1679) in favour of the Catholic communities in those places where they had been re-established by Louis XIV in the interval.

Text of the Treaty of Ryswick between the Emp. Leopold and Louis XIV, pr., with comm., in H. Vast, *Les Grands Traités du règne de Louis XIV*, ii (1898), pp. 228–53, this stipulation occurring on p. 232; most imp. sections of Treaty repr. in E. Reich (ed.), *Select Documents Illustrating Mediaeval and Modern History* (1905), pp. 25–32, with this stipulation, p. 26 f. C. T. G. von Scheurl in *P.R.E.* (ed. 3), xvii (1906), p. 273 f., s.v. 'Ryswicker Klausel'.

S

SA, MANOEL DE (c. 1530–96), Portuguese theologian. He entered the *Jesuit novitiate at Coimbra in 1545. In 1551 he became professor of philosophy at Alcalá and in 1557 was called to teach theology at the Roman College. *Pius V appointed him a member of the *Septuagint Commission. The last years of his life he spent in apostolic works at *Loreto and Genoa. Besides several Scriptural Commentaries he published, in 1595, *Aphorismi Confessariorum*, a manual of casuistry in dictionary form which was temporarily placed on the *Index in 1603 for allowing confession and absolution to be made by letter, but in its corrected edition of 1607–8 enjoyed great authority among moral theologians.

Sommervogel, vii (1896), cols. 349–54, and ix (1900), col. 829. R. Brouillard, S.J., in *D.T.C.*, xiv (pt. 1; 1939), cols. 425–8, s.v. 'Sa (Emmanuel)', with bibl.

SABAOTH (Heb. צְבָאוֹת; Gk. Σαβαώθ). This Hebrew word, which denotes 'armies' or 'hosts', is preserved untranslated in the phrase 'Lord of Sabaoth' in the ordinary English version of the *Te Deum and in the NT (Rom. 9. 29, Jas. 5. 4). For its meaning and bibl., see *Lord of Hosts*.

SABAS, St. (439–532), monk. A native of Mutalaska in Cappadocia, after leading the life of a monk and solitary in several places in the East, in 478 he founded a large *laura* (still extant as 'Mar Saba') in Palestine in the wild country between *Jerusalem and the Dead Sea (the Wadi en-Nar). With reluctance he accepted ordination to the priesthood (then not usual for monks) in 491, and in 493 the Patr. of Jerusalem created him superior of all the hermits in Palestine. A strong supporter of theological orthodoxy, he took a prominent part in the campaign against *Origenism and *Monophysitism. A *typicon* circulates under his name in the E. Church. Feast day, 5 Dec.

The principal authority is the life by *Cyril of Scythopolis, pr., with Lat. tr., by J. B. *Cotelier, *Ecclesiae Graecae Monumenta*, iii (Paris, 1686), pp. 220–376; modern ed. by E. *Schwartz in T.U., xlix (pt. 2; 1939), pp. 85–200. *B.H.G.*, p. 226 f. (Nos. 1608–10). History of the Laura of St. Sabas (in Gk.) by J. Phocylides (Alexandria, 1927). H. *Leclercq, O.S.B., in *D.A.C.L.*, xv (pt. 1; 1950), cols. 189–211, s.v., with full bibl. on the churches and monastery.

SABAS, St., Patron St. of Serbia. See *Sava, St.*

SABATIER, AUGUSTE (1839–1901), French Protestant theologian. He was professor of reformed dogmatics at Strassburg university from 1867 to 1873, and from 1877 at the newly established Protestant theological faculty at *Paris. He propagated the theories of F. D. E. *Schleiermacher and A. *Ritschl in France, applied the methods of historical criticism to the NT, and, esp. by his interpretation of Christian dogma as the symbolism of religious feelings, exercised a profound influence not only on French Protestantism but also in Catholic theological circles, thus helping to prepare the *Modernist Movement. Among his best-known works are *L'Apôtre Paul* (1870; Eng. trans., 1891), *La Vie intime des dogmes* (1890), *Esquisse d'une philosophie de la religion* (1897; Eng. trans., 1897), and his posthumous *Les Religions d'autorité et la religion de l'esprit* (1903; Eng. trans., 1904).

E. Ménégoz, 'The Theology of Auguste Sabatier of Paris' in *Expository Times*, xv (1903–4), pp. 30–4 (tr. from the French). G. B. Stevens, 'Auguste Sabatier and the Paris School of Theology' in *Hibbert Journal*, i (1903), pp. 553–68.

SABATIER, PAUL (1858–1928), *Calvinist Pastor and Franciscan scholar. Born at Strassburg, after studying letters at Besançon and Lille and medicine at Montpellier, he enrolled himself in the Protestant Faculty of Theology at Paris, where Auguste *Sabatier and E. *Renan were among his teachers. From 1885 to 1889 he held a pastoral cure at St. Nicholas, Strassburg. He then became Pastor at St.-Cierge-la-Serre, where he began his studies on St. *Francis, to which he had been stimulated by Renan. Soon compelled by frail health to give up his pastoral work, he devoted the rest of his life solely to his researches, spending long periods in Italy, esp. at *Assisi. His *Vie de St. François* (1893), depicting the mission of the Saint as a renewal of the medieval Church in the light of the 'pure Gospel', was based on a close study of the sources, brilliant in presentation and penetrating in its psychological understanding. The work was widely read, but, on account of its liberal outlook, was soon put on the *Index (8 June 1894).

Sabatier's further researches continued to give great impetus to Franciscan studies. He brought to light much important new material, notably the *Speculum Perfectionis*, the *Tractatus de Indulgentia S. Mariae de Portiuncula* of Brother Bartolo of Assisi and the *Regula Antiqua* of the Third Franciscan Order, though some of his contentions on the primitive sources, notably his attempt to give priority to those ascribed to Brother Leo, have been generally rejected. He also directed two series of publications, *Collection de documents pour l'histoire religieuse et littéraire du moyen-âge* (1898–1909) and *Opuscules de critique historique* (1901–1919). In 1902 he founded the 'Società Internazionale di Studi Francescani' at Assisi and in 1908 the British Society of Franciscan Studies at London. He was also an active sympathiser with the RC *Modernist Movement, on which he delivered a course of Jowett Lectures in London in 1908 (publd. later in the year).

Eng. tr. of Sabatier's *Vie de S. François d'Assise* by L. Houghton (1894). A. G. Little, 'Paul Sabatier, Historian of

St. Francis' in *Franciscan Papers, Lists and Documents* (Publications of the University of Manchester, No. cclxxxiv, Historical Series No. lxxxi, 1943), Lecture XI (delivered in 1929), pp. 179–88.

SABATIER, PIERRE (1682 – 1742), *Maurist scholar. After joining the *Benedictine Order at *Reims in 1700, he went to *St.-Germain-des-Prés, where he was trained in historical method by T. *Ruinart. His monumental work, the fruit of many years' research, was a virtually exhaustive collection of the material for the *Old Latin (i.e. pre-*Vulgate) text of the Bible. It was published posthumously as *Bibliorum Sacrorum Latinae Versiones Antiquae* (3 vols., fol., 1743[–9]) at Reims, whither the author had been transferred in 1727 on account of his supposed *Jansenist tendencies. Despite the great amount of work done on the textual criticism of the Bible, esp. since the middle of the 19th cent., it has not been superseded.

[R. P. Tassin, O.S.B.,] *Histoire littéraire de la congrégation de Saint-Maur* (1770), pp. 617–21. A. Manser, O.S.B., in *L.Th.K.*, ix (1937), col. 48, s.v., with bibl.

SABBATARIANISM. Excessive strictness in the observance of the Divinely ordained day of rest. In its more rigorous form it is a peculiar development of the English and Scottish Reformation, being unknown on the Continent even among *Calvinists. The beginning of 17th cent. Sabbatarianism is connected with the publication of Nicholas Bound's *True Doctrine of the Sabbath* in 1595, which advocated its strict enforcement on OT lines. The book caused a lively controversy, which assumed political importance when *James I issued his *Book of *Sports* (1618), enjoining cessation of work but allowing lawful recreation. James's *Book* roused a storm of protest, and was burned by Parliament in 1643. The Puritan Sabbath was imposed by successive Acts of legislation (1644, 1650, 1655) prohibiting any kind of recreation on Sunday, even going for a walk. After the Restoration observance was slightly relaxed when under *Charles II the Act for the Better Observance of the Lord's Day (1677) was passed which, though it forbade all work and travel by horse or boat on Sunday, was silent on recreations. Under the influence of the *Evangelical Revival at the end of the 18th cent. rigorism took a new lease of life by the *Lord's Day Observance Act, drawn up by Bp. B. *Porteus in 1781, which laid down that any place of entertainment or debate where admission was gained by payment of money should be closed to use on Sunday. In Scotland Sabbatarianism was carried to extremes from the beginning of the 17th cent., all recreation including even books and music not strictly religious being disallowed. Here, as well as in England, relaxation has been progressive since the latter part of the 19th cent. The Puritan point of view is to-day represented by the Lord's Day Observance Society, which opposed the Sunday Performances Bill of 1931 and successfully agitated against the opening of theatres on Sunday during World War I and the Fun Fair at Battersea on Sundays in the Festival of Britain of 1951. See also *Sunday*.

Full bibl. of the older literature (which, though abundant, is very repetitive) in R. Cox, *The Literature of the Sabbath Question* (2 vols., Edinburgh, 1865). E. W. *Hengstenberg, *Ueber den Tag des Herrn* (1852); R. Cox, *Sabbath Laws and Sabbath Duties* (1853); J. A. Hessey, *Sunday*. Its Origin, History and Present Obligation (Bampton Lectures for 1860; 1860). On the 'Law relating to Sunday' see W. F. Craies in *E.B.* (ed. 11), xxvi (1911), pp. 95–8, s.v. 'Sunday' (part). See also bibl. to *Sunday*.

SABBATH. The seventh day of the Jewish week. It was to be sanctified by complete abstinence from work (Ex. 20. 10) and marked by the doubling of the daily sacrifices (Num. 28. 9 f.) and special gatherings for worship (Lev. 23. 2 f.). The particular distinction of the seventh day is probably connected with the phases of the moon. Its origin is accounted for in a double way. Acc. to Ex. 20. 11 and 31. 17 it represents the rest God took on the seventh day from His work of Creation, whereas acc. to Deut. 5. 15 it is kept in remembrance of the deliverance from Egypt. The Sabbath served the twofold purpose of being a day set apart for the worship of God (Ex. 31. 13–17) as well as for the rest and recreation of man, esp. slaves, and cattle (Deut. 5. 14). The prohibition of work was regulated by detailed prescription, forbidding e.g. the gathering of manna, cooking (Ex. 16. 22–30), and the lighting of fire (Ex. 35. 3). In the *Maccabean period regulations became increasingly strict, and pious Jews let themselves be killed rather than defend their lives on the Sabbath (1 Macc. 2. 32–8). In our Lord's time, even activities such as healing (e.g. Mt. 12. 10) and plucking of ears of corn (Mt. 12. 1 f.) were forbidden. One of the Pharisees' chief grievances against Christ was that He declared the Sabbath to have been made for man and not vice versa (Mk. 2. 27), thus freeing men from an obligation which had become intolerable. Though the early Christians largely continued to keep the seventh day as a day of rest and prayer, the fact that the Resurrection and the Coming of the Holy Ghost had taken place on the first day of the week soon led to the widespread observance of the *Sunday (Acts 20. 7), which became the general practice of the Church in the first cents. Only a few post-Reformation sects such as the *Seventh Day Adventists observe the Sabbath instead of the Sunday.

The details of later Jewish Sabbath observance are set out in the *Mishnah tractate 'Shabbath'. Eng. tr. of Tractate Shabbath with notes by W. O. E. Oesterley (Translations of Early Documents, Series III, S.P.C.K., 1927). J. Hehn, *Siebenzahl und Sabbat bei den Babyloniern und in Altem Testament* (Leipziger semitische Studien, ii, Hft. 5; 1907). K. *Budde, 'The Sabbath and the Week' in *J.T.S.*, xxx (1928–9), pp. 1–15; J. Meinhold, 'Zur Sabbathfrage' in *Z.A.T.W.*, xlviii (1930), pp. 121–38; reply by K. Budde, ib., pp. 138–45. S. R. *Driver in *H.D.B.*, iv (1902), pp. 317–23, s.v.; W. Lotz in *P.R.E.* (ed. 3), xvii (1906), pp. 283–91, s.v.; H. Lesêtre in *Dict. Bibl.*, v (1912), cols. 1291–1302, s.v.' Sabbat'; H. Webster–T. G. Pinches–I. *Abrahams–G. Margoliouth in *H.E.R.E.*, x (1918), pp. 885–94, s.v.

SABBATICAL YEAR. The one year in seven which the *Mosaic legislation (Ex. 21. 2–6, Deut. 15. 1–3, 15. 12–18, 31. 10–13, Lev. 25, &c.) ordered to be observed as a 'Sabbath', i.e., requiring the land to remain fallow and all debtors and Israelite slaves to be freed. In Lev. 25 a simultaneous fallow year is prescribed; but in the older strata of the *Pentateuch, it seems to have been intended that each husbandman and slave-owner should be at liberty to decide which seventh year he would observe, so that the whole land should not go out of cultivation at once. See also *Jubilee, Year of.*

G. Harford-Battersby in *H.D.B.*, iv (1902), pp. 323–6, s.v.; H. Lesêtre in *Dict. Bibl.*, v (1912), cols. 1302–6, s.v. 'Sabbatique (année)'. See also commentaries to Deut., ad loc.

SABBATINE PRIVILEGE. An indulgence granted to the *Carmelite Order. On the basis of a bull, 'Sacratissimo uti culmine', ascribed to *John XXII (1322), which was held to rest on an apparition of the BVM, certain privileges were granted to the Carmelite Order and its confraternities. They include unfailing salvation and early release from Purgatory through the intervention of the BVM (esp. release on *Saturdays, Our Lady's day), provided certain conditions such as wearing the brown *scapular, keeping certain fasts, and reciting the *Little Office of the BVM, are observed. The Sabbatine Privilege has been confirmed by several Popes, e.g. by *Pius XI in 1922. The authenticity of the original bull was widely contested in the 16th and 17th cents., esp. by the Jesuit D. *Papebroch, and some violent controversies ensued. Its spuriousness is now admitted even by Carmelites themselves, e.g. B. Zimmerman in his *Monumenta Historica Carmelitana* (Lérins, 1907). It prob. dates from the latter half of the 15th cent.

A note of the bull of John XXII occurs in G. Mollat, *Jean XXII (1316–1334)*. Lettres communes analysées d'après les registres dits d'Avignon et du Vatican, iv (1910), p. 169 (No. 16193). B. Zimmerman, O.D.C., *Monumenta Historica Carmelitana* (Lerins, 1907), pp. 356–63. K. Bihlmeyer in *L.Th.K.*, ix (1937), col. 51 f., s.v. 'Sabbatina'; B. Xiberta, Ord. Carm., in *E.C.*, x (1953), col. 1512, s.v. 'Sabatino, Privilegio'. See also bibl. to *Simon Stock, St.*

SABELLIANISM. An alternative title for the Modalist form of *Monarchianism (q.v.). It is so named from Sabellius, of whom, however, very little is known. He was prob., like his fellow-Monarchians *Noetus and *Praxeas, an early 3rd cent. theologian of Roman origin, though he is described by later 4th-5th cent. Gk. writers (*Basil, *Timothy of Constantinople) as belonging to Libya or the Pentapolis.

SABINA, St. (c. 126), Roman martyr. Acc. to her late and untrustworthy *acta*, she was a widow of Umbria who was converted by the virtuous life of her servant, Serapia, a native of Antioch in Syria. Both Sabina and Serapia were arrested in the persecution under Hadrian, and Serapia beaten to death while Sabina was discharged on account of her rank.

A year later, however, Sabina was again apprehended and martyred at Rome. There seems no probability even of the existence of such a saint. The *acta* were perhaps fabricated to account for the church of St. Sabina (originally 'titulus Sabinae', later 'titulus Sanctae Sabinae') on the Aventine Hill, which is believed to contain her relics. Feast-day, 29 Aug. She is commemorated by name in the canon of the *Ambrosian Rite.

On SS. Sabina and Serapia, *AA.SS.*, Aug. VI (1743), pp. 496–504; cf. also H. *Delehaye, S.J., in his ed. of the *Hieronymian Martyrology (*AA.SS.*, Nov. II (pt. 2; 1931), p. 475). J. P. Kirsch, *Die römischen Titelkirchen im Altertum* (Studien zur Geschichte und Kultur des Altertums, ix, Hftt. 1–2; 1918), pp. 163–6.

On the church, J. J. Berthier, *L'Église de Sainte-Sabine à Rome* (Rome, 1918); id., *Le Couvent de Sainte-Sabine à Rome* (ib., 1912). C. Descement, *Mémoire sur les fouilles exécutées à Santa-Sabina, 1855–1857* (1863); A. Muñoz, *Il restauro della basilica di Santa Sabina* (1938). J. P. Kirsch, op. cit., pp. 96–100. H. I. Marrou, 'Sur les origines du titre romain de Sainte-Sabine' in *Archivum Fratrum Praedicatorum*, ii (1932), pp. 316–25. M. D. Darsy, O.P., in *D.A.C.L.*, xv (pt. 1; 1950), cols. 218–38, s.v. 'Sabine (Basilique de Sainte-).

SACCAS, AMMONIUS. See *Ammonius Saccas.*

SACCOS. See *Sakkos.*

SACHEVERELL, HENRY (c. 1674–1724), High Church divine and pamphleteer. Born at Marlborough, he was educated at the Grammar School and at Magdalen College, Oxford, where he became a Fellow in 1701. In 1705 he was elected chaplain of St. Saviour's, Southwark (now Southwark Cathedral). On 15 Aug. 1709 he preached the assize sermon at Derby and on 5 Nov. 1709 before the Lord Mayor at *St. Paul's. On both these occasions he upheld the doctrine of non-resistance and emphasized in violent language the perils facing the Church from the Whig government's policy of toleration and allowance of *Occasional Conformity. In the latter sermon he also openly attacked G. *Burnet, Bp. of *Salisbury. In Dec. 1709 the Commons condemned the sermons as seditious and, despite the opposition of the Tories and of many Whigs, as well as strong feeling in the country, Sacheverell was impeached for high crimes and misdemeanour. The sentence (suspension from preaching for three years) was so light as to be a triumph for the accused and he became a popular hero. When the three years had passed, Sacheverell preached on Palm Sunday, 1713, to a packed gathering at St. Saviour's, Southwark. The sermon sold for £100 and had a very wide circulation. In 1713 he was presented by Queen *Anne, who had openly shown him sympathy, to the living of St. Andrew's, Holborn.

Although the fall of the Whigs in 1710 was largely the result of the impeachment of Sacheverell, he would prob. not have made his mark in history had he not become the champion of the High Church and Tory Parties. Among his pamphlets were *Character of a Low Churchman* (1701) and *The Rights of the*

Church of England (1705; with Edmund Perkes).

J. R. *Bloxam, *Register of Magdalen* (1879), pp. 98–110. F. Madan, *A Bibliography of Dr. Henry Sacheverell* (1884). W. Hunt in *D.N.B.*, 1 (1897), pp. 80–3: W. H. Hutton in *D.E.C.H.*, p. 529 f.

SACRAMENT. Acc. to the *Catechism of the BCP, 'an outward and visible sign of an inward and spiritual grace given unto us, ordained by Christ Himself, as a means whereby we receive the same and a pledge to assure us thereof'; or more briefly, acc. to St. *Thomas Aquinas, 'the sign of a sacred thing in so far as it sanctifies men' (*signum rei sacrae in quantum est sanctificans homines*). The Lat. *sacramentum* orig. meant an oath, esp. the soldier's oath of allegiance, and traces of this meaning survive in early Christian literature (e.g. *Tertullian, *Ad Martyres* 3). But the main factor in determining Christian usage was its employment in the Lat. NT to render the Gk. μυστήριον ('mystery').

In Christian theology, the scope of what the word comprises has varied widely. St. *Augustine, who defined it as 'the visible form of invisible grace' or 'a sign of a sacred thing', applied it to *formulae* such as the Creed and the Lord's Prayer; and this wide application was maintained into the Middle Ages. *Hugh of St.-Victor (d. 1141) in his 'De Sacramentis Christianae Fidei' enumerated as many as thirty Sacraments, dividing them into three groups. In *Peter Lombard (*Sentences*, Bk. 4, dist. i, num. 2), the seven which have become traditional, viz. *Baptism, *Confirmation, the *Eucharist, *Penance, Extreme *Unction, *Order, and *Matrimony, are enumerated. This list was accepted by St. Thomas and formally affirmed at the Councils of *Florence (1439; in the 'Decretum pro Armenis') and *Trent (1545–63). Acc. to the Council of Trent (Sess. VII) all seven Sacraments were instituted by Christ; but in the case of some of the Sacraments (notably Confirmation, Extreme Unction, Matrimony) there is much disagreement among RC theologians as to the occasion when Christ instituted them. The sevenfold enumeration of the Sacraments is accepted also by the E. Church.

From early times a special rank among the Sacraments was given to Baptism and the Eucharist, both of which are clearly referred to in the Gospels (Mt. 28. 19; 26. 26–29). In Art. 25 of the C of E they are differentiated as the 'two Sacraments ordained of Christ our Lord in the Gospel' as distinct from the other 'five commonly called Sacraments', which are 'such as have grown partly of the corrupt following of the Apostles, partly are states of life allowed in the Scriptures; but yet have not like nature of Sacraments with Baptism and the Lord's Supper, for that they have not any visible sign or ceremony ordained of God'. In modern times Anglican theologians generally have adopted a more positive attitude towards the five lesser Sacraments, and teaching not widely different from that of the Council of Trent is often held.

The theological significance of the Sacraments lies in: (1) The exhibition of the principle of the Incarnation. By the embodiment of spiritual reality in material form an appropriate counterpart of the union of God with man in the Person of Christ is made patent. (2) Their expression of the objectivity of God's action on the human soul. The reception of God's gifts is normally dependent not on changing subjective feelings, but on obedience to the Divine will. (3) As ordinances mediated through the Church, their essentially social structure. They are the means whereby the union of God and man consequent on the Incarnation is perpetuated in Christ's mystical Body of His Church, its members incorporated in Him, and through Him united to one another.

Acc. to traditional Catholic theology, a distinction, orig. due to *William of Auxerre (d. c. 1235), is made between the 'matter' (*materia*) and the 'form' (*forma*) of the Sacraments, the matter being the undetermined material element (in Baptism, water; the Eucharist, the bread and wine) and the form the consecratory words (in Baptism, the pronouncement of the Triple Formula; in the Eucharist, the words 'This is My Body', 'This is my Blood'). The right matter and the right form, used with the right *intention, are among the minimal conditions for the 'validity' of the Sacrament. Where given conditions are all present the due performance of the acts is sufficient to ensure that the Sacraments will normally convey grace, since acc. to Catholic theology the validity of the Sacraments is independent of the worthiness or unworthiness of the minister and hence their working is normally *ex opere operato*. Nevertheless they do not convey grace to the recipient if he is not rightly disposed. In the absence of faith and repentance he may put an impediment (*obex*) in the way of the grace which would naturally flow from the Sacrament. In such cases the Sacramental act, though 'valid', is not 'efficacious'.

Three of the Sacraments, viz. Baptism, Confirmation, and Orders, are held to imprint an abiding mark or *character (*character indelebilis*) on the soul and therefore cannot be repeated. When there is uncertainty as to whether or not a person has already received these Sacraments, they are administered 'conditionally'.

Among the Protestant Churches the *Quakers and the *Salvation Army are the only two large bodies which wholly repudiate Sacraments. In general, though the technicalities of Sacramental theology are less developed, the greatest importance is often attached to Baptism and the Lord's Supper. The comparative rarity with which the latter is celebrated in some Protestant Churches is often matched with a correspondingly high degree of seriousness and devotion in its reception. Great emphasis is laid on the belief that the Sacraments are expressive of the Word.

See also entries on the separate Sacraments.

Introductory modern studies include P. T. *Forsyth, *Lectures on the Church and the Sacraments* (1917); A. J. Tait,

The Nature and Functions of the Sacraments (1917); O. C. *Quick, *The Christian Sacraments* (1927); J. W. C. Wand, *The Development of Sacramentalism* (1928); B. Leeming, S.J., *Principles of Sacramental Theology* (1956). F. Gavin, *The Jewish Antecedents of the Christian Sacraments* (1928). J. C. Lambert, *The Sacraments in the New Testament* (Kerr Lectures for 1903; 1903). F. *Probst, *Sakramente und Sakramentalien in den drei ersten christlichen Jahrhunderten* (1872). J. B. *Franzelin, S.J., *Tractatus de Sacramentis in Genere* (Rome, 1868); P. Schanz, *Die Lehre von den heiligen Sakramenten der katholischen Kirche* (1893); J. B. Sasse, *Institutiones Theologiae de Sacramentis Ecclesiae* (2 vols., Freiburg i.Br., 1897–8); N. Gihr, *Die heiligen Sakramente der katholischen Kirche* (Theologische Bibliothek, 2 vols., 1918–21). T. Spačil, S.J., *Doctrina Theologiae Orientis Separati de Sacramentis in Genere* (Orientalia Christiana Analecta, cxiii; 1937). J. de Ghellinck, S.J., and others, *Pour l'histoire du mot 'Sacramentum'* (S.S.L., iii; 1924). Other studies include those of P. B. Bull, C. R. (London, 1915), W. M. Clow (ib., 1934), C. R. Smith (ib., 1927), A. L. Lilley (ib., 1928), and M. M. Philipon, O.P. (Bruges, 1945; Eng. tr., 1956). R. G. Parsons–T. A. Lacey–H. E. Jacobs–J. Stalker in *H.E.R.E.*, x (1918), pp. 902–15, s.v. 'Sacraments, Christian'; A. Michel in *D.T.C.*, xiv (pt. 1; 1946), cols. 485–644, s.v. 'Sacrements', with further bibl. See also bibl. to separate Sacraments. D. M. Baillie, *The Theology of the Sacraments and Other Papers* (1957), pp. 37–124.

SACRAMENT HOUSE. A shrine-like receptacle for the *reservation of the Blessed Sacrament. It developed from the stone niche in the wall ('*aumbry') which after the introduction of the Feast of *Corpus Christi (1264) began to take the shape of a small tower, the central part of which was done in open-work. These Sacrament Houses, which were popular esp. in Germany, Belgium, and France, were frequently decorated with ornamental reliefs representing the Last Supper, the Passion, and other subjects. From the 16th cent. they were more and more replaced by the *Tabernacle and their use is now allowed only in a few churches, esp. in Germany, by Papal indult.

J. Hertkens, *Die mittelalterlichen Sakraments-Häuschen* (1908). Braun, *C.A.*, ii, 585–97 passim. G. Lill in *L.Th.K.*, ix (1937), col. 98 f., s.v. 'Sakramentshäuschen', with illustrations. See also works cited under *Reservation*.

SACRAMENTALS. Certain religious practices and objects akin to the *Sacraments (q.v.) but differing in being held not to have been instituted by Christ and therefore of relatively much less importance. Their number is undetermined, but they are sometimes classified under the six heads of praying, anointing, eating, confessing, giving, and blessing ('orans', 'tinctus', 'edens', 'confessus', 'dans', 'benedicens'). They include the *sign of the cross, the saying of *grace at meals, the *Confiteor recited at Mass and in the Divine Office, *vestments, lights, palms and ashes, the *Stations of the Cross, *litanies, the *Angelus, the *rosary, the Solemnization of *Matrimony (as contrasted with Matrimony itself), the *Churching of Women, and so on. RC theologians hold that they do not convey grace *ex opere operato*, but assist the soul in the removal of venial sin, mitigate (if rightly used) the temporal punishment due to sin, and convey in certain circumstances temporal benefits.

Popular account in M. Donovan, *Sacramentals* (1925). F. *Probst, *Sakramente und Sakramentalien in den drei ersten christlichen Jahrhunderten* (1872), pp. 16–96. Much material also in A. Franz, *Die kirchlichen Benediktionen im Mittelalter*

(2 vols., 1909). H. *Leclercq, O.S.B., in *C.E.*, xiii (1912), p. 292 f., s.v.; A. Gaboardi in *E.C.*, x (1953), cols. 1555–8, s.v. 'Sacramentali'.

SACRAMENTARIANS. The name which M. *Luther gave to those theologians (esp. H. *Zwingli and J. *Oecolampadius) who maintained that the Bread and Wine of the *Eucharist were the Body and Blood of Christ in only a 'sacramental', i.e. metaphorical, sense. The word thus came to be commonly used in the 16th cent. for all those who denied the doctrine of the *Real Presence of Christ in the Eucharist. It has occasionally been applied also in other senses.

SACRAMENTARY (Lat. *Liber Sacramentorum*). In the W. Church, the liturgical book in use down to the 13th cent. which contained the *Canon of the Mass and the proper *Collects and other prayers for use throughout the year, but not the *Epistles or *Gospels, nor those parts of the rite (e.g. the *Gradual) which were sung. The *Leonine, *Gelasian, and *Gregorian Sacramentaries, which are the chief sources for the early history of the Roman Mass, are the best known Sacramentaries. From the 9th cent. onwards, the desirability of having all the parts of the service in a single book led to the gradual replacement of the Sacramentary by the *Missal.

Older editions of the texts include G. M. *Tommasi, *Codices Sacramentorum* (Rome, 1680); id., *Antiqui Libri Missarum* (ib., 1691); L. A. *Muratori, *Liturgia Romana Vetus* (2 vols., Venice, 1748); J. A. *Assemani, *Codex Liturgicus Ecclesiae Universae* (13 vols., Rome, 1749–66). For more recent edd., see under separate Sacramentaries. The Sacramentaries are described in all histories of the Roman liturgy. On the Sacramentaries generally, L. Delisle, *Mémoire sur d'anciens sacramentaires* (1886); F. *Probst, *Die ältesten römischen Sakramentarien und Ordines* (1892); E. Bourque, *Étude sur les sacramentaires romains* (vol. i, Studi di Antichità Cristiana, xx, 1948; vol. ii, Bibliothèque Théologique de Laval, Quebec, 1952 ff.), with extensive bibl. V. Leroquais, *Les Sacramentaires et les missels manuscrits des bibliothèques publiques de France* (1924; with plates). M. Andrieu, 'Quelques Remarques sur le classement des sacramentaires' in *J.L.W.*, xi (1931), pp. 46–66. L. Eisenhofer in *L.Th.K.*, ix (1937), cols. 93–7, s.v. 'Sakramentar'; H. *Leclercq, O.S.B., in *D.A.C.L.*, xv (pt. 1; 1950), cols. 242–85, s.v. 'Sacramentaires'; A. Bugnini in *E.C.*, x (1953), cols. 1558–69, s.v. 'Sacramentario'. See also bibl. to *Gelasian*, *Gregorian*, and *Leonine Sacramentaries*; to *Missal*; and to *Ordines Romani*.

SACRED COLLEGE. The corporation of the *cardinals in the RC Church which since *c.* 1150 has been known as a 'Collegium'. Its 70 members comprise six cardinal bishops, 50 cardinal priests, and 14 cardinal deacons, with a Dean (the Bp. of Ostia) at the head, a Sub-dean (the Bp. of Porto), and a chamberlain to administer revenues. Its chief duties are to elect the Pope and act as his privy council. Its present constitution dates from 1586.

SACRED HEART. Devotion to the physical heart of Jesus, though theologically defined and officially practised only since the 18th cent., can be traced back to the Middle Ages. It seems to have sprung from the cult of the Wound in the Side. It is to be met with in the treatise 'Vitis mystica', attributed to St. *Bernard and also to St. *Bonaventure, extracts from which were incorporated in the present Office of the Feast, and the devotion appears richly developed in the visions of St. *Mechtilde (d. 1298) and St. *Gertrude (d. c. 1303). But the devotion was long confined to a relatively small number of mystics and saints, e.g. *Julian of Norwich and St. *Frances of Rome. A new departure was made in the 16th cent. when the devotion extended from the visions of the mystics to the regular practice of many given to the ascetic life, and it was fostered esp. by the *Carthusians. A little later the *Jesuits became its most ardent advocates in France and St. *Francis of Sales imbued with it his *Visitandines, and these two orders worked together to obtain for the Sacred Heart a place in the official as well as the popular life of the Church. The first to provide an elaborate theological and liturgical foundation for both devotion and feast, however, was St. John *Eudes (q.v.). But his efforts remained without much response until the famous visions (1673–1675) of the Visitandine nun, St. *Margaret Mary Alacoque, which gave a definite shape to the object of the devotion and its practices. Its most prominent feature was reparation for the outrages committed against the Divine Love, esp. in the Blessed Sacrament. From that time it became one of the most popular RC devotions, though its liturgical observance was not permitted until 1765, when *Clement XIII authorized the Mass and Office of the Feast. It is observed on the Friday after the octave of *Corpus Christi. In 1856 *Pius IX extended the Feast to the universal Church; in 1889 *Leo XIII raised it to a *Double of the First Class, and ten years later solemnly consecrated all mankind to the Sacred Heart. The Mass and Office of the Feast were revised by *Pius XI in 1928 when it received a privileged octave.

J. Croiset, *La Dévotion au Sacré-Cœur de N.S. Jésus-Christ* (Lyons, 1691; 3rd and definitive ed., 1694; Eng. tr. from Italian, London, 1863; modern Eng. tr. from 1694 ed., Dublin and London, 1949); J. de Galliffet, S.J., *De Cultu Sacrosancti Cordis Dei et Domini Nostri Jesu Christi* (Rome, 1726; Fr. tr., 1732). J. B. Terrien, S.J., *La Dévotion au Sacré-Cœur de Jésus d'après les documents authentiques et la théologie* (1893). J. V. Bainvel, *La Dévotion au Sacré-Cœur de Jésus* (1906; Eng. tr., 1924). D. Chastelain, *De Cultu Eucharistici Cordis Jesu.* Historia—Doctrina—Documenta (Paris, 1928). J. Bainvel in *C.E.*, vii (1910), pp. 163–7, s.v. 'Heart of Jesus. Devotion to the'; id. in *D.T.C.*, iii (1908), cols. 271–351, s.v. 'Cœur Sacré de Jésus (Dévotion au)', with bibl.; L. Penzo in *E.C.*, iv (1950), cols. 1059–64, s.v. 'Cuore di Gesù', with bibl.

SACRIFICE. Sacrifice is fundamentally the offering of a material, esp. a living, creature to the Deity. It is a very widespread feature of religion, incl. that of the early Hebrews.

Already in the earliest portions of the OT, Sacrifice is a recognized human institution (cf. the sacrifice of Cain and *Abel, Gen. 4. 3–5), acceptable to God, esp. in the form of animal, but not human, sacrifice. Animal sacrifice, comprising the 'Peace Offering' (in which the worshippers shared in the flesh) and the 'Burnt Offering' (when none of the flesh was eaten),

was the regular observance; but cereal, oil, and wine were also offered. It was due to God as His right. It maintained, or if necessary restored, a right relation of man to Jehovah, and also, on occasion, could solemnly initiate a new relationship. Notably was this last the case in the fundamental covenant established between God and Israel at *Sinai (Ex. 24. 4–8).

After the settlement in Canaan, sacrificial observances became more elaborate (Mic. 6. 6 f., Is. 1. 11–14). They also became contaminated with Canaanite religion, esp. at the *High Places (Hos. 4. 12–14). The current sacrificial worship was strongly denounced by the 8th-7th cent. Prophets (*Hosea, *Amos, *Micah, *Isaiah), though it is more probable that the Prophets rejected the current amoral ritual than that they completely repudiated sacrifice as such. In the next cent. the reforms of King Josiah (640–608 B.C.), based on the prescriptions of the Book of Deut., prohibited sacrifice except at the one sanctuary of *Jerusalem; and when the City was destroyed at the Exile (586), Jewish sacrifices temporarily ceased altogether.

After the Exile the ritual traditions, duly safeguarded, modified, and codified under the control of the Levitical priesthood, were embodied in the final form of the *Pentateuch, esp. in *Leviticus (q.v.). Apart from a brief interruption by *Antiochus Epiphanes (168), this sacrificial system was practised in the restored *Temple until its destruction in A.D. 70. Meanwhile the spread of the *Diaspora and the rise of the *Synagogue led to a widespread form of non-sacrificial worship. It became increasingly recognized that the cardinal requirement of God was a right intention in the worshipper (Hos. 6. 6, cf. Pss. 40. 6–8, 51. 16 f.) rather than material offerings, and that a 'pure offering' might be made to God even 'among the Gentiles' (Mal. 1. 11).

In the NT Christ appears to have tolerated the current practice of sacrifice (cf. Matt. 5. 23 f., 8. 4); but He quoted with approval the teaching of Hosea subordinating 'sacrifice' to 'mercy' (Matt. 9. 13, 12. 7: cf. Hos. 6. 6). Also by announcing the imminent end of the Temple (Mk. 13. 2, &c.) and its worship (Jn. 4. 20–3), He looked forward to the speedy ending of the Levitical sacrifices. At the Institution of the *Eucharist, which took place in the sacrificial context of the *Passover (whether on 14 Nisan or 15 Nisan) and with reference to the covenant-sacrifice of Exod. 24. 4–8, He pointed to the sacrificial quality of His death (cf. Mk. 10. 45), speaking of the shedding of His Blood in a New Covenant 'for the remission of sins'. Both St. *John the Baptist (Jn. 1. 29) and the Evangelist (Jn. 19. 14 and 36) appear to imply that Christ, as the 'Lamb of God', is Himself a Sacrificial Victim, a doctrine endorsed by St. *Paul in 1 Cor. 5. 7, and made more explicit in Eph. 5. 2 (cf. also 1 Pet. 1. 19, 1 Jn. 2. 2), while Rev. 13. 8 emphasizes the eternal nature of the Lord's Sacrifice. The author of *Hebrews (q.v.) stresses the High Priesthood of Christ who by His perfect obedience in the voluntary offering of Himself (9. 26, cf. 10. 5 ff.) made 'one sacrifice for sins for ever' (10. 12), in contrast to the deficiencies of the OT sacrifices, and he compares the Lord's Passion to the sin-offering (13. 11 f.).

The implications of these Biblical ideas are developed by the Fathers who stress esp. the uniqueness of Christ's sacrifice in that He was (1) a voluntary victim, (2) a victim of infinite value, and (3) also Himself the Priest. The Patristic teaching on these matters has been endorsed by subsequent theology. See also *Atonement*.

The chief development of the Patristic and Medieval period was in regard to the *Eucharist (q.v.) From early times the Eucharistic Offering was called a sacrifice in virtue of its immediate relation to the Sacrifice of Christ (e.g. by *Serapion of Thmuis). While it can also be said that in the Eucharist Christ is sacrificed 'again', yet St. *Thomas Aquinas insisted that the Mass was itself an 'immolation' only in so far as it was an 'image' of the Passion which was the 'real immolation' (*S.T.* III. lxxxiii. 1). In rejecting the doctrine of 'the Sacrifices of Masses', the Anglican Article XXXI is perhaps more concerned to deny the idea, current in the Middle Ages, of the repeated 'immolation' of Christ than to repudiate belief in the Eucharistic Sacrifice altogether. See also *Eucharist*.

In accordance with such passages as Ps. 40. 6-8 and Rom. 12. 1, Christian theology has commonly asserted that the individual's conscious obedience, active or passive, to the will of God may be a form of sacrifice which can be offered to God the Father in imitation of, and in union with, the Sacrifice of Christ.

E. O. James, *Origins of Sacrifice* (1933). W. R. *Smith, *Lectures on the Religion of the Semites* (1889), pp. 196-419; ed. 3 by S. A. *Cook (1927), pp. 213-440, with full notes; S. C. Gayford, *Sacrifice and Priesthood* (1924); G. B. *Gray, *Sacrifice in the Old Testament* (posthumous, 1925); W. O. E. Oesterley, *Sacrifices in Ancient Israel* (1937). W. P. Paterson in *H.D.B.*, iv (1902), pp. 329-49, s.v.; E. O. James-C. A. F. Rhys Davids-E. Anwyl-J. A. MacCulloch-L. R. Farnell-E. Edwards-M. Revon-M. Gaster-T. H. Weir-R. A. S. Macalister-S. G. Youngert in *H.E.R.E.*, xi (1920), pp. 1-38, s.v.; A. Gaudel in *D.T.C.*, xiv (pt. 1; 1939), cols. 662-92, s.v., all with bibl.

SACRILEGE. Strictly a violation or contemptuous treatment of a person, thing, or place, publicly dedicated to the worship of God. Moral theologians hold that it may be either personal, i.e. directed against a person in holy orders or a religious (e.g. ill-treatment or sins against chastity), or real, i.e. committed against a thing, esp. the Sacraments (e.g. treating irreverently the Blessed Sacrament or administering or receiving the sacraments in a state of mortal sin), or local, i.e. committed in a holy place (e.g. homicide in a church). Sacrilege is held to be a grave sin in itself, though venial if the matter be trivial. It is dealt with in the various parts of canon law treating of sacred persons and things. In everyday language the term is used more vaguely, though in a sense similar to that of moral theology.

The subject is regularly treated in works on moral theology. N. Iung in *D.T.C.*, xiv (pt. 1; 1939), cols. 692-703, s.v. 'Sacrilège'.

SACRING BELL. A bell, also known as a 'Sanctus bell', which is rung at *Mass to focus the people's attention. This use of a bell, esp. at the *Elevation of the Elements, dates from the 12th cent., and is required both at the *Sanctus and at the Elevation by the *Ritus Servandus in the modern Roman *Missal. In the W. Church, the bell is now ordinarily also rung at other moments of the Mass, e.g. at the *Offertory (in some countries) and at the words 'Domine non sum dignus', but this is a matter of custom rather than of prescription.

H. Thurston, S.J., 'The Bells of the Mass' in *The Month*, cxxiii (1914), pp. 389-401. Braun, *C.A.*, pp. 573-80. P. Browe, S.J., 'Die Elevation in der Messe' in *J.L.W.*, ix (1929), esp. pp. 37-40, with reff. Jungmann, *M.S.*, ii (ed. 1949), p. 160; Eng. tr., ii (ed. 1955), p. 131, with reff.

SACRISTAN. The term is used either (1) for a sexton or (2), more commonly, for the sacrist or official who has charge of the contents of a church, esp. those used in Divine worship such as sacred vessels, vestments, &c. He may be in holy orders, as is usual in a cathedral, or a layman.

SACRISTY (Lat. *sacristia*, *sacrarium*, or *secretarium*; Gk. διακονικόν). A room annexed to a church or chapel for keeping the sacred vessels and for the vesting of priests and other clerics. Sacristies were introduced *c*. 400 in Syria as annexes to the apse; in the Middle Ages they came to be built behind or on either side of the high altar. In large conventual churches and cathedrals they often consist of a suite of separate rooms for the higher and the lower clergy and for lay servers. They are furnished with chests, cupboards, and a table for vestments, liturgical books, and vessels, a basin for the washing of hands, a *prie-dieu*, and a crucifix. In early times the sacristy was often used for the permanent reservation of the Blessed Sacrament, and it is commonly still so used for the purpose when the Blessed Sacrament is removed from the church between Good Friday and the First Mass of Easter Day. In current Anglican usage, the room where the clergy vest is often known as the (priests') vestry, the term sacristy tending to be restricted to vestries in churches with an elaborate ceremonial, where a larger number of liturgical objects need to be stored.

SADDUCEES. A Jewish politico-religious sect, opposed to the '*Pharisees'. The name is probably derived from the high priest Zadok (2 Sam. 8. 17). The party originated at the time of the *Hasmoneans, and stood for the interests of the priestly aristocracy and the rich. Though never popular, they exercised a great political influence from the reign of John Hyrcanus (B.C. 135-104) onwards, and in the time of our Lord were the most important party in Palestine after the Pharisees. To maintain their power and privileges they favoured Hellenizing tendencies and were opposed to excessive religious strictness. Their chief doctrinal characteristics were their repudiation of oral tradition and the acceptance of the written Law only. Thus they rejected belief in retribution in an after-life and in the resurrection of the body (Mt. 22. 23), and also the existence of angels and spirits (Acts 23. 8). In the NT they took a leading part against Jesus, whose work they feared would cause trouble with the Roman power and whose doctrines they attacked (Mt. 22. 23–33, &c.); and though less in touch with Him than the Pharisees, they were largely instrumental in bringing about His death, for the chief priests and elders mentioned in the Passion narrative belonged for the most part to their sect. They also repeatedly attacked the Apostles for teaching the Resurrection of Christ (Acts 4. 1–3; 5. 17; cf. 23. 6–10). After the fall of *Jerusalem they disappear from history.

For works dealing with the Pharisees and the Sadducees, together, see also bibl. to Pharisees. G. Hölscher, *Der Sadduzäismus* (1906); R. Leszynsky, *Die Sadduzäer* (1912). P. Z. Lauterbach, 'The Sadducees and Pharisees. A Study of their Respective Attitudes towards the Law' in *Studies in Jewish Literature issued in Honor of Prof. Kaufman Kohler* (Berlin, 1913), pp. 176–98; G. H. Box, 'Who were the Sadducees?' in *The Expositor*, Ser. 8, xv (1918), pp. 19–38; id., 'Scribes and Sadducees in the New Testament', ib., pp. 401–11, and xvi (1918), pp. 55–69. J. W. Lightley, *Jewish Sects and Parties in the Time of Jesus* (1925), pp. 11–78 ('Pharisees and Sadducees'). T. W. Manson, 'Sadducee and Pharisee: the Original Significance of the Name' in *Bulletin of the John Rylands Library*, xxii (1938), pp. 144–59, esp. pp. 144–53. E. *Schürer, *Geschichte des jüdischen Volkes im Zeitalter Jesu Christi*, ii (ed. 4, 1907), pp. 475–89, with bibl. pp. 447–9. H. L. Strack–P. Billerbeck, *Kommentar zum Neuen Testament aus Talmud und Midrash*, iv (1928), pp. 339–52. A. E. Cowley in *E.Bi.*, iv (1903), cols. 4234–40, s.v.; K. Kohler in *J.E.*, x (1905), pp. 630–3, s.v.; H. Lesêtre in *Dict. Bibl.*, v (1912), cols. 1337–45, s.v. 'Sadducéens'.

SADHU, The. See *Sundar Singh, Sadhu.*

SADOLETO, JACOPO (1477–1547), cardinal. A classical and philosophical scholar and favourite of Card. O. Caraffa, he was appointed secretary of *Leo X in 1513, and in 1517 Bp. of Carpentras. A man of pure and blameless character and unselfish zeal, he soon became one of the most influential ecclesiastics of his time, one of his chief concerns being the reconciliation of the Protestants. In 1536 he was made cardinal by *Paul III together with R. *Pole, and in 1537 he became a member of the special commission for the reform of the Church and the preparation of a General Council. At the same time he endeavoured unsuccessfully to win back P. *Melanchthon (1537) and the city of Geneva (1539) to the Catholic faith. In 1542 as Papal legate he failed to effect a reconciliation between the French King Francis I and the Emp. *Charles V. During his last years he was among the most trusted advisers of Paul III, constantly advocating reform. Among his writings are the treatises *De Peccato Originali* and *De Exstructione Ecclesiae Catholicae* as well as a commentary on Romans, which was forbidden at Rome until its doctrine of grace, which was suspected of *Semi-Pelagianism, had been corrected in the *Augustinian sense.

Works [ed. D. Raustius] (Mainz, 1607), with life by A. Florebelli prefixed [no pagination]; also ed. in 4 vols., Verona, 1737–8. Eng. tr. of his *De Pueris Recte Instituendis* by E. T. Campagnac–K. Forbes (London, 1916). Modern studies by A. Joly (Caen, 1856), G. von Schulthess-Rechberg (Zürich, 1909), and S. Ritter, *Un umanista teologo* (Rome, 1912). J. E. Sandys, *A History of Classical Scholarship*, ii (1908), p. 115 f. H. Jedin in *L.Th.K.*, ix (1937), col. 70 f., s.v.; F. Gagliuolo in *E.C.*, x (1953), col. 1611 f., s.v.; both with further bibl. Life by R. M. Douglas (Cambridge, Mass., 1959).

SAHIDIC (see also *Bohairic, Fayumic*). The dialect of *Coptic used in Upper (i.e. Southern) Egypt early in the Christian era. The Scriptures were translated into Sahidic prob. as early as the 3rd or even the end of the 2nd cent. In recent years a large number of papyrus fragments of this version have been discovered, so that it is now possible, by piecing their witness together, to construct an almost continuous NT in which, at any rate in the Gospels, most passages are supported by as many as three authorities. Notable longer NT MSS. are an almost complete Acts (also containing Deuteronomy and Jonah; early 4th cent., Brit. Mus. Or. 7594), and a nearly complete John (Library of the *British and Foreign Bible Society). The text of the Sahidic version has both '*Neutral' and '*Western' elements, though the extent of the Western element is less considerable than used to be supposed. The older name among scholars for 'Sahidic' was **Thebaic**, from Thebes, the chief city in Upper Egypt.

The standard edition of the Sahidic NT is that of G. Horner (7 vols., Oxford, 1911–24).

ST. ALBANS. A church has existed at Verulam on the site of the reputed martyrdom of St. *Alban from at least the time of *Bede; and *c.* 794 King Offa founded a monastery here in expiation of the murder of St. *Ethelbert, King of the East Angles, which soon became one of the most famous in the country. In 1077 Paul of Caen, the first Norman abbot, began to rebuild it. Its wealth continued to increase, esp. after *Hadrian IV gave it precedence over all other English monasteries and exempted it from episcopal jurisdiction. At the Reformation the church was bought from *Edward VI (1553) for use as a parish church. In 1877 a see of St. Albans was constituted, by taking Hertford, Essex, and N. Woolwich from *Rochester to make the new diocese; and the abbey became the new cathedral church. In 1914, Essex and N. Woolwich were transferred to the new see of Chelmsford, while the county of Bedford was added by compensation to St. Albans. See also *Matthew Paris.*

Thomas Walsingham, *Gesta Abbatum Monasterii Sancti Albani*, ed. H. T. Riley (3 vols., R.S., 1867–9); fuller text of the St. Alban's Chronicle, 1406–1420, ed. from Bodley MS. 462 by V. H. Galbraith (Oxford, 1937). John Amundesham, *Annales Monasterii S. Albani*, ed. H. T. Riley (2 vols., R.S., 1870–1). *Chronica Monasterii S. Albani. Registra Quorundam Abbatum Monasterii S. Albani, qui Saeculo XVmo floruere*, ed. id. (2 vols., ib., 1872–3). W. *Dugdale, *Monasticon Anglicanum*, ii (ed. 1819), pp. 178–255). P. Newcome, *The History of the Ancient and Royal Foundation, called the Abbey of St. Alban . . . from the Foundation thereof in 793, to its Dissolution in 1539* (2 pts., bound in one, 1793–5). I. C. Buckler–C. A. Buckler, *A History of the Architecture of the Abbey Church of St. Alban, with especial reference to the*

Norman Structure (1847). E. Beckett, *St. Alban's Cathedral and its Restoration* (1885). L. F. R. Williams, *History of the Abbey of St. Alban* (1917). T. Perkins, *The Cathedral Church of St. Albans* (Bell's Cathedral Series, 1903). C. R. Peers-W. Page, and others in *V.C.H.*, Hertfordshire, ii, ed. W. Page (1908), pp. 469–515. W. Levison, 'St. Alban and St. Albans' in *Antiquity*, xv (1941), pp. 337–59. A. L. Poole–G. Crosse in *D.E.C.H.* (1912), pp. 530–2, s.v.

ST. ASAPH. The foundation of this diocese, now a see in the Anglican Province of *Wales, is prob. to be ascribed to St. *Kentigern (*c.* 560), after whose favourite disciple and successor, St. *Asaph (q.v.), the see took its name. Like the other Welsh sees, it was in origin a monastic settlement of the Celtic type. The present diocese includes the counties of Flint and Denbigh and portions of four other adjacent counties. The present cathedral is largely the work of Bp. Redman (*c.* 1480); the choir was rebuilt *c.* 1770; and the whole restored by G. G. *Scott (1869–75). Notable Bishops of St. Asaph include *Geoffrey of Monmouth (1152–4), R. *Pecock (1444–50), I. Barrow, the elder (1670–80), W. *Beveridge (1704–8), and S. *Horsley (1802–6).

'Summi Libri Rubei Asaphensis communiter dicti "Llyfr Coch Asaph", exscrpt. ex Originali 26° Octobris 1602' in *Collectanea Topographica et Genealogica*, ii (1835), pp. 255–79; 'Index to "Llyfr Coch Asaph" copied out of a MS. in the Bishop's Library at St. Asaph', ed. G. Roberts in *Archaeologia Cambrensis*, Third Series, xiv (1868), pp. 151–66, 329–40, with notes pp. 433–43. The Registers of the thirteen ancient parishes of the Diocese in the County of Shropshire, ed. W. P. W. Phillimore–W. G. D. Fletcher–D. R. Thomas (Shropshire Parish Register Society, 8 vols. bound in 11, 1899–1922). B. Willis, *A Survey of the Cathedral Church of St. Asaph and the Edifices belonging to it* (1720; enlarged ed. by E. Edwards, 2 vols., 1801). D. R. Thomas, *Esgobaeth Llanelwy*. A History of the Diocese of St. Asaph (1874). Id., *St. Asaph* (Diocesan Histories, 1888); P. B. I. Bax, *The Cathedral Church of Saint Asaph* (Bell's Cathedral Series, 1904). J. Fisher in *D.E.C.H.* (1912), pp. 532–5, s.v.

SAINT-CYRAN, ABBÉ DE (1581–1643), Jean Duvergier de Hauranne, one of the authors of *Jansenism. A pupil of Justus Lipsius at the *Jesuit College at Louvain, and then a fellow-student at Paris (1604–10) and Bayonne (1611–17) with C. *Jansen, with whom he made a close friendship, he was attracted to St. *Augustine's writings, the theology of which he preferred to the prevailing scholasticism. In 1617 he settled for a time at Poitiers where he was secretary to the Bishop de la Rocheposay. In 1620 he was created Abbot of Saint-Cyran and henceforward lived mainly in Paris, seeking out all the chief personalities of the time (*Vincent de Paul, J. J. *Olier, G. Tarisse, P. de *Bérulle). He made it his object to reform Catholicism on Augustinian lines, largely in the hope of defeating Protestantism with its own weapons. From 1623 he became closely associated with the influential *Arnauld family and with *Port Royal, and from 1633 as spiritual counsellor of the convent exercised an immense religious influence. Between 1617 and 1635 he was the recipient of a long series of letters from Jansen (publd. at Louvain, 1654). His power led *Richelieu to consider him a dangerous character, and from 1638 until Richelieu's death in 1643 he was incarcerated in the donjon

at Vincennes, where he wrote his *Lettres chrétiennes et spirituelles* (publd. 1645). He was held in great veneration by later Jansenists who looked up to him as a martyr. His writings include *Somme des fautes . . . du P. Garasse* (1626), an attack on the Jesuits; *Petrus Aurelius de Hierarchia Ecclesiastica* (1631), a plea for the rights of the episcopate against the Papacy, partly based on M. Antonio de Dominis's *De Republica Christiana*; *Chapelet secret du très saint sacrement* (1632); and *Théologie familière* (1642).

C. Lancelot, *Mémoires touchant la vie de M. de S. Cyran* (2 vols., Cologne, 1738). J. Lafferrière, *Étude sur Jean Dwergier de Hauranne, abbé de Saint-Cyran* (Louvain, 1912). J. Orcibal, *Les Origines du jansénisme* (Bibliothèque de la *R.H.E.*, xvi), ii and iii, Jean Duvergier de Hauranne, abbé de Saint-Cyran et son temps (1947–8). H. Lindau, 'Saint Cyran. Ein Beitrag zu seiner Charakteristik' in *Z.K.G.*, xxxvi (1916), pp. 405–23. Bremond, iv, 36–175. C. Constantin in *D.T.C.*, iv (1911), cols. 1967–75, s.v. 'Du Vergier', with reff. to sources. See also bibl. to *Jansenism* and *Port Royal*.

ST. DAVIDS. Acc. to tradition a monastery was founded at Menevia by St. *David (6th cent.), the Patron of *Wales, which was thereafter called St. Davids. The early history is fragmentary and uncertain, but a succession of bishops followed. In 1115 Bernard the Norman was elected bishop and the see became suffragan to *Canterbury. The shrine of St. David became famous, and was visited by William I, Henry II, Edward I, and his queen Eleanor; and, acc. to an inscription found on the shrine by Abp. Peckham (1240–1292), two pilgrimages to St. Davids were the equivalent of one to Rome. To-day only the stone base of the shrine survives, but the reputed relics of St. David are preserved close by. The present beautiful cathedral was begun by Bp. Peter de Leia (1176–98). Among his successors were Henry Gower (1328–47), the 'Menevian *Wykeham', who built the stone rood-screen and the fine episcopal palace (now in ruins); Henry *Chichele (1408–14), afterwards Abp. of Canterbury; W. *Barlow (1536–48), the chief consecrator of Abp. M. *Parker (1559); and W. *Laud (1621–6). The official title of the Bishop of St. Davids is 'Episcopus Menevensis'.

The Episcopal Registers of the Diocese of St. David's, 1397 to 1518, ed., with Eng. tr., by R. F. Isaacson (Cymmrodorion Record Series No. vi, vols. i and ii, 1917; vol. iii, A Study of the Published Registers by R. A. Roberts, 1920). J. W. Willis-Bund (ed.), *An Extent of all the Lands and Rents of the Lord Bishop of St. David's, made by Master David Faunceys, Chancellor of St. David's . . . in Year of Our Lord 1326*. Usually called the Black Book of St. David's (ib., No. v; 1902). B. Willis, *A Survey of the Cathedral Church of St. David's, and the Edifices belonging to it as they stood in the Year 1715* (1717). G. W. Manby, *The History and Antiquities of the Parish of Saint David, South Wales . . . to which is annexed a correct List of the Archbishops, Bishops, etc., who have filled the See* (1801). W. B. Jones–E. A. Freeman, *The History and Antiquities of Saint David's* (1856). P. A. Robson, *The Cathedral Church of Saint David's* (Bell's Cathedral Series, 1907). F. Morgan in *D.E.C.H.* (1912), pp. 535–9, s.v.

ST.-DENIS. The *Benedictine abbey at St.-Denis, four miles north of *Paris, which was founded *c.* 625 and contained the reputed shrine of St. Denis (see *Dionysius, St.* [3]), was for centuries the richest and most important in France. As it became the regular burying-place of the kings of France and other French princes and nobles, it long enjoyed royal favour, and over the high altar was suspended the 'Oriflamme' of the kings of France (originally the banner of the abbey). Here St. *Joan of Arc hung up her arms in 1429, and *Henry IV renounced his Protestantism in 1593. Early in the 17th cent. it was constituted the chief abbey of an independent Benedictine congregation, but in 1633 it was attached to the *Maurists. The abbey (which had been reduced to the rank of a priory in 1691 by Louis XIV) was dissolved and sacked at the Revolution (1792-3), but the buildings were restored under Napoleon III, and are now a 'national monument'.

The best ed. of the book of Abbot *Suger (q.v.), *Sugerii Abbatis Sancti Dionysii Liber*, is that, with Eng. tr. and introd., by E. Panofsky (Princeton, 1946). J. Doublet, O.S.B., *Histoire de l'abbaye de S.-Denys en France* (1625); M. Félibien, O.S.B., *Histoire de l'abbaye royale de Saint-Denys en France* (1706). [F.] de Guilhermy, *Monographie de l'église royale de St.-Denis*. Tombeaux et figures historiques (1848). W. M. Conway, 'The Abbey of Saint-Denis and its ancient Treasures' in *Archaeologia*, lxvi (1915), pp. 103-58. S. McK. Crosby, *The Abbey of St.-Denis, 475-1122*, i (Yale Historical Publications, History of Art, 3; New Haven, Conn., 1942); id., *L'Abbaye royale de Saint-Denis* (1953), with 130 photographs by P. Devinoy.

ST. GALL. See *Gall, St.*

ST.-GERMAIN-DES-PRÉS. An abbey in Paris on the south bank of the Seine. It was founded in the 6th cent. and originally dedicated to the Holy Cross and St. *Vincent, but later it assumed the name of its benefactor, St. *Germanus of Paris, who was buried in its church. In the 17th cent. it gained great celebrity when it adopted the *Maurist reform and became the headquarters of such scholars as J. *Mabillon and B. de *Montfaucon. Most of the abbey was destroyed by fire during the French Revolution, but its fine collection of MSS. was saved, and mostly passed in 1795-6 to the Bibliothèque Nationale.

H. *Leclercq, O.S.B., in *D.A.C.L.*, vi (pt. 2; 1925), cols. 1102-50, s.v. 'Germain-des-Prés (Saint-)', with reff. L. H. Cottineau, O.S.B., *Répertoire topo-bibliographique des abbayes et prieurés* (Mâcon, 1935), col. 2710 f.

ST.-MAUR, Congregation of. See *Maurists*.

ST.-OMER. The *Jesuit college of St.-Omer in Artois was founded by R. *Parsons *c.* 1592 for the education of the English RC laity and, in the first ten years of its existence, numbered already over a hundred pupils. After a fire in 1684 it was rebuilt on a large scale. When, in 1762, the Parliament of Paris ordered the expulsion of the Jesuits and the Society transferred their school to Bruges, the buildings at St.-Omer were used for the preparatory school of the English clergy at *Douai until they removed to England in 1795. The house at St.-Omer was afterwards sold to the French Government and used for secular purposes.

ST. PATRICK'S PURGATORY. A place of pilgrimage on Station Island, in Lough Derg in Donegal. Acc. to tradition, St. *Patrick saw here a vision which promised all who should visit the sanctuary in penitence and faith a plenary indulgence for their sins and, if their confidence did not fail, a sight of the torments of the damned and the joys of the redeemed. The place has been a place of pilgrimage from far and wide at least since the 13th cent.

Various MSS. containing the legend in different forms have been edited, mainly in specialized periodicals; details are given in a collection of the legends, tr. into Eng. by S. Leslie, *Saint Patrick's Purgatory. A Record from History and Literature* (1932), with bibl., pp. 195-215. T. Wright, *St. Patrick's Purgatory* (1844). P. de Félice, *L'Autre Monde. Mythes et légendes. Le Purgatoire de saint Patrice* (Montauban thesis; Paris, 1906), pp. 3-92. The legend is also discussed in J. Healy, Abp. of Tuam, *The Life and Writings of Saint Patrick* (Dublin, 1905), pp. 656-67, and other works on St. Patrick, and Purgatory (qq.v.). W. H. Grattan-Flood in *C.E.*, xii (1911), p. 580, s.v. 'Purgatory, Saint Patrick's'.

ST. PAUL'S CATHEDRAL, London. A church was built *c.* 607 by *Ethelbert, King of Kent, as a cathedral for St. *Mellitus, first Bp. of London. This was rebuilt in stone between 675 and 685 by St. *Erconwald, whose shrine attracted pilgrims throughout the Middle Ages. The Saxon building, the scene of many of the early synods of the English, was burnt in a great fire which destroyed much of London in 1087. The new Norman cathedral was begun in the same year and completed in 1332. The largest building in England, it was 690 ft. long and covered an area of 3½ acres. The spire, 498 ft. high, was completed in 1315. The Bishop's Palace adjoined the NW. corner of the Nave. In the NE. part of the Close stood 'St. Paul's Cross', originally a rallying-place for Folk-moots, but from the mid-13th cent. until 1633 the national centre for religious and political proclamations, sermons and disputations. It was destroyed in 1643. During W. *Laud's episcopate (1628-33) a restoration of St. Paul's was begun with Inigo *Jones as architect, but this ceased under the Commonwealth, when the Nave became a cavalry barrack and the Lady Chapel a preaching-house. The old building, already ruinous, perished in the Great Fire of 1666.

The present Cathedral, designed by Sir Christopher *Wren, combines with much success the classical style with a traditionally gothic ground-plan. Rebuilding began in 1675, the choir was opened for service in 1697, and the whole was completed by 1710. The restrained Baroque of the interior was enriched considerably by the woodwork of Grinling Gibbons (1648-1720) and the ironwork of Jean Tijou (fl. 1690-1711). Later generations have removed Wren's fine organ-screen and filled the vaulting and saucer-domes of the E. end with mosaics. Since 1906, the SW. chapel, formerly the *Consistory Court, has been the religious centre of the Most Distinguished Order of St. Michael and St. George. In the crypt are the tombs of Lord Nelson and the Duke of Wellington and of

Wren with its famous inscription *Lector si monumentum requiris circumspice*. Because of its position St. Paul's is frequently the scene of great national services. Notable Deans include J. *Colet, A. *Nowell, J. *Overall, J. *Donne, W. *Sancroft, E. *Stillingfleet, J. *Tillotson, H. H. *Milman, H. L. *Mansel, R. W. *Church, R. *Gregory and W. R. *Inge.

W. *Dugdale, *The History of St. Paul's Cathedral in London from its Foundation Untill these Times* (1658). W. Sparrow Simpson (ed.), 'The Charter and Statutes of the College of the Minor Canons in S. Paul's Cathedral, London', in *Archaeologia*, xliii (1871), pp. 165–200; id. (ed.), *Registrum Statutorum et Consuetudinum Ecclesiae Sancti Pauli Londinensis* (London, 1873); id. (ed.), *Documents Illustrating the History of S. Paul's Cathedral* (Camden Society, New Series, xxvi; 1880); Marion Gibbs (ed.), *Early Charters of the Cathedral Church of St. Paul, London* (ib., Third Series, lviii; 1939). H. M. Milman, *Annals of S. Paul's Cathedral* (1868); W. Longman, *A History of the Three Cathedrals Dedicated to St. Paul in London* (1873); W. Sparrow Simpson, *Chapters in the History of Old S. Paul's* (1881); id., *S. Paul's Cathedral and City Life*. Illustrations of Civil and Cathedral Life from the Thirteenth to the Sixteenth Centuries (1894); W. M. Sinclair, *Memorials of St. Paul's Cathedral* (1909). G. L. Prestige, *St. Paul's in its Glory*. A Candid History of the Cathedral 1831–1911 (S.P.C.K., 1955); Jane Lang, *Rebuilding St. Paul's after the Great Fire of London* (1956). A. Dimock, *The Cathedral Church of Saint Paul* (Bell's Cathedral Series, 1900); S. A. Warner, *St. Paul's Cathedral* (S.P.C.K., 1926). On the clergy, and others, connected with St. Paul's, G. Bolton, *The Dome of Devotion* [1938]. Collection of studies edd. W. R. Matthews–W. M. Atkins (London, 1957).

ST. PAUL'S OUTSIDE THE WALLS,

Rome (San Paolo fuori le Mura). The church, one of the four 'Major *Basilicas', lies on the W. side of the *Ostian Way about 1½ miles beyond the Porta S. Paolo. The original edifice, erected by *Constantine over the relics of St. *Paul (324) was rebuilt as a large basilica in the late 4th cent. (completed by the Emp. Honorius, 395); this latter suffered little change until it was destroyed by fire on 15 July 1823, with only the triumphal arch and its mosaics surviving. The present building, which conforms closely to the plan of the earlier basilica, was consecrated on 10 Dec. 1854, two days after the Definition of the *Immaculate Conception. Until the Reformation the Kings of England were honorary members of the Chapter and the Abbot of the monastery a Prelate of the Order of the Garter (hence the insignia of the garter incorporated in the arms of the church). The basilica has long been served by *Benedictines.

N. M. Nicolai, *Della basilica di S. Paolo* (1815). I. Schuster, *La basilica e il monasterio di S. Paolo fuori le Mura*. Note storiche (1934). J. P. Kirsch, 'Der Ort des Martyriums des hl. Paulus' in *R.Q.*, ii (1888), pp. 233–47. S. Pesarini, 'La basilica di S. Paolo sulla *Via Ostiense* prima delle innovazioni del sec. XVI' in *Studi romani*, i (1913), pp. 386–427. L. de Bruyne, *L' antica serie di ritratti papali della basilica di S. Paolo fuori le Mura* (Studi di Antichità cristiana, vii; 1934). U. Benigni in *C.E.*, xiii (1912), pp. 369 f., s.v.; E. Josi in *E.C.*, ix (1952), col. 719 f., s.v. 'Paolo, Apostolo. VI. Archeologia'. See also works cited under *Rome, Churches of*.

ST. PETER'S, Rome.

The present 16th cent. building replaced a much older basilican structure, erected by *Constantine (d. 337) on the supposed site of St. *Peter's crucifixion. After it had fallen into serious disrepair by the later Middle Ages, *Nicholas V (1447–55) planned to replace it by a new church in the form of a Latin cross, selecting Bernardo Rosselino (1409–64), the restorer of the church of St. *Francis at *Assisi, as architect. Little had been done when the work was suspended on Nicholas's death. It was resumed under *Julius II (1503–13), who laid the first stone on 11 April 1506, and continued by a succession of architects—Bramante (d. 1514), *Raphael (d. 1520), Peruzzi (d. 1536), Sangallo (d. 1546) —all in turn making drastic changes in the design. The dome followed closely a design of *Michelangelo (d. 1564). By a radical change in plan the nave was lengthened under *Sixtus V to accommodate a vast congregation; the effect of this extension was to spoil the view of the dome from the Piazza. The building was finished in 1614 and consecrated by *Urban VIII on 18 Nov. 1626. Since 1940 extensive excavations have been made under the basilica, and it is claimed that the remains of a shrine dating from the early 3rd cent., if not earlier, have been recovered.

St. Peter's, which is the largest church in Christendom (length, 619 ft.; *St. Paul's Cathedral, London, *c.* 517 ft.), contains the remains of over 130 Popes. The traditional burial-place of St. Peter is the *confessio* under the high altar. The baldachino over the high altar, supported on four massive spiral columns of bronze, is the work of G. L. Bernini (1598–1680). Around the base of the dome are inscribed the words *Tu es Petrus . . . cœlorum* (from Mt. 16. 18 f.). See also *Vatican*.

The literature is dispersed in accordance with the various interests (historical, archaeological, architectural, liturgical, &c.) involved. A. Valentini, *La patriarcale basilica vaticana* (2 vols., 1845–55); F. M. Mignanti, *Istoria della sacrosanta patriarcale basilica vaticana* (2 vols., 1867); P. M. Letarouilly, *Le Vatican et la basilique de Saint-Pierre de Rome* (2 vols., 1882). D. A. Mortier, O.P., *Saint-Pierre de Rome*. Histoire de la basilique vaticane et du culte du tombeau de saint Pierre (Tours, 1900). H. Chéramy, *Saint-Pierre de Rome*. De la tombe apostolique à la basilique moderne (1933). In English there is a description of the church in A. S. Barnes, *St. Peter in Rome and his Tomb on the Vatican Hill* (1900), pp. 158–391. The official report of the recent excavations was issued under the title *Esplorazioni sotto la confessione di San Pietro in Vaticano eseguite negli anni 1940–1949: relazioni a cura di B. M. Apollonij Ghetti–A. Ferrua, S.J.– E. Josi–E. Kirschbaum, S.J.* (2 vols., 1951). Jocelyn Toynbee–J. W. Perkins, *The Shrine of St. Peter and the Vatican Excavations* (1956). H. I. Marrou in *D.A.C.L.*, xv (pt. 2; 1953), cols. 3290–334, s.v. 'Vatican (Fouilles du)', with reff. E. Josi in *E.C.*, xii (1954), cols. 1053–97, s.v. 'Vaticano. III: Zona archeologica e basilica', with further bibl. See also bibl to *Rome, Churches of*.

SAINT-SIMON, CLAUDE HENRI DE

ROUVROY (1760–1825), one of the earliest exponents of French socialism. He was a native of Paris and came from a noble family. His education was directed by J. le R. *d'Alembert. After fighting on the side of the Americans in the War of Independence, he led a life of adventure in Holland, Spain, and other European countries. In the French Revolution of 1789 he abandoned his titles and changed his name. During the following years he took part in successful financial enterprises, which were to help him to his ideal of service to humanity, but some of his plans having failed, he was reduced to great poverty. From 1797 his interest in science and the reorganization of society rapidly increased, and he worked out the ideas which he later embodied esp. in *L'Industrie* (1817), *L'Organisateur* (1819; a periodical), *Du système industriel* (1821), and *Catéchisme des industriels* (1823–4). In these works he developed and expounded his thesis that only the industrial classes work for the moral and physical welfare of mankind and that they should be preferred to those who have hitherto been privileged. In the last years of his life his thought turned into more religious channels and was expressed in the *Nouveau Christianisme* (1825). The one Divine principle in Christianity is that men must behave as brothers towards each other, i.e. must organize society in the way that will be most advantageous to the majority. Religion, therefore, ought to provide a speedy amelioration of the lot of the poorest. A truly Christian priest will regard dogma and cult as negligible accessories and give his chief attention to morals and social betterment.

This teaching, which won little following in Saint-Simon's lifetime, was later propagated by his disciples, esp. O. Rodrigues, S. A. Bazard, and B. P. Enfantin. In the two collective volumes, *Exposition de la doctrine de Saint-Simon* (1829 and 1830), Bazard and Enfantin sought to substitute for the traditional structure of society a religious system of social solidarity with the object of the progressive disappearance of the leisured classes and the abolition of all privileges, including interest and inheritance. This Saint-Simonian tendency to generalize and unify everything eventually led his disciples, esp. Enfantin, to a pantheism that divinized the universe and the carnal instincts of man and resulted in a semi-religious sect given to immorality. In 1832 Enfantin was imprisoned; but the ideas of his master exercised a great influence not only in France but also in other Continental countries and in England.

Saint-Simon was one of the first representatives of positive science, industrialism, and socialism as well as the apostle of a new humanitarian lay religion, whose suggestions were destined to a great future in the 19th and early 20th cents. For a time A. *Comte, the Positivist leader, was under his influence.

Works in *Œuvres de Saint-Simon et d'Enfantin* publiées par membres du conseil institué par Enfantin (47 vols., Paris, 1865–78), vols. xv, xviii–xxiii, xxxvii–xlv, and xlvii, with Notice Historique in vol. i, pp. 1–133. Selected Writings ed., with Eng. tr., by F. M. H. Markham (Oxford, 1952). A. J. Booth, *Saint-Simon and Saint-Simonism*. A Chapter in the History of Socialism in France (1871); P. A. Janet, *Saint-Simon et le saint-simonisme* (Bibliothèque de Philosophie contemporaine, 1876); [J.]G. Weill, *Saint-Simon et son œuvre* (1894); S. Charléty, *Essai sur l'histoire du saint-simonisme* (Paris thesis, 1896; revised ed., 1931); M. Leroy, *La Vie véritable du Comte Henri de Saint-Simon* (1925). E. M. Butler, *The Saint-Simonian Religion in Germany*. A Study of the Young German Movement (1926). J. Tonneau in *D.T.C.*, xiv (pt. 1; 1939), cols. 769–99, s.v. 'Saint-Simon et saint-simonisme'.

ST. SOPHIA. See *Santa Sophia*.

SAINT-SULPICE, Society of. The congregation of secular priests founded by J. J. *Olier in the parish of St.-Sulpice, *Paris, in 1642 with the aim of forming a zealous clergy, esp. suited to be directors of seminaries. The Society, which spread to Canada in 1657, was granted Papal approbation in 1664. Under its second Superior General, A. de Bretonvilliers (1657–76), it received its constitutions, which were further elaborated by his successor, L. Tronson (1676–1700), who also developed the Sulpician method of prayer and asceticism. Acc. to their rule, modelled on that of the *Oratory and adapted to the double purpose of studies and spiritual formation, the members of the Society take no vows, keep their property, which they are expected to use in the spirit of poverty, and live in close community with their pupils, whose spiritual and other exercises they share.

St.-Sulpice soon gained a profound influence on the ecclesiastical life of France, to which it gave a great number of bishops. After a period of partial eclipse during the French Revolution, it was restored soon after the *Concordat of 1801 by its resolute Superior General J. A. Emery, who, in 1791, had opened a house in Baltimore. Though again hard hit by the anti-ecclesiastical legislation in France of 1903 and 1906, the Society still trains many of those destined for the French priesthood and has provinces in Canada and the U.S.A.

The theology of St.-Sulpice, which is solid and traditional, is deeply imbued with *Thomism. Its spirituality follows the lines of the French School, professed by its founder, Olier, and laid down in the ascetical textbooks of Tronson. Past members of the Society include B. Joubert, who prepared new editions of the *Missal (1777) and the *Breviary (1778), F. Vigouroux, the author of *La Bible et les découvertes modernes* (1877) and editor of the *Dictionnaire de la Bible* (1895–1912), P. Pourrat whose *La Spiritualité chrétienne* (1917) is a standard work on the history of spirituality, and M. Lepin, author of *L'Idée du sacrifice de la messe* (1926).

H. Joly, *La Compagnie de Saint-Sulpice* (1914); J. Montval, *Les Sulpiciens* (1934). C. G. Herbermann, *The Sulpicians in the United States* (New York, 1916). L. Bertrand, P.S.S., *Bibliothèque sulpicienne, ou Histoire littéraire de la compagnie de Saint-Sulpice* (3 vols., 1900). Bremond, iii, 419–507. C. Hamel, *Histoire de l'église de Saint-Sulpice* (1900). Heimbucher, ii, 586–92.

ST.-VICTOR, Abbey of. See *Victorines*.

SAINTE-CHAPELLE, The, *Paris. The chapel built *c.* 1245 by St. *Louis IX to house the *Crown of Thorns and other relics of the Passion, and richly endowed by successive kings of France. It was desecrated in 1791, restored to the cult in 1837, and again secularized and dismantled in 1906. This masterpiece of Gothic architecture is the work of Pierre de Montereau, and though zealously restored in the 19th cent. by E. E. Viollet-le-Duc (1814–79), J. B. A. Lassus (1807-57), and others, still contains much beautiful medieval glass.

F. de Guilhery, *La Sainte-Chapelle de Paris après les restaurations commencées par M. Duban . . . terminées par M. Lassus* (1857). Id., *Description de la Sainte-Chapelle* (1867). C. Desmaze, *La Sainte-Chapelle du Palais de Justice de Paris* (1873); E. Pottet, *La Sainte-Chapelle de Paris, 1246-1912* (1912). H. Stein, *Le Palais de Justice et la Sainte-Chapelle de Paris* (1912), pp. 191-239; F. Gebelin, *La Sainte-Chapelle et la Conciergerie* (Petites Monographies des Grands Édifices de la France, 1931), pp. 1-86. A. Vidier, 'Le Trésor de la Sainte-Chapelle. Inventaires' in *Mémoires de la Société de l'Histoire de Paris et de l'Ile-de-France*, xxxiv (1907), pp. 199-324, xxxv (1908), pp. 189-339. See also works cited s.v. *Paris*.

SAINTS, Devotion to the. The practice of venerating and invoking the Saints has long been a regular element in Catholic devotion. OT adumbrations of the custom are found in, e.g., the efficacy with Jehovah of the intercession of His friends on earth (e.g. Gen. 18. 16–31). There would seem to be a much clearer anticipation in 2 Macc. where *Judas Maccabaeus sees Onias and *Jeremiah in a dream 'with outstretched hands invoking blessings on the whole body of the Jews' (15. 12).

In the NT the gift of special privileges to certain persons in the next world is indicated in Christ's promises to the Apostles (Mt. 19. 28). Support for the intercession of the dead on behalf of the living is found in the parable of Dives and Lazarus (Lk. 16. 19–31). Other NT references are the description of the saints of the Old Covenant as a 'cloud of witnesses' (Heb. 12. 1), which Christians are to imitate (13. 7), and the martyrs who pray before the throne of God (Rev. 6. 9 f.) and receive white robes (7. 14–17) as a reward of their martyrdom. But the principal theological basis of the practice is St. Paul's doctrine of the Mystical Body of Christ, in which all members have their particular office (Rom. 12. 4–8) as 'fellow citizens with the saints, and of the household of God' (Eph. 2. 19). It is the implications of this teaching about the Church rather than specific references to the subject that are commonly held by its advocates to constitute the Biblical foundation of devotion to the saints.

For the pre-Nicene period, literary evidence for the practice continues scanty, though the 'Odes of *Solomon' (2nd cent.) and the (largely *Gnostic) Apocryphal Acts of the Apostles attest a developing cult. The first incontrovertible documentary witness is the 'Martyrium *Polycarpi' (*c.* 156), where his followers express their intention of 'celebrating the birthday of his martyrdom' in days to come. The practice was furthered by the growing cultus of the relics of those who had suffered death for their faith. Besides the actual martyrs, those who had survived their sufferings ('confessores') were also paid special honours, and their power of intercession after death asserted e.g. by St. *Cyprian. *Origen was apparently the first of the Fathers to give the cult of martyrs an express theological foundation. He placed it within the doctrine of the Communion of Saints and taught that the prayer of the saints is efficacious in so far as the faithful follow in their footsteps.

From the 4th cent. devotion to the saints spread rapidly. St. *Cyril of Jerusalem dis-

tinguished the saints commemorated at the Eucharistic Sacrifice who offer our prayer to God from the ordinary dead who would be benefited by the sacrifice. The same distinction is found by St. *Chrysostom, who exhorted his hearers to have confidence in the intercession of the martyrs. About the same time the ranks of these accounted saints were enlarged by the addition of 'confessors' and 'virgins', on the ground that a life of renunciation and holiness might equal the devotion of those who had actually died for Christ. Thus ascetics such as St. *Antony and bishops such as St. *Athanasius and St. Chrysostom were soon venerated in the E., and in the W. St. *Augustine was honoured as a saint at Carthage before 475. The abuses connected with the cultus met, however, with occasional opposition, e.g. from *Vigilantius (q.v.). Later theologians sought to rebut the charge of idolatry by a distinction between the worship of God, expressed in the Gk. word λατρεία, and the cult of honour and imitation due to the saints, expressed in the term δουλεία. Among later Fathers who contributed to the theology of the cultus were St. *Leo, St. *Gregory the Great, and St. *John of Damascus. St. Leo affirmed that the saints as our special intercessors obtain for us the mercy of God by their prayers; St. Gregory, who did much to further the cultus, exhorted the faithful in his 'Dialogues' to place themselves under the protection of the saints; and St. John of Damascus stressed the theocentric character of the cult.

Liturgical developments followed popular devotion and the current of Patristic teaching. The mention of saints in the Mass is already attested by St. *Augustine (*De Civ. Dei*, XXII. 10). From the 5th cent. onwards *diptychs of martyrs and confessors found a place in the *Gallican, *Mozarabic, and *Celtic liturgies, and from the 6th cent. also in the *Roman Mass. From the 8th cent. the lives of the saints were read at *Mattins. In the beginning of the Middle Ages their cult was greatly extended through the conversion of the barbarians. The Irish monks, themselves influenced by the E., spread it to England, and thence to the Continent. From the 9th cent. saints' lives and edificatory sermons, often resting on very slender historical evidence, enjoyed increasing popularity and Councils frequently found it necessary to curb the excesses and superstitions of popular devotion. The fervour of even such preachers as St. *Peter Damian, St. *Anselm, and St. *Bernard needed some measure of correction from the great 13th cent. Scholastics.

The large amount of superstition surrounding the practice in the later Middle Ages had led the *Bogomiles and *Waldensians to attack the practice, and at the Reformation it was fiercely repudiated, esp. by the *Zwinglians and *Calvinists, on the ground that it was not explicitly recommended in Scripture. In the *Thirty-Nine Articles (art. 22) of the C of E the 'Romish doctrine' on the subject is designated 'a fond thing vainly invented'; but it is debated by modern Anglican theologians whether the Article forbids the invocation of saints altogether, or only condemns exaggerations in the RC Church. Under the influence of the *Oxford Movement, the practice has been widely revived in the C of E in recent times, though the early Tractarians viewed the veneration of the saints with considerable misgivings.

In the RC Church the practice is everywhere upheld. The Council of *Trent, however, treated the subject with studied moderation, the bishops being merely asked to remind the faithful to address themselves to the saints to obtain their assistance in winning the favours of God and Christ. The post-Tridentine theologians carried on and developed the teaching of the Schoolmen. The modern cult of the saints in the RC Church is regulated by canon law (*CIC*, can. 1255–6; 1276–8), which recommends the veneration of the saints and esp. of our Lady. The attitude of the E. Churches to the subject is closely akin to that of Rome. See also *Beatification, Canonization.*

On the history of the Cult of the Saints: I. C. Trombelli, *De Cultu Sanctorum* (2 vols., Bologna, 1740–3); E. Lucius–G. Anrich, *Die Anfänge des Heiligenkults in der christlichen Kirche* (1904; Protestant); H. *Delehaye, S.J., *Les Origines du culte des martyrs* (Brussels, 1912; ed. 2, Subsidia Hagiographica, 20, 1933); id., *Sanctus*, Essai sur le culte des martyrs dans l'antiquité (Subsidia Hagiographica, 17, 1927). P. Dörfler, *Die Anfänge der Heiligenverehrung nach den römischen Inschriften und Bildwerken* (Veröffentlichungen aus dem kirchen-historischen Seminar München, IV. Reihe, ii; 1913). On the theological principles involved, D. *Stone, *The Invocation of Saints*. An Article reprinted, with slight Additions, from the *Church Quarterly Review* [for Jan. 1899] (1903); J. P. Kirsch, *Die Lehre von der Gemeinschaft der Heiligen im christlichen Altertum* (1900; Eng. tr. [1911]); H. F. Stewart, *Doctrina Romanensium de Invocatione Sanctorum*. Being a Brief Enquiry into the Principles that underlie the Practice of the Invocation of Saints (London, S.P.C.K., 1907). H. Thurston, S.J., in *H.E.R.E.*, xi (1920), pp. 51–9, s.v. 'Saints and Martyrs (Christian)'; P. Séjourné, O.S.B., in *D.T.C.*, xiv (pt. 1; 1939), cols. 870–978, s.v. 'Saints (Culte des)'. Much material will be found also in the *Analecta Bollandiana* (q.v.). See also bibls. to *Martyr* and *Martyrology*.

SAKKOS (Gk. σάκκος). In the Eastern Church, an embroidered liturgical vestment similar in form to the *dalmatic in the West. It prob. dates from the 11th cent. It is the chief Eucharistic vestment of those of high rank and was orig. confined to Archbishops and Metropolitans. It is now worn instead of the *phelonion (q.v.) by all Bishops in many countries, e.g. *Russia, Bulgaria, and *Ruthenia.

SALAMANCA, School of. See *Salmanticenses.*

SALESIANS. The Society of St. *Francis de Sales, founded near Turin in 1859 by St. John *Bosco for the Christian perfection and education of boys and young men of the poorer classes, esp. with a view to their ordination. About 1845 St. John began to gather them together in what he termed 'festive oratories' and night schools, with a view to fighting the irreligious doctrines of the day. A religious congregation of priests and teachers came into being to develop the work, and in 1859 began to live on a rule drawn up by

St. John two years earlier. In 1874 the rule was approved by *Pius IX, and the Society eventually spread to many parts of the world, including England. It has several thousand members—priests and lay brothers. A sister congregation of Daughters of Our Lady Help of Christians was founded by St. John in 1872, out of a small community started independently in 1852 at Mornese, for similar work among girls, and now has some 7,000 members altogether.

E. Ceria, *Annali della Società Salesiana* [1841–1921] (4 vols., Turin (1941–51); also other specialized works by the same author. Heimbucher, ii, 392–9 and 667; and on the female order, pp. 641 f. and 661. E. Marsh, Salesian, in *C.E.*, xiii (1912), p. 298 f., s.v. 'Salesian Society'; V. M. Kreyenbühl, Salesian, in *L.Th.K.*, ix (1937), col. 115 f., s.v. 'Salesianer'; L. Castano, Salesian, in *E.C.*, xi (1953), col. 870 f., s.v. 'Società Salesiana di San Giovanni Bosco'. See also lives of *Bosco, St. John*, cited s.v.

SALETTE, La. See *La Salette.*

SALISBURY. From the see originally founded in 634 by St. *Birinus at *Dorchester in Oxfordshire sprang the later sees of *Winchester, *Sherborne, Ramsbury, and Salisbury. Herman, Bp. of Ramsbury, who united the dioceses of Ramsbury and Sherborne in 1058, transferred the see to Old Sarum in 1075. Here his successor, St. *Osmund, built a cathedral, constituted a chapter, and drew up offices, which perhaps formed the basis of the *Sarum Rite. Richard *Poore, the seventh Bp. of Old Sarum, moved the see to New Sarum or Salisbury in 1218, and laid the foundation of the new cathedral (of the BVM) on 28 Apr. 1220. The Lady Chapel was consecrated in 1225 in the presence of St. *Edmund, afterwards Abp. of Canterbury, and the cathedral completed in 1266. Built throughout in the Early English style, it is a rare example of architectural unity. Cloisters and chapterhouse were added later. The spire, built about 1300, is the highest in England.

C. T. Flower–M. C. B. Dawes (edd.), *Registrum Simonis de Gandavo, Diocesis Saresbiriensis, A.D. 1297–1315* (*Canterbury and York Society, xl and xli; 1934). W. H. Rich Jones (ed.), *Vetus Registrum Sarisberiense alias dictum Registrum S. Osmundi Episcopi* (2 vols., R.S., 1883–4); id., *Fasti Ecclesiae Sarisberiensis*, or a Calendar of the Bishops, Deans, Archdeacons, and Members of the Cathedral Body at Salisbury from the Earliest Times to the Present (1879); id.–W. D. Macray, *Charters and Documents Illustrating the History of the Cathedral, City and Diocese of Salisbury in the Twelfth and Thirteenth Centuries, selected from the Capitular and Diocesan Registers* (R.S., 1891). E. A. Dayman–W. H. Rich Jones (edd.), *Statutes of the Cathedral Church of Sarum* (privately printed, Bath, 1883); C. *Wordsworth–D. Macleane (edd.), *Statutes and Customs of the Cathedral Church of the Blessed Virgin Mary of Salisbury* (1915), incl. Eng. tr. C. Wordsworth (ed.), *Ceremonies and Processions of the Cathedral Church of Salisbury* (Cambridge, 1901). R. L. Poole, 'The Muniments of the Dean and Chapter of Salisbury' in the *Historical Manuscripts Commission Report on Manuscripts in Various Collections*, i (1901), pp. 338–88; id., 'The Records of the Bishop of Salisbury', ib., iv (1907), pp. 1–12. S. M. Lakin, *A Catalogue of the Library of the Cathedral Church of Salisbury* (1880). [R. Rawlinson], *The History and Antiquities of the Cathedral-Church of Salisbury and the Abbey-Church of Bath* (1719), pp. iii–xvi, 1–161, and 269–351. W. Dodsworth, *An Historical Account of the Episcopal See and Cathedral Church of Salisbury* (1814). S. H. Cassan, *Lives and Memoirs of the Bishops of Sherborne and Salisbury, from the Year 705 to 1824* (Salisbury, 1824). G. W[hite], *The Cathedral Church of Salisbury* (Bell's Cathedral Series, 1896); J. M. J. Fletcher, *The Story of Salisbury Cathedral* (1933). G. Crosse in *D.E.C.H.* (1912), pp. 539–43, s.v.

SALISBURY or SARUM, Use of. The local medieval modification of the Roman rite in use at the cathedral church of Salisbury, traditionally ascribed to St. *Osmund (d. 1099) but really much later. The *Consuetudinary, i.e. the cathedral statutes and customs and a complete directory of services, were compiled by Richard le *Poore (d. 1237). The 'New Use of Sarum' was a further (14th cent.) revision, effecting certain changes in the Calendar. In the later Middle Ages the Sarum Use was increasingly followed, in whole or in part, in other dioceses, and in 1457 stated to be in use in nearly the whole of England, Wales, and Ireland. In 1543 the *Canterbury Convocation imposed the Sarum *Breviary on the whole province, and the books of the Sarum rite furnished the Reformers with their main material for the First (1549) BCP of *Edward VI, in the Preface to which (the section now headed 'Concerning the Service of the Church') the Sarum use appears as one of the local variations which the new standard order was to replace. In the years preceding the Reformation the output of Sarum books was enormous. The much increased knowledge which has followed their discovery and reediting in modern times has led to the revival of Sarum customs and ornaments in many English cathedral and parish churches.

Missale ad Usum Insignis et Praeclarae Ecclesiae Sarum, ed. F. H. Dickinson (Burntisland, 1861–83); *The Sarum Missal* done into English by A. Harford Pearson (1863; ed. 2, 1884); *Breviarium ad Usum Insignis Ecclesiae Sarum,* ed. F. Procter et C. Wordsworth (3 vols., 1879–86); W. H. *Frere, *The Use of Sarum,* I: The Sarum Customs (1898), II: The Ordinal and Tonal (1901); C. Wordsworth, *Ceremonies and Processions of the Cathedral Church of Salisbury* (1901); J. W. Legg, *The Sarum Missal edited from Three Early MSS* (1916). *Manuale ad usum percelebris ecclesie Sarisburiensis,* ed. J. Collins (H.B.S. xci; 1960).

SALMANTICENSES. The customary name for the authors of the *Cursus theologicus Summam d. Thomae complectens,* a group of Discalced *Carmelites who taught at Salamanca between 1600 and 1725. The authors were anonymous, but their identity is now well established; they were Antonio de la Madre de Dios (c. 1585–c. 1640), Domingo de Sta Teresa (1600–54), Juan de la Anunciación (1633–1701), and three others. The *Cursus,* which took 70 years to complete (1631–1701), is a gigantic Commentary on the 'Summa' of St. *Thomas Aquinas, undertaken to provide a sound basis of theological teaching for the friars of the *Teresian reform. It was conceived on the same lines as the philosophical course (*Cursus Complutensis*) done by their college at Alcalá, and was supplemented by the *Cursus Salmanticensis Theologiae Moralis* (publd. in its complete form, 1717–24).

F. Stegmüller in *L.Th.K.,* ix (1937), col. 121 f.; T. Deman, O.P., in *D.T.C.,* xiv (pt. 1; 1939), cols. 1017–31, s.v. 'Salamanque (Théologiens de)', with bibl.; Ambrogio di Santa Teresa in *E.C.,* x (1953), col. 1681 f., also with bibl.

SALMASIUS, CLAUDIUS (1588–1653), Claude Saumaise, French classical scholar. At Paris, where he studied from 1604, he made the friendship of I. *Casaubon and was converted to *Calvinism. In 1608 he edited two 14th cent. tracts against the primacy of the Pope. After publishing various classical works, including an edition of Solinus's 'Polyhistor' (1629), he succeeded to the chair of J. J. *Scaliger (d. 1609) at *Leyden in 1632. Here he wrote two books defending the compatibility of *usury with Christian principles, *De usuris liber* (1638) and *De modo usurarum* (1639), and a *Defensio regia pro Carolo I* (1649) which provoked J. *Milton's celebrated and successful reply, *Pro populo anglicano defensio* (1651). In 1650 he accepted an invitation to visit the court of Queen *Christina of Sweden, but soon afterwards returned to Holland.

Letters ed. A. Clément (Leyden, 1656), with life of Salmasius prefixed (pp. iii–lxiv). There also exists a MS. life by Philibert de la Mare, which was used by P. Papillon, *Bibliothèque des auteurs de Bourgogne* (Dijon, 1745), pp. 247–287 [incl. full list of Salmasius's works]. G. Laubmann in *P.R.E.* (ed. 3), xvii (1906), pp. 397–9, s.v.; unsigned art. in *E.B.* (ed. 11), xxiv (1911), p. 81, s.v.

SALMON, GEORGE (1819–1904), mathematician and theologian. He was educated at *Trinity College, Dublin, of which he became a Fellow in 1841, Regius professor of divinity in 1866, and provost in 1888. He was ordained priest in 1845. A strong Protestant, Salmon co-operated with R. *Whately in writing the *Cautions for the Times* (1853), intended as a reply to the *Tracts for the Times* (1833–41). His lectures on the *Infallibility of the Church,* first published in 1888, were a defence of Protestant principles against the tenets of the Church of Rome, and well illustrate at once his skill, his vigour, and his humour, as a controversialist. In his widely read *Introduction to the New Testament* (1885), he was more concerned to refute critical theories than to produce a handbook of reference. His distinguished work as a mathematician cannot be described here. Salmon also took a prominent part in the reconstruction of the Irish Church after its disestablishment in 1870.

J. H. *Bernard in *D.N.B.,* Second Suppl., iii (1912), pp. 251–4.

SALOME. (1) The daughter of Herodias mentioned in Mk. 6. 22, &c. (2) A woman who followed Jesus to *Jerusalem, Mk. 15. 40, 16. 1. From Mt. 27. 56 she seems to have been the mother of St. *James and St. *John, the sons of Zebedee. Sometimes she is identified also with the sister of the BVM (Jn. 19. 25). See *Marys in the NT* (4).

SALONICA. See *Thessalonica.*

SALT. Owing to its preservative quality salt was a sign of purity and incorruptibility, esp. among the Semitic peoples. As such, it served to confirm contracts and friendship, the covenant between Jehovah and Israel on *Sinai, e.g., being called a 'covenant of salt' in Num. 18. 19. This symbolism, taken together with its seasoning properties, explains our Lord's saying 'Ye are the salt of the earth'

(Mt. 5. 13, cf. also Mk. 9. 50), where the salt represents Christian wisdom and integrity, as also in Col. 4. 6. The ritual use of salt is very old and widespread. It was prescribed in the OT for every oblation (Lev. 2. 13) and played an important part in the sacrifices of the Greeks and Romans. In the W. Church the ceremony of the Roman ritual of offering blessed salt to the *catechumen before baptism is probably a transformation of the old pagan Roman custom of placing a few grains of salt on the lips of an infant on the 8th day after his birth to chase away the demons. Salt is also used for the preparation of *holy water and in the ceremonial of the consecration of altars and churches.

V. Hehn, *Das Salz.* Eine kulturhistorische Studie (1873; ed. 2 by O. Schader, 1901). A. Franz, *Die kirchlichen Benediktionen im Mittelalter,* i (1909), pp. 154–92 and 221–9; L. Eisenhofer, *Handbuch der katholischen Liturgik,* i (1932), pp. 304–6, and ii (1933), pp. 247 f., 269 f., 279, and 455–60. W. E. Scudamore in *D.C.A.,* ii (1880), p. 1838 f., s.v. W. Robertson *Smith–A. R. S. Kennedy in *E.Bi.,* iv (1903), cols. 4247–50, s.v. F. Hauck in *T.W.B.,* i (1933), p. 229, s.v. 'ἅλας', with bibl.

SALTMARSH, JOHN (d. 1647), preacher and writer. He crowded much controversy into a short life of some 35 years. *C.* 1639 he became rector of Heslerton, Yorks, and was at first an ardent supporter of episcopacy and conformity; but his opinions gradually changed and he became equally ardent in advocating complete religious liberty. In 1644 he was appointed to the sequestered rectory of Brasted, Kent, and in 1646 became chaplain in Fairfax's army. All the time he was pouring forth a stream of books and pamphlets of which the best known are *Holy Discoveries* (1640) and *Sparkles of Glory* (1647).

W. Schenk, *The Concern for Social Justice in the Puritan Revolution* (1948), pp. 85–9. L. F. Solt, 'John Saltmarsh: New Model Army Chaplain' in *J.E.H.,* ii (1951), pp. 69–80. A. Gordon in *D.N.B.,* l (1897), pp. 220–2.

SALTUM, Per. See *Per Saltum.*

SALUTARY ACT. In RC theological terminology a human act which contributes to the salvation of the person performing it. To be 'salutary', it must be carried out in a state of grace and with the co-operation of the will, i.e. it must not be a purely instinctive reaction.

SALVATION ARMY, The. An extensive international Christian organization for evangelistic and social work. It was founded by W. *Booth (q.v.) in 1865, received its present form and title in 1878, and from that time spread rapidly all over the world. It is organized on a strictly military basis, with a 'General' at its head. On W. Booth's death (1912), his son, William Bramwell Booth, succeeded to the Generalship on his father's death, but since 1931 the General has been elected by the High Council, consisting of commanders and other leading officers. 'Unquestioning obedience' is required from all members of the Army, which is divided into 'territories', acc. to the national frontiers of the respective countries, which,

in their turn, are subdivided into 'provinces' and 'divisions'. The religious teaching of the Salvation Army is largely in harmony with traditional evangelical belief, but rejects all Sacraments and stresses esp. the moral side of Christianity. It enjoins complete self-denial on all its followers. The technique of producing conversions is aggressive and emotional and makes extensive use of public testimony and penance; its realistic methods of presenting religion to the people, in which open-air meetings with brass bands and banners play an important part, differ greatly from those of other Christian bodies. The Army carries on a great variety of social activities, including all kinds of rescue work, care of criminals and drunkards, soup kitchens, workers' hostels and night shelters, as well as hospitals and schools. The Army, which is esp. strong in the U.S.A., has its headquarters in London.

R. Sandall, *The History of the Salvation Army* (3 vols, 1947–55).

SALVATOR NOSTER. The bull of *Sixtus IV, dated 3 Aug. 1476, granting an indulgence to the church of Saintes. It is the first instance of the issue of an indulgence granting plenary remission of sins for the dead (*plenarium remissionem per modum suffragii*).

Text in *Archives historiques de la Saintogne et de l'Aunis,* x (1882), pp. 56–69. The clauses concerning the souls in purgatory also pr. in H. Lea, *A History of Auricular Confession and Indulgences in the Latin Church,* iii (1896), p. 585 f., with discussion, pp. 345–51, and extracts from other allied documents, pp. 586–96; extracts of the text repr. in Kidd, p. 3 f. (No. 2). A. Teetaert, O.F.M.Cap., in *D.T.C.,* xiv (pt. 2; 1941), col. 2210 f., s.v. 'Sixte IV'. See also works cited under *Indulgences.*

SALVE REGINA (Lat., 'Hail, Holy Queen'). One of the oldest Marian *antiphons, recited in the W. Church at the end of the canonical hours. It is among the most widely used Catholic prayers to the BVM, owing its popularity to its tender devotional language and beautiful plain-song. The earliest MS. evidence for it dates from the end of the 11th cent., when it is mentioned in connexion with the old pilgrim shrine of Le Puy-en-Velay (therefore called 'Antiphona de Podio') in the chronicle of Alberick of Trois - Fontaines. The authorship is uncertain, though from the 15th cent. it has generally been attributed to *Herimannus Contractus (d. 1054). The final words ('O clemens', &c.), traditionally assigned to St. *Bernard, are found in earlier MSS. and are therefore probably an integral part of the anthem.

The Salve Regina, from 1135 onwards frequently sung at processions in *Cluny, soon penetrated into other religious orders such as the *Cistercians and *Dominicans, by whom it is still sung all through the year after *Compline. In 1884 *Leo XIII ordered it to be said after *Low Mass; and in the Roman and Monastic Breviaries it is recited from the First *Vespers of *Trinity Sunday till *None of the Saturday before *Advent Sunday.

Critical ed. of text by G. M. Dreves, *Lateinische Hymnendichter des Mittelalters,* ii (A.H.M.A., 1; 1907), p. 318 f.

J. de Valois, *En marge d'une antienne*. Le 'Salve Regina' (1912). H. Thurston, S.J., 'The Salve Regina' in *The Month*, cxxviii (1918), pp. 248–60 and 300–14; text (without illustrations) repr. in his *Familiar Prayers*, ed. P. Grosjean, S.J. (1953), No. vii, pp. 115–45, with reff. A. Manser, O.S.B., in *L.Th.K.*, ix (1937), col. 137 f., and I. Cecchetti in *E.C.*, x (1953), cols. 1719–21, both with full bibl.

SALVIAN (*c.* 400–*c.* 480), 'Massiliensis', ecclesiastical writer. Born, prob. near *Cologne, of a noble Christian family, he married a pagan, Palladia, who thereupon became a Christian. Later they separated by mutual agreement so that both could devote themselves more exclusively to religion, and Salvian lived henceforward at *Lérins (from *c.* 424) and Marseilles (from *c.* 439). His chief work was his 'De Gubernatione Dei', a treatise in 8 books in which, by contrasting the vices of decadent Roman civilization with the virtues of the victorious barbarians, he used the latter as a witness to God's judgement on society and as an incentive for Christians to purity of life and faith in Providence. Though somewhat deficient in criticism, his book is valuable as social history. There are also extant a treatise 'Ad Ecclesiam' (on almsgiving) and 9 letters.

Works repr. from ed. of S. *Baluze in J. P. Migne, *PL*, liii, 25–238; crit. edd. by F. Pauly in C.S.E.L., viii (1883), and by C. Halm in *M.G.H.*, Auctores Antiquissimi, i (pt. 1; 1887). Eng. tr. of his *De Gubernatione Dei* by Eva M. Sandford (Records of Civilization. Sources and Studies; New York, 1930), with notes on early edd. of his works. M. Pellegrino, *Salviano di Marsiglia* (Lateranum, N.S., vi; fascc. 1–2; 1940). G. Bardy in *D.T.C.*, xiv (pt. 1; 1939), cols. 1056–8, s.v. 'Salvien', with bibl.

SAMARIA. The capital of the kingdom of *Israel, i.e. of the 'Ten [northern[Tribes', founded by King Omri (*c.* 880 B.C.) and captured by the Assyrians in 722 B.C. (2 Kgs. 18. 9 ff.). The name was also used for the kingdom itself (e.g. Hos. 7. 1), and thus came to denote the territory, west of the Jordan, bounded by *Galilee on the north and *Judaea on the south. On the death of *Herod the Great it was assigned to Archelaus whence on Archelaus's banishment it passed to the province of Syria. The hostility of the Jews to the Samaritans was proverbial (Jn. 4. 9, 8. 48). The Lord's sympathy to them is shown in the parables of the Good Samaritan (Lk. 10. 33) and the Ten Lepers (Lk. 17. 16). Apparently St. *Philip the Evangelist was the first to preach the Gospel to them.

G. A. *Smith, *The Historical Geography of the Holy Land* (ed. 25, 1931), pp. 323–63. J. A. Montgomery, *The Samaritans* (Philadelphia, 1907); J. E H. Thomson, *The Samaritans. Their Testimony to the Religion of Israel* (1919). M. Gaster, *The Samaritans* (Schweich Lectures for 1923; 1925). L. Heidet in *Dictionnaire de la Bible*, v (1912), cols. 1413–21, s.v., with bibl. On the city of Samaria: G. A. Reisner–C. S. Fisher–D. G. Lyon, *Harvard Excavations at Samaria, 1908–1910* (2 vols., Cambridge, Mass., 1924). J. W. Crowfoot–Kathleen M. Kenyon–E. L. Sukenik, *The Buildings at Samaria* (1942). R. W. Hamilton, *Guide to Samaria-Sebaste* (Jerusalem, 1944).

SAMARITAN PENTATEUCH, The. A slightly divergent form of the *Pentateuch in Hebrew, current since pre-Christian times among the Samaritans. It is the only part of the OT accepted by the Samaritans, who possibly received it from the Jews at the time of *Nehemiah (cf. Neh. 13. 23–31). Where it differs from the *Massoretic (i.e. the standard Jewish) text, it seems usually to be inferior in value. Though the differences for the most part are only verbal, they sometimes accord with the more developed ideas of reverence of a later date, e.g. in the substitution of 'an angel' for 'God' in the sentence 'God met Balaam' (Num. 23. 4). A notable difference is the name of the Samaritan holy mountain, Mt. Gerizim, for Mt. Ebal in Deut. 27. 4. No MS. appears to be older than the 13th cent.

The text was first made known in Europe in 1616 by the traveller Pietro della Valle, who brought home a copy from Damascus, now preserved in the *Vatican Library. The text was first publd. in the Paris *Polyglott of 1645 and repr. by B. *Walton in the London Polyglott of 1657; also ed. separately by B. Blayney (Oxford, 1790); best ed. by A. von Gall (5 pts., Giessen, 1914–18) (eclectic text, which makes no use of older MSS., preserved at Nablus). W. *Gesenius, *De Pentateuchi Samaritani Origine, Indole et Auctoritate* (Halle, 1815; denies its usefulness for OT text). P. Kahle, 'Untersuchungen zur Geschichte des Pentateuchtextes' in *Theologische Studien und Kritiken*, lxxxviii (1915), pp. 399–439, esp. 'I. Der Pentateuch der Samaritaner', pp. 402–10. C. W. Dugmore, 'Two Samaritan MSS. in the Library of Queens' College, Cambridge' in *J.T.S.*, xxxvi (1935), pp. 131–46. R. H. Pfeiffer, *Introduction to the Old Testament* (New York, [1948]; London, 1954), pp. 101–4. E. König in *H.D.B.*, v (extra vol.; 1904), pp. 68–72, s.v.; P. Nober, S.J., in *E.C.*, x (1953), cols. 1736–40, s.v. 'Samaritano, Pentateuco'.

SAMSON (prob. 11th cent. B.C.) Hebrew hero, enemy of the Philistines and traditionally the last of the great 'judges'. Acc. to Jgs. 13. 2–16. 31 he was the son of Manoah, of the tribe of Dan, born in answer to prayer and bound throughout his life by a *Nazarite vow. He was endowed with prodigious strength, which enabled him to perform various remarkable exploits (e.g. slaying a lion and moving the gates of Gaza). After marrying a Philistine woman who betrayed him, he wrought havoc among the Philistines from whom he escaped by his own strength both when surrendered by the men of Judah and when surrounded while visiting a harlot at Gaza. He at last fell victim to his consuming passion for Delilah, to whom he revealed that the secret of his strength lay in his hair. The Philistines put out his eyes, but Samson was granted his revenge in pulling down the pillars of the temple when three thousand Philistines were assembled. The name 'Samson' (Heb. Shimshom) means 'solar', and some would see in Samson the hero of a solar myth, derived either from the form of his name, or that of his burial-place (Bethshemesh). In acc. with the scheme of the editor of the Book of Judges, he is said to have 'judged' Israel for 20 years (15. 16 and 16. 31), but the account in general contains nothing to suggest that he was a deliverer of Israel. He was, however, regarded as a recipient of divine favour and in the NT his faith is commended (Heb. 11. 32). In later literature he is the hero of J. *Milton's *Samson Agonistes* (1671) and one of G. F. *Handel's oratorios (1743).

See commentaries on *Judges*, cited s.v., notably C. F. *Burney, *The Book of Judges* (1918), with bibl. p. 335, and additional note pp. 391–408 ('The Mythical Element in the Story of Samson'). G. G. Roskoff, *Die Simsonsage nach ihrer Entstehung, Form und Bedeutung und der Heraclesmythus* (1860). H. Stahn, *Die Simsonsage* (1908). A. Smythe Palmer, *The Samson Saga and its Place in Comparative Religion* (1913). V. Zapletal, O.P., *Der biblische Samson* (Fribourg, 1906). K. *Budde in *H.D.B.*, iii (1900), pp. 377–381, s.v.; W. R. *Smith–T. K. *Cheyne in *E.Bi.*, iv (1903), cols. 4268–70, s.v.

SAMSON, St. (*c.* 490–?565), Bp. of Dol. A native of Wales, who had embraced the monastic life, he was ordained by St. *Dubritius. His repute for piety and as a miracle-worker was such that he was compelled to retire first to the banks of the Severn and later to Cornwall and finally to Brittany in search of solitude. Having landed near Dol, he built a monastery there, and was subsequently consecrated bishop, though Dol did not become an established episcopal see til the 9th cent. Feast day, 28 July.

Anon. life, poss. 7th cent., first pr. by J. *Mabillon, also in *AA.SS.*, Jul. VII (1729), pp. 573–93; crit. ed. by R. Fawtier (Bibliothèque de l'École des Hautes Études, cxcvii; 1912); Eng. tr. of text by T. Taylor ('Translations of Christian Literature'; 1925). F. Duine, 'La Vie de saint Samson, à propos d'un ouvrage récent' in *Annales de Bretagne*, xxviii (1913), pp. 332–56; R. Fawtier, 'Saint Samson abbé de Dol. Réponse à quelques objections', ib., xxxv (1923), pp. 137–86. F. C. *Burkitt in *J.T.S.*, xxvii (1926), pp. 42–57.

SAMUEL, Books of. The two Books of Samuel were originally a single Book, which was divided for convenience by the compilers of the *Septuagint, who also grouped the Books of Samuel with those of *Kings under the one single title of the '[Four] Books of the Reigns'. The English title follows the Hebrew, and is due to the important part played in the opening chapters by the prophet Samuel, in the establishment of the monarchy in Israel. The Books are the primary authority for the history of the Israelite people in the crucial years of the 11th–10th cents. B.C. After relating the history of Samuel, the writer sets down a description of the reigns of *Saul (*c.* 1025–1010 B.C.) and *David (*c.* 1010–974). Three ancient poems lie embedded in the narrative: Hannah's prayer (1 Sam. 2. 1–10), David's lament (2 Sam. 1. 19–27), David's song of triumph (2 Sam. 22). As might be expected in such a work, various sources have been used by the compiler, some of them being named, others not. The Hebrew text survives in a very corrupt state, and in reconstructing the original much assistance may be gained from the Greek version.

Commentaries by A. F. Kirkpatrick (2 vols., Camb. Bib., AV, 1880–1; RV, 1930), H. P. Smith (I.C.C., 1899), A. R. S. Kennedy (Cent. Bib., 1905), W. Nowack (H.K.A.T., Abt. 1, Bd. iv, pt. 2, 1902; sep. pagination), K. *Budde (K.H.C., Abt., viii; 1902), P. Dhorme, O.P. (Études bibliques, 1910), W. Caspari (K.A.T., vii, 1926). S. R. *Driver, *Notes on the Hebrew Text and the Topography of the Books of Samuel* (1890); O. Eissfeldt, *Die Komposition der Samuelisbücher* (1931). R. Press, 'Der Prophet Samuel. Eine traditionsgeschichtliche Untersuchung' in *Z.A.T.W.*, lviii (1938), pp. 177–225. J. F. Stenning in *H.D.B.*, iv (1902), pp. 381–91, s.v.

SANATIO IN RADICE (Lat. 'healing at the root'). In canon law, the process whereby

an invalid 'marriage' is validated retrospectively, i.e. from the moment at which the 'marriage' was solemnized. Unless special provision is made for *sanatio in radice*, the marriage is validated only from the moment at which the *impediment is dispensed. In the absence of such retrospective validation, the full legitimacy of children born before validation would not be secured. Under RC canon law (*CIC*, can. 1141) *sanatio in radice* can be granted only by the see of Rome.

N. Iung in *D.T.C.*, xiv (pt. 1; 1939), cols. 1063–74, s.v., with reff. to docc., incl. the Replies of the *Holy Office on the subject. See also bibl. to discussions in RC handbooks of moral theology.

SANBENITO. The yellow penitential garment, provided with a red cross front and back, which the Spanish *Inquisition ordered to be worn by those who had confessed heresy. It was so named from its resemblance in shape to a Benedictine *scapular.

SANCHEZ, THOMAS (1550–1610), Spanish moral theologian. He entered the *Jesuit Order in 1567 and was appointed master of novices at Granada, where he also taught moral theology and canon law. He became famous for his *Disputationes de sancto matrimonii sacramento* (1602), a comprehensive work on the moral and canonical aspects of matrimony which enjoyed high authority in the 17th cent. One volume of its Venetian edition was placed on the *Index because of the omission of a passage, displeasing to the Venetian Republic, defending the legitimization of illegitimate children by the Pope without interference of the civil authorities. In the *Opus Morale in Praecepta Decalogi* (1613), published posthumously, he undertook to expound a system of casuistry based on the Decalogue, but he did not go beyond the Second Commandment. Much later Sanchez was attacked as a *laxist by B. *Pascal in his *Lettres provinciales*, but he seems only to have shared some erroneous opinions, e.g. on *mental reservation, with other *probabilists of his time.

Collected ed. of his works, 7 vols., Venice, 1740. Sommervogel, vii (1896), cols. 530–7. A. Astrain, S.J., *Historia de la Compañia de Jesús en la asistencia de España*, iv (1913), p. 65. M. Petrocchi, *Il problema del lassismo nel secolo XVII* (1953), passim. R. Brouillard, S.J., in *D.T.C.*, xiv (1939), cols. 1075–85, s.v.

SANCROFT, WILLIAM (1617–93), Abp. of *Canterbury. He was educated at Emmanuel College, Cambridge, where he was a Fellow from 1642 till 1651, when he was ejected by the *Puritans. At the *Restoration he was appointed chaplain to *Charles II, in 1662 master of his college, and in 1664 Dean of York. Later, in 1664, he became Dean of St. Paul's, in which capacity he warmly collaborated with C. *Wren in the rebuilding of the cathedral. In 1678 he succeeded G. *Sheldon in the see of Canterbury. His attempts to bring James, Duke of York, back to the C of E having failed, he radically altered the *Coronation service in 1685 so that the

Communion could be omitted. His action as leader of the *Seven Bishops who opposed the *Declaration of Indulgence in 1688 led to his imprisonment in the Tower, but on trial he was acquitted. After James's flight he refused, however, to recognize William of Orange as rightful king, was suspended from office on 1 Aug. 1689, and on 1 Feb. 1690 deprived of his archbishopric as a '*Nonjuror'. His later years were spent in retirement. The *Fur Praedestinatus* (orig. anon.; ed. 1651 ascribed to Sancroft) was an attack on *Calvinism.

A small collection of his *Occasional Sermons* was publd., London, 1694. Life by G. D'Oyly (2 vols., London, 1821), with repr., in appendix, of the *Fur Praedestinatus*, ii, 173–228. *Modern Policies, taken from Machiavel, Borgia, and other Choice Authors, by an Eye-Witness* (orig. publd. London, 1652), pp. 229–436, and two of his letters, pp. 437–46. C. R. L. Fletcher, 'Some Troubles of Archbishop Sancroft' in *Proceedings of the Huguenot Society of London*, xiii (1926), pp. 209–61, with calendar of some of his correspondence in the Tanner Collection [Bodleian Library], pp. 255–61. W. H. *Hutton in *D.N.B.*, i (1897), pp. 244–50; id. in *D.E.C.H.*, p. 543 f. See also works cited under *Seven Bishops* and *Nonjurors*.

SANCTA CLARA, FRANCISCUS A. See *Davenport, Christopher*.

SANCTORALE. The section of a *Missal or *Breviary (sometimes made into a separate book) which supplies the Masses or offices peculiar to the festivals of particular saints, with the exception of those occurring at Christmastide (which are in the *Temporale).

SANCTUARY (Gk. ἱερατεῖον, or, more commonly, βῆμα). The part of the church containing the altar (or, if there be several altars, the high altar). In Byzantine churches it is enclosed by the *iconostasis. It is sometimes termed the 'presbytery', as being the portion of the church properly reserved to the clergy.

SANCTUARY, Right of. In the Middle Ages this was of two kinds, ecclesiastical and secular. The former had developed out of the usage that a criminal who had taken refuge in a church might not be removed from it, but was allowed to take an oath of abjuration before the coroner and proceed to a seaport appointed by the latter. If within 40 days he refused to adopt this procedure, he might be forcibly extricated for justice. The privilege was understood not to extend to sacrilege or high treason. Sometimes those claiming the privilege of sanctuary had to touch a particular object in the church (in early times, often the altar). The sanctuary-stool ('frith-stool') survives at *Hexham, the sanctuary-knocker at *Durham and elsewhere.

Secular and jurisdictional sanctuary relied upon royal grant, and in theory at least might be held to apply to every franchise where the lord had *jura regalia* and the king's writ did not run. This institution is frequently confused with ecclesiastical sanctuary, since criminals commonly repaired to a church in

a franchise, esp. in the great ecclesiastical liberties like *Beverley, *Durham, and Tynemouth. Such sanctuaries as these latter certainly promoted social disorder in the later Middle Ages. At the Reformation the privilege of sanctuary was drastically curtailed. In 1540 *Henry VIII limited it to seven cities, viz. *Wells, *Westminster, Northampton, Manchester, *York, Derby and Launceston. A petition from Manchester against the nomination led to *Chester being substituted. By an act of *James I (1623), sanctuary for crime was finally abolished altogether, though it lingered on for civil processes until 1723.

S. Pegge, 'A Sketch of the History of the Asylum, or Sanctuary, from its Origin to the Final Abolition of it in the Reign of James I' in *Archaeologia*, viii (1787), pp. 1–44. N. M. Trenholme, *The Right of Sanctuary in England* (University of Missouri Studies, vol. i, No. 5; 1903). J. C. Cox, *The Sanctuaries and Sanctuary Seekers of Mediaeval England* (1911). G. Le Bras in *D.H.G.E.*, iv (1930), cols. 1035–47, s.v. 'Asile'; E. Herman and L. R. Misserey in *Dictionnaire de droit canonique*, i (1935), cols. 1084–9 and 1089–1104, s.vv. 'Asile dans l'Église orientale (Le Droit de)' and 'Asile en Occident' respectively, all with detailed bibl.

SANCTUS. The hymn of adoration which follows the *Preface in the *Eucharist and begins with the words 'Holy, Holy, Holy'. It is probably referred to by St. *Clement of Rome (1 Cor. 34. 6 f.) and *Origen (Hom. in Is. 1. 2). Based on the Lat. of the medieval rite, it runs in the BCP 'Holy, Holy, Holy, Lord God of Hosts; Heaven and Earth are full of Thy Glory; Glory be to Thee, O Lord, Most High'. The words of the '*Benedictus qui venit' (i.e. 'Blessed is He that cometh in the name of the Lord, Hosanna in the Highest'), which completed it, were omitted in the 1552 and subsequent English Prayer Books. Originally it was not separated from the *canon which follows immediately afterwards (in the BCP, the Prayer of *Humble Access has been interpolated at this point); but the practice of the congregation and choir joining in the words of the Sanctus led to a division here and the canon proper has come to be looked on as a separate item. At *High Mass, the *deacon and *subdeacon commonly go up to the altar for the Sanctus and, standing respectively on the right and left of the celebrant, say it in a low voice with him while the choir are engaged in singing it.

A. *Baumstark, 'Trishagion und Qeduscha' in *J.L.W.*, iii (1923), pp. 18–32. Jungmann, *M.S.*, ii (ed. 1952), pp. 161–173, with reff. to ancient lit. and further bibl. A. *Fortescue in *C.E.*, xiii (1912), p. 432–4, s.v.

SANCTUS BELL. See *Sacring Bell*.

SANCTUS CANDLE. The rubrics of the *Roman Missal require that at the Epistle side of the altar an additional candle be lighted at the *Sanctus, and that it be left burning until after the Communion. The custom seems to have originated at the end of the Middle Ages; but, despite the rubric, it is not generally observed in modern times. It is in use, however, among the *Dominicans.

SANDALS, Episcopal. The low shoes with leather soles and the upper part of embroidery which are worn by bishops in the W. Church exclusively at solemn Pontifical Masses and other functions (e.g. Ordination) performed during them. Except in Rome they are usually adorned with a small cross. Their use goes back certainly to the 5th cent. Liturgical stockings ('*caligae*'), now of the liturgical colour of the day, are also worn with them.

Braun, *L.G.*, pp. 384-424. J. Braun, S.J., in *C.E.*, xiii (1912), p. 434 f., s.v.

SANDAY, WILLIAM (1843-1920), English NT scholar. He was educated at Repton, and at Balliol and Corpus Christi Colleges, Oxford. In 1876 he was appointed principal of Hatfield Hall, Durham, and in 1882 recalled to Oxford as Dean Ireland's professor of exegesis, where he remained for the rest of his life. From 1895 to 1919 he was Lady Margaret professor of divinity. Hesitant in decision, he warmly defended his convictions when once his mind had been made up; and his influence went far to winning Anglican clergy to the acceptance of modern methods of NT study. Though his long projected Life of Christ was never achieved, the plan bore fruit in a large number of books conceived as subsidiary studies. Among his writings are *The Authorship and Historical Character of the Fourth Gospel* (1872); *The Gospels in the Second Century* (1876); *Inspiration* (*Bampton Lectures, 1893); *Commentary on Romans* (1895, in conjunction with A. C. *Headlam); *Outlines of the Life of Christ* (1905; reprinted from J. *Hastings' *Dictionary of the Bible*); *Christologies, Ancient and Modern* (1910); and *Oxford Studies in the Synoptic Problem* (in conjunction with other Oxford scholars, 1911); *Novum Testamentum S. Irenaei* (in collaboration with C. H. *Turner and others, 1923).

Obituary notice by W. *Lock in *J.T.S.*, xxii (1921), pp. 97-104, with bibl. of his published works by A. Souter, pp. 193-205. C. H. Turner in *D.N.B.*, *1912-1921*, pp. 482-4.

SANDEMANIANS. See *Glasites*.

SANDERS, NICHOLAS (c. 1530-81), RC controversialist and historian. Educated at Winchester and New College, Oxford, he graduated in 1551 and lectured on canon law. After the accession of *Elizabeth I he fled to the Continent (1559) and was ordained priest at Rome c. 1560. In 1561 he accompanied Cardinal S. *Hosius to the Council of *Trent and later on missions to Poland, Prussia, and Lithuania. In 1565 he went to Louvain, where he became professor of theology and, in connexion with the controversy aroused by Bp. J. *Jewel's *Apology*, published *The Supper of the Lord* (1565), *A Treatise of Images* (1566), *The Rock of the Church* (1567), and *De Visibili Monarchia Ecclesiae* (1571). The last of these, resuming the general ideas of St. *Augustine's *De Civitate Dei*, gives a comprehensive view of the Church from its first adumbrations at the beginnings of humanity and defends its monarchical government; it also throws much incidental light on the sufferings endured by RCs under Elizabeth. Called to Rome in 1572, he became consultor to *Gregory XIII on English affairs. In 1573 he went to Spain to induce *Philip II to make war on Elizabeth, and in 1579 he went to Ireland as Papal agent to cause an insurrection against the government. After two years of continual failure he died as a fugitive, probably of exhaustion. His unfinished work *De Origine ac Progressu Schismatis Anglicani* was edited by E. Rishton in 1585 and translated by D. Lewis in 1877. Though sharply criticized at the time, it is now admitted to be accurate in many of its controverted statements.

J. H. Pollen, S.J. (ed.), 'Dr. Nicholas Sanders' Report to Cardinal Moroni, n.d., ? May 1561' in *Catholic Record Society Miscellanea*, i (*Catholic Record Society, i; 1905), pp. 1-23, with Eng. tr. pp. 24-47. Id., 'Dr. Nicholas Sanders' in *E.H.R.*, vi (1891), pp. 36-47. T. M. Veech, *Dr. Nicholas Sanders and the English Reformation, 1530-81* (Université de Louvain, Recueil de Travaux publiés par les Membres des Conférences d'Histoire et de Philologie, Sér. 2, fasc. xxxii; 1935), with bibl. T. G. Law in *D.N.B.*, l (1897), pp. 259-62.

SANDERSON, ROBERT (1587-1663), Bp. of *Lincoln. Educated at Rotherham Grammar School and Lincoln College, Oxford, of which he became a Fellow in 1606, he was ordained in 1611 and held several livings, as well as prebendal stalls at Southwell and Lincoln. Gaining the favour of W. *Laud, he was appointed a royal chaplain in 1631 and Regius professor of divinity at Oxford in 1642. During the Civil War he was deprived of his professorship and for a time imprisoned. In 1660 he was reinstated and soon afterwards consecrated to the see of Lincoln. He took a leading part in the *Savoy Conference of 1661 and drafted the preface to the new (1662) Prayer Book. His best known work is his *Nine Cases of Conscience Occasionally Determined* (1678), one of the most notable contributions to moral theology in its age. His other writings include: *Logicae Artis Compendium* (1618); *De Juramenti Promissorii Obligatione* (lectures in 1646; publd. 1670); and *De Obligatione Conscientiae* (lectures in 1647; published 1660).

An Eng. tr. of Sanderson's *De Obligatione Conscientiae* by R. Codrington was also publd., London, 1660; ed. with Eng. comm. and abridged tr. by W. Whewell, Cambridge, 1851; Eng. tr. with preface by C. *Wordsworth, Lincoln, 1877. Collected ed. of his works by W. Jacobson (6 vols., Oxford, 1854), with repr. of the famous life by I. *Walton, orig. publd. London, 1678, in vol. vi, pp. 265-350. Modern study by G. Lewis ('English Theologians', ed. S. L. Ollard-N. Spens, London, 1924). J. H. Legge in *D.N.B.*, l (1897), p. 265 f., with further reff.

SANDYS, EDWIN (c. 1516-88), Abp. of *York. A graduate of St. John's College, Cambridge, he became master of St. Catharine's Hall in 1547, vicar of Caversham in 1548, canon of *Peterborough in 1549, and vice-chancellor of Cambridge university in 1553, in all these posts doing his utmost to further the principles of the English Reformation. A supporter of Lady Jane Grey, he was imprisoned in the Tower in July 1553, but eventually escaped to the Continent. On *Elizabeth I's accession he returned, and was appointed subsequently to the sees of *Worcester (1559), London (1570), and *York (1575). A fervent and learned opponent of Romanist practices, with personal leanings towards Puritanism, he came on several occasions into collision with his clergy. He was one of the translators of the *Bishops' Bible.

Sandys issued a collection of his sermons, London, 1585; ed. T. Whitaker (ib., 1812), with life, pp. i–lxiv; also ed., with other miscellaneous pieces, by J. Ayre (*Parker Society, 1841), with biographical introduction, pp. i–xxxii. Further letters in H. Robinson (ed.), *The Zürich Letters*, i (Parker Society, 1842), pp. 3–6, 72–5, 145 f., 264–6, 294–7, 311–13 and 331–3. W. A. J. Archbold in *D.N.B.*, l (1897), pp. 283–6.

SANHEDRIN. The supreme council and highest court of justice at *Jerusalem in NT times. The name is a Heb. form of the Gk. συνέδριον, 'council', though in Gk. sources the Sanhedrin is also designated by the words βουλή (*Josephus, *Bell. Jud.*, II, xvi, 5), γερουσία (Acts 5. 21) and πρεσβυτέριον (Lk. 22. 66, Acts 22. 5). Its origin is obscure, but it certainly goes back behind Roman times when it was given a definite place in the administration of Palestine. It consisted of 71 members (cf. Num. 11. 16). It was usually dominated by members of the priestly aristocracy, but it also included laymen, such as Scribes and *Pharisees, who were probably co-opted for life. The NT implies that it was presided over by the *High Priest (Mt. 26. 57, Acts 24. 1). Rabbinic sources, however, make no mention that such a position belonged to the High Priest and refer to its president by such expressions as 'the Head of the House of Justice'. The Sanhedrin dealt with the religious problems of the whole Jewish world, collected taxes, and acted as a civil court for Jerusalem. Having the right (prob.) to try capital cases (Josephus, *Antiq.*, XIV, ix, 3 f.; Mt. 26. 3 f., Acts 4. 5, 6. 12, 22. 30), it pronounced sentence of death on Christ. After the destruction of Jerusalem in A.D. 70, when it came to an end in its original form, some of its duties were taken over by the Pharisees at Jamnia and later at Tiberias.

Much information is contained in the Tractate 'Sanhedrin' of the *Mishnah (q.v.). E. *Schürer, *Geschichte des jüdischen Volkes im Zeitalter Jesu Christi*, ii (ed. 3, 1898), pp. 188–214. On the disputed right of the Sanhedrin to inflict the death-sentence, cf. U. Holzmeister, S.J., 'Zur Frage der Blutgerichtsbarkeit des Synedriums' in *Biblica*, xix (1938), pp. 43–59 and 151–74. W. Bacher in *H.D.B.*, iv (1902), cols. 397–402, s.v.; W. Kohler in *D.A.C.*, ii (1918), pp. 454–7, s.v.; U. Kahrstedt in *P.W.*, 2te Reihe, iv (pt. 2; 1932), cols. 1333–50, s.v. Συνέδριον; J. Schmid in *L.Th.K.*, ix (1937), cols. 940–3, s.v. 'Synedrium'.

SANKEY, IRA DAVID (1840–1908). See *Moody, Dwight Lyman*.

SANTA CLAUS. An American corruption of the Dutch form of St. *Nicholas, Bp. of Myra, widely venerated as the patron of children. The custom of making Christmas gifts in his name was introduced in America by the Dutch Protestants at New Amsterdam and thence into England. In some countries, e.g. parts of Germany, small presents are given to children on his feast day, 6 Dec.

SANTA MARIA MAGGIORE, Rome. The celebrated *basilica on the Esquiline Hill was founded by Pope *Liberius (352–366). The present structure was erected under Sixtus III (432–40). Acc. to a medieval tradition, commemorated in the Feast of Our Lady of the Snows (5 Aug.), the site was indicated by the BVM, who one August night left her footprints in a miraculous fall of summer snow. Though smaller than the other early basilicas (Old St. Peter's, S. Paolo fuori le Mura, and the *Lateran), it is the largest of the eighty churches in Rome dedicated to our Lady. Among the treasures of the church are the reputed remains of parts of the manger in which Christ was born.

A. Valentini, *La patriarcale basilica liberiana illustrata* (Rome, 1839). E. Josi in *E.C.*, x (1953), cols. 1228–31, s.v. 'Roma. V: Topographia, vi. Le chiese mariane, 1', with full bibl. of modern literature, col. 1230 f. See also *Rome, Churches of*.

SANTA SOPHIA. The famous church at *Constantinople, dedicated to the 'Holy *Wisdom' (i.e. the Person of Christ), was built under *Justinian by Anthemius of Tralles and Isidore of Miletus between 532 and 537 and consecrated in 538. One of the most perfect examples of Byzantine architecture, its chief feature is the enormous dome, supported by piers, arches, and pendentives, and pierced by 40 windows, which crowns the basilica. In 1453 the church was converted into a mosque by the Turks, and the mosaics which adorned its interior were covered up and partly destroyed. They were restored in 1847–9 by the Italian architect Fossati and, since 1931, under American direction, esp. by T. Whittemore.

W. R. Lethaby–H. Swainson, *The Church of Sancta Sophia, Constantinople*. A Study of Byzantine Building (1894). E. M. Antoniades, Ἔκφρασις τῆς Ἁγίας Σοφίας (3 vols., Athens, 1907–9). V. R. Zaloziecky, *Die Sophienkirche in Konstantinopel und ihre Stellung in der abendländischen Architektur* (Studi di Antichità Cristiana, xii; 1936). A. M. Schneider, *Die Hagia Sophia zu Konstantinopel* (Bilderhefte Antiker Kunst herausgegeben vom Archäologischen Institut des Deutschen Reiches, vi; [1938]). T. Whittemore, *The Mosaics of St. Sophia at Istanbul* (Byzantine Institute, 4 vols., 1933–52). See also works cited under *Constantinople*.

SANTIAGO DE COMPOSTELA. See *Compostela*.

SARABAITES. A name, of doubtful derivation, given in the early Church to a class of ascetics who dwelt either in their own houses or in small groups near cities and acknowledged no monastic superior. Their mode of life seems to have been regarded with disfavour, notably by St. *Benedict, who refers to them adversely in the first chapter of his rule.

Comm. on rule of St. Benedict (q.v.), esp. that by P. Delatte, O.S.B. (Eng. tr., 1921), pp. 30–2. J. *Bingham, *Origines Ecclesiasticae*, VII, ii, 4.

SARACENS (Lat. *Saracenus*, from Gk. Σαρακηνός, perh. from Arabic *Sharqi*, 'an oriental'). A word used by medieval writers of the Arabs generally and later applied to the infidel and Mohammedan nations against whom the crusaders fought. In his *De Haeresibus Compendium*, 101 (*PG*, xciv, 764 AB) St. *John of Damascus identifies the Saracens with the Ishmaelites, giving a curious etymology as though the word were Σάρρας κένοι, i.e., the descendants of Hagar the Ishmaelite whom *Sarah* sent away *empty*. The term was not used by the Mohammedans themselves. See *Islam*.

SARAPION, St. See *Serapion, St.*

SARAVIA, HADRIAN à (1531–1613), Protestant divine. Born at Hesdin in Artois of Hispano-Flemish Protestant parents, he became pastor at Antwerp, where he assisted in the drafting of the *Belgic Confession (1561). The religious disturbances in the Low Countries having compelled him to transfer his residence to the *Channel Islands, he here acted as assistant minister at St. Peter's, Guernsey. Later he became master of the Grammar School at Southampton, and then returned to Holland, where he was made professor of divinity at *Leyden. In 1585 he again left the Low Countries for England, was appointed rector of Tattenhill (1588), and in 1591 he became a prebendary of *Gloucester. From now onwards he was a zealous champion of episcopacy, esp. in his *De Diversis Gradibus Ministrorum Evangelii* (1590), which led to a controversy with T. *Beza. Incidentally the book was among the earliest Protestant writings to stress the claims of the heathen on the preaching of the Gospel. In 1595 Saravia became vicar of Lewisham and in 1610 of Great Chart. A cultured and studious man, he was a close friend of R. *Hooker and I. *Casaubon. He was also one of the translators of the AV of the Bible.

A Collection of some of his writings was publ. as *Diversi Tractatus Theologici* (London, 1611). His treatise, *De Sacra Eucharistia*, ed. with Eng. tr. by G. A. *Denison (1855), with notes on the author, pp. vii–xxviii. G. W. Sprott in *D.N.B.*, l (1897), pp. 299–301, s.v., with reff.

SARCOPHAGUS. Sarcophagi, i.e. stone coffins, usually adorned with bas-reliefs, were much used down to the Byzantine period for the burial of both pagans and Christians. Till a late date Christians continued to adorn them with pagan designs; but from the 4th cent. Christian designs also became common. The Christian subjects illustrated were, however, strictly limited in number, the most popular being *Jonah and the whale, *Moses striking the rock, the apprehension of *Peter, and one or two of our Lord's miracles. Most of the extant Christian sarcophagi are to be found in Italy, esp. in the *Lateran Museum and at *Ravenna. There are also many at *Arles.

G. Wilpert, *I sarcofagi cristiani antichi* (3 vols., bound in 5, 1929–36).

SARDICA, Council of (mod. Sofia). A Council summoned *c.* 343 by the Emps. *Constans and Constantius principally to settle the orthodoxy of St. *Athanasius. It was intended that it should be an Oecumenical Council, but the E. bishops on arrival refused to attend on the ground that Athanasius, whom the E. had deposed, was being regarded by the W. as a proper member of the synod. The W. bishops therefore met by themselves, under the presidency of *Hosius of Cordova. They confirmed the restoration of Athanasius, acquitted *Marcellus of Ancyra of heresy, and restored Asclepas, Bp. of Gaza, who had been deposed by a Synod of *Antioch. The Council is famous for the disciplinary canons which it passed, chief among which are the provisions constituting the Bp. of Rome a court of appeal for accused bishops in certain circumstances. The canons of Sardica were at one time held to be canons of *Nicaea and were quoted as such by Pope *Zosimus in a letter sent in 418 to a Council of *Carthage.

The documents connected with the Council, incl. the text of the canons (both Gk. and Lat. versions), will be found in Hardouin, i, cols. 635–84, and Mansi, iii (Florence, 1759), cols. 1–140. Convenient ed. of canons only in Lauchert, pp. 51–72. Critical ed. of Lat. text of canons [incl. Gk. text in parallel column] in *E.O.M.I.A.*, I, ii, 3 (1930), pp. 441–560. Hefele–Leclercq, i (pt. 2; 1907), pp. 733–823. J. *Friedrich's criticism of the authenticity of the canons was decisively answered by C. H. *Turner, 'The Genuineness of the Sardican Canons', in *J.T.S.*, iii (1902), pp. 370–97. On the disputed question on the original language of the canons, cf. G. R. von Hankiewicz, 'Die Kanones von Sardika. Ihre Echtheit und ursprüngliche Gestalt' in *Zeitschrift der Savigny-Stiftung für Rechtsgeschichte*, xxxiii (Kan. Abt., ii; 1912), pp. 44–99 [argues Gk. text original], and E. *Schwartz, 'Der griechische Text der Kanones von Serdika in *Z.N.T.W.*, xxx (1931), pp. 1–35 [Lat. original]. On the Sardican Creed, F. *Loofs, *Das Glaubensbekenntnis der Homousianer von Sardika* (*Abh.* (Berl.), 1909, Hft. 1). On the Sardican encyclicals, J. Zeiller, 'Donatisme et arianisme. La Falsification donatiste des documents du concile arien de Sardique' in *Académie des Inscriptions et Belles-Lettres. Comptes-Rendus des séances de l'année 1933* (1933), pp. 65–73; I. Gelzer, 'Das Rundschreiben der Synode von Serdika' in *Z.N.T.W.*, xl (1941), pp. 1–24. H. Hess, *The Canons of the Council of Sardica, A.D. 343* (Oxford, 1958). G. Bardy in Fliche–Martin, iii (1936), pp. 123–30. Id. in *D.T.C.*, xiv (pt. 1; 1939), cols. 1109–14, s.v. 'Sardique (Concile de)'.

SARPI, PAOLO (1552–1623), **Fra Paolo**, *Servite theologian. A native of *Venice, he entered the Servite Order in 1565 or 1566, and was elected Provincial in 1579. From 1585 to 1588 he was Procurator-General. His relations with leading Protestants aroused the suspicion of the Curia, which opposed several times his appointment to an episcopal see. In the struggle between Venice and *Paul V (1606–7) he defended the interests of the Republic, which appointed him its theological consultor in 1606. Largely owing to his influence the interdict placed on Venice remained without effect, and his violent anti-Papal activities resulted in his excommunication in 1607. In the same year an abortive attempt to murder him was made, possibly by his ecclesiastical enemies. Despite his excommunication he remained theological counsellor to the Republic and exercised his priestly functions until his death. His most important work is the *Istoria del Concilio Tridentino* first published, in English, at London in 1619, under the name of 'Pietro Soave Polan' (an anagram of 'Paolo Sarpi Veneto'). It is based on much authentic material but, lacking in objectivity, it represents the Council as being solely a conspiracy against the reform of the Church. Sarpi's general attitude favoured the Protestants, and he was also keenly interested in the new scientific movement.

Works collected in 5 vols., bound in 6 (Venice, 1677), with life by Fulgentio Micanzio, Ord. Serv. (orig. publd. Leyden, 1646) in vol. i, pp. 1–326; standard ed. 8 vols. (Helmstadt-Verona, 1761–8); modern ed. by M. D. Busnelli-G. Gambarin–R. Amerio . . . in the series 'Scrittori d' Italia' (Bari, 1931 ff.). A. Bianchi-Giovini, *Biografia di Frà Paolo Sarpi* (2 vols., Brussels, 1836); P. de Balan, *Frà Paolo Sarpi* (Venice, 1887). Arabella G. Campbell, *The Life of Fra Paolo Sarpi* (1869); A. Robertson, *Fra Paolo Sarpi, the Greatest of the Venetians* [1894]. F. A. Yates, 'Paolo Sarpi's "History of the Council of Trent"' in *Journal of the Warburg and Courtauld Institutes*, vii (1944), pp. 123–44. P. Tschackert in *P.R.E.* (ed. 3), xvii (1906), pp. 486–8, s.v.; E. Amann in *D.T.C.*, xiv (pt. 1; 1939), cols. 1115–21, s.v.; H. Jedin in *E.C.*, x (1953), col. 1928 f., s.v., with further bibl.

SARTRE, JEAN PAUL. See *Existentialism*.

SARUM; SARUM RITE. See *Salisbury; Salisbury, Use of.*

SATAN. In the Hebrew-Christian tradition, the supreme embodiment of evil, also the *Devil (q.v.). The word is from the Heb. שָׂטָן (satan), 'adversary', esp. one who plots against another. In the OT it is used of an angelic being hostile to God, esp. in the later Books (Job, Chr., Zech., Ps. 119). The older form of the word 'Satanas' (Gk. Σατανᾶς), usual in the Greek NT and the *Vulgate, is found in J. *Wycliffe, but was abandoned in the English Bible from W. *Tyndale onwards.

SATIS COGNITUM. The encyclical issued by Pope *Leo XIII on 29 June 1896, on the subject of religious unity. While professing an ardent desire for the reunion of Christendom, it insisted that it was possible only on the basis that the Pope was recognized as the sole source of jurisdiction in the Church and hence the necessary centre of unity. The bull '*Apostolicae Curae' (13 Sept.), pronouncing *Anglican Ordinations invalid, followed shortly afterwards.

The text is in *Leonis Papae XIII Allocutiones, Epistolae, Constitutiones*, vi (1900), pp. 156–89. Critique in E. Denny, *Papalism*. The Claims of the Papacy as set forth in the Encyclical *Satis Cognitum* (1912).

SATISFACTION. An act of reparation for an injury committed. In Christian theology it is usually applied to the payment of a penalty due to God on account of sin. St. *Anselm first gave the term theological currency in reference to the *Atonement (q.v.) by interpreting Christ's death as a sufficient vicarious satisfaction for the sins of the world, which was possible because of the sinlessness of His human nature and its hypostatic union with the Second Person of the Trinity.

In Catholic moral theology satisfaction is

held to be a necessary element of the virtue and sacrament of penance, in addition to contrition and confession. The term was used by *Tertullian and *Cyprian of the reparation made for sin by fasting, almsgiving, and other good works, which were already in Scripture regarded as means of averting Divine punishment (cf. Dan. 4. 27, Lk. 16. 9). It became part of the penitential practice of the early Church which enjoined such works before giving absolution. With the gradual attenuation of penances and the practice of giving absolution before satisfaction was made, the distinction between the forgiveness of the fault and the satisfaction due to it after forgiveness was worked out more clearly, the classical example, adduced by St. *Augustine, being the penance inflicted on David after Nathan had pronounced God's forgiveness (2 Sam. 12. 13, 14). Thus *satisfactio operis* came to be regarded as a necessary means of avoiding punishment in purgatory after the sin itself had been remitted by sacramental absolution, and this doctrine, which had been repeatedly formulated by *Peter Lombard and the later Schoolmen, was defended by the Council of *Trent.

On non-Christian conceptions, L. Vannicelli, O.F.M., in *E.C.*, xi (1953), cols. 884–7, s.v. 'Soddisfazione (nella etnologia)', with bibl. On its place in the Christian Sacrament of Penance, cf. St. *Thomas Aquinas, *Summa Theologica*, Suppl. qqu. 12–15. Also R. S. Franks in *H.E.R.E.*, xi (1920), pp. 207–210, s.v.; P. Galtier, S.J., in *D.T.C.*, xiv (pt. 1; 1939), cols. 1129–210, s.v. See also bibl. to *Penance*.

SATORNILUS. See *Saturninus*.

SATURDAY. The Jewish '*Sabbath' (q.v.) and the day of the week on which Christ's body rested in the tomb. In the W., Saturday was observed as a fast day as early as the 3rd cent., but never so in the E. The reason of the fasting was probably the extension of the Friday fast (*superponere jejunium*) which was subsequently reduced to a semi-fast on both days. In modern times the Saturday fast, except during *Lent and on the *Ember Days, became more and more restricted to Italy and Rome, where it was eventually abolished in 1918. Down to the 5th cent. Mass was not celebrated on that day at Rome and Alexandria, nor apparently elsewhere in the W. In most of the E. Church, on the other hand, the opposition to Judaism led it to be distinguished from the 4th cent. onwards by the celebration of the Liturgy, which in Lent is still confined to Saturday and Sunday.

The special connexion of Saturday with Our Lady is a medieval development. Usually mystical reasons are given for it, such as the Sabbath rest of the Word in Mary. It finds liturgical expression in the recitation of the 'Office of Our Lady' on Saturday, a practice supposed to have been introduced by *Urban II at the Council of Clermont in 1096. In the pre-Tridentine MS. breviaries this office (*Officium BMV in Sabbato*) was said in addition to the ferial office; the present custom, acc. to which it is said instead of the ferial office on all Saturdays throughout the year on which there occurs no feast above the rank of a simple, no day within an Octave, and no privileged feria (Advent, Lent, Vigils, Ember days), is due to *Pius V and *Clement VIII.

SATURDAY, Holy. See *Holy Saturday.*

SATURNINUS (2nd cent.), also 'Satornilus', Syrian *Gnostic. Apparently the only authority is St. *Irenaeus (*Haer.* I, xxii), on whom later references to this heretic (*Hippolytus, *Philosoph.*, vii. 28; Ps.-*Tertullian, *Praescr.*, 3; *Epiphanius, *Haer.*, 23; *Philaster, *Haer.*, 31; &c.) depend. He is said to have been a pupil of Menander, the Samaritan heretic (himself the disciple of *Simon Magus), and to have taught in *Antioch. He held that the origin of things was to be sought in a Father unknown to all, who created a series of angels and other supernatural beings who in turn created man. As originally formed, man was a powerless entity who wriggled on the ground like a worm (ὡς σκώληκος σκαρίζοντος) until a Divine spark set him on his feet. The God of the Jews was one of the creator angels, and the Supreme Father sent the Saviour to destroy this God and to redeem such as were endowed with the Divine spark. These fantastic cosmological speculations have close affinities with those of *Ophites with which are doubtless historically linked. In ethics Saturninus rejected marriage and the use of animal food.

G. *Salmon in *D.C.B.*, iv (1887), p. 587 f., s.v.; R. Liechtenhan in *P.R.E.* (ed. 3), xvii (1906), p. 491 f., s.v. 'Satornil'; G. Bardy in *D.T.C.*, xiv (pt. 1; 1939), col. 1310 f., s.v. 'Satornil'. See also bibl. to *Gnosticism.*

SATYRUS, St. (d. 375 or 377). Elder brother of St. *Ambrose, whose household and property he administered. He was evidently a much-loved and gentle character. When Satyrus died, Ambrose preached the funeral oration 'De Excessu Fratris'. Feast day, 17 Sept.

St. Ambrose's 'De Excessu Fratris' is repr. in J. P. Migne, *PL*, xvi, 1289-354.

SAUMAISE, CLAUDE. See *Salmasius, Claudius.*

SAVA, St. (c. 1176-1235), also Sabas, patron of Serbia. Rastko was the third son of Stephen Nemanya, founder of a strong Serbian dynasty who united the Serbs into a nation. In 1191 he secretly went to Mt. *Athos, where he became a monk under the name of Sava. In 1196 his father followed him after abdicating in favour of Sava's elder brother, Stephen. Here on Mt. Athos father and son founded the Serbian monastery of Hilandar which became the centre of Serbian culture in the Middle Ages. In 1208 Sava returned to Serbia, where, as archimandrite of the monastery of Studenica, he took an active part in the political and

religious life of the country. He opposed his brother's policy, who, in 1216, had himself crowned king with the help of the Pope, and, in 1219, he succeeded in establishing an independent Serbian Church, of which he was consecrated the first archbishop by the Patr. of Nicaea. He organized the Church by establishing several bishoprics, devoted himself to the education of the country, and built and embellished many churches. In 1229 he made a pilgrimage to Palestine, and in 1233 went there again to obtain the recognition of the Bulgarian patriarch from those of Alexandria, Jerusalem, and Antioch. He died on his way back in Tirnovo in Bulgaria. Feast day in the Serbian Church, 14 Jan.

J. T. Marnavitius in *AA.SS.*, Jan. I (1647), pp. 979-83. Brief modern account in English by A. *Butler, *The Lives of the Saints* (ed. H. Thurston, S.J.), i (1926), p. 181. J. Turk in *L.Th.K.*, ix (1937), col. 198, with bibl. (mainly Eastern European).

SAVIGNY, Abbey of, Normandy (dept. Manche). In 1105 Vitalis of Mortain, a canon of the collegiate church of St.-Évroul, established a hermitage in the Forest of Savigny. After a time some of the hermits felt a call to follow the *Benedictine Rule in its primitive strictness and Vitalis obtained from Rudolf, Count of Fougères, some grants of land. The new house, which in its customs kept some distinctive practices, e.g. the wearing of grey habits, rose to high repute, esp. under the Abbots Geoffrey (1122-38) and Serlon (1140-1153); and daughter monasteries were founded in France (*La Trappe), England (Furness, Quarr), Ireland, and elsewhere. In 1147, Serlon integrated the houses into the *Cistercian Order (confirmed by Pope *Eugenius III, 10 Apr. 1148), though they continued to retain certain peculiarities. In the later Middle Ages the orig. Abbey of Savigny declined and community life finally came to an end during the French Revolution.

C. Auvray, O.S.B., *Histoire de la congrégation de Savigny*, ed. A. Laveille (3 vols., Rouen, 1896-8). L. Guilloreau, O.S.B., 'Les Fondations anglaises de l'abbaye de Savigny' in *Revue Mabillon*, v (1909), pp. 290-335. L. H. Cottineau, O.S.B., *Répertoire topo-bibliographique des abbayes et prieurés* (Mâcon, 1935), cols. 2965-7, with full bibl. E. M. Obrecht, O.C.R., in *C.E.*, xiii (1912), p. 489, s.v.

SAVILE, HENRY (1549-1622), Warden of Merton College, Oxford, and Provost of Eton. He was educated at Brasenose College, became a Fellow of Merton in 1565, and soon acquired a wide reputation as a Greek scholar, mathematician, historian, and antiquarian. In 1578 he travelled in Europe, collecting MSS., and on his return was appointed Greek tutor to Queen *Elizabeth I. In 1585 he was elected Warden of Merton, which greatly flourished under his rule. In 1596 he asked for, and obtained from the Queen, the provostship of Eton, although, not being in holy orders, he was not qualified under the statutes. In 1604 he was named as one of the scholars appointed to prepare the AV of the Bible. In 1610-13 he published in 8 folio vols. his celebrated edition of the works of St. *Chrysostom, based on a collation of the best available MSS. and earlier editions, and still of great value for determining the correct text of many of St. Chrysostom's treatises. It was printed at Savile's private press at Eton, at his own charges (£8,000), in type imported from Holland. He also helped in the foundation of the *Bodleian Library, to which he afterwards presented many MSS. and printed books; and he founded at Oxford professorships of geometry and astronomy.

W. Carr in *D.N.B.*, 1 (1897), pp. 367-70, s.v., with reff.

SAVONAROLA, GIROLAMO (1452-98), Italian preacher and reformer. Educated at Ferrara, he entered the *Dominican Order at *Bologna in 1474, where from the first he led a life of fervent asceticism. In 1482 he moved to the priory of San Marco at Florence, and here attracted great attention as a preacher by his passionate denunciations of the immorality of the Florentines and of the contemporary clergy. Believing himself inspired, he prophesied on the future of the Church and on other subjects, often in apocalyptic language. Elected prior in 1491, he slighted Lorenzo the Magnificent whose end he predicted accurately, supported Charles VIII of France, in whom he saw the instrument of God for the reform of the Church, during his Italian campaign in 1494-5, and established a kind of theocratic democracy in Florence. The principles of this government, which included a thorough moral reform of the city, are laid down in his 'Rule and Government of the City of Florence'. His severity, however, made him many enemies, and in 1495 *Alexander VI summoned him to Rome to give an account of his prophecies. As he refused to leave Florence on grounds of health and personal danger, the Pope forbade him to preach; and when Savonarola continued his attacks on the Curia and Alexander himself, he was excommunicated (1497). The friar, believing himself directly charged by God and therefore entitled to disobey ecclesiastical authority, disregarded the excommunication and demanded a General Council which should depose the Pope. His position, however, was already shaken by the hostility of many citizens and other religious orders, esp. the *Franciscans, one of whom proposed an ordeal by fire between himself and one of Savonarola's followers in order to disprove his prophecies. But the ordeal did not take place, and the people now turned against the Dominican and imprisoned him together with two of his brethren. Put to the torture, he confessed to have acted not by Divine inspiration but for personal motives, a confession which he soon retracted. He was hanged as a schismatic and heretic on the market-place of Florence. Among his many writings 'The Triumph of the Cross' is a remarkable apology of orthodox Catholicism. His theological treatises follow the lines of Thomist doctrine. His character has been variously judged. Whilst he has sometimes been venerated almost as a saint, e.g. by St. *Catherine dei Ricci, others would see in him only a fanatic.

Modern edd. of various of his Sermons by G. Baccini (Florence, 1889), P. Villari-E. Casanova (ib., 1898), F. Cognasso-R. Palmarocchi ('Documenti di Storia Italiana', Perugia and Venice, 3 vols. bound in 4, 1930-5) and of his letters by R. Ridolfi (Florence, 1933). Anthology ed. M. Ferrara, *Predichi e scritti* (Milan, 1930). 16th cent. life attributed to P. Burlamacchi ed. R. Ridolfi (Florence, 1937). F. T. Perrens, *Jérôme Savonarola, sa vie, ses prédications, ses écrits* [c. 1853]; R. R. Madden, *The Life and Martyrdom of Savonarola, Illustrative of the History of Church and State* (2 vols., 1853). P. Villari, *La storia di Girolamo Savonarola e de' suoi tempi* (2 vols., 1859-61; Eng. tr., 1863); J. Schnitzer, *Quellen und Forschungen zur Geschichte Savonarolas* (4 vols., 1902-10). P. Misciattelli, *Savonarola* (1925; Eng. tr., 1929). R. Rudolfi, *Studi savonaroliani* (1935); id., *Vita di Girolamo Savonarola* (2 vols., 1952). M. Ferrara, *Savonarola* (2 vols., 1952).

SAVOY CONFERENCE, The. The conference which sat by royal warrant, dated 25 March 1661, at the Savoy in the Strand from 15 April until 24 July 1661, to review the BCP. It consisted of twelve bishops, twelve presbyterian divines, and nine assessors from each party. The Presbyterians vainly hoped to gain concessions which would enable them to remain members of the Established Church. The bishops, led by G. *Sheldon, Bp. of London (though Accepted Frewen, Abp. of York, was nominal president), ignored R. *Baxter's alternative service-book and his appeal that ministers not episcopally ordained should not be required to seek reordination. In reply to the Presbyterian *Exceptions (q.v.) to the BCP, the bishops made only 17 trivial concessions, 15 of which were embodied in the BCP of 1662. The Presbyterians could not accept the 1662 Book and about 2000 were deprived of their livings.

Proceedings of the Commission for the Revision of the Book of Common Prayer (1661). E. *Cardwell, *A History of Conferences and other Proceedings connected with the Revision of the Book of Common Prayer from the Year 1558 to the Year 1690* (1840), chs. vi and vii. R. Baxter, *A Petition for Peace* (1661). F. E. *Brightman in *D.E.C.H.*, pp. 548-50, s.v.

SAVOY DECLARATION, The. A statement of *Congregational principles and polity of a moderate type, drawn up at a Conference held at the Chapel of the old Savoy Palace in 1658 by representatives of 120 churches. It consists of a Preface, a Confession of Faith closely akin to the *Westminster Confession, and a Platform of Discipline. The first is largely an apology for the divisions of the Reformed Churches as contrasted with the 'dull and stupid peace' of the Church of Rome and a plea for toleration of the Congregational form of Church government side by side with Presbyterianism. The second professes the modified *Calvinism of the Westminster Confession, with a few alterations, e.g. rejecting the power of civil authority to punish heresy. The third part, which treats of the Institution of Churches, declares that all necessary power is vested in each individual Church and repudiates the institution, by Christ, of a wider organization.

Text repr. in P. *Schaff, *A History of the Creeds*, iii (1877), pp. 707-29, with introd. in vol. i (1877), pp. 829-33. See also works cited under *Congregationalism*.

SAWTREY, WILLIAM (d. 1401), *Lollard. As a priest at Lynn, Norfolk, he was summoned before his bishop in 1399, to answer charges of heresy; and after ministering in London, he was charged before Abp. T. *Arundel in 1401 with heresies concerning the adoration of the cross, *transubstantiation, and other matters. He appealed to the King in Parliament, and also made a defence from the NT and St. *Augustine. On the ground that he had relapsed into heresies which he had abjured in 1399, he was burned, being the first to suffer under the statute '*De Haeretico Comburendo'.

A. M. Cooke in *D.N.B.*, l (1897), p. 380 f.

SAXA RUBRA, Battle of. See *Milvian Bridge, Battle of the.*

SAXON CONFESSION, The (1551). The Protestant Confession of Faith drawn up in 1551 by P. *Melanchthon at the Emperor's request for the Council of *Trent. It followed the main lines of the *Augsburg Confession of 1530 but, with all hope of reconciliation between Catholic and Protestant over, was less conciliatory. The distinctive Protestant doctrines were elaborated round the two Articles in the *Apostles' Creed on the forgiveness of sins and the Church. The former article was held to exclude merit and justification by works, the latter to prove the Church to be a spiritual though visible communion of believers in Christ. The sacramental character of the Eucharistic gifts was asserted to be confined to their use in the service. Unlike the Augsburg Confession, the Saxon Confession bore the signatures of theologians only, among them, besides Melanchthon himself, J. *Bugenhagen and G. *Major.

Lat. and Germ. texts pr. among P. Melanchthon's collected works ed. E. H. Bindseil, xxviii (Corpus Reformatorum, xxviii; Brunswick, 1860), cols. 369–568, with introd. cols. 327–68. Lat. text only also pr. in *Sylloge Confessionum sub Tempus Reformandae Ecclesiae Editarum* (Oxford, 1804), pp. 199–287. P. *Schaff, *A History of the Creeds of Christendom*, i (1877), pp. 340–3.

SAYCE, ARCHIBALD HENRY (1845–1933), English oriental scholar. He was elected Fellow of Queen's College, Oxford, in 1869, and from 1891 to 1915 was professor of Assyriology at Oxford. He was a member of the company which produced the RV of the OT. After 1885 he was almost wholly absorbed in the history of religion, particularly of Egypt, Babylon, and Israel, and in this connexion he travelled and explored extensively in the E. His many publications included works on the Hittites, Hebrews, Assyrians, Babylonians, and Egyptians. In several of them, notably *The 'Higher Criticism' and the Verdict of the Monuments* (1894), he defended the Mosaic authorship of the *Pentateuch.

A. H. Sayce, *Reminiscences* (1923). B. Gunn in *D.N.B.*, *1931–1940*, pp. 786–8.

SAYINGS OF JESUS, The. Two series of sayings ('Logia', λόγυα) ascribed to Christ which were found among the *Oxyrhynchus Papyri (Nos. 1, 654). When first published in 1897 and 1904 respectively, they were believed to stand in close relation to the canonical Gospels, and it was even suggested that they were part of the supposed lost common source of Mt. and Lk. known to NT scholars as '*Q'. Subsequent study has tended to show that they are derived from an apocryphal work, probably of *Gnostic provenance, and/or from the 'Gospel acc. to the *Hebrews' (q.v.). See also *Thomas, Coptic Gospel of St.*

B. P. Grenfell–A. S. Hunt, ΛΟΓΙΑ ΙΗΣΟΥ, *Sayings of Our Lord from an early Greek Papyrus* (1897); id., *New Sayings of Jesus and Fragments of a Lost Gospel* (1904); H. G. Evelyn White, *The Sayings of Jesus* (1920).

SAYINGS OF THE JEWISH FATHERS, The. See *Pirqe Aboth.*

SCALA SANCTA (also known as the **Scala Pilati**). A staircase of twenty-eight Tyrian marble steps near the *Lateran church at *Rome. Tradition affirms that they were the steps descended by Christ after His condemnation to death and brought to the W. by St. *Helena from the palace of *Pilate in *Jerusalem. Now covered with wood, they are a popular place of *pilgrimage in Rome, pilgrims making the ascent on their knees. At the top of the steps is the 'Sancta Sanctorum' chapel (1278), the only surviving piece of the old Lateran Palace.

H. Thurston, S.J., *The Holy Year of Jubilee* (1900), pp. 185–91, with full reff. L. Oliger, O.F.M., in *C.E.*, xiii (1912), p. 505 f., s.v.

SCALIGER, JOSEPH JUSTUS (1540–1609), French scholar. He was a native of Agen and studied Greek and oriental languages at Paris, where he became a *Calvinist in 1562. After travelling in Italy (1565) and England and Scotland (1566), between 1567 and 1570 he fought on the side of the *Huguenots. From 1572 to 1574 he was professor at *Geneva. The following years he spent in private research until, in 1593, he became the successor of J. Lipsius at *Leyden university, which he made a European centre of philological studies though he did not lecture himself. His editions of Latin authors such as Festus (1575), Catullus, Tibullus, Propertius (1577), and others were a new departure in the field of textual criticism. His greatest claim to fame, however, is his *De Emendatione Temporum* (1583) by which he established the modern science of chronology, though his attacks on the newly introduced *Gregorian Calendar and on the genuineness of *Dionysius the Areopagite earned him the hostility of the *Jesuits. In 1606 followed the *Thesaurus Temporum* containing a brilliant partial reconstruction of the 'Chronicon' of *Eusebius of Caesarea. D. *Petavius's great work, *De Doctrina Temporum* (1627), directed against Scaliger whom it corrected, carried on his ideas.

The chief sources for his life are his *Epistolae* (Leyden, 1627) and his *Lettres françaises inédites* (ed. P. Tamizey de Larroque, Agen and Paris, 1879). *Autobiography of*

Joseph Scaliger. With autobiographical Selections from his Letters, his Testament and the Funeral Orations by Daniel Heinsius and Dominicus Baudius. Tr. . . . with introd. and notes by G. W. Robinson (Harvard Translations, Camb., Mass., 1927; good collection of material. 'Autobiography', however, very brief, on pp. 29–33). Life by J. Bernays (Berlin, 1855). [M. Pattison] 'J. J. Scaliger' in *Quarterly Review*, cviii (1860), pp. 34–81, review of J. Bernays's book; repr., with long extension from Pattison's MSS., in M. Pattison, *Essays*, i (1889), pp. 132–243. J. E. Sandys *History of Classical Scholarship*, ii (1908), pp. 199–204. R. C. Christie–J. E. Sandys in *E.B.* (ed. 11), xxiv (1911), pp. 284–6, s.v. 'Scaliger (2)'.

SCANDINAVIA, Christianity in. See *Denmark; Norway;* and *Sweden, Christianity in.*

SCAPULAR (Lat. *scapulare* from *scapulae,* 'shoulder-blades'). A short cloak consisting essentially of a piece of cloth worn over the shoulders and hanging down in front and behind. It is usually from 14 to 18 inches wide with its two ends reaching almost to the feet, and forms part of the regular monastic habit. The Rule of St. *Benedict (cap. 55) prescribes its use for the monks when engaged in manual labour and the rules of some religious orders require it to be worn also throughout the night. By a natural symbolism it is taken to denote the 'yoke of Christ' (*jugum Christi,* cf. Mt. 11. 29 f.). A vesture of very much smaller dimensions (known as 'the smaller scapular') is worn by persons living in the world who have become affiliated to the religious orders, e.g. *tertiaries. In the RC Church important privileges have been attached to wearing the smaller scapular.

Comms. on rule of St. Benedict (q.v.), esp. by P. Delatte, O.S.B. (Eng. tr., 1921), p. 349 f. P. Oppenheim, O.S.B., *Das Mönchskleid im christlichen Altertum* (R.Q. Supplementheft, xxviii; 1931), esp. pp. 139–42. P. E. Magennis, Ord. Carm., *The Scapular Devotion.* Origin, Legislation and Indulgences attached to the Scapular (Dublin, 1923). H. Thurston, S.J., 'Scapulars' in *The Month,* cxlix (1927), pp. 481–8, and cl (1927), pp. 44–58. J. Hilgers, S.J., in *C.E.,* xiii (1912), pp. 508–14, s.v.

SCARAMELLI, GIOVANNI BATTISTA (1687–1752), Italian spiritual writer. He entered the *Jesuit Order in 1706 and was ordained priest in 1717. From 1722 onwards he was chiefly engaged on giving missions and retreats in the Pontifical States. He expounded his spiritual teaching in three works *Direttorioascetico* (1752), *Discernimento de' spiriti* (1753), and *Direttorio mistico* (1754). In his Ascetic Directory, which has long been regarded as a classic, Scaramelli examines the nature of Christian perfection and the means of attaining it. His books were designed primarily for the use of spiritual directors.

Eng. tr. of *Direttorio ascetico* by W. Eyre (4 vols., Dublin, 1870; ed. 2, London, 1879–81). O. Marchetti, S.J., 'Un opera inedita su di una mistica del 700 attribuita al P. Scaramelli, S.J.' in *Archivum Historicum Societatis Jesu,* ii (1933), pp. 230–57. L. A. Hogue, S.J., 'The *Direttorio mistico* of J. B. Scaramelli, S.J.', ib., ix (1940), pp. 1–39. Sommervogel, vii, cols. 689–94 (incomplete). Pourrat, iv, 439–42. L. A. Hogue, S.J., in *D.T.C.,* xiv (pt. 1; 1939), cols. 1259–63, s.v.

SCETE. The south portion of the *Nitrian desert which lies to the west of the mouths of the Nile, celebrated in the 4th and 5th cents.

as a centre of monasticism. Among the most celebrated of its monks were Pambo and *Macarius the Egyptian.

H. *Leclercq, O.S.B., in *D.A.C.L.,* xv (pt. 1; 1950), cols. 994–1002.

SCHAFF, PHILIP (1819–93), German American theologian and Church historian. Born in Switzerland, he was educated at *Tübingen, Halle, and Berlin, and became professor first in the German Reformed Seminary at Mercersburg, Pennsylvania (1844), and later in *Union Theological Seminary, New York (1870). He saw through the press an immense body of theological literature. The most extensive of his original writings was his *History of the Christian Church* (12 vols., 1883–93), a popular work from the standpoint of Evangelical liberalism, hortatory rather than scientific in tone. He edited, among other compendious works, the *Religious Encyclopaedia* (3 vols., 1882–4), an American adaptation of J. J. *Herzog's *Realencyclopädie* (12 vols., 1908–12), and the sets of patristic translations known as the *Nicene and post-Nicene Fathers* (Series I, 28 vols., 1886–9; Series II, 14 vols., of varying merit, 1890–1900); and he compiled a valuable collection of credal documents in *The Creeds of Christendom* (3 vols., 1877). From 1870 he was president of the American committee which co-operated with the British committee responsible for the *Revised Version of the Bible. As an exponent of the 'Mercersburg Theology', he was closely associated in outlook with J. W. Nevin (q.v.).

David S. Schaff (son), *The Life of Philip Schaff* (New York, 1897). Id. in *P.R.E.* (ed. 3), xvii (1906), pp. 515–22, s.v. H. E. Starr in *Dict. Amer. Biog.,* xvi (1935), p. 417 f.

SCHEEBEN, MATTHIAS JOSEPH (1835–1888), German Catholic theologian. He was educated at the *Gregorian university in Rome (1852–9), ordained priest in 1858, and was professor of dogma at the seminary at *Cologne from 1860 to his death. Already in his first speculative work *Natur und Gnade* (1861), he outlined his doctrine of the supernatural, which he describes as a participation in the Being of God, and popularized this conception in *Die Herrlichkeiten der göttlichen Gnade* (1863, an independent version of a work of the 17th cent. author, E. Nieremberg), which had an immediate success and was translated into many languages. In his profound, though sometimes obscure, *Mysterien des Christenthums* (1865) he attempted to build up the whole organism of Christian doctrine, viewed as a supernatural cosmos with the mystery of the Blessed Trinity as its centre. In the following years his dogmatic work was interrupted by the controversies raised by the impending *Vatican Council, in which he took a vigorous part as one of the chief opponents of J. J. I. von *Döllinger and a passionate defender of Papal Infallibility. Between 1873 and 1887 he wrote his *Handbuch der katholischen Dogmatik,* a work of immense erudition, based on Thomist principles but also making extensive use of the Fathers as well as of modern theologians. Scheeben, whose influence on modern theology is still growing, stood for the rights of supernatural faith against the rationalist and naturalistic tendencies of 18th and 19th cent. theology which had been rife esp. in Germany and Austria.

Gesammelte Schriften, ed. J. Höfer (8 vols., Freiburg i.Br., 1941 ff.). Fr. tr. of part of his *Die Mysterien des Christentums* by A. Kerkvoorde, O.S.B., as *Le Mystère de l'Église* (Unam Sanctam, xv; 1946), with introd., pp. 5–75; full tr. (Paris [*c.* 1947]). J. Hertkens, *Professor M. J. Scheeben. Leben und Wirken eines katholischen Gelehrten im Dienste der Kirche* (1892). K. Feckes and others, *M. J. Scheeben* (1935). Eng. tr. of *Die Mysterien des Christentums* by C. Vollert, S.J. (St. Louis, Mo., 1946), and of *Natur und Gnade* by id. (ibid. and London, 1954). G. Fritz in *D.T.C.*, xiv (pt. 1; 1939), cols. 1270–4, s.v.; A. Piolanti in *E.C.*, xi (1953), col. 33 f., s.v., with further bibl.

SCHEFFLER, JOHANNES. See *Angelus Silesius.*

SCHELLING, FRIEDRICH WILHELM JOSEPH VON (1775–1854), German Idealist philosopher. He was the son of a Württemberg pastor and was educated at the *Tübingen Stift, where G. W. F. *Hegel was one of his elder contemporaries. From 1798 to 1803 he taught at Jena, where he was brought into close contact with the leaders of the *Romantic Movement, and from 1803 at the university of Würzburg. Difficulties with the government led him to retire to Munich in 1806. From 1820 to 1826 he lectured at Erlangen, and in 1827 he became professor at the newly founded university of Munich. In 1841 he was called to Berlin to counteract the influence of Hegel's disciples.

Schelling never elaborated a consistent philosophical system. His constantly changing views owed much to his vivid imagination and were also greatly influenced by current scientific doctrines which, however, he only imperfectly understood. In his early years he was under the influence of J. G. *Fichte and thus mediately of I. *Kant. In his first important work, *Vom Ich als Prinzip der Philosophie* (1795), he acknowledged only one reality, the infinite and absolute Ego, of which the universe was the expression. In his *Ideen zu einer Philosophie der Natur* (1797) and *Von der Weltseele* (1798), this abstract pantheism was modified in favour of his conception of 'Naturphilosophie', acc. to which nature was an absolute being which works unconsciously, though purposively. The problem of the relation of nature to spirit later gave rise to his 'Identitätsphilosophie', expounded esp. in *Darlegung des Systems der Philosophie* (1802) and *Bruno, oder über das göttliche und natürliche Prinzip der Dinge* (1802). Acc. to this philosophy, which shows strong traces of B. *Spinoza, both nature and spirit are but manifestations of one and the same being, absolute identity being the ground of all things. In his subsequent speculations he became more and more influenced by *Neoplatonist and *theosophist speculations, esp. by J. *Boehme. Thus in *Philosophie und Religion* (1804) he explained the universe as a Fall of the ideas into matter and redemption as a

return to the world of ideas. His attempt in *Philosophische Untersuchungen über das Wesen der menschlichen Freiheit* (1809) to reconcile Christianity with his philosophy was carried on later in his Berlin lectures (publd. 1856–8). Here he distinguished three elements in God: (1) the blind primeval necessary being; (2) the three potentialities of the Divine Essence, viz. unconscious will (material cause), rational will (efficient cause), and unity of the two (final cause of creation); (3) the Three Persons who evolve from the three potentialities by overcoming the primeval being. In the history of Christianity he also distinguished three periods, viz. the Petrine or Catholic, the Pauline or Protestant, and the Johannine or the Church of the future.

Schelling exercised a profound influence on German thought. His earlier teaching was the point of departure of Hegel's system, and many elements of his nature and religious philosophy were taken up and transformed by E. von *Hartmann.

Sämmtliche Werke collected and ed. by his son, K. F. A. von Schelling (14 vols., Stuttgart, 1856–61). His Munich lectures 'Zur Geschichte der neueren Philosophie' ed. A. *Drews (Leipzig, 1902). Correspondence, Speeches, &c., ed. O. Braun, Leipzig, 1908. Among the many studies of his system may be mentioned G. A. C. Frantz, *Schelling's Positive Philosophie* (3 vols., 1879–80); J. Watson, *Schelling's Transcendental Idealism* (1882); E. von Hartmann, *Schelling's Philosophisches System* (1897); H. Sueskind, *Der Einfluss Schellings auf die Entwicklung von Schleiermachers System* (1909); W. Metzger, *Die Epochen der Schellingschen Philosophie v. 1795–1802* (1911); E. Bréhier, *Schelling* ('Les Grands Philosophes', 1912). R. Kroner, *Von Kant bis Hegel*, i (1921), pp. 535–612, ii (1924), pp. 1–141. N. Hartmann, *Die Philosophie des deutschen Idealismus*, i (1923), pp. 122–186, with bibl. p. 279 f. H. Knittermeyer, *Schelling und die romantische Schule* (Geschichte der Philosophie in Einzeldarstellungen, Abt. vii: Die Philosophie der neuesten Zeit i.Band xxx–xxxi; 1929). Bibliography by J. Jost (Bonn, 1927). Überweg, iv, 35–67, with bibl. pp. 674–77. R. Adamson–J. M. Mitchell in *E.B.* (ed. 11), xxiv (1911), pp. 316–19.

SCHELSTRATE, EMMANUEL (1649–92), Belgian Church historian and canonist. A native of Antwerp, he early specialized in the study of Christian antiquities. Through his publications, in which he defended the rights of the Holy See, he attracted the attention of *Innocent XI, who made him Prefect of the *Vatican Library and later canon of the *Lateran and of St. Peter's. Among his writings are *Antiquitas Illustrata circa Concilia Generalia et Provincialia* (1678), in which he undertook to prove the antiquity of the Roman primacy, and the *Acta Constantiensis Concilii* (1683), defending the supremacy of the Pope over the Council against the *Gallican Articles of 1682. In the considerable controversy created by the latter, J. B. *Bossuet and A. *Arnauld took sides against the author. In the *De disciplina arcani* (1685) he developed the view that the 'discipline of the secret', i.e. the secrecy exacted by Christ, the Apostles and their successors, explained the relative weakness of the evidence for the doctrines of the Person of Christ and the Sacraments in the Primitive Church.

The primary authority for Schelstrate's life is the introd. to vol. ii of his *Antiquitas Illustrata* (Rome, 1697; i.e. five years after his death), written by an unknown Roman friend of the author. L. Ceyssens, O.F.M., *La Correspondance d'Emmanuel Schelstrate, préfet de la bibliothèque vaticane, 1683–1692* (Bibliothèque de l'Institut Historique Belge de Rome, fasc. 1; 1949); this vol. has a valuable study of Schelstrate with full bibl. reff. in its introd. (esp. pp. 18–90). J. Mercier in *D.T.C.*, xiv (pt. 1; 1939), cols. 1278–80, s.v., also with bibl. reff.

SCHENUDI. See *Shenoute*.

SCHISM (Gk. σχίσμα, 'tear' or 'rent').

Formal and wilful separation from the unity of the Church. In a technical sense the word is first met with in St. *Irenaeus (adv. Haer.*, IV, xxxiii, 7). Early instances of schismatic bodies are the *Novatianists and *Donatists. RC theologians account all those out of communion with the Pope, the supreme head of the Church, in a state of schism. It is distinguished from heresy in that the separation involved is not at basis doctrinal; whereas heresy is opposed to faith, schism is opposed to charity. Schism does not entail the loss of orders. A bishop in schism can ordain and a priest in schism can celebrate the Eucharist. The term 'schism' is also often used by Anglican and Protestant theologians of divisions within the Church, e.g. of that between Anglicanism and Roman (or Orthodox) Catholicism. See also *Reunion, Oecumenical Movement*.

T. A. *Lacey, *Unity and Schism* (1917).

SCHISM ACT, The.

The Act (12 Anne, St. II, c. 7) passed in 1714 by the English Parliament under the Tory leadership of Bolingbroke forbidding dissenters to keep schools or engage in tuition. The Act was repealed in 1719 by 5 Geo. I, c. 4.

The principal clauses of the Act are pr. in W. C. Costin–J. S. Watson (edd.), *The Law and Working of the Constitution. Documents*, i (1952), pp. 121–3.

SCHLATTER, ADOLF (1852–1939), Protestant theologian.

Born at *St. Gall in Switzerland, he taught first at Berne (1880–8), and later was professor at Greifswald (1888–93), Berlin (1893–8), and Tübingen (1898–1922). He held that the only sound foundation of Systematic Theology lay in Biblical exegesis, and also vigorously opposed all idealistic interpretations of the Christian faith. In these and other respects he anticipated the *Dialectical Theology of K. *Barth. His work on the Fourth Gospel exercised considerable influence on E. C. *Hoskyns. His writings (none trans. into English during his lifetime) include *Der Glaube im Neuen Testament* (1885), *Erläuterungen zum Neuen Testament* (3 vols., 1887–1904), *Die philosophische Arbeit seit Cartesius* (1906), *Das christliche Dogma* (1911), *Andachten* (1927). Schlatter was also the editor of *Beiträge zur Förderung christlicher Theologie*.

R. Brezger, *Der Schrifttum von Professor D. A. Schlatter* (Beiträge zur Förderung christlicher Theologie, xl, Hft. 2; 1938). A. Schlatter, *Die Entstehung der Beiträge zur Förderung christlicher Theologie und ihr Zusammenhang mit meiner theologischen Arbeit* (ib., xxv, Hft. 1; 1920). Theodor Schlatter (ed.), *Adolf Schlatters Rückblick auf seine Lebensarbeit. Zu seinem hundertsten Geburtstag* (Sonder-

heft to the *Beiträge*, 1952). Memorial volume to A. Schlatter and W. Lütgert by P. Althaus–G. Kittel–H. Strathmann (Beiträge, xl, Hft. 1; 1938).

SCHLEGEL, FRIEDRICH (1772–1829),

*Romantic author and Catholic apologist. From 1793 onwards, he devoted himself entirely to literary pursuits. His early leanings were towards Greek ideals, as revealed in his *Von den Schulen der griechischen Poesie* (1796). Before long, however, he abandoned classicism and became an enthusiast for medieval poetry and the reigning German idealism, esp. the ideas of J. G. *Fichte and F. W. J. *Schelling. In 1797 he settled in Berlin where he became one of the leaders of the Romantic Movement. His next years were devoted to lectures at Jena, Dresden, and Paris, and the study of Oriental languages and literature. In 1808 he and his wife, Dorothea, a daughter of Moses Mendelssohn, were converted to the RC Church. From now on Schelling became an advocate of Catholic principles. In lectures on literature and modern history which he gave at Vienna (1810–12) he defended the medieval Imperial idea against the Napoleonic state; and, in association with F. X. von Baader and St. Clement Maria *Hofbauer, he sought to restore the national life of Austria and Germany on a Catholic basis. When circumstances led him to despair of a reform of the state on these lines, he looked to literature and philosophy for a renewed Catholicism. His *Philosophie der Geschichte* (2 vols., 1829) contained the lectures given to these ends at Vienna in 1828. Philosophically, Schlegel after he became a Catholic was a severe critic of the *pantheism of G. W. F. *Hegel. His own philosophy, based on *Plato rather than *Aristotle, had affinities with some forms of *Ontologism.

Collected works ed., 10 vols., Vienna, 1822–5; Eng. tr. of selected writings by E. J. Millington (Bohn's Standard Library, London, 1849). F. [D. E.] *Schleiermacher, *Vertraute Briefe über Lucinde* (1800). I. Rouge, *Frédéric Schlegel et la genèse du romantisme allemand* (1904); id., *Erläuterungen zu F. Schlegel's Lucinde* (1905). W. Glawe, *Die Religion Friedrich Schlegels* (1906). L. Wirz, *Friedrich Schlegels philosophische Entwicklung* (Grenzfragen zwischen Theologie und Philosophie, xiii; 1939). Überweg, iv, 128–33, with bibl. p. 685 f. G. Fritz in *D.T.C.*, xiv (pt. 1; 1939), cols. 1492–5.

SCHLEIERMACHER, FRIEDRICH DANIEL ERNST (1768–1834), German theologian.

A native of Breslau in Silesia, he was the son of a Reformed army chaplain, and after his parents' conversion to the *Herrnhuter Brethren, was educated at their college at Niesky and their seminary at Barby. Finding the teaching imparted at Barby too narrow for his independent intellect, he entered the university of Halle in 1787, where he was introduced to the philosophy of I. *Kant and *Aristotle. In 1790 he accepted a post as tutor to a noble family in W. Prussia. Ordained to the ministry in 1794, he was appointed Reformed preacher at the Charité at Berlin, where he came into close contact with representatives of the *Romantic Movement, esp. F. *Schlegel. In 1799 he published his famous *Reden über die Religion* (Eng. trans., *Religion, Speeches to its Cultured Despisers*, 1893). In this work, which shows the influence of B. *Spinoza, G. W. *Leibniz, and I. Kant, he attempts to win the educated classes back to religion which he defines romantically as 'a sense and taste for the infinite'. Contending that religion was based on intuition and feeling (*Anschauung und Gefühl*) and independent of all dogma, he saw its highest experience in a sensation of union with the infinite. In 1800 followed the *Monologen*, a preliminary to his later work on ethics. In 1804 he became professor of theology at Halle, but left it in 1807, after the Prussian defeat, and went to Berlin, where he was appointed preacher at the Dreifaltigkeitskirche in 1809 and dean of the Theological Faculty of the newly founded university in 1810. As such he played an influential part in the Prussian war against Napoleon, esp. through his stirring sermons. From 1819 he was chiefly occupied with his most important work, published in 1821–2 under the title *Der christliche Glaube nach den Grundsätzen der evangelischen Kirche im Zusammenhang dargestellt*, which is the chief source for his theology. Here he defines religion as the feeling of absolute dependence, which finds its purest expression in monotheism. The variety of forms which this feeling assumes in different individuals and nations accounts for the diversity of religions, of which Christianity is the highest, though not the only true one. He died on 12 Feb. 1834.

Schleiermacher's strong emphasis on feeling as the basis of religion, inherited from his Herrnhut education, was at once a reaction from contemporary German rationalism and from the regnant formalist orthodoxy. His influence on Protestant thought was enormous; generations of theologians, among whom were authorities such as A. *Ritschl, A. von *Harnack, and E. *Troeltsch, built on, developed, and modified his ideas. Recently, however, his influence has been diminished by a powerful reaction, connected esp. with the names of K. *Barth and E. *Brunner who oppose to Schleiermacher's 'feeling' the Scriptural principle of the Reformers.

The high regard in which Schleiermacher was held in Germany throughout the 19th cent. is well illustrated by the large literature on him. Collected ed. of his writings, ed. Berlin, 32 vols., 1834–64. Collected correspondence publd., 4 vols., Berlin, 1858–63, of which there is an Eng. tr. of vols. i and ii, 1860; selected correspondence [ed. M. Rade], Jena, 1906. Correspondence with J. C. Gass, ed. Berlin, 1852. Crit. edd. of his *Reden über die Religion* by G. C. B. Pünjer, Brunswick, 1879; also by R. *Otto (Jubiläumsausgabe), Göttingen, 1899; of the *Monologen* by F. M. Schiele, Philosophische Bibliothek, lxxxiv; Leipzig, 1902. *Friedrich Schleiermachers Aesthetik*, ed. from unpubld. sources by R. Odebrecht (Berlin–Leipzig, 1931); *Friedrich Schleiermachers Dialektik* also ed. from unpubld. sources by id. (Leipzig, 1942). Eng. tr. of Schleiermacher's essay on St. Luke's Gospel by C. *Thirlwall, London, 1825; of his *Reden über die Religion* by J. *Oman, ib., 1893; of 'Selected Sermons' by Mary F. Wilson, ib., 1890; of the *Monologen* by H. L. Friess, Chicago, 1926; and of *Der christliche Glaube* by H. R. Mackintosh–J. S. Stewart, Edinburgh, 1928. Studies on Schleiermacher in English by R. Munro (Paisley, 1903), G. Cross (Chicago, 1911), W. B. Selbie ('The Great Christian Theologies', 1913), J. A. Chapman (London, 1932), and R. B. Brandt (New York, 1941), with bibl. The innumerable studies on him in German include lives by D. Schenkel (Elberfeld, 1868) and W. *Dilthey (2 vols., Berlin, 1870). E. Troeltsch and others, *Schleiermacher, der Philosoph des Glaubens* (Moderne Philosophie, vi; 1910). R. Odebrecht,

Schleiermachers System der Aesthetik (1932). H. Lindroth, *Schleiermachers Religionsbegrepp* (Uppsala Universitets Arsskrift, 1926, Teologi, i, and 1930, Teologi, i). E. Brunner, *Die Mystik und das Wort*. Der Gegensatz zwischen moderner Religionsauffassung und christlichen Glauben dargestellt an der Theologie Schleiermachers (1924). Überweg, iv, 112–28 and 682–5 (full bibl.). Recent literature noted by H. Mulert in *Zeitschrift für Theologie und Kirche*, N.F., xiv (1933), pp. 370–8, xv (1934), pp. 77–88 and 256–73. O. Kirn in *P.R.E.* (ed. 3), xvii (1906), pp. 587–617, s.v., with additional bibl. by A. Hauck–H. Hering, ib., xxiv (1913), p. 454 f.; W. B. Selbie in *H.E.R.E.*, xi (1920), pp. 236–9; G. Wobbermin in *R.G.G.* (ed. 2), v (1931), cols. 170–9; L. Cristiani in *D.T.C.*, xiv (pt. 1; 1939), cols. 1495–1508.

SCHMALKALDIC ARTICLES (1537). The doctrinal statement drawn up by M. *Luther at the behest of Johann Friedrich, Elector of Saxony, for presentation to the projected General Council convoked by *Paul III to Mantua for 23 May 1537. It consisted of (1) a statement of the doctrines of the Creeds, very brief as outside controversy; (2) a long section on 'the office and work of Christ, or our redemption', attacking such practices and institutions as the *Mass ('the greatest and most horrible abomination'), *purgatory ('a Satanic delusion'), the *Pope ('Antichrist'), the Invocation of *Saints, and *Monasticism; and (3) a final section on matters on which Protestants were themselves divided, e.g. the *Eucharist. On 23 Feb. 1537 an assembly of Lutheran princes and theologians at Schmalkalden in Thuringia approved the Articles as well as a much more moderate Appendix, added by P. *Melanchthon at the Assembly's request, conceding to the Pope as a matter of human right jurisdiction over the other bishops of Christendom and adopting a markedly conciliatory attitude towards the Papacy. The Articles were issued from the press by Luther (but without Melanchthon's Appendix, which had exposed its author to violent abuse from the stricter *Lutherans) as *Artikel christlicher Lehre* in 1538, and in 1580 incorporated in the 'Book of *Concord'. The title *Articuli Smalcaldici* is first met with in 1553.

Text pr. among the works of Luther, e.g. in the Weimar ed., l (1914), pp. 192–254, with introd., pp. 160–91; also ed., with Melanchthon's appendix, by H. Volz in the *Bekenntnisschriften der evangelisch-lutherischen Kirche* (Göttingen, 1930), pp. 407 ff. H. Volz, 'Luthers Schmalkaldische Artikel und Melanchthons *Tractatus de Potestate Papae*' in *Theologische Studien und Kritiken*, ciii (1931), pp. 1–70. Id. (ed.), *Drei Schriften gegen Luthers Schmalkaldische Artikel von Cochläus, Witzel und Hoffmeister* (Corpus Catholicorum, xviii; 1932). P. *Schaff, *A History of the Creeds*, i (1877), pp. 253–7. Further bibl. in Schottenlöher, i (1933), p. 586 f. (Nos. 13675–87). T. Kolde in *P.R.E.* (ed. 3), xvii (1906), pp. 640–645, s.v. 'Schmalkaldische Artikel'.

SCHMALKALDIC LEAGUE. The alliance concluded in the town hall at Schmalkalden on 27 Feb. 1531 between the Protestant groups in Germany in self-defence against *Charles V's 'Recess of Augsburg' (19 Nov. 1530). It united the *Lutherans and the *Zwinglians, as well as the N. and S. German princes, and soon became a strong anti-Hapsburg force. It was T. *Cromwell's wish that England should join the confederates, but this wish was not realized.

SCHMIDT, BERNARD. See *Smith, Bernard*.

SCHMIEDEL, PAUL WILHELM (1851–1935), NT scholar. He taught successively at Jena (1873–93) and, as professor of NT Theology, at Zürich (1893–1923). His principal writings were *Das vierte Evangelium gegenüber den drei ersten* (1906; Eng. trans., *The Johannine Writings*, 1908) and his short but much discussed *Die Person Jesu im Streit der Meinungen der Gegenwart* (1906). He also contributed extensively to the (British) *Encyclopaedia Biblica* (1899–1903), including the notable art. 'Gospels'. He is best known through his celebrated attack on a small group of critics (A. Kalthoff, W. B. Smith, J. M. Robertson) who denied the historical existence of Christ. On the basis of nine crucial passages in the Gospels ('die Grundsäulen eines wahrhaft wissenschaftlichen Lebens Jesu'), viz. Mk. 3. 21 and 31–35, Mk. 13. 32, Mk. 10. 18, Mt. 12. 32, Mk. 15. 34, Mk. 8. 12, Mk. 6. 5 f., Mt. 11. 5, and Mt. 16. 5–12, which could not be the invention of the primitive Church, he argued that the historicity of Jesus was put beyond dispute. On the other hand, he was himself one of the most radical of critics and professed that his Christian faith would be unaffected even if Christ's historicity were disproved.

A. Meyer, 'Zu Prof. Dr. Schmiedels 70. Geburtstag' in *Protestantische Monatshefte*, xxv (1921), pp. 161–7 (with portrait); R. Steck, 'Professor Schmiedels Grundsäulen des Lebens Jesu und ihre amerikanische Bestreitung', ib., pp. 167–72.

SCHOLA CANTORUM (Lat., 'a school of singers'). In the worship of the early Church all music was rendered by the clergy with the assistance of the congregation, but gradually the practice of having a body of trained singers was introduced. At *Rome the Schola was established on a sound basis by *Gregory the Great (d. 604), and several of his successors were trained in it. From Rome the custom spread rapidly over W. Christendom, the Roman chant being brought to England by St. *Benedict Biscop (d. 690) and St. *Wilfrid (d. 709). The modern descendant of the Schola is the cathedral choir school and, in certain monasteries (notably *Solesmes), those monks whose special work is the study of the ecclesiastical chant. The term 'Schola Cantorum' is also used for the place where the chant is taught.

SCHOLARIUS, GEORGE. See *George Scholarius*.

SCHOLASTICA, St. (c. 480–c. 543), sister of St. *Benedict of Nursia. Almost all that is known of her comes from a brief passage in St. *Gregory the Great's 'Dialogues' (ii, 33 f.). She established a convent at Plombariola, a few miles from *Monte Cassino where brother and sister met annually for the discussion of spiritual matters. Feast day, 10 Feb. She is invoked against storms.

I. Cecchetti in *E.C.*, xi (1953), col. 141, s.v. See also lives of *St. Benedict*, s.v.

SCHOLASTICISM. In its strict etymological sense Scholasticism is the educational tradition of the Medieval Schools. As now understood it may be described as a method of philosophical and theological speculation which aims at a better understanding of revealed truths, that is, as an attempt by intellectual processes, by analogy and by defining, co-ordinating, and systematizing the data of faith, to attain to a deeper penetration into the inner meaning of Christian doctrine. Consequently, philosophy has a great part to play in Scholastic thought, and there is a Scholastic philosophy as much as a Scholastic theology.

The theoretical foundations of Scholasticism were already laid by St. *Augustine and *Boethius. In his *De Doctrina Christiana* St. Augustine urged the need for dialectics in the study of Christian doctrine, while in the *De Praedestinatione Sanctorum* he formulated, as it were, the programme of Scholasticism. Setting out from the notion that 'to believe is to ponder with assent' (*credere est cum assensione cogitare*), he reached the maxim: 'Understand so that you may believe, Believe so that you may understand' (*ergo intellige ut credas, crede ut intelligas*). Boethius by his translations of, and commentaries on, *Aristotle and *Porphyry, opened the door which later introduced medieval thinkers to their first knowledge of logic, while his *Opuscula Sacra* indicated the way in which philosophy should come to the aid of theology. *Cassiodorus, a follower of Boethius, pointed in a different direction. In his *Institutiones Divinarum et Humanarum Litterarum* he propounded a plan of studies for his monastery at Vivarium which put the seven liberal arts at the basis of all secular and sacred learning. This programme, followed later by *Alcuin and *Rabanus Maurus, led to the flourishing *Carolingian renaissance, and by insisting on the *Trivium* (Grammar, Rhetoric, and Dialectic) and the *Quadrivium* (Arithmetic, Geometry, Astronomy, and Music) also did much to prepare the way for the philosophical and theological speculation of the Middle Ages.

John Scotus *Erigena in the 9th cent. was one of the first to put St. Augustine's teaching into practice by stating clearly the distinction between *auctoritas* (Holy Scripture) and *ratio* (reason). Holy Scripture is still the main source of our knowledge of God; but it is the duty of reason, illuminated by God, to investigate and expound the Christian data supplied by authority. Moreover, by reviving interest in Boethius's translations of the logical treatises of Aristotle and translating the pseudo-*Dionysian *corpus*, he played a fundamental part in the moulding of medieval thought. The study of the *trivium*, and especially of dialectic, kept alive in the 10th cent. in the monastic schools which were spread all over Europe, developed and expanded in the 11th cent. and also led to the establishment of the *Cathedral schools. It gave rise to a twofold controversy, that between the *Realists and *Nominalists on the problem of Universals and that between dialecticians and anti-dialecticians. One consequence was that *Berengar of Tours, relying solely on dialectics and applying its use to all theological matters (*per omnia ad dialecticam confugere*), came to uphold views contrary to Christian dogma. By the middle of the 11th cent., however, the service that dialectic, used in due moderation, could render to theology was widely recognized. Masters such as *Lanfranc, Alger of Liége and others, distinguishing between use and abuse, showed that dialectic could be skilfully employed in theological disputations without imperilling the faith.

At the end of the 11th cent. St. *Anselm's great achievement was to formulate the programme of Scholasticism. Following the traditional teaching, esp. that of St. Augustine, he asserted the right of reason to inquire into revealed truths, not in the sense that by rational reasoning we acquire the knowledge of faith, but because it seems reprehensible if, once established in the faith, we make no effort to understand what we believe. His guiding principles, which remained the fundamental rules of every Schoolman, found expression in such positions as: a distinction between understanding (*intelligere*) and belief (*credere*); 'I believe that I may understand' (*credo ut intelligam*); the constant endeavour to understand what we believe (*intelligere quod credimus*); and quest of faith for intellectual formulation (*fides quaerens intellectum*).

The impulse given by St. Anselm of Canterbury was developed in the 12th cent. in the school of St. *Anselm of Laon and of his brother, Ralph. Here we find in the 'Sentences', a selection of dogmatic, moral, ascetic topics grouped under special headings, the first systematic arrangement of theological questions. Authority (*auctoritas*), the argument from Biblical and Patristic sources, is still predominant; but we also perceive here a timid endeavour to use the argument from reason (*ratio*). A more important innovation is the appearance of the *quaestio* with its arguments for and against. Despite its elementary and crude character, it was this technique and method that in the long run gave the chief impetus to classical Scholasticism.

To *Abelard belongs the merit of perfecting this technique. He did this by the unreserved application to theology of the dialectic method, based on the *quaestio* and *interrogatio* and on the *disputatio*; he also achieved the first theological synthesis, co-ordinating the whole of theology under the headings, *fides, caritas, sacramentum*. The schools of *Chartres and St. *Victor also had an important share in moulding Scholasticism. *Hugh of St.-Victor in particular, by his skilful use of secular learning, saved the scholastic method, which had been somewhat compromised by certain rash applications of Abelard and *Gilbert de La Porrée. All these achievements are summed up in *Peter Lombard's *Sentences*, which until the 16th cent. was, after the Bible, the text-book of the theological schools.

Of decisive importance at this stage was the introduction into Western Europe of the works of Aristotle. Although the main treatises were already translated from the Greek and Arabic in the 12th cent., their real influence was felt only in the 13th. At the same period the translations of the great Arabic commentators, *Avicenna and *Averroes, and other philosophical writings, reached the schools. From the new material arose three currents of thought. First, the so-called Augustinians who, though using Aristotelian terminology and some of his ideas, refused to accept what they considered to be in opposition to St. Augustine. Second, the Latin Averroists, under the leadership of *Siger of Brabant and Boethius of Dacia, who adhered strictly to Aristotelian doctrines, as interpreted by Averroes and the Arabian commentators, even when in opposition to Catholic teaching. It was left, third, to the *Dominicans to establish a harmony between St. Augustine and Aristotle, which, foreshadowed by St. *Albert the Great, was accomplished by his disciple, St. *Thomas Aquinas, in his '*Summa Theologica', the crowning achievement of Scholastic Theology. Following the usual method of presenting a doctrine in argument, counter-argument, and solution, he drew the line between faith and reason with the utmost clarity, securely establishing their connexion and showing the completion of the one by the other.

The work of St. Thomas found its most vigorous contemporary critic in the Franciscan *Duns Scotus. In opposition to the Dominican School, with its Aristotelian emphasis on the intellect, Scotus and the Franciscan School stressed the Augustinian primacy of the will. From now on Scholasticism declined rapidly. *William of Occam, though drawing on the work of Duns Scotus, went far beyond him and taught a Nominalism which undermined all belief in the possibility of objective knowledge. Such teaching was a leading factor in the dissolution of medieval Scholasticism, and certain aspects of it exercised a decisive influence on the theology of the Protestant Reformers.

Scholasticism, which had never wholly lost its vitality esp. in the Latin countries and continued to be generally taught in the *curricula* of the RC theological seminaries, has been revivified in modern times. In the 19th and 20th cents. it has become increasingly important as a reaction against a destructive subjectivism, particularly after *Leo XIII in his encyclical '*Aeterni Patris' (1879) strongly recommended the study of St. Thomas to all RC priests and scholars. Since then Neo-Thomism has spread chiefly in France and Belgium, where J. *Maritain and Cardinal *Mercier are among its best-known exponents. It has recently attracted much attention also in Britain and America, and not only among Roman Catholics.

The very large literature, much of it of high quality, is mainly the work of RC scholars. For edd. of the texts, see bibliographies to the chief Scholastics, incl. those mentioned above. There is an important collection of monographs, incl. some crit. texts, founded by C. Baeumker, *Beiträge zur Geschichte der Philosophie des Mittelalters* (Münster i.W., 1891 ff.). The older histories of Scholastic philosophy include those of A. Stöckl (3 vols., Mainz, 1864–6), B. Hauréau (2 vols., Paris, 1850; much extended, 2 vols., 1872–1878); more recent are the works of M. de Wulf (Louvain-Paris, 1900; ed. 6, 3 vols., 1934–47; Eng. tr. of ed. 6, 1952 ff.), and F. Überweg, *Grundriss der Geschichte der Philosophie*, ii (ed. 11 by B. Geyer, 1928); briefer are E. *Gilson, *La Philosophie au moyen-âge* (Collection Payot, 1922; ed. 2, much extended, 1944); F. Copleston, S.J., *Medieval Philosophy* (1952); E. Gilson, *History of Christian Philosophy* (New York, 1955; London, 1955). R. L. Poole, *Illustrations of the History of Medieval Thought in the Department of Theology and Ecclesiastical Politics* (1884; ed. 2, with revised title, 1920). M. *Grabmann, *Die Geschichte der scholastischen Methode* (2 vols., 1909–11); id., *Die Geschichte der katholischen Theologie seit dem Ausgang der Väterzeit* (Herders theologische Grundrisse, 1933); A. M. Landgraf, *Einführung in die Geschichte der theologischen Literatur der Frühscholastik* (1948); id., *Dogmengeschichte der Frühscholastik* (1952 ff.). A. J. Macdonald, *Authority and Reason in the Early Middle Ages* (Hulsean Lectures, 1931–2; 1933). O. Lottin, O.S.B., *Psychologie et morale aux XIIᵉ et XIIIᵉ siècles* (1942 ff.). G. Paré–A. Brunet–P. Tremblay, *La Renaissance du XIIᵉ siècle*. Les écoles et l'enseignement (Publications de l'Institut d'Études Médiévales d'Ottawa, iii; 1933). P. Glorieux *La Littérature quodlibétique de 1260 à 1326* (Bibliothèque Thomiste, v, xxi; 1925–35). Id., *Répertoire des maîtres en théologie au XIIIᵉ siècle* (Études de Philosophie médiévale, xvii, xviii; 1933–4); suppl. by V. Doucet, O.F.M., in *A.F.H.*, xvii (1934), pp. 531–64 and 584–9; F. Stegmüller, *Repertorium Commentariorum in Sententias Petri Lombardi* (2 vols., Würzburg, 1947; suppl. by V. Doucet, O.F.M., Quaracchi, 1954). On the history of Logic in the Middle Ages, the classical study is C. Prantl, *Geschichte der Logik im Abendlande* (4 vols., 1855–70), esp. vols. ii–iv. Periodicals dealing largely with scholastic philosophy, often with bibl. of current literature, include the *Revue thomiste* (Paris, 1893 ff., with separate *Bulletin thomiste*, 1924 ff.), *Revue néo-scolastique* (Louvain, 1894 ff.; since 1946, *Revue philosophique de Louvain*), *Revue des Sciences philosophiques et théologiques* (vols. i–ii, Le Saulchoir, 1907–8, iii ff., Paris, 1909 ff.), *Scholastik* (Freiburg i.Br., 1926 ff.), *Recherches de théologie ancienne et médiévale* (Louvain, 1929 ff.), with separate Bulletin, and *Mediaeval Studies* (New York–London, 1939 ff.); also other publications of the 'Institute [from 1940, Pontifical Institute] of Mediaeval Studies of the University of Toronto', 1929 ff. A. S. *Pringle-Pattison [–X.] in *E.B.* (ed. 11), xxiv (1911), pp. 346–56, s.v.; S. H. Mellone in *H.E.R.E.*, xi (1920), pp. 239–249, s.v.; C. Fabro in *E.C.*, xi (1953), cols. 121–40, s.v. 'Scolastica'.

SCHOLIA (plur. of Gk. σχόλιον). Notes, esp. of a critical, grammatical, or explanatory kind, inserted in the margins of an ancient MS. Their use was a regular practice in the Greek schools of later classical antiquity, and, probably through the contact between pagan and Christian culture at Alexandria, they were introduced by Christian scholars into the MSS. of Biblical and ecclesiastical texts.

SCHOOL OF ENGLISH CHURCH MUSIC. See *Royal School of Church Music*.

SCHOOLMEN. The teachers of philosophy and theology at the medieval European universities, then usually called 'schools', of which *Paris and *Oxford were pre-eminent. From the 13th cent. many of their greatest representatives belonged to the *Mendicant Orders, among the most famous being the Dominicans St. *Albert the Great and St. *Thomas Aquinas, and the Franciscan St. *Bonaventure and *Duns Scotus. See *Scholasticism*.

SCHOOLS, Cathedral. See *Cathedral Schools*.

SCHOOLS, Sunday. See *Sunday Schools*.

SCHOPENHAUER, ARTHUR (1788–1860), German philosopher. The son of a wealthy Danzig merchant, he was apprenticed to a Hamburg firm by his father in 1804, but went to Göttingen university in 1809 and to Berlin in 1811, where he attended the lectures of J. G. *Fichte and F. D. E. *Schleiermacher. He was a great admirer of I. *Kant, whose only authentic interpreter he professed himself to be, and was also influenced by the nature philosophy of J. W. Goethe and F. W. J. *Schelling. The problem of combining Kant's criticism with the positive view of life of Goethe and Schelling led him to construct a philosophical system which he expounded in his chief work, *Die Welt als Wille und Vorstellung* ('1819' [really 1818]; ed. 2, 1834). After its completion he travelled in Italy and in 1820 accepted a lectureship at Berlin university which, however, proved a failure. In 1831 he fled from the cholera to Frankfurt, where he spent the latter part of his life in embittered seclusion, publishing only a few works, the chief of which were *Die beiden Grundprobleme der Ethik* (1841) and *Parerga und Paralipomena* (1851).

Schopenhauer may be regarded as the classic exponent of Pessimism. The ultimate Reality was Will (Gk. θέλημα, 'impulse', 'striving'; rather than βούλησις, 'the capacity to determine'), which extends far beyond the range of conscious life. Its extinction by pity for creatures and the mortification of the passions was the sovereign remedy for the ills of existence; and Schopenhauer claimed that his teaching was in so far essentially at one with that of the Christian mystics. Meanwhile, as a stage towards this goal, he found a transient place of rest in the realms of art, poetry, and above all music. In the formulation of his ethical doctrines he was considerably influenced by Buddhism, though he never made any pretence of practising himself the Buddhist maxims.

Schopenhauer's philosophy, which achieved recognition only at the end of his life, influenced R. Wagner and F. *Nietzsche (in his early years), and was continued and modified by E. von *Hartmann and A. *Drews. It was one of the chief anti-Christian systems in Germany in the 19th cent.

Collected work ed. by his pupil, J. Frauenstädt, 6 vols., Leipzig, 1873–4. Posthumous writings ed. id., ib., 1864; others ed. E. Grisebach from MSS. in the Royal Library at Berlin, Leipzig [1896]. Correspondence ed. L. Scheemann, Leipzig, 1893. Eng. tr. of his principal work, *The World as Will and Idea*, by R. B. Haldane–J. Kemp, 3 vols., 1883–6; ed. 8, 1937. Selected essays tr. E. H. Bax, Bohn's Philological Library, 1891; another selection, *The Wisdom of Schopenhauer*, ed. W. Jekyll, 1911. Studies in German by W. von Gwinner (Leipzig, 1862), O. Busch (Heidelberg, 1877; ed. 2, Munich, 1878), J. Volkelt (Stuttgart, 1900; ed. 3, 1907). Studies in English by Helen Zimmern (1876; rev. ed., 1932), W. Caldwell (Edinburgh, 1896), T. Whittaker (Philosophies Ancient and Modern, 1909), F. Copleston, S.J. (Bellarmine Series, xi, 1946). G. Simmel, *Schopenhauer und Nietzsche* (1907). *Schopenhauer-Lexikon*, ed. J. Frauenstädt, 2 vols., Leipzig, 1871. C. Gebhardt, *Schopenhauer-Bilder* (1913). Überweg, iv, 133–47, with bibl. pp. 686–90. W. Wallace [–X.] in *E.B.* (ed. 11), xxiv (1911), pp. 372–6, s.v.

SCHRADER, EBERHARD (1836–1908), Assyriologist. A pupil of H. E. W. *Ewald, he became professor of OT in turn at Zürich

(1863), Giessen (1870), and Jena (1873); and later professor of Semitic studies at Berlin (1875). He was a leading authority in the field of Assyriology, and did pioneer work in bringing its findings to bear on OT problems. The most important of his writings was *Die Keilinschriften und das Alte Testament* (1872; ed. 3 by H. Zimmern and H. Winckler, 1902; Eng. trans. by O. C. Whitehouse, 1889).

E. Meyer, 'Gedächtnisrede auf Eberhard Schrader' in *Abh.* (Berl.), 1909, Gedächtnisrede I.

SCHÜRER, EMIL (1844–1910), German NT scholar. After lecturing in theology at Leipzig from 1869 to 1878, he was appointed professor at Giessen in 1878, went to Kiel in 1890, and held a chair of NT exegesis at Göttingen from 1895. In 1876 he founded the *Theologische Literaturzeitung* which he edited together with A. *Harnack from 1881. His principal work is the *Lehrbuch der Neutestamentlichen Zeitgeschichte* (1874), published since its 2nd edition (1886–7) under the title *Geschichte des jüdischen Volkes im Zeitalter Jesu Christi* (Eng. trans., *A History of the Jewish People in the Time of Jesus Christ*, 5 vols., 1890–1; later editions [not translated] are fuller and better). This monumental treatise gives a detailed and carefully substantiated account of the political history and the religious and social customs and beliefs as well as of the religious and profane literature of the Jewish people from the time of the *Maccabeans to the wars under Trajan, and is still the standard text-book.

Obituary notice by A. *Harnack in *T.L.Z.*, xxxv (1910), cols. 289–92. A. B. Titius in *P.R.E.* (ed. 3), xxiv (1913), pp. 460–6.

SCHÜTZ, HEINRICH (1585–1672), German composer. The Latin form 'Sagittarius', is also found. From 1609 to 1612 he studied music at *Venice, became court organist at Cassel in 1612, and from 1617 was court conductor at Dresden. Apart from secular works he wrote much Church music, and is esp. famous for his *Passion music, which is remarkable for its dramatic qualities. He was one of the greatest exponents of the musical *baroque and exercised a profound influence on J. S. *Bach and other later composers esp. in Germany. Both Catholic and Protestant Church music are deeply indebted to him, the former esp. for his Latin motets. His works include the *Symphoniae Sacrae*, i (1629) and ii (1647), the *Geistliche Konzerte* (1636–9), and *Geistliche Chormusik* (1648).

Collected ed. of his musical works by P. Spitta and others (18 vols., Leipzig, 1885–1927); letters and other writings ed. E. H. Müller (Ratisbon, 1931). Modern studies by A. Pirro (Paris, 1913) and E. H. Müller (Leipzig, 1925; much briefer). A. C. Lewis in *Grove's Dictionary of Music and Musicians* (ed. 5 by E. Blom), vii (1954), pp. 642–50, s.v., with bibl. by J. H. Davies, pp. 650–2.

SCHWABACH, Articles of (1529), the first of the *Lutheran Confessions. These 17 Articles were based on the collection of 15 Articles considered and, with one exception (that on the Eucharist), adopted at the Colloquy of *Marburg (3 Oct. 1529). The revision was due to M. *Luther, assisted by P. *Melanchthon, J. *Jonas, J. *Brenz, and others. On 16 Oct. 1529 they were accepted at Schwabach by the Elector and George, Margrave of Brandenburg-Ansbach, as admitting to membership of the Lutheran League of the N. German States. They were later taken as the basis of the first part of the *Augsburg Confession (1530).

Text of the articles pr. among the works of P. Melanchthon in the *Corpus Reformatorum* founded by C. G. Bretschneider, xxvi, ed. H. E. Bindseil (Brunswick, 1857), cols. 151–60, with introd. cols. 129–50. P. *Schaff, *The History of the Creeds*, i (ed. 2, London, 1878), p. 228 f. Schottenloher, iv (1938), p. 599 (Nos. 42437–44). T. Kolde in *P.R.E.* (ed. 3), xviii (1906), p. 1 f., s.v. 'Schwabacher Artikel'.

SCHWARTZ, EDUARD (1858–1940), classical philologist and *Patristic scholar. A native of Kiel, he was educated at Göttingen, Bonn (under H. Usener), and Greifswald (under U. von Wilamowitz-Moellendorff). He held a succession of Professorships in German universities, among them Strassburg (1897–1902; 1913–18), Göttingen (1902–9; here he was closely associated with J. *Wellhausen), and Munich (1919 onwards). His early training, philological rather than theological, gave the stamp to his Patristic work. He published editions of *Tatian's 'Oratio ad Graecos' (1888), *Athenagoras (1891), and *Eusebius's 'Ecclesiastical History' (1903–9, in collaboration with T. *Mommsen), the Pseudo-*Athanasian *Sermo Major de Fide* (1924), *Cyril of Scythopolis (1939), and other Patristic texts. His main work, the *Acta Conciliorum Oecumenicorum*, was a grandly planned edition of the Greek Councils, based on extended MS. researches. Publication began in 1914 and, after interruption through the war, was actively prosecuted from 1922 onwards; it was mostly completed at the time of his death. It provided, for the first time, a critical edition of the 'Acts' of *Ephesus (431) and *Chalcedon (451), besides portions of the later Councils. It was in many respects the Greek counterpart of C. H. *Turner's *Monumenta*, the last part of which, after Turner's death (1930), Schwartz saw through the press (1939). His important collection of papers on Athanasius in the *Nachrichten* of the Göttingen Gesellschaft (1904–11) inaugurated a new era in Athanasian studies. His other writings include a paper maintaining the early death of *John, the son of Zebedee (1904), *Kaiser Konstantin und die christliche Kirche* (1913; ed. 2, 1936), and a paper on the so-called 'Counter-Anathemas' of *Nestorius (1923). Among his many papers subsidiary to his edition of the Councils was an important study of the *Theodosian Collection.

There is much autobiographical material in Schwartz's own *Vergangene Gegenwärtigkeiten* (1938). A. Rehm, *Eduard Schwartz' wissenschaftliches Lebenswerk* (Sb. (Bayr.), 1942, Hft. 4), with list of his works, pp. 67–75. Appreciation in English by C. H. Turner, 'Eduard Schwartz and the *Acta Conciliorum Oecumenicorum*' in *J.T.S.*, xxx (1929), pp. 113–120. *Gesammelte Schriften*, ed. E. Schwartz, K. Aland, and W. Eltester (Berlin, 1938 ff.).

SCHWARZERD, PHILIPP. See *Melanchthon, Philipp*.

SCHWEGLER, ALBERT (1819–57), German Patristic scholar and philosopher. At the university of Tübingen, which he had entered in 1836, he came under the influence of F. C. *Baur, and from the standpoint of the *Tübingen School published *Der Montanismus und die christliche Kirche des zweiten Jahrhunderts* (1841). His other writings in the field of Patristics, all written from the same point of view, include a *Geschichte des nachapostolischen Zeitalters* (2 vols., 1846) and an edition of the '*Clementine Homilies' (1847). He also wrote extensively on the history of philosophy and on Roman history.

E. Zeller, 'Drei deutsche Gelehrte: 1. Albert Schwegler' in *Vorträge und Abhandlungen*, II (1877), pp. 329–63. W. S. Teuffel in *Allgemeine Deutsche Biographie*, xxxiii (1891), p. 327 f.

SCHWEITZER, ALBERT (b. 1875), German theologian, physician, and organist. He was born at Kaisersberg in Alsace and educated at Strassburg University, completing his studies at Berlin and Paris. In 1899 he became pastor at Strassburg. In *Das Messianitäts- und Leidensgeheimnis* (1901; Eng. trans. *The Mystery of the Kingdom of God*, 1925) he expounded what was to be the leading idea of his theological work, viz. that Our Lord's teaching centred in His conviction of the imminent end of the world. The book made a great stir, and shortly after its publication he became lecturer at Strassburg University (1902) and principal of a theological college. In 1906 appeared his brilliant *Von Reimarus zu Wrede* (Eng. trans., *The Quest of the Historical Jesus*, 1910). After a review of previous attempts at interpreting the Life of Christ (G. E. *Lessing, D. F. *Strauss, J. E. *Renan, O. Pfleiderer, and W. *Wrede), all of which he held to be inadequate, he expounded an interpretation on the basis of 'thoroughgoing eschatology'. He held that Christ shared with His contemporaries the expectation of a speedy end of the world and, when this proved a mistake, concluded that He Himself must suffer in order to save His people from the tribulations preceding the last days. In 1911 there followed *Die Geschichte der paulinischen Forschung* (Eng. trans., *Paul and his Interpreters*, 1912), in which Schweitzer applied similar eschatological principles to the theology of St. Paul. In the same year he took his medical degree, and in 1913 gave up a career of great academic distinction to devote himself at Lambaréné (French Equatorial Africa) to the care of the sick natives and to missionary activities. Having been interned in France in 1917, he returned to Strassburg in 1918. In 1921 he published his widely read reminiscences, *Zwischen Wasser und Urwald* (Eng. trans., *On the Edge of the Primeval Forest*, 1922). In 1923 appeared his *Kulturphilosophie*, summing up his views on ethics as 'reverence for life'. In 1924 he went back to Lambaréné and restored his destroyed hospital.

After his return (1927) he completed his work on St. Paul, *Die Mystik des Apostels Paulus* (1930, Eng. trans., 1931), which is built on the thesis that 'Being in Christ', interpreted as the 'physical union between Christ and the elect', is the centre of the Pauline teaching and is to be distinguished from 'God mysticism', which attains to God directly without the mediation of Christ. In 1954 he delivered the Nobel Peace Prize address in Oslo.

Schweitzer has exercised a widespread influence on Continental as well as on English and American Protestant theology, though his view of Our Lord's Person aroused much opposition not only among conservative, but also among liberal Protestant theologians. He is also an accomplished musician and interpreter of J. S. Bach, on whom he wrote a monograph (1908; Eng. trans., 1911), and his organ recitals have found an enthusiastic public.

Collections of Autobiographical reminiscences publd. as *Aus meiner Kindheit und Jugendzeit* (1924; Eng. tr. by C. T. Campion as *Memoirs of Childhood and Youth*, 1924); *Aus meinem Leben und Denken* (1931; Eng. tr. by id. as *My Life and Thought*, 1933); and *Afrikanisches Tagebuch, 1939–45* (1946). Studies by O. Kraus (Berlin, 1926; Eng. tr., 1944), G. Seaver (London, 1944), id. (ib., 1947), J. M. Murry (ib., 1948), and J. Feschotte (ib., 1954). M. Schlunk in *R.G.G.* (ed. 2), v (1931), cols. 339–41, with bibl.

SCHWENKFELDIANS. The followers of the Silesian Reformation theologian, Caspar Schwenkfeld (1490–1561).

Schwenkfeld, essentially a mystic by temperament, was much impressed by the writings of J. *Tauler and M. *Luther, and in 1522 made a pilgrimage to *Wittenberg. He soon found, however, that he could not give unreserved assent to many of the Protestant doctrines. He believed the tenet of justification by faith created serious moral dangers; he was unable to accept the Lutheran doctrine of the Eucharist; and he sought to introduce among his followers a strict rule of Church discipline. The opposition which his teaching met with from both Catholics and Protestants led him to leave his native Silesia in 1529 for Strassburg and other cities in S. Germany. He gradually came to hold also a doctrine of the deification of Christ's humanity, and in 1540 issued an elaborate account (*Konfession und Erklärung*) of his beliefs on the subject, with a reply to his opponents. Its theses were at once repudiated by the main body of orthodox Protestants, and a few years later Schwenkfeld finally withdrew from the Lutheran Church. After much further persecution from both Church and state he died at Ulm on 10 Dec. 1561.

After his death his small band of disciples, who called themselves the 'Confessors of the Glory of Christ', continued to propagate his teaching, publishing many of his writings from his MSS. They continued to exist in Silesia till 1826, and a branch of their disciples, which established itself at Philadelphia, Pa., in 1734, still survives.

Their writings and letters are appearing in the *Corpus Schwenckfeldianorum* (1907 ff.; 13 vols., to 1937); 'Letters and Treatises, 1530–33' and '1534–38', ed. C. D. Hartranft

(Leipzig, 1914–16), the 'Letters and Treatises, 1552–4' by E. E. Schultz Johnson, S. G. Schultz, and L. Kriebel (ib., 1935). Schwenkfeld's correspondence with *Philip of Hesse ed. J. L. French (London, 1908). H. W. Kriebel, *The Schwenckfelders in Pennsylvania* (Lancaster, Pa., 1904). E. *Troeltsch, *Die Soziallehren der christlichen Kirchen* (1912), pp. 881–5 (Eng. tr., 1931, pp. 756–9). See also R. H. Grützmacher in *P.R.E.* (ed. 3), xviii (1906), pp. 72–81, and artt. in *R.G.G.* (ed. 2), v (1910), cols. 354–6, with further bibl.

SCIENCE, Christian. See *Christian Science.*

SCIENTIA MEDIA

(Lat., 'mediate knowledge'). A term coined by the *Jesuit theologian, L. *Molina, in his attempt to reconcile God's foreknowledge with human freewill. It designates the knowledge which God has of 'futuribilia', i.e. of things which are not, but which would be if certain conditions were realized, and thus are *intermediate* between mere possibilities and actual future events. Acc. to Molinist teaching this mediate knowledge is independent of the decree of the Divine Will. This thesis was keenly contested by the *Thomists and remains one of the chief differences between the systems of theology in the *Jesuit and *Dominican Orders. See also *Molinism.*

G. de Henao, S.J., *Scientia Media Historice Propugnata* (Lyons, 1655); id., *Scientia Media Theologice Defensata* (Lyons, 1674). F. Stegmüller in *L.Th.K.*, ix (1937), col. 385 f., s.v., with bibl.

SCILLITAN MARTYRS, The.

Seven men and five women of Scillium in North Africa who were executed in 180, by order of the proconsul Saturninus, for refusal to renounce Christianity and to swear by the 'genius' of the Roman Emperor. Their 'Passio', which is authentic, is a valuable document for the persecutions of the 2nd cent. It shows the pagan authorities eager to obtain a recantation and the martyrs steadfast in their refusal; and it is the first documentary evidence of Christianity in N. Africa. Later a basilica was built over their tomb where St. *Augustine preached three sermons. Feast day, 17 July.

Text of 'Acta' in *AA.SS.*, Jul. IV (1725), pp. 204–16; also in R. Knopf, *Ausgewählte Märtyrerakten* (ed. 3, Sammlung ausgewählter kirchen- und dogmengeschichtlicher Quellenschriften, N.F., iii; 1929), p. 28 f. J. A. *Robinson, *The Passion of S. Perpetua* (Texts and Studies, I (2), Cambridge, 1891), with 'The Acts of the Scillitan Martyrs', pp. 106–21 (incl. orig. Lat. text, with Gk. version and later Lat. recension). Eng. tr. with notes in E. C. E. Owen, *Some Authentic Acts of the Early Martyrs* (1927), pp. 71–4. P. Franchi de' Cavalieri, 'Le reliquie dei martiri scillitani' in *R.Q.*, x (1903), pp. 209–21. Bardenhewer, ii, 675–8; J. Quasten, *Patrology*, i (Utrecht, 1950), p. 178 f., with further bibl. J. P. Kirsch in *L.Th.K.*, ix (1937), col. 386, s.v.

SCINTILLA ANIMAE

(Lat., 'spark of the soul'). A metaphorical expression current in mystic literature, esp. in the writings of Master *Eckhart, for the element in the soul (also 'ground' or 'apex'), in which its union with God is achieved.

S.C.M. See *Student Christian Movement.*

SCONE, Perthshire.

Ancient Scottish religious centre and once the capital of a Pictish kingdom. At an assembly held here in 908, the Scottish king, Constantine, swore to protect the Church, and recognized the Bp. of St. Andrews as primate. In 1115 an abbey of *Augustinian canons, succeeding an earlier foundation, was settled there by King Alexander I (1107–24). All the kings of Scotland, from Malcolm IV (1153) onwards, were crowned at Scone. The Stone of Destiny, on which the Celtic kings were crowned, was brought to *Westminster Abbey by Edward I in 1296. It was traditionally believed to be that on which *Jacob laid his head at *Bethel (Gen. 28.11). In the night of 24–25 Dec. 1950 it was removed from the Abbey by unknown hands. It was restored to its place early in 1952.

The *Liber Ecclesie de Scon* was ed. by W. Smythe for the Bannatyne Society, vol. lxxxii, Edinburgh, 1843. M. E. C. Walcott, *Scoti-Monasticon*. The Ancient Church of Scotland (1874), esp. pp. 313–16. W. F. Skene, *The Coronation Stone* (1869). J. Hilton, 'The Coronation Stone at Westminster Abbey' in *Archaeological Journal*, liv (1897), pp. 201–24. See also bibl. to *Coronation Rite.*

SCORY, JOHN

(d. 1585), successively Bp. of *Chichester and *Hereford. Originally a Cambridge *Dominican, he became a secular clerk in 1538 at the *Dissolution of the Monasteries and was appointed in 1551 to the see of *Rochester and in 1552 to that of Chichester. At the accession of *Mary Tudor, Scory was deprived of his see, but submitted and recanted. Nevertheless he left England, going first to Emden and then to Geneva. In 1558 he returned and was in the next year appointed Bp. of Hereford, which see he held until his death. He was a wealthy, able, and not over-scupulous prelate. He assisted at M. *Parker's consecration (and hence figured prominently in the *Nag's Head Fable) and is thus held to be one of the channels through which the episcopal succession was preserved in the C of E.

W. A. J. Archbold in *D.N.B.*, li (1897), p. 8 f., s.v., with further reff. See also H. N. Birt, O.S.B., *The Elizabethan Religious Settlement* (1907), pp. 241, 246, 248, 362–70 and passim.

SCOTISM.

The system of Scholastic philosophy expounded by the *Franciscan teacher, *Duns Scotus (q.v.), and defended in the later Middle Ages, esp. in the Franciscan Order.

SCOTLAND, Christianity in.

The first known Christian missionary to Scotland was the Briton, St. *Ninian, who had come under the influence of St. *Martin of Tours. He built the first stone church in Scotland, Candida Casa, at Whithorn (397), from which he carried on a widespread mission among the Picts. The next great evangelist was St. *Columba, a Scot from Ireland, who used *Iona as the headquarters of his missionary labours (563–97). The Columban monks, through St. *Aidan (c. 635), created a new centre at *Lindisfarne, from which they evangelized the northern English. The Celtic Church represented by these men was monastic and missionary; the heads of its communities were presbyter-abbots not bishops; it was independent of Rome and maintained peculiar usages, e.g. the date of *Easter and the *tonsure were different from those of the Roman Church. The declaration of the Synod of *Whitby (664) in favour of the Roman Easter was a prelude to the decline of the Celtic Church's influence in England and the gradual adoption of Roman usages in the North.

From the dark age that long shrouded the Scoto-Pictish Church it eventually emerged as a united body under a national bishop, whose seat was at Dunkeld from the middle of the 9th cent. to the beginning of the 10th, when it was transferred to St. Andrews. The Romanization of the Scottish Church was completed under the influence of Queen *Margaret (d. 1093), the devout exile driven from England by the Norman Conquest, and her sons, esp. David I in whose reign (1124–53) diocesan episcopacy was extended, Roman monastic orders introduced, and many monastic houses built by the munificent king. The chief features of the medieval period were the constant affirmation of independence by the Scottish Church against the claims of *Canterbury and *York to supremacy, the establishment of provincial councils, the arrival of the friars in the 13th cent., the patriotic part played by the Church in the wars with England, the founding of the universities of St. Andrews (c. 1411), Glasgow (1450–1), and Aberdeen (1494), the erection of archiepiscopal sees (St. Andrews, 1472; Glasgow, 1492), the deterioration of the Church, and the forebodings of the Reformation.

Among those who prepared the way for the Reformation were the exponents of *Wycliffite doctrines; their story is marked by the martyrdoms of Resby (1406) and Crawar (1433) and the citation of the *Lollards of Kyle before the Abp. of Glasgow (1494). The first wave of the Reformation proper was *Lutheran, the second was Swiss. Heretical books were smuggled into Scotland in spite of an Act of Parliament (1525) against their importation. Patrick *Hamilton, who had been in Germany, was burnt at the stake in St. Andrews (1528) for his advocacy of Lutheran principles and his death increased the number of reformers. The policy and campaigns of England under *Henry VIII and *Edward VI added to the pro-Reformation forces but also created patriotic opposition. Cardinal *Beaton led the anti-English party, but his responsibility for the martyrdom of G. *Wishart (1546) led to his murder shortly afterwards. Wishart's mantle fell upon the shoulders of J. *Knox who, after his labours in England, Frankfurt, and Geneva, ultimately returned to lead the Calvinistic party, now strongly supported by the Lords of the Congregation.

In 1560 the reformed Church of Scotland was established on *Presbyterian lines. It prepared a Confession of Faith (see *Scottish Confession*) and a 'Book of *Discipline' (1560) and soon adopted the Anglo-Genevan 'Book of *Common Order' as its liturgical directory,

but not until twenty years afterwards were presbyteries systematically erected. To make up for the dearth of ministers at first, it was deemed expedient to appoint *superintendents and readers. Soon after the death of Knox (1572) the mantle of leadership was borne by the doughty advocate of high Presbyterianism, A. *Melville. Intimate associations existed between Scottish Presbyterians and the English *Puritans who, led by T. *Cartwright and W. *Travers, sought by 'Scottizing for Discipline'—to use R. *Bancroft's phrase—to presbyterianize the C of E, but were frustrated by *Elizabeth I and her agent J. *Whitgift.

For more than a hundred years the fortunes of Scottish Presbyterians ebbed and flowed owing to the determination of the Stuart kings to make the Kirk episcopal. Now the Crown was dominant and pro-episcopal Acts were passed (1584); now the Kirk came into power again and Presbyterianism was ratified (1592). For some decades the policy of *James VI & I prevailed, Episcopacy being established by the Scottish Parliament in 1612. The Five Articles of *Perth, which enjoined such usages as kneeling at Communion and the observance of holy days, were passed by a packed Assembly in 1618. The imposition of the Prayer book, known as W. *Laud's liturgy, brought the conflict between the Kirk and *Charles I to a head in 1637. In the following year the pro-Presbyterian National Covenant was subscribed and the Glasgow General Assembly, the first free assembly for thirty years, swept Episcopacy away. In 1643 the alliance between the Scottish Covenanters and the Long Parliament was cemented by the *Solemn League and Covenant, and the southern Parliament, aiming, under Scottish influence, at Presbyterian uniformity for the British Isles, convened the *Westminster Assembly (q.v.). The *Directory of Church Government, the Directory of Public *Worship, the *Westminster Confession and the *Westminster Catechisms (qq.v.) were formerly accepted as standards by the Church of Scotland.

After the Restoration Episcopacy was reestablished and a bitter and bloody struggle between Scottish Episcopalians and Presbyterians ensued. At the Revolution the Church of Scotland became Presbyterian once more (1690) and has remained so ever since. Chiefly owing to the infringement of popular rights by the Patronage Act of 1712 the Church was weakened by secessions in the 18th cent. (Original Secession, 1733; Relief, 1761) and by the *Disruption (q.v.) of 1843 when nearly a third of its ministers and members left the Establishment and formed the *Free Church. Among notable modern features of Scottish Presbyterian history may be mentioned foreign and colonial missionary enterprise, Church extension at home, increased interest in Church worship and architecture, the transfer of Church schools to civil authorities (1872), the abolition of patronage (1874), and the relaxation of the terms of credal subscription. The 19th cent. witnessed a growing movement in favour of the union of the different Presbyterian Churches in Scotland. The chief unions took place in 1847 (Secession and Relief to form United Presbyterian), 1900 (United Presbyterian and Free to form *United Free), and 1929 (United Free and Church of Scotland under the name of the latter). Each union had its unyielding remnant who continued in their former ways, e.g. Free Church, 1900, and United Free Church, 1929.

The overwhelming majority of the population of Scotland belong to the Church of Scotland, which is Presbyterian, national, endowed, and free. Its spiritual independence has been recognized and patrimony secured by Acts of Parliament (1921, 1925). From those who adhered to Episcopacy at the Revolution settlement (1690) arose the Episcopal Church in Scotland which after years of repression and suspicion, largely owing to its Jacobite predilections, is now free to make its distinctive contribution to Scottish religious life. It is in full communion with the C of E, but is autonomous, has its own Prayer Book and is governed by bishops, the chief of whom is called *Primus. The RC Church retains its hold on the descendants of those in the Highlands who were never deeply influenced by Reformation principles; and it also flourishes among those of Irish extraction in industrial Lowland areas.

G. Grub, *An Ecclesiastical History of Scotland from the Introduction of Christianity to the Present Time* (4 vols., Edinburgh, 1861); J. Cunningham, *The Church History of Scotland from the Commencement of the Christian Era to the Present Century* (2 vols., Edinburgh, 1859; ed. 2, continued, 1882). A. B. Scott, *The Pictish Nation.* Its People and its Church (1918). J. Ritchie, *Reflections on Scottish Church History* (1927); J. D. Rose, *Scotland's True Glory.* The Story of the Church of Scotland from the Earliest Times to the Present Day [1934]. A. R. MacEwen, *A History of the Church in Scotland* [379–1560] (2 vols., [1913]–1918); J. A. Duke, *History of the Church of Scotland to the Reformation* (1937). A. B. Scott, *The Rise and Relations of the Church of Scotland* (Edinburgh, 1932); J. A. Duke, *The Columban Church* (1932). G. A. Frank Knight, *Archaeological Light on the Early Christianizing of Scotland* (2 vols., 1933). W. D. Simpson, *Saint Ninian and the Origins of the Christian Church in Scotland* (1940). J. Dowden, *The Medieval Church in Scotland.* Its Constitution, Organisation and Law (Glasgow, 1910); id., *The Bishops of Scotland.* Being Notes on the Lives of all the Bishops under each of the Sees prior to the Reformation (Glasgow, 1912). The primary authorities for the period of the Reformation are the histories of J. *Knox and J. *Spottiswode (qq.v.). D. Calderwood (d. 1650), *The History of the Kirk of Scotland* (ed. T. Thomson; Wodrow Society, 8 vols., 1842–9). G. D. Henderson, *Religious Life in Seventeenth Century Scotland* (1937). A. J. Campbell, *Two Centuries of the Church of Scotland, 1707–1929* (Hastie Lectures; Paisley, 1930). J. R. Fleming, *A History of the Church in Scotland, 1843–1874* (Edinburgh, 1927); id., *A History of the Church in Scotland, 1875–1929* (ib., 1933). H. Scott, *Fasti Ecclesiae Scoticanae.* The Succession of Ministers in the Church of Scotland from the Reformation (3 vols., Edinburgh, 1866–71; new ed., 8 vols., Edinburgh, 1915–28, with additional vol., 1950). W. Perry, *The Oxford Movement in Scotland* (1933). D. Maclean, *The Counter-Reformation in Scotland, 1560–1930* [1931]. Janet G. MacGregor, *The Scottish Presbyterian Polity.* A Study of its Origins in the Sixteenth Century (Edinburgh thesis; 1926). C. L. Warr, *The Presbyterian Tradition.* A Scottish Layman's Handbook (1933). J. T. Cox, *Practice and Procedure in the Church of Scotland* (1934). M. B. Macgregor, *The Sources and Literature of Scottish Church History* (Glasgow, 1934). Recent lit. includes J. H. S. Burleigh, *A Church History of Scotland* (1960). G. Donaldson, *The Scottish Reformation* (1960). The Scottish liturgies of 1637 and 1764 are printed in W. J. Grisbrooke, *Anglican Liturgies of the Seventeenth and Eighteenth Centuries* (Alcuin Club Collections, xl, 1958), pp. 163–82 and 333–48, with comm. pp. 1–18 and 150–9.

SCOTT, GEORGE GILBERT (1811–78), ecclesiastical architect. He was the grandson of T. *Scott, the Biblical commentator (q.v.). A native of Gawcott, Bucks, he had an Evangelical upbringing, and studied architecture under James Edmeston and Robert Smirke, who discouraged his predilection for Gothic. But his acquaintance with Benjamin *Webb, the secretary of the (High Church) *Cambridge Camden Society, and with A. W. N. *Pugin led him to an intensified study of the principles of Gothic art; and his first notable church in that style was St. Giles at Camberwell. In 1840 he was selected as architect for the Martyrs' Memorial, Oxford, from which time he became the most prominent ecclesiastical architect in England. In 1844 he won a competition for the *Lutheran church of St. Nicholas at Hamburg, executed in 13th cent. German Gothic. From 1847 he frequently travelled on the Continent, utilizing his studies esp. of French Gothic for restoration as well as original work in Great Britain. Among cathedrals he was entrusted with work of restoration at *Ely, *Hereford, *Salisbury, and *Gloucester. In 1849 he was appointed architect to the Dean and chapter of *Westminster Abbey. His later works include the Albert Memorial and the mosaic pavement of *Durham Cathedral. In his 'restorations', for which he was famous, he met with resistance owing to his too ready preference for his own designs to the original plans, and the Society for the Protection of Ancient Buildings was founded to oppose the methods of restoration of which Scott was the leading promoter. Well-known ecclesiastical architects who were trained in his office include G. E. *Street and G. F. Bodley (1827–1907).

His grandson, GILES GILBERT SCOTT (b. 1880) is also a distinguished architect. His works include the Anglican cathedral at *Liverpool, the New Library at Cambridge, and the New Bodleian Library and the New Buildings and Chapel at Lady Margaret Hall, Oxford.

George Gilbert Scott, *Personal and Professional Recollections*, ed. by his son, G. Gilbert Scott (1879), with introd. by J. W. *Burgon, pp. ix–xx. List of his works from 1847 to the time of his death in *The Builder*, xxxvi (1878), p. 360. P. Waterhouse in *D.N.B.*, li (1897), pp. 19–23, s.v.

SCOTT, ROBERT (1811–87), Greek lexicographer. Educated at Shrewsbury and at *Christ Church, Oxford, he was elected a Fellow of Balliol in 1835 and master (with B. *Jowett, who succeeded him at the next election, as rival candidate) in 1854. From 1861 to 1870 he was also Dean Ireland's professor of exegesis, and from 1870 till his death Dean of *Rochester. He is remembered esp. through the famous Lexicon which he edited in conjunction with H. G. *Liddell (q.v. for particulars). His other publications include *Twelve Sermons* (1851) and *Sermons preached before the University of Oxford* (1860).

H. Craik in *D.N.B.*, li (1897), p. 65 f.

SCOTT, THOMAS (1747–1821), Biblical commentator. The son of John Scott (d. 1777), a grazier, Thomas was apprenticed to a surgeon at Alford, Lincs, but after quick dismissal for some misconduct was employed for some nine years in menial work on the land. Eventually he was ordained deacon in 1772 by the Bp. of *Lincoln and held a succession of curacies, in 1781 succeeding John *Newton, whose acquaintance he had made earlier, at Olney. From 1801 till his death he was rector of Aston Sandford, Bucks. In his *Force of Truth* (1779) he set out the stages in which his theological beliefs developed from a *Unitarian rationalism to a fervent *Calvinism. His chief work, however, was his *Commentary on the Bible*, issued in weekly numbers between 1788 and 1792. It was remarkable for its endeavour to discover the message of each section of the Bible for his own soul and a persistent refusal to shirk difficulties by falling back on historical or pietistic disquisitions. It had an enormous circulation, though Scott, who shared but few of the financial profits, continued a poor man. J. H. *Newman in the *Apologia* testifies to Scott as the influence 'to whom (humanly speaking) I almost owe my soul'.

Collected editions of his works were published at Buckingham in 1805–8 (5 vols.) and in 1823–5 (10 vols.). A. Gordon in *D.N.B.*, li (1897), pp. 73–5.

SCOTTISH CONFESSION, The (Lat., *Confessio Scotica*).

The first Confession of Faith of the reformed Church of Scotland. It was adopted by the Scottish Parliament in 1560 and remained the confessional standard until superseded by the *Westminster Confession in 1647. It had been drawn up in four days by J. *Knox and five other ministers in 25 articles, and is a typical Calvinistic document. *Justification by faith is assumed; the doctrine of *election is affirmed; the real presence in Communion is emphasized and *transubstantiation and the view that the elements are bare signs are condemned. The Kirk is defined as Catholic; it consists of the elect, and outside of it there is no salvation. The notes of the true Kirk on earth are not lineal descent or numbers, but the true preaching of the Word, and the right administration of the sacraments and of discipline. Civil magistrates are stated to be the lieutenants of God, whose duty it is to conserve and purge the Church when necessary; but supreme authority is ascribed to the Word of God.

A supplement to the Confession, also known as the 'Second Scottish Confession' or the 'National Covenant', of a strongly anti-Roman character, was issued and subscribed in 1581.

P. Schaff, *The Creeds of Christendom* (1877), iii, 479–85. K. *Barth's *Gifford Lectures (*The Knowledge of God and the Service of God according to the Teaching of the Reformation*, 1938) are in the form of a commentary on the 1560 Confession.

SCOTUS, DUNS.

See *Duns Scotus*.

SCOTUS, ERIGENA.

See *Erigena*.

'SCOURGE OF GOD', The.

See *Attila*.

SCREENS.

Partitions of wood, stone, or iron, dividing a church into two or more parts. Chancel- or choir-screens, separating the *choir from the *nave, may be high, solid, and elaborate, as the 15th cent. screens at Amiens, *Chartres, *Canterbury, and *York, or, as in Italy in early times, quite low. In the latter form they were sometimes provided with *ambones on either side. When a chancel-screen is surmounted by a cross ('rood'), it is termed a 'rood-screen'.

J. B. Thiers, *Dissertations ecclésiastiques, sur les principaux autels des églises, les jubés des églises, la clôture du chœur des églises* (1688), Dissertation des jubés des églises (separate pagination). A. W. *Pugin, *A Treatise on Chancel Screens and Rood Lofts, their Antiquity, Use and Symbolic Signification* (1851); F. Bond, *Screens and Galleries in English Churches* (1908); A. Vallance, *English Church Screens*. Being Great Roods, Screenwork and Rood-Lofts of Parish Churches in England and Wales (1936); id.–E. T. Long, *Greater English Screens*. Being Great Roods, Screenwork and Rood-Lofts in Cathedrals, Monastic and Collegiate Churches in England and Wales (1947). J. C. Cox, *English Church Fittings, Furniture and Accessories* [1928], pp. 133–53. G. W. O. Addleshaw–F. Etchells, *The Architectural Setting of Anglican Worship* (1948), pp. 37–63.

SCRIPTORIUM.

The room, esp. in a monastery, which was set apart for the scribes to copy MSS. The necessary utensils were provided by a person known as the 'armarius'. As the scriptorium of a particular monastery (or group of monasteries) often adopted a characteristic script, its affiliations can be of great value to palaeographers in assigning the date and place to a MS. A good instance of such a characteristic style of writing is the school of Tours, and of illumination that of *Winchester.

SCRIVENER, FREDERICK HENRY AMBROSE (1813–91), NT textual critic.

Educated at Trinity College, Cambridge, he held a number of parochial appointments. From 1846 to 1856 was head master of Falmouth School. He made a very comprehensive study of the text of the NT, publishing collations and detailed descriptions of a large number of (esp. minuscule) MSS., some of them hitherto unexamined. His *Plain Introduction to the Criticism of the NT*, of which the 1st edition appeared in 1861 (listing some 1,170 MSS.) and the 4th (posthumous, ed. by E. Miller) in 1894 (listing over 3,000), is still a valuable book of reference, though his attempt to defend the *textus receptus has now been almost universally abandoned.

E. C. Marchant in *D.N.B.*, li (1897), p. 126, s.v.

SCROFULA, Touching for.

See *King's Evil, Touching for*.

SCROPE, RICHARD LE (c. 1350–1405), Abp. of *York.

Of noble family, he was ordained priest in 1377, became chancellor of Cambridge university in 1378, and went to Rome in 1382 where he was made auditor of the Curia. He was appointed Bp. of Coventry and *Lichfield in 1386 and, at the request of Richard II, was translated to the Abpric. of

York in 1398. Though he acquiesced in the abdication of the King in 1399 and assisted at the enthronement of Henry IV, he soon grew discontented with the latter's government and favoured Northumberland's revolt to which his reputation of holiness gave additional weight. He also composed a manifesto demanding justice, security, and lighter taxation, and gathered an army of dissatisfied citizens whom he led against the royal troops. He was tricked, however, into disbanding his followers by the Earl of Westmorland, who feigned compliance with his demands for reform, and arrested and irregularly sentenced to death at the command of the King. At his tomb in York Minster miracles were soon believed to take place, and he was popularly venerated as a saint though his cult was never formally approved.

Miscellanea relating to Abp. Scrope in J. Raine (ed.), *The Historians of the Church of York and its Archbishops*, ii (R.S., 1886), pp. 292–311; account of the proceedings against him, ib., iii (1894), pp. 288–91, and letters deprecating the worship at his shrine, pp. 291–4. Life by continuator of chronicle of Thomas Stubbs (perhaps William Melton, 1496–1528), ib., ii, 428–33. Short life by N. H. Nicolas in his ed. of the Scrope and Grosvenor Roll, *The Controversy between Sir Richard Scrope and Sir Robert Grosvenor in the Court of Heraldry, MCCCLXXXV–MCCCXC*, ii (1832), pp. 121–6. J. H. Wylie, *History of England under Henry IV*, ii (1894), pp. 192–211, 226–9, and 236–42. J. Solloway, *Archbishop Scrope* ('York Minster Tracts', No. 15, [1928]). J. Tait in *D.N.B.*, li (1897), pp. 144–7, s.v., with reff. to original sources.

SCRUPLES (Lat. *scrupulus*, 'small sharp stone'). In *moral theology, unfounded fears that there is sin where there is none. Scrupulosity may be the result of much ascetic reading of a rigorist tendency, but more often is the outcome of nervous disturbances. It usually manifests itself in the fear of having consented to sinful imaginations and desires, of having made incomplete confessions, and of being unworthy of the reception of the sacraments. It may also err with regard to duties which it is prone to see where they do not exist. Scrupulosity, which often inclines the penitent to refuse submission to the judgement of his confessor, may lead to the sins of obstinacy and despair, or, conversely, to self-indulgence. The scrupulous, who are discouraged from making minute confessions, are usually counselled to disregard their scruples and to act in obedience to the advice of a prudent spiritual director.

SCRUTINY (Lat. *scrutinium*). In the early Church a term applied to the formal testing to which *catechumens were subjected before their baptism. The word came to be used also of the corresponding examination of candidates for holy orders.

SEA, Forms of Prayer to be used at. In the BCP, a small collection of prayers and anthems for use in various circumstances at sea. The forms include a prayer to be used daily in the Royal Navy, prayers for use in a storm and before battle, thanksgivings for deliverance from storm and for victory, and directions for general confession and absolution in serious danger. The first special prayers for use at sea were put out as a supplement to the *Directory for Public *Worship*, issued by the Long Parliament in 1645, and the forms now prescribed were first included in the BCP of 1662.

F. Procter–W. H. *Frere, *A New History of the Book of Common Prayer* (1901), pp. 162, 199, 246, and esp. 644 f. F. S. Horan in *P.B.D.*, p. 745 f., s.v.

SEABURY, SAMUEL (1729–96), first bishop of the *Protestant Episcopal Church of America. After studying theology at Yale university and medicine at Edinburgh, he was ordained priest by the Bp. of *Lincoln in 1753 and served as a missionary in New Brunswick, later holding livings near New York. Remaining loyal to the British Government in the War of Independence, he engaged in controversy in the three 'Farmer's Letters' with Alexander Hamilton and for a time (in 1775) suffered imprisonment. He was elected bishop in 1783; but as his inability, now that the States were independent, to take the Oath of Allegiance precluded his consecration by English bishops, arrangements were made that he should obtain his episcopal orders from Scotland. Seabury was accordingly consecrated at Aberdeen on 14 Nov. 1784. Later, by his co-operation in the consecration of Bp. T. J. Claggett of Maryland, the Scottish and English successions were united. An able organizer and administrator, he was one of the pioneers of the American Protestant Episcopal Church.

E. E. Beardsley, *Life and Correspondence of the Right Reverend Samuel Seabury* (Boston, 1881; abridged ed. as *The Life of Samuel Seabury*, London, 1884). William Jones Seabury (great grandson), *Memoir of Bishop Seabury* (New York and London, 1908). C. K. Vance in *Dict. Amer. Biog.*, xvi (1935), pp. 528–30.

SEAL OF CONFESSION. The absolute obligation not to reveal anything said by a penitent using the Sacrament of *Penance. The obligation includes not only the confessor, but interpreter, bystander, eavesdropper, persons finding and reading lists of sins obviously drawn up for the purpose of the confession, and indeed everyone except the penitent himself. It covers all sins, *venial as well as *mortal, and any other matter the revelation of which would grieve or damage the penitent, or would lower the repute of the sacrament. The obligation arises from a tacit contract between penitent and confessor, from its necessity for the maintenance of the use of the sacrament by the faithful, and from canon law. The obligation covers direct and indirect revelation, e.g. unguarded statements from which matters heard in confession could be deduced or recognized, and admits of no exception, no matter what urgent reasons of life and death, Church or state, may be advanced. The RC ruling on the seal (*Sacramentale sigillum*) is to be found in C.I.C., can. 889.

B. Kurtscheid, O.F.M., *Das Beichtsiegel in seiner geschichtlichen Entwicklung* (1912; Eng. trans. as *A History of the Seal of Confession*, 1927).

SEBALDUS, St., patron saint of Nuremberg. His date (8th–11th cent.) is disputed and nothing certain is known of him, but he is traditionally believed to have lived as a hermit and preacher near Nuremberg. His tomb is attested as a place of pilgrimage from 1072, when miracles were reported to have taken place at it and a church was built over it. From 1300 to 1377 the famous Sebalduskirche was built, and in 1425 the city obtained his formal canonization from *Martin V. His relics rest in the celebrated shrine of Peter Vischer (1508–19), and his name was inserted in the *Roman martyrology in 1927. Feast day, 19 Aug.

His Acta, of uncertain date, mainly recording miracles, pr., with introd., together with the proper of the Mass for his Feast, in *AA.SS.*, Aug. III (1737), pp. 762–77. J. B. Stamminger, *Franconia Sancta. Das Leben der Heiligen und Seligen des Frankenlandes*, i (Würzburg, 1881), pp. 534–52. A. Feulner, *Peter Vischers Sebaldusgrab in Nürnberg* (Munich, 1924). The decree of the Sacred Congregation of Rites inserting his name in the Roman Martyrology is pr. in *A.A.S.*, xix (1927), p. 154 f.

SE-BAPTISTS (Lat. *se baptizare*, 'to baptize oneself'). In the 17th cent. a name occasionally given to the followers of John *Smyth (the 'Se-Baptist', q.v.), who after baptizing himself established a church at Amsterdam in 1609.

SEBASTE, The Forty Martyrs of. Forty Christian soldiers of the '*Thundering Legion' who were martyred at Sebaste in Lesser Armenia during the Licinian persecution (*c.* 320) by being left naked on the ice of a frozen pond, with baths of hot water on the banks as a temptation to apostatize. The place of one who gave way was taken by a heathen soldier of the guard, who was immediately converted. The martyrdom is narrated by St. *Basil of Caesarea and St. *Gregory of Nyssa; and their ashes, which were recovered by the Empress *Pulcheria, were very greatly venerated in the E. Feast day in the E., 9 Mar.; in the W., 10 Mar.

Besides the descriptions in Basil, *Hom.* 19 ('In sanctos quadraginta Martyres'; J. P. Migne, *PG*, xxxi, 507–26), and Greg. Nyss., 'In Laudem SS. Quadraginta Martyrum' (J. P. Migne, *PG*, xlvi, 749–88), there survive an ancient Gk. *Passio* (not contemporary; ed. O. von Gebhardt, *Acta Martyrum Selecta*, Berlin, 1902, pp. 171–81) and a *Testamentum* (διαθήκη; Gk. and Old Slavonic; ed. N. Bonwetsch, *Das Testament der vierzig Märtyrer*, 1897). P. F. de Cavalieri, 'I quaranta martiri di Sebastia' in *Note agiografiche*, vii (S.T., xlix; 1928), pp. 155–84 (retracting his earlier views).

SEBASTIAN, St. Roman martyr who is believed to have suffered death during the *Diocletianic Persecution. He is mentioned by the *Chronographer of 354 and in the *Hieronymian Martyrology, and his remains probably gave the name to the Basilica San Sebastiano on the *Appian Way. Acc. to later legend, he was sentenced by the Emp. Diocletian to be shot by archers (hence the representations of him in late medieval and renaissance art as a young man transfixed by arrows), but through the attentions of a widow, named Irene, he recovered from this ordeal and unexpectedly presented himself before the Emperor, who caused him to be clubbed to death. Feast day, 20 Jan.

Gk. text of Martyrium in J. P. Migne, *PG*, cxvi, 793–816. *AA.SS.*, Jan. II (1643), pp. 257–96. F. Fornari, *S. Sebastiano extra Moenia* (Amici della Catacombe, iv; 1934). J. P. Kirsch–K. Hofmann in *L.Th.K.*, ix (1937), cols. 391–3, with bibl.

SECKER, THOMAS (1693–1768), Abp. of *Canterbury. Won over from Dissent to the C of E, he was passed with celerity through Exeter College, Oxford, and deacon's orders, and was ordained priest in 1723. Standing in high favour with Queen Caroline, he was made rector of St. James's, *Westminster, in 1733, and Bp. of Bristol in addition in 1735. In 1737 he became Bp. of *Oxford, in 1750 Dean of *St. Paul's, and from 1758 till his death was Abp. of Canterbury. Secker was among the better prelates of his age. Though he disliked the enthusiasm of the *Methodists, he admired their piety, and he favoured the dispatch of bishops to the American colonies. He stood for tolerance and good sense in general, and thoroughly eschewed the theology of B. *Hoadly. He published a large number of his sermons, which though of no outstanding merit reflect his sober and judicious outlook.

Beilby Porteus, *A Review of the Life and Character of Dr. Thomas Secker* [1770]. J. H. Overton in *D.N.B.*, li (1897), pp. 170–3.

S.E.C.M. See *Royal School of Church Music*.

SECOND ADAM. A title of Christ, the new Head of redeemed humanity, as contrasted with the 'first Adam', the original member and type of fallen man. The conception goes back to St. *Paul (Rom. 5. 14, 1 Cor. 15. 45), whose expression, however, is not the 'second' but the 'last Adam' (ὁ ἔσχατος Ἀδάμ). St. Paul was perhaps influenced by the notion of the 'heavenly Man' in the Book of *Enoch (so, e.g., A. E. J. Rawlinson).

SECOND COMING. See *Parousia*.

SECRET. A prayer said silently by the celebrant at *Mass after the '*Orate Fratres' and before the *Preface. It varies with the *Proper, and follows the rules of the *Collects, the last secret invariably ending with the words 'per omnia saecula saeculorum' which are said or sung aloud. It is a true offertory prayer, being the original and only one mentioned in the Roman (e.g. the *Gelasian and dependent) Sacramentaries. The name prob. derives from the fact that the prayer is said silently, a practice first recorded in France in the middle of the 8th cent. Prob. for this reason it is not preceded by 'Oremus'.

Jungmann, *M.S.*, ii (ed. 1949), pp. 108–17, with reff.

SECRÉTAN, CHARLES (1815–95), Swiss Protestant philosopher and theologian. A native of Lausanne, he studied at Munich under F. W. J. *Schelling and Franz Baader

(1765-1841), under whose joint influence he was led to a speculative and mystical view of religion. He held professorships at Lausanne (1839-45; where he lost his post in the latter year for political reasons), Neuchâtel (1850-66), and again at Lausanne (from 1866). With his older contemporary, A. R. *Vinet (1797-1847), he was one of the leaders of liberal Swiss Protestant thought in the 19th cent. As his outlook matured he increasingly emphasized, under Kant's influence, the moral significance of faith and the importance of freedom. Among his works were *Philosophie de la liberté* (2 vols., 1849; later edd., much altered, 1866, 1879), *La Raison et le christianisme* (1863), *La Civilisation et la croyance* (1887), and *Essais de philosophie et de littérature* (1896; posthumous).

L. Secrétan, *Charles Secrétan. Sa vie et ses œuvres* (1911). F. Pillon, *La Philosophie de Charles Secrétan* (1898). E. Plasshoff-Lejeune in *P.R.E.* (ed, 3), xviii (1896), pp. 114-8.

SECRETS OF ENOCH, Book of the, also known as 'II Enoch' or 'the Slavonic Enoch', an apocryphal work orig. written in Greek and prob. dating from the first century A.D. For further details, see *Enoch, Books of*.

SECTARY. The term was applied in the 17th and 18th cent. esp. to Protestant Non-conformists in England. Occasionally it is used in modern writers of those whose zeal for their own religious body is considered excessive.

SECULAR ARM. In *canon law, a term used to describe the state or any lay power when intervening in ecclesiastical cases. This intervention has been generally of two kinds, (1) unsought, (2) sought, by the Church. (1) Resort has often been made by individuals to the lay authorities to interfere with or hinder the processes of ecclesiastical jurisdiction. In the RC Church such action is now punished by excommunication and is a case specially reserved to the Apostolic See (see *Reserved Cases*). It has frequently been invoked as an appeal *tamquam ab abusu*, i.e. an appeal to the secular arm to see that justice is done, on the ground that the ecclesiastical authorities have been guilty of a miscarriage of justice. (2) The Church has not felt justified in imposing in her own tribunals penalties which involve mutilation or death, but the Church courts have had to deal with some cases, chiefly those of heresy, in which it was felt that sterner punishments were needed than they could impose. The assistance of the secular arm was therefore sought and, after trial by an ecclesi-astical judge, the condemned prisoner was handed over to the secular authorities for punishment. In the Middle Ages this course of action, which was common, was a fruitful source of dispute between the two powers as to the proper method of procedure, and in particular as to whether there should be a second trial in a secular court.

For the action of the secular arm in the trial and punishment of clerks see *Benefit of Clergy*.

R. Naz in *D.D.C.*, ii (1937), col. 980 f., s.v. 'Bras séculier (Appel au)'; R. Laprat, ib., cols. 981-1060, s.v. 'Bras séculier (Livraison au)'. See also works cited under *Inquisition*.

SECULAR CLERGY. The term, which seems to have been first used in the 12th cent., is used of priests living in the world, to distin-guish them from the 'regular clergy', i.e. members of religious orders, who live acc. to a rule. Secular priests are bound by no vows, may possess property, and owe canonical obedience to their bishops. Acc. to RC canon law, they are bound to celibacy. They take precedence of the regular clergy of equal rank.

SECULARISM. The term, which was first used *c.* 1850 by G. J. Holyoake (1817-1906), denotes a system which seeks to interpret and order life on principles taken solely from this world, without recourse to belief in God and a future life. Holyoake's ideas were later developed into extreme atheism by being cast into a more logical form by C. *Bradlaugh. Apart from its negative attitude to Christianity and religion in general, secularism advocated on the positive side social progress and the amelioration of material conditions for the working classes. The term is now widely used in a more general sense for the modern tendency to ignore, if not to deny, the prin-ciples of supernatural religion in the inter-pretation of the world and existence.

SEDE VACANTE (Lat., 'the see being vacant'). The period during which a diocese is without its bishop. In the C of E during such vacancy the archbishop of the province is guardian of the spiritualities of the diocese, which are administered under his commission. The temporalities are in the custody of the King. During a vacancy in the Papal See, the administration of the RC Church is in the hands of the 'Cardinal Camerlengo', the Chamberlain at the Vatican.

SEDIA GESTATORIA. The portable throne on which the Pope is carried by 12 footmen (*palafrenieri*), dressed in red uniforms, on certain prescribed solemn occasions.

SEDILIA (Lat., 'seats'). The seats of the celebrant, deacon, and subdeacon, on the south side of the chancel, usually three in number. They were introduced in England *c.* the 12th cent. and are used during those parts of the Eucharist and the Divine Office at which the ministers are allowed to sit, e.g. at the singing of the *Kyrie, *Creed, and *Gloria, and while the Psalms and the Lessons are chanted. In England they were usually stone benches built into a niche in the wall, whereas on the Continent and in modern English churches wooden seats (*scamna*) are more common. In the Middle Ages they were often richly carved and surmounted by arches or canopies.

SEDULIUS SCOTUS (9th cent.), poet and scholar. A native of *Ireland, he came to Liége in 848 where he found a patron in Bp. Hartgar and established an important Irish centre of culture. He also enjoyed the favour of the Emp. Lothair I, who probably entrusted him with the education of his sons, Lothair and Charles, and for one of whom his 'Liber de Rectoribus Christianis' on the art of government seems to have been written. Besides his numerous poems on religious and secular subjects he published several theological works, among them commentaries on St. Paul and St. Matthew, which, however, are compilations lacking in originality.

His Commentaries on the Pauline Epp., 'Liber de Rectoribus Christianis', and some other theological works are collected in J. P. Migne, *PL*, ciii, 9–352; his Comm. on Matt. is not yet published. Poems ed. L. Traube in *M.G.H.*, Poetae, iii (1896), pp. 151–240. S. Hellmann, *Sedulius Scottus* (Quellen und Untersuchungen zur lateinischen Philologie des Mittelalters, i, Hft. 1; 1906), with text of 'Liber de Rectoribus Christianis', pp. 19–91, and certain other fragments. Further letter probably to be attributed to him ed. E. Dümmler in *M.G.H.*, Epistolae, vi (1925), p. 206. G. *Morin, O.S.B., 'Une Révision du psautier sur le texte grec par un anonyme du neuvième siècle' in *R. Bén.*, x (1893), pp. 193–7. G. Martini, 'Un codice sconosciuto del "De Rectoribus Christianis" di Sedulio Scoto' in *Bullettino dell' Istituto Storico Italiano per il Medio Evo e Archivio Muratoriano*, l (1935), pp. 49–62. H. Pirenne, 'Sedulius de Liége' in *Mémoires couronnés et autres mémoires publiés par l'Académie Royale des Sciences, des Lettres et des Beaux-Arts de Belgique*, Collection in 8o, xxxii (1882), Lettres, No. 4. Manitius, i, 315–23; Raby, pp. 193–6. J. F. Kenney, *The Sources for the Early History of Ireland*, i (Records of Civilization, 1929), pp. 553–69 ('The Circle of Sedulius'). W. Turner in *C.E.*, xiii (1912), p. 680 f., s.v.; I. Cecchetti in *E.C.*, xi (1953), col. 228 f., s.v. 'Sedulio Scoto'.

SEE. Properly, the official 'seat' (*sedes*) or 'throne' (*cathedra*) of a *Bishop. This seat, which is the earliest of the Bishop's insignia, normally stands in the *Cathedral of the Diocese; hence the town or place where the Cathedral is located is also itself known as the Bishop's see. See also *Holy See*.

SEEKERS. A small *Puritan sect of the early 17th cent., also called 'Legatine-Arians' (from three of the earliest Seekers by the name of Legate) or 'Scattered Flock'. They believed that no true Church had existed since the spirit of *Antichrist became uppermost in the Church, and that God would in His own time ordain new Apostles or Prophets to found a new Church. They did not think it right to hasten on this process, with the result that they were vehemently opposed by the *Anabaptists. In their quietistic outlook they had many affinities with the *Quakers. Bartholomew Legate (*c.* 1575–1612), one of their preachers, was burnt at Smithfield for heresy. The Seekers of a later generation exercised considerable influence during the Commonwealth period.

R. M. Jones, *Studies in Mystical Religion* (1909), pp. 449–469; W. C. Braithwaite, *The Beginnings of Quakerism* (1912), esp. pp. 25–7, 58–65, and 78–97. R. M. Jones in *H.E.R.E.*, xi (1920), p. 350 f., s.v., with reff. See also bibl. s.v. 'Friends, Society of'.

SEELEY, JOHN ROBERT (1834–95), historian. The son of R. B. Seeley, an author and publisher (1798–1886), J. R. Seeley was educated at Christ's College, Cambridge, and in 1863 appointed professor of Latin at University College, London. His book *Ecce Homo* (1865; q.v.) at once made him famous. Later he supplemented this by an essay *Natural Religion* (1882) which was designed to reconcile the claims of Christianity with those of natural science, though he denied that the supernatural was an integral part of the Christian faith. In 1869 he was appointed professor of modern history at Cambridge where he exercised a stimulating influence as a teacher. His later writings were on purely historical subjects, among them his widely read *Expansion of England* (1883).

Memoir by G. W. Prothero prefixed to Seeley's *The Growth of British Policy*, i (1895), pp. vii–xxii. Id. in *D.N.B.*, li (1897), pp. 190–3, s.v.

SEGNERI, PAOLO (1624–94), Italian preacher. Having entered the *Jesuit Order in 1637, he was ordained priest in 1653. He is reckoned the greatest pulpit orator of Italy after St. *Bernardino of Siena and *Savonarola. Though his sermons show occasional lapses in taste, he was very successful in uniting a vigorous and ordered exposition of his argument with a powerful emotional appeal. His most famous collection of sermons is his *Quaresimale* (i.e. those delivered in *Lent), first published at Florence in 1679. In the matter of moral theology he opposed both *Probabiliorist and *Quietist doctrines.

Early collected edd. of his works in 2 vols., Parma, 1700–1701; 4 vols., Venice, 1712, and 3 vols., Parma, 1714; several later edd. *Lettere inedite*, ed. G. Boero (Naples, 1848); further *Lettere inedite di P. Segneri al granduca Cosimo Terzo* [ed. S. Giamini] (Florence, 1857). P. T. Venturi, S.J. (ed.), 'Lettere inedite di Paolo Segneri di Cosimo III e di Giuseppe Agnelli intorno la condanna dell' opera segneriana la "Concordia"' in *Archivio storico italiano*, Ser. 5, xxxi (1903), pp. 127–65. The brief life by G. Massei, S.J. (Venice, 1701), is also pr. in the edd. of his works; Eng. tr. ed. F. W. *Faber, Cong. Orat., London, 1851. G. Minozzi, *Paolo Segneri* (Il pensiero cristiano, i, 2 vols., Amatrice, 1949). V. Socini, *Il p. Paolo Segneri (1624–1694) nella storia farnese a Parma con lettere e documenti inediti* (Parma, 1924). G. Marzot, *Un classico della controriforma, Paolo Segneri* (Saggi di letteratura ital., x; Palermo, 1950). Sommervogel, vii (1896), cols. 1050–89, and ix (1900), col. 849. R. Brouillard in *D.T.C.*, xiv (pt. 2; 1951), cols. 1771–5, s.v.; C. Testore in *E.C.*, xi (1953), cols. 239–41, s.v., for further litt.

SÉGUIER, PIERRE (1588–1672), Chancellor of France from 1635 (with some interruptions) until his death. A keen patron of literature, he possessed one of the finest private collections of (esp. Greek) MSS. then in existence. Séguier's great-grandson, H. C. du Cambout de Coislin, Bp. of Me:z from 1697 to 1732, into whose hands his library had passed, commissioned the *Maurist scholar, B. de *Montfaucon, to make a catalogue of it, which he issued in 1715 as *Bibliotheca Coisliniana olim Segueriana*. In 1732 the MSS came into the possession of the abbey of *St.-Germain-des-Prés, whence those which survived the fire at the abbey in 1794 passed to the Bibliothèque Nationale.

Life by R. Kerviler (Paris, 1874).

SEISES, Dance of the. The religious dance performed before the Blessed Sacrament in Seville Cathedral every day in the *Octaves of *Corpus Christi and of the Immaculate *Conception of the BVM. It is executed by a group of boys, of whom there were formerly (as their name implies; seis='six') only six, but are now ten.

SELBORNE, First Earl of. See *Palmer, Roundell.*

SELDEN, JOHN (1584–1654), author of the *History of Tithes.* Educated at Hart Hall, Oxford, he was admitted to the bar at the Inner Temple in 1612, but never made the practice of law more than incidental to his life. He sat in several parliaments, being M.P. for Oxford University in the Long Parliament. A moderate *Puritan, he became in 1643 a member of the *Westminster Assembly of Divines. His learning was prodigious. In his *History of Tithes* (1618) he upheld their legal, but denied their Divine, right, and in consequence the book was suppressed and its author forbidden to reply to any of his antagonists. Among his other historico-legal writings are *Jani Anglorum Facies Altera* (1610), *The Duello* (1610; a history of trial by combat), *Mare Clausum* (1635, but for the most part written much earlier; a reply to H. *Grotius's *Mare Liberum,* 1609), and *Privileges of Baronage* (1642). Selden was also one of the foremost oriental scholars of his day and the author of *De Diis Syris* (1617). The greater part of his valuable collection of books passed to the *Bodleian Library. His *Table Talk* (1689), the utterances of his last twenty years, was compiled by his amanuensis, Richard Milward.

Opera Omnia, ed. D. *Wilkins (3 vols. bound in 6, London, 1726), with life by id. in vol. i, pt. 1, pp. i–lvi. Modern ed. of his *Table Talk* by F. Pollock (London, 1927), with account of his life by E. Fry (repr. from *D.N.B.,* li (1897), pp. 212–14, s.v.), pp. 153–85, and introd., pp. vii–xxiv. G. W. Johnson, *Memoirs of the Life of John Selden and Notices of the Political Contest during his Time* (1835). J. Aitkin, *The Lives of John Selden, Esq., and Archbishop Usher* (1812), pp. 1–199. H. D. Hazeltine, 'Selden as a Legal Historian: A Comment in Criticism and Appreciation' in *Festschrift Heinrich Brunner zum siebzigsten Geburtstag dargebracht von Schülern und Verehrern* (1910), pp. 579–630. A. W. Ward, 'Selden's Table Talk' in A. W. Ward–A. R. Waller (edd.), *The Cambridge History of English Literature,* viii (1912), pp. 321–7. D. M. Barratt, 'The Library of John Selden and its later History' in *Bodleian Record,* iii (1951), pp. 128–42, 208–13 and 256–74.

SELEUCEIA, Synod of. See *Ariminum and Seleuceia, Synods of.*

SELLON, PRISCILLA LYDIA (c. 1821–1876), restorer of the religious life in the C of E. She was the daughter of W. R. B. Sellon, Commander R.N. When about to leave England for her health on New Year's Day, 1848, she was led to change her plans at the last moment by a public appeal of H. *Phillpotts, Bp. of Exeter, for work among the degraded and destitute of Plymouth, Devonport, and Stonehouse. Here she was gradually joined by others, who, with the help of E. B.

*Pusey, created a community life (the 'Devonport Sisters of Mercy'), set up schools and orphanages and heroically tended the sick in the cholera epidemic of 1848. Their conventual mode of life soon provoked local opposition, but the support of Phillpotts (who, however, withdrew from the office of 'visitor' in 1852) enabled them to continue. In 1856 Miss Sellon united her community with the Sisters of the Holy Cross at Osnaburgh Street, Regent's Park, and assumed the title of Abbess of the combined sisterhood of the 'Society of the Most Holy Trinity' (present headquarters at Ascot Priory, Berks). In her last years Miss Sellon suffered severely from paralysis. In 1867 she visited Honolulu, where she founded St. Andrew's Priory. She died at West Malvern.

T. J. Williams, *Priscilla Lydia Sellon* (1950).

SELWYN, GEORGE AUGUSTUS (1809–1878), first Bp. of *New Zealand. Educated at Eton and St. John's College, Cambridge, he was ordained deacon in 1833 and made missionary Bishop of New Zealand in 1841. He was a *Tractarian in his convictions, whose formal protest against a clause in the civil Letter Patent professing to 'give him power to ordain' signalled the beginnings of a less Erastian conception of the Colonial Episcopate. He had a very marked effect on the future of the New Zealand Church, for settling the constitution of which he was himself largely responsible. Returning to England in 1867, he was appointed in 1868 to the see of Lichfield and held this office till his death.

His son, JOHN RICHARDSON SELWYN (1844–1898), was Bp. of Melanesia (1877–89) and master of Selwyn College, Cambridge (1890–1898), which had been founded in memory of his father in 1881.

Lives by H. W. Tucker (2 vols., London, 1879), G. H. Curteis (ib., 1889), and Louise Creighton (ib., 1923). R. Bayne in *D.N.B.,* li (1897), p. 232 f.; R. H. Codrington in *D.E.C.H.,* p. 550 f.

SEMIARIANISM. The teaching of the theologians who gathered round *Basil of Ancyra from c. 356 onwards and upheld a doctrine of Christ's Sonship intermediate between that of orthodoxy and *Arianism. Other members of the group were *Macedonius of Constantinople, *George of Laodicea, *Eustathius of Sebaste, and Eleusius of Cyzicus. Over against ὁμοούσιος, they took as their watchword ὁμοιούσιος; but the whole tendency of the group was towards orthodoxy. They were sympathetically treated by St. *Athanasius at the Alexandrine Council of 362, and by their theological influence on the *Cappadocian Fathers' contributed largely to the reaffirmation of orthodoxy at the Council of Constantinople in 381.

The chief work is J. Gummerus, *Die homöusianische Partei bis zum Tode des Konstantius.* Ein Beitrag zur Geschichte des arianischen Streites in den Jahren 356–61 (1900). Much useful material also in H. M. *Gwatkin, *Studies of Arianism* (ed. 2, 1900). G. Rasneur, 'L'Homoiousianisme dans ses rapports avec l'orthodoxie' in *R.H.E.,* iv (1903), pp. 189–206, 411–31. F. J. Foakes Jackson in *H.E.R.E.*, xi (1920), pp. 374–6, s.v.; É. Amann in *D.T.C.*, xiv (pt. 2; 1941), cols. 1790–6, s.v. 'Semi-Ariens'. See also bibl. to *Arianism*.

SEMI-DOUBLES. Feasts in the Roman Calendar which rank below *Doubles and above *Simple Feasts. By a decree of the Sacred Congregation of *Rites dated 23 Mar. 1955, the rank of Semi-Double was abolished, feasts which had ranked hitherto as such being reduced to Simples. For the classification of feasts, see also *Doubles*.

SEMINARY. The term is sometimes used to describe Anglican *Theological Colleges (q.v.), but is more usually kept for the corresponding institutions in the RC Church. The Council of *Trent ordered the establishment of a seminary in every diocese and this has remained roughly the rule of the RC Church. The rules concerning seminaries are to be found in *CIC*, cans. 1352–71. Seminaries are of different kinds, diocesan, interdiocesan, provincial, and pontifical, acc. to the authority which establishes them and has jurisdiction over them.

SEMI-PELAGIANISM. The doctrines on human nature upheld by a group of theologians in the 4th and 5th cents., who, while not denying the necessity of *Grace for salvation, maintained that the first steps towards the Christian life were ordinarily taken by the human will and that Grace supervened only later. Their position was roughly midway between the radically opposed doctrines of St. *Augustine and *Pelagius. (It should be added that the term 'Semi-Pelagian', which is modern, was orig. coined by the followers of D. *Banez for the doctrines of the Jesuit, L. *Molina; in this sense it is now extinct.)

These teachings first took definite shape in the writings of *Cassian of Marseilles *c.* 420 and received widespread support esp. in the monasteries in the S. of Gaul. They developed mainly in opposition to St. Augustine's later writings, which taught an extreme form of predestination, infallible perseverance, and a 'numerous clausus' of the elect. When after Augustine's death (430) these doctrines continued to be championed by his disciple, St. *Prosper of Aquitaine, they were fiercely attacked in two writings of Gallic *provenance*, the 'Objectiones Vincentianae', almost certainly by St. *Vincent of Lérins, and in the 'Capitula Gallorum'. Prosper replied in two no less violent works 'Contra Collatorem' and 'Responsiones ad Capitula Objectionum Gallorum'. After this the controversy subsided, though Semi-Pelagianism continued to be the dominant teaching in Gaul for several generations.

Early in the 6th cent. the controversy broke out afresh over the 'De Gratia Dei', a Semi-Pelagian writing of *Faustus of Riez (q.v.), composed *c.* 470. Its author had long been dead, but the work was denounced as heretical both at *Constantinople and Rome by the

Scythian monks under John Maxentius. Its critics gained the support of St. *Fulgentius of Ruspe and of St. *Caesarius of Arles; and through their agency Semi-Pelagian (as well as Pelagian) doctrines were formally condemned by the Council of *Orange of 529. From then onwards the Augustinian teaching on grace was generally accepted in orthodox Western theology.

For an extended treatment, see the classical study of H. *Noris, *Historia Pelagiana* (Padua, 1673), pp. 158–338. F. Wörter, *Beiträge zur Dogmengeschichte des Semipelagianismus* ('1898' [1897]); id., *Zur Dogmengeschichte des Semipelagianismus* (Kirchengeschichtliche Studien, v, Hft. 2; 1899). F. A. *Loofs in *P.R.E.* (ed. 3), xviii (1906), pp. 192–203, s.v. 'Semipelagianismus'; É. Amann in *D.T.C.*, xiv (pt. 2; 1941), cols. 1796–1850, s.v. 'Semi-Pélagiens'. See also bibl. to *Pelagianism* and to the entries on the Semi-Pelagians mentioned in the text.

SEMI-QUIETISM. A name sometimes applied to the doctrines of Abp. *Fénelon and other spiritual writers who, though not sufficiently unorthodox to come under the censures attaching to *Quietism and quite free from its anti-ecclesiastical and antimoral elements, manifest certain quietist tendencies.

SEMLER, JOHANN SALOMO (1725–91), *Lutheran theologian and Biblical critic. Born at Saalfeld in Thuringia, he studied at Halle, where he later became Prof. of Theology (1753–91). He soon rejected the *Pietism of his youth for a rationalistic position which he termed 'liberalis theologia'. One of the first German theologians to apply the critico-historical method to the study of the Biblical *Canon and Text, he reached many novel, and often unorthodox, conclusions, at some points anticipating F. C. *Baur. He held, however, that Christian ministers should be required to make external profession of all traditional doctrine. In this matter, finding himself at variance with G. E. *Lessing in the controversy over the *Wolfenbüttel Fragments, he directed against Lessing his *Beantwortung der Fragmente eines Ungekannten* (1779). In his last years he interested himself in scientific, alchemistic, and theosophical studies. His principal treatises are *Historiae Ecclesiasticae Selecta Capita* (3 vols., Halle, 1767–9), *Abhandlung von freier Untersuchung des Canon* (4 parts, Halle, 1771–5), *Commentarii Historici de Antiquo Christianorum Statu* (2 vols., Halle, 1771–2), and *Versuch eines fruchtbaren Auszugs der Kirchengeschichte* (3 vols., Halle, 1773–8).

Autobiography, 2 vols., Halle, 1781–2, with list of his writings. H. Hoffmann, *Die Theologie Semlers* (1905); P. Gastrow, *Johann Salomo Semler in seiner Bedeutung für die Theologie* (1905); L. Zscharnack, *Lessing und Semler. Ein Beitrag zur Entstehungsgeschichte des Rationalismus und der kritischen Theologie* (1905). Id. in *R.G.G.* (ed. 2), v (1931), col. 427 f., s.v., with further bibl.

SEMPRINGHAM. In S. Lincolnshire, the mother-house of the Order founded by St. *Gilbert of Sempringham (d. 1189; q.v.). Gilbert was in early life an incumbent of the parish.

SENECA, LUCIUS ANNAEUS (*c.* 4 B.C.–A.D. 65), Roman moralist. A native of Cordova, he studied at *Rome under the *Stoic Attalus, and entered on a career at the bar. Under the Emp. *Claudius he was banished for several years to Corsica (41–49). After his recall by Agrippina he became the tutor of the future Emp. Nero. In the earlier part of Nero's reign he exercised much influence, being granted a suffect consulate *c.* 56; later he was charged by Nero with taking part in Piso's conspiracy and forced to take his own life. Seneca's brother, *Gallio (q.v.), who was Proconsul of Achaia, is mentioned in Acts 18. 12.

Seneca's writings include a collection of so-called 'Dialogues', among them 'De Providentia', 'De Ira', 'De Beata Vita' (imperfect), 'De Tranquillitate Animi', 'De Brevitate Vitae'; a set of 124 'Epistulae Morales' addressed to Lucilius; the 'Apocolocyntosis', a skit on the deification of the Emp. Claudius; and the 'Naturales Quaestiones', a treatise on natural phenomena which was widely read in the Middle Ages. He also wrote some Tragedies. His writings represent Stoicism at its best and have been much studied by Christian apologists for the similarities as well as the contrasts of their moral teaching with the Gospel ethic.

There is also in existence an apocryphal correspondence of fourteen letters between Seneca (eight letters) and St. *Paul (six letters). Their commonplace manner and colourless style show that they cannot be the work of either the moralist or of St. Paul. They are prob. the same letters as those known to St. *Jerome (*De Vir. Illustr.* xii), who on the strength of them reckons Seneca a Christian, and to St. *Augustine (*Ep.* cliii. 14), though some critics have denied the identification and assigned the extant letters to a much later date. The oldest MSS. date from the 9th cent., and the text is transmitted in a corrupt state.

There have been innumerable editions of Seneca's works, beginning with the *editio princeps* of B. Romerus, Naples, 1475. Modern lives by R. Waltz (Paris, 1909) and C. Marchesi (Messina, 1920). M. Baumgarten, *Lucius Annaeus Seneca und das Christenthum* (1895). E. Albertini, *La Composition dans les ouvrages philosophiques de Sénèque* (1923). Überweg, i, 488 f., 491–3, with bibl. pp. 158*–162*. R. D. Hicks–'X' in *E.B.* (ed. 11), xxiv (1911), p. 637 f., s.v.; E. P. Barker in *O.C.D.*, p. 827 f., s.v. 'Seneca (2)'.

Edd. of Seneca's Correspondence with St. Paul by F. X. Kraus in *T.Q.*, xlix (1867), pp. 603–24; by F. Haase in *Senecae Opera*, Suppl. 1902 (Teub.), pp. 74–9, and by C. W. Barlow (Rome, 1938). Eng. tr. in M. R. James, *The Apocryphal New Testament* (1924), pp. 480–4. T. *Zahn, *Geschichte des neutestamentlichen Kanons*, ii (pt. 2; 1892), pp. 612–22; P. de Labriolle, *La Réaction païenne*. Étude sur la polémique antichrétienne du Ier au VIe siècle (1934), pp. 25–8. On the relations between St. Paul and the real Seneca see J. B. *Lightfoot, 'St. Paul and Seneca' in *Philippians* (1868), pp. 268–331; K. Deissner, *Paulus und Seneca* (Beiträge zur Förderung christlicher Theologie, Bd. xxi (2), 1917); and P. Benoît, O.P., 'Sénèque et Saint Paul' in *R. Bibl.*, liii (1946), pp. 7–35.

SENS, Councils of. Of the many provincial Councils held at Sens (e.g. in A.D. 601, 833, 845, 1141, 1225, 1461, 1485), the most renowned is that of 1141 (or perh. 1140) under Abp. Henri le Sanglier, which condemned *Abelard for heresy. Abelard forthwith appealed to Pope Innocent II against its sentence.

On the council of 1141, Hardouin, vi (pt. 2), cols. 1219–24; Mansi, xxi (Venice, 1776), cols. 559–70. Hefele–Leclercq, v (pt. 1; 1912), pp. 747–90. M. Deutsch, *Die Synode von Sens 1141 und die Verurteilung Abälards* (1880). E. Vacandard, 'Chronologie abélardienne; la date du concile de Sens: 1140' in *R.Q.H.*, l (1891), pp. 235–45. See also works cited under *Abelard, P.*, and *Bernard, St.*

SEPARATISTS. As a title, first applied to the followers of R. *Browne and later to the *Independents (*Congregationalists) and others who separated from the C of E.

SEPTUAGESIMA (Lat., 'the seventieth [day before Easter]'). The third Sunday before *Lent and hence the ninth before *Easter. The name, which first occurs in the *Gelasian Sacramentary, seems not very appropriate, as the Sunday indicated is in fact only 64, and not 70, days before Easter; but perhaps it was coined by reckoning back the series 'septuagesima', 'sexagesima', 'quinquagesima', from Quinquagesima Sunday, which is exactly 50 days from Easter. Liturgically it marks a stage towards the Lent fast. In the W. purple vestments are worn from that day onwards until *Holy Week and the word 'Alleluia' is not used again in the offices or at Mass until Lent is over. The traditional OT Lessons on Septuagesima are the Creation Narratives in Gen. 1 and 2.

C. Callewaert, 'L'Œuvre liturgique de S. Grégoire. La septuagésime et l'alléluia' in *R.H.E.*, xxxiii (1937), pp. 306–326; G. *Morin, O.S.B., 'La Part des papes du sixième siècle dans le développement de l'année liturgique' in *R. Bén.*, lii (1940), pp. 1–14, pp. 1–8 being relevant; J. Froger, O.S.B., 'Les Anticipations du jeûne quadragésimal' in *Mélanges de Science religieuse*, iii (1946), pp. 207–34; A. Chavasse, 'Temps de préparation à la Pâques d'après quelques livres liturgiques romains' in *Rech. S.R.*, xxxvii (1950), pp. 125–45 esp. V, 'La "Septantaine" ou Septuagésime', pp. 143–5. H. *Leclercq, O.S.B., in *D.A.C.L.*, xv (pt. 1; 1950), cols. 1262–6, s.v.

SEPTUAGINT, The. ('LXX.') The most influential of the Greek versions of the Heb. OT. Jewish tradition asserts it was written for Ptolemy Philadelphus (285–246 B.C.), who desired a translated copy of the Hebrew Law for his famous Library at Alexandria (see *Aristeas, Letter of*) and engaged 72 translators (hence the title 'Septuagint') for the work. Gradually the story was improved, and Ptolemy's name was connected not only with the Pentateuch, but with all the OT. Little credence is now given to these traditions. Internal evidence indicates that the LXX was really the work of several Alexandrian Jewish translators, in some cases more than one scholar sharing a Hebrew Book, and that the work of translation extended over a considerable period. A passage in the preface to the Greek version of Ecclus. suggests that at its date (132 B.C.) the Greek OT as we now know it was virtually complete.

The LXX differs from the Hebrew Bible in the order of the Biblical books and in its greater extent. The threefold grouping into the 'Law', the 'Prophets', and the 'Writings' is abandoned, and several other Books, which are not found in the OT but which circulated among Greek-speaking Jews, are included.

The latter, known as the '*Apocrypha' in the English Bible, include Wisdom, Ecclesiasticus, Judith, Tobit, and Baruch. Also the text of the LXX differs considerably at many points from the corresponding Hebrew. Thus the LXX of Job is about one-sixth shorter than the Hebrew; there are important omissions in 1 Sam. and Jer.; and there are considerable differences in order in Jer. and Ezek.

The early Christian Church inherited the LXX version of the Scriptures, and the NT writers commonly quoted the OT Books from the LXX. In Mt. 1. 23, where the *Immanuel prophecy of Is. 7. 14 is cited in the LXX form, the Greek is particularly relevant since it here renders the Hebrew word 'almah ('a young woman of marriageable age') by παρθένος ('a virgin'). Commonly, however, the differences between the Hebrew and LXX are only verbal. It must also be noted that in a number of NT passages the Hebrew is followed against the LXX.

In post-NT times, the Christian Fathers down to the later 4th cent. almost all regarded the LXX as the standard form of the OT and seldom referred to the Hebrew. *Origen, however, was greatly interested in the relation of the LXX to the Hebrew and the other Greek versions. The LXX was also the basis of the '*Old Latin Version(s)' of the OT. It was St. *Jerome's *Vulgate that first provided Christians with a version of the OT Scriptures direct from their original language, and did most to dispel the belief, common in the early Church, that the LXX was verbally inspired.

The LXX exists in a large number of MSS., uncial and minuscule, as well as in a number of important, though not very extensive, papyrus fragments (esp. the *Chester Beatty Papyri). The MSS. include the *Codex Sinaiticus, where, however, only about a third of the OT survives; the *Codex Vaticanus, with Gen. 1. 1–46. 28, and a few other portions wanting; and the *Codex Ephraemi, of which only 64 leaves from the poetical books remain.

The complete LXX was printed for the first time in Cardinal *Ximenes' *Complutensian Polyglott (1514–17), the Latin Vulgate being placed between the Hebrew on the left and the LXX on the right ('tanquam duos hinc et inde latrones, medium autem Jesum'). Later editions are those of A. Manutius (1518); 'Auctoritate Sixti V Pont. Max.' (Rome, 1586); J. E. *Grabe (Oxford, 1707–20); R. Holmes–J. Parsons (Oxford, 1798–1827); H. B. *Swete (Cambridge, 1887–94); A. E. Brooke, N. McLean, and H. St. J. Thackeray (Cambridge, 1906 ff.); A. Rahlfs (Stuttgart, 1935).

E. *Hatch–H. A. Redpath, A Concordance to the Septuagint (2 vols., 1897; suppl., 1906). H. St. J. Thackeray, A Grammar of the Old Testament in Greek according to the Septuagint (vol. i, all publ., 1909). H. B. Swete, An Introduction to the Old Testament in Greek (1900, rev. by R. R. Ottley, 1914). R. R. Ottley, Handbook to the Septuagint (1920). P. de *Lagarde, 'Septuaginta Studien' in Abh. (Gött.), xxxvii (1891), pp. 3–92, and xxxviii (1892), pp. 3–102. A. Rahlfs (ed.), Septuaginta-Studien (3 vols., 1904–11). F. G. Kenyon, The Text of the Greek Bible (1937), pp. 24–65. Mitteilungen des Septuaginta-Unternehmens der Gesellschaft der Wissenschaften zu Göttingen (5 vols., Berlin, 1910–32).

E. *Nestle in H.D.B., iv (1902), pp. 437–54, s.v.; F. C. *Burkitt in E.Bi., iv (1903), col. 5016 f., s.v. 'Text and Versions'.

SEPULCHRE, Holy. See Holy Sepulchre.

SEQUENCE (Lat. sequentia).

In the Liturgy, a rhythm sung on certain days between the *Gradual and the *Gospel. The word seems to have been applied originally to the series of notes on which the final a of the *Alleluia was sung. As time went on, a syllabic text was introduced as a basis of this music, and by an easy change the word was transferred from the melody to the text of the composition, which gradually came to resemble a hymn in form. In medieval times a large number of sequences were in regular use. Many of these have survived in the rites of the religious orders, e.g. the *Dominican, but in the Roman Missal their number has now been reduced to five. These are the well-known '*Victimae paschali' (at *Easter), the '*Veni, sancte Spiritus' (at *Whitsun), the '*Lauda Sion' (at *Corpus Christi), the '*Dies Irae' (at *All Souls'), and the '*Stabat Mater' (on the two Feasts of Our Lady's *Seven Sorrows). The last-named was not added till 1727.

Nine volumes of Sequentiae Ineditae are published in A.H.M.A., viz. vols. viii, ix, x, xxxiv, xxxvii, xxxix, xl, xlii, and xliv (1890–1904); others are printed in other volumes in the same series. N. Gihr, Die Sequenzen des römischen Messbuches dogmatisch und ascetisch erklärt (1887). Jungmann, M.S., i (ed. 1949), pp. 538–44; Eng. tr., pp. 436–41, with reff. Raby (ed. 1953), pp. 210–19, with bibl. p. 479.

SERAPHIC ORDER, The.

Another name for the *Franciscan Order (q.v.). The name commemorates St. Francis's vision on Mount Alverna in which he saw a seraph from heaven impressing the stigmata on his body.

SERAPHIM.

The supernatural creatures, each with six wings, which *Isaiah in his inaugural vision saw hovering above the throne of Jehovah (Is. 6. 2–7). Unless they are to be identified with the fiery serpents mentioned in Num. 21. 6 ff., Deut. 8. 15, Is. 14. 29, and Is. 30. 6, which in the Heb. text are denoted by formally the same word, they are not mentioned elsewhere in the OT. If this identity be allowed, the Seraphim in Is. presumably had some resemblance to serpents.

From an early date Christian interpreters held the 'Seraphim' to be a category of *angels, and considered them counterparts of the '*Cherubim; hence their occurrence together in the *Preface of the Roman Mass and also in the *Te Deum. The further view, which was widely accepted among Christian exegetes, that the Heb. word 'seraphim' was connected with a root meaning 'to burn' led to the notion that they were esp. distinguished by the fervour of their love. As such they came to be ranked highest in the nine orders of angels (the cherubim filling the next place).

O.E.D., viii (pt. 2; 1914), p. 490 f., s.v. J. Strachan in H.D.B., iv (1902), p. 458 f., s.v. See also comm. to Is. 6. 2 ff.

SERAPION, St. (d. 211), Bp. of *Antioch from 199. Though one of the chief theologians of his age, little is known of him. His writings, of which only a few fragments survive, include a letter to Caricus and Pontius against *Montanism, a work addressed to one Domninus who had lapsed during persecution, and a letter withdrawing his earlier permission to the Church of Rhossus to read the 'Gospel of St. *Peter', on the ground that he had now discovered it to be *Docetic. Feast day, 30 Oct.

The principal ancient authorities are *Eusebius, *H.E.* v, xix and vi, xii, and *Jerome, *De Viris Illustribus*, 31. The fragments are collected in M. J. *Routh, *Reliquiae Sacrae*, i (ed. 2), pp. 447–62.

SERAPION, St. (d. after 360), Bp. of Thmuis in the Nile delta from *c.* 339. He was the close friend and protégé of St. *Athanasius, probably his junior in age; and before he became bishop had been a monk and a companion of St. *Antony, who left in his will one of his two sheepskin cloaks to Serapion and the other to Athanasius. Athanasius selected him for a difficult mission to the Emp. Constantius, and addressed to him a series of important doctrinal letters on the Divinity of the Holy Ghost. Serapion composed some literary works, notably a treatise against the *Manichees; and an early 'Sacramentary' which has come down under his name was probably his compilation. He also corresponded with the heresiarch *Apollinarius, then still orthodox. Feast day, 21 Mar.

Crit. ed. of 'Serapion of Thmuis against the Manichees' by R. P. Casey (Harvard Theological Studies, No. 15, Cambridge, Mass., 1931); older uncrit. text, with other items of Serapion, in J. P. Migne, *PG*, xl, 895–942 (from A. *Gallandi). 'Sacramentary' (or 'Euchologion'), which survives in the single 11th cent. MS. Athos Laura 149, ed. by G. Wobbermin, *Altchristliche liturgische Stücke aus der Kirche Ägyptens nebst einem dogmatischen Brief des Bischofs Serapion von Thmuis* (T.U., xvii. 3b; 1898); also ed. by F. E. *Brightman in *J.T.S.*, i (1899–1900), pp. 88–113, 247–77. Eng. tr. (based on Wobbermin's ed. 1) by J. *Wordsworth (*Bishop Sarapion's Prayer-book*; Early Church Classics, S.P.C.K., 1899). Eng. ed. of Athanasius's Epp. to Serapion, with introd. and notes, by C. R. B. Shapland (1951). A. Peters, O.F.M., 'Het Tractaat van Serapion van Thmuis tegen de Manichaeën' in *Sacris Erudiri*, ii (1949), pp. 55–94. B. *Capelle, O.S.B., 'L'Anaphore de Sérapion. Essai d'exégèse' in *Muséon*, lix (1946), pp. 425–43. Bardenhewer, iii, 98–102. G. Bardy in *D.T.C.*, xiv (pt. 2; 1941), cols. 1908–12, s.v.

SERGEANT, JOHN (1622–1707), RC controversialist. He was educated at St. John's College, Cambridge, and afterwards became secretary to T. *Morton, Bp. of *Durham. Later he became a RC. After study at the English College, Lisbon, he was ordained to the priesthood, and in 1652 was attached to the English Mission. The remainder of his life was spent in controversy, for which he had marked gifts. Indeed there was hardly any Protestant writer of standing whose views Sergeant did not attack. The titles of some 34 pamphlets by Sergeant are listed under his name in the *D.N.B.*

His 'Literary Life' written by himself is publ. in *Catholicon*, ii (1816), pp. 132–6, 169–76, 217–24, iii (1816), pp. 9–16, 55–64, 97–104, and 121–7, with introd. in ii, pp. 129–31. T. Cooper in *D.N.B.*, li (1897), pp. 251–3, s.v.

SERGIUS (d. 638), Patr. of *Constantinople from 610 and the most influential exponent of *Monothelitism. He was of Syrian origin. After elevation to the Patriarchal See he became the trusted adviser of Emp. *Heraclius, who confided the capital to his care during his absence in his wars with the Persians. To reconcile the disaffected Monophysites Sergius, in his search for a Christological formula acceptable both to them and to the adherents of the Dyophysite *Chalcedonian orthodoxy, began to teach Two Natures but only one 'activity' (ἐνέργεια) in Christ. On being opposed by St. *Sophronius of Jerusalem, he referred the case to Pope *Honorius I, who in his reply used the unfortunate expression 'one will'. Sergius now modified his teaching to the affirmation of only one will (μία θέλησις) in Christ. This doctrine was promulgated by the Emperor in the famous '*Ecthesis' (q.v.), of which Sergius was the author. Two synods held at Constantinople in 638 and 639 approved this teaching, which was, however, condemned by the Council of Constantinople in 681. Sergius is believed to have introduced several liturgical innovations, and an old tradition ascribes to him the authorship of the famous hymn known as the '*Acathistos'.

V. Grumel, A.A., *Les Régestes des actes du patriarcat de Constantinople*, i, fasc. i (1932), pp. 113–18 (Nos. 279–93), with reff. Krumbacher, pp. 671–3. See also bibl. to *Monothelitism*, esp. artt. by V. Grumel.

SERGIUS, St. (d. 701), Pope from 687. A native of *Antioch, he was educated at Palermo. On the death of his predecessor, Pope Conon (686–7), Sergius was elected in the face of two rival candidates with the support of the mass of the clergy and people. He took an active part in several English matters. He baptized Caedwalla, King of the West Saxons (689), consecrated St. *Willibrord, Bp. of the Frisians (Nov. 695), and ordered St. *Wilfrid to be restored to his see (*c.* 700). He strongly resisted the attempt of the Emp. Justinian II (685–95) to secure his support for the *Trullan Council (692) which would have placed Constantinople on an ecclesiastical level with Rome and was saved by the Roman populace from being forcibly conveyed to the Eastern capital. He made various liturgical innovations, notably the singing of *Agnus Dei in the Mass and the introduction of a litany and processions on the four chief feasts of Our Lady. He also did much for the restoration of the Roman basilicas. Feast day, 8 Sept.

Jaffé, i, 244 f. *L.P.* (Duchesne), i, 371–82. F. Görres, 'Justinian II und das römische Papsttum' in *B.Z.*, xvii (1908), pp. 432–54, esp. pp. 440–54. J. Gay, 'Quelques Remarques sur les papes grecs et syriens avant la querelle des iconoclastes (678–715)' in *Mélanges offerts à M. Gustave Schlumberger*, i (1924), pp. 40–54. Mann, i (pt. 2; 1902), pp. 77–104. E. Caspar, *Geschichte des Papsttums*, ii (1933), pp. 624–36; Fliche–Martin, v (1938), pp. 407–9. É. Amann in *D.T.C.*, xiv (pt. 2; 1941), cols. 1913–16, s.v. 'Serge Ier'; A. Amore, O.F.M., in *E.C.*, xi (1953), col. 384 f., s.v. 'Sergio I', with further bibl. See also bibl. to *Trullan Synod*.

SERGIUS, St. (1314–92), Russian monastic reformer and mystic. His original name was Bartholomew. He was born at Rostov, and when a boy fled with his family to Radonež, nr. Moscow. He founded in the neighbourhood, with his brother Stephen, the famous monastery of the Holy Trinity, and thereby reestablished the community life which had been lost in Russia through the Tartar invasion. When his brother opposed his reforms, Sergius, though abbot, retired into seclusion, but was later restored. He had great influence over all classes, stopped four civil wars between Russian princes, and inspired the resistance of Prince Dmitri which saved Russia from the Tartars (1380). In 1378 he refused the metropolitan see. Altogether, Sergius founded forty monasteries. He was canonized before 1449, and is regarded as the greatest of Russian saints. Feast day, 25 Sept.

The primary authority is the life written by Epiphanius the Wise, one of his monks, which was shortened and revised in the 15th cent. by a Serbian monk, Pachomius. Abridged Eng. tr. in G. P. Fedotov (ed.), *A Treasury of Russian Spirituality* (1950), pp. 54–83, with introd. pp. 50–3, and notes pp. 487–9. N. Zernov, *St. Sergius: Builder of Russia* (New York, 1939), also with Eng. tr. of Life, by A. Delafeld, as pt. 3 (ptt. 1 and 2 also publ., London, [1939]).

SERGIUS PAULUS. The proconsul of *Cyprus who, acc. to Acts 13. 4–12, having invited St. *Paul and St. *Barnabas to preach before him on their first missionary journey and seen the miracle done by St. Paul on the sorcerer Bar-Jesus, 'believed' (ἐπίστευσεν). He is perhaps the Paulus mentioned as proconsul in a Cypriot inscription of this time.

A. C. *Headlam in *H.D.B.*, iii (1900), p. 731, s.v. 'Paulus, Sergius'; J. E. Roberts in *D.A.C.*, ii (1918), p. 471, s.v. 'Sergius Paulus'.

SERMO GENERALIS. The ceremony at which the final decision in trials of heretics by the *Inquisition was pronounced, usually with great solemnity. After a short exhortation, the 'sermo' proper, the secular officials assisting at the ceremony vowed obedience to the Inquisitor; then were published the 'decrees of mercy', i.e. mitigations of earlier sentences; and lastly the penalties imposed on those found guilty at the present trial were announced. The proceedings closed with the turning-over of the guilty to the secular arm. The term 'Sermo Generalis' has come to be replaced in more recent usage by '*auto-da-fé'.

SERMON ON THE MOUNT, The. The Lord's discourse in Mt. 5–7 setting forth the principles of the Christian ethic. It includes the eight (or, acc. to another counting, nine) *Beatitudes (5. 3–12) and the *Lord's Prayer (6. 9–13). The Mountain (cf. Mt. 5. 1) is traditionally Karn Hattin. A shorter discourse of similar content, sometimes known as the 'Sermon on the Plain', is recorded in Lk. 6. 20–49 [cf. 6. 17].

The only Patristic treatment of the subject as a separate work is St. *Augustine, 'De Sermone Domini in Monte' (*PL*, xxxiv, 1229–1308); Eng. tr. by J. J. Jepson, with introd. and notes (Ancient Christian Writers, v; 1948). F. A. G. *Tholuck, *Philologisch-theologische Auslegung der Bergpredigt Christi nach Matthäus, zugleich ein Beitrag zur Begründung einer rein-biblischen Glaubens- und Sittenlehre*

(1833; Eng. tr., 1834–7); E. Achelis, *Die Bergpredigt nach Matthaeus und Lucas exegetisch und kritisch untersucht* (Bielefeld, 1875); W. B. *Carpenter, *The Great Charter of Christ. Being Studies in the Sermon on the Mount* (1895; homiletic); C. *Gore, *The Sermon on the Mount* (1896; also homiletic); B. W. Bacon, *The Sermon on the Mount. Its Literary Structure and Didactic Purpose* (1902). K. Bornhäuser, *Die Bergpredigt. Versuch einer zeitgenössischen Auslegung* (Beiträge zur Förderung christlicher Theologie, Reihe 2, vii; 1923); C. Stange, 'Zur Ethik der Bergpredigt' in *Zeitschrift für systematische Theologie*, ii (1924), pp. 37–74; G. Kittel, 'Die Bergpredigt und die Ethik des Judentums', ib., iii (1925), pp. 555–94; A. Runestam, 'Das ethische Problem der Bergpredigt', ib., iv (1926–7), pp. 555–72; H. Windisch, *Der Sinn der Bergpredigt* (1929; ed. 2, 1937); M. *Dibelius, *The Sermon on the Mount* (New York, 1940). T. Soiron, O.F.M., *Die Bergpredigt Jesu. Formgeschichtliche, exegetische und theologische Erklärung* (Freiburg i.Br., 1941). W. D. Davies, *The Setting of the Sermon on the Mount* (1963). J. *Moffatt in *E.Bi.*, iv (1903), cols. 4375–91, s.v.; C. W. Votaw in *H.D.B.* Extra vol. (1904), pp. 1–45, with bibl. See also commentaries to *Luke* and *Matthew*, Gospels of.

SERPENT, The Brazen. See *Brazen Serpent, The.*

SERVANT SONGS. The four passages in *Deutero-Isaiah (Is. 42. 1–4, 49. 1–6, 50. 4–9, and 52.13–53.12) describing the person and character of the 'Servant of the Lord'. Christian theology has traditionally interpreted them as a prophecy of the Incarnate Christ. From the rise of modern Biblical scholarship until the last years of the 19th cent. it was the prevalent opinion that the original reference of the passages was to the nation of Israel, or some element in it, which was depicted by the Prophet as Jehovah's Servant. Since 1892, when B. Duhm challenged this interpretation in his celebrated commentary on Is., there have been many attempts to identify the Servant with some historical individual, e.g. Zerubbabel, Jehoiachin, Cyrus, or even *Moses, while in 1921 S. Mowinckel contended (though he abandoned the theory later) that it was the Prophet himself. Among British OT scholars, prevalent opinion (J. Skinner, H. W. *Robinson, C. R. North, H. H. Rowley) still identifies the Servant with Israel in some form.

There is a vast literature. Among the more important items are S. R. *Driver–A. Neubauer, *The Fifty-Third Chapter of Isaiah according to the Jewish Interpretation* (2 vols., 1876–77); F. Giesebrecht, *Beiträge zur Jesajakritik* (1890), pp. 146–85; M. Schian, *Die Ebed-Jahwe-Lieder in Jes. 40–66* (Halle Diss., 1895); L. Laue, *Die Ebed-Jahwe Lieder ... untersucht* (Wittenberg, 1898); K. *Budde, *Die sogennanten Ebed-Jahwe-Lieder in Jes. 40–55* (1900); F. Giesebrecht, *Der Knecht Jahves des Deuterojesaia* (1902); F. Feldmann, *Der Knecht Gottes in Isaias Kap. 40–55* (1907); R. H. *Kennett, *The 'Servant of the Lord'* (1911); S. Mowinckel, *Der Knecht Jahwäs* (Giessen, 1921); L. Köhler, *Deuterojesaja (Jesaja 40–55) stilkritisch untersucht* (Beiheft der *Z.A.T.W.*, xxxvii; 1923); A. S. *Peake, *The Servant of Jahweh and other Lectures* (Manchester, 1931); W. E. Barnes, 'Cyrus the "Servant of Jehovah"' in *J.T.S.*, xxxii (1931), pp. 32–9; O. Eissfeldt, *Der Gottesknecht bei Deutero-Jesaja* (Beiträge zur Religionsgeschichte des Altertums, ii; 1933); J. Begrich, *Studien zu Deuterojesaja* (Beiträge zur Wissenschaft vom Alten und Neuen Testament, 4. Folge; xxv; 1938); C. R. North, *The Suffering Servant in Deutero-Isaiah* (1948; ed. 2, 1956), with valuable bibl. pp. 240–53; H. H. Rowley, *The Servant of the Lord and Other Essays* (1952), pp. 1–88; O. Eissfeldt, 'Neue Forschungen zum Ebed-Jahwe Problem' in *T.L.Z.*, lxviii (1943), cols. 273–80. H. *Gunkel in *R.G.G.* (ed. 1), iii (1912), cols. 1540–3, s.v. 'Knecht Jahwes'; id., ib. (ed. 2), iii (1929), cols. 1100–3, s.v. 'Knecht Jahwes'; H. Zimmerli–J. Jeremias in *T.W.B.*, v (1954), pp. 650–713, s.v. 'παῖς θεοῦ'. The subject is also discussed in all commentaries on Isaiah (qq.v.).

SERVATUS LUPUS. See *Lupus, Servatus.*

SERVER. In the W. Church a minister in the sanctuary, esp. at the Eucharist. He may be either a boy or an adult man, but not a woman, though when no male person is available a woman (lay or religious) may answer a Mass at the altar-rails. His principal duties are to make the responses, move the altar-book from side to side as required, bring the bread and wine to the altar at the *Offertory, to minister the *Lavabo and *Ablutions and to ring the *Sanctus bell. He normally wears cassock and surplice.

SERVETUS, MICHAEL (1511–53), physician and heretic. A native of Tudela in Navarre, he studied at Saragossa and Toulouse and travelled in Italy and Germany, where he met P. *Melanchthon and M. *Bucer. His Biblical studies having led him to abandon the dogma of the Trinity, he published his conclusions in a provocative but earnest treatise *De Trinitatis Erroribus Libri VII* (1531). The book shocked his Protestant friends, and he went to *Paris, where he studied medicine. From 1541 to 1553 he was physician to the Abp. of Vienne. In these years he entered into a secret correspondence with J. *Calvin who, however, soon repudiated his anti-Trinitarian views. In 1553 appeared anonymously his principal work, *Christianismi Restitutio*, in which he expounded his doctrines in full. He denied the Trinity and the true Divinity of Christ, whose humanity he regarded as a compound of three elements, viz. (1) the Logos, conceived as the model of all created things, though not really Divine, (2) the soul, and (3) the human body. Servetus's authorship was denounced to the Catholic *Inquisition by a friend of Calvin and he was imprisoned, but escaped to Geneva, possibly counting on the support of an anti-Calvinist party. Calvin, however, had him arrested and, having refused to recant, he was burnt as a heretic at Champel on 27 Oct. 1553.

Eng. tr. of his *Two Treatises on the Trinity* by E. M. Wilbur (Harvard Theological Studies, xvi; 1932), with life, pp. xix–xxviii, and bibl. W. H. Drummond, *The Life of Michael Servetus, the Spanish Physician* (1848). H. Tollin, *Charakterbild Michael Servets* (1876); id., *Das Lehrsystem Michael Servets genetisch dargestellt* (3 vols., 1876–8); A. van der Linde, *Michel Servet, een Brandoffer der Gereformeerde Inquisitie* (Groningen, 1891), with bibl. R. Willis, *Servetus and Calvin* (1877). J. Goyanes, *Miguel Serveto. Teólogo, geógrafo y médico, descubridor de la circulacíon de la sangre quemado vivo en Ginebra en 1553* (1933). D. Cuthbertson, *A Tragedy of the Reformation*, being the authentic Narrative of the History and Burning of the 'Christianismi Restitutio', 1553, with a succinct Account of the Controversy between Michael Servetus, its Author, and the Reformer, John Calvin (1912). R. H. Bainton, 'The Present State of Servetus Studies' in *The Journal of Modern History*, iv (1932), pp. 72–92, with detailed bibl. B. Riggenbach–E. Lachenmann in *P.R.E.* (ed. 3), xviii (1906), pp. 228–36, s.v. 'Servet, Michael'; L. Cristiani in *D.T.C.*, xiv (pt. 2; 1941), cols. 1967–72, s.v. 'Servet, Michel', with reff.

SERVICE, Divine. See *Divine Service.*

SERVILE WORK (Lat. *opus servile*, Lev. 23, Num. 28 and 29 passim, Vulg.), a term applied specifically to work which is forbidden on *Sundays or Holy Days, as the work of slaves, in contrast with liberal work, that of free men. Taken in early times to cover agricultural and mechanical work, by the 13th cent., when the prohibition was becoming increasingly unpopular, attempts were made to define it (after St. *Augustine, *In Jo.*, iii. 19; J. P. Migne, *PL*, xxxv. 1404) as work which made a man the slave of sin or had the appearance of making him such. In modern RC canon law (*CIC*, can. 1248) the term is still used. It is frequently interpreted as work in which the body plays a greater part than the mind.

SERVITES, The Order of (*Ordo Servorum BVM*). The Order was founded in 1240 by seven wealthy Florentine city councillors who had left the world seven years earlier in order to devote themselves entirely to the service of the BVM. They adopted a black habit and the Rule of St. *Augustine, with some additions from the *Dominican constitutions. The Order developed rapidly, esp. after it had been officially sanctioned by a bull of Benedict XI in 1304. Its most influential member in early days was St. Philip Benizi (1233–85), under whose generalship Servite missionaries were sent as far as India. The Servite nuns (Second Order) were founded by two of Benizi's penitents about the time of his death; they are chiefly contemplative. The nuns of the *Third Order were founded by St. Juliana Falconieri in 1306; they devote themselves to the care of the sick and the poor and to the education of children. The principal Servite devotion is to the Sorrowful Virgin in whose honour they recite the Rosary of the Seven Dolours. The Feast of the Seven Founders is on 12 Feb.

A. Gianius, O.S.M., *Annales Sacri Ordinis Fratrum Servorum B. Mariae Virginis* (Florence, 1618; ed. 2 with continuation by A. M. Garbio, O.S.M., 3 vols., Lucca, 1719–1725). *Monumenta Ordinis Servorum Sanctae Mariae*, ed. A. Morini, O.S.M.–P. Soulier, O.S.M., and others [to 1750] (20 vols., Brussels and Rome, 1897–1930). A. P. M. Piermejus, *Memorabilia Sacri Ordinis Servorum B.M.V.* (4 vols., Rome, 1927–34). P. Panichelli, *I setto patriarchi*. Storia dei SS. fondatori della ordine dei Servi di Maria (Turin, 1933). Heimbucher, i, 576–88, with bibl. A. M. Rossi, O.S.M., in *E.C.*, xi (1953), col. 410 f., s.v. 'Servi di Maria', with bibl.

SERVUS SERVORUM DEI (Lat., 'the servant of God's servants'). A title of the Pope employed in official documents. It was first used by St. *Gregory the Great (590–604) and has been in general use since the time of *Gregory VII (1073–85).

K. Schmitz, *Ursprung und Geschichte der Devotionsformeln bis zu ihrer Aufnahme in die fränkische Königsurkunde* (Kirchenrechtliche Abhandlungen ed. U. Stutz, Hft. 81; 1913), ch. v, 'Servus Servorum Dei', pp. 120–39. W. Levison, 'Zur Vorgeschichte der Bezeichnung Servus Servorum Dei' in *Zeitschrift der Savigny-Stiftung für Rechtsgeschichte*, Kan. Abt., vi (1916), pp. 384–6.

SESSION. See *Kirk-session.*

SETH, ANDREW. See *Pattison, Andrew Seth Pringle-.*

SETTLEMENT, Act of. The Act (12 & 13 Will. III, c. 2) passed in 1701 to settle the Crown on the Electress Sophia of Hanover. Since William III had no children, Princess *Anne's only surviving child had died in infancy, and the son of *James II was a Papist, the hereditary rights of the descendants of *Charles I were set aside and the succession vested in Sophia of Hanover, daughter of Elizabeth of Bohemia who was the daughter of *James I. Thus the title of the present monarch rests not so much on hereditary right as on Parliamentary settlement. The opportunity was also taken to extend the provisions of the Bill of Rights and to ordain that all future sovereigns should 'join in Communion with the Church of England as by law established'.

Text in Gee-Hardy, No. cxxiv, pp. 664–70; C. G. Robertson, *Select Statutes, Cases and Documents* (1904), No. xx, pp. 87–92; and in W. C. Costin-J. S. Watson, *The Law and Working of the Constitution*, i (1952), No. xxxvi, pp. 92–6.

SEUSE, HEINRICH. See *Henry Suso, Blessed*.

SEVEN BISHOPS, Trial of. The Trial arose out of *James II's decree that his *Declaration of Indulgence should be read in all churches on 20 and 27 May 1688 (London) or 3 and 10 June (elsewhere). W. *Sancroft, Abp. of *Canterbury, summoned a meeting, and a protest was drawn up by six divines and six other bishops, viz. W. Lloyd of *St. Asaph, F. Turner of *Ely, J. Lake of *Chichester, T. *Ken of *Bath and Wells, T. White of *Peterborough, and J. Trelawney of Bristol. Their petition was presented on 18 May. The protest, received with wild enthusiasm throughout the country, seemed to James 'a standard of rebellion'. The seven bishops were imprisoned in the Tower on 8 June and tried in Westminster Hall on 29 June on a charge of seditious libel. By ten o'clock on the next day even the King's Brewer (to his sorrow a juryman) had consented to the verdict of 'Not Guilty'.

Full account in T. B. Howell, *A Complete Collection of State Trials and Proceedings for High Treason and other Crimes and Misdemeanours*, xii (1812), cols. 183–434, with other docs. cols. 433–524. Chief relevant docs. in C. G. Robertson, *Select Statutes, Cases and Documents to Illustrate English Constitutional History, 1660–1832* (1904), Case ix, pp. 249–67; extracts of the case also in W. C. Costin-J. S. Watson, *The Law and the Working of the Constitution*. Documents, 1660–1914, i (1952), pp. 258–71. W. H. *Hutton, *The English Church from the Accession of Charles I to the Death of Anne* (1903), pp. 227–31; id. in *D.E.C.H.* (1912), p. 553 f., s.v. 'Seven Bishops'.

SEVEN CHURCHES, The. The churches in Asia Minor to which the letter of St. *John, incorporated in Rev. (1–3), was addressed, viz. *Ephesus, Smyrna, *Pergamum, *Thyatira, Sardis, *Philadelphia, and *Laodicea. A separate message for each of these churches, appropriate to its particular temporal and spiritual condition, was revealed to John.

W. M. *Ramsay, *The Letters to the Seven Churches of Asia and their Place in the Plan of the Apocalypse* (1904). See also comm. on Revelation, cited s.v.

SEVEN CORPORAL ACTS OF MERCY. See *Corporal Works of Mercy*.

SEVEN DEACONS. The title traditionally given to the 'seven men of honest report, full of the Holy Ghost and wisdom' who, as related in Acts 6. 1–6, were appointed to 'serve tables', i.e. to administer the temporal concerns of the Church. Their names were *Stephen, *Philip, Prochorus, Nicanor, Timon, Parmenas, and Nicolas. Their appointment has been commonly held to be the institution of the order of *deacons in the Christian Church, and for many centuries the practice obtained at Rome of restricting the number of its deacons to seven.

S. Bibel, O.F.M., 'De Septem Diaconis (Acts 6, 1–7)' in *Antonianum*, iii (1928), pp. 129–50. See also comm. on Acts, cited s.v.

SEVEN DEADLY SINS. They are: (1) Pride; (2) Covetousness; (3) Lust; (4) Envy; (5) Gluttony; (6) Anger; (7) Sloth ('Accidie').

*Cassian, *Coll.*, v, 10, gives a list of eight sins (dejection and accidie counting as two); the traditional number of seven is found in St. *Gregory the Great, *Moralia in Job*, xxxi, 45 (where *tristitia* takes the place of *accidie*). St. *Thomas Aquinas, *Summa Theologica*, II (1), qu. lxxxiv, art. 4. Further reff. in K. E. *Kirk, *The Vision of God* (1931), p. 201 f. (Note 4 f.). O. Zöckler, *Askese und Mönchtum*, i (1897), pp. 253–6. K. E. Kirk, *Some Principles of Moral Theology and their Application* (1920), pp. 265–7.

SEVEN GIFTS OF THE HOLY GHOST. They are: (1) Wisdom; (2) Understanding; (3) Counsel; (4) Fortitude; (5) Knowledge; (6) Piety; (7) Fear of the Lord. The list is taken from Is. 11. 2 (*Vulgate text, which adds *pietas* to the six in the AV and RV).

A. Mitterer, 'Die sieben Gaben des Hl. Geistes nach der Väterlehre' in *Z.K.T.*, xlix (1925), pp. 529–66. K. Schlütz, *Is. 11. 2. Die sieben Gaben des Heiligen Geistes in den ersten vier Jahrhunderten* (Alttestamentliche Abhandlungen, xi, Hft. 4; 1932). A. Gardeil, O.P., in *D.T.C.*, iv (1911), cols. 1728–81, s.v. 'Dons du Saint-Esprit'; R. Garrigou-Lagrange, O.P., in *E.C.*, iv (1950), cols. 1861–5, s.v. 'Doni dello Spirito Santo', with bibl.

SEVEN LIBERAL ARTS. The group of sciences which formed the staple of secular education esp. in the earlier Middle Ages, consisting of the elementary *Trivium (grammar, rhetoric, and dialectic) and the more advanced *Quadrivium (music, arithmetic, geometry, and astronomy). This grouping derived from Martianus Capella (early 5th cent.), who drew it up on the basis of the ninefold arrangement of Varro by excluding architecture and medicine, but it did not become generally established until the time of *Alcuin. In practice considerably more was covered by the three disciplines of the Trivium than their titles might suggest, e.g. classical and philological study as well as the technical rules of grammar were comprised under 'grammar'. It was not till the student had completed his studies in the 'liberal arts' that he was held competent to proceed to theology.

SEVEN PENITENTIAL PSALMS, The.
Psalms 6, 32, 38, 51, 102, 130, and 143. They
were in liturgical use from early Christian
times, and in the later Middle Ages they were
ordered to be recited after *Lauds on Fridays
in *Lent. They are now prescribed for occasional use, e.g. at the consecration of churches.
The BCP appoints them as Proper Psalms for
*Ash Wednesday, the first three at *Matins,
Ps. 51 at the *Commination, and the last
three at *Evensong. They were also used in
the English *Coronation Service before the
revision of 1603.

SEVEN SACRAMENTS, The. Since the
12th cent. the RC Church has held the number
of the sacraments to be seven, viz. *Baptism,
*Confirmation, *Eucharist, *Absolution, Ex-
treme *Unction, *Ordination, and *Matrimony.
Though the beginnings of these rites can all be
traced back to very much earlier times, it was
through the teaching of *Peter Lombard in
his 'Sentences' (c. 1150) that the belief gained
general credence that these particular seven
constituted a set different in kind from all
other religious rites (see Sacramentals). Their
sevenfold number was given formal definition
at the Council of *Trent (Sess. VII, can. 1).
Most of the Reformed Churches rejected this
enumeration, coming to hold that there were
only two sacraments, viz. Baptism and the
Eucharist. The E. Church, however, has
accepted the W. enumeration. For further
discussion, see Sacrament.

SEVEN SLEEPERS OF EPHESUS.
Seven Christian young men who are said to
have been walled up in a cave when taking
refuge during the *Decian persecution (c.
A.D. 250) and to have been awakened under the
Emp. *Theodosius II (d. 450), as a proof of
the *resurrection of the dead. The legend was
certainly known in the E. and the W. in the
6th cent., as both *Jacob of Sarug (d. 521)
and St. *Gregory of Tours record it. It probably arose in a Syriac-speaking Church in
connexion with the *Origenist controversies
over bodily resurrection. The alleged tomb
of the Sleepers was much visited by pilgrims
from all parts of the world before the Turkish
conquest of Asia Minor. Feast day, 27 July.

I. Guidi (ed.), 'Testi orientali inediti sopra i Sette Dormi-
enti di Efeso' in Atti della R. Accademia dei Lincei. Memorie
della classe di scienze morali, storiche e filologiche, Ser. iii,
xi (1884), pp. 343-445, with It. tr.; crit. ed. of the version
of Gregory of Tours by B. Krusch in Anal. Boll., xii (1893),
pp. 371-387. M. Huber, O.S.B., 'Textbeiträge zur Sieben-
schläferlegende des Mittelalters' in Romanische Forschungen,
xxvi (1909), pp. 462-583 and 825-36. Id., Die Wander-
legende von den Siebenschläfern. Eine literargeschichtliche
Untersuchung (1910), with reff. J. Koch, Die Siebenschlä-
ferlegende, ihr Ursprung und ihre Verbreitung. Eine mytholo-
gisch-literaturgeschichtliche Studie (1883). E. Honigmann,
Patristic Studies (Studi e Testi, clxxiii; 1953), No. 17, 'Stephen
of Ephesus (April 15, 448–Oct. 29, 451) and the Legend of
the Seven Sleepers', pp. 125–68. I. Guidi in H.E.R.E., xi
(1920), pp. 428-30, with reff.; H. *Leclercq, O.S.B., in
D.A.C.L., xv (pt. 1; 1950), cols. 1251–62, s.v. 'Sept Dormants
d'Éphèse'.

SEVEN SORROWS OF THE BVM. Acc.
to the Roman Breviary, our Lady's Sorrows

were the following: (1) at the prophecy of
*Simeon; (2) at the flight into Egypt; (3) at the
loss of the Holy Child; (4) on meeting our
Lord on the way to Calvary; (5) at standing at
the foot of the Cross; (6) at the taking down of
Christ from the Cross; (7) at His burial. The
Seven Sorrows are commemorated on two
separate feast days—the Friday after *Passion
Sunday (made of universal observance by
*Benedict XIII in 1727) and 15 Sept. (first
granted to the *Servites in 1668, and in 1814
extended by *Pius VII to the whole RC
Church).

SEVEN VIRTUES. They are (1) Faith;
(2) Hope; (3) Charity; (4) Justice; (5) Prudence;
(6) Temperance; (7) Fortitude. The first
three are the '*Theological Virtues', the
remaining four the '*Cardinal Virtues'.

SEVEN WORDS FROM THE CROSS.
They are (1) 'Father forgive them; for they
know not what they do' (Lk. 23. 34); (2)
'To-day shalt thou be with Me in paradise'
(Lk. 23. 43); (3) 'Woman, behold thy son! . . .
Behold thy Mother' (Jn. 19. 26 f.); (4) 'Eli, Eli,
lama sabachthani? [that is to say,] My God,
My God, why hast Thou forsaken Me?' (Mt.
27. 46; cf. Mk. 15. 34); (5) 'I thirst' (Jn. 19. 28);
(6) 'It is finished' (Jn. 19. 30); (7) 'Father, into
Thy hands I commend My spirit' (Lk. 23. 46).

SEVENTH-DAY ADVENTISTS. A sec-
tion of the *Adventists who, after the expected
Second Coming of Christ failed to be realized
in 1844, constituted themselves a separate body.
In deference to the views of Mrs. Rachel D.
Preston, who had been a Seventh-Day Baptist
before joining the Adventist connexion, they
began to observe the OT Sabbath as the weekly
day of rest and praise instead of Sunday. In
England its beginnings as an organized community go back to a mission started at Southampton by W. Ing in 1878. They are a
staunchly Protestant body, believing that the
Scriptures provide the unerring rule of faith
and practice and that the return of Christ to
earth is imminent. They demand from their
members a life of strict temperance (abstinence
from alcohol, tobacco, and, in certain communities, also tea and coffee), the observance
of the Sabbath from Friday sunset to Saturday
sunset, and adult baptism which is by total
immersion.

The vast literature issued by the Adventists includes
M. E. Olsen, A History of the Origin and Progress of the
Seventh Day Adventists (Washington, D.C., 1925); E. E.
Howell, The Great Advent Movement (ib., 1935); A. W.
Spalding, Captains of the Host (ib., 1949); id., Christ's Last
Legion (ib., 1949); Le R. E. Froom, The Prophetic Faith of
Our Fathers, esp. vol. iii (ib., 1946), pp. 263–751, and vol. iv
(1954). On their early history, F. D. Nichol, The Midnight
Cry (ib., 1944); on their doctrine, W. L. Emmerson, The
Bible Speaks (Watford, [1942]), and D. E. Rebot (ed.), Our
Firm Foundation (2 vols., Washington, D.C., 1953). D. E.
Robinson, The Story of Our Health Message. The Origin,
Character, and Development of Health Education in the
Seventh Day Adventist Church (Nashville, Tennessee,
1943).

SEVENTY WEEKS. Acc. to a prophecy in Dan. 9. 20-7, an Anointed One (i.e. *Messiah) will arise, and then be 'cut off', in a predestined period of 'seventy weeks', and afterwards *Jerusalem and its *Temple be destroyed. Biblical scholars are generally agreed that by the 'seventy weeks' is meant '70 weeks [i.e. "sevens"] of years', viz. 490 years, and that the Prophet is here reinterpreting the 70 years of Jer. 25. 11 f. In Christian tradition the prophecy has frequently been referred to the coming of Christ at the Incarnation, but there is little doubt that the primary reference, at least, is to the Jewish High Priest and the desecration of the Temple in 166 B.C.

SEVERIAN (*fl. c.* 400), Bp. of Gabala. A strong opponent of St. *Chrysostom, he played a leading part at *Constantinople in the events leading up to the Synod of the *Oak in 403. He is chiefly important as an exegete of the *Antiochene School. His writings include a collection of six Homilies on the *Hexaemeron*, other sermons on Genesis, a set of nine Homilies which have come down in Armenian and several catena fragments. Many of these survive under the name of St. Chrysostom.

His writings have not been collected. His six Homilies on the Hexaemeron are repr. in J. P. Migne, *PG*, lvi, 429-500; Hom. de Serpente, ib., cols. 499-516; Hom. de Sigillis, ib., lxiii, 531-44. Catena fragments from Severian's Commentaries on the Pauline Epp. in K. Staab, *Die Pauluskommentare aus der griechischen Kirche* (1933), pp. 213-351. Fifteen Armenian Homilies ed. J. B. Aucher, Venice, 1827 (several of these, however, are spurious). J. Zellinger, *Die Genesishomilien des Bischofs Severian von Gabala* (Alttestamentliche Abhandlungen, vii, Hft. 1; 1916); id., *Studien zu Severian von Gabala* (Münsterische Beiträge zur Theologie, viii; 1926). Recently B. Marx has ascribed other homilies among the Chrysostomica to Severian in '*Severiana* unter der *Spuria Chrysostomi* bei Montfaucon-Migne' in *O.C.P.*, v (1939), pp. 281-367. Bardenhewer, iii, 363-5; Altaner (ed. 1951), p. 289 f. E. Venables in *D.C.B.*, iv (1887), p. 625 f.; H. *Lietzmann in *P.W.*, Reihe 2, ii (pt. 2; 1923), cols. 1930-2, s.v. 'Severian (17)'; G. Bardy in *D.T.C.*, xiv (pt. 2; 1941), cols. 2000-6, s.v. 'Sévérien de Gabala'; E. Peterson in *E.C.*, xi (1953), cols. 463, s.v. 'Severiano'.

SEVERINUS, St. (d. 482), 'Apostle of Austria'. He was in early life a monk in the East. After the death of *Attila in 453, he came to Noricum Ripense, then overrun by barbarian invaders, and though never himself a bishop, he rallied the Church, founded two monasteries, and organized relief work, in this way winning the respect of the barbarians (particularly Odoacer) and moderating their cruelty. His body was taken to Lucullanum, nr. Naples, where his companion *Eugippius wrote his Life in 511. Feast day, 8 Jan. He is the patron of wine-dressers.

Acc. to the Roman Martyrology, his feast-day, Jan. 8, is also observed as that of another Severinus, Bp. of Naples, 'brother of Bl. Victorinus, Martyr'. As no Bishop of Naples of this name is known to have existed, there is perhaps some confusion with St. Severinus, the Apostle of Austria.

The principal authority is the life by Eugippius pr. J. P. Migne, *PL*, lxii, 1167-2000; crit. ed. P. Knoell (C.S.E.L., ix, pt. 2; 1886); Eng. tr. by G. W. Robinson ('Harvard Translations'; Cambridge, Mass., 1914). R. Schweizar, *Studien*

über das Handschriften-Verhältnis der Vita S. Severini des Abtes Eugippius (Prager Studien aus dem Gebiete der Geschichtswissenschaft ed. A. Bachmann, Hft. i; 1898). 'Historia Translationis Auctore Ioanne Diacono' in *AA.SS.*, Jan. I (1643), pp. 1098-1103. A. Baudrillart, *Saint Séverin, apôtre de Norique* ('Les Saints'; 1908). P. Dörfler, *Severin, der Seher von Norikum.* Dichtung und Geschichte (ed. 2, 1947).

SEVERUS (*c.* 465-538), *Monophysite Patr. of *Antioch. He studied at Alexandria and Berytus, was baptized in 488, and later became a monk. C. 508 he went to *Constantinople, where he succeeded in securing the support of Emp. Anastasius (491-518) for the persecuted Monophysite monks, and in 512 was made Patr. of Antioch in place of the deposed Flavius II. On Justin I's accession (518), he was deposed, took refuge with Timothy IV, the Monophysite Patr. of Alexandria, and after the failure of an attempted reconciliation under *Justinian, was excommunicated by a synod at Constantinople in 536. Severus was the leading theologian of the moderate Monophysites. Many of his works, still not completely edited, survive, including 125 homilies and 400 letters. They are mainly preserved in Syriac. His Life to the year 512 was written by his friend *Zacharias the Scholastic ('Rhetor').

Severus's *Liber contra Impium Grammaticum* [sc. against a certain John, an upholder of the *Chalcedonian Christology] was ed. J. Lebon (C.S.C.O., Scriptores Syrici, Series quarta, iv-vi; 1929-38); his *Orationes ad Nephalium* by id. (ib., vii; 1949) (incl. his 'Critique of the Tome of Julian' and 'Refutation of the Propositions'); writings against the extreme Monophysite, *Julian of Halicarnassus, partly ed. A. Sanda, Beirut, (1931); an Anti-Julianist Pastoral (c. A.D. 530) ed. R. Draguet [from Brit. Mus. Add. 14663] in *Muséon*, xl (1927), pp. 75-92; there are other writings against Julian still unpublished. Of his 125 Cathedratical Homilies, which survive in the Syr. tr. of *Jacob of Edessa, the first, that for his enthronization, ed., with Fr. tr., by M. A. Kugener in *Oriens Christianus*, ii (1902), pp. 265-82; others [lii-lvii] ed., with Fr. tr., by R. Duval in *P.O.*, iv (1908), pp. 5-94 (fasc. 1); [lviii-lxix] by M. Brière, ib., viii (1912), pp. 211-394 (fasc. 2); [lxx-lxxvi] ib., xii (1919), pp. 5-164 (fasc. 1); [lxxvii] by M. A. Kugener-E. Triffaux, ib., xvi (1922), pp. 765-862 (fasc. 5); [lxxviii-lxxxiii] by M. Brière, ib., xx (1929), pp. 277-432 (fasc. 2); [xcix-ciii] by I. Guidi, ib., xxii (1930), pp. 207-312 (fasc. 2); [lxxxiv-xc] by M. Brière, ib., xxiii (1932), pp. 5-176 (fasc. 1); [xci-xciii] ib., xxv (1943), pp. 5-174 (fasc. 1); [xciii-cxix] ib., xxvi (1949), pp. 263-450 (fasc. 3). Severus's 'Sixth Book of Letters', ed. E. W. Brooks (2 vols., Text and Translation Society, 1902-4); further Letters, ed. id., with Eng. tr., in *P.O.*, xii (1919), pp. 165-342 (fasc. 2), and xiv (1920), pp. 1-310 (fasc. 1). His Hymns, in the translation of Jacob of Edessa, ed., with Eng. tr., by E. W. Brooks, ib., vi (1911), pp. 5-179 (fasc. 1), and vii (1911), pp. 597-802 (fasc. 5). The 'Anaphora' traditionally (but wrongly) ascribed to Severus ed. H. W. Codrington (Pontificio Istituto per gli Studi Orientali, Rome, 1939). Lives by Zacharias Scholasticus and by John of Beith Aphthonia, with other relevant documents, ed. M. A. Kugener, with Fr. tr., in *P.O.*, ii (1907), pp. 5-115 and 203-400 (fascc. 1 and 3). The most important modern study is J. Lebon, *Le Monophysisme sévérien* (Louvain, 1909). A. Grillmeier, S.J.-H. Bacht, S.J. (edd.), *Das Konzil von Chalkedon* (3 vols., 1951-4), passim (see index, iii, 968 f.). On the attempt of J. Stiglmayr, S.J., to equate the Pseudo-Areopagite with Severus, see bibl. to *Dionysius* (6). A. *Baumstark, 'Das Kirchenjahr in Antiocheia zwischen 512 und 518' in *R.Q.*, xi (1897), pp. 31-66, xiii 1899, pp. 305-23. A. Baumstark, *Geschichte der syrischen Literatur* (1922), see index, p. 376; Bardenhewer, v, 1-5; Altaner (ed. 1951), p. 457 f. K. Bihlmayer in *L.Th.K.*, ix (1937), cols. 508-10, s.v.; G. Bardy in *D.T.C.*, xiv (pt. 2; 1941), cols. 1988-2000.

SEVERUS, GABRIEL, Metropolitan of Philadelphia. See *Gabriel Severus*.

SEVERUS SULPICIUS. See *Sulpicius Severus.*

SEWELL, WILLIAM (1804–74), Anglican divine. Educated at *Winchester and Merton College, Oxford, where he had a brilliant academic career, he was elected a Petrean Fellow of Exeter College in 1827. He was one of the ablest and most learned of those in general sympathy with the *Tractarian Movement in its earlier days, though after the publication of *Tract No. 90* in 1841, he dissociated himself from the movement. He remained a High Churchman, and in 1847 founded St. Peter's College, Radley, as a school where strict Anglican principles were to be inculcated. He was also the author of many theological and classical writings.

L. James, *A Forgotten Genius.* Sewell of St. Columba's and Radley (1945). G. C. Boase in *D.N.B.*, li (1897), p. 290 f.

SEXAGESIMA (Lat., 'the sixtieth [day before Easter]'). The second Sunday before *Lent and hence the eighth before *Easter. Its name, formed on the analogy of *Quinquagesima and *Septuagesima (qq.v.), goes back certainly to the 6th cent. It is also known in the W., from the opening words of the *introit, as Exsurge Sunday. The traditional OT Lesson for this Sunday is the narrative of the *Fall (Gen. 3).

A. Chavasse, 'Temps de préparation à la Pâques d'après quelques livres liturgiques romains' in *Rech. S.R.*, xxxvii (1950), pp. 125–45, esp. IV., 'La "Soixantaine" ou Sexagésime', pp. 130–43. See also bibl. to *Septuagesima*.

SEXT (1). 'Liber Sextus Decretalium', the Book of *Canon Law promulgated by *Boniface VIII in 1298. This 'Sixth Book' contains the *Decretals posterior to the five books compiled by *Gregory IX (1234), the material being similarly arranged. The bulk of the texts are from the Decretals of Boniface VIII himself, notably the bull '*Clericis laicos' (under the title 'De immunitate'), the rest from those of the successors of Gregory IX and the two Councils of *Lyons in 1245 and 1274. The legislation in the Sext, as in most collections of canon law, covers a wide range of miscellaneous subjects and also reflects the growing tendency to centralization in the later medieval Church.

The standard text is that of E. Friedberg (ed.), *Corpus Juris Canonici*, ii (Leipzig, 1881), cols. 929–1124. P. Torquebiau in *D.D.C.*, iv (1949), cols. 632–5, s.v. 'Corpus Juris Canonici III', with list of principal commentators and other bibl. reff.

SEXT (2). The 'Little Hour' of the Breviary Office appointed to be recited at noon. See also *Terce* and *None*.

SEYMOUR, EDWARD. See *Somerset, Duke of.*

SHAFTESBURY, ANTHONY ASHLEY COOPER (1801–85), **7th Earl of**, social reformer and factory legislator. He was edu-

cated at Harrow and Christ Church, Oxford, and in 1826 entered on his Parliamentary career as a member of the Conservative Party. His main concern was with the amelioration of the conditions of the working classes, in whose interests he often pursued an independent line of policy. A personal investigation of the London slums in 1846 bore fruit in the Ten Hours' Bill of 1847 and the Factory Act of 1874, for both of which he was largely responsible. He also took up the cause of women and children in the mines and collieries, as well as young chimney sweeps, for whose protection he introduced the Climbing Boys Act. He was for a long time chairman of the Ragged School Union, and in 1872 he laid the foundation stone of Shaftesbury Park Estate at Battersea. He was a fervent *Evangelical, who hated Ritualism and attacked Rationalism. Though a supporter of *Catholic Emancipation, he opposed the *Maynooth Endowment. He was for many years president of the *British and Foreign Bible Society and took a deep interest in the work of the London City Mission, the *C.M.S., and the *Y.M.C.A. He was also the trusted adviser of Lord Palmerston for the appointment of bishops and other high preferments in the C of E.

E. Hodder, *The Life and Work of the Seventh Earl of Shaftesbury* (3 vols., 1886), with extracts from his diaries passim. J. L. Hammond–B. Hammond, *Lord Shaftesbury* (1923); [Evelyn] Barbara Blackburn, *Noble Lord.* The Life of the Seventh Earl of Shaftesbury (1949). Other studies by H. Frith (London, 1887), R. E. Pengelly (ib. [1902]), and M. G. Higham (S.C.M.; 1945). J. Wesley Bready, *Lord Shaftesbury and Social-Industrial Progress* (1926). W. G. Blaikie in *D.N.B.*, xii (1887), pp. 133–7, s.v. 'Cooper'.

SHAKERS, also 'The United Society of Believers in Christ's Second Appearing' or 'The Millennial Church', or 'Alethians', an early communistic and pacifist body which took its origin during a *Quaker revival in England in 1747. The original leaders, James and Jane Wardley, were succeeded by Ann Lee, known as Mother Ann, who came to be regarded as 'The female principle in Christ', Jesus being the 'Male principle', and in whom the Second Coming was fulfilled. Under the influence of persecution she led a band of six men and two women to U.S.A. in 1774, where they settled in the woods of Watervliet, near Albany, N.Y. Going about preaching and faith-healing Mother Ann founded many new communities. Their numbers were greatly increased in 1780 by converts from an independent religious revival near New Lebanon. After Mother Ann's death in 1784, the leadership passed into the hands of Joseph Meecham and Lucy Wright.

The name 'Shakers' is derived from the shaking by which under the stress of spiritual exaltation they were possessed during their meetings. They rose at a common hour, wore uniform dress, took their meals together, and, in the case of the advanced or 'Senior Order', held property in common. They insisted on confession before admission, abstained from alcohol, and discouraged smoking; but foremost in their teaching was the high value that they put on celibacy. Marriage, however, was not absolutely forbidden. They also claimed to have special powers over disease, which they regarded as due to sin, and they encouraged separation from the world, to attain which they lived in large 'families' of 30 to 90, under a hierarchical form of government, each family with its own house. At one time there were about 5,000 Shakers in U.S.A., but in 1930 only a twentieth of that number. They claim to have spent nothing on police, lawyers, judges, poor-houses, or penal institutions.

F. W. Evans, *Shakers. Compendium of the Origin, History, Principles, Rules and Regulations, Government, and Doctrines of the United Society of Believers in Christ's Second Appearing* (New York, 1859), and other works by this author. C. E. Robinson, *A Concise History of the United Society of Believers called Shakers* (East Canterbury, New Hampshire [c. 1893]). Anna White–Leila S. Taylor, *Shakerism. Its Meaning and Message* (Columbus, Ohio, 1904). C. E. Shears, *Gleanings from Old Shaker Journals* (Boston, Mass., 1916). Marguerite F. Melcher, *The Shaker Adventure* (Princeton, New Jersey, 1941). Julia Neal, *By their Fruits. The Story of Shakerism in South Union, Kentucky* (Chapel Hill, N.C., 1947). E. D. Andrews, *The People Called Shakers* (New York, 1953). J. P. MacLean, *A Bibliography of Shaker Literature* (privately pr., Columbus, Ohio, 1905). R. B. Taylor in *H.E.R.E.*, iii (1910), pp. 781–3, s.v. 'Communistic Societies of America. 2'.

SHAKESPEARE, JOHN HOWARD (1857–1928), *Baptist preacher and organizer. After a fifteen years' pastorate at *Norwich, he became secretary of the Baptist Union in 1898 and gradually won for himself a leading position in the religious world. He made the Baptist Union a highly influential organization, and was mainly responsible for founding the Baptist World Alliance (1905) and the Federal Council of the *Free Churches (1919), and securing the appointment of Baptist and Congregational chaplains in the army. His book, *The Churches at the Cross Roads* (1918), is a moving and powerful plea for the reunion of Christendom.

Geoffrey Shakespeare (son), *Let Candles Be Brought* (1947), ch. xvii, pp. 335–47.

SHAMMAI, School of. The disciples of Shammai, a leading rabbinical teacher of the time of Christ. In contrast with the School of *Hillel, the Shammaites interpreted the Mosaic Law strictly and rigidly, following the unbending attitude of their founder. Their intolerance of any intercourse with Gentiles brought them into frequent conflict with the Roman authorities in Palestine. In the *Sanhedrin, which represented Jewish officialdom, the Shammaites, with the help of the *Zealots, the party of extreme Jewish patriots, succeeded in winning a temporary victory over the Hillelites. At the reorganization of the Sanhedrin after A.D. 70, however, the moderation of the School of Hillel prevailed.

Bibl. as for School of Hillel, q.v., except A. Hyman, *Toldoth Tannaim Ve'Amoraim* (Heb., London, 1910), p. 1118 f.

SHARP, JAMES (1613–79), Abp. of St. Andrews. He was educated at King's College, Aberdeen, and being out of sympathy with the

O.D.C.C.–2 S

more radical *Covenanters, went to England in 1639. After his return he was appointed professor of philosophy at St. Andrews (1643) and minister of Crail, Fifeshire (1648). When the Scottish Kirk was divided into resolutioners and protestors he took sides with the former and soon became one of their leaders. In 1651 he joined General G. Monck, who was then planning to effect the Restoration, and began to work secretly for the re-establishment of Episcopacy while outwardly protesting his loyalty to the Kirk. The services he thus rendered to the King's cause were rewarded by his appointment to the see of St. Andrews in 1661. As such he took severe measures to abolish Presbyterianism and supported the oppressive policy of J. M. Lauderdale, an attitude which roused the bitter resentment of his opponents. In 1668 James Mitchell made an attempt to shoot him, and when, in 1678, Mitchell was finally executed, the hatred against him increased, and in the next year he was brutally murdered by a party of Fife lairds and farmers.

'Twenty Four Letters written to James Sharp . . . by the Duke and Duchess of Lauderdale and by Charles Maitland, Lord Hatton, 1660–1672', ed. J. Dowden in *Miscellany of the Scottish History Society*, i (Scottish History Society, xv; 1893), pp. 229–92. A number of polemical accounts of his murder were published at the time of his death; further contemporary account by James Russell appended to J. Kirkton, *The Secret and True History of the Church of Scotland from the Restoration to the Year 1678* (1817), pp. 403–82. T. Stephen, *The Life and Times of Archbishop Sharp* (1839). J. Willcock, 'Sharp and the Restoration Policy in Scotland' in *Transactions of the Royal Historical Society*, New Series, xx (1906), pp. 149–69. T. F. Henderson in *D.N.B.*, li (1897), pp. 404–7.

SHARP, JOHN (1645–1714), Abp. of *York. Educated at Christ's College, Cambridge, he became rector of St. Giles-in-the-Fields in 1675 and Dean of *Norwich in 1681. A strong High Churchman, he refused to read the *Declaration of Indulgence of 1688. In 1689, however, he took the oaths to William and Mary, but announced that he would not accept any bishopric vacated by a *Nonjuror during the lifetime of the former occupant. In 1691 he accepted the see of York on the death of Thomas Lamplugh, and his episcopate was notable for the high standard of duty which marked it (e.g. in his distribution of patronage). Queen *Anne, who greatly respected him, made him her spiritual adviser.

Life by Thomas Sharp (son), ed. T. Newcome, publd. 2 vols., London, 1825. A. T. Hart, *The Life and Times of John Sharp, Archbishop of York* (*Church Historical Society; 1949). G. Le G. Norgate in *D.N.B.*, li (1897), pp. 408–11.

SHAXTON, NICHOLAS (c. 1485–1556), Bp. of *Salisbury. Educated at Cambridge, he was one of the committee appointed by the university in 1530 to consider the royal divorce. He thereby obtained the patronage of Anne Boleyn, while the favour of T. *Cromwell and his own advocacy of the Royal Supremacy enabled him to survive her downfall unharmed. He soon developed pronounced Protestant views. In 1535 he was made Bp. of Salisbury, but resigned his see in 1539, in protest against the *Six Articles. During the rest of the reign his position was precarious, and in 1546 he was arrested with Anne *Askew and others, and charged with heretical views on the Eucharist. He saved himself from the stake by a recantation, apparently quite sincere, since he maintained a Catholic position throughout the reign of *Edward VI. Under *Mary he was appointed a suffragan to the Bp. of *Ely, and took part in the examination of certain Protestants on trial for heresy.

J. *Gairdner in D.N.B., li (1897), pp. 452–4, s.v., with reff.

SHEER THURSDAY. An old name for *Maundy Thursday, perhaps from 'skere' or 'sheer' (='clean', 'free from guilt'), with reference to the practice of receiving absolution or (alternatively) of ceremonially washing the altars of the church on that day.

SHEKINAH (Heb., שְׁכִינָה 'dwelling'). The word (not found in the OT) was used by the Jews of God's visible Presence, conceived as 'dwelling' among men. The *Rabbis often employed it as a periphrasis for the name of 'God' in cases where it was desired to avoid anthropomorphism. Hence in the *Targums, Is. 6. 5 becomes 'Mine eyes have seen the glory of the Shekinah of the King of the World'. In the NT the word 'glory' (δόξα) seems occasionally to contain a reference to the Jewish Shekinah, notably in the coupling together of 'glory' and God's 'dwelling' among men in Jn. 1. 14 ('And the Word became flesh, and dwelt among us, and we beheld His glory').

J. T. Marshall in H.D.B., iv (1902), pp. 487–9, s.v.

SHELDON, GILBERT (1598–1677), Abp. of *Canterbury. Educated at Trinity College, Oxford, he was elected Fellow of All Souls in 1622 and ordained in the same year. In 1626 he was made Warden of All Souls and became an active supporter of W. *Laud's reforms at Oxford. During this period he also held in plurality several country livings. In 1638 he was put on the reforming commission which visited Merton College. A strong Royalist, he took part in the negotiations for the Uxbridge treaty of 1644 and in 1647 was with the King at Newmarket and Carisbrooke. In 1648 he was ejected from All Souls and spent some months in prison. During most of the Commonwealth he lived in retirement in the Midlands. Eventually, in 1659, he was restored to his Wardenship. In 1660 he became Bp. of London and Master of the Savoy, and in 1661 the *Savoy Conference, met at his lodgings. While W. *Juxon lived he was virtually primate and succeeded him at Canterbury on his death in 1663. As Archbishop he worked hard for the re-establishment of Laudian religious principles. He also carried through the arrangement with Clarendon whereby the Convocations ceased to tax the clergy (1664). Throughout his life he was devoted to his uni-

versity, and from 1667 to 1669 he was Chancellor. The Sheldonian Theatre at Oxford was built at his expense. His papers are preserved in the *Bodleian Library.

N. Salmon (anon.), The Lives of English Bishops from the Restauration to the Revolution (pt. 1; 1731), pp. 10–47. V. Staley, The Life and Times of Gilbert Sheldon [1913]. R. S. Bosher, The Making of the Restoration Settlement (1951), passim. W. H. Hutton in D.N.B., lii (1897), pp. 24–6.

SHEMA, The. (Heb. שְׁמַע, 'hear'). The Jewish confession of faith. Its name is derived from the first word of the first of the three Scriptural passages of which it consists, viz. Deut. 6. 4–9, 11. 13–21, Num. 15. 37–41. These are preceded and followed by a number of benedictions, which perhaps emanated from *Essene circles and were added by the Great *Synagogue. The Shema, which is mentioned as a well-known observance in the *Mishnah (Berakoth, 2) and was doubtless known to Our Lord (cf. Mk. 12. 29), is to be recited every morning and evening by all Jewish men and is included among the passages inscribed in the phylacteries.

J. D. Eisenstein in J.E., xi (1905), p. 266 f., s.v.

SHEMONE ESRE. See Eighteen Benedictions.

SHENOUTE (d. c. 450), or 'Shenudi', Abbot of Athribis in Egypt. In 370 he entered the White Monastery, nr. Schâg, under his uncle Pgôl, where he became superior c. 388. His community greatly increased, the numbers being given as 2,200 monks and 1,800 nuns. His government was very severe, esp. in the punishments which included flogging and imprisonment for light faults, and he added many austerities to the more humane rule of *Pachomius. One of his most important innovations was the introduction of a written profession of obedience for his religious, probably elicited by the frequent cases of revolt and insubordination. He also allowed his older monks to live apart as hermits. An organizer rather than a theologian, Shenoute accompanied St. *Cyril of Alexandria to the Council of *Ephesus in 431, where he played an important part opposing *Nestorius. He knew Greek, but wrote in Coptic. The letters, homilies, and apocalypses attributed to him, of which many are spurious, are written in a fiery style and deal chiefly with monastic concerns and with exhortations to practise virtue and avoid vice. Feast day in the Coptic Church, 1 July.

Life and Works ed. J. Leipoldt (C.S.C.O., Ser. II, Scriptores Coptici, ii, 1906 (life by his pupil Besa); iv, 3, 1908, with Lat. tr. by H. Wiesmann, 1931; and v, 4, 1913, with Lat. tr. by H. Wiesmann, 1936). E. Amélineau, Œuvres de Schenoudi (Coptic text and Fr. tr.; 2 vols., 1907–14). J. Leipoldt, Schenute von Atripe und die Entstehung des national-ägyptischen Christentums (T.U., xxv, Hft. 1; 1903). Bardenhewer, iv, 98–100; Altaner (ed. 1951), p. 228 f.

SHEOL (Heb. שְׁאוֹל), in the OT, the underworld, the place of the departed spirits. Several derivations of the word have been given, e.g.

(1) from a root meaning 'to ask', and hence referred to Sheol as the place of inquiry or scrutiny, or (2) from a root denoting 'to be hollow'. In the AV it is translated variously as 'hell', 'grave', or 'pit'. The notion reflects an undeveloped and shadowy belief in the future life which was gradually superseded by the more defined beliefs of later Judaism. The conception was widely held in early Semitic mythology and in the OT closely linked with similar Babylonian beliefs.

A. Jeremias, *Die babylonisch-assyrischen Vorstellungen vom Leben nach dem Tode* (1887), pp. 106–26. Friedrich *Delitzsch, *Das Land ohne Umkehr*. Die Gedanken der Babylonier-Assyrer über Tod und Jenseits (1911). J. Kroll, *Gott und Hölle*. Der Mythos vom Descensuskampfe (Studien der Bibliothek Warburg, xx; 1932), passim. P. Dhorme, O.P., 'Le Séjour des morts chez les Babyloniens et chez les Hébreux' in *R. Bibl.*, xvi (1907), pp. 59–78; id., 'L'Idée de l'au-delà dans la religion hébraïque' in *Revue de l'Histoire des Religions*, cxiii (1941), pp. 113–42. W. O. E. Oesterley, *Immortality and the Unseen World* (1921), esp. pp. 80–94. R. H. *Charles, *A Critical History of the Doctrine of a Future Life* (1899), see index p. 426. A. Romeo in *E.C.*, xi (1953), cols. 349–53, s.v. 'Šĕ'ôl.'

SHEPHERD OF HERMAS, The. The treatise of the sub-Apostolic Christian writer, *Hermas (q.v.). It was so named from the angel who, in the form of a shepherd, is recorded to have communicated to Hermas some of its contents. The identification of Hermas himself with the Shepherd, found in some later writers, seems to have arisen from mere confusion.

For bibl. see *Hermas*.

SHEPPARD, HUGH RICHARD LAWRIE (1880–1937), popularly 'Dick Sheppard', vicar of St. Martin-in-the-Fields, London. He was educated at Marlborough, Trinity Hall, Cambridge, and Cuddesdon, ordained deacon in 1907 to Oxford House, Bethnal Green, and in 1911 became curate of St. George's, Hanover Square, London, with the charge of St. Mary's, Bourdon Street, and later of the Grosvenor Chapel. In 1914 he was appointed vicar of St. Martin-in-the-Fields. His religious enthusiasm and personal attractiveness won the affection of innumerable people in all stations of life, esp. after the growth of broadcasting, of which he was the first to sense the full possibilities as a Christian influence. He made his church, with its unique 'parish magazine', the *St. Martin's Review*, the best-known parish church in the British Empire. A keen enthusiast for ecclesiastical reform on unconventional lines, Sheppard identified himself with the Life and Liberty Movement in its earlier stages, and later his ideals for reform were embodied in *The Human Parson* (1924) and the very widely read *The Impatience of a Parson* (1927). Ill-health compelled his resignation of St. Martin's in 1926. From 1929 to 1931 he was Dean of *Canterbury and for a brief space (1934–5) Canon of *St. Paul's. In his last years he was an ardent upholder of the Pacifist cause and devoted his chief energies to its propagation. In 1934 he sent a letter to the press, inviting those who agreed with him to send him a post-card stating that they renounced war and would never again, directly or indirectly, sanction another; and in 1936 he followed up the great response to it by founding the Peace Pledge Union (P.P.U.). He also defended his pacifism in *We say 'No': The Plain Man's Guide to Pacifism* (1935).

R. Ellis Roberts, *H. R. L. Sheppard*. Life and Letters (1942). C. H. S. Matthews, *Dick Sheppard*. Man of Peace (Modern Christian Revolutionaries, n.d.). C. Jenkins in *D.N.B., 1931–1940*, p. 809 f.

SHERBORNE. St. *Aldhelm established the seat of the Bp. of W. Wessex here in 705, and founded a church and school. In 978 Bp. Wulfsey introduced the Benedictine Rule, himself becoming the first abbot. In 1058 the see was united with Ramsbury, and in 1075 moved to Old *Sarum. The church was rebuilt in the 12th cent., and again, after a serious fire, in the 15th. At the *Dissolution in 1536, the parishioners purchased the abbey for a parish church, while the conventual buildings (13th, 14th, and 15th cents.) were handed over to the school, which was refounded (1550), with a new charter from *Edward VI. The church is a fine example of the Perpendicular style, with notable fan-tracery in the choir. A Bishopric of Sherborne, suffragan to *Salisbury, was founded in 1928.

On the abbey, see W. *Dugdale, *Monasticon Anglicanum*, i (ed. 1817), pp. 331–41; Muriel M. C. Calthrop in *V.C.H.* Dorset, ii, ed. W. Page (1908), pp. 62–70

SHERLOCK, THOMAS (1678–1761), Bp. of London. He was educated at Eton and St. Catherine's Hall, Cambridge, where he was elected Fellow in 1698, and was Master from 1714 to 1719. In 1704 he had succeeded his father as Master of the Temple and held the office till 1753. Here he established a great reputation as a preacher. In the *Bangorian Controversy he was strongly opposed to B. *Hoadly, thereby temporarily losing his influence at court. He was subsequently in turn Bp. of *Bangor (1728–34), of *Salisbury (1734–48), and of London (1748–61). The most celebrated of his writings was his *Trial of the Witnesses of the Resurrection of Jesus* (1729, anon.), a highly characteristic apologetic writing of its age. In ecclesiastical politics he endeavoured to maintain against nearly all his contemporaries the ideals of the previous century.

E. F. Carpenter, *Thomas Sherlock* (*S.P.C.K. for C. H. S., 1936). W. H. *Hutton in *D.N.B.*, lii (1897), pp. 93–5.

SHERLOCK, WILLIAM (1641–1707), Dean of *St. Paul's. He was a native of Southwark, educated at Eton and Peterhouse, Cambridge, and in 1669 became rector of St. George's, Botolph Lane, London. In 1674 he published *The Knowledge of Jesus Christ, and Union with Him*, in which he attacked Puritan spirituality, esp. the contention of J. *Owen that the mercy of God can be known only through Christ. In his *Case of Resistance* (1684) he upheld the *Divine Right of Kings and inculcated the duty of passive obedience. In 1685 he was made master of the Temple. In the Revolution of 1688 he sided with the *Nonjurors, and the *Practical Discourse concerning Death* (1689), the most popular of his works, reflects the emotions of this period. In 1690 he published the *Vindication of the Doctrines of the Trinity and of the Incarnation*. A violent controversy with R. *South and others followed, in which he was charged with teaching Tritheism. In the same year he took the oath, an action which he defended in the *Case of Allegiance* (1691), and in 1691 he was made Dean of St. Paul's. In 1695 his Trinitarian views, propagated at Oxford by J. *Bingham, were condemned by the Hebdomadal Council, and in his *Present State of the *Socinian Controversy* (1698) Sherlock abandoned most of his earlier theological doctrines.

Sermons Preached upon Several Occasions (1700; ed. 4, 2 vols., 1755); several repr. in T. S. Hughes, *Summaries of the Sermons and Discourses of the Most Eminent British Divines* (1834), pp. 1–276. Sherlock's *Practical Discourse of Religious Assemblies* (1681) ed. by H. Melvill (1840), with preface, pp. v–xx. A. Gordon in *D.N.B.*, lii (1897), pp. 95–7.

SHEWBREAD (Heb. לֶחֶם הַפָּנִים; Gk. ὁ ἄρτος τῆς προθέσεως. The English word was adopted by W. *Tyndale from M. *Luther's *Schaubrot*). The twelve loaves which, acc. to the practice of the Jewish *Temple, were prepared from the finest flour and, arranged in two piles, set out weekly beside the altar of incense 'before the Lord'. When they were removed for renewal at the end of the week, only the priests might eat them (cf. Lev. 24. 9, Mk. 2. 26). The practice, which is first referred to in 1 Sam. 21. 2–6 (*David at the sanctuary of Nob), was doubtless a survival from the naïve primitive custom of putting out food for the god (cf. the Roman *lectisternia*). Acc. to 1 Kgs. 7. 48, the Table of Shewbread was among the furnishings of *Solomon's Temple. The use of the Shewbread was restored by *Judas Maccabaeus after Antiochus Epiphanes' desecration of the Temple (2 Macc. 10. 3). At the destruction of the Temple under Titus in A.D. 70, the Table was rescued and its transport to Rome by captured Jews is prominently depicted on the Arch of Titus. It eventually reached *Constantinople whence it was sent back to *Jerusalem under *Justinian (d. 565). It probably perished in the sack of Jerusalem by Chosroes in 614.

A. R. S. Kennedy in *H.D.B.*, iv (1902), pp. 495–7, s.v.

SHIBBOLETH (Heb. שִׁבֹּלֶת). A word used by Jephthah as a test to distinguish the Gileadites from the Ephraimites, who could not pronounce it (Jgs. 12. 4 ff.). In modern usage it denotes a sectarian or party catchword.

SHORTENED SERVICES ACT. See *Uniformity, Act of, Amendment Act* (1872).

SHORTHOUSE, JOSEPH HENRY (1834–1903), author of *John Inglesant*. Born at Birmingham, the son of *Quaker parents, he was attracted to Anglicanism under the influence of J. *Ruskin and the Pre-Raphaelites and baptized at St. John's, Ladywood, in 1861. From 1866 to 1876, in the intervals of an active business life, he was constantly brooding over and working on *John Inglesant*, which he wrote down piecemeal. Finishing it at Llandudno in 1876, he was unable to find a publisher and had it printed privately in 1880. Shortly afterwards, Mrs. Humphry Ward brought it to the notice of A. Macmillan who published it in 1881. It at once attracted very wide interest, among its admirers being W. E. *Gladstone, C. M. *Yonge, T. H. *Huxley, H. E. *Manning and E. S. *Talbot. The delicacy and charm with which John Inglesant's spiritual pilgrimage is portrayed, its sympathetic understanding of the religious life of the 17th cent., and its vivid delineation of the community at *Little Gidding, made it, apart from its high literary qualities, a powerful *apologia* for Anglicanism.

Shorthouse also wrote some other works, but they were without merit and have long been forgotten.

Life and Letters of J. H. Shorthouse. Edited by his Widow (2 vols., 1905). T. Seccombe in *D.N.B.*, 1901–1911, iii, 309 f.

SHRINE (Lat. *scrinium*, 'chest'). In its original sense the word is applied to *reliquaries (q.v.), but is now commonly used either of sacred images of special importance usually kept in a church, or of any holy place, esp. one connected with *pilgrimages (q.v.). Among famous English medieval shrines are those of Our Lady of *Walsingham (recently rebuilt), of St. *Edward the Confessor at *Westminster Abbey, of St. Thomas *Becket at *Canterbury and St. *Cuthbert at *Durham.

SHROUD, Holy. See *Holy Shroud*.

SHROVE TUESDAY. The day immediately preceding *Ash Wednesday, so named from the 'shriving', i.e. confession and absolution, of the faithful on that day.

SIAN-FU STONE. See *Sigan-Fu Stone*.

SIBYLLINE ORACLES, The. A collection of oracles worked up by Jewish and Christian authors in imitation of the pagan 'Sibylline Books'. They consist of fifteen books, three of which (9, 10, and 15) are missing. Books 1 and 2 give an account of the history of the world, in prophetic form, from the beginning of the world to the fall of Rome. Book 3 contains a defence of Jewish monotheism, together with another history of the world and apocalyptic prophecies. Books 4 and 5 deal with Roman history of Neronian times from the Jewish point of view, whereas Book 6 is a hymn to Christ. Book 7 is a conglomeration of eschatological prophecies and moral and ritual precepts. Book 8 treats of the nature of

Christ and of His second birth. Books 11 to 14 are of less religious interest, giving yet another account of world history of more or less imaginative character. The whole collection, which is written in hexameters, is preceded by a prose prologue affirming that the oracles are utterances of Greek Sibyls of various periods.

Many of the Fathers, e.g. *Theophilus of Antioch and *Clement of Alexandria, accepted this view of the Oracles and drew from them arguments in defence of Christianity. Modern critics, however, assign them to Jewish and Christian authors; for, though genuine Greek oracles are inserted in some places, the tendency of the whole is monotheistic and Messianic. They are evidently cast in their particular form to gain the pagan world to Jewish or Christian doctrines. The dates of the Jewish portions of the collection range from the *Maccabean period to the time of Hadrian, and these were freely used by the Christian *Apologists of the 2nd cent. The Christian additions seem to date from not earlier than the 3rd cent. Books 3–5 in their present form are probably mainly Jewish, of which the third, the oldest, is generally attributed to an Egyptian Jew writing c. 140 B.C., whilst the contents of Books 4 and 5 demand a date after the destruction of Jerusalem in A.D. 70. The other books, which are either of Christian origin or heavily interpolated in the Christian sense, are generally assigned to the 3rd cent., Books 11–14 to the 4th. The hymn to Christ (Book 6) has sometimes been held to be *Gnostic and 2nd cent. The work, which reflects contemporary popular theology, had considerable influence on *Lactantius and was known to St. *Augustine, who quotes a short passage in his 'De Civitate Dei' (xviii. 23).

Crit. ed. by J. Geffcken (G.C.S., 1902); more recent ed., with Germ. tr., by E. A. Kurfess [Munich, 1951]. Books iii–v also ed., with Ital. tr., by A. Pincherle (Rome, 1922). Eng. tr. of portion of Book ii (190–338) in M. R. James, *The Apocryphal New Testament* (1924), 521–4; further fragments of Book ii and Books iii–v are tr. into Eng., with comm. by H. C. O. Lanchester in R. H. *Charles (ed.), *The Apocrypha and Pseudepigrapha of the Old Testament*, ii (1913), pp. 368–406; Eng. tr. of Books iii–v by H. N. Bate (Translations of Early Documents, Series 2, Hellenistic-Jewish Texts, S.P.C.K., 1918). J. Geffcken, *Komposition und Entstehungszeit der* Oracula Sibyllina (T.U., xxiii, Hft. 1; 1902). E. *Schürer, *Geschichte des jüdischen Volkes im Zeitalter Jesu Christi*, iii (ed. 4, 1909), pp. 555–92. Bardenhewer, ii, 708–13; Altaner (ed. 1951), p. 68 f. J. Quasten, *Patrology*, i (Utrecht, 1950), pp. 168–70, with bibl. to date. B. Bischoff, 'Die lateinischen Übersetzungen und Bearbeitungen aus den Oracula Sibyllina' in *Mélanges Joseph de Ghellinck*, i (Museum Lessianum, Section Historique, xiii; 1951), pp. 121–47. J. R. *Harris in *H.D.B.* Extra Vol. (1905), pp. 66–8, s.v.; W. *Bousset in *P.R.E.* (ed. 3), xviii (1906), pp. 265–80, s.v. 'Sibyllen und sibyllinische Bücher'; [A.] Rzach in *P.W.*, Zweite Reihe ii (pt. 2; 1923), cols. 2117–69, s.v. 'Sibyllinische Orakel'; J. B. Frey in *Dict. Bibl.*, Suppl., i (1928), cols. 423–8, s.v. 'Apocryphes de l'Ancien Testament 12'; É. Amann in *D.T.C.*, xiv (pt. 2; 1941), cols. 2027–32, s.v. 'Sibyllins (Livres)'.

SICARD (1160–1215), Bp. of Cremona, historian, canonist, and liturgist. A native of Cremona, he was appointed Canon of Mainz in 1183 and Bp. of Cremona in 1185. Having won the confidence of *Frederick I, he played a considerable part in Lombard politics and was entrusted with several missions to Rome. In 1212–13 he was employed by the Pope on behalf of *Frederick II against Otto IV. His principal works are his *Chronicon*, a history of the world orig. up to 1201, revised and continued up to 1213, which is a primary authority for the Crusade of Frederick I; his *Summa Canonum*, a collection of canons based on the *Decretum Gelasianum*; and his *Mitrale*. The last of these, a moralistic and allegoristic interpretation of places, ceremonies and vestments, throws important light on contemporary liturgical practice.

The best ed. of his *Chronicon* is that of O. Holder-Egger in *M.G.H.*, Scriptores, xxxi (1904), pp. 22–181, with bibl. reff.; the *Mitrale* is pr. in J. P. Migne, *PL*, ccxiii, 13–436. E. Komorowski, *Sicard, Bischof von Cremona* (Diss., Königsberg, 1881). S. Kuttner, 'Zur Biographie des Sicardus von Cremona' in *Zeitschrift der Savigny-Stiftung für Rechtsgeschichte*. Kanonistische Abteilung, xxv (1936), pp. 476–8, with valuable reff. O. Holder-Egger, 'Einiges zur Quellenkritik der Chronik Sicards' in *N.A.*, xxvi (1900), pp. 471–555; id., 'Ueber die verlorene grössere Chronik Sicards von Cremona', ib., xxix (1904), pp. 177–245. P. G. Ficker, *Der Mitralis des Sicardus nach seiner Bedeutung für die Ikonographie des Mittelalters* (Leipzig Diss., 1889; also pr. as Beiträge zur Kunstgeschichte, N.F., ix; 1889). J. Sauer, *Symbolik des Kirchengebäudes und seiner Ausstattung in der Auffassung des Mittelalters* (1902), pp. 22–8 and passim. A. Franz, *Die Messe im deutschen Mittelalter* (1902), pp. 448–52.

SICILIAN VESPERS, The. A general massacre of the French in Sicily on 30 March 1282, the signal for which was the tolling of the bell for *Vespers. The number of the victims was prob. between 3000 and 4000.

M. Amari, *La guerra del vespero siciliano* (2 vols., Paris, 1843; Eng. tr., 3 vols., 1850). O. Cartellieri, *Peter von Aragon und die sizilianische Vesper* (Heidelberg, 1904). H. D. Sedgwick, *Italy in the Thirteenth Century*, ii (1913), pp. 134–40. For further bibl. see G. Cipolla, 'Les Vêpres siciliennes. Compte-Rendu des principales publications parues à propos du septième centenaire célébré à Palerme le 31 mars 1881' in *R.H.*, xxi (1883), pp. 135–47.

SICK, Visitation of the (B.C.P.). See *Visitation of the Sick (B.C.P.).*

SICKINGEN, FRANZ VON (1481–1523), German knight. A native of Ebernburg near Worms, he became the leader of bands of 'Landsknechte' with whose help he conducted many feuds, ostensibly in the cause of the weak and oppressed, but always accompanied by plunder and cruelty. He warred against the cities of Worms and Metz and also fought in the service of Francis I of France and the German Emperor. Having supported the election of *Charles V he was made Imperial Councillor in 1519. Under the influence of Ulrich von *Hutten he embraced the Reformation, defended J. *Reuchlin, and offered his castles as places of refuge to the Protestants. He also aided the Reformers by literary activities and supported M. *Luther in the hope of wresting their power from the spiritual princes and of increasing the strength of the knights. In 1522 he led an army against the Abp. o Trier, but the campaign was a failure, and in 1523 the archbishop and other princes laid a siege against his castle of Landstuhl. In the defence he was mortally wounded and capitulated shortly before his death.

Studies by E. de Bouteiller (Metz, 1860), H. Ulmann (Leipzig, 1872), F. P. Bremer (Strassburg, 1885) and K. H. Rendenbach (Historische Studien, ccxxv; 1933). Further bibl. in Schottenloher, ii (1935), pp. 274-6 (Nos. 20010-67).

SIDETES, PHILIP. See *Philip Sidetes.*

SIDGWICK, HENRY (1838-1900), moral philosopher. A cousin of Abp. E. W. *Benson, he was educated at Rugby and Trinity College, Cambridge, and in 1859 elected a Fellow of his college. Here he taught classics and (after 1869) moral philosophy. He gave strong support to the movement for abolishing religious tests at Cambridge, and in 1869, through feeling no longer able to subscribe himself, resigned his fellowship as a public protest. From 1883 till his death he held the Knightbridge professorship at Cambridge. Sidgwick took a keen and active interest in many fields, —university administration, psychical research, morality, politics, and the admission of women students to the university. His *Methods of Ethics* (1874), a thorough, if inconclusive, study of moral philosophy on mainly *hedonistic lines, exercised considerable influence, e.g. on H. *Rashdall and C. D. Broad. Sidgwick's other writings include *The Ethics of Conformity and Subscription* (1871), *The Principles of Political Economy* (1883), *Outlines of the History of Ethics* (1886), and *The Elements of Politics* (1891).

His posthumous writings include *Lectures on the Ethics of T. H. Green, Mr. H. Spencer and J. Martineau* (1902), *The Development of European Polity* (1903), *Miscellaneous Essays and Addresses* (1904) and *Lectures on the Philosophy of Kant and other Philosophical Lectures and Essays* (ed. J. Ward, 1905). Arthur Sidgwick (brother) and Mrs. E. M. Sidgwick, *Henry Sidgwick. A Memoir* (1906). L. Stephen, 'Henry Sidgwick' in *Mind*, x (1901), pp. 1-17. F. H. Hayward, *The Ethical Philosophy of Sidgwick* (1901); C. D. Broad, *Five Types of Ethical Theory* (1930), ch. vi (pp. 143-256). L. Stephen in *D.N.B.*, Suppl. iii (1901), pp. 342-5 [date of Sidgwick's death incorrectly given].

SIDONIUS APOLLINARIS, St. (c. 432-c. 480), statesman, author and Bp. of Clermont. A member of an aristocratic family of the Lyonnais, he received a good classical education at Arles (perh. also at Lyons) and became the friend and pupil of *Claudianus Mamertus of Vienne. *C.* 450 he married Papianilla, a daughter of the future Emp. Avitus (455-6), and about the same time entered upon a political career. In 456 he published an elaborate panegyric on his father-in-law for which he was rewarded by a statue in the Forum of Trajan. After the overthrow of Avitus by Ricimer and Emp. Majorian, he obtained the favour of the latter through another panegyric. On Majorian's fall he retired for a time from public life, but resumed it in 467 with a mission to Emp. Anthemius, being soon made prefect of Rome (468-9). In 469, when probably still a layman, he was elected Bp. of Clermont, partly in order to defend the country against the Goths. He accepted the episcopal office with reluctance and humility, abandoned

poetry, became a benefactor of monks, and distributed much of his wealth in charities. His strenuous efforts did not avert the occupation of Clermont by the Visigoths under Euric in 475 after repeated sieges, and he himself was exiled and imprisoned. Freed in 476 and reinstated in his diocese, he spent the leisure of his remaining years in making a collection of his letters.

Sidonius may be regarded as the last representative of classical culture. His poems, of which twenty-four are still extant, lack poetical inspiration but show great technical skill. They are formed on the models of *Virgil and Horace and filled with pagan mythology. His letters, though of little religious depth and marred by verbosity, are a valuable source for the history of his time. A work 'Contestatiuncula', probably a collection of his Eucharistic prayers made by St. *Gregory of Tours, has been lost. He was venerated as a saint in Gaul. Feast day, 23 Aug. (in modern editions of the *Roman Martyrology, 21 Aug.).

Editio princeps by E. Vinetus (Lyons, 1552). Improved ed. by J. *Sirmond, S.J., Paris, 1614; new ed., 1652; repr. in J. P. Migne, *PL*, lviii, 435-752. Crit. ed. by C. Luetjohann (completed by F. Leo and T. *Mommsen; *M.G.H.*, Auctores Antiquissimi, viii; 1887). Poems and letters, with Eng. tr., ed. W. B. Anderson (Loeb., vol. i, 1936). Eng. tr. of Letters ed. O. M. Dalton (2 vols., Oxford, 1915). C. E. Stevens, *Sidonius Apollinaris and his Age* (1933), with bibl. H. Rutherford, *Sidonius Apollinaris. L'homme politique, l'écrivain, l'évêque* (Mémoires de l'Académie des Sciences, Belles-Lettres et Arts de Clermont-Ferrand, xxxviii; 1938), with bibl. Bardenhewer, iv, 652-8; Altaner (ed. 1951), p. 449 f. A. Klotz in *P.W.*, 2te Reihe, ii (pt. 2; 1923), cols. 2230-8, s.v. 'Sidonius (1); G. Bardy in *D.T.C.*, xiv (pt. 2; 1941), cols. 2033-5.

SIGAN-FU STONE, The. An early *Nestorian monument, discovered in 1625 at Sigan-Fu (officially Sian-Fu) in NW China. It is a slab, 7½ ft. high by 3 ft. wide, which was set up in A.D. 781. The inscription, mainly in Chinese, contains (1) an allusive statement of Christian doctrine; (2) a description of the arrival in 635 at Sigan-Fu, then the capital of the Tang dynasty, of a missionary from Tuts'in named Olopan and of the imperial privileges which he was granted. After relating how Olopan became a 'Guardian of the Empire' and 'Lord of the Great Law', there follows an account of the fortunes of the Church down to the reign of Tih-tsung (780-3); (3) an epitome of (2) in octosyllabic verse; and (4) a series of short additions in *Syriac in the Estrangelo character. The stone is the most considerable witness extant to the growth of Christianity in the Far East before the 13th cent. In 1907 a replica of the stone was made by the Danish traveller, Frits v. Holm, and deposited in 1908 in the Metropolitan Museum of Art, New York.

F. v. Holm, *The Nestorian Monument* (Chicago, 1909).

SIGEBERT OF GEMBLOUX (c. 1030-1112), medieval chronicler. He was a monk of the *Benedictine abbey of Gembloux, taught for more than 20 years at the school of St. Vincent at Metz, and returned to Gembloux c. 1071. His two principal works are the

'Chronicon' (from 381 to 1111), in which he uses an immense wealth of sources, but without much critical discernment, though from 1024 he relied more on first-hand information, and 'De Viris Illustribus', an ecclesiastical literary history in biographies with an air of great erudition. He is also the author of a history of the early abbots of Gembloux (*Gesta Abbatum Gemblacensium*), as well as of a number of hagiographical works mainly intended for edification and of little historical value. In the great struggle between the Empire and the Papacy he took the side of *Henry IV against *Gregory VII, whose reforms he thought inopportune and whose policy he attacked in several pamphlets. He also wrote against Pope *Paschal II.

Collection of his works in J. P. Migne, *PL*, clx, 57–834 (incl. repr. ed. of the *Chronicon* from L. C. Bethmann in *M.G.H.*, Scriptores, vi (1844), pp. 300–74). His *Apologia contra eos qui calumniantur Missas Coniugatorum Sacerdotum* was first pr. by E. Sackur in *M.G.H.*, Libelli de Lite Imperatorum et Pontificum Saeculis XI. et XII, ii (1892), pp. 436–464; his *Passio Sanctae Luciae Virginis* and his *Passio Sanctorum Thebeorum* were pr. in full by H. Dümmler in *Abh.* (Berl.), 1893, Abh. i. Crit. ed. of *Sigeberti Gemblacensis Chronographiae Auctarium Affligemense* by P. Gorissen (Verhandelingen van de Koninklijke Vlaamse Academie voor Wetenschappen, Letteren en Schone Kunsten van België, Klasse der Letteren, Verhandeling No. 15; 1952). S. Hirsch, *De Vita et Scriptis Sigeberti* (Berlin, 1841). A. Cauchie, *La Querelle des investitures dans les diocèses de Liége et de Cambrai* (2 pts. 1890–1), passim. E. de Moreau, S.J., *Histoire de l'Église en Belgique*, ii (ed. 2, Museum Lessianum, Section Historique, ii, 1945), pp. 83–6, 95–9, 156–8, 277–81, and 285 f. M. Schulz, 'Zur Arbeitsweise Sigeberts von Gembloux im Liber de Scriptoribus Ecclesiasticis' in *N.A.*, xxxv (1910), cols. 563–71. L. Brigué in *D.T.C.*, xiv (pt. 2; 1941), cols. 2035–41, s.v.

SIGER OF BRABANT (c. 1235–c. 1282), *Averroist philosopher. After holding a canonry at St. Martin's Cathedral, Liége, he taught philosophy in the faculty of arts at *Paris from c. 1266 to 1277, where he became the leader of the Averroistic movement. His doctrines were condemned (though not under Siger's name) by Stephen Tempier, Bp. of Paris (1268–79), in 1270 and again in 1277. In the latter year he was cited for heresy before Simon Duval, the Grand Inquisitor of France. He forthwith fled from Paris and retired to Orvieto, where he was assassinated by his secretary, apparently in a fit of insanity, between 1281 and 1284. The view of older historians (e.g. J. Echard) that in his later years Siger accepted Thomistic doctrines rests on a mistaken identification of Siger of Brabant and Siger of Courtrai.

Siger's works, mostly only recovered in recent times, include *De Anima Intellectiva* (acc. to M. Chossat and F. van Steenberghen, a reply to St. Thomas' *De Unitate Intellectus*; P. Mandonnet and earlier scholars put the dependence the other way), *Questiones Naturales* and *Quaestiones Logicales*, six *Impossibilia*, *De Aeternitate Mundi* and Commentaries on various Aristotelian writings (*De Anima, Physica, Meteorologica, De Juventute et Senectute*, &c.; mainly discovered by M.*Grabmann). An epitome of Siger's teaching is to be found in the lists of propositions condemned by Tempier in 1270 and 1277.

Siger has been a much disputed personality from his own day. *Dante (*Paradiso*, X, 133–7) even placed him with St. Thomas among the Doctors of the Church. In general he closely followed the Averroistic interpretation of Aristotle, maintaining as necessary conclusions of philosophy the unity of the intellect in the human race, the eternity of the world, psychological determinism and the denial of retribution after death. He also held that God, the 'uncaused cause' (*causans non causatum*), was the necessary origin of the world and that He was ignorant of future contingents. He apparently adopted a position closely akin to that of the 'double truth', viz. that the same tenet might be true in theology but false in philosophy. But he made the proviso that where faith and philosophy were at variance, it was the former which was to be followed, and he perhaps left the status of philosophical truths unresolved.

P. Mandonnet, O.P., *Siger de Brabant et l'averroïsme latin au 13e siècle* (Collectanea Friburgensia, viii, 1899; 2nd ed. enlarged in 2 vols., 'Les Philosophes belges', vi, 1911, and vii, 1908). M. Grabmann, 'Mitteilungen über scholastische Funde in der Bibliotheca Ambrosiana zu Mailand' in *T.Q.*, xciii (1911), p. 544 f. F. van Steenberghen, *Siger de Brabant d'après ses œuvres inédites* (2 vols., 'Les Philosophes belges', xii, 1931, and xiii, 1942); id., *Les Œuvres et la doctrine de Siger de Brabant* (Académie Royale de Belgique. Classe de Lettres. Mémoires, xxxix, fasc. 3, 1938). P. Delhaye, *Siger de Brabant. Questions sur la physique d'Aristote* ('Les Philosophes belges', xv, 1941). C. A. Graiff, O.S.B., *Siger de Brabant. Questions sur la métaphysique* (Philosophes médievaux, i, 1948). M. Chossat, S.J., 'S. Thomas d'Aquin et Siger de Brabant' in *Revue de Philosophie*, xiv (1914), pt. 1, pp. 553–75. P. Glorieux in *D.T.C.*, xiv (pt. 2; 1941), cols. 2041–56, s.v.

SIGN OF THE CROSS. From the time of *Tertullian Christian writers testify to the use of the 'sign of the Lord', partly as sanctifying every action in daily life from rising in the morning to retiring at night, partly as an encouragement in temptation and trial, and partly as a means of mutual recognition in times of persecution. From early times the sign was also employed in *Baptism and *Confirmation, and its use was then extended to the liturgical blessings of persons and things. In the early centuries the sign was drawn upon the forehead by the thumb or finger of the right hand. In later times it has been made by drawing the right hand from forehead to breast, and then from shoulder to shoulder, returning to the centre afterwards. It is usual in the W. Church to make the cross-stroke from left to right, in the E. from right to left.

H. Thurston, S.J., 'The Sign of the Cross' in *The Month*, cxviii (1911), pp. 586–602, repr. in his *Familiar Prayers*, ed. P. Grosjean, S.J. (1953), pp. 1–21, with reff. E. Beresford-Cooke, *The Sign of the Cross in the Western Liturgies* (*Alcuin Club Tracts, vii; 1907), with reff. F. Dölger, *Antike und Christentum*, iii (1932), 'Das Segnen der Sinne mit dem Eucharistie', pp. 231–44. A. Rücker, 'Die Kreuzzeichen in der westsyrischen Messliturgie' in *Pisciculi*. Studien zur Religion und Kultur des Altertums Franz Joseph Dölger zum sechzigsten Geburtstag dargeboten von Freunden, Verehren und Schülern (Antike und Christentum Ergänzungsband, i; 19)37pp. 245–5.1

SILAS, St. A prominent early Christian disciple. He was St. *Paul's companion on his first visit to Macedonia and *Corinth (Acts

15. 22-40, 2 Cor. 1. 19), and St. Paul associated him with himself and *Timothy in writing to the Thessalonians (1 & 2 Thess. 1. 1), giving his name in the form 'Silvanus'. This led some of the Fathers to distinguish between the two, making Silas Bp. of Corinth and Silvanus Bp. of Thessalonica. Silas, who is probably identical with St. Peter's amanuensis Silvanus (1 Pet. 5. 12), acc. to tradition died in Macedonia. Feast day, 13 July; in the Greek calendar, 30 July.

A. Stegmann, *Silas als Missionar und 'Hagiograph'*. Eine exegetische Studie (1917). L. Radermacher, 'Der erste Petrusbrief und Silvanus' in *Z.N.T.W.*, xxv (1926), pp. 287-99.

SILENCE, The Argument from (Lat. *argumentum e silentio*).
The deduction from the absence of any known reference to a subject in the extant writings of a particular author that he was ignorant of it. Many 19th cent. critics of historic Christianity carried it to extreme lengths. In a famous set of articles (1874-7) criticizing *Supernatural Religion* (anon., by W. R. Cassels; 3 vols., 1874-7), in which the argument had been extensively used, J. B. *Lightfoot showed that it is unsafe to employ it, except in the most compelling cases.

SILESIUS, ANGELUS. See *Angelus Silesius*.

SILOAM, The Pool of.
A pool or reservoir at *Jerusalem, mentioned several times in the OT, and almost certainly the modern *Birket Silwān*. In the NT it is referred to only twice, viz. in the incident of the man born blind (Jn. 9. 1 ff.), whom Christ told to go and wash in this pool, and in Christ's mention of the fall of a tower 'in Siloam' (Lk. 13. 4). In the latter reference, part of the city wall, which ran near the pool, may be intended. The pool *Birket Silwān* receives, through an underground conduit probably made by King Hezekiah, its waters from the 'Virgin's Spring' (*Ain Sitti Maryam*) on the other side of the eastern hill of Jerusalem. Since the 4th cent. it has been a place of pilgrimage for Christians.

T. Tobler, *Die Siloahquelle und der Oelberg* (1852), pp. 1-58. H. Vincent, O.P.-F. M. Abel, O.P., *Jérusalem*, ii (1914), pp. 861-4, with reff. C. W. Wilson in *H.D.B.*, iv (1902), p. 515 f., s.v., with details of reports of the important excavations undertaken in the late 19th cent. under the auspices of the *Palestine Exploration Fund.

SILVESTER. See *Sylvester*.

SILVIA OF AQUITAINE.
A relative of the Roman prefect, Rufinus. Her sole interest to the Church historian lies in the fact that she was considered to be the authoress of the 'Pilgrimage of *Etheria' (q.v.), by F. Gamurrini, who discovered the work in MS. in 1884. In 1903, however, Dom M. Férotin identified the writer with a Spanish nun, Etheria, and this view is now generally accepted.

SIMEON.
(1) In the OT, one of the Hebrew patriarchs, the ancestor of the tribe of the same name. (2) In the NT, the aged and devout Jew who took the infant Christ in his arms in the *Temple at *Jerusalem and spoke the words known as the '*Nunc Dimittis' (Lk. 2. 25-35). (3) In Acts 15. 14, apparently for St. *Peter (elsewhere 'Simon Peter'), though St. *Chrysostom, perhaps correctly, sees here a reference to the Simeon of Lk. 2.

SIMEON, the New Theologian (949-1022).
Though destined for the Imperial service, he embraced the monastic life at the *Studios at an early age. He soon left this monastery, however, because of its lax observance, and was later, for *c.* 25 years, abbot of the monastery of St. Mamas at *Constantinople. He eventually became the most outstanding of Byzantine medieval mystics. Belonging to the tradition of *Evagrius, *Maximus Confessor, and *John Climacus, he taught that 'deification', or sharing in the Divine essence through grace, was the crown of spiritual endeavour. His appellation 'the New' or 'Younger Theologian' ranks him as second in Byzantine estimation to St. *Gregory Nazianzen, 'The Theologian' *par excellence*.

There is no satisfactory ed. of Simeon's writings, which have to be studied in MSS. Some of his Hymns in the orig. Gk, with unsatisfactory Modern Gk. tr. of his other works, were publ. by Dionysius Zagoraios, Venice, 1790 (repr. 'Syros' (Smyrna), 1886). 'Kephalaia', ed. Nicodemus of Agioritis and Macarius of Corinth, in *Philocalia* (Venice, 1782; ed. 2, Athens, 1893); repr. in J. P. Migne, *PG*, cxx, 604-88. Further passages from Hymns, ed. P. Maas, 'Aus der Poesie des Mystikers Symeon' in *Festgabe Albert Ehrhard* (Bonn, 1922), pp. 328-41. Crit. ed. of 'Catechetical Sermons', with Eng. tr., in preparation by Joan M. Hussey and B. Krivocheine. Life by Nicetas Stethatos ed. I. Hausherr, S.J., with Fr. tr. by G. Horn, S.J. (*Orientalia Christiana*, xii; 1928; fasc. 45). B. Krivocheine, 'The Brother-Loving Poor Man. The Mystical Autobiography of St. Symeon the New Theologian' in *Christian East*, N.S., ii (1953-4), pp. 216-27. J. Gouillard, A.A., in *D.T.C.*, xiv (pt. 2; 1941), cols. 2941-56, s.v. 'Syméon le Jeune'.

SIMEON OF DURHAM (c. 1060-1130),
chronicler. He was a monk of the *Benedictine monastery of *Durham, where he was professed in 1085 or 1086 and later became precentor. His first work, inspired by *Bede, was his 'Historia Ecclesiae Dunelmensis', written between 1104 and 1108, which brings the history of the see of Durham down to 1096. After that he wrote a general history of England, 'Historia regum Anglorum et Dacorum', wholly based on earlier writers, except for the contemporary period between 1119 and 1129. The latter was continued by Richard and John of *Hexham.

Opera Omnia, ed. T. Arnold (R.S., 2 vols., 1882-5), with biog. introd. pp. ix-xv. Eng. tr. of his Historical Works by J. Stevenson (The Church Historians of England, iii, pt. 2; 1855). Preface by I. H. Hinde to his ed. of *Symeonis Dunelmensis Opera et Collectanea*, i (all publ.; Surtees Society, li, 1868), pp. v-lv. C. L. Kingsford in *D.N.B.*, lii (1897), p. 254 f.

SIMEON METAPHRASTES (fl. c. 960),
also known as **Logothetes**, Byzantine hagiographer. Nothing is known of his life. He owes his fame to his collection of saints' lives

('Menologion') compiled, it is said, at the bidding of the Emperor. A few of the lives were simply copied from older collections, but most of them worked over ('metaphrased', hence his name) to make them acceptable in style and manner of presentation to the taste of his time. They were not, however, subjected to criticism, the historical errors of the models being reproduced in the new versions, as the interest of the author was chiefly moral and devotional. His work was frequently added to in later times. Among other writings attributed to Simeon are a chronicle and collections of sayings from St. *Basil and other Fathers. The Orthodox Church honours him as a saint. Feast day, 28 Nov.

Texts (many only in mod. Lat. trss.) collected in J. P. Migne, *PG*, cxiv–cxvi. For general orientation, see *B.H.G.* (ed. 1909), esp. pp. 267–92 ('Synopsis Metaphrastica'); but since 1909 several more Gk. texts have been publd. (cf. *D.T.C.*, xiv, pt. 2, 1941, col. 2971). H. *Delehaye, S.J., 'La Vie de saint Paul le Jeune et la chronologie de Métaphraste' in *R.Q.H.*, liv (1893), pp. 49–85; id., *Lives of St. *Alypius, pp. lxxvi–lxxxv and 148–94). A. Ehrhard, *Überlieferung und Bestand der hagiographischen Literatur der griechischen Kirche*, ii (T.U., li, 1938), pp. 306–717. Artt. by V. Laurent, A.A., in *L.Th.K.*, ix (1937), cols. 564 f., s.v., and by J. Gouillard, A.A., in *D.T.C.*, xiv (2; 1941), cols. 2959–71, s.v. 'Syméon Logothète', both with bibl.

SIMEON STOCK, St. See *Simon Stock, St.*

SIMEON STYLITES, St. (*c.* 390–459).
The first of the *stylites or pillar ascetics. He was born on the Syrian border of Cilicia. Having migrated to *Antioch, he became an anchorite in the neighbourhood of the city at the age of *c.* 16, and by his austerities gathered round him a company of followers. After ten years of anchoretic life he built a pillar, at first low, but gradually increased to a height of forty cubits, and lived on the top of it until his death, occupied in adoration and intercession. This novel austerity attracted to him a continuous stream of pilgrims, and was widely imitated. Both by personal intercourse and by correspondence, Simeon exercised considerable influence upon the world of his time, converting pagans, awakening the careless, reconciling enemies, and urging the cause of *Chalcedonian orthodoxy. Feast day, 1 Sept. in the E., 5 Jan. in the W.

AA.SS., Jan. I (1643), pp. 261–86, with Lat. texts only. Of the early lives, the most trustworthy is the account in *Theodoret (*Hist. Rel.*, 26). This was used, and the narrative carried to a later date, in the less reliable Gk. Life by a monk Antony (to which a Coptic Life is nearly related). Its Gk. text was first pr. from a St. Petersburg MS. by A. Papadopoulos-Kerameos (St. Petersburg, 1907). There is also a Syriac Life, which is closely followed by a Georgian text. H. *Lietzmann, *Das Leben des heiligen Simeon Stylites* (T.U., xxxii, 4, 1908), with texts and full crit. discussion. H. *Delehaye, S.J., *Les Saints stylites* (1923), pp. i–xxxix. P. Peeters, S.J., 'St. Syméon Stylite et ses premiers biographes' in *Anal. Boll.*, lxi (1943), pp. 29–71. Bardenhewer, iv, 311–15, with bibl.

SIMEON OF THESSALONICA (d. 1429),
Abp. of Thessalonica. Little is known of his life except that he favoured the Venetians who had bought Thessalonica in 1423 and opposed the surrender of the city to the Turks. He was

one of the most influential authors of his age. His principal work is a 'Dialogue against all Heresies and on the One Faith' (Διάλογος κατὰ πασῶν τῶν αἱρέσεων καὶ περὶ τῆς μόνης πίστεως), which reflects his predominating interest in the mystical interpretation of the Byzantine cultus. It consists of a shorter treatise on doctrine, dealing chiefly with the Trinity and with Christology, and a longer second part on the Liturgy and the Sacraments. The polemical passages envisage the Jews, *Bogomils, Mohammedans, and the Church of Rome. Among his other works are a treatise 'On the Holy Temple' (Περὶ τοῦ θείου Ναοῦ), also mainly a symbolical explanation of the ritual, and an exposition of the *Niceno-Constantinopolitan Creed ('Ερμηνεία συνοπτική).

His writings, edited by *Dositheus (Jassy, 1683), are reprinted in J. P. Migne, *PG*, clv. M. Jugie, A.A., in *D.T.C.*, xiv (pt. 2; 1941), cols. 2976–94, s.v. 'Syméon de Thessalonique'.

SIMEON, CHARLES (1759–1836), leader of
the *Evangelical Revival. He was educated at Eton and King's College, Cambridge, where he became a Fellow in 1782. In 1783 he was ordained priest, and in the same year was appointed vicar of Holy Trinity, Cambridge, holding this incumbency till his death. At an early date he had come under the influence of the two *Venns and his whole future ministry was strongly coloured by his Evangelical experience. At first he was met by hostility both in the university and among his congregation, but his pastoral zeal broke down all opposition. He became a leading figure in the Missionary Movement, being one of the founders of the *C.M.S. (1799) and a prominent supporter of the *British and Foreign Bible Society; and he was frequently consulted by the East India Company on the choice of their chaplains. He was also the founder of a body of trustees (the Simeon Trustees) for securing and administering Church patronage in accordance with his principles.

H. C. G. *Moule, *Charles Simeon* (1892); Charles Smyth, *Simeon and Church Order* (1940). A. R. Buckland in *D.N.B.*, lii (1897), pp. 255–7; G. W. E. Russell in *D.E.C.H.*, pp. 558–560.

SIMILITUDO DEI (Lat., 'likeness of God').
Acc. to a distinction based on a traditional exegesis of Gen. 1. 26, that element in man's being as originally constituted which he lost through the Fall. See *Imago Dei*.

SIMON, St., Apostle. One of the twelve
Apostles, called by *Matthew and *Mark 'the Cananaean' and by *Luke 'the Zealot', two terms which represent the same Hebrew word. Of his personal history nothing certain is known, beyond the inference from Lk. that he had once been a member of the *Zealots. The apocryphal 'Passion of Simon and Jude' relates the preaching and martyrdom of these two Apostles in Persia. In the W. the two are always coupled in the ecclesiastical calendar and in dedications of churches. Feast of Sts. Simon and Jude, 28 Oct. See also *Simons in the N.T.*

AA.SS., Oct. XII (1867), pp. 421–36. J. S. Hoyland, *Simon the Zealot* (1941; an imaginative reconstruction of the Gospel narrative, conceived as the supersession of Jewish nationalism). J. Freundorfer in *L.Th.K.*, ix (1937), col. 570 f.

SIMON MAGUS.

Acc. to Acts 8. 9–24, a sorcerer, known as 'the Power of God which is called Great', who practised in *Samaria in the time of the Apostles. Having professed Christianity and been baptized, he was later rebuked by St. *Peter for trying to obtain spiritual powers from the Apostles for money (hence the term '*Simony'). This in substance is all that is recorded in the NT.

In the 2nd–3rd cents. there existed a quasi-Christian sect of a *Gnostic cast which was supposed to have taken its origin from him. *Justin Martyr, followed by other writers, says that its founder, Simon, was a native of Gitta in Samaria, who came to Rome in the time of Emp. Claudius (A.D. 41–54). He affirms that Simon was honoured by his disciples as a god and that he taught a Gnostic type of doctrine. Simon was said by St. *Hippolytus and others to have come into conflict with St. Peter again at Rome, and to have perished dramatically there through a failure of his magic powers. He later figures in the '*Clementine Homilies' and 'Recognitions', and also in ancient and medieval legends from which, perhaps, that of Faust evolved. The most probable view seems that the heresiarch, Simon of Gitta, though a genuinely historical person, was in fact a different person from the Simon Magus of Acts, and that he really lived in the 2nd cent.

On the NT account see commentaries on Acts, cited s.v., esp. E. Jacquier (Paris, 1926), pp. 254–67. The base of the statue which Justin Martyr (*Apol.* i. 26) records that he saw in Rome erected to the honour of Simon (acc. to Justin, inscribed 'Simoni Deo Sancto') was recovered in 1574; it was really dedicated, not to Simon, but, as the actual inscription showed ('Semoni Sanco Deo Fidio'), to a Sabine god. On Simon's place in Gnosticism, L. Cerfaux, 'La Gnose simonienne' in *Rech. S.R.*, xv (1925), pp. 489–511, and xvi (1926), pp. 5–20, 265–85, and 481–503. G. *Salmon in *D.C.B.*, iv (1887), pp. 681–8; A. C. *Headlam in *H.D.B.*, iv (1902), pp. 520–7; G. N. L. Hall in *H.E.R.E.*, xi (1920), pp. 514–25; H. *Lietzmann in *P.W.*, Zweite Reihe, iii (1929), cols. 180–184; S. Lösch in *L.Th.K.*, ix (1937), col. 572 f.; É. Amann in *D.T.C.*, xiv (pt. 2; 1941), cols. 2130–40, s.v. 'Simon le Magicien'.

SIMON PETER, St.

See *Peter, St.*

SIMON STOCK, St.

(c. 1165–1265), also 'Simeon Stock' and 'Simon Anglus' General of the *Carmelites. One of the first Englishmen to join the Carmelites when they settled in Britain, he became at a great age the sixth General of the order (1247). During his term of office the order increased rapidly, esp. in England; and he was responsible for obtaining Papal approbation for the alterations which it had undergone since leaving Palestine (see *Carmelites*). The name 'Stock' is perhaps derived from the legend that as a young man he lived a hermit's life inside a tree-trunk. Feast day, 16 May.

A. Monbrun, *Vie de saint Simon de Stock, sixième général des Carmes, fondateur de la confrérie du Saint-Scapulaire,* suivie de la bulle sabbatine du pape Jean XXII (Clermont-Ferrand, 1869). F. M. Xiberta, Ord. Carm., *De Visione Sancti Simonis Stock* (Bibliotheca Sacri Scapularis, i; Rome, 1950). B. Zimmerman, O.D.C., (ed.), *Monumenta Historica Carmelitana* (Lerins, 1907), pp. 313–22.

SIMON OF SUDBURY

(d. 1381), Abp. of *Canterbury. Born at Sudbury in Suffolk, he studied at the university of *Paris, and later became chaplain to Innocent VI, who appointed him Bp. of London in 1361. He was very soon playing a prominent part as a diplomatist and politician, being an adherent of John of Gaunt, Duke of Lancaster. In 1375 he was translated to Canterbury, and two years later crowned Richard II. He seems to have been reluctant to take proceedings against J. *Wycliffe until ordered to do so by the Pope, and then was not extreme in his measures. In 1380 he became chancellor and was responsible for the imposition of a poll tax. When in 1381 a great rising of the Commons took place, the Kentish rioters spoiled the archbishop's lands, released from prison John *Ball, the excommunicated priest, and attacked the Tower where Sudbury had taken refuge with the King. He resigned the chancellorship, but this did not avail to save him, and on Friday, 14 June 1381, the mob captured and beheaded him. The archbishop met his death bravely and was by many regarded as a martyr.

R. C. Fowler (ed.), *Registrum Simonis de Sudbiria, Diocesis Londoniensis A.D. 1362–1375* (*Canterbury and York Society, xxxiv and xxxviii; 1927–38), with introd. by C. Jenkins in vol. ii, pp. v–lxv. W. Hunt in *D.N.B.*, lv (1898), pp. 146–9, s.v. 'Sudbury, Simon of'; W. H. *Hutton in *D.E.C.H.* (1912), p. 575, s.v. 'Sudbury, Simon of'.

SIMON, RICHARD

(1638–1712), Biblical scholar. From 1662 to 1678 he was a member of the French *Oratory. After extensive studies in oriental languages, he published in 1678 his *Histoire critique du Vieux Testament*, in which he denied that *Moses was the author of the *Pentateuch, arguing from the existence of duplicate accounts of the same incident and the variations of style. He is thus generally regarded as the founder of OT criticism. For his boldness Simon was expelled from his order. Much of his work, however, was written in the interests of orthodoxy against B. *Spinoza's OT theories, and Simon continued throughout his life to have the interests of Catholicism at heart. He was strongly opposed to *Jansenism. He lived later at Rouen and at Dieppe, where he wrote several works on the NT.

Of older books the best is the Life by K. H. Graf (Jena, 1847). There is no modern Life. A. Bernus, *Richard Simon et son Histoire critique du Vieux Testament* (Diss., Lausanne, 1869); H. Margival, *Essai sur Richard Simon et la critique biblique au XVIIe siècle* (1900); F. Stummer, *Die Bedeutung Richard Simons für die Pentateuchkritik* (Alttestamentliche Abhandlungen, iii, 4; 1912). A. Bernus, *Notice bibliographique sur Richard Simon* (Basle, 1882); A. Molien in *D.T.C.*, xiv (pt. 2, 1941), cols. 2094–118, s.v., with bibl.

SIMONS, MENNO.

See *Mennonites*.

SIMONS IN THE NT.

Besides (1) Simon *Peter the Apostle, (2) *Simon the Apostle, called 'Zelotes' or 'the Cananaean', and (3)

*Simon Magus, there is mention in the NT of (4) Simon, one of the *Brethren of the Lord, who has been identified with (2) but is almost certainly distinct, also (5) Simon of Cyrene, a passer-by who was compelled to bear the cross of Christ on the way to His crucifixion (Mk. 15. 21, &c.); (6) Simon the *Pharisee, in whose house Christ was anointed by 'a woman which was a sinner' (Lk. 7. 36–50); (7) Simon the leper, in whose house at *Bethany Christ was anointed by an unnamed woman (Mk. 14. 3–9), sometimes identified with *Mary of Bethany; and (8) Simon, a tanner, with whom St. Peter lodged at Joppa (Acts 9. 43).

SIMONY. The term, which is derived from *Simon Magus (cf. Acts 8. 18–24), denotes the purchase or sale of spiritual things. The legislation of the early Councils shows that simony became frequent in the Christian Church after the age of the persecutions. The Council of *Chalcedon (451) forbade ordination to any order for money. St. *Gregory the Great later vigorously denounced the same evil. It came to be very widespread in the Middle Ages, esp. in its form of traffic in ecclesiastical preferment, which was frequently forbidden, e.g. by the Third *Lateran Council (1179). It was treated in detail by St. *Thomas Aquinas and again strenuously opposed by the Council of *Trent. In post-Reformation England the English *Canons of 1604 exacted an oath from all ordinands and recipients of benefices to the effect that their offices had not been obtained by simoniacal transactions. The system of ecclesiastical patronages led almost inevitably to simony in a large number of cases, an evil partly remedied by the English Benefices Act of 1898, inaugurated by Abp. E. W. *Benson, which, among other anti-simoniacal provisions, forbade sales of next presentations.

A. Leinz, *Die Simonie. Ein kanonistische Studie* (1902); N. A. Weber, *A History of Simony in the Christian Church from the Beginning to Death of Charlemagne, 814* (Baltimore, 1909); R. A. Ryder, *Simony.* An historical Synopsis and Commentary (Catholic University of America Canon Law Studies, lxv, 1931). A. Bride in *D.T.C.*, xiv (pt. 2, 1941), cols. 2141–60, s.v. 'Simonie'.

SIMPLE FEASTS. Feasts of the lowest rank in the Roman Calendar. They are characterized by having no Second Vespers and only one *nocturn with three lessons at *Mattins. For the classification of feasts, see *Doubles.*

SIMPLICIANUS, St. (d. 400), Bp. of Milan. He is first heard of at *Rome between 350 and 360, where he was instrumental in bringing about the conversion of *Victorinus. Shortly afterwards he became tutor to St. *Ambrose, and when in 373 his pupil was elected bishop, Simplicianus also removed to Milan to prepare him for baptism and ordination. Later he played an important part in St. *Augustine's conversion by recounting the story of Victorinus, and some of Augustine's early treatises were addressed to him. In 397 he succeeded

Ambrose as Bp. of Milan. Feast day, 16 Aug. (sometimes, 13).

The chief early sources are Augustine, *Confessions*, viii. 1–12, and *Gennadius, *De Viris Illustribus*, 36. H. W. Phillpott in *D.C.B.*, iv (1887), p. 688 f., with further reff.

SIMPLICIUS, St. (d. 483), Pope from 468. He was born at Tivoli. During his pontificate, which was marked by the fall of the W. Empire (476), the rule of Odoacer (an *Arian) as king of Italy, and the spread of the *Monophysite heresy, he considerably advanced the jurisdictional claims and prestige of the Roman see. In the E. he successfully intervened in defence of the *Chalcedonian formula against its Monophysite critics. He also ably organized the ecclesiastical affairs of the city, where he established several new churches, including S. Stefano Rotondo on the Celian Hill. See *Rome, Churches of.* Feast day, 2 Mar.

Several of his letters are repr. from the conciliar collections in J. P. Migne, *PL*, lviii, 35–62; fourteen from the Collectio Avellana also ed. O. Guenther in C.S.E.L., xxv (pt. 1; 1895), pp. 124–55. P. Jaffé, *Regesta Pontificum Romanorum*, i (ed. 2 by W. Wattenbach, Leipzig, 1885), pp. 77–80. V. Grumel, A.A., *Les Régestes des actes du patriarcat de Constantinople*, i, fasc. i (Istanbul, 1932), pp. 64–9. L.P. (Duchesne), i, 1886, pp. 92 f. and 249–51. É. Amann in *D.T.C.*, xiv (pt. 2; 1941), cols. 2161–4, s.v., with reff.

SIMULTANEUM. The term was originally used in the 16th cent. in Germany for the authorization of two or more religious communions in the same territory. It gradually came to be restricted to the simultaneous right of two congregations differing in their faith to use a single ecclesiastical building. Special provisions for this practice were made in the Peace of *Ryswick (1697). Fresh arrangements for the joint use of churches were drawn up by the Prussian state after the *Vatican Council of 1870 for the newly formed *Old Catholics and the RCs, but on 12 Mar. 1873 *Pius IX expressly forbade RCs to use the churches given by the government to the Old Catholics.

SIN. The purposeful disobedience of a creature to the known will of God. Unlike moral evil it is a fundamentally theological conception.

In the OT sin is represented as a constant factor in the experience both of God's people and the world from the first transgression of *Adam and *Eve in the Garden of Eden (Gen. 3) onwards. Its power was aggravated rather than diminished by the moral and ceremonial precepts in the Law of *Moses, which both increased the occasions of sin and developed a keener sense of moral responsibility (cf. Rom. 7. 13). The teaching of the Prophets with its emphasis on the heinousness of injustice (Am. 5. 11–25), lack of mercy (Hos. 4. 1), and idolatry (Am. 5. 4–5, Is. 1. 10–17) deepened the sense of sin in another way. The Pss. and Jer., by their stress on the heart as the seat of sin, were marked by their penetrating insights into its personal and emotional effects. In the *Wisdom literature classifications of the virtues and vices are met with, parallel to those in the popular philosophy of Hellenistic times.

In the NT the Hebrew and Jewish teaching on sin is summed up and deepened by the clear recognition that its roots lie in a man's character (Mt. 5. 21–5; 15. 18). St. *Paul expounds it as a breach of the natural law written in the conscience of man (Rom. 2. 14–16) and asserts its universality. St. *James stresses its origin in the human will and the personal responsibility of each man for his own sins. In the Johannine writings sin is seen to consist esp. in disbelief in Christ and the consequent judgement.

Later theology, though it introduced many formal distinctions, has added little if anything to what is implicit in the NT. In the 2nd cent. an acute problem was raised by the question of serious post-Baptismal sins which certain theologians held to be never, or only once (*Hermas, *Tertullian), forgivable; but this rigorism was soon generally abandoned for a more lenient view. The Fathers held varying beliefs in the universality or otherwise of sin, e.g. St. *Athanasius believed that there were sinless lives both before and after Christ. In the early 5th cent. *Pelagius raised the fiercest of all controversies on the nature of *original sin (q.v.) and grace. St. *Augustine's part in the conflict, combined with his own religious experience, issued in an intense personal perception of the gravity of sin. Yet on the theological issue St. Augustine emphatically rejected the *Manichean doctrine that evil was a substance and the created universe inherently wicked, opposing to it the *Platonic view that sin was in essence privative (privatio boni). In this teaching he exercised a decisive influence on the medieval doctrine of sin.

In the 8th-9th cents. the prevalence of feudal notions and the development of the penitential system fostered in many quarters a somewhat external view of sin. For each sin due satisfaction was to be paid in a measurable quantity of penance. But under the influence of such teachers as St. *Anselm and the *Victorines a fundamentally personal view of sin reasserted itself. The regularization of confessional practice also led to the elaboration of a corpus of *moral theology in St. *Thomas Aquinas and other writers. For the long dispute as to whether or not the BVM was conceived without sin, see Immaculate Conception.

The Reformers were largely concerned to reject the external view of sin which they saw in the later Middle Ages. The doctrine of *justification by faith only was held by M. *Luther to be the one solvent for every external view of sin. The *Calvinistic teaching on *predestination brought vividly before the imagination of countless Protestants the terrifying consequences of sin. In the 17th cent. the doctrine of sin in the *Jansenist movement in the RC Church had close affinities with the teaching of the Reformers, while in the Protestant Churches certain *Arminian tenets had much in common with Catholic teaching. Among Catholic theologians, the intensive cultivation of moral theology since the 16th cent. has led to such precise distinctions as those currently drawn between *mortal and *venial, and between *formal and *material, sin (qq.v.).

Since the end of the 17th cent. there has been little further development of the doctrine of sin. Under the secularizing influences of the Aufklärung attempts were made to remove sin from its religious setting and interpret it as moral evil ('philosophic sin'). The liberalistic optimism of the 19th cent. led to the virtual elimination of the notion of sin from much popular religious teaching. Early in the present century the Freudian psychology was invoked in attempts to explain sin in non-moral terms. More recently the recognition of demonic forces in contemporary civilization has led to a renewed theological emphasis on the gravity of sin in the spirit of St. Augustine and the Reformers (*Dialectical Theology, &c.).

See also Atonement, Penance, Redemption, Seven Deadly Sins.

Modern works in English directly on the subject include J. *Tulloch, The Christian Doctrine of Sin (1877); F. R. Tennant, The Origin and Propagation of Sin (*Hulsean Lectures, 1902); id., The Sources of the Doctrines of the Fall and Original Sin (1903); id., The Concept of Sin (1912); T. A. *Lacey, Nature, Miracle and Sin (1916); P. Green, The Problem of Evil (1920); R. S. Moxon, The Doctrine of Sin (1922); E. J. Bicknell, The Christian Idea of Sin and Original Sin (1922); N. P. *Williams, The Ideas of the Fall and of Original Sin (*Bampton Lectures for 1924; 1927). E. R. Bernard in H.D.B., iv (1902), pp. 528–36, s.v.; artt. in H.E.R.E., xi (1920), pp. 528–71, esp. H. R. *Mackintosh on 'Sin (Christian)' pp. 538–44; T. Deman, O.P., in D.T.C., xii (pt., 1; 1933), cols. 140–275, s.v. 'Péché'; G. Quell–G. Bertram–G. Stählin–W. Grundmann in T.W.B., i (1933), pp. 267–320, s.v. 'ἁμαρτάνω, ἁμάρτημα, ἁμαρτία', with extensive bibl. reff.

SINAI. The mountain in the desert between Egypt and Palestine where the Law was given by *Moses (Ex. 19. 1 ff.). From very ancient times it was regarded as the sacred mountain of *Jehovah (Deut. 33. 2, Jgs. 5. 5). The region of the traditional Sinai (now Jebel Musa) became an early centre of Christian *monasticism, the present monastery dedicated to St. *Catherine of Alexandria claiming to have been built on the site to which her body was miraculously transported.

A. P. *Stanley, Sinai and Palestine in connection with their History (1856), ch. i, 'The Peninsula of Sinai', pp. 3–62. M. J. *Lagrange, O.P., 'Le Sinaï biblique' in R. Bibl., viii (1899), pp. 369–92. D. Nielsen, 'The Site of the Biblical Mount Sinai' in Journal of the Palestine Oriental Society, vii (Jerusalem, 1927), pp. 187–208; L. H. Vincent, O.P., 'Un Nouveau Sinaï biblique' in R. Bibl., xxxix (1930), pp. 73–83. L. Prévost, Le Sinaï hier-aujourd'hui. Étude topographique, biblique, historique, archéologique (1937). A. Legendre in Dictionnaire de la Bible, v (1908), cols. 1751–83, s.v., with bibl.

C. N. Papamichalopoulos, Ἡ μονὴ τοῦ Ὄρους Σινᾶ (Athens, 1932), with docc. M. H. L. Rabino, Le Monastère de Sainte-Catherine du Mont Sinaï. Souvenirs épigraphiques des anciens pèlerins (Cairo, 1935). For further bibl., G. Hofmann in E.C., xi (1953), col. 660, s.v.

SINAI, Patriarchate of. The smallest autocephalous Church of the Orthodox Communion. It is ruled by the 'Abp. of Mt. Sinai', the abbot of the monastery of St. Catherine on the mountain, who has jurisdiction over a few daughter-houses and cells and a small number of Arabs who live in the vicinity of the monastery. The independence of the Church was proclaimed in 1575 and confirmed in 1782. The archbishop must always be consecrated by the Patr. of *Jerusalem, who in consequence has often tried, though with little success, to assert a certain supremacy over the Church.

SINAITICUS, CODEX. See *Codex Sinaiticus.*

SION. See *Zion.*

SION COLLEGE, London. An ecclesiastical institution founded by Thomas White (1550?–1624), who left £3,000 to purchase premises for a 'college' for a 'corporation' or guild of the clergy of London and its suburbs, with almshouses for 20 people attached. To the original hall, chapel, and almshouses in London Wall, a library was added by the donation of John Simpson, White's executor. The College was moved to the Victoria Embankment in 1886 and now functions chiefly as a theological and historical library.

E. H. Pearce, *Sion College and Library* (1913).

SI QUIS (Lat., 'if anyone'). The public notice issued on behalf of a candidate for a benefice, holy orders, &c., which requires any objectors to come forward.

SIRICIUS, St. (*c.* 334–99), Bp. of *Rome from 384. His pontificate is of importance as marking a new stage in the development of Papal authority. His epistle to Himerius, Bp. of Tarragona (385), advocating a relatively lenient treatment of public penitents, is the first of the Papal *decretals. He held a synod at Rome in 386 which passed nine canons on matters of ecclesiastical discipline that were sent to the African Church. He also took active steps towards preventing the Church in E. Illyria from becoming subject to the jurisdiction of *Constantinople. In 390 he dedicated the new *basilica of St. Paul on the *Ostian Way, and in 392 condemned* Jovinian. Feast day, 26 Nov.

Letters ed. P. *Coustant, O.S.B., *Epistolae Romanorum Pontificum,* i (Paris, 1721), cols. 623–700; repr. in J. P. Migne, *PL,* xiii, 1131–96. Jaffé, i, 40–2. *L.P.* (Duchesne), i, 216 f. On the events of his pontificate, E. Caspar, *Geschichte des Papsttums,* i (1930), pp. 257–85. J. Barmby in *D.C.B.,* iv (1887), pp. 696–702, s.v. E. Amann in *D.T.C.,* xiv (pt. 2; 1941), cols. 2171–4, s.v. 'Sirice'; A Amore, O.F.M., in *E.C.,* xi (1953), col. 756 f., s.v. 'Siricio'.

SIRMIUM, Blasphemy of. The doctrinal formula published in Latin by the Council of Sirmium of 357, setting forth the teaching of the extreme *Arian party. All mention of the term 'substance' (*substantia, quae Graece usia appellatur*) and its compounds (including the *Homoousion) in Trinitarian speculation was forbidden, and the subordination of the Son to the Father asserted. Its promulgation marked the turning point in the history of the Arian controversy. It takes its name from the description of it in St. *Hilary of Poitier's 'De synodis' as the *Exemplum blasphemiae apud Sirmium.*

The text is in A. Hahn, *Bibliothek der Symbole und Glaubensregeln der alten Kirche* (ed. 3, 1897), § 161, pp. 199–201.

SIRMOND, JACQUES (1559–1651), French *Jesuit scholar. Having entered the Society of Jesus in 1576, he was professor of literature and rhetoric at the Collège de Clermont from 1581 to 1590, where he numbered St. *Francis of Sales among his pupils. From 1590 to 1608 he was secretary to the General of the Jesuits, C. *Aquaviva, at Rome, and while there assisted C. *Baronius in his historical works. After returning to France he became rector of the Paris College (1617) and later confessor to Louis XIII (1637–43). From 1610 onwards he published the works which established his fame as one of the greatest scholars of his century. Esp. important are his editions of the Fathers, which include St. *Fulgentius's 'De veritate praedestinationis et gratiae' (1612), the works of *Paschasius Radbertus (1618) and *Theodoret of Cyrrhus (1642), the 'Opuscula' of *Eusebius of Caesarea (1643), and *Rufinus's 'De Fide' (1650). His other writings include *Concilia Antiqua Galliae* (1629), a dissertation *Dionysii Parisiensis et Dionysii Areopagitae discrimen* (1641) which raised a long-drawn-out controversy owing to its attack on the traditional identification of the two *Dionysii, and various polemical works.

Opera Varia nunc primum collecta (not quite complete), ed. by J. de La Baune, S.J. (5 vols., fol., Paris, 1696, with brief biography; repr. Venice, 1728), H. *Valesius, *Oratio in Obitum J. Sirmondi* (Paris, 1651). Sommervogel, vii (1896), pp. 1237–61. P. Galtier, S.J., in *D.T.C.,* xiv (pt. 2; 1941), cols. 2186–93.

SISTERS OF MERCY. (1) A name widely used in the 19th cent. of members of any (esp. Anglican) religious community engaged in nursing or similar work. A penitentiary conducted by such sisters was known as a 'House of Mercy'. (2) A RC sisterhood founded in *Dublin in 1827.

SISTINE CHAPEL. The principal chapel of the *Vatican Palace, so called because it was built for Pope *Sixtus IV (1471–84). It is used for the principal Papal ceremonies and also by the cardinals for the election of a new Pope when the see is vacant. The chapel is celebrated for the frescoes by *Michelangelo and other artists on its walls and ceiling, chief among them being Michelangelo's *Last Judgement* covering the altar wall.

E. Steinmann, *Die Sixtinische Kapelle* (2 vols., 1901–5), with plates (2 vols., 1901–5). C. de Tolnay, *Michelangelo,* ii (Princeton, 1945), The Sistine Ceiling, incl. full bibl.

SISTINE MADONNA (Madonna di S. Sisto). One of *Raphael's best-known works, depicting the Virgin and Child floating on the clouds of heaven, between St. *Sixtus II and

St. *Barbara, while two angels gaze upwards at them from below. It was painted in Rome c. 1515, and placed over the high altar of the Benedictine abbey church of San Sisto at Piacenza. By reason of the idealism of its form and its vision-like grace it has been pronounced the 'sublimest lyric of the art of Catholicity' (J. A. Symonds). It is now at Dresden.

SIX ARTICLES, The (1539). The Articles imposed in June 1539 at the King's bidding by 31 Hen. VIII, c. 14, popularly known as 'the Whip with Six Strings', to prevent the spread of Reformation doctrines and practices. They (1) maintained *transubstantiation and (2) *communion in one kind, (3) enforced clerical *celibacy, (4) upheld *monastic vows and (5) defended private *Masses and (6) *auricular confession. The bill was introduced into the Lords by the Duke of Norfolk, and all the lay peers were subservient. A minority of the bishops, however, resisted. Nicholas Shaxton (c. 1485–1556), Bp. of *Salisbury, and H. *Latimer, Bp. of *Worcester, resigned their sees, and T. *Cranmer sent his wife back to Germany. In operation the act turned out to be less severe than its critics feared, as its requirements were widely ignored even by those holding high ecclesiastical office.

Text in Gee–Hardy, pp. 303–19 (No. lxv); the Articles, without the rest of the Act, repr. in Bettenson, p. 328 f.

SIX POINTS, The. The *Eastward Position, Eucharistic *Vestments, the *Mixed Chalice, *Altar Lights, Unleavened *Bread at the *Eucharist, and *Incense. Their introduction into the C of E followed a campaign, set on foot c. 1870 under the indirect influence of the *Oxford Movement, to restore these and many similar ceremonial usages. Their crystallization into 'six points' dates from a resolution of the *English Church Union, proposed by T. T. *Carter and passed at the annual meeting of the Union on 15 June 1875. See also Purchas Judgement, Lincoln Judgement.

SIX-PREACHERS. In *Canterbury Cathedral the Six preachers established by *Henry VIII to represent the new learning. They were required to preach every saints' day, not being a Sunday, and to travel round the diocese. They still receive a wood and forage allowance and now preach once a year. Under the new statutes of Canterbury Cathedral, a Six-preacher holds office for five years only, renewable for five years, and he is paid for the sermons actually delivered.

SIXTUS II, St. (d. 258), or 'Xystus', Pope. On his accession in 257 to the Roman see, he resumed relations with St. *Cyprian and the Churches of Africa and Asia Minor, which had been broken off under his predecessor St. *Stephen I on account of the controversy on the validity of heretical baptism. Sixtus himself, however, continued the Roman practice of not rebaptizing heretics. He suffered martyrdom under the second edict of Emp. Valerian (Aug. 258) and was buried in the catacomb of St. Callistus. He was one of the most highly venerated of early martyrs. His name is found in the Roman calendar of the middle of the 4th cent. and still stands in the *Canon of the Mass. Feast day, 6 Aug.

He is to be distinguished from an earlier St. Sixtus (I), who was Bp. of Rome c. 117–c. 127. Feast-day, 6 Apr.

Jaffé, i, 21 f. L.P. (Duchesne), i, 155 f. AA.SS., Aug. II (1735), pp. 124–42; also Nov. II (pt. 2; 1931), p. 420 f., with full reff. P. Corssen, 'Der Schauplatz der Passion des römischen Bischofs Sixtus II' in Z.N.T.W., xvi (1915), pp. 147–66, with reff.; P. F. de' Cavalieri, Note agiografiche, vi (S.T., xxxiii; 1920), No. 4, 'Un recente studio sul luogo del martirio di S. Sisto II', pp. 145–78. É. Amann in D.T.C., xiv (pt. 2; 1941), cols. 2194–6, s.v. 'Siste II'; H. *Leclercq, O.S.B.,–M. Combet-Farnoux in D.A.C.L., xv (pt. 1; 1950), cols. 1501–15, s.v. 'Siste II', with bibl.; A. Amore, O.F.M., in E.C., xi (1953), col. 778 f., s.v. 'Sisto II'. On the Sayings of a pagan moralist Sextus, wrongly ascribed to the Pope, cf. lit. cited in Bardenhewer ii, p. 643 f.

SIXTUS IV (1414–84), Pope from 1471. Born of a poor family, Francesco della Rovere entered the *Franciscan Order, where he became a successful lecturer, General in 1464, and cardinal in 1467. Elected Pope in 1471, he undertook a crusade against the Turks, but with little success, and soon turned almost entirely to Italian politics and the aggrandizement of his family. With him the nepotism of the Renaissance Popes entered its worst stage and the spiritual interests of the Church were almost wholly relegated to the background. His nephews, one of whom was the later Pope *Julius II, implicated the Pope in political intrigues with the Italian cities, esp. in the conspiracy of the Pazzi, which resulted in the murder of Giuliano de' Medici and a war with Florence (1478–80). His nepotism also led to considerable confusion of the Papal finances and troubles in the Pontifical States. Besides increasing the privileges of the Franciscans and other Mendicant orders and furthering the cult of the BVM, Sixtus was a great protector of arts and scholarship. He founded the Sistine Choir, built the *Sistine Chapel, and enriched the *Vatican Library. Sixtus was unfortunate in his training and his circumstances. His extravagance arose from his inexperience as a member of a Mendicant Order and from the want of any worthy relatives on whom to exercise his natural generosity. For in his personal life he appears to have been blameless and also a passable theologian.

Life attributed to B. Platina (d. 1481) in L. A. *Muratori (ed.), Rerum Italicarum Scriptores, iii (pt. 2; Milan, 1724), cols. 1053–68. L. *Pastor, The History of the Popes from the Close of the Middle Ages (Eng. tr.), iv (1894), pp. 197–471; A. Fliche–V. Martin (edd.), Histoire de l'Église, xv (1951), esp. pp. 74–90. E. Franz, Sixtus IV und die Republik von Florenz (1880). E. Müntz, 'Un Mécène italien au XVe siècle. Les Lettres et les arts à Rome pendant le règne de Sixte IV' in Revue des Deux Mondes, xlviii (1881), pp. 154–192. C. Bauer, 'Studi per la storia delle finanze papali durante il pontificato di Sisto IV' in Archivio della R. Società di Storia Patria, l (1927), pp. 314–404. A. Teetaert, O.Cap., in D.T.C., xiv (pt. 2; 1941), cols. 2199–217, s.v., with full bibl. P. Paschini in E.C., xi (1953), cols. 780–2, s.v. 'Sisto IV', with bibl.

SIXTUS V (1521-90), Pope from 1585. The son of a gardener, Felice Peretti was educated by the *Franciscans of Montalto, where he took the habit at the age of 12. Ordained priest in 1547, he soon became a famous preacher and a friend of St. *Ignatius Loyola and St. *Philip Neri. He was appointed Consultor of the *Inquisition and professor at the Roman University in 1560, and general of his order and Bp. of S. Agata in 1566. In 1570 he was created cardinal by *Pius V, whose confessor he was. He was Bp. of Fermo from 1571 to 1577 and in 1585 was elected Pope. The five years of his pontificate were devoted to far-reaching reforms in the government of the Church and of the Papal States, carried through by ruthless methods. He rigorously suppressed brigandage in his territories and put the Papal finances on a sound basis by the sale of certain offices, the setting-up of more '*montes', and additional taxes. Continuing the reform of the Curia, he fixed the number of cardinals at 70, and by the bull 'Immensa Aeterni' of 1588 established 15 cardinalitial congregations (see *Roman Congregations*). In his European policy he endeavoured to uphold the balance of the Catholic powers, and thus distrusted the ambitions of *Philip II who wished to split up France. A patron of art and scholarship, Sixtus V was esp. concerned with the embellishment of Rome, though he had scant appreciation of its antiquities. He built the *Lateran Palace and the *Vatican Library, had the cupola of St. Peter's finished, and supplied the city with drinking water, the 'Acqua Felice', which was conducted over a distance of 20 miles. The current text of the *Vulgate (the 'Sistine') is that of the edition which he inaugurated, though many errors in its readings were eliminated under *Clement VIII.

Bullarum, Diplomatum et Privilegiorum Sanctorum Romanorum Pontificum Taurinenis Editio, viii (Naples, 1883), pp. 563-1025, and ix (Turin, 1865), pp. 1-381. 'Acta Consistoralia' in *Analecta Juris Pontificii*, ix (Rome, Paris, and Brussels, 1872), cols. 841-74. G. Cugnoni, 'Documenti chigiani concernenti Felice Peretti, Sisto V' in *Archivio della Società Romana di Storia Patria*, v (1882), pp. 1-32, 210-304, and 542-89. C. Leti, *Vita di Sisto V* (3 vols., Amsterdam, 1721; Eng. tr., 1724); C. Tempesti, *Storia della vita e geste di Sisto Quinto* (1754); J. A. de Hübner, *Sixte-Quint* (2 vols., 1870; Germ. tr., 1932). S. Klein, *Sixtus der Fünfte* nach dem grösseren Werke des Barons von Hübner bearbeitet (Sammlung historicher Bildnisse, x, 1873). E. A. Segretain, *Sixte-Quint et Henri IV* (1861). M. de Boüard, 'Sixte-Quint, Henri IV et la Ligue. La Légation du Cardinal Caetani en France (1589-1590)' in *R.Q.H.*, cxvi (1932), pp. 59-140. Pastor, xxi (1932) and xxii (1932), pp. 1-312. A. Teertaert, O.F.M.Cap. in *D.T.C.*, xiv (pt. 2; 1941), cols. 2217-38, s.v. 'Sixte-Quint', with full bibl.; G. B. Picotti in E.C., xi (1953), cols. 780-7, s.v. 'Sisto V', with bibl.

SLAVERY. A state of servitude by which a man is the property of another man. It is opposed on the one hand to human dignity, which does not allow a person to be treated as a chattel, and violates a man's rights to liberty of conscience, integrity of soul and body, and the stability of family life, and, on the other hand, tends to breed vice and cruelty in the owner. In the OT, however, a mitigated form of slavery was tolerated by the Mosaic Law (Ex. 21. 1-11, Lev. 25. 44-55), and in NT times it was an integral part of the social system whose sudden abolition would have reduced the Roman Empire to chaos. There is no explicit teaching on the subject in the Gospels, but the spiritual equality of men as children of the same Father, together with the *Golden Rule and our Lord's affection for the poor and oppressed, provided the principles which were slowly to penetrate the nascent Christian society. They were formulated by St. Paul, who recognized neither bond nor free in Christ (Gal. 3. 28, 1 Cor. 12. 13, Col. 3. 11), though he did not condemn slavery but rather strove to imbue both masters and slaves with the new Christian spirit of charity which was finally to abolish the institution itself. This teaching is most conspicuous in his Ep. to Philemon and in the exhortations of Col. 3. 22-4. 1 and Eph. 6. 5-9. A similar attitude was prevalent in the early Church until the 3rd cent., Christian masters and slaves, who shared in the same sacraments, being still more closely drawn together by their common sufferings often culminating in martyrdom. From *Constantine onwards the Imperial legislation followed the Christian sentiment and many mitigations were introduced, esp. in the 6th cent., by *Justinian. Slaves who, with the consent of their masters, became priests were automatically freed, whereas entrance into the religious life did not even presuppose this consent. After the christianization of N. and E. Europe slavery was gradually transformed into the much milder institution of serfdom, which in its turn slowly disappeared in and after the Renaissance. A cruel form of slavery, however, reappeared after the fall of *Constantinople in 1453, when the Turks reduced large numbers of Christians to a servitude which was only mitigated by the devoted work of the religious orders such as the *Trinitarians, the *Mercedarians, and St. *Vincent de Paul's 'Congregation of the Mission'. A renewed outbreak of slave-owning among Christians took place after the discovery of America, when the Spanish, Portuguese, and British settlers made slaves of the Indians and later also introduced negro slaves from Africa despite the steady resistance of the missionaries, esp. the *Dominicans and the *Jesuits who set up a model colony without slaves in Paraguay, and despite the condemnations of successive Popes, e.g. *Paul III in 1537, *Pius V in 1567, and *Urban VIII in 1639. In the 18th cent. the movement against slavery was taken up by the *Quakers, esp. W. *Penn, who abolished slavery in Pennsylvania, and philanthropists like T. Clarkson and W. *Wilberforce. The slave trade was made illegal in 1808, and slavery was finally suppressed in the British Empire in 1833. In the U.S.A. at the conclusion of the Civil War in Dec. 1865, a constitutional amendment for ever prohibited slavery throughout the States.

The question of slavery has been much discussed by theologians. Acc. to several of the Fathers, e.g. St. *Gregory of Nazianzus and St. *Augustine, it was a state of life which was consequent on the Fall; acc. to St. *Thomas Aquinas it was a chastisement. It has been admitted as, theoretically, not contrary to the natural law by later theologians such as L. *Lessius and J. De *Lugo, if arising from contract, birth, in punishment for a crime or as the result of a just war. It is now generally condemned on account of the almost inevitable abuses accompanying it and of its opposition to the spirit of the Gospel.

J. K. Ingram, *A History of Slavery and Serfdom* (1895). A. Katz, *Christentum und Sklaverei* (Vienna, [1926]). A. Rivière, *L'Église et l'esclavage* (1846); P. Allard, *Les Esclaves chrétiens, depuis les premiers temps de l'Église jusqu'à la fin de la domination romaine en Occident* (1876); H. Wallon, *Histoire de l'esclavage dans l'antiquité* (3 vols., 1879); T. *Zahn, *Sklaven aus dem Leben der alten Kirche* (1894), Ch. 2, 'Sklaverei und Christentum in der alten Kirche', pp. 62–105. J. Dutilleul in *D.T.C.*, v (1913), cols. 457–520, s.v. 'Esclavage', with bibl.; L. D. Agate in *H.E.R.E.*, xi (1920), pp. 601–12, s.v. 'Slavery, Christian', with bibl.; N. Turchi, A. Penna, F. Crosara, E. Degano in *E.C.*, xi (1953), cols. 48–58, s.v. 'Schiavitù', with bibl. For the history of the abolition of slavery in the British Empire see also lives of W. Wilberforce, &c.

SLAVONIC BOOK OF ENOCH, The.
See *Enoch, Books of.*

SLEIDANUS, JOHANNES (1506–56),
annalist of the German Reformation. Born at Schleiden near Aachen, he studied classics at Liége and *Cologne and jurisprudence at *Paris and Orléans. Adopting Protestant views (exact date unknown) of a *Calvinist type, in 1536 he entered the service of the Bellay brothers, who were in correspondence with the *Schmalkaldic League, and in 1540–1 he was employed in diplomatic missions for the French crown. In 1544 M. *Bucer persuaded *Philip of Hesse to appoint him historiographer of the Reformation. When war interrupted his work, *Edward VI at T. *Cranmer's intercession gave him a stipend in England (1551). But he soon returned to the Continent, where he represented a group of S. German cities at the Council of *Trent (1551–52) and took part in the negotiations of the German Protestants with Henry II of France in 1552. In 1554 he was appointed Prof. of Law at Strassburg where he completed his *De Statu Religionis et Reipublicae Carolo V Caesare Commentarii* (2 vols. [Strassburg], 1555; Eng. trans. by J. Daws, 1560). Its large collection of documents makes it the chief contemporary source for the period, though its author's impartiality met with little favour from his contemporaries, Protestant or Catholic. His other writings include a Latin version of Bucer's *Shorter Catechism* (1544).

Briefwechsel ed. H. Baumgarten (Strassburg, 1881). Id., *Über Sleidans Leben und Briefwechsel* (1878); W. Friedensburg, *Johannes Sleidanus* (Leipzig, 1935), with reff. G. Kawerau in *P.R.E.* (ed. 3), xviii (1906), pp. 443–7, s.v., with bibl. to date. Further bibl. in Schottenloher, ii (1935), pp. 279–81 (Nos. 20151–78).

SLESSOR, MARY (1848–1915), missionary
of the *United Presbyterian Church. Born in Aberdeen, she spent her early life in work in a factory. In 1875 she offered herself for service in Africa to the Foreign Missions Board of her Church, and the next year sailed for the Calabar coast of West Africa. Here she

gained great influence with the native population, not least in successfully bringing to an end many tribal abuses (twin murder, human sacrifice, witchcraft, cruelty). In 1905 the Government, recognizing her authority, invested 'Ma Slessor' (as she was popularly called) with the powers of a magistrate, which she continued to exercise until her death.

Life by W. P. Livingstone (London, 1915).

SMALKALDIC ARTICLES, LEAGUE.
See *Schmalkaldic Articles, League.*

SMART, PETER (1569–c. 1652), *Puritan
iconoclast. Educated at *Westminster School and at Broadgates Hall and *Christ Church, Oxford, he was appointed Headmaster of *Durham Grammar School in 1598. In 1609 he became rector of Boldon, Co. Durham, and also a prebendary of *Durham Cathedral, where in 1614 he was promoted to the fourth stall. He strongly resisted the introduction by Richard Neile, Bp. of Durham (1617–28), of High Church ornaments into Durham cathedral and on 27 July 1628 preached a violent sermon against J. *Cosin, one of the chief promoters of the advanced ceremonial, which was published as *The Vanity and Downfall of Superstitious Popish Ceremonies* (1628). Smart was at once brought before the *High Commission of *York and on 2 Sept. suspended. Early in 1629 the case was removed to the Southern High Commission, but it was referred back to York in 1630, and in 1631 Smart degraded, fined £500, and, on refusing to pay, imprisoned. He remained in custody until 1641 when the Long Parliament declared his imprisonment void, ordered the prosecution of Cosin and restored Smart to his preferments. In 1643 he took the *Solemn League and Covenant. In his last years he was given various sequestered benefices.

G. W. Kitchin, *Seven Sages of Durham* (1911), pp. 97–132. A. Gordon in *D.N.B.*, lii (1897), p. 392 f.; L. Pullan in *D.E.C.H.*, p. 560 f., s.v.

'SMECTYMNUUS'.
The professed writer of a book publd. in March 1641 to defend the *Presbyterian theory of the Christian ministry in reply to Bp. J. *Hall's *Humble Remonstrance.* The name was made up of the initials of its five real authors, viz. Stephen Marshall, Edmund *Calamy, Thomas Young, Matthew Newcomen, and William Spurstow. The form 'Smectymnuan' was used both of the actual composers of the treatise and for others who accepted its views. On its publication J. Hall replied with a *Defence of that Remonstrance,* while in May 1641 J. *Milton, who had prob. had a hand in the orig. Smectymnun work, defended 'Smectymnuus' in *Of Reformation touching Church Discipline in England and the Causes that hitherto have hindered it.*

SMITH, BERNARD (c. 1630–1708), usually
called 'Father Smith', organ builder. He was a native of Germany (his original name was

Schmidt) who came to England before 1660, where he was appointed organ-maker in ordinary to *Charles II. In 1660 he built a new organ for *Westminster Abbey and in 1664 one for *Wells Cathedral, followed by others. In 1676 he became organist to St. Margaret's, Westminster, where he had installed an organ in 1675. In 1680 he finished the instrument for *Christ Church, Oxford, and in 1685 that for *Durham Cathedral. In the same year his organ, built in competition with Renatus Harris, was accepted by the Temple Church, and in 1694 he was entrusted with that of *St. Paul's Cathedral, which was installed in 1697, after dissensions with C. *Wren over its position and the size of its case. His last work was the organ for Trinity College, Cambridge, which was uncompleted at his death. His organs, of which more than forty existed, are famous for the quality of their material and their purity of tone.

A. Freeman, *Father Smith, otherwise Bernard Schmidt* (1926).

SMITH, GEORGE ADAM (1856–1942), OT scholar. Born at Calcutta and educated at Edinburgh, *Tübingen, and Leipzig, he became minister of Queen's Cross Free Church, Aberdeen, in 1882, professor of OT at the United Free Church College at Glasgow in 1892 and Principal of the university of Aberdeen in 1909. He travelled extensively in Egypt, Syria, and Palestine. His writings include the *Book of Isaiah* (Expositor's Bible, 2 vols., 1888–90); *The Preaching of the Old Testament to the Age* (1893); *Historical Geography of the Holy Land* (1894, 25th ed. 1931, still unsurpassed); *The Twelve Prophets* (Expositor's Bible, 2 vols., 1896–7); *Life of Henry *Drummond* (1898); *Jerusalem* (2 vols., 1907); *The Early Poetry of Israel* (Schweich Lectures, 1912); *Deuteronomy* (Cambridge Bible, 1918); and *Jeremiah* (1923).

Lilian Adam Smith, *George Adam Smith*. A Personal Memoir and Family Chronicle (1943).

SMITH, JOHN (c. 1554–1612), **The Se-Baptist.** See *Smyth, John*.

SMITH, JOHN (1618–52), *Cambridge Platonist. He was educated in the *Puritan foundation of Emmanuel College, Cambridge, where B. *Whichcote was his tutor. In 1644 he was transferred to Queens' College and here lectured. Under the influence of Whichcote and the study of *Plato and *Plotinus he became one of the leading Cambridge Platonists, upholding spiritual religion against the acrimonious theological disputes of his age. His work was cut short by his early death. S. *Patrick, a warm admirer, preached his funeral sermon.

His *Select Discourses*, ed. John Worthington (London, 1660), with a sermon preached at his funeral and a short account of his life and death by Simon Patrick, pp. 483–526; ed. 4 revised by H. G. Williams (Cambridge, 1859). J. *Tulloch, *Rational Theology and Christian Philosophy in England in the Seventeenth Century*, ii (1872), pp. 121–92;

F. J. Powicke, *The Cambridge Platonists*. A Study (1926), ch. iii, pp. 87–109. J. B. Mullinger, *The University of Cambridge*, iii (1911), pp. 630–7.

SMITH, WILLIAM ROBERTSON (1846–1894), Scottish theologian and Semitic scholar. Educated at Aberdeen, Edinburgh, Bonn, and Göttingen, he became professor of oriental languages and OT exegesis at the Free Church College, Aberdeen, in 1870. In 1875 he was made a member of the company for the RV of the OT. About the same time his articles in the 9th edition of the *Encyclopaedia Britannica* began to appear, and henceforward Smith was in the centre of the storm provoked by the Higher Criticism of the OT. His writings having been severely criticized by a committee of the General Assembly of the Free Church as undermining belief in the inspiration of the Bible, in 1881 he was removed from his chair. He spent the rest of his life at Cambridge, where he was elected in 1885 a Fellow of Christ's College. Of his two celebrated books, *The OT in the Jewish Church* (1881) and *The Prophets of Israel* (1882; ed. 2, by T. K. *Cheyne, 1895), both series of lectures, the former popularized among English readers J. *Wellhausen's theory of the structure and date of the Pentateuch and of the development of the Israelite religion, while the latter expounded on this basis the life and teaching of the early prophets. Later Smith extended his researches into the whole field of Semitic religion. Through his *The Religion of the Semites* (1889; ed. 3, by S. A. *Cook, 1927) his thesis that the original leading idea in sacrifice was that of Communion with the Deity rather than propitiation became widely known and accepted, though it is now generally recognized to be an over-simplification.

Collection of his *Lectures and Essays* (mainly unpubl.) ed. J. S. Black–G. Chrystal (London, 1902). Idd., *The Life of William Robertson Smith* (1902). J. S. Black in *D.N.B.*, liii (1898), pp. 160–2, s.v.

SMITHFIELD, in London, originally Smoothfield. The place was noted formerly as the site of executions, esp. during the Reformation period, when in the 'fires of Smithfield' during *Mary Tudor's reign about 300 heretics were burned there. It is now famous as a meat market.

SMYTH, or SMITH, JOHN (c. 1554–1612), the 'Se-baptist' and reputed founder of the *General Baptists. Educated at Christ's College, Cambridge, of which he was afterwards a Fellow, he was ordained in the C of E. He became a *Puritan preacher at *Lincoln (1603–5) and later *Separatist pastor in Gainsborough (1606). He led a company of exiles to Amsterdam c. 1608 and there, after baptizing himself (hence the name Se-Baptist), established in 1609 the first modern *Baptist Church. He styled his community 'The Brethren of the Separation of the Second English Church at Amsterdam'. Membership consisted of such as had confessed their faith in baptism. From now onwards Smyth passed increasingly under *Mennonite influence. He died in Amsterdam in 1612. In the same year a company of his associates returned to London to establish the first Baptist Church in Great Britain. Among Smyth's writings were *A True Description out of the Word of God of the Visible Church* (1589), *A Pattern of True Prayer* (1605; on the *Lord's Prayer), and *The Differences of the Churches of the Separation* (1608).

Collected ed. of his works by W. T. Whitley (Tercentenary ed. for the Baptist Historical Society, 2 vols., Cambridge, 1915), with life, vol. i, pp. xvii–cxxii. T. Cooper in *D.N.B.*, liii (1898), pp. 68–70, with further reff.

SOBORNOST (from Russian *sobor*, 'assembly' or 'synod'). A term with no exact English equivalent, sometimes translated 'conciliatory', to denote the quality needed for charitable collaboration, as expressed, e.g., in the attitude of the Russian Church to the Liturgy as corporate worship, with stress on the co-operation of the people. Orthodox Russians claim 'sobornost' as a special characteristic of their Church, contrasted with the emphasis on authority in the RC Church and the individualism of the Protestant communions.

SOCIALISM, Christian. See *Christian Socialism.*

SOCIETY FOR PROMOTING CHRISTIAN KNOWLEDGE. See *S.P.C.K.*

SOCIETY FOR THE PROPAGATION OF THE GOSPEL. See *S.P.G.*

SOCIETY OF FRIENDS. See *Friends, Society of.*

SOCIETY OF JESUS. See *Jesuits.*

SOCIETY OF ST. JOHN THE EVANGELIST ('S.S.J.E.'). The Anglican society of mission priests, popularly known as the '*Cowley Fathers'. It was founded in 1865 by R. M. *Benson, then vicar of St. James's, Cowley, and is thus the oldest Anglican society for men religious. While a life of prayer and discipline under the monastic vows is its first object, the society is also occupied in missionary and educational works. It is now constituted in three congregations—English, American, and Canadian—each with its own superior and chapter, and there are houses in Oxford, London, Poona, Cape Town, Cambridge (Mass.), and elsewhere. The mother house of the Society is the Mission House, Marston Street, Oxford. Although primarily a society of priests, lay brothers are admitted.

SOCINUS. The Latinized name of two Italian religious teachers, uncle and nephew.

(1) LELIO FRANCESCO MARIA SOZINI (1525–1562), a native of Siena, came of a cultivated family. He was educated by his father, Mariano Sozini, junior (1482–1556), himself a jurist, at *Bologna, to be a lawyer. Finding that his real interests were in theology he made his way to Venice, then the headquarters of Protestantism in Italy. In 1547 he came also under the influence of Camillo, a Sicilian mystic of liberal views, at Chiavenna. Between 1547 and 1550 he was received by the Reformers in several countries (Switzerland, France, England, and Holland), and from 1548 to 1550 settled in Switzerland. Later he visited *Wittenberg, where for a time he was the guest of P. *Melanchthon, and later Poland. Changed political conditions drew him back to Italy in 1552 where he endeavoured to win his nephew (see below) over to his beliefs. Early in 1554 he left Italy again for Switzerland. At Geneva, where he made the acquaintance of J. *Calvin, he was challenged on the doctrine of the Trinity; he satisfied H. *Bullinger, but reserved to himself the right to further inquiry. His surviving writings include a Confession of Faith (1555) and *De Sacramentis Dissertatio* (1560). He died at Zürich.

(2) FAUSTO PAOLO SOZZINI (1539–1604; he spelled his name with two z's), nephew of the preceding, was also a native of Siena. His early education was neglected. In 1562 he published a work on St. John's Gospel, denying the essential divinity of Christ; by 1563 he had rejected the natural immortality of man. From 1565 to 1575 he was in the service of Isabella de' Medici, daughter of the Grand Duke of Tuscany, where he conformed, at least outwardly, to Catholicism. After a period of theological study and discussion at Basle, where he wrote *De Jesu Christo Servatore* (1578) against the Evangelical teaching of the Reformers, he made his way to Klausenburg in Transylvania in 1578, in the hope that his liberal teachings would be welcomed under the anti-Trinitarian ruler, John Sigismund. In fact his services were enlisted to moderate the extreme anti-Trinitarianism of the Bishop, Francis David (1510–79). In 1579 he passed to Poland where he spent the rest of his life and did much to spread moderate *Unitarian doctrines among the upper classes. But when he acknowledged the authorship of some of his anonymous writings, the masses revolted against him and on Ascension Day, 1598, he was forced to flee from Cracow. He spent his last years at Luclawice. See also *Racovian Catechism* and *Unitarianism.*

(1) C. F. Illgen, *Vita Laelii Socini* (Leipzig, 1814); E. Burnat, *Lelio Socin* (Vevey, 1894).
(2) The works of Faustus Socinus [ed. by his grandson, Andreas Wiszowaty] (Bibliotheca Fratrum Polonorum quos Unitarios vocant i et ii, Amsterdam, 1656), with life written by Samuel Przipcovius in 1636 prefixed to vol. i [no pagination]; this life was repr., with Eng. annotations by 'E. S.' (Manchester, 1912). J. Toulmin, *Memoirs of the Life, Character, Sentiments and Writings of Faustus Socinus* (1827). P. Lecler, *Fauste Socin* (Geneva thesis, 1885); D. M. Cory, *Faustus Socinus* (Boston, Mass., 1932), with bibl. to date. Full modern study by G. Pioli, *Fausto Socino. Vita, opere, fortunata* (Modena, 1952). On the two Socini, L. Cristiani in *D.T.C.*, xiv (pt. 2; 1941), cols. 2326–34, s.v.

Socinianisme'; M. Bendiscioli in *E.C.*, xi (1953), cols. 874–6, s.v. 'Socini (Sozzini), Lelio e Fausto'. See also bibl. to *Unitarianism*.

SOCRATES (*c.* 380–450), 'Scholasticus', Greek Church historian. He was a native of *Constantinople, where he became a lawyer (σχολαστικός). His Church History, in seven Books, each covering the life of one of the Emperors, was designed as a continuation of *Eusebius's treatise and extends from the abdication of *Diocletian (305) to 439. It draws on *Rufinus and also on Gelasius of Caesarea. After publishing it, Socrates became possessed of the writings of St. *Athanasius, which apprised him of Rufinus's historical blunders, and he accordingly drastically revised the work. Only this later edition survives. For information about the ecclesiastical Councils he made extensive use of a collection of documents issued *c.* 375 by the *Macedonian, Sabinus of Heraclea. In general Socrates' history is objective and lucidly written, but its treatment is rather colourless and the author has few theological interests. He shows a certain sympathy with the *Novatianists and gives special attention to events connected with Constantinople. See also *Sozomen*.

Ed. princeps by R. *Stephanus (Paris, 1544). An excellent ed. for its date by H. *Valesius (Paris, 1668); revisions by W. Reading (Cambridge, 1720; repr. J. P. Migne, *PG*, lxvii, 9–842) and R. Hussey (3 vols., Oxford, 1853). Hussey's text was repr. by W. *Bright (Oxford, 1878). A modern crit. text is badly needed. Eng. tr. by A. C. Zenos in N.P.N.C.F., Ser. 2, vol. ii, 1890. F. Geppert, *Die Quellen des Kirchenhistorikers Sokrates Scholastikus* (1898). Bardenhewer, iv, 137–41. G. Loeschcke in *P.R.E.* (ed. 3), (1906), pp. 481–6, s.v.; W. Eltester in *P.W.*, 2te Reihe, iii (pt. 1; 1927), cols. 893–901, s.v.; E. Peterson in *E.C.*, xi (1953), col. 883, s.v.

SODALITY (Lat. *sodalis*, 'companion'). In the RC Church, a common designation for a guild established for the furtherance of some religious purpose by mutual action or assistance.

SÖDERBLOM, NATHAN (1866–1931), *Lutheran Abp. of *Upsala and chief promoter of the '*Life and Work' Movement. A native of Trönö, nr. Söderhamn, he studied at Upsala and was ordained in 1893. In the same year he published *The Religion of Luther* (Swedish), whose great admirer he was. In 1894 he was appointed chaplain to the Swedish legation in *Paris, where he pursued the study of comparative religion, esp. of *Zoroastrianism. In 1901 he became Prof. at Upsala, continuing to lecture in Paris from time to time, and from 1912 to 1914 he also held a lecturership at Leipzig. In 1914 he was appointed Abp. of Upsala despite the opposition of the more conservative elements in the Swedish Church. He was a prominent supporter of the reunion movement and the leading figure in the *Stockholm Conference (1925), his aim being to organize the practical co-operation of the Christian Churches esp. in social questions without consideration of doctrinal differences. His own theological beliefs were largely influenced by A. *Sabatier, A. *Ritschl, and

other representatives of Liberal Protestantism.

Söderblom's religious outlook was essentially constructive, despite its challenge to the older orthodoxy. His sense of personal religion went deep. Of his books, only comparatively few have been translated into English. In *The Nature of Revelation* (1903, Eng. trans., 1933) he defended the position of 'Higher Criticism', maintaining that the scientific study of the history of religion will lead to a sure knowledge of God. He criticized here the dogma of the two natures of Christ as unacceptable for modern men and also formulated one of his leading ideas, viz. that God's Revelation is restricted neither to the Bible nor to the Church but continues in history throughout the ages. In his treatise *Gudstrons Uppkomst* (1914) he argued that the idea of holiness rather than the conception of God was at the basis of religion. Among his other works are *Christian Fellowship* (Eng. trans., 1923) and *The Living God* (1933; Gifford Lectures for 1931). He encouraged the liturgical movement in the Swedish Church and was also influenced by Catholic modernist authors such as A. *Loisy and F. *von Hügel.

Tal och Skrifter (5 vols., Stockholm, 1933). Lives in Swedish by T. Andrae (Uppsala, 1931), in Danish by M. Neiiendam (Copenhagen, 1933). Brief sketch by Y. Brilioth prefixed to Eng. tr. of Söderblom's Gifford Lects. (1933). P. Katz, *Nathan Söderblom. Ein Führer zu kirchlicher Einheit* (1925; Eng. tr. with additions, 1949). J. G. H. Hoffmann, *Nathan Soederblom. Prophète de l'oecuménisme* (Geneva, 1948). M. Pribilla, S.J., 'Söderblom und die ökumenische Bewegung' in *Stimmen der Zeit*, cxxii (1931), pp. 295–310; H. Dorr, 'Söderbloms Beitrag zur Offenbarungsfrage' in *Zeitschrift für Theologie und Kirche*, N.F., xvii (1936), pp. 169–90.

SODOM AND GOMORRAH. Acc. to Gen. 19. 24 f. two of the 'Cities of the Plain' (prob. S. of the *Dead Sea) which were destroyed by fire from heaven for their wickedness. Our Lord proclaimed that in the Day of Judgement even more severe punishment would be meted out to cities which rejected the Gospel than to Sodom and Gomorrah (Mt. 10. 15).

M. G. Kyle, *Exploration at Sodom. The Story of Ancient Sodom in the Light of Modern Research* (popular; [1928]). On the question of the location of Sodom, F. M. Abel, O.P., 'Histoire d'une controverse' in *R. Bibl.*, xliii (1931), pp. 388–400, with reff. to earlier litt.; cf. also other artt. by the same author in earlier numbers of the review; M. J. *Lagrange, O.P., 'Le Site de Sodome d'après les textes', ib., xliv (1932), pp. 489–514; F. C. Clapp, 'The Site of Sodom and Gomorrah' in *American Journal of Archaeology*, New Series, xl (1936), pp. 323–44, also with reff.; J. P. Harland, 'Sodom aud Gomorrah' in *The Biblical Archaeologist*, v (1942), pp. 17–32, and vi (1943), pp. 41–54. G. A. *Smith, *The Historical Geography of the Holy Land* (ed. 25, 1931), pp. 504–10; W. F. Albright, *The Archaeology of Palestine and the Bible* (1932), pp. 133–7.

SODOR AND MAN. The present Anglican diocese of Sodor and Man consists of the Isle of Man. The original diocese of Sodor (from 'Sudreys', i.e. Southern Isles, as distinct from the Northern Isles of Orkney and Shetland), which seems to date from the time of *Edward the Confessor (d. 1066), included, besides the Isle of Man, the Hebrides and other islands west of Scotland. In early days it was probably suffragan to *York, but when in 1152 Cardinal Nicolas, afterwards Pope *Hadrian IV, organized the Norwegian Church at the Council of Nidaros, Sodor became a suffragan see to Nidaros (Trondhjem). The Scottish islands were detached in 1334. Since 1542 the diocese of Sodor has been in the province of York, but it has its own *Convocation. The termination 'and Man' was apparently added in error by a 17th cent. legal draughts-man. The Prayer Book was issued in Manx in 1765, the Bible in 1772. In 1895 a *chapter was constituted with four canons, the bishop being dean. The bishop has a seat in the House of Lords, but no vote. Of the bishops of Sodor and Man the most renowned is the saintly T. *Wilson (bishop 1698–1755). The cathedral (in ruins), dedicated to St. *Ger-manus, stands on St. Patrick's Isle (now united to the mainland), near Peel.

The principal source for the early history of the Isle of Man is the *Chronica Regum Manniae et Insularum* (ed. P. A. Munich, Manx Society, xxii and xxiii; 1874, with Eng. tr.); facsimile ed. from Cod. Julius A. VI in Brit. Mus. (Douglas, 1924). W. Harrison (ed.), *The Old Historians of the Isle of Man*; Camden, Speed, Dugdale, Cox, Wilson, Willis and Crosse (Manx Society, xviii; 1871). A. W. Moore–J. Rhŷs (edd.), *The Book of Common Prayer in Manx Gaelic*. Being translations made by Bishop Phillips in 1610, and by the Manx Clergy in 1765 (2 vols., 1895). B. Willis, *A Survey of the Cathedrals of York, Durham, Carlisle, Chester, Man, Lichfield, Hereford, Worcester, Gloucester and Bristol*, i (1727), pp. 359–70. A. W. Moore, *Sodor and Man* (Diocesan Histories, 1893). P. M. C. Kermode, *Manx Crosses* (1907); E. A. Jones, *The Old Church Plate of the Isle of Man* (1907). E. W. Watson in *D.E.C.H.* (1912), pp. 346–9, s.v. 'Man, Isle of, Church in'.

SOHM, RUDOLPH (1841–1917), jurist and Protestant Church historian.

He taught law first at Göttingen, and later as Professor at Freiburg i.Br. (1880), Strassburg (1872), and Leipzig (1887). His chief theological works were *Verhältnis von Staat und Kirche* (1873), *Kirchenrecht* (vol. i, 1892; vol. ii, posthumously ed. by E. Jacobi and O. Mayer, 1923), and *Wesen und Ursprung des Katholizismus* (1909). In these and other writings he developed the view that, while the Church was wholly spirit-ual, law was wholly secular; hence the develop-ment of canon law ('Catholicism') was an abandonment of the primitive ideal of the Church, which was a fundamentally '*charis-matic' body. Sohm also compiled a manual, *Kirchengeschichte im Grundriss* (1888; Eng. tr. *Outlines of Church History*, 1895).

Festgabe für Rudolph Sohm (Munich, 1914). W. Lowrie, *The Church and its Organisation in Primitive and Catholic Times*. An Interpretation of Rudolph Sohm's *Kirchenrecht* (1904); W. Schmidt, 'Worte zum Gedächtnis an Rudolf Sohm' in *Ber.* (Sächs.), lxix, Hft. 8 (1917), pp. 15*–34*. H. Barion, *Rudolf Sohm und die Grundlegung des Kirchenrechts* (1931). Critique of Sohm's theses in A. *Harnack, *Ent-stehung und Entwicklung der Kirchenverfassung und des Kirchenrechts* (1910; Eng. tr., 1910); O. Scheel, 'Zur urchrist-lichen Kirchen- und Verfassungsproblem' in *Theologische Studien und Kritiken*, lxxxv (1912), pp. 403–57.

SOISSONS, Councils of.

The two principal Councils are:

(1) 1092. The Council was convened by Raynaldus, Abp. of *Reims, against the *nomi-nalist, *Roscellinus, who was accused of teach-ing *Tritheism. Roscellinus asserted that *Lanfranc and *Anselm, then abbot of Bec, shared his views; but the latter sent a letter to be read at the Council, denying the charge and professing the Catholic faith. Roscellinus was condemned by the Council and recanted, though he later declared that he had done so only through fear of the populace.

(2) 1121. The Council was held by the Papal legate, Conon, Bp. of Palestrina, in order to censure *Abelard's work 'De Unitate et Trinitate Divina'. Conceived as an attack on Roscellinus's Tritheistic teaching, it con-tained itself the opposite error of *Sabellianism. Abelard was not permitted to dispute about it, but forced to burn his book. Our infor-mation about the Council comes from the partisan account in Abelard's own 'Historia Calamitatum'.

(1) Hardouin, vi (pt. 2), cols. 1695–1700; Mansi, xx (Venice, 1775), cols. 741–4. Hefele–Leclercq, v (pt. 1; 1912), pp. 365–7.
(2) Hardouin, vi (pt. 2), cols. 1103–6; Mansi, xxi (Venice, 1726), cols. 265–70. Hefele–Leclercq, v (pt. 1; 1912), pp. 593–602. See also bibl. to *Abelard, P.

SOLEMN LEAGUE AND COVENANT.

The agreement between the Scots and the English Parliament in 1643. Its professed aims were the maintenance of the *Presbyterian Church of Scotland, the reformation of the Church of England, the uniformity of the Churches of the British Isles, the extirpation of popery and prelacy (i.e. episcopacy), the preservation of the rights of Parliaments and the liberties of the kingdoms, the defence of the King's just power and the suppression of the malignants who sought to divide him from his people. It was also a pact of mutual defence and a covenant of penitents with their God. The English Parliamentarians in their struggle with the Royalists were specially anxious for a civil league; the Scots emphasized the re-ligious side of the agreement. It was formally accepted by the General Assembly of the Church of Scotland on 17 Aug. 1643, and by the English Commons and the *Westminster Assembly on 25 Sept. 1643. Shortly after-wards, the proceedings of the Westminster Assembly took a pro-Presbyterian turn and for a time the English allies became nominal 'Covenanters'; but after the Scottish army had helped to turn the tide at Marston Moor (2 July 1644) and the rise of O. *Cromwell and the *Independents to power the Covenant became a dead letter in England. It continued longer, however, to be a living document in Scotland, where it was renewed in 1648 and subscribed by *Charles II in 1650 and 1651.

Text in Gee–Hardy, pp. 569–74 (No. cvii). See also bibl. to *Westminster Assembly.

SOLESMES.

The seat of a famous Benedic-tine monastery, dedicated to St. Peter, in the department of Sarthe, France. It was founded in 1010, but in modern times its history goes back to Dom Prosper *Guéranger who settled there with five other priests in 1833. In 1837 *Gregory XVI constituted it an abbey and head of the French Benedictine congregation with Guéranger as its first abbot. Under his influence it became, and has remained, a centre of the *Liturgical Movement in France, taking a notable part in the revival and development of liturgical music. After being several times ejected by force by the French Government, the monks were finally expelled from France in 1901 under the anticlerical legislation, and for several years *Quarr Abbey in the Isle of Wight was their headquarters. They returned to Solesmes in 1922. Solesmes has numbered among its members many eminent scholars, notably Dom J. B. *Pitra (1812–89), Dom P. Cagin (1847–1923), Dom. F. *Cabrol (1855–1937), Dom H. *Quentin (1872–1935), and Dom A. *Wilmart (1876–1941).

H. Quentin, O.S.B., *Notice historique sur l'abbaye de Solesmes*, suivie d'une courte description de l'église abbatiale et ses sculptures (Tours, 1924). N. Rousseau, *L'École grégorienne de Solesmes, 1833–1910* (Tournai, 1910). G. Cozien, O.S.B., *L'Œuvre de Dom Guéranger* (Solesmes, 1933; with illustrations of the Abbey). F. Cabrol, O.S.B., 'L'Œuvre historique et littéraire de Solesmes et de la Congrégation de France (1833–1933)' in *Revue Mabillon*, xxiii (1933), pp. 249–65.

SOLIFIDIANISM. The doctrine of *Justification by faith alone (*sola fides*), proclaimed by the Protestant Reformers against the Medieval teaching of the merit of good works. It was orig. based on M. *Luther's translation of Rom. 3. 28 where he rendered πίστει by *allein durch den Glauben* ('only by faith').

SOLIPSISM (Lat. *solus*, 'alone', and *ipse*, 'oneself'). The philosophical belief that the individual self is the only existent and that all other selves are illusions. It is doubtful whether any philosopher has ever held this extreme form of theoretical egotism; its chief use in philosophical debate is to reduce opponents to absurdity. The word is less commonly applied to the doctrine that the self is the only object of real knowledge, without prejudice to the existence of other selves. Either doctrine is a particular form of 'Subjective Idealism'.

SOLOMON (d. *c*. 933 B.C.). King of Israel from *c*. 970 B.C. No such clear picture of his personality is to be found in the OT as we have of his father, *David, whom he succeeded. The impression made by the account in 2 Kgs. 1–11 is of an oriental despot, honoured for his wealth and wisdom and round whose name much legendary material has gathered. This reputation, which is responsible for the later attribution to him of the Books of *Proverbs, *Canticles, *Ecclesiastes, and the *Wisdom of Solomon, has probably coloured the history in 2 Kings. His reign marked the zenith of ancient Israel's prosperity and saw the organization of the kingdom on new lines. The *Temple, with the erection of which his name is esp. associated in subsequent history, was part of a grandiose building scheme intended to make Jerusalem a worthy capital for a kingdom which he determined should rank among the great powers. With such ends in view, he made a marriage alliance with the reigning

Pharaoh and, by strengthening the friendly relations established by David with Hiram, King of Tyre, obtained from Phoenicia the skill and materials needed for his building schemes (5. 1–12) and the experienced sailors to direct a short-lived naval experiment (9. 26–8). His other enterprises include a trade in horses with Egypt (10. 28–9), the fortifying of strategic cities (9. 15–19), and the establishment of a standing army (10. 26). But to finance his projects Solomon had to impose on his subjects a system of levies and forced labour, and the resulting discontent led, after his death, to the secession of the ten northern tribes under Jeroboam. In this, the compiler of the Books of Kings saw Divine retribution for Solomon's apostasy in his later years, which is ascribed to the influence of his foreign wives.

The main discussions will be found in Histories of Israel and commentaries on 1 Kgs. J. Garstang, *The Heritage of Solomon* (1934; on the sociology of ancient Palestine generally). J. Hornell, 'Naval Activity in the Days of Solomon and Rameses III' in *Antiquity*, xxi (1947), pp. 66–73. R. Flint in *H.D.B.*, iv (1902), pp. 559–69.

SOLOMON, Odes of. This pseudepigraphical work contains forty-two short hymns, of the same general character as the canonical Psalms. Mention of it occurs in lists of Christian books from the 6th cent. onwards, but until the discovery (1908) by J. R. *Harris of a Syriac MS. containing the Odes and Psalms of Solomon, the only known fragments of it were (1) five of the Odes included in the *Gnostic *Pistis Sophia (where the Odes are treated as of almost equal authority with the Pss. of David) and (2) a short quotation in *Lactantius. The Odes are perhaps a Christian adaptation of a Jewish work, but more probably wholly Christian in origin; and though containing thoughts and expressions which lend themselves to a Gnostic interpretation, they are not unorthodox. If Christian, they were almost certainly written in Syria or Palestine in the 1st (J. R. Harris) or 2nd (J. H. *Bernard) cent. A.D. It is disputed whether the original language was Greek or Syriac. In these Psalms, the terms used of '*Wisdom' in the Wisdom Literature are freely applied to Christ. Though there are few references to our Lord's life, the descent into Hades is described in some detail in more than one place; but the doctrine of the Holy Spirit is undeveloped and the word 'Church' nowhere occurs. One suggestion is that they were baptismal hymns, used ritually on the days of *Lent as part of the final preparation of catechumens for baptism.

Syriac text of Odes and Psalms of Solomon ed., with Eng. tr., by J. R. Harris (Cambridge, 1909; ed. 2, with facsimile, 1911); also ed., with facsimile of the whole MS., by id.-A. Mingana (Manchester, &c., 1916; Eng. tr. and notes, 1920). Eng. tr., with notes, publd. by [J.] R. Harris, *An Early Christian Psalter* (London, 1909). Further Eng. tr., with introd. and notes, by J. H. Bernard (Texts and Studies, viii, No. 3, Cambridge, 1912). W. Frankenberg, *Das Verständnis der Oden Salomos* (Beiheft zur *Z.A.T.W.*, xxi; 1911). R. H. *Connolly, 'The Odes of Solomon: Jewish or Christian?' in *J.T.S.*, xiii (1912), pp. 298–309. G. Kittel, *Die Oden Salomos überarbeitet oder einheitlich?* (Beiträge zur Wissenschaft vom Alten Testament, xvi; 1914). J. Quasten, *Patrology*, i (Utrecht, 1950), pp. 160–8.

SOLOMON, Psalms of. Mention of this Jewish *Pseudepigraphical collection of 18 Psalms occurs after the list of OT and NT Books in the catalogue at the beginning of *Codex Alexandrinus (A), as well as in later lists of canonical Books, but the Psalms had little influence on early Christian literature. Though extant only in Greek (and in a Syriac translation of the Greek), almost all scholars are agreed that they were written in Hebrew. Certain historical allusions indicate the date. A period of prosperity has been brought to an end by foreign invasion and the capture of Jerusalem; Jewish kings are condemned as usurpers; and the description of the invader seems most readily to refer to Pompey; and thus the Psalms can be assigned with considerable confidence to the post-*Maccabean age and prob. to the years 70–40 B.C. The Psalms depict the nation as divided into two classes, 'the righteous' (almost entirely the *Pharisees to which party the author belongs) and the 'sinners' (the *Sadducees), while the writer sees in the catastrophes that have overcome his country Divine retribution for national sin. The last two Psalms are esp. significant as predicting the coming of a Messiah of the house of David who will cleanse Jerusalem, punish sinners, subdue the nations hostile to Israel and rule in righteousness.

Crit. ed. of Gk. text with Eng. tr. by H. E. *Ryle–M. R. James (Cambridge, 1891); also by O. von Gebhardt (T.U., xiii, Hft. 2; 1895). Syriac text first ed., along with that of the Odes of Solomon, with Eng. tr. by J. R. *Harris (Cambridge, 1909; ed. 2, with additions, 1911); also ed. with facsimile, [J.] R. Harris–A. Mingana (Manchester, &c., 1916, with Eng. tr. and notes, 1920). Gk. text also pr., with notes of main Syriac variations, Fr. tr. and comm. by J. Viteau (Documents pour l'Étude de la Bible, 1911). Eng. tr. and comm. by G. B. *Gray in R. H. *Charles (ed.), The Apocrypha and Pseudepigrapha of the Old Testament, ii (1913), pp. 625–52. W. Frankenberg, Die Datierung der Psalmen Salomos (Beiheft zur Z.A.T.W., i; 1896). K. G. Kuhn, Die älteste Textgestalt der Psalmen Salomos insbesondere auf Grund der syrischen Übersetzung neu untersucht (Beiträge zur Wissenschaft vom Alten Testament, Folge 4, xxi; 1937). J. Begrich, 'Der Text der Psalmen Salomos' in Z.N.T.W., xxxviii (1939), pp. 131–64. M. R. James in H.D.B., iv (1902), p. 162 f., s.v. 'Psalms of Solomon'; J. B. Frey in Dict. Bibl., Suppl. i (1928), cols. 390–6, s.v. 'Apocryphes de l'Ancien Testament 4', with further bibl.

SOLOMON, The Song of, also known as 'The Song of Songs' (i.e. the supreme song; cf. 'Holy of Holies', 'Vanity of Vanities') or as 'Canticles', OT Book included among the *Hagiographa. It is prob. an anthology of love poems of varying length, ascribed to *Solomon and his beloved (the 'Shulamite') and their friends. The Book, however, must be much later than the time of Solomon; its vocabulary (many late words) and place in the *Canon suggest that it dates from c. 2nd cent. B.C. In the Hebrew Bible it is the first of the five *Megilloth and it was read by the Jews on the eighth day of *Passover.

From an early date Jewish and Christian exegetes alike have interpreted the Book allegorically. Indeed, apart from such interpretation it would be hard to justify its inclusion in the Biblical Canon. Rabbi *Akiba (d. 132) already protested strongly against a literal interpretation of its contents. In the *Talmud it is interpreted as an allegory of God's dealings with the congregation of Israel. Christian exegetes from St. *Hippolytus onwards have seen in it a description of God's relations with the Church or the individual soul; and it was already the subject of a commentary in this sense by *Origen. This interpretation became esp. congenial to a long succession of mystics, beginning with St. *Dionysius the Areopagite, and received classical form in St. *Bernard's eighty-six homilies on Canticles. Among later interpreters of it in this sense were R. *Rolle, St. *Teresa of Ávila and St. *John of the Cross (esp. in his 'Spiritual Canticle'). Indeed among Christian interpreters *Theodore of Mopsuestia seems to have been alone until modern times in upholding a literal exegesis. This was revived in the 16th cent. by Sebastian *Castellio and the *Anabaptists and it is now very generally allowed that the original character of the work was erotic.

Commentaries by A. Harper (Camb. Bib., AV, 1902), G. C. Martin (Cent. Bib. on Prov., Eccles., Song of Sol., 1908, pp. 287–355), K. *Budde (K.H.C., xviii, on Song of Sol., Ruth, Lam., Eccles. Est., 1898, pp. 1–48), C. Siegfried (H.K.A.T., Abt. 2, Bd. iii, Theil 2, on Eccles. and Song of Sol., 1898, pp. 78–126), G. Pouget–J. Guitton (Études bibliques, 1934) and M. Haller (H.A.T., Reihe 1, Bd. xviii, on Ruth, Song of Sol., Eccles., Lam., Est., 1940, pp. 21–46). Older commentaries, with dramatic interpretations, include those of G. H. A. von *Ewald (Göttingen, 1826), E. *Renan (Paris, 1860), F. [J.] *Delitzsch (Biblischer Commentar über das Alte Testament, Theil 4, Bd. iv, on Song of Sol. and Eccles., 1875, pp. 3–161; Eng. tr. 1877, pp. 1–161). M. Jastrow, The Song of Songs. Being a Collection of Love Lyrics of Ancient Palestine (1921; imaginative). W. H. Schoff (ed.), The Song of Songs. A Symposium (Philadelphia, 1924). W. Wittekindt, Das Hohe Lied und seine Beziehungen zum Istarkult [1926]. T. J. Meek, 'Canticles and the Tammuz Cult' in The American Journal of Semitic Languages and Literature, xxxix (1922–3), pp. 1–14. H. H. Rowley, 'The Interpretation of the Song of Songs' in J.T.S., xxxviii (1937), pp. 337–63; id., 'The Song of Songs. An Examination of Recent Theory' in The Journal of the Royal Asiatic Society, 1938, pp. 251–76. P. A. Vaccari, S.J., 'Il cantico dei cantici nelle recenti pubblicazioni' in Biblica, ix (1928), pp. 443–57.

SOLOMON, Wisdom of. See Wisdom of Solomon.

SOLOVIEFF, VLADIMIR (1853–1900), Russian philosopher and theologian. After lecturing on philosophy at Moscow in 1875 and holding a post in the ministry of education at St. Petersburg from 1877 to 1881, he devoted himself entirely to writing. In 1873 he became an intimate friend of F. *Dostoievsky, on whose religious ideas he exercised considerable influence. Down to 1881 he shared the ideas of the religiously minded Slavophils, including their antipathy to the RC Church; but further study and the desire for visible unity led him to modify his attitude, and from that time he regarded the union of the Churches as the main task of Russia, desiring to conserve the characteristic values of E. and W. During this period he wrote a profound ascetical book on the spiritual foundations of life (1882–4) and carried on negotiations with Bp. J. G. *Strossmayer for reunion between the Orthodox and RC Churches. In 1889 he published La Russie et *l'Église universelle* in which he proclaimed his Catholic ideal. It met with violent opposition in Russia, and when forbidden by the Holy Synod to write on religious questions he confined himself to politics and philosophy. In 1896 he was received into the RC Church, but without abandoning his critical attitude.

In his philosophical and religious ideas he was strongly influenced by German thought, esp. G. W. F. *Hegel and the nature philosophers J. *Böhme and F. W. J. *Schelling. He sought to combine their pantheism with the Christian doctrine of the Incarnation. He admitted into his system, however, Gnostic elements and upheld the existence of a female principle, 'Sophia' or the world-soul. Solovieff also wrote fine religious poetry. His influence, esp. among the refugees from the 1917 Revolution, did much to turn the Russian intellectuals from their 19th cent. materialism and nihilism to a definitely religious and Christian view of the world.

Works publ. in 9 vols., St. Petersburg, 1901–3, and 10 vols., ib., 1911–14. Letters publ., ib., 4 vols., 1908–23. There are Eng. trr. of *War and Christianity* with introd. by S. Graham (London, 1915); *War, Progress and the End of History*, tr. by A. Bakshy (ib., 1915), with biog. notice by H. Wright, pp. vii–xii; *The Justification of the Good*, tr. by N. A. Duddington (ib., 1918); *Plato*, tr. by R. Gill (ib., 1935), with note by J. Lavrin, pp. 5–21; *God, Man and the Church*, tr. by D. Attwater (ib. [1938]); *Lectures on Godmanhood*, tr. by P. Zouboff (New York, 1944), with introd. pp. 11–77; *The Meaning of Love*, tr. by Jane Marshall (London, 1945); and of *Russia and the Universal Church*, tr. by H. Rees (ib., 1948). There is also *A Solovyov Anthology* arranged by S. L. Frank, tr. by N. Duddington (1950), with introd. pp. 9–31. M. d'Herbigny, *Un Newman russe*. Vladimir Soloviev (1911; Eng. tr., 1918). D. Strémooukoff, *Vladimir Soloviev et son œuvre messianique* (1935). F. Muckermann, S.J., *Wladimir Solowiew* (1945). K. Pfleger, *Geister die um Christus ringen* (1934; Eng. tr., 1936), ch. 7 (pp. 223–65 of Eng. tr.); N. Zernov, *Three Russian Prophets* (1944), pp. 116–51.

SOMASCHI, The. An order of clerks regular in solemn vows who follow the Rule of St. *Augustine. They were founded in 1532 by St. *Jerome Emiliani at Somasca in N. Italy to work among the poor and afflicted, and formally constituted by Pope *Pius V in 1568. They still flourish in Italy, where they conduct schools and orphanages.

L' ordine dei Chierici Regolari Somaschi nel IV centenario della sua fondazione (Rome, 1928). Heimbucher, ii, 110–112, with reff. G. B. Pigata in *E.C.*, xi (1953), cols. 952–4, s.v.

SOMERSET, Duke of (c. 1506–1552), Protector of England. Edward Seymour, Earl of Hertford (1537) and Duke of Somerset (1547), was a brother of Jane Seymour, third wife of *Henry VIII. From 1524 onwards he held a succession of offices in the royal household. He played an important part in the Scottish campaign of 1544, and in 1545–6 successfully commanded the English forces in France. The fall of the Howards left him the leading figure in the Council when his nephew succeeded as *Edward VI. As protector to the young King he pressed on the reforming cause in the English Church, while attempting to coerce the Scots into co-operation. The offence given by his liberal agrarian policy and his failure to repress the risings of 1549 contributed largely to his deprival of the protectorship in Jan. 1550 and his ultimate execution on a charge of conspiracy against his rival and successor, Warwick.

A. F. Pollard, *England under the Protector Somerset* (1900), with bibl. Id. in *D.N.B.*, li (1897), pp. 299–310, s.v. 'Seymour, Edward', with notes on unpublished material. See further bibl. s.v. *Edward VI*.

SON OF MAN. In the NT, a title of Christ. With one exception (Acts 7. 56) it is found only in the Gospels and here always on the Lord's lips.

Its uses in the Gospels may be classified as: (1) of One who is to appear at the Last Judgement 'coming with the clouds of heaven' (Mk. 14. 62; cf. Dan. 7. 13) or 'sitting on the throne of His glory' (Mt. 19. 28), as Judge of the World (Jn. 5. 27). In these passages, which derive their meaning from the associations of popular eschatology, the identification of the phrase with Jesus during His earthly life would not be natural to His hearers; (2) passages where it relates to the future sufferings, death, and Resurrection of the Messiah (e.g. Mt. 17. 22, cf. 20. 28; Mk. 8. 31; Jn. 3. 14); (3) passages where it unambiguously refers to Christ Himself, e.g. Mt. 8. 20, 11. 19. In some cases the parallel passage in another Gospel has 'I' or 'Me' (cf. Lk. 6. 22 and Mt. 5. 11; Lk. 12. 8 and Mt. 10. 32).

The meaning of the phrase must be sought in its Jewish ancestry. The corresponding Hebrew phrase is often just a synonym for 'man', i.e. a human being (e.g. Num. 23. 19, Ps. 8. 4, Ezek. 2. 1). But gradually it took on a technical meaning, largely, it would seem, under the influence of Dan. 7. 2–14 where the 'one like unto a son of man' (Dan. 7. 13, RV) coming 'with the clouds of heaven' was apparently a symbolic representative of the ideal Israel and only secondarily a real heavenly person. It is widely held, however, that under the influence of this passage the 'Son of Man' mentioned in the Similitudes of *Enoch (1st cent. B.C.) is the heavenly Messiah, who will be revealed at the last day and that this and one or two other such passages are the source of its use in many contexts in the Gospels. It is just possible that the Primal or Heavenly Man (*Urmensch*) who figures in Oriental mythology and folk-lore was also a contributory influence. A number of recent English scholars, following T. W. Manson, have argued that in the Gospels the word had a 'communal' sense (on the ground that it is based wholly on Dan. 7. 13) and was indicative of the Messianic Community.

In traditional exegesis of the Gospels the term 'Son of Man' signifies esp. the humility of Christ's incarnate manhood as contrasted with the majesty of His Divinity denoted by 'Son of God'. But as we have seen, the original associations of the phrase 'Son of Man' were connected with the Messiah's supernatural destiny rather than His humiliation. It has been suggested that the Lord chose it rather than any phrase referring to His Davidic Messiahship, e.g. 'Son of David', because its associations were less fixed and narrowly nationalistic, and also perhaps because if literally understood it could be referred to the coming in humility which would precede the appearance in glory and judgement traditionally associated with the title.

Important modern discussions include H. *Lietzmann, *Der Menschensohn* (1896); W. *Bousset, *Kyrios Christos* (1913), esp. pp. 1–27; D. Völter, *Die Menschensohn-Frage neu untersucht* (Leiden, 1916); Nils Messel, *Der Menschensohn in den Bilderreden des Henoch* (Beiheft zur Z.A.T.W., xxxv; 1922); J. M. Creed, 'The Heavenly Man' in *J.T.S.*, xxvi (1924–5), pp. 113–36. C. H. Kraeling, *Anthropos and Son of Man. A Study in the Religious Syncretism of the Hellenistic Orient* (Columbia University Oriental Studies, xxv; 1927; esp. in ref. to the 'Anthropos' in Manichaean, Hellentic and West Gnostic, Mandaean, and Jewish sources). *Otto, *Reich Gottes und Menschensohn* (1934), pp. 124–220 (Eng. tr., pp. 159–261). W. Manson, *Jesus the Messiah* (1943), esp. Appendix D ('The Heavenly Man Redemption Myth'), pp. 174–90. J. Y. Campbell, 'The Origin and Meaning of the Term Son of Man' in *J.T.S.*, xlviii (1947), pp. 145–55. M. Black, 'Unsolved New Testament Problems. The "Son of Man" in the Old Biblical Literature' in *The Expository Times*, lx (1948–9), pp. 11–15. C. H. *Dodd, *The Interpretation of the Fourth Gospel* (1953), pp. 241–9. V. Taylor, *The Names of Jesus* (1953), pp. 25–35. S. R. *Driver in *H.D.B.*, iv (1902), pp. 579–89, s.v. with bibl.; G. P. Gould in *D.C.G.*, ii (1908), pp. 659–65, s.v.

SONG OF SONGS, The. See *Solomon, The Song of.*

SONG OF THE THREE CHILDREN, The.

A short 'Book' of the *Apocrypha. In the *Septuagint and *Vulgate, where its 68 verses are treated as part of the canonical Book of *Daniel (into which they are inserted after Dan. 3. 23), the Song purports to be an expansion of the story of the three young Hebrew exiles thrown into the fiery furnace by Nebuchadnezzar. The Book consists of (1) the Prayer of Azarias, a petition for national deliverance, and (2) the canticle used in Christian worship under the name of the '*Benedicite'. Neither of these, however, apart from a single verse (66) in the Benedicite, seems to have any immediate relevance to the story of the three young men of Dan., and hence they are generally supposed to have been written originally for some other occasion.

Gk. text in H. B. *Swete, *The Old Testament in Greek*, ii (ed. 1912), pp. 515–23. Eng. tr. and comm. by W. H. Bennett in R. H. *Charles (ed.), *The Apocrypha and Pseudepigrapha of the Old Testament*, i (1913), pp. 625–37. W. H. Daubney, *The Three Additions to Daniel. A Study* (1906), pp. 17–99. C. Kuhl, *Die drei Männer im Feuer* (Beiheft zur Z.A.T.W., lv; 1930). W. O. E. Oesterley, *An Introduction to the Books of the Apocrypha* (1935), pp. 272–9. E. *Schürer, *Geschichte des jüdischen Volkes im Zeitalter Jesu Christi*, iii (ed. 4, 1909), pp. 453–8, with detailed bibl. to date (on the additions to Daniel). R. H. Pfeiffer, *History of New Testament Times with an Introduction to the Apocrypha* (New York, 1949; London, 1954), pp. 444–8, with further reff. J. T. Marshall in *H.D.B.*, iv (1902), pp. 754–6, s.v. 'Three Children, Song of the'. See also Catholic commentaries on Daniel and bibl. to *Benedicite* and *Apocrypha.*

SONGS OF ASCENT or SONGS OF DEGREES. See *Gradual Psalms.*

SONGS OF PRAISE,

a 'national' hymnal designed for the use of Christians of all denominations, first published in 1925. The General Editor was P. *Dearmer (1867–1936) and the Musical Editors Martin Shaw (b. 1875) and R. Vaughan Williams (b. 1872). It aimed at an improved literary and artistic quality in the words, introducing many poems which had hitherto not found a place in hymnals. Theologically its standpoint was markedly liberal; considerable place was found for the social aspects of religion; and a high standard of musical taste was set. In 1931 it was superseded by a second edition in which the liberal element in the book was carried to a much greater extreme. Many of the hymns were altered, and sometimes rewritten, to eliminate expressions of dogmatic faith, esp. those concerned with the Atonement, and references to penitence, fasting, and the sterner side of Christian practice generally were removed. Though *Songs of Praise* continues to be widely used for inter-denominational purposes, e.g. in schools, its use as a hymnal adapted to the needs of regular Anglican worship has declined.

P. Dearmer, *Songs of Praise Discussed*. A Handbook to the Best-known Hymns and to Others Recently Introduced (1933), with notes on the Music by A. Jacob.

SOPHIA, St. See *Santa Sophia.*

SOPHRONIUS, St.

(c. 560–638), Patr. of *Jerusalem from 634. His identity with Sophronius, 'the Sophist', seems now beyond dispute. He was a monk first in Egypt (c. 580), later near the Jordan, and finally (from 619) at Jerusalem. From 633 onwards he was the chief opponent of *Monothelitism then being defended by Cyrus, Patr. of Alexandria. He wrote extended Lives of the two Alexandrian saints, Cyrus and John, believed to have been martyred in the *Diocletianic Persecution, and some of his sermons, as well as several poems, have also survived. Shortly before his death he witnessed the capture of Jerusalem by the Saracens under Caliph Omar in 637. Feast day, 11 Mar.

Collection of his works in J. P. Migne, *PG*, lxxxvii (3), 3147–4014, with life repr. from *AA.SS.*, 3125–46. S. Vailhé, A.A., 'Sophrone le Sophiste et Sophrone le Patriarche' in *Revue de l'Orient chrétien*, vii (1902), pp. 360–85, and viii (1903), pp. 32–69 and 356–87. Bardenhewer, v, 36–41; Altaner, p. 695 f., with bibl. G. Bardy in *D.T.C.*, xiv (pt. 2; 1941), cols. 2379–83, s.v. 'Sophrone de Jérusalem'; E. Peterson in *E.C.*, xi (1953), col. 906 f., s.v. 'Sofrone', with full bibl.

SORBONNE.

The most famous college of the old university of *Paris, originally known as the Collegium Pauperum Magistrorum. It was founded c. 1257 by Robert de Sorbon, confessor of St. *Louis, for the education of advanced students aspiring to the theological doctorate. Among its many benefactors was St. Louis himself, who gave part of the site. It was favoured by the Popes, and Clement IV granted it Papal approbation in 1268. The house was governed by a 'provisor', assisted by the 'bursars', to whom were added the 'socii' without a 'burse' and the 'hospites'. In addition to these were the 'beneficiarii', supported by the college to perform menial offices for the Fellows. The reputation of the Sorbonne, whose examinations were famous for their severity, soon became such that its membership was sought not only by most theological doctors of Paris but also by many otherwise prominent personalities. The college also came to be consulted on theological and even political questions from all parts of Christendom. From 1554 it was the regular meeting-place of the Theological Faculty, and from this date the name Sorbonne was popularly applied to this faculty. From the later Middle Ages the Sorbonne had favoured *Gallican tendencies, and in the 17th and 18th cents. it vigorously defended the '*Gallican Articles'. It opposed the bull '*Unigenitus' (1713), thus losing its influence with Rome, and also fought the *probabilist moral theology and the educational aims of the *Jesuits. On the other hand, it stoutly defended Catholic principles against the Reformation theology and the Rationalist philosophy of the 18th cent. The Sorbonne was suppressed in 1792, but re-established as the Theological Faculty of the university by Napoleon in 1808. Its professors and graduates, however, were obliged to subscribe to the Gallican Articles, a condition which drew away most theological students to *St.-Sulpice and the diocesan seminaries. The faculty was finally abolished in 1882, but the name, 'Sorbonne', is still in general use for the modern University of Paris.

Important docc. in the *Chartularium Universitatis Parisiensis*, ed. H. *Denifle, O.P.–A. Chatelain (4 vols., Paris, 1889–97). J. Duvernet, *Histoire de la Sorbonne dans laquelle on voit l'influence de la théologie sur l'ordre social* (2 vols., bound in one, 1790). O. Gréard, *Nos Adieux à la vieille Sorbonne* (1893), with docc. A. Franklin, *La Sorbonne. Ses origines, sa bibliothèque, les débuts de l'imprimerie à Paris et la succession de Richelieu* (1875). H. *Rashdall, *The Universities of Europe in the Middle Ages*, i (new ed. by F. M. Powicke–A. B. Emden, 1936), pp. 507–9, with bibl. p. 497. J. Bonnerot, *La Sorbonne. Sa vie, son rôle, son œuvre à travers les siècles* (1927).

SORROWFUL MYSTERIES, The Five. The second chaplet of the *Rosary consisting of (1) the Agony in Gethsemane, (2) the Scourging, (3) the Crowning with Thorns, (4) the Carrying of the Cross, and (5) the Crucifixion.

SOTERIOLOGY (Gk. σωτηρία, 'salvation'). The section of Christian theology which treats of the saving work of Christ for the world. It includes not only the doctrines of the *Atonement and of *Grace, but also (a) the doctrine of human nature as affected by the *fall and by *sin, which is the presupposition of Christ's work, and (b) the doctrine of man's final destiny as the result of that work (see *Resurrection, Heaven, Hell).

SOTO, DOMINIC (1494–1560), *Dominican theologian. A native of Spain who was a student at Alcalá and at Paris, he entered the Dominican Order at Burgos in 1524. Here he taught in his convent for 7 years until appointed in 1532 to a chair of theology at Salamanca university. This office he continued to hold until 1545, when *Charles V chose him as Imperial Theologian for the Council of *Trent, where he ably expounded the *Thomistic teaching on grace and original sin. After spending some time in Germany as confessor to *Charles V, he returned to Salamanca in 1550, where he was elected in 1552 to the principal chair of theology in succession to Melchior *Cano. His writings include, besides his *Summulae* (a manual of logic, 1529), commentaries on *Aristotle (1544–5), on the Ep. to the Romans (1550), and on the *Sentences* (1557–60).

A. M. Viel, O.P., 'Dominique Soto, 1494–1560. Étude historico-doctrinale' in *Revue thomiste*, xii (1904), pp. 151–66, and xiii (1905), pp. 174–93. Valuable series of studies by V. Beltrán de Heredia, O.P., in *La Ciencia tomista*, xliii (1931), pp. 357–73, and xliv (1931), pp. 28–54; xlv (1932), pp. 35–49 and 177–93; xlviii (1933), pp. 41–67; lvii (1938), pp. 38–67 and 281–302; lxi (1941), pp. 133–62; lxiii (1942), pp. 113–47, and lxv (1943), pp. 59–82. F. Stegmüller, 'Zur Gnadenlehre des spanischen Konziltheologen Domingo de Soto' in G. Schreiber (ed.), *Das Weltkonzil von Trient*, i (1951), pp. 169–230. Quétif–Échard, ii, 171–4. V. Beltrán de Heredia, O.P., in *D.T.C.*, xiv (pt. 2; 1941), cols. 2423–2431, s.v.

SOUBIROUS, BERNADETTE. See *Bernadette, St.*

SOUL. No precise teaching about the soul received general acceptance in the Christian Church until the Middle Ages. The Scriptures are explicit only on the facts of the distinction between soul and body, the creation of the soul of the first man by the Divine breath, and its immortality. St. Paul's teaching on the existence in the human person of body, soul, and spirit (cf. 1 Thess. 5. 23) seems to imply a 'trichotomy' rather than the 'dichotomy' of body and soul of later times; but in his language he is not entirely consistent, and spirit sometimes denotes the principle of supernatural life in contrast to the natural life of the soul, and on other occasions signifies the higher powers (intellect and will), as opposed to the lower faculties (emotions, &c.).

The indefiniteness of Scriptural teaching, in conjunction with the confusion in pagan philosophy where materialistic, pantheistic, and dualistic conceptions were held side by side, was reflected in the writings of the early Fathers. Thus *Tertullian, supporting his view by the material imagery of the parable of Dives and Lazarus, held the corporeity of the soul, an error from which even St. *Irenaeus does not seem to have been entirely free. *Origen, on the other hand, was led by his strongly *Platonist leanings to affirm its pre-existence and explained its confinement in a body as a punishment for sins committed in its previous incorporeal state. In the post-Nicene period, these divergences largely disappeared. St. *Gregory of Nyssa and St. *Augustine found in the soul an image of the Trinity (*Noverim Te, noverim me*), and in

*Nemesius and *Maximus Confessor the doctrine of the Schoolmen is already developed in its main aspects.

Acc. to St. *Thomas Aquinas, who follows *Aristotle in his definition of the human soul, the soul is an individual spiritual substance, the 'form' of the body. Both, body and soul together, constitute the human unity, though the soul may be severed from the body and lead a separate existence, as happens after death. The separation, however, is not final, as the soul, in this differing from the angels, was made for the body. As it is purely spiritual, the soul is not, as *Traducianism affirms, a product of the generative, and therefore entirely material, powers of man, but each individual soul is a new creation of God, infused into the body destined for it ('Creationism').

This Scholastic teaching is that which has received the widest acceptance in the Christian Church. Among orthodox *Lutheran and *Calvinistic theologians, however, Traducianism has been commonly preferred to Creationism, as conforming more nearly with the Reformation tenet of the depravity of human nature. Modern Christian theologians tend to consider the doctrine of the soul not *per se*, but in relation to the whole Biblical doctrine of man.

SOUTER, ALEXANDER (1873–1949), NT and Patristic scholar. He was educated at Aberdeen and Gonville and Caius College, Cambridge, where he came under the influence of the Latinist, J. E. B. Mayor. From 1903 to 1911 he was professor of NT Greek at Mansfield College, Oxford, and from 1911 to 1937 Regius Professor of Humanity (in succession to W. M. *Ramsay) at Aberdeen. He came to acquire an unrivalled knowledge of early Christian Latin. His writings include *A Study of Ambrosiaster* (1905; after G. *Morin, Souter held that *Ambrosiaster was an ex-Jew, Isaac), an edition of the Pseudo-Augustinian *Quaestiones Veteris et Novi Testamenti* (C.S.E.L., 1908), translations and notes on treatises of *Tertullian, and three works on *Pelagius's 'Expositions on St. Paul's Epistles' (1922, 1926, 1931). He also cooperated with W. *Sanday in studies on the text of the NT and vigorously maintained (with F. J. A. *Hort against C. H. *Turner) a late date (370–420) for the Latin version of *Irenaeus. Of a more popular character were three manuals widely used by students—his *critical apparatus* to the Greek NT (1910), a short manual on the text and canon of the NT (1913), and a scholarly pocket-lexicon to the Greek NT (1916). His valuable *Glossary of Later Latin* (1949) was published posthumously.

SOUTH, ROBERT (1634–1716), English divine. Educated at Westminster under R. Busby and at Christ Church, Oxford, he was for a time in sympathy with *Presbyterianism. In 1658, however, he secretly took Orders. He held a varied succession of offices, becoming Public Orator of Oxford (1660), domestic chaplain to Lord Clarendon (1660), Prebendary of *Westminster (1663), chaplain to the Duke of York (1667), canon of Christ Church (1670), and rector of Islip, Oxon (1678). His sermons, smart, witty, and often sarcastic, became exceedingly popular, but his outspokenness precluded him from higher preferment, though in 1713 he was apparently offered, but declined, the see of *Rochester. In 1689 he opposed the *Toleration Act and for a time hesitated before taking the Oath, and in 1710 he sided with H. *Sacheverell. For several years he controverted with vigour W. *Sherlock's dubiously orthodox teaching on the *Trinity, publishing in 1693 some *Animadversions* on Sherlock's *Vindication* (1690) and in 1695, in answer to a reply by Sherlock, *Tritheism Charged* (both anonymous).

South himself began the publication of his *Sermons Preached on Several Occasions* (Oxford, 1679; new edd., with further sermons, London, 1692, and 3 vols., ib., 1697–8). Posthumous Works, Lat. and Eng., publd. 2 vols., London, 1717, incl. his will and memoir of his life and writings. The many later edd. of his sermons include five additional vols., London, 1744; also collected ed., 7 vols., Oxford, 1823. Selection of his writings under the title *The Wisdom of Our Fathers* [1867], with memoir, pp. v–xxiv. His sermon on 'Man Created in God's Image' repr. in D. Macleane (ed.), *Famous Sermons by English Preachers* (1911), pp. 120–34, with biographical introd., pp. 117–20. A. Gordon in *D.N.B.*, liii (1898), pp. 275–7; W. H. *Hutton in *D.E.C.H.*, pp. 569 f., s.v.

SOUTH AFRICA, Christianity in. Some measure of Christianity was brought to South Africa in the 15th cent. by the Portuguese, who were the first explorers, but their interests were chiefly in the exploitation of the country and its people, and their missionary work was limited and unsuccessful. The Dutch, who ruled Cape Colony in the 18th cent., were hostile to missionary work, and discouraged the *Moravian missions which attempted to start work, even compelling them to close down for a time. They reopened in 1792. The *L.M.S. started work in 1799. When the British occupied Cape Town in 1806, they found two RC missionaries, whom they promptly expelled, and RC missions were not able seriously to restart work until 1837. Much pioneer work was done by R. *Moffat.

The character of Christian work in S. Africa during the past hundred years has been determined by two principal facts, the existence of a large white community (though not large proportionately to the native population), made up principally of English and Dutch settlers, and the vast scope, given by the enormous size of the sub-continent and the gradual opening-up of communications, for evangelistic work among the native population. The first fact has caused the establishment and organization of a settled Church in many places, with duties other than those of missionary propaganda; and so the Dutch Reformed Church (Calvinist) and the Anglican Church of the Province of South Africa exist as local institutions rather than as European mission outposts. The second fact, the immensity of the field, has made room for missionary activity of religious bodies and societies from almost every country of W. Christendom, RC, Anglican, and Protestant. Besides the bodies noted earlier, and the continuous evangelistic work of the Dutch Reformed Church and the Church of the Province of South Africa, American, German, French, Finnish, Swiss, Scandinavian, Scottish, and English Protestant missions have all been at work for varying periods, in particular the *Methodists, who first arrived in 1814. The *S.P.G., whose work is now partly merged with that of the Church of the Province, arrived in 1821. RCs have also been active, esp. in the Rhodesias, where, in addition to the Oblates of Mary Immaculate, who are responsible for RC missions in most of the rest of S. Africa, the English and Polish *Jesuits are engaged. The Dutch Reformed Church predominates in the Transvaal and the Orange Free State. Missions exist also in the countries of Bechuanaland, Basutoland, and Swaziland, French Protestants being the earliest (in 1833) to enter Basutoland, while S.W. Africa was reached by German missions, Catholic and Protestant, between 1832 and 1834.

The missionaries and Church authorities in S. Africa have been rightly sensitive of the fact that in the early days Christianity and exploitation often went hand in hand in Africa, and have striven hard to remove this stigma from themselves. John Philip of the L.M.S. earned much disfavour in the early days of missions in the last century through his outspoken support of native rights. And in modern times the Church, though hesitant at times, has often strongly opposed state policy and social custom where the interests of the African appear to have been thrust aside.

The Church of the Province of South Africa is an independent province of the Anglican Communion, with an archiepiscopal see at Cape Town, founded in 1847, and over a dozen other dioceses. The BCP is used, in its 1662 edition, with the exception of the Lectionary, as the use of the English Revised Lectionary of 1922 was made obligatory in 1924. An Alternative *Eucharistic Liturgy was approved by the Provincial Synod in 1919, and a complete provincial Prayer Book was issued in 1954. Religious communities, both of men and women, are perhaps more active in South Africa than in any other Anglican province.

J. Du Plessis, *A History of Christian Missions in South Africa* (London, 1911). C. Lewis–G. E. Edwards, *Historical Records of the Church of the Province of South Africa* (ib., 1934). A. T. Wirgman, *The History of the English Church and People in South Africa* (ib., 1895); A. H. Baynes, *South Africa* (Handbooks of English Church Expansion, 1908). H. L. Clarke, *Constitutional Church Government in the Dominions beyond the Seas and other Parts of the Anglican Communion* (1924), pp. 320–91. C. C. Martindale, S.J., *African Angelus.* Episodes and Impressions (London, 1932); Father Agathangelus, O.F.M. (ed.), *The Catholic Church and Southern Africa* (Cape Town, 1951), pp. 109–80. G. B. A. Gerdener, *Boustowwe vir die Geskiedenis van die Nederduits-Gereformeerde Kerk in die Transgariep* (Cape Town, 1930). H. D. van Broekhuizen (ed.), *Die Wordingsgeskiedenis van die Hollandse Kerke in Suid-Afrika, 1652–1804* (Amsterdam, 1922); A. Moorrees, *Die Nederduitse Gereformeerde*

Kerk in Suid-Afrika, 1652–1872 (Cape Town, 1937). W. C. Holden, *A Brief History of Methodism and of Methodist Missions in South Africa* (London, 1877); J. Whiteside, *History of the Wesleyan Methodist Church of South Africa* (ib., 1906). Latourette, iii, 245 f.; v, 319–81, with bibl. pp. 471–506 passim; and vii, 224–30, with bibl. notes. P. Hinchliff, *The South African Liturgy* (Cape Town, 1959).

SOUTH INDIA, Church of. The Church inaugurated on 27 Sept. 1947 by the union of three religious bodies: (1) the (*Anglican) Church of India, Burma, and Ceylon, in respect to four of its dioceses, viz. Madras, Tinnevelly, Travancore and Cochin, and Dornakal; (2) the South India Province of the *Methodist Church; (3) the South India United Church, itself the result of a movement which brought *Presbyterian, *Congregational, and Dutch Reformed bodies into organic union in 1908 and was joined in 1919 by the Malabar District of the Basel Mission, which draws its foreign workers from Continental *Lutheran and *Reformed Churches. The new Church, which numbers about one million, is based doctrinally on the *Lambeth Quadrilateral (1888) and claims to be a united and visible Church, in which the Congregational, Presbyterian, and Episcopal elements are preserved. Though it is not yet wholly episcopal, there are provisions in the plan the outcome of which may be that at the end of an interim period of 30 years its presbyters will be all episcopally ordained.

The union is the fruit of negotiations which began at a historic conference at Tranquebar in May 1919, when the 33 participants (31 Indians, 1 American, and 1 Englishman, almost all ministers of varying denominations) determined to remedy the evils arising from divisions to Christian Mission work in India. The 1920 *Lambeth Conference *Appeal to all Christian People* quickened hopes, and a Joint Committee of the three bodies concerned was set up. The challenge to traditional Catholic order in the proposed arrangement led to much controversy and many delays; but the 1930 Lambeth Conference gave general encouragement to the scheme, believing that Catholic principles would be sufficiently safeguarded. The scheme was later subjected to considerable revision, and in 1947, if one vote had been differently cast, the union would have been delayed. The 1948 Lambeth Conference gave the union a measure of approval, though it expressed the hope that certain parts of the constitution of the new Church, which had caused anxiety, might be reconsidered. In the Nandyal district of S. India some 40,000 Anglicans refused to join the Church. In 1955 a state of 'limited intercommunion' between the Church of South India and the C of E was approved by the Canterbury and York Convocations.

G. K. A. Bell, *Documents on Christian Unity* (3 vols., 1924–48; Nos. 71–81, 139–43, 147, and 204–8); W. J. Sparrow Simpson, *South Indian Schemes* (1930); Trevor Jalland, *The Bible, the Church and South India* (1944); J. E. L. Newbigin, *The Reunion of the Church.* A Defence of the South India Scheme (1948); J. J. Willis and others, *Towards a United Church, 1913–1947* (1947); B. Sundkler, *Church of South India.* The Movement towards Union, 1900–1947 (1954).

SOUTH SEAS, Christianity in the. In 1776 a RC mission was sent by the Viceroy of Peru to Tahiti, but withdrew after a few months. The *L.M.S. (London Missionary Society) sent out evangelists who started work in the Society Islands in 1796 and in Tahiti in 1797, and rapidly extended it. Among their pioneers were John Williams and James Harris of the New Hebrides, who suffered martyrdom at Erromanga in 1839. The L.M.S., whose work has been more persistent and widespread in the Pacific than that of any other society, now serve the Cook and Samoan groups, the Tokelau Islands, the Ocean and Nauru Islands, and the Polynesians, while in Papua the work, which began in 1871, has greatly extended. *Presbyterians share with the L.M.S. the honour of repeated fatal attempts between 1839 and 1848 to settle among the most savage of the cannibal tribes. *Lutherans work in New Guinea, and the Paris Missionary Society (Protestant) in the French possessions. The Australian Methodists and the South Sea Evangelicals also have scattered missions. For the missionary work performed by the *Reformed Presbyterian Church of *Scotland, see also *Paton, J. G.

RC missions entered the field in many places early in the 19th cent., esp. in Polynesia. They have posts in Papua, the Gilbert Islands, Samoa, New Guinea, and the French possessions. The work is chiefly in the hands of the newer missionary orders, and is mostly supplied from France and America. The heroic work of Father *Damien (d. 1889) in the leper colony at Molokai, Hawaii, is well known. RCs, Episcopalians, and the Board of Commissioners (Protestant) direct from the U.S.A. many missions, esp. in the Hawaian Islands and adjacent parts of the Pacific. There are also missions from *Japan.

Anglican work in the South Seas began under G. A. *Selwyn, appointed first Bp. of New Zealand in 1841. One of his disciples, J. C. *Patteson, first Bp. of Melanesia (1861), suffered martyrdom in 1871. At present Anglican missions cover a very wide area, and the dioceses of Melanesia and Polynesia form part of the Province of New Zealand. Australia and New Zealand, with some help from England, maintain these dioceses.

The task which confronted missionaries in these seas was one of the hardest in missionary history, from the difficulties of communication and the extreme savagery of the inhabitants, many of whom were cannibals. The civilization and tranquillity which is now general is due almost entirely to the labours of Christian missionaries, whose heroism has led very many to martyrdom even down to recent times.

J. Williams, *A Narrative of Missionary Enterprises in the South Sea Islands* (London, 1837); J. Hutton, *Missionary Life in the Southern Seas* (ib., 1874). J. Colwell (ed.), *A Century in the Pacific* (ib., 1914), pt. iv, 'Missionary', pp. 409–585. E. S. Armstrong, *The History of the Melanesian Mission* (ib., 1900). R. Lovett, *The History of the London Missionary Society, 1795–1895*, i (1899), pp. 117–474; N. Goodall, *History of the London Missionary Society, 1895–1945* (1954), esp. pp. 352–411, and bibl. refs., p. 592; Latourette, v, 198–263, with bibl. pp. 471–506 passim, and vii, 192–9, with bibl. notes.

SOUTHCOTT, JOANNA (1750–1814), religious fanatic. After beginning life as a dairymaid to her father, she became a domestic servant. In 1791 she joined the *Methodist Society 'by Divine command', and in the following year proclaimed that she was the woman of Rev. 12. She thereupon proceeded to 'seal' the 144,000 elect at a charge varying from 12s. to 21s., but when one was hanged for murder in 1809 no further 'sealing' was done. She had a habit of writing and sealing prophecies, and R. T. *Davidson, when Abp. of Canterbury, was constantly being requested to open a box said to contain them. When opened in 1927 (not by the Archbishop), its contents were found to include a woman's nightcap and a lottery ticket. Among her 60 publications were *Prophecies announcing the Prince of Peace* (1814), to whom she was to have given birth in 1814, and the *Book of Wonders* (1813–14). She died of brain disease.

Her own writings are the primary source for her life. *General Index to the Writings of Joanna Southcott* (London, [1805]). Life by D. Hughson (pseudonym of Edward Pugh, London, 1814; very critical). G. R. Balleine, *Past Finding Out. The Tragic Story of Joanna Southcott and her Successors* (1956). A. Seymour, *The Express* (2 vols.; 1909; sympathetic). G. K. A. Bell, *Randall Davidson* (1935), ii, 1099–201. A. Gordon in *D.N.B.*, liii (1898), pp. 277–9 s.v., with further bibl.

SOUTHWELL. St. *Paulinus is said to have founded a collegiate church here *c.* 630. The present cathedral church of St. Mary the Virgin was begun in the reign of Henry I and has a fine Norman nave and transepts, and a 13th cent. *chapter-house. The early collegiate foundation developed into a college of secular canons, which was dissolved by *Henry VIII in 1540, refounded in 1585, and again dissolved in 1841. In 1884 the church became the cathedral of the new Diocese of Southwell, consisting roughly of the counties of Derbyshire and Nottinghamshire. In 1927, the former was separated off when the Diocese of Derby was constituted. In 1935 the Diocese was transferred from the Province of *Canterbury to that of *York.

A. F. Leach (ed.), *Visitations and Memorials of Southwell Minster* (Camden Society, Second Series, xlviii; 1891); T. M. Blagg (ed.), *Seventeenth Century Parish Register Transcripts Belonging to the Peculiar of Southwell* (Thoroton Society, Record Series, i; 1903); A. H. Thompson (ed.), 'The Certificates of the Chantry Commissioners for the College of Southwell in 1546 and 1548' in *Transactions of the Thoroton Society*, xv (1900), pp. 63–158. W. D. Macray, 'The Manuscripts of Southwell Cathedral' in the *Twelfth Report of the Historical Manuscripts Commission, Appendix*, Part ix (1891), pp. 539–52. W. *Dugdale, *Monasticon Anglicanum*, vi (pt. 3, ed. 1830), pp. 1312–23. W. Dickinson Rastall, *A History of the Antiquities of the Town and Church of Southwell* (1787). A. Dimock, *The Cathedral Church of Southwell* (Bell's Cathedral Series, 1898). J. C. Cox in *V.C.H. Nottingham*, ii. ed. W. Page (1910), pp. 152–61. A. H. Thompson, 'The Cathedral Church of the Blessed Virgin Mary, Southwell' in *Transactions of the Thoroton Society*, xv (1900), pp. 15–62. G. Crosse in *D.E.C.H.* (ed. 3, 1948), p. 582 f., s.v.

SOUTHWELL, ROBERT (*c.* 1561–95), RC poet and martyr. He was a native of Norfolk, educated by the *Jesuits at *Douai and *Paris, and entered the order in 1580 after a two years' novitiate. In 1584 he was ordained priest and made prefect of studies at the English College in Rome. In 1586 he was sent on the English mission. He first stayed with Lord Vaux of Harrowden and, though closely watched, gained many conversions through his piety and winning manner. In 1589 he became chaplain to Anne, Countess of Arundel, and established relations with her husband, imprisoned in the Tower. During his missionary activities he spent most of his time in hiding in London or in RC country houses where he stayed in disguise and under assumed names. In 1592 he was betrayed by Anne Bellamy, the daughter of Richard Bellamy, a Catholic whom he had visited at Harrow. He was confined first at the gatehouse at *Westminster and later in the Tower. After three years of imprisonment he was hanged and quartered as a traitor. He was beatified in 1929. Feast day, 21 Feb.

Collections of his verse were published immediately after his death entitled St. Peter's Complaint with other Poems and Maeoniae (both 1595). Among his prose treatises are An Epistle of Comfort, The Triumphs over Death, Mary Magdalen's Tears, and A Humble Supplication to Her Majesty, all written in 1591 and at first circulated in manuscript. They were designed esp. to encourage Catholics under persecution. His poems, most of which were probably written in prison, soon became popular both with Catholics and Protestants. They give utterance to deep religious feeling, though his vivid imagination led him to use extensively the fanciful conceits favoured by the poets of his time.

Southwell's Prose Works ed. W. J. Walter (London, 1828); standard ed. of his Poems by A. B. Grosart ('The Fuller Worthies Library', London, 1872), with introd., pp. xxxv–c; modern ed. (selections) by Mrs. Ivo [Christobel M.] Hood, The Book of Robert Southwell, Priest, Poet, Prisoner (1926), with introd., pp. 1–77. His Spiritual Exercises and Devotions (Lat. text) first ed. by J. M. de Buck, S.J., with Eng. tr. by P. E. Hallett (London, 1931). Modern ed. of An Humble Supplication to her Maiestie by R. C. Bald (Cambridge, 1953). A. Possoz, S.J., Vie du Père Robert Southwell de la Compagnie de Jésus, martyrisé en Angleterre sous Élisabeth (1866). Rose A. Morton, S.S.J., An Appreciation of Robert Southwell (University of Philadelphia thesis; Philadelphia-London, 1929). P. Janelle, Robert Southwell the Writer. A Study in Religious Interpretation (Paris thesis, Clermont-Ferrand; also London, 1935). Modern life by C. Devlin (London, 1956). J. G. MacLeod, 'Robert Southwell, Scholar, Poet and Martyr' in The Month, xxxi (1877), pp. 439–56; H. Thurston, S.J., 'Catholic Writers and Elizabethan Readers', parts 2 and 3, ib., lxxxiii (1895), pp. 231–45 and 383–99. J. H. McDonald, The Poems and Prose Writings of Robert Southwell, S.J. A Bibliographical Study (Roxburghe Club, 1937). S. Lee in D.N.B., liii (1898), pp. 294–9, with reff. to original sources. Further bibl. in C.B.E.L., i, 421 f. and 685.

SOZOMEN (early 5th cent.), Salmaninius Hermias Sozomen, Church historian. Little is known of his life beyond the facts that he was a native of Bethelia, nr. Gaza in Palestine, that he was educated by monks, and that, after travelling extensively, he settled at *Constantinople as a lawyer. Here he conceived the idea of continuing *Eusebius of Caesarea's 'Church History' down to his own day. His work, in nine Books, covers the period 323 to 425. He drew extensively upon his elder contemporary, *Socrates; his historical grasp was weaker, but he reports certain subjects, e.g. the spread of

Christianity among the *Armenians, Saracens, and Goths, much more fully. Also, he had more sense of style than Socrates. Though orthodox in intention, he reveals little understanding of the issues at stake in the dogmatic controversies.

Text ed. by R. *Stephanus, H. *Valesius, and W. Reading, as for Socrates (q.v.). W. Reading's ed. repr. in J. P. Migne, PG, lxvii, 843–1630. Revision by R. Hussey (3 vols., Oxford, 1860). G. Schoo, Die Quellen des Kirchenhistorikers Sozomenos (1911). J. Bidez, La Tradition manuscrite de Sozomène et la Tripartite de Théodore le Lecteur (T.U., xxxii. 2b; 1908); cf. also id. in Sb. (Berl.), 1935, No. 18. P. *Batiffol, 'Sozomène et Sabinos' in B.Z., vii (1898), pp. 265–84. G. Loeschcke in P.R.E. (ed. 3), xviii (1906), pp. 541–7; W. Eltester in P.W., 2te Reihe, iii (pt. 1; 1927), cols. 1240–8; G. Bardy in D.T.C., xiv (pt. 2; 1941), cols. 2469–71, all s.v.

SPAIN, Christianity in. Spain was reached very early by Christian missionaries, acc. to tradition by St. *Paul (q.v.) and St. *James. *Prudentius (4th cent.) says that there were Spanish martyrs in all the ten great persecutions. Early Spanish councils are those of *Elvira (c. 300), Saragossa (380), and *Toledo (400). In the 5th cent. the *Arian Visigoths overran the land, but at the Third Council of Toledo (589) their king, Recared, accepted Catholicism.

In the 8th cent. the Moslem Moors conquered Spain, and were only checked from entering the Frankish kingdom by *Charles Martel's victory at Tours (732). About 100 years later the persecution of the Christians of Spain began. The Christian reconquest, which began with the victory at Calatañazor in 1002, was completed only by the reduction of Granada in 1492. As the reconquest proceeded, French influences became increasingly felt, e.g. in church buildings and the founding of religious orders, esp. those of the *Cluniac reform; and as early as the 11th cent. the Roman rite nearly everywhere replaced the ancient *Mozarabic rite, which has lingered, however, until the present day at Toledo. The 12th cent. saw the arrival of the *Cistercians and the military orders, the latter gaining great influence in Spain. In the 13th cent. came the *Carmelites, *Dominicans, and *Franciscans.

The later Middle Ages were marked by the introduction of the *Inquisition, an institution congenial to the Spanish temperament. It was largely fostered by the civil power as a means of checking the Jews, whose numbers, wealth, and frequent intrigues with the Moors were causing alarm. In the Great Schism Spain played a leading part on the side of the antipopes, until the time of the Council of *Constance (1415).

In 1494, after the union of the kingdoms of Aragon and Castile and the complete expulsion of the Moors, the title of 'Catholic Majesty' was conferred by *Alexander VI upon the King of Spain. Under the Emp. *Charles V, who was also King of Spain from 1519 to 1555, the power of the country reached its height. Not only was its influence in Europe unparalleled, but it had won an Empire in the New World, equalled only by *Portugal. The adhesion of Spain to the Papacy in the conflicts of the 16th cent. thus became a political factor of the first importance, while the moderating influence of the Spanish bishops at the Council of *Trent did much to shape the *Counter-Reformation. It was an age of unparalleled mystics (St. *Teresa of Ávila, St. *John of the Cross, *Luis of Granada). Under *Philip II (reigned 1555–98) the decay of Spanish power began, and steadily continued in the succeeding centuries.

Political and religious liberalism appeared in Spain, under French influence, c. 1800. It has never come to terms with the traditional Spanish spirit, which in both spheres is strongly reactionary. The result has been a century and a half of unrest, war, and alternation of extremes, down to the civil war of 1936–39. In these conflicts the Church has been allied with the conservative side, while the opposing forces, from freemasonry in the early 19th cent. to communism in the mid-20th, have been almost consistently anti-religious.

Non-RC Christianity, for which toleration only became effective in 1910, is of the smallest importance in Spain. Protestantism received some encouragement by the disestablishment and restriction of the RC Church in the Revolution of 1931, but its fortunes were again reversed by the settlement of 1939.

H. Florez, cont. by M. Risco, A. Merino, J. de la Canal, S. de Barnanda, V. de la Fuente, and C. R. Fort, *España sagrada*. Theatro geográphico-histórica de la Iglesia de España (51 vols., 1747–1879; index by A. Gonzáles, 1918). V. de la Fuente, *Historia eclesiástica de España* (3 vols., 1855; ed. 2, 6 vols., 1873–5); P. B. *Gams, *Die Kirchengeschichte von Spanien* (3 vols., 1862–79). F. Meyrick, *The Church in Spain* (1892). P. Kehr, *Papsturkunden in Spanien*. Vorarbeiten zur Hispania Pontificia (*Abh.* (Gött.), N.F., xviii, 2; xxii, 1; 1926–8). Z. García Villada, S.J., *Historia eclesiástica de España* [to 1085] (3 vols. bound in 5, 1929–36). H. *Leclercq, O.S.B., *L'Espagne chrétienne* (1906). A. K. Ziegler, *Church and State in Visigothic Spain* (Catholic University of America Diss., Washington, 1930). J. Vincke, 'Kirche und Staat in Spanien während des Spätmittelalters' in *R.Q.*, xliii (1935), pp. 35–53. H. C. Lea, *A History of the Inquisition in Spain* (4 vols., 1906–7), and other works. A. de Castro, *Historia de los protestantes españoles* (1851; Eng. tr., 1851); E. Schäfer, *Beiträge zur Geschichte des spanischen Protestantismus und der Inquisition im sechzehnten Jahrhundert* (3 vols., 1902). C. A. Garcia–K. G. Grubb, *Religion in the Republic of Spain* (1933; evangelical survey). J. Vincke in *L.Th.K.*, ix (1937), cols. 703–12, s.v. 'Spanien'; G. F. Alonso and I. Rotoli in *E.C.*, xi (1953), cols. 1042–55, s.v. 'Spagna, Storia ecclesiastica', and 'Condizione giuridica della Chiesa', and A. Neppi, cols. 1075–80, s.v. 'Arte sacra', with bibl. See also bibl. to *Inquisition* and to the various religious orders.

SPALATIN, GEORG (1484–1545), German humanist and reformer. Georg Burkhardt was born at Spalt (hence his name) nr. Nuremberg, studied at Erfurt, and from 1505 to 1508 taught at the monastery of Georgenthal. In 1508 he was ordained priest and in 1509 was appointed tutor to the sons of the Prince Elector, *Frederick the Wise of Saxony. He soon won the Elector's confidence and became his secretary and librarian. In 1511 he was sent to *Wittenberg, where he became acquainted with M. *Luther, under whose guidance he began to study the Bible. His scholarship came to be much valued at the Saxon court, and it was mainly through Spalatin's influence that the hesitating Elector was gained to the

ideas of the Reformer. In 1518 he accompanied Frederick to the Diet of *Augsburg, and in 1521 to *Worms. In 1525 he advocated the complete abolition of Catholicism in Saxony. In the same year he married and went to Altenburg, where he carried through the reform. Under Frederick's successor, John (1525–32), he continued to foster the Reformation, being chiefly engaged in the visitation of schools and churches. His later years were darkened by melancholy. Besides translations of writings of Luther, P. *Melanchthon, and *Erasmus, he compiled *Annales Reformationis* (ed. 1718) and *Chronicon et Annales* [1463–1525]. He also conducted an extensive correspondence with Luther, whose confidant he was, but only Luther's replies survive.

An edition of his *Historischer Nachlass und Briefe* was undertaken by C. Neudecker–L. Preller (vol. i only, the life of Frederick the Wise, publd., Jena, 1851). A Seeheim, *Georg Spalatin als sächsischer Historiograph* (1876; low estimate of Spalatin's competence as a historian). Several studies by G. Berbig (Halle, 1906 ff.; uncritical). I. Höss, *Georg Spalatin, 1484–1545* (Weimar, 1956). F. Müller in *Allgemeine deutsche Biographie*, xxxv (1893), pp. 1–29, s.v.; T. Kolde in *P.R.E.* (ed. 3), xviii (1906), pp. 547–53, s.v. Further bibl. in Schottenloher, ii, 284–6 (Nos. 20266–96).

SPALATRENSIS. See *De Dominis, Marco Antonio*.

SPANISH ARMADA. See *Armada, Spanish*.

SPARROW, ANTHONY (1612–85), Bp. of *Norwich. He was a Fellow of Queens' College, Cambridge, from 1633 till his expulsion by the *Puritans in 1644. For a sermon preached on confession and absolution in 1637, he was brought into the Vice-Chancellor's court, but successfully defended by W. *Juxon, Bp. of London. At the Restoration, when he became Archdeacon of Sudbury, he appears to have taken an influential part in the revision of the BCP. In 1662 he was appointed President of his college, in 1667 was made Bp. of *Exeter, and in 1676 translated to Norwich. He was a keen High Churchman throughout his life, best known through his *Rationale or Practical Exposition of the Book of Common Prayer* (earliest extant edition, 1657; many times reprinted), the object of which was to show that the C of E service was neither 'old superstitious Roman dotage' nor 'schismatically new'.

His *Rationale* was ed., with some of his minor works, to which are prefixed the lives of the Compilers of the Liturgy, by Samuel Downes (London, 1722), and repr. by J. H. *N[ewman] (Oxford, 1839), with preface, pp. i–iv; extracts in P. E. More–F. L. Cross (edd.), *Anglicanism* (1935), Nos. 220 and 234, pp. 501 f. and 521 f. W. P. Courtney in *D.N.B.*, liii (1898), p. 313 f., s.v.

S.P.C.K. The 'Society for Promoting Christian Knowledge'. It was founded by T. *Bray and four laymen in 1698 'to promote and encourage the erection of charity schools in all parts of England and Wales; to disperse, both at home and abroad, Bibles and tracts of religion; and in general to advance the honour of God and the good of mankind, by promoting Christian knowledge both at home and in the other parts of the world by the best methods that should offer'. Its educational and missionary work is still vigorously carried on, although partly taken over since by the *National Society and the *S.P.G. Through its agency many Church schools and teachers' Training Colleges have been built at home and on the mission field. The Society also has an important publishing house, which issues literature in book and pamphlet form on theological and other subjects.

W. O. B. Allen–E. McClure, *Two Hundred Years*. The History of the Society for Promoting Christian Knowledge, 1698–1898 (1898). W. K. L. Clarke, *A Short History of S.P.C.K.* (1919). Id., 'Two Hundred and Fifty Years of S.P.C.K.' in *Theology*, li (1948), pp. 163–6. E. McClure (ed.), *A Chapter in English Church History*. Being the Minutes of the Society for Promoting Christian Knowledge for the Years 1698–1704, together with Abstracts of Correspondents' Letters during Part of the same Period (1888). Mary Clement, *The S.P.C.K and Wales, 1699–1740*. The History of the S.P.C.K. in Wales from its Foundation to the Early Years of the Welsh Methodist Movement (C.H.S., 1954), with bibl. W. K. Lowther Clarke, *A History of the S.P.C.K.* (London, S.P.C.K., 1959).

SPEAKER'S COMMENTARY, The. A Commentary on the whole Bible, edited by F. C. Cook (1810–89), at the instance of J. E. Denison (1800–73), who was Speaker of the House of Commons from 1857 to 1872. It was published in 10 vols. between 1871 and 1881. Its object was the defence of a conservative attitude to Scripture, to combat the liberalism of *Essays and Reviews* (1860) and similar writings. Cook was assisted by many eminent scholars and theologians, but his work suffered from a somewhat narrow purpose and the Commentary is now almost entirely superseded.

SPEIER, Diets of. See *Speyer, Diets of.*

SPENCER, HERBERT (1820–1903), philosophical and scientific thinker. The son of a schoolmaster, he was practically self-taught. From 1837 to 1846 he was a civil engineer on the railway. Two years later he became connected with the *Economist* and afterwards with the *Westminster Review*. His two earliest writings were *Social Statics* (1851) and *Principles of Psychology* (1855). In 1860 he announced a systematic series of philosophical treatises; they included *First Principles* (1862), *Principles of Biology* (1867), *Principles of Psychology* (1872), and *Principles of Sociology* (1877). From 1886 to 1891 Spencer's health prevented his writing, but in 1893 he completed *Principles of Ethics*.

Spencer was the chief exponent of *Agnosticism in 19th-cent. England. He divided all reality into the knowable (the province of science) and the unknowable (that of religion). He asserted that man could not only be conscious of the unknowable, but that knowledge itself was finally dependent upon the unknowable, and that the Absolute is the fundamental reality behind all things. Nevertheless the Absolute could not be known in the strict sense of the word. Spencer also affirmed his belief in progress as a supreme law of the universe. All his writings were characterized by an extreme individualism.

Autobiography (2 vols., 1904; posthumous). D. Duncan, *The Life and Letters of Herbert Spencer* (1908, with full bibl.). F. H. Collins, *An Epitome of the Synthetic Philosophy* (1889; suppl. 1894; Pref. by H. Spencer). Studies by H. Macpherson (London, 1900), Josiah Royce (New York and London, 1904), J. A. Thomson ('English Men of Science', 1906), W. H. Hudson (London, 1908), and H. [S. R.] Elliot ('Makers of the Nineteenth Century', 1917). W. H. Hudson, *An Introduction to the Philosophy of Herbert Spencer* (New York, 1894; London, 1895; rev. ed., 1904); H. *Sidgwick, *Lectures on the Ethics of T. H. Green, Mr. Herbert Spencer and J. Martineau* (1902), pp. 135–312. H. S. R. Elliot in *D.N.B., 1901–1911*, iii, 360–69.

SPENCER, JOHN (1630–93), English Hebraist. He was a native of Bocton, Kent. In 1645 he became a scholar of Corpus Christi, Cambridge, of which he was elected a Fellow *c.* 1655 and Master in 1667. In 1677 he became Dean of *Ely. After publishing a treatise on the *Urim and Thummim (1669), which he believed to be of Egyptian origin, he devoted himself chiefly to Hebrew studies. The result was his principal work, *De Legibus Hebraeorum, Ritualibus et earum Rationibus libri tres* (1685). Though, owing to the state of contemporary oriental studies, he had to rely almost entirely on second-hand information furnished mainly by the Bible, the classical authors, and the Fathers, he can claim to be the founder of the study of *comparative religion. He endeavoured to trace the connexions between the religious rites of the Hebrews and those of other Semitic peoples, and his work remains a permanent contribution to the subject. His new departure in OT scholarship caused his orthodoxy to be suspected, and his opinions, being too far in advance of his time, were severely criticized and exercised no immediate influence. His work, however, was taken up in the 19th cent. by such scholars as J. *Wellhausen and W. Robertson *Smith.

His Works were reissued at Cambridge (rev. by L. Chappelow), 2 vols., 1727. T. Cooper in *D.N.B.*, liii (1898), p. 359 f.

SPENER, PHILIPP JAKOB (1635–1705), founder of German *Pietism (q.v.). Born of devout Protestant parents at Rappoltsweiler in Alsace, he studied history and philosophy at Strassburg (1651–53). When on a visit to Switzerland, the influence of J. de Labadie (see *Labadists) gave his religion a personal and interior turn, and Spener became increasingly aware of a call to revivify the *Lutheran Church with evangelical fervour. He was appointed minister successively at Strassburg (1663) and Frankfurt (1666). At Frankfurt he introduced 'Collegia Pietatis', devotional meetings which gathered twice weekly in his house, and also issued his *Pia Desideria (1675, s.v.) and his *Erklärung der christlichen Lehre nach der Ordnung des Kleinen Katechismus Luthers* (1677), based on his instructions on the Catechism. His independent outlook, added to his endeavours to give the laity a real part in Church life, offended many of the clergy, and when the ecclesiastical authorities had become openly hostile, he gladly accepted an invitation to Dresden as court preacher (1686). Here in Saxony he gained the warm support of A. H. *Franke (q.v.) and P. Anton, who instituted their 'Collegia Philobiblica'; but he came into conflict with the theological faculty at Leipzig. In 1691 he migrated to Berlin, where he was appointed Rector of the Nikolaikirche, finding an influential ally in the Elector of Brandenburg (King Frederick I of Prussia from 1701). His movement, by this time known as 'Pietism', made rapid progress, and in 1694 the University of Halle was founded, largely under his influence. Though he met with ever increasing opposition from Lutheran orthodoxy, the movement won many ardent supporters. In 1695 J. Deutschmann's *Christuslutherische Vorstellung*, composed for the theological faculty at *Wittenberg, charged Spener with 283 heads of heretical teaching. In 1698 Spener withdrew from the struggle and devoted his last years mainly to pastoral work. His enthusiasm for the reform of the Lutheran Church and his insistence on the inner religious life of the individual had a deep and mainly beneficent influence on German Protestantism. Spener also wrote *Das geistliche Priesterthum* (1677), *Die allgemeine Gottesgelehrtheit aller gläubigen Christen und rechtschaffenen Theologen* (1680), *Natur und Gnade* (1687), *Letzte theologische Bedencken* (1711), and other works.

Life by P. Grünberg (3 vols., Göttingen, 1893–1906). Recent studies by W. Grün (Würzburg, 1934) and H. Bruns (Marburg, 1937). H. Leube, 'Die Entscheidungsjahre der Reformbestrebungen P. J. Speners' in *Neue kirchliche Zeitschrift*, xxxvi (1925), pp. 155–74. K. D. Schmid, 'Labadie und Spener' in *Z.K.G.*, xlvi (1927), pp. 566–83. P. Grünberg in *P.R.E.* (ed. 3), xviii (1906), pp. 609–22; H. Leube in *R.G.G.* (ed. 2), v (1931), col. 685 f.

SPEYER (Spires), Diets of (1526 and 1529).

(1) The Diet of June 1526 marked a new stage in the consolidation of reforming influences in Germany. Instructions sent by *Charles V from Spain in the previous March forbidding all innovations and requiring the enforcement of the Edict of *Worms (1521) were set aside on the ground of his war with the Papacy which had broken out in the interval. The Diet determined that each Prince should order ecclesiastical affairs in his state in acc. with his own conscience.

(2) By the end of 1528 a Catholic reaction had set in, provoked by *Philip of Hesse's repressive measures and his invocation of foreign (French and Hungarian) aid. In response to an appeal from the Pope, Charles V issued a mandate on 30 Nov. 1528 summoning the Diet to Speyer on 21 Feb. 1529. The proceedings were controlled by a strong and well-organized Catholic majority who passed legislation to end all toleration of *Lutherans in Catholic districts. On 19 April six Princes and fourteen cities made a formal 'protest' addressed to the Archduke Ferdinand, defending freedom of conscience and the right of minorities. Henceforward the Reformers were known as 'Protestants'.

(1) W. Friedensburg, *Der Reichstag zu Speier 1526 im Zusammenhang der politischen und kirchlichen Entwicklung Deutschlands im Reformationszeitalter* (Historische Untersuchungen herausgegeben J. Jastrow, v; 1887). J. Ney, *Der Reichstag zu Speier 1526* (Sammlung gemeinverständlicher wissenschaftlicher Vorträge, lxxv; 1889). T. J. Ney in *P.R.E.* (ed. 3), xviii (1906), pp. 589–94, s.v. 'Speier, Reichstage in, 1'. Further bibl. in Schottenloher, iii (1936), p. 15 f. (Nos. 2796ob–74).

(2) J. Ney, 'Geschichte des Reichstages zu Speier im Jahre 1529' in *Mittheilungen des historischen Vereins der Pfalz*, viii (1879), pp. 1–368; also issued separately, Halle, 1880, with primary docc., pp. 291–362. Some of these docc. are translated into Eng. in Kidd, pp. 239–45 (No. xxxii). J.|Kühn, *Die Geschichte des Speyer Reichstags 1529* (Schriften des Vereins für Reformationsgeschichte, xlvii, Hft. 1; 1929). E. Mayer, *Der Speierer Reichstag 1529* (Speyer, 1929). T. J. Ney in *P.R.E.*, loc. cit., pp. 594–603, s.v. 'Speier, Reichstage in, 2'. Further bibl. in Schottenloher, iii (1936), pp. 16–18 (Nos. 27975–28010).

S.P.G.

The 'Society for the Propagation of the Gospel in foreign parts'. This Anglican society was formed in 1701 to assist in the missionary work initiated by the *S.P.C.K. Authorized by Convocation, and incorporated by Royal Charter, it had two main objects before it: (1) to provide the ministrations of the Church for British people overseas; and (2) to evangelize the non-Christian races of the world. In pursuance of these aims the work of the Society has grown in importance and extent and carried the Gospel to British settlers as well as to the heathen all over the globe. Among its financial responsibilities are 60 and more overseas dioceses, and included in its ranks are many non-European workers, besides nearly 1,000 European missionaries.

C. F. Pascoe, *Two Hundred Years of the S.P.G.* [1701–1900]. Based on a Digest of the Society's Records (1901). H. P. Thompson, *Into All Lands*. A History of the Society for the Propagation of the Gospel in Foreign Parts, 1701–1950 (1951).

SPINCKES, NATHANIEL (1653–1727),

*Non-juror. The son of a Northamptonshire rector, he was educated locally and at Trinity and Jesus Colleges, Cambridge. Ordained priest in 1678, he became chaplain to the first Duke of Lauderdale (d. 1682), curate and lecturer at St. Stephen's, Walbrook (1682–5), rector of Peakirk-cum-Glinton (Northants), and in 1687 a prebendary and rector of St. Martin's, *Salisbury. On his refusal to take the oath of *allegiance to William and Mary he was deprived in 1690. In 1713 he was consecrated Bishop by G. *Hickes, but took no title. In the dispute about the *usages, he advocated the retention of the BCP as it then was rather than a return to the First Book of *Edward VI. A man of considerable learning, proficient in Greek, Latin, Anglo-Saxon, and French, with some knowledge of Oriental languages, he was much revered for his personal sanctity. He wrote five treatises on the Roman controversy, one against the French prophets, one against B. *Hoadley, and several against the Usagers, but he is esp. remembered for his sermons and devotional works, which include *A Sick Man Visited* (1712) and a collection of prayers and meditations from L. *Andrewes, W. *Laud, T. *Ken, and others entitled '*The True Church of England Man's Companion to the Closet* with a preface by N. Spinckes' (1721), commonly known as 'Spinckes's Devotions'. He was a close friend of G. Hickes, R. *Nelson, and J. *Kettlewell.

J. Blackbourne, *The Life of the R. Reverend Mr. Nathanael Spinckes* (1731). J. H. Overton, *The Nonjurors* (1902), pp. 129-33 and 384 f.; id. in *D.N.B.*, liii (1898), p. 405 f.

SPINOZA, BARUCH (BENEDICT DE) (1632–77), Dutch Jewish philosopher. He was born in Amsterdam of Portuguese parents. From an early age he was prob. familiar with the works of G. *Bruno, *Maimonides, R. *Descartes, T. *Hobbes, and others who fostered in him religious unorthodoxy, and in 1656 he was expelled by the Synagogue and compelled to leave Amsterdam. He went to Rijnsburg and several other places, at last to the Hague (1670), earning his living by grinding lenses. During his lifetime only a treatise on Descartes (1663) and the *Tractatus Theologico-politicus* (1670) were published. His principal work, the *Ethica ordine geometrico demonstrata*, appeared posthumously (Amsterdam, 1677). It is in five parts: 'De Deo', 'De Natura et Origine Mentis', 'De Origine et Natura Affectuum', 'De Servitute Humana, seu de Affectuum Viribus', and 'De Potentia Intellectus, seu de Libertate Humana'. Spinoza also wrote a *Tractatus Politicus* and a *Tractatus de Intellectus Emendatione* (both first publd. with the *Ethica*, 1677). Several of his letters have also survived.

Spinoza is to be accounted the most thorough-going modern exponent of *pantheism. The foundation of his system is his idea of God as the substance which is 'causa sui' or 'natura naturans' from which follows logically the world as 'natura naturata'. This substance is infinite, with an infinite number of attributes of which, however, only two, thought (*cogitatio*) and extension (*extensio*), are known to man. All individual things are modes of these two attributes, being either bodies or ideas, between which there is a perfect parallelism. The human mind is part of the Divine impersonal intellect which works acc. to necessity. Thus Spinoza denies both freedom and will, the permanence of personality and immortality. The highest human activity is the loving contemplation of the necessity in God (*amor Dei intellectualis*), which becomes possible after the complete victory over the passions among which Spinoza numbers such Christian virtues as humility and penitence. The conceptions of a personal God and an immortal soul being ruled out, Spinoza's religious ideas developed in the *Tractatus* are purely rationalist. His studies on the Bible, carried on from the same point of view, have made him one of the fathers of the modern historical criticism of the Bible. Spinoza's influence on European philosophy was at its height in the 19th cent., esp. in Germany, where F. D. E. *Schleiermacher, F. W. J. *Schelling, G. W. F. *Hegel, and others owed much to his teaching.

The best and fullest ed. of his works is that of J. van Vloten–J. P. N. Land (2 vols., The Hague, 1882-3). Eng. trr. of the *Ethics* and other works by R. H. M. Elwes

(Bohn's Philological Library, 1883); of *Ethics* also by W. H. *White (London, 1883) and by A. Boyle (Everyman's Library, [1910]). Correspondence tr. and ed. A. Wolf (London, 1928). Studies in English by F. Pollock (London, 1880), J. *Martineau (ib., 1882), J. *Caird (Blackwood's Philosophical Classics, 1888), R. MacKeon (New York, 1928), L. Roth (Leaders of Philosophy, London, 1929), H. A. Wolfson (2 vols., Cambridge, Mass., 1934), S. Hampshire (Pelican Books, 1951) and others. L. Brunschvicq, *Spinoza* (Paris, 1894; ed. 3, extended, with title *Spinoza et ses contemporains*, 1923). H. H. Joachim, *A Study of the Ethics of Spinoza* (1901); id., *Spinoza's Tractatus de Intellectus Emendatione*. A Commentary (1940; posthumous). H. F. Hallett, *Aeternitas*. A Spinozistic Study (1930). Überweg, iii, 269-94, with bibl. pp. 664-72. A. S. Pringle *Pattison in *E.B.* (ed. 11), xxv (1911), pp. 687-91, s.v. There is a 'Societas Spinozana' at The Hague which issues a *Chronicon Spinozanum* (The Hague, 1921 ff.).

SPIRES, Diets of. See *Speyer, Diets of*.

SPIRIDION, St. See *Spyridon, St.*

SPIRIT. In Christian theology the word denotes : (1) The intelligent and immaterial part of man or the human *soul in general, whether united with the body in life or separated from it in death, and esp. that aspect of it which is concerned with religious truth and action and is directly susceptible to Divine influence. (2) An order of being which is superhuman in the sense that it is not subject to the limits of time, space, and a bodily frame. In this sense God Himself is said in Scripture to be spirit (in contrast with 'flesh', i.e. humanity). (3) One of the creatures belonging to this order, whether good or evil, i.e. angels or demons. In accord with popular beliefs of the time, certain forms of disease, esp. lunacy and epilepsy, were attributed in the early Christian centuries to the presence of evil or 'unclean' spirits in the human body (see *Exorcism). (4) The Third Person of the *Trinity (see *Holy Spirit, The*).

SPIRIT, Brethren of the Free. See *Brethren of the Free Spirit*.

SPIRITISM. See *Spiritualism*.

SPIRITUAL EXERCISES, The. The famous treatise of St. *Ignatius Loyola, drafted at Manresa and much revised and expanded through the greater part of his life. It contains a series of meditations and rules designed to lead souls to conquer their passions and give themselves to God. This result is obtained by systematic consideration of sin and its consequences (first week, *deformata reformare*), the Kingdom of Christ (second week, *reformata conformare*) culminating in the 'Two Standards', the Passion (third week, *conformata confirmare*), and the risen and glorified Lord (fourth week, *confirmata transformare*). The special characteristic of these meditations and the main ground why they have been an invaluable help for souls is their successful employment in combination of sense impressions, imagination, and understanding, in actuating the will towards the pursuit of perfection. Besides the points for meditation the work contains a wealth of ascetic advice which has led it to be considered an almost indispensable manual of spiritual direction. The Exercises, originally meant to extend over 4 weeks, but which may be compressed into 10 days or an even shorter time, are to-day prescribed in the RC Church for all candidates for orders, and are widely used by many others.

Crit. ed., with introd., notes, and bibl., in *Monumenta Historica Societatis Jesu*, Ser. 2, vol. 1, Madrid, 1919. Eng. tr., with comm. by W. H. Longridge, S.S.J.E., London, 1919. Earlier edd. and trr., &c., listed in Sommervogel, v (1894), cols. 59–75. A. Brou, S.J., *Les Exercices spirituels de S. Ignace de Loyola*. Histoire et psychologie [1922]. R. Debauche, S.J., and others, *Les Exercises spirituels de saint Ignace à l'occasion du 4ᵉ centenaire de leur approbation* (Cahiers de la *Nouvelle Revue théologique*, v, 1949). I. Iparraguirre, S.J., *Historia de la práctica de los ejercicios espirituales de San Ignacio de Loyola* (Bibliotheca Instituti Historici S.I., iii, Bilbao–Rome, [1946 ff.]), with full bibl. Handbooks on the subject in English designed primarily for retreat conductors include the works of H. V. Gill, S.J. (Dublin, 1935), and H. S. Box (London, 1939). Pourrat, iii, 36–65. See also bibl. to *Ignatius Loyoln*.

SPIRITUAL FRANCISCANS. Before St.

*Francis's death two groups, (1) those led by *Elias of Cortona who wished to mitigate the rule of poverty and remodel the order, and (2) the 'Zealots' or 'Spirituals' who wished to maintain the original manner of life, could be distinguished. The latter group became more apparent as the original simplicity of the Franciscan rule was progressively modified, the decretal 'Quo elongati' (1230), e.g., allowing any one to give alms to the order provided it was given to a *nuncius*, chosen by the donor or the order, who would buy the goods required, whilst any surplus money was given into the administration of a so-called 'spiritual friend'. The influence of the teaching of *Joachim of Fiore, whose works under the title, the *Eternal Gospel*, were published in 1254 by a young Franciscan, Gerard of Borgo San Donnino, also encouraged the Spirituals to take an extreme position. For a time, under the generalship of *John of Parma (1247–57), this rigid view was officially accepted in the order.

By the end of the 13th cent. a compromise, implicit in the teaching of St. *Bonaventura who held that all property left to the friars was the property of the Church and that they were permitted to use things necessary for their life and work (*usus pauper*), had been arrived at and was embodied in Nicholas III's decretal 'Exiit qui Seminat' (1279). The solution proved unacceptable, however, to the Spirituals, esp. as the Constitutions of the Chapter-Generals of the time indicate that the abuses denounced by the Spirituals were spreading. The conflict was renewed under Clement V (1310–12; see *Ubertino of Casale*), as a result of which Nicholas's decretal was reaffirmed in 'Exivi de Paradiso' (1312). Meanwhile the Spirituals, now led by Angelo Clareno in the March of Ancona and by P. J. *Olivi in Provence, maintained an intransigent position, and even employed force to seize certain possessions of the Conventuals. Pope *John

XXII, in consequence, resorted to rigorous measures, enjoining them to obey authority under penalty of excommunication and burning four of their number as heretics (1318). But within two or three years the controversy relating to the poverty of Christ again threatened to create a schism within the order, and the danger was increased when the Spirituals were aided by the forces of Louis of Bavaria and the able pen of *William of Occam. As a result the Pope followed up his previous condemnation in the bulls 'Sancta Romana' (1317; here they had been first called '*Fraticelli') and 'Gloriosam Ecclesiam' (1318) by the publication of the decretals, 'Ad Conditorem Canonum' (1322), which affirmed that complete renunciation of possessions did not necessarily constitute the perfect life, and 'Cum Inter Nonnullos' (1323), which declared that the Spirituals' doctrine of the absolute poverty of Christ and his Apostles, both individually and corporately, was heretical. The conflict continued. The Fraticelli and the *Béghards of Provence continued to hold the Spirituals' views, while the whole question of *usus facti* and *dominium* gave rise to *FitzRalph's 'De Pauperie Salvatoris', perhaps the best argued attack on their position. In the face of persecution the numbers dwindled, but the movement itself gave an impetus to the rise of a more rigorous group of the Franciscan Order, the Friars of the Strict Observance (*Osservanti*) who later received papal recognition.

F. von Ehrle, S.J., 'Die Spiritualen, ihr Verhältniss zum Franciscanerorden und zu den Fraticellen' in *Archiv für Litteratur- und Kirchengeschichte des Mittelalters*, i (1885), pp. 509–69; ii (1886), pp. 106–64; iii (1887), pp. 553–623, and iv (1888), pp. 1–190, with full reff. D. S. Muzzey, *The Spiritual Franciscans* (Columbia University thesis, New York, 1907). K. Balthasar, *Geschichte des Armutsstreites im Franziskanerorden bis zum Konzil von Vienne* (Vorreformations-geschichtliche Forschungen, vi; 1911). Decima L. Douie, *The Nature and the Effect of the Heresy of the Fraticelli* (Publications of the University of Manchester, ccxx; Historical Series, lxi; 1932). Heimbucher, i, 697–709, with bibl. L. Oliger, O.F.M., in *D.T.C.*, xiv (pt. 2; 1941), cols. 2522–49, s.v. 'Spirituels', with detailed bibl. A. Ghinato in *E.C.*, xi (1953), cols. 1151–3, s.v. 'Spirituali'. See also bibl. to *Franciscan Order* and to *Fraticelli*.

SPIRITUAL HEALING. The expression,

occasionally used as a synonym of psychotherapy, is properly confined to the attempt to heal the whole personality by prayer and sacramental means, sometimes combined with religious suggestion. Among the methods in general use are *unction and the laying on of hands. Most of those who practise such methods believe that the patient should at the same time make full use of medical skill, but a minority holds that spiritual means should alone be sufficient. It is a common practice among Anglicans to give Absolution and Communion immediately before the anointing. Although bodily healing is not normally expected as a result of unction in the Roman Communion, many miraculous cures are claimed at *Lourdes and other places of pilgrimage. The laying on of hands as a '*sacramental' should be distinguished from the use of a natural gift of healing which does not depend on its possessor being a Christian; but it may be added that such a gift may most profitably be used when combined with Christian suggestion. The possession of the gift of healing was regarded in the early Church as a recommendation in candidates for holy orders.

The *Lambeth Conference of 1920 (Resolution 63) asked the Abp. of *Canterbury to appoint a committee to consider and report upon 'the use of prayer with the Laying on of Hands, of the Unction of the Sick, and other spiritual means of Healing'; the report of the committee appointed under the chairmanship of the Bp. of *Oxford was publd. under the title The Ministry of Healing (S.P.C.K., 1924), with 'Forms of Service suggested for use at the Anointing of the Sick', pp. 38–43. The many discussions of the subject include introductions by P. *Dearmer, Body and Soul (1909); G. Rhodes (ed.), Medicine and the Church. Being a Series of Studies on the Relationship between the Practice of Medicine and the Church's Ministry to the Sick (1910); W. F. Cobb Spiritual Healing (1914); H. Anson, Spiritual Healing. A Discussion of the Religious Elements in Physical Health (1923); H. H. *Henson, Notes on Spiritual Healing (1925); J. R. Pridie, The Church's Ministry of Healing (S.P.C.K., 1926); T. W. Crafer (ed.), The Church and the Ministry of Healing (S.P.C.K., 1934); A. G. Ikin, The Background of Spiritual Healing. Psychological and Religious (1937), and other works by this author; L. D. Weatherhead, Psychology, Religion and Healing (1951). The subject is treated historically in G. G. Dawson, Healing, Pagan and Christian (S.P.C.K., 1935), pp. 112–308 on the Christian period. Evelyn Frost, Christian Healing. A Consideration of the Place of Spiritual Healing in the Church of Today in the Light of the Doctrine and Practice of the Ante-Nicene Church (1940). See also bibl. to Unction and Visitation of the Sick.

SPIRITUAL WORKS OF MERCY, The. There are traditionally seven: (1) converting the sinner; (2) instructing the ignorant; (3) counselling the doubtful; (4) comforting the sorrowful; (5) bearing wrongs patiently; (6) forgiving injuries; (7) praying for the living and the dead. See also Corporal Works of Mercy.

SPIRITUALISM, also 'Spiritism'. A system of (often superstitious) beliefs and practices the purpose of which is to establish communication with the spirits of the dead. Necromancy is an element common to most primitive and many higher religions, an early example occurring in 1 Sam. 28. 8. In its modern form Spiritualism dates from the occult experiences of the American Fox family in 1848, and soon spread to England and the Continent as a reaction against the prevalent materialism. It professes to make contact with the souls of the departed chiefly by means of mediums, accompanied by table turning, automatic writing, and other devices. It has found adherents, also, among professed scholars such as O. Lodge, F. W. H. Myers, and W. F. Prince. The scientific study of these phenomena has been extensively pursued in Great Britain by the Society for Psychical Research (founded 1882). After ruling out conscious or unconscious fraud, of which almost all famous mediums have been convicted, and phenomena susceptible of a natural explanation, e.g. by the abnormal qualities of the medium, there remains a certain number of striking cases such as the foreseeing of free actions and otherwise incalculable events. The theory that such

phenomena are due to preternatural, i.e. demonic, agencies has been advanced by certain Christian theologians who point to the fact that the alleged messages from the beyond are generally hostile to Christian doctrine and of no moral or spiritual value. The practice of Spiritualism is denounced by Scripture (Dt. 18. 11) and by all parts of the Christian Church. In England, and esp. in U.S.A., the cult is highly organized, and has been much exploited for commercial ends.

There is an immense literature on the subject. More serious studies in English include E. Gurney–F. W. H. Myers–F. Podmore, Phantasms of the Living (2 vols., 1886); F. Podmore, Studies in Psychical Research (1897); id., Modern Spiritualism. A History and Criticism (2 vols., 1902); F. W. H. Myers, Human Personality and its Survival after Bodily Death (2 vols., 1903); F. Podmore, The Newer Spiritualism (1910); O. J. Lodge, Raymond, or Life and Death, with examples of the evidence for survival of memory and affection after Death (1916); A. C. Doyle, A History of Spiritualism (2 vols., 1926); H. Price, Fifty Years of Psychical Research. A Critical Survey (1939), with bibl. G. Lawton, The Drama of Life after Death. A Study of the Spiritualist Religion (Columbia University thesis; London, 1933), with bibl. H. Thurston, S.J., The Church and Spiritualism (Milwaukee, Wisc., 1933); G. W. Butterworth, Spiritualism and Religion (S.P.C.K., 1944). F. C. S. Schiller in H.E.R.E., xi (1920), pp. 805–8, s.v. 'Spiritism'; L. Roure, S.J., in D.T.C., xiv (pt. 1; 1941), cols. 2507–22, s.v. 'Spiritisme', both with further bibl. See also the Proceedings of the Society for Psychical Research (London, 1882 ff.) and the Journal of the same body (ib., 1884 ff.).

SPITTA, FRIEDRICH (1852–1924), German Protestant theologian. Born at Wittingen in Hanover, he became lecturer at Bonn in 1880, professor of NT and pastoral theology at Strassburg in 1887, and prof. at Göttingen in 1919. He was keenly interested in Church music and the renewal of liturgical life in German Protestantism, and from 1895 joint editor with J. Smend (1857–1930) of the Monatsschrift für Gottesdienst und kirchliche Kunst. His best-known work is Zur Geschichte und Litteratur des Urchristentums (3 vols., 1891–1901 [–1907]). He also wrote Das Johannes Evangelium als Quelle der Geschichte Jesu (1910) and Die synoptische Grundschrift (1912), both based on the method of source analysis. Among his many other writings are Der Gottesdienst des Urchristentums (1901), Studien zu Luthers Liedern (1906), Jesus und die Heidenmission (1909) and Die Auferstehung Jesu (1918).

A. Meyer in R.G.G. (ed. 2), v (1931), col. 704, s.v.

SPONSOR. Another name for a *godparent at a *baptism.

SPOON, Liturgical. In the E. rites, a spoon is used for giving communion, a portion of the consecrated Host being dipped in the chalice and the two species then conveyed on the spoon to the communicant. In the W. spoons are sometimes used to measure the water at the mixing of the chalice. Mention of them, however, in inventories of Church property is not proof that they have any liturgical significance. See also Fistula.

Rohault, iv [c. 1887], pp. 185–8. Braun, C.A., pp. 265–79, and plate 142, Fig. 565. H. *Leclercq, O.S.B., in D.A.C.L., iii (pt. 2; 1914), cols. 3172–83, s.v. 'Cuiller', with bibl.

SPORTS, The Book of.

SPORTS, The Book of. A declaration defining the recreations permissible on Sunday first issued in 1617 by *James I for the use of the magistrates in Lancs., and extended in the following year to the whole country with instructions to ministers to read it from the pulpit. It was reissued in 1633 by *Charles I, who deprived all clergy who refused to publish it. It permitted archery and dancing, and was designed to counteract the growing *Sabbatarianism fostered by the *Puritans. It derived such legal force as it possessed from the ecclesiastical supremacy conferred on the Crown in 1559; its publication aroused considerable opposition, culminating in its being publicly burnt by order of Parliament in 1643.

Modernized version of text in E. Cardwell, *Documentary Annals of the Reformed Church of England*, ii (1839), pp. 188–93; repr. in P. E. More–F. L. Cross (edd.), *Anglicanism* (1935), No. 261, pp. 565–8. R. W. Henderson, *The King's Book of Sports in England and America* (repr. from the Bulletin of the New York Public Library of November, 1948). M. Levy, *Der Sabbath in England*. Wesen und Entwicklung des englischen Sonntags (Kölner anglistische Arbeiten, xviii; 1933), pp. 192–206, with greater part of Eng. text, pp. 193–5. See also lives of James I cited s.v.

SPOTTISWOODE, JOHN

SPOTTISWOODE, JOHN (1565–1639), Abp. of St. Andrews and historian. He was educated at Glasgow University and embraced an ecclesiastical career in 1583 as a staunch supporter of strict Presbyterianism. When, however, at the end of the century the relations between King and Kirk deteriorated his attitude changed and he became an adherent of the royal policy. In 1603 he accompanied *James I to London and was appointed Abp. of Glasgow. He did not receive episcopal consecration, however, until 1610, when, with two other Scottish bishops, he was consecrated (*per saltum*, on High Anglican principles) at London House. He became the chief agent of the King for suppressing the political influence of the Kirk, being a convinced advocate of *Erastian principles. In 1610 he was Moderator of the Assembly which limited the presbyteries, and in 1615 was translated to St. Andrews. At the General Assembly of the Kirk in 1618 he made himself Moderator without election, and succeeded in imposing the so-called Five Articles of *Perth (q.v.), heavy penalties being inflicted on ministers who refused to conform. In 1635 *Charles I appointed him Chancellor, and as such he gave loyal, if reluctant, support to the introduction of the Liturgy which he regarded as inexpedient. After the riots in 1637 he petitioned the King to desist from his policy, and when, in 1638, the *National Covenant had been signed he fled to Newcastle. He was deposed by the Assembly some months later on a series of unjustified charges, including adultery, incest, and sacrilege. His chief works are *Refutatio Libelli de Regimine Ecclesiae Scoticanae* (1620) and *The History of the Church of Scotland* [to 1625] (1655; rev. ed., G. *Burnet, 1677; new ed., 3 vols., 1847–51), an amply documented official history reflecting the writer's position in the struggle.

Life prefixed to the first ed. of his *History* (1655), ascribed in the fourth ed. (1677) to B. *Duppa, and another by M. Russell prefixed to the latter's ed. of the *History* publd. for the Spottiswoode Society (3 vols., 1847–51), i, pp. xxix–cxxxvi. The fourth ed. of his *History* (1677) contains an appendix by G. *Burnet, with addit. information to date. T. F. Henderson in *D.N.B.*, liii (1898), pp. 412–15. Study by I. Dunlop in R. S. Wright (ed.), *Fathers of the Kirk* (1960), pp. 48–61.

SPURGEON, CHARLES HADDON

SPURGEON, CHARLES HADDON (1834–1892), *Baptist preacher. The descendant of several generations of *Independent ministers, he was born at Kelvedon, Essex, and became a Baptist in 1850. In the same year he preached his first sermon, and in 1852 he was appointed pastor of the Baptist congregation at Waterbeach. In 1854 he went to Southwark, where his sermons drew such crowds that a new church, the Metropolitan Tabernacle in Newington Causeway, had to be built for him. Apart from his preaching activities he founded a pastor's college, an orphanage, and a colportage association for the propagation of uplifting literature. Spurgeon was a strong Calvinist. He had a controversy in 1864 with the *Evangelical party of the C of E for remaining in a Church that taught Baptismal Regeneration, and also estranged considerable sections of his own community by rigid opposition to the more liberal methods of Biblical exegesis. These differences led to a rupture with the Baptist Union in 1887. He owed his fame as a preacher to his great oratorical gifts, humour, and shrewd common sense, which showed itself esp. in his treatment of contemporary problems. Among his works are *The Saint and his Saviour* (1857), *Commenting and Commentaries* (1876) and numerous volumes of sermons (translated into many languages).

Spurgeon's Autobiography, compiled from his Diary, Letters, and Records, by his wife [Susannah Spurgeon] and private secretary [Rev. W. J. Harrald] (4 vols., London, 1897–1900). Letters ed. Charles Spurgeon, son (London, [1923]). Full life by G. H. Pike (3 vols., London, [1892–3]). The many other studies include those of W. Williams (London, 1895), C. Ray (ib., 1903), W. Y. Fullerton (ib., 1920), and J. C. Carlile (ib., 1933). A. R. Buckland in *D.N.B.*, liii (1898), pp. 433–5.

SPY WEDNESDAY.

SPY WEDNESDAY. The Wednesday before *Good Friday, so named as the day on which *Judas Iscariot betrayed Christ (Mt. 26. 14–16).

SPYRIDON, St.

SPYRIDON, St., also 'Spiridion' (d. c. 348), Bp. of Tremithus in *Cyprus. He was a simple peasant who acc. to tradition had suffered in the *Diocletianic Persecution, and after becoming bishop had attended the Council of *Nicaea (though his name is not found in the episcopal lists of signatures). He was certainly present at the Council of *Sardica (c. 343). His life gathered to it many legends. Acc. to one, some thieves trying one night to rob him of his sheep discovered their hands tied miraculously behind their backs and were set free by Spyridon the next morning; acc. to another, he recovered a valuable ornament by the prayers of his deceased daughter, Irene (*Socrates, *H.E.*, I, xii; *Sozomen, *H.E.*, I, xi). Later writers attribute to him the recitation of the Creed at Nicaea that converted the heathen philosopher who had mocked at the Christian faith. Feast day, in the E., 12 Dec.; in the W., 14 Dec.

A Life, apparently the work of Leontius of Naples, survives only in an adapted form in *Simeon Metaphrastes (PG, cxvi, 417–68). H. Engberding, O.S.B., in L.Th.K., ix (1937), col. 744 f.; cf. Bardenhewer, v, col. 138 f.

S.S.J.E. See *Society of St. John the Evangelist.*

STABAT MATER DOLOROSA. A hymn of unknown date descriptive of the Sorrows of the BVM at the Cross. Suggested authors are *Innocent III (d. 1216), St. *Bonaventure (d. 1274), and *Jacopone da Todi (d. 1306). It gradually came into liturgical use in the later Middle Ages, and since 1727 the Roman Missal has prescribed it as a *sequence for the two feasts of the *Seven Sorrows of the BVM and in the corresponding Breviary offices. It is also used at the devotions of the *Stations of the Cross. Its popularity is reflected in the many English translations (among them 'At the Cross her station keeping') and the variety of musical settings (e.g. of G. P. da *Palestrina, F. J. Haydn, A. Dvořák, &c.). Another hymn, 'Stabat Mater speciosa', apparently modelled on the 'dolorosa', which describes the sorrows of the BVM at the manger in *Bethlehem, was also widely popular, though this hymn was never used liturgically.

Crit. ed. of text in C. Blume, S.J.–H. M. Bannister (edd.), Liturgische Prosen des Übergangsstiles und der zweiten Epoche insbesondere die dem Adam von Sanct Victor zugeschriebenen (A.H.M.A., liv; 1915), pp. 312–18. C. Carbone, L' inno del dolore mariano 'Stabat Mater'. Studi critico-dogmatico-litterari (1911). C. Blume, S.J., 'Der Sänger der Sequenz auf die "Schmerzensreiche Mutter" ' in Stimmen der Zeit, lxxxix (1915), pp. 592–8. Raby, pp. 437–40, with bibl. p. 484 f.

STABILITY (Lat. *stabilitas loci*). The vow taken by every monk under the Rule of St. *Benedict to remain till death attached to the monastery of his profession. The vow, which fosters the dependence of the monks on their abbot, was in keeping with St. Benedict's conception of the monastery as a large family, and has in fact exercised a potent and continuous influence in moulding the character of Benedictine monasticism.

Rule of St. Benedict, cap. lviii, 'De Disciplina Suscipiendorum Fratrum'. See also commentaries cited under Benedict, St., Rule of.

STAFF, Pastoral. See *Crosier.*

STAFFORD, ANTHONY (1587–1645?), devotional writer. He was educated at Oriel College, Oxford. He is known as the author of *The Female Glory; or the Life and Death of Our Blessed Lady, the Holy Virgin Mary, God's Own Immaculate Mother* (1635), of which the language of exalted adulation addressed to the BVM and an engraving depicting the *Assumption gave great offence to the *Puritans, esp.

when the work was licensed and defended by W. *Laud.

The book was edited and reprinted in 1860 by Orby Shipley (ed. 4, 1869).

STAINER, JOHN (1840–1901), organist and composer. He was born at Southwark, became a chorister of *St. Paul's in 1849, and organist of St. Benedict and St. Peter, Paul's Wharf, in 1854. In 1857 he was appointed organist at St. Michael's, Tenbury, where he completed his studies under F. Gore Ouseley. In 1860 he became organist of Magdalen College, Oxford, and in 1861 organist to the university. Having been appointed organist at St. Paul's Cathedral in 1872, he carried out important reforms in its service music, which became famous for beauty and reverence under his direction. He helped to found the Musical Association in 1874, and in 1881 became principal of the National Training School for Music. From 1889 to 1899 he was professor of music in the university of Oxford, and from 1900 to his death Master of the Musicians' Company. His principal works were oratorios and cantatas, among them St. Mary Magdalen, performed at the *Gloucester Festival of 1887, *The Crucifixion* (1887), and *The Story of the Cross* (1893). His anthems include 'Lead, kindly Light', 'O clap your Hands', and 'I saw the Lord'. He also composed hymn tunes, many of which are reproduced in *Hymns, Ancient and Modern. In 1899 he published *Dufay and his Contemporaries,* on the development of harmony and counterpoint in the 15th cent., and in 1902 appeared his *Early Bodleian Music* (2 vols., posthumous). His compositions show influences from various schools, notably J. S. *Bach, early English composers, and F. Mendelssohn, and though these are not always completely assimilated, his music is remarkable for its rich melody and power of expression.

F. G. E[dwards], 'John Stainer' in The Musical Times, xlii (1901), pp. 297–309. W. G. McNaught in D.N.B., 1901–1911, pp. 377–9, s.v.; G. Grove [with later additions] in Grove's Dictionary of Music and Musicians (ed. 5 by E. Blom), viii (1954), p. 39 f.

STALLS. The fixed seats for the clergy and others on both sides of the choirs of cathedral and certain other churches. They are usually separated by high projecting arms, often richly carved, and sometimes surmounted by canopies. The seats can frequently be turned back, disclosing a bracket called a '*misericord' (sometimes carved with a grotesque design). Knightly orders have stalls for their members, the Knights of the Garter, e.g., having stalls assigned to them in St. George's Chapel, Windsor. See also *Installation.*

F. Bond, Wood Carvings in English Churches, ii (1910), pp. 1–100.

STANISLAUS, St. (1030–79), Patron of Poland. The son of a noble family, he was educated at Gnesen, and perh. at *Paris, and became Bp. of Cracow in 1072. In imposing strict discipline in his diocese, he soon came into conflict with King Boleslav II whom he repeatedly reproved for his scandalous conduct. Eventually he excommunicated the King, and Boleslav, acc. to tradition, slew him with his own hand while he was offering Mass. He was canonized by *Innocent IV in 1253, and his first biography, which is full of purely legendary material, dates from that time. In 1904 a Polish historian, T. Wojciechowski, provoked much discussion by alleging, in a work on Poland in the 11th cent., that Stanislaus had rightly been put to death for treason. Feast day, 7 May (at Cracow, 8 May).

Two early lives, with miracles cited in procedure for canonization, ed. W. Ketrzyński in *Monumenta Poloniae Historica*, iv (Lwów, 1884), pp. 238–438; excerpts ed. M. Perlbach in *M.G.H.*, Scriptores, xxix (1892), pp. 501–17. 15th-cent. life by J. Dlugossius printed in *AA.SS.*, May II (1680), pp. 200–80. *B.H.L.* (pt. 2, 1901), p. 1134 f., Nos. 7832–43. T. Wojciechowski, *Szkice Historyczne Jedenastego Wieku* (ed. 3, 1950), pp. 221–340, passim, and introd. by A. Gieysztor, pp. 17–19.

STANLEY, ARTHUR PENRHYN (1815–1881), Broad Church Anglican divine. He was educated at Rugby under T. *Arnold and felt his master's influence all his life. In 1834 he went up to Balliol College, Oxford, and in 1838 was elected a Fellow of University College. In the ecclesiastical struggles of the period he consistently advocated toleration for both *Tractarian and liberal extremes. He was Canon of *Canterbury from 1851 to 1858, professor of ecclesiastical history at Oxford from 1856 to 1864, and Dean of *Westminster from 1864 till his death. He made it his aim at Westminster to make the Abbey a national shrine for all, irrespective of dogmatic creed, and gave much offence to orthodox Churchmen by his invitation to all the scholars who had produced the RV, among them a Unitarian, to receive Holy Communion in the Abbey. In the *Colenso case he did not agree with the bishop, but was strongly opposed to disciplinary action against him. His publications include *Life and Correspondence of Dr. Arnold* (1844), *Sermons on the Apostolical Age* (1847), *Memorials of Canterbury* (1854), *Commentary on the Epistles to the Corinthians* (1855), *Sinai and Palestine* (1856), *Three Lectures on the Study of Ecclesiastical History* (1857), *Canterbury Sermons* (1859), *Lectures on the History of the Eastern Church* (1861), *Lectures on the History of the Jewish Church* (3 parts, 1863–76).

Letters and Verses of Arthur Penrhyn Stanley, D.D., between the Years 1829 and 1881, ed. R. E. Prothero (London, 1895). R. E. Prothero–G. G. Bradley, *The Life and Correspondence of Arthur Penrhyn Stanley* (2 vols., 1893). Modern memoir, with further letters ed. A. V. Baillie-H. Bolitho, *A Victorian Dean* (1930). R. E. Prothero in *D.N.B.*, liv (1898), pp. 44–8; G. W. E. Russell in *D.E.C.H.*, p. 571 f.

STANLEY, HENRY MORTON (1841–1904), explorer, administrator, author, and journalist. His original name was John Rowlands, but in 1859 he took the name of Henry Morton Stanley, after his adoptive father. Appointed in 1868 foreign correspondent to the *New York Herald*, he left Zanzibar on 21 Mar.

1871 to seek D. *Livingstone, and they met on the following 10 Nov. This expedition led to various other journeys of exploration between 1873 and 1889, in the course of which he discovered and reported on the nature of over two million sq. miles of the interior of Africa. His communications with the *C.M.S. during his crossing of Africa from east to west in 1874–7 led to the beginning of mission work in Uganda, and his discoveries probably did more than those of any other man to make Christian missionary work possible in the heart of the Continent.

Autobiography ed. by Dorothy Stanley, widow (London, 1909), with life continued from his Journal and Notes, pp. 219–539, and list of his works, which contain much autobiographical material, p. 540. Authorized life by F. Hird (London, [1935]). Other lives by H. W. Little (London, 1890), J. Wassermann (Berlin, 1932; Eng. tr., 1932); shorter lives by A. Montefiore–Brice (London, [1907]), P. Price (ib., [1931]) and A. J. A. Symons ('Great Lives', London, 1933), and, with that of Livingstone, by M. Douglas (London, 1900). W. Hoffmann, *With Stanley in Africa* (1938). C. L. Skinner in *Dict. Amer. Biog.*, xvii (1935), pp. 509–13.

STANTON, ARTHUR HENRY (1839–1913), Anglo-Catholic priest. He was educated at Trinity College, Oxford, and in 1862 ordained to the title of St. Alban's, Holborn, where he remained as a curate for 50 years. The depth and sincerity of his religious faith, combined with his personal attractiveness, won him the confidence of thousands of men in one of the roughest parts of London, while his eloquent and powerful preaching made a great appeal to people of all classes. Like many other Anglo-Catholic priests of that time, he met with much opposition at the hands of the more official elements in the Church.

Faithful Stewardship and other Sermons, ed. E. F. Russell (London, 1916), and *Last Sermons in S. Alban's, Holborn*, ed. id. (ib., [1916]), both ed. from report of a shorthand writer. Further collection of *Sermon Outlines* from his own Manuscripts, ed. id. (2 vols., ib., 1917–19). Life by G. W. E. Russell (London, 1917). E. F. Russell in *D.N.B.*, *1912–1921*, p. 506 f.

STAPELDON, WALTER DE (1261–1326), Bp. of *Exeter. Born at Annery in Devon, he became professor of canon law at Oxford and chaplain to *Clement V. In 1308 he was consecrated to the see of Exeter. As Lord Treasurer (from 1320) he reformed the royal exchequer; he helped to rebuild Exeter Cathedral, and founded Stapeldon Hall, which became Exeter College, Oxford. He was murdered by the London mob for his association with the misgovernment of Edward II.

Register ed. F. C. Hingeston-Randolph (1892). G. Oliver, *Lives of the Bishops of Exeter* (1861), pp. 54–70. C. W. Boase, *Register of . . . Exeter College, Oxford* (O.H.S., xxvii; 1894), pp. iii–v; W. K. Stride, *Exeter College* (1900), pp. 1–11. J. P. V. D. Balsdon, 'Walter de Stapeldon and the Founding of Exeter College' in *Devon and Cornwall Notes and Queries*, xvii (1933), pp. 147–52. F. C. Hingeston-Randolph in *D.N.B.*, liv (1898), p. 92 f., s.v.

STAPLETON, THOMAS (1535–98), RC controversialist. He was a native of Henfield in Sussex and educated at Winchester and New College, Oxford. He became a prebendary of *Chichester under *Mary in 1558, but fled on *Elizabeth's accession to Louvain, where he studied theology. Returning to England, he declined to renounce the authority of the Pope, was deprived of his prebend in 1563, and went back to Louvain. In 1569 he met W. *Allen at *Douai, where he took part in the foundation of the *English College and was appointed professor of divinity. In 1590 he was given by *Philip II the professorship of Scripture at Louvain as the successor of M. *Baius. Shortly afterwards he became Dean of Hilverenbeck, and in 1597 *Clement VIII made him *protonotary apostolic. Stapleton was an able, skilful and erudite controversialist. The circumstances of his time led him to treat esp. of the relation of the Pope to the temporal power, a matter in which he ascribed more limited rights to the Pope than many RC writers. He was a prolific author. Among his more important works are the *Principiorum Fidei Doctrinalium Demonstratio* (1578) on the authority of the Church and *Apostolic succession; *Tres Thomae* (1588), viz. the Apostle, St. Thomas *Becket, and St. Thomas *More; and *Auctoritatis Ecclesiasticae Defensio* (1592), directed against W. *Whitaker.

Lat. tr. of his Eng. works publ. 4 vols., Paris, 1620, with brief life by T. Holland in vol. i (no pagination). Mod. ed. of his Eng. tr. of *Bede's *Historia Ecclesiastica* (orig. publ. Antwerp, 1565; Oxford, 1930; also ed. P. Hereford, London, 1935); Eng. tr. of his Lat. life of Sir Thomas More from *T es Thomae* (orig. publ. Douai, 1588) by P. E. Hallett (London, 1928). J. F. Ledoux, 'De Vita et Scriptis Thomae Stapleton Oratio' in *Annuaire de l'Université Catholique de Louvain* (1865), pp. 290–312. T. Cooper in *D.N.B.*, liv (1898), pp. 101–4, s.v.

STAR OF BETHLEHEM, The. The star seen by the wise men 'in the east' at the birth of Christ and which 'went before them till it came and stood over where the young child was' [i.e. at *Bethlehem] (Mt. 2. 1–11). Several attempts have been made to connect the star with unusual astronomical phenomena at the time, J. *Kepler, e.g., calculating that there was a conjunction of the planets, Jupiter and Saturn, in 7 B.C.; but such rationalizations of the story have now been generally abandoned.

STARETZ. In the Russian Church a religious leader who is sought out as a spiritual counsellor because of his exceptional personal holiness. He has no formal position in the ecclesiastical hierarchy, but owes his authority to his spiritual gifts. He is usually a monk and often has no settled abode. The Russian word meant orig. just 'an old man'.

STAROVERY. Another name for the Russian sect of the *Old Believers (q.v.).

STATE PRAYERS. In the BCP, the prayers for the Sovereign and the Royal Family towards the end of *Mattins and *Evensong.

F. Streatfeild, *The State Prayers and other Variations in the Book of Common Prayer* (1950), pp. 9–30.

STATE SERVICES. In the C of E, the services appointed to commemorate days of national rejoicing or deliverance. Since the Reformation the rubrics have required the anniversary of the reigning sovereign's accession to be so observed. In the 17th cent., services to mark the *Gunpowder Plot (5 Nov.), the beheading of *Charles I (30 Jan.), and the birth and return of *Charles II (both 29 May) were drawn up. Though these services have never been an integral part of the BCP, and thus did not fall under the provisions of the Acts of *Uniformity, they were formerly printed at the end of the Book. In 1859 all except the 'Accession Service' were withdrawn.

STATES OF THE CHURCH. Those parts of Italy and the territory of *Avignon and Venaissin in France which at one time acknowledged the temporal sovereignty of the Papacy. Some of these lands, which were a special gift to the Basilica of *St. Peter at Rome, were also known as the '*Patrimony of St. Peter' (q.v.). Their beginnings date from the edict of *Constantine in 321, which declared the Church capable of holding and transmitting property, but their possession constantly involved the Popes in temporal disputes, which added nothing to their spiritual authority. See also *Stephen II* and *Donation of Constantine*.

In 1791 the Papal territories situate in France were lost to the new republic, and by 1861 the Papacy was left with Rome alone, all the rest having been absorbed in the kingdom of Italy. In 1870 Rome itself was lost and the Pope withdrew into the *Vatican. By the Law of *Guarantees the new secular state allotted to the Pope a pension and declared the basilicas and palaces of the *Lateran and Vatican and the country seat of *Castel Gandolfo to be extraterritorial. The Popes refused to accept this settlement, but in 1929 the *Lateran treaty between Pius XI and Fascist Italy contained an agreement on much the same lines and constituted the 'Vatican City' a separate state.

For the early history of the Papal States see bibl. to *Patrimony of St. Peter*. W. Barry, *The Papal Monarchy from St. Gregory the Great to Boniface VIII, 590–1303* (1902). G. Ermini, 'La libertà comunale nello Stato della Chiesa da Innocenzo III all' Arbornoz (1198–1367)' in *Archivio della Società Romana di Storia Patria*, xlix (1926), pp. 5–126. M. Brosch, *Geschichte des Kirchenstaats* [1500–1800] (Geschichte der europäischen Staaten, xli and xliii, 1880–2). J. *Hergenröther, *Der Kirchenstaat seit der französischen Revolution* (1860). L. C. Farini, *Lo stato romano dall' anno 1815 all' anno 1850* (2 vols., 1850; Eng. tr., 4 vols., 1851–4, vols. i–iii being tr. by W. E. *Gladstone). G. Mollat, *La Question romaine de Pie VI à Pie XI* (Bibliothèque de l'Enseignement de l'Histoire Ecclésiastique, 1932), with bibl. Id., 'La Question romaine sous Grégoire XVI et Pie IX' in *Rev. S.R.*, xxvi (1952), pp. 132–42. G. Schnürer in *C.E.*, xiv (1912), pp. 257–68, s.v.; G. Mollat in *E.C.*, xii (1954), cols. 1272–83, s.v. 'Stato pontificio'. Much material is also to be found in all histories of the Papacy, e.g. that of L. von *Pastor. See also bibl. to *Lateran Treaty* and under individual Popes.

STATION DAYS. Certain days, still marked in the Roman Missal, on which the Pope formerly celebrated Mass in the so-called 'station churches' in Rome. The solemnity was enhanced by processions of clergy and people from one church, called 'collecta', to the station church ('statio' being from early times the term for the Christian assemblies of worship) where the Pope was to offer Mass, while litanies and other prayers were recited on the way. Acc. to tradition it was St. *Gregory the Great who assigned its special church to each of the station days which were marked in the *Sacramentaries, and comprised all Marian feasts and the ferias of Lent. To these days were later added the Ember Days, the Sundays in Advent and from Septuagesima, the Octaves of Easter and Pentecost and certain other feasts and vigils, 84 days in all. The Papal Station Masses fell into disuse esp. during the exile of the Popes at *Avignon, but traces of the ancient custom survive in the indulgences attached to visits to the station churches under certain conditions. Among the most famous of the station churches are *Santa Maria Maggiore for the First Sunday in Advent, the First and Third Mass on Christmas Day, and Easter Day, the church of St. John *Lateran for Holy Saturday, and Santa Sabina, established by *Urban VIII for Ash Wednesday, where the Popes distributed the ashes to the people. The station Masses were also imitated by some churches outside Rome, e.g. at Milan. See also Rome, Churches of.

H. Grisar, S.J., 'Die Stationsfeier und der erste römische Ordo' in Z.K.T., ix (1885), pp. 385–422. Id., Das Missale im Lichte römischer Stadtgeschichte. Stationen, Perikopen, Gebräuche (1925). J. P. Kirch, 'Origine e carattere primitivo delle stazioni liturgiche di Roma' in Atti della Pontificia Accademia Romana di Archeologia, Ser. iii, Rendiconti, iii (1925), pp. 123–41. Id., Die Stationskirchen des Missale Romanum (Ecclesia Orans, xix; 1926). R. Hierzegger, 'Collecta und Statio. Die römischen Stationsprozessionen im frühen Mittelalter' in Z.K.G., lx (1936), pp. 511–54. J. Bonsirven, 'Notre Statio liturgique est-elle empruntée au culte juif?' in Rech. S.R., xv (1925), pp. 258–66. G. Löw, C.S.S.R., in E.C., xi (1953), cols. 1291–7, s.v. 'Stazione liturgica', with further bibl.

STATIONS OF THE CROSS. A series of 14 pictures or carvings, designed for devotional purposes, which depict incidents in the last journey of Christ from *Pilate's house to His entombment. They are commonly arranged round the walls of a church, and it is a popular devotion, esp. during *Lent and *Passiontide, to visit the stations in order, reciting prayers and meditating on each incident. The devotion probably arose out of the practice, attested from an early date, of pilgrims at *Jerusalem following the traditional route from Pilate's house to *Calvary and wishing to reproduce an analogous devotion at home. Its currency dates from the later Middle Ages when it was popularized esp. by the *Franciscans, but the final selection of incidents was not settled until the 18th–19th cents. In the RC Church many *indulgences are attached to the devotion. The 14 incidents of which the stations now consist are: (1) Christ is condemned to death; (2) Christ receives the cross; (3) His first fall; (4) He meets His Mother; (5) *Simon of Cyrene is made to bear the cross; (6) Christ's face is wiped by *Veronica; (7) His second fall; (8) He meets the women of Jerusalem; (9) His third fall; (10)

He is stripped of His garments; (11) He is nailed to the cross; (12) Christ dies on the cross; (13) His body is taken down from the cross; (14) His body is laid in the tomb.

H. Thurston, S.J., The Stations of the Cross. An Account of their History and Devotional Purpose (1906), with reff.

STATUTA ECCLESIAE ANTIQUA (Lat., 'the Ancient Statutes of the Church'). A set of 104 (or 102) canons, dealing mainly with matters of ecclesiastical discipline. They are preserved in very many ancient MSS. Acc. to the *Hispana collection of canons, they were the decrees of the Fourth Council of Carthage of 398, and they are constantly cited as such. Probably they were really drawn up in Gaul, perhaps in the neighbourhood of Arles, in the latter part of the 5th cent. Some modern scholars have tried to connect them with St. *Caesarius of Arles.

The canons, which will be found in all the principal edd. of the Councils under the 'Council of Carthage of 398', have come down in two forms. In the Hispana form (J. P. Migne, PL, lxxxiv, 199–208) they are divided into 104 canons; in another (and apparently more authentic form, PL, lvi, 879–89) there are 102 canons. F. *Maassen, Geschichte der Quellen und der Literatur des kanonischen Rechts, i (1870), pp. 382–94. Hefele–Leclercq, ii (pt. 1; 1908), pp. 102–20. A. Malnory, Saint Césaire, évêque d'Arles (Paris thesis, 1894; also publd. in the Bibliothèque de l'École des Hautes Études, ciii, 1894), pp. 50–62, in defence of Caesarius' authorship; G. *Morin, O.S.B., 'Les Statuta Ecclesiae Antiqua, sont-ils de Saint Césaire d'Arles?' in R. Bén., xxx (1913), pp. 334–42. H. Moureau in D.T.C., ii (1905), cols. 1806–10, s.v. 'Carthage (Canons du soi-disant IV concile de).

STATUTES OF PROVISORS. See Provisors, Statutes of.

STEEN, CORNELIS CORNELISSEN VAN DEN. See Cornelius a Lapide.

STEIN, EDITH (1891–1942), in religion Teresa Benedicta a Cruce, *Carmelite nun. A native of Breslau, of Jewish family, she studied at Göttingen and Freiburg i.Br. under E. Husserl and became a leading figure of the *Phenomenological School. Having lost faith in her ancestral religion in early childhood, she was received into the RC Church in 1922, and from then on sought to interpret Phenomenology from a Thomist standpoint. She took the Carmelite habit at Echt in Holland in 1933; during the occupation of the country by the Nazis she was taken to Poland and put to death in a gas-chamber. Her philosophical publications include 'Beiträge zur philosophischen Begründung der Psychologie und der Geisteswissenschaften' in Jahrbuch für Philosophie und phänomenologische Forschung, v (1922), pp. 1–283, and 'Eine Untersuchung über den Staat', ib., vii (1925), pp. 1–123. Most of her later works remained unpublished at her death.

Collected works ed. L. Gelber–R. Leuven, O.C.D. (Louvain, 1950 ff.). Biography by Sr. Teresa Renata de Spiritu Sancto, Prioress of Carmelite Convent, Cologne (Nuremberg, 1948; Eng. tr., 1952). Hilda C. Graef, The Scholar and the Cross. The Life and Work of Edith Stein (1955).

STEINER, RUDOLF (1861–1925), founder of *Anthroposophy (q.v.) The son of a station-master and apparently given a Catholic up-bringing, he studied natural science at Vienna University and from 1890 to 1897 he was engaged on the Weimar ed. of the works of J. W. Goethe. In the next years he sought to elaborate a scientific method of studying the world of spirit and lectured widely on his con-clusions. He was co-editor for a time of a literary magazine, and in 1902 he became the leader of a German section of the *Theo-sophical Society, but rejected the predomin-antly Eastern associations of the main body. In 1913 Steiner founded the Anthroposophical Society as an independent association, building the Gotheanum at Dornach near Basle as its headquarters. His aim was to develop the faculty of spirit cognition inherent in ordinary people and to put them into touch with the spiritual world from which materialism had long estranged them. He taught the original nobility of the human spirit and a doctrine of immortality, but he seems to have found no place in his system for belief in God. His extensive writings, which were mostly founded on his lectures, include *Die Philosophie der Freiheit* (1894; Eng. tr., 1916), *Das Christen-thum als mystische Tatsache* (1902), *Die Geheim-wissenschaft* (1910), *Vom Menschenrätsel* (1916), and *Von Seelenrätseln* (1917).

The principal authority for his life is Steiner's autobio-graphy, written when he was about 60; it was publd. at Dornach, 1925; Eng. tr., London, 1928. Details of his lectures by A. Arenson, *Ein Führer dürch die Vortragszyklen Rudolf Steiners* (1–50) (3 vols., 1930).

'STEPHANUS' (Estienne). A family of scholar-printers who worked at *Paris and Geneva in the 16th and 17th cents. The two best-known are:

(1) ROBERT ESTIENNE (1503–59), prin-ter to Francis I. He is famous chiefly for his editions of the Scriptures and for his *Thesaurus Linguae Latinae*, first published in 1532, and for long a standard work. In his Latin Bibles, of which those of 1528, 1532, and 1540 are of special importance, he tried to follow as closely as possible the original text of St. *Jerome. Of his editions of the Hebrew OT the chief are those of 1539 and 1544–6. In 1544 he began to print Greek, first using the famous Gara-mond type in his *editio princeps* of *Eusebius's *Historia Ecclesiastica*. Among his later editions of the Fathers is that of *Justin Martyr (1551). His most important edition of the Greek NT is that of 1550. It was the earliest to contain a critical apparatus, and its text is almost identical with the '*textus receptus' (q.v.). His annotations to his Bibles provoked severe attacks from the *Sorbonne, which led him to flee to Geneva in 1551 where he became a *Calvinist. In his NT, published at Geneva in the same year, he introduced the division into verses arranged by himself, which is still used to-day. He subsequently published many of J. Calvin's works.

(2) HENRI ESTIENNE (1528–98), Robert's eldest son, who took over his father's establishment at Geneva. He published

several *editiones principes*, including works by *Athenagoras, *Athanasius (spurious), and *Synesius. His fame rests chiefly on his *Thesaurus Linguae Graecae* (5 vols., 1572), a work of outstanding erudition which remained indispensable to generations of Greek scholars and was twice republished in the 19th cent. (London, 1815–25; Paris, 1831–63).

M. Maittaire, *Stephanorum Historia, Vitas Ipsorum ac Libros Complectens* (London, 1709). A. A. Renouard, *Annales de l'imprimerie des Estienne, ou histoire de la famille des Estienne et de ses éditions* (2 vols., 1837–8). A. J. Bernard, *Les Estienne et les types grecs de François Ier* (1856). H. Stein (ed.), 'Nouveaux Documents sur les Estienne, imprimeurs parisiens (1517–1665)' in *Mémoires de la Société de l'Histoire de Paris et de l'Ile-de-France*, xxii (1895), pp. 249–95. W. Kothe, 'Die Druckerfamilie der Estienne (Stephanus)' in *Zeitschrift für Bücherfreunde*, ix (pt. 1; 1905/6), pp. 179–87. G. A. Crapelet, *Robert Estienne, imprimeur royal, et le roi Fran ois I* (1839). R. Heurtebize in *Dict. Bibl.*, ii (1899), cols. 1982–4, s.v. 'Estienne, Robert'. L. J. Feugère, *Essai sur la vie et les ouvrages de Henri Estienne* (1853). [A.] Elizabeth Armstrong, *Robert Estienne, Royal Printer* (1954).

STEPHEN, St. (d. *c.* 35), protomartyr and, acc. to tradition, the first deacon. Most prob-ably a Hellenistic Jew, he was one of the 'the seven' Apostles to 'serve tables' in *Jerusalem (Acts 6. 5). He also took part in the preaching and performed many miracles (Acts 6. 8 ff.), thus incurring the hostility of the Jews who accused him to the *Sanhedrin. There he delivered the great dis-course reproduced in Acts 7. 2–53, setting out by a recapitulation of Israel's history that God does not depend on the Temple, which he had been accused of blaspheming, and that Christ was the prophet announced by *Moses, whom the Jews had killed. Incensed at his denuncia-tions, his accusers, apparently without formal trial, had him stoned acc. to the Mosaic Law, the witnesses laying their clothes at the feet of Saul, the future St. Paul, on whom Stephen's death made a deep impression. He died con-fessing Christ and asking forgiveness for his persecutors, and was buried by 'devout men' (Acts 8. 2). His tomb was not known until its discovery by the priest Lucian in 415. His feast has been celebrated on 26 Dec. from the end of the 4th cent., while a second feast, 'Inventio S. Stephani', commemorating the finding of his relics, is also kept on 3 Aug. A church was built in his honour outside the Damascus Gate by the Empress Eudocia in 455–60. Its ruins were discovered by the *Dominicans in 1882 and a new church erected on the site. St. Stephen was one of the most popular saints of the Middle Ages, esp. on the Continent. He is also commemorated in the *Canon of the Roman Mass.

For St. Stephen himself the main material is to be found in commentaries on Acts, cited s.v., esp. that of E. Jacquier (Paris, 1926), pp. 194–245. On the church at Jerusalem, M. J. *Lagrange, O.P., *Saint Étienne et son sanctuaire à Jérusalem* (1894); C. Mommert, *Saint Étienne et ses sanc-tuaires à Jérusalem* (Jerusalem, &c., 1912); [L.] H. Vincent, O.P.–F. M. Abel, O.P., *Jérusalem*, ii (1914), pp. 743–804. H. *Leclercq, O.S.B., in *D.A.L.C.*, v (1922), cols. 624–71, s.v. 'Étienne (Martyre et sépulture de saint)'; F. M. Abel, O.P., in *Dict. Bibl.*, Suppl. ii (1934), cols. 1132–46, s.v. 'Étienne (Saint)'; A. P. Frutaz–A. Romeo in *E.C.*, xi (1953), cols. 1298–1304, s.v. 'Stefano, Santo', with further bibl. M. Simon, *St. Stephen and the Hellenists in the Primitive Church* (1958).

STEPHEN I, St. (d. 257), Pope from 12 May 254. He was a Roman by birth of the *gens Julia* and successor to Pope Lucius I. On his accession he (with St. *Cyprian) was at once pressed by Faustinus, Bp. of Lyons, to intervene in the affairs of S. Gaul where Marcian, Bp. of Arles, had embraced *Novatianist doctrines. Soon afterwards he also intervened in *Spain in another dispute arising out of the *Decian Persecution. Later he became involved in a long and bitter dispute with Cyprian over the validity of Baptism by heretics, which Cyprian, with the support of three African councils and Firmilian, Bp. of Caesarea in Cappadocia, held to be null and void; and Stephen even refused to see a delegation from Carthage in 256. Acc. to the (unreliable) *Liber Pontificalis*, he introduced the rule that clerics should wear special clothes at their ministrations. He is traditionally reckoned a martyr, but on insufficient evidence. Feast day, 2 Aug.

Two letters ascribed to Pope Stephen I are pr. in J. P. Migne, *PL*, iii, 1033–44. Jaffé, p. 20 f. The principal sources are Cyprian, *Epp.*, lxvii–lxxv; *Eusebius, *H.E.*, vii, 2–5; and *L.P.* (Duchesne), i, 68 and 154. *AA.SS.*, Aug. I (1733), pp. 112–46, incl. Lat. text of 'Acta', pp. 139–46; 'Acta' translated into Lat. from Armenian text by P. Martin in *Anal. Boll.*, i (1882), pp. 470–84. J. Ernst, *Stephan I und der Ketzertaufstreit* (Forschungen zur christlichen Literatur-und Dogmengeschichte, v, Hft. 4; 1905); id., 'Die Stellung der römischen Kirche zur Ketzertauffrage vor und unmittelbar nach Papst Stephan I' in *Z.K.T.*, xxix (1905), pp. 258–98. H. Koch, 'Zwei Erlasse Papst Stephans I in sprachgeschichtlicher Beleuchtung' in *Philologus*, lxxxvi (1930), pp. 128–32. H. K. Mann in *C.E.*, xiv (1912), p. 288, s.v.; A. Clerval in *D.T.C.*, v (1913), cols. 970–3, s.v. 'Étienne (1) Ier (Saint)'.

STEPHEN II (III), (d. 757) Pope from 752. (He is sometimes counted the third of his name, 'Stephen II' having died four days after his election.) Under him the Papacy finally freed itself from the weakened Byzantine power and became allied with the rising Frank dynasty, a fact which was to determine the relations between Church and Empire for several centuries. When the Lombard king, Aistulf, in defiance of a treaty concluded with Stephen shortly before, besieged Rome, the Pope, after turning in vain to the Byzantine Emperor for help, crossed the Alps to ask the assistance of the Frankish king, *Pepin. After obtaining from him the much discussed 'Donation' of Quiercy (754), Stephen returned to Rome, which was finally delivered from the Lombard threat by Pepin's second campaign in 756. See also *Patrimony of St. Peter*.

Letters preserved in the Codex Carolingus (ed. W. Gundlach in *M.G.H.*, Epistolae, iii (1892), pp. 487–507). Jaffé, i, 271–7. *L.P.* (Duchesne), i, 1886, pp. 440–62. G. Schnürer, 'Der Verfasser der *Vita Stephani II* im *Liber Pontificalis*' in *Hist. J.*, xi (1890), pp. 425–38. C. Rodenburg, *Pippin, Karlmann und Papst Stephan II* (Historische Studien, clii; 1923). L. Levillain, 'L'Avènement de la dynastie carolingienne et les origines de l'état pontifical (749–757)' in *Bibliothèque de l'École des Chartes*, xciv (1933), pp. 225–95. M. Buchner, *Das Vizepapsttum des Abtes von St.-Denis. Studien zur 'Offenbarung des Papstes Stephan II' ('Revelatio') und ihrem Anhang ('Gesta')* (1928). L. *Duchesne, *Les Premiers Temps de l'état pontifical* (ed. 2, 1904), pp. 52–78. Mann, i (pt. 2; 1902), pp. 289–330; Fliche–Martin, v (1938), pp. 423–30. A. Clerval in *D.T.C.*, v (1913), cols. 973–5, s.v. 'Étienne II ou III'; G. Mollat in *E.C.*, xi (1953), col. 1308 f., s.v. 'Stefano II (III)'.

STEPHEN III (IV) (d. 772), Pope from 768. Elected as the candidate of the Frankish party after the expulsion of the usurper Constantine II, he held a synod at the *Lateran (769) to regularize the situation created by Constantine's irregular election and ordinations, which were declared null. The same synod excluded laymen from the Papal elections, confirmed the veneration of images, and anathematized the *iconoclastic Synod of 754. In the following years the Pope tried in vain to prevent a marriage between *Charlemagne and the daughter of the Lombard king, Desiderius, but finally abandoned the Franks and allied himself with the Lombards, a policy revoked by his successor *Hadrian I.

Letters preserved in the Codex Carolingus (ed. W. Gundlach in *M.G.H.*, Epistolae, iii (1892) pp. 558–67). Jaffé, i, 285–8. *LP* (Duchesne), i, 468–85; L. *Duchesne, *Les Premiers Temps de l'état pontifical* (ed. 2, 1904), pp. 123–33. Mann, i (pt. 2, 1902), pp. 361–93. Hefele–Leclercq, iii (pt. 2; 1910), pp. 452–73. A. Clerval in *D.T.C.*, v (1913), cols. 975–7, s.v. 'Étienne III ou IV'; G. Mollat in *E.C.*, xi (1953), col. 1309 f., s.v. 'Stefano III (IV)'.

STEPHEN, St. (975–1038), first king of *Hungary. He became a Christian, with his father, in 985, and on his accession to the Hungarian throne in 997 set out to christianize his country, a work which was partly undone by his pagan successors. A strong supporter of the Papacy, he obtained in 1001 a royal crown from the Pope, part of which is incorporated into the crown preserved at Budapest. At about the same date he established episcopal sees throughout Hungary. He was canonized in 1083 together with his son, St. Emeric. His feast is kept on 2 Sept.; but in Hungary 20 Aug., the day of the translation of his relics, is his principal festival.

Two early lives (prob. 11th cent.), known as the Vita Maior and the Vita Minor, ed. W. Wattenbach in *M.G.H.*, Scriptores xi (1854), pp. 224–42. A 12th cent. life by Hartwick, perh. Bp. of Veszprem, pr. in *AA.SS.*, Sept. I (1746), pp. 562–75, with other material, pp. 456–562. E. Horn, *Saint Étienne, roi apostolique de Hongrie* ('Les Saints', 1899). R. F. Kaindl, 'Studien zu den ungarischen Geschichtsquellen', I: 'Ueber das Verhältniss der Hartvici Eps. Vita S. Stephani zu der Vita Maior und Vita Minor' in *Archiv für österreichische Geschichte*, lxxxi (pt. 1; 1894), pp. 325–37. On the question of the supposed bull granted by Pope *Sylvester II and the crown, L. L. Kropf, 'Pope Sylvester II and Stephen I of Hungary' in *E.H.R.*, xiii (1898), pp. 290–295. On his son Emeric, *AA.SS.*, Nov. II (pt. 1; 1894), pp. 477–91, which includes discussion of sources for the history of the father.

STEPHEN HARDING, St. (d. 1134), abbot of *Cîteaux. He was educated at the abbey of *Sherborne in Dorsetshire. After travelling in France and Italy, he withdrew to Molesme, where he led a life of extreme austerity until, in 1098, he went with part of the community to Cîteaux. There, after being in turn sub-prior and prior, he was elected abbot in 1109. Owing to poverty and the severity of the rule, the monastery was faced with the danger of dying out when, in 1112, St. *Bernard with 30 followers joined the monks, whose sudden increase of numbers soon necessitated other foundations. In order to maintain the original austerity and uniform government, Stephen drew up the 'Carta Caritatis' which established the system of regular visitations and General Chapters. The oldest history of the order, the 'Exordium Cisterciensis Coenobii', is also commonly attributed to him. Besides being a great organizer he was a competent Biblical scholar, as is shown by his emendations of the *Vulgate text destined for the use of Cîteaux. He was canonized in 1623. Feast day, 17 Apr.; in the order, 16 July.

Works ascribed to him, with life from *AA.SS.*, repr. in J. P. Migne, *PL*, clxvi, 1361–1510. Standard ed. of 'Exordium Cisterciensis Coenobii' and 'Carta Caritatis' (prob. not by Stephen Harding in its present form) by P. Guignard, *Les Monuments primitifs de la règle cistercienne* (Analecta Divionensia, x, Dijon, 1878), pp. 59–75 and 77–84 respectively. Life [by J. B. *Dalgairns] (The Lives of English Saints written at the suggestion of J. H. *Newman, 1844; ed. 2 by A. W. Hutton, i, 1900, pp. 3–214). G. de Beaufort, 'La Charte de charité cistercienne' in *R.H.E.*, xlix (1954), pp. 391–433, with reff. to other discussions of its authorship. On the Exordium see J. A. Lefèvre, 'Que savons-nous du Cîteaux primitif?' ib., li (1956), pp. 5–41, with reff. to recent literature.

STERCORANISTS. Persons who asserted that the Blessed Sacrament is digested and evacuated by the recipient. Although they are written of as a sect, there appears to be no evidence that such a sect ever existed.

The name, prob. of 12th cent. origin (from Lat. *stercus*, 'dung'), is found in connexion with the *Berengarian controversies. C. M. *Pfaff, *Dissertatio Theologica de Stercoranistis Medii Aevi, tam Latinis, quam Graecis* (Tübingen, 1750). O. Zöckler–A. Hauck in *P.R.E.* (ed. 3), xix (1907), p. 9 f., s.v. 'Sterkoranisten', with further bibl.; also *O.E.D.* s.v.

STERILIZATION. The sterilization of criminals and defectives by a surgical operation depriving them of the power of begetting children is condemned by Christian moralists and by the RC Church in particular in *Pius XI's Encyclical *Casti Connubii* (31 Dec. 1930).

STERN, HENRY AARON (1820–85), missionary to the Jews. Born of Jewish parents at Unterreichenbach in Hessen-Cassel, he was educated at Frankfurt and Hamburg. Having entered on a commercial career he went to London, where he received Christian baptism in 1840, and in 1842 began to prepare for service as a missionary. In 1844 he was ordained deacon by M. S. *Alexander, Bp. of *Jerusalem, on his way to Baghdad, and for some ten years he conducted itinerant missionary work among the Jews of Mesopotamia, Persia, and Kurdistan. He was ordained priest in 1849 on a visit to London. From 1853 to 1856 and again from 1857 to 1859 he was at *Constantinople. In 1859 and 1862 he made journeys to Abyssinia, where he did notable work among the black Falasha Jews. Anti-European feeling led to the imprisonment of Stern and his fellow-Europeans by King Theodore of Abyssinia in 1864, and only the approach of a British army secured his release in 1868. Somewhat broken in health, he spent the rest of his life in missionary activity in London where many conversions and baptisms took place. His publications include *Dawning of Light in the East* (1854) and *The Captive Missionary* (1868).

Life by A. A. Isaacs (London, 1886). Popular sketch by E. C. Dawson ('Splendid Lives Series', ib., [1901]). W. G. D. Fletcher in *D.N.B.*, liv (1898), pp. 195–7.

STERNHOLD, THOMAS (d. 1549), versifier of the Psalms. Educated at Cardinal College (*Christ Church), Oxford, he entered the King's service and became a court favourite as one of the grooms of the robes. In 1544 he was elected M.P. for Plymouth. His claim to fame rests on his metrical version of the Psalms. A first edition (undated) containing 19 Pss. appeared in 1547; it was dedicated to *Edward VI. A second edition with 37 Pss. was issued posthumously in 1549. In 1557 there appeared a third edition with seven further Pss. by 'J. H.' (John Hopkins, a Suffolk clergyman, d. 1570); and the collection, in the complete edition printed by John *Day in 1562, became generally known as 'Sternhold and Hopkins'. For the most part Sternhold used the familiar ballad metre of 'Chevy Chase', a fact which partly accounts for the popularity of psalm-singing in Elizabethan times.

J. Holland, *The Psalmists of Great Britain*, i (1843), pp. 91–105. M. Patrick, *Four Centuries of Scottish Psalmody* (1949), pp. 27–30. Detailed account of his early edd. of the metrical psalter, composed in conjunction with J. Hopkins, in W. *Beveridge, *A Defence of the Book of Psalms collected into English Metre, by Thomas Sternhold, John Hopkins and Others* (1710). H. L. Bennett in *D.N.B.*, liv (1898), p. 223 f., s.v.

STERRY, PETER (?1613–72), *Puritan divine. He was a native of Surrey and educated at Emmanuel College, Cambridge, where he was elected a Fellow in 1636. In 1643 he was one of the fourteen divines proposed by the House of Lords for the *Westminster Assembly, and from 1645 preached frequently before the Houses of Parliament. In 1649 he was appointed one of O. *Cromwell's chaplains. After the Protector's death he retired to Hackney, where he took pupils and devoted himself to literary work. Sterry's theology was a mixture of *Calvinism and *Neo-Platonism. The former is to be seen in his emphasis on the will of God to the virtual exclusion of secondary causes and human free will, the latter in his conception of the world as emanating from God and, through the Fall and Redemption by Christ, returning to God and to its own original beauty. He was influenced by J. *Böhme, and in an age of sectarian strife was an ardent advocate of mutual tolerance founded in Christian love. Among his more important works, all written in a fine prose, are *A Discourse of the Freedom of the Will* (1675) and *The Rise, Race and Royalty of the Kingdom of God in the Soul of Man* (1683).

V. de Sola Pinto, *Peter Sterry, Platonist and Puritan, 1613–1672. A Biographical and Critical Study with Passages selected from his Writings* (1934). F. J. Powicke, *The Cambridge Platonists. A Study* (1926), ch. v, pp. 174–192. C. Fell Smith in *D.N.B.*, liv (1898), p. 224 f.

STEVENS, WILLIAM (1732–1807), Anglican religious writer. He was born at Southwark, and educated at Maidstone together with his cousin, G. *Horne. He later became partner of a hosier and studied theology in his leisure time. He belonged to the circle of '*Hutchinsonians' and acquired an extensive knowledge of the Scriptures, the early Fathers, and such Anglican divines as L. *Andrewes and J. *Taylor. His works were chiefly pamphlets, collected as Οὐδενὸς Ἔργα ('Nobody's Works') in 1805. One of his best-known studies is *An Essay on the Nature and Constitution of the Church* (1773), in which he defended episcopacy and the legislative power of the Church. He also edited the works of W. *Jones of Nayland (12 vols., 1801) to which he prefixed a Life written by himself in the style of I. *Walton.

J. A. Park, *Memoirs of William Stevens, Esq.* (anon., 1812; enlarged ed. with name of author, 1859). G. Le G. Norgate in *D.N.B.*, liv (1898), p. 233.

STICHARION (Gk. στιχάριον). The liturgical tunic, usually of coloured stuff, worn in the Eastern Church and comparable with the *alb in the West.

Braun, *L.G.*, pp. 92–101.

STICHERON (Gk. στιχηρόν). In the Eastern Church a brief liturgical hymn which is attached to a verse (στίχος) of a Psalm or other Scriptural passage and develops its principal idea.

STICHOMETRY. The practice, dating from at least 300 B.C., of computing the length of a MS. from the number of lines. In the MSS. of the Greek classics the standard line (στίχος) contained 16 syllables; but when stichometric reckoning came to be applied to Biblical MSS., it seems that a 15-syllable line was sometimes used for the Gospels. Among the oldest extant Biblical stichometric tables is the list of the Pauline Epistles in the *Codex Sinaiticus.

STIGAND (d. 1072), Abp. of *Canterbury. After filling the see of *Winchester from 1047, he was appointed Abp. of Canterbury in 1052 in succession to Robert of Jumièges, who had been outlawed by the witan. His primacy, however, was not recognized at Rome till 1058, and then by Benedict X, who in the following year was himself deposed as a schismatic Pope. As Stigand's position thus became uncertain, it provided a pretext for William I's invasion in 1066, though after William had established himself, Stigand submitted and assisted at the coronation. In 1070 he was deposed on a number of charges, and succeeded by *Lanfranc.

W. Hunt, *A History of the English Church from its Foundation to the Norman Conquest*, 597–1066 (1899), pp. 402 and 405–13. F. M. Stenton, *Anglo-Saxon England* (1943), pp. 459–61, 559 f., 616, 651–3. W. Hunt in *D.N.B.*, liv (1898), p. 369 f., with reff.

STIGMATIZATION. The reproduction of the wounds of the Passion of Christ in the human body. It is a phenomenon usually accompanied by other manifestations of the same category, such as levitation, *bilocation, and telepathic faculties, as well as by abnormal physical states such as lameness or blindness not due to organic causes, and almost complete abstinence from food and sleep. Stigmata may either be invisible, i.e. the stigmatized person experiences only the pain without any exterior signs, or visible, in which case they normally consist of wounds or blood blisters on hands, feet, and near the heart, also on the head (Crown of Thorns) or shoulders and back (carrying of the Cross and Scourging). They do not become septic and resist ordinary treatment, but are liable to periodical bleedings, mostly on Fridays and during Lent and Passion-tide. Various natural explanations have been advanced; and though it is widely held that supernatural influences have to be admitted in many cases, a certain abnormal physical predisposition, acted upon by a deeply religious mind imbued with an extraordinary devotion to the Passion of our Lord, would seem to account for much in these phenomena. The official attitude of the RC Church has always been guarded, and stigmatization has never been made a reason for *canonization; among the more than 330 known stigmatized there are only some 60 saints and beati. None of them appear before the 13th cent., when the growing devotion to the suffering Christ seems to have occasioned their appearance. The first saint known to have received the stigmata is St. *Francis of Assisi; but since then cases have been numerous, esp. among women. Some of the best known are St. *Catherine of Siena (invisible), St. *Catherine of Genoa, Anna Katharina *Emmerick, St. Gemma *Galgani, and Therese *Neumann. The Stigmata of St. Francis are commemorated by a feast on 17 Sept.

A. Imbert-Gourbeyre, *La Stigmatisation, l'extase divine et les miracles de Lourdes* (2 vols., 1894), esp. vol. i, and vol. ii, pp. 1–231. H. Thurston, S.J., *The Physical Phenomena of Mysticism* (posthumously ed. J. H. Crehan, S.J., 1952), pp. 32–129 (various essays repr. from scattered sources, with corrections). G. Wunderle, *Zur Psychologie der Stigmatisation* (1938). Jeanne Danemarie [pseudonym for Marthe Ponet-Bordeaux], *Le Mystère des stigmatisés de Catherine Emmerich à Thérèse Neumann* (1933; Eng. tr., 1934). É. Amann in *D.T.C.*, xiv (pt. 2; 1941), cols. 2616–24, s.v. 'Stigmatisation'.

STILLINGFLEET, EDWARD (1635–99), Bp. of *Worcester. He was born at Cranborne in Dorset and educated at St. John's College, Cambridge, of which he became a Fellow in 1653. In 1657 he was appointed rector of Sutton, Bedfordshire, and in 1665 rector of St. Andrew's, Holborn, where he soon made a name as a preacher. Having won the favour of *Charles II he was given several preferments, becoming Archdeacon of London in 1677 and Dean of *St. Paul's in 1678. He was less esteemed under *James II, but after the Revolution of 1689 he was immediately appointed Bp. of Worcester.

Stillingfleet was a man of *Latitudinarian views. His first book, the *Irenicum* (1659), advocated a union between *Episcopalians and

*Presbyterians. While opposing Nonconformity, it treated forms of Church government as inessential. The work was re-edited in 1662 with an appendix, in which Stillingfleet propounded the view that the Church was a society distinct from the state with its own rights and privileges. In the same year he published *Origines Sacrae*, an apologetic work dealing with the Divine authority of Scripture. In 1664 he replied to the *Jesuit account of the controversy between W. *Laud and J. *Fisher in his *Rational Account of the Grounds of the Protestant Religion*. The book had a great success and was followed by other controversial writings against RCs, *Socinians and J. *Locke. Stillingfleet held Locke's *Essay Concerning Human Understanding* (1690) to be detrimental to the Trinitarian faith and published three pamphlets in reply (1696–7). His famous *Origines Britannicae* (1685) deal with the sources of the British Church. His *Sermons*, of which several volumes were published, enjoyed a long popularity.

Works (6 vols., London, 1709–10), with life [by R. Bentley] in vol. i, pp. 1–46. J. Nankinvell, 'Edward Stillingfleet, Bishop of Worcester 1689–99' in *Transactions of the Worcestershire Archaeological Society*, xxii for 1945 (1946), pp. 16–34; sep. publd. with list of his ordinations appended (1946). W. H. *Hutton in *D.N.B.*, liv (1898), pp. 375–8; id. in *D.E.C.H.* (1912), p. 574 f.

STOCK, St. SIMON. See *Simon Stock, St.*

STOCKHOLM CONFERENCE (1925). It grew out of an appeal for peace and fellowship sent out by Christian leaders in several neutral countries at the outset of the First World War (1914), followed by a further appeal by N. *Söderblom, Abp. of Upsala, in June 1917 for an immediate conference. After the end of the war, plans were made and the Universal Christian Conference on *Life and Work eventually met at Stockholm, 19–30 Aug. 1925, to promote Christian influences on political, social, and economic life in the modern world. The four Presidents were the Abp. of Upsala, the Abp. of *Canterbury (with F. T. Woods, Bp. of *Winchester, as his deputy), the Patriarch of *Constantinople (with S. Germanos, Abp. of Thyateira, as his deputy), and Dr. A. J. Brown of New York from America. Over 500 representatives, drawn from most of the larger religious bodies except the RC Church, took part. The subjects of the discussions were: The Purpose of God for Humanity and the Duty of the Church; The Church and Economic and Industrial Problems; The Church and International Relations; The Church and Christian Education; and Methods of Co-operative and Federative Efforts by the Christian Communions. The conference issued a 'Message', but no official findings. Its work was carried further in the conferences of *Oxford (1937) and *Amsterdam (1948).

G. K. A. Bell (ed.), *The Stockholm Conference 1925*. The Official Report of the Universal Christian Conference on Life and Work held in Stockholm, 19–30 August, 1925 (1926).

STOICISM. A Greco-Roman school of philosophy, founded at *Athens by Zeno of Citium (335–263 B.C.). His chief pupil was Cleanthes of Assos (331–232), whose work was carried on by Chrysippus of Soli (*c.* 280–207). The system may be described as a form of materialistic pantheism or monism in contrast to *Platonic idealism on the one hand and *Epicurean hedonism on the other. The Stoics believed in law—the law of nature and the law of conscience or duty. To them God is the immanent all-pervading energy by which the natural world is created and sustained. He is also the world reason or '*Logos' which manifests itself in the order and beauty of the world. To the Stoics the good man is the wise man, and his wisdom consists in conformity to nature, i.e. in living according to the law of the universe embodied in the Divine reason. This 'life according to nature' was open to all men, even to slaves. Stoic ethics had a wide and tonic influence in the Greco-Roman world, and its religious spirit is well illustrated in the famous 'Hymn to Zeus' of Cleanthes. The Stoic *Seneca was reputed to have engaged in correspondence with St. *Paul.

Fragments of earlier Stoics collected in H. von Arnim, *Stoicorum Veterum Fragmenta* (4 vols. [vol. iv, index], Teub., 1903–24). For the editions of Seneca, Epictetus and Marcus Aurelius, see s.vv. Studies in English include E. V. Arnold, *Roman Stoicism* (1911); R. D. Hicks, *Stoic and Epicurean* (1911); E. R. Bevan, *Stoics and Sceptics* (1913; four lectures); R. M. Wenley, *Stoicism and its Influence* (1924). A. Dyroff, *Die Ethik der alten Stoa* (1897); M. Pohlenz, *Die Stoa*. Geschichte einer geistigen Bewegung (2 vols., 1948–9). Überweg, i, 410–31, 475–83, 486–503, with bibl. pp. 125*–30*, 149*–56*, 157*–67*. R. D. Hicks in *E.B.* (ed. 11), xxv (1911), pp. 942–51, s.v.; E. V. Arnold in *H.E.R.E.*, xi (1920), pp. 860–4, s.v.

STOLBERG, FRIEDRICH LEOPOLD, Graf zu (1750–1819), poet. A member of the German poets' circle, Goettinger Hain, he was an admirer and imitator of J. G. *Klopstock and a friend of J. W. Goethe, and became a translator of Homer, Aeschylus, and other classical authors. After filling the posts of envoy of the Protestant Prince Bp. of Lübeck to the Danish court (1777), of Danish envoy to Berlin (1789), and other offices, he was received into the RC Church in 1800. His most important work after his conversion is the *Geschichte der Religion Jesu Christi* in 15 vols. (1806–18), an influential though not always scholarly history of Christianity from OT times to the death of St. *Augustine. Among his numerous poetical and prose works a Life of *Alfred the Great (1817) and the devotional *Büchlein von der Liebe* (1819) became popular among his contemporaries.

Gesammelte Werke der Brüder Christian und Friedrich Leopold Grafen zu Stolberg (20 vols., Hamburg, 1820–5; ed. 2, 1827). T. Menge, *Der Graf Friedrich Leopold und seine Zeitgenossen* (2 vols., 1862); J. Janssen, *Friedrich Leopold Graf zu Stolberg*, grösstentheils aus dem bisher noch ungedruckten Familiennachlass dargestellt (2 vols., 1876–1877); id., *Friedrich Leopold Graf zu Stolberg. Sein Entwicklungsgang und sein Wirken im Geiste der Kirche* (1882; ed. 4 by L. von *Pastor, 1910). H. Jansen (ed.), *Briefe aus dem Stolberg- und Novalis-Kreis* (1932), with full introd. E. Schmidt in *Allgemeine Deutsche Biographie*, xxxvi (1893), pp. 350–67, s.v. 'Stolberg-Stolberg: Friedrich Leopold', with literature to date; P. Wittmann in *C.E.*, xiv (1912), p. 299 f., s.v.

STOLE. A liturgical vestment, consisting of a strip of silk *c*. 8 ft. long and 4 ins. wide. Its origin is doubtful. It was possibly first used in the manner of a neckcloth or a handkerchief in the E., where the deacon's stole is first mentioned in the 4th cent. In the W. it is first attested for Spain in the 6th cent. When it came to Rome in the 8th cent. it was worn under the dalmatic, whereas in the E. it was worn outside, as it still is in the *Ambrosian Rite of Milan. The priest's stole is not mentioned in the E. till the 8th cent., but was in general use in the W. from the 9th, when the priests of the Frankish Empire were bidden always to wear it as a sign of their calling, e.g. by the Synod of Mainz in 813. At Rome the stole was originally called 'orarium', the *stola* being Gallican and introduced into Italy *c*. 11th cent.

The stole has become the distinctive vestment of the deacon, who wears it like a sash over the left shoulder, its ends being fastened together under the right arm. It is, however, also a regular vestment of the priest, who wears it round the neck. When worn in conjunction with the other Eucharistic vestments, its ends are crossed over the breast, otherwise they fall straight down in front. Acc. to Latin practice, the bishop always wears it in this latter way. Besides its use at Mass, it is also worn when touching the Blessed Sacrament, when administering the Sacraments, and very generally when preaching. Its colour depends on that of the other vestments and on the occasion, e.g. when hearing confessions the priest wears a purple stole. In the E. rite the priest's stole is called an '*epitrachelion', that of the deacon an '*orarion' (qq.v.). See also *Broad Stole*.

Braun, *LG*, pp. 562–620. J. Braun, S.J., *Handbuch der Paramentik* (1912), pp. 154–64. Id. in *C.E.*, xiv (1913), p. 301 f. s.v.

STONE, DARWELL (1859–1941), *Anglo-Catholic theologian. Educated at Merton College, Oxford, he was ordained deacon in 1883, and after a short period of parish work at Ashbourne (1883–4) became vice-principal (1885) and later principal (1888) of Dorchester (Oxon.) Missionary College. From 1909 to 1934 he was principal of Pusey House, Oxford. Throughout his adult life he was a strenuous upholder of High Church principles, defending the more traditional theology of R. W. *Church and H. P. *Liddon against the teaching of the *Lux Mundi* School. In later life he became increasingly the leader of the Anglo-Catholic Movement in the C of E. He was strongly opposed to the project of Prayer Book revision. Stone's writings were characterized by wide and accurate learning and fairness towards his opponents. Among the chief were *Holy Baptism* (1899), *Outlines of Christian Dogma* (1900), *The Christian Church* (1905), a *History of the Doctrine of the Holy Eucharist* (1909), and *The Reserved Sacrament* (1917). From 1915 till his death he was editor of the projected *Lexicon of Patristic Greek*.

F. L. Cross, *Darwell Stone, Churchman and Counsellor* (1943).

STONYHURST COLLEGE. One of the largest RC schools in England. Conducted by the *Jesuit Fathers, it traces its origin back to Elizabethan days when a college for English boys was founded at St.-Omer (1592), and subsequently transferred to Bruges (1762) and Liége (1773). In 1794 it moved to Stonyhurst Hall in Lancashire. The standard of education is that of the great public schools. Stonyhurst Observatory has been made famous by many astronomers of European reputation.

A. Hewitson, *Stonyhurst College, Past and Present* (Preston, 1870). J. Gerard, S.J., *Stonyhurst College. Its Life Beyond the Seas, 1592–1794, and on English Soil, 1794–1894* (Centenary Record. Belfast, 1894). G. Gruggen, S.J.–J. Keating, S.J., *Stonyhurst. Its Past History and Life in the Present* (1901). A. Rimmer, *Stonyhurst Illustrated* (1884). Hubert Chadwick, *St. Omers to Stonyhurst* (1962). F. Irwin, S.J., in *C.E.*, xiv (1912), p. 309 f., s.v.

STORCH, NICHOLAS (d. 1530), *Anabaptist. A Saxon clothmaker, he became leader of the *Zwickau Prophets (q.v.) after T. *Münzer's flight. Later he and his associates, having been compelled to leave Zwickau, arrived at *Wittenberg (1521). Here their success was only temporary, and Storch is next met with in West Thuringia in 1523 and at Strassburg in 1524. After the collapse of Münzer's rebellion (1525), he fled to Silesia; then to Poland, where he established an Anabaptist sect; and finally to Bavaria, where he died. He taught that, since all godly men were under the direct influence of the Holy Spirit, a ministerial and sacramental Church was unnecessary, and that the Church was shortly to suffer violent purification.

R. Bachmann, *Niclas Storch, der Anfänger der Zwickauer Wiedertäufer* (Zwickau, 1880). Schottenloher, ii (1935), p. 307 (Nos. 20732–5). See also bibl. to *Zwickau Prophets*.

STOUP (O.E. *stéap*). A basin near the entrance of a church containing *holy water with which the faithful may sprinkle themselves. Holy-water fonts were perhaps originally derived from the fountains in the *atrium of the old basilicas, in which those who entered washed their hands and faces. They began to come into more general use with the custom of sprinkling the people with holy water at the Sunday Mass, which was introduced in the middle of the 9th cent. The stoups are of various forms, either let into the wall or standing on a socle, and often richly ornamented. In England they were usually of stone and built into a small niche, and many specimens are preserved in pre-Reformation churches. Their use is universal in RC churches and has been widely revived in the C of E in recent times.

F. Bond, *The Chancel of English Churches* (1916), Appendix, 'The Holy Water Stoup', pp. 255–8. H. *Leclercq, O.S.B., in *D.A.C.L.*, ii (pt. 1, 1910), pp. 758–71, s.v. 'Bénitier'.

STOWE MISSAL. The oldest known Massbook of the early Irish Church, formerly preserved at Stowe House in Bucks. It contains, besides extracts from St. John's Gospel, an *Ordinary and *Canon of the Mass, propers for three special Masses, an office of Baptism and of the Visitation of the Sick, a treatise in Irish on the ceremonies of the Mass, and three short Irish spells. It has been variously dated from the 6th to the 10th cents. It is now in the Library of the Royal Irish Academy at Dublin (D. II. 3).

G. F. Warner, *The Stowe Missal* (*Henry Bradshaw Society, 2 vols., 1906, 1915).

STRABO, WALAFRID. See *Walafrid Strabo.*

STRATFORD, JOHN DE (d. 1348), Abp. of *Canterbury. He was a native of Stratford-on-Avon. After being Archdeacon of *Lincoln and Dean of the Court of *Arches, he succeeded in getting himself appointed Bp. of *Winchester in 1323, a step which temporarily lost him the favour of Edward II. In 1327 he drew up the six articles against Edward II and counselled him to abdicate. From 1330, the year in which he was first appointed Chancellor by Edward III, he was the chief adviser of the young King, and in 1333 became Abp. of Canterbury. The following years were mainly spent in political affairs, including repeated negotiations with France. When, in 1340, Edward returned from an unsuccessful expedition to Flanders, Stratford's enemies attributed to him the failure and the King brought a series of charges against him. Stratford, however, inspired by the example of St. Thomas *Becket, stood firm and finally obtained recognition of the principle that peers should be tried only by their equals in full Parliament. Though soon reconciled to the King, he retired from political life and devoted himself to his ecclesiastical duties. He was a benefactor of Stratford-on-Avon, where his devotion to Becket led him to establish a chantry in his honour in the parish church and to endow a college of priests.

W. F. *Hook, *Lives of the Archbishops of Canterbury*, iv (1865), pp. 1–79. C. L. Kingsford in *D.N.B.*, lv (1898), pp. 30–2, s.v., with reff.

STRAUSS, DAVID FRIEDRICH (1808–1874), German theologian. A native of Ludwigsburg in Württemberg, in 1821 he entered the seminary at Blaubeuren, where he was a pupil of F. C. *Baur, and in 1825 went to the *Tübingen Stift. Here he came under the influence of F. D. E. *Schleiermacher (with whose doctrines he later lost sympathy) and of G. W. F. *Hegel's philosophy. After studying in Berlin, he was appointed in 1832 'repetent' at the Stift and lecturer on Hegelian philosophy at Tübingen university. His famous *Leben Jesu*, in which he applied the 'myth theory' to the life of Christ, appeared in 1835–6. The book denied the historical foundation of all supernatural elements in the Gospels, which were assigned to an unintentionally creative legend (the 'myth'), developed between the death of Christ and the writing of the Gospels in the 2nd cent. The growth

of primitive Christianity was to be understood in terms of the Hegelian dialectic. The work, which exercised a deep influence on subsequent German Protestant theology, roused a storm of indignation and led to Strauss's dismissal from his post at Tübingen. In 1839 an attempt to obtain for him a Professorship of Theology at Zürich came to nothing. His next work, *Die christliche Glaubenslehre* (2 vols., 1840–1) is a polemical history of Christian doctrine from the NT and the Fathers to its dissolution in Hegelian philosophy. Strauss now turned his attention to politics and, in the literary sphere, to biography. His writings of this period include *Ulrich von Hutten* (3 vols., 1858–60) and *Hermann Samuel Reimarus* (1862). In 1864 he published a slightly more positive version of his first work, *Leben Jesu für das deutsche Volk*, and in 1865 *Der Christus des Glaubens und der Jesus der Geschichte* (1865), an attack on Schleiermacher's attempt to combine the 'historical Jesus' with the 'Christ' of dogma. His last work, *Der alte und der neue Glaube* (1872; Eng. trans., *The Old Faith and the New*, 1873), is essentially a negation of Christianity in favour of scientific materialism and rejects human immortality.

Gesammelte Schriften (incomplete), ed. E. Zeller (12 vols., Bonn, 1876–8); *Ausgewählte Briefe*, ed. id. (ib., 1895); *Briefwechsel zwischen Strauss und Vischer*, ed. A. Rapp (Veröffentlichungen der deutschen Schillergesellschaft, xviii and xix; 1952–3). E. Zeller, *David Friedrich Strauss in seinem Leben und seinen Schriften* (1874; Eng. tr., 1874); A. Hausrath, *David Friedrich Strauss und die Theologie seiner Zeit* (2 vols., 1876–8); T. Ziegler, *David Friedrich Strauss* (2 vols., Strassburg, 1908). A. *Schweitzer, *Von Reimarus zu Wrede* (1906), pp. 67–119 (Eng. tr., *The Quest of the Historical Jesus*, 1910, pp. 68–120). T. Ziegler in *P.R.E.* (ed. 3), xix (1907), pp. 76–92, s.v.; P. Nober, S.J., in *E.C.*, xi (1953), cols. 1407–12, s.v., with further bibl.

STREET, GEORGE EDMUND (1824–81), architect. A native of Woodford, Essex, he was educated at Mitcham and Camberwell. He soon developed an enthusiastic interest in ecclesiastical architecture and, obtaining an appointment under G. G. *Scott, became a leader in the Gothic revival. In 1849 he set up an office of his own and, after making the acquaintance of B. *Webb, became a member of the *Ecclesiological Society. His first successes were several churches in the West country, esp. Cornwall. After some good work for W. J. *Butler at Wantage, where he resided from 1850, he was appointed Diocesan Architect by S. *Wilberforce, Bp. of *Oxford. He continued to travel extensively to study French and German churches, and in 1855 his design for the new cathedral at Lille only just missed acceptance. He was the architect of the Crimea Memorial Church at *Constantinople (1864–9). Meanwhile at home he had carried through a large number of churches and institutions, among them St. Peter's, Plymouth, Cuddesdon Theological College, the Convent at East Grinstead, St. Peter's, Bournemouth, the nave of Bristol Cathedral, St. Mary Magdalene's, Paddington, All Saints', Clifton, and St. Margaret's, Liverpool. He was the first to make modern students of architecture aware of the glories of the church of Santiago of *Compostela, mainly through his *Gothic Architecture in Spain* (1865). The apex of his influence was marked by the invitation to design the new Law Courts in the Strand, which he did not live to see completed.

Arthur Edmund Street (son), *Memoir of George Edmund Street, R.A.* (1888; with complete list of Street's works). P. Waterhouse in *D.N.B.*, lv (1898), pp. 42-5.

STREETER, BURNETT HILLMAN (1874-1937), NT scholar. He was educated at Queen's College, Oxford, and was a Fellow from 1905 to 1933 and Provost from 1933 to 1937. His researches into the *Synoptic problem, notably in *Oxford Studies in the Synoptic Problem* (ed. W. *Sanday, 1911), went far towards winning the assent of English Biblical scholarship to the priority of St. Mark's Gospel and the existence of ' *Q'. In 1924 he published a large-scale work, *The Four Gospels*, in which he set out his conclusions on the *Caesarean text of the NT and *Proto-Luke. He also took a keen interest in the problems confronting the Christian faith in its relations with the modern outlook on life. In *Reality* (1926) he sought to correlate science with theology. His other publications included essays in *Foundations* (1912), *Concerning Prayer* (1916), *Immortality* (1917), *The Spirit* (1919), and *Adventure* (1926), all of which he edited. In 1932 he delivered a course of *Bampton lectures on *The Buddha and the Christ*. He was an active supporter of the *Student Christian Movement and of the *Modern Churchmen's Union, and also (at the end of his life) of the *Oxford Group Movement.

L. W. Grensted in *D.N.B., 1931-40*, pp. 836-8, s.v.

STREITGESPRÄCHE (Ger., 'controversial discussions'). In *form-critical analysis, R. *Bultmann's designation for the group of *apophthegmata in the Gospels, introduced by a controversial pronouncement by Christ's enemies. The Question on the Tribute Money (Mk. 12. 13-17) is a characteristic instance.

STRIGEL, VICTORINUS (1524-69), Reformation theologian. A native of Kaufbeuren in Swabia, he was educated at Freiburg and later at *Wittenberg, where he was much influenced by P. *Melanchthon. After teaching for a time at Erfurt, in 1548 he became first professor and rector of the new school at Jena, founded by the followers of J. A. *Ernesti. Here he expounded, in opposition to the strict Lutheranism of M. *Flacius, more moderate and conciliatory doctrines and defended a form of *synergism. At Weimar in Aug. 1560 he found himself involved in a disputation in the presence of the court on the relation of the human will to divine grace in the work of conversion. The five heads of discussion—*de libero arbitrio, de definitione legis et evangelii, de *Majorismo, de *Adiaphorismo*, and *de academica ἐποχή*—indicate the points at which Strigel's teaching departed from the stricter

Lutheranism, it being opposition to Strigel at Weimar that led Flacius to the formula that original sin is the substance of the natural man. In 1563 he was appointed professor at Leipzig, but four years later opposition to his liberal outlook led to his withdrawal, and he became a professor at Heidelberg. He wrote extensively on philological and historical as well as on theological subjects, though many of his works were not published till after his death. They include a commentary on almost the whole Bible.

Collection of his *Opuscula Quaedam Theologica*, publ. Hanover, 1598. V. A. Nordman, *Victorinus Strigelius als Geschichtslehrer* (Helsingfors thesis, Åbo, 1930), with reff. to earlier litt. G. Kawerau in *P.R.E.* (ed. 3), xix (1907), pp. 97-102, s.v.

STRONG, THOMAS BANKS (1861-1944), Dean of *Christ Church, Oxford. Educated at Westminster and at Christ Church, he was ordained deacon in 1885, priest in 1886, and was successively Student (1888-1901) and Dean (1901-20) of Christ Church, Bp. of *Ripon (1920-5) and Bp. of Oxford (1925-37). As Vice-Chancellor (1913-17) during the First World War, he took a leading part in bringing the needs of the nation before the university. Theologically his sympathies were with the *Lux Mundi School, but he had a great dislike of its *Anglo-Catholic developments. He wrote a *Manual of Theology* (1892), *Christian Ethics* (Bampton Lectures, 1896), *The Doctrine of the Real Presence* (1899), *Authority in the Church* (1903), and *Religion, Philosophy and History* (1923); and he edited C. *Bigg's *Origins of Christianity* (1909). A talented musician, he wrote some hymn tunes, among them 'Peckwater' and 'Hebdomadal', and edited, in conjunction with Basil Harwood, organist of Christ Church (1892-1909), *The Oxford Hymn Book* (1908).

Harold Anson, *T. B. Strong*, Bishop, Musician, Dean, Vice-Chancellor (London, 1949).

STROSSMAYER, JOSEPH GEORG (1815-1905), Bp. of Diakovár. Born in Croatia of a family of German descent, he was ordained priest in 1838, and in 1847 became professor of canon law at Vienna. In 1850 he was appointed Bp. of Diakovár. Despite his German ancestry, he was a keen pan-Slavist, who led the movement which issued in the formation of Yugoslavia after the war of 1914-1918. At the *Vatican Council of 1869-70 he was one of the most outstanding opponents of the definition of Papal infallibility, and, on 22 Mar. 1870, occasioned a 'scene 'at the Council by his ill-timed defence of Protestantism. Until Oct. 1871 he continued to maintain relations with J. J. I. v. *Döllinger and J. H. *Reinkens, but on 26 Dec. 1872 finally published the Vatican decrees in his official diocesan journal.

F. Šišić (ed.), *Korespondencija Racki-Strossmayer* (Zagreb, 4 vols., 1928-31); id., *Josi Juraj Strossmayer*. Dokumenti i Korespondencija (ib., 1933 ff.). A. Loiseau, 'La Politique de Strossmayer' in *Le Monde slave* (Mars, 1927), pp. 379-405. C. Butler, O.S.B., *The Vatican Council*, i (1930), pp. 134 f., 189 f., 270-5, and ii (1930), p. 175, and passim.

STRYPE, JOHN (1643–1737), English Church historian. He was a native of London, educated at St. Paul's School and at Jesus College and Catharine Hall, Cambridge, and in 1669 was appointed curate and lecturer at Leyton, Essex. From 1689 to 1724 he was lecturer at Hackney, and in 1711 he was given the sinecure of West Tarring, Sussex. He formed a very fine collection of Tudor documents, now in the Harleian and Lansdowne MSS. of the British Museum. His historical works deal chiefly with the Reformation period, the principal one being the *Memorials of Thomas Cranmer* (1694, ed. for the Eccl. Hist. Soc. in 3 vols., 1848–54). Among the others are *Annals of the Reformation in England* (4 vols., 1709–31), *Life and Acts of Matthew Parker* (1711), and *Ecclesiastical Memorials* (3 vols., 1721). The wealth of documentary material on which his works are based renders them invaluable to the student of the period, despite their bad arrangement, cumbersome style, and frequent errors. He also edited J. Stow's *Survey of London* (1720).

Modern repr. of his historical and biographical works, 19 vols. bound in 25, Oxford, 1812–24; index to this ed. [by R. F. Laurence] (2 vols., ib., 1828). G. Goodwin in *D.N.B.*, lv (1898), p. 67–9.

STUBBS, JOHN (*c.* 1543–1591), *Puritan fanatic. A native of Norfolk, he was educated at Trinity College, Cambridge. In 1574 he published an Eng. trans. of the *Lives of the Archbishops of Canterbury* which John Joscelyn (1529–1603), M. *Parker's secretary, had incorporated in the Archbishop's *De Antiquitate Britannicae Ecclesiae* (1572). Somewhat later Stubbs became a strong opponent of Catholicism. In Aug. 1579 he published *The Discovery of a Gaping Gulf whereinto England is like to be swallowed by another French Marriage if the Lord forbid not the Banns by letting Her Majesty see the Sin and Punishment thereof*, an attack on *Elizabeth's proposed marriage with Henry, Duke of Anjou. Stubbs, his publisher and his printer, were all sentenced and the first two had their right hands cut off (3 Nov. 1579), though Stubbs continued to protest his loyalty to the Queen. After 18 months' imprisonment in the Tower he was set free. In 1589 he became M.P. for Great Yarmouth. His other writings include a reply (apptly. unpublished) to W. *Allen's *Defence of the English Catholics* (1584) and an English version of some of T. *Beza's Meditations on the Psalms (publd. 1582).

A. F. Scott Pearson, *Thomas Cartwright and English Puritanism* (1925), pp. 185 f. and 305 f. L. Stephen in *D.N.B.*, lv (1898), p. 119 f., s.v., with reff.

STUBBS, WILLIAM (1825–1901), ecclesiastical historian and Bp. of *Oxford. A native of Knaresborough, Yorks, he was educated at Ripon Grammar School and through C. T. *Longley's influence nominated a servitor at *Christ Church, Oxford. In 1848 he was elected a Fellow of Trinity College. While rector of Navestock (1850–66) he laid the

basis of his immense historical learning. From 1866 to 1884 he was Regius professor of modern history at Oxford, and from 1879 to 1884 also a Canon of *St. Paul's. Later he became Bp. of *Chester (1884–9) and of *Oxford (1889–1901).

Stubbs was the greatest British historian of his time. He contributed 19 volumes to the Rolls Series of *Chronicles and Memorials*, among them the *Gesta Regum* of *William of Malmesbury (1867), the *Gesta Regis Henrici II* (1867), Roger Hoveden's *Chronica* (4 vols., 1868–71), the *Memorials of St. Dunstan* (1874), and the *Historical Works of Gervase of Canterbury* (1879–80). His *Constitutional History of England* (3 vols., 1873–8), which takes its subject down to 1485, with its companion vol. of *Select Charters* (1870), became classics. His other works included *Registrum Sacrum Anglicanum* (1858, ed. 2, 1897; chronological lists of the English Bishops), *Councils and Ecclesiastical Documents relating to Great Britain and Ireland* (3 vols., 1869–73, with A. W. Haddan), and several sets of mainly posthumous lectures, including *Lectures on European History* (1904), *Germany in the Early Middle Ages, 476–1250* (1908), and *Germany in the Later Middle Ages, 1250–1500* (1908). A collection of his ordination addresses was published (also posthumously) in 1901.

W. H. *Hutton (ed.), *Letters of William Stubbs, Bishop of Oxford* (1904). T. F. Tout in *D.N.B.*, *1901–1911*, pp. 444–51.

STUDD, CHARLES THOMAS (1862–1931), missionary. He was the son of a retired planter, Edward Studd, who was converted in 1877 at a mission of D. L. *Moody (1837–99) and I. D. Sankey (1840–1908). He was educated at Eton and Trinity College, Cambridge, where he was famed for his cricketing prowess. Edward Studd's conversion influenced his three sons and 'C. T.' (as he came to be called) volunteered for missionary work in China. As one of the 'Cambridge Seven', his intentions aroused much interest and enthusiasm, and laid the seeds of the Student Volunteer Movement. Sailing for China under the *China Inland Mission in 1885, he followed the early practice of that Mission by living in Chinese fashion. Ill-health compelled him to return in 1894. In 1900 he sailed for India, where he was the pastor of an undenominational Church at Ootacamund until he was again forced to return through sickness. Stirred by the need of missionary pioneer work in Central Africa, he sailed, contrary to medical advice, for the heart of Africa in 1910, and continued to work there till his death. On being joined by recruits in 1912, he founded the 'Heart of Africa Mission'. As this work developed, 'C. T.' conceived the idea of a 'World Evangelization Crusade' for the occupation by missionaries of the unevangelized areas of the world; the Crusade has since extended its activities to S. America and elsewhere.

Lives by T. B. Walters (London, 1930) and N. P. Grubb (ib., 1933). N. [P.] Grubb, *After C. T. Studd* (1939).

STUDDERT-KENNEDY, GEOFFREY ANKETELL (1883–1929), Anglican priest. Of Irish descent, he was educated at Leeds Grammar School, Trinity College, Dublin, and Ripon Clergy College, and in 1908 was ordained deacon. After holding curacies at Rugby and Leeds, he became vicar of St. Paul's, *Worcester (1914–21), and Chaplain to the Forces (1916–19). His vivid faith, the fruit of a deep sacramentalism, was reflected in a warmth of character which endeared him to the men in the trenches (where he won the affectionate title of 'Woodbine Willie', from a brand of cigarettes he distributed) and made him the best-known padre in the Great War of 1914–1918. The unconventionality of his views (e.g. his belief in God's passibility and his dissatisfaction with certain elements in the traditional Christian moral code), which helped to gain him a wide hearing, were the expression of a solid theology. In 1922 he was appointed rector of St. Edmund, King and Martyr, Lombard Street. He continued his mission preaching, constantly travelling about and working in association with the *Industrial Christian Fellowship. His books, popular in form, include *Rough Rhymes* (1918), *The Hardest Part* (1918), *The Wicket Gate* (1923), and *The Word and the Work* (1925).

J. K. Mozley (ed.), *G. A. Studdert-Kennedy*. By his friends (1929).

STUDENT CHRISTIAN MOVEMENT ('S.C.M.'). The British section of a world-wide fellowship of students who 'desire to understand the Christian faith and live the Christian life'. It developed out of several independent movements at Cambridge and elsewhere in the later years of the 19th cent. By study-circles, conferences, and camps, it seeks to bring Christian students of all denominations together, to instruct them in the Christian faith and to enable them to witness to the outside world. From the first an integral part of its work has been the 'Student Volunteer Missionary Union', which aims at fostering missionary work abroad, and it has taken its full share in the international association known as the World Student Christian Federation. From its activity in promoting the issue of literature addressed to students, originally publications of small cost and of practical purpose, there has developed a considerable religious publishing house (S.C.M. Press, Ltd., London). As a body drawing membership from all (non-RC) Christian communions the Movement has cultivated an outlook closely akin to that of the *Oecumenical Movement, many of whose leaders had earlier been associated with the S.C.M.

T. Tatlow *The Story of the Student Christian Movement of Great Britain and Ireland* (S.C.M., 1933). E. Fenn, *Learning Wisdom*. Fifty Years of the Student Christian Movement (ib., 1939). Ruth Rouse, *The World's Student Christian Federation*. A History of the First Thirty Years [viz. 1895–1924] (ib., 1948), with bibl.

STUDIOS. The famous monastery of *Constantinople, dedicated to St. *John the

Baptist. It stood in the west of the city, not far from the Golden Horn. Acc. to tradition founded in 463 by the former Roman consul, Studios, its monks followed the rule of the '*Acoemetae', who organized their psalmody so as to ensure its perpetual recitation by part of the community. They became famous as zealous upholders of orthodoxy, and defended the decrees of *Chalcedon against the Monophysite patriarch, *Acacius (484–519). Driven from their monastery by the persecution of Constantine Copronymus (718–75), only few of them returned after his death.

A new period began for Studios under St. *Theodore who became its abbot in 799. He introduced a new rule, based on that of St. *Basil, in which manual work played a far greater part than hitherto, and a strict discipline, esp. in regard to enclosure, poverty, and the exclusion of women from the monastery, was introduced. From his time Studios became the centre and model of E. monasticism and the monks of Mount *Athos, e.g., formed their life on its basis. It became esp. famous for its school of copyists and artists, and very many of its ancient hymns are still in use in the Greek Church. During the *Iconoclastic Controversy it supplied the most ardent defenders of images. Destroyed by the *Crusaders in 1204, the monastery was rebuilt in 1290, but again severely damaged by the Turks in 1453. To-day its church is a mosque. The religious life of Studios, however, was revived by the metropolitan, A. Szeptyckij, who founded an organization of E. monks acc. to the Rule of St. Theodore of Studios in 1906.

Extracts from the Rule ('Constitutiones Studianae') from Vat. gr. 2029 in J. P. Migne, *PG*, xcix, 1703–20. E. Marin, *De Studio Constantinopolitano* (Paris, 1897). On the form of the name, H. *Delehaye, S.J., 'Studion-Studios' in *Anal. Boll.*, lii (1934), p. 64 f. E. Candal, S.J., in *E.C.*, xi (1953), col. 1441 f., s.v. 'Studiti'.

STUDIUM GENERALE. A name widely current from the middle of the 14th cent. for what is now a university. At first the term denoted any 'school of general resort' (H. *Rashdall) which set out to attract students from all parts and possessed one or more of the higher faculties, viz. theology, law, and medicine. Of the early *studia generalia*, the most celebrated were those at *Paris (for theology and arts), *Bologna (for law), and Salerno (for medicine). By the end of the 13th cent., the privilege, granted by the Pope or Emperor, of conferring the *ius ubique docendi* ('the right of teaching everywhere') had become the special mark of the *studium generale*.

H. Rashdall, *The Universities of Europe in the Middle Ages* (new ed. by F. M. Powicke–A. B. Emden, 3 vols., 1939), esp. vol. i, pp. 6–17.

STUNDISTS (Russ. *štundisty*; cf. Ger. *Stunde*, 'devotional hour'). Certain Russian evangelical sects which trace their origin to a group of Bible students, founded near Odessa *c.* 1845 under the influence of a pastor Bonekemper. In 1871 they became separated into several divisions, and in more recent times have come increasingly under *Baptist influence.

STURM, JOHANNES (1507–89), Protestant Reformer and educationalist. Educated at Liége at the School of the *Brethren of the Common Life and at Louvain university, he joined himself to the French humanists and lectured on the classics at *Paris from 1530 to 1536. Having become a Protestant under M. *Bucer's influence, he went to Strassburg in 1537, where he took an active part in furthering the Reformation. His interest in education did much to make the city one of the foremost educational centres of Europe, and in 1538 a gymnasium on a humanistic model devised by Sturm was established with himself as rector. In 1564 an academy followed. In 1581 Sturm was expelled from Strassburg for his liberalism and inter-confessional sympathies by the strict *Lutherans, but eventually allowed to return. His writings included a Life of the German humanist, B. *Rhenanus.

C. Schmidt, *La Vie et les traveaux de Jean Sturm* (1855), with careful chronological lists of Sturm's writings, pp. 314–331. W. Sohm, *Die Schule Johannes Sturms und die Kirche Strassburgs in ihren gegenseitigen Verhältnis* (Historische Bibliothek, xxvii; 1912). C. Schmidt–J. Ficker in *P.R.E.* (ed. 3), xix (1907), pp. 109–13; C. Testore, S.J., in *E.C.*, xi (1953), col. 1449 f. Schottenloher, ii (1935), p. 315 f. (Nos. 20926–52).

STYLITE (Gk. στῦλος, 'pillar'). In the early Church a solitary who lived on the top of a pillar. Their pillars would vary in height, and the platforms, sometimes made more habitable by a small hut, were generally provided with a parapet against which the Stylite would lean for his scanty sleep. His food was usually supplied by disciples or admirers. Apart from prayer they gave much time to spiritual instruction, to reconciling enemies, and often to theological controversies. They considered St. *Simeon Stylites (q.v.) their founder. There are many instances of such ascetics from the 5th to the 10th cents., and isolated examples down to modern times. They flourished esp. in Syria, Mesopotamia, Egypt, and Greece.

H. *Delehaye, S.J., 'Les Stylites' in *Compte-Rendu du Troisième Congrès Scientifique International des Catholiques, tenu à Bruxelles du 3 au 8 septembre 1894*, v (1895), pp. 191–232; also printed in *R.H.Q.*, lvii (1895), pp. 52–103. Id., *Les Saints stylites* (Subsidia Hagiographica, xiv; 1923), with general bibl. in note to p. cxvii f. B. Kötting, *Peregrinatio Religiosa* (Münster i.W., 1950), pp. 113–31. S. V[ailhé], 'Les Stylites de Constantinople' in *É.O.*, i (1897–8), pp. 303–7. Heimbucher, i, 107–9.

SUAREZ, FRANCISCO DE (1548–1617), Spanish *Jesuit theologian. From 1564 to 1570 he studied philosophy and theology at Salamanca, and subsequently taught at several Spanish colleges of his order. From 1580 to 1585 he lectured on the 'Summa' of St. *Thomas Aquinas at the Roman College, and from 1585 to 1593 on the Incarnation and the Sacraments at the Jesuit College at Alcalá. Here he wrote his first work *De Verbo Incarnato* (1590), a commentary on the first 26 questions of the third part of the 'Summa',

noted esp. for its attempt to reconcile the Thomist view of the Redemption as the final cause of the Incarnation with that of *Duns Scotus, who held the manifestation of the perfection of the Divine work of creation to be its final cause, so that even without the Fall the Incarnation would have taken place. *De Mysteriis Vitae Christi* followed in 1592, and in 1597 appeared his *Disputationes Metaphysicae*, one of the principal textbooks on the subject in which he combined the teaching of Aristotle with that of St. Thomas. The work, which exercised a considerable influence also on Protestant contemporary philosophers, is important esp. for its new method, as it no longer closely follows Aristotle in the sequence of thought but gives an independent systematic treatment adapted to the needs of the modern Christian thinker. In 1597 *Philip II called Suarez to the university of Coimbra, where he lectured until 1616. In 1599 he published his *Varia Opuscula Theologica*, occasioned by the controversy on grace (*De auxiliis*) between the Jesuits and *Dominicans. In it, as in his *De vera intelligentia auxilii efficacis* of 1605 (publd. 1655), he proposed in the system called *Congruism a solution of the problem of the relation between human freedom and Divine grace on *Molinist lines. Acc. to Suarez, God does not, as the Thomists teach, cause man's free acts, but, foreseeing them by His special knowledge called '*scientia media', brings about the salvation of the elect by giving them those graces ('gratia congrua') of which he foresees that they will make good use in certain given circumstances. The teaching provoked much opposition but is now the prevalent doctrine among non-Thomist RC theologians. In 1608–1609 he published *De Virtute et Statu Religionis*, a fundamental work on the religious state with special reference to the Society of Jesus, and in 1612 *De Legibus* (which became of paramount importance for jurists and legislators on the Continent and in America) in the form of a Commentary on the 19 relevant questions of the 'Summa', in which he expounded the principles of natural and international law. It was followed, in 1613, by the *Defensio Fidei*, directed against the C of E, which was burned in London and banned by the Parliament of Paris for teaching doctrines prejudicial to the power of the state. His last great works on grace, published posthumously in three parts as *De necessitate gratiae* (1619), *De gratia habituali* (1619), and *De gratia actuali* (1651), elaborated and systematized the teaching given in his earlier writings.

The salient points in which Suarez departs from Thomism are regarded by some scholars as forming a system of his own, called 'Suarism'. Among its chief features are the conception of the individual as the object of direct Divine and human intellectual cognition, the pure potentiality of matter, and the conceptual, not real, distinction in created beings of essence and existence. Suarez is usually considered the greatest theologian of the Society of Jesus and was called by *Paul V 'Doctor eximius et pius'.

Collected ed. of his *Opera*, 23 vols., Venice, 1740–51; new ed. by D. M. André, 28 vols., Paris, 1856–78. Photographic reproductions from the original editions of *Selections from Three Works*: De Legibus ac Deo Legislatore, 1612; Defensio Fidei Catholicae et Apostolicae adversus Anglicanae Sectae Errores, 1613; De Triplici Virtute Theologica, Fide, Spe, et Charitate, 1621, with list of errata and Eng. tr. by Gwladys L. Williams–A. Brown–J. Waldron–H. Davis, S.J., and introd. by J. B. Scott (2 vols., Classics of International Law, xx; 1944). Good general modern study by R. de Scorraille, S.J., *François Suarez de la Compagnie de Jésus d'après ses lettres, ses autres écrits inédits et un grand nombre de documents nouveaux* (2 vols., [1912–13]). J. H. Fichter, *Men of Spain*. Francis Suarez (New York, 1940). The vast number of more specialized studies, of which there is an extensive list in *D.T.C.*, cited infra, include L. Mahieu, *François Suarez*. Sa philosophie et les rapports qu'elle a avec sa théologie (1921); P. Dupont, S.J., *Liberté humaine et concours divin d'après Suarez* (1936). Sommervogel, vii (1896), cols. 1661–1687, s.v. P. Monnot, S.J.,–P. Dupont, S.J.,–R. Brouillard, S.J., in *D.T.C.*, xiv (pt. 2; 1941), cols. 2638–2728, s.v., with bibl.

SUBCINCTORIUM.

An ecclesiastical vestment resembling the *maniple, which is now reserved to the Pope. He wears it on his left side, attached to his *girdle, when celebrating a solemn pontifical Mass. In the Middle Ages it was worn also by bishops (a usage which persisted at Milan until the 16th cent.) and occasionally by priests. Its original purpose was to secure the *stole to the girdle.

Braun, *L.G.*, pp. 117–24.

SUBDEACON.

In the RC Church a person in the lowest of the three *major orders. The Subdiaconate was not instituted by Christ but by the Church, and the conferring of the order is thus regarded as a *Sacramental rather than a true *Sacrament. The earliest mention of a 'subdeacon' is in a letter of Pope *Cornelius to Fabius of Antioch (255), while the correspondence of St. *Cyprian attests the existence of subdeacons in Africa at the same time. Until the 13th cent. the subdiaconate was regarded as a *minor, not a major, order.

Candidates for the order must have entered on their 22nd year and after ordination are bound to celibacy and the recitation of the *Breviary. A subdeacon is one of the three sacred ministers at *High Mass, when his functions are to prepare the bread and wine and the vessels, to assist the deacon, to chant the Epistle, to present the chalice and paten at the offertory and pour water in the chalice, and to remove the vessels from the altar after the communion. At the present day, however, the part of the subdeacon at High Mass is generally taken by a person in deacon's or priest's orders. The subdiaconate exists in the E. Church as a minor order. In the C of E it was given up with the other minor orders in the 16th cent., though in recent times proposals have occasionally been made to restore it. It has been restored in certain Anglican missionary dioceses.

H. Reuter, *Das Subdiakonat: dessen historische Entwicklung und liturgischkanonistische Bedeutung* (1890). F. Wieland, *Die genetische Entwicklung der sog. Ordines Minores in den drei ersten Jahrhunderten* (Römische Quartalschrift, Supplementheft, vii; 1897), pp. 18–48. A. Michel in *D.T.C.*, xiv (pt. 2; 1941), cols. 2459–66, s.v. 'Sous-Diacre'; H. *Leclercq, O.S.B., in *D.A.C.L.*, xv (1953), cols. 1619–26, s.v. 'Sous-Diacre', with reff.

SUBIACO (Lat. *Sublacum*).

A town some 40 miles east of Rome, famous as the site of the grotto where St. *Benedict settled on his retirement from the world. It became the cradle of the *Benedictine Order. Before his death St. Benedict founded 12 separate monasteries in the vicinity. The present monastery is the principal house of the *Cassinese Congregation of Primitive Observance.

P. Egidi–G. Giovannoni–F. Hermanin–V. Federici, *I monasteri di Subiaco* (2 vols., 1904). Cherubino Mirzio, O.S.B., *Cronaca Sublacense* (ed. L. Allodi, O.S.B., Rome, 1885). 'Chronicon Sublacense, sive Catalogus Abbatum Monasterii Sublacensis ab Anno circiter DXCV usque ad MCCCXC' by an anonymous monk, ed. L. A. *Muratori, *Rerum Italicarum Scriptores*, xxiv (Milan, 1738), pp. 927–66; new ed. by R. Morghen in G. Carducci–V. Fiorini–P. Fedele's ed. of Muratori, xxiv, part 6; Bologna, 1927. L. Allodi–G. Levi (edd.), *Il Regesto Sublacense del secolo XI* (Biblioteca della R. Società Romana di Storia Patria, 1885). L. Allodi, O.S.B. (ed.), *Consuetudines et Caeremoniae Regularis Observantiae Monasterii Sublacensis* (Subiaco, 1902). B. Albers, O.S.B., 'Une Nouvelle Édition des "Consuetudines Sublacenses"' in *R. Bén.*, xix (1902), pp. 183–204. B. Trifone, O.S.B. (ed.), 'Documenti Sublacensi' in *Archivio della R. Società Romano di Storia Patria*, xxxi (1908), pp. 101–120. B. Camm, O.S.B., *Pilgrim Paths in Latin Lands* (1923), pp. 1–46. L. H. Cottineau, O.S.B., *Répertoire topo-bibliographique des abbayes et prieurés* (Mâcon, 1935), col. 3099 f., s.v. F. Mershman in *C.E.*, xiv (1913), p. 321 f., s.v.; E. Josi–G. Avanzi in *E.C.*, xi (1953), cols. 1459–64, s.v., with bibl.

SUBINTRODUCTAE (Gk. συνείσακτοι).

In the early Church, women who lived associated with men in spiritual marriage. *Hermas seems to be familiar with the practice, and later *subintroductae* existed at *Antioch under *Paul of Samosata and at *Constantinople under St. *Chrysostom. The practice, with its obvious dangers, was opposed by St. *Cyprian, St. Chrysostom, and others, and forbidden by the canons of the Councils of *Elvira (can. 27), *Ancyra (can. 19), and *Nicaea (can. 3; A.D. 325). There is a certain analogy with the practice centuries later in the Irish mixed monasteries of monks and nuns. *Philo attests the existence of a similar institution among the *Therapeutae (q.v.)

H. Achelis, *Virgines Subintroductae*. Ein Beitrag zu 1 Kor. vii (1902). H. Koch, *Virgines Christi* (T.U., xxxi, Hft. 2; 1907, pp. 59–112). P. de Labriolle, 'Le "Mariage spirituel" dans l'antiquité chrétienne' in *Revue historique*, cxxxvii (1921), pp. 204–25. H. Achelis in *P.R.E.* (ed. 3), xix (1907), pp. 123–7, s.v.; id. in *H.E.R.E.*, i (1908), pp. 171–80, s.v. 'Agapetae'; E. Magnin in *D.D.C.*, i (1935), cols. 311–15, s.v. 'Agapètes'; A. Ferrua, S.J., in *E.C.*, i (1948), col. 426 f., s.v. 'Agapete'.

SUBLAPSARIANISM.

Also known as 'Infra-' or 'Post-lapsarianism'. In contrast to *Supralapsarianism (q.v.), the form of the *Calvinistic doctrine of *Predestination which holds that it was only after the *Fall that God decreed the election or non-election of individual men to salvation. This less rigid teaching on predestination has been commonly current among Calvinists, esp. since the Synod of *Dort (1618).

SUBMERSION (also 'total immersion' or,

loosely, 'immersion'). The form of *Baptism in which the water completely covers the candidate's body. It is still the method practised in the Orthodox and several of the other E. Churches, as well as in the *Ambrosian rite. On the basis of Rom. 6. 3–11 it has been generally supposed to have also been the custom of the early Church, but this view has been challenged by C. F. Rogers from the evidence of primitive pictorial representations and measurements of surviving early baptismal fonts.

C. F. Rogers, 'Baptism and Christian Archaeology' in *Studia Biblica et Ecclesiastica*. Essays chiefly in Biblical and Patristic Criticism by Members of the University of Oxford, v (1903), pp. 239–361; id., 'Baptism by Affusion in the Early Church' in *J.T.S.*, vi (1905), pp. 107–10, with reff. See also bibl. to *Baptism*.

SUBMISSION OF THE CLERGY. The act whereby the English *Convocations surrendered, on 15 May 1532, to the demands made by *Henry VIII. The clergy promised to make no new *canon without royal licence, and to submit the existing canons to a committee of 32, half lay and half clerical and all to be chosen by the King, for revision. Its effect was to make the King supreme in all ecclesiastical causes. Less than two years later (Jan. 1534), the submission of the clergy was incorporated into an Act of Parliament (25 Hen. VIII, c. 19), which coupled it with the restraint of appeals to Rome. See also *Reformatio Legum Ecclesiasticarum*.

Text in Gee–Hardy, pp. 176–8 (No. xlviii); also repr. in Bettenson, p. 305 f.

SUBORDINATIONISM. A heretical form of Trinitarian teaching which regards either the Son as subordinate to the Father or the Holy Ghost as subordinate to both. During the first three centuries subordinationist tendencies are found in several otherwise orthodox Fathers, e.g. St. *Justin, St. *Irenaeus, *Clement of Alexandria, and (esp.) *Origen. They were due partly to *Gnostic influences which led to stress on the unbridgeable gulf between the Deity and creation, but also to a one-sided interpretation of Biblical passages such as Prov. 8. 22 and Jn. 14. 28, and to the fear of compromising monotheism. In an explicit form Subordinationism was taught by *Arius and his followers, who held that the Son was God not by nature but by grace and was created by the Father, though before the creation of the world. It was attacked by St. *Athanasius and formally condemned by the Council of *Nicaea in 325. In the latter 4th cent. Subordinationism was applied to the Holy Ghost by the *Pneumatomachians, who interpreted Jn. 15. 26 as teaching that the Holy Ghost is the creature of the Son. The heresy was condemned by the Council of *Constantinople in 381.

SUBSTANCE (Lat. *substantia*). (1) The word has played a continuous and important part in philosophy since *Aristotle, who in the *Categories* distinguished between first and second substances (πρώτη οὐσία, δευτέρα οὐσία). The former was the individual, which can neither exist in another nor be predicated of another; the latter was the universal which does not as such exist in another, though it may be predicated of another. These distinctions were taken over by the *Scholastic philosophers. In general *substantia* was the permanent, underlying reality as contrasted with its changing and visible accidents. In modern times, R. *Descartes defined substance as that which needed nothing else for its existence; there were two kinds of substances, —absolute substance, viz. God, and created substances (unextended mind and extended matter). For B. *Spinoza substance was whatever needed nothing else for its conception. The sole substance was the eternal and infinite substance, God, whose essence implied His existence. For G. W. *Leibniz the monads were substances.

(2) In the Christian doctrine of the Godhead, the word is used to express the underlying Being, by which all Three Persons are One. The earliest theologian to make extensive use of the word *substantia* in this connexion was *Tertullian; but the common view that he was largely influenced by its legal meaning ('a piece of property') is exaggerated. At first, besides οὐσία, the Greek-speaking Church widely used ὑπόστασις in a closely similar sense, a usage favoured by the apparent etymological equivalence of ὑπο-στασις and *substantia*; and this identity was accepted at *Nicaea (325) and is common in *Athanasius. But under the influence of the *Arian Controversy, and esp. the *Cappadocian Fathers, οὐσία and ὑπόστασις became generally distinguished, οὐσία being confined to the meaning 'substance', whereas ὑπόστασις became the accepted equivalent of the Latin *persona*. See also *Homoousios, Homoiousios*.

(3) In the Middle Ages the word filled an important place in the theology of the *Eucharist, where the substance of the Eucharistic species was contrasted with their '*Accidents' (q.v.). For the history of the doctrine see *Transubstantiation*.

SUBUNISTS. The party in Bohemia in the 15th cent. which defended against the *Utraquists the practice of communion in one kind (*sub una specie*).

SUBURBICARIAN DIOCESES (Lat. *suburbium*, 'suburb'). The seven dioceses in the immediate vicinity of Rome, viz. Albano, Frascati, Ostia, Palestrina, Porto and Santa Rufina (united in 1120), Sabina and Poggio Mirteto (divided in 1841, reunited in 1925), and Velletri. The occupants of these sees are the six '*Cardinal Bishops', the senior of whom holds in conjunction with his own see that of Ostia, to which is annexed the office of 'Dean of the Sacred College'. The Suburbicarian Dioceses are very small, but very ancient. Their bishops had the right of taking part in the election of the Pope probably as early as the 11th cent.

P. F. Kehr, *Regesta Pontificum Romanorum*. Italia Pontificia sive Repertorium Privilegiorum et Litterarum a Romanis Pontificibus ante Annum MCLXXXXVIII Italiae, Ecclesiis, Monasteriis, Civitatibus Singulisque Personis Concessorum, ii (Berlin, 1907), pp. 14–74. G. Phillips, *Kirchenrecht*, iv (1864), pp. 145–220. U. Benigni in *C.E.*, xiv (1912), p. 324 f., s.v. See also works cited under *Cardinal*.

SUCCENTOR. In cathedral churches of the 'Old Foundation', the title usually given to the deputy of the *Precentor. He is generally a *minor canon. At *York there are two Succentors, the one subject to the canons and the other the principal member of the corporation of vicars-choral. At *Lichfield, the holder of the office is called the 'Subchanter'.

SUCCESSION, Apostolic. See *Apostolic Succession*.

SUDBURY, SIMON. See *Simon of Sudbury*.

SUETONIUS. Roman historian and secretary to Emp. Hadrian (117–38). He was apparently one of the first pagan writers to mention Christianity, the following passage from his 'Life of Claudius' (25. 4) being generally held to refer to the early Christians: 'Since the Jews constantly made disturbances at the instigation of Chrestus, he [i.e. Claudius] expelled them from Rome' (*Iudaeos impulsore Chresto assidue tumultuantes Roma expulit*).

The best ed. of his Lives of the Caesars is that of M. Ihm (Teub., 1908), which is repr., with Eng. tr. by J. C. Rolfe (Loeb, 2 vols., 1914); of his other works that by A. Reifferscheid (Leipzig, 1860). A. Macé, *Essai sur Suétone* (1900). Index Verborum by A. A. Howard–C. N. Jackson (Cambridge, Mass., 1922). On the significance of his words quoted, see W. M. *Ramsay, *The Church in the Roman Empire* (1893), pp. 230–2, 240, 257 f., 267, 271–4, 276 f. G. Funaioli in *P.W.*, II. Reihe, iv (pt. 1; 1931), s.v., cols. 593–641; J. C. Rolfe in *O.C.D.*, p. 865 f., s.v. 'Suetonius (2) Tranquillus'.

SUFFICIENT GRACE. In the RC theology of grace, grace which, in contrast to *efficacious grace (q.v.), does not meet with adequate co-operation on the part of the recipient, and hence fails to achieve the result for which it was bestowed. In the *Dominican view (D. *Bañez), it required a further Divine motion ('efficacious grace') to produce a salutary act. The *Jesuit view (L. *Molina), on the other hand, was that 'sufficient grace' was really adequate to produce such a result, needing only the consent of human free will to become efficacious. Both sufficient and efficacious grace are different forms of 'actual grace'.

SUFFRAGAN BISHOP. The title is used in two senses, viz. for:

(1) Any Bishop in relation to his *Archbishop or *Metropolitan, by whom he may be summoned to assist at synods and give his 'suffrage'.

(2) An assistant Bishop appointed to help the Bishop of the diocese. The first instance of the office in England is from 1240. From the end of the 14th cent. to the Reformation

appointments of such assistant bishops were frequent and made by the Pope. An Act of 1534 (26 Hen. VIII, cap. 14) named twenty-six specific places (Thetford, Ipswich, Colchester, Dover, Guildford, and so on) as sees from which Bishops Suffragan would take their titles. When a diocesan Bishop was desirous of a suffragan, he was to recommend two candidates to the King who was to have power to nominate one of them to any see in the list specified within the same province and to present him to the Archbishop, in letters patent under the great seal, for consecration within three months. The suffragan depended for his authority and fees on the commission of the diocesan, which was presumed to lapse on the death or translation of the latter and was renewable only at the pleasure of his successor. The Act was repealed under *Mary (1554; 1 & 2 Ph. and M., cap. 8), but restored under *Elizabeth (1559; 1 Eliz., cap. 1). After the consecration of seventeen suffragan Bishops in the 16th cent. it lapsed in 1592, though the existence of Bishops suffragan is assumed in the *Canons of 1604. In 1870, in the face of strong demands, suffragan Bishops were consecrated under the same act for Nottingham (for the diocese of *Lincoln) and Dover (for that of *Canterbury). The Suffragans' Nomination Act of 1888 (51 & 52 Vict., cap. 56) empowered the Crown, by order in council, to make additions to the list of places from which Suffragan Bishops might take their titles.

Henry VIII's Act of 1534 is repr. in Gee–Hardy, pp. 253–5 (No. lix). W. *Stubbs, *Registrum Sacrum Anglicanum. An Attempt to Exhibit the Course of Episcopal Succession in England* from the Records of the Church (1858), esp. pp. 142–9 (Appendix V: 'Suffragans and Bishops in Partibus'). R. *Phillimore, *The Ecclesiastical Law of the Church of England*, i (ed. 2 by W. G. F. Phillimore, 1895), pp. 75–86 ('Bishops without Sees').

SUGER (c. 1081–1151), Abbot of *St.-Denis, near Paris. Of humble origin, he entered the Abbey of St.-Denis c. 1091, where he was a fellow-student of King Louis VI. In 1106 he became secretary to the Abbot. In 1107 he was nominated Provost of Berneval in Normandy and in 1109 of Toury. In 1118 Louis VI sent him to the court of Pope Gelasius II at Maguelonne; and later he spent some time at the court of *Callixtus II. On returning from Italy (1122) he became Abbot of St.-Denis. In the next year he went to Rome again to attend the (Ninth) General Council of the *Lateran. In his first years as Abbot he was chiefly concerned with matters of state, but from 1127 to 1137 devoted himself to the thorough reform and reorganization of his monastery. During Louis VII's absence on the Second *Crusade, which Suger personally opposed, he was one of the regents, discharging his duties with such success that Louis on his return rewarded him with the title of 'Father of the Country'.

Suger's two panegyrics on Louis VI and Louis VII (the latter in its present form a revision by a Burgundian monk of *St.-Germain-des-Prés) are primary historical sources for his age. His new church at St.-Denis (consecrated 1144), of which he has left an account in his 'Libellus de Consecratione Ecclesiae S. Dionysii', was the first building in the Gothic style. His methods of monastic government are set out in his 'Liber de Rebus in Administratione sua gestis'.

Œuvres complètes, ed. A. Lecoy de La Marche (Societé de l'Histoire de France; 1867), with 12th-cent. life by Père Guillaume, O.S.B., pp. 377–411. Eng. tr. of his 'Sancti Dionysii Liber' by E. Panofsky, *Abbot Suger on the Abbey Church of St.-Denis and its Art Treasures* (Princeton, 1946). F. A. Gervaise, O.S.B., *Histoire de Suger* (3 vols., 1721). A. Huguenin, *Étude sur l'abbé Suger* (thesis; 1855). O. Cartellieri, *Abt Suger von Saint-Denis, 1081–1151* (Historische Studien Hft., xi; 1898). M. Aubert, *Suger* ('Figures monastiques'; 1950), with reff.

SUICER, JOHANN KASPAR (1620–84), author of the *Thesaurus Ecclesiasticus*. He was a Reformed theologian, a native of Frauenfeld in Switzerland. Educated at the French academies of Montauban and Saumur (1640–1643), he taught Latin, Greek, and Hebrew at Zürich from 1644 and was professor of Greek at the Collegium Carolinum from 1660 to 1683. After publishing several works on Greek linguistics, he brought out his famous *Thesaurus Ecclesiasticus e Patribus Graecis Ordine Alphabetico* in 1682 (2 vols., Amsterdam), of which a 2nd enlarged edition appeared in 1728. The work, which shows immense erudition and extensive reading of patristic literature, is still indispensable to students of the vocabulary of the Greek Fathers and of Greek ecclesiastical institutions.

His son, JOHANN HEINRICH SUICER (1646–1705), who in 1683 succeeded his father at the Collegium Carolinum, wrote a *Compendium Physicae Aristotelico-Cartesianae* (Amsterdam, 1685) and other works.

A. Schweizer–P. Schweizer in *P.R.E.* (ed. 3), xix (1907), p. 149 f.

SUIDAS (*c.* 1000 A.D.), 'Greek lexicographer'. The traditional supposition that the Greek Lexicon which passes under this name was the work of a certain 'Suidas', is, however, prob. mistaken, the name (properly ἡ Σοῦδα) being apparently derived from a Lat. word meaning 'fortress', i.e. an armoury of information. The Lexicon, both a dictionary and an encyclopaedia, was compiled *c.* 1000 from many ancient texts, abridgements, and scholia (Homer, Aristophanes, the Palatine Anthology, an epitome of Hesychius of Miletus), including several sources now lost, and also drew, for its lexical entries, on glossaries and word-lists. Much of its historical material came from the Chronicle of *George Hamartolos (9th cent.) and the Excerpts of Constantine Porphyrogenitus (912–59). Its contents are largely of indifferent value, but certain items stand apart as of great historical value. The whole work is an important witness to the interests and learning of late Byzantine culture.

Editio princeps of the lexicon [by D. Chalcondyles], Milan, 1499; later edd. by A. E. Porteus (with Lat. tr., 2 vols., Geneva, 1619), L. Kusterus (3 vols., Cambridge, 1705), T. *Gaisford (3 vols., Oxford, 1834), G. Bernhardy (2 vols. in

4 parts, Halle, 1853), I. Bekker (Berlin, 1854) and modern crit. ed. by Ada Adler (5 vols., Lexicographi Graeci, Leipzig, 1928–38). A. Adler in *P.W.*, Zweite Reihe, iv (pt. 1; 1931), cols. 675–717, s.v.

SULPICE, St. See *Saint Sulpice*.

SULPICIUS SEVERUS (*c.* 363–*c.* 420/5), historian and hagiographer. Descended from a noble house of Aquitaine, he practised as an advocate, and, after the early death of his wife *c.* 392, retired into solitude as a monk under the influence of St. *Martin of Tours; acc. to *Gennadius, he also became a priest and, in his later days, was temporarily influenced by *Pelagianism. The most famous of his extant writings are his 'Chronicle' (finished *c.* 403) and the 'Life of St. Martin', written during the lifetime of the saint but published only some time after his death. The former, written in elegant and easy Latin, is a summary of sacred history from the creation of the world to A.D. 400, intended as a textbook for educated Christian readers. It shows remarkable critical sense and is an important source esp. for the history of *Priscillianism. The 'Life of St. Martin', on the other hand, which is inspired by deep devotion to its hero, suffers from credulousness and inordinate prevalence of the miraculous element. It became at once extremely popular and a much-imitated model of medieval hagiography.

Editio princeps of his collected works by V. Giselinus (Antwerp, 1574); also ed. H. da Prato, (2 vols., Verona, 1741–54), repr. in J. P. Migne, *PL*, xx, 95–248, with 'carmina' attributed to him in lxxiv, 671 f.; works also ed. C. Halm (C.S.E.L., i, 1866). Eng. tr. by A. Roberts in L.N.P.N.F., Ser. 2, xi (1894), pp. 3–122. Crit. ed. of his Chronicle, with Fr. tr., by A. Lavertujon (2 vols., Paris, 1896–9); Fr. tr. of his life of St. Martin by P. Monceaux (Paris, 1926; Eng. tr., 1928). F. Mouret, *Sulpice Sévère à Primulac* (1907). P. Hyltén, *Studien zu Sulpicius Severus* (Lund, 1940). Bardenhewer, iii, 421–7; Altaner, p. 206 f. G. Bardy in *D.T.C.*, xiv (pt. 2; 1941), cols. 2760–2, s.v. 'Sulpice Sévère'. See also bibl. to *Martin, St.*

SUMMA. Originally a title of reference books on various subjects, the term, as used by medieval writers, came to denote a compendium of theology, philosophy, and canon law. These compendia were normally used as textbooks in the Schools, much like the earlier *Sentences. The 'Summae' divide their subjects into a great number of questions, usually following a more or less generally accepted order, and use the dialectical method of evolving a theme by affirmation and contradiction. The most famous 'Summae' are the 'Summa Theologica' and the 'Summa contra Gentiles' of St. *Thomas Aquinas; but well-known Summae were also produced by *William of Auxerre, *Alexander of Hales, St. *Albertus Magnus, and many others.

'SUMMA THEOLOGICA'. The chief dogmatic work of St. *Thomas Aquinas (q.v.). It is a vast structure of treatises, questions, and articles, which falls into three parts. The First Part ('Prima') treats of God considered in Himself and as the principle of creation, the first half of the Second Part ('Prima Secundae') of God as the end of man, its second half ('Secunda Secundae') of man's return to God, and the Third Part ('Tertia') of Christ as the way of man to God. The First and Second Parts date from 1265 to 1271, the Third from 1271 onwards. The concluding sections of the Tertia, which deal with the Sacraments and the Last Things, were left unfinished, the missing parts being supplied by *Reginald of Piperno, who used the relevant parts of St. Thomas's 'Commentary on the Sentences' for their completion.

For bibl. see *Thomas Aquinas, St.*

SUMMI PONTIFICATUS. The *encyclical issued by *Pius XII on 20 Oct. 1939 expounding the bearing of Catholic principles on such matters as the growth of secularism, the brotherhood of man, the state and the family, state-worship and international confidence, and *Catholic Action, and summoning Christians to a renewed devotion to the *Sacred Heart.

Lat. text in *A.A.S.*, xxxi (1939), pp. 413–53, with Italian tr., pp. 454–80; Fr. tr., pp. 481–509, Spanish tr., pp. 510–37; Eng. tr., pp. 538–64; and Germ. tr., pp. 565–94. Further Eng. tr., under the title *Darkness over the World*, made by R. A. Knox from the Lat. (*Catholic Truth Society pamphlet, 1939), repr. in G. D. Smith (ed.), *Selected Letters and Addresses of Pius XII* (C.T.S., 1949), pp. 3–45. A. Piolanti in *E.C.*, xi (1953), col. 1519 f., s.v.

SUMNER, CHARLES RICHARD (1790–1874), Bp. of *Winchester. A younger brother of J. B. *Sumner (q.v.), he was educated at Eton and Trinity College, Cambridge, and ordained deacon in 1814. In 1820 he was introduced to George IV, to whom he owed his subsequent rapid preferment. Having been appointed Chaplain to the King, he was made Canon of *Worcester in 1822 and of *Canterbury in 1825. In 1826 he was consecrated to the see of *Llandaff, which he held in plurality with the deanery of *St. Paul's, and in 1827 he was translated to Winchester by order of the King. He lost the royal favour by voting for the *Catholic Emancipation Bill in 1829, an action he regretted in later life. He was an *Evangelical in his sympathies and as such opposed R. D. *Hampden's appointment to the see of *Hereford. He lent his support, however, to S. *Wilberforce and to G. Moberly (1803–85), Bp. of *Salisbury. In 1850 he strongly protested against the restoration of the RC hierarchy. A very capable and successful administrator, he furthered in his diocese the establishment of Poor Schools, better conditions for the agricultural labourers, and the building of churches and parsonages. His literary works include the *Ministerial Character of Christ Practically Considered* (1824) and an annotated translation of J. *Milton's *De Doctrina Christiana* (2 vols., 1825). In 1869 he resigned his see through ill-health, to be succeeded by S. Wilberforce.

Life by his son, George Henry Sumner (London, 1876). W. P. Courtney in *D.N.B.*, lv (1898), pp. 165–8.

SUMNER, JOHN BIRD (1780–1862), Abp. of *Canterbury. Elder brother of C. R. *Sumner, he was born at Kenilworth and educated at Eton and King's College, Cambridge, of which he was elected a Fellow in 1801. In 1802 he became assistant master at Eton, and was ordained in 1803. After holding several benefices he was nominated Bp. of *Chester in 1828. Though a convinced Evangelical, he voted for the *Catholic Emancipation Bill in 1829. Later he opposed the *Oxford Movement. He was an able administrator of his diocese, which he enriched by causing many churches and schools to be built. In 1848 he was appointed Abp. of Canterbury. Though rejecting the theology of R. D. *Hampden's Bampton Lectures, he did not oppose his consecration as Bp. of *Hereford, in which he himself took part. In the controversy concerning the *Gorham Case he denied that Baptismal Regeneration was a fundamental doctrine of the C of E. In 1852 it fell to him to preside over the Upper House of *Convocation when, for the first time for 135 years, it met again for business. His numerous writings, which were highly esteemed in Evangelical circles, include *Apostolical Preaching* (1815), based on the Pauline Epp.; *A Treatise on the Records of the Creation* (2 vols., 1816), founded on the Mosaic account in Genesis; and *The Evidence of Christianity* (1824), in which he argued from the vitality of Christianity to its Divine origin; as well as several volumes of Sermons.

G. H. Sumner, *Life of Charles Richard Sumner* (1876), pp. 402–5. W. P. Courtney in *D.N.B.*, lv (1898), pp. 168–70, s.v.

SUN, Canticle of the. See *Canticle of the Sun.*

SUNDAR SINGH, SADHU (1889–c. 1929), Indian Christian and mystic. Born of wealthy Sikh parents, he was converted to Christianity by a vision on 18 Dec. 1904, baptized in the C of E at Simla in 1905, and donned the robe of a Sadhu (i.e. 'holy man') in an endeavour to present Christianity in a Hindu form. In his early travels he covered the Punjab, Kashmir, Baluchistan, and Afghanistan, and in 1908 made his first visit to evangelize Tibet. A visit to Madras in 1918 introduced him to the world at large, and his fame was enhanced by travels in the West in 1920 and 1922. He expected death at 33, the age at which Christ died, and was disappointed that he lived on. Despite ill-health, he persisted in his strenuous work in Tibet. He was last heard of in April 1929.

B. H. *Streeter and A. J. Appasamy, *The Sadhu* (1921); C. F. Andrews, *Sadhu Sundar Singh* (1934).

SUNDAY. Its English name derives from the old pagan 'dies solis' (Gk. ἡλίου ἡμέρα), the day consecrated to the sun, which was given a Christian interpretation and referred to Christ, the Sun of Righteousness (Mal. 4. 2). In Rev. it is called the Day of the Lord, κυριακὴ ἡμέρα

(1. 10), the Latin translation of which, 'Dominica', is the name used in the calendars of the W. Church. Already in NT times Sunday began to replace the Jewish Sabbath. St. *Paul and the Christians of Troas assembled on the first day of the week 'to break bread' (Acts 20. 7) and the Apostle bids his converts put by their alms on this day (1 Cor. 16. 2). The chief reason for the substitution of the Sunday for the Sabbath was the commemoration of the Resurrection, mentioned already by St. *Ignatius, which gives the day its joyful character; thus there is to be no fasting or kneeling on this day. *Justin Martyr connects it also with the first day of Creation, and St. *Isidore of Seville, much later, with the Coming of the Holy Ghost. This association with the Three Divine Persons led to its being esp. dedicated to the Trinity, a connexion reflected in its liturgical celebration, e.g. in the *Preface of the Trinity assigned in the W. Church to all the Sundays of the year that have no special Preface of their own.

The observance of Sunday as a day of rest consecrated esp. to the service of God began to be regulated both by ecclesiastical and civil legislation from the 4th cent. It was enjoined by the Council of *Elvira (c. 306; can. 21), and by *Constantine in a law promulgated in 321, commanding the abstention from work, including legal business, for townspeople, though permitting farm labour. The Council of *Laodicea (c. 380; can. 29) enjoined abstention from work as far as possible. From the 6th to the 13th cents. the ecclesiastical legislation became more and more strict, enforcing also assistance at Mass, and was helped by the infliction of severe penalties by the civil authorities, e.g. by the Anglo-Saxon king Ine and by *Alfred the Great. From the 13th cent. onwards the custom of allowing dispensations became widespread. Present-day Catholic practice in the W. requires the faithful to hear Mass on Sundays and to abstain from *servile work, except in cases where either or both would cause grave inconvenience, e.g. when no church is available at a reasonable distance, or where pressing needs make relaxation from servile work undesirable.

The Protestant Churches did not at first introduce special Sunday legislation; but the abuse of Sunday soon led to a reaction. In England the new attitude to Sunday was much influenced by Nicholas Bound's *True Doctrine of the Sabbath* (1595), which identified the Christian Sunday with the Jewish Sabbath. Despite King James's defence of the traditional Sunday pleasures in his *Book of *Sports* (1618), rigorist views gained ground and found classical expression in the legislation of the Long Parliament and the *Westminster standards. While the Restoration brought much relaxation, the Act of 1677, by reducing Sunday labour, furthered its rigorist observance. The early 18th cent. was marked by greater liberty, but through the influence of the Evangelical Revival stricter observance was once more enforced by the Act of 1781. In the 19th cent. Sunday was still a day mainly

devoted to duties of piety, but the increasing secularization of life in the present century has considerably reduced its religious observance, while, on the other hand, considerations of social well-being have made the cessation of work on Sunday a matter increasingly encouraged by the civil authorities. See also *Sabbatarianism*.

J. A. Hessey, *Sunday. Its Origin, History and Present Obligation* (Bampton Lectures for 1860; 1860). T. *Zahn, *Geschichte des Sonntags vornehmlich in der alten Kirche* (1878). S. V. McCasland, 'The Origin of the Lord's Day' in *Journal of Biblical Literature*, xlix (1930), pp. 65–82. A. Barry in *D.C.A.*, ii (1880), pp. 1042–53, s.v. 'Lord's Day'; O. Zöckler in *P.R.E.*, xviii (1906), pp. 521–9, s.v. 'Sonntagsfeier'; M. G. Glazebrook in *H.E.R.E.*, xii (1921), pp. 103–11, s.v.

SUNDAY LETTER. In ecclesiastical calendars that one of the seven letters A to G, allotted to the days of the year in rotation (1 Jan. = A, &c.), which coincides with the Sundays in a given year. Knowledge of it enables the user to discover at a glance on what day of the week any calendarial date in that year will fall. It is ascertained by a simple arithmetical calculation, as described, e.g., in the 'Table to Find Easter Day' prefixed to the BCP. A leap year necessarily has two Sunday letters, the change in the BCP calendar falling on 29 Feb., but in older forms of the calendar on 25 Feb. (vi. Kal. Mar.; hence 'bissextile years').

SUNDAY SCHOOLS. Schools, mainly for children, in which instruction, now primarily religious instruction, is given on Sunday; they are usually held in conjunction with a parish or congregation. Although there are isolated earlier examples of schools for poor children on Sundays, the movement owed its success to Robert *Raikes (q.v.), who, along with the local incumbent (T. Stock), engaged four women in 1780 to instruct the children of *Gloucester in reading and the Church Catechism on Sundays. Partly owing to the publicity which Raikes gave to the enterprise in his *Journal*, his example was soon followed in many parts of England and later on the Continent and in America. On the initiative of a group of City gentlemen, the Sunday School Union, an interdenominational body, was founded in 1803 to improve methods, fill gaps, and help with supplies of books and material for Sunday schools in the London area. In other large towns similar associations known as 'auxiliaries' were formed, affiliated to the central Union. The Union received much support, esp. in Evangelical and Nonconformist circles.

With the increase of general education in the 19th cent. the Sunday Schools devoted themselves more exclusively to religious education. Partly as a result of the *Oxford Movement, there grew up a desire among Anglicans to introduce more specifically C of E teaching into the Sunday Schools, and in 1843 a new society, the Sunday School Institute, was formed (incorporated in 1910). With the enhanced standard of general education which followed the 1870 Act, it became necessary to initiate greater organization among the Sunday school teachers, who were, by now, mainly voluntary workers. Under the auspices of the Sunday School Union a training college for teachers was founded in 1907 at Selly Oak, Birmingham; the Sunday School Institute opened St. Christopher's College, Blackheath, in 1909 for similar purposes. The Sunday Schools of the C of E are partly organized on a diocesan basis; those sponsored by the Sunday School Union on a national basis; both provide summer schools, teachers' courses and conferences, as well as material help with literature and other necessities.

A number of histories of individual schools have been written but there is little on the movement as a whole. Catharine R. Newby, *The Story of Sunday Schools*. Robert Raikes and After [1930; very brief]; D. P. Thomson (ed.), *The Sunday School in the Modern World* [c. 1924]; G. H. Archibald, *The Modern Sunday School*. Its Psychology and Method [1926] and other works of this author. W. C. R. Hicks in *Chambers's Encyclopaedia*, xii (ed. 1950), p. 284 f., s.v. See also lives of *Raikes, R.*

SUNG MASS. See *Missa Cantata*.

SUPEREROGATION, Works of. In RC *moral theology, acts which are not enjoined as of strict obligation, and therefore are not simply good as opposed to bad, but better as opposed to good ('opera meliora'). Thus the '*counsels of evangelical perfection' are held to be not of duty but of supererogation. The term, which goes back to the Latin translation of Lk. 10. 35 ('quodcumque supererogaveris'), was probably not used in its present technical sense until the Middle Ages, when 'opera supererogationis' were treated in the works of *Alexander of Hales, St. *Thomas Aquinas, and others. The doctrine, for which the story of the rich young ruler (Mt. 19. 16–22) and St. Paul's teaching on virginity (1 Cor. 7) are usually adduced in evidence, was repudiated by the Reformers and in the Anglican Article XIV which asserts that 'works of supererogation cannot be taught without arrogancy and impiety'.

Commentaries on the Thirty-Nine Articles, cited s.v., Art. XIV, esp. E. C. S. Gibson, *The Thirty-Nine Articles*, ii (1897), pp. 424–38.

SUPERINTENDENTS. In the reformed Church of Scotland, the officials appointed under the *First Book of *Discipline* (1560) to oversee the districts roughly corresponding to the old dioceses. They would appear to have been temporary office-bearers chosen, owing to the great dearth of ministers, to settle and organize the churches under their care. It has been much disputed whether their appointment implies t at the Church of Scotland was originally Episcopalian. While they enjoyed a measure of superiority over other ministers, they differed from diocesan bishops, in being admitted to office by fellow-presbyters, in not possessing exclusive power of ordination, and in being subject to the control and censure of the other ministers regularly associated with them.

In the *Lutheran Churches, which in this matter supplied a model for the Scottish superintendents, Church officials of this name were created from an early date for similar reasons and with similar functions. In the Scandinavian countries the title of 'Bishop' was retained. In accordance with the principles of Lutheran polity they were to be appointed by, and responsible to, the civil powers. See also *General Superintendent*.

SUPERIOR. One who has authority over others by virtue of his ecclesiastical rank. The term is commonly used of the heads of the religious orders and congregations, though it is not in general use in those (esp. older) orders of monks and canons which consisted originally of independent houses. In some of the more recent bodies of religious, esp. of women, it has become a title.

SUPPER, The Last. See *Last Supper*.

SUPPRESSION OF THE MONASTERIES. See *Dissolution of the Monasteries*.

SUPRALAPSARIANISM (or 'Antelapsarianism'). The form of the *Calvinistic doctrine of *Predestination which maintains that God decreed the election and non-election of individual men before the *Fall of *Adam. *Calvin himself regarded Divine Predestination as an inscrutable mystery; for though he held that the elect, being sinners, were favoured beyond their merit, and that the non-elect, being also sinners, received just treatment acc. to their merit, he did not presume to elaborate the whole subject. It was his followers who boldly asserted such doctrines as supralapsarianism. Though logical consistency may appear to favour the supralapsarian position, the milder *sublapsarian doctrine (q.v.) has been generally dominant among Calvinists, esp. since the Synod of *Dort (1618).

SUPREMACY, Act of. The Act passed in Nov. 1534 (26 Hen. VIII, c. 1) confirming to the King and his successors the title of 'the only supreme head in earth of the Church of England, called *Anglicana Ecclesia'*. It was repealed by *Mary (1 & 2 Philip and Mary, c. 8) and the repeal was confirmed by *Elizabeth I. But Elizabeth's new Act of Supremacy (1 Eliz., c. 1), the first act of her reign (1559), restored the Henrician legislation in a revised form. The monarch's title just quoted was dropped, however, and the Queen declared to be 'the only supreme governor of this realm, and of all other her highness's dominions and countries, as well in all spiritual or ecclesiastical things or causes as temporal'. The election of bishops by *congé d'élire* was restored, and an oath of obedience to the Crown in things ecclesiastical as well as civil imposed on all clergymen and public officials. The act was an assertion of the monarch's responsibility before God for the welfare of the Church, and annexed 'for ever' the power of reforming abuses to the crown.

The text of the Act of 1534 is repr. in Gee–Hardy, p. 243 f. (No. lv); the repeal by Mary of this and other ecclesiastical legislation of the previous reigns is pr. ib., pp. 385-415 (No. lxxvi), esp. p. 390; and the Act restoring the Queen's Supremacy under Elizabeth, ib., pp. 442-58 (No. lxxix).

SURIN, JEAN JOSEPH (1600-65), French mystic and spiritual writer. In 1616 he entered the *Jesuit Order, where he came under the influence of Louis Lallemant (1587-1635). Having been sent as a man of great spiritual power to Loudun in 1636 to exorcize some *Ursulines believed to be possessed by the devil, he underwent in the result a series of mysterious trials and sufferings which have been variously interpreted as possession or as a purely pathological state. These experiences, which went on for 20 years without, however, completely precluding his activities as a preacher, writer, and spiritual director, were followed by a period of mystic exaltation. His principal work, the *Catéchisme spirituel* (1659), published without his knowledge, was, in its Italian translation, placed on the Index in 1695 during the controversy between F. *Fénelon and J. B. *Bossuet. Surin's spiritual doctrine, expressed also in his *Les Fondements de la vie spirituelle* (1667), *Dialogues spirituels* (1704-9), and several other works, insists on the necessity of purification by self-abnegation and suffering. It advocates the practice of the presence of God and the prayer of contemplation in which the soul, abandoned to the direction of the Holy Spirit, loses itself in the love of God. The *Fondements* was published by E. B. *Pusey in a version 'adapted' for C of E readers in 1844.

List of works with notices of edd. and translations to date in Sommervogel, vii (1896), cols. 1704-16, and ix (1900), col. 868. H. M. Boudon, *L'Homme de Dieu*. En la personne du R. Père Jean-Joseph Seürin (Chartres, 1683; modern ed. 2 vols., Lyons, 1826). Bremond, v (1920), pp. 148-310; Pourrat, iv (ed. 3, 1928), pp. 85-107, with note on edd. of his works. M. Olphe-Galliard, S.J., in *D.T.C.*, xiv (pt. 2; 1941), cols. 2834-42, s.v., with further reff.

SURPLICE (Lat. *superpelliceum*, 'over a fur garment'). A liturgical vestment of white linen, with wide sleeves. It was originally a loose choir vestment substituted for the narrow-sleeved alb because it was better suited for wear over the fur coats customary in northern countries, hence its name. From the 12th cent. it came to be the distinctive dress of the lower clergy and to be used by priests outside Mass. At first a tunic reaching to the feet, it became steadily shorter until, in the 18th cent. on the Continent, it just covered the hips, the sleeves also being reduced in size. To-day this form, usually called the *cotta, is used esp. in the RC Church beside the older, wide-sleeved form, reaching to the knees. The surplice is worn by all clerics and is also used by laymen, e.g. in choir, when serving Mass, acting as acolytes, &c. In the C of E the BCP of 1552 made it the only prescribed vestment of the clergy, but the '*Ornaments Rubric' ordering it was removed in later editions. Its use caused much controversy in the reign of *Elizabeth I, but was insisted upon by Abp. M. *Parker in his *Advertisements*. Can. 58 of 1604 orders the wearing of the surplice for ministers during Divine service

and when administering the sacraments, and can. 17 enjoins it also on students in colleges other than clerics on certain days. The question whether a surplice should be worn by a cleric when preaching in the pulpit was widely agitated in the 19th cent. in connexion with the Ritualist Movement. Its use in the C of E is now almost, if not quite, universal. See also *Vestiarian Controversy*.

Braun, *L.G.*, pp. 135-48. J. Braun, S.J., in *C.E.*, xiv (1912), p. 343 f., s.v. V. Staley in *P.B.D.* (1912), p. 774 f., s.v. See also bibl. to *Ornaments Rubric*.

SURPLICE FEES. The fees which are payable to the incumbent of a parish for marriages and burials. They are his by right, whoever performs the service, and he pays income-tax on them as part of the income of the benefice.

SURROGATE. In ecclesiastical usage, the word is applied esp. to a clergyman or other person appointed by the bishop as his deputy to grant licences for marriages without banns.

SURSUM CORDA (Lat., 'Lift up your hearts'). In the Eucharistic liturgy the words addressed by the celebrant to the congregation immediately before the *Preface. The reply is: 'We lift them up unto the Lord'. Its use, which is universal, is attested as early as St. *Cyprian (252) in the W. and as St. *Cyril of Jerusalem in the E.

Jungmann, *M.S.*, ii (ed. 1949), pp. 133-40; Eng. tr., ii, pp. 110-15.

SUSANNA, Book of. In the English Bible one of the smaller Books of the *Apocrypha. In the LXX it follows the Book of Daniel (of which the *Vulgate reckons it the thirteenth chapter). In the *Old Latin it precedes the 1st chapter of Daniel. There is no agreement among scholars as to whether it was originally written in Greek, Hebrew, or Aramaic. The Book tells in 64 verses of the false accusation of adultery brought against Susanna by the two elders, her condemnation, and her final deliverance by the sagacity of Daniel. In the Christian era the incident became the symbol of the saved soul, and as such is to be met with already in the paintings of the *Catacombs and on early *sarcophagi. It became again a favourite subject of art in the Renaissance, esp. the bathing scene, which has also been painted by P. P. Rubens, *Rembrandt, and others, as well as by many modern artists.

Gk. texts in H. B. *Swete (ed.), *The Old Testament in Greek*, iii (ed. 1912), pp. 576-85. Eng. tr., with commentary and reff. to other edd. of texts by D. M. Kay in R. H. *Charles (ed.), *The Apocrypha and Pseudepigrapha of the Old Testament*, i (1913), pp. 638-51. W. H. Daubney, *The Three Additions to Daniel*. A Study (1906), pp. 101-77. W. Baumgartner, 'Susanna. Die Geschichte einer Legende' in *Archiv für Religionsgeschichte*, xxiv (1926), pp. 259-80; id., 'Der weise Knabe und die des Ehebruchs beschuldigte Frau', ib. xxvii (1929), p. 187 f. J. T. Marshall in *H.D.B.*, iv (1902), pp. 630-2, s.v. On early representations in art, H. *Leclercq, O.S.B., in *D.A.C.L.*, xv (pt. 2; 1953), cols. 1742-1752, s.v. 'Suzanne', with reff. See also Catholic commentaries to Daniel and bibl. to *Apocrypha*.

SUSANNA, St. (3rd cent.), Roman martyr. Acc. to legend, she was a woman of noble birth and great beauty, a niece of Pope Caius (283–296), and was put to death for refusing to marry a pagan relative of *Diocletian. Her 'Acts' seem to be a working-over of what was orig. an edifying tale. Since the 5th cent., her name has been attached to one of the *tituli at Rome. Feast day, 11 Aug.

AA.SS., Aug. II (1734), pp. 624–32, with part 2 of the Acta and other material; part 1, ib., Feb. III (1658), pp. 61–4 L. *Duchesne, 'Les Légendes de l'Alta Semita' in *Mélanges d'Archéologie et d'Histoire*, xxxvi (1916–17), pp. 27–56, esp. pp. 33–42; J. P. Kirsch, *Die römischen Titelkirchen im Altertum* (Studien zur Geschichte und Kultur des Altertums, ix, Hft. 1 and 2; 1918), pp. 70–4; P. Franchi de' Cavalieri, *Note agiografiche*, vii (S.T., xlix, 1928), pp. 185–202.

SUSO, HENRY. See *Henry Suso*.

SUTTON, CHRISTOPHER (*c.* 1565–1629), devotional writer. Educated at Hart Hall and Lincoln College, *Oxford, he held several livings in the eastern counties. In 1605 he became a Canon of *Westminster and in 1618 of *Lincoln. His devotional books, written with much fervour, enjoyed great popularity. The most used was *Godly Meditations upon the Most Holy Sacrament of the Lord's Supper* (1613), in which, deprecating controversy, he sought to defend a doctrine of Christ's presence in the Eucharist midway between *Transubstantiation and the teaching of H. *Zwingli, maintaining that while consecration effected no change in the substance of the elements it radically altered their use. The book was reissued by J. H. *Newman with a fresh preface in 1838 and became popular for some years with the *Tractarians. Sutton's *Disce Mori* (1600) and *Disce Vivere* (1608) were also reissued in the 19th cent.

His *Disce Vivere* was repr. from the 1602 ed. with A Memoir of his Life by J. E. Tyler (1847), pp. iii–xxii.

SUVERMERIAN. A word applied by the Saxon Reformers to certain Swiss Protestant extremists. It arose from an attempted Latinization (*Swermeros*) of the Germ. *Schwärmer* ('fanatical enthusiasts'). It has recently been brought to general notice through its (apparently somewhat inaccurate) use by C. H. Smyth of the Eucharistic doctrine of T. *Cranmer in *Cranmer and the Reformation under Edward VI* (1926).

On the term see review of C. H. Smyth by E. W. Watson in *J.T.S.*, xxviii (1926–7), p. 204.

SWAINSON, CHARLES ANTHONY (1820–87), English theologian. A native of Liverpool, he was educated at Trinity College, Cambridge, and became a Fellow of Christ's College in 1841. He was ordained priest in 1844 and was appointed principal of the theological college at *Chichester in 1854. In 1864 he became Norrisian professor of divinity at Cambridge, was elected master of Christ's College in 1881, and vice-chancellor of the university in 1885. In 1858 he published his *Hulsean Lectures on *The Creeds of the Church*, in which he discussed the authority of the Creeds on the basis of Biblical teaching and in their relation to private judgement. It was followed in 1875 by his important work, *The Nicene and Apostles' Creed*, which was the fruit of many years' work on MSS. in Continental libraries. It included an account of the *Athanasian Creed which Swainson dated between 860 and 870 and believed to consist of two separate documents. In 1884 appeared his edition of *The Greek Liturgies*, a standard collection of texts, parts of which are still indispensable to the student of Greek liturgiology.

S. Cheetham in *D.N.B.*, lv (1898), p. 191 f., s.v.

SWASTIKA (Skt. *svastika*, 'well-being', 'fortune'; Lat. *crux gammata*; Fr. *croix gammée*; Germ. *Hakenkreuz*). A symbol of great antiquity, in the form of a cross of equal arms each of which is bent in the shape of a hook. It was probably in origin a charm for attracting good luck and averting misfortune and has also been explained as a symbol of fertility or as representing the wheel of the sun, though the latter interpretation has been commonly rejected in recent times. It appears already on the vases of Mussiân Tepe (nr. Susa, in Elamite country) *c.* 4000–3000 B.C., among the German tribes *c.* 1000 B.C., and is found as a widespread ornament in China, Japan—esp. in Buddhist art—and America in the Christian era. From the middle of the 3rd cent. A.D. it appears in the Roman catacombs, but apparently without any symbolic or Christian reference. It is also to be found on medieval embroidery and brasses, e.g. at Lewknor, Oxfordshire. In recent times, owing to the mistaken idea that it is an old Teutonic sign confined to the Aryan peoples, it was adopted as the official symbol of the National Socialist Party in Germany, with special emphasis on its anti-Semitic significance.

T. Wilson, 'The Swastika. The earliest known Symbol and its Migrations' in *Annual Report of . . . the . . . Smithsonian Institution for the Year ending June 30, 1894* (Washington, D.C., 1896), pp. 757–1011, with bibl. J. Lechler, *Vom Hakenkreuz*. Die Geschichte eines Symbols (1921; ed. 2, 1934). O. Hupp, *Runen und Hakenkreuz*. Eine archäologische Studie mit heraldischen Schlussfolgerungen (1921). J. Hösl in *L.Th.K.*, iv (1932), col. 793 f., s.v. 'Hakenkreuz'.

SWEDEN, Christianity in. The evangelization of Sweden started in the 9th cent., when at the request of some Swedish nobles St. *Anskar (801–65) was sent from the Frankish court. His work, however, was destroyed by civil wars. The systematic conversion of the country began in the 11th cent., largely from England, and was not complete till the middle of the 12th. In 1104 the see of *Lund received metropolitical rank, while *Upsala became an archbishopric in 1164. In the later Middle Ages the position of the bishops and clergy was highly privileged. They were exempt from civil burdens, and from the oath to the civil authority, while at the same time they amassed great riches and held considerable political power. The greatest figure in the ecclesiastical history of the time was St. *Bridget of Sweden (c. 1303-1373), founder of the *Brigittine Order.

The Reformation in Sweden was gradual, and of an entirely individual character. The national leader, Gustavus Vasa, who in 1521 headed the war of independence against Denmark, was no doubt led to join the movement by the undue wealth and influence of the clergy. But although in 1524 relations were formally broken off with the Roman Curia, and Olaus *Petri, a pupil of *Luther, began to teach under the protection of Gustavus, the ancient episcopal succession was deliberately kept through Petrus Magni, who in that year was consecrated Bp. of Västerås at Rome, and the old forms of service were retained for many years. A tentative Swedish Mass appeared in 1531, but did not immediately replace the Latin Mass, portions of the two being freely interchanged. In general, the result of the policy of Olaus Petri and of his brother Laurentius Petri (Abp. of Upsala, 1531-73) was the establishment of Lutheran dogma concurrently with the retention of Catholic Church order; and the Swedish Church, though holding the basic doctrine of justification by faith, has never used the word 'Lutheran' in its official title.

King John III (reigned 1569-92) made some attempts to reunite the Swedish Church with Rome, but these were unsuccessful, as were also the Calvinist designs of his successor, Charles IX, under whom, in 1593, the Swedes for the first time adopted the *Augsburg Confession, and so formally committed themselves to Lutheran dogma. In the Swedish Constitution of 1809 it was provided that the King and members of the Government must belong to the Swedish Church.

In the 19th cent. the Swedish Church suffered from a wave of *latitudinarianism, which was succeeded, about the time of the abolition of the Test Acts in 1858, by an evangelical revival which encouraged the growth of dissenting chapels, and in the Church itself almost destroyed sacramental religion.

The 20th cent. has seen the beginnings of a Church revival, partly through sympathetic intercourse with England. The recognition of the Church as the Mystical Body of Christ, of the value of the historical ministry, of the sacraments, and of liturgical worship, is beginning slowly to reappear, though Lutheran dogma is considered more fundamental than Church order, and the closest kinship is felt with the Lutheran bodies of Finland, Norway, Denmark, and Germany. Among outstanding 20th-cent. Swedish theologians are Abp. N. *Söderblom and Bp. G. *Aulén. The latter, with Anders Nygren, has done much to revive Lutheran theology. The Swedish Church has played a prominent part in the Oecumenical Movement.

At present the Church of Sweden numbers as its members 96 per cent of the population. Of the other 4 per cent about half belongs to the Swedish Mission Society, the members of which, in spite of nominal adherence to the Swedish Church, have their own preachers and sacraments; the rest are *Baptists, *Salvationists (though these use the sacraments of the Church of Sweden), *Pentecostalists, *Methodists, and RCs.

The state, while tolerating all religions, gives special protection to the Established Church, which controls religious teaching in the state schools. It has its own Kyrkomöte, or Convocation, without the consent of which no laws on Church matters may be passed by Parliament.

In English there is a good survey by J. *Wordsworth, *The National Church of Sweden* (Hale Lectures, 1910; 1911). Other general works by J. H. Swinstead, *The Swedish Church and Ours* (S.P.C.K., 1921), and H. M. Waddams, *The Swedish Church* (S.P.C.K., 1946). C. J. A. Oppermann, *The English Missionaries in Sweden and Finland* (C.H.S., 1937), with bibl. Eng. tr. of the *Handbok för Svenska Kyrkan* (the service book containing the orders for administering the Sacraments, the forms for Morning and Evening Prayer and the Occasional Offices) by E. E. Yelverton, *The Swedish Rite* (Translations of Christian Literature, Series III, Liturgical Texts, S.P.C.K., 1921). Id., *The Mass in Sweden*. Its Development from the Latin Rite from 1531 to 1917 (H.B.S., lvii; 1920). C. M. Butler, *The Reformation in Sweden* (New York, 1883). F. Siegmund-Schultze (ed.), *Ekklesia*. Eine Sammlung von Selbstdarstellungen der christlichen Kirchen, ii, Die skandinavischen Länder, pt. 1, Die Kirche in Schweden (5. Lieferung des Gesamtwerkes; 1935), with bibl. H. Reuterdahl, *Svenska Kyrkans Historia* (4 vols., Lund, 1838-66). H. Wijkmark, *Svensk Kyrko-historia* (Stockholm, 1928 ff.). H. Holmquist-H. Pleijel (edd.), *Svenska Kyrkans Historia* (Uppsala, 1933 ff.). C. A. Cornelius, *Svenska Kyrkans Historia efter Reformationen* (2 parts, Upsala, 1886-7). J. Martin, *Gustave Vase et la Réforme en Suède* (1906); H. Biaudet (ed.), *Le Saint Siège et la Suède durant la seconde moitié du XVIe siècle*. Notes et documents [1570-76] (Helsingfors, 1906); id., *Le Saint Siège et la Suède durant la seconde moitié du XVIe siècle*. Études politiques [1570-76] (Paris, 1907). Numerous specialized studies in H. Pleijel (ed.), *Samlingar och Studier till Svenska Kyrkans Historia* (Stockholm, 1940 ff.). There are also many vols. devoted to Swedish Church history in the *Uppsala Universitets Årsskrift* (Uppsala, 1865 ff.). H. Holmquist-G. Aulén in *P.R.E.* (ed. 3), xviii (1906), pp. 17-43, s.v. 'Schweden'; E. Newman in *R.G.G.* (ed. 2), v (1931), cols. 326-37, s.v. 'Schweden'.

SWEDENBORG, EMANUEL (1688-1772), orig. Swedberg, Swedish scientist and mystical thinker. He was the son of Jesper Swedberg, who later became professor of theology at Upsala and Bp. of Skara. After studying at Upsala and extensive travels in England (where he was influenced by Henry *More, J. *Locke, and I. *Newton) and elsewhere, he was appointed by Charles XII to a post on the Swedish Board of Mines (1716). Endowed with unusual mental fertility and inventiveness and considerable mathematical ability, he anticipated many subsequent hypotheses and discoveries (nebular theory, magnetic theory, machine-gun, aeroplane). He is also claimed as the founder of crystallography. As time went on he became increasingly concerned to show by purely scientific (esp. physical) analysis that the Universe had a fundamentally spiritual structure, notably in *Prodromus Philosophiae Ratiocinantis de Infinito et Causa Finali Creationis* (1734). In the next years further proof of this supremacy of the spiritual was found in biological and physiological studies.

In 1743–5 Swedenborg's outlook underwent a sudden development. He became conscious of direct contact with the angels and the spiritual world, partly in dreams and supernatural visions, but also in his normal waking life. He felt that the Lord was commissioning him to make known his doctrines to mankind at large. The agency was to be the New Church, organized not as a body separate from the existing Churches, but as a spiritual fraternity of all those of whatever ecclesiastical allegiance who accepted his doctrines. In 1747 he resigned his position on the Board of Mines and embarked on intensive study of the Scriptures. He spent the rest of his life in Sweden, Holland, and London, writing assiduously in defence of his teachings, but also maintaining his purely scientific interests to the end. He died in London on 29 March 1772 and was buried in the Swedish Church in Princes Square. In 1908 his remains were removed to Stockholm by arrangement with the Swedish Government.

Among the earliest disseminators of his teaching were two C of E clergymen, Thomas Hartley (d. 1784), rector of Winwick, Lancs., and John Clowes (1743–1831), vicar of St. John's, Manchester. Lancashire has remained a centre of Swedenborgian influence in England. Clowes (esp.) was averse to a new organization and, like Swedenborg himself, wished to propagate the teaching in the existing churches. The formal creation of the New Jerusalem Church was the work of five ex-Wesleyan preachers in London (7 May 1787). Since 1815 conferences have been held annually. In Gt. Britain the Church now has a membership of some 6,000–7,000. Small branches of the New Church exist on the Continent, in the U.S.A., and in Australia.

Swedenborg's combination of pantheistic and theosophic doctrines does not admit of brief summary. Of his voluminous expositions the most comprehensive was *Arcana Coelestia* (8 vols., 1756). Among others were *The Earths in the Universe* (1758), *The New Jerusalem and its Heavenly Doctrine* (1758), *Heaven and Hell* (1758), *Divine Love and Wisdom* (1763; perhaps the best epitome of his system), *The Apocalypse Revealed* (1766), and *The True Christian Religion* (1771). Among his earliest critics was I. *Kant, whose *Träume eines Geistersehers* (1766) was directed against him.

Photo-lithographed ed. of his works by R. L. Tafel (10 vols., Stockholm, 1869–70); also ed. in 18 vols., ib., 1901–16. *Posthumous Tracts* tr. from Lat. into Eng. by J. J. G. Wilkinson (London, 1847). A facsimile ed. of his *Memorabilia seu Diarium Spirituale ab Anno 1747 ad Annum 1765* was publ. at Stockholm (3 vols., 1901–5); Eng. tr. of the Diary by G. Bush–J. H. Smithson (5 vols., London, 1883–1902). J. Hyde, *A Bibliography of the Works of Emanuel Swedenborg Original and Translated* (1906). *The Swedenborg Concordance. A Complete Work of Reference to the Theological Writings of Emanuel Swedenborg Based on the Original Latin Writings of the Author, Compiled, Edited and Translated* by J. F. Potts (6 vols., London, 1888–1902). R. L. Tafel (ed. and tr.), *Documents Concerning the Life and Character of Emanuel Swedenborg* (2 vols., bound in 3, 1875–7). W. White, *Swedenborg. His Life and Writings* (1856); G. Trobridge, *A Life of Emanuel Swedenborg*. With a Popular Exposition of his Philosophical and Theological Teachings (1912). S. Toksvig, *Emanuel Swedenborg. Scientist and Mystic* (1949). E. Benz, *Swedenborg im Deutschland*. F. C. Oetingers und Immanuel Kants Auseinandersetzung mit der Person und Lehre Emanuel Swedenborgs (Auflage 2000; 1947); id., *Emanuel Swedenborg. Naturforscher und Seher* (1948). Popular life by E. A. Sutton, *The Happy Isles* (1938). L. B. de Beaumont in *H.E.R.E.*, xii (1921), pp. 129–32, s.v.

SWETE, HENRY BARCLAY (1835–1917), Biblical and patristic scholar. He was educated at King's College, London, and Gonville and Caius College, Cambridge. From 1882 to 1890 he was professor at King's College, London, and from 1890 until 1915 Regius professor of divinity at Cambridge. He achieved great success in fostering theological study, esp. at Cambridge; and among the many co-operative projects with which he was directly concerned were the *Journal of Theological Studies* (1899 ff.), the series of Cambridge Patristic Texts and the Cambridge Handbooks of Liturgical Study, the Central Society of Sacred Study (C.S.S.S., for the encouragement of theological study among Anglican clergy), and the (still unfinished, 1957) 'Lexicon of Patristic Greek'. He also edited *Essays on the Early History of the Church and Ministry* (posthumous, 1918), with important contributions by J. A. *Robinson, C. H. *Turner, W. H. *Frere, F. E. *Brightman, and others. His own writings include 2 vols. on the History of the Doctrine of the Holy Spirit (1909, 1912), editions of *Theodore of Mopsuestia's commentary on the Minor Epistles of St. Paul (1880–2) and of the text of the *Septuagint (3 vols., 1887–94), and commentaries on St. Mark (1898) and the Apocalypse (1906.)

'M. B. K.'–'H. G.'–'J. F. B.-B.', *Henry Barclay Swete. . . A Remembrance* (1918); this reprints, with additions, on pp. 163–92, a bibliography of Swete's publd. works by C. H. Turner–A. Rogers, orig. publd. in *J.T.S.*, xix (1918) pp. 1–19. J. H. Srawley in *D.N.B.*, 1912–1921, pp. 520–2.

SWIFT, JONATHAN (1667–1745), Dean of St. Patrick's, *Dublin (from 1713), and English satirist. Only the more definitely religious aspects of his career can be noted here. Ordained priest in Ireland in 1695, he remained faithful to the C of E and opposed alike to the N. Irish and Scottish *Presbyterians and to English Dissenters. In politics he was a Whig, but was persuaded to write against the *Occasional Conformity Act (1708) and frequently found difficulty in supporting his party in its leanings towards Nonconformists. His great powers of satire were used to religious ends in his *Argument to Prove the Inconvenience of Abolishing Christianity* (1708). He hated injustice and condemned the English misgovernment of Ireland, attacking even the Irish Bishops, but retaining the confidence of the common people. He wrote pamphlets against G. *Burnet, Bp. of *Salisbury, and A. *Collins, the *Deist. He is most popularly remembered as the author of *Gulliver's Travels* (1726). His works (nearly 100) were, with one exception, published anonymously.

Principal edd. of his works by J. Hawkesworth (14 vols., London, 1755–79), with account of life of the author in vol. i, pp. 9–40; by T. Sheridan (17 vols., ib., 1784), with life as vol. i, also issued separately; by W. Scott (19 vols., Edinburgh, &c., 1814), with memoirs as vol. i; of his prose works by Temple Scott (12 vols., London, 1897–1908), with biog. introd. by W. E. H. Lecky in vol. i, pp. xiii–xci; of his poems by H. Wilson (3 vols., Oxford, 1937), with bibl.; and of his Correspondence by F. E. Ball (6 vols., London, 1910–14). Lives and studies by H. Craik (London, 1882), L. Stephen ('English Men of Letters'; 1882; J. C. Collin (London, 1893); C. van Doren (ib., 1931), W. D. Taylor (ib., 1933); M. M. Rossi–J. M. Hone (ib., 1934); B. Newman (ib., 1937); and B. Ackworth (ib., 1947). S. Gwynn, *The Life and Friendships of Dean Swift* (1933). R. W. Jackson, *Jonathan Swift, Dean and Pastor* (S.P.C.K., 1939); C. Looten, *La Pensée religieuse de Swift et ses antinomies* (1935). H. Teerink, *A Bibliography of the Writings in Prose and Verse of Jonathan Swift* (The Hague, 1937). H. Williams in *C.B.E.L.*; il (1940), pp. 581–96. L. Stephen in *D.N.B.*, lv (1898), pp. 204–27.

SWISS GUARD (*Guardia Svizzera Pontificia*). The military guardians of the Papal Palace. The corps was instituted by Pope *Julius II (1503–13), with whom the cantons of Zürich and Lucerne entered into an agreement to supply 250 guardsmen. It now consists of about 100 men, recruited from all the Swiss cantons. The parade uniform of the Guard, which was designed by *Michelangelo, is composed of tunic, breeches, and stockings of wide and gaily coloured red, yellow, and dark blue stripes. See also *Noble Guard, Palatine Guard*.

P. Krieg, *Die päpstliche Schweizergarde* (Zürich, 1948). J. Repond, *Le Costume de la garde suisse pontificale et la renaissance italienne* (Rome, 1917). E. Hampoole, O.P., 'The Papal Swiss Guards' in *The American Catholic Quarterly Review*, xxxvii (1912), pp. 286–309 and 369–87. G. Felice in *E.C.*, vi (1951), col. 1206 f., s.v. 'Guardia Svizzera Pontificia', with bibl. and illustr.

SWITHIN, St. (d. 862), also 'Swithun', Bp. of *Winchester. He was the trusted adviser of Egbert, King of Wessex, whose son, Ethelwulf, he educated. It appears that he was consecrated Bp. of Winchester by Ceolnoth, Abp. of *Canterbury, in 852. Originally buried outside the walls of the minster, his body was translated to a shrine within the cathedral in the 10th cent. In 1093 it suffered a further translation when Bp. Walkelin's new cathedral was erected. At the Reformation (1538) the shrine was destroyed. The popular tradition that the weather on St. Swithin's day (15 July) will be that of the next forty days is of uncertain origin.

Account of his translation and miracles by Lanfrid, monk of the old minster, Winchester, written before 1006, and life by *Goscelin, together with other material on his cult, pr. in *AA.SS.*, Jul. I (1719), pp. 322–7. Crit. edd. of full text from different MSS. by E. P. Sauvage, of the former in *Anal. Boll.*, iv (1885), pp. 367–410, and of the latter, ib., vii (1888), pp. 373–86. Some leaves on St. Swithin in an Anglo-Saxon MS. extant at Gloucester, *c.* 985, ed. with modern Eng. tr. by J. Earle, *Gloucester Fragments*, i (1861), with 'An Essay on the Life and Times of St. Swithin', pp. 21–56. The principal later authority is *William of Malmesbury, *Gesta Pontificum* (ed. N. E. S. A. Hamilton, R.S., 1870, pp. 160–2 and 167 f.).

'SWORD OF THE SPIRIT'. A RC social movement inaugurated by Card. A. *Hinsley in 1940. It was designed as an organization for unifying international Catholic social efforts by 'prayer, study, and action' with a view to promoting justice in war and in the peace which was to follow, on the basis of *Pius XII's 'Five Peace Points' and the requirements of the *Natural Law. These aims, set forth in detail in many of the writings of C. Dawson, vice-president of the movement, were shared by Christians of other denominations and were stated in a letter to *The Times* (21 Dec. 1940) signed by the Abps. of Canterbury (C. G. *Lang) and York (W.*Temple), Card. Hinsley, and the moderator of the Free Churches (W. H. Armstrong). The collaboration between RCs and other groups was, however, restricted in 1941 when full membership of the 'Sword' was confined to RCs and the non-RC communions set up a separate organization under the title 'Religion and Life', the two movements being connected by a Joint Committee.

SYLLABUS ERRORUM. A set of eighty theses, already condemned in earlier pronouncements (encyclicals, allocutions, etc.) of *Pius IX and promulgated as erroneous with '*Quanta Cura' (q.v.) on 8 Dec. 1864. The suggestion of comprehensive attack on modern errors seems to have originated with V. G. Pecci, Bp. of Perugia (later *Leo XIII) at the Council of Spoleto in 1849. The basis of the Syllabus was a list of 85 errors in a Pastoral Instruction (1860) of O. P. Gerbet, Bp. of Perpignan (1853–64), which, modified in turn into a catalogue of 61 theses with corresponding censures, was approved by an assembly of Bishops at Rome in 1862.

The Syllabus was disposed under ten heads dealing with: I, Pantheism, Naturalism and Absolute Rationalism (1–7); II, Moderate Rationalism (8–14); III, Indifferentism and Latitudinarianism (15–18); IV, Socialism, Communism, secret societies, Bible societies and Liberal-clerical societies (various earlier documents); V, The Church and its Rights (19–38); VI, Civil Society and its relation to the Church (39–55): VII, Natural and Christian Ethics (56–64); VIII, Christian Marriage (65–74); IX, The Temporal Power of the Pope (75–6); and X, Modern Liberalism (77–80). The last (the 80th) of the rejected propositions is the (often misunderstood) thesis that the 'Roman Pontiff can and ought to reconcile and adjust himself with progress, liberalism and modern civilization' (80). The covering letter issued with the Syllabus and 'Quanta Cura' seemed to make it dogmatically binding.

Its issue was greeted with a storm of protest, e.g. from W. E. *Gladstone. In France publication of the Syllabus and Encyclical were forbidden on 1 Jan. 1865, though the prohibition was withdrawn shortly afterwards. F. A. P. *Dupanloup's *La Convention du 15 septembre et l'encyclique du 8 décembre* (1865), which purported to interpret each condemnation in the light of its original context, did much to mitigate consternation. Many of its fundamental doctrines were embodied in the Dogmatic Constitution *De Fide Catholica* at the *Vatican Council of 1870. In the later years of the 19th cent. the Syllabus was the bulwark of the Ultramontane party in the RC Church.

Text in *A.S.S.*, iii (1867), pp. 168–76, and in *Pii IX Pontificis Acta*, Pars Prima, iii (no date), pp. 701–17; repr. in Denz.–Bann. (ed. 1928), pp. 465–73. J. B. Bury, *History of the Papacy in the Nineteenth Century* (ed. R. H. Murray, 1930), esp. Lectures i and ii, pp. 1–46.

SYLVESTER, St., Bp. of Rome from 314 to 335. He filled the see of Rome at a very important era in the history of the Church, but very little is known of him. He occupies, however, an important place in later legend, which asserts that he baptized Emp. *Constantine (cleansing him from physical leprosy) at the Baptistery of the *Lateran and established the Lateran church as the cathedral of Rome on territory given him by the Emperor. He is also the reputed recipient of the *Donation of Constantine, which provided him with wide temporal rights over the Church. Though he did not himself attend the Council of *Nicaea (325), he was represented by two legates, Vitus and Vincentius. Feast day, 31 Dec.

Jaffé, i, 28–30. *L.P.* (Duchesne), i, 170–201; see also pp. cix–xx. W. Levison, 'Konstantinische Schenkung und Silvester-Legende' in *Miscellanea Francesco Ehrle*, ii (S.T., xxxviii; 1924), pp. 159–247, with full reff. E. Caspar, *Geschichte des Papsttums*, i (1930), pp. 115–30. É. Amann in *D.T.C.*, xiv (pt. 2; 1941), cols. 2068–75, s.v. 'Silvestre I'; A. Amore, O.F.M., in *E.C.*, xi (1953), col. 596 f., s.v. 'Silvestro I'. J. P. Kirsch in *L.Th.K.*, ix (1937), col. 559 f., s.v., for further bibl. See also bibl. to *Donation of Constantine.*

SYLVESTER II (*c.* 940–1003), Pope from 999. A native of Auvergne, Gerbert was educated at the *Benedictine monastery of Aurillac and later at the episcopal school of Ausona (Vich) in Spain, where he acquired an unrivalled knowledge of mathematics. Having gained fame as teacher at the cathedral school of *Reims, he became secretary of Abp. Adalbero, and, after the deposition of the latter's successor by the synod of St.-Basle-de-Verzy, Abp. of Reims in 991. As John XV did not recognize his election, he joined Emp. Otto III in Italy in 996, through whose influence he obtained the Abpric. of *Ravenna in 998 and was elected Pope in 999. He at once became one of the most ardent defenders of Papal prerogatives, esp. against the anti-Roman tendencies of the Church in France which he himself had professed as Abp. of Reims. He fully reinstated his deposed predecessor in that see, initiated measures against simony and concubinage of the clergy, organized the Church in Poland and Hungary by erecting Gnesen and Gran into archiepiscopal sees, and gave the title of king to St. *Stephen of Hungary. In 1001 he was obliged to leave Rome on account of a revolt against the Emperor, after whose death in the following year he returned to the city.

Sylvester II was a gifted scholar who endeavoured to give reason its place by the side of revelation. He was one of the first medieval philosophers to elaborate the dialectical method and has been credited with attempting a synthesis between *Plato and *Aristotle. His mathematical, astronomical, and other scientific knowledge was much admired by his contemporaries and even believed to be acquired by magic. In the treatise 'De corpore et sanguine Christi' which is probably to be ascribed to him is reasserted, in a somewhat mitigated form, the Eucharistic teaching of *Paschasius Radbertus.

Opera Omnia in J. P. Migne, *PL*, cxxxix, 57–338; modern ed. with notes and biog. introd. by A. Olleris (Clermont, 1867); *Lettres de Gerbert* (983–997) ed. J. Havet (Collection de Textes pour servir à l'Étude et à l'Enseignement d'Histoire; 1869); his *Opera Mathematica*, ed. N. Bubnov (Berlin, 1899). Jaffé, i, 496–501. *L.P.* (Duchesne), ii, 263 f. C. F. Hock, *Gerbert oder Papst Sylvester II und sein Jahrhundert* (1837; Fr. tr., with additional docc., 1842). F. Picavet, *Gerbert un pape philosophique d'après l'histoire et d'après la légende* (1897). J. Leflon, *Gerbert. Humanisme et chrétienté au X*^e^ *siècle* (1946), with full bibl. R. Allen, 'Pope Sylvester II' in *E.H.R.*, vii (1892), pp. 625–68. Mann, v (1910), pp. 1–120. É. Amann in Fliche–Martin, vii (1940), pp. 68–77. Id. in *D.T.C.*, xiv (pt. 2; 1941), cols. 2075–83, s.v. 'Silvestre II', with bibl.

SYLVESTRINES. A small religious order which follows a rule akin to that of St. *Benedict, but with special emphasis on the vow of poverty. It was founded in 1231 by St. Sylvester Gozzolini (d. 1267; feast day, 26 Nov.). Its houses, which are independent of the confederation of Benedictine Congregations, have been mainly confined to Italy, though since 1855 it has conducted a mission in Ceylon.

[H. Helyot], *Histoire des ordres monastiques, religieuses et militaires*, vi (1718), pp. 170–8; Heimbucher, i, 211 f. with bibl.

SYMEON. See *Simeon.*

SYMMACHUS (later 2nd cent.). An *Ebionite, perhaps of *Samaria, who made a fresh translation of the OT into Greek. Unlike *Aquila, he preferred a readable style and palatable rendering to verbal accuracy, modifying esp. the anthropomorphic expressions of the Hebrew text. The extant fragments of his work are hence of limited use for critical purposes. His version was incorporated by *Origen into his *Hexapla. Symmachus seems also to have written a lost commentary on the Ebionite Gospel, in which he criticized the canonical Gospel acc. to St. Matthew.

The chief ancient reff. are *Eusebius, *H.E.*, vi, 17; *Jerome, *De Vir. Ill.*, liv [under *Origen]; *Epiphanius, *De Mensuris et Ponderibus*, xvi. G. *Mercati, *L' età di Simmaco l' interprete e S. Epifanio* (Modena, 1892). H. B. *Swete, *Introduction to the Old Testament in Greek* (1900), pp. 49–53. Bardenhewer, i, 379 f. J. Gwynn in *D.C.B.*, iv (1887), p. 748 f., s.v. 'Symmachus (2)'; H. A. Redpath in *H.D.B.*, iv (1902), p. 865 f., s.v. 'Versions, Greek (2)'; J. Schmid in *L.Th.K.*, ix (1937), col. 933.

SYMMACHUS, St. (d. 514), Pope from 498. A native of Sardinia, Symmachus was appointed Pope by the majority to oppose the concessions to the Emp. and Patr. of *Constantinople advocated by the party of his predecessor, Anastasius II, which elected against him the archpriest, Laurentius. As the validity of the election of Symmachus was confirmed by the Gothic King, *Theodoric, the partisans of Laurentius cast suspicion upon the Pope's personal character, accused him of simony and of celebrating Easter at the wrong date, and occupied most of the Roman churches. In 501 the King summoned a council of bishops (the 'Palmary Synod') to Rome to deal with these charges, but Symmachus, who had been attacked on the way, refused to appear. The synod, on the other hand, declared itself incompetent to pronounce him guilty and asserted him to be the rightful Pope. Theodoric, however, allowed Laurentius to return to Rome and Symmachus was restricted to St. Peter's, though he had the support of the majority of the people and, among others, the Abps. of Milan and *Ravenna. The troubles, which led to much bloodshed in the city, lasted till 506. In 507, owing to the good offices of the Alexandrine deacon, Dioscurus, Theodoric withdrew his opposition. During the latter part of his reign Symmachus devoted himself to the defence of the Catholic faith against the *Henoticon of *Zeno, upheld by Emp. Anastasius, and against the *Manicheans, whom he expelled from Rome. He confirmed the primatial rights of *Arles over the Gallican and Spanish Churches and sent the pallium to *Caesarius, its archbishop, who was thus the first bishop outside Italy to receive the privilege. He also liberally assisted the poor and the African Catholics who were persecuted by the *Arians, and embellished many Roman churches, esp. St. Peter's. Among his liturgical innovations were the singing of *Gloria in excelsis on Sundays and the feasts of martyrs (but only by bishops). During his reign *Dionysius Exiguus compiled his collection of Latin canons and the so-called 'Symmachian Forgeries', a collection of writings intended to prove from spurious precedents that the Pope cannot be judged by any man, were also issued. Feast day, 19 July.

Epistolae et Decreta in A. Thiel (ed.), Epistolae Romanorum Pontificum Genuinae, i (Brunswick, 1867), pp. 641–738; Acts of the Synods held in Rome in 499, 501, and 502 also ed. T. *Mommsen in M.G.H., Auctores Antiquissimi, xii (1894), pp. 395–455. Jaffé, i, 96–100. L.P. (Duchesne), i, 260–8; see also pp. cxxxiii–xl. W. von Pölnitz, O.S.B., 'A propos des synodes apocryphes du pape Symmaque' in R.H.E., xxxii (1936), pp. 81–8; A. Alessandrini, 'Teodorico e Papa Simmaco durante lo scisma laurenziano' in Archivio della R. Deputazione Romana di Storia Patria, lxvii (1944), pp. 152–207. E. Caspar, Geschichte des Papsttums, ii (1933), pp. 87–129; Fliche–Martin, iv (1937), pp. 341–52. F. X. Seppelt in L.Th.K., ix (1937), cols. 933 f., s.v., with bibl. É. Amann in D.T.C., xiv (1941), cols. 2984–90, s.v. 'Symmaque (Saint)'; A. Amore, O.F.M., in E.C., xi (1953), cols. 629–31, s.v. 'Simmaco'. Further bibl. in Altaner (ed. 1950), p. 415.

SYNAGOGUE (Gk. συναγωγή). It would appear that the Jews introduced Synagogues as their regular meeting-places for worship after the Babylonian exile (6th cent. B.C.), when, owing to the Dispersion, they could no longer take part in Temple-worship, even at the annual festivals. By NT times the Synagogue was well established, and it has remained a characteristic feature of Jewry down to the present day.

The worship of the Synagogue, unlike that of the Temple, was non-sacrificial. It consisted chiefly in readings from the Law and, to a less extent, from the Prophets, accompanied by prayers, canticles, and sometimes a sermon. The most important piece of its furniture was the '*Ark', a kind of cupboard in which the sacred rolls of the Scriptures were kept. At least ten males were required for public worship, and certain officials were responsible for the various duties. The Gospels mention the synagogues of *Nazareth (Lk. 4. 16) and *Capernaum (Mk. 1. 21).

Among early studies C. *Vitringa, De Synagoga Vetere Libri Tres (Franeker, 1696; abridged Eng. tr., 1842). W. O. E. Oesterley–G. H. Box, The Religion and Worship of the Synagogue (1907); I. Elbogen, Der jüdische Gottesdienst in seiner geschichtlichen Entwicklung (1913), pp. 444–510 ('Organisation des jüdischen Gottesdienstes'); S. Krauss, Synagogale Altertümer (1922); A. Menes, 'Tempel und Synagogue' in Z.A.T.W., l (1932), pp. 268–76. H. Kohl–C. Watzinger, Antike Synagogen in Galiläa (1916); E. L. Sukenik, Ancient Synagogues in Palestine and Greece (Schweich Lectures for 1930; 1934); id. [tr. from the Heb. by H. Danby], The Ancient Synagogue of Beth Alpha (fol., Jerusalem–Oxford, 1932). R. Krautheimer, Mittelalterliche Synagogen (1927). G. *Dalman in P.R.E. (ed. 3), vii (1899), pp. 7–19, s.v. 'Gottesdienst, Synagogaler'; W. Backer in H.D.B., iv (1902), pp. 636–43, s.v.; L. N. Dembitz in J.E., xi (1905), pp. 619–31, s.v. 'Synagogue'; J. Jacobs, ib., pp. 631–40, s.v. 'Synagogic Architecture'; R. W. Moss in D.C.G., ii (1908), pp. 689–92, s.v.; K. Kohler in D.A.C., ii (1918), pp. 541–5, s.v.; I. Elbogen in R.G.G. (ed. 2), v (1931), cols. 947–9, s.v.

SYNAGOGUE, Great. Acc. to Jewish tradition, a legislative body of 120 members which was established in *Jerusalem in the time of *Ezra and *Nehemiah (5th cent. B.C.). Its activities were held to have been largely concerned with the fixing of the *canon and text of the Hebrew Scriptures. The grounds for supposing that such a permanently constituted body ever existed, however, are unconvincing, the oldest reference to it being in the Jewish treatise *Pirqe Aboth (3rd cent. A.D.).

A. *Kuenen, 'Over de Mannen der Groote Synagoge' in Verslagen en Mededeelingen der Koninklijke Akademie van Wetenschapen, Afdeeling Letterkunde, vi (Amsterdam, 1877), pp. 207–48*. S. Krauss, 'The Great Synod' in J.Q.R., x (1898), pp. 347–77. J. A. Selbie in H.D.B., iv (1902), p. 643 f., s.v.; W. Bacher in J.E., xi (1905), pp. 640–643, s.v.; both with bibl.

SYNAPTE (Gk. συναπτή, 'joined together'). In the E. Church, a prayer composed of a number of suffrages 'linked together', corresponding to the W. '*Litany'. Synaptai are recited by the deacon outside the *Iconostasis, near the outset of the Liturgy of St. Chrysostom, the choir responding 'Kyrie Eleison'.

SYNAXARION (Gk. συναξάριον). (1) In the E. Church, a short account of a saint or feast appointed to be read at the early morning service of *Orthros. (2) The book which contains, inter alia, these passages, arranged acc. to the calendar ('The Greater Synaxarion'). (3) Another book which merely enumerates the feasts to be observed every day, with a reference to the appropriate Biblical lessons ('The Lesser Synaxarion'). Confusion arises through these various uses, and H. *Delehaye recommends that the word be confined to senses (1) and (2).

SYNAXIS (Gk. σύναξις, 'an assembly' or 'congregation', a word cognate with and equivalent to συναγωγή, 'synagogue', the use of which was avoided by Christian writers, doubtless on account of its Jewish associations). The term is applicable to any assembly for public worship and prayer, inclusive of the Eucharist or 'liturgical synaxis', and is so used in the E. Church. In the W. it was used in early times esp. of the 'aliturgical synaxis', or non-Eucharistic service, consisting of Psalms, lessons from Scripture, and prayers, out of which the Divine *Office and pre-anaphoral rite (*Vormesse*, 'Pre-Mass') are held to have developed.

SYNCELLUS (a hybrid word: Gk. σύν +Lat. *cella*; i.e. literally, a person who shares a cell with someone else). In the Byzantine Church, an ecclesiastic who lived continually with a bishop, esp. in the capacity of a domestic chaplain and in order to bear witness to the purity of the bishop's moral life. In the W. St. *Augustine of Canterbury is said by *Leo III to have been the *syncellus* of St. *Gregory the Great. In later times, the word was used of a dignitary associated as counsellor with a prelate, who subsequently succeeded to his office.

SYNCELLUS, GEORGE (*fl. c.* 800). See *George Syncellus*. He is often referred to simply as 'Syncellus'.

SYNCRETISM. The attempt to combine different or opposite doctrines and practices, esp. in reference to philosophical and religious systems. The term came into prominence in the 17th cent. when it was applied to the teaching of G. *Calixtus who undertook to unite the Reformation Churches in Germany with each other and with the Catholic Church on the basis of the Apostles' Creed and the doctrine of the first five cents. It is also frequently applied to the unifying cultural forces in the Mediterranean civilization of the Hellenistic and Roman periods, and in the history of religion to any fusion of various beliefs and practices, e.g. to some tendencies in pre-Christian Judaism. In the RC theology of grace the term is used of attempts to combine *Thomist and *Molinist teaching.

SYNDERESIS. See *Synteresis*.

SYNEISAKTOI. See *Subintroductae*.

SYNERGISM. The teaching of P. *Melanchthon that in the act of conversion the human will can co-operate with the Holy Spirit and God's grace. By insisting that the primary cause of such conversion is the Holy Spirit and not the will Melanchthon rebutted the charge of *Pelagianism which his opponents raised against him. His teaching had many points of contact with the *Semi-pelagianism (*Cassian, &c.) of the 5th cent. The long controversy provoked by Melanchthon only ended with the publication of the 'Formula of *Concord' in 1577.

SYNESIUS (*c.* 370–*c.* 414), Bp. of Ptolemais. A native of Cyrene and descended from an ancient family, he was brought up a pagan and studied at Alexandria under the celebrated *Neo-Platonist philosopher, *Hypatia. In 403 he married a Christian wife, with the blessing of *Theophilus, Patr. of Alexandria. Having won the confidence and affection of his fellow-Alexandrians by a successful embassy to the Imperial court at *Constantinople, he was chosen *c.* 410 Bp. of Ptolemais, although probably as yet not even baptized. At first he hesitated, wishing to continue living with his wife and to retain certain of his philosophical beliefs, e.g. in the pre-existence of the soul and the eternity of the world; but eventually, without engaging himself to give up either his wife or his doctrines, he was consecrated by Theophilus. A series of domestic and other tragedies marked his episcopate, though he did not survive to witness the murder of Hypatia in 415.

Synesius's writings, all from his pre-Christian period but breathing a sincere spirituality, include *De Providentia*, a political pamphlet describing life at Constantinople; *De Regno*, a speech depicting the ideal Roman Emperor, delivered before Arcadius in 399; *De Dono Astrolabii*, a book with which he accompanied the gift of an astrolabe; *Calvitii Encomium*, a satire on the sophists in the form of a eulogy on baldness; *Dion*, a defence of a life of learning and the enjoyment of reasonable pleasures against the advocates of extreme asceticism; and *De Insomniis*, on the causes and meanings of dreams. Synesius also wrote many letters, as well as a collection of hymns in the Doric dialect.

Only complete ed. by D. *Petavius (Paris, 1612), repr. in J. P. Migne, *PG*, lxvi, 1021–756. Modern ed. (without Letters and Hymns) by J. G. Krabinger, Landshut, 1850; of Letters in R. Hercher (ed.), *Epistolographi Graeci* (Paris, ed. F. Didot, 1873), pp. 638–739. Crit. ed. of hymns by N. Terzaghi (2 vols., Rome, 1939–44; with commentary). Eng. tr. of Letters by A. FitzGerald (London, 1926); of Essays and Hymns by id. (2 vols., London, 1930). On Synesius's life and works, studies by Alice Gardner (The Fathers for English Readers, S.P.C.K., 1886), W. S. Crawford (London, 1901), G. Grützmacher (Leipzig, 1913), and C. Lacombrade (Paris, 1951). J. Stiglmayr, S.J., 'Synesius von Kyrene, Metropolit der Pentapolis' in *Z.K.T.*, xxxviii (1914), pp. 509–63. W. Fritz, *Die Briefe des Bischofs Synesius von Kyrene* (1898); id., 'Die handschriftliche Überlieferung der Briefe des Bischofs Synesius' in *Abh.* (Bayr.), xxiii (1909), pp. 319–98. Bardenhewer, iv, 110–122; Altaner (ed. 1951), p. 241 f. T. R. Halcomb in *D.C.B.*, iv (1887), pp. 756–80, s.v. 'Synesius (2)'; W. Möller–G. Krüger in *P.R.E.* (ed. 3), xix (1907, pp. 235–9, s.v.; H. *Leclercq, O.S.B., in *D.A.C.L.*, viii (pt. 2; 1929), cols. 2851–2855, s.v. 'Lettres chrétiennes. Iii. Lettres de Synésius'; H. von Campenhausen in *P.W.*, Zweite Reihe iv (pt. 2; 1932), cols. 1362–5, s.v. 'Synesios'.

SYNOD. See *Council*.

SYNODICON. The term is applied:

(1) In a general sense to a synodal act or a collection of such acts (e.g. W. *Beveridge's *Synodicon*, 1672).

(2) To a liturgical text for use in the E. Church on the 'Feast of *Orthodoxy'. Composed by Patr. Methodius I *c.* 843 for the new feast, it was worked over by Sergius II *c.* 1000 and since then has been frequently modified by excising old names and inserting new ones. Its form is akin to a litany, and it contains a series of praises for the heroes of orthodoxy and for Emperors and bishops, followed by anathemas against numerous heresies. In modern times it is not customary to recite it publicly *in extenso*.

The text of the Synodicon is pr. in Mansi, xiii (Florence, 1767), cols. 812-20 (under the year 1027); also in J. P. Migne, *PG*, cxx, 728-36. In its current official form it is contained in editions of the *Triodion for the First Sunday in Lent (e.g., ed. Rome, 1879, pp. 240-6). A. Michel in *L.Th.K.*, ix (1937), col. 950, s.v., with bibl.

SYNOPTIC PROBLEM, The. The problem of the literary relations between the three 'Synoptic Gospels' (Mt., Mk., Lk.), which arises from the occurrence of large areas of common subject-matter and often similar phrasing in more than one Gospel. That this parallelism, of varying degrees of closeness, must be accounted for by their literary interdependence is nowadays almost universally held by scholars. There is also wide, but less complete, agreement:

(1) That Mk. is the earliest of the Gospels and was used as a framework by both Mt. and Lk.;

(2) That the non-Marcan material common to Mt. and Lk. is derived from a single lost source, known to critics as '*Q' (q.v.);

(3) That the authors of Mt. and Lk. used further written sources for the matter peculiar to each of them. Whether each of the Evangelists had only one or more than one such source is debated. Without prejudging this question, scholars commonly use the letters 'M' and 'L' to denote this material.

Among the many elaborations and modifications of these widely accepted theories are:

(1) The *Proto-Luke Theory orig. propounded by B. H. *Streeter;

(2) The view, defended by T. *Chapman, O.S.B., and B. C. Butler, O.S.B., and officially upheld by the RC *Biblical Commission, that Mt. was the earliest Gospel;

(3) The view that the Lucan 'Passion Narrative' is from a source independent of that of those of Mt. and Mk. The disproportionate length of the Passion Narratives in any case suggests that they once had a separate existence;

(4) The belief that the 'Infancy Narratives' in Mt. 1 f. and Lk. 1 f. (which have no counterpart in Mk.) are entirely independent.

V. Taylor, *The Gospels*: A Short Introduction (1930); B. H. Streeter, *The Four Gospels* (1924); J. C. Hawkins, *Horae Synopticae* (1899); [Oxford] *Studies in the Synoptic Problem*, ed. W. *Sanday (1911). From the RC side, J. Chapman, *Matthew, Mark and Luke* (ed. J. M. T. Barton, 1937). For parallel texts of the three Gospels in English see J. M. Thompson, *The Synoptic Gospels* (1910); for the Greek Text, A. Huck, *Synopse der drei ersten Evangelien* (1892 and later; 9th ed., with English Introduction, etc., by F. L. Cross, 1935).

SYNTERESIS, also 'Synderesis'. A technical term used by St. *Thomas Aquinas (e.g. 'De Veritate', q. 17. a. 2) and other Scholastic theologians for our knowledge of the first principles of moral action. It appears to derive from a scribal error in St. *Jerome's 'Commentary on Ezekiel' (on Ezek. 1. 7) where συντήρησις (not attested elsewhere in this sense) occurs as a corruption of συνείδησις, the normal Greek word for 'conscience'. The medieval mystics, e.g. Master *Eckhart, sometimes identify it with the mysterious ground of the soul where the mystic union takes place.

H. Appel, *Die Lehre der Scholastiker von der Synteresis* (1891); O. Renz, *Die Syntheresis nach dem heiligen Thomas von Aquin* (1911).

SYRIAC. The Syriac language is a branch of Aramaic, which was spoken in *Edessa and its neighbourhood from shortly before the beginning of the Christian era. It was extensively used in the early Church owing to the active Christian communities in those parts. From an early date it was employed in translations of the Bible (see *Diatessaron*; *Old Syriac*; *Peshitta*; *Syro-hexaplar*), translations of other works from the Greek, and for original Syriac compositions. After the religious divisions in the 5th cent. it continued in general use both among the East Syrians (*Nestorians) and the West Syrians (*Monophysites or *Jacobites). Like *Hebrew, its alphabet is derived from the so-called Phoenician alphabet and is fundamentally consonantal. There are three forms of script, Estrangelo, Nestorian, and Jacobite (or Serto).

The surviving literature, which dates mainly from the 2nd to the 8th cents. A.D., is almost wholly Christian. The Syriac Versions of the Bible are of exceptional value to the textual critic of the Scriptures on account of their early date and the natural accuracy of Syriac scholars. A large number of Gk. patristic works survive only in Syriac. These (generally very literal) versions sometimes make it possible to recover the Greek with an approach to certainty. Among the most important Syriac authors were *Aphraates and St. *Ephrem Syrus. After the 5th cent. orig. compositions became rare and the literature consists almost wholly of translations. When Arabic became the current vernacular, Syriac increasingly became an artificial language.

The most important collections of Syriac MSS. are now preserved in the *Vatican and the British Museum. Notable editors of Syriac texts include the *Assemani, W. *Cureton, W. Wright, G. *Bickell, R. Duval, P. Bedjan, Cong. Orat., I. E. Rahmani, E. W. Brooks, R. Graffin, F. Nau, J. B. Chabot, and A. *Baumstark.

The chief modern collections of printed texts include many items in the series *Horae Semiticae* (London, 1903 ff.), others issued by the Text and Translation Society (London,

1902 ff.); others in *P.O.*; *Patrologia Syriaca* (Paris, 1894 ff.); *C.S.C.O.*, Scriptores Syri (Paris, Leipzig, &c., 1907 ff.); also texts and translations in *Woodbrooke Studies*. Christian Documents in Syriac, Arabic, and Garshūni, ed. and tr. by A. Mingana (7 vols., Cambridge, 1927–34). *Thesaurus Syriacus* by R. P. Smith (2 vols., Oxford, 1879; supplement by J. P. Margoliouth, 1927); *Lexicon Syriacum* by C. Brockelmann (Edinburgh–Berlin, 1895; ed. 2, Halle, 1928). *Compendious Syriac Dictionary* by J. P. Margoliouth (Oxford, 1903). *Dictionary of the Dialects of Vernacular Syriac* by A. J. Maclean (ib. 1901). Lexicon to Syriac NT by W. Jennings–U. Gantillon (ib., 1926). *Kurzgefasste syrische Grammatik* by T. Nöldeke (Leipzig, 1880; Eng. tr. as *Compendious Syriac Grammar* by J. A. Crichton, 1904); shorter *Syrische Grammatik* by C. Brockelmann (Berlin, &c., 1899; many subsequent edd.); *Grammatik der neu-syrischen Sprache* by T. Nöldeke (Leipzig, 1868); *Grammar of the Dialects of Vernacular Syriac* by A. J. Maclean (Cambridge, 1895). R. Duval, *Traité de grammaire syriaque* (1881). G. Bickell, *Conspectus Rei Syrorum Literariae* (Munster, 1871); W. Wright, *A Short History of Syriac Literature* (1894); R. Duval, *La Littérature syriaque* (1899); A. Baumstark, *Geschichte der syrischen Literatur mit Ausschluss der christlich-palästinenischen Texte* (1922); J. B. Chabot, *Littérature syriaque* (1935). On Palestinian Syriac, see F. C. *Burkitt, 'Christian Palestinian Literature' in *J.T.S.*, ii (1901), pp. 174–85, with bibl. Id., 'The Old Lectionary of Jerusalem' ib., xxiv (1923), pp. 415–24. N. McLean in *E.B.* (ed. 11), xxvi (1911), pp. 310–17, s.v. 'Syriac Literature'.

SYRIAC VERSIONS OF THE BIBLE.

(1) *Old Testament*. The principal are: (a) The *Peshitta* version, made originally by Jews, probably in the early 2nd cent., for the Jewish community at Edessa. Used also by the primitive Christian community of *Edessa, it was later revised in certain parts (notably in the Psalter and the Prophets) under the influence of Greek Christianity so as to harmonize with the *Septuagint. (b) The *Syro-Hexaplar*, a close rendering of *Origen's text of the *Septuagint made at Alexandria *c.* 616–17 by the *Monophysite bishop, Paul of Tella.

(2) *New Testament*. In early times the Gospels were known in two forms: (a) The *Evangelión da-Mĕhallĕtē*, or 'Gospel of the Mixed', a Syriac version of *Tatian's *Diatessaron; and (b) the *Evangelión da-Mĕpharrĕshē*, or 'Gospel of the Separated' (i.e. the four Gospels), known as the 'Old Syriac'. It is probable that the 'Gospel of the Separated' was made not earlier than 200, and that the 'Syriac Diatessaron' is prior to and independent of it. It exists in two MSS.—the 'Curetonian' and the 'Sinaitic'. There is also evidence for the existence of an Old Syriac version of Acts and the Pauline Epistles. The Old Syriac NT is generally held to have been the basis of the NT *Peshitta* revision.

Subsequently to the Peshitta, two further versions of the NT were made: (c) the *Philoxenian*, in 508, which included the books omitted from the Peshitta canon, and (d) the *Harklean*, in 616, a revision of the Philoxenian and more literal than its predecessor in rendering the Greek. With the exception of the books omitted from the Peshitta, the Philoxenian version has perished.

The Peshitta remains the authorized version of the Syriac-speaking Churches.

Introductory account in A. *Souter, *The Text and Canon of the New Testament* (ed. 2, by C. S. C. Williams, 1954), pp. 50–8, with bibl. p. 227. For further bibl. see artt. on separate items cited above.

SYRIAN CATHOLICS.

A body of *Uniat Christians descended from the Syrian *Jacobites (*Monophysites). In the latter part of the 16th cent. relations were established between the Syrian Jacobite Church and the Papacy, which led to some conversions in the 17th cent., and the election of a Catholic, Andrew Akhidjan, to the see of Aleppo in 1656. The Catholics lived, however, a precarious existence and seem to have virtually disappeared soon after 1700. The present Church traces its existence to the accession of Mar Michael Garweh, who had become a RC, to the Abpric. of Aleppo in 1783, since when a Catholic minority has co-existed with the Jacobites in Syria. In 1830 their existence as a separate body was formally recognized by the Turks. The Patr., Ignatius Ephrem II Rahmani (1898–1929), has become known in the W. as a scholar of distinction through his edition of the *Testamentum Domini* (1899). Their membership, which since the war of 1914–18 has declined considerably, is said to be now some 50,000.

D. Attwater, *The Catholic Eastern Churches* (Milwaukee, Wisc., revised ed., 1935), pp. 163–79. S. Vailhé, A.A., in *D.T.C.*, i (1903), cols. 1430–3, s.v. 'Antioche, V. Patriarcat syrien catholique'; I. Ziade, ib., xiv (pt. 2; 1946), cols. 3017–3088, s.v. 'Syrienne (Église), esp. cols. 3023 f. (Droit Canonique), 3025–8 (Liturgie, with reff. to edd. of texts), and 3078–80 (Hiérarchie). For edd. of liturgical texts see also A. *Baumstark, *Liturgie comparée* (ed. 3, 1953), p. 244 f.

SYRIAN TEXT, The.

The name applied by B. F. *Westcott and F. J. A. *Hort to an edition of the Greek text of the NT which was made, as they held, in or near *Antioch in Syria *c.* A.D. 300, and of which *Lucian of Antioch was the probable author. It is, in the main, the text found in the great majority of the Greek MSS. of the NT which come from the Byzantine period, and is hence the immediate ancestor of the *Byzantine Text (q.v.).

SYRO-CHALDAEANS.

An alternative name for the *Chaldean Christians, i.e. the descendants of the ancient *Nestorian Church now in communion with the see of Rome.

SYRO-HEXAPLAR, The.

The translation into *Syriac of the Greek text of the *Septuagint contained in *Origen's *Hexapla, which was made in 616–17 by Paul, the *Jacobite Bp. of Tella in Mesopotamia. It was produced with great care and accuracy, preserving Origen's critical symbols. As most of it survives, while nearly all the Greek text of the original Hexapla is lost, it is an important witness to the text of the OT.

One of the extant MSS is in the *Ambrosiana, in two vols., of which vol. ii [Job–Mal.] was ed. by A. M. Ceriani, *Monumenta Sacra et Profana*, vii (Milan, 1874; photo-lithographic text). The principal sections of the text not pr. by Ceriani ed., from various MSS., in P. de *Lagarde, *Bibliothecae Syriacae* (Göttingen, 1892), pp. 1–256. A. *Baumstark,

Geschichte der syrischen Literatur (1922), pp. 186–8. On the liturgical use of the Syro-Hexaplar, cf. A. Baumstark, *Nichtevangelische syrische Perikopenordnungen des ersten Jahrtausends* (Liturgiegeschichtliche Forschungen, iii; 1921), pp. 88–100. Bardenhewer, ii, 117. J. Fischer in *L.Th.K.*, ii (1931), col. 312 f., s.v. 'Bibelübersetzungen, IV. 2'.

SYRO-MALABAR CHURCH. See *Malabar Christians.*

SYZYGY (Gk. συζυγία, 'pair'). A word current among the *Gnostics, notably *Valentinus, for a pair of cosmological opposites, e.g. male and female. It was held that the universe had come into being through the interaction of such opposites (somewhat after the fashion of the *Hegelian doctrine of thesis and antithesis).

T

TABERNACLE (Jewish). The portable
shrine constructed under *Moses' direction
during the wilderness wanderings. The fullest
account of its structure is contained in Exod.
25–31 and 35–40, where it is described as consisting of an inner shrine (the 'Holy of Holies')
which housed the *Ark and an outer chamber
(the 'Holy Place') which contained the seven-
branched lampstand, the table for the *shewbread, and the altar of incense. These were
surrounded by an enclosure in which stood the
altar of sacrifice and the whole was set up in
the midst of the camp.

The Tabernacle was held to embody the
presence of God in the midst of His people,
the symmetry and harmony of its parts
to express the Divine perfection and the careful gradation of the courts and of the service
to reflect the Divine holiness. Acc. to modern
Biblical critics, the description of it in Exod.
25–31 and 35–40 is the work of the Priestly
school of writers of far later date than Moses
and reflects the structure of the Temple of
*Solomon. There is an independent and
briefer account of the Tabernacle in Exod. 33.
7–10 where it is called the 'tent of meeting'.
Acc. to this account it was pitched outside the
camp and was the centre towards which the
people directed their worship, and at its door
was to be seen the pillar of cloud, the symbol
of the Divine presence.

The principal material is to be found in comm. on Exodus,
cited s.v., ad locc., and in discussions on the *Pentateuch,
q.v. Studies devoted to the Tabernacle include W.
Neumann, *Die Stiftshütte in Bild und Wort* (1861); C. Schick,
*Die Stiftshütte, der Tempel in Jerusalem und der Tempelplatz
der Jetztzeit* (1896), pp. 3–51. E. Sellin, 'Das Zelt Jahwes' in
*Alttestamentliche Studien Rudolf Kittel zum 60. Geburtstag
dargebracht* (Beiträge zur Wissenschaft vom Alten Testament, xiii; 1913), pp. 168–92; R. Hartmann, 'Zelt und Lade'
in *Z.A.T.W.*, xxxvii (1918), pp. 209–44, esp. pp. 209–35;
[G.] von Rad, 'Zelt und Lade' in *Neue kirchliche Zeitschrift*,
xlii (1931), pp. 476–98. J. Morgenstern, 'The Tent of
Meeting' in *Journal of the American Oriental Society*, xxxviii
(1918), pp. 125–39; id., 'The Ark, the Ephod and the Tent'
in *Hebrew Union College Annual*, xvii (1942–3), pp. 153–265,
and xviii (1943–4), pp. 1–52, esp. pp. 17–47 of the latter
vol. M. F. Cross, 'The Tabernacle. A Study from an
Archaeological and Historical Aspect' in *The Biblical
Archaeologist*, x (1947), pp. 45–68. There is also a popular
reconstruction in English by W. Brown, *The Tabernacle and
its Priests and Services described and considered in relation to
Christ and the Church* (1871). B. F. *Westcott, *The Epistle
to the Hebrews* (1889), pp. 233–40 ('The General Significance
of the Tabernacle'). A. R. S. Kennedy in *H.D.B.*, iv (1902),
pp. 653–68, s.v.; R. Kittel in *P.R.E.* (ed. 3), xix (1907),
pp. 33–42, s.v. 'Stiftshütte'.

TABERNACLE (Christian). The ornamental receptacle for the vessels containing
the Blessed Sacrament in churches of the
Roman rite. Derived from the Lat. *tabernaculum* (='tent') and used of a variety of
canopied structures in the church building, the
word came to be applied esp. to the box set in
the middle of the altar which, from the 16th
cent. onwards, gradually superseded earlier
types of receptacles used for this purpose, e.g.
hanging *pyxes and *Sacrament - houses.

Except in cathedral and monastic churches, the
Tabernacle stands on the High Altar. The
interior is either gilded or covered with white
silk, and the exterior is veiled with the
canopeum. Except in a few cases, other
methods of *reservation have been forbidden
since 1863 in the RC Church.

F. Raible, *Der Tabernakel einst und jetzt. Eine historische
und liturgische Darstellung der Andacht zur aufbewahrten
Eucharistie* (1908). Braun, *C.A.*, ii (1924), pp. 632–47. E.
Maffei, *La Réservation eucharistique jusqu'à la Renaissance*
(1942). G. *Dix, *A Detection of Aumbries* (1942), passim.
J. Braun, S.J., in *C.E.*, xiv (1914), p. 424.

TABERNACLES, The Feast of. With the
*Passover and *Pentecost, one of the three
great feasts of the Jewish year. It was the
harvest-home, or 'feast of ingathering at end of
the year' (Exod. 23. 14–16), lasted 7 days, and
was followed by a solemn 8th day of 'holy
convocation'. During the feast the people
dwelt in booths (i.e. 'tabernacles') in commemoration of the sojourn in the wilderness
(cf. Lev. 23. 34 ff., 39 ff., Neh. 8. 14 ff., Jn.
7. 2, 37). The last and greatest feast of the
year, it was sometimes referred to as 'the feast'
par excellence (cf. Jn. 5. 1 RV). Its ceremonial
included the use of lights and libations of water
(cf. Jn. 7. 38, 8. 12).

W. O. E. Oesterley–G. H. Box, *The Religion and Worship
of the Synagogue* (1907), pp. 368–74; G. F. Moore, *Judaism
in the First Centuries of the Christian Era, the Age of the
Tannaim*, ii (Cambridge, Mass., 1927), pp. 43–51; W. O. E.
Oesterley, 'Early Hebrew Festival Rituals' in S. H. Hooke
(ed.), *Myth and Ritual* (1933), pp. 111–46, esp. pp. 120–46.
On the supposed connexion between the Feast of Taber-
nacles and the Semitic New Year Feasts, see also H. N.
Snaith, *The Jewish New Year Festival.* Its Origins and
Development (S.P.C.K., 1947), passim, and A. R. Johnson,
Sacral Kingship in Ancient Israel (Cardiff, 1955), esp. pp.
49–63. A. T. Chapman in *H.D.B.*, iv (1902), p. 668 f., s.v.;
H. G. Friedmann in *J.E.*, xi (1905), pp. 656–62, s.v.

TABLE, Communion. See *Communion
Table*.

TABLE PRAYERS. A term apparently
first found in the 19th cent. for the prayers
from the Communion service said at the
altar (or 'Holy Table') when there was no
administration of the Communion. In all the
forms of the English BCP, provision is made
(in slightly varying form) for such prayers.
The term seems to be no longer in use.

TABLET, The. RC weekly, founded in 1840
in London by Frederick Lucas, a barrister and
recent convert. It was later edited by Rev. H.
(later Cardinal) *Vaughan. With the *Dublin
Review* (1836) it is one of the two oldest RC
periodicals in England.

TABORITES. The extreme party of *Hussites, so named from Mount Tabor, their fortified stronghold south of Prague. They gained

ascendancy after the death of King Wenceslaus (1419), and, under their leader Zizka, began to spread the 'Kingdom of God' by force
of arms. Through Zizka's military genius
and the fanatical devotion of his followers
the far superior armies sent against them
were repeatedly defeated. After Zizka's death
(1424) they split into two main parties, the
more moderate of which joined the Catholics
after the Compactata of Prague (1433; see
*Utraquism); the radicals, under Procopius the
Bald, suffered a crushing defeat at Lipany in
1434.

The Taborites scorned all reasoned theology.
They had no churches and kept no feast days;
they rejected *transubstantiation; their priests
wore lay clothes and blessed bread and wine
at an ordinary table while the people said the
Lord's Prayer. They professed extreme social
doctrines, demanding the abolition of oaths,
courts of justice, and all worldly dignities, and
shrank from no cruelty in carrying out their
ideas. After the Battle of Lipany the party
disappeared from history.

F. C. Heymann, *John Žižka and the Hussite Revolution*
(Princeton, N.J., 1955). See also bibl. to *Hussites*.

TACITUS, CORNELIUS (*c.* 55–120),
Roman historian. Despite his eminence as a
historian and man of letters, nothing is known
of Tacitus beyond allusions in his writings and
some correspondence from the younger Pliny.
His surviving works, in their probable chronological order, are: (1) *Dialogus de Oratoribus*
(*c.* 77, date disputed); (2) Life of Agricola,
Tacitus' father-in-law (*c.* 98); (3) the *Germania*
(98); (4) his *Histories* (finished by *c.* 116); and
(5) his *Annals* (roughly same date).

In his *Annals* XV, 44, Tacitus mentions the
persecution of the Christians by *Nero who,
he says, made them scapegoats for the fire of
Rome (A.D. 64). Though Tacitus himself
held them guiltless of this charge, he believed
their religion a pernicious superstition (*exiti-
abilis superstitio*). He asserts that some were
thrown to dogs, some crucified, and some
burned in Nero's gardens. The passage contains one of the earliest witnesses in non-
Christian literature to the Crucifixion.

Modern ed. of his works by E. Koestermann (Teubner ed.,
2 vols., 1936); Eng. tr. by A. J. Church–W. J. Brodribb (3
vols., 1864–9). *Opera Minora*, ed. H. Furneaux (O.C.T.,
1900); *Annales*, ed. C. D. Fisher (ib., 1906), and *Historiae*,
ed. id. (ib., 1910). G. Boissier, *Tacite* (1903); C. Marchesi,
Tacito (Messina and Rome, 1924). A. Profumo, *Le fonti ed
i tempi dello incendio neroniano* (1905), passim. See also
bibl. to *Nero*.

TAIT, ARCHIBALD CAMPBELL (1811–
1882), Abp. of *Canterbury. Of Presbyterian
upbringing, Tait was educated at Glasgow
university and at Balliol College, Oxford,
where he was confirmed by Bp. R. *Bagot in
1830. From 1834 to 1842 he was a Fellow of
Balliol. In 1841 he was one of the Four Tutors
who publicly protested against Tract 90 (see
Tractarianism), and henceforward, despite
personal friendship with many of its leaders,
he was strongly opposed to the Anglo-
Catholic Movement. In 1842 he succeeded

T. *Arnold as headmaster of Rugby and in
1849 became Dean of *Carlisle. In 1856, at
the personal request of the Queen, he was
appointed Bp. of London, where his Broad
Church sympathies became much more prominent. He joined the other Bishops, however,
in publicly deprecating *Essays and Reviews*
(1860). In 1858 he had alienated the sympathies of the High Church party by withdrawing the licence of Alfred Poole, curate of
St. Barnabas, Pimlico, for his practice of hearing
confessions. In 1868 he succeeded C. T.
*Longley as Abp. of Canterbury. Though a
staunch upholder of the Establishment in
England, he came to the view that W. E.
*Gladstone's policy in *Ireland was inevitable,
and used the gifts of his statesmanship to secure
the best terms possible for the disestablished
Church of Ireland. He sought, but without
success, to abolish the recitation of the *Athanasian Creed in Divine service (1871–2). The
*Public Worship Regulation Act (1874) was
mainly his creation, though he objected to its
final form and later became convinced that its
practical working was a failure.

Life by R. T. *Davidson (son-in-law)–W. Benham (2 vols.,
London, 1891). W. H. Fremantle in *D.N.B.*, lv (1898), pp.
292–9.

TALBOT, EDWARD STUART (1844–
1934), Bp. of *Winchester. He was educated
at Christ Church, Oxford, where in 1866 he
was elected a Student. In 1870 he became
first Warden of *Keble College, Oxford.
Nearly twenty years later he exchanged
academic for parish work; and from 1888 to
1895 he had a very successful incumbency as
vicar of Leeds. In 1895 he became Bp. of
*Rochester, where his main work was the
division of the Diocese and the creation of the
see of Southwark of which he was enthroned
bishop in 1905. From 1911 to 1924 he was
Bp. of *Winchester. Closely associated in his
earlier years with C. *Gore, he was theologically a member of the School of *Lux
Mundi* (1889), to which he had contributed
the essay on 'The Preparation in History for
Christ', and throughout his life exercised great
influence in furthering moderate High Church
principles. Like other members of the *Lux
Mundi* School, he was a keen advocate of social
reform.

His three sons were:

(1) EDWARD KEBLE TALBOT (1877–1949),
who joined the *Community of the Resurrection at Mirfield in 1910 (Superior, 1922–40).

(2) NEVILLE STUART TALBOT (1879–1943),
who after army service in the Boer War,
became Chaplain of Balliol College, Oxford
(1909), Bp. of Pretoria (1920), and Vicar of St.
Mary's, Nottingham (1933). He contributed
an essay on 'The Present Situation' to *Foundations*.

(3) GILBERT TALBOT (1891–1915), who was
killed in action (30 July 1915) on the Ypres
salient. 'Talbot House' (popularly '*Toc H',
q.v.) was founded in his memory.

There is much autobiographical material in Edward
Stuart Talbot's *Memoirs of Early Life* (1924). Life by

Gwendolen Stephenson (S.P.C.K., London, 1936). A. Mansbridge, *Edward Stuart Talbot and Charles Gore* (1935), pp. 1–27 and 71–90. John Sankey in *D.N.B.*, *1931–1940*, p. 844 f.

Edward Keble Talbot's *Retreat Addresses*, ed. Lucy Menzies (S.P.C.K., London, 1954), with introd., pp. 7–16; miscellaneous writings in G. P. H. Pawson, C.R. (ed.), *Edward Keble Talbot. His Community and his Friends* (ib., 1954), with memoir, pp. 11–33. Memoir of Neville Stuart Talbot by F. H. Brabant (London, 1949).

TALL BROTHERS, The (Gk. ἀδελφοὶ μακροί). The four monks, Dioscorus (Bp. of Hermopolis Minor), Ammonius, Eusebius, and Euthymius, who led the *Origenist Movement in Egypt at the end of the 4th cent. In 399 they made their way from the *Nitrian Desert to Alexandria to defend Origenist views against their new opponent, *Theophilus, Patr. of Alexandria. Failing to get satisfaction, they proceeded to *Constantinople, where they continued their propaganda and even gained the support of St. *Chrysostom.

The chief source is *Sozomen, *Hist. Eccl.* viii. 12.

TALLEYRAND-PÉRIGORD, CHARLES MAURICE DE (1754–1838), Prince of Benevento, Bp. of Autun, and statesman. Ordained priest in 1779, he was made Bp. of Autun in 1789. After short hesitation, he joined the cause of the Revolution and became a member of the Constitutional Assembly, taking the oath to the *Civil Constitution and consecrating persons prepared to do likewise to fill the vacated bishoprics. In 1791 he was constrained to resign his see, and in 1792 was excommunicated. The same year he undertook an embassy to London to win support for the Revolution, but shortly afterwards lost the favour of the Government and had to flee to the U.S.A. Regaining favour, in 1796 he became Foreign Minister. After the *Concordat of 1801 *Pius VII readmitted him to lay communion. Henceforward he was Napoleon's principal agent in making treaties, except between 1809 and 1814, when he was in disgrace. In 1814 he took charge of the provisional Government, and in that year and the next he was instrumental in preserving the territorial integrity of France in the peace treaties. He retired from active political life in 1815, but later lent his support to Louis Philippe (1830–48) in his bid for the throne, and was by him made Ambassador to England, a post which he held from 1830 to 1834. On his death-bed he signed, in the presence of the Abbé F. A. P. *Dupanloup, a solemn repudiation of his errors and misdeeds against the Church.

[C. J. V. A.] de Broglie (ed.), *Mémoires du Prince de Talleyrand* (5 vols., 1891–2; Eng. tr., 5 vols., 1891–2). G. Pallain (ed.), *Correspondance inédite du Prince de Talleyrand et du Roi Louis XVIII pendant le congrès de Vienne* (1881; Eng. tr., 2 vols., 1881); id. (ed.), *Correspondance diplomatique de Talleyrand. La mission de Talleyrand à Londres en 1792* (1889); id. (ed.), *Correspondance diplomatique de Talleyrand. La ministère de Talleyrand sous le Directoire* (1891); id. (ed.), *Correspondance diplomatique de Talleyrand. Ambassade de Talleyrand à Londres, 1830–1834* (pt. 1, 1891). P. Bertrand (ed.), *Lettres inédites de Talleyrand à Napoléon, 1800–1809* (1889). Full life by G. Lacour-Gayet (3 vols., Paris, 1928–32). Other modern studies include those of A. Duff Cooper (London, 1932), A. F. Saint-Aulaire (Paris,

1936; Eng. tr., 1937) and L. Madelin (Paris, 1944; Eng. tr., 1948). C. Brinton, *The Lives of Talleyrand* (1937), with *bibliographie raisonnée*.

TALLIS, THOMAS (d. 1585), organist and composer, the 'Father of English Cathedral Music'. He was organist of Waltham Abbey before its dissolution in 1540, and soon after was appointed a Gentleman of the Chapel Royal. By this time his unprinted compositions were already in use, but his first works to be printed were 5 anthems, which appeared in 1560. He lived in his later years on the income of leases granted him by Queen *Mary (1557) and *Elizabeth I (1577) and the monopoly granted by Elizabeth to Tallis and W. *Byrd of music-printing for 21 years. His vocal works are his principal compositions. They are mostly set to Latin words, but also include a number of settings of the Anglican service, which, in their simplicity of form, are a reaction against the complications of plainchant, and also mark the point at which the ancient modes were changing into the modern keys. Tallis's 'Responses', taken from a complete service and popularized in the 19th cent., are his best-known composition. He also wrote several hymn tunes, some of which, in certain instances adapted, appear in modern hymn-books.

H. Davey, *History of English Music* [1908], pp. 144–8 and passim. E. H. Fellowes–D. W. Stevens in *Grove's Dictionary of Music and Musicians* (ed. 5 by E. Blom), viii (1954), pp. 294–300, s.v., with list of his works. H. Davey in *D.N.B.*, lv (1898), pp. 348–51.

TALMUD. The Jewish compilation which embodies the *Mishnah, or oral teaching of the Jews, and the *Gemara, or collection of discussions on the Mishnah. It dates from the early cents. of the Christian era, and contains a heterogeneous body of rules and reflections, the spiritually sublime being often juxtaposed to the crudely material. There are two recensions—the so-called 'Jerusalem Talmud', giving the discussions of the Palestinian *Rabbis, which survives only in an incomplete form, and the *Babylonian Talmud', which is three times as large as the Palestinian and is the more important in Jewish estimation. Most Jews still consider the Talmud an authoritative guide and companion to the spiritual life. To Christian as well as to Jew it is valuable for the light it throws on the background of the OT and the NT, while in modern Israel increasing importance is being attached to the (Palestinian) Talmud.

Best standard edd. of texts, *Talmud Babli* in 20 vols. Wilna, 1880–6; Eng. tr. ed. by I. Epstein (35 vols., London, 1935–52); Germ. tr., with *variae lectiones*, by L. Goldschmidt (9 vols., Berlin, 1897–1935); *Talmud Yerushalmi* in 8 vols., Wilna, 1922; first tr., into Fr., by M. Schwab (11 vols., Paris, 1878–89). S. Schechter, *Studies in Judaism*, Second Series (1908), pp. 102–25; Third Series (1924), pp. 143–237; D. Wright, *The Talmud* (1932). H. L. Strack, *Einleitung in Talmud und Midrasch* (1887; ed. 5, 1930; Eng. tr., Philadelphia, 1945). M. Berlin–S. J. Zevin, *Ensiklopedia Talmudith* (Hebr., Jerusalem, 1947 ff).

TAMBARAM CONFERENCE. The Missionary Conference, convened by the International Missionary Council, which met at

Tambaram, nr. Madras, from 12 to 29 Dec. 1938. Its membership of 471, drawn from 69 different countries and all the more important non-RC communions, was esp. remarkable for its strong representation from the younger Churches, the white delegates being actually in a slight minority. The chairman of the Conference was John R. *Mott, with Dr. William Paton as Secretary.

The Tambaran Series: I. *The Authority of the Faith*; II. *The Growing Church*; III. *Evangelism*; IV. *The Life of the Church*; V. *The Economic Basis of the Church*; VI. *The Church and the State*; VII. *Addresses and other Records* [with list of members]. 7 vols. (all 1939).

TAMETSI. The *Tridentine decree (Sess. XXIV, cap. i; 1563) prescribing the formal mode of celebrating matrimony. It aimed at suppressing clandestinity and was passed after long debates by a majority of 133 to 59. It laid down that in places where the decree was promulgated, a marriage between baptized persons (whether Catholics or not) was valid only when it took place in the presence of the parish priest or of the local Ordinary, or a priest appointed by one of these, and at least two witnesses. As its effect in Protestant countries would have been to reduce all unions between men and women to illicit cohabitations, it was prescribed that before coming into operation in any parish the decree had to be formally published in that parish. Hence it was normally not published in Protestant countries, e.g. it was never brought into operation anywhere in England, Scotland, or Wales. None the less it led to many complications and in 1908 it was finally superseded by other provisions of *Ne Temere (q.v.).

The text is pr. in the edd. of the decrees of the Council of Trent, e.g. in *Concilium Tridentinum*. Diariorum, Actorum, Epistularum, Tractatuum Nova Collectio. Edidit Societas Goerresiana, ix, ed. S. Ehses (Freiburg i.Br., 1924), p. 968 f.; also, with Fr. tr., in Hefele–Leclercq, x (pt. 1; 1938), pp. 554–8. The principal part is also pr. in Denn.–Bann. (ed. 1952), p. 344 f. (Nos. 990–2). See also works on *Matrimony* by RC authors and bibl. to *Trent, Council of*.

TAMMUZ. A Babylonian deity, commonly regarded as the equivalent of the Greek Adonis. Originally associated with Sun-worship, the deity became the Divine personification of the annual decay and revival of vegetation in autumn and spring. The chief feature of the cultus was ceremonial lamentation, a reference to which occurs at Ezek. 8. 14.

S. [H.] Langdon, *Tammuz and Ishtar* (1914). M. Witzel, O.F.M., *Tammuz-Liturgien und Verwandtes* (Analecta Orientalia, x; 1935). T. G. Pinches in *H.E.R.E.*, xii (1921), 187–91, s.v., with bibl.; K. Preisendanz in *P.W.*, Reihe 2, iv (pt. 2; 1932), cols. 2139–48, s.v.; A. Romeo in *E.C.*, xi (1953), col. 1722 f., s.v., with further bibl.

TANNER, THOMAS (1674–1735), English antiquary and divine. Born at Market Lavington, Wilts, he was educated at Queen's College, Oxford, where he formed a lifelong friendship with E. *Gibson, and elected Fellow of All Souls in 1696. In 1695 he published his *Notitia Monastica*, an erudite account of the

medieval religious houses in England and Wales (enlarged edition publd. by his brother, John Tanner, in 1744). In 1698 he became private chaplain to John Moore, then Bp. of *Norwich, who appointed him chancellor of his diocese in 1701. Having become Canon of *Ely in 1713, he returned to Oxford as Canon of *Christ Church in 1724. In 1732 he became Bp. of *St. Asaph. His second great work, the *Bibliotheca Britannico-Hibernica*, an enlargement of J. Leland's *De Scriptoribus*, was published posthumously by D. *Wilkins in 1748. Based on extensive research into medieval bibliography, it aims at giving a comprehensive account of all British writers down to the beginning of the 17th cent., and has long remained the standard work on the subject. He bequeathed to the *Bodleian Library his valuable collection of MSS., most of which had formerly belonged to Abp. W. *Sancroft. They contain a number of important papers relating to the time of the civil wars.

A. Hackman (ed.), *Catalogi Codicum Manuscriptorum Bibliothecae Bodleianae Pars Quarta*. Codices Viri Admodum Reverendi Tomae Tanneri (1860). C. McNeill, *The Tanner Letters*. Original Documents and Notices of Irish Affairs in the Sixteenth and Seventeenth Centuries Extracted from the Collection in the Bodleian Library, Oxford (Dublin, 1943). D. C. Douglas, *English Scholars* (1939), pp. 199–207 and passim. W. P. Courtney in *D.N.B.*, lv (1898), pp. 359–362.

TANQUEREY, ADOLF ALFRED (1854–1932), dogmatic theologian. Born at Blainville, Normandy, he was educated at Saint-Lô, Coutances, *Saint-Sulpice de Paris and Rome. In 1878 he was ordained priest and entered the Society of Saint-Sulpice. He taught at Rodez from 1879 to 1887, at Baltimore, U.S.A., from 1887 to 1902, and at Saint-Sulpice de Paris from 1902 to 1905. From 1915 to 1926 he was superior of the Solitude (a training centre for novices) at Issy, retiring to Aix in 1927.

His *Synopsis Theologiae Dogmaticae* (3 vols., 1894–6) and his *Synopsis Theologiae Moralis et Pastoralis* (3 vols., 1902–5), condensed in his *Brevior Synopsis Theologiae Dogmaticae* (1911) and his *Brevior Synopsis Theologiae Moralis et Pastoralis* (1913), have had a wide circulation. They provide a large body of useful and generally reliable information within a manageable compass. His other published works include *Précis de théologie ascétique et mystique* (1932) and contributions to various Catholic periodicals.

F. Cimetier in *D.T.C.*, xv (pt. 1; 1946), col. 47 f.

TANTUM ERGO. The last two verses of St. *Thomas Aquinas's Eucharistic hymn ''*Pange Lingua Gloriosi', and the second of the hymns used at *Benediction in the RC Church. The practice of inclining the head at the words 'veneremur cernui' is general, but not laid down in any rubrics. There are several English translations, the best known beginning 'Therefore we before Him bending'.

TARASIUS, St. (d. 806), Patr. of *Constantinople from 784. He was an uncle or great-uncle of *Photius and chief secretary of the Empress Irene II, at whose instigation, though only a layman, he was uncanonically elected patriarch. He at once embarked on a policy of restoring good relations between the Byzantine Church and the W. and persuaded the Empress to convoke, in concert with the Pope, *Hadrian I, a General Council which sat at *Nicaea in 787 under his own presidency. After its successful conclusion he became involved in a series of difficulties, consequent on his supposed tolerance of simony and his lack of energy in the divorce affair of Irene's son, Constantine VI. On being violently attacked for laxity by *Theodore of Studios and his rigorous monks, he deposed the priest who had performed the ceremony of Constantine's second marriage. In 802 he crowned as Emperor Nicephorus, who had dethroned Irene. After his death he was venerated as a saint. Feast day, 25 Feb.

A few of his letters and a sermon which have survived are repr. from J. D. *Mansi in J. P. Migne, *PG*, xcviii, 1423-1500. V. Grumel, A.A., *Les Régestes des actes du patriarcat de Constantinople*, vol. i, fasc. ii (Istanbul, 1936), pp. 12-22, Nos. 350-73. Lat. tr. of life by his disciple Ignatius, pr. in *AA.SS.*, Feb. III (1658), pp. 576-90, repr. in J. P. Migne, op. cit., 1385-424; Gk. text first ed. by I. A. Heikel in *Acta Societatis Scientiarum Fennicae*, xvii (Helsingfors, 1891), pp. 389-439. Theophanes, *Chronographia* (ed. C. de Boor, i, Leipzig, 1885, pp. 457-63, 470 f., 480 f., 500). On the 7th Council of Nicaea, Hefele-Leclercq, iii (pt. 2; 1910), pp. 741-804. R. Janin, A.A., in *D.T.C.*, xv (pt I; 1946), cols. 54-7, s.v. 'Taraise'.

TARGUM. The name, meaning 'interpretation', given to the Aramaic translations or paraphrases of the OT made when Hebrew had ceased to be the normal medium of speech among the Jews. They were the outcome of the explanatory oral matter which for a long time had been unofficially added to the Scripture lections in the worship of the *synagogue. Officially sanctioned Targums were produced first in Babylon and later in Palestine, the most famous being the Targum of Onkelos on the *Pentateuch, and the Targum of Jonathan on the Prophets, both of which were in use in the 3rd cent. A.D. All the books of the OT were so treated except Ezra, Nehemiah, and Daniel, which already contained large sections in Aramaic.

Editio princeps of Targum of Onkelos, Bologna, 1482. Modern ed. by A. Berliner (Berlin, 1884). Both the Targum of Onkelos and that of Jonathan are pr. in the London *Polyglott. M. Ginsburger (ed.), *Das Fragmententhargum* (*Thargum Jeruschlami zum Pentateuch*) (1899); id. (ed.), *Pseudo-Jonathan* (*Thargum Jonathan ben Usiël zum Pentateuch nach der Londoner Handschrift* (*Brit. Mus.; add. 27031*) (1903); F. Praetorius (ed.), *Das Targum zum Buch der Richter in jemenischer Überlieferung* (1900); J. F. Stenning (ed.), *The Targum of Isaiah* (1949; incl. Eng. tr.). R. H. Melamed, 'The Targum to Canticles according to six Yemen MSS.compared with the "Textus Receptus" (ed. de Lagarde)' in *J.Q.R.*, N.S., x (1919-20), pp. 377-410; xi (1920-1), pp. 1-20; xii (1921-2), pp. 57-117. P. [E.] Kahle, *Masoreten des Westens*, ii (Beitr'ge zur Wissenschaft vom Alten und Neuen Testament, 3 Folge, xiv; 1930), pp. 1*-13* and 1-66 ('Das Palästinische Pentateuchtargum'). Id., *The Cairo Geniza* (Schweich Lectures, 1941), esp. pp. 118-32. B. J. Roberts, *The Old Testament Text and Versions* (Cardiff, 1951), pp. 197-213 (ch. xiv: 'The Aramaic Targumim'). E. *Schürer, *Geschichte des jüdischen Volkes im Zeitalter Jesu Christi*, i

(ed. 4, 1901), pp. 147-56, with bibl. M. Jastrow, *A Dictionary of the Targumim, the Talmud Babli and Yerushalmi and the Midrashic Literature* (2 vols., 1886-1903). W. Volck-E. Nestle in *P.R.E.* (ed. 3), iii (1897), pp. 103-110, s.v. 'Bibelübersetzungen, 12. Jüdisch-aramäsche Übersetzungen (Targumim)', with bibl.; T. Walker in *H.D.B.*, iv (1902), pp. 678-83, s.v., with bibl.; E. Mangenot in *Dict. Bibl.*, v (1912), cols. 1995-2008, s.v. 'Targums'; A. *Baumstark in *L.Th.K.*, ii (1931), cols. 307-9, s.v. 'Bibelübersetzungen III', with further bibl. reff. to edd.

TARSICIUS, St. (3rd-4th cent.), martyr. Tradition states that he was killed in *Rome by the mob while bearing the Blessed Sacrament rather than surrender it to profanation. He is first mentioned in one of *Damasus' *Epigrammata*, where a comparison with St. *Stephen (Acts 6) suggests that he may have been a deacon. Acc. to a 6th cent. tradition, he took the Sacrament as an acolyte to certain Christian prisoners. His relics were originally located in the catacombs of S. Callisto, though they were later claimed by San Silvestro in Capite. Feast day, 15 Aug. A fraternity dedicated to him, fostering the cult of the Blessed Sacrament, received Papal approval in 1920. The incident of his death figures in N. *Wiseman's *Fabiola*.

AA.SS., Aug. III (1737), p. 201. A. Ferrua, S.J. (ed.), *Epigrammata Damasiana* (Rome, 1942), Elogium 15, pp. 117-19, with reff. J. M. Lambert, *Étude historique et critique sur saint Tharsicius, acolyte* (Rome, 1890). J. Wilpert, *Die Papstgräber und die Cäciliengruft in der Katakombe des hl. Kallistus* (1909), pp. 92-4 and 96-8; O. *Marucchi, 'La questione del sepolcro del papa Zeffirino e del martire Tarsicio in seguito ad una ultima scoperto' in *Nuovo Bullettino di Archeologia cristiana*, xvi (1910), pp. 205-25.

TARSUS. Pompey made this ancient city of Asia Minor the capital of the Roman province of Cilicia in 67 B.C. It became the seat of a famous *Stoic philosophical school and was the birthplace of St. *Paul (Acts 9. 11; 21. 39; 22. 3). In Christian times it was an episcopal see, and included among its bishops Helenus (*fl. c.* 250), the opponent of *Paul of Samosata, and *Diodore (Bp. 378-*c.* 390), the Antiochene exegete and theologian.

W. M. *Ramsay, *The Cities of St. Paul* (1907), pp. 85-244. W. Ruge in *P.W.*, Zweite Reihe, iv (pt. 2; 1932), cols. 2413-2439, s.v. 'Tarsos (3)'.

TASSO, TORQUATO (1544-95), Italian poet. Educated at *Venice and Padua, he published his first poem *Rinaldo* in 1562, and in 1565 entered the service of Cardinal Luigi d'Este at Ferrara. Here most of his time was given to his great epic *Gerusalemme liberata*, a poem on the First Crusade, written in the grave style characteristic of the *Counter-Reformation and completed in 1574. From that time he suffered much from religious scruples as well as from the criticisms directed against his work. As he became increasingly tormented by a kind of persecution mania and subject to violent outbursts, the Duke of Ferrara had him confined in an asylum in 1579. During this imprisonment he composed numerous prose dialogues on philosophical subjects. On his liberation in 1586, he went to Mantua and from there to various other Italian cities, spending his last years in writing

Gerusalemme conquistata (1592), an attempt to satisfy the critics of the earlier work, to which it is much inferior, and the *Sette giornate*, a blank verse epic of the Creation. He died shortly before receiving the crown of the Poet Laureate intended for him by *Clement VIII.

The best collected ed. of his works is that of G. Rosini, 33 vols., Pisa, 1821-32. There are crit. edd., by L. Bonfigli, of *Gerusalemme liberata* (Scrittori d' Italia, Bari, 1930); of *Gerusalemme conquistata* (2 vols., ib., 1934); and of *Rinaldo* (ib., 1936). A number of his works have been translated into English. E. Donadoni, *Torquato Tasso*. Saggio critico (2 vols., Florence, 1920); L. Tonelli, *Tasso* (Storia e pensiero, Turin, 1935). Life in Eng. by R. Milman (2 vols., London, 1850); W. Boulting, *Tasso and his Times* (1907). C. Previtera, *La poesia e l' arte di Torquato Tasso* (Messina-Milan, 1936); G. Getto, *Interpretazione del Tasso* (Naples, 1951). Id. in *E.C.*, xi (1953), cols. 1784-94, s.v., with bibl. U. Bosco in *Enciclopedia italiana*, xxxiii (1937), pp. 308-17, with extensive bibl.

TATE, NAHUM (1652-1715), and **BRADY, NICHOLAS** (1659-1726), authors of the *New Version of the Psalms* (1696). Both were Irish Protestant clergymen, educated at Trinity College, Dublin, Brady also at Christ Church, Oxford. Tate, who had written the second part of *Absalom and Achitophel* (1682) under J. *Dryden's direction, besides a large number of works of indifferent merit, including alterations of some of Shakespeare's plays, became Poet Laureate in 1692. Brady was chaplain to William III, Mary, and Queen *Anne, and held a number of benefices; among his works was a translation of *Virgil's *Aeneid* in blank verse (1726). Their joint work, the *New Version*, is a versification of the Psalter acc. to the artificial taste of the period, sacrificing the literal method of previous versions to the principle of contemporary literary refinement. There are, however, a number of simpler and more poetical pieces, such as 'Through all the changing scenes of life' (Ps. 34) and 'As pants the hart' (Ps. 42) which have made their way into modern hymn-books. Two slightly differing editions of the version, which were both printed in 1698, were the standard texts of later reissues. This *New Version*, though at first not favourably received, gradually supplanted the older rendering of T. *Sternhold and J. Hopkins. It was constantly reprinted during the next hundred years and down to the early 19th cent. was in almost universal use.

W. Hunt in *D.N.B.*, vi (1886), p. 192 f., s.v. 'Brady'; H. L. Bennett, ib., lv (1898), p. 379 f., s.v. 'Tate'. W. J. Austin-J. Ralf, *The Lives of the Poets-Laureate* (1853), pp. 196-222, esp. pp. 214-19; on the other works of Tate, E. K. Broadus, *The Laureateship*. A Study of the Office of Poet Laureate in England with some account of the Poets (1921), pp. 88-101, and *C.B.E.L.*, ii (1940), p. 428 f.

TATIAN (*c.* 160), Christian Apologist and *Gnostic. A native of Assyria, he was educated in Greek rhetoric and philosophy. He became a Christian in Rome between 150 and 165 and was a pupil of St. *Justin Martyr, but soon showed leanings to heretical opinions. *c.* 172 he went into the E. where he is said to have founded the Gnostic sect of the *Encratites. He is the author of an apology, usually called 'Oratio ad Graecos'. It is a passionate

defence of the venerable age and Divine purity of Christianity combined with a violent attack on Greek civilization, which is represented as a mass of evil, incompatible with the Christian faith. His chief claim to fame is the ''Diatessaron' (q.v.), a history of the life of Christ compiled from the four Gospels which was used in the Syriac Church until the 5th cent., when *Rabbula of Edessa perhaps replaced it by the *Peshitta version because its author was a heretic. Among his literary opponents were St. *Irenaeus, *Tertullian, *Clement of Alexandria, St. *Hippolytus and *Origen. It is possible that the memory of him in the Syriac Church was preserved under the name of *Addai (q.v.).

The best edd. of Tatian's 'Oratio ad Graecos' are those by J. C. T. Otto (Corpus Apologetarum Christianorum, vi; Jena, 1851), E. *Schwartz (T.U., iv, Hft. 1; 1888), and E. J. Goodspeed (*Die ältesten Apologeten* (1914), pp. 266-305). Eng. tr. by B. P. Pratten in A.N.C.L., iii (1867), pp. 3-48 (incl. other fragments). Bardenhewer, i, 262-73; Altaner (ed. 1951), p. 95 f. J. Quasten, *Patrology*, i (Utrecht, 1950), pp. 220-8. E. Fascher in *P.W.*, Zweite Reihe, iv (pt. 2; 1932), cols. 2468-71, s.v. 'Tatianus(9)'; G. Bardy in *D.T.C.*, xv (pt. 1; 1946), cols. 59-66, s.v. 'Tatien'; F. Bolgiani in *E.C.*, xi (1953), cols. 1807-12, s.v. 'Taziano'. See also bibl. to *Diatessaron*.

TATTAM, HENRY (1789-1868), Coptic scholar. He held a succession of Anglican benefices, and in 1845 was appointed Archdeacon of Bedford. On travels in Egypt he recovered from the *Nitrian desert several important Coptic and Syriac MSS., now in the British Museum, among them the 5th cent. codex of the *Old Syriac text of the Gospels which W. *Cureton identified in 1847 and published in 1858.

Miss Platt (stepdaughter), *Journal of a Tour through Egypt, the Peninsula of Sinai, and the Holy Land in 1838, 1839* (2 vols., privately printed, 1841-2). W. Wright, *Catalogue of the Syriac Manuscripts in the British Museum, acquired since the Year 1838*, iii (1872), esp. pp. xi-xiii and xvi-xxv. T. Cooper in *D.N.B.*, lv (1898), p. 386 f., s.v., for full list of his works.

TAULER, JOHANN (*c.* 1300-61), German *Dominican mystic. He entered the Order of Preachers at Strassburg in 1315, where he prob. came under the influence of Master *Eckhart and *Henry Suso. He later became famous as a preacher and director, esp. of nuns, and during the Black Death in 1348 devoted himself completely to the sick, a fact which still more increased his popularity. During a stay at Basle (1338-43), he was brought into close relations with the '*Gottesfreunde'. His popularity caused many spurious works to be ascribed to him; but, apart from two letters, only a number of sermons can be regarded as certainly genuine. They contain his mystic teaching, which, firmly grounded in *Thomist doctrine, is eminently practical. He emphasizes the indwelling of God in the human soul, and describes in detail the Mystic Way, which he conceives as consisting chiefly in the practice of the virtues, esp. humility and abandonment to the will of God. Union is to be desired not so much for its own sake as for the results it produces in the soul, which are an increase of charity and the strength to lead a life of suffering and self-sacrifice. His sermons were highly esteemed by M. *Luther.

Editio princeps of his sermons, Leipzig, 1498; fuller ed. of his works, Cologne, 1543; Lat. tr., ib., 1548. First crit. ed. of his sermons by F. Vetter (Deutsche Texte des Mittelalters, xi; 1910); also ed. after the important Cod. Vindobonensis 2744, with variants of other edd. by A. L. Corin (Bibliothèque de la Faculté de Philosophie et Lettres de l'Université de Liége, xxxiii, xlii, &c., 1924 ff.). G. I. Lieftinck, De Middelnederlandsche Tauler-handschriften (Groningen, 1936), with selected texts and facsimilies. Eng. tr. of his sermons by W. Elliott (Brookland Station, Washington, D.C., 1910); of selections by Susanna Winkworth (London, 1857). C. Schmidt, Johannes Tauler von Strassburg. Beitrag zur Geschichte der Mystik und des religiösen Lebens im vierzehnten Jahrhundert (Hamburg, 1841). H. S. *Denifle, O.P., Taulers Bekehrung kritisch untersucht (Quellen und Forschungen zur Sprach- und Culturgeschichte der Germanischen Völker, xxxvi; 1879). A. Chiquot, Histoire ou légende?, Jean Tauler et le "Meisters/Buoch" (Strassburg-Paris [1922; here ascribed to Rulman Merswin]). D. Helander, Johann Tauler als Prediger (Lund, &c., 1923). A. Korn, Tauler als Redner (Forschungen und Funde, xxi; 1928). K. Grunewald, Studien zu Johannes Taulers Frömmigkeit (Beiträge zur Kulturgeschichte des Mittelalters und Renaissance, xliv; 1930). F. W. Wentzlaff-Eggebert, Studien zur Lebenslehre Taulers (Abh. (Berl.), 1939, Hft. 15). X. de Hornstein, Les Grands Mystiques allemands du XIV° Siècle (1922), pp. 159–220. J. M. Clark, The Great German Mystics (1949), pp. 36–54, with bibl., pp. 114–17. Quétif-Échard, i, 677–9. K. Löffler in C.E., xiv (1912), p. 465 f., s.v.; P. Pourrat, P.S.S., in D.T.C., xv (pt. 2; 1946), cols. 66–79, s.v., with bibl.

TAUROBOLIUM. A rite first found in the West in connexion with the worship of Venus and later particularly associated with that of Cybele and Attis, in which the recipient descended into a ditch and was bathed in the blood of a bull slain above him. It appears to have originated in Asia Minor and spread to the West in the 2nd cent. A.D. The view that it influenced the Christian theology of Baptism (*Religionsgeschichtliche Schule, K. *Lake) seems wholly unfounded. It rested on a single late text taurobolio criobolioq. in aeternum renatus (I.L.S., 4152), which (if there is any connexion) may well have borrowed from Christianity.

A description of the rite is to be found in *Prudentius, Peristephanon, x, lines 1011–50. H. Oppermann in P.W. (Zweite Reihe, v (pt. 1; 1934), 16–21, s.v. 'Taurobolia'.

TAUSEN, HANS (1494–1561), Reformer, the 'Danish Luther'. A peasant's son, he became a monk at Antvorskov, and travelling abroad was attracted by the teaching of the Dutch humanists. In 1523 he studied at *Wittenberg, where he came under the influence of M. *Luther. The result was that on his return to *Denmark he was imprisoned for teaching novel doctrines. After his release he preached reform at Viborg, discarded his friar's habit, and, on becoming chaplain to King Frederick I (1526), he married and proceeded to employ Danish in the Church services. In 1529, following his appointment by the King to preach at Copenhagen, he secured the support of the Danish National Assembly (Herredag) against J. Rönne, Bp. of Roëskilde. A Confession of Faith in 43 articles was then drawn up by Tausen and his supporters. Three years later, when Rönne had turned the Herredag against him, Tausen was convicted of heresy, but

as he saved the bishop from the violence of the enraged mob, his only punishment was a warning to modify his opinions. In the immediately following years, Tausen's Confession was set aside in favour of the more moderate *Augsburg Confession, which was made the basis of the Danish Reformation. In 1542 Tausen was appointed to the see of Ribe.

Selection of his Writings ed. H. F. Rördam (Copenhagen, 1870). L. Schmitt, S.J., Johannes Tausen oder der dänische Luther (Cologne, 1894). F. Nielsen in P.R.E. (ed. 3), xix (1907), pp. 459–62.

TAVERNER'S BIBLE. The English translation of the Bible issued in 1539 by Richard Taverner (1505?–75). It was a revision of *Matthew's Bible, published in 1537. As Taverner was a good Greek scholar, but not a Hebraist, his work was far better in the NT than in the OT. The edition never became popular as M.*Coverdale's officially sponsored '*Great Bible' (1539) appeared in the same year.

H. H. Hutson–H. R. Willoughby, 'The Ignored Taverner Bible of 1539' in The Crozer Quarterly, xvi (1939), pp. 161–76. B. F. *Westcott, A General View of the History of the English Bible (1868), pp. 110–13, 269–71, with Taverner's variants collated with other edd. of the Bible, pp. 408–13. Darlow-Moule, i (1903), p. 20 f. On Taverner himself, A. *Wood, Athenae Oxonienses (ed. 3 by P. Bliss), i (1813), cols. 419–24; A. F. Pollard in D.N.B., lv (1898), pp. 393–6.

TAYLOR, ALFRED EDWARD (1869–1945), Anglican philosopher. Educated at New College, Oxford, he was successively Fellow of Merton College (1891–8), Lecturer in Greek and philosophy at Owens College, Manchester (1896–1903), professor of logic and metaphysics at McGill University, Montreal (1903–8), and professor of moral philosophy at St. Andrews (1908–24) and at Edinburgh (1924–41). Though a commentator and philosophical man of letters rather than an original systematic thinker he became a considerable intellectual and religious power. His writings, most of which are packed with information and suggestive judgements, include The Problem of Conduct (1901), Elements of Metaphysics (1903), Varia Socratica (1911), Plato. The Man and his Work (1926), A Commentary on Plato's Timaeus (1928), The Faith of a Moralist (2 vols., 1930; *Gifford Lectures at St. Andrews for 1926–8), The Laws of Plato (1934), Philosophical Studies (1934; with studies of Aeschines, *Proclus, St. *Thomas Aquinas, Francis Bacon and others); The Christian Hope of Immortality (1938), and Does God Exist? (1945). He also contributed the art. 'Theism' to J. *Hastings' Encyclopedia of Religion and Ethics (vol. xii, 1921) and that on 'The Vindication of Religion' to Essays Catholic and Critical (1926); and he frequently wrote for the Proceedings of the Aristotelian Society and Mind.

W. D. Ross, 'Alfred Edward Taylor, 1869–1945' in Proceedings of the British Academy, xxxi (1945), pp. 407–22, with bibl. of his works, pp. 422–4.

TAYLOR, JAMES HUDSON (1832–1905), founder of the *China Inland Mission. He was a medical man who felt the call to be a missionary (1849) and sailed for China in 1853 under the auspices of the Chinese Evangelization Society. Despite many obstacles, among them ill-health which forced him to return in 1860, he carried on his work for China, and in 1865 founded the interdenominational China Inland Mission (q.v.). In 1866, accompanied by his family and a small staff, he went back to China, where he travelled extensively, heroically facing many difficulties, and conforming as much as possible to Chinese habits of life. A man of indomitable faith and great personal devotion, he carried the missionary work into the heart of the country and ensured its continuance by recruiting a large number of helpers. His books include *China; its Spiritual Need and Claims* (1865), *A Retrospect* (1894), and *Union and Communion* (1894).

H. and G. Taylor (son and daughter-in-law), *Hudson Taylor in Early Years. The Growth of a Soul* (1911); Idd., *Hudson Taylor and the China Inland Mission. The Growth of a Work of God* (1918). Idd., *Hudson Taylor's Spiritual Secret* (1932). M. Broomhall, *The Man Who Believed God. Hudson Taylor* (1936).

TAYLOR, JEREMY (1613–67), Anglican bishop and writer. He was a native of Cambridge and educated at Gonville and Caius College, of which he was elected a Fellow in 1633. Having been ordained in the same year he went to London to preach in the place of a friend, where he attracted the notice of Abp. W. *Laud who nominated him to a fellowship at All Souls, Oxford, in 1635. Shortly afterwards he was appointed chaplain to *Charles I. Owing to his friendship with the Franciscan, Christopher *Davenport, he was suspected of Roman tendencies, of which he cleared himself in a ' Gunpowder Sermon' at Oxford in 1638. In the same year he was made rector of Uppingham, which he left in 1642 to become a chaplain in the Royalist army. After imprisonment for a short time he retired to Wales in 1645, where he lived as chaplain to Lord Carbery at Golden Grove. Many of Taylor's best works were written here, among them the *Liberty of Prophesying* (1647), a plea for *toleration; the two devotional treatises, *The Rule and Exercise of Holy Living* (1650) and *The Rule and Exercise of Holy Dying* (1651); the *Golden Grove* (1655); and the *Unum Necessarium* (1655), a treatise on sin and repentance. In 1658 he went to Lisburn in NE. Ireland as a lecturer, and in 1660 was appointed Bp. of Down and Connor and vice-chancellor of Dublin university, which he restored to order. In the same year he published his *Ductor Dubitantium*, a comprehensive manual of *moral theology. In 1661 he received the further see of Dromore. His episcopate was much troubled by the *Presbyterians who refused submission, and whom he treated with considerable harshness, as also the RCs, against whom he wrote his *Dissuasive from Popery* (1664), a violent invective against Roman Catholicism.

Taylor's fame to-day rests almost entirely on his devotional writings, esp. *Holy Living* and *Holy Dying*. They are characteristic expressions of Anglican spirituality in their balanced sobriety and their insistence on a well-ordered piety which stresses temperance and moderation in all things. They have become classics esp. for their beautiful prose, combining transparent lucidity with rhetorical vigour and powerful imagery, qualities which also made him one of the most celebrated preachers of his day. He was less felicitous as a theologian. The *Unum Necessarium* roused a violent controversy by reason of its alleged *Pelagianism and minimizing treatment of Original Sin. In his controversial writings he defended Episcopalianism against the Presbyterians (*Of the Sacred Order and Offices of Episcopacy*, 1642) and attacked the RC doctrine of *Transubstantiation (*The Real Presence . . . proved against . . . Transubstantiation*, 1654), himself holding a view of the *Real Presence which comes near to the *Receptionist or *Virtualist doctrines. The work he accounted of most value was his *Ductor Dubitantium*, a compendium of casuistry based on both RC and Continental Protestant authors, and intended to guide the Anglican clergy in the practice of confession. Despite its solid erudition it was long disregarded, but in recent times it has received some attention.

Whole Works, ed. R. *Heber (15 vols., London, 1822), with life of author by id., vol. i, pp. ix–ccciii; rev. by C. P. Eden (10 vols., ib., 1847–54), with life by R. Heber, vol. i, pp. ix–ccl. C. J. Stranks, *The Life and Writings of Jeremy Taylor* (1952). Other lives and studies by H. K. Bonney (London, 1815), R. A. Willmott (ib., 1847), E. H. May (ib., 1892), G. Worley (ib., 1904), E. Gosse ('English Men of Letters', 1904), and W. J. Brown ('English Theologians', 1925). H. H. *Henson, 'Jeremy Taylor' in W. E. Collins (ed.), *Typical English Churchmen*, (The Church Historical Society, lxv; 1902), pp. 123–46. T. Wood, *English Casuistical Divinity During the Seventeenth Century with Special Reference to Jeremy Taylor* (1952). The liturgy which Taylor composed for Anglican congregations under the Commonwealth is repr. by W. J. Grisbrooke, *Anglican Liturgies of the Seventeenth and Eighteenth Centuries* (Alcuin Club Collections, xl, 1958), pp. 183–200, with comm., pp. 19–36.

TAYLOR, JOHN (1694–1761), Dissenting divine and Hebrew scholar. After studying at the academy at Whitehaven for the training of Presbyterian and Congregational ministers, he was ordained by dissenting ministers and worked at *Norwich where he founded the Octagon Chapel (1754). In 1757 he was appointed divinity tutor at Warrington Academy. His greatest work of scholarship was his *Hebrew Concordance*, publd. by subscription in 1754–7. Based on that of J. Buxtorf, it was designed to serve also the purposes of a lexicon, and marked an important advance in the study of Hebrew roots. In matters of theology, Taylor tended increasingly towards an *Arian view of the Person of Christ and to a denial of the fact of Original Sin. His influential *Scripture Doctrine of Original Sin* (1740), which had a wide circulation in England, Scotland, and America, did much by undermining the foundations of the *Calvinistic system to prepare the way for the *Unitarian Movement in American Congregationalism.

A. Gordon in *D.N.B.*, lv (1898), p. 439 f., with reff.

TEACHING OF THE TWELVE APOSTLES, The. See *Didache*.

TE DEUM. A Latin hymn to the Father and Son, in rhythmical prose. Since the 9th cent. tradition has assigned its composition to Sts. *Ambrose and *Augustine at the latter's baptism, but this account of its origin is almost universally rejected by modern scholars. It is widely thought to be the work of *Niceta of Remesiana (as was first suggested by Dom G. *Morin). Verses 22 ff. are suffrages, early appended to the original. Its use in the offices is already referred to in the Rules of St. *Caesarius of Arles and of St. *Benedict, and in the RC Church it has remained an integral part of *Mattins, at least on festal days. The BCP prescribes its use daily at Mattins, with the *Benedicite as an alternative. It has often been set to music for use on occasions of thanksgiving, e.g. G. F. *Handel's 'Dettingen Te Deum'.

J. *Wordsworth, *The 'Te Deum'* (1902). A. E. Burn, *The Hymn* Te Deum *and its Author* (1926). P. Cagin, O.S.B., *L'Euchologie latine*, i, Te Deum ou Illatio? Contribution à l'histoire de l'euchologie latine à propos des origines du Te Deum (Solesmes, 1906). G. Morin, O.S.B., 'Nouvelles Recherches sur l'auteur du *Te Deum*' in *R. Bén.*, xi (1894), pp. 49–77; id., 'Le *Te Deum*, type anonyme d'anaphore latine préhistorique?', ib., xxiv (1907), pp. 180–223. P. Siffrin in *E.C.*, xi (1953), col. 1862 f., s.v., with bibl. Dekkers, No. 650, p. 116, for reff. to artt. on text; Altaner, p. 342.

TE IGITUR (Lat., 'Thee, therefore'). The opening words of the *Canon of the Roman Mass, and hence also the name for the first section of the canon. It asks God to accept and bless the Eucharistic offerings, and offers intercession for the whole Church, including the Pope, the Diocesan Bishop (these two mentioned by name), and all the faithful. The representation of the Crucifixion immediately preceding it in *Missals was apparently in origin a pictorial elaboration of the initial T of *Te Igitur*.

A. Ebner, *Quellen und Forschungen zur Geschichte und Kunstgeschichte des* Missale Romanum *im Mittelalter* (1896), pp. 443–9; V. Leroquais, *Les Sacramentaires et les missels manuscrits des bibliothèques publiques de France* (4 vols., 1924), esp. vol. i, pp. xxxiii–xxxvii, with reff. Jungmann, *M.S.* (ed. 1949), ii, 180–5; Eng. tr., ii (1955), pp. 147–52.

TEILO, St. (6th cent.), patron saint and Bp. of *Llandaff. It is difficult to deduce from the mass of mutually conflicting later traditions anything certain about his life. He is credited with having been consecrated bishop at *Jerusalem while on a pilgrimage to Palestine and (a less unlikely tradition) with having visited St. *Samson at Dol. He is also said to have succeeded St. *Dubritius in the see of Llandaff when the latter retired to Bardsey in 495. His reputation for piety and pastoral devotion was such that three churches laid claim to possess his bones. The dispute was settled (it is said) when two additional identical corpses were provided supernaturally. Feast day, 9 Feb.

An account of his life is included in the *Liber Landavensis* (first publd. by W. J. Rees for the Welsh MSS. Society, 1840, pp. 92–111; re-ed. by I. G. Evans from the Gwysaney MS., 1893, pp. 97–117). Lat. text also publd. with crit. notes by J. Loth, 'La Vie de saint Teliau d'après le livre de Llandaf' in *Annales de Bretagne*, ix (1893), pp. 81–5, 277–86, 438–46, and x (1894), pp. 66–77.

TEINDS. The Scottish equivalent of *tithes. Regarded as the patrimony of the Church and a separate estate and not a burden on the land, they were payable by the *heritors to the minister of a parish, at first in kind and later in money. The system was terminated by Act of Parliament in 1925.

TELEMACHUS, St. Acc. to *Theodoret (*Hist. Eccl.* v, 26), Telemachus was an E. monk who seeking to put an end to the gladiatorial shows at Rome, entered the arena in person on 1 Jan. 391 to separate the combatants, and was killed by the spectators. The act is said to have led Emp. Honorius to abolish the games. In the *Hieronymian Martyrology he is called 'Almachius'. Feast day, 1 Jan.

The sole sources are Theodoret, *H.E.*, v, 26, and a note in the *Hieronymianum. H. *Delehaye, S.J., 'Saint Almachius ou Télémaque' in *Anal. Boll.*, xxxiii (1914), pp. 421–8. G. *Morin, 'Le Dragon du Forum romain, sa légende et son histoire' in *R. Bén.*, xxxi (1919), pp. 321–6. J. P. Kirsch in *D.H.G.E.*, ii (1914), col. 630 f., s.v. 'Almachius', with further bibl. St. Telemachus is also the subject of an unpublished poem by C. G. *Rossetti.

TELEOLOGY (Gk. τέλος, 'end'). The word, probably coined by C. *Wolff in 1728, denotes the science of ends or final causes. It is esp. applied to the doctrine, inherent in every organic and non-mechanistic interpretation of the universe, that it embodies design and purpose. This doctrine, taught by *Plato and *Aristotle, acc. to whom God is both the First Cause and the Last End of the world, was taken over by Christian theology and forms the basis of the modern argument from design (also known in the 18th cent. as the 'physico-theological argument' and by recent philosophers as the 'teleological argument') for the existence of God. In its classical form (e.g., in W. *Paley's *Evidences*), it sets out from the observation that every biological species is apparently designed to serve its own needs and argues therefrom to an intelligent Creator. Under the influence of C. *Darwin, E. *Haeckel, and the general trend of 19th cent. science, the traditional form of the argument has been abandoned. But in a modified form the argument still retains its validity, on the ground that the very survival of life in conflict is evidence of purpose. Foremost among modern biologists who on purely scientific grounds have defended teleological doctrine is H. Driesch.

For a modern presentation of the teleological argument, see W. R. Matthews, *The Purpose of God* (1935).

TELESIO, BERNARDINO (1508–88), Italian humanist. A native of Cosenza, nr. Naples, he studied philosophy, mathematics, and natural science at Padua and Rome, becoming a strong critic of the *Aristotelian philosophy. At Rome he enjoyed for a while the patronage of *Paul IV, who offered him the Archbishopric of Cosenza. In 1566 he returned to Naples and founded a scientific society ('Academia Telesiana'). His doctrines, much influenced by the early Greek nature philosophers (esp. Parmenides), were based on an extreme empiricism; but he gradually built up a speculative system in which the Aristotelian doctrine of matter and form was replaced by one of matter and force. His principal treatise was *De Rerum Natura iuxta Propria Principia* (pt. i, Rome, 1565; pt. ii, Naples, 1587); others were *De Somno, De Cometis et Lacteo Circulo*, and *De Iride* (ed. together, A. Persius, Venice, 1590). Among his disciples were T. *Campanella and G. *Bruno (qq.v.). In 1606 most of his writings were placed on the *Index.

Modern ed.of *De Rerum Natura* by V. Spampanato (vol. i, Modena, 1910; vol. ii, Genoa, 1913; vol. iii, Rome, 1923). Modern studies by E. Troilo (Modena, 1910; ed. 2, Rome, 1924), G. *Gentile (Bari, 1911; ed. 2, 1923; with bibl.) and G. Soleri (Brescia, 1944). N. Abbagnano, *Bernardino Telesio e la filosofia del rinascimento* (1941). E. Zavattari, *La visione della vita nel rinascimento e Bernardino Telesio* (1923). Überweg, iii, 38, 42 f., with bibl., p. 631. G. Soleri in *E.C.*, xi (1953), cols. 1873–5, s.v.

TELESPHORUS, (d. *c.* 137) Bp. of Rome from *c.* 127. St.*Irenaeus (ap. Eusebius, *H.E.*, V. xxiv. 14) mentions that he always observed Easter on Sundays, as against the *Quartodeciman practice, and that he suffered death by martyrdom (*Haer*. III. iii. 3). He is thus the only 2nd cent. Pope whose martyrdom is well attested. Feast day, in the E., 22 Feb.; in the W., 2 or 5 Jan.

Jaffé, i, 6. The principal authority is *L.P.* (Duchesne), i, 129 f. É. Amann in *D.T.C.*, xv (pt. 1; 1946), col. 82, s.v. 'Télesphore'; A. P. Frutaz in *E.C.*, xi (1953), col. 1872, s.v. 'Telesforo'.

TELL EL-AMARNA TABLETS. A collection of ancient inscriptions, discovered in 1887 at Tell el-Amarna, the site of the former royal city of Akhnaton, Egyptian ruler of the early 14th cent. B.C. They are written in Akkadian cuneiform script, and consist chiefly of letters, many of them from Canaanite kings to their Egyptian suzerain, complaining of the attacks on Palestine of invading forces from the north and the east. Among these invaders mention is made of the Habiru, who are commonly identified with the Hebrews, and among the letters are some from an early ruler of Urusalim (i.e. *Jerusalem) named Arad-hiba.

Edd. of the Tablets in Cuneiform by O. Schroeder (2 vols., Leipzig, 1914–15); in transliteration with Eng. tr. by H. Winckler (London, 1896); in transliteration with Germ. tr. by J. A Knudtzon (Vorderasiatische Bibliothek, ii, 1908–1915); in transliteration with Eng. tr. by S. A. B. Mercer (2 vols., Toronto, 1939), with bibl. information about scattered tablets, i, p. xiii f. On the site, T. E. Peet–C. J. Woolley, *The City of Akhenaten*, i (Egyptian Exploration Society, 1923), ii (ib., 1933) and iii (in two parts, ib., 1951). W. M. F. Petrie, *Syria and Egypt from the Tell el-Amarna Letters* (1898).

TEMPERANCE (Lat. *temperantia*, used by Cicero to render *Plato's σωφροσύνη), restraint of the appetites and passions in accordance with reason. One of the four *cardinal virtues,

and indeed, acc. to the moralists, the most fundamental of them as that on which the other three depend, it was inculcated by the Gk. philosophers, esp. *Plato and the *Stoics. In the NT, the Gk. noun σωφροσύνη, translated in the AV by 'soberness' or 'sobriety', occurs three times (Acts 26. 25, 1 Tim. 2. 9 and 15), in each case as an adjunct to godliness. The adjective σώφρων, translated indiscriminately as 'sober', 'temperate,' or 'discreet', is listed among the attributes proper to a bishop (1 Tim. 3. 2 and Tit. 1. 8), to old men (Tit. 2. 2) and aged women (Tit. 2. 5). (Elsewhere in the NT, the AV 'temperance' is a rendering of ἐγκράτεια, 'self-control').

For the Christian, temperance in its physical aspects is linked with the need for self-control of the body, regarded as a 'temple of the Holy Ghost'. The Gk. teaching influenced *Origen and the *Cappadocian Fathers, while the conception was developed, under the influence of Cicero, esp. by St. *Ambrose and St. *Augustine; it was further elaborated by St. *Thomas Aquinas. Moral theologians commonly subdivide it into several other virtues, e.g. abstinence, chastity, and modesty. The 'temperance societies', founded to foster abstinence from alcoholic drinks, date from the 19th cent.

A. Michel in *D.T.C.*, xv (pt. 1; 1946), cols. 94–9, s.v.

TEMPLARS. Also 'Knights Templar' and 'Poor Knights of Christ', a military order founded in 1118 after the capture of *Jerusalem by *Godfrey of Bouillon (1099) to defend it from the Moslems. The original nucleus consisted of Hugo of Payens, a Knight of Champagne, and eight companions who bound themselves by a solemn vow in the presence of the Patriarch of Jerusalem. Baldwin I (d. 1118) gave them a house near Solomon's *Temple. At first they lived on alms; but in 1127 Hugo journeyed to the West to obtain ecclesiastical approbation and recruits, and their fortunes rapidly changed. At the Council of Troyes (1128), under the influence of St. *Bernard, they adopted a form of the *Cistercian Rule.

In the following years the Templars rose in influence and wealth, soon having settlements in nearly every country in Christendom. They introduced solemn forms of initiation and an elaborate organization ('*preceptories'); the four ranks of 'knights', 'chaplains', 'sergeants', and 'craftsmen'). Their devotion was undoubted, but their military effectiveness was limited by the jealousy of the clergy of the Holy Land and also of the Knights of St. John (*Hospitallers). They built several castles (at once monasteries and cavalry barracks) of which notable ruins still remain (e.g. Safèd, 1140; Karak of the desert, 1143; and Castle Pilgrim, 1217). Though they could not avert the Fall of Jerusalem in 1187, they continued to prosper through most of the 13th cent. Their supporters loaded them with great wealth, which was deposited in their 'temples' at Paris and London, while their integrity and credit led them to be much trusted also as bankers. In the later years of the 13th century their influence began to wane. Their indifference to death was a constant strain on the *morale* of what was a military as well as a monastic body and they were often faced with insufficient numbers to repair their enormous losses; and their interference in the government of Jerusalem was resented. But they continued to fight until the end; and at the Fall of Acre (1291), which brought Christian power in Palestine to an end, the Master of the Temple, who led the besieged, was killed.

The Templars now suffered a sudden reversal of fortune. At the Council of *Lyons (1274), St. *Louis had made an unsuccessful attempt to end the rivalry of Templars and Hospitallers by incorporating them into a single order. But it was the combined energies of Philip the Fair and *Clement V in the early years of the 14th cent. which brought the power of the Templars to an end. During his quarrel with *Boniface VIII Philip had, indeed, entered into a formal treaty with Hugo de Perand, general visitor of the French Templars (1303); but the temptation to lay hands on their wealth was too great for the King. Finding an accomplice in an apostate Italian Templar, he brought against them charges of immorality, superstition, and heresy. He also won over to his aid Clement V. Both King and Pope freely used torture to procure confessions of guilt; and the Order was finally suppressed by Clement V at the Council of *Vienne in 1312. The innocence of the Templars, vigorously championed by *Dante, has been a matter of prolonged controversy, but is now generally admitted.

The headquarters of the English branch of the Order was for a long time in London, S. of the Strand (now the Inner and Middle Temple). The orig. Temple Church, dating from 1185, was, in common with other churches of the Templars, a round structure on the model of the Church of the *Holy Sepulchre in *Jerusalem. A nave (or choir) was added in 1240. It was severely damaged in air raids in 1941.

Rule ed. H. de Curzon (Societé de l'Histoire de France, Paris, 1886), and, with Germ. tr., ed. G. Schnürer (Studien und Darstellungen aus dem Gebiete der Geschichte. Im Auflage der Görres-Gesellschaft und in Verbindung mit der Redaktion des Historischen Jahrbuches, iii, Hftt. 1–2; 1903). Marquis d'Albon (ed.), *Cartulaire générale de l'ordre du Temple (1119?–1150* (1913; fasc. complémentaire, 1922); E. G. Léonard, *Introduction au cartulaire manuscrit du Temple (1150–1317) constitué par le marquis d'Albon* (1930). Other docc. in H. Michelet (ed.), *Procès des templiers* (Collection de documents inédits sur l'histoire de France, Première Série, Histoire politique, 2 vols., 1841–51). Most of the older literature is controversial. In English there are two studies, by C. G. Addison, *The History of the Knights Templars, the Temple Church and the Temple* (1842; revised ed., 1852), and G. A. Campbell, *The Templars. Their Rise and Fall* (1937), with bibl. Other more important works include K. Schottmüller, *Der Untergang des Templer-Ordens* (2 vols., 1887); H. Prutz, *Entwicklung und Untergang des Tempelherrenordens* (1888); M. Lavocat, *Procès des frères et de l'ordre du Temple d'après des pièces inédites publiées par M. Michelet et des documents imprimés anciens et nouveaux* (1888); J. Gmelin, *Schuld oder Unschuld des Templerordens?* (2 vols., 1893); H. Finke, *Papsttum und Untergang des Templerordens* (Vorreformationsgeschichtliche Forschungen, iv and v; 1907). G. Lizerand, *Clément V et Philippe IV le Bel* (1910), passim; id. (ed.), *Le Dossier de l'affaire des templiers* (incl. Fr. tr. and introd.; Les Classiques de l'histoire de France au moyen-âge, 1923). J. Piquet, *Des Banquiers au moyen-âge. Les Templiers. Étude de leurs opérations financiers* (1939). B. A. Lees (ed.), *Records of the Templars in England in the Twelfth Century*. The Inquest of 1185, with Illustrative Charters and Documents (1935). M. Dessubré, *Bibliographie de l'ordre des Templiers, imprimés et manuscrits* (Bibliothique des Initiations Modernes, v; 1928). W. A. Phillips–T. A. Archer in *E.B.* (ed. 11), xxvi (1911), pp. 591–600, s.v.; C. Moeller in *C.E.*, xiv (1912), pp. 493–5, s.v.

TEMPLE, The. Although the idea of a national shrine of the Jews at *Jerusalem was conceived by *David, the first Temple dates from the reign of *Solomon (c. 970–933 B.C.). This building became the central sanctuary of Jewish religion, and here alone, acc. to the legislation of *Deuteronomy, could sacrificial worship be offered. It was destroyed by the Babylonians in 586 B.C., and its rebuilding was envisaged by *Ezekiel, and undertaken in 520 B.C. at the instigation of *Haggai and *Zechariah. This structure (the 'Second Temple') suffered desecration at the hands of *Antiochus Epiphanes, but was rededicated under *Judas Maccabaeus. The grandest of Temple buildings was put up by *Herod the Great, his chief motive being a bid for popular approval. This was the Temple standing in our Lord's day, the scene of the Cleansing, and of His teaching during the days before the Betrayal. In Roman times the custody of the Temple was left in the hands of the *High Priest, assisted by priests officiating by rota. With the destruction of Jerusalem by the Romans in A.D. 70 the Temple worship ceased. The site is now occupied by a Moslem shrine. See also *Jerusalem; Dome of the Rock.

All attempted reconstructions of the Temple are necessarily highly conjectural. The more important reliable modern discussions include W. Nowack, *Lehrbuch der hebräischen Archäologie*, ii (1894), pp. 25–53 and 71–83, with full bibl. reff. to earlier literature. K. Möhlenbrink, *Der Tempel Salomos*. Eine Untersuchung seiner Stellung in der Sakralarchitektur des alten Orients (Beiträge zur Wissenschaft vom Alten und Neuen Testament, Folge 4, vii; 1932). J. de Groot, *Die Altäre des salomonischen Tempelhofes*. Eine archäologische Untersuchung (ib., N.F., vi; 1924). J. F. Hollis, *The Archaeology of Herod's Temple* (London thesis, London, 1934). T. W. Davies in *H.D.B.*, iv (1902), pp. 695–716, s.v.; I. Benzinger in *E.Bi.*, iv (1903), cols. 4923–56, s.v.; J. D. Eisenter–G. A. Barton in *J.E.*, xii (1906), pp. 81–101, s.v.

TEMPLE, FREDERICK (1821–1902), Abp. of *Canterbury. Born at Santa Maura in the Ionian Islands, he was educated at Blundell's School, Tiverton, and at Balliol College, Oxford, where B. *Jowett, A. C. *Tait, and W. G. *Ward were among his tutors. He was much interested in the *Tractarian Movement, but never attached himself to it; and gradually welcoming liberal principles, he condemned the attempted censure of both W. G. Ward and R. D. *Hampden. In 1846 he was ordained deacon and in 1847 priest, both by S. *Wilberforce. He continued to teach for a time at Balliol, where he became an advocate of Educational Reform, and in 1850 he submitted evidence before the Oxford University Reform Commission. From 1857 to 1869 he was Headmaster of Rugby, where he did much to increase the prestige of the school and also became increasingly prominent in the education movement. In 1860 he wrote on 'The Education of the World' for *Essays and Reviews* (q.v.). This paper, though wholly inoffensive from the standpoint of orthodoxy, brought him much obloquy through the extremities of some of his fellow-contributors. Hence when in 1869 he was offered the Bishopric of *Exeter, the nomination was received with fierce opposition, but he was consecrated on 21 Dec. 1869 and, characteristically, only consented to withdraw his essay from future editions of *Essays and Reviews* after the event. In his diocese he did much to foster Church Schools and was also a leading figure in the temperance movement. In 1885 he was translated to London where it fell to him to take an important part in the Royal Jubilee celebrations (1887) and in the *Lincoln Judgement (1892). In his later years he became increasingly involved in conflict with the High Church party. In 1897 he was translated to *Canterbury. His archiepiscopate was marked by the Queen's Golden Jubilee of 1897, the notable *Lambeth Conference of the same year and the issue of the *Lambeth Opinions (q.v.) of 1899–1900. His writings include an impressive set of *Bampton Lectures on *The Relations between Religion and Science* (1884) and several vols. of Sermons.

E. G. Sandford (ed.), *Memoirs of Archbishop Temple* by Seven Friends (2 vols., 1906); last section (Editor's Supplement), with extracts from other parts, repr. as E. G. Sandford, *Frederick Temple*. An Appreciation (1907).

TEMPLE, WILLIAM (1881–1944), Abp. of *Canterbury. The second son of F. *Temple, he was successively Exhibitioner of Balliol College (1900), Fellow of Queen's College, Oxford (1904), Headmaster of Repton (1910), Rector of St. James's, Piccadilly (1914), Canon of Westminster (1919), Bp. of Manchester (1921), Abp. of *York (1929), and Abp. of Canterbury (1942). While still a layman, he formed lasting interests in educational and social work, esp. through the Workers' Educational Association and the *Student Christian Movement. He contributed to *Foundations* (1912; q.v.) and was among the leaders of the 'Life and Liberty Movement' calling for a degree of autonomy for the C of E which was substantially granted by the *Enabling Act (1919). In 1923 he became a member (from 1925, Chairman) of the Archbishops' Commission which in 1938 produced the report on *Doctrine in the Church of England*. As Abp. of York (1929–42), he became increasingly prominent in the national life, esp. through his lively concern with social, economic, and international questions, though remaining independent of organized parties, both political and religious. He also gave whole-hearted support to the *Faith and Order and *Life and Work Movements and to the *Oecumenical Movement generally. In 1941 he was active in calling, and presided over, the *Malvern Conference. His short period as Abp. of Canterbury (23 Apr. 1942–26 Oct. 1944) was overshadowed by the War of 1939–45 and by ill-health, but it was remarkable, *inter alia*, for his participation, with Card. A.

*Hinsley and the Moderator of the Free Church Council, in the issue of a statement of principles which should guide a post-war settlement, and for his public speeches and broadcasts.

Temple was trained as a philosopher under E. *Caird, and the Neo-*Hegelian position from which he set out coloured all his later thinking, though he gradually developed into an independent thinker and philosopher of some significance. His principal works include *Mens Creatrix* (1917), *Christus Veritas* (1924), and *Nature, Man and God* (*Gifford Lectures for 1932–3 and 1933–4; 1934), *Readings in St. John's Gospel* (1939; Second Series, 1940; devotional studies) and *Christianity and Social Order* (Penguin Special; 1942). Of his other published works, many originated as lectures or addresses.

Life and Letters by F. A. Iremonger (1948). *Some Lambeth Letters, 1942–1944* (selected from W. Temple's correspondence), ed. F. S. Temple (1963).

TEMPORALE. The section of a *Missal or *Breviary (sometimes made into a separate book) which supplies the variable parts of the *Masses, *Offices, and a few other closely connected services, for the whole of the ecclesiastical year, except in so far as they are provided for in the *Sanctorale.

TEMPTATION. The etymology of the Lat. word (*temptatio*), of which the Heb. (מַסָּה) and Greek (πειρασμός) equivalents are neutral in flavour, suggests 'trying' or 'proving'. This primary sense is retained in the idea of the children of Israel's tempting God (Ex. 17. 2), of God's tempting *Abraham (Gen. 22. 1), and in Jas. 1. 2 f.: 'Count it all joy when ye fall into divers temptations, knowing this, that the trial of your faith worketh patience'. Perhaps it was by an extension of this usage that the word was applied to the persecutions of the early Christians. It is also possible that this is the meaning of the word in the *Lord's Prayer.

Elsewhere in the NT, as in present-day usage, the word has the implication of incitement to sin. St. *Augustine distinguished temptation which tended to issue in sin (*tentatio deceptionis* or *seductionis*) from temptation which merely put to the proof (*tentatio probationis*). Both he and St. *Gregory the Great divided the former into the three stages of suggestion, delight, and consent (*suggestio, delectatio, consensus*). In this, the classical sense, temptation seems to be a part of universal experience which already attacked our first parents before the *Fall. But, although St. *Paul warns his readers against committing acts which though innocent in themselves might be a temptation to others, he nowhere implies that inclination to wrongful action is sinful before consent.

Acc. to St. *James, temptation is inherent in free-will, but God does not permit it beyond what the soul can bear. He warns his readers against regarding God as its author (Jas. 1. 13). The three traditional sources of temptation are the world, the flesh, and the devil. Although in the OT the tempter is regularly depicted as personal, the Lord also points to the weakness of the flesh as a cause of temptation (Mt. 26. 41), while St. James holds that lust is its main source (Jas. 1. 14 f.).

Modern psychologists, who frequently interpret sin mainly as psychological disorder, often teach that the forms of temptation rooted in the appetites are primarily natural instincts, which as such ought, at least to some extent, to be satisfied. They are apt to regard many forms of mental temptation, notably those which may lead to scruples and illusions, as of a much more serious nature. Since temptation is heightened by resistance, they frequently advocate circumvention rather than direct defence as the best means of avoiding repression. For the Christian moralist, the fundamental ethical facts remain unaffected by these psychological analyses. Rightly appreciated these analyses can be of positive service to him in assisting him to a better estimation of the roots of moral action and enabling him to see where moral responsibility really lies.

See also foll. entry.

The subject is regularly treated in works on Moral Theology. J. H. Horn, Πειρασμός. Die Versuchung des Gläubigen in der griechischen Bibel (Beiträge zum Wissenschaft vom Alten und Neuen Testament, Vierte Folge, xx; 1937). R. Brouillard in D.T.C., xv (pt. 1; 1946), cols. 116–27, s.v. 'Tentation', with bibl.; H. Seesemann in T.W.B., vi ('1954'), pp. 23–37, s.v. 'πεῖρα κτλ.', with further bibl.

TEMPTATION OF CHRIST. The Temptation of Christ in the wilderness after His baptism is recorded in Mt. 4. 1–11, Lk. 4. 1–13, Mk. 1. 13. Three particular temptations are described in Mt. and Lk., viz. (1) to use His power as Son of God to turn stones into bread to satisfy His hunger; (2) to cast Himself down from a pinnacle of the Temple, i.e. to put God to an arbitrary test and to stage a spectacular miracle; and (3) to obtain from the devil power over all the kingdoms of the world by falling down and worshipping him, i.e. to desert His true mission for the sake of power unworthily obtained. In Lk. the last two temptations are mentioned in the reverse order. It is a matter of Christian faith that though Christ was 'tempted in all points like as we are', He was 'yet without sin' (Heb. 4. 15).

St. *Thomas Aquinas, Summa Theologica, iii, 41. H. J. C. Knight, The Temptation of Our Lord considered as related to the Ministry and as a Revelation of His Person (Hulsean Lectures, 1905–6; 1907). F. *Spitta, Zur Geschichte und Litteratur des Urchristentums, iii (pt. 2; 1907), pp. 1–108 ('Die Versuchung Jesu'); P. Ketter, Die Versuchung Jesu nach dem Berichte der Synoptiker (Neutestamentliche Abhandlungen, vi, Hft. 3; 1918); H. J. Vogels, 'Die Versuchungen Jesu' in Biblische Zeitschrift, xvii (1926), pp. 238–55; J. M. Vosté, O.P., De Baptismo, Tentatione et Transfiguratione Jesu (Studia Theologiae Biblicae Novi Testamenti, ii; Rome; 1934), pp. 51–114; E. Fascher, Jesus und der Satan. Eine Studie zur Auslegung der Versuchungsgeschichte (Hallische Monographien herausgegeben O. Eissfeldt, x; 1949). R. Schnackenburg, 'Der Sinn der Versuchung Jesu bei den Synoptikern' in T.Q., cxxxii (1952), pp. 297–326. H. Seesemann in T.W.B., vi ('1954'), pp. 33–7, s.v. 'πεῖρα κτλ. C. III. Die Versuchungen Jesu', with bibl, See also commentaries to the Gospels.

TEMPUS CLAUSUM (Lat., 'closed time'). The seasons in the Christian year in which owing to their solemn and penitential character marriages may not normally be solemnized. The prohibition is already found for *Lent in the 52nd canon of the Council of *Laodicea (4th cent.). Later it was extended to *Advent (Council of Beneventum in 1091) and from the first of the *Rogation Days to the first Sunday after *Pentecost (Council of Nîmes, 1284). There was, however, no uniform practice until the Council of *Trent, which defined the forbidden season as extending from the first Sunday of Advent to the *Epiphany and from *Ash Wednesday to *Low Sunday (Sess. 24, cap. 10). In the new RC canon law it extends only from the first Sunday of Advent to Christmas Day and from Ash Wednesday to Easter Day (CIC, can. 1108). This legislation does not refer to the marriage ceremony itself, which may take place at any time of the year, but only to its solemnization by the Nuptial Mass and Blessing. For sufficient reasons, however, even the solemnization may be permitted by the Ordinaries during the closed time. In such cases the bride and groom are admonished to abstain from undue display.

TEN ARTICLES, The (1536). The first Articles of faith issued by the C of E during the Reformation period. They were adopted by *Convocation in 1536 at the desire of *Henry VIII. The three Sacraments of Baptism, Penance, and the Eucharist are upheld. The Eucharistic presence is called both corporal and substantial, but *transubstantiation is not mentioned. Justification is said to be attained by contrition and faith joined with charity. Images are to be retained as representative of virtue, but are not to be worshipped. The intercession of the saints may be sought. Prayers and Masses for the dead are enjoined. The Articles were superseded in 1537 by 'The *Bishops' Book' (q.v.).

Text in C. Hardwick, A History of the Articles of Religion (1851), pp. 231–48, with discussion, pp. 39–59.

TEN COMMANDMENTS, The. See Commandments, The Ten.

TEN THOUSAND MARTYRS, The. Two groups of 'Ten Thousand Martyrs' are named in the '*Roman Martyrology': (1) On 22 June, In monte Ararath, passio sanctorum martyrum decem millia crucifixorum. The reference here is a purely legendary record of 10,000 soldiers, crucified with their leader, Acacius, on Mount Ararat. Some of their reputed relics were brought to the W. at the time of the *Crusades. (2) On 18 Mar. Nicomediae sanctorum decem millium martyrum qui pro Christi confessione gladio percussi sunt. This entry would seem to relate to those who suffered at the beginning of the *Diocletianic Persecution (303). Though the number has doubtless been rounded to a conventional figure and is almost certainly exaggerated, both *Eusebius (Hist. Eccl.

VIII, vi) and *Lactantius (*De Mortibus Persecut.* XV) indicate that it was very large.

The legends will be found with commentary in *AA.SS.*, Jun. IV (1707), pp. 175–88, and Mar. II (1668), p. 617. J. P. Kirsch in *L.Th.K.*, x (1938), col. 1049 f., s.v. 'Zehntausend Märtyrer', with bibl.

TEN TRIBES, The. The ten of the twelve Hebrew tribes which at the death of *Solomon (933 B.C.) separated from the two tribes of Judah and Benjamin to form the kingdom of Israel, while the two latter formed the kingdom of Judah. At the conquest of Israel by the Assyrians in 721, many of the more prosperous of its people were deported to Assyria (2 Kgs. 17. 1–6), though the bulk of the population remained in Palestine. The descendants of those taken into exile were either merged in the Gentile population of the Assyrian empire or else became part of the later Jewish *Diaspora. The theory upheld by '*British Israelites' that the lost Ten Tribes were the ancestors of the British nation is without historical basis.

TEN YEARS' CONFLICT, The (1833–43). In the Church of *Scotland, the conflict which culminated in the *Disruption of 1843. The struggle, which arose out of the claim of certain of the laity to an effective say in the choice of their ministers, began in 1833 when a motion in the General Assembly that a majority of dissentient voices should veto the presentee of the patron was lost by a narrow margin. In the Assembly of 1834, however, the Popular party gained the ascendancy over the 'Moderates' and, on the motion of Lord Moncreiff, the Veto Act passed. The new situation created great legal difficulties, and when the Veto Act was applied, e.g. at Auchterarder and Marnoch, and the patron and his presentee brought their cases into the law courts, the Scottish Court of Session (1838) and later the House of Lords (1839) pronounced the Veto Act *ultra vires*. The Assembly, dominated by the evangelical popular party now led by T. *Chalmers, were none the less defiant. In 1841 the Popular party deposed ministers of the Strathbogie Presbytery who adhered to the law of the land, and in their 'Claim of Rights' (1842) they affirmed the Church's spiritual independence. The government of the day continued to regard the Popular party as rebellious subjects, and in 1843 the climax came when about one-third of the ministers and members of the Church seceded and formed the *Free Church of Scotland (q.v.).

R. Buchanan, *The Ten Years' Conflict* (2 vols., 1849). See also works cited under *Scotland, Christianity in*.

TENEBRAE. In the W. Church, the *Mattins and *Lauds of the last three days of *Holy Week. The service is sung by anticipation on the three preceding evenings. The name, which literally means 'darkness', is probably derived from the very ancient ceremony of extinguishing one by one the lights in the church as the service proceeds. During the greater part of the service, the only light is derived from a set of 15 (since the later Middle Ages) candles fitted on to a '*hearse', which are put out one by one at the end of each of the Psalms and the 15th at the end of the *Benedictus. The service concludes with Psalm 51 ('*Miserere'), recited in complete darkness. The office has dramatic reference to the death of Christ and His descent into Hades.

H. Thurston, S.J., *Lent and Holy Week* (1904), pp. 238–73. M. Andrieu, *Les Ordines Romani du haut moyen-âge*, iii (S.S.L., xxiv; 1951), pp. 313–20. H. Thurston, S.J., in *C.E.*, xiv (1912), p. 506, s.v.

TENISON, THOMAS (1636–1715), Abp. of *Canterbury. Educated at *Norwich and Corpus Christi College, Cambridge, he was ordained privately in 1659 by B. *Duppa, and after other parochial work was appointed in 1680 to St. Martin-in-the-Fields, where he gained a considerable reputation as a preacher. In 1687 he engaged in a public controversy with Fr. Andrew Pulton, S.J. At the same time he made zealous efforts to reunite the more moderate Protestant Nonconformists with the C. of E., though he supported the protest of the *Seven Bishops against the *Declaration of Indulgence. In 1692 he became Bp. of *Lincoln, and in 1695 Abp. of Canterbury, where he at once revived the Archbishop's Court. In 1701 he took a prominent part in the foundation of *S.P.G. He fell into disfavour under *Anne, because of his pronounced Whig and *Low Church views, and for the same reasons was a zealous supporter of the Hanoverian succession. J. *Evelyn wrote in praise of his generosity, modesty, prudence, and piety, while J. *Swift spoke of him as 'a very dull man who had a horror of anything like levity in his clergy, especially of whist'. Besides sermons and pamphlets, he wrote *The Creed of Mr. Hobbes examined* (1670) and *Baconia, or Certain Genuine Remains of Lord Bacon* (1679).

Memoirs of the Life and Times of the Most Reverend Father in God, Dr. Thomas Tennison [1715]. E. [F.] Carpenter, *Thomas Tenison, Archbishop of Canterbury*. His Life and Times (C.H.S., 1948). W. H. *Hutton in *D.N.B.*, lvi (1898), pp. 57–60.

TEPHILLIN (תְּפִלִּין). The Jewish name for *phylacteries. It is the plural of *tephillah*, a 'prayer'.

TERAPHIM. Religious images, mentioned in Gen. 31. 19, which were popularly venerated by the Israelites in pre-exilic times. The narrative of 1 Sam. 19. 13 would imply that at least their upper part had human shape. They are now generally held to have been household gods of some kind, used also for purpose of divination (Ezek. 21. 21, Zech. 10. 2). In Hos. 3. 4 they are associated with the *ephod, where they are perhaps regarded as legitimate implements of religion, whereas in 2 Kgs. 23. 24 their use is condemned by Josiah. In later times they seem to have gradually disappeared from Israelite worship.

See commentaries to Biblical passages cited and works cited, s.v. *Ephod.* G. F. Moore in *E.Bi.*, iv (1903), col. 4974 f., s.v.; W. Baudissin in *P.R.E.* (ed. 3), xix (1907), pp. 514–18, s.v., with reff.

TERCE, SEXT, NONE. Together with *Prime, the 'Little Hours' of the Divine Office, appointed to be recited at the third, sixth, and ninth hours respectively. The old Jewish times for prayer played a considerable part in the devotion of the early Christians (cf. Acts 3. 1, 10. 9), and are attested as hours of private prayer by *Clement of Alexandria, *Cyprian, and others. It was not until the 5th cent., however, that, under the influence of monasticism, the public recitation of prayers at these times became general. Acc. to the modern Roman Breviary, Terce, Sext, and None, which are all of like structure, consist of three Psalms, preceded by Pater, Ave, versicle, and (almost) unchanging hymn, and followed by a chapter with responsory, prayer, and the usual concluding versicles. Ferial prayers are inserted before the prayer on the ferias of Lent, Advent, and certain Vigils and other fast days.

The principal work is contained in histories of the *Breviary, q.v. C. Callewaert, 'De Parvis Horis Romanis ante Regulam S. Benedicti' in *Collationes Brugenses*, xxix (1929), pp. 481–92, repr. in his *Sacris Erudiri* (Steenbrugge, 1940), pp. 119–26. L. Eisenhofer, *Handbuch der katholischen Liturgik*, ii (1933), pp. 527–37 ('Die kleinen Horen'); M. Righetti, *Manuale di storia liturgica*, ii (Milan, 1946), pp. 584–6. F. *Cabrol, O.S.B., in *C.E.*, xi (1911), p. 97 f., s.v. 'None'; id., ib., xiii (1912), p. 747 f., s.v. 'Sext'; id., ib., xiv (1912), p. 514 f., s.v. 'Terce'; H. *Leclercq, O.S.B., in *D.A.C.L.*, xii (pt. 2; 1936), cols. 1554–7, s.v. 'None'; id., ib., xv (pt. 1; 1950), cols. 1396–9, s.v. 'Sexte et Tierce'.

TERESA OF ÁVILA, St. (1515–82), Spanish *Carmelite nun and mystic. Teresa was descended from an old Spanish family. She was educated by *Augustinian nuns and in 1533 entered the Carmelite monastery of the Incarnation ('mitigated observance') at Ávila. A mysterious illness obliged her to return to her family, but on her recovery she re-entered her convent where she began to lead a rather lax life. On the advice of her confessor she resumed mental prayer, but it was not until 1555 that she was finally converted to a life of perfection, while praying before a statue of Christ scourged at the pillar. Her mystic life began soon afterwards with Divine locutions and an intellectual vision of Christ. In 1557 St. *Peter of Alcantara became temporarily her confessor and her first ecstasy occurred about the same time. In order to lead a more mortified life she wanted to found a house where the primitive rule would be strictly observed. This plan she carried out in the face of strong opposition and in 1562 St. Joseph was founded at Ávila. During her stay there, the quietest time of her life, she wrote her first work, *The Way of Perfection.* The subsequent years from 1567 to her death were filled with labours for the establishment of houses of the primitive rule ('Discalced *Carmelites') both for nuns and for friars, an undertaking in which she received much assistance from St. *John of the Cross, (q.v.). Despite violent opposition from the Calced Carmelites and several of the

ecclesiastical authorities, her work proceeded, and at the same time her religious life deepened until it reached the state of 'spiritual marriage' (1572). In the intervals between her foundations she wrote, under obedience to her confessors, *Foundations, Life, The Interior Castle,* and several smaller books. After her last foundation at Burgos (1582) under the greatest difficulties and privations, she fell ill and died at Alva on 4 Oct. She was canonized 1622, in and her feast is kept on 15 Oct.

St. Teresa's importance is twofold. As the reformer of the Carmelite Order her work has survived in the great number of Discalced monasteries which venerate her as their foundress. She was a woman of strong character, shrewdness, and great practical ability. As a spiritual writer her influence was epoch-making because she was the first to point to the existence of states of prayer intermediate between discursive meditation and ecstasy ('quiet' and 'union') and to give a scientific description of the entire life of prayer from meditation to the so-called mystic marriage. Her combination of mystic experience with ceaseless activity as a reformer and organizer make her life the classical instance for those who contend that the highest contemplation is not incompatible with great practical achievements.

Editio princeps of her works by L. de León (Salamanca, 1588; incomplete); crit. edd. by V. de la Fuente (2 vols., Biblioteca de Autores Españoles, liii and lv; 1861–2) and by Silverio de Santa Teresa, O.C.D. (6 vols., Burgos, 1915–19, Letters, 3 vols., 1922–4, in Biblioteca Mística Carmelitana', i–ix; Eng. tr. by E. A. Peers of the Works, 3 vols., 1946, and of the Letters, 2 vols., 1951). Photographic facsimiles of St. Teresa's autographs, with introd. by V. de la Fuente, of her Life (Madrid, 1873), and of the Foundations (ib., 1880). Early lives by Diego de Yépès (Madrid, 1587) and F. de Ribera, S.J. (Salamanca, 1590; Lat. tr., Cologne, 1620). *AA.SS.*, Oct. VII (1845), pp. 109–790, with Lat. tr. of life by F. de Ribera, pp. 539–725. H. J. Coleridge, *The Life and Letters of St. Teresa* ('Quarterly Series', 3 vols., 1881–8); (Mrs.) G. C. Graham, *Santa Teresa* (2 vols., 1894). H. Joly, *Sainte Thérèse* ('Les Saints', 1902; Eng. tr., 1903). H. H. Colville, *Saint Teresa of Spain* (1909); *The Life of Saint Teresa* taken from the Fr. of 'A Carmelite Nun' by Alice Lady Lovat [1912]. Silverio de Santa Teresa, O.C.D., *Santa Teresa, síntesis suprema de la raza* (1939; Eng. tr., 1947); E. A. Peers, *Mother of Carmel.* A Portrait of St. Teresa of Jesus (1945). R. Hoornaert, *Ste Térèse écrivain.* Son milieu, ses facultés, son œuvre (1922; Eng. tr. of 3rd ed., abridged, 1931). G. Etchegoyen, *L'Amour divin.* Essai sur les sources de sainte Thérèse (Bibliothèque de l'École des Hautes Études Hispaniques, iv; 1923). V. Sackville-West, *The Eagle and the Dove* (1943), pp. 7–100. Pourrat, iii, 187–268. P. Pourrat, P.S.S., in *D.T.C.*, xv (pt. 1; 1946), cols. 552–73, s.v. 'Thérèse, Sainte', with full bibl. on early sources. A. Mager in *L.Th.K.*, x (1938), cols. 90–5, s.v. 'Theresia v. Jesus' with further bibl.

TERESA OF LISIEUX, St. (1873–97), *Carmelite nun. The youngest daughter of Louis Martin, a devout watchmaker of Alençon, she was drawn towards religious perfection at an early age. In spite of opposition, she obtained permission to enter the Carmelite convent at Lisieux at the age of 15. She was professed in 1890, and was assistant novice-mistress from 1893. In 1896 she was prevented from joining the Carmelites in *China by the first of a series of haemorrhages. She died of tuberculosis on 30 Sept. 1897.

At the command of her superiors she wrote her autobiography, *L'Histoire d'une âme.*

The spread of her fame was largely due to the decision of the prioress to circulate a revised version of this, together with details of her death, to all Carmelite houses. Miracles of healing and prophecy were soon reported in sufficient number to realize her promise, 'Je vais faire tomber un torrent de roses'. By 1907 an account of them was appended to her biography. Proceedings for her beatification were initiated in the court of Bayeux in 1910 and moved to Rome in 1918, her cause being exempted from the fifty years' delay imposed by Canon Law. On 25 Apr. 1923 her beatification was proclaimed by *Pius XI and her bones solemnly translated to the convent. On 17 May 1925 she was canonized under the name of 'Saint Teresa of the Child Jesus and the Holy Face'. Her feast is kept 3 Oct.

Owing to the continued increase in the number of pilgrims of all nations, it was decided in 1926 to erect a large basilica at Lisieux. The popularity of her cult was largely due to her appeal to the ordinary people of her age, to whom her life showed that the attainment of sanctity was practicable, not only through extreme mortification, but through continual renunciation in small matters. She is popularly known in England as 'The Little Flower' from the sub-title of her autobiography. In 1929 Pius XI named her patroness of foreign missions and all works directed to Russia. In 1947 she was joined with Joan of Arc as patroness of France.

Her autobiography was first publd. at Lisieux in 1899; many subsequent edd.; Eng. tr., 1901; more recent tr. by T. N. Taylor, 1927. Letters ed. A. Combes, Lisieux, 1948; Eng. tr., New York, 1948. *Pluies des roses* (6 vols., Lisieux, 1913–25). A. P. Laveille, *Sainte Thérèse de l'Enfant Jésus* (1873–1897), *d'après les documents officiels du Carmel de Lisieux* (1925; Eng. tr., 1928). The large number of other lives include studies by H. Petitot, O.P. (1922; Eng. tr., 1927), H. *Ghéon (Paris, 1934; Eng. tr., 1934), H. U. von Balthasar (Olten, 1950; Eng. tr., 1953), and V. Johnson (London, 1953). A. Combes, *Introduction à la spiritualité de sainte Thérèse de l'Enfant Jésus* (1946; enlarged ed., 1948; Eng. tr. of 1946 ed., 1950); id., *Sainte Thérèse de l'Enfant Jésus*. Contemplation et apostolat (1949). Id., *La Problème de L'Histoire d'une âme et des œuvres complètes de S. Thérèse de Lisieux* (1950), and other works by this author.

TERMINISM. (1) The doctrine that God has ordained a definite period or 'term' in the life of every individual at the end of which he loses his opportunity of achieving salvation. The belief was defended by J. G. Böse (*c.* 1662–1700) in his *De Termino Salutis* (1698) and much cherished in *Pietist circles, and also upheld by Adam Rechenberg (1642–1721); but it met with fierce opposition from orthodox *Lutherans. (2) By philosophers, the word is occasionally used as another name for *Nominalism (q.v.).

TERRITORIALISM. A theory of Church government formerly held by certain Protestant theologians, acc. to which the civil authority had the right to determine the religious doctrines of its subjects. It is summarized in the formula *cuius regio eius religio*. The opposite view was often known as *Collegialism.

TERSANCTUS. An alternative name for the *Sanctus ('Holy, Holy, Holy'), sung or recited in the *Eucharistic Liturgy. The word is sometimes used also for the *Trisagion in the *Reproaches on *Good Friday.

TERSTEEGEN, GERHARD (1697–1769), German Protestant devotional writer. Born at Moers, near Düsseldorf, he underwent a conversion in a circle of *Pietists at the age of 20. Under the influence of ascetic and *quietist ideas, he retired into solitude and earned his living as a ribbon weaver. Having established in 1727 his Pilgrims' Hut at Otterbeck, near Mülheim, in order to realize his spiritual ideals in a kind of religious community, he abandoned his profession in 1728 and devoted himself entirely to the career of a director of souls and devotional meetings. Besides many translations, chiefly from French *Quietist writers, he published poems and hymns under the title *Geistliches Blumen-Gärtlein inniger Seelen* (1729) and, from 1733 to 1753, *Auserlesene Lebensbeschreibungen heiliger Seelen*, a set of selected biographies of Catholic mystics, in which, however, he explicitly denounced their 'sensual religion'. His influence spread throughout Germany, Holland, and Scandinavia, though his activities were temporarily hampered by the Prussian anti-conventicle laws of 1740. His piety was highly individualistic, e.g. he refused to partake of Holy Communion together with worldly or godless people. To-day he is chiefly known for his hymns, remarkable for their poetical charm and a deep spirituality which expresses itself esp. in adoration of the Divine Majesty and a tender love for the Saviour. Many of them, e.g. '*Brunn alles Heils*' ('Thee fount of blessing') and '*Gott ist gegenwärtig*' ('Lo, God is here'), have been translated into English.

Gesammelte Schriften, 8 vols., Stuttgart, 1844–6; separate collections of his *Dichtungen*, ed. E. W. Schimmelbusch, 3 vols., Düsseldorf, 1897, and of his *Geistliche Leider*, ed. W. Nelle, Gütersloh, 1897. Modern anthology ed. T. Klein, Munich, 1925. Various of his hymns tr. into Eng. by Frances Bevan, *Hymns of Ter Steegen, Suso and Others* (1895); id., *Hymns of Ter Steegen and Others* (1897). The basic study is that of G. Kerlen (Mülheim a.d. Ruhr, 1851). W. Blankenagel, *Tersteegen als religiöser Erzieher* (Emsdetten, 1934). In Eng. there is a life by H. E. Govan (London, 1898, with selections of his writings) and a popular sketch by W. E. Oliphant (publd. by the *Salvation Army, London, 1905). E. Simons in *P.R.E.* (ed. 3), xix (1907), pp. 530–7, s.v.

TERTIANSHIP. Also known as the **Schola Perfectionis.** In the *Jesuit Order a period of intensive training in piety undergone a year or two after ordination to the priesthood before admission to final vows. It is of the nature of a second *novitiate and intended to re-establish the candidate in religious fervour after the relaxation in discipline which follows his ordination. It begins with a 30 days' *retreat, and lasts for somewhat under a year.

TERTIARY. Member of a 'Third Order' (q.v.). The institution came into existence in the 13th cent., when the need was felt to afford lay people opportunities for self-dedication in religion in accordance with the spirit of the great *Mendicant orders. The term 'tertiary' is now popularly used only of those members living in the world to distinguish them from 'Regular Tertiaries' who live in community. Acc. to RC canon law 'Secular Tertiaries are those persons who in the world strive after Christian perfection, under the guidance of, and in harmony with the spirit, of some Order, in a manner compatible with the life in the world and acc. to rules approved by the Holy See' (*CIC*, can. 702). The most important are the *Franciscan, *Dominican, and *Carmelite Tertiaries, who are under the direction of priests of their respective First Orders. They have to make a *novitiate and are clothed with the habit of the order, which, however, is now worn only on prescribed occasions and hardly ever in public, a *scapular worn under the ordinary clothes taking its place. Tertiaries observe a rule and recite a liturgical *office, usually the Divine Office or the Little Office of Our Lady, or certain other prescribed prayers. They also keep special fasts and have their own spiritual privileges, such as *indulgences. They are not bound by vow, but make a solemn promise; they may not leave the order or join another without grave cause, nor may they belong to more than one at a time. Normally, but not always, they form chapters under the leadership of a priest. The aims of the Third Orders differ acc. to the spirit of their First Orders. Thus the Franciscans are specially interested in the practice of charity and social works, whereas the Dominicans and Carmelites lay greater stress on works of penance. For the practices of 'Regular Tertiaries', see *Third Order*.

TERTULLIAN, QUINTUS SEPTIMIUS FLORENS (*c.* 160–*c.* 220), African Church Father. A native of Carthage, he received a solid pagan education and later became a lawyer, probably living in *Rome. Having been converted to Christianity in 195 or 196 he returned to Carthage, where he became a catechist and, acc. to St. *Jerome, a priest. His rigorist views led him to sympathize with *Montanism, and *c.* 207 he officially joined the sect. He later founded his own party, the Tertullianists, who survived until the 4th cent.

Tertullian was the author of a long list of apologetic, theological, controversial, and ascetic works in Latin, as well as of a few writings in Greek. Of the former most have been preserved only in one MS., the 9th cent. 'Codex Agobardinus' (Par. lat. 1622), whereas the latter have all been lost. His celebrated defence of Christianity, the 'Apologeticum' (*c.* 197), is addressed to the prefects of the Roman provinces and deals chiefly with the absurdity of the accusations brought against the Christians. He maintains that the Christians are good citizens, who refuse Divine honours to the Emperor because of their monotheistic religion. He then gives a vivid description of life in the Christian communities, which only increase

under persecution, acc. to his famous formula 'semen est sanguis Christianorum'. A kind of complement to the 'Apologeticum' is the exquisite little work 'De Testimonio Animae' in which he argues that the human soul is Christian by nature, 'anima naturaliter Christiana'. His polemical treatise, 'De Praescriptione Haereticorum' (*c.* 200), contains an exposition of the Catholic principles of tradition and authority, by which he denies all heresy the right to interpret the Scriptures. The Bible is the possession of the Church, to whom alone the truth has been handed down by Christ and the Apostles. Of his works against individual heresies the most important are those 'Against *Marcion' (207 onwards) and 'Against *Praxeas' (after 213). The former is a lucid exposition of the unity of God and the identity of Christ with the Jewish Messiah against Gnostic dualism, the latter an attempt to elaborate the orthodox doctrine of the Trinity against *Patripassianism. In it for the first time the term 'Trinity' is applied to the Three Divine Persons. Of his ascetical and practical works 'De Baptismo' (*c.* 198–200) and 'De Poenitentia' (*c.* 203) are esp. valuable for the light they shed on the respective practices of the early Church in regard to *Baptism and *Penance. 'De Corona Militum' (211) and 'De Idolatria' (*c.* 211–12), on the other hand, are already saturated with the Montanist spirit which would debar Christians of the Empire from most professions because of their connexion with paganism. The same rigorism appears in most other works of this last period, notably in 'De Pudicitia' (*c.* 217–22), in which he attacked Pope *Callistus for teaching that capital sin was forgiven after canonical penance. What appears to be the first Christian writing on psychology is his 'De Anima' (*c.* 210), in which he stresses the unity of the soul and its life, though, owing to his anti-Gnostic prepossessions, he assigns to it a certain corporality. The same trend towards materialism leads him into affirming *Traducianism as the mode of the propagation of the soul. Cogent reasons have been adduced for attributing to him also the editing of the 'Passio SS. Perpetuae et Felicitatis'.

Tertullian was the first Christian theologian to write in Latin. Despite his rugged and difficult style, which is the expression of a passionate and even violent character, he may be said to have created the language of W. theology, which owes its characteristic precision to his legally trained mind. The fact of his *Montanism did not prevent him from remaining dogmatically orthodox in most respects, and his contributions to the elucidation of the Trinitarian and Christological doctrines place him beside St. *Augustine as the greatest W. theologian of the patristic period.

The earliest collected ed. of Tertullian's writings was that of Beatus *Rhenanus (Basle, 1521); this and other 16th cent. edd. were based on several 11th cent. MSS. now lost. Later edd. by J. Pamelius (Antwerp, 1579), J. S. *Semler (6 vols., Halle, 1769–76), and F. Oehler (3 vols., Leipzig. 1851–4). Crit. edd. in course of publication in C.S.E.L. (edd. A. Reifferscheid, E. Kroymann, H. Hoppe, &c., 1890 ff.) and in Corpus Christianorum (edd. J. G. P. Borleffs

TEST ACT

E. Dekkers, O.S.B., &c., 1952 ff.). The many edd. of single works include: *Apologeticum*, ed. J. E. B. Mayor–A. *Souter (Camb.idge, 1917), J. P. Waltzing–A. Severyns (Collection des Universités de la France, 1929), and J. P. Waltzing (Paris, 1931, with comm.); *Ad Nationes*, ed. J. G. P. Borleffs (Leiden, 1929); *De Testimonio Animae*, ed. W. A. J. C. Scholte (Amsterdam, 1934); *De Praescriptione Haereticorum*, ed. P. de Labriolle (Paris, 1907); *De Anima*, ed. J. H. Waszink (Amsterdam, 1933; more elaborate ed., ib., 1947); *De Spectaculis*, ed. A. Boulenger (Paris, 1933); *De Baptismo*, ed. R. F. Refoulé (S.C., xxxv; 1952). Eng. tr. by S. Thelwall, P. Holmes and others (A.N.C.L., vii, xi, xv, and xviii, 1869–70); also of *De Oratione* and *De Baptismo* by A. Souter (S.P.C.K., London, 1919); of *De Resurrectione Carnis* by id. (ib., 1922); and of various moral treatises by W. P. Le Saint, S.J. (Ancient Christian Writers, xiii; 1951).

P. Monceaux, *Histoire littéraire de l'Afrique chrétienne*, i (1901), pp. 177–461; A. d'Ales, S.J., *La Théologie de Tertullien* (1905). K. Adam, *Der Kirchenbegriff Tertullians* (1907). B. B. Warfield, *Studies in Tertullian and Augustine* (1930). E. Dekkers, O.S.B., *Tertullianus en de Geschiednis der Liturgie* (1947). J. P. Waltzing, *Le Codex Fuldensis de Tertullien* (Bibliothèque de la Faculté de Philosophie et Lettres de l'Université de Liége, xxi; 1914–17). H. Hoppe, *Syntax und Stil des Tertullian* (1903). Bardenhewer, ii, 377–442; Altaner (ed. 1951), pp. 122–34; J. Quasten, *Patrology*, ii (Utrecht, 1953), pp. 246–340. G. Bardy in *D.T.C.*, xv (pt. 1; 1946), cols. 130–71, s.v. 'Tertullien'; M. Pellegrino in *E.C.*, xi (1953), cols. 2025–33, s.v. 'Tertulliano', with bibl. of recent publications.

TEST ACT, The.

The Act (25 Car. II, c. 2) passed in 1673 requiring all holders of office under the crown (*inter alia*) to receive the sacrament of the Eucharist acc. to the usage of the C of E, to take the Oaths of Supremacy and Allegiance to the King, and to make the '*Declaration against Transubstantiation'. Among its first effects was the resignation by *James (II), Duke of York, of his post of Lord High Admiral. The Act remained in force till 1829.

Text in Gee–Hardy, No. cxx, pp. 632–40; part also in Bettenson, pp. 405–7.

TESTAMENT, Old and New.

See *Old Testament* and *New Testament*.

TESTAMENT OF OUR LORD IN GALILEE,

also known as **The Epistle of the Apostles** (*Epistula Apostolorum*). This *apocryphal document, dating from *c.* 150 and written in the form of an encyclical sent out by the eleven Apostles after the Resurrection, purports to record conversations between the Apostles and the Risen Christ. It was written in Greek, but survives, as far as is known, only in *Ethiopic, *Coptic (in an incomplete form), and, in the case of a single leaf, in Latin. It was apparently directed against the *Gnostics and probably emanated from Asia Minor or Egypt. It is to be distinguished from *Testamentum Domini* (q.v.).

C. Schmidt, *Gespräche Jesu mit seinen Jüngern nach der Auferstehung* (T.U., xliii, 1919); review by G. Bardy in *R. Bibl.*, xxx (1921), pp. 110–34. Eth. text, ed., with introd. and Fr. tr., by L. Guerrier–S. Grébaut in *P.O.*, ix, pp. 141–236 (fasc. 3). Eng. tr. with short introd. in M. R. James, *The Apocryphal New Testament* (1924), pp. 485–503. I. Delazer, O.F.M., 'Disquisitio in Argumentum Epistolae Apostolorum' in *Antonianum*, iii (1928), pp. 369–406; id., 'De Tempore Compositionis Epistolae Apostolorum', ib., iv (1929), pp. 257–92 and 387–430. Altaner (ed. 1950), p. 60 f., with bibl.; J. Quasten, *Patrology*, i (Utrecht, 1950), pp. 150–3.

TESTAMENTS OF THE TWELVE PATRIARCHS, The.

A pseudepigraphical writing modelled on the 'Testament of *Jacob' in Gen. 49. It professes to relate in its 12 books the message that each of the 12 sons of Jacob gave to his descendants on his deathbed. Its purpose is chiefly to give moral encouragement and spiritual consolation to its readers, whose confidence is claimed by revelations *ex post facto* prophetic of the later history of the different Israelite tribes. Certain passages, clearly of Christian origin, are generally held to be interpolations into what was originally a Jewish writing. R. H. *Charles seems to have demonstrated that the book was originally written in Hebrew. It survives, however, only in Greek and in Old Armenian and Old Slavonic, with portions in other languages. Charles also argued that the bulk of it dates from the *Maccabean period (2nd cent. B.C.), and that even in pre-Christian times it received additions, these by the hand of an anti-Maccabean writer.

Editio princeps of Gk. text by J. E. *Grabe (ed.), *Spicilegium SS. Patrum*, i (Oxford, 1698), pp. 145–253; the ed. of A. *Gallandi is repr. in J. P. Migne, *PG*, ii, 1037–150. Crit. edd. by R. Sinker (Cambridge, 1869, with appendix, ib., 1879) and R. H. Charles (Oxford, 1908). Eng. tr. by R. H. Charles (London, 1908); there is also an Eng. tr., with notes and other material, in id., *The Apocrypha and Pseudepigrapha of the Old Testament*, ii (1913), pp. 282–367. M. De Jonge, *The Testaments of the Twelve Patriarchs* (Theologische Bibliotheek; xxv; Assen, Holland, 1953; also publ. by the Manchester University Press), with detailed bibl. p. 170 f. R. Sinker, *A Descriptive Catalogue of the Editions of the Printed Text of the Versions of the* Testamenta XII Patriarcharum (Cambridge, 1910). J. B. Frey in *Dict. Bibl.*, Suppl. i (1928), cols. 380–90, s.v. 'Apocryphes de l'Ancien Testament, 3', with bibl.

TESTAMENTUM DOMINI.

A short early Christian treatise professing to be in the words of Christ Himself. It contains detailed regulations on matters of ecclesiastical order and church building, and a complete liturgy. It was originally written in Greek, probably in the 4th–5th cents., but survives only in a Syriac translation made in the 7th cent. apparently by *Jacob of Edessa. It was probably a private compilation and hence does not represent the official practice of any Church. Later it became incorporated in a collection known as the 'Clementine Octateuch' which circulated among the Syrian *Monophysites.

The work has close literary connexions with Hippolytus's *Apostolic Tradition*, the *Apostolic Constitutions*, and other early Church Orders. *Editio princeps* of complete Syr. text by Mgr Ignatius Ephraem II Rahmani (Mainz, 1899; with Lat. tr.). J. Cooper–A. J. Maclean, *The Testament of the Lord* (1902; Eng. tr. with useful notes). F. X. Funk, *Das Testament unseres Herrn und die verwandten Schriften* (1901). É. Amann in *D.T.C.*, xv (pt. 1; 1946), cols. 194–200.

TETRAGRAMMATON, The.

The technical term for the four-lettered Hebrew word, יהוה (i.e. 'JHVH'), usually translated in the AV and RV 'the Lord'. Owing to its sacred character the Jews avoided uttering it when reading the Scriptures and substituted 'Adonai', i.e. the Hebrew word for 'Lord'. To call the reader's attention to this substitution, the vowel-points of 'Adonai' were inserted in Hebrew MSS. into the letters of the Tetragrammaton, and since the 16th cent. the bastard word '*Jehovah', obtained by fusing the vowels of the one word with the remaining letters of the other, has become established. The original pronunciation of the Tetragrammaton is now commonly thought to be represented in English by 'Yahweh'.

For bibl. see *Yahweh*.

TETRAPOLITAN CONFESSION, The.

A Protestant Confession of Faith drawn up by M. *Bucer and W. *Capito conjointly at the Diet of *Augsburg (1530) and presented to the Emperor on 9 July 1530, in the name of the four S. German cities of Strassburg, Memmingen, Lindau, and Constance. Its purpose was to prevent a rupture in German Protestantism. Its doctrinal formulae, though they had some *Zwinglian affinities, were based on those of the Augsburg Confession, a copy of which had been secretly transmitted to its compilers.

The text is in H. A. Niemeyer, *Collectio Confessionum in Ecclesiis Reformatis Publicatarum* (Leipzig, 1840), pp. 740-70. E. F. K. Müller in *P.R.E.* (ed. 3), xix (1907), pp. 559-64, s.v. 'Tetrapolitana, confessio', with bibl.

TETZEL, JOHANN (c. 1465-1519), German preacher of *indulgences. c. 1490 he became a *Dominican friar at Leipzig. In 1516, when the indulgence was issued for the rebuilding of *St. Peter's, Rome, Tetzel was appointed subcommissary for the regions of Magdeburg and Halberstadt. His rough-and-ready eloquence commended it widely, but his commercialism and the extravagance with which he supported the popular opinion that a mere money payment could be applied with unfailing effect to deliver a soul from purgatory caused great scandal. Though not permitted to preach at *Wittenberg (as the indulgence had been forbidden in Saxony), Tetzel preached at the neighbouring town of Jüterbog which lay just outside Saxony, and after hearing him here M. *Luther was stimulated to the issue, on 31 Oct. 1517, of his Ninety-Five Theses. Tetzel took up the challenge in two sets of counter - theses. The attempt of C. von *Miltitz in 1519 to restrain Tetzel in the interests of conciliation proved a failure.

The best modern study is that of N. Paulus (Mainz, 1899), with other works of this author cited in Schottenloher, *vide infra*. P. Mandonnet, O.P., 'Jean Tetzel et sa prédication des indulgences' in *Revue thomiste*, vii (1899), pp. 481-496, and viii (1900), pp. 178-93. H. G. Ganss in *C.E.*, xiv (1912), pp. 539-41, s.v. Further bibl. in Schottenloher, ii (1935), pp. 324-6 (Nos. 21132-74). See also works cited s.v. *Indulgences*.

TEUTONIC ORDER. An order of German knights, priests, and serving brothers. It originated in a tent hospital established by pilgrims from Bremen and Lübeck before Acre in 1189. Its rule, founded on that of the Order of St. *John, was confirmed by Clement

III on 6 Feb. 1191. In 1197 the order spread to Europe and, in 1198, it added the conquest of the infidels after the model of the *Templars to its nursing activities. Its first Grand Master, Hermann of Salza (1210 – 39), was given Prussia and made a prince of the Empire by *Frederick II in 1226, in exchange for help against the pagan Prussians; and under him and his successors the order conquered large parts of the Baltic provinces and Russia where it introduced Christianity and German colonists. After the fall of Acre in 1291 the residence of the Grand Master was transferred to *Venice and in 1309 to the fortress of Marienburg in E. Prussia. From the 15th cent. the order declined, owing to the superiority of the Poles under Wladislaw II Jagiello who defeated the knights in the battle of Tannenberg in 1410. In 1466 the order had to cede most of its territory except E. Prussia which it kept as a Polish fief. When, in 1525, the Grand Master *Albert of Brandenburg became a Protestant, Prussia was secularized, whereat the knights who remained Catholic transferred the seat of the order to Mergentheim. The end of its existence in Germany was brought about by Napoleon in 1809, but it continued in Austria with an archduke as Grand Master until 1923. In 1929 it received a new rule which once more established its strictly religious character. It devotes itself chiefly to work in schools and hospitals. There is a Protestant branch of the order at Utrecht.

E. Joachim–W. Hubatsch (edd.), *Regesta Historico-Diplomatica Ordinis S. Mariae Theutonicorum, 1198-1524* (4 vols., Göttingen, 1948-50). [G. E. J. de Wal,] *Essai sur l'histoire de l'ordre teutonique* (4 vols., 1784-6). F. Salles, *Annales de l'ordre teutonique ou de Sainte-Marie-de Jérusalem* (1887). A. Reiterer, *Das deutsche Kreuz*. Geschichte des deutschen Ritter-Ordens (Graz, 1922). H. von Treitschke, *Das Deutsche Ordensland Preussen* (1862; Eng. tr., 1942). E. Caspar, *Hermann von Salza und die Gründung des Deutschordensstaats in Preussen* (Tübingen, 1924). E. Maschke, *Der deutsche Orden und die Preussen*. Bekehrung und Unterwerfung in der preussischen baltischen Mission des 13. Jahrhunderts (Historische Studien, clxxvi; 1928). H. G. Plum, *The Teutonic Order and its Secularization* (thesis, Iowa, 1906). F. C. Woodhouse, *The Military Religious Orders in the Middle Ages* (1879), pp. 261-92. H. Prutz, *Die geistlichen Ritterorden* (1908), pp. 101-41. A. B. Boswell in *C. Med. H.*, vii (1932), pp. 248-69. Heimbucher, i, 617-620, and ii, 661, with bibl. E. Barker in *E.B.* (ed. 11), xxvi (1911), pp. 676-9, s.v.; C. Moeller in *C.E.*, xiv (1912), p. 541 f., s.v. See also bibl. to *Crusades*.

TEWKESBURY ABBEY. The place derives its name from Theoc, a hermit of the 8th cent. In 980 it became a cell of the Benedictine abbey of Cranborne and in 1103 independent. The magnificent abbey church, now the parish church of Tewkesbury, was completed in 1123. It underwent restoration by G. G. *Scott in 1875-9, and of recent years the fabric has been much repaired.

Annales Monasterii de Theokesberia, 1066-1263, ed. H. R. Luard, *Annales Monastici*, i (Rolls Series, 1864), pp. 43-180, with introd. pp. xv-xxvii. W. *Dugdale, *Monasticon Anglicanum*, ii (ed. 1819), pp. 53-87. *A Cursory Disquisition on the Conventual Church of Tewkesbury and its Antiquities* (1818). J. H. Blunt, *Tewkesbury Abbey and its Associations* (1875); H. J. L. J. Massé, *The Abbey Church of Tewkesbury with some Account of the Priory Church of Deerhurst, Gloucester* (1900), pp. 3-102. Rose Graham in W. Page (ed.), *V.C.H.*, Gloucester, ii (1907), pp. 61-6, with reff.

TEXTE UND UNTERSUCHUNGEN.

The abbreviated title of the series of *Texte und Untersuchungen zur Geschichte der altchristlichen Literatur*, the famous studies of early Christian literature. The first series, containing 15 vols., was published from 1882 onwards under the original editorship of O. von Gebhardt and A. *Harnack. A new series ('Neue Folge', 1897–1906), also comprising 15 vols., made the *Texte* the organ for publishing studies subsidiary to the edition of the Greek Fathers issued by the Prussian Academy (*Die Griechischen Christlichen Schriftsteller*). A third series ('Dritte Reihe'), edited by A. Harnack and C. Schmidt, was begun in 1907. Among its most notable publications are A. Resch's *Agrapha* (1906), A. Harnack's *Marcion* (1920), and F. *Loofs' *Paulus von Samosata* (1924).

TEXTUS RECEPTUS (Lat., 'the Received

Text'). The Greek text of the NT ordinarily contained in printed editions down to the later decades of the 19th cent. It takes its name from a casual phrase in the preface of the 2nd (1633) *Elzevir edition ('Textum *ergo habes, nunc ab omnibus* receptum, *in quo nihil immutatum aut corruptum damus*'). This text, which closely followed that of T. *Beza (1565), was substantially that of D. *Erasmus (1516), the *Complutensian Polyglott (NT printed 1514, publd. 1522) and esp. R. *Stephanus (1550). It is in substance the *Byzantine text contained in the great majority of the MSS. and underlies the AV of the English Bible. Critically it is far inferior to that of, e.g., *Westcott and Hort (1881), which is in substance that presupposed by the RV.

THADDAEUS, St. Acc. to tradition he has

been identified with the *Jude 'not Iscariot' of Jn. 14. 22 and 'Judas of James' of Lk. 6. 16 and Acts 1. 13, the name 'Thaddaeus', which occurs in Mt. 10. 3 and Mk. 3. 18 (in some MSS. also '*Lebbaeus') being used to distinguish him from the traitor (Iscariot). He is generally believed to be one of the *Brethren of the Lord and the author of the Ep. of *Jude. Tradition also frequently confuses him with *Addai, one of the Seventy, who plays an important part in the *Abgar Legend. In modern times St. Judas Thaddaeus has become a very popular saint in the RC Church and is much invoked in circumstances of special difficulty. Feast day together with St. Simon, 28 Oct.

Passio, which purports to be the work of Abdias, a disciple of St. Thaddaeus and first Bp. of Babylon, pr. in R. A. *Lipsius–M. Bonnet, *Acta Apostolorum Apocrypha*, i (Leipzig, 1891), pp. 273–8, with introd. pp. cvi–cx. A. S. *Peake in *D.A.C.*, i (1915), p. 658, s.v. 'Jude, the Lord's Brother'. See also introd. to comms. on Epistle of Jude, cited s.v., and bibl. to *Brethren of the Lord*.

THADDEUS, THE DOCTRINE OF. See

Addai, The Doctrine of.

THANKSGIVING, General. See *General

Thanksgiving*.

THEANDRIC ACTS (Gk. θεανδρικαὶ

ἐνέργειαι). The term was coined by *Dionysius the Areopagite (Ep. 4) to denote the characteristic activity of the God-man. It was often misused by *Monophysites and *Monothelites (e.g. *Severus of Antioch) in support of their theories of the one nature and the one will in Christ, but was defended by St. *Maximus the Confessor as presupposing the two natures, whose union and interaction it was meant to emphasize.

THEATINES, religious order. Founded in

Rome in 1524, as 'Clerks Regular of the Divine Providence', by two members of the Roman Oratory of Divine Love, St. *Cajetan and Gian Pietro Caraffa (Bp. of Chieti, or 'Theate'; afterwards Pope *Paul IV), the order aimed at the reform of the Church from the grave abuses and scandals then corrupting it. The Theatines were not allowed to have any property, or to beg; they observe the strictest austerity of life; and their habit was distinguished from that of the secular clergy only by their white socks. Within ten years other houses of Theatines had been established in Italy, and the order soon spread into Spain and Central Europe. By their zeal and piety they played an important part in the *Counter-Reformation. In 1583 a congregation of Theatine nuns was founded in Italy under the direction of the Theatine fathers; but the order never obtained wide extension.

G. B. del Tufo, *Historia della religione de' padri chierici regolari* (2 vols., 1609–16); G. Silos, C.R., *Historia Clericorum Regularium a Congregatione Condita* (3 parts, Rome and Parma, 1650–66). B. Ferro, C.R., *Istoria delle missioni de' chierici regolari teatini* (2 vols., Rome, 1704–5). Heimbucher, ii, 97–106. F. Andreu, C.R., in *E.C.*, xi (1953), cols. 1814–17, s.v. 'Teatini'. See also lives of St. Cajetan and Pope Paul IV, cited s.vv.

THEBAIC VERSION. See *Sahidic*.

THEBAID, The. The upper part of the Nile

valley (named after its capital, Thebes) which from the 3rd cent. onwards was the cradle of Christian monasticism. Acc. to St. *Jerome the first ascetic in the region was St. *Paul of Thebes (c. 230–341). The monks, who at first practised the most extreme asceticism and lived as solitaries, became increasingly organized into communities, mainly through the efforts of St. *Antony and St. *Pachomius.

THEBAN LEGION, The. The Christian

legion from the *Thebaid which acc. to tradition was massacred under Emp. Maximian at St.-Maurice-en-Valais. See *Maurice, St.*

THECLA, St. An early Christian virgin.

The tradition concerning her derives from the 'Acts of *Paul and Thecla' (q.v. for details), acc. to which she was converted by St. Paul at Iconium. W. M. *Ramsay and others have contended that these 'Acts' contain a nucleus of genuine history, though it is difficult to separate fact from legend. A large church was built over Thecla's supposed tomb at Meriamlik, near Seleucia, and she was greatly venerated in both E. and W. though apparently never much at Rome. Feast day in the W., 23 Sept.; in the E., 24 Sept.

The main bibl. on St. Thecla is listed under *Paul and Thecla, Acts of.* L. Radermacher, *Hippolytus und Thekla.* Studien zur Geschichte von Legende und Kultus (*Sb.* (Wien), clxxxii; 1916), pp. 51–69 and 121–6. H. *Delehaye, S.J., 'Les Recueils antiques de miracles des saints § 7. Les Miracles de Ste Thècle' in *Anal. Boll.*, xliii (1925), pp. 49–57, with reff. M. Armellini, 'Das wiedergefundene Oratorium u. Coemeterium der H. Thecla an der *Via Ostiensis*' in *R.Q.*, iii (1889), pp. 343–53. H. *Leclercq, O.S.B., in *D.A.C.L.*, xv (pt 2; 1953), cols. 2225–36, s.v. 'Thècle (Sainte)', with reff.

THEISM (from Gk. Θεός, 'God'). The term, prob. first employed by R. *Cudworth in the preface to his *Intellectual System* (1678), was originally used as an opposite to atheism, and only later acquired its present definite meaning to denote a creed distinct also from *Pantheism and esp. from *Deism (q.v.). Theism, as the word is currently employed, may be said to denote a philosophical system which accepts a transcendent and personal God who not only created but also preserves and governs the world, the contingency of which does not exclude miracles and the exercise of human freedom. Theism, therefore, leaves room for the Christian revelation and is in its various forms the view of the world common to all orthodox Christian philosophers, and, in a less perfect form, also required by the Jewish and Mohammedan religions. Apart from certain aberrations, usually of a pantheistic character, Theism was the basis of Christian philosophy down to modern times. Relegated to the background by the Deistic philosophy of the 18th cent. and the *Hegelianism and materialism of the 19th, it has again found many competent and convinced exponents in the modern world.

Modern works defending Theism include R. Flint, *Theism* (Baird Lecture for 1876; 1877); A. J. *Balfour, *The Foundations of Belief* (1895); A. C. *Fraser, *Philosophy of Theism* (*Gifford Lectures for 1894–6; 2 vols., 1895–6); F. *von Hugel, *Eternal Life* (1912), passim; A. J. Balfour, *Theism and Humanism* (Gifford Lectures for 1914; 1915); C. C. J. *Webb, *Studies in the History of Natural Theology* (1915), and other works; W. R. Sorley, *Moral Values and the Idea of God* (Gifford Lectures for 1914 and 1915; 1918); E. L. Mascall, *He Who Is.* A Study in Traditional Theism (1943); A. M. Farrer, *Finite and Infinite* (1943). M. Heinze in *P.R.E.* (ed. 3), xix (1907), pp. 585–95, s.v. 'Theismus'; A. E. *Taylor in *H.E.R.E.*, xii (1921), pp. 261–87, s.v.; G. van der Leeuw–T. Steinmann in *R.G.G.* (ed. 2), v (1931), cols. 1089–95, s.v. 'Theismus'. See also bibl. to *Philosophy of Religion.*

THEMISTIANS. See *Agnoetae.*

THEOBALD (d. 1161), also 'Tedbald', Abp. of *Canterbury. A descendant of a Norman family, he became a monk at *Bec, prior in 1127, and abbot in 1137. In 1138 he became Abp. of Canterbury, receiving the *pallium at Rome, where he had attended the Second *Lateran Council (1137). In the struggle between Stephen and Matilda he hesitated for

some time, but finally decided in Stephen's favour and crowned him in 1141. As Innocent II had made *Henry of Blois, and not himself, Papal legate, frequent disputes arose, e.g. over the consecration of the future St. *William of York whose appointment as archbishop Theobald opposed, and over questions of jurisdiction with the monks of Christ Church, Canterbury. Though Henry was not reappointed legate on the death of Innocent (1143), the office was not conferred on Theobald till *c.* 1150, and then probably at the recommendation of St. *Bernard of Clairvaux, who highly valued him. When, in 1148, he defied Stephen and attended the Council of *Reims, his property was seized and he himself exiled. In consequence *Eugenius III laid England under an interdict, but the king and country were reconciled in the same year. In 1151 Theobald, as Papal legate, held a Council in London. In 1152 he refused to crown Stephen's son, Eustace, and had to flee to Flanders. Soon recalled, he reconciled Stephen and Henry of Anjou in 1153. On Stephen's death (1154), he crowned Henry king and recommended to him the future St. Thomas *Becket as chancellor. His own secretary, *John of Salisbury, was his chief adviser during his last years. Theobald was of a deeply religious nature as well as an able administrator, and during his pontificate the position and influence of the Church in England were greatly strengthened.

Some of his letters are pr. among the correspondence of John of Salisbury (q.v.). Brief 'Compendium Vitae', written at Bec, pr. among the works of *Lanfranc (q.v.); ed. J. A. Giles, i (Oxford, 1844, pp. 337–9, repr. in J. P. Migne, *PL*, cl. 733 f.). A. Saltmann, *Theobald of Canterbury* (University of London Historical Studies, ii; 1956), with text of charters, &c. W. Hunt in *D.N.B.*, lvi (1898), pp. 113–18, with reff.

THEOCRACY (Gk. θεοκρατία, 'government of God'). The term was coined by Flavius *Josephus (*Contra Apionem*, ii, 16) to denote the political organization of the Jewish people, as the purest example of a theocracy. Before the institution of the kingship in Israel, Jehovah was the supreme ruler of the Hebrews, whose laws constituted at the same time religious and civil obligations. Even after the election of a king this state of things virtually remained in force, the kings being vicegerents of Jehovah and under His immediate guidance, while a more complete theocracy was created after the Exile when the monarchy disappeared. A theocratic form of government was also known to many ancient peoples, e.g. in Egypt and Tibet, where kings appeared as representatives or even incarnations of the Deity, and it is intrinsic in the Mohammedan religion. In the history of Christianity attempts at the realization of the theocratic ideal were made by the medieval Popes, esp. *Gregory VII, and again by J. *Calvin at Geneva. The influence of the OT model of government on Calvinist political doctrines is the source of the theocratic features in O. *Cromwell's Commonwealth and in Scottish Presbyterianism.

THEODICY (Gk. Θεός, 'God', and δίκη, 'justice'), etymologically the justification of God. The word was coined by G. W. *Leibniz who used it as the title of his *Essais de Théodicée sur la Bonté de Dieu* (1710), and since then it has been applied to that part of natural theology which is concerned to defend the goodness and omnipotence of God against objections arising from the existence of evil in the world. The question itself, i.e. the origin and meaning of evil, has occupied philosophers and theologians from early times. Attempts at solving it have been made in many religions, e.g. in Brahmanism, Buddhism, and *Manicheism, both on dualistic and pantheistic lines, and in the philosophic systems of *Plato and the *Stoics. *Origen explained it by the abuse of the freedom of the creatures, an interpretation since then developed in many forms, notably by St. *Thomas Aquinas. The problem, less prominent in very religious eras, was much discussed in the period of the *Aufklärung, and Leibniz's work was an answer to P. *Bayle's brilliantly developed thesis that the existence of evil is incompatible with the goodness and omnipotence of God. Leibniz who, in contrast to St. Thomas, regarded this world as the best of all possible worlds, held that evil is a necessary element like the shade in a picture, throwing into relief the beauty and harmony of the whole. This optimistic view was shared by most 18th cent. thinkers, e.g. by Lord Shaftesbury and A. Pope. In the 19th cent. Theodicy came to be more and more regarded in connexion with the entire complex of *Natural Theology, of which it is now sometimes used as a synonym.

THEODORA I (c. 500–47), wife of *Justinian I, who married her in 523. Solemnly crowned co-regnant Empress in 527, she exercised a very great influence upon the complicated theological controversies of the time. Her sympathies were on the side of the *Monophysite party, and it was probably mainly through her influence that Justinian adopted his reactionary religious policy which, esp. in the dispute over the *Three Chapters, sought to conciliate the Monophysites even at the expense of the *Chalcedonian decrees. Although, acc. to the (unreliable) evidence of the 'Anecdota' of *Procopius, she had lived a very dissolute life in her earlier years, she was undoubtedly a woman of outstanding intellect and learning, and as Empress she is said to have been a moral reformer. Her firm character was shown in her vigorous support of her husband in the Nika insurrection (532). Her portrait in mosaic is to be seen in the church of San Vitale at *Ravenna.

C. Diehl, *Théodora. Impératrice de Byzance* (Paris, ed. 3, c. 1904); H. Sladelmann, *Theodora von Byzanz* (2 vols., 1927). W. G. Holmes, *The Age of Justinian and Theodora*, esp. i (1905), pp. 321–49, and ii (1907), passim. L., *Duchesne, 'Les Protégés de Théodora' in *Mélanges d'Archéologie et d'Histoire*, xxxii (1915), pp. 57–79.

THEODORE THE LECTOR (early 6th cent.), Church historian who lived at *Con-

stantinople. He wrote two historical treatises: (1) a 'Tripartite History', composed of extracts from the Histories of *Socrates, *Sozomen, and *Theodoret; and (2) a work composed by himself carrying the history down to the time of Justin I (d. 527). The former work has survived in part, though the extant parts have never been fully published; of the latter only fragments have been preserved.

Of the 'Tripartite History' (4 Books), Bks. I and II survive in Cod. Marc. 344 and excerpts in Cod. Bodl. Barocc. 142. In 7th–8th cent. an Epitome of the Church History (2, above) was compiled; fgmts. of this are embodied in the Byzantine Chronographers. Fgmts. of Theodore, first publd. by H. *Valesius (1673), repr. from 1720 ed. (Valesius-Reading) in J. P. Migne, *PG*, lxxxvi (1), 165–228. New fragments ed. by E. Miller (1876), A. Papadopoulos-Kerameus (1901), and F. Diekamp (1903). H. G. Opitz in *P.W.*, ii (5), cols. 1869–81.

THEODORE OF MOPSUESTIA (c. 350–428), Antiochene theologian and Biblical exegete. He studied rhetoric at *Antioch under Libanius; but in 369, with his friend St. John *Chrysostom, he entered the school of *Diodore in a monastery at Antioch, where he remained for nearly ten years. In 392 he became Bp. of Mopsuestia. The rest of his life he spent in his see, gaining a wide reputation for learning and orthodoxy. In his Biblical commentaries he used scientific, critical, philological, and historical methods, following Diodore in rejecting the Alexandrian use of allegorical interpretations. His account of the Fall of man includes positions superficially like those of *Pelagianism. His doctrine concerning the Incarnation was condemned at the Councils of *Ephesus (431) and *Constantinople (553), while his psychological analysis of human personality, influenced by a hostile reaction against *Apollinarianism, seems to have dictated certain *Nestorian formulae, which, however, he tried sincerely to explain in a Catholic sense.

The modern texts of Theodore's works are scattered. Collection of his commentaries on NT ed. O. F. Fritzsche (Zürich, 1847), repr., together with commentaries on the Twelve Prophets and others from A. *Mai (ed.), *Nova Patrum Bibliotheca*, vii, pt. 1 (Rome, 1854), and other material, in J. P. Migne, *PG*, lxvi, 9–1020. Crit. edd. of his Commentaries on Minor Epp. of St. Paul (fragmentary) by H. B. *Swete (2 vols., Cambridge, 1880–2); fragments on St. Paul collected in K. Staab, *Pauluskommentare aus der griechischen Kirche aus Katenenhandschriften gesammelt* (Neutestamentliche Abhandlungen, xv, 1933), pp. 113–212; commentary on Pss. i–lxxx ed. R. Devreesse (S.T., xciii; 1939); fragments of Gk. text of comm. on St. John's Gospel ed. id., *Essai sur Théodore de Mopsueste* (ib., cxli; 1948), appendix, pp. 287–419; Syr. text ed. from Paris MS. by J. B. Chabot (Paris, 1887); crit. text, with Lat. tr., by J. M. Vosté, O.P. (C.S.C.O., Scriptores Syri, Series quarta, iii, 1940). Catecheses (Syr. text and Eng. tr.) ed. A. Mingana (Woodbrooke Studies, v (on Nicene Creed), 1932; and vi (on the *Lord's Prayer and the Sacraments of Baptism and the Eucharist), 1933); also photographically repr. from MS. Mingana Syr. 561 (Selly Oak Colleges' Library, Birmingham) with Fr. tr. and introd. by R. Tonneau, O.P.–R. Devreesse (S.T., cxlv; 1949). L. Pirot, *L'Œuvre exégétique de Théodore de Mopsueste* (Scripta Pontificii Instituti Biblici, 1913). J. M. Vosté, O.P., 'Le Commentaire de Théodore de Mopsueste sur Saint Jean, d'aprés la version syriaque' in *R. Bibl.*, xxxii (1923), pp. 522–51. Bardenhewer, iii, 312–22; Altaner (ed. 1951), pp. 276–8. H. B. Swete in *D.C.B.*, iv (1887), pp. 934–48, s.v. 'Theodorus (26)'; H. G. Opitz in *P.W.*, Zweite Reihe, v (pt. 2; 1934), cols. 1881–90, s.v. 'Theodorus (49)'; É. Amann in *D.T.C.*, v (pt. x; 1946), cols. 235–79, s.v. Further studies by R. A. Greer (London, 1961) and R. A. Norris (Oxford, 1963).

THEODORE OF RAÏTHU (*fl. c.* 550), monk at the monastery of Raïthu on the Gulf of Suez. He was the author of a Προπαρασκευή (*Praeparatio*), defending the Christological formulae of St. *Cyril of Alexandria (d. 444) and of the *Chalcedonian Council (451) alike and attacking the doctrines of his contemporaries, *Severus of Antioch and *Julian of Halicarnassus. The treatise outlines the chief Christological heresies from *Manes to Severus, while in its later sections it deals with specifically philosophical problems. J. P. Junglas has argued (perh. mistakenly) that Theodore was also the author of the 'De Sectis' traditionally ascribed to *Leontius of Byzantium.

The only complete pr. text of the 'Praeparatio' is the crit. ed. in F. Diekamp, *Analecta Patristica* (Orientalia Christiana Analecta, No. 117, 1938), ch. x: Theodorus von Raïthu, pp. 173–222; text of treatise, pp. 185–222. Portions of the text in J. P. Migne, *PG*, xci, 1484–504. J. P. Junglas, *Leontius von Byzanz* (Paderborn, 1908), pp. 16–20. M. Richard in *D.T.C.*, xv (pt. 1; 1946), cols. 282–4, s.v.

THEODORE OF STUDIOS, St. (759–826), monastic reformer. The son of pious parents of *Constantinople, he early came under the influence of his uncle, St. Plato, abbot of Saccudium, under whose direction he embraced the religious life *c.* 780. He was ordained priest by the patriarch *Tarasius in 787, and in 794 was made abbot of Saccudium in the place of Plato who resigned in his favour. In 796 he was one of the most influential opponents of the adulterous marriage of Constantine VI and separated from the communion of Tarasius who had tolerated it. The result was that his monks were scattered and he himself was banished to Thessalonica; but in the next year he was recalled after the Emperor's mother, Irene, had deposed her son. In 799 he and the greater part of his community went from Saccudium, where they had been exposed to the raids of the Saracens, to the old monastery of *Studios at Constantinople which had become almost extinct. The energy and organizing genius of Theodore soon made it the centre of the monastic life of the E. The conferences in which he expounded to his monks the principles of the religious life embody his austere and noble ideals. In the controversy under the next Emp., Nicephorus I (802–11), about the reinstitution of the priest Joseph who had blessed Constantine's second marriage by the new patriarch, Theodore was again banished (809). From his exile he appealed to Pope *Leo III, but without success. After the Emperor's death in 811 Theodore returned. In 813 Leo V ascended the throne and, reviving the *Iconoclastic policy of Constantine V, exiled Theodore, its most vigorous opponent. In 815 Theodore was taken to Metopa in N. Phrygia, and subsequently to Boneta in Anatolia and to Smyrna, where he was closely confined and frequently ill-treated, though he succeeded in writing numerous letters (many of them still extant) to encourage his followers. He also sent appeals to the Pope, Paschal I, who wrote to the Emperor on the question of image worship. After Leo's assassination in

820, Theodore was recalled by his successor, Michael, who pursued a policy of toleration, but prohibited image-worship in the capital. Theodore therefore could not permanently return to his monastery and spent his last years outside Constantinople, largely on the peninsula of Tryphon. A man of austere sanctity and iron will, a vigorous defender of the independence of the Church, and a genius of religious legislation, Theodore of Studios was one of the finest representatives of Byzantine monasticism. His writings include a 'Short' and a 'Long Catechesis', an Exposition of the Liturgy of the Presanctified, a number of spiritual orations, a list of canonical penances, several polemical works directed against the Iconoclasts, and poetry and correspondence. He is widely venerated esp. in the E. Feast day, 11 Nov.

There is no complete ed. of his works, that projected by the *Maurists not having been carried through. His letters and various dogmatic works ed. J. *Sirmond, *Opera Varia*, v (Venice, 1696); further texts ed. A. *Mai, *N.P.B.*, v (Rome, 1849), with notice by L. *Allatius in vol. vi (ib., 1853), part 2, pp. 158–68; these items are repr. in J. P. Migne, *PG*, xcix. Further letters and fragments ed. J. P. Cozza Luzi, *N.P.B.*, viii (Rome, 1871), part 1, pp. 1–244, and sermons, ib., ix (ib., 1888), part 1, pp. 1–318 ('Short Catechesis'), and part 2, pp. 1–217 ('Long Catechesis'); hymns ed. J. B. *Pitra, *Analecta Sacra Spicilegio Solesmensi*, i (Paris, 1876), pp. 336–80. Modern studies by C. Thomas (Osnabrück, 1892), G. A. Schneider (Kirchengeschichtliche Studien, v, Hft. 3; 1900), Alice Gardner (London, 1905), [B.] E. Marin ('Les Saints'; 1906), and A. P. Dobroklonskij (in Russian; 2 vols., Odessa, 1913–14). I. Hausherr, S.J., 'Saint Théodore Studite, l'homme et l'ascète' in *Orientalia Christiana*, vi (1926), pp. 1–87. Krumbacher, pp. 147–51 and 712–15. É. Amann in *D.T.C.*, xv (pt. 1; 1946), cols. 287–98, s.v. 'Théodore (16), Le Studite', with further reff.

THEODORE OF TARSUS, St. (*c.* 602–90), Abp. of *Canterbury. He was an Asiatic Greek, educated at *Tarsus and *Athens. While not yet a subdeacon he was recommended to Pope *Vitalian for the Abpric. of Canterbury by *Hadrian, an African monk to whom the see had been offered. Vitalian consecrated him in 668; but the Pope, fearing that his orthodoxy might be corrupted by his Greek upbringing, arranged for *Benedict Biscop and Hadrian to accompany him to Britain. After a visitation of the whole of England, he set about reforming the government of the Church by dividing dioceses and extending the episcopate. In 673 he summoned, and presided over, the first important synod of the whole English Church at *Hertford, and in 680 he held another great synod at *Hatfield where a declaration of orthodoxy was drawn up and forwarded to Rome at the request of Pope *Agatho. By such methods he unified the English Church and established the metropolitical authority of the see of Canterbury. He also did much to prepare the way for the parochial system. His active interference in the diocese of York created serious difficulties with St. *Wilfrid (q.v. for details). Though he remained throughout his life a devoted scholar, none of his writings survive. The 'Penitential' traditionally attributed to Theodore is of a later date. Feast day, 19 Sept.

The principal sources are *Bede, *H.E.*, esp. iv. 1–v. 8; cf. notes in ed. C. Plummer, ii (Oxford, 1891), ad locc.; and Eddius's life of St. *Wilfred, ed. J. Raine, *The Historians of the Church of York and its Archbishops*, i (R.S., 1879), pp. 1–103. The Penitential was first pr. in full by F. W. H. Wasserschleben, *Die Bussordnungen der abendländischen Kirche* (Halle, 1851), pp. 182–219, with other decrees, pp. 145–81; Penitential also in A. W. Haddan–W. *Stubbs (edd.), *Councils and Ecclesiastical Documents Relating to Great Britain and Ireland*, iii (1871), pp. 173–213; other decrees of his archiepiscopate, pp. 114–72. P. Fournier, 'Les Capitula du Pseudo-Théodore et le décret de Burchard de Worms' in *Florilegium ou recueil de travaux d'érudition dédiés à M. le marquis Melchior de Vogüé* (1909), pp. 241–55; F. Liebermann, 'Zur Herstellung der Canones Theodori Cantuariensis' in *Zeitschrift für Savigny-Stiftung für Rechtsgeschichte*, xliii (Kanon. Abt., xii; 1922), pp. 387–409; P. W. Finsterwalder, *Die Canones Theodori Cantuariensis*. Über ihre Überlieferungsformen (Untersuchungen zu den Bussbüchern des 7., 8., und 9. Jahrhunderts, i; 1929); G. Le Bras, 'Notes pour servir à l'histoire des collections canoniques, V: 'Judicia Theodori' in *Revue historique de Droit français et étranger*, Série 4e (1931), pp. 95–115. W. Stubbs in *D.C.B.*, iv (1887), pp. 926–32, s.v. 'Theodorus (7)'; W. Hunt in *D.N.B.*, lvi (1898), pp. 122–6; É. Amann in *D.T.C.*, xv (pt. 1; 1946), cols. 229–31, s.v. 'Théodore (6) de Cantorbéry'.

THEODORET (*c.* 393–*c.* 458), Bp. of Cyrrhus. A native of *Antioch, he was educated in its monastery schools. After distributing his property among the poor, he entered the monastery of Nicerte *c.* 416. Consecrated Bp. of Cyrrhus in Syria against his will in 423, he governed his diocese with great wisdom and munificence, at the same time indefatigably fighting paganism and heresy. He soon became involved in the Christological controversy between *Nestorius and *Cyril of Alexandria, in the latter of whose anathematisms he believed he detected a new version of *Apollinarianism. As a personal friend and admirer of Nestorius, he became one of the foremost defenders of the Antiochene Christology, and in a polemical work against Cyril maintained a duality in Christ and accepted the title '*Theotokos' only in a figurative sense. After the Council of *Ephesus (431) he continued to oppose Cyril and the decision of the Council, though Cyril accepted (433) a declaration of faith which had prob. been composed (432) by Theodoret himself. In 448, when accused by Cyril's successor, *Dioscorus, of dividing Christ 'into two Sons', he drew up another confession of faith in which he plainly asserted the unity of Christ and anathematized anyone who did not recognize the BVM as θεοτόκος. In spite of this, Dioscorus anathematized him and obtained Imperial edicts forbidding him to leave his diocese (448) and to come to the Council held at Ephesus in 449 unless summoned. This Council, the so-called '*Latrocinium', deposed Theodoret, who was forced into exile. The new Emp., Marcian, summoned him to the Council of *Chalcedon (451), where he reluctantly anathematized Nestorius. It seems that he spent his last years in the peaceful administration of his diocese. A century later his writings against Cyril became the subject of the '*Three Chapters Controversy' and were condemned by the Council of *Constantinople in 553.

Only a comparatively small number of Theodoret's works has come down to us. In his 'Graecarum Affectionum Curatio', one of

the finest Christian apologies, he places side by side the Christian and the pagan answers to the fundamental religious questions such as the nature of God and of man, sacrifice, the end of the world, &c. The 'Eranistes' is a treatise against the *Monophysites, which asserts the immutability and impassibility of the Divine nature in Christ and the unconfused coexistence of the Divine and human natures in Him. His exegetical works, which deal with a large number of OT Books, e.g. the *Octateuch, Kings and Chronicles, Psalms, Song of Solomon, and the Major and Minor Prophets, are among the finest specimens of the Antiochene School and remarkable for their lucidity and erudition. His historical works include a 'Religious History', i.e. a collection of biographies of monks, a 'Church History', which continues the work of *Eusebius down to 428, and is esp. valuable for the numerous authentic documents used in it, and a 'Compendium of Heretical Fables', which gives first-hand information on *Arianism, *Nestorianism, and *Eutychianism.

Theodoret's Christological opinions have been a matter of controversy, but it seems to be conceded by most scholars that he held Nestorian views at least till 434–5 and possibly until Chalcedon, but abandoned them at the latest after 451.

Collected works ed. J. *Sirmond, S.J. (4 vols., Paris, 1642); suppl. vol. ed. J. *Garnier, S.J. (Paris, 1684), repr. with additions by J. L. Schulze and J. A. Noesselt in J. P. Migne, *P.G.*, lxxx–lxxxiv. There are separate editions of the *Graecarum Affectionum Curatio* by J. Raeder (Leipzig, Teubner, 1904), *Eccl. Hist.* by T. *Gaisford (Oxford, 1854), and L. Parmentier (G.C.S., 1911), his Commentary on Isaiah by A. Möhle (Mitteilungen des Septuaginta-Unternehmens der Gesellschaft der Wissenschaften zu Göttingen, v, Berlin, 1932). N. N. Glubokovskii, *The Blessed Theodoret*, Bishop of Cyrus (in Russian, 1890). Theodoret has been the subject of several imp. studies by Marcel Richard (1934 ff.). Bardenhewer, iv, 219–47; Altaner (ed. 1950), pp. 295–7. H. G. Opitz in *P.W.*, Zweite Reihe, v (pt. 2; 1934), cols. 1791–1801; G. Bardy in *D.T.C.*, xv (pt. 1; 1946), cols. 299–325.

THEODORIC (*c.* 455–526), King of the Ostrogoths from 475, and of the Romans from 493. Having spent his boyhood and youth as a hostage at *Constantinople, he became successively the powerful ally and insatiable enemy of Emp. *Zeno, until he was commissioned by the latter (487) to overthrow the usurper Odoacer, then King of Italy. Having achieved this end, Theodoric proceeded to rule, in effective independence of the Emperors, over his subject Arian Goths and Catholic Romans. He refrained from persecuting national or religious minorities, carried out legal, social, and economic reforms, and patronized the arts; and his reign of 33 years was marked by great prosperity. Under the name of Dietrich von Bern (i.e. 'Theodoric of Verona') he figures in the *Nibelungenlied*.

The chief source for his life is the *Cassiodori Senatoris Variae* ed. by T. *Mommsen, *M.G.H.* Auctores Antiquissimi, xii (1894). T. Hodgkin, *Theodoric the Goth*. The Barbarian Champion of Civilisation (Heroes of the Nations, 1891).

THEODORIC OF CHARTRES. See *Thierry of Chartres*.

THEODOSIAN CODE, The.

In 435, abandoning a more ambitious project, *Theodosius II instructed a commission to codify, with any necessary adaptations to new circumstances, all general constitutions enacted since *Constantine I. The Code, compiled in Latin, was promulgated to the E. on 15 Feb. 438, with effect from 1 Jan. 439, and was accepted as authoritative by the W. Henceforward, E. and W. legislated separately, and the Code was still used by the W. after its supersession in the E. by *Justinian. The laws are arranged chronologically under topical *tituli* in 16 books. Book XVI, which deals with religious affairs, contains the laws that banned paganism and penalized heresy, as well as those regulating the position of the clergy and determining the relation between Church and state.

The standard ed. is that of T. *Mommsen (Berlin, 1905); Books I–VIII also ed. P. Krüger (ib., 1923–6). W. K. Boyd, *The Ecclesiastical Edicts of the Theodosian Code* (New York, 1905).

THEODOSIAN COLLECTION, The.

The compilation of esp. canonical documents in the *Verona Chapter MS. lx (58), subscribed with the name of Theodosius the Deacon. It contains *inter alia* an epistle from a Roman synod under *Damasus in 372 to the Catholic bishops in the E., 10 canons of the Council of *Carthage of 421, a Paschal cycle, some letters sent from the Council of *Sardica to Egypt, the 'Historia Acephala' relating to St. *Athanasius, and some important documents concerning the *Melitian Schism at Alexandria. As none of these items is found elsewhere, the collection is one of unique interest. Among other items (27 in all, acc. to the usual reckoning) are the canons of *Nicaea and other Councils in various Latin versions. Some of its contents were published by S. *Maffei, its discoverer, and later instalments have been issued by the *Ballerini, F. *Maassen, C. H. *Turner, and E. *Schwartz. The thesis, first propounded by Turner, that the Collection goes back to the mission sent by Carthage to the E. in 419 in connexion with the Apiarius affair has received a wide measure of acceptance.

[F.] S. Maffei, 'Monumenti ecclesiastici del quarto secolo cristiano non piu venuti in luce: conservati in codice antichissimo del Capitolo veronese' in *Osservazioni letterarie*, iii (Verona, 1738), pp. 7–92; text repr. in Maffei's *Istoria Teologica* (Trent, 1742), pt. 2, pp. 254–72, with description, pp. 75–7. P. Ballerini–G. Ballerini (edd.), *Leonis Magni Opera*, iii (Venice, 1757), pp. cxxiv–cxxix, 105–27, 434–46, 581–622, 649–53. F. Maassen, *Geschichte der Quellen und der Literatur des canonischen Rechts im Abendlande*, i (1870), pp. 546–51. A. Reifferscheid, 'Bibliotheca Patrum Latinorum Italica', section 'LX. 58. memb. 8. foliorum 126. Saec. VIII' in *Sb.* (Wien), xlix (1865), pp. 35–40. C. H. Turner, 'The Verona Manuscripts of Canons: The Theodosian MS. and its Connection with St. Cyril' in *The Guardian*, l (pt. 2; 1895), p. 1921 f.; cf. also *E.O.M.I.A.*, i (fasc. 2, pt. 3, 1930), p. 623 f. A. Spagnolo, 'Intorno all' origine dei testi di diritto canonico contenuti in un codice della Biblioteca Capitolare di Verona' in *Atti della R. Accademia delle Scienze di Torino*, xxxii (1896), pp. 509–24. E. Schwartz, 'Zur Geschichte des Athanasius', part II, in *Nachr.* (Gött.), 1904, pp. 357–91; id., 'Ueber die Sammlung des Cod. Veronensis LX' in *Z.N.T.W.*, xxxv (1936), pp. 1–23. W. Telfer, 'The Codex Verona LX (58)' in *H.T.R.*, xxxvi (1943), pp. 169–246.

THEODOSIUS I (the 'Great'), Roman Emperor

from 379 to 395. After repelling barbarian attacks on Britain and suppressing revolt in Africa, his father, the Spanish general, Count Theodosius, was executed, for reasons now unknown, in 376. In 379, however, his son was created co-Augustus by Gratian. In secular affairs he defeated and pacified the Goths after their victory at Hadrianople (378). Ecclesiastically he continued Gratian's policy and founded the orthodox Christian state. *Arianism and other heresies became legal offences, sacrifice was forbidden, and paganism almost outlawed. The Emperor's penitent submission to St. *Ambrose after the massacre at Thessalonica (390) foreshadows *Canossa. The senatorial attempt to restore at Rome the 'Altar of Victory' (384) failed, and Theodosius sealed his work by defeating Arbogast's puppet-king, Eugenius, who would have tolerated paganism.

The principal sources include Aurelius Victor, *Epitome*, 48; Pacatus, *Panegyricus Theodosio Aug. dictus*; and St. Ambrose, *De Obitu Theodosii Oratio* and *Ep.* 51. 4; and the 5th-cent. Church Historians. A. Güldenpenning and J. Ifland, *Der Kaiser Theodosius der Grosse* (1878); G. Rauschen, *Jahrbücher der christlichen Kirche unter dem Kaiser Theodosius dem Grossen* (1897). W. Ensslin, *Die Religionspolitik des Kaisers Theodosius d. Gr.* (*Sb.* (Bayr.), 1953, Hft. 2). N. Q. King, *The Emperor Theodosius and the Establishment of Christianity* (1961). G. T. Stokes in *D.C.B.*, iv (1887), pp. 959–64, s.v. 'Theodosius (2) I'.

THEODOSIUS II (401–50), grandson of

*Theodosius I, E. Roman Emperor from 408. He is significant in religious history by his foundation of the university of Constantinople (425), his summoning of the Council of *Ephesus (431), and his enactment of the *Theodosian Code (q.v.). Though pious by nature, he was politically incompetent, being dominated at one stage by *Simeon Stylites, and later in his reign by his minister, Chrysaphius, who secured his support for the *Monophysites. He died on 28 July 450 after a fall from his horse.

A. Güldenpenning, *Geschichte des oströmischen Reiches unter den Kaisern Arcadius und Theodosius II* (1885). G. T. Stokes in *D.C.B.*, iv (1887), pp. 964–7, s.v. 'Theodosius (3) II'.

THEODOTION (2nd cent. A.D.), editor of

a Greek version of the OT. Hardly anything is known with certainty about him. St. *Irenaeus refers to him as a Jewish proselyte, St. *Jerome as an *Ebionite Christian, and St. *Epiphanius as a follower of *Marcion. His translation is a revision of the *Septuagint made with the help of the Hebrew, and has special value for the texts of Jer., Job, and Dan. In *Origen's *Hexapla, his text was placed next after the Septuagint; from this source considerable fragments survive.

H. B. *Swete, *An Introduction to the Old Testament in Greek* (1900), pp. 42–9. J. Gwynn in *D.C.B.*, iv (1887), pp. 970–9, s.v.

THEODOTUS (2nd cent.), *Gnostic.

A follower of *Valentinus, he is known from the fragments preserved by *Clement of Alexandria in the *Excerpta ex Theodoto* found among Clement's writings.

The *Excerpta* are printed in all the editions of Clement. Separate editions by R. P. Casey ('Studies and Documents', 1934) and F. M. M. Sagnard, O.P. (*Sources chrétiennes*, 1948; excellent notes).

THEODOTUS, the Cobbler or Leather-seller (2nd cent.), Adoptionist *Monarchian. He came from Byzantium to Rome under Pope *Victor (*c.* 189–98), proclaiming that Jesus was a man who was anointed with the Holy Ghost at His baptism and thus became Christ. He was excommunicated by Victor. His disciples, who were known as 'Theodotians', included his namesake, 'Theodotus the Money-changer' (early 3rd cent.), who was condemned by Pope *Zephyrinus (198–217).

The primary sources are *Hippolytus, *Philosoph.*, vii, 35 f., and x, 23 f., and *Eusebius, *H.E.*, v, 28. See also *Epiphanius, *Haer.*, 54 f., where the sect is described under the name of 'Melchisedekians'. A. *Harnack in *P.R.E.* (ed. 3), xiii (1903), pp. 311–18, s.v. 'Monarchianismus'. G. Bardy in *D.T.C.*, x (pt. 1; 1928), cols. 513–16, s.v. 'Melchisédéciens'.

THEODOTUS (d. *c.* 445), Bp. of Ancyra. At first a supporter of *Nestorius, he became one of his most determined adversaries, taking a prominent part on the Cyrilline side at the Council of *Ephesus (431). At the (Nestorian) Council of Tarsus (432) he was anathematized. Among his writings were: (1) Six Books against Nestorius (lost); (2) an 'Explanation of the Creed of Nicaea', maintaining that Nestorian teaching was already condemned by the Creed of 325; and (3) various 'Sermons' (partly lost), incl. one for *Christmas (which was read at the Council of Ephesus) and another for the *Purification (εἰς τὰ φῶτα). These last are important early witnesses to the existence of these two Feasts. A long panegyric ascribed to him on 'The Martyrdom and Miracles of St. *George' is certainly spurious.

He is not to be confused with St. Theodotus of Ancyra, a martyr in the *Diocletianic Persecution, commemorated in the *Roman Martyrology on 18 May.

Works in J. P. Migne, *PG*, lxxvii, 1309–1432 (from A. *Gallandi). Bardenhewer, iv, 197–200. G. Bardy in *D.T.C.*, xv (pt. 1; 1946), cols. 328–30.

THEODULF (*c.* 750–821), Bp. of Orléans. A native of Spain and of Gothic descent, he attracted the attention of *Charlemagne, who made him abbot of *Fleury and Bp. of Orléans (before 798). In 798 he was sent, together with Leidrad of Lyons, as a royal legate on a visitation tour to the South of France. He took part in the trial of St. *Leo III in 800 and in the same year received the pallium. After the death of Charlemagne he was accused of conspiracy with King Bernard of Italy against Louis the Pious, and was deposed in 818 and exiled to Angers.

Theodulf was one of the leading theologians of the Frankish Empire. Among his writings are a work on the Holy Ghost, 'De Spiritu Sancto', in which he defended the *Filioque, and a treatise on Baptism, and probably also expositions of the Mass and the Creed. He was, moreover, a poet of ability. His 'Carmina', with their descriptions of the court of Charlemagne, are of great historic interest, as is also his 'Versus contra Judices', in which he recorded his impressions of his visitation of 798 and sharply criticized the harshness of the Frankish Law. Of his hymns the 'Gloria, laus et honor' ('All glory, laud and honour') became the *Palm Sunday Processional of the W. Church. As a bishop he was devoted to his diocese, in which he carried out many reforms. He introduced parish schools, raised the standard of worship, and did much for ecclesiastical architecture and art. He favoured esp. the production of illuminated MSS. of the Bible and sought to improve the text of the *Vulgate. Some scholars also attribute to him the authorship of the '*Caroline Books'.

His works, ed. J. *Sirmond, S.J. (Paris, 1646), repr. in J. P. Migne, *PL*, cv, 191–380. The best edition of his Poems is that of E. Duemmler in *M.G.H.*, Poetae, i (1881), pp. 437–581 (text pp. 445–581). Studies by L. Baunard (Orléans, 1860) and C. Cuissard (in *Mémoires de la Société Archéologique et Historique de l'Orléanais*, xxiv (1892), pp. 1–351). Raby, pp. 171–7. Manitius, i (1911), pp. 537–43.

THEOGNOSTUS (d. *c.* 282), *Alexandrian ecclesiastical writer. He was head of the *Catechetical School, probably in succession to *Dionysius and before (not after, as *Philip of Side asserts) Pierius. He elaborated a system of theology on *Origenist lines in seven books of 'Hypotyposes' (Ὑποτυπώσεις) of which an account is preserved by *Photius (Cod. 106). Quotations also survive in St. *Athanasius (*Ep.* iv *ad Sarapionem*, 11; *De Decretis*, 25) and St. *Gregory of Nyssa (*Contra Eunom.*, III, iii). Despite his subordinationist language on the Son derived from Origen, Athanasius could appeal to his support against the *Arians.

The fragments are printed in J. P. Migne, *PG*, x, 235–242. A. *Harnack, Die Hypotyposen des Theognost (*T.U.* xxiv, 3, Leipzig, 1903). L. B. Radford, *Three Teachers of Alexandria*: Theognostus, Pierius, Peter (1908), pp. 1–43.

THEOLOGIA CRUCIS (Lat., 'Theology of the Cross'). The name given by M. *Luther to the theological principle that our knowledge of the Being of God must be derived from the study of Christ in His humiliation and the sufferings He underwent on the cross. He opposed it to a *theologia gloriae* ('theology of glory') which would maintain with the *Scholastic theologians that a true knowledge of God can be obtained from the study of nature.

THEOLOGIA GERMANICA. A late 14th cent. anonymous mystical treatise, apparently written at Sachsenhausen, nr. Frankfurt a.M., by a priest of the *Teutonic Order. In its mystical doctrine it follows the Dionysian tradition of the great Dominicans, Master *Eckhart and J. *Tauler, counselling poverty of spirit and abandonment to God as the means of transformation by love into participation of the Divine nature. M. *Luther, who supervised its first printed edition (1518), was much influenced by the book in his early period, and found in it his own opposition to good works and his views on individual religion. Later it was enthusiastically admired by the *Pietists, and, in the English translation of Susanna Winkworth, had a considerable vogue in Great Britain. The treatise has frequently been suspected of pantheism, but apart from a few misleading expressions its doctrine is perfectly orthodox and now generally recognized as such by Catholic theologians.

Crit. ed. of text by F. Pfeiffer (Stuttgart, 1851); Eng. tr. by Susanna Winkworth, pref. by C. *Kingsley (London, 1854); rev. by J. Bernhart (New York, 1949; London, 1950), with introd. pp. 9–109. F. G. Lisco, *Die Heilslehre der Theologia deutsch* (1857); Maria Windstosser, *Étude sur la 'Théologie germanique'* (1911); J. Paquier, *Un Mystique allemand au XIV siècle*. L'orthodoxie de la Théologie germanique (1922). K. Müller, 'Zum Text der Deutschen Theologie' in *Z.K.G.* (1930), pp. 307–35. F. Cohrs in *P.R.E.* (ed. 3), xix (1907), pp. 626–31.

THEOLOGICAL COLLEGES (Anglican). In these Colleges candidates receive their final preparation for ordination. Before the 19th cent. various attempts were made to establish theological colleges in England, notably by Matthew Sutcliffe, Dean of Exeter, in 1609, by G. *Burnet, Bp. of Salisbury (d. 1715), and by T. *Wilson, Bp. of Sodor and Man, in 1700; but nothing in the way of a permanent foundation was accomplished. In 1816 St. Bees' College was founded by G. H. Law, Bp. of Chester, for non-university men, and in 1825 the *C.M.S. started a college at Islington for those of its candidates who were not graduates. Neither of these colleges has survived. The oldest existing seminary is the Queen's College, Birmingham, which was founded in 1828 for medical and theological students, and in 1934 was reconstituted for theology alone. Chichester Theological College was established in 1839, and after that date others followed rapidly.

F. W. B. Bullock, *A History of Training for the Ministry of the Church of England in England and Wales from 1800 to 1874* (St. Leonards-on-Sea, 1955). Id., *The History of Ridley Hall, Cambridge* (2 vols., 1941–53), with general information, esp. Introduction on 'Theological Colleges of the Church of England before 1875' in vol. i, pp. 1–17. A notable history of a particular foundation is [W.] O. Chadwick, *The Founding of Cuddesdon* (1954). S. L. Ollard in *D.E.C.H.*, pp. 587–91, s.v.

THEOLOGICAL VIRTUES, The. A title given to the three virtues of faith, hope, and charity, which are grouped together by St. *Paul (1 Cor. 13. 13; cf. 1 Thess. 1. 3, Gal. 5, 5–6, Col. 1. 4–5) as the basis of the Christian life. They are so named in contradistinction to the 'natural' or 'Cardinal Virtues' (q.v.). Their place in the life of grace and their relations to each other were much studied by the Schoolmen, esp. St. *Thomas Aquinas.

A. Michel in *D.T.C.*, xv (pt. 2; 1950), cols. 2739–99, s.v. 'Vertu', esp. cols. 2782–4 ('vii, Vertus théologales').

THEOLOGISCHE LITERATURZEITUNG. A German theological periodical, founded in 1876 by E. *Schürer and A. *Harnack largely in the interests of *Ritschlian theology and devoted entirely to reviews of current theological literature. It was published fortnightly till the end of 1938, and from 1939 monthly.

THEOLOGY (Gk. θεολογία), lit. the 'Science of God'. In its Christian sense it is the science of the Divinely revealed religious truths. Its theme is the Being and Nature of God and His Creatures and the whole complex of the Divine dispensation from the Fall of Adam to the Redemption through Christ and its mediation to men by His Church, including the so-called natural truths of God, the soul, the moral Law, &c., which are accessible to mere reason. Its purpose is the investigation of the contents of belief by means of reason enlightened by faith (*fides quaerens intellectum*) and the promotion of its deeper understanding. Catholic theology differs from Protestant theology in that it also admits the authority of tradition, the utterances of which are accounted binding, whereas Protestant theology, in so far as it is conservative, is circumscribed by the Biblical revelation. Liberal Protestant theologians, however, recognize the existence of no revelation except in so far as it is confirmed by the conscience and reason of the believer. In the course of time theology has developed into several branches, among them dogmatic, historical, and practical theology. The methods of classification of the sub-disciplines, however, fluctuate in different theological systems.

THEOPASCHITES (Gk. θεοπασχῖται, i.e. 'those who hold that God suffered'), a name applied, already by their contemporaries, to a group of 6th-cent. *Monophysite theologians. They first appeared at *Constantinople in 519, where their supporters (John Maxentius and some Scythian monks) defended the formula 'One of the Trinity was crucified'. Their orthodoxy was upheld by the Emp. *Justinian and *Leontius of Byzantium. The formula was rejected, however, by the Patr. of Constantinople, and (with some hesitation) by Pope *Hormisdas.

THEOPHANY. An appearance of God in visible form, temporary and not necessarily material (cf. e.g. Exod. 33. 20 ff.). Such an appearance is to be contrasted with the *Incarnation, in which there was a permanent union between God and complete manhood (body, soul, and spirit). In early Christian times the word was in regular use in an orthodox sense, e.g. for the Feast of the *Epiphany in the *Gelasian Sacramentary.

THEOPHILANTHROPISTS. A *Deistic sect founded in France during the reign of the Directory under the patronage esp. of the Director L. M. La Réveillière-Lépeaux (1753–1824). Its tenets were set forth in a pamphlet by J. B. Chemin-Dupontès (Paris, Sept. 1796) under the title of *Manuel des théophilanthropes*, the three articles of its creed being belief in

God, virtue, and immortality. At first the movement seemed likely to spread and was given the use of ten churches in Paris by the Directory; but after the re-establishment of Catholicism by the *Concordat of 1801 it soon lost ground, and in 1802 Napoleon restored its churches to Catholic worship. Some attempts were made to revive it later in the 19th cent., but without success.

J. Brugerette in *D.T.C.*, xv (pt. i, 1946), cols. 518–23, s.v.

THEOPHILUS, St. (later 2nd cent.), Bp. of *Antioch and one of the 'Christian *Apologists'. Of his writings, only his 'Apology', in three books addressed to Autolycus, has survived. Its purpose was to set before the pagan world the Christian idea of God and the superiority of the doctrine of *creation over the immoral myths of the Olympian religion. Theophilus developed the doctrine of the *Logos a stage further than any of his Christian predecessors, distinguishing between the λόγος ἐνδιάθετος, the intelligence of the Father, and the λόγος προφορικός, the Word brought forth externally in order to create. He is also the first theologian to use the word 'Triad' (τριάς) of the Godhead. Among his (lost) treatises were writings against *Marcion and Hermogenes. F. *Loofs endeavoured to show that considerable portions of his work against Marcion were incorporated in *Irenaeus's 'Treatise Against Heresies', but his contention has won little support.

The sole MS. authority for the 'Ad Autolycum' is Cod. Marcianus 496 (saec. xi), all other known MSS. being direct descendants. *Editio princeps* by J. Frisius and C. Gesner (Zürich, 1546). Crit. ed., J. C. T. Otto, *Corpus Apologetarum*, viii (ed. 3, Jena, 1861); also ed. G. Bardy, with Fr. tr. by J. Sender (*S.C.*, xx; 1948). J. P. Migne, *PG*, vi, 1023–168. Eng. tr. in A.N.C.L., vol. iii (1867), pp. 49–133. F. *Loofs, *Theophilus von Antioch und die anderen theologischen Quellen bei Irenäus* (T.U., xlvi (2), 1930). R. M. Grant, 'Theophilus of Antioch to Autolycus' in *H.T.R.*, xl (1947), pp. 227–56. E. Rapisarda in *E.C.*, xi (1953), col. 1952 f., s.v.

THEOPHILUS (d. 412), Patriarch of Alexandria from 385. He was the uncle of St. *Cyril, who succeeded him. In his first years as patriarch he took an active part in suppressing the remnants of paganism in his city, in 391 destroying the temple of Serapis; but later his main ambition seems to have been the furtherance of the prestige of his see, sometimes by unscrupulous methods. A fierce campaign against *Origenism, involving him in an attack on the *Tall Brothers, was encouraged by jealousy of the see of *Constantinople and St. *Chrysostom, its bishop. The *Copts and Syrians, who consider him a saint, celebrate his feast on 15 and 17 Oct. respectively.

Works ed. by A. *Gallandi in *Bibliotheca Veterum Patrum*, vii (1770), pp. 601–53, repr. in J. P. Migne, *PG*, lxv, 29–68 and 401–4. Further letters, ib., *PL*, xxii, 758–69, 773–90, 792–812, and 813–28. M. Richard, 'Une Homélie de Théophile d'Alexandrie sur l'institution de l'Eucharistie' in *R.H.E.*, xxxiii (1937), pp. 46–56; id., 'Les Écrits de Théophile d'Alexandrie' in *Le Muséon*, lii (1939), pp. 35–50. Bardenhewer, iii, 115–17; Altaner (ed. 1950), p. 240. H. G. Opitz in *P.W.*, 2. Reihe, v (pt. 2, 1934), cols. 2149–65.

THEOPHYLACT (11th cent.), Byzantine exegete. A native of Euboea, he was a pupil of Michael *Psellus, and for a time the tutor of Constantine Porphyrogenitus, son of Michael VII. *C.* 1078 he was made Abp. of Achrida in the country of the Bulgarians, whose lack of civilization was a source of constant suffering to him, as is revealed in his letters. His principal work is a series of commentaries on several OT Books and on the whole of the NT except Rev. They are marked by lucidity of thought and expression and closely follow the Scriptural text. At the same time they insist on practical morality in the manner of St. *Chrysostom, whom Theophylact took as a model. In matters of exegesis Theophylact was largely influenced by earlier writers such as the so-called '*Oecumenius', esp. in Acts and the Catholic Epistles, as well as by his contemporary, *Euthymius Zigabenus. In the question of the Schism he adopted a conciliatory position, defending in his Περὶ ὧν ἐγκαλοῦνται Λατῖνοι the Catholic attitude to *Images and the use of Unleavened *Bread in the Eucharist. Among his other works are many homilies, still partly unprinted, letters, a book on the 'training of princes' (παιδεία βασιλική), largely drawn from older sources, written for his pupil, a panegyric on Emp. Alexis Comnenus, and two iambic poems.

Works [ed. F. Foscari], 4 vols., Venice, 1754–63, repr. in J. P. Migne, *PG*, cxxiii–cxxvi; prefaced by useful 'Dissertatio' by J. F. Bernard María de Rubeis, O.P., repr. in *PG*, cxxiii, 9–130. Alice Leroy-Molinghen, 'Les Lettres de Théophylacte de Bulgarie à Grégoire Taronite' in *Byzantion*, xi (1936), pp. 589–92; id., 'Prolégomènes à une édition critique des "Lettres" de Théophylacte de Bulgarie' ib., xiii (1938), pp. 253–62. Krumbacher, pp. 133–5, 463 f. R. Janin, A.A., in *D.T.C.*, xv (pt. 1; 1946), cols. 536–8, s.v.

THEOSOPHY (Gk. Θεός, 'God', σοφία, 'wisdom'). In its wider application the term has been used for any intuitive knowledge of the Divine, and as such covers a number of religious and philosophical systems closely akin to pantheism and natural mysticism. Thus the teaching of Buddha, *Plotinus, and the *Gnostics in antiquity, and of John Scotus *Erigena, J. *Boehme (the 'Teutonic Theosopher'), E. *Swedenborg, and others in more modern times may be called Theosophy.

In a more restricted sense the word is now commonly applied to the movement instigated by the Russian adventuress, H. P. Blavatsky, who, together with Col. H. S. Olcott, founded the Theosophical Society in New York in 1875. Three years later they went to India, and in 1882 Adyar (near Madras) became their headquarters. After Mme Blavatsky's death (1891) Mrs. A. Besant was made its leader. It soon spread to Europe where it gained adherents in many countries, esp. in Germany (see *Anthroposophy*). Theosophy purports to derive its teaching from Indian sacred books, such as the Upanishads and Sutras, and from Indian Mahatmas. A mixture of pantheism, magic, and rationalism, it teaches the transmigration of souls, the brotherhood of men irrespective of colour and creed, and complicated systems of psychology and cosmology.

Theosophists deny both a personal God and personal immortality, but advocate universal toleration of all religions as well as of atheism. They regard Christ as purely human and consequently deny the validity of the Christian Revelation.

The very extensive Theosophical literature includes the studies of H. S. Olcott, *Theosophy*. Religion and Occult Science (1885); H. P. Blavatsky, *The Key to Theosophy* (1889); id., *The Secret Doctrine* (ed. 2, 3 vols., 1888–97), and many other studies by this author; Annie Besant, *The Ancient Wisdom*. An Outline of Theosophical Teachings (1897); id., *Popular Lectures on Theosophy* [1910], and many other works of this author; C. W. Leadbeater, *An Outline of Theosophy* (1902), and many other works of this author; Lilian Edger, *The Elements of Theosophy* (1903); Ethel M. Mallet, *First Steps in Theosophy* (1905). Critical studies include R. Guénon, *Le Théosophisme*. Histoire d'une pseudo-religion (Bibliothèque Français de Philosophie; 1921); T. Mainage, O.P., *Les Principes de la théosophie*. Étude critique (1922; Eng. tr., 1927); W. S. Urquhart, *Theosophy and Christian Thought* [1922]; L. de Grandmaison, *Théosophie et l'anthroposophie* (1939). P. Oltramare, *L'Histoire des idées théosophiques dans l'Inde* (Annales du Musée Guimet. Bibliothèque d'Études, xxiii and xxxi; 1906–23). Josephine Ranson, *A Short History of the Theosophical Society* (Adyar, 1938). T. Besterman, *A Dictionary of Theosophy* (1927). There is also much information about the modern theosophical movement in the lives of Annie Besant by 'Geoffrey West' [pseud.] (London, 1929), Gertrude M. Williams (ib. [1931]), and T. Besterman (ib., 1934). The numerous periodical publications of the Theosophical Society include *Theosophist* (Madras, 1879 ff.) and the *Theosophical Quarterly* (New York, 1903 ff.). Annie Besant in *H.E.R.E.*, xii (1921), pp. 300–4, s.v. 'Theosophical Society'; P. Oltramare, ib., pp. 304–15, s.v.; J. Brugerette in *D.T.C.*, xv (pt. 1; 1946), cols. 540–52, s.v. 'Théosophie'.

THEOTOKOS (Gk. θεοτόκος, Lat. *Deipara*), the 'God-bearer', title of the BVM. The word was used of the Virgin by the Greek Fathers from *Origen onwards (perh. even by *Hippolytus) and increasingly became a popular term of devotion. In 429 it was attacked by *Nestorius and his supporters as incompatible with the full humanity of Christ, and the word 'Christotokos' proposed in its place. It found, however, a zealous champion in St. *Cyril of Alexandria and was formally upheld at the Councils of *Ephesus (431) and *Chalcedon (451). Henceforward its orthodoxy was generally undisputed in the Church. In the W. the usual equivalent in practice was not *Deipara*, which corresponded to it etymologically, but *Dei Genitrix* ('Mother of God'), with its somewhat different emphasis.

J. H. *Newman, *Select Treatises of St. Athanasius* (ed. 2, 1881), ii, 210–15. F. J. Dölger in *Antike und Christentum*, i (1929), pp. 118–23 ['Zum Theotokos-Namen']; H. Rahner, S.J., 'Hippolyt von Rom als Zeuge für den Ausdruck Θεοτόκος' in *Z.K.T.*, lix (1935), pp. 73–81; cf. id., ib., lx (1936), pp. 577–90.

THERAPEUTAE (Gk. θεραπευταί, 'physicians', 'devotees', hence 'those who worship God'), a pre-Christian monastic community of Egyptian Jewish ascetics. The only real authority for their practice and beliefs is *Philo's *De Vita Contemplativa*, where they are contrasted with the *Essenes, who lived a more active life. They were severe in their discipline, abjured money, and lived in seclusion near Alexandria and above Lake Mareotis. They prayed at sunrise and at sunset; devoted themselves assiduously to the allegorical study

of the OT; and met together only for Sabbath-worship and during the great festival corresponding to Pentecost, when bands of men and women danced and sang throughout the night. Virtually nothing is known of their history. Their interest lies largely in their being an example of a pre-Christian monastic system. *Eusebius (*H.E.*, II, xvii) mistakenly regarded them as a Christian sect.

F. C. *Conybeare (ed.), *Philo: About the Contemplative Life, or the Fourth Book of the Treatise concerning Virtues* (1895; text, with defence of its genuineness). P. E. Lucius, *Die Therapeuten und ihre Stellung in der Geschichte der Askese*. Eine kritische Untersuchung der Schrift *De Vita Contemplativa* (Strassburg, 1879; maintained Philo's treatise was a 3rd-cent. Christian forgery). P. Wendland, 'Die Therapeuten und die philonische Schrift vom beschaulichen Leben' in *Jahrbücher für classische Philologie*, Supplement-band, xxii (1896), pp. 693–772. J. *Moffatt in *H.E.R.E.*, xii (1921), pp. 315–19, with bibl.

THERESA OF ÁVILA, St. See *Teresa of Ávila, St.*

THÉRÈSE OF LISIEUX, St. See *Teresa, St., of Lisieux.*

THERMARION (Gk. θερμάριον). In the E. Church, a vessel for the warm water used in the Eucharistic rite for mixing with the species of wine after its consecration and in the washing of altars at their dedication.

THESSALONIANS, Epistles to the. The two Epp. were most probably written by St. Paul from Corinth on his first visit to the city (*c.* 51) and are the earliest of his letters, unless it be argued that Gal. was written before them. The main purpose of the First Epistle, remarkable for the affectionate solicitude of the Apostle for his converts, is to set their minds at rest on the fate of the dead members of the community. He assures them that, at the Second Coming of Christ, those who have died in the Lord will rise first and then, together with the living, be united to Christ; he declines, however, to make pronouncements on the time and circumstances of these events, but bids his readers watch and be sober in faith, hope, and charity.

The Second Epistle, following shortly afterwards, was also occasioned by the eschatological preoccupations of the Thessalonians, many of whom had become over-excited by their belief in the immediately impending *Parousia and neglected their ordinary duties. Paul reminds them of his former teaching, acc. to which the apostasy and the 'Son of Perdition' (see *Antichrist*) must come first, but teaches that there is still something or someone 'that restraineth' (2. 6, τὸ κατέχον; 2. 7, ὁ κατέχων). This has been very differently interpreted; the most widely accepted critical explanation regards the term as referring to the Roman Empire under Claudius, whereas in the more traditional view it applies to a supernatural power, such as e.g. St. *Michael.

The authenticity of the First Epistle, once questioned by F. C. *Baur, is now generally accepted. That of the Second Epistle is still rejected by some scholars, despite its early attestation as one of St. Paul's letters by the time of St. *Irenaeus and its place in the *Muratorian Canon as well as in *Marcion's Collection. The chief objections are the alleged incompatibility of the eschatological teaching of the two epp. and their different tone, but these arguments are to-day largely regarded as artificial.

The more valuable Patristic commentaries include those of St. John *Chrysostom (*PG*, lxii, 391–500); *Theodore of Mopsuestia (fragments, ib., lxvi, 931–6); *Theodoret (ib., lxxxii, 628–73) and *John of Damascus (ib., xcv, 905–29); further list in *D.T.C.*, cited below. Modern commentaries include that of J. *Jewel (London, 1583); also those of G. G. Findlay (Camb. Bib., 1891; revised commentary for Camb. Bib., Gk. text, 1904), J. *Denney (The Expositor's Bible, London, 1892), G. Wohlenberg (Kommentar zum Neuen Testament ed. T. *Zahn, xii; 1903), G. Milligan (Cambridge, 1908), E. von *Dobschütz (K.E.K., x, ed. 7, 1909), M. *Dibelius (Hb. N.T., iii, pt. 2, 1911, with Philippians, pp. 1–43), J. E. Frame (I.C.C., 1912), J. M. Vosté (in Lat., Rome–Paris, 1917), A. Plummer (2 vols., London, 1918), E. J. Bicknell (West. Comm., 1932), F. Amiot (with Gal., Verbum Salutis, xiv; Paris, 1946, pp. 245–383), and W. Neill (Moff. Comm., 1950). F. C. Baur, *Paulus, der Apostel Jesu Christi. Sein Leben und Wirken, seine Briefe und seine Lehre* (1845), pp. 480–99 (Eng. tr., vol. ii, 1875, pp. 85–97). E. H. Askwith, *An Introduction to the Thessalonian Epistles* (1902). W. *Wrede, *Die Echtheit des zweiten Thessalonicherbriefs* (T.U., xxiv, Hft. 2; 1903). W. Hadorn, *Die Abfassung der Thessalonicherbriefe in der Zeit der dritten Missionsreise des Paulus* (Beiträge zur Förderung christlicher Theologie, xxiv, Hft. 2–3; 1919). Full Comm. by B. Rigaux, O.F.M. (Études Bibliques, 1956). W. Lock in *H.D.B.*, iv (1902), pp. 743–9, s.v.; D. Buzy–A. Burnot in *D.T.C.*, xv (pt. 1; 1946), cols. 573–610, s.v. 'Thessaloniciens (Épîtres aux)'.

THESSALONICA. The modern Salonica in Macedonia, it was founded *c*. 315 B.C. by Cassander, perhaps on the site of the ancient Thermae, and called after his wife, Thessalonica (step-sister of Alexander the Great). Under the Romans it became the virtual capital of the province and an important centre of trade. In the first Civil War it was the headquarters of Pompey and the Senate. Its rulers were known as 'politarchs' (cf. Acts 17. 6). In A.D. 50 or 51 St. *Paul visited the city, preached on three 'Sabbaths' in the synagogue, and founded the second Christian community in Europe, chiefly from the Greeks and proselytes (Acts 17), which was renowned for its orthodoxy and steadfastness in the succeeding period. (For his two letters to the *Thessalonians, see previous entry). Their early martyrs included St. Agape, with her sisters Chionia and Irene, St. Agathopus, and St. Demetrius (later the patron of the city). Acc. to *Origen (on Rom. 16. 23), the first Bp. of Thessalonica was Gaius (cf. 1 Cor. 1. 14, Acts 19. 29). In the late 4th or early 5th cent. the creation of a Papal vicariate of Thessalonica enabled Rome to retain ecclesiastical control of Illyria, which had been transferred politically to the Eastern Empire. In 732 *Leo III, the Isaurian, made Thessalonica and all Illyrian sees dependent on the Patriarchate of *Constantinople.

Notable Abps. of later date included St. Joseph, brother of St. *Theodore of Studios, Basil of Achrida (1145–*c*. 1169), Eustathius of Thessalonica (d. *c*. 1193), and *Gregory Palamas. From 1430 to 1912 Thessalonica

was governed by the Turks, and many of its beautiful churches, which still preserve much of their old mosaic work, were turned into mosques. Since 1912 the city has again been Greek. It is the seat of a Greek orthodox metropolitan and an orthodox Bulgarian bishop. A Latin Vicariate Apostolic was established in 1926.

L. *Duchesne, 'L'Illyricum ecclésiastique' in *B.Z.*, (1892), pp. 531–50; S. L. Greenslade, 'The Illyrian Churches and the Vicariate of Thessalonica, 378–95' in *J.T.S.* xlvi (1945), pp. 17–30. E. Oberhummer in *P.W.*, 2te Reihe, vi (pt. 1; 1936), cols. 143–63.

THEUDAS. The leader of an unsuccessful Jewish insurrection, mentioned in Acts 5. 36, where his date is given as before 'the days of the enrolment', i.e. A.D. 6 or 7. In *Josephus (*Ant.* XX, v, 1) a Theudas occurs in connexion with a Jewish rebellion in A.D. 45 or 46, but there is some doubt as to the authenticity of the name in this passage, which may have been inserted later. Many modern Biblical scholars hold, however, that the reference in Acts is an anachronism, arising out of St. Luke's careless reading of the passage in Josephus. It is objected that this implies an impossibly late date for Acts. Other explanations are to suppose an error on the part of Josephus or to assume the existence of two rebels of the same name.

M. Krenkel, *Josephus und Lukas* (1894), pp. 162–74. F. J. Foakes Jackson and K. *Lake (edd.), *The Beginnings of Christianity*, ii (1922), pp. 312 (H. Windisch), and 356 (H. J. Cadbury and Editors). S. J. Case in *D.A.C.*, ii (1918), p. 575 f., with bibl. reff.

THIERRY OF CHARTRES (d. after 1151), medieval philosopher and theologian. A Breton by birth and a younger brother of *Bernard of Chartres, he became a 'Magister' of the school of *Chartres in 1121 and *c*. 1124 went to *Paris, where he counted *John of Salisbury among his pupils. In 1136 he became Archdeacon of Dreux and in 1141 succeeded *Gilbert de La Porrée as Archdeacon and Chancellor of Chartres. In 1148 he took part in the synod of *Reims which condemned Gilbert and also attended the Diet of Frankfurt in the following year. At some date between 1151 and 1156 he retired into a monastery, prob. *Cistercian, and nothing further is known of his life.

Thierry of Chartres was one of the leading and most original exponents of the Platonist tendencies of the school of Chartres. In his treatise 'De Sex Dierum Operibus' he interpreted the Genesis account of creation acc. to *Plato's 'Timaeus', regarding the Divine form as the form of all things ('forma divina omnium rerum forma est'), without, however, understanding the Platonic formulae in a *Pantheistic sense. In the work of creation he assigned the four *Aristotelian causes to the Persons of the *Trinity, the Father being the efficient cause, the Son the formal, and the Holy Ghost—also identified with Plato's world-soul—the final cause, whereas Divinely created matter was the material cause. In his Commentary on

*Boethius's 'De Trinitate' he further developed his Trinitarian doctrine, tending here to interpret it in a rationalistic way as capable of being deduced from the considerations of the unity, the Father, which leads to equality, the Son, and thence to the bond between the two, the Holy Ghost. He also wrote a commentary on Cicero's 'De Inventione' and made a collection of texts for the study of the seven liberal arts known as the 'Heptateuchon'.

Thierry's 'De Sex Dierum Operibus' was ed. by B. Hauréau in *Notices et extraits des manuscrits de la Bibliothèque Nationale*, xxxii (pt. 2; 1888), pp. 167–86; repr. in id. (ed.), *Notices et extraits de quelques manuscrits latins de la Bibliothèque Nationale*, i (1890), pp. 45–70; text also partly pr. in W. Jansen, *Der Kommentar des Clarenbaldus von Arras zu Boëthius* De Trinitate (Breslauer Studien zur historischen Theologie, viii; 1926), pp. 106*–12*. Jansen also identified as Thierry's Commentary on Boethius a treatise beginning with the words 'Librum hunc', which he printed ib., pp. 3*–25*; this ascription, though generally accepted, has been disputed by N. M. Haring in *Mediaeval Studies*, xv (1953), p. 215, who holds that Thierry's commentary is to be found in the Paris Bibl. Nat. MS. Lat. 14489, of which extracts were publd. by J. M. Parent, O.P., *La Doctrine de la création dans l'École de Chartres* (Publications de l'Institut d'Études Médiévales d'Ottawa, viii; 1938), pp. 178–205. Extracts from his commentary on Cicero's 'De Inventione' have been pr. by W. H. D. Suringar, *Historia Critica Scholiastarum Latinorum*, i (Leyden, 1834), pp. 213–52, and P. Delhaye in *Mediaeval Studies*, xi (1949), pp. 97–9. The Prologue of the 'Heptateuchon' ed. E. Jeaunneau in *Mediaeval Studies*, xvi (1954), pp. 171–5; the plan is pr. and discussed in A. Clerval, *Les Écoles de Chartres au moyen-âge* (1895), pp. 220–223. See also pp. 254–9, and on his followers pp. 188–94. A. Vernet, 'Une Épitaphe inédite de Thierry de Chartres' in *Recueil de travaux offerts à M. Clovis Brunel*, ii (Mémoires et Documents publiés par la Société de l'École de Chartes, xii; 1955), pp. 660–70. Überweg, ii, 233–5, with further bibl. p. 704; Manitius, iii, 198–202; E. *Gilson, *History of Christian Philosophy in the Middle Ages* (1955), pp. 145–8, with bibl. p. 621 f.

THIRD ORDERS. Religious organizations affiliated usually to one of the *Mendicant orders, and so called to distinguish them from the First and Second Orders, of fully professed men and women, respectively. A member of a Third Order may be either living in the world, and is then usually called a '*Tertiary' (q.v.), or in community. The latter, or 'Regular Tertiaries', date from the later 13th cent., and arose from the desire of great numbers of 'Secular Tertiaries' to lead a community life. At first these convents followed the special rule for seculars of their respective orders ; but from the 15th cent. many of them took vows. To-day all members of the regulated Third Orders live under vows, and, in the case of nuns, are often as strictly enclosed as their Sisters of the Second Orders. Both Brothers (or Fathers) and Sisters of the Third Orders devote themselves to all kinds of works of mercy, esp. nursing, teaching, and missionary activities. The most important Third Orders belong to the religious families of *Franciscans and *Dominicans, but others, e.g. *Carmelites, *Servites, and *Augustinian Friars, also have a large number of convents of Regular Tertiaries. For the rules and practices of 'Secular Tertiaries', see entry *Tertiary*.

THIRD ROME. A title given esp. by Russian Christians to Moscow in the belief that the privileges which formerly belonged to

Rome and *Constantinople (the 'New Rome') had been committed to the city. The first instance of its use appears to be in a letter of the monk Philotheus to the Grand Duke Basil III (1505–33).

THIRLBY, THOMAS (1506?–70), successively Bp. of *Westminster (1540), *Norwich (1550), and *Ely (1554). A Cambridge man who was favoured by T. *Cranmer, he became a chaplain to *Henry VIII, and first and only bishop of the new see of Westminster (suppressed 1550). In 1549 he opposed the First Prayer Book of *Edward VI and the Act of *Uniformity, but accepted them when passed, despite his strong Catholic sympathies. He was naturally in high favour under *Mary, but under *Elizabeth I refused the Oath of Supremacy and was deposed and afterwards imprisoned.

T. Cooper in *D.N.B.*, lvi (1898), pp. 135–8, s.v., with reff.

THIRLWALL, CONNOP (1797–1875), historian and Bp. of *St. David's. After a very precocious childhood he was educated at Trinity College, Cambridge, where he became a Fellow in 1818. After studying law at Lincoln's Inn he entered on an ecclesiastical career, and in 1828 was ordained priest. In 1832 he was appointed assistant tutor at Trinity College, but in 1834 he was compelled to resign owing to his denunciation of compulsory attendance at chapel in the course of the controversy over the admission of Dissenters to the universities. In the same year he was offered the living of Kirby Underdale, Yorks, where he began his chief work, the *History of Greece* (8 vols., 1835–44). In 1840 Lord Melbourne appointed him Bp. of St. David's. He learned Welsh, restored Church life in his diocese, and took part in all the ecclesiastical questions of the day in a liberal and unbiased spirit. He supported the grant to *Maynooth (1845) and the removal of the civil disabilities of the Jews (1848), and urged the disestablishment of the Irish Church (1869). He also permitted Bp. J. W. *Colenso to preach in his diocese. His important 'Charges', delivered between 1842 and 1872 (publd. in *Remains Literary and Theological*, 3 vols., 1877–8), deal with these and other subjects such as the question of *Essays and Reviews*, the *Ritualist controversy, and the *Vatican Council.

Thirlwall's *Letters, Literary and Theological*, ed. J. J. S. Perowne–L. Stokes (London, 1881); his *Letters to a Friend* [a young Welshman] ed. A. P. *Stanley (ib., 1881). Modern life by John Connop Thirlwall (great-great-great nephew) (S.P.C.K., London, 1936). J. W. Clark in *D.N.B.*, lvi (1898), pp. 138–41.

THIRTEEN ARTICLES, The (1538). A MS. in Latin entitled *A Book containing Divers Articles de Unitate Dei et Trinitate Personarum, de Peccato Originali, &c.* which was discovered among some papers that belonged to Abp. T. *Cranmer. It appears to have been drawn up as a basis for negotiations, or was perhaps a record of doctrines actually agreed upon, between a small body of conservative *Lutheran divines, invited to England by *Henry VIII in 1538, and an English committee of three bishops and four doctors. The articles were closely modelled upon the *Augsburg Confession.

Text in C. Hardwick, *A History of the Articles of Religion* (1861), pp. 251–63, with discussion, pp. 60–73. See also bibl. to *Cranmer, T.*

THIRTY-NINE ARTICLES, The. The set of doctrinal formulae finally accepted by the C of E in its attempt to define its dogmatic position in relation to the controversies of the 16th cent. The earlier stages were the *Ten Articles (1536), the *Bishops' Book (1537), the *Six Articles (1539), the *King's Book (1543), and the *Forty-Two Articles (1553). In 1563 Convocation, by slightly revising the last named, issued the first text of the Thirty-Nine Articles. But, before they were printed, No. 29 ('Of the Wicked which eat not the Body of Christ') was excised, probably to conciliate the Romanists, and a preamble to No. 20, asserting the authority of the Church to decree rites and ceremonies, was added. Both alterations are attributed to *Elizabeth I personally. In 1571 No. 29 was restored, as the Romanists had now finally seceded. In their final form the Articles gained synodical approval through Convocation.

The Thirty-Nine Articles are not a statement of Christian doctrine in the form of a creed, nor the exposition of a creed already accepted. They are, rather, short summaries of dogmatic tenets, each article dealing with some point raised in current controversies and laying down in general terms the Anglican view. Though not ostensibly vague, they avoid unduly narrow definition. Much variety of interpretation has been put upon many of them without improperly straining the text, and probably this licence was deliberately intended by their framers. They seek esp. to define the Anglican position with regard to medieval corruptions of Catholic teaching, to orthodox RC doctrine, to *Calvinism, and to *Anabaptist teachings. Among typical points it may be noticed that Art. 28 excludes both *Transubstantiation (in the sense in which it is there defined) and *Zwinglian Eucharistic doctrine, but can be interpreted in terms either of a doctrine of the *Real Presence or of *Receptionism. Art. 6 declares that 'Holy Scripture containeth all things necessary to salvation'; the Creeds are to be accepted because they may be proved by Scripture (Art. 8); and General Councils are declared to be not of themselves infallible (Art. 21). Predestination is discussed in Art. 17, the masterly ambiguity of which is seen when it is compared with other professions of faith such as the Presbyterian *Westminster Confession (1647). The position of the Sovereign and civil power in relation to the Church is set out in the concluding Articles.

Subscription to the Articles has never been required of any but the clergy and, until the 19th cent., members of the universities of Oxford and Cambridge. Since 1865, the clergy have been required only to affirm that the doctrine of the C of E as set forth in the BCP and the Articles is agreeable to the Word of God, and to undertake not to teach in contradiction of them, instead of giving a more particular subscription as before.

E. C. S. Gibson, *The Thirty-Nine Articles* (2 vols., 1896–7); B. J. Kidd, *The Thirty-Nine Articles* (2 vols., 1899). E. J. Bicknell, *A Theological Introduction to the Thirty-Nine Articles* (1919; chiefly of doctrinal interest). For *Tractarian views on the Articles, J. H. *Newman, *Tract 90* (1841) and A. P. *Forbes, *The Thirty-Nine Articles* (1867).

THIRTY YEARS WAR, The (1618–48). The series of religious and political wars between Catholic and Protestant Continental states and powers, fought out in Central Europe in the 17th cent. Foremost among its manifold causes were the internal decay of the Empire and the continued religious unrest after the Peace of *Augsburg in 1555. The war began with the revolt of the Bohemians against the Emperor, and the '*Defenestration of Prague'. The first part of the war (1618–23) was carried on chiefly in Bohemia and the Palatinate. The Bohemians, who had set up Frederick V of the Palatinate, the so-called 'Winter King', in opposition to Emp. Ferdinand II, were defeated in the Battle at the White Hill (1620) by the armies of the Catholic League under the Imperial general, Tilly, and Maximilian of Bavaria. Frederick was put to the ban of the Empire, Maximilian conquered the Upper Palatinate, and this stage of the war ended with the capture of the Calvinistic stronghold of Heidelberg by Tilly (1622) and the restoration of Catholicism in the conquered territories.

War broke out anew in 1623. Shifting to Lower Saxony, it was conducted with Dutch and English support, with Wallenstein as the chief leader on the Imperial side. After his victory, in 1626, over Ernest of Mansfeld, and Christian IV of Denmark's defeat at the hands of Tilly (1626), the Peace of Lübeck was concluded in 1629. In the same year the Emperor issued the Edict of Restitution which ordered the restoration of all ecclesiastical property unlawfully appropriated by the Protestants since 1552. Its strict execution roused much opposition among the Protestants, while many Catholics were alienated from the Emperor by the extravagances of Wallenstein's army. In 1630 Wallenstein himself was dismissed.

The third stage of the war, which now became a European conflict, began with the landing of *Gustavus Adolphus in Pomerania in 1630. Encouraged by Cardinal A. J. du P. *Richelieu, whose anti-Spanish policy led him to support all opponents of the Imperial power at Vienna, the Swedish invasion was a mainly political adventure, though it incidentally saved German Protestantism. In 1631 Tilly conquered Magdeburg, but was defeated in the same year at Breitenfeld and killed in 1632. Wallenstein, who had been recalled by the Emperor, was defeated in the battle at Lützen, but Gustavus Adolphus himself was killed (1632). The next two years were taken up with negotiations, while the Protestant leader, Bernard of Weimar, took Ratisbon and laid waste Bavaria without opposition from Wallenstein, who was murdered in 1634. In the same year Imperial and Bavarian troops gained a decisive victory at Nördlingen, which led to the Treaty of Prague (1635) between the Emperor and the majority of the Protestant estates.

The Swedes, however, continuing to resist, were now openly joined by France and the war entered on its final and most violent stage (1635–48). After years of fighting with varying success in E. and W. Germany, the French position became increasingly advantageous, esp. owing to the weakening of Spain by internal discord. The demand for peace in Germany grew increasingly insistent and in 1644 negotiations were opened with the French at Münster and with Sweden at Osnabrück, and the Peace of *Westphalia (q.v.) was at last concluded in 1648. As a result the ecclesiastical state of the Empire as it was in 1624 was restored, except for the secularization—a term then used for the first time—of a considerable part of ecclesiastical property, which was distributed among the several powers as compensation for their participation in the war. The decrees of the Religious Peace of Augsburg were reinforced and extended to the *Calvinists, and Catholics and Protestants given equal political rights.

Among the chief effects of the Thirty Years War was an enormous strengthening of the power of France. The corresponding weakening of Germany and Spain hastened the final breaking-up of the Empire and decided the future of Europe in succeeding centuries. The religious, moral, and economic anarchy which it produced in Central Europe had the same far-reaching consequences, and accounts for much in the subsequent religious and social developments on the Continent.

Important docc. pr. in the collection of *Briefe und Acten zur Geschichte des Dreissigjährigen Krieges in den Zeiten des vorwaltenden Einflusses der Wittelsbacher* . . . herausgegeben durch die histor. Commission bei der Königl. Academie der Wissenschaften (11 vols., Munich, 1870–1909). Modern studies include A. Gindely, *Geschichte des Dreissigjährigen Krieges* (4 vols., 1869–80); also a shorter study by the same author with the same title (Das Wissen der Gegenwart, i, iii, v; 1882; Eng. tr., 2 vols., New York, 1884; London, 1885); S. R. Gardiner, *The Thirty Years War* (Epochs of Modern History, 1874); E. Charvériat, *Histoire de la guerre de Trente Ans* (2 vols., 1878); O. Klopp, *Der Dreissigjährige Krieg bis zum Tode Gustav Adolfs, 1632* (3 vols. in 4 parts, 1891–6); G. Winter, *Geschichte des Dreissigjährigen Krieges* (Allgemeine Geschichte in Einzeldarstellungen herausgegeben von W. Oncken, iii; 1893); H. G. R. Reade, *Sidelights on the Thirty Years War* (3 vols., 1924); Cicely V. Wedgwood, *The Thirty Years War* (1938); G. Pagès, *La Guerre de Trente Ans* (1939). A. W. Ward in *C.M.H.*, iv (1906), pp. 1–255 and 364–433, with bibl. to date, pp. 801–72, incl. good discussion of sources.

THOLUCK, FRIEDRICH AUGUST GOTTREU (1799–1877), German Protestant theologian. He was educated at Breslau and Berlin, where he studied esp. oriental languages, but under the influence of *Pietist friends and J. A. W. *Neander he turned to theology. From 1820 to 1826 he lectured at Berlin and in 1826 became professor at Halle university,

where he remained to his death, except for a short appointment as embassy chaplain at Rome from 1827 to 1829. In 1823 appeared his influential work *Die Lehre von der Sünde und dem Versöhner, oder die wahre Weihe des Zweiflers*, which was widely translated and did much to check the spread of Rationalism in Germany. It was followed by a commentary on Romans (1824), a collection of the writings of oriental mystics (*Blütensammlung aus der morgenländischen Mystik*, 1825), and further commentaries on St. John (1827), the Sermon on the Mount (1833), and Hebrews (1836), which are written from a moralist and apologetical rather than an exegetical point of view. His other works include the devotional *Stunden christlicher Andacht* (1839), *Die Propheten und ihre Weissagungen* (1861) which was highly valued by E. B. *Pusey, and a history of Rationalism (1865). Tholuck, who through his pastoral work among the students exercised a profound influence on his contemporaries, was a representative of the '*Vermittlungstheologie' (q.v.), combining personal piety with far-reaching disregard of dogma. Despite their theological divergences, he was a lifelong friend of Pusey, who had become acquainted with Tholuck in 1825, and whose first work, *The Theology of Germany* (1828), is largely based on Tholuck's ideas.

Gesammelte Werke (11 vols., Gotha, 1862–73). Life by L. Witte (2 vols., Bielefeld and Leipzig, 1884–6); briefer sketches by M. Kähler (Halle, 1877) and C. H. Rennecke (Rostock, 1878). M. Kähler in *P.R.E.* (ed. 3), xix (1907), pp. 695–702.

THOMAS, St., Apostle.
He is mentioned as one of the Twelve in all four Gospels. In St. John, where his name is translated as Δίδυμος (Gk., 'twin'), he appears in three episodes, viz. offering to die with Jesus on His way to Bethany (Jn. 11. 16), interrupting the last discourse with his question 'We know not whither thou goest, how know we the way?' (14. 5), and, lastly, doubting the Resurrection unless he were to touch the wounds of the Risen Lord (20. 25–8). After Christ's appearance he confesses his faith in the words 'My Lord and my God' and is thus the first to confess explicitly His Divinity. Acc. to an early tradition mentioned by *Eusebius (*Hist. Eccl.* III, i) and others, he evangelized the Parthians, whereas another tradition, derived from the Gnostic 'Acts of *Thomas' (where he is called 'Judas Thomas' as generally by the Syrians), asserts that he brought the Gospel to *India where he was martyred. The Syrian Christians of *Malabar, who call themselves 'Christians of St. Thomas', have a tradition which they strongly defend that they were evangelized by the Apostle, who later was martyred and buried at Mylapore, nr. Madras. The 'Thomas Cross', an ancient stone cross (6th–8th cent.) with a problematical inscription, is preserved in the church which marks the place where his body is held to have rested before its translation to *Edessa in the 4th cent. His relics are now supposed to be at Ortona in the Abruzzi, where they are still venerated. In

the Roman Martyrology the place where he died is given as Calamina. As yet it has not been identified, but it has sometimes been connected with Mylapore. Feast day, 21 Dec.; in the Syrian Church, 3 July.

For the several apocryphal writings that have circulated under his name, see the following entries.

For discussions of the evidence in the NT, see commentaries on the Gospels. For later traditions, see bibl. to *Thomas, Acts of.*

THOMAS, Acts of St. (Περίοδοι Θωμᾶ). An apocryphal book of great length which recounts in 13 'Acts' the missionary activities of the Apostle Thomas ('Judas Thomas'). It tells how Gundaphorus, one of the kings of India, wishing for a magnificent palace, sent his merchant Abbanes to Syria to obtain a skilled architect. At *Jerusalem Abbanes met Jesus, the carpenter's son, who recommended to him His 'slave', Thomas, and Thomas agreed to go back with him to Syria. Thomas gave away the large sums of money with which Gundaphorus provided him to the poor, and soon convinced him that his money was being used to build a far nobler palace in heaven than the earthly building for which it had been intended. Gundaphorus and many others were thereupon converted. After further missionary work, accompanied by healing miracles, in the neighbouring lands of King Misdaeus, Thomas was persecuted for his success in persuading Mygdonia to cease marriage relationships with her husband, Charisius, and finally was pierced with spears. The Apostle's bones were taken back shortly afterwards to Mesopotamia. Contained in the 'Acts' are four poems,—an 'Ode to Sophia' (6, 7), two hymns relating to Baptism (27), and the Eucharist (50), and a famous Hymn to the Redeemer (108–13; formerly, but probably wrongly, called the 'Hymn of the Soul').

The work, which was in origin a *Gnostic composition and apparently written before the middle of the 3rd cent., survives in several Syriac and Greek MSS. The complicated relation of the Syriac and Greek texts is held by most scholars to point to a Syriac original. If so, the most likely place of origin is Edessa. Parts of the Acts survive also in Latin and Ethiopic; and there exists also an Armenian version. It would appear that from the surviving texts most of the Gnostic elements have been removed to make the work acceptable to Catholic readers, though its origin is betrayed, e.g., by its continual depreciation of marriage.

Syriac text ed. W. Wright, *Apocryphal Acts of the Apostles* (1871), i, 171–333; Eng. tr., ii, 146–298; Eng. tr. of older fragments by Mrs. Agnes Smith Lewis, *The Mythological Acts of the Apostles* (Horae Semiticae, iv; 1904), pp. 223–41. Best ed. of the Gk. text in R. A. *Lipsius–M. Bonnet, *Acta Apostolorum Apocrypha*, ii (pt. 2; Leipzig, 1903), pp. 99–291. Eng. tr. in M. R. James, *The Apocryphal New Testament* (1924), pp. 364–438. A. A. Bevan, *The Hymn of the Soul contained in the Syriac Acts of St. Thomas* (re-edited with Eng. tr.; Texts and Studies, v, No. 3, Cambridge, 1897); G. Hoffmann, 'Zwei Hymnen der Thomasakten' in *Z.N.T.W.*, iv (1903), pp. 273–309. K. Macke, 'Syrische Lieder gnostischen Ursprungs. Eine Studie über die apokryphen syrischen Thomasacten' in *T.Q.*, lvi (1874),

pp. 3–70. F. C. *Burkitt, 'The Original Language of the Acts of Judas Thomas' in *J.T.S.*, i (1900), pp. 280–90; id., 'Another Indication of the Syriac Origin of the Acts of Thomas', ib., iii (1902), pp. 94–6. G. E. Medlycott, *India and the Apostle Thomas.* An Inquiry, with a critical analysis of the *Acta Thomae* (1905), pp. 213–97. F. Wilhelm, *Deutsche Legenden und Legendare.* Texte und Untersuchungen zu ihrer Geschichte im Mittelalter (1907). J. Dahlmann, S.J., *Die Thomas-Legende und die ältesten historischen Beziehungen des Christentums zum fernen Osten im Lichte der indischen Altertumskunde* (Stimmen aus Maria Laach Ergänzungsheft, cvii; 1912). W. *Bousset, 'Manichäisches in den Thomasakten' in *Z.N.T.W.*, xviii (1918), pp. 1–39. J. N. Farquhar, 'The Apostle Thomas in North India' in *Bulletin of the John Rylands Library*, x (1926), pp. 80–111; id.,'The Apostle Thomas in South India', ib., xi (1927), pp. 20–50. G. Bornkamm, *Mythos und Legende in den apokryphen Thomas-Akten* (1933). R. H. *Connolly, 'A Negative Golden Rule in the Syriac Acts of Thomas' in *J.T.S.*, xxxvi (1935), pp. 353–7. D. S. Margoliouth, 'Some Problems of the "Acta Judae Thomae" ' in *Essays in Honour of Gilbert Murray* (1936), pp. 249–59. Bardenhewer, ii, 579–84; J. Quasten, *Patrology*, i (Utrecht, 1950), p. 139 f., with bibl. É. Amann in *Dict. Bibl.* Suppl. i (1928), cols. 500–4, s.v. 'Apocryphes du Nouveau Testament III (5)'; G. Bornkamm in *P.W.*, Zweite Reihe, vi (pt. 1; 1936), cols. 316–23, s.v. 'Thomas (1)'.

THOMAS, Apocalypse of St. An apocryphal eschatological treatise, probably written by a *Manichaean at the end of the 4th cent. and referred to in the *Gelasian Decree. It had long been lost, but was rediscovered early in this cent. and edited by P. Bihlmeyer in the *Revue Bénédictine* in 1911. This Latin text is probably the original. There exist several Anglo-Saxon versions.

Text ed. on the basis of MS. Monacensis Clm 5463 by P. Bihlmeyer, O.S.B., 'Un Texte non interpolé de l'Apocalypse de Thomas' in *R. Bén.*, xxviii (1911), pp. 270–82. It was also ed. by M. Förster from two Anglo-Saxon revisions of the text in 'Der Vercelli-Codex CXVII nebst Abdruck einiger altenglischer Homilien der Handschrift' in *Festgabe für Lorenz Morsbach* (Studien zur englischen Philologie 50; 1913), pp. 20–179; this text being pr. pp. 116–37. A reconstructed text is the basis of the trs. in M. R. James, *The Apocryphal New Testament* (1924), pp. 555–62. See also id., 'Revelatio Thomae' in *J.T.S.*, xi (1909–10), pp. 288–90. J. Quasten, *Patrology*, i (Utrecht, 1950), p. 149 f.

THOMAS, Coptic Gospel of St. See p. 1384.

THOMAS, Syriac Gospel of St. An early apocryphal writing, prob. of *Gnostic origin, mentioned as heretical by St. *Hippolytus (*Ref.* v. 7) and *Origen (*Hom. I in Luc.*). In the form in which it now survives it seems to be an abbreviated and expurgated version of the original Gnostic book. Its collection of stories of the boyhood of Christ presents us with an unedifying picture of a conceited, and frequently even malicious, child who uses his miraculous powers for the satisfaction of his whims. The work is extant in two Greek recensions as well as in Latin, Slavonic, and Syriac versions.

The two Gk. and the Lat. versions ed. C. *Tischendorf, *Evangelia Apocrypha* (Leipzig, 1853), pp. 134–70; ed. 2 (1876), pp. 140–80; Eng. tr. in M. R. James, *The Apocryphal New Testament* (1924), pp. 49–65, with appendix from other sources, pp. 66–70, and introd., incl. Eng. tr. of Patristic reff., pp. 14–16. Syriac text ed., with Eng. tr., by W. Wright, *Contributions to the Apocryphal Literature of the New Testament* (1865), pp. 1–16 of the Syriac; Eng. tr., pp. 6–11. Gk. text also ed., with Fr. tr., by C. Michel-P. Peeters, S.J. (edd.), *Évangiles apocryphes* (Textes et Documents pour l'Étude du Christianisme; 1911), pp. 162–189, with introd., pp. xxiii–xxxii; Fr. tr. of Lat. and Syriac texts, ib., (1914), pp. 290–311. L. Conrady, 'Das Thomasevangelium. Ein wissenschaftlicher Versuch', in *Theologische Studien und Kritiken*, lxxvi (1903), pp. 377–459.

M. R. James, 'The Gospel of Thomas' in *J.T.S.*, xxx (1929), pp. 51–4. W. Lüdtke, 'Die slavonischen Texte des Thomas-Evangeliums' in *Byzantinisch-neugriechische Jahrbücher*, vi (1928), pp. 490–508. Bardenhewer, i, 530–3. J. Quasten, *Patrology*, i (Utrecht, 1950), pp. 123–5.

THOMAS AQUINAS, St. (*c.* 1225–74), also 'Doctor Communis' and 'Doctor Angelicus', *Dominican philosopher and theologian. He was born at Roccasecca, the youngest son of Count Landulf of Aquino, who was related to the Emperor and the King of France. At the age of five he was sent to the neighbouring *Benedictine school at *Monte Cassino where he was destined by his parents for the abbacy. In 1240 he proceeded to Naples to finish his arts course. Here he was attracted to the ideal of an intellectual apostolate and resolved to seek admission to the recently founded Dominican Order. His family, who strongly opposed his intention, held him prisoner for 15 months at Roccasecca, but without weakening his determination; and in April 1244 he joined the Order. From the autumn of 1245 until 1248 he was at *Paris, where he came under the powerful influence of St. *Albertus Magnus, who introduced him to *Aristotle; and in 1248 he accompanied Albert to the newly established Dominican *studium generale* at Cologne. (The chronology of this part of his life is, however, somewhat uncertain.) In 1252 he returned to Paris and became lecturer at the Dominican Convent of St.-Jacques. Here he wrote his 'Contra Impugnantes Dei Cultum' in defence of the Mendicant Orders, then being attacked by the secular doctors of the University of Paris, led by William of St.-Amour. He became Master of Theology in 1256. In 1259 he was sent to Italy, where he taught as 'lector curiae' at Anagni and Orvieto (1259–65), at Santa Sabina and the Dominican *studium generale* at Rome (1265–7), and at Viterbo (1267–9). He was recalled to Paris in 1269. Here he combated the opposed philosophical doctrines of *Siger of Brabant, John *Peckham, and Stephen Tempier, Bp. of Paris. In 1272 he moved to Naples to set up a Dominican school, where he laboured hard at his 'Summa Theologica'. He died on 7 Mar. 1274 at the *Cistercian monastery of Fossanuova on his way to the Council of *Lyons. Several propositions drawn from his writings were condemned by Tempier in 1277, by Abp. *Kilwardby (a Dominican) in 1277, and by Abp. Peckham in 1284. The *Franciscan Order for a time forbade its members to study his works. In 1278 the General Chapter of the Dominicans officially imposed his teaching on the Order, and in 1323 he was canonized by John XXII. His body rests at Toulouse. Feast day, 7 Mar.

The extent of St. Thomas's writings, esp. in view of their compact thought and expression, is immense. From his first Paris period come several writings of less intrinsic importance, among them 'De Ente et Essentia' (1252–3; against *Avicebron), the 'Commentary on the *Sentences*' (1254–6, still influenced by the older Scholastic teaching), and the 'Quaestiones Disputatae de Veritate' (1256–9). The next group of writings embody his philosophy, which is

expounded in the form of Commentaries esp. on *Aristotle ('De Interpretatione', 'Analytica posteriora', 'Metaphysica', 'Ethica', 'De Anima', 'Parva Naturalia', 'De Generatione et Corruptione', 'Politica', and others). He also commented on the '*Liber de Causis' (probably after 1268, q.v.), *Dionysius the Areopagite ('De Divinis Nominibus') and *Boethius ('De Hebdomadibus', 'De Trinitate'). Much of his theology and spirituality is contained in his exegetical Commentaries on the Gospels (known as the 'Catena Aurea'), the Epistles, Isaiah, Jeremiah, the Psalms, and Job. His work found its culmination in the two 'Summae'. The earlier 'Summa contra Gentiles', of which the autograph survives in the *Vatican, was designed as a text-book for missionaries. Apparently written at the instigation of *Raymond of Pennafort, it contained a defence of natural theology against the Arabians. The *Summa Theologica' (q.v.), the highest achievement of medieval theological systematization and the accepted basis of modern RC theology, was the latest of his works and unfinished at his death. The 'Quaestiones Disputatae' and 'Quaestiones Quodlibetales' go over parts of the ground of the 'Summae', often in fuller detail. Among St. Thomas's other writings are 'De Substantiis Separatis' (against Avicebron), 'De Unitate Intellectus contra Averroistas' (against *Siger of Brabant), and 'De Regimine Principum' (partly spurious).

St. Thomas's philosophy received its characteristic shape under the influence of the recently recovered metaphysical writings of Aristotle. He thus carried to completion a process already well advanced by St. Albert. The way for the abandonment of much traditional Platonist teaching had, indeed, been already prepared in the previous century by the conceptualism of *Abelard and others. To secure a correct text of Aristotle, St. Thomas persuaded his friend, *William of Moerbecke, to revise the existing translations or prepare new ones. Yet St. Thomas was never rigidly bound by the *dicta* of Aristotle. And at a deeper level he continued to uphold many fundamental Platonist doctrines which had come down from St. *Augustine and Dionysius the Areopagite.

Fundamental in St. Thomas's teaching is his sharp distinction between reason and faith. If in a large area reason is paramount, many of the fundamental Christian verities (the Trinity, the Incarnation, the creation of the world in time, original sin, purgatory, the resurrection of the body, etc.) lie wholly beyond its province. But while such doctrines cannot be established by reason they must not be considered contrary to reason. Indeed, up to a point reason can often indicate their probability and rebut arguments designed to overthrow them. Such doctrines reach us through revelation, which is embodied in Scripture and in the consistent teaching of the Fathers. As their province is that of faith, where primacy (*principalitas*) belongs to the will, not to the intellect, their acceptance by the believer is a matter for moral decision. On the other hand, such truths as the existence of God, His eternity and simplicity, His creative power and providence, can be discovered by the natural reason altogether apart from revelation.

In his theory of knowledge, St. Thomas accepts the Aristotelian maxim that since all knowledge presupposes an essential likeness between knower and known and man's nature is corporeal as well as intellectual, cognition necessarily sets out from sense-perception (*nihil in intellectu quod non prius fuerit in sensu*). This belief gave St. Thomas's arguments for the existence of God their characteristic shape. An argument to be valid for us must start from the facts of the natural world. It is true that since essence and existence are identical in God, God's existence is a necessary consequence of His nature, i.e. for a purely intelligent being (the angels, or God Himself) the *ontological argument would be valid. But for the human intellect such an argument necessarily fails, since man cannot obtain that clear notion of God which the argument presupposes. On the other hand, it is possible to construct arguments of absolute cogency for the being of God on the basis of sense-perception. St. Thomas elaborates these with great detail, most fully in the 'Summa contra Gentiles' (I, 12, and 13) and the 'Summa Theologica'. For an account of these, see *Quinque Viae*.

Running through St. Thomas's system is the Aristotelian antithesis of potency and act. He held that the idea of 'primary matter' or pure potency, existing without form, was self-contradictory, a notion which even God could not bring into being. God, on the other hand, was 'pure act' (*actus purus*), since in Him every possible perfection was wholly realized. Intermediate in the scale of being were created things, composed of potency and act.

Closely related is the other Aristotelian antithesis of matter and form. Matter is the principle of individuation. While all the individuals in a species have the same form, the matter is proper to each particular individual. In the case of the angels, which are non-material beings, dwelling in the ninth and highest heaven, the *empyreum* or *primum mobile*, the normal principle of individuation is wanting. Hence acc. to St. Thomas, after *Avicenna, each angel is a separate species (*quot sunt ibi individua, tot sunt ibi species*).

Less original, but no less thoroughly elaborated, was St. Thomas's theology. The Incarnation and the Sacraments claimed his special interest. On controverted matters he tended to follow the tradition of his Order, and by the sharpened form which he imposed on Dominican tenets did much to propagate them. Against the Franciscans he maintained that the Incarnation would not have taken place apart from the Fall and that the BVM was not immaculately conceived. He paid much attention to the conditions governing Christ's human knowledge. He held that all seven Sacraments were instituted by Christ, that the Eucharist was the highest of them (*sacramentum sacramentorum*), and that as the

ultimate purpose of the Sacrament of Order was the Eucharist, the Priesthood was the highest of the seven orders, and the Episcopate therefore not a separate order. For the elaboration of the doctrine of transubstantiation, which had been formally defined at the Fourth *Lateran Council of 1215 shortly before his time, he employed the Aristotelian philosophy of substance and accidents. The *concomitance of the Body and Blood of Christ in both Eucharistic species afforded theological justification for communion in one kind.

In 1264 Urban IV entrusted St. Thomas with the composition of the office for the newly instituted Feast of *Corpus Christi. His hymns for the purpose are masterpieces in doctrinal precision, economy of expression, and metrical skill. They include the Sequence, 'Lauda Sion Salvatorem' (q.v.) for the *Mass, 'Pange lingua gloriosi' (q.v.) for the First *Vespers, and 'Verbum Supernum Prodiens' for *Lauds. Their merits were immediately recognized, and in the RC Church portions of the two last-named are still in regular use at the service of *Benediction.

The RC Church has accepted the substance of St. Thomas's teaching as its official doctrine. He was declared 'Doctor of the Church' by *Pius V in 1567. After a period of eclipse, a new era for Thomism was inaugurated by *Leo XIII's bull *Aeterni Patris (1879; q.v.) which enjoined his study on all theological students. In 1880 he was made patron of all Catholic Universities and on 29 June 1923, the sixth centenary of his canonization, his authority as a teacher was reiterated by *Pius XI in *Studiorum Ducem*. The *Codex (*CIC*, cans. 589. 1 and 1366. 2) makes the study of St. Thomas obligatory on all students of philosophy and theology. Among the classical exponents of Thomism were John *Capreolus ('Princeps Thomistarum'; 1380–1444), Thomas *Cajetan (1469–1534), Sylvester of Ferrara (1474–1528), and *John of St. Thomas (1589–1644). Recent exponents of his doctrines include A. Gardeil, O.P., E. *Gilson, M. *Grabmann, R. Garrigou-Lagrange, O.P., P. Mandonnet, O.P., J. *Maritain, and E. L. Mascall.

The principal modern edd. of his works are those of Parma, 25 vols., 1852–75; the 'Vives' ed. by S. E. Fretté and others (34 vols., Paris, 1871–80), and the sumptuous critical ed. 'iussu impensaque Leonis XIII' (Rome, 1882 ff.). There are a vast number of edd. and trr. of individual works and selections, and a very extensive modern literature. General studies concerned expressly with the Angelic Doctor include those of C. Jourdain (2 vols., Paris, 1858), K. Werner (3 vols., Ratisbon, 1858–9), P. Rousselot, [S.J.] (Paris, 1908; Eng. tr., 1935), A. D. Sertillanges, O.P. (Les Grands Philosophes, 2 vols., 1910; ed. 2, 1940; and other works of this author), E. Gilson (Strassburg, 1919; ed. 5, Paris, 1944; Eng. tr., 1924), F. Olgiati (Pubblicazioni della Università Cattolica del Sacro Cuore, Serie Prima, i, fasc. 1; 1923; Eng. tr., 1925), E. de Bruyne (Études philosophiques et religieuses, 1928), M. C. *D'Arcy, S.J. (Leaders of Philosophy, 1930), H. Meyer (Bonn, 1938; Eng. tr., 1944), G. Vann, O.P. (London, 1940), R. Garrigou-Lagrange, O.P. (Paris, 1946), and M. D. Chenu, O.P. (Université de Montréal. Publications de l'Institut d'Études Médiévales, xi; 1950). M. Grabmann, *Die echten Schriften des hl. Thomas von Aquin* (B.G.P.M., xxii, Hftt. 1–2; 1920; ed. 2, as *Die Werke des Hl. Thomas von Aquin*, ib., 1931; ed. 3, ib., 1949). A. Whitacre, O.P., and others, *St. Thomas Aquinas*. Being Papers read at the Celebrations of the Sixth Centenary of the Canonization of St. Thomas Aquinas held at Manchester, 1924 (1925); *Xenia Thomistica* a pluribus Orbis Catholici Viris Eruditis praeparata quae Sancto Thomae Aquinati . . . anno ab eius canonizatione sexcentesimo devotissime offert . . . L. Theissling, O.P., ed. S. Szabó, O.P. (3 vols., Rome, 1925). C. C. J. *Webb, *Studies in the History of Natural Theology* (1915), pp. 233–91. R. J. Deferrari–M. I. Barry, C.D.P., *A Lexicon of St. Thomas Aquinas* based on the *Summa Theologica* and selected passages of his other works (5 fascc., Baltimore, Md., 1948–9). P. Mandonnet, O.P.–J. Destrez, O.P., *Bibliographie thomiste* (Bibliothèque thomiste, i; 1921); V. J. Bourke, *Thomistic Bibliography, 1920–1940* (St. Louis, Mo., 1945). P. Wyser, O.P., *Thomas von Aquin* (Bibliographische Einführungen in das Studium der Philosophie herausgegeben v. I. M. Bochenski, xiii–xv; 1950); id., *Der Thomismus* (ib., xv–xvi; 1951). Überweg, ii, 419–45, with further bibl. pp. 743–57. D. J. Kennedy, O.P., in *C.E.*, xiv (1912), pp. 663–76, s.v.; M. Grabmann in *L.Th.K.*, x (1938), cols. 112–21, s.v. 'Thomas von Aquin'; P. A. Walz, O.P.–P. M. R. Gagnebet–L. B. Gillon, O.P.–C. Spicq–G. Geenen, O.P., in *D.T.C.*, xv (pt. 1; 1946), cols. 618–761, s.v. 'Thomas d'Aquin'; R. Garrigou-Lagrange, O.P., ib., cols. 823–1024, s.v. 'Thomisme'; C. Fabro, C.P.S., in *E.C.*, xii (1954), cols. 252–97, s.v. 'Tommaso d' Aquino'; all with extensive bibl. There are also a number of periodicals very largely devoted to studies connected with St. Thomas; a selection is listed s.v. *Scholasticism*.

THOMAS BECKET OF CANTERBURY, St. See *Becket, St. Thomas*

THOMAS BRADWARDINE. See *Bradwardine, Thomas*.

THOMAS OF CANTILUPE, St. See *Cantilupe, St. Thomas of*.

THOMAS OF CELANO (c. 1190–1260), the earliests of St. *Francis' biographers. Having joined St. Francis's band of friars c. 1214, he wrote two Lives of the saint (d. 1226), the first in 1228 at the command of *Gregory IX and the second in 1246–7 at the instance of the General of his order. They were followed in 1250–3 by the 'Tractatus de Miraculis S. Francisci'. Written in the rhythmical prose that delighted his age, these biographies were deservedly admired for their elegance, but their historicity has been challenged in modern times. Thomas was also the author of the 'Legend' of St. *Clare (1255), and, acc. to an uncertain tradition, of the *Dies Irae (q.v.).

Crit. edd. of the two lives and miracles of St. Francis by Eduardus Alenconiensis, O.F.M.Cap. (E. d'Alençon, Rome, 1906), and by the Franciscans of Quaracchi in *Analecta Franciscana*, x (1926–41), pp. 1–331, with introd. pp. iii–xlii; earlier edd. by S. Rinaldi (Rome, 1806), L. Amoni (Assisi, 1879, and Rome, 1880), and H. G. Rosendale (London, 1904). Eng. tr. of the two lives of St. Francis by A. G. F. Howell (London, 1908). The Legend of St. Clare is pr. in the *AA.SS.*, Aug. II (1735), pp .754–67; Eng. tr. by P. Robinson, O.F.M. (London, 1910); also ed. from MS. 338 of the Bibl. Communale of Assisi by F. Pennachi (Assisi, 1910). V. Facchinetti, *Tommaso da Celano, il primo biografo di S. Francesco* (Quaracchi, 1918). J. R. H. Moorman, *The Sources for the Life of St. Francis of Assisi* (Publications of the University of Manchester, No. cclxxiv, Historical Series, No. lxxix; 1940), esp. pp. 61–81 and 110–28. M. Bihl, O.F.M., 'Disquisitiones Celanenses' in *A.F.H.*, xx (1927), pp. 433–96, xxi (1928), pp. 3–54 and 161–205. A. G. Little, 'Some Recently Discovered Franciscan Documents and their Relation to the Second Life of Celano and the *Speculum Perfectionis*' in *Proceedings of the British Academy*, xii (1926), pp. 147–78. See also bibl. to *St. Francis of Assisi* and *Dies Irae*.

THOMAS CHRISTIANS. See *Malabar Christians*.

THOMAS OF HEREFORD, St. See *Cantilupe, St. Thomas of*.

THOMAS À JESU (1564–1627), spiritual author. Influenced by the writings of St. *Teresa, Díaz Sánchez de Ávila entered the *Carmelite Order in 1587, where he soon held the offices of professor of theology at Seville, prior at Saragossa, and provincial of Old Castile. After establishing a strictly eremitical life in several Carmelite monasteries, he was called to Rome in 1607 by *Paul V, in order to further the missionary activities in his order; but his efforts were frustrated by the opposition of the Spanish and Italian superiors. The literary results of the enterprise, however, the treatises *Stimulus Missionum* (1610) and *De Procuranda Salute omnium Gentium* (1613), in which he outlined his missionary theory, contributed largely to the foundation of the Congregation 'De *Propaganda Fide' (1622). His works on mysticism, *De Contemplatione Divina* (1620) and *Divinae Orationis Methodus* (1623), are remarkable for the clarity and sureness of their doctrine, presenting the teaching of St. Teresa in the form of Scholastic treatises.

Opera Omnia, publd. in 2 vols. bound in 1, Cologne, 1684. B. M. Zimmerman, C.D., *Les Saints déserts des Carmes déchaussés* (1927), pp. 46–60. E. A. Peers, *Studies of the Spanish Mystics*, ii (1930), pp. 279–306, with bibl. pp. 447–452. S. Salaville, A.A., 'Un Précurseur de la Propagande et un âpotre des missions, le P. Thomas de Jésus' in *Études carmélitaines*, v (1920), pp. 301–23. José de Jesús Crucificado, O.C.D., 'El Tomás de Jesús, escritor místico' in *Ephemerides Carmeliticae*, iii (1949), pp. 305–49, and iv (1950), pp. 149–206; Gabriel de Ste-Marie-Magdaleine, O.C.D., 'Thomas de Jésus et la contemplation acquise' in *Revue d'Ascétique et de Mystique*, xxv (1949), pp. 3–17.

THOMAS À KEMPIS (c. 1380–1471), ascetical writer. Thomas Hemerken, acc. to the usual and most probable tradition the author of the '*Imitation of Christ' (q.v.), was born at Kempen, nr. Cologne, of poor parents. After education at Deventer at the school of the *Brethren of the Common Life, he entered in 1399 the house of the *Canons Regular at the Agnietenberg, nr. Zwolle (one of the daughter-houses of *Windesheim), of which his elder brother, John, was co-founder and prior, and in 1406 took the habit. Here he lived for almost the whole of the rest of his life, writing, preaching, and copying MSS., and widely sought after as a spiritual adviser. His writings, though of many different kinds,—ascetical, homiletic, poetical, biographical, &c.—are all pervaded by the devotional spirit which finds its classical expression in the 'Imitation'. They include *Orationes et Meditationes de Vita Christi*, *Vallis Liliorum*, and *Hospitale Pauperum*.

Opera et Libri Vite Fratris Thome a Kempis by H. Rosweyden, ed. [P. Danhausser] (Nuremberg, 1494); revised ed. by H. Sommalius, S.J. (Antwerp, 1601); crit. ed. by M. J. Pohl (7 vols., Freiburg i.Br., 1902–22; vol. 8 wanting). Eng. tr. from ed. by M. J. Pohl of *Prayers and Meditations on the Life of Christ* by W. Duthoit (London, 1904); of *The Founders of the New Devotion* by J. P. Arthur (ib. 1905); of *The Chronicle of the Canons Regular of Mount St. Agnes* by id. (ib., 1906); of *Sermons to the Novices Regular* by V. Scully, C.R.L. (ib., 1907), and of *Meditations and Sermons on the Incarnation, Life and Passion of Our Lord* by id. (ib., 1907).

S. Kettlewell, *Thomas à Kempis and the Brothers of the Common Life* (2 vols., 1882). F. R. Cruise, *Thomas à Kempis*. Notes of a Visit to the Scenes in which his Life was spent, with some account of the examination of his relics (1887). V. Scully, C.R.L., *Life of the Venerable Thomas à Kempis* (1901); D. Butler, *Thomas à Kempis. A Religious Study* (1908). J. Mooren, *Nachrichten über Thomas à Kempis, nebst einem Anhange von meistens noch ungedruckten Urkunden* (Krefeld, 1855). See further bibl. to *Imitation of Christ*.

THOMAS OF MARGA (9th cent.), *Nestorian historian. In 832 he entered the celebrated Nestorian monastery of Beth-'Abhe, c. 25 miles E. of Mosul. Later he became secretary to the Patriarch Abraham (837–50), by whom he was created Bp. of Marga. Finally he became Metropolitan of Beth-Garmai. He wrote c. 840 his *Book of Governors*, a history of his monastery, but embodying also biographies of monks from various places in Mesopotamia, and one of the chief authorities for the earlier history of the Nestorian Church.

Thomas's 'Book of Governors' (Liber Superiorum), ed. E. A. W. Budge (2 vols., London, 1893; Syr. text with Eng. tr. in vol. ii) and P. Bedjan, Cong. Miss. (Paris, 1901). W. Wright, *A Short History of Syriac Literature* (1894), p. 219 f.; A. *Baumstark, *Geschichte der syrischen Literatur* (1922), p. 233 f.

THOMAS MORE, St. See *More, St. Thomas.*

THOMISM. The systematized expression of the (esp. philosophical) doctrines of St. *Thomas Aquinas (q.v.), particularly as developed in the RC Church in the *Dominican Order.

THOMPSON, FRANCIS (1859–1907), RC poet. A native of Preston, he was originally intended for the priesthood and educated at Ushaw, but later unsuccessfully studied medicine at Manchester. In 1885 he went to London, where he lived for three years in almost complete destitution, occasionally selling newspapers and matches. In 1888 his poetic gifts were discovered by Wilfrid Meynell, then editor of the Catholic magazine *Merry England*, who remained his friend and benefactor throughout his life. His first volume of *Poems*, published in 1893, contained the exquisite cycle 'Love in Dian's Lap', dedicated to Alice *Meynell, and his best-known poem, 'The Hound of Heaven', almost autobiographical in its arresting description of the pursuit of the soul by God. His *Sister Songs* (1895) and *New Poems* (1897) contain the magnificent 'Orient Ode', 'The Mistress of Vision', and 'To any Saint', poems in which the asceticism of the mystic, the beauty of the liturgy, and a sacramental conception of nature are blended into a unity. His poetry, though sometimes marred by an excessive use of neologisms, archaical words, and difficult allusions, has close affinities with that of the '*Metaphysical School' of the 17th cent. Its occasional obscurity rarely prevents it from conveying the central thought, and in its profound spirituality and love of children and the simple things of life has a genuine Franciscan ring, fostered by the poet's long stay (1893–7) near the Franciscan monastery at Pantasaph. After 1897 he wrote almost no more poetry. Among his prose works are *Health and Holiness; A Study of the Relations between Brother Ass the Body and his Rider the Soul* (1905; with Preface by G. *Tyrrell), a *Life of St. Ignatius Loyola* and an *Essay on Shelley* (latter both posthumous, 1909).

Works (3 vols., 1913). E. Meynell, *The Life of Francis Thompson* (1913); R. L. Mégroz, *Francis Thompson* (1927); Viola Meynell, *Francis Thompson and Wilfrid Meynell* (1952); R. M. Gautrey, '*This Tremendous Lover.*' An Exposition of the *Hound of Heaven* (1932). E. Meynell in *D.N.B., 1901–1911*, p. 502 f. B. I. Evans in *C.B.E.L.*, iii, p. 326 f.

THORESBY, JOHN (d. 1373), Abp. of *York. After executing several missions for W. Melton, Abp. of York (1317–40), and holding a number of ecclesiastical positions, he became Master of the Rolls in 1341, and Keeper of the Privy Seal in 1345, and was employed by Edward III to treat with France in 1346 and with Scotland in 1357, and to be guardian of the kingdom in 1355. In 1347 he became Bp. of *St. David's, and in 1349 of *Worcester. From 1349 to 1356 he was Chancellor of England, and from 1351 to 1373 Abp. of York. It was mainly through his instrumentality that the ancient dispute as to the respective privileges of Canterbury and York was settled, the Pope directing, on 22 Feb. 1354, that the Abp. of York should be the 'Primate of England' and the Abp. of Canterbury the 'Primate of All England'.

A few of his Constitutions are printed in D. *Wilkins (ed.), *Concilia Magnae Britanniae et Hiberniae*, iii (1737), pp. 663, 666–79; his will in J. Raine (ed.), *The Historians of the Church of York and its Archbishops*, iii (R.S., 1894), pp. 281–4. W. H. Dixon–J. Raine (ed.), *Fasti Eboracenses*. Lives of the Archbishops of York, i (1863), pp. 449–94, with eight of his letters, pp. 377–80. Life by Thomas Stubbs (14th cent.) in J. Raine, op. cit., ii (R.S., 1886), pp. 419–21. C. L. Kingsford in *D.N.B.*, lvi (1898), pp. 280–2, s.v., with further reff.

THORN, Conference of (1645). A conference (*colloquium caritativum*), of 26 *Catholic, 28 *Lutheran, and 24 *Calvinist theologians, convened in the Rathaus at Thorn on 28 Aug. 1645 on the proposal of Vladislav IV, King of Poland (1632–48), to bring about religious reunion. Among the participants were J. A. *Comenius, A. *Calovius, and G. *Calixtus (who on being rejected by the Lutherans ranked himself a Calvinist). Though discussions continued until the end of Nov., no result was achieved, largely because the Lutherans believed that the Catholics' only interest was to sever them from the Calvinists and the Protestant cause. Hence it was described as in fact *colloquium irritativum*.

Acta Conventus Thoruniensis Celebrati Anno 1645 (Warsaw, 1646); F. Jacobi, 'Das liebreiche Religionsgespräch zu Thorn 1645' in *Z.K.G.*, xv (1895), pp. 345–63. B. Tschackert in *P.R.E.* (ed. 3), xix (1907), pp. 745–51.

THORNDIKE, HERBERT (1598–1672), Anglican theologian. Probably a native of Suffolk, he was educated at Trinity College,

Cambridge, of which he became a Fellow in 1620. Ordained priest *c.* 1627, he held various offices in his college. In 1642 he became rector of Barley in Herts, but was ejected in 1643, as also from his fellowship at Trinity in 1646. In 1660 he was reinstated in both offices, and in the following year was appointed Prebendary of *Westminster. His first important theological work is his *Discourse of the Government of Churches* (1641), in which he defended the Apostolic origin of episcopal government against the Presbyterians. It was followed by the treatise *Of Religious Assemblies and the Public Service of God* (1642), upholding the worship of the C of E against the Puritans. In *A Discourse of the Right of the Church in a Christian State* (1649) he endeavoured to elucidate the relations between Church and State, stressing the supranational character of the former but conceding to the latter a certain authority over it. From 1652 to 1657 he helped in editing B. *Walton's *Polyglott Bible*, working chiefly on the Syriac texts. His principal work is *An Epilogue to the Tragedy of the Church of England* (1659), which consists of three parts: I, The Principles of Christian Truth; II, The Covenant of Grace; III, The Laws of the Church. In it he looks for a unified Christendom on the basis of the first six General Councils, conceding a certain superiority to the Pope with prescriptive rights over the W. Church. The third part contains his Eucharistic teaching. He rejects what he calls the 'Socinian' (=*Zwinglian), *Calvinistic, and *Lutheran doctrines as well as *Transubstantiation, to which, however, he is more sympathetic than most of his contemporaries. Acc. to his own view, the mystical but objective Presence of the Body and Blood of Christ is added to the substance of bread and wine by the consecration, which, however, is not effected by the words of Institution, but by the use of prayer. Thorndike's significance was for long forgotten, until he was rediscovered by the *Tractarians.

Works in *L.A.C.T.* (6 vols., bound in 9, 1844–54; with Life in vol. vi by A. W. Haddan, pp. 153–266). T. A. *Lacey, *Herbert Thorndike, 1598–1672* (1929). J. B. Mullinger in *D.N.B.*, lvi (1898), pp. 290–2.

THORVALDSEN, BERTEL (1770–1844), Danish sculptor. Educated at the School of Art at Copenhagen, he went to Rome in 1797, where he lived until 1838. His art is saturated with the classical ideal of beauty, which is prominent also where he deals with Christian subjects. His most famous religious work is the monumental group of Christ and His Apostles (1821–42) in the Frue Kirke at Copenhagen; the beautiful figure of the Risen Christ, His hands extended in blessing, has often been imitated. Among his other religious works are the tomb of Pope *Pius VII in St. Peter's (1830) and an Entrance of Christ into Jerusalem.

J. M. Thiele, *Den Danske Billedhugger Bertel Thorvaldsen og hans Vaerker* (4 vols., Copenhagen, 1831–50); id., *Thorvaldsens Biographi* (4 vols., ib., 1851–6; much abridged Eng. adaptation by M. R. Bernard, 1865); E. Plon, *Thor-*

valdsen. Sa vie et son œuvre (1867; Eng. tr., 1874); S. Müller, *Thorvaldsen*. Hans Liv og hans Vaerker (Copenhagen, 1893); T. Oppermann, *Thorvaldsen* (3 vols., ib., 1924–1930). The numerous smaller studies include that of S. Trier (Copenhagen, 1903). 'A. P.'-H. Vollmer in *Allgemeines Lexikon der bildenden Künstler von der Antike bis zur Gegenwart* begründet von U. Thieme–F. Becker, xxxiii (ed. H. Vollmer, 1939), pp. 94–100, s.v. 'Thorvaldsen', with detailed bibl.

THOU, JACQUES AUGUSTE DE. See *De Thou, Jacques Auguste.*

THREE CHAPTERS, The (τὰ τρία κεφάλαια). The three subjects condemned by the Emp. *Justinian in an edict of 543–4, viz. (1) the person and works of *Theodore of Mopsuestia, (2) the writings of *Theodoret against *Cyril of Alexandria, and (3) the letter of *Ibas of Edessa to Maris. As all three were sympathetic to *Nestorius, Justinian issued the edict in the hope of conciliating the *Monophysites by a display of anti-Nestorian zeal. The E. patriarchs assented, but in the W. the Emperor's interference was unpopular, and on the ground that it was opposed to the *Chalcedonian decrees, Pope *Vigilius refused at first to approve the edict. After being summoned to *Constantinople, however, Vigilius eventually issued in 548 his 'Iudicatum' to *Menas, the Patr. of Constantinople, which condemned the Three Chapters, but upheld the Chalcedonian decisions. After a storm of protest in the W., Vigilius deemed it best to withdraw his 'Iudicatum' and await a General Council. At the Fifth General Council, which met at *Constantinople in 553, the Three Chapters, and indirectly Vigilius, were condemned, though the Council also asserted the intention of the E. to remain in communion with Rome. In a 'Constitutum', issued in 554, Vigilius declared his submission to the Council's decision and his successor, Pelagius I, followed his example, though a serious schism in the W. resulted. Justinian's policy, which was in fact an attack on the *Antiochene theology and the decisions of Chalcedon, failed even of its purpose of reconciling the Monophysites.

The main documents will be found with the Acta of the Fifth General Council, pr. in the Conciliar collections. Latin theologians who wrote expressly in defence of the 'Three Chapters' include *Facundus of Hermiane and *Fulgentius Ferrandus [Ep. vi], qq.v., also Pope Pelagius I (556–61). L. *Duchesne, *L'Église au sixième siècle* (1925), pp. 185–218. R. Devreesse, 'Le Début de la querelle des Trois-Chapitres' in *Rev. S.R.*, xi (1931), pp. 543–65. Hefele–Leclercq, iii (pt. 1; 1909), pp. 1–156, passim. J. P. Junglas in *L.Th.K.*, iii (1931), col. 450 f., s.v. 'Dreikapitelstreit'; E. Amann in *D.T.C.*, xv (pt. 2; 1950), cols. 1868–1924, s.v. 'Trois-Chapitres (Affaire des)'. See also bibl. to *Constantinople, Second Council of* (553).

THREE CHILDREN, Song of the. See *Song of the Three Children.*

THREE DENOMINATIONS, The. A title applied to the *Presbyterian, *Congregationalist, and *Baptist Churches, the ministers of which in London and Westminster formed an association in 1727 for the purpose of joint political action.

THREE HOURS' SERVICE, The. An extra-liturgical service on Good Friday. It was instituted by the *Jesuits on the occasion of an earthquake at Lima in 1687, and is now widely observed esp. in Anglican churches as well as in some RC churches. It is held during the three hours of our Lord's Passion from noon till 3 p.m., and usually consists of seven sermons on the Seven Words from the Cross, with the intervals filled with hymns and prayers.

A. Mesia, S.J., *Devoción á la Tres Horas de Agonía de Nuestro Redentor Jesú Cristo* (1687; Eng. tr., London, 1806, reprinted with historical introd. by H. Thurston, S.J., as *The Devotion of the Three Hours' Agony on Good Friday*, 1899).

THREE WITNESSES, The. See *Johannine Comma*.

THUNDERING LEGION, The. When in the Danubian campaigns of the Emp. *Marcus Aurelius (172) a sudden rainstorm saved the Roman army from drought and defeat, Christians (e.g. *Justin, *Tertullian, *Eusebius) attributed this to the prayers of Christian members of the 'Legio XII Fulminata', claiming that the Emperor had admitted this in a letter to the Senate. The miracle is also referred to by pagan writers, e.g. Dio Cassius, though without reference to the Christian setting. On the column of M. Aurelius, in Rome, Jupiter Pluvius is represented as the benefactor. The mistranslation 'thundering' for 'thunder-struck' led to the elaborations that a thunderbolt had destroyed the enemy. As the name 'Fulminata' for the Legion dates from the time of Augustus (d. A.D. 14), it had no connexion originally with the incident here mentioned. The 'Thundering Legion' again appears in the legend of the Forty Martyrs of *Sebaste (q.v.).

Good discussion of the legend, with text and Eng. tr. of the letter of Marcus Aurelius to the Senate and further reff., in J. B. *Lightfoot, *The Apostolic Fathers*, part 2, i (1885), pp. 469–76. G. T. Stokes in *D.C.B.*, iv (1887), p. 1023 f., s.v.; H. *Leclercq, O.S.B., in *D.A.C.L.*, v (pt. 2; 1923), cols. 2692–703, s.v. 'Fulminata (Légion XIIᵉ). Further bibl. reff. listed by J. P. Kirsch in *L.Th.K.*, vii (1934), col. 452, s.v. 'Legio Fulminata'.

THURIBLE (Lat. *thus* or *tus*, 'incense'). A metal vessel for the ceremonial burning of *incense. In the usual form of thurible the container is suspended on chains from which it can be swung during the incensation. The thurible is also known as a 'censer'.

Rohault, v (1887), pp. 149–69. Braun, *A.G.*, pp. 598–632, with plates 126–37. H. *Leclercq, O.S.B., in *D.A.C.L.*, v (pt. 1; 1922), cols. 21–33, s.v. 'Encensoir'; J. Sauer in *L.Th.K.*, viii (1936), cols. 651–4, s.v. 'Rauchfass'.

THURIFER. A person appointed to carry the *thurible at religious ceremonies and services. He is sometimes attended by a boy bearing the incense-boat (the 'boat boy'), sometimes he carries this also himself.

THURNEYSEN, EDUARD (1888–), Swiss Protestant theologian. A native of Wallenstadt, after working among the Christian youth at Zürich, he was pastor successively at Leutwil in Aargau (1913), Bruggen near St. Gall (1920), and the Münster at Basel (1927). From 1913 onwards he was intimately associated with K. *Barth, and largely contributed to the elaboration of the *Dialectical Theology, with the pastoral and social applications of which he was esp. concerned. His writings include *Dostojewski* (1921), *Komm' Schöpfer Geist* (sermons, in collaboration with K. Barth, 1924), *Christoph Blumhardt* (1926), *Das Wort Gottes und die Kirche* (collected essays, 1927), and *Die Lehre von der Seelsorge* (1948). He was also one of the editors of the Barthian periodical *Zwischen den Zeiten* (1923 onwards).

THURSDAY, Holy or Maundy. See *Maundy Thursday*.

THYATIRA, city in N. Lydia. It is one of the 'Seven Churches' addressed in Rev. (2. 18–29) and the birthplace of St. Paul's convert Lydia, 'a seller of purple' (Acts 16. 14), one of the industries for which the town was noted. In Rev. its Christian community is upbraided for tolerating a 'Jezebel' in their midst who teaches them 'to commit fornication and to eat things sacrificed to idols' (2. 20), probably an adherent of the sect of the *Nicolaitans who introduced pagan elements into Christian worship. In the beginning of the 3rd cent. Thyatira was a stronghold of *Montanism. Its bishop, Sozon, took part in the Council of *Nicaea (325), and another bishop, Basil, is mentioned in 879. The modern city, named Ak-Hissar, has a small Christian population.

W. M. *Ramsay in *H.D.B.*, iv, pp. 757–9; id., *The Letters to the Seven Churches of Asia* (1904), pp. 316–53.

TIARA, extra-liturgical Papal headdress. First mentioned in the 'Vita' of Pope Constantine (708–15), it was in its original form a kind of white Phrygian cap, called 'camelaucum', worn as a sign of the Papal prerogative. Not later than the 11th cent. a coronet was placed round its lower rim, to which were added in the 13th cent. two lappets hanging down at the back. Under *Boniface VIII the tiara was adorned with a second coronet, possibly to symbolize the twofold power of the Papacy, and under Benedict XI (1303–4) or *Clement V (1305–14) a third coronet was added. At the same time the tiara increased in bulk, and in the 15th cent. it attained its modern shape resembling a beehive. It is worn by, or carried in front of, the Pope at important non-liturgical functions such as Papal processions and at solemn acts of jurisdiction, e.g. solemn dogmatic definitions.

Braun, *L.G.*, pp. 498–508. E. Müntz, 'La Tiare pontificale du VIIIᵉ au XVIᵉ siècle' in *Mémoires de l'Institut National de France*. Académie des Inscriptions et Belles-Lettres, xxxvi (1898), pp. 235–324; C. Sachsse, 'Tiara und Mitra der Päpste' in *Z.K.G.*, xxxv (1914), pp. 481–501. J. Braun, S.J., in *C.E.*, xiv (1913), p. 714 f., s.v.

TICONIUS. See *Tyconius*.

TIELE, CORNELIS PETRUS (1830–1902), Dutch theologian. A *Remonstrant pastor, he became professor of religious history, a chair specially founded for him, at *Leyden university, and here during the years of his professorship (1877–1901) exercised a great influence on the development of the study of comparative religion, esp. in Holland. Among the best known of his many books are *Geschiedenis van den Godsdienst tot aan de Heerschappij der Wereldgodsdiensten* (1876; Eng. trans. by J. E. *Carpenter as *Outlines of the History of Religion*, 1877) and his *Gifford Lectures on *The Elements of the Science of Religion* (1897–9). The fruit of a vast knowledge of ancient languages and history and prodigious industry, they became widely used on account of their lucid and orderly arrangement.

P. D. Chantepie de la Saussaye, 'Cornelis Petrus Tiele, 16 December 1830–11 Januari 1902' in *Koninklijke Akademie van Wetenschappen*, Jaarboek 1902, pp. 125–54. S. Cramer in *P.R.E.* (ed. 3), xix (1907), pp. 766–75.

TIERCE. See *Terce*.

TIGURINUS, Consensus. See *Consensus Tigurinus*.

TIKHON (1865–1925). Basil Ivanovitch Belavin, the first Patriarch of the Russian Church since 1700. The son of a village priest, he studied theology at the ecclesiastical academy of St. Petersburg and was successively Bp. of Lublin in 1897, of Alaska in 1898, of Yaroslav in 1907, and of Vilna in 1914. In Apr. 1917 he became metropolitan of Moscow, and in Nov. 1917 was elected patriarch, though with very circumscribed powers, by the Panrussian Council. Though not an eminent scholar or Church politician, his courage and humility gave him the moral authority needed in the subsequent difficult years. In 1919 he anathematized all who persecuted the Church and called upon the people to resist, but in the same year he imposed neutrality on the clergy in the civil war between the Reds and the Whites and refused to give his blessing to the latter. Owing to resistance to the State policy of confiscating Church property during the famine of 1921–2 he was banished to a monastery, but, owing to English political pressure, was not brought to trial. During his absence the state-supported schismatic 'Living Church' was set up, which called a council in 1923 to depose him and gained many adherents. In the same year Tikhon signed a declaration professing loyalty to the Soviet Government, which gained him less intolerable conditions, and he was allowed to live in the Don monastery at Moscow and to officiate in the churches of the capital. Owing to his personal influence many schismatics returned to the Patriarchal Church, and his death was the occasion of great popular demonstrations of veneration and affection.

Prince P. M. Volkonsky, 'La Reconstitution du patriarcat en Russie. Mgr Tykhon, patriarche de Moscou et de toute la Russie' in *É.O.*, xx (1921), pp. 195–219. M. d'Herbigny, S.J., *Après la mort du patriarche Tykhon*. Les patriarcats de Constantinople et de Moscou. Projets anglo-orthodoxes de Concile Œcuménique, Grecs et Russes en Europe et en Amérique (Orientalia Christiana [Analecta] xv, vol. iv, No. 2; 1925). E. Goudal, 'Les Églises russes. Origines.—Situation actuelle' in *É.O.*, xxvii (1928), pp. 45–67. A. Wuyts, S.J., *Le Patriarcat russe au concile de Moscou de 1917–1918* (Orientalia Christiana Analecta, cxxix; 1941). M. Spinka, *The Church in Soviet Russia* (New York–London, 1956).

TILLEMONT, LOUIS SÉBASTIEN LE NAIN DE (1637–98), French Church historian. He was educated at *Port-Royal under P. *Nicole, and early developed a taste for history, beginning research work at the age of 18. Leaving Port-Royal in 1656, in 1661 he entered the seminary of Beauvais, but was not ordained priest till 1676. He then returned to Port-Royal, but had to leave it in 1679 and retired to his estate at Tillemont, nr. Paris. Though of *Jansenist leanings, he did not take part in the controversy, but divided his time between his studies and works of piety. His fame as an ecclesiastical historian rests on his *Mémoires pour servir à l'histoire ecclésiastique des six premiers siècles* (16 vols., 1693–1712), a work of enormous erudition, following the development of the Church from the beginnings of Christianity to the year 513. Its narrative consists almost entirely of patristic material, linked together by a minimum of connecting text, with questions of chronology, authorship, &c., relegated to the learned critical notes appended to each volume. For comprehensiveness the work has never been surpassed, though its lack of elegance in style and arrangement has prevented it from finding a wider public. Tillemont also wrote a separate treatise on the history of the Emperors and other princes during those same centuries (6 vols., 1690–1738). His materials for a Life of St. *Louis were not published until 1847–1851 (6 vols.).

[M. Tronchai, Tillemont's secretary,] *Idée de la vie et de l'esprit de Mr. Le Nain de Tillemont* (Nancy, 1706); repr., with *Réflexions de M. Le Nain de Tillemont sur divers sujets de morale* (Cologne, 1711). Bremond, iv (1920), pp. 258–80. A. Momigliano, 'La formazione della moderna storiographia sull' impero romano', sect. 2, in *Rivista storica italiana*, Ser. v, i (1936), pp. 38–44, with reff. G. Bardy in *D.T.C.*, xv (pt. 1; 1946), cols. 1029–33, s.v.

TILLICH, PAUL (b. 1886), Protestant theologian. The son of a *Lutheran pastor, he studied at Berlin, Tübingen and Halle (1904–1908). During the First World War he served as an army chaplain. In 1924 he became professor of theology at Marburg, in 1925 at the Technical Hochschule at Dresden, and in 1929 professor of philosophy at Frankfurt. Compelled by his connexion with the Religious Socialists to leave Germany in 1933, he settled in the U.S.A. where he was appointed professor of philosophical theology at the *Union Theological Seminary, New York. In 1940 he became an American national. His thought has been much influenced by K. *Barth and *Existentialism; and he is recognized as one of the leading contemporary exponents of Protestantism.

Tillich is a prolific writer. Among the more considerable of his works are *Ideen zur einer Theologie der Kultur* (1921), *Das System der Wissenschaften* (1923), *Kirche und Kultur* (1924), *Die religiöse Lage der Gegenwart* (1926, Eng. trans. 1932); *The Interpretation of History* (1936), *The Protestant Era* (Chicago, 1948), and *The Shaking of the Foundations* (sermons; New York, 1948; S.C.M., 1949); the most important is prob. his *Systematic Theology* (2 vols., 1951–1957). He is also the author of innumerable essays. In 1955 he became Professor at Harvard Divinity School.

C. W. Kegley–R. W. Bretall (edd.), *The Theology of Paul Tillich* (New York, 1952), with bibl. V. A. Demant, 'A Theologian on Historical Existence' in *Christendom*, vii, No. 28 (Oxford, Dec., 1937); R. H. Daubney, 'A Preface to Paul Tillich' in *C.Q.R.*, cl (1950), pp. 1–36.

TILLOTSON, JOHN (1630–94), Abp. of *Canterbury. He was educated at, and later Fellow of, Clare Hall, Cambridge. In 1661 he was present at the *Savoy Conference, as a watcher on the Nonconformist side. In 1688 he helped the *Seven Bishops to draw up their reasons for refusing to read the *Declaration of Indulgence of *James II. In 1689 he was appointed Dean of *St. Paul's, and in the same year became a member of the commission for revising the BCP and the *Canons. He wished to be rid of the *Athanasian Creed and held *Zwinglian doctrines about the *Eucharist. The advocates of the policy of comprehension for Nonconformists proposed him in 1689 as *Prolocutor of the Lower House of Convocation, but he was heavily defeated. In 1691, with some reluctance through the circumstances of W. *Sancroft's deposition, he accepted the see of Canterbury. His archepiscopate was undistinguished. His policy was dictated by hatred of the RC Church and a desire to include all Protestant dissenters other than *Unitarians in the C of E. A famous preacher, he was a pattern on which the 18th cent. divines modelled their sermons. He was the first married Abp. of Canterbury since M. *Parker (d. 1575).

Sermons, ed. R. Barker (14 vols., 1695–1704), and as *Works*, ed. with life by T. Birch (3 vols., 1752). *The Golden Book of Tillotson*. Selection ed. by J. *Moffatt (1926). A. Gordon in *D.N.B.*, lvi (1898), pp. 392–8.

TIMOTHY, St. St. *Paul's companion on his Second Missionary Journey and later one of his most intimate friends and the addressee of two of his epp. A native of Lystra, he was the son of a mixed marriage between a Jewess, Eunice, and a heathen, and was circumcised by St. Paul (Acts 16. 3) in order to placate the Jews. Among the missions with which the Apostle entrusted him were that to the *Thessalonians to encourage them under persecution (1 Thess. 3. 2) and that to *Corinth to confirm the converts in the faith (1 Cor. 4. 17). He afterwards was together with St. Paul in *Rome (Col. 1. 1, Philem. 1. 1, Phil. 1. 1) and became his representative at *Ephesus (1 Tim. 1. 3) and, acc. to *Eusebius, the first bishop of that city. The 4th cent. *Acta S. Timothei*, of which

there has been some confirmation from recent excavations, narrate his martyrdom on 22 Jan. 97 at the hands of the pagans when he opposed the 'Katagogia', the licentious festivities of Diana. His supposed relics were translated to *Constantinople in 356. Feast day, 24 Jan.; in the Greek and Syrian Churches, 22 Jan.

Gk. text of *Acta* ed. H. Usener (Bonn. diss. [1877]). R. A. *Lipsius, *Die apokryphen Apostelgeschichten und Apostellegenden*, ii (pt. 2; 1884), pp. 372–400, with further notes in Ergänzungsheft (1890), p. 86 f. W. Michaelis, *Die Gefangenschaft des Paulus in Ephesus und das Itinerar des Timotheus* (Neutestamentliche Forschungen, Reihe 1, Hft. iii; 1925). A. *Jülicher in *P.R.E.* (ed. 3), xix (1907), pp. 781–8, s.v. 'Timotheus, der Apostelschüler'; R. A. Falconer in *D.A.C.*, ii (1918), p. 582 f., s.v.; E. Fascher in *P.W.*, Zweite Reihe, vi (pt. 2; 1937), cols. 1342–54, s.v. 'Timotheus (20)'. See also introductions to commentaries cited in following entry, and commentaries to Acts, &c.

TIMOTHY AND TITUS, Epistles to. The term '*Pastoral Epistles' (q.v.), under which these three epp. of St. Paul are generally known, dates from the 18th cent., having probably been first used by the German theologian, Paul Anton, in lectures delivered at Halle in 1726–7. They were written at a period in St. Paul's life not covered by the account given in Acts, and presuppose a release from his first imprisonment and further missionary activities. The First to Timothy was sent from Macedonia, that to Titus while on a journey to Nicopolis, and the Second to Timothy from another imprisonment in Rome, shortly before his death. They were probably all written during the last year of his life.

The chief subjects dealt with in these Epistles are the appointment and duties of Church ministers and certain doctrinal novelties. In 1 Tim. St. Paul, after exhorting his disciple to deal firmly with the innovators (1), orders the institution of public prayers and defines the respective functions of men and women within the life of the community (2). The necessary qualities of bishops and deacons having been set out in detail (3), St. Paul returns to the suppression of false teaching (4), gives instructions for the enrolment of widows and the rule of elders (5), and concludes with various moral exhortations. In 2 Tim. the Apostle encourages his disciple in hardships and difficulties (1–2. 13), telling him to avoid useless discussions with false teachers (2. 15–26) and reminding him that in the last days impostors will abound (3), against whom he must stand firm (4. 1–8). The ep. ends with personal news and requests. The Ep. to Titus differs little in point of content from the other two Pastorals. It deals first with the qualities required in the elders (1), goes on to define the duties of various classes of society such as old men, old women, slaves, &c. (2), and finally sums up the Christian virtues and warns against indulging in vain questionings.

The mention of false teachers in the epp. has given rise to many explanations. Very probably the errors envisaged were Judaizing speculations on genealogies and the Law as found in pseudepigraphical writings such as the Book of *Jubilees. The Pastorals are esp.

valuable for the light they shed on contemporary Church organization and discipline, which they show still in a fluctuating state. The 'bishops' (ἐπίσκοποι) have not yet the monarchical position of the time of St. *Ignatius, and are frequently also called 'elders' (πρεσβύτεροι), whereas the term 'deacon' (διάκονος) seems to mean only 'helper, assistant' and not yet a definite grade in the order of the ministry.

Since F. D. E. *Schleiermacher (1807) and F. C. *Baur (1835) the authenticity of the Pastorals has been frequently denied by NT critics, though their Pauline authorship had been unquestionably received from the time of St. *Irenaeus and *Tertullian. The chief arguments brought against them are that they cannot be fitted into the framework of St. Paul's life as known from Acts, and their difference of vocabulary from that of the other Pauline letters. In spite of this, however, Pauline elements are so evident that a theory was formed by E. *Renan, followed by A. *Harnack, J. *Moffatt, P. N. Harrison, and others, acc. to which genuine Pauline notes are incorporated in the epp. in order to give them Apostolic authority. Thus P. N. Harrison finds five such fragments (2 Tim. 1. 16–18, 3. 10 f., 4. 1, 2a, 5b, 6–8, 18b, 19, 21b, 22a; 4. 13–15, 20, 21a; 4. 16–18; 4. 9–12, 22b; Tit. 3. 12–15); but scholars differ as to what these authentic parts are.

The Epp. were the subject of commentaries by St. John *Chrysostom (PG, lxii, 501–700), *Ambrosiaster (PL, xvii, 461–503), and J. *Calvin (Geneva, 1563; modern Eng. tr., 1856). Important modern commentaries include those of F. D. E. Schleiermacher (on 1 Tim., Berlin, 1807), F. C. Baur (Stuttgart, 1835), H. P. *Liddon (on 1 Tim., privately printed, 1877; publd., London, 1897), H. J. Holtzmann (Leipzig, 1880), B. *Weiss (K.E.K., N.T, xi, ed. 5, 1885), H. von Soden (Handcommentar zum Neuen Testament bearbeitet H. J. Holtzmann, &c., iii. 1, 1891, pp. 151–250), J. H. *Bernard (Camb. Bib., Gk. text, 1899), G. Wohlenberg (Kommentar zum Neuen Testament ed. T. *Zahn, xiii; Leipzig, 1906), M. *Dibelius (Hb. N.T., iii, pt. 2, 1913, pp. 133–222), E. F. Brown (West. Comm., 1917), R. St. J. Parry (Cambridge, 1920), W. *Lock (I.C.C., 1924), E. F. Scott (Moff. Comm., 1936), R. Falconer (Oxford, 1937), C. Spicq, O.P. (Études bibliques, 1947), with detailed bibl., A. Boudou, S.J. (Verbum Salutis, xv; Paris, 1950), E. K. Simpson (London, 1954), and C. K. Barrett (Oxford, 1963). J. B. *Lightfoot, Biblical Essays (1893), pp. 397–418 ('The Date of the Pastoral Epistles'). T. Zahn, Einleitung in das Neue Testament, i (1899), pp. 398–489 (Eng. tr., ii, 1909, pp. 1–133). P. N. Harrison, The Problem of the Pastoral Epistles (1921), with full bibl., pp. 179–84; W. Michaelis, Pastoralbriefe und Gefangenschaftsbriefe. Zur Echtheitsfrage der Pastoralbriefe (Neutestamentliche Forschungen, Reihe 1, Hft. vi; 1930). W. Lock in H.D.B., iv (1902), pp. 743–9, s.v.; A. Médebeille in D.T.C., xv (pt. 1; 1946), cols. 1036–1121, s.v. 'Timothée et Tite (Épîtres à)'.

TIMOTHY (d. 517), Patr. of *Constantinople. He was in charge of the cathedral ornaments of Constantinople till 511 when, on the deposition of Macedonius II, the Emp. Anastasius I made him patriarch. After some initial hesitation, he became a strong defender of the *Monophysite doctrine and in 512 provoked a riot through adding to the '*Trisagion' the Monophysite formula 'Who wast crucified for us'. At a synod in 515 he formally condemned the Chalcedonian teaching and afterwards worked in conjunction with *Severus of Antioch. The regular use of the *Nicene Creed in the Liturgy at Constantinople is ascribed by

*Theodore the Lector to Timothy; it had probably been introduced earlier at Antioch by *Peter the Fuller.

The Gk. text of his work Περὶ τῶν προσερχομένων τῇ ἁγίᾳ ἐκκλησίᾳ ('De Receptione Haereticorum') was first pr. by J. Meursius, Varii Divini, i (Leyden, 1619), pp. 111–30; also pr., with Lat. tr., by J. B. *Cotelier, Ecclesiae Graecae Monumenta, iii (Paris, 1686), pp. 377–424, repr. in J. P. Migne, PG, lxxxvi (1), 11–74. É. Amann in D.T.C., xv (pt. 1; 1946), col. 1139 f., s.v. 'Timothée de Constantinople'.

TIMOTHY AELURUS (d. 477), *Monophysite Patriarch of Alexandria. His name 'Aelurus' (Gk. αἴλουρος, 'weasel') was given him by his opponents because of his small stature. He became patriarch in 457 after his predecessor Proterius had been lynched by the mob, but being unacceptable to the majority of bishops, was banished by the Emp. Leo I in 460. During his exile he wrote much to propagate Monophysitism, but also anathematized *Eutyches because, unlike Eutyches, he held that the Body of Christ was of the same substance as other human bodies. He was recalled to Alexandria by the Emp. Basiliscus in 475, where he died before another decree of banishment by the Emp. *Zeno could be carried out. Of his writings three letters are extant in a Syriac translation. A collection of treatises and letters against the Council of *Chalcedon, also in Syriac, goes under his name, as well as an Armenian version of a similar work. In the *Coptic Church he is venerated as a saint, his feast day being 31 July.

Sermo and fragments ascribed to him by A. *Mai are printed among the works of Timothy (III) of Alexandria in J. P. Migne, PG, lxxxvi (1), 269–76. Bardenhewer, iv, 79–82. H. G. Opitz in P.W., Zweite Reihe, vi (pt. 2; 1937), cols. 1355–7, s.v. 'Timotheos (24)'.

TINDAL, MATTHEW (1655–1733), one of the leading *Deists. Educated at Lincoln and Exeter colleges, Oxford, he was elected a Fellow of All Souls in 1678. For a short time in *James II's reign he became a RC, but returned to the C of E at Easter, 1688. He called himself a 'Christian Deist', and his book, The Rights of the Christian Church asserted against the Romish and all other Priests who claim an Independent Power over it (1706), written in defence of a rationalistic and *Erastian position, created a considerable stir. Author, publisher, and printer were prosecuted, but four editions were printed. Tindal then issued A Defence of the Rights of the Christian Church (1709), which was burned, together with H. *Sacheverell's sermon, in 1710 by the common hangman, by order of the House of Commons. It was denounced for several years, as it was thought to undermine the Christian religion. He replied at the end of his life by Christianity as old as the Creation, or the Gospel a Republication of the Religion of Nature (1730), which became the 'Bible' of Deism. It sought to show that, common to all rational creatures 'there's a law of nature or reason, absolutely perfect, eternal, and unchangeable; and that the design of the Gospel was not to add to, or take from this law', but to free men from superstition.

E. C[urll], *Memoirs of the Life and Writings of Matthew Tindal . . . with a History of the Controversies wherein he was engaged* (1733); *The Religious, Rational, and Moral Conduct of Matthew Tindal . . . in a letter to a Friend* by a Member of All Souls College (1735). J. Leland, *A View of the Principal Deistical Writers that have Appeared in England in the Last and Present Century,* i (1754), pp. 144–76. L. Stephen, *History of English Thought in the Eighteenth Century,* i (1876), pp. 134–63. G. C. Joyce in *H.E.R.E.,* iv (1911), pp. 535–7, s.v. 'Deism'. L. Stephen in *D.N.B.,* lvi (1898), pp. 403–5.

TINDAL, WILLIAM. See *Tyndale, William.*

TINTERN ABBEY, in Monmouthshire. It was founded by Walter de Clare in 1131 for French *Cistercian monks from the Abbey of L'Aumône. The magnificent abbey church was built in the late 13th cent., but the subsequent history of the monastery was uneventful, and when it was dissolved in 1536 there were only 13 monks left. The ruins of Tintern Abbey, in scenery which inspired W. *Wordsworth to one of his finest poems, are among the most beautiful in England. The roofless church, with its delicately traced windows, shows the transitional Gothic style to perfection. The rest of the abbey has, for the most part, disappeared.

W. *Dugdale, **Monasticon Anglicanum,* v (ed. 1825), pp. 265–73. [C. Heath,] *Descriptive Accounts of Tintern Abbey: Selected from the Most Esteemed Writers on that Beautiful Ruin: with . . . a correct translation of the charters of the Earls of Pembroke and Norfolk, whose ancestors founded the Monastery in the Year 1131* (1798). On the daughter house of the same name in Co. Wexford, see P. H. Hore, *History of the Town and County of Wexford* (1901), pp. 3–151.

TIPPET (Lat., *liripipium*). A broad black scarf worn by Anglican clergy in choir over the surplice. It may be of silk if its wearer is a graduate, but in other cases is of stuff. It was evolved, it seems, from the long ends of the hood which hung down from the shoulders in front, and was not originally confined to the clergy. There has been much dispute as to what vesture was denoted by the word in the 16th and 17th cents., some antiquarians holding that it was then used of a garment identical with the ordinary graduate's hood, except in the matter of shape and material. Can. 74 of 1604 orders all the clergy to wear the tippet as part of their ordinary apparel, and can. 58 allows non-graduates to wear it as a substitute for the hood. The custom of confining it to dignitaries and chaplains is without authority.

TISCHENDORF, CONSTANTIN (1815–1874), NT textual critic. From 1859 he was nominally professor of theology at Leipzig. Between 1840 and 1860 he visited many libraries in Europe and the Near East in search of MSS., the most famous of his finds being his dramatic discovery of the *Codex Sinaiticus (q.v.). Besides careful editions of several important Biblical MSS. (e.g. of *Codex Ephraemi, 1843–5; *Codex Amiatinus, 1850; Codex Claromontanus, 1852), he published between 1841 and 1869 eight editions of the Greek text of the NT with a full critical

apparatus of the variant readings. The last edition of this work, the '*octava critica maior*', remains by reason of the abundance of its data the standard book of reference for the text of the NT.

J. E. Volbeding, *Constantin Tischendorf in seiner fünfundzwanzigjährigen schriftstellerischen Wirksamkeit* (1862). C. R. Gregory, 'De Tischendorfio' prefixed to the *editio octava critica maior* of Tischendorf's Gk. N.T., iii (1894), pp. 3–22, with list of his works. L. Schneller (son-in-law), *Tischendorf-Erinnerungen.* Merkwürdige Geschichte einer verlorenen Handschrift (1927; Eng. tr., 1939 [popular]). G. Bertheau in *P.R.E.* (ed. 3), xix (1907), pp. 788–97, s.v., with bibl.

TISSOT, JAMES JOSEPH JACQUES (1836–1902), French Bible illustrator. Having studied art at Paris, he became a painter of fashionable women. When the Commune seized power in 1871 he fled to England. Here he became known by his caricatures for *Vanity Fair* and as a portrait and genre painter. Later he returned to Paris where his art underwent a complete change owing to an experience of conversion, and henceforth he devoted himself to the illustration of the Life of Christ for which purpose he made comprehensive studies in Palestine. His *Vie de Notre-Seigneur Jésus-Christ* (1896) is a series of *c.* 350 water-colours, representing the scenes of the Gospel in a fresh and unconventional style which abandons the traditional types. It was followed by an unfinished sequence of illustrations to the OT which, however, are inferior in quality to the earlier work.

An edition of the OT (Gen.–Job, with some additions) in Fr., incorporating Tissot's illustrations, was publd., with preface by A. D. Sertillanges, 2 vols., Paris, 1904; with text in English, 2 vols., London, 1904. J. Laver, '*Vulgar Society*'. The Romantic Career of James Tissot, 1836–1902 (1936). Unsigned art. in *Allgemeines Lexikon der bildenden Künstler von der Antike bis zur Gegenwart* begründet U. Thieme–F. Becker, xxxiii (ed. H. Vollmer, 1939), pp. 218–220, s.v., with detailed bibl.

TITHES. The clergy were maintained in early times by receiving one-quarter of the offerings of the laity, the remaining three-quarters going to the upkeep of the fabric of the church, to the relief of the poor, and to the bishop. At a date which cannot be precisely determined this system was superseded by tithes, the payment of a tenth part of all the produce of lands. At first the owner of the land might pay the tithe to what clergy he pleased. Probably they were usually paid to the bishop, who distributed them among his clergy. But, as the parochial system developed, the tithes of each parish were allotted to its own 'parson', often by the action of the lord of the manor, who in this way provided the endowment necessary for securing the right to build a church on his estate. In time this allocation of tithes became the general law. In England we find the payment of tithes strongly enjoined by a synod held in 786, and enforced by law in 900. Tithes were of three sorts, 'praedial', of the fruits of the ground, 'personal', of the profits of labour, and 'mixed', arising partly of the ground and partly of the industry of man. They were further divided into 'great' and 'small', the 'great' being the tithes of the major crops (wheat, oats, &c.) and the 'small' the tithes of minor produce (lambs, chicken, &c.).

The incumbent, when entitled to the whole tithes of a parish, was termed a '*rector'. By the system of appropriations the tithes of a parish appropriated belonged to the 'appropriator'. He was compelled to provide and endow a clergyman to reside on the parish and perform the ecclesiastical duties. The endowment of this clergyman, called the 'vicar', usually took the form of a portion of the glebe, together with the small tithes, because they were troublesome to collect. If there were both a rector (or appropriator) and a vicar, the rector normally had the great tithes and the vicar the small.

Originally and in theory all land in England was subject to tithe, but for varying reasons many lands were discharged from payment. The most frequent method of payment came to be by composition, or a fixed annual money payment in lieu of tithe. This became so general that the amount of the payment was fixed by legislation, dependent on the varying price of corn. In 1918, however, an Act of Parliament stabilized the value of tithe for seven years, irrespective of any fluctuation in the price of corn, and in 1925 steps were taken to extinguish all tithe rent charges by ordering that of the £105 which by the 1918 Act every £100 of tithe was worth, £4 : 10s. should be paid into a sinking fund, which by the end of a period of eighty-five years would have accumulated sufficient funds to redeem the whole of the tithe rent charges in the country. This process was accelerated in 1936 by a further Act which immediately extinguished all tithe rent charges and authorized the Treasury to issue in return tithe redemption stock to such an amount as would yield interest equivalent to the rent charge. In return an annuity was charged upon the land, for a period of sixty years, of £91 11s. 2d. for every £100 of tithe rent charge on agricultural land, and of £105 on non-agricultural land. These annuities are collected by the Commissioners of Inland Revenue. They are a state tax on certain lands, which after sixty years will disappear. Thus there is now in England no such thing as tithe.

The payment of tithe has been held to be enjoined not merely by ecclesiastical law, but by natural and divine law—by natural law because it is essential to the maintenance of religion, which is enjoined by the natural law; by divine law because the payment of tithes is specifically ordered in the OT, and implied in the NT (e.g., Deut. 14. 22; Mt. 10. 10, 23. 23; 1 Cor. 9. 7). But it is also held, that though tithes must be paid by natural and divine law, it is a matter for the Church to determine by whom they shall be paid and of what they shall consist. Hence it would appear that the natural and divine law is not broken if tithes as such are abolished, provided that there be some offerings or oblations in their stead sufficient to maintain the practice of religion.

That these arguments have lost most of their strength in the secularized society of modern times is reflected in the recent legislation mentioned above.

The classical study is J. *Selden, The History of Tithes (1618). On the practical aspects of the older legislation, J. Godolphin, Repertorium Canonicum: or An Abridgement of the Ecclesiastical Laws of this Realm (ed. 2, London, 1680), pp. 344–464, and R. *Phillimore, The Ecclesiastical Law of the Church of England (ed. 2 by W. G. F. Phillimore), ii (1895), pp. 1147–237; and for the modern legislation, H. W. Cripps, A Practical Treatise on the Law Relating to the Church and Clergy (ed. 8 by K. M. Macmorran, 1937), pp. 450–99, and R. W. Frazier, The Tithe Act, 1936, and the Rules Thereunder (1936). H. W. Clarke, A History of Tithes (1891). E. W. Watson in D.E.C.H., pp. 592–7, s.v.; ed. 3, with supplement (1948), pp. 607–12.

TITIAN (c. 1476–1576), Tiziano Vecellio or Vecelli, Venetian painter. He was a pupil of Gentile and Giovanni Bellini and in his early years much influenced by Giorgione, though he cultivated a more monumental style. To this period belongs what is perhaps his most religious work, the Tribute Money (c. 1515), esp. famous for the face of Christ with its impressive blending of sweetness and majesty. After Bellini's death (1515), Titian became the acknowledged head of the Venetian school and was connected with many European monarchs, e.g. *Charles V and Francis I. One of his most famous paintings of this time is the Assumption (Venice), a monumental work of high craftsmanship but without deeper religious feeling, whereas the Ecce Homo (1543), the Crowning with Thorns (Louvre), and the stirring St. Peter Martyr (destroyed in 1867), are fraught with tragic emotion. In his later years his compositions are remarkable for an increasing devotion to dramatic effects. His St. Sebastian (Leningrad), the Entombment (Louvre; another at the Prado), and the Annunciation (Venice) are all vivid scenes with much beauty in colouring and form, though lacking the interior spirit characteristic of medieval religious painting.

Reproductions of his paintings (in black and white), with introd. by O. Fischel (Klassiker der Kunst, iii; 1904; ed. 5, enlarged [c. 1947]). H. Tietze, Tizian. Leben und Werk (2 vols., Phaidon Press, Vienna, 1936, vol. 2 being plates with reprod., some in colour; this latter vol. also publd., with introd. in English, Phaidon Press, London, 1937). Other modern studies include those by J. A. Crowe–G. B. Cavalcaselle (2 vols., London, 1877), G. Gronau (Berlin, 1900; Eng. tr., 1904), C. Ricketts (London, 1910), and W. Suida (Rome, 1933). L. Hourticq, La Jeunesse de Titien (1919). T. Hetzer in Allgemeines Lexikon der bildenden Künstler von der Antike bis zur Gegenwart begründet von U. Thieme–F. Becker, xxxiv (ed. H. Vollmer; 1940), pp. 158–72, s.v. 'Vecellio, Tiziano', with detailed bibl. A. Morassi in E.C., xii (1954), cols. 167–76, s.v. 'Tiziano, Vecellio'.

TITLE (Lat. titulus). At least since the 3rd cent., this term has been used to designate the older churches of *Rome. As several clergy were attached to each titulus, all of whom were provided with revenues for their personal maintenance, allocation to a 'Title' at ordination came to mean the provision of maintenance, which otherwise was the personal responsibility of the Pope or ordaining bishop. From this, the term has acquired the general sense of a definite spiritual charge or office with guarantee of maintenance, without appointment to which a bishop may not ordinarily ordain a man, unless he is prepared personally to support him until such time as he can prefer him to a 'Living'. The C of E rule concerning Titles is contained in can. 33 of 1604.

J. P. Kirsch, *Die römischen Titelkirchen im Altertum* (Studien zur Geschichte und Kultur des Altertums, ix, Hft. 1 and 2, 1918); L. *Duchesne, 'Les Titres presbytéraux et les diaconies' in *Mélanges d'Archéologie et d'Histoire*, vii (1887), pp. 217-43.

TITUS, St. A disciple of St. *Paul who calls him 'my true child after a common faith' (Tit. 1. 4). He first appears on the journey to the Apostles' Council at *Jerusalem (Gal. 2. 1) and was later sent on difficult missions to *Corinth (2 Cor. 8. 6, 16 f., 23) and left behind in Crete to organize the Church there. Thence the Apostle ordered him to meet him at Nicopolis in Epirus (Tit. 3. 12) and afterwards sent him to Dalmatia (2 Tim. 4. 10). He is believed to have returned to Crete, of which, acc. to *Eusebius, he was the first bishop. His body was believed to rest at Gortyna, the ancient capital of the island, whence the head was brought to *Venice after the invasion of the Saracens in 823, where it has since been venerated in St. Mark's. Feast day in the Greek and Syrian Churches, 25 Aug.; in the Latin Church, 4 Jan. In the RC Church, the feast was transferred to 6 Feb. by *Pius IX to avoid coincidence with the Octave of the Holy Innocents.

The main literature is to be found in commentaries to the Epistle addressed to Titus, cited s.v. *Timothy and Titus, Epistles to*. R. A. *Lipsius, *Die apokryphen Apostelgeschichten und Apostellegenden*, ii (pt. 2; 1884), pp. 401–6. A. von *Harnack, 'Der apokryphe Brief des Paulusschülers Titus "De Dispositione Sanctimonii"' in *Sb.* (Berl.), 1925, pp. 180–213. A. *Jülicher in *P.R.E.* (ed. 3), xix (1907), pp. 798–800, s.v.; R. A. Falconer in *D.A.C.*, ii (1918), p. 595 f., s.v.; E. Fascher in *P.W.*, Zweite Reihe, vi (pt. 2; 1937), cols. 1579–86, s.v. 'Titus (4)'.

TITUS, Epistle to St. See *Timothy and Titus, Epistles to*.

TITUS (4th cent.), Bp. of Bostra. Little is known of his life except that he was involved in a controversy with the Emp. *Julian, who ordered his expulsion, and that he took part in a synod at *Antioch, in 363, which sent a letter to the Emp. *Jovian recognizing the Nicene Creed. His name has survived through his authorship of a voluminous treatise against the *Manichaeans. In its first part he gives the Christian solution of the problem of evil based on the ideas of Divine Providence and human free will; in the second he defends the OT and denounces the Manichaean falsifications of the NT. The first half of the treatise is preserved in the Greek original, but the whole now exists only in a Syriac version. Both were edited by P. A. de *Lagarde in 1859, who recognized in the Greek text an interpolation which has been identified as a work of *Serapion of Thmuis. Titus is also the author of a work on St. Luke in the form of homilies, fragments of which have survived in later *catenae*.

Gk. text first publd. by J. *Basnage, *Thesaurus Monumentorum Ecclesiasticorum et Historicorum*, i (Antwerp, 1725), pp. 56–162; repr. from A. *Gallandi in J. P. Migne, *PG*, xviii, 1065–204; crit. ed. by P. A. de Lagarde (Berlin, 1859). Syriac text ed. id. (ib., 1859). J. Sickenberger, *Titus von Bostra. Studien zu dessen Lukashomilien* (T.U., xxi, Hft. 1; 1901). R. P. Casey, 'The Text of the Anti-Manichaean Writings of Titus of Bostra and Serapion of Thmuis' in *H.T.R.*, xxi (1928), pp. 97–111. Bardenhewer, iii, 269–273; Altaner (ed. 1950), p. 268. R. P. Casey in *P.W.*, Zweite Reihe, vi (pt. 2; 1937), cols. 1586–91, s.v. 'Titus (5) v. Bostra'; É. Amann in *D.T.C.*, xv (pt. 1; 1946), col. 1143 f., s.v. 'Tite de Bostra'.

TOBIT, Book of. One of the apocryphal books of the OT. It relates the story of Tobit, a pious Jew of the captivity of Nineveh, who, in pursuit of his good works became poor and blind in his old age. He prayed to God to deliver him, and, remembering a debt due to him from a friend in Media, sent his son Tobias there with a companion who later revealed himself as the angel *Raphael. After rescuing his kinswoman, Sarah, from the power of a demon with the assistance of the angel, who also recovered the debt and finally helped to cure old Tobit of his blindness, Tobias married her. Tobias's dog (5. 16) is the only dog favourably mentioned in Scripture.

The chief purpose of the story is to inculcate that God is faithful to such Jews as are faithful to Him and to recommend virtue, esp. almsgiving and the burial of the dead. The book exists in Greek, Latin, Syriac, Aramaic, and Hebrew versions. Its original language was Aramaic or Hebrew, and its date probably *c.* 200 B.C. Until modern times it was generally regarded as historical, but many now consider it a piece of folklore, the story of the grateful dead, and find traces of Persian demonology. The more conservative view would admit an historical kernel, enriched by additions and legendary traits. Owing to its intrinsic charm Tobit has been one of the most popular books of the Bible. It was frequently quoted by the Fathers from the time of St. *Polycarp (Phil. 10), and was a favourite of Christian art, its principal scenes being represented already in the Catacombs.

The Gk. text is pr. in edd. of the Septuagint (q.v.); for edd. of the Lat. text see bibl. to *Old Latin Versions*, also A. Neubauer, cited below; Hebr. text ed. S. *Münster (Basle, 1542); Hebr. and Syriac text also in B. *Walton's London Polyglott of 1657; Aramaic text ed. A. Neubauer (Oxford, 1878). Modern commentaries include those of D. C. Simpson in R. H. *Charles (ed.), *The Apocrypha and Pseudepigrapha of the Old Testament*, i (1913), pp. 174–241, A. Schulte (Biblische Studien, xix, Hft. 2; 1914) and M. M. Schumpp, O.P. (Exegetisches Handbuch zum Alten Testament begründet J. Nikel, xi; Münster, i.W., 1933). J. Müller, *Beiträge zur Erklärung und Kritik des Buches Tobit* (Beiheft zur *Z.A.T.W.*, xiii, 1908, pp. 1–53). D. C. Simpson, 'The Chief Recensions of the Book of Tobit' in *J.T.S.*, xiv (1913), pp. 516–30. E. *Schürer, *Geschichte des jüdischen Volkes im Zeitalter Jesu Christi*, iii (ed. 4; 1908), pp. 237–47; R. H. Pfeiffer, *History of New Testament Times with an Introduction to the Apocrypha* (New York, 1949; London, [1954]), pp. 258–84, with bibl. p. 534. A. Clamer in *D.T.C.*, xv (pt. 1; 1946), cols. 1153–76, s.v. 'Tobie (Livre de)', with further reff.

TOC H. A Christian fellowship embracing men of all ages over 16, of all classes, denominations, and political opinions. Its Women's Association covers the same ground among women. It originated in Talbot House, a soldiers' club opened in 1915 at Poperinghe in Belgium under the Rev. P. B. Clayton, M.C., a C of E chaplain, and named after Lt. Gilbert Talbot, son of E. S. *Talbot (q.v.). In 1920 Toc H (the army signallers' method of pronouncing T H) was refounded in London and spread rapidly through Britain and English-speaking countries. It was incorporated by Royal Charter, 14 Dec. 1922. It is organized in branches and has a number of residential houses ('Marks'). The close fellowship finds its natural outlet in a great variety of Christian social service.

P. T. B. Clayton, *Tales of Talbot House*. Everyman's Club in Poperinghe and Ypres, 1915–1918 (1919); P. W. Monie, *Toc H under Weigh* [1927]. M. Harcourt, *Tubby Clayton*. A Personal Saga (1953).

TOKEN, Communion. See *Communion Token.*

TOLAND, JOHN (1670–1722), *Deistical writer. He was a RC Irishman who became a Protestant at the age of 16. In 1687 he entered Glasgow university, and after spending some time in English Protestant families, probably as tutor, was sent to *Leyden where he studied Divinity under F. Spanheim. In 1694 he went to Oxford, where in 1695 he finished his *Christianity not Mysterious* (publd. 1696). In it he asserted that neither God Himself nor His revelation are above the comprehension of human reason, and attributed the mysteries of Christianity to the intrusion of pagan conceptions and the machinations of priestcraft. The work roused great indignation and was condemned and caused to be burned by the Irish Parliament in 1697, and Toland fled from Ireland, whither he had returned, to England to avoid imprisonment. In 1698 he published a *Life of Milton*. A passage of this book, which was believed to cast doubt on the authenticity of the NT, caused great scandal, and Toland replied in his *Amyntor, or a Defence of Milton's Life* (1699), stating that the passage in question referred to the apocryphal writings, of which he gave a remarkable list. In 1701 he defended the Act of Succession in his book *Anglia Libera*, which won him the favour of the electress Sophia, and during the next years he visited several times the courts at Hanover and Berlin. He was admitted to the intimate circle of the Prussian Queen Sophie Charlotte to whom he addressed several letters (*Letters to Serena*, 1704), one of which became famous through its attempt to prove that motion is essential to matter. From 1707 to 1710 he travelled on the Continent and, after returning to England, wrote many polemical pamphlets, directed esp. against *High churchmen and Jacobites. In 1718 appeared his *Nazarenus*, a treatise on the *Ebionites, and in 1720 *Tetradymus*, a collection of essays dealing, among other things, with the natural explanation of Scripture miracles. In the same year he published his *Pantheisticon*, a kind of pagan liturgy in imitation of Christian services, in which he expounded a *pantheistic creed, the term

'pantheist' having first been used by him in 1705. Though not an original thinker, Toland was one of the most influential representatives of Deism, and his books largely contributed to later discussions on the relations between reason and revelation and the genuineness of the NT books.

A Collection of Several Pieces of Mr. John Toland, now first published from his Original Manuscripts (2 vols., 1726), with Memoir of his Life and Writings [by P. Desmaizeaux], vol. i, pp. iii–xcii. *An Historical Account of the Life and Writings of the late Eminently Famous Mr. John Toland by one of his most intimate friends* (1722). G. Berthold, *John Toland und der Monismus der Gegenwart* (1876); A. Lantoine, *Un Précurseur de la franc-maçonnerie: John Toland, 1670–1722* (1927). L. Stephen, *History of English Thought in the Eighteenth Century*, i (1876), pp. 101–11, and passim; E. Sayous, *Les Déistes anglais et le christianisme principalement depuis Toland jusqu'à Chubb, 1696–1738* (1882), ch. ii, pp. 47–75. G. C. Joyce in *H.E.R.E.*, iv (1911), p. 534 f., s.v. 'Deism'. L. Stephen in *D.N.B.*, lvi (1898), pp. 438–42.

TOLEDO, Councils of. Some 30 ecclesiastical Councils took place at Toledo (*Concilia Toletana*) between the 5th and 16th cents., the canons of the earlier of which are preserved in the *Hispana Collection. They include the 'First' (400), directed against *Priscillianism; the 'Third' (589), when King Reccared formally renounced the *Arian Creed; the 'Fourth' (633) under St. *Isidore of Seville, which issued important liturgical regulations; and the 'Twelfth' (681), which established the primacy of the See of Toledo in the Spanish Church. For the liturgy of Toledo, see *Mozarabic Rite.*

Best text of the canons of the earlier Councils (1–17) in *Collectio Canonum Ecclesiae Hispanae ex Probatissimis ac Pervetustis Codicibus nunc primum in lucem edita a Publica Matritensi Bibliotheca* [ed. F. A. Gonzalez] (Madrid, 1808), cols. 321–598, repr. in J. P. Migne, *PL*, lxxxiv, 327–562. Eng. tr. of some of the canons, with introd., in E. H. Landon, *A Manual of the Councils of the Holy Church* (ed. 2 by P. Landon), ii [1893], pp. 151–69. On the first, third, fourth, and twelfth councils, Hefele–Leclercq, ii (pt. 1; 1908), pp. 122–5; iii (pt. 1; 1909), pp. 222–8, 279–81, and 540–6. J. A. de Aldama, S.J., *El Símbolo Toledano I* (Analecta Gregoriana, vii; 1934); J. Madoz, S.J., 'Le Symbole du IVe concile de Tolède' in *R.H.E.*, xxxiv (1938), pp. 5–20. A. Michel in *D.T.C.*, xv (pt. 1; 1946), cols. 1176–208, s.v. 'Tolède (Conciles de)'. See also works cited under *Spain, Christianity in.*

TOLEDO, Rite of. An alternative name for the *Mozarabic Rite (q.v.), the use of which now survives in one of the chapels of Toledo cathedral.

TOLERATI (Lat., 'tolerated persons'). The technical name in *canon law for those *excommunicate persons with whom the faithful are permitted to have intercourse of a non-religious kind. They are thus distinguished from the *vitandi.

TOLERATION. Religious toleration is the leaving undisturbed of those whose faith and practice is other than one's own. It is generally held to merit commendation when it issues from respect for the natural rights of the human person to freedom of belief, but condemnation when it is due to mere indifference.

Christianity, which claims to be the only true religion, has always been dogmatically intolerant. Dissent ('heresy') within its own ranks has been anathematized time and again in the history of the Church. St. *Augustine went so far as to demand corporal punishment for heretics and schismatics; and this became the normal procedure in the Middle Ages when, owing to the intimate connexion between Church and state, Catholic and citizen were virtually synonymous terms, and the heretic was thus considered a revolutionary endangering the foundations of society. The regular penalty in the Middle Ages was death.

The Renaissance, with its religious indifference, and the Reformation, by its revolt against the authority of the Papacy, established the conditions for the future development of the practice of toleration. The Reformers themselves, however, e.g. M. *Luther, T. *Beza, and esp. J. *Calvin, were as intolerant to dissentients as the RC Church, and the maxim of the Peace of *Augsburg (1555) ('cuius regio eius religio') which recognized only one religion, either Catholicism or Lutheranism, in a state to the exclusion of all others, was virtually the principle adopted also in England under *Elizabeth I in favour of the C of E. In the 17th cent. the most notable instances of practical toleration were the colonies of Maryland, founded by Lord Baltimore in 1632 for persecuted Catholics, which offered asylum also to Protestants, and of Rhode Island, founded by Roger *Williams (q.v.).

In England the advocates of religious toleration long continued to be in a minority, but it was demanded esp. by *Baptists, *Congregationalists, and *Quakers, and defended by J. *Milton in his *Areopagitica* (to the exclusion, however, of RCs) and by such divines as W. *Chillingworth, J. *Hales, and J. *Taylor and the *Latitudinarians. It virtually became the policy of the state by the Act of Toleration (q.v.) of 1689, which excluded only RCs and Unitarians. In the same year J. *Locke published his first *Letter concerning Toleration*, to be followed by three others, denying the state all right of interference in religious matters and demanding toleration for all except RCs and atheists.

In the 18th cent. the prevalent religious indifferentism of the *Aufklärung* led to the demand of equal liberty for all religions, and the view of life, enunciated by such writers as J.-J. *Rousseau and *Voltaire in France and G. E. *Lessing in Germany and proclaimed by the American Bill of Rights of 1776, became general. Thence it made its way into the ideas of the French Revolution of 1789, and in the 19th cent. became the accepted policy of most European states. It has, however, become apparent that the principle of freedom for religion is easily changed into that of freedom from religion, and thus the modern problem is not so much one of toleration for other religious convictions as that of the preservation of religion in view of the general indifference and secularization of life.

TOLERATION, Edict of (313). See *Milan, Edict of*.

TOLERATION ACT. The Act of 1689 (1 Will. & Mary, c. 18) granting freedom of worship to dissenters on certain prescribed conditions. Its real purpose was to unite all Protestants under William III against the deposed RC *James II. It exempted from the penalties of existing statutes against conventicles persons who took the Oaths of *Allegiance and Supremacy (though Dissenters continued to be barred from civil office until 1828; see *Corporation* and *Test Acts*) and relieved dissenting ministers from religious disabilities provided that, in addition to the oaths, they signed the *Thirty-nine Articles (except two requiring Infant Baptism). *Quakers might make an *affirmation instead of taking the oaths. Roman Catholics and disbelievers in the Trinity did not benefit under this Act.

Text in Gee–Hardy, pp. 654–64 (No. cxxiii).

TOLSTOY, LEO (1828–1910), Russian novelist and social reformer. From 1845 to 1847 he studied at the university of Kazan, but did not take a degree. Under the influence of J.-J. *Rousseau's writings he became an enthusiast for social reform, anxious to relieve the miseries of the serfs. In 1851 he joined the Russian army. His *Tales from Sebastopol* (1855) at once attracted literary notice. In this period he also began the serial publication of his autobiographical fragments (1852–6), describing the mental struggles of his youth. He left the army in 1855 and from 1857 to 1861 travelled in Germany, France, Italy, Switzerland, and England, studying educational methods and writing in support of reforms; and he established schools on his estates in which the children were given the utmost liberty. In 1862 he married Sophia Behrs, by whom he had 13 children. In the next years there followed his two most famous novels, *War and Peace* (1864–9) and *Anna Karenina* (1873–7). After 1877 he renounced his literary ambitions, believing them to be incompatible with his deepest convictions. All his later works were on moral and religious subjects and his output was considerable. He was deeply influenced by a close study of A. *Schopenhauer's writings and became very critical of the formalism of the Orthodox Church, which eventually excommunicated him in 1901. He sought to live in great simplicity, renouncing his property and the happiness of family life, engaging in manual labour and striving ceaselessly for the relief of social distress during the great famine of 1891–2. In 1895 he actively took up the cause of the persecuted *Doukhobors, writing in their defence his last great novel *Resurrection* (1899).

Tolstoy's religious teaching in its latest phase claimed to be a following of the Gospels when the miraculous and other irrelevancies are set aside. The key was to be found in the *Sermon on the Mount, which could be resolved into five wholly new commandments, viz.: (1) the suppression of anger, even righteous indignation, and living in peace with all men; (2) the complete exclusion of sex relationships outside marriage; (3) the wrongfulness of oaths; (4) non-resistance to evil and the consequent refusal to act as judges or police officers; (5) unreserved love of one's enemies. These, and not the doctrines of the Atonement, the Resurrection, the Trinity and personal immortality, were the central tenets of the Christian message. He did not accept the divinity of Christ and he believed that man's greatest good consisted in the fulfilment of God's will that men should love one another. The increase of love in individuals would do away with the evils of the existing order and lead to the establishment of the kingdom of God in the world.

Eng. tr. of his works ed. L. Wiener (24 vols., London-Boston, Mass., 1904-5, incl. life by the translator in vol. xxiv, pp. 205-317, and bibl. to date of works in Eng., Germ., and Fr., pp. 403-35; but includes some works not by Tolstoy); better Eng. tr., mainly by A. Maude–Louise Maude (Tolstoy Centenary Edition, ed. A. Maude, 21 vols., London, 1928-37). Life by A. Maude, 2 vols., London, 1908-10; abridged ed., ib., 1918; full Life also repr. in Centenary ed., vols. i-ii. Many of his works have also been translated separately and are available in popular edd.; several are included in 'The World's Classics'. C. A. Behrs's *Recollections of Count Tolstoy* were tr. into Eng. by C. E. Turner (London, 1893); the *Reminiscences of Tolstoy* by his son, Count Ilya Tolstoy, were tr. into Eng. by G. Calderon (ib., 1914); a number of articles on Tolstoy by members of his family collected by R. Fülöp–Miller were tr. into Eng. under the title *Family Views of Tolstoy*, ed. A. Maude (1926). A life, written with Tolstoy's co-operation, by P. Birukoff was publd. in 4 vols., Moscow, 1906-23; Eng. tr. of vol. i, 1906; an abridged version was tr. into Eng. in 1911. There is a wide range of studies on Tolstoy; those available in English include the works of C. E. Turner (London, 1888), C. H. Perris (ib., 1898), R. Rolland (Paris, 1911; Eng. tr., 1911), G. R. Noyes (London, 1919), J. Lavrin (ib., 1924), A. I. Nazaroff (ib., 1930, with bibl.), D. Leon (ib., 1944, also with bibl.), and E. J. Simmons (Boston, 1946; London, 1949).

TOME OF DAMASUS. See *Fides Damasi*.

TOME OF LEO, The. The letter sent by Pope *Leo I (*Ep.* 28) to *Flavian, Patr. of *Constantinople, on 13 June 449, also called Epistola Dogmatica. Basing himself on the teaching of the Fathers, esp. *Tertullian and St. *Augustine, St. Leo expounds with remarkable clarity, precision, and vigour the Christological doctrine of the Latin Church. Acc. to it Jesus Christ is One Person, viz. the Divine Word, in whom are two natures, the Divine and the human, permanently united, though unconfused and unmixed. Each of these exercises its own particular faculties, but within the unity of the Person. Hence follows the '*communicatio idiomatum', so that it can truly be said that the Son of Man descended from heaven, and that the Son of God was crucified. The letter, which was directed esp. against the heresy of *Eutyches, was given formal authority by the Council of *Chalcedon (451) as the classical statement of the Catholic doctrine of the Incarnation: 'Peter has spoken through Leo'. Later it was constantly used in the controversies with the Monophysites.

Text in P. and H. *Ballerini's ed. of Leo, i (1753), cols. 793-838 repr. J. P. Migne, *PL*, liv, 755-82. Crit. ed. in *A.C.O.*, II, 2, i (1932), pp. 24-33; also by C. Silva-Tarouca, S.J. (Rome, 1932), Gk. text in *A.C.O.*, II, 1, i (1933), pp.

10-20; on this cf. G. L. Prestige, 'The Greek Translation of the *Tome* of St. Leo', in *J.T.S.*, xxxi (1929-30), p. 183 f. P. Mouterde, S.J., 'Les Versions syriaques du tome de saint Léon' in *Mélanges de l'Université Saint-Joseph, Beyrouth*, xvi (1932), pp. 121-65, with Syr. text pp. 146-65.

TOMMASI, GIUSEPPE MARIA (1649-1713), liturgical scholar. The eldest son of the Duke of Palma, he resigned his claims as an heir in favour of his younger brother in 1664 and entered the Order of the *Theatines where he was professed in 1666. After studying at Messina, Rome, and Palermo, he was ordained priest in 1673 and henceforth devoted himself completely to Biblical, patristic, and above all liturgical studies, leading at the same time a life of great austerity. Of his numerous publications, many of them under the pseudonym of 'J. M. Carus', his editions of the ancient *Sacramentaries and *Missals are esp. valuable. They include the *Codices Sacramentorum Nongentis Annis Vetustiores* (1680) which comprises Gallican books and contains the *editiones principes* of the '*Missale Gothicum' and the '*Missale Francorum', the *Responsalia et Antiphonaria Romanae Ecclesiae a Sancto Gregorio Magno disposita* (1686), and *Antiqui Libri Missarum Romanae Ecclesiae* (1691), as well as several editions of the Psalter and of Biblical texts used in the liturgy of the first ten centuries. A project for a reformed and much simplified *Breviary was probably written in 1706 (ed. J. W. Legg in the publications of the *Church Historical Society, 1904). Tommasi was made cardinal in 1712 and beatified in 1803. Commemoration, 24 Mar.

An edition of his works was begun by J. Bianchini (Rome, 1741; vol. i (in parts) only publd.); new ed. by A. F. Vezzozi, Theatine (7 vols., ib., 1747-54); continued with his *Institutiones Theologicae*, ed. id., 4 vols., ib., 1769), with life prefixed to vol. i. *Opuscoli inediti*, ed. G. *Mercati (S.T., xv; 1905). Lives by A. Borromeo (Venice, 1713) and D. Bernino (Rome, 1714). H. *Leclercq, O.S.B., in *D.A.C.L.*, xv (1953), col. 2428 f., s.v.

TONGUES, Gift of. See *Glossolalia*.

TONSURE. The shaving of part or all of the hair of the head, prescribed in the RC Church by canon law (cf. *CIC*, 136) for all clerics except in places where, as in England and the U.S.A., it is not in accordance with popular usage. The cutting of the hair, a religious ceremony of many E. peoples, became a generally received custom in 4th and 5th cent. monasticism and thence was introduced into the W. as the form of admission to the clerical state, distinct from Minor Orders, in the 6th and 7th cents. There were three styles of tonsure: the W., leaving a fringe of hair round the head, often regarded as symbolizing the crown of thorns; the E., shaving the whole head; and the Celtic, in which the hair is shaven in front of a line running from ear to ear. Acc. to modern RC custom, dating from the 16th cent., the secular clergy shave only a small round space at the crown of the head, whereas the tonsure of the religious is usually much larger, varying in size in the several orders. In the rite of tonsure by which a lay-

man is admitted to the clerical state, the bishop or his delegate cuts some hair at five places of the head of the candidate and invests him with the surplice.

Classical study by G. Chamillard, *De Corona, Tonsura et Habitu Clericorum Locuples cum veterum tum recentiorum Canonum, Pontificarumque Constitutionum etc. Collectio* (Paris, 1659). E. *Martène, *De Antiquis Ecclesiae Ritibus*, ii (Rouen, 1700), pp. 294–301 (Lib. I, cap. viii, art. 7; 'De Tonsura Clericali'); id., *De Antiquis Monachorum Ritibus* (Lyons, 1690), pp. 723–35 (Lib. V, cap. vii: 'De Tonsura et Rasura Fratrum'). There is a useful appendix by J. Smith to his ed. of *Bede, *H.E.* (Cambridge, 1722), pp. 705–15 (Appendix No. IXb., 'De Tonsura Clericorum'), repr. in J. P. Migne, *PL*, xcv, 327–32. The best modern study is that of P. Gobillot, 'Sur la tonsure chrétienne et ses prétendues origines païennes' in *R.H.E.*, xxi (1925), pp. 399–451. F. E. Warren in *D.C.A.*, ii (1880), p. 1989 f., s.v.; C. Neudecker–A. Hauck in *P.R.E.* (ed. 3), xix (1907), pp. 836–9, s.v. 'Tonsur'; J. A. MacCulloch in *H.E.R.E.*, xii (1921), p. 385 f., s.v.; A. Michel in *D.T.C.*, xiv (pt. 1; 1946), cols. 1228–35, s.v.; H. *Leclercq, O.S.B., in *D.A.C.L.*, xv (pt. 2; 1953), cols. 2430–43, s.v. See also commentaries on the *Codex Juris Canonici*, ad loc.

TOPHET. A place or object in the valley of Hinnom, immediately to the south-west of *Jerusalem, where human sacrifices were burned by idolatrous Israelites in the worship of Moloch (2 Kgs. 23. 10, Jer. 7. 31, &c.).

TOPLADY, AUGUSTUS MONTAGUE (1740–78), author and hymn writer. He was a native of Farnham, Surrey, and educated at Westminster School and Trinity College, *Dublin. He was ordained priest in 1764 and in 1768 became vicar of Broad Hembury in Devonshire. At first he fell under J. *Wesley's influence, but in 1758 he was converted to extreme *Calvinist opinions and henceforward bitterly attacked Wesley. His position was set out in his most important prose work, *The Historic Proof of the Doctrinal Calvinism of the Church of England* (1774), in which he developed his subject from the *Apostolic Fathers downwards. He also wrote on the same subject *The Church of England Vindicated from the Charge of *Arminianism* (2 vols., 1769). Toplady, however, is remembered esp. for his hymns, of which he published several collections. His well-known 'Rock of Ages' first appeared in the *Gospel Magazine* in 1775; though the tradition that he wrote it while sheltering in the Mendips from a storm is without foundation.

Works publd. 6 vols., London, 1794, with memoir [by W. Row] in vol. i, pp. 1–125; new ed., 6 vols., ib., 1825. Separate ed. of his *Hymns and Sacred Poems on a Variety of Divine Subjects* (London, 1860). Life by T. Wright ('The Lives of British Hymnwriters', ii; 1911). H. L. Bennett in *D.N.B.*, lvii (1899), pp. 57–9.

TORAH (Heb. תּוֹרָה). Term in use, esp among the Jews, for the Mosaic Law embodied in the Pentateuch which regulated the religious, moral, and social life of Israel. The word probably comes from a root meaning 'to throw', *torah* being the decision obtained by the priest through the casting of the sacred lot. Although the word could be used of the teaching of the Prophets (e.g. Is. 8. 16), of the precepts of parents (e.g. Prov. 1. 8, 4. 2), and of the utterances of wise men (e.g. Prov. 13. 14),

for all of which the OT writers characteristically claim a Divine origin, it was pre-eminently the function of the priests to give 'torah' or instruction in the Will of God (e.g. Jer. 18. 18), and it was for their failure in, or misuse of, this office that the Prophets denounced them (e.g. Mic. 3. 11, Zeph. 3. 4). By a natural development, 'torah' came to be used also of written collections of such priestly decisions (e.g. Hos. 8. 12), and so of the Pentateuch as containing the Mosaic legislation, as well as of individual laws within that legislation (e.g. Lev. 7. 1).

TORGAU ARTICLES, The. A memorandum summarizing the disciplinary and ceremonial demands of the four Reformers, M. *Luther, P. *Melanchthon, J. *Bugenhagen, and J. *Jonas. It was compiled in Mar.-Apr. 1530, and handed in by the Kurfürst John to the Diet of *Augsburg. The name is misleading, as no gathering at Torgau of the four theologians mentioned ever took place.

Text in *Corpus Reformatorum*, xxvi (1858), pp. 171–200. T. Brieger, 'Die Torgauer Artikel' in *Kirchengeschichtliche Studien Hermann Reuter zum 70. Geburtstag gewidmet* (1888), pp. 265–320. See also bibl. to *Augsburg Confession*.

TORQUEMADA, JUAN DE (1388–1468), 'Turrecremata', Spanish theologian. In 1403 he entered the *Dominican Order. In 1417 he accompanied his provincial to the Council of *Constance and from there went to Paris to finish his studies. Having been prior of the houses of his order at Valladolid and Toledo, he was made master of the Sacred Palace by *Eugenius IV in 1431 and Papal theologian at the Council of *Basle in 1433. He took an active part in the negotiations with the Bohemians and with the Greeks on the question of reunion, was created Cardinal of St. Sixtus in 1439, and till the end of his life had a decisive share in ecclesiastical Papal policy. His most important works are the 'Commentarii in Decretum Gratiani' (publd. 1519) on canon law, and the 'Summa de Ecclesia' (publd. 1489), a systematic treatise on the Church, defending the infallibility and plenitude of the spiritual power of the Pope, but taking only a moderate view of his temporal power. An edition of his treatise *De Veritate Conceptionis B. Virginis* (1547; rejecting the *Immaculate Conception) was issued by E. B. *Pusey in 1869.

S. Lederer, *Der spanische Cardinal Johann von Torquemada, sein Leben und seine Schriften* (1879). J. F. Stockmann, *Joannis de Turrecremata, O.P., Vita eiusque Doctrina de Corpore Christi Mystico* (Bologna, 1951). V. Beltrán de Heredia, O.P., 'Coleccion de documentos inéditos para illustrar la vida del Cardenal Juan de Torquemada, O.P.' in *Archivum Fratrum Praedicatorum*, vii (1937), pp. 210–45. R. Creytens, O.P., 'Raphaël de Pornaxio, O.P., auteur du "De Potestate Papae et Concilii Generalis" faussement attribué à Jean de Torquemada, O.P.', ibid. xiii (1943), pp. 108–37. Quétif–Échard, i, pp. 837–43. A. Michels in *D.T.C.*, xv (pt. 1; 1946), cols. 1235–9.

TORQUEMADA, TOMÁS DE (1420–98), Spanish Grand Inquisitor. A nephew of Juan de *Torquemada, he entered the Dominican Order at Valladolid at an early age. He subsequently became prior at Segovia, an office he retained for 22 years, and confessor to *Ferdinand and *Isabella of Spain. As Christianity in the country was at that time much troubled by the great numbers of Jewish Marranos and Mohammedan Moriscos, *Sixtus IV, in 1478, permitted the monarchs to establish the *Inquisition in their realm. After being made assistant inquisitor in 1482, Torquemada was appointed Grand Inquisitor in 1483. He set up tribunals in various cities and in 1484 laid down directions for the guidance of Inquisitors which he later expanded in his chief work 'Compilación de las Instrucciones de la santa Inquisición' (publd. 1576). His methods, which have often been accused of inhuman cruelty, were in accordance with the customs of his time which included torture in its normal judicial procedure. The number of burnings during his term of office, formerly greatly exaggerated, is now usually given as about 2,000. Torquemada was also chiefly responsible for the expulsion of the Jews from Spain in 1492 as an alternative to their being baptized.

E. de Molènes (ed.), *Documents inédits*. Torquemada et l'inquisition, la Jurisprudence du saint-office, l'Enfant de la Guardia, le Cœur et l'Hostie, Sortilèges et vénéfices, Sentences et autodafés, l'Expulsion des Juifs, les Procès à la mort (1897). R. Sabatini, *Torquemada and the Spanish Inquisition* (1913); E. Lucka, *Torquemada und die spanische Inquisition* [1926]; T. Hope, *Torquemada, Scourge of the Jews* (1939). Quétif–Échard, i, 892 f.

TORRES, FRANCISCO, also 'Turrianus' (c. 1504–84), patristic scholar and RC controversialist. After studying at Salamanca he went to Rome, where he became a well-known controversial author. From 1562 to 1563 he was at the Council of *Trent as Papal theologian. In 1563 he brought out the first edition of the '*Apostolic Constitutions', attributing them to St. *Clement of Rome. In 1566 he entered the *Jesuit Order, and later was appointed professor at the Roman College, where he was one of the scholars entrusted with the revision of the official *Vulgate. He sought to defend the authenticity of the '*Apostolic Canons', the *False Decretals, and the 80 *Nicene Canons, all of them spurious, as well as that of the (genuine) Acts of the Sixth and Seventh General Councils. He was a very voluminous writer, but he had little critical sense. In his controversial writings he upheld the *Immaculate Conception, the superiority of the Pope over Councils, and the Divine origin of episcopal authority.

Sommervogel, viii (1898), cols. 113–26. J. P. Grausem, S.J., in *D.T.C.*, xv (pt. 1; 1946), col. 1239 f., s.v., with bibl.

TOSEFTA (Heb., 'supplement'). A collection of early Jewish tradition (also *baraita*, i.e. 'outside') of the same character as and contemporary with, but not incorporated in, the *Mishnah (q.v.). Like the Mishnah it has six main divisions, each of which is subdivided into tractates. It contains a much larger proportion of *Haggadic elements than the Mishnah.

Eng. trans. of the Tractates *Sanhedrin* (S.P.C.K., 1919), *Berakoth* (id., 1921) and *Sukkah* (id., 1925), in each case with the corresponding Mishnah Tractate. J. Z. Lauterbach in *J.E.*, xii (1906), pp. 206–8.

TOTAL DEPRAVITY. A term in common use esp. in *Calvinism to express the extreme wretchedness of man's condition as the result of the *Fall. It emphasizes the belief that this result was not a mere loss or *deprivation* of a supernatural endowment possessed by unfallen man, but a radical corruption or *depravation* of his whole nature, so that apart from Christ he can do nothing whatever pleasing to God. Even his reason has been radically vitiated, so that, acc. to Calvinism, all natural knowledge of God (such as obtains in the system of St. *Thomas Aquinas) is held to be impossible.

TOTAL IMMERSION. See *Submersion*.

TOTEMISM. A phenomenon partly social, partly magical (or, acc. to some, religious), found among primitive peoples, by which the members of a tribe believe themselves to be associated with and named after a species of animal or plant. It is commonly held that the totem has a holy and sacrosanct nature and is therefore an object of worship, and that its flesh is untouchable save at a tribal feast where the eponymous animal is ritually slain and eaten by the members of the tribe who thus identify themselves with their god. A theory has been put forward that totemism is an early phase of all religion, and it has been suggested that the prevalence of animal and plant names among Canaanite place-names and the fact that the tribes of Israel were descended from Leah ('wild cow') and Rachel ('ewe') indicate a totemic ancestry for the religion of the Hebrews and therefore for Christianity; but the evidence for this thesis is altogether too slender to give it any show of probability.

J. G. Frazer, *Totemism and Exogamy*. A Treatise on Certain Early Forms of Superstition and Society (4 vols., 1910; Supplementary vol., *Totemica*, 1937); A. Lang, *The Secret of the Totem* (1905); W. R. *Smith, *Lectures on the Religion of the Semites*. The Fundamental Institutions (1889; ed. 3 rev. by S. A. *Cook, 1927). E. S. Hartland in *H.E.R.E.*, xii (1921), pp. 393–407, s.v.

TOUCHING FOR THE KING'S EVIL. See *King's Evil, Touching for the*.

TOWER OF BABEL. See *Babel, Tower of*.

TRACT (Liturgical). The chant sung or recited at Mass on certain penitential days instead of the *Alleluia. It is already mentioned in the oldest Roman *Ordines. It was originally the Psalm chanted after the second Lesson, but this was later supplanted by the Alleluia, though preserved on days of penance and mourning. It differs from the *Gradual in that it is chanted without a responsory (Lat. *tractim*, 'straight through'), but acc. to recent scholars its name is probably not derived from this, as formerly assumed, but is connected with the Greek εἱρμός ('train', 'series'), a technical term of Greek musical theory denoting a typical tune by which the several parts of a hymn are joined together. Some tracts such as that of the First Sunday in *Lent and of *Palm Sunday have preserved almost the whole Psalm, whereas most others have been reduced to a few verses. The tract is said on the Sundays from Septuagesima till Easter and on the Mondays, Wednesdays, and Fridays of Lent; also on the Saturdays in Ember Weeks (when it replaces the Gradual), and in Masses for the Dead.

Jungmann, *M.S.*, i (ed. 1949), p. 531 f.; Eng. tr., i (1951), p. 430 f.).

TRACT (Propagandist) (Lat. *tractare*, 'to treat of the matter'). A pamphlet, usually issued with a religious or moral purpose. Its early history is obscure, but many medieval works, e.g. the lesser English works of J. *Wycliffe, come under this heading. The religious controversies of the 16th and 17th cents. stimulated the production of tracts which often (e.g. under the Commonwealth) reached vast proportions. The abusive *Marprelate Tracts* (1588) are an instance from the age of *Elizabeth I. The *Bangorian Controversy also inspired a number of tracts. On the *Tracts for the Times* (1833–45) see foll. entry. Various tract societies have been formed, among them the *S.P.C.K. (1698) and the *Religious Tract Society (1799).

TRACTARIANISM. A name for the earlier stages of the *Oxford Movement, derived from the *Tracts for the Times* issued under its aegis. The purpose of the tracts was to disseminate Church principles 'against Popery and Dissent'. The first, written by J. H. *Newman and published with two others on 9 Sept. 1833, was a 4-page leaflet entitled 'Thoughts on the Ministerial Commission respectfully addressed to the Clergy' and containing a defence of the Apostolic Succession. Others followed rapidly and on 21 Dec. appeared E. B. *Pusey's first tract ('Thoughts on the Benefits of the System of Fasting enjoined by our Church'; No. 18 of the series). The other tract writers included J. *Keble, J. W. Bowden (1798–1844), A. P. *Perceval, R. H. *Froude, C. *Marriott, and I. *Williams. They secured a wide circulation, and their influence, as the first public utterances of the Oxford Movement, was enormous. Their form gradually changed from brief leaflets to learned treatises. On 25 Jan. 1841 Newman's famous Tract 90 ('Remarks on Certain Passages in the Thirty-Nine Articles') appeared; the storm which it provoked brought the series to an end.

The Tracts were issued in bound volumes as follows: vol. i, numbers 1–46 (1834); ii, numbers 47–70 (1836); iii, numbers 71–77 (1836); iv, numbers 78–82 (1838); v, numbers 83–88 (1840). For the reputed authors of the Tracts see the lists by H. P. *Liddon in *Life of Edward Bouverie Pusey*, iii (1894), Appendix, pp. 473–80, and J. W. *Burgon, *Lives of Twelve Good Men* (1891), Appendix D, pp. 475–6. See also bibl. on *Oxford Movement*.

TRACTATUS ORIGENIS (Lat. 'Tractates of Origen'). A collection of twenty Homilies

on the Scriptures, nineteen of them on OT texts, first publd. in 1900 by P. *Batiffol and A. *Wilmart, O.S.B. In the 10th cent. Orléans MS. and the 12th cent. St.-Omer MS. where they are preserved, they are ascribed to *Origen. Batiffol held that their Gk. originals were really the work of Origen; but it is now generally agreed, following G. *Morin's earlier view, that they were the work of *Gregory, Bp. of Elvira (q.v.).

P. Batiffol–A. Wilmart, O.S.B., *Tractatus Origenis de Libris SS. Scripturarum* (Paris, 1900). G. Morin, O.S.B., 'Les Nouveaux *Tractatus Origenis* et l'héritage littéraire de l'évêque espagnol Grégoire d'Illiberis' in *Revue d'Histoire et de Littérature religieuses*, v (1900), pp. 145–61. Hugo Koch, 'Zu Gregors von Elvira Schrifttum und Quellen' in *Z.K.G.*, li (1932), pp. 238–72. Altaner (ed. 1950), p. 324.

TRACTORIA. Originally a 'letter of summons' (from Lat. *trahere*, 'to convey', i.e. by the *cursus publicus* or postal service), the word was applied also to letters containing the decisions of Councils. It is used esp. of the (lost) 'Epistola Tractoria' of *Zosimus (417–418), in which that Pope reversed his previous support of *Pelagianism.

The chief fragments of Zosimus's *Ep. Tractoria* are preserved in *Augustine, *Ep.* 190. 23, and in *Prosper of Aquitaine, *Auctoritates*, cap. 9; repr. with others in J. P. Migne, *PL*, xx. 693–5.

TRADITIO SYMBOLI (Lat., the 'delivery' or 'handing over of the Creed'). During early times candidates for baptism, who were mainly adults, were subjected to a long course of instruction before admission to the sacrament. Their training was both practical and doctrinal, as in modern 'Confirmation classes', and the latter part of it consisted of explanations of the Creed. This was the 'delivery' or *traditio*, made by the teacher to the candidates, who thus 'received the creed' into their own keeping. At their baptism they were required to recite and profess the Creed, thus 'returning it' (*redditio symboli*) to the presiding bishop.

TRADITION. In the early Christian Fathers, tradition (παράδοσις, *traditio*) means the revelation made by God and delivered by Him to His faithful people through the mouth of His prophets and apostles. It does not mean something 'handed down' but something 'handed over'. Similarly in the NT the word, or its corresponding verb, is applied equally to the betrayal of Christ by *Judas to the Jews, and to the delivery of Christian teaching by St. *Paul to his converts. The tradition was at first called 'apostolic', because delivered by the apostles to the Churches which they founded, and later also 'ecclesiastic', because delivered again in each generation by the Church's teachers to their people. Its substance was held to consist of the central facts and beliefs crystallized in the creeds of the great orthodox bishoprics. From the beginning of the 3rd cent. the tradition was sometimes expressly identified with the Gospel record contained in Scripture. The occasional references in early Christian literature to an 'unwritten tradition' left by the apostles appear to relate not to any body of information independent of Scripture, but to the evidence of primitive Christian institutions and customs which confirms Scriptural teaching.

In a more modern sense, tradition means the continuous stream of explanation and elucidation of the primitive faith, illustrating the way in which Christianity has been presented and understood in past ages. It is, that is, the accumulated wisdom of the past. Sometimes, again, it means simply customs and ideas which have grown up imperceptibly and been accepted more or less uncritically. All tradition in these modern senses needs to have its true value proved by the double test— (1) whether it is in accordance with the principles embodied in divine revelation, and (2) whether it can be justified by right reason.

In the Reformation era the relation of unwritten tradition to the Scriptural revelation was the subject of acute controversy between Protestants and Catholics. As against the Protestant notion of the sole-sufficiency of the Bible, the Council of *Trent (Sess. IV, 8 Apr. 1546) laid down that Scripture and tradition were to be received by the Church as of equal authority (*pari pietatis affectu ac reverentia*). An extreme expression of the view that the whole of Catholic tradition is embodied in the Papacy is the saying attributed to *Pius IX, *Sono la tradizione* ('I am tradition'). See also entry *Traditionalism*.

J. B. *Bossuet, *Défense de la tradition et des saints pères* (2 vols., 1763); J. B. *Franzelin, *Tractatus de Divina Traditione et Scriptura* (Rome, 1870); J. Bainvel, *De Magisterio Vivo et Traditione* (Paris, 1905); M. Winkler, *Der Traditionsbegriff des Urchristentums bis Tertullian* (1897). G. L. Prestige, 'Tradition' in *Fathers and Heretics* (1940), pp. 1-46; W. *Sanday and N. P. *Williams, *Form and Content in the Christian Tradition*. A Friendly Discussion (1916); C. H. *Turner, *Catholic and Apostolic* (1931). A. M. *Fairbairn (*Congregationalist), *Catholicism: Roman and Anglican* (1899); C. J. Cadoux, *Catholicism and Christianity*. A Vindication of Progressive Protestantism (1928); A. Deneffe, S.J., *Der Traditionsbegriff* (Münsterische Beiträge zur Theologie, Heft xviii, 1931); O. Cullmann, *The Early Church* (1956), pp. 55–99.

TRADITION OF THE INSTRUMENTS.
See *Instruments, Tradition of the*.

TRADITIONALISM.
In its strict sense a theory proposed by a group of 19th cent. RC thinkers, acc. to which all metaphysical, moral, and religious knowledge is based on a primitive revelation of God to man handed down in an unbroken tradition. Denying to human reason the power of attaining by itself to any truths, esp. those of natural theology, it makes an act of faith in a revealed tradition the origin of all knowledge. It was historically a reaction from 18th cent. rationalism in the direction of the other extreme and flourished chiefly in France and Belgium. Among its advocates were L. G. A. de Bonald (1754–1840) and F. R. de *Lamennais and of esp. influence was the latter's *Essai sur l'indifférence en matière de religion* (4 vols., 1817–23) with its doctrine of the 'sens commun'. To restore belief to the modern world the Traditionalists aimed at removing it from discussion by individual reason and at imposing it by the authority of the common consent of mankind, which, acc. to Lamennais, is invested with infallibility. Modified forms of the doctrine were held by L. E. M. Bautain (1796–1867), A. Bonnetty (1798-1879), and G. C. *Ubaghs (q.v.) and the philosophers of the Louvain school. Though the insistence on the social nature of man and on the importance of tradition in religion were orthodox elements in the teaching of Traditionalism, its fundamental distrust of human reason could not but eventually lead to scepticism. It was officially condemned by a number of decrees, and finally ruled out as a possible Catholic system by the constitution 'De fide catholica' at the *Vatican Council of 1870.

The word is also used less strictly by liberal theologians, usually with a more or less opprobrious *nuance*, of what they consider unduly conservative beliefs.

The condemnations of E. Bautin and A. Bonnetty are conveniently repr. in Denz.–Bann. (ed. 1952), pp. 451 f. (Nos. 1622–7) and 462 f. (Nos. 1649–52). J. Lupus, *Le Traditionalisme et le rationalisme examinés au point de vue de la philosophie et de la doctrine catholique* (3 vols., Liége, 1858). J. Henry, 'Le Traditionalisme et l'ontologisme à l'université de Louvain (1835–1865)' in *Annales de l'Institut Supérieur de Philosophie* [at Louvain], v (1924), pp. 41–149, with bibl. reff. G. M. Sauvage in *C.E.*, xv (1912), p. 13 f., s.v.; E. Basadonna in *E.C.*, xii (1954), cols. 395–7, s.v. 'Tradizionalismo'.

TRADITORS.
The name given in Africa in early times to Christians who surrendered the Scriptures when their possession was forbidden in the persecution of *Diocletian. The controversy between Catholics and *Donatists which followed the persecution was centred chiefly in the refusal of the Donatists to recognize *Caecilian, Bp. of Carthage, on the ground that he was consecrated by traditors.

TRADUCIANISM
(Lat. *tradux*, 'shoot', 'sprout'). The theory acc. to which the human soul is transmitted by the parents to the children. The term is sometimes restricted to the crudely materialistic view which asserts that this happens in the physical act of generation, and then distinguished from opinions, which refrain from dogmatizing on this point, collectively styled 'Generationism'. Traducianism was advocated by some of the Fathers, e.g. St. *Gregory of Nyssa and esp. *Tertullian in his 'De Anima' (chs. 23–41) in order to explain *Original Sin, and also by St. *Augustine, though he understood it as a spiritual generation. Pope Anastasius II condemned the theory in his ep. to the Gallican bishops (498). In the Middle Ages *Creationism (q.v.) was the almost universally accepted doctrine, but in the 19th cent. Traducianism was revived in a modified form by several RC theologians, e.g. A. *Rosmini, who argued that the parents generate a sensitive soul which God changes by illumination into a spiritual one. The theory in its crude form is incompatible with the spiritual nature of the soul, but even in the attenuated form of Generationism is widely held to be heretical.

A. Michel in *D.T.C.*, xv (part 1; 1946), cols. 1350–65.

TRAHERNE, THOMAS (c. 1636–74), English *Metaphysical poet and divine. Probably a native of Hereford, he entered Brasenose College, Oxford, in 1652, which he left after taking his degree in 1656. In 1657 he became rector of Credenhill, nr. Hereford, and in 1667 private chaplain to Sir Orlando Bridgman, Lord Keeper of the Seals, and 'minister' in the parish of Teddington. Only one work, *Roman Forgeries* (1673), a controversial treatise on forged documents of the RC Church, appeared before his death. His *Christian Ethics*, issued in 1675 and still almost unknown, is an eloquent description of Christian virtue, though sometimes over-subtle in discussing theological niceties. In 1699 a friend published a little devotional book of Traherne, *A Serious and Pathetical Contemplation of the Mercies of God*, but his poems, for which he is now famous, remained in MS. until they were publd. by B. Dobell in 1903. They were followed in 1908 by four *Centuries of Meditations*, a collection of reflections on ethics and religion. Traherne, who was an ardent admirer and constant reader of the *Neo-Platonist 'Hermes Trismegistos', is the least orthodox of the metaphysical poets. From his essentially optimistic and 'vitalistic' conception of experience, the elements of sin and suffering are almost entirely excluded. His poetry, remarkable for a penetrating sense of the glory of nature and childhood, is clearly pantheistic in feeling. Among his more famous poems are 'The Rapture' and 'An Hymn upon St. Bartholomew's Day'.

Poems ed. B. Dobell (London, 1903) and, with orig. spellings and further poems, by Gladys I. Wade (ib., 1932). *Centuries of Medidations*, also ed. B. Dobell (ib., 1908). Studies by G. E. Willett (Cambridge, 1919), [Hilda] Q. Iredale (Oxford, 1935) and Gladys I. Wade (Princeton, N.J., 1944). F. E. Hutchinson in *C.B.E.L.*, i, p. 462 f.

TRANSCENDENTALS. In *Scholastic philosophy, the transcendentals (*transcendentalia, transcendentia*) were those properties which belonged to all objects, whatever their nature. St. *Thomas Aquinas held that there were six: reality (*res*), being (*ens*), truth (*verum*), goodness (*bonum*), being something (*aliquid*), and unity (*unum*). They were so named on the ground that they 'transcended' the Aristotelian categories.

TRANSENNA (Lat., properly a 'net'). In ecclesiastical architecture, a wall, usually of marble, which is pierced with holes in a regular pattern. Apart from purely ornamental purposes, transennae were also used to surround the tomb of a martyr (e.g. in the confessio, and thus to enable the worshipper to see it, and sometimes also touch it, through the grating.

TRANSFIGURATION, The. The appearing of the Lord in glory during His earthly life, related in the first three Gospels (Mt. 17. 1–13, Mk. 9. 2–13, Lk. 9. 28–36), and alluded to in 2 Pet. 1. 16–18. This vision of our Lord, transfigured, with *Moses and *Elijah, was witnessed by Sts. *Peter, *James, and *John, and is described by the Evangelists as an historic event, with striking agreement as to the main outline and understandable differences in the details which they record. Tradition locates it on Mount Tabor, but many scholars prefer Mount Hermon, and some have even suggested the Mount of *Olives. The event was significant as showing the testimony of the Jewish Law and Prophets to the Messiahship of Christ, as furnishing a further Divine proclamation of our Lord's Sonship, and as foreshadowing His future glory. In the Calendar, the Feast of the Transfiguration is observed on 6 Aug. It originated in the E. Church, where it appears to have been at first a local and unofficial feast, but it had become widely adopted before A.D. 1000. In the W., where the feast was not introduced till a much later date, its general observance goes back to 1457 when *Callistus III ordered its universal celebration in commemoration of the victory gained over the Turks at Belgrade on 6 Aug. 1456.

L. P. Crawfurd, *The Transfiguration*. A Manifestation of God in Man (1912); G. H. Boobyer, *St. Mark and the Transfiguration Story* (1942); H. Riesenfeld, *Jésus transfiguré*. L'Arrière-plan du récit évangélique de la transfiguration de Notre-Seigneur (Acta Seminarii Neotestamentici Upsaliensis, xvi, 1947); A. M. Ramsey, *The Glory of God and the Transfiguration of Christ* (1949).

TRANSITORIUM. A prayer in the *Ambrosian Rite corresponding to the *Communion Anthem in the Roman Mass. It is apparently so named because the celebrant passes over (*transit*) to the south side of the altar to recite it.

TRANSLATION. In ecclesiastical contexts the word is used in various senses:

(1) The transference of the relics of a saint either from their original place of burial into an altar tomb or shrine, or from one shrine to another. The solemnities connected with it frequently gave rise to a new liturgical feast. Thus the translation of St. Thomas *Becket, observed on 7 July, commemorates the reburial of the saint's relics at *Canterbury on 7 July 1220.

(2) The transference to a later day of a feast with which a feast of higher rank coincides. Acc. to the reformed Breviary of *Pius X, it is only permitted for Doubles of the First and Second Class.

(3) In canon law the transference of a cleric from one ecclesiastical office to another. The translation of a bishop from one see to another was forbidden by the can. 15 of the Council of *Nicaea (325), but the decree was never rigorously adhered to, and in the Middle Ages the translation of bishops became one of the prerogatives of the Popes and the practice has continued down to modern times.

TRANSMIGRATION OF SOULS. See *Metempsychosis*.

TRANSUBSTANTIATION. In the theology of the *Eucharist, the conversion of the whole substance of the bread and wine into the whole substance of the Body and Blood of Christ, only the *accidents (i.e. the appearances of the bread and wine) remaining. The word was in widespread use in the later part of the 12th cent., and at the *Lateran Council of 1215 belief in Transubstantiation was defined as *de fide*; but the elaboration of the doctrine was not achieved till after the acceptance of the *Aristotelian metaphysics later in the 13th cent. when it found classical formulation in the teaching of St. *Thomas Aquinas. At the Council of *Trent (sess. xiii, cap. 4) the medieval doctrine was reaffirmed, but with a minimum of technical philosophical language. Since the 13th cent the E. Church has used the word μετουσίωσις to denote an essentially identical doctrine and has given it formal approval, e.g. at the Synod of *Jerusalem of 1672. See also *Declaration against Transubstantiation*.

TRAPPISTS. Popular name for the Reformed *Cistercians of the Strict Observance. This reform had been introduced by Abbot A. J. Le B. de *Rancé (q.v.) at *La Trappe in 1664, whose 'Réglement' was confirmed by *Innocent XI in 1678 and *Clement XI in 1705. The reform at first was restricted to La Trappe and two other monasteries, but the expulsion of the monks during the French Revolution led to Trappist foundations in many other countries not only of Europe but also in China, Japan, U.S.A., and elsewhere. During the 18th and 19th cents. several different observances developed which were united by *Leo XIII in 1893 and 1902, and their constitutions confirmed in 1925. The Cistercian abbey of Mount St. Bernard in Leicestershire, founded by A. M. P. *de Lisle, follows the Trappist reform, and there is a house of Trappist nuns at Stapehill in Dorset.

The chief characteristics of the order are the emphasis on liturgical worship, which, including Mass, Divine Office, Office of the BVM, and, on certain days, Office of the Dead, takes about seven hours, absolute silence with no allowance for recreation, and community life with no cells but a common dormitory. Fleshmeat, fish, and eggs are at all times forbidden. Apart from liturgical prayer and contemplation the monks devote themselves to manual, esp. agricultural, labour and to theological studies, but never to parish work. Their habit is white with a black scapular and cowl, that of the lay brothers brown. The women's branch of the Cistercian reform ('Trappistines') follows the same rules as the monks and its houses are usually under their direction.

E. de Mier, *Los Trapenses*. Apuntes históricos de la Trapa (Madrid, 1912). A. Le Bail, O.S.B., *L'Ordre de Cîteaux*. 'La Trappe' (Les Ordres religieux, 1924); C. Grolleau–G. Chastel, *L'Ordre de Cîteaux*. La Trappe (Les Grandes Ordres monastiques et instituts religieux, 1932). A. Limagne, *Les Trappistes en Chine* (Paris, 1911). F. L. Holmes, *The Voice of Trappist Silence* (New York, 1941). Y. Estienne, *Les Trappistines*. Cisterciennes de la stricte

observance (1937). Heimbucher, i, 363–73. E. M. Obrecht in *C.E.*, xv (1912), pp. 24–6, s.v., with reff. to earlier lit.

TRAVERS, WALTER (*c.* 1548–1643), *Puritan divine. He was educated at Christ's College, Cambridge, and elected a Fellow of Trinity in 1567. Having formed a friendship with T. *Beza on a visit to Geneva, Travers returned to England an acknowledged leader of the movement of Reform. Owing to his unwillingness to subscribe the *Thirty-Nine Articles, he was refused a licence to preach and returned to the Continent, where he was ordained to serve the English congregation at Antwerp. In 1581 he became afternoon lecturer at the Temple and two years later would have been made Master had he not declined to receive orders in the C of E. Continuing as afternoon lecturer, he was soon engaged in a controversy with R. *Hooker, the new Master, which lasted until he was inhibited by J. *Whitgift. In 1595 he was made first provost of *Trinity College, Dublin. His principal work, the *Ecclesiasticae Disciplinae et Anglicanae Ecclesiae ab illa Aberrationis plena e verbo Dei et dilucida Explicatio* (publd. anon. at La Rochelle in 1574 and simultaneously in an Eng. trans. by T. *Cartwright), in which he defended the Presbyterian form of Church government as of Dominical institution, exercised a determinative influence on the policy of the Puritan Reformers, who came to accept it as authoritative.

R. G. Usher (ed.), *The Presbyterian Movement in the Reign of Queen Elizabeth as Illustrated by the Minute Book of the Dedham Classis, 1582–1586* (Camden Society, 3rd Series, viii; 1905), esp. pp. lxvii, with reff., 5, 13, 19, and 21. J. Hunt, *Religious Thought in England from the Reformation to the End of the Last Century*, i (1870), pp. 61–5. J. B. Mullinger, *The University of Cambridge*, ii (1884), pp. 262–4, 291 f., 302–5, 355 f., with Appendix on the *Disciplina*, pp. 631–3. R. G. Usher in *D.E.C.H.* (1912), p. 601, s.v.

TRAVERSARI, AMBROGIO (*c.* 1386–1439), also Fra Ambrogio, Italian humanist. In 1400 he entered the *Camaldolensian Order at the monastery of Sta Maria degli Angioli at Florence, and in 1431 became its General. A scholar of refined taste, he was fired by his possession of a splendid collection of Greek patristic MSS. to translate many of the Greek Fathers into Latin. He also fostered movements for reforming the Church and for bringing about reunion between E. and W. Though never formally canonized, he is commemorated on 20 Nov.

Epistolae et Orationes, ed. P. Canneto, with life by L. Mehus, Florence, 1759. F. P. Luiso, *Riordinamento dell' Epistolario di Ambrogio Traversari con lettere inedite e note storico-cronologiche* (3 fascc., Florence, 1898–1903). Twelve further letters ed. L. Bertalot in *R.Q.*, xxix (1915), pp. *91–*106. A. Dini Traversari, *Ambrogio Traversari e i suoi tempi* (Florence, 1912), incl. text of the *Hodoeporicon*. P. Richard in *D.H.G.E.*, ii (1914), cols. 1127–9, s.v. 'Ambrogio Traversari'; C. Somigli in *E.C.*, xii (1954), col. 453 f., s.v., with bibl. For his part at the Council of Florence, and his trr. into Gk., see works cited under *Florence, Council of*.

TREACLE BIBLE, The. A popular title for M. *Coverdale's '*Great Bible' (q.v.; 1539) from its rendering of Jer. 8. 22, 'There is no more *triacle* [AV, 'balm'] in Gilead'.

TRECANUM. (From Gk. τρικάνων, 'triple canon'). In the *Gallican liturgy the title of the Communion chant. It consisted in an act of faith in the Trinity. The name is found already in pseudo-*Germanus of Paris.

TRE FONTANE. This monastery, now *Trappist, is some 3 miles south of Rome and the traditional site of St. *Paul's martyrdom. Acc. to legend, St. Paul's head, on severance from his body, rebounded from the ground at three points, from which issued the three springs that give the site its name.

Dom Marie Gabriel [Montbet], Abbé d'Aiguebelle, *L'Abbaye des Trois Fontaines située aux Eaux-Salviennes, près de Rome, et dédiée aux saints martyrs Vincent et Anastase* (1869). A. Sartorio, 'L' abbazia cistercense delle Tre Fontane' in *Nuova Antologia*, clxvii (5) (1913), pp. 50–65.

TREGELLES, SAMUEL PRIDEAUX (1813–75), Biblical scholar. A boy of exceptional talent, he devoted his spare time while at the Neath Abbey Iron Works, Glamorgan, to learning Greek, Aramaic, Hebrew, and Welsh. Returning to his native Falmouth, he joined the *Plymouth Brethren, although he subsequently became a *Presbyterian. In 1838 Tregelles formed the design for a new critical text of the NT which should replace the '*textus receptus', and was thenceforward engaged in the collation of Greek texts, making very extensive travels for the purpose. His *Account of the Printed Text* appeared in 1854, to be followed by the publication of all the NT, with the exception of Rev., by 1870. From 1862 Tregelles was in receipt of a Civil List pension.

F. G. Kenyon, *Handbook to the Textual Criticism of the New Testament* (1901), pp. 82–100 passim and 248 f. E. C. Marchant in *D.N.B.*, lvii (1899), p. 170 f.; C. Bertheau in *P.R.E.* (ed. 3), xx (1908) pp. 90–5, s.v., with further reff.

TREMELLIUS, JOHN IMMANUEL (1510–80), Hebrew scholar. The son of a Ferrarese Jew, he was educated at the university of Pavia and converted to Christianity in 1540 through the influence of R. *Pole. In 1541 he was persuaded by *Peter Martyr to become a Protestant and, leaving Italy, he taught at Strassburg under Johannes *Sturm. After the peace of *Schmalkalden he came to England at the invitation of Abp. T. *Cranmer (1547), and in 1549 succeeded Paul Fagius as the King's Reader of Hebrew at Cambridge university. Having returned to the Continent on the death of *Edward VI (1553), he became professor of OT studies at the university of Heidelberg in 1561. In 1577 he was expelled by Louis VI, the Lutheran Count Palatine, on account of his *Calvinistic opinions, and finally appointed by the Duc de Bouillon as a teacher of Hebrew at his newly founded college at Sedan. Tremellius's greatest work is his translation of the Bible from Hebrew and Syriac into Latin, which was for long the standard Protestant Latin translation. The NT with the Syriac text and the Latin translation appeared in 1569. It was followed,

between 1575 and 1579, by a Latin translation of the OT in 5 parts. Among his other works are a Hebrew and Greek Catechism (1551) and a Chaldean and Syriac Grammar (1569).

W. Becker, *Immanuel Tremellius, ein Proselytenleben im Zeitalter der Reformation* (1887). T. J. Ney in *P.R.E.* (ed. 3), xx (1908), pp. 95–8, s.v.

TRENCH, RICHARD CHENEVIX (1807–1886), Abp. of *Dublin. Educated at Harrow and Trinity College, Cambridge, he was ordained deacon in 1832, and for a brief time was curate at Hadleigh to H. J. *Rose. Later he became rector of Itchenstoke (1844–5), professor of divinity at *King's College, London (1846–58), Dean of *Westminster (1856–63), and finally Abp. of Dublin (1863–84). His two books on the Gospels, *Notes on the Parables of our Lord* (1841) and *Notes on the Miracles of our Lord* (1846), at once scholarly and stimulating, created a fresh interest in the Gospels in many quarters. Trench also took a keen interest in philology, the fruits of which included his *Study of Words* (1851) and *Synonyms of the NT* (1854). He also exercised a decisive influence in the early stages of the *Oxford English Dictionary*. In addition, he wrote much religious poetry. As Abp. of Dublin he vigorously opposed W. E. *Gladstone's proposals for disestablishing the Irish Church. His other publications include *Sacred Latin Poetry* (1849), *Gustavus Adolphus* (1865), *Studies in the Gospels* (1867), *Plutarch* (1873) and *Lectures on Mediaeval Church History* (1877), and many volumes of sermons and poetry.

Letters and Memorials [ed. by M. Trench] (2 vols., 1888). R. Bayne in *D.N.B.*, lvii (1899), pp. 191–4.

TRENT, Council of (1545–63). This Council, reckoned by RC theologians the Nineteenth *Œcumenical Council, was the most impressive embodiment of the ideals of the *Counter-Reformation.

The spread of Protestantism and the drastic need of moral and administrative reforms within the RC Church led to widespread demand among Catholics for a Universal Council, but disputes between *Charles V and others who favoured such action, and the Popes, who were generally averse from it, long prevented a move. At last *Paul III summoned a council to Mantua for 23 May 1537, but the plan fell through owing to French resistance. In 1538 further proposals for a council at Vicenza were frustrated by the unexpected indifference of the Emperor. In 1542 the Pope again convoked the Council, this time to Trent. After yet another postponement it eventually met on 13 Dec. 1545. At the outset it was a very small assembly, composed of three legates, one cardinal, four archbishops, twenty-one bishops, and five generals of orders. *Period I* (1545–7; Sessions I–VIII). As it was decided that voting should be by individual heads rather than (as at *Constance, 1415) by nations, the pro-Papal Italian bishops had a preponderating influence. The principal preliminary, whether the Council should first discuss dogma or disciplinary reform, was settled by the compromise that the subjects should be treated concurrently.

At Session III (4 Feb. 1546), the *Niceno-Constantinopolitan Creed was formally re-affirmed as the basis of faith. At Session IV (8 Apr. 1546) the equal validity of Scripture and *Tradition as sources of religious truth, the sole right of the Church to interpret the Bible, and the authority of the text of the *Vulgate were asserted. The decrees of Session V (17 June 1546) on *Original Sin and of Session VI (13 Jan. 1547) on *Justification and Merit struck at the root of the Protestant system. No decision was reached, however, on the points in dispute on these matters in the Catholic schools. At Session VII (3 Mar. 1547) the theology of the Sacraments in general was defined. The institution of all seven by Christ and their necessity to salvation was affirmed. Baptism and confirmation were also treated in detail and a number of decrees on administrative reforms were also passed.

Meanwhile, renewed political tension between Charles V and the Pope hindered progress. An epidemic at Trent offered a pretext for transferring the Council to *Bologna (Session VIII, 11 Mar. 1547). The Council was now virtually suspended for four years, until *Julius III (1550–5) re-convoked the assembly to Trent.

Period II (1551–2; Sessions IX–XIV). Important decisions were reached at Session XIII (11 Oct. 1551) on the *Eucharist and at Session XIV (25 Nov. 1551) on *Penance and Extreme *Unction. *Transubstantiation was affirmed and the *Lutheran, *Calvinist, and *Zwinglian Eucharistic doctrines repudiated. The Protestants present demanded renewed discussion of the subjects previously defined, the release of the bishops from their oaths of allegiance to the Papacy, and the supremacy of General Councils over the Pope.

The revolt of the princes against Charles V led to the suspension of the Council on 28 Apr. 1552. Under the austere and violently anti-Protestant *Paul IV (1555–9, Caraffa) there was no hope of its reassembly, and it first met again ten years later under his more tolerant successor, *Pius IV.

Period III (1562–3; Sessions XV–XXV). When the Council reassembled on 18 Jan. 1562, all hope of conciliating the Protestants had gone and the *Jesuits were now a strong force. The proceedings were henceforward hampered by struggles between the Papal and the opposition bishops, Imperial, Spanish, and French. A far-reaching plan of reform, devised by the Emp. Ferdinand II and advocated by Cardinal Guise (Charles de Lorraine), failed. The papal party largely owed its success to the diplomatic skill of the legate, Cardinal G. *Morone. At Session XXI (16 July 1562), the subject of Eucharistic Communion was treated and the presence of the undivided Christ under either species (*concomitance*) and the denial of the chalice to the laity affirmed. Session XXII (17 Sept. 1562)

issued a series of important definitions on the sacrificial doctrine of the Mass. Session XXIII (15 July 1563) dealt with Orders and Session XXIV (24 Nov. 1563) with the Sacrament of Matrimony. Other work was done on the reform of the *Index and the residence of bishops. Of great practical significance was the legislation establishing clerical seminaries, and regulating the appointment of bishops, provincial and diocesan synods, preaching of sermons, &c. Finally, Session XXV (3–4 Dec. 1563) dealt cursorily with *Purgatory, the *Invocation of Saints, the veneration of *relics and *images, and *Indulgences.

The Council ended on 4 Dec. 1563. The decrees were confirmed in a body on 26 Jan. 1564 by Pius IV, who in the same year published the 'Profession of the Tridentine Faith', a brief summary of doctrine, generally known as the Creed of Pius IV.

Several important works, which the Council recommended or initiated but could not effectually carry through, were handed over to the pope for completion. The revision of the *Vulgate, ordered at Trent in 1546, was concluded under *Clement VIII in 1592; and *Pius V founded the Congregation of the *Index in 1571 to carry out other unfinished work, having himself issued the *Catechism of the Council of Trent (1566) and revised the *Breviary (1568).

Though the Council failed to satisfy the Protestants and its reforms were less comprehensive than many Catholics had hoped for, it had established a solid basis for the renewal of discipline and the spiritual life in the RC Church, which emerged from Trent with a clearly formulated doctrinal system and an enhanced religious strength for the subsequent struggle with Protestantism.

The *Acta* of the Council ed. A. Theiner (2 vols., Leipzig, 1874); the decrees have frequently been repr.; the more important are readily accessible in Denz.–Bann. (ed. 1952), pp. 278–349 (Nos. 782–1000); Eng. tr. of canons and decrees by J. Waterworth (London, 1888). The principal collections of documents are J. Le Plat (ed.), *Monumentorum ad Historiam Concilii Tridentini Illustrandam Spectantium Collectio* (7 vols., Louvain, 1781–7) and the *Concilium Tridentinum*. Diariorum, Actorum, Epistolarum, Tractatuum nova Collectio. Edidit Societas Goerresiana (Freiburg i.Br., 1901 ff.). Modern ed. of Spanish documents in *Concilium Tridentinum Hispanicum* (Valladolid, 1951 ff.). Early histories by P. *Sarpi, *Servite (under the pseudonym of P. S. Polano), *Historia del Concilio Tridentino* (London, 1619; Eng. tr. by Nathaniel Brent, Warden of Merton College, Oxford, Oxford, 1620; very hostile), and S.Pallavicino, S.J., *Istoria del Concilio di Trento* (2 vols., Rome, 1656–7; reply to preceding work). Full account of recent work in Hefele–Leclercq, ix (by P. Richard, 2 parts, 1930–1) and x (pt. 1, by A. Michel, 1938); H. Jedin, *Geschichte des Konzils von Trient* (1949 ff.; Eng. tr., 1957 ff.); G. Schrieber (ed.), *Das Weltkonzil von Trient*. Sein Werden und Wirken (2 vols., 1951). Shorter study by K. D. Schmidt, *Studien zur Geschichte des Konzils von Trient* (1925). Older works include L. Maynier, *Étude historique sur le Concile de Trente* (1874); J. A. Froude, *Lectures on the Council of Trent, delivered at Oxford, 1892–3* (1896); H. Swoboda, *Das Konzil von Trient*. Sein Schauplatz, Verlauf und Ertrag (Festgabe der österreichischen Leo-Gesellschaf zum XXIII. Internationalen Eucharistischen Kongress; 1912). V. Martin, *Le Gallicanisme de la réforme catholique*. Essai historique sur l'introduction en France des décrets du Concile de Trente, 1563–1615 (1919). H. E. Symonds, C.R., *The Council of Trent and Anglican Formularies* (1933). R. V. Laurence in *C.M.H.*, ii (1903), pp. 639–89, with bibl. pp. 818–24. L. Cristiani in Fliche–Martin, xvii (1948), pp. 13–242. A. Michel in *D.T.C.*, xv (pt. 1; 1946), cols. 1414–1508, s.v.

'Trente (Concile de)'. J. P. Kirsch in *C.E.*, xv (1912), pp. 30–35, s.v.; H. Jedin in *L.Th.K.*, x (1938), cols. 275–84, s.v.; id. in *E.C.*, xii (1954), cols. 465–80, s.v. 'Trento, Concilio di', all with further bibl. See also bibl. to *Counter-Reformation*.

TRENTAL. A set of thirty *Requiem Masses for the repose of a soul, whether said on a single or on successive days. The word was also formerly in occasional use for a Mass or other service (also 'Month's Mind') on the thirtieth day after death or burial.

TREUGA DEI. See *Truce of God*.

TRIAD (Gk. τριάς). A word first used of the *Trinity in the Godhead by *Theophilus of Antioch, who names as the Triad 'God and His Word and His Wisdom' (*ad Autol.* ii, 15).

TRIDENTINE. Having reference to the Council of *Trent (*Concilium Tridentinum*), 1545–63.

TRIDUUM SACRUM (Lat., 'the sacred three days'). The three concluding days of *Holy Week commemorating the Last Supper, Passion, and Death of Christ, i.e. *Maundy Thursday, *Good Friday, and *Holy Saturday.

TRIERS, The. The body of commissioners, appointed by O. *Cromwell under an Act of 20 Mar. 1654, 'for the approbation of all public preachers and lecturers before their admission to benefices'. It consisted of 38 members, 29 clerics, and 9 laymen, drawn from various religious bodies.

The Act is pr. in Gee-Hardy, pp. 577–82 (No. cxi).

TRIMMER, SARAH (1741–1810), authoress, known as 'Good Mrs. Trimmer'. Sarah Kirby was born at Ipswich, where her father, J. J. Kirby (1716–74), was an artist of some standing. While still a young girl, she counted many famous men among her friends, e.g. Dr. S. *Johnson, T. Gainsborough, and W. Hogarth. She married in 1762 and had six sons and six daughters, whom she educated herself except for the boys' classics. She later interested herself esp. in the establishment of *Sunday schools, a project which she ventilated in her book *The Oeconomy of Charity* (1786). In 1793 began her connexion with the *S.P.C.K., which published two of her books in the same year, *The Abridgment of the Old Testament* and *The Abridgment of the New Testament*, which were designed as text-books for charity schools. The best known of her writings, *The History of the Robins* (1786; originally in *Fabulous Histories*), long remained a favourite children's book for the better classes, whereas her numerous school books were intended for the instruction of the poor. She was a woman of great piety and assiduous in visiting the poor.

Some Account of the Life and Writings of Mrs. Trimmer (2 vols., 1814) contains mainly extracts from her private journals. Elizabeth Lee in *D.N.B.*, lvii (1899), p. 231 f.

TRINITARIAN. A person who believes in the doctrine of the Holy *Trinity, esp. as contrasted with a *Unitarian. In the 15th and 16th cents., however, the word was occasionally applied to those who held heretical, as opposed to orthodox, views on the Trinity.

TRINITARIANS (Order of the Most Holy Trinity). This order was founded in 1198 at Cerfroid in the diocese of Meaux by St. *John of Matha (d. 1213) and St. Felix of Valois (d. 1212) with the approval of *Innocent III. Its members, also known as 'Mathurins', followed an austere form of the *Augustinian Rule, wearing a white habit with a cross 'flory' (upright *red*, crossbar *blue*) on the *scapular and cappa. They devoted themselves esp. to the ransoming of countless captives, and at the height of their influence in the 15th cent. they possessed about 800 houses. In 1596, a reform called the Barefooted Trinitarians was started in Spain by Fr. Juan Bautista of the Immaculate Conception. It became a distinct order and is the only body of Trinitarians that now survives (with under 500 members; headquarters at St. Crisogono in Trastevere, Rome). The brethren are engaged in education, nursing, and the ransoming of negro slaves. Nuns of the same name, devoted to works of mercy, have been affiliated to the order from early times. The Barefooted Trinitarian Sisters date from 1612.

Acta Ordinis S. Trinitatis, vol. i (Rome, 1919–23) includes important primary docc. P. Deslandres, *L'Ordre des Trinitaires pour le rachat des captifs* (2 vols., Toulouse, 1903). Antoninus ab Assumptione, Ord. Trinit., *Les Origines de l'ordre de la Très Sainte Trinité d'après les documents* (Rome, 1925). Id., *Ministorum Generalium Ordinis SS. Trinitatis Series* (Isola del Liri, 1936). Id., *Diccionario de Escritores Trinitarios de España y Portugal* (2 vols., Rome, 1898–9), and other works of this author. Heimbucher, i, 448–55, and ii, 658, with reff. to earlier literature.

TRINITY, Doctrine of the. The central dogma of Christian theology, viz. that the One God exists in Three Persons and One Substance. This doctrine is held to be a mystery in the strict sense, in that it can neither be known by unaided human reason apart from revelation, nor cogently demonstrated by reason after it has been revealed. On the other hand it is maintained that, though the mystery is above reason, it is not contrary to it, for it is not incompatible with the principles of rational thought.

Though the word 'Trinity', first used in its Greek form τριάς by *Theophilus of Antioch (c. A.D. 180), is not found in Scripture, the conception is there both implicitly and explicitly. Christian theology has seen adumbrations of the doctrine in such OT texts as the narrative of the apparition of the three men to *Abraham (Gen. 18), the threefold *Sanctus of *Isaiah's vision (Is. 6. 3), and the frequent mention of God, His Wisdom, and His Spirit, side by side in the Sapiential Books. It is held to be explicitly taught in some passages of the NT, esp. in the baptismal formula of Mt. 28. 19, where the singular εἰς τὸ ὄνομα, used in connexion with the Three Persons each linked with the other by καί, seems to indicate clearly the Unity in Trinity. Other passages from the *Synoptics, if less convincing, are also sometimes adduced in evidence, such as the threefold manifestation of the Divinity at the baptism of Christ in the Jordan (Mt. 3. 16) and the *Annunciation (Lk. 1. 35), whereas in the Johannine discourses after the Last Supper the mutual relations between the Father, the Son, and the Holy Ghost ('*Paraclete') are brought out with great clarity (cf. esp. Jn. 14. 11, 16 f., and 26). In the Epp. the Trinitarian formula is employed in 1 Pet. 1. 2 and 2 Cor. 13. 14; and in 1 Cor. 12. 4–6 the juxtaposition of 'the same Spirit', 'the same Lord', and 'the same God, who worketh all things in all' seems to indicate at least implicitly a co-equal Trinity.

This NT teaching was taken over by the early Church and set out in the Creeds (at first, the '*Apostles' Creed') and doxologies, as well as in the individual confessions of faith of the martyrs, without regard to the theological problems involved. Where the doctrine was elaborated, as e.g. in the writings of the *Apologists, the language remained on the whole indefinite, and, from a later standpoint, was even partly unorthodox. Sometimes it was not free from a certain *subordinationism, more rarely, as in the case of *Hermas, the Persons of the Trinity, esp. the Second and the Third Persons, were confused. The former tendency was chiefly due to the insistence of the Fathers that the First Person was the principle of the other Two and that the generation of the Son was a 'voluntary' act against the emanationist vagaries of the *Gnostics. Such considerations led *Origen to the subordinationism which marked one side of his teaching; but on the other hand he was the first theologian to formulate the doctrine of the Eternal Generation of the Son, so that St. *Athanasius, no less than his opponents, was able to appeal to his authority. At the Council of *Nicaea (A.D. 325) and at *Constantinople (A.D. 381) the dogma was defined in its simplest outlines in the face of pressing heresies. Against *Sabellianism the real distinction, and against *Arianism and *Macedonianism the co-equality and co-eternity, of the Three Divine Persons were affirmed. The Persons differ only in origin in that the Father is ungenerated, the Son is generated by the Father, and the Holy Ghost proceeds from the Father through the Son (a doctrine later repudiated by *Photius in favour of the procession of the Spirit from the Father only), and the Inner-Trinitarian Procession thus resembles, as it were, a straight line.

In the W., the doctrine was developed in a somewhat different manner. Starting not from the difference of the Persons, as did many of the more philosophically minded Greek Fathers, but from the unity of the Substance, it readily safeguarded the co-equality of the Persons. The Procession of the Holy Ghost was attributed equally to the Father and the Son, and so, in the W., the Trinitarian symbol was not the line, but the triangle. The chief exponent of the teaching of the Latin Church during the patristic period was St. *Augustine, esp. in his 'De Trinitate', whose great contribution was the comparison of the two processes of the Divine Life (the later 'Filiation' and 'Spiration') to the analogical processes of human self-knowledge and self-love. His conception of the generation of the Son as the act of thinking on the part of the Father was based on *Tertullian, whereas the explanation of the Holy Ghost as the mutual love of the Father and the Son was the fruit of his own reflections. This so-called 'psychological theory of the Trinity' was taken over from him and developed by medieval Scholasticism. In its more formal aspects, medieval teaching on the Trinity reasserted the doctrines of the *Athanasian Creed (q.v.). It received classical exposition in the writings of St. *Thomas Aquinas.

The Trinitarian teaching thus elaborated by the Scholastics, though challenged in the 17th cent. by *Socinianism and *Unitarianism, has remained the common inheritance of subsequent W. theology.

Discussions of the doctrine of the Trinity figure in all works on Christian Dogmatics and in writings concerned with the nature of God. Modern studies devoted to the subject as a whole include F. C. Baur, *Die christliche Lehre von der Dreieinigkeit und Menschwerdung Gottes in ihrer geschichtlichen Entwicklung* (3 vols., 1841–3); T. de Régnon, S.J., *Études de théologie positive sur la Sainte Trinité* (4 vols., 1892–8); J. R. Illingworth, *The Doctrine of the Trinity apologetically considered* (1907); J. Lebreton, S.J., *Histoire du dogme de la Trinité* (Bibliothèque de Théologie Historique, 2 vols., 1910–28; Eng. tr. of vol. i; 1939); E. Hugon, O.P., *Le Mystère de la Très Sainte Trinité* (1912); A. E. J. Rawlinson (ed.), *Essays on the Trinity and the Incarnation* (1928); P. Galtier, S.J., *De SS. Trinitate in se et in nobis* (Paris, 1933); A. d'Alès, S.J., *De Deo Trino* (ib., 1934); G. L. Prestige, *God in Patristic Thought* (1936), passim; L. Hodgson, *The Doctrine of the Trinity* (Croall Lectures, 1942–3; 1943); C. Welch, *The Trinity in Contemporary Theology* (1953). G. Bardy–A. Michel in *D.T.C.*, xv (pt. 2; 1950), cols. 1545–1855, s.v. 'Trinité', with detailed bibl.

TRINITY COLLEGE, DUBLIN. The (one) College in the University of *Dublin, founded 1591. Membership was long confined to Anglicans but religious tests were eventually abolished in 1873. Since 1903 women have been admitted to degrees. The College is governed by a Provost and Fellows and is represented in the Dail Eireann. The library has a very valuable collection of Irish and other MSS, among them the '*Book of Kells' (A.1.6; q.v.).

J. P. Mahaffy, J. W. Stubbs, R. Ball, T. K. Abbott, U. R. Burke, W. M. Dixon and E. P. Wright, *The Book of Trinity College, Dublin* (1892); J. P. Mahaffy, *An Epoch in Irish History*. Trinity College, Dublin, its Foundation and Early Fortunes, 1591–1660 (1903). G. D. Burtchaell and T. U. Sadleir (edd.), *Alumni Dublinenses*. A Register of the Students, Graduates, Professors and Provosts of Trinity College, in the University of Dublin (1924; revised and continued, 1935). *A Handbook to Trinity College*. Authorized by the Board (1929).

TRINITY SUNDAY. The Sunday following *Pentecost which was originally kept only as the *Octave of Whitsun. It was not till the Middle Ages that the Sunday was at all widely observed as a separate feast in honour of the

Holy Trinity. Its observance, introduced to mark the conclusion of the liturgical commemorations of the life of Christ and the descent of the Holy Spirit by a celebration embracing God in all three Persons, was universally enjoined by Pope *John XXII in 1334. The feast became specially popular in England, perhaps by its association with St. Thomas *Becket, who was consecrated bishop on that day (1162). The restriction of the feast to a single day by the absence of an octave is appropriate to the Unity of the Godhead which the feast commemorates. In the *Sarum Missal, and in the ancient rites of the *Carmelite and *Dominican orders, Sundays are reckoned after Trinity, and not after Pentecost as in the Roman Rite.

A. Klaus, O.F.M., *Ursprung und Verbreitung der Dreifaltigkeitsmesse* (1938). F. *Cabrol, O.S.B., 'Le Culte de la Trinité dans la liturgie de la fête de la Trinité' in *E.L.*, xlv (1931), pp. 270–8. P. Browe, S.J., 'Zur Geschichte des Dreifaltigkeitsfestes' in *Archiv für Liturgiewissenschaft*, i (1950), pp. 65–81.

TRIODION (Gk. τριῴδιον). In the E. rite, a liturgical book containing the variable portions of the services from the 4th Sunday before *Lent till the Saturday before *Easter. It is so named because during this season the *canons ordinarily contain only three odes (ᾠδαί) instead of the usual nine.

H. Engberding, O.S.B., in *L.Th.K.*, x (1938), col. 293 f., s.v.

TRIPLE CANDLESTICK. The candlestick used acc. to the Latin Rite at the 'Lumen Christi', in the liturgy of *Holy Saturday, to hold the three candles, which are successively lighted in the course of the procession up to the altar. It is commonly mounted on a long pole. A triple candlestick is also used in the E. Church for episcopal blessings.

TRISAGION (Gk. τρισάγιον, 'thrice holy'). The chant 'Holy God, Holy and mighty, Holy and immortal, have mercy upon us', found in all the ancient E. liturgies at some point between the lections. It occurred also in the *Gallican Liturgy, and thence passed into the Roman Rite where it is sung as part of the *Reproaches on Good Friday. The earliest datable occurrence of it is in the Acts of the Council of *Chalcedon (451).

A. *Baumstark, 'Trishagion und Queduscha' in *J.L.W.*, iii (1923), pp. 18–32. L. Brou, O.S.B., 'Études sur la liturgie mozarabe. Le Trishagion de la Messe d'après les sources manuscrits' in *E.L.*, lxi (1947), pp. 309–34.

TRITHEISM. The heretical teaching about the Trinity which denies the unity of substance in the Three Divine Persons. The name is esp. applied to the teaching of a group of 6th-cent. *Monophysites, the best known of whom was John Philoponus, the commentator on *Aristotle. By his identification of person and nature Philoponus was led to affirm three Divine substances in the Trinity. His tritheism, however, seems to have been of a speculative rather than a practical character,

for he did not actually abandon his Christian faith. In the Middle Ages the extreme *Nominalism of *Roscellinus and the exaggerated *Realism of *Gilbert de La Porrée caused both these Schoolmen to be accused of teaching tritheistic doctrines; and they were condemned by the Councils of *Soissons (1092) and of *Reims (1148) respectively. Gilbert's doctrines later influenced *Joachim of Fiore and issued in the clear definition of the numerical unity of the Divine Nature by the Fourth *Lateran Council (1215). A more recent exponent of tritheistic teaching was A. *Günther who, in his struggle against *Hegelian pantheism, affirmed the existence of three absolute realities in the Trinity, distinct from each other and bound together only by a unity of origin. Popular ideas about the Trinity, in intention orthodox, often tend to be tritheistic in expression.

TRITHEMIUS (1462–1516), Abbot of Sponheim. He was so named from his birthplace, Trittenheim, on the Moselle. After harsh treatment at the hands of his stepfather, he fled to Würzburg, where his intellectual powers developed rapidly and he came into close contact with the humanist movement. A chance visit to the monastery of Sponheim in 1482 led him to join the community, and in 1483 he was elected its abbot. He rapidly brought about its reform, collecting a library of MSS. which soon made it one of the most famous in Europe. In 1506, however, through dissensions caused by the stringency of his discipline, he was induced to resign his abbacy, and for his last ten years presided over the Scottish abbey of St. Jakob at Würzburg. His writings include many useful historical compilations, e.g. *De Viris Illustribus Germaniae* (1495); works on natural science and magic, e.g. *Steganographia* (publd. 1606); and some fine sermons.

Theological writings first publd. at Mainz, 1604 and 1605; Historical writings at Frankfurt, 1601; Letters at Dresden, 1536. Studies by I. Silbernagl (Landshut, 1868) and W. Schneegans (Kreuznach, 1882). P. Séjourné, O.S.B., in *D.T.C.*, xv (pt. 2; 1950), cols. 1862–7.

TRITO-ISAIAH. A word coined by B. Duhm in 1892 for the author of the last eleven chapters of Isaiah (56–66), in the belief that they were written by a later prophet than the 6th cent. 'Deutero-Isaiah' who wrote chs. 40–55. The term is also in current use for chs. 56–66 themselves, even when they are not held to be the work of a single individual.

TRIUMPHANT, The Church. The body of Christians in heaven, i.e., the perfected saints, distinguished from those still on earth (*militant), and those in *Purgatory (*expectant). See *Communion of Saints*.

TRIVIUM. The medieval name for the group of three sciences consisting of grammar, rhetoric, and dialectic, which together constituted the inferior group of the *Seven Liberal Arts.

TROAS. A city of NW. Asia Minor visited several times by St. Paul. It was on his first visit here that he saw the vision of 'a man of Macedonia' which led him to carry the Gospel into Europe (Acts 16. 8–11).

TROELTSCH, ERNST (1865–1923), theologian and philosopher. A native of Augsburg, he taught theology successively at Göttingen (1891–2), Bonn (1892–4), and Heidelberg (1894–1915). From 1915 until his death he was professor of the history of philosophy and civilization at Berlin. In theological outlook, he was much influenced by A. *Ritschl, in philosophy by the Neo-Kantians Wilhelm Windelband (1848–1915) and Heinrich Rickert (1863–1936) and in the religious understanding and assessment of culture by W. *Dilthey.

Troeltsch's principal works were *Vernunft und Offenbarung bei Johann Gerhard und Melanchthon* (1891), *Die Absolutheit des Christentums und die Religionsgeschichte* (1901), *Psychologie und Erkenntnistheorie in der Religionswissenschaft* (1905), *Die Bedeutung des Protestantismus für die Entstehung der modernen Welt* (1906; Eng. trans., *Protestantism and Progress*, 1912), *Die Soziallehren der christlichen Kirchen und Gruppen* (1912; Eng. trans., 2 vols., 1931), *Augustin, die christliche Antike und das Mittelalter* (1915), *Der Historismus und seine Probleme* (1922), and *Christian Thought. Its History and Application* (1923). Among close students of Troeltsch in Great Britain were F. *von Hügel and C. C. J. *Webb.

Gesammelte Schriften, 4 vols., Tübingen, 1912–25. E. Vermeil, *La Pensée religieuse de Ernst Troeltsch* (Études d'Histoire et de Philosophie religieuses, ii; 1922). W. [E.] Köhler, *Ernst Troeltsch* (Tübingen, 1941). E. Spiess, *Die Religionstheorie von Ernst Troeltsch* (RC study, 1927). Überweg, iv, 600–5, with bibl. p. 722.

TROPARION (Gk. τροπάριον). In the Greek Liturgies and Office Books, a short hymn celebrating the event or saint commemorated in the office for the day. Its use at Alexandria is attested as early as *c.* 400. Many Troparia were written in praise of the BVM. From the 9th cent., a liturgical book ('Tropologium') filled with these compositions is met with.

E. [J.] Wellesz, *A History of Byzantine Music and Hymnography* (1949), pp. 144–52. L. Clugnet, *Dictionnaire grec-français des noms liturgiques* (1895), pp. 153–5, s.v. 'τροπάριον'. Bardenhewer, iv, 130–2, ('Tropariendichter'). A. Raes, S.J., in *E.C.*, xii (1954), col. 571 f.

TROPE. In W. Church, a short series of words added as an amplification and embellishment to the text of the Mass or of the Breviary Office to be sung by the choir. Tropes tended to go out of fashion about the 12th cent., when their place was taken by *sequences, and they were finally discontinued at *Pius V's revision of the Missal (1570). The 'Troper' was at first a collection of such tags; but later the word was used of a Book of Sequences. The oldest known Troper, the St.-Martial Troper (Cod. Par. 1240), dates from the 10th cent.

See W. H. *Frere, *The Winchester Troper* (Henry *Bradshaw Society, 1894), esp. Introd.

TROPHIMUS, St. (1) Acc. to Acts 20. 4, 21. 29, a Gentile disciple of St. *Paul. He was an Ephesian, who accompanied the Apostle on part of his Third Missionary Journey and to *Jerusalem where St. Paul's introduction of Trophimus into the Temple was the chief ground of the riot. He is also mentioned at 2 Tim. 4. 20 ('Trophimus I left at Miletus sick'). In the Gk. *Menology he is reckoned one of the Seventy (cf. Lk. 10. 1) and commemorated with St. Aristarchus (cf. Acts 19. 29, &c.) and St. *Pudens on 14 Apr.

(2) St. Trophimus, traditionally reckoned the first Bp. of Arles, is a quite independent figure. He is first mentioned in 417 in an Ep. of Pope *Zosimus to Patroclus, Bp. of Arles, as an early preacher of the Gospel sent from Rome to Gaul. Acc. to St. *Gregory of Tours he was one of the Bishops who came to Gaul with St. *Dionysius of Paris. He was later identified with the Trophimus of the NT and since the Middle Ages has been highly venerated at Arles. Feast day, 29 Dec.

(1) See comm. to Acts, cited s.v., and to Titus, Epistle to, cited s.v. *Timothy and Titus, Epistles to*. W. F. Boyd in *D.A.C.*, ii (1918), p. 620 f., s.v.
(2) L. *Duchesne, *Fastes épiscopaux de l'ancienne Gaule*, i (1894), p. 246 f., with reff. E. Caspar, *Geschichte des Papsttums*, i (1930), esp. pp. 347 f. and 449 f. L. Levillain, 'Saint Trophime, confesseur et métropolitain d'Arles et la Mission des Sept en Gaule. Étude d'un texte de Grégoire de Tours et d'un passage de la Passion de Saint Saturnin' in *Revue d'Histoire de l'Église de France*, xiii (1927), pp. 145–189. S. A. Bennett in *D.C.B.*, iv (1887), p. 1055, s.v.

TRUCE OF GOD (Lat. *pax, treuga Dei*). In medieval times, a suspension of hostilities ordered by the Church on certain days and during certain seasons. The institution goes back to attempts to remedy the feudal anarchy of the 11th cent. By a canon of the Council of Elne of 1027, the conduct of hostilities between Saturday night and Monday morning was forbidden. At a later date *Advent and *Lent were also brought within the Truce.

TRULLAN SYNOD. The synod held in 692 by the E. bishops to pass disciplinary canons to complete the work of the Fifth (553) and Sixth (680) General Councils (hence its other name of Πενθέκτη, 'Quinisext', or Fifth-Sixth, Council). It sat in the domed room ('trullus') of the Emp. Justinian II's palace at *Constantinople, where the Sixth General Council (681) had also met. The disciplinary decrees of the synod were rejected by the Pope and, though by no means completely observed in the E., served to accentuate the growing division between W. and E. practice. They are sometimes quoted (wrongly) as having been passed by the Sixth General Council, and as such seem to have received some sort of recognition by Pope *Hadrian I (772–95). The subjects legislated on included clerical marriage, ecclesiastical dress, the age of ordination, and affinity and other impediments to matrimony.

There survive only the Council's allocution to the Emperor and the 102 Canons, with the signatures of the participants of the Council. Hardouin, iii, cols. 1645–1712; Mansi, xi

(Florence, 1765), cols. 929–1006. Text of canons also pr. in Lauchert, pp. 97–139. Hefele-Leclercq, iii (pt. 1; 1909), pp. 560–81. L. *Duchesne, *L'Église au VIᵉ siècle* (1925), pp. 477–80. L. Bréhier in Fliche-Martin, v (1938), pp. 193–196 and 475 f. G. Fritz in *D.T.C.*, xiii (pt. 2; 1937), cols. 1581–97, s.v. 'Quinisexte (Concile)'. See also bibl. to *Sergius I.*

TRUMPETS, Feast of. A Jewish feast kept on the first day of Tishri (Oct.), the observance of which is ordained in Lev. 23. 24 and Num. 29. 1. It is now regarded by the Jews as New Year's Day ('Rosh ha-Shanah'), though Ezek. 40. 1 puts the beginning of the year on the 10th Tishri.

TRURO. The Anglican diocese of Truro was created in 1877, out of the Archdeaconry of Cornwall, previously in the diocese of *Exeter. In pre-Norman times the Cornish Church had been independent, and it is probable that the British bishops who assisted in St. *Chad's consecration (664) were Cornish. In 931 the Cornish Church was finally incorporated with the English Church and Cornwall became an English diocese. In 1027 it was annexed to the see of *Crediton, and in 1050 the see of the united diocese was fixed at Exeter. In 1877 when Truro became the see of the reconstituted diocese, E. W. *Benson became its first bishop. The fine cathedral church of St. Mary, designed by J. L. *Pearson in the early English style and incorporating the south aisle of the old parish church, was begun in 1880 and completed in 1910. The Community of the Epiphany, founded *c.* 1880 by G. H. Wilkinson, the second Bishop of Truro, when Vicar of St. Peter's, Eaton Square, London, has its Mother House at Truro.

A. B. Donaldson, *The Bishopric of Truro.* The first twenty-five years, 1877–1902 (1902).

TÜBINGEN. The university for Württemberg, founded in 1477, soon grew in importance and numbered many celebrities among its early teachers, e.g. G. *Biel and P. *Melanchthon (1514–18). When Württemberg was made Protestant by Duke Ulrich in 1534–5, Tübingen became a centre of *Lutheran orthodoxy and increased the number and standard of its students through the famous 'Stift', a kind of public school at which later G. W. F. *Hegel and F. W. J. *Schelling were educated. In the 18th cent. G. C. Storr founded the older 'Tübingen School' of theology. Its chief characteristic was a 'Biblical Supranaturalism', which put the guarantee of Christ and the Apostles in the place of the orthodox Protestant doctrine of the inspiration of Scripture and regarded the Bible as the exclusive source and law book of Christianity, from which the tenets of faith were to be derived by purely deductive methods. In the early part of the 19th cent. another school of theology was formed under the influence of Hegel, F. C. *Baur being its leader and chief representative (see *Tübingen School*). In 1817 a Catholic faculty of theology was opened which soon became one of the most important centres of Catholic scholarship in Germany, counting among its members J. A. *Möhler and K. J. *Hefele and, in recent times, K. Bihlmeyer and K. Adam. The Catholic school has been characterized by a combination of the historical and speculative methods, and by its emphasis on the need for relating modern thought to the data of the faith.

H. *Rashdall, *The Universities of Europe in the Middle Ages*, ii (ed. F. M. Powicke–A. B. Emden, 1936), pp. 278–80, with full bibl. H. Hermelink, *Die theologische Fakultät in Tübingen vor der Reformation 1477–1534* (1906). Accounts of the Catholic theological school at Tübingen will be found in E. Vermeil, *Jean-Adam Möhler et l'école catholique de Tubingue, 1815–1840* (1913), and K. Adam, 'Die katholische Tübinger Schule' in *Hochland*, xxiv (pt. 2; 1927), pp. 581–601.

TÜBINGEN SCHOOL. A school of German NT theologians founded by F. C. *Baur. Among its most prominent members were Eduard Zeller, who edited its organ, the *Tübinger Theologische Jahrbücher* (1842–57), and A. *Hilgenfeld who continued it as the *Zeitschrift für wissenschaftliche Theologie* (1858–1914). The principal endeavour of the School was to apply G. W. F. *Hegel's conception of development to primitive Christianity. The early Church was held to be divided into 'Petrinists' (Jewish Christians) and 'Paulinists' (Gentile Christians), the cleavage between them being healed only in the later 2nd cent. ('Catholicism'). This state of things is reflected in the books of the NT, several of which represent the views of one or other of the parties, the bulk, however, being products of the 2nd cent. synthesis and therefore of practically no historical value for the period to which they profess to refer. These theories were expressed most vigorously in A. *Schwegler's *Nachapostolisches Zeitalter* (1846), which assigns to Mk. a date later than St. *Justin Martyr, and sees in Baptism and the Episcopate substitutes introduced by the Judaizers for circumcision and the aristocracy of Israel respectively. The school was at the height of its influence in the forties of the 19th cent., but it soon lost its prestige through the discrepancy between its axioms and historical fact. A. *Ritschl, who for a time belonged to the group, later founded a school of its own. Since A. *Harnack the Tübingen position has been generally abandoned.

The chief sources are, besides the writings of its leading members (qq.v.), the *Theologische Jahrbücher* mentioned above. R. W. Mackay, *The Tübingen School and its Antecedents* (1863). E. Zeller, *Vorträge und Abhandlungen* (1865), pp. 267–353 ('Die Tübinger historische Schule').

TUCKNEY, ANTHONY (1599–1670), *Puritan divine. He was educated at Emmanuel College, Cambridge, where he was elected Fellow in 1619. In 1633 he became vicar of Boston, Lincs. In 1643 he was nominated to the *Westminster Assembly, where as chairman of committee he took a leading part in the drawing-up of its doctrinal formularies, the section on the Decalogue in the 'Larger Catechism' being his work. He then became master successively of Emmanuel

(1645) and St. John's (1653) colleges, Cambridge, and in 1656 also Regius professor of divinity. After the Restoration he was superseded in his mastership and his chair, and passed the rest of his life in retirement. He published little and his chief works are posthumous, but his four letters to B. *Whichcote, published with the replies as an appendix to the latter's *Moral and Religious Aphorisms* (1753), illustrate the strength of his Puritan convictions, his fear of the rationalistic tendencies of the *Cambridge Platonists, and his charity towards the opinions of his opponents.

Forty Sermons upon Several Occasions, ed. by his son, Jonathan Tuckney (London, 1676); *Praelectiones Theologicae*, ed. id. (Amsterdam, 1679), with short biogr. preface by W. D[illingham] (no pagination). 'Eight Letters of Dr. Anthony Tuckney and Dr. Benjamin Whichcote' are appended to Whichcote's *Moral and Religious Aphorisms* ed. S. Salter (1753; separate pagination), with preface, pp. i–xl. J. *Tulloch, *Rational Theology and Christian Philosophy in England in the Seventeenth Century*, ii (1872), pp. 47, 53–5, and 59–84; J. B. Mullinger, *The University of Cambridge*, iii (1911), pp. 529–32, 576–8, 591–4 and passim. F. J. Powicke, *The Cambridge Platonists. A Study* (1926), pp. 54–9. A. Gordon in *D.N.B.*, lvii (1899), pp. 286–8.

TULCHAN BISHOPS (Gaelic, *tulachan*, 'little hillock'). Term contemptuously applied to the titular bishops introduced by the Scottish *Presbyterians after the Covenant of Leith (1572). They were to be responsible to the General Assembly; but, evading ecclesiastical control, they became merely tools of the lay nobles who drew the revenues of their sees. On his return from Geneva (1574), A. *Melville condemned episcopacy in any form as unscriptural and incompatible with a pure Church. The bishops had disappeared by 1580.

TULLOCH, JOHN (1823–86), Scottish theologian. Ordained in the Church of Scotland, he became in 1854, after several years' parochial work, Principal and professor of theology at St. Mary's College, St. Andrews. From about 1875 he was the most prominent member of his Church, and in 1878 was elected *Moderator. He is chiefly remembered for the prominent part he took in trying to awaken a spirit of liberal orthodoxy in the Church of Scotland. He sought to defend its comprehensiveness in doctrine and did not wish its members to be bound to the letter of its credal formularies. His most important treatise was his *Rational Theology and Christian Philosophy in England in the Seventeenth Century* (2 vols., 1872).

Memoir by Mrs. [M. O. W.] Oliphant (Edinburgh, 1888). T. Bayne in *D.N.B.*, lvii (1899), pp. 307–10.

TUNICLE. In the W. rite the outer liturgical garment of the *subdeacon. It is also worn by the bishop under his *dalmatic and *chasuble. It seems to have developed out of the ordinary overcoat (*tunica*) of the later Empire, though without the usual girdle. St. *Gregory I (*Ep.* ix. 26) suppressed it at Rome, but it survived elsewhere and was reintroduced at Rome *c.* A.D. 1000. Its further development was closely parallel with that of the dalmatic. The tunicle formerly differed from it in possessing no *clavi* or stripes of coloured material and in having narrower sleeves, but the two garments are now identical.

Braun, *L.G.*, pp. 247–305. J. Braun, S.J., *Handbuch der Paramentik* (1912), pp. 108–19; id. in *C.E.*, xv (1912), p. 87 f., s.v. 'Tunic', with bibl.

TUNKERS, also known as Dunkers, Dunkards (from Old Germ., *tunken*, 'to dip') and as German Baptists, a Protestant sect so named from its distinctive baptismal rite. Originating in Germany in 1708 under Alexander Mack (1679–1735), they quickly gathered adherents in Germany, Holland, and Switzerland; but persecution compelled them to emigrate to America (1719–29), where they have been settled ever since. In the 1880s the Tunkers became divided into Progressives and Conservatives ('Old Church'). They reject infant baptism, insist on total immersion, accompany the celebration of the Lord's Supper with an *agape*, refuse to take oaths or to bear arms, discourage litigation, and disallow statistics as savouring of pride. Since 1908 their official title has been 'Church of the Brethren'.

M. G. Brumbaugh, *A History of the German Baptist Brethren in Europe and America* (Mount Morris, Ill., 1899). J. L. Gillin, *The Dunkers*. A Sociological Interpretation (Columbia University thesis; New York, 1906). J. H. Moore in S. M. Jackson (ed.), *The New Schaff-Herzog Encyclopedia of Religious Knowledge*, iv (1909), pp. 24–7; D. W. Kurtz in *E.B.* (ed. 14, revised), x (1939), p. 208 f., s.v. 'German Baptist Brethren'.

TUNSTALL, CUTHBERT (1474–1559), Bp. of *Durham. He was educated at Cambridge and Padua. His interest in learning won him the friendship of Abp. W. *Warham, who appointed him his chancellor in 1511. After holding a series of preferments and being employed on various political missions by *Henry VIII, he was made Bp. of London in 1522 and translated to Durham in 1530. In the divorce question he was one of the counsel of the Queen, but during the following years, though continuing sympathetic to Catholic doctrine, he lacked strength of purpose. He yielded in the matter of the Royal Supremacy after first opposing it, and introduced into his diocese the religious changes confirmed by Parliament. In 1537 he was made president of the Council of the North, but continued to take an active part in ecclesiastical affairs, writing in favour of auricular confession, using his influence to keep the '*Bishops' Book' (1537) as Catholic as possible, and assisting with the preparation of the '*Great Bible' of 1539. Under *Edward VI his position became more and more difficult. In 1547 he voted against the abolition of *chantries, and in 1549 against the Act of *Uniformity and the Act permitting priests to marry. In 1551 he was imprisoned in his house in London, where he wrote his treatise *De Veritate Corporis et Sanguinis Domini Nostri Jesu Christi in Eucharistia* (publd. at

Paris, 1554), a careful exposition of Catholic Eucharistic doctrine. In 1552 he was tried by a lay commission for high treason and deprived of his bishopric, but reinstated by *Mary in 1554, when he refrained from taking part in the persecution of Protestants. On the accession of *Elizabeth I he refused to take the Oath of Supremacy and declined to consecrate M. *Parker to the Abpric. of Canterbury (1559). He was then deprived of his see and kept a prisoner in *Lambeth Palace under the care of Parker, where he died shortly afterwards.

The Register of his Durham episcopate was ed. and calendared by Gladys Hinde (Surtees Society, clxi for 1951; 1952; pp. 1–131, with introd., pp. xi–xxxv). A collection of *Certain Godly and Devout Prayers* written by Tunstall in Lat. were translated into Eng. by Thomas Paynell, Augustinian Friar (London, 1558; ed. R. Hudleston, O.S.B., 'Orchard Books', extra series, i, 1925). Full life by C. Sturge (London, 1938). Brief sketch by G. H. Ross-Lewin (Typical English Churchmen, series ii, 1909, pp. 135–66). A. F. Pollard in *D.N.B.*, lvii (1899), pp. 310–15; H. Gee in *D.E.C.H.*, pp. 603–5, s.v.

TURNER, CUTHBERT HAMILTON

(1860–1930), *Patristic and NT scholar. Educated at *Winchester and at New College, Oxford, he was a Fellow of Magdalen from 1889 until his death. In 1920 he was elected Dean Ireland's professor of exegesis at Oxford in succession to W. *Lock. An early interest in chronology bore fruit in 'The Day and Year of St. *Polycarp's Martyrdom [Saturday, 22 Feb. 156]', in *Studia Biblica*, II (1890), pp. 105–55; this was followed by a comprehensive article 'Chronology of the NT' in J. *Hastings' *Dictionary of the Bible*, i. (1898). His main life-work was *Ecclesiae Occidentalis Monumenta Iuris Antiquissima*, an edition of the early Latin ecclesiastical canons. Six fascicules (1899–1930) appeared at intervals during his life; the concluding 7th fascicule came out in 1939, leaving the work still incomplete. The textual evidence for the different Latin versions was presented with immense thoroughness and the work also led Turner to several important subsidiary studies, notably papers on the canons and other subjects in the *Journal of Theological Studies*, to which Turner was a constant contributor. In conjunction with W. *Sanday (d. 1920) and others he investigated the Biblical text of St. *Irenaeus, the fruits of which studies eventually appeared in 1923. His writings also include a revision of C. *Gore's *The Church and the Ministry* (1919), an important essay on 'The Apostolic Succession' in *Essays on the Early History of the Church and the Ministry* (1918; edited by H. B. *Swete, d. 1917), some papers on 'Marcan Usage' in the *Journal of Theological Studies*, and 'St. Mark' in the S.P.C.K. Commentary (1928).

Catholic and Apostolic. Collected Papers by ... Cuthbert Hamilton Turner, ed. by H. N. Bate (1933), with Memoir by id., pp. 1–65. H. N. Bate in *D.N.B.*, 1922–1930, pp. 861–4.

TURRECREMATA, JUAN DE; TOMÁS DE. See *Torquemada, Juan de; Tomás de.*

TUTIORISM. The system of moral theology (also termed **Rigorism**), acc. to which, in cases of doubt or perplexity, the 'safer opinion' (*opinio tutior*; i.e. that in favour of the moral principle) must be followed unless there is a degree of probability amounting to moral certitude in the 'less safe opinion' (*opinio minus tuta*; i.e. that against the principle). A kind of Tutiorism was the normal position held by Catholic moral theologians before the notion of 'probability' achieved its full development in the 17th and 18th cents. As against *Probabilism, many of the Jansenists (e.g. P. *Nicole) maintained Tutiorist doctrines; but the system was obsolescent by 1690, when the *Inquisition included statements of Tutiorism in a list of condemned rigorist propositions. Its critics urge that the system, if strictly practised, would render life intolerable, its requirement of absolute certainty before taking action making moral decisions in many cases impossible.

TWELFTH NIGHT. The evening preceding Twelfth Day (the *Epiphany), twelve days after *Christmas, formerly kept as a time of merry-making and associated with many old customs such as taking down the Christmas decorations. In Herefordshire there was a tradition of lighting twelve bonfires, representing the Twelve Apostles, to secure a blessing on the fruits of the earth, and similar practices prevailed elsewhere. The 'Twelfth Cake' was an ornamented cake made for the occasion, containing a bean or coin, the drawer of which became the 'King' or 'Queen' of the festivities.

TWELVE APOSTLES, Teaching of the. See *Didache*.

TWELVE ARTICLES, The. The main charter of the *Peasants' Revolt, in the form of 'Twelve Articles' adopted at Memmingen in Mar. 1525. Among the peasants' demands were the right to appoint their own pastors, control over tithes, abolition of serfdom, proper rights in the matters of fishing (in streams, but not in ponds), game, and woodcutting, just conditions of work and rent, justice in the courts and abolition of *Todfall* ('heriot', i.e. the usage whereby the landlord appropriated the most valuable chattel of a deceased tenant). For the most part the claims were moderate, esp. when compared with the extremities to which the peasants soon pushed their demands; and in a final article it was stated that nothing would be required except in so far as it could be shown to conform with the will of God. M. *Luther formally professed his agreement with the Articles, though he opposed the attempt to achieve their demands by revolt.

Text in H. Böhmer, *Urkunden zur Geschichte des Bauernkrieges und der Wiedertäufer* (H. *Lietzmann (ed.), *Kleine Texte*, No. 50/51, 1910), pp. 3–10; Eng. tr. in Kidd, No. 83, pp. 174–9.

TWELVE PATRIARCHS, Testaments of the. See *Testaments of the Twelve Patriarchs.*

TYCHICUS. A disciple of St. *Paul. He was a native of Asia (Acts 20. 4) who accompanied St. Paul on his third missionary journey, and in his captivity; and he was the bearer of the letters to *Colossae (Col. 4. 7 f.) and *Ephesus (Eph. 6. 21 f.). He is also referred to at 2 Tim. 4. 12 and Tit. 3. 12. Several cities claim him as bishop, while some martyrologies make him a deacon. Feast day in the E., 9 Dec.; in the W., 29 Apr.

TYCHON, Patriarch. See *Tikhon, Patriarch.*

TYCONIUS (d. *c.* 400), *Donatist theologian. He seems to have been a layman of considerable importance in his community, but was attacked for his catholicizing views by the Donatist bishop, Parmenian (*c.* 378), and condemned by a Donatist Council at *Carthage *c.* 380; he remained, however, a member of his sect. His condemnation was probably caused by two works, 'De Bello Intestino Libri Tres' and 'Expositiones Diversarum Causarum', now lost, in which he seems to have taught that the Church must be a society spread over the whole earth and contain both good and bad. Tyconius's chief work was his 'Liber Regularum' (*c.* 380) which propounded seven rules for the interpretation of Scripture, which St. *Augustine, who greatly esteemed him despite his being a Donatist, incorporated in his 'De Doctrina Christiana'; hence they played an important part in medieval exegesis. His Commentary on Rev., which consistently followed a spiritual line of interpretation, is partly preserved in a compilation by the Spanish presbyter, Beatus of Liebana (*c.* 776).

Editio princeps of the 'Liber Regularum' by J. J. Grynaeus, *Monumenta Patrum Orthodoxographa* (Basle, [1569]), pp. 1352–87; the 'Rules' are also repr. from a later ed. in J. P. Migne, *PL*, xviii, 13–66. Discussion and crit. text in F. C. *Burkitt, *The Book of Rules of Tyconius* (Texts and Studies, iii, pt. 1, Cambridge, 1894). H. A. Sanders (ed.), *Beati in Apocalypsin Libri XII* (Papers and Monographs of the American Academy in Rome, vii, 1930). On his commentary on the Apocalypse see also J. Haussleiter, 'Die lateinische Apokalypse der alten Afrikanischen Kirche' in T. *Zahn, *Forschungen zur Geschichte des neutestamentlichen Kanons und der altkirchlichen Literatur,* iv (1891), pp. 1–244. T. Hahn, *Tyconius-Studien* (Studien zur Geschichte der Theologie und der Kirche, vi, Hft. 2; 1900). P. Monceaux, *Histoire littéraire de l'Afrique chrétienne,* v (1920), pp. 165–219. Bardenhewer, iii, 495–8; Altaner (ed. 1951), p. 326. E. Dinkler in *P.W.,* Zweite Reihe, vi (pt. 1; 1936), cols. 849–56, s.v. 'Ticonius'; G. Bardy in *D.T.C.,* xv (pt. 2; 1950), cols. 1932–4, s.v.

TYNDALE, WILLIAM (1494?–1536), translator of the Bible and Reformer. A native of Gloucestershire, he studied from 1510 to 1515 at Magdalen Hall, Oxford, and later at Cambridge. *C.* 1522 he conceived the project of translating the Bible; but when C. *Tunstall, Bp. of London, refused his support, Tyndale went to Germany and settled at Hamburg (1524), never to return to his own country.

The printing of his first translation, which was begun at *Cologne in 1525, was interrupted by the local magistrates, but completed at Worms the same year. On its arrival in England in 1526, it was bitterly attacked by Abp. W. *Warham, C. Tunstall, and T. *More. Tyndale spent most of his remaining years in the English House at Antwerp, where he frequently revised the NT. His other writings include *A Prologue on . . . Romans* (1526), *Parable of the Wicked Mammon* (1528), and *Obedience of a Christian Man* (1528). In theology, he insisted on the authority of Scripture and, like M. *Luther, on justification by faith, though his Eucharistic teaching resembled that of H. *Zwingli. He wrote also against T. *Wolsey and the 'Divorce' (*Practice of Prelates,* 1530) and against T. More, his ablest opponent. Besides his frequently revised NT, Tyndale printed translations of the Pentateuch (1530) and Jonah (1531), and left Josh.–2 Chr. in MS. His Biblical translations, made direct from the Greek and Hebrew into straightforward, vigorous English, remain the basis of both the AV and the RV. In 1535 he was arrested, imprisoned at Vilvorde, nr. Brussels, and strangled and burnt at the stake prob. on 6 Oct. 1536.

Collection of his works publd. London, 1573. Doctrinal Treatises ed. H. Walter (*Parker Society, 1848); selections from his works ed. S. L. Greenslade (London, 1938). Modern lives by R. Demaus (London [1872]) and J. F. Mozley (ib., 1937). *Tyndale Commemoration Volume,* reproducing substantial parts of Tyndale's Revised Testament of 1534 (London, 1939), with brief life by J. F. Mozley, pp. 224–40, and essay on 'Tyndale's Influence on English Literature' by J. R. Coates, pp. 241–55. E. I. Carlyle in *D.N.B.,* lvii (1899), pp. 424–30. See also bibl. to *Bible* (English Versions).

TYPES (Gk. τύποι, 'examples', 'figures'). In theology, the foreshadowings of the Christian dispensation in the events and persons of the OT. Just as Christ Himself could refer to *Jonah as a symbol of His *Resurrection, so St. *Paul found in the Israelites' crossing of the *Red Sea (1 Cor. 10. 1–6) the 'type' of baptism, while to the author of the Ep. to the Hebrews *Melchizedek was the foreshadowing of Christ (Heb. 7). A Christian type differs from an allegory in that the historical reference is not lost sight of. Types are looked upon, however, as having a greater significance now than was apparent in their pre-Christian OT context. Typology, with an increasingly allegorical emphasis, was much employed in the early Church, esp. by the *Alexandrine Fathers, for whom almost everything in the OT was capable of interpretation by this method.

Modern studies in Biblical typology include W. J. Phythian-Adams, *The Fulness of Israel.* A Study of the Meaning of Sacred History (Warburton Lectures for 1935–1937; 1938); L. Goppelt, *Typos.* Die typologische Deutung des Alten Testaments im Neuen (Beiträge zur Förderung christlicher Theologie, xliii; 1939); J. Daniélou, S.J., *Sacramentum Futuri.* Études sur les origines de la typologie biblique (1940); A. G. Hebert, S.S.M., *The Throne of David.* A Study of the Fulfilment of the Old Testament in Jesus Christ and His Church (1941); H. Riesenfeld, *Jésus transfiguré.* L'arrière-plan du récit évangélique de la Transfiguration de Notre-Seigneur (Acta Seminarii Neotestamentici Upsaliensis, xvi; 1948). P. Lundberg, *La Typologie baptismale dans l'ancienne Église* (ib., x; 1942).

TYPICON (Gk. τυπικόν).   In the E. Church, a liturgical manual which indicates how the services are to be recited during the ecclesiastical year, with directions as to the rules to be followed when two or more feasts fall on the same day.

TYPOS, The.   The Imperial edict issued by Constans II in Sept. 647 or 648 to supersede *Heraclius's *Ecthesis.   With a view to securing peace, it forbade anyone to assert either *Monothelite or *Dyothelite beliefs, and required that teaching should be limited to what had been defined in the first Five Oecumenical Councils.   The refusal of Pope *Martin I (649–55; q.v.) to accept it led to his deposition.

The text is preserved in the Acts of the Lateran Council of 649; pr. in Hardouin, iii, col. 824 f., with Lat. tr. cols. 823–6.   Hefele–Leclercq, iii (pt. 1; 1909), pp. 432–4.   Fliche–Martin, v (1938), p. 166.   See also further bibl. to *Martin I*.

TYRANNICIDE.   The murder of a tyrant whose rule has become insupportable.   On the ethical question, three opinions have been current among Christians:
(1) Those who hold that the sixth commandment is to be interpreted as forbidding killing in any form, e.g. in police action or in war, naturally believe Tyrannicide to be included in the prohibition.
(2) Those who (e.g. on a basis of Rom. 13. 1 f.) hold that force is by Divine authority wholly invested in the *de facto* civil government also believe Tyrannicide to be morally unjustifiable.
(3) Those who hold that rebellion, including Tyrannicide, is defensible and right in circumstances where, if the oppressor were an alien, war would be justified, and provided that the grievance is considerable, that the circumstances offer no milder means of redress, and that the killing is not simply an act of revenge. Such is the general view of Catholic moral theologians.

A. Bride in *D.T.C.*, xv (pt. 2; 1950), cols. 1988–2016, s.v.

TYRE AND SIDON.   The two chief cities of the Phoenicians, on the coast of Syria.   In OT times they carried on a lucrative maritime trade, and the Israelites knew them as rich heathen neighbours, from whom in the time of King Ahab (c. 875–853 B.C.) the worship of the Tyrian *Baal was introduced into Israel, and combated by *Elijah (1 Kgs. 16. 31 ff., 18. 18 ff.).   The district of Tyre and Sidon was visited by Christ, who healed a Gentile woman there (Mk. 7. 24 ff.) and the two towns were referred to by Him as outstanding instances of places of unbelief (Mk. 3. 8, Lk. 6. 17).   Tyre was held by the *Crusaders, 1124–1291.

F. C. Eiselen, *Sidon. A Study in Oriental History* (Columbia University Oriental Studies, iv; New York, 1907); W. B. Fleming, *The History of Tyre* (Columbia University thesis; ib., x; 1915).   G. M. Mackie in *H.D.B.*, iv (1902), pp. 823–5, s.v. 'Tyre' and 980 f., s.v. 'Zidon'; H. Guthe in *P.R.E.* (ed. 3), xviii (1906), pp. 280–302, s.v. 'Sidonier', with postscript in xxiv (1913), p. 503 f.; [E.] Honigmann in *P.W.*, Zweite Reihe, ii (pt. 2; 1923), cols. 2216–29, s.v. 'Sidon'; L. Hennequin in *Dict. Bibl.*, Suppl. iii

(1938), cols. 439–47, s.v. 'Fouilles en Phénicie, 88. Saida (Sidon)' and '90. Sour (Tyr)', with reff. to reports of recent excavations; [O.] Eissfeldt in *P.W.*, Zweite Reihe, vi (pt. 2; 1948), cols. 1876–1907, s.v. 'Tyros (3)'.

TYRRELL, GEORGE (1861–1909), English *Modernist theologian.   He was a native of Dublin, of Evangelical upbringing, and educated at Trinity College.   At an early age he had come under High Church influence, esp. that of R. *Dolling, and was later received into the RC Church (1879).   In 1880 he entered the *Jesuit novitiate and in 1891 was priested and became lecturer in moral theology at *Stonyhurst.   In 1896 he was transferred to Farm Street, the principal church of his order in London, where he was a sought-after confessor and made a name by writing, publishing two collections of Meditations, *Nova et Vetera* (1897) and *Hard Sayings* (1898), and a series of Conferences, *On External Religion* (1899).   His friendship with F. *von Hügel led to his acquaintance with the writings of H. *Bergson, M. *Blondel, L. *Laberthonnière, and A. *Loisy, which contributed to his increasing hostility to *Scholasticism and his stress on the anti-intellectual and experiential aspects of religion.   From 1899 he moved further and further from traditional RC orthodoxy, notably in an article on hell, entitled 'A Perverted Devotion', which appeared in the *Weekly Register* (1899).   Though its publication led to his removal from Farm Street and his retirement to the Jesuit mission house at Richmond in Yorkshire, Tyrrell did not cease to feel a strong attraction to the devotional aspects of Catholicism, for which he continued to work as a keen apologist.   In 1900 he wrote *Oil and Wine* (printed 1902; new preface, 1907), another book of meditations, but its immediate publication was prohibited by his episcopal superiors on account of its immanentist tendencies.   In 1901 he published *The Faith of the Millions* and in 1903 his *Lex Orandi*, his last work to appear with an '*Imprimatur'.   After he had in vain asked for his secularization (1905), the final rupture with the Society of Jesus came in 1906, following the publication of extracts from an anon. 'Letter to a Professor' by the *Corriere della Sera*.   This writing, in which he contrasted living faith with dead theology, he published with amplifications in 1906 as *A Much Abused Letter*.   Though expelled from his order and suspended 'a divinis', Tyrrell continued his literary activities.   *Lex Credendi* (1906) is for the most part a devotional exposition of the 'Our Father' with a strong anti-intellectual and anti-theological bias, and *Through Scylla and Charybdis* (1907) a collection of essays which reflected his increasing sympathy with a thoroughgoing symbolism. After *Pius X's issue of the encyclical 'Pascendi', Tyrrell wrote two letters of protest to *The Times* of 30 Sept. and 1 Oct. 1907; they drew upon him the minor excommunication. In 1908 Tyrrell published his *Medievalism*, a bitter attack on Card. D. J. *Mercier and a violent denunciation of the contemporary RC Church.   His posthumous work, *Christianity* *at the Cross-Roads* (1909), questioned whether Christianity was the final religion and held out hopes of a universal religion of which Christianity was but the germ. Tyrrell died with the last rites of the Church, but was refused Catholic burial. His remains were deposited

in the Anglican churchyard at Storrington, where H. *Bremond took part in the funeral.

Maude D. Petre, *Autobiography and Life of George Tyrrell* (2 vols., 1912); id. *Letters* (1920); J. L. May, *Father Tyrrell and the Modernist Movement* (1932); A. *Loisy, *Georges Tyrrell et Henri Bremond* (1936).

Addendum to p. 1351

THOMAS, Coptic Gospel of St. This apocryphal Gospel, orig. written in Greek, was found in a Coptic version among the papyri dug up at Nag-Hammadi in Upper Egypt in 1945–6. It is now preserved in the Coptic Museum at Old Cairo. The Greek original perhaps dates from *c.* 150, the Coptic, which contains some additions, from *c.* 400. In its heading, the Gospel professes to have been written down by 'Didymus Judas Thomas'. It is not, like the canonical Gospels, historical in form, but consists of a series of pithy sayings and parabolic discourses of Jesus. Some of its 114 items have points of contact with the sayings in 'Q' (q.v.), though where parallels exist, the sayings in Thomas are secondary. It has been thought possible that it preserves a few

sayings of the Lord not found in the canonical Gospels which ultimately go back to genuine tradition; but its contents hardly warrant the extravagant claims made for it when it first became generally known in 1959. There are significant literary parallels with certain of the (Greek) *Oxyrhynchus papyri, viz. Nos. 1, 654 and 655 (see *Sayings of Jesus*). Apparently the work is of Gnostic *provenance*.

The Coptic text was orig. issued in a photographic edition by Pahor Labib at Cairo in 1956. Ed. princeps of printed text, with Eng. tr. by A. Guillaumont and others, London, 1959. R. M. Grant and D. N. Freedman, *The Secret Sayings of Jesus* (1960; trans., notes and discussion). R. McL. Wilson, *Studies in the Gospel of Thomas* (1960), with bibl. B. Gärtner, *The Theology of the Gospel of Thomas* (1961); H. E. W. Turner and H. Montefiore, *Thomas and the Evangelists* (Studies in Biblical Theology, xxxv, 1962).

U

UBAGHS, GERHARD CASIMIR (1800–1875), chief representative of the *Traditionalist *Ontologism of Louvain. He became professor of philosophy at Louvain in 1834 and from 1846 onwards was editor of the *Revue Catholique*, the principal organ of Ontologism. Among his most important works are his *Logicae seu Philosophiae Rationalis Elementa* (1834), *Ontologiae seu Metaphysicae Generalis Elementa* (1835), and *Theodiceae seu Theologiae Naturalis Elementa* (1841) in which he expounds a mitigated Traditionalism acc. to which the knowledge of metaphysical and moral truths is based on a primitive Divine teaching handed on by oral tradition. This teaching he combined with the Ontologist doctrine of the direct contemplation of God by the intellect in the 'objective ideas'. Though his books were not placed on the *Index, his teaching was censured by the *Holy Office on 21st Sept. 1864, and soon afterwards Ubaghs submitted and resigned his chair. See also *Traditionalism*.

J. Jacops, 'Notice sur la vie et les travaux de M. le Chanoine G. C. Ubaghs, Professeur Émérite à la Faculté de Philosophie et Lettres de l'Université Catholique de Louvain' in *Annuaire de l'Université catholique de Louvain* (1876), pp. 417–66. J. Henry in *Biographie nationale* publiée par l'Académie Royale des Sciences, des Lettres et des Beaux-Arts de Belgique, xxv (1930–2), p. 890 f., s.v. See also works cited under *Traditionalism*.

UBERTINO OF CASALE (1259–c. 1330), a leader of the '*Spiritual Franciscans' (q.v.). He became a *Franciscan in 1273, studied at *Paris, and returned to Italy as a preacher and lecturer. Here *John of Parma and Peter John *Olivi, then leading figures among the Spirituals, with whom he became acquainted, gained a strong influence on him. In 1305 he wrote his principal work, 'Arbor vitae crucifixae Jesu Christi', a collection of apocalyptic ideas and thoughts on the Church and society, full of invective against *Boniface VIII and Benedict XI. From 1306 to 1308 he was chaplain to Cardinal N. Orsini, pontifical legate in N. and Central Italy, and in 1310 was called to *Avignon by *Clement V to defend the Spirituals in the controversy on poverty. Having failed to obtain the erection of convents and provinces for his party, he was allowed, in 1317, to be transferred to the *Benedictines of Gembloux. In 1322 *John XXII asked his opinion in the question of 'theoretical poverty', then a matter of dispute between the *Dominicans and the Franciscans. Two years later he was still at the Curia, in the service of Cardinal Orsini. He fled, however, in 1325, probably because accused of heresy; in 1328 he was prob. among the Franciscans who accompanied Louis the Bavarian on his journey to Rome; and in 1329 he seems to have preached against John XXII at Como. Nothing is known of his death. He is mentioned by *Dante in canto xii of the 'Paradiso', and was venerated by the *Fraticelli of the 15th cent.

F. Callaey, *L'Idéalisme franciscain spirituel au XIVᵉ siècle*. Étude sur Ubertin de Casale (Université de Louvain. Recueil de travaux publiés par les membres des Conférences d'Histoire et de Philologie, fasc. 28, 1911). Earlier lives by J. C. Huck (Freiburg i.Br., 1903) and E. Knoth (Marburg, 1903). See also P. Godefroy in *D.T.C.*, xv (pt. 2; 1950), 2021–34, s.v.

UBIQUITARIANISM. The doctrine held by M. *Luther and many of his followers that Christ in His human nature is everywhere present. Luther employed it, e.g. in his two writings *Das diese Worte Christi*, '*Das ist mein Leib*', *noch fest stehen wider die Schwarmgeister* (1527) and *Bekenntnis vom Abendmahl Christi* (1528), to uphold his belief in the real presence of Christ in the Eucharist; and it was formally defended by J. *Brenz at a Lutheran synod at Stuttgart in 1559.

UDALL, JOHN (c. 1560–92), also 'Uvedale', *Puritan pamphleteer and Hebrew scholar. Matriculating at Christ's College, Cambridge, in 1578, he was chiefly educated at Trinity College, where he became strongly inclined to Puritanism. While curate of Kingston-on-Thames (1584–8) he was charged before the Court of *High Commission in 1586 for his critique of Episcopacy. In 1588 he published anonymously a widely read pamphlet on *The State of the Church of England, laid open in a Conference between Diotrephes a Bishop, Tertullus a Papist, Demetrius a Usurer, Pandochus an Innkeeper and Paul a Preacher of the Word of God*. Suspected of complicity in the *Marprelate Tracts, he was summoned before the Privy Council in 1589. In 1590, on his refusal to clear himself on oath, he was found guilty of the authorship of *A Demonstration of the Truth of that Discipline which Christ hath Prescribed for the Government of His Church* [1588]; but the sentence of felony was not executed. He died in prison in Southwark, shortly after his pardon had been procured.

He published several volumes of his sermons, including *Amendment of Life* [1584], *The True Remedy against Famine and Wars* [1588], and *The Combat between Christ and the Devil* (1588). In 1593 his *Commentary upon the Lamentations of Jeremy* (anon.) was published posthumously. In the same year there appeared at *Leyden his *Key to the Holy Tongue*, which comprised a Hebrew Grammar translated from *Peter Martyr and a Hebrew dictionary of his own compilation; the work was highly valued by *James I.

The State of the Church of England was repr. by E. Arber (The English Scholar's Library of Old and Modern Works, v, 1880); *A Demonstration of the Truth of that Discipline which Christ hath Prescribed*, also ed. id. (ib., ix, 1880). S. Lee in *D.N.B.*, lviii (1899), pp. 4–6, s.v., with reff.

UDALL, NICHOLAS (c. 1505–56), also 'Uvedale', reformer and dramatist. Born at Southampton, he was admitted a scholar of

*Winchester in 1517 and of Corpus Christi College, Oxford, in 1520, where he became a probationary Fellow *c.* 1525. His *Lutheran sympathies prob. forced him to leave Oxford in 1529 and prevented his proceeding to M.A. until 1534. In 1533 he joined John Leland (d. 1552) in the composition of verses for the coronation of Anne Boleyn. He was appointed Headmaster of Eton in 1534, but dismissed in 1541 on charges of complicity in the theft of silver images and college plate and of unsuitable behaviour, which led to a short imprisonment in the Marshalsea. In 1547, with the patronage of Catherine Parr, he was appointed to assist with Princess (later Queen) *Mary in translating the first volume of the *Paraphrases* of *Erasmus (publ. 1548). Through the favour of *Edward VI he became a Canon of *Windsor in 1551 and in 1553 he became rector of Calborne (Isle of Wight). Possibly because of his association with Mary over the translation of Erasmus's *Paraphrases* he remained in favour in the next reign, continuing to write for the Court stage and *c.* 1555 becoming Headmaster of *Westminster (in succession to Alexander *Nowell).

Udall is a significant example of the influence of Protestantism on the new humanist movement. His other published works include translations of Erasmus's *Apophthegms* (1542), of *Peter Martyr's *Tractatio de Sacramento Eucharistiae* (*c.* 1550), and of T. Gemini's *Compendiosa Totius Anatomiae Delineatio* (1553). His play *Ezekias*, performed before *Elizabeth in 1564, has been lost. His *Ralph Roister Doister*, however, a Christmas comedy, originally written for a London school, prob. between 1545 and 1552 (publd. 1567), although lost since the 16th cent., was recovered in the early 19th cent. and has been frequently reprinted.

Ralph Roister Doister ed. for the Shakespeare Society by W. D. Cooper (London, 1847), with memoirs of Nicholas Udall, pp. xi–xxiv. Later edd. include those of W. C. Hazlitt (London, 1874), W. H. Williams–P. A. Robin (London, 1901), J. S. Farmer (ib., 1906, with notes on his other dramatic works), C. G. Child (ib., 1913; with introd.) and G. Scheurweghs (Materials for the study of Old English Drama, ed. H. de Vocht, xvi, Louvain, 1939), with biographical introd. pp. xi–l. N. Pocock (ed.), *Troubles Connected with the Prayer Book of 1549* (Camden Society, New Series, xxxvii; 1884), pp. xx–xxv. S. Lee in *D.N.B.*, lviii (1899), pp. 7–9, s.v. F. S. Boas–A. W. Reed in *C.B.E.L.*, i, p. 519 f.

U.I.O.D.G. (sometimes **I.O.D.G.**), i.e. the initial letters of (*ut*) *in omnibus Deus glorificetur* ('that God may be glorified in all things'), one of the mottoes of the *Benedictine Order. It occurs in the 'Rule of St. Benedict', ch. 57.

ULLATHORNE, WILLIAM BERNARD (1806–89), RC Bp. of Birmingham. He was a direct descendant of St. Thomas *More. After over three years as a cabin-boy, Ullathorne entered the *Benedictine monastery at *Downside in 1824. He was ordained priest in 1831 and, in 1832, volunteered for the mission in *Australia, of which he was made *Vicar General. He organized the RC Church there,

working esp. among the convicts whose cause he defended vigorously during a stay in England. His tract *The Catholic Mission in Australasia* (1837), as the first popular attack on the convict system, earned him much hostility in Australia. In 1840 he returned to England and in the next year was put in charge of the Benedictine mission at Coventry, where, with the help of Mother Margaret Mary Hallahan (1803–68), the future foundress of the *Dominican convent at Stone, he developed the religious life of the RC parish. Having repeatedly refused a see in Australia, he was appointed *Vicar Apostolic for the Western District of England in 1846. Transferred to the Central District in 1848, he took an active part in the negotiations for establishing the hierarchy in England. During these years he worked together with Cardinal N. *Wiseman to bring about the fusion of the old Catholics with the recent Oxford converts and the Italian priests of the modern congregations, taking up an intermediate position and forming a firm friendship with J. H. *Newman. On the restoration of the hierarchy in 1850 he became Bp. of Birmingham, and later engaged in the controversies about the *Rambler and E. B. *Pusey's *Eirenicon* (1866). At the *Vatican Council, though a firm *Ultramontane, he occupied an independent position and was a member of the deputation on ecclesiastical discipline. In 1888, he resigned his see and became titular archbishop. His most popular work, the *Autobiography*, ending with the year 1851, which was written in 1868–9 and revised in the last year of his life, was published together with his letters in 1891–2.

Cuthbert Butler, O.S.B., *The Life and Times of Bishop Ullathorne* (2 vols., 1926); id., *The Vatican Council. The Story told from inside in Bishop Ullathorne's letters* (2 vols., 1930). T. Cooper in *D.N.B.*, lviii (1899), pp. 19–21.

ULPHILAS (*c.* 311–383), Apostle of the Goths. Of Cappadocian ancestry, he was completely at one with the Goths, among whom he was born, both in language and sympathy. He spent much of his life as a young man at *Constantinople, and *c.* 341 was consecrated bishop in the city by *Eusebius (formerly Bp. of Nicomedia), then bishop of the capital. Shortly afterwards he returned to his native country to spend the rest of his life as a keen missionary, at first beyond the confines of the Empire, and later among Goths settled in Moesia II. He translated the Bible into the *Gothic language for the first time, omitting (acc. to *Philostorgius) only the Books of Kings, as their warlike deeds might have a bad influence upon a nation so fond of war as the Goths. Through his connexions with Eusebius of Nicomedia, he was led into *Arianism; and it was esp. through his influence that for several centuries the Goths continued attached to that heresy. A confession of faith, *Homoean in character, of which Ulphilas was the author, has survived in an imperfect form.

G. Waitz, *Über das Leben und die Lehre des Ulphila* (1840); F. Kauffmann, *Aus der Schule des Wulfila* (Texte und

Untersuchungen zur altgermanischen Religionsgeschichte, i, 1899). On his version of the Bible, Studies by G. W. S. Friedrichsen: Gospels, Oxford, 1926; Epistles, Oxford, 1939. For his Confession of Faith, see A. Hahn, *Bibliothek der Symbole* (ed. 3, 1897), § 198 (p. 270 f.). Bardenhewer, iii, 594 f.

ULRICH, St. (*c.* 890–973), Bp. of Augsburg from 923. He took a very prominent part in the political and ecclesiastical history of his times, upholding a high standard of clerical morality and giving his strong support to the policy and reforms of the Emp. Otto I. He is the first person who is known to have been formally canonized by a Pope, John XV pronouncing him a saint at the *Lateran synod of 29 Jan. 993. A considerable cultus developed around him. In the cent. after his death, a forged letter was put into circulation in which he was represented as opposed to clerical celibacy. Feast day, 4 July.

A *Sermo Synodalis* of Ulrich is repr. from P. *Labbé in J. P. Migne, *PL*, cxxxv, 1071–4. The 'Epistola de Continentia Clericorum' ascribed to him is ed. L. de Heinemann in *M.G.H.*, Libelli de Lite Imperatorum et Pontificum Saeculis XI et XII, i (1891), pp. 254–60. The principal source for his life is the biography by his contemporary, Gebhard, Provost of Augsburg Cathedral, pr. in *AA.SS.*, Jul. II (1721), pp. 97–131; repr. from the *Acta Sanctorum Ordinis Sancti Benedicti in J. P. Migne, op. cit., 1009–70; also ed. G. Waitz in *M.G.H.*, Scriptores, iv (1841), pp. 377–425. The life by Bernard of *Reichenau (d. 1248), tr. into German *c.* 1200, ed. in Germ. and Lat. by J. A. Schmeller (Munich, 1844). Studies by P. I. Braun (Augsburg, 1796; see also other works by the same author), J. N. Stützle (ib., 1860), C. Raffler (ib., 1866), and U. Schmid (ib., 1901). E. W. Kemp, *Canonization and Authority in the Western Church* (1948), p. 57 f. A. Vogel–A. Hauck in *P.R.E.* (ed. 3), xx (1908), pp. 211–13, s.v.; A. Bigelmair in *L.Th.K.*, x (1938), cols. 365–8, s.v.

ULRICH, St. (d. 1154). See *Wulfric, St.*

ULTRAMONTANISM. The name widely given to a tendency in the RC Church which favours the centralization of authority and influence in the papal Curia, as opposed to national or diocesan independence. The word is found as early as the 11th cent., but opinions differ as to whether it was used in an ecclesiastical as distinguished from a geographical sense before the rise of *Gallicanism in France in the 17th cent. In this cent. and the next, Ultramontanism became a definite point of view which gained more and more power as national and centrifugal movements such as *Gallicanism, *Jansenism, and *Josephinism became discredited either as involved in definite heresy or as lending countenance to the new liberal and anti-Christian movements of which the French Revolution of 1789 was the logical and most systematic expression. The 19th cent., therefore, saw the triumph of the Ultramontane cause, since there rallied to it all those elements in the RC Church which were most opposed to the rising theological liberalism of the age. In France the Gallican party was overpowered by the reproach of having conformed to the Revolution; in Germany the Ultramontanes seized the part of defenders of the Church against the interference of the state in spiritual affairs; in England the new missionary element among the RCs, little

hampered by national traditions of the past, had every inducement, in spite of opposition from the hereditary RC families, to support to the utmost the policy of the Curia. The stages of the triumph of Ultramontanism were roughly as follows:

1814. The revival of the *Jesuit Order, which was always the mainstay of curial as opposed to local authority.

1864. The issuing by *Pius IX of the *Syllabus, in which Catholicism and any form of liberalism were held to be incompatible.

1870. The declaration by the *Vatican Council that the Pope is infallible, when he makes, by virtue of his office, a solemn pronouncement on faith or morals. (This declaration, though not conceding the claim of administrative infallibility which many Ultramontanes would have wished, marks a substantial triumph for their point of view.)

F. Nielsen, *Pavedømmet i den nittende Hundredaar* (2 vols., 1876, ed. 2 revised, 1895–8; Eng. tr., *The History of the Papacy in the XIXth Century*, 2 vols., 1906); J. B. Bury, *History of the Papacy in the Nineteenth Century* (1930).

U.M.C.A. The (Anglican) Universities Mission to Central Africa. It was founded in response to the appeal made by D. *Livingstone in the Senate House at Cambridge in 1857 and has since received the continuous response of the universities. The first head of the Mission was Bp. C. F. Mackenzie. After an unsuccessful attempt to establish work in the Zambezi valley, the Mission was moved in 1864 to the island of Zanzibar, a centre of the Arab slave trade. Here, with five boys from a slave dhow, began a work which has always taken a foremost place, the training of a native ministry. In 1873, largely owing to the influence on public opinion of reports from the Mission, the Sultan of Zanzibar was persuaded to abolish slavery and the foundation stone of Christ Church, the cathedral of Zanzibar, was laid on the site of the slave market. In the same year work was re-established on the mainland which was gradually extended through the area now covered by the five dioceses of Zanzibar, Nyasaland (1892), Northern Rhodesia (1910), Masasi (1926), and S.W. Tanganyika (1952). The Community of the Sacred Passion, founded in 1910 by Bp. F. *Weston for his diocese of Zanzibar, has its mother house at Magila and now numbers African as well as English women among its members.

R. Keable, *Darkness or Light* (1912); G. H. Wilson, *History of the Universities' Mission to Central Africa* (1936).

UNA SANCTA (Lat. 'One Holy'). Two of the *notes of the Church in the Nicene Creed, and often used, esp. in quite recent times, substantivally for the Church, usually with emphasis upon its corporate aspect.

UNAM SANCTAM. The Bull (so named from its opening words) which *Boniface VIII issued on 18 Nov. 1302 during his quarrel with Philip IV of France, declaring that there was 'One Holy Catholic and Apostolic Church' outside which there was 'neither salvation nor remission of sins'. It strongly emphasized the position of the Pope as the Supreme Head of the Church; and it maintained that to reject his authority was to cease to belong to the Church. It further declared that the 'temporal sword' and the 'spiritual sword' were alike committed to the Church. Of these the spiritual sword was in the hands of the clergy, while the temporal sword was delegated to the secular authority, to be wielded on behalf of the Church and under its direction. Since what was spiritual was greater than what was temporal, the temporal power was to be subject to the spiritual, which was itself subject only to the judgement of God. As the authority of the spiritual power had been divinely granted to St. *Peter and his successors, to oppose it was to oppose the law of God Himself. The Bull concluded by affirming that it was necessary to salvation for every human creature to be subject to the Roman Pontiff. Although the text of the Bull contained nothing new, it brought to a point the ever-growing claims of the Papacy and marks the zenith of medieval Papal ecclesiastical polity.

Crit. ed. of text in G. Digard–M. Faucon–A. Thomas–R. Fawtier (edd.), *Les Registres de Boniface VIII* (Bibliothèque des Écoles Françaises d'Athènes et de Rome, Ser. 2, iv), iii (1921), No. 5382, cols. 888–90; operative portions in Mirbt, No. 372, p. 210 f.; Eng. tr. in Bettenson, pp. 159–61. T. S. R. Boase, *Boniface VIII* (1933), esp. ch. xii, pp. 313–337; J. Rivière, *Le Problème de l'Église et de l'État au temps de Philippe le Bel* (S.S.L., viii, 1926), esp. pp. 79–91, 150–5.

UNCIAL SCRIPT. A form of majuscule script used for books in Greek and Latin from about the 4th to the 8th cents. A.D. Greek examples are the *Codices Sinaiticus, Vaticanus and Alexandrinus; Latin examples are the Codex of *Eusebius of Vercelli and the *Codices Fuldensis and Amiatinus (qq.v.). Its name is derived from a passage in *Jerome's preface to Job, but its present meaning is that assigned to it by the *Maurist authors of the *Nouveau Traité de diplomatique* (1765).

UNCONDITIONED, The. The term used by William Rowan Hamilton (1805–65) for the supposed entity which was the condition of the universe and by some equated with God.

UNCREATED LIGHT. In the *Hesychast system, the mystical light of God's visible Presence (also known as the **Light of Tabor**) which the soul was held to be capable of apprehending by submitting to an elaborate process of ascetic purification and devotion. Its attainment was considered the highest end of man on earth. See also *Hesychasm*.

UNCTION. The process of anointing with oil with a religious significance, usually by a bishop or priest, e.g. at the *Coronation of a King. In the RC and Eastern Orthodox Churches, Unction is used both at *Baptism and *Confirmation. The word is most commonly applied, however, to the Sacrament of the Unction of the Sick, sometimes called

Extreme Unction (*unctio extrema*), though the name is repudiated in the E. Church. The word 'extreme' may refer to the fact that the Unction is the last of three Sacramental Unctions, or to the fact that it is usually administered when the patient is *in extremis*.

In the NT the anointing of the sick is referred to in Mk. 6. 13 and Jas. 5. 14 f. There is a prayer for the Blessing of Oil in St. *Hippolytus's *Apostolic Tradition*, 5, and in the *Euchologion* of St. *Serapion of Thmuis (d. *c.* 365). From the 5th cent. references are more frequent. *Innocent I, in his Ep. to Decentius of Eugubium (416), describes a rite of unction with both spiritual and physical effects from which those undergoing canonical penance are excluded. In St. *Caesarius of Arles the rite is found in connexion with the reception of Holy Communion; *Bede represents it as a well established custom; and from the 10th cent. it is frequently discussed in connexion with the theology of the Sacraments. Since *Peter Lombard, the first known author to use the term 'extreme unction', it has been numbered among the Seven Sacraments. Acc. to the developed medieval doctrine, as expounded by St. *Thomas, the remote matter of the Sacrament is olive oil consecrated by the bishop, its proximate matter the anointing of the five senses, its form prayer, and its minister the priest. The Council of *Trent reaffirmed the medieval doctrine and against the Reformers asserted the sacramental character of the rite. See also *Viaticum*.

In the first seven centuries recovery from illness was commonly expected as a result of unction, and in the RC Church it is still given 'for the health of soul and body', though in practice bodily recovery is not ordinarily looked for. It is administered to those who have attained the age of reason once during each illness when there is danger of death, by anointing with prayer the eyes, ears, nose, lips, hands, and feet.

In the Greek Church the rite is called *Euchelaion* (Gk. εὐχέλαιον, 'oil of prayer') and administered in church by seven, five, or three priests. Here its primary end is held to be the physical cure, though it is in fact frequently received as a preparation for Communion even by those who are not ill.

In the First English BCP (1549) a form of unction was included in the Order for the Visitation of the Sick for use 'if the sick person desire'. It contained an accompanying prayer for healing of body and mind, forgiveness, and spiritual strengthening. In 1552 and later versions of the BCP there has been no provision for unction. Recently a desire for its restoration has been widely expressed in the Anglican Communion. The revised Scottish and American Prayer Books (1929) and the Alternative Book of Occasional Offices authorized for the Province of South Africa all make provision for unction of the sick, and in 1935 a 'Form of Unction and the Laying on of Hands' was approved by the Convocations of *Canterbury and *York 'for provisional use subject to due diocesan sanction'.

Modern works include F. W. Puller, S.S.J.E., *The Anointing of the Sick in Scripture and Tradition, with some Consideration of the Numbering of the Sacraments* (C.H.S., lxxvii; 1904); J. Kern, S.J., *De Sacramento Extremae Unctionis Tractatus Dogmaticus* (Ratisbon, 1907); J. B. Bord, *L'Extrême-Onction d'après l'épître de saint Jacques (v. 14–15) examinée dans la tradition* (Museum Lessianum, Section théologique; 1923). C. de Clercq, 'Ordines Unctionis Informi des IXe et Xe siècles' in *E.L.*, xliv (1930), pp. 100–122; P. Browe, S.J., 'Die letzte Ölung in der abendländischen Kirche des Mittelalters' in *Z.K.T.*, lv (1931), pp. 515–561. E. Jacquemier, 'L'Extrême-Onction chez les Grecs' in *É.O.*, ii (1898–9), pp. 193–203. K. M. Rallis, Περὶ τῶν μυστηρίων τῆς μετανοίας καὶ τοῦ εὐχελαίου κατὰ τὸ δίκαιον τῆς ὀρθοδόξου ἀνατολικῆς ἐκκλησίας (1905). T. Spáčil, S.J., *Doctrina Theologiae Orientis Separati de Sacra Infirmorum Unctione* (Orientalia Christiana, xxiv, Hft. 2; No. 74; 1931); with bibl. L. Eisenhofer, *Handbuch der katholischen Liturgik*, ii (1933), pp. 344–55. C. Ruch–L. Godefroy in *D.T.C.*, v (1913), cols. 1897–2022, s.v. 'Extrême-Onction' H. *Leclercq, O.S.B., in *D.A.C.L.*, v (1922), cols. 1029–37, s.v. 'Extrême-Onction'; A. Baumeister in *L.Th.K.*, vii (1935), cols. 714–17, s.v. 'Ölung'; H. Leclercq, O.S.B., in *D.A.C.L.*, xii (pt. 2; 1936), cols. 2116–30, s.v. 'Onction'. See also bibl. to *Spiritual Healing* and *Visitation of the Sick*.

UNDERHILL, EVELYN (1875–1941), exponent of the mystical life. The daughter of a distinguished barrister, she was educated at *King's College, London, and later travelled much on the Continent. In 1907 she underwent an experience of religious conversion and in her spiritual struggles turned to the study of the mystics. The first literary fruit of her newly awakened interest was her well-known book *Mysticism* (1911; ed. 13, 1940). Its range extended from St. *Teresa to J. *Boehme and from Christian mystical experience to *Neo-Platonist speculations, and its comprehensive approach to religious experience at once made it a standard work. In 1911 she came under the influence of F. *von Hügel, and about the same time began to undertake individual spiritual direction. Among her books of this period are *The Path of Eternal Wisdom* (1911) and *The Spiral Way* (1912), symbolic interpretations of the *Stations of the Cross and the Mysteries of the *Rosary, both published under the pseudonym 'John Cordelier'. They were followed by *The Mystic Way* (1913), *Practical Mysticism* (1914), *The Essentials of Mysticism* (1920) and *The Life of the Spirit and the Life of To-day* (1922). From 1924 onwards she was a much sought-after retreat conductor, and in 1927 she was made a Fellow of King's College, London. *Worship* (1936) embodied her general outlook in a broad review of the subject. Among her translations and editions were *The Cloud of Unknowing* (1912), *Walter Hilton's Scale of Perfection* (1923) and *Eucharistic Prayers from the Ancient Liturgies* (1939). She also wrote a study of *Jacopone da Todi (1919). In her later years she was a keen pacifist.

The Letters of Evelyn Underhill, edited with an Introd. by C. [W. S.] *Williams (1943). *Collected Papers of E. Underhill*, ed. L. Menzies (1946). Life by Margaret [B.] Cropper (S.P.C.K., 1958).

UNIAT CHURCHES. The Churches of Eastern Christendom in communion with *Rome, which yet retain their respective languages, rites, and canon-law in accordance with the terms of their union; these last in most cases provide for *Communion under both kinds, *baptism by *immersion, and marriage of the clergy. The term 'Uniat' (Lat. *Unio*, so Polish *Unia*) was first used by the opponents of the Union of *Brest-Litovsk (1595), and, while consistently disowned by the Churches concerned, has among RCs retained a slightly hostile flavour. The main groups covered by the designation are the *Maronites (united 1182), the *Syrians under the Patriarch of *Antioch, and the *Malankarese (1930), all of the Antiochene rite; the *Armenians under the Patriarch of Cilicia (united 1198–1291 and 1741); the *Chaldeans (1551) and the *Malabarese (before 1599) of the Chaldean rite; the *Copts (1741) and *Ethiopians (1839), both of the Alexandrine rite, and of the Byzantine rite the Polish *Ruthenians (1595), the *Hungarians (1595), Yugoslavs (1611), the Podcarpathian Ruthenians (1652), the Rumanians (1701), the Melkites (1724), and certain Bulgars (1860) and *Greeks (1860). Of these the largest body is the Ukrainians. The term is also applied to the Italo-Greek-Albanian community of S. Italy which, although never separated from Rome, is permitted to follow similar practices. In 1946 the Uniats of the Ukraine and in 1948 those of Rumania were separated from the RC Church and joined to the *Russian and Rumanian Orthodox Churches respectively. The total number of Uniats in 1950 was estimated at about eight-and-a-quarter millions. See also under separate groups.

D. Attwater, *The Catholic Eastern Churches* (Milwaukee, 1937). C. de Clercq, *Les Églises unies d'Orient* (Bibliothèque Catholique des Sciences Religieuses; 1934). S. Gaselee, *The Uniats and their Rites* (*Alcuin Club Tracts, xvi; 1925). B. J. Kidd, *The Churches of Eastern Christendom from A.D. 451 to the Present Time* [c. 1927], ch. xviii, pp. 457–63 and 521 f. J. Hajjar, *Des chrétiens uniates du Proche-Orient* (1962). On the Melkites and Uniats of S. Italy, A. *Fortescue, *The Uniate Eastern Churches*, ed. G. D. Smith (1923).

UNIFORMITY, Acts of. There were four: (1) *The Act of 1549*. This Act (2 & 3 Edw. VI. c. 1), passed on 21 Jan. 1549, imposed the exclusive use of the First BCP of *Edward VI from the ensuing *Whitsunday (9 June) in the 'celebration of the Lord's Supper, commonly called the Mass' and in all public services. Holders of benefices who did not comply were punishable for a first offence with forfeiture of a year's income and six months' imprisonment, for a second offence with deprivation and a year's imprisonment, and for a third offence with imprisonment for life. Penalties of the same order were imposed for depraving or speaking against the Book. The public services were to be in English with the exception that at the universities 'for the encouragement of learning' all services other than the Mass might be said in Latin, Greek, or Hebrew; and in private use of the Book everyone was at liberty to use these languages as he wished. Only eight bishops and three lay peers voted against the Bill.

(2) *The Act of 1552* (5 & 6 Edw. VI. c. 1). The First Book, which was a compromise, having proved a failure, this further Act was passed on 9 Mar.–14 Apr. 1552. It stated

that owing to doubts occasioned by the interpretation of the 'very godly order' of the first Act the Book had been revised; and its use was ordered from *All Saints' Day following. Absence from church on Sundays and Holy Days by all not reasonably hindered was now made punishable by ecclesiastical censures and attendance at any other form of service by imprisonment.

(3) *The Act of 1559* (1 Eliz. c. 2). This Act, after repealing the legislation of the previous reign reimposing the forms of worship in use under *Henry VIII, ordered the use of the Book of 1552, with a few catholic modifications, from 24 June 1559. The penalties for depraving the Book were increased, and absence from church made punishable by a fine of twelve pence as well as ecclesiastical censures. Such ornaments of the church and the minister were to be retained 'as was in this Church of England by authority of Parliament in the second year of' Edward VI 'until other order shall be therein taken by the authority of the Queen's Majesty'.

(4) *The Act of 1662* (13 & 14 Car. II. c. 4). As part of the Restoration settlement, a Bill for reintroducing the BCP passed the Commons in July 1661, but as the *Convocations did not complete the revision of the Book until December, the Bill was again considered in 1662. The Book itself (i.e. the BCP still in use), which was annexed to the Bill, was not discussed by either Commons or Lords. The Bill received the Royal Assent on 19 May. Before the ensuing St. *Bartholomew's Day (24 Aug.), all ministers were required publicly to assent to the Book, from which day its exclusive use was ordered. Ministers not episcopally ordained by that date were to be deprived. All ministers and schoolmasters were also required to make a declaration of the illegality of taking up arms against the King and to repudiate the *National Covenant (q.v.). Some 2,000 Presbyterian ministers who refused to conform were ejected from their livings.

This Act still remains in force. It has been modified at a few points by the '*Clerical Subscription Act' (1865, q.v.), the '*Universities Test Act' (1871, q.v.), the 'Table of Lessons Act' (1871) and the 'Act of Uniformity Amendment Act' (1872; see following art.).

The texts are pr. in Gee–Hardy as follows: (1) pp. 358–66 (No. lxix); (2) pp. 369–72 (No. lxxi); (3) pp. 458–67 (No. lxxx); and (4), pp. 600–19 (No. cxvii), with further reff.

UNIFORMITY, Act of, AMENDMENT ACT (1872). More generally known as the 'Shortened Services Act'. This Act (35 & 36 Vict. c. 35), passed by Parliament after its approval by the *Convocations of *Canterbury and *York, provides for the optional use of shortened forms of Morning and Evening Prayer, as additional services, in parish churches on Sundays and certain other days, and in cathedrals on any day, and as substitutes for the full services in parish churches on week-days. The chief omissions sanctioned are the Exhortation 'Dearly beloved brethren', all but one of the appointed *Psalms, one of the

*Canticles, and the State Prayers. It also provides that Morning Prayer, the Litany, and the Communion Service may be recited separately, and not necessarily as a continuous service.

For exact details, see the 'Schedule' to the Act, printed in R. *Phillimore, *Ecclesiastical Law* (ed. 2, 1895), i, pp. 757–61.

UNIGENITUS (1343). The bull of Clement VI, issued on 27 Jan. 1343, which gave official approval to the teaching of the Schoolmen that *Indulgences owed their efficacy to the Pope's dispensation of the accumulated *merit of the Church. In 1518 Cardinal T. de Vio *Cajetan accused M. *Luther of contravening its contents.

Text in *Corpus Iuris Canonici*, ed. A. Friedberg, ii (Leipzig, 1881), cols. 1304–6. Abbreviated text in Mirbt, No. 385, pp. 224–5.

UNIGENITUS (1713). The Constitution of *Clement XI, publd. 8 Sept. 1713, condemning 101 propositions extracted from P. *Quesnel's *Réflexions morales sur le Nouveau Testament.* About half these propositions contain doctrine previously condemned in the works of M. *Baius (1567) and C. *Jansenius (1653). Most of the others are reactionary criticisms of modern developments in Catholic faith and practice. Many French Jansenists appealed from Clement's verdict to a 'future Council'.

Text in *Bullarum, Diplomatum et Privilegiorum Sanctorum Romanorum Pontificum Taurinensis Editio*, xxi (1871), No. clxxxvii, pp. 567–75; abbrev. text in Denz.–Bann. (ed. 1928), pp. 371–9. J. Parguez, *La Bulle Unigenitus et le jansénisme politique* (1936); J. F. Thomas, *La Querelle de l'Unigenitus* (1950). J. Carreye, P.S.S., in *D.T.C.*, xv (pt. 2; 1950), cols. 2061–162, s.v. 'Unigenitus (Bulle)'.

UNION OF BREST. See *Brest, Union of.*

UNION OF CHRISTENDOM. See *Reunion.*

UNION THEOLOGICAL SEMINARY, New York City. An institution for the training of ministers founded in 1836, by the independent action of 'New School' Presbyterians, for 'men of moderate views' of any denomination. It has always encouraged critical studies and advocated toleration. Temporarily under Presbyterian control after 1870, in 1892–3 it reclaimed its independence and refused to dismiss the 'heretic' professor, C. A. *Briggs. Its professors have been outstanding men, and have recently included many British (esp. Scots) scholars.

UNITARIANISM. A type of Christian thought and religious observance which rejects the doctrines of the Trinity and the Divinity of Christ in favour of the unipersonality of God. Unitarians have no formal creed. Originally, their teaching was based on Scriptural authority, but J. *Martineau (1805–1900) in England and T. *Parker (1810–1860) in U.S.A. led the way from Biblical to rational unitarianism. Hence reason and conscience have now become the criteria of belief and practice for Unitarians. Owing to their belief in the abiding goodness of human nature, they are critical of the orthodox doctrines of the Fall, the Atonement, and eternal punishment.

Though the unipersonality of God was voiced in the early Church in the various forms of *Monarchianism, modern Unitarianism dates historically from the Reformation era. It soon attracted adherents among those of extreme reforming views, esp. in the sects. Probably its earliest exponent was Martin Cellarius (1499–1564), a pupil of J. *Reuchlin, who defended Unitarian views in *De Operibus Dei* (Strassburg, 1527). Other early Unitarians were J. *Valdés (at least in sympathy), M. *Servetus, and B. *Ochino. As an organized community, it became established in the 16th–17th cents. in Poland, Hungary, and England.

In Poland George Blandrata, a Piedmontese physician, became leader of an active group of Unitarians in 1558. They continued to grow until 1565, when anti-Trinitarians were excluded from the synod of the Reformed Church and henceforward compelled to hold their own synods as the 'Minor Church'. From 1579 until his death (1604) Faustus *Socinus led the party. In 1605 the *Racovian Catechism (q.v.) was issued. Towards the middle of the 17th cent. they had to face strong opposition. In 1638 the *Jesuits secured the suppression of the Unitarian college at Racow; in 1658 Socinians were expelled from the realm and all traces of Unitarianism disappeared from Poland.

In Hungary Blandrata, who arrived in the country in 1563, was also largely responsible for the spread of anti-Trinitarianism, and the King himself, John Sigismund, was converted. But after Sigismund's death (1570) the sect was persecuted. In 1638 the Unitarians put forward a common confession and were recognized as a legitimate religion.

In England John *Biddle (q.v.; 1615–1662) is generally reckoned the father of Unitarianism. He published Unitarian tracts and in 1652–4 and 1658–62 held conventicles in London. Rather more than a hundred years later J. *Priestley defended Unitarian principles in his *Appeal to the Serious and Candid Professors of Christianity* (1770). But until T. *Lindsey seceded from the C of E in 1773 and formed for the first time a Unitarian denomination, there was only one other Unitarian conventicle in England. In 1774 Lindsey opened Essex Chapel in London. Penal Acts continued in force against Unitarians until 1813. In the 18th cent. Unitarian views were also widely accepted by Dissenting congregations, esp. among the English *Presbyterians. The long disputes as to the endowments of chapels, once orthodox but now in the hands of the Unitarians, were ended in 1844 by the *Nonconformist Chapels Act, which allowed the Unitarians to keep chapels founded on an Open Trust where over 25 years' usage could be proved for their opinions.

In America the first definitely Unitarian congregation was King's Chapel, Boston. In 1785, it adopted a form of the American liturgy, revised to meet the needs of the Unitarians. In the early 19th cent. Unitarianism was also adopted in *Congregationalist Churches. Its ethical and philosophical aspects were emphasized in different ways by W. E. *Channing and R. W. *Emerson. In more recent times it has exercised a pervasive influence in American religion, notably through the Divinity School at Harvard University as reconstituted under Charles W. Eliot (1869–1909).

Collection of the works of F. Socinus, J. Crellius, J. Stichling, and L. Wolzogen in the *Bibliotheca Fratrum Polonorum quos Unitarios Vocant* (8 vols., Amsterdam, 1656). F. S. Bock, *Historia Antitrinitariorum, maxime Socinianismi et Socinianorum* (2 vols., Königsberg, 1774–8). F. Trechsel, *Die Protestantischen Antitrinitarier vor Faustus Socin* (2 vols., 1839–44); O. Fock, *Der Socianismus nach seiner Stellung in der Gesammtentwickelung des christlichen Geistes* (2 vols., Kiel, 1847). J. H. Allen, *An Historical Sketch of the Unitarian Movement since the Reformation* (New York, 1894), J. E. *Carpenter (ed.), *Freedom and Truth*. Modern Views of Unitarianism (1925). H. Gow, *The Unitarians* ('The Faiths', 1928). E. M. Wilbur, *A History of Unitarianism*. Socinianism and its Antecedents (Cambridge, Mass., 1946); id., *A History of Unitarianism in Transylvania, England, and America* (ib., 1952). R. Wallace, *Antitrinitarian Biography: or Sketches of the Lives and Writings of Distinguished Antitrinitarians . . . to the Close of the Seventeenth Century*. To which is prefixed a History of Unitarianism in England during the same period (3 vols., 1850). G. Bonet-Maury, *Des origines de christianisme unitaire chez les Anglais* (1881; Eng. tr., 1884). Herbert John McLachlan, *Socinianism in Seventeenth-Century England* (1951); Herbert McLachlan, *The Unitarian Movement in the Religious Life of England*. Its Contribution to Thought and Learning. 1700–1900 (1934); R. V. Holt, *The Unitarian Contribution to Social Progress in England* (1938). H. McLachlan, *The Methodist Unitarian Movement* (Publications of the University of Manchester, Historical Series, xxxiii; 1919). J. H. Allen in J. H. Allen–R. Eddy, *A History of the Unitarians and the Universalists in the United States* (American Church History Series, x; 1894), pp. 1–249; G. W. Cooke, *Unitarianism in America*. A History of its Origin and Development (Boston, Mass., 1902). W. J. Kühler, *Socinianisme in Nederland* (Leiden, 1912); J. C. van Slee, *De Geschiednis van het Socinianisme in Nederlanden* (Haarlem, 1914). J. E. Carpenter in *H.E.R.E.*, xii (1921), pp. 519–27, s.v. (also issued separately, London, 1922).

UNITAS FRATRUM. The Latinized form of the Czech *jednota bratrská* ('society of brethren'), the title assumed by the branch of the *Hussites known as the *Bohemian Brethren (q.v.).

UNITED FREE CHURCH OF SCOTLAND. The Church formed in 1900 by the union of the *United Presbyterian Church and the *Free Church of Scotland. In 1929 it united with the Established Church of Scotland.

UNITED METHODIST CHURCH. The branch of Methodism formed in 1907 by the union of the *Methodist New Connexion, the *Bible Christians, and the *United Methodist Free Churches (qq.v.), and itself embodied in the *Methodist Church (q.v.) in 1932.

The possibility of reunion in Methodism was discussed throughout the 19th cent. and towards its end negotiations between various bodies took place. In 1901 the third Methodist Ecumenical Conference recommended that reunion in British Methodism was desirable and in 1902 active steps to that end were taken. Although other Methodist Churches were consulted and agreed in principle to the plan of reunion, only the above-named three churches took part in the union of 1907.

The constitution accepted for the new Church closely followed that common to all branches of Methodism. Central government was in the hands of a conference meeting annually and presided over by a president elected each year. The missionary and social activities of the uniting churches were maintained and increased.

The success of the union increased the desire for wider reunion in Methodism, and proposals in this direction were made by the Wesleyan Conference in 1913. In 1932 the United Methodist Church finally united with the *Wesleyan and *Primitive Methodist Church to form a Methodist Church including almost the whole of English Methodism.

See foll. entry and bibliography to *Methodist Churches.*

UNITED METHODIST FREE CHURCHES. One of the bodies which went to form the *United Methodist Church in 1907. It originated in the amalgamation of smaller communities which had broken away from *Wesleyan Methodism. In every case the reason for division was not doctrinal but constitutional, the Free Churches embodying the most democratic elements of Methodism.

The *Protestant Methodists*, formed in 1827, arose from discontent of long standing with the government of the Methodist Church. The great power vested in the annual Conference of ministers was oppressive to those who wished the laity to have a share in the government of their Church, and feeling ran high when Dr. Jabez *Bunting (q.v.) asserted at the Conference: 'Methodism knows nothing of democracy; Methodism hates democracy as it hates sin'. The immediate occasion of their secession was trifling—the erection of an organ at Brunswick Chapel, Leeds. After much dissension the Protestant Methodists were founded at Leeds, with a few associated societies, mostly in Yorks.

The next group, the *Wesleyan Methodist Association*, was formed in 1835 through a dispute about the founding of a Theological Institution for the training of ministers. The principal ground of offence was that the Conference had acted contrary to its constitution and not consulted the people before taking a step of such importance; objections to the theological institution as such was of secondary importance. The expulsions which followed led to the formation of the new democratic association. In 1836 it was joined by the 'Protestant Methodists' and a year later by a small body of secessionists at Derby.

Further dissension was brought to a head at the Wesleyan Conference of 1849. For some years Methodism had been disturbed by the circulation of anonymous pamphlets, known as the Fly Sheets, containing accusations of favouritism, narrowness, and the mismanagement of Connexional funds against the predominant party in Methodism. Vigorous and, as some thought, unjust, steps were taken to discover their authors, and finally, in the Conference of 1849, three ministers were expelled for refusing to answer questions. At the same time some 80,000 members left the Wesleyan Church. At first they were content to agitate for reform in Wesleyanism; but when it became apparent that they would not gain their end, a separate body, the *Wesleyan Reformers*, was formed.

After several years of discussion, largely on the subject of their constitution, the 'Wesleyan Methodist Association' and the 'Wesleyan Reformers' united in 1857, taking the name of the 'United Methodist Free Churches'. Peace and a settled constitution contributed to solid progress both in England and in foreign missions. As early as 1837 the Wesleyan Association had commenced work in Jamaica, in 1851 the first missionary had been sent to Australia. In both West and East Africa missions were established and maintained in spite of much hardship. From 1864 stations were supported in China.

The constitution adopted by the United Methodist Free Churches reflects the opposition to autocratic rule by the ministry which led to their separation from the parent Church. The annual Assembly, unlike the Wesleyan Conference, was not composed wholly of ministers. It was composed, with the exception of a very small number of officials elected at the previous Assembly, of representatives elected by their own circuits. In organization an endeavour was made to combine the congregational with the connexional system, and great authority was given to the circuits in dealing with their own affairs, e.g. the Assembly did not determine the circuits to which ministers should be appointed.

In 1907 the United Methodist Free Churches united with the *Methodist New Connexion and the *Bible Christians to form the *United Methodist Church.

G. Eayrs in W. J. Townsend–H. B. Workman–G. Eayrs (edd.), *A New History of Methodism*, i (1919), pp. 514–51.

UNITED PRESBYTERIAN CHURCH. The Church formed in Scotland in 1847 by the union of two earlier groups, the *United Secession Church and the Relief Synod. In 1900, apart from a very small minority (the *Wee Frees), the United Presbyterians united with the Free Church of Scotland to form the *United Free Church of Scotland.

UNITED SECESSION CHURCH. The Church formed in Scotland in 1820 by the fusion of the 'Old Lights' and the 'New Lights', the two groups into which the *Burghers divided in the later 18th cent. In 1847 it united with the Relief Synod to form the *United Presbyterian Church (q.v.).

UNITED SOCIETY FOR CHRISTIAN LITERATURE.

A Society founded in 1935 by the fusion of the *Religious Tract Society (q.v.), the Christian Literature Society for India and Africa (founded 1858), and the Christian Literature Society for China (founded 1884) for the spread of the Christian faith through literature in Britain and overseas. It is the proprietor of the general and religious publishing house, the Lutterworth Press, London.

G. Hewitt, *Let the People Read*. A Short History of the United Society for Christian Literature, Religious Tract Society, 1799, Christian Literature Society for India and Africa, 1858, Christian Literature Society for China (British Support), 1887 (1949). Annual Reports (London, 1937 ff.).

UNITED STATES OF AMERICA, Christianity in.

Of the earliest colonial settlements that of Virginia was under Royal and therefore Anglican auspices; while those of New England, which were founded by minority groups who wished to escape from the religious Establishment in England, were strongly *Puritan. The '*Pilgrim Fathers' who settled Plymouth Bay Colony in 1620 were *Independents from the start. The founders of Massachusetts (1628) were Anglicans of the Puritan party, but on settling in America they ordained their own minister (1629). In general, while the Church government of the New England colonies was *Congregational, their theology and ecclesiastical polity were *Presbyterian, with Church and State in close relations on the Genevan model. Until the end of the 17th cent. no other form of Church order was tolerated, and civic rights depended on Church membership. Church establishments, with payment of clergy from taxes, lasted in three states until the early 19th cent. Rhode Island was an exception; from its foundation it tolerated all Protestants except *Quakers, and *Baptists esp. found a home there. New York (formerly New Amsterdam) was at first the seat of a Dutch Reformed Church, but in 1664 Anglicanism was introduced by the British. Maryland was the only colony founded by RCs, and this became officially Anglican in 1702. Pennsylvania, founded in 1682 by W. *Penn, was created as a centre for Quakers (whose actual numbers, however, were not large). With neighbouring colonies, it received many Scots and Irish Presbyterians, and several bodies of German Protestants (*Lutherans, *Mennonites, *Moravians, etc.), before c. 1750. The Southern colonies mainly had Anglican establishments but tolerated dissenters; Baptists, and later *Methodists, became numerous in them.

In the 18th cent. strict Calvinism was represented by Jonathan *Edwards (1703–58) and other leading New England divines, and a revival of evangelical fervour within the traditional New England Protestantism (the '*Great Awakening') coincided with the visit of G. *Whitefield in 1740; but in the decades preceding the Declaration of Independence (1776) *Deism and rationalism increased, and the resultant outlook, rather than any Protestant

sectarianism, found embodiment in the Constitution, which forbade the imposition of any religious test on holders of federal office, and precluded Congress (in the First Amendment) from passing any law regarding the establishment of religion. In this way the fundamental principle of complete separation of Church and State, which has always been regarded as part of the American way of life, was laid down. In law all religious bodies are purely private associations of citizens. The tradition of public life, like the Declaration of Independence, does not hesitate to assume belief in God, but no particular confession of faith or religious tradition may be officially sponsored.

In the late 18th and early 19th cent. the prevailing rationalistic outlook encouraged the spread of *Unitarianism within New England Congregationalism and its organization as a separate denomination. Its growth was made possible by the Congregational polity, which allowed the majority in any congregation to determine its doctrinal standards and retain Church property despite alterations of faith. Consequently in New England Unitarianism shares with orthodox Congregationalism the oldest church-buildings and the prestige of antiquity. In the early 19th cent. Baptist and Methodist churches also multiplied, their loose forms of Church order and itinerant ministry being esp. adaptable to the conditions of an expanding population and the advancing western frontier. Methodism had reached America before the Revolution and the first Methodist Conference was held in 1773. It was J. *Wesley's sense of the impossibility of the Anglican ministry filling the needs of America which led him to ordain ministers and a superintendent for America in 1784, and thus bring about the decisive break of Methodism from the C of E. Although the question was several times mooted, the English bishops had always refused (or believed themselves unable under the Establishment) to consecrate a Bishop for the American colonies, and the growth and work of the C of E in America was long hampered by the absence of an episcopate. The C of E was further weakened in Revolutionary times by its connexion with the English government and the fact that many of the clergy (all of whom had necessarily to be ordained in England, even if American by birth) were of English origin or loyalist in sympathy. Consequently some left the country at the Revolution, but sufficient clergy and laity remained in America to form the *Protestant Episcopal Church (q.v.). Thereafter it shared in the growth of other Christian bodies and even increased more than some of the larger denominations, relatively to its initial numbers. The RC Church also had no Bishop in the United States at the Revolution. J. *Carroll, who had become the first Prefect Apostolic in 1784, was appointed Bishop (of Baltimore) in 1789 and consecrated in England in 1790. RC numbers, small at that date, were greatly swelled in the 19th cent. by immigration from Ireland and Central and Southern Europe. They were further increased by the expansion of the Union, which brought within it traditionally Catholic areas such as Louisiana, New Mexico, and the originally Spanish parts of the Southwest. Protestant immigrants from Continental Europe swelled the numbers of denominations of non-British origin, such as the Lutheran and *Reformed Churches, which are separately organized for different national groups, such as Swedish, Norwegian, and Slovak, as well as German, Lutherans. Various national Eastern Orthodox Churches and the Polish *Old Catholic (or National Catholic) Church were also brought to America. Separatist movements in various Protestant denominations arose, one of the most important in its results being that of Thomas and Alexander *Campbell, which became the denomination of *Disciples of Christ. Another purely American sect is the *Mormons (Latter Day Saints), founded by Joseph Smith in 1830, the original members of which migrated from New York State via Ohio to Utah, where they set up their own community, still centred on Salt Lake City. In 1879 the *Christian Science body (Churches of Christ Scientist) was founded in Boston, and has become influential in upper- and middle-, rather than working-class circles, esp. in the North-east.

In the 1840s both the Baptist Convention and the Methodist Conference were divided on the issue of slavery, the Southern (slave-holding) parties seceding in 1844 and 1845 respectively. The Presbyterian Church was divided only in 1861, when a separate General Assembly was set up in the Confederate States. 'The Methodist Church' and 'The Methodist Church South' were reunited in 1939, but there remain (1957) the Northern Baptist, the National Baptist, and the Southern Baptist Conventions, of which the Southern is the largest. 'The Presbyterian Church in the U.S.A.' and 'The Presbyterian Church in the U.S.' are also separate bodies, the latter being the Southern branch, and in this case the smaller. There are also two minor Presbyterian Churches. The Episcopalians in the Confederate States organized themselves separately during the Civil War but their secession was not recognized by the General Convention, to which they returned after the war. In addition to the main bodies mentioned, there have sprung up a number of smaller Baptist and Methodist Churches; many of these are negro in origin and membership. The Negro Baptist Church is the largest negro Church and there are also two 'African Methodist' Churches and one 'Coloured Methodist' Church of considerable size. There are also several smaller Protestant bodies of less definite denominational ancestry, many of them evangelical and missionary, with memberships of several hundred thousand, as well as a large number of independent, separatist, and specialized groups. The over-all figures of membership of religious bodies for 1953-4 show an increasing proportion of the total population—about 97½ million, or 60 per cent. Of these,

RCs number about 32 million (19½ per cent), Protestants about 57 million (35 per cent), practising Jews 5½ million (3 per cent), the remainder miscellaneous. Of the major denominations, Baptists of all organizations number about 18 million (Southern Baptists over 8 million, Negro Conventions 7 million), Methodists about 11½ million ('The Methodist Church' 9 million), Lutherans nearly 7 million, Presbyterians just over 3½ million, Episcopalians just over 2½ million, Disciples of Christ just under 2 million, Congregationalists 2¼ million. The Eastern Churches have a total membership of nearly 2 million, of which the Greek Orthodox numbers 1 million. Although RCs are a strong and influential body and, compared with England, a larger percentage of the population, the preponderating religious sentiment of the country is Protestant in outlook, with an undogmatic and optimistically liberal trend. Biblical Fundamentalism, however, has been powerful and is still relatively stronger than in England. The RC Church has its main strength in the cities, and so far has drawn its hierarchy largely from Americans of Irish stock, and its membership from those of Irish, Polish, Italian, West German, or other Catholic European ancestry. It has been relatively more occupied with the pastoral care and the progressive Americanization of these immigrant groups, and less with Catholics of English stock, than in England, and conversions from Protestantism are relatively less frequent.

All religious bodies, particularly the larger and wealthier Protestant Churches, have been active in promoting educational and philanthropic institutions, including colleges and universities, of which there are a great many of nominal or real religious affiliations, in addition to state and independent institutions. American Christians have also been very active in missionary work, in China, Africa, India, the Near East, and elsewhere; China in particular is a field of special concern to the American Churches. The emphasis on mission work has often, particularly in the 20th cent., been medical and educational, rather than purely evangelistic, and has been backed by generous supplies of money and technical equipment. American missions in many cases undertook to supply the needs of European missions which were cut off from home support by the war of 1939-45.

The theological outlook in the Protestant Churches has been greatly influenced by liberalism. At the universities Biblical criticism and archaeology have flourished more than dogmatic theology. In the later 1930s and 1940s, however, there has been a growth of interest in and respect for dogma, and a theology of crisis and judgement has challenged the former evolutionary outlook: Reinhold *Niebuhr of *Union Theological Seminary has been prominent in this respect. There has also been a revival of interest in *Thomism which has not been confined to RCs. The *Œcumenical Movement, represented originally by the conferences on *Faith and Order and on

*Life and Work and now by the *World Council of Churches, has from the first received considerable support from America, which was strongly represented at the *Amsterdam Assembly of 1948 and gave generously to the expenses of the Movement; this was followed in 1954 by a notable meeting of the Assembly of the World Council at Evanston, near Chicago. Within the United States, likewise, in spite of the fact that there still are over 250 denominations and sects, there has been an increasing trend toward inter-denominational co-operation and even federation, as shown by the excellent work of the Federal Council of the Churches of Christ in North America. In respect to actual organic union there has been more reluctance; yet there have been significant gains both in reunion of schismatic groups, especially among Methodists and Presbyterians, and in mergers of denominations, notably in Congregational and Evangelical groups. Outstanding examples are the merger of the Congregationalist Church and the Christian Church (1931) in the General Council of Congregational and Christian Churches; and of the Evangelical Synod of North America and the Reformed Church in the United States (1934) as the Evangelical and Reformed Church; in 1956 the two bodies thus formed completed arrangements to merge in 'the United Church of Christ'; another union is that of the Evangelical Church and the United Brethren in Christ (1946).

The American Church History Series, ed. P. *Schaff and others (13 vols., New York, 1893–7). R. Baird, Religion in the United States of America. Or an Account of the Origin, Progress, Relations to the State and Present Condition of the Evangelical Churches in the United States (1844). D. Dorchester, Christianity in the United States from the First Settlement down to the Present Time (New York, 1888); L. W. Bacon, A History of American Christianity (1899). H. K. Rowe, A History of Religion in the United States (New York, 1924); W. W. Sweet, The Story of Religions in America (ib., 1930; revised ed., [1939]), with bibl.; W. L. Sperry, Religion in America (1945). J. W. Platner and others, The Religious History of New England (King's College Chapel Lectures, Cambridge, Mass.,–London, 1917). W. W. Sweet, Religion in Colonial America (New York, 1943). P. G. Mode, The Frontier Spirit in American Christianity (New York, 1923). T. C. Hall, The Religious Background of American Culture (Boston, Mass., 1930). W. W. Sweet, Religion in the Development of American Culture, 1765–1840 (New York, 1952). E. F. Humphrey, Nationalism and Religion in America, 1774–1789 (Boston, Mass., 1924). W. A. Brown, Church and State in Contemporary America (New York, 1936). A. P. Stokes, Church and State in the United States (3 vols., ib., 1950). O. W. Elsbree, The Rise of the Missionary Spirit in America, 1790–1815 (Williamsport, Pa., 1928). J. G. Shea, History of the Catholic Church in the United States (4 vols., New York, 1886–92). T. Roehmer, O.F.M.Cap., The Catholic Church in the United States (1950). A. B. Bass, Protestantism in the United States (New York, [1929]); A. L. Drummond, Story of American Protestantism (1949). J. M. Mecklin, The Story of American Dissent (New York, 1934). A. R. Wentz, The Lutheran Church in American History (Philadelphia, Pa., [1923]). W. W. Sweet, Methodism in American Church History (New York, [1933]). W. Walker, A History of the Congregational Churches in the United States of America (New York, 1894); G. G. Atkins, History of American Congregationalism (Boston, Mass., 1942). R. M. *Jones, The Quakers in the American Colonies (1911). E. T. Clark, The Small Sects in America (Nashville, [1937]). H. M. Morais, Deism in Eighteenth Century America (New York, 1934). P. G. Mode, Source Book and Bibliographical Guide for American Church History (Menasha, Wisc., [1921]). Latourette, vi (1941), pp. 175–456, with bibl. pp. 463–96, and vii (1945), pp. 122–156. N. R. Burr, A Critical Bibliography of Religion in America (2 vols., Princeton, 1961).

UNITIVE WAY, The. (Via Unitiva). The third and last stage of the spiritual life. Acc. to Christian mystical writers, when the soul has been purified in the *Purgative and enlightened in the *Illuminative Way it enters on the Way of Union with God. It is generally held, however, that there is no hard-and-fast dividing line, and elements from the illuminative and even purgative stages may appear also in the unitive life. Its special marks are found in the habitual practice of the virtues, frequently to a heroic degree, and the graces of passive *contemplation.

'UNIVERS, L'' The organ of the violently *Ultramontane opinions of L. *Veuillot, who took over its editorship in 1843. Though many Catholics were offended by its virulent tone, it forced the anticlerical French Government to make some concessions to the Church, esp. in the much-debated issue of religious education. In its later days its claims for the Church and the Papacy exceeded those commonly defended even at Rome. The paper was suppressed by the French Government in 1860 for publishing *Pius IX's encyclical 'Nullis certe', but it was revived in 1867, only to be again suppressed in 1874.

UNIVERSALISM. (1) The anti-nationalist teaching of certain of the later Hebrew prophets (e.g. *Deutero-Isaiah, *Jonah) that God's purposes covered not only the Jewish race but also at least some men of other nations.

(2) The doctrine, also known as ἀποκατάστασις, that hell is in essence purgative and therefore temporary and that all intelligent beings will therefore in the end be saved. See Apocatastasis.

UNIVERSALS. In metaphysics, general concepts, representing the common elements belonging to individuals of the same genus or species. The medieval doctrine of universals traces its origin to Greek philosophy, esp. to *Porphyry's 'Introduction to the Categories of Aristotle', which poses three questions, viz. whether the universals exist substantially or only in the human mind; if the former, whether they have bodies or are disembodied beings; and lastly whether they exist separated from the objects of sense or only in them. These problems were combined with the question treated by *Boethius whether the universals are things ('res') or only names ('voces', 'nomina'), and acc. to the answer given philosophers subscribed to the systems of either *Realism or *Nominalism (qq.v.) which were developed in manifold variations during the Middle Ages. Among the best-known representatives of early Realism are John Scotus *Erigena, St. *Anselm, and *William of Champeaux, whereas in the 13th cent. St. *Thomas and *Duns Scotus developed a doctrine which has come to be known as

'Moderate Realism'. Among the Nominalist opponents of the earlier forms of Realism were *Roscellinus and *Abelard, whilst the Realist system of the 13th cent. was attacked by *William of Occam, Gabriel *Biel, and others.

UNIVERSITIES' MISSION TO CENTRAL AFRICA. See *U.M.C.A.*

UNIVERSITY TESTS ACT (1871). By this Act (34 & 35 Vict. c. 26) it was laid down that no person taking any degree other than a degree in divinity, or holding lay, academical, or collegiate offices, should henceforward be required to subscribe any article or formulary of faith.

UNKNOWABLE, The. A term applied by H. *Spencer in his *First Principles* (1862) to the ultimate cause of all things. In a new effort to reconcile science with religion, Spencer assigned to the former the sphere of the knowable, to the latter that of the unknowable, though he held that both science and religion agreed 'in the assertion of a Reality utterly inscrutable in nature'. See also *Agnosticism.*

UNKNOWING, The Cloud of. See *Cloud of Unknowing, The.*

UNLEAVENED BREAD. See *Bread, Leavened and Unleavened.*

UPPER ROOM, THE. See *Cenaculum, The.*

UPSALA. Long after the introduction of Christianity into *Sweden by St. *Anskar, Old Upsala (now a neighbouring town to the north) continued a centre of pagan religious rites. In 1164 Pope *Alexander III made it the head of an ecclesiastical province, separate from *Lund. The see was transferred from Old Upsala to its present site (Aros) under Abp. Folke (1274–7). The cathedral, still the largest church in Sweden, dates from 1287 to 1435. The archbishop, who from the middle of the 15th cent. until the Reformation bore the title of 'Primate of Sweden' ('Primas Sueciae'), is still accorded a certain primacy, though his position is now only that of a 'primus inter pares'. The university, modelled on that of *Bologna, was founded in 1477, and became in the 19th cent. the home of a liberal and 'Low Church' theology as contrasted with the orthodoxy of Lund. Among its most notable bishops of recent times was N. *Söderblom (d. 1931).

The 'Historia Pontificum Metropolitanae Ecclesiae Upsalensis' of Johannes Magnus Gothus (Rome, 1560) is conveniently pr. in the *Scriptores Rerum Svecicarum Medii Aevi,* iii (pt. 2; Upsala, 1871), pp. 1–97, with other material pp. 97–102. G. Kallstenius, *Blad ur Uppsalasangens*

Historia (Stockholm, 1913). N. J.-E. Söderberg, *Studier till Uppsala Domkyrkas Historia* (3 pts., Kyrkohistoriska Föreningen Skrifter, Ser. 1, Arg. xxxv and xxxvi; 1936–7). G. Boëthius–A. L. Romdahl, *Uppsala Domkyrka, 1258–1435* (1935). C. Annerstedt, *Upsala Universitets Historia* [1477–1792] (3 vols. in 6 parts, 1877–1914, + register by E. Colliander, 1931; in Swedish). G. Armfelt in *C.E.,* xv (1912), p. 207 f., s.v. 'Upsala, Ancient See of'; K. Hoeber, ib., p. 208, s.v. 'Upsala, University of'; E. Newman in *R.G.G.* (ed. 2), v (1931), cols. 1402–4, s.v.; J. Metzler, S.J., in *L.Th.K.,* x (1938), cols. 426–8, s.v. See also works cited under *Sweden, Christianity in.*

URBAN II (*c.* 1042–99), Pope from 1088. Odo of Lagery studied at *Reims under St. *Bruno, who afterwards became his most trusted adviser. Having early been canon and archdeacon, he entered the monastery of *Cluny *c.* 1070, where he became prior. He was later called to Rome by *Gregory VII, who made him Cardinal Bp. of Ostia in 1078. Sent as Papal legate to France and Germany, he held a synod at Quedlinburg in Saxony in 1085, at which the *antipope, Guibert of Ravenna (Clement III), was anathematized. Elected to the Papacy in 1088, he expressed his intention of adhering closely to the principles of Gregory VII, which he did, though in a more measured and diplomatic form than his predecessor. The three great difficulties of his pontificate were the antipope, the interference of secular princes in the question of *investiture, and the simony and incontinence of the clergy. Owing to the presence in the city of Guibert and his followers, Urban could not at first enter Rome. He held a Council at Melfi in 1089 which promulgated 16 canons against simony, lay investiture, and clerical marriage. In the same year his position was temporarily strengthened by the marriage of his ardent supporter, Matilda of Tuscany, with Guelph V of Bavaria, which enabled Urban to enter Rome and expel Guibert. The latter was brought back, however, by *Henry IV in 1090, and Urban was once more an exile in S. Italy. But from 1093 Henry's power began to weaken, esp. through the defection of his son, Conrad, who went over to the Pope and was crowned king of Italy. In the same year Urban re-entered Rome and took possession of the *Lateran in 1094. In 1095 he held two Councils at Piacenza and *Clermont, whose chief object was the general reform of the Church, esp. on the subjects of simony and clerical marriage. At Clermont the '*Truce of God' was proclaimed a law of the Church, and Philip I of France, who had put away his queen Bertha and married Bertrada, wife of the Count of Anjou, was anathematized. Having received an appeal for help against the Seljuk Turks from the Greek Emperor, Alexius I Comnenus, Urban proclaimed the First *Crusade. His call, which was received with enthusiasm by the people, initiated the great medieval Crusading movement that was to become a source of strength and prestige to the Papacy. Having returned to Rome in 1096 he held a synod at the Lateran and, in 1098, one at Bari with the object of healing the E. schism. At the latter St. *Anselm defended the *Filioque clause against the Greeks.

Urban died in 1099 before the news of the capture of *Jerusalem by the Crusaders could reach him. Urban's cult was sanctioned in 1881. Feast day, 29 or 30 July.

Although Urban's registers have been lost, 304 of his letters are pr. in J. P. Migne, *PL*, cli, 283–552. Jaffé, i, 657–701, and ii, 713 and 752 f. Life by Peter of Pisa in *L.P.* (Duchesne), ii (1892), p. 293 f. Brief modern study by M. F. Stern, *Zur Biographie des Papstes Urbans II* (1883); full life by L. Paulot, *Un Pape français*. Urbain II (1903). B. Leib, *Rome, Kiev et Byzance à la fin du XIe siècle*. Rapports religieux des Latins et des Gréco-Russes sous le pontificat d'Urbain II (1924). W. Holtzmann, 'Die Unionsverhandlungen zwischen Kaiser Alexios I und Papst Urban II im Jahre 1089' in *B.Z.*, xxviii (1928), pp. 38–66. R. Crozet, 'Le Voyage d'Urbain II et ses négotiations avec le clergé de France (1095–1096)' in *Revue historique*, clxxv (1937), pp. 271–310. Mann, vii (1910), pp. 245–346; A. Fliche in Fliche–Martin, viii (1946), pp. 199–337, both with bibl. Hefele–Leclercq, v (pt. 1, 1912), pp. 337–465. É. Amann in *D.T.C.*, xv (pt. 2; 1950), cols. 2269–85, s.v. 'Urbain II'; G. Mollat in *E.C.*, xii (1954), col. 905 f., s.v. 'Urbano II'. See also works cited under *Crusades*.

URBAN V (1309–70), Pope from 1362. Guillaume de Grimoard, born at Grisac in Languedoc of a noble family, became a *Benedictine monk at the priory of Chirac and studied at *Paris and *Avignon. After ordination, he taught canon law at Montpellier and Avignon and later became Vicar General at Clermont and Uzès. In 1352 Clement VI named him Abbot of St.-Germain-d'Auxerre and entrusted him with several legations in Italy; in 1361 he was appointed Abbot of St.-Victor at Marseilles; and in 1362 was elected Pope. In many ways the best of the Avignon Popes, Urban seriously undertook the reform of the Church, esp. with regard to the distribution of benefices. He made peace with Barnabo Visconti in 1364, and endeavoured to suppress the *condottieri* in France and Italy, but without success. His plans for a Crusade against the Turks, despite the temporary occupation of Alexandria by Peter de Lusignan in 1365, came to nothing. In 1365 the German Emperor, Charles IV, urged him to return to Rome, and after Cardinal Albornoz had reconquered the States of the Church, Urban went to Italy in 1367, disregarding the remonstrances of the French court and cardinals who feared the loss of their influence on the Curia. He was enthusiastically received by the Roman people and began at once to restore the badly neglected city and to establish discipline among clergy and laity. In 1368 he crowned the consort of Charles IV German Empress, and in 1369 received the Greek Emperor, John V Palaeologus, into communion. In the same year Perugia revolted and war broke out between England and France, two facts which added weight to the wish of Urban's advisers to go back to Avignon. Against the admonitions of St. *Bridget, who foretold his early death if he were to leave Rome, he returned to France in 1370, where he died soon after. Urban was a great benefactor of the universities and generously assisted poor scholars. His cult was confirmed in 1870. Feast day, 19 Dec.

A. Fierens–C. Tihou (edd.), *Lettres d'Urbain V, 1362–1370* (Analecta Vaticano-Belgica, ix and xv; 1928–32); P.

Lecacheux–G. Mollat (edd.), *Lettres secrètes et curiales du pape Urbain V (1362–1370) se rapportant à la France* (Bibliothèque des Écoles Françaises d'Athènes et de Rome, Sér. 3, 1955); M. Dubrulle (ed.), *Les Registres d'Urbain V* (ib., 1926 ff.; (fasc. 1 only publd. to date); M. H. Laurent (ed.), *Urbain V (1362–1370)*. Lettres communes (ib., 1954 ff.). A. Fierens (ed.), *Suppliques d'Urbain V, 1362–1370* (Analecta Vaticano-Belgica, vii; 1914). E. *Baluze, *Vitae Paparum Avenionensium*, ed. G. Mollat, i (1914), pp. 349–414. Modern lives by J. B. Magnan (Paris, 1862), M. Chaillon ('Les Saints', 1911), and E. de Lanouvelle (Paris, 1928, with bibl.). J. M. Prou, *Étude sur les relations politiques du pape Urbain V avec les rois de France Jean II et Charles V* (Bibliothèque des Hautes Études, lxxvi; 1888). J. P. Kirsch, *Die Rückkehr der Päpste Urban V und Gregor XI von Avignon nach Rom* (Quellen und Forschungen aus dem Gebiete der Geschichte, vi; 1898), pp. 1–165. G. Mollat, *Les Papes d'Avignon* (ed. 9, 1950), esp. pp. 109–22, with bibl. R. Webster, O.S.B., in *C.E.*, xv (1912), pp. 214–16, s.v.; G. Mollat in *D.T.C.*, xv (pt. 2; 1950), cols. 2295–302, s.v. 'Urbain V', with extensive bibl.; G. Tabacco in *E.C.*, xii (1954), col. 908 f., s.v. 'Urbano V'.

URBAN VI (1318–89), Pope from 8 Apr. 1378. Bartolommeo Prignano became Abp. of Acerenza in 1363 and was translated to Bari in 1377. On the death of *Gregory XI (1378), under whom he had been head of the Papal chancery, he was elected Pope under pressure from the Roman populace who demanded an Italian. Hitherto he had been an ecclesiastic noted for his austerity and his aptitude for affairs, but his pontificate became a series of grave imprudences and extravagances, frequently attributed to partial mental derangement. During the first months of his reign he estranged the cardinals by his violent and over-bearing manner, his irritation culminating in the threat to establish an Italian majority in the Sacred College. The French members therefore, in Aug. 1378, announced the nullity of the election on account of its having been performed under duress, and in Sept., by electing Clement VII (Robert of Geneva) as antipope, began the Great Schism in the West. Among Clement's adherents was Queen Joanna of Naples whom Urban excommunicated (1380), putting in her place Charles of Durazzo. With him, too, he soon began to quarrel, and personally led an expedition against him during which he was captured (1383–4). After his escape, Urban had six of his cardinals tortured and five of them executed for conspiracy. From that time the conquest of Naples became his chief preoccupation, but a second expedition in 1386 was frustrated by the unreliability of his troops. He appointed the *Holy Year to be celebrated every 33 years and on 6 Apr. 1389 extended the Feast of the *Visitation of the BVM to the whole Catholic Church (decree publd. by Boniface IX, 9 Nov. 1389).

The principal authority is *Dietrich of Niem (d. 1418), *De Schismate*, Book 1 (ed. G. Erler, Leipzig, 1890), pp. 7–123. 'Aktenstücke zur Geschichte des Papstes Urban VI' mitgeteilt von H. B. Sauerland in *Historisches Jahrbuch*, xiv (1893), pp. 820–32. T. Lindner, 'Papst Urban VI' in *Z.K.G.*, iii (1879), pp. 409–28 and 524–46. L. *Pastor, *The History of the Popes from the Close of the Middle Ages* (Eng. tr.), i (1891), pp. 117–37. G. Mollat in *D.T.C.*, xv (pt. 2; 1950), cols. 2302–5, s.v. 'Urban VI', with detailed bibl. See also works cited under *Great Schism*.

URBAN VIII (1568–1644), Pope from 1623. Maffeo *Barberini, descendant of one of the oldest Florentine families, distinguished himself early by his literary activities. Having been twice Papal Nuncio in France he became titular Abp. of *Nazareth in 1604, Cardinal in 1606, and Bp. of Spoleto in 1608. In 1617 *Paul V appointed him legate of *Bologna and prefect of the Segnatura di Giustizia. He was elected in 1623, and, though essentially a 'political' Pope, was a zealous promoter of ecclesiastical reforms. By canonizing and beatifying a number of saints, e.g. Elizabeth of Portugal (1625) and Francis *Borgia (1624), and by approving new religious orders such as the *Visitation (1626) and St. *Vincent de Paul's *Lazarists (1632), he encouraged the religious life. He fostered missionary efforts by founding the Urban College of *Propaganda in 1627 and in the same year gave its final form to the bull '*In coena Domini' which consisted of a number of excommunications against heretics and others, ordered to be read on every *Maundy Thursday. His decrees on *Canonization (1625; confirmed by brief of 1634) are still observed to-day, and the revised Breviary which he issued in 1632 remained in force till the Breviary Reform of *Pius X (1912). He also revised the *Missal and the *Pontifical and much reduced the number of *Feasts of Obligation (1642). Under him G. *Galilei was condemned for the second time (1633), and the '*Augustinus' of *Jansenius declared heretical by the bull 'In eminenti' of 1642. Urban, who was much interested in military matters, had St. Angelo and Civitavecchia fortified and built the new Fort Urban. From 1625 he favoured the policy of Cardinal *Richelieu against the House of Habsburg and deprived the Catholic League of sufficient subsidies against the Protestant powers, an attitude that earned him the unfounded reproach of sympathizing with *Gustavus Adolphus and estranged the Emperor; on the other hand he tried to prevent the alliance between France and Sweden (1631), thus straining the relations with Richelieu. Urban's greatest fault was his nepotism, which lost him the sympathies of the Romans and involved him in an unfortunate war against the Duke of Parma (1642-4). He established close contact with the English Court through *Henrietta Maria by means of his agents, G. Panzani (1634) and G. Conn (1638), in a vain endeavour to re-establish the RC Church in England. Urban VIII was a highly gifted classical scholar. His Latin poems were published at Paris in 1623 and often reprinted.

The official acts of his pontificate are pr. in the *Bullarum, Diplomatum et Privilegiorum Sanctorum Romanorum Pontificum Taurinensis Editio*, xiii (Turin, 1858), xiv (ib., 1858), and xv (ib., 1858), pp. 1–428. Modern introd. in Eng. by W. N. Weech, *Urban VIII* (Lothian Prize Essay for 1903; 1905). F. *Gregorovius, *Urban VIII im Widerspruch zu Spanien und dem Kaiser* (1879). A. Leman, *Urbain VIII et la rivalité de la France et de la Maison d'Autriche de 1631 à 1635* (Mémoires et Travaux publiés par les professeurs des Facultés Catholiques de Lille, xvi; 1920). R. Quazza, 'L' elezione di Urbano VIII nelle relazioni dei diplomatici mantovani' in *Archivio della R. Società Romana di Storia Patria*, xlvi ('1922' [1923]) pp. 5–47. O. Pollak, *Die Kunsttätigkeit unter Urban VIII* (2 vols., Quellenschriften zur Geschichte der Barockkunst in Rom, 1928–[31]). R. Aubanel, *Le Génie sous la tiare. Urbain VIII et Galilée*

(1929). G. Hofmann, S.J., *Griechische Patriarchen und römische Päpste*. Untersuchungen und Texte, iii, 1. Theophanes III Patriarch von Jerusalem und Papst Urban VIII (Orientalia Christiana, xxx, Pt. 1 [No. 84]; 1933). J. Grisar, 'Päpstliche Finanzen, Nepotismus und Kirchenrecht unter Urban VIII' in *Xenia Piana* (Rome, 1943), pp. 207–366 (also separately publd. as Miscellanea Historiae Pontificiae xiv; 1943). Pastor, xxviii and xxix (both 1938). M. Ott in *C.E.*, xv (1912), pp. 218–21, s.v.; G. Mollat in *D.T.C.*, xv (pt. 2; 1950), col. 2305 f., s.v. 'Urbain VIII'; R. Ciasca in *E.C.*, xii (1954), cols. 912–16, s.v. 'Urbano VIII'. See also bibl. to *Thirty Years War*.

URBI ET ORBI (Lat., 'to the City [i.e. of Rome] and for the World'). A phrase used esp. of the solemn blessing which the Pope imparts from time to time from the balcony of one of the Roman basilicas (now from *St. Peter's church). The custom, which fell into abeyance after 1870, was revived by *Pius XI after his election in 1922.

URBS BEATA HIERUSALEM. A 6th–7th cent. hymn celebrating the Heavenly Jerusalem in terms suggested by Rev. 21. In medieval Breviaries it was the office hymn for the dedication of a church. In the revised Roman Breviary of 1632, its crude rhythm was changed into quantitative iambic metre beginning 'Coelestis Urbs Jerusalem', and much of its beauty was lost. As now printed in Breviaries and Hymnals it consists of two parts, the first four stanzas (with an added doxology) being used for *Vespers, the second part, beginning 'Angularis fundamentum' (in the revised version: 'Alto ex Olympi vertice') for *Lauds. Of the many Eng. transs. of the original hymn, J. M. *Neale's 'Blessed City, Heavenly Salem' is probably the best known.

Text, with introd., notes, and reff., in A. S. Walpole, *Early Latin Hymns* (1922), No. 119, pp. 377–80.

URBS SION AUREA. A set of extracts from the 'Hora novissima, tempora pessima' of *Bernard of Cluny (q.v.) in use as a well-known hymn ('Jerusalem the Golden '). The familiar Eng. rendering is by J. M. *Neale. The hymn is not to be confused with that of the preceding entry.

URGESCHICHTE (Ger., 'pre-history'). A term much used in the *Dialectical Theology for events which, from the standpoint of faith, are seen to be the means of God's direct supernatural revelation to man, though viewed from the human angle they appear merely as historical occurrences. This use of the word apparently derives from F. *Overbeck.

URIEL. Acc. to Jewish apocryphal writings, one of the four chief *archangels. In the Bk. of *Enoch he is said to have charge of Tartarus.

URIM AND THUMMIM. Prob. orig. 'lots', used in early Heb. divination to interpret the will of God to the people. There are several reff. in the OT, and from the *Septuagintal text of 1 Sam. 14. 41 it would seem that the lots were cast so as to yield a negative or affirmative answer to the question posed. Their nature is not stated; but the Arabic custom of divination by headless arrows, with the alternatives written on them (cf. Ex. 28. 30) may indicate the procedure followed.

Their divinatory use is nowhere mentioned after the time of *Solomon, presumably because it was replaced by the living voice of the Prophets, who disapproved of all mechanical oracles (cf. Hos. 4. 12), and Ez. 2. 63 and Neh. 7. 65 expressly suggest that such divination had ceased in post-exilic times. The inclusion of Urim and Thummim in the breastplate worn by the *High Priest in later times (cf. Ex. 25. 30, Lev. 8. 8), was prob. a traditional survival. They were numbered by the Rabbis among the five things no longer possessed by the Second Temple; by the time of *Josephus they were so little understood as to be confused with the breastplate itself.

Etymologically the meaning of the words, which was unknown to the ancient translators of the Bible, is obscure. In RV marg. they are rendered 'the Lights and the Perfections'. It has been suggested (G. R. Driver) that 'Urim' is to be connected with a word meaning 'to give oracular response'.

A. R. S. Kennedy in *H.D.B.*, iv (1902), pp. 838–41, s.v.; G. F. Moore in *E.Bi.*, iv (1903), cols. 5235–7, s.v., with bibl.; E. F. Kautzsch in *P.R.E.* (ed 3), xx (1908), pp. 328–36, s.v., also with bibl. See also works cited under *Ephod*.

URMARCUS (Ger. 'primitive Mark'), a supposed early and lost draft of St. *Mark's Gospel. The case for its existence is based partly on apparent signs of revision in the Gospel as we have it, partly on the study of the other *Synoptists (Mt. and Lk.) which (it is argued) presuppose knowledge of a variant, and earlier, form of Mk. The theory, which has been defended in various forms by J. *Weiss, H. von Soden, E. Wendling, and W. Bussmann, has never had much following (rejected by F. C. *Burkitt, B. H. *Streeter, V. Taylor).

E. Wendling, *Urmarcus* (1905); id., *Die Entstehung des Marcus-Evangeliums* (1908). F. C. *Burkitt, *The Gospel History and its Transmission* (1906), pp. 40–61. N. P. *Williams, *Studies in the Synoptic Problem* (ed. W. *Sanday, 1911), pp. 387–421 (a critique of Wendling). A. E. J. Rawlinson, *The Gospel according to St. Mark* (West. Comm., 1925), p. xli. f. See also other commentaries to *Mark*, *Gospel of St.*, cited s.v.

URSACIUS (*fl. c.* 335–71), Bp. of Singidunum (now Belgrade). Leader with *Valens, Bp. of Mursa, of the *Arians in the W. See *Valens*.

URSULA, St. The legend of the martyr St. Ursula and her 11,000 virgins developed from the veneration of some nameless virgin martyrs at *Cologne. Its earliest basis is a 4th–5th cent. inscription formerly at Cologne, acc. to which a certain Clematius restored an old basilica on the site where holy virgins had shed their blood for Christ. The next mention of the martyrs occurs in a sermon of the 8th or 9th cent. in honour of several thousand virgins who had perished in the persecution of Maximian. Acc. to a later form of the story, Ursula, whose name now came to be affixed to their leader, was a British princess who, accompanied by 11,000 virgins, went on a pilgrimage to Rome, and on her return was massacred with her companions at Cologne by the Huns. This legend, which existed in two versions, called from their opening words 'Fuit tempore' (10th cent.) and 'Regnante Domino' (before 1112), was a favourite of the Middle Ages, and the discovery, in 1106, of a burial ground near the church of St. Ursula, believed to contain the relics of the martyrs, gave rise to many further embellishments. St. Ursula became the patron of many educational institutes; in modern times her name is chiefly known through the teaching order of the *Ursulines (q.v.). In the Roman liturgy her feast is now only commemorated. Feast day, 21 Oct.

Texts ed., with full discussion, by V. de Buck, S.J., in *AA.SS.*, Oct. IX (1858), pp. 73–303. W. Levison, 'Das Werden der Ursula-Legende' in *Bonner Jahrbücher*, cxxxii (1927), pp. 1–164; also separately issued, Cologne, 1928. Extensive reff. to other literature in the discussion of Levison's book by M. Coens in *Anal. Boll.*, xlvii (1929), pp. 89–110. Studies in English include M. (Mrs. T. F.) Tout, 'The Legend of St. Ursula and the Eleven Thousand Virgins' in *Historical Essays by Members of Owens College, Manchester*, ed. T. F. Tout–J. Tait (1902), pp. 17–56. On the representation of the legend in art, G. de Tervarent, *La Légende de sainte Ursule dans la littérature et l'art du moyen-âge* (2 vols., 1931). A. Poncelet, S.J., in *C.E.*, xv (1912), pp. 225–8, s.v., with bibl.; A. Bigelmair in *L.Th.K.*, x (1938), cols. 452–4, s.v.; S. Moschini Marconi in *E.C.*, ix (1952), cols. 377–80, s.v. 'Orsola'.

URSULINES. The oldest and most considerable teaching order of women in the RC Church. It was founded at Brescia in 1535 by St. *Angela Merici as a society of virgins dedicated to Christian education, but living in their own homes. Approved by *Paul III in 1544, community life and simple vows were introduced in 1572 by *Gregory XIII at the instigation of St. *Charles Borromeo. In 1612 *Paul V allowed the Ursulines of Paris solemn vows and strict enclosure, and convents erected on these lines and following the modified Rule of St. *Augustine multiplied esp. in France and Canada. The growth of the order was temporarily stopped by the French Revolution but continued again in the 19th cent. In 1900 at a Congress at Rome of Ursulines from all over the world, the union was effected of a great number of convents belonging to different congregations in the 'Roman Union'. Its members take simple perpetual vows, but many convents which have remained independent have solemn vows and Papal enclosure. The habit is black with large sleeves and a black veil for the professed, and a white veil for novices and lay sisters. On profession, its members used to take a fourth vow to devote themselves to education, besides the usual three vows of religion. One of their most famous members was the mystic, Marie *Guyard

('Mary of the Incarnation'), foundress of the house at Quebec.

Annales de l'ordre de Ste Ursule . . . avec une préface par M. C. Ste-Foi (2 vols., Clermont Ferrand, 1857). V. Postel, *Histoire de sainte Angèle Merici et de tout l'ordre des Ursulines depuis sa fondation jusqu'au pontificat de S.S. Léon XIII* (2 vols. bound in 1, 1878). M. Aron, *Les Ursulines* (Les Grands Ordres monastiques et instituts religieux; 1937). A. Bertout, *Les Ursulines de Paris sous l'ancien régime* (1936); H. Albisser, *Die Ursulinen zu Luzern.* Geschichte, Leben und Werk, 1659–1847 (Stans, 1938). *Les Ursulines des Trois Rivières* (3 vols. Three Rivers, Canada, 1888–98; vol. 4, Quebec, 1911); *Les Ursulines de Québec* (4 vols., Quebec, 1864–6). P. G. Roy, *A travers l'histoire des Ursulines de Québec* (Lévis, 1939). C. J. Beaumier, *L'Union romaine des Ursulines d'après les documents pontificaux* (Three Rivers, 1951). Heimbucher, i, 628–39, and ii, 661, with bibl. M. V. Boschet, O.S.U., in *E.C.*, ix (1952), cols. 380–7, s.v. 'Orsoline', with further bibl.

USAGERS. The section of the *Nonjurors who in 1719 accepted the Communion Service which had been newly drawn up by J. *Collier, T. *Brett, and T. Deacon on the basis partly of the primitive Christian liturgies and partly of the 1549 BCP. They were so named from four 'usages' which the new rite contained, viz. (1) the *mixed chalice; (2) prayers for the dead; (3) a prayer for the descent of the Holy Ghost on the elements (see *Epiclesis*); and (4) an Oblatory prayer. The schism between the 'Usagers' and 'Non-usagers' was healed in 1732.

J. H. Overton, *The Nonjurors.* Their Lives, Principles, and Writings (1902), pp. 290–308, 321 f., 443–5; H. Broxap, *The Later Non-Jurors* (1924), pp. 35–65 and passim.

USE. In liturgiology, a local modification of the standard (esp. the Roman) rite. In Latin Christendom, such uses arose partly through the absorption of *Gallican features by the Roman Rite as it spread through Europe and partly through later local developments in the Roman Rite itself. These uses, which differed from the Roman Rite only in details, were gradually consolidated and codified in metropolitan and diocesan cathedrals and in some of the religious orders and, after ritual books came to be printed, were often used over wide areas. In the Preface to the BCP of 1549, where the five uses of *Hereford, *York, *Lincoln, *Bangor, and *Salisbury are referred to, it was ordered that 'from henceforth all the whole realm shall have but one use'. In the RC Church all uses, except those which could prove an existence of two centuries (notably the *Ambrosian use at *Milan, the *Mozarabic use at Toledo, and those of some religious orders), were abolished by the Council of *Trent.

USSHER, JAMES (1581–1656), Abp. of *Armagh. Educated at the newly founded *Trinity College, Dublin, he was ordained in 1601, and appointed chancellor of St. Patrick's Cathedral in 1606, and first professor of divinity at Dublin in 1607. Subsequently he became Bp. of Meath (1621) and Abp. of Armagh (1625). A scholar and historian of vast learning, he was intimate with most of the English writers and divines of the day and was an authority on such diverse topics as the letters of St. *Ignatius of Antioch (of which he distinguished the 7 genuine from the later spurious ones, whose existence had previously discredited them all) and the early history of Ireland. Although a *Calvinist in theology, he was not unfriendly with W. *Laud, and advised *Charles I against the execution of Strafford. After the Irish rebellion of 1641 he remained in England, endeavouring to bring about a reconciliation between Churchmen and Dissenters. So great was his repute for scholarship, tolerance, and sincerity, that on his death he was given a state funeral in *Westminster Abbey by O. *Cromwell. See also *Irish Articles* (1615).

Ussher's published writings include: *A Discourse of the Religion anciently professed by the Irish* (1623); *Gotteschalci et Predestinaianæ Controversiæ . . . Historia* (1631); *Britannicarum Ecclesiarum Antiquitates* (1639); *The Original of Bishops* (1641); *Polycarpi et Ignatii Epistolæ* (1644); *A Body of Divinity* (1645; publd. by J. Downham); *De Romanæ Ecclesiæ Symbolo Apostolico . . . Diatriba* (1647); *De Græca Septuaginta Interpretum Versione Syntagma* (1655); *Chronologia Sacra* (1660; ed. T. *Barlow); *The Power communicated by God to the Prince* (1661); *Historia Dogmatica Controversiæ inter Orthodoxos et Pontificios de Scripturis* (1690; ed. H. *Wharton). His *Annales Veteris et Novi Testamenti* (1650–4) are said to be the source of the dates later inserted in the margins of the AV of the Bible (edd. 1701 onwards).

Works ed. C. R. Elrington–J. H. Todd (17 vols., Dublin–London, 1847–64), with life by C. R. Elrington in vol. i, pp. 1–324. Selected extracts from his writings by P. E. More–F. L. Cross (edd.), *Anglicanism* (1935), pp. 69–71 (No. xxxii), 134–7 (No. lxviii), 257 f. (No. cxi), 286–8 (No. cxxvi), 488–494 (No. ccxi), 608 f. (No. cclxxvi), 649 (No. cccvi), and 691 f. (No. cccxxvii). Early lives by N. Bernard (Ussher's chaplain; London, 1656) and R. Parr (also chaplain; ib., 1686, important for letters). Modern study by J. A. Carr, *The Life and Times of James Ussher, Archbishop of Armagh* (1895). A. Gordon in *D.N.B.*, lviii (1899), pp. 64–72.

USUARD, Martyrology of. The most widely circulated of the *martyrologies in the Middle Ages and the basis of the current '*Roman Martyrology'. Its compiler, Usuard (d. *c.* 875), who was commissioned for the work by Charles the Bald, was a Benedictine monk of the abbey of *St.-Germain-des-Prés at Paris. He seems to have based his work on the somewhat earlier Martyrology of *Ado of Vienne (d. 875). It was edited at Paris in 1718 by Dom Jacques Bouillart from a MS. contemporary with its compiler and possibly the autograph.

The most important earlier edd. are those of J. Molanus (Louvain, 1563 and 1573, and Antwerp, 1583) and J. B. du Sollier, S.J. (*A.A.SS.*, Jun. VII, 1714, and Venice, 1745, repr. in J. P. Migne, *PL*, cxxiii, 453–992, and cxxiv, 9–860). *Histoire littéraire de la France*, v (1740), pp. 436–45, with lists of other edd. H. *Quentin, O.S.B., *Les Martyrologes historiques du moyen-âge* (1908), passim (see index). P. Grosjean, S.J., 'Sur les éditions de l'Usuard de Jean Molanus' in *Anal. Boll.*, lxx (1952), pp. 327–33. É. Amann in *D.T.C.*, xv (pt. 2; 1950), cols. 2313–16, s.v. 'Usuard'.

USURY. The exacting of interest was forbidden in the OT in the case of Jewish debtors (Ex. 22. 25, Deut. 23. 19 f.). The NT is not explicit on the subject, but during the patristic age all lending on interest was forbidden to clerics by the Councils of *Arles (314) and *Nicaea (325). The first Council of *Carthage (348) and the Council of Aix (789) objected to this method of making profit even in the case of laymen; and in the Decree of *Gratian, and subsequently at the Third *Lateran Council (1179) and the Second of *Lyons (1274), the practice was formally condemned, though it was allowed to the Jews by the Fourth Lateran Council of 1215. The condemnation was justified by the medieval view of money as solely a medium of exchange for articles of consumption, the use of which is adequately repaid by the return of a sum equal to that which was lent. This doctrine, founded on *Aristotle's theory of the 'barren' nature of money, was elaborated by the Schoolmen, esp. St. *Thomas Aquinas (S.T. II/IIae q. 78, art. 1) and held sway in the RC Church till the 19th cent. It was re-stated, e.g., by *Benedict XIV in 1745.

With the rise of capitalism the principle had to be gradually abandoned. M. *Luther and H. *Zwingli, as well as the 16th cent. Anglican divines, still condemned the lending of money for interest, but J. *Calvin permitted it in the case of wealthy debtors, and the civil legislation, which had hitherto followed canon law, began to provide for moderate charges of interest in England in 1571, in Germany in the same century, but in many Continental countries much later, in France e.g. not until 1789. To-day money is no longer thought of, as in the Middle Ages, as a barren means of exchange but as capital productive of wealth like other property. Since the exaction of a reasonable interest for its loan has been tolerated by the Christian Church, the term 'usury' has tended to be restricted to excessive rates.

Modern studies include M. Weber, 'Die protestantische Ethik und der "Geist" des Kapitalismus' in *Archiv für Sozialwissenschaft und Sozialpolitik*, xx (1905), pp. 1–54, and xxi (1905), pp. 1–110; Eng. tr., London, 1930; E. *Troeltsch, *Die Soziallehren der christlichen Kirchen und Gruppen* (1911; abridged Eng. tr., 2 vols., 1931); R. H. Tawney, *Religion and the Rise of Capitalism* (Holland Memorial Lectures for 1922; 1926). T. P. McLaughlin, C.S.B., 'The Teaching of the Canonists on Usury (XII, XIII and XIV Centuries)' in *Mediaeval Studies*, i (1939), pp. 81–146, and ii (1940), pp. 1–22. B. N. Nelson, *The Idea of Usury* (Princeton, N.J., 1949), with bibl. J. Dow in *H.E.R.E.*, xii (1921), pp. 550–5, s.v. 'Usury (Christian)'; A. Bernard–G. Le Bras–H. du Passage, S.J., in *D.T.C.*, xv (pt. 2; 1950), cols. 2316–90, s.v. 'Usure', with reff.

UTICA, The Martyrs of. A group of early African martyrs of uncertain date who suffered at the Massa Candida (lit. 'White Farm'). The place, misunderstood as 'White Lump', gave rise to the legend that in the time of Valerian (c. 258) they were thrown alive into slaking quicklime and their bodies reduced to a white mass of powder. Acc. to St. *Augustine (*Serm.* 306, preached on their anniversary) there were 153 (cf. Jn. 21. 11), and the

massacre took place at Utica, 35 miles from Carthage, though the *Roman Martyrology increases the number to 300 and assigns it to Carthage. *Prudentius, who extols the purity (*candor*) of their souls reflected in the whiteness (*candor*) of their bodies, prob. had a decisive influence on the legend. Feast day, 24 Aug.

Prudentius, *Peristephanon*, xiii, lines 76–87; Augustine, *Sermones*, cccvi and cccxi. 10; also *Sermones post Maurinos reperti*, ed. *G. Morin, O.S.B. (Miscellanea Agostiniana, i, Rome, 1930), p. 645 f. (No. xiv); also *Enarrationes in Pss.*, xlix. 9, and cxliv. 17; and among the Ps.-Augustian sermones No. cccxvii. P. Monceaux, 'Les Martyrs d'Utique et la légende de la "Massa Candida"' in *Revue archéologique*, Sér. 3, xxxvii (1900), pp. 404–11; F. P. de' Cavalieri, 'I martiri della Massa Candida' in *Nuove Note agiografiche* (S.T., ix; 1902), pp. 39–51. H. *Leclercq, O.S.B., in *D.A.C.L.*, x (pt. 2; 1932), cols. 2649–53, s.v. 'Massa Candida', and xv (pt. 2; 1953), col. 2878 f., s.v. 'Utique'; A. Amore, O.F.M., in *E.C.*, viii (1952), col. 284, s.v. 'Massa Candida', with further bibl.

UTILITARIANISM. The doctrine in ethics which identifies the good with happiness and maintains those actions to be right which bring the greatest happiness to the greatest number. In principle it was maintained by T. *Hobbes, B. de Mandeville, D. *Hume, and C. A. Helvetius, but it came into prominence with J. Bentham, J. S. Mill, and the Philosophical Radicals. H. *Rashdall sought to interpret the Christian ethic as an 'Ideal Utilitarianism'.

J. S. Mill's classical defence of the doctrine was orig. publd. in three articles in *Fraser's Magazine*, lxiv (1861; pt. 2), pp. 391–406 (Oct.), 525–34 (Nov.), 659–73 (Dec.); they were reissued in book form as *Utilitarianism* (1863). L. Stephen, *The English Utilitarians* (3 vols., 1900). E. Albee, *A History of English Utilitarianism* (1902). Good account by A. W. Hastings in *H.E.R.E.*, xii (1921), pp. 558–567.

UTRAQUISM. The Hussite doctrine that the laity, like the clergy, should receive the Holy Communion under the forms of both bread and wine (*sub utraque specie*). It was first formally defended by Jacob of Mies, a professor of the university of Prague, in 1414. John *Huss did not personally press the thesis, but, despite condemnation at the Councils of *Constance (1415) and *Basle (1432), it was maintained by his followers, including the more moderate group of them (who were also called *Calixtines, from their demand for the cup, *calix*). Communion in both kinds was conceded to the laity by the Compactata of Prague (1433), which, though formally cancelled by *Pius II in 1462, were maintained by the Bohemian Diet until 1567.

See bibl. to *Calixtines*.

UTRECHT, Declaration of. The Profession of Faith which is the doctrinal basis of the *Old Catholic Church. It was drawn up by an assembly of the Old Catholic bishops at Utrecht on 24 Sept. 1889. Professing adherence to the beliefs of the primitive Church, esp. as formulated in the decrees of the *Oecumenical Councils down to A.D. 1000, it is mainly concerned with controverting the specific doctrines of the RC Church. Among the formulae repudiated are the decrees on the Papacy of the *Vatican Council of 1870, the dogma of the *Immaculate Conception, the encyclicals '*Unigenitus' and '*Auctorem fidei', and the *Syllabus of 1864. Positively it maintains the sacrificial element in the *Eucharist and the *Real Presence, though

without mention of the propitiatory nature of sacrifice or of *transubstantiation.

The text is printed in the *Report* of the *Lambeth Conference for 1930, pp. 142-4.

UVEDALE, JOHN and NICHOLAS. See *Udall, John* and *Nicholas.*

V

VAISON, Councils of. Two important ecclesiastical synods were held at Vaison (Dept. Vaucluse, S.E. France):

(1) On 13 Nov. 442. It enacted ten canons which provided *inter alia* that clergy should receive the *chrism at Easter from their own bishops (can. 3), that any unwilling to accept the judgements of their Bishop should resort to the Synod (can. 5) and that there should be no intimacy with those hostile to the Bishop (can. 6). It also regulated the adoption of children (cans. 9 and 10). Acc. to St. *Ado, Abp. of Vienne (9th cent.), his predecessor, Nectarius of Vienne, presided at the Council.

(2) 5 Nov. 529. It enacted five canons of liturgical import, ordering the frequent repetition of *Kyrie Eleison in the office and at Mass (can. 3), the regular use of prayer for the Pope (can. 4) and of *Sicut erat* after *Gloria Patri* (can. 5). Twelve Bishops were present, among them St. *Caesarius of Arles.

(1) Hardouin, i, cols. 1787–90; Mansi, vi (Florence, 1761), col. 451 f. Hefele–Leclercq, ii (pt. 1; 1908), pp. 454–60.
(2) Hardouin, ii, cols. 1105 f.; Mansi, viii (Florence, 1762), cols. 725–8. Hefele–Leclercq, ii (pt. 2; 1908), pp. 1110–15.

VALDÉS, JUAN DE (*c.* 1500–41), Valdesso, Spanish humanist and religious writer. He was a native of Cuenca in Castile, came to Italy in 1531, and was *camerario* of *Clement VII in 1533. From 1534 he lived at Naples, in the service of Cardinal Ercole Gonzaga. Here he became the spiritual centre of a group of prominent men and women anxious for reform and spiritual revival in the Church, to whom belonged, among others, Giulia Gonzaga and Vittoria Colonna. Though he remained a Catholic, he paved the way for Protestant ideas by his emphasis on religious feeling and his disregard of ecclesiastical authority; and after his death many of his friends, among them *Peter Martyr and B. *Ochino, left the Catholic Church. Besides an important work on the Spanish language *Didlogo de la lengua* (publd. 1737) he wrote a number of devotional books, many of them remarkable for their penetrating spiritual insight and considerable charm of exposition. Among them are the *Didlogo de doctrina cristiana* (1529) and the *Alfabeto cristiano* (1536), the latter a study in Christian perfection written for Giulia Gonzaga. Valdés also wrote commentaries and made translations from the Hebrew Psalter and parts of the NT. The *Ciento y diez consideraciones* (1550), containing letters and essays collected by his friends, was translated into English by N. *Ferrar (1638).

His twin brother, ALFONSO DE VALDÉS (*c.* 1500–32), who became Chancellor to the Emp. *Charles V, was also a noted humanist. After the capture of Rome in 1527 he wrote a *Didlogo de Lactancio y in Arcadiano* (publd.

1529; Eng. tr., 1590) to justify the Imperial sack of the city, in which he violently attacked the political system of the Papacy; he was also the author of the *Didlogo de Mercurio y Carón* (1529), a satire against the Curia, containing a defence of Catharine of Aragon, but primarily intended to show the perfidy of King Francis I of France in his dealings with the Emperor; this last work has traditionally, but apparently erroneously, been attributed to Juan.

Modern edd. of Juan de Valdés's *Didlogo de las lenguas* with introd. and notes by Janet H. Perry (London, 1927); also by J. F. Montesinos (Madrid, 1928); of his *Alfabeto cristiano* by B. *Croce (Bari, 1938); photographic repr. of the 1529 ed. of his *Didlogo de doctrina cristiana* with introd. and notes by M. Bataillon (Coimbra, 1925). Unpubld. Letters to Card. Gonzaga, ed. J. F. Montesinos (Anejos de la *Revista de Filología española*, xiv, 1931). Modern Eng. tr. by J. T. Betts of his *Alfabeto cristiano* (London, 1861); of *XVII Opuscula* (ib., 1882), of his commentaries on Matt. (ib., 1882), on 1 Cor. (ib., 1882), on Rom. (ib., 1883), and on Pss. 1–41 (posthumous, Edinburgh, 1894). Modern edd. of Alfonso de Valdés's *Didlogo de Lactancio* by J. F. Montesinos (Madrid, 1928) and *Didlogo de Mercurio y Carón* by id. (ib., 1929); modern Eng. tr. of the former by J. E. Longhurst (Albuquerque, New Mexico, 1952). The 19th cent. biographies tend to confuse the lives of the two brothers. Those available in English include B. B. Wiffen, *Life and Writings of Juan de Valdés* (1865), with Eng. tr. of his *Ciento y diez consideraciones* by J. T. Betts, pp. 195–583; E. Boehmer, *Bibliotheca Wiffeniana*, i (1874), pp. 63–130 ('Juan and Alfonso de Valdés'). Other lives of Alfonso and Juan by E. Stern (Strassburg thesis, Strassburg, 1869), F. Caballero (Conquenses Illustres, iv; Madrid, 1875) and M. Carrasco (Geneva, 1880). Modern life of Juan de Valdés by E. Cione (Bari, 1938), with good bibl. pp. 117–81. J. E. Longhurst, *Erasmus and the Spanish Inquisition*. The Case of Juan de Valdés (University of New Mexico Publications in History, i; Albuquerque, New Mexico, 1950), with bibl. pp. 97–114. M. Bataillon, 'Alonso de Valdés, auteur du "Didlogo de Mercurio y Carón" ' in *Homenaje ofrecido a Menéndez Pidal*, i (1925), pp. 403–15. P. Paschini in *E.C.*, xii (1954), col., 964 f., s.v.

VALENCE, Councils of. Of the many Councils held at Valence in Dauphiné, the three most important were:

(1) 12 July 374. A Council of thirty bishops, summoned to deal with various disciplinary problems, among them the refusal of Acceptus to become Bp. of Forum Iulii (Fréjus). It issued four disciplinary canons. Can. 1 forbade the ordination of digamists, can. 2 easy penance to lapsed virgins, and can. 3 absolution until death to those who had lapsed to idolatry or received second baptism. Can. 4 dealt with clerics who falsely accused themselves of crime to escape office.

(2) *c.* 530. Its Acts are lost, and it is uncertain whether it was held before or after the Council of *Orange (529). Like the latter, it was directed against *Pelagianism and *Semi-Pelagianism. Its president was *Cyprian of Toulon, who represented St. *Caesarius of Arles.

(3) 8 Jan. 855. The Council was convoked by the Emp. Lothair (817–55) to try the Bp. of Valence on various counts. It then proceeded to discuss *Predestination, upholding against *Hincmar of Reims and the Council of *Quiercy

1403

(853) 'Double Predestination' and rejecting the view that the Redemptive Work of Christ extended to the whole human race.

(1) Hardouin, i, cols. 795–8; Mansi, iii (Florence, 1759), cols. 491–500; Lauchert, pp. 181–3. Hefele-Leclercq, i (pt. 2; 1907), p. 982.
(2) Hardouin, ii, col. 1103 f.; Mansi, viii (Florence, 1762), cols. 723–6. Hefele-Leclercq, ii (pt. 2; 1908), p. 1110, with further reff. See also works cited s.v. *Orange, Council of*.
(3) Hardouin, v, cols. 87–96; Mansi, xv (Venice, 1770), cols. 1–16. Hefele-Leclercq, iv (pt. 1; 1911), pp. 204–10, and iv (pt. 2; 1911), pp. 1326 and 1390–8, with further reff. See also works cited s.v. *Hincmar*.

VALENS (4th cent.), Bp. of Mursa, who with *Ursacius, Bp. of Singidunum, was an *Arian leader in the W. Pupils of *Arius, they became bitter enemies of St. *Athanasius whom they opposed, e.g. at the Council of Tyre in 335. After retracting their charges at the Council of Milan in 347, owing to a temporary change in the policy of the Emp. Constantius, they resumed their opposition to him at *Arles in 353 and at Milan in 355, and at Sirmium (357) maintained the extreme Arian ('Anomoean') position. Again in acc. with Imperial policy they took up a compromising attitude at the Synod of *Ariminum in 359 where they were responsible for the victory of the *Homoean party. Though frequently excommunicated in the W. Church, they seem to have retained considerable influence at the court of Constantius. The last mention of Valens dates from 367.

There are scattered reff. in *Hilary of Poitiers, *Athanasius, *Socrates, and *Sozomen. Fragments of a treatise of Hilary, 'Adv. Valentem et Ursacium', known to St. *Jerome (*De Vir. Ill.*, 100), survive; text in J. P. Migne, *PL*, x, 627–724; crit. ed. by A. L. Feder, S.J., in *C.S.E.L.*, vol. 65 (1916), pp. 39–193. J. P. Jungklas in *L.Th.K.*, x (1938), col. 448 f., s.v. 'Ursacius'.

VALENTINE, St. The commemoration of 14 Feb. appears to refer to two Valentines, a Roman priest martyred on the Flaminian Way under the Emp. Claudius (*c.* 269) and a Bp. of Terni (Interamna) who was taken to Rome and martyred, and whose remains were later conveyed back to Terni. Though the surviving accounts of both martyrdoms are clearly legendary, there are indications that each contains a nucleus of fact; and it is just possible that the kernel of truth in the two legends refers to a single person. The traditional association of St. Valentine's day with courtship and the choosing of a 'Valentine' of the opposite sex is connected perhaps with certain customs of the pagan festival of Lupercalia (mid-Feb.) at Rome, or with the natural season, not with any tradition concerning either saint of the name.

'Acta' of both SS. Valentine in *AA.SS.*, Feb. II (1658), pp. 751–62. Note on the SS. Valentine in *Anal. Boll.*, xi (1892), pp. 471–3. E. M. Fusciardi, *Vita di S. Valentino, V. e M., patrono di Terni*. Con messa, novena, triduo e preghiere (Terni, 1936). O. *Marucchi, *Il cimitero e la basilica di S. Valentino* (1890); H. Grisar, S.J., *Geschichte Roms und der Päpste im Mittelalter*, i (1901), pp. 655–9 ('Kirche und Friedhof des heiligen Valentin an der Via Flaminia. Neuere Ausgrabungen'), Eng. tr., iii (1912), pp. 131–7. J. P. Kirsch in *L.Th.K.*, x (1938), col. 478 f., s.v. 'Valentin', with further bibl.

VALENTINUS (2nd cent.), founder of a *Gnostic sect ('Valentinians'). Acc. to St. *Irenaeus and others he was a native of Egypt, whose disciples claimed that he had been educated by Theodas, a pupil of St. *Paul. He lived at Rome from *c.* 136 to *c.* 165, where he seceded from the Church; then he perh. went to *Cyprus. He secured a wide following. His system, which is known only in the developed and modified form given to it by his disciples, is founded on the Platonic conception of a parallelism between the world of ideas ($\pi\lambda\eta\rho\omega\mu\alpha$) and the world of phenomena ($\kappa\epsilon\nu\omega\mu\alpha$). Its main features are an elaborate doctrine of aeons forming a succession of pairs or '*syzygies'. Their ultimate offspring, which came into being by the fall of Sophia, one of the lowest aeons, was the *Demiurge, the God of the OT, who created the visible world. The redemption was effected by the aeon Christ, who united Himself to the man Jesus at His Baptism to bring men the gnosis. This gnosis, however, is given only to the 'pneumatics', i.e. the Valentinians, who through it enter into the *pleroma*, whereas the Catholics or 'psychics' by faith and good works attain only to the middle realm of the Demiurge, and the 'hylics' (i.e., the rest of mankind), being all engrossed in matter, are given over to eternal perdition.

Valentinus was prob. the most influential of the Gnostics and had a very large following (*frequentissimum collegium inter haereticos*, *Tertullian, *Adv. Valentin.* i). Several of his disciples founded schools of their own. They included, in the E.,* Theodotus, and in the W., Mark (see *Marcosians*), *Heracleon, and Florinus. See also *Jung Codex*.

The newly recovered Coptic Gnostic texts from Nag-Hammadi (see *Jung Codex*) promise to throw much light on the Valentinians. The chief Christian sources are Irenaeus, *Adv. Haer.*, i, passim, and iii, 4; Tertullian, *Adv. Valentinianos*; Clement of Alexandria, *Stromateis* (several reff.); Epiphanius, *Haer.*, xxxi, xxxiii f., and lvi; Hippolytus, *Philos.*, vi. 20–55; Pseudo-Tertullian, *Adversus Omnes Haereses*, iv [=*De Praescriptione*, xlix]; Eusebius, *H.E.*, iv. 11. Fragments assembled with introd. in A. *Hilgenfeld, *Die Ketzergeschichte des Urchristenthums* (1884), pp. 283–316, 461–522; also in W. Völker, *Quellen zur Geschichte der christlichen Gnosis* (1932), pp. 57–141. Comprehensive study by F. M. M. Sagnard, O.P., *La Gnose valentinienne et le témoignage de saint Irénée* (Études de Philosophie médiévale, xxxvi; 1947). Other important studies include G. Heinrici, *Die valentinianische Gnosis und die heilige Schrift* (1871), R. A. Lipsius, 'Valentinus und seine Schule' in *Jahrbücher für protestantische Theologie* (1887), pp. 585–658, O. *Dibelius, 'Studien zur Geschichte der Valentinianer' in *Z.N.T.W.*, ix (1908), pp. 230–47, 329–40, C. Barth, *Die Interpretation des Neuen Testaments in der valentinianischen Gnosis* (T.U., xxxvii, Hft. 3; 1911), W. Foerster, *Von Valentin zu Herakleon*. Untersuchungen über die Quellen und die Entwicklung der valentinianischen Gnosis (Beihefte zu *Z.N.T.W.*, vii; 1928). G. Quispel, 'The Original Doctrine of Valentine' in *Vigiliae Christianae*, i (1947), pp. 43–73. Bardenhewer, i, 358–64; Altaner (ed. 1951), p. 106. R. A. Lipsius in *D.C.B.*, iv (1887), pp. 1076–99, s.v. 'Valentinus (1)'; E. Preuschen in *P.R.E.* (ed. 3), xx (1908), pp. 395–417, s.v. 'Valentinus, Gnostiker'; G. Bardy in *D.T.C.*, xv (pt. 2; 1950), cols. 2497–519, s.v. 'Valentin'.

VALERIAN, St. (d. *c.* 460), Bp. of Cemele (now Cimiez, nr. Nice) in S. Gaul. He was probably a monk of *Lérins before he became bishop. The only facts known of his life are that he was present at the Councils of Riez (439) and *Vaison (442), and upheld the ancient jurisdictional claims of the see of *Arles against Pope *Leo the Great. He was the author of twenty homilies which, apart from one already known ('De bono disciplinae'), were discovered by J. *Sirmond in a *Corbie MS. early in the 17th cent. Their subjects are mainly moral and ascetic. Written in a highly rhetorical but effective style, they are valuable for the light they throw on the history of their age. Valerian was also the author of an 'Epistola ad Monachos de Virtutibus et Ordine Doctrinae Apostolicae'. Theologically he seems to have inclined to *Semi-Pelagianism. Feast day, 23 July.

'Homiliae' and 'Epistolae', first ed. J. Sirmond, S.J., Paris, 1612; repr. in J. P. Migne, *PL*, lii, 691–758. Bardenhewer, iv, 572 f. C. F. Arnold in *P.R.E.* (ed. 3), xx (1908), pp. 418–20; J. Zellinger in *L.Th.K.*, x (1938), col. 482, s.v.

VALESIUS, HENRICUS (1603–76), French historian. Henri Valois was a native of Paris, who, after being educated by the *Jesuits at Verdun and Paris, spent nearly all his life in the capital. In 1630 he abandoned a career in law to devote himself exclusively to learning. In his earlier years he issued editions of many classical authors, including Ammianus Marcellinus (1636). In 1650 he began an intensive study of the early ecclesiastical historians, which bore fruit in his celebrated editions of the Church histories of *Eusebius (1659), *Socrates and *Sozomen (1668), and *Theodoret and *Evagrius (1673).

His edd. of Eusebius, Socrates, Sozomen, Theodoret, and Evagrius were reissued at Amsterdam, 3 vols., 1695–1700, and are repr. in J. P. Migne, *PG* (see under separate authors); they were revised by W. Reading (3 vols., Cambridge, 1720). His Minor works ed. P. Burmann, *Henri Valesii . . . Emendationum Libri Quinque et de Critica Libri Duo* (Amsterdam, 1740). Life by his brother, Adrian Valesius, was appended to a Lat. tr. of his ed. of Eusebius, Socrates, &c., publd. at Paris, 1677, pp. i–viii; repr. in G. Bates, *Vitae Selectorum Aliquot Virorum* (London, 1681), pp. 719–33; by P. Burmann, op. cit. (no pagination); and by W. Reading, op. cit., iii, 615–22. E. *Schwartz (ed.), *Eusebius Werke*, Band ii, Teil 3 (G.C.S.; 1909), pp. xliii–xlv. H. Hurter, S.J., *Nomenclator Literarius Theologiae Catholicae*, iv (Innsbruck, 1910), cols. 173–7. P. Lejay in *C.E.*, xv (1912), p. 263 f., s.v. 'Valois, Henri'; E. Amann in *D.T.C.*, xv (pt. 2; 1950), col. 2526 f., s.v. 'Valois, Henri de'.

VALIDATION OF MARRIAGE. A marriage null by reason of defective consent or some *diriment impediment can be validated in canon law (a) by simple renewal of consent or (b) by dispensation. Simple renewal of consent is sufficient when the marriage is null because of defective consent or when the impediment has ceased to exist. If the nullity was well known, the renewal must be public; if secret, it may be private. But if the marriage is null because of a persisting removable diriment impediment, the marriage may be validated by a simple dispensation followed by renewal of consent. In certain cases, esp. where a renewal of consent is difficult to obtain, a marriage can be validated by a *sanatio in radice (q.v.).

VALLA, LORENZO (*c.* 1406–57), Italian humanist. Ordained priest in 1431, he accepted a chair of eloquence at Pavia, but he had to leave the city in 1432 owing to quarrels with the jurists of the university. After several years of wandering from place to place he was received by King Alfonso I of Naples *c.* 1436, who was his protector for the next ten years. In 1447 he went to Rome where he became 'scriptor' and later Apostolic Secretary, and in 1450 professor of eloquence at the university.

His first earliest work of importance, *De voluptate* (1431), is a dialogue between representatives of the *Stoic, *Epicurean, and Christian views, in which he defends the pleasure of the senses as the greatest good, though not perfectly attainable in this life. Valla soon became one of the first exponents of modern historical criticism. He proved the spuriousness of the '*Donation of *Constantine' in *De falso Credita et Ementita Constantini Donatione Declamatio* (1440), which also contained a bitter attack on the temporal power of the Papacy. He also undertook a critical comparison between the *Vulgate and the Greek NT in *Collatio Novi Testamenti* (1444). He was a violent opponent of Scholasticism, the method of which he ridiculed in *Dialecticae Disputationes contra Aristotelicos* (printed 1499). In *De libero arbitrio* (printed 1493) he denies the possibility of understanding the harmony of God's omnipotence with human free will, and *De Professione Religiosorum* (not printed until 1869) was a sustained critique of the ideals of the religious life. His *De Elegantiis Linguae Latinae* (1442) long remained a standard work on humanist Latin.

Valla's novel and audacious views, which caused him to be suspect of heresy, had a deep influence on Renaissance scholars and also on the Reformers; and his writings were held in high esteem, esp. by M. *Luther.

Works, publ. Basle, 1540. Modern edd. of his *De Constantini Donatione*, with Eng. tr. by C. B. Coleman (New Haven, 1922) and by W. Schwahn (Teubn. ed., 1928) and of his *De Libero Arbitrio* by M. Anfossi (Opuscoli Filosofici Testi e Documenti Inediti o Rari Pubblicati da Giovanni Gentile, vi; Florence, 1934). G. Mancini, *Vita di Lorenzo Valla* (1891). L. Barozzi–R. Sabbadini, *Studi sul Panormita e sul Valla* (Pubblicazioni del R. Istituto di Studi Superiori Practici di Perfezionamento in Firenze, Sezione di Filosofia e Filologia, xxv; 1891). J. Vahlen, 'Laurentii Vallae Opuscula Tria' in *Sb.* (Wien), lxi (1869), pp. 7–66, 357–444, and lxii (1869), pp. 93–149; also publd. separately, ib., 1869. M. v. Wolff, *Lorenzo Valla* (1893). W. Schwahn, *Lorenzo Valla* (Diss., Berlin, 1896). J. E. Sandys, *A History of Classical Scholarship*, ii (1908), pp. 60–70, with reff. U. Benigni in *C.E.*, xv (1912), p. 257 f., s.v.

VALLARSI, DOMENICO (1702–71), editor of St. *Jerome's writings. He was a native of *Verona, where he spent most of his life. His edition of Jerome (11 vols., 1734–42), was considerably superior to that of the *Maurists (Paris, 1693–1706), and, except for individual works, has not been superseded.

His ed. of the works of Jerome was repr. in J. P. Migne, *PL*, xxii–xxx; the ed. of the works of St. *Hilary, in which Vallarsi assisted F. S. *Maffei (Verona, 1730), was repr. ib., ix, x; the first vol. of his ed. of the works of *Rufinus (Verona, 1745; vol. 2 not publd.), was repr. ib., xxi, 45–632. L. Federici, *Elogi istorici de' più illustri ecclesiastici veronesi*, iii (Verona, 1819), pp. 134–48. É. Amann in *D.T.C.*, xv (pt. 2; 1950), col. 2525, s.v.

VALLEY OF JEHOSHAPHAT, The.
See *Jehoshaphat, The Valley of.*

VALLUMBROSAN ORDER. A religious
order, so named from the mother-house at
Vallombrosa, some 20 miles E of Florence.
The order was founded *c.* 1036 by St. *John
Gualbert (d. 1073) to follow the *Benedictine
Rule, and confirmed by Victor II in 1055.
After the death of their founder, the Vallumbrosan monks spread rapidly, having more than
50 abbeys at the end of the 12th cent. and over
80 by 1500, most of them in Italy. In the 15th
cent. a reform of the order through *Cassinese
Benedictines was instigated by *Eugenius IV,
and another was effected in the 17th cent.
by Bl. John Leonardi. The mother-house
at Vallombrosa was burnt by the soldiers of
*Charles V in 1527. After being rebuilt in
1637, it was plundered by Napoleon's troops
in 1808 and finally suppressed by the Italian
Government in 1866. Owing to these misfortunes the order declined, though it still has
a few houses in Italy, governed by abbots
who are now elected and hold office for four
years.

The Vallumbrosan rule is based on that
of St. Benedict, but with greater stress on
austerity and penance. It represents a mixture
of the cenobitic and eremitic life; and as it
is strictly contemplative, enforcing perpetual
silence, poverty, and enclosure, the manual
work is done by lay brothers, the Vallumbrosan monks, indeed, being among the first
to adopt this institution. The order has been
noted for its contributions to ascetical literature, art, and science, and for a time counted
G. *Galileo among its novices.

There exists also an order of Vallumbrosan
nuns, who trace their origin to St. Bertha
Bardi (d. 1163), but whose real foundress was
St. Humilitas (d. 1310); they still have a few
houses, at Florence and elsewhere in Italy.

F. Tarani, *L' ordine vallombrosano* (Florence, 1921). T.
Sala, *Dizionario storico biografico di scrittori, letterati ed
artisti dell' ordine di Vallombrosa* (ib., 1929). Heimbucher,
i, 320–5. R. Webster, O.S.B., in *C.E.*, xv (1912), p. 262 f.,
s.v., with reff. to earlier litt.

VALOIS, HENRI DE. See *Valesius, Henricus.*

VALOR ECCLESIASTICUS. The official
valuation of ecclesiastical and monastic
revenues made in 1535. It became necessary
through the legislation of *Henry VIII, and
esp. the second *Annates Act of 1534 (26 Hen.
VIII, c. 3) whereby the first-fruits of every
benefice, which had formerly been paid to the
Pope, together with a tenth of the annual
income, were appropriated to the crown. Its
importance to the ecclesiastical historian, with
its details of every benefice, may be compared
with that of the Domesday Survey of 1086 to
the student of secular history. It became
popularly known as the 'Kings' Books'.

It was ed. by J. Caley for the Record Commission (6 vols.,
1810–34), with general introd. by J. Hunter, in vol. i, pp.

i–viii. A. Savine, 'English Monasteries on the Eve of the
Dissolution' in *Oxford Studies in Social and Legal History*, ed.
P. Vinogradoff, i (1909), pp. 1–217, esp. Book I, pp. 1–75.
S. L. Ollard in *D.E.C.H.* (1912), p. 609, s.v.

VAMPING HORN. A species of trumpet
used in churches for humming harmonies
('vamping') to fill out the insufficient body of
sound from the other instruments. Its use
dates from the latter half of the 17th cent. and
it survived in a few places till the middle of the
19th. Examples may be seen at East Leake
(Notts) and Charing (Kent). The notion that
vamping horns were used for summoning the
congregation to church seems erroneous.

VAN DEN STEEN, CORNELIS CORNE-
LISSEN. See *Cornelius a Lapide.*

VAN ESPEN, ZEGER BERNHARD (1646–
1728), Belgian canonist. A native of Louvain,
he was ordained priest in 1673 and became
professor of canon law at Louvain university
in 1675. His comprehensive knowledge soon
made him a much-consulted adviser of princes
and bishops, and his works, the most important
of which is *Jus Ecclesiasticum Universum* (2
vols., 1700), are remarkable for their learning
and lucidity. Van Espen vigorously defended *Gallican theories and was an ardent
upholder of secular power against religious
authority. In the question of the 'Chapter of
Utrecht' he gave his opinion in favour of the
validity of the ordination of a *Jansenist bishop,
an act which led to his suspension *a divinis*
and deprivation of his academic functions in
1728. Summoned by the Abp. of Utrecht to
retract, he fled to the Jansenist colony at
Amersfoort where he died soon afterwards.
All his works were placed on the *Index in
1704, and again in 1714 and 1732.

Best collected ed. of works [by J. Barre] (4 vols., 'Louvain'
[Paris], 1753); [id.,] *Supplementum ad Varias Collectiones
Operum clar. viri Z. B. van Espen* (Brussels, 1758). Anon.
life by G. du Parc de Bellegarde (Louvain, 1767; also
appended to supplementary vol. of works [separate pagina-
tion]). Later study by F. Laurent (Brussels, 1860). E. [W.]
Kemp, 'Zeger Bernhard Van Espen' in *Theology*, xlix
(1946), pp. 194–200, with further reff. A. Depreester in
D.D.C., v (1953), cols. 457–61, s.v. 'Espen'.

VAN EYCK, HUBERT (*c.* 1366–1426) and
JAN (*c.* 1390–1441), Flemish painters. They
were natives of Maeseyck, in the diocese of
Liége. Hubert later went to Ghent where he
began the famous altar-piece, *The Adoration of
the Lamb*, for the cathedral of St. Bavon. Jan,
who was probably a pupil of his brother,
became court painter of Philip the Good of
Burgundy in 1425 and settled at Bruges.

The *Adoration*, which Jan finished in 1432, is
one of the masterpieces of Christian art, combining the allegorical treatment of the Middle
Ages with a hitherto unknown naturalism and
delight in picturesque detail. The work, based on
the Apocalypse, consists of of over 200 figures,
grouped on several panels round the central
figure of the Lamb, standing on the altar and

adored by processions of saints. The work has had a varied history. It was hidden from the Protestant iconoclasts from 1566 to 1587 and in 1794 transferred to Paris. In 1816 the central piece was restored to Ghent and in 1821 its side parts removed to Berlin, whence they were brought back to Ghent in 1919.

J. van Eyck also painted several Madonnas and other works. All are remarkable for their brilliant colouring, produced by a new technique. Though he had hardly any disciples, his influence was paramount among the painters of N. and W. Europe for a hundred years and may be traced down as far as the naturalism of P. P. Rubens and *Rembrandt.

The very extensive literature includes general studies of the two brothers by W. H. J. Weale (London, 1908; ed. 2, assisted by M. W. Brockwell, ib., 1912), E. Durand-Gréville (Brussels, 1910), [W.] M. Conway (London, 1921), A. Schmarsow (Kunstgeschichtliche Monographien, xix; 1924), and L. Baldass (Phaidon Press, London, 1952). The existence of Hubert van Eyck has occasionally in modern times been emphatically denied, notably by E. Renders, *Hubert van Eyck.* Personnage de légende (1933); id., *Jean Van Eyck. Son œuvre, son style, son évolution et la légende d'un frère peintre* (Bruges, 1935); and id., *Jean Van Eyck et le polyptyque.* Deux problèmes résolus (ib., 1950). This thesis has been more tentatively accepted by others. The legend on the painting ascribing the *Adoration of the Lamb* to Hubert has been subject to much critical examination; the results of various laboratory tests conducted under the direction of P. Coremans were publd. at Antwerp, 1953. There is much other controversial literature on the subject. Good reprods., with commentary by L. van Puyvelde (Paris-Brussels, 1946; Eng. tr., 1947). O. Kerber, *Hubert van Eyck. Die Verwandlung der mittelalterlichen in die neuzeitliche Gestaltung* (1937). E. Panofsky, *Early Netherlandish Painting* (Charles Eliot Norton Lectures, 1947-8; Cambridge, Mass., 1953), i, 178-246, with notes, pp. 427-57, and illustrations, ii, plates 109-68. Useful bibl. reff. in M. W. Brockwell, *The Van Eyck Problem* (1954). M. J. Friedländer in *Allgemeines Lexikon der bildenden Künstler von der Antike bis zum Gegenwart* begründet von U. Thieme-F. Becker, xi, ed. U. Thieme (1915), pp. 129-33, s.v. 'Eyck'.

VAN MANEN, WILLEM CHRISTIAAN (1842–1905), Dutch Biblical critic. After studying at Utrecht and holding pastorates in the Dutch Reformed Church, he was professor of Old Christian literature and NT exegesis at *Leyden from 1885 till his death. He was also co-editor of the *Theologisch Tijdschrift.* The opinions of van Manen, who was among the most radical Biblical critics of the 19th cent., attracted attention more as curiosities than for their intrinsic importance. He maintained, e.g., that all the NT writings belong to the Sub-Apostolic period. His methods are most fully exhibited in his *Paulus* (3 vols., 1890–6), in which he rejected the authenticity of St. Paul's Epistles, arguing that they were the creation of a group of theologians who sought to transform primitive Christianity, which was originally a movement in Judaism, into a universal religion, with a system closely akin to *Gnosticism. He admitted that there was a historic St. Paul, totally unlike the author of the Epp., but why he was taken by this school as its patron must, van Manen held, remain an insoluble mystery. Van Manen's views became widely known in Great Britain through his contributions to the *Encyclopaedia Biblica* (ed. T. K. *Cheyne and J. S. Black, 1899–1903).

T. Whittaker, *The Origins of Christianity with an Outline of van Manen's Analysis of the Pauline Literature* (1904; ed. 3, 1914, with additional prologue, pp. xi–xxxii; ed. 4 revised 1933). A. Meyer in *R.G.G.* (ed. 2), iii (1929), col. 1958 f., s.v. 'Manen, W. C. van'.

VAN MILDERT, WILLIAM (1765–1836), Bp. of *Durham. Of Dutch descent, he was appointed Regius professor of divinity at Oxford in 1813, made Bp. of *Llandaff in 1819, Dean of *St. Paul's (in plurality) in 1820, and Bp. of Durham in 1826. He was the last Bp. of Durham with palatine rank, and was one of the founders of the university of Durham (1832). His chief works were *An Historical View of the Rise and Progress of Infidelity* (*Boyle Lectures, 2 vols., 1806) and an elaborate edition of the *Works* of D. *Waterland (10 vols., 1823–8), prefaced by a Life.

A Collection of his *Sermons on Several Occasions and Charges* (Oxford, 1838), with Memoir by C. Ives, pp. 3–158. W. P. Courtney in *D.N.B.*, lviii (1899), p. 1333 f.

VANE, HENRY (1613–62), English politician. To distinguish him from his father, Henry Vane (1589–1655), he is commonly known as 'the Younger'. He was educated at Westminster and at Magdalen College, Oxford, and for a time travelled abroad, esp. in France and Switzerland, where he found encouragement for his already latent anti-episcopal and anti-monarchical views. On returning to England, he decided to emigrate to America where he became Governor of Massachusetts (1636). Before long he came back again and was appointed co-treasurer of the Navy, elected M.P., for Hull and made a knight (1640). In the Long Parliament he was a vigorous and bitter opponent of W. *Laud and Strafford, and one of the commissioners chiefly responsible for the *Solemn League and Covenant. He strongly disliked, however, the Presbyterian system of state-enforced discipline. He became a member of the Council of State in 1649 and its president in 1652, but latterly lost influence, owing to his opposition to O. *Cromwell's dictatorial methods. At the Restoration he was arrested, imprisoned, tried, and executed on Tower Hill, 14 July 1662.

[G. Sikes,] *The Life and Death of Sir Henry Vane* (1662). Modern lives by J. K. Hosmer (London, 1888), W. W. Ireland (ib., 1905), and J. Willcock (ib., 1913). C. H. Firth in *D.N.B.*, lviii (1899), pp. 116–29.

VANGEON, HENRI LÉON. See *Ghéon, Henri.*

VÁSQUEZ, GABRIEL. See *Vázquez, Gabriel.*

VATICAN. The modern Papal residence in Rome on the ancient 'Mons Vaticanus', once adorned with the Circus of Nero. A Papal domicile is said to have been erected near the court of the old basilica of St. Peter's by Pope *Symmachus (498–514). An earlier residence on the site was rebuilt by *Innocent III (c. 1200) and extended by Nicholas III (1277–1280). During the *Avignonese captivity

(1308–77) it fell into disrepair; but as the *Lateran palace had also been seriously damaged by fire in 1309, the Vatican became the principal Papal residence after the return in 1377. The first *conclave was held here in the following year. Little of the existing building is earlier than the 15th cent. In 1410 *John XXIII restored the covered passage to the Castle of S. Angelo and in 1447 *Nicholas V began an extensive plan of building which included administrative offices and residences for the cardinals. This programme was actively carried into effect by Nicholas's successors. *Sixtus IV erected the *Sistine Chapel (1473–1481), Innocent VIII the Belvedere (c. 1490), *Julius II and *Leo X Bramante's *cortile* and the *stanze* of *Raphael and *Paul III the *Sala Regia*. For the building of the basilica, see *St. Peter's*. The present palace was completed by *Clement VIII (d. 1605), the Braccio Nuovo (designed by Raffael Stern) by Pius VII in 1821. By the Law of Guarantees (13 May 1871) the Vatican, the Lateran, and the Papal villa at *Castel Gandolfo were granted extra-territoriality, and additional privileges were conceded by the Lateran Treaty of 1929. The celebrated Library ('Bibliotheca Apostolica Vaticana') is administered by a Cardinal Prefect. Among its more famous collections of MSS. are the *Palatini* (presented by the elector Maximilian on the capture of Heidelberg; 1623), the *Reginenses* (formerly the property of Queen *Christina of Sweden; 1690), and the *Ottoboniani* (purchased by *Alexander VIII, Ottobuoni; incorporated, 1746). See also *Codex Vaticanus*.

Much information is to be found in the many good guides to the Vatican palace, intended in the first place for tourists. There are also countless monographs on the various collections. Modern general works include C. Cecchelli, *Il Vaticano. La basilica, i palazzi, i giardini, le mura* [1928]. F. Ehrle, S.J.–H. Egger, *Der vaticanische Palast in seiner Entwicklung bis zur Mitte des XV. Jahrhunderts* (Studi e Documenti per la Storia del Palazzo Apostolico Vaticano ed. F. Ehrle, S.J.–H. Egger, ii; 1935). There are good catalogues to many of the MSS. collections in the library. The Gk. catalogues are listed in M. Richard, *Répertoire des bibliothèques et des catalogues des manuscrits grecs* (Publications de l'Institut de Recherche et d'Histoire des Textes, i; 1948), p. 92 f.; the Lat. ones by P. O. Kristeller, 'Latin Manuscript Books before 1600: a Bibliography of the Printed Catalogues of Extant Collections' in *Traditio*, vi (1948), pp. 227–317, 311 f. There are also numerous studies on Vatican MSS. in S.T. P. M. Baumgarten in *C.E.*, xv (1912), pp. 276–302, s.v.; G. Caraci–P. A. D'Avack–E. Josi–D. R. de Campos–F. Magi–P. Maarschalkerweerd, O.F.M.–N. Del Ré–N. Vian–G. Junkes, S.J.–P. García,S.J., in *E.C.*, xii (1954), cols. 1040–140, s.v. 'Vaticano'. See also bibls. to *St. Peter's, Rome; Sistine Chapel*.

VATICAN COUNCIL. The Council held at Rome in 1869–70 and reckoned in the RC Church as the Twentieth *Oecumenical Council. Convoked by *Pius IX by a bull of Indiction dated 29 June 1868, it was planned to deal with a vast variety of subjects including faith and dogma, ecclesiastical discipline and canon law, religious orders, oriental Churches and foreign missions, and the relations between the Church and the civil powers. Even before the Council began, two bodies of opinion stood out clearly. The majority party, usually designated the '*Ultramontanes', were in favour of

the heightening of Papal authority and of the definition of Papal Infallibility. They included such distinguished laymen, as W. G. *Ward in England and L. *Veuillot in France, and, among members of the Council, Abps. H. E. *Manning of Westminster and V. A. Dechamps of Malines, and Bps. L. Pie of Poitiers and I. von Senestréy of Ratisbon. The liberal minority was represented by J. H. *Newman in England and J. J. I. von *Döllinger in Bavaria, and, among the members of the Council, by F. *Dupanloup, Bp. of Orléans, and most German and many Austrian and American bishops. Of the governments none except the Russian, which forbade the Catholic bishops to attend, interfered with the Council; the French attitude, one of benevolent neutrality, was largely influenced by E. Ollivier (1825–1913), the French premier, who later embodied his views in *L'Église et l'État au concile du Vatican* (2 vols., 1879).

After elaborate preparations the Council began with a pre-synodal congregation on 2 Dec. 1869 at which Pius IX nominated the presidents. It was followed by the issue of the brief 'Multiplices inter' which established the procedure, acc. to which the Pope had the right of proposing questions (*ius proponendi*), though bishops might suggest subjects for discussion to congregations set up for this purpose. Four Deputations, on dogma, on ecclesiastical discipline, on religious orders, and on the oriental Churches, were appointed.

The business of the Council was opened by Pius IX on 8 Dec. 1869 in the presence of nearly 700 bishops. It began with a discussion on the schema *De fide* which had been drawn up against rationalism, naturalism, materialism, pantheism, and kindred errors. While this schema, which was criticized as too cumbrous, was being revised by the Deputation on dogma, the Council discussed matters of ecclesiastical discipline with special reference to canon law and repeatedly listened to the desire for a reform of the *Breviary.

In Feb. 1870 the procedure which had proved very slow was hastened by new regulations. Long debates were prevented by the application of closure and the quicker method of voting by standing up was adopted. Both measures were later much criticized by the minority. The revised constitution on Faith, 'Dei Filius', was laid before the Council on 1 Mar., and after detailed discussion was promulgated in its final form on 24 Apr. It consists of a prooemium deploring the pantheism, materialism, and atheism of the time, followed by four chapters on God the Creator of all things, on Revelation, on Faith, and on Faith and Reason. The respective spheres of reason and faith were defined, esp. with a view to excluding *Traditionalism and other doctrines anathematized in the appended canons.

The public announcement that the question of Papal Infallibility was to be discussed at the Council had been made on 6 Mar. After some controversy it was decided that this subject and the Primacy of the Pope, both of which divided the members of the Council, should be dealt with before the other points of the schema 'De Ecclesia'. From 27 Apr. the Deputation on dogma worked on the schema 'De Romano Pontifice'; and the debate on the 'opportunity' of the definition, which lasted from 13 May to 3 June, was ended by closure. In the debate on the Primacy which followed, the point to which the minority esp. objected was the definition of the Pope's jurisdiction as ordinary, immediate, and truly episcopal. In the debate on Infallibility, the minority party desired to see the Pope's Infallibility linked more closely with the Infallibility of the Church by the use of some such expression as St. *Antonino of Florence's formula that the Pope 'using the counsel and seeking for the help of the universal Church' cannot err. The Infallibility debate was closed on 4 July. On 13 July the definition received 451 placets, 88 non-placets, and 62 placets juxta-modum, and at the Fourth Public Session on 18 July the constitution '*Pastor Aeternus' was passed by 533 placets to 2 non-placets, the remainder of the minority having abstained from voting. The definition as finally accepted disappointed the extremists of both sides. It stated plainly the Infallibility of the Roman Pontiff, affirming that his definitions are 'irreformable of themselves, and not from the consent of the Church', but it restricted this Infallibility only to those occasions 'when he speaks *ex cathedra*, that is, when in discharge of the office of Pastor and Doctor of all Christians, by virtue of his supreme Apostolic authority he defines a doctrine regarding faith or morals to be held by the Universal Church'.

On 19 July, the day after the promulgation, war broke out between France and Prussia, and the removal of the French troops from Rome and the Italian occupation of the city brought the Council to an end. It was formally suspended on 20 Oct. 1870.

The definitions of the Council, which were accepted by all the minority bishops, roused serious opposition only in Germany and Austria. In these countries some small groups organized themselves as the '*Old Catholics', and in Germany the opposition of Bismarck to the increased consolidation of Papal power issued in the *Kulturkampf*. J. J. I. von Döllinger, who had vigorously opposed the Council throughout, esp. in his articles in the *Augsburger Allgemeine Zeitung* and his book *The Pope and the Council* (1869), also refused to submit and was excommunicated, though he did not join the Old Catholic body. The chief result in Austria was the renouncing of the Concordat by the state.

In the RC Church itself, the result of the definition of the Papal primacy and Infallibility was the final settlement of the controversies that began at the Council of *Constance (1415) and had been sustained by *Gallican theologians in later times, while the constitution 'Dei Filius' provided the principles on which Catholicism was soon to make its stand against the infiltration of *Modernism into its own ranks.

Acta et Decreta Sacrosancti Concilii Oecumenici Vaticani cum permultis aliis Documentis ad Concilium eiusque Historiam Spectantibus auctoribus Presbyteris S.J. e Domo BVM sine Labe Conceptae ad Lacum (Collectio Lacensis Conciliorum Recentiorum, vii; Freiburg i.Br., 1892); Mansi (continuation), xlix-liii (Arnhem-Leipzig, 1923-7). Some of the more important decrees are also pr. in Denz.-Bann. (ed. 1952), pp. 491-508 (Nos. 1781-1840); also in Mirbt, pp. 456-66 (No. 605 f.). E. Cecconi, *Storia del concilio ecumenico vaticano* (2 vols. in 4 parts, to end of second session 1872-9; all publd.). J. *Friedrich, *Geschichte des vatikanischen Konzils* (3 vols., 1877-87); T. Granderath, S.J., *Geschichte des vatikanischen Konzils*, ed. K. Kirch, S.J. (3 vols., 1903-6). F. Mourret, *Le Concile du Vatican* (1919). E. Campana, *Il concilio vaticano* (2 vols., Lugano, 1926). [E.] C. Butler, O.S.B., *The Vatican Council*. The Story Told from Inside in Bishop Ullathorne's Letters (2 vols., 1930). T. *Mozley, *Letters from Rome on the Occasion of the Oecumenical Council, 1869-1870* (1891; hostile). H. E. *Manning, *The True Story of the Vatican Council* (1877). E. Ollivier, *L'Église et l'État au concile du Vatican* (2 vols., 1879). A. Vacant, *Études théologiques sur les constitutions du concile de Vatican, d'après les actes du concile* (2 vols., 1895). J. Brugerette-É. Amann in *D.T.C.*, xv (pt. 2; 1950), cols. 2536-85, s.v. 'Vatican (Concile du)'.

VAUDOIS. See *Waldenses*.

VAUGHAN, CHARLES JOHN (1816-97), Dean of *Llandaff. Educated at Rugby under T. *Arnold and at Trinity College, Cambridge, he was ordained in 1841. From 1844 to 1859 he was Headmaster of Harrow, where he greatly improved the discipline and prestige of the school. After declining the Bpric. of *Rochester he became vicar of Doncaster in 1860, where he undertook to prepare graduates for ordination. He carried on this work all through his life, so that by his death over 450 young men, popularly known as 'Vaughan's Doves', had gone through his training. In 1869 he became Master of the Temple, where he deliberately upheld the traditional Christian beliefs against contemporary critical views. In 1879 he became Dean of Llandaff, where his sympathies with Nonconformity gained him considerable influence in S. Wales, and he took an active part in the foundation of the University College at Cardiff (1883/4). Vaughan was a notable preacher who combined force and lucidity of expression with warmth of feeling and conviction. Among his numerous publications are commentaries on Rom. (1859), Phil. (1885), and Heb. (1890) and collections of sermons, including *Lessons of Life and Godliness* (1862) and *Words from the Gospels* (1863).

Vaughan left strict instructions that no biography should be published. Brief sketch by F. D. How, *Six Great Schoolmasters* (1904), pp. 138-80 ('Charles J. Vaughan, D.D., Headmaster of Harrow, 1844-1859'). C. E. Vaughan in *D.N.B.*, lviii (1899), pp. 159-61.

VAUGHAN, HENRY (1622-95), 'Silurist', English poet. Born near Brecon of an ancient Welsh family he was entered at Jesus College, Oxford, in 1638, where he was an ardent supporter of *Charles I. He left without taking a degree, studied medicine in London and *c*. 1645 began to practise at Brecknock, and from *c*. 1650 at his native place Newton-by-Usk. About this time a spiritual transformation took place in his life, partly due perhaps to the death of a brother and a severe illness. The poetical outcome was the *Silex Scintillans*

(2 parts, 1650 and 1655), a collection of spiritual poems, influenced by G. *Herbert, which are marked by an atmosphere of intense and sustained religious fervour. The first volume of *Silex* was followed in 1652 by *The Mount of Olives*, a small collection of prayers and meditations, and in 1654 by *Flores Solitudinis*, translations from J. E. Nieremberg (1595–1658) and St. *Eucherius, with a Life of St. *Paulinus of Nola by Vaughan himself. Apparently through the neglect of his works by the public, he published nothing after the second volume of the *Silex* except a heterogeneous collection of verse, which was brought out by one of his friends, 'J. W.' (prob. John Williams), under the title *Thalia Rediviva*, in 1678. Vaughan is usually numbered among the '*metaphysical' poets of the 17th cent., but his style is simpler and his thought less abstract than that of e.g. J. *Donne or T. *Traherne. He exercised a considerable influence on W. *Wordsworth whose 'Ode on Intimations of Immortality' reflects Vaughan's poem, 'The Retreat'.

A. B. Grosart (ed.), *The Works . . . of Henry Vaughan* (4 vols., 1871), with 'Essay on the Life and Writings of Henry Vaughan' in vol. ii, pp. ix–ci; work also ed., with full crit. app., by L. C. Martin (2 vols., Oxford, 1914). E. K. Chambers (ed.), *The Poems of Henry Vaughan, Silurist* (2 vols., 1896), with introd. by H. C. Beeching in vol. i, pp. xvii–lii. F. E. Hutchinson, *Henry Vaughan. A Life and Interpretation* (1947), with reff. R. Sencourt, *Outflying Philosophy. A Literary Study in the Religious Element in the Poems and Letters of John Donne and in the Works of . . . Henry Vaughan* [1925], pp. 133–238. E. Blunden, *On the Poems of Henry Vaughan. Characteristics and Intimations* (1927); E. Holmes, *Henry Vaughan and the Hermetic Philosophy* (1932). E. L. Marilla, *A Comprehensive Bibliography of Henry Vaughan* (University of Alabama Studies, No. 3; 1948). F. E. Hutchinson in *C.B.E.L.*, i (1940), p. 461 f. See also works cited under *Metaphysical Poets*.

VAUGHAN, HERBERT (1832–1903), Abp. of *Westminster. Descended of an old English RC family, Vaughan was ordained to the priesthood at Lucca in 1854. For a time he was vice-president of the seminary of St. Edmund's College, Ware. Having conceived the idea of founding a college in England to train missionaries, he toured S. America in 1863–5 to raise money for the purpose. In 1866 he founded St. Joseph's College, Mill Hill, whose members were commissioned to work among the coloured population of the United States. At the height of the controversies prior to the *Vatican Council, he bought the *Tablet* (1868) and for three years acted as editor, championing the *Ultramontane cause. In 1872 he was appointed Bp. of Salford, and in 1892 Abp. of Westminster. He became a cardinal in 1893. The most notable events of Vaughan's archiepiscopacy were his obtaining the permission of the authorities at Rome for RCs to attend the ancient English universities, the building of *Westminster Cathedral (begun, 1895), the discussions regarding *Anglican ordinations, which ended in their condemnation by *Leo XIII (1896), and his activities in connexion with the Education Bill of 1902, which recognized his main thesis, viz. that all schools, whether sectarian or public schools, are equally the concern of the state.

Of Vaughan's family, six of his eight brothers became priests, and all six sisters entered convents. His eldest brother, ROGER WILLIAM BEDE VAUGHAN (1834–83), was educated at *Downside and entered the *Benedictine Order in 1851. Appointed Prior of St. Michael's, Belmont, nr. Hereford, in 1862, in 1873 he was consecrated with the title of Abp. of Nazianzen as coadjutor to the Abp. of Sydney, whom he succeeded in 1877. BERNARD JOHN VAUGHAN (1847–1922), who was educated at Stonyhurst and entered the *Jesuit Order in 1866, was a notable preacher. Several volumes of his Sermons have been published.

S. Leslie (ed.), *Letters of Herbert Cardinal Vaughan to Lady Herbert of Lea, 1867 to 1903* (1942). Life of Herbert Vaughan by J. G. Snead-Cox (2 vols., London, 1910; abridged ed., 1934); much shorter life by P. Thureau-Dangin (Paris, 1911). J. G. Snead-Cox in *D.N.B.*, 1901–1911, iii (1912), pp. 550–4.
Of Roger William Bede Vaughan there is a memoir [by J. C. Hedley] in *The Downside Review*, iii (1884), pp. 1–27; T. Cooper in *D.N.B.*, lviii (1899), p. 177 f. Life of Bernard John Vaughan, by C. C. Martindale, S.J. (London, 1923).

VÁZQUEZ, GABRIEL (1549–1604), less correctly Vásquez, Spanish theologian. From his birthplace, Belmonte, he is sometimes known as **Bellomontanus**. He became a *Jesuit in 1569, and taught moral theology in the universities of Madrid, Ocaña, and Alcalá. He spent six years (1585–91) in Rome, but returned thence to Alcalá where he taught till his death. His most important work is his commentary (*Commentarii ac Disputationes*) on the Summa of St. *Thomas Aquinas (8 vols. in all; 1598–1615), largely directed in its details against the theses of his co-Jesuit, F. *Suarez. In the discussion then raging as to the doctrine of grace, he opposed to the *Congruism of F. *Suarez and R. *Bellarmine a strictly *Molinist position. His learning was immense; but it was often squandered on the discussion of useless questions and the defence of eccentric theories.

A. Astrain, S.J., *Historia de la Compañía de Jesús en la assistencia de España*, iv (1913), pp. 68–73. F. Stegmüller, 'Zur Prädestinationslehre des jungen Vásquez' in *B.G.P.M.*, Supplementband iii (Halbband 2; 1935), pp. 1287–311. J. A. de Aldama, S.J. (ed.), 'Un parecer inédito del P. Gabriel Vázquez sobre la doctrina augustiniana de la gracia eficaz' in *Estudios eclesiásticos*, xxiii (1949), pp. 515–20. Sommervogel, viii (1898), cols. 513–19. J. Hellin, S.J., in *D.T.C.*, xv (pt. 2; 1950), cols. 2601–10, s.v., with further bibl.

VECCHIONI. The members of an ancient guild at Milan officially known as the 'Scuola di S. Ambrogio' and consisting of 10 old men and 10 old women. Four of them (two of each sex) make public offerings of bread and wine on behalf of the laity at the solemn celebration of the (*Ambrosian) Liturgy in Milan Cathedral. The ceremony is a survival of the primitive offerings in kind by the faithful at Mass.

VEDAST, St. (d. 539), also 'Vaast', Bp. of Arras. He was ordained to the priesthood at Toul, where he was deputed to prepare King *Clovis I, returning from his victory over the

Alemanni, for baptism. For a time he assisted St. *Remigius in his mission work among the Franks at *Reims. C. 499 he was consecrated Bp. of Arras, where he successfully established Christianity; and he was also charged with the diocese of Cambrai. He was venerated in England as 'St. Foster' (cf. the church of St. Vedast in Foster Lane, London). Feast day, 6 Feb.

Two medieval lives, the one ascribed to St. Jonas of Bobbio (7th cent.), the other by *Alcuin, in *AA.SS.*, Feb. I (1658), pp. 792–80; crit. ed. by B. Krusch in *M.G.H.*, Scriptores Rerum Merovingicarum, iii (1896), pp. 399–427. Id., 'Die ältere V. Vedastis und die Taufe Chlodovechs' in *Mittheilungen des Instituts für österreichische Geschichtsforschung*, xiv (1893), pp. 427–42. Gertrude Sparrow Simpson–W. Sparrow Simpson, *The Life and Legend of S. Vedast* (1896); E. Guilbert, *S. Vaast, fondateur de l'église d'Arras* (Arras, 1928).

VEIL (1), Christian headdress. The veil, the customary feminine headdress among many ancient peoples, was worn by the Roman matron as a mark of distinction from the unmarried woman. In the Christian Church it was given to consecrated virgins by the bishop from the 3rd cent., as the symbol of their spiritual marriage to Christ. Since then it has come to be considered the most important part of the religious habit of women (cf. the expression 'to take the veil'). In most orders and congregations the veil of the professed sister is black, that of the novice white, but other colours, e.g. blue, are possible. Some modern congregations, such as the Sisters of Charity of St. *Vincent de Paul, dispense with it altogether. In the C of E female candidates usually wear a white veil at *Confirmation.

VEIL (2), liturgical cloths for covering various objects, e.g. the *chalice veil (q.v.), the veil used for the *ciborium while containing the sacred species, and the *humeral veil (q.v.). Acc. to a custom of the W. Church, traceable as far back as the 11th cent., all crucifixes, statues, and pictures are veiled during *Passiontide. In the Middle Ages the veiling lasted throughout *Lent, when the veils were usually white. In modern RC practice, it is from *Vespers preceding *Passion Sunday to the *Gloria in excelsis of the first Mass of *Easter, and violet veils are used except for the crucifix on the high altar on *Maundy Thursday, which is veiled in white.

VENANTIUS FORTUNATUS, St (c. 535–c. 600), Latin poet. An Italian by birth, he was educated at *Ravenna, and later became secretary to Queen Radegund in her convent at Poitiers (c. 567). C. 600 he was appointed Bp. of Poitiers. A fluent versifier, he composed 11 books of occasional poems, a metrical Life of St. *Martin of Tours, Lives of 11 other Gallic saints (in prose), an elegy 'De Excidio Thuringiae', and some fine hymns, notably '*Vexilla Regis' and '*Pange Lingua gloriosi'. Feast Day, 14 Dec.

Editio princeps of his poems publ. Cagliari, 1573; fuller edd. of his works by C. Brouwer, S.J. (Mainz, 1603), and M. A. Luchi, O.S.B. (2 vols., Rome, 1786–7), repr. in J. P. Migne, *PL*, lxxxviii, 59–592, with addition, cols. 592–6; crit. ed. by F. Leo–B. Krusch in *M.G.H.*, Auctores Antiquissimi iv (2 ptt. 1881–5). W. Meyer, *Der Gelegenheitsdichter Venantius Fortunatus* (*Abh*. (Gött.), N.F., iv, Nr. 5; 1901). G. M. Dreves, *Hymnologische Studien zu Venantius und Rabanus Maurus* (Veröffentlichungen aus dem kirchenhistorischen Seminar München, III. Reihe, Nr. 3; 1908), pp. 1–54. R. Koebner, *Venantius Fortunatus. Seine Persönlichkeit und seine Stellung in der geistigen Kultur des Merowinger-Reiches* (1915). D. Tardi, *Fortunat.* Étude sur un dernier représentant de la poésie latine dans la Gaule mérovingienne (Paris thesis, 1927). S. Blomgren, *Studia Fortunatiana* (Uppsala Universitets Årsskrift, 1933, Filosofi, Språkvetenskap och Historiska Vetenskaper, i, 1933 (in Band 2 of 1933), and ib., 1934, iii, 1934 (in Bd. 2 of 1934)). B. de Gaiffier, 'S. Venance Fortunat, évêque de Poitiers. Les témoignages de son culte' in *Anal. Boll.*, lxx (1952), pp. 262–84. Raby, pp. 86–95, with bibl. p. 489. Bardenhewer, v, 367–77; Altaner (ed. 1951), p. 451 f.

VENERABLE. (1) In the RC Church, a title bestowed on a departed person when a certain stage in the process of *Beatification has been reached. In 1913 *Pius X fixed this stage as the publication of the official decree that the subject of the process had exercised all the virtues to an heroic degree or had suffered martyrdom. Formerly the title was popularly given on the introduction of the case before the Sacred Congregation of Rites, and was the occasion for great celebrations; but now all that is then allowed is a special service of thanksgiving. In a less limited sense the word is used of other persons of marked holiness of life, esp. the 'Venerable *Bede'.

(2) In the C of E, the proper address of an *archdeacon.

VENERATION OF THE CROSS. A ceremony of the Latin Rite for *Good Friday, sometimes also called **Creeping to the Cross,** in which clergy and people, kneeling, kiss a crucifix, usually on the sanctuary steps. The ceremony originated in the veneration of the relics of the true cross in *Jerusalem (mentioned in the 'Pilgrimage of *Etheria'), whence it spread to other places which claimed to possess relics. In earlier times its observance was not confined to Good Friday. An analogous ceremony, consisting in a solemn procession, veneration, and elevation of the cross, takes place in the E. Church on *Holy Cross Day (14 Sept.)

H. Thurston, S.J., *Lent and Holy Week* (1904), pp. 345–62. L. Eisenhofer, *Handbuch der katholischen Liturgik*, i (1932), pp. 528–30.

VENI CREATOR (Lat. 'Come Creator'). A hymn to the Holy Ghost, prob. composed in the Frankish Empire in the 9th cent. and frequently attributed to *Rabanus Maurus. It was used as the Vespers Hymn of *Whitsuntide from the 10th cent., and from the 12th cent. came to be substituted during the Octave of the feast for the usual hymn of Terce, 'Nunc Sancte nobis Spiritus'. It is also widely used outside Pentecost, e.g. at the ordination of priests and the consecration of bishops, and at the consecration of churches. The best known English version is that of Bp. J. *Cosin, 'Come, Holy Ghost, Our souls inspire', included since 1662 in the Anglican *Ordinal (to replace the earlier version in the 1550 Rite). Other versions of the 'Veni Creator' are due to J. *Dryden, R. *Mant, F. W. *Faber, and E. *Caswall.

Crit. text by G. M. Dreves, *Lateinische Hymnendichter des Mittelalters*, ii (A.H.M.A., l; 1907), p. 193 f. S. G. Pimont, *Les Hymnes du bréviaire romain*, ii (1884), No. xx, pp. 125–43. A. *Wilmart, O.S.B., 'L'Hymne et la Séquence du Saint-Esprit' in *La Vie et les Arts liturgiques*, x (1924), pp. 395–401, repr. in his *Auteurs spirituels et textes dévots du moyen-âge latin* (1932), pp. 37–45. Raby, p. 183.

VENI SANCTE SPIRITUS. The
*Sequence, sometimes called the 'Golden Sequence', for *Whitsunday and the following six days. Its authorship is now usually attributed to Stephen *Langton (not *Innocent III). The most popular Eng. transs. are those of J. M. *Neale ('Come, Thou Holy Paraclete') and E. *Caswall ('Holy Spirit, Lord of Light').

Crit. text with notes by C. Blume, S.J.-H. M. Bannister, *Liturgische Prosen des Übergangsstiles und der zweiten Epoche insbesondere die dem Adam von Sanct Victor zugeschriebenen* (A.H.M.A., xliv; 1915), pp. 234–9. H. Thurston, S.J., 'Notes on Familiar Prayers. IV, 'The *Veni, Sancte Spiritus* of Cardinal Langton' in *The Month*, cxxi (1915), pp. 602–16, repr. in his *Familiar Prayers* (ed. J. H. Crehan, S.J., 1953), pp. 54–72. A. *Wilmart, O.S.B., *Auteurs spirituels et textes dévots du moyen-âge latin* (1932), pp. 37–45 ('L'Hymne et la Séquence du Saint-Esprit'). Raby, pp. 342–4.

VENI, VENI, EMMANUEL ('O Come, O
Come, Emmanuel'). The origins of both the words and the music of this well-known hymn (*A.M.* 49, *E.H.* 8), a versification of the *O-Antiphons (q.v.), are very obscure. The words have been traced back to the *Psalteriolum Cantionum Catholicarum* (Cologne, 1710). (J. M. *Neale's ascription of it to the 12th cent. seems wholly unfounded). The tune, which first appeared in the *Hymnal Noted* (1854), is possibly founded on a reminiscence of a plainsong phrase.

The text of the words is pr. in H. A. Daniel (ed.), *Thesaurus Hymnologicus*, ii (Leipzig, 1844), p. 336, and in J. M. Neale (ed.), *Hymni Ecclesiae e Breviariis quibusdam et Missalibus Gallicanis, Germanis, Hispanis, Lusitanis desumpti* (Oxford, 1851), p. 57 f. P. *Dearmer, *Songs of Praise Discussed* (1933), p. 43 f. For other Eng. trr. see J. Julian in J. Julian (ed.), *A Dictionary of Hymnology* (ed. 2, 1907), p. 74, s.v. 'Antiphon', with additional note p. 1551; J. Mearns, ib., p. 1721, s.v.

VENIAL SIN. In moral theology, a sin
which, though it disposes the soul to death and is the greatest of all evils except *mortal sin (q.v.), unlike mortal sin, does not wholly deprive the soul of sanctifying grace. On the basis of 1 Jn. 5. 16 the Fathers posited two classes of sins (*mortalia seu capitalia* as opposed to *levia*; St. *Augustine) differing in gravity, but the modern distinction goes back to the Schoolmen, esp. St. *Thomas Aquinas (*S. Theol.*, II (1), qq. 88, 89). It was formally approved (against M. *Luther) at the Council of *Trent (Sess. VI, cans. 23, 25, 27). Acc. to

the theology of Penance, there is no obligation to confess venial sins when resorting to the Sacrament.

VENICE. The present see of Venice goes back
to the bishopric, founded in 774, on the isle of Olivolo, later known as Castello. It belonged to the patriarchate of Grado, the relations of which to the see of Castello were finally settled under Marco II Michele (1225–35). In 1327 Jacopo Albertini, Bp. of Castello, who was an adherent of Louis of Bavaria, crowned Louis with the Iron Crown and was deposed in consequence. Half a century later Giovanni Piacentini (1376–78) met with the same fate for supporting the antipope Clement VII. Angelo Corrario, Bp. of Olivolo from 1380 to 1390, became Patr. of *Constantinople and in 1406 Pope under the name of Gregory XII. Owing to constant disputes between the patriarch of Grado and the see of Olivolo both were suppressed and replaced by the patriarchate of Venice in 1451, St. Lawrence Giustiniani being the first Patr. of Venice (1433–56). The *Tridentine reforms were introduced into the diocese by Giovanni Trevisano (1560), and later by Laurentius Priuli (1591–1600), who restored the cathedral and founded a seminary. The patriarchate was reorganized in 1818. Among its most important prelates of recent times were the learned Thomist, D. Agostini (1877–91), and Giuseppe M. Sarto (1893–1903), the future Pope *Pius X.

The most famous church of Venice is San Marco, originally the chapel of the Doges. Destined to receive the relics of St. *Mark, it was begun *c.* 830 and completed in 883. Burned down in 976, it was rebuilt after the model of the Basilica of the Apostles at Constantinople from 1063 to 1071. Its plan forms a Greek cross of equal arms, the centre and each of the arms being surmounted by a dome. The interior is richly decorated with many-coloured marbles and mosaics, dating from the end of the 11th to the 17th cents. The retable of the high altar is the famous Pala d' oro, a magnificent 10th cent. piece of goldsmiths' and jewellers' art, with additions dating from the 12th to the 15th cents., representing Christ surrounded by angels, prophets, and saints. The treasury contains a unique collection of plate and jewellery, mostly of Byzantine origin. Immediately in front of the church stands the celebrated campanile, built in 1329 and rebuilt in 1910 after its fall in 1902. Since 1807 San Marco has been the cathedral church of the patriarchate in place of S. Pietro di Castello.

Among other famous Venetian churches are the *Franciscan Santa Maria Gloriosa (1250–1338) for which *Titian painted an *Assumption*, and the *Dominican S. Giovanni e Paolo (1333–90) with the tombs of the Doges. Of the many religious orders that have houses in Venice the *Armenian Benedictine Congregation of the *Mechitarists is esp. remarkable; their convent on the island of San Lazzaro is a centre of Armenian education.

G. Cappelletti, *Storia della repubblica di Venezia dal suo principio sino al suo fine* (13 vols., 1850–5); S. Romanin, *Storia documentata di Venezia* (10 vols., 1853–61). W. C. Hazlitt, *The Venetian Republic. Its Rise, its Growth, and its Fall*, 421–1797 (2 vols., 1900); H. Kretschmayr, *Geschichte von Venedig* (3 vols., 1905–34); E. Musatti, *Storia di Venezia* (2 vols., 1914–15); A. Battistella, *La repubblica di Venezia ne' suoi undici secoli di storia* (1921); R. Cessi, *Storia della repubblica di Venezia* (Bibliotheca Storica Principato, xxiii and xxvi; 1944–6). Mrs. Aubrey Richardson, *The Doges of Venice* (1914). T. Okey, *Venice and its Story* (1903); H. A. Douglas, *Venice on Foot* (1907); E. Hutton, *The Pageant of Venice* (1922). F. Ughelli, Ord. Cist., *Italia sacra*, v (Rome, 1652), cols. 1225–406; G. Capelletti, *Le chiese d'Italia*, ix (1853), pp. 105–489. F. Schillmann, *Venedig. Geschichte und Kultur Venetiens* (1933). There are copious illustrations of *La basilica di San Marco in Venezia*, ed. F. Ongania with various others (15 vols., 1881–6). *Archivio veneto* (Venice, 1871 ff.). H. F. Brown in *E.B.* (ed. 11), xxvii (1911), pp. 995–1007; V. Piva-P. Paschini-M. Muraro in *E.C.*, xii (1954), cols. 1205–21, s.v. 'Venezia', with further bibl.

VENITE. Ps. 95 [Vulg. 94], from its first words ('Venite exultemus'). In the Rule of St. *Benedict (ch. 9), it is prescribed at the 'vigil' (i.e. the night service which became commonly known as *Mattins), whence it found its way into the Roman and Sarum *Breviaries, and in 1549 it was set in its familiar place in the BCP at the beginning of Mattins. The version of the BCP is that of the '*Great Bible'. The stern language of the concluding four verses led the revisers of the BCP of 1927–8 to propose their excision.

VENN, HENRY (1725–97), *Evangelical divine. In 1749 he was elected a Fellow of Queens' College, Cambridge, and after holding several curacies, he became vicar of Huddersfield from 1759 to 1771. Here his piety and zeal made a great impression and he became one of the founders of the *Clapham Group. His *The Complete Duty of Man* (1763) was very popular in his day. Forced by ill-health to retire from Huddersfield in 1771, for the rest of his life he held the living of Yelling in Hunts. His son, John Venn (1759–1813), also a prominent Evangelical and rector of Clapham from 1792 till his death, was one of the founders of the *C.M.S.

H. Venn (grandson, ed.), *The Life and a Selection from the Letters of the late Rev. Henry Venn* (1834), with Memoir of his life mainly by John Venn (son), pp. 1–57, and list of his works, pp. 58–60. See also bibl. s.v. 'Clapham Sect'. J. Venn in *D.N.B.*, lviii (1899), p. 207 f. M. [M.] Hennell, *John Venn and the Clapham Sect* (1958).

VERGER. Strictly the official who carries a mace or 'verge' (Lat. *virga*) before a dignitary. Today the term is commonly used for one who takes care of the interior fabric of the church. In the *Sarum Rite the verger headed the procession. The form 'virger', formerly also in general use, has been occasionally revived in a few places.

VERGIL. See *Virgil*.

VERGILIUS OF SALZBURG, St. See *Virgilius of Salzburg, St.*

VERMIGLI, PIETRO MARTIRE. See *Peter Martyr*.

VERMITTLUNGSTHEOLOGIE. A school of 19th cent. German Protestant theologians. The name derives from a memorandum drawn up by F. Lücke in 1827 and published in 1828 in the first issue of the *Theologische Studien und Kritiken*, the leading organ of the movement. Among its chief representatives were A. *Neander, K. I. *Nitzsch, F. A. G. *Tholuck, J. P. *Lange, J. A. *Dorner, R. *Rothe, H. L. *Martensen, and W. *Beyschlag. All endeavoured in various ways to combine the traditional Protestantism of the Reformation Confessions with modern science, philosophy and theological scholarship. Most of them owed much to F. D. E. *Schleiermacher. The mediating aspirations of the school were vigorously attacked by A. *Ritschl and his disciples, and, more recently, by the theologians of the school of K. *Barth.

F. Traub in *R.G.G.* (ed. 2), v (1931), cols. 1548–51, s.v. For further bibl. see under separate representatives of the school.

VERNAZZA, BATTISTA (1497–1587), *Augustinian canoness and mystic. She was the daughter of Ettore Vernazza, the friend and disciple of St. *Catherine of Genoa (who was Battista's godmother). From 1510 till her death she lived in a convent at Genoa. She wrote letters, some verses, many 'Spiritual Discourses' or homilies, and some 'Colloquies' on her mystical experiences. She is believed to be the final redactor of the Life and so-called *Works* of St. Catherine, and the writer of the 'Spiritual Dialogue' which they incorporate.

Opere spirituali della Vergine di Cristo Donna Battista da Genova, ed. D. Gaspare da Piacenza, 3 vols., Venice, 1588; additional vol. iv, Verona, 1602; ed. 6, 6 vols., Genoa, 1755. F. *von Hügel, *The Mystical Element of Religion as Studied in Saint Catherine of Genoa and her Friends*, i (1908), pp. 336–67. Umile Bonzi de Genova, O.F.M.Cap., 'La Vénérable Battista Vernazza' in *Revue d'Ascétique et de Mystique*, vii (1935), pp. 147–79. G. I. Scatena, C.R.L., in *E.C.*, xii (1954), col. 1287 f., s.v., with further bibl.

VERONA. The beginnings of Christianity in Verona are described in the legendary 9th cent. 'Carmen Pipinianum', which gives a list of its churches and of its early bishops. As its first bishop the city venerates St. Euprepius (probably 3rd cent.). Its first historically attested bishop is Lucilius, who took part in the Council of *Sardica in 343. Its patron is St. *Zeno (c. 362–c. 371). Among its later bishops were Nottingus (c. 840), who opposed the monk, *Gottschalk; Francesco Condulmer (1439), who founded the College of Acolytes; and L. Lippomano (1548–58), who was one of the presidents of the Council of *Trent. An important synod was held at Verona in 1184, which introduced the episcopal inquisition. Till 1752 the see was suffragan of Aquileia, then of Udine, and since 1818 of *Venice. Among the famous churches of the city are the cathedral (12th cent.), which possesses a celebrated collection of MSS. in the Chapter Library and also houses *Titian's painting of the Assumption; S. Zeno Maggiore, also 12th cent.; and the 13th cent. *Dominican church, S. Anastasia. The city suffered severely in the spring of 1945 in the Second World War.

'Annales Veronenses Antiqui', ed. C. Cipolla in *Bullettino dell' Istituto Storico Italiano*, xxix (1908), pp. 7–81. G. Venturi, *Compendio della storia sacra e profana di Verona* (Verona, 1820); C. Cipolla, *Compendio della storia politica di Verona* (ib., 1899); A. M. Allen, *A History of Verona* (1910); L. Simeoni, *Verona* (Rome, 1929). F. Ughello, *Italia sacra*, v (Rome, 1653), cols. 523–1090. P. F. Kehr, *Regesta Pontificum Romanorum*. Italia Pontificia sive Repertorium Privilegiorum et Litterarum a Romanis Pontificibus ante Annum MCLXXXXVIII Italiae Ecclesiis Monasteriis Civitatibus Singulisque Personis Concessorum, vii (pt. 1; Berlin, 1923), pp. 212–304. G. B. G. Biancolini, *Notizie storiche delle chiese di Verona* (8 vols., 1749–71). On the Council of 1184, Hardouin, vi, pt. 2, cols. 1881 f.; Mansi, xxii (Venice, 1778), cols. 487–94; Hefele–Leclercq, v (pt. 2; 1913), pp. 1117–27. G. Turrini in *E.C.*, xii (1954), cols. 1289–98, s.v., with further bibl.

VERONICA, St. A woman of Jerusalem who, acc. to a legend (prob. of French origin) first found in its present form in the 14th cent., offered her head-cloth to Our Lord to wipe the blood and sweat from His face on the way to Calvary. He returned it with His features impressed upon it.

The name is applied in a late version of the 'Acts of *Pilate' to the woman 'diseased with an issue of blood' (Mt. 9. 20–22). In this account she is said to have cured the Emp. Tiberius with a miraculous portrait of Christ. *Giraldus Cambrensis mentions that she had long wanted to see Him, and that, accepting a cloth, He returned it with His features impressed upon it. He applies the word 'veronica' to the cloth, suggesting *vera εἰκών* ('true image') as its etymology. Matthew Paris also applies the name to the portrait, but says that it was so called after the woman at whose request the Lord's features were impressed upon it. A portrait professing to be the original imprint, which seems to have been at Rome since the 8th cent., was translated by *Boniface VIII to St. Peter's in 1297. The relic at Rome was greatly venerated throughout the Middle Ages, esp. in the 14th and 15th cents., and Milan and Jaen also claimed possession of the original headcloth. The incident now occupies a recognized position in the *Stations of the Cross. Although St. Veronica is not mentioned in the Roman martyrology, her feast is kept 12 July.

The identification of Veronica with the woman 'with an issue of blood' occurs in ch. vii of the Acts of Pilate (ed. C. Tischendorf, *Evangelia Apocrypha*, ed. 2, Leipzig, 1876, p. 239, with note; Eng. tr. in M. R. James, *The Apocryphal New Testament*, 1924, p. 102); the account of the cure of the Emp. Tiberius is preserved in the Lat. legend of the Death of Pilate (text in C. Tischendorf, op. cit., p. 456 f.; Eng. tr. in M. R. James, op. cit., p. 157 f., with further information, p. 158 f.). Giraldus Cambrensis, *Speculum Ecclesiae*, cap. vi (*Opera*, ed. J. S. Brewer, R.S., 1873, p. 278 f.); Matthew Paris, *Chronica Majora*, ed. H. R. Luard, iii (R.S., 1876), p. 7 f. *A.A.SS.*, Feb. I (1668), pp. 449–57, and Jul. III (1723), pp. 273–9. E. von Dobschütz, *Christusbilder. Untersuchungen zur christlichen Legende* (T.U., xviii, 1899), ch. 4, 'Die Veronica-Legende', pp. 197–263, with docc. and bibl. pp. 250*–335* and 157**–203**. K. Pearson, *Die Fronica. Ein Beitrag zur Geschichte des Christusbildes im Mittelalter* (Strassburg, 1887); J. Palme, *Die christlichen Veronicalegenden des XII. Jahrhunderts, ihr Verhältnis unter einander und zu den Quellen* (Prague, 1892). P. Perdrizet, 'De la Véronique et de sainte Véronique' in *Seminarium Konda-*

kovianum (Prague, 1932), pp. 1–15. H. *Leclercq, O.S.B., in *D.A.C.L.*, xv (pt. 2; 1953), cols. 2962–6, s.v. 'Véronique'; A. P. Frutaz in *E.C.*, xii (1954), cols. 1299–303, s.v.

VERSICLE. A short sentence, often taken from the Pss., which is said or sung antiphonally in Christian worship. It is answered by a 'response' on the part of the congregation or other half of the choir. Thus, in the services of *Mattins and *Evensong in the BCP, the words 'O Lord, open Thou our lips' and 'And our mouth shall shew forth Thy praise' are respectively versicle and response.

VESPERALE. (1) A liturgical book containing the psalms, hymns, &c., used at *Vespers with their appropriate chants. For convenience the corresponding items at *Compline are also commonly added.

(2) In the W. Church, the cloth spread over the altar when not in use to keep the white linen altar-cloths free from dirt and dust. It is so named from the practice of turning the front part of it back when the altar is being censed at Vespers.

VESPERS. The Evening Office of the W. Church. Together with *Lauds it is the oldest of the '*Day hours', but it was originally part of the Night Office, also called 'lucernarium' (Gk. λυχνικόν), because candles were lit at its celebration. From the time of St. *Benedict, the office was recited earlier in the evening, before dark, and since the later Middle Ages in the afternoon and in *Lent even before midday. The structure of the office resembles that of Lauds, with five psalms (in the *Monastic Breviary, four) and their antiphons, followed by a short lesson (Capitulum), hymn, the canticle '*Magnificat', collect, and concluding versicles; on the ferias of Advent and Lent, on certain Vigils and on Ember Days the 'preces feriales' are added after the Magnificat. The custom of celebrating feast days by two Vespers, the first being said on the previous day, the second on the feast itself, dates from the early Middle Ages. Acc. to the present Roman Rite all Sundays and feasts of double rank have a first and second Vespers; in the case of concurrence of the first and second Vespers of succeeding feasts, the celebration is regulated by elaborate rules acc. to the rank of the feasts. Vespers is together with Lauds the most important hour of the Day Office and frequently celebrated with great solemnity, culminating in the chanting of the Magnificat during which the celebrant incenses the altar. The service of Evensong in the BCP has been partly formed on the model of Vespers, with important additions from *Compline.

P. *Batiffol, *Histoire du bréviaire romain* (1893), esp. pp. 84–8 (ed. 3, 1911, pp. 108–14; Eng. tr., 1912, pp. 70–4). C. Callewaert, *Sacris Erudiri* (1940), No. v, 'Vesperae Antiquae in Officio praesertim Romano', pp. 91–117. 'D. G. M.' [perh. Dom. G. *Morin] in *D.A.C.L.*, xv (pt. 2; 1953), cols. 2939–49, s.v. 'Vêpres'. See also works cited under *Breviary*.

VESPERS, Sicilian. See *Sicilian Vespers.*

VESTIARIAN CONTROVERSY, The.
The dispute concerning clerical dress begun
under *Edward VI, which under *Elizabeth I
became one of the foundations of the *Puritan
party. Already discussed before the publication of the First BCP of Edward VI (1549),
the question of vestments became acute when
R. *Hooper, on being nominated to the
Bpric. of *Gloucester (1550), refused to be
consecrated in the surplice and rochet prescribed in the BCP. Although he eventually
agreed to wear the appropriate vestments on
public occasions, considerable laxity seems to
have existed for the rest of the reign.

The restoration of vestments in 1559, and
esp. the vestments in the Chapel Royal, excited opposition. Acc. to the *Interpretations*
of 1560, an order apparently issued by the
Bishops, a cope was to be worn in the celebration of Holy Communion and a surplice at
other times. Strong opposition to any vestments was voiced in the Convocation of 1563.
After the failure of M. *Parker's attempts in
1564 to reach a compromise with the most
learned of the returned exiles, he issued his
Advertisements (q.v.) in 1566 and required the
use of a 'four-cornered cap, a scholar's gown
priestly and in the church a linen surplice' and
a cope in cathedral and collegiate churches.
Thirty-seven of the London clergy who refused
to promise compliance were deprived. Serious
disturbances followed. Parker tried to enforce
the *Advertisements* in other dioceses, but, with
the Bishops divided, laxity remained. Polemical literature and some bitterness continued
throughout the reign.

The controversy was of purely ministerial
origin, concerning a subject which one party
regarded as indifferent and therefore fit for
the legislation of the magistrate and the other
a matter of real importance because of its
connexion with Popery. In the end most of
the latter group, on the advice of the Continental reformers, acquiesced. Such opposition
as remained was based less on the use of vestments as such than on the claim to freedom of
conscience against the attempts of the Bishops
to enforce conformity, and, before the end of
the 16th cent., had become merged in the
disputes about Church government.

W. H. *Frere, *The English Church in the Reigns of Elizabeth and James I* (1904), pp. 54–6, 59, 111–25. See also lives
of Parker, Matthew, cited s.v.

VESTMENTS. The distinctive dress worn
by the clergy when performing the liturgical
and other services of the Church. This dress
did not, as formerly believed, derive from the
vestments of the Aaronic priesthood, but
originated in the ordinary secular costume of
the world of antiquity in which the early
Church grew up. During the first centuries a
better kind of dress was probably set aside for
the sacred functions, but the development of
a specific priestly costume took place only
between the 4th and 9th cents., one of the chief
reasons being the abandonment of long tunics
and mantles by laymen and their continued use
in the Church. By the 10th cent. the principal

liturgical vestments and their use had been
established in the W. as they are current to-
day. From the 10th to the 13th cents. further
minor additions and alterations were made.
The *surplice was introduced as a substitute
for the *alb on many occasions, the *chasuble
came to be almost reserved to the celebration of Mass, and the *tunicle became the
distinctive vestment of the *subdeacon. In the
same period the bishops, owing to their
enhanced importance in the medieval world,
received additional vestments such as *sandals,
*mitre, and *gloves. Since the 13th cent. the
vestments have varied in form and material,
the general tendency being towards reducing
their size for the sake of convenience. Their
shape and adornments are dependent on the
artistic style and taste of the period. To-day
a distinction is made between the cut back
'Roman' and the more ample and flowing
'Gothic' style, the *Liturgical Movement advocating a return to the fuller forms of the Middle
Ages.

In the RC Church the material and colour
of vestments are regulated by detailed legislation. Mass vestments must be specially
blessed, a custom going back as far as the 9th
cent., and certain prayers are recited while
they are being put on. From the Middle Ages
the Mass vestments have been endowed with
symbolical meaning, being variously interpreted as signifying the Passion of Christ or the
priestly virtues.

The principal vestments of the E. Church
are similar to those of the W., though tunicle,
dalmatic, and some others are not represented,
whereas there is no equivalent of *epigonation
and *epimanikion in the W. See also *Cope,
Eucharistic Vestments,* and *Ornaments Rubric.*

J. Braun, S.J., *Die liturgische Gewandung im Occident und
Orient nach Ursprung und Entwicklung, Verwendung und
Symbolik* (1907). H. Norris, *Church Vestments.* Their
Origin and Development (1949; uncritical). C. E. Pocknee,
Liturgical Vesture, Its Origins and Development (1960). F. E.
*Brightman in *D.E.C.H.*, p. 611 f., s.v.; H. *Leclercq,
O.S.B., in *D.A.C.L.*, xv (pt. 2; 1953), cols. 2989–3007, s.v.
'Vêtement', with bibl.

VESTRY. A room in or attached to a church
in which the vestments, vessels, and other
requisites for Divine worship are kept and in
which the clergy vest. From the fact that it was
here that the parishioners formerly met to
transact the business of the parish, the word
came to be used both of the body of parishioners
and of the actual meeting. By the Local
Government Act of 1894 and subsequent
legislation, the vestries in the C of E lost all
their powers except those concerned with the
administration of the church and of ecclesiastical charities. In 1921 the administration
of the church passed to the newly formed
*Parochial Church Councils, though the
vestries continue to share with the Parochial
Church Meeting the right of electing *churchwardens. In the *Protestant Episcopal Church
of the U.S.A., every parish has a 'vestry', consisting of the incumbent, two wardens, and a
number of 'vestrymen'. This vestry is responsible for the financial administration of the

parish and exercises control over the appointment of the incumbent (subject to the bishop's approval).

VEUILLOT, LOUIS (1813–83), *Ultramontane French journalist. Born at Boynes in Loiret, of poor parents, he entered journalism in 1831, editing the *Mémorial de la Dordogne* at Périgueux from 1832 to 1836 and the *Charte de 1830* at Paris from 1836 to 1838. Converted at Rome to a living Catholic faith in 1838, in 1843 he became editor until his death of the *Univers*, a newspaper at that time of little importance, which increased in authority and acquired an international significance through his defence of the Church. The violence of his views led to his imprisonment in 1844. From 1860 to 1867 the *Univers* was suspended for continual opposition to the Austrian policy of Napoleon as endangering the temporal sovereignty of the Pope, but Veuillot continued in books and pamphlets to advocate his views, esp. his dislike of attempts to reconcile religion with modern ideas and his belief in Papal Infallibility. During the Council of 1869 he was so closely in the confidence of the Pope that the *Univers* became an almost official organ. During the siege of 1870 Veuillot elected to remain in Paris.

His brilliant and incisive style, together with his single-minded devotion to Catholicism, made him one of the foremost defenders of the Church in 19th cent. France. In his original stand for the freedom of Catholic teaching, he was supported by the majority of French Catholics, but from *c.* 1844, when he defended the temporal sovereignty of the Papacy, and esp. when he advocated Papal Infallibility, he was opposed not only by free-thinkers but also by moderate Catholics such as F. *Dupanloup. His published works include *Le Parfum de Rome* (1861), *Les Satires* (1863), *Les Odeurs de Paris* (1866) and *Rome pendant le Concile* (2 vols., 1872) as well as 18 vols. of *Mélanges* (1842–75).

Collected ed. of his works by François Veuillot, nephew (Paris, 1924 ff.). The fundamental life is that by Eugène Veuillot (brother), continued by François Veuillot (4 vols., Paris, 1899–1913). The numerous other studies include those of E. Tavernier, Veuillot's secretary and later editor of *L'Univers* (Paris, 1913), E. Lecigne (ib., 1913), G. Bontoux (ib., 1914), M. M. McDevitt (ib., 1935), François Veuillot (ib. [1937]), and E. Gauthier, *Le Vrai Louis Veuillot* [1939]. E. Gauthier, *Le Génie satirique de Louis Veuillot* [1953]. P. Fernessole, *Les Origines littéraires de Louis Veuillot, 1813–43* (1923); id., *Bio-bibliographie de la jeunesse de Louis Veuillot, 1813–1843* (2 parts of a thesis, 1923). E. Tavernier in *C.E.*, xv (1912), pp. 394–6, s.v.; É. Amann in *D.T.C.*, xv (pt. 2; 1950), cols. 2799–835, s.v.

VEUSTER, JOSEPH DE. See *Damien, Father.*

VEXILLA REGIS. The Latin hymn by *Venantius Fortunatus celebrating the mystery of Christ triumphant on the tree of the Cross. In the Roman Rite it is sung at *Vespers during *Passiontide and on the *Invention (3 May) and *Exaltation (14 Sept.) of the Holy Cross.

The fine Eng. trans., 'The royal banners forward go', is due to J. M. *Neale.

Crit. ed. by G. M. Drews, *Lateinische Hymnendichter des Mittelalters*, ii (A.H.M.A., l; 1907), p. 284; text, with notes and introd., also in A. S. Walpole, *Early Latin Hymns* (1922), No. 34, pp. 173–7. S. G. Pimont, *Les Hymnes du bréviaire romain*, iii (1884), No. xiii, pp. 30–46. A. Manser, O.S.B., in *L.Th.K.*, x (1938), col. 588, s.v. for further bibl.

VIA APPIA. See *Appian Way.*

VIA DOLOROSA. The route in *Jerusalem which Christ is believed to have followed from the judgement - hall of *Pilate, where He received the sentence of death, to Mount *Calvary, the site of the Crucifixion. It is marked by fourteen 'Stations of the Cross', and it is the traditional custom for *Franciscans resident in Jerusalem to conduct devotions along it every Friday.

VIA MEDIA (Lat. 'The Middle Way'). A term in use esp. by J. H. *Newman and other *Tractarians for the *Anglican system as a middle road between 'Popery' and 'Dissent'. This conception of Anglicanism is already found in English divines of the 17th cent., e.g. G. *Herbert and S. *Patrick.

VIA OSTIENSIS. See *Ostian Way.*

VIANNEY, J.-B. M. St. See *Curé d'Ars, The.*

VIATICUM (Lat., 'provision for a journey'; Gk. ἐφόδιον). The Holy Communion given to those in likelihood of immediate death to strengthen them with grace for their journey into eternity. Acc. to W. usage it can be given at any time of the day and the ordinary regulation requiring fasting from the preceding midnight is dispensed.

VICAR. (Lat., *vicarius*, 'a substitute'). In the C of E, the priest of a parish where the *tithes have been appropriated. The institution goes back to medieval times, when churches were appropriated e.g. to monasteries, which received the revenues, and employed first one of their monks to perform the duties of the *rector, and later a secular priest, called a vicar, who acted as the substitute for the religious house. For his maintenance about one-third of the tithes were set apart ('Vicarial' or 'small tithes'), the remainder ('Rectorial' or 'great tithes') being reserved for the monastery. When the monasteries were dissolved, the King granted the rectorial tithes to others, who became known as lay impropriators or lay rectors. As the parish priest a vicar has exactly the same spiritual status as a rector, and the forms of *institution and *induction are identical, since in both cases he holds his full spiritual jurisdiction from the bishop. He also holds the freehold of church, churchyard, vicarage, and glebe, with the exception of the chancel, of which the freehold, though not the possession, is commonly said to belong to the rector. In common parlance, the title 'Vicar' is also used of incumbents who are legally *Perpetual Curates' (q.v.).

VICAR APOSTOLIC. The name given to a RC titular bishop in Christian and missionary countries where the normal hierarchy is not established (e.g. *Iceland, *Sweden, *China) or the ordinary jurisdiction of the bishop is impeded. He performs the spiritual functions of a diocesan bishop and has generally the same rights and delegated powers. The RC community in England was ruled by Vicars Apostolic until the '*Papal Aggression' of 1850.

VICAR OF CHRIST, The. A title of the Roman Pontiff dating from the 8th cent. From the 13th cent. it completely superseded the older title, 'Vicar of St. *Peter'. It expresses his claim to universal jurisdiction in virtue of Christ's words to St. Peter, 'Feed my lambs. . . . Feed my sheep' (Jn. 21. 16 ff.). Down to the 9th cent., other bishops sometimes called themselves Vicars of Christ, though probably not as a formal title.

A. *Harnack, 'Christus Praesens—Vicarius Christi. Eine kirchengeschichtliche Skizze' in *Sb.* (Berl.), 1927, pp. 415–446. M. Maccarone, *Vicarius Christi.* Storia del titolo papale (Lateranum, N.S., xviii; 1952), with reff.

VICAR GENERAL. An official whom a bishop deputes to represent him in the exercise of his jurisdiction. He may appoint more than one Vicar General or none at all, acc. to circumstances. In early times his functions were mostly performed by the *archdeacons, but by the end of the 13th cent. the office had become well established and its duties were exactly defined in the *Sext of *Boniface VIII. No member of a *mendicant order was permitted to fill the office.

In the C of E the office is nowadays ordinarily committed to the *Chancellor of the Diocese, together with that of *Official Principal. In *Sodor and Man, however, it survives as a separate office. Each archbishop also has a Vicar General who holds a court for the confirmation of bishops which 'praeconizes' opposers to appear and produce evidence against the validity of the election or the qualifications of the elected candidate. In the RC Church the office is in regular use. For the present legislation, see *C.I.C.*, cans. 366–71.

VICELIN, St. (c. 1090–1154), 'Apostle of Holstein'. A native of Hameln, he studied at the Paderborn cathedral school and from 1123 to 1126 in France. He was ordained priest by St. *Norbert in 1126 and in the same year was sent by Adalbero, Bp. of Bremen, as a missionary to the pagan Wagrians. From 1127 he worked in Holstein, and despite constant revolts of the Wend population founded the monasteries of *Augustinian Canons at Neumünster and Faldera and a great number

of other churches. After the unfortunate Crusade of the Wends in 1147 had destroyed all his labours, he was consecrated Bp. of Oldenburg in 1149, but not recognized by Henry the Lion. The ensuing political dissensions darkened his last years until he became completely paralysed two years before his death. Feast day, 12 Dec.

The principal sources are Helmold of Bosau, *Chronica Slavorum* capp. 42–79 (ed. B. Schmeidler, Scriptores Rerum Germanicarum, 1909, pp. 84–149), and a metrical life ascribed to Sidon of Neumünster and a letter of the same Sidon (pr. by B. Schmeidler, ib., pp. 219–45). R. Hampt, *Nachrichten über Wizelin den Apostel der Wagern und seine Kirchenbauten* (3 vols., 1913–16). F. Hestermann, *Sankt Vizelin, Apostel der Holsten und Wagrier* (Dülmen i. Westf., 1926).

VICO, GIOVANNI BATTISTA (1668–1744), Italian jurist and philosopher. The son of a Neapolitan bookseller, he was educated in a *Jesuit school and at Naples University, where he became Prof. of Rhetoric in 1697. In 1734 he was appointed historiographer to Charles III. He died after a period of mental disturbance.

Vico's chief work was his *Principii di una scienza nuova d' intorno alla natura comune delle nazioni* (1725; ed. 2, much enlarged, 1730). The treatise was one of the first attempts in modern times to expound a philosophy of history, though Vico restricted the scope of the science to the study of particular peoples and races, and never elaborated a world view. He was much influenced in his mental development by *Plato, St. *Augustine, F. *Bacon, and H. *Grotius, and very critical of the non-historical rationalism of R. *Descartes. In his metaphysical doctrines he showed kinship with his older contemporary, G. W. *Leibniz.

Believing that religion, marriage, and the cult of the dead were the primal things common to all mankind, Vico constructed his metaphysics of history on a religious basis, radically opposed to the principles of utilitarianism and rationalism of later times. He held that nations rise and fall in cycles, and that their development takes place acc. to a threefold pattern: the first the age of the gods, corresponding to theocratic law and hieroglyphic script; the second the heroic age, where might is right and language is symbolic; and the last the human age, where the right rests with reason and writing is alphabetical.

Vico's philosophy of history began to be appreciated in the later 18th cent., and in recent times has exercised a considerable influence on such thinkers as B. *Croce, who interpreted him on Hegelian lines, and on J. *de Maistre.

Collected ed. of Vico's works by G. Ferrari, 6 vols., Milan, 1835–7; fuller ed. by G. de Steffano, 8 vols., Naples, 1858–1869; works also ed. G. *Gentile–F. Nicolini–B. Croce (Scrittori d'Italia, xi, lxvii, cxii, cxiii, cxxxv, clx–clxii, clxviii, clxxiv, and clxxxiii, Bari, 1914–41). Eng. tr. of autobiography by M. H. Fisch–T. G. Bergin (Ithaca, N.Y., 1944), and of *Scienza nuova* by idd. (ib., 1948). G. Ferrari, *Vico et l'Italie* (1839). R. Flint, *Vico* (Blackwood's Philosophical Classics, ix; 1884). B. Croce, *La filosofia di Giambattista Vico* (Saggi Filosofici, ii; Bari, 1911; Eng. tr. by R. G. Collingwood, 1913). G. Gentile, *Studi vichiani* (Messina, 1915). B. Croce, *Bibliografia vichiana*, ed. F. Nicolini (2 vols., Naples, 1947–8). Überweg, iii, 341, 346 f., 682 f.

VICTIMAE PASCHALI (Lat., 'To the Paschal Victim'). The Easter *Sequence in the W. Church. It is a short, dramatic hymn celebrating Christ's triumphant conquest of death, and was composed by *Wipo (d. *c.* 1050), a hymn-writer of Burgundy (or Swabia).

Crit. ed. of text in C. Blume, S.J. (ed.), *Sequentiae Ineditae.* Liturgische Prosen des Mittelalters, iv (A.H.M.A., xxxiv; 1900), No. 23, p. 27 f. E. Arens, 'Wipos Oster-Sequenz' in *Theologie und Glaube*, xviii (1926), pp. 149–54.

VICTOR I, St. (d. 198), Pope from 189. Acc. to the '*Liber Pontificalis' he was an African by birth. His name is chiefly connected with the *Quartodeciman controversy, for the settlement of which he ordered synods to be held throughout Christendom. He himself assembled a Council at *Rome and threatened *Polycrates of Ephesus and other bishops of Asia Minor with excommunication if they refused to give up their practice of keeping *Easter on 14 Nisan instead of the following Sunday. When he actually carried out his threat, St. *Irenaeus and other bishops blamed his severity, but the fact that the churches in Asia Minor remained in communion with Rome would suggest that the Pope took back his sentence. The whole incident is an important step in the history of the Papal supremacy. Among other incidents of Victor's pontificate were the deposition of the presbyter Florinus for defending *Valentinian doctrines and the excommunication of the leather merchant, *Theodotus, the founder of Dynamic *Monarchianism. Acc. to St. *Jerome, Victor was the first Latin ecclesiastical writer, but it seems that he wrote nothing but his encyclicals, which would naturally have been issued in both Latin and Greek. Though venerated as a martyr in the Liturgy, he appears to have died before the persecution under Septimius Severus. Feast day, 28 July.

Jaffé, i, 11 f. The principal authorities are *L.P.* (ed. Duchesne), i (1886), p. 137 f., and *Eusebius, *H.E.*, v, 23 f. E. Caspar, *Geschichte des Papsttums von den Anfängen bis zur Höhe der Weltherrschaft*, i (1930), esp. 19–22. Fliche-Martin, ii (1935), pp. 90–3, with bibl. p. 87. É. Amann in *D.T.C.*, xv (pt. 2; 1950), cols. 2862 f., s.v.; A. Amore, O.F.M., in *E.C.*, xii (1954), col. 1541 f., s.v. 'Vittore I'. See also bibl. to Paschal Controversy.

VICTOR (5th cent.), presbyter of *Antioch. He wrote a Gk. commentary on Mk., really a compilation from earlier exegetical writings (*Origen, *Titus of Bostra, *Theodore of Mopsuestia, *Chrysostom, *Cyril of Alexandria) on Mt., Lk., and Jn. He was also the author of a similar work on Jer., preserved only in *catena* fragments.

No critical, or even complete, text exists. Older editions of Victor's Commentary on Mk. by P. Possinus, S.J. (Rome, 1673), C. F. Matthaei (Moscow, 1775), and J. A. *Cramer, *Catenae in Evangelia S. Matthaei et S. Marci* (Oxford, 1840), pp. 259–447. Modern discussion of problems in J. Reuss, *Matthäus-, Markus- und Johannes-Katenen nach den handschriftlichen Quellen untersucht* (Neutestamentliche Abhandlungen, xviii, Hftt. 4–5; 1941), pp. 118–41. Bardenhewer, iv, 255–7; Altaner (ed. 1951), p. 465. G. Bardy in *D.T.C.*, xv (pt. 2; 1950), cols. 2872–4, s.v.

VICTOR, St. (d. 554), Bp. of Capua from 541. He was the author of many writings, including a treatise on Noah's ark ('Reticulus') and a *Paschal cycle; but his most celebrated work is a Harmony of the Gospels, made on the basis of the *Vulgate text, the so-called *Codex Fuldensis (q.v.). Feast day, 17 Oct.

Apart from the 'Codex Fuldensis', Victor's writings survive only in fragments. Texts collected by J. B. *Pitra from 'De Reticulo seu de Arca Noe' in *Spicilegium Solesmense*, i (1852), pp. 287–9; from 'De Cyclo Paschali', ib., pp. 296–301; from 'De Resurrectione Domini', ib., p. liv. Bardenhewer, v, 277 f. G. Bardy in *D.T.C.*, xv (pt. 2; 1950), cols. 2874–6. See also bibl. to Codex Fuldensis.

VICTOR (late 5th cent.), 'Vitensis', Bp. of Vita in N. Africa. He wrote 'Historia Persecutionis Africanae Provinciae', a history of the persecution of the Catholic Church in Africa by the Arian Vandals under Gaiseric and Huneric (429–84). Its 2nd and 3rd books, based on contemporary material and the author's own experiences, are of special value as giving not only a trustworthy account of the historical events, but also a vivid picture of the political and religious civilization of the country. The work, which was written *c.* 485 in exile, contains several official documents, notably the 'Notitia Africae' of 484, i.e. a list of the Catholic bishops of the African Vandal Empire. The 'Passio Septem Monachorum', added to the history in some older editions, is not by Victor but belongs to a later period.

Editio princeps of his 'Historia' by Jehan Petit, Paris, *c.* 1500. Later ed. by T. *Ruinart, O.S.B., Paris, 1694, repr., with dissertations by J. *Sirmond, S.J., and others, in J. P. Migne, *PL*, lviii, 125–434. Crit. edd. by C. Halm in *M.G.H.*, Auctores Antiquissimi, iii (pt. 1; 1879), and M. Petschenig in C.S.E.L., vii, 1881. A. Schönfelder, *De Victore Vitensi Episcopo* (Breslau Diss., 1899). H. I. Marrou, 'Diadoque de Photiké et Victor de Vita' in *Revue des Études anciennes*, xlv (1943), pp. 225–32. L. *Duchesne, *Histoire ancienne de l'Église*, iii (1910), pp. 625–45; Eng. tr. (1924), pp. 430–41. Bardenhewer, iv, 550–2. G. Bardy in *D.T.C.*, xv (pt. 2; 1950), col. 2881 f., s.v.

VICTORINES. The *canons regular of the former abbey dedicated to St. *Victor at *Paris. The house was founded by *William of Champeaux (the most famous scholar of his day and teacher of *Abelard) and built in 1113 at the cost of King Louis VI. The 'customs' of the house, which were drawn up under the influence of St. *Bernard, acquired considerable prestige. But though the Victorines enjoyed great respect, they never became large in numbers. Many famous scholars, mystics, and poets were found in their ranks, esp. during the 12th cent., among them, *Hugh of St.-Victor, *Richard of St.-Victor, and *Walter of St.-Victor (qq.v.). The abbey became extinct at the outbreak of the French Revolution.

F. Bonnard, *Histoire de l'abbaye royale et de l'ordre des chanoines réguliers de Saint-Victor de Paris* (2 vols., [1904–8]. Heimbucher, i, 413–16.

VICTORINUS, St. (d. *c.* 304), Bp. of Pettau (Poetovio) in Pannonia. Acc. to St. *Jerome he was martyred, probably under *Diocletian. Victorinus was the first exegete of the W. Church, but nearly all his works are lost, probably on account of his *millenarianist tendencies, which caused them to be condemned as apocryphal by the '*Decretum Gelasianum'. He followed *Origen and other Greek commentators, but St. Jerome finds fault with both his style and his erudition. Of his many commentaries only that on Rev. survives. It has come down in a 15th cent. *Vatican MS. (Ottob. lat. 3288 A) and in a working over of it by St. Jerome. The treatise 'De Fabrica Mundi', though not, as formerly believed, part of his commentary on Gen., is almost certainly also to be assigned to him. The attribution of the Pseudo-Tertullianic 'Adversus omnes haereses', (De Praesc., 46-53), to Victorinus (A. *Harnack) is improbable. Acc. to E. *Schwartz, however, Victorinus translated it from a Greek original. Feast day, 2 Nov.

The only crit. text is that of J. Haussleiter in C.S.E.L., xlix (1916). Older texts, with prolegomena, partly repr. in J. P. Migne, PL, v, 281-344. Bardenhewer, ii, 657-63; Altaner (ed. 1951), p. 152 f. J. Haussleiter in P.R.E. (ed. 3), xx (1908), pp. 614-19; G. Bardy in D.T.C., xv (pt. 1; 1950), cols. 2882-7; E. Peterson in E.C., xii (1954), col. 154 f., s.v. 'Vittorino di Pettau' for further bibl.

VICTORINUS AFER, CAIUS (or FABIUS) MARIUS (4th cent.), rhetor and theologian. A native of Africa, he taught in Rome, where he gained a great reputation. About the middle of the century he became a Christian, resigned his rhetorship under *Julian in 362 (an event which excited much comment, and contributed towards determining Augustine to follow his example in 386), and wrote theological works against the *Arians. His style is very obscure, and his doctrine deeply influenced by *Neo-Platonism. But his considerable power as a metaphysician, and his determined use of rationalist methods in theology, made him an important figure. Both in method and in conclusions he occasionally anticipates Augustinian positions, e.g. in his treatment of the Pauline doctrine of *justification.

In his pagan period Victorinus commented extensively on Cicero; translated some writings of *Aristotle and the 'Isagoge' of *Porphyry, and prob. also part of *Plotinus's 'Enneads'; and wrote some original philosophical works. His Christian writings include 'Liber de Generatione Verbi Divini', 'Adversus Arium Libri IV', 'De Homoousio Recipiendo', 'In Epistolas B. Pauli', 'Liber ad Justinum Manichaeum', and 'De Verbis Scripturae'. He also wrote some poems, among them three Hymns to the Trinity and 'De Machabaeis'.

A critical text of Victorinus's theological works by P. Henry, S.J., to appear in S.C., is in preparation [1957]. The only collected edition is in J. P. Migne, PL, viii, 993-1310; this is a compilation from earlier edd. of particular works by J. *Sirmond, S.J., J. *Mabillon, O.S.B., A. *Mai and others. Older studies by G. Koffmane (Breslau diss., 1880) and G. Geiger (2 parts, Metten, 1888-9). E. Benz, Marius Victorinus und die Entwicklung der abendländischen Willensmetaphysik (1934). A. *Souter, The Earliest Commentaries on the Epistles of St. Paul (1927), pp. 8-38. P. Henry, S.J., Plotin et l'Occident (S.S.L., xv; 1934), pp. 44-62. P. Monceaux, Histoire littéraire de l'Afrique chrétienne, iii (1905), pp. 373-422. Bardenhewer, iii, 460-8; Altaner (ed. 1951), p. 321 f. C. *Gore in D.C.B., iv (1887), pp. 1129-38, s.v. 'Victorinus (6)'; P. Séjourné, O.S.B., in D.T.C., xv (pt. 2; 1950), cols. 2887-954, s.v. His treatises on the Trinity ed. P. Henry, S.J., with Fr. tr. by P. Hadot (S.C. lxviii-lxix, 1960).

VICTRICIUS, St. (c. 330-c. 407), Bp. of Rouen from c. 380. At the age of 17 he entered the army. Becoming a Christian not long afterwards, he renounced the military profession as incompatible with his new faith and, acc. to St. *Paulinus of Nola, narrowly escaped execution on a charge of desertion. He is next heard of as Bp. of Rouen, where he became a zealous defender of the faith against pagans and heretics, and undertook mission work as far afield as Flanders, Hainault, and Brabant. He visited Rome, and also in his later years Britain to settle some ecclesiastical dispute. He was the recipient from Pope *Innocent I c. 405 of the celebrated decretal ('Liber Regularum') on disciplinary matters. One of his sermons, 'De laude sanctorum', survives. He became the close friend of St. Paulinus of Nola and of St. *Martin of Tours. Feast day, 7 Aug.

The Liber de Laude Sanctorum is pr. in J. P. Migne, PL, xx, 443-58; crit. ed. by [E. P.] Sauvage-A. Tougard (Paris, 1895). The principal source for his life is the two letters by Paulinus of Nola, Epistolae, xviii (ed. W. Hartel, C.S.E.L., xxxix, 1894, pp. 128-37) and xxxvii (ib., pp. 316-323). The letter from Innocent to Victricius is repr. in J. P. Migne, PL, xx, 469-81. E. Vacandard, Saint Victrice, évêque de Rouen ('Les Saints', 1903). A. *Wilmart, O.S.B., 'Un Manuscrit oublié de l'opuscule de saint Victrice' in R. Bén., xxxi (1919), pp. 333-42, with reff. E. de Moreau, 'S. Victrice de Rouen, apôtre de la Belgica Secunda' in Revue belge de Philologie et d'Histoire, v (1926), pp. 71-79. G. Bardy in D.T.C., xv (pt. 2; 1950), cols. 2954-6, s.v. 'Victrice de Rouen'.

VIDI AQUAM (Lat., 'I beheld water'). In the W. Church, the anthem sung in Eastertide during the aspersing of the congregation at the beginning of the principal Mass on Sundays, in place of the *Asperges sung during the rest of the year. The words 'Vidi Aquam' are the opening words of the *antiphon, a combination of verses from Ezek. 47. The psalm verse is Ps. 118. 1.

L. Eisenhofer, Handbuch der katholischen Liturgik, i (1932), p. 479 f.

VIENNE, Council of (1311-12). The Fifteenth *Oecumenical Council, summoned by *Clement V in 1308 primarily to deal with the question of the *Templars, who were being accused of heresy and immorality by those who coveted their wealth. The Council, which eventually met at Vienne on 16 Oct. 1311, also aimed at providing assistance for the Holy Land and reforming the Church. The majority of the Council at first held that the evidence against the Templars was insufficient. But owing to the transference of the Papacy to *Avignon the Council was under French dominance; and when Philip IV of France appeared with an army before Vienne in Feb. 1312, the Pope by an administrative ordinance suppressed the Order in the bull 'Vox Clamantis' (22 Mar. 1312), and this was promulgated at the next session of the Council. The King then undertook to go on a Crusade within six years. On the question of *Franciscan poverty the Council decided in favour of the more austere party. It also issued a large number of miscellaneous decrees, relating inter alia to the *Beguines and the *Inquisition, which were partly incorporated later in the '*Clementines' by *John XXII. In the event Philip IV never went on the Crusade, but appropriated to his own use the tithe levied for the purpose, and also managed to obtain much of the property of the Templars.

Hardouin, vii, cols. 1321–62; Mansi, xxv (Venice, 1782), cols. 367–426. F. Ehrle, S.J., 'Zur Vorgeschichte des Concils von Vienne' in *Archiv für Litteratur- und Kirchengeschichte des Mittelalters*, ii (1886), pp. 353–416 and 672, and iii (1887), pp. 1–195. Id., 'Ein Bruchstück der Acten des Concils von Vienne', ib., iv (1888), pp. 361–470. Hefele-Leclercq, vi (pt. 2; 1915), pp. 643–719, with bibl. to date. E. Müller, *Das Konzil von Vienne, 1311–1312. Seine Quellen und seine Geschichte* (Vorreformationsgeschichtliche Forschungen, xii; 1934), with further reff. J. Leclercq, O.S.B., in *D.T.C.*, xv (pt. 2; 1950), cols. 2973–9, s.v. See also works cited under *Templars*.

VIGIL. Nocturnal services of prayer, frequently ending with the Eucharistic celebration, were common in the first Christian cents. and are attested by *Pliny in his letter to Trajan (c. 111–13) and described in the 'Peregrinatio *Etheriae'. Without parallel in the public worship of the Synagogue, the reason for their introduction was possibly the widespread belief that the Second Coming would take place at midnight. Vigils were kept esp. before *Easter, when, acc. to *Tertullian, they lasted throughout the night (*Ad uxor.* ii, 4), and *Whitsun, as well as on Sundays and the feasts of the martyrs, in which cases they normally comprised only the beginning (Vespers) and the end of the night. From the later of these services, which began at the first cock-crow, the offices of *Mattins and *Lauds developed. From the 4th and 5th cents., on account of frequent abuses, the Vigils of the people became restricted to the early hours, i.e. before nightfall. From the 8th cent., the custom of anticipating the Vigils became prevalent. At first confined to the afternoon of the preceding day, fast, office, and Mass of the Vigil were gradually transferred to the morning (c. 14th cent.), so that the whole day became a 'profestum'. In the C of E there are 16 feasts which are provided with a Vigil, the list closely following that of the *Sarum Rite. Acc. to modern RC practice, Vigils are never observed for feasts introduced later than the 12th cent., with the one exception of the Feast of the *Immaculate Conception, to which *Leo XIII assigned a Vigil in 1879; only the Vigils of Whitsun, the Assumption, All Saints, and Christmas are fast days; and only those of Christmas and Whitsun can never be ousted by a major feast. In the *Ambrosian Liturgy only the Vigils of Christmas and Whitsun have Masses of their own, and in the *Mozarabic Rite there is only one Vigil, viz. that of Christmas.

A. Gastoué, *Les Vigiles nocturnes* (Science et Religion, ccxcv; 1908). L. Eisenhofer, *Handbuch der katholischen Liturgik*, i (1932), p. 589, ii (1933), pp. 500–17. W. Caspari, 'Untersuchungen zum Kirchengang im Altertum, II' in *Z.K.G.*, xxix (1908), pp. 125–53, esp. pp. 130–53. C. Callewaert, 'De Vigiliarum Origine' in *Collationes Brugenses*, xxiii (1923), pp. 425–66, repr. in his *Sacris Erudiri* (Steenbrugge, 1940), No. xxxi, pp. 329–33. A. *Baumstark-O. Heiming, [O.S.B.,] *Nocturna Laus.* Typen frühchristlicher Vigilienfeier und ihr Fortleben vor allem im römischen und monastischen Ritus (Liturgiegeschichtliche Quellen und

Forschungen xxxii; 1957). H. *Leclercq, O.S.B., in *D.A.C.L.*, xv (pt. 2; 1953), cols. 3108–13, s.v. 'Vigiles'; P. Siffrin O.S.B., in *E.C.*, xii (1954), col. 1414 f., s.v. 'Vigilia'. See also bibl. to *Mattins*.

VIGILANTIUS (*fl. c.* 400), a presbyter of Aquitaine. Most of our knowledge of him comes from his bitter opponent, St. *Jerome, who nicknamed him 'Dormitianus' (i.e. 'the dormant', instead of 'the vigilant'). He was a native of Calagurris in Aquitania. Having paid Jerome a visit at *Bethlehem which ended in a quarrel, Vigilantius on his return to the W. attacked Jerome as an *Origenist. Jerome replied with his 'Contra Vigilantium' (406), accusing his adversary of rejecting such practices as the cult of the saints and martyrs, the observance of vigils, and celibacy and monasticism. As Jerome's writings against him are full of invective and his opponent's replies have not survived, the justice of these allegations cannot be assessed. It is possible that Vigilantius did not go further than attack certain excesses which threatened the practice of asceticism at that period.

Jerome also attacked him in *Epp.* 61 (ad Vigilantium) and 109 (ad Riparium). A. Réville, *Vigilance de Calagurris. Un chapitre de l'histoire de l'ascétisme monastique* (Paris, 1902). G. Bardy in *D.T.C.*, xv (pt. 2; 1950), cols. 2992–4, s.v.

VIGILIUS (d. 555), Pope from 537. Of a noble Roman family, he was a deacon in 531, when Boniface II nominated him his successor. The nomination, however, was nullified in 532 as uncanonical and in 535–6 Vigilius became *apocrisiarius at the court of *Constantinople. Here, induced, it is said, by the Empress Theodora, he promised his help to restore the deposed *Monophysite patriarch, Anthimus, and to condemn the Council of *Chalcedon. In 537 the legitimate Pope Silverius was deposed with the help of the Byzantine commander Belisarius, and Vigilius consecrated in his place. The new Pope, however, neither reinstalled Anthimus nor did he favour Monophysitism. The letter addressed by him to the deposed Monophysite patriarchs Anthimus, Severus, and Theodosius is probably a forgery, and in letters to *Justinian and *Menas of Constantinople he decisively upheld the doctrine of Chalcedon. The Emperor's religious policy soon involved him in the *Three Chapters Controversy (q.v.) raised by Justinian's edict of 543–4, which condemned writings of *Theodore of Mopsuestia, *Theodoret, and *Ibas of Edessa. Vigilius, in accordance with the opinion of the W., refused at first to assent to the condemnation in which he saw a repudiation of Chalcedon. But, brought to Constantinople by order of Justinian, he repudiated the Three Chapters after considerable resistance and waverings in his 'Iudicatum' of 548, though not without reservations in favour of the Council of Chalcedon. His capitulation met with violent opposition in the W. The Pope was even excommunicated at a synod at Carthage, presided over by its bishop, Reparatus, and in consequence he retracted the 'Iudicatum'.

After his protest against another Imperial edict in 551 he fled to Chalcedon, and in 553 refused to preside at the Council of *Constantinople. He again declined to condemn the Three Chapters in the 'Constitutum', in the drawing-up of which his deacon, the future Pope Pelagius I, had a large share. The Council, however, finally condemned the Three Chapters, leaving intact the authority of Chalcedon. Pressed by the Emperor, who would not allow him to return to Rome unless he accepted the decrees of Constantinople, Vigilius consented to them after six months' consideration and departed for Italy in 555, dying before he reached Rome.

The case of Pope Vigilius was adduced at the *Vatican Council by the opponents of Papal *Infallibility. It is generally held by RC theologians that Infallibility was not involved and that the condemnation of the Three Chapters was in itself justified on account of their *Nestorian tendencies, though inopportune under the circumstances.

Correspondence and decrees in J. P. Migne, *P.L.*, lxix, 12–328. Jaffé, i, 117–24. *L.P.* (ed. Duchesne), i (1886), pp. 296–302. F. Savio, S.J., 'Il Papa Vigilio (537–555)' in *Civiltà cattolica*, 18e Ser., xii (1903), pp. 5–26, 551–64 and 660–78. L. *Duchesne, *L'Église au VIe siècle* (1925), pp. 151–218. E. Caspar, *Geschichte des Papsttums von den Anfängen bis zur Höhe der Weltherrschaft*, ii (1933), pp. 229–286; Fliche–Martin, iv (1937), pp. 457–79. G. Krüger in *P.R.E.* (ed. 3), xx (1908), pp. 633–40, s.v.; É. Amann in *D.T.C.*, xv (pt. 2; 1950), cols. 2994–3005, s.v., with further bibl. P. Paschini in *E.C.*, xii (1954), col. 1416, s.v. See also bibl. to *Three Chapters*.

VIGILIUS (*fl. c.* 500), Bp. of Thapsus. Banished from Africa in 484 by the Arian king, Huneric, he fled to Constantinople. His chief work, 'Against Eutyches', attacks *Monophysitism and defends the *Tome of St. *Leo and the *Chalcedonian Definition. Of several anti-Arian works, only the 'Dialogue against Arians, Sabellians, and Photinians' is extant. Other writings, notably a 'De Trinitate', have been wrongly attributed to him, while P. *Quesnel held that he was the author of the *Athanasian Creed.

Works ed. P. F. Chifflet, S.J. (Dijon, 1664), repr. in J. P. Migne, *PL*, lxii, 93–544. G. Ficker, *Studien zu Vigilius von Thapsus* (1897). Bardenhewer, iv, 553–7. G. Ficker in *P.R.E.* (ed. 3), xx (1908), pp. 640–4, s.v.; G. Bardy in *D.T.C.*, xv (pt. 2; 1950), cols. 3005–8.

VILATTE, JOSEPH RENÉ (1854–1929), '*episcopus vagans'. A Frenchman by birth, he joined the RC Church on several separate occasions, to leave it each time for a different Protestant denomination. In 1892, on the authority of an apparently forged bull, he was consecrated at Colombo in Ceylon by Abp. Alvarez, a schismatic from the Church of Antioch, as *Old Catholic bishop in America, and took the name of 'Mar Timotheos'. He himself consecrated a large number of bishops who have been recognized by no other Christian body. In 1898 he ordained 'Father *Ignatius' to the priesthood at Llanthony.

J. Parisot, O.S.B., *Monseigneur Vilatte, fondateur de l'Église Vieille-Catholique aux États-Unis d'Amérique* (Tours, 1899). H. R. T. Brandreth, O.G.S., *Episcopi Vagantes and the Anglican Church* (1947), pp. 31–44, with bibl. p. 72 f.

VILMAR, AUGUST FRIEDRICH CHRISTIAN (1800–60), *Lutheran theologian. A native of Solz in Kurhessen, he held a number of pastoral and administrative appointments until in 1855 he was appointed professor of theology at Marburg. He was a vigorous opponent of all forms of rationalism, upholding dogmatic and confessional Lutheranism by opposing to the prevalent 'theology of rhetoric' (as he termed it) a 'theology of facts' ('*Theologie der Tatsachen*'). He defended the retention of the ancient creeds in worship. In addition to a widely read *Geschichte der deutschen Nationalliteratur* (1845; ed. 26, 1905), he wrote many theological works, largely dealing with the contemporary situation in Church politics. He also compiled a hymnbook (*Kleines evangelisches Gesangbuch*, 1838) embodying improved ideals in hymnology.

Selected Essays ed. K. Ramge, Munich [1939]. Studies by J. H. Leimbach (Hannover, 1875) and W. Hopf (2 vols., Marburg, 1912–13). P. Dietz, *Dr. August Friedrich Christian Vilmar als Hymnolog* (ib., 1899). J. Haussleiter in *P.R.E.* (ed. 3), xx (1908), pp. 649–61, s.v.; P. Glaue in *R.G.G.* (ed. 2), v (1931), cols. 1588 f., s.v.

VINCENT, St. (4th cent.), the proto-martyr of Spain. Acc. to a tradition of the late 4th cent. onwards, referred to by St. *Augustine and by *Prudentius, St. Vincent was educated and ordained deacon by Valerius, Bp. of Saragossa, and suffered in the *Diocletianic persecution. The details surrounding his death were considerably developed in later times. Feast day, 22 Jan.

Prudentius, *Peristephanon*, v; St. Augustine, *Sermones*, 274–7; *Sermo in Natali S. Vincentii Martyris* attributed to *Leo I (Sermo XII in J. P. Migne, *PL*, liv, 501–6). A 'Passio Sancti Vincentii Levitae', which Ruinart suggested was used by St. Augustine, is printed in T. *Ruinart, O.S.B., *Acta Primorum Martyrum Sincera et Selecta* (Paris, 1689), pp. 387–404; various 'Acta S. Vincentii Martyris' in *Anal. Boll.*, i (1882), pp. 259–78, incl. the 'Passio Brevior', more prob. used by St. Augustine, pp. 260–2. *AA.SS.*, Jan. II (1647), pp. 397–414. S. Hurault, *Saint Vincent, martyr, patron de vignerons et son culte dans le diocèse de Châlons* (Châlons-sur-Marne, 1910). P. Allard, *La Persécution de Dioclétien et le triomphe de l'Église*, i (1890), pp. 237–41 and 246–50. A. de Waal, 'Zum Kult des hl. Vinzenz von Saragossa' in *R.Q.*, xxi (1907), pp. 135–8. K. Hofmann in *L.Th.K.*, x (1938), cols. 636 f., s.v. 'Vinzenz', with further bibl.

VINCENT OF BEAUVAIS (*c.* 1190–1264), medieval encyclopaedist. He probably entered the *Dominican Order at Paris *c.* 1220 and moved to Beauvais *c.* 1229. Later he was brought into close relations with King *Louis IX and lived, at least for a time, at the monastery of Royaumont, nr. Paris. His encyclopaedia, the 'Speculum Majus', composed between 1247 and 1259, consisted of three parts—a 'Speculum Naturale', a 'Speculum Doctrinale', and a 'Speculum Historiale'—and set out to be a compendium of the whole range of knowledge accessible to his time, in 80 books and 9,885 chapters. He is estimated to have drawn upon some 450 authors and 2,000 writings. A supposed fourth part of the 'Speculum', a 'Speculum Morale', is by a later writer. His other writings include a treatise (compiled at the behest of Queen Margaret),

'De eruditione seu modo instruendorum filiorum regalium'.

His *Speculum Historiale* was publd. at Strassburg by J. Mentelin, 4 vols., 1473; his son-in-law, A. Rusch, also publd. at Strassburg the *Speculum Historiale*, 3 vols., c. 1473, and the *Speculum Doctrinale* and the *Speculum Naturale* separately not later than 1478; the *Speculum Morale* was publd. by J. Mentelin, ib., 1476. The latest ed. of the *Speculum Maius* is that of the Benedictines of *Douai, 4 vols., Douai, 1624. Collected *Opuscula* publd. at Basle, 1481. Crit. ed. of the *De Eruditione* by A. Steiner (Mediaeval Academy of America Publication No. 32; Cambridge, Mass., 1938). Parts of Vincent's works are still unpubld. B. L. Ullman, 'A Project for a New Edition of Vincent of Beauvais' in *Speculum*, viii (1933), pp. 312–26, with discussion of existing edd. J. B. Bourgeat, *Études sur Vincent de Beauvais* (Paris thesis, 1856). L. Lieser, *Vincenz von Beauvais als Kompilator und Philosoph*. Eine Untersuchung s. Seelenlehre im *Speculum Maius* (1928). M. Daunou, 'Vincent de Beauvais' in *Histoire littéraire de la France*, xviii (1835), pp. 449–519; L. Delisle, 'Miroir historial de Vincent de Beauvais', ib., xxxii (1898), p. 547 f. E. Boutaric, 'Vincent de Beauvais et la connaissance de l'antiquité classique au treizième siècle' in *R.Q.H.*, xvii (1875), pp. 5–57. Dr. Gass, 'Zur Geschichte der Ethik. Vincenz von Beauvais und das *Speculum Morale*' in *Z.K.G.*, i (1877), pp. 365–96, ii (1876), pp. 332–65 and 510–36. Quétif-Échard, i, 212–40. Überweg, ii, 380, with bibl. p. 733. H. Peltier in *D.T.C.*, xv (pt. 2; 1950), cols. 3026–33, s.v.

VINCENT FERRER, St. (c. 1350–1419), *Dominican mission preacher. In 1367 he entered the Dominican house at Valencia, his native town. Through his close acquaintance with Cardinal Pedro de Luna (afterwards *Benedict XIII) he became for a time a warm enthusiast for the *Avignonese Papacy, and later was Benedict XIII's confessor at Avignon. From 1399 to 1409 he undertook a highly effective series of missionary travels, visiting such centres as Marseilles, Geneva, Lausanne, and Freiburg, and collecting around him large crowds of followers, many of whom were stirred to flagellation and other severe forms of penance. He is credited with having performed a large number of miracles. In his later years he took a prominent part in the movement for ending the Papal schism. He died at Vannes in Brittany. He was canonized in 1455. Feast day, 5 Apr.

Works ed. P. H. D. Fages, O.P. (2 vols., Paris, 1909). Process of canonization, also ed. id., ib., 1904; id., *Notes et documents de l'histoire de saint Vincent Ferrier* (1905). Id., *Histoire de saint Vincent Ferrier* (2 vols., 1894). M. M. Gorce, O.P., *Saint Vincent Ferrier, 1350–1419* (Paris thesis, 1923); id., *Les Bases de l'étude historique de saint Vincent Ferrier* (Thèse Complémentaire, Paris, 1923). S. Brettle, *San Vicente Ferrer und sein literarischer Nachlass* (Vorreformationsgeschichtliche Forschungen, x; 1924). H. Finke, 'Die Quaresma-Predigten des heiligen Vicente Ferrer, 1413' in *Festschrift Gustav Schnürer zum 70. Geburtstag gewidmet* (1930), pp. 24–38. H. *Ghéon, *Saint Vincent Ferrier* (1940; Eng. tr., 1939). M. M. Gorce, O.P., in *D.T.C.*, xv (pt. 2; 1950), cols. 3033–45, s.v. 'Vincent Ferrier (Saint)'.

VINCENT OF LÉRINS, St. (d. before 450), the author of the 'Commonitorium'. Little is known of his life. He became a monk on the island of *Lérins, where as a *Semi-Pelagian he opposed *Augustinianism, and was probably the object of *Prosper of Aquitaine's 'Responsiones ad capitula objectionum Vincentianarum'. His surviving 'Commonitorium', which was written under the pseudonym 'Peregrinus' to provide a guide in the determination of the true Catholic faith, embodies the famous *Vincentian Canon. Despite his emphasis on tradition he maintained that the final ground of Christian truth was Holy Scripture, and that the authority of the Church was to be invoked only to guarantee its right interpretation. He did not, however, preclude a development in matters of doctrine, maintaining that in the process of history the truth of Scripture often became more fully explicated. A second commonitorium which he wrote has not survived. Feast day, 24 May.

Among the innumerable edd. of the Commonitorium the more recent include those of A. *Jülicher (Freiburg i.Br., 1895), G. Rauschen (Florilegium Patristicum, v, Bonn, 1906) and R. S. Moxon (Cambridge Patristic Texts, 1915). Of the older texts, the best was the 17th cent. ed. by E. *Baluze (Paris, 1663, also 1669, 1684; repr. in J. P. Migne, *PL*, l, 637–86). Eng. trr. by C. A. Heurtley (N.P.N.C.F., ser. 2, xi, 1894, pp. 123–59), T. H. Bindley ('Early Church Classics', 1914) and others. *Excerpta Vincentii Lirinensis según el Códice de Ripoll, No. 151*, ed., with introd., by J. Madoz, S.J. (Estudios Onienses, ser. 1, vol. i; Madrid, 1940). Id., *El concepto de la tradición en S. Vincente de Lerins* (Analecta Gregoriana, v; Rome, 1933). Bardenhewer, iv, 579–82; Altaner (1950), p. 403 f.; both with bibl. J. Zellinger in *L.Th.K.*, x (1938), col. 632 f., s.v.; G. Bardy in *D.T.C.*, xv (pt. 2; 1950), cols. 3045–55, s.v.; G. Madoz, S.J., in *E.C.*, xii (1954), col. 1440 f., s.v. 'Vicenzo di Lérins'; all with bibl.

VINCENT DE PAUL, St. (c. 1580–1660), founder of the *Lazarist Fathers and the 'Sisters of Charity'. Born of a peasant family at Ranquine in SW. France, he studied theology at Toulouse and was ordained priest in 1600. Captured by pirates in 1605 he was for two years a slave in Tunisia, but in 1607 escaped to *Avignon. In 1609 he went to Paris and here, coming under the influence of P. de *Bérulle, resolved to devote his life entirely to works of charity. From 1613 to 1625 he was tutor in the household of Count de Gondi, General of the galleys, where he did much to relieve the lot of the prisoners. During this time he founded Confraternities of charity for both men and women, and in 1625 the Congregation of the Mission, usually called 'Lazarists' (or 'Vincentians'), for the giving of missions esp. among country people and for the training of the clergy. Eight years later he carried out a project cherished already by St. *Francis de Sales, by founding, together with St. Louise de Marillac, the 'Sisters of Charity', the first congregation of women without enclosure entirely devoted to the care of the sick and the poor. In 1643 the Queen Regent, Anne of Austria, appointed him a member of Louis XIV's Council of Conscience during the King's minority, and during the Wars of the Fronde he used his influence to become the organizer of far-reaching relief work among the suffering populations. St. Vincent de Paul was also one of the most uncompromising opponents of *Jansenism and took an active part in furthering its condemnation. He was canonized in 1737. Feast day, 19 July. In 1833, the 'Society of St. Vincent de Paul' was founded by F. *Ozanam and others in defence of Catholic truth against free-thinkers.

P. Coste, C.M. (ed.), *Saint Vincent de Paul, correspondance, entretiens, documents* (14 vols., 1920–5); Eng. trr. of selected letters and addresses as *St. Vincent de Paul and*

Mental Prayer (1925), of further letters (1937), and of the Conferences of St. Vincent de Paul to the Sisters of Charity (4 vols., 1938–40), all by J. Leonard, C.M. L. Abelly, La Vie du vénérable serviteur de Dieu, Vincent de Paul (1664). P. Collet, La Vie de saint Vincent de Paul (2 vols., 1748). U. Maynard, Saint Vincent de Paul. Sa vie, son temps, ses œuvres, son influence (4 vols., 1860); L. E. Bougaud, Histoire de saint Vincent de Paul (2 vols., 1889; Eng. tr., 2 vols., 1899). Ella K. Sanders, Vincent de Paul, Priest and Philanthropist (1913). P. Coste, C.M., Le Grand Saint du grand siècle, Monsieur Vincent (3 vols., 1932; Eng. tr., 3 vols., 1934–5). Other studies by A. Loth (Paris, 1880), E. de Broglie ('Les Saints', 1897), H. Déplanque (Paris, 1936) and J. Calvet (Paris, 1948; Eng. tr., 1952), with bibl. Bremond, iii (1921), pp. 222–57, with reff.; Eng. tr., iii (1936), pp. 193–222; Pourrat, iii (1925), pp. 575–86; Eng. tr., iii (1927), pp. 387–94.

VINCENT, WILLIAM (1739–1815), Dean of *Westminster. He was educated at Westminster School and Trinity College, Cambridge, and, after holding several ecclesiastical appointments, became head master of Westminster in 1788. He took a special interest in the religious education of the pupils, and in 1801 published his Defence of Public Education in reply to charges brought against head masters of neglecting this duty. In 1802 he was made Dean of Westminster, among his chief activities being the restoration of Henry VII's Chapel in Westminster Abbey (1807–1821). He is known esp. for his works on comparative geography and ancient navigation, including his commentary on Arrian's Voyage of Nearchus (1797) and The Periplus of the Erythraean Sea (2 parts, 1800 and 1805).

Collection of his Sermons on Faith, Doctrines and Public Duties (London, 1817), with life by R. Nares (previously publd. in substance in The Classical Journal, xiii (1816), pp. 221–6, and xiv (1816), pp. 190–215) prefixed to the Sermons, pp. xi–lxxv; further vol. of Sermons ed. W. Thornton (London, 1836). G. Le G. Norgate in D.N.B., lviii (1899), pp. 363–5.

VINCENTIAN CANON, The. The threefold test of Catholicity laid down by St. *Vincent of Lérins in his 'Commonitorium' (II. 3), viz. quod ubique, quod semper, quod ab omnibus creditum est ('what has been believed everywhere, always, and by all'). By this triple test of oecumenicity, antiquity, and consent, the Church is to differentiate between true and false traditions. The order of the tests is to be noted, as the canon was very frequently misquoted with 'antiquity' (quod semper) first by English writers in the 19th cent.

VINCI, LEONARDO DA. See Leonardo da Vinci.

VINCIBLE IGNORANCE. In moral theology, the converse of *invincible ignorance (q.v.).

VINEAM DOMINI SABAOTH. The Constitution issued by Clement XI on 16 July 1705 against the French *Jansenists. Besides confirming the three earlier Papal bulls—'*Cum Occasione' (1653), 'Ad Sanctam' (1656), and 'Regiminis Apostolici' (1664)—it maintained that the Pope could determine questions

of historic fact (the case in point being whether or not certain propositions, condemned by the Pope, were in fact contained in *Jansen's *Augustinus) as well as matters of doctrine, and that when such a determination had been made by the Pope, it must be accepted 'by the heart' of the believer, and not merely received 'with a respectful silence'. As its issue was believed to infringe the liberties of the French clergy, Louis XIV accompanied its promulgation in France with a Declaration maintaining the prerogatives of the bishops.

The orig. text, which incorporates the earlier bulls mentioned above, is pr. in Bullarum, Diplomatum et Privilegiorum Sanctorum Pontificum Taurinensis Editio, xxi (Turin, 1871), pp. 233–6; part repr. in Denz.-Bann. (ed. (1952), p. 390 f. (No. 1350). M. Ott in C.E., xv (1912), p. 445 f., s.v.; B. Matteucci in E.C., xii (1954), col. 1446 f., s.v. See also works cited under Gallicanism and Jansenism.

VINEGAR BIBLE. A popular name for the fine folio edition of the Bible, printed at Oxford in 1716–17 by John Baskett (d. 1742), the King's Printer. The headline of Lk. 20 reads 'The Parable of the Vinegar' instead of 'The Parable of the Vineyard'.

Darlow–Moule, No. 735 f., i, 259 f.

VINES, RICHARD (1600? – 56), *Puritan divine. Educated at Magdalene College, Cambridge, where he became a good Greek scholar, he was a schoolmaster at Hinckley (c. 1624–42) and non-resident rector of Weddington (1628–42) and Caldecote, Warwickshire (1630–42). On 30 Nov. 1642 he preached on the fast day before the House of Commons and in the next few years took a leading part in the reform of Church government and liturgy. In 1643 he was nominated a member of the *Westminster Assembly where he became a member of the committee which drafted the Confession; he was also intruded as rector of St. Clement Danes. In 1644 he became Master of Pembroke College, Cambridge, whence Benjamin Laney had been ejected. In the same year he was put on the Parliamentary Committee of Accommodation, and, though episcopally ordained, defended *Presbyterian ordinations. He was opposed, however, to lay elders as Church governors. In 1645 he was present at negotiations between King and Parliament at Uxbridge for peace and also exchanged his London rectory for that of Watton, Herts. In 1648 he took part in the written discussion on episcopacy with *Charles I in the Isle of Wight; but though he and the King held each other in mutual esteem and he himself had become opposed to the growing power of the *Independents, he felt too deeply committed to Presbyterianism to moderate his views. In 1649 he opposed the abolition of the kingly office and the House of Peers, and being ejected from Pembroke College and Watton Rectory he became minister of St. Lawrence Jewry. Several of his sermons were published, mostly posthumously, but they scarcely represent his great learning and theological powers.

XII Sermons Preached upon Several Public Occasions: By . . . Mr. Richard Vines (1658), To which is adjoined the Sermon preached at his funeral by Mr. Thomas Jacomb (originally publd. 1656; sep. pagination). S. Clarke, *The Lives of Sundry Eminent Persons in this Later Age* (1683), pp. 48–56. B. Brook, *The Lives of the Puritans*, iii (1813), pp. 230–5. A. Gordon in *D.N.B.*, lviii (1899), pp. 369–71, s.v.

VINET, ALEXANDRE RUDOLF (1797–1847), Swiss Reformed theologian. A native of Ouchy, nr. Lausanne, he taught French language and literature at Basle from 1817, where he came under the influence of W. M. L. *De Wette, and was ordained minister in 1819. He became professor of practical theology at Lausanne in 1837, where he remained till 1847, when he attached himself to the newly constituted Free Church in Canton Vaud. He was a strenuous defender of liberty of worship and the separation of Church and state and advocated these principles in his *Mémoire sur les libertés des cultes* (1826), *Essai sur la manifestation des convictions religieuses* (1842), and *Du socialisme considéré dans son principe* (1846). His conception of Christianity was thoroughly individualistic, the seat of religion being the conscience and dogma important only in so far as it issued in moral action. Vinet gave forceful expression to these views in his sermons, collected in *Discours sur quelques sujets religieux* (1831 and 1841), which have had a lasting influence on Swiss and French Protestants, owing to their combination of classic form with modern scholarship and warmth of feeling. Shortly after his death appeared his brilliant *Études sur Blaise *Pascal* (1848), with whom Vinet had certain affinities in his emphasis on the heart as the chief organ of religion and in his use of psychology in apologetics. Other formative influences on his theology were I. *Kant and T. *Erskine. He has sometimes been designated the 'Swiss Schleiermacher'.

Œuvres publ. under the auspices of the Société d'Édition Vinet, founded 23 April, 1908, with introd. by various authors (Lausanne and Paris, 1910 ff.). Selected works tr. into Germ., ed. E. Staehelin (4 vols., Zürich, 1944–5); selections ed. P. Bridel, *La Pensée de Vinet* (Lausanne, 1944), with reff. E. Rambert, *Alexandre Vinet*. Histoire de sa vie et ses ouvrages (1875). Laura M. Lane, *The Life and Writings of Alexander Vinet* (1890). E. Scherer, *Alexandre Vinet*. Notice sur sa vie et ses écrits (1852). L. Molines, *Études sur Alexandre Vinet*. Critique littéraire (1890). A. Ruegg in *P.R.E.* (ed. 3), xx (1908), pp. 680–92, s.v., with further bibl.

VIO, THOMAS DE. See *Cajetan, Cardinal*.

VIRET, PIERRE (1511–71), early Protestant Reformer. A native of Orbe in Switzerland, he studied theology at Paris. In 1531 he came under the influence of the Reformer G. *Farel, who ordained him a preacher, and in 1533 Viret became his assistant at Geneva. From 1536 onwards he worked in the interests of Protestantism, mainly in Lausanne. In 1559 he was appointed a preacher in Geneva but two years afterwards went to France, where at Nîmes, Lyons, Orange, and elsewhere he took an active and leading part in the affairs of the French Reformed Church. The chief of his writings was his *Instruction chrestienne*

en la doctrine de la Loy et l'Évangile (3 vols., Geneva, 1564), a popularized version of Calvinistic doctrine in dialogue form.

His letters were publ. in A. L. Herminjard (ed.), *Correspondance des réformateurs* (9 vols., 1866–97), passim. J. Barnaud (ed.), *Quelques Lettres inédites de Pierre Viret* (1911). *Pierre Viret d'après lui-même*. Pages extraites des œuvres du réformateur à l'occasion du 4ᵉ centenaire de sa naissance (Lausanne, 1912). J. Barnaud, *Pierre Viret*. Sa vie et son œuvre (1911). P. Godet, *Pierre Viret* (Lausanne, 1892). H. Vuilleumier, *Notre Pierre Viret* (ib., 1911). C. Schmidt–C. Schetzler in *P.R.E.* (ed. 3), xx (1908), pp. 693–5, s.v.

VIRGER. See *Verger*.

VIRGIL (70–19 B.C.), Roman poet. Almost from the time of its publication, the *Aeneid* was employed as a school textbook throughout the Roman Empire. It was therefore impossible for W. Christian writers to escape the study of Virgil; and, from the 4th cent. onwards, evidence of this is to be found in the publications of Christian Virgilian centos, in the adoption by St. *Augustine of Virgilian historico-political conceptions, and in innumerable reminiscences of Virgil in all Christian Latin literature. Two considerations help to explain the unique position, among pagan classics, accorded to Virgil by the Fathers: first, the moral characteristics evinced by the poet, esp. in the *Aeneid*, which earned him the reputation of *anima naturaliter Christiana*, whom only the historical accident of dates separated from Christianity; and secondly, the Messianic interpretation imposed upon the 4th *Eclogue*. From the scholastic use of his works derives the common medieval conception of Virgil as a sage and magician; from his supposed affinities with Christianity came a loftier idealization, best expressed in the all-but-saintly guide of *Dante's allegorical journey.

The editions and translations of all Virgil's works are innumerable, while the literature is immense. Recent general studies on Virgil in English include T. R. Glover, *Studies in Virgil* (1904); T. Frank, *Vergil*. A Biography (1922); and W. F. J. Knight, *Roman Vergil* (1944). Studies more specifically concerned with his religious significance include J. B. Mayor–W. W. Fowler–R. S. Conway, *Virgil's Messianic Eclogue*. Its Meaning, Occasion, and Sources (1907); T. F. Royds, *Virgil and Isaiah*. A Study of the Pollio with translations, notes, and appendices (1918); C. Bailey, *Religion in Virgil* (1935). D. Comparetti, *Virgilio nel medio evo* (2 vols., Leghorn, 1872; Eng. tr., 1895); J. W. Spargo, *Virgil the Necromancer* (Harvard Studies in Comparative Literature x; Cambridge, Mass., 1934). M. N. Wetmore, *Index Verborum Vergilianus* (New Haven, Conn.–London, 1911).

VIRGILIUS OF SALZBURG, St. (c. 700–784), 'Apostle of Carinthia'. An Irishman—the Gaelic form of his name was 'Fergal'—he was one of the most learned men of his age, esp. in mathematical matters. The facts of his early life are uncertain; but acc. to one tradition, he was at first a monk of Aghaboe, where he later became abbot. Having made his way to the Continent in 743, for several years he governed the diocese of Salzburg without becoming bishop. St. *Boniface, who disapproved of this ecclesiastical arrangement no less than of some of Virgilius's scientific doctrines, went so far as to accuse him to Pope *Zacharias of heresy for holding the existence of the antipodes. He was eventually consecrated in 755 (or, less probably, in 767) to the see of Salzburg. He has been held in continuous repute in his diocese and was canonized by *Gregory IX in 1233. Feast day, 27 Nov.

The 'Gesta Sancti Hrodberti Confessoris' attributed to Virgilius, ed. by F. M. Mayer in *Archiv für Oesterreichische Geschichte*, lxiii (1882), pp. 606–8. A 12th cent. life ed. G. H. Pertz in *M.G.H.*, Scriptores xi (1854), pp. 86–95; of greater historical importance is the epitaph by *Alcuin, ib., Poetae, i (1881), p. 340. L. Gougaud, O.S.B., *Les Saints irlandais hors d'Irlande* (Bibliothèque de la Revue d'Histoire Ecclésiastique, xvi; 1932), ch. xl, pp. 170–2. F. S. Betton, S.J., *St. Boniface and St. Virgil.* A Study from the Original Sources of Two Supposed Conflicts (Benedictine Historical Monographs, ii; Washington, 1927). H. Krabbo, 'Bischof Virgil von Salzburg und seine kosmologischen Ideen' in *Mittheilungen des Instituts für Oesterreichische Geschichtsforschung*, xxiv (1903), pp. 1–28; H. Van der Linden, 'Virgile de Salzbourg et les théories cosmographiques au VIIIe siècle' in *Bulletin de l'Académie de Belgique.* Classe des Lettres (1914), pp. 163–87. É. Amann in *D.T.C.*, xiv (pt. 2; 1950), cols. 3093–7, s.v.

VIRGIN BIRTH OF CHRIST, The. The belief that Jesus Christ had no human father, but was conceived by the Blessed Virgin Mary by the power of the Holy Spirit is clearly stated in the two narratives of Christ's Infancy recorded in the Gospels (Mt. 1 f. and Lk. 1 f.), and has been a consistent tenet of orthodox Christian theology. It is also implied in the *Apostles' Creed. It has generally been regarded by Christian theologians as altogether congruous with the Catholic doctrine of the *Incarnation, with its stress on the uniqueness of Christ.

In early times, the fact was questioned only by a few heretical sects (*Psilanthropists, *Adoptionists). Within the last hundred years, however, it has been challenged by a number of liberal theologians on such grounds as: (1) a general suspicion of everything miraculous and in particular the belief that the LXX of Is. 7. 14 (παρθένος, 'virgin'), as an inexact rendering of the Heb., gave rise to, or at least promoted, the legend; (2) the absence of reference to the Virgin Birth in other parts of the NT, notably the Christological teaching of the Epp. and the Fourth Gospel; and (3) the contention that it would have been more congruous with the full Humanity of Christ for His Birth to have been like that of other men. It is answered: (1) that belief in miracle is integral to the Christianity of the NT and, as regards the supposed influence of Is. 7. 14, the more circumstantial account of the Birth of Christ in Lk. (as contrasted with that in Mt.) is in no way associated with this OT passage; (2) it was the kind of fact which from its nature would at first have become known in the Church much less rapidly than the public facts of the Lord's life; and (3) it is rash to suppose that the Son of God needed two parents in order to assume human nature. Yet it should be observed that the acceptance of Christ's Divine Sonship is not theologically dependent on the fact that He was not the son of Joseph, and in any case the doctrine of the Virgin Birth is to be clearly distinguished from that of the Incarnation itself.

Modern works defending the traditional belief include C. *Gore, *Dissertations on Subjects connected with the Incarnation* (1895), pp. 3–68; W. M. *Ramsay, *Was Christ born at Bethlehem?* A Study on the Credibility of St. Luke (1898); J. Orr, *The Virgin Birth of Christ* (1907); G. H. Box, *The Virgin Birth of Jesus* (1916); and J. G. Machen, *The Virgin Birth of Christ* (1930). The belief was rejected by P. Lobstein, *Études christologiques.* Dogme de la naissance miraculeuse du Christ (1890; Eng. tr., 1903); also by P. W. Schmiedel in *E.Bi.*, iii (1902), cols. 2954–66, s.v. 'Mary', and H. Usener, ib., cols. 3340–52, s.v. 'Nativity (–Narratives)'. A useful critical examination of the NT evidence in V. Taylor, *The Historical Evidence for the Virgin Birth* (1920; no conclusion drawn and belief must be determined by dogmatic considerations). J. A. MacCulloch in *H.E.R.E.*, xii (1921), pp. 623–6, s.v., with bibl. See also commentaries to Gospels, ad locc., and bibl. to *Incarnation*.

VIRGIN MARY, The Blessed. See *Mary, The Blessed Virgin*.

VIRTUALISM. A form of *Eucharistic doctrine acc. to which while the bread and wine continue to exist unchanged after consecration, the faithful communicant receives together with the elements the virtue or power of the Body and Blood of Christ. Its classical exponent was J. *Calvin.

VIRTUES, Cardinal. See *Cardinal Virtues*.

VIRTUES, Theological. See *Theological Virtues*.

VISIGOTHIC RITE, The. Another name, used e.g. by Dom M. Férotin (1855–1914), for the *Mozarabic Rite in use in Spain during its dominance by the Visigoths (5th–7th cents.).

VISITANDINE ORDER. See *Visitation, Order of the*.

VISITATIO LIMINUM APOSTOLORUM. See *Ad Limina Apostolorum*.

VISITATION, Episcopal. Episcopal Visitations are designed for the periodic inspection of those temporal and spiritual affairs of a diocese under the bishop's control. From the 6th cent., such visitations were regulated by several ecclesiastical councils. Triennial visitation, which was the usual medieval practice, was exacted by the Anglican *Canons of 1603 (can. 60). Biennial visitation is the minimum stipulated by the Council of *Trent. In the later Middle Ages, when the work of visitation was already conducted by commissaries of the bishop, there developed elaborate legal forms centring in the presentation of offenders by both clergy and laity, to whom articles of inquiry had been previously administered. The cases were then tried by canon law in much the same form as that of the *consistory court. The Abps. of *Canterbury and *York have the right to visit all the dioceses within their respective provinces, e.g. W. *Laud in 1634 instituted a visitation of all his suffragan dioceses. See also *Charge*.

VISITATION OF OUR LADY, The.

The feast, observed on 2 July, commemorates the Blessed Virgin's visit to her cousin *Elizabeth, recorded in Lk. 1. 39–56. It made its first appearance in the 13th cent. when it was introduced into the *Franciscan Order by the General Chapter of 1263 at the instigation of St. *Bonaventure. Its extension to the universal Church in order to obtain the end of the Great Schism was decided upon by *Urban VI and prescribed by Boniface IX in 1389, but accepted only by the part of the Church under his obedience. The Council of *Basle, in 1441, again ordered its celebration, and *Pius V finally established it for the whole RC Church. It was inserted as a *Black Letter Day into the calendar of the 1662 BCP.

F. G. Holweck in *C.E.*, xv (1912), p. 480 f., s.v.; G. Löw, C.SS.R.–W. Wehr in *E.C.*, xii (1954), cols. 1499–502, s.v. 'Visitazione di Maria Santissima'.

VISITATION ORDER,

also known as the Visitandines or Salesian Sisters. The order of contemplatives founded in 1610 by St. *Francis of Sales and St. *Jane Frances de Chantal. It was designed for women unable to bear the austerities of the older orders and devoted itself to the special cultivation of humility, gentleness, and sisterly love. Originally the Visitandines were a congregation with simple vows. Only the novices were strictly enclosed, while the professed sisters went out on works of mercy, esp. nursing the sick. But this innovation was received unfavourably by the Abp. of Lyons, D. S. de Marquemont, who refused to admit the sisters to his diocese unless they kept to the enclosure. St. Francis gave way, and on 23 Apr. 1618 Pope *Paul V constituted the congregation an order with full privileges ('Ordo Visitationis BMV'). It was solemnly approved by *Urban VIII in 1626. The 'constitutions' drawn up by St. Francis were an adaptation of the *Augustinian Rule, with the characteristic substitution of the *Little Office of Our Lady for the Canonical Hours. The mother-house at Annecy has a primacy of honour among the houses of the order, but each house retains its independence and is under the jurisdiction of the diocesan bishop. Besides cultivating the contemplative life, the Sisters of the Visitation now devote themselves chiefly to education. Their habit is black, with a black veil for the choir sisters and a white one for lay sisters and novices. The most notable saint of the order is St. *Margaret Mary Alacoque, whose visions had a large share in the institution of the Feast of the *Sacred Heart.

C. F. Ménestrier, S.J., *Projet de l'histoire de l'ordre de la Visitation de Sainte-Marie* (Annecy, 1701). *La Visitation Sainte-Marie* (Les Grands Ordres religieux, Paris, 1923); E. Lecouturier, *La Visitation* (Les Grands Ordres monastiques et instituts religieux, 1935). F. A. *Gasquet, O.S.B., *The Order of the Visitation. Its Spirit and its Growth in England* [1910]. F. M. de Chaugy, *Les Vies des quatres premières mères de l'ordre de la Visitation Sainte-Marie* (1659; repr. as vol. i of the Œuvres historiques de la Mère Françoise-Madeleine de Chaugy, 1892); also other works by this author. For the early history of the order see also *The*

Life of Jeanne Charlotte de Bréchard by the Sisters of the Visitation, Harrow (1924). Heimbucher, i, 641–6, with bibl. R. Perrin, O.S.F.S., in *C.E.*, xv (1912), pp. 481–3, s.v.

VISITATION OF THE SICK, The.

The 'Order for the Visitation of the Sick' in the BCP follows in arrangement that in the *Sarum *Manual, but with considerable omissions, e.g. of the *Seven Penitential Psalms formerly recited on the way to the sick person's house. In the 1662 Book, the minister of the parish, after an opening versicle and response on entering the sick person's presence, says the Lord's Prayer, followed by further versicles and responses, collects for the sick man's faith, repentance, and perseverance, an exhortation (added in 1549, and partly based on the *Homilies* of 1547), a profession of faith in the articles of the Apostles' Creed in an interrogatory form, an exhortation to confession of sin, followed by a form prescribed for priestly absolution, a further collect for the sick man's forgiveness, Psalm 71, 'O Saviour of World', a final collect, and the Blessing (in the form in Num. 6. 24–26). Four occasional collects are appended. In the 1549 Book provision was also made for the *unction of the sick man, but this has been omitted since 1552. In the 1927–1928 Book the service was much revised and modernized. The 'Communion of the Sick' included in the BCP from 1549 onwards as a separate item provides for a celebration in the sick-room (as against Communion from the Reserved Sacrament), with a special collect, Epistle (Heb. 12. 5), and Gospel (Jn. 5. 24).

F. Procter–W. H. *Frere, *A New History of the Book of Common Prayer* (1919), esp. pp. 622–9. C. Harris, 'Visitation of the Sick' in W. K. L. Clarke–C. Harris (edd.), *Liturgy and Worship*. A Companion to the Prayer Books of the Anglican Communion (1932), pp. 472–541; id., 'The Communion of the Sick, Viaticum, and Reservation', ib., pp. 541–615. Forms of Service for 'Unction and the Laying-on of Hands' and for 'the Laying-on of Hands without Unction' were approved by both Houses of the *Convocation of Canterbury on 6 June 1935; they are repr. in A. F. Smethurst–H. R. Wilson (ed.), *Acts of the Convocations of Canterbury and York . . . passed since . . . 1921* (1948), pp. 72–83; for somewhat similar provision made by both Houses of the Convocation of York, see ib., pp. 83–6. See also bibll. to *Unction* and *Spiritual Healing*.

VITALIAN

(d. 672), Pope from 657. Despite the strained relations between Rome and *Constantinople during the *Monothelite controversy, he kept on good terms with the E. during the earlier part of his pontificate, exchanging the customary compliments with the E. Emp. Constans II, at his consecration, and receiving him at Rome in 663. Later, however, Vitalian's name was removed from the *Diptychs at Constantinople for his adhesion to 'Dyothelite', i.e. orthodox, views. It was he who consecrated *Theodore of Tarsus as Abp. of *Canterbury in 668. Feast day, 27 Jan.

Jaffé, i (1885), pp. 235–7. L.P. (Duchesne), i (1886), pp. 343–5. Mann, i (pt. 2; 1902), pp. 1–16, with notes on sources. E. Caspar, *Geschichte des Papsttums von den Anfängen bis zur Höhe der Weltherrschaft*, ii (1933), pp. 580–586, 588 f., 600, and 681 f. É. Amann in *D.T.C.*, xv (pt. 2, 1950), cols. 3115–17, s.v. 'Vitalien'.

VITALIS, St. St. *Ambrose relates that in 393 he discovered at *Bologna, with the assistance of the local bishop, Eusebius, the bones of Sts. Agricola and Vitalis which lay buried in the Jewish cemetery there, and that both Vitalis and Agricola (whose slave Vitalis was) had suffered death together. The cult of Vitalis spread rapidly through W. Christendom and famous churches were dedicated to his honour at *Ravenna (5th cent.; rebuilt in 6th) and *Rome (5th cent., formerly the basilica of the *titulus Vestinae*). Two historically value-less later accounts of the death of St. Vitalis exist, in one of which he is associated not with Agricola, but his wife Valeria. Feast days: Vitalis and Valeria, 28 Apr.; Vitalis and Agricola, 4 Nov.

F. Savio, S.J., 'Due lettere falsamente attribuite a S. Ambrogio' in *Nuovo Bullettino di Archeologia cristiana*, iii (1897), pp. 153–77. On the legend associating St. Vitalis with Agricola, see also *AA.SS.*, Nov. II (pt. 1; 1894), pp. 233–53; H. *Delehaye, S.J., 'L'Hagiographie ancienne de Ravenne' in *Anal. Boll.*, xlvii (1929), pp. 5–30, esp. pp. 7–10; id., *Les Origines du culte des martyrs* (ed. 2, Subsidia Hagiographica, xx, 1933), esp. p. 324 f. and 328 f. On the legends associating St. Vitalis with Valeria, id., 'Trois Dates du calendrier romain' in *Anal. Boll.*, xlvi (1928), sect. 2, 'Saint Vital (28 avril)', pp. 55–9.

VITANDI (Lat., 'persons to be avoided'). The technical name in *canon law for those *excommunicated persons with whom mem-bers of the Church are debarred from having any kind of intercourse. They are distinguished from the **tolerati* with whom relations of a personal kind are allowed. Unless he has laid violent hands on the person of the Pope, in which case *ipso facto* he is *vitandus*, an offender acquires this status only when he has been expressly so named by the Roman see. For these rulings see *CIC*, cans. 2258, 2259 and 2343.

VITORIA, FRANCISCO DE (c. 1485–1546), Spanish theologian. He entered the *Dominican Order *c.* 1502 and studied at the Convent of S. Pablo, Burgos, and from 1506 to 1512, partly under Peter Crockart (d. 1514), at Paris, where he was ordained priest in 1509. There he taught arts and philosophy at the Convent of St. James from 1512 to 1517, and in 1523 became 'doctor theologiae'. After his return to Spain he lectured on theology at Valladolid from 1523 to 1526, and from 1526 held the first chair of theology at the university of Salamanca.

Vitoria may be considered a forerunner of the '*Salmanticenses'. By substituting the 'Summa Theologica' of St. *Thomas for Peter *Lombard's 'Sentences' as the theological text-book, he inaugurated a new school at Salamanca, which under his pupils Dominic *Soto, Andreas de Vega (1498–1560), Melchior *Cano, and others, became the chief university in Europe in the 16th cent. for the study of Scholasticism. A humanist as well as a philo-sopher and theologian, he developed a method which, without disregarding philosophical speculation, made the Scriptures and the Fathers the foundation of theological teaching.

He is often also regarded to-day as the 'Father of International Law', and at some points H. *Grotius was dependent on him. In his famous 'Relectiones', Conferences given be-tween 1527 and 1540, he dealt *inter alia* with the chief problem of his day in international morality, viz. the conquest of the Indies. He was critical of the Spanish methods of coloniza-tion in America and also laid down the con-ditions of a just war. On this last matter, basing himself on St. *Augustine and St. Thomas, he confined legitimate warfare to the redressing of a wrong received; and, indeed, he went further than St. Thomas, in holding that no war would be permissible if it should bring serious evil to Christendom and the world at large.

The early edd. of Vitoria's writings are very rare, and part of his work is still unpubld. Modern edd. of his com-mentary on the Secunda Secundae of St. Thomas by V. Beltrán de Heredia, O.P. (Bibliotheca de Teólogos Españoles, 1932 ff.); of the sections 'De Indis' and 'De Jure Belli' of his *Relectiones Theologicae XII* (orig. publd. at Lyons, 1557) by H. F. Wright, with introd. by E. Nys, and Eng. tr. and photographic reproduction of the 1696 ed. (The Classics of International Law; Washington, D.C., 1917); the same sections also ed. with Germ. tr. by W. Schätzel (Die Klas-siker des Völkerrechts, ii; 1952); the *Relectiones* also repr. from various early edd., with photographic repr. of MSS., by L. G. A. Getino (3 vols., [Madrid,] 1933–5). V. Beltrán de Heredia, O.P., *Los manuscritos del Maestro Fray Francisco de Vitoria* [1928]. C. Barcia Trelles, *Francisco de Vitoria, fundator del derecho internacional* (Valladolid, 1928); L. G. A. Getino, *El Mro. Francisco de Vitoria* (1930); J. B. Scott, *Francisco de Vitoria and his Law of Nations* (The Spanish Origin of International Law; 1934); V. Beltrán de Heredia, O.P., *Francisco de Vitoria* (Barce-lona, 1939). F. Stegmüller, *Francisco de Vitoria y la doctrina de la gracia en la escuela salmantina* (Biblioteca histórica de la Biblioteca Balmes, Ser. 2, x; 1934). R. C. Gonzales, O.P., *Francisco de Vitoria. Estudio bibliográfico* (Buenos Aires, 1946). Quétif–Echard, ii, 128–30. F. Stegmüller in *L.Th.K.*, x (1938), cols. 656–8, s.v.; V. Beltrán de Heredia, O.P.–J. G. Menéndez-Rigada, O.P., in *D.T.C.*, xv (pt. 2; 1950), cols. 3117–44, s.v.; A. Piolanti in *E.C.*, v (1951), cols. 1607–9, s.v. 'Francesco da Vitoria', for further bibl.

VITRINGA, CAMPEGIUS (c. 1659–1722), Biblical exegete. A native of Leeuwarden in Friesland, he was educated at Franeker and *Leyden Universities and in 1680 was offered a teaching post at Franeker. Here he lectured with great success for the rest of his life, re-peatedly refusing to leave the town for a more prominent position at Utrecht. His fame rests on his Biblical exegesis, which, though inspired by the *Calvinistic orthodoxy of his age, succeeded in interpreting the sacred text with unusual freshness and penetration. His principal work was a commentary on Isaiah (2 vols. fol., Leeuwarden, 1714, 1720). Among his other writings were *De Synagoga Vetere* (1696; Eng. trans., *The Synagogue and the Church*, 1842) and *Anakrisis Apocalypseos Ioannis Apostoli* (1705).

E. F. Kautzsch in *P.R.E.* (ed. 3), xx (1908), pp. 705–8, s.v., with bibl.

VITUS, St. (perh. 303), martyr. The common legend about him is much later, and exists in several forms. He is generally supposed to have been born of pagan parents in Lucania, S. Italy, and secretly brought up as a Christian by Crescentia, his nurse, and Modestus, her husband, all three being martyred under *Diocletian. St. Vitus is invoked against sudden death, hydrophobia, and the convulsive disorder known as St. Vitus' dance. The association of his cultus with bodily health appears already in the *Gelasian Sacramentary, and an early S. Italian Gospel *pericope appointed for his feast (Mt. 9. 35–10. 1) connects him with the cure of sickness and of demonic possession. He is one of the 14 *auxiliary saints. Feast day, 15 June.

AA.SS., Jun. II (1699), pp. 1013–42; B.H.L., ii, 1257–1259 (Nos. 8711–23), and Suppl., p. 308 f. Text of the *Translatio S. Viti* also ed. F. Stentrup in F. Philippi (ed.), *Abhandlungen über Corveyer Geschichtsschreibung* (Veröffentlichungen der historischen Kommission für Westfalen, 1906), pp. 51–100 (text, pp. 75–100). H. Königs in *L.Th.K.*, x (1938), cols. 658–60, s.v., with bibl.

VLADIMIR, St. (956–1015), the Apostle of the Russians and Ruthenians. Though he was a grandson of St. Olga, he was brought up a pagan. In 978 he took Kiev from his elder brother, and subsequently conquered Polotsk, subjugated large districts of White Russia, and was involved in many other wars. Having assisted the Greek Emp. Basil II in quelling a revolt, he married c. 987 the Emperor's sister, Anne. Henceforth he was an ardent promoter of Christianity and erected many churches and monasteries; but his work of evangelism owed much of its success to physical compulsion, and those who refused baptism were heavily punished. Vladimir's later years were troubled by insurrections of his sons by his former pagan wives, and he died on an expedition against one of them. Feast day, 15 July.

The principal authority is the chronicle attributed to Nestor, monk of Kiev (11th–12th cent.); Eng. tr., with introd. and notes of edd. in Russian and Germ. and Fr. trr., by S. H. Cross in *Harvard Studies and Notes in Philology and Literature*, xii (1930), pp. 77–309; (text, pp. 178–214). N. de Baumgarten, *Saint Vladimir et la conversion de la Russie* (Orientalia Christiana, vol. xxvii, fasc. 1; Num. 79; 1932), with full bibl.

VOETIUS, GISBERT (1589–1676), Dutch Reformed theologian. A native of Heusden in Holland, he was educated at the university of *Leyden, where he was deeply influenced by F. *Gomar. Having been preacher at Vlijnen (1611) and Heusden (1617), he took a prominent part in the Synod of *Dort (1618), everywhere combating *Arminianism and defending an uncompromising *Calvinistic predestinationism. In 1634 he was appointed professor of theology and oriental languages at Utrecht, and in 1637 also pastor of the Reformed Church there. A man of strong convictions and violently hostile to everything Catholic, he was involved in frequent controversies. He defended strict Calvinism against the freer school represented by J. *Cocceius, carried on bitter and often unfair attacks against R. *Descartes, and at the end of his life quarrelled with J. de *Labadie because of his separatist tendencies. Though of great influence during his lifetime, Voetius did not form a theological school. His writings include *Politica-Ecclesiastica* (4 vols., Amsterdam, 1663–1676) and *Diatribe de Theologia* (Utrecht, 1668).

Life by A. C. Duker (3 vols.+index vol., Leyden, 1897–1915). M. Bouwman, *Voetius over het Gezag der Synoden* (1937). J. J. van Oosterzee–S. D. van Veen in *P.R.E.* (ed. 3), xx (1908), pp. 717–25.

VOLTAIRE, pseudonym of **François-Marie Arouet** (1694–1778), French writer. Educated by the Paris *Jesuits, he embarked on a literary career in which his brilliant and malicious wit soon gained him both admirers and enemies. In 1717 he was imprisoned in the Bastille for ridiculing the Regent, but shortly afterwards his first tragedy, *Œdipe*, established his reputation as an author. A quarrel with the Chevalier de Rohan led to his second imprisonment, followed by his exile in London from 1726 to 1729. Here he came into contact with *Deism and the English *Aufklärung which decisively influenced his future development. In his *Lettres philosophiques sur les Anglais* (1734) he contrasted favourably the rationalistic currents in England of H. St. J. Bolingbroke and J. *Locke to the reactionary outlook of France and made a violent attack on B. *Pascal. When the book was publicly burnt in Paris he fled to Cirey in Lorraine, the country house of Mme de Châtelet, where he wrote his *Traité de métaphysique* (1734), a recommendation of Deism, as well as completed several of his best plays, among them *Alzire* (1736) and *Mahomet* (1741) and the blasphemous epic on St. *Joan of Arc, *La Pucelle* (1739; publd. 1755). From 1750 to 1752 he lived at the court of Frederick II of Prussia, and in 1758 bought the estate of Ferney, on the Swiss frontier, where he led the life of a country gentleman. To this last period belong *Essai sur les mœurs* (1756) and *Candide* (1759). Both are filled with hatred of orthodox Christianity and marked by a pessimism which, in the face of the presence of evil in the world, denies the Christian conception of a good and omnipotent God. Voltaire did not, however, subscribe to atheism, against which he urged the argument from design, and he strongly recommended a Deistic religion (*Théisme*), regarding belief in the existence of God and personal immortality as necessary for the government of the masses. Throughout his life he was violently opposed to the Catholic Church against which he directed his slogan 'Écrasez l'infâme', and in whose institutions he saw nothing but deceit, superstition, and fanaticism, though he seems to have preserved a certain regard for the human personality of Christ. Voltaire's character was a strange mixture 'made up', in the words of T. B. Macaulay, 'of mean and great, of foul and fair', his generally destructive influence being offset by the courageous defence of innocent victims of the régime he hated, such as the Huguenot, Jean Calas, and his unwearied insistence on progressive reforms.

Voltaire's works have frequently been ed. and individually tr. into English. The extensive literature includes, besides the well-known life by J. Morley (London, 1872), studies by G. Desnoiresterres (8 vols., Paris, 1867–76), E. Champion (ib., 1893), L. Crouslé (2 vols., ib., 1899), S. G. Tallentyre (2 vols., London, 1903), G. Lanson ('Les Grands Écrivains français', 1906), R. Aldington (London, 1925), A. Bellessort (Paris, 1925), H. N. Brailsford (H.U.L., 1935), A. Noyes (London, 1936; tries to prove Voltaire a good Catholic), N. L. Torrey (New York, 1938), J. Charpentier (Paris, 1938), R. Naves (ib., 1942; and earlier works), and Ira O. Wade (Princeton, N.J., 1947; and other works by this author). G. Bengesco, *Voltaire*. Bibliographie de ses œuvres (4 vols., 1882–90); Mary M. H. Barr, *A Century of Voltaire*. A Bibliography of Writings on Voltaire, 1825–1925 (New York, 1929). C. Constantin in *D.T.C.*, xv (pt. 2; 1950), cols. 3387–471, s.v.

VOLUNTARY. A piece of music played on the organ at the beginning or end of (and, occasionally, during) a religious service. Those played at the beginning and close are sometimes distinguished as the In- and Out-Voluntaries.

VOLUNTARYISM. Esp. in *Scotland, the doctrine that the Church ought to be spiritually independent of the State. It rests on the theses that the establishment of a particular denomination is unjust and that State endowments are devitalizing.

VON HARNACK, ADOLF. See *Harnack, Adolf*.

VON HOFFMANN, J. C. K. See *Hoffmann, J. C. K.*

VON HÜGEL, Baron FRIEDRICH (1852–1925), RC theologian and philosopher. He was born at Florence, the elder son of Carl Alexander Anselm, Baron von Hügel (1795–1870), and of Elizabeth, *née* Farquharson, a Scottish Presbyterian lady who was a convert to the RC Church. After a cosmopolitan education he settled in England in 1867. In 1870 an attack of typhus left him deaf and permanently weakened in health. After a religious crisis he was brought to a firm faith at Vienna through the influence of Raymond Hocking, a Dutch *Dominican (1870). He married in 1873 and for the rest of his life lived at Hampstead (1876–1903) and Kensington (1903–25), though he constantly travelled abroad. In 1884 he met for the first time the Abbé Henri Huvelin at *Paris, who made a profound spiritual impression on him.

Meanwhile von Hügel had become a keen student of science (esp. geology), philosophy, Biblical criticism and religious history. Having become convinced of the critical view of the OT, he defended it in 1897 in a Congress at Fribourg (Switzerland). He found himself in growing accord with the cultural and liberalizing tendencies in the RC Church and several of the leaders of the *Modernist Movement (A. *Loisy, G. *Tyrrell) became his lifelong friends. In 1905 he founded the London Society for the Study of Religion, which brought him into touch with thinkers and scholars of the most diverse views. In 1908 he published *The Mystical Element of Religion as studied in St. Catherine of Genoa and her Friends*. This was followed in 1910 by an article on St. John's Gospel in the *Encyclopaedia Britannica* (ed. 11) and in 1912 by his book *Eternal Life*. In 1921 appeared his *Essays and Addresses on the Philosophy of Religion*; a Second Series followed in 1926, after his death. He was appointed *Gifford Lecturer at Edinburgh for 1924–6, but owing to ill-health was unable to deliver the course; portions of it were published posthumously in *The Reality of God* (1931).

Among the problems with which von Hügel constantly wrestled were the relation of Christianity to history (in which field he found a kindred spirit in E. *Troeltsch), the place of human culture in the Christian life, the Christian conception of time, and the significance of eschatology for the modern world. He saw the Institutional, the Intellectual, and the Mystical as the three abiding elements in religion. In his earlier life he had much sympathy with the activist philosophy of M. *Blondel, but believing that the essence of religion was 'adoration', he came in his later years to emphasize the Divine transcendence and the 'givenness' of faith. 'The Baron' became one of the chief religious influences in cultured circles in England, more so outside the RC Church than within it, though his 'Modernism' escaped formal condemnation. The confidence which he inspired as a spiritual counsellor may be clearly discerned in his published correspondence.

Von Hügel's *Selected Letters, 1896–1924*, ed. B. Holland (1927), with Memoir by id., pp. 1–68; *Letters from Baron Friedrich von Hügel to a Niece*, ed. Gwendolen Greene (1928), with introd., pp. vii–xlv. Much of his correspondence with G. Tyrrell is pr. in Maude D. Petre, *Von Hügel and Tyrrell. The Story of a Friendship* (1937). Life by M. de la Bedoyère (London, 1951). L. V. Lester-Garland, *The Religious Philosophy of Baron F. von Hügel* (1933); A. H. Dakin, *Von Hügel and the Supernatural* (S.P.C.K., 1934); M. Nédoncelle, *La Pensée religieuse de Friedrich von Hügel, 1852–1925* (Paris thesis, 1935; Eng. tr., 1937); A. A. Cock, *A Critical Examination of von Hügel's Philosophy of Religion* (London thesis, [1953]). C. C. J. *Webb in *D.N.B., 1922–1930*, pp. 874–6.

VORSTIUS (Konrad von der Vorst) (1569–1622), *Arminian theologian. He was a native of *Cologne. After abandoning his early intention of entering business, he studied theology at Heidelberg, and later proceeded to Basle and Geneva, where he greatly impressed T. *Beza by his abilities. In 1596 he accepted a teaching post at Count Arnold of Bertheim's academy at Steinfurt. Certain of his writings gave rise to a charge of *Socinianism; but having successfully cleared himself before the Theological Faculty at Heidelberg, he continued to teach at Steinfurt, where his reputation rose from year to year. In 1610, after the death of J. *Arminius, he accepted, after much hesitation, a call by J. Uitenbogaert to the vacant chair at *Leyden. In the same year he had issued a treatise against R. *Bellarmine and also a work, *Tractatus Theologicus de Deo, sive de Natura et Attributis Dei*, which at once provoked attention on account of its rationalist tendencies. Strict Calvinists led by F. *Gomar pronounced it heretical; the

Heidelberg theologians, and even A. *Saravia, professed themselves shocked; and when *James I's attention was drawn to it he drew up a list of its theological errors and instructed Ralph Winwood, British Ambassador at the Hague, to oppose Vorstius's appointment. Vorstius in consequence found himself compelled to retire from Leyden to Gouda (1612). Meanwhile he increased suspicion by translating certain of the works of F. *Socinus; and at the Synod of *Dort (1618–19) he was condemned as a heretic and banished from the States General. He was the author of a long series of writings, including a commentary on most of St. Paul's Epp. (posthumous, 1631). He was more sympathetic to the Fathers than most Protestant theologians of his age.

A. Schweizer, 'Conradus Vorstius. Vermittlung der reformirten Centraldogmen mit den socinianischen Einwendungen' in *Theologische Jahrbücher*, xv (1856), pp. 435–486, and xvi (1857), pp. 153–84. J. C. G. Neudecker–S. D. van Veen in *P.R.E.* (ed. 3), xx (1908), pp. 762–4, s.v. See also bibl. to *Dort, Synod of*.

VOSS, GERHARD JAN (1577–1649), Dutch humanist theologian. Born in Germany, he was educated at *Leyden, where he formed a life-long friendship with H. *Grotius. In 1600 he became rector of the high school at Dort and in 1615 regent of the College of the States-General at Leyden. Though his scholarly temper was averse to the religious controversies of the time, he became involved in the disputes between the *Remonstrants and their opponents; and as himself suspected of Remonstrant leanings, he was compelled to resign his post in 1619. In 1622 he accepted a professorship of rhetoric and chronology, and later also of Greek, at Leyden university. He twice refused a call to Cambridge, but accepted a non-residential prebend at *Canterbury Cathedral from Abp. W. *Laud, being installed in 1629, and made a D.C.L. at Oxford. In 1632 he was appointed professor of general and Church history at the newly founded Athenaeum at Amsterdam.

Voss's *Historia Pelagiana* (1618), *Dissertationes Tres de Tribus Symbolis* (1642), and *Libri IV de Theologia Gentili* (1642) were all solid contributions to learning. In the second he decisively disproved the traditional authorship of the *Athanasian Creed. He was also one of the first scholars to apply the historical method to Christian dogmatics.

His son, ISAAK VOSS (1618–89), who became a residentiary Canon of Windsor in 1673, was also a classical and ecclesiastical historian of much erudition. He edited Pomponius Mela (1658), Marcus Junianus Justinus (1664) and Catullus (1684) and also zealously defended the genuineness of St. *Ignatius's Epistles.

Collected ed. of G. J. Voss's *Opera*, publd. in 6 vols., Amsterdam, 1695–1701. P. Colomesius (ed.), *Gerardi Joan. Vossii et Clarorum Virorum ad eum Epistolae* (London, 1690). J. E. Sandys, *A History of Classical Scholarship*, ii (1908), pp. 307–9. C. Sepp–S. D. van Veen in *P.R.E.* (ed. 3), xx (1908), pp. 764–8.
On Isaak Voss see J. E. Sandys, op. cit., p. 322 f., with reff.; J. Zellinger in *L.Th.K.*, xii (1938), col. 700 f., s.v., with further bibl.

VOTIVE MASSES. The *Masses provided in the Latin Missals for such special occasions and objects as the election of a Pope or the restoration of peace, or in honour of the BVM, of the Passion of our Lord, or of the Blessed Sacrament. A Votive Mass is chosen by the priest at his discretion, or at the request of others, and there are fixed rules prescribing the days on which Votives are forbidden. Besides ordinary Votives, there are Solemn Votive Masses (for a 'grave cause'), which are usually prescribed by the bishop for some special reason. These are normally sung as *High Masses, and may take the place of the Mass proper to the day on many days when ordinary Votives are forbidden (e.g. on most Sundays, though not on the greatest festivals). Other special Votives are those 'for bridegroom and bride' ('*Nuptial Mass') and for the dead ('*Requiem').

VOWEL POINTS. In common with other Semitic languages *Hebrew was originally written without signs for the vowels. In course of time their absence was remedied by using certain consonants as vowel letters, and later, when the language was no longer spoken and there was a danger of the true pronunciation being forgotten, by introducing 'vowel points'. This vocalization, attributed to the *Massoretes and dating from the 6th and 7th cents. A.D., is a fairly accurate, though not infallible, indication of the primitive pronunciation. The vowel points are superimposed on the consonantal text, i.e. they are placed immediately above, below, or within the consonants. Unvocalized texts are still produced, notably for synagogue use. Similar points are used to harden the pronunciation of certain consonants and to distinguish the letters 'Sin' (שׂ) and 'Shin' (שׁ), which are otherwise identical.

VOWS. Solemn and voluntary promises to perform something not otherwise required but believed to be acceptable to the person to whom the vows are made. Such promises to the Deity are common in many religions, esp. in a propitiatory connexion.

In the OT vows are sometimes explicitly dependent upon the performance of certain favours by Jehovah (e.g. the oath of Jacob at Bethel, Gen. 28. 20–22; Hannah's dedication of Samuel, 1 Sam. 1. 11), others appear to have been made unconditionally (cf. Ps. 132. 2–5). In the former case the vow was conceived less as a payment than as an offering of thankfulness (cf. the custom which still survives in some countries of vowing the model of a ship after deliverance from shipwreck). The idea of sacrifice behind the vow is most clearly seen in the ritual governing the vows of the *Nazarites (q.v.), which were prob. in origin an extension of such vows of self-dedication as are found in Ps. 132 and in *Saul's prohibition against eating before sundown (1 Sam. 14. 24). The obligation to fulfil a vow once undertaken could be very solemn, as appears in the case of Jephthah's daughter (Jg. 11. 30–39). This obligation was emphasized in the Law (Deut. 23. 21–3), though it was recognized that things unlawful should not be offered to Jehovah even in fulfilment of a vow (Deut. 23. 18). In Lev. 27. 1–8 ('*P'; c. 5th cent.), however, a system was elaborated whereby persons under vows might evade a direct offering of themselves by the payment of a fixed sum (cf. Num. 8, 10–16); things vowed might be redeemed by the payment of their value together with an extra sum in compensation.

In the NT Christ condemned the Jewish rule which enabled a man to escape his duty to his parents on the pretext of a vow (Mk. 7. 9–13), thus emphasizing that the matter of a vow pleasing to God must itself be acceptable. St. *Paul is recorded to have been on one occasion himself under a vow (Acts 18. 23) and on another to have aided others to fulfil one (Acts 21. 23 f.). Vows of virginity, which were taken from a very early date, may be implied in 1 Cor. 7.

Acc. to Catholic moral theologians a vow to be valid must be freely made by a person who is of age (18 years in the RC Church), be within the bounds of possibility of performance and tending to some future good. By definition it cannot relate to matters of precept. With the development of monasticism the threefold vow of poverty, chastity, and obedience, taken on entering the religious life, came to occupy special prominence. Those most commonly taken outside religious profession include vows to go on a pilgrimage, vows of chastity, and vows dedicating property, but they may cover a variety of subjects. A vow may be private, in which case it is usually taken with the consent of a confessor, or public, when it is accepted in the name of the Church by a legitimate authority, such as an Abbot receiving a vow of profession. Since c. the 13th cent. *canon law has also distinguished between 'simple' and 'solemn' vows. The exact scope of the distinction is disputed, but acc. to a common view the solemnity of vows is determined by their irrevocable acceptance. In practice the distinction is determined in the RC Church by whether a vow is instituted and accepted as solemn by the Church. Actions opposed to simple vows are prohibited under pain of sin; those contrary to solemn vows are, acc. to canon law, invalid. Thus a marriage attempted by a person under solemn vows is regarded as non-existent. Solemn vows and vows to the advantage of a third party without his consent are in the RC Church dispensed very rarely and only by the Pope or an agent appointed by him for the purpose.

P. Séjourné, O.S.B., in *D.T.C.*, xv (pt. 2; 1950), cols. 3182–281, s.v. 'Vœu, Vœu∷ de Religion'.

VOYSEY, CHARLES (1828–1912), Theistic preacher. He was educated at St. Edmund Hall, Oxford. After ordination in the C of E he held a number of curacies in London and elsewhere, at one of which (St. Mary's, Victoria Docks) he preached a sermon denying the doctrine of eternal punishment. From 1864 to 1871 he was vicar of Healaugh, nr. Tadcaster. Here his heterodox opinions led to his citation before the Chancellor of *York, and the sentence of deprivation which followed was upheld on his appeal to the Privy Council. Removing to London, Voysey began holding services in St. George's Hall, Langham Place, and founded the 'Theistic Church', whose headquarters from 1885 were in Swallow Street, off Regent Street. On Voysey's death some of his followers formed a schism, the 'Free Religious Movement'.

D. Wright in *D.N.B.*, *1912–1921*, p. 545 f., s.v.

VULGATE. The Latin version of the Bible (*editio vulgata*) most widely used in the West. It was the work of St. *Jerome, who compiled it at the command of Pope *Damasus (382). The Gospels were finished in 384, the whole of the NT perhaps before 386 (acc. to J. *Chapman c. 391), and the complete Bible c. 404. Its original purpose was to end the great differences of text in the *Old Latin MSS. circulating in the later 4th cent.

In the NT Jerome's revision was most radical in the Gospels where, esp. through the assimilation of the Gospels to each other, confusion was greatest. Here he apparently used a Greek MS. closely akin to the *Codex Sinaiticus. In the later Books of the NT his alterations were much less drastic and many Old Latin readings were preserved.

In revising the Latin text of the OT, Jerome began with the Psalms. In his earliest recension (the '*Roman Psalter', q.v.) his changes were slight and based wholly on the (Greek) *Septuagint. A second recension (the '*Gallican Psalter' q.v.) was more thorough, though here again the basis was the Septuagint. But meanwhile, Jerome's growing studies in Hebrew had convinced him of the superiority of the original, and in the course of some 15 years he revised the whole of the OT on the basis of Hebrew MSS. This included a third recension of the Psalter (the 'Hebrew Psalter') which, however, never won general acceptance, so that in modern Vulgate Bibles the 'Gallican Psalter' is ordinarily printed. Of the Greek Apocryphal Books, Jerome never revised Wisdom, Ecclus., nor (probably) Maccabees. He also stated that he passed over ('*praetermisimus') Baruch, since it was neither read nor reckoned by the Hebrews.

When it first appeared, the new version had to face considerable opposition through the long and sacred associations of the earlier texts. Even when these prejudices were overcome, it was liable to easy corruption by the reminiscence of Old Latin readings, so much so that these corruptions, increased by scribal errors, threatened within a few generations to destroy Jerome's achievement. From *Cassiodorus onwards attempts were made to standardize the text, notably by *Alcuin (commissioned by *Charlemagne), *Theodulf of Orléans, and Hartmut of St. Gall. A fresh, but defective, standard text (the 'Exemplar

Parisiense') was put forth by the University of Paris in the 13th cent. Further efforts to preserve a standard text were made by the various '*Correctoria' (q.v.).

The first printed edition was the *Mazarin (or 'Gutenberg') Bible (1456). A great many printed editions followed. The first critical text was that of Robert *Stephanus (Paris, 1528). At its Fourth Session (8 Apr. 1546) the Council of *Trent pronounced the Vulgate the only authentic Latin text of the Scriptures, and an edition eventually issued under the authority of *Sixtus V in 1590 was intended to be definitive. As, however, it contained many errors, existing copies, as far as possible, were called in and a revised text issued in 1592 by *Clement VIII, with some 3,000 corrections. Since, however, Sixtus had declared in his Bull authorizing the 1590 edition that that alone was the approved edition and its text was unalterable, the revised edition of 1592 bore the title-page: *Biblia Sacra Vulgatae Editionis Sixti Quinti Pont. Max. jussu recognita atque edita*, though it is commonly known as the 'Clementine edition'.

Later research has shown that the Clementine edition departs at many points from Jerome's text, and several attempts have been made to revise it. An emended text was printed by D. *Vallarsi in 1734: but owing to Papal prohibitions against further emendation of the Bible, he included it in his edition of Jerome as the 'Divina Biblioteca'. A fresh edition projected by R. *Bentley was never

completed. A critical edition of the NT, begun by John *Wordsworth (d. 1911) and H. J. White (d. 1934) was publd. in the years 1889–1954. The RC Church has also recently adopted a more liberal attitude to the Clementine edition and in 1908 *Pius X appointed a Commission with F. A. *Gasquet as president to produce a new edition. Publication began with Genesis at the Vatican Press in 1926, and is in progress.

Editions of the Clementine Vulgate are innumerable. Besides the two critical texts (Papal Commission; J. Wordsworth–H. J. White) there is a convenient students' edition, *Novum Testamentum Latine*. Editio Minor (Oxford, 1911) by H. J. White. S. Berger, *Histoire de la Vulgate pendant les premiers siècles du moyen-âge* (1893). F. Stummer, *Einführung in die lateinische Bibel* (1928). H. *Quentin, O.S.B., *Mémoire sur l'établissement du texte de la Vulgate*, i, Octateuque (Collectanea Biblica Latina, vi; Rome–Paris, 1922). J. *Chapman, O.S.B., *Notes on the Early History of the Vulgate Gospels* (1908); H. J. Vogels, *Vulgatastudien*. Die Evangelien der Vulgata, untersucht auf ihre lateinische und griechische Vorlage (Neutestamentliche Abhandlungen, xiv, Hftt. 2–3; 1928); H. Glunz, *Britannien und Bibeltext*. Der Vulgatatext der Evangelien in seinem Verhältnis zu irisch-angelsächsischen Kultur des Frühmittelalters (Kölner anglische Arbeiten, xii; 1930); id., *History of the Vulgate in England from Alcuin to Roger Bacon*. Being an Inquiry into the Text of some English Manuscripts of the Vulgate Gospels (1933). C. H. *Turner (ed.), *The Oldest Manuscript of the Vulgate Gospels* [St. Gall MS 1395] (1931; Turner prob. overestimated the importance of this MS.). Beryl Smalley, *The Study of the Bible in the Middle Ages* (1941; ed. 2, 1952), passim. H. F. D. Sparks, 'The Latin Bible' in H. W. Robinson (ed.), *The Bible in its Ancient and English Versions* (1940), pp. 100–27. W. E. Plater–H. J. White, *A Grammar of the Vulgate* (1926). H. J. White in *H.D.B.*, iv (1902), pp. 873–90, s.v.; F. Stummer in *L.Th.K.*, x (1934), cols. 703–6, s.v. See also *Codex Amiatinus* and *Codex Fuldensis*.

W

WACE, HENRY (1836–1924), Dean of *Canterbury. He was educated at Rugby and Brasenose College, Oxford, and ordained in 1862. In 1863 he became a regular contributor to *The Times* and, after holding several ecclesiastical appointments, was made chaplain (1872), and later preacher (1880), of Lincoln's Inn. In 1879 he was *Bampton Lecturer at Oxford. In 1883 he was appointed principal of *King's College, London, and in 1896 rector of St. Michael's, Cornhill. From 1903 till his death he was Dean of Canterbury. Wace was a staunch Evangelical and supporter of the Reformation settlement, an admirer of M. *Luther, and equally opposed to the modern methods of 'higher criticism' of the Bible and to the High Church attempts at revising the BCP. He was the editor, with W. Smith, of the *Dictionary of Christian Biography* (4 vols., 1880–6), with P. *Schaff of the second series of the *Nicene and Post-Nicene Fathers* (14 vols., 1890–1900), and with C. A. Buchheim of *Luther's Primary Works* (1896). His own writings include lectures on *The Gospel and its Witnesses* (1883), *Sermons on the Sacrifice of Christ* (1898), and *The Bible and Modern Investigations* (1903), as well as numerous articles in newspapers and periodicals.

A. Cochrane in *D.N.B.*, 1922–1930, p. 876 f., s.v.

WADDING, LUKE (1588–1657), *Franciscan historian. A native of Waterford, he made his profession in the Franciscan Order at Matozinhos, nr. Oporto, in 1608, studied at Lisbon and Coimbra, and was ordained priest in 1613. In 1617 he became president of the Irish College at Salamanca, and in 1618 theologian to the Spanish Embassy sent to Rome to promote the definition of the *Immaculate Conception. His studies led to his *Legatio Philippi III et IV pro definienda controversia Immaculatae Conceptionis* (1624). In 1625 he founded the College of St. Isidore at Rome for Irish Franciscans, and in 1627 the Ludovisian College for the Irish secular clergy. Under Wadding these colleges became the centres of a flourishing school of *Scotist Theology at Rome and led him to edit, in collaboration with others, a corrected text of the complete works of *Duns Scotus (16 vols., 1639; new ed., 26 vols., 1891–5). His principal work was his *Annales Ordinis Minorum* (8 vols., 1625–54; latest ed., 25 vols., 1931–5), a valuable collection of material on the earlier history of the Franciscan Order. He also edited the works and lives of other Franciscan authors, among them John Guallensis (1655).

Life by Francis Harold (nephew) originally printed in Epitome to *Annales* (Rome, 1662), prefixed to *Annales*, i (ed. 2, Rome, 1731), pp. i–clxxx. J. A. O'Shea, O.S.F., *The Life of Father Luke Wadding* (Dublin, 1885). F. Casolini, *Luca Wadding, O.F.M. L' annalista dei Francescani* (Milan, 1936). G. Cleary, *Father Luke Wadding and St. Isidore's College, Rome* (Rome, 1925). Detailed account of modern

Quaracchi ed. of Annales (1931–5) by M. Bihl, O.F.M., in *A.F.H.*, xxviii (1935), pp. 273–9 and 579–82, with notes on other relevant material analysed by the Irish MSS. Commission, pp. 556–60.

WAILING WALL, The. A part of the western wall of the modern Haram-es-Sherif ('Noble Sanctuary') in *Jerusalem. Acc. to Jewish tradition, it is a section of the original wall of Solomon's *Temple. Jews have been accustomed, probably since the Middle Ages, to lament here the downfall of the Temple and the Holy City and to pray, esp. on the *Sabbath (Friday evenings and Saturdays), for their restoration.

WAKE. A vigil, and hence a holiday. The name (from Lat. *vigilia*) was originally applied to the all-night *vigil kept, from Anglo-Saxon times onwards, before certain holy-days, but it early came to refer to the feasting and merry-making on the holy-day itself, and then (by the 16th cent.) to a fair held annually at the festival of the local patron saint. The word survives as the name of annual local holidays of two or three days observed by a whole town or village in the Northern and West Midland districts of England. In Ireland a wake is a vigil and feast at a funeral.

WAKE, WILLIAM (1657–1737), Abp. of *Canterbury. Educated at *Christ Church, Oxford, he went to Paris as chaplain of the English ambassador in 1682, an office to which he owed his acquaintance with *Gallicanism. After his return to England in 1685 he held various ecclesiastical appointments, being made Canon of Christ Church in 1689 and Dean of *Exeter in 1703. In 1705 he became Bp. of *Lincoln, and in 1716 Abp. of Canterbury. From 1717 to 1720 he was engaged in negotiations with representatives of Gallicanism, notably L. E. *Dupin, on a plan of reunion between the C of E and the French Church, in which both parties showed themselves ready for concessions. The death of Dupin in 1719, however, checked the project, which would probably have proved unacceptable in any case to both the English and the French clergy. A man of liberal views, Wake was in sympathy with the Nonconformists, and even advocated changes in the BCP to meet their difficulties, though he opposed, in 1718, a bill for modification of the *Corporation and *Test Acts. Among his numerous writings the most important is the *State of the Church and Clergy of England* (1703), a history of English ecclesiastical synods which was intended as a reply to F. *Atterbury's theories of Convocation. His *Principles of the Christian Religion* (1700), a commentary on the Church Catechism, became very popular. Wake bequeathed his valuable collections and library to Christ

Church, which also possesses a large number of his unpublished manuscripts.

Definitive Life by N. Sykes (2 vols., Cambridge, 1957). J. H. Lupton, *Archbishop Wake and the Project of Union (1717–20) between the Gallican and Anglican Churches* (1896); E. Préclin, *L'Union des Églises gallicane et anglicane*. Une tentative au temps de Louis XV. P.-F. le Courayer (de 1681 à 1732) et Guillaume Wake (1928). J. H. Lupton in *D.N.B.*, lviii (1899), p. 445 f., s.v., with reff.

WALAFRID STRABO (*c.* 808–49), i.e. 'Walafrid the Squinter', German theological writer. Educated at the monastery of *Reichenau, and later under *Rabanus Maurus at *Fulda (where he established a lifelong friendship with *Gottschalk), he became Abbot of Reichenau in 838. Before long he was compelled to flee to Speyer, apparently because he had supported Lothair against Charles the Bald on the latter's accession in 840. In 842, however, he was restored to his monastery. He wrote a large number of works, both in poetry and prose, and both secular and religious. Of his theological treatises the most important is his *De Exordiis et Incrementis quarundam in Observationibus Ecclesiasticis Rerum*, a handbook on matters of liturgical and archaeological interest, of great value for the light it throws on the religious practice of his time. The *Glossa Ordinaria*, a laborious compilation from the commentaries of the early Church Fathers on the Bible, has traditionally been assigned to him, but it now appears that not more than a fraction of it, if indeed any at all, is Walafrid's work. His poems include the lives of a number of saints.

Works collected in J. P. Migne, *PL*, cxiii, cxiv, incl. the *Glossa Ordinaria*; crit. edd. of his verse, with the *Visio*, by E. Duemmler in *M.G.H.*, Poetae, ii (1884), pp. 259–473; of his *Liber de Exordiis et Incrementis* by G. Knoepler (Munich, 1890). A. Jundt, *Walafrid Strabon. L'homme et le théologien* (Paris thesis; Cahors, 1900); L. Eigl, *Walahfrid Strabo. Ein Mönch- und Dichterleben* (Vienna, 1908). H. Sierp, 'Walafrid Strabos Gedicht über den Gartenbau' in K. Beyerle (ed.), *Die Kultur der Abtei Reichenau*, ii (1925), pp. 756–72. On other aspects of his life and work, K. Beyerle, ib., i (1925), pp. 92–108, K. Künstle, ib., ii (1925), pp. 706–10 and A. Bergmann, ib., pp. 712–38. K. Beyerle, 'Das Briefbuch Walahfrid Strabos' in *Historische Aufsätze Aloys Schulte zum 70. Geburtstag gewidmet* (1927), pp. 82–96. B. Bischoff, 'Eine Sammelhandschrift Walahfrid Strabos' in *Aus dem Welt des Buches*. Festgabe zum 70. Geburtstag von Georg Leyh (Beiheft zum Zentralblatt für Bibliothekenswesen, lxxv; 1950), pp. 30–48. On the authorship of the *Glossa Ordinaria*, see B. Smalley in *R.T.A.M.*, vii (1935), pp. 235–62, viii (1936), pp. 24–60, and ix (1937), pp. 365–400. J. de Blic, S.J., 'L'Œuvre exégétique de Walafrid Strabon et la Glossa Ordinaria', ib., xvi (1949), pp. 5–28. M. L. W. Laistner, *Thought and Letters in Western Europe A.D. 500 to 900* (1931), pp. 193, 230 f., 252, 260, 276, and 284–7. H. Peltier in *D.T.C.*, xv (pt. 2; 1950), cols. 3498–505, s.v. 'Walafrid Strabon'; P. Nober in *E.C.*, xii (1954), cols. 961–3, s.v. 'Valafrid Strabone', for further bibl.

WALBURGA, St. (*c.* 710–79), sister of St. *Willibald and St. Winnebald (d. 761) and Abbess of Heidenheim. Born in England and educated at the abbey at Wimborne, she went at the wish of St. *Boniface to assist in his mission work in Germany. On Winnebald's death she assumed the direction of his double-monastery at Heidenheim, and remained there till her death. Her feast day is observed on 25 Feb. and 1 May. The coincidence of the latter date with an old pagan feast commemorating the beginning of summer, with rites protecting

from witchcraft, has given to 1 May the name 'Walpurgis [i.e. Walburga's] Night', e.g. in Goethe's *Faust*.

AA.SS., Feb. III (1658), pp. 511–72; extracts 'Ex Wolfhardi Haserensis Miraculis S. Waldburgis Monheimensibus' also ed. O. Holder-Egger in *M.G.H.*, Scriptores, xvi (pt. 1; 1887), pp. 535–55. Francesca M. Steele, *The Life of Saint Walburga* [1921]. A. Zimmermann, O.S.B., in *L.Th.K.*, x (1938), col. 727 f., s.v. 'Waldburga', with full bibl. See also bibl. to St. Willibald, for whom the sources are historically more reliable.

WALCH, JOHANN GEORG (1693–1775), German Protestant theologian. In 1718 he became professor in the philosophical, and in 1724 in the theological, faculty at Jena. He belonged to the Orthodox School. Among many writings was *Historische und theologische Einleitung in die religiösen Streitigkeiten welche sonderlich ausser der ev.-lutherischen Kirche entstanden* (5 vols., 1733–6). He also produced an edition of M. *Luther's works in 24 vols. (1740–52). Two of his sons, Johann Ernst Immanuel Walch (1725–78) and Christian Wilhelm Franz Walch (1726–84), were also distinguished theologians.

W. Moeller–G. Kawerau in *P.R.E.* (ed. 3), xx (1908), pp. 792–7; xxiv (1913), p. 624.

WALDEN, ROGER (d. 1406), Abp. of *Canterbury. A native of Essex, he rose to a position of importance in the *Channel Islands and held livings at Fenny Drayton, Leicestershire, and Burton in Kendale. In 1387 he became Archdeacon of *Winchester and from then onwards, under court influence, advanced rapidly. From 1387 to 1392 he was treasurer of Calais. In 1395 he was created Treasurer of England and, continuing to hold numerous other preferments, Dean of *York. On *Arundel's banishment in 1397 Richard II secured his provision to the see of Canterbury from the Pope; but when Arundel returned with Henry of Lancaster (1399), Walden's property was plundered and his register destroyed. On 10 Jan. 1400 he was committed to the Tower on a charge of complicity in the Epiphany plot against Henry IV, but liberated about a month later. In 1405 he succeeded Robert Braybrooke as Bp. of London. He died at Much Hadham, Herts, on 6 Jan. 1406. A MS. collection of chronological tables (Cotton MS. Julius B. XIII), known as the 'Historia Mundi', has been wrongly attributed to him.

J. H. Wylie, *History of England under Henry the Fourth*, iii (1896), pp. 123–8. J. Tait in *D.N.B.*, lix (1899), pp. 24–6, s.v., with further reff.

WALDENSES, also 'Vaudois'. This small Christian community, which still survives in Piedmont ('Chiesa Evangelica Valdese'), had its origin in the 'poor men of Lyons' organized in the 12th cent. by Peter Waldo of Lyons (d. 1217), from whom it took its name. The view that 'Waldenses' was derived from the Lat. *vallis* ('valley') is a more recent invention. The obscurities which surround the early history of the community have been increased by the claims of the Waldenses themselves and of some older Protestant historians on their behalf that they preserved a pure and uncorrupted form of primitive Christianity. It was argued that their Church was founded by St. *Paul on his way to Spain (so *Olivetan, T. *Beza); or that their separate existence dated from the time of *Constantine (d. 337) when the Catholic Church was corrupted by *Sylvester's acceptance of temporal wealth and power (so certain of the early Waldenses, as reported by the inquisitor Moneta); or (a less fantastic view) that their origin was to be traced to the reforming work of *Claudius of Turin (J. Leger, A. Muston). Hardly more probable is the view that they were an offshoot of the *Albigenses (G. S. Faber).

The early evidence for Waldo and the Poor Men of Lyons comes from their opponents, notably a certain 'Anonymus Laudunensis'. It would seem that Waldo, a rich merchant of Lyons, on hearing the words of Mt. 19. 21, distributed his property to the poor, and, adopting the life of a mission-preacher and mendicant, soon attracted followers. The first settlements were on the French side of the Alps. Waldo's attacks on the worldliness of the Church quickly provoked opposition. An appeal for ecclesiastical recognition at the Third Lateran *Council (1179) failed and in 1184 a Council of Verona, presided over by Pope Lucius III, put them under the ban. Forced to organize themselves as a separate body they appointed their own ministers who administered the Eucharist (but only once a year) and drew up a code of life. Waldo had also made for his followers a translation of the NT into Provençal.

They rapidly grew in numbers and were scattered by persecution through Provence, Dauphiné, Piedmont, Lombardy, and parts of Germany and Spain. In 1209 a crusade against them was instituted by *Innocent III; in 1211 some 80 Waldenses of both sexes were burnt at Strassburg; and in 1237 a bull of *Gregory IX to the Abp. of Tarragona caused 15 to be burnt in Spain as heretics. The Franciscans, *David of Augsburg and Berthold of Regensburg, wrote against them. In Bohemia, where Waldo had died, a strong Waldensian community grew up, which later became fused with the *Hussites. From an early date the various Waldensian communities were divided by doctrinal differences, notably on the validity of Sacraments dispensed by unworthy ministers. By the 15th cent. their chief centre was in Savoy, where they suffered severe persecution from the ruling House.

In the 16th cent. contact was quickly made with the Reformers. In 1522 the Bohemian Hussites (then often known as 'Waldenses') made overtures to M. *Luther. A little later the Waldenses proper of the Cottian Alps approached the S. German and Swiss Reformers. In 1532 a synod was held at Chanforans in the valley of the Angrogne which was attended by Protestant representatives, among them G. *Farel and Olivetan. It adopted a new Confession of Faith which included the doctrine of predestination; formally renounced all recognition of the RC Church; accepted

clerical marriage; and ordered communal worship to be henceforward open and public. For a brief space they enjoyed in Piedmont a relative measure of freedom and built many churches ('temples'). A fierce attack was made on them under Charles Emmanuel II, Duke of Savoy, which, largely through J. *Milton's famous sonnet (1655), aroused much feeling in England and led to O. *Cromwell's proclamation of a solemn fast and active intervention. The outcome was twenty years' liberty, secured at last by the 'Patente of Turin' (14 Feb. 1664). After the revocation of the Edict of *Nantes (1685) many were compelled to cross the mountains in terrible conditions to Switzerland. Their outward circumstances improved in the 18th cent., but they were still not allowed to hold real property nor to have physicians of their own faith. After some vacillation, Napoleon granted them a constitution in May 1805, which was abolished, however, by Victor Emmanuel in 1814; and it was not until 1848 that Charles Albert gave them real political and religious freedom. Meanwhile they received much active encouragement from various non-Roman Churches. Their existence was brought to the notice of many Englishmen by W. S. Gilly's *Narrative of an Excursion to the Mountains of Piedmont and Researches among the Vaudois or Waldenses* (1824), and J. C. Beckwith (1789–1862), an officer who lost a leg at Waterloo, was induced by this book to settle among them and devote his life to their welfare. Beckwith established 120 schools and secured the reintroduction of the Italian language (in place of French) in their services. Their membership to-day is said to be about 20,000. Their ministers have long been known as *barbes (q.v.). They possess a theological school which was founded at Torre Pellice near Turin and moved in 1861 to Florence and in 1920 to Rome.

The relevant passage from the Chronicle of the 'Anonymus Laudunensis', ed. G. Waitz in M.G.H., Scriptores, xxvi (1882), pp. 447–9. Classical works by S. Morland, *The History of the Evangelical Churches of the Valleys of Piedmont* (1658; the author had been Cromwell's emissary to Piedmont), and J. Leger, *Histoire générale des Églises évangéliques de Piedmont, ou Vaudoises* (Leyden, 1669). More recent studies include W. Jones, *The History of the Waldenses* (1812; revised ed., 2 vols., 1816); A. Monastier, *Histoire de l'Église vaudoise depuis son origine, et des Vaudois du Piedmont jusqu'à nos jours* (2 vols., 1847; Eng. tr., 1848); A. Muston, *L'Israël des Alpes*. Première histoire complète des Vaudois du Piédmont et de leur colonies (4 vols., 1851; Eng. tr., 2 vols., 1857;) J. A. Wylie, *History of the Waldenses* [1880]; A. Bérard, *Les Vaudois*. Leur histoire sur deux versants des Alpes du IVe siècle au XVIIIe (Lyons, 1892). More critical works include Emilio Comba, *Histoire des Vaudois d'Italie* (1887; Eng. tr., 1889); id., *Storia de' Valdesi* (1893); Ernesto Comba, *Storia dei Valdesi* (Torre Pellice, 1923; revised ed., 1930); and J. Jalla, *Histoire des Vaudois des Alpes et de leurs colonies* (Pignerol, 1926). W. Dieckhoff, *Die Waldenser im Mittelalter*. Zwei historische Untersuchungen (1851); J. J. *Herzog, *Die romanischen Waldenser* (1853); W. Preger, 'Beiträge zur Geschichte der Waldesier im Mittelalter' in *Abh.* (Bayr.), Hist. Cl., xiii (1877), Abt. 1, pp. 179–250; id., 'Ueber die Verfassung der französischen Waldesier in der älteren Zeit' ib., xix (1891), Abt. 3, pp. 639–711. M. Viora, *Storia delle leggi sui Valdesi di Vittorio Amadeo II* (1930). G. B. Watts, *The Waldenses in the New World* (Durham, N.C., 1941). J. H. Todd, *The Books of the Vaudois*. The Waldensian Manuscripts preserved in the Library of Trinity College, Dublin (1865). A. Armand-Hugon–G. Gonnet, *Bibliografica valdese* (Torre Pellice, 1953). H. Böhmer in *P.R.E.* (ed. 3), xx (1908), pp. 799–840, s.v. 'Waldenser', with details of sources and bibl. to date; W. F. Adeney in *H.E.R.E.*, xii (1921), pp. 663–73, s.v. 'Waldenses'; L. Cristiani in *D.T.C.*, xv (pt. 2; 1950), cols. 2586–600, s.v. 'Vaudois'.

WALDENSTRÖM, PAUL PETER (1838–1917), Swedish preacher and Free Churchman. As a young man he held various teaching appointments. In 1864 he was ordained a pastor. Attaching himself to the revival movement of C. O. Roserius (d. 1868), he succeeded him as editor of the *Pietisten*, a widely circulating revivalist newspaper. In various writings between 1872 and 1875 he put forward a theory of the *Atonement inconsistent with *Lutheran Orthodoxy; man had to be reconciled to God, not God to man, and God sent His Son, not in wrath but in love. He also rejected the doctrine that when Christ died His atoning work was finished. A long controversy ensued, and Waldenström became the founder of the largest sectarian movement in Sweden. In 1905 he took over the direction of the separatist Swedish Mission Society (Svenska Missionsförbundet), which, besides work in Sweden, established missions in the Congo, China, and Chinese Turkestan. From 1884 to 1905 he was a member of the Swedish *Riksdag*.

Collected Sermons, 2 vols., Stockholm, 1918–19; Memoirs, 1838–75. ed. B. Nyrén (ib., 1928). There are English translations by J. G. Princell, with notes and introdd., of Waldenström's meditations on *The Blood of Jesus* (Chicago, 1888) and on *The Reconciliation* (ib., 1888). Studies by N. P. Ollén (Stockholm, 1917), ed. A. Ohldén (Uppsala, 1917), E. Leufvén (ib., 1920), E. Newman (Stockholm, 1932) and W. Bredberg (Uppsala, 1948). C. Olsson, *Försoningen enlight C. O. Rosenius och P. Waldenström* (1928). E. Newman in *R.G.G.* (ed. 2), v (1931), col. 1748, s.v.

WALES, Christianity in. The early date of the beginning of Welsh Christianity is indicated by the fact that, of the four ancient dioceses of *St. Davids, *St. Asaph, *Bangor, and *Llandaff, each covers roughly the territory of one of the four pre-Roman tribes. Certainly Roman missionaries were at work in the 4th cent., and the independent parts of Wales were completely christianized in the following three centuries by Celtic missionaries. The same period saw also the foundation of numerous Celtic monasteries, and was the great age of the Welsh saints, of whom *David, *Teilo, *Deiniol, and *Asaph are perhaps the best known. The meeting of Celtic bishops with St. *Augustine *c.* 603 failed to produce any union between the Celtic Christians and the new mission; but gradually between the Synod of *Whitby (664) and the end of the 12th cent. various parts of the Celtic Church made submission to Canterbury, and a formal claim to supremacy over the whole of Wales was made by Abp. *Baldwin in his tour of the Welsh sees in 1188, and generally accepted, in spite of the efforts of *Giraldus Cambrensis, Bp. elect of St. Davids, who was in 1203 finally compelled to make submission.

The *Reformation settlement was generally accepted in Wales, though a few recusants remained among the gentry. *Elizabeth pursued the policy of appointing Welsh bishops, and encouraging the use of the vernacular. The growth of *Puritanism in Wales was slow, and the first dissenting chapel (*Independent) was opened by W. *Wroth at Llanfaches, Monmouthshire, in 1638. In the Civil War, Wales was royalist and High Church. After the Restoration the decay of Welsh Church life began, chiefly through the continued appointment of English non-resident dignitaries and the kindred abuses of pluralism and nepotism. In this period a great work was done in promoting popular education by Griffith *Jones (1683–1761), who began to catechize in the vernacular, and by means of numerous charity schools taught Welshmen to read the Scriptures in their own language. See also *Welsh Bible and Prayer Book*.

The influence of the established Church was at its lowest in the early years of the 19th cent., when the separation of the *Methodist revivalists (1811), longer delayed than in England, carried away the majority of the population of the principality. In the half-century which followed, Dissent grew rapidly, and a small RC body grew up also in the industrial areas, formed by immigrant Irish; but in the history of the established Church the only important event was the founding of St. David's College, Lampeter, in 1822.

The estrangement of the majority of Welshmen from Anglicanism eventually brought about the Disestablishment of the Welsh Church in 1920. Since then a separate province has existed, the bishops being appointed by representative electors. There are now six sees, Monmouth, and Swansea and Brecon, having been added to the original four. One of the diocesan bishops is elected to the rank of archbishop. The Disestablishment appears to have added to the influence and numbers of the Church in Wales. Of Free Church bodies, the Presbyterians (formerly '*Calvinistic Methodists') are the most numerous; many other denominations flourish. The RCs, though a vigorous community, are few in number, and consist chiefly of Irish, with some French communities which settled in Wales in 1903.

There are a number of studies in Welsh. Works in English include H. W. Clarke, *A History of the Church of Wales* (1896); A. G. Edwards, *Landmarks in the History of the Welsh Church* (1912); J. E. de Hirsch-Davies, *A Popular History of the Church in Wales from the Beginning to the Present Day* (1912); D. A. Jones, *A History of the Church in Wales* (Carmarthen, 1926). A. W. Wade-Evans, *Welsh Christian Origins* (Oxford, 1934). E. J. Newell, *A History of the Welsh Church to the Dissolution of the Monasteries* (1895). C. A. H. Green, *The Setting of the Constitution of the Church in Wales* (1937). J. E. de Hirsch-Davies, *Catholicism in Mediaeval Wales* (1916). D. Attwater, *The Catholic Church in Modern Wales. A Record of the Past Century* (1935). T. Rees, *History of Protestant Nonconformity in Wales from its Rise to the Present Time* (1861; enlarged ed., 1883). H. E. Lewis, *Nonconformity in Wales* (1904). There is also much information in the Report of the Royal Commission on the Church of England and Other Religious Bodies in Wales and Monmouthshire (Parliamentary Papers, England, 1910, vols. xiv–xix [Cd. 5432–9]). G. Williams, *The Welsh Church from Conquest to Reformation* (Cardiff, 1962). See also bibl. to *Celtic Church*; also to *Methodism*, &c.

WALL, WILLIAM (1647–1728), Anglican theologian. Educated at Queen's College, Oxford, he became vicar of Shoreham, Kent, in 1674, and rector of Milton-next-Gravesend in 1708. His chief work is *The History of Infant Baptism* (2 vols., 1705). Designed to combat the arguments of the *Baptists against Infant Baptism, it consisted in a learned exposition of the teaching of the Fathers, supported by ample quotations and taking into account recent controversies. It has remained the English classic on the subject. His other works include *Brief Critical Notes, especially on the Various Readings of the New Testament Books* (1730) and *Critical Notes on the Old Testament* (1734).

The History of Infant Baptism . . . Together with Mr. Gale's Reflections, and Dr. Wall's Defence, ed. H. Cotton (4 vols., Oxford, 1835–6), with introd. vol. i, pp. v–xxvii; an abridged ed. of the History was publ. by W. H. Spencer (London, 1848). T. Cooper in *D.N.B.*, lix (1899), p. 97, s.v., with reff.

WALLOON CONFESSION (1561), The.
See *Belgic Confession, The.*

WALSINGHAM (Norfolk), place of pilgrimage. A replica of the Holy House of *Nazareth, said to have been built there in the 11th cent., made the Walsingham pilgrimage one of the most important in England in the Middle Ages. The shrine was destroyed in 1538; but the pilgrimage has been revived in the present century both by Anglicans and RCs.

D. *Erasmus, Pilgrimages to Saint Mary of Walsingham and St. Thomas of Canterbury, tr. into Eng. by J. G. Nichols (1849), pp. 11–43 and 82–110. The Foundation of the Chapel of Walsingham, orig. pr. by Richard Pynson (c. 1493), repr. in H. Huth (ed.), Fugitive Tracts Series, i (1875), No. 2 (separate pagination). H. P. Feasey, O.S.B., Our Ladye of Walsingham. A History of the World-renowned Shrine and Priory of the Blessed Virgin at Walsingham in Norfolk (Weston-super-Mare, 1901); H. M. Gillet, Walsingham and its Shrine (1934); J. C. Dickinson, The Shrine of Our Lady of Walsingham (1956). J. Lee Warner, 'Walsingham Priory' in The Archaeological Journal, xiii (1856), pp. 115–33; T. J. Pettigrew, 'Walsingham Priory' in The Journal of the British Archaeological Association, xxxvi (1880), pp. 129–36. J. C. Cox in V.C.H., Norfolk, ii, ed. W. Page (1906), pp. 394–401, with reff.

WALTER, HUBERT. See *Hubert Walter.*

WALTER DE STAPELDON. See *Stapeldon, Walter de.*

WALTER OF ST.-VICTOR (d. after 1180), prior of the *Augustinian Canons of St.-Victor (See *Victorines*). He is the author of a highly controversial work 'Contra Quattuor Labyrinthos Franciae' (after 1179) which was directed chiefly against *Abelard (whom he believed to have written the 'Sententiae Divinitatis'), *Peter Lombard, Peter of Poitiers (d. 1205), and *Gilbert de La Porrée. Its violent attack on the dialectical method had little effect on his contemporaries.

The 'Contra Quattuor Labyrinthos Franciae', ed. P. Glorieux in Archives d'Histoire doctrinale et littéraire du Moyen-Age, xix for 1952 (1953), pp. 187–335. H. *Denifle, O.P., 'Die Sentenzen Abaelards und die Bearbeitungen seiner Theologia vor Mitte des 12. Jhs. I. Walter von St. Victor und die Sententiae Divinitatis' in Archiv für Litteratur- und Kirchen-Geschichte des Mittelalters, i (1885), pp. 404–17. R. Studeny, S.V.D., 'Walter of St.-Victor and the Apologia de Verbo Incarnato' in Gregorianum, xviii (1937), pp. 579–85. J. Chatillon, 'Un Sermon théologique

de Gauthier de Saint-Victor égaré parmi les œuvres du Prieur Richard' in Revue du Moyen-Age latin, viii (1952), pp. 43–50. J. de Ghellinck, S.J., Le Mouvement théologique du XII⁵ siècle (Études d'Histoire des Dogmes et d'ancienne Littérature ecclésiastique, 1914), pp. 158–60 and 268 f. (ed. 2, Museum Lessianum, Section Historique, x, 1948, pp. 260–3 and 404 f.).

WALTON, BRIAN (c. 1600–61), Bp. of *Chester and editor of the 'London *Polyglott Bible'. He was educated at Magdalene College and Peterhouse, Cambridge, and ordained in 1623. In 1628 he became rector of St. Martin's Orgar in London, where he took an active part in the controversy between the clergy and the citizens on the subject of the city tithes. His over-zealous defence of the claims of the clergy, added to his pronounced Laudian sympathies, led to his being accused in Parliament and deprived of his livings (1641). After a short term of imprisonment he resided at Oxford for some years. The *Biblia Sacra Polyglotta*, which is among the first books in England to have been printed by subscription, was begun in 1653, and its six vols. of OT, Apocrypha, NT, and appendices were completed in 1657. Altogether nine languages are represented, though no individual book of the Bible is printed in more than eight versions. The work, which has not yet been superseded, is esp. useful because of its lucid arrangement. It was criticized by J. *Owen in his *Considerations*, to which Walton replied in an able defence entitled *The Considerator Considered* (1659). Walton's merits as a scholar were officially recognized at the Restoration, when he was appointed Bp. of Chester in 1660.

H. J. Todd, Memoirs of the Life and Writings of the Right Rev. Brian Walton, Lord Bishop of Chester (2 vols., 1821). A. Fox, John Mill and Richard Bentley. A Study of the Textual Criticism of the New Testament, 1675–1729 (1954), pp. 47–9 and passim. D. S. Margoliouth in D.N.B., lix (1899), pp. 268–71, s.v.

WALTON, IZAAK (1593–1683), English author. A native of Stafford, he went to London, where he settled as an ironmonger in the parish of St. Dunstan's (c. 1514) and soon became a friend of the vicar, J. *Donne. A strong High Churchman and Royalist, he retired from business after the battle of Marston Moor (1644), and spent most of the rest of his life as a welcome guest in the families of many eminent ecclesiastics, e.g. with G. *Morley, Bp. of Winchester, at Farnham Castle. His *Compleat Angler* (1653) breathes the simplicity, charm, and gentle piety of his nature-loving soul. He made a notable contribution to Christian biography in his Lives of J. Donne (1640), H. Wotton (1651), R. *Hooker (1665), G. *Herbert (1670), and R. *Sanderson (1678). Based on personal knowledge and extensive investigation, they are remarkable for their beauty of expression and sincerity and for their author's understanding of his subjects. They are also valuable to the historian as contemporary documents.

R. H. Shepherd (ed.), Waltonia. Inedited Remains in Verse and Prose of Izaak Walton (London, 1878). *The Compleat Angler, the Lives of Donne, Wotton, Hooker, Herbert and Sanderson, with Love and Truth and Miscellaneous*

Writings, ed. G. [L.] Keynes (London, 1929). Lives also ed. G. Saintsbury (World's Classics, 1927) and S. B. Carter (London, 1951), with introd., pp. xi–xxi. S. Martin, *Izaak Walton and his Friends* (1903). T. Zouch, *The Life of Isaac Walton*; including Notices of his Contemporaries (1823); E. Marston, *Thomas Ken and Izaak Walton*. A Sketch of their Lives and Family Connection (1908), pp. 81–213. C. J. Sisson, *The Judicious Marriage of Mr. Hooker and the Birth of* The Laws of Ecclesiastical Polity (1940), pp. lx–xiv and passim. A. Lang [–X.] in *D.N.B.*, lix (1899), pp. 273–7.

WANDERING JEW, The. A Jew who, acc. to popular legend, taunted Christ on His way to crucifixion and was doomed to wander over the earth till the Last Day. The legend, which first appeared in a pamphlet published in 1602, professedly at *Leyden, immediately became popular throughout the Protestant world and was known in Britain by 1625. Recorded meetings with the Jew in various places and at various dates range from one at Hamburg in 1542 (mentioned in the original pamphlet) to one at Salt Lake City in 1868; but whether they were purely fictitious or some impostor played the part is uncertain. There existed in the 13th cent. a somewhat similar legend. Roger of Wendover, e.g., chronicles that some natives of Armenia who visited England in 1228 alleged that St. *Joseph of Arimathaea had been recently seen in their own country under the name of 'Cartaphilis', and that he had confessed to having taunted Christ as He went to His death.

M. D. Conway, *The Wandering Jew* (1881). L. Neubaur, *Die Sage vom Ewigen Juden untersucht* (1884; revised ed., 1893); G. Paris, *Légendes du moyen-âge* (1903), pp. 149–221. W. Zirus, *Der ewige Jude in der Dichtung vornehmlich in der englischen und deutschen* (Palaestra, clxii; 1928), and other works of this author. G. K. Anderson, 'The Wandering Jew Returns to England' in *The Journal of English and Germanic Philology*, xlv (1946), pp. 237–50, incl. repr. of 1602 pamphlet mentioned in art. above; id., 'Popular Survivals of the Wandering Jew in England', ib., xlvi (1947), pp. 367–82; id., 'The Neo-Classical Chronicle of the Wandering Jew' in *Publications of the Modern Language Association of America*, lxiii (1948), pp. 199–213.

WAR, Christian Attitude to. It has always been recognized that in a world wholly governed by Christian principles war would be ruled out as at variance with the moral teaching of Christ, esp. as contained in the *Sermon on the Mount (Matt. 5–7), and the theology of the *Incarnation. But since Christians are also citizens of a secular order in which the exercise of force is necessary to maintain the authority of law it has been widely, but far from universally, held that the method of war and the active participation of Christians in it are on occasion morally defensible and even praiseworthy. In early times when the form of civil government was essentially pagan, some ecclesiastical enactments were made which seemed to forbid Christians to take part in military service (St. *Hippolytus's *Ap. Trad.* 17–19; *Nicaea, can. 12), while *Tertullian (*de corona militis*; from his *Montanist period) and *Lactantius (*Div. Inst.* 6. 20. 16) also expressly condemned it. On the other hand, there were numbers of Christians in the army from the 2nd cent. onwards (see *Thundering Legion*, also *Theban Legion*).

From the time of *Constantine, Christians

were less troubled by scruples about participation in war. St. *Augustine defended it when undertaken for the good of society (*Ep.* 138, ad Volusianum), arguing that it was justified when the end of war is peace (*Ep.* 189, ad Bonifacium). The Crusades are the classical instance of warfare in defence of supposed religious ends. But the constant wars of all kinds in which Christians in the Middle Ages found themselves engaged led to a discrimination by moral theologians between wars in which a Christian legitimately could and could not participate. St. *Thomas lays down three conditions for a 'just war', viz. (i) it must be on the authority of the sovereign (*auctoritas principis*); (ii) the cause must be just (*justa causa*); and (iii) the belligerents should have a rightful intention (*recta intentio*), intending the advancement of good or the avoidance of evil. (*S.Th.*, II, ii, q. 40, *de bello*). Similar lists of conditions were drawn up by other medieval moralists. F. de *Vitoria (d. 1546) insisted on the further condition, of which much has been made by recent Catholic moralists, that the war must be waged by 'proper means' (*debito modo*). The Anglican Reformers dealt with the subject briefly in the *Thirty-Nine Articles (art. 37; note *justa bella* in the Lat. text).

In modern times, 'Absolute Pacifism', i.e. the doctrine that warfare is in all circumstances forbidden by the Gospel, has been upheld by the *Anabaptists, the *Quakers and L. *Tolstoy. Recently, esp. in Great Britain, it has been widely defended on humanitarian, and sometimes even on frankly hedonistic, grounds as well as on Christian principles. Leading exponents of it in the inter-War years (1918–1939) were C. J. Cadoux, H. R. L. *Sheppard, and C. E. Raven. Another group of (mainly RC) moralists (F. Stratmann, G. Vann, E. I. Watkin, E. *Gill) has argued against the permissibility of participation in modern warfare on the ground that a 'just war' is nowadays not possible, since e.g. the means (bombing of civilians, &c.) are never 'proper' (*debito modo*). On the other hand, there has been abundant criticism of pacifism by Christians in all countries, as well by those whose judgement might be held to be influenced by nationalist leanings or (in the case of highly placed Churchmen) official position as by many others whose integrity is beyond suspicion (W. *Temple, R. *Niebuhr, A. D. Lindsay).

G. H. C. Macgregor, *The New Testament Basis of Pacifism* (1936); C. J. Cadoux, *The Early Christian Attitude to War* (1919); R. Regout, S.J., *La Doctrine de la guerre juste de saint Augustin à nos jours* (1935); J. Eppstein, *The Catholic Tradition of the Law of Nations* (1935); F. Stratmann, O.P., *The Church and War* (Eng. trans., 1928); H. R. L. Sheppard, *We Say No!* (1934); C. E. Raven, *War and the Christian* (1938); H. Beevor, *Peace and Pacifism* (1938); N. Micklem, *May God Defend the Right!* (1939); G. Vann, O.P., *Morality and War* (1939); R. Niebuhr, *Why the Christian Church is not Pacifist* (1940); *This War and Christian Ethics*. A Symposium ed. by A. Sampson (1940).

WAR, Participation of Clergy in. Since the Middle Ages clerics in *major orders have been expressly forbidden to take a direct part in the shedding of blood. The prohibition was based on the grounds that it was unseemly for the ministers of the altar to shed blood and that the military life was detrimental to the discharge of pastoral duties. This teaching is embodied in the present RC canon law (*CIC*, can. 141). In the modern state, however, clerics are permitted to conform to the *force majeure* of military law both in peace-time and in war. The C of E has commonly upheld the medieval discipline, though ecclesiastical penalties have not been imposed on the few clerics who have entered the services and such clerics have been allowed to resume their clerical life when the war has ended.

WARBURTON, WILLIAM (1698–1779), Bp. of *Gloucester. After being apprenticed for five years to an attorney, he decided on an ecclesiastical career and was ordained priest in 1727. He held various livings, was made Dean of Bristol in 1757, and Bp. of Gloucester in 1759. As an editor of Shakespeare and the friend and champion of A. Pope, he played a conspicuous part in the literary world of his time and became involved in innumerable controversies. His first theological work of importance was *The Alliance between Church and State* (1736), a defence of the existing Establishment, in which, following the principles of J.*Locke, he argued that while the Church, by accepting the protection of the state, must abandon its own independence, the toleration of those who differ from it in doctrine and worship should be allowed. In his most famous book, *The Divine Legation of Moses* (2 vols., 1737–41), he professed to uphold the Divine origin of the Mosaic Law against the *Deists by the singular argument that it contained no doctrine of eternal life. The doctrine of future rewards and punishments being essential to the well-being of humanity, its absence from the OT can only be explained by a special Divine inspiration. This eccentric argumentation involved him in a series of controversies. The 'enthusiasm' of *Methodism being esp. repugnant to him, he published in 1762 *The Doctrine of Grace* against J.*Wesley. Warburton's works are remarkable for paradox rather than for scholarship, and his arrogance in the conduct of his literary feuds made him many enemies. He is, however, more creditably remembered for having preached against the slave trade as early as 1766.

Works, ed. R. Hurd (7 vols., London, 1788); id., *A Discourse by Way of General Preface to the Quarto Edition of Bishop Warburton's Works, Containing some Account of the Life, Writings and Character of the Author* (1794). J. S. Watson, *Life of Warburton* (1863). J. N. *Figgis, 'William Warburton' in W. E. Collins (ed.), *Typical English Churchmen from Parker to Maurice* (1902), No. 9, pp. 215–53. A. W. Evans, *Warburton and the Warburtonians*. A Study in some Eighteenth-Century Controversies (1932).

WARD, MARY (1585–1645), foundress of the Institute of the '*English Ladies' (q.v.). Born at Mulwith in Yorkshire, she entered the Convent of the *Poor Clares of *St.-Omer in 1606. In 1609, wanting a more active life, she founded, with five other Englishwomen, a religious congregation on the model of the *Jesuit Order, seeking to provide for the education of and an active apostolate among women. After opening houses in Liége, *Cologne, Vienna, and elsewhere, she went to Rome in 1629 to secure Papal approval for her enterprise. As her project was conceived on untraditional lines, involving freedom from enclosure and the choir office, as well as from episcopal jurisdiction, and thus ran counter to the decree of *Pius V enjoining solemn vows and strict enclosure on all religious houses of women, her institute was suppressed in 1630, and in 1631 she herself was imprisoned in the Convent of Poor Clares at Munich. On regaining her liberty she returned to Rome, and, after securing the approval of *Urban VIII reopened her houses on slightly different lines. Later she went back to England, where she spent her remaining years. Among her Foundations is the present Bar Convent at *York, orig. established near *Fountains in 1642 and transferred to Micklegate Bar in 1686.

M. C. E. Chambers–H. J. Coleridge, *The Life of Mary Ward, 1585–1645* ('Quarterly Series', xxxv and lii; 1882–5). Other lives by M. Salome, I.B.V.M. (London, 1901), and anon., with introd. by F. A. *Gasquet (ib., 1909). M. Philip, I.B.V.M., *Companions of Mary Ward* (1939).

WARD, SETH (1617–89), Bp. of *Salisbury. He was educated at Sidney Sussex College, Cambridge, where he became a Fellow in 1640, but was deprived of his fellowship in 1644 for his opposition to the ''Solemn League and Covenant'. In 1649, however, he took the oath to the English Commonwealth when he became Savilian professor of astronomy at Oxford, and was one of the group of natural scientists at Oxford which foreshadowed the Royal Society, of which Seth later became one of the original members. The fruits of his scientific studies included two works *In Ismaelis Bullialdi Astronomiae Philolaicae Fundamenta Inquisitio Brevis* (1653) and *Astronomia Geometrica* (1656), in which he expounded a theory of planetary motions, and a philosophical controversy with T. *Hobbes. Resigning his professorship in 1660, he subsequently held several ecclesiastical offices. He was consecrated Bp. of *Exeter in 1662 and translated to Salisbury in 1667. In 1671 he became Chancellor of the Order of the Garter, being the first Anglican bishop to hold this office. In both dioceses he did much for the improvement of the cathedral. He was also a determined opponent of the dissenters and as a vigorous supporter of the *Conventicle and *Five Mile Acts, he was so severe that the Nonconformists brought an unsuccessful petition against him in 1669. Among his theological works are *A Philosophical Essay towards an Eviction of the Being and Attributes of God* (1652) and *Seven Sermons* (1673); he also edited several works of Samuel Ward, Master of Sidney Sussex College, Cambridge, (d. 1643), a strong *Calvinist, to whom Seth was not related.

Life by W. Pope (London, 1697), repr. with brief addenda, but some omissions, in S. H. Cassan, *Lives and Memoirs of the Bishops of Sherborne and Salisbury* (1824), pt. 2, pp. 31–163. Further points and corrections by J. E. B. Mayor, 'Seth Ward' in *Notes and Queries*, 2nd Series, vii (1859), p. 269 f. E. I. Carlyle in *D.N.B.*, lix (1899), pp. 336–40.

WARD, WILFRID (1856–1916), biographer and RC critic. The son of W. G. *Ward, he was trained for the priesthood but, not finding his vocation here, took up literary work. After controversial writings against H. *Spencer and F. *Harrison, he first wrote his father's Life in two separate books, *W. G. Ward and the Oxford Movement* (1889) and *W. G. Ward and the Catholic Revival* (1893). A biography of Card. N. *Wiseman followed in 1897. Under his direction, the *Dublin Review* (of which he became editor in 1906) rose to distinguished rank among the quarterlies. In his Life of J. H. *Newman (dealing almost wholly with the RC period of his life; 2 vols., 1912), he showed considerable sympathy with the *Modernist Movement, and in so far departed from the rigidly orthodox opinions of his father.

Last Lectures, ed. Josephine and Maisie Ward (widow and daughter) (1918), with introd. study by his widow, pp. vii–lxxi. Shane Leslie in *D.N.B.*, *1912–1921*, p. 552 f.

WARD, WILLIAM GEORGE (1812–82), theologian and philosopher. He held a fellowship of Balliol College, Oxford, from 1834 to 1845, during which period he became an ardent follower of J. H. *Newman. He was among the keenest of logicians, and pushed *Tractarian principles to their furthest extremes. In 1844 he published *The Ideal of a Christian Church*, strongly praising the RC Church. In 1845 he was deprived of his degrees for heresy and in the same year entered the RC Church. From 1851 to 1858 he was lecturer in moral philosophy at St. Edmund's College, Ware. In later life he was a supporter of the *Ultramontane party, upholding Papal Infallibility and maintaining fiercely anti-liberal views. He successfully opposed Newman's scheme to open a RC college in Oxford. In the last thirty years of his life he was constantly engaged in controversial writing.

Wilfrid Ward [q.v.], *W. G. Ward and the Oxford Movement* (1889) and *W. G. Ward and the Catholic Revival* (1893). J. M. Rigg in *D.N.B.*, lix (1899), pp. 344–8.

WARHAM, WILLIAM (c. 1450–1532), Abp. of *Canterbury. He was educated at *Winchester and New College, *Oxford, of which he became a Fellow in 1475. After taking his doctor's degree, he went to London in 1488 where he practised in the Court of *Arches. A rapid career followed. He was in turn moderator in the civil law school at Oxford (c. 1490), precentor of *Wells (1493), Master of the Rolls (1494), and Archdeacon of Huntingdon (1496), and employed on several notable commercial and diplomatic missions, esp. between 1496 and 1502, when he became Bp. of London. Nominated Abp. of Canterbury by *Julius II in 1503, he received the pallium in 1504, after having been made Lord

Chancellor by Henry VII in the same year. From this time he took a leading part in all affairs of national importance. He was also a recognized patron of the New Learning. In 1506 he negotiated the King's marriage to Margaret of Savoy, and in the same year was elected chancellor of Oxford university. In 1509 he crowned *Henry VIII and Catharine of Aragon, and in 1515 conferred the cardinal's hat on T. *Wolsey who, in the same year, replaced him as Lord Chancellor.

After Wolsey's appointment as Papal legate (1518) official friction between archbishop and legate was continuous, though their personal relations remained friendly. In 1527 he was Wolsey's assessor in the secret inquiry into the validity of the King's marriage, and later the chief of the counsel for the Queen whom, however, he in no way assisted. In 1530 he signed the petition to the Pope asking him to grant the King the divorce, his attitude in the matter being probably decided by the King's threat to destroy all ecclesiastical authority in the country unless his wishes were complied with. When, in 1531, the English clergy were bidden to acknowledge Henry as the Supreme Head of the Church, Warham introduced the amendment 'so far as the law of Christ will allow'. In 1532 he formally though ineffectually protested against all Acts of Parliament prejudicial to the authority of the Pope. He was a generous benefactor, esp. to scholars (D. *Erasmus, &c.), but without sympathy for the Protestant movement.

The principal sources are the State Papers and Calendars of the State Papers of the reigns of Henry VII and Henry VIII. The only life is that in W. F. *Hook, *Lives of the Archbishops of Canterbury*, vi (1888), pp. 155–421. Mary Bateson, 'Archbishop Warham's Visitation of Monasteries, 1511' in *E.H.R.*, vi (1891), pp. 18–35. J. Gairdner in *D.N.B.*, lix (1899), pp. 378–83.

WARTBURG. The 12th cent. castle near Eisenach in Thuringia where M. *Luther was hidden for safety after being seized (with his own connivance) by the Elector Friedrich on his way home from the Diet of *Worms in 1521. In his letters he described the Wartburg as his '*Patmos'; and during his ten months' residence he prepared his translation of the NT and also issued a number of polemical works.

WATCH TOWER BIBLE AND TRACT SOCIETY. See *Jehovah's Witnesses*.

WATER. See *Holy Water*.

WATERLAND, DANIEL (1683–1740), Anglican theologian. He was educated at Magdalene College, Cambridge, of which he became a Fellow in 1704 and Master in 1713. In 1717 he was appointed chaplain to the King and in 1722 chancellor of the diocese of *York. In the following years he received many preferments, becoming a Canon of *Windsor in 1727 and Archdeacon of Middlesex in 1730. He took an active part in the theological controversies of his time, esp. those on the Divinity of Christ and the Trinity, on *Deism, and on the *Eucharist. His principal works were *A Vindication of Christ's Divinity* (1719), directed against S. *Clarke; *Eight Sermons in Defence of the Divinity of Our Lord Jesus Christ* (1720), his most popular work, in which he argued that the Divinity of Christ in no way impaired the unity of the Godhead; *A Critical History of the *Athanasian Creed* (1723), in which he maintained that St. *Hilary of Arles was the author of the Creed; *Scripture Vindicated* (finished 1732), against M. *Tindal's *Christianity as Old as Creation*, in which he defended the OT accounts of the Fall, of the origin of circumcision, and of the sacrifice of Isaac against the attacks of the Deists; *The Nature, Obligation and Efficacy of the Christian Sacraments* (1732); and his *Review of the Doctrine of the Eucharist* (1737). In this last work he sought to steer a middle course between the high views of the *Real Presence represented by T. *Brett and other *Nonjurors, and the minimizing opinions of *Socinians and Deists. The Eucharist was a commemorative and representative service, which possessed a sacrificial aspect from the remembrance of Christ's death, and the sacramental Presence was to be understood as the virtue and grace of our Lord's Body and Blood communicated to the worthy receiver. Waterland was a theologian of considerable learning, widely read not only in the Fathers but also in RC and Continental Protestant theologians, though hostile alike to philosophy and mysticism. His influence did much to restore sound Trinitarian teaching against the Arianizers, and his intermediate position in the Eucharistic controversy was for long widely accepted in the C of E.

Collected ed. of his Works publd. in 10 vols., Oxford, 1823, with 'Review of the Author's Life and Writings' by W. *van Mildert as vol. i, pt. 1. J. M. Rigg in *D.N.B.*, lix (1899), pp. 446–8.

WATSON, RICHARD (1737–1816), Bp. of *Llandaff. He was educated at Trinity College, Cambridge, where he became Fellow in 1760. In 1764 he was elected professor of chemistry, a subject of which he then knew nothing but in which he soon became an adept, and in 1769 a Fellow of the Royal Society. In 1771 he became Regius Prof. of Divinity. In 1776 he published a reply to E. *Gibbon's attack on Christianity which Gibbon himself commended for its candour. In 1779 he was made Archdeacon of *Ely, and in 1782 Lord Shelburne offered him, as a known opponent of the American War, the see of Llandaff. Proposals for radical ecclesiastical reforms, including a redistribution of church revenues, brought him into disfavour with the government and put an end to his hopes of a better see. He settled at Calgarth Park in Westmorland, where he devoted himself largely to forestry and agriculture. He continued to write, issuing in 1796 *An Apology for the Bible* against T. *Paine, and in 1798 a work encouraging resistance to the French

claims. He was one of the most versatile men of his age.

Anecdotes of the Life of Richard Watson . . . written by himself at different Intervals and revised in 1814, ed. Richard Watson, son (London, 1817). A. Gordon in *D.N.B.*, lx (1899), pp. 24–7, with further reff.

WATTS, ISAAC (1674–1748), Nonconformist hymn-writer. A native of Southampton, he was educated at the local grammar-school, where his unusual abilities induced a local benefactor to offer him a university education. He preferred, however, to enter the Dissenting Academy at Stoke Newington (1690–4), the high educational standard of which left a permanent mark on his mind. After holding a post as a private tutor, he was appointed assistant (1699) and then full pastor (1702) to the *Independent congregation at Mark Lane, London. But Watts's health deteriorated from 1703 onwards, and his pastoral duties devolved increasingly on his assistant. In 1712 he resigned and spent the rest of his life at Abney Park, Stoke Newington. In his later years he seems to have inclined towards *Unitarianism. In 1719 he opposed the imposition of the doctrine of the *Trinity on dissenting ministers.

Watts deservedly merits a very high place among English hymn-writers. His hymns reflect his strong and serene faith and did much to make hymn-singing a powerful devotional force, esp. in Nonconformity, where hitherto the use of music in worship, apart from the *Metrical Psalms, had been regarded with suspicion. They include many still in common use, among them, 'Jesus shall reign where'er the sun', 'When I survey the wondrous Cross', and 'Our God, our help in ages past'. The two principal collections were *Hymns and Spiritual Songs* (1707) and *The Psalms of David* (1719). His other writings include *Horae Lyricae* (1706; poems), *Divine Songs* (1715; the first children's hymn-book), *The Improvement of the Mind* (1741), and a number of educational manuals, among them a *Logic* (1725).

Works ed. D. Jennings–P. *Doddridge (6 vols., London, 1753), 'with some account of the Author's life and character' in vol. i, pp. iii–x; repr. with corrections (6 vols., ib., 1810–1811), with memoirs of the Life of the Author by G. Burder, vol. i, pp. ix–lxxx. New ed. of his *Horae Lyricae* (London, 1837), with memoir by R. Southey, pp. i–lii. Abridged ed. of his *A Guide to Prayer* (originally publd. 1715) by H. Escott (London, 1948). T. Gibbons, *Memoirs of the Rev. Isaac Watts* (1830); T. Milner, *The Life, Times and Correspondence of the Rev. Isaac Watts* (1834); E. P. Hood, *Isaac Watts. His Life and Writings, his Homes and Friends* [c. 1875]. A. P. Davies, *Isaac Watts. His Life and Works* (New York, 1943; London, 1948). B. L. Manning, *The Hymns of Wesley and Watts* (1942), pp. 78–105. *Hymns and Spiritual Songs, 1707–1748*, ed. Selma L. Bishop (London, 1962). H. Escott, *Isaac Watts Hymnographer* (1962). H. L. Bennett in *D.N.B.*, lx (1899), pp. 67–70.

WAYNFLETE, WILLIAM. See *William of Waynflete*.

WAZO (980/90–1048), Bp. of Liége. Educated at the abbey school of Lobbes, he was appointed head of the cathedral school of Liége in 1008 on the recommendation of *Notker, and dean in 1015. Later he became provost, and in 1042 he was elected bishop. A man of great energy and austere habits, he was a faithful adherent of the Emperor, Henry III, whose rights he defended against Henry I of France. In the incipient conflict between Papacy and empire, however, he upheld the superiority of the spiritual authority, denied the Emperor the right to interfere in the appointment of bishops, and generally defended the independence of the Church. Having warned Henry before the Synod of Sutri that no one could judge the Pope save God, he regarded the deposition of Gregory VI as unjustifiable.

The chief source is the account written shortly after his death by Anselm of Liége, which forms the last part of Anselm's continuation of the *Gesta Episcoporum Tungrensium et Leodiensium* begun by Heriger of Lobbes; it is ed. R. Koepke in *M.G.H.*, Scriptores, vii (1846), pp. 210–34; repr. from E. *Martène in J. P. Migne, *PL*, cxlii, 725–64. A. Bittner, *Wazo und die Schulen von Lüttich* (Breslau Diss., 1879). R. Huysmans, *Wazo van Luik in de Ideeënstrijd zijner Dagen* (Nimegen, 1932). A. Fliche, *La Réforme grégorienne*, i (S.S.L., vi, 1924), pp. 113–28. C. Mirbt in *P.R.E.* (ed. 3), xxi (1908), pp. 32–4, s.v.; É. Amann in *D.T.C.*, xv (pt. 2; 1950), cols. 3520–4, s.v. 'Wazon de Liége'.

WEARMOUTH AND JARROW. The twin *Benedictine abbeys between the Tyne and the Wear, St. Peter at Wearmouth and St. Paul at Jarrow, founded respectively in 674 and 682 by St. *Benedict Biscop, soon became one of the chief centres of learning and culture in W. Christendom. Benedict himself and Ceolfrid, deputy Abbot of Jarrow, who made numerous journeys to Rome, were great collectors of books which formed the nucleus of the celebrated library at Jarrow. The '*Codex Amiatinus', which Ceolfrid presented to the Pope in 715, was written at Jarrow early in the 8th cent.; and for a time the '*Codex Fuldensis' was preserved here. The abbeys were made widely known through the writings of the Venerable *Bede (d. 735), who was educated there and carried on the traditions of scholarship. In 867–70 they were destroyed by the Danes, but restored *c.* 1074 by Aldwin, former prior of Winchcombe. He and two of his friends settled there for a time, and soon the monasteries began to flourish once more, later becoming cells to the priory of *Durham. The houses were secularized in the Reformation, and to-day part of their site is occupied by the parish churches.

J. Raine (ed.), *The Inventories and Account Rolls of the Benedictine Houses or Cells of Jarrow and Monk-Wearmouth* (Surtees Society, xxix; 1854). W. *Dugdale, *Monasticon Anglicanum*, i (ed. 1817), pp. 501–4. H. E. Savage, 'Jarrow Church and Monastery' in *Archaeologia Aeliana*, xxii (1900), pp. 30–60. Margaret E. Cornford in *V.C.H.*, Durham, ii, ed. W. Page (1907), pp. 81–5, with reff.

WEBB, BENJAMIN (1819–85), ecclesiologist. In 1838 he entered Trinity College, Cambridge, and while still an undergraduate founded with J. M. *Neale the *Cambridge Camden Society for the revival of ecclesiology. In this and other ways he did much to promote the revival of ritual that followed the *Oxford Movement, though Webb himself was a strictly moderate ceremonialist and never wore the Eucharistic vestments. From 1862 till his death he held the living of St. Andrew's, Wells Street, London, which became famed for its music and parochial organizations. See also foll. entry.

C. C. J. *Webb, 'Benjamin Webb' in *C.Q.R.*, lxxv (1913), pp. 329–48. Id. in *D.N.B.*, lx (1899), p. 96 f., with further reff.

WEBB, CLEMENT CHARLES JULIAN (1865–1954), *Anglican religious philosopher. The son of Benjamin *Webb, he was educated at *Christ Church, Oxford. From 1889 to 1922 he was a Fellow of Magdalen College, Oxford, and from 1920 to 1930 (the first) Oriel (now Nolloth) Prof. of the Philosophy of the Christian Religion at Oxford. His philosophical writings include *Problems in the Relations of God and Man* (1911) and two sets of *Gifford Lectures, *God and Personality* (1918) and *Divine Personality and Human Life* (1920). His standpoint was in essentials that of Orthodox Theism, with stress on the ultimate significance of Personality against the *pantheism of *Hegelian Idealism. Webb also made important contributions to the study of medieval philosophy, incl. critical editions of *John of Salisbury's *Policraticus* (2 vols., 1909) and *Metalogicon* (1929). Among his other writings were *Religious Thought in the Oxford Movement* (1928), *John of Salisbury* (1932), and *A Study of Religious Thought in England from 1850* (1933; Olaus Petri Lectures).

C. C. J. Webb, *Religious Experience*. A Public Lecture delivered . . . on Friday 19 May 1944, . . . with a Foreword by L. W. Grensted . . . together with a Bibliography of his published Writings (1945).

WEDNESDAY (originally so named in English after the Norse god, 'Woden' or 'Odin'). From early times, as is shown by the *Didache (8. 1), Wednesday, the day on which the Lord was betrayed, was together with *Friday a Christian fast day, as it still is in *Embertide. In the time of *Tertullian (*De Oratione*, 14), the Eucharist was celebrated on both these days in Africa, as was the custom later elsewhere. In Alexandria, however (Soc., *H.E.*, v, 22), and also in Rome until the 5th cent., there was only a service of prayers and lessons similar to the Ante-Communion of the BCP, and the Liturgy of the *Presanctified is still the principal service of the E. Orthodox Churches on Wednesdays and Fridays in *Lent. In modern RC practice abstinence from flesh meat is prescribed in England for the Wednesdays, as well as the Fridays, of Lent, in addition to the daily fast.

WEE FREES. The minority of the *Free Church of Scotland which refused to countenance the action of the rest of their number in uniting in 1900 with the *United Presbyterian Church to form the *United Free Church.

WEEK. The week as a liturgical institution derived from the Jewish observance of the *Sabbath day. The conception of a day of rest specially dedicated to God was taken over by the first Christians, but soon transferred to the first day of the week (Acts 20. 7, 1 Cor. 16. 2) in honour of the *Resurrection. The Jewish fasts on Tuesday and Thursday were translated to *Wednesday, the day of the Betrayal, and *Friday, the day of the Crucifixion (Didache 8), events still marked in the Latin Rite by the character of the Psalms recited on these days in the *Office. Thursday as a day of rejoicing on account of the *Ascension and of the Institution of the Eucharist came into prominence in the early Middle Ages. About the same time *Saturday began to be dedicated to our Lady, and later other days, too, had their particular devotion, e.g. Monday became the day of the Holy Souls.

Possibly in NT times (cf. Rev. 1. 10), and certainly very early, the first day of the week was known as ἡ ἡμέρα κυριακή or τοῦ Κυρίου ('the Lord's Day'), but the other days retained their Jewish designations, viz. ἡμέρα δευτέρα ('second day', i.e. 'Monday'), &c. In Latin these became dies dominica, feria secunda, &c., with sabbatum for Saturday. As fast days, Wednesday and Friday came to be known in the W. as 'stationes' (see Station Days). The planetary names, which had been introduced into Roman usage shortly before the Christian era, were occasionally used by early Christian authors, but almost entirely in writings intended for non-Christians. They did not come into general Christian currency till late in the 3rd cent. The English names are the Teutonic equivalents of the Roman planetary names.

WEEK, Holy. See Holy Week.

WEEKS, Feast of. The Jewish celebration (Exod. 23. 16) of the completion of the grain harvest. It was held on the 50th day (hence the Greek title 'Pentecost') after the offering of the barley-sheaf at the feast of unleavened bread (i.e. in the late spring or early summer). Two loaves of leavened bread were presented as a 'wave-offering', accompanied by a 'peace-offering', a 'burnt-offering', and a 'sin-offering'. The fullest account in the OT of the ceremonies surrounding it is in Lev. 23. 9–21. In later times the feast was regarded both by Jews (e.g. *Maimonides) and Christians (e.g. *Jerome, *Augustine) as commemorating the Giving of the Law on Sinai (Exod. 20).

WEIGEL, VALENTIN (1533–88), *Lutheran mystical writer. From 1567 he was pastor at Zschopau, nr. Chemnitz. Not till the 17th cent., however, when from 1609 onwards his writings (not all genuine) were printed at Halle, did his doctrines become generally known. These books consisted esp. of attacks on the 'Bibliolaters' (Buchstabentheologen) and of cosmological speculations incompatible with dogmatic Lutheranism. In the history of mysticism his ideas, largely the outcome of the prolonged study of such writers as *Dionysius

the Areopagite and *Paracelsus, are important for the considerable influence which they exercised on J. *Boehme.

J. O. Opel, Valentin Weigel (Leipzig, 1864). A. Israel, M. Valentin Weigels Leben und Schriften (Zschopau, 1888). H. Maier, Der mystische Spiritualismus Valentin Weigels (Beiträge zur Forderung christlicher Theologie, xxix, Hft. 4; 1926). A. Koyré, 'Un Mystique protestant. Maître Valentin Weigel' in Revue d'Histoire et de Philosophie religieuses [viii] (1928), pp. 227–48 and 329–48. F. Schiele, 'Zu den Schriften Valentin Weigels' in Z.K.G., xlviii (1929), pp. 380–9. H. Längin, 'Grundlinien der Erkenntnislehre Valentin Weigels' in Archiv für Geschichte der Philosophie, xli (1932), pp. 435–78. W. Zeller, Die Schriften Valentins Weigels. (Historische Studien, ccclxx; 1940). R. H. Grützmacher in P.R.E. (ed. 3), xxi (1908), pp. 37–44, s.v.

WEISS, BERNHARD (1827–1918), German NT critic and theologian. Educated at the universities of Königsberg, Halle, and Berlin, he became professor of NT exegesis at Kiel (1863–77) and Berlin (1877–1908). In his Lehrbuch der biblischen Theologie des NT (1868; Eng. trans., Biblical Theology of the NT, 1882–3), he distinguished in the NT a number of different doctrinal systems which he analysed and classified under four heads (Teaching of Jesus, Original Apostolic Christianity, Paulinism, Post-Paulinism). His critical foundations were on the whole conservative, though he upheld the priority of Mk. before it was generally allowed. His Das Leben Jesu (1882; Eng. trans., The Life of Christ, 1883) became a standard book. He was also the author of a long series of studies and commentaries on the books of the NT, esp. the Gospels, and undertook many of the later editions of the commentaries of H. A. W. *Meyer. These were notable for their careful exegesis, their attention to the history of interpretation, and their interest in the *Synoptic Problem. He also issued a critical edition of the NT text (3 parts, 1894–1900; ed. 2, 1902–5).

His autobiography, Aus neunzig Lebensjahren, 1827 bis 1918, ed. Hansgerhard Weiss (Leipzig, 1927). Theologische Studien (Festschrift to Weiss on his 70th birthday, with contributions by C. R. Gregory, A. *Harnack and others, Göttingen, 1897). A. Meyer in R.G.G. (ed. 2), v (1931), col. 1810 f., s.v.

WEISS, JOHANNES (1863–1914), German NT scholar. The son of Bernhard *Weiss, he was educated at the universities of Marburg, Berlin, Göttingen, and Breslau, and became professor of NT exegesis at Göttingen (1895) and Heidelberg (1908). His Die Predigt Jesu vom Reiche Gottes (1893) was the first attempt at a consistent eschatological interpretation of the Gospel, defending the thesis that the central purpose of Christ's mission was to proclaim the imminence of a transcendental Kingdom of God, in which He Himself was to be manifested as the Messiah. He further elaborated this view in his Kommentar zum Lukasevangelium (1893) and elsewhere. In Paulus und Jesus (1909), Christus, die Anfänge des Dogmas (1909), and in his last and most comprehensive work, Das Urchristentum (1917; completed by R. Knopf; Eng. trans. by F. C. Grant and others, 1937), he traced the growth of early Christianity. In his article 'Literaturgeschichte des NT' in Religion in Geschichte und Gegenwart

(1912), he expounded for the first time the principles of *Form-criticism which were elaborated later by M. *Dibelius, his successor at Heidelberg, R. *Bultmann, his pupil, and others. He also edited, and contributed to, *Die Schriften des Neuen Testaments* (1905 ff.).

F. C. *Burkitt, 'Johannes Weiss. In Memoriam' in *H.T.R.*, viii (1915), pp. 291–5. A. Meyer in *R.G.G.* (ed. 2), v (1931), col. 1811, s.v.; J. Schmid in *L.Th.K.*, x (1938), col. 798 f., s.v., with further reff.

WELLHAUSEN, JULIUS (1844–1918),
Biblical critic and orientalist. A native of Hameln, he studied under H. G. A. *Ewald at Göttingen, where he became Privatdozent in 1870. In 1872 he became professor of OT at Greifswald, but in 1882 resigned his chair on conscientious grounds. In the same year he became Privatdozent in Semitics at Halle and later Prof. in Semitics at Marburg (1885–1892) and Göttingen (1892–1913). After original study of the texts of *Samuel (1871) and other parts of the OT, he devoted the greater part of his life to *Higher Criticism on lines foreshadowed by E. Reuss. He elaborated the problem of the structure of *Genesis by a close analysis of *J and *E (qq.v.), while his thesis on the relative dating of the component documents of the Pentateuch, acc. to which *P (the 'Priestly Code') was the latest, completely transformed OT studies. It established the gradual development of Hebrew religion from a nomadic stage through that of the Prophets to the religion of the Law. His influence was consolidated by the researches of a long series of disciples (e.g. K. *Budde, C. F. *Burney and G. B. *Gray) and his conclusions were generally accepted by Protestant scholars by the first decades of the 20th century. In his later years he devoted himself largely to a critical study of the NT on similar lines. He upheld the priority of the Gospel of St. *Mark over '*Q', its composite nature and its original Aramaic form. In spite of his insight into philological problems, his conclusions in the NT field met with less ready acceptance, though his pregnant commentaries on the Gospels laid down many of the lines for the later development of *form criticism.

His most important works on the OT are *Die Geschichte Israels* (1878; ed. 2 issued as *Prolegomena zur Geschichte Israels*, 1883; Eng. tr. 1885) and *Die Komposition des Hexateuchs und der historischen Bücher des Alten Testaments* (1885). His other writings on the OT include *Die Pharisäer und Sadduzäer* (1874) and *Israelitische und jüdische Geschichte* (1894). His chief works on the NT were *Das Evangelium Marci* (1903), *Das Evangelium Matthäi* (1904), *Das Evangelium Lucae* (1904), *Einleitung in die drei ersten Evangelien* (1905), *Das Evangelium Johannis* (1908) and *Kritische Analyse der Apostelgeschichte* (1914).

K. Marti (ed.), *Studien zur semitischen Philologie und Religionsgeschichte Julius Wellhausen zum siebzigsten Geburtstag am 17. Mai 1914 gewidmet* (Beiheft zur *Z.A.T.W.*, xxvii; 1914). E. *Schwartz, 'Julius Wellhausen' in *Nachr.* (Gött., Gesch. Mitt., 1918); pp. 43–70. M. Kegel, *Los von Wellhausen!* (1923; Eng. tr., *Away from Wellhausen!*, 1924). W. Baumgartner, 'Wellhausen und der heutige Stand der

alttestamentlichen Wissenschaft' in *Theologische Rundschau*, ii (1930), pp. 287–307. H. *Gunkel in *R.G.G.* (ed. 2), v (1931), cols. 1820–2, s.v., with bibl.

WELLS. Acc. to local tradition, a college of secular canons under the shelter of *Glastonbury Abbey was founded at Wells by King Ina *c.* 705. Two centuries later, in 905, a Bishopric was erected by King Edward the Elder (reigned, 901–24). The see was removed to *Bath *c.* 1090 by Bp. John of Tours (or 'John de Villula', 1088–1122). After a long struggle between the monastic chapter of Bath and the secular chapter of Wells an arrangement for a joint see of Bath and Wells was made *c.* 1140 whereby both chapters took part in the election of the Bishop. Since *c.* 1256 he has borne the present title of 'Bishop of Bath and Wells'.

The present cathedral was begun *c.* 1186 under Bp. Reginald Fitz-Jocelyn (1174–91) and the main structure finished in 1239. The magnificent West front, with its 600 figures (angels; saints; Saxon, Norman, and Plantagenet Kings and Queens) and 48 reliefs, is attributed to Bp. Jocelyn (1206–42). In the 14th cent. the octagonal chapter house, the Lady chapel and the central tower were all added, as well as the three inverted arches at the crossing; these last, introduced to give strength to the central piers, are the most striking interior feature of the building. The *misericords in the stalls contain some fine woodwork of the 15th cent.

The Theological College at Wells was founded in 1840. Its members are partly housed in the ancient Vicars' Close.

The Cathedral MSS. were calendared by J. A. Bennett (Historical Manuscripts Commission, Tenth Report, 1885, Appendix, pt. 3); the Records of the Dean and Chapter by W. H. B. Bird–W. P. Baildon (Historical Manuscripts Commission, 2 vols., 1907–14). D. M. Clerk, 'Wells Cathedral' in *Somerset Archaeological Society Proceedings*, i (pt. 1; 1851), pp. 65–88, with docc. pp. 176–80. E. A. Freeman, *History of the Cathedral Church of Wells* (1870); H. E. Reynolds (ed.), *Wells Cathedral. Its Foundation, Constitutional History and Statutes* (1881); P. *Dearmer, *The Cathedral Church of Wells* (1898). T. S. Holmes, 'The Cathedral of Wells' in *V.C.H.*, Somerset ii, (ed. W. Page (1911), pp. 162–9. For editions of Episcopal Registers, see bibl. to *Bath and Wells*.

WELLS, EDWARD (1667–1727), mathematician and theological writer. Having graduated from Christ Church, Oxford, in 1690, he held several pastoral appointments, becoming rector of Bletchley in 1716. Between 1709 and 1719 he published an edition of the Greek text of the NT, with an Eng. trans. and notes, in which for the first time a complete NT was printed with the *textus receptus abandoned in favour of readings from better MSS.

His *A Historical Geography of the Old and New Testament* (orig. publd. as two separate works, 3 vols., 1708), republd. in 2 vols., Oxford, 1801; his *The Rich Man's Duty to Contribute Liberally to the Building, Rebuilding, Repairing, Beautifying, and Adorning of Churches* (ed. 2; 1717), republd. Oxford, 1840, with introd. by J. H. *N[ewman], pp. iii–vi. T. Cooper in *D.N.B.*, lx (1899), p. 227 f., s.v., with reff.

WELSH BIBLE AND PRAYER BOOK.
In 1567 the New Testament first appeared in Welsh, translated from the Greek mainly by

William Salesbury (c. 1529–95). It served as the basis for the complete Bible published in 1588 by William Morgan (c. 1547–1604), Bp. of *St. Asaph. This was revised by Richard Parry (1560–1623; Morgan's successor in the see of St. Asaph), probably with the help of John Davies (1570–1644), his chaplain, and published in 1620. This Bible, which used the language of the bards, was an important formative influence on the Welsh prose language. It is the Welsh Bible in general use to-day.

The English Prayer Book of 1559 was translated into Welsh by Richard Davies (1501–81), Bp. of *St. Davids, and appeared in 1567. The Psalms were translated direct from the Hebrew, and the first lesson continued to be read in English. A translation of the new Book of 1662 which was provided for in the Act of *Uniformity appeared in 1664. Several improvements have been added since, but the 1664 Book remains in essence that still in use. In 1770 there was issued an edition with 54 fine plates, considered the most beautifully printed Welsh book of the 18th cent. Like the Welsh Bible, the Prayer Book has played a large part in fixing the Welsh language.

J. Ballinger, The Bible in Wales (1906), with bibl. of Welsh Bibles [by J. I. Jones] appended (separately paged, pp. 1–90). Darlow–Moule, iv (1911), pp. 1657–85. Life of Bp. Morgan by W. Hughes (S.P.C.K., 1891). A. O. Evans, A Chapter in the History of the Welsh Book of Common Prayer, or Letters which were written preparatory to the Revised Edition of 1841 (3 vols., Bangor, 1922), with general introduction, i, pp. xiii–xxxix. W. Muss-Arnolt, The Book of Common Prayer among the Nations of the World (S.P.C.K., 1914), pp. 69–76 (ch. vii, 'Richard Davies and the Welsh Translations'). A. O. Evans, A Memorandum on the Legality of the Welsh Bible and the Welsh Version of the Book of Common Prayer (Cardiff, 1925).

WENCESLAS, St. (c. 907–29), Bohemian prince and martyr. The son of Duke Wratislaw and Drahomira, he received a good Christian education, supervised by his grandmother, St. Ludmilla. After the death of his father (c. 920) his mother became regent, but her violent actions so estranged the people that Wenceslas took over the government, probably c. 922. Himself a man of much piety, he worked for the religious and cultural improvement of his people which he sought to bring into closer connexion with the W. world, and for this reason entertained friendly relations with Germany. It was probably this policy as well as the dissatisfaction of the pagan elements among his subjects which, in 929, led to his being murdered by his brother Boleslav. He was soon venerated as a martyr, and Boleslav himself had his relics translated to the Church of St. Vitus, at Prague, c. 932. From 985 his feast is known to have been observed in Bohemia, whose patron he became. From the year 1000 his picture appeared on Bohemian coins, and the Crown of St. Wenceslas came to be the symbol of Czech independence. The name of the saint has become familiar in England through J. M. *Neale's Christmas carol 'Good King Wenceslas', but its contents are wholly imaginative. Feast day, 28 Sept.

AA.SS., Sept. VII (1760), pp. 770–844. J. Pekař Die Wenzels- und Ludmila-Legenden und die Echtheit Christians (1906), with modern ed. of texts. Other primary texts listed in B.H.L., ii (1900–1901), pp. 1273–5, Nos. 8821–44, and Suppl. (1911), p. 311 f. A. Naegle, Der heilige Wenzel, der Landespatron Böhmens (1928); F. Dvornik, Zivot svalého Václava (1929; Germ. tr., 1929). In Eng. there is a short pamphlet based on the researches of J. Hanush, canon of Prague (d. 1928), tr. and abridged by A. Christitch (*Catholic Truth Society, c. 1930). G. Weisskopf in L.Th.K., x (1938), cols. 822–4, s.v. 'Wenzel', with bibl.

WERBURGH, St. (d. c. 699), English abbess. The daughter of the Mercian king, Wulfhere, and St. Ermenilda, Werburgh entered the *Benedictine abbey of *Ely, where she became abbess, and was later instigated by King Ethelred to reform the monasteries of nuns in his kingdom. She also established new monasteries at Trentham and Hanbury (in Staffordshire) and at Weedon (in Northants). She was renowned for her holy life and many miracles were reported to have occurred at her tomb. For fear of the Danes her body was removed to *Chester in 875. Her shrine, of which fragments are still to be seen in Chester Cathedral, was destroyed during the reign of *Henry VIII. Her Life was written by *Goscelin c. 100 years after her death, but the account is mostly legendary. Feast day, 3 Feb.

Life by Goscelin pr. in AA.SS., Feb. I (1658), pp. 386–90; Florence of Worcester, Chronicon ex Chronicis (ed. B. Thorpe, London, i, 1848, p. 32). Metrical life by Henry Bradshaw (d. 1513), orig. publ. 1521, ed. by E. Hawkins (Chetham Society Old Series, xv; 1848) and C. Horstmann (E.E.T.S., Original Series, lxxxviii; 1887). J. Tait (ed.), The Chartulary or Register of the Abbey of St. Werburgh, Chester, i (Chetham Society New Series, lxxix; 1920, pp. viii–xiv.

WESEL, JOHN OF. See John of Wesel.

WESLEY, CHARLES (1707–88), eighteenth child of Samuel, and brother of John, *Wesley. Educated at Westminster School and *Christ Church, Oxford, he became an active member of the Oxford *Methodists. After ordination in 1735 he accompanied his brother to Georgia (also 1735), where he acted as secretary to Governor Oglethorpe; he returned to England in 1736. Like John he came under the influence of Peter Böhler and the *Moravians and experienced conversion on Whitsunday (21 May) 1738. Entering on the itinerant ministry in the next year, he occupied himself in preaching and travelling until 1756. Eventually, in 1771, he settled in London where he took turns in preaching at the City Road Chapel. He was the most gifted and indefatigable hymn-writer that England has ever known (over 5,500 hymns in all), and like his brother understood their immense importance for missionary, devotional, and instructional purposes. The first collection, entitled Hymns and Sacred Poems (with the original form of 'Hark! the herald angels sing' and 'Hail the day that sees Him rise'), appeared in 1739, to be quickly followed by others, all professedly the joint work of the two brothers. Other favourites include 'Jesu, Lover of my soul', 'Love divine, all loves excelling', the Advent hymn 'Lo! He comes, with clouds descending', and the Eucharistic hymn 'Author of life divine'. A more balanced and livelier character than his brother, Charles Wesley remained faithful to the C of E and was much irritated by John's ordinations.

His *Journal*, with selections from his Correspondence and Poetry, ed. T. Jackson (2 vols., London, 1849), with introd. in vol. i, pp. iii–xliv; first part (1736–9) also publd. in The Finsbury Library [1919]. J. Telford (ed.), *The Treasure House of Charles Wesley*. A Short Anthology of the Evangelical Revival (1933). T. Jackson, *The Life of the Rev. Charles Wesley* (2 vols., 1841). J. Telford, *The Life of the Rev. Charles Wesley* ([1887]; revised ed., 1900); J. Whitehead, *The Life of the Rev. John Wesley* . . . To which is prefixed . . . the Life of the Rev. Charles Wesley, i (1893), pp. 97–374. Other studies by D. M. Jones (London [1919]) and F. L. Wiseman (New York, 1932; London, 1933). J. E. Rattenbury, *The Evangelical Doctrines of Charles Wesley's Hymns* (1941); B. L. Manning, *The Hymns of Wesley and Watts* (1942), pp. 32–77. F. L. Wiseman, 'Charles Wesley and the Hymnwriters of Methodism' in W. J. Townsend–H. B. Workman–G. Eayrs (edd.), *A New History of Methodism*, i (1909), pp. 237–50. R. Green, *The Works of John and Charles Wesley*. A Bibliography; containing an exact account of all the publications issued by the Wesley Brothers (1896). A. Gordon in *D.N.B.*, lx (1899), pp. 298–302.

WESLEY, JOHN (1703–91), founder of the *Methodist Movement. The fifteenth child of the Rev. Samuel Wesley (1662–1735), rector of Epworth, Lincs, and his wife, Susannah, he was educated at the Charterhouse and *Christ Church, Oxford. In 1726 he was elected to a fellowship at Lincoln College, Oxford, and also acted for a time (1727–9) as curate to his father. At Oxford he gathered round him a group of earnest, devout, and scholarly Christians who became known as the 'Holy Club', 'Bible Moths', or 'Methodists', and included his brother, Charles *Wesley, and G. *Whitefield (qq.v.). At this period he came much under the influence of W. *Law (whom he visited), H. *More (d. 1687), and other mystics. In 1735 he set out with his brother, Charles, on a missionary journey to Georgia under the auspices of the *S.P.G., but his preaching (esp. against the slave-trade and gin) and inexperience alienated the colonists and he soon returned home (1737). His friendship with the *Moravian, Peter Böhler, who convinced him that he lacked 'that faith whereby alone we are saved', and a visit (1738) to the Moravian colony at *Herrnhut, had a profound effect on his religious life. He had the experience of conversion on 24 May 1738 at the reading of M. *Luther's Preface to the Ep. to the Romans at a meeting in Aldersgate Street. Henceforth his professed object was 'to promote as far as I am able vital practical religion and by the grace of God to beget, preserve, and increase the life of God in the souls of men', and the rest of his life was spent in evangelistic work.

Finding the churches closed to him, Wesley began field-preaching to the Kingswood colliers in 1739. His success soon led him to organize a body of lay pastors to follow up his evangelism. After 1742 Wesley widened the sphere of his activity, covering the whole of the British Isles, among his chief centres being the Foundery at Moorfields, Bristol, Newcastle-on-Tyne, and Macclesfield. His annual journeyings averaged 8,000 miles on horseback; he wrote thousands of letters and preached innumerable sermons; and despite the hostility of many Churchmen he was nearly always greeted with enthusiasm. In 1744 he held a conference of lay preachers which later became an annual event, and for which a legal constitution was eventually provided in 1784. In 1747 he visited Ireland for the first time; in 1751 he made the first of twenty-two visits to Scotland. From small beginnings in 1760 the Methodist system gradually developed also in America. In 1768 a Methodist Chapel was opened in New York. The needs of this new field induced Wesley to ordain Dr. Thomas Coke (1747–1814), a Welshman and graduate of Jesus College, Oxford, Superintendent or Bishop, and also to instruct Coke to ordain Francis *Asbury (1745–1816) in America as his colleague. Wesley himself still wished the Movement to take place within the C of E, but an increasingly independent system grew up. At the time of Wesley's death there were 294 preachers and 71,668 members in Great Britain, 19 missionaries and 5,300 members on mission stations, and 198 preachers and 43,265 members in America. Less of a *Calvinist than most of his followers, Wesley's opposition to the strict Calvinist view of election had led to a break with G. Whitefield in 1741.

Wesley was a man of the greatest courage and persistence, with a vast capacity for leadership and organization. His personality was magnetic, his piety and charity uncontestable. His conversation was admired by Dr. Samuel *Johnson. His marriage with Maria Vazeille, a widow of very different temperament from his own, proved unhappy. Although his brother Charles was a more gentle and attractive character and Whitefield a greater preacher, John Wesley was beyond doubt the central figure in the rise of Methodism as well as one of the greatest Christians of his age.

Wesley himself ed. a collection of his works, 32 vols., Bristol, 1771–4; the more important later edd. include ed. 3, by T. Jackson, 14 vols., London, 1829–31, and ed. 11, also by T. Jackson, 15 vols., ib., 1856–62, with life by J. Becham in vol. i, pp. i–xlix. The standard ed. of his Journals, which extend from 1735 to 1790, is that of N. Curnock, 8 vols., London, 1909–16; of his Letters by J. Telford, 8 vols., ib., 1931; of his Sermons by E. H. Sugden, vol. i, only publd., ib., 1921. Lives by J. Hampson (3 vols., London, 1791), T. Coke–H. Moore (ib., 1792), J. Whitehead (2 vols., ib., 1793–6), R. Southey (2 vols., ib., 1820, and many later edd.), H. Moore (2 vols., ib., 1824–5), R. Watson (ib., 1831), Julian Wedgwood (ib., 1870), L. Tyerman (3 vols., ib., 1870–1871; with much fresh material), R. D. Urlin (ib., 1870), J. H. Rigg (ib., 1875; ed. 2, 1891), J. Telford (ib., 1886), J. H. Overton (ib., 1891), R. Green (*Religious Tract Society, 1905), C. T. Winchester (London, 1906), W. H. Fitchett (ib., 1906), G. Eayrs (ib., 1926), W. H. *Hutton ('Great English Churchmen', 1927), G. C. Cell (New York, 1935), R. Pike (London, 1938), and F. J. McConnell (New York–London, 1939). There is also a series of important studies by J. S. Simon (5 vols., London, 1921–34). Maldwyn [L.] Edwards, *John Wesley and the Eighteenth Century*. A Study of his Social and Political Influence (1933). J. B. Green, *John Wesley and William Law* (1945). W. R. Cannon, *The Theology of John Wesley*, with special Reference to the Doctrine of Justification (New York, 1946); H. Lindström, *Wesley and Sanctification*. A Study in the Doctrine of Salvation (Stockholm, 1946). Maldwyn [L.] Edwards, *Family Circle*. A Study of the Epworth Household in Relation to John and Charles Wesley (1939). V. H. H. Green, *The Young Mr. Wesley* (1961). A. Gordon in *D.N.B.*, lx (1899), pp. 303–14. See also works cited under *Methodism*.

WESLEY, SAMUEL SEBASTIAN (1810–1876), English composer and organist. He was a son of the composer Samuel Wesley (1766–1837), who was himself a son of Charles *Wesley. A boy soprano of the Chapel Royal from 1819, he afterwards became organist of *Hereford Cathedral (1832–5), of *Exeter Cathedral (1835–42), of Leeds Parish Church (1842–9), of *Winchester Cathedral (1849–1865), and of *Gloucester Cathedral (1865–76). He conducted the Three Choirs' Festival in 1834 and four times from 1865 to 1874. His compositions include such well-known anthems as 'The Wilderness' and 'Blessed be the God and Father'.

G. W. Spink, 'Samuel Sebastian Wesley: A Biography' in *The Musical Times*, lxxviii (1937), pp. 44–6, 149 f., 239 f., 245–7, 438 f., and 536–8. E. Walker, *A History of Music in England* (1907), pp. 263–6. F. G. Edwards in *D.N.B.*, lx (1899), pp. 320–2, s.v.; H. S. Oakeley in *Grove's Dictionary of Music and Musicians*, ed. 4 by H. C. Colles, v (1940), p. 702 f., with list of his publd. works.

WESLEYAN METHODISTS. See *Methodism* and other artt. there listed.

WESSEL (*c.* 1420–89), Dutch theologian. (He is also known as **Gansfort**, the name 'Wessel' having been given to him at his baptism; the designation 'John Wessel' by which he is sometimes described, appears to have arisen through confusion with *John of Wesel). Educated by the *Brethren of the Common Life at Deventer, he was influenced by *Plato, St. *Augustine, and St. *Thomas Aquinas. For 16 years he studied and taught at Paris, where he defended the side of *Nominalism against *Realism, more, however, it appears, on ecclesiastical than on philosophical grounds. Later he visited Italy, where he came into contact with the Renaissance humanism, and finally returned home for his last years. He is commonly regarded by German Protestant writers as one of the 'Reformers before the Reformation'; since in his attitude to the Papacy, to the authority of the Church, and to the superstitious tendencies of his age, he shared many of the sentiments of M. *Luther.

A collection of his writings ed. M. *Luther (n. pl. d. [c. 1521]); later ed., Basle, 1522. Complete works publ. Groningen, 1614. E. W. Miller, *Wessel Gansfort, Life and Writings* (2 vols., Papers of the American Society of Church History, i and ii; New York and London, 1917), with Eng. tr. by J. W. Scudder of his Correspondence in vol. i, pp. 231–333, of his treatise 'concerning the Blessed Sacrament of the Eucharist and the Hearing of the Mass' in vol. ii, pp. 3–70, and of the Farrago, pp. 75–315, and full bibl. C. Ullmann, *Reformatoren vor der Reformation*, book 4, vol. ii (ed. 2, 1866), pp. 236–557; Eng. tr. (1885), pp. 263–615. J. *Friedrich, *Johann Wessel* (1862). M. van Rhihn, *Wessel Gansfort* (The Hague, 1917); id., *Studiën over Wessel Gansfort en zijn Tijd* (1933). A. Hyma, *The Christian Renaissance*. History of the 'Devotio Moderna' (New York, 1925), ch. 6.

WESSENBERG, IGNAZ HEINRICH VON (1774–1860), *Febronianist reformer. Educated at Augsburg by ex-Jesuits, and later at Dillingen (where he struck up a friendship with J. M. Sailer, 1751–1832), and Würzburg, in 1795 he made the acquaintance of K. v. Dalberg (1744–1817). In 1802, though only a subdeacon, he was appointed by Dalberg, now Coadjutor Prince-Bp. of Constance, his *vicar general. He became an increasingly warm advocate of Febronianist principles and aimed at the creation of a National German Church, largely independent of Rome. As early as 1802 he began a monthly review, *Geistliche Monatsschrift* (1802–4), which was replaced after two years by the less aggressive *Konstanzer Pastoralarchiv* (1804–27). Among his reforms were the raising of standards in the clerical seminaries, frequent gatherings of the clergy for mutual encouragement, bi-weekly religious instruction in the state schools, systematic provision for the blind and deaf-mute, and the establishment of an inter-confessional house of refuge. His *Josephinistic principles and writings met with much opposition at Rome. In support of his cause he accompanied Dalberg to Paris in 1811 and in 1814–15 attended the Congress of Vienna as Dalberg's deputy, but without positive result. During his absence in Vienna, Rome separated the Swiss portion of the diocese from Constance and shortly afterwards brought pressure on Dalberg to depose Wessenberg. Though Dalberg obeyed, he sought Wessenberg's appointment as his Coadjutor with the right of succession. The acceptance of this proposal by the Government of Baden was invalidated by Rome. When, on Dalberg's death (1817), the chapter elected Wessenberg as vicar and administrator of the diocese, *Pius VII again resisted the appointment and refused Wessenberg an audience at Rome. From now onwards Wessenberg, in open disobedience to the Pope, acted as administrator until 1827, when the diocese of Constance, which had been suppressed in 1821 by the bull 'Provida sollersque', was incorporated into that of Freiburg. In 1833, he retired into private life. Wessenberg was a very voluminous writer. His publications included a large treatise, *Die grossen Kirchenversammlungen des 15. und 16. Jahrhunderts in Bezug auf die Kirchenverbesserung* (4 vols., 1840), but they lacked solidity and are without enduring value.

Life by J. Beck (Freiburg i.Br., 1862; put on *Index on 11 June 1866). A. Rösch, *Das religiöse Leben in Hohenzollern unter dem Einfluss des Wessenbergianismus, 1800–1850* (1908). M. Ott in *C.E.*, xv (1912), p. 590 f.; L. Zscharnack in *R.G.G.* (ed. 2), v (1931), col. 1880, s.v., with bibl.; C. Gröber in *L.Th.K.*, x (1938), cols. 835–9.

WEST AFRICA, Christianity in. The first Europeans arriving in W. Africa were a poor witness to Christianity, for the settlements on the coast from the 15th to the early 19th cents. had no purpose but exploitation. This object was ruthlessly pursued in the slave trade, by which thousands of Africans were kidnapped and transported to America. The Portuguese arrived in the 15th cent., and at that date began the missions in Angola which still continue. But serious mission work on the west coast only began when the slave trade ended in the early 19th cent. Since then the various occupying nations have offered no deliberate obstacle, though the conduct of nominal white Christians, seen perhaps at its worst in the brutalities perpetrated in the Belgian Congo in the early years of the 20th cent., did not commend Christianity. French and Portuguese RC missionary societies have established posts in practically the whole region. The first Anglican diocese was established in 1852 and others followed. In French territory, the French Evangelicals are also working, while in Belgian Congo, American Baptists and Presbyterians have missions. In the vast territory of Nigeria various Free Church missions are at work, as well as the *C.M.S.; Methodists have many missions in Gambia, the Gold Coast, and Dahomey; and American Baptists are active in Portuguese territory. The missions in Liberia are almost exclusively American (RC, Episcopalian, and Protestant). In French W. Africa there is also a mission of Anglicans from the W. Indies, under *S.P.G. direction.

Since the war of 1939–45 the Gold Coast (since 1957, Ghana) and Nigeria have advanced towards self-government. The existing Anglican dioceses (except Liberia) were organized in 1951 as the Province of West Africa and several new dioceses were set up; of 14 bishoprics (diocesan and assistant) in 1956, 8 were held by Africans. Since 1948 the University College of Ghana and University College, Ibadan, provide higher education including some theological studies, and leadership in Christian, as in secular, affairs is likely to become increasingly African.

J. Du Plessis, *The Evangelisation of Pagan Africa. A History of Christian Missions to the Pagan Tribes of Central Africa* (Cape Town, &c. [c. 1930]), pp. 61–249. C. P. Groves, *The Planting of Christianity in Africa*, i (to 1840; Lutterworth Library, xxvi; 1948), pp. 197–218 and 275–311. H. L. Clarke, *Constitutional Church Government in the Dominions Beyond the Seas and in other Parts of the Anglican Communion* (1924), pp. 412–17. Latourette, v, 419–60, and vii, 238–49. See also bibl. to *C.M.S.*

WEST INDIES, Christianity in the. The West Indies were originally colonized chiefly by the Spanish, English, and French. Nearly all the aboriginal population was exterminated by the conquerors, though a small number remains. Mostly, however, they were replaced by negro slaves imported from Africa. In the islands which were Spanish or French, the RC Church came with the invaders, and in many such, even though now under British rule (e.g. Trinidad, Dominica, and St. Lucia), most of the islanders belong nominally to that faith. In the British islands, including St. Vincent and Grenada, which were won very early from France and Spain, the Anglican Church was established, as in England. From time to time in the 17th and 18th cents. attempts were made by individual Anglicans to evangelize the negroes, e.g. the establishment of *Codrington Missionary Training College, Barbados, in 1714–42, but the planters and some of the official chaplains were hostile to such work, and even more so to the missionary efforts of the *Moravians, *Methodists, *Presbyterians, and *Baptists, which nevertheless had some

success. In the 19th cent., however, Anglicans awoke to their responsibility. In 1824 the first two bishoprics of Jamaica and Barbados were set up, and by 1852 the work of evangelization was so far advanced that the Church in the West Indies was able to assume responsibility for the Rio Pongas Mission in West Africa, which it still maintains. Later in the century the Anglican Church was disestablished everywhere except in Barbados. The Province was constituted in 1883.

With the liberation of the slaves (1833) came a new problem. The evangelization of the Orientals, esp. Indians and Chinese, brought to the islands to supply the need for cheap hired labour, proved extremely difficult. But among these, as among the negroes, progress has been made, and Anglicans, RCs, and Protestants alike have for many years begun to build up a native ministry.

A. Caldecott, *The Church in the West Indies* (Colonial Church Histories, 1898). J. B. Ellis, *The Diocese of Jamaica* (1913). H. L. Clarke, *Constitutional Church Government in the Dominions beyond the Seas and other Parts of the Anglican Communion* (1924), pp. 259–315. F. D. Walker, *The Call of the West Indies*. The Romance of Methodist Work and Opportunity in the West Indies and Adjacent Regions [1933]. Latourette, v, 48–61, and vii, 162–4, with bibl. notes.

WESTCOTT, BROOKE FOSS (1825–1901), Bp. of *Durham. He was educated at King Edward VI's School at Birmingham under J. Prince Lee, where he became the lifelong friend of J. B. *Lightfoot and E. W. *Benson, and at Trinity College, Cambridge. Ordained in 1851, in 1852 he became assistant master at Harrow under C. J. *Vaughan, where he published a series of theological works, including the 1st edition of his *History of the New Testament Canon* (1855), the *Introduction to the Study of the Gospels* (1860), and a *History of the English Bible* (1868). In 1869 he left Harrow for a residentiary canonry at *Peterborough Cathedral, which he retained when, in 1870, he was elected Regius professor of divinity at Cambridge. Here he prepared together with F. J. A. *Hort the celebrated critical edition of the Greek NT, published in 1881. It was followed by his three great commentaries on St. John's Gospel (1881), on the Epp. of St. John (1883), and on the Ep. to the Hebrews (1889), the fruit of his Cambridge lectures. At the same time he devoted much of his energy to the training of his students and to the encouragement of missions, the Cambridge Clergy Training School (now 'Westcott House') and the Cambridge Mission to Delhi owing their existence to his inspiration and direction. In 1890 he was consecrated Bp. of Durham, where he made social problems his special concern, one of his most successful efforts being his mediation in the coal strike of 1892. In the same year he published his doctrinal work *The Gospel of Life*, which was followed by several volumes of collected sermons and addresses, among them *The Incarnation and Common Life* (1893) and *Christian Aspects of Life* (1897).

Westcott's fame as a scholar rests chiefly on

his edition of the NT and on his great commentaries. The former has been recognized as fundamental by both English and Continental theologians. If he was not gifted with Hort's outstanding acumen in this field, his share in the work was probably equal to that of his collaborator. His commentaries follow the traditional views as regards authorship and date. Despite a marked inclination to oversubtle distinctions, they are esp. esteemed for their penetrating insight into the spiritual meaning of the text, assisted by a judicious use of patristic exegesis. In theology he owed much to F. D. *Maurice. His doctrinal works, esp. *The Gospel of the Resurrection* (1866) and *The Gospel of Life*, though less satisfactory owing to lack of precision and difficulty of language, promoted a deeper understanding, in the C of E, of the implications of the Incarnation and the Resurrection. He sought to put the Divine Person of God made Man rather than a juridical view of the Atonement or a merely ethical understanding of the Sermon on the Mount in the centre of Christian experience.

Arthur Westcott (son), *Life and Letters of Brooke Foss Westcott* (2 vols., 1903). Shorter life by J. Clayton ('Leaders of the Church, 1800–1900', ed. G. W. E. Russell, 1906); brief sketch by A. G. B. West, *Memories of Brooke Foss Westcott* (1936). V. H. Stanton in *D.N.B.*, *1901–1911*, pp. 635–41.

WESTERÅS, The Ordinance of. The regulations passed by the Diet of Westerås which Gustavus Vasa assembled on 24 June 1527 to carry through the Protestant Reformation in *Sweden. Their effect was to transfer to the crown the enormous power hitherto possessed by the Swedish episcopate, to alienate its property, and to make the Church completely subservient to the King.

Text in *Svenska Riksdagsakter jämte andra handlingar som höra till statsforfattningens historia under tidehvarfvet 1521–1718*, i, ed. E. Hildebrand–O. Alin (1887), pp. 89–95; Eng. tr. in Kidd, pp. 234–6 (No. ci). See also works on the Reformation in Sweden, cited under *Sweden, Christianity in*.

WESTERN TEXT OF THE NT. An early form of the Greek text of the NT, so named by B. F. *Westcott and F. J. A. *Hort because the chief authorities for it were of Western *provenance*, viz. some Graeco-Latin MSS., the *Old Latin, and quotations in the Latin Fathers. Since Westcott and Hort's day, many fresh and geographically widely separated evidences of a similar text have been found, e.g. the Sinaitic *Old Syriac, and for a time textual critics designated all these texts collectively as 'Western'. But as it is becoming clear that these other recently recovered ('unrevised') texts are less closely related than are the Graeco-Latin manuscripts and their Latin allies among themselves, the term 'Western' is now tending to be confined to the witnesses to which Westcott and Hort originally applied it.

The Western text reflects changes, some accidental and others deliberate, which the NT text suffered before A.D. 150. In contrast with the *Caesarean, *Neutral, and *Byzantine texts, which seem to be consciously revised

witnesses, the Western is apparently an unrevised text. Scholars are now agreed (against Westcott and Hort) that it cannot be disregarded in attempting to reach the original NT text. Though it cannot be made the basis, its readings have often to be considered and sometimes adopted.

In the Gospels, the peculiarities of the Western text often arose from the desire to make the texts of the various Gospels identical in places where they are similar. Through this tendency to assimilate parallel passages, many omissions as well as additions to the original text have resulted. In some cases, however, the Western text preserves the correct text against other witnesses, e.g. at Mt. 9. 34, 21. 44; Lk. 22. 19b–20, 62, 24. 12, 40; Jn. 12. 8; Rom. 16. 25–27; and it has sometimes resisted the tendency to assimilate passages where other witnesses have succumbed. Notable additions in the Gospel of Lk. preserved only in the Western text include 6. 4 (man working on the Sabbath), 22. 43 f. (the angel and sweat at the Agony in the Garden), 23. 34 ('Father, forgive them' at the Crucifixion), and 24. 51b (the Ascension). In Acts the differences between the Western and the other texts are at their greatest. In this Book no agreement has been reached among scholars as to how far each is original. In the Epistles differences are much smaller, but here, as in the Gospels, the Western text is sometimes clearly correct.

Important discussions in B. F. Westcott–F. J. A. Hort, *The New Testament in the Original Greek*, ii (1881); B. H. *Streeter, *The Four Gospels* (1924); F. J. Foakes Jackson–K. *Lake (edd.), *The Beginnings of Christianity*, Part I, vol. iii (1926; The Text of Acts, by J. H. Ropes); C. H. *Turner, 'Western Readings in the Second Half of St. Mark's Gospel' in *J.T.S.*, xxix (1928), pp. 1–16; A. C. Clark, *The Acts of the Apostles* (1933); F. [G.] Kenyon, 'The Western Text in the Gospels and Acts' in *Proceedings of the British Academy*, xxiv (1938), pp. 287–315. M. J. *Lagrange, O.P., *Introduction à l'étude du Nouveau Testament*, Deuxième Partie, i: La Critique textuelle; ii: La Critique rationnelle (1935), pp. 42–82, 389–409.

WESTMINSTER ABBEY. Acc. to a legend, not mentioned by *Bede and prob. of 13th cent. origin, a Benedictine abbey was founded in Thorney Island in 616 and miraculously consecrated by St. *Peter, the patron of the Church. The abbey is mentioned in a charter of *Offa, dated 785, of which, however, the authenticity has been challenged. Acc. to *William of Malmesbury it was restored by St. *Dunstan. The rebuilding and restoration of the abbey were undertaken by *Edward the Confessor in commutation of a vow to go on a pilgrimage to Rome, the new choir and transepts being dedicated in 1065. The nave, begun *c.* 1100, was completed by 1163, when, after the canonization of Edward the Confessor (1161), his relics were translated to a shrine in the choir. A much larger chapel at the East End seems to have been undertaken in 1220, when various extensions were planned. Henry III in 1245 began the erection of the present church in the French style. By 1269, when the relics of Edward the Confessor were translated to the shrine behind the High Altar, the eastern part of the church had been completed.

Work on the nave, continued in 1375, was finished c. 1505. By 1519 the chapel planned by Henry VII as a shrine for *Henry VI had been added. The western towers, designed by C. *Wren and modified by N. Hawksmoor (1661–1736), were completed between 1740 and 1750. The present choir-screen (reredos) was erected in 1867 after the designs of G. G. *Scott (d. 1878).

The Benedictine foundation of Edward the Confessor soon became one of the richest abbeys in the country, largely through the veneration accorded to the last Anglo-Saxon king. As a royal foundation it occupied a special position in relation to the reigning sovereigns, and it was under the protection of the Holy See. From pre-Norman times until the reign of *James I it enjoyed wide rights of *sanctuary. Abbot Laurence (abbot c. 1158–1175) obtained the right to wear a mitre and complete exemption from the jurisdiction of the Bp. of London. Notable Abbots include, Edwin (abbot 1047–71), Gilbert Crispin (abbot 1085–1117), Simon Langham (abbot 1349–62), Nicholas Lytlington (abbot 1362–86), and John Islip (abbot 1500–32).

In 1540 the monastery was dissolved and a collegiate church under a Dean with twelve prebendaries was founded, W. Boston (abbot 1532–40) becoming the first Dean (1540–49). The abbey became a Royal Peculiar, retaining its independence of the see of London. At the same time most of the monastic quarters, rebuilt after a fire in 1298, were appropriated for the school founded by *Henry VIII in 1540. In the same year a bishopric was established under T. *Thirlby, covering most of the county of Middlesex; it was suppressed in 1550. A Benedictine community under J. Feckenham (d. 1584) was reinstated by *Mary in 1556; it was dissolved in 1559 when *Elizabeth restored the collegiate church. From the time of J. Dolben (Dean 1662–83) to that of S. *Horsley (Dean 1793–1801) the Deanery was held in conjunction with the see of *Rochester. In 1840 the number of prebendaries was reduced from twelve to six. Notable Deans include L. *Andrewes (Dean 1601–5), J. *Williams (Dean 1620–45), J. *Ireland (Dean 1816–42), R. Chenevix *Trench (Dean 1856–63) and A. P. *Stanley (Dean 1864–81). J. Thynne, sub-dean from 1834 to 1880, did much to improve the standard of worship in the abbey.

Notable features in the abbey include the fan-vaulting in the chapel of Henry VII, the chantry of Abbot Islip, the mosaic pavement in the sanctuary, the Coronation Chair and Stone of *Scone (q.v.), the mural paintings of St. Christopher and the Incredulity of St. Thomas in the South Transept, the 11th cent. chapel of the Pyx in the cloisters and the tombs of numerous sovereigns from Henry III to George II and celebrities of all kinds, esp. since the 18th cent. Since the time of William I, who chose the place because of its association with Edward the Confessor, it has been the traditional place for the Coronation of the Sovereign, the abbot or dean having a special part in the ceremony. Until 1547 the House of Commons frequently sat in the 13th-cent. octagonal Chapter House. Almost throughout its history the abbey has retained a unique position as a centre of the national life.

A. P. Stanley, *Historical Memorials of Westminster Abbey* (1868); H. F. Westlake, *Westminster Abbey* (2 vols., 1923); id., *The Story of Westminster Abbey* (1924); W. R. Lethaby, *Westminster Abbey Re-examined* (1925); J. Perkins, *Westminster Abbey. Its Worship and Ornaments* (*Alcuin Club Collections*, xxxiii, xxxiv, and xxxviii, 1938–52); id., *Westminster Abbey. Benedictine Monastery and Collegiate Church* [1945]; A. Fox, *Westminster Abbey* [1951]. W. R. Lethaby, 'Medieval Paintings at Westminster' in the *Proceedings of the British Academy*, xiii (1927), pp. 123–51; W. A. Pantin, 'Medieval Westminster' in J. McCann, O.S.B., and C. Cary-Elwes, O.S.B. (edd.), *Ampleforth and its Origins* (1952); pp. 29–52. R. B. Rackham, C.R.-L. E. Tanner in *D.E.C.H.* (ed. 1948), pp. 645–50. Cf. also W. *Dugdale,*Monasticon Anglicanum*, i (ed. 1817), pp. 265–330.

WESTMINSTER ASSEMBLY (1643).

The synod appointed by the Long Parliament to reform the English Church. A bill passed on 15 Oct. 1642 convening a body of divines having failed to receive the Royal Assent, Parliament issued on 12 June 1643 an ordinance to the same effect. The conference consisted of 151 nominated members,—30 lay assessors (named first) and 121 divines. Among the laymen were such notable persons as J. Pym, J. *Selden, Bulstrode Whitelock, and H. Vane. The ecclesiastics were carefully selected from men of widely diverse views. They fell into four groups: (1) *Episcopalians*, a group of four bishops (R. Brownrigg of *Exeter, J. Prideaux of *Worcester, J. *Ussher of *Armagh, and T. Westfield of Bristol) and five D.D.'s (D. Featley, H. *Hammond, R. Holdsworth, G. *Morley, and R. *Sanderson); (2) *Presbyterians*, much the largest group, which included E. *Calamy, E. *Reynolds (later Bp. of *Norwich), A. *Tuckney, W. Twisse, and R. *Vines; (3) a small group of *Independents* of disproportionate influence, through the favour of Oliver *Cromwell and the Army—among them were Thomas Goodwin and Philip Nye; and (4) *Erastians* such as J. *Lightfoot. Out of loyalty to the King the Episcopalians practically never attended the sessions. It should be noted that despite its importance in the history of the Presbyterian Churches, the Assembly was in no sense a creation of Presbyterianism, nor indeed a Church court at all.

It met originally on 1 July 1643 in the Henry VII Chapel of *Westminster Abbey. When the autumn weather set in, it moved to the Jerusalem Chamber, which was thereafter its regular meeting-place. After the adoption of the *Solemn League and Covenant (q.v.), it was increased by five clerical and three lay Commissioners from Scotland. Between 1 July 1643 and 22 Feb. 1649, it held 1163 sessions; but the last mention of the presence of the Scottish Commissioners is on 9 Nov. 1647. Under the Commonwealth meetings continued at very irregular intervals down to 1653, mainly for the trial of ministers. The Assembly was never formally dissolved.

The Assembly began by revising the *Thirty-Nine Articles. But the appearance of the Solemn League and Covenant led to the construction of a wholly new formula, the celebrated *Westminster Confession (q.v.). At the same time the Assembly prepared the Directory of Public *Worship (q.v.) and the two *Westminster Catechisms (q.v.). The proceedings were long delayed by violent controversies between Presbyterians and Independents over the Sacraments and the jurisdiction of Church courts, and between Presbyterians and Erastians over Church censures.

Although only partially and temporarily accepted in England, the documents issued were approved by the Church of Scotland and came into general use throughout the Presbyterian world. In the present constitution of the Church of Scotland they are expressly mentioned as subordinate standards.

A. F. Mitchell, *The Westminster Assembly* (1883); W. Beveridge, *A Short History of Westminster Assembly* (1904); S. W. Carruthers, *The Everyday Work of the Westminster Assembly* (1943).

WESTMINSTER CATECHISMS.

The two Catechisms ('Larger' and 'Shorter') compiled by the *Westminster Assembly. They were completed in the autumn of 1647 and, with slight changes, approved by Parliament on 15 Sept. 1648. Meanwhile the Larger Catechism had been adopted by the General Assembly at Edinburgh on 20 July, the Shorter on 28 July.

The Larger Catechism, partly based on J. *Ussher's *Body of Divinity* (1645), was mainly the work of A. *Tuckney. It is in essence a popular restatement of the teaching of the Westminster Confession. It suffers from being in places unnecessarily elaborate, e.g. in its specification of what is commanded and forbidden in the Ten Commandments.

The Shorter Catechism, which came to fill a much more important place in Presbyterianism, was probably also largely the work of A. Tuckney, who was assisted by John Wallis. It opens with the well-known Question and Answer: 'What is the chief end of man?' 'Man's chief end is to glorify God and to enjoy Him for ever.' Its didactic usefulness is increased by its method, since the answer always embodies the question and forms a sentence complete in itself. It has been in regular use among *Congregationalists and *Baptists as well as Presbyterians.

The Catechisms have often been reprinted. The Shorter, with Latin translation, is in P. *Schaff, *The Creeds of Christendom*, iii (1882), pp. 676–704.

WESTMINSTER CATHEDRAL.

The cathedral of the RC Abp. of Westminster, dedicated to the *Precious Blood of Our Lord Jesus Christ. The building was proposed in 1865, begun in 1895 under Card. H. *Vaughan and opened for his funeral in 1903. It was consecrated by Abp. (later Card.) Francis Bourne in 1910. It was designed by J. F. Bentley (1839–1902) in 'early Christian-Byzantine style' and executed mainly in red brick. The principal features are the spaciousness of the nave, the massive ciborium over

the High Altar, the interior decoration of marble and mosaic (still incomplete), and the domed campanile, 284 ft. high.

W. de L'Hôpital, *Westminster Cathedral and its Architect* (2 vols., 1919). *Westminster Cathedral*, ed. by the Administrator (1930); *A Popular Guide to Westminster Cathedral* (*Catholic Truth Society [1930]). See also Life of H. Vaughan (cited, s.v.) and E. Oldmeadow, *Francis Cardinal Bourne* (2 vols., 1940–4), passim.

WESTMINSTER CONFESSION.

The profession of *Presbyterian faith set forth by the *Westminster Assembly. Originally the Assembly had been directed to revise the *Thirty-Nine Articles of the C of E in a Puritan direction and changes were made with the help of the *Lambeth Articles of 1595 and the *Irish Articles of 1615. But when Art. XV was reached, the *Solemn League and Covenant appeared presupposing uniformity of doctrine between England and Scotland and, under Scottish influence, Parliament ordered the suspension of the revision on 12 Oct. 1643 and the framing of 'a Confession of Faith for the three Kingdoms, according to the Solemn League and Covenant'. The task was entrusted to a large commission; it took 27 months in all and was completed on 4 Dec. 1646. After revision it was finally approved by Parliament on 20 June 1648. Meanwhile the General Assembly at Edinburgh had ratified it on 27 Aug. 1647.

The Confession expounded in 33 chapters all the leading articles of the Christian Faith from the creation of the world to the last judgement. It taught emphatically the Calvinistic doctrine of election, though it recognized freedom of the will and 'the liberty or contingency of second causes' in the Divine decrees. It distinguished the two covenants, that of works made with *Adam and his posterity and that of grace made in Christ with believers, with its offer of free salvation on condition of faith. The distinction between the invisible and the visible Church was upheld. Great stress was laid on the identification of the Jewish Sabbath with the Christian Sunday (*dies dominica*) and the due observance of the Sabbath rest.

The Confession at once established itself as the definitive statement of Presbyterian doctrine in the English-speaking world. It exercised a deep influence on other groups of Calvinists. Several of the 17th cent. *Baptist Confessions are simply adaptations of it.

S. W. Carruthers, *The Westminster Confession of Faith. Being an Account of the Preparation and Printing of its Seven Leading Editions* (Presbyterian Historical Society of England. Extra Publications No. 2 [1937]), with crit. ed. of text, pp. 89–157. Text, with Lat. vers., also pr. in H. B. Smith–P. Schaff (edd.), *The Creeds of the Evangelical Protestant Churches* (1877), pp. 598–673.

WESTON, FRANK (1871–1924),

Anglican Bp. of Zanzibar. After several years' work in slum parishes in England, he joined the *U.M.C.A. in 1898, and was appointed principal of St. Andrew's Training College, Kiungani, in 1901. Here he learned to live among Africans as one of themselves, and to understand their point of view as few English-men have done. In 1908 he was consecrated to the see of Zanzibar. He is chiefly remem-bered for the occasions in which he figured in controversy. Of these the most notable were (1) the *Kikuyu Dispute (1913), and (2) his severance of relations with the Bp. of Hereford (J. *Percival) in 1915, after the appointment of B. H. *Streeter to a canonry at Hereford. In 1920 he largely inspired the appeal for Chris-tian unity put out by the *Lambeth Con-ference, and in the same year appeared his protest against forced labour in Africa, entitled *Serfs of Great Britain*. In 1923 he presided at the Second Anglo-Catholic Congress, where his personality made a great impression. Of his writings the most important is *The One Christ* (1907), an expression of the *Kenotic view of the Incarnation.

H. Maynard Smith, *Frank, Bishop of Zanzibar* (1926). Id. in *D.N.B.* (*1922–1930*), p. 902 f.

WESTPHALIA, Peace of (1648). The treaty terminating the *Thirty Years' War. Strictly it was a pair of treaties concluded by the Empire on 24 Oct. 1648; the one with France at Münster in Westphalia and the other with Sweden and the Protestant states at Osna-brück. Besides many territorial decisions, the *Augsburg Formula of 'cuius regio eius religio' was accepted as the basis of ecclesiastical settlement. The principle was to apply also to the *Calvinists, but with the proviso that in the hereditary dominions of the Hapsburgs the situation on 1 Jan. 1624 (in Württemberg, Baden, and the Palatinate on 1 Jan. 1618) should be regulative. Princes were restrained from changing their religion and the Roman see restricted from interference in religious matters in Germany. These last two provi-sions led to *Innocent X's bull, 'Zelo Domus Dei' (26 Nov. 1648) strongly denouncing the treaty. In the long run its constitutional, territorial, and ecclesiastical changes helped to hasten the dissolution of the Holy Roman Empire.

Text of Treaty of Münster pr. in J. Dumont, *Corps universel diplomatique du droit des gens*, vi (pt. 1; Amster-dam, 1738), pp. 450–61; of that of Osnabrück, ib., pp. 469–490. Treaty of Münster also pr., with introd., in H. Vast *Les Grands Traités du règne de Louis XIV*, i (1893), pp. 1–64. Pope Innocent X's Bull 'Zelo Domus Dei' pr. in the *Bulla-rum, Diplomatum et Privilegiorum Sanctorum Romanorum Pontificum Taurinensis Editio*, x (Turin, 1868), pp. 603–6. Extracts from the treaties repr. in Mirbt, pp. 378–81, and of Innocent's Bull, p. 382 f. (Nos. 518–27 and 529). Eng. tr. of the religious clauses of the Peace and of Innocent's Bull in S. Z. Ehler–J. B. Morrall (edd.), *Church and State Through the Centuries* (1954), pp. 189–98. J. G. von Meiern (ed.), *Acta Pacis Westphalicae Publica oder Westphälische Friedens-Handlungen und Geschichte* (6 vols., Hanover, 1734–6, +Register, 1740). [J. Dumont (ed.)] *Négociations secrètes touchant la paix de Munster et d'Osnaburg: ou Recueil général des préliminaires, instructions, lettres, mémoires* etc. concernant ces négociations depuis leur commencement en 1642 jusqu'à leur conclusion en 1648 (4 vols., The Hague, 1725–6). J. S. Pütter, *Geist des Westphälischen Friedens . . . historisch und systematisch dargestellt* (1795). F. Philippi and others, *Der Westfälische Friede*. Ein Gedenk-buch zur 250. jähr. Wiederkehr des Tages seines Abschlus-ses am 24. Oktober 1648 (1898). F. Kopp–E. Schulte, *Der Westfälische Friede*. Vorgeschichte, Verhandlungen, Folgen (1940). A. Rapisardi Mirabelli, *Le Congrès de Westphalie . . . au point de vue de l'histoire du droit des gens* (Bibliotheca Visseriana, viii; 1929). M. Ritter, 'Das römische Kirchen-recht und der Westfälische Friede' in *H.Z.*, ci (1908), pp.

253–82. J. B. Sägmüller, 'Der Begriff des *exercitium religionis publicum, exercitium religionis privatum* und der *devotio domestica* im Westfälischen Frieden' in *T.Q.*, xc (1908), pp. 255–79. See also works cited under *Thirty Years War*.

WETSTEIN, J. J. See *Wettstein, J. J.*

WETTE, W. M. L. DE. See *De Wette, W. M. L.*

WETTSTEIN, JOHANN JAKOB (1693–1754), NT critic. A native of Basle, where he became a Protestant pastor, he was twice removed from his office on the charge of *Socinianism. From 1733 onwards he was professor at Amsterdam. His edition of the Greek NT (2 vols., 1751–2), which marked a great advance on its predecessors, included in the critical apparatus innumerable important variants, hitherto unrecorded, and also the *sigla* for denoting the MSS. since then in common use. On a visit to England in search of MSS. in 1716, he made the acquaintance of R. *Bentley who gave him considerable encouragement, though a rupture occurred between them a few years later.

C. L. Hulbert-Powell, *J. J. Wetstein* (Church Historical Society, [1938]).

WEYMOUTH NEW TESTAMENT. An English version of the NT, translated from the Greek by R. F. Weymouth (1822–1902), a *Baptist who was for several years headmaster of Mill Hill School, and first published in 1903 under the title *The New Testament in Modern Speech*. It was the fruit of many years' intensive study in textual criticism. Besides the translation, each book is provided with a short introduction, and there are footnotes to the text.

WHARTON, HENRY (1664–95), English medievalist. A native of Worstead in Norfolk, he was educated at Caius College, Cambridge. In 1686–7 he assisted W. *Cave in the com-pilation of his *Historia Literaria*, and in 1688 published several controversial writings, among them *A Treatise on the Celibacy of the Clergy* and *The Enthusiasm of the Church of Rome*, as well as an edition of Reginald *Pecock's *Treatise proving Scripture to be the Rule of Faith*. In the same year he became domestic chaplain to Abp. W. *Sancroft and began the work which made him famous, the *Anglia Sacra*. Though committed by his connexion with Sancroft to the cause of the *Nonjurors he took the oaths in 1689. He thus estranged his former friends without gaining the favour of the new authorities, and his ecclesiastical career thereby came to an end. In 1691 he published the two volumes of his *Anglia Sacra*, which placed him among the founders of English medieval scholarship. They contain a history, down to the Reformation, of the English sees whose cathedrals were served by regulars. The first volume deals with the dioceses and gives editions of medieval chronicles, whereas the second is chiefly a collection of medieval texts bearing on the lives of English bishops. In it are printed for the first time, e.g., *William of Malmesbury's 'Life of St. *Wulfstan' and *John of Salisbury's 'Life of St. *Anselm'. The work, which is still indispensable to medieval studies, was severely criticized by G. *Burnet, who disparaged antiquarian erudition. Among its defects are rather arbitrary abbreviations of the sources and minor inaccuracies, but these do not detract from its importance. A third volume, intended to deal with the cathedrals served by secular clergy, and only partly finished, is inferior to the other two. Many of his unpublished MSS. are preserved in *Lambeth Palace Library.

Fourteen Sermons Preached . . . before William Sancroft . . . in the Years M DCLXXXVIII, M DCLXXXIX. (1697), with life of the author (no pagination); One and Twenty Sermons Preached . . . in the Years M DCLXXXIX, M DCXC (1698). 'Excerta ex Vita MS. Henrici Whartoni, A.M., a Seipso Scripta' printed in G. D'Oyly, The Life of William Sancroft, ii (1821), pp. 103–74. D. C. Douglas, English Scholars (1939), ch. vii, pp. 175–96. W. H. *Hutton in D.N.B., lx (1899), pp. 404–7.

WHATELY, RICHARD (1787–1863), Anglican Abp. of *Dublin. Educated at Oriel College, Oxford, he became successively Fellow of Oriel (1811), vicar of Halesworth (1822), principal of St. Alban Hall, Oxford (1825), Drummond professor of political economy (1829), and Abp. of Dublin (1831). He was one of the best known of the '*Noetics', an anti-*Erastian, and an anti-*Evangelical; and almost certainly the author of Letters on the Church by an Episcopalian (1826), which had considerable influence on J. H. *Newman, for a time his vice-principal at St. Alban Hall. Later Whately became a vigorous opponent of the *Tractarians. His best known writings were his Historic Doubts relative to Napoleon Buonaparte (1819), an attempted reductio ad absurdum of the principles of D. *Hume; his Elements of Logic (1826), over many generations a standard text-book for students; his Elements of Rhetoric (1828); and his Introductory Lectures on Political Economy (1831-2). As Abp. of Dublin, he took an active part in the religious and political life of *Ireland, and did valuable work as a Commissioner of National Education. It was on his advice that Lord John Russell nominated R. D. Hampden (q.v.) to the Regius Professorship of Divinity at Oxford.

E. J. Whately (daughter; ed.), Miscellaneous Remains from the Commonplace Book of Richard Whately (1864). Id., Life and Correspondence of Richard Whately (2 vols., 1866). W. J. Fitzpatrick, Memoirs of Richard Whately . . . with a Glance at his Contemporaries and Times (2 vols., 1864). J. M. Rigg in D.N.B., lx (1899), pp. 423–9.

WHEATLY, CHARLES (1686-1742), English divine. Educated at St. John's College, Oxford, he was elected a Fellow of his college in 1707. He resigned his fellowship in 1713 and held various parochial appointments until his death. He is remembered by his commentary on the BCP, first published in 1710 as The Church of England Man's Companion, or a Rational Illustration of the *Harmony . . . and Usefulness of the Book of Common Prayer* and a standard work until well into the 19th cent. He also wrote The Nicene and Athanasian Creeds (1738).

Fifty Sermons on Several Subjects and Occasions (3 vols., London, 1746), with preface by J. Berriman in vol. i (no pagination); his A Rational Illustration of the Book of Common Prayer and Administration of the Sacraments, ed., with notes, by G. E. Corrie (Cambridge, 1858). E. I. Carlyle in D.N.B., lx (1899), p. 435, s.v.

WHICHCOTE, BENJAMIN (1609 – 83), Provost of King's College, Cambridge. A native of Stoke, Salop, he entered Emmanuel College, Cambridge, in 1628, becoming Fellow in 1633 and tutor in 1634. Ordained deacon and priest simultaneously in 1637, he was appointed Sunday afternoon preacher at Trinity Church, Cambridge, where his preaching met with immediate success. On his marriage (1643) he retired to a college living at North Cadbury, Somerset. The following year, as a result of the Parliamentary reform of the University, he returned as Provost of King's College, but alone among the newly appointed heads of houses avoided subscribing to the *National Covenant. Vice-Chancellor for 1650–1, in 1655 he advised O. *Cromwell on the question of toleration of the Jews. At the *Restoration he was ejected by royal command, but was restored to favour in 1662 on accepting the Act of *Uniformity. From 1662 he held the cure of St. Anne's, Blackfriars, until the church was burnt in 1666. In 1668 he was appointed vicar of St. Lawrence, Jewry; while the church was being rebuilt he preached frequently before the Corporation of London in the Guildhall Chapel.

Whichcote was one of the leading *Cambridge Platonists (q.v.). A sermon preached at the Commencement of 1650 involved him in a controversy with his old tutor and friend, A. *Tuckney. Averse to the pessimistic view of human nature prevalent among the *Puritans, he exalted man as a child of reason. He saw in reason the test of Scripture, maintained that some matters on which good men disagreed were insoluble, and pleaded for freedom of thought; and he was charged at different times with *Latitudinarianism, *Arminianism, and *Socinianism. His works, nearly all posthumous, include Θεοφορούμενα Δόγματα, or Some Select Notions of B. Whichcote (1685), Select Sermons (with preface by the third Earl of Shaftesbury, 1689), Several Discourses (ed. by J. Jeffery 1701) and Moral and Religious Aphorisms (ed. by J. Jeffery, 1703).

Works (4 vols., Aberdeen, 1751), with short life in vol. i, pp. i–viii; selections from his Select Sermons and Aphorisms in E. T. Campagnac (ed.), The Cambridge Platonists (1901), pp. 1–75, with introd., pp. ix–xxvii; his Moral and Religious Aphorisms, ed. S. Salter (London, 1753), with 'Eight Letters of Dr. Antony Tuckney and Dr. Benjamin Whichcote' appended (separate pagination), with introd. preface, pp. i–xl; Aphorisms reprinted (London, 1930), with introd. by W. R.*Inge, pp. iii–x. J. *Tulloch, Rational and Religious Philosophy in England in the Seventeenth Century, ii (1872), ch. ii, pp. 45–116; B. F. *Wescott, 'Benjamin Whichcote' in A. Barry (ed.), Masters in English Theology (1877), pp. 147–173. F. J. Powicke, The Cambridge Platonists. A Study (1926), ch. ii, pp. 50–86. J. B. Mullinger, The University of Cambridge, iii (1911), pp. 296 f., 531 f., 567–70, 589–96 and passim. Id. in D.N.B., lxi (1900), pp. 1–3.

WHISTON, WILLIAM (1667–1752), mathematician and theologian. Educated at Clare Hall, Cambridge, he was appointed chaplain to J. Moore, Bp. of *Norwich (1696), and vicar of Lowestoft (1698). In 1703 he succeeded I. *Newton as Lucasian professor of mathematics at Cambridge. His Arianizing views, however, caused him to be expelled from the university in 1710, and in 1747 he finally deserted the C of E and joined the *General Baptists. He wrote a large number of treatises, many of them of a startlingly paradoxical kind, which include his *New Theory of the Earth* (1696), *Accomplishment of Scripture Prophecies* (1708; in which he affirms that all prophecies have but one meaning), *Primitive Christianity Revived* (4 vols., 1711), *Life of Samuel *Clarke* (1730), and *Primitive New Testament* (1745). He is best remembered now by his translation of *Josephus, with many useful notes and dissertations (1737; very often reprinted).

The principal sources for his life are the *Memoirs of the Life and Writings of Mr. William Whiston . . . written by himself* (1733) and his *An Account of the Convocation's Proceedings with Relation to Mr. Whiston* (1711). L. Stephen in *D.N.B.*, lxi (1900), pp. 10–14, s.v.; G. Crosse in *D.E.C.H.* (1912), p. 629 f.

WHITAKER, WILLIAM (1548–95), *Puritan divine. A nephew of A. *Nowell, he was educated at St. Paul's School, London, and Trinity College, Cambridge, where in 1571 he was elected to a Major Fellowship. In 1580 he became Regius professor of divinity and in 1586 master of St. John's College. A strict *Calvinist, he exercised a wide influence by his devotion to learning and his impartiality. A strong anti-Romanist, he held that the Pope was *antichrist and attacked the writings of R. *Bellarmine and T. *Stapleton. In the last year of his life he was mainly responsible for drafting the *Lambeth Articles, though at one or two points J. *Whitgift softened the extreme Calvinism of Whitaker's original text. His writings include Greek versions of the BCP (1569) and of Nowell's *Larger Catechism* (1573).

Opera Theologica (2 vols., Geneva, 1610), with life [by A. Assheton], in vol. i, pp. 698–704. R. Churton, *The Life of Alexander Nowell* (1809), esp. pp. 325–34; J. B. Mullinger, *The University of Cambridge*, ii (1884), pp. 293, 322–6, 339 f. and passim.

WHITBY, The Synod of (664). (The O. Eng. name was Streanaeshalch). The chief question settled at this synod was the date of Easter (see *Paschal Controversy*), which divided the Christians of Northumbria from those in the South. The former, represented by King Oswy and the bishops St. *Colman and St. *Chad, followed the Irish custom, which claimed to be the custom of St. *John, whereas the latter, led by St. *Wilfrid, had adopted the Roman system. Accounts of the proceedings of the synod given by St. *Bede and Eddius state that, while Colman appealed to the custom of St. John, Wilfrid quoted the authority of St. *Peter and the decisions of

the Council of *Nicaea. The controversy was settled by King Oswy, who decided to follow St. Peter, as being the keeper of the keys of the Kingdom of Heaven. Thus England severed her connexion with the old Irish Church in favour of Rome, and, though the *Celtic Churches still hesitated for some time before accepting the decision, the Synod of Whitby virtually ended the Paschal Controversy in the West.

The principal sources are *Bede, *H.E.*, iii, 25 (cf. notes to ed. C. Plummer, Oxford, 1896, i, pp. xxxix–xli, ii, pp. 146 and 188–92), and Eddius's life of St. Wilfrid, x, ed. J. Raine, *The Historians of the Church of York and its Archbishops*, i (R.S., 1879), pp. 14–16. Hardouin, iii, cols. 993–8; Mansi, xi (Florence, 1765), cols. 67–72; A. W. Haddan–W. *Stubbs (edd.), *Councils and Ecclesiastical Documents Relating to Great Britain and Ireland*, iii (1871), pp. 100–6. W. *Bright, *Chapters of Early English Church History* (1878), pp. 193–200. J. L. G. Meissner, *The Celtic Church in England after the Synod of Whitby* (1929), pp. 7–18 (ch. 2. 'The Synod of Whitby and its Immediate Results'). See also works cited under *Paschal Controversy*.

WHITBY, DANIEL (1638–1726), English divine. Educated at Trinity College, Oxford, of which he was elected a Fellow in 1664, he was appointed in 1668 to a prebendal stall at *Salisbury, and in 1669 became rector of St. Edmund's Church in that city. He gained notoriety for his hostility to Popery, for his desire for reconciliation with the Nonconformists, and for his provocative writings, the best known of which were *The Protestant Reconciler* (1682; subsequently publicly burnt at Oxford) and *Last Thoughts* (1727). This last showed that Whitby was a *Unitarian in his later years. His most considerable work was a *Paraphrase and Commentary on the NT* (2 vols., 1703). He also wrote in defence of B. *Hoadley in the *Bangorian Controversy.

Extracts from Whitby's writings in P. E. More–F. L. Cross (edd.), *Anglicanism. The Thought and Practice of the Church of England, Illustrated from the Religious Literature of the Seventeenth Century* (1935), Nos. 57, 95, 118, 294, pp. 116 f., 221 f., 270–2, and 634 f. A. A. Sykes, 'A Short Account of Dr. Whitby. To which is Added, A Catalogue of his Works' prefixed to ed. 2 of Whitby's *Last Thoughts* (1728), pp. i–xvi. A. Gordon in *D.N.B.*, lxi (1900), pp. 28–30, s.v., with reff.

WHITCHURCH, EDWARD (d. 1561), *Protestant printer. A citizen of London, he became a warm adherent of the Reformed doctrines and in 1537 associated himself with R. *Grafton (q.v.) for circulating *Matthew's Bible (printed at Antwerp). In 1538 he and Grafton gave M. *Coverdale financial assistance in printing his NT at Paris and in 1539 published the *Great Bible at Greyfriars House in London. Seven editions had appeared by 1541, some copies bearing Whitchurch's, others Grafton's name. In 1543, with six other printers, they were imprisoned for Protestantism, but released four weeks later. In the last years of *Henry VIII's reign they continued to print religious books such as *Primers. Under *Edward VI, Whitchurch printed both the First (1549) and Second (1552) Prayer Books.

S. Lee in *D.N.B.*, lxi (1900), p. 30 f., s.v.; E. G. Duff, *A Century of the English Book Trade* (1905), p. 169, s.v. H. R.

Plomer, *A Short History of English Printing, 1476–1900* (1915), pp. 57–9. See also bibls. s.v. 'Grafton' and 'Great Bible'.

WHITE FATHERS (Fr. *Pères Blancs*). The Society of Missionaries of Africa was founded by Abp. Charles Lavigerie (1825–92) at Algiers in 1868. It is composed of secular priests and coadjutor brothers living in community without vows, but bound by solemn oath to lifelong work in the African mission and obedience to their superiors. They wear a white tunic and a mantle or burnous with a rosary round the neck. Their constitutions were approved by the Holy See in 1885 and confirmed in 1908. The White Fathers devote themselves to a thorough four years' preparation of the Africans for baptism and to the subsequent training of converts for trades, agriculture, missionary work, and for the priesthood. They began their missions in Algeria and Tunisia but soon extended them to Central and E. Africa, often meeting with violent opposition. Apart from their missionary achievements the White Fathers have done much for the abolition of slavery, for the improvement of agriculture, and for the scientific exploration of Africa.

T. Frey, *Die Gesellschaft der Missionare von Afrika in ihren 50-jähr. Bestehen* (Trier, 1918). J. Bouniol, W.F., *The White Fathers and their Mission* ([1929]; based on T. Frey, op. cit.). *La Société des Missionnaires d'Afrique (Pères Blancs)* (Les Ordres religieux; 1924); P. Lesourd, *Les Pères Blancs du Cardinal Lavigerie* (Les Grands Ordres monastiques et instituts religieux; 1935). R. Vanlande, *Chez les Pères Blancs* (1928). Heimbucher, ii, 623–30. G. Cottino in *E.C.*, viii (1952), col. 1090 f., s.v. 'Missionari d' Africa'.

WHITE FRIARS. The *Carmelite friars, so called from their white cloaks and *scapulars. The term has been applied, less accurately, to the *Premonstratensians or White Canons.

WHITE LADIES. A name popularly given to the following religious orders, from their white habits: (1) The Sisters of the Presentation of Mary, a teaching order founded at Theuyts, Ardèche, in France in 1796, by Marie Rivier, for the education of young girls. The mother-house is at Saint-Andéol, Ardèche. Since 1853 they have been established also in Canada. (2) The *Magdalens (q.v.). (3) In medieval England the *Cistercian nuns, the designation still surviving here and there in the place-name 'Whiteladies'.

WHITE MONKS. The *Cistercian monks, so named from the colour of their habit, which was of undyed wool.

WHITE SISTERS. (1) The Congregation of the Missionary Sisters of Our Lady of Africa was founded by Abp. C. Lavigerie in 1869 to assist the *White Fathers (q.v.) and was recognized by the Pope in 1909. They have simple perpetual vows, no lay sisters, and devote themselves chiefly to teaching, nursing, and the training of native sisters. They are under the spiritual direction of the White Fathers, who are also responsible for their safety in the missions.

(2) The Congregation of the Daughters of the Holy Ghost, usually called White Sisters from their white habit, was founded at St.-Brieuc in Brittany in 1706. Its chief objects are the education of children and the care of the sick. They spread rapidly esp. during the 19th cent., but were driven from many of their houses in France by the legislation of 1902. They have numerous convents in Belgium, England, and the U.S.A.

(1) Heimbucher, ii, 630–2, with bibl. K. Hofmann in *L.Th.K.*, x (1938), col. 808, with bibl. col. 809, s.v. 'Weisse Väter'; G. Cottino in *E.C.*, viii (1952), col. 1105 f., s.v. 'Missionarie di Nostra Signora d' Africa'. See also works cited s.v. *White Fathers*.
(2) C. Lemercier, *Notice sur la congrégation des Filles du Saint-Esprit, 1706–1850* (Saint-Brieuc, 1888). Heimbucher, ii, 499 f. J. T. Murphy in *C.E.*, vii (1910), p. 417 f., s.v. 'Holy Ghost, Religious Congregations of the'.

WHITE, FRANCIS (*c.* 1564–1638), Bp. of *Ely. Educated at Gonville and Caius College, Cambridge, he was ordained priest in 1588, and after filling several livings was appointed Dean of *Carlisle in 1622. He became bishop successively of Carlisle (1626), *Norwich (1629), and Ely (1631). He was a prominent anti-Papist disputant. In 1617 he published *The Orthodox Faith and Way to the Church* (1617), in answer to a RC treatise entitled *White dyed Black*, and in 1622 he was engaged by *James I to support W. *Laud in presenting the Anglican case in a formal dispute with the Jesuit, 'John *Fisher'. His final works, *A Treatise of the Sabbath Day* (1635), dedicated to Laud, and *An Examination and Confutation of . . . a Briefe Answer to a late Treatise of the Sabbath Day* (1637; the unnamed author of the *Brief Answer* was Richard Byfield, *c.* 1598–1664) were both written to refute the *Sabbatarian tendencies of his time.

Extracts from White's works repr. in P. E. More–F. L. Cross (edd.), *Anglicanism. The Thought and Practice of the Church of England, Illustrated from the Religious Literature of the Seventeenth Century* (1935), pp. 8 f., 46, 58 f., 132–4, 415, 437, 441 f., 514 f., 559, 573 f., 634. A. Gordon in *D.N.B.*, lxi (1900), p. 34 f., s.v., with reff.

WHITE, JOSEPH BLANCO (1775–1841), theological writer. Born in Seville of an Irish RC family, he was ordained to the priesthood in 1800; but, becoming troubled by religious doubts, he came to England in 1810 and later became an Anglican. For a time he was attached to Oriel College, Oxford, where he became intimate with R. *Whately and was well known among the *Tractarians. Later he was again afflicted with doubts and, under the influence of J. *Martineau, became a *Unitarian. His writings include the *Letters from Spain* (1822), *Practical and Internal Evidence against Catholicism* (1825), and *Second Travels of an Irish Gentleman in Search of a Religion* (1833), and the sonnet 'Night and Death'.

J. H. Thom, *The Life of the Rev. J. B. White* (3 vols., 1845).

WHITE, WILLIAM HALE. The author of the writings of 'Mark *Rutherford' (q.v.).

WHITEFIELD, GEORGE (1714–70), *Methodist evangelist. Born at *Gloucester of humble parentage, he was sent as a servitor to Pembroke College, Oxford, where he came under the influence of John and Charles *Wesley. He was ordained deacon in 1736 and followed the Wesleys to Georgia where he founded an orphanage. On returning to England shortly afterwards, primarily to obtain priest's orders, he began large open-air meetings. His fervent and eloquent preaching soon attracted notice and his evangelistic tours, during which he collected large sums for his Georgian orphanage, met with a remarkable response, esp. in South Wales and Scotland. His activities were frowned on by ecclesiastical authority, esp. as his markedly *Calvinist theology appeared less orthodox than that of the Wesleys. In 1739 he began the publication of his *Journal*. In 1741 he set up a chapel at Moorfields, Bristol, and later through the patronage of Selina, Countess of *Huntingdon, opened a Tabernacle in Tottenham Court Road, London. His labours, which included several visits to America, wore down his health and he died a relatively early death. He was the most striking orator of the *Methodist revival, but less successful as an organizer than the Wesleys. His theology was more rigid and made a less general appeal, but his influence in awakening the religious conscience of the 18th cent. went very deep.

His *Journal* and collections of his sermons have frequently been reprinted. Works pr. in 6 vols., London, 1772, with life by J. Gillies prefixed; this life was also issued separately, London, 1772. Other lives by R. Philip (London, 1837), J. R. Andrews (ib., 1864), J. P. Gledstone (ib., 1871), L. Tyerman (2 vols., ib., 1876–7), and A. D. Belden (ib., [1930]). R. Austin, 'Bibliography of the Works of George Whitefield' in *Proceedings of the Wesley Historical Society*, x (1916), pp. 169–84 and 211–23. A. Gordon in *D.N.B.*, lxi (1900), pp. 85–92; G. Croȿe in *D.E.C.H.*, p. 630 f., s.v.

WHITGIFT, JOHN (c. 1530–1604), Abp. of *Canterbury. Educated at Queens' College and Pembroke Hall, Cambridge, he was elected a Fellow of Peterhouse in 1555, ordained in 1560, and became later Lady Margaret (1563) and Regius (1567) professor of divinity, master of Pembroke Hall (1567), master of Trinity College (1570), Dean of *Lincoln (1571), and Bp. of *Worcester (1577). His opposition as master of Trinity and Regius professor to the *Puritan, T. *Cartwright, had brought him to the notice of *Elizabeth, who in 1583 nominated him Abp. of Canterbury in succession to the Puritan, E. *Grindal. His desire for a strong and unified C of E, impervious alike to Papal influence and Puritan views of Church government, was reflected in his 'Six Articles' of 1583. In repressing Puritanism (*Marprelate Tracts, &c.) he made great use of the Ecclesiastical Commission, summoning before it suspects for interrogation on oath. He also vigorously opposed the Puritan attempt of 1584–5 to impose upon the Church a Presbyterian form of government. Though a determined advocate

of episcopacy and ritual uniformity, he was theologically a *Calvinist (*Lambeth Articles of 1595). In his later years he concerned himself with various administrative reforms, e.g. fostering learning among the clergy, abolishing non-residence, and reforming the ecclesiastical courts. He is commemorated by the Whitgift schools and almshouses at Croydon, which he founded and endowed.

Works ed. J. Ayre (*Parker Society, 3 vols., 1851–3), with biographical memoir in vol. iii, pp. v–xxiii. Early life by G. Paule, Controller of his Household (London, 1612). The fullest source, however, is the life by J. *Strype (London, 1718; new ed., 3 vols., Oxford, 1822). D. W. Garrow, *The History and Antiquities of Croydon* (1818), with sketch of the life of John Whitgift appended, pp. 209–336. P. M. Dawley, *John Whitgift and the Reformation* (Hale Lectures; New York, 1954; London, 1955); V. J. K. Brook, *Whitgift and the English Church* (1957). S. Lee in *D.N.B.*, lxi (1900), pp. 129–37; W. H. *Frere in *D.E.C.H.*, p. 630 f., s.v.

WHITSUNDAY. The Feast of the Descent of the Holy Ghost upon the Apostles on the 50th day after Easter (see *Pentecost*). It ranks, after *Easter, as the second festival in the Church. Its celebration at *Jerusalem in the late 4th cent. is described in the 'Peregrinatio *Etheriae'. In the W., the Vigil of Pentecost soon became a secondary date for baptisms with a ceremonial closely resembling that of *Holy Saturday except for the omission of the blessing of the new fire and the candle; the number of the OT lessons in the Roman Missal is six. That the feast itself has been kept with an Octave from early times is shown by the '*Apostolic Constitutions' (5. 20) and the *Gelasian and *Gregorian Sacramentaries, but the following Sunday, now *Trinity Sunday, is not reckoned as the Octave Day. Monday and Tuesday within the Octave rank in the Latin Church as Doubles of the First Class, in the BCP as '*Red Letter days', and Wednesday, Friday, and Saturday are *Ember Days. The liturgical colour of the feast is red, and during Mass throughout the Octave the Sequence, '*Veni Sancte Spiritus', is said and at *Terce the hymn, '*Veni Creator'. In most of the W. Church the Sundays between Whitsunday and Advent are reckoned as 'Sundays after Pentecost', but the C of E, following the *Sarum Use, reckons them from Trinity Sunday, as do also the *Dominicans.

J. A. Jungmann, S.J., 'Pfingstoctav und Kirchenbusse in der römischen Liturgie' in *Miscellanea Liturgica in honorem L. Cuniberti Mohlberg*, i (Bibliotheca Ephemerides Liturgicae, xxii; 1948), pp. 169–82. G. Kretschmar, 'Himmelfahrt und Pfingsten' in *Z.K.G.*, lxvi (1956), pp. 209–53. E. Venables in *D.C.A.*, ii (1880), p. 1618 f., s.v. 'Pentecost'; H. *Leclercq, O.S.B., in *D.A.C.L.*, xiv (pt. 1; 1939), cols. 260–74, s.v. 'Pentecôte'; A. P. Frutaz in *E.C.*, ix (1952), cols. 1156–60, s.v. 'Pentecoste. II. Liturgia'.

WHITTIER, JOHN GREENLEAF (1807–1892), American *Quaker poet. After working as a journalist up to the age of 25, he became the poet-seer of the Anti-Slavery Movement, writing many poems in the cause of liberation, and suffering from mob-violence and political hate. His fervent Christianity, which shone through all his work, was esp. evident in such poems as 'The Crucifixion', 'The Call of the Christian', and 'My Soul and I'. He is the author of several hymns, among them 'Dear Lord and Father of mankind', 'Immortal love for ever full', and 'O Lord and Master of us all'.

Collected ed. of his Works, 7 vols., London, 1888–9; Poetical Works also publd. Cambridge, Mass., 1895, with biog. sketch by H. E. S[cudder], pp. xi–xix, and ed. W. G Horder, London, 1892; ed. 2, ib., 1904. *Selected Poems* (World's Classics, 1913). S. T. Pickard, *Life and Letters of John Greenleaf Whittier* (2 vols., Cambridge, Mass., 1894; London, 1895). Other studies by W. S. Kennedy (Boston, Mass., 1882; also New York, 1892), F. H. Underwood (Boston, 1884), T. W. Higginson ('English Men of Letters', 1902), G. R. Carpenter ('American Men of Letters', Boston, 1904), G. K. Lewis (London, [1913]), and A. Mordell (Boston, 1933). Bibliography by T. F. Currier (Cambridge, Mass., 1937). W. M. Payne in W. P. Trent–J. Erskine–S. P. Sherman–G. van Doren (edd.), *A History of American Literature*, ii (Cambridge, Eng., 1919), pp. 42–54, with good bibl. by F. H. Ristine, pp. 436–51.

WHITTINGHAM, WILLIAM (*c.* 1524–1579), Dean of *Durham. Educated at Brasenose College, Oxford, he was elected a Fellow of All Souls in 1545 and two years later moved to Christ Church. His *Calvinistic views having forced him to flee from England in *Mary's reign, he took a leading part in the organization of the English congregation at Frankfurt, where he supported J. *Knox against R. *Cox, and, on Knox's defeat, followed him to Geneva. Here he succeeded him as minister in 1559, although he had apparently received no ordination of any kind. Returning to England in the following year, he was made Dean of Durham in 1563. His iconoclasm and repeated failures to conform to the BCP led eventually to an attempt by E. *Sandys, Abp. of *York, to deprive him on the ground that he had not been validly ordained, but he died before the proceedings were concluded. His chief literary work was in the field of Biblical translation. In 1557 he published at Geneva an English version of the NT and he also took a leading part in the production of the *Geneva Bible, remaining behind to supervise its completion when most of the translators returned to England on Mary's death. He also rendered into metre a number of Psalms, the Lord's Prayer, and the Decalogue. He was prob. the author of *A Brief Discourse of the Troubles begun at Frankfort*, A.D. 1554 (1574).

A Brief Discourse of the Troubles at Frankfort, repr. from the Blackletter ed. of 1575 (London, 1846), with introd. by J. P[etheram], pp. iii–xiv, also repr. in D. Laing (ed.), *The Works of John Knox*, iv (1855), pp. 9–40, and ed. by E. Arber ('A Christian Library', i; 1907). Contemporary life ed. from MS. by A. *Wood in *Bodleian Library, Oxford (MS Wood E 64, Art. 5) by M. A. Everett Green in *The Camden Miscellany*, vi (1871), pp. 1–40, with other relevant material, pp. 41–6. Brief notes on the question of his ordination in E. Denny, *The English Church and the Ministry of the Reformed Churches* (*Church Historical Society, Tract lvii; 1900), pp. 59–62, with reff. A. F. Polland in *D.N.B.*, lxi (1900), pp. 150–3. S. L. Ollard in *D.E.C.H.* (1912), p. 632 f., s.v.

WHOLE DUTY OF MAN, The. This devotional manual, first published *c.* 1658 and formerly very widely used, contains seventeen discourses, mainly on matters of Christian morals, 'one whereof being read every Lord's Day, the whole may be read over thrice in the year'. The identity of the author is not known with certainty, but among those to whom it has been ascribed are H. *Hammond (who

certainly contributed the prefatory letter signed 'H. H.'), J. *Fell, and (with most probability) R. *Allestree. Its moral standards are exacting, though adapted to life in the world.

WICHERN, JOHANN HINRICH (1808–1881), founder of the German *Innere Mission. A native of Hamburg, he studied theology at Göttingen and Berlin, where he came under the influence of J. A. W. *Neander and F. D. E. *Schleiermacher. After his return to Hamburg he was deeply moved by the neglect from which the children suffered in the poor quarters of the city, and in 1833 founded an institute, the Rauhes Haus, based on the principle of family education, to provide for their spiritual and material needs. Under Wichern's powerful personality and educational gifts the house soon began to expand, and in 1842 he established a training-house of helpers. From 1844 he edited a periodical, *Die Fliegenden Blätter aus dem Rauhen Hause*, which became the central organ of all charitable undertakings in the German Protestant Churches. At his suggestion all these activities were co-ordinated in the central organization of the Innere Mission at the first congress of the Evangelical Churches (*Erster evangelischer Kirchentag*) at *Wittenberg in 1848. In 1857 he was entrusted with the Prussian prison reform, and in 1858 he founded the Johannisstift at Spandau, nr. Berlin, on the model of the Rauhes Haus. In the wars of 1864, 1866, and 1870–1 he and his 'Brothers' organized a service of assistance to the wounded, the Felddiakonie. In 1872 Wichern returned to the Rauhes Haus, where his last years were spent in illness.

Collected writings ed. Johannes Wichern (son)–F. Mahling (6 vols., Hamburg, 1901–8). Diaries of his earlier years ed. M. Gerhardt with title *Der junge Wichern* (1925). Lives by F. Oldenberg (2 vols., Hamburg, 1882–7) and M. Gerhardt (3 vols., ib., 1927–31), M. Hennig, *Das Lebenswerk Wicherns* (ib., 1908). F. J. Leenhardt, *La Mission intérieure et sociale de l'Église d'après Wichern, 1808–1881* [1931]. H. Rahlenbeck in *P.R.E.* (ed. 3), xxi (1908), pp. 219–24; F. Mahling in *R.G.G.* (ed. 2), v (1931), col. 1901 f.

WICLIF, JOHN. See *Wycliffe, John.*

WIDOWS. In NT times widows had an acknowledged claim to the charity of their fellow-Christians (Acts 6. 1). Before long they acquired, like virgins, a recognized status and privileges in the Church, though they do not seem to have been ordained or to have taken specific vows. 1 Tim. 5. 3–16, which contains a detailed account of what was expected of widows, restricted the privileges to those over 60, younger women being recommended to remarry. The early history of the office was closely connected with that of the *Deaconess (q.v.).

J. Mayer (ed.), *Monumenta de Viduis Diaconissis Virginibusque Tractantia* (Florilegium Patristicum, xlii; Bonn, 1938), with bibl. C. H. *Turner, 'Ministries of Women in the Primitive Church. Widow, Deaconess and Virgin in the First Four Christian Centuries', in *The Constructive Quarerly*, vii (1919), pp. 434–59, esp. pp. 435–42 and 457–9; repr. in *Catholic and Apostolic*, ed. H. N. Bate (1931), No. xi, pp. 316–51, esp. pp. 317–28 and 349–51. J. Viteau,

'L'Institution des diacres et des veuves' in *R.H.E.*, xxii (1926), pp. 513–37. K. Pieper in *L.Th.K.*, xii (1938), col. 950 f., s.v. 'Witwen', with further bibl.

WIED, HERMANN VON. See *Hermann of Wied*.

WILBERFORCE, ROBERT ISAAC (1802–1857), *Tractarian divine. The second son of W. *Wilberforce, he was educated at Oriel College, Oxford, where he was elected a Fellow in 1826 and was brought into close association with J. H. *Newman and R. H. *Froude. He gradually acquired an extensive theological knowledge which made him one of the most learned of the Tractarians. In 1841 he was appointed Archdeacon of the East Riding. From *c.* 1843 he was in close personal relations with H. E. *Manning, then rector of Lavington, and carried on with him an extended theological correspondence which was largely concerned with the Roman claims. On 1 Nov. 1854 he was received into the RC Church at Paris. At the time of his death he was preparing for the priesthood. Besides the Life of his father, which he published in conjunction with his brother, Samuel, in 1838, his writings included *The Doctrine of the Incarnation* (1848), *The Doctrine of Holy Baptism* (1849), and *The Doctrine of the Holy Eucharist* (1853).

A. R. Ashwell–Reginald G. Wilberforce, *Life of the Right Reverend Samuel Wilberforce* (3 vols., 1880–2), passim. F. Legge in *D.N.B.*, lxi (1900), pp. 201–4, s.v., with further reff.

WILBERFORCE, SAMUEL (1805–73), successively Bp. of *Oxford and *Winchester. The third son of W. *Wilberforce, he was educated at Oriel College, Oxford, and in 1828 ordained deacon. From 1830 to 1840 he was rector of Brighstone in the Isle of Wight. The repute of his eloquence and pastoral efficiency led to his appointment by the Prince Consort, in 1840, as one of his chaplains, which was the beginning of his influence at court. After holding the living of Alverstoke in Hants from 1840, he was appointed Dean of *Westminster in 1845 and later in the same year Bp. of Oxford. Though at first viewed with suspicion both by Evangelicals and *Tractarians, esp. E. B. *Pusey, he soon gained general confidence by the many reforms he introduced in his diocese. He encouraged the building of churches and the formation of Anglican sisterhoods, and himself founded Cuddesdon Theological College (1854). He also established the system of Lenten missions and interested himself in the education of the poor. The effective methods of pastoral administration adopted in his diocese were widely imitated elsewhere. In 1869 Wilberforce was translated to Winchester. One of his main achievements in his last years was his initiation of the revision of the AV. On 19 July 1873 he was killed by a throw from his horse.

Life by A. R. Ashwell–Reginald G. Wilberforce [son] (3 vols., London, 1880–2), incl. extensive extracts from his diaries and correspondence. Shorter life, based on the above, by R. [G.] Wilberforce (London, 1888). Further lives by G. W. Daniell (London, 1891), R. G. Wilberforce

('Leaders of the Church, 1800–1900', ed. G. W. E. Russell, 1905) and J. C. Hardwick, *Lawn Sleeves. A Short Life of Samuel Wilberforce* (1933). J. W. *Burgon, *Lives of Twelve Good Men*, ii (1888), pp. 1–70 ('Samuel Wilberforce: The Remodeller of the Episcopate'). F. Legge in *D.N.B.*, lxi (1900), pp. 204–8; G. W. E. Russell in *D.E.C.H.*, pp. 633–6, s.v.

WILBERFORCE, WILLIAM (1759–1833), philanthropist and advocate of the abolition of the slave trade. A native of Hull, he was educated at St. John's College, Cambridge. In 1780 he became M.P. for Hull, later for Yorkshire, and formed an intimate friendship with W. Pitt, whose devoted supporter he became. In 1784–5 he travelled on the Continent. Under the influence of his NT reading he was converted to *Evangelicalism and determined to lead henceforth a strictly Christian life. In this purpose he was guided by John Newton, who opposed his wish to take Holy Orders and persuaded him to serve the cause of Christianity in Parliament, a vocation for which he was particularly well fitted by his oratorical gifts. In 1787 he founded a society for the reformation of manners. About the same time, under the influence of T. *Clarkson, he began to interest himself in the slave trade, which he determined to take up in Parliament. In 1797 he settled at Clapham where he became a prominent member of the '*Clapham Sect'. His *Practical View of the Prevailing Religious System of Professed Christians* (1797), a call to take seriously the duties of a Christian, esp. those of repentance and hatred of sin, enjoyed great popularity and established his reputation as the acknowledged leader of the Evangelical party. He contributed generously to the charities of Hannah *More and helped in the foundation of the *Church Missionary Society (1798) and the Bible Society (1803). Throughout these years the abolition of the slave trade continued to be his chief concern, and after many vicissitudes the Bill, which had repeatedly been refused passage in the Lords, finally became law in 1807. Later he supported the movement for the complete abolition of slavery, which was effected by the Emancipation Act of 1833, shortly before his death. In 1813 he defended *Catholic Emancipation; he also advocated the introduction of English missionaries into *India and long championed the cause of *Sunday observance. In 1825 he resigned his seat in Parliament owing to failing health.

W. Wilberforce had four sons and three daughters. For *Robert Isaac Wilberforce* and *Samuel Wilberforce* see preceding entries. HENRY WILLIAM WILBERFORCE (1807–73), his youngest son, was received into the RC Church in 1850. From 1854 to 1863 he edited the *Catholic Standard*.

William Wilberforce's *Family Prayers*, ed. Robert Isaac Wilberforce (son; London, 1834); *Correspondence*, ed. id.–Samuel Wilberforce (sons; ib., 1840); *Private Papers*, ed. A. M. Wilberforce (ib., 1897). The principal authority is the life by Robert Isaac Wilberforce–Samuel Wilberforce (5 vols. bound in 3, London, 1838; condensed ed., ib., 1868). The best modern study is that of R. Coupland (Oxford, 1923). Other lives by J. S. Harford (London, 1864), J. C. Colquhoun (ib., 1866), and J. Stoughton (ib., 1880). L. Stephen in *D.N.B.*, lxi (1900), pp. 208–17.

WILFRID, St. (634–709), Bp. of *York. He was the son of a Northumbrian thegn, and was educated at the monastery of *Lindisfarne. Dissatisfied, however, with the *Celtic way of religious life, he studied the Roman form at *Canterbury and, later, at Rome itself, whither he accompanied St. *Benedict Biscop in 654. Having spent three years at Lyons, where he received the tonsure in the Roman manner, he returned to England and, being made Abbot of *Ripon, introduced the Benedictine Rule. At the Synod of *Whitby (664) he was largely responsible for the victory of the Roman party in the question of dating *Easter. Shortly afterwards he was consecrated Bp. of York at Compiègne by twelve Frankish bishops, to avoid consecration by the Celtic bishops whom he regarded as schismatical. On his return (666), which had been delayed, he found his see occupied by St. *Chad and retired to Ripon, but was put in possession of it by St. *Theodore of Canterbury in 669. When in 678 Theodore divided the diocese of York into four sees without Wilfrid's consent, he departed for Rome to appeal against the high-handed procedure, spending a year on the way preaching in Frisia. Though the synod, assembled by the Pope, declared in his favour, on his return to England he was imprisoned, and later retired to Sussex, where he carried out successful missionary work among the heathen population. Having become reconciled to Theodore, he was once more reinstated in his see, which he held from 686 to 691. When disputes with King Aldfrith compelled him to flee again, the King of Mercia asked him to administer the vacant see of *Lichfield. When, in 703, a synod called by Abp. Brihtwold of Canterbury decreed that he should resign his see of York and retire to Ripon, he went once more to Rome to appeal to the Holy See. Though his claims were completely vindicated, he agreed, on his return, to resign in favour of St. *John of Beverley, contenting himself with the see of *Hexham, and spending the last years of his life in his monastery at Ripon. A great defender of Papal authority, Wilfrid, despite many setbacks, succeeded in bringing England into closer touch with Rome, and in replacing the existing Celtic usages in the N. of England by the Roman liturgy, and Celtic by Benedictine monasticism. Feast day, 12 Oct.

Life by his disciple, Eddius Stephanus of Ripon, ed. J. Raine, *The Historians of the Church of York and its Archbishops*, i (R.S., 1879), pp. 1–103, with introd., pp. xxxi–xxxviii; modern ed., with Eng. tr. and notes, by B. Colgrave (Cambridge, 1927). Later authorities include *Bede, *H.E.*, v, 19, notes to ed. by C. Plummer, ii (Oxford, 1896), pp. 315–29; metrical life ascribed to Frithegode (12th cent.), and life by *Eadmer, with 'Brevilogium Vitae Sancti Wilfridi' also ascribed to Eadmer, printed in J. Raine, op. cit., pp. 105–59, 161–226, and 227–37 respectively, with introd. pp. xxxix–l, and notes on further sources, p. 1 f. B. W. Wells, 'Eddi's Life of Wilfrid' in *E.H.R.*, vi (1891), pp. 535–50. [F. W. *Faber,] 'St. Wilfrid, Bishop of York' in [J. H. *Newman, ed.] *Lives of the English Saints* (London, 1844; ed. 2 by A. W. Hutton, i [1901], pp. 217–449). G. F. Browne, *Theodore and Wilfrith* (1897); J. S. Fletcher, *The Life and Work of St. Wilfrid of Ripon, Apostle of Sussex* (Chichester, 1925); W. H. *Hutton, *St. Wilfrid* (York Minster Historical Tracts, No. 5; 1927). W. *Bright, *Chapters of Early English Church History* (1878), pp. 187–

200, 209–11, 280–308, 367–416, and 432 f. F. M. Stenton, *Anglo-Saxon England* (The Oxford History of England, ii; 1943), pp. 123 f., 132–45. J. Raine in *D.C.B.*, iv (1887), pp. 1179–85.

WILKES, PAGET (1871–1934), Protestant missionary in Japan. The son of an Anglican clergyman, Wilkes was educated at Lincoln College, Oxford, where he associated with the Oxford Inter-Collegiate Christian Union, well known in his day for its evangelistic fervour and missionary zeal. In 1897 he sailed for Japan under the *C.M.S. to work with B. F. Buxton, the C.M.S. pioneer. Here he formed the idea of a Japanese Evangelistic Band (J.E.B.) which, free of ecclesiastical organization, would be directed towards aggressive evangelism and the spread of Scriptural holiness; and in 1903 the J.E.B. was established under the name of the 'One by One Band' of Japan, with its centre at Kobe. Apart from a few visits to England, Wilkes spent all his active life in Japan, pursuing his missionary work with unabating fervour. His best-known works (translated into many languages) are *The Dynamic of Service* (1920), *The Dynamic of Faith* (1921), and *The Dynamic of Redemption* (1923).

M. W. Dunn Pattison (Wilkes's sister), *Ablaze for God: The Life Story of Paget Wilkes* (1936).

WILKINS, DAVID (1685–1745), editor of the 'Concilia'. His parentage was German and his name anglicized from Wilke. After studying at several Continental universities, he became professor of Arabic at Cambridge in 1724. His patron, Abp. W. *Wake, had meanwhile made him Librarian at *Lambeth Palace and in due course secured for him several promotions, including the rectory of Hadleigh, a prebend at *Canterbury, and the archdeaconry of Suffolk. A pioneer in oriental studies and in Anglo-Saxon, Wilkins was a versatile, though by modern standards somewhat inaccurate, scholar. His reputation rests principally upon his *Concilia Magnae Britanniae et Hiberniae* (4 vols., 1737), a monumental collection of documents which remains a standard source work for the British and Irish ecclesiastical councils.

D. C. Douglas, *English Scholars* (1939), pp. 276–84. E. F. Jacob, 'Wilkins's *Concilia* and the Fifteenth Century' in *Transactions of the Royal Historical Society*, 4th Ser., xv (1932), pp. 91–131. J. M. Rigg in *D.N.B.*, lxi (1900), p. 260 f., s.v., with reff.

WILKINS, JOHN (1614–72), Bp. of *Chester. Born at Fawsley, Northants, he studied at New Inn Hall and at Magdalen Hall, Oxford. In 1637 he was appointed Vicar of Fawsley, but soon resigned and held a succession of private chaplaincies. He became increasingly interested in the new scientific movement. In 1638 he published *The Discovery of a World in the Moon*, which argued the moon's habitability; in 1640 followed *A Discourse concerning a New Planet*, maintaining that the earth was a planet. From not later than 1645 he was a regular member of the group which met in London for the furtherance of scientific knowledge

(R. *Boyle's 'Invisible College'). As his sympathies during the Civil War had been with the Parliamentarians, the Visitors made him Warden of Wadham College, Oxford, in 1648. Here his tolerant disposition won warm approval and attracted to Oxford a brilliant group of scientists, including many of his former London associates, which used to meet in Wilkins's rooms in Wadham. In 1659 he was appointed Master of Trinity College, Cambridge, but he was deprived at the Restoration (1660). He was given a succession of benefices, among them the Rectory of Cranford, Middlesex (1660), the Vicarage of St. Lawrence Jewry, London (1662), and the Deanery of the collegiate church of *Ripon (1663). But his chief interests remained the furtherance of science and philosophy; and when the Royal Society received its charter from Charles II (15 July, 1662), Wilkins, who had been largely instrumental in its foundation, became its first secretary. In 1668 he became Bp. of Chester, where he advocated the toleration of dissenters. Wilkins was a strong upholder of natural theology. He held that it was the conflicting contentions of fanatics and sceptics which were the main cause of unbelief. His writings include *Mathematical Magick, or the Wonders that may be performed by Mechanical Geometry* (1648), *A Discourse concerning the Gift of Prayer* (1649), *An Essay towards a real Character and a Philosophical Language* (1668), and *On the Principles and Duties of Natural Religion* (1678; posthumous).

P. A. Wright Henderson, *The Life and Times of John Wilkins* (1910). F. Sanders in *D.N.B.*, lxi (1900), pp. 264–7.

WILLEHAD, St. (d. 789), Bp. of Bremen. A native of Northumbria, he was probably educated at *York. Apparently inspired by the examples of St. *Boniface and St. *Willibrord, he set out with the approval of King Alhred and a Northumbrian synod for missionary work in Frisia between 765 and 774 and for a time preached at Dockum. In 780 *Charlemagne sent him to preach to the Saxons at Wigmodia near the North Sea; but shortly afterwards his work was brought to an end by an insurrection under the Saxon chief, Widukind, in 782. After a journey to Rome, he returned for a time to Willibrord's abbey of Echternach, where he devoted himself to copying MSS. Later, when Charlemagne had restored peace, Willehad resumed his activities at Wigmodia. In 787 he was consecrated Bishop at Worms and took up his residence at Bremen where he built a cathedral (dedicated to St. Peter, 1 Nov. 789). A few days later he succumbed to a fever. Feast day, 8 Nov.

The principal source is a life written prob. between 838 and 860 by a cleric of Bremen (commonly, but apparently erroneously, attributed to St. *Anskar); best ed. in *AA.SS.*, Nov. III (1910), pp. 842–6; Book of Miracles by St. Anskar, ib., pp. 847–51, with valuable introd. by A. Poncelet, S.J., ib., pp. 835–42. O. H. May (ed.), *Regesten der Erzbischöfe von Bremen*, i, Lieferung 1 (Veröffentlichungen der Historischen Kommission für Hannover, Oldenburg, Braunschweig, Schaumburg-Lippe und Bremen, xi; 1928), pp. 1–4. Modern lives by E. Wulf (Breslau, 1889) and A. Tappehorn

(Dülmen, 1901). G. H. Klippel–A. Hauck in *P.R.E.* (ed. 3), xxi (1908), pp. 302–4, s.v. In English there is an article by J. Gommack in *D.C.B.*, iv (1887), p. 1186 f., s.v.

WILLIAM OF AUVERGNE (c. 1180–1249), also 'William of *Paris', French Scholastic philosopher and theologian. In 1223 he became a Canon of *Notre-Dame, and in 1228 Bp. of Paris. He was a protector of the *Mendicant Orders, an adversary of pluralism, and an influential personality at the court of St. *Louis. His prolific writings mainly form a vast philosophico-theological encyclopaedia, 'Magisterium Divinale' (between 1223 and 1240), consisting of 'De Trinitate', 'De Universo', 'De Anima', 'Cur Deus Homo', 'De Fide et Legibus', 'De Sacramentis', and 'De Virtutibus'. William drew esp. on *Aristotelian material, then available in the commentaries of *Avicebron and *Avicenna, which he used, however, with considerable freedom and severity. He largely prepared the way for later Scholasticism by teaching a moderate form of *Realism, being among the first Schoolmen to recognize a real distinction between essence and existence, but his efforts to combine *Neo-Platonism with Aristotelian ideas did not always issue in a coherent synthesis. He strongly opposed the superstitions, esp. on the subject of astronomy, rife among his contemporaries.

Collected ed. of his Works publd. at Nuremberg, 2 vols. 1496; also ed. J. D. Trajanun (Venice, 2 vols., 1591); the most complete ed. is that of J. B. Le Feron (anon., 2 vols., Orléans, 1674). His treatise *De Bono et Malo* was first ed. by J. R. O'Donnell, C.S.B., in *Medieval Studies*, viii (1946), pp. 245–99. The *De Immortalitate Animae*, an anonymous work prob. wrongly ascribed to him, ed.G. Bülow (B.G.P.M., ii, Hft. 3; 1897). N. Valois, *Guillaume d' Auvergne . . .* Sa vie et ses ouvrages (1880). M. Baumgartner, *Die Erkenntnislehre des Wilhelm von Auvergne* (B.G.P.M., ii, Hft. 1; 1893). A. Masnovo, *Da Guglielmo d' Auvergne a S. Tomaso d' Aquino* (3 vols., 1930–45). J. Kramp, 'Des Wilhelm von Auvergne "Magisterium Divinale"' in *Gregorianum*, i (1920), pp. 538–616; ii (1921), pp. 42–103 and 174–95, incl. text. E. *Gilson, 'La Notion d'existence chez Guillaume d'Auvergne' in *Archives d'Histoire doctrinale et littéraire du Moyen-Age*, xv for 1946 (1942), pp. 55–91; P. Glorieux, 'Le Tractatus Novus De Poenitentia de Guillaume d'Auvergne' in *Miscellanea Moralia in Honorem Arthur Janssen*, ii (Bibliothecæ Ephemeridum Theologicarum Lovaniensium, Ser. I, iii [1949]), pp. 551–65. Überweg, ii, 363–6, with bibl. p. 730 f. P. Vernet in *D.T.C.*, vi (1920), cols. 1967–76, s.v. 'Guillaume d'Auvergne', with bibl.

WILLIAM OF AUXERRE (d. 1231), Scholastic theologian. At one time Archdeacon of Beauvais, he later taught at *Paris. He became a member of the Commission appointed by *Gregory IX in 1231 to examine and amend the physical treatises of *Aristotle, the reading of which had been unreservedly forbidden by the university of Paris in 1210. He is himself important as one of the first to make use of the doctrines of the newly discovered Aristotle, esp. in his chief work, the 'Summa Aurea'. This, though still influenced by the 'Sentences' of *Peter Lombard and accepting the validity of the *Ontological Argument soon to be rejected, showed much originality and, in its turn, influenced John of Treviso, one of the first Dominican theologians.

The *Summa Aurea* was publd. at Paris, 1500 and 1518, and Venice, 1591; his other works remain unpubld. P. Glorieux, *Répertoire des maîtres en théologie de Paris au XIII* siècle, i (1933), p. 293 f. C. Ottaviano, *Guglielmo d' Auxerre* (d. 1231). La vita, le opere, il pensiero (Rome [1930]). P. Mandonnet, O.P., 'Date de la mort de Guillaume d'Auxerre (3 Nov. 1231)' in *Archives d'Histoire doctrinale et littéraire du Moyen-Age*, vii (1935), pp. 39–46. Überweg, ii, 363, with bibl. p. 730. S. Vanni Rovighi in *E.C.*, vi (1951), col. 1253, s.v. 'Guglielmo d' Auxerre', with further bibl.

WILLIAM OF CHAMPEAUX (*c.* 1070–1121), Scholastic philosopher.

After studying under *Anselm of Laon, and (probably) hearing *Roscellinus at Compiègne, he began to teach in the cathedral schools of Paris (1095), whence he was driven (1108) by *Abelard's ridicule of his exaggerated *realism. In retirement at the (then) priory of Saint-Victor, he appears to have modified his extreme doctrines, and by his lectures there to have laid the foundations of the *Victorine school. In 1112 he became Bp. of Châlons. In his last years he seems to have abandoned the distinctive tenets of realism altogether, though without elaborating any significant philosophical alternative.

Some of William of Champeaux's writings in J. P. Migne, *PL*, clxiii, 1039–72. G. Lefèvre, *Les Variations de Guillaume de Champeaux et la question des universaux.* Étude suivie de documents originaux (Travaux et Mémoires de l'Université de Lille, vi, No. 20; 1898; mainly texts). E. Michaud, *Guillaume de Champeaux et les écoles de Paris aux XII* siècle (1867). H. Weisweiler, S.J., 'L'École d'Anselme de Laon et de Guillaume de Champeaux. Nouveaux documents' in *R.T.A.M.*, iv (1932), pp. 237–69 and 371–91, with reff. to earlier litt.; id., 'Le Recueil des sentences "Deus de cuius Principio et Fine Tacetur" et son remaniement', ib., v (1933), pp. 245–74. Id., *Das Schrifttum der Schule Anselms von Laon und Wilhelms von Champeaux in deutschen Bibliotheken* (B.G.P.M., xxxiii, Hftt. 1–2; 1936), incl. a number of texts. Überweg, ii, 209–11, with bibl. p. 701 f. H. Weisweiler, S.J., in *L.Th.K.*, x (1938), col. 894 f., s.v. 'Wilhelm v. Champeaux', with further bibl.

WILLIAM OF CONCHES (*c.* 1080–*c.* 1154), medieval philosopher.

He was a pupil of *Bernard of Chartres, whose efforts to encourage the study of the profane sciences and literature in the interests of a Christian humanism he sought to further. His writings, of which his 'Philosophia Mundi' and his 'Dragmaticon' became the most popular, deal mainly with natural philosophy. The former treatise was attacked by *William of St.-Thierry for its supposed *Modalistic view of the Trinity. William of Conches' other writings include glosses on Priscian's 'Institutiones Grammaticae', *Plato's 'Timaeus', Macrobius's 'In Somnium Scipionis', and *Boethius's 'Consolatio Philosophiae'. A work on ethics, 'Moralium Dogma Philosophorum', has also been attributed to him.

The only ed. of the 'Dragmaticon' is that of G. Gratarolus publd. under the title *Dialogus de Substantiis Physicis . . .* confectus a Willelmo Aneponymo . . . [and other works] (Strassburg, 1567), pp. 1–312. The 'Philosophia Mundi' is pr. among the works of *Bede in *PL*, xc, 1127–78, and among those of *Honorius of Autun, ib., clxxi, 39–102. Part of the text of his gloss on Boethius was ed. C. Jourdain in *Notices et extraits des manuscrits de la Bibliothèque Impériale*, xx (pt. 2; 1862), pp. 40–82; J. M. Parent, O.P., *La Doctrine de la création dans l'École de Chartres* (Publications de l'Institut d'Études Médiévales d'Ottawa, viii; 1938), pp. 115–77, incl. further extracts of the text of the gloss on Boethius, pp. 124–36, and of that on the 'Timaeus', pp. 142–77. The 'Moralium Dogma Philosophorum' is pr. among the works of *Hildebert of Lavardin in J. P. Migne,

PL, clxxi, 1007–56; modern ed., attributing it to William of Conches, by J. Holmberg (Arbeten utgivna met Understöd av Vilhelm Ekmans Universitetsfond, Uppsala, 1929). R. L. Poole, *Illustrations of the History of Political thought in the Departments of Theology and Ecclesiastical Politics* (1884), pp. 346–59 (Excursus VI on the Writings of William of Conches). L. Thorndike, *A History of Magic and Experimental Science during the first Thirteen Centuries of Our Era*, ii (New York, 1923), pp. 50–65; M. *Grabmann, *Handschriftliche Forschungen und Mitteilungen zum Schrifttum des Wilhelm von Conches und zu Bearbeitungen seiner naturwissenschaftlichen Werke* (*Sb.* (Bayr.), 1935, Hft. 10); H. Flatten, *Die Philosophie des Wilhelm von Conches* (Koblenz, 1929); T. Gregory, *Anima Mundi.* La filosofia di Guglielmo di Conches e la Scuola di Chartres (Pubblicazioni dell' Istituto di Filosofia dell' Università di Roma, iii; 1955). L. Thorndike, 'More Manuscripts of the *Dragmaticon* and *Philosophia* of William of Conches' in *Speculum*, xx (1945), pp. 84–7. A. Vernet, 'Un Remaniement de la *Philosophia* de Guillaume de Conches' in *Scriptorium*, i (1946–7), pp. 243–59. M.D. Chenu, 'Nature ou histoire? Une controverse exégétique sur la création au XIIe siècle' in *Archives d'Histoire doctrinale et littéraire du Moyen-Age*, xx (for 1953; 1954), pp. 25–30. The authorship of the 'Moralium Dogma Philosophorum' is still much disputed. Its attribution to William of Conches is upheld by P. Delhaye, 'Une Adaptation du *De Officiis* au XIIe siècle. Le *Moralium Dogma Philosophorum*', in *R.T.A.M.*, xvi (1949), pp. 227–58, xvii (1950), pp. 5–28, and id., *Gauthier de Châtillon est-il l'auteur du* Moralium Dogma? (Analecta Medievalia Namurcensia, iii; [1953]); it is rejected by J. R. Williams, 'The Authorship of the *Moralium Dogma Philosophorum*' in *Speculum*, vi (1931), pp. 392–411, by P. Glorieux, 'Le *Moralium Dogma Philosophorum* et son auteur' in *R.T.A.M.*, xv (1948), pp. 361–366, by R. A. Gauthier, O.P., 'Pour l'attribution à Gauthier de Châtillon du *Moralium Dogma Philosophorum*' in *Revue du Moyen-Age latin*, vii (1951 pp. 19–64, and id., 'Les Deux Récensions du *Moralium Dogma Philosophorum*' ib., ix (1953 [publd. 1956]), pp. 171–260. The attribution to William of Conches of a 'Tertia Philosophia' partly pr. by C. Ottaviano, *Un brano inedito della "Philosophia" di Guglielmo di Conches* (Collezione di Testi Filosofici inediti e rari, i, Naples, 1935), pp. 19–52, has been disproved by T. Gregory, 'Sull' attribuzione a Guglielmo di Conches di un rimaneggiamento della *Philosophia Mundi*' in *Giornale critico della Filosofia italiana*, xxx (1951), pp. 119–25. Überweg, ii, 237 f., with bibl. p. 704.

WILLIAM OF MALMESBURY (*c.* 1080–*c.* 1143), the chief English historian of his generation.

He appears to have spent most of his life at the monastery at *Malmesbury, where he was offered, but declined, the abbacy in 1140. His work, though credulous and often careless in its chronology, is not without literary merits. His two most important books were his 'Gesta Regum Anglorum' (1120) and his 'Gesta Pontificum Anglorum' (1125), which, as their titles imply, dealt respectively with the secular and ecclesiastical history of England. They were considerably revised both by William himself and, after his death, by others. William also wrote several theological works, including a treatise on 'The Miracles of the Virgin' and an abridged edition of the 'De Ecclesiasticis Officiis' of *Amalarius of Metz.

Most of his Works, collected from various edd., in J. P. Migne, *PL*, clxxix, 945–1774, with fragments also pr. ib., cxxvii, 375–84. Crit. edd. of his *De Gestis Pontificum Anglorum* by N. E. S. A. Hamilton (R.S., 1870); of his *Vita Sancti Dunstani* in W. *Stubbs (ed.), *Memorials of Saint Dunstan* (ib., 1874), pp. 250–324, with introd., pp. xxxv–xxxvii; of his *De Gestis Regum Anglorum* by id. (2 vols., ib., 1887–9), with introd. prefaces in vol. i, pp. xi–xclvii, and vol. ii, pp. xv–cxlii, with reff.; Eng. tr. of last by J. A. Giles ('Bohn's Antiquarian Library', 1866); of his *Vita Wulstani* by R. R. Darlington (first full ed., Camden Society, 3rd Series, xl; 1928]; Eng. tr. by J. H. F. Peile (Oxford, 1934). Modern Eng. tr. of his work 'On the Antiquity of the Church of *Glastonbury', by H. F. Scott Stokes (Glastonbury, 1932).

WILLIAM OF MOERBEKE (c. 1215–86), philosopher. He was the most important of the translators of *Aristotle into Latin in the Middle Ages. A Flemish *Dominican, he was *penitentiary at the Apostolic See under Popes Clement IV (1265–8) and Gregory X (1271–6), and in 1278 became Abp. of *Corinth. With his translation c. 1260 of Aristotle's 'Politics' from the Greek, he embarked on a series of editions and versions of ancient Greek writings, incl. works of the Aristotelian commentators, Alexander of Aphrodisias and Simplicius, as well as of Proclus and Hero of Alexandria. The autograph of some of his translations survives in a Vatican MS. (Cod. Ottob. lat. 1850). He was a close personal friend of St. *Thomas Aquinas.

Some of his trr. of Aristotle were publd. in the 16th cent.; Quétif-Échard, i, 388–90, with list of edd. to date; P. Glorieux, *Répertoire des maîtres en théologie de Paris au XIIIe siècle*, i (1933), pp. 119–22, for MSS. and edd. of works; much of his work is still unpubld. M. *Grabmann, *Guglielmo di Moerbeke, O.P., il traduttore delle opere di Aristotele* (Miscellanea Historiae Pontificiae, vol. xi, Collectionis totius N. 20; 1946). L. Minio-Paluello, 'Guglielmo di Moerbeke, traduttore della *Poetica* d' Aristoteli (1278)' in *Rivista di Filosofia neo-scolastica*, xxxix (1947), pp. 1–17; id., 'Henri Aristippe, Guillaume de Moerbeke et les traductions latines médiévales des "Météorologiques" et du "De Generatione et Corruptione" d'Aristote' in *Revue philosophique de Louvain*, xlv (1947), pp. 206–35. Überweg, ii, 348 f., with bibl. p. 728.

WILLIAM OF NORWICH, St. (1132–44), supposed victim of a Jewish ritual murder. A tanner's apprentice at *Norwich, he was enticed from home on Monday in Holy Week, 1144, and, on Holy Saturday six days later, his body found with marks of violence in a neighbouring wood. Acc. to Thomas of Monmouth, a monk of Norwich and the only authority for the legend, William had been crucified and murdered by the Jews during the Passover. This story was substantiated by a converted Jew, Theobald, who asserted that, acc. to Jewish religious tradition, a Christian must be sacrificed every year to obtain the deliverance of the people. This is the first known case of the blood accusation against the Jews; but as the authorities took no action, the account is open to much suspicion.

The cult of William of Norwich dates from the translation of his body from the chapter-house of the monks, where it had been buried, to the cathedral (1151) amidst a wave of religious enthusiasm. Many visions and miracles were reported to have taken place at his tomb, and throughout the Middle Ages he enjoyed great popularity. Feast day at Norwich, 26 Mar.; commemoration elsewhere, 25 Mar.

The Life by Thomas of Monmouth was ed., with Eng. tr., full introd., and notes, by A. Jessop-M. R. James (Cambridge, 1896). John Capgrave's version of the Legend, which depends on Thomas of Monmouth, is repr. in *AA.SS.*, Mar. (1668), p. 590 f. R. Webster in *C.E.*, xv (1912), p. 635 f., s.v.

WILLIAM OF OCCAM (c. 1300–c. 1349), *Nominalist philosopher, 'Doctor Invincibilis'. A native of Ockham in Surrey, William early entered the *Franciscan Order and studied and taught at Oxford. He never became a 'magister', but remained an 'inceptor' (hence 'Venerabilis Inceptor'), prob. owing to the accusation of teaching dangerous doctrines by John Lutterell, the chancellor of the university. After he had completed his 'Commentaries on the Sentences', he was summoned to *Avignon to give an account of his teaching, and while there he became interested in the controversy on poverty then agitating the Franciscans. Taking the side of the *Spirituals against Pope *John XXII, he fled from Avignon to Louis of Bavaria in 1328, in whose service he remained till 1349. C. 1330 he wrote his 'Opus nonaginta dierum', a violent attack against the Pope on the question of poverty, and in 1331 he was sentenced to expulsion from his order and perpetual imprisonment, having been excommunicated since 1328. During the next years other writings against the Pope and in favour of the Imperial policy followed, among them the 'Compendium Errorum Johannis Papae XXII' (c. 1334–8), 'Dialogus super Dignitate Papali et Regia' (c. 1338–42), and 'Tractatus de Imperatorum et Pontificum Potestate' (c. 1347). It seems that, towards the end of his life, he took steps to be reconciled to the Church.

William of Occam was a vigorous, critical, and independent thinker, and the principal advocate of *Nominalism in the 14th cent. One of his main principles, usually known as 'Occam's razor', was that beings should not be multiplied without necessity ('entia non sunt multiplicanda praeter necessitatem'). He denied all reality to *universals, which, acc. to him, have existence only in the thinking mind and not in individual things. Hence science had to do not with things but with concepts, and words ('voces') conveying these concepts. As only individual things existed, the normal means of acquiring knowledge was not abstraction, but intuition; while the subjective character of intuition and the merely notional, not real, character of science led ultimately to agnosticism. Thus Occam denied the possibility of proving either the existence or the attributes of God and held that the distinction between the latter was merely nominal. He taught an extreme form of *Augustinian and *Scotist doctrines, maintaining that the Divine will was the cause of all things and its own rule, i.e. that God did not will things because they were good, but that they were good because He willed them.

Occam's theories, though never officially condemned by Rome, were at first proscribed at Paris, where, however, he later found his most convinced adherents such as John *Buridan, Peter *d'Ailly, and John *Gerson. In separating faith from reason and confining to faith such truths as the being and attributes of God, he prepared the way for the Reformers. M. *Luther esp. was much influenced by his teaching. His political theories played an important part in the development of the Conciliar Movement of the 14th and 15th cents. He advocated a radical separation of the Church from the world, denied the Pope all temporal authority, and conceded large powers to the laity and their representatives. His ideal may be described as a modified Papal monarchy combined with a system of national Churches.

Many of his philosophical treatises were frequently printed in the 15th and 16th centt., but some have remained unpublished and many (esp. his philosophical writings) are not available in modern edd. Crit. ed. of his *Opera Politica* by J. G. Sikes and others (Manchester, 1940 ff.). There are also modern edd. of his *De Imperatorum et Pontificum Potestate* by C. K. Brampton (Oxford, 1927); of his *Epistola ad Fratres Minores* by id. (ib., 1929); of his *De Sacramento Altaris*, with Eng. tr., by T. B. Birch (Burlington, Ia., 1930); of his *Breviloquium de Potestate Papae* by L. Baudry (Études de Philosophie médiévale, xxiv; 1937); of his *Breviloquium de Principatu Tyrannico* by R. Scholtz (Schriften des Reichsinstituts für ältere deutsche Geschichtskunde, viii; 1944); of his *Tractatus de Praedestinatione et de Praescientia Des et de Futuris Contingentibus* by P. Boehner, O.F.M. (Franciscan Institute Publications, ii; 1945); of his *Summa Logicae* by id. (ib., Text Series, ii, 1951 ff.); M. *Grabmann (ed.), *Quaestio de Universali secundum Viam et Doctrinam Guilelmi de Ockham . . . ex Cod. Vatic. Palat. 998* (Opuscula et Textus Historiam Ecclesiae eiusque Vitam atque Doctrinam Illustrantia, Series Scholastica, x; 1930); the *Tractatus de Principiis Theologiae* attributed to William of Ockham, ed. L. Baudry (Études de Philosophie médiévale, xxiii; 1936); the *Tractatus de Successivis*, also attributed to him, ed. P. Boehner, O.F.M. (Franciscan Institute Publications, i; 1944). S. U. Zuidema, *De Philosophie van Occam in zijn Commentar op de Sententien* (2 vols., Hilversum, 1936), with extensive extracts. P. Boehner, O.F.M., 'The Text Tradition of Ockham's *Ordinatio*' in *The New Scholasticism*, xvi (1942), pp. 203–41; id., 'The Notitia Intuitiva of Non-Existents according to William of Ockham, with a critical Study of the Text of Ockham's Reportatio and a revised edition of Rep. II. Q. 14–15' in *Traditio*, i. (1943), pp. 223–75; id., 'The Metaphysics of William of Ockham' in *The Review of Metaphysics*, i, No. 4 (1948), pp. 59–86, all with extracts. Eng. tr. of extracts from the *Quodlibeta* in R. McKeon, *Selections from Medieval Philosophers*, ii (1931), pp. 360–421, with introd. pp. 351–9. S. C. Tornay, *Ockham Studies and Selections* (La Salle, Ill., 1938). N. Abbagnano, *Guglielmo di Ockham* (Lanciano, 1931); L. Baudry, *Guillaume d'Occam* (Études de Philosophie médiévale, xxxix, &c., 1949 ff.), with good bibl. C. Basoli, *Guglielmo d' Occam* (Biblioteca di Cultura, l; 1953). E. A. Moody, *The Logic of William of Ockham* (1935; uncritical). G. Giacon, S.J., *Guglielmo di Occam* Pubblicazione dell' Università Cattolica del S. Cuore [Milan], ser. 1, xxxiv; 2 vols. 1941). A. Hamman, O.F.M., *La Doctrine de l'Église et de l'État chez Occam* (Études de Science religieuse, i; 1942). G. de Lagarde, *La Naissance de l'esprit laïque au déclin du moyen-âge*, iv–vi (1942–6). R. Guelly, *Philosophie et théologie chez Guillaume d'Ockham* (Louvain, 1947). G. Martin, *Wilhelm von Ockham*. Untersuchungen zur Ontologie der Ordnungen (1949). *Wilhelm Ockham (1349–1949)*. Aufsätze su seiner Philosophie und Theologie (Franziskanische Studien, xxxii; 1950), with bibl. for the period 1919–49 by V. Heynck, O.F.M., pp. 164–83. Überweg, ii, 571–83, with bibl. p. 781 f.; É. *Gilson, *History of Christian Philosophy in the Middle Ages* (1954), pp. 489–99. P. Vignaux in *D.T.C.*, xi (pt. 1; 1931), cols. 733–84, s.v. 'Nominalisme II. Le Nominalisme du XIVe siècle'; É. Amann, ib., cols. 864–904, s.v. 'Occam', with bibl.

WILLIAM OF ST.-THIERRY (*c.* 1085–*c.* 1148), Scholastic philosopher. Of noble descent, he was born at Liége and educated at *Reims at the *Benedictine house of St.-Nicasius, which he afterwards entered. In 1119 he was elected abbot of St.-Thierry, near Reims, but left it in 1135 to enter as a simple monk the newly founded *Cistercian monastery of Signy in the forest of the Ardennes. Although drawn to the contemplative life, he devoted himself to theological study. He was a close friend of St. *Bernard, to whom he first pointed out in a letter the defects in *Abelard's views on the *Trinity and *Redemption, which he afterwards attacked in his

Disputatio adversus Petrum Abaelardum. His writings, both ascetical and didactic, were remarkable for their wide knowledge of the Bible and the Fathers; they were mainly directed to a defence of the traditional Catholic position. Besides admirable commentaries on the *Song of Songs, the Ep. to the *Romans and other Scriptures, they include treatises *De Natura et Dignitate Amoris, De Contemplando Deo* (attributed to St. Bernard), *De Natura Corporis et Animae, De Sacramento Altaris* (dedicated to St. Bernard), and *Speculum Fidei*. The famous *Epistola ad Fratres de Monte Dei de Vita Solitaria* has often, prob. correctly, been attributed to him. He planned a life of St. Bernard, but never completed it.

Opera ed. B. Tissier, Ord. Cist., *Bibliotheca Patrum Cisterciensium*, iv (Bonnefontaine, 1662), pp. 1–237; repr. in J. P. Migne, *PL*, clxxx, 201–726; other works among those of St. Bernard, ib., clxxxii, 531–3, and clxxxiv, 307–436. Modern ed., with Fr. tr., of his *Meditativae Orationes* by M. M. Davy (Bibliothèque des Textes Philosophiques; 1934), and of the *Epistola ad Fratres de Monte dei* by id. (Études de Philosophie médiévale, xxix; 2 vols., 1940); Eng. tr. of this last by W. Shewring, ed. J. McCann, O.S.B., 1930); modern ed., with Fr. tr., of his *Speculum Fidei* by J. M. Déchanet, O.S.B. (Bibliothèque de Spiritualité médiévale; 1946). Life by an anonymous author (d. 1148), ed. A. Poncelet, S.J., 'Vie ancienne de Guillaume de Saint-Thierry' in *Mélanges Godefroid Kurth*, i (1908), pp. 85–96. F. Clément, O.S.B., in *Histoire littéraire de la France*, xii (1763), pp. 312–33. H. Kutter, *Wilhelm von St. Thierry. Ein Repräsentant der mittelalterlichen Frömmigkeit* (1898). A. Adam, *Guillaume de Saint-Thierry*. Sa vie, et ses œuvres (Lyons thesis; Bourg, 1923). J. M. Béchanet, O.S.B., 'Aux Sources de la Spiritualité de Guillaume de Saint Thierry' in *Collectanea Ordinis Cisterciensium Reformatorum*, v (1938), pp. 187–98, 262–78; id., *Guillaume de Saint-Thierry. L'homme et son œuvre* (Bibliothèque Médiévale; 1942). L. Bouyer, Cong. Orat., *La Spiritualité de Cîteaux* (1955; Eng. tr. 1958), chs. iv and v. Überweg ii, 257 f., with bibl. p. 708.

WILLIAM OF TYRE (*c.* 1130–*c.* 1185), Abp. of Tyre, chronicler. He was born in Palestine, prob. of European (poss. Italian) parents of the merchant class, ordained priest before 1161 and studied in Europe before 1163. After returning to Tyre, he was appointed Archdeacon of Tyre in 1167 by Amaury, king of Jerusalem (1163–74), with an enhanced stipend on condition that he wrote the official 'History' of the reign ('Gesta Amaurici'). In 1168 he was sent on a diplomatic mission to *Constantinople and in 1169 summoned to *Rome to answer charges of an obscure nature preferred by his Archbishop. He was appointed tutor to Amaury's son, Baldwin (later Baldwin IV), in 1170 and Chancellor in 1174. In May 1175 he was consecrated Abp. of Tyre. In the next few years he took an important part in government. He led the ecclesiastical delegation from Jerusalem to the *Lateran Council of 1179, where he obtained some restriction of the independence of military orders from the local hierarchy, and was entrusted by *Alexander III with a mission to Constantinople in connexion with the union of the East and West. On his return to Palestine (1180) dynastic changes excluded him from power. He continued, and prob. in 1182 revised, his 'History', adding the prologue in 1184.

William of Tyre's *Historia Rerum in Partibus Transmarinis Gestarum*, comprising the 'Gesta

Regum' (begun *c.* 1170) and the 'Gesta Amaurici', covers the period from 1095 (Preaching of First *Crusade) to 1184. It is the primary authority from 1127 (where Fulcher of Chartres ends), and from *c.* 1144 is a contemporary record. Although the chronology is at times confused, the work is marked by insight, tolerance, impartiality and the careful sifting of evidence from a wide range of sources, as well as by the clear delineation of the physical and mental features of the characters portrayed. Unlike most medieval chronicles, it is arranged under topics, not chronologically. It was translated into French in the 12th or 13th cent., and in this form had a wide circulation. Another work by William of Tyre, the 'Gesta Orientalium Principum', partly based on the Arabic chronicle of Said-ibn-Batrik (d. 940), Patr. of Alexandria, has been lost.

Lat. text of History first printed at Basle, 1549; repr· from ed. of J. Bongars (Hanover, 1611) in J. P. Migne, *PL*, cci, 200–892; Lat. text, with old Fr. tr. [ed. A. Beugnot–A. Prévost] in *Recueil des historiens des croisades*. Historiens occidentaux, i (Paris, 2 pts., 1844); Eng. tr., with notes and full bibl., by E. A. Babcock–A. C. Krey (2 vols., 'Records of Civilization', xxxv; 1943), with introd., vol. i, pp. 3–49; 13th cent. Fr. version, ed. P. Paris (2 vols., Paris, 1879). H. Prutz, 'Studien über Wilhelm von Tyrus' in *N.A.*, viii (1883), pp. 93–132. A. C. Krey, 'William of Tyre. The Making of an Historian in the Middle Ages' in *Speculum*, xvi (1941), pp. 149–66. F. Lundgreen, *Wilhelm von Tyrus und der Templerorden* (Historische Studien, Hft. xcvii; 1911); M. Salloch, *Die lateinische Fortsetzung Wilhelms von Tyrus* (Berlin Diss.; 1934). See also works cited under *Crusades*.

WILLIAM OF WAYNFLETE (*c.* 1395–1486), Bp. of *Winchester. Probably educated at Winchester College and New College, Oxford, in 1426 he was ordained priest and also appointed master of St. Mary Magdalen Hospital, nr. Winchester. He was made provost of the newly founded Eton College by *Henry VI in 1443. On Henry's recommendation he succeeded Cardinal H. *Beaufort as Bp. of Winchester in 1447, and in 1448 obtained licence for founding a hall at Oxford, dedicated to St. Mary Magdalen, in order to foster the study of theology and philosophy; in 1457 it was refounded as Magdalen College. As a moderate Lancastrian and a favourite of the King, he took an increasingly prominent part in public affairs. He treated with Jack Cade in 1450, and made terms with the Yorkists in 1452. In 1456 Henry appointed him Chancellor, and in the next year he was assessor in the trial of Bp. R. *Pecock. He resigned the Chancellorship in 1460 and soon after acquiesced in the accession of Edward IV, receiving the royal pardon in 1466, in 1469, and again in 1471, after renewed support of Henry VI. Thenceforward he was frequently at court and finished building Eton College and Magdalen.

There is a short panegyrical life by J. Budden (Oxford, 1602; repr. by W. Bales (ed.), *Vitae Selectorum Aliquot Virorum qui Doctrina, Dignitate aut Pietate Inclaruere* (London, 1681), pp. 51–89); some further information added by P. *Heylin in *Memorial of Bishop Waynflete*, ed. J. R. *Bloxam (Caxton; Society, 1851). Fuller modern life by R. Chandler (London, 1811). I. S. Leadham in *D.N.B.*, lx (1899), pp. 85–9, s.v. 'Waynflete'; A. F. Leach in *D.E.C.H.*, p. 619 f., also s.v. 'Waynflete'.

WILLIAM OF WYKEHAM (1324–1404), Bp. of *Winchester. He was born of a poor family at Wickham, Hants, and educated at Winchester. He passed *c.* 1343 from the service of the Constable of Winchester Castle into that of Edward III, who appointed him chaplain and rector of Irstead, Norfolk, in 1349. In 1356 he became clerk of the royal works at Henley and Easthampstead and surveyor of the works at Windsor. He was also responsible for the erection of Queenborough Castle in the Isle of Sheppey. Although not priested until 1362, between 1357 and 1363 he was presented to a large number of benefices, mostly without cure of souls. In 1364 he became Keeper of the Privy Seal. Elected Bp. of Winchester in 1366, he was consecrated in 1367 and became Chancellor in the same year. Being blamed for the disasters of the French war, he was driven from office during an attack of anti-clericalism in 1371. He devoted himself to the organization of his diocese, the reform of abuses, esp. in religious houses, and the plans for his future academic foundations. In 1376, owing to the hostility of John of Gaunt, he was accused in Parliament of malversation. Although found guilty on only one minor count, he was deprived of the temporalities of his see and also expelled from court. Although restored to favour before the death of Edward III and declared guiltless by Richard II in 1377, he took little further interest in politics. As a member of the commission of regency appointed in 1386 and as Chancellor from 1389 to 1391, he endeavoured to exercise a moderating influence both on the lords appellant and the King. He also restrained the persecutions of the *Lollards by Abp. *Chichele, though he had little sympathy with J. *Wycliffe's teaching.

At Oxford he founded a college of 100 members dedicated to St. Mary, but soon known as New College, for which he obtained a royal and papal charter of foundation in 1379 (formally opened, 1386). At Winchester he established a school for 70 poor scholars to feed his Oxford foundation (Papal bull, 1378; royal charter, 1382). This college, which was the first independent and self-governing school in the country, was opened in 1394.

His episcopal Register, ed. T. F. Kirby (2 vols., Hampshire Record Society, 1896–9). G. H. Moberly, *Life of William of Wykeham* (1887), with two brief lives written shortly after his death, the one prob. by Dr. Thomas Aylward, one of his executors, the other perh. by Robert Heete (d. 1422), pp. 286–92 and 293–308 respectively. [T. Martin,] *Historica Descriptio Complectens Vitam ac Res Gestas Beatissimi Viri Guilliemi Wicami* (London, 1597). R. Lowth, *The Life of William of Wykeham* (1758; short supplement, 1759). M. E. C. Walcott, *William of Wykeham and his Colleges* (1852), esp. 'The Life of William of Wykeham', pp. 3–100. G. C. Heseltine, *William of Wykeham. A Commentary* (1932), with bibl. J. Tait in *D.N.B.*, lxiii (1900), pp. 225–231; A. F. Leach in *D.E.C.H.*, pp. 659–61, both s.v. 'Wykeham'.

WILLIAM OF YORK, St. (d. 1154), Abp. of *York. William Fitzherbert, of noble birth, was a chaplain of King Stephen and by 1138 (prob. by 1130) Canon and Treasurer of York Minster. Elected Abp. of York by a majority of the Chapter in 1142, he received the temporalities of the see from the king, but, being accused of simony by the *Cistercians, was refused consecration by *Theobald, Abp. of *Canterbury. Both sides appealed to Innocent II, who, in 1143, decided that William might be consecrated if he was cleared by the oath of himself and the Dean of York. Prob. consecrated by *Henry of Blois in 1143, he ruled his diocese conscientiously, but failed to obtain from Card. Hincmar the *pallium which Lucius II sent to him in 1145 before the Pope's death. Forced to go to Rome in 1147, he sold some of the treasures of York for his expenses. Prob. under the influence of St. *Bernard, *Eugenius III suspended him from the exercise of his episcopal functions until the Dean of York (now Bp. of *Durham) cleared him in person, having previously done so by proxy. After William's relatives had attacked the abbey of *Fountains, where Henry Murdac, the rival candidate, was abbot, William was deposed by the Council of *Reims in 1147. Taking refuge with Henry of Blois, he lived in great austerity at *Winchester until the death of Eugenius in 1153, when he appealed for restoration. On the death of Henry Murdac in the same year, Anastasius IV restored him and gave him the pallium. As he entered York in 1154, the bridge collapsed, but the victims escaped uninjured, supposedly through his sanctity and prayers. He promised restitution to Fountains and was respected in his diocese. He died a month after his return, possibly by poison. Buried in York Minster, he was regarded as a martyr and miracles were reported at his tomb. He was canonized by *Honorius III in 1227; his relics were translated to a shrine behind the High Altar in 1284. The St. William window in York Minster was erected to his honour in 1421. Feast day, 8 June; that of his translation, 8 Jan., until 1478 when it was transferred to the first Sunday after *Epiphany. His cult remained local.

The earliest sources, besides the letters of St. Bernard (q.v. for edd.), are the contemporary accounts by William of Newburg, *Historia Rerum Anglicarum* (ed. R. Howlett, i, R.S., 1884, pp. 55–7 and 79–81) and (up to 1153) John of Hexham's continuation of Symeon of Durham's *Historia Regum* (*Symeonis Monachi Opera Omnia*, ed. T. Arnold, ii, R.S., 1885, pp. 306 f., 311, 313–21). An anonymous life, preserved in a 13th cent. MS. in the Harleian collection (2, fols. 76–88), is pr. in J. Raine, *Historians of the Church of York and its Archbishops*, ii (R.S., 1886), pp. 270–91, with introd. p. xviii f.; the account in the chronicle attributed to Thomas Stubbs (14th cent.), pr. ib., pp. 388–97, is mainly based on the anonymous life; additions to Hugh the Chanter are pr. ib., pp. 220–7; also an account of certain miracles 'out of a table in the Revestry in the Cathedral Church of York' are ed. from a Bodleian MS., ib., pp. 531–80. R. L. Poole, 'The Appointment and Deprivation of St. William, Archbishop of York' in *E.H.R.*, xlv (1930), pp. 273–81; [M.] D. Knowles, O.S.B., 'The Case of Saint William of York' in *The Cambridge Historical Journal*, v (1935–37), pp. 162–77 and 212–14, with bibl.; C. H. Talbot, 'New Documents in the Case of Saint William of York', ib., x (1950–2), pp. 1–15; A. Morey, 'Canonist Evidence in the Case of St. William of York', ib., p. 352 f. T. F. Tout in *D.N.B.*, xix (1889), pp. 173–6, s.v. 'Fitzherbert, William'.

WILLIAMS, CHARLES WALTER STANSBY (1886–1945), poet and theological writer. Educated at *St. Albans and at University College, London, he worked from

1908 until his death in the London publishing business of the Oxford University Press. After some early poetry and plays, of which he later came to think poorly, he began to publish novels, largely devoted to supernatural themes, among them *War in Heaven* (1930), *Descent into Hell* (1937) and *All Hallows' Eve* (1944); and also a play, *Thomas Cranmer of Canterbury*. Of his theological writings prob. the most significant was *The Descent of the Dove* (1939), an unconventional and penetrating study of the Church as governed by the activity of the Holy Spirit in history. His poetic achievement culminated in his two volumes on the Arthurian theme, *Taliessin through Logres* (1938) and *The Region of the Summer Stars* (1944), in which he employed an original and highly personal technique to interpret the inter-relation of romantic and theological ideas. Both in London and later in Oxford (in 1939–45) Williams by his life and writings did much, like his fellow-Anglicans, T. S. *Eliot and C. S. Lewis (b. 1898), to commend Christianity in a Catholic and sacramental form to many who would have been unmoved by conventional apologetic.

Williams's unfinished prose work 'The Figure of Arthur' was edited, with a commentary on his Arthurian poems, by C. S. Lewis and publd. as *Arthurian Torso* (1948). *Essays Presented to Charles Williams*, by D. Sayers and others, with preface by C. S. Lewis (1947). Selected essays ed. with biogr. and critical introd. by Anne Ridler (London, 1958). *Collected Plays*, with introd. by J. Heath-Stubbs (1963). G. W. S. Hopkins in *D.N.B., 1941–1950*, p. 958 f., s.v.

WILLIAMS, ISAAC (1802–65), *Tractarian poet and theologian. He was educated at Harrow and Trinity College, Oxford, where he was drawn into the Tractarian Movement through the influence of J. *Keble. He was ordained priest in 1831, became tutor of Trinity College in 1832 and dean in the next year, and about the same time curate to J. H. *Newman at St. Mary's. Besides contributing poetry to the *Lyra Apostolica* (1836) he wrote the famous Tract 80 on 'Reserve in Communicating Religious Knowledge', which lost him the election to the chair of poetry (1842). The defeat caused him to withdraw from Oxford and spend the rest of his life in retirement, occupied chiefly with writing sermons and poetry. Among his best-known poetical writings are *The Cathedral* (1838), interpreting Gothic architecture as a symbol of Christian doctrine, and *The Baptistery* (1842), containing an attack on the RC Church. He also wrote a *Devotional Commentary on the Gospel Narrative* (8 vols., 1869–70).

The Autobiography of Isaac Williams, ed. Sir G. Prevost (1892). W. P. Courtney in *D.N.B.*, lxi (1900), pp. 408–11.

WILLIAMS, JOHN (1582–1650), Abp. of *York. Descended from an ancient Welsh family, he was educated at St. John's College, Cambridge, where he was elected Fellow in 1603. Through the patronage of *James I and Chancellor Ellesmere, he received a large accumulation of benefices, including the Bpric. of *Lincoln (1621), and in addition the Lord Keepership. His accommodating and intriguing character occasioned the dislike of *Charles I and W. *Laud, leading to heavy fines in 1637 and 1639 in the Star Chamber. During the Long Parliament Williams headed a party of compromise in the Lords, and recovering royal favour, was translated to York in 1641. He proved an assiduous royalist throughout the Civil War, but was allowed to spend his last years in retirement in Wales.

J. E. B. Mayor (ed.), 'Letters of Archbishop Williams, with documents relating to him' in *Antiquarian Communications*; Being Papers Presented at the Meetings of the Cambridge Antiquarian Society, ii (1864), pp. 25–66, iii (1879), pp. 61–106; B. H. Beedham (ed.), 'The Unpublished Correspondence between Archbishop Williams and the Marquis of Oxford' in *Archaeologia Cambrensis*, Ser. 3, xv (1869), pp. 305–43. J. Hacket, *Scrinia Reserata*. A Memorial Offered to the Deservings of John Williams (1693). Life by A. Philips (Cambridge, 1700). R. D. Roberts, *Mitre and Musket*. John Williams, Lord Keeper, Archbishop of York, 1582–1650 (1938), with bibl. S. R. Gardiner in *D.N.B.*, lxi (1900), pp. 414–20.

WILLIAMS, JOHN (1796–1839), missionary of the *L.M.S. Born in London, after a commercial education he was accepted in 1816 by the L.M.S., which had chosen the Pacific Isles for its earliest work. In 1817 he sailed for Eimeo, one of the Society Islands, near Tahiti, and in 1818, for Huahine, where he opened a chapel and also published a code of laws. In 1822 he went further afield, visiting the Cook Islands and translating portions of the Bible into the Raratongan language. His sphere of activity also embraced the Friendly Islands. On 20 Nov. 1839 he landed at Dillon's Bay, Erromanga, to be promptly killed and eaten by the natives in retaliation for cruelties once inflicted on them by some English sailors. He is chiefly notable for the burst of missionary enthusiasm that the news of his death aroused in England. A succession of ships of the name *John Williams* have been employed furthering the evangelization of the Pacific Islands.

There is much autobiographical material in his *A Narrative of Missionary Enterprises in the South Sea Islands* (1837). E. Prout, *Memoirs of the Life of the Rev. John Williams* (1843). Other lives by J. J. Ellis (London [1890]), C. Northcott (ib., 1939), and E. Prater (ib., 1947). E. I. Carlyle in *D.N.B.*, lxi (1900), pp. 423–5.

WILLIAMS, NORMAN POWELL (1883–1943), Anglican theologian. Educated at *Durham School and at *Christ Church, Oxford, he was elected a Fellow of Magdalen College in 1906. In 1909 he was ordained priest. From 1909 to 1927 he was Chaplain-Fellow of Exeter College, and from 1927 until his death Lady Margaret Prof. of Divinity and Canon of Christ Church. A leading Anglo-Catholic theologian, he expounded his main positions in his contributions to *Essays Catholic and Critical* ('The Origins of the Sacraments', 1927), *Northern Catholicism* ('The Theology of the Catholic Revival', 1933), and *The Study of Theology* ('What is Theology?', 1939). Among his principal works were *The Ideas of the Fall and of Original Sin* (1927; *Bampton Lectures for 1924) and *The Grace of God* (1930).

E. W. Kemp, *N. P. Williams* (1954; memoir, with sermons). Id. in *D.N.B.*, 1941–1950, p. 959 f., s.v.

WILLIAMS, ROGER (c. 1604–83), champion of religious toleration. Educated at Pembroke College, Cambridge, and apparently ordained in the C of E, he sailed for N. America in 1630 in search of religious liberty. When he discovered that restrictions on religious freedom existed also at Boston, he set up a schismatic Church. He soon found himself in conflict with the civil powers, and in 1635 was ordered to leave Massachusetts and took refuge with the Indians who dwelt beyond the confines of the state, where he founded a settlement to which he gave the name 'Providence' (1636). In 1639 he established there the first Baptist church in the colonies. In 1643 he came back to England to try to secure a title for the new colony, and in the following year his friend, Sir Henry *Vane, procured him the desired charter, and Williams returned. While in England he published anonymously his vigorous pamphlet in defence of religious liberty, *The Bloody Tenent of Persecution* (1644). The constitution of his colony (later 'Rhode Island') included wide religious latitude, and when the *Quakers came to America in 1656 Williams granted them political toleration, though he sharply attacked their doctrines. He was the friend of the American Indians, whose language he learned.

Lives by O. S. Straus (New York, 1894), E. J. Carpenter (New York, 1909), A. B. Strickland (Boston, Mass. [c. 1919]), Emily Easton (ib., 1930), J. E. Ernst (New York, 1932), and S. H. Brockunier (New York, 1940). J. E. Ernst, *The Political Thought of Roger Williams* (University of Washington Publications in Language and Literature, vi. 1, 1929). S. H. Brockunier in *Dict. Amer. Biog.*, xx (1936), pp. 286–9.

WILLIAMS, ROWLAND (1817–70), Anglican scholar. He was educated at Eton and King's College, Cambridge, of which he became a Fellow in 1839. Ordained priest in 1843, he was appointed tutor at King's College, and, in 1850, vice-principal and professor of Hebrew at St. David's College, Lampeter. In 1856 he published his most important work, *Christianity and Hinduism*. In 1860 Williams contributed an article dealing with Biblical criticism to *Essays and Reviews*, which caused him to be prosecuted for heterodoxy by the Bp. of Salisbury (W. K. *Hamilton). The Court of *Arches having sentenced him to one year's suspension, the sentence was annulled by the Privy Council in 1864. Having left Lampeter in 1862, he retired to the living of Broad Chalke, nr. Salisbury.

Life and Letters of Rowland Williams, D.D., ed. by his widow (2 vols., 1874). Id. in *D.N.B.*, lxi (1900), pp. 450–3.

WILLIBALD, St. (700–86), Bp. of Eichstätt. He was related through his mother to St. *Boniface. After education at an otherwise unknown monastery at Waltham in Hants, he made a pilgrimage to Rome in 722 with his father, St. Richard, who died on the way at Lucca, and his brother, St. Winnebald (Wynbald). In 724 he set out from Rome for the East (Sicily, Cyprus, Palestine, Tyre, *Constantinople), where he met with much courteous treatment from the Moslems.

He eventually arrived back at *Monte Cassino in 730, where he spent the next ten years in retirement. In 740 he was again in Rome whence Gregory III sent him to Germany. Boniface ordained him priest (741) and shortly afterwards Bp. of Eichstätt (742). Before 750, with the assistance of Winnebald, who had in the meantime been an active missionary in Thuringia, he founded a double monastery at Heidenheim in Württemberg, of which his sister, St. *Walburga (q.v.), became Abbess after Winnebald's death. He continued until his death actively consolidating the Church in Franconia. His body still lies in the cathedral of Eichstätt. Feast day, 7 July.

St. Willibald's life of St. Boniface is pr. in the collections of the early lives of St. Boniface, cited s.v.; there is an Eng. tr. by G. W. Robinson (Harvard Transactions, Cambridge, Mass., 1916). St. Willibald's *Vita* is contained in the 'Hodoeporicon', an early and reliable history of his travels, written by a nun of Heidenheim, who was a relative of St. Willibald; text, with introd., and other material, in *AA.SS.*, Jul. II (1731), pp. 485–519; better ed. O. Holder-Egger in *M.G.H.*, Scriptores, xv (pt. 1; 1887), pp. 86–106; Eng. tr. by [W. R. B.] Brownlow (Palestine Pilgrims' Text Society, 1891). F. Heidingsfelder (ed.), *Die Regesten der Bischöfe von Eichstätt* (Veröffentlichungen der Gesellschaft für Fränkische Geschichte, VI Reihe, 1915 ff.), pp. 1–15 [1915]. W. Grothe, *Der heilige Richard und seine Kinder* (Berlin diss., 1908). B. Bischoff, 'Wer ist die Nonne von Heidenheim?' in *Studien und Mitteilungen zur Geschichte des Benediktiner-Ordens*, xlix (1931), p. 387 f. [the nun's name was Hugeburc, concealed under a cryptogram in Clm. 1086]. M. Coens, 'Légende et miracles du roi S. Richard' in *Anal. Boll.*, xlix (1931), pp. 353–84 (text of *Vita Sancti Richardi*, pp. 385–97; but the introd. contains information and valuable texts on St. Willibald). A. M. Cooke in *D.N.B.*, lxii (1900), p. 12 f., s.v.; A. Hauck in *P.R.E.* (ed. 3), xxi (1908), pp. 338–40, s.v.; F. Heidingsfelder in *L.Th.K.*, x (1938), col. 918 f., s.v.

WILLIBRORD, St. (658–739), 'Apostle of Frisia'. A native of Northumbria, he was educated by the monks of *Ripon under the direction of St. *Wilfrid. In 678 he went to the Irish abbey of Rathmelsigi (probably Mellifont, Co. Louth), where he remained for 12 years and was ordained priest. In 690, with about a dozen companions, he made his way as a missionary to W. Frisia. In 693, on a visit to Rome, he secured Papal support for his mission, and on a second visit, in 695, was consecrated Abp. of the Frisians by Pope *Sergius. On his return *Pepin granted him a seat for his cathedral just outside Utrecht, and in 698 he founded the monastery of Echternach in Luxembourg which became an important missionary centre. In 714 he was temporarily driven from Utrecht by Duke Radbod but despite this and other difficulties Willibrord continued his mission work with success, receiving at one stage the co-operation of St. *Boniface and making his way as far as *Denmark, Heligoland, and Thuringia. Feast day, 7 Nov.

The Society of St. Willibrord, founded *c.* 1910, exists to promote closer relations between the C of E and the *Old Catholic Churches.

Prose and metrical lives by *Alcuin pr. in *AA.SS.*, Nov.III (1910), pp. 435–57, with other primary material, pp. 458–500, and excellent introd. by A. Poncelet, S.J., pp. 414–35, incl. reff. to earlier works; prose life of Alcuin also ed. id. in *M.G.H.*, Scriptores Rerum Merovingicarum, vii (pt. 1; 1913), pp. 81–141. 'Miracula' also ed. W. Levison in *M.G.H.*, Scriptores, xxx (pt. 2; 1934), pp. 1368–71, with further reff. A. Grieve, *Willibrord, Missionary in the*

Netherlands, 691–737 (1923), with English tr. of Alcuin's prose life, pp. 97–126. G. H. Verbist, *Saint Willibrord, apôtre des Pays-Bas et fondateur d'Echternach* (Université de Louvain. Recueil des Travaux publiés par les membres des Conférences d'Histoire et de Philologie, Sér. 2, lix; 1939). Further lives by M. A. Erens, O.Praem. (Tongerloo, 1939), and C. Wampach (Luxembourg, 1953). Facsimile ed of *The Calendar of St. Willibrord*, ed. H. A. Wilson (H.B.S., lv; 1918).

WILMART, ANDRÉ (1876–1941), *Patristic scholar. A native of Orléans, he studied under P. *Batiffol, with whom he published the *Tractatus Origenis* (1900). In 1901 he entered the *Benedictine Order at *Solesmes and was ordained priest in 1906. His demonstration (1906) that the *Tractatus* were the work of *Gregory of Elvira helped to establish his reputation. From now on he contributed constantly to the *Revue Bénédictine*. His main interests were Latin patristics (esp. the Carolingian epoch) and also Latin (esp. *Gallican) liturgies, here stimulated by his friendship with E. *Bishop. His longer works include *L'Ancien Cantatorium de l'église de Strasbourg* (1928), an edition of twelve sermons of St. *Augustine in the *Miscellanea Agostiniana* (vol. i, 1930), and *Auteurs spirituels et textes dévots du moyen-age latin* (1932). In the field of liturgy special importance attaches to his discovery that the letters attributed to St. *Germanus, hitherto a primary authority for the Gallican rite, were spurious, and to his edition of the *Bobbio Missal (1924).

J. B. Odier–L. Brou, O.S.B.–A. Vernet, *Bibliographie sommaire des travaux du père André Wilmart* (Sussidi Eruditi, v; 1953), with biogr. introd. pp. 7–10, docc. on his life pp. 13–27, and list of obituary notices p. 10.

WILSNACK. A former place of pilgrimage nr. *Wittenberg. After a fire in the church of Wilsnack in 1383 three consecrated hosts were said to have been found unharmed, but marked with drops of blood. The alleged miracle, followed by striking answers to prayer and other extraordinary events, soon drew crowds of pilgrims to the spot, which made of the small village a prosperous town. Though frequently suspected of fraud, e.g. by J. *Huss (1405) and *Nicholas of Cusa (1451), the pilgrimage was encouraged by *Eugenius IV (1447) and *Nicholas V (1453), and continued to flourish until, in 1552, Wilsnack became Protestant and the miraculous hosts were burned by Joachim Ellefeld, an Evangelical preacher.

E. Breest, 'Das Wunderblut von Wilsnack, 1383–1552. Quellenmässige Darstellung seiner Geschichte' in *Märkische Forschungen*, xvi (1881), pp. 193–248. B. Hennig, 'Kurfürst Friedrich II und das Wunderblut zu Wilsnack' in *Forschungen zur Brandenburgischen und Preussischen Geschichte*, xix (pt. 2; 1906), pp. 73–104. G. Wentz in *Germania Sacra* herausg. von Kaiser-Wilhelm-Institut für deutsche Geschichte, i (pt. 2; 1933), pp. 116–19, with full bibl. p. 7 f. G. Kawerau in *P.R.E.*, xxi (1908), pp. 346–50, s.v.

WILSON, THOMAS (1663–1755), Bp. of *Sodor and Man. Born at Burton, Cheshire, he was educated at Trinity College, *Dublin, for the medical profession. After ordination as deacon in 1686, he became curate to his uncle at Newchurch Kenyon, Lancs. (1687), and chaplain to the ninth Earl of Derby (1692). In 1697, after refusing a valuable plurality, he was persuaded by the Earl of Derby to accept the see of Sodor and Man. He was consecrated in 1698, installed in St. German's cathedral, Peel, and, taking up his residence at Kirkmichael, held the bishopric for the rest of his long life. He promptly set himself to raise the standards of spiritual life and pastoral efficiency in the island, and was also active as church-builder, farmer and founder of public libraries under the scheme of T. *Bray. His assiduous administration of Church discipline, based on his Ecclesiastical Constitutions of 1704, which inflicted public penance for slander, perjury, immorality, and other offences, drew him into acrimonious legal disputes, notably during the governorship of Alexander Horne (1713–23), on whose wife Wilson had imposed penance for slander. In 1722 he suspended his archdeacon, R. Horrobin, for heresy and on Horrobin's appeal to the governor, Wilson was convicted and imprisoned for a time. When in 1724 the case was finally decided in his favour, Wilson was offered, but declined, the see of *Exeter in compensation. Theologically he had many affinities with the *Nonjurors. His devotional writings, esp. his *Sacra Privata* (posthumous, ed. C. Cruttwell, 1781), long enjoyed a wide circulation; and his *Principles and Duties of Christianity* (projected 1699, first printed 1707; 'the Manx Catechism') was the first book printed in Manx. Many of his sermons were also published.

He was commemorated in the Isle of Man by the 'Bishop Wilson Theological College' (closed, 1943) at Kirkmichael.

Works ed. C. Cruttwell (2 vols., London, 1781), with life by id., vol. i, pp. iii–xcvi; also in L.A.C.T. (7 vols., bound in 8, 1847–63), with life by J. *Keble, vol. i (pts. 1 and 2). H. Stowell, *The Life of . . . Thomas Wilson* (1819). A. Gordon in *D.N.B.*, lxii (1900), pp. 248–51.

WINCHELSEA, ROBERT OF (d. 1313), Abp. of *Canterbury. He studied arts at Paris, where he became master and rector of the university, and later theology at Oxford, where he was chancellor in 1288. He was appointed Archdeacon of Essex in 1283, and elected Abp. of Canterbury in 1292, but, owing to the vacancy of the Papal chair, not confirmed by Rome till 1294. An energetic upholder of ecclesiastical rights, he soon became involved in a struggle with Edward I, chiefly on the subject of taxation of the clergy, forbidden by *Boniface VIII's bull '*Clericis laicos' of 1296. His refusal to contribute towards the expenses of the French war led to the temporary confiscation of his property in 1297 and won him praise from the Pope. His strong hostility to the King's Treasurer, Walter Langton, Bp. of *Lichfield, caused further deterioration in his relations with Edward; but the King revenged himself on Winchelsea when, in 1305, his vassal Bertrand de Goth became Pope as *Clement V and at his remonstrances suspended the archbishop, who then made his way to the Papal court at Bordeaux. After Edward I's death in 1307, Winchelsea returned to his see at the request of Edward II, but soon found himself again in opposition to the King. Despite ill-health, he continued to take an active part in politics during his last years, and assisted the barons in their struggle against Edward by frequent excommunications of their enemies. Though insisting on his official dignity, in his personal life he was affable and cheerful, of ascetic habits and regular in his spiritual duties, a hard worker and a zealous administrator of his diocese. Miracles were said to have taken place at his tomb in Canterbury Cathedral, but several efforts at obtaining his canonization came to nothing.

Registrum Roberti Winchelsey, Archiepiscopi Cantuariensis ed. Rose Graham (*Canterbury and York Society, li and lii, 1942–56). A. G. Little–F. Pelster, S.J., *Oxford Theology and Theologians c. A.D. 1282–1302* (O.H.S., xcvi; 1934), esp. pp. 122 f. and 137–45. P. Glorieux in *D.T.C.*, xv (pt. 2; 1950), col. 3553, s.v. for reff. to MS sources. T. F. Tout in *D.N.B.*, lxii (1900), pp. 155–61, s.v., with reff.

WINCHESTER. Apart from legends of very dubious authority, the history of Christianity in Winchester begins with the transference of the bishopric of Wessex thither from *Dorchester, Oxon, in the later 7th cent. The political importance of the city, coupled with the fame of St. *Swithin (852–62), assisted the growth in power of the see. St. *Ethelwold (963–84) replaced the secular canons, who had formerly ruled the cathedral, by *Benedictine monks, under a prior, with the bishop as titular abbot. He and his successor, St. *Alphege (984–1005), enlarged the cathedral. Half a century later it was wholly rebuilt by Walkelin (1070–98) on a new site in the Norman style. The transepts survive, but the remainder was gradually transformed from Norman to Gothic. *Henry of Blois (1129–71), the brother of King Stephen, made some important additions to the buildings. He brought from Hyde Abbey the remains of Saxon kings, now in the mortuary-chests around the *presbytery; erected two episcopal residences, Wolvesey Castle, now in ruins, and Farnham Castle, which was razed by Henry III, but rebuilt for *Charles I; and founded the Hospital of St. Cross, the best extant example of a medieval English almshouse. Godfrey de Lucy (1189–1204) built the retro-choir and Lady-chapel of the cathedral in the Early English style (much altered later). The perpendicular nave was the work of William of Edington (1345–66) and *William of Wykeham (1367–1404), who also founded the college (1387–93). The magnificent stone reredos dates from the later part of the 15th cent. At the Dissolution (1539) William Kingsmill, the last prior, became the first Dean of the new foundation.

The see of Winchester ranks fifth among the English bishoprics (after *Canterbury, *York, London, and *Durham) and the bishop always has a seat in the Lords (irrespectively of his seniority). He is also Prelate of the Order of the Garter, and Provincial Chancellor of Canterbury. Among former Bps. of Winchester of note are *William of Waynflete (1447–86), Richard *Foxe (1501–28), T.

*Wolsey (1529–30), S. *Gardiner (1531–50 and 1553–55), L. *Andrewes (1619–26), B. *Duppa (1660–2), G. *Morley (1662–84), C. R. *Sumner (1827–69), S. *Wilberforce (1869–1873), E. H. *Browne (1873–1890), R. T. *Davidson (1895–1903), H. E. *Ryle (1903–1910), E. S. *Talbot (1911–24), and C. F. Garbett (1932–42). In 1499 the *Channel Islands were transferred to Winchester from the diocese of *Salisbury, though they first came under the effective authority of Winchester in the reign of *Elizabeth I. By the creation of the new sees of Guildford and Portsmouth in 1927, the diocese of Winchester was much reduced in size. It now comprises only the western portions of Hants and the Channel Islands.

C. Deedes (ed.), *Registrum Johannis de Pontissara, Episcopi Wyntoniensis A.D. MCCLXXXII–MCCCIV* (*Canterbury and York Society, xix and xxx; 1915–24); A. W. Goodman (ed.), *Registrum Henrici Woodstock Diocesis Wintoniensis A.D. 1305–16* (ib., xliii; 1940); F. J. Baigent (ed.), *The Registers of John de Sandale and Rigaud de Asserio, Bishops of Winchester, 1316–1323* (Hampshire Record Society, [viii]; 1897); F. T. Kirby (ed.), *Wykeham's Register* (ib., [xi and xiii]; 1896); F. T. Madge–H. Chitty (edd.), *Registrum Thome Wolsey Cardinalis Ecclesiae Wintoniensis Administratoris* (Canterbury and York Society, xxxii; 1926); H. Chitty–H. E. Malden (edd.), *Registra Stephani Gardiner et Johannis Poynet Episcoporum Wintoniensium* (ib., xxxvii; 1930). G. W. Kitchin–F. T. Madge (edd.), *Documents Relating to the Foundation of the Chapter of Winchester A.D. 1541–1547* (Hampshire Record Society, [i]; 1889); W. R. W. Stephens–F. T. Madge (edd.), *Documents Relating to the History of the Cathedral Church of Winchester in the Seventeenth Century* (ib., [x]; 1897). G. W. Kitchin (ed.), *Compotus Rolls of the Obedientiaries of St. Swithun's Priory, Winchester* (ib., [v]; 1892). W. de Gray Birch (ed.), *Liber Vitae*. Register and Martyrology of New Minster and Hyde Abbey, Winchester (ib., [vi]; 1892). 'Thomae Rudborne Monachi Wintonienis Historia Major de Fundatione et Successione Ecclesiae Wintoniensis' and other material in H. *Wharton, *Anglia Sacra*, i (1691), pp. 179–326; 'Annales Monasterii de Wintonia (A.D. 519–1277)', also in H. R. Luard (ed.), *Annales Monastici*, ii (Rolls Series, 1865), pp. 1–125, with introd. pp. ix–xxix. A. W. Goodman (editor into English), *Chartulary of Winchester Cathedral* (Winchester, 1927); id.–W. H. *Hutton (edd.), *The Statutes Governing the Cathedral Church of Winchester given by King Charles I* (Oxford, 1925). *The Pipe Roll of the Bishopric of Winchester for the Fourth Year of the Pontificate of Peter des Roches, 1208–1209*, ed. under the supervision of H. Hall (Studies in Economics and Political Science, ed. W. A. S. Hewins; 1903). S. Gale, *The History and Antiquities of the Cathedral Church of Winchester* (1715); J. Milner, *The History Civil and Ecclesiastical and Survey of the Antiquities of Winchester* (2 vols. bound in one [1798]), esp. ii, pp. 11–157; J. Britton, *The History and Antiquities of the See and Cathedral Church of Winchester* (1817). S. H. Cassan, *The Lives of the Bishops of Winchester from Birinus, the first Bishop of the West Saxons, to the Present Time* (2 vols., 1827). R. Willis, 'The Architectural History of Winchester Cathedral' in *Proceedings of the Annual Meeting of the Archaeological Institute of Great Britain and Ireland at Winchester, September, MDCCCXLV* (1846), No. 2. J. Vaughan, *Winchester Cathedral*. Its Monuments and Muniments [c. 1919]. P. W. Sergeant, *The Cathedral Church of Winchester* (Bell's Cathedral Series, 1903). E. G. Selwyn, *The Story of Winchester Cathedral* (1934). W. *Dugdale, *Monasticon Anglicanum*, esp. i (ed. 1817), pp. 189–218. On the Priory of St. Swithun, Winchester, New Minster and Nunnaminster, or the Abbey of St. Mary, Winchester, J. C. Cox in *V.C.H.*, Hants and Isle of Wight, ii, ed. H. Doubleday–W. Page (1903), pp. 106–26; on the Cathedral, C. R. Peers–H. Brakspear, ib., v, ed. W. Page (1912), pp. 50–9. C. W. C. Oman in *D.E.C.H.* (1912), pp. 643–7, s.v.

WINDESHEIM, near Zwolle, in Holland. Here a house of *Augustinian Canons was established in 1387 under the direction of *Florentius Radewyns by six of G. de *Groote's disciples who had received their religious formation at Eemstein, a foundation of the community of John *Ruysbroeck (q.v.). Their constitutions were approved by Boniface IX in 1395, and under their second great prior, John Vos (1391–1424), they formed, with three other Dutch monasteries, the 'Congregation of Windesheim'. They were joined in 1413 by the seven houses of the Groenendael Congregation, and in 1430 by the Congregation of Neuss. Throughout the 15th cent. the congregation grew rapidly, esp. in the Netherlands, W. and N. Germany, and Switzerland. Their fervent aspirations to religious perfection, notably under the saintly priors I. *Busch (d. 1479) and John Mauburnus ('John of Brussels', d. 1501), became an example to many other communities.

The Canons of Windesheim were the chief monastic representatives of the '*Devotio Moderna' (q.v.). Their influence also reached out to the secular clergy and the laity, whom they exhorted to frequent Communion and veneration of the Blessed Sacrament. They included many fine scholars, copyists, and illuminators, and among their members were *Thomas à Kempis, the probable author of the *Imitation of Christ*, and G. *Biel, the 'last German Schoolman'. In the 16th cent. the Congregation suffered great losses and all the Dutch houses were destroyed, Windesheim itself in 1581. It was reorganized under a Prior General in 1573 and continued to exist in Belgium and the Catholic parts of Germany until the secularization of the monasteries in 1802.

Statuta Capituli Windesemensis ([Windesheim], 1508); *Ordinarius Divini Officii pro Ordine Canonicorum Regularium Capituli sive Congregationis Wyndesemensis* (Deventer, 1521); *Regula Beati Augustini Episcopi cum Constitutionibus Canonicorum Regularium Capituli Windesemensis* (Utrecht, 1553); *Acta Capituli Windeshemensis*, [1387–1611], ed. S. van der Woude (Kerkhistorische Studien behorende bij het Nederlands Archief voor Kerkgeschiedenis, vi; The Hague, 1953), with detailed bibl. reff. I. Busch, *Chronicon Windesemense*, ed H. Rosweyde., S., J., Antwerp, 1621; also ed. K. Grube, *Geschichtsquellen der Provinz Sachsen und angrenzender Gebiete*, xix (1886), pp. 1–375. J. C. van Slee, *De Klostervereeniging te Windesheim* (Leiden, 1874); J. G. R. Acquoy, *Het Kloster te Windesheim en zijn Invloed* (3 vols., Utrecht, 1875–80). H. Schmidt–S. D. van Veen in *P.R.E.* (ed. 3), xxi (1908), pp. 363–8, s.v. 'Windesheim, Das Kloster von'. See also bibl. to *Brethren of the Common Life* and *Devotio Moderna*.

WINDISCH, HANS (1881–1935), NT scholar. He became a Privatdozent at Leipzig in 1908. Later he held professorships at *Leyden (1914–29), Kiel (1929–35), and Halle (1935). He was a leading member of the *Religionsgeschichtliche Schule. Among his writings were *Taufe und Sünde im ältesten Christentum bis auf Origenes* (1908); *Die Frömmigkeit Philos und ihre Bedeutung für das Christentum* (1909); *Der Sinn der Bergpredigt* (1929), and commentaries on the Catholic Epistles (Hb. N.T., 1911; ed. 2, 1930), and Heb. (ib., 1913; ed. 2, 1931), and on 2 Cor. (K.E.K., 1924).

WINDSOR, St. George's Chapel. The 'Royal Free Chapel of Windsor', constituted by Edward III to take charge of the shrine of the Order of the Garter (founded c. 1348), received its statutes from William of Edington,

Bp. of *Winchester (1346–66), on 30 Nov. 1352. Originally it was designed to consist of a warden (later 'Dean'), 12 canons, 13 vicars, 4 clerks, 6 choristers, 24 Poor Knights and a verger; but the ideal was never fully realized. The present fine perpendicular chapel, with its elaborate stone vaulting, dates from 1475–1508. In 1840 the canons were reduced to four (later to three), while the minor canons, as the vicars came to be called, have also been gradually reduced to three. The chapter is under the direct jurisdiction of the Sovereign, which is exercised through the Lord Chancellor. Until the Marriage Act of 1822, the Dean possessed the right of granting faculties for marriage licences and for proving wills.

W. H. St. J. Hope, *Windsor Castle*. An Architectural Survey, ii (1913), pp. 375–477. S. L. Ollard, *Fasti Wynde-sorienses*. The Deans and Canons of Windsor (Historical Monographs relating to St. George's Chapel, ed. S. L. Ollard, 1950); E. H. Fellowes, *The Vicars or Minor Canons of His Majesty's Free Chapel of St. George in Windsor Castle* (ib., [1945]); id., *Organists and Masters of the Choristers of St. George's Chapel in Windsor Castle* (ib., [1939]). E. A. Jones, *The Plate of St. George's Chapel, Windsor Castle* (ib., 1939); M. F. Bond, *The Inventories of St. George's Chapel, Windsor Castle, 1384–1667* (ib., 1947); A. K. B. Roberts, *St. George's Chapel, Windsor Castle, 1348–1416*. A Study in early Collegiate Administration (London thesis, ib. [1947]), and other volumes in this series. H. W. Blackburne–M. F. Bond, *The Romance of St. George's Chapel, Windsor Castle* (1933). W. St. J. Hope in *V.C.H.*, Berks, iii, ed. W. Page–P. H. Ditchfield–J. H. Cope (1923), pp. 36–41. S. L. Ollard in *D.E.C.H.* (ed. 3, 1948), pp. 667–9, s.v.

WINDTHORST, LUDWIG (1812–91), German Catholic politician. The descendant of a well-known Hanoverian family, he studied law at Göttingen and Heidelberg and settled as a lawyer at Osnabrück in 1836. In 1848 he became Councillor at the Hanoverian supreme Court of Appeal at Celle, and in 1849 entered on a political career, twice becoming Minister of Justice (1851–3 and 1862–5). Having acquiesced in the enforced union of Hanover with Prussia in 1866, he became a member of the N. German Diet in 1867 and later of the German Reichstag. In 1871 he helped to found the *Centre Party whose leader he remained till his death. The growth of the party, which was constantly harassed by the bitter opposition of O. von Bismarck, was due chiefly to his devotion and initiative. He played a prominent part in the *Kulturkampf, and, after Bismarck's change of policy, was reconciled to the Chancellor in 1879. He had a considerable share in the negotiations for the repeal of the *May Laws, and, after Bismarck's retirement (1888), his relations with the new Emperor, William II, became very friendly. His last political success was the defeat of the School Bill in 1891.

Ausgewählte Reden (3 vols., Osnabrück, 1901–2). Studies by J. N. Knopp (Männer der Zeit, hrsg. J. Zeitler, Dresden, 1898), E. Hüsgen (Cologne, 1907) and, slighter, by A. Reumont (Führer des Volkes, iii; Munich, 1913). G. Bazin, *Windthorst*. Ses alliés et ses adversaires [1896]. F. Rachfahl in *Allgemeine Deutsche Biographie*, lv (1910), pp. 97–104, s.v.; J. W. Headlam in *E.B.* (ed. 11), xxvii (1911), p. 715 f., s.v.

WINER, JOHANN GEORG BENEDIKT (1789–1858), German theologian. From 1832 he was professor of theology at Leipzig. His celebrity rests on his NT Greek grammar (*Grammatik des neutestamentlichen Sprachidioms*), first publd. in 1822. It went through a large number of editions, and was several times translated into English, e.g. by W. F. *Moulton (1870). Its elaborate collection of material is still valuable, though Winer's conclusions have been largely invalidated by increased knowledge of Hellenistic Greek.

G. Lechler in *P.R.E.* (ed. 3), xxi (1908), pp. 368–71, s.v.

WINFRID or WINFRITH, St. See *Boniface, St.*

WINIFRED, St. (d. *c.* 650), in Welsh 'Gwenfrewi', the patron saint of N. Wales. Acc. to legends (late and not worthy of credence) she was a maiden of great beauty and attainments, who was sought in marriage by the Prince Caradog of Hawarden. For refusing his advances, she was wounded (or killed) by him, but miraculously healed (or restored to life) by her uncle, St. *Beuno. A spring marked the scene, the present Holywell (Welsh, 'Tre Ffynnon') in Flintshire, and here Winifred established a nunnery of which she became abbess. In 1138 her relics were translated to Shrewsbury and in 1398 her feast was ordered to be observed throughout the province of *Canterbury. Holywell, for many centuries a famous place of pilgrimage, has continued to attract sufferers down to modern times; Dr. S. *Johnson saw people bathing there on 3 Aug. 1774. Feast day, 3 Nov.

The principal sources include a life preserved principally in the Brit. Mus. MS. Cott. MS. Claud. A.5, attributed to Elerius, a monk, in the year 660 (actually *c.* 12th cent.), pr. in W. J. Rees, *Lives of the Cambro-British Saints* (Published for the Welsh MSS. Society, 1853), pp. 198–209, and a life by Robert, prior of Shrewsbury, principally preserved in the Bodleian MS. Laud. Misc. 114, saec. XII (*c.* 1139); they are both pr. in *AA.SS.*, Nov. I (1887), pp. 702–8, and 708–31 respectively, with introd. and other material, pp. 691–701 and 732–59. Eng. tr. of life attributed to Elerius, with abridgment of life by Robert of Shrewsbury, by J. Dalton (London, 1857). Collection of later material, mainly in English, ed. C. de Smedt, S.J., in *Anal. Boll.*, vi (1887), pp. 305–52. Life by Philip Metcalfe, S.J. (no place, 1712; modern ed. by H. Thurston, S.J., London, 1917).

WIPO (d. *c.* 1050), hymn writer. Apparently a native of Burgundy or Swabia, he became priest and chaplain to the Emps. Conrad II and Henry III. He wrote much verse, the greater part of which has been lost. There survive a 'Tetralogus', a eulogy of *Henry II (d. 1024); his 'Proverbs', a series of maxims for Prince Henry; and, best known, the '*Victimae paschali laudes', the *sequence for Easter Day. His 'Gesta Chuonradi Imperatoris' is one of the principal sources for the reign of the Emp. Conrad II (1024–39).

Crit. ed. of his works by H. Bresslau (Scriptores Rerum Germanicarum in usum Scholarum, Hanover and Leipzig, 1915), with introd. and reff.; except for the Easter Sequence, they were ed. G. H. Pertz in *M.G.H.*, Scriptores, xi (1853), pp. 243–75. Id., 'Über Wipos Leben und Schriften' in *Abh.* (Berl.) for 1851 (1852), pp. 215–33. W. Pflüger, 'Wipos *Vita Chuonradi Imperatoris*' in *N.A.*, ii (1877), pp. 129–55; R. Holtzmann, 'Wipo und die schwäbische Weltchronik', ib., xxxv (1910), pp. 55–104. M. Manitius, *Geschichte der lateinischen Literatur des Mittelalters*, ii (1923), pp. 318–28, with bibl. Raby, pp. 217–19. See also bibl. to *Victimae Paschali Laudes*.

WISDOM. In the OT wisdom, whether human or Divine, occupies a prominent place. Human wisdom, of which esp. *Solomon is the representative, extends over a diversity of subjects, examined esp. in the so-called 'Wisdom Literature'. They range from the fundamental principles of virtuous living to practical details such as advice on education and the choice of friends, all, however, subjected to the fear of the Lord, which is the beginning of wisdom. Divine Wisdom, on the other hand, is manifest in creation and Providence which guides nations and individuals (Wisd. 10–19). It is more than a mere quality and tends increasingly to become a hypostasis, so esp. in Prov. 8 and Wisd. 7. 22 ff., foreshadowing the Logos of St. John. The 'Wisdom Literature' is generally reckoned to include Prov., Job, Eccles., Ecclus., and Wisd. (qq.v.), to which Cant. and Pss. are sometimes added.

In the NT Divine Wisdom is incarnate in Christ, whom St. Paul calls 'the wisdom of God' (1 Cor. 1. 24), 'in whom are all the treasures of wisdom and knowledge hidden' (Col. 2. 3). At the same time it is intimately connected with the Holy Ghost, one of whose gifts it is. Many of the Greek Fathers, following the terminology of the OT and St. Paul, use 'Wisdom' as a synonym for the Incarnate Word or Logos, as in the dedication of the Church of *Santa Sophia ('Holy Wisdom') at *Constantinople. In *Gnostic thought, which saw in Wisdom a Divine emanation and a cause of the creation and redemption of the world, the conception played an important part, and was understood in the various systems as the spouse of the Logos, the mother of the Demiurge, &c. In medieval theology the term was chiefly applied to the gift of the Holy Ghost.

In its connexion with the Deity, Wisdom has again been made a subject of speculation in the thought of modern Russian authors such as V. *Soloviev and S. *Bulgakov. These authors distinguish a created from an uncreated wisdom, which together form the unity of God and the world, and which, in their teaching, is closely connected with the Platonic World-soul, the *Theotokos, and the Holy Ghost.

WISDOM OF SOLOMON, The. This *Deuterocanonical Book, which does not lend itself to exact analysis, can be divided roughly into three parts. The opening chapters (1. 1–6. 8) describe the different destinies awaiting the righteous and the wicked. In opposition to the 'ungodly', who maintain that, since this life is all, the only sensible course is to live for pleasure, the writer maintains that the righteous will be rewarded by a blessed immortality while the ungodly will certainly be punished. The section seems to be a reply to Eccles. 7. 15, against which Wisd. 4. 7–9, 17–19 seem ex-

pressly directed. The second part (6. 9–9. 18) contains the meditation on Wisdom which has given the Book its name. Wisdom is 'a breath of the power of God, and a clear effluence of the Almighty' (7. 25), and she comes forth from God to dwell among men that she may make those who receive her 'friends of God, and prophets' (7. 27); and the section ends with *Solomon's prayer for Wisdom (9). The last part of the Book (10–19) gives a review of Israel's history down to the *Exodus, interrupted in 13–15 by a description of the origin and evils of idolatry. The good fortune of Israel's forefathers and the disasters overtaking their enemies, attributed in 10 to the activity of Wisdom, are used to illustrate the theories that 'by what things their foes were punished, by the same they in their need were benefited' (11. 5), and that 'wherewithal a man sinneth, by the same also shall he be punished' (11. 16).

The ascription of the Book to Solomon has long been questioned and is now generally believed by critics to be a literary device. The Book shows the blending of Jewish religion and Greek philosophy characteristic of Alexandrian theology and was almost certainly written by an Alexandrian Jew. It was written in a time of persecution (2. 12, 19 f.), and 14. 16–17 suggests that the persecution had arisen through refusal to participate in Emperor-worship. Most of the commentators of the 19th cent. took these allusions as indicating a date in the Ptolemaic period and put the Book in the 2nd or 1st cent. B.C., but some more recent commentators follow F. W. *Farrar in dating it *c.* A.D. 40 in the reign of Caligula. The unity of the Book has been challenged by some critics, but their case is not established.

The Book has had a great influence on Christian thought. The majority of critics explain the undoubted resemblances to it in passages of the Pauline Epistles (e.g. Rom. 9. 21–23, cf. Wisd. 12. 12–18; Eph. 6. 11–17, cf. Wisd. 5. 17–20) as due to direct use made of it by St. Paul, and there are probable reminiscences of it in Heb. (e.g. 1. 3, cf. Wisd. 7. 26), Jas. (2. 6, cf. Wisd. 2. 10), 1 Pet. (1. 6 f., cf. Wisd. 3. 5 f.), and Jn. (17. 3, cf. Wisd. 15. 3). In later writers, the terms used of the Divine Wisdom are freely applied to Christ and so passed into the vocabulary of Christian theology.

Modern commentaries include those of W. J. Deane (Oxford, 1881), F. W. Farrar in H. *Wace, Apocrypha, i (Speaker's Commentary, 1888), pp. 403–534, J. A. F. Gregg (Camb. Bib., RV, 1909), P. Heinisch (Exegetisches Handbuch zum Alten Testament hergeb. J. Nikel, xxiv; 1912), A. T. S. Goodrick (Oxford Church Bible Commentary, 1913), S. Holmes in R. H. *Charles (ed.), *The Apocrypha and Pseudepigrapha of the Old Testament*, i (1913), pp. 518–68. F. Feldmann (Die heilige Schrift des Alten Testamentes, vi, Abh. 4; 1926), and J. von Fichtner (H.A.T., Reihe 2, vi; 1938). P. Heinisch, *Die griechische Philosophie im Buch der Weisheit* (Alttestamentliche Abhandlungen, i, Hft. 4; 1908); H. Bückers, C.SS.R., *Die Unsterblichkeitslehre des Weisheitsbuches* (ib., xiii, Hft. 4; 1938). R. H. Pfeiffer, *History of New Testament Times with an Introduction to the Apocrypha* (New York, [1949], London, [1954]), pp. 313–51, with bibl. p. 535. L. Bigot in *D.T.C.*, xiv (pt. 1; 1939), cols. 703–44, s.v. 'Sagesse (Livre de)', with further bibl. See also works cited, s.v. *Apocrypha*.

WISEMAN, NICHOLAS PATRICK STEPHEN (1802–65), English cardinal. The son of Anglo-Irish parents, he was rector of the English College at Rome from 1828 to 1840. His considerable knowledge of oriental languages also secured him a position at the *Vatican Library. On a visit to England in 1835–6, he gave some lectures on the RC faith which attracted much attention. In 1840 he returned to England as coadjutor to Bp. Walsh, *Vicar Apostolic of the Midland District, and from 1847 to 1850 he was himself Vicar Apostolic of the London District. When in 1850 the RC hierarchy was restored in England, Wiseman was appointed cardinal and the first Abp. of Westminster. His original pastoral letter, sent 'From the Flaminian Gate' (7 Oct. 1850), aroused in England great fears and hostility, but on his return to England from Rome he succeeded by tact in allaying suspicion. A believer in *Ultramontane methods of devotion, he was much opposed by the older school of English RCs. His attitude towards the *Oxford Movement was always sympathetic, although latterly the policy for which he was officially responsible, esp. under the influence of H. E. *Manning, became more rigid. His eagerness for a religious culture on a Catholic basis is seen in his foundation of the *Dublin Review (q.v.) in 1836. Wiseman also published a widely read novel, *Fabiola, or the Church of the Catacombs* (1854). R. Browning's *Bishop Blougram's Apology* was said to have been directed against him.

W. *Ward, *The Life and Times of Cardinal Wiseman* (2 vols., 1897). Modern Life by B. Fothergill, London, 1963. C. Kent in *D.N.B.*, lxii (1900), pp. 234–6.

WISHART, GEORGE (c. 1513–46), Scottish Reformer. The facts of his early life are obscure. Charged with heresy in 1538, he fled to England, where a similar accusation was preferred against him in 1539. After travelling on the Continent and studying for some time at Corpus Christi College, Cambridge, he returned to Scotland in 1543 and was probably the Wishart who approached the English government in 1544 with a view to the murder of Card. D. *Beaton. In 1544 he began active propaganda on behalf of Reformed doctrines, going from place to place in great danger of his life and denouncing current abuses. In this work he was assisted by J. *Knox. He was apprehended by Bothwell at Ormiston in Jan. 1546, soon afterwards transferred to Edinburgh Castle, and burnt by Beaton at St. Andrews on 1 Mar. 1546. He made an English translation of the '*Helvetic Confession' which was published posthumously (prob. 1548).

The primary authorities include J. Knox, *History of the Reformation in Scotland* (ed. W. C. Dickinson, 2 vols., London, 1949, vol. i, pp. 60–72), and for his trial and death, Robert Lindesay of Pitscottie (c. 1532–c. 1578), *Historie and Chronicles of Scotland* (ed. Æ. J. G. Mackay, Scottish Text Society, xlii and xliii, with glossary and index, lx, 1899–1911, vol. ii, pp. 52–82, with notes, p. 421 f.), and J. *Foxe, *Acts and Monuments* (ed. G. Townsend, vi, 1846, pp. 625–36). Notes by D. Laing appended to his ed. of *The Works of John Knox*, i (The Woodrow Society, 1864), pp. 534–7. C. Rogers, 'Memoir of George Wishart, the Scottish Martyr' in *Transactions of the Royal Historical Society* [Original Series], iv (1876), pp. 260–363, with Eng. tr. of his Helvetian Confession, pp. 319–28. Æ. Macray in *D.N.B.*, lxii (1900), pp. 248–51.

WITCHCRAFT. The malevolent exercise of preternatural powers, esp. by women, attributed to a connexion with demons. The narrative of the witch of Endor (1 Sam. 28. 7–25) and the condemnations of witchcraft in the Old (Exod. 22. 18, Deut. 18. 10) and New Law (Gal. 5. 20) have sometimes been adduced as Scriptural proof of its existence. In the patristic age *Tertullian (*Apol.* 22) and St. *Augustine (*De Civ. Dei*, xxi, 6) believed in it. On the other hand, the belief was opposed by many of the Fathers, e.g. St. *Hippolytus, St. *Chrysostom, and St. *Caesarius of Arles.

In the early Middle Ages, *Charlemagne punished the persecution of witches, which had been a feature of the old Roman Law; *Rabanus Maurus and many bishops of the 10th and 11th cents. wrote against it, and *Gregory VII forbade the killing of women for supposed crimes such as causing storms and epidemics. But the popular superstition, resting in part on old pagan beliefs, did not die out, and it was given a fresh impetus by Arabic and Jewish magic introduced into Europe through the *Crusades and by the exaggerated teaching of the *Cathari on the evil principle; and on occasion it influenced the speculations of the Schoolmen. Popes Alexander IV (1258), and later *John XXII (1320), permitted the *Inquisition to deal with cases of witchcraft if connected with heresy, and, esp. in Germany, secular courts also punished these supposed crimes with exile and often with cruelty and burning. Mass persecutions, however, began to take place only in the later 15th cent. In 1484 Innocent VIII encouraged the Inquisitors to take severe measures against witches, and the appearance of the *Malleus Maleficarum* ('Hammer of Witches') in 1487 or 1488, which described their alleged practices such as witches' sabbaths, intercourse with the devil, transformations into animals and malicious spells cast on men and cattle, greatly increased superstition and persecution. The 16th cent. Reformers, with their often exaggerated belief in the power of the devil, further contributed to the evil, as did the unrest stirred up by the religious wars. In England large numbers of women were hanged for witchcraft during the Commonwealth, and only at the end of the 17th cent. did persecution begin to lessen, though it had been repeatedly denounced for over a hundred years, e.g. by the Calvinist doctor, J. Weyer, in his *De Praestigiis Daemonum* (1563), the Jesuit F. von Spee in *Cautio Criminalis* (1631), and many others. Under the influence of the *Aufklärung the persecution of witches practically ceased. The last trials for witchcraft in England took place in 1712 in *Scotland in 1722, and on the Continent in Switzerland in 1782 and in Posen in 1793.

M. Summers, *The History of Witchcraft and Demonology* ('History of Civilization', 1926), with bibl.; id., *The Geography of Witchcraft* (ib., 1927). *Materials Toward a History of Witchcraft* collected by H. C. Lea, arranged and ed. A. C Howland (3 vols., Philadelphia and London, 1939).

C. [W. S.] *Williams, *Witchcraft* (London, 1941); P. Hughes, *Witchcraft* (ib., 1952). J. Français, *L'Église et la sorcellerie* (Bibliothèque de Critique religieuse, 1910). Margaret A. Murray, *The Witch-Cult in Western Europe* (1921); G. L. Kittredge, *Witchcraft in Old and New England* (Cambridge, Mass., and London, 1928). W. Notestein, *A History of Witchcraft in England from 1558–1718* (Washington and London, 1911). C. L'E. Ewen (ed.), *Witch Hunting and Witch Trials*. The Indictments for Witchcraft from the Records of 1373 Assizes held for the Home Circuit, A.D. 1559–1736 (1929); id., *Witchcraft and Demonianism*. A Concise Account derived from Sworn Depositions in the Courts of England and Wales (1933); id., *Witchcraft in the Star Chamber* (privately printed, 1938). C. Hole, *Witchcraft in England* (popular, 1945). P. Séjourné in *D.T.C.*, xiv (pt. 2; 1941), cols. 2340–417, s.v. 'Sorcellerie'.

WITELO (b. *c.* 1230), medieval philosopher and scientist. A native of Silesia, he studied philosophy and science at Padua (*c.* 1260–8) and later went to Viterbo, where he became the friend of the translator of *Aristotle, *William of Moerbeke, to whom he dedicated his treatise on optics, 'Perspectiva' (between 1270 and 1277). On his later life there is no certain information. Two of his other treatises, 'De Natura Daemonum' and 'De Primaria Causa Paenitentiae', have recently been discovered, but the further works of Witelo which are cited in the 'Perspectiva' are still unknown.

Witelo's 'Perspectiva', which had a great influence on later scientists, e.g. J. *Kepler, is based for the greater part on the Arabic scholar, Alhazen. It is esp. interesting on account of its psychological doctrines, which are akin to modern views on association and the subconscious. In its metaphysical teaching it is *Neo-Platonist, recognizing two orders of being, intellectual substances and corporeal things, which are connected by the bond of causality and both emanate from the Divine Light. His theories on the dynamics of light, which he regards as the first of sensible forms ('lumen . . . primum omnium formarum sensibilium'), have much in common with the doctrines of Robert *Grosseteste and Roger *Bacon.

C. Baeumker, *Witelo, ein Philosoph und Naturforscher des XIII. Jahrhunderts* (B.G.P.M., iii, Hft. 2; 1908), incl. text of the *Liber de Intelligentiis*, pp. 1–71, and of the *Perspectiva* (previously publd. at Nuremberg, 1535 and 1551, and at Basle, 1572), pp. 127–79. Id., 'Zur Biographie des Philosophen und Naturforschers Witelo' in *Hist. J.*, xxxiii (1912), pp. 359–61. A. Birkenmajer, 'Études sur Witelo' in the *Bulletin international de l'Académie Polonaise des Sciences et des Lettres*. Classe de Philologie, Classe d'Histoire et de Philosophie for 1918 (1920), pp. 4–6; for 1919, 1920 (1922–4), pp. 354–60; for 1922 (1925), pp. 6–9. C. Baeumker, 'Zur Frage nach Abfassungszeit und Verfasser des irrtümlich Witelo zugeschriebenen *Liber de Intelligentiis*' in *Miscellanea Francesco Ehrle*, i (S.T., xxxvii; 1924), pp. 87–102. Überweg, ii, pp. 474–7, with bibl. p. 761. M. *Grabmann in *L.Th.K.*, x (1938), col. 944 for further bibl.

WITNESSES, The Three. See *Johannine Comma*.

WITTENBERG, since 1922 officially known as **Lutherstadt Wittenberg**, the cradle of the *Reformation. At its university (founded, 1502; united with that of Halle, 1815) M. *Luther became professor in 1508. On 31 Oct. 1517 he affixed his Ninety-Five Theses to the door of the Schlosskirche, declaiming

against the medieval doctrine of *Indulgences; and at the beginning of 1522 Protestant public worship was celebrated here for the first time, in the parish church. The *Augustinian monastery in the town, where Luther lived first as a monk and later with his family, is now fitted up as a museum (Lutherhaus). Both Luther and P. *Melanchthon are buried in the Schlosskirche.

WITTENBERG, Concord of (1536). An agreement reached by *Lutheran and *Zwinglian theologians in the disputed doctrine of the *Eucharist. After a preliminary conference between M. *Bucer and P. *Melanchthon at Cassel in Dec. 1534, a large and representative body of divines, including M. *Luther himself, met at Wittenberg in May 1536, where a doctrinal statement drawn up by Melanchthon, which set forth an essentially Lutheran doctrine of the Eucharist, though without insistence on *ubiquity, was accepted. The reunion thus achieved soon collapsed, however, largely through the refusal of the Swiss Zwinglians to accept the 'Concord'.

Text pr. among P. Melanchthon's collected works ed. C. G. Bretschneider, iii (Corpus Reformatorum, iii, Brunswick, 1836), cols. 75–7; mostly repr. in Kidd, p. 318 f. (No. 127); Eng. tr. of most of text in D. *Stone, *A History of the Doctrine of the Holy Eucharist*, ii (1909), p. 46 f. T. Kolde in *P.R.E.* (ed. 3), xxi (1908), pp. 383–99, s.v. 'Wittenberger Konkordie'. Further bibl. in Schottenloher, iv (1938), p. 381 (Nos. 39213a–39216).

WOLFENBÜTTEL FRAGMENTS, The. The title under which G. E. *Lessing issued between 1774 and 1778 seven extracts from the long (unpubld.) work in which H. S. *Reimarus (1694–1768; q.v.) had attacked historic Christianity. The most famous of them was the last, entitled *Von dem Zwecke Jesu und seiner Jünger* (1778), in which Reimarus interpreted the purpose of Christ's work, as set down in the Gospels, in terms of *eschatology. Widespread attention was again drawn to it by A. *Schweitzer's *Von Reimarus zu Wrede* (1906; Eng. trans., *The Quest of the Historical Jesus*, 1910).

For bibliography, see *Reimarus, H. S.*

WOLFF, CHRISTIAN (1679–1754), less correctly 'Wolf', German philosopher. In 1706 he became professor of mathematics and natural science at Halle, then a stronghold of *Pietism. In an attempt to systematize the principles of G. W. *Leibniz, he developed a comprehensive system of philosophy. His supreme confidence in reason offended the Pietists, who eventually persuaded Frederick William I to expel him from Halle in 1723, urging on the monarch that the spread of Wolff's teaching would be subversive of military discipline since its determinism would justify desertion from the army. Wolff spent his exile at *Marburg. On the accession of Frederick the Great (1740), one of the new king's first acts was to recall Wolff, who re-entered Halle on 6 Dec. 1740 in triumph. Wolff's system won great popularity and was in substance that taught in most of the German universities in the latter half of the 18th cent. It also provided the background of the Critical Philosophy of I. *Kant. Wolff wrote a very long series of treatises (in form text-books), the earlier ones in German and the later in Latin. Among the latter were a Logic (1728), an Ontology (1730), a Cosmology (1731), Psychologies (1731–4), a Natural Theology (1736–7), an Ethics (1750–3), and an Economics (1750). Together they covered nearly the whole field of speculative philosophy.

There is no collected ed. of Wolff's works. Wolff himself assembled his *Kleine Schriften*, 6 vols., Halle, 1736–40. Autobiography first ed. by H. Wuttke, Leipzig, 1841. Wolff finds a place in all histories of modern German philosophy. Studies on his general doctrines by F. W. Kluge (Breslau, 1831), H. Pichler (Leipzig, 1910), J. Baumann (ib., 1910), and E. Kohlmeyer (Göttingen, 1911). W. Arnsperger, *Christian Wolff's Verhältnis zu Leibniz* (1897). Überweg, iii, 448–54, with bibl. p. 703. H. Stephan in *P.R.E.* (ed. 3), xxi (1908), pp. 452–64.

WOLFGANG, St (*c.* 924–94), Bp. of *Ratisbon. Of Swabian descent, he was educated at the celebrated monastery of *Reichenau on an island in Lake Constance and later became a teacher in the cathedral school at Trier. In 964 he entered the *Benedictine Order at *Einsiedeln. Consecrated to the see of Ratisbon in 972, he soon became an ardent and successful reformer. His feast (31 Oct.) is widely observed in Central Europe.

The principal sources are the works of two monks of St. Emmeran, Ratisbon: Arnold of Vohburg on St. Emmeran, Book ii (written *c.* 1037), and a life of St. Wolfgang by Otho (written *c.* 1052), which is more lively but less reliable; the best of ed. of both these sources, with other material, and introd. and commentary by H. *Delehaye, S.J., in *AA.SS.*, Nov. II (pt. 1; 1894), pp. 527–97. Festschrift to mark the ninth centenary of his death, ed. J. B. Mehler (Ratisbon, 1894). Other modern studies by I. Zibermayr (Linz, 1924) and O. Häfner (Rottenburg a/N., 1930). A. Hauck in *P.R.E.* (ed. 3), xxi (1908), pp. 494–6, s.v.; U. Schmid in *C.E.*, xv (1912), p. 682 f., s.v.; A. Zimmermann, O.S.B., in *L.Th.K.*, x (1938), cols. 960–2, s.v., with further bibl.

WOLSEY, THOMAS (*c.* 1474–1530), cardinal. Of middle-class birth, he was educated at *Oxford, elected Fellow of Magdalen College *c.* 1497, and ordained priest in 1498. He soon held a number of benefices, becoming one of the domestic chaplains of Henry Dean, Abp. of *Canterbury, in 1502, and chaplain to Henry VII in 1507. He retained the royal favour under his successor, *Henry VIII, became a privy counsellor in 1511, and Bp. of *Lincoln in 1514. In 1514 he was also appointed Abp. of *York, and in 1515 was created cardinal. A month later he was made Lord Chancellor of England, now wielding an almost royal power. His main interest was foreign politics, in which he frequently changed sides, skilfully holding the balance of power between the Empire and France, in a boldly conceived attempt to make England the arbiter of Europe. Though he himself was in favour of friendship with France, he had to sign a secret treaty of alliance with the Emperor (1521). The latter, however, on the death of *Leo X (1521), as well as on that of *Hadrian VI (1523), failed to exercise his influence to get

Wolsey elected Pope. In the meantime the cardinal, though retaining the royal favour, had made himself enemies throughout the country by his ruthless methods of obtaining money for the war with France, as well as by his arrogance and pomp. When, in 1527, Henry began to take steps to obtain his divorce, Wolsey, though opposed to the scheme, endeavoured by all means to further the King's wishes. His plan to induce the Pope to cede to himself authority to decide the case proved a failure, however, and the cardinal, unable to obtain the Papal dispensation necessary for the divorce, was blamed by Anne Boleyn and, through her, incurred the King's displeasure. In 1529 he pleaded guilty to a *praemunire, being the first English prelate to accept the jurisdiction of a secular court. In the same year he had to resign the Great Seal and to give up all his property to the King, though later his archbishopric was restored to him. His last months, devoted to his diocese and to deeds of charity, were embittered by the knowledge that the King intended to suppress the two colleges he had founded at Ipswich and Oxford. Of these the latter, the present *Christ Church (q.v.) survived, in somewhat different form. Owing to a denunciation by his Italian doctor, he was arrested on a charge of high treason in Nov. 1530, but died soon afterwards on his way to London. A statesman rather than a Churchman, Wolsey had devoted his life to the aggrandizement of his king and country, fostering the development of royal absolutism in politics as well as in ecclesiastical matters; but his dream of making England the chief factor in European politics remained unrealized in his age.

Registrum Thome Wolsey Cardinalis Ecclesie Wintoniensis Administratoris transcribed by F. T. Madge–H. Chitty, ed., with introd., by H. Chitty (*Canterbury and York Society, xxxii, 1926). The primary sources for his official policies are the calendars of the state papers for the reign of Henry VIII (cited s.v.). Important docc. connected with the divorce in S. Ehses (ed.), *Römische Dokumente zur Geschichte der Ehescheidung Heinrichs VIII von England* (Quellen und Forschungen aus dem Gebeite der Geschichte . . . herausgegeben von der Görres-Gesellschaft, ii; Paderborn, 1893). The primary authority for his personal life is the record of George Cavendish (1500–*c.* 1561), pr. as *The Negotiations of Thomas Wolsey, the Great Cardinall of England* (1641); this life has very frequently been republished; standard ed. by S. W. Singer (2 vols., 1825; ed. 2, 1827); the latest ed. is that publd. at Chipping Camden, 1930. The best modern life is that of A. F. Pollard (London, 1929). Other lives by R. Fiddes (London, 1724), J. Grove (4 vols., ib., 1742–4), M. *Creighton (ib., 1888), E. L. Taunton (ib., 1902), H. Belloc (ib., 1930), and A. Sampson (ib., 1935; popular). T. W Cameron, 'The Early Life of Thomas Wolsey' in *E.H.R.*, iii (1888), pp. 458–77; J. *Gairdner, 'The Fall of Cardinal Wolsey' in *Transactions of the Royal Historical Society*, N.S., xiii (1899), pp. 75–102. Id. in *D.N.B.*, lxii (1900), pp. 325–43, s.v. See also bibl. to *Henry VIII*.

WOOD, ANTHONY (1632–95), antiquary and historian of *Oxford. In his later years he called himself 'Anthony à Wood'. He lived for most of his life in a house opposite the gate of Merton College, of which he became a member in 1647. He was an assiduous collector of facts, and, though his judgements were often prejudiced, his writings contain a mine of information about the university of Oxford and very many of its otherwise little-known members. In 1674 he issued *Historia et Antiquitates Universitatis Oxoniensis*, printed in two folios at the expense of John *Fell, and in 1691–2 his *Athenae Oxonienses; An Exact History of all the Writers and Bishops who have had their Education in the University of Oxford from 1500 to 1690, to which are added the Fasti or Annals for the said time* (also in two folios).

His *Athenae Oxonienses . . . to which are added the Fasti, or Annals of the said University*, ed. P. Bliss (5 vols., London, 1813–20), with his autobiography in vol. i, pp. i–cxxv, and T. *Hearne's account of him, pp. cxxvii–cxxx. His *Survey of the Antiquities of the City of Oxford* (composed in 1661–6), ed. A. Clark (O.H.S., xv, xvii, xxvii; 1889–99); *The Life and Times of Anthony Wood, Antiquary of Oxford, 1632–1695, described by himself*, ed. id. (ib., xix, xxi, xxvi, xxx, xl; 1891–1900); abridged ed. by L. Powys (London, 1932). A. Clark in *D.N.B.*, lxii (1900), pp. 349–53.

WOOD, CHARLES LINDLEY, 2nd Viscount Halifax. See *Halifax, Second Viscount*.

WOODARD, NATHANIEL (1811–91), founder of the 'Woodard Schools'. He was born at Basildon Hall, Essex, educated at Magdalen Hall, Oxford, and ordained in 1841. While a curate in East London he became convinced of the necessity of establishing public schools which would provide a sound middle-class education on a definite Anglican basis. When, in 1847, he was appointed curate at New Shoreham, he founded his first day school, and in 1848 outlined his ideas in his *Plea for the Middle Classes*, which aroused much controversy, but also received warm approval. In the same year he established the St. Nicolas Society for the realization of his plans, and many schools were founded, among them St. Nicolas's, Lancing (1848), and St. John's, Hurstpierpoint (1850). Woodard's organizing abilities, combined with his devoted service, won him wide moral and financial support, esp. among High Church-men, and in recognition of his work he was made Canon of Manchester and rector of St. Philip's, Salford, in 1870. In 1873 he founded Denstone, the first of the Midland Schools, in 1880 King Alfred's School, Taunton, and in 1887 a girls' school at Bangor (N. Wales).

Life by J. Otter (London, 1925). K. E. *Kirk, *The Story of the Woodard Schools* (1937). J. A. Atkinson in *D.N.B.*, lxii (1900), pp. 383–5; A. L. Woodard in *D.E.C.H.*, p. 649, s.v.

WOOLMAN, JOHN (1720–72), American *Quaker preacher. A native of Northampton, nr. Burlington, N.J., U.S.A., he led a long campaign against slavery from 1743 till his death, constantly travelling among the Quaker communities in America in support of negro rights. In 1772 he crossed to England to further the interests of his cause and died at *York a few weeks after his arrival. His writings, remarkable for their unadorned sincerity and restrained but strong religious feeling, are among the best literary expressions of the Quaker ideal. The best known, his *Journal* (1774), records Woolman's 'Life, Gospel-Labours and Christian Experiences' from 1756 till his death.

The *Journal*, as well as Woolman's other writings, has been often reprinted. J. G. *Whittier issued an edition, with Introduction (1871). More recent is that of V. D. Scudder in Everyman's Library, also with Introduction (1910). W. Teignmouth Shore, *John Woolman. His Life and our Times* (1913).

WOOLSTON, THOMAS (1670–1733), *Deistical writer. Educated at Sidney Sussex College, Cambridge, he was elected a Fellow of his college in 1691 and after ordination held a succession of college appointments. In various writings he defended the *Origenistic modes of exegesis of the OT, and in some polemical writings upheld the *Quakers as their modern exponents. His provocative methods led to the loss of his Fellowship in 1721, whereupon Woolston announced his intention of founding a new sect. He entered the lists on the Deistical side in the controversy between A. *Collins and Edward Chandler (c. 1668–1750, Bp. of *Durham from 1730) with his *A Moderator between an Infidel and an Apostate* (1725). This was soon followed by two supplements in which he maintained that the Virgin Birth and the Resurrection were allegories.

Collection of his Works in 5 vols., London, each work being separately paginated and dated, incl. [T. Stackhouse?,] *The Life of Mr. Woolston, with an Impartial Account of his Writings* (London, 1733); C. C. Woog, *De Vita et Scriptis Thomae Woolstoni* (Leipzig, 1743). *Memoirs of the Life and Writings of Mr. William *Whiston, containing Memoirs of Several of his Friends also Written by himself* (ed. 2, 1749), pp. 231–5. J. Leland, *A View of the Principal Deistical Writers that have Appeared in England in the Last and Present Century*, i (1754), pp. 126–43. L. Stephen, *History of English Thought in the Eighteenth Century* (2 vols, 1876), esp. vol. i, pp. 230–8; E. Sayous, *Les Déistes anglais et la christianisme principalement depuis Toland jusqu'à Chubb, 1696–1738* (1882), pp. 122–45. A Gordon in *D.N.B.*, lxii (1900), pp. 437–9.

WORCESTER. The diocese was founded c. 680 on the initiative of St. *Theodore of Canterbury for the tribe of the Hwicce, when the diocese of Mercia was divided into five. The cathedral church, first dedicated to St. Peter but later to our Lady, was richly endowed by the Mercian kings. The secular canons, who originally served it, were gradually replaced by *Benedictine monks (c. 974–7), under St. *Oswald, who also completed the building of the cathedral in 983. Destroyed by the Danes in 1041, it was rebuilt by St. *Wulfstan (1084–9), but the only remaining parts of his work are the crypt and a few walls, much of it having perished by fire and by the fall of the central tower in 1175. In 1218 the cathedral, which contained the tomb of King John between the shrines of St. Oswald and St. Wulfstan, was restored and reconsecrated. In the course of time several alterations were made in its structure, the choir being a particularly fine example of the Early English style, whereas the nave, re-done in the 14th cent., shows chiefly Perpendicular work. The subsequent history of the see was uneventful. From 1497 to 1534 it was held by absentee Italian bishops who were the King's representatives at Rome. The monastery was suppressed in 1540 and a secular chapter founded in 1542, the last of the priors, Henry Holbeach, becoming the dean. Among the better-known Bps. of Worcester are, besides those already named, St. *Dunstan, H. *Latimer, J. *Hooper, J. *Gauden, J. *Earle, E. *Stillingfleet, and C. *Gore.

Episcopal Register for the periods of vacancy of the See ('Registrum Sede Vacante'), 1301-1435, ed. J. W. Willis Bund (Worcestershire Historical Society, 3 vols., 1893-7); Registers of Godfrey Giffard [Bp. 1268-1301], ed. id. (ib., 2 vols., 1902); of William Ginsborough [Bp. 1303-7], ed. id. (ib., 1907); of Walter Reynolds [Bp. 1308-13], ed. R. A. Wilson (ib., 1927); of Thomas de Cobham [Bp. 1317-27], ed. E. H. Pearce (ib., 1930). E. S. Fegan (ed.), *Journal of Prior William More* [1518-36] (ib., 1914). J. M. Wilson, *The Liber Albus of the Priory of Worcester*. Parts i and ii, Priors John de Wyke, 1301-17, and Wulfstan de Bransford, 1317-39 (ib., 1919). M. Hollings (ed.), *The Red Book of Worcester containing Surveys of the Bishop's Manors and other Records chiefly of the Twelfth and Thirteenth Centuries* (ib., 4 pts., 1934-50). J. M. Wilson (ed.), *Accounts of the Priory of Worcester for the Year . . . 1521-2*, and J. H. Bloom-S. G. Hamilton, *A Catalogue of the Rolls of Obedientiaries* (ib., 1907); J. M. Wilson-C. Gordon (edd.), *Early Compotus Rolls of the Priory of Worcester* (ib., 1908); S. G. Hamilton (ed.), *Compotus Rolls of the Priory of Worcester of the XIVth and XVth Centuries* (ib., 1910). C. Price (ed.), *Liber Pensiorum Prioratus Wigorn*. Being a Collection of Documents Relating to Pensions from Appropriated Churches and other Payments Receivable by the Prior and Convent of Worcester and to the Privileges of the Monastery (ib., 1925). I. Atkins, *The Early Occupants of the Office of Organist and Master of the Choristers of the Cathedral Church of Christ and the Blessed Virgin Mary, Worcester* (ib., 1918). W. Thomas, *A Survey of the Cathedral Church of Worcester*: with an Account of the Bishops thereof from the Foundation of the See to the Year 1660 (1736). J. Noake, *The Monastery and Cathedral of Worcester* (1866). W. *Dugdale, *Monasticon Anglicanum*, i (ed. 1817), pp. 567-622. E. F. Strange, *The Cathedral Church of Worcester* (Bell's Cathedral Series, 1900). W. M. Ede, *The Cathedral Church of Christ and the Blessed Virgin Mary of Worcester*. Its Monuments and their Stories (Worcester, 1925). R. Willis, 'The Architectural History of the Cathedral and Monastery at Worcester' in *The Archaeological Journal*, xx (1863), pp. 83-132, 254-72, and 301-18. M. M. C. Calthrop in *V.C.H.*, Worcs, ed. J. W. Willis-Bund-W. Page, ii (1906), pp. 94-112, and F. M. Stenton-H. Brakspear in iv (1924), pp. 394-408. H. W. Yeatman-Biggs in *D.E.C.H.* (1912), pp. 649-53, s.v.

WORD OF GOD. See *Logos*.

WORDSWORTH, CHRISTOPHER (1807-1885), Bp. of *Lincoln.

He was the youngest son of Christopher Wordsworth (1774-1846), Master of Trinity College, Cambridge, and thus a nephew of W. *Wordsworth, the poet. After a brilliant career at his father's college at Cambridge, he was elected a Fellow in 1830. From 1836 to 1844 he was Headmaster of Harrow, and later held various ecclesiastical appointments till consecrated Bp. of Lincoln in 1869. Throughout his life he remained a conservative High Churchman, with great veneration for the early Church Fathers. He compiled a Commentary on the whole Bible (NT, 1856-60; OT, 1864-70) which had a wide circulation in its day, being esp. valued for its large range of homiletic material. In *patristics, perhaps his most important study was *St. Hippolytus and the Church of Rome* (1853), a reply to C. C. J. Bunsen's book (1852). He also wrote a series of hymns, published in *The Holy Year* (1862), of which several are still in frequent use, among them 'Gracious Spirit, Holy Ghost', 'Hark! the sound of holy voices', 'See the Conqueror mounts in triumph' and 'Songs of thankfulness and praise'.

He publd. a collection of his works as *Miscellanies Literary and Religious* (3 vols., 1879). J. H. Overton-Elizabeth Wordsworth (daughter), *Christopher Wordsworth, Bishop of Lincoln, 1807-1885* (1888). A. C. Benson, *The Leaves of the Tree*. Studies in Biography (1911), ch. 11, 'Bishop Wordsworth of Lincoln', pp. 260-83. J. H. Overton in *D.N.B.*, lxiii (1900), pp. 9-11.

WORDSWORTH, JOHN (1843-1911), Bp. of *Salisbury.

The elder son of Christopher Wordsworth, Bp. of *Lincoln (q.v.), he was educated at *Winchester and New College, *Oxford, became a Fellow of Brasenose College in 1867, and a prebendary of Lincoln in 1870. One of the best Latin scholars of his day, he worked assiduously from 1878 onwards at producing a critical edition of the *Vulgate NT (Mt. to Acts publd. 1889-1905; minor edition of whole, 1911). In 1881 he was *Bampton Lecturer, and from 1883 to 1885 the first Oriel professor of the Interpretation of Scripture. From 1885 till his death he was Bp. of Salisbury. As a bishop he proved an invaluable adviser to Abp. E. W. *Benson (with whom he was intimate) and an enthusiastic worker in the cause of Reunion, esp. with the *Swedish and *Old Catholic Churches. To the latter end he published two treatises on the validity of Anglican Ordinations, *De successione episcoporum in ecclesia anglicana* (1890) and *De validitate ordinum anglicanorum* (1894). In 1897 he composed the Latin *Responsio* sent by the Abps. of *Canterbury and *York in reply to '*Apostolicae curae'. His other writings include *The Ministry of Grace* (1901) and *The National Church of Sweden* (1911).

Life by E. W. Watson (London, 1915). Id. in *D.N.B.*, 1901-1911, iii, pp. 705-7.

WORDSWORTH, WILLIAM (1770-1850), English poet.

He was educated at St. John's College, Cambridge, and went to France in 1791-2 where he became a radical in politics and sympathized with the revolutionaries. In these years he went through a period of moral laxity and religious unbelief. After his return to England he devoted himself entirely to poetry. In 1797 began his friendship with S. T. *Coleridge, and in 1798 the two published jointly *Lyrical Ballads* which contain the famous 'Lines above Tintern Abbey'. Wordsworth's chief aim in this collection, which was a landmark in English poetry, was to bring out the deeper spiritual meaning in everyday persons and events, a task for which he was particularly fitted by his capacities for minute observation and for the detection of the emotional qualities in commonplace things. In 1799 he settled at Grasmere. Among his later works are *The Prelude*, his spiritual autobiography (completed 1805), and the *Poems in Two Volumes* (1807), containing the famous 'Ode to Duty' and 'Ode on the Intimations of Immortality'. In the poetry written after 1810 there is a marked decline of poetic power, e.g. in much of *The Excursion* (1814), on which he had been working for many years. The great inspiration of Wordsworth's art being nature, which he invested with spiritual qualities, brought his thought sometimes near to *pantheism. In his later years, however, he returned to a more orthodox form of creed. His *Ecclesiastical Sonnets* (1822), which give an account of the Church in England from the introduction of Christianity to the reign of *Charles I, are an eloquent expression of his devotion to the C of E, containing, at the same time, a fair appreciation of medieval English Catholicism. He was in sympathy with the *Oxford Movement and esp. with J. *Keble, whose *Christian Year* he admired. Having been little valued in his youth, Wordsworth's genius came to be recognized in his later years, and he was made Poet Laureate in 1843.

Edd. of Poems publd. by Wordsworth himself include those of 1807 (2 vols., London; reprinted by T. Hutchinson, 1897, and ed. H. Darbishire, Oxford, 1914), 1827 (5 vols., London), 1832 (4 vols., London), and 1849-50 (7 vols., ib.). Important posthumous ed. in 6 vols., London, 1857; repr. as the Centenary Edition, 6 vols., 1870; edd. by J. Morley (London, 1888), by E. Dowden (7 vols., London, &c., 1892–1893), by T. Hutchinson (Oxford, 1895; not quite complete), by [D.] W. Knight (8 vols., London, 1896), and by E. de Selincourt (6 vols., Oxford, 1940-4). Prose Works, ed. A. B. Grosart (3 vols., London, 1876) and [D.] W. Knight (2 vols., ib., 1896). [D.] W. Knight (ed.), *Letters of the Wordsworth Family from 1787 to 1855* (3 vols., 1907). Christopher *Wordsworth, *Memoirs of William Wordsworth* (2 vols., 1851). J. Searle [i.e. Philips], *Memoirs of William Wordsworth* (1852); E. P. Hood, *William Wordsworth*. A Biography (1856); J. M. Sutherland, *William Wordsworth*. The Story of his Life with critical remarks on his Writings (1887). Elizabeth Wordsworth, *William Wordsworth* (1891). D. W. Rannie, *Wordsworth and his Circle* (1907). E. H. Sneath, *Wordsworth, Poet of Nature and Poet of Man* (1912); W. Harper, *William Wordsworth*. His Life, Works and Influence (2 vols., 1916). A. Beatty, *William Wordsworth, His Doctrine and Art in their historical Relations* (University of Wisconsin Studies in Language and Literature, xvii; 1922). C. H. Herford, *Wordsworth* (1930); H. Read, *Wordsworth* (Clark Lectures, 1929-30; 1930). E. Smith, *An Estimate of Wordsworth by his Contemporaries, 1793-1822* (1932). H. I'Anson Fausset, *The Lost Leader*. A Study of Wordsworth (1933). E. C. Batho, *The Later Wordsworth* (1933). A. D. Martin, *The Religion of Wordsworth* (1936). T. J. Wise, *A Bibliography of the Writings in Prose and Verse of William Wordsworth* (1916). H. King-E. de Selincourt in *C.B.E.L.*, iii (1940), pp. 165–72.

WORLD COUNCIL OF CHURCHES, The.

The 'fellowship of Churches which accept our Lord Jesus Christ as God and Saviour', formally constituted at *Amsterdam on 23 Aug. 1948. The organization arose from the fusion of the two earlier movements, '*Life and Work' and '*Faith and Order', the first practical steps being taken at their respective conferences at *Oxford and *Edinburgh in 1937. Further stages were a conference at Utrecht in 1938, where a constitution was drafted, and the first World Conference of Christian Youth at Amsterdam (Aug. 1939). The Council set up a Central Committee, which meets annually. It has held Assemblies at Evanston, Ill. (1954), and New Delhi, India (1961). The membership now comprises nearly all the major non-RC Christian bodies, Protestant, Anglican, and Orthodox, including (since 1961) the Patriarchate of Moscow. In 1961 the International Missionary Council (see *Edinburgh Conference* (1910)) was integrated in the World Council of Churches.

WORLD'S EVANGELICAL ALLIANCE.

See *Evangelical Alliance*.

WORMS, Concordat of (1122),

also the 'Pactum Calixtinum'. The agreement which was reached between Pope *Callistus II and the Emp. Henry V on 23 Sept. 1122, putting an end to the *Investiture Controversy. It professed to maintain the rights of both parties in the matter of filling the German, Burgundian, and Italian sees. The Church was to have full freedom in episcopal elections, and investiture with the ring and crozier, symbolizing ecclesiastical jurisdiction, was to be combined with consecration. On the other hand, elections were to take place in the presence of the Emperor, who was to have the right to settle any disputed cases, and also to give temporal investiture by the sceptre.

Text ed. G. H. Pertz in *M.G.H.*, Leges, ii (1837), p. 75 f.; conveniently repr. in Mirbt, p. 161 f. (No. cccv), with bibl. reff.; Eng. tr. in Bettenson, p. 154 f., and in S. Z. Ehler-J. B. Morrall (edd.), *Church and State Through the Centuries* (1954), p. 48 f. E. Bernheim, *Zur Geschichte des Wormser Concordates* (1878); D. Schäfer, *Zur Beurteilung des Wormser Konkordats* (*Abh.* (Berl.), 1905, Hft. 1); E. Bernheim, *Das Wormser Konkordat und seine Vorurkunden hinsich.lich Entstehung, Formulierung, Rechtsgültigkeit* (Untersuchungen zur Deutschen Staats- und Rechtsgeschichte, lxxxi; 1906); H. Rudorff, *Zur Erklärung des Wormser Konkordats* (Quellen und Studien zur Verfassungsgeschichte des Deutschen Reiches, i, Hft. 4; 1906). See also works cited under *Investiture Controversy*.

WORMS, Diet of (1521).

The most celebrated of the long series of Imperial diets held at Worms, at which M. *Luther defended his doctrines before the Emp. *Charles V. It took place in the Bischofshof from 27 Jan. to 25 May. The Papal legate, *Aleander, who had arrived at Worms on 30 Nov. 1520, having put the case against Luther on 13 Feb. 1521, Luther was then summoned and arrived on 16 Apr. On 18 Apr. he made his final refusal to recant his doctrines, acc. to an early tradition concluding his answer with the famous words 'Hie stehe ich. Ich kan nicht anders. Gott helff mir. Amen.' Charles V having announced on the following day his resolve to take firmer measures against his doctrines, Luther departed from Worms on 26 Apr. On 25 May his teachings were formally condemned in the Edict of Worms.

Many of the primary docc. are pr. in P. Balan (ed.), *Monumenta Reformationis Lutherana ex Tabulariis S. Sedis Secretis, 1521-1525* (Ratisbon, 1883); extracts from these and other collections, with further reff., in Kidd, pp. 79-89 (Nos. xxxix-xlvi). J. Friedrich, 'Der Reichstag zu Worms im Jahre 1521 nach den Briefen des päpstlichen Nuntius Hieronymus Aleander' in *Abh.* (Bayr.), hist. Cl., xi, Abt. 3 (1870), pp. 55-146. T. Brieger, *Aleander und Luther, 1521*. Die vervollständigten Aleander-Depeschen nebst Untersuchungen über den Wormser Reichstag (Quellen und Forschungen zur Reformation, i; 1884); A. Hausrath, *Aleander und Luther auf dem Reichstage zu Worms* (1897). N. Paulus, 'Zur Geschichte des Wormser Reichstages von 1521' in *Hist. J.*, xxxix (1919), pp. 269-77. P. Kalkoff, *Der Wormser Reichstag von 1521* (1922), with full reff. Detailed bibl. in Schottenloher, iii (1938), pp. 12-14 (Nos. 27923-50), with reff. to other lists of specialized items, and on the Edict of Worms, ib., iv (1938), p. 753 f. (Nos. 44534-42). See also works cited under *Aleander; Luther, M.*; and *Reformation*.

WORMS, Disputation of (1540-1).

The colloquy arranged, after the failure of the Conference of *Hagenau (q.v.), with a view to reuniting the Catholics and Protestants in Germany. The conference met on 25 Nov.

1540, with eleven representatives on each side. After a long debate on procedure, it was finally agreed that one theologian should speak for each party, J. *Eck being selected by the Catholics and P. *Melanchthon by the Protestants. In Jan. 1541 an agreed formula was reached on the disputed matter of *original sin; but on 18 Jan. it was decided to end the discussions at Worms in view of the forthcoming Reichstag at *Ratisbon.

L. von *Pastor, *Die kirchlichen Reunionsbestrebungen während der Regierung Karls V* (1879), pp. 198–217. W. Friedensburg, 'Zur Geschichte des Wormser Convents, 1541' in *Z.K.G.*, xxi (1901), pp. 112–27. O. Clemen, 'Epigramme auf Teilnehmer am Wormser Religionsgespräch 1540/41', ib. I (1931), pp. 441–54. G. Kawerau in *P.R.E.* (ed. 3), xxi (1908), pp. 489–92, s.v. 'Wormser Religionsgespräche I'. Further bibl. in Schottenloher, iv (1938), p. 538 f. (Nos. 41404–16).

WORMS, Synod of (1076). The synod convened by the Emp. *Henry IV to defend his claims during the *Investiture controversy with Pope *Gregory VII. Henry invited to the assembly, which met on 24 Jan. 1076, the Abps. of Mainz and Trier and a large number of other (mainly German) bishops. It issued a strong anti-Papal statement, charging Gregory with many serious crimes and calling upon the people of Rome to depose him; and an offensively worded letter was despatched by Henry to the Pope personally. As a result, the Pope excommunicated Henry shortly afterwards.

Relevant texts ed. L. Weiland in *M.G.H.*, Leges, Sect. iv, Constitutiones et Acta Publica Imperatorum et Regum, i (1893), pp. 106–13. G. Meyer von Knonau (ed.), *Jahrbücher des deutschen Reiches unter Heinrich IV und Heinrich V*, ii (1894), pp. 613–28. A. Fliche, *La Réforme grégorienne*, iii (S.S.L., xvi; 1937), pp. 50–9, with important notes. See also works cited under *Investiture Controversy*.

WORSHIP, Directory of Public (1645). The 'Directory for the Public Worship of God', compiled by the *Westminster Assembly (q.v.), was designed on *Presbyterian principles to replace the BCP. An Ordinance requiring its use was passed by both houses of Parliament on 4 Jan. 1645. For the most part it contained general instructions rather than set forms of service. The principal service consisted of prayers, two lessons, Psalms and a sermon. The Holy Communion was to follow the morning sermon, with the people seated round the Holy Table. Instructions were provided for Baptism, visitation of the sick, and a form of marriage, but the burial of the dead was to be performed without ceremony, and feast days, apart from Sunday, were abolished. Penalties for using the BCP or failure to follow the Directory were imposed on 26 Aug. 1645.

The 'Ordinance for taking away the Book of Common Prayer, and for establishing and putting into execution of the Directory for the Public Worship of God' [incl. text of Directory] is pr. in C. H. Firth–R. S. Rait (edd.), *Acts and Ordinances of the Interregnum, 1642–1660* (1911), pp. 582–607.

WOUNDS, The Five Sacred. Though the Passion narratives of the Gospels expressly record only the opening of the Lord's side, the piercing of His hands and feet, a normal practice in contemporary crucifixions, is attested in the Resurrection appearances (Lk. 24. 39 and Jn. 10. 10 and 27). Acc. to Catholic theology the Five Wounds continue to be visible on the glorified body of Christ. Devotion to them developed in the Middle Ages, esp. under the influence of St. *Bernard's love for the human Person of our Lord and His Passion, and was fostered by the *stigmatization of St. *Francis of Assisi. Preference was soon given to the wound in the side from which the Church and the Sacraments, esp. Baptism ('water') and Eucharist ('blood'), were said to have sprung, and which led gradually to the cult of the *Sacred Heart. In the 14th and 15th cents. prayers to the Five Wounds became numerous in popular religious literature. A feast was instituted which is still observed in some places on the Fourth Friday in *Lent, *Portugal adopted the emblem on her coat of arms, the members of the *Pilgrimage of Grace wore it on their clothes, and the 'wells of pity' were engraved on many English rings in the 15th cent. To-day the devotion is fostered esp. by the *Passionists, and their Rosary of the Five Wounds approved by the Popes in 1823 and 1851. The Wounds are symbolized by the five signs of the cross over the Host after the Consecration in the Mass, by the five grains of incense in the *Paschal Candle, and by the five crosses on the altar stone.

L. Gougaud, O.S.B., *Dévotions et pratiques ascétiques du moyen-âge* (Pax, xxi; 1925), pp. 78–128 (Eng. tr., 1927, pp. 80–130). A. Franz, *Die Messe im deutschen Mittelalter* (1902), pp. 155–61 and 703 f. G. F. Holweck in *C.E.*, xv (1912), p. 714 f., s.v.; K. Hofmann in *L.Th.K.*, xii (1938), additional page inserted between cols. 708 and 709, s.v. 'Wunden Christi', with further bibl. See also works cited under *Sacred Heart* and *Stigmatization*.

WRATH OF GOD, The. An anthropomorphic phrase for the Divine attitude towards sin. Wrath is predicated of God only metaphorically, as the human passions have no equivalents in the purely spiritual Divine substance. The expression is frequent in the Bible, esp. in the OT (e.g. Exod. 15. 7, Ps. 2. 12), where wrath is attributed to God not only when He punishes sinners but also when He sends trials to the just (e.g. Job 14. 13). In the NT the wrath of God is particularly connected with the Judgement on the Last Day which St. *Paul calls the 'day of wrath' (Rom. 2. 5, cf. ib. 1. 18 and Mt. 3. 7), a conception elaborated in the Book of Rev., esp. under the metaphors of the 'wrath of the Lamb' (6. 16) and the 'winepress of the fierceness of the wrath of Almighty God' (19. 15).

Patristic discussion in *Lactantius' *De Ira Dei*. A. Ritschl, *De Ira Dei* (Bonn, 1859). F. W. Weber, *Vom Zorn Gottes* (Erlangen, 1862; with introd. essay by Franz *Delitzsch). M. Pohlenz, *Vom Zorne Gottes*. Eine Studie über den Einfluss der griechischen Philosophie auf das alte Christentum (Forschungen zur Religion und Literatur des Alten und Neuen Testaments, xii; 1909). G. Bornkamm, 'Die Offenbarung des Zornes Gottes (Rom. 1–3)' in *Z.N.T.W.*, xxxiv (1935), pp. 239–62. See also comm. to Romans, cited s.v., ad loc. J. Orr in *H.D.B.*, i (1898), pp. 97–9, s.v. 'Anger (Wrath) of God'; R. Kübel–A. Rüegg in *P.R.E.* (ed. 3), xxi (1908), pp. 719–29, s.v. 'Zorn Gottes'; T. B. Kilpatrick in *H.E.R.E.*, i (1908), pp. 477–82, s.v. 'Anger (Wrath) of God'; H. Kleinkert–O. Grethier–J. Fichtner–E. Sjöberg–G. Stählin–O. Procksch in *T.W.B.*, v (1954), pp. 382–448, s.v. 'ὀργή', with bibl.

WREDE, WILHELM (1859–1906), German NT scholar. He was professor of NT at Breslau from 1895 till his death. In his chief contribution to NT studies, *Das Messiasgeheimnis in den Evangelien* (1901), he challenged the current critical view that St. Mark's Gospel was an unadorned record of historic fact and almost uninfluenced by the dogmatic beliefs of its author. Wrede also maintained that Jesus in His earthly life did not claim to be the Messiah, and that the Gospel story is a reading-back of later beliefs about His Person into the narrative. In a small book on St. *Paul (*Paulus*, 1905), written in a similar vein of scepticism, he maintained that the Christian religion received its essential form largely through St. Paul's radical transformation of the teaching of Christ. Of his many writings on NT literary problems perhaps the most important was *Die Echtheit des zweiten Thessalonicherbriefes* (1903).

Wrede's *Vorträge und Studien*, ed. Adolf Wrede (brother; Tübingen, 1907), with introd., pp. iii–xiv. A. *Schweitzer, *Geschichte der Leben-Jesu-Forschung* (ed. 2, 1913), pp. 368–89 (Eng. tr. of ed. 1, 1910, pp. 328–49). J. *Kaftan, *Jesus und Paulus. Eine freundschaftliche Streitschrift gegen . . . Wrede* (1906). A. *Jülicher in *P.R.E.* (ed. 3), xxi (1908), pp. 506–10.

WREN, CHRISTOPHER (1632–1723), architect of *St. Paul's Cathedral. Educated at Wadham College, Oxford, he was elected to a fellowship at All Souls in 1653 and in 1657 appointed professor of astronomy at Gresham College, London. Three years later he became Savilian professor of astronomy at Oxford, and in 1661 assistant, and later full, surveyor-general. He was one of the founders, and from 1680 to 1682 president, of the Royal Society. He soon proved himself a consummate draughtsman, with as keen a grip on practice as on theory. His architectural designs for the chapel of Pembroke College, Cambridge (1663), and the Sheldonian Theatre, Oxford (1664), having disclosed his marked ability, he was chosen, after the Great Fire of 1666, as one of the rebuilders of the city. Besides his greatest work, St. Paul's Cathedral, begun in 1675 and completed in 1716, Wren was also responsible for building 52 churches, 36 company halls, the Monument (1671–8), the Chelsea Hospital (1682), Trinity College Library, Cambridge (1677), and perh. the (Old) Ashmolean Museum, Oxford (1683), in addition to other important works.

Parentalia: or Memoirs of the Family of the Wrens: . . . but chiefly of Sir Christopher Wren. . . . Compiled by his son Christopher (London, 1750), pp. 181–368; *Life and Works of Sir Christopher Wren, from the Parentalia or Memoirs of his son Christopher* [ed. E. J. Enthover] (London and New York, [1903]). Lives and studies by J. Elmes (London, 1823), L. Phillimore (ib., 1881), A. Stratton (Liverpool, 1897), L. Milman (London, 1908), L. Weaver (ib., 1923), C. Whitaker-Wilson (ib., 1932), J. Lindsey (ib., 1951), M. S. Briggs (ib., 1953), E. Sekler (ib., 1956) and V. Fürst (ib., 1956). *Sir Christopher Wren, A.D. 1632–1723.* Bicentenary Memorial Volume published under the Auspices of the Royal Institute of British Architects (1923). P. Waterhouse and others, *Sir Christopher Wren, 1632–1723* (1923). Publications of the Wren Society (Oxford, 1924 ff.). F. C. Penrose in *D.N.B.*, lxiii (1900), pp. 80–94.

WROTH, WILLIAM (*c.* 1575–1642), the first Welsh Nonconformist pastor. Educated at Oxford, he became rector of Llanfaches in Monmouthshire in 1611, and after a sudden conversion in 1620 became famous as a Puritan preacher. In 1635 he was summoned before the Court of *High Commission, but his case was delayed. In 1639, however, after he had ceased to hold his living, he established at Llanfaches with some associates the first separatist church in Wales.

WULFILA. See *Ulphilas.*

WULFRIC, St. (d. 1154), also 'St. Ulrich', anchorite. He was born at Compton, nr. Bristol, and ordained priest to the charge of Deverill, nr. Warminster. After a conversion attributed to an interview with a beggar, who told him the contents of his purse and prophesied a life of sanctity for him, he returned to Compton. He was enclosed *c.* 1125 in a cell at Haselbury, Somersetshire, where he practised severe austerities and became renowned for his prophecies and miracles, e.g. that at his prayers the suit of mail which he wore was once cut with scissors as cloth. The statement that he was a *Cistercian seems to rest on a confusion. His cult was mainly confined to the south-west of England, and he was never formally canonized. Feast day, 20 Feb.

Earliest account, written during his lifetime, by Henry of Huntingdon, *Historia Anglorum*, ix, 23 (ed. T. Arnold, R.S., 1879, p. xxix f.). Life by John, Abbot of Ford, prob. written between 1180 and 1190, ed. M. Bell, O.S.B. (Somerset Record Society, xlvii; 1933), with full introd.

WULFSTAN (d. 1023), Abp. of *York from *c.* 1002. Like his two predecessors, he held the see of York in plurality with that of *Worcester. (He is not to be confused with the Wulfstan of the foll. entry.) The fact that he was buried at *Ely suggests that he was at one time a monk there and he may have been Bp. of London from 996 to 1002. He was one of the best writers in Old English, probably surpassed only by his correspondent, *Aelfric. Among his writings is an examination of the principles of civil and ecclesiastical government which influenced later legislators, e.g. Canute. He is best known, however, for a homily, in alliterative English prose bearing the MS. Latin title: '*Lupi Sermo ad Anglos quando Dani maxime prosecuti sunt eos, quod fuit anno 1014*'. In it he vividly depicted the miseries of the time, ascribing them to God's judgement on the wickedness of all classes.

Sermons ed. A. [S.] Napier (Sammlung Englischer Denkmäler in kritischen Ausgaben, iv, Abt. 1; 1883). Crit. ed. of 'Sermo Lupi ad Anglos' by Dorothy Whitelock (Methuen's Old English Library, 1939), with introd. Id., 'A Note on the Career of Wulfstan the Hermit' in *E.H.R.*, lii (1937), pp. 460–5; id., 'Archbishop Wulfstan, Homilist and Statesman' in *Transactions of the Royal Historical Society*, Fourth Series, xxiv (1942), pp. 25–45. K. Jost, *Wulfstanstudien* (Schweizer Anglistische Arbeiten, xxiii; 1950), with detailed bibl. In Eng. there are also the more specialized artt. by D. Whitelock, 'Wulfstan and the so-called Laws of Edward and Guthrum', in *E.H.R.*, lvi (1941), pp. 1–21; id., 'Wulfstan and the Laws of Cnut', ib., lxiii (1948), pp. 433–52. Homilies, ed. Dorothy Bethurum (Oxford, 1957), with introd. and notes.

WULFSTAN, St. (*c.* 1009–95), also 'Wulstan', Bp. of *Worcester. After ordination he spent some 25 years in a monastery at Worcester, where he became greatly respected for his humility and asceticism. Elected Bp. of Worcester in 1062, he accepted the office with extreme reluctance, but having resigned himself to it, administered the diocese with great effectiveness till his death. Largely through uncertainty as to the status of the see of Worcester in relation to *Canterbury and *York, Wulfstan found himself opposed at the beginning of his episcopate to both archbishops; but later *Lanfranc was won by the simple goodness of Wulfstan, and together they suppressed the slave trade between England and Ireland. In the secular struggles of the time he assisted William I against the Barons and William II against the Welsh. His Life was written by Coleman, a monk of Worcester. Feast day, 19 Jan.

The Old English Life by Coleman, written between 1095 and 1113, has not survived; a Lat. rendering by *William of Malmesbury ed. R. R. Darlington (Camden Society, 3rd Series, xl; 1928; Eng. tr., Oxford, 1934). [R. W. *Church], 'St. Wulstan' in *Lives of the English Saints* [ed. J. H. *Newman] (London, 1844; ed. 2, by A. W. Hutton, v [1901], pp. 3–50). J. W. Lamb, *Saint Wulstan, Prelate and Patriot. A Study of his Life and Times* (C.H.S., 1933), with bibl.

WURTEMBERG CONFESSION, The. A
Protestant confession of faith in 35 articles, compiled in 1552 by J. *Brenz on the model of the *Augsburg Confession for presentation to the Council of *Trent. It contained some *Calvinist elements, but it was predominantly Lutheran, with certain approximations (in view of its purpose) to the specifically Catholic position. Use was made of it by Abp. M. *Parker in preparing the Thirty-Eight Articles of 1563 (see *Thirty-Nine Articles*).

Text in H. Heppe (ed.), *Die Bekenntnisschriften der altprotestantischen Kirche Deutschlands* (Cassel, 1855), pp. 491–554. J. Rauscher (ed.), *Württemberg und das Augsburgische Glaubensbekenntnis* (Blätter für Württembergische Kirchengeschichte, iv; Stuttgart, 1930), pp. 70–89. P. *Schaff, *A History of the Creeds of Christendom*, i (1877), pp. 343 f. and 627–9, with table illustrating the connexion with the Thirty-Nine Articles. See also works cited s.v. *Thirty-Nine Articles*.

WYCLIFFE, JOHN (c. 1329–84), English
reformer. Born of a manorial family at Wycliffe-on-Tees, near Richmond, he was educated at Oxford and appears as Master of Balliol College c. 1360. He is probably to be identified with the Wycliffe appointed in 1365 Warden of Canterbury Hall (now incorporated in Christ Church) and deprived when the secular clergy in the Hall were expelled by Abp. Simon Langham (1336–8) in favour of the regulars. In 1361 he was appointed vicar of Fillingham, in 1368 of Ludgershall, and finally in 1374 of Lutterworth, where he held the incumbency until his death (31 Dec. 1384), although throughout he spent much time at Oxford. He also held the prebend of Aust in the Collegiate Church of Westbury-on-Trym. In 1374 he was one of the envoys who negotiated the dispute on papal provisions and reservations at Bruges.

Wycliffe early gained a reputation as a philosopher. He vigorously attacked the *Nominalism of *Duns Scotus and *William of Occam.

Even in his earliest works he ridiculed on philosophical grounds the notion of annihilation. He rose to fame through the doctrine of 'lordship' or 'dominion' in his two books, 'De Dominio Divino' and 'De Civili Dominio', where he insisted that lordship depended on grace and that since the present sinful state of the Church precluded true lordship, disendowment and the confiscation of ecclesiastical property were demanded. His other thesis, that everyone in a state of grace has true lordship, may have been used to justify the Peasants' Rebellion of 1381; but, though the revolt undoubtedly damaged respect for Wycliffe among the upper classes, there is little to show that Wycliffe had anything to do with it. His attitude towards the Church itself grew more and more radical as the Great Schism, and with it the deterioration in Papal prestige, continued. In 'De Potestate Papae' (c. 1379) he maintained that the Pope's claims were ill founded in Scripture, that his salvation was no more certain than that of any other man, and that the sole criterion of his acts was their conformity with the Gospel. His language became increasingly violent. The Pope and the hierarchy began to figure as antichrist and his adherents as the 'twelve daughters of the diabolical leech'. In addition, he castigated the monks with their 'red and fat cheeks and great bellies', and fiercely attacked the worship of saints, pluralities, non-residence, pilgrimages, and other abuses.

Wycliffe also hotly contested certain of the medieval doctrines. In 'De Eucharistia' he questioned *transubstantiation, maintaining that in the Eucharist the substance of the bread and wine remained after the consecration, while Christ was in the sacrament 'not by way of multiplication, but virtually only, as a king is in every part of his kingdom' (not *substantialiter et corporaliter*, but *vere et realiter, virtualiter et sacramentaliter*). In the Bible, which he urged should be read in English, he found the one criterion for Christian action or belief, and to this end he began to translate it into English, a work carried on by his disciples, *Nicholas of Hereford and J. *Purvey. Every humble and holy man was to be free to read and interpret the Scriptures for himself. For further details see *Bible* (English Versions, 1).

In bulls issued in 1377, Gregory XI pronounced against eighteen Wycliffite errors, of a political rather than a theological nature, and in 1382 the Blackfriars Council of London (the '*Earthquake Synod') further condemned his teaching. Yet the final step was not taken until the Council of *Constance (1415) passed judgement on 267 errors, culled from his works, ordered his writings to be burned, and his bones to be dug up. The last injunction was not actually fulfilled until 1428.

Wycliffe has been called the 'Morning Star of the Reformation'. Although in many respects he was essentially the medieval scholar, he expounded doctrines which, especially when popularized by his Poor Preachers and later *Lollards, cut at the roots of the medieval theocracy and at current faith and dogma. His main direct influence was in Bohemia and Central Europe where his views were propagated by J. *Huss and his followers. See also *Lollards*.

His Lat. works are being publd. by the Wyclif Society (London, 1883 ff.); among those not included in this collected ed. are the *Tractatus de Officio Pastorali*, ed. G. V. Lechler (Leipzig, 1863); *Trialogus*, ed. id. (Oxford, 1869), and *De Christo et suo Antichristo*, ed. R. Buddensieg (Gotha, 1880). *Select English Works* (with some wrong attributions), ed. T. Arnold (3 vols., Oxford, 1867–71) and *English Works . . . hitherto Unprinted*, ed. F. D. Matthew (E.E.T.S., lxxiv; 1880); *Selections*, ed. H. E. Winn (Oxford, 1929). The primary source, apart from his own works, is the *Fasciculi Zizaniorum* attributed to Thomas *Netter (q.v.). There is much documentary material in J. Lewis, *The History of the Life and Sufferings of . . . John Wicliffe* (1720; new ed. repr. from copy with author's corrections, 1820). The best modern studies are those of G. [V.] Lechler (2 vols., Leipzig, 1873; Eng. tr. by P. Lorimer, 2 vols., 1878, revised ed., with additional material, [1884]) and H. B. Workman (2 vols., Oxford, 1926). Shorter studies by L. Sergeant (Heroes of the Nations, 1893), J. N. *Figgis (Typical English Churchmen, Series ii, 1909, pp. 3–46), and D. Hague (London, 1909; enlarged ed., 1935). H. J. Wilkins, *Was John Wycliffe a Negligent Pluralist? . . .* (1915), pp. 1–67. J. H. Dahmus, *The Prosecution of John Wyclif* (New Haven, Conn.–London, 1952), with bibl. R. L. Poole, *Wycliffe and Movements for Reform* (1893), pp. 61–112. K. B. McFarlane, *John Wycliffe and the Beginnings of English Nonconformity* ('Teach Yourself History', [1952]). W. W. Shirley, *A Catalogue of the Original Works of John Wyclif* (Oxford, 1865; rev. ed. by J. Loserth, [1924]). S. H. Thomson, *The Order of Writing of Wyclif's Philosophical Works* (Prague, 1929).

J. A. Robson, *Wyclif and the Oxford Schools* (Cambridge, 1961). B. L. Manning in *C. Med. H.*, vii (1932), pp. 486–507 (ch. xvi), with good bibl. pp. 900–7. J. Loserth in *P.R.E.* (ed. 3), xxi (1908), pp. 225–44, s.v. 'Wiclif und der Wiclifismus'; H. *Rashdall in *D.N.B.*, lxiii (1909), pp. 202–223, with discussion of literature to date. See also works cited under *Bible (English Versions)*, and *Lollards*.

WYCLIFFITES. See *Lollards*.

WYNFRITH, St. See *Boniface, St.*

WYTTENBACH, THOMAS (1472–1526), Swiss Reformer. A native of Biel (Bienne), Switzerland, after studying at *Tübingen, he became a lecturer at Basel, where H. *Zwingli was one of his pupils. Here he came under the influence of the Humanist Movement and the new methods of Biblical Study. After long ecclesiastical disputes at Biel, he eventually settled there as pastor in 1515 and from 1523 publicly supported the Reformation. Marriage in 1524 led to his deposition. Wyttenbach died soon afterwards, and it was left to his successor at Biel, Jakob Würben, to carry through the Reformation in the city.

F. A. Haller–H. Hermelink in *P.R.E.* (ed. 3), xxi (1908), pp. 574–7, s.v.; O. E. Strasser in *R.G.G.* (ed. 2), v (1931), col. 2056, s.v., with bibl.

X

XAVIER, St. FRANCIS. See *Francis Xavier, St.*

XIMÉNEZ DE CISNEROS, FRANCISCO (1436–1517), Cardinal Abp. of Toledo. A native of Torrelaguna in Castile, after studying at Alcalá de Henares and Salamanca, he spent some years in Rome, returning to Spain in 1465 with a letter from Sixtus IV, which provided him with the archpriestship of Uzeda in 1473. His diocesan, Carillo, Abp. of Toledo, who was offended by the appointment, incarcerated him, but in 1480 eventually gave way. Ximénez, restored to his benefice, promptly exchanged it for a chaplaincy in the diocese of Siguenza, where Cardinal Mendoza (later Abp. of Toledo) made him his vicar general. After fulfilling this office with distinction, he unexpectedly gave it up to become an *Observantine friar and entered the convent of San Juan de los Reyes at Toledo, recently founded by *Ferdinand and *Isabella. His life of extreme austerity soon attracted large crowds of penitents and he took refuge in a remote monastery, living for considerable periods as an anchorite.

In 1492 a new epoch in his life began when he reluctantly accepted the office of confessor to Queen Isabella to whom he had been recommended by Mendoza. His advice was soon sought on affairs of state as well as on strictly spiritual matters. In 1494 he was appointed under the Queen's influence Provincial of the *Franciscans in Castile and in the face of formidable opposition carried through drastic reforms esp. among the *Conventuals. On the death of Mendoza (1495), he succeeded, again with great reluctance, to the Archbishopric of Toledo, the primatial and most influential see in Spain, and an office which carried with it the High Chancellorship of Castile. Behind the outward splendour of his position, Ximénez continued to live a severely ascetic life. In 1499 he followed the court to Granada where he was active in promoting measures to convert the Moors.

On the death of Isabella (24 Nov. 1504), Ferdinand resigned his title of King of Castile, and Ximénez was faced with the delicate political task of establishing concord between Ferdinand and his son-in-law, the Archduke Philip of Burgundy, who succeeded to the throne. Ferdinand eventually agreed to retire from Castile. On the sudden death of Philip in 1506, Ximénez found himself the virtual ruler of Castile, until Ferdinand returned from Naples in Aug. 1507, bringing for the Archbishop a cardinal's hat. In 1509 he led a Spanish force to Oran in Morocco for purposes partly religious and partly territorial. On the death of Ferdinand (23 Jan. 1516), Ximénez became regent of Castile during the minority of the later *Charles V (q.v.). Intrigues at home and in Flanders, where Charles was then living, made his position extremely difficult, but his vigorous measures enabled him to maintain his authority. On his way to meet Charles, who had landed in Asturias and virtually dismissed him from his office, he died at Roa on 8 Nov. 1517, not without a suspicion of poison.

In addition to his services to the Church, Ximénez was a zealous patron of learning. In 1500 he founded on a lavish scale out of his private income the university of Alcalá (opened 1508), to which he brought distinguished scholars from Paris, Bologna, and Salamanca. At Toledo he revived the *Mozarabic Rite and endowed a chapel in the cathedral for its survival. His chief contribution to scholarship was the famous *Complutensian Polyglott (q.v.; Lat. 'Complutum', i.e. Alcalá).

The principal materials are to be found in Alvaro Gómez de Castro, *De Rebus Gestis a F. Ximenio Cisnerio* (fol. 'Compluti' [Alcalá], 1569). There is also an account written by a member of the Cardinal's household, J. de Vallejo, *Memorial de la vida de Fray Francisco Jimenes de Cisneros*, first ed. A. de la Torre y del Cerro (Madrid, 1913). Other eary lives by E. de Robles (Toledo, 1604), M. Baudier (Paris, 1635), J. Marsollier (Toulouse, 1694), and [V.] E. Fléchier (Paris, 1693; also 2 vols., Amsterdam, 1693). Important modern studies by C. J. *Hefele (Tübingen, 1844: Eng. tr., 1860) and [Jerónimo López de Alvarez de Toledo y del Hierro], Conde de Cedillo (3 vols., Madrid, 1921–8). Other studies by J. P. R. Lyell (London, 1917, wi'h good bibl.), R. Merton (ib., 1934), and J. García Mercadal (ed. 2, Madrid, 1941). W. Starkie, *Grand Inquisitor. Being an Account of Cardinal Ximines de Cisneros and his Times* (1940; popular). L. F. de Retana, C.SS.R., *Cisneros y su siglo* (2 vols., 1929–30).

XYSTUS. See *Sixtus*.

Y

YAH, abbreviation of *Yahweh (q.v.). This form of the word is confined to poetical passages in the OT.

YAHWEH. One of the proper names of the Hebrew Deity, traditionally rendered in English as '*Jehovah' (q.v.). It probably represents the correct original pronunciation of the *Tetragrammaton, which was lost through the Jews having regularly substituted in reading the word '*Adonai' from motives of reverence. The traditional explanation of the name is given in Ex. 3. 14 f. (cf. 6. 2 f.); but the word is almost certainly more ancient and of disputed derivation.

S. R. *Driver, 'Recent Theories on the Origin and Nature of the Tetragrammaton' in *Studia Biblica*. Essays in Biblical Archaeology and Criticism, i (1885), pp. 1–20. C. F. *Burney (ed.), *The Book of Judges* (1918), 'Yahweh or Yahu originally an Amorite Deity', pp. 243–53. G. R. Driver, 'The Evidence for the Name "Yahweh" Outside the Old Testament' in D. C. Simpson (ed.), *Old Testament Essays*. Papers Read Before the Society for Old Testament Studies . . . (1927), pp. 18–24. T. J. Meek, *Hebrew Origins* (Haskell Lectures for 1933–4; 1936), pp. 85–115 and passim. W. F. Albright, *From the Stone Age to Christianity* (Baltimore, 1940), esp. pp. 197–207. H. H. Rowley, *From Joseph to Joshua*. Biblical Traditions in the Light of Archaeology (Schweich Lectures for 1948; 1950), pp. 148–63, with reff.

YEAR, Liturgical. In the W., the Christian Year is based on the week and the two festivals of *Easter and *Christmas. Easter, by its Pass-over connexion, forms a link with the Jewish liturgical calendar, which is lunar; Christmas was fixed in the 4th cent. to coincide with the pagan observance of the winter solstice which, acc. to the Roman calendar, fell at that time on 25 Dec., and thus is a link with the Roman civil year which began on 1 Jan., and is solar.

The liturgical year begins with the first Sunday in *Advent, i.e. that nearest to the Feast of St. Andrew (30 Nov.). There are four Sundays in Advent and either one or two Sundays after Christmas bridge the gap to the *Epiphany (6 Jan.). Sundays are reckoned 'after Epiphany' until *Septuagesima, *Sexagesima and *Quinquagesima, which receive their names from the approximate number of days before Easter. *Ash Wednesday introduces the forty days of *Lent with its six Sundays, and five Sundays 'after Easter' lead up to *Ascension Day with its following Sunday and *Pentecost (or *Whitsunday), the end of Eastertide. In the RC Church the Sundays from Pentecost to Advent are usually numbered 'after Pentecost' but in the Anglican Church they are reckoned, as in the *Sarum Use, 'after *Trinity', i.e. the Sunday after Pentecost.

The liturgical year of the Orthodox Church of the East, which is based on Easter, falls into three parts, τριῴδιον (the ten weeks before Easter), πεντηκοστάριον (the paschal season), and ὀκτώηχος (the rest of the year).

N. Nilles, S.J., *Kalendarium Manuale Utriusque Ecclesiae Orientalis et Occidentalis* (2 vols., Innsbruck, 1896–7). K. A. H. Kellner, *Heortologie oder das Kirchenjahr und die Heiligenfeste in ihrer geschichtlichen Entwicklung* (1901). J. Dowden, *The Church Year and Kalendar* (1910). F. *Cabrol, O.S.B., *Les Origines liturgiques* (1906). A. A. McArthur, *The Evolution of the Christian Year* (1953). G. *Dix, O.S.B., *The Shape of the Liturgy* [1945], ch. xi, pp. 303–96; A. *Baumstark, *Liturgie comparée* (ed. 3 by B. Botte, O.S.B., 1953), ch. ix., pp. 168–93 [Eng. tr., 1958, pp. 152–74]. H. Thurston, S.J., in *C.E.*, iii (1908), pp. 158–66, s.v. 'Calendar'.

YEW SUNDAY. A medieval name for *Palm Sunday, derived from the custom of carrying branches of yew (as a substitute for palm) in the liturgical procession.

YIDDISH. A language which is in essence a combination of *Hebrew or *Aramaic and Low German. It originated in the early Middle Ages as a result of a migration of Jews from the Rhineland to E. Europe, Poland, and Russia. Written in Hebrew characters, the words were at first mainly German, but later Hebrew, Aramaic, and even Russian and Polish words found their way into the vocabulary. It is still spoken, and there is a considerable literature.

M. Mieses, *Die Jiddische Sprache* (1924).

Y.M.C.A. ('Young Men's Christian Association'). An association founded in London in 1844 by George Williams (1821–1905) out of his meetings for prayer and Bible-reading. It has always had an essentially lay and interdenominational character, and in recent years has become increasingly inter-confessional. Its object is to win young men and boys for Jesus Christ by uniting them in fellowship through activities designed to develop and train their powers of body, mind, and spirit, and to enable them to serve God and their fellows. Full members are committed to the Christian way of life, including the obligations of witness and service: Associate members are not bound by the same obligations, but share the facilities provided, although they do not control policy or management. Most Y.M.C.A.s do their work in club buildings in which provision is made for social amenities, for programmes of religious, educational, and physical activities, and in many large cities for hostels as well. But an increasingly important sphere of Y.M.C.A. work lies in its service to the wider community—men and women of H.M. Forces at home and overseas, apprentices and trainees, its farm training and sea training schemes, its residential college courses for industrial leadership, its national camps and holiday centres. The membership of the World's Alliance of Y.M.C.A.s numbers between three and four millions. Its extensive work for prisoners of war and displaced persons as well as for belligerents in two World Wars has been deservedly praised. See also *Y.W.C.A.*

L. L. Doggett, *History of the Young Men's Christian Association* (New York, 1922). C. P. Shedd and others,

History of World's Alliance of Young Men's Christian Associations (S.P.C.K., 1955). R. C. Morse, *History of the North American Young Men's Association* (New York, 1913); C. H. Hopkins, *History of the Y.M.C.A. in North America* (ib., 1951).

YOGA. A Sanskrit word meaning 'union', and by extension 'contemplation'. The name is applied in a technical sense to a Hindu system of philosophy aiming at the union of the soul with the Divine Spirit by means of concentration to the exclusion of all sense perception. The earliest known description of the system occurs in the Upanishads (5th cent. B.C.); the technique was fully developed by Patanjali in the Yogasutras (either 2nd cent. B.C. or 5th cent. A.D.). Modern adherents have tended to substitute a system of health culture for the asceticism of the original teachers.

R. Garbe in *H.E.R.E.*, xii (1921), pp. 831–3, s.v.

YOM KIPPUR (יוֹם הַכִּפֻּרִים). The Hebrew name of the *Day of *Atonement* (q.v.).

YONGE, CHARLOTTE MARY (1823–1901), novelist. She was born at Otterbourne, near *Winchester, where she lived throughout her life. Imbued by her father with great devotion to the Church, she taught for 71 years in the village Sunday school. When in 1835 J.*Keble became vicar of Hursley (with which parish Otterbourne was then united) she soon fell under his influence, became an enthusiastic supporter of the *Oxford Movement, and determined to apply her remarkable talents as a story teller to spreading the faith in fiction. Her first success was *The Heir of Redclyffe* (1853). Among those which followed were *Heartsease* (1854), *The Daisy Chain* (1856), *The Trial* (1864), *The Pillars of the House* (1873), and *Magnum Bonum* (1879). Miss Yonge also wrote Lives of Bp. J. C. *Patteson (2 vols., 1873) and of Hannah *More (1888), and from 1851 onwards she edited *The Monthly Packet*, a periodical which aimed esp. at commending Anglican ideals to young women. She issued in all some 160 books.

Collected ed. of her *Novels and Tales* (16 vols., London, 1879–80). C. Coleridge, *Charlotte Mary Yonge*. Her Life and Letters (1903), with text of her autobiography of her childhood and early youth, pp. 1–119, and list of her works, pp. 355–68. Ethel Romanes, *Charlotte Mary Yonge*. An Appreciation (1908). G. Battiscombe, *Charlotte Mary Yonge*. The Story of an Uneventful Life (1943). M. Mare-A. C. Percival, *Victorian Best Seller*. The World of Charlotte M. Yonge (1947).

YORK. From 79 to 427 York was ruled by the Romans, who made it their capital of Britain. The first mention of a Bp. of York occurs in the acts of the Council of *Arles (314). The original Christian community was destroyed in the Saxon invasion. Christianity was restored in the 7th cent.; in 625 St. *Paulinus was consecrated Bp. of York. He baptized King Edwin in 627 and received the *pallium in 631, but in 633 there was another pagan invasion; Paulinus fled to *Rochester,

and during the next decades York was under the care of the Celtic bishops of *Lindisfarne. The see was finally restored in 664, when St. *Wilfrid was consecrated bishop, who introduced Roman usages and favoured *Benedictine monasticism. In 735, under *Egbert, the brother of the King, the see was raised to archiepiscopal dignity and its archbishops became the primates of the Northern Province. Egbert also founded the famous School of York; among its pupils were his successor Ethelbert and the famous scholar *Alcuin. Under the first Norman Archbishop, Thomas of Bayeux (1070–1100), began the long drawn-out struggle for precedence between *Canterbury and York. In 1071, in a discussion at Rome between *Lanfranc of Canterbury and Thomas of York, Pope *Alexander II decided in favour of the former, who was to consecrate the Archbishops of York and receive their oath of obedience. But in 1118 Thurston, Abp.-elect of York, refused to submit and appealed to *Callistus II, who consecrated him and released him and his successors from the supremacy of Canterbury. The controversy continued during the following centuries and was finally settled by Innocent VI (1352–62), who decided that the Abp. of Canterbury was to have precedence and the title of 'Primate of All England', and that the Abp. of York should be styled 'Primate of England'. Either archbishop was allowed to carry his cross in the other's province. Among the later pre-Reformation archbishops were Thomas *Arundel (1388–96), who fought Wycliffites and Lollards, the popular Richard *Scrope (1398–1405) who was executed because he took the part of Richard II in the rebellion against Henry IV, Cardinal C. *Bainbridge (1508–14), and T. *Wolsey (1514–30). The suppression of the religious houses caused the famous Yorkshire rising known as the *Pilgrimage of Grace (q.v.) in 1536–37, which resulted in the ruthless destruction of monasteries throughout the diocese, among them the Benedictine Abbeys St. Mary's York (founded 1078), and Whitby, the Cistercian Abbeys of *Fountains, *Rievaulx and Sawley, and the Augustinian monastery of Bolton. In the 17th cent. York became a stronghold of *Puritanism and in the 18th of *Methodism. Among the best known of its post-Reformation archbishops are E. *Grindal, E. *Sandys, T. *Herring, C. G. *Lang, and W. *Temple.

The cathedral, York Minster, dedicated to St. Peter, stands on the site of the basilica built by St. Edwin, which was destroyed in the rebellion against the Normans in 1069. The fine present building, in Early English and Decorated Gothic, dates from 1230 to 1744.

Registers of Walter Gray [Abp. 1215–55], ed. J. Raine (Surtees Society, lvi; 1872); of Walter Giffard [Abp. 1266–79], ed. W. Brown (ib., cix; 1904); of William Wickwane [Abp. 1279–85], ed. id. (ib., cxiv; 1907); of John le Romeyn [Abp. 1286–96] and Henry Newark [Abp. 1296–99], ed. id. (ib., cxxiii and cxxviii; 1913–17); of Thomas Corbridge [Abp. 1300–4], ed. id. (ib. cxxxviii and cxli; 1925–8); and of William Greenfield [Abp. 1306–15], ed. id.-A. H. Thompson (ib., cxlv, cxlix, cli, clii, and cliii; 1931–40). J. Raine (ed.), *The Fabric Roll of York Minster* (ib., xxxv; 1859). 'York Statutes' in H. Bradshaw-C. *Wordsworth (edd.), *Statutes of Lincoln Cathedral*, ii (1897), pp. 90–135. J. Raine (ed.), *The Historians of the Church of York and its Archbishops* (3 vols., R.S., 1879–94). W. H. Dixon–J. Raine, *Fasti Eboracenses*. Lives of the Archbishops of York, i (1863). F. Drake, *Eboracum, or the History and Antiquities of the City of York* (1736), esp. Book II, 'The History and Antiquities of the Church of York', pp. 399–627. J. Browne, *The History of the Metropolitan Church of St. Peter, York* (2 vols., 1847). W. *Dugdale, *Monasticon Anglicanum*, vi, pt. 3 (ed. 1830), pp. 1172–1209. R. Willis, 'The Architectural History of York Cathedral' in *Memoirs Illustrative of the History and Antiquities of the County and City of York, Communicated to the Archaeological Institute of Great Britain and Ireland held at York, July 1846* (1848), No. 9. G. Benson, *Handbook to the Cathedral Church of St. Peter, York* [1893]. A. Clutton-Brock, *The Cathedral Church of York* (Bell's Cathedral Series, 1899). A. H. Thompson in *V.C.H.* Yorks, iii, ed. W. Page (1913), pp. 375–382. W. R. Lethaby, 'Archbishop Roger's Cathedral at York and its stained glass' in *The Archaeological Journal*, lxxii (1915), pp. 37–48. A. H. Thompson, *The Building of York Minster* (York Minster Historical Tracts, No. 2; 1927). H. Gee in *D.E.C.H.* (1912), pp. 662–6, s.v.

YOUNG, PATRICK (1584–1652), Biblical and Patristic scholar. He was educated at St. Andrews. After incorporation at Oxford in July 1605, he was ordained and became a chaplain at All Souls College. A year or two later he settled in London where he was appointed Royal Librarian and prob. assisted *James I in preparing the Latin edition of his Works which appeared in 1619. From 1623 to 1647 he was rector of Hayes, Middlesex. In 1633 he published from the *Codex Alexandrinus, which had reached the Royal Library from Cyril *Lucar in 1628, the *editio princeps* of St. *Clement of Rome's *Ep. I ad Cor.* and in 1637 a folio *Catena Graecorum Patrum in Jobum* on the basis of two Bodley MSS.; but these works, though important, embody only a fraction of his great erudition. On his title-pages he Latinized his name as 'Patricius Junius'.

Letters calendared and ed. J. Kemke (Sammlung Bibliothekswissenschaftlicher Arbeiten, ed. K. Dziatzko, xii; 1898), with life, pp. v–xxix. '*Catalogus Librorum Manuscriptorum Bibliothecae Wigorniensis' made in 1622–1623 by Patrick Young*, ed. I. Atkins–N. R. Ker (Cambridge, 1944). Life in T. Smith, *Vitae Quorundam Eruditissimorum et Illustrium Virorum* (London, 1707; sep. pagination). A. H. Millar in *D.N.B.*, lxiii (1900), p. 385 f.

YULE. The word, of Teutonic ancestry, which etymologically seems to imply 'noise' or 'clamour', was prob. originally applied to a Scandinavian feast of obscure origin, possibly connected with the turn of the year, and hence in Old English to the season of Dec. and Jan. In later usage it came to denote *Christmas and its attendant festivities. Except in the north of England the term is now archaic: but it is still found in compounds such as 'yule-log' connected with old-fashioned Christmas celebrations. Until the middle of the 19th cent. it was also used as an exclamation of joy and revelry at Christmastide.

YVO, St., of Chartres. See *Ivo, St., of Chartres.*

Y. W. C. A. ('Young Women's Christian Association'). This is a very similar movement to the *Y.M.C.A. (q.v.). It was founded in 1855 by two women simultaneously—Miss Robarts, who in the South of England began a Prayer Union, and Lady Kinnaird, who in London opened homes and institutes for young business women. The two organizations united in 1877.

Anna V. Rice, *A History of the World's Young Women's Christian Association* (New York, 1948). F. Kinnaird in *H.E.R.E.*, xii (1921), pp. 838–41, s.v. 'Young Women's Christian Association'.

Z

ZABARELLA, FRANCESCO (1360–1417), Italian canonist. Having studied jurisprudence at *Bologna, he taught canon law at Florence from 1385 to 1390 and at Padua from 1390 to 1410, being at the same time employed in both the Paduan and the Venetian diplomatic services. Called to Rome by Boniface IX to tender advice in the matter of the Great Schism, he took part in the Council of *Pisa in 1409. Though not in major orders, he received the Bpric. of Florence in 1410, which he resigned on being created cardinal by *John XXIII in 1411. After supporting John at the Council of Rome in 1412–13, he conducted the negotiations with the Emp. Sigismund for the Council of *Constance. His courageous conduct at the Council, which he continued to attend after John XXIII had fled (1415), contributed largely to the final healing of the schism. Though a supporter of John, he advised the Pope to abdicate, and until his death made continuous efforts to bring about the election of a new Pope. His collection of proposals for ending the schism entitled 'De schismate' (1402–8) was first printed in 1545. It was placed on the Index, however, because it asserted the supremacy of the General Council over the Pope. His writings on canon law, the 'Lectura super *Clementinis' and the 'Commentaria in libros *Decretalium', long remained standard works.

G. Vedova, *Memorie intorno alla vita ed alle opere del cardinale F. Zabarella* (Padua, 1829). Lives by A. Kneer (Münster Diss., 1891; vol. i only) and G. Zouta (Padua, 1915). See also works cited under *Constance, Council of*.

ZACCHAEUS. The chief 'publican' (tax-collector), who was the subject of an incident related in Lk. 19. 1–10. Having climbed a sycamore tree to see Christ pass through *Jericho, he was called by name to come down and give Him lodging in his house.

ZACHARIAH. The father of St. *John the Baptist. A Jewish priest, he received a vision in the *Temple promising him and his aged wife, *Elisabeth, a son, who would be 'filled with the Holy Ghost, even from his mother's womb' (Lk. 1. 15). He celebrated the birth of the child and the coming redemption of Israel in the '*Benedictus'. Acc. to later tradition he was murdered in the Temple at the command of Herod. Feast day, 5 Nov.

ZACHARIAS, St. (d. 752), Pope from 741. He was a Greek of Calabria by birth. Revising the policy of his predecessor, Gregory III, he gave up the alliance with Duke Trasamund of Spoleto, and, through his personal influence, induced Liutprand, King of the Lombards, to return four cities and all her patrimonies to the Church. He also obtained a twenty years'

truce, caused the King to abandon his attack on *Ravenna and persuaded him to restore what he had already taken of its possessions. His relations with the Frankish kingdom were very cordial, esp. through the influence of St. *Boniface, to whose missionary activities and reforms he gave full support. He confirmed the deposition of the last Merovingian, Childeric III, and had *Pepin and his consort solemnly anointed by Boniface. In the matter of images he vigorously denounced the *Iconoclastic policy of the Emp. Constantine Copronymus, to whom he addressed two important letters on the subject. Zacharias held synods at Rome in 743 and 745, the latter confirming the condemnation of the two heretics, Adalbert and Clement, by St. Boniface. He made a Greek translation of the 'Dialogues' of St. *Gregory the Great which was widely read in the E. Feast day, 5 Mar.

Two Letters ed. W. Gundlach in *M.G.H.*, Epistolae, iii (1892), pp. 479–87, 709–11. Jaffé, i, 262–70. *L.P.* (ed. Duchesne), i (1886), pp. 426–39. E. Caspar, *Geschichte des Papsttums von den Anfängen bis zur Höhe der Weltherrschaft*, ii (1933), esp. 710–23 and 731–40. Mann, i (pt. 2; 1902), pp. 225–88; Fliche–Martin, v (1938), pp. 419–23, with reff. F. X. Seppelt in *L.Th.K.*, xii (1938), col. 1021 f., s.v., with bibl.; E. Amann in *D.T.C.*, xv (pt. 2; 1950), cols. 3671–5, s.v.; G. Mollat in *E.C.*, xii (1954), col. 1760, s.v. 'Zaccaria', for further bibl.

ZACHARIAS SCHOLASTICUS (d. after 536), also 'Zacharias of Mitylene' and 'Zacharias Rhetor', *Monophysite divine. He was a native of Maiuma, nr. Gaza, and hence known, with *Procopius and *Aeneas of Gaza, as one of the 'Gaza Triad'. *C.* 492 he became a lawyer at *Constantinople and is known to have been in later life Bp. of Mitylene. His most important work was a Church History, valuable for the years 450–91. It survives in *Syriac embedded in a later compilation. Zacharias was also the author of biographies of *Severus of Antioch, Peter the Iberian and others; of a dialogue, 'De Opificio Mundi', directed against the *Neo-Platonists; and of a Disputation against the *Manichees.

His 'De Opificio Mundi', the only writing of Zacharias which survives complete in Gk., was ed., with Lat. tr. and notes, by C. Barth (Leipzig, 1655; with Aeneas of Gaza's 'De Immortalitate Animae', pp. 164–326); it was repr. from the ed. of A. *Gallandi, *Bibliotheca Veterum Patrum*, xi (Venice, 1776), pp. 266–92, in J. P. Migne, *PG*, lxxxv, 1011–44. Better ed. by D. F. Boissonade, Paris, 1836 (with the 'De Immortalitate Animae' of Aeneas of Gaza, pp. 79–152; with notes, pp. 317–460). A Gk. fragment of his Disputation against the Manichees is pr., with Lat. tr., by J. B. *Pitra, *Analecta Sacra et Classica Spicilegio Solesmensi*, v (pt. 1; Rome, 1888), pp. 66–71. His 'Church History', incorporated in a later Syriac Chronicle in which alone it survives, ed. J. P. N. Land, *Anecdota Syriaca*, iii (Leyden, 1870), pp. 1–340; crit. ed., with Lat. tr., by E. W. Brooks (C.S.C.O., Syriaci Scriptores, Series III, v–vi, 1919–24); Eng. tr. by F. J. Hamilton–E. W. Brooks (London, 1899). Syriac trr. of lives of Severus of Antioch ed. J. Spannuth (Wissenschaftliche Beilage zum Programm des Königlichen Gymnasiums zu Kiel; Göttingen, 1893); also ed., with Fr. tr., by M. A. Kugener in *P.O.*, ii (1907), pp. 5–115; of an Egyptian monk named Isaias, ed. J. P. N. Land, op. cit.

pp. 346–56; also ed. E. W. Brooks, *Vitae Virorum apud Monophysitas Celeberrimorum* (C.S.C.O., Syriaci Scriptores, Series III, xxv; 1907), pp. 3–16, with Lat. tr., pp. 3–10; of a fragment of life of Peter the Iberian, ib., p. 18, with Lat. tr. p. 12. M. A. Kugener, 'La Compilation historique de Pseudo-Zacharie le Rhéteur' in *Revue de l'Orient chrétien*, v (1900), pp. 201–14 and 461–80; id., 'Observations sur la vie de l'ascète Isaïe et sur les vies de Pierre l'Ibérien et de Théodore d'Antinoë par Zacharie le Scolastique' in *B.Z.*, ix (1900), pp. 464–70. T. Nissen, 'Eine christliche Polemik gegen Julians Rede auf den König Helios', ib., xl (1940), pp. 15–22. E. Honigmann, *Patristic Studies* (S.T., clxxiii; 1953), pp. 194–204 (No. XXI: 'Zacharias of Mitylene'). Bardenhewer, v, 112–16. G. Krüger in *P.R.E.* (ed. 3), xxi (1908), pp. 593–8, s.v. 'Zacharias Scholasticus'; G. Bardy in *D.T.C.*, xv (pt. 2; 1950), cols. 3676–80, s.v. 'Zacharie le Rhéteur'.

ZADOKITE FRAGMENTS. See *Damascus Fragments*.

ZAHN, THEODOR (1838–1933), NT and Patristic scholar.

Born at Mörs, he was Privatdozent (1868) and Extraordinary Professor (1871) at Göttingen and Professor successively at Kiel (1877), Erlangen (1878), Leipzig (1888) and Erlangen (again, 1892). He retired in 1909. His standpoint was that of sober conservatism and all his work was characterized by a vast erudition and great thoroughness. His long series of studies on the NT *Canon, embodied in his *Geschichte des neutestamentlichen Kanons* (2 vols., 1888–92) and the successive fascicules of *Forschungen zur Geschichte des neutestamentlichen Kanons* (10 parts, 1881–1929), contained much pioneer work. He edited a Commentary on the NT, to which he himself contributed the volumes on Mt. (1903), Lk. (1913), Jn. (1908), Acts (2 vols., 1919–21), Rom. (1910), Gal. (1905) and Rev. (2 vols., 1924–6); and also wrote an Introduction to the NT (2 vols., 1897–9; Eng. trans., 3 vols., 1909). His studies in the field of Patristics included *Marcellus von Ancyra* (1867), *Der Hirt des Hermas untersucht* (1868), *Ignatius von Antiochien* (1873) and the *Acta Joannis* (1880). With A. *Harnack and O. von Gebhardt he edited *Patrum Apostolicorum Opera* (ed. major, 1875–8; ed. minor, 1877). Among his many works addressed to a less specialized public were *Konstantin der Grosse und die Kirche* (1876), *Geschichte des Sonntags vornehmlich in der alten Kirche* (1879) and *Skizzen aus dem Leben der alten Kirche* (1894).

Festschriften for Theodor Zahn, Leipzig, 1908, with contributions by N. Bonwetsch and others; and ib., 1928, with contributions by P. Bachmann and others. *Zahnbibliographie* (ib., 1918). E. Stange (ed.), *Die Religionswissenschaft der Gegenwart in Selbstdarstellungen*, i (1925), last item (28 pp.). A. Meyer in *R.G.G.* (ed. 2), v (1931), col. 2070 f., s.v.

ZEALOTS. A Jewish party of revolt.

Acc. to *Josephus (*Bell. Jud.* IV, iii, 9), they were followers of John of Gischala who, after resisting the Romans in Galilee, escaped to *Jerusalem, where they wrested the city from the more moderate party and inspired the fanatical resistance which led to its destruction by the Romans in A.D. 70. They have been commonly identified with (1) the followers of Judas of Gamala who led a revolt at the time of the census of Quirinius (A.D. 6) and who, acc. to Josephus, was the 'author of the fourth sect of Jewish philosophy' whose members 'agree in all things with the Pharisaic notions' but 'have an inviolable attachment to liberty, and say that God is their only ruler and lord' (*Antiq.* XVIII, i, 6) and (2) the Sicarii who, in the unsettled period before the outbreak of the Jewish war, tried to achieve their ends by assassinating their political opponents. The epithet ζηλωτής ('zealot'), applied in Lk. 6.15 to Simon, one of the Twelve, is an accurate translation of an Aramaic word, derived from a root meaning 'to be zealous', which in Mk. 3. 18 is transliterated καναναῖος ('Cananean'); it may mean that Simon belonged to the Zealot party, which in that case must have been already in existence in the lifetime of Jesus. But it may equally well be a description of his character, 'the zealous'.

The chief reff. in Josephus are *Antiq.* xviii. 1, 6 and *Bell. Jud.* iv, 3, 9, iv, 4, 7 and vii, 8, 1. E. *Schürer, *Geschichte des Volkes im Zeitalter Jesu Christi*, i (ed. 4, 1910), pp. 617–634; but cf. F. J. Foakes Jackson-K. *Lake in idd. (edd.), *The Beginnings of Christianity*, i (1920), pp. 421–5 (Appendix A: 'The Zealots'). J. W. Lightley, *Jewish Sects and Parties in the Time of Jesus Christ* (1925), pp. 323–95. See also commentaries on Mt. 10. 4. K. Kohler in *J.E.*, xii (1906), pp. 639–43, s.v.; F. Sieffert in *P.R.E.* (ed. 3), xxi (1908), pp. 655–7, s.v. 'Zeloten'; A. Stumpff in *T.W.B.*, ii (1935), pp. 886–9, s.v. ζηλόω. 'C. Der Zelotismus'.

ZECHARIAH, Book of.

One of the *Minor Prophets. The book falls into two distinct sections, chs. 1–8 and 9–14.

The former, written by Zechariah (cf. Ezra 5. 1, 6. 14) himself, dates from the spring of 519 B.C. (1. 7) and the winter of 518/7 B.C. (7. 1). The Jews had returned from exile *c.* 537, but the *Temple was not yet restored (cf. Hag. 1. 4–2. 5). After a short introductory prophecy (1. 1–6) there follow accounts of eight visions: (1) 1. 7–17, four horsemen, signifying messengers, who report that the whole earth is quiet: nevertheless the prophet declares that God will shortly act to end the desolation of Jerusalem which has now lasted for nearly 70 years; (2) 1. 18–21, four horns broken by four smiths, signifying the destruction of heathen powers; (3) 2. 1–13, the man with a measuring line, shewing that the future glory of Jerusalem will not be limited by a city-wall but that she will be a holy city for all nations; (4) 3. 1–10, the cleansing of Joshua the High Priest (cf. Ez. 5. 2, Hag. 1. 1, Ecclus. 49. 12) from his 'filthy garments' (i.e. the removal of the nation's guilt) and his investiture with new dignity, in view of the near advent of the expected prince of David's line, foretold by Isaiah (Is. 11. 1) and Jeremiah (Jer. 23. 5); (5) 4. 1–14, a seven-branched candlestick (Israel) supplied with oil (brightness, grace) from two olive-trees, which are explained as two 'sons of oil', i.e. anointed persons who are prob. the High Priest and the Davidic prince (see art. *Messiah*). The latter seems to be identified with the person of Zerubbabel, the contemporary head of the royal line of

Judah (cf. 1 Chr. 3. 1–19, Ez. 5. 2, Hag. 1. 1), who is exhorted to complete the restoration of the Temple. The remaining visions show (6) 5. 1–4, a flying roll, symbolizing the curse which will light on evil-doers throughout the land; (7) 5. 5–11, a woman, named 'Wickedness', carried away in an *ephah* (a large dry measure) from the holy land to a far country; and (8) 6. 1–8, four chariots representing four winds (or spirits) carrying God's judgements to the four corners of the earth. Joshua the High Priest (perh. the original text referred also, or only, to Zerubbabel here) is to be crowned as Messiah (6. 9–15). In chs. 7–8 Zechariah declares that the observance of fasts should give place to true righteousness, and prophesies the future glory of Judah when the *Diaspora should be gathered in and the Gentiles seeking God should voluntarily join themselves to the Jews.

Chs. 9–11 and 12–14, which each begin (like the following Book of *Malachi) with the descriptive title *massah*, i.e. prophetic utterance (AV and RV, 'burden'), are probably to be considered anonymous prophecies relating to different circumstances, and different in style, from the work of Zechariah. They contain examples of a developed *eschatology (e.g. ch. 14) and allusions to events, often obscure but apparently best explained by reference to the history of the period of the *Maccabees, esp. in the case of 9. 13, which refers to strife between Jews and Greeks.

Commentaries by H. G. Mitchell (I.C.C. on Hag., Zech., Mal., and Jon., 1912, pp. 81–362) and W. E. Barnes (Cam. Bib., RV, 1917). J. W. Rothstein, *Die Nachtgesichte des Sacharja*. Studien zur Sacharjaprophetie und jüdische Geschichte im ersten nachexilischen Jahrhundert (Beiträge zur Wissenschaft vom Alten Testament, viii; 1910); J. Kremer, *Die Hirtenallegorie im Buche Zacharias auf ihre Messianität hin untersucht* (Alttestamentliche Abhandlungen, xi, Hft. 2; 1930). K. Marti, 'Die Zweifel an der prophetischen Sendung Sacharjas' in *Studien zur semitischen Philologie und Religionsgeschichte Julius Wellhausen zum siebzigsten Geburtstag . . . gewidmet* (Beihefte zur Z.A.T.W., xxvii, 1914), pp. 279–97. J. *Wellhausen in E.Bi., iv (1903), cols. 5391–5, s.v. Further commentaries under *Minor Prophets*.

ZENO, St. (d. *c.* 375), Bp. of *Verona from 362. Beyond the fact that Zeno was an African by birth, very little is known of him. His sermons ('Tractatus') have affinities with the writings of such Africans as *Tertullian and *Cyprian, but, as they did not come into circulation until the earlier Middle Ages, they were unknown to St. *Jerome and *Gennadius. The 8th cent. Life by the Veronese presbyter Coronatus is devoid of historical value. He is commonly represented in art with a fish. Feast day, 12 Apr.

Editio princeps of his sermons by A. Castellanus, O.P.–J. de Lenco (Venice, 1508); more accurate ed. by P. and H. *Ballerini (Verona, 1739), repr. in J. P. Migne, *PL*, xi, 253–528; modern ed. by J. B. C. Giuliari (Verona, 1883). F. A. Schütz, *S. Zenonis, Episcopi Veronensis, Doctrina Christiana* (Leipzig, 1854); A. Bigelmair, *Zeno von Verona*. Habilitationsschrift (1904). A. Grazioli, 'S. Zenone di Verona' in *Scuola cattolica*, lxviii (1940), pp. 174–99; B. Pesci, O.F.M., 'De Christianarum Antiquitatum Institutionibus in Sancti Zenonis Veronensis Episcopi Sermonibus' in *Antonianum*, xxiii (1948), pp. 33–42. G. Bardy in *D.T.C.*, xv (pt. 2; 1950), cols. 3685–90, s.v. 'Zénon', with bibl.

ZENO (*c.* 450?–91), Emperor of the E. from 474. His life was a tissue of treachery and violence, and his reign a succession of disastrous wars against his relations and ministers, and against the Ostrogoths (see *Theodoric). He took an active, but ill-advised, part in attempting to remedy some of the evil consequences of the *Monophysite heresy; but his *Henoticon (482) did nothing to bring about the reunion for which it was devised, and occasioned a new schism between Constantinople and Rome.

Accounts of his reign in J. B. Bury, *A History of the Later Roman Empire from Arcadius to Irene*, i (1889), esp. pp. 250–60, and G. Ostrogorsky, *Geschichte des byzantinischen Staates* (1940), pp. 36–9. E. W. Brooks, 'The Emperor Zenon and the Isaurians' in *E.H.R.*, viii (1893), pp. 209–38. R. J. Neumann in *P.R.E.* (ed. 3), xxi (1908), pp. 663–5, s.v.

ZEPHANIAH, Book of. This prophecy claims to have been delivered by Zephaniah, a descendent of (King?) Hezekiah, in the reign of Josiah, King of Judah (d. 608 B.C.). The prophet announces the approaching judgement of all nations including Judah in the coming Day of the Lord, but he holds out the hope of future conversion among the heathen and of a faithful remnant among the Jews (1. 2–3. 8). He concludes by encouraging Jerusalem to rejoice in the loving providence of God (3. 9–20). The prophecy, as originally delivered, probably belongs to the years immediately before the reformation of Josiah in 621 B.C., and gives some valuable information on religion and society in Jerusalem and Judah at that time. From the religious point of view, the Book is evidence of Zephaniah's deep moral sense, of his awareness of the sin of his people, and of his implicit faith in the justice of God in the expected day of judgement. The opening words of the well-known Christian hymn '*Dies irae, dies illa' are taken from the *Vulgate version of 1. 15–16.

Commentaries by A. B. *Davidson (Camb. Bibl., AV, on Nah., Hab., and Zeph., 1896, pp. 95–139), J. M. P. Smith (I.C.C. on Mic., Zeph., Nah., Hab., Obad., and Joel, 1912, pp. 159–263), and G. G. V. Stonehouse (West Comm. on Zeh., Nah., and Hab., 1929, pp. 1–72). F. Schwally, 'Das Buch Ssefanja, eine historisch-kritische Untersuchung' in *Z.A.T.W.*, x (1890), pp. 165–240; C. H. *Cornill, 'Die Prophetie Zephanjas' in *Theologische Studien und Kritiken*, 1916, pp. 297–332. J. A. Selbie in *H.D.B.*, iv (1902), pp. 974–7, s.v.; T. K. *Cheyne in *E.Bi.*, iv (1903), cols. 5402–9, s.v. Further commentaries under *Minor Prophets*.

ZEPHYRINUS, St. (d. 217), Pope. He succeeded St. *Victor as Bp. of Rome in 198, but despite his long pontificate relatively little is known of him. His critic, St. *Hippolytus, described him as a simple man without education (ἀνὴρ ἰδιώτης καὶ ἀγράμματος). In his office he was closely associated with his deacon, *Callistus, who succeeded him as Pope. Hippolytus charged him with laxity in enforcing discipline and failure to assert his authority sufficiently in repressing the heresies (esp. *Sabellianism) then prevalent in the Roman Church. Zephyrinus excommunicated, however, the two *Theodoti who defended the cause of 'Dynamic *Monarchian-ism'. He is traditionally commemorated (on insufficient grounds) as a martyr. Feast day, 26 Aug.

Jaffé, i, 12. *L.P.* (ed. Duchesne), i (1886), p. 139 f. A. v. *Harnack, 'Die älteste uns im Wortlaut bekannte dogmatische Erklärung eines römischen Bischofs (Zephyrin bei Hippolyt, *Refut.* IX. 11)' in *Sb.* (Berl.), 1923, pp. 51–7; B. *Capelle, O.S.B., 'Le Cas du pape Zéphyrin' in *R. Bén.*, xxxviii (1926), pp. 321–30; K. G. Preysing, 'Echtheit und Bedeutung der dogmatischen Erklärung Zephyrins (Hippolyt. *Philos.* IX. 11, 3)' in *Z.K.T.*, lii (1928), pp. 225–30. J. Wilpert, 'Beiträge zur christlichen Archäologie', xii, 'Das Mausoleum des hl. Zephyrin' in *R.Q.*, xxii (1908), pp. 183–195; O. *Marucchi, 'La questione del sepolcro del papa Zefirino e del martire Tarsicio in sequito ad una ultima scoperta' in *Nuovo Bulletino di Archeologia cristiana*, xvi (1910), pp. 205–25; P. F. de' Cavalieri, *Note agiografiche*, iv (S.T., xxiv; 1912), sect. iv, 'Del sepolcro di S. Zefirino', pp. 69–76. E. Caspar, *Geschichte des Papsttums von den Anfängen bis zur Höhe der Weltherrschaft*, i (1930), pp. 22–4 and 38–40. Fliche–Martin, ii (1935), esp. p. 103. Altaner (ed. 1950), p. 109. É. Amann in *D.T.C.*, xv (pt. 2; 1950), col. 3690 f., s.v.; E. Josi in *E.C.*, xii (1954), col. 1785 f., s.v. 'Zefirino'.

ZIGABENUS, EUTHYMIUS. See *Euthymius Zigabenus.*

ZILLERTHAL EVANGELICALS. A body of Protestants, resident in the Zillerthal, one of the principal valleys of the Tyrol, who seceded from the RC Church in 1829 and the following years. Religious and social boycott from the RC clergy and laity culminated in a decree from the provincial estates of the Tyrol, ordering all nonconformists to leave the country. On appeal to Frederick William III of Prussia in 1837, they were allowed to sell their possessions and settle at Erdmannsdorf in Prussian territory, where they were assisted by a grant from the Prussian government.

F. C. Arnold in *P.R.E.* (ed. 3), xxi (1908), pp. 675–8, with bibl.

ZINZENDORF, NIKOLAUS LUDWIG GRAF VON (1700–60), founder of the *Herrnhuter 'Brüdergemeine'. A native of Dresden, he was educated at A. H. *Francke's Adelspädagogium and at *Wittenberg university (1716–19). He then travelled in Holland and France, where Card. L. A. *de Noailles became his friend, and in 1721 he entered the service of the Saxon Government. His chief interest, however, was evangelization. He organized religious assemblies in his home, and from 1722 received on one of his estates Protestant emigrants from Austria, many of whom were descendants of the *Bohemian Brethren. Giving up his Government post in 1727, he henceforward devoted himself entirely to the spiritual care of this colony called Herrnhut. Before long he was attacked as an innovator by *Lutheran orthodoxy, but his beliefs were examined and approved in 1734, though he was subsequently exiled from Saxony in 1736. During the following years he travelled in Europe and America, accompanied by a band of disciples called the Pilgrims' Community. In 1737 he received *Moravian episcopal consecration from the Berlin court preacher, D. E. Jablonski, and later founded communities in

the Baltic Provinces, Holland, England, the W. Indies, and N. America. He was permitted to return to Saxony in 1747, where, during the next two years, the Herrnhuter passed through a period of emotional upheaval. From 1749 to 1755 he propagated his ideas in England, the Moravian Episcopal Church ('Unitas fratrum') having been recognized by Act of Parliament in 1749. His last years were spent in pastoral work at Herrnhut.

Opposed alike to the unbelieving rationalism and the barren Protestant orthodoxy of his time, Zinzendorf proclaimed a 'religion of the heart', based on an intimate fellowship with the Saviour, whose Person, conceived as creator, sustainer, and redeemer of the world, completely dominated his theology. The striving for a felt experience of this fellowship was not always free from excessive emotionalism, which shows itself in many of his poems and in the almost playful Herrnhut cult of the Five Wounds. Originally meaning to realize his religious ideals within the framework of the different Protestant Churches, he was forced by circumstances to give his work a separate organization, though he continued it in close connexion with Lutheranism. His emphasis on the place of feeling in religion infused new life into Protestant orthodoxy and, esp. through F. D. E. *Schleiermacher, profoundly influenced 19th cent. German theology.

Zinzendorf publd. his autobiography under the title Περὶ ἑαυτοῦ. Das ist naturelle Reflexiones über allerhand Malerien [c. 1748]. Life by A. G. Spangenberg (8 Thle, [Barby,] 1772–5; abridged Eng. tr., 1838). L. K. von Schrautenbach, *Der Graf von Zinzendorf und die Brüdergemeine seiner Zeit* (written in 1782; ed. F. W. Kölbing, Gnadau, 1851). Modern lives by [E. V.] F. Bovet (2 vols., Paris, 1860; Eng. tr., 1865) and J. R. Weinlick (Abingdon, Ill., 1956). H. Plitt, *Zinzendorfs Theologie* (3 vols., 1869–71). B. Becker, *Zinzendorf im Verhältniss zu Philosophie und Kirchentum seiner Zeit* (1886). O. Uttendörfer, *Zinzendorfs Weltbetrachtung* (1929); id., *Zinzendorfs religiöse Grundgedanken* (Herrnhut, 1935); and other writings by id. W. Bettermann, *Theologie und Sprache bei Zinzendorf* (1935). L. Aalen, *Den Unge Zinzendorfs Teologi* (Oslo, 1952), with bibl. B. Becker–J. T. Müller in *P.R.E.* (ed. 3), xxi (1908), pp. 679–703, s.v.; W. Bettermann in *R.G.G.* (ed. 2), v (1931), cols. 2118–21, s.v.; L. Cristiani in *D.T.C.*, xv (pt. 2; 1950), cols. 3695–704, s.v. See also bibl. to *Moravian Brethren*; also histories of Pietism, cited s.v.

ZION. The citadel of *Jerusalem, taken by *David from the Jebusites (2 Sam. 5. 6–7). It was probably situated on the eastern ridge of the city, south of the site of the *Temple. The name came to signify God's holy hill at Jerusalem (Ps. 2. 6), Jerusalem itself (Is. 1. 27), and allegorically the heavenly city (Heb. 12. 22, Rev. 14. 1).

ZITA, St. (c. 1215–72), the patroness of domestic servants. At the age of 12 she entered the service of the Fatinelli family at Lucca, where she remained till her death. Misunderstood and maltreated at first, she later won, by her religious fervour, the respect, and even veneration, of the family. She was canonized in 1696. Feast day, 27 Apr.

The principal authority is the life by Fatinellus de Fatinellis (anon.) printed in *AA.SS.*, Apr. III (1675), pp. 499–509. Modern lives by A. Guerra (Lucca, 1875) and J. G. Ledóchowski (Vienna, 1911). On the ref. to St. Zita in *Dante's Inferno, see F. P. Luiso, *L'Anziano di Santa Zita* (Lucca, 1927); cf. B. de Gaiffier in *Anal. Boll.*, xlviii (1930), p. 229 f.

ZONARAS, JOHANNES (12th cent.), Byzantine canonist and historian. After holding high positions at *Constantinople in the Imperial administration, he retired from the court during the reign of John II Comnenus (1118–43) and spent the rest of his life in monastic retirement on the small island of Niandro. The chief of his writings, a universal History (Ἐπιτομὴ τῶν Ἱστοριῶν) in 18 books, preserves much material that would otherwise be lost. It extends to 1118, and includes events of which Zonaras was himself an eye-witness. He also wrote a Commentary on Greek *canon law, starting with the *Apostolic Canons, notable for the aptness and directness of his comments. It is possible that portions of the canonical writings traditionally attributed to *Balsamon are also to be ascribed to Zonaras. His other works include a commentary on the poems of St. *Gregory of Nazianzus and a hymn to the Blessed Virgin (Κανὼν εἰς τὴν ὑπεραγίαν Θεοτόκον).

His Epitome of History, ed. M. Pinder–R. Büttner-Wobst (3 vols., C.S.H.B., 1841–97); also by L. Dindorf (6 vols., Teubn., 1868–76). Collected ed. in J. P. Migne, *PG*, cxxxiv and cxxxv, 9–438. Krumbacher, pp. 370–6, with bibl. P. Meyer in *P.R.E.* (ed. 3), xxi (1908), pp. 715–19; É. Amann in *D.T.C.*, xv (pt. 2; 1950), cols. 3705–8, both s.v.

ZOROASTRIANISM. The system of religious doctrine ascribed to Zoroaster (Zarathrustra) which in later times became the dominant religion of Iran and under the Sassanian dynasty (211–640) the official State teaching.

Of Zoroaster himself next to nothing is known with certainty. The *Gathas* (as contrasted with the later and mainly legendary *Avesta*, q.v.) probably incorporate historical material on his life. From these it would seem that his sphere of activity was Eastern Iran. His date is much disputed. Eduard Meyer put it at *c.* 1000 B.C.; but more recent scholars have put him much later, A. Christensen at between 650 and 600 B.C. and J. Hertel and E. Herzfeld (on the basis of the equation of Vistaspes, the protector of Zoroaster, with Hystaspes, father of Darius I) at between 550 and 523.

Zoroaster's teaching was apparently not a creation of his own, but at most a reform of earlier doctrines. He taught that the world was made by one 'Wise Lord' (*Ahura Mazda* or *Ormuzd*) with the help of his holy Spirit (*Spenta Mainyu*) and six other divine spirits or attributes of God. These spirits work against the Evil Spirit (*Angra Mainyu* or *Ahriman*), who is also helped by six other spirits, and tempt man to wrong. After the life on earth of a virgin-born Saviour (*Saoshyant*) God will finally triumph over evil, and all souls eventually pass over the 'bridge of decision' (from which some must first fall into purifying flames) and enjoy eternal bliss. He stressed the importance of discovering and setting forth

the truth, and showed the value of mercy; yet he allowed his king Vistashpa to use force in propagating his ideas. His religious ideas proved too exalted for the next generation in Persia, which reverted to polytheism, but they are sometimes held to have influenced *Jewish apocalyptic and (less probably) the NT (so R. *Otto). In a modified form they have been partly preserved by the Parsees.

There is a very considerable literature, much of it publd. in Bombay. General studies include those of A. V. W. Jackson, *Zoroaster the Prophet of Ancient Iran* (New York-London, 1899), and id., *Zoroastrian Studies* (New York, 1928); J. H. Moulton, *Early Zoroastrianism* (Hibbert Lectures for 1912; 1913), and id., *The Treasure of the Magi.* A Study of Modern Zoroastrianism (1917); L. Mills, *Our Own Religion in Ancient Persia* (Leipzig, 1913), and other works; M. N. Dhalla, *Zoroastrian Theology from the Earliest Times to the Present Day* (New York, 1914), id., *Zoroastrian Civilization from the Earliest Times to the Downfall of the last Zoroastrian Empire*, 651 (ib., 1922), and id., *Our Perfecting World.* Zarathustra's Way of Life (ib., &c., 1930); J. Hertel, *Die Zeit Zoroasters* (Indo-Iranische Quellen, i, 1924), and other more specialized works of this author; M. M. Dawson, *The Ethical Religion of Zoroaster* (New York, 1931); J. W. Waterhouse, *Zoroastrianism* ('Great Religions of the East', 1934; more popular); E. Herzfeld, *Zoroaster and his World* (2 vols., Princeton, N.J., 1947). E. Meyer, *Ursprung und Anfänge des Christentums*, ii (1921), pp. 58–94; C. Autram, *Mithra, Zoroastre et la préhistoire aryenne du christianisme* (Bibliothèque Historique, 1935), pp. 137–269. C. *Gore, *The Philosophy of the Good Life* (*Gifford Lectures for 1929–30; 1930), pp. 32–57. K. Geldner in *E.B.* (ed. 11), xxviii (1911), pp. 1039–43, s.v. 'Zoroaster'; A. J. Carnoy in *H.E.R.E.*, xii (1921), pp. 862–8, s.v., with bibl.

ZOSIMUS (d. 418), Bp. of Rome from 417. He was a Greek by birth. His brief pontificate was marked by blunders, which are in sharp contrast with the high claims he made for his office. Thus his unconsidered attempt to establish a vicariate of Arles, in disregard of already existing metropolitical rights in Gaul, had to be abandoned by his successor. His policy also twice suffered defeats in Africa. Led by St. *Augustine, the African Church compelled him to retract in his *Tractoria his favourable judgement of *Pelagianism; and he was again out-manœuvred when, citing as *Nicene and therefore of oecumenical authority a canon which properly belonged to the Council of *Sardica (343), he tried to quash the sentence passed on the African priest *Apiarius by the Bp. of Sicca. Several of his letters survive. Feast day, 26 Dec.

Epp. ed. P. *Coustant, O.S.B., *Epistolae Romanorum Pontificum*, i (1721), cols. 933–1006; repr. J. P. Migne, *PL*, xx, 639–704. *L.P.* (ed. Duchesne), i, 225 f. E. Caspar, *Geschichte des Papsttums von den Anfängen bis zur Höhe der Weltherrschaft*, i (1930), pp. 344–60. G. Bardy in Fliche-Martin, iv (1937), pp. 248–51. Bardenhewer, iv, 614 and 616. É. Amann in *D.T.C.*, xv (pt. 2; 1950), cols. 3708–16, s.v.; P. Paschini in *E.C.*, xii (1954), col. 1823 f., s.v.

ZOSIMUS (later 5th cent.), Greek historian. He held an administrative post at *Constantinople. His history of the Roman Empire, in six Books, going down to 410 and probably written after 425, is one of the primary sources for the secular history of the 4th cent. Though based throughout on earlier histories, it has a special interest because, without intentional distortion of facts, Zosimus consistently developed a pagan and anti-Christian view of his subject-matter, attributing, e.g., the decline of the Empire as much to the neglect of the old religion as to any political cause. His account of ecclesiastical affairs also serves as an occasional corrective to the better-known accounts in Christian writers.

Ed. princeps of Gk. text by F. Sylburg (Frankfurt, 1590). Crit. ed. by L. Mendelssohn (Leipzig, 1887), with prolegomena; Eng. tr., London, 1814. W. von Christ, Geschichte der griechischen Literatur (ed. W. Schmid–O. Stählin), II, ii (ed. 6, 1924), p. 1037 f.

ZUCCHETTO. The small round skull-cap used by certain RC ecclesiastics. It has been customarily worn since the 13th cent., and varies in colour with the different grades of the hierarchy, the *Pope wearing white, *cardinals red, *bishops violet, and others black. It is worn at *Mass, except during the *canon.

ZÜRICH CONSENSUS. See Consensus Tigurinus.

ZWICKAU PROPHETS. A group of early *Anabaptists which sought to realize the rule of the elect in a community at Zwickau, an industrial town in Saxony. The chief were N. *Storch, T. Drechsel, and M. Thomä. They claimed immediate Divine inspiration, maintained apocalyptic ideas, and rejected infant baptism and other traditional doctrines and practices. They removed to *Wittenberg, where they established themselves at Christmastide 1521. Here they gained the interest of P. *Melanchthon, and their followers rapidly grew in influence; but they were promptly put down by M. *Luther on his return to Wittenberg in March 1522.

Brief reports on the Zwickau Prophets drawn up for the Kurfürst Friedrich by P. *Melanchthon and N. von Amsdorf, ed. C. G. *Bretschneider, Corpus Reformatorum, i (Halle, 1834), cols. 533–55. N. Müller, 'Die Wittenberger Bewegung, 1521 und 1522' in Archiv für Reformationsgeschichte, vi (1908/9), pp. 161–226, 261–325, 385–469, vii (1909/10), pp. 185–224, 233–93, 353–412, viii (1910/11), pp. 1–43; also separately issued, Leipzig, 1911.

ZWINGLI, ULRICH (or HULDREICH) (1484–1531), Swiss Reformer. A native of Wildhaus in the Toggenburg valley, canton St. *Gall, Switzerland, he was educated at Berne (1498–1500), Vienna (1500–2), and Basle (under T. *Wyttenbach, 1502–6). He was ordained priest in 1506, and from 1506 to 1516 was pastor at Glarus. Already a devoted admirer of D. *Erasmus, he gave himself up at Glarus largely to humanistic studies, taught himself Greek and prob. the rudiments of Hebrew, learned St. Paul's Epp. by heart, and read the Fathers. In 1513 and 1515 he served as military chaplain to Swiss mercenaries in the Papal service and was present at the Battle of Marignano (13–14 Sept. 1515). In 1516 he left Glarus for *Einsiedeln, where the pilgrimage abuses at the famous shrine quickened his desire for reform; he also deepened his knowledge of the Greek NT with the aid of D. *Erasmus's newly published editio princeps (1516) and improved his technique as a preacher. On 11 Dec. 1518 he was

elected minister at Zürich, where he remained for the rest of his life. Here, in an important office, he sought to carry through his political and religious ideals and met with strong local support. The rupture with ecclesiastical authority came gradually. The real beginning of the Reformation in Switzerland was Zwingli's lectures on the NT in 1519. Attacks in his sermons on Purgatory, Invocation of Saints, and Monasticism soon followed. He seems to have owed little directly to M. *Luther, of whose influence he always betrayed some jealousy. In April 1522 appeared his first Reformation tract, Von Erkiesen and Fryheit der Spysen, and later in the same year (22 Aug.) Architeles, advocating the liberation of believers from the control of the Papacy and bishops. The Bp. of Constance's Vicar General (Johann *Faber), sent to Zürich to deal with the situation, was silenced in a public disputation on 29 Jan. 1523, when Zwingli successfully upheld 67 theses before an audience of some 600. The sole basis of truth was the Gospel, and the authority of the Pope, the Sacrifice of the Mass, the Invocation of Saints, times and seasons of fasting, and clerical celibacy were rejected. The city council gave Zwingli their full support and the Minster Chapter was reconstituted in independence of episcopal control. Matters were carried further at a second disputation on 26 Oct. 1523, which led to Zwingli's Eine kurze christliche Inleitung expounding for the clergy the relations between the Gospel and the Law. Shortly afterwards steps were taken to abolish the Mass (eventually suppressed at Zürich in Apr. 1525) and remove images and pictures from churches. On 2 Apr. 1524 Zwingli publicly celebrated his marriage with Anna Meyer (née Reinhard) in the cathedral.

It was at this stage that Zwingli began to develop his characteristic Eucharistic teaching ('Zwinglianism'). In 1522 he still accepted the traditional view of the Eucharist, but in a letter to Matthäus Alber of Reutlingen (16 Nov. 1524) he upheld a purely symbolic interpretation, which he developed further in Commentarius de Vera and Falsa Religione (1525). The ensuing conflict with Luther led to the fruitless Colloquy of *Marburg (Sept.–Oct. 1529). Every form of the carnal presence of Christ in the Eucharist, whether by *transubstantiation, *consubstantiation, or *impanation, was rejected as 'Capernaitic' (Jn. 6. 51–3. 59). To Zwingli's great disappointment, the division went so deep that any union of the Protestant forces was impossible. In these years he was also engaged in active disputes with the *Anabaptists and acquiesced when the Council of Zürich put one of their leaders to death by drowning in 1527.

Meanwhile, the movement had spread to other parts of Switzerland. In a public theological disputation at Berne in Jan. 1528 Zwingli successfully upheld ten theses (see *Berne Theses), and the canton joined the movement. Basel, St. Gall, and Schaffhausen followed shortly afterwards. The movement met, however, with fierce resistance elsewhere, notably in the five Forest Cantons (Lucerne,

Zug, Schwyz, Uri, Unterwalden). War was only just avoided in 1529 and finally broke out in 1531 when the Forest Cantons made a sudden and unexpected descent on Zürich. They were met by a small force at Cappel where Zwingli, who as chaplain carried the banner, was killed (11 Oct. 1531).

Collected edd. of his works by R. Walther, 4 vols., Zürich, 1539; 4 vols., ib., 1545, and 3 vols., ib., 1581; ed. M. Schuler–J. Schulthess (8 vols., ib., 1829–42); ed. E. Egli–G. Finsler and others (Corpus Reformatorum, lxxxviii ff., 1904 ff.). Selections of his writings tr. into Eng. by S. M. Jackson (Philadelphia, Pa., 1901); also by G. W. Bromiley, *Zwingli and Bullinger* (Library of Christian Classics, xxiv. 1953), pp. 47–279, with introd., pp. 13–40. Life by O. *Myconius, written in 1532, publd. Basel, 1536. Modern lives by J. J. Hottinger (Zürich, 1842; Eng. tr., 1856), R.

Christoffel (Leben und ausgewählte Schriften der Väter und Begründer der reformirten Kirche, i; 1857; Eng. tr., 1858), C. Mörikofer (2 vols., Leipzig, 1867–9), R. Staehelin (2 vols., Basel, 1895–7), S. M. Jackson (New York–London, 1901), and O. Farner (Zürich, 1943 ff.). Shorter studies by S. Simpson (London, 1903) and O. Farner (Zürich, 191 ; Eng. tr., 1952). A. Baur, *Zwinglis Theologie. Ihr Werden und ihr System* (2 vols., 1885–9). W. Köhler, *Zwingli und Luther. Ihr Streit über das Abendmahl nach seinen politischen und religiösen Beziehungen* (Quellen und Forschungen zur Reformationsgeschichte, vi and vii; 1924–1953), and other works of this author. *Zwingliana*. Mitteilungen zur Geschichte Zwinglis und der Reformation, herausgegeben von der Vereinigung für das Zwinglimuseum in Zürich (Zürich, 1897 [1904] ff.). G. Finsler, *Zwingli-Bibliographie* (Zürich, 1897). E. Güder–R. Stähelin–E. Egli in *P.R.E.* (ed. 3), xxi (1908), pp. 774–815, s.v.; L. Cristiani in *D.T.C.*, xv (pt. 2; 1950), cols. 3716–44, s.v. 'Zwingli'; J. V. M. Pollet, O.P., ib., cols. 3745–928, s.v. 'Zwinglianisme'.